ROSAI AND ACKERMAN'S

Surgical Pathology

NINTH EDITION

Commissioning Editor: Michael Houston
Project Development Manager: Joanne Scott
Project Manager: Naughton Project Management, Aoibhe O'Shea
Design Manager: Sarah Russell
Illustration Manager: Mick Ruddy
Illustrator: Lynda Payne

Cover illustrations: Volume 1: Fig. 5.21
Volume 2: Fig. 5.40

ROSAI AND ACKERMAN'S
Surgical Pathology

Juan Rosai MD

Chairman, Department of Pathology
National Cancer Institute
Milan, Italy

Professor, Department of Pathology
Weill Medical College of
Cornell University
New York, New York, USA

NINTH EDITION

 Mosby

An Affiliate of Elsevier

MOSBY
An Affiliate of Elsevier

Previous editions copyrighted 1953, 1959, 1964, 1968, 1974, 1981, 1989, 1996
© 2004, Elsevier Inc. All rights reserved.

First edition 1953   Fifth edition 1974
Second edition 1959   Sixth edition 1981
Third edition 1964   Seventh edition 1989
Fourth edition 1968   Eighth edition 1996

Part ISBN-13: 9789996000485
Part ISBN-10: 9996000486
Set ISBN-13: 978-0-323-01342-0
Set ISBN-10: 0-323-01342-2

British Library Cataloguing in Publication Data
A catalogue record for this book is available from the British Library

Library of Congress Cataloging in Publication Data
A catalog record for this book is available from the Library of Congress

Notice
Medical knowledge is constantly changing. Standard safety precautions must be
followed, but as new research and clinical experience broaden our knowledge, changes
in treatment and drug therapy may become necessary or appropriate. Readers are
advised to check the most current product information provided by the manufacturer of
each drug to be administered to verify the recommended dose, the method and duration
of administration, and contraindications. It is the responsibility of the practitioner,
relying on experience and knowledge of the patient, to determine dosages and the best
treatment for each individual patient. Neither the Publisher nor the authors assume any
liability for any injury and/or damage to persons or property arising from this
publication.
The Publisher

 **ELSEVIER** your source for books,
journals and multimedia
in the health sciences
www.elsevierhealth.com

Printed in China
Last digit is the print number: 07 06 05 04 03

The
publisher's
policy is to use
**paper manufactured
from sustainable forests**

To my sons,
Alberto, Carlos, and Johnny

And my grandson,
John

Contents

VOLUME 2

Preface
to the ninth edition

The eight years that have elapsed between this and the previous edition have seen momentous changes taking place in the practice of surgical pathology. Immuno-histochemistry has continued its notable expansion and has become an indispensable adjunct for the practice of the specialty. It has truly transformed the practice of surgical pathology in a fashion that no other special technique has done before or after. Newcomers to the specialty take it for granted when ordering their panels, without pausing to think that only thirty years ago none of it was available to the brave pathologists who based all of their diagnoses and their histogenetic con-siderations on patterns of growth and cell shapes seen in hematoxylin-stained slides, with occasional modest help provided by one or other special stain.

We are now in the midst of another transformation, resulting from the application to surgical pathology specimens of the enormous amount of new knowledge derived from the genetic molecular revolution. The potential, and in some instances, already tangible benefits of this technology are too obvious to be emphasized. It may instead be instructive to reflect on the effect that this barrage of new information is having on the approach to surgical pathology by the new generation of practitioners, and the danger that the tradition of meticulous gross and microscopic examination upon which surgical pathology has been built may be gradually eroding. Some of this may be inevitable and is perhaps not altogether undesirable, yet the amount of information that this time-honored examination can still provide is so rich and dependable that one recoils at the thought of its being ignored or slighted. On that basis, this edition dutifully incorporates the many promising results reached with the new technologies (emphasizing the few in which a clinical validation has occurred), but always matches them against the results and conclusions derived from the morphology-based approach that has served pathologists so well for so long.

Another important change that has taken place during this period concerns the increasing demands for standardization, obedience of regulatory controls, and legal accountability, which have prompted various professional organizations to produce sets of guidelines to help pathologists navigate this increasingly complicated system.

Yet another significant development concerns the pervasive influence acquired by electronic information systems in practically all activities that take place in the surgical pathology laboratory, rendering some degree of computer literacy indispensable to those wishing to practice the specialty.

It has not been easy to accommodate this rapidly changing and continuously expanding universe in the confines of the covers of this book. The amount of information that has to be reviewed, even if often of a merely confirmatory or plainly repetitive nature, is monumental, and the trend for subspecialization of surgical pathology—each with its own rites and language—has accelerated. The sum of these factors has made the production of this book a heavy burden, to the point of making one wonder whether it had grown beyond the capabilities of an individual. Yet, as you can see, don't ask me how, another edition has been completed, once again for the most part written by one author, in the continuing hope that whatever expertise is inevitably missing as a result may be compensated by what somebody referred to as "the ultimate simplicity of one voice speaking." Along those lines, a constant attempt has been made to preserve as much as possible of the pragmatic flavor initially given to this work by its peerless begetter, Dr. Lauren V. Ackerman (1905–1993).

This goal of coherence notwithstanding, it was obvious that there were highly specialized areas that could not have been covered adequately without the contribution of experts. I was fortunate in being able to secure the collaboration of the outstanding individuals listed on the Contributors' page for this purpose, and I am very grateful to them for their generosity in lending their considerable expertise to this effort.

A book that has gone through so many editions is bound to contain strata of text and illustrative material that have been contributed by someone or other at some point and then been covered by other strata, but whose source will still be identifiable to the initiated. Among the many such past contributors, I would like to mention Dr. Morton E. Smith (Chapter 30), Dr. Robert E. Vickers

(Chapter 6), and Dr. John Morrow (sections on Information systems in surgical pathology and Model for an automated anatomic pathology system, Chapter 1).

Thanks are also due to the many colleagues and associates who generously contributed illustrative material from their own files or personal publications. Among them, I would like to single out for the magnitude of their contributions the following: Dr. Robin A. Cooke, from Brisbane, Australia; Dr. Robert Erlandson, from South Berlington, Vermont; Dr. Fabio Facchetti, from Brescia, Italy; Dr. Pedro J. Grases Galofrè, from Barcelona, Spain; and Ms. Loredana Alasio, Chief Cytotechnologist in my Department of Pathology at the Cancer Institute in Milan.

Each of the editions of this book in which I have been involved has been written at a different place: the Fifth at Washington University, the Sixth at the University of Minnesota, the Seventh at Yale University, the Eighth at Memorial Sloan-Kettering Cancer Center, and the present at the National Cancer Institute in Milan. In each place I have learned a great deal from my colleagues and have incorporated many of their comments and suggestions. I am most grateful to the countless staff pathologists, pathology residents, and pathology fellows from each of these places who have unwittingly contributed to the book in this fashion. I suspect that some of them will recognize themselves in some of the statements.

Once again, the contribution made by my wife, Dr. Maria Luisa Carcangiu, has been colossal. It encompassed every aspect of the book production, beginning with psychologic support in the many moments of near collapse to the chore of performing many of my departmental responsibilities in order to allow me to put the final touches to the project, not to speak of the thoughts that were generated during the course of our innumerable exchanges of opinions at work and at home.

The secretarial staff at the Institute has been most supportive. I must confess I was a little apprehensive when all this started in view of the relative inexperience of the person chosen for the transcription task and her less than perfect knowledge of the English language. The way Maria Morelli rose to the task was astounding. After a few stressful initiation chapters, she was typing my handwritten pages (yes, I still did it with pencil and paper) with a speed and accuracy of the kind I have rarely witnessed anywhere, not to speak of the enthusiasm and devotion she threw into the effort. Thanks are also due to Gianni Roncato, the Department's photographer, for his skillful and dedicated contribution to this effort.

So, here it is for you, my fellow surgical pathologist, hoping that it will provide you with some assistance in carrying out our demanding, stressful, wonderful job.

Juan Rosai, MD
Milan, 2004

Preface
to the first edition

This book can be only an introduction to the vast field of surgical pathology: the pathology of the living. It does not pretend to replace in any way the textbooks to general pathology, its purpose being merely to supplement them, assuming that the reader has a background in or access to those texts. The contents are not as complete as they might be because emphasis has been placed on the common rather than the rare lesions and are, to a great extent, based on the author's personal experiences.

This book has been written for the medical student as well as for those physicians who are daily intimately concerned with surgical pathology. This must of necessity include not only the surgeon and the pathologist, but also those physicians in other fields who are affected by its decisions, such as the radiologist and the internist. Gross pathology has been stressed throughout with an attempt to correlate the gross findings with the clinical observations. The many illustrations have been selected as typical of the various surgical conditions, although in a few instances the author has been unable to resist showing some of the more interesting rare lesions he has encountered. Concluding each chapter there is a bibliography listing those references which are not only relatively recent and readily available, but also those which will lead the reader to a more detailed knowledge of the subject.

Dr. Zola K. Cooper, Assistant Professor of Pathology and Surgical Pathology, has written one of the sections on Skin, and Dr. David E. Smith, Assistant Professor of Pathology and Surgical Pathology, has written the chapter on Central Nervous System. Both of these members of the Department are particularly well qualified for their respective roles because of their background and present responsibilities in these fields. Their efforts on my behalf are most gratefully acknowledged.

Many members of the Surgical Staff at Barnes Hospital have given much help both knowingly and unwittingly. I am particularly grateful to Dr. Charles L. Eckert, Associate Professor of Surgery, for letting me bother him rather constantly with my questions and for giving freely of his experience. Dr. Richard Johnson, who succeeded me as Pathologist at the Ellis Fischel State Cancer Hospital, agreeably made available all the material there, and Dr. Franz Leidler, Pathologist at the Veterans Hospital, has been most cooperative.

Thanks must be given to Dr. H.R. McCarroll, Assistant Professor of Orthopedics, for constructively criticizing the chapter on Bone and Joint, and to Dr. C.A. Waldron for helping me with the chapters related to the Oral Cavity. Among other faculty friends and colleagues who were especially helpful, I would like to mention Dr. Carl E. Lischer, Dr. Eugene M. Bricker, Dr. Heinz Haffner, Dr. Thomas H. Burford, Dr. Carl A. Moyer, Dr. Evarts A. Graham, Dr. Robert Elman, Dr. Edward H. Reinhard, Dr. J. Albert Key, Dr. Glover H. Copher, Dr. Margaret G. Smith, and Dr. Robert A. Moore.

Mr. Cramer K. Lewis, of our Department of Illustration, has been very patient with my demands, and his efforts and skill have been invaluable. Miss Marion Murphy, in charge of our Medical Library, and her associates gave untiringly of their time.

Because of recent advances in anesthesia, antibiotics, and pre- and postoperative care, modern surgery permits the radical excision of portions or all of various organs. There is a need today for contemplative surgeons, men with a rich background in the fundamental sciences, whether chemistry, physiology, or pathology. The modern surgeon should not ask himself, "Can I get away with this operation?" but rather, "What does the future hold for this patient?" It is hoped that this book may contribute in some small fashion toward the acquisition of this attitude.

Lauren V. Ackerman, MD
St. Louis, Missouri, USA

List of Contributors

Chapter 13: Liver (Non-neoplastic diseases)
Valeer J. Desmet, MD PhD
Emeritus Professor of Pathology
Universitair Ziekenhuis St Rafael
Leuven, Belgium

Chapter 17: Kidney (Non-neoplastic diseases)
Nelson G. Ordòñez, MD
Professor of Pathology
The University of Texas M.D.Anderson Cancer Center
Houston, Texas, USA

Chapter 23: Bone Marrow
Richard D. Brunning, MD
Professor Emeritus
Department of Laboratory Medicine and Pathology
University of Minnesota Medical School
Minneapolis, Minnesota, USA

Chapter 28: Central Nervous System
Marc K. Rosenblum, MD
Chairman, Department of Pathology
Memorial Hospital
Memorial Sloan-Kettering Cancer Center;
Professor of Pathology
Weill Medical College
Cornell University
New York, New York, USA

Chapter 28: Peripheral Nerves; Skeletal Muscle;
Chapter 29: Pituitary Gland
Juan M. Bilbao, MD
Staff Neuropathologist
Sunnybrook and Women's College Health Sciences Centre
North York, Ontario, Canada;
Office of the Chief Coroner for Ontario, Canada;
Associate Professor of Pathology
University of Toronto Medical School
Toronto, Ontario, Canada

Lee-Cyn Ang, MBBS, FRCPC, FRCPath
Director of Neuropathology
Department of Pathology
London Health Sciences Centre and
University of Western Ontario
London, Ontario, Canada

19 Female reproductive system

Vulva
Vagina
Uterus—cervix

Uterus—corpus
Fallopian tube
(including broad and round ligaments)

Ovary
Placenta

Vulva

Normal anatomy

The vulva is composed of the following anatomic structures: mons pubis, clitoris, labia minora, labia majora, vulvar vestibule and vestibulovaginal bulbs, urethral meatus, hymen, Bartholin's and Skene's glands and ducts, and vaginal introitus.[1,4]

The *labia majora* are lined by keratinized skin containing all the cutaneous adnexa: hair follicles, sebaceous glands, apocrine glands, and sweat (eccrine) glands.[3] The *labia minora* are covered by nonkeratinized stratified squamous epithelium on their vestibular surfaces but have a thin keratinized layer on their lateral side. Skin adnexa are usually absent in them, but on occasions one encounters both sweat and sebaceous glands.

Bartholin's gland is the major vestibular gland and has a tubuloalveolar structure. It is made up of acini composed of mucus-secreting columnar cells and a duct lined by transitional epithelium.[2] *Minor vestibular glands* are of simple tubular type and are lined with a mucus-secreting columnar epithelium that merges with the stratified squamous epithelium of the vestibule.

Skene's or periurethral glands are analogous to the male prostate gland; they are lined by a pseudostratified mucus-secreting columnar epithelium that merges with the transitional-type epithelium of the ducts, which in turn joins with the stratified squamous epithelium of the vestibule.

The *hymen* is lined by nonkeratinized stratified squamous epithelium on both surfaces.

The *clitoris* contains erectile tissue similar to that in the corpora cavernosa of the penis.

Most of the vulvar lymphatics drain to the superficial inguinal nodes, but those in the clitoris empty directly into the deep chain.

Congenital abnormalities

Ectopic mammary tissue can occur in the vulvar region, along the primitive milk line that extends in the embryo from the axilla to the groin. This tissue is subject to many of the physiologic and pathologic changes that occur in the normally situated breast. These include swelling and secretion of milk during pregnancy, cysts,[14] fibroadenoma,[5,12] (Fig. 19.1) phylloides tumor,[6,13] and carcinoma.[8,10,11,14] The

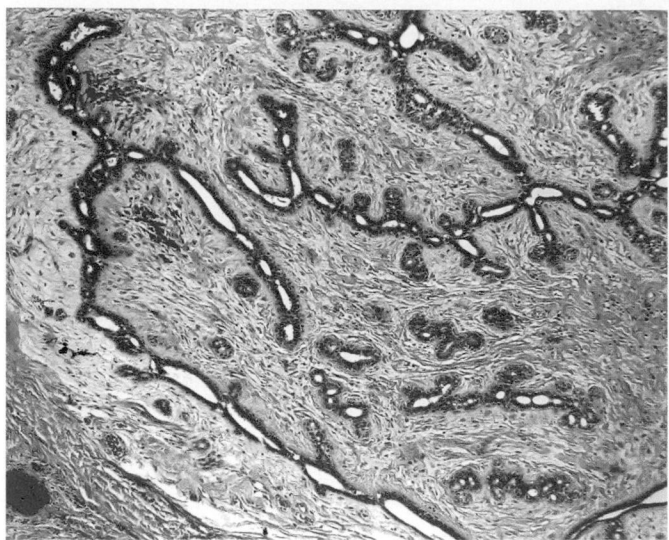

Fig. 19.1 Fibroadenoma of vulva arising from ectopic breast tissue.

latter has been reported in association with bilateral breast carcinoma.[9] Most of the carcinomas have been of ductal type, including some of its variants (such as mucinous carcinoma).[7] In addition, it is likely that ectopic mammary tissue is the source of the common benign vulvar tumor known as papillary hidradenoma (see p. 1493).

Inflammatory diseases

Syphilis in women often manifests itself initially in the vulvar region. The fully developed syphilitic chancre is composed microscopically of plasma cells, lymphocytes, and histiocytes and is covered by a zone of ulceration infiltrated by neutrophils and necrotic debris. The microscopic appearance is not entirely specific, but the combination of numerous plasma cells and endarteritis should alert to the diagnosis. Sometimes, the possibility of syphilis is first suggested on the basis of the microscopic examination of an enlarged inguinal lymph node if this node shows a combination of capsular and pericapsular fibrosis, follicular hyperplasia, plasma cell infiltration, and endarteritis. The latter feature, which represents the most useful clue to the diagnosis, is particularly well seen in or outside the nodal capsule (see Chapter 21).

Granuloma inguinale (donovanosis) is a chronic infection caused by *Calymmatobacterium granulomatis*, a gram-negative, non-motile, encapsulated bacillus.[17,26] It begins as a soft elevated granulomatous area that enlarges very slowly by peripheral extension and ulcerates. Microscopically, there is a dense dermal inflammatory infiltrate composed of histiocytes and plasma cells, with a scattering of small abscesses.[30] The diagnosis rests on the demonstration of Donovan bodies, which are seen as small round encapsulated bodies inside the cytoplasm of the histiocytes. They can be seen in H&E sections but are best demonstrated with the Giemsa or Warthin–Starry stains. Pronounced pseudo-epitheliomatous hyperplasia, which may accompany chronic lesions, should be distinguished from the very rare squamous cell carcinoma that may arise in such areas.[15] The infection can spread to the retroperitoneum and simulate a soft tissue neoplasm.[16]

Lymphogranuloma venereum is a venereal disease produced by *Chlamydia* organisms corresponding to serotypes L1, L2, and L3.[25,27] It mainly affects lymph vessels and lymphoid tissue. The initial small ulcer at a site of venereal contact is often unnoticed. The first clinical manifestation is swelling of inguinal lymph nodes caused by stellate abscesses surrounded by pale epithelioid cells.[22] There is extensive scarring as the disease progresses, often leading to fistulas and strictures of the urethra, vagina, and rectum. The diagnosis can be confirmed by intradermal skin test (Frei test), complement fixation test, or immunofluorescence.[19] Serum immunoglobulin levels are usually markedly elevated. Rainey[29] reported 11 cases of squamous cell carcinoma or adenocarcinoma engrafted on lymphogranulomatous strictures. Most of the tumors were located in the anorectal area.

Crohn's disease can involve the vulvar region.[23,24,33] In some cases, the vulvar lesions are associated with perineal disease and fistula formation, but in others they are separated from the anal lesions by normal tissue. Grossly, erythematous areas appear that later ulcerate. Microscopically, noncaseating granulomas may be found. The process reported as *vulvitis granulomatosa* is probably related to Crohn's disease in that some of the patients have subsequently developed either intestinal Crohn's disease or cheilitis granulomatosa.[20]

Behçet's disease can, rarely, involve the vulvar region, where it presents as a microscopically nonspecific ulceration.[21,32]

Necrotizing fasciitis of the vulva may be seen in diabetic women and is associated with a high mortality rate; wide excision of the diseased tissue is the treatment of choice.[31]

Vulvar vestibulitis is a disorder characterized microscopically by a chronic inflammatory infiltrate predominantly involving the mucosal lamina propria and the periglandular/periductal connective tissue of the vestibular region.[28] There is no evidence of human papilloma virus (HPV) involvement.[18]

So-called "chronic vulvar dystrophies"

There exists a group of vulvar diseases that are pathogenetically unrelated but that have several features in common at the clinical level. They usually present as irregular patchy areas of thickened skin, often accompanied by severe pruritus. The color is usually white, in which case the clinically descriptive term *leukoplakia* has traditionally been used. In other instances, the lesions are red or a mixture of both colors. They are easily traumatized and excoriated. In some of these lesions the vulvar soft tissues are atrophied and shrunken, in which case the term *kraurosis* has been employed.

In the presence of a lesion with some of these clinical features, it is essential to reach a specific diagnosis, and this often necessitates the performance of a biopsy.[41] Multiple biopsies are necessary if the lesion is large or varies in appearance from place to place. The differential diagnosis includes the following categories:

1 Specific dermatoses such as psoriasis, lichen planus, or lichen simplex chronicus (see Chapter 4).[34]
2 Squamous intraepithelial lesions (see p. 1487).
3 So-called "chronic vulvar dystrophy." In turn, this highly questionable term[34,43] encompasses two diseases, which, although sometimes coexisting, should be regarded as separate: lichen sclerosus and keratosis.

Lichen sclerosus (et atrophicus) of the vulva may occur in any age group, including children[39] (Fig. 19.2). In the latter group, the vulvar region represents the most common location, and there is a high incidence of spontaneous involution at the time of puberty.[42] The microscopic features are similar but not identical to those seen in this disorder when it occurs elsewhere in the skin (see Chapter 4) (Fig. 19.3). It has been stated that the minimal histologic criteria for the microscopic diagnosis of lichen sclerosus are the presence of a vacuolar interface reaction pattern in conjunction with dermal sclerosis (homogenized and hyalinized eosinophilic collagen bundles) of any thickness in between the inflammatory infiltrate and the epithelium of vessel walls.[36] In the early stages, lichen sclerosus may be difficult to distinguish from lichen planus.[37] The overlying epidermis is characteristically atrophic, but on occasions it may show foci of pseudoepitheliomatous hyperplasia.[44] The curious fact

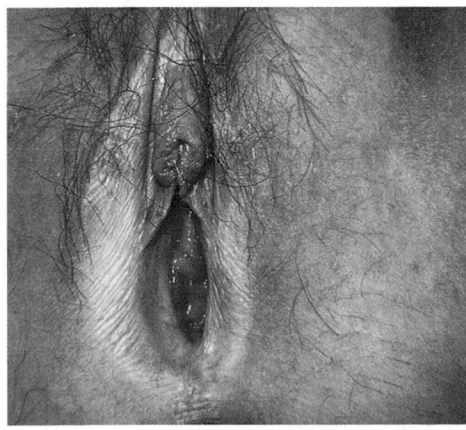

Fig. 19.2 Clinical appearance of vulvar lichen sclerosus.

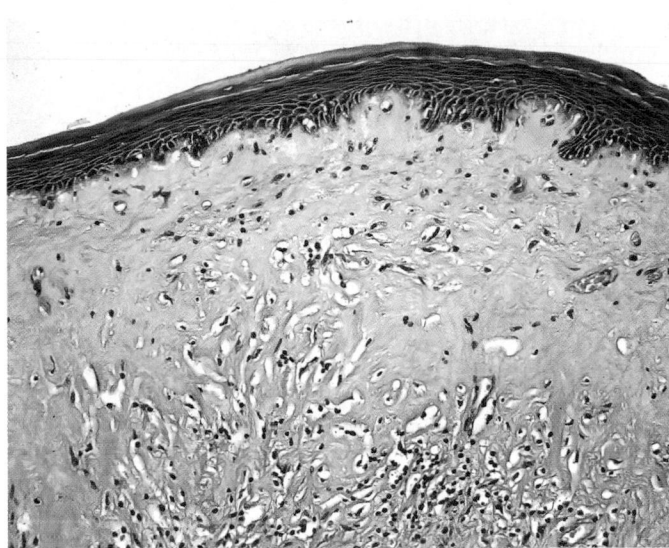

Fig. 19.3 Lichen sclerosus et atrophicus of vulva. A thick hypocellular edematous layer is bounded by atrophic epidermis on one side and inflamed stroma on the other.

that the dermal lymphocytic infiltrate shows a monoclonal gamma-T-cell receptor rearrangement has been documented.[45]

A highly controversial issue is the possible precancerous nature of lichen sclerosus. In one series, squamous cell carcinoma developed in only one of 92 patients,[38] and in another it was found in 12 (4%) of 290 patients followed for a mean period of 12.5 years.[48] The consensus is that if an increased risk exists, it must be of a very low magnitude.[35] The cases of lichen sclerosus associated with carcinoma show thickening of the epidermis and some degree of basal atypia (especially in the areas adjacent to the carcinoma), suggesting that there is a superimposed vulvar intraepithelial neoplasia (VIN).[47] This is supported by the fact that cases of carcinoma-associated lichen sclerosus tend to show an overexpression of p53.[35]

Keratosis (squamous hyperplasia) is characterized microscopically by acanthosis, prominent stratum granulosum, and hyperkeratosis, often associated with mild dermal chronic inflammatory infiltrate (Fig. 19.4). An important criterion for the use of this term without a qualifier is the *absence of atypia*. If this criterion is followed, keratosis will not be found to be a precancerous condition, a belief supported by the fact that such lesions are not clonal and are devoid of *p53* mutations.[40]

Occasionally, the features of lichen sclerosus and squamous cell hyperplasia are seen to coexist, in which case the term *mixed vulvar dystrophy* has been used.[46] Furthermore, the changes of VIN are sometimes superimposed on any of these conditions. Failure to appreciate the existence of these various combinations is probably responsible for the widely different figures given regarding the precancerous connotations of these various entities.[46]

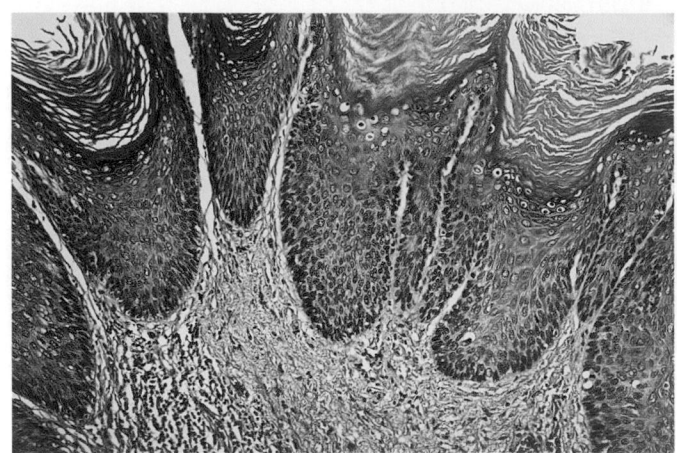

Fig. 19.4 Marked squamous cell hyperplasia (keratosis) of vulva associated with papillomatosis and chronic inflammation of the underlying stroma. There is no significant atypia.

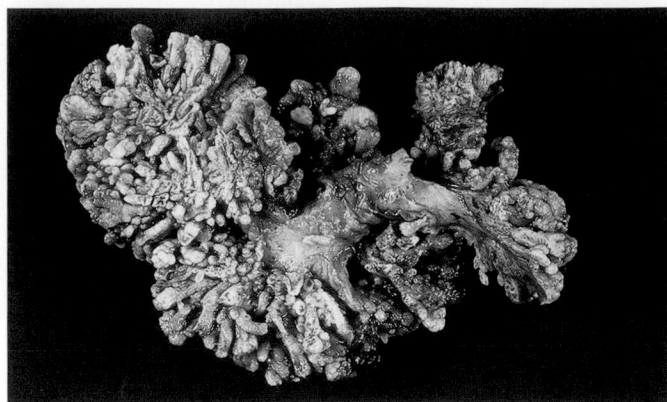

Fig. 19.5 Large condyloma of vulva.

Human papilloma virus and vulvar pathology

The role of HPV in vulvar pathology is analogous to the one it plays in the vagina and cervix, and is discussed in connection with the latter (see p. 1530). In the vulva, this includes condyloma (acuminatum and flat), VIN, invasive squamous cell carcinoma (including those of the urethra), and verrucous carcinoma.[49]

From a practical standpoint, it is important to classify these conditions separately in view of their widely different natural history and treatment.

Condyloma and seborrheic keratosis

Vulvar **condyloma** is a venereal disease caused by HPV, usually type 6. The better known form is **condyloma acuminatum,** which is characterized grossly by one or several soft elevated masses of variable size (Fig. 19.5). Microscopically there is a complicated papillary arrangement of well-differentiated undulating squamous epithelium supported by delicate, well-vascularized connective tissue stalks containing mononuclear inflammatory cells (mainly CD4+ and CD8+ cells)[54] (Figs 19.6 and 19.7).

The other form of condyloma, which is actually much more common, is the **flat condyloma** (not to be confused with the *condyloma latum* of syphilis). The cytologic features are similar in both forms. Koilocytosis of the malpighian epithelium (see p. 1530) and lymphocytic infiltration of the stroma are regular features (Fig. 19.8). Koilocytosis refers to the combination of perinuclear cytoplasmic clearing and crinkling of the nuclear membrane (nuclear "raisins"). As a rule, this change is not as florid in vulvar condylomas as it tends to be in condylomas of the cervix. A typical condyloma shows minimal

Fig. 19.6 Whole mount of condyloma acuminatum of vulva.

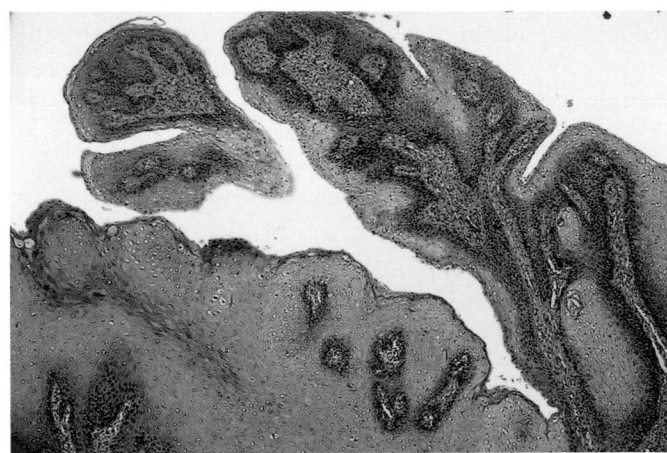

Fig. 19.7 Papillomatous shape of vulvar condyloma.

basal or parabasal cell atypia, orderly maturation, and a smooth transition to koilocytotic intermediate and superficial cells; mitoses may be numerous but are all typical.[50,56] In contrast, the lesions of VIN exhibit abnormal

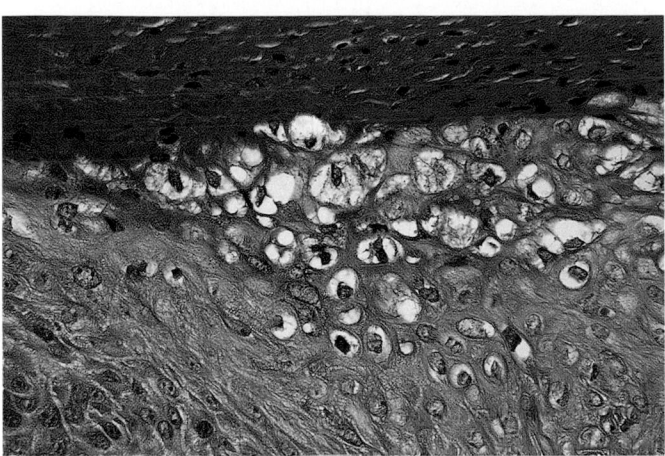

Fig. 19.8 Prominent koilocytotic changes in vulvar epithelium.

mitoses and nuclear pleomorphism, enlargement, and hyperchromasia in the basal and parabasal cell layers (see later section). The increased proliferative activity of condyloma (in contrast to fibroepithelial polyp and squamous papilloma) can be easily appreciated with the MIB-1 stain.[57] The DNA content of condylomas is diploid and polyploid (including tetraploidy and octaploidy), in contrast to the aneuploid pattern seen in most cases of VIN.[59]

Sometimes one sees verrucopapillary vulvar lesions in children or adults that lack the cytologic markers of condyloma; these are often referred to as *squamous papillomas* and usually contain genital HPV types by PCR.[52] Conversely, there may be multinucleated atypia of the epithelial squamous cells associated with reactive conditions in the absence of HPV infection.[53] Another vulvar lesion which needs to be discussed here is the process morphologically indistinguishable from cutaneous seborrheic keratosis, which in this particular location is frequently associated with HPV infection.[51a] The differential diagnosis of condyloma also includes a lesion characterized by *epidermolytic hyperkeratosis*, which could be related to Darier's disease or represent a form of Hailey–Hailey disease.[58] The acantholysis is usually suprabasal, but we have also seen it at the level of the granular layer.

The traditional therapy for condyloma consisted of podophyllin application. Microscopically, this results in epidermal pallor, necrosis of keratinocytes, and marked increase in mitosis; these changes wane after 72 hours and are essentially gone by 1 week.[60] Occasionally, similar microscopic changes are seen in the absence of podophyllin therapy.[55] The treatment of choice of these lesions at present is with carbon dioxide laser.[51]

Squamous intraepithelial lesions

The spectrum of abnormalities seen in atypical proliferative squamous lesions of the vulvar skin and generically designated as **vulvar intraepithelial neoplasia (VIN)** is wider than that exhibited by equivalent lesions in the vagina (VAIN) or cervix (CIN).[67,73] Traditionally, they have been segregated into subtypes on the basis of clinical and pathologic features.[64,78] However, both the International Society for the Study of Vulvovaginal Disease and the International Society of Gynecological Pathologists recommend the use of the term VIN and the avoidance of eponymous terminology.

The type of VIN traditionally known as **Bowen's disease** presents as a slightly elevated, plaque-like lesion with a red velvety appearance (Fig. 19.9).[61] It is usually centered in the labia majora, and it may extend to the perineum and anus. Microscopically, there is hyperkeratosis and parakeratosis, acanthosis, and a variable number of multinucleated dyskeratotic cells and abnormal mitoses involving the entire thickness of the epidermis, therefore corresponding to a CIN III-type lesion (Fig. 19.10). The acrotrichium (intraepidermal portion of the hair follicle) is often involved, whereas the acrosyringium (intraepidermal portion of the sweat gland) is usually spared.[77,80] On occasion, the tumor cells

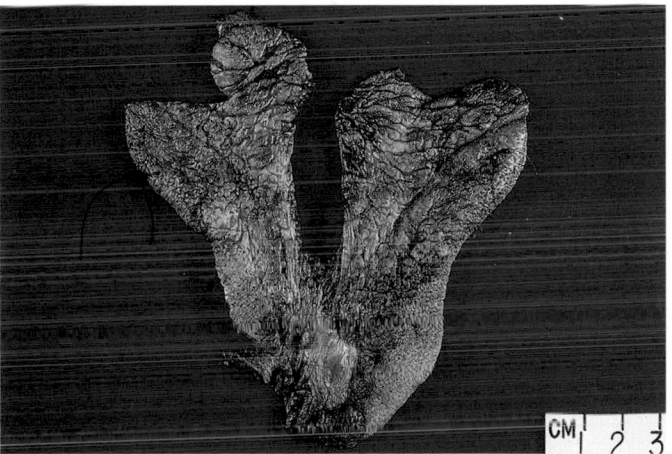

Fig. 19.9 Skinning vulvectomy specimen performed for vulvar intraepithelial neoplasia (VIN).

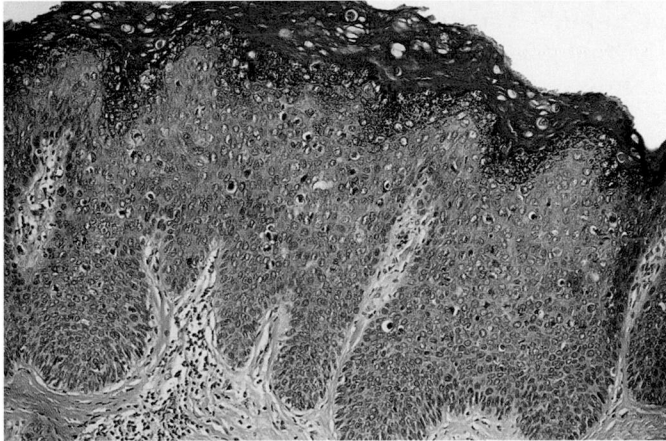

Fig. 19.10 Typical microscopic appearance of VIN III. This form is traditionally known as Bowen's disease.

are arranged in a nested pattern, simulating Paget's disease.[79] The majority of these lesions are aneuploid, and there is a strong association with HPV-16.[68,84]

The type of VIN designated as **bowenoid papulosis** presents as multiple, often pigmented, papules in or near the vulva of young patients. Clinically, they resemble verrucae, small condylomas, or nevi, but microscopically they show a degree of cytologic atypia approaching that of Bowen's disease.[74] The distinction is largely made on clinical grounds, but some microscopic differences have been described, the most important being that in bowenoid keratosis the dysplastic cells are present in a background of relatively orderly epithelial maturation and that the acrotrichium is usually spared.[77,83] Spontaneous regression has been observed, and response to conservative therapy is the rule, even if recurrences are common.[62]

The similarities in morphologic appearance, ploidy pattern and p53 expression between Bowen's disease and bowenoid papulosis, their occasional coexistence,[63] and the fact that both are statistically associated with HPV[86] suggest an etiologic and pathogenetic link between the two. This has led to the proposal to group them under the term *bowenoid dysplasia*[83] and incorporate them into the VIN concept while still acknowledging the important differences they exhibit in age of appearance and risk of development of invasive carcinoma.[69] According to this proposal, such lesions could be diagnosed as VIN, Bowen's disease type and VIN, bowenoid papulosis type, respectively. Another proposed morphologic approach is to divide VIN into two types: warty or bowenoid (which includes both Bowen's disease and bowenoid papulosis) and basaloid or undifferentiated. The latter type, which resembles CIN III, shows a lesser degree of association with HPV than the warty type.[76] Yet another scheme, which is the one currently favored, is to divide VIN into *classic type* (which includes Bowen's disease, bowenoid papulosis, warty VIN, carcinoma in situ, and basaloid VIN) and a *variant*, simplex, or differentiated type.[67] The latter, which is characterized by maturation, variable degrees of hyperplasia, keratinization and parabasal atypia, usually lacks HPV and shows overexpression of p53.[73,87]

Low-grade VIN (VIN1) is usually associated with low-risk viral types; its recognition is aided by MIB-1 staining.[74a]

Clonality studies have shown that low-grade lesions (including bowenoid papulosis) tend to be polyclonal, whereas high-grade lesions (including classic Bowen's disease) are usually clonal.[70,85] Alas, clonality has also been detected in keratosis (squamous hyperplasia) without atypia and even in lichen sclerosus.[82]

The importance of VIN resides in its putative role as precursor of invasive squamous cell carcinoma, particularly in view of the fact that its incidence is on the increase, especially among young women.[71] The evidence for a causal relationship is very strong,[75] with several studies showing a parallel increase in the incidence of two conditions and a heightening of the risk with increased degrees of VIN.[72] It has been stated that, if left untreated, VIN III will progress into invasive carcinoma in approximately 10% of cases, but the rate of transformation varies widely among the different series.[81] The therapy of VIN depends on the age of the patient and the size, configuration, and distribution of the lesions.[81] Localized lesions can be treated by wide local excision or skinning vulvectomy.[65] A relationship has been found between positive margins and local recurrence.[66]

Invasive squamous cell carcinoma

General features

Squamous cell carcinoma accounts for approximately 95% of the malignant tumors of this organ. The mean age at presentation is between 60 and 74 years.[94] Risk factors include number of lifetime sexual partners, cigarette smoking, immunodeficiency, and genital granulomatous disease.[90–92] Vulvar carcinoma is frequently associated with malignant tumors elsewhere in the lower genital tract, notably the uterine cervix.[95] This has led to the hypothesis that the epithelium of the entire lower genital tract (cervix, vagina, vulva, and perianal area) reacts as a single tissue field to certain carcinogenic stimuli, particularly HPV infection.[98,99]

On the basis of epidemiologic and virologic studies, it has been proposed that there are two types of vulvar carcinoma: the most common occurring in older women, not related to HPV, microscopically typical keratinizing squamous cell carcinomas, and associated with keratosis (epithelial hyperplasia); and the other occurring in younger women, frequently HPV-positive, often with a basaloid or warty histology, and associated with VIN (see p. 1487).[88,89,93,96,97,100]

Morphologic, histochemical, immunohistochemical, and molecular genetic features

Invasive squamous cell carcinoma of the vulva arises most commonly on the labia majora but may be found on the labia minora or in the region of the clitoris[101,102] (Fig. 19.11). Microscopically, most cases have a well-differentiated appearance, although those located in the clitoris tend to be more anaplastic (Fig. 19.12A,B). VIN and keratosis are often present at the margins.[108]

Some high-grade squamous cell carcinomas show focal areas of glandular differentiation, analogous to those sometimes seen in squamous cell carcinomas of other organs, and others show pseudoglandular features as a result of acantholysis (Fig. 19.12C). Basaloid squamous cell carcinoma is discussed on p. 1494.[104]

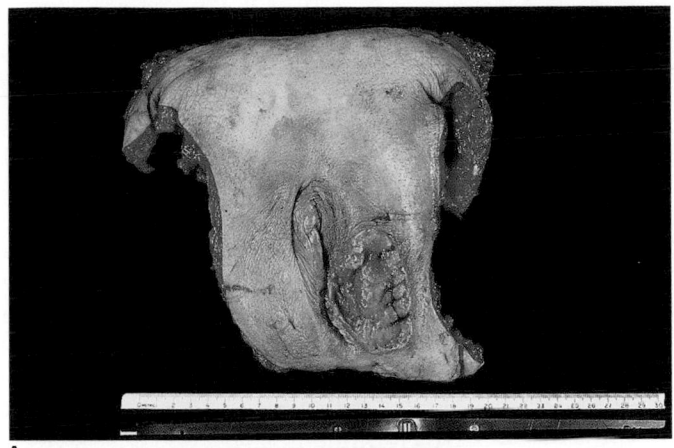

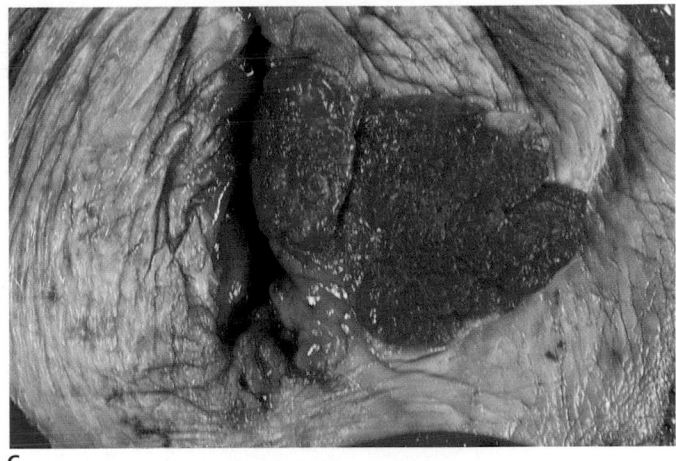

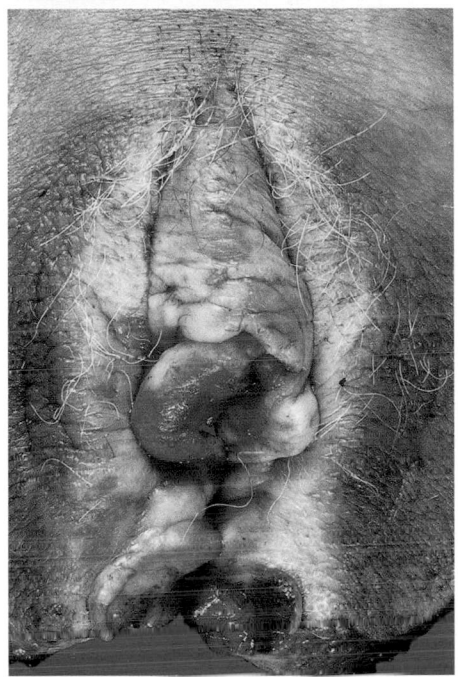

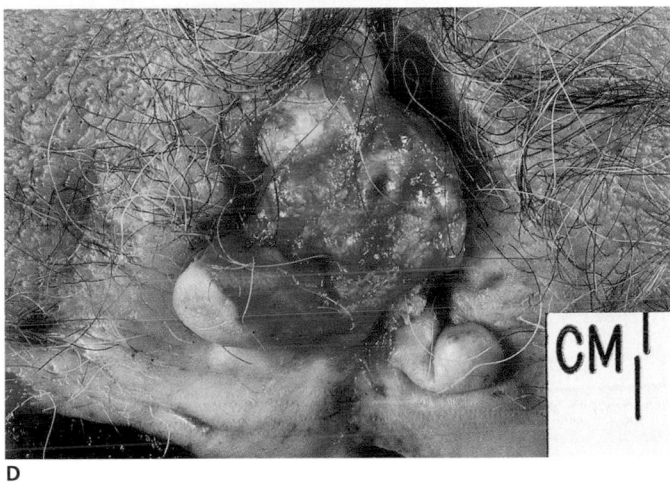

Fig. 19.11 Gross appearance of invasive squamous cell carcinoma of vulva: **A**, tumor of labium majus; **B**, tumor of clitoris, **C**, tumor involving both labia; **D**, huge tumor mass involving all vulvar structures.

The immunohistochemical features of vulvar squamous cell carcinoma are not distinctive. Cytogenetically, loss in 3p and 4p and gain in 3q have been found with increased frequency.[103] The pattern seems to be similar in HPV-positive and HPV-negative cases,[107] and between the invasive component and the adjacent VIN when the latter is present.[106] At the molecular level, aberrations in the expression pattern of several cell cycle-associated proteins have been noted.[109]

p53 overexpression seems to be a late event in vulvar carcinogenesis, and Rb does not seem to play a significant role.[105]

Spread and metastases

Regional lymph node metastases occur in approximately 20% of cases.[112] Tumors of the labia spread first to inguinal lymph nodes, whereas those located in the clitoris may metastasize directly into the deep nodes. It should be noted that ulceration and inflammation in vulvar carcinoma often lead to reactive enlargement of inguinal lymph nodes, which may be confused clinically with metastatic disease.

Lately, the technique of sentinel lymph node biopsy has been introduced as a staging criterion and therapeutic guide for vulvar carcinoma.[110] Preliminary results suggest that the procedure is highly accurate in predicting the inguinofemoral lymph node status of those patients.[111]

Therapy

The usual treatment of invasive carcinoma is radical vulvectomy with bilateral radical inguinal lymph node dissection.[114] Iliac lymphadenectomy and pelvic exenteration are reserved for advanced cases.[117] Conversely, early cases can be treated with a more conservative approach in the form of wide local excision[115]; it has been

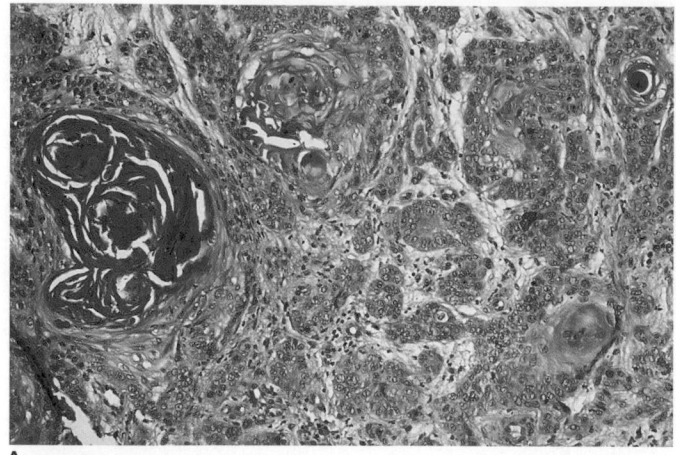

A

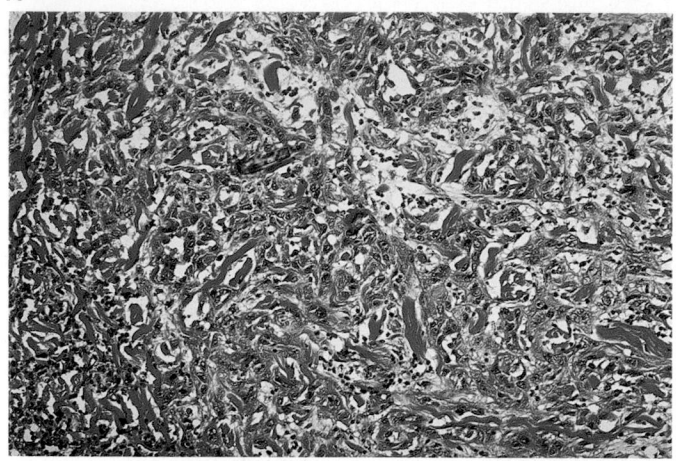

B

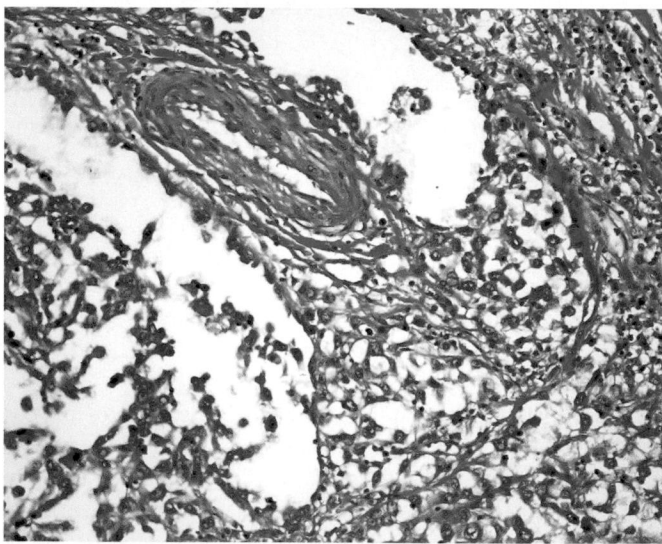

C

Fig. 19.12 Microscopic appearance of invasive squamous cell carcinoma of vulva: **A**, well-differentiated tumor; **B**, poorly differentiated tumor; **C**, acantholytic variety, resulting in pseudoglandular formations.

shown that leaving a 1-cm tumor-free surgical margin results in a high rate of local control.[116] Alternative methods include radiation therapy alone and the combination of wide local excision and radiation therapy.[113,118]

Prognosis

The overall 5-year survival rate in patients treated for vulvar squamous cell carcinoma has been in the 50% to 75% range in most large series.[122,126,134]

The most important prognostic factors are included in the staging system and are represented by tumor diameter, depth of invasion, and lymph node status.[122,124,126,127,129,131] The latter is by far the most significant parameter. In cases with involved nodes, the presence of extracapsular spread and large size of the metastatic focus are poor prognostic indicators.[125,133] Infiltrative margins and vascular invasion in the primary tumor correlate with the incidence of nodal metastases.[121,135] A well-differentiated cytologic appearance and the presence of a keratotic skin with VIN-type changes at the edge of the cancer have been associated with a significantly better prognosis in some series.[123,128]

The observation has also been made that carcinomas associated with a prominent fibromyxoid stromal response are associated with an older age group, poorer survival rate, and more extensive lymph node metastases.[119]

DNA ploidy status and p53 protein overexpression do not have an independent prognostic significance.[120,130,132]

Microinvasive carcinoma

The term **microinvasive carcinoma** has been applied to vulvar carcinomas in which the depth of penetration is less than 5 mm (Fig. 19.13). Some authors have suggested that inguinal lymphadenectomy be foregone in these patients because of the low incidence of lymph node metastases.[143] However, enough exceptions have been reported to cast serious doubts on the wisdom of this recommendation[138,140] and on the very use and definition of the term.[136,137,139,141,144] Perhaps the only invasive carcinomas for which conservative surgery is indicated are those that are both well differentiated and very superficial (3 mm or less).

The point has been made that the presence of eosinophils in VIN may represent a clue to the presence of early invasion, which, therefore, should be searched for with particular care in those areas.[142]

Other microscopic types

Verrucous carcinoma is a reasonably distinctive type of squamous cell carcinoma of the vulva, similar to its more common counterpart in the upper aerodigestive tract. It may grow to huge dimensions, has a typical exophytic appearance, and infiltrates locally (Figs 19.14 and 19.15). Metastases are practically nonexistent,[147,148] and therefore inguinal lymphadenectomy is not necessary.

The differential diagnosis of verrucous carcinoma includes condyloma acuminatum and conventional squamous cell carcinoma. It is distinguished from the former by its generally larger size and the presence of

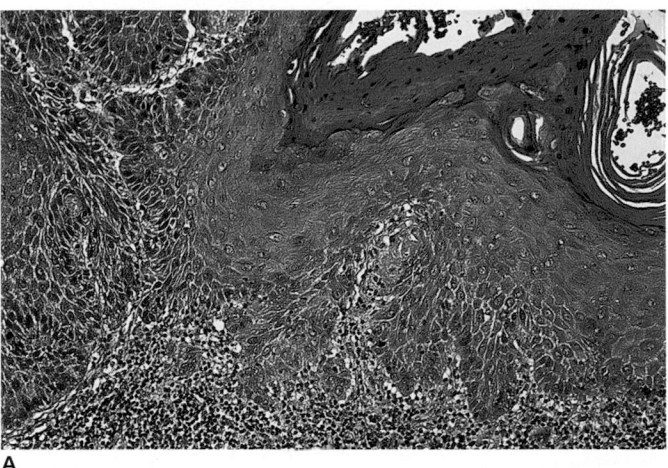
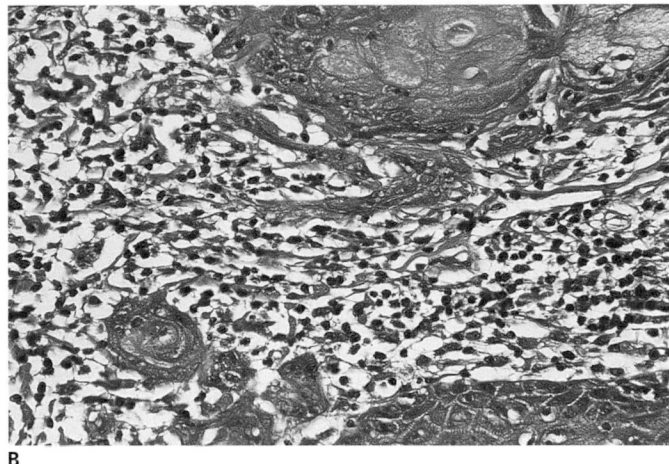

Fig. 19.13 Microinvasive squamous cell carcinoma: **A**, low-power appearance; **B**, high-power view, showing small clusters of tumor cells detaching from the in situ component and invading a heavy inflamed stroma.

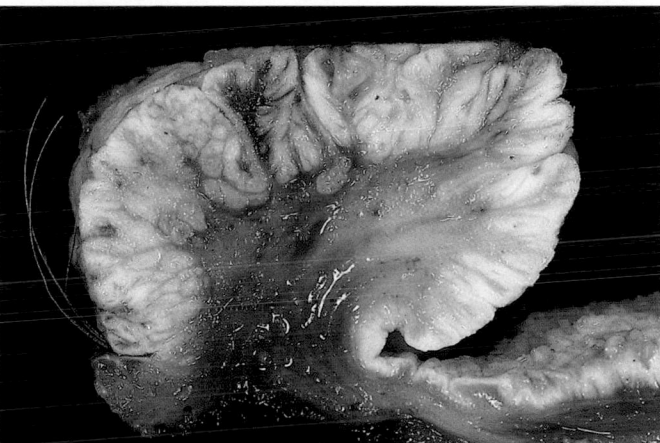

Fig. 19.14 Cut surface of verrucous carcinoma of vulva. (Courtesy of Dr Pedro J Grases Galofrè; from Grases Galofrè PJ: Patologia ginecològica., Bases para el diagnòstico morfològico, Barcelona, Masson, 2002)

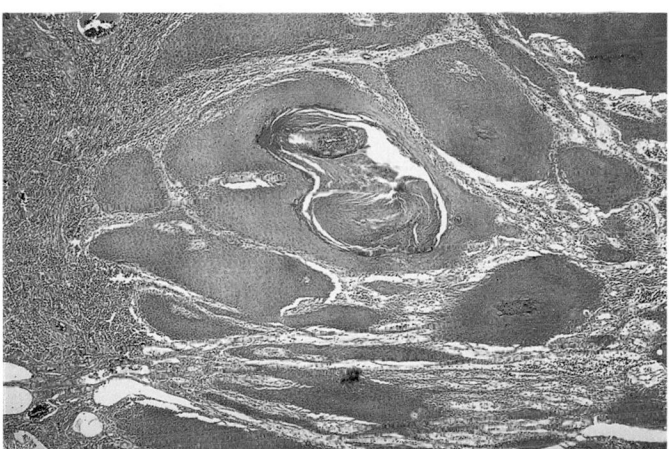

Fig. 19.15 Bulbous pegs of well-differentiated squamous cells infiltrate the stroma in vulvar verrucous carcinoma.

club-shaped fingers of epithelium invading the underlying stroma in a well-circumscribed ("pushing") fashion.[150] The distinction from squamous cell carcinoma rests entirely on two criteria, which often go together: the presence of cytologic atypia and/or a clearly infiltrative pattern of growth. The occurrence of either of these features removes the lesion from the verrucous carcinoma category and puts it into the squamous cell category. Immunohistochemically, staining for keratin is more uniform and homogeneous in verrucous carcinoma than in squamous cell carcinoma.[146] Tumors having the overall appearance of verrucous carcinoma but exhibiting focal squamous cell features as previously defined are designated by some as *hybrid carcinomas*.

Warty carcinoma should not be used as a synonym for verrucous carcinoma, despite the fact that the gross appearance of the latter has sometimes been described as "warty." The term warty carcinoma, if used at all, should be reserved for the squamous cell carcinomas in which the tumor cells display marked pleomorphism, enlargement, atypia, and multinucleation. These features are often associated with koilocytotic atypia in the adjacent epithelium. HPV DNA is often detected in these tumors.[149]

Lymphoepithelioma-like carcinoma has been described in the vulvar region, but the single reported case was negative for Epstein–Barr virus (EBV).[145]

Paget's disease

Paget's disease is a malignant tumor of the vulva that could be viewed either as a sweat gland carcinoma arising primarily from the intraepidermal portion of the glands (acrosyringium) or as a carcinoma of multipotential cells located along the epidermal basal layer that differentiate along glandular (sweat gland) lines, the latter explanation being the most likely. Clinically, it presents as a crusting, elevated scaling erythematous rash in the labia majora, labia minora, and/or perineal skin (Fig. 19.16). Microscopically, the epidermis contains large pale tumor cells that form solid nests, glandular

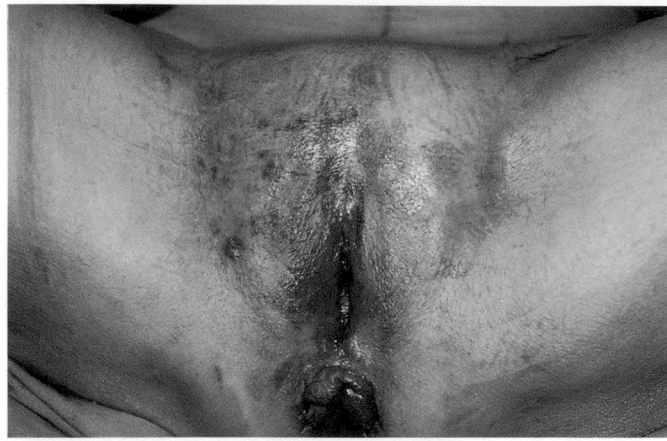

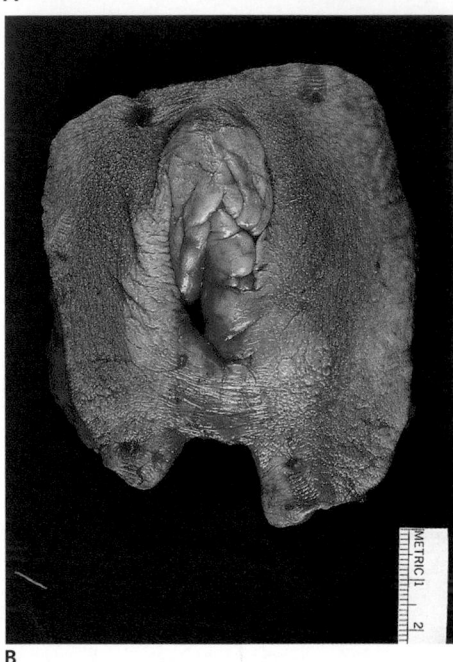

Fig. 19.16 A and **B,** Clinical and gross appearance of vulvar Paget's disease. In both cases the disease is very extensive.

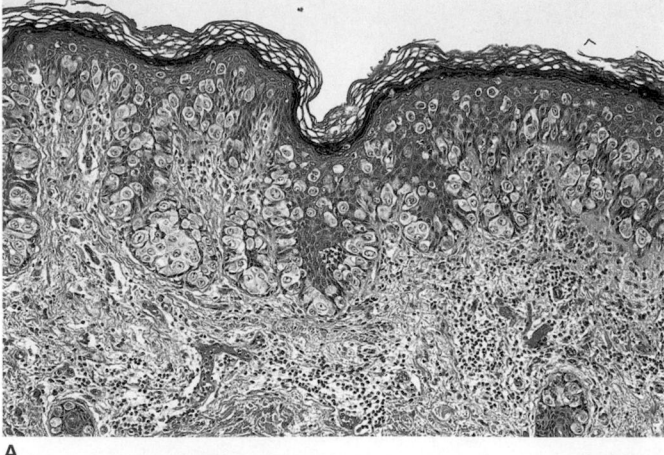

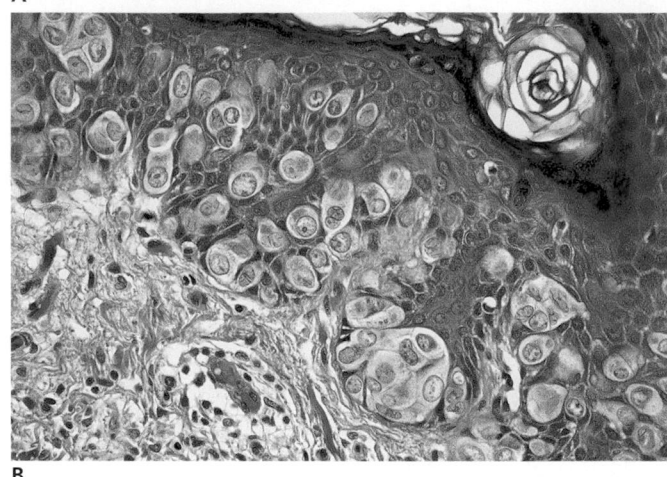

Fig. 19.17 A and **B,** Low- and medium-power appearances of vulvar Paget's disease. The large clear tumor cells are distinct from the malpighian layer.

spaces, or a continuous layer along the epidermal basement membrane and also in pilosebaceous structures and sweat ducts (Fig. 19.17). A cleft often develops between the row of malignant cells and the overlying keratinocytes, resulting in a low-power appearance sometimes reminiscent of an acantholytic suprabasal bulla. Paget's disease can also be misinterpreted as malignant melanoma. It should be noted that the presence of melanin granules in some tumor cells *does not* rule out the diagnosis of Paget's disease. Histochemically, some or all of the tumor cells contain acidic mucus, as evidenced by their positivity for Mayer's mucicarmine and aldehyde fuchsin stains.[165] Immunohistochemically, these mucins are positive for MUC1 and MUC5AC, the latter in striking contrast with Paget's disease of the breast.[171,183] They are also reactive for HGM-45, a marker associated with gastric surface mucous cells.[170] Vulvar Paget's disease also expresses

keratin, EMA, CEA, B72.3, GCDF-15, and a marker of apocrine differentiation[169,175,176,180,181] (Fig. 19.18). S-100 protein is positive in one third of the cases, and HMB-45 is negative.[161,177] Vulvar Paget's disease lacks estrogen and progesterone receptors, but it frequently expresses androgen receptor.[157,159]

Regarding the keratins, the usual profile of vulvar Paget's disease is CK7+/CK20–.[160,179] If it is instead CK20+ (and GCDFP-15 negative), the possibility of an internal malignancy (especially of urothelial nature) should be suspected.[160,182] Confirmation of the latter can be obtained with uroplakin-III immunostains.[154] The ultrastructural features are indicative of glandular rather than keratinocytic or melanocytic differentiation.[178] Overexpression of c-*erb*B-2 oncoprotein and of the *ras* oncogene product p21 has been found in about half the cases.[168,174]

As already indicated, Paget's disease of the vulva differs in several respects from Paget's disease of the breast. The latter is nearly always associated with an underlying carcinoma, which may be intraductal or invasive, and the intraepidermal malignant cells are more often than

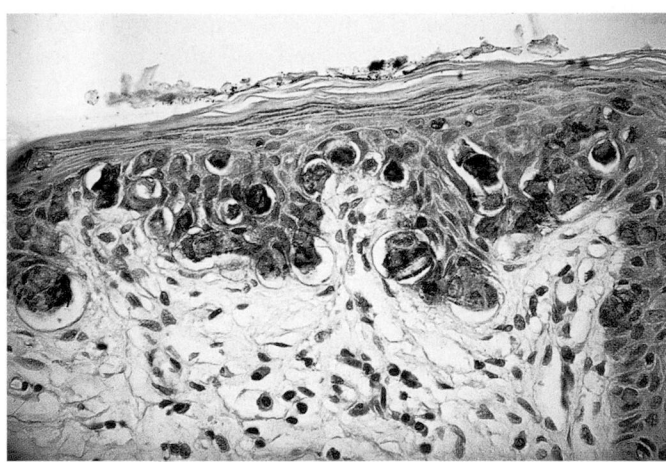

Fig. 19.18 Strong EMA immunoreactivity in cells of Paget's disease.

not mucin-negative. In contrast, the majority of the cases of vulvar Paget's disease are not associated with an invasive underlying carcinoma and are usually (although not always) positive for mucin stains, as previously recorded.[151,166,167] The incidence of underlying invasive carcinoma in vulvar Paget's disease ranges from zero to 30% depending on the series,[156,158,172] with some of the invasive cases being in the microinvasive or minimally invasive (>1 mm) category.[155] It has been claimed that stromal invasion in Paget disease is correlated with p53 overexpression.[183a] Occasionally, Paget's disease is seen in association with VIN, in keeping with its presumed origin from multipotential epidermal basal cells.[164] These cases should be distinguished from the reactive keratinocytic proliferation that sometimes accompanies Paget's disease—not always an easy task.[153]

If no invasive component is found in the resected specimen, the prognosis is good. Metastases do not occur under these circumstances, although local recurrence may supervene, sometimes in the form of invasive carcinoma.[155,163] Therefore, excision should include a margin of normal skin and the underlying subcutaneous tissue. Unfortunately, the microscopic extent of the disease is often greater than that suspected from clinical examination, and this should be taken into account at the time of surgery.[162] Frozen sections are useful to determine the status of the margins[152]; however, this is only minimally related to the incidence of local recurrence.[155] In some instances local recurrence has been seen in the vulvar split-thickness skin graft.[173] Cases of Paget's disease with an invasive component beyond the microinvasive stage have a high incidence of nodal involvement.[155]

Other epithelial tumors

Hidradenoma papilliferum is a benign vulvar tumor that usually presents as a small, well-circumscribed nodule covered by normal skin. Occasionally, it ulcerates through the skin and clinically may simulate carcinoma. Microscopically, it has a complex papillary glandular pattern, with stratification and some degree of pleomorphism; a myoepithelial layer is always apparent (Fig. 19.19). Traditionally, this tumor has been regarded as of sweat gland derivation. However, its remarkable morphologic and immunohistochemical similarity with intraductal papilloma of breast and nipple adenoma suggests an origin from ectopic mammary tissue (see p. 1483). All acceptable examples of this tumor have behaved in a benign fashion.[195,204] However, a case of intraductal carcinoma of mammary-type apocrine epithelium has been reported arising from this tumor.[197]

Benign lesions of skin adnexal type occur in the vulva. These include *syringoma* (Fig. 19.20), *chondroid syringoma* (benign mixed tumor),[186,201] *benign pilar tumor*,[185] *warty*

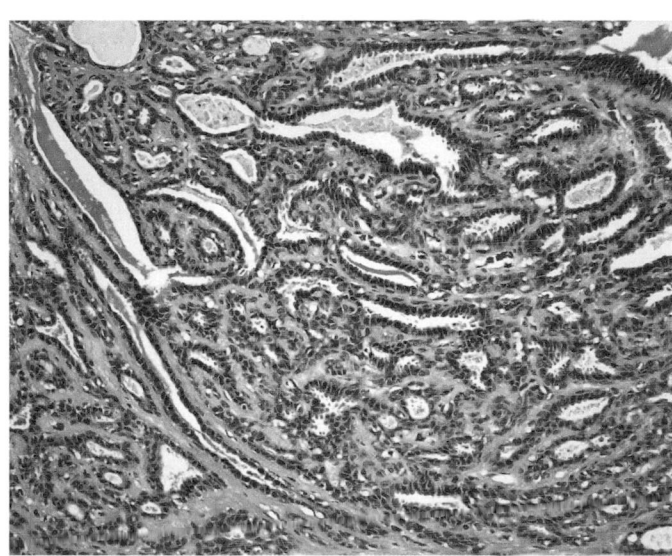

Fig. 19.19 Hidradenoma papilliferum of vulva. This tumor probably arises from ectopic breast tissue.

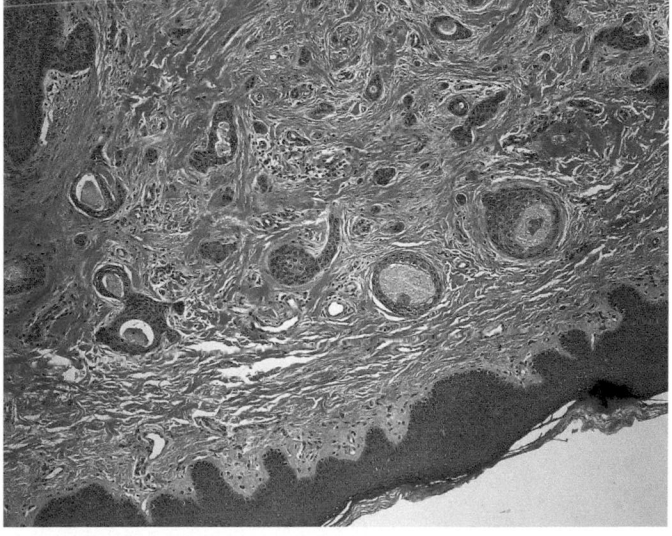

Fig. 19.20 Syringoma of vulva. The tadpole-shaped structures are characteristic.

dyskeratoma,[190] *inverted follicular keratosis,*[202] and *keratoacanthoma.*[200]

Basal cell carcinoma of the vulva usually presents as nodular masses in the labia majora of elderly patients; it may grow very large and ulcerate.[189,192] Its microscopic appearance and behavior are the same as those of basal cell carcinomas elsewhere in the skin; solid, keratotic, and adenoid types have been described (Fig. 19.21). The differential diagnosis includes basaloid carcinoma (see later section) and the basaloid changes sometimes seen as a component of Bowen's disease and invasive squamous cell carcinoma. It should be remembered that, as elsewhere in the skin, basal cell carcinoma may exhibit abrupt squamous differentiation of possible follicular type, a change that does not affect the natural history of the lesion; such tumors should not be referred to as basosquamous carcinomas.

The incidence of nodal metastases in vulvar basal cell carcinoma is extremely low and is largely restricted to the deeply invasive lesions.[198]

Basaloid (squamous cell) carcinoma has an appearance analogous to its counterpart in the upper aerodigestive tract. Peripheral palisading is prominent; in some cases there is a well-developed adenoid cyst-like appearance (Fig. 19.22). These features suggest an early differentiation toward adnexal glandular structures and establish a link with basaloid tumors of other sites.[184,196]

Merkel cell carcinoma has been reported in the vulva, sometimes in association with Bowen's disease.[187,188] Its behavior has been very aggressive.[194]

Sweat gland carcinoma of the vulva, exclusive of Paget's disease, is exceptional; it may present with a variety of morphologic patterns and should be distinguished from metastatic adenocarcinoma.[203] A case has been described showing mucinous and neuroendocrine features,[199] another with features of *malignant myoepithelioma,*[193] and another resembling *polymorphous low-grade adenocarcinoma* of salivary glands.[204a]

Sebaceous carcinoma can occur in the vulva; its appearance is similar to that of its more common counterpart in the head and neck region.[191]

Melanocytic tumors

Melanocytic nevi occur in the vulva, particularly in the labia majora. Those seen in adults are nearly always of intradermal or compound type. Sometimes, a prominent junctional component is seen in nevi of younger women, in which the enlarged junctional nests vary in size, shape, and position, and may lead to an overdiagnosis of malignant melanoma.[207,221] The term *(atypical) genital*

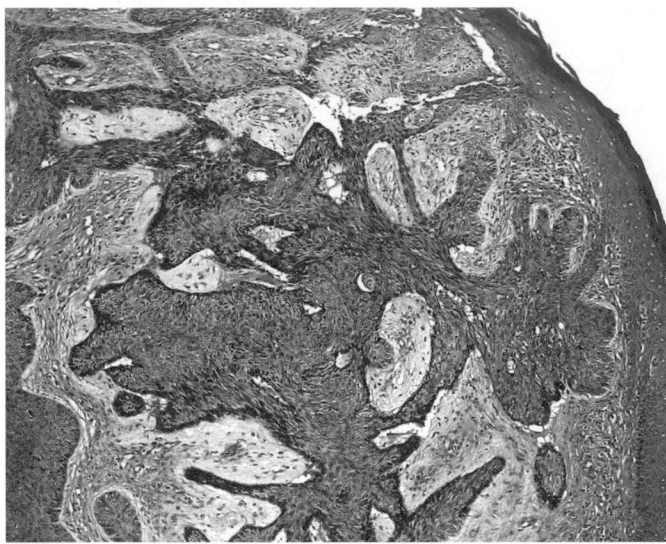

Fig. 19.21 Basal cell carcinoma of vulva. It is important to distinguish this tumor from squamous cell carcinoma, especially the basaloid variant of the latter.

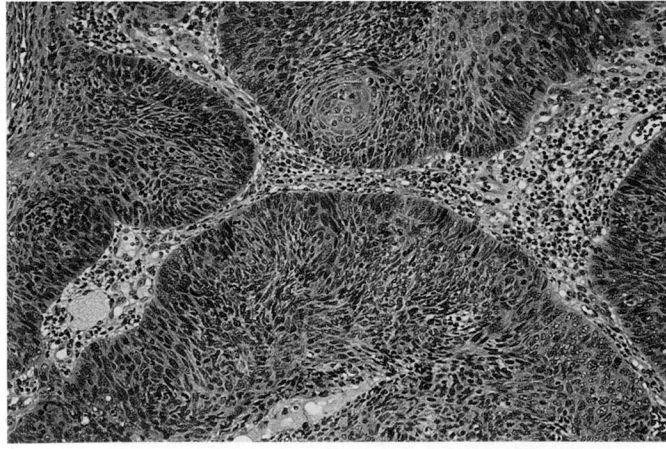

Fig. 19.22 Basaloid squamous cell carcinoma of vulva showing peripheral palisading and deep basophilic staining pattern.

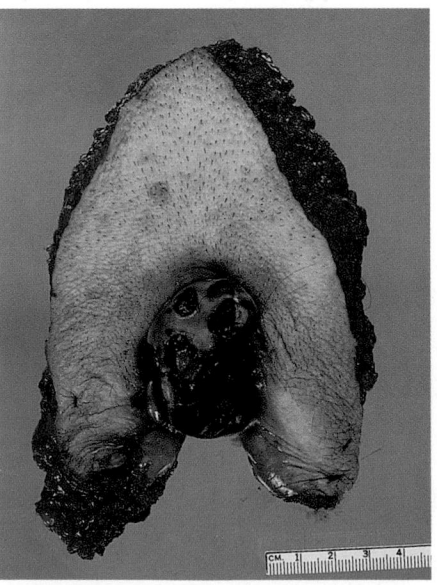

Fig. 19.23 Gross appearance of vulvar malignant melanoma. The tumor is large, polypoid, deeply pigmented, and ulcerated.

nevus is sometimes employed for this microscopically troublesome lesion.[208]

Malignant melanoma is the second most common malignant tumor of the vulva, following squamous cell carcinoma and representing roughly 10% of all malignant tumors at this site.[212,215] The large majority of the patients are older than 50 years at the time of diagnosis, a fact of great importance in the differential diagnosis with genital nevus.[218,219] Most lesions are advanced (Clark's level III or IV) at the time of diagnosis[223] (Fig. 19.23). The microscopic appearance is similar to that of cutaneous melanoma (see Chapter 4) (Fig. 19.24A). Sometimes the tumor is formed of spindle cell growing in fascicles and simulating sarcoma (Fig. 19.24B). The usual treatment is radical vulvectomy with bilateral inguinal lymph node dissection, but small lesions with depths of ≤1.75 mm may be treated with wide local excision.[209–211,214] The overall 5-year survival rate is approximately 35%.[206,217] Lymph node status, level or thickness of the primary tumor, and ulceration are the most important prognostic parameters.[205,213,216,217,220,226] There is some suggestion that the DNA ploidy pattern may also provide prognostic information.[224] Curiously, some cases of vulvar melanomas have been found to be associated with HPV.[222]

Malignant blue nevus of the vulva leading to ovarian metastases has been recorded.[225]

Aggressive angiomyxoma and related lesions

Aggressive angiomyxoma is a soft tissue neoplasm that usually arises within the perineum. It often presents as a vulvar mass and clinically simulates a Bartholin's gland cyst[227,244] (Fig. 19.25). Most patients are in the second or third decade of life, but cases have also been reported in children.[229,247] A similar tumor has been described in the scrotal region in males.[234]

Grossly, the appearance is edematous and ill defined (Fig. 19.26). Microscopically, a hypocellular stroma devoid of atypicality or mitotic activity is seen intermingling with sizable vessels having dilated lumina and frequent hyaline thickening of the adventitia (Fig. 19.27). This tumor is distinguished from the more common and innocuous fibroepithelial polyp described below because of its larger size, deeper location, and lack of bizarre stromal cells. The ultrastructural and immunohistochemical features are those of primitive mesenchymal cells focally exhibiting myoid traits.[236a,243] Stains for acidic mucins are only weakly

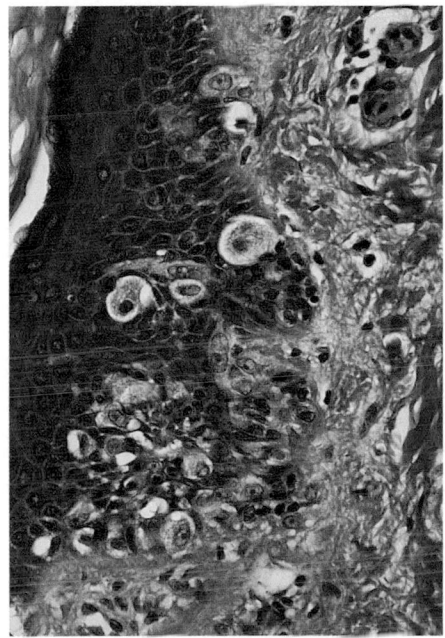

A

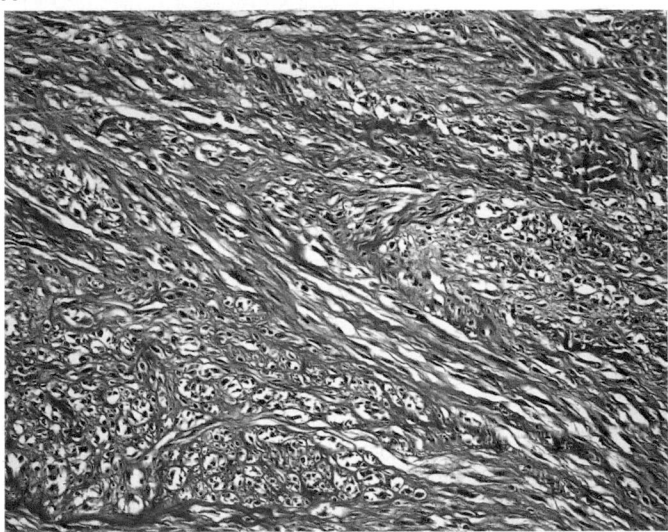

B

Fig. 19.24 Malignant melanoma of vulva: **A**, superficially spreading type, showing typical intraepidermal growth of pagetoid cells; **B**, melanoma growing in the form of fascicles of spindle cells and simulating a mesenchymal neoplasm.

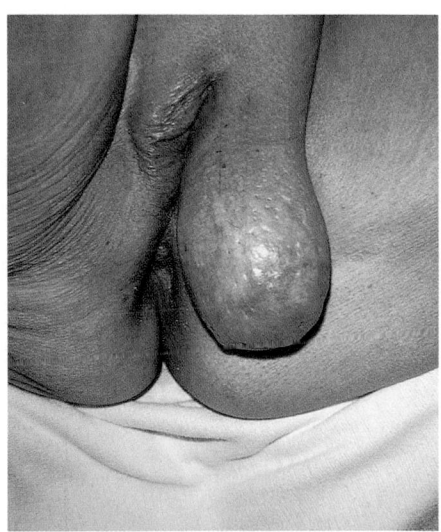

Fig. 19.25 Aggressive angiomyxoma protruding in a polypoid fashion through one of the labia.

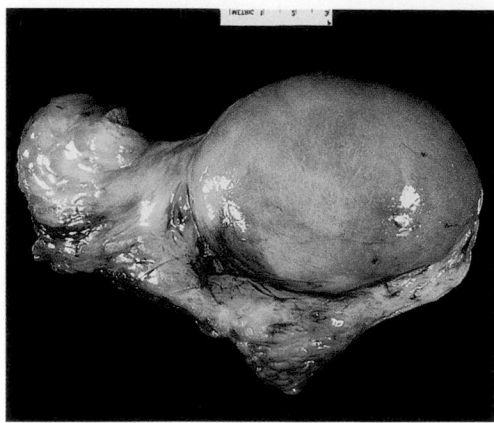

Fig. 19.26 Cut surface of vulvar aggressive angiomyxoma. The tumor is soft, gelatinous, and encapsulated.

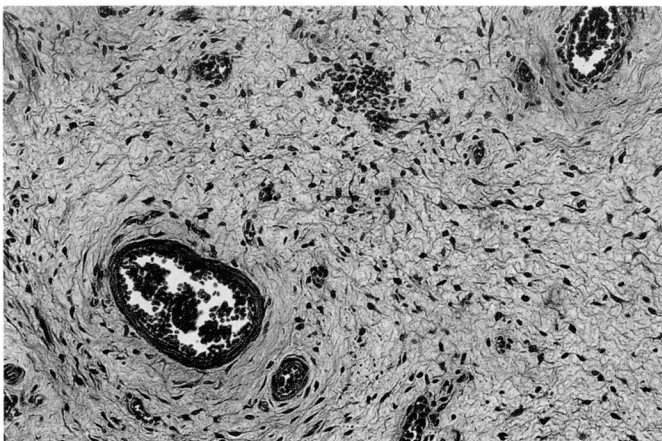

Fig. 19.27 Microscopic appearance of aggressive angiomyxoma. The lesion is hypocellular and features large-sized vessels.

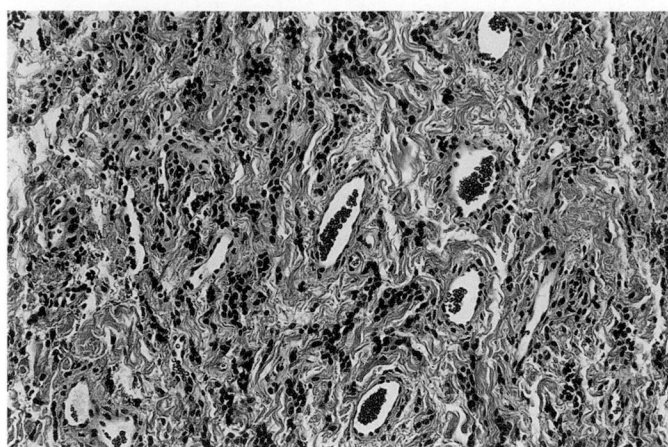

Fig. 19.28 Vulvar angiomyofibroblastoma. Rows of small oval cells are separated by fibrous strands.

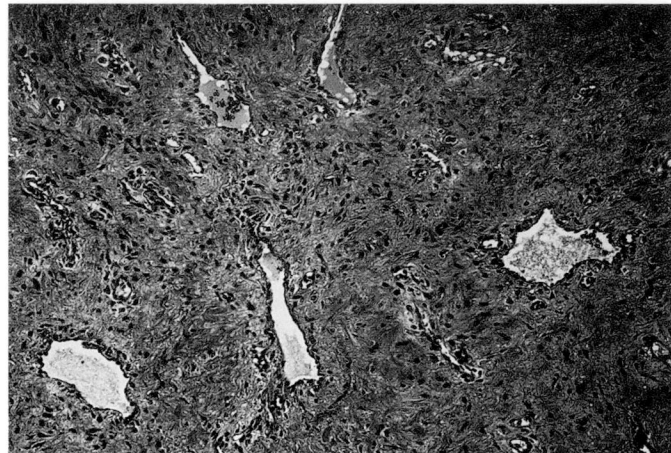

Fig. 19.29 Angiofibroma of vulva. The microscopic appearance is reminiscent of nasopharyngeal angiofibroma. (Slide courtesy of Dr. Robert E. Scully, Boston, MA)

positive, suggesting that this tumor is more edematous than myxoid; as a matter of fact, the differential diagnosis includes vulvar hypertrophy with lymphedema.[245] A case analyzed cytogenetically showed a chromosomal translocation involving the region 12q14–15.[235]

Recurrence in the ischiorectal and retroperitoneal spaces is common, probably because of the difficulties encountered in achieving a complete surgical excision.[228,241] In addition, two typical cases have been reported in association with lung metastases.[227a,242]

Angiomyofibroblastoma is a benign vulvar tumor characterized by alternating hypercellular and hypocellular areas admixed with small blood vessels.[230,231,246] Spindle and plump stromal cells aggregate around the vessels (Fig. 19.28). These cells are immunoreactive for vimentin, desmin, and hormone receptors, but usually not for actin or keratin.[236,237] There may be a component of mature adipose tissue.[234,235] The behavior is benign, with an extremely low rate of local recurrence, but a case with sarcomatous transformation ("angiomyofibrosarcoma") has been reported.[238]

The typical example of myofibroblastoma differs from aggressive angiomyxoma by virtue of its circumscribed borders, higher cellularity, abundance of blood vessels, plump stromal cells, minimal stromal mucin, and rarity of red blood cell extravasation.[230,233] However, enough common features and transitions occur between it and aggressive angiomyxoma to suggest that they are closely related entities.[232,240,243]

Cellular angiofibroma has well-circumscribed margins, like angiomyofibroblastoma. Microscopically, it is composed of uniform, bland, spindle mesenchymal cells accompanied by numerous thick-walled vessels and inconspicuous islands of mature fat (Fig. 19.29). The tumor is cellular and can be mitotically active.[239] Once again, it is hard to escape from the suspicion that this tumor is histogenetically related to the others described in this section.

Other tumors and tumorlike conditions

Fibroepithelial polyp is a superficially located lesion composed of a loose myxoid stroma covered by normal squamous epithelium. Bizarre, stellate, frequently multinucleated cells may be present[248,257,287] (Fig. 19.30). Some lesions are moderately hypercellular. The combination of hypercellularity and bizarre tumor cells may result in overdiagnosis.[283] As in other sites where this lesion occurs, desmin immunoreactivity may be present.[275]

Smooth muscle tumors of both benign and malignant types occur.[280] The leiomyomas include a myxoid variety that can simulate aggressive angiomyxoma,[276] and the leiomyosarcomas include epithelioid and myxoid variants.[277,294] Nielsen et al.[280] evaluated the tumors on the basis of size (≥5 cm), infiltrative margins, mitoses (≥5/10 HPF), and moderate to severe cytologic atypia. Tumors that had three or all four of these features were regarded as leiomyosarcomas, tumors that had none or one of the features were called leiomyomas, and tumors that had two features were designated atypical leiomyomas.

Many other types of nonepithelial tumors and tumorlike conditions have been described in the vulva, most of them of soft tissue type.[279,285] They include *endometriosis, hemangioma, lymphangioma* (which may clinically simulate warts),[274] *angiokeratoma,*[272] *epithelioid hemangioendothelioma,*[293] *glomus tumor*[265,292] and *glomangiomyoma,*[252,292] *angiosarcoma,*[282] *hemangiopericytoma/solitary fibrous tumor*[265a,292] (Fig. 19.31), benign and malignant *granular cell tumors* (some with accompanying pseudoepitheliomatous hyperplasia)[289,302] (Fig. 19.32), *schwannoma,*[263] *neurofibroma(tosis),*[258,262] *malignant peripheral nerve sheath tumor,*[296,297] *sclerosing lipogranuloma,*[266] *yolk sac tumor,*[256] *rhabdomyosarcoma*[260,261] (usually occurring in children and belonging to the embryonal/botryoid variety), *benign lymphoid hyperplasia,*[267] *malignant lymphoma,*[264] *verruciform xanthoma,*[290] *Langerhans' cell histiocytosis,*[250,273] *nodular fasciitis,*[286] *postoperative spindle cell nodule,*[269] *malignant fibrous histiocytoma,*[295] *dermatofibrosarcoma protuberans*[251,253] (including cases with fibrosarcomatous transformation[259]), *Ewing's sarcoma/PNET,*[300] *synovial sarcoma,*[281] *fibromatosis/desmoid tumor* (sometimes

associated with pregnancy),[249,278] *atypical lipomatous tumor,*[283] a lesion resembling *lipoblastoma,*[268] *malignant lymphoma,*[299] *paraganglioma,*[254] *alveolar soft part sarcoma,*[291] and *epithelioid sarcoma.*[298]

The latter tumor is of importance because of its relatively high frequency at this site and the fact that it tends to run a more aggressive course here than in its usual location in the distal extremities. This may at least partially result from the fact that this tumor, when located in the vulva, often exhibits rhabdoid features, known to be associated with an aggressive course.[301] As a matter of fact, it may be difficult to decide whether to designate a given vulvar tumor as an epithelioid sarcoma or as a malignant rhabdoid tumor.[270,288] The term proximal-type epithelioid sarcoma has been employed for this particular situation, of which the vulva is a prime example (see Chapter 25).

Metastases to the vulva usually originate from the cervix (almost 50%), endometrium, kidney, or gastrointestinal tract.[255] Most are expressions of generalized disease.[271] The labius majus is the most common location.[276a]

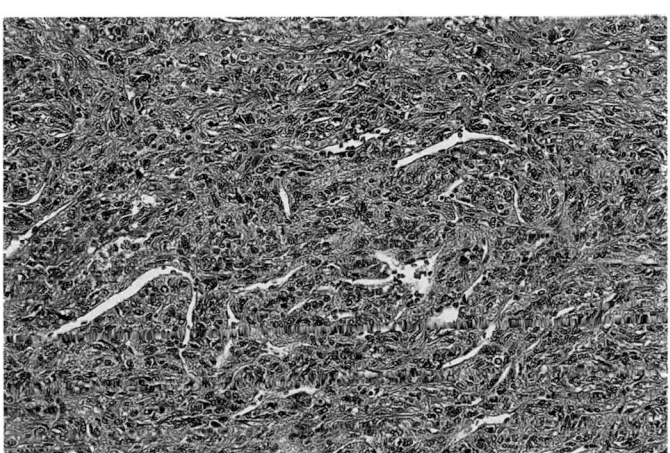

Fig. 19.31 A rare example of hemangiopericytoma/solitary fibrous tumor involving soft tissues of vulva.

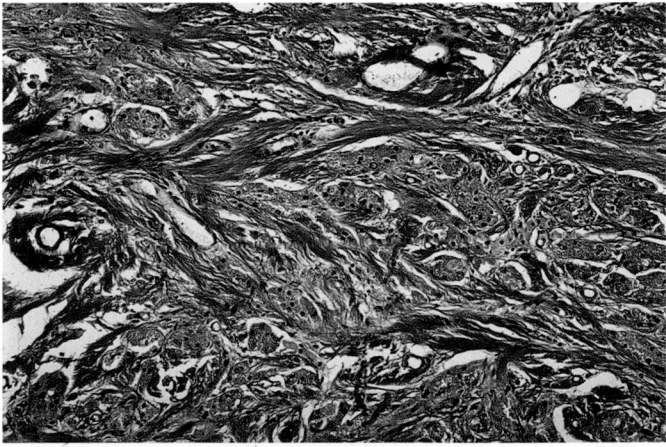

Fig. 19.32 Granular cell tumor of vulva.

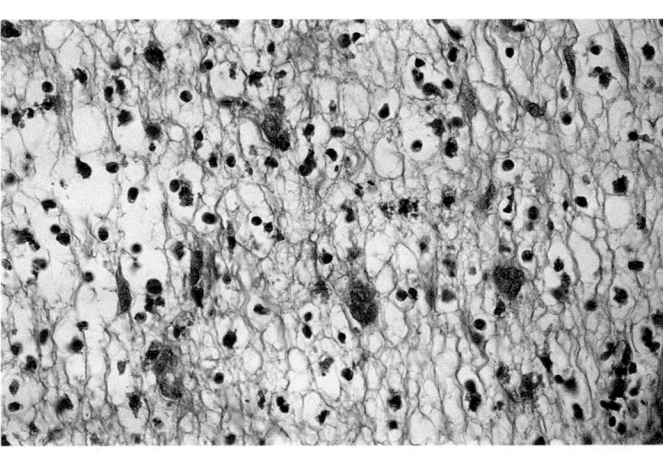

Fig. 19.30 Vulvar polyp containing reactive stromal cells, some of which are multinucleated.

Lesions of Bartholin's glands and related structures

Cysts and abscesses of Bartholin's glands are the result of chronic bacterial inflammation, especially from gonorrhea.[325] The lining of the cyst, which is usually of transitional or squamous type, can be destroyed partially or totally by the inflammatory infiltrate. The nature of the cyst can be established by the presence of residual mucinous glands in the fibrotic and inflamed connective tissue that forms the cyst wall. The secretion product is a nonsulfated sialomucin.[321] Sometimes, extravasation of this mucus into the stroma may induce changes similar to those seen in "mucocele" of the oral cavity.[313] The cyst may be treated by excision or marsupialization.[303] Exceptionally, the inflammatory infiltrate is found to have the features of *malakoplakia*.[320]

Mucous cysts of the *vulvar vestibule* are usually solitary and lined by mucin-producing columnar cells.[314]

Benign tumors and tumorlike conditions of this area include adenoma of minor vestibular glands (which may well represent focal hyperplastic changes secondary to trauma and inflammation),[304] nodular hyperplasia, adenoma, adenomyoma,[316] mucinous cystadenoma,[307] and papilloma.[310]

Carcinomas of Bartholin's gland may take the form of squamous cell carcinoma (the most common) (Fig. 19.33), adenocarcinoma, transitional cell carcinoma (Fig. 19.34), salivary gland-type basal cell adenocarcinoma, small cell carcinoma, and adenoid cystic carcinoma[308,309,311,312,315,317–319,322–324] (Fig. 19.35). Lymph node metastases are common. HPV is often found in the

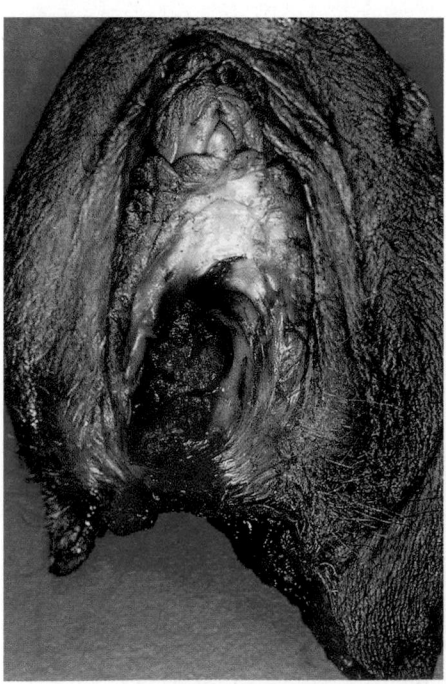

Fig. 19.33 Large carcinoma arising from Bartholin's gland.

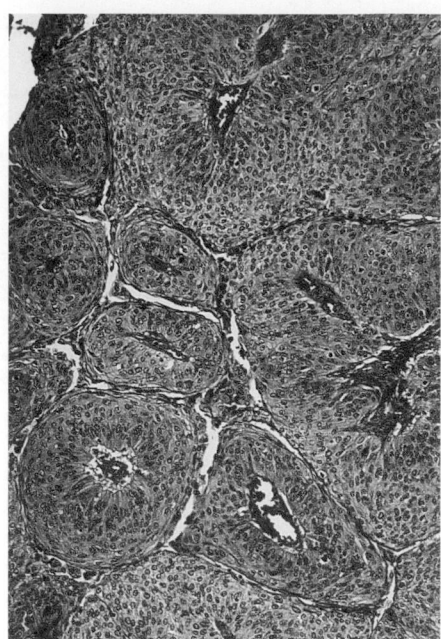

Fig. 19.34 Bartholin's gland carcinoma of transitional cell type.

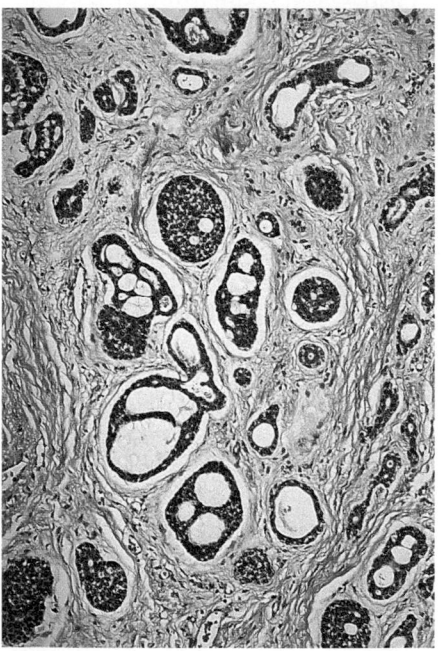

Fig. 19.35 Bartholin's gland carcinoma of adenoid cystic type.

squamous cell type.[312] The overall survival rate is in the neighborhood of 60%.[305,306]

Lesions of the female urethra

Urethral caruncle has the appearance of a small raspberry protruding from the meatus; it bleeds easily and may become infected. It occurs only in the female urethra and is not a true neoplasm but rather a reactive polypoid lesion. Microscopically, chronic inflammatory cells, dilated vessels, and hyperplastic epithelium are seen in varying proportions. Mistaken diagnoses of malignancy can result from overinterpretation of islands of reactive epithelium or scattered bizarre stromal or lymphoid cells.[353] There is a tendency for these lesions to recur following excision, probably because of persistence of the original inciting factors.

Prolapse of the urethral mucosa can occur in childhood and clinically simulate a vulvovaginal neoplasm.[329]

So-called **nephrogenic (mesonephric) adenoma** is a metaplastic change resulting from inflammation rather than a true neoplasm. It is microscopically similar to the more common lesions located in the bladder neck.[332,343] Similarly, an occurrence in the urethra of mucinous epithelium of *colonic* type can also be explained on a metaplastic basis, although a congenital origin is also possible.[335]

Villous adenoma has been reported in the urethra in association with tubulovillous adenoma and adenocarcinoma of the rectum.[340]

Urethral carcinoma occurs in elderly patients and presents with bleeding or dysuria.[328,336] The majority of the cases arise from the meatus, at the junction of the transitional and squamous epithelium. In a series of 35 cases, 19 were anterior (vulvourethral), 4 were posterior (vesicourethral), and 12 involved the entire urethra.[348]

Microscopically, most urethral carcinomas are of squamous cell type.[376,341] Other types include transitional cell carcinoma, columnar/mucinous adenocarcinoma,[339] signet ring adenocarcinoma,[349] and clear cell (mesonephroid) adenocarcinoma.[345,352] Interestingly, nearly half of the carcinomas reported as arising in urethral diverticula have been adenocarcinomas of either conventional or clear cell type.[330,331] Some of the urethral adenocarcinomas have been associated with adenomatous hyperplasia of the periurethral glands.[327] HPV has been detected by PCR techniques in a high proportion of urethral carcinomas.[351]

The prognosis of urethral carcinoma is relatively poor, except when the disease is limited to the anterior portion of the urethra.[338] In one large series, the 5-, 10-, and 15-year actuarial survival rates were 41%, 31% and 22%, respectively.[333] The usual treatment is radiation therapy,[333,347,350] but, depending on their size and location, they can also be treated by surgery alone or surgery plus irradiation.[334,342]

Leiomyoma of the urethra, although extremely unusual, is the most common type of benign mesenchymal tumor at this site.[348a]

Malignant melanoma of the urethra is a highly aggressive neoplasm that is treated by total urethrectomy with bilateral inguinal lymph node dissection.[337,346]

Malignant lymphoma can exceptionally present as a urethral tumor.[344]

Metastatic tumors in the urethra usually originate in other portions of the female genital tract, particularly endometrium.[341]

References

Normal anatomy

1 McLean JM. Anatomy and physiology of the vulvar area. In Ridley CM (ed.): The vulva. New York, 1988, Churchill Livingstone.

2 Rorat E, Ferenczy A, Richart RM. Human Bartholin gland, duct, and duct cyst. Arch Pathol 1975, **99**: 367–374.

3 van der Putte SC. Anogenital "sweat" glands. Histology and pathology of a gland that may mimic mammary glands. Am J Dermatopathol 1991, **13**: 557–567.

4 Wilkinson EJ, Hardt NS. Vulva. In Sternberg S (ed.): Histology for pathologists, ed. 2. Philadelphia, 1997, Lippincott-Raven, pp. 851–866.

Congenital abnormalities

5 Burger RA, Marcuse PM. Fibroadenoma of the vulva. Am J Clin Pathol 1954, **24**: 965–968.

6 Chulia MT, Paya A, Niveiro M, Ceballos S, Aranda FI. Phyllodes tumor in ectopic breast tissue of the vulva. Int J Surg Pathol 2001, **9**: 81–83.

7 Chung-Park M, Zheng Liu C, Giampoli EJ, Emery JD, Shalodi A. Mucinous adenocarcinoma of ectopic breast tissue of the vulva. Arch Pathol Lab Med 2002, **126**: 1216–1218.

8 Di Bonito L, Patriarca S, Falconieri G. Aggressive "breast-like" adenocarcinoma of vulva. Pathol Res Pract 1992, **188**: 211–214.

9 Guerry RL, Pratt-Thomas HR. Carcinoma of supernumerary breast of vulva with bilateral mammary cancer. Cancer 1976, **38**: 2570–2574.

10 Rose PG, Roman LD, Reale FR, Tak WK, Hunter RE. Primary adenocarcinoma of the breast arising in the vulva. Obstet Gynecol 1990, **76**: 537–539.

11 Simon KE, Dutcher JP, Runowicz CD, Wiernik PH. Adenocarcinoma arising in vulvar breast tissue. Cancer 1988, **62**: 2234–2238.

12 Sington JD, Manek S, Hollowood K. Fibroadenoma of the mammary-like glands of the vulva. Histopathology 2002, **41**: 563–565.

13 Tbakhi A, Cowan DF, Kumar D, Kyle D. Recurring phylloides tumor in aberrant breast tissue of the vulva. Am J Surg Pathol 1993, **17**: 946–950.

14 van der Putte SC. Mammary-like glands of the vulva and their disorders. Int J Gynecol Pathol 1994, **13**: 150–160.

Inflammatory diseases

15 Alexander LJ, Shields TL. Squamous cell carcinoma of the vulva secondary to granuloma inguinale. Arch Dermatol 1953, **67**: 395–402.

16 Barnes R, Masood S, Lammert N, Young RH. Extragenital granuloma inguinale mimicking a soft-tissue neoplasm. A case report and review of the literature. Hum Pathol 1990, **21**: 559–561.

17 Bassa AG, Hoosen AA, Moodley J, Bramdev A. Granuloma inguinale (donovanosis) in women. An analysis of 61 cases from Durban, South Africa. Sex Transm Dis 1993, **20**: 164–167.

18 Chadha S, Gianotten WL, Drogendijk AC, Schultz WC, Blindeman LA, van der Meijden WI. Histopathologic features of vulvar vestibulitis. Int J Gynecol Pathol 1998, **17**: 7–11.

19 Douglas CPL. Lymphogranuloma venereum and granuloma inguinale of the vulva. J Obstet Gynaecol Br Commonw 1962, **69**: 871–880.

20 Guerrieri C, Ohlsson E, Rydén G, Westermark P. Vulvitis granulomatosa. A cryptogenic chronic inflammatory hypertrophy of vulvar labia related to cheilitis granulomatosa and Crohn's disease. Int J Gynecol Pathol 1995, **14**: 352–359.

21 Haidopoulos D, Rodalakis A, Stefanidis K, Blachos G, Sotiropoulou M, Diakomanolis E. Behcet's disease: part of the

differential diagnosis of the ulcerative vulva. Clin Exp Obstet Gynecol 2002, **29**: 219–221.

22 Koteen H. Lymphogranuloma venereum. Medicine (Baltimore) 1945, **24**: 1–69.

23 Kremer M, Nussenson E, Steinfeld M, Zuckerman P. Crohn's disease of the vulva. Am J Gastroenterol 1984, **79**: 376–378.

24 Lavery HA, Pinkerton JHM, Sloan J. Crohn's disease of the vulva. Two further cases. Br J Dermatol 1985, **113**: 359–363.

25 Mabey D, Peeling RW. Lymphogranuloma venereum. Sex Transm Infect 2002, **78**: 90–92.

26 O'Farrell N. Donovanosis. Sex Transm Infect 2002, **78**: 452–457.

27 Oriel JD. Infective conditions of the vulva. In Ridley CM, Neill SM (eds): The vulva, ed. 2. Oxford, 1999, Blackwell Science, pp. 71–120.

28 Prayson RA, Stoler MH, Hart WR. Vulvar vestibulitis. A histopathologic study of 36 cases, including human papillomavirus in situ hybridization analysis. Am J Surg Pathol 1995, **19**: 154–160.

29 Rainey R. The association of lymphogranuloma inguinale and cancer. Surgery 1954, **35**: 221–235.

30 Ramdial PK, Kharsany AB, Reddy R, Chetty R. Transepithelial elimination of cutaneous vulval granuloma inguinale. J Cutan Pathol 2000, **27**: 493–499.

31 Roberts DB. Necrotizing fascitis of the vulva. Am J Obstet Gynecol 1987, **157**: 568–571.

32 Sakane T, Takeno M, Suzuki N, Inaba G. Behcet's disease. N Engl J Med 1999, **341**: 1284–1291.

33 Vettraino IM, Merritt DF. Crohn's disease of the vulva. Am J Dermatopathol 1995, **17**: 410–413.

So-called "chronic vulvar dystrophies"

34 Ambros RA, Malfetano JH, Carlson JA, Mihm MC. Non-neoplastic epithelial alterations of the vulva: recognition assessment and comparisons of terminologies used among the various specialities. Mod Pathol 1997, **10**: 401–408.

35 Carlson JA, Ambros R, Malfetano J, Ross J, Grabowski R, Lamb P, Figge H, Mihm MC. Vulvar lichen sclerosus and squamous cell carcinoma: a cohort, case control, and investigational study with historical perspective; implications for chronic inflammation and sclerosis in the development of neoplasia. Hum Pathol 1998, **29**: 932–948.

36 Carlson JA, Lamb P, Malfetano J, Ambros RA, Mihm MC. Clinicopathologic comparison of vulvar and extragenital lichen sclerosus: histologic variants, evolving lesions, and etiology of 141 cases. Mod Pathol 1998, **11**: 844–854.

37 Fung MA, LeBoit PE. Light microscopic criteria for the diagnosis of early vulvar lichen sclerosus: a comparison with lichen planus. Am J Surg Pathol 1998, **22**: 473–478.

38 Hart WR, Norris JH, Helwig EB. Relation of lichen sclerosus et atrophicus of the vulva to development of carcinoma. Obstet Gynecol 1975, **45**: 369–377.

39 Janovski NA, Ames S. Lichen sclerosus et atrophicus of the vulva. A poorly understood disease entity. Obstet Gynecol 1963, **22**: 697–708.

40 Kim YT, Thomas NF, Kessis TD, Wilkinson EJ, Hedrick L, Cho KR. p53 mutations and clonality in vulvar carcinomas and squamous hyperplasias: evidence suggesting that squamous hyperplasias do not serve as direct precursors of human papillomavirus-negative vulvar carcinomas. Hum Pathol 1996, **27**: 389–395.

41 Kiryu H, Ackerman AB. A critique of current classification of vulvar diseases. Am J Dermatopathol 1990, **12**: 377–392.

42 Laseano EF, Montes LF,Mazzini MA, Lichen sclerosus et atropicus in childhood. Report of 6 cases.Obstet Gynecol 1964, **24**: 872–877.

43 Lawrence WD. Non-neoplastic epithelial disorders of the vulva (vulvar dystrophies). Historical and current perspectives. Pathol Annu 1993, **28** (Pt 2): 23–51.

44 Lee ES, Allen D, Scurry J. Pseudoepitheliomatous hyperplasia in lichen sclerous of the vulva. Int J Gynecol Pathol 2002, **22**: 57–62.

45 Regauer S, Reich O, Beham-Schmid C. Monoclonal gamma-T-cell receptor rearrangement in vulvar lichen sclerosus and squamous cell carcinomas. Am J Pathol 2002, **160**: 1035–1045.

46 Rodke G, Friedrich EG Jr, Wilkinson EJ. Malignant potential of mixed vulvar dystrophy (lichen sclerosus associated with squamous cell hyperplasia). J Reprod Med 1988, **33**: 545–550.

47 Scurry J, Whitehead J, Healey M. Histology of lichen sclerosus varies according to site and proximity to carcinoma. Am J Dermatpathol 2002, **23**: 413–418.

48 Wallace HJ. Lichen sclerosus et atrophicus. Trans St. John's Hosp Dermatol Soc 1971, **57**: 9–30.

Human papilloma virus and vulvar pathology

49 Sawchuk WS. Vulvar manifestations of human papillomavirus infection. Dermatol Clin 1992, **10**: 405–414.

Condyloma and seborrheic keratosis

50 Crum CP, Fu YS, Levine RU, Richart RM, Townsend DE, Fenoglio CM. Intraepithelial squamous lesions of the vulva. Biologic and histologic criteria for the distinction of condylomas from vulvar intraepithelial neoplasia. Am J Obstet Gynecol 1982, **144**: 77–83.

51 Ferenczy A. Laser treatment of patients with condylomata and squamous carcinoma precursors of the lower female genital tract. CA Cancer J Clin 1987, **37**: 334–347.

51a Hongwei B, Cviko A, Granter S, Yuan L, Betensky RA, Crum CP. Immunophenotypic and viral (Human papillomavirus) correlates of vulvar seborrheic keratosis. Hum Pathol 2003, **34**: 559–564.

52 McLachlin CM, Kozakewich H, Craighill M, O'Connell B, Crum CP. Histologic correlates of vulvar human papillomavirus infection in children and young adults. Am J Surg Pathol 1994, **18**: 728–735.

53 McLachlin CM, Mutter GL, Crum CP. Multinucleated atypia of the vulva. Report of a distinct entity not associated with human papillomavirus. Am J Surg Pathol 1994, **18**: 1233–1239.

54 McMillan A, Bishop PE, Fletcher S. An immunohistological study of condylomata acuminata. Histopathology 1990, **17**: 45–52.

55 Nucci MR, Genest DR, Tate JE, Sparks CK, Crum CP. Pseudobowenoid change of the vulva: a histologic variant of untreated condyloma acuminatum. Mod Pathol 1996, **9**: 375–379.

56 Nuovo GJ, O'Connell M, Blanco JS. Levine RU, Silverstein SJ. Correlation of histology and human papillomavirus DNA detection in condyloma acuminatum and condyloma-like vulvar lesions. Am J Surg Pathol 1989, **13**: 700–706.

57 Pirog EC, Chen YT, Isacson C. MIB-1 immunostaining is a beneficial adjunct test for accurate diagnosis of vulvar condyloma acuminatum. Am J Surg Pathol 2000, **24**: 1393–1399.

58 Quinn TR, Young RH. Epidermolytic hyperkeratosis in the lower female genital tract: an uncommon simulant of mucocutaneous papillomavirus infection – a report of two cases. Int J Gynecol Pathol 1997, **16**: 163–168.

59 Shevchuk MM, Richart RM. DNA content of condyloma acuminatum. Cancer 1982, **49**: 489–492.

60 Wade TR, Ackerman AB. The effects of resin of podophyllin on condyloma acuminatum. Am J Dermatopathol 1984, **6**: 109–122.

Squamous intraepithelial lesions

61 Abell MR, Gosling JRG. Intraepithelial and infiltrating carcinoma of the vulva. Bowen's type. Cancer 1961, **14**: 318–329.

62 Berger BW, Hori Y. Multicentric Bowen's disease of the genitalia. Spontaneous regression of lesions. Arch Dermatol 1978, **114**: 1698–1699.

63 Bergeron C, Neghashfar Z, Canaan C, Shah K, Fu Y, Ferenczy A. Human papillomavirus type 16 in intraepithelial neoplasia

(bowenoid papulosis) and coexistent invasive carcinoma of the vulva. Int J Gynecol Pathol 1987, **6:** 1–11.

64 Crum CP, Liskow A, Petras P, Keng WC, Frick HC II. Vulvar intraepithelial neoplasia (severe atypia and carcinoma in situ). A clinicopathologic analysis of 41 cases. Cancer 1984, **54:** 1429–1434.

65 Forney JP, Morrow CP, Townsend DE, DiSaia PJ. Management of carcinoma in situ of the vulva. Am J Obstet Gynecol 1977, **127:** 801–806.

66 Friedrich EG Jr, Wilkinson EJ, Fu YS. Carcinoma in situ of the vulva. A continuing challenge. Am J Obstet Gynecol 1980, **136:** 830–843.

67 Hart WR. Vulvar intraepithelial neoplasia: historical aspects and current status. Int J Gynecol Pathol 2001, **20:** 16–30.

68 Hording U, Daugaard S, Junge J, Lundvall F. Human papillomavirus and multifocal genital neoplasia. Int J Gynecol Pathol 1997, **15:** 230–234.

69 Husseinzadeh N, Newman NJ, Wesseler TA. Vulvar intraepithelial neoplasia. A clinicopathological study of carcinoma in situ of the vulva. Gynecol Oncol 1989, **33:** 157–163.

70 Inagaki H, Nonaka M, Eimoto T. Bowenoid papulosis showing polyclonal nature. Diagn Mol Pathol 1999, **7:** 122–126.

71 Jones RW. Vulval intraepithelial neoplasia: current perspectives. Eur J Gynaecol Oncol 2001, **22:** 393–402.

72 Joura EA, Losch A, Haider-Angeler MG, Breitenecker G, Leodolter S. Trends in vulvar neoplasia. Increasing incidence of vulvar intraepithelial neoplasia and squamous cell carcinoma of the vulva in young women. J Reprod Med 2000, **45:** 613–615.

73 Kaefner HK, Tate JE, McLachlin CM, Crum CP. Vulvar intraepithelial neoplasia. Morphological phenotype, papillomavirus DNA, and coexisting invasive carcinoma. Hum Pathol 1995, **26:** 147–154.

74 Kimura A. Condylomata acuminata with pigmented papular lesions. Dermatologica 1980, **160:** 390–397.

74a Logani S, Lu D, Quint WGV, Ellenson L, Pirog EC. Low-grade vulvar and vaginal intraepithelial neoplasia: correlation of histologic features with human papillomavirus DNA detection and MIB-1 immunostaining. Mod Pathol 2003, **16:** 735–741.

75 Naik R, Cross P, de Barros Lopes A, Robson P, Monaghan J. Lectins in the vulva II. Vulvar intraepithelial neoplasia and squamous cell carcinoma. Int J Gynecol Pathol 1998, **17:** 162–170.

76 Park JS, Jones RW, McLean MR, Currie JL, Woodruff JD, Shah DV, Kurman RJ. Possible etiologic heterogeneity of vulvar intraepithelial neoplasia. A correlation of pathologic characteristics with human papillomavirus detection by in situ hybridization and polymerase chain reaction. Cancer 1991, **67:** 1599–1607.

77 Patterson JW, Kao GF, Graham JH, Helwig EB. Bowenoid papulosis. A clinicopathologic study with ultrastructural observations. Cancer 1986, **57:** 823–836.

78 Prat J. Pathology of vulvar intraepithelial lesions and early invasive carcinoma. Hum Pathol 1991, **22:** 877–883.

79 Raju RR, Goldblum JR, Hart WR. Pagetoid squamous cell carcinoma in situ (pagetoid Bowen disease) of the external genitalia. Int J Gynecol Pathol 2003, **22:** 127–135.

80 Shatz P, Bergeron C, Wilkinson EJ, Arseneau J, Ferenczy A. Vulvar intraepithelial neoplasia and skin appendage involvement. Obstet Gynecol 1989, **74:** 769–774.

81 Sykes P, Smith N, McCormick P, Frizelle FA. High-grade vulval intraepithelial neoplasia (VIN 3): a retrospective analysis of patient characteristics, management outcome and relationship to squamous cell carcinoma of the vulva 1989-1999. Aust N Z J Obstet Gynaecol 2002, **42:** 69–74.

82 Tate J, Mutter G, Boynton K, Crum C. Monoclonal origin of vulvar intraepithelial neoplasia and some vulvar hyperplasia. Am J Pathol 1997, **150:** 315–322.

83 Ulbright TM, Stehman FB, Roth LM, Ehrlich CE, Ransburg RC. Bowenoid dysplasia of the vulva. Cancer 1982, **50:** 2910–2919.

84 van Beurden M, ten Kate FW, Tjong-A-Hung SP, de Craen AJ, van der Vange N, Lammes FB, ter Schegget J. Human papillomavirus DNA in multicentric vulvar intraepithelial neoplasia. Int J Gynecol Pathol 1998, **17:** 12–16.

85 Wada H, Enomoto T, Yoshino K, Ozaki K, Kurachi H, Nomura T, Murata Y, Kim N, Weinrich S, Lea-Chou E, Lopez-Uribe D, Shroyer KR. Immunohistochemical localization of telomerase hTERT protein and analysis of clonality in multifocal vulvar intraepithelial neoplasia. Am J Clin Pathol 2000, **114:** 371–379.

86 Walts AE, Koeffler HP, Said JW. Localization of p53 protein and human papillomavirus in anogenital squamous lesions. Immunohistochemical and in situ hybridization studies in benign, dysplastic, and malignant epithelia. Hum Pathol 1993, **24:** 1238–1242.

87 Yang B, Hart WR. Vulvar intraepithelial neoplasia of the simplex (differentiated) type: a clinicopathologic study including analysis of HPV and p53 expression. Am J Surg Pathol 2000, **24:** 429–441.

Invasive squamous cell carcinoma
General features

88 Andersen WA, Franquemont DW, Williams J, Taylor PT, Crum CP. Vulvar squamous cell carcinoma and papillomaviruses. Two separate entities? Am J Obstet Gynecol 1991, **165:** 329–335.

89 Bloss JD, Liao SY, Wilczynski SP, Macri C, Walker J, Peake M, Berman ML. Clinical and histologic features of vulvar carcinomas analyzed for human papillomavirus status. Evidence that squamous cell carcinoma of the vulva has more than one etiology. Hum Pathol 1991, **22:** 711–718.

90 Brinton LA, Nasca PC, Mallin K, Baptiste MS, Wilbanks GD, Richart RM. Case-control study of cancer of the vulva. Obstet Gynecol 1990, **75:** 859–866.

91 Carter J, Carlson J, Fowler J, Hartenbach E, Adcock L, Carson L, Twiggs LB. Invasive vulvar tumors in young women. A disease of the immunosuppressed? Gynecol Oncol 1993, **51:** 307–310.

92 Crum CP. Carcinoma of the vulva. Epidemiology and pathogenesis. Obstet Gynecol 1992, **79:** 448–454.

93 Fox H, Wells M. Recent advances in the pathology of the vulva. Histopathology 2003, **42:** 209–216.

94 Hopkins MP, Nemunaitis-Keller J. Carcinoma of the vulva. Obstet Gynecol Clin North Am 2001, **28:** 791–804.

95 Jimerson GK, Merrill JA. Multicentric squamous malignancy involving both cervix and vulva. Cancer 1970, **26:** 150–153.

96 Kim YT, Thomas NF, Kessis TD, Wilkinson EJ, Hedrick L, Cho KR. p53 mutations and clonality in vulvar carcinomas and squamous hyperplasias: evidence suggesting that squamous hyperplasias do not serve as direct precursors of human papillomavirus-negative vulvar carcinomas. Hum Pathol 1996, **27:** 389–395.

97 Kurman RJ, Trimble CL, Shah KV. Human papillomavirus and the pathogenesis of vulvar carcinoma. Curr Opin Obstet Gynecol 1992, **4:** 582–585.

98 Mitchell MF, Prasad CJ, Silva EG, Rutledge FN, McArthur MC, Crum CP. Second genital primary squamous neoplasms in vulvar carcinoma. Viral and histopathologic correlates. Obstet Gynecol 1993, **81:** 13–18.

99 Sherman KJ, Daling JR, Chu J, McKnight B, Weiss NS. Multiple primary tumours in women with vulvar neoplasms. A case-control study. Br J Cancer 1988, **57:** 423–427.

100 Toki T, Kurman RJ, Park JS, Kessis T, Daniel RW, Shah KV. Probable non-papillomavirus etiology of squamous cell carcinoma of the vulva in older women. A clinicopathologic study using in situ hybridization and polymerase chain reaction. Int J Gynecol Pathol 1991, **10:** 107–125.

Morphologic, histochemical, immunohistochemical, and molecular genetic features

101 Czernobilsky B, Gat A, Evron R, Dgani R, Ben-Hur H, Lifschitz-Mercer B. Carcinoma of the clitoris. A histologic study with cytokeratin profile. Int J Gynecol Pathol 1995, **14:** 274–278.

102 Dvoretsky PM, Bonfiglio TA. The pathology of vulvar squamous cell carcinoma and verrucous carcinoma. Pathol Annu 1986, 21(Pt 2): 23–45.

103 Jee KJ, Kim YT, Kim KR, Kim HS, Yan A, Knuutila S. Loss in 3p and 4p and gain 3q are concomitant aberrations in squamous cell carcinoma of the vulva. Mod Pathol 2001, 14: 377–381.

104 Lasser A, Cornog JL, Morris JM. Adenoid squamous cell carcinoma of the vulva. Cancer 1974, 33: 224–227.

105 Lerma E, Matias-Guiu X, Lee SJ, Prat J. Squamous cell carcinoma of the vulva: study of ploidy, HPV, p53, and pRB. Int J Gynecol Pathol 2002, 18: 191–197.

106 Lin MC, Mutter GL, Trivijisilp P, Boynton KA, Sun D, Crum CP. Patterns of allelic loss (LOH) in vulvar squamous carcinomas and adjacent non-invasive epithelia. Am J Pathol 1998, 152: 1313–1318.

107 Pinto AP, Lin MC, Mutter GL, Sun D, Villa LL, Crum CP. Allelic loss in human papillomavirus-positive and -negative vulvar squamous cell carcinoma. Am J Pathol 1999, 154: 1009–1015.

108 Zaino RJ, Husseinzadeh N, Nahhas W, Mortel R. Epithelial alterations in proximity to invasive squamous carcinoma of the vulva. Int J Gynecol Pathol 1982, 1: 173–184.

109 Zamparelli A, Mascuillo V, Bovicelli A, Santini D, Ferrandina G, Minimo C, Terzano P, Costa S, Cinti C, Ceccarelli C, Mancuso S, Scambia G, Bovicelli L, Giordano A. Expression of cell-cycle-associated proteins pRB2/p 130 and p27kip1 in vulvar squamous cell carcinomas. Hum Pathol 2001, 32: 4–9.

Spread and metastases

110 Cady B. Sentinel lymph node procedure in squamous cell carcinoma of the vulva. J Clin Oncol 2000, 18: 2795–2797.

111 de Hullu JA, Hollema H, Piers DA, Herheijen RH, Van Diest PJ, Mourits MJ, Aalders JG, van der Zee AG. Sentinel lymph node procedure is highly accurate in squamous cell carcinoma of the vulva. J Clin Oncol 2000, 18: 2811–2816.

112 Figge DC, Tamimi HK, Greer BE. Lymphatic spread in carcinoma of the vulva. Am J Obstet Gynecol 1985, 152: 387–394.

Therapy

113 Coleman RL, Santoso JT. Vulvar carcinoma. Curr Treat Options Oncol 2000, 1: 177–190.

114 Creasman WT, Phillips JL, Menck HR. The National Cancer Data Base Report on early stage invasive vulvar carcinoma. The American College of Surgeons Commission on Cancer and the American Cancer Society. Cancer 1997, 80: 505–513.

115 Hacker NF, Van der Velden J. Conservative management of early vulvar cancer. Cancer 1993, 71: 1673–1677.

116 Heaps JM, Fu YS, Montz FJ, Hacker NF, Berek JS. Surgical-pathologic variables predictive of local recurrence in squamous cell carcinoma of the vulva. Gynecol Oncol 1990, 38: 309–314.

117 Hopkins MP, Morley GW. Pelvic exenteration for the treatment of vulvar cancer. Cancer 1992, 70: 2835–2838.

118 Perez CA, Grigsby PW, Galakatos A, Swanson R, Camel HM, Kao MS, Lockett MA. Radiation therapy in management of carcinoma of the vulva with emphasis on conservation therapy. Cancer 1993, 71: 3707–3716.

Prognosis

119 Ambros RA, Melfetano JH, Mihm MC. Clinicopathologic features of vulvar squamous cell carcinomas exhibiting prominent fibromyxoid stromal response. Int J Gynecol Pathol 1996, 15: 137–145.

120 Ballouk F, Ambros RA, Malfetano JH, Ross JS. Evaluation of prognostic indicators in squamous carcinoma of the vulva including nuclear DNA content. Mod Pathol 1993, 6: 371–375.

121 Binder SW, Huang I, Fu YS, Hacker NF, Berek JS. Risk factors for the development of lymph node metastasis in vulvar squamous cell carcinoma. Gynecol Oncol 1990, 37: 9–16.

122 Donaldson ES, Powell DE, Hanson MB, van Nagell JR. Prognostic parameters in invasive vulvar cancer. Gynecol Oncol 1981, 11: 184–190.

123 Gosling JRG, Abell MR, Prolette BM, Loughrin TD. Infiltrative squamous cell (epidermoid) carcinoma of vulva. Cancer 1961, 14: 330–343.

124 Heaps JM, Fu YS, Montz FJ, Hacker NF, Berek JS. Surgical-pathologic variables predictive of local recurrence in squamous cell carcinoma of the vulva. Gynecol Oncol 1990, 38: 309–314.

125 Homesley HD. Lymph node findings and outcome in squamous cell carcinoma of the vulva (editorial). Cancer 1994, 74: 2399–2402.

126 Homesley HD, Bundy BN, Sedlis A, Yordan E, Berek JS, Jahsan A, Mortel R. Assessment of current International Federation of Gynecology and Obstetrics staging of vulvar carcinoma relative to prognostic factors for survival (a Gynecologic Oncology Group study). Am J Obstet Gynecol 1991, 164: 997–1003.

127 Homesley HD, Bundy BN, Sedlis A, Yordan E, Berek JS, Jahsan A, Mortel R. Prognostic factors for groin node metastasis in squamous cell carcinoma of the vulva (a Gynecologic Oncology Group study). Gynecol Oncol 1993, 49: 279–283.

128 Husseinzadeh N, Wesseler T, Schneider D, Schellhas H, Nahhas W. Prognostic factors and the significance of cytologic grading in invasive squamous cell carcinoma of the vulva. A clinicopathologic study. Gynecol Oncol 1990, 36: 192–199.

129 Husseinzadeh N, Zaino R, Nahhas WA, Mortel R. The significance of histologic findings in predicting nodal metastases in invasive squamous cell carcinoma of the vulva. Gynecol Oncol 1983, 16: 105–111.

130 Kagie MJ, Kenter GG, Tollenaar RA, Hermans J, Trimbos JB, Fleuren GJ. p53 protein overexpression, a frequent observation in squamous cell carcinoma of the vulva and in various synchronous vulvar epithelia, has no value as a prognostic parameter. Int J Gynecol Pathol 1997, 16: 124–130.

131 Kunschner A, Kanbour AI, David B. Early vulvar carcinoma. Am J Obstet Gynecol 1978, 132: 599–606.

132 Lerma E, Matias-Guiu X, Lee SJ, Prat J. Squamous cell carcinoma of the vulva: study of ploidy, HPV, p53, and pRB. Int J Gynecol Pathol 2002, 18: 191–197.

133 Paladini D, Cross P, Lopes A, Monaghan JM. Prognostic significance of lymph node variables in squamous cell carcinoma of the vulva. Cancer 1994, 74: 2491–2496.

134 Perez CA, Grigsby PW, Galakatos A, Swanson R, Camel HM, Kao MS, Lockett MA. Radiation therapy in management of carcinoma of the vulva with emphasis on conservation therapy. Cancer 1993, 71: 3707–3716.

135 Ross MJ, Ehrmann RL. Histologic prognosticators in stage I squamous cell carcinoma of the vulva. Obstet Gynecol 1987, 70: 774–784.

Microinvasive carcinoma

136 Buckley CH, Butler EB, Fox H. Vulvar intraepithelial neoplasia and microinvasive carcinoma of the vulva. J Clin Pathol 1984, 37: 1201–1211.

137 Buscerna J, Woodruff JD, Parmley TH, Genadry R. Carcinoma in situ of the vulva. Obstet Gynecol 1980, 55: 225–230.

138 Dipaola GR, Gomez-Rueda N, Arrighi L. Relevance of microinvasion of carcinoma of the vulva. Obstet Gynecol 1975, 45: 647–649.

139 Dvoretsky PM, Bonfiglio TA, Helmkamp BF, Ramsey G, Chuang C, Beecham JB. The pathology of superficially invasive, thin vulvar squamous cell carcinoma. Int J Gynecol Pathol 1984, 3: 331–342.

140 Nakao CY, Nolan JF, DiSaia PJ, Futoran R. Microinvasive epidermoid carcinoma of the vulva with an unexpected natural history. Am J Obstet Gynecol 1974, 120: 1122–1123.

141 Sedlis A, Homesley H, Bundy BN, Marshall R, Yordan E, Hacker

N, Lee JH, Whitney C. Positive groin lymph nodes in superficial squamous cell vulvar cancer. A gynecologic oncology group study. Am J Obstet Gynecol 1987, **156:** 1159–1164.

142 Spiegel GW. Eosinophils as a marker for invasion in vulvar squamous neoplastic lesions. Int J Gynecol Pathol 2002, **21:** 108–116.

143 Wharton JT, Gallager S, Rutledge FN. Microinvasive carcinoma of the vulva. Am J Obstet Gynecol 1974, **118:** 159–162.

144 Wilkinson EJ, Rico MJ, Pierson KK. Microinvasive carcinoma of the vulva. Int J Gynecol Pathol 1982, **1:** 29–39.

Other microscopic types

145 Axelsen SM, Stamp IM. Lymphoepithelioma-like carcinoma of the vulvar region. Histopathology 1995, **27:** 281–283.

146 Brisigotti M, Moreno A, Murcia C, Matias-Guiu X, Prat J. Verrucous carcinoma of the vulva. A clinicopathologic and immunohistochemical study of five cases. Int J Gynecol Pathol 1989, **8:** 1–7.

147 Japaze H, Van Dinh T, Woodruff JD. Verrucous carcinoma of the vulva. Study of 24 cases. Obstet Gynecol 1982, **60:** 462–466.

148 Kraus FT, Perez-Mesa C. Verrucous carcinoma. Clinical and pathologic study of 105 cases involving oral cavity, larynx and genitalia. Cancer 1966, **19:** 26–38.

149 Kurman RJ, Toki T, Schiffman MH. Basaloid and warty carcinomas of the vulva. Distinctive types of squamous cell carcinoma frequently associated with human papillomaviruses. Am J Surg Pathol 1993, **17:** 133–145.

150 Partridge EE, Murad T, Shingleton HM, Austin JM, Hatch KD. Verrucous lesions of the female genitalia. I. Giant condylomata. Am J Obstet Gynecol 1980, **137:** 412–418.

Paget's disease

151 Alguacil-Garcia A, O'Connor R. Mucin-negative biopsy in extra-mammary Paget's disease. A diagnostic problem. Histopathology 1989, **15:** 429–431.

152 Bergen S, Di Saia PJ, Liao SY, Berman ML. Conservative management of extramammary Paget's disease of the vulva. Gynecol Oncol 1989, **33:** 151–156.

153 Brainard J, Hart WR. Proliferative epidermal lesions associated with anogenital Paget's disease. Am J Surg Pathol 2000, **24:** 543–552.

154 Brown HM, Wilkinson EJ. Uroplakin-III to distinguish primary vulvar Paget disease from Paget disease secondary to urothelial carcinoma. Hum Pathol 2002, **33:** 545–548.

155 Crawford D, Nimmo M, Clement PB, Thomson T, Benedet JL, Miller D, Gilks CB. Prognostic factors in Paget's disease of the vulva: a study of 21 cases. Int J Gynecol Pathol 1999, **18:** 351–359.

156 Curtin JP, Rubin SC, Jones WB, Hoskins WJ, Lewis JL Jr. Paget's disease of the vulva. Gynecol Oncol 1990, **39:** 374–377.

157 Diaz de Leon E, Carcangiu ML, Prieto VG, McCue PA, Burchette JL, To G, Norris BA, Kovatich AJ, Sanchez RL, Krigman HR, Gatalica Z. Extramammary Paget's disease is characterized by the consistent lack of estrogen and progesterone receptors but frequently expresses androgen receptor. Am J Clin Pathol 2000, **113:** 572–575.

158 Fenn ME, Morley GW, Abell MR. Paget's disease of vulva. Obstet Gynecol 1971, **38:** 660–670.

159 Fujimoto A, Takata M, Hatta N, Takehara K. Expression of structurally unaltered androgen receptor in extramammary Paget's disease. Lab Invest 2000, **80:** 1465–1471.

160 Goldblum JR, Hart WR. Vulvar Paget's disease: a clinicopathologic and immunohistochemical study of 19 cases. Am J Surg Pathol 1997, **21:** 1178–1187.

161 Guarner J, Cohen C, De Rose PB. Histogenesis of extramammary and mammary Paget cells. An immunohistochemical study. Am J Dermatopathol 1989, **11:** 313–318.

162 Gunn RA, Gallager HS. Vulvar Paget's disease. A topographic study. Cancer 1980, **46:** 590–594.

163 Hart WR, Millman JB. Progression of intraepithelial Paget's disease of the vulva to invasive carcinoma. Cancer 1977, **40:** 2333–2337.

164 Hawley IC, Husain F, Pryse-Davies J. Extramammary Paget's disease of the vulva with dermal invasion and vulval intra-epithelial neoplasia. Histopathology 1991, **18:** 374–376.

165 Helm KF, Goellner JR, Peters MS. Immunohistochemical stains in extramammary Paget's disease. Am J Dermatopathol 1992, **14:** 402–407.

166 Helwig EB, Graham JH. Anogenital (extramammary) Paget's disease. A clinicopathological study. Cancer 1963, **16:** 387–403.

167 Jones RE Jr, Austin C, Ackerman AB. Extramammary Paget's disease. A critical reexamination. Am J Dermatopathol 1979, **1:** 101–132.

168 Keatings L, Sinclair J, Wright C, Corbett IP, Watchorn C, Hennessy C, Angus B, Lennard T, Horne CH. c-erbB-2 oncoprotein expression in mammary and extramammary Paget's disease. An immunohistochemical study. Histopathology 1990, **17:** 243–247.

169 Kohler S, Smoller BR. Gross cystic disease fluid protein-15 reactivity in extramammary Paget's disease with and without associated internal malignancy. Am J Dermatopathol 1996, **18:** 118–123.

170 Kondo Y, Kashima K, Daa T, Fujiwara S, Nakayama I, Yokoyama S. The ectopic expression of gastric mucin in extramammary and mammary Paget's disease. Am J Surg Pathol 2002, **26:** 617–623.

171 Kuan SF, Montag AG, Hart J, Krausz T, Recant W. Differential expression of mucin genes in mammary and extramammary Paget's disease. Am J Surg Pathol 2001, **25:** 1469–1477.

172 Lee SC, Roth LM, Ehrlich C, Hall JA. Extramammary Paget's disease of the vulva. A clinicopathologic study of 13 cases. Cancer 1977, **39:** 2540–2549.

173 Misas JE, Larson JE, Podezaski E, Manetta A, Mortel R. Recurrent Paget disease of the vulva in a split-thickness graft. Obstet Gynecol 1990, **76:** 543–544.

174 Mori O, Hachisuka H, Nakano S, Sasai Y, Shiku H. Expression of ras p21 in mammary and extramammary Paget's disease. Arch Pathol Lab Med 1990, **114:** 858–861.

175 Nadji M, Morales AR, Girtanner RE, Ziegels-Weissman J, Penneys NS. Paget's disease of the skin. A unifying concept of histogenesis. Cancer 1982, **50:** 2203–2206.

176 Olson DJ, Fujimura M, Swanson P, Okagaki T. Immunohistochemical features of Paget's disease of the vulva with and without adenocarcinoma. Int J Gynecol Pathol 1991, **10:** 285–295.

177 Reed W, Oppedal BR, Eeg Larsen T. Immunohistology is valuable in distinguishing between Paget's disease, Bowen's disease and superficial spreading malignant melanoma. Histopathology 1990, **16:** 583–588.

178 Roth LM, Lee SC, Ehrlich CE. Paget's disease of the vulva. A histogenetic study of five cases including ultrastructural observations and review of the literature. Am J Surg Pathol 1977, **1:** 193–206.

179 Smith KJ, Tuur S, Corvette D, Lupton BP, Skelton HG. Cytokeratin 7 staining in mammary and extramammary Paget's disease. Mod Pathol 1997, **10:** 1069–1074.

180 Urabe A, Matsukuma A, Shimizu N, Nishimura M, Wada H, Hori Y. Extramammary Paget's disease. Comparative histopathologic studies of intraductal carcinoma of the breast and apocrine adenocarcinoma. J Cutan Pathol 1990, **17:** 257–265.

181 Watanabe S, Ohnishi T, Takahashi H, Ishibashi Y. A comparative study of cytokeratin expression in Paget cells located at various sites. Cancer 1993, **72:** 3323–3330.

182 Wilkinson EJ, Brown HM. Vulvar Paget disease of urothelial origin: a report of three cases and a proposed classification of vulvar Paget disease. Hum Pathol 2002, **33:** 549–554.

183 Yoshii N, Kitajima S, Yonezawa S, Matsukita S, Setoyama M,

Kanzaki T. Expression of mucin core proteins in extramammary Paget's disease. Pathol Int 2002, **52:** 390–399.

183a Zhang C, Xhang P, Sung J, Lawrence WD. Overexpression of p53 is correlated with stromal invasion in extramammary Paget's disease of the vulva. Hum Pathol 2003, **34:** 880–885.

Other epithelial tumors

184 Abell MR. Adenocystic (pseudoadenomatous) basal cell carcinoma of vestibular glands of vulva. Am J Obstet Gynecol 1963, **86:** 470–482.

185 Avinoach I, Zirkin HJ, Glezerman M. Proliferating trichilemmal tumor of the vulva. Case report and review of the literature. Int J Gynecol Pathol 1989, **8:** 163–168.

186 Carneiro SJC, Gardner HL, Knox JM. Syringoma. Three cases with vulvar involvement. Obstet Gynecol 1972, **39:** 95–99.

187 Chen KTK. Merkel's cell (neuroendocrine) carcinoma of the vulva. Cancer 1994, **73:** 2186–2191.

188 Copeland LJ, Cleary K, Sneige N, Edwards CL. Neuroendocrine (Merkel cell) carcinoma of the vulva. A case report and review of the literature. Gynecol Oncol 1985, **22:** 367–378.

189 Cruz-Jimenez PR, Abell MR. Cutaneous basal cell carcinoma of vulva. Cancer 1975, **36:** 1860–1868.

190 Duray PH, Merino MJ, Axiotis C. Warty dyskeratoma of the vulva. Int J Gynecol Pathol 1983, **2:** 286–293.

191 Escalonilla P, Grilli R, Canamero M, Soriano ML, Farina MDC, Manzarbeitia F, Sainz R, Matsukura T, Requena L. Sebaceous carcinoma of the vulva. Am J Dermatopathol 1999, **21:** 468–472.

192 Fetsch JF, Laskin WB, Tavassoli FA. Superficial angiomyxoma (cutaneous myxoma): a clinicopathologic study of 17 cases arising in the genital region. Int J Gynecol Pathol 1998, **16:** 325–334.

193 Hinze P, Feyler S, Berndt J, Knolle J, Katenkamp D. Malignant myoepithelioma of the vulva resembling a rhabdoid tumour. Histopathology 1999, **35:** 50–54.

194 Loret de Mola JR, Hudock PA, Steinetz C, Jacobs G, Macfee M, Abdul-Karim FW. Merkel cell carcinoma of the vulva. Gynecol Oncol 1993, **51:** 272–276.

195 Meeker JH, Neubecker RD, Helwig EF. Hidradenoma papilliferum. Am J Clin Pathol 1962, **37:** 182–195.

196 Merino MJ, LiVolsi VA, Schwartz PE, Rudnicki J. Adenoid basal cell carcinoma of the vulva. Int J Gynecol Pathol 1982, **1:** 299–306.

197 Pelosi G, Martignoni G, Bonetti F. Intraductal carcinoma of mammary-type apocrine epithelium arising within a papillary hydradenoma of the vulva. Report of a case and review of the literature. Arch Pathol Lab Med 1991, **115:** 1249–1254.

198 Perrone T, Twiggs LB, Adcock LL, Dehner LP. Vulvar basal cell carcinoma. An infrequently metastasizing neoplasm. Int J Gynecol Pathol 1987, **6:** 152–165.

199 Rahilly MA, Beattie GJ, Lessells AM. Mucinous eccrine carcinoma of the vulva with neuroendocrine differentiation. Histopathology 1995, **27:** 82–86.

200 Rhatigan RM, Nuss RC. Keratoacanthoma of the vulva. Gynecol Oncol 1985, **21:** 118–123.

201 Rorat E, Wallach RC. Mixed tumors of the vulva. Clinical outcome and pathology. Int J Gynecol Pathol 1984, **3:** 323–328.

202 Roth LM, Look KY. Inverted follicular keratosis of the vulvar skin: a lesion that can be confused with squamous cell carcinoma. Int J Gynecol Pathol 2001, **19:** 369–373.

203 Wick MR, Goellner JR, Wolfe JT III, Su WPD. Vulvar sweat gland carcinomas. Arch Pathol Lab Med 1985, **109:** 43–47.

204 Woodworth H Jr, Dockerty MB, Wilson RB, Pratt JH. Papillary hidradenoma of the vulva. A clinicopathologic study of 69 cases. Am J Obstet Gynecol 1971, **110:** 501–508.

204a Young S, Leon M, Talerman A, Teresi M, Emmadi R. Polymorphous low-grade adenocarcinoma of the vulva and vagina: a tumor resembling adenoid cystic carcinoma. Int J Surg Pathol 2003, **11:** 43–49.

Melanocytic tumors

205 Benda JA, Platz CE, Anderson B. Malignant melanoma of the vulva. A clinical pathologic review of 16 cases. Int J Gynecol Pathol 1986, **5:** 202–216.

206 Bradgate MG, Rollason TP, McConkey CC, Powell J. Malignant melanoma of the vulva. A clinicopathological study of 50 women. Br J Obstet Gynaecol 1990, **97:** 124–133.

207 Christensen WN, Friedman KJ, Woodruff JD, Hood AF. Histologic characteristics of vulvar nevocellular nevi. J Cutan Pathol 1987, **14:** 87–91.

208 Clark WH Jr, Hood AF, Tucker MA, Jampel RM. Atypical melanocytic nevi of the genital type with a discussion of reciprocal parenchymal-stromal interactions in the biology of neoplasia. Hum Pathol 1998, **29:** S1–S24.

209 Das Gupta T, D'Urso J. Melanoma of female genitalia. Surg Gynecol Obstet 1964, **119:** 1074–1078.

210 Dunton CJ, Kautzky M, Hanau C. Malignant melanoma of the vulva: a review. Obstet Gynecol Surv 1995, **50:** 739–746.

211 Irvin WP Jr, Legallo RL, Stoler MH, Rice LW, Taylor PT Jr, Anderson WA. Vulvar melanoma: a retrospective analysis and literature review. Gynecol Oncol 2001, **83:** 457–465.

212 Jaramillo BA, Ganjei P, Averette HE, Sevin B-U, Lovecchio JL. Malignant melanoma of the vulva. Obstet Gynecol 1985, **66:** 398–401.

213 Johnson TL, Kumar NB, White CD, Morley GW. Prognostic features of vulvar melanoma. A clinicopathologic analysis. Int J Gynecol Pathol 1986, **5:** 110–118.

214 Look KY, Roth LM, Sutton GP. Vulvar melanoma reconsidered. Cancer 1993, **72:** 143–146.

215 Panizzon RG. Vulvar melanoma. Semin Dermatol 1996, **15:** 67–70.

216 Podratz KC, Symmonds RE, Taylor WF, Williams TJ. Carcinoma of the vulva. Analysis of treatment and survival. Obstet Gynecol 1983, **61:** 63–74.

217 Raber G, Mempel V, Jackisch C, Hudeiker M, Heinecke A, Kurzl R, Glaubita M, Rompel R, Schneider HP. Malignant melanoma of the vulva: report of 89 patients. Cancer 1996, **78:** 2353–2358.

218 Ragnarsson-Olding B, Johansson H, Rutqvist LE, Ringborg U. Malignant melanoma of the vulva and vagina. Trends in incidence, age distribution, and long-term survival among 245 consecutive cases in Sweden 1960–1984. Cancer 1993, **71:** 1893–1897.

219 Ragnarsson-Olding BK, Kanter-Lewensohn LR, Lagerlof B, Nilsson BR, Ringborg UK. Malignant melanoma of the vulva in a nationwide, 25-year study of 219 Swedish females: clinical observations and histopathologic features. Cancer 1999, **86:** 1273–1284.

220 Ragnarsson-Olding BK, Nilsson BR, Kanter-Lewensohn LR, Lagerlof B, Ringborg UK. Malignant melanoma of the vulva in a nationwide, 25-year study of 219 Swedish females: predictors of survival. Cancer 1999, **86:** 1285–1293.

221 Rock B. Pigmented lesions of the vulva. Dermatol Clin 1992, **10:** 361–370.

222 Rohwedder A, Philips B, Malfetano J, Kredentser D, Carlson JA. Vulvar malignant melanoma associated with human papillomavirus DNA: report of two cases and review of literature. Am J Dermatopathol 2002, **24:** 230–240.

223 Ronan SG, Eng AM, Briele HA, Walker MJ, Das Gupta TK. Malignant melanoma of the female genitalia. J Am Acad Dermatol 1990, **22:** 428–435.

224 Scheistroen M, Trope C, Koern J, Pettersen EO, Abeler VM, Kristensen GB. Malignant melanoma of the vulva. Evaluation of prognostic factors with emphasis on DNA ploidy in 75 patients. Cancer 1995, **75:** 72–80.

225 Spatz A, Zimmermann U, Bachollet B, Pautier P, Michel G, Duvillard P. Malignant blue nevus of the vulva with late ovarian metastasis. Am J Dermatopathol 1998, **20:** 408–412.

226 Tasseron EW, van der Esch EP, Hart AA, Brutel de la Riviere G,

Aartsen EJ. A clinicopathological study of 30 melanomas of the vulva. Gynecol Oncol 1992, **46**: 170–175.

Agressive angiomyxoma and related lesions

227 Bégin LR, Clement PB, Kirk ME, Jothy S, McCaughey WTE, Ferenczy A. Aggressive angiomyxoma of pelvic soft parts. A clinicopathologic study of nine cases. Hum Pathol 1985, **16**: 621–628.

227a Blandamura S, Cruz J, Vergara LF, Puerto IM, Ninfo V. Aggressive angiomyxoma: a second case of metastasis with patient's death. Hum Pathol 2003, **34**: 1072–1074.

228 Fetsch JF, Laskin WB, Lefkowitz M, Kindblom LG, Meis-Kindblom JM. Aggressive angiomyxoma: a clinicopathologic study of 29 female patients. Cancer 1996, **78**: 79–90.

229 Fetsch JF, Laskin WB, Tavassoli FA. Superficial angiomyxoma (cutaneous myxoma): a clinicopathologic study of 17 cases arising in the genital region. Int J Gynecol Pathol 1998, **16**: 325–334.

230 Fletcher CD, Tsang WY, Fisher C, Lee KC, Chan JK. Angiomyofibroblastoma of the vulva. A benign neoplasm distinct from aggressive angiomyxoma. Am J Surg Pathol 1992, **16**: 373–382.

231 Fukunaga M, Nomura K, Matsumoto K, Doi K, Endo Y, Ushigome S. Vulval angiomyofibroblastoma. Clinicopathologic analysis of six cases. Am J Clin Pathol 1997, **107**: 45–51.

232 Granter SR, Nucci MR, Fletcher CD. Aggressive angiomyxoma: reappraisal of its relationship to angiomyofibroblastoma in a series of 16 cases. Histopathology 1997, **30**: 3–10.

233 Hisaoka M, Kouho H, Aoki T, Daimaru Y, Hashimoto H. Angiomyofibroblastoma of the vulva. A clinicopathologic study of seven cases. Pathol Int 1995, **45**: 487–492.

234 Iezzoni JC, Fechner RE, Wong LS, Rosai J. Aggressive angiomyxoma in males. A report of four cases. Am J Clin Pathol 1995, **104**: 391–396.

235 Kazmierczak B, Wanschura S, Meyer-Bolte K, Caselitz J, Meister P, Bartnitzke S, Van de Ven W, Bullerdiek J. Cytogenetic and molecular analysis of an aggressive angiomyxoma. Am J Pathol 1995, **147**: 580–585.

236 Laskin WB, Fetsch JF, Tavassoli FA. Angiomyofibroblastoma of the female genital tract: analysis of 17 cases including a lipomatous variant. Hum Pathol 1997, **28**: 1046–1055.

236a Martinez MA, Ballestin C, Carabias E, Lois CG. Aggressive angiomyxoma: an ultrastructural study of four cases. Ultrastruct Pathol, 2003, **27**: 227–233.

237 Nielsen GP, Rosenberg AE, Young RH, Dickersin GR, Clement PB, Scully RE. Angiomyofibroblastoma of the vulva and vagina. Mod Pathol 1996, **9**: 284–291.

238 Nielsen GP, Young RH, Dickersin GR, Rosenberg AE. Angiomyofibroblastoma of the vulva with sarcomatous transformation ("angiomyofibrosarcoma"). Am J Surg Pathol 1997, **21**: 1104–1108.

239 Nucci MR, Granter SR, Fletcher CD. Cellular angiofibroma: a benign neoplasm distinct from angiomyofibroblastoma and spindle cell lipoma. Am J Surg Pathol 1997, **21**: 636–644.

240 Ockner DM, Sayadi H, Swanson PE, Ritter JH, Wick MR. Genital angiomyofibroblastoma. Comparison with aggressive angiomyxoma and other myxoid neoplasms of skin and soft tissue. Am J Clin Pathol 1997, **107**: 36–44.

241 Rotmensch EJ, Kasznica J, Hamid MA. Immunohistochemical analysis of hormone receptors and proliferating cell nuclear antigen in aggressive angiomyxoma of the vulva. Int J Gynaecol Obstet 1993, **41**: 171–179.

242 Siassi R, Papadopoulos T, Matzel KE. Metastasizing aggressive angiomyxoma. N Engl J Med 1999, **341**: 1772 (letter to the Editor).

243 Skalova A, Michal M, Husek K, Zamecnik M, Leivo I. Aggressive angiomyxoma of the pelvioperineal region. Immunohistological and ultrastructural study of seven cases. Am J Dermatopathol 1993, **15**: 446–451.

244 Steeper TA, Rosai J. Aggressive angiomyxoma of the female pelvis and perineum. Report of nine cases of a distinctive type of gynecologic soft tissue neoplasm. Am J Surg Pathol 1983, **7**: 463–475.

245 Vang R, Connelly JH, Hammill HA, Shannon RL. Vulvar hypertrophy with lymphedema: a mimicker of aggressive angiomyxoma. Arch Pathol Lab Med 2000, **124**: 1697–1699.

246 Vasquez MD, Ro JY, Park YW, Tornos CS, Ordonez NG, Ayala AG. Angiomyofibroblastoma: a clinicopathologic study of eight cases and review of the literature. Int J Surg Pathol 1999, **7**: 161–170.

247 White J, Chan YF. Aggressive angiomyxoma of the vulva in an 11-year-old girl. Pediatr Pathol 1994, **14**: 27–37.

Other tumors and tumorlike conditions

248 Abdul-Karim FW, Cohen RE. Atypical stromal cells of lower female genital tract. Histopathology 1990, **17**: 249–253.

249 Allen MV, Novotny DB. Desmoid tumor of the vulva associated with pregnancy. Arch Pathol Lab Med 1997, **121**: 512–514.

250 Axiotis CA, Merino MJ, Duray PH. Langerhans cell histiocytosis of the female genital tract. Cancer 1991, **67**: 1650–1660.

251 Barnhill DR, Boling R, Nobles W, Crooks L, Burke T. Vulvar dermatofibrosarcoma protuberans. Gynecol Oncol 1988, **30**: 149–152.

252 Blandamura S, Florea G, Brotto M, Salmaso R, Castellan L. Periurethral glomangiomyoma in women: case report and review of the literature (Letter). Histopathology 2000, **36**: 571–572.

253 Bock JE, Andreasson B, Thorn A, Holck S. Dermatofibrosarcoma protuberans of the vulva. Gynecol Oncol 1985, **20**: 129–135.

254 Colgan TJ, Dardick I, O'Connell G. Paraganglioma of the vulva. Int J Gynecol Pathol 1991, **10**: 203–208.

255 Dehner LP. Metastatic and secondary tumors of the vulva. Obstet Gynecol 1973, **42**: 47–57.

256 Dudley AG, Young RH, Lawrence WD, Scully RE. Endodermal sinus tumor of the vulva in an infant. Obstet Gynecol 1983, **61**: 76S–78S.

257 Elliott GB, Elliott JDA. Superficial stromal reactions of lower genital tract. Arch Pathol 1973, **95**: 100–101.

258 Gersell DJ, Fulling KH. Localized neurofibromatosis of the female genitourinary tract. Am J Surg Pathol 1989, **13**: 873–878.

259 Ghorbani RP, Malpica A, Ayala AG. Dermatofibrosarcoma protuberans of the vulva: clinicopathologic and immunohistochemical analysis of four cases, one with fibrosarcomatous change, and review of the literature. Int J Gynecol Pathol 1999, **18**: 366–373.

260 Hays DM, Raney RB Jr, Lawrence W Jr, Gehan EA, Soule EH, Tefft M, Maurer HM. Rhabdomyosarcoma of the female urogenital tract. J Pediatr Surg 1981, **16**: 828–834.

261 Hays DM, Shimada H, Raney RB Jr, Tefft M, Newton W, Crist WM, Lawrence W Jr, Ragab A, Beltangady M, Maurer HM. Clinical staging and treatment results in rhabdomyosarcoma of the female genital tract among children and adolescents. Cancer 1988, **61**: 1893–1903.

262 Hood AF, Lumadue J. Benign vulvar tumors. Dermatol Clin 1992, **10**: 371–385.

263 Huang HJ, Yamabe T, Tagawa H. A solitary neurilemmoma of the clitoris. Gynecol Oncol 1983, **15**: 103–110.

264 Kaplan MA, Jacobson JO, Ferry JA, Harris NL. T-cell lymphoma of the vulva in a renal allograft recipient with associated hemophagocytosis. Am J Surg Pathol 1993, **17**: 842–849.

265 Katz VL, Askin FB, Bosch BD. Glomus tumor of the vulva. A case report. Obstet Gynecol 1986, **67**: 43S–45S.

266 Kempson RL, Sherman AI. Sclerosing lipogranuloma of the vulva. Report of a case. Obstet Gynecol 1968, **101**: 854–856.

267 Kernen JA, Morgan ML. Benign lymphoid hamartoma of the vulva. Report of a case. Obstet Gynecol 1970, **35**: 290–292.

268 Lae ME, Pereira PF, Keeney GL, Nascimento AG. Lipoblastoma-like tumour of the vulva: report of three cases of a distinctive mesenchymal neoplasms of adipocytic differentiation. Histopathology 2002, **40:** 505–509.

269 Manson CM, Hirsch PJ, Coyne JD. Post-operative spindle cell nodule of the vulva. Histopathology 1995, **26:** 571–574.

270 Matias C, Nunes JF, Vicente LF, Almeida MO. Primary malignant rhabdoid tumour of the vulva. Histopathology 1990, **17:** 576–578.

271 Mazur MT, Hsueh S, Gersell DJ. Metastases to the female genital tract. Analysis of 325 cases. Cancer 1984, **53:** 1978–1984.

272 McNeely TB. Angiokeratoma of the clitoris. Arch Pathol Lab Med 1992, **116:** 880–881.

273 Meehan SA, Smoller BR. Cutaneous Langerhans cell histiocytosis of the genitalia in the elderly: a report of three cases. J Cutan Pathol 1998, **25:** 370–374.

274 Mu XC, Tran TA, Dupree M, Carslon JA. Acquired vulvar lymphangioma mimicking genital warts. A case report and review of the literature. J Cutan Pathol 1999, **26:** 150–154.

275 Mucitelli DR, Charles EZ, Kraus FT. Vulvovaginal polyps. Histologic appearance, ultrastructure, immunocytochemical characteristics, and clinicopathologic correlations. Int J Gynecol Pathol 1990, **9:** 20–40.

276 Nemoto T, Shinoda M, Komatsuzaki K, Hara T, Kojima M, Ogihara T. Myxoid leiomyoma of the vulva mimicking aggressive angiomyxoma. Pathol Int 1994, **44:** 454–459.

276a Neto AG, Deavers MT, Silva EG, Malpica A. Metastatic tumors of the vulva. A clinicopathologic study of 66 cases. Am J Surg Pathol 2003, **27:** 799–804.

277 Newman PL, Fletcher CD. Smooth muscle tumours of the external genitalia. Clinicopathological analysis of a series. Histopathology 1991, **18:** 523–529.

278 Nielsen GP, Young RH. Fibromatosis of soft tissue type involving the female genital tract: a report of two cases. Int J Gynecol Pathol 1998, **16:** 383–386.

279 Nielsen GP, Young RH. Mesenchymal tumors and tumor-like lesions of the female genital tract: a selective review with emphasis on recently described entities. Int J Gynecol Pathol 2001, **20:** 105–127.

280 Nielsen GP, Rosenberg AE, Koerner FC, Young RH, Scully RE. Smooth-muscle tumors of the vulva: a clinicopathological study of 25 cases and review of the literature. Am J Surg Pathol 1996, **20:** 779–793.

281 Nielsen GP, Shaw PA, Rosenberg AE, Dickersin GR, Young RH, Scully RE. Synovial sarcoma of the vulva: a report of two cases. Mod Pathol 1997, **9:** 970–974.

282 Nirenberg A, Ostor AG, Slavin J, Riley CB, Rome RM. Primary vulvar sarcomas. Int J Gynecol Pathol 1995, **14:** 55–62.

283 Nucci MR, Young RH, Fletcher CD. Cellular pseudosarcomatous fibroepithelial stromal polyps of the lower female genital tract: an underrecognized lesion often misdiagnosed as sarcoma. Am J Surg Pathol 2000, **24:** 231–240.

284 Nucci MR, Fletcher CD. Liposarcoma (atypical lipomatous tumors) of the vulva: a clinicopathologic study of six cases. Int J Gynecol Pathol 1998, **17:** 17–23.

285 Nucci MR, Fletcher CD. Vulvovaginal soft tissue tumors: update and review. Histopathology 2000, **36:** 97–108.

286 O'Connell JX, Young RH, Nielsen GP, Rosenberg AE, Bainbridge TC, Clement PB. Nodular fasciitis of the vulva: study of six cases and literature review. Int J Gynecol Pathol 1997, **16:** 117–123.

287 Ostor AG, Fortune DW, Riley CB. Fibroepithelial polyps with atypical stromal cells (pseudosarcoma botryoides) of vulva and vagina. A report of 13 cases. Int J Gynecol Pathol 1988, **7:** 351–360.

288 Perrone T, Swanson PE, Twiggs L, Ulbright TM, Dehner LP. Malignant rhabdoid tumor of the vulva. Is distinction from epithelioid sarcoma possible? A pathologic and immunohistochemical study. Am J Surg Pathol 1989, **13:** 848–858.

289 Robertson AJ, McIntosh W, Lamont P, Guthrie W. Malignant granular cell tumour (myoblastoma) of the vulva. Report of a case and review of the literature. Histopathology 1981, **5:** 69–79.

290 Santa Cruz J, Martin SA. Verruciform xanthoma of the vulva. Am J Clin Pathol 1979, **71:** 224–228.

291 Shen J-T, D'Ablaing G, Morro CP. Alveolar soft part sarcoma of the vulva. Report of first case and review of literature. Gynecol Oncol 1982, **13:** 120–128.

292 Sonobe H, Ro JY, Ramos M, Diaz I, Mackay B, Ordóñez NG, Ayala AG. Glomus tumor of the female external genitalia. A report of two cases. Int J Gynecol Pathol 1994, **13:** 359–364.

293 Strayer SA, Yum MN, Sutton GP. Epithelioid hemangioendothelioma of the clitoris. A case report with immunohistochemical and ultrastructural findings. Int J Gynecol Pathol 1992, **11:** 234–239.

294 Tavassoli FA, Norris HJ. Smooth muscle tumors of the vulva. Obstet Gynecol 1979, **53:** 213–217.

295 Taylor RN, Bottles K, Miller TR, Braga CA. Malignant fibrous histiocytoma of the vulva. Obstet Gynecol 1985, **66:** 145–148.

296 Terada KY, Schmidt RW, Roberts JA. Malignant schwannoma of the vulva. A case report. J Reprod Med 1988, **33:** 969–972.

297 Thomas WJ, Bevan HE, Hooper DG, Downey EJ. Malignant schwannoma of the clitoris in a 1-year-old child. Cancer 1989, **63:** 2216–2219.

298 Ulbright TM, Brokaw SA, Stehman FB, Roth LM. Epithelioid sarcoma of the vulva. Evidence suggesting a more aggressive behavior than extra-genital epithelioid sarcoma. Cancer 1983, **52:** 1462–1469.

299 Vang R, Medeiros LJ, Malpica A, Levenback C, Deavers M. Non-Hodgkin's lymphoma involving the vulva. Int J Gynecol Pathol 2000, **19:** 236–242.

300 Vang R, Taubenberger JK, Mannion CM, Bijwaard K, Malpica A, Ordonez NG, Tavassoli FA, Silver SA. Primary vulvar and vaginal extraosseous Ewing's sarcoma/peripheral neuroectodermal tumor: diagnostic confirmation with CD99 immunostaining and reverse transcriptase-polymerase chain reaction. Int J Gynecol Pathol 2000, **19:** 103–109.

301 Weissmann D, Amenta PS, Kantor GR. Vulvar epithelioid sarcoma metastatic to the scalp. A case report and review of the literature. Am J Dermatopathol 1990, **12:** 462–468.

302 Wolber RA, Talerman A, Wilkinson EJ, Clement PB. Vulvar granular cell tumors with pseudocarcinomatous hyperplasia. A comparative analysis with well-differentiated squamous carcinoma. Int J Gynecol Pathol 1991, **10:** 59–66.

Lesions of Bartholin's glands and related structures

303 Andersen G, Christensen S, Detlefsen GU, Kern-Hansen P. Treatment of Bartholin's abscess. Marsupialization versus incision, curettage and suture under antibiotic cover. A randomized trial with a 6-months follow-up. Acta Obstet Gynecol Scand 1992, **71:** 59–62.

304 Axe S, Parmley T, Woodruff JD, Hlopak B. Adenomas in minor vestibular glands. Obstet Gynecol 1986, **68:** 16–18.

305 Balat O, Edwards CL, Delclos L. Advanced primary carcinoma of the Bartholin gland: report of 18 patients. Eur J Gynecol Oncol 2001, **22:** 46–49.

306 Cardosi RJ, Speights A, Fiorica JV, Grendys EC Jr, Hakam A, Hoffman MS. Bartholin's gland carcinoma: a 15-year experience. Gynecol Oncol 2001, **82:** 247–251.

307 Chapman GW Jr, Hassan N, Page D, Mostoufi-Zadeh M, Leyman D. Mucinous cystadenoma of Bartholin's gland. A case report. J Reprod Med 1987, **32:** 939–941.

308 Copeland LJ, Sneige N, Gershenson DM, McGuffee VB, Abdul-Karim F, Rutledge FN. Bartholin gland carcinoma. Obstet Gynecol 1986, **67:** 794–801.

309 Copeland LJ, Sneige N, Gershenson DM, Saul PB, Stringer CA, Seski JC. Adenoid cystic carcinoma of Bartholin gland. Obstet Gynecol 1986, **67:** 115–120.

310 Enghardt MH, Valente PT, Day DH. Papilloma of Bartholin's gland duct cyst. First report of a case. Int J Gynecol Pathol 1993, **12**: 86–92.

311 Felix A, Nunes JF, Soares J. Salivary gland-type basal cell adenocarcinoma of presumed Bartholin's gland origin: a case report. Int J Gynecol Pathol 2002, **21**: 194–197.

312 Felix JC, Cote RJ, Kramer EE, Saigo P, Goldman GH. Carcinomas of Bartholin's gland. Histogenesis and the etiological role of human papillomavirus. Am J Pathol 1993, **142**: 925–933.

313 Freedman SR, Goldman RL. Mucocele-like changes in Bartholin's glands. Hum Pathol 1978, **9**: 111–114.

314 Friedrich EG Jr, Wilkinson EJ. Mucous cysts of the vulvar vestibule. Obstet Gynecol 1973, **42**: 407–414.

315 Jones MA, Mann EW, Caldwell CL, Tarraza HM, Dickersin GR, Young RH. Small cell neuroendocrine carcinoma of Bartholin's gland. Am J Clin Pathol 1990, **94**: 439–442.

316 Koenig C, Tavassoli FA. Nodular hyperplasia, adenoma, and adenomyoma of Bartholin's gland. Int J Gynecol Pathol 1998, **17**: 289–294.

317 Leuchter RS, Hacker NF, Voet RL, Berek JS, Townsend DE, Lagasse LD. Primary carcinoma of the Bartholin gland. A report of 14 cases and review of the literature. Obstet Gynecol 1982, **60**: 361–368.

318 Milchgrub S, Wiley EL, Vuitch F, Albores-Saavedra J. The tubular variant of adenoid cystic carcinoma of the Bartholin's gland. Am J Clin Pathol 1994, **101**: 204–208.

319 Mossler JA, Woodard BH, Addison A, McArty KS. Adenocarcinoma of Bartholin's gland. Arch Pathol Lab Med 1980, **104**: 523–526.

320 Paquin ML, Davis JR, Weiner S. Malacoplakia of Bartholin's gland. Arch Pathol Lab Med 1986, **110**: 757–758.

321 Rorat E, Ferenczy A, Richart RM. Human Bartholin gland, duct and duct cyst. Histochemical and ultrastructural study. Arch Pathol 1975, **99**: 367–374.

322 Rosenberg P, Simonsen E, Risberg B. Adenoid cystic carcinoma of Bartholin's gland. A report of five new cases treated with surgery and radiotherapy. Gynecol Oncol 1989, **34**: 145–147.

323 Scinicariello F, Rady P, Hannigan E, Dinh TV, Tyring SK. Human papillomavirus type 16 found in primary transitional cell carcinoma of the Bartholin's gland and in a lymph node metastasis. Gynecol Oncol 1992, **47**: 263–266.

324 Wheelock JB, Goplerud DR, Dunn LJ, Oates JF III. Primary carcinoma of the Bartholin gland. A report of ten cases. Obstet Gynecol 1984, **63**: 820–824.

325 Wilkinson EJ. Pathology of the vulva and vagina. In Wilkerson EJ (ed.): Contemporary issues in surgical pathology, vol. 9. New York, 1986, Churchill Livingstone.

Lesions of the female urethra

326 Amin MB, Young RH. Primary carcinomas of the urethra. Semin Diagn Pathol 1997, **14**: 147–160.

327 Baxendine-Jones JA, Wedderburn AW, Smart CJ, Theaker JM. Primary adenocarcinoma of the female urethra associated with adenomatous hyperplasia of the periurethral glands. J Urol Pathol 1998, **9**: 233–239.

328 Benson RC, Tunca JC, Buchler DA, Uehling DT. Primary carcinoma of the female urethra. Gynecol Oncol 1982, **14**: 313–318.

329 Capraro VJ, Bayonet-Rivera NP, Magoss I. Vulvar tumor in children due to prolapse of urethral mucosa. Am J Obstet Gynecol 1970, **108**: 572–575.

330 Clayton M, Siami P, Guinan P. Urethral diverticular carcinoma. Cancer 1992, **70**: 665–670.

331 Evans KJ, McCarthy MP, Sands JP. Adenocarcinoma of a female urethral diverticulum. Case report and review of the literature. J Urol 1981, **126**: 124–126.

332 Furusato M, Takaki K, Joh K, Suzuki M, Chiba S, Nakata Y, Kakimoto S, Aizawa S, Ishikawa E. Nephrogenic adenoma in female urethra. Acta Pathol Jpn 1983, **33**: 1009–1015.

333 Garden AS, Zagars GK, Delclos L. Primary carcinoma of the female urethra. Results of radiation therapy. Cancer 1993, **71**: 3102–3108.

334 Grigsby PW, Corn BW. Localized urethral tumors in women. Indications for conservative versus exenterative therapies. J Urol 1992, **147**: 1516–1520.

335 Jarvi OH, Marin S, de Boer WGRM. Further studies of intestinal heterotopia in urethral caruncle. Acta Pathol Microbiol Immunol Scand (A) 1984, **92**: 469–474.

336 Johnson DE, O'Connell JR. Primary carcinoma of female urethra. Urology 1983, **21**: 42–44.

337 Kim CJ, Pak K, Hamaguchi A, Ishida A, Arai Y, Konishi T, Okada Y, Tomoyoshi T. Primary malignant melanoma of the female urethra. Cancer 1993, **71**: 448–451.

338 Mayer R, Fowler JE Jr, Clayton M. Localized urethral cancer in women. Cancer 1987, **60**: 1548–1551.

339 Meis JM, Ayala AG, Johnson DE. Adenocarcinoma of the urethra in women. A clinicopathologic study. Cancer 1987, **60**: 1038–1052.

340 Morgan DR, Dixon MF, Harnden P. Villous adenoma of urethra associated with tubulovillous adenoma and adenocarcinoma of rectum. Histopathology 1998, **32**: 87–89.

341 Mostofi FK, David CJ Jr, Sesterhenn IA. Carcinoma of the male and female urethra. Urol Clin North Am 1992, **19**: 347–358.

342 Narayan P, Konety B. Surgical treatment of female urethral carcinoma. Urol Clin North Am 1992, **19**: 373–382.

343 Odze R, Begin LR. Tubular adenomatous metaplasia (nephrogenic adenoma) of the female urethra. Int J Gynecol Pathol 1989, **8**: 374–380.

344 Ohsawa M, Mishima K, Suzuki A, Hagino K, Doi J, Aozasa K. Malignant lymphoma of the urethra. Report of a case with detection of Epstein-Barr virus genome in the tumor cells. Histopathology 1994, **24**: 525–529.

345 Oliva E, Quinn TR, Amin MB, Eble JN, Epstein JI, Srigley JR, Young RH. Primary malignant melanoma of the urethra: a clinicopathologic analysis of 15 cases. Am J Surg Pathol 2000, **24**: 785–796.

346 Oliva E, Young RH. Clear cell adenocarcinoma of the urethra: a clinicopathologic analysis of 19 cases. Mod Pathol 1997, **9**: 513–520.

347 Prempee T, Amornmarn R, Patanaphan V. Radiation therapy in primary carcinoma of the female urethra. Part II. An update on results. Cancer 1984, **54**: 729–733.

348 Rogers RE, Burns B. Carcinoma of the female urethra. Obstet Gynecol 1969, **33**: 54–57.

348a Saad AG, Kaouk JH, Kaspar HG, Khauli RB. Leiomyoma of the urethra: report of three cases of a rare entity. Int J Surg Pathol 2003, **11**: 123–126.

349 Suzuki K, Morita T, Tokue A. Primary signet ring cell carcinoma of female urethra. Int J Urol 2001, **8**: 509–512.

350 Wegnaupt K, Gerstner GJ, Kucera H. Radiation therapy for primary carcinoma of the female urethra. A survey over 25 years. Gynecol Oncol 1984, **17**: 58–63.

351 Wiener JS, Walther PJ. A high association of oncogenic human papillomaviruses with carcinomas of the female urethra. Polymerase chain reaction-based analysis of multiple histological types. J Urol 1994, **151**: 49–53.

352 Young RH, Scully RE. Clear cell adenocarcinoma of the bladder and urethra. A report of three cases and review of the literature. Am J Surg Pathol 1985, **9**: 816–826.

353 Young RH, Oliva E, Saenz Garcia JA, Bhan AK, Clement PB. Urethral caruncle with atypical stromal cells simulating lymphoma or sarcoma – a distinctive pseudoneoplastic lesion of females: a report of six cases. Am J Surg Pathol 1996, **20**: 1190–1195.

Vagina

Normal anatomy

The vagina is a tubular structure derived from the paired müllerian ducts that extend from the vestibule of the vulva to the uterus.[3,4] It is composed of three main layers: mucosa, muscularis, and adventitia. The mucosa is composed of stratified squamous epithelium resting on loose connective tissue stroma. The squamous epithelium can be divided, as in the exocervix, into three main zones: basal, intermediate, and superficial.[2] This epithelium is responsive to steroid hormones, its appearance depending on the age of the patient and the time of the menstrual cycle.[3]

The subepithelial stroma or lamina propria contains elastic fibers and a rich venous and lymphatic network. Polygonal to stellate stromal cells—some multinucleated—may be present. These cells are immunoreactive for desmin and hormone receptors but not for actin.

The wolffian (mesonephric) duct in the vagina is represented by *Gartner's duct*,[4] which runs deeply along the lateral vaginal walls. Microscopically, this usually appears in the form of a small single duct, sometimes surrounded by a cluster of small glands, all of them lined by a simple cuboidal epithelium. The presence of inspissated eosinophilic secretion in the lumen is a characteristic feature of these remnants.

The lymphatic drainage of the vagina is rather complex. The vessels in the upper anterior wall join those of the cervix and terminate in the medial chain of the external iliac nodes (interiliac nodes). Those in the posterior vagina drain into deep pelvic, rectal, and aortic nodes. Some of those of the lower vagina (including the hymenal portion) go to the interiliac nodes; others traverse the paravesical spaces and drain into the inferior gluteal nodes. Finally, the vessels that anastomose with those from the vulva drain to the femoral nodes.[1,2]

Adenosis and related lesions

Adenosis of the vagina was originally described as a partial or complete conversion of the vaginal mucosa from squamous to endocervical-type glandular epithelium[18]

(Fig. 19.36), but the concept was later expanded to embrace the presence of any müllerian-type glandular epithelium in the vagina. Sandberg[17] found occult vaginal adenosis in 9 (41%) of 22 vaginas from postpubertal girls obtained at autopsy but in none of 13 prepubertal patients. Kurman and Scully[11] obtained similar results, suggesting that vaginal adenosis can arise on a congenital basis but that steroid hormones probably play a stimulatory role in their development. Excess mucous discharge is the most common complaint in the symptomatic cases. Grossly, adenosis appears as red granular spots or patches that do not stain with Lugol's solution. Microscopically, the glands may be mucin secreting and similar to those of the endocervix (most commonly) or have a lining resembling tubal or endometrial mucosa[8] (Fig. 19.37).

Depending on the relative amounts of these components, a *mucinous (endocervical)* and a *tuboendometrial* form of vaginal adenosis have been described. Exceptionally, intestinal metaplasia is encountered.[12] The glandular-type epithelium of vaginal adenosis may be in the lamina propria or it may line the surface of the vagina. As a result, it can be identified in cytologic smears, which represent a useful means for the detection of this disorder.[16] Chronic inflammation and squamous metaplasia (mature, immature, or atypical) are common

Fig. 19.36 Whole-mount view showing a sharply delimited portion of vagina covered by glandular epithelium in vaginal adenosis.

accompanying features (Fig. 19.38). The latter, which is poor in cytoplasmic glycogen, can obliterate the glandular lumen and appear as a peg continuous with the surface, a feature that may be misinterpreted as vaginal intraepithelial neoplasia (VAIN) or even squamous cell carcinoma.[14] One should be aware, however, that lesions with the features of VAIN can superimpose themselves on foci of adenosis; the identifying features are the same as those described for similar lesions in the chapter on the uterine cervix.

Sometimes the squamous metaplasia is so extensive that the only evidence of a preexisting adenosis is found in the form of rare intercellular pools or intracellular droplets of mucin, as shown by mucicarmine or other mucin stains. It has been suggested that, as these women grow older, vaginal adenosis regresses by the process of squamous metaplasia.[15]

Microglandular hyperplasia can develop within lesions of vaginal adenosis following the use of oral contraceptives; it is important not to confuse this benign lesion with clear cell adenocarcinoma.[16]

A causal relationship between vaginal adenosis and exposure in utero to diethylstilbestrol (DES) has been documented. The reported incidence of adenosis in the exposed population has varied from 35% to more than 90% in the different series.[5] It has been shown that the incidence of vaginal adenosis and related colposcopic abnormalities is close to 100% if the drug is begun during or before the eighth week of pregnancy and only 6% if it is begun during the fifteenth week or later.[19] The microscopic features of adenosis in women exposed in utero to DES are identical to those seen in unexposed women.[6,13]

Transverse ridges and other structural anomalies are also related to DES administration.[9,10] They are found in the upper vagina or cervix in about one fourth of the exposed population and have been described as cockscomb cervix, rims, collars, hoods, and pseudopolyps. Microscopically, the ridge is composed of a core of fibrous tissue lined by mucinous epithelium, metaplastic squamous epithelium, or, rarely, tubal or endometrial epithelium. Although both vaginal adenosis and clear cell carcinoma are related to DES exposure (see p. 1512), it seems that the potential for the development of carcinoma from adenosis is exceedingly small.

DES-related lesions featuring immature squamous metaplasia, atypical metaplasia, and VAIN I usually revert to normal following biopsy or therapy; lesions in the VAIN II or III categories (usually characterized by an aneuploid DNA pattern by microspectrophotometry) tend to persist and recur after biopsy or therapy.[7]

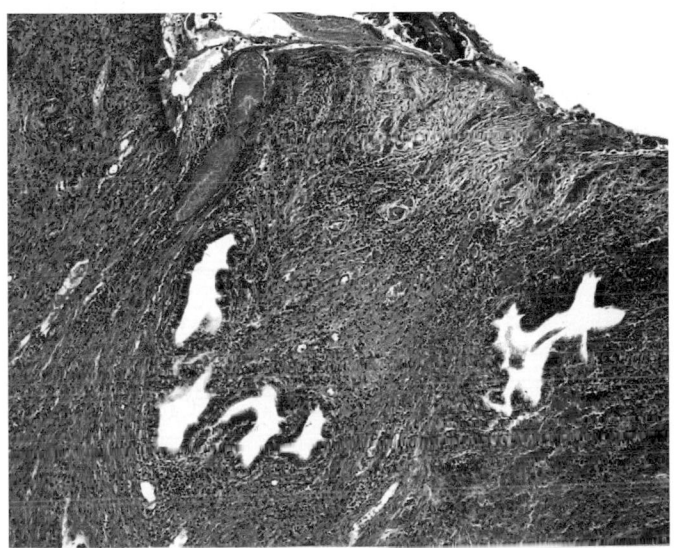

Fig. 19.37 Vaginal adenosis of tuboendometrial type beneath an ulcerated surface. Other areas of this specimen showed adenocarcinoma arising from the adenosis.

Other non-neoplastic lesions

The adult vagina is impervious to most bacterial infections. However, the overgrowth of facultative and anaerobic bacterial flora may result in a condition known as *bacterial vaginosis*. Microscopically, the most important finding is the presence of squamous cells covered with coccobacilli ("clue cells").[26] Indolent infections caused by *Trichomonas vaginalis* and *Candida albicans* are relatively common, especially during pregnancy.[28] **Lymphogranuloma venereum** can involve the vagina during the late stage of the disease and result in stricture. **Xanthogranulomatous reactions**[29] and **malakoplakia**[21] may occur as a result of unusual bacterial infections and lead to pseudotumor formation or strictures (Fig. 19.39). The use of *tampons* can result in gross vaginal ulcers.[22]

Occasionally, following vaginal hysterectomy, the **tubal fimbria** may become entrapped in the healing vaginal apex, a finding that must not be confused with a neoplastic process.[20] The clinical presentation is that of "granulation tissue" at the vaginal apex, usually appearing within 6 months following a hysterectomy.[27]

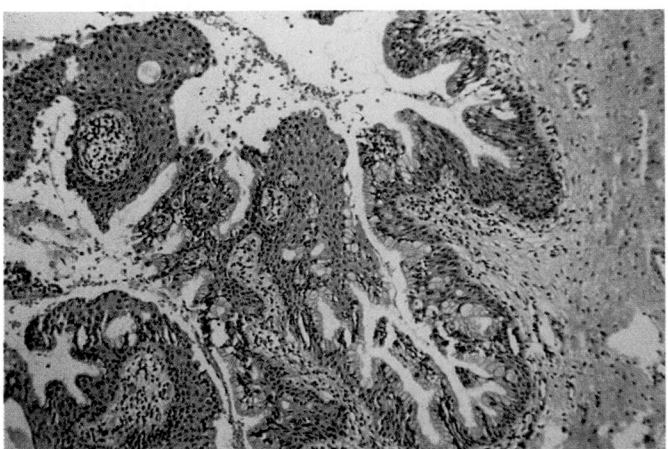

Fig. 19.38 Extensive squamous metaplasia in vaginal adenosis.

Occasionally, the tubal prolapse is associated with an exuberant stromal response with an angiomyofibroblastic appearance, a feature which adds to the diagnostic difficulty.[25a]

Endometriosis and the related condition known as **endocervicosis** occur in the vagina, but less commonly than in other portions of the genital tract.[25] Most cases are seen in connection with episiotomy scars.

Cysts of the vagina can be of several different types.[23] The most common is the *epithelial inclusion cyst*, lined by squamous epithelium and sometimes resulting from surgery or trauma. Another common type is characterized by a simple lining of mucin-secreting, tall columnar, nonciliated epithelium of endocervical type, sometimes associated with focal squamous metaplasia; this has been designated *müllerian cyst* and can be found anywhere in the vagina (Fig. 19.40). *Mesonephric (Gartner's duct) cyst* is rare; it is located in the anterolateral or lateral vaginal wall and is lined by low cuboidal epithelial cells, sometimes ciliated, that do not secrete

mucin. Other rare cystic lesions of the vagina include *urothelial cysts* (located in the suburethral portion and probably arising from paraurethral glands and Skene's ducts), *emphysematous vaginitis*,[23,24] and the already mentioned *endometriosis*.

Benign epithelial tumors

Intramural papilloma having a branching configuration and a lining of a single layer of cuboidal cells has been rarely described in children. It may present in the surface as polyps or intramurally. It is sometimes referred to as *mesonephric papilloma*, but ultrastructural studies suggest that the lesion is instead of müllerian derivation.[36] *Papillary müllerian cystadenofibroma* of the vagina is probably a histogenetically closely related tumor.[33]

Squamous papilloma may be seen in the adult vagina but less commonly than in the cervix. Many of the cases are probably of viral (human papilloma virus; HPV) etiology.

Tubulovillous adenoma of the vagina morphologically similar to its colorectal counterpart has been described.[31]

Benign mixed tumor (spindle cell epithelioma) is usually located in or near the hymenal ring. It is composed of small stromal-type spindle cells intermixed with mature squamous cells and glands lined by mucinous epithelium[32,34] (Fig. 19.41). Ultrastructural and immunohistochemical studies have conclusively proved its epithelial nature.[30] There is also immunoreactivity for CD34, bcl-2, and CD99.[35] The lesion is benign, but it may recur locally.[30,37]

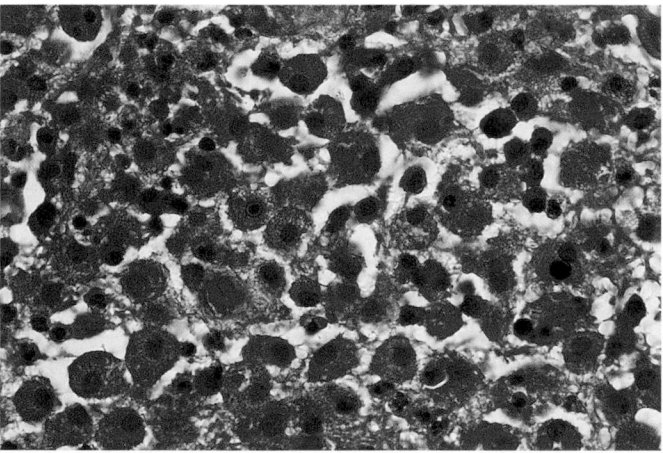

Fig. 19.39 Malakoplakia of vagina. This PAS stain shows numerous histiocytes containing particulate material in their cytoplasm.

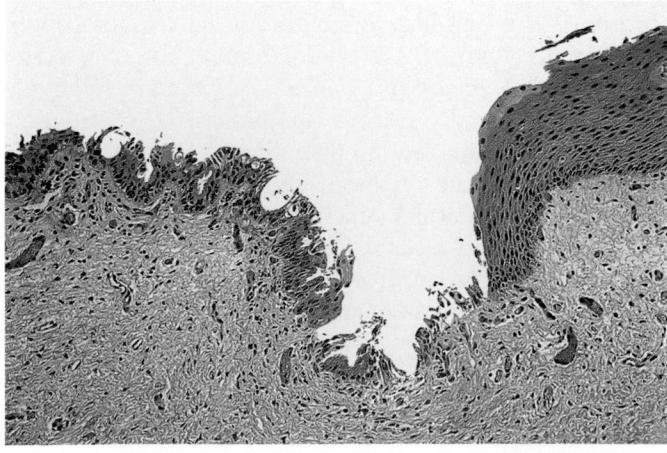

Fig. 19.40 Vaginal cyst lined by müllerian epithelium connecting with surface squamous epithelium.

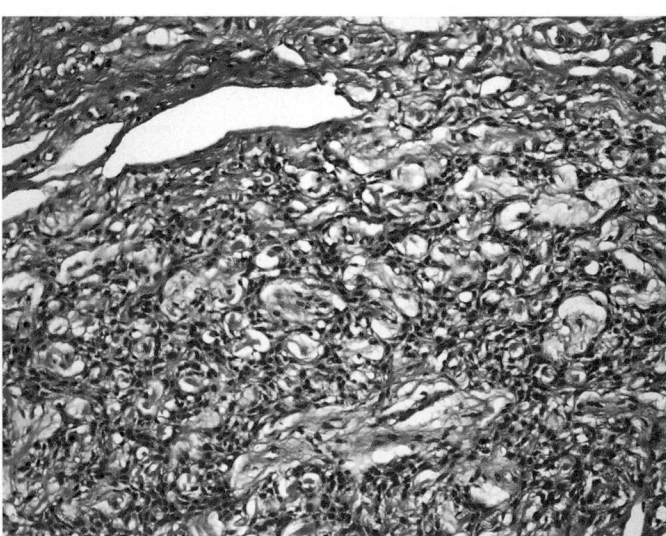

Fig. 19.41 So-called "benign mixed tumor of vagina." The plexiform pattern of growth seen in this field is characteristic of the entity.

Fig. 19.42 Vaginal intraepithelial neoplasia (VAIN) III. This is the type traditionally known as in situ squamous cell carcinoma.

Squamous intraepithelial lesions

Atypical squamous epithelial lesions of the vagina have been designated as *vaginal intraepithelial neoplasia* (VAIN), borrowing the terminology from the analogous lesions in the cervix (CIN)[44] (Fig. 19.42). It should be noted that the vaginal lesions usually arise from native squamous epithelium, in contrast to most cervical cases, which originate from *metaplastic* squamous epithelium. VAIN is multifocal in about one half of cases and very frequently associated with concomitant, subsequent, or prior (in situ or invasive) neoplasms of the lower genital tract.[38,40,42] The upper third of the vagina is the most common site, in which case the vaginal and cervical lesions may be confluent.[43] The type of treatment depends largely on the extent of the disease and may consist of local excision, partial or total vaginectomy, CO_2 laser therapy, or administration of topical 5-fluorouracil.[39–41]

It is important not to overdiagnose transitional cell metaplasia as VAIN, the criteria for the differential diagnosis being the same as for the uterine cervix.[45]

Invasive squamous cell carcinoma

Primary carcinoma of the vagina is much less common than carcinoma of the vulva or cervix.[47,57,64] It is largely a disease of the elderly. HPV has been incriminated as a possible causative agent, as it has been for microscopically similar tumors of cervix and vulva.[53,56,58]

Since most carcinomas involving the vagina represent direct extension from cervical carcinomas, only vaginal tumors that spare the uterine cervix are regarded as primary. Those involving both areas are classified as cervical carcinomas with vaginal extension, regardless of the relative proportion of involvement.

Up to 20% of the patients successfully treated for CIN or invasive squamous cell carcinoma of the cervix will have abnormal cytologic smears from the vagina, and some will develop a similar tumor in the vagina at a later date.[59] The latter event seems to be more common in those patients who were treated by irradiation alone than in those who had only surgery, and the average interval is 5 or 6 years.[48,59] Therefore, patients who had cervical carcinoma should have follow-up examinations for the rest of their lives, with special attention to the possibility of a vaginal recurrence of the cervical tumor or a new primary vaginal carcinoma. The area for biopsy may be detected by colposcopy, Schiller's test, or multiple smears taken from all sectors of the vagina.[54] Vaginal carcinoma can also develop following hysterectomy for benign disease; therefore regular Papanicolaou tests are still indicated after this operation.[46]

Most primary vaginal carcinomas are grossly nodular or ulcerative[73] (Fig. 19.43). The upper third and the anterior or lateral walls are the most common sites of origin.[69] A few cases have arisen in surgically constructed neovaginas.[67,71]

Microscopically, approximately 95% of vaginal carcinomas are conventional squamous cell carcinomas of varying degrees of differentiation, their morphologic appearance duplicating that of their more common cervical and vulvar counterparts (Fig. 19.44).

Vaginal carcinoma is usually treated by a combination of external and intracavitary radiation[55,66,70]; local excision can be employed for small tumors[60] and radical surgery for selected cases located in the upper vaginal third or posterior wall.[50,52] The overall 5-year survival rate is between 40% and 50%.[52,65,68] The prognosis is closely related to the stage of the disease[60,62] and is similar whether the patient has a previously treated cervical carcinoma or not.[61] In the series from the National Cancer Data Base, the relative 5-year survival was 96% for stage 0, 73% for stage I, 58% for stage II, and 36% for stages III

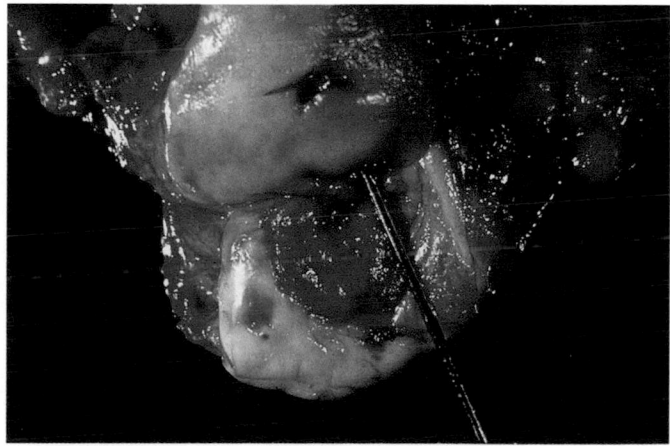

Fig. 19.43 Invasive squamous cell carcinoma resulting in a large ulcerated mass.

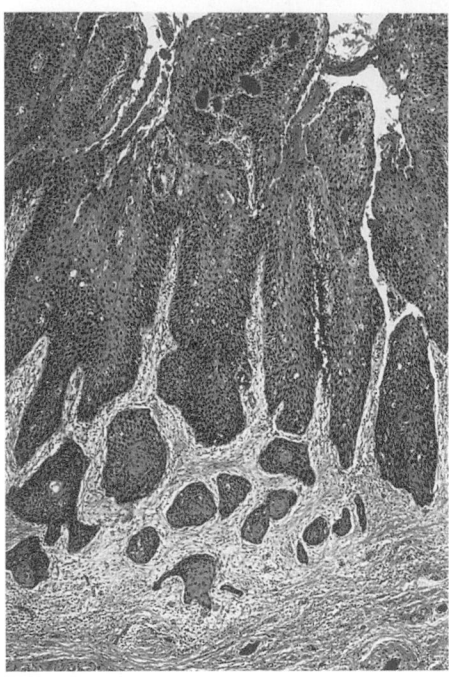

Fig. 19.44 Well-differentiated squamous cell carcinoma of vagina invading the superficial stroma.

and IV.[49] Most recurrences occur within 1 year of therapy and carry an ominous prognosis. Upper lesions tend to recur locally, whereas lower lesions are more commonly associated with pelvic sidewall and distal recurrence.[72]

The existence of *microinvasive (superficially or minimally invasive) carcinoma* as a distinct clinical entity in the vagina has been proposed, but the concept faces the same theoretic and practical difficulties for a precise definition as in the vulva (see p. 1490).[63] As in the case of the grossly invasive tumors, some of the reported examples have followed treatment for cervical carcinoma.[51]

Clear cell (adeno)carcinoma

Clear cell (adeno)carcinoma is also known as mesonephroid (adeno)carcinoma, both terms being preferable to the older designation, *mesonephric carcinoma*.[81,84] It characteristically occurs in the anterior or lateral wall of the upper vagina or in the uterine cervix of children, adolescents, and young adults. The average age at the time of diagnosis is 17 years. It is extremely rare before the age of 12 and after the age of 30 years, but there is a second smaller peak at age 70 years.[77] In two thirds of the patients, there is a history of prenatal exposure to DES or related nonsteroid estrogens.[82,85,92] However, the risk of carcinoma in the exposed population is low: it has been estimated to be 1 in 1000.[78,85] It has been found to be higher for those patients whose mothers began therapy before the twelfth week of pregnancy.[79]

Steroid estrogens do not seem to be associated with this complication. Most patients present with vaginal bleeding or discharge, but 16% of those studied by Herbst et al.[80] were asymptomatic. There is a very common association with vaginal adenosis, cervical ectropion, and occasional coexistence of transverse vaginal or cervical ridges. These features strongly suggest the existence of a DES-related disturbance in the development of the lower müllerian tract. Grossly, the larger tumors may involve most of the vagina. The majority are polypoid and nodular; others are flat or ulcerated, with an indurated or granular surface.[88] Most of the tumors are only superficially invasive at the time of diagnosis.

Microscopically, there are tubules and cysts lined by clear cells alternating with more solid areas and papillary formations[86] (Fig. 19.45). Mitotic figures are variable but usually scanty. The tumor cells have an abundant clear cytoplasm because of the presence of glycogen and sometimes fat. Intracytoplasmic mucin is either absent or scanty. Hobnail-shaped cells are frequently seen protruding into the glandular lumen. These cells can be detected by cytologic examination,[76,90] but about one fourth of patients will have a negative vaginal smear. The microscopic differential diagnosis needs to be made primarily with microglandular hyperplasia, which can occur in areas of vaginal adenosis, and the Arias-Stella reaction related to pregnancy or progestational agents. It is of interest that whereas the lesions of vaginal adenosis are usually strongly positive for mucin stain, this is almost never the case for the cells of clear cell adenocarcinoma. The explanation given is that this tumor tends to arise from the tuboendometrial rather than the mucinous form of adenosis; support for this interpretation comes from a study showing tuboendometrial epithelium in 95% of clear cell adenocarcinomas (usually in greater concentrations at the margin of the tumor) and the presence of atypical changes in 80% of them.[89]

The immunohistochemical profile of these tumors is characterized by consistent positivity for CK7, CAM 5.2, 34βE12, CEA, CD15, vimentin, bcl-2, and CA-125; variable positivity for estrogen receptors and HER2/*neu*; and negativity for CK20 and progesterone receptors.[91]

Ultrastructurally, the appearance of clear cell carcinoma is very similar regardless of the architecture or cytologic features as seen by light microscopy and is comparable to the clear cell carcinomas of the endometrium and ovary seen in older women.[75]

At the genetic molecular level, there is widespread instability in these tumors, as manifested by somatic mutation of microsatellite repeats.[74]

The prognosis is relatively good. Small, asymptomatic tumors usually are cured by surgery. Tumors that are large, that are close to the resection margins, or that have penetrated more than 3 mm into the wall tend to recur locally.[87] Metastases occur to pelvic lymph nodes (and sometimes those in the supraclavicular region) and lungs. In the series of Herbst et al.,[80] 24% of the patients developed persistent or recurrent disease, and 16% have

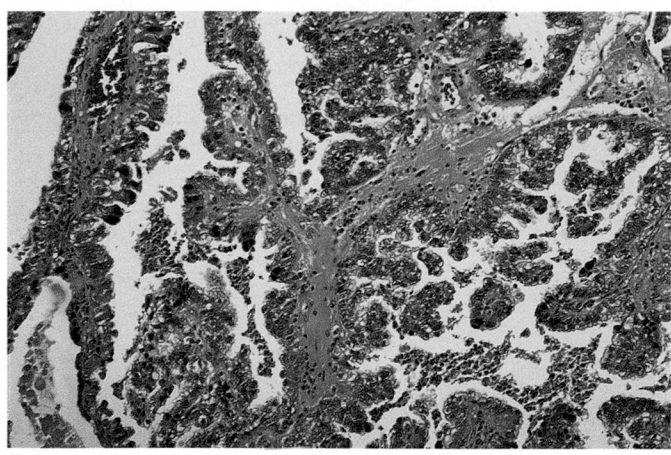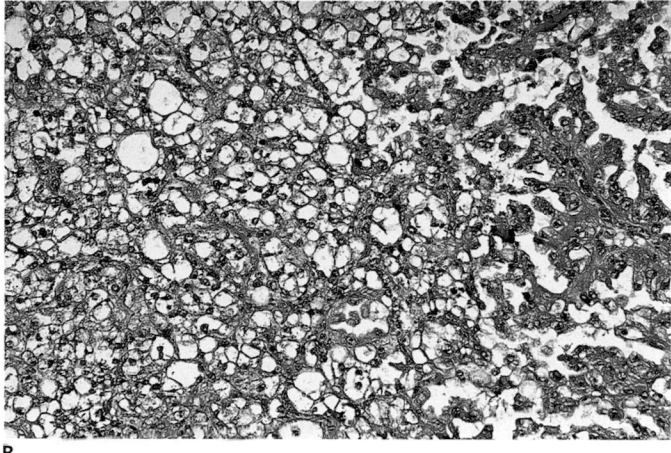

A   B

Fig. 19.45 Clear cell carcinoma of vagina. A, Papillary pattern; B, Prominent clear cell features.

died. The recurrences can occur very late after the treatment of the primary tumor.[83]

Other carcinoma types

Verrucous carcinoma is an extremely well-differentiated variant of squamous cell carcinoma. Like its vulvar and cervical counterparts, it invades locally but is practically never associated with lymph node metastases. The local spread can be quite extensive and reach the rectum and coccyx.[111] It should be distinguished from condyloma acuminatum, which may rarely involve the vagina; the criteria are the same as those described in the section on the vulva. **HPV** has been demonstrated in some cases of vaginal verrucous carcinoma.[107]

Spindle cell (sarcomatoid) carcinoma has an appearance analogous to that more often seen in tumors of the upper aerodigestive tract[112,118] (Fig. 19.46). It should be kept separate from **malignant mixed müllerian tumor,** which can also occur in the vagina,[109] even if both tumors probably represent epithelial malignant neoplasms with sarcoma-like features.

Mucinous adenocarcinoma of vagina has been described in middle-aged and elderly patients, occasionally arising on the basis of endocervicosis.[105] Its microscopic features are indistinguishable from those of its more common endocervical counterpart.[96] In a few reported cases, the appearance has been reminiscent of enteric epithelium.[97,121]

Mesonephric (wolffian) adenocarcinoma is an exceptionally rare tumor located paravaginally, along the course of the wolffian-derived ducts of Gartner.[101]

Endometrioid adenocarcinoma is thought to arise on the basis of vaginal endometriosis.[100] This is also the presumed origin for most cases of adenocarcinomas located in the rectovaginal septum and having no mucosal involvement of either the vagina or rectum; this supposition is based on the fact that endometriosis is sometimes

detected together with or preceding the carcinoma,[99] and because of the well-known predilection of this condition for the rectovaginal septum.[122]

Small cell neuroendocrine carcinoma can occur in the vagina, either in a pure form or associated with squamous or glandular elements.[94,102,103,106] One case has been reported in a background of atypical adenosis.[110] As in other sites where this tumor type occurs, there is usually electron microscopic and immunohistochemical evidence of neuroendocrine differentiation.[98,115,120] Most cases have been treated by a combination of radiation therapy and chemotherapy.[102]

Other carcinoma types that have been described in the vagina are *transitional cell carcinoma*[93] (including a page-

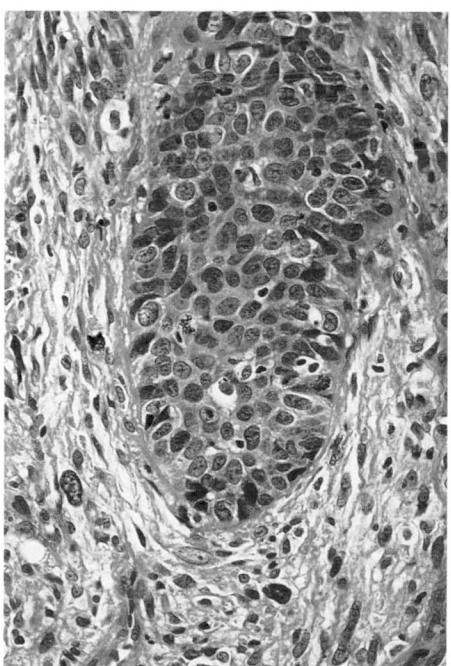

Fig. 19.46 Spindle cell (sarcomatoid) carcinoma of vagina. Elongated cells with a mesenchymal-like appearance surround a well-defined nest having a clear-cut epithelial appearance.

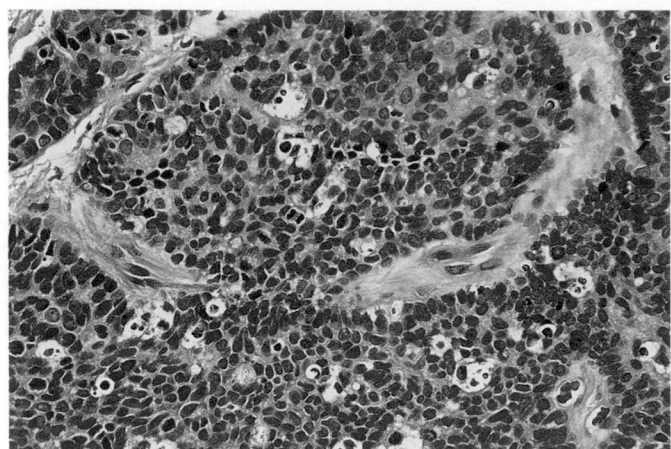

Fig. 19.47 Basaloid carcinoma of vagina.

toid form and a variant described as papillary squamotransitional[114,117]), *serous papillary adenocarcinoma*,[113] *lymphoepithelioma-like carcinoma*[95,104] and *basaloid carcinoma* (Fig. 19.47).

Malignant mixed tumor of the vagina (not to be confused with the neoplasm discussed on p. 1510) is characterized microscopically by a biphasic pattern of glands and spindle cells. Its superficial resemblance to synovial sarcoma has led some observers to erroneously propose a mesenchymal origin for this neoplasm.[108] Indeed, the tumor has been referred to as "synovioid."[119] Some of the cases have been located in the upper lateral portion, and the possibility that they may arise from Gartner's ducts or related mesonephric rests has been suggested.[116]

Mesenchymal tumors and tumorlike conditions

Fibroepithelial polyps may be seen in adult women (especially during pregnancy) or in neonates.[150] They are probably not true neoplasms but rather manifestations of hormone-induced localized hyperplasia of the loose subepithelial connective tissue zone[124]; others may represent the end stage of granulation tissue[136] (Fig. 19.48). Microscopically, they are formed of a central fibrovascular core and a covering of normal-appearing squamous epithelium (Fig. 19.49). Sometimes the stroma is markedly edematous[124]; in other instances it is hypercellular and/or contains scattered highly atypical stromal cells of stellate shape[123,131,145,153] (Fig. 19.50). These stromal cells are immunoreactive for vimentin, desmin, and steroid receptors but usually not for actin.[137,146] The clinical appearance, nuclear atypia, and desmin immunoreactivity may lead to a mistaken diagnosis of botryoid rhabdomyosarcoma or other types of malignant tumor.[150,152] The slow pace of growth at the clinical level and the fact that a cambium layer, epithelial invasion,

and cross striations are absent are among the distinguishing features.

Aggressive angiomyxoma can present as a protruding intravaginal mass and extend through the paravaginal soft tissue.[160] This entity is more fully described on p. 1495.

Angiomyofibroblastoma, superficial myofibroblastoma, and **solitary fibrous tumor** are other types of benign mesenchymal neoplasms of fibroblastic/myofibroblastic nature that have been reported in the vagina.[143,149,162] The angiomyofibroblastoma has an appearance identical to that of its vulvar counterpart, and the superficial myofibroblastoma represents a minor

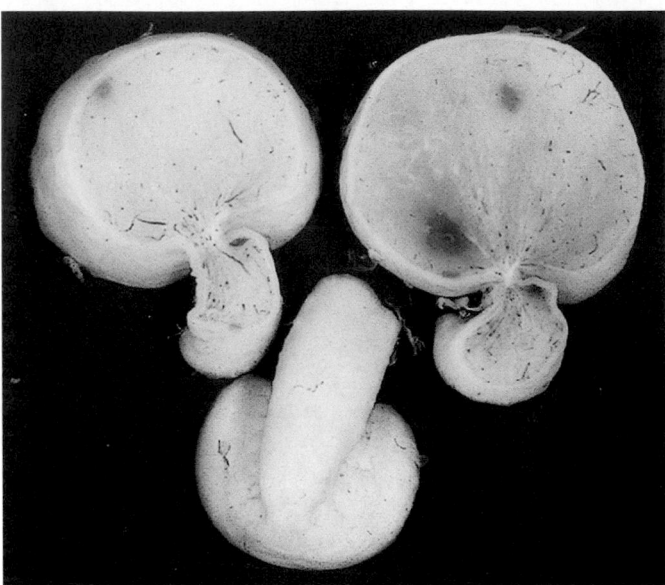

Fig. 19.48 Curious mushroom-like appearance of vaginal fibroepithelial polyp. (Courtesy of Dr Pedro J Grases Galofrè; from Grases Galofrè PJ: Patologia ginecològica., Bases para el diagnòstico morfològico, Barcelona, Masson, 2002)

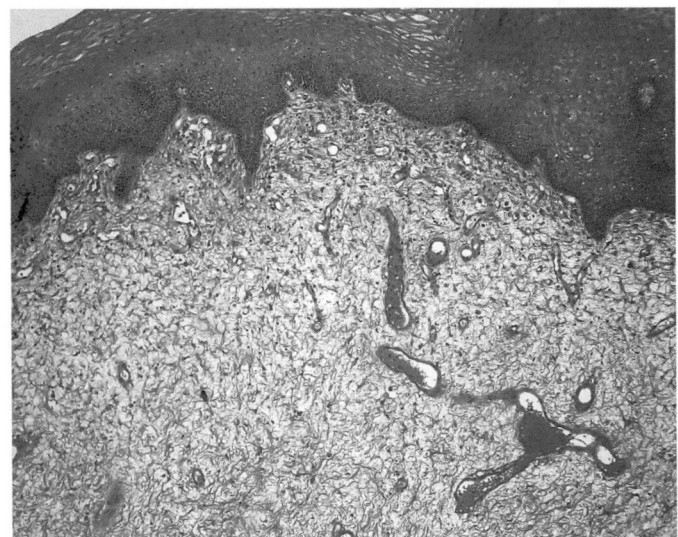

Fig. 19.49 Fibroepithelial polyp of vagina showing loose fibrovascular stroma covered by slightly thickened but otherwise unremarkable squamous epithelium.

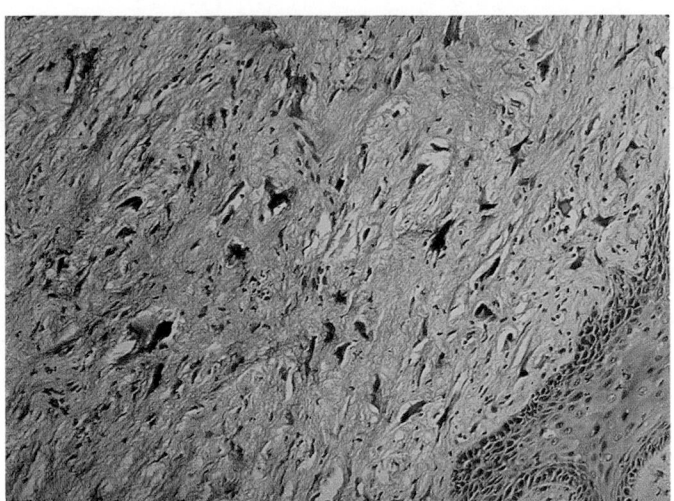

Fig. 19.50 Atypical benign stromal cells in a vaginal polyp.

variation on the theme of benign polypoid tumors of the hormonally responsive mesenchymal cells of the region.[151]

Postoperative spindle cell nodule is a pseudosarcomatous vaginal lesion that occurs a few weeks following hysterectomy or some other surgical procedure in the region and presents as a small friable reddish mass in the vaginal vault.[156,164] Microscopically, it shows ulceration, granulation tissue, and a very hypercellular spindle cell proliferation characterized by a fascicular pattern of growth, many mitotic figures, and numerous extravasated red blood cells, resulting in a Kaposi's sarcoma-like appearance[156] (Fig. 19.51). It may be confused with sarcoma (particularly leiomyosarcoma) and sarcomatoid carcinoma. Immunohistochemically, there may be reactivity for low-molecular-weight keratin, which may contribute to the misinterpretation of the lesion. Clues to its recognition are the distinctly fascicular pattern, the Kaposi's sarcoma-like areas, the absence of pleomorphism, the fact that the mitoses—although abundant—are all typical, and, most important, the history of a recent operation in the area.

Leiomyoma is the most common benign mesenchymal tumor of the vagina.[151,161] The patients are adults, and any region of the vagina can be affected. A peculiar case has been seen containing paraganglioma-like tissue within.[147]

Leiomyosarcoma can attain a large size and ulcerate.[132] The majority of the cases manifest their malignancy only through local recurrence. The criteria of malignancy used by Tavassoli and Norris[161] were the presence of moderate to marked atypism and 5 or more mitotic figures per 10 high-power fields. Poorly differentiated tumors are associated with a high mortality rate.[157]

Rhabdomyoma presents as a polypoid mass.[127] All of the reported cases have occurred in adult patients, an important differential point with botryoid rhabdomyosarcoma, discussed below. Microscopically, the lesion

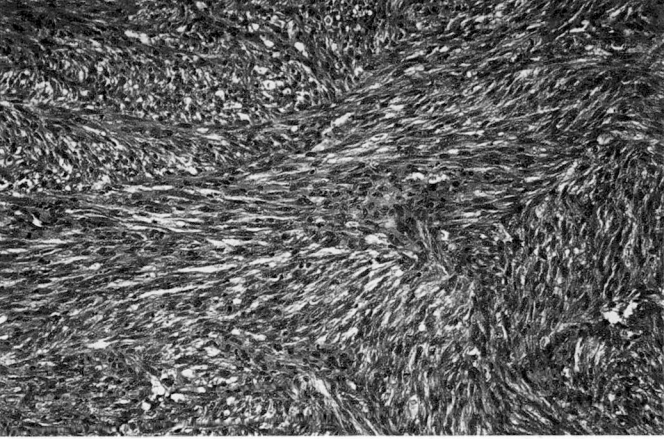

A

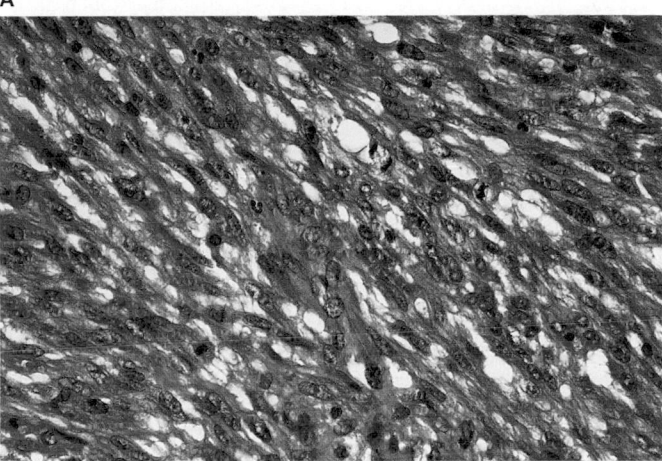

B

Fig. 19.51 A and **B**, Medium- and high-power views of postoperative spindle cell nodule. The lesion is extremely cellular and mitotically active, but there is little pleomorphism.

consists of interweaving and haphazardly oriented bundles of spindle- to strap-shaped cells, some with cross striations[135] (Fig. 19.52). Mitoses are scanty or absent, and there is no concentration of neoplastic cells beneath the epithelium.

Other benign mesenchymal tumors that have been reported in the vagina are *hemangioma, hemangiopericytoma,*[142] *glomus tumor,*[159] *benign "triton" tumor,*[125] *angiomyolipoma,*[130] *schwannoma,*[133] and neurofibroma.[134]

Botryoid rhabdomyosarcoma (sarcoma botryoides) is a rare polypoid invasive tumor that usually arises from the anterior vaginal wall[139] (Fig. 19.53). Approximately 90% of cases occur in girls under 5 years of age, with close to two thirds appearing during the first 2 years. Grossly, it presents as a conglomerate of soft polypoid masses resembling a bunch of grapes—hence its name.

Microscopically, a myxoid stroma is seen containing undifferentiated round or spindle cells (Fig. 19.54). Some of these cells contain a bright eosinophilic granular cytoplasm suggestive of rhabdomyoblastic differentiation. Their racquet- or strap-shaped form mimics that of the cells seen during normal muscle embryogenesis. Cross

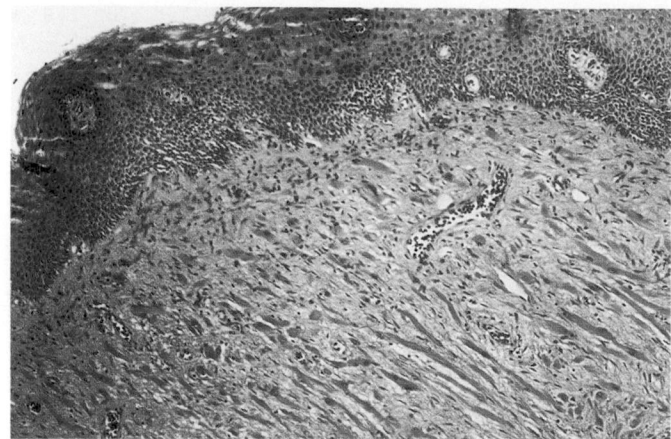

A

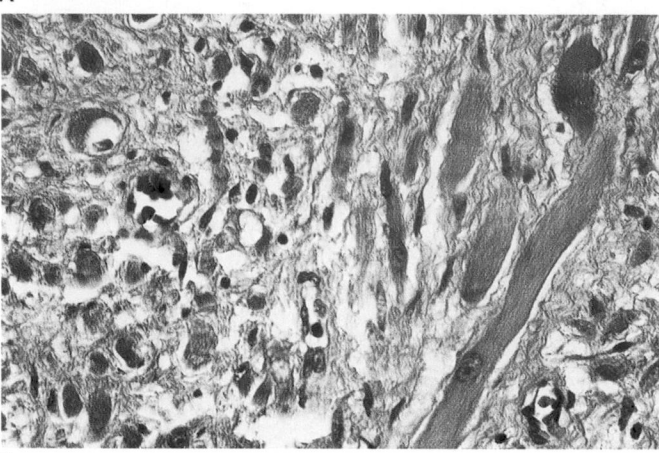

B

Fig. 19.52 A and **B,** Vaginal rhabdomyoma composed of bundles of mature skeletal muscle cells scattered in the stroma beneath normal squamous epithelium.

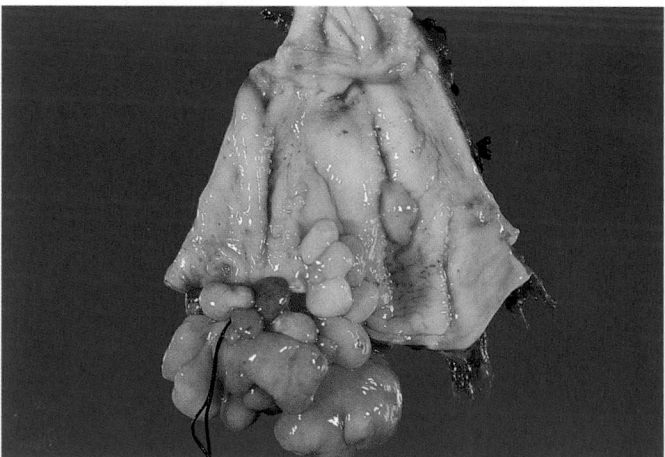

Fig. 19.53 Botryoid rhabdomyosarcoma of vagina. The grape-like configuration of this lesion is characteristic.

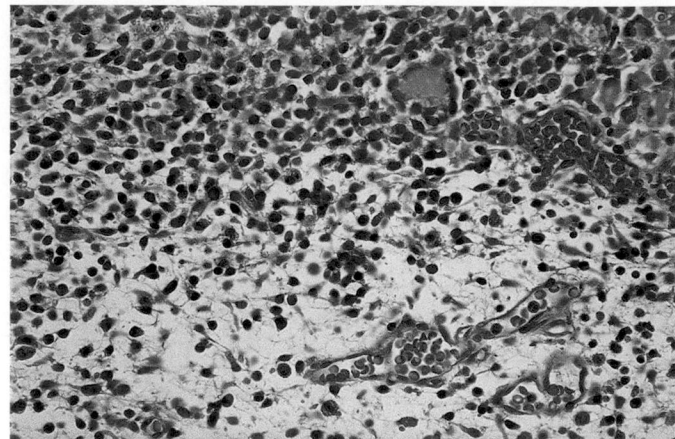

Fig. 19.54 Microscopic appearance of embryonal rhabdomyosarcoma. The differential diagnosis is that of small round cell tumors.

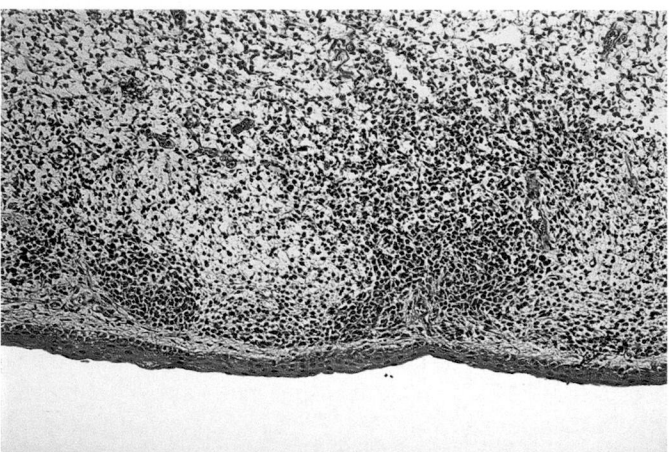

Fig. 19.55 So-called "cambium layer" beneath non-neoplastic epithelium in botryoid rhabdomyosarcoma.

striations may or may not be present. An important diagnostic feature is the crowding of the tumor cells around blood vessels and, most important, beneath the squamous epithelium. The latter results in a distinctive subepithelial dense zone (the "cambium layer" of Nicholson) (Fig. 19.55). Invasion of the overlying epithelium can be seen. Foci of neoplastic cartilage may be found; these tend to occur in older patients and/or in tumors located higher in the vagina or cervix, and they are said to be associated with a better prognosis. Botryoid tumors are currently regarded as a variation in the growth pattern of embryonal rhabdomyosarcoma, due to their location immediately beneath an expansile epithelial lining. They cause death more often by direct extension than by distant metastases.[144] Of the 15 autopsied cases reviewed by Hilgers et al.,[141] the tumor was confined to the pelvis in about half.

The treatment of this tumor, traditionally consisting of radical surgery,[140,158] is now primarily based on chemotherapy, which can be combined with radiation therapy and/or surgery depending on the circumstances.[138]

Other primary sarcomas that have been reported in the vagina are *stromal sarcoma* of endometrial type,[154] *malignant peripheral nerve sheath tumor,*[154] *angiosarcoma*[155] (sometimes arising as a complication of radiation therapy[128]), *alveolar soft part sarcoma,*[126,129,148] and Ewing's sarcoma/PNET.[163]

Melanocytic tumors

Malignant melanoma can occur as a primary vaginal tumor in elderly patients.[167,172,174,175] It presents as a soft polypoid mass, blue or black, frequently ulcerated (Fig. 19.56). Most cases are located in the lower one third and in the anterolateral aspect.[165] Microscopically, the appearance is the same as that of the cutaneous melanomas, although they tend to show greater anaplasia and pleomorphism (Fig. 19.57). An intraepithelial component of lentiginous appearance ("junctional activity") should be looked for to substantiate a local origin, although this feature can be destroyed by the tumor ulceration. The prognosis is extremely poor.[168,169,171] The melanocytes that have been identified in 3% of normal vaginas[173] most likely represent the cell of origin of this neoplasm, sometimes through a preceding stage of melanosis or atypical melanocytic hyperplasia.[166,170]

Blue nevus of the ordinary type can present as a primary vaginal lesion.[176]

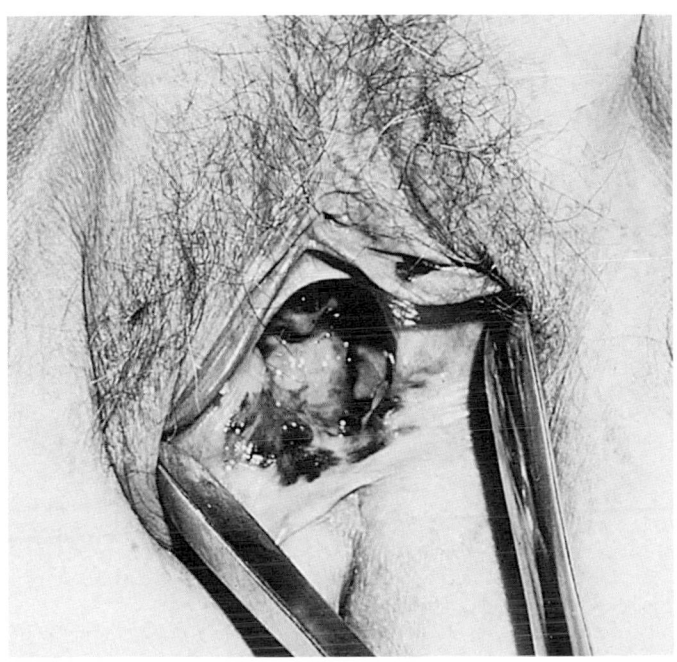

Fig. 19.56 Malignant melanoma of vagina. (From Norris HJ, Taylor HD. Melanomas of the vagina. Am J Clin Pathol 1966, 46: 420–426)

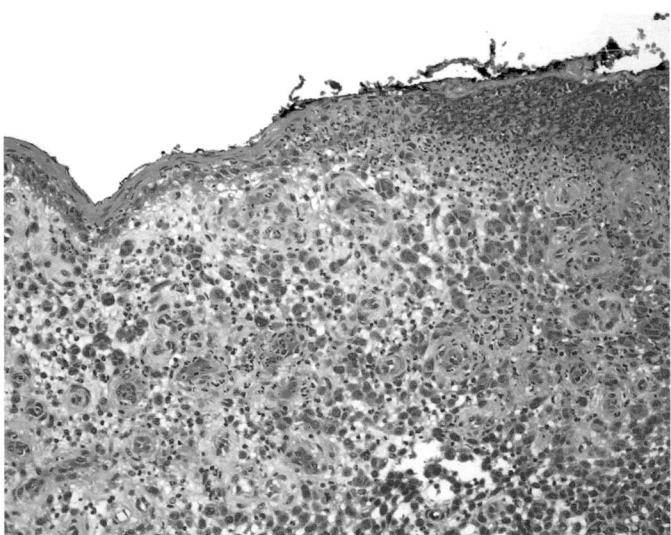

Fig. 19.57 Malignant melanoma of vagina. The tumor has an undifferentiated appearance, is largely amelanotic, and has an ulcerated surface.

Other primary tumors

Yolk sac tumor (endodermal sinus tumor) typically affects infants under 2 years of age and is more commonly located in either the posterior wall or the fornices.[180,190] Clinically, it can simulate botryoid rhabdomyosarcoma.[184] Microscopically, the most important differential diagnosis is with clear cell (adeno)carcinoma, a tumor with which it has been confused in the past. Immunohistochemically, reactivity for α-fetoprotein favors yolk sac tumor, and reactivity for Leu-M1 favors clear cell carcinoma.[191] In early series, most patients with vaginal yolk sac carcinoma died with generalized metastases,[185] but the combination of surgical excision and multidrug chemotherapy (sometimes with the addition of radiation therapy) has resulted in several long-term cures.[183,187]

Malignant lymphoma can affect the vagina secondarily or sometimes as the only site of involvement; nearly all cases are of non-Hodgkin's type.[179,182,186] The largest group is represented by diffuse large B-cell lymphomas.[189] A case has been reported in association with malakoplakia.[188] Vaginal involvement can also occur in *acute granulocytic leukemia* (granulocytic sarcoma).[182]

Other primary tumors of the vagina, both exceptionally rare, are *Brenner's tumor*,[177,178] and *female adnexal tumor of probable wolffian origin*.[181]

Metastatic tumors

Metastatic carcinoma to the vagina arises most commonly in the uterine cervix and endometrium, followed by the ovary, large bowel, and kidney.[193,194,196] Some cases represent direct extension, and others are distant metastases. The metastases from endometrial adenocarcinoma are often submucosal and located in the upper third of the organ. The routine practice of preoperative radiation therapy for uterine adenocarcinomas associated with uterine enlargement has reduced their frequency.

Other tumors that can metastasize to vagina are malignant melanoma[192] and malignant trophoblastic neoplasms, including epithelioid trophoblastic tumor.[195]

References

Normal anatomy

1 Hafez ESE, Evans TN (eds): The human vagina. New York, 1978, North-Holland.

2 Krantz KE. The gross and microscopic anatomy of the human vagina. Ann NY Acad Sci 1959, 83: 89–104.

3 Robboy SJ, Bentley RC. Vagina. In Sternberg S (ed.): Histology for pathologists, ed. 2. Philadelphia, 1997, Lippincott-Raven, pp. 867–878.

4 Ulfelder H, Robboy SJ. The embryological development of the human vagina. Am J Obstet Gynecol 1976, 126: 769–776.

Adenosis and related lesions

5 Antonioli DA, Burke L. Vaginal adenosis. Analysis of 325 biopsy specimens from 100 patients. Am J Clin Pathol 1975, 64: 625–638.

6 Chattopadhyay I, Cruickshan DJ, Packer M. Non diethylstilbesterol induced vaginal adenosis – a case series and review of literature. Eur J Gynecol Oncol 2001, 22: 260–262.

7 Fu YS, Reagan JW, Richart RM, Townsend DE. Nuclear DNA and histologic studies of genital lesions in diethylstilbestrol-exposed progeny. I. Intraepithelial squamous abnormalities. Am J Clin Pathol 1979, 72: 503–520.

8 Hart WR, Townsend DE, Aldrich JO, Henderson BE, Roy M, Benton B. Histopathologic spectrum of vaginal adenosis and related changes in stilbestrol-exposed females. Cancer 1976, 37: 763–775.

9 Herbst AL, Poskanzer DC, Robboy SJ, Friedlander L, Scully RE. Prenatal exposure to stilbestrol. A prospective comparison of exposed female offspring with unexposed controls. N Engl J Med 1975, 292: 334–339.

10 Jefferies JA, Robboy SJ, O'Brien PC, Bergstralh EJ, Labarthe DR, Barnes AB, Noller KL, Hatab PA, Kaufman RH, Townsend DE. Structural anomalies of the cervix and vagina in women enrolled in the Diethylstilbestrol Adenosis (DESAD) Project. Am J Obstet Gynecol 1984, 148: 59–66.

11 Kurman RJ, Scully RE. The incidence and histogenesis of vaginal adenosis. An autopsy study. Hum Pathol 1974, 5: 265–276.

12 Merchant WJ, Gale J. Intestinal metaplasia in stilboestrol-induced vaginal adenosis. Histopathology 1993, 23: 373–376.

13 Robboy SJ, Hill EC, Sandberg EC, Czernobilsky B. Vaginal adenosis in women born prior to the diethylstilbestrol era. Hum Pathol 1986, 17: 488–492.

14 Robboy SJ, Scully RE, Welch WR, Herbst AL. Intrauterine diethylstilbestrol exposure and its consequences. Pathologic characteristics of vaginal adenosis, clear cell adenocarcinoma, and related lesions. Arch Pathol Lab Med 1977, 101: 1–5.

15 Robboy SJ, Szyfelbein WM, Goellner JR, Kaufman RH, Taft PD, Richard RM, Gaffey TA, Prat J, Virata R, Hatab PA, McGorray SP, Noller KL, Townsend D, Lobarthe D, Barnes AB. Dysplasia and cytologic findings in 4589 young women enrolled in Diethylstilbestrol Adenosis (DESAD) Project. Am J Obstet Gynecol 1981, 140: 579–586.

16 Robboy SJ, Welch WR. Microglandular hyperplasia in vaginal adenosis associated with oral contraceptives and prenatal diethylstilbestrol exposure. Obstet Gynecol 1977, 49: 430–434.

17 Sandberg EC. The incidence of distribution of occult vaginal adenosis. Trans Pac Coast Obstet Gynecol Soc 1967, 35: 36–48.

18 Siders DB, Parrott MH, Abell MR. Gland cell prosoplasia (adenosis) of vagina. Am J Obstet Gynecol 1965, 91: 190–203.

19 Sonek M, Bibbo M, Wied GL. Colposcopic findings in offspring of DES-treated mothers as related to onset of therapy. J Reprod Med 1976, 16: 65–71.

Other non-neoplastic lesions

20 Bilodeau B. Intravaginal prolapse of the fallopian tube following vaginal hysterectomy. Am J Obstet Gynecol 1982, 143: 970–971.

21 Chalvardjan A, Picard L, Shaw R, Davey R, Cairns JD. Malacoplakia of the female genital tract. Am J Obstet Gynecol 1980, 138: 391–394.

22 Danielson RW. Vaginal ulcers caused by tampons. Am J Obstet Gynecol 1983, 146: 547–548.

23 Deppisch LM. Cysts of the vagina. Classification and clinical correlations. Obstet Gynecol 1975, 45: 632–637.

24 Kramer K, Tobón H. Vaginitis emphysematosa. Arch Pathol Lab Med 1987, 111: 746–749.

25 Martinka M, Allaire C, Clement PB. Endocervicosis presenting as a painful vaginal mass: a case report. Int J Gynecol Pathol 2002, 18: 274–276.

25a Michal M, Rokyta Z, Mejchar B, Pelikan K, Kummel M, Mukensnabl P. Prolapse of the fallopian tube after hysterectomy associated with exuberant angiomyofibroblastic stroma response: a diagnostic pitfall. Virchows Arch 2000, 437: 436–439.

26 Robboy SJ, Welch WR. Selected topics in the pathology of the vagina. Hum Pathol 1991, 22: 868–878.

27 Silverberg SG, Frable WJ. Prolapse of fallopian tube into vaginal vault after hysterectomy. Histopathology, cytopathology, and differential diagnosis. Arch Pathol 1974, 97: 100–103.

28 Sobel JD. Vaginal infections in adult women. Med Clin North Am 1990, 74: 1573–1602.

29 Strate SM, Taylor WE, Forney JP, Silva FG. Xanthogranulomatous pseudotumor of the vagina. Evidence of a local response to an unusual bacterium (mucoid Escherichia coli). Am J Clin Pathol 1983, 79: 637–643.

Benign epithelial tumors

30 Branton PA, Tavassoli FA. Spindle cell epithelioma, the so-called mixed tumor of the vagina. A clinicopathologic, immunohistochemical, and ultrastructural analysis of 28 cases. Am J Surg Pathol 1993, 17: 509–515.

31 Fox H, Wells M, Harris M, McWilliam LJ, Anderson GS. Enteric tumours of the lower female genital tract. A report of three cases. Histopathology 1988, 12: 167–176.

32 Fukunaga M, Endo Y, Ishikawa E, Ushigome S. Mixed tumor of the vagina. Histopathology 1997, 28: 457–461.

33 Kerner H, Munichor M. Papillary mullerian cystadenofibroma of the vagina. Histopathology 1997, 30: 84–86.

34 Sirota RL, Dickersin GR, Scully RE. Mixed tumors of the vagina. Am J Surg Pathol 1981, 5: 413–422.

35 Skelton H, Smith KJ. Spindle cell epitheliomas of the vagina shows immunohistochemical staining supporting its origin from a primitive/progenitor cell population. Arch Pathol Lab Med 2001, 125: 547–550.

36 Ulbright TM, Alexander RW, Kraus FT. Intramural papilloma of the vagina. Evidence of müllerian histogenesis. Cancer 1981, 48: 2260–2266.

37 Wright RG, Buntine DW, Forbes KL. Recurrent benign mixed tumor of the vagina. Gynecol Oncol 1991, 40: 84–86.

Squamous intraepithelial tumors

38 Aho M, Vesterinen E, Meyer B, Purola E, Paavonen J. Natural history of vaginal intraepithelial neoplasia. Cancer 1991, 68: 195–197.

39 Audet-Lapointe P, Body G, Vauclair R, Drouin P, Ayoub J. Vaginal intraepithelial neoplasia. Gynecol Oncol 1990, 36: 232–239.

40 Benedet JL, Sanders BH. Carcinoma in situ of the vagina. Am J Obstet Gynecol 1984, 148: 695–700.

41 Caglar H, Hertzog RW, Hreshchyshyn MM. Topical 5-fluorouracil treatment of vaginal intraepithelial neoplasia. Obstet Gynecol 1981, 58: 580–583.

42 Kanbour AI, Klionsky B, Murphy AI. Carcinoma of the vagina following cervical cancer. Cancer 1974, 34: 1838–1841.

43 Nwabineli NJ, Monaghan JM. Vaginal epithelial abnormalities in

patients with CIN. Clinical and pathological features and management. Br J Obstet Gynaecol 1991, **98**: 25–29.

44 Sherman ME, Paull G. Vaginal intraepithelial neoplasia. Reproducibility of pathologic diagnosis and correlation of smears and biopsies. Acta Cytol 1993, **37**: 699–704.

45 Weir MM, Bell DA, Young RH. Transitional cell metaplasia of the uterine cervix and vagina: an underrecognized lesion that may be confused with high-grade dysplasia: a report of 59 cases. Am J Surg Pathol 1997, **21**: 510–517.

Invasive squamous cell carcinoma

46 Bell J, Sevin B-U, Averette H, Nadji M. Vaginal cancer after hysterectomy for benign disease. Value of cytologic screening. Obstet Gynecol 1984, **64**: 699–702.

47 Benedet JL. Vaginal malignancy. Curr Opin Obstet Gynecol 1991, **3**: 73–77.

48 Choo YC, Anderson DG. Neoplasms of the vagina following cervical carcinoma. Gynecol Oncol 1982, **14**: 125–132.

49 Creasman WT, Phillips JL, Menck HR. The National Cancer Data Base Report on cancer in the vagina. Cancer 1998, **83**: 1033–1040.

50 Davis KP, Stanhope CR, Garton GR, Atkinson EJ, O'Brien PC. Invasive vaginal carcinoma. Analysis of early-stage disease. Gynecol Oncol 1991, **42**: 131–136.

51 Eddy GL, Singh KP, Gansler TS. Superficially invasive carcinoma of the vagina following treatment for cervical cancer. A report of six cases. Gynecol Oncol 1990, **36**: 376–379.

52 Houghton CRS, Iversen T. Squamous cell carcinoma of the vagina. A clinical study of the location of the tumor. Gynecol Oncol 1982, **13**: 365–372.

53 Ikenberg H, Runge M, Goppinger A, Pfeiderer A. Human papillomavirus DNA in invasive carcinoma of the vagina. Obstet Gynecol 1990, **76**: 432–438.

54 Kanbour AI, Klionsky B, Murphy AI. Carcinoma of the vagina following cervical cancer. Cancer 1974, **34**: 1838–1841.

55 Kucera H, Vavra N. Radiation management of primary carcinoma of the vagina. Clinical and histopathological variables associated with survival. Gynecol Oncol 1991, **40**: 12–16.

56 Macnab JCM, Walkinshaw SA, Cordiner JW, Clements JB. Human papillomavirus in clinically and histologically normal tissue of patients with genital cancer. N Engl J Med 1986, **315**: 1052–1058.

57 Manetta A, Gutrecht EL, Berman ML, Di Saia PJ. Primary invasive carcinoma of the vagina. Obstet Gynecol 1990, **76**: 639–642.

58 Merino MJ. Vaginal cancer. The role of infectious and environmental factors. Am J Obstet Gynecol 1991, **165**: 1255–1262.

59 Murad TM, Durant JR, Maddox WA, Dowling EA. The pathologic behavior of primary vaginal carcinoma and its relationship to cervical cancer. Cancer 1975, **35**: 787–794.

60 Perez CA, Arneson AN, Dehner LP, Galakatos A. Radiation therapy in carcinoma of the vagina. Obstet Gynecol 1974, **44**: 862–872.

61 Perez CA, Arneson AN, Galakatos A, Samanth HK. Malignant tumors of the vagina. Cancer 1973, **31**: 36–44.

62 Peters WA III, Kumar NB, Morley GW. Carcinoma of the vagina. Factors influencing treatment outcome. Cancer 1985, **55**: 892–897.

63 Peters WA III, Kumar NB, Morley GW. Microinvasive carcinoma of the vagina. A distinct clinical entity? Am J Obstet Gynecol 1985, **153**: 505–507.

64 Piura B, Rabinovich A, Cohen Y, Glezerman M. Primary squamous cell carcinoma of the vagina: report of four cases and review of the literature. Eur J Gynecol Oncol 1998, **19**: 60–63.

65 Prempree T, Viravathana T, Slawson RG, Wizenberg MJ, Cuccia CA. Radiation management of primary carcinoma of the vagina. Cancer 1977, **40**: 109–118.

66 Reddy S, Lee MS, Graham JE, Yordan EL, Phillips R, Saxena VS,

67 Hendrickson FR, Wilbanks GD. Radiation therapy in primary carcinoma of the vagina. Gynecol Oncol 1987, **26**: 19–24.

67 Rotmensch J, Rosenshein N, Dillon M, Murphy A, Woodruff JD. Carcinoma arising in the neovagina. Case report and review of the literature. Obstet Gynecol 1983, **61**: 534–538.

68 Rubin SC, Young J, Mikuta JJ. Squamous carcinoma of the vagina. Treatment complications and long-term follow-up. Gynecol Oncol 1985, **20**: 346–353.

69 Rutledge F. Cancer of the vagina. Am J Obstet Gynecol 1967, **97**: 635–655.

70 Spirtos NM, Doshi BP, Kapp DS, Teng N. Radiation therapy for primary squamous cell carcinoma of the vagina. Standford University experience. Gynecol Oncol 1989, **35**: 20–26.

71 Steiner E, Woernle F, Kuhn W, Beckmann K, Schmidt M, Pilch H, Knapstein PG. Carcinoma of the neovagina: case report and review of the literature. Gynecol Oncol 2002, **84**: 171–175.

72 Tarraza MH Jr, Muntz H, Decain M, Granai OC, Fuller A Jr. Patterns of recurrence of primary carcinoma of the vagina. Eur J Gynaecol Oncol 1991, **12**: 89–92.

73 Whelton J, Kottmeier HL. Primary carcinoma of the vagina. A study of a Radium-hemmet series of 145 cases. Acta Obstet Gynecol Scand 1962, **41**: 22–40.

Clear cell (adeno)carcinoma

74 Boyd J, Takahashi H, Waggoner SE, Jones LA, Hajek RA, Wharton JT, Liu FS, Fujino T, Barrett JC, McLachlan JA. Molecular genetic analysis of clear cell adenocarcinomas of the vagina and cervix associated and unassociated with diethylstilbestrol exposure in utero. Cancer 1996, **77**: 507–513.

75 Dickersin GR, Welch WR, Erlandson R, Robboy SJ. Ultrastructure of 16 cases of clear cell adenocarcinoma of the vagina and cervix in young women. Cancer 1980, **45**: 1615–1624.

76 Hanselaar AG, Boss EA, Massuger LF, Bernheim JL. Cytologic examination to detect clear cell adenocarcinoma of the vagina or cervix. Gynecol Oncol 1999, **75**: 338–344.

77 Hanselaar A, van Loosbroek M, Schuurbiers O, Helmerhosrt T, Bulten J, Bernheim J. Clear cell adenocarcinoma of the vagina and cervix: an update of the Central Netherlands Registry showing twin age incidence peaks. Cancer 1997, **79**: 2229–2236.

78 Herbst AL, Anderson D. Clear cell adenocarcinoma of the vagina and cervix secondary to intrauterine exposure to diethylstilbestrol. Semin Surg Oncol 1990, **6**: 343–346.

79 Herbst AL, Anderson S, Hubby MM, Haenszel WM, Kaufmann RH, Noller KL. Risk factors for the development of diethylstilbestrol-associated clear cell adenocarcinoma. A case-control study. Am J Obstet Gynecol 1986, **154**: 814–822.

80 Herbst AL, Robboy SJ, Scully RE, Poskanzer DC. Clear-cell adenocarcinoma of the vagina and cervix in girls. Analysis of 170 registry cases. Am J Obstet Gynecol 1974, **119**: 713–724.

81 Herbst AL, Scully RE. Adenocarcinoma of the vagina in adolescence. A report of 7 cases including 6 clear-cell carcinomas (so-called mesonephromas). Cancer 1970, **25**: 745–757.

82 Herbst AL, Ulfelder H, Poskanzer DC. Adenocarcinoma of the vagina. Association of maternal stilbestrol therapy with tumor appearance in young women. N Engl J Med 1971, **284**: 878–881.

83 Jones WB, Tan LK, Lewis JL Jr. Late recurrence of clear cell adenocarcinoma of the vagina and cervix. A report of three cases. Gynecol Oncol 1993, **51**: 266–271.

84 Matias-Guiu X, Lerma E, Prat J. Clear cell tumors of the female genital tract. Semin Diagn Pathol 1998, **14**: 233–239.

85 Melnick S, Cole P, Anderson D, Herbst A. Rates and risks of diethylstilbestrol-related clear-cell adenocarcinoma of the vagina and cervix. An update. N Engl J Med 1987, **316**: 514–516.

86 Nordqvist SRB, Fidler WJ Jr, Woodruff JM, Lewis JL. Clear cell adenocarcinoma of the cervix and vagina. A clinicopathologic study of 21 cases with and without a history of maternal ingestion of estrogens. Cancer 1976, **37**: 858–871.

87 Robboy SJ, Herbst AL, Scully RE. Clear-cell adenocarcinoma of the vagina and cervix in young females. Analysis of 37 tumors that persisted or recurred after primary therapy. Cancer 1974, **34**: 606–614.

88 Robboy SJ, Scully RE, Welch WR, Herbst AL. Intrauterine diethylstilbestrol exposure and its consequences. Pathologic characteristics of vaginal adenosis, clear cell adenocarcinoma, and related lesions. Arch Pathol Lab Med 1977, **101**: 1–5.

89 Robboy SJ, Young RH, Welch WR, Truslow GV, Prat J, Herbst AL, Scully RE. Atypical vaginal adenosis and cervical ectropion. Association with clear cell adenocarcinoma in diethylstilbestrol-exposed offspring. Cancer 1984, **54**: 869–875.

90 Taft PD, Robboy SJ, Herbst AL, Scully RE. Cytology of clear-cell adenocarcinoma of the genital tract in young females. Report of 95 cases from the registry. Acta Cytol (Baltimore) 1974, **18**: 279–290.

91 Vang R, Whitaker BP, Farhood AI, Silva EG, Ro JY, Deavers MT. Immunohistochemical analysis of clear cell carcinoma of the gynaecologic tract. Int J Gynecol Pathol 2001, **20**: 252–259.

92 Welch WR, Prat J, Robboy SJ, Herbst AL. Pathology of prenatal diethylstilbestrol exposure. Pathol Annu 1978, **13**(Pt 1): 201–216.

Other carcinoma types

93 Bass PS, Birch B, Smart C, Theaker JM, Wells M. Low-grade transitional cell carcinoma of the vagina. An unusual cause of vaginal bleeding. Histopathology 1994, **24**: 581–583.

94 Chafe W. Neuroepithelial small cell carcinoma of the vagina. Cancer 1989, **64**: 1948–1951.

95 Dietl J, Horny HP, Kaiserling E. Lymphoepithelioma-like carcinoma of the vagina. A case report with special reference to the immunophenotype of the tumor cells and tumor-infiltrating lymphoreticular cells. Int J Gynecol Pathol 1994, **13**: 186–189.

96 Ebrahim S, Daponte A, Smith TH, Tiltman A, Guidozzi F. Primary mucinous adenocarcinomas of the vagina. Gynecol Oncol 2001, **80**: 89–92.

97 Fox A, Wells M, Harris M, McWilliam LJ, Anderson GS. Enteric tumours of the lower female genital tract. A report of three cases. Histopathology 1988, **12**: 167–176.

98 Fukushima M, Twiggs LB, Okagaki T. Mixed intestinal adenocarcinoma. Argentaffin carcinoma of the vagina. Gynecol Oncol 1986, **23**: 387–394.

99 Granai CO, Walters MD, Safaii H, Jelen I, Madoc-Jones H, Moukhtar M. Malignant transformation of vaginal endometriosis. Obstet Gynecol 1984, **64**: 592–595.

100 Haskel S, Chen SS, Spiegel G. Vaginal endometrioid adenocarcinoma arising in vaginal endometriosis. A case report and literature review. Gynecol Oncol 1989, **34**: 232–236.

101 Hinchey WW, Silva EG, Guarda LA, Ordonez NG, Wharton JT. Paravaginal Wolffian duct (mesonephros) adenocarcinoma. A light and electron microscopic study. Am J Clin Pathol 1983, **80**: 539–544.

102 Hopkins MP, Kumar NB, Lichter AS, Peters WA, Morley GW. Small cell carcinoma of the vagina with neuroendocrine features. A report of three cases. J Reprod Med 1989, **34**: 486–491.

103 Kaminski JM, Anderson PR, Han AC, Mitra RK, Rosenblum NG, Edelson MI. Primary small cell carcinoma of the vagina. Gynecol Oncol 2003, **88**: 451–455.

104 McCluggage WG. Lymphoepithelioma-like carcinoma of the vagina. J Clin Pathol 2001, **54**: 964–965.

105 McCluggage WG, Price JH, Dobbs SP. Primary adenocarcinoma of the vagina arising in endocervicosis. Int J Gynecol Pathol 2001, **20**: 399–402.

106 Miliauskas JR, Leong AS. Small cell (neuroendocrine) carcinoma of the vagina. Histopathology 1992, **21**: 371–374.

107 Okagaki T, Clark BA, Zachow KR, Twiggs LB, Ostrow RS, Pass F, Faras AJ. Presence of human papillomavirus in verrucous carcinoma (Ackerman) of the vagina. Immunocytochemical,

ultrastructural, and DNA hybridization studies. Arch Pathol Lab Med 1984, **108**: 567–570.

108 Okagaki T, Ishida T, Hilgers RD. A malignant tumor of the vagina resembling synovial sarcoma. A light and electron microscopic study. Cancer 1976, **37**: 2306–2320.

109 Peters WA III, Kumar NB, Anderson WA, Morley GW. Primary sarcoma of the adult vagina. A clinicopathologic study. Obstet Gynecol 1985, **63**: 699–704.

110 Prasad CJ, Ray JA, Kessler S. Primary small cell carcinoma of the vagina arising in a background of atypical adenosis. Cancer 1992, **70**: 2484–2487.

111 Ramzy I, Smout MS, Collins JA. Verrucous carcinoma of the vagina. Am J Clin Pathol 1976, **65**: 644–653.

112 Raptis S, Haber G, Ferenczy A. Vaginal squamous cell carcinoma with sarcomatoid spindle cell features. Gynecol Oncol 1993, **49**: 100–106.

113 Riva C, Fabbri A, Facco C, Tibiletti MG, Guglielmin P, Capella C. Primary serous papillary adenocarcinomas of the vagina: a case report. Int J Gynecol Pathol 1998, **16**: 286–290.

114 Rose PG, Stoler MH, Abdul-Karin FW. Papillary squamotransitional cell carcinoma of the vagina. Int J Gynecol Pathol 1998, **17**: 372–375.

115 Rusthoven JJ, Daya D. Small-cell carcinoma of the vagina. A clinicopathologic study. Arch Pathol Lab Med 1990, **114**: 728–731.

116 Shevchuk MM, Fenoglio CM, Lattes R, Frick HC II, Richart RM. Malignant mixed tumor of the vagina probably arising in mesonephric rests. Cancer 1978, **42**: 214–233.

117 Singer G, Hohl MK, Hering F, Anabitarte M. Transitional cell carcinoma of the vagina with pagetoid spread pattern. Hum Pathol 1998, **29**: 299–301.

118 Steeper TA, Piscioli F, Rosai J. Squamous cell carcinoma with sarcoma-like stroma of the female genital tract. Clinicopathologic study of four cases. Cancer 1983, **52**: 890–898.

119 Takehara M, Hayakawa O, Itoh E, Sagae S, Suzuki Kudo R. A case of a malignant mixed tumor in the vagina. J Obstet Gynaecol Res 1998, **24**: 7–11.

120 Ulich TR, Liao S-Y, Layfield L, Romansky S, Cheng L, Lewin KJ. Endocrine and tumor differentiation markers in poorly differentiated small-cell carcinoids of the cervix and vagina. Arch Pathol Lab Med 1986, **110**: 1054–1057.

121 Yaghsezian H, Palazzo JP, Finkel GC, Carlson JA Jr, Talerman A. Primary vaginal adenocarcinoma of the intestinal type associated with adenosis. Gynecol Oncol 1992, **45**: 62–65.

122 Young EE, Gamble CH. Primary adenocarcinoma of the rectovaginal septum arising from endometriosis. Report of a case. Cancer 1969, **24**: 597–601.

Mesenchymal tumors and tumorlike conditions

123 Abdul-Karim FW, Cohen RE. Atypical stromal cells of lower female genital tract. Histopathology 1990, **17**: 249–253.

124 al-Nafussi AI, Rebello G, Hughes D, Blessing K. Benign vaginal polyp. A histological, histochemical and immunohistochemical study of 20 polyps with comparison to normal vaginal subepithelial layer. Histopathology 1992, **20**: 145–150.

125 Azzopardi JG, Eusebi V, Tison V, Betts CM. Neurofibroma with rhabdomyomatous differentiation. Benign "triton" tumour of the vagina. Histopathology 1983, **7**: 561–572.

126 Carinelli SG, Giudici MN, Brioschi D, Cefis F. Alveolar soft part sarcoma of the vagina. Tumori 1990, **76**: 77–80.

127 Chabrel CM, Beilby JOW. Vaginal rhabdomyoma. Histopathology 1980, **4**: 645–651.

128 Chan WW, Sen Gupta SK. Postirradiation angiosarcoma of the vaginal vault. Arch Pathol Lab Med 1991, **115**: 527–528.

129 Chapman GW, Genda J, Williams T. Alveolar soft-part sarcoma of the vagina. Gynecol Oncol 1984, **18**: 125–129.

130 Chen KT. Angiomyolipoma of the vagina. Gynecol Oncol 1990, **37**: 302–304.

131 Chirayil SJ, Tobon H. Polyps of the vagina. A clinico-pathologic study of 18 cases. Cancer 1981, **47**: 2904–2907.

132 Ciaravino G, Kapp DS, Vela AM, Fulton RS, Lum BL, Teng NN, Roberts JA. Primary leiomyosarcoma of the vagina. A case report and literature review. Int J Gynecol Cancer 2000, **10**: 340–347.

133 Ellison DW, Mac Kenzie IZ, McGee JO. Cellular schwannoma of the vagina. Gynecol Oncol 1992, **46**: 119–121.

134 Gersell DJ, Fulling KH. Localized neurofibromatosis of the female genitourinary tract. Am J Surg Pathol 1989, **13**: 873–878.

135 Gold JH, Bossen EH. Benign vaginal rhabdomyoma. A light and electron microscopic study. Cancer 1976, **37**: 2283–2294.

136 Halvorsen TB, Johannesen E. Fibroepithelial polyps of the vagina. Are they old granulation tissue polyps? J Clin Pathol 1992, **45**: 235–240.

137 Hartmann CA, Sperling M, Stein H. So-called fibroepithelial polyps of the vagina exhibiting an unusual but uniform antigen profile characterized by expression of desmin and steroid hormone receptors but no muscle-specific actin or macrophage markers. Am J Clin Pathol 1990, **93**: 604–608.

138 Hays DM, Shimada H, Raney RB Jr, Tefft M, Newton W, Crist WM, Lawrence W Jr, Ragab A, Beltangady M, Maurer HM. Clinical staging and treatment results in rhabdomyosarcoma of the female genital tract among children and adolescents. Cancer 1988, **61**: 1893–1903.

139 Hays DM, Shimada H, Raney RB Jr, Tefft M, Newton W, Crist WM, Lawrence W Jr, Ragab A, Maurer HM. Sarcomas of the vagina and uterus. The Intergroup Rhabdomyosarcoma Study. J Pediatr Surg 1985, **20**: 718–724.

140 Hilgers RD. Pelvic exenteration for vaginal embryonal rhabdomyosarcoma. A review. Obstet Gynecol 1975, **45**: 175–180.

141 Hilgers R, Malkasian GD Jr, Soule EH. Embryonal rhabdomyosarcoma (botryoid type) of the vagina. A clinicopathologic review. Am J Obstet Gynecol 1970, **107**: 484–502.

142 Hiura M, Nogawa T, Nagai N, Yorishima M, Fujiwara A. Vaginal hemangiopericytoma. A light microscopic and ultrastructural study. Gynecol Oncol 1985, **21**: 376–384.

143 Laskin WB, Fetsch JF, Tavassoli FA. Superficial cervicovaginal myofibroblastoma: fourteen cases of a distinctive mesenchymal tumor arising from the specialised subepithelial stroma of the lower female genital tract. Hum Pathol 2001, **32**: 715–725.

144 Leuschner I, Harms D, Mattke A, Koscielniak E, Treuner J. Rhabdomyosarcoma of the urinary bladder and vagina: a clinicopathologic study with emphasis on recurrent disease: a report from the Kiel Pediatric Tumor Registry and the German CWS study. Am J Surg Pathol 2001, **25**: 856–864.

145 Miettinen M, Wahlstrom T, Vesterinen E, Saksela E. Vaginal polyps with pseudosarcomatous features. A clinicopathologic study of seven cases. Cancer 1983, **51**: 1148–1151.

146 Mucitelli DR, Charles EZ, Kraus FT. Vulvovaginal polyps. Histologic appearance, ultrastructure, immunocytochemical characteristics, and clinicopathologic correlations. Int J Gynecol Pathol 1990, **9**: 20–40.

147 Naidoo P. Vaginal leiomyoma with heterologous paragangliomatous elements. Int J Surg Pathol 2001, **8**: 359–365.

148 Nielsen GP, Oliva E, Young RH, Rosenberg AE, Dickersin GR, Scully RE. Alveolar soft-part sarcoma of the female genital tract. A report of nine cases and review of the literature. Int J Gynecol Pathol 1995, **14**: 283–292.

149 Nielsen GP, Rosenberg AE, Young RH, Dickersin GR, Clement PB, Scully RE. Angiomyofibroblastoma of the vulva and vagina. Mod Pathol 1996, **9**: 284–291.

150 Norris HJ, Taylor HB. Polyps of the vagina. Cancer 1966, **19**: 227–232.

151 Nucci MR, Fletcher CD. Vulvovaginal soft tissue tumors: update and review. Histopathology 2000, **36**: 97–108.

152 Nucci MR, Young RH, Fletcher CD. Cellular pseudosarcomatous fibroepithelial stromal polyps of the lower female genital tract: an underrecognized lesion often misdiagnosed as sarcoma. Am J Surg Pathol 2000, **24**: 231–240.

153 Ostor AG, Fortune DW, Riley CB. Fibroepithelial polyps with atypical stromal cells (pseudosarcoma botryoides) of vulva and vagina. A report of 13 cases. Int J Gynecol Pathol 1988, **7**: 351–360.

154 Peters WA III, Kumar NB, Anderson WA, Morley GW. Primary sarcoma of the adult vagina. A clinicopathologic study. Obstet Gynecol 1985, **63**: 699–704.

155 Prempree T, Tang C-K, Hatef A, Forster S. Angiosarcoma of the vagina. A clinicopathologic report. A reappraisal of the radiation treatment of angiosarcomas of the female genital tract. Cancer 1983, **51**: 618–622.

156 Proppe KH, Scully RE, Rosai J. Postoperative spindle cell nodules of genitourinary tract resembling sarcomas. A report of eight cases. Am J Surg Pathol 1984, **8**: 101–108.

157 Rastogi BL, Bergman B, Angervall L. Primary leiomyosarcoma of the vagina. A study of five cases. Gynecol Oncol 1984, **18**: 77–86.

158 Rutledge F, Sullivan MP. Sarcoma botryoides. Ann NY Acad Sci 1967, **142**: 694–708.

159 Spitzer M, Molho L, Seltzer VL, Lipper S. Vaginal glomus tumor. Case presentation and ultrastructural findings. Obstet Gynecol 1985, **66**: 86S–88S.

160 Steeper TA, Rosai J. Aggressive angiomyxoma of the female pelvis and perineum. Report of nine cases of a distinctive type of gynecologic soft tissue neoplasm. Am J Surg Pathol 1983, **7**: 463–475.

161 Tavassoli FA, Norris HJ. Smooth muscle tumors of the vagina. Obstet Gynecol 1979, **53**: 689–693.

162 Vadmal MS, Pellegrini AE. Solitary fibrous tumor of the vagina. Am J Dermatopathol 2000, **22**: 83–86.

163 Vang R, Taubenberger JK, Mannion CM, BiJwaard K, Malpica A, Ordonez NG, Tavassoli FA, Silver SA. Primary vulvar and vaginal extraosseous Ewing's sarcoma/peripheral neuroectodermal tumor: diagnostic confirmation with CD99 immunostaining and reverse transcriptase-polymerase chain reaction. Int J Gynecol Pathol 2000, **19**: 103–109.

164 Young RH, Clement PB. Pseudoneoplastic lesions of the lower female genital tract. Pathol Annu 1989, **24**(Pt 2): 189–226.

Melanocytic tumors

165 Borazjani G, Prem KA, Okagaki T, Twiggs LB, Adcock LL. Primary malignant melanoma of the vagina. A clinicopathological analysis of 10 cases. Gynecol Oncol 1990, **37**: 264–267.

166 Bottles K, Lacey CG, Miller TR. Atypical melanocytic hyperplasia of the vagina. Gynecol Oncol 1984, **19**: 226–230.

167 Chung AF, Casey MJ, Flannery JT, Woodruff JM, Lewis JL Jr. Malignant melanoma of the vagina. Report of 19 cases. Obstet Gynecol 1980, **55**: 720–727.

168 Gupta D, Neto AG, Deavers MT, Silva EG, Malpica A. Metastatic melanoma of the vagina: clinicopathologic and immunohistochemical study of three cases and literature review. Int J Gynecol Pathol 2003, **22**: 136–140.

169 Hasumi K, Sakamoto G, Sugano H, Kasuga T, Masubuchi K. Primary malignant melanoma of the vagina. Study of four autopsy cases with ultrastructural findings. Cancer 1978, **42**: 2675–2686.

170 Kerley SW, Blute ML, Keeney GL. Multifocal malignant melanoma arising in vesicovaginal melanosis. Arch Pathol Lab Med 1991, **115**: 950–952.

171 Morrow CP, DiSaia PJ. Malignant melanoma of the female genitalia. A clinical analysis. Obstet Gynecol Surv 1976, **31**: 233–271.

172 Neven P, Shepherd JH, Masotina A, Fisher C, Lowe DG. Malignant melanoma of the vulva and vagina: a report of 23 cases presenting in 10-year period. Int J Gynecol Cancer 1994, **4**: 379–383.

173 Nigogosyan G, De La Pava S, Pickren JW. Melanoblasts in the vaginal mucosa. Origin for primary malignant melanoma. Cancer 1964, **17**: 912–913.

174 Norris HJ, Taylor HB. Melanomas of the vagina. Am J Clin Pathol 1966, **46**: 420–426.

175 Ragnarsson-Olding B, Johansson H, Rutqvist LE, Ringborg U. Malignant melanoma of the vulva and vagina. Trends in incidence, age distribution, and long-term survival among 245 consecutive cases in Sweden 1960–1984. Cancer 1993, **71**: 1893–1897.

176 Tobon H, Murphy AI. Benign blue nevus of the vagina. Cancer 1977, **40**: 3174–3176.

Other primary tumors

177 Ben-Izhak O, Munichor M, Malkin L, Kerner H. Brenner tumor of the vagina. Int J Gynecol Pathol 1998, **17**: 79–82.

178 Chen KTK. Brenner tumor of the vagina. Diagn Gynecol Obstet 1981, **3**: 255–258.

179 Chorlton I, Karnei RF Jr, Norris HJ. Primary malignant reticuloendothelial disease involving the vagina, cervix, and corpus uteri. Obstet Gynecol 1974, **44**: 735–748.

180 Copeland LJ, Sneige N, Ordonex NG, Hancock KC, Gershenson DM, Saul PB, Kavanagh JJ. Endodermal sinus tumor of the vagina and cervix. Cancer 1985, **55**: 2558–2565.

181 Daya D, Murphy J, Simon G. Paravaginal female adnexal tumor of probable wolffian origin. Am J Clin Pathol 1994, **101**: 275–278.

182 Harris NL, Scully RE. Malignant lymphoma and granulocytic sarcoma of the uterus and vagina. A clinicopathologic analysis of 27 cases. Cancer 1984, **53**: 2530–2545.

183 Kohorn EI, McIntosh S, Lytton B, Knowlton AH, Merino M. Endodermal sinus tumor of the infant vagina. Gynecol Oncol 1985, **20**: 196–203.

184 Lopes LF, Chazan R, Sredni ST, de Camargo B. Endodermal sinus tumor of the vagina in children. Med Pediatr Oncol 1999, **32**: 377–381.

185 Norris HJ, Bagley GP, Taylor HB. Carcinoma of the infant vagina. A distinctive tumor. Arch Pathol 1970, **90**: 473–479.

186 Perren T, Farrant M, McCarthy K, Harper P, Wiltshaw E. Lymphomas of the cervix and upper vagina. A report of five cases and a review of the literature. Gynecol Oncol 1992, **44**: 87–95.

187 Rutledge F, Sullivan MP. Sarcoma botryoides. Ann NY Acad Sci 1967, **142**: 694–708.

188 Skinnider BF, Clement PB, MacPherson N, Gascoyne RD, Viswanatha DS. Primary non-Hodgkin's lymphoma and malakoplakia of the vagina: a case report. Hum Pathol 1999, **30**: 871–874.

189 Vang R, Medeiros LJ, Silva EG, Gershenson DM, Deavers M. Non-Hodgkin's lymphoma involving the vagina: a clinicopathologic analysis of 14 patients. Am J Surg Pathol 2000, **24**: 719–725.

190 Young RH, Scully RE. Endodermal sinus tumor of the vagina. A report of nine cases and review of the literature. Gynecol Oncol 1984, **18**: 380–392.

191 Zirker TA, Silva EG, Morris M, Ordonez NG. Immunohistochemical differentiation of clear-cell carcinoma of the female genital tract and endodermal sinus tumor with the use of alpha-fetoprotein and Leu-M1. Am J Clin Pathol 1989, **91**: 511–514.

Metastatic tumors

192 Gupta D, Malpica A, Deavers MT, Silva EG. Vaginal melanoma: a clinicopathologic and immunohistochemical study of 26 cases. Am J Surg Pathol 2002, **26**: 1450–1457.

193 Mazur MT, Hsueh S, Gersell DJ. Metastases to the female genital tract. Analysis of 325 cases. Cancer 1984, **53**: 1978–1984.

194 Nerdrum TA. Vaginal metastasis of hypernephroma. Report of three cases. Acta Obstet Gynecol Scand 1966, **45**: 515–524.

195 Ohira S, Yamazaki T, Hatano H, Harada O, Toki T, Konishi I. Epithelioid trophoblastic tumor metastatic to the vagina: an immunohistochemical and ultrastructural study. Int J Gynecol Pathol 2001, **19**: 381–386.

196 Stander RW. Vaginal metastases following treatment of endometrial carcinoma. Am J Obstet Gynecol 1956, **71**: 776–779.

Uterus—cervix

Normal anatomy

The cervix is the lower portion of the uterus, which connects this organ to the vagina through the endocervical canal. It is divided into a portion that protrudes into the vagina (*portio vaginalis*) and one that lies above the vaginal vault (*supravaginal portion*). The outer surface of the portio vaginalis is known as the exocervix or ectocervix, and the portion related to the endocervical canal corresponds to the endocervix. The opening of the endocervical canal onto the exocervix is known as the *external os*, whereas the grossly indistinct upper limit of the endocervical canal is designated the *internal os*.[3]

Most of the exocervix is covered by nonkeratinizing squamous epithelium that in child-bearing age is composed of three layers: basal cell, midzone (stratum spongiosum), and superficial. The portion of the midzone immediately above the basal layer, referred to as the *suprabasal layer*, is well demonstrated with silver stains; according to some authors, the real "stem cells" of the cervical squamous mucosa are located in this layer rather than in the basal layer.[12] The morphologic appearance of the various layers varies with age; in the postmenopausal period the cells are atrophic and exhibit a high nucleocytoplasmic ratio. These changes should not be misinterpreted as evidence of cervical intraepithelial neoplasia (CIN).

Histochemically, the cells above the basal layer show variable amounts of glycogen, readily appreciated in sections with a PAS stain and clinically by the application of the iodine (Lugol or Schiller's) test. Immunohistochemically, the cells of the basal layer are positive for low-molecular-weight keratin and tissue polypeptide antigen (TPA) but not for high-molecular-weight (epidermal type) keratin or for involucrin.[4,5,9–11] The latter two markers become positive in the cells above the basal layer. Basal cells are also immunoreactive for estrogen receptors.[6]

The glandular mucosa of the endocervix is formed by a layer of columnar mucus-secreting cells, the histochemical reactivity for the mucin depending on the time of the menstrual cycle.[2] These cells rest on a normally inconspicuous layer of subcolumnar "reserve" cells, which are also positive for TPA.[4] These "reserve" cells (in particular, those located at or near the squamocolumnar junction) are primarily involved in the processes of squamous metaplasia, CIN, and carcinoma. The glandular epithelium is immunoreactive for estrogen receptors.[6] In addition to lining the surface, it invaginates into the stroma to produce elongated clefts (usually less than 5 mm deep but sometimes as deep as 1 cm or more), usually referred to as endocervical glands.

The area where the squamous and glandular epithelia meet is known as the squamocolumnar junction (Fig. 19.58). It should be noted that this junction is not located

Fig. 19.58 Transition zone of uterine cervix between exocervical squamous cells and endocervical mucin-producing glandular epithelium.

in the anatomic external os but rather in the adjacent exocervix, a fact that renders it easily accessible to the colposcope. The portion of endocervical mucosa covering the exocervix is sometimes referred to as *ectropion* and, inaccurately, as *erosion*. This is a very unstable region, in which replacement of one epithelium for another repeatedly occurs, a process that Robert Meyer allegorically referred to as "the fight of the epithelia." Today, this area is more prosaically known as the *transformation zone*.

Scattered endocrine cells are found in both the normal endocervix and exocervix,[1,8] and melanocytes are occasionally detected along the exocervical basal layer.[7]

The stroma of the cervix is mainly made up of fibrous tissue admixed with elastic fibers and scattered smooth muscle fibers.

Remnants and ectopias

Mesonephric rests are remnants of the wolffian ducts that are found surrounded by the endocervical stroma in about a third of women. They are composed of tubules

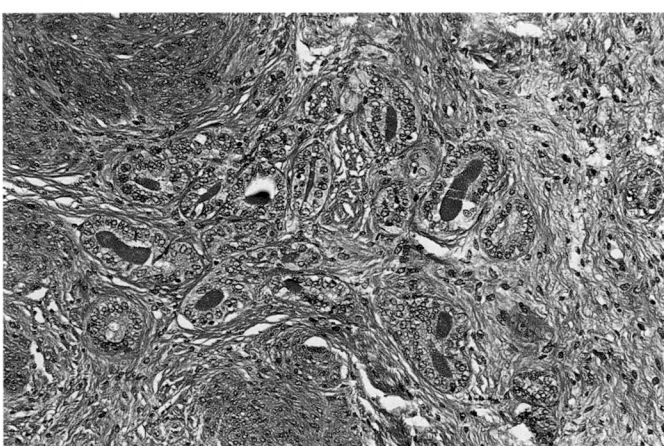

A

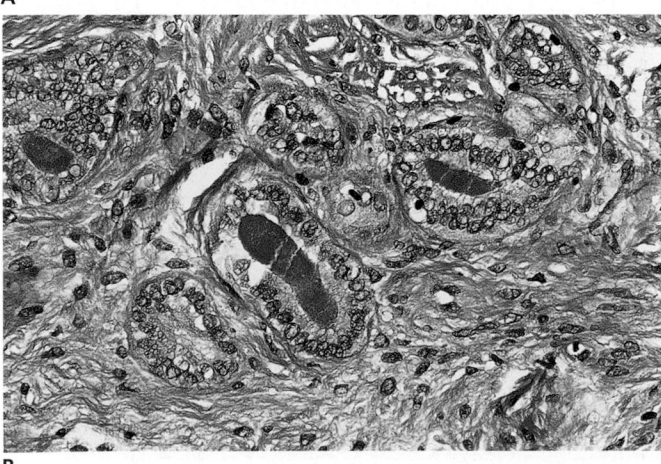

B

Fig. 19.59 A and **B,** Florid mesonephric rests in endocervix. Note the eosinophilic inspissated secretion in the glandular lumen, an important diagnostic clue.

lined by a single row of cuboidal cells; they typically contain an inspissated deeply eosinophilic secretion in the lumen (Fig. 19.59).

Ectopic tissues sometimes found in the cervix include *cutaneous adnexa* (sebaceous glands and hair follicles),[15] prostatic tissue (sometimes referred to as "female prostate"),[13,14] and *mature cartilage islands*.[16] The latter (which may be metaplastic rather than ectopic) should not be confused with the cartilaginous component of a mixed müllerian tumor or a botryoid rhabdomyosarcoma.

Squamous and other metaplasias

Various types of metaplastic changes of the cervical epithelium occur, their appearance being related to the type of mucosa affected. Squamous metaplasia, by far the most common (to the point that some regard it as a normal finding) is centered on the transformation zone; transitional metaplasia involves the exocervical squamous epithelium; and tubal, tuboendometrial, and intestinal metaplasia affect the glandular epithelium of the endocervix.

The term **squamous metaplasia** is used to designate the focal or extensive replacement of the mucus-secreting glandular epithelium by stratified squamous epithelium, which, in its late stage, is morphologically indistinguishable from the epithelium normally lining the exocervical portion (Fig. 19.60). The pathogenesis of this process, also known as *prosoplasia*, has been a subject of a heated controversy over the years. It is now generally agreed

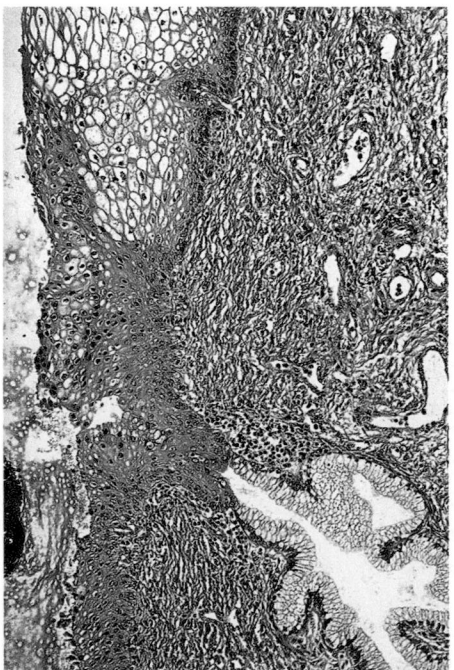

Fig. 19.60 Squamous metaplasia of endocervix involving surface epithelium and glandular openings.

that it most commonly arises on the basis of proliferation and metaplasia of reserve cells. It is possible that in other instances it results from direct ingrowth into the endocervical mucosa of mature native squamous epithelium from the exocervix, possibly as a healing mechanism of a true cervical erosion.[26] Strictly speaking, the latter is not a metaplastic process but rather one of "squamous epithelization." However, it is common usage to employ the term squamous metaplasia regardless of the presumed mechanism for the change.

Some degree of squamous metaplasia is present in almost every uterine cervix during the child-bearing years. Most commonly, the process involves only the superficial epithelium and is recognized by the presence of squamous epithelium overlying endocervical glands. In other instances, it affects the glandular component as well, resulting in a complex microscopic appearance that can be confused with invasive carcinoma by the inexperienced (Fig. 19.61).

Ultrastructural and immunohistochemical markers of squamous epithelium appear *pari passu* with the morphologic changes.[22,35] Variations on this theme, probably representing various stages within a continuum, have been described as *reserve cell hyperplasia* and as *immature, intermediate,* and *mature squamous metaplasia.*[18] A further nuance is *atypical immature metaplasia*, a lesion combining the features of immature metaplasia with some degree of cytologic atypia.[18] Cases carrying this diagnosis are associated with a wide range of Ki-67 indices and variable human papilloma virus (HPV) status, suggesting that this designation is used for a heterogeneous group of conditions rather than a well-defined entity.[20,23,34]

All of the above changes are characterized by a flat architecture, and are, therefore, different from the condyloma and other papillary processes described on p. 1486, including so-called "papillary immature metaplasia (immature condyloma)."

Although most cervical carcinomas arise in areas of the cervix that sometime in the past had been involved by squamous metaplasia; the latter process has no premalignant connotations per se. Actually, it is so common and insignificant that, unless quite extensive and/or involving the glandular component, we tend to ignore it altogether in our pathology reports.

A somewhat different appearance is seen often in the cervix of prolapsed uteri. The clinical appearance is usually referred to as "leukoplakic." Microscopically, the process involves mainly the exocervical portion and is characterized by the appearance of granular and horny layers in the epithelium. This process, which is also unrelated to carcinoma, is best designated as *keratosis.* Sometimes this epithelium contains scattered large pale cells, a change that has been dignified by the term *pagetoid dyskeratosis.*[37]

Transitional metaplasia is seen in the exocervix of older women and it is often associated with atrophy. It morphologically resembles transitional (urothelial) epithelium, and it involves the entire thickness of the mucosa. The nuclei are oval and devoid of atypical features. Their long axes, which are arranged perpendicularly to the surface, often exhibit longitudinal grooves[21,38] (Fig. 19.62). Immunohistochemically, there is positivity for CK13, CK17, and CK18, as in the normal urothelium, but not for CK20.[24] This condition has proved controversial, inasmuch as some authorities regard it as nothing less than an atrophic form of CIN.[30] However, the sum of morphologic, cell kinetics, and follow-up data do not support this alternative interpretation.[28,32]

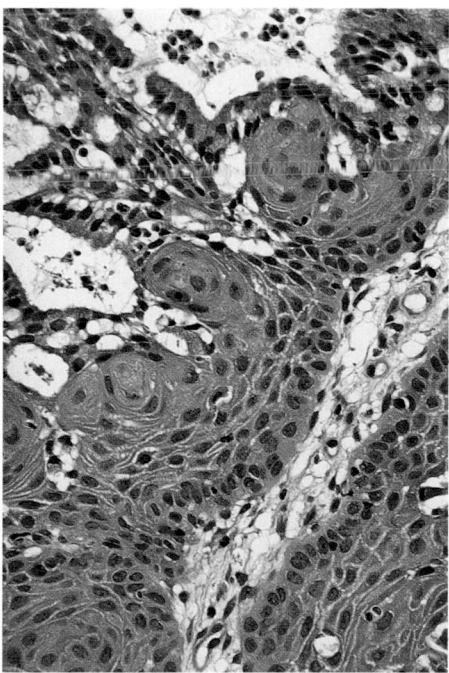

Fig. 19.61 Complex pattern resulting from cervical squamous metaplasia. It may result in an overdiagnosis of squamous cell carcinoma.

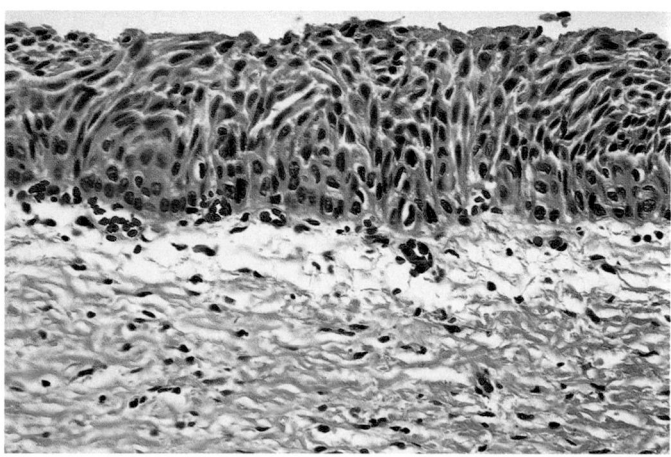

Fig. 19.62 Typical appearance of cervical intraepithelial neoplasia (CIN) III (carcinoma in situ).

Tubal metaplasia is diagnosed when a specimen from the endocervix (usually from the upper portion) is found to contain all three cell types found in the normal fallopian tube (i.e., ciliated, secretory, and intercalated)[27,36] (Fig. 19.63). In many instances, the appearance of the metaplastic epithelium combines features of tubal and endometrial mucosa, in which case the term *tuboendometrial (tuboendometrioid) metaplasia* is employed.[17,31,39] Diagnostic difficulties may result from the fact that these glands may be deeply seated, irregularly shaped, cystically dilated, and/or accompanied by a hypercellular, edematous, or myxoid stroma.[33] Staining for MIB-1(Ki-67) is of some help in the differential diagnosis from in situ and invasive endocervical adenocarcinoma.[31] Tubal metaplasia is often found after conization, and it has

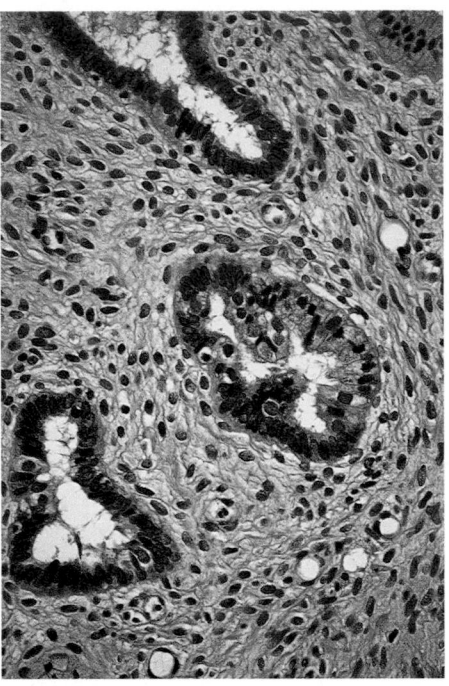

Fig. 19.63 Tubal metaplasia of endocervix. Some of the lining cells are ciliated.

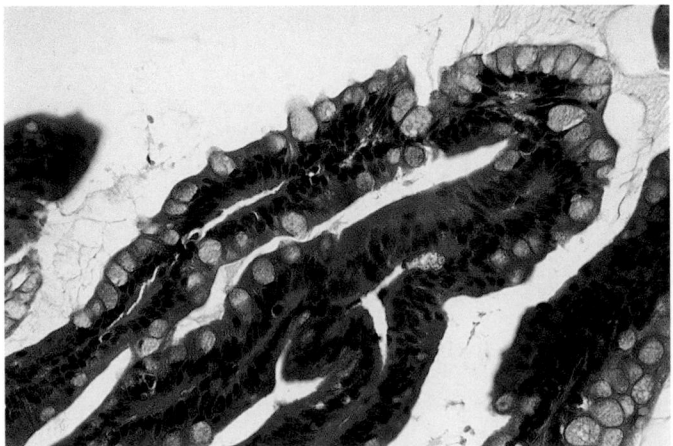

Fig. 19.64 Intestinal metaplasia of cervix. There are numerous goblet cells. This is a very unusual finding.

therefore been suggested that it represents aberrant differentiation following injury.[25] This condition can be identified in cytologic preparations.[19]

Intestinal metaplasia is a much rarer condition, which may be accompanied by extravasation of mucin into the stroma[40] (Fig. 19.64).

Atypical oxyphilic metaplasia is characterized by the presence of large cuboidal or polygonal epithelial cells with dense eosinophilic, focally vacuolated cytoplasm and variable nuclear atypia in the endocervical glands. This rare change seems to be of benign nature.[29]

Inflammatory lesions

Chronic cervicitis is an extremely common condition in adult females, at least at the microscopic level. It affects preferentially the squamocolumnar junction and endocervix, and it may be accompanied by hyperemia, edema, fibrosis, and metaplastic changes in the epithelium. The etiology is variable.[54] In most cases the disease is asymptomatic, but it is of importance because it may lead to endometritis, salpingitis, and "pelvic inflammatory disease" through ascending intraluminal spread, chorioamnionitis, and other complications during pregnancy, and it may also play a role in the initiation or promotion of cervical neoplasia.

Herpes simplex infection of the cervix is now recognized as a relatively common occurrence. The microscopic appearance at the time of biopsy is usually that of an intense nonspecific inflammation with ulceration (Fig. 19.65A). Only rarely are diagnostic multinucleated squamous cells with intranuclear inclusions encountered[53] (Fig. 19.65B). The diagnosis can be confirmed by immunocytochemical demonstration of the viral antigen.[41,51]

Chlamydia trachomatis **infection** is now recognized as the most common venereal disease in the Western world. The microscopic appearance in the cervix is that of a chronic nonspecific inflammation, with reactive epithelial atypia and sometimes prominent formation of lymphoid follicles.[49,57] The organisms are not visible in routine histologic slides and only with difficulty in cytologic preparations, but they can be detected by immunocytochemical techniques.[57] Culture isolation is regarded as the standard for diagnosis of active infection. Chlamydial cervicitis can be associated with CIN, but there is no evidence of a causal relationship.[52]

Syphilis can affect the cervix, usually in the form of a primary chancre.[56]

Amebiasis may produce a polypoid and ulcerated mass in the cervix clinically simulating carcinoma, and it may also engraft itself upon a preexisting cervical carcinoma.[42,47]

Actinomycosis of the cervix occurs, but it needs to be distinguished from the more common pseudoactinomy-

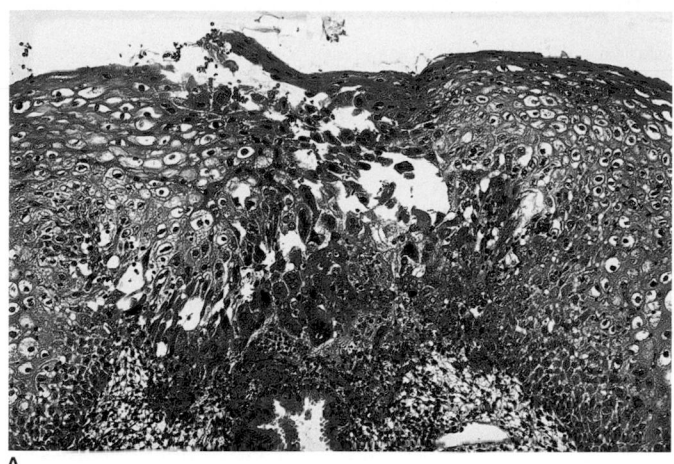
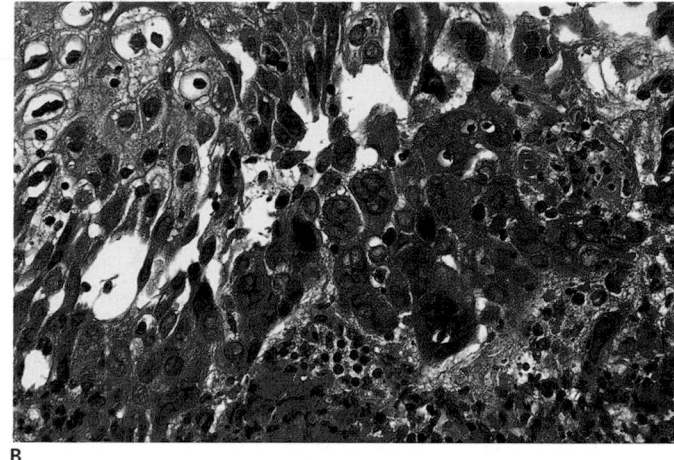

Fig. 19.65 A and **B**, Low- and high-power appearance of herpes simplex infection of cervix. Multinucleated epithelial cells and intranuclear inclusions are evident in the high-power view.

cotic radiate granules that may form around microorganisms or biologically inert substances.[45]

Bilharziasis (schistosomiasis), common in Africa and Central America, can involve any portion of the female genital tract, including the cervix.[44]

Malakoplakia occurs rarely in the cervix, sometimes in association with disease in the uterine corpus, renal pelvis, or kidney.[46]

Ceroid granuloma of the type more commonly seen in the gallbladder has, exceptionally, been found to involve the cervix.[43,55]

Localized arteritis of the cervix has been described, accompanied by inflammation and ulceration, and apparently restricted to this anatomic site.[48,50]

Non-neoplastic glandular lesions

Endocervical polyps are not true neoplasms but probably the result of chronic inflammatory changes ("chronic polypoid cervicitis"). They are usually small but may reach several centimeters in diameter. Microscopically, dilated endocervical glands are seen in an edematous, inflamed, and fibrotic stroma. The surface epithelium usually shows squamous metaplasia. CIN can develop from these polyps but not more so than in the cervix as a whole. Occasionally, the configuration of these polyps is that of a branching papillary structure, in which case the term *papillary endocervicitis* is employed[80] (Fig. 19.66). This lesion is to be distinguished from so-called "superficial cervicovaginal myofibroblastoma," which is equally benign and perhaps histogenetically related.[69]

Nabothian cysts are thought to develop from blockage of the endocervical glands secondarily to inflammation and associated changes; they appear grossly as cystic spaces filled with mucoid material and microscopically as cystically dilated glands lined by a flattened epithelium, sometimes focally absent. Occasionally they extend

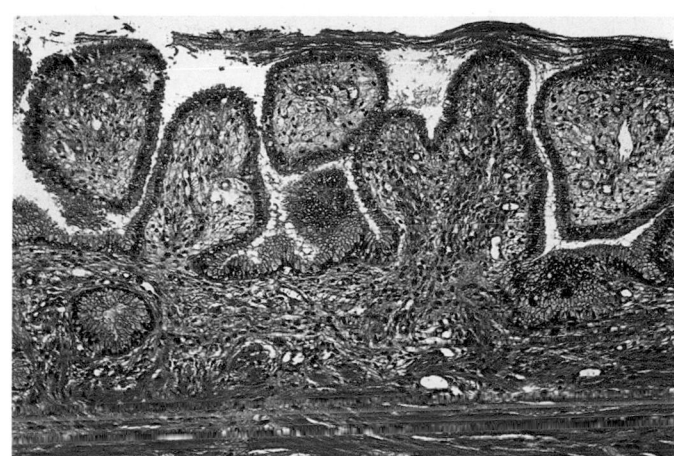

Fig. 19.66 Chronic endocervicitis resulting in a papillary configuration at the surface. This pattern is sometimes referred to as papillary endocervicitis.

deeply into the cervical wall, a phenomenon that should not be mistaken for malignancy.[59]

Tunnel clusters, as originally described by Fluhmann, are the result of localized proliferation of endocervical glands (clefts), with side channels growing out from them. This may be accompanied by dilatation resulting from the accumulation of inspissated, deeply eosinophilic secretion in the lumen[75] (Fig. 19.67). Tunnel clusters have been divided into type A (noncystic) and type B (cystic). Sometimes the former are accompanied by a florid glandular proliferation and a certain degree of atypia. However, they retain a lobular configuration and mitotic activity is practically nil.[66]

Microglandular hyperplasia of the endocervical epithelium was originally described in women using oral contraceptive drugs and, less frequently, during pregnancy.[68,79] However, it can also be seen in the absence of these conditions and even in postmenopausal patients.[58] As a matter of fact, the very relationship between microglandular hyperplasia and oral contraception or other hormonal perturbations has been questioned.[62] Microscopically, the typical case is characterized by a complex proliferation of small glands lined by flat epithelial cells with little or no atypia (Fig. 19.68). Accompanying squamous metaplasia is frequent, resulting in a complex microscopic picture that may be confused with carcinoma. Additional features that may lead to overdiagnosis include areas of solid proliferation, pseudoinfiltrative pattern, signet ring cells, focal atypia, and occasional mitotic figures[81] (Fig. 19.69). The intervening stroma invariably shows chronic inflammation. There is usually no immunocytochemical reactivity for CEA, a useful feature in the differential diagnosis with endocervical adenocarcinoma.[78]

The **Arias-Stella reaction,** as seen during pregnancy, can involve the endocervical glands. The nuclear abnormalities are similar to those seen more commonly in the endometrial mucosa and should not be confused with malignancy.[60,71,73] In contrast to clear cell carcinoma, the Arias-Stella reaction does not form a mass lesion, lacks a desmoplastic stromal response, and does not have an infiltrative pattern.[72a]

Diffuse laminar endocervical glandular hyperplasia is a non-neoplastic condition characterized by a proliferation of medium-sized, evenly spaced, well-differentiated glands within the inner third of the cervical wall, sharply separated from the underlying stroma, and often accompanied by chronic inflammation[67] (Fig. 19.70); it

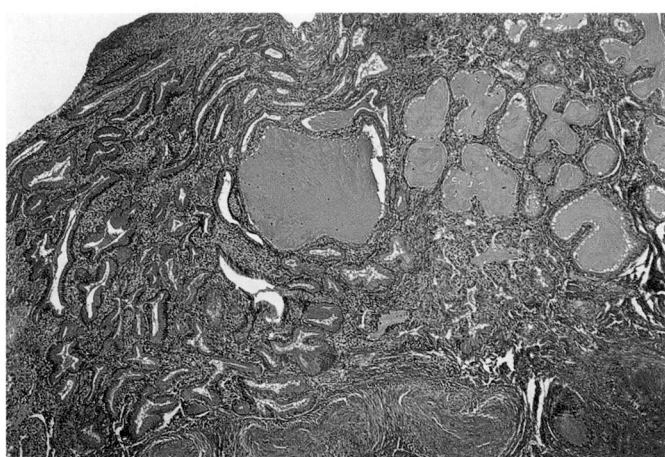

Fig. 19.67 Cervical tunnel clusters of predominantly cystic type.

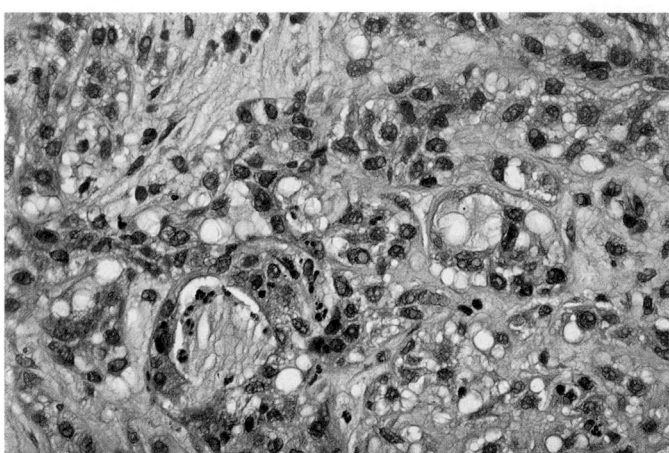

Fig. 19.69 Predominantly solid form of microglandular adenosis. This variety is particularly likely to be overdiagnosed as a malignant process.

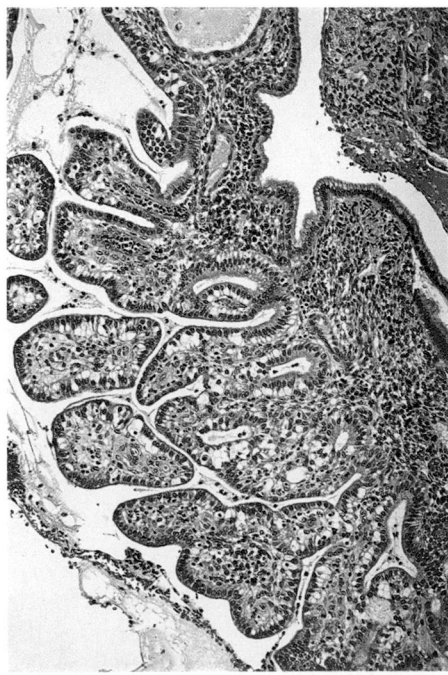

Fig. 19.68 Microglandular adenosis of cervix. The papillary configuration seen here is common in this condition.

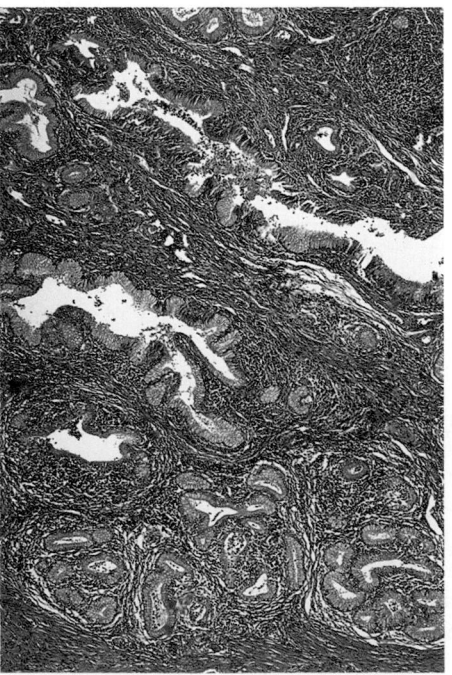

Fig. 19.70 Diffuse laminar endocervical hyperplasia. The glands are medium-sized, evenly spaced, and well differentiated.

should not be confused with adenoma malignum, from which it is distinguishable because of the fact that stromal infiltration, desmoplastic stromal response, and cytologic atypia are absent.[71]

Lobular endocervical glandular hyperplasia is characterized by a distinctly lobular proliferation of small to medium-sized glands, often centered around a larger central gland.[72] In contrast to adenoma malignum, this lesion lacks irregular stromal infiltration, desmoplastic stromal response, and significant cytologic atypia. Interestingly, the phenotype of this process is similar to that of pyloric glands.[70]

Mesonephric duct rests (already mentioned on p. 1524) can undergo cystic dilatation or be affected by florid and even atypical hyperplastic changes[63,65,76,81] (Fig. 19.71). This hyperplasia may have a lobular, diffuse, or ductal pattern[61] (Fig. 19.72). Rare malignant tumors arising from these structures also occur (see p. 1545). Mesonephric remnants are also rarely involved by CIN.[74]

It is doubtful whether the rare benign polypoid lesion found in the cervix and vagina of young children and described as *mesonephric papilloma* is related to these remnants.[64,77] Microscopically, it is a superficially located lesion composed of delicate connective tissue stalks covered by a layer of cuboidal cells and is probably of müllerian derivation.

Non-neoplastic stromal lesions (including endometriosis and related processes)

Multinucleated stromal giant cells can be present beneath the cervical epithelium and be mistaken for a malignancy. They are often accompanied by edema and may result in a vaguely polypoid-appearing lesion.[84,87] These cells are of a reactive fibroblastic/myofibroblastic nature and analogous to those seen in other sites covered by mucosal membranes, such as the vulva, vagina, anus, oral cavity, and nasal cavity.[82,90]

Decidual reaction in the cervix during pregnancy usually presents as multiple, small, yellowish or red elevations of the cervical mucosa. They are soft and friable and bleed easily with trauma. Rarely, they develop into fungating masses difficult to distinguish grossly from carcinoma.[85] Microscopically, the decidual cells are characterized by abundant pale granular cytoplasm and bland nuclei (Fig. 19.73). Immunostains for keratin are negative.

Placental site nodule appears as a well-defined hyalinized lesion located immediately beneath the mucosa.[93] It is composed of intermediate trophoblasts exhibiting cytoplasmic vacuolization.[91,95] Some nuclear atypia may be present. This lesion can be confused with carcinoma and with neoplastic cartilage. Immunohistochemically, the trophoblastic cells are reactive for keratin (another factor that may lead to a mistaken diagnosis of malignancy) but also for human placental lactogen (see p. 1748).

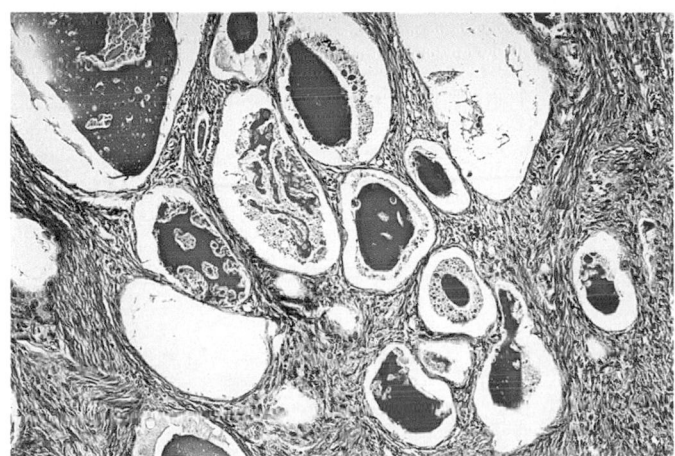

Fig. 19.71 Mesonephric glands embedded within the stroma of the uterine cervix exhibiting cystic dilatation. The presence of a dense eosinophilic secretion is characteristic.

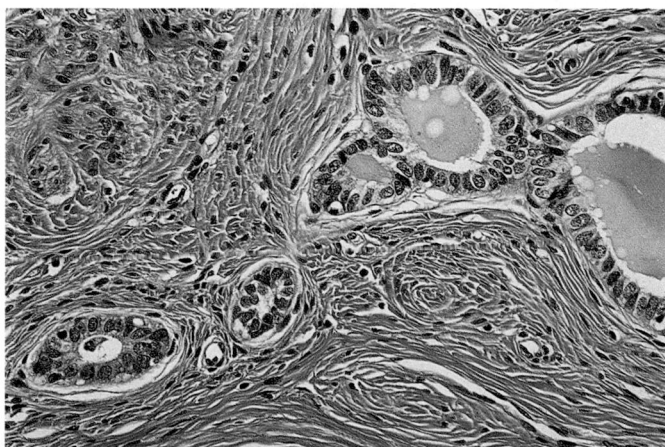

Fig. 19.72 Hyperplastic mesonephric rests with mild atypia.

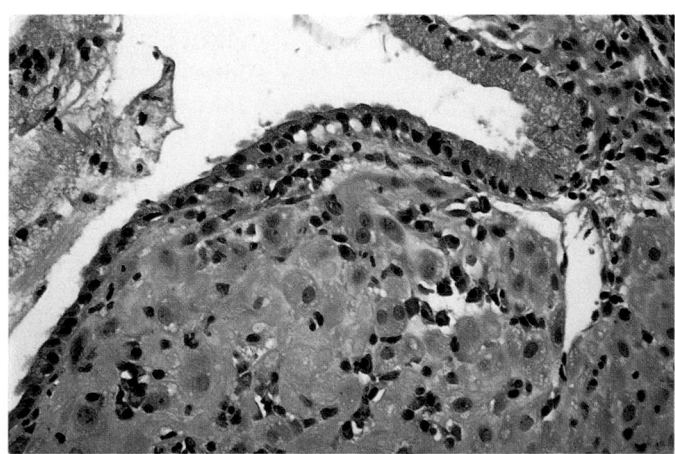

Fig. 19.73 Focus of ectopic cervical decidual reaction.

Endometriosis of the cervix presents as blue or reddish nodules and may result in abnormal uterine bleeding. Both endometrial glands and stroma are needed to establish the diagnosis. However, the proportion of the two components may vary greatly from case to case. On occasion, the process is composed almost exclusively of endometrial stroma ("stromal endometriosis") and may be confused with a neoplasm.[86] Another source of confusion arises when the endometriosis is superficial, in which case it may be overinterpreted as endocervical glandular dysplasia or adenocarcinoma in situ, one of the reasons being that it may be mitotically active.[83] It differs from tuboendometrial metaplasia of the endocervix because of the concomitant presence of endometrial-type stroma, however scarce. A lesion with an appearance resembling a miniature uterus in the cervix ("uterus-like mass") has been interpreted as a form of superficial endometriosis with florid smooth muscle metaplasia.[89] A bizarre variation on the theme is represented by **endocervicosis**, which can present as a deep-seated cervical mass simulating endocervical adenocarcinoma.[94]

Necrobiotic granulomas resembling tuberculosis or rheumatoid nodules have been seen following cervical surgery.[88] They are probably histologically and pathogenetically analogous to those described postoperatively in the prostate (see Chapter 18).

Florid mesenchymal reactions can develop from the cervical stroma as a result of various surgical interventions and lead to confusion with sarcoma.[92] Some of these have a nodular fasciitis-like appearance and may be looked upon as the genitourinary equivalent of this soft tissue lesion.

Human papilloma virus (HPV) and the lower female genital tract

HPV has been linked to many types of cervical diseases, ranging from the relatively innocuous condyloma acuminatum (see p. 1531) to the sometimes fatal invasive squamous cell carcinoma.[110,131,149] HPV comprises a family of DNA viruses, of which more than 60 types have been characterized, the most common being types 6 and 11. It can be detected by electron microscopy (as intranuclear crystalline and occasionally filamentous inclusions), but its specific identification depends on immunohistochemical or molecular virologic analysis with in situ or Southern blot hybridization.[105,113,122,127,137,141,159] The latter test is currently regarded as the "gold standard" for the detection of HPV. The main competitor is the Hybrid Capture HPV test, a signal-amplified hybridization microplate-based array designed to detect close to 20 HPV genotypes using two probe cocktails for high-risk and low-risk groups, respectively (see below).[121]

HPV infection of the cervix is transmitted venereally, and it has a predilection for the metaplastic squamous epithelium. It may remain dormant for long periods or become productive, with release of infectious virus in the terminally differentiated squamous epithelium.

The morphologic hallmark of HPV infection of the cervical squamous epithelium (as first described by two Finnish workers, Esco Purola and Eeva Savia) is *koilocytosis*, also known as *koilocytotic atypia* (two terms coined by Leopold Koss and Grace Durfee). This change is thought to be related to expression of the viral E4 protein and the disruption that this causes in the cytoplasmic keratin matrix.[140] The koilocyte is a superficial or intermediate mature squamous cell characterized by a sharply outlined perinuclear vacuolation, dense- and irregular-staining peripheral cytoplasm, and an enlarged nucleus with an undulating (raisin- or prune-like) nuclear membrane and a rope-like chromatin pattern[128] (Fig. 19.74). Binucleation and multinucleation can occur.[142] It is important that these nuclear changes—which may be accompanied by either a diploid or polyploid nuclear DNA distribution[153]—be present somewhere in the lesion for the diagnosis of koilocytosis (and, by inference, HPV infection) to be made, or else other forms of cytoplasmic clearing (notably those related to glycogen accumulation) will be mistakenly included in this category.[132,154] This is particularly the case for the condition known as *postmenopausal squamous atypia*, in which perinuclear halos can be very prominent.[123] Indeed, there is evidence that the overdiagnosis of HPV infection on the basis of the microscopic appear-

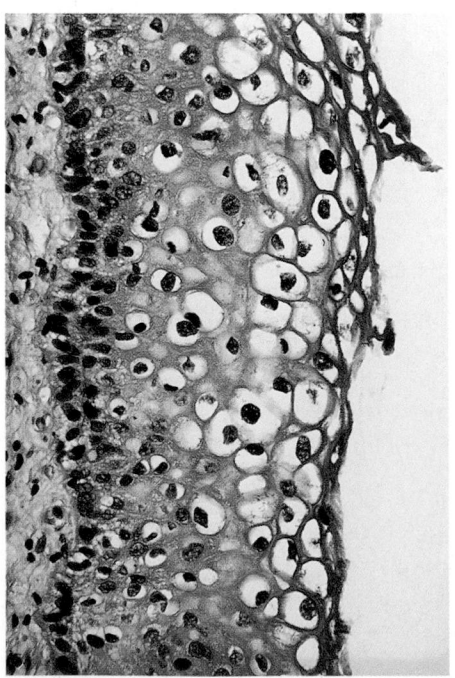

Fig. 19.74 Koilocytotic changes in cervical squamous epithelium. These are diagnostic of HPV infection.

ance of cervical biopsies is frequently made.[96] This is not to imply that HPV infection does not occur in the absence of koilocytosis, because it certainly does. Sometimes, the only abnormality seen in HPV-infected cells is nuclear enlargement, and occasionally there are no detectable changes at all.[107,138,158]

The most difficult and clinically significant problem that these HPV-induced cervical lesions pose is in relation to the differential diagnosis, coexistence, and possible causation of CIN and invasive carcinoma.[98,99,109,116,157] It seems obvious, in retrospect, that many cases diagnosed in the past as mild or moderate dysplasia (CIN I and II) would now be reported as HPV-induced koilocytotic atypia.[101] It has also become apparent that HPV-associated lesions are often seen together with (or preceding those of) CIN or, sometimes, invasive cervical carcinoma.[134,139,150] Actually, the high frequency of this association on a worldwide basis,[102] the topographic continuity between the two processes,[145] and the respective age distributions of the affected populations[111] all suggest an underlying dependence and perhaps a continuum between the two.[120,148] This concordance is not apparent between cervical carcinoma and other infections of the cervix.[103] The association between HPV and cervical neoplasia is particularly strong for squamous cell tumors, but it has also been documented for both in situ and invasive adenocarcinoma[108,114,115,129,155] and for adenosquamous carcinoma.[125] The HPV proteins E6 and E7 are thought to play an important role in this process by their interaction with the p53 protein and the Rb-susceptibility gene product, respectively.[106,140,149]

Following the realization that koilocytotic atypia equals HPV infection, an attitude took hold in some quarters that the presence of this change in a cervical biopsy was indicative of a benign process. This is not necessarily the case. These biopsies should be evaluated according to the standard criteria applied to CIN. The added presence of the HPV-associated component should be mentioned in the diagnosis but should not modify the diagnostic or clinical approach toward them.[124]

The features in a cervical biopsy exhibiting the signs of HPV infection that indicate the additional presence of CIN are the presence of atypia along the basal layers, a disorderly pattern of maturation, and abnormal mitotic figures.[156,160] A definite association exists between high-degree atypia (CIN III), an aneuploid DNA pattern, p53 overexpression, and the presence of HPV type 16.[112,117,118,151] Along similar lines, the presence of the HPV-16 genome has been documented in most invasive cervical carcinomas and in histologically normal neighboring epithelium.[130]

Currently, HPVs are divided into major categories depending on their level of association with CIN and invasive squamous cell carcinoma. The "high-risk" ("carcinogenic") types are primarily 16 and 18, but also 31, 33, 35, 39, 45, 51, 52, 56, 58, 59, 68, 73, and 82. HPV types 26, 53, and 66 have been classified as "probably high-risk", and HPV types 6, 11, 40, 42, 43, 44, 54, 61, 70, 72, 81, and CP6108 are included in the "low-risk category."[136] Typing of the viral strain is now being used together with cytology for cervical screening,[119,147] and there is great hope that the various HPV vaccines currently being tried will have a considerable impact on the incidence of the disease.[104,126] It is of interest that the probability of finding direct evidence of HPV infection in cervical squamous intraepithelial lesions decreases proportionally to the degree of atypia, reaching low levels in CIN III.[100,144] These findings have been explained by postulating that an intact squamous epithelium is needed for virus replication.

It should be mentioned here that Epstein–Barr virus (EBV), often present in cervical carcinoma and once thought to be of importance in its genesis, is not currently believed to play a causative role.[146]

Condyloma acuminatum is a grossly polypoid lesion characterized microscopically by papillomatosis, acanthosis, koilocytosis, and a variable degree of inflammatory infiltration of the stroma. An undulating appearance of the epithelium is a characteristic feature on low-power examination. A mild degree of atypia in the squamous component is common and need not be mentioned; if more severe, it should be evaluated and graded as for the flat squamous intraepithelial lesions (i.e., condyloma with CIN II or III).

Condyloma acuminatum is an HPV-induced lesion (see p. 1530); HPV-6 and HPV-11 are found in 70% to 90% of the cases, but occasionally other types—such as HPV-16—are encountered. When the latter is the case, high-grade cytologic atypia is often found.

Other morphologic manifestations of HPV infection of the cervix (which are actually much more common than condyloma acuminatum) include lesions variously described as *flat, spiked,* and *inverted condyloma* and *warty atypia.*[155] Many HPV infections are clinically inapparent. Microscopically, these clinically different lesions share the following features: relatively normal basal cell layer, expanded or hyperplastic parabasal cell layer, orderly maturation, mitotic activity (but few or no abnormal mitoses), and koilocytosis (Fig. 19.75). The proliferation rate of condyloma is higher than that of inflamed or metaplastic cervical squamous epithelium,[135] and is particularly elevated in the presence of high-risk HPV types.[133]

Immature condyloma (papillary immature metaplasia) is the name given to a lesion with a cellular composition similar to immature squamous metaplasia (see p. 1486) but having a filiform papillary configuration.[152] It is believed to be produced by HPV-6 or 11 infection.

Squamous papilloma is a polypoid lesion composed of a fibrovascular stalk covered by mature squamous epithelium. It has also been designated as fibroepithelial

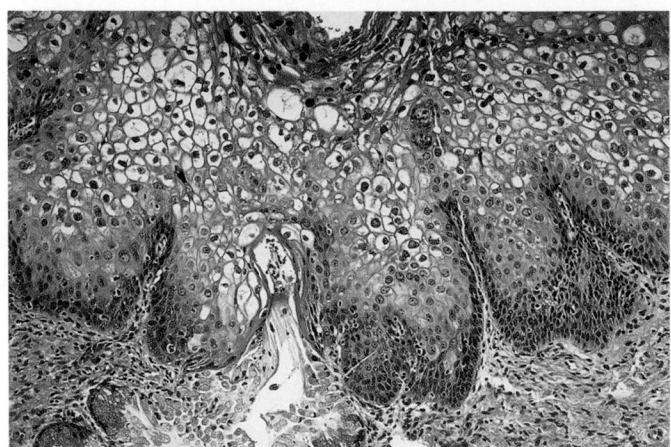

Fig. 19.75 HPV-induced cervical lesion characterized by acanthosis, papillomatosis, and koilocytotic changes.

papilloma, fibroepithelioma, and ectocervical polyp. Microscopically, the lack of an arborizing pattern and—most important—the absence of koilocytotic changes distinguish this lesion from condyloma acuminatum. The nature of this process is not clear; in at least some instances, squamous papilloma probably represents condyloma in which the recognizable morphologic changes of HPV infection have subsided. The differential diagnosis also includes the papillary form of CIN (in which case the atypical changes present in the epithelium of the polypoid lesion are also seen in the adjacent flat epithelium),[143] verrucous carcinoma (see p. 1539), and well-differentiated squamous cell carcinoma (see p. 1535).

Inverted transitional cell papilloma, similar to its more common bladder counterpart, has been recently described in the cervix.[97] It is probably not related to HPV and is included here only because it enters into the differential diagnosis with the other polypoid benign lesions of this region.

Tumors

Cervical intraepithelial neoplasia (CIN)

The terminology of cervical intraepithelial lesions composed of squamous epithelium and thought to represent the precursors of invasive carcinoma has evolved over the years and continues changing today. The concept is of great practical and historical importance, since it represents the main model on which the theory of the existence of morphologically identifiable precursor lesions of cancer has been built (a general model that, one should add, has found strong support from molecular studies).[222] The basic premises are the following:

1 Nearly all invasive cervical carcinomas are preceded by a stage in which the abnormal cells are confined to the epithelium (intraepithelial stage).[185]

2 These intraepithelial lesions share many of the cytologic features of the invasive stage, mainly manifested by enlargement, irregularities, and hyperchromasia of the nuclei; increase in mitotic activity; and alteration of the maturation pattern. There is also a diminution or absence of cytoplasmic glycogen, this being the reason for the decrease or lack of staining in the iodine (Lugol or Schiller's) test.

3 A continuous range of morphologic abnormalities exists among these lesions, which provide a rough indication of the likelihood with which they would evolve into invasive carcinoma if left untreated.[206] These morphologic abnormalities correlate with immunohistochemical cytogenetic, DNA ploidy, cell proliferation, and molecular changes.[169,172,197,226,229] For instance, autoradiographic studies have shown a continuum in the proportion of cells in DNA synthesis, their number paralleling the degree of atypia.[218] Low-grade lesions usually have a euploid or polyploid pattern, whereas high-grade lesions are generally aneuploid.[165,208,214] A similar relationship has been found among morphologic aberrations and proliferating cell nuclear antigen (PCNA),[201,223] nucleolar organizer region,[190,230] and aberrant expression of various keratins,[224,225] p53 protein,[161,178,211] p16INK4a expression[160a] and *ras* oncogene.[219] The available evidence suggests the existence of a sequence of events that in some cases leads to progression to a full-blown invasive malignancy but in others stops at a given stage or possibly regresses altogether. The often held assumption that the most severe forms will *inevitably* lead to invasive carcinoma is unproven and unprovable.[191,203] The milder forms are particularly unstable.[175,216] In one study, follow-up evaluation after conservative therapy showed regression in 62% of the cases, persistence in 22%, and progression to a more severe lesion in 16%.[204] The more severe lesions regress less frequently and may persist for long periods. In a classic study, Petersen[209] studied the course of 127 untreated patients with such severe lesions. Invasive carcinoma had developed in 11% at the end of 3 years, in 22% at the end of 5 years, and in 33% at the end of 9 years.

4 In the large majority of cases, the process does not affect the native squamous epithelium of the exocervix but rather areas of squamous metaplasia located at the transformation zone and in its endocervical side.[183] It practically always involves the surface epithelium, as well as the glandular elements, but by definition shows no stromal invasion. It often ends abruptly, and its extent is highly variable. Occasionally it seems to consist of only a minute focus removable by a simple biopsy; more commonly, it involves large areas of the cervix. Extension up the endocervical canal is particularly common,[180] but it may also grow along the portio and upper vagina[174,212,228] or extend into mesonephric remnants.[221] In exceptional instances, it has been seen

to extend into the vagina to the introitus or into the endometrial cavity and even the fallopian tubes.[187,210,220] Sometimes, the intraepithelial change as seen in a cervical biopsy represents only the peripheral manifestation of a more proximally located invasive carcinoma that is diagnosed only by endocervical curettage.

5 The microscopic criteria for the diagnosis of these lesions should be the same regardless of the circumstances. This is true if they are found in the pregnant woman; such changes do not routinely regress postpartum, despite early statements to the contrary. It is also true if they are found following treatment of invasive squamous cell carcinoma with radiation therapy, a change found in approximately one fourth of the patients and sometimes referred to as **postirradiation atypia or dysplasia**.[195] The available evidence suggests that this is not merely a reaction of a previously normal epithelium to the radiation but rather the expression of a basically abnormal mucosa. Indeed, postirradiation dysplasia appearing within 3 years after treatment is associated with poor prognosis.[233]

All of the previously listed basic tenets have been accepted, the current controversy centering on the num-

ber of recognizable steps within that range (2, 3, or 4) and the best terminology to use for them (Figs 19.76 to 19.80).

The classic approach, unchallenged for half a century, has been that of designating these lesions as either dysplasia or carcinoma in situ. The term *dysplasia* was used

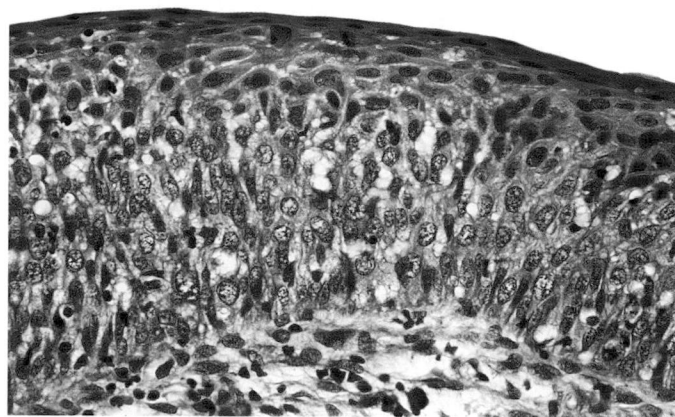

Fig. 19.78 CIN III (moderate dysplasia). There is proliferation and atypia in the lower two thirds, but some surface maturation is still apparent.

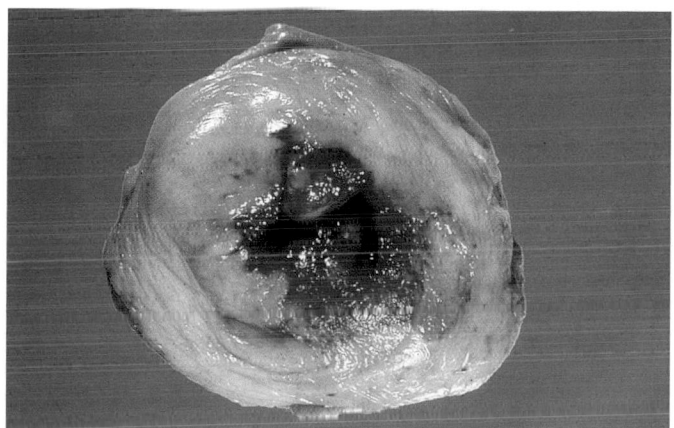

Fig. 19.76 Gross appearance of carcinoma in situ (CIN III) extensively involving the uterine cervix. (Courtesy of Dr. Hector Rodriguez-Martinez, Mexico City)

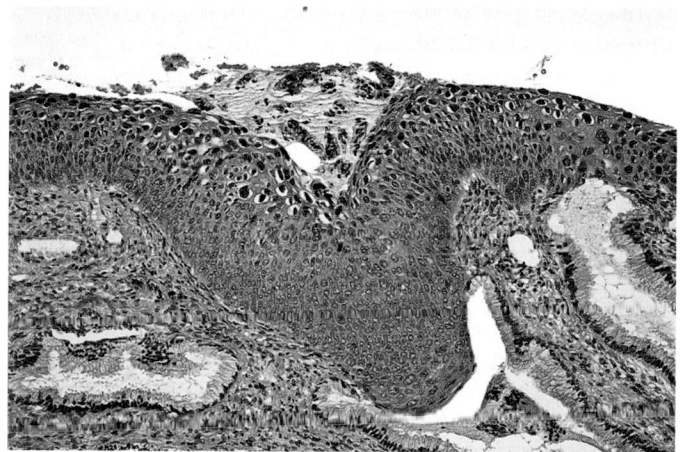

Fig. 19.79 Extensive involvement by CIN III of surface epithelium and glands of endocervix.

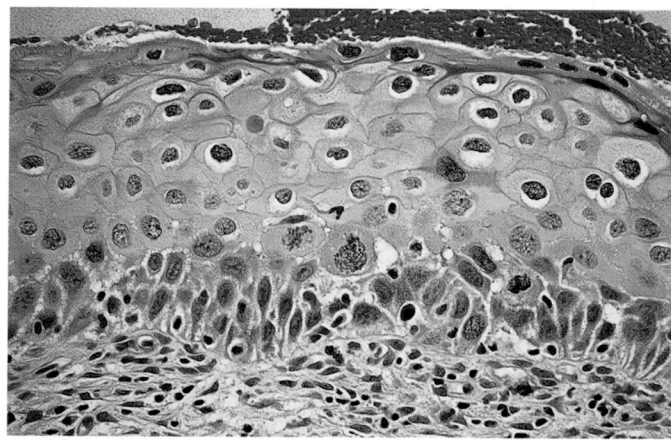

Fig. 19.77 CIN I accompanied by koilocytotic atypia.

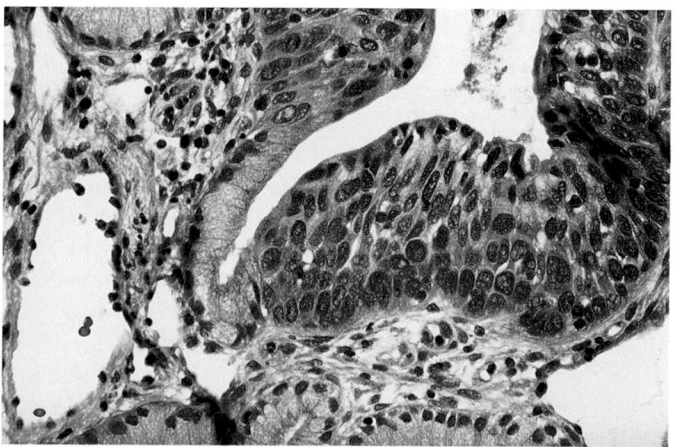

Fig. 19.80 Partial replacement of endocervical glandular epithelium by CIN III.

when the atypical cytologic features mentioned were accompanied by a partial retention of the normal maturation pattern and a preservation of the organization of the basal layer.[167,177] By contrast, the term *carcinoma in situ* was employed when there was no differentiation at any level (despite some occasional flattening of the surface cells) and the basal cell was disorganized.[189,193,213] Dysplasia was further subdivided into mild, moderate, and severe, depending on the severity of the changes. Carcinoma in situ was further subdivided by some authors into parabasal cell (51%), keratinizing cell (37%), pleomorphic cell (3%), and small cell (1.5%) types.[231]

Most of the seminal studies documenting the relationship between these changes and the development of invasive carcinoma have been done using this terminology, which, however, came under attack on the grounds that it implies a significant biologic difference between dysplasia and carcinoma in situ that probably does not exist and also because it may lead to a radically different approach to therapy (i.e., follow-up with cytologic studies in the case of dysplasia as opposed to surgical therapy for carcinoma in situ), which does not seem justified.[222] That the difference between severe dysplasia and carcinoma in situ is based on rather subtle and subjective criteria, and that these criteria vary according to the individual pathologist and institution has been repeatedly proved.[179,182,184]

In the hope of eliminating at least some of these problems, the alternative term *cervical intraepithelial neoplasia* (CIN) was proposed, with a subdivision into three grades: CIN I as the equivalent of mild dysplasia, CIN II of moderate dysplasia, and CIN III of severe dysplasia and carcinoma in situ.[214] When it seemed as if this terminology was finally on its way to replacing that of dysplasia/carcinoma in situ,[166,168,181,227] a new one was proposed, referred to as the Bethesda classification.[186,205] In this scheme, which was originally designed for cervical cytologic specimens (see p. 1532) but which some would like to see applied also to histologic samples[171] the preferred generic term is *squamous intraepithelial lesion* (SIL), with a subdivision into low and high grades. The low-grade lesion corresponds to CIN I (as well as some HPV-induced lesions that do not qualify as CIN; see p. 1531), whereas the high-grade lesion corresponds to CIN II and III.

One of the rationales for this new approach is the problem represented by the difficulty often encountered in distinguishing CIN I from HPV-related flat condylomatous changes and the overdiagnosis of CIN that can occur as a result.[162] A suggested way to deal with this problem within the context of the CIN terminology is to designate those doubtful cases as either "borderline CIN"[176] or "CIN with HPV-related changes."[215] Whichever scheme is ultimately chosen, one hopes that it will be applied to both cytologic and histologic specimens.

At a practical level, and regardless of the terminology used, these lesions can be safely treated by conization, electrodiathermy, cryosurgery, laser, or the more recent loop electrosurgical excision, all of them done under colposcopic guidance, assuming that a proper cytologic follow-up can be assured.[170,192,198,200,202,232] In most series, conization has resulted in control of even the most severe forms in over 90% of the patients.[188,194] In making the final decision regarding the timing and type of therapy for this group of lesions, the microscopic diagnosis is only one of the factors to be considered, albeit a very important one. The extension of the lesion, age of the patient, parity, and the desire to have more children all have to be considered. Both the surface and the possible depth of involvement have to be taken into account. Anderson and Hartley[163] calculated that destruction of tissue to a depth of 2.92 mm would eradicate all involved glands in 95% of the patients, whereas destruction to a depth of 3.8 mm would eradicate 99.7%. Whether all patients with low-grade CIN require therapy remains a contentious issue.[217]

The pathologic report of a cervical biopsy specimen containing this group of lesions should include the degree of abnormality according to the agreed terminology for that institution, the presence or absence of endocervical gland involvement, and the presence or absence of HPV-related or any other associated changes. The report on a conization specimen should also include the status of the surgical margins, of which the endocervical one is the most important. Positive margins and involved glands are independent predictors of residual or recurrent disease.[173,196,207]

Once the pathologist has made the diagnosis of CIN in a cervical biopsy, it is the responsibility of the gynecologist to determine the presence or absence of invasive carcinoma, especially in the case of the high-grade lesions. Thorough cervical sampling and the proper sectioning of tissue should establish whether or not invasive carcinoma exists. If the later is found, conventional methods of therapy may be instituted. Whenever the therapy is conservative, long-term follow-up (longer than 5 years) with periodic cytologic examination is imperative. In one series, patients with continuing abnormal cytology after initial treatment of CIN III (carcinoma in situ) were found to be 25 times more likely to develop invasive carcinomas than women with normal follow-up cytology.[199]

In addition to HPV-related koilocytotic atypia, the differential diagnosis of CIN includes florid squamous metaplasia and transitional metaplasia (see p. 1524). It should also be mentioned that the iodine test, used to delineate the extent of cervical disease prior to conization, can induce shrinkage, cytoplasmic eosinophilia and vacuolization, and pyknosis in the epithelial cells (particularly when they are abnormal).[164]

Microinvasive squamous cell carcinoma

Invasive squamous cell carcinomas in which the depth of stromal invasion is minimal (5 mm or less) have been

gous to that sometimes encountered in carcinomas of the lung and other sites.[293] These tumors have been variously referred to as mucoepidermoid carcinoma (a misleading term), adenosquamous carcinoma (less objectionable but not ideal), and squamous (cell) carcinoma with mucin secretion.[286] Whatever term one may wish to employ, it is important to regard this tumor as a morphologic variation on the theme of squamous cell carcinoma rather than as an adenocarcinoma (see p. 1540). Indeed, its behavior seems to be the same as that of the squamous cell carcinoma lacking mucin secretion, and therefore the utility of mucin stains in these circumstances is very limited.[293]

Immunohistochemical and molecular genetic features

Immunohistochemically, squamous cell carcinomas of the cervix express keratins (nearly 100% of the cases), CEA (90%),[295] p63 (a homolog of p53 preferentially expressed in basal and immature cervical squamous epithelium),[305] and blood group antigens.[304] The range of keratins found in the tumor varies somewhat depending on the subtype, but it is very wide.[303] There may also be reactivity for cathepsin B (although not as frequently as in adenocarcinoma),[301] for β-human chorionic gonadotrophin (β-hCG),[297] and for parathyroid hormone-related gene (although these tumors rarely give rise to hypercalcemia).[296]

The expression of estrogen receptor is decreased in cervical carcinoma when compared with that of the normal cervical mucosa, whereas that of progesterone receptor is increased.[298,300]

In contrast to the situation in many other human malignancies, the p53 gene is rarely mutated in cervical squamous cell carcinoma; this is also true for the biologically related MDM2 gene.[299]

Aneuploidy has been the rule in DNA studies of cervical squamous cell carcinoma, but there is often considerable heterogeneity within the same lesion.[302]

Spread and metastases

Cervical carcinoma spreads characteristically by direct extension to the vagina, corpus (endometrium or myometrial wall), parametrium, lower urinary tract, and uterosacral ligaments[307,311] (Fig. 19.85).

Lymph node metastases are also common. The pattern of involvement generally proceeds in a sequential fashion. The first station is represented by the paracervical, hypogastric, obturator, and external iliac groups and the second by the sacral, common iliac, aortic, and inguinal groups.[308] The incidence of nodal involvement is directly related to the stage of the disease. Hematogenous metastases were rare in older series, but, with better control of the local lesion, they have increased in frequency.[311] Lungs (9%) and bones (4%) are the most common sites.[306,309,310] Ovarian metastases are less common than with endometrial adenocarcinoma, but they do occur.[312]

Treatment

Invasive carcinomas of the cervix can be treated by surgery, irradiation, or a combination of both modalities.[316,322,327] The choice depends on the extent of the tumor, the general condition of the patient, and the expertise available at the institution where the patient is treated. Early lesions can be treated just as effectively with hysterectomy or intracavitary radium[315,317]; for stage IIa lesions, irradiation alone and a combination of irradiation and surgery have yielded equivalent results in randomized studies.[325] If an occult invasive cervical carcinoma is found in a specimen from a simple hysterectomy done for another reason, additional therapy is indicated, usually in the form of a radical reoperation.[320]

Lack of prompt response (within 1 to 3 months) to radiation therapy is a predictor of likely recurrence and an indicator that adjuvant chemotherapy should be considered.[318] The latter has also been tried to increase the number of operable patients and as a postoperative measure, with some encouraging preliminary results.[319]

In cases of postirradiation relapse of cervical carcinoma, pelvic exenteration should be seriously considered because a considerable number of the patients will have the persistent tumor confined to the pelvis.[323] This operation removes all pelvic viscera and lateral pelvic lymph node-bearing tissue. At laparotomy, the surgeon should examine the upper abdomen carefully, particularly the periaortic area, for evidence of spread outside the pelvis. Any suspicious lymph nodes or liver nodules should be submitted to the pathologist for frozen section before the operative procedure is begun. Gross appraisal of enlarged extrapelvic nodes is unreliable, whereas frozen section examination is a highly accurate procedure.[313] The study of the surgical specimen should include a careful examination of the lymph nodes, the lateral edges of the resection, and the local extent of the tumor. Microscopically, the nodes, vessels, and adjacent organs should be examined for evidence of tumor. The finding of greater prognostic relevance in the pathologic evaluation of pelvic exenteration specimens is the presence or absence of lymph node metastases.[326]

Other indications for pelvic exenteration are locally invasive carcinoma of the rectum, severe pelvic irradiation necrosis, and recurrent carcinoma of the endometrium. The 5-year survival rate for patients undergoing this formidable procedure for postirradiation persistence of carcinoma of the cervix is notably high considering the circumstances; it was approximately 25% in early series[314,321] and has reached the remarkable figure of 73% at one institution.[324]

Prognosis

The prognosis of cervical carcinoma is related to the following parameters:

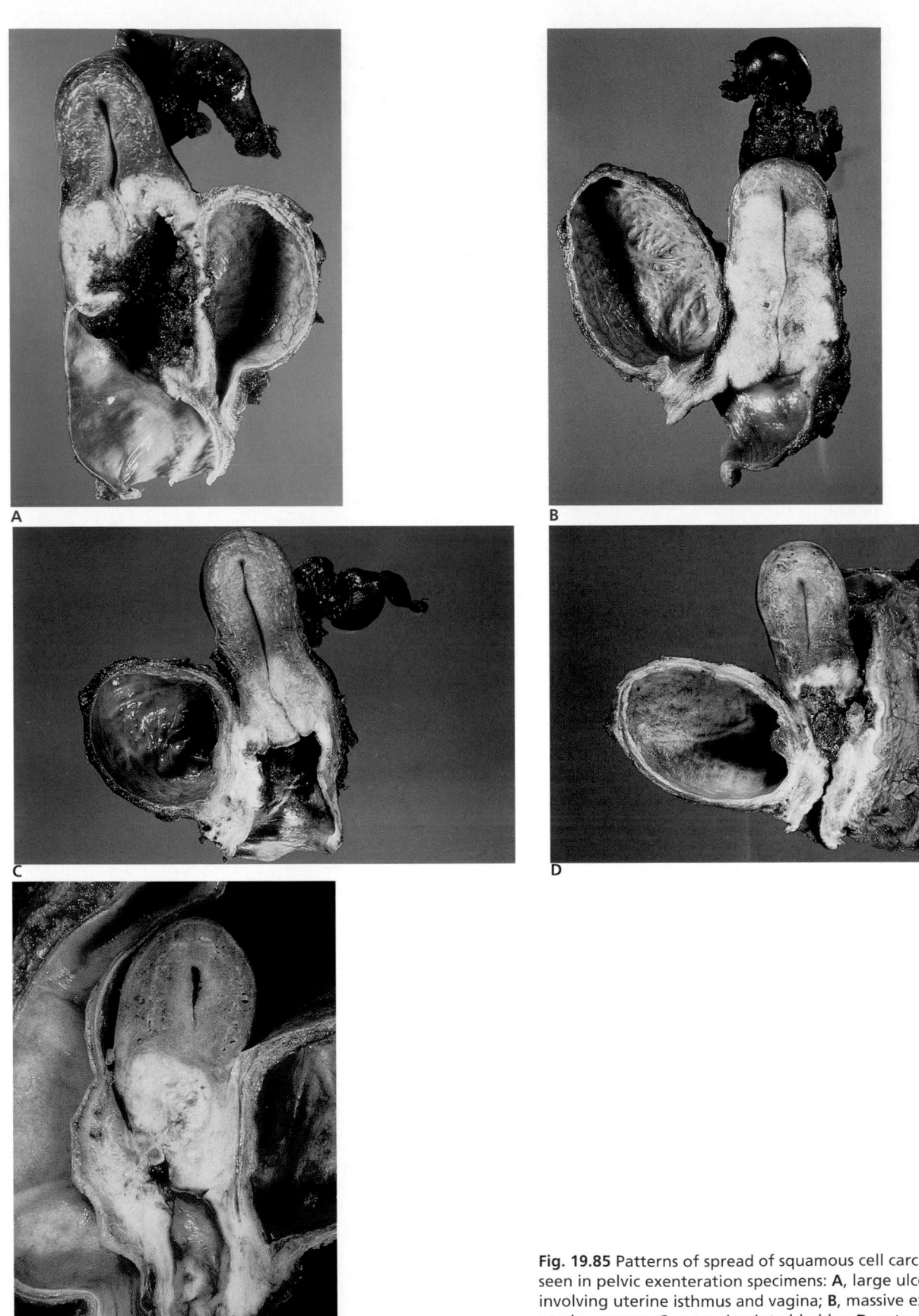

Fig. 19.85 Patterns of spread of squamous cell carcinoma of cervix as seen in pelvic exenteration specimens: **A**, large ulcerated tumor involving uterine isthmus and vagina; **B**, massive extension into uterine corpus; **C**, extension into bladder; **D**, extension into bladder and rectum; **E**, extension into rectal wall, with impingement into rectal mucosa. (**A** to **D**, Courtesy of Dr. Hector Rodriguez-Martinez, Mexico City, Mexico)

1 *Clinical stage.*[328] As for most other human malignancies, this is the most important prognostic determinator.

2 *Nodal status.* This is another crucial predictor, which is incorporated into the staging scheme.[338,346]

3 *Size* of the largest involved node[340] and *number* of positive nodes.[341]

4 *Size of the primary tumor*, as determined by measurement of the tumor's greatest diameter[343,350] or by volumetric techniques.[331]

5 *Depth of invasion.*[339,347,352,356]

6 *Endometrial extension.* The presence of this feature decreases the survival rate by a factor of 10% to 20%.[349]

7 *Parametrial involvement*, as detected microscopically.[342]

8 *Blood vessel invasion.*[330,355,364]

9 *Microscopic grade.* Whether the degree of tumor differentiation as evaluated in routinely stained sections correlates with survival independently from staging remains a controversial issue.[357,358] If a correlation exists, it must be minimal indeed, whether one uses the Reagan–Ng or the Broders' method of grading.[359,364]

10 *Microscopic type.* A similar comment applies to this parameter, which is roughly related to microscopic grade. Some authors have found a better prognosis with the large cell nonkeratinizing type and a worse prognosis with the small cell type,[363] but others have found no correlation between microscopic classification and prognosis.[333,334]

11 *Tumor-associated tissue eosinophilia (TATE).* Presence of numerous mature eosinophils in the inflammatory infiltrate of cervical carcinoma has been associated with an improved survival in one study[329] and a worse survival in another.[362] At other sites, this feature is generally regarded as a good prognostic sign.

12 *Keratin profile* as evaluated immunohistochemically. No predictive value seems to be attached to this parameter.[361]

13 *Cell proliferation index.* High S-phase rates as determined by flow cytometry are correlated to both a poorly differentiated histologic appearance and decreased short-term survival.[360]

14 *Angiogenesis.* There is no evidence of a correlation between microvessel density and prognosis.[353]

15 *HPV.* It has been claimed that HPV is a major determinant of the course of cervical cancer.[336] In one series, the 5-year disease free survival was 100% for patients with intermediate risk HPV, 58% for patients with HPV-16-positive tumors, and 38% for patients with HPV-18-positive tumors.[344] It has been further claimed that lack of detection of HPV in the tumor cells is a poor prognostic sign.[351]

16 *Others.* Stromal infiltration by S-100 protein-positive Langerhans' cells,[345] allelic loss on chromosome 1,[332] and expression of c-*erb*B-2,[335,348] *ras* oncogene,[354] and Tn antigen (a precursor of MN blood group antigen)[337] have all been found to relate to an unfavorable outcome. It remains to be determined how many of these parameters will prove to have independent prognostic value.

Other microscopic types

Verrucous carcinoma is a highly differentiated variant of squamous cell carcinoma with a polypoid pattern of growth, an extremely well-differentiated cytologic appearance, and a capacity for local invasion but not for metastatic spread. Some cases have been found to extend into the endometrial cavity.[378] Verrucous carcinoma should be distinguished both from condyloma acuminatum and from ordinary squamous cell carcinoma with a prominent papillary pattern of growth.[365,376] The general gross and microscopic features of this tumor are described in Chapter 4.

Spindle cell carcinoma (sarcomatoid carcinoma; squamous cell carcinoma with sarcoma-like stroma; carcinosarcoma) is morphologically analogous to the homonymous tumor in the upper aerodigestive tract.[377] It may contain osteoclast-like giant cells,[375] and there is often evidence of HPV infection.[369] The recognizable epithelial component of this tumor, when present, is of squamous type; this is in contrast with mixed müllerian tumor, in which that component is usually glandular (p. 1599). It is advisable to keep these tumors (both of which can occur in the cervix) in separate categories, although both of them probably represent carcinomas with a sarcoma-like component.

Basaloid (squamous cell) carcinoma is characterized by prominent peripheral palisading, an infiltrative growth pattern, and minimal stromal reaction[367] (Fig. 19.86). The behavior of this tumor is aggressive, as is also the case with the homonymous neoplasm in the upper

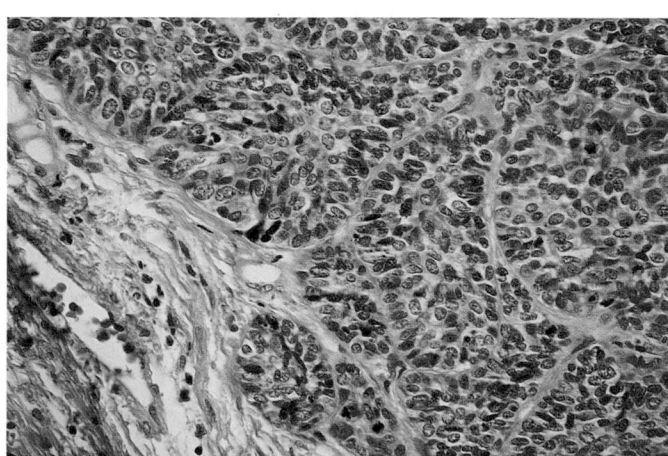

Fig. 19.86 Basaloid squamous cell carcinoma of uterine cervix. The tumor grows in the form of well-defined nests showing peripheral palisading.

aerodigestive tract. It is, therefore, very important to clearly separate this tumor from the adenoid cystic carcinomas and adenoid basal carcinomas discussed on p. 1494.[368]

Lymphoepithelioma-like carcinoma resembles its more common counterpart in the upper respiratory tract by virtue of the large size of the tumor cells, vesicular nuclei with prominent nucleoli, syncytial appearance, and heavy lymphocytic infiltration.[370,374,380] Some cases have been found to secrete β-hCG, as is also occasionally the case with conventional squamous cell carcinoma.[366] The possible association of this tumor with either EBV or HPV remains controversial.[373,379] This tumor type shows considerable overlap with the *circumscribed* type of cervical carcinoma described by Japanese authors (Fig. 19.87).[371]

Transitional cell carcinoma having an appearance similar to the homonymous tumor located in the bladder or ovary can occur in the cervix. It needs to be distinguished from *inverted transitional cell papilloma*, which has also been reported in this location. It also needs to be differentiated from papillary squamous cell carcinoma (see p. 1488). The latter is not always an easy task, since the transitional-like and squamous-like areas of these tumors often blend with each other. The term *papillary squamotransitional cell carcinoma* has been proposed for the tumors having an obvious hybrid composition.[372]

Fig. 19.87 Whole-mount appearance of well-circumscribed cervical carcinoma with a polypoid pattern of growth. Stromal invasion is minimal.

Adenocarcinoma

Primary adenocarcinomas make up 5% to 15% of all carcinomas of the cervix. This percentage is higher in Jewish women,[397] and it has been suggested that its relative incidence is on the rise in the general population, particularly in young women.[415,419,420,422,429] An association has been found between the long-term use of oral contraceptives and the development of endocervical neoplasia in young patients,[393,428] but this has been contested by others.[401]

An association between endocervical adenocarcinoma and ovarian mucinous adenocarcinoma (and occasionally even tubal adenocarcinoma) has also been recorded.[400,410]

The tumor presents no distinguishing gross characteristics (Fig. 19.88). Microscopically, the most common pattern is that of a well-differentiated glandular pattern with mucin secretion, some of which can leak into the stroma[406,418,423,431–433] (Fig. 19.89). However, the degree of differentiation varies, and poorly differentiated forms exist. In addition to the mucin-secreting appearance, which recapitulates the histology of the normal endocervix, cervical carcinomas can have an endometrioid or a papillary serous appearance; these are discussed in the section dealing with Variants (see p. 1542).

Histochemically, Alcian blue and mucicarmine-positive material is found intracellularly in nearly all cases of conventional cervical adenocarcinoma.[423] The staining pattern is different from that of normal endocervical glands but similar to that of in situ adenocarcinoma.[395] Keratins, EMA, and CEA are consistently expressed, whereas vimentin is not.[385–387,408] Another marker that is generally present is p16 (ink4a), which links this tumor to HPV infection.[417] Estrogen and progesterone receptors are expressed in only one fourth of the cases.[392] Overexpression of p53 is frequent.[384,413] Markers common to gastric, intestinal, and pancreatobiliary epithelial cells (such as M1 and cathepsin E) are commonly present.[424] Cervical adenocarcinomas have also been shown to contain argyrophilic cells,[409] a variety of peptide hor-

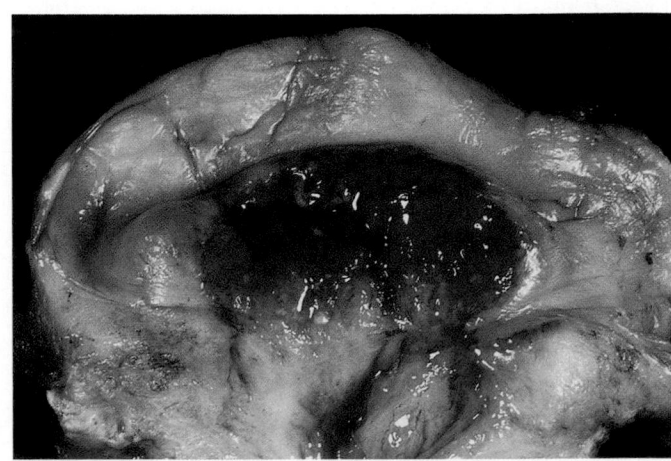

Fig. 19.88 Gross appearance of endocervical adenocarcinoma.

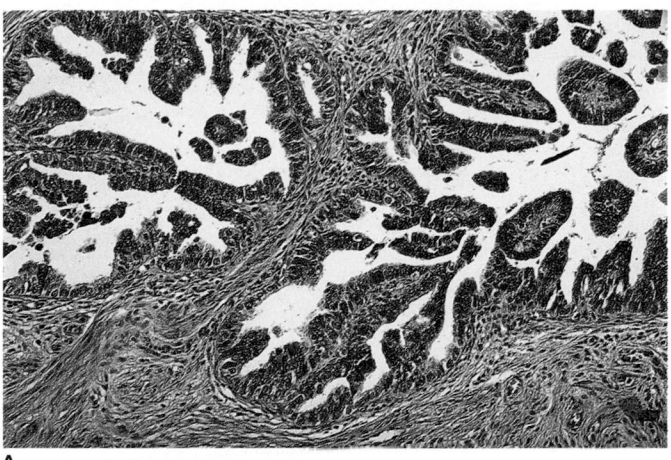 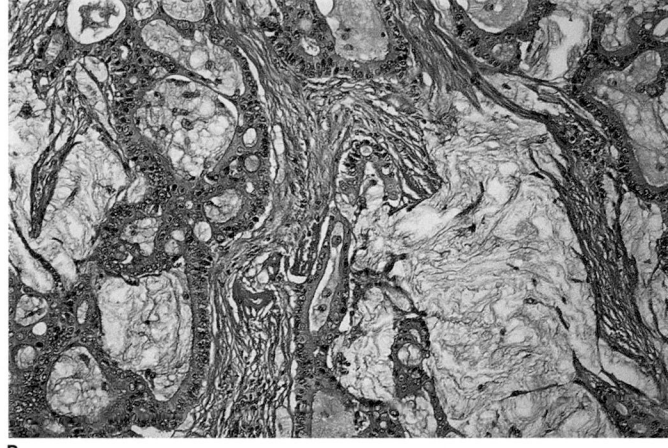

A   **B**

Fig. 19.89 Microscopic appearance of conventional (**A**) and mucinous (**B**) adenocarcinoma of cervix.

mones,[427] and the enzyme amylase.[396] Basement membrane, as investigated immunohistochemically with type IV collagen or laminin, may be present around the tumor cell even in the invasive tumors, but usually in a discontinuous fashion.[426,430]

HPV infection (particularly 16 and 18) is found in most endocervical adenocarcinomas.[391,425] The few negative tumors tend to be nonmucinous and occur in older women.[425]

The prognosis in cervical adenocarcinoma depends on the clinical stage, amount of tumor (as determined by tumor volume), microscopic grade, and nodal status.[382,390,399,402,405,414] In most series, the overall prognosis has been less favorable than for the squamous cell counterpart.[399,407,416] There is not much difference among the various histologic subtypes,[381] although the endometrioid variety is said to behave slightly better.[471] The presence of nodal metastases is an ominous prognostic sign.[383] Increased serum levels of CA-125 and overexpression of c-*erb*B-2 and nm23-H1 proteins have also been found to represent poor prognostic factors,[388,403,412] whereas expression of p21 has been associated with a favorable outcome.[411]

The preferred therapies are radiation alone or a combination of radiation and surgery.[389,394,398] The incidence of residual tumor in the hysterectomy specimens after intracavitary treatment is much higher than for squamous cell carcinoma.[404]

Differential diagnosis with endometrial adenocarcinoma

The differential diagnosis between endocervical and endometrial adenocarcinoma can be very difficult, whether the tumor has a conventional mucin-secreting pattern or whether it belongs to one of the variants mentioned later in this chapter.[434,440] Features that favor a primary endocervical origin are the following:

1 Presence of in situ adenocarcinoma in the cervical glands

2 Diffuse and abundant intracellular mucin and CEA, since these two markers tend to be present only focally and luminally in endometrial tumors[436,437,439]
3 Negativity for vimentin[435]
4 Negativity or only weak positivity for estrogen or progesterone receptors[437,438]
5 Presence of HPV by in situ hybridization.[438]

Markers of no utility for this purpose are CK7, CK20, 34βE12, and EMA.[435,437]

In situ and microinvasive adenocarcinoma

The documentation of the existence of an in situ stage of cervical carcinoma has lagged behind that of squamous cell carcinoma, but is now widely accepted.[453,459] Instances of glandular dysplasia have also been described,[451,452,454,466] with the ensuing proposal to group the dysplastic and the in situ adenocarcinomatous lesions under the term "cervical intraepithelial glandular neoplasia,"[446,465] a concept that remains controversial.[447,450] Some of the in situ lesions have been shown to precede the development of invasive adenocarcinoma, just as squamous carcinoma in situ (CIN III) precedes invasive carcinoma of the same type.[443] Cytologic atypia (manifested by nuclear hyperchromasia and pleomorphism) and increased mitotic figures are the two most important identifying features (Fig. 19.90). The presence of numerous apoptotic bodies is another diagnostic clue.[442] The mucins secreted by the in situ malignant glands may be similar to those of the normal endocervical mucosa or may resemble the pattern of intestinal goblet cells.[446] Most lesions are positive for CEA, less than half for keratin, and one tenth for secretory component, those figures being lower than for the invasive tumors.[449] The cell proliferative index (as measured by MIB-1) is increased, there is an abnormal expression of cell cycle-related molecules, and the expression of hormone receptors is either decreased or absent.[456]

An important differential diagnosis of in situ cervical adenocarcinoma is with tubal or tubal–endometrial

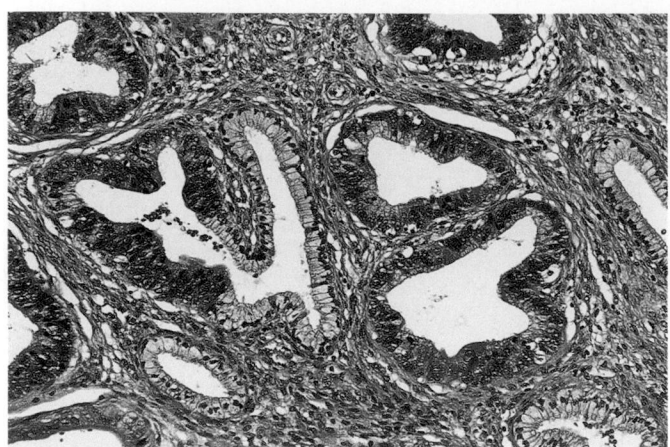

Fig. 19.90 Adenocarcinoma in situ with partial preservation of endocervical glands.

hyperplasia, further complicated by the fact that a tubal type of in situ endocervical adenocarcinoma has been described.[462] Immunohistochemically, the carcinoma tends to be negative for vimentin, diffusely positive for p16 (ink4), generally negative for bcl-2, and usually exhibits a high proliferative index with MIB-1.[444,458] The generally strong positivity for p16 (ink4) supports a strong association of in situ cervical adenocarcinoma with HPV infection.[461]

Almost half of the invasive cervical adenocarcinomas and approximately 75% of their in situ counterparts have an associated CIN of the conventional squamous type of the overlying epithelium.[445,457,464]

Conization is the treatment of choice for in situ adenocarcinoma of the cervix.[441] The status of the margins is not a particularly accurate indicator of the adequacy of excision.[448]

Microinvasive cervical adenocarcinoma has been defined along lines similar to those previously agreed upon for microinvasive squamous cell carcinoma. Terms such as "early stage" and "early invasive" have also been used.[455,460,463] The usual criterion used for its recognition is the presence in an in situ adenocarcinoma of a focus of stromal invasion not exceeding 5 mm in depth.[455,460] The treatment is dependent upon the horizontal extent and whether vascular invasion is present or absent.[466]

Morphologic variants of cervical adenocarcinoma

Endometrioid adenocarcinoma closely resembles its endometrial and ovarian counterparts.[522] It can be extremely well differentiated,[476,537] and can be seen in association with a synchronous or metachronous endometrioid carcinoma in the ovary.[506] The incidence of this tumor type seems to be on the rise.[468] The differential diagnosis includes endometrioid adenocarcinoma of the endometrium, which can be accompanied by a very deceptive pattern of cervical spread.[531a]

Papillary serous carcinoma is analogous in appearance to the homonymous uterine and ovarian neoplasm,

including the common occurrence of psammoma bodies.[528,539]

Adenoma malignum (minimal deviation adenocarcinoma) is a type of cervical adenocarcinoma so well differentiated structurally and cytologically that it can be diagnosed only as malignant because of the presence of distorted glands with irregular outlines deeply positioned in the cervix and the fact that a portion of the infiltrating tumor is associated with a stromal response[485,503,505,518] (Fig. 19.91). In addition, about half of the cases have small foci with a less well differentiated appearance. Vascular and perineurial invasion may be present. The mucin produced is predominantly of neutral type.[496] Ultrastructurally, some authors claim to have identified gastric phenotypes among the tumor cells,[498] a fact that has been supported histochemically.[533] A minor component of argyrophilic cells can be detected in most of the cases.[485] The fact that these tumors, like the more obvious adenocarcinomas, are CEA positive is of importance in the differential diagnosis with benign lesions such as microglandular hyperplasia.[516,530] Parenthetically, there is no convincing evidence that adenoma malignum and conventional cervical adenocarcinoma are causally related to microglandular hyperplasia.[501] The differential diagnosis also includes endocervical-type *cervical adenomyoma*,[486] and the condition known as *florid deep glands*, in which atypia, architectural disarray, and desmoplastic stromal reaction are lacking.[477]

Adenoma malignum usually lacks evidence of high-risk HPV and *p53* mutations.[534]

Adenoma malignum constitutes approximately 1% of all endocervical adenocarcinomas. Some cases are associated with the Peutz–Jeghers syndrome,[485,538] and mutations of the *STK11* gene (a tumor suppressor gene responsible for this syndrome) have been found in over half of the cases of this tumor type.[509]

Villoglandular (papillary) adenocarcinoma presents as an exophytic polypoid lesion with papillae lined by

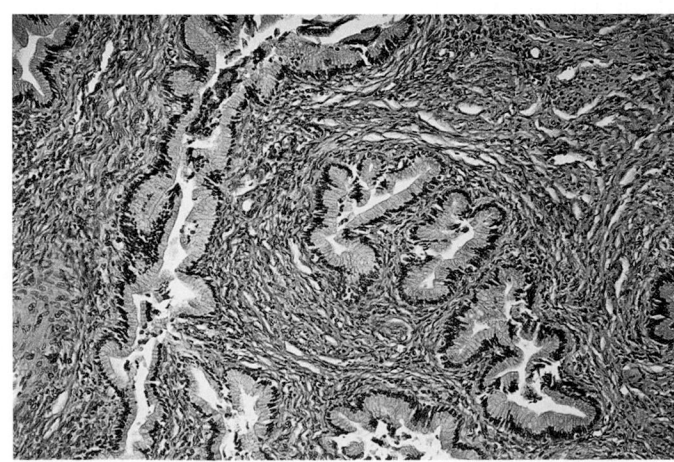

Fig. 19.91 So-called "adenoma malignum" (minimal deviation adenocarcinoma) of cervix.

endocervical, endometrial, or intestinal-type epithelium showing mild atypia (Fig. 19.92). The appearance of the superficial portion is similar to that of colorectal villous adenoma.[494] Most cases are associated with adenocarcinoma in situ and/or CIN,[502] and there is usually evidence of HPV infection.[500] The prognosis is excellent.[536]

Adenosquamous (mixed) carcinoma combines the patterns of adenocarcinoma with a well-defined squamous component[471] (Figs 19.93 and 19.94). This tumor

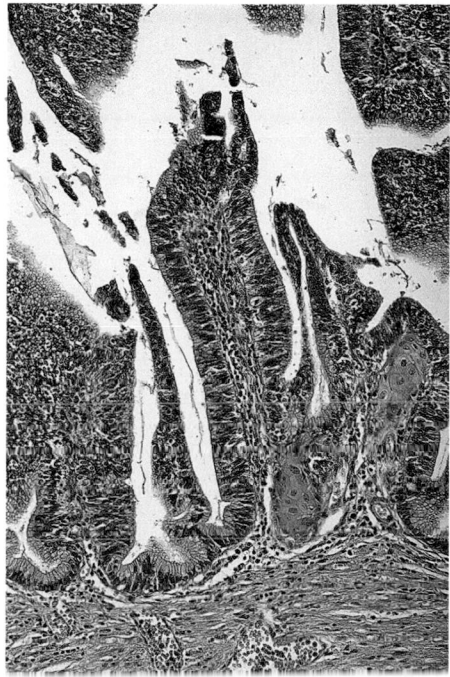

Fig. 19.92 Villoglandular variant of endocervical adenocarcinoma. The architecture is reminiscent of colorectal villous adenoma.

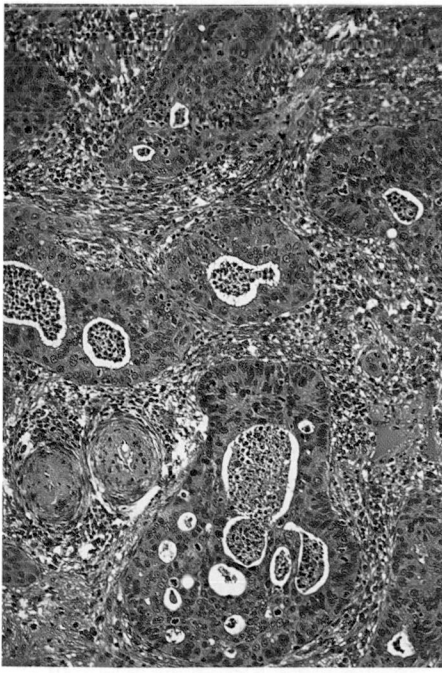

Fig. 19.93 Adenosquamous carcinoma of cervix.

type seems to be particularly common during pregnancy.[487] It is likely that the cell of origin of adenosquamous carcinomas and most adenocarcinomas of the cervix is the same as for the ordinary squamous cell carcinoma (i.e., the subcolumnar reserve cell).[472,508,521]

Adenocarcinoma as previously defined should be distinguished from squamous cell carcinoma without glandular formations but with histochemically demonstrable intracellular mucin (see p. 1536).[532]

Adenosquamous carcinomas have been shown in some series to have a worse overall prognosis than pure squamous cell carcinoma or adenocarcinoma, at least in advanced-stage lesions.[478a] This is probably due to the fact that most of them are poorly differentiated tumors,[483] as supported by the greater proportion of high-ploidy stem cells found in these lesions when subjected to DNA analysis.[482] However, when compared grade by grade and stage by stage with adenocarcinomas and squamous cell carcinomas, no prognostic differences are found.[475,493]

Auersperg et al.[169] have shown that most cervical carcinomas that appear undifferentiated at the light microscopic level still exhibit traits of squamous and/or glandular differentiation at the ultrastructural level.

Glassy cell carcinoma has been described as a distinct type of poorly differentiated adenosquamous carcinoma.[488] It occurs in a younger age group (mean age, 41 years) than other cervical neoplasms and often has been associated with pregnancy. The tumor cells have a moderate amount of cytoplasm with a ground glass or finely granular appearance, a prominent eosinophilic and PAS-positive cell wall, and large nuclei with prominent nucleoli.

Mitoses are numerous. A prominent inflammatory infiltrate, often rich in eosinophils, is regularly seen in the adjacent stroma, and this may be accompanied by peripheral blood eosinophilia.

In pure cases of glassy cell carcinoma, glandular or squamous differentiation is absent, although it can be

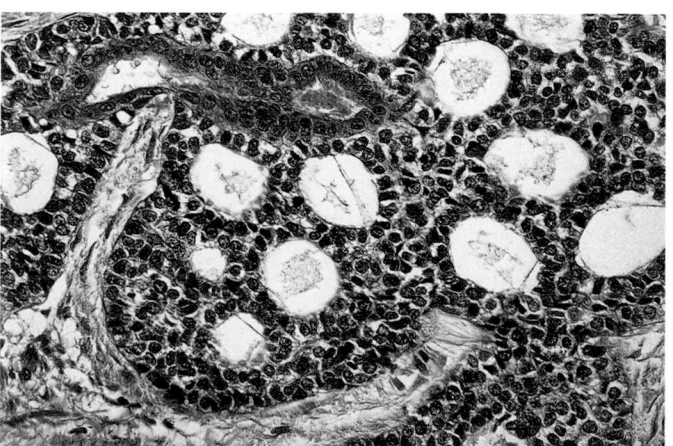

Fig. 19.94 Adenoid cystic carcinoma of cervix with a typical cribriform pattern of growth.

consistently detected by ultrastructural examination.[535] Other cases show an admixture with mucin-producing adenocarcinoma and/or clear-cut squamous foci, raising the question whether it is justified to regard glassy cell carcinoma as a distinct entity.[474,513] The immunohistochemical keratin profile is similar to that of reserve cells or immature squamous cells of cervix.[507] The prognosis is poor, a fact probably related to its poorly differentiated nature.[512,519]

Adenoid cystic carcinoma is a specific variant of cervical adenocarcinoma that tends to occur in elderly multigravid black women[484] and that is associated with a particularly poor prognosis.[481,497] The morphologic appearance is similar to that of the homonymous tumors of salivary glands (Fig. 19.95). Like the former, it may be cribriform (the most common pattern) or grow in a predominantly solid fashion.[467]

Adenoid basal carcinoma should be distinguished

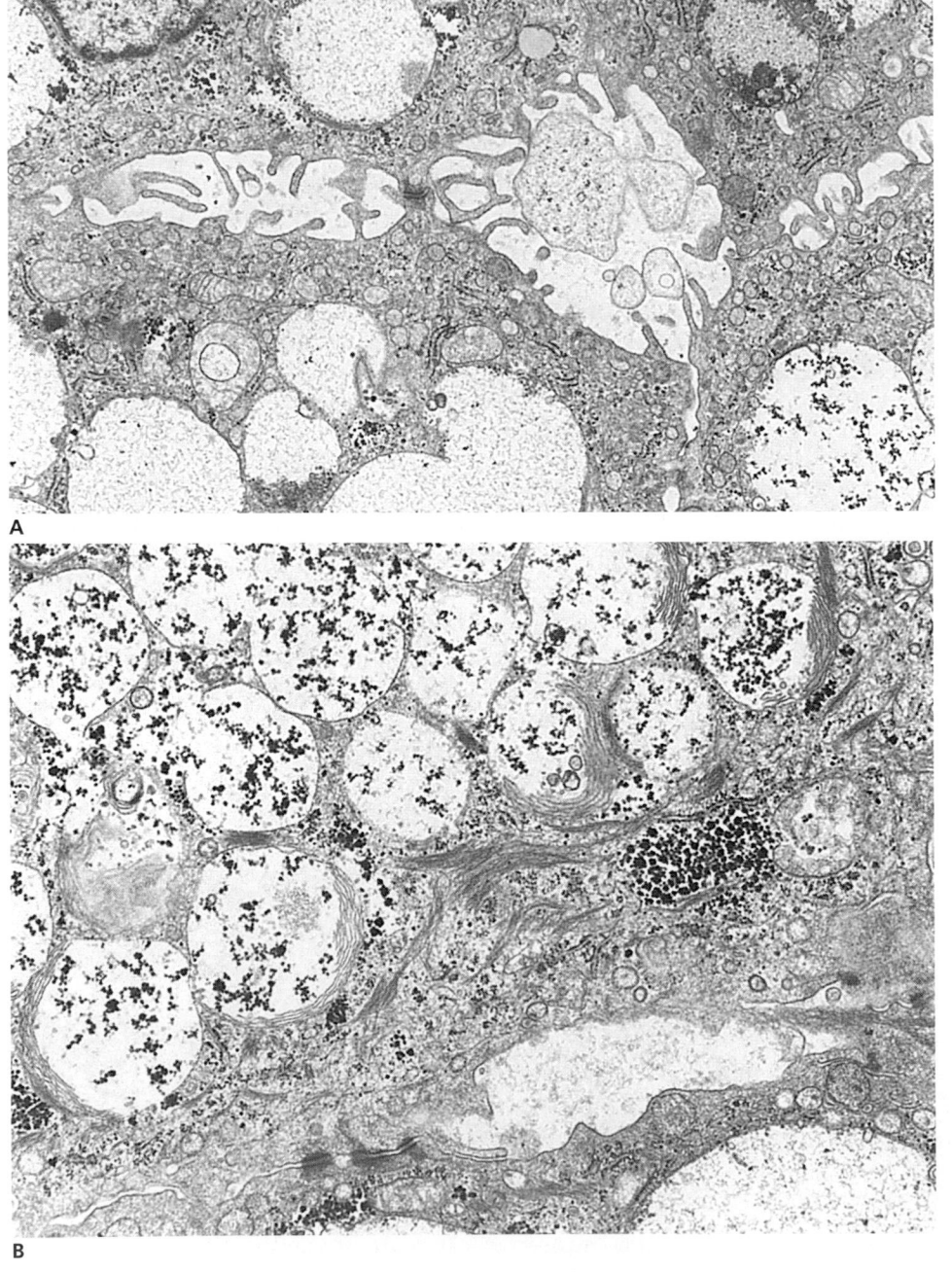

A

B

Fig. 19.95 A and **B**, Ultrastructural appearance of adenosquamous carcinoma of cervix. **A**, Large mucous secretory vacuoles, true lumen formation, and scattered glycogen may be noted in tumor cells. **B**, Note the presence of tonofilaments in addition to secretory products.

both from adenoid cystic carcinoma and from basaloid (squamous cell) carcinoma (see p. 1494). Although it shares many phenotypical features with adenoid cystic carcinoma,[489] it is a very low grade lesion, in contrast with the two neoplasms with which it can be confused. It is usually discovered incidentally, it does not produce a mass lesion, and it has never resulted in metastases.[470,480] The consistent presence of HPV-16 has been documented.[499] The lesion blends with the process that has been called *adenoid basal hyperplasia*. Brainard et al.[470] have proposed grouping these two conditions under the term *adenoid basal epithelioma* to emphasize their indolent nature.

Clear cell carcinoma (formerly called *mesonephric carcinoma*) of the cervix is of müllerian rather than of mesonephric origin.[514] The presence of in situ changes in the area of the squamocolumnar junction in some of the cases[524] and the electron microscopic features[478] seem to provide conclusive evidence for this interpretation. Glands lined by large cells with abundant clear cytoplasm are characteristic[479] (Fig. 19.96). "Hobnail" cells are common, as are intraglandular papillary projections. Grossly, the tumor is usually exophytic. This is the most common form of cervical carcinoma in young females, although it occurs in all age groups,[490,517] and it shows a second peak at age 70 years.[492] The prognosis is relatively good. In the 13 cases studied by Hart and Norris,[495] the actuarial survival rate was 55% at 5 years and 40% at 10 years. The relationship with intrauterine diethylstilbestrol exposure and other features of this tumor are the same as for the analogous vaginal neoplasms.[491,520,526] It is

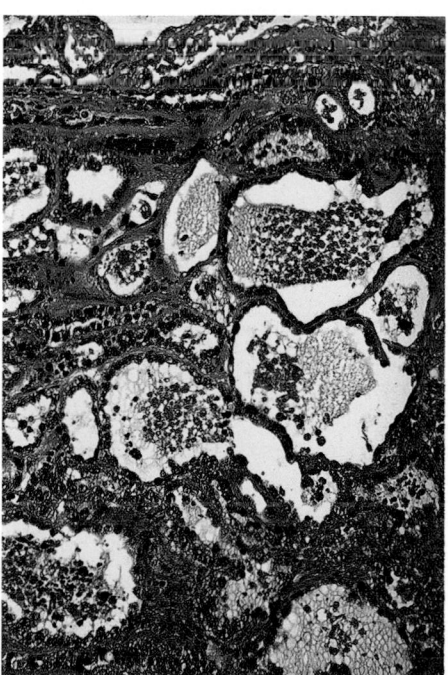

Fig. 19.96 Clear cell adenocarcinoma of cervix showing tubular, microcystic, and tubulocystic features.

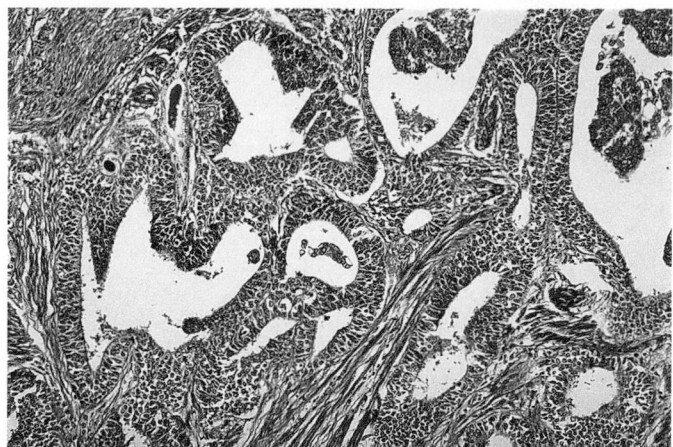

Fig. 19.97 Mesonephric gland carcinoma of cervix.

also evident, however, that morphologically identical cases occur in the absence of exposure to this hormone, particularly in older women.[504]

Mesonephric (adeno)carcinoma is a very rare tumor. Most of the cases that have been reported as such in the past probably represent müllerian type adenocarcinomas or yolk sac tumors. True mesonephric carcinomas are often found adjacent to mesonephric hyperplasia (sometimes florid and atypical) and may exhibit a variety of patterns, such as ductal (resembling endometrioid adenocarcinoma), small tubular, retiform, solid, sex-cord-like, and spindle[473,510,523] (Fig. 19.97). The immunohistochemical profile is similar to that of mesonephric rests, and includes positivity for CD10 and calretinin,[515a,529] two interesting but not entirely specific findings.[529]

Other variants of endocervical adenocarcinoma, all of them exceedingly rare, are a microcystic type,[531] a type associated with Paget's disease,[470a] a signet ring type,[515] a small intestinal (enteric) type,[511,525] and a type with choriocarcinomatous and hepatoid differentiation.[527]

Neuroendocrine carcinoma

A small number of cervical carcinomas exhibit various degrees of neuroendocrine differentiation, as detected by conventional morphologic, ultrastructural, histochemical, and/or immunohistochemical criteria. These tumors have been variously called (atypical) carcinoid tumor, argyrophil cell carcinoma, (extrapulmonary) small cell carcinoma, (neuro)endocrine carcinoma, and carcinoma with (neuro)endocrine differentiation, the choice in terminology depending on the degree of differentiation of the tumor, the extent of endocrine features present, and the observer's bias[552,564] (Fig. 19.98). It is probably preferable to use terms similar to those employed at other sites for morphologically similar tumors, i.e., typical carcinoid tumor (almost nonexistent in the cervix), atypical carcinoid tumor, small cell neuroendocrine carcinoma, and

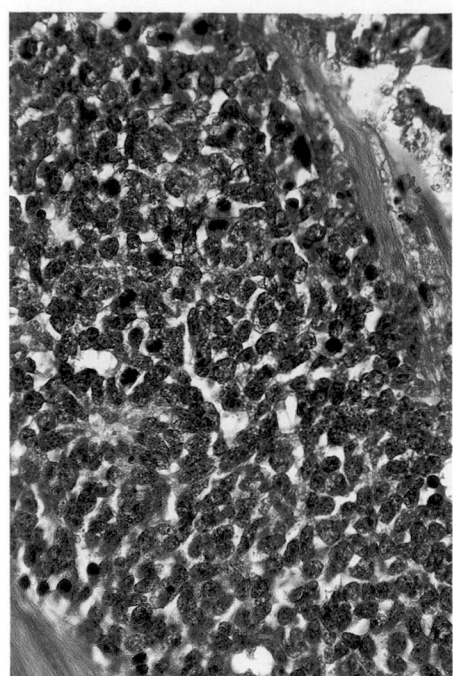

Fig. 19.98 High-grade neuroendocrine carcinoma of cervix of small cell type.

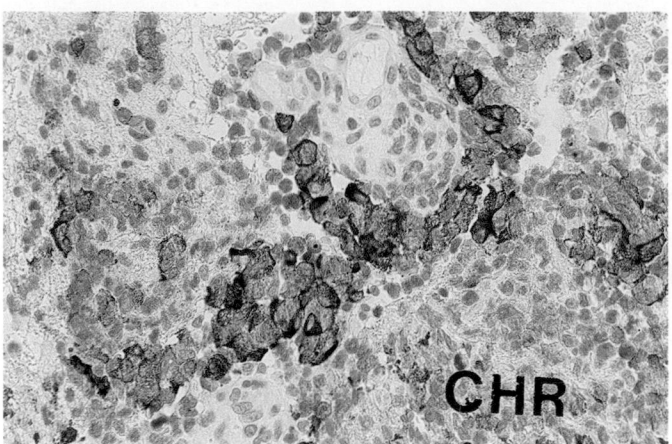

Fig. 19.99 Strong focal immunoreactivity for chromogranin in neuroendocrine carcinoma of cervix.

large cell neuroendocrine carcinoma.[541,546,548] Another analogy with other sites worth mentioning is that sometimes one finds neuroendocrine markers in cervical carcinomas of conventional type, a fact that should not result in a change of their designation.[545]

The age distribution of neuroendocrine carcinomas of the cervix is the same as for squamous cell carcinoma. They also show a similar association with HPV.[540,557,563] The carcinoid syndrome is invariably absent, but some cases have been seen in association with Cushing's syndrome,[555] and with inappropriate secretion of antidiuretic hormone (ADH).[553] In contrast to squamous cell carcinoma, CIN changes in the adjacent epithelium are extremely rare.[542,563] A possible precursor lesion in the form of endocrine cell hyperplasia of the cervix has been identified.[544]

The better differentiated members of this group have an organoid arrangement, with trabecular, insular, glandular, and spindle patterns of growth. Most cases are pure, but others are combined with squamous cell carcinoma[562] or adenocarcinoma.[551,559,561] Some of these combined tumors have been referred to as amphicrine carcinomas.[549]

Argyrophilic (but not argentaffin) granules can be demonstrated in many of the cases, particularly the better differentiated ones. Amyloid may be deposited in the stroma. Ultrastructurally, a variable number of dense-core secretory granules are found in all but the most undifferentiated types. Immunohistochemically, positivity may be found for neuron-specific enolase, chromogranin (but only in the better differentiated examples), synaptophysin, 5-hydroxytryptamine (sero-

tonin), other generic neuroendocrine markers,[565,566] and a variety of peptide hormones[567] (Fig. 19.99). They also commonly express keratin (befitting their epithelial nature) and CEA.[567] At the genetic molecular level, there is frequent loss of heterozygosity at 3p and 11p,[556,557] and loss of Rb protein expression.[550]

The large majority of these cervical neoplasms are histologically and clinically aggressive. Mitoses and areas of necrosis are common, and the prognosis is generally poor.[540] A definite relationship exists between degree of microscopic differentiation and clinical behavior, the outcome being particularly bleak for the small cell carcinomas.[547,554,558] Naturally, there is also a close relationship between clinical stage and prognosis.[543] The treatment, especially for high-grade lesions, usually consists of a combination of surgery, radiation therapy, and chemotherapy.[560]

Cytology

The broadest and most successful application of clinical cytology has been in the diagnosis of invasive carcinoma of the uterine cervix and precursor lesions through the technique. First described by Aureli Babès, a Rumanian pathologist, and popularized by George Papanicolaou at Cornell University and universally known as the Pap test[581,589] (Fig. 19.100). Today, it is widely used both as a screening test in asymptomatic populations and in the follow-up of patients with cervical carcinomas treated by either conservative surgery or irradiation.[576a,584]

Mass cytologic screening has shifted the presentation of cervical carcinoma from the clinical to the preclinical stage. This is an established fact, the statement that the incidence of cervical carcinoma was already declining prior to the introduction of this diagnostic method notwithstanding. Incidentally, the accuracy of the latter statement has been disputed.[575] Following mass screening, there has been a reduction of 38% to 57% in the overall incidence of invasive carcinoma and a reduction

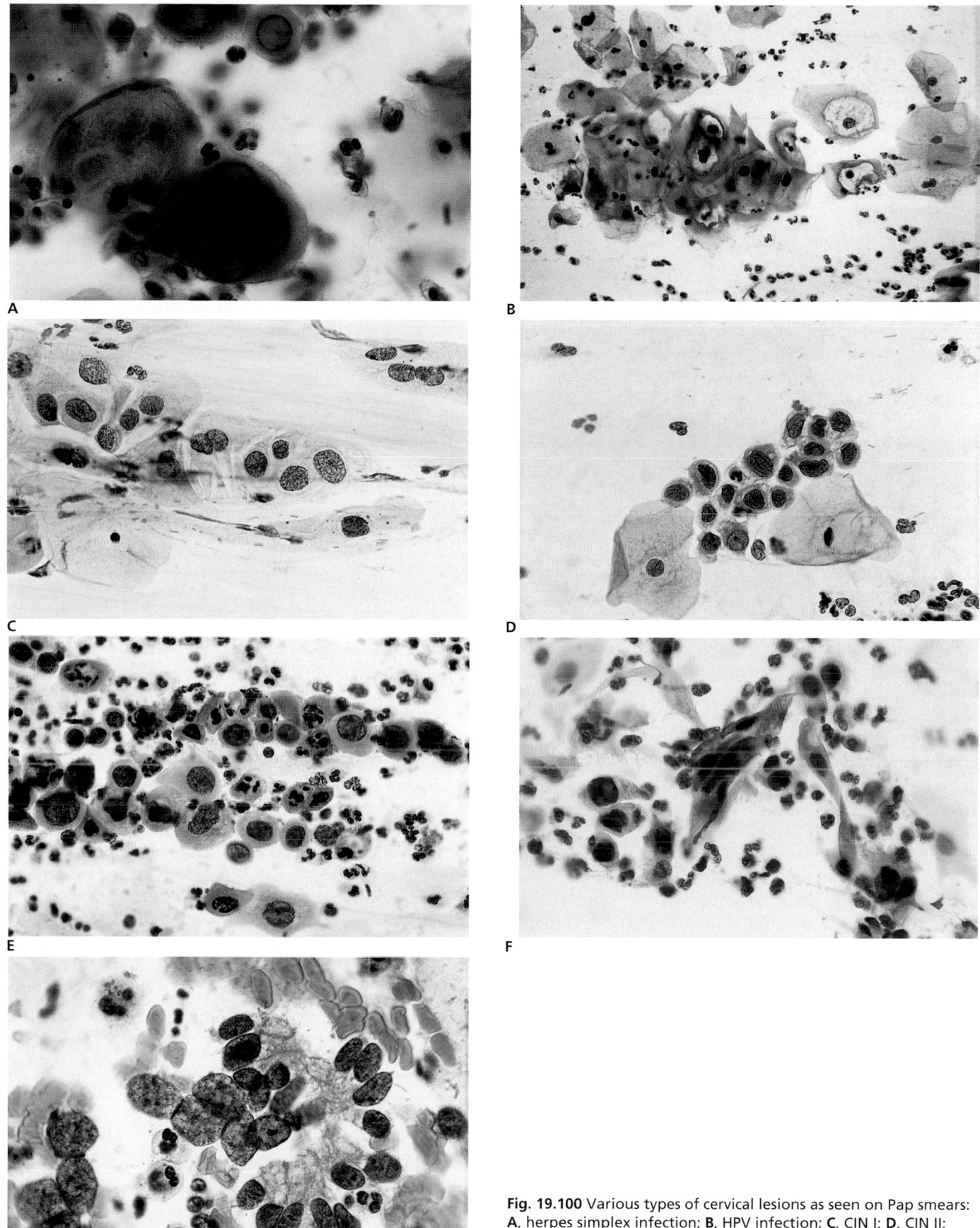

Fig. 19.100 Various types of cervical lesions as seen on Pap smears: **A**, herpes simplex infection; **B**, HPV infection; **C**, CIN I; **D**, CIN II; **E**, CIN III; **F**, invasive squamous cell carcinoma; **G**, adenocarcinoma. (Courtesy of L. Alasio, Milan, Italy)

of 67% in the incidence of clinically evident carcinoma (stages Ib to IV).[571,576] Whereas in the prescreening era invasive carcinoma contributed approximately 80% of all diagnosed cases, at the present time it makes up less than 20% of the cases, the remaining being carcinomas in the intraepithelial (CIN) stage.[575] This has resulted in an increased cure rate for the screened population and in an increase in the survival times for the patients with invasive carcinoma.[573,575,576] In an often quoted article, Christopherson and Scott[572] reported a 70% decrease in the mortality from carcinoma of the uterine cervix between 1970/1971 and 1955/1956 in women younger than 60 years of age.

The diagnostic accuracy of cervical cytology is high, as was already amply demonstrated in several large studies done in the 1960s.[585,599] However, in the evaluation of some remarkably high figures, one cannot escape the suspicion that they might have been influenced by the fact that the same person diagnosed the cytology specimen and the cervical biopsy. To avoid subconscious bias, it is better for these two functions to be performed by two different individuals. Seybolt[590] demonstrated this fact by distributing 25 problem cases to eight authorities in cytopathology and requesting them to interpret the cytology slides independently of the histology. There was no universal agreement in any case, and in some instances the disagreements were quite disparate. The conclusion from this survey was that it is not always possible to determine the exact histologic change in the cervix on the basis of the cytology smear. However, a more important demonstration was that if a cervical abnormality was present, this was detected by cytologic examination in the large majority of the cases.

Careful attention to technical factors is essential to achieve good results. The smear should be promptly fixed and carefully stained. Air-dried smears are grossly inadequate in this regard. Even if squamous cells can be rehydrated, they never exhibit the fine structural details of wet-fixed material; glandular cells are even more distorted. It is also highly desirable that the specimen be secured by a trained individual. Self-made samples, obtained with a pipette, are not nearly so satisfactory. Invasive carcinoma is detected at almost the same rate as with the material obtained by the physician, but the accuracy is considerably lower. Furthermore, the percentage of unsatisfactory specimens approaches 20%.[580] It is also important for the detection of early carcinoma that an endocervical sample obtained by the use of a special brush[579] be examined in addition to the ordinary specimen from the exocervix and vaginal pool.

Special techniques are also applicable to cytology smears, including immunohistochemistry, in situ hybridization, and DNA cytometry.[574] For instance, it has been shown that MIB-1 staining of cervical smears improves the diagnostic accuracy of cervical low-grade intraepithelial lesions.[586,601]

The terminology used in cervicovaginal cytology has evolved over the course of years, sometimes adapting names from the histopathology lexicon but more often devising some of its own. Papanicolaou's original system had five "classes" of increasing atypia. Although this nomenclature fulfilled a very important role in the establishment of the technique, it was eventually abandoned because of the vagueness of the information provided. A "class III" smear, for instance, could represent anything from a CIN II (moderate dysplasia) to an invasive carcinoma. Therefore, it was progressively replaced in the 1960s by the nomenclature then in vogue among histopathologists (i.e., negative, benign atypia, dysplasia [mild, moderate, or severe] carcinoma in situ, and invasive carcinoma).[590,591] During the 1970s, many institutions switched to the CIN system for both cytologic and histologic specimens (see p. 1532). In 1988, a proposal was made at a meeting in Bethesda to classify squamous intraepithelial lesions (SIL) in the following categories: (1) atypical squamous cells of undetermined significance (ASCUS), (2) low-grade SIL, (3) high-grade SIL, and (4) squamous cell carcinoma.[583,594,598] In this scheme, low-grade SIL corresponds to HPV-associated cellular changes, mild dysplasia, and CIN I, whereas high-grade SIL corresponds to moderate and severe dysplasia, carcinoma in situ, and CIN II and III. The rationale for grouping HPV-related changes (koilocytosis) and CIN I within the low-grade SIL group is based on the many similarities that exist between the lesions, which makes their separation difficult. A similar reasoning lies behind the decision to combine CIN II and III lesions in the category of high-grade SIL. The term "atypical squamous cells of undetermined significance" (ASCUS) was proposed at the same meeting for cases in which the findings do not fulfill the criteria for either benign reactive change or SIL; as such, it has a more restricted meaning than the traditional terms "atypia" and "inflammatory atypia."

The system has been criticized on several grounds, one of them being the claim that it leads to overtreatment of many individuals whose smears are placed in the low-grade SIL category.[570,578] Partly as a response to these criticisms, the system was revised in 2001 in order to facilitate triage of women for more intensive screening only when a strong suspicion of a high-grade lesion is present.[593,595] The current categories are the following:

1 Atypical squamous cells:
   a Of unknown significance (ASC-US)
   b Cannot exclude high-grade squamous intraepithelial lesion (ASC-H)
2 Low-grade squamous intraepithelial lesion (LGSIL)
3 High-grade squamous intraepithelial lesion (HGSIL).

The recommendation is for women with ASC-US to be managed using a program of two repeat cytology tests, immediate colposcopy, or DNA testing for high-risk types of HPV.[600]

The great success of the Pap test has led to overexpectations on the part of clinicians and the public at large and the unreasonable demand that every case of carcinoma be detected with it. One should not forget that it is and will remain a *screening* test and that—as such—it will inevitably be associated with a "false-negative rate."[587,596] The reasons include inadequacy of the sample, insufficient time devoted to screening, human fatigue, and inadequate interpretation by the screener and/or pathologist.[582,588,592] Of these, the latter represents only a minor fraction of all cases, as has been repeatedly demonstrated.[589,592]

The areas of innovation in cervical cancer screening consist of the technologies of liquid based-cytology (ThinPrep; AutoCite), computer assisted screening (AutoPap; PapNet), and molecular testing for high-risk HPV[568,569,574a,577,597] (see p. 1530 and Chapter 3). An even more sophisticated technique recently applied to cytologic specimens is the detection of genomic amplification of the human telomerase gene (TERC) as an independent screening test for HSIL.[578a]

Other tumors and tumorlike conditions

Carcinomas of one type or another comprise approximately 99% of all primary cervical malignancies. The remaining 1% is made up of a large variety of neoplasms.

Botryoid rhabdomyosarcoma (a variant of embryonal rhabdomyosarcoma) presents in children and adolescents as a myxoid polypoid mass covered by attenuated epithelium[611,616,641] (Figs 19.101 and 19.102). The appearance is generally similar to that of the homonymous vaginal tumor. However, some of the cervical cases occurring in older patients have been seen to contain cartilage and to be associated with a better prognosis[618] (Fig. 19.103).

Mixed müllerian tumors also present as polypoid masses but generally occur in much older patients, the average age in one series being 65 years.[615] Some tumors look identical to their more common uterine counterparts, but in others the recognizable epithelial component has an adenoid basal or squamous appearance.[615,644] When the latter is the case, the appearance blends with that of spindle cell (sarcomatoid) carcinoma.

Müllerian adenosarcoma[634] and **stromal sarcoma** of endometrial type also occur in the cervix (Fig. 19.104), the former sometimes featuring foci of ovarian sex-cord-like structures[630]; this includes the better differentiated and presumably benign variant of this tumor originally described as *papillary adenofibroma*.[603,661]

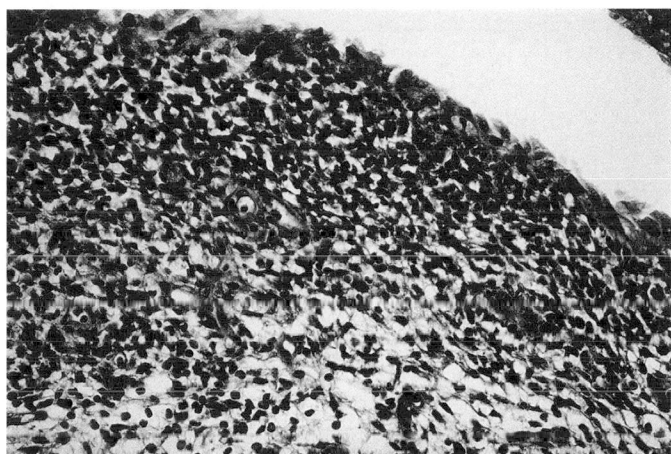

Fig. 19.102 Cambium layer beneath cervical epithelium in botryoid rhabdomyosarcoma of cervix.

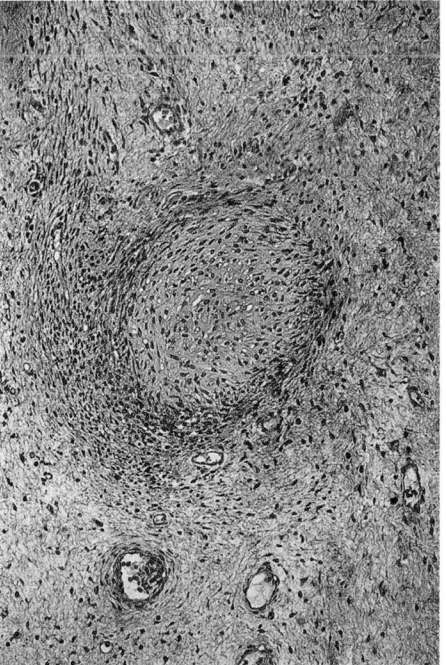

Fig. 19.103 Cartilage formation in botryoid rhabdomyosarcoma. This feature is more commonly seen in cervical than in vaginal examples of this tumor type.

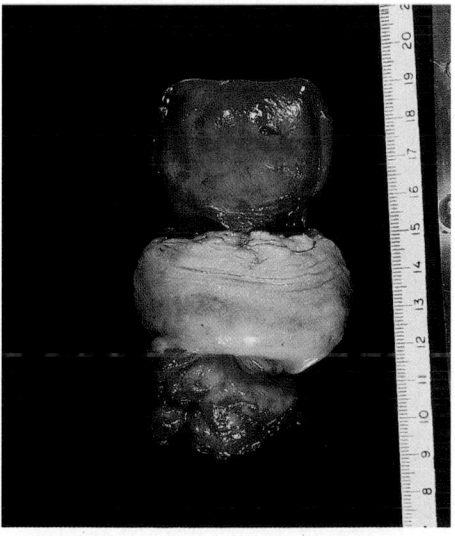

Fig. 19.101 Botryoid rhabdomyosarcoma of cervix protruding in the form of grapelike masses.

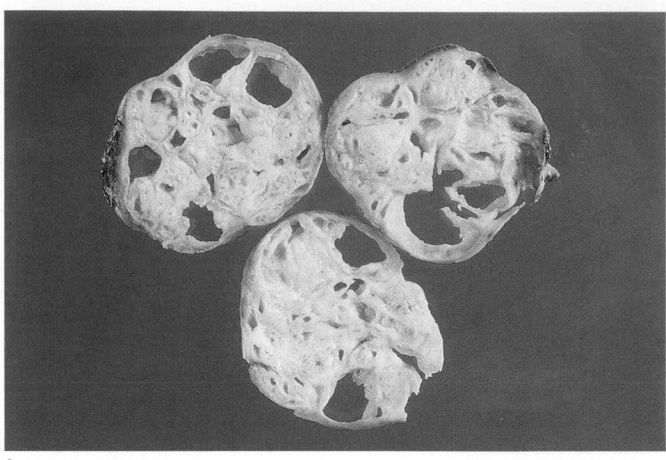

A

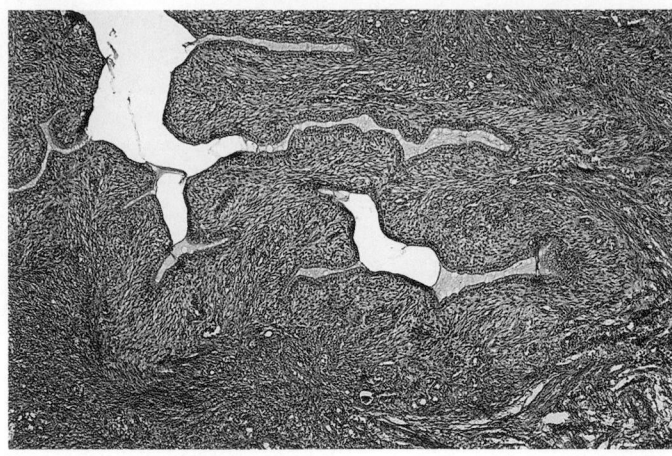

B

Fig. 19.104 A and **B**, Müllerian adenosarcoma of cervix. **A**, Gross appearance. This tumor was extremely well differentiated and qualified as an adenofibroma. **B**, Microscopic appearance of another case. The appearance is reminiscent of phylloides tumor of breast. (**A**, Courtesy of Dr. Juan Segura, San José, Costa Rica)

Smooth muscle tumors, both benign and malignant, also occur in the cervix (Fig. 19.105).[654] The diagnostic criteria are the same as for those in the uterine corpus, but the ratio may be slightly different (comparatively more leiomyosarcomas are found in the cervix). Some of the reported leiomyosarcomas have been of the myxoid variety,[623] and others have had a xanthomatous appearance.[626]

Other primary cervical tumors and tumorlike conditions include *teratoma*,[628,636] *glial polyp (glioma)*, and *ganglioneuroma*[642]; *yolk sac (endodermal sinus) tumor* (closely simulating the clinical appearance of botryoid rhabdomyosarcoma)[617]; *choriocarcinoma*[639]; *sebaceous carcinoma*[658]; *extrarenal Wilms' tumor*[608]; *traumatic (amputation) neuroma*[607] (some occurring post partum)[655]; *neurofibroma*[624]; *schwannoma*[627] (including the pigmented variety)[653]; *malignant peripheral nerve sheath tumor*[609,635]; *pigmented neuroectodermal tumor of infancy*[652]; *melanosis* (sometimes developing after cryotherapy for CIN)[619,631,659]; *blue nevus*[648,656] (Fig. 19.106); *cellular blue nevus*; *malignant melanoma*[613,638] (including the desmoplastic variety[633]); *benign mesenchymoma*[657]; *hemangioma*[637] (Fig. 19.107); *glomus tumor*[605]; *angiosarcoma*[614]; *osteosarcoma*[610]; *alveolar soft part sarcoma*[622,647,650]; and *Ewing's sarcoma/PNET*.[612,643]

Malignant lymphomas of the cervix present with vaginal bleeding and a subepithelial mass without obvious ulceration; most are diffuse large B-cell lymphomas and many are accompanied by extensive fibrosis[606,620,621,629,649] (Fig. 108). An important differential diagnosis is with lymphoma-like lesions resulting from focally florid lymphoid proliferation associated with chronic cervicitis or as an expression of infectious mononucleosis[660]; these are identified by the polymorphic nature of the infiltrate (including mature plasma cells, small lymphocytes, and neutrophils), surface ulceration, minimal or no sclerosis, and evidence of polyclonality by immunoperoxidase staining. *Granulocytic sarcoma (chloroma)*,[602,651] *Hodgkin's*

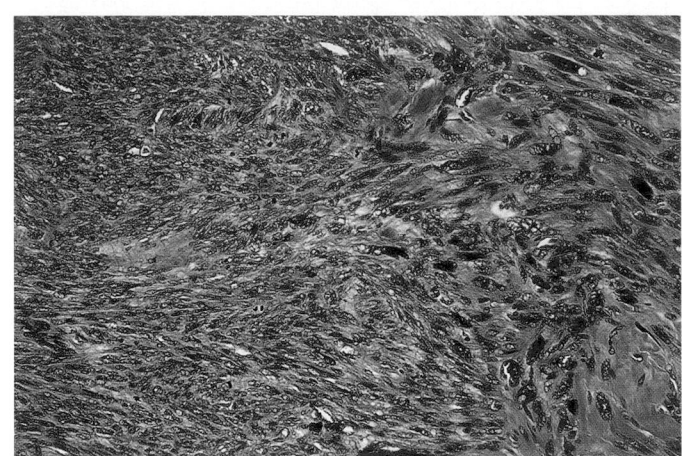

Fig. 19.105 Poorly differentiated leiomyosarcoma of cervix.

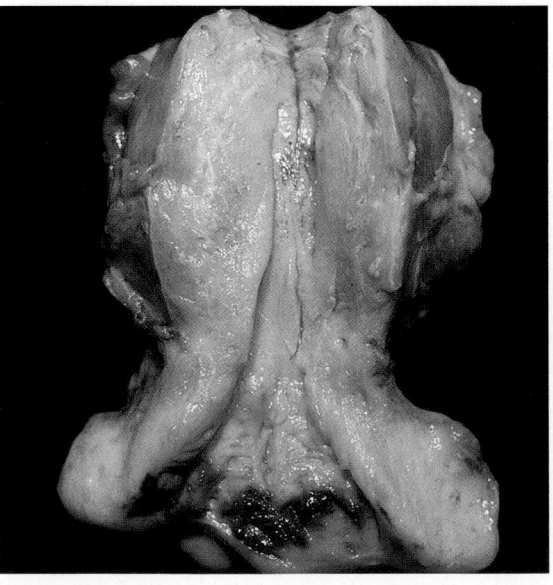

Fig. 19.106 Gross appearance of blue nevus of cervix. (Courtesy of Dr. Luis Spitale, Cordoba, Argentina)

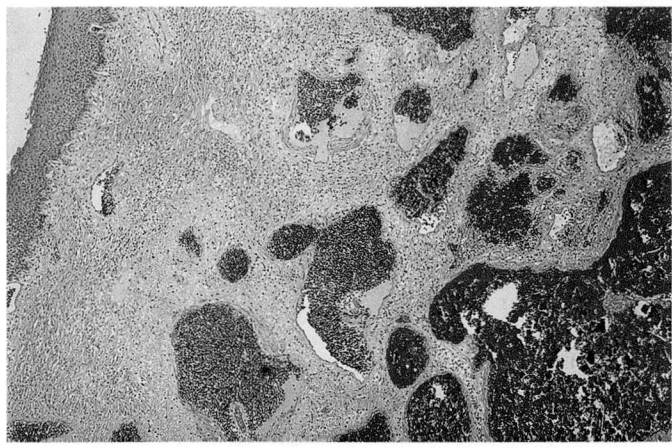

Fig. 19.107 Cavernous hemangioma of cervix, a most unusual occurrence.

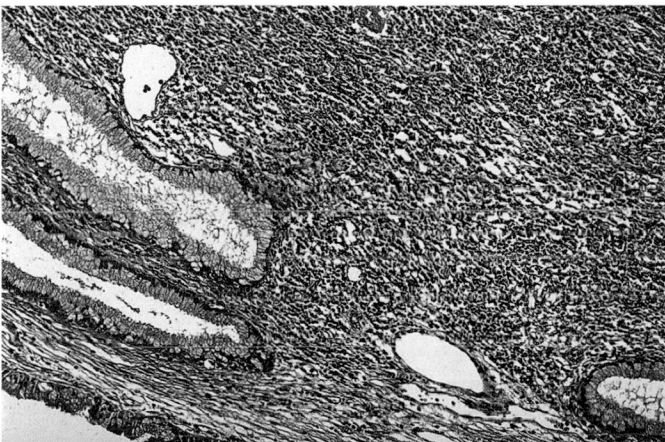

Fig. 19.108 Diffuse large cell lymphoma of cervix growing between normal endocervical glands.

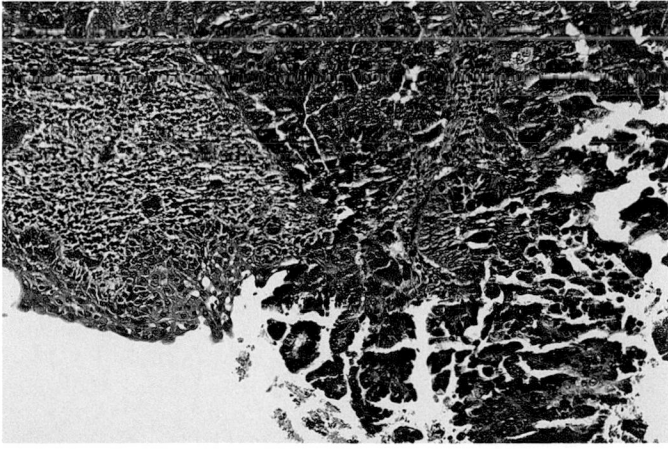

Fig. 19.109 Serous papillary carcinoma of ovary metastatic to cervix.

disease, inflammatory pseudotumor,[604] localized *amyloidosis,*[625] and *Rosai–Dorfman disease* (sinus histiocytosis with massive lymphadenopathy)[646] can also present initially as a cervical mass.

Metastatic carcinomas to the cervix (excluding direct invasion from endometrial carcinoma) can originate from genital or extragenital organs; the most common

sites are the ovary, large bowel, stomach, breast, and kidney[632,640] (Fig. 19.109). Some of them simulate clinically and pathologically the appearance of primary cervical carcinoma. Knowledge of the clinical findings may make this mistake avoidable.

An exceptional event is represented by a coating of the endocervical (and endometrial) mucosa by metastatic mucinous tumor of the appendix, a phenomenon somewhat analogous to that seen in pseudomyxoma peritonei and pseudomyxoma ovarii.[645]

References

Normal anatomy

1 Fetissof F, Serres G, Arbeille B, de Muret A, Sam-Giao M, Lansac J. Argyrophilic cells and ectocervical epithelium. Int J Gynecol Pathol 1991, **10:** 177–190.
2 Gilks CB, Reid PE, Clement PB, Owen DA. Histochemical changes in cervical mucus-secreting epithelium during the normal menstrual cycle. Fertil Steril 1989, **5:** 286–291.
3 Hendrickson MR, Kempson RL. Normal histology of the uterus and fallopian tubes. In Sternberg S (ed.): Histology for pathologists, ed. 2. Philadelphia, 1997, Lippincott-Raven, pp. 879–928.
4 Loning T, Kuhler C, Caselitz J, Stegner HE. Keratin and tissue polypeptide antigen profiles of the cervical mucosa. Int J Gynecol Pathol 1983, **2:** 105–112.
5 Malecha MJ, Miettinen M. Patterns of keratin subsets in normal and abnormal uterine cervical tissues. An immunohistochemical study. Int J Gynecol Pathol 1992, **11:** 24–29.
6 Nonogaki H, Fujii S, Konishi I, Nanbu Y, Ozaki S, Ishikawa Y, Mori T. Estrogen receptor localization in normal and neoplastic epithelium of the uterine cervix. Cancer 1990, **66:** 2620–2627.
7 Osamura RY, Watanabe K, Oh M. Melanin-containing cells in the uterine cervix. Histochemical and electron-microscopic studies of two cases. Am J Clin Pathol 1980, **74:** 239–242.
8 Remadi S, MacGee W, Mégevand E, Chappuis P, Redard M, Seemayer TA. Resident neuroendocrine cells in the normal ectoendocervical epithelium: an immunohistochemical study of 100 cases using a microwave heating technique. Int J Surg Pathol 1997, **5:** 19–24.
9 Smedts F, Ramaekers F, Troyanovsky S, Pruszczynski M, Robben H, Lane B, Leigh I, Plantema F, Vooijs P. Basal-cell keratins in cervical reserve cells and a comparison to their expression in cervical intraepithelial neoplasia. Am J Pathol 1992, **140:** 601–612.
10 Warhol MJ, Antonioli DA, Pinkus GS, Burke L, Rice RH. Immunoperoxidase staining for involucrin. A potential diagnostic aid in cervicovaginal pathology. Hum Pathol 1982, **13:** 1095–1099.
11 Whittaker JR, Samy AM, Sunter JP, Sinha DP, Monaghan JM. Cytokeratin expression in cervical epithelium. An immunohistological study of normal, wart virus-infected and neoplastic tissue. Histopathology 1989, **14:** 151–160.
12 Zwillenberg LO. At 40 years of the 'Golden Chain'. Which are the stem cells in ectocervical epithelium? Gynecol Obstet Invest 1999, **46:** 247–251.

Remnants and ectopias

13 Nucci MR, Ferry JA, Young PR. Ectopic prostatic tissue in the uterine cervix: a report of four cases and review of ectopic prostatic tissue. Am J Surg Pathol 2000, **24:** 1224–1230.
14 Rath-Wolfson L, Koren R, Amiel A, Pardo J, Gal R. The "female prostrate" in cervix uteri: a case report. Appl Immunhistochem 1998, **6:** 50–53.

15 Robledo M, Vazquez J, Contreras-Mejuto F, Lopez-Garcia G. Sebaceous glands and hair follicles in the cervix uteri. Histopathology 1992, **21**: 278–279.

16 Roth E, Taylor HB. Heterotopic cartilage in the uterus. Obstet Gynecol 1966, **27**: 838–844.

Squamous and other metaplasias

17 al-Nafussi A, Rahilly M. The prevalence of tubo-endometrial metaplasia and adenomatoid proliferation. Histopathology 1993, **22**: 177–179.

18 Crum CP, Egawa K, Fu YS, Lancaster WD, Barron B, Levine RU, Fenoglio CM, Richart RM. Atypical immature metaplasia (AIM). A subset of human papilloma virus infection of the cervix. Cancer 1983, **51**: 2214–2219.

19 Ducatman BS, Wang HH, Jonasson JG, Hogan CL, Antonioli DA. Tubal metaplasia. A cytologic study with comparison to other neoplastic and non-neoplastic conditions of the endocervix. Diagn Cytopathol 1993, **9**: 95–103.

20 Duggan MA. Cytologic and histologic diagnosis and significance of controversial squamous lesions of the uterine cervix. Mod Pathol 2000, **13**: 252–260.

21 Egan AJM, Russell P. Transitional (urothelial) cell metaplasia of the uterine cervix: morphological assessment of 31 cases. Int J Gynecol Pathol 1997, **16**: 89–98.

22 Feldman D, Romney SL, Edgcomb J, Valentine T. Ultrastructure of normal, metaplastic, and abnormal human uterine cervix. Use of montages to study the topographical relationship of epithelial cells. Am J Obstet Gynecol 1984, **150**: 573–688.

23 Geng L, Connolly DC, Isaacson C, Ronnett BM, Cho KR. Atypical immature metaplasia (AIM) of the cervix: is it related to high-grade squamous intraepithelial lesion (HSIL)? Hum Pathol 1999, **30**: 345–351.

24 Harnden P, Kennedy W, Andrew AC, Southgate J. Immunophenotype of transitional metaplasia of the uterine cervix. Int J Gynecol Pathol 1999, **18**: 125–129.

25 Ismail SM. Cone biopsy causes cervical endometriosis and tubo-endometrioid metaplasia. Histopathology 1991, **18**: 107–114.

26 Johnson LD, Easterday CL, Gore H, Hertig AT. Histogenesis of carcinoma in situ of the uterine cervix. A preliminary report of the origin of carcinoma in situ in subcylindrical cell anaplasia. Cancer 1964, **17**: 213–229.

27 Jonasson JG, Wang HH, Antonioli DA, Ducatman BS. Tubal metaplasia of the uterine cervix. A prevalence study in patients with gynecologic pathologic findings. Int J Gynecol Pathol 1992, **11**: 89–95.

28 Jones MA. Transitional cell metaplasia and neoplasia in the female genital tract: an update. Adv Anat Pathol 1999, **5**: 106–113.

29 Jones MA, Young RH. Atypical oxyphilic metaplasia of the endocervical epithelium: a report of six cases. Int J Gynecol Pathol 1997, **16**: 99–102.

30 Koss LG. Traditional cell metaplasia of cervix: a misnomer. Am J Surg Pathol 1998, **22**: 774–776.

31 McCluggage WG, Maxwell P, McBride HA, Hamilton PW, Bharucha H. Monoclonal antibodies Ki-67 and M1B1 in the distinction of tuboendometrial metaplasia from endocervical adenocarcinoma and adenocarcinoma in situ in formalin-fixed material. Int J Gynecol Pathol 1995, **14**: 209–216.

32 Mittal K, Mesia A, Demopoulos RI. MIB-1 expression is useful in distinguishing dysplasia from atrophy in elderly women. Int J Gynecol Pathol 1999, **18**: 122–124.

33 Oliva E, Clement PB, Young RH. Tubal and tubo-endometrioid metaplasia of the uterine cervix. Unemphasized features that may cause problems in differential diagnosis – A report of 25 cases. Am J Clin Pathol 1995, **103**: 618–623.

34 Park JJ, Genest DR, Sun D, Crum CP. Atypical immature metaplastic-like proliferations of the cervix: diagnostic

35 Puts JJG, Moesker O, Kenemans P, Vooijs GP, Ramaekers FCS. Expression of cytokeratins in early neoplastic epithelial lesions of the uterine cervix. Int J Gynecol Pathol 1985, **4**: 300–313.

36 Suh KS, Silverberg SG. Tubal metaplasia of the uterine cervix. Int J Gynecol Pathol 1990, **9**: 122–128.

37 Val-Bernal JF, Pinto J, Garijo MF, Gomez MS. Pagetoid dyskeratosis of the cervix: an incidental histologic finding in uterine prolapse. Am J Surg Pathol 2000, **24**: 1518–1523.

38 Weir MM, Bell DA, Young RH. Transitional cell metaplasia of the uterine cervix and vagina: an underrecognized lesion that may be confused with high-grade dysplasia: a report of 59 cases. Am J Surg Pathol 1997, **21**: 510–517.

39 Yeh IT, Bronner M, Li Volsi VA. Endometrial metaplasia of the uterine endocervix. Arch Pathol Lab Med 1993, **117**: 734–735.

40 Young RH, Clement PB. Pseudoneoplastic glandular lesions of the uterine cervix. Semin Diagn Pathol 1991, **8**: 234–249.

Inflammatory lesions

41 Adams RL, Springall DR, Levene MM. The immunocytochemical detection of herpes simplex virus in cervical smears. A valuable technique for routine use. J Pathol 1984, **143**: 241–247.

42 Albores-Saavedra J, Rosas-Uribe A, Altramirano-Dimas M, Brandt H. Cancer with superimposed amebiasis. Am J Clin Pathol 1968, **49**: 677–682.

43 al Nafussi AI, Hughes D, Rebello G. Ceroid granuloma of the uterine cervix. Histopathology 1992, **21**: 282–284.

44 Berry A. A cytopathological and histopathological study of bilharziasis of the female genital tract. J Pathol Bacteriol 1966, **91**: 325–338.

45 Bhagavan BS, Ruffier J, Shinn B. Pseudoactinomycotic radiate granules in the lower female genital tract. Relationship to the Splendore-Hoeppli phenomenon. Hum Pathol 1982, **13**: 898–904.

46 Chen KTK, Hendricks EJ. Malakoplakia of the female genital tract. Obstet Gynecol 1985, **65**: 84S–87S.

47 Cohen C. Three cases of amoebiasis of the cervix uteri. J Obstet Gynaecol Br Commonw 1973, **80**: 476–479.

48 Crow J, McWhinney N. Isolated arteritis of the cervix uteri. Br J Obstet Gynaecol 1979, **86**: 393–398.

49 Kiviat NB, Paavonen JA, Wolner-Hanssen P, Critchlow CW, Stamm WE, Douglas J, Eschenbach DA, Corey LA, Holmes KK. Histopathology of endocervical infection caused by *Chlamydia trachomatis*, herpes simplex virus, *Trichomonas vaginalis*, and *Neisseria gonorrhoeae*. Hum Pathol 1990, **21**: 831–837.

50 Marrogi AJ, Gersell DJ, Kraus FT. Localized asymptomatic giant cell arteritis of the female genital tract. Int J Gynecol Pathol 1991, **10**: 51–58.

51 Marsella RC, Buckner SB, Bratthauer GL, O'Connor DM, O'Leary TJ. Identification of genital herpes simplex virus infection by immunoperoxidase staining. Appl Immunohistochem 1995, **3**: 184–189.

52 Mitao M, Reumann W, Winkler B, Richart RM, Fujiwara A, Crum CP. Chlamydial cervicitis and cervical intraepithelial neoplasia. An immunohistochemical analysis. Gynecol Oncol 1984, **19**: 90–97.

53 Naib ZM, Nahmias AJ, Josey WE. Cytology and histopathology of cervical herpes simplex infection. Cancer 1966, **19**: 1026–1031.

54 Paavonen J, Critchlow CW, DeRouen T, Stevens CE, Kiviat N, Brunham RC, Staam WE, Kuo CC, Hyde KE, Corey L, Eschenbach DA, Holmes KK. Etiology of cervical inflammation. Am J Obstet Gynecol 1986, **154**: 556–564.

55 Pikarsky E, Maly B, Maly A. Ceroid granuloma of the uterine cervix. Int J Gynecol Pathol 2002, **21**: 191–193.

56 Tchertkoff V, Ober WB. Primary chancre of cervix uteri. NY State J Med 1966, **66**: 1921–1924.

57 Winkler B, Crum CP. Chlamydia trachomatis infection of the

female genital tract. Pathogenetic and clinicopathologic correlations. Pathol Annu 1987, **22**(Pt 1): 193–223.

Non-neoplastic glandular lesions

58 Chumas JC, Nelson B, Mann WJ, Chalas E, Kaplan CG. Microglandular hyperplasia of the uterine cervix. Obstet Gynecol 1985, **66**: 406–409.

59 Clement PB, Young RH. Deep nabothian cysts of the uterine cervix. A possible source of confusion with minimal-deviation adenocarcinoma (adenoma malignum). Int J Gynecol Pathol 1989, **8**: 340–348.

60 Cove H. The Arias-Stella reaction occurring in the endocervix in pregnancy. Recognition and comparison with an adenocarcinoma of the cervix. Am J Surg Pathol 1979, **3**: 567–568.

61 Ferry JA, Scully RE. Mesonephric remnants, hyperplasia, and neoplasia in the uterine cervix. A study of 49 cases. Am J Surg Pathol 1990, **14**: 1100–1111.

62 Greeley C, Schroeder S, Silverberg SG. Microglandular hyperplasia of the cervix. A true "pill" lesion? Int J Gynecol Pathol 1995, **14**: 50–54.

63 Inai K, Arihiro K, Tokuoka S, Katsube Y, Fujiwara A. Mesonephric duct hyperplasia of the uterus. Report of two cases and three other cases of mesonephric duct remnant with findings of mucin histochemistry and lectin binding immunohistochemistry. Acta Pathol Jpn 1989, **39**: 457–464.

64 Janovski NA, Kasdon EJ. Benign mesonephric papillary and polypoid tumors of the cervix in childhood. J Pediatr 1963, **63**: 211–216.

65 Jones MA, Andrews J, Tarraza HM. Mesonephric remnant hyperplasia of the cervix. A clinicopathologic analysis of 14 cases. Gynecol Oncol 1993, **49**: 41–47.

66 Jones MA, Young RH. Endocervical type A (noncystic) tunnel clusters with cytologic atypia: a report of 14 cases. Am J Surg Pathol 1996, **20**: 1312–1318.

67 Jones MA, Young RH, Scully RE. Diffuse laminar endocervical glandular hyperplasia. A benign lesion often confused with adenoma malignum (minimal deviation adenocarcinoma). Am J Surg Pathol 1991, **15**: 1123–1129.

68 Kyriakos M, Kempson RL, Konikov NF. A clinical and pathologic study of endocervical lesions associated with oral contraceptives. Cancer 1968, **22**: 99–110.

69 Laskin WB, Fetsch JF, Tavassoli FA. Superficial cervicovaginal myofibroblastoma: fourteen cases of a distinctive mesenchymal tumor arising from a specialized subepithelial stroma of the lower female genital tract. Hum Pathol 2001, **32**: 715–725.

70 Mikami Y, Hata S, Melamed J, Fujiwara K, Manabe T. Lobular endocervical glandular hyperplasia is a metaplastic process with a pyloric gland phenotype. Histopathology 2001, **39**: 364–372.

71 Nucci MR. Tumor-like glandular lesions of the uterine cervix. Int J Gynecol Pathol 2002, **21**: 347–359.

72 Nucci MR, Clement PB, Young RH. Lobular endocervical glandular hyperplasia, not otherwise specified: a clinicopathologic analysis of thirteen cases of a distinctive pseudoneoplastic lesion and comparison with fourteen cases of adenoma malignum. Am J Surg Pathol 1999, **23**: 886–891.

72a Nucci MR, Young RH. Arias-Stella reaction of the endocervix: a study of 14 cases with emphasis on its varied morphology. Mod Pathol 2003, **16**: 203a.

73 Rhatigan RM. Endocervical gland atypia secondary to Arias-Stella change. Arch Pathol Lab Med 1992, **116**: 943–946.

74 Samaratunga H, Beresford A, Davison A. Squamous cell carcinoma in situ involving mesonephric remnants. A potential diagnostic pitfall. Am J Surg Pathol 1994, **18**: 1265–1269.

75 Segal GH, Hart WR. Cystic endocervical tunnel clusters. A clinicopathologic study of 29 cases of so-called adenomatous hyperplasia. Am J Surg Pathol 1990, **14**: 895–903.

76 Seidman JD, Tavassoli FA. Mesonephric hyperplasia of the uterine cervix. A clinicopathologic study of 51 cases. Int J Gynecol Pathol 1995, **14**: 293–299.

77 Selzer I, Nelson HM. Benign papilloma (polypoid tumor) of the cervix uteri in children. Report of 2 cases. Am J Obstet Gynecol 1962, **84**: 165–169.

78 Speers WC, Picaso LG, Silverberg SG. Immunohistochemical localization of carcinoembryonic antigen in microglandular hyperplasia and adenocarcinoma of the endocervix. Am J Clin Pathol 1983, **79**: 105–107.

79 Taylor HB, Irey NS, Norris HJ. Atypical endocervical hyperplasia in women taking oral contraceptives. JAMA 1967, **202**: 637–639.

80 Young RH, Clement PB. Pseudoneoplastic glandular lesions of the uterine cervix. Semin Diagn Pathol 1991, **8**: 234–249.

81 Young RH, Scully RE. Atypical forms of microglandular hyperplasia of the cervix simulating carcinoma. A report of five cases and review of the literature. Am J Surg Pathol 1989, **13**: 50–56.

Non-neoplastic stromal lesions (including endometriosis and related processes)

82 Abdul-Karim FW, Cohen RE. Atypical stromal cells of lower female genital tract. Histopathology 1990, **17**: 249–253.

83 Baker PM, Clement PB, Bell DA, Young RH. Superficial endometriosis of the uterine cervix: a report of 20 cases of a process that may be confused with endocervical glandular dysplasia or adenocarcinoma in situ. Int J Gynecol Pathol 2002, **18**: 198–205.

84 Clement PB. Multinucleated stromal giant cells of the uterine cervix. Arch Pathol Lab Med 1985, **109**: 200–202.

85 Clement PB, Young RH, Scully RE. Nontrophoblastic pathology of the female genital tract and peritoneum associated with pregnancy. Semin Diagn Pathol 1989, **6**: 372–406.

86 Clement PB, Young RH, Scully RE. Stromal endometriosis of the uterine cervix. A variant of endometriosis that may simulate a sarcoma. Am J Surg Pathol 1990, **14**: 449–455.

87 Elliott GB, Elliott JDA. Superficial stromal reactions of lower genital tract. Arch Pathol 1973, **95**: 100–101.

88 Evans CS, Goldman RL, Klein HZ, Kohout ND. Necrobiotic granulomas of the uterine cervix. A probable postoperative reaction. Am J Surg Pathol 1984, **8**: 841–844.

89 Fukunaga M. Uterus-like mass in the uterine cervix: superficial cervical endometriosis with florid smooth muscle metaplasia? Virchows Archiv 2001, **438**: 302–305.

90 Hariri J, Ingemanssen JL. Multinucleated stromal giant cells of the uterine cervix. Int J Gynecol Pathol 1993, **12**: 228–234.

91 Huettner PC, Gersell DJ. Placental site nodule. A clinicopathologic study of 38 cases. Int J Gynecol Pathol 1994, **13**: 191–198.

92 Kay S, Schneider V. Reactive spindle cell nodule of the endocervix simulating uterine sarcoma. Int J Gynecol Pathol 1985, **4**: 255–257.

93 Van Dorpe J, Moerman P. Placental site nodule of the uterine cervix. Histopathology 1997, **29**: 379–382.

94 Young RH, Clement PB. Endocervicosis involving the uterine cervix: a report of four cases of a benign process that may be confused with deeply invasive endocervical adenocarcinoma. Int J Gynecol Pathol 2001, **19**: 322–328.

95 Young RH, Kurman RJ, Scully RE. Placental site nodules and plaques. A clinicopathologic analysis of 20 cases. Am J Surg Pathol 1990, **14**: 1001–1009.

Human papilloma virus (HPV) and the lower female genital tract

96 Abadi MA, Ho GY, Burk RD, Romney SL, Kadish AS. Stringent criteria for histological diagnosis of koilocytosis fail to eliminate overdiagnosis of human papillomavirus infection and

cervical intraepithelial neoplasia Grade 1. Hum Pathol 1998, **29:** 54–59.

97 Albores-Saavedra J, Young RH. Transitional cell neoplasms (carcinomas and inverted papillomas) of the uterine cervix. A report of four cases. Am J Surg Pathol 1995, **19:** 1138–1145.

98 Ambros RA, Kurman RJ. Current concepts in the relationship of human papillomavirus infection to the pathogenesis and classification of precancerous squamous lesions of the uterine cervix. Semin Diagn Pathol 1990, **7:** 158–172.

99 Arends MJ, Wyllie AH, Bird CC. Papillomaviruses and human cancer. Hum Pathol 1990, **21:** 686–698.

100 Bergeron C, Barrasso R, Beaudenon S, Flamant P, Croissant O, Orth G. Human papillomaviruses associated with cervical intraepithelial neoplasia. Great diversity and distinct distribution in low- and high-grade lesions. Am J Surg Pathol 1992, **16:** 641–649.

101 Binder MA, Cates GW, Emson HE, Valnicek SJ, MacLachlan TB, Schmidt EW, Popkin DR, Ferenczy A. The changing concepts of condyloma. A retrospective study of colposcopically directed cervical biopsies. Am J Obstet Gynecol 1985, **151:** 213–219.

102 Bosch FX, Manos MM, Muñoz N, Sherman M, Jansen AM, Peto J, Schiffman MH, Moreno V, Kurman R, Shah KV. International Biological Study on Cervical Cancer (IBSCC) Study Group: Prevalence of human papillomavirus in cervical cancer. A worldwide perspective. J Natl Cancer Inst 1995, **87:** 796–802.

103 Boyle CA, Lowell DM, Kelsey JL, Li Volsi VA, Boyle KE. Cervical intraepithelial neoplasia among women with papillomavirus infection compared to women with *Trichomonas* infection. Cancer 1989, **64:** 168–172.

104 Cain JM, Howett MK. Preventing cervical cancer. Science 2000, **288:** 1753–1794.

105 Chapman WB, Lorincz AT, Willett GD, Wright VC, Kurman RJ. Evaluation of two commercially available in situ hybridization kits for detection of human papillomavirus DNA in cervical biopsies. Comparison to Southern blot hybridization. Mod Pathol 1993, **6:** 73–79.

106 Chen JJ, Reid CE, Band V, Androphy EJ. Interaction of papillomavirus E6 oncoproteins with a putative calcium-binding protein. Science 1995, **269:** 529–531.

107 Colgan TJ, Percy ME, Suri M, Shier RM, Andrews DF, Lickrish GM. Human papillomavirus infection of morphologically normal cervical epithelium adjacent to squamous dysplasia and invasive carcinoma. Hum Pathol 1989, **20:** 316–319.

108 Cooper K, Herrington CS, Lo ES, Evans MF, McGee JO. Integration of human papillomavirus types 16 and 18 in cervical adenocarcinoma. J Clin Pathol 1992, **45:** 382–384.

109 Crum C. Genital papillomaviruses and related neoplasms. Causation, diagnosis and classification (Bethesda). Mod Pathol 1994, **7:** 138–145.

110 Crum CP. Contemporary theories of cervical carcinogenesis: the virus, the host, and the stem cell. Mod Pathol 2000, **13:** 243–251.

111 Crum CP, Egawa K, Barron B, Fenoglio CM, Levine RU, Richart RM. Human papilloma virus infection (condyloma) of the cervix and cervical intraepithelial neoplasia. A histopathologic and statistical analysis. Gynecol Oncol 1983, **15:** 88–94.

112 Crum CP, Ikenberg H, Richart RM, Gissman L. Human papilloma virus type 16 and early cervical neoplasia. N Engl J Med 1984, **310:** 880–883.

113 Delvenne P, Fontaine M, Delvenne C, Nikkels A, Boniver J. Detection of human papillomaviruses in paraffin-embedded biopsies of cervical intraepithelial lesions. Analysis by immunohistochemistry, in situ hybridization, and the polymerase chain reaction. Mod Pathol 1994, **7:** 113–119.

114 Duggan MA, Benoit JL, McGregor SE, Inoue M, Nation JG, Stuart GCE. Adenocarcinoma in situ of the endocervix. Human papillomavirus determination by dot blot hybridization and polymerase chain reaction amplification. Int J Gynecol Pathol 1994, **13:** 143–149.

115 Farnsworth A, Laverty C, Stoler MH. Human papillomavirus messenger RNA expression in adenocarcinoma in situ of the uterine cervix. Int J Gynecol Pathol 1989, **8:** 321–330.

116 Franco EL, Rohan TE, Villa LL. Epidemiologic evidence and human papillomavirus infection as a necessary cause of cervical cancer. J Natl Cancer Inst 1999, **91:** 506–511.

117 Franquemont DW, Ward BE, Andersen WA, Crum CP. Prediction of "high-risk" cervical papillomavirus infection by biopsy morphology. Am J Clin Pathol 1989, **92:** 577–582.

118 Genest DR, Stein L, Cibas E, Sheets E, Zitz JC, Crum CP. A binary (Bethesda) system for classifying cervical cancer precursors. Criteria, reproducibility, and viral correlates. Hum Pathol 1993, **24:** 730–736.

119 Graf A, Cheung AL, Hauser-Kronberger C, Dandachi N, Tubbs RR, Dietze O, Hacker GW. Clinical relevance of HPV 16/18 testing methods in cervical squamous cell carcinoma. Appl Immunohistochem Mol Morphol 2000, **8:** 300–309.

120 Ho GYF, Burk RD, Klein S, Kadish AS, Chang CJ, Palan P, Basu J, Tachezy R, Lewis R, Romney S. Persistent cervical dysplasia. J Natl Cancer Inst 1995, **87:** 1365–1371.

121 Jenkins D. Diagnosing human papillomaviruses: recent advances. Curr Opin Infect Dis 2001, **14:** 53–62.

122 Johnson TL, Kim W, Plieth DA, Sarkar FH. Detection of HPV 16/18 DNA in cervical adenocarcinoma using polymerase chain reaction (PCR) methodology. Mod Pathol 1992, **5:** 35–40.

123 Jovanovic AS, McLachlin CM, Shen L, Welch WR, Crum CP. Postmenopausal squamous atypia. A spectrum including "pseudo-koilocytosis." Mod Pathol 1995, **8:** 408–412.

124 Kaufman R, Koss LG, Kurman RJ, Meisels A, Okagaki T, Patten SF, Reid R, Richart RM, Wied GL. Statement of caution in the interpretation of papilloma virus-associated lesions of the epithelium of uterine cervix. Am J Obstet Gynecol 1983, **146:** 125.

125 Kenny MB, Unger ER, Chenggis ML, Costa MJ. In situ hybridization for human papillomavirus DNA in uterine adenosquamous carcinoma with glassy cell features ("glassy cell carcinoma"). Am J Clin Pathol 1992, **98:** 180–187.

126 Koutsky LA, Ault KA, Wheeler CM, Brown DR, Barr E, Alvarez FB, Chiacchierini LM, Jansen KU. A controlled trial of human papillomavirus type 16 vaccine. N Engl J Med 2002, **347:** 1645–1651.

127 Kurman RJ, Sanz LE, Jenson AB, Perry S, Lancaster WD. Papillomavirus infection of the cervix. I. Correlation of histology with viral structural antigens and DNA sequences. Int J Gynecol Pathol 1982, **1:** 17–28.

128 Lee KR, Minter LJ, Crum CP. Koilocytotic atypia in Papanicolaou smears: reproducibility and biopsy correlations. Cancer 1997, **81:** 10–15.

129 Leminen A, Paavonen J, Vesterinen E, Wahlstrom T, Rantala I, Lehtinen M. Human papillomavirus types 16 and 18 in adenocarcinoma of the uterine cervix. Am J Clin Pathol 1991, **95:** 647–652.

130 Macnab JCM, Walkinshaw SA, Cordiner JW, Clements JB. Human papilloma virus in clinically and histologically normal tissue of patients with genital cancer. N Engl J Med 1986, **315:** 1052–1058.

131 Milde-Langosch K, Riethdorf S, Loning T. Association of human papillomavirus infection with carcinoma of the cervix uteri and its precursor lesions: theoretical and practical implications. Virchows Arch 2000, **437:** 227–233.

132 Mittal KR, Chan W, Demopoulos RI. Sensitivity and specificity of various morphological features of cervical condylomas. An in situ hybridization study. Arch Pathol Lab Med 1990, **114:** 1038–1041.

133 Mittal K, Demopoulos RI, Tata M. A comparison of proliferative activity and atypical mitoses in cervical condylomas with various HPV types. Int J Gynecol Pathol 1998, **17:** 24–28.

134 Mittal KR, Miller HK, Lowell DM. Koilocytosis preceding squamous cell car cinoma in situ of uterine cervix. Am J Clin Pathol 1987, **87**: 243–245.

135 Mittal K, Palazzo J. Cervical condylomas show higher proliferation than do inflamed or metaplastic cervical squamous epithelium. Mod Pathol 1998, **11**: 780–783.

136 Munoz N, Bosch Z, de Sanjose S, Herrero R, Castellsangué X, Shah KV, Snijders PJF, Meijer CJ. Epidemiologic classification of human papillomavirus types associated with cervical cancer. N Engl J Med 2003, **348**: 518–527.

137 Nagai N, Nuovo G, Freidman D, Crum CP. Detection of papillomavirus nucleic acids in genital precancers with the in situ hybridization technique. Int J Gynecol Pathol 1987, **6**: 366–379.

138 Nuovo GJ. Human papillomavirus DNA in genital tract lesions histologically negative for condylomata. Analysis by in situ, Southern blot hybridization and the polymerase chain reaction. Am J Surg Pathol 1990, **14**: 643–651.

139 Nyeem R, Wilkinson EJ, Grover LJ. Condylomata acuminata of the cervix. Histopathology and association with cervical neoplasia. Int J Gynecol Pathol 1982, **1**: 246–257.

140 Paquette RL, Lee YY, Wilczynski SP, Karmakar A, Kizaki M, Miller CW, Koeffler HP. Mutations of p53 and human papillomavirus infection in cervical carcinoma. Cancer 1993, **72**: 1272–1280.

141 Poljak M, Seme K, Gale N. Detection of human papillomaviruses in tissue specimens. Adv Anat Pathol 1999, **5**: 216–234.

142 Prasad CJ, Sheets E, Selig AM, McArthur MC, Crum CP. The binucleate squamous cell. Histologic spectrum and relationship to low-grade squamous intraepithelial lesions. Mod Pathol 1993, **6**: 313–317.

143 Qizilbash AH. Papillary squamous tumors of the uterine cervix. A clinical and pathologic study of 21 cases. Am J Clin Pathol 1974, **61**: 508–520.

144 Richart RM, Nuovo GJ. Human papillomavirus DNA in situ hybridization may be used for the quality control of genital tract biopsies. Obstet Gynecol 1990, **75**: 223–226.

145 Saito K, Saito A, Fu YS, Smotkin D, Gupta J, Shah K. Topographic study of cervical condyloma and intraepithelial neoplasia. Cancer 1987, **59**: 2064–2070.

146 Sasagawa T, Shimakage M, Nakamura M, Sakaike J, Ishikawa H, Inoue M. Epstein-Barr virus (EBV) genes expression in cervical intraepithelial neoplasia and invasive cervical cancer: a comparative study with human papillomavirus (HPV) infection. Hum Pathol 2000, **31**: 318–326.

147 Sawaya GF, Brown AD, Washington AE, Garber AM. Clinical practice. Current approaches to cervical-cancer screening. N Engl J Med 2001, **344**: 1603–1607.

148 Schiffman MH, Bauer HM, Hoover RN, Glass AG, Cadell DM, Rush BB, Scott DR, Sherman ME, Kurman RJ, Wacholder S, et al. Epidemiologic evidence showing that human papillomavirus infection causes most cervical intraepithelial neoplasia. J Natl Cancer Inst 1993, **85**: 958–964.

149 Stoler MH. Human papillomaviruses and cervical neoplasia: a model for carcinogenesis. Int J Gynecol Pathol 2000, **19**: 16–28.

150 Syrjanen KJ. Human papillomavirus (HPV) infections of the female genital tract and their associations with intraepithelial neoplasia and squamous cell carcinoma. Pathol Annu 1986, **21**(Pt 1): 53–89.

151 ter Harmsel B, van Belkum A, Quint W, Pronk A, Kuijpers J, Ramaekers F, Tandon A, Smedts F. p53 and human papilloma virus type 16 in cervical intraepithelial neoplasia and carcinoma. Int J Gynecol Pathol 1995, **14**: 125–133.

152 Trivijitslip P, Mosher R, Sheets EE, Sun D, Crum CP. Papillary immature metaplasia (immature condyloma) of the cervix: a clinicopathologic analysis and comparison with papillary squamous carcinoma. Hum Pathol 1998, **29**: 641–648.

153 Vallejos H, Delmistro AD, Kleinhaus S, Braunstein JD, Halwer M, Koss LG. Characterization of human papilloma virus types in condylomata acuminata in children by in situ hybridization. Lab Invest 1987, **56**: 611–615.

154 Ward BE, Burkett B, Petersen C, Nuckols ML, Brennan C, Birch LM, Crum CP. Cytologic correlates of cervical papillomavirus infection. Int J Gynecol Pathol 1990, **9**: 297–305.

155 Willett GD, Kurman RJ, Reid R, Greenberg M, Jenson AB, Lorincz AT. Correlation of the histologic appearance of intraepithelial neoplasia of the cervix with human papillomavirus types. Emphasis on low grade lesions including so-called flat condyloma. Int J Gynecol Pathol 1989, **8**: 18–25.

156 Winkler B, Crum CP, Fujii T, Ferenczy A, Boon M, Braun L, Lancaster WD, Richart RM. Koilocytotic lesions of the cervix. The relationship of mitotic abnormalities to the presence of papillomavirus antigens and nuclear DNA content. Cancer 1984, **53**: 1081–1087.

157 Wright TC Jr, Richart RM. Role of human papillomavirus in the pathogenesis of genital tract warts and cancer. Gynecol Oncol 1990, **37**: 151–164.

158 Yang GC, Demopoulos RI, Chan W, Mittal KR. Superficial nuclear enlargement without koilocytosis as an expression of human papillomavirus infection of the uterine cervix: an in situ hybridization study. Int J Gynecol Pathol 1992, **1**: 283–287.

159 Zehbe I, Rylander E, Edlund K, Wadell G, Wilander E. Detection of human papillomavirus in cervical intraepithelial neoplasia, using in situ hybridisation and various polymerase chain reaction techniques. Virchows Arch 1996, **428**: 151–157.

160 Ziol M, Di Tomaso C, Biaggi A, Tepper M, Piquet P, Carbillon L, Uzan M, Guettier C. Virological and biological characteristics of cervical intraepithelial neoplasia grade I with marked koilocytotic atypia. Hum Pathol 1998, **29**: 1068–1073.

Tumors

Cervical intraepithelial neoplasia (CIN)

160a Agoff SN, Lin P, Morihara J, Mao C, Kiviat NB, Koutsky LA. P16^{INK4a} expression correlates with degree of cervical neoplasia: a comparison with Ki-67 expression and detection of high-risk HPV types. Mod Pathol 2003, **16**: 665–673.

161 Akasofu M, Oda Y. Immunohistochemical detection of p53 in cervical epithelial lesions with or without infection of human papillomavirus types 16 and 18. Virchows Arch 1995, **425**: 593–602.

162 Al-Nafussi AI, Colquhoun MK. Mild cervical intraepithelial neoplasia (CIN 1). A histological overdiagnosis. Histopathology 1990, **17**: 557–561.

163 Anderson MC, Hartley RB. Cervical crypt involvement by intraepithelial neoplasia. Obstet Gynecol 1980, **55**: 546–550.

164 Benda JA, Lamoreaux J, Johnson SR. Artifact associated with the use of strong iodine solution (Lugol's) in cone biopsies. Am J Surg Pathol 1987, **11**: 367–374.

165 Bibbo M, Dytch HE, Alenghat E, Bartels PH, Wied GL. DNA ploidy profiles as prognostic indicators in CIN lesions. Am J Clin Pathol 1989, **92**: 261–265.

166 Buckley CH, Butler EB, Fox H. Cervical intraepithelial neoplasia. J Clin Pathol 1982, **35**: 1–13.

167 Christopherson WM. Dysplasia, carcinoma in situ, and microinvasive carcinoma of the uterine cervix. Hum Pathol 1977, **8**: 489–501.

168 Christopherson WM, Gray LA Sr. Dysplasia and preclinical carcinoma of the uterine cervix. Diagnosis and management. Semin Oncol 1982, **9**: 265–279.

169 Cooper K, Haffajee Z, Taylor L. Bcl-2 immunoreactivity, human papillomavirus DNA, and cervical intraepithelial neoplasia. Mod Pathol 1999, **12**: 612–617.

170 Coppleson M, Pixley E, Reid B. Colposcopy. A scientific and practical approach to the cervix in health and disease. Springfield, IL, 1971, Charles C Thomas, Publisher.

171 Crum CP. Symposium part 1: should the Bethesda system terminology be used in diagnostic surgical pathology? Int J Gynecol Pathol 2002, **22**: 5–12.

172 de Boer CJ, van Dorst E, van Krieken H, Jansen-van Rhijn CM, Warnaar SO, Fleuren GJ, Litvinov SV. Changing roles of cadherins and catenins during progression of squamous intraepithelial lesions in the uterine cervix. Am J Pathol 1999, **155**: 505–515.

173 Demopoulos RI, Horowitz LF, Vamvakas EC. Endocervical gland involvement by cervical intraepithelial neoplasia grade III. Predictive value for residual and/or recurrent disease. Cancer 1991, **68**: 1932–1936.

174 Foote FW Jr, Stewart FW. The anatomical distribution of intraepithelial epidermoid carcinomas of the cervix. Cancer 1948, **1**: 431–440.

175 Fox CH. Biologic behavior of dysplasia and carcinoma in situ. Am J Obstet Gynecol 1967, **99**: 960–974.

176 Fox H, Buckley CH. Current problems in the pathology of intra-epithelial lesions of the uterine cervix. Histopathology 1990, **17**: 1–6.

177 Fu YS, Reagan JW, Richart RM. Definition of precursors. Gynecol Oncol 1981, **12**: S220–S231.

178 Giannoudis A, Herrington CS. Differential expression of p53 and p21 in low grade cervical squamous intraepithelial lesions infected with low, intermediate, and high risk human papillomaviruses. Cancer 2000, **89**: 1300–1307.

179 Govan ADT, Haines RM, Langley FA, Taylor CW, Woodcock AS. Changes in the epithelium of the cervix uteri. J Obstet Gynaecol Br Commonw 1968, **73**: 883–896.

180 Gusberg SB, Moore DB. The clinical pattern of intraepithelial carcinoma of the cervix and its pathologic background. Obstet Gynecol 1953, **2**: 1–14.

181 Heatley MK. How should we grade CIN? Histopathology 2002, **40**: 377–390.

182 Holmquist ND, McMahan CA, Williams OD. Variability in classification of carcinoma in situ of the uterine cervix. Arch Pathol 1967, **84**: 334–345.

183 Howard L, Erickson CC, Stoddard LD. A study of the incidence and histogenesis of endocervical metaplasia and intraepithelial carcinoma. Cancer 1951, **4**: 1210–1223.

184 Ismail SM, Colclough AB, Dinnen JS, Eakins D, Evans DM, Gradwell E, O'Sullivan JP, Summerell JM, Newcombe R. Reporting cervical intra-epithelial neoplasia (CIN). Intra- and interpathologist variation and factors associated with disagreement. Histopathology 1990, **16**: 371–376.

185 Johnson LD, Nickerson RJ, Easterday CL, Stuart RS, Hertig AT. Epidemiologic evidence for the spectrum of change from dysplasia through carcinoma in situ to invasive cancer. Cancer 1968, **22**: 901–914.

186 Joste NE, Rushing L, Granados R, Zitz JC, Genest DR, Crum CP, Cibas ES. Bethesda classification of cervicovaginal smears: reproducibility and viral correlates. Hum Pathol 1996, **27**: 581–585.

187 Kanbour AI, Stock RJ. Squamous cell carcinoma in situ of the endometrium and fallopian tube as superficial extension of invasive cervical carcinoma. Cancer 1978, **42**: 570–580.

188 Killackey MA, Jones WB, Lewis JL. Diagnostic conization of the cervix. Review of 460 consecutive cases. Obstet Gynecol 1986, **67**: 766–770.

189 Klavins JV. Intra-epithelial carcinoma with differentiated surface cells and dysplasia. Definition and separation of these lesions. Acta Cytol (Baltimore) 1963, **7**: 351–356.

190 Kobayashi I, Matsuo K, Ishibashi Y, Kanda S, Sakai H. The proliferative activity in dysplasia and carcinoma in situ of the uterine cervix analyzed by proliferating cell nuclear antigen immunostaining and silver-binding argyrophilic nucleolar organizer region staining. Hum Pathol 1994, **25**: 198–202.

191 Kolstad P, Klein V. Long-term follow-up of 1121 cases of carcinoma in situ. Obstet Gynecol 1976, **48**: 125–129.

192 Kolstad P, Stafl A. Atlas of colposcopy. Baltimore, 1972, University Park Press.

193 Kraus FT. Gynecologic pathology. St. Louis, 1967, C.V. Mosby, p. 174.

194 Kreiger JS, McCormack LJ. Graded treatment for in situ carcinoma of the uterine cervix. Am J Obstet Gynecol 1968, **101**: 171–182.

195 Lesack D, Wahab I, Gilks CB. Radiation-induced atypia of endocervical epithelium: a histological, immunohistochemical and cytometric study. Int J Gynecol Pathol 1997, **15**: 242–247.

196 Livasy CA, Maygarden SJ, Rajaratnam CT, Novotny DB. Predictors of recurrent dysplasia after a cervical loop electrocautery excision procedure for CIN-3: a study of margin, endocervical gland, and quadrant involvement. Mod Pathol 1999, **12**: 233–238.

197 Lopez-Ferrer A, Alameda F, Barranco C, Garrido M, de Bolòs C. MUC4 expression is increased in dysplastic cervical disorders. Hum Pathol 2001, **32**: 1197–1202.

198 Matseoane S, Williams SB, Navarro C, Hedriana H, Mushayandebvu T. Diagnostic value of conization of the uterine cervix in the management of cervical neoplasia: a review of 756 consecutive patients. Gynecol Oncol 1992, **47**: 287–291.

199 McIndoe WA, McLean MR, Jones RW, Mullins PR. The invasive potential of carcinoma in situ of the cervix. Obstet Gynecol 1984, **64**: 451–458.

200 McIndoe GA, Robson MS, Tidy JA, Mason WP, Anderson MC. Laser excision rather than vaporization. The treatment of choice for cervical intraepithelial neoplasia. Obstet Gynecol 1989, **74**: 165–168.

201 Mittal KR, Demopoulos RI, Goswami S. Proliferating cell nuclear antigen (cyclin) expression in normal and abnormal cervical squamous epithelia. Am J Surg Pathol 1993, **17**: 117–122.

202 Montz FJ, Holschneider CH, Thompson LD. Large-loop excision of the transformation zone. Effect on the pathologic interpretation of resection margins. Obstet Gynecol 1993, **81**: 976–982.

203 Murphy WM, Coleman SA. The long-term course of carcinoma in situ of the uterine cervix. Cancer 1976, **38**: 957–963.

204 Nasiell K, Roger V, Nasiell M. Behavior of mild cervical dysplasia during long-term follow-up. Obstet Gynecol 1986, **67**: 665–669.

205 National Cancer Institute Workshop. The 1988 Bethesda System for reporting cervical/vaginal cytologic diagnoses. JAMA 1988, **262**: 931–932.

206 Ostor AG. Natural history of cervical intraepithelial neoplasia. A critical review. Int J Gynecol Pathol 1993, **12**: 186–192.

207 Paterson-Brown S, Chappatte OA, Clark SK, Wright A, Maxwell P, Taub NA, Raju KS. The significance of cone biopsy resection margins. Gynecol Oncol 1992, **46**: 182–185.

208 Perticarari S, Presani G, Michelutti A, Facca MC, Alberico S, Mandruzzato GP. Flow cytometric analysis of DNA content in cervical lesions. Pathol Res Pract 1989, **185**: 686–688.

209 Petersen O. Spontaneous course of cervical precancerous conditions. Am J Obstet Gynecol 1956, **72**: 1063–1071.

210 Pins MR, Young RH, Crum CP, Leach IH, Scully RE. Cervical squamous cell carcinoma in situ with intraepithelial extension to the upper genital tract and invasion of tubes and ovaries: report of a case with human papilloma virus analysis. Int J Gynecol Pathol 1998, **16**: 272–278.

211 Pollanen R, Soini Y, Vahakangas K, Paakko P, Lehto VP. Aberrant p53 protein expression in cervical intra-epithelial neoplasia. Histopathology 1993, **23**: 471–474.

212 Przybora LA, Plutowa A. Histological topography of carcinoma in situ of the cervix uteri. Cancer 1959, **12**: 263–277.

213 Reagan JW, Seidemann IL, Saracusa Y. Cellular morphology of

carcinoma in situ and dysplasia or atypical hyperplasia of the uterine cervix. Cancer 1953, **6**: 224–235.

214 Richart RM. Cervical intraepithelial neoplasia. Pathol Annu 1973, **8**: 301–328.

215 Richart RM. A modified terminology for cervical intraepithelial neoplasia. Obstet Gynecol 1990, **75**: 131–133.

216 Richart RM, Barron BA. A follow-up study of patients with cervical dysplasia. Am J Obstet Gynecol 1969, **105**: 386–393.

217 Richart RM, Wright TC Jr. Controversies in the management of low-grade cervical intraepithelial neoplasia. Cancer 1993, **71**: 1413–1421.

218 Rubio CA, Lagerlöf B. Autoradiographic studies of dysplasia and carcinoma in situ in cervical cones. Acta Pathol Microbiol Scand (A) 1974, **82**: 411–418.

219 Sagae S, Kudo R, Kuzumaki N, Hisada T, Mugikura Y, Nihei T, Takeda T, Hashimoto M. Ras oncogene expression and progression in intraepithelial neoplasia of the uterine cervix. Cancer 1990, **66**: 295–301.

220 Salm R. Superficial intra-uterine spread of intra-epithelial cervical carcinoma. J Pathol 1969, **97**: 719–723.

221 Samaratunga H, Beresford A, Davison A. Squamous cell carcinoma in situ involving mesonephric remnants. A potential diagnostic pitfall. Am J Surg Pathol 1994, **18**: 1265–1269.

222 Sherman ME, Kurman RJ. Intraepithelial carcinoma of the cervix: reflections on half a century of progress. Cancer 1998, **83**: 2243–2246.

223 Shurbaji MS, Brooks SK, Thurmond TS. Proliferating cell nuclear antigen immunoreactivity in cervical intraepithelial neoplasia and benign cervical epithelium. Am J Clin Pathol 1993, **100**: 22–26.

224 Smedts F, Ramaekers F, Leube RE, Keijser K, Link M, Vooijs P. Expression of keratins 1, 6, 15, 16, and 20 in normal cervical epithelium, squamous metaplasia, cervical intraepithelial neoplasia, and cervical carcinoma. Am J Pathol 1993, **142**: 403–412.

225 Smedts F, Ramaekers F, Robben H, Pruszczynski M, van Muijen G, Lane B, Leigh I, Vooijs P. Changing patterns of keratin expression during progression of cervical intraepithelial neoplasia. Am J Pathol 1990, **136**: 657–668.

226 Southern SA, McDicken IW, Herrington CS. Loss of cytokeratin 14 expression is related to human papillomavirus type and lesion grade in squamous intraepithelial lesions of the cervix. Hum Pathol 2002, **32**: 1351–1355.

227 Suprun HZ, Schwartz J, Spira H. Cervical intraepithelial neoplasia and associated condylomatous lesions. A preliminary report on 4,764 women from northern Israel. Acta Cytol (Baltimore) 1985, **29**: 334–340.

228 Takeuchi A, McKay DB. The area of the cervix involved by carcinoma in situ and anaplasia (atypical hyperplasia). Obstet Gynecol 1960, **15**: 134–145.

229 Tendler A, Kaufman HL, Kadish AS. Increased carcinoembryonic antigen expression in cervical intraepithelial neoplasia grade 3 and cervical squamous cell carcinoma. Hum Pathol 2000, **31**: 1357–1362.

230 Thickett KM, Griffin NR, Griffiths AP, Wells M. A study of nucleolar organizer regions in cervical intraepithelial neoplasia and human papillomavirus infection. Int J Gynecol Pathol 1989, **8**: 331–339.

231 Tweeddale DN, Roddick JW. Histologic types of squamous-cell carcinoma in situ of the cervix. Obstet Gynecol 1969, **33**: 35–40.

232 Walton LA, Edelman DA, Fowler WC Jr, Photropulos GJ. Cryosurgery for the treatment of cervical intraepithelial neoplasm during the reproductive years. Obstet Gynecol 1980, **55**: 353–357.

233 Wentz WB, Reagan JW. Clinical significance of postirradiation dysplasia of the uterine cervix. Am J Obstet Gynecol 1970, **106**: 812–817.

Microinvasive squamous cell carcinoma

234 Benson WL, Norris HJ. A critical review of the frequency of lymph node metastasis and death from microinvasive carcinoma of the cervix. Obstet Gynecol 1977, **49**: 632–638.

235 Brudenell M, Cox BS, Taylor CW. The management of dysplasia, carcinoma in situ and microcarcinoma of the cervix. J Obstet Gynaecol Br Commonw 1973, **80**: 673–679.

236 Burghardt E, Girardi F, Lahousen M, Pickel H, Tamussino K. Microinvasive carcinoma of the uterine cervix (International Federation of Gynecology and Obstetrics Stage IA). Cancer 1991, **67**: 1037–1045.

237 Burke TW. Factors affecting recurrence and survival in stage I carcinoma of the uterine cervix. Oncology (Huntingt) 1992, **6**: 111–119.

238 Christopherson WM, Gray LA, Parker JE. Microinvasive carcinoma of the uterine cervix. A long-term follow-up study of eighty cases. Cancer 1976, **38**: 629–632.

239 Clement PB, Scully RE. Carcinoma of the cervix. Histologic types. Semin Oncol 1982, **9**: 251–264.

240 Copeland LJ, Silva EG, Gershenson DM, Morris M, Young DC, Wharton JT. Superficially invasive squamous cell carcinoma of the cervix. Gynecol Oncol 1992, **45**: 307–312.

241 Creasman WT, Fetter BF, Clarke-Pearson DL, Kaufmann L, Parker RT. Management of stage IA carcinoma of cervix. Am J Obstet Gynecol 1985, **153**: 164–172.

242 Fennell RH. Review. Microinvasive carcinoma of the uterine cervix. Obstet Gynecol Surv 1978, **33**: 406–411.

243 Genadry R, Olson J, Parmley T, Woodruff JD. The morphology of the earliest invasive cell in low genital tract epidermoid neoplasia. Obstet Gynecol 1978, **51**: 718–722.

244 Hartveit F, Sandstad E. Stromal metachromasia. A marker for areas of infiltrating tumour growth? Histopathology 1982, **6**: 423–428.

245 Hasumi K, Sakamoto A, Sugano H. Microinvasive carcinoma of the uterine cervix. Cancer 1980, **45**: 928–931.

246 Jones WB, Mercer GO, Lewis JL Jr, Rubin SC, Hoskins WJ. Early invasive carcinoma of the cervix. Gynecol Oncol 1993, **51**: 26–32.

247 Kudo R, Sato T, Mizuuchi H. Ultrastructural and immunohistochemical study of infiltration in microinvasive carcinoma of the uterine cervix. Gynecol Oncol 1990, **36**: 23–29.

248 Langley FA, Crompton AC. Epithelial abnormalities of the cervix uteri. New York, 1973, Springer-Verlag.

249 Lehman MH Jr, Benson WL, Kurman RJ, Park RC. Microinvasive carcinoma of the cervix. Obstet Gynecol 1976, **48**: 571–578.

250 Margulis RR, Ely CW Jr, Ladd JE. Diagnosis and management of stage IA (microinvasive) carcinoma of cervix. Obstet Gynecol 1967, **29**: 529–538.

251 Morris M, Mitchell MF, Silva EG, Copeland LJ, Gershenson DM. Cervical conization as definitive therapy for early invasive squamous carcinoma of the cervix. Gynecol Oncol 1993, **51**: 193–196.

252 Mussey E, Soule EH, Welch JS. Microinvasive carcinoma of the cervix. Am J Obstet Gynecol 1969, **104**: 738–744.

253 Ng ABP, Reagan JW. Microinvasive carcinoma of the uterine cervix. Am J Clin Pathol 1969, **52**: 511–529.

254 Ostor AG. Studies on 200 cases of early squamous cell carcinoma of the cervix. Int J Gynecol Pathol 1993, **12**: 193–207.

255 Richards CJ, Furness PN. Basement membrane continuity in benign, premalignant and malignant epithelial conditions of the uterine cervix. Histopathology 1990, **16**: 47–52.

256 Roche WD, Norris HJ. Microinvasive carcinoma of the cervix. The significance of lymphatic invasion and confluent patterns of stromal growth. Cancer 1975, **36**: 180–186.

257 Rubio CA, Söderberg G, Einhorn N. Histological and follow-up studies in cases of micro-invasive carcinoma of the uterine cervix. Acta Pathol Microbiol Scand (A) 1974, **82**: 397–410.

258 Sevin BU, Nadji M, Averette HE, Hilsenbeck S, Smith D, Lampe

B. Microinvasive carcinoma of the cervix. Cancer 1992, **70:** 2121–2128.

259 Simon NL, Gore H, Shingleton HM, Soong S-J, Orr JW, Hatch KD. Study of superficially invasive carcinoma of the cervix. Obstet Gynecol 1986, **68:** 19–24.

260 Stewart CJ, McNicol AM. Distribution of type IV collagen immunoreactivity to assess questionable early stromal invasion. J Clin Pathol 1992, **45:** 9–15.

261 Ueki M, Okamoto Y, Misaki O, Seiki Y, Kitsuki K, Ueda M, Sugimoto O. Conservative therapy for microinvasive carcinoma of the uterine cervix. Gynecol Oncol 1994, **53:** 109–113.

262 van Nagell JR, Greenwell N, Powell DF, Donaldson ES, Hanson MB, Gay EC. Microinvasive carcinoma of the cervix. Am J Obstet Gynecol 1983, **145:** 981–991.

Invasive squamous cell carcinoma

General features

263 Cannistra SA, Niloff JM. Cancer of the uterine cervix. N Engl J Med 1996, **334:** 1030–1038.

264 Devesa SS. Descriptive epidemiology of cancer of the uterine cervix. Obstet Gynecol 1984, **63:** 605–612.

265 Devesa SS, Young JL Jr, Brinton LA, Fraumeni JF Jr. Recent trends in cervix uteri cancer. Cancer 1989, **64:** 2184–2190.

266 Hawes SE, Kiviat NB. Are genital infections and inflammation cofactors in the pathogenesis of invasive cervical cancer? J Nat Cancer Inst 2002, **94:** 1592–1593.

267 Herrero R, Brinton LA, Reeves WC, Brenes MM, Tenorio F, de Britton RC, Gaitan E, Garcia M, Rawls WE. Sexual behavior, venereal diseases, hygiene practices, and invasive cervical cancer in a high-risk population. Cancer 1990, **65:** 380–386.

268 Kristensen GB, Holm R, Abeler VM, Trope CG. Evaluation of the prognostic significance of cathepsin D, epidermal growth factor receptor, and c-erbB-2 in early cervical squamous cell carcinoma: an immunohistochemical study. Cancer 1996, **78:** 433–440.

269 Kushima M, Fujii H, Murakami K, Ota H, Matsumoto T, Motoyama T, Kiyokawa T, Ishikura H. Simultaneous squamous cell carcinomas of the uterine cervix and upper genital tract: loss heterozygosity analysis demonstrates clonal neoplasms of cervical origin. Int J Gynecol Pathol 2001, **20:** 353–358.

270 Larsen NS. Invasive cervical cancer rising in young white females. J Natl Cancer Inst 1994, **86:** 6–7.

271 La Vecchia C, Franceschi S, Decarli A, Fasoli M, Gentile A, Parazzini F, Regallo M. Sexual factors, venereal diseases, and the risk of intraepithelial and invasive cervical neoplasia. Cancer 1986, **58:** 935–941.

272 Maiman M, Fruchter RG, Serur E, Remy JC, Feuer G, Boyce J. Human immunodeficiency virus infection and cervical neoplasia. Gynecol Oncol 1990, **38:** 377–382.

273 Miyazaki K, Yamaguchi K, Tohya T, Ohba T, Takatsuki K, Okamura H. Human T-cell leukemia virus type I infection as an oncogenic and prognostic risk factor in cervical and vaginal carcinoma. Obstet Gynecol 1991, **77:** 107–110.

274 Nair BS, Pillai R. Oncogenesis of squamous carcinoma of the uterine cervix. Int J Gynecol Pathol 1992, **11:** 47–57.

275 Piver MS. Invasive cervical cancer in the 1990s. Semin Surg Oncol 1990, **6:** 359–363.

276 Rapp F, Jenkins FJ. Genital cancer and viruses. Gynecol Oncol 1981, **12:** S25–S41.

277 Rellihan MA, Dooley DP, Burke TW, Berkland ME, Longfield RN. Rapidly progressing cervical caner in a patient with human immunodeficiency virus infection. Gynecol Oncol 1990, **36:** 435–438.

278 Sasagawa T, Shimakage M, Nakamura M, Sakaike J, Ishikawa H, Inoue M. Epstein-Barr virus (EBV) genes expression in cervical intraepithelial neoplasia and invasive cervical cancer: a comparative study with human papillomavirus (HPV) infection. Hum Pathol 2000, **31:** 318–326.

279 Schwartz LB, Carcangiu ML, Bradham L, Schwartz PE. Rapidly progressive squamous cell carcinoma of the cervix coexisting with human immunodeficiency virus infection: clinical opinion. Gynecol Oncol 1991, **41:** 255–258.

280 Wong KY, Collins RJ, Srivastava G, Pittaluga S, Cheung AN, Wong LC. Epstein Barr virus in carcinoma of the cervix. Int J Gynecol Pathol 1993, **12:** 224–227.

Morphologic features

281 Aho HJ, Talve L, Maenpaa J. Acantholytic squamous cell carcinoma of the uterine cervix with amyloid deposition. Int J Gynecol Pathol 1992, **11:** 150–155.

282 Benda JA. Pathology of cervical carcinoma and its prognostic implications. Semin Oncol 1994, **21:** 3–11.

283 Bostrom SG, Hart WR. Carcinomas of the cervix with intense stromal eosinophilia. Cancer 1981, **47:** 2887–2893.

284 Brinck U, Jakob C, Bau O, Fuzesi L. Papillary squamous cell carcinoma of the uterine cervix: report of three cases and a review of its classification. Int J Gynecol Pathol 2000, **19:** 231–235.

285 Clement PB, Scully RE. Carcinoma of the cervix. Histologic types. Semin Oncol 1982, **9:** 251–264.

286 Colgan TJ, Auger M, McLaughlin JR. Histopathologic classification of cervical carcinomas and recognition of mucin-secreting squamous carcinomas. Int J Gynecol Pathol 1993, **12:** 64–69.

287 Gondo T, Ishihara T, Kawano H, Uchino F, Takahashi M, Iwata T, Matsumoto N, Yokota T. Localized amyloidosis in squamous cell carcinoma of uterine cervix. Electron microscopic features of nodular and star-like amyloid deposits. Virchows Arch [A] 1993, **422:** 225–231.

288 Heller PB, Barnhill Dr, Mayer AR, Fontaine TP, Hoskins WJ, Park RC. Cervical carcinoma found incidentally in a uterus removed for benign indications. Obstet Gynecol 1986, **67:** 187–190.

289 Kapp DS, LiVolsi VA. Intense eosinophilic stromal infiltration in carcinoma of the uterine cervix. A clinicopathologic study of 14 cases. Gynecol Oncol 1983, **16:** 19–30.

290 Miller BE, Copeland LJ, Hamberger AD, Gershenson DM, Saul PB, Herson J, Rutledge FN. Carcinoma of the cervical stump. Gynecol Oncol 1984, **18:** 100–108.

291 Morrison C, Catania F, Wakely P, Nuovo GJ. Highly differentiated keratinising squamous cell cancer of the cervix: a rare, locally aggressive tumor not associated with human papillomavirus or squamous intraepithelial lesions. Am J Surg Pathol 2001, **25:** 1310–1315.

292 Ng ABP, Atkin NB. Histological cell type and DNA value in the prognosis of squamous cell cancer of uterine cervix. Br J Cancer 1973, **28:** 322–331.

293 Samlal RA, Ten Kate FJ, Hart AA, Lammes FB. Do mucin-secreting squamous cell carcinomas of the uterine cervix metastasise more frequently to pelvic lymph nodes? A case-control study. Int J Gynecol Pathol 1998, **17:** 201–204.

294 Tsang WY, Chan JK. Amyloid-producing squamous cell carcinoma of the uterine cervix. Arch Pathol Lab Med 1993, **117:** 199–201.

Immunohistochemical and molecular genetic features

295 Bychkov V, Rothman M, Bardawil WA. Immunocytochemical localization of carcinoembryonic antigen (CEA), alpha-fetoprotein (AFP), and human chorionic gonadotropin (HCG) in cervical neoplasia. Am J Clin Pathol 1983, **79:** 414–420.

296 Dunne FP, Rollason T, Ratcliff WA, Marshall T, Heath DA. Parathyroid hormone-related protein gene expression in invasive cervical tumors. Cancer 1994, **74:** 83–89.

297 Hameed A, Miller DS, Muller CY, Coleman RL, Albores-Saavedra J. Frequent expression of beta-human chorionic gonadotropin (beta-hCG) in squamous cell carcinoma of the cervix. Int J Gynecol Pathol 1999, **18:** 381–386.

298 Kanai M, Shiozawa T, Xin L, Nikaido T, Fujii S.

Immunohistochemical detection of sex steroid receptors, cyclins and cyclin-dependent kinases in the normal and neoplastic squamous epithelia of the uterine cervix. Cancer 1998, **82**: 1709–1719.

299 Kessis TD, Slebos RJ, Han SM, Shah K, Bosch XF, Munoz N, Hedrick L, Cho KR. p53 gene mutations and MDM2 amplification are uncommon in primary carcinomas of the uterine cervix. Am J Pathol 1993, **143**: 1398–1405.

300 Konishi I, Fujii S, Nonogaki H, Nanbu Y, Iwai T, Mori T. Immunohistochemical analysis of estrogen receptors, progesterone receptors, Ki-67 antigen, and human papillomavirus DNA in normal and neoplastic epithelium of the uterine cervix. Cancer 1991, **68**: 1340–1350.

301 Mitchell KM, Hale RJ, Buckley CH, Fox H, Smith D. Cathepsin-D expression in cervical carcinoma and its prognostic significance. Virchows Arch [A] 1993, **422**: 357–360.

302 Nguyen HN, Sevin BU, Averette HE, Ramos R, Ganjei P, Perras J. Evidence of tumor heterogeneity in cervical cancers and lymph node metastases as determined by flow cytometry. Cancer 1993, **71**: 2543–2550.

303 Smedts F, Ramaekers F, Link M, Lauerova L, Troyanovsky S, Schijf C, Voojis GP. Detection of keratin subtypes in routinely processed cervical tissue. Implications for tumour classification and the study of cervix cancer aetiology. Virchows Arch 1994, **425**: 145–155.

304 To ACW, Soong S-J, Shingleton HM, Gore H, Wilkerson JA, Hatch KD, Phillips D, Dollar JR. Immunohistochemistry of the blood group A, B, H isoantigens and Oxford Ca antigen as prognostic markers for stage IB squamous cell carcinoma of the cervix. Cancer 1986, **58**: 2435–2439.

305 Wang TY, Chen BF, Yang YC, Chen H, Wang Y, Cviko A, Quade BJ, Sun D, Yang A, McKeon FD, Crum CP. Histologic and immunophenotypic classification of cervical carcinomas by expression of the p53 homologue p63: a study of 250 cases. Hum Pathol 2001, **32**: 479–486.

Spread and metastases

306 Barmeir E, Langer O, Levy JI, Nissenbaum M, DeMoor NG, Blumenthal NJ. Unusual skeletal metastases in carcinoma of the cervix. Gynecol Oncol 1985, **20**: 307–316.

307 Benedetti-Panici P, Maneschi F, D'Andrea G, Cutillo G, Rabitti C, Congiu M, Coronetta F, Capelli A. Early cervical carcinoma: the natural history of lymph node involvement redefined on the basis of thorough parametrectomy and giant section study. Cancer 2000, **88**: 2267–2274.

308 Henriksen E. The lymphatic spread of carcinoma of the cervix and the body of the uterus. Am J Obstet Gynecol 1949, **58**: 924–942.

309 Ratanatharathorn V, Powers WE, Steverson N, Han I, Ahmad K, Grimm J. Bone metastasis from cervical cancer. Cancer 1994, **73**: 2372–2379.

310 Tellis CJ, Beechler CR. Pulmonary metastasis of carcinoma of the cervix. A retrospective study. Cancer 1982, **49**: 1705–1709.

311 Uqmakli A, Bonney WA Jr, Palladino A. The nonlymphatic metastases of carcinoma of the uterine cervix. A prospective analysis based on laparotomy. Cancer 1978, **41**: 1027–1033.

312 Young RH, Gersell DJ, Roth LM, Scully RE. Ovarian metastases from cervical carcinomas other than pure adenocarcinomas. A report of 12 cases. Cancer 1993, **71**: 407–418.

Treatment

313 Bjornsson BL, Nelson BE, Reale FR, Rose PG. Accuracy of frozen section for lymph node metastasis in patients undergoing radical hysterectomy for carcinoma of the cervix. Gynecol Oncol 1993, **51**: 50–53.

314 Bricker EM, Butcher HR Jr, Lawler WH Jr, McAfee CA. Surgical treatment of advanced and recurrent cancer of the pelvic viscera.

An evaluation of ten years' experience. Ann Surg 1960, **152**: 388–402.

315 Hamberger AD, Fletcher GH, Wharton JT. Results of treatment of early stage I carcinoma of the uterine cervix with intracavitary radium alone. Cancer 1978, **41**: 980–985.

316 Holtz DO, Dunton C. Traditional management of invasive cervical cancer. Obstet Gynecol Clin North Am 2002, **29**: 645–657.

317 Hopkins MP, Morley GW. Radical hysterectomy versus radiation therapy for stage IB squamous cell cancer of the cervix. Cancer 1991, **68**: 272–277.

318 Jacobs AJ, Faris C, Perez CA, Kao MS, Galakatos A, Camel HM. Short-term persistence of carcinoma of the uterine cervix after radiation. An indicator of long-term prognosis. Cancer 1986, **57**: 944–950.

319 Jones WB. New approaches to high-risk cervical cancer. Advanced cervical cancer. Cancer 1993, **71**: 1451–1459.

320 Kinney WK, Egorshin EV, Ballard DJ, Podratz KC. Long-term survival and sequelae after surgical management of invasive cervical carcinoma diagnosed at the time of simple hysterectomy. Gynecol Oncol 1992, **44**: 24–27.

321 Kiselow M, Butcher HR, Bricker EM. Results of the radical surgical treatment of advanced pelvic cancer. Ann Surg 1967, **166**: 428–437.

322 Morgan LS, Nelson JH. Surgical treatment of early cervical cancer. Semin Oncol 1982, **9**: 312–330.

323 Morley GW. Pelvic exenterative therapy and the treatment of recurrent carcinoma of the cervix. Semin Oncol 1982, **9**: 331–340.

324 Morley GW, Hopkins MP, Lindenauer SM, Roberts JA. Pelvic exenteration, University of Michigan. 100 patients at 5 years. Obstet Gynecol 1989, **74**: 934–943.

325 Perez CA, Camel HM, Kao MS, Hederman MA. Randomized study of preoperative radiation and surgery or irradiation alone in the treatment of stage IB and IIA carcinoma of the uterine cervix. Final report. Gynecol Oncol 1987, **27**: 129–140.

326 Perez-Mesa C, Spjut HJ. Persistent postirradiation carcinoma of cervix uteri. A pathologic study of 83 pelvic exenteration specimens. Arch Pathol 1963, **75**: 462–474.

327 Thar TL, Million RR, Daly JW. Radiation treatment of carcinoma of the cervix. Semin Oncol 1982, **9**: 299–311.

Prognosis

328 Baltzer J, Lohe KJ. What's new in prognosis of uterine cancer? Pathol Res Pract 1984, **178**: 635–641.

329 Bethwaite PB, Holloway LJ, Yeong ML, Thornton A. Effect of tumour associated tissue eosinophilia on survival of women with stage IB carcinoma of the uterine cervix. J Clin Pathol 1993, **46**: 1016–1020.

330 Boyce JG, Fruchter RG, Nicastri AD, DeRegt RH, Ambiavagar PC, Reinis M, Macasaet M, Rotman M. Vascular invasion in stage I carcinoma of the cervix. Cancer 1984, **53**: 1175–1180.

331 Burghardt E, Baltzer J, Tulusan AH, Haas J. Results of surgical treatment of 1028 cervical cancers studied with volumetry. Cancer 1992, **70**: 648–655.

332 Cheung TH, Chung TKJ, Poon CS, Hampton GM, Wand VW, Wong YF. Allelic loss on chromosome 1 is associated with tumor progression of cervical carcinoma. Cancer 1999, **86**: 1294–1298.

333 Goellner JR. Carcinoma of the cervix. Clinicopathologic correlation of 196 cases. Am J Clin Pathol 1976, **66**: 775–785.

334 Gunderson LL, Weems WS, Hebertson RM, Plenk HP. Correlation of histopathology with clinical results following radiation therapy for carcinoma of the cervix. Am J Roentgenol Radium Ther Nucl Med 1974, **120**: 74–87.

335 Hale RJ, Buckley CH, Fox H, Williams J. Prognostic value of c-*erb*B-2 expression in uterine cervical carcinoma. J Clin Pathol 1992, **45**: 594–596.

336 Herrington CS, Wells M. Can HPV typing predict the behaviour of cervical epithelial neoplasia? Histopathology 1997, **31**: 301–303.

337 Hirao T, Sakamoto Y, Kamada M, Hamada S, Aono T. Tn antigen, a marker of potential for metastasis of uterine cervix cancer cells. Cancer 1993, **72**: 154–159.

338 Hopkins MP, Morley GW. Prognostic factors in advanced stage squamous cell cancer of the cervix. Cancer 1993, **72**: 2389–2393.

339 Inoue T. Prognostic significance of the depth of invasion relating to nodal metastases, parametrial extension, and cell types. A study of 628 cases with stage IB, IIA, and IIB cervical carcinoma. Cancer 1984, **54**: 3035–3042.

340 Inoue T, Chihara T, Morita K. The prognostic significance of the size of the largest nodes in metastatic carcinoma from the uterine cervix. Gynecol Oncol 1984, **19**: 187–193.

341 Inoue T, Morita K. The prognostic significance of number of positive nodes in cervical carcinoma stages IB, IIA, and IIB. Cancer 1990, **65**: 1923–1927.

342 Inoue T, Okumura M. Prognostic significance of parametrial extension in patients with cervical carcinoma stages IB, IIA, and IIB. A study of 628 cases treated by radical hysterectomy and lymphadenectomy with or without postoperative irradiation. Cancer 1984, **54**: 1714–1719.

343 Kamura T, Tsukamoto N, Tsuruchi N, Saito T, Matsuyama T, Akazawa K, Nakano H. Multivariate analysis of the histopathologic prognostic factors of cervical cancer in patients undergoing radical hysterectomy. Cancer 1992, **69**: 181–186.

344 Lombard I, Vincent-Salomon A, Validire P, Zafrani B, de la Rochefordiere A, Clough K, Favre M, Pouillart P, Sastre-Garau X. Human papillomavirus genotype as a major determinant of the course of cervical cancer. J Clin Oncol 1998, **16**: 2613–2619.

345 Nakano T, Oka K, Takahashi T, Morita S, Arai T. Roles of Langerhans' cells and T-lymphocytes infiltrating cancer tissues in patients treated by radiation therapy for cervical cancer. Cancer 1992, **70**: 2839–2844.

346 Noguchi H, Shiozawa I, Sakai Y, Yamazaki T, Fukuta T. Pelvic lymph node metastasis of uterine cervical cancer. Gynecol Oncol 1987, **27**: 150–158.

347 Obermair A, Wanner C, Bilgi S, Speiser P, Reisenberger K, Kaider A, Kainz C, Leodolter S, Breitenecker G, Gitsch G. The influence of vascular space involvement on the prognosis of patients with stage IB cervical carcinoma: correlation of results from hematoxylin and eosin staining with results from immunostaining for factor VIII-related antigen. Cancer 1998, **82**: 689–696.

348 Oka K, Nakano T, Arai T. c-erbB-2 Oncoprotein expression is associated withpoor prognosis in squamous cell carcinoma of the cervix. Cancer 1994, **73**: 664–671.

349 Perez CA, Camel HM, Askin F, Breaux S. Endometrial extension of carcinoma of the uterine cervix. A prognostic factor that may modify staging. Cancer 1981, **48**: 170–180.

350 Perez CA, Grigsby PW, Nene SM, Camel HM, Galakatos A, Kao MS, Lockett MA. Effect of tumor size on the prognosis of carcinoma of the uterine cervix treated with irradiation alone. Cancer 1992, **69**: 2796–2806.

351 Riou G, Favre M, Jeannel D, Bourhis J, Le Doussal V, Orth G. Association between poor prognosis in early-stage invasive cervical carcinomas and non-detection of HPV DNA. Lancet 1990, **335**: 1171–1174.

352 Robert ME, Fu YS. Squamous cell carcinoma of the uterine cervix – a review with emphasis on prognostic factors and unusual variants. Semin Diagn Pathol 1990, **7**: 173–189.

353 Rutgers JL, Mattox TF, Vargas MP. Angiogenesis in uterine cervical squamous cell carcinoma. Int J Gynecol Pathol 1995, **14**: 114–118.

354 Sagae S, Kuzumaki N, Hisada T, Mugikura Y, Kudo R, Hashimoto M. ras Oncogene expression and prognosis of

355 Sakuragi N, Takeda N, Hareyama H, Fujimoto T, Todo Y, Okamoto K, Takeda M, Wada S, Yamamoto R, Fujimoto S. A multivariate analysis of blood vessel invasion as predictor of ovarian and lymph node metastases in patients with cervical carcinoma. Cancer 2000, **88**: 2578–2583.

356 Samlal RA, van der Velden J, Ten Kate FJ, Schilthuis MS, Hart AA, Lamnes FB. Surgical pathology factors that predict recurrence in stage IB and IIA cervical carcinoma patients with negative pelvic lymph nodes. Cancer 1997, **80**: 1234–1240.

357 Smiley LM, Burke TW, Silva EG, Morris M, Gershenson DM, Wharton JT. Prognostic factors in stage IB squamous cervical cancer patients with low risk for recurrence. Obstet Gynecol 1991, **77**: 271–275.

358 Stendahl U, Eklund G, Willen R. Prognosis of invasive squamous cell carcinoma of the uterine cervix. A comparative study of the predictive values of clinical staging IB-III and a histopathologic malignancy grading system. Int J Gynecol Pathol 1983, **2**: 42–54.

359 Stock RJ, Zaino R, Bundy BN, Askin FB, Woodward J, Fetter B, Paulson JA, DiSaia PJ, Stehman FB. Evaluation and comparison of histopathologic grading systems of epithelial carcinoma of the uterine cervix; Gynecologic Oncology Group studies. Int J Gynecol Pathol 1994, **13**: 99–108.

360 Strang P. Cytogenetic and cytometric analyses in squamous cell carcinoma of the uterine cervix. Int J Gynecol Pathol 1989, **8**: 54–63.

361 van Bommel PF, Kenemans P, Helmerhorst TJ, Gallee MP, Ivanyi D. Expression of cytokeratin 10, 13, and involucrin as prognostic factors in low stage squamous cell carcinoma of the uterine cervix. Cancer 1994, **74**: 2314–2320.

362 van Driel WJ, Hogendoorn PC, Jansen FW, Zwinderman AH, Trimbos JB, Fleuren GJ. Tumor-associated eosinophilic infiltrate of cervical cancer is indicative for a less effective immune response. Hum Pathol 1996, **27**: 904–911.

363 Wentz WB, Lewis GC Jr. Correlation of histologic morphology and survival in cervical cancer following radiation therapy. Obstet Gynecol 1965, **26**: 228–232.

364 Zaino RJ, Ward S, Delgado G, Bundy B, Gore H, Fetter G, Ganjei P, Frauenhoffer E. Histopathologic predictors of the behavior of surgically treated stage IB squamous cell carcinoma of the cervix. A Gynecologic Oncology Group study. Cancer 1992, **69**: 1750–1758.

Other microscopic types

365 Brinck U, Jakob C, Bau O, Fuzesi L. Papillary squamous cell carcinoma of the uterine cervix: report of three cases and a review of its classification. Int J Gynecol Pathol 2000, **19**: 231–235.

366 Coleman RL, Lindberg G, Muller CY, Miller DS, Hameed A. Ectopic production and localization of beta-human chorionic gonadatropin in lymphoepithelioma-like carcinoma of the cervix: a case report. Int J Gynecol Pathol 2000, **19**: 179–182.

367 Daroca PJ Jr, Dhorandhar HN. Basaloid carcinoma of uterine cervix. Am J Surg Pathol 1980, **4**: 235–239.

368 Grayson W, Cooper K. A reappraisal of "basaloid carcinoma" of the cervix, and the differential diagnosis of basaloid cervical neoplasms. Adv Anat Pathol 2002, **9**: 290–300.

369 Grayson W, Taylor LF, Cooper K. Carcinosarcoma of the uterine cervix: a report of eight cases with immunohistochemical analysis and evaluation of human papillomavirus status. Am J Surg Pathol 2001, **25**: 338–347.

370 Halpin TF, Hunter RE, Cohen MB. Lymphoepithelioma of the uterine cervix. Gynecol Oncol 1989, **34**: 101–105.

371 Hasumi K, Sugano H, Sakamoto G, Masubuchi K, Kubo H. Circumscribed carcinoma of the uterine cervix, with marked lymphocytic infiltration. Cancer 1977, **39**: 2503–2507.

372 Koenig C, Turnicky RP, Kankam CF, Tavossoli FA. Papillary

squamotransitional cell carcinoma of the cervix: a report of 32 cases. Am J Surg Pathol 1997, **21**: 915–921.

373 Matorell MA, Julian JM, Calabuig C, Garcia-Garcia JA, Perez-Valles A. Lymphoepithelioma-like carcinoma of the uterine cervix. Arch Pathol Lab Med 2002, **126**: 1501–1505.

374 Mills SE, Austin MB, Randall ME. Lymphoepithelioma-like carcinoma of the uterine cervix. A distinctive, undifferentiated carcinoma with inflammatory stroma. Am J Surg Pathol 1985, **9**: 883–889.

375 Pang LC. Sarcomatoid squamous cell carcinoma of the uterine cervix with osteoclast-like giant cells: report of two cases. Int J Gynecol Pathol 1998, **17**: 174–177.

376 Randall ME, Andersen WA, Mills SE, Kim JAC. Papillary squamous cell carcinoma of the uterine cervix. A clinicopathologic study of nine cases. Int J Gynecol Pathol 1986, **5**: 1–10.

377 Steeper TA, Piscioli F, Rosai J. Squamous cell carcinoma with sarcoma-like stroma of the female genital tract. Cancer 1983, **52**: 890–898.

378 Tiltman AJ, Atad J. Verrucous carcinoma of the cervix with endometrial involvement. Int J Gynecol Pathol 1982, **1**: 221–226.

379 Tseng CJ, Pao CC, Tseng LH, Chang CT, Lai CH, Soong YK, Hsueh S, Jyu-Jen H. Lymphoepithelioma-like carcinoma of the uterine cervix: association with Epstein-Barr virus and human papillomavirus. Cancer 1997, **80**: 91–97.

380 Weinberg E, Hoisington S, Eastman AY, Rice DK, Malfetano J, Ross JS. Uterine cervical lymphoepithelial-like carcinoma. Absence of Epstein-Barr virus genomes. Am J Clin Pathol 1993, **99**: 195–199.

Adenocarcinoma

381 Alfsen GC, Thorensen S, Kristensen GB, Skovlund E, Abeler VM. Histopathological subtyping of cervical adenocarcinoma reveals increasing incidence rates of endometrioid tumors in all age groups: a population based study with review of all nonsquamous cervical carcinomas in Norway from 1966 to 1970, 1976 to 1980, and 1986 to 1990. Cancer 2000, **89**: 1291–1299.

382 Angel C, Du Beshter B, Lin JY. Clinical presentation and management of stage I cervical adenocarcinoma. A 25 year experience. Gynecol Oncol 1992, **44**: 71–78.

383 Berek JS, Hacker NF, Fu Y-S, Sokale JR, Leuchter RC, Lagasse LD. Adenocarcinoma of the uterine cervix. Histologic variables associated with lymph node metastasis and survival. Obstet Gynecol 1985, **65**: 46–52.

384 Cina SJ, Richardson MS, Austin RM, Kurman RJ. Immunohistochemical staining for Ki-67 antigen, carcinoembryonic antigen, and p53 in the differential diagnosis of glandular lesions of the cervix. Mod Pathol 1997, **10**: 176–180.

385 Cohen C, Shulman G, Budgeon LR. Endocervical and endometrial adenocarcinoma. An immunoperoxidase and histochemical study. Am J Surg Pathol 1982, **6**: 151–157.

386 Cooper P, Russell G, Wilson B. Adenocarcinoma of the endocervix. A histochemical study. Histopathology 1987, **11**: 1321–1330.

387 Dabbs DJ, Geisinger KR, Norris HT. Intermediate filaments in endometrial and endocervical carcinomas. The diagnostic utility of vimentin patterns. Am J Surg Pathol 1986, **10**: 568–576.

388 Duk JM, De Bruijn HW, Groenier KH, Fleuren GJ, Aalders JG. Adenocarcinoma of the uterine cervix. Prognostic significance of pretreatment serum CA 125, squamous cell carcinoma antigen, and carcinoembryonic antigen levels in relation to clinical and histopathologic tumor characteristics. Cancer 1990, **65**: 1830–1837.

389 Eifel PJ, Burke TW, Delclos L, Wharton JT, Oswald MJ. Early stage I adenocarcinoma of the uterine cervix. Treatment results in patients with tumors less than or equal to 4 cm in diameter. Gynecol Oncol 1991, **41**: 199–205.

390 Eifel PJ, Morris M, Oswald MJ, Wharton JT, Delclos L. Adenocarcinoma of the uterine cervix. Prognosis and patterns of failure in 367 cases. Cancer 1990, **65**: 2507–2514.

391 Ferguson AW, Svoboda-Newman SM, Frank TS. Analysis of human papillomavirus infection and molecular alterations in adenocarcinoma of the cervix. Mod Pathol 1998, **11**: 11–18.

392 Fujiwara H, Tortolero-Luna G, Mitchell MF, Koulos JP, Wright TC. Adenocarcinoma of the cervix: expression and clinical significance of estrogen and progesterone receptors. Cancer 1997, **79**: 505–512.

393 Gallup DG, Abell MR. Invasive adenocarcinoma of the uterine cervix. Obstet Gynecol 1977, **49**: 596–603.

394 Greer BE, Figge DC, Tamimi HK, Cain JM. Stage IB adenocarcinoma of the cervix treated by radical hysterectomy and pelvic lymph node dissection. Am J Obstet Gynecol 1989, **160**: 1509–1513.

395 Griffin NR, Wells M. Characterisation of complex carbohydrates in cervical glandular intraepithelial neoplasia and invasive adenocarcinoma. Int J Gynecol Pathol 1994, **13**: 319–329.

396 Griffin NR, Wells M, Fox H. Modulation of the antigenicity of amylase in cervical glandular atypia, adenocarcinoma in situ and invasive adenocarcinoma. Histopathology 1989, **15**: 267–279.

397 Gusberg SB, Corscaden JA. The pathology and treatment of adenocarcinoma of the cervix. Cancer 1951, **4**: 1066–1072.

398 Hopkins MP, Schmidt RW, Roberts JA, Morley GW. The prognosis and treatment of stage I adenocarcinoma of the cervix. Obstet Gynecol 1988, **72**: 915–921.

399 Hopkins MP, Sutton P, Roberts JA. Prognostic features and treatment of endocervical adenocarcinoma of the cervix. Gynecol Oncol 1987, **27**: 69–75.

400 Jackson-York GL, Ramzy I. Synchronous papillary mucinous adenocarcinoma of the endocervix and fallopian tubes. Int J Gynecol Pathol 1992, **11**: 63–67.

401 Jones MW, Silverberg SG. Cervical adenocarcinoma in young women. Possible relationship to microglandular hyperplasia and use of oral contraceptives. Obstet Gynecol 1989, **73**: 984–989.

402 Kaspar HG, Dinh TV, Doherty MG, Hannigan EV, Kumar D. Clinical implications of tumor volume measurement in stage I adenocarcinoma of the cervix. Obstet Gynecol 1993, **81**: 296–300.

403 Kihana T, Tsuda H, Teshima S, Nomoto K, Tsugane S, Sonoda T, Matsuura S, Hirohashi S. Prognostic significance of the overexpression of c-erbB-2 protein in adenocarcinoma of the uterine cervix. Cancer 1994, **73**: 148–153.

404 Kjorstad KE, Bond B. Stage IB adenocarcinoma of the cervix. Metastatic potential and patterns of dissemination. Am J Obstet Gynecol 1984, **150**: 297–299.

405 Kleine W, Rau K, Schwoeorer D, Pfleiderer A. Prognosis of the adenocarcinoma of the cervix uteri: a comparative study. Gynecol Oncol 1989, **35**: 145–149.

406 Konishi I, Fujii S, Nanbu Y, Nonogaki H, Mori T. Mucin leakage into the cervical stroma may increase lymph node metastasis in mucin-producing cervical adenocarcinomas. Cancer 1990, **65**: 229–237.

407 Korhonen MO. Adenocarcinoma of the uterine cervix. Prognosis and prognostic significance of histology. Cancer 1984, **53**: 1760–1763.

408 Kudo R, Sasano H, Koizumi M, Orenstein JM, Silverberg SG. Immunohistochemical comparison of new monoclonal antibody 1C5 and carcinoembryonic antigen in the differential diagnosis of adenocarcinoma of the uterine cervix. Int J Gynecol Pathol 1990, **9**: 325–336.

409 Lee SJ, Rollason TP. Argyrophilic cells in cervical intraepithelial glandular neoplasia. Int J Gynecol Pathol 1994, **13**: 131–132.

410 LiVolsi VA, Merino MJ, Schwartz PE. Coexistent endocervical adenocarcinoma and mucinous adenocarcinoma of ovary. A clinicopathologic study of four cases. Int J Gynecol Pathol 1983, **1**: 391–402.

411 Lu X, Toki T, Konishi I, Nikaido T, Fujii S. Expression of p21WAF1/CIP1 in adenocarcinoma of the uterine cervix: a possible immunohistochemical marker of a favorable prognosis. Cancer 1998, **82:** 2409–2417.

412 Mandai M, Konishi I, Koshiyama M, Komatsu T, Yamamoto S, Nanbu K, Mori T, Fukumoto M. Altered expression of nm23-H1 and c-erbB-2 proteins have prognostic significance in adenocarcinoma but not in squamous cell carcinoma of the uterine cervix. Cancer 1995, **75:** 2523–2529.

413 McCluggage WG, McBride HA, Maxwell P, Bharucha H. Immunohistochemical detection of p53 and bcl-2 proteins in neoplastic and non-neoplastic endocervical glandular lesions. Int J Gynecol Pathol 1997, **16:** 22–27.

414 Matthews CM, Burke TW, Tornos C, Eifel PJ, Atkinson EN, Stringer CA, Morris M, Silva EG. Stage I cervical adenocarcinoma. Prognostic evaluation of surgically treated patients. Gynecol Oncol 1993, **49:** 19–23.

415 Miller BE, Flax SD, Arheart K, Photopulos G. The presentation of adenocarcinoma of the uterine cervix. Cancer 1993, **72:** 1281–1285.

416 Moberg PJ, Einhorn N, Silfversward C, Soderberg G. Adenocarcinoma of the uterine cervix. Cancer 1986, **57:** 407–410.

417 Negri G, Egarter-Vigl E, Kasal A, Romano F, Haitel A, Mian C. P16 INK4a is a useful marker for the diagnosis of adenocarcinoma of the cervix uteri and its precursors: an immunohistochemical study with immunocytochemical correlations. Am J Surg Pathol 2003, **27:** 187–193.

418 Nguyen GK, Daya D. Cervical adenocarcinoma and related lesions. Cytodiagnostic criteria and pitfalls. Pathol Annu 1993, **28**(Pt 2): 53–75.

419 Parazzini F, La Vecchia C. Epidemiology of adenocarcinoma of the cervix. Gynecol Oncol 1990, **39:** 40–46.

420 Reagan JW. Cellular pathology and uterine cancer. Ward Burdick Award Address. Am J Clin Pathol 1974, **62:** 150–164.

421 Saigo PE, Cain JM, Kim WS, Gaynor JJ, Johnson K, Lewis JL. Prognostic factors in adenocarcinoma of the uterine cervix. Cancer 1986, **57:** 1584–1593.

422 Shorrock K, Johnson J, Johnson IR. Epidemiological changes in cervical carcinoma with particular reference to mucin-secreting subtypes. Histopathology 1990, **17:** 53–57.

423 Sorvari TE. A histochemical study of epithelial mucosubstances in endometrial and cervical adenocarcinomas. With reference to normal endometrium and cervical mucosa. Acta Pathol Microbiol Scand 1969, **207**(Suppl): 1–85.

424 Tenti P, Romagnoli S, Silini E, Zappatore R, Giunta P, Stella G, Carnevali L. Cervical adenocarcinomas express markers common to gastric, intestinal, and pancreatobiliary epithelial cells. Pathol Res Pract 1994, **190:** 342–349.

425 Tenti P, Romagnokli S, Silini E, Zappatore R, Spinillo A, Giunta P, Cappelini A, Vesentini N, Zara C, Carnevali L. Human papillomavirus types 16 and 18 infection in infiltrating adenocarcinomas of the cervix. PCR analysis of 138 cases and correlation with histologic type and grade. Am J Clin Pathol 1996, **106:** 52–56.

426 Toki N, Kaku T, Tsukamoto N, Matsumura M, Saito T, Kamura T, Matsuyama T, Nakano H. Distribution of basement membrane antigens in the uterine cervical adenocarcinomas. An immunohistochemical study. Gynecol Oncol 1990, **38:** 17–21.

427 Ueda G, Yamasaki M, Inoue M, Tanaka Y, Hiramatsu K, Inoue Y, Abe Y. Immunohistochemical demonstration of peptide hormones in cervical adenocarcinomas with argyrophil cells. Int J Gynecol Pathol 1984, **2:** 373–379.

428 Valente PT, Hanjani P. Endocervical neoplasia in long-term users of oral contraceptives. Clinical and pathologic observations. Obstet Gynecol 1986, **67:** 695–704.

429 Vesterinen E, Forss M, Nieminen U. Increase of cervical adenocarcinoma. A report of 520 cases of cervical carcinoma including 112 tumors with glandular elements. Gynecol Oncol 1990, **33:** 49–53.

430 Yavner DL, Dwyer IM, Hancock WW, Ehrmann RL. Basement membrane of cervical adenocarcinoma. An immunoperoxidase study of laminin and type IV collagen. Obstet Gynecol 1990, **76:** 1014–1019.

431 Young RH, Clement PB. Endocervical adenocarcinoma and its variants: their morphology and differential diagnosis. Histopathology 2002, **41:** 185–207.

432 Young RH, Scully RE. Invasive adenocarcinoma and related tumors of the uterine cervix. Semin Diagn Pathol 1990, **7:** 205–227.

433 Zaino RJ. Glandular lesions of the uterine cervix. Mod Pathol 2000, **13:** 261–274.

Differential diagnosis with endometrial adenocarcinoma

434 Caron C, Tetu B, Laberge P, Bellemare G, Raymond PE. Endocervical involvement by endometrial carcinoma on fractional curettage. A clinicopathological study of 37 cases. Mod Pathol 1991, **4:** 644–647.

435 Castrilon DH, Lee KR, Nucci MR. Distinction between endometrial and endocervical adenocarcinoma: an immunohistochemical study. Int J Gynecol Pathol 2002, **21:** 4–10.

436 Cohen C, Shulman G, Budgeon LR. Endocervical and endometrial adenocarcinoma. An immunoperoxidase and histochemical study. Am J Surg Pathol 1982, **6:** 151–157.

437 McCluggage WG, Sumathi VP, McBride HA, Patterson A. A panel of immunohistochemical stains, including carcinoembryonic antigen, vimentin, and estrogen receptor, aids the distinction between primary endometrial and endocervical adenocarcinomas. Int J Gynecol Pathol 2002, **21:** 11–15.

438 Staebler A, Sherman ME, Zaino RJ, Ronnett BM. Hormone receptor immunohistochemistry and human papillomavirus in situ hybridisation are useful for distinguishing endocervical and endometrial adenocarcinomas. Am J Surg Pathol 2002, **26:** 998–1006.

439 Tamimi HR, Gown AM, Kim-Deobald J, Figge DC, Greer BE, Cain JM. The utility of immunocytochemistry in invasive adenocarcinoma of the cervix. Am J Obstet Gynecol 1992, **166:** 1655–1661.

440 Zaino RJ. The fruits of our labours: distinguishing endometrial from endocervical adenocarcinoma. Int J Gynecol Pathol 2002, **21:** 1–3.

In situ and microinvasive adenocarcinoma

441 Andersen ES, Arffmann E. Adenocarcinoma in situ of the uterine cervix. A clinico-pathologic study of 36 cases. Gynecol Oncol 1989, **35:** 1–7.

442 Biscotti CV, Hart WR. Apoptotic bodies: a consistent morphologic feature of endocervical adenocarcinoma in situ. Am J Surg Pathol 1998, **22:** 434–439.

443 Boon ME, Baak JPA, Kurver PJH, Overdiep SH, Verdonk GW. Adenocarcinoma in situ of the cervix. An underdiagnosed lesion. Cancer 1981, **48:** 768–773.

444 Cameron RI, Maxwell P, Jenkins D, McCluggage WG. Immunohistochemical staining with MIB1, bcl2, and p16 assists in the distinction of cervical glandular intraepithelial neoplasia from tubo-endometrial metaplasia, endometriosis and microglandular hyperplasia. Histopathology 2002, **41:** 313–321.

445 Colgan TJ, Lickrish GM. The topography and invasive potential of cervical adenocarcinoma in situ, with and without associated dysplasia. Gynecol Oncol 1990, **36:** 246–249.

446 Gloor E, Hurlimann J. Cervical intraepithelial glandular neoplasia (adenocarcinoma in situ and glandular dysplasia). A correlative study of 23 cases with histologic grading, histochemical analysis of mucins, and immunohistochemical determination of the affinity for four lectins. Cancer 1986, **58:** 1272–1280.

447 Goldstein NS, Ahmad E, Hussain M, Hankin RC, Perez-Reyes N. Endocervical glandular atypia. Does a preneoplastic lesion of adenocarcinoma in situ exist? Am J Clin Pathol 1998, **110:** 200–209.

448 Goldstein NS, Mani A. The status and distance of cone biopsy margins as a predictor of excision adequacy for endocervical adenocarcinoma in situ. Am J Clin Pathol 1998, **109:** 727–732.

449 Hurlimann J, Gloor E. Adenocarcinoma in situ and invasive adenocarcinoma of the uterine cervix. An immunohistologic study with antibodies specific for several epithelial markers. Cancer 1984, **54:** 103–109.

450 Ioffe OB, Sagae S, Moritani S, Dahmoush L, Chen TT, Silverberg SG. Should pathologists diagnose endocervical preneoplastic lesions "less than" adenocarcinoma in situ? Int J Gynecol Pathol 2002, **22:** 18–21.

451 Jaworski RC. Endocervical glandular dysplasia, adenocarcinoma in situ, and early invasive (microinvasive) adenocarcinoma of the uterine cervix. Semin Diagn Pathol 1990, **7:** 190–204.

452 Jaworski RC, Pacey NF, Greenberg ML, Osborn RA. The histologic diagnosis of adenocarcinoma in situ and related lesions of the cervix uteri. Adenocarcinoma in situ. Cancer 1988, **61:** 1171–1181.

453 Jones MW, Silverberg SG. Cervical adenocarcinoma in young women. Possible relationship to microglandular hyperplasia and use of oral contraceptives. Obstet Gynecol 1989, **73:** 984–989.

454 Lee KR, Flynn CE. Early invasive adenocarcinoma of the cervix. Cancer 2000, **89:** 1048–1055.

455 Lee KR, Sun D, Crum CP. Endocervical intraepithelial glandular atypia (dysplasia): a histopathologic, human papillomavirus, and MIB-1 analysis of 25 cases. Hum Pathol 2000, **31:** 656–664.

456 Lu X, Shiozawa T, Nakayama K, Toki T, Nikaido T, Fujii S. Abnormal expression of sex steroid receptors and cell cycle-related molecules in adenocarcinoma in situ of the uterine cervix. Int J Gynecol Pathol 1999, **18:** 109–114.

457 Maier RC, Norris HJ. Coexistence of cervical intraepithelial neoplasia with primary adenocarcinoma of the endocervix. Obstet Gynecol 1980, **56:** 361–364.

458 Marques T, Andrade LA, Vassallo J. Endocervical tubal metaplasia and adenocarcinoma in situ: role of immunohistochemistry for carcinoembryonic antigen and vimentin in differential diagnosis. Histopathology 1996, **28:** 549–550.

459 Muntz HG, Bell DA, Lage JM, Goff BA, Feldman S, Rice LW. Adenocarcinoma in situ of the uterine cervix. Obstet Gynecol 1992, **80:** 935–939.

460 Ostor AG. Early invasive adenocarcinoma of the uterine cervix. Int J Gynecol Pathol 2000, **19:** 29–38.

461 Riethdorf L, Riethdorf S, Lee KR, Cviko A, Loning T, Crum CP. Human papillomavirus, expression of p16INK4A, and early endocervical glandular neoplasia. Hum Pathol 2002, **33:** 899–904.

462 Schlesinger C, Silverberg SG. Endocervical adenocarcinoma in situ of tubal type and its relation to atypical tubal metaplasia. Int J Gynecol Pathol 1999, **18:** 1–4.

463 Teshima S, Shimosato Y, Kishi K, Kasamatsu T, Ohmi K, Uei Y. Early stage adenocarcinoma of the uterine cervix. Histopathologic analysis with consideration of histogenesis. Cancer 1985, **56:** 167–172.

464 Weisbrot IM, Stabinsky C, Davis AM. Adenocarcinoma in situ of the uterine cervix. Cancer 1972, **29:** 225–233.

465 Wells M, Brown LJR. Glandular lesions of the uterine cervix. The present state of our knowledge. Histopathology 1986, **10:** 777–792.

466 Zaino RJ. Adenocarcinoma in situ, glandular dysplasia, and early invasive adenocarcinoma of the uterine cervix. Int J Gynecol Pathol 2002, **21:** 314–326.

Morphologic variants of cervical adenocarcinoma

467 Albores-Saavedra J, Manivel C, Mora A, Vuitch F, Milchgrub S, Gould E. The solid variant of adenoid cystic carcinoma of the cervix. Int J Gynecol Pathol 1992, **11:** 2–10.

468 Alfsen GC, Kristensen GB, Skovlund E, Pettersen EO, Abeler VM. Histologic subtype has minor importance for overall survival in patients with adenocarcinoma of the uterine cervix: a population-based study of prognostic factors in 505 patients with nonsquamous cell carcinomas of the cervix. Cancer 2001, **92:** 2471–2483.

469 Auersperg N, Erber H, Worth A. Histologic variation among poorly differentiated invasive carcinomas of the human uterine cervix. J Natl Cancer Inst 1973, **51:** 1461–1477.

470 Brainard JA, Hart WR. Adenoid basal epitheliomas of the uterine cervix: a reevaluation of distinctive cervical basaloid lesions currently classified as adenoid basal carcinoma and adenoid basal hyperplasia. Am J Surg Pathol 1998, **22:** 965–975.

470a Carinelli S, Scarfone G, Bianco V. Paget's disease of the cervix. Mod Pathol 2003, **16:** 184a.

471 Choo YC, Naylor B. Coexistent squamous cell carcinoma and adenocarcinoma of the uterine cervix. Gynecol Oncol 1984, **17:** 168–174.

472 Christopherson WM, Nealon N, Gray LA Sr. Noninvasive precursor lesions of adenocarcinoma and mixed adenosquamous carcinoma of the cervix uteri. Cancer 1979, **44:** 975–983.

473 Clement PB, Young RH, Keh P, Östör AG, Scully RE. Malignant mesonephric neoplasms of the uterine cervix. A report of eight cases, including four with a malignant spindle cell component. Am J Surg Pathol 1995, **19:** 1158–1171.

474 Costa MJ, Kenny MB, Hewan-Lowe K, Judd R. Glassy cell features in adenosquamous carcinoma of the uterine cervix. Histologic, ultrastructural, immunohistochemical, and clinical findings. Am J Clin Pathol 1991, **96:** 520–528.

475 Costa MJ, Kenny MB, Judd R. Adenocarcinoma and adenosquamous carcinoma of the uterine cervix. Histologic and immunohistochemical features with clinical correlation. Int J Surg Pathol 1994, **1:** 181–190.

476 Costa MJ, McIlnay KR, Trelford J. Cervical carcinoma with glandular differentiation. Histological evaluation predicts disease recurrence in clinical Stage I or II patients. Hum Pathol 1995, **26:** 829–837.

477 Daya D, Young RH. Florid deep glands of the uterine cervix. Another mimic of adenoma malignum. Am J Clin Pathol 1995, **103:** 614–617.

478 Dickersin GR, Welch WR, Erlandson R, Robboy SJ. Ultrastructure of 16 cases of clear cell adenocarcinoma of the vagina and cervix in young women. Cancer 1980, **45:** 1615–1624.

478a Farley JH, Hickey KW, Carlson JW, Rose GS, Kost ER, Harrison TA. Adenosquamous histology predicts a poor outcome for patients with advanced-stage, but not early-stage, cervical carcinoma. Cancer 2003, **97:** 2196–2202.

479 Fawcett KJ, Dockerty MB, Hunt AB. Mesonephric carcinoma of the cervix uteri. Clinical and pathologic study. Am J Obstet Gynecol 1966, **95:** 1068–1079.

480 Ferry JA, Scully RE. "Adenoid cystic" carcinoma and adenoid basal carcinoma of the uterine cervix. A study of 28 cases. Am J Surg Pathol 1988, **12:** 134–144.

481 Fowler WC Jr, Miles PA, Surwit EA, Edelman DA, Walton LA, Photopulos GJ. Adenoid cystic carcinoma of the cervix. Obstet Gynecol 1978, **52:** 337–342.

482 Fu YS, Reagan JW, Fu AS, Janiga KE. Adenocarcinoma and mixed carcinoma of the uterine cervix. II. Prognostic value of nuclear DNA analysis. Cancer 1982, **49:** 2571–2577.

483 Fu YS, Reagan JW, Hsiu JG, Storaasli JP, Wentz WB. Adenocarcinoma and mixed carcinoma of the uterine cervix. Cancer 1982, **49:** 2560–2570.

484 Gallager HS, Simpson CB, Ayala AG. Adenoid cystic carcinoma

of the uterine cervix. Report of 4 cases. Cancer 1971, **27:** 1398–1402.

485 Gilks CB, Young RH, Aguirre P, De Lellis RA, Scully RE. Adenoma malignum (minimal deviation adenocarcinoma) of the uterine cervix. A clinicopathological and immunohistochemical analysis of 26 cases. Am J Surg Pathol 1989, **13:** 717–729.

486 Gilks CB, Young RH, Clement PB, Hart WR, Scully RE. Adenomyomas of the uterine cervix of endocervical type: a report of ten cases of a benign cervical tumor that may be confused with adenoma malignum [corrected]. Mod Pathol 1996, **9:** 220–224.

487 Glücksmann A. Relationships between hormonal changes in pregnancy and the development of "mixed carcinoma" of the uterine cervix. Cancer 1957, **10:** 831–837.

488 Glücksmann A, Cherry CP. Incidence, histology, and response to radiation of mixed carcinomas (adenocanthomas) of the uterine cervix. Cancer 1956, **9:** 971–979.

489 Grayson W, Taylor LF, Cooper K. Adenoid cystic and adenoid basal carcinoma of the uterine cervix: comparative morphologic, mucin, and immunohistochemical profile of two rare neoplasms of putative 'reserve cell' origin. Am J Surg Pathol 1999, **23:** 448–458.

490 Hameed K. Clear-cell carcinoma of the uterine cervix. Am J Obstet Gynecol 1968, **101:** 954–958.

491 Hanselaar AG, Van Leusen ND, De Wilde PC, Vooijs GP. Clear cell adenocarcinoma of the vagina and cervix. A report of the Central Netherlands Registry with emphasis on early detection and prognosis. Cancer 1991, **67:** 1971–1978.

492 Hanselaar A, van Loosbroek M, Schuurbiers O, Helmerhorst T, Bulten J, Bernheim J. Clear cell adenocarcinoma of the vagina and cervix: an update of the central Netherlands registry showing twin age incidence peaks. Cancer 1997, **79:** 2229–2236.

493 Harrison TA, Sevin BU, Koechli O, Nguyen HN, Averette HE, Penalver M, Donato DM, Nadji M. Adenosquamous carcinoma of the cervix. Prognosis in early stage disease treated by radical hysterectomy. Gynecol Oncol 1993, **50:** 310–315.

494 Hart WR. Symposium Part II: special types of adenocarcinoma of the uterine cervix. Int J Gynecol Pathol 2002, **21:** 327–346.

495 Hart WR, Norris HJ. Mesonephric adenocarcinomas of the cervix. Cancer 1972, **29:** 106–113.

496 Hayashi I, Tsuda H, Shimoda T. Reappraisal of orthodox histochemistry for the diagnosis of minimal deviation adenocarcinoma of the cervix. Am J Surg Pathol 2000, **24:** 559–562.

497 Hoskins WJ, Averette HE, Ng ABP, Yon JL. Adenoid cystic carcinoma of the cervix uteri. Report of six cases and review of literature. Gynecol Oncol 1979, **7:** 371–384.

498 Ishii K, Hidaka E, Katsuyama T, Ota H, Shiozawa T, Tzuchiya S. Ultrastructural features of adenoma malignum of the uterine cervix: demonstration of gastric phenotypes. Ultrastruct Pathol 2000, **23:** 375–381.

499 Jones MW, Kounelis S, Papadaki H, Bakker A, Swalsky PA, Finkelstein SD. The origin and molecular characterization of adenoid basal carcinoma of the uterine cervix. Int J Gynecol Pathol 1998, **16:** 301–306.

500 Jones MW, Kounelis S, Papadaki H, Bakker A, Swalsky PA, Woods J, Finkelstein SD. Well-differentiated villoglandular adenocarcinoma of the uterine cervix: oncogene/tumor suppressor gene alterations and human papillomavirus genotyping. Int J Gynecol Pathol 2000, **124:** 110–117.

501 Jones MW, Silverberg SG. Cervical adenocarcinoma in young women. Possible relationship to microglandular hyperplasia and use of oral contraceptives. Obstet Gynecol 1989, **73:** 984–989.

502 Jones MW, Silverberg SG, Kurman RJ. Well-differentiated villoglandular adenocarcinoma of the uterine cervix. A clinicopathological study of 24 cases. Int J Gynecol Pathol 1993, **12:** 1–7.

503 Kaku T, Enjoji M. Extremely well-differentiated adenocarcinoma ("adenoma malignum") of the cervix. Int J Gynecol Pathol 1983, **2:** 28–41.

504 Kaminski PF, Maier RC. Clear cell adenocarcinoma of the cervix unrelated to diethylstilbestrol exposure. Obstet Gynecol 1983, **62:** 720–727.

505 Kaminski PF, Norris HJ. Minimal deviation carcinoma (adenoma malignum) of the cervix. Int J Gynecol Pathol 1983, **2:** 141–152.

506 Kaminski PF, Norris HJ. Coexistence of ovarian neoplasms and endocervical adenocarcinoma. Obstet Gynecol 1984, **64:** 553–556.

507 Kato N, Katayama Y, Kaimori M, Motoyama T. Glassy cell carcinoma of the uterine cervix: histochemical, immunohistochemical, and molecular genetic observations. Int J Gynecol Pathol 2002, **21:** 134–140.

508 Kudo R, Sagae S, Hayakawa O, Ito E, Horimoto E, Hashimoto M. Morphology of adenocarcinoma in situ and microinvasive adenocarcinoma of the uterine cervix. A cytologic and ultrastructural study. Acta Cytol 1991, **35:** 109–116.

509 Kuragaki C, Enomoto T, Ueno Y, Sun H, Fujita M, Nakashima R, Ueda Y, Wada H, Murata Y, Toki T, Konishi I, Fujii S. Mutations in the STK11 gene characterize minimal deviation adenocarcinoma of the uterine cervix. Lab Invest 2003, **83:** 35–45.

510 Lang G, Dallenbach-Hellweg G. The histogenetic origin of cervical mesonephric hyperplasia and mesonephric adenocarcinoma of the uterine cervix studied with immunohistochemical methods. Int J Gynecol Pathol 1990, **9:** 145–157.

511 Lee KR, Trainer TD. Adenocarcinoma of the uterine cervix of small intestinal type containing numerous Paneth cells. Arch Pathol Lab Med 1990, **114:** 731–733.

512 Littman P, Clement PB, Henriksen B, Wang CC, Robboy SJ, Taft PD, Ulfelder H, Scully RE. Glassy cell carcinoma of the cervix. Cancer 1976, **37:** 2238–2246.

513 Maier RC, Norris HJ. Glassy cell carcinoma of the cervix. Obstet Gynecol 1982, **60:** 219–224.

514 Matias-Guiu X, Lerma E, Prat J. Clear cell tumors of the female genital tract. Semin Diagn Pathol 1998, **14:** 233–239.

515 Mayorga M, Garcia-Valtuille A, Fernàndez F, Val-Bernal JF, Cabrera E. Adenocarcinoma of the uterine cervix with massive signet-ring cell differentiation. Int J Surg Pathol 1997, **5:** 95–100.

515a McCluggage WG, Oliva E, Herrington CS, McBride H, Young RH. CD10 and calretinin staining of endocervical glandular lesions, endocervical stroma and endometrioid adendocarcinomas of the uterine corpus: CD10 positivity is characteristic of, but not specific for, mesonephric lesions and is not specific for, endometrial stroma. Histopathology 2003, **43:** 144–150.

516 Michael H, Grawe L, Kraus FT. Minimal deviation endocervical adenocarcinoma. Clinical and histologic features, immunohistochemical staining for carcino-embryonic antigen, and differentiation from confusing benign lesions. Int J Gynecol Pathol 1984, **3:** 261–276.

517 Nordqvist SRB, Fidler WJ Jr, Woodruff JM, Lewis JL Jr. Clear cell adenocarcinoma of the cervix and vagina. A clinicopathologic study of 21 cases with and without a history of maternal ingestion of estrogens. Cancer 1976, **37:** 858–871.

518 Norris HJ, McCauley KM. Unusual forms of adenocarcinoma of the cervix. An update. Pathol Annu 1993, **28**(Pt 1): 73–95.

519 Pak HY, Yokota SB, Paladugu RR, Agliozzo CM. Glassy cell carcinoma of the cervix. Cytologic and clinicopathologic analysis. Cancer 1983, **52:** 307–312.

520 Robboy SJ, Herbst AL, Scully RE. Vaginal and cervical abnormalities related to prenatal exposure to diethylstilbestrol (DES). In Blaustein A (ed.): Pathology of female genital tract. New York, 1977, Springer-Verlag, pp. 87–101.

521 Rollason TP, Cullimore J, Bradgate MG. A suggested columnar

cell morphological equivalent of squamous carcinoma in situ with early stromal invasion. Int J Gynecol Pathol 1989, **8**: 230–236.

522 Rombaut RP, Charles D, Murphy A. Adenocarcinoma of the cervix. A clinico pathologic study of 47 cases. Cancer 1966, **19**: 891–900.

523 Rosen Y, Dolan TE. Carcinoma of the cervix with cylindromatous features believed to arise in mesonephric duct. Cancer 1975, **36**: 1739–1747.

524 Roth LM, Hornback NB. Clear-cell adenocarcinoma of the cervix in young women. Cancer 1974, **34**: 1761–1768.

525 Savargaonkar PR, Hale RJ, Pope R, Fox H, Buckley CH. Enteric differentiation in cervical adenocarcinomas and its prognostic significance. Histopathology 1993, **23**: 275–277.

526 Scully RE, Robboy SJ, Welch WR. Pathology and pathogenesis of diethylstilbestrol-related disorders of the female genital tract. In Herbst AL (ed.): Intrauterine exposure to diethylstilbestrol in the human. Chicago, IL, 1978, American College of Obstetricians and Gynecologists, pp. 8–22.

527 Shintaku M, Kariya M, Shime H, Ishikura H. Adenocarcinoma of the uterus cervix with choriocarcinomatous and hepatoid differentiation: report of a case. Int J Gynecol Pathol 2000, **19**: 174–178.

528 Shintaku M, Ueda H. Serous papillary adenocarcinoma of the uterine cervix. Histopathology 1993, **22**: 506–507.

529 Silver SA, Devouassoux-Shisheboran M, Mezzetti TP, Tavassoli FA. Mesonephric adenocarcinomas of the uterine cervix: a study of 11 cases with immunohistochemical findings. Am J Surg Pathol 2001, **25**: 379–387.

530 Steeper TA, Wick MR. Minimal deviation adenocarcinoma of the uterine cervix ("adenoma malignum"). An immunohistochemical comparison with microglandular endocervical hyperplasia and conventional endocervical adenocarcinoma. Cancer 1986, **58**: 1131–1138.

531 Tambouret R, Bell DA, Young RH. Microcystic endocervical adenocarcinomas: a report of eight cases. Am J Surg Pathol 2000, **24**: 369–374.

531a Tambouret R, Clement PB, Young RH. Endometrial endometrioid adenocarcinoma with a deceptive pattern of spread to the uterine cervix. A manifestation of stage IIB endometrial carcinoma liable to be misinterpreted as an independent carcinoma or a benign lesion. Am J Surg Pathol 2003, **27**: 1080–1088.

532 Thelmo WL, Nicastri AD, Fruchter R, Spring H, Di Maio T, Boyce J. Mucoepidermoid carcinoma of uterine cervix stage IB. Long-term follow-up, histochemical and immunohistochemical study. Int J Gynecol Pathol 1990, **9**: 316–324.

533 Toki T, Shiozawa T, Hosaka N, Ishii K, Nikaido T, Fujii S. Minimal deviation adenocarcinoma of the uterine cervix has abnormal expression of sex steroid receptors, CA125, and gastric mucin. Int J Gynecol Pathol 1997, **16**: 111–116.

534 Toki T, Zhai YL, Park JS, Fujii S. Infrequent occurrence of high-risk human papillomavirus and of p53 mutation in minimal deviation adenocarcinoma of the cervix. Int J Gynecol Pathol 2002, **18**: 215–219.

535 Ulbright TM, Gersell DJ. Glassy cell carcinoma of the uterine cervix. A light and electron microscopic study of five cases. Cancer 1983, **51**: 2255–2263.

536 Young RH, Scully RE. Villoglandular papillary adenocarcinoma of the uterine cervix. A clinicopathologic analysis of 13 cases. Cancer 1989, **63**: 1773–1779.

537 Young RH, Scully RE. Minimal-deviation endometrioid adenocarcinoma of the uterine cervix. A report of five cases of distinctive neoplasm that may be misinterpreted as benign. Am J Surg Pathol 1993, **17**: 660–665.

538 Young RH, Welch WR, Dickersin GR, Scully RE. Ovarian sex-cord tumor with annular tubules. Cancer 1982, **50**: 1384–1402.

539 Zhou C, Gilks CB, Hayes M, Clement PB. Papillary serous carcinoma of the uterine cervix: a clinicopathologic study of 17 cases. Am J Surg Pathol 1998, **22**: 113–120.

Neuroendocrine carcinoma

540 Abeler VM, Holm R, Nesland JM, Kjorstad KE. Small cell carcinoma of the cervix. A clinicopathologic study of 26 patients. Cancer 1994, **73**: 672–677.

541 Albores-Saavedra J, Gersell D, Gilks B, Henson DE, Lindberg G, Santiago H, Scully RE, Silva E, Sobin LH, Tavassoli FJ, Travis WD, Woodruff JM. Terminology of endocrine tumors of the uterine cervix: results of workshop sponsored by the College of American Pathologists and the National Cancer Institute. Arch Pathol Lab Med 1997, **121**: 34–39.

542 Ambros RA, Park JS, Shah KV, Kurman RJ. Evaluation of histologic, morphometric, and immunohistochemical criteria in the differential diagnosis of small cell carcinomas of the cervix with particular reference to human papillomavirus types 16 and 18. Mod Pathol 1991, **4**: 586–593.

543 Chan JK, Loizzi V, Burger RA, Rutgers J, Monk BJ. Prognostic factors in neuroendocrine small cell cervical carcinoma: a multivariate analysis. Cancer 2003, **97**: 568–574.

544 Chan JK, Tsui WM, Tung SY, Ching RC. Endocrine cell hyperplasia of the uterine cervix. A precursor of neuroendocrine carcinoma of the cervix? Am J Clin Pathol 1989, **92**: 825–830.

545 Chavez-Bianco A, Taja-Chayeb L, Cetina L, Chanona-Vilchis G, Trejo-Becerill C, Perez-Cardenaz E, Segura-Pacheco B, Acuna-Gonzales C, Duenas-Gonzales A. Neuroendocrine marker expression in cervical carcinomas of non-small cell type. Int J Gynecol Pathol 2002, **21**: 368–374.

546 Conner MG, Richter H, Moran CA, Hameed A, Albores-Saavedra J. Small cell carcinoma of the cervix: a clinicopathologic and immunohistochemical study of 23 cases. Ann Diagn Pathol 2002, **6**: 345–348.

547 Gersell DJ, Mazoujian G, Mutch DG, Rudloff MA. Small-cell undifferentiated carcinoma of the cervix. A clinicopathologic, ultrastructural, and immunocytochemical study of 15 cases. Am J Surg Pathol 1988, **12**: 684–698.

548 Gilks CB, Young RH, Gersell DJ, Clement PB. Large cell (neuroendocrine) carcinoma of the uterine cervix: a clinicopathologic study of 12 cases. Am J Surg Pathol 1997, **21**: 905–914.

549 Hammar SP, Insalaco SJ, Lee RB, Bockus DE, Remington FL, Yu A. Amphicrine carcinoma of the uterine cervix. Am J Clin Pathol 1992, **97**: 516–522.

550 Herrington CS, Graham D, Southern SA, Bramdev A, Chetty R. Loss of retinoblastoma protein expression is frequent in small cell neuroendocrine carcinoma of the cervix and is unrelated to HPV type. Hum Pathol 1999, **30**: 906–910.

551 Husain AN, Gattuso P, Abraham K, Castelli MJ. Synchronous adenocarcinoma and carcinoid of the uterine cervix. Immunohistochemical study of a case and review of literature. Gynecol Oncol 1990, **33**: 125–128.

552 Ibrahim NBN, Briggs JC, Corbishley CM. Extrapulmonary oat cell carcinoma. Cancer 1984, **54**: 1645–1661.

553 Ishibashi-Ueda H, Imakita M, Yutani C, Ohmichi M, Chiba Y, Kubo T, Waki M. Small cell carcinoma of the uterine cervix with syndrome of inappropriate antidiuretic hormone secretion. Mod Pathol 1996, **9**: 397–400.

554 Johannessen JV, Capella C, Solcia E, Davy M, Sobrinho-Simões M. Endocrine cell carcinoma of the uterine cervix. Diagn Gynecol Obstet 1980, **2**: 127–134.

555 Jones HW III, Plymate S, Gluck FB, Miles PA, Greene JF Jr. Small cell non-keratinizing carcinoma of the cervix associated with ACTH production. Cancer 1976, **38**: 1629–1635.

556 Man YG, Mannion C, Kuhls E, Moinfar F, Bratthauer GL, Albores-Saavedra J, Tavassoli FA. Allelic losses at 3p and 11p are

detected in both epithelial and stromal components of cervical small-cell neuroendocrine carcinoma. Appl Immunohistochem Mol Morphol 2001, **9:** 340–345.

557 Mannion C, Park WS, Man YG, Zhuang Z, Albores-Saavedra J, Tavassoli FA. Endocrine tumors of the cervix: morphologic assessment, expression of human papillomavirus, and evaluation for loss of heterozygosity on 1p, 3p, 11q and 17p. Cancer 1998, **83:** 1391–1400.

558 Miller B, Dockter M, el Torky M, Photopulos G. Small cel carcinoma of the cervix: a clinical and flow-cytometric study. Gynecol Oncol 1991, **42:** 27–33.

559 Mullins JD, Hilliard GD. Cervical carcinoid ("argyrophil cell" carcinoma) associated with an endocervical adenocarcinoma. A light and ultrastructural study. Cancer 1981, **47:** 785–790.

560 Sevin BU, Method MW, Nadji M, Lu Y, Averette HA. Efficacy of radical hysterectomy as treatment for patients with small cell carcinoma of the cervix. Cancer 1996, **77:** 1489–1493.

561 Silva EG, Kott MM, Ordonez NG. Endocrine carcinoma intermediate cell type of the uterine cervix. Cancer 1984, **54:** 1705–1713.

562 Stahl R, Demopoulos RI, Bigelow B. Carcinoid tumor within a squamous cell carcinoma of the cervix. Gynecol Oncol 1981, **11:** 387–392.

563 Stoler MH, Mills SE, Gersell DJ, Walker AN. Small-cell neuroendocrine carcinoma of the cervix. A human papillomavirus type 18-associated cancer. Am J Surg Pathol 1991, **15:** 28–32.

564 Tateishi R, Wada A, Hayakawa K, Hongo J, Ishii S, Terakawa N. Argyrophil cell carcinomas (apudomas) of the uterine cervix. Light and electron microscopic observations of 5 cases. Virchows Arch [A] 1975, **366:** 257–274.

565 Ueda G, Shimizu C, Shimizu H, Saito J, Tanaka Y, Inoue M, Tanizawa O. An immunohistochemical study of small-cell and poorly differentiated carcinomas of the cervix using neuroendocrine markers. Gynecol Oncol 1989, **34:** 164–169.

566 Ueda G, Yamasaki M, Inoue M, Tanaka Y, Inoue Y, Abe Y, Tanizawa O: Immunohistochemical demonstration of HNK-1-defined antigen in gynecologic tumors with argyrophilia. Int J Gynecol Pathol 1986, **5:** 143–150.

567 Ulich TR, Liao S-Y, Layfield L, Romansky S, Cheng L, Lewin KJ. Endocrine and tumor differentiation markers in poorly differentiated small cell carcinoids of the cervix and vagina. Arch Pathol Lab Med 1986, **110:** 1054–1057.

Cytology

568 Baldwin P, Laskey R, Coleman N. Translational approaches to improving cervical screening. Nat Rev Cancer 2003, **3:** 217–226.

569 Ball C, Madden JE. Update on cervical cancer screening. Current diagnostic and evidence-based management protocols. Postgrad Med 2003, **113:** 59–70.

570 Bonfiglio TA. Atypical squamous cell of undetermined significance: a continuing controversy. Cancer 2002, **96:** 125–127.

571 Christopherson WM, Mendez WM, Ahuja EM, Lundin FE, Barker JE. Cervix cancer control in Louisville, Kentucky. Cancer 1970, **26:** 29–38.

572 Christopherson WM, Scott MA. Trends in mortality from uterine cancer in relation to mass screening. Acta Cytol (Baltimore) 1977, **21:** 5–9.

573 Cramer DW. The role of cervical cytology in the declining morbidity and mortality of cervical cancer. Cancer 1974, **34:** 2018–2027.

574 Davey DD, Gallion H, Jennings CD. DNA cytometry in postirradiation cervical-vaginal smears. Hum Pathol 1992, **23:** 1027–1031.

574a de Cremoux P, Coste J, Sastre-Garau X, Thioux M, Bouillac C, Labbé S, Cartier I, Ziol M, Dosda A, Le Galès C, Molinié V, Vacher-Lavenu M-C, Cochand-Priollet B, Vielh P, Magdelénat H.

Efficiency of the hybrid capture 2 HPV DNA test in cervical cancer screening. Am J Clin Pathol 2003, **120:** 442–499.

575 Dickinson L, Mussey ME, Kurland LT. Evaluation of the effectiveness of cytologic screening for cervical cancer. II. Survival parameters before and after inception of screening. Mayo Clin Proc 1972, **47:** 545–549.

576 Dickinson L, Mussey ME, Soule EH, Kurland LT. Evaluation of the effectiveness of cytologic screening for cervical cancer. I. Incidence and mortality trends in relation to screening. Mayo Clin Proc 1972, **47:** 534–544.

576a Ducatman BS, Wang HH. The PAP smear: controversies in practice. London, 2002, Arnold Publishers.

577 Felix JC, Amezcua C. In vitro adjuncts to the pap smear. Obstet Gynecol Clin North Am 2002, **29:** 685–699.

578 Herbst AL. The Bethesda System for cervical/vaginal cytologic diagnoses. A note of caution (editorial). Obstet Gynecol 1990, **76:** 449–450.

578a Heselmeyer-Haddad K, Janz V, Castle PE, Chaudhri N, White N, Wilber K, Morrison L, Auer G, Burroughs FH, Sherman ME, Ried T. Detection of genomic amplification of the human telomerase gene (TERC) in cytologic specimens as a genetic test for the diagnosis of cervical dysplasia. Am J Pathol 2003, **163:** 1405–1416.

579 Hoffman MS, Sterghos S Jr, Gordy LW, Gunasekaran S, Cavanagh D. Evaluation of the cervical canal with the endocervical brush. Obstet Gynecol 1993, **82:** 573–577.

580 Klinken L, Koch F, Albrechtsen R. Comparison of pipette and smear methods in population screenings for carcinoma of the uterine cervix. Dan Med Bull 1972, **19:** 138–140.

581 Koss LG. Diagnostic cytology and its histopathologic bases, ed. 3. Philadelphia, 1979, J.B. Lippincott.

582 Koss LG. The Papanicolaou test for cervical cancer detection. A triumph and a tragedy. JAMA 1989, **261:** 737–743.

583 Luff RD. The Bethesda System for reporting cervical/vaginal cytologic diagnoses. Report of the 1991 Bethesda workshop. The Bethesda System Editorial Committee. Hum Pathol 1992, **23:** 719–721.

584 Nguyen GK, Nguyen-Ho P, Husain M, Husain EM. Cervical squamous cell carcinoma and its precursor lesions: cytodiagnostic criteria and pitfalls. Anat Pathol 1998, **1:** 139–164.

585 Patten SF. Diagnostic cytology of the uterine cervix. Baltimore, 1969, Williams & Williams.

586 Pirog EC, Baergen RN, Soslow RA, Tam D, DeMattia AE, Chen YT, Issacson C. Diagnostic accuracy of cervical low-grade squamous intraepithelial lesions is improved with MIB-1 immunostaining. Am J Surg Pathol 2001, **26:** 70–75.

587 Ramzy I, Mody DR. Gynecologic cytology. Practical considerations and limitations. Clin Lab Med 1991, **11:** 271–292.

588 Robertson JH, Woodend B. Negative cytology preceding cervical cancer: causes and prevention. J Clin Pathol 1993, **46:** 700–702.

589 Schneider V, Henry MR, Jimenez-Ayala M, Turnbull LS, Wright TC, International Consensus Conference on the fight against cervical cancer, IAC Task Force, Chicago, Illinois, USA. Cervical cancer screening, screening errors, and reporting. Acta Cytol 2001, **45:** 493–498.

590 Seybolt JF. Thoughts on "the numbers game." Acta Cytol (Baltimore) 1968, **12:** 271–273.

591 Seybolt JF, Johnson WD. Cervical cytodiagnostic problems. A survey. Am J Obstet Gynecol 1971, **109:** 1089–1103.

592 Sherman ME, Kelly D. High-grade squamous intraepithelial lesions and invasive carcinoma following the report of three negative Papanicolaou smears. Screening failures or rapid progression? Mod Pathol 1992, **5:** 337–342.

593 Smith JH. Bethesda 2001. Cytopathology 2002, **13:** 4–10.

594 Solomon D. The Bethesda Sytem for reporting cervical/vaginal cytologic diagnosis. An overview. Int J Gynecol Pathol 1991, **10:** 323–325.

595 Solomon D, Davey D, Kurman R, Moriarty A, O'Connor D, Prey M, Raab S, Sherman M, Wilbur D, Wright T Jr, Young N; Forum Group Members; Bethesda 2001 Workshop. The 2001 Bethesda System: terminology for reporting results of cervical cytology. JAMA 2002, 287: 2114–2119.

596 Spitzer M. In vitro conventional cytology historical strengths and current limitations. Obstet Gynecol Clin North Am 2002, 29: 673–683.

597 Stoler MH. Advances in cervical screening technology. Mod Pathol 2000, 13: 275–284.

598 The Bethesda System for reporting cervical/vaginal cytologic diagnosis: revised after the second National Cancer Institute Workshop, April 29-30, 1991. Acta Cytol 1993, 37: 115–124.

599 Wied GL, Legorreta G, Mohr D, Rauzy A. Cytology of invasive cervical carcinoma and carcinoma in situ. Ann NY Acad Sci 1962, 97: 759–766.

600 Wright TC Jr., Cox JT, Massad LS, Twiggs LB, Wilkinson EJ, ASCCP Sponsored Consensus Conference. 2001 Consensus Guidelines for the management of women with cervical cytological abnormalities. JAMA 2002, 287: 2120–2129.

601 Zeng Z, Del Priore G, Cohen JM, Mittal K. MIB-1 expression in cervical Papanicolau tests correlates with dysplasia in subsequent cervical biopsies. Appl Immunohistochem Mol Morphol 2002, 10: 15–19.

Other tumors and tumorlike conditions

602 Abeler V, Kjorstad KE, Langholm R, Marton PF. Granulocytic sarcoma (chlorma) of the uterine cervix. Report of two cases. Int J Gynecol Pathol 1983, 2: 88–92.

603 Abell MR. Papillary adenofibroma of the uterine cervix. Am J Obstet Gynecol 1971, 110: 991–993.

604 Abenoza P, Shek Y, Perrone T. Inflammatory pseudotumor of the cervix. Int J Gynecol Pathol 1994, 13: 80–86.

605 Albores-Saavedra J, Gilcrease M. Glomus tumor of the uterine cervix. Int J Gynecol Pathol 1999, 18: 69–72.

606 Aozasa K, Saeki K, Ohsawa M, Horiuchi K, Mishima K, Tsujimoto M. Malignant lymphoma of the uterus. Report of seven cases with immunohistochemical study. Cancer 1993, 72: 1959–1964.

607 Barua R. Post-cone biopsy traumatic neuroma of the uterine cervix. Arch Pathol Lab Med 1989, 113: 945–947.

608 Bell DA, Shimm DS, Gang DL. Wilms' tumor of the endocervix. Arch Pathol Lab Med 1985, 109: 371–373.

609 Bernstein HB, Broman JH, Apicelli A, Kredentser DC. Primary malignant schwannoma of the uterine cervix: a case report and literature review. Gynecol Oncol 1999, 74: 288–292.

610 Bloch T, Roth LM, Stehman FB, Hull MT, Schwenk GR Jr. Osteosarcoma of the uterine cervix associated with hyperplastic and atypical mesonephric rests. Cancer 1988, 62: 1594–1600.

611 Brand E, Berek JS, Nieberg RK, Hacker NF. Rhabdomyosarcoma of the uterine cervix. Sarcoma botryoides. Cancer 1987, 60: 1552–1560.

612 Cenacchi G, Pasquinelli G, Montanaro L, Cesaroli S, Vici M, Bisceglia M, Giangaspero F, Martinelli GN, Derenzini M. Primary endocervical extaosseous Ewing's sarcoma/PNET. Int J Gynecol Pathol 1998, 17: 83–88.

613 Clark KC, Butz WR, Hapke MR. Primary malignant melanoma of the uterine cervix: case report with world literature review. Int J Gynecol Pathol 2002, 18: 265–273.

614 Clement PB. Miscellaneous primary tumors and metastatic tumors of the uterine cervix. Semin Diagn Pathol 1990, 7: 228–248.

615 Clement PB, Zubovits JT, Young RH, Scully RE. Malignant mullerian mixed tumors of the uterine cervix: a report of nine cases of a neoplasm with morphology often different from its counterpart in the corpus. Int J Gynecol Pathol 1998, 17: 211–222.

616 Copeland LJ, Gershenson DM, Saul PB, Sneige N, Stringer CA, Edwards CL. Sarcoma botryoides of the female genital tract. Obstet Gynecol 1985, 66: 262–266.

617 Copeland LJ, Sneige N, Ordonez NG, Hancock KC, Gershenson DM, Saul PB, Kavanagh JJ. Endodermal sinus tumor of the vagina and cervix. Cancer 1985, 55: 2558–2565.

618 Daya DA, Scully RE. Sarcoma botryoides of the uterine cervix in young women: a clinicopathological study of 13 cases. Gynecol Oncol 1988, 29: 290–304.

619 Deppisch LM. Cervical melanosis. Obstet Gynecol 1983, 62: 525–526.

620 Ferry JA, Young RH. Malignant lymphoma, pseudolymphoma, and hematopoietic disorders of the female genital tract. Pathol Annu 1991, 26(Pt 1): 227–263.

621 Ferry JA, Young RH. Malignant lymphoma of the genitourinary tract. Curr Diagn Pathol 1997, 4: 145–169.

622 Foschini MP, Eusebi V, Tison V. Alveolar soft part sarcoma of the cervix uteri. A case report. Pathol Res Pract 1989, 184: 354–358.

623 Fraga M, Prieto O, Garcia-Caballero T, Beiras A, Forteza J. Myxoid leiomyosarcoma of the uterine cervix. Histopathology 1994, 25: 381–383.

624 Gersell DJ, Fulling KH. Localized neurofibromatosis of the female genitourinary tract. Am J Surg Pathol 1989, 13: 873–878.

625 Gibbons D, Lindberg GM, Ashfaq R, Saboorian MH. Localized amyloidosis of the uterine cervix. Int J Gynecol Pathol 1998, 17: 368–371.

626 Grayson W, Fourie J, Tiltman AJ. Xanthomatous leiomyosarcoma of the uterine cervix. Int J Gynecol Pathol 1998, 17: 89–90.

627 Gwavava NJ, Traub AL. A neurilemmoma of the cervix. Br J Obstet Gynaecol 1980, 87: 444–446.

628 Hanai J, Tsuji M. Uterine teratoma with lymphoid hyperplasia. Acta Pathol Jpn 1981, 31: 153–159.

629 Harris NL, Scully RE. Malignant lymphoma and granulocytic sarcoma of the uterus and vagina. A clinicopathologic analysis of 27 cases. Cancer 1984, 53: 2530–2545.

630 Hirschfield L, Kahn LB, Chen S, Winkler B, Rosenberg S. Müllerian adenosarcoma with ovarian sex cord-like differentiation. Cancer 1986, 57: 1197–1200.

631 Hytiroglou P, Domingo J. Development of melanosis of uterine cervix after cryotherapy for epithelial dysplasia. A case report and brief review of the literature on pigmented lesions of the cervix. Am J Clin Pathol 1990, 93: 802–805.

632 Imachi M, Tsukamoto N, Amagase H, Shigematsu T, Amada S, Nakano H. Metastatic adenocarcinoma to the uterine cervix from gastric cancer. A clinicopathologic analysis of 16 cases. Cancer 1993, 71: 3472–3477.

633 Ishikura H, Kojo T, Ichimura H, Yoshiki T. Desmoplastic malignant melanoma of a uterine cervix: a rare primary malignancy in the uterus mimicking a sarcoma. Histopathology 1998, 33: 93–94.

634 Jones MW, Lefkowitz M. Adenosarcoma of the uterine cervix. A clinicopathological study of 12 cases. Int J Gynecol Pathol 1995, 14: 223–229.

635 Keel SB, Clement PB, Prat J, Young RH. Malignant schwannoma of the uterine cervix: a study of three cases. Int J Gynecol Pathol 1998, 17: 223–230.

636 Khoor A, Fleming MV, Purcell CA, Seidman JD, Ashton AH, Weaver DL. Mature teratoma of the uterine cervix with pulmonary differentiation. Arch Pathol Lab Med 1995, 119: 848–850.

637 Kondi-Pafiti A, Kairi-Vassilatou E, Spanidou-Carvouni H, Kontongianni K, Dimopoulou K, Goula K. Vascular tumors of the female genital tract: a clinicopathological study of nine cases. Eur J Gynaecol Oncol 2003, 24: 48–50.

638 Kristiansen SB, Anderson R, Cohen DM. Primary malignant melanoma of the cervix and review of the literature. Gynecol Oncol 1992, 47: 398–403.

639 Lee JD, Chang TC, Lai YM, Hsueh S, Soong YK. Choriocarcinoma of the cervix. Acta Obstet Gynecol Scand 1992, 71: 479–481.

640 Lemoine NR, Hall PA. Epithelial tumors metastatic to the uterine cervix. A study of 33 cases and review of the literature. Cancer 1986, **57**: 2002–2005.

641 Loughlin KR, Retik AB, Weinstein HJ, Colodny AH, Shamberger RC, Delorey M, Tarbell N, Cassady JR, Hendren WH. Genitourinary rhabdomyosarcoma in children. Cancer 1989, **63**: 1600–1606.

642 Luevano-Flores E, Sotelo J, Tena-Suck M. Glial polyp (glioma) of the uterine cervix. Report of a case with demonstration of glial fibrillary acidic protein. Gynecol Oncol 1985, **21**: 385–390.

643 Malpica A, Moran CA. Primitive neuroectodermal tumor of the cervix: a clinicopathologic and immunohistochemical study of two cases. Ann Diagn Pathol 2002, **6**: 281–287.

644 Mathoulin-Portier MP, Pernault-Llorca F, Labit-Bouvier C, Charafe E, Martin F, Hassoun J, Jacquemier J. Malignant mullerian mixed tumor of the uterine cervix and adenoid cystic component. Int J Gynecol Pathol 1998, **17**: 91–92.

645 Moore WF, Bentley RC, Kim KR, Olatidoye B, Gray SR, Robboy SJ. Goblet-cell mucinous epithelium lining the endometrium and endocervix: evidence of a metastasis from an appendiceal primary tumor through the use of cytokeratin-7 and -20 immunostains. Int J Gynecol Pathol 1998, **17**: 363–367.

646 Murray J, Fox H. Rosai-Dorfman disease of the uterine cervix. Int J Gynecol Pathol 1991, **10**: 209–213.

647 Nielsen GP, Oliva E, Young RH, Rosenberg AE, Dickersin GR, Scully RE. Alveolar soft-part sarcoma of the female genital tract. A report of nine cases and review of the literature. Int J Gynecol Pathol 1995, **14**: 283–292.

648 Patel DS, Bhagavan BS. Blue nevus of the uterine cervix. Hum Pathol 1985, **16**: 79–86.

649 Perren T, Farrant M, McCarthy K, Harper P, Wiltshaw E. Lymphomas of the cervix and upper vagina: a report of five cases and a review of the literature. Gynecol Oncol 1992, **44**: 87–95.

650 Sahin AA, Silva EG, Ordonez NG. Alveolar soft part sarcoma of the uterine cervix. Mod Pathol 1989, **2**: 676–680.

651 Seo IS, Hull MT, Pak HY. Granulocytic sarcoma of the cervix as a primary manifestation. Case without overt leukemic features for 26 months. Cancer 1977, **40**: 3030–3037.

652 Sobel N, Carcangiu ML. Primary pigmented neuroectodermal tumor of the uterine cervix. Int J Surg Pathol 1994, **2**: 31–36.

653 Terzakis JA, Opher E, Melamed J, Santagada E, Sloan D. Pigmented melanocytic schwannoma of the uterine cervix. Ultrastruct Pathol 1990, **14**: 357–366.

654 Tiltman AJ. Leiomyomas of the uterine cervix: a study of frequency. Int J Gynecol Pathol 1998, **17**: 231–234.

655 Tiltman AJ, Duffield MS. Postpartum microneuromas of the uterine cervix. Histopathology 1996, **28**: 153–156.

656 Uehara T, Izumo T, Kishi K, Takayama S, Kasuga T. Stromal melanocytic foci ("blue nevus") in step sections of the uterine cervix. Acta Pathol Jpn 1991, **41**: 751–756.

657 Volpe R, Canzonieri V, Gloghini A, Carbone A. "Lipoleiomyoma with metaplastic cartilage" (benign mesenchymoma) of the uterine cervix. Pathol Res Pract 1992, **188**: 799–801.

658 Yamazawa K, Ishikura H, Matsui H, Seki K, Sekiya S. Sebaceous carcinoma of the uterine cervix: a case report. Int J Gynecol Pathol 2002, **22**: 92–94.

659 Yilmaz AG, Chandler P, Hahm GK, O'Toole RV, Niemann TH. Melanosis of the uterine cervix: a report of two cases and discussion of pigmented cervical lesions. Int J Gynecol Pathol 1999, **18**: 73–76.

660 Young RH, Harris NL, Scully RE. Lymphoma-like lesions of the lower female genital tract. A report of 16 cases. Int J Gynecol Pathol 1985, **4**: 289–299.

661 Zaloudek CJ, Norris HJ. Adenofibroma and adenosarcoma of the uterus. Cancer 1981, **48**: 354–366.

Uterus—corpus

Normal anatomy

The adult nulliparous uterus is a hollow, pear-shaped organ that weighs 40 to 80 g and measures 7 to 8 cm along its longest axis. It is divided into the *cervix* (discussed in the preceding section of this chapter) and the *corpus*. The portion of the corpus cephalad to a line connecting the insertion of the fallopian tubes is the *fundus*. The two lateral regions of the fundus associated with the intramural portion of the fallopian tubes are referred to as the *cornua*. The portion of the corpus that connects with the cervix is called the *isthmus* or *lower uterine segment*.

The uterine cavity has a triangular shape and a length of approximately 6 cm. It is lined by the endometrial mucosa, which constitutes the inner layer (endometrium) of the organ. It is surrounded by a thick muscular layer (myometrium) and a serosal covering, the latter extending to the point of peritoneal reflection (which is lower in the posterior than the anterior aspect).

The uterine lymph vessels drain to a rich network of lymph nodes, the main groups being parametrial and paracervical; internal (hypogastric), external and common iliac; periaortic; and inguinal.

The endometrial mucosa is made up of glands and stroma. It is divided into a deeply seated *basal* layer and a superficial *functional* layer. The basal layer is the equivalent of the reserve cell layer of other epithelia and is responsible for the regeneration of the endometrium following menstruation. It is made up of weakly prolifer-

ative glands and spindled stroma. The functional layer is subdivided into two strata, the *compactum* (toward the surface) and the *spongiosum* (close to the basalis). The stroma is mainly composed of endometrial stromal cells (whose appearance changes considerably during the menstrual cycle, see later section) and vessels (of which the spiral arterioles are the most distinctive). Other components include the stromal granulocyte (thought to be either a subpopulation of either T lymphocytes or macrophages) and inconstant stromal foamy cells (lipid-containing cells of disputed histogenesis).

During child-bearing age, the normal endometrium undergoes a series of sequential changes in the course of the ovulatory cycle that prepare it to receive the ovum[9] (Fig. 19.110). If the ovum is not fertilized, the proliferative endometrium is cast off by menstruation, and the cycle repeats itself. A normal endometrial cycle is associated with changes in both endometrial glands and stroma that allow the pathologist to diagnose microscopically the phase of the menstrual cycle.[14] In a series of classic articles, Noyes et al[15–17] set forth specific criteria by which an accurate dating of the endometrium was made possible (Fig. 19.111 and box).

In general, the changes are quite uniform throughout the functional endometrium.[15] When this is not the case, the dating should be based on the most advanced area rather than on the average morphologic picture.[16] The surface epithelium is less responsive to the hormonal influences than the glandular epithelium. Radioautographic studies have shown that cell proliferation is highest on the eighth to tenth day in the upper third of the functional

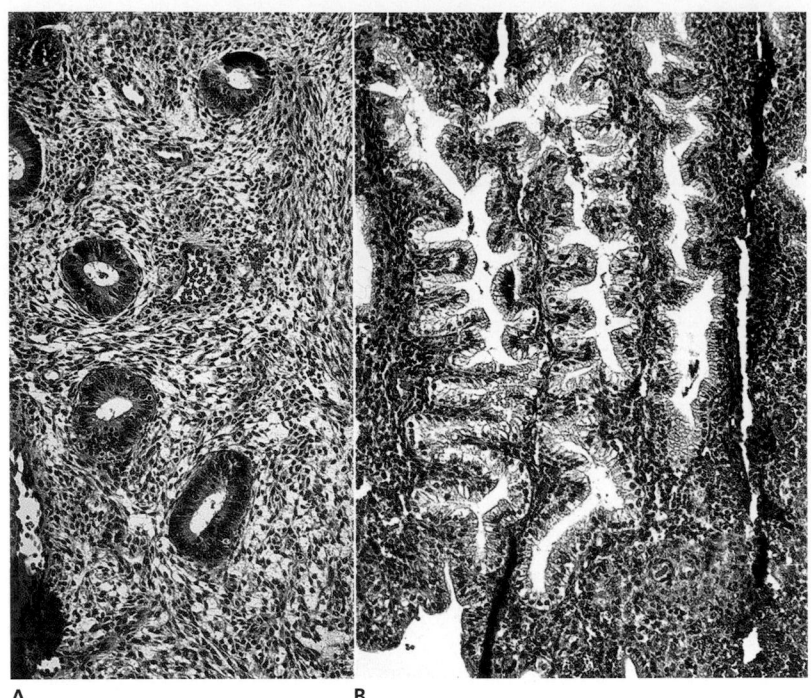

A   B

Fig. 19.110 Normal endometrium: A, proliferative; B, secretory.

Microscopic features for dating endometrium

Proliferative phase

Early (fourth–seventh day)—thin regenerating surface epithelium; straight, short, narrow glands; compact stroma, with some mitotic activity and large nuclei

Mid (eighth–tenth day)—columnar surface epithelium; longer, curving glands; variable amount of stromal edema; numerous mitoses in naked nuclei of stroma

Late (eleventh–fourteenth day)—undulant surface; tortuous glands showing active growth and pseudostratification; moderately dense, actively growing stroma

Secretory phase

36–48 hours after ovulation—no microscopic changes apparent

Sixteenth day—subnuclear vacuolation of epithelium appears

Seventeenth day—orderly row of nuclei with homogeneous cytoplasm above them and large vacuoles below

Eighteenth day—vacuoles decrease in size; nuclei approach base of cell

Nineteenth day—few vacuoles; appearance of intraluminal secretion

Twentieth day—peak of acidophilic intraluminal secretion

Twenty-first day—tissue edema appears rather abruptly

Twenty-second day—edema reaches its peak

Twenty-third day—spiral arterioles become prominent

Twenty-fourth day—collections of predecidual cells appear around arterioles

Twenty-fifth day—predecidua appears under surface epithelium

Twenty-sixth day—predecidua appears as solid sheet of well-developed cells; polynuclear cell infiltration appears

Twenty-seventh day—polynuclear infiltration becomes prominent; areas of focal necrosis and hemorrhage begin to appear

Twenty-eighth day—necrosis and hemorrhage prominent

layer and that it decreases to nearly zero levels by the nineteenth day.[8] For subnuclear vacuolation to be regarded as evidence of ovulation, it should be present in at least 50% of the functional glands present in the section. A markedly compact stroma may simulate predecidua. One of the earlier signs of the menstrual phase (and also of pathologic crumbling of the stroma) is the presence of nuclear dust at the base of the glandular epithelium.[7] Neutrophils, which are seen in large numbers in areas of tissue degradation (beginning on day 26) are very rare during the other days of the cycle; they should be distinguished from the already mentioned stromal granulocytes, which do not stain for chloroacetate esterase.[18]

The nuclear crowding, squamoid appearance, and focal cytoplasmic acidophilia seen in late menstrual and postcurettage specimens should not be confused with a malignant or other pathologic process. The possibility of overdiagnosis is even greater in the rare instances in which the menstrual endometrium is seen within the lumen of blood vessels.[4] It should be noted that endometrial tissue can also be found in myometrial vessels independently from menstruation.[19]

The basal layer of the endometrium is not subject to the influence of progesterone. Therefore, if biopsies are taken in the premenstrual phase for evidence of secretory activity (ovulation) and contain only the basal layer, a proper evaluation cannot be made. Similarly, the mucosa of the lower uterine segment responds only sluggishly to the hormonal stimulations and should be disregarded for dating purposes.[8] This mucosa gradually merges with that of the endocervix; the hybrid endometrial–endocervical appearance of both glands and stroma allows its recognition in D&C specimens.

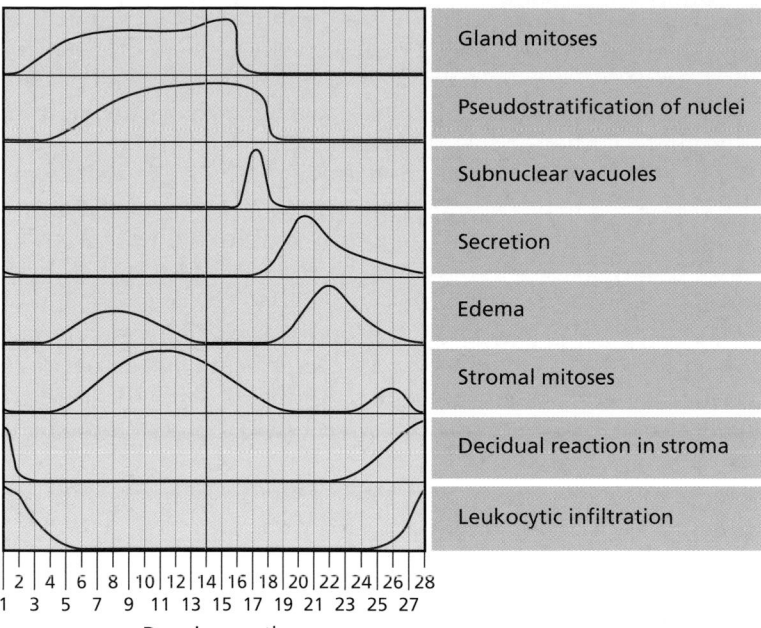

	Gland mitoses
	Pseudostratification of nuclei
	Subnuclear vacuoles
	Secretion
	Edema
	Stromal mitoses
	Decidual reaction in stroma
	Leukocytic infiltration

2 4 6 8 10 12 14 16 18 20 22 24 26 28
1 3 5 7 9 11 13 15 17 19 21 23 25 27
Days in month

Fig. 19.111 Cyclic changes in endometrium. Approximate relationship of useful microscopic changes. (After Latour, from the classic article by Noyes RW, Hertig AT, Rock J. Dating the endometrial biopsy. Fertil Steril 1950, **1**: 3–25)

Biopsies to determine anovulatory cycles are most informative when performed approximately 2 days before the expected onset of menstruation.

The reappearance of glandular secretion and stromal edema once predecidual reaction is established—leading to the simultaneous presence of these three features in an endometrial specimen—is evidence that a fertilized ovum has implanted; this pattern is referred to as *gestational hyperplasia*.[10] An exaggerated expression of this phenomenon is the *Arias-Stella reaction*, in which secretory or proliferative changes in the endometrial glands are accompanied by prominent nuclear changes, manifested by hyperchromasia and marked enlargement (Fig. 19.112). Normal and abnormal mitoses may also be present.[2] These changes are almost always focal and may also occur in the cervix, endocervical polyps, adenomyosis, and endometriosis.[1] They are more often seen in postabortion curettings (present in 20 to 70% of cases and

persisting for weeks), but they are also seen in normal orthotopic or ectopic pregnancies, hydatidiform mole, choriocarcinoma, and (very rarely) following the administration of exogenous hormones.[3,6,11] In hydatidiform mole and choriocarcinoma, the nuclei of the endometrial cells may attain gigantic sizes. The most important differential diagnosis is with so-called in situ and clear cell types of endometrial adenocarcinoma.

Another interesting pregnancy-related endometrial alteration (often associated with the Arias-Stella reaction) is the focal appearance of optically clear nuclei in the glandular cells, simulating viral inclusions; these are due to the replacement of normal chromatin by a fine filamentous network that is immunoreactive for biotin.[12,20,21]

Exceptionally, decidual reaction is seen in the postmenopausal endometrium in the absence of an exogenous or endogenous source of progesterone excess.[5]

The myometrium has a rich network of vessels in its midportion; this landmark, which can be recognized grossly, has been used to subdivide the uterine wall into subvascular, vascular, and supravascular regions. A peculiar vascular architecture sometimes encountered in the myometrium is that of arteries apparently free-floating within cleft-like spaces, which have been interpreted as venous channels.[13]

Curettage and biopsy

Tissue from the endometrial cavity taken for diagnostic purposes has been traditionally obtained by *dilatation* of the cervical canal and *curettage* of the endometrial cavity (D&C). As a sampling technique, it is unsurpassed. If properly performed, very few endometrial lesions (perhaps only those located deep in a cornu) should escape

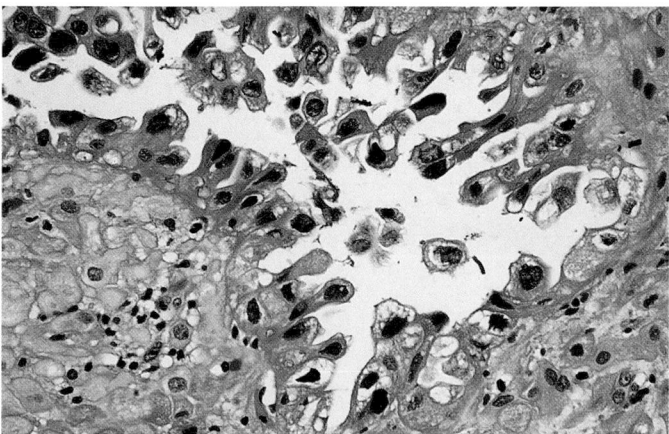

Fig. 19.112 Arias-Stella reaction in endometrial mucosa. This is not to be confused with a malignant condition.

detection. It has been regarded for a long time as the method of choice for the detection and typing of lesions presumed to be localized, such as polyps and carcinoma.[29] Information about endocervical extension of an endometrial neoplasm can be obtained by performing a *fractional curettage* (i.e., a separate sampling from the endometrial and endocervical cavities during the same procedure). The endocervical specimen should be obtained first so as to minimize contamination from the endometrium. However, even when this precaution is taken, small isolated tumor fragments may be found in endocervical specimens in cases without actual infiltration of the cervix. Therefore, it is our policy to report the presence of endocervical extension of a tumor *only* if cancer and normal endocervical glands are seen *in the same fragment*. Otherwise, we simply record the presence of carcinoma in the material submitted from the endocervix and let the clinician decide whether this is significant on the basis of the findings at the time of curettage.

Regeneration of the endometrium proceeds very rapidly after curettage. Complete restoration occurs in 2 or 3 days in most instances.[30] Exceptionally, intrauterine adhesions develop, resulting in amenorrhea and other menstrual abnormalities. This condition, known as *Asherman's syndrome*, is seen most often after postpartum or postabortal curettages and is thought to be the result of a subclinical uterine infection.[23,26]

Endometrial biopsy is a safe alternative to D&C for the evaluation of infertile or dysmenorrheic patients.[22,27] In addition, this procedure (as carried out with various suction devices) has become the choice method for the initial approach to patients with suspected endometrial hyperplasia or carcinoma.[24] Kahler et al.,[28] in a pioneer study of 160 patients, demonstrated that, when the endometrial biopsy was performed successfully (137 patients), the tissue obtained was truly representative of the endometrium in all but six, as proved by subsequent D&C or hysterectomy. Furthermore, no endometrial carcinoma was missed when sufficient tissue was obtained. A meta-analysis study with the use of the Pipelle showed a detection rate for endometrial adenocarcinoma of 99.6% in postmenopausal women and 91% in the premenopausal group.[25] Another issue is the accuracy of the grading of endometrial carcinoma done in a biopsy when compared with that seen in the hysterectomy specimen. In one study, the concordance was 45% for grade I, 63.3% for grade II, and 75.6% for grade III, the overall concordance being 64.5%.[31]

Effects of hormone administration

Estrogen therapy

Exogenous administration of estrogen preparations exposes the cycling or postmenopausal endometrium to a potent stimulus.[39] Endometrial hyperplasia is present in 15% to 30% of postmenopausal women receiving estrogen therapy alone, with some of the cases having an atypical pattern.[33,38,40] Furthermore, several case-control population studies have linked the exogenous administration of estrogens to the subsequent appearance of endometrial adenocarcinoma.[32,34] The risk is said to be four to eight times greater in this population.[36,41] The addition of progestin to the medication protects the endometrium and reduces the incidence of hyperplasia and carcinoma.[37]

Fortunately, the large majority of these tumors are well differentiated and superficial and are associated with an excellent prognosis compared with those occurring in postmenopausal women unexposed to exogenous estrogens.[35]

Progestational agents

Owing to the widespread use of progestational agents for therapeutic and contraceptive purposes, a new endometrial morphology has emerged.[44,48] The pathologist should be thoroughly familiar with the variety of changes that the "pill" may induce in the endometrium in order not to confuse them with pathologic conditions. The effect of these agents is exerted on the glands and stroma and differs more according to the regimen used than to the actual drug employed.[47] In the *combined program*, pills of the same mixture, representing a combination of progestogen and estrogen, are taken on consecutive days. They can be administered *continuously* for therapeutic purposes or *cyclically* (for 20 or 21 days with 7-day or 8-day intervals) for contraception or therapy.[44] In the *sequential program*, no longer used, predominantly estrogenic pills were taken for 14 to 16 days followed by progestin-dominant pills for 5 or 6 days. The changes described are those to be expected in a previously normal endometrium.

In the **continuous combined program**, the glands are small, straight, and inactive, with no mitoses or secre-

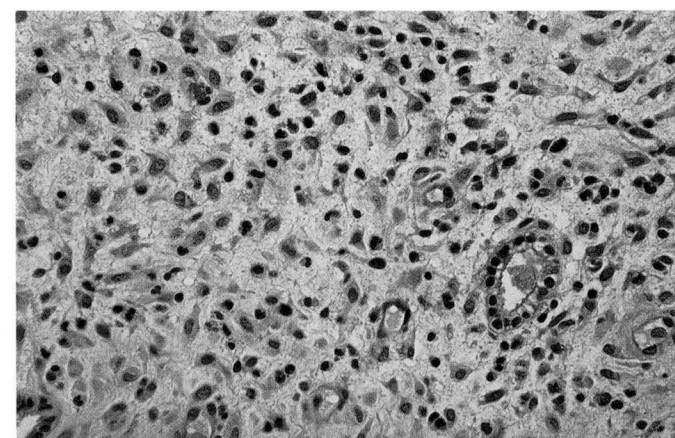

Fig. 19.113 Typical appearance of endometrium after long-term administration of contraceptive pills. The glands are sparse and atrophic, whereas the stroma is prominent and has decidual features.

tion. The stroma is very prominent and edematous, is infiltrated by some neutrophils, and shows striking pseudodecidual changes[42] (Fig. 19.113). The latter, which may appear as fragments of frankly necrotic decidua, are distinguished from the decidua of pregnancy by the completely atrophic glandular pattern. The stromal reaction can be very florid. Foci of endometriosis respond in a similar manner. This must be kept in mind whenever lesions of any pelvic organ are being evaluated microscopically, especially by frozen section.

In the **cyclic combined program**, the glands show little or no evidence of proliferation. There is a short, poorly developed stage of secretory activity, reaching a peak around the fourteenth or fifteenth day, followed by regression of the glands.[49] Pseudodecidual changes appear in the stroma around the twentieth day of the cycle (fifteenth day of treatment). Development of spiral arterioles is inhibited. After prolonged therapy, glandular secretion and stromal pseudodecidual changes become inconspicuous or recede altogether. The stroma acquires an atrophic, fibroblast-like appearance and may form characteristic small polypoid projections covered by atrophic surface epithelium. On very rare occasions, focal glandular changes of the Arias-Stella type may appear in patients taking contraceptive pills. In most cases, discontinuation of the hormones results in a restoration of a normal endometrial pattern in a matter of weeks.

The **sequential program** more nearly parallels the normal cycle and results in a somewhat similar endometrial morphology.[46] The glands show signs of proliferation, followed by tortuosity and the appearance of well-developed secretory changes. The stroma shows inconspicuous pseudodecidual changes. Thus the endometrial morphology on the twenty-sixth day of a cycle induced by sequential therapy (the day after treatment is completed) is roughly analogous to that of the eighteenth or nineteenth day of a normal menstrual cycle. Regressive changes and crumbling of stroma, resulting in withdrawal bleeding, occur soon thereafter.

The sequential program was discontinued in the United States and Canada in 1976 because of several reports suggesting that it promoted the development of endometrial adenocarcinoma.[43,51,52] This complication is probably not the direct result of the hormones being administered sequentially but rather a result of the difference in net estrogenic effect with the combined preparations. Most of these tumors are well differentiated and very superficial, and the prognosis generally has been good.

There are other complications resulting from the prolonged use of contraceptive pills, regardless of the program used. Early studies in England and in the United States have shown an increased incidence of thrombophlebitis and pulmonary embolism.[50,53] Morphologically, the vascular changes are widely distributed and involve arteries and veins. They include thrombi and intimal thickening with endothelial proliferation.[45]

With present regimens, the incidence of these complications has decreased substantially.

Tamoxifen

Tamoxifen is a synthetic anti-estrogen used in the treatment of breast carcinoma. It has an anti-estrogenic effect on the endometrium when competing with ovarian estrogen secretion, but also a paradoxical estrogenic effect in the absence of ovarian estrogen secretion.[56,59] It is associated with an increased frequency of proliferative endometrial lesions, including hyperplasias, polyps, and malignant tumors,[55,57] but the latter are not seen often enough to justify routine endometrial biopsies in this population.[54]

According to Kennedy et al.,[58] the most characteristic features of tamoxifen-associated endometrial lesions are polarized glands along the long axis of polyps, a cambium layer, frequent and diverse metaplasias, staghorn glands, small glands, and myxoid degeneration. They felt that none of these features was diagnostic, but that their combined presence strongly suggested tamoxifen exposure. In terms of special studies, tamoxifen-associated endometrial adenocarcinomas are said to be characterized by a lower expression of estrogen receptor-alpha, higher expression of progesterone receptor, and more frequent expression of estrogen receptor-beta than spontaneous tumors.[59a]

Endometritis

Acute endometritis is usually seen in association with abortion, the postpartum state, or instrumentation. Gonococcal endometritis is rarely seen by the pathologist because of its very transient nature. It should be remembered that neutrophils are normally present in the endometrium on days 26, 27, and 28.[92]

Chronic endometritis, characterized by an infiltrate of lymphocytes and plasma cells, may follow pregnancy or abortion, be the result of an intrauterine device (IUD), or be accompanied by mucopurulent cervicitis and/or pelvic inflammatory disease (PID).[90,94] If the diagnosis is suspected clinically, cultures should be taken. The most common symptoms are vaginal bleeding and pelvic pain.[94] It should be emphasized that lymphoid follicles, with or without germinal centers, are a normal occurrence in the functional layers of the endometrial mucosa and, therefore, should not be considered as evidence of chronic endometritis. Actually, some authors believe that they are more common in normal than in abnormal endometria.[97] Therefore, identification of plasma cells constitutes the most important criterion for the diagnosis of chronic endometritis, whether by conventional criteria or—as suggested by some—by immunostaining the sections for immunoglobulins,[71] CD38,[84] VS38,[84] or syndecan-1[62] (Fig. 19.114).

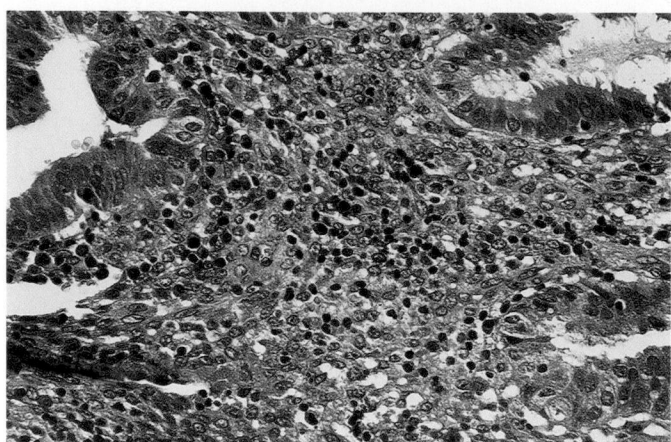

Fig. 19.114 Chronic endometritis showing an inflammatory infiltrate rich in lymphocytes and plasma cells.

The possibility of inflammation should be suspected—and plasma cells searched for—whenever there is an absence of a normal cyclic pattern, a focal mononuclear infiltrate, inflammatory cells in the glandular lumina, dense stroma, a stellate stromal pattern of proliferation, or foci of necrosis or calcification (Fig. 19.115). Glandular alterations commonly accompany the inflammatory reaction, to the point that endometrial dating becomes impossible. The presence of neutrophils in the endometrial surface is a good predictor of PID, especially if combined with plasma cells in the endometrial stroma.[83]

The myometrium is usually spared in most types of endometritis (sarcoidosis excluded) unless the inflammation is very severe.

Intrauterine devices inserted for the purpose of contraception result in many biologic changes.[70,99] In an old series, only 29% of symptomatic patients and 40% of asymptomatic patients with a polyethylene IUD had a normal endometrial appearance on biopsy.[88] The most common change is focal or extensive chronic endometri-

tis, which may be accompanied by necrosis and squamous metaplasia.[93,96] On occasion, the inflammation spreads through the fallopian tubes to produce PID and sometimes tubo-ovarian abscesses.[102,104] One of the agents involved in the inflammatory process is *Actinomyces*[65,68,87] (Fig. 19.116). The organisms can be detected in microscopic sections or in cytology preparations,[78] but care should be exercised in distinguishing them from pseudoactinomycotic radiate granules; the latter lack central branching filaments and diphtheroid forms.[66]

Pyometra refers to the accumulation of pus within the endometrial cavity. It is the consequence of the combined effect of obstruction and infection. Whiteley and Hamlett[105] reviewed 35 cases in postmenopausal patients. Only five were secondary to carcinoma; the remaining 30 were the result of benign cervical stricture originating from senile atresia, surgery, or cauterization.

Hematometra is the accumulation of blood within the endometrial cavity, usually as a result of cervical occlusion. This may lead to the disappearance of the endometrial mucosa and its replacement by sheets of lipid-containing histiocytic cells, a process known as *histiocytic* or *xanthogranulomatous endometritis* when diffuse and as *nodular histiocytic hyperplasia* when localized[67,82]; these are not to be confused with the more common histiocytic reaction seen in the stroma of endometrial adenocarcinomas, whether spontaneously or following irradiation.[95]

Sometimes the histiocytes are found to contain a yellowish-brown cytoplasmic pigment, in which case the term *ceroid-containing histiocytic granuloma* has been used.[98]

Endometrial tuberculosis is rare in the United States but still common in other parts of the world. Menstrual disturbances are common. The microscopic diagnosis is based on the demonstration of acid-fast bacilli in tuber-

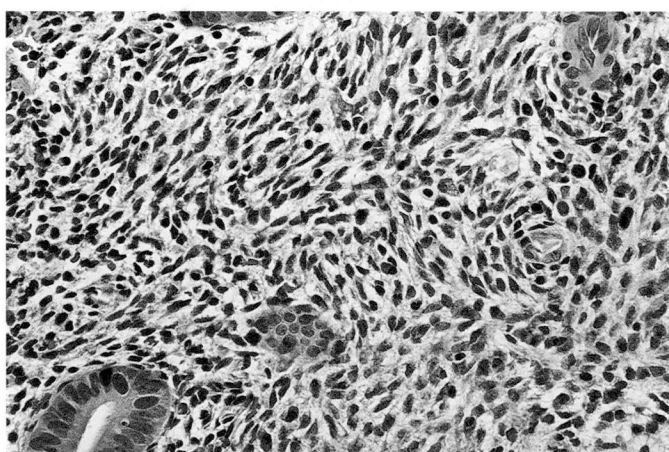

Fig. 19.115 The oval to spindle and occasionally stellate shape of endometrial stromal cells is a clue to the diagnosis of chronic endometritis.

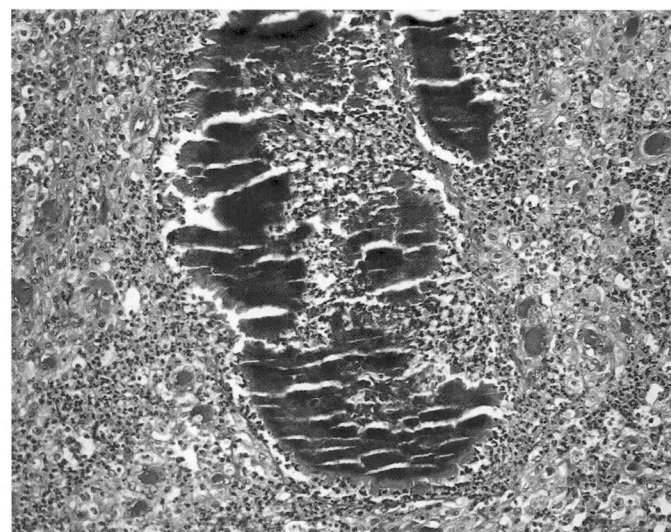

Fig. 19.116 IUD-related uterine actinomycosis. The disease had spread to the pelvic cavity.

cles or culture. The presence of plasma cells and leukocytes probably results from secondary infection.[77] Tubercles may be missed unless multiple levels of curettings are examined. Since the granulomas tend to concentrate in the superficial functional layers of the endometrium, it is recommended that the biopsy be taken during the late secretory phase.

Chlamydial infection is now recognized as a major sexually transmitted disease; cases associated with endometritis have been identified through the immunohistochemical demonstration of chlamydial antigens in endometrial epithelial cells[89,106] or by PCR.[101] These cases are associated with severe acute and/or chronic inflammation. Plasma cells tend to be very numerous; as a matter of fact, it has been proposed that the presence of these cells is linked to *Chlamydia* infection.[91]

Viral infection of the endometrium is probably more common than generally suspected. Cytomegalovirus endometritis and diffuse papillomatosis (condyloma) have both been documented[72,103]; the former can have a granulomatous quality.[75]

Coccidioidomycosis of the uterus has been reported in the United States in a few cases as a localized infection; it probably results from a clinically inapparent and completely resolved primary lung infection.[69,79]

Focal necrotizing endometritis is the name that has been proposed for a patchy necrotizing endometrial process seen in premenopausal women and devoid of plasma cells; it remains to be seen whether this is a bona fide entity.[64]

Postoperative granulomas of the endometrium have been described following endometrial ablation procedures; they may be thought of as the female counterpart of those seen in the prostate or bladder following TUR.[60,100]

Malakoplakia of the endometrium has been reported, sometimes in a recurrent fashion and sometimes in association with endometrial adenocarcinoma.[86]

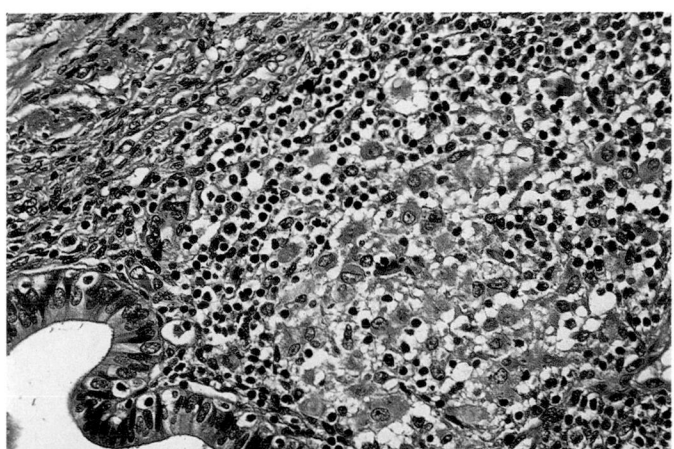

Fig. 19.117 Noncaseating granuloma in endometrial mucosa consistent with sarcoidosis.

Sarcoidosis of the uterus occurs, but it remains a diagnosis of exclusion[80] (Fig. 19.117). In contrast to tuberculosis, the granulomatous reaction usually spreads to the myometrium.[73] Granulomatous endometritis can also follow hysteroscopic resection of the endometrium.[61]

Giant cell arteritis may involve the uterus and other female genital organs of elderly women, either as an isolated finding or as part of a generalized process.[63,74,76] The former event is more frequent than the latter,[76] but sometimes female genital tract disease is the first manifestation of systemic periarteritis nodosa.[85]

Follicular myometritis has been described as a component of inflammatory pelvic disease.[81]

Metaplasia

The endometrial glands and stroma are subject to a variety of metaplastic changes, many of them hormonally induced. They are often accompanied by hyperplastic changes in the endometrial glands but can occur independently from them and, therefore, need to be evaluated separately. They should not be regarded by themselves as evidence for the existence of a neoplastic process. At the same time, it should be realized that endometrial metaplasias, like endometrial hyperplasias, tend to be associated with endometrial adenocarcinoma and that they are more common in populations at high risk for the development of endometrial carcinoma (such as those in the United States) than in low-risk populations (such as those in Japan).[118] An unexpected and somewhat perplexing finding is the presence of p53 overexpression—as detected immunohistochemically—in a significant number of metaplasias of various morphologic subtypes, albeit in a weak and heterogeneous fashion.[121] These metaplasias include:

1　**Squamous metaplasia.** This can be encountered in normal or hyperplastic endometrium, sometimes in association with leiomyoma or uterine polyps.[111] Frank keratinization is very rare (*ichthyosis uteri*). A more common finding is the presence of nonkeratinizing squamoid cells occurring either diffusely (adenoacanthosis)[112] or in the form of berry-like aggregates (morules)[114] (Fig. 19.118A,B). Most are seen in premenopausal women, in those receiving exogenous hormones, or in association with polycystic ovarian disease.[110,119] This change is distinguished from well-differentiated endometrial adenocarcinoma with squamous metaplasia ("adenoacanthoma") because of the benign appearance of the glandular elements.[116]

2　**Ciliated cell (tubal) metaplasia.** Scattered ciliated cells are normally present in the endometrial mucosa; when markedly increased in number, the appearance resembles that of a fallopian tube, and the term listed above is used[125] (Fig. 19.119). Ciliated cell metaplasia

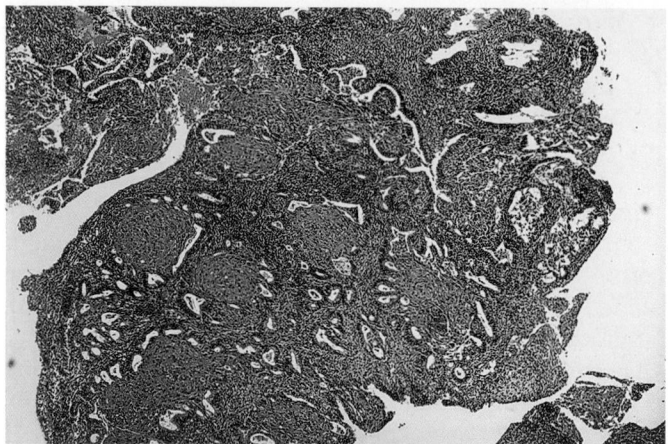

A

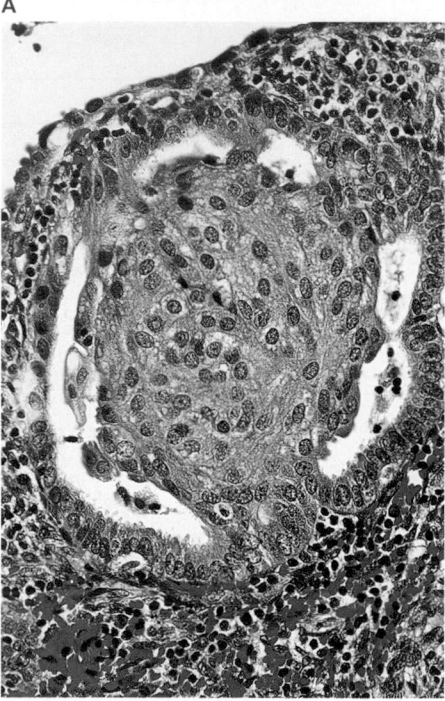

B

Fig. 19.118 A and **B**, Squamous metaplasia of endometrium with morule formation.

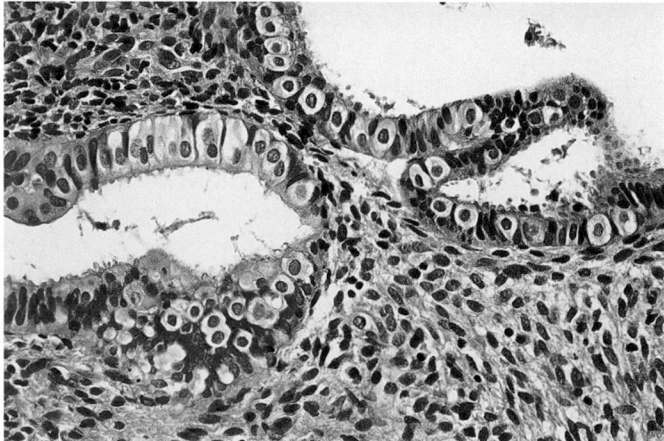

Fig. 19.119 Tubal metaplasia of endometrial mucosa. All three cell types that make up the normal mucosa of the fallopian tube can be recognized.

may be seen in an otherwise normal organ but occurs more commonly in the setting of endometrial hyperplasia.

3 **Papillary metaplasia** (syncytial papillary hyperplasia, papillary syncytial change). This alteration is characterized by the presence of syncytial to papillary aggregates of eosinophilic cells along the surface epithelium (Fig. 19.120). It is often seen in association with prolonged estrogen stimulation.[122] It has been variously regarded as a metaplastic change, a hyperplastic change, and a retrogressive alteration associated with acute endometrial breakdown.[115,129]

4 **Mucinous metaplasia.** In this condition, the endometrial mucosa reverts to a pattern morphologically, histochemically and ultrastructurally similar to that of the endocervical mucosa[113,124] (Fig. 19.121). The main differential diagnosis is with the mucinous variant of endometrial adenocarcinoma.[120]

5 **Eosinophilic (oxyphilic; oncocytic) metaplasia.** This is another estrogen-induced lesion, characterized by strong acidophilia of the cytoplasm.[107] It is distinguished from atypical endometrial hyperplasia and the exceptionally rare oncocytic carcinoma by the absence of atypical nuclear features.[116,117,126]

6 **Hobnail and clear cell (mesonephric or mesonephroid) metaplasia.** In these closely related metaplastic changes, the epithelium is clear, with tall cells having apically located nuclei (Fig. 19.122). The differential diagnosis is with clear cell (mesonephroid) adenocarcinoma).[117]

7 **Intestinal metaplasia.** In this exceptionally rare form, the endometrium resembles intestinal mucosa.[128]

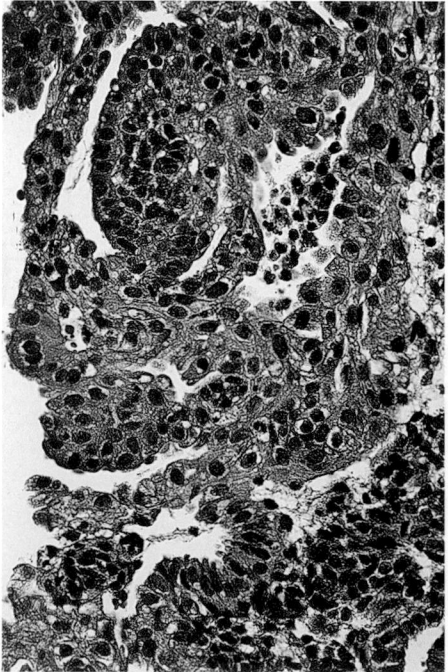

Fig. 19.120 Papillary (syncytial) metaplasia of endometrium.

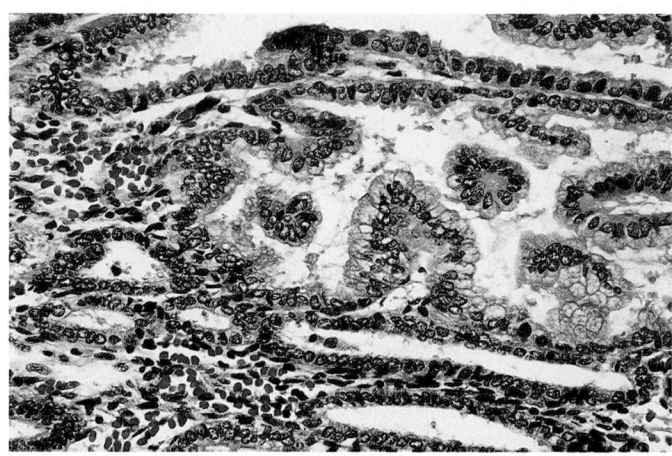

Fig. 19.121 Mucinous metaplasia of endometrium. Note the basal location of the nuclei and the mucin-containing cytoplasm of the columnar cells.

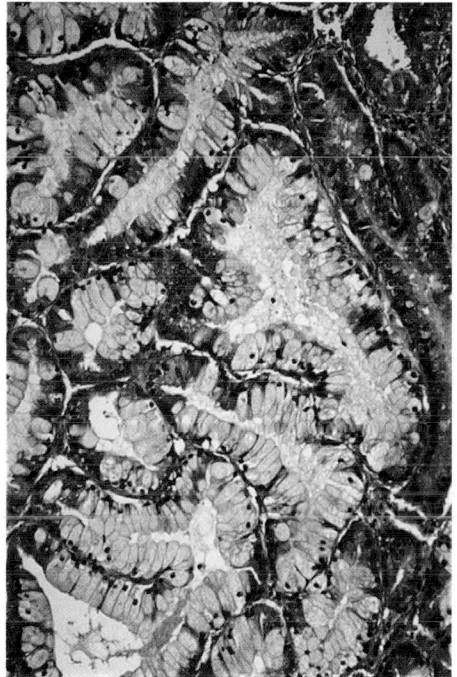

Fig. 19.122 Clear cell metaplasia of endometrium. The cytoplasm has a finely granular quality.

8 Stromal metaplasia. This includes the formation within the endometrial stroma of islands of smooth muscle,[109] cartilage,[123] and bone.[108] It should be noted that in some instances the presence of cartilage or bone is the result of retained fetal parts.[127]

Adenomyosis and endometriosis

Adenomyosis refers to the presence of islands of endometrial glands and stroma deep within the myometrium, whereas *endometriosis* is the term employed for the occurrence of endometrial tissue outside the uterus. These two disorders are usually regarded as closely related, but their microscopic appearance—and probably their pathogenesis—is somewhat different. Furthermore, they often occur independently of each other. In most cases, adenomyosis is made up of the nonfunctional (basal) layer of the endometrium, is sometimes (and perhaps frequently) connected with the mucosa, and has been viewed by some as representing a complex form of endometrial diverticulosis. Endometriosis, on the other hand, is composed of the functional layers of the endometrium. As such, it goes through proliferative, secretory, and menstrual changes similar to those of its orthotopic counterpart. However, studies using conventional morphologic techniques, immunohistochemistry, and cell proliferation markers have shown that the endometriotic lesions are consistently more proliferative than the normally located endometrium, both during the menstrual cycle and in postmenopause.[133,149,172] Accordingly, markers associated with the secretory phase (such as CD44s) tend to be decreased in these lesions.[160] Adenomyosis is rare in postmenopausal women, except for the tamoxifen-associated cases, which tend to show stromal fibrosis, glandular dilatation, and various metaplastic changes.[155]

Many pathogenetic theories have been proposed over the years for endometriosis: origin from congenital müllerian or wolffian rests, implantation of endometrium (spontaneous or induced by hysterosalpingography), lymphatic or hematogenous spread, and serosal metaplasia.[151] Different pathogenetic routes may be operative depending on the nature and location of the lesion, but a metaplastic change of the secondary müllerian system represented by the pelvic mesothelium is probably the most common and important mechanism.[159] Interestingly, endometriotic cysts have been found to be clonal on evaluation of X-chromosome inactivation.[171]

Both endometriosis and adenomyosis may result in pelvic pain, characteristically associated with the menstrual period. Between 30 and 40% of women with endometriosis are infertile, but the exact mechanism remains obscure. Exceptionally, adenomyosis may lead to rupture at the time of pregnancy.

Adenomyosis results grossly in an enlarged and globular uterus because of the myometrial hypertrophy that regularly accompanies it.[139,153] The diagnosis may be suspected on cut section in the presence of depressed small cystic lesions in obvious but ill-defined bulging zones of muscle hypertrophy (Fig. 19.123). In elderly women, the uterus may appear atrophic despite extensive adenomyosis. Leiomyomas in uteri with adenomyosis may themselves be involved by the process.

Microscopically, the diagnosis of adenomyosis depends on the thresholds used by the individual pathologist, some of which are very liberal indeed.[166] The interphase between endometrium and myometrium is normally an irregular one, without interposition of a

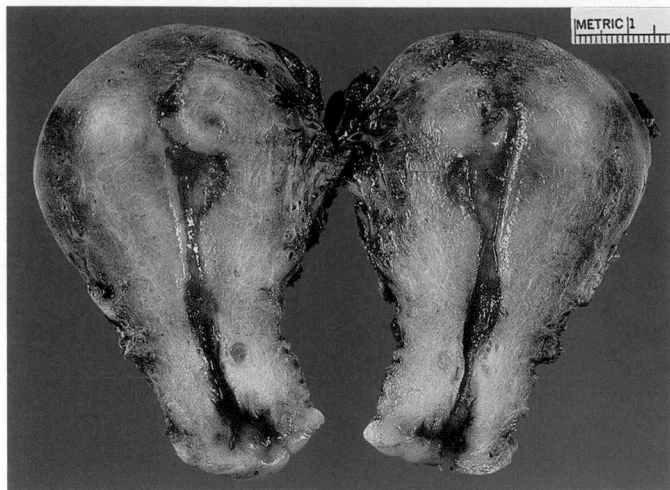

Fig. 19.123 Gross appearance of uterus involved by adenomyosis. The wall is irregularly thickened and contains small hemorrhagic foci.

submucosal layer; invaginations of the endometrial basal layer into the superficial portions of the myometrium should be regarded as a normal finding. By convention, the diagnosis of adenomyosis should be reserved for those cases in which endometrial glands and stroma are seen in the myometrium at a distance of at least one low-power field from the endometrial–myometrial junction (Fig. 19.124).

Microscopically, the endometrium of adenomyosis usually has a proliferative appearance, consistent with its basal layer nature. When the normally located endometrium is in the secretory phase, this is also true for one fourth of the foci of adenomyosis.[156] These foci can be involved by any of the diseases affecting the orthotopic endometrium, including hyperplasia and adenocarcinoma.[173] It is important to recognize this phenomenon, lest a case of in situ or superficial endometrial adenocarcinoma associated with similar changes in the foci of adenomyosis be misinterpreted as a deeply inva-

sive malignancy.[144] Some small islands of adenomyosis are made up predominantly of endometrial stroma (*stromal adenomyosis, incomplete adenomyosis* or *adenomyosis with sparse glands*)[133a] (Fig. 19.125); however, any sizable intramyometrial focus composed entirely of endometrial stroma is likely to represent an endometrial stromal sarcoma.[143]

Endometriosis is thought to occur in 1% to 7% of women in the United States.[132,162] It can be located in the cervix, vagina, vulva, rectovaginal septum, ovary, fallopian tubes, uterine ligaments, appendix, small and large bowel, bladder and ureters, pelvic peritoneum, hernia sacs, lymph nodes, kidney, and skin, and even within skeletal muscles, peripheral nerves, pleura, lung, and nasal cavity (Figs 19.126 and 19.127). The specific features as they pertain to the various sites are discussed in the respective chapters. Spontaneous cutaneous endometriosis is limited to the umbilicus and inguinal area.[169] In other locations, such as the lower abdominal wall, it practically always arises in surgical scars (particularly those from cesarean sections).

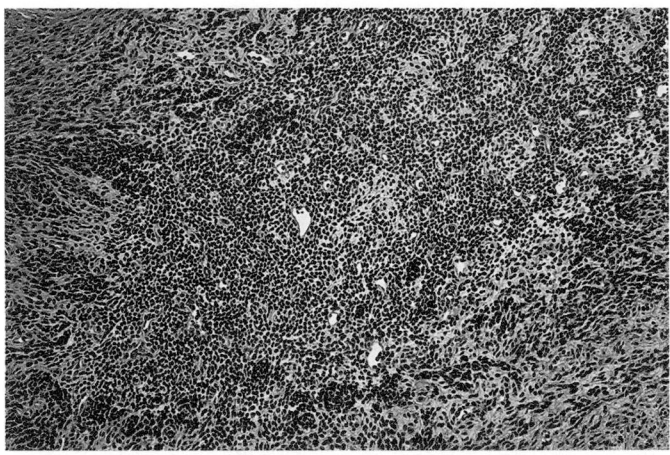

Fig. 19.125 So-called "stromal adenomyosis." An ill-defined island of endometrial stroma is deeply embedded within the myometrium.

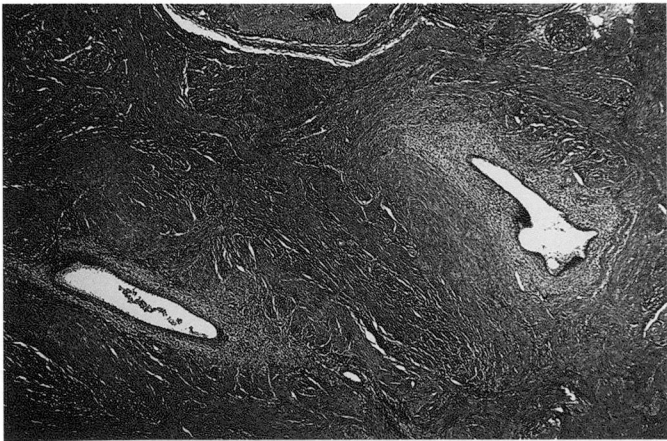

Fig. 19.124 Intramyometrial foci of endometrial glands and stroma in adenomyosis.

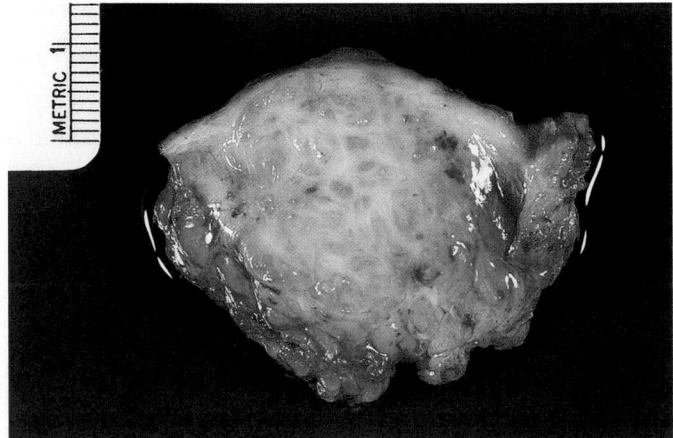

Fig. 19.126 Gross appearance of endometriosis involving the anterior abdominal wall.

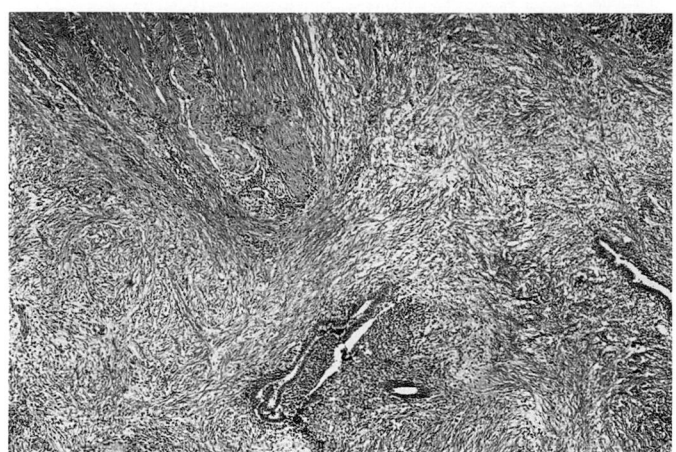

Fig. 19.127 Endometriosis involving the umbilical region.

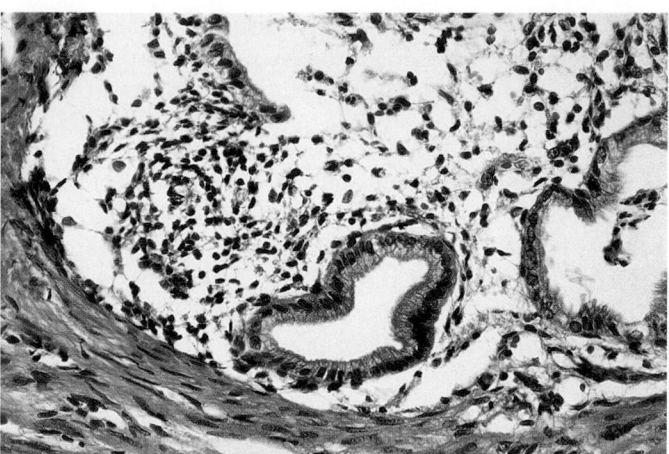

Fig. 19.128 So-called "endocervicosis." The stroma has an endometrium-like quality, but the glands are of endocervical type.

Grossly, endometriosis appears as bluish cystic nodules, often surrounded by fibrosis. Exceptionally, it may present as multiple polypoid masses grossly simulating a neoplastic process (*polypoid endometriosis or endometriotic polyposis*).[157]

Microscopically, endometrial glands and stroma are seen, often embedded in a dense fibrous mass exhibiting signs of fresh and old hemorrhage.[136] The stromal component of endometriosis can undergo smooth muscle metaplasia.[141] Along those lines, it is still being argued whether the nodular lesion resembling a miniature uterus, which can be found in several places within the peritoneal cavity, is a peculiar variant of endometriosis with smooth muscle metaplasia of the stroma or a malformation of the müllerian ducts.[130,146]

Other morphologic variations of endometriosis, some of which can be of confusing interpretation, include a micronodular stromal form, stromal elastosis, prominent myxoid changes, and perineurial invasion.[137,138a,164] Endometriotic foci can undergo prominent mucinous metaplasia, a change that can result in a mistaken diagnosis of well-differentiated mucinous adenocarcinomas. Such change has been interpreted as a metaplasia toward endocervical-type epithelium and designated as *endocervicosis*[136] (Fig. 19.128).

Although well-documented cases of endometriosis of lymph nodes exist, most cases so designated are made up of glands lined by ciliated or nonciliated cuboidal epithelium unaccompanied by stroma, limited to the capsule or cortical area of the node[140]; as such, they are more reminiscent of fallopian tube than endometrial epithelium and are better designated as *endosalpingiosis*. They have been found in approximately 14% of nodes in females but practically never in males.[147]

Endosalpingiosis is particularly frequent in the pelvic peritoneum in connection with ovarian surface tumors and is discussed on page 1678. It can also present in the form of a florid cystic mass and involve the uterine wall in a transmural fashion.[138]

The combination of endometriosis with endocervicosis and/or endosalpingiosis is sometimes referred to as müllerianosis.[167]

Endometriosis, like adenomyosis, is subject to any of the metaplastic, hyperplastic, and atypical changes that may supervene in the orthotopic endometrium.[142,165] More importantly, it may undergo malignant transformation.[145,148] The most common forms are endometrioid and clear cell carcinoma,[134,157,170] but endometrial stromal sarcoma and malignant mixed müllerian tumor have also been reported.[131,135]

Benign and borderline tumors of either serous or endometrioid nature can also develop, both from conventional endometriosis and from endosalpingiosis.[154,158,161,163]

The most common sites for endometriosis-related neoplasms are ovary, pelvic peritoneum, rectovaginal septum, and intestinal wall.[168,170]

The treatment of endometriosis may be hormonal or surgical depending on the circumstances.[150] It is believed that the laparoscopic ablation of minimal and mild endometriosis enhances fecundity in infertile women.[152]

Dysfunctional uterine bleeding and hyperplasia

Normal menstruation is defined as the bleeding from secretory endometrium—associated with an ovulatory cycle—not exceeding a length of 5 days. Any bleeding not fulfilling these criteria is referred to as an **abnormal uterine bleeding**. Some of these are the result of an identifiable lesion, such as endometriosis, submucous myoma, endometrial polyp, or cancer, particularly in the postmenopausal patient. In most series, approximately 5% to 15% of the cases of postmenopausal bleeding are due to endometrial carcinoma and a similar proportion to endometrial polyps.[202,213] The only finding on D&C in over half of postmenopausal bleeders is an atrophic endometrium[185]; vascular degenerative changes in the uterine blood vessels have been suggested as a possible etiology in these cases.[204]

Bleeding not associated with an organic cause in women of child-bearing age belongs to the large and somewhat nebulous category known as **dysfunctional uterine bleeding**. Examination of specimens obtained on D&C or endometrial biopsy is a continuous source of frustration for the pathologist. Sometimes, provided with minimal clinical information or material taken at an inappropriate moment in the menstrual cycle, one is unable to recognize any abnormality. At most, changes can be detected that only confirm what the gynecologist already knows—i.e., that the patient has an abnormal bleeding. These include the presence of fibrin clumps in the endometrial stroma (a finding not usually present in the normal menstrual endometrium),[214] the identification of fragmented pieces with dense stromal cellularity (a process known as *stromal crumbling*), and the presence of an increased number of apoptotic bodies at the base of the glands.[220]

On the other hand, if a thorough clinical study is available, examination of a correctly timed biopsy can be quite informative.[186,187] Cases of dysfunctional uterine bleeding can be divided into two large categories: those associated with ovulation and the more numerous ones in which ovulation has not occurred. A hybrid group in which ovulatory and anovulatory cycles alternate is frequently seen in premenopausal patients.

In the ovulatory group, bleeding may occur because of an *inadequate proliferative phase*. This is recognized by a disparity between the endometrial pattern observed and that expected from the time of the cycle (i.e., an endometrium chronologically in the fourteenth day with a morphologic appearance suggestive of the fourth to seventh day) or by the fact that the morphologic signs of proliferation (such as pseudostratification of nuclei or mitotic activity) are inconspicuous.

Bleeding resulting from an *inadequate secretory phase* (underdeveloped secretory endometrium, luteal phase inadequacy) is recognized by analogous criteria. Traditionally, it has been recommended that the curetting or biopsy should be obtained on the twelfth postovulatory day or 2 days prior to the expected menstruation, but some authors believe that an earlier biopsy taken on the seventh or eighth postovulatory day may be more informative.[184,206] According to Noyes,[212] biopsies should be taken of at least two menstrual cycles, and both the basal temperature shift and the onset of succeeding menses should be used as points of reference to time the length of the secretory phase. The "date" obtained from the endometrial biopsy should be more than 2 days retarded before the diagnosis of underdeveloped secretory endometrium is entertained. A minor accompanying morphologic change that has been described is the pres-ence of elongated, hyperchromatic nuclei in the glandu-lar cell.[222] Hormone administration often corrects this defect.[192,206]

Another type of defect seen in the ovulatory group of bleeders is known as *irregular shedding of the endometrium*. The term refers to a regularly recurring menorrhagia in which the bleeding phase of the cycle requires 7 days or more for completion, without subse-quent prolongation of the cycle. This is due to a lag in the shedding of the secretory endometrium, which is normally completed by the fourth day of menstrua-tion.[203] The tissue should be obtained 5 or more days after the onset of menstrual bleeding, the diagnosis depending on the detection of retained secretory endometrium in addition to fragmented menstrual and/or early proliferative endometrium.

The term *membranous dysmenorrhea* is given to a rare condition characterized by the painful passage of an endometrial cast of the uterus during the first few days of menstruation. This cast has the microscopic appear-ance of decidua. The disease is thought to result from a hyperprogestational response and may be induced by the administration of high doses of progesterone.[195]

An *anovulatory cycle* can be recognized, at its earliest stage, by finding a proliferative endometrium at a time of the cycle when a secretory pattern would be expected. Most commonly, the prolonged unremitting estrogen stimulation results in **endometrial hyperplasia**. All gra-dations of this phenomenon occur, ranging from one distinguished only with difficulty from a normal exu-berant proliferative endometrium (so-called *disordered proliferative endometrium*) to an atypical one that app-roaches the appearance of adenocarcinoma.[208] Many classifications of endometrial hyperplasia have been pro-posed over the years (see box on p. 1581). The one that is currently preferred and which has been sanctioned by the World Health Organization (WHO) was originally proposed by Kurman and Norris.[200] It takes into account both the architectural and cytologic features, in the sense of dividing the hyperplasias into *simple* and *complex* on the basis of the architecture, and subdividing each into *typical* and *atypical* on the basis of their cytology (Fig. 19.129A to C). This classification scheme has been criti-cized on the basis of its complexity and poor reproducibility index.[217,226] The alternative proposal is to reduce the four categories to two. The first is endometrial hyperplasia, viewed as a benign lesion, easily treated with hormones, and with a negligible risk for the devel-opment of carcinoma; the second (called endometrial neoplasia by one group and endometrial intraepithelial neoplasia by another) is regarded as a premalignant condition with a high risk (approximately 30%) of trans-formation into an invasive carcinoma.[181,188,207] The WHO committee that met in 2002 acknowledged the criticisms of the Kurman–Norris scheme, but felt that no other classification system is ready to replace it at present. A

Comparison of some proposed classifications of endometrial hyperplasia
Campbell and Barter (1961)[183]
Benign hyperplasia
Atypical hyperplasia, type I
Atypical hyperplasia, type II
Atypical hyperplasia, type III
Beutler, Dockerty, and Randall (1963)[182]
Cystic proliferation
Glandular hyperplasia
Glandular hyperplasia with atypical epithelial proliferation
Gusberg and Kaplan (1963)[196]
Mild adenomatous hyperplasia
Moderate adenomatous hyperplasia
Marked adenomatous hyperplasia
Gore and Hertig (1966)[194]
Cystic hyperplasia
Adenomatous hyperplasia
Anaplasia
Carcinoma in situ
Vellios (1972)[223]
Cystic hyperplasia
Adenomatous hyperplasia
Atypical hyperplasia
Tavassoli and Kraus (1978)[221]
Cystic hyperplasia
Adenomatous hyperplasia
Atypical hyperplasia
Hendrickson and Kempson (1980)[197]
Hyperplasia
Without atypia
With mild atypia
With moderate atypia
With severe atypia
Kurman and Norris (1986)[200]
Hyperplasia
Simple
Complex
Atypical hyperplasia
Simple
Complex

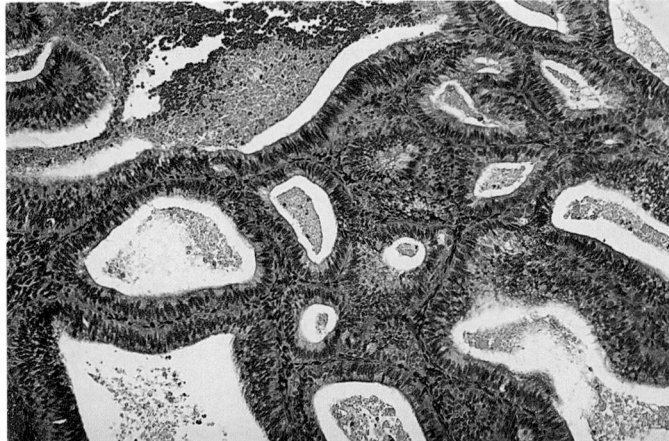

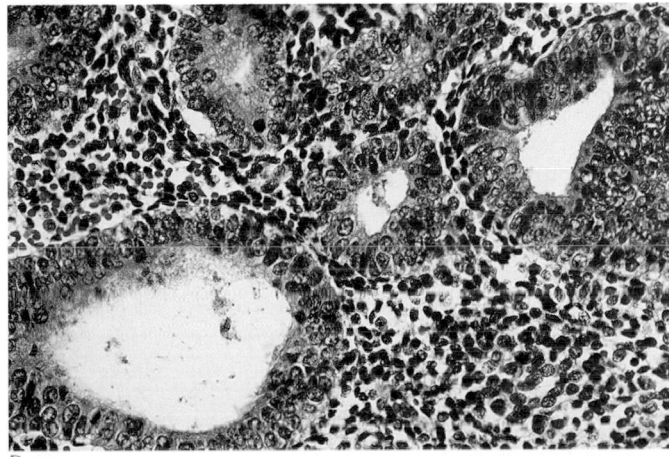

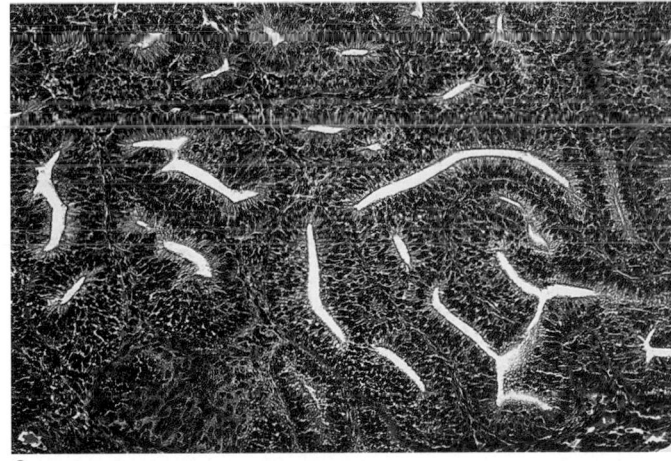

Fig. 19.129 Various types of endometrial hyperplasia: **A**, simple without atypia; **B**, simple with atypia; **C**, complex.

particular concern of the panel was that the category of simple atypical hyperplasia was poorly reproducible and of rare occurrence; however, the decision was made to retain it.[209]

Regardless of the classification scheme used, a comment should be made on the significance of *cystic* endometrial glands, in the sense that they are not necessarily diagnostic of hyperplasia. To be sure, they have traditionally been associated with the form of hyperplasia called simplex in the WHO scheme (the old "swiss cheese" hyperplasia). However, some cystic endometrial glands are not hyperplastic, and some are downright atrophic, as confirmed by MIB-1 staining.[175] The latter condition, known as *cystic endometrial atrophy*, was referred to in the past as "retrogressive hyperplasia",

under the impression that it represented the end stage of a previous cystic hyperplasia.

Endometrial hyperplasia is most commonly seen during the perimenopausal period. However, it can also be encountered in younger patients, even adolescent ones.[201] Some of these develop as the result of estrogenic stimulation in Stein–Leventhal syndrome and in estrogen-secreting ovarian neoplasms.

The distinction between a case of severe hyperplasia and a well-differentiated adenocarcinoma can be very difficult, largely because of the fact that endometrial hyperplasia and carcinoma represent different points in a disease continuum at the morphologic, ultrastructural, immunocytochemical, and molecular genetic levels.[179,190,193,197,218] Microscopic features favoring carcinoma include marked pleomorphism with loss of polarity, complex ramification of disorderly arranged glands, extensive papillary formations, confluent glandular pattern with a solid or cribriform appearance, and desmoplastic stroma (Table 19.1).[198,199,211,215,216] Fox and Buckley[191] have remarked on the importance of true intraglandular cellular bridges devoid of stromal support and the presence of neutrophils and nuclear debris within glandular lamina. Whether quantitative morphology (particularly nuclear morphometry), immunohistochemistry, flow cytometry, or other techniques will assist or replace conventional morphology in this difficult problem remains to be seen.[176–178,189,205,210]

In a frequently quoted study, Gore and Hertig[194] designated an endometrial pattern characterized by endometrial glands composed of large cells with abundant eosinophilic cytoplasm as *carcinoma in situ*. Since the assumption that this change inevitably progresses to invasive adenocarcinoma has never been proved and since this alteration has, on occasion, been reversed by hormone manipulations,[219] this and similar patterns[174,219] are now regarded by most as morphologic variants of endometrial hyperplasia with or without associated metaplastic changes.[211,221] Indeed, it is not unusual to see metaplastic changes of various types (squamous, ciliated, clear cell, and others) superimposed on a picture of endometrial hyperplasia. As already stated (see p. 1575), it is important for them to be evaluated separately and for the hyperplasia to be classified independently from them.

An endometrium does not necessarily become hyperplastic because it contains a metaplastic change; similarly, a hyperplastic endometrium does not become necessarily malignant because it is accompanied by focal metaplasia of squamous or some other type. Another lesion that is sometimes confused with hyperplasia (and which may actually represent a localized hyperplastic process) is adenomatous polyp, a lesion recognized by its dense fibrotic stroma and thick-walled vessels[225] (see p. 1583).

The term **atypical secretory hyperplasia** has been applied to a pattern of architectural abnormalities and cellular atypia within a secretory endometrium, with the atypical glands resembling those seen in the sixteenth to seventeenth day of the normal cycle.[180,224] This change should be distinguished from the Arias-Stella reaction and from hormonally treated conventional endometrial hyperplasia. The natural history of this condition is not well known. Judging from our experience, it would seem that a conservative therapeutic approach is justified.

Relationship with carcinoma

The relationship between hyperplasia and carcinoma has been a hotly debated subject.[232,236,237,241] On the basis of the considerable collective experience that has accumulated on the subject, the following statements can be safely made:

1 Most cases of endometrial carcinoma of the endometrioid type are preceded by a stage of hyperplasia. This is especially true in the younger woman and/or in cases of the better differentiated tumors, in which this sequence approaches 100%. In the classic series of Hertig and Sommers,[233] published in 1949, *all* patients with endometrial adenocarcinoma who had adequate material from curettage examined 15 years or less before the development of adenocarcinoma had an abnormal endometrial pattern.

Table 19.1 Differential microscopic criteria between endometrial hyperplasia and adenocarcinoma

Microscopic criteria	Adenomatous hyperplasia	Atypical hyperplasia	Adenocarcinoma
Nuclei			
Profiles	Smooth and oval	Irregular	Irregular
Size	Uniform	Large, variable	Large, variable
Nucleoli	Small, round	Large, irregular	Large, irregular, spiculated
Mitoses	Numerous in stroma and glands	Numerous	Variable
Cytoplasm	Abundant, amphophilic	Sometimes scant; may be very abundant, with dense eosinophilia	Scant, pale, amphophilic
Glands			
Lining epithelium	Tall columnar, single layered	Stratification, loss of polarity	Loss of polarity
Profiles	Dilated, irregular, with outpouching and infoldings	Irregular, with intraglandular tufting *but no bridging*	Irregular, with cribriform pattern and intraglandular bridging
Size	Variable	Variable	Variable
Stroma	Usually abundant, cellular	Scant, with crowding	Scant

Adapted from Tavassoli F, Kraus FT. Endometrial lesions in uteri resected for atypical endometrial hyperplasia. Am J Clin Pathol 1978, **70**: 770–779.

2 Overall, relatively few patients with hyperplasia will subsequently develop cancer. Therefore, the mere presence of hyperplasia is not a basis for hysterectomy.

3 The more severe the hyperplasia, the more likely it is to be followed by carcinoma.[238] This is particularly true in regard to the *cytologic* changes, even if these assume even greater significance when coupled with *architectural* changes.[234] This correlation has been demonstrated both using conventional morphologic evaluation and with morphometric techniques.[227]

In the case of simple hyperplasia (which is often accompanied by cystic changes), the risk is very small. Thus, in an old series of 544 premenopausal women followed for periods ranging up to 24 years, less than 0.4% developed carcinoma.[235] Conversely, the incidence of carcinoma in women with complex and atypical hyperplasia has been in the neighborhood of 15% and has reached 30% in some series.[228,229,231,234] Tavassoli and Kraus[230] analyzed the pathologic findings in 48 hysterectomy specimens resected usually within 1 to 6 months after a diagnosis of atypical endometrial hyperplasia (including so-called "adenocarcinoma in situ") had been made in a curettage specimen. Lesions interpreted as well-differentiated adenocarcinomas were found in 12 instances (25%). In only one case was there myometrial extension, and this measured only 2 mm. Persistent hyperplasia was found in most of the other cases. The authors concluded that, although atypical endometrial hyperplasia poses a threat of carcinoma, this can easily be eliminated by either medical (progestogen therapy) or surgical (hysterectomy) means. The great efficacy of hormonal therapy in controlling most cases of endometrial hyperplasia and in avoiding hysterectomy in surgically high-risk postmenopausal patients has been repeatedly demonstrated.[230,239]

Tumors

Endometrial polyps

The large majority of endometrial polyps are not true neoplasms but probably represent circumscribed foci of hyperplasia, possibly due to a decreased expression of hormone receptors in the stromal component.[254] Grossly, they protrude into the endometrial cavity and often exhibit secondary changes (Fig. 19.130). The glands usually show some degree of cystic change. They may be lined by an active pseudostratified epithelium containing mitotic figures or, in the postmenopausal patient, by a flat, inactive epithelium (Fig. 19.131).

The glands and stroma of the polyp are unresponsive to progesterone stimulation and retain their integrity throughout the menstrual cycle. In material obtained from D&C, where usually only fragments of the polyp are obtained, the distinction with endometrial hyperplasia is made by examining the stroma. In the latter condition,

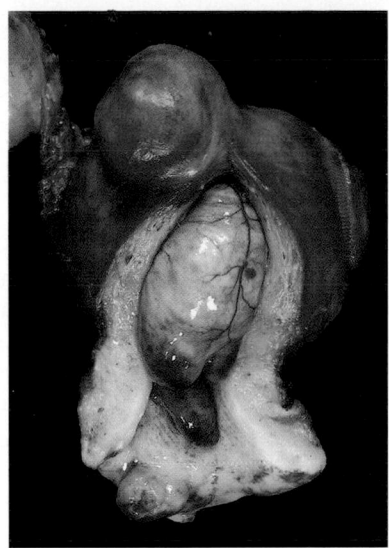

Fig. 19.130 Huge endometrial polyp filling the endometrial cavity. There is also a smaller endocervical polyp and a subserosal leiomyoma. (Courtesy of Dr Pedro J Grases Galofrè; from Grases Galofrè PJ: Patologia ginecològic. Bases para el diagnòstico morfològico, Barcelona, Masson, 2002.)

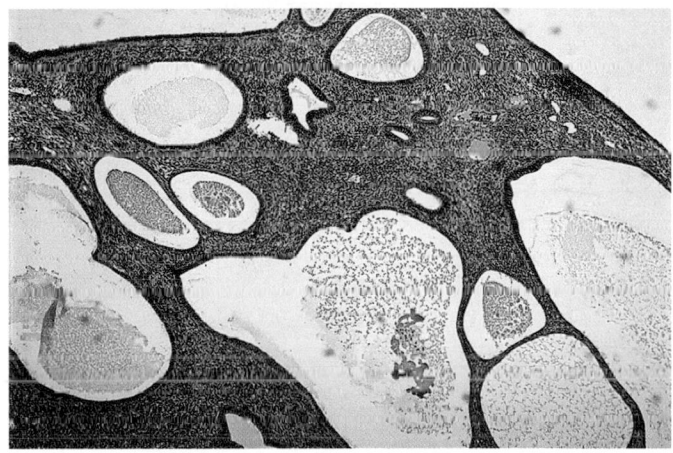

Fig. 19.131 Low-power appearance of endometrial polyp showing cystically dilated glands and a fibrous stroma with thick-walled vessels.

the stromal cells are active, with large vesicular nuclei and occasional mitotic figures, whereas the stroma of a polyp is composed of spindle (fibroblast-like) cells, contains abundant extracellular connective tissue, and has large blood vessels with thick walls. On occasion, however, the stroma is more cellular and mitotically active, i.e., similar to that of endometrial hyperplasia.[248] Some polypoid lesions exhibit either simple or complex hyperplastic papillary endometrial proliferations, and it is a matter of individual choice whether to regard them as localized forms of endometrial hyperplasia or endometrial polyps with hyperplastic changes.[250] Furthermore, endometrial polyps with a typical appearance often coexist with endometrial hyperplasia. All of these observations point to a shared pathogenesis for these two lesions.

Exceptionally, endometrial polyps contain scattered atypical (bizarre) stromal cells.[244,257]

Endometrial polyps occur with increased frequency after tamoxifen exposure. These are characteristically multiple, large and fibrotic, and may exhibit stromal decidualization and mucinous metaplasia[243,249,255] (Fig. 19.132A,B) (see p. 1573). At the molecular level, they are said to exhibit a higher frequency of k-*ras* mutations.[247a]

Rarely, polyps composed of functional endometrium are encountered. The diagnosis is made on the gross features of the lesion rather than on the microscopic pattern of glands and stroma and is, therefore, difficult or even impossible to make on a D&C specimen.

Malignant transformation of endometrial polyps is an exceptional but well documented occurrence. Some of these cases present in the form of in situ or invasive serous carcinomas[252a] (see also p. 1586).

Endometrial polyps having smooth muscle fibers (not connected with blood vessel walls) in addition to the customary glands and stroma are designated as **adenomyomatous polyps** (polypoid adenomyomas).[247] They have a characteristic hard consistency and a grayish color (Fig. 19.133A,B). An important variation on the theme is the **atypical polypoid adenomyoma** (atypical polypoid adenomyofibroma).[251,252,258] These tend to occur in premenopausal women (average age, 40 years) and present with abnormal uterine bleeding (Fig. 19.134). Some are associated with Turner's syndrome.[242] Microscopically, they are identified by the fact that the glands occurring between the endometrial stroma and smooth muscle exhibit varying degrees of hyperplasia and atypia, sometimes approaching the appearance of carcinoma in situ ("of low malignant potential") (Fig. 19.135A,B).[251] The danger is to misdiagnose them as adenocarcinomas with myometrial invasion. The behavior is generally benign, but cases have been seen with local recurrences, carcinomatous transformation,[246,256] and coexistent endometrial or ovarian endometrioid carcinoma.[245,253]

At the molecular level, atypical polypoid leiomyomas share several alterations with complex glandular hyperplasias.[254a]

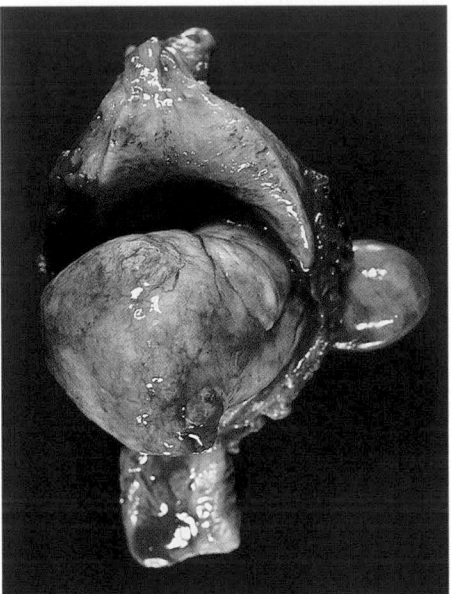

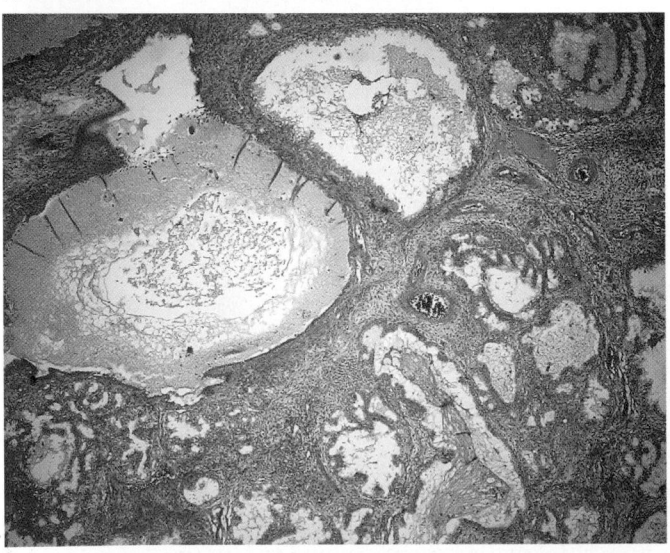

Fig. 19.132 Tamoxifen-related endometrial polyp: **A**, gross appearance; **B**, microscopic appearance.

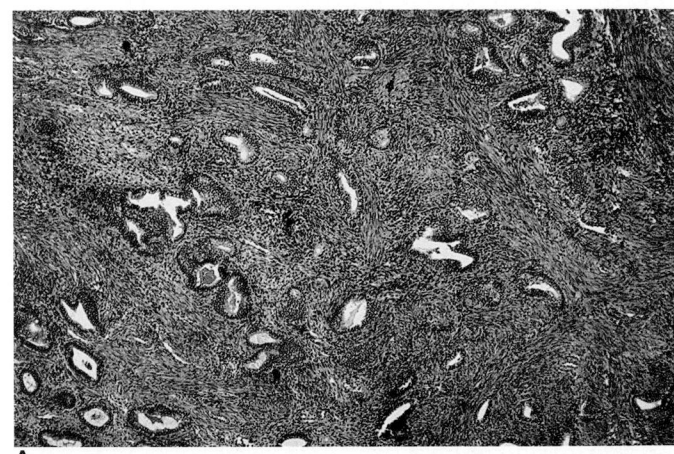

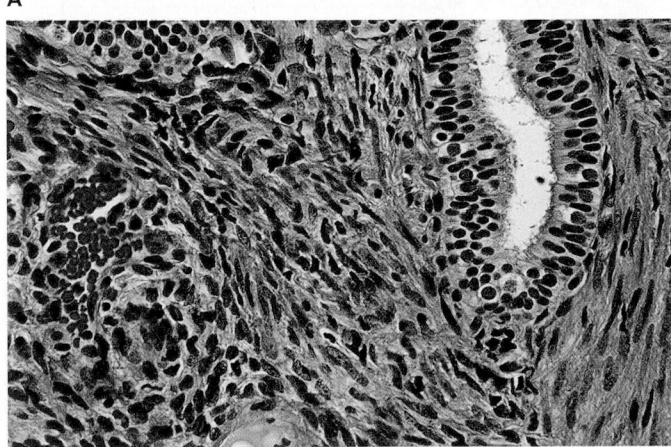

Fig. 19.133 A and **B**, Low- and high-power appearance of adenomyomatous polyp.

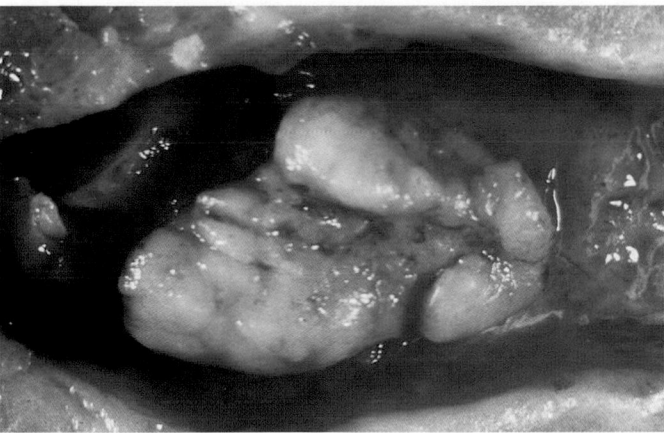

Fig. 19.134 Atypical polypoid adenomyoma. The gross appearance is not substantially different from that of an ordinary polyp.

Endometrial carcinoma

General and clinical features

Carcinoma of the endometrium is the most common gynecologic malignancy in developed countries.[279] The highest incidence rates are in the United States and Canada, but in recent years there has been a decline in incidence and mortality. It typically occurs in elderly individuals, 80% of the patients being postmenopausal at the time of diagnosis.[274] However, it can occur in any age group and has even been reported in association with intrauterine pregnancy.[275]

It is currently believed that endometrial carcinoma can be divided in two distinct types on the basis of their pathogenesis: one—by far the more common—occurring as a result of excess estrogenic stimulation and developing against a background of endometrial hyperplasia[267] and the other developing de novo.[259,262,278] Patients at high risk for the first category include the obese, diabetic, hypertensive, and infertile; those with failure of ovulation (including Stein–Leventhal syndrome) and dysfunctional bleeding; longstanding estrogen users; breast cancer patients treated with tamoxifen (see below); those with severe degrees of endometrial hyperplasia; and—to a much lesser degree—those with functioning granulosa cell tumors and thecomas.[266,272,276]

In the majority of patients with Stein–Leventhal syndrome, the endometrial pathology is that of hyperplasia and, as such, it will regress with medical therapy.[268] However, a few well-documented cases of carcinoma have been reported; these have almost always been of a well-differentiated nature, and myometrial invasion, if present at all, has been minimal. It has been pointed out that the lesion may be reversible when treated by curettage followed by therapy directed toward reestablishment of ovulation, and a conservative approach to these patients has been recommended.[264] In support of this policy, it has been pointed out that not a single case of well-differentiated adenocarcinoma in a patient with

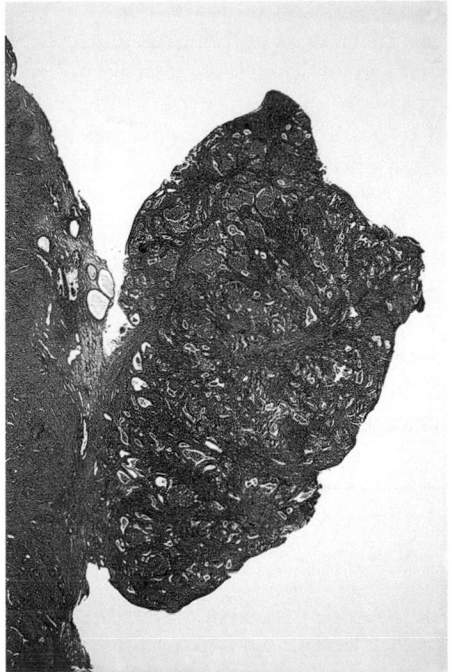

A

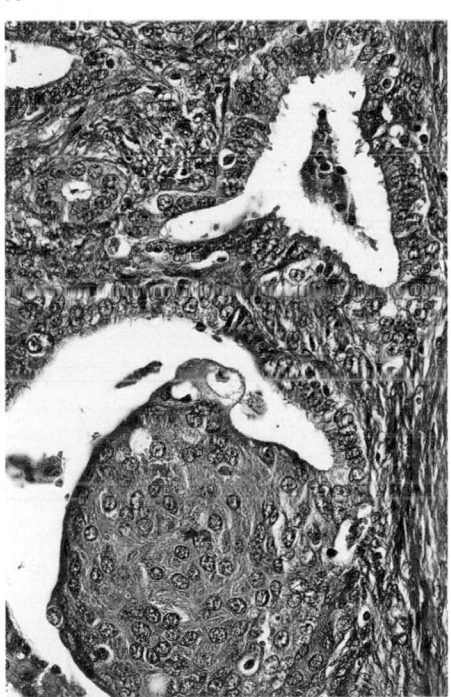

B

Fig. 19.135 A and **B**, Whole-mount and high-power appearance of atypical polypoid adenomyoma. Note the glandular architectural complexity, metaplastic changes, and atypia.

Stein–Leventhal syndrome has been proved to metastasize, recur locally, or cause death. The situation is quite similar regarding the relationship between endometrial pathology and functioning ovarian tumors (see p. 1698).

Gonadal dysgenesis (Turner's syndrome) can also be associated with endometrial adenocarcinoma, usually of the well-differentiated type. McCarty et al.[269] found 13 reported cases; 11 patients had received replacement estrogen therapy, usually in high doses and for prolonged periods. It is not clear whether this association represents a complication of long-term estrogen exposure or a rare expression of the Turner phenotype. Interestingly, almost two thirds of the carcinomas exhibited squamous differentiation.[260]

Some cases of endometrial carcinoma, of either endometrioid or papillary serous types, have been seen years after pelvic irradiation for some other condition, but whether these are spontaneous or radiation-induced is not clear.[271,273]

Patients who receive tamoxifen as long-term treatment for breast carcinoma are at an increased risk for the development of endometrial adenocarcinoma[261,265]; of particular concern is the fact that in two series a significant number of these cases were high-grade tumors associated with a poor prognosis.[263,270,277]

Pathologic features

Grossly, carcinoma of the endometrium may form broad-based polypoid masses or infiltrate diffusely into the myometrium (Fig. 19.136A,B). In general, extensive myometrial invasion is accompanied by clinically detectable uterine enlargement. However, notable exceptions occur; sometimes deep myometrial extension is accompanied by a normal-sized uterus, the pattern of growth resembling that of adenoma malignum of cervix.[299] This pattern has also been described as "minimal deviation invasive."[295]

Endometrial carcinoma can develop in any anatomic region of the mucosa. Tumors developing in younger women have a greater tendency to involve the lower uterine segment (isthmus).[288] Parenthetically, tumors thought to have arisen in the isthmus are included among the endometrial rather than the cervical carcinomas.[293] Small carcinomas restricted to a cornu can be missed by a biopsy or even a D&C.

Microscopically, approximately 80% of endometrial malignant epithelial tumors are conventional adenocarcinomas, which are usually divided into well (grade I, 50%), moderately (grade II, 35%), and poorly differentiated (grade III, 15%) tumors (Fig. 19.137A to C). The FIGO 3-grade system is primarily based on the growth pattern (relative proportion of glandular and solid areas), but it also makes provisions for nuclear atypia.[306] An alternative 2-grade system (low grade and high grade), mainly based on architectural criteria, has been recently proposed.[297]

The better differentiated tumors closely recapitulate the light and electron microscopic features of the non-neoplastic endometrium,[282,287] hence the term "endometrioid" that is used for them. Over a quarter of the endometrioid carcinomas have papillary (villoglandular) foci, either on the surface or in the invasive areas[280,281] (Fig. 19.137D). These tumors should be sharply separated from the much more aggressive papillary

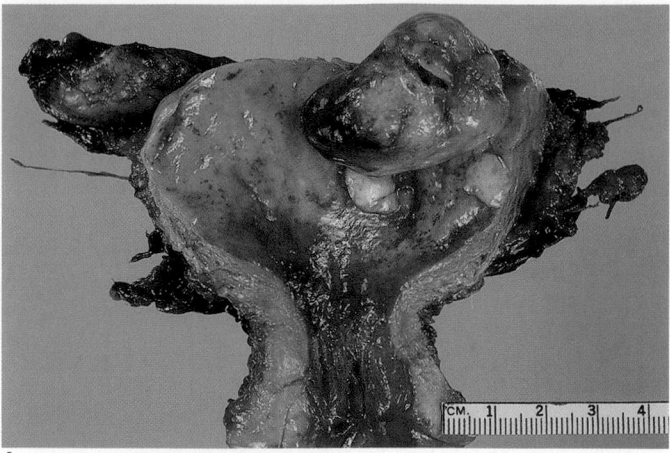

A

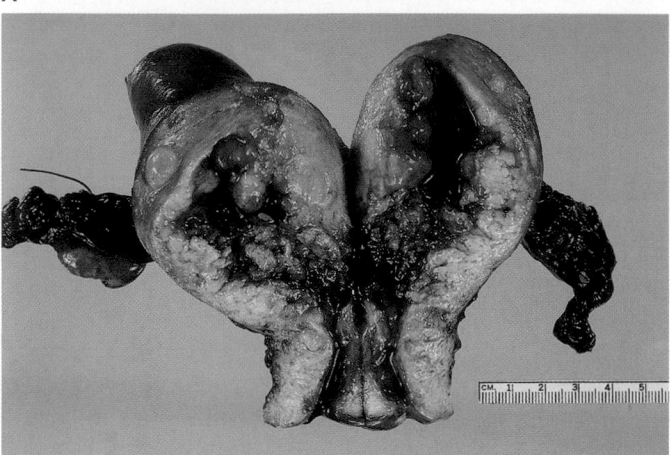

B

Fig. 19.136 A and **B**, Gross appearances of endometrioid adenocarcinoma. The tumor shown in **A** is polypoid, whereas that depicted in **B** is highly infiltrating.

serous carcinomas (see p. 1589).[283,284,305] A further variation on the theme is represented by the endometrioid adenocarcinoma containing small nonvillous papillae. These papillae can arise either from an otherwise unremarkable endometrioid carcinoma or from the villous projections of the villoglandular variant of this tumor.[300] It should also be noted that the most superficial portions of endometrial adenocarcinomas can exhibit patterns closely simulating various hyperplastic and metaplastic conditions of the endometrial mucosa.[292]

The stroma of endometrial adenocarcinoma usually has a desmoplastic quality. It may contain collections of foamy cells, probably the result of tumor necrosis and a good marker for the presence of carcinoma.[290] However, these cells can also be seen in hyperplasia and in the absence of proliferative epithelial changes. Their immunophenotype corresponds to that of histiocytes rather than endometrial stromal cells.[304] They are fat positive and mucin negative, in contrast to the mucin-positive macrophages sometimes seen in the stroma of benign endometrial polyps.[303]

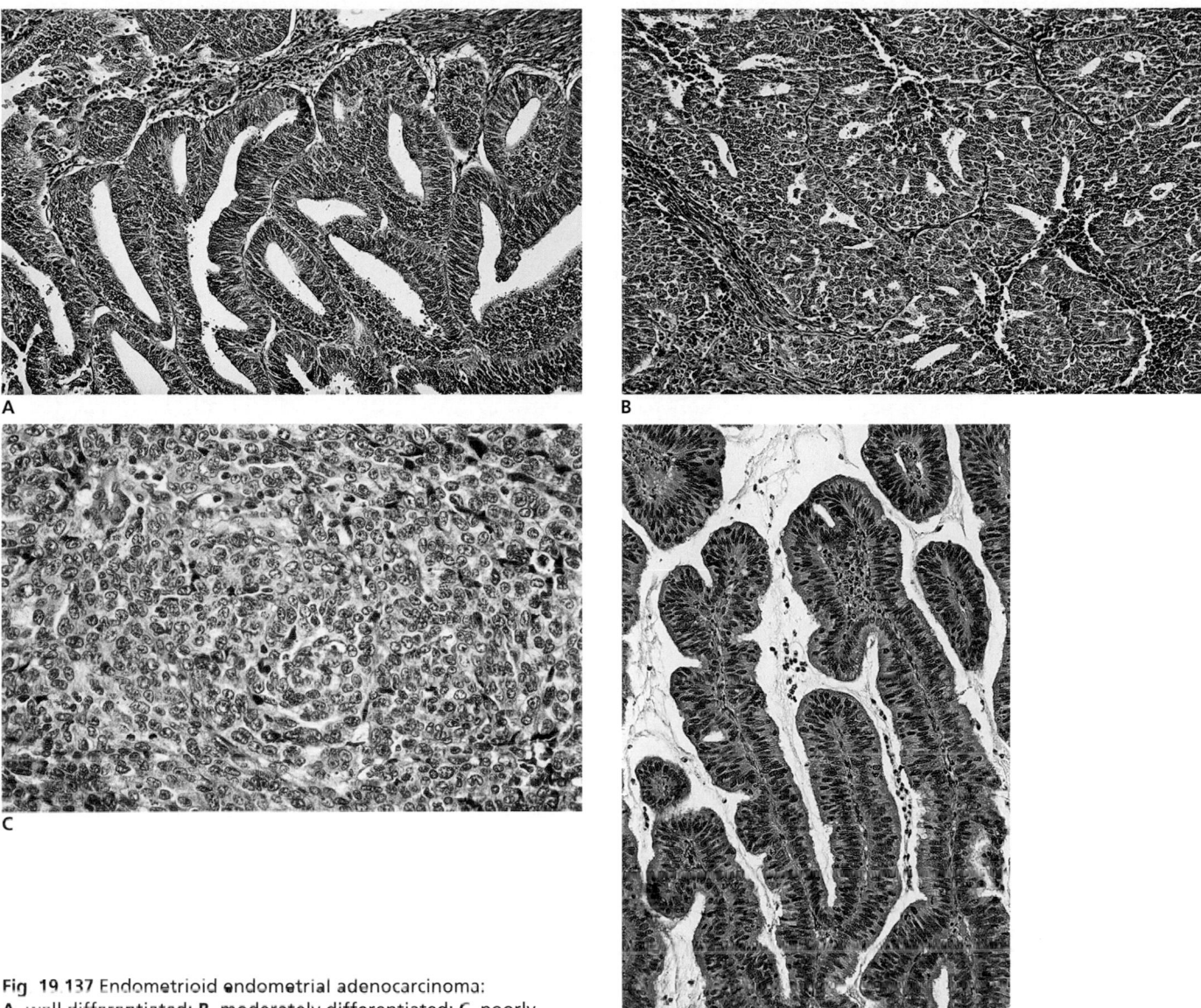

Fig 19.137 Endometrioid endometrial adenocarcinoma:
A, well differentiated; **B**, moderately differentiated; **C**, poorly
differentiated; **D**, with villoglandular pattern of growth.

The non-neoplastic endometrium of a uterus harboring an endometrioid adenocarcinoma is often hyperplastic and only exceptionally exhibits a normal proliferative or secretory pattern; when it does, the assumption has been made that the carcinoma has arisen in a "progesterone-refractory" mucosal area.[302]

The frequency and extent of myometrial invasion by carcinoma are directly related to the microscopic grade of the tumor.[298] Care should be exercised to distinguish true myometrial extension by carcinoma from expansion of the endometrial–myometrial junction and from atypical or malignant changes involving preexisting foci of adenomyosis[291]; the latter condition is recognized by the presence of endometrial stroma around the intramyometrial proliferating glandular foci.[289] It has been proposed that CD10 immunostaining can help in this distinction by highlighting the endometrial stroma associated with the adenomyosis when present.[301] However, a warning has been sounded to the effect that CD10 immunoreactivity can also be found around foci of invasive adenocarcinoma.[304a] Extension of the endometrial carcinoma into the cervix occurs in over 10% of cases, usually by direct invasion,[286,296] but allegedly also by implantation following D&C.[285] This extension may be grossly evident or become apparent only on microscopic examination; it may involve the surface only, the fibrous stroma, or both.[294,296] The presence and type of cervical extension—which influences the staging of the tumor—is best detected by fractional curettage; care should be exercised in distinguishing bona fide cervical extension from isolated tumor fragments, or else a high false-positive rate will occur.[294]

The differential diagnosis between endometrial and endocervical carcinoma is discussed on p. 1541.

Variants and other microscopic types

Numerous morphologic forms of endometrial adenocarcinoma have been described. Some, such as adenoacanthoma, adenosquamous carcinoma, secretory carcinoma, and ciliated carcinoma, are thought to represent variants of ordinary ("endometrioid") adenocarcinoma. Others, notably papillary serous carcinoma, clear cell carcinoma, and mucinous adenocarcinoma, are regarded as being of nonendometrioid type, although any of them can be seen coexisting with endometrioid adenocarcinoma.

Adenoacanthoma is the term traditionally given to the well-differentiated endometrioid adenocarcinoma containing similarly well-differentiated (benign appearing) squamous elements derived from metaplasia of the tumor glands (Fig. 19.138). Its natural history closely parallels that of the ordinary adenocarcinoma of a similar degree of differentiation lacking squamous changes.[374]

Adenosquamous (mixed) carcinoma refers to the endometrioid carcinoma containing *malignant-appearing* squamous elements[345] (Fig. 19.139). In some series the incidence of this tumor type has been notably high—up to 30% of all uterine carcinomas and on the rise[345,346]—but this was not our experience or that of others.[310,324] Patients with adenosquamous carcinoma are said to have a worse prognosis than those with adenocarcinoma or adenoacanthoma. However, several studies have shown that, stage by stage and grade by grade, there are no prognostic differences between pure adenocarcinoma, adenoacanthoma, and adenosquamous carcinoma.[357,373] Therefore, it would appear that the bad reputation that the latter tumors have is the result of the fact that most of them are basically high-grade adenocarcinomas, whereas the reverse is true for the adenoacanthomas. In other words, once an endometrial adenocarcinoma is clinically staged and microscopically graded into well-differentiated, intermediate, and poorly differentiated categories, the presence and appearance of a focal squamous component would seem immaterial.[373] Morphologic studies have suggested—and immunocytochemical studies have supported—the notion that adenoacanthoma and adenosquamous carcinoma represent a spectrum of squamous metaplasia in a single tumor type rather than two independent entities.[368]

Glassy cell carcinoma is a special type of adenosquamous carcinoma that has occasionally been reported in the endometrium; its appearance is similar to that of its more common cervical counterpart.[316,323]

Secretory carcinoma is characterized by neoplastic glands having subnuclear vacuolization resembling that of a normal 17-day secretory endometrium and accompanied by a late secretory pattern in the adjacent noninvolved endometrium[363] (Fig. 19.140). This tumor is not believed to be a specific type of endometrial carcinoma but rather the expression of a pattern that may be present diffusely or focally in a well-differentiated endometrioid carcinoma, usually as a result of progesterone stimulation. It should be distinguished from the clear cell carcinoma described later.[315,337]

Ciliated carcinoma is an extremely rare variant of endometrial adenocarcinoma that is composed predomi-

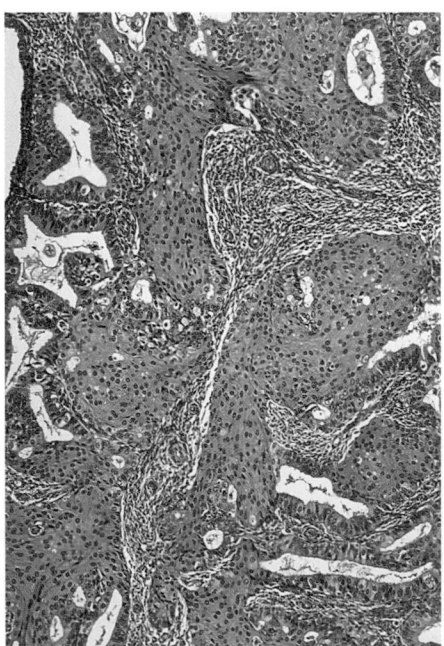

Fig. 19.138 Well-differentiated endometrioid adenocarcinoma with squamous metaplasia (so-called "adenoacanthoma").

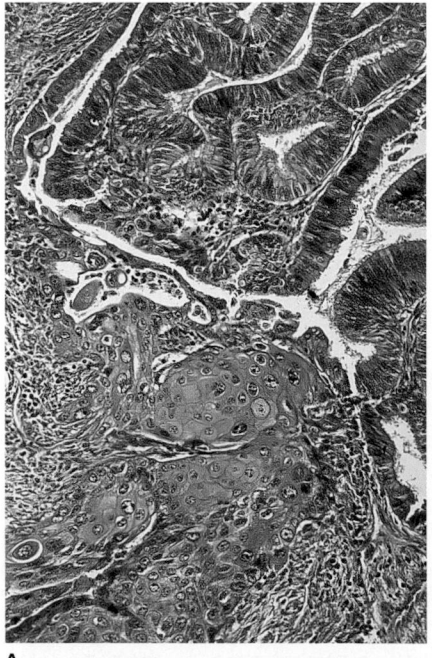

A

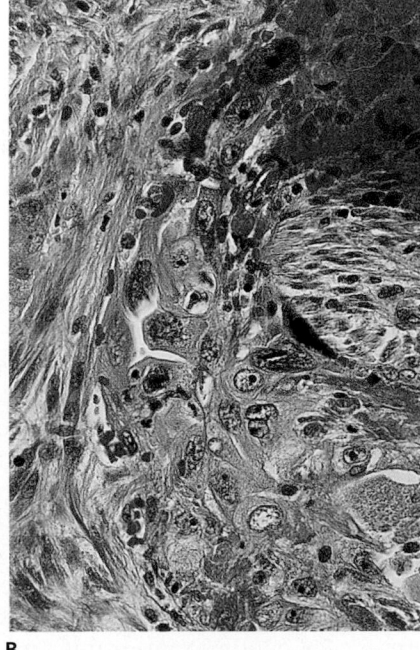

B

Fig. 19.139 A and **B**, Endometrial adenocarcinoma of endometrioid type with squamous metaplasia. In contrast to the case shown in Fig. 19.138, the squamous component has markedly atypical cytologic features.

nantly of ciliated cells[325]; it needs to be distinguished from the much more common ciliated cell metaplasia (see p. 1575).

Mucinous adenocarcinoma is a tumor subtype characterized by abundant mucin secretion[343] (Fig. 19.141). It is distinguished from mucinous metaplasia by virtue of its architectural and cytologic atypia, although on occasions the carcinomas exhibit a deceptively bland appearance.[364a] It should be noted that scattered foci of mucin positivity are often found in ordinary endometrial adenocarcinoma and that they are not necessarily an indication of endocervical origin.[362] The distinction between endometrial mucinous adenocarcinoma and primary endocervical adenocarcinoma—which is further discussed on p. 1541—cannot be made on the basis of morphologic or histochemical features but rather depends on differential biopsy and fractional curettage.[354] Parenthetically, some of the histochemical features of the mucin produced by these tumors suggest the existence of enteric differentiation.[340]

On occasion, endometrial adenocarcinomas of mucinous or mixed mucinous–endometrioid type exhibit a conspicuous *microglandular* pattern associated with eosinophilic mucinous intraluminal secretion and prominent acute inflammation, the overall picture simulating the appearance of endocervical microglandular hyperplasia.[372,375]

Papillary serous carcinoma (formerly also known as tubal carcinoma) is a highly aggressive form of endometrial adenocarcinoma closely resembling ovarian papillary serous carcinoma[322,326,333] (Fig. 19.142). It is characterized by a complex papillary pattern of growth, a high degree of cytologic atypia (pleomorphism, hyperchromasia, giant nucleoli), numerous mitoses, extensive necrosis, psammoma bodies (30% of the cases), and prominent myometrial invasion (Fig. 19.143). It should be distinguished from the already mentioned (and much more common) endometrial adenocarcinoma with a villoglandular pattern of growth, with which it shares several architectural features[317] (see p. 1586). A key aspect in this regard is the consistently high-grade nature of its cytologic features, which are also apparent on Pap smears.[336] It should be mentioned here that psammoma bodies are not necessarily indicative of a papillary serous-type tumor, since occasionally they are also seen in endometrioid carcinomas.[348a]

Uterine papillary serous carcinoma can coexist with endometrioid adenocarcinoma of the uterus or serous carcinoma of the ovary,[312] be confined to an endometrial polyp, or be entirely intramucosal[312,314,358,359,369] (Fig. 19.144). Some cases have been described following radiation therapy for carcinoma of the cervix.[348]

Clear cell carcinoma is composed of large clear cells with distinct cellular margins containing variable but usually large amounts of glycogen[337,342] (Fig. 19.145). The papillary formations and "hobnail" cells found in this

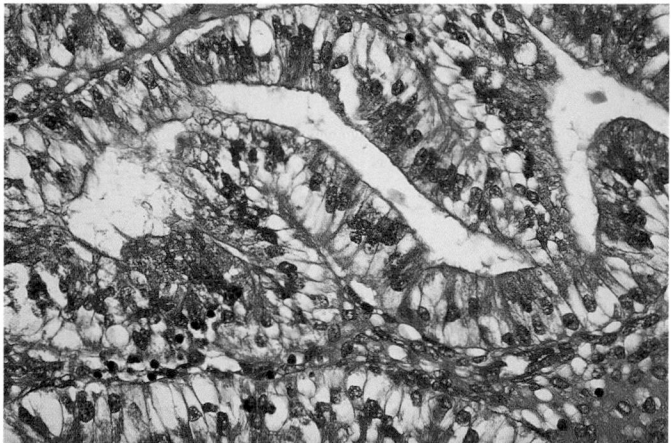

Fig. 19.140 Secretory carcinoma of endometrium. This well-differentiated lesion is a variant of endometrioid adenocarcinoma and is composed of cells with abundant clear to finely granular cytoplasm. It should be distinguished from clear cell carcinoma.

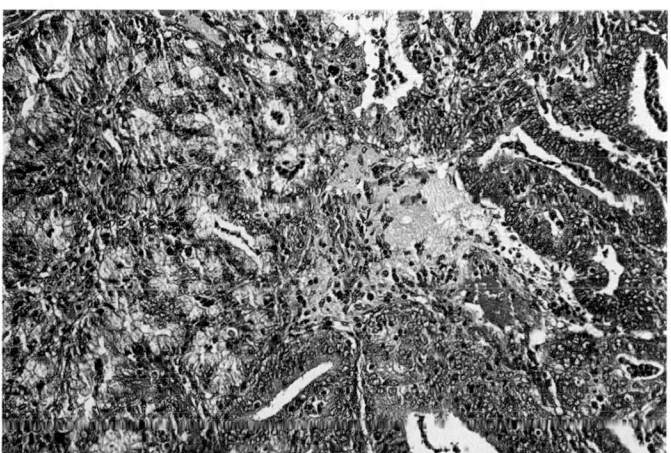

Fig. 19.141 Endometrial adenocarcinoma of mucinous type.

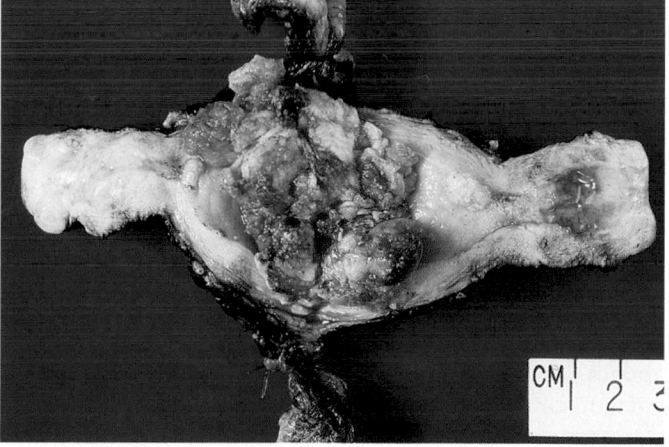

Fig. 19.142 Gross appearance of papillary serous carcinoma of endometrium. The neoplasm fills the endometrial cavity.

variant of adenocarcinoma resemble those seen in the ovarian, cervical, and vaginal tumors that carry the same name. Their presence in superficial endometrial carcinomas, as a focal change in ordinary adenocarcinomas, and, exceptionally, even in benign endometrial polyps[337]

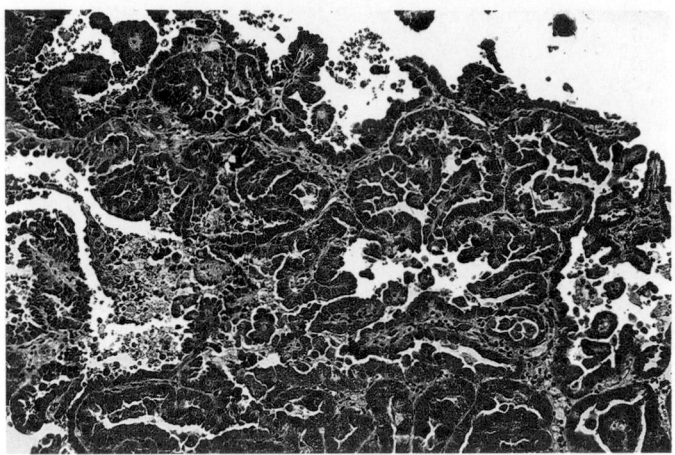

A

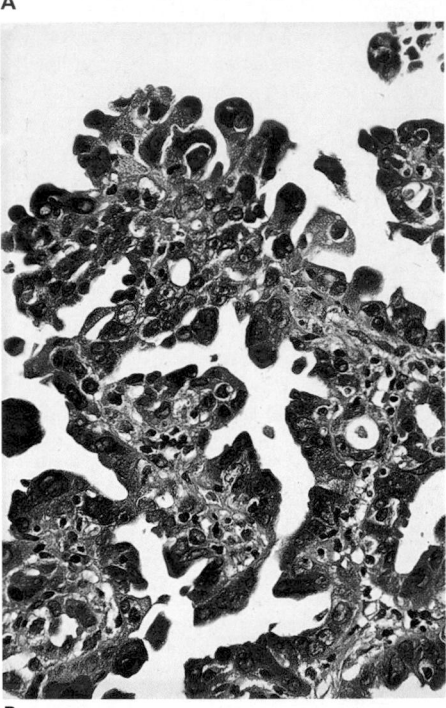

B

Fig. 19.143 A and **B**, Low- and high-power appearance of serous carcinoma. Note the high nuclear grade.

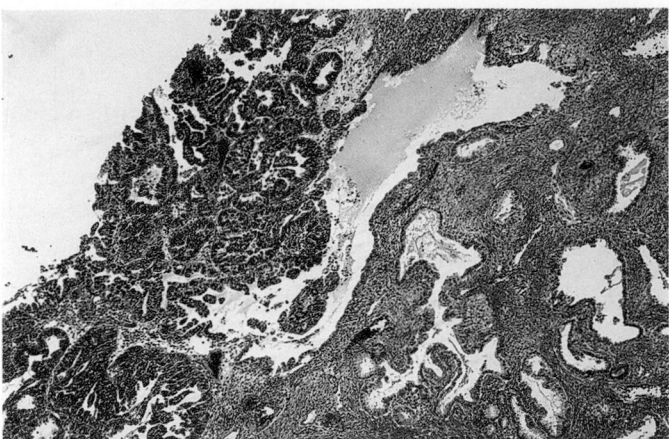

Fig. 19.144 Serous carcinoma limited to the superficial portion of a tamoxifen-related endometrial polyp.

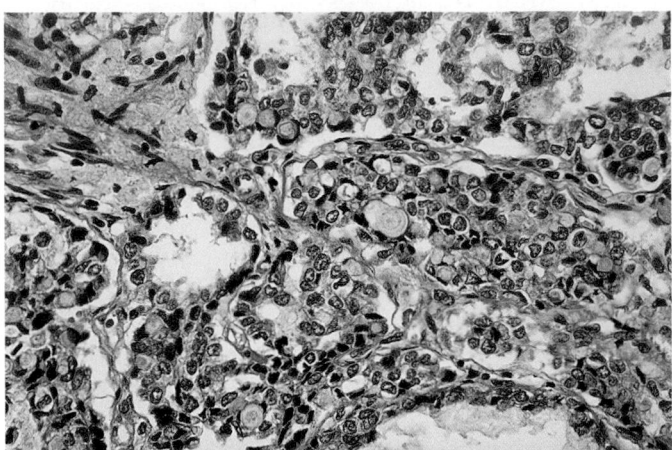

Fig. 19.145 Clear cell carcinoma of endometrium.

and otherwise normal endometria[319] clearly speaks in favor of a müllerian rather than a mesonephric histogenesis (Fig. 19.146). The ultrastructural and immunohistochemical features of this tumor are also supportive of this interpretation.[338,353,355,365] Most patients are postmenopausal, and there seems to be no relationship with intrauterine diethylstilbestrol exposure, as there is for somewhat similar tumors occurring in the vagina and cervix.

Although earlier articles emphasized the similarities that clear cell carcinoma bears with ordinary ("endometrioid") adenocarcinoma,[337,360] the current belief is that it is more closely related to papillary serous carcinoma, both in terms of morphology and natural history.[313,341]

Small cell (neuroendocrine) carcinoma usually presents grossly as bulky (sometimes polypoid), ill defined,

and invasive (Fig. 19.147). Microscopically, its appearance is similar to that of its more common cervical counterpart (Fig. 19.148). It may be associated with areas of ordinary adenocarcinoma or be seen as a component of mixed müllerian tumor[329,349] (Fig. 19.149). Immunohistochemically, there is usually reactivity for NSE and low-molecular-weight keratin, and sometimes also for chromogranin and synaptophysin. Dense-core secretory granules can be detected ultrastructurally. The behavior is very aggressive.[366] As in the lung, cervix, and other sites, tumors with similar high-grade neuroendocrine features but composed of cells of intermediate or large size exist.[308] In this context, it should be noted that a minor population of endocrine cells—as detected with argyrophilic stains—is present in 25% to 50% of otherwise typical endometrial adenocarcinomas.[311,361] Some of these cells have been found to contain chromogranin, NSE, 5-hydroxytryptamine (5-HT; serotonin), somatostatin, adrenocorticotrophic hormone (ACTH), and indolamines.[309,331]

Squamous cell carcinoma occurring in the endometrium in a pure form is extremely rare[307,332] and it is, therefore, particularly important in this instance to rule out the alternative possibility of extension of a cervical

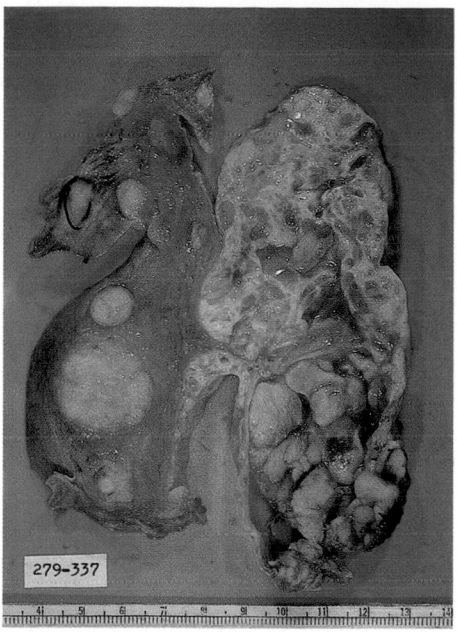

Fig. 19.146 Gross appearance of a clear cell carcinoma involving a large endometrial polyp. (Courtesy of Dr. Juan José Segura, San José, Costa Rica)

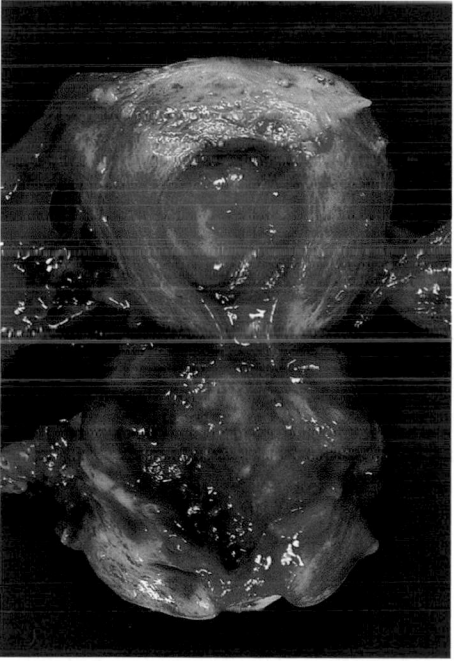

Fig. 19.147 Gross appearance of small cell neuroendocrine carcinoma of endometrium. The tumor is red and fleshy, and has a soft consistency.

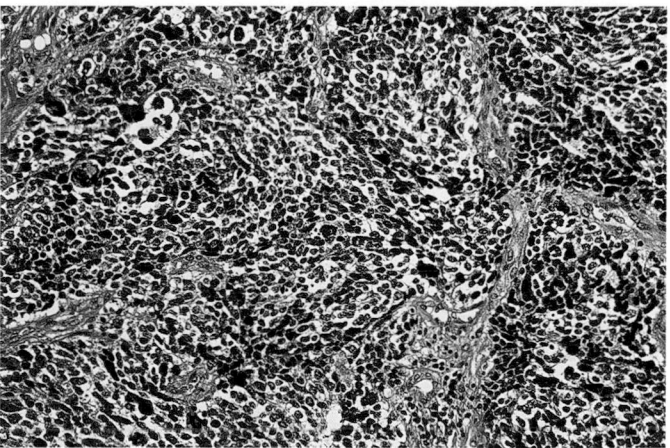

Fig. 19.148 Small cell neuroendocrine carcinoma of endometrium showing a diffuse pattern of growth.

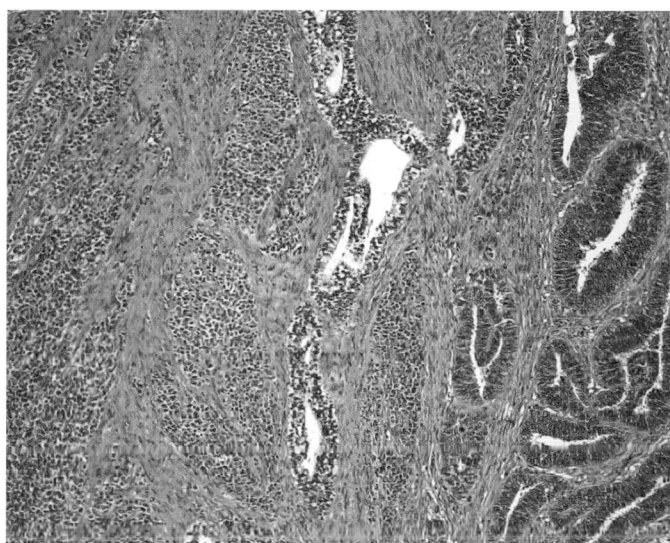

Fig. 19.149 Small cell neuroendocrine carcinoma of endometrium admixed with endometrioid adenocarcinoma. This is a common combination.

carcinoma.[350] Some cases have developed in elderly patients with pyometra, presumably on the basis of a preexisting endometrial squamous metaplasia.[327] Others have occurred in association with mucinous glands of presumably heterotopic cervical origin.[370] One reported case was associated with *spindle cell (sarcomatoid)* changes,[371] and another was of the *verrucous type*.[356]

Giant cell carcinoma is a rare pleomorphic form of high-grade endometrial adenocarcinoma featuring poorly cohesive sheets and nests of bizarre multinucleated giant cells.[334]

Endometrial carcinoma with trophoblastic (chorio-carcinomatous) differentiation should be distinguished from the tumor just mentioned and from gestational choriocarcinoma.[335] The multinucleated syncytiotro-phoblast-like cells present in the tumor are strongly immunoreactive for hCG.[351]

Oxyphilic cell carcinoma is a rare variant of endo-metrioid carcinoma characterized by a predominant or exclusive component of large eosinophilic (oxyphilic) cells.[352]

Endometrioid carcinoma with sertoliform (sex cord-like) differentiation similar to that more commonly seen in ovarian endometrioid tumors has been reported.[318,364] This is to be distinguished from the uterine tumors resembling ovarian sex-cord tumors.

Transitional cell carcinoma has architectural and cytologic features similar to those of urothelial carcinoma, but it retains a müllerian profile. It is almost always admixed with one or another of the more conventional patterns.[320,339]

Hepatoid adenocarcinoma has been reported as arising from the endometrium, in association with α-fetoprotein production.[328]

Signet ring cell adenocarcinoma has been described as a primary uterine tumor.[344] Before making this diagnosis, all attempts should be made to rule out the alternative possibilities of metastasis (particularly from breast and stomach) and of vacuolated decidual cells and stroma histiocytes simulating signet ring cells.[330]

Lymphoepithelioma-like carcinoma looks like its homonym in other sites. The few reported cases have not shown evidence of EBV infection.[367]

Rhabdoid tumor of the uterus represents, in at least some of the cases, a dedifferentiated form of endometrial adenocarcinoma, as is strongly suggested by its occasional coexistence with a conventional adenocarcinoma appearance.[321]

Mesonephric carcinoma of the endometrium, i.e., a tumor truly derived from wolffian remnants and, therefore, unrelated to the clear cell carcinoma described above (which in the past was inaccurately called mesonephric) has been described once, presenting as a myometrial mass.[347]

Cytology

Unfortunately, the success of mass screening in reducing invasive cervical carcinoma has not had quite the same effect on endometrial carcinoma.[378] The routine Pap smear is not as effective for the detection of this tumor,[377] the positive rate being only 50%.[377] With cervical scrapings, this rate is 60%, and with vaginal pool material it reaches 75%.[385,387] The presence of normal endometrial cells in a cervical cytologic specimen should raise the possibility of endometrial hyperplasia or carcinoma and is an indication for histologic examination of the endometrium.[382] Several cytologic methods have been employed to increase the positive rate, such as endometrial aspiration, tampon smear, endometrial lavage, endometrial brushing, the jet-wash technique, and suction curettage.[376,379–381] Of these, the latter is preferred by many because of its high degree of accuracy and patient acceptance.[379] However, the widespread applicability of any of these methods to mass screening still remains problematic.[383,384,386]

Histochemical and immunohistochemical features

Immunohistochemically, endometrial adenocarcinomas of the conventional (endometrioid) type are positive for keratin (especially keratins 7, 8, 18, and 19),[398,399] vimentin (65% to over 80% of cases),[390,391] CEA (although less so than cervical carcinomas and generally limited to areas of squamous metaplasia),[406] CA-125,[400] IgA and secretory component,[404] *Ulex europaeus*, agglutinin I, and amylase (12% of cases).[405] Coexpression of keratin and vimentin is common.[401] Some tumor cells have also been found to contain GFAP.[399]

Estrogen and progesterone receptors, as detected by biochemical analysis or immunocytochemistry, are present in most cases of endometrial adenocarcinoma.[388,394] Endometrioid carcinoma shows the highest degree of positivity for both receptors, followed by papillary serous carcinoma and clear cell carcinoma.[392] High-grade adenosquamous carcinomas are consistently negative.[397] In endometrioid carcinoma and most of its variants, the presence of hormone receptors correlates with FIGO stage, FIGO grade, and nuclear grade.[396] Degrees of estrogen and progesterone receptor positivity are often similar.[389] Overexpression of HER2/*neu* is present in approximately 20% of endometrial carcinomas.[402] Expression of CD114 (c-kit), as evaluated immunohistochemically, has been found in about half of the adenocarcinomas, while it is present in over 90% of normal proliferative endometria.[393] GLUT-1, a facilitative glucose transporter, is aberrantly expressed in most atypical hyperplasias and adenocarcinomas, but allegedly not in normal endometrium or in simple or complex hyperplasias without atypia.[407] Expression of the cell adhesion molecules β-catenin and E-cadherin is related to histotype, in the sense that both tend to be present in endometrioid carcinoma and absent in papillary serous carcinoma.[403]

A recent finding of diagnostic significance is that WT-1, which is nearly always positive in papillary serous tumor of the ovary and its metastases, is generally negative in papillary serous tumor of the endometrium,[395] as well as in other types of primary endometrial carcinoma.[407a]

Molecular genetic features

The four major genetic abnormalities that have been detected in endometrioid adenocarcinomas are microsatellite instability and mutations in the *PTEN*, k-ras, and β-catenin genes, whereas nonendometrioid carcinomas (notably the papillary serous type) often have *p53* mutations and loss of heterozygosity on several chromosomes.[408,411,417,418,424,425,426] An inverse relation has been found between p53 overexpression and hormone receptor status.[413,415] These differences have been interpreted as probably indicative of different pathogenetic mechanisms for the two major types of endometrial neoplasia.[410,414,416,422]

Other genetic abnormalities that have been documented in endometrial adenocarcinoma include decreased expression of p21 (waf1/cip1, a nuclear protein that binds to cyclin-dependent kinase complexes),[419] decreased expression of β1C integrin (member of a group of ubiquitous cell adhesion molecules involved in maintaining normal tissue morphology,[416a] overexpression of COX-2 in the poorly differentiated forms,[412] loss of expression of DCC,[420] downregulation of Rb2/p130,[423] and high telomerase activity in the high-grade tumors.[409]

DNA aneuploidy is present in approximately one quarter of the cases; positive tumors tend to be of advanced surgical stage and higher microscopic grade, associated with deeper myometrial invasion, and accompanied by lymph node metastases. As expected, aneuploidy is the rule in papillary serous carcinoma.[421]

Spread and metastases

The two obvious sites of local spread of endometrial carcinoma are the myometrium and the cervix, both of these having important prognostic connotations[434,343a] (see p. 1594). The most common sites of extrauterine spread in endometrial adenocarcinoma of the endometrioid type are the pelvic and para-aortic lymph nodes and the ovaries (see next section). Nodal metastases occur in approximately 5% to 25% of clinically stage I tumors and are more likely to occur in invasive high-grade tumors (even if such tumors are superficial), in large sized and/or deeply invasive tumors regardless of grade, in tumors with cervical extension, and in tumors with vascular invasion.[428,430,433]

Papillary serous carcinoma has a propensity for lymph vessel permeation. Involvement of peritoneal surfaces (particularly in the pelvis) occurs early in the disease, and can be present even at the intraepithelial stage.[434] In these cases, molecular analysis has shown that the disease is clonal, suggesting origin at a single site with secondary early spread.[427,432,434a]

The most common sites of recurrence of endometrial carcinoma are the vaginal vault and pelvis. Papillary serous carcinoma characteristically spreads throughout the abdominal cavity in a fashion similar to that of ovarian serous carcinoma. Metastases of this tumor in the bladder can simulate a primary neoplasm of this organ.[435]

Distant metastases of endometrial carcinoma are more common in the lung, liver, bone, central nervous system, and skin. The latter tend to occur in the head and neck region, particularly the scalp.

On occasion, the keratin present in endometrial carcinoma with squamous metaplasia desquamates into the uterine cavity and from there travels via the fallopian tube to produce implants in the peritoneal surface, leading to the formation of foreign body granulomas.[479] This finding should not be regarded as evidence of metastatic disease in the absence of viable neoplastic cells. Follow-up data on these patients suggest that these keratin granulomas have no prognostic significance and that they should be distinguished from viable tumor implants.[431]

Coexistent uterine and ovarian carcinoma

Approximately 8% of endometrial carcinomas are accompanied by a simultaneous ovarian carcinoma. When they are of similar microscopic types—which is usually the case—it becomes difficult to decide whether there are two independent tumors or whether one of the sites represents a metastasis. Features favoring a metastatic nature for the ovarian tumor include the following: smaller size, bilateral involvement, multinodular pattern of growth, presence of associated surface implants, and prominent lymphatic or vascular invasion within the ovarian stroma.[439] Immunohistochemical and DNA flow cytometric studies have proved of only limited value in this context.[439] On the other hand, molecular studies done for the evaluation of clonality (loss of heterozygosity, *PTEN* mutations, microsatellite instability) have provided more pertinent information.[447a] The results of these combined evaluations seem to indicate that both situations occur but that—at least in the case of endometrioid tumors—there is a greater number of independent primary uterine and ovarian neoplasms than of endometrial tumors metastasizing to the ovary.[436–438,440]

Treatment

The usual treatment of endometrial carcinoma is total abdominal hysterectomy with bilateral salpingo-oophorectomy. Whenever feasible, this should be supplemented by surgical staging (including biopsies of pelvic and para-aortic lymph nodes) if any of the following is present: greater than 50% myometrial invasion, grade III tumor, cervical involvement, extrauterine spread, unfavorable histologic component (serous, clear cell, or undifferentiated), or palpably enlarged nodes.[450] Radiation therapy, which until recently was administered routinely in conjunction with surgery (either preoperatively or postoperatively), is no longer favored, except for patients with poor prognostic factors that put them at a high risk of recurrence.[451] Tumor sterilization by radiation, as determined by histopathologic study of the hysterectomy specimen, was often obtained for tumors limited to the endometrium but only rarely for tumors invading the myometrium.[449] Progestational agents, although not curative, occasionally induce striking temporary regressions in the primary tumor as well as in the metastases.[442,444] Well-differentiated lesions are more likely to respond; this is in keeping with the fact that, as already indicated, an association exists between microscopic degree of differentiation and presence of estrogen and progesterone receptors.

The treatment of papillary serous carcinoma consists of hysterectomy with bilateral salpingo-oophorectomy, omentectomy, and surgical staging, the latter including peritoneal cytology and pelvic and para-aortic lymph node sampling. This is usually followed by adjuvant therapy, except for the minimally invasive tumors.[443,445–447,452]

Tumor relapse may appear in the form of local recrudescence (50%), distant metastases (28%), or both (21%); the median interval is between 1 and 2 years.[441] Local recurrences can be treated successfully with aggressive radiation therapy.[448]

Prognosis

Factors of prognostic importance in endometrial adenocarcinoma are the following:

1 *Tumor stage*, as defined by the FIGO system.[461,462,483] This refers to the surgical stage, since the clinical stage frequently underestimates the extent of disease.[498] The surgical staging includes a search for intraperitoneal microscopic tumor dissemination, as evaluated on cytologic preparations, supplemented if necessary with immunohistochemistry.[459]

2 Level of *infiltration* of the myometrial wall, as incorporated into the staging system. Tumors with invasion of over one half of the myometrium fare worse than those invading less than one half.[465,470,473,475] Among the latter (stage IB tumors), there is no significant difference between those that invade up to one third and those that invade greater than one third but less than one half.[453]

3 *Microscopic grade* of differentiation, as defined by the FIGO system.[473,484,491,496] As already stated, originally this system was primarily based on architectural rather than nuclear features, except for the papillary serous and clear cell types, which are by definition high-grade tumors.[500] The addition of a nuclear parameter to the FIGO system has improved its prognostic significance.[457] A relationship exists between microscopic grade and level of invasion (well-differentiated tumors being more superficial), but there is also a correlation between grade and survival within a given stage.[482]

4 *Cervical extension*. This is associated with a somewhat worse prognosis, regardless of the nature or extent of the change.[468,480]

5 *Estrogen dependence*. As a group, tumors associated with—and probably resulting from—chronic estrogenic stimulation have a better prognosis than the others. This includes most tumors in young patients (<40 years) and those associated with Stein–Leventhal syndrome, functioning ovarian tumors, and exogenous estrogen administration.[458,479,489] Along the same lines, adenocarcinomas associated with hyperplasia in the residual endometrium have a better prognosis than those lacking this feature.[458]

6 *Microscopic type*. Among the various morphologic variants, the papillary serous type and clear cell types are the most aggressive, with a definite tendency for upper abdominal spread for the former. Adenosquamous carcinomas are also highly malignant, but this is probably only a reflection of the fact that they are poorly differentiated tumors. Conversely, the excellent prognosis associated with grade I endometrioid adenocarcinoma, adenoacanthoma, and secretory carcinoma probably relates to their well-differentiated nature.[465,494,499]

7 *Lymph vessel invasion*. Tumor permeation of lymph vessels is a poor prognostic sign,[472] particularly if severe (diffuse or multifocal).[471]

8 *Blood vessel invasion*. The presence of blood vessel invasion is an important prognostic factor in stage I adenocarcinoma[477]; this feature has often been found to be associated with perivascular lymphocytic infiltration.[454]

9 *Hormone receptor status*. Multivariate analyses have shown that the estrogen receptor status (whether measured biochemically or immunohistochemically) is a significant predictor of recurrence and survival.[464,467,469]

10 *p53 overexpression*. This parameter has been found to be associated with tumor type, grade, and stage.[456,488,490]

11 *HER2/neu expression*. Intense overexpression of this oncogene is said to be associated with a poor overall survival.[474]

12 *Epidermal growth factor receptor*. Expression of this marker is said to correlate with microscopic grade and a shorter survival rate.[485]

13 *DNA ploidy*. Aneuploid tumors are associated with high microscopic grade, high clinical stage, and poor prognosis; it has been claimed that tumor aneuploidy has independent prognostic value.[455,463,476,481,497] In some studies, it has proved to be one of the most important predictors of outcome, together with age and tumor stage.[486]

14 *Cell proliferation*. The degree of tumor cell proliferation, as determined by S-phase fraction, was found in one series to be a strong predictor of outcome.[492] High mitotic rate has also been found to be a sign of aggressiveness in stage I grade I adenocarcinomas.[495]

15 *Rb gene*. It has been claimed that the presence of decreased levels of pRb2/p130 is associated with an increased risk of recurrence and tumor death, independent of tumor stage and ploidy status.[493]

16 *Angiogenesis*. In one study, vessel density was found to be an independent prognostic factor in endometrial carcinoma.[478]

17 *Others*. Parameters said to be indicative of favorable outcome are vimentin positivity,[466] Langerhans' cell infiltration,[466] low expression of p170 (a cell cycle-related antigen),[460] and absence of *hMLH1* (a mismatch repair gene).[487]

Endometrial stromal tumors

Tumors composed of endometrial stroma tend to occur in middle-aged women (average age, 45 years) and often present with vaginal bleeding.[518]

Microscopically, both types are composed of uniform small cells closely resembling those of the endometrial stroma, individually enveloped by reticulin fibers, which characteristically encircle small vessels that resemble spiral arterioles (Fig. 19.150). Other commonly encountered features include foci of hyalinization and scattered foamy cells.[548] Morphologic variations (other than those described in greater detail below) include the presence of a prominent fibrous or myxoid component,[542] and of a component of epithelioid cells with abundant eosinophilic cytoplasm.[540]

The similarity of the tumor cells to normal endometrial stromal cells is also evident ultrastructurally and phenotypically[502,513]; these cells contain estrogen and progesterone receptors, and the tumors respond to administration of progestins.[546,551,552] Their immunohistochemical profile is variable. Reactivity for vimentin is the rule, positivity for actin is common, reactivity for keratin and desmin is focal and inconstant, and negativity for S-100 protein is universal.[512,517,520]

Two recently described markers that promise to be of importance in the identification and differential diagnosis of these tumors are CD10 (consistently positive) and h-caldesmon (consistently negative, in contrast to smooth muscle tumors, see below).[508,534,537,545]

Endometrial stromal tumors have been divided according to the type of margins into: (1) a benign category (endometrial stromal nodule) having pushing margins, and (2) a malignant category (endometrial stromal sarcoma) having infiltrating margins.[526,536,539]

Endometrial stromal nodules appear grossly as solitary sharply circumscribed masses of soft consistency and a characteristic yellow-to-orange color (Fig. 19.151). They do not invade veins, lymphatics, or the myometrium. The prognosis is excellent; recurrence did not occur in any of the 60 cases studied by Tavassoli and Norris,[550] even when some irregularities in the margin, high mitotic counts, or glandular foci were present. Cases in which the irregularities at the margins are pronounced but which lack the typical, usually extensive infiltration of the endometrial stromal sarcomas listed below have been referred to as *endometrial stromal tumors with limited infiltration*.[514] Their behavior seems to be as favorable as that of the conventional stromal nodules.

Endometrial stromal sarcomas, traditionally designated *endolymphatic stromal myosis*, infiltrate the myometrium and have a particular tendency to permeate lymph vessels (Figs 19.152 and 19.153). The latter feature sometimes can be detected grossly by the presence of yellowish, ropy, or ball-like masses filling dilated channels. They may also present as polypoid masses (Fig. 19.154). The local invasion may extend into the broad ligament,

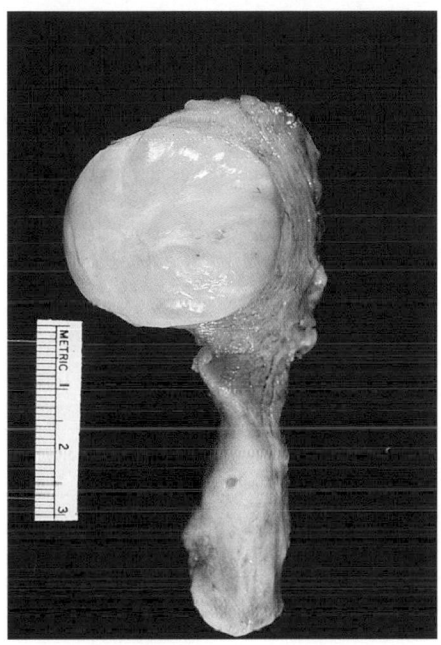

Fig. 19.151 Endometrial stromal nodule. The lesion is characteristically well circumscribed and has a yellow color.

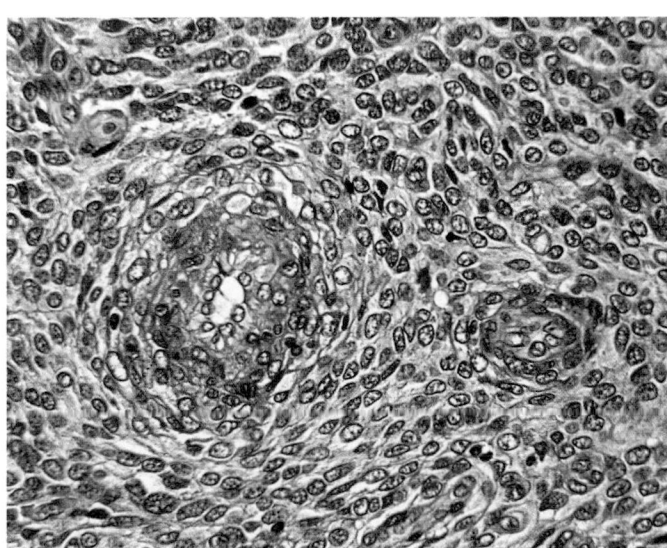

Fig. 19.150 Typical microscopic appearance of endometrial stromal tumor, showing bland oval cells arranged concentrically around spiral arterioles.

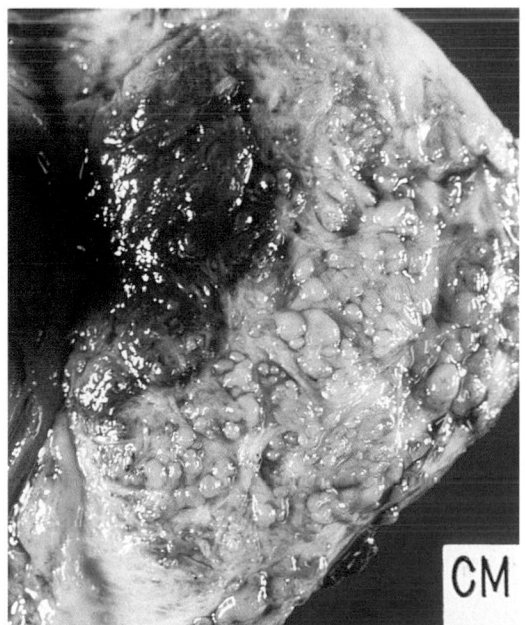

Fig. 19.152 Low-grade endometrial stromal sarcoma showing diffuse permeation of the myometrium in the form of small nodules bulging on the cut surface.

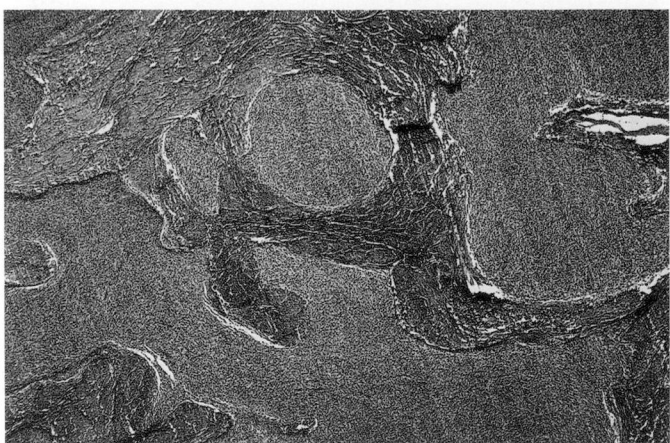

Fig. 19.153 Typical low-power appearance of endometrial stromal sarcoma.

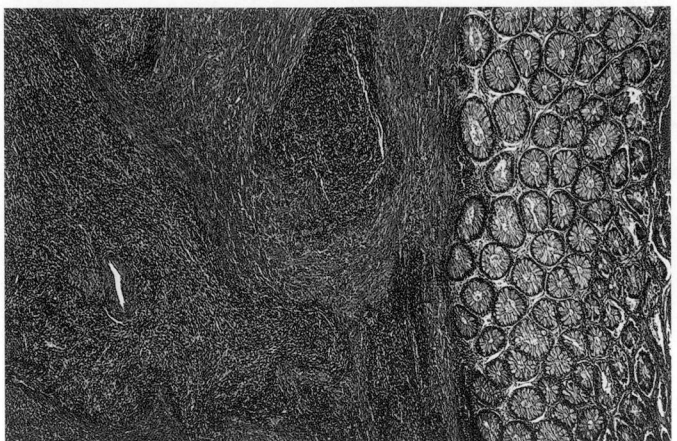

Fig. 19.155 Endometrial stromal sarcoma metastatic to wall of large bowel.

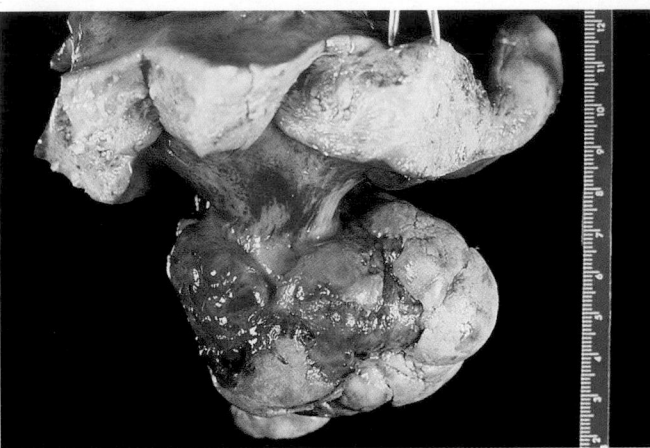

Fig. 19.154 Low-grade endometrial stromal sarcoma presenting as a huge polypoid mass within the endometrial cavity. This pattern of growth is unusual in this tumor type.

tubes, and ovaries. Their low-power appearance is very distinctive, in the sense of showing extensive myometrial permeation by sharply defined tumor islands with pointed edges, somewhat reminiscent of those seen (in an altogether different context) in thymoma.

The proposal had been made to subdivide endometrial stromal sarcoma into low-grade and high-grade types on the basis of their mitotic count (<10 versus ≥10 mitoses/10 HPF, respectively), after a substantial difference in outcome between the two groups was noted.[536] However, more recent and larger series have not supported such a sharp distinction, the tendency at present being to designate the whole group as endometrial stromal sarcoma, to regard mitotic activity as one of the morphologic factors to evaluate for prognostic purposes, and to reserve the term high-grade endometrial sarcoma for an altogether different tumor, to be discussed below.

As thus defined, the natural history of endometrial stromal sarcoma is characterized by slow clinical progression, repeated local recurrences (in the pelvis, ovary, intestinal wall, other intra-abdominal sites, and anterior abdominal wall), and occasional metastases[501] (Figs 19.155 and 19.156A,B). A remarkable case has been described involving the placenta.[525]

Size of the tumor, extrauterine extension, and mitotic activity are important prognostic features. Stromal neoplasms less than 4 cm in diameter practically never recur, and tumors confined to the uterus at the time of the initial surgery very rarely do so, regardless of the variety to which they belong. As already indicated, there is a relationship between mitotic activity and outcome, but this does not seem to be as significant as previously believed.[507] DNA ploidy analysis is also thought to have prognostic significance.[504,515,522]

A particularly interesting and difficult issue concerns the relationship and differential diagnosis between endometrial stromal tumors and smooth muscle tumors (not too surprising considering their histogenetic closeness), as already hinted at by the fact that even in non-neoplastic conditions one can see foci of smooth muscle "metaplasia" in the endometrial stroma and foci of endometrial stroma (not connected to adenomyosis) in the myometrium. Regarding the differential diagnosis, which is mainly with the epithelioid cellular variant of smooth muscle tumors, features that favor a diagnosis of endometrial stromal tumor are: multinodular pattern of growth, spiral-type arterioles (some with hyalinized walls), lack or inconspicuousness of large thick-walled vessels and cleft-like spaces, immunoreactivity for CD10, and lack of reactivity for h-caldesmon, desmin and oxytocin receptor.[508,514,533a,537,541]

A related issue concerns the fact that a certain number of mesenchymal uterine tumors show features of *both* endometrial stromal and smooth muscle differentiation. If the latter is present in the form of an inconspicuous focus in the midst of an otherwise typical endometrial stromal tumor, it can be ignored for diagnostic purposes.[554] If sizable (one third or more of the tumor mass), the neoplasm is referred to as **combined smooth mus-**

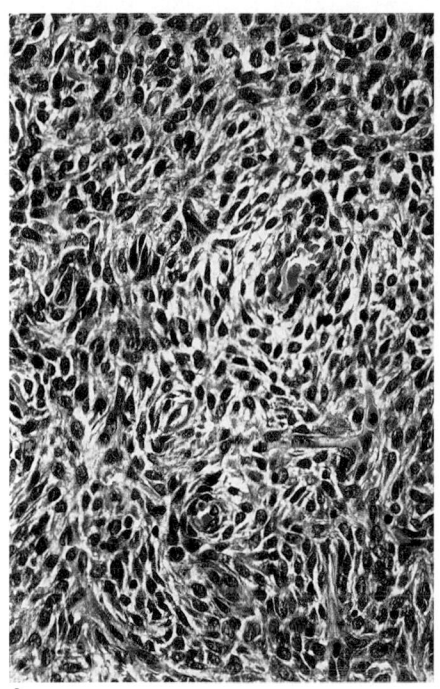
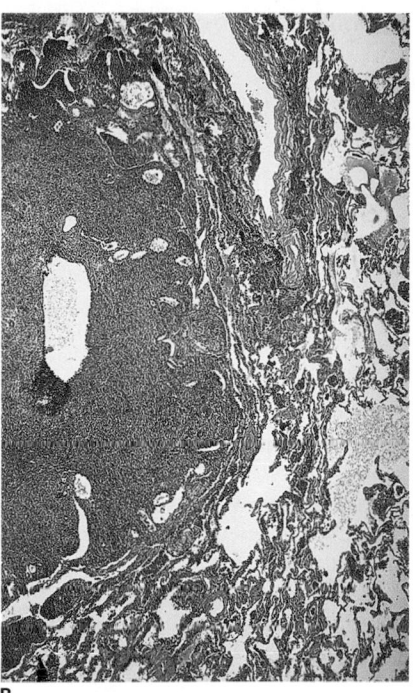

Fig. 19.156 A and **B**, Low- and high-power appearance of endometrial stromal sarcoma metastatic to lung. This lesion may be misdiagnosed as spindle carcinoid tumor, hemangiopericytoma, or solitary fibrous tumor.

cle–stromal tumor[538,550]; this is probably equivalent to the *(nodular) stromomyoma* of the older literature.[544] The areas with the smooth muscle component often show collagen deposition with a characteristic "starburst" pattern. Behaviorally, these tumors seem to be closer to endometrial stromal than to smooth muscle tumors, and—on the whole—very indolent.[538] A further variation on the theme is represented by the exceptional case exhibiting both smooth and skeletal muscle differentiation; it is important not to confuse this lesion with a malignant mixed müllerian tumor.[533]

Epithelial-like formations may appear in endometrial stromal tumors in the form of solid masses, glandular structures, or anastomosing cords. Clement and Scully[509] likened these formations to those of ovarian sex-cord neoplasms (particularly granulosa cell tumors) and have referred to the tumors containing them as **uterine tumors resembling ovarian sex-cord tumors** (Fig. 19.157A). Their immunohistochemical and ultrastructural profile has varied considerably in the various reported series, ranging from myogenous to epithelial.[532,549] However, at least some of the cases have shown a phenotype consistent indeed with a sex-cord line of differentiation, including reactivity for inhibin, CD99, and A13.[505,528] Uterine tumors in which these structures predominate have generally behaved in a benign fashion.[509]

The uterine neoplasm known as **plexiform tumor** or **tumorlet** and variously claimed to be of endometrial stromal,[530] myofibroblastic,[519] and smooth muscle derivation[521,524] is a closely related variation, and it is, therefore, not surprising that similar histogenetic arguments have been raised (Fig. 19.157B). The ultrastructural[521] and

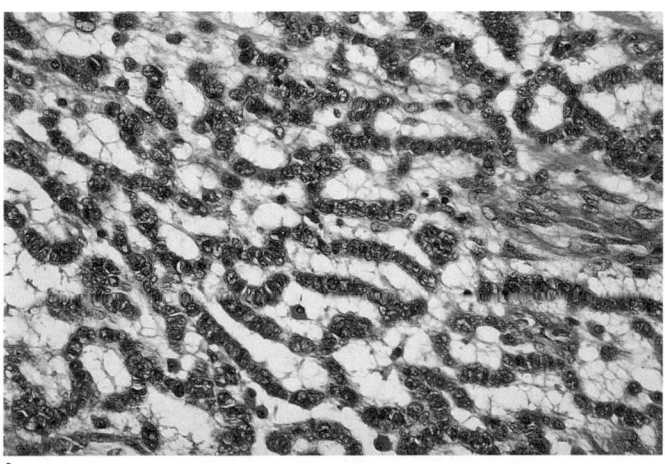
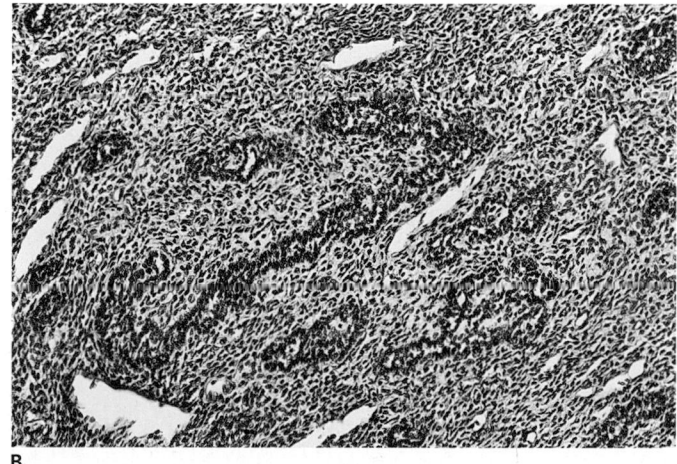

Fig. 19.157 A Endometrial stromal sarcoma with structures resembling ovarian sex cord tumors. **B**, So-called "plexiform tumor" of the uterus. This lesion is probably related to endometrial stromal neoplasms, but its histogenesis is still controversial.

immunohistochemical evidence (actin and desmin positivity[506,530]) clearly points toward a smooth muscle nature. This lesion is always an incidental finding, it usually measures less than 1 cm, and its behavior is always benign.

A different type of epithelium-like formation that can be seen in endometrial stromal tumor is represented by **endometrioid glandular foci** having a benign, atypical, or carcinomatous appearance[510] (Fig. 19.158).

Exceptionally, an endometrial stromal tumor may be seen in a uterus that also contains an endometrial adenocarcinoma. As a matter of fact, the two tumors can collide with each other.[529] It is important not to misinterpret this phenomenon as a malignant mixed müllerian tumor.

Tumors with the appearance of endometrial stromal neoplasms may be found in the cervix,[535] ovary (see p. 1705), pelvis, and retroperitoneum.[553] Some of these are seen in association with endometriosis, from which presumably they have arisen.[547] These extrauterine tumors may have any of the morphologic features and variations described in connection with the uterine neoplasms, including ovarian sex cord-like structures and endometrioid glandular proliferation.[531]

A note of caution is in order. Before making a diagnosis of primary extrauterine endometrial stromal tumor, one should make an effort to rule out a metastasis from a uterine lesion, knowing that these metastases are often solitary and that they can occur years or decades after the excision of the original tumor, which (to complicate things further) might have been misdiagnosed as a peculiar-looking smooth muscle tumor.[503,527] We have seen many such cases in several locations, mainly lung but also intestinal wall, retroperitoneum, and even deep soft tissues of extremity, in which diagnoses of hemangiopericytoma, monophasic synovial sarcoma, solitary fibrous tumor, lymphangioleiomyomatosis, and mesenchymal

cystic hamartoma were made.[523] Clues to the diagnosis are the multinodularity as seen on very low power, the uniformly bland appearance of the oval tumor cells, the presence of spiral arteriole-like vessels, and the deposition of coarse collagen fibers among the tumor cells.[539] Immunohistochemical reactivity for estrogen and progesterone receptors and for CD10 will provide confirmatory evidence. The best protection against missing this diagnosis is simply to think about the entity when it occurs in an unexpected place, a situation to which Dr Lauren V. Ackerman used to refer as "the man from Istanbul."[543]

Poorly differentiated endometrial (stromal) sarcoma shows a marked degree of nuclear pleomorphism and atypicality and lacks the vascular pattern and other distinctive features of endometrial stromal sarcoma (Fig. 19.159). It is an altogether different neoplasm, which

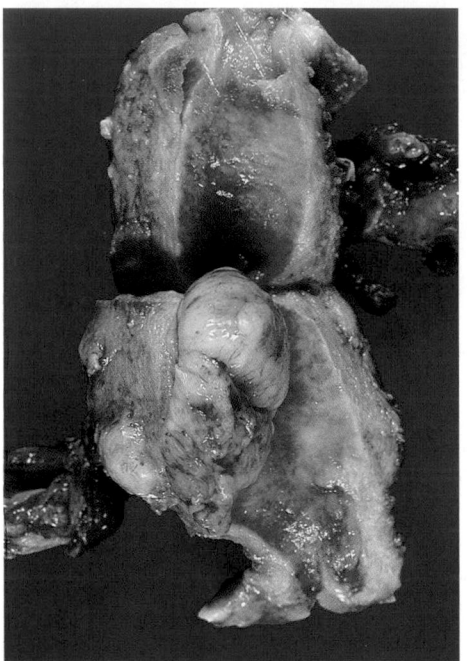

A

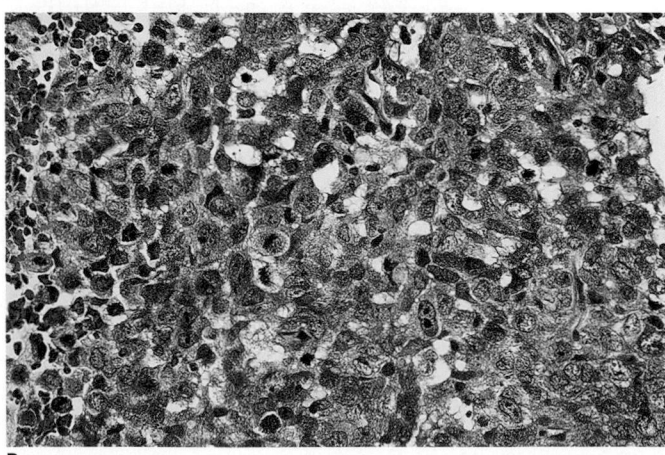

B

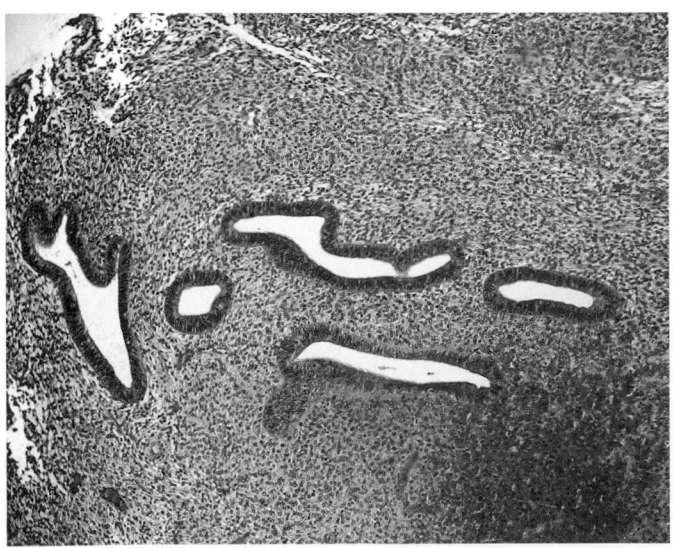

Fig. 19.158 Peritoneal metastasis from endometrial stromal sarcoma accompanied by benign endometrioid glands.

Fig. 19.159 A and **B**, Gross and microscopic appearance of high-grade endometrial sarcoma.

behaves in a very aggressive manner and which may actually have a closer relationship to malignant mixed müllerian tumor, the sarcoma-like component of which it greatly resembles.[511,516,518,555]

Malignant mixed müllerian tumor (carcinosarcoma)

Malignant mixed müllerian tumors (MMMTs) are practically always seen in postmenopausal patients, although exceptions occur.[560] They present with uterine bleeding and enlargement. The usual location is the uterine body, particularly the posterior wall in the region of the fundus.[557,581,583] Grossly, they present as large, soft, polypoid growths involving the endometrium and myometrium, sometimes protruding from the cervix (Fig. 19.160). Foci of necrosis and hemorrhage are common.

Microscopically, the characteristic feature of MMMTs is the *admixture of carcinomatous and sarcoma-like elements*, resulting in a characteristic biphasic appearance. The carcinomatous component is usually of glandular type, whether endometrioid, clear cell, or papillary serous.[588] As a rule, it has a poorly differentiated appearance and is of a high-grade nature; therefore, a careful search for stromal elements should be carried out whenever such patterns are found in an endometrial D&C, particularly if accompanied by extensive necrosis and hemorrhage. Squamous cell, undifferentiated, and primitive neuroectodermal patterns may also be seen.[572,594] Cases have also been described with melanocytic[556] and yolk sac differentiation.[587]

The appearance of the sarcomatous component is the basis for the time-honored division of these neoplasms into a homologous and a heterologous variety. In the former, the malignant stroma is formed either by round cells resembling those of the endometrial stroma or by spindle cells resembling leiomyosarcoma or fibrosarcoma. In the latter, specific heterologous mesenchymal elements (such as skeletal muscle, cartilage, bone, or fat) also are present (Fig. 19.161). Identification of cross striations, or of skeletal muscle markers by immunocytochemistry, is required to document the presence of a rhabdomyosarcomatous component (Fig. 19.162A to C). In some cases this component is so prominent as to overgrow the epithelial elements and to mimic a pure rhabdomyosarcoma.[565] Conversely, the malignant sarcoma-like component may be so inconspicuous in such a specimen as to be missed altogether, the lesion being misdiagnosed as an ordinary adenocarcinoma. This is particularly the case for the peritoneal metastases, in which the stromal component is often scanty or altogether absent. Since the epithelial elements can form papillae, be accompanied by psammoma bodies, and have all the other features of papillary serous carcinoma, a confusion with metastatic ovarian carcinoma may occur. Parenthetically, cases have been reported of coexistent uterine MMMT and ovarian serous adenocarcinoma.[576] Exceptionally, a rhabdoid component is present.[580]

The fact that the epithelial component of an MMMT is the one showing the greatest capability for invasion and metastases — also indirectly indicated by its greater microvessel density when compared with the sarcoma-like component[567,595] — suggests that these tumors should be primarily regarded as carcinomas rather than sarcomas, employing a reasoning analogous to that currently accepted for carcinomas with sarcoma-like stroma of the upper aerodigestive tract and other sites.[558,588,591] Immunohistochemical and ultrastructural studies support this view: keratin is always detectable in the

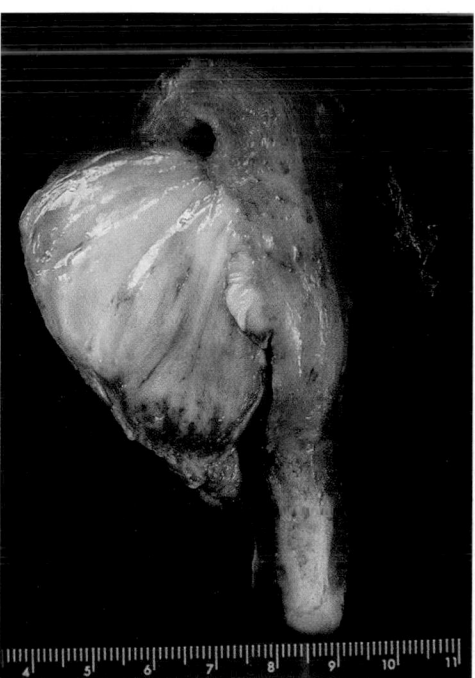

Fig. 19.160 Malignant mixed müllerian tumor of uterus resulting in a huge polypoid mass.

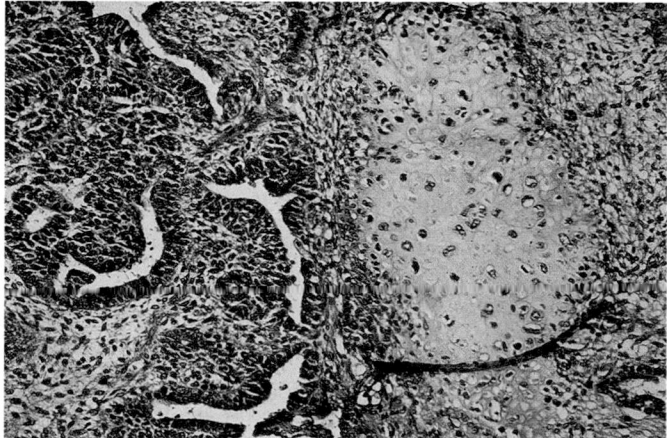

Fig. 19.161 Glandular and mesenchymal components of mixed müllerian tumor. Heterologous elements in the form of cartilage are present.

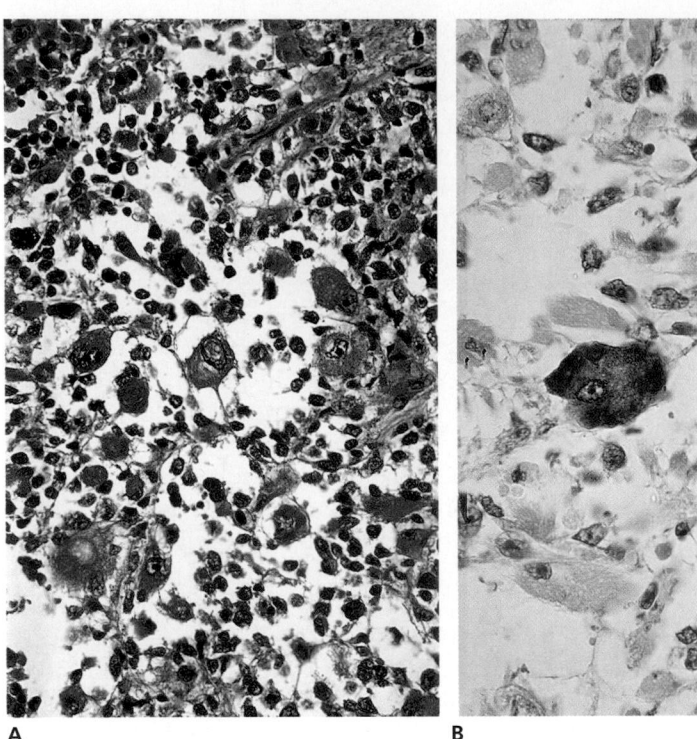

A   B

Fig. 19.162 Skeletal muscle elements in mixed müllerian tumor, seen on H&E stain (**A**) and following immunostaining for myoglobin (**B**). *continued opposite*

epithelial areas, but is also present in the sarcomatous component in over half of the cases[571]; by electron microscopy, hybrid epithelial/stromal cells coexist with those having purely epithelial or stromal features.[563,578] An additional supportive finding is the concordant pattern of p53 staining and type of mutation in the carcinomatous and sarcomatous areas, which would be difficult to explain if these tumors were biclonal.[562,575,577] Other markers that have been encountered in MMMTs are CD10 (in the sarcoma-like component)[579] and HER2/*neu*.[561]

MMMTs are easily distinguished from teratomas by their occurrence in an older age group and by the absence of skin appendages, glia, thyroid, and other tissue; however, as already noted, they may exceptionally contain neuroectodermal elements.[572] They should also be clearly separated from botryoid rhabdomyosarcoma (sarcoma botryoides). The latter term should be reserved for the tumor of childhood or adolescence arising from the cervix or vagina that exhibits skeletal muscle differentiation but lacks a carcinomatous component.

MMMTs are highly aggressive neoplasms, perhaps more so than even the higher grades and the more unfavorable variants of endometrial carcinoma.[570] Extension into the pelvis, lymphatic and vascular permeation, and distant lymph-borne and blood-borne metastases are all common. If the tumor has extended to the serosa of the uterus or beyond at the time of surgery, the prognosis is hopeless. The only patients with some chance of cure are those in whom the tumor is restricted to the inner half of the myometrium at the time of surgery. This determination implies a thorough sampling of the hysterectomy specimen by the pathologist. Unfortunately, over one half of these patients will harbor occult metastatic disease.[593]

In several series, tumors having only homologous stromal elements (called "carcinosarcomas" by Norris and Taylor[583]) have been found to have a slightly better prognosis than those with heterologous elements.[581,583,585] It should be pointed out, however, that the difference between the two is small, in some series absent altogether, and far outweighed by the stage of the disease.[559,569,590] Taking everything into account, we need to conclude once again that staging remains the most important predictor of prognosis.[573] Abdominal hysterectomy with bilateral salpingo-oophorectomy and pelvic lymphadenectomy is the treatment of choice, usually followed by adjuvant therapy. The response to radiation therapy and chemotherapy has been generally poor, although some encouraging reports have appeared.[574] The most common sites of recurrent disease are lung and abdominal cavity.[589]

Norris and Taylor[582] made the disturbing observation that 30% of patients with heterologous MMMTs and 13% of those with homologous tumors that they studied had a history of previous irradiation to the pelvic area, usually given for some benign disorder. The median interval between irradiation and the time of diagnosis of the tumor was 16.4 years, both in their series and in that of Doss et al.[566] Postirradiation uterine sarcomas tend to occur in a younger age group and spread earlier to the pelvis than comparable tumors not related to irradiation.[568,592]

MMMTs and other sarcoma-like malignant uterine

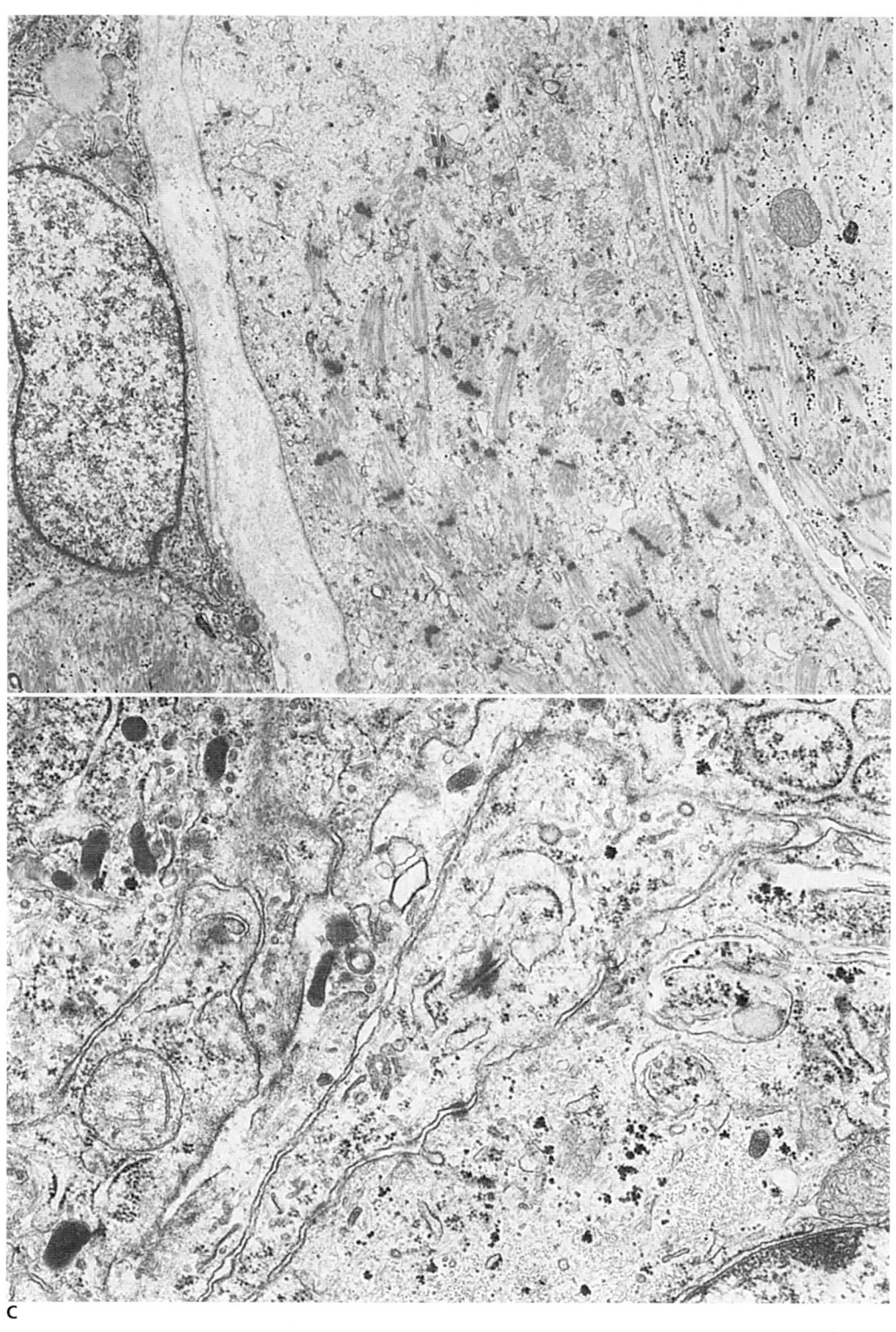

Fig. 19.162 *continued* C, Mixed müllerian tumor. A, Area of rhabdomyosarcomatous differentiation. Note Z-band formation. B, Area showing epithelial differentiation; paranuclear microfilaments similar to those of endometrioid endometrial carcinoma are present.

tumors have also been seen in association with chronic estrogenic stimulation (ovarian thecoma, polycystic ovarian disease, and prolonged estrogen therapy).[584]

MMMTs can arise in extrauterine locations, the most common sites being ovary and pelvic structures. Their morphologic and immunohistochemical features are similar to those of their uterine counterparts.[564,586]

Müllerian adenosarcoma and related tumors

Müllerian adenosarcoma is a distinctive type of uterine tumor, generally regarded as a low-grade variant of MMMT.[598,601,609] Like the latter, it usually presents in elderly individuals as a bulky polypoid growth filling the endometrial cavity, less commonly as an intramural nodule (Fig. 19.163). Microscopically, it is also composed

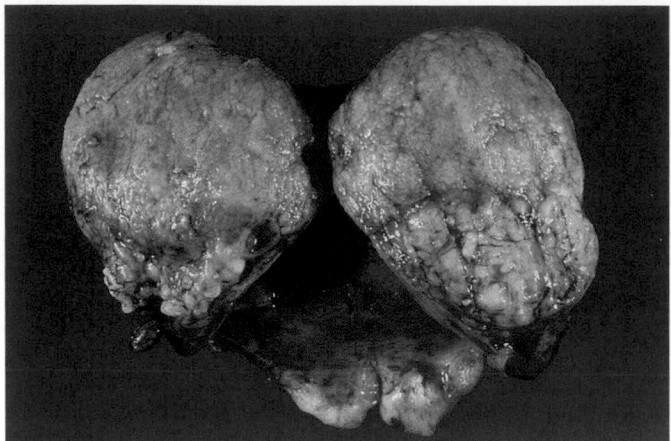

Fig. 19.163 Müllerian adenosarcoma. The tumor shows a lesser degree of necrosis and hemorrhage than the usual malignant mixed müllerian tumor.

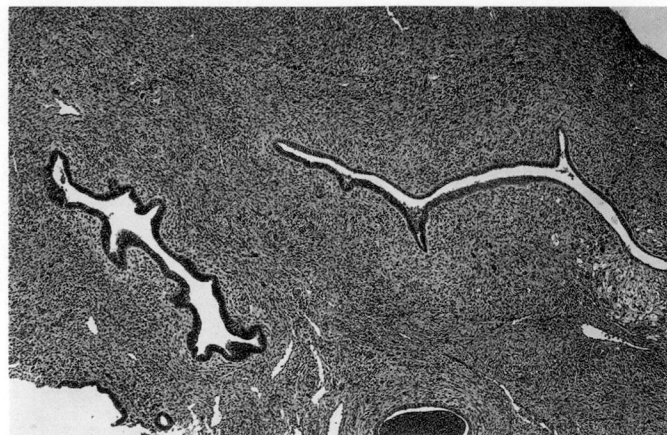

A

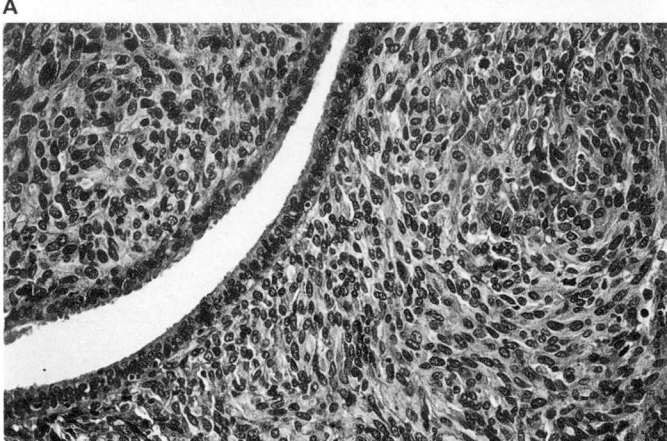

B

Fig. 19.164 **A** and **B**, Low- and high-power view of müllerian adenosarcoma. The resemblance to phylloides tumor of breast is obvious.

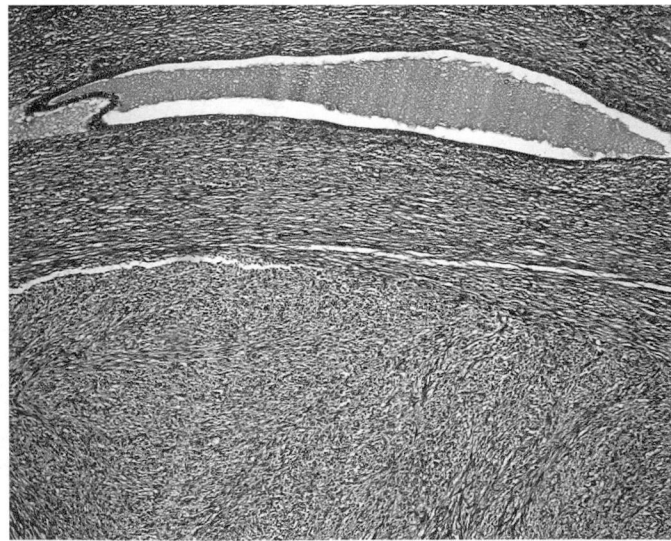

Fig. 19.165 Müllerian adenosarcoma (top) with sarcomatous overgrowth (bottom).

of an admixture of epithelial and stromal elements. Its distinguishing feature is the fact that the epithelial (glandular) component appears benign, giving to the lesion a sometimes striking similarity to phylloides tumor of the breast (Fig. 19.164). The stromal elements usually resemble endometrial stroma by light and electron microscopic examination.[605,610] As a rule, they do not appear as bizarre and undifferentiated as in the classic MMMT, although multinucleated giant cells and heterologous elements occur in approximately 20% of cases. The latter are usually of skeletal muscle type, but peculiar components such as angiosarcoma have also been observed.[596,611] Extensive areas of stromal fibrosis may result in a deceptively benign appearance.[601]

We prefer to view müllerian adenosarcomas not as a type of MMMT but rather as a variant of endometrial stromal sarcoma having the capacity to induce the formation and/or proliferation of glands. Support for this interpretation comes from the fact that smooth muscle metaplasia and sex cord-like differentiation (two well-known features of endometrial stromal sarcomas) have occasionally been found in them.[600,604,607] Additional support is provided by the cases in which a typical adenosarcoma is overgrown by a pure sarcoma having a higher grade and exhibiting a higher mitotic rate than the sarcomatous component of the associated adenosarcoma (Fig. 19.165). This development is analogous to that well known to occur in phylloides tumor of the breast, a fact that strengthens the analogy between the two models. These *müllerian adenosarcomas with sarcomatous overgrowth* behave in an aggressive fashion and are often associated with postoperative recurrence or metastases and a fatal outcome.[597,609]

Cases of müllerian adenosarcomas have been reported in association with tamoxifen therapy.[603] Also of interest is the report of a cluster of cases of uterine müllerian adenosarcomas with sarcomatous overgrowth that has been detected in the Washington, D.C., metropolitan area.[614]

Uterine adenofibroma and the related conditions papillary adenofibroma, papillary cystadenofibroma,

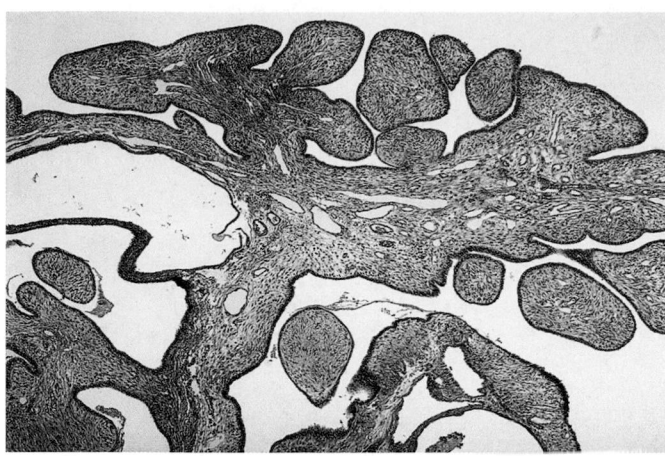

Fig. 19.166 Papillary adenofibroma of uterus. This lesion represents the lower end of the müllerian adenosarcoma spectrum.

lipoadenofibroma, and adenomyomatosis[606,608,615,617,618] are regarded as the benign counterparts of müllerian adenosarcoma, but the dividing line between the two groups is not sharp (Fig. 19.166). As a matter of fact, tumors with the characteristic features of uterine adenofibroma have occasionally been found to invade myometrium and pelvic veins.[602] The problems in separating them are analogous to those encountered in trying to separate benign from malignant phylloides tumors of the breast. Criteria found to be useful in distinguishing müllerian adenosarcomas from müllerian adenofibromas include two or more stromal mitoses per 10 HPF, marked stromal cellularity, and significant stromal cell atypia.[598] Cases have been reported of papillary adenofibroma involved by adenocarcinoma.[612]

Like MMMTs and endometrial stromal sarcomas, müllerian adenosarcomas can arise outside the uterine corpus. Cases have been described in the cervix, ovary, round and broad ligaments, and pelvic wall.[599,616]

A tumor purported to be the morphologic counterpart of müllerian adenosarcoma—i.e., composed of malignant epithelium and benign stroma—has been reported under terms such as *müllerian carcinofibroma* or *carcinomesenchymoma*.[613] The analogy is ingenious but probably unwarranted.

Leiomyoma

Leiomyomas of the uterus are extremely common neoplasms. The overall incidence is between 4% and 11%, but it rises to nearly 40% in women over the age of 50 years. Clinically apparent lesions are less common in parous than nulliparous women and premenopausal than postmenopausal women.[642] They are known to shrink after menopause; this is associated both with fibrosis and with a reduction in the size of the individual tumor cells.[624,625] The normal myometrium of leiomyoma-containing uteri expresses higher levels of estrogen receptors, a fact that may be related to their pathogene-sis.[643] Leiomyomas are much more common in black women, in whom they have a tendency to be very numerous (Fig. 19.167).

Many of these tumors are small and go undetected; a systematic and meticulous study of 100 consecutive hysterectomy specimens revealed leiomyomas in 77 of them, 84% of the tumors being multicentric.[623]

These tumors occur subserosally, intramurally, or submucosally (Fig. 19.168) and produce symptoms referable to their size and location. The conventional teaching (which, like most conventional teachings, is only partially true) is that the submucous tumors produce metrorrhagia (because of endometrial ulceration), the intramural ones result in menorrhagia (because they interfere with myometrial contraction), and the subserosal ones usually remain asymptomatic. They may become large enough to block the ureters, interfere with pregnancy, or cause inflammatory complications. In rare instances, uterine leiomyomas have been associated with polycythemia, which regressed after the tumor was excised.[639]

Submucosal tumors often result in secondary endometrial changes that range from gland distortion to atrophy and ulceration. They may fill the endometrial cavity and emerge from the cervical canal as polypoid growths ("myoma nascens"). Under these circumstances, their surface is usually ulcerated and infected, the gross appearance thus simulating that of a malignant neoplasm.

It is difficult to make a diagnosis of leiomyoma when only a few small fragments of smooth muscle are present in a curettage specimen. Unless these fragments show an

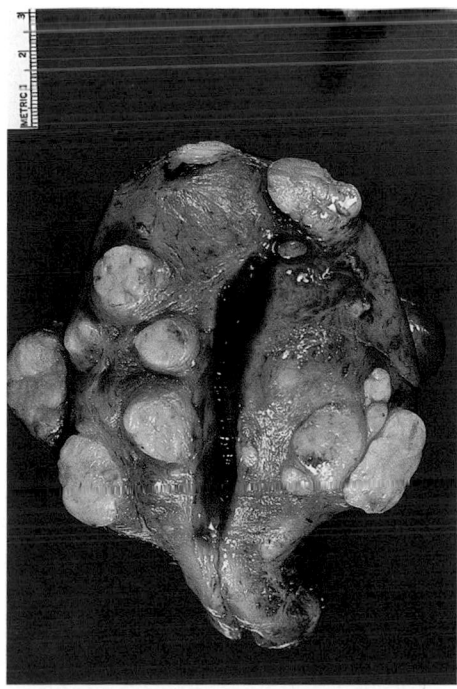

Fig. 19.167 Multiple uterine leiomyomas.

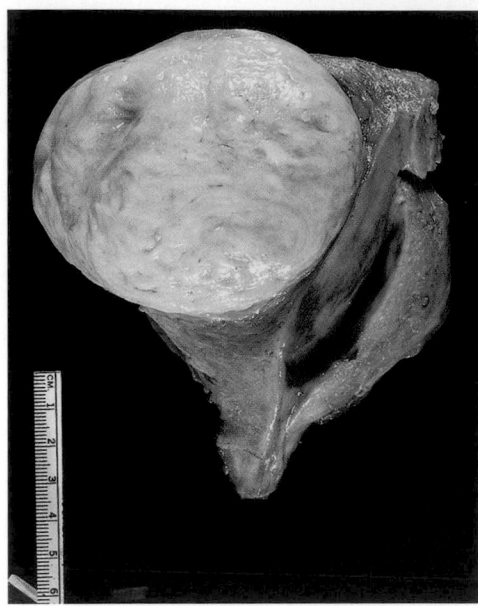

Fig. 19.168 Large uterine leiomyoma with intramural and subserous involvement.

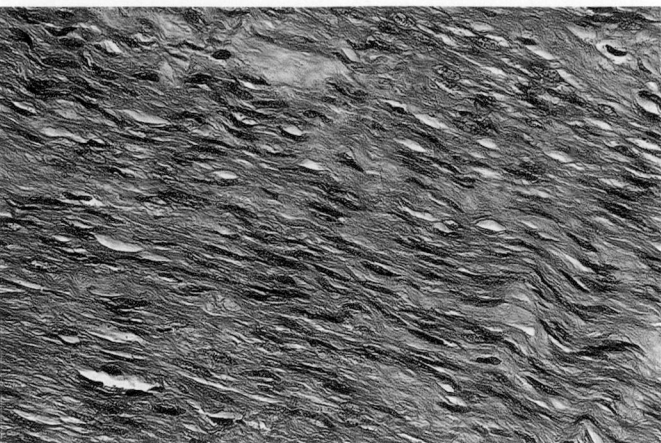

Fig. 19.169 Elongated spindle cells with fibrillary acidophilic cytoplasm in the usual type of uterine leiomyoma.

obvious increase in cellularity or definite hyaline changes, one is unable in most instances to decide whether they originated in a submucosal leiomyoma or whether they represent normal superficial myometrium curetted out by a vigorous operator.

Grossly, the cut surface of a typical leiomyoma has a raw silk appearance. Microscopically, the tumor is formed by interlacing bundles of smooth muscle cells separated by a greater or lesser amount of well-vascularized connective tissue (Fig. 19.169). Ultrastructurally, the features are those of smooth muscle cells with varying degrees of differentiation.[632] The stroma may contain a scattering of lymphocytes. Mast cells are often conspicuous, in contrast with leiomyomas of other sites.[634,637] On average, they are more numerous in cellular and bizarre leiomyomas than in either ordinary leiomyomas or leiomyosarcomas.[641]

Cytogenetic alterations are common in uterine leiomyomas. The most consistent are rearrangements of 6p, del(7q), +12, and +(12:14).[629,640] These have led to the discovery that disruptions or dysregulations of the high-mobility proteins HMGIC and HMGIY contribute to the development of these tumors.[631,635]

The treatment of uterine leiomyomas (including that of most of the many variants listed later) varies depending on the size and number of lesions, the age of the patient, and her desire to have children. Most asymptomatic leiomyomas need not be excised. Malignant transformation is such a rare event in these tumors that for practical purposes it can be disregarded.[638] Symptomatic neoplasms can be treated by hysterectomy or, in the case of patients who desire to become pregnant, by myomectomy.[620] Medical therapy includes administration of gonadotropin-releasing hormone analogs, such as leuprolide acetate depot. This may result in a decrease in the size of the leiomyoma—probably as a result of ischemic injury and cellular atrophy[626]—but it does not result in significant pleomorphism or increased mitotic activity.[621,627,628,644] The decrease in cell size and increase in collagenization have also been documented at the ultrastructural level.[630] Other authors have reported tumor infiltration by lymphocytes of predominantly T-cell type[619,633] and vasculitis.[680a] Immunohistochemically, leuprolide-treated leiomyomas show a decrease in cell proliferation indices and in hormone receptor expression.[645]

Another treatment modality for uterine leiomyoma is arterial embolization. This results in massive necrosis, sometimes accompanied by calcification, thrombosis, and a foreign body-type reaction to the injected material.[622,636]

Leiomyoma variants

Many variations on the basic theme previously described exist. Most of these are the result of secondary changes and are detectable in approximately 65% of cases. These include hyaline degeneration (63%), mucoid or myxomatous degeneration (19%), calcification (8%), cystic changes (4%), and fatty metamorphosis (3%). There is no relation between symptomatology and the presence of these changes.[689]

Red degeneration (present in 3% of cases) can result in abdominal pain, vomiting, and fever. This change is characterized grossly by a bulging surface and a homogeneous dark red appearance, and microscopically by extensive coagulative necrosis. It is often associated with pregnancy or the use of contraceptive drugs (Fig. 19.170).

Apoplectic leiomyoma is pathogenetically related to red degeneration. It is seen in patients taking birth-control pills and is characterized by stellate zones of recent hemorrhage within nodules of hypercellular smooth muscle, with few or no mitotic figures.[684]

Hydropic degeneration is characterized by the accu-

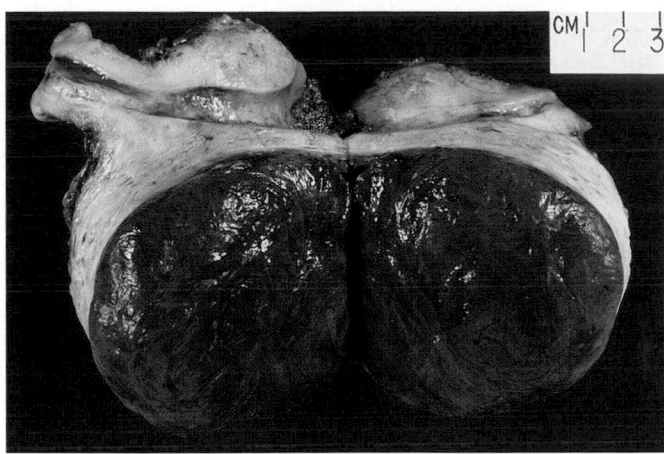

Fig. 19.170 This uterine leiomyoma has undergone massive red degeneration.

mulation of edema fluid, often associated with collagen deposition. It may have a diffuse, perinodular, or other pattern[656,657] (Figs 19.171 and 19.172). The appearance may simulate intravenous leiomyomatosis or myxoid leiomyosarcoma.[656] Regarding the latter, leiomyomas with hydropic degeneration have a delicate filigree pattern rather than thick fascicles, and the extracellular material is edema fluid rather than mucopolysaccharides.

Leiomyoma with lymphoid infiltration may simulate a malignant lymphoma because of the massiveness of the inflammatory component, which is made up of small lymphocytes, immunoblasts, and plasma cells. Germinal centers may be present. The surrounding myometrium is relatively unaffected.[663,666] A variation on the theme is represented by the leiomyomas with a heavy infiltration by eosinophils.[701] Some of these leiomyomas with infiltration by inflammatory cells had been treated with leuprolide.

Cellular leiomyoma is a term reserved for those tumors having increased cellularity but no coagulative necrosis, atypia, or an excessive number of mitotic figures (Fig. 19.173). Their natural history seems to be the

same as for the ordinary leiomyoma. The differential diagnosis includes leiomyosarcoma and endometrial stromal neoplasms.[688] At the cytogenetic level, cellular leiomyoma has been found to be accompanied by loss of almost the entire short arm of chromosome 1.[658a]

Atypical, bizarre, symplasmic, or pleomorphic leiomyoma contains bizarre tumor cells with variation in size and shape, hyperchromatic nuclei, and multinucleated forms but no coagulative necrosis or increased mitotic activity (Fig. 19.174).[660] Rarely, the entire tumor is composed of such cells. It may occur spontaneously but is often seen in patients taking progestin compounds.[662,691]

Mitotically active leiomyoma refers to tumors having from 5 to 15 mitotic figures per 10 HPF but lacking coagulative necrosis or cytologic atypia[687,692] (Fig. 19.175). They are discussed in more detail on p. 1611.

Granular cell change may exceptionally develop in uterine leiomyoma. We have seen a case of multiple

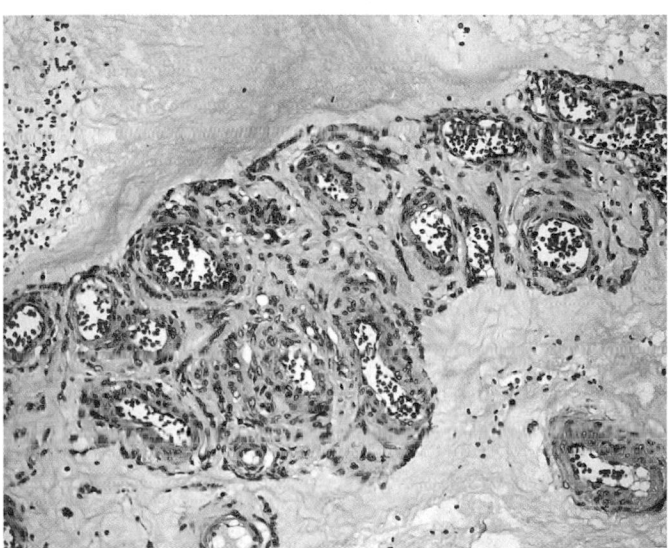

Fig. 19.172 So-called "perinodular hydropic degeneration" in uterine leiomyoma.

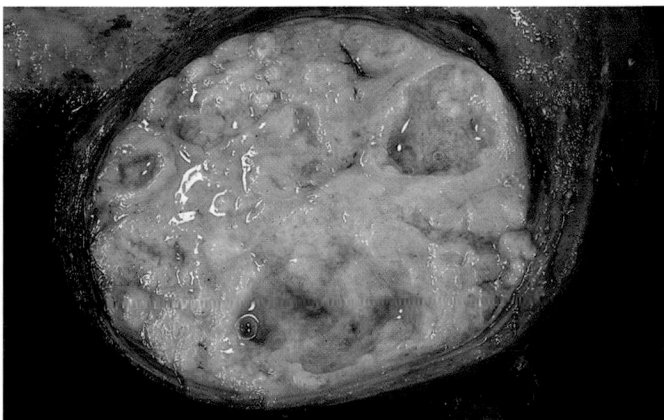

Fig. 19.171 Leiomyoma with edematous (hydropic) changes leading to the formation of cystic cavities. (Courtesy of Dr Pedro J Grases Galofrè; from Grases Galofrè PJ: Patologia ginecològic. Bases para el diagnòstico morfològico, Barcelona, Masson, 2002.)

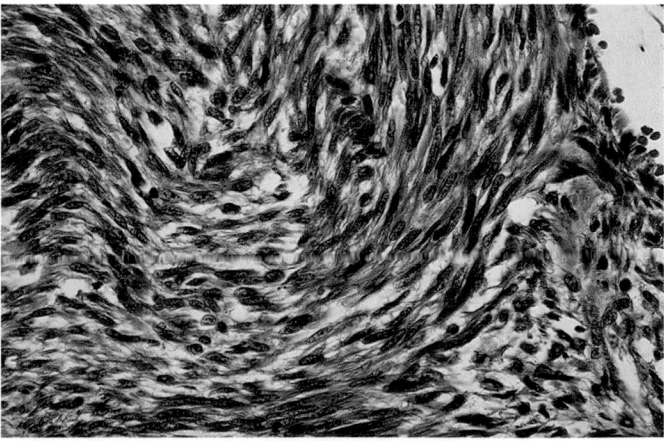

Fig. 19.173 Cellular leiomyoma. There is no pleomorphism, undue mitotic activity, or necrosis.

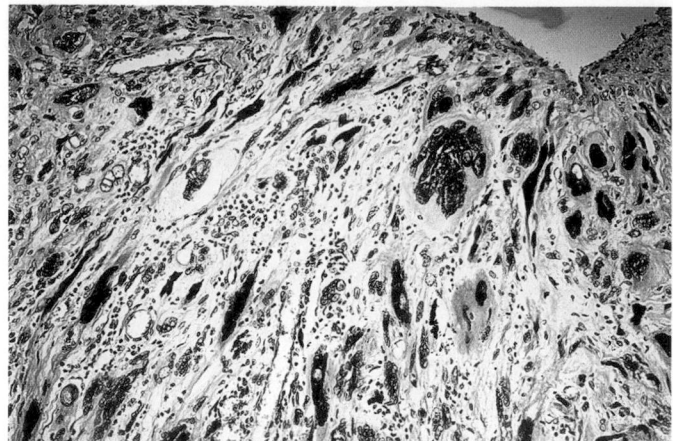

A

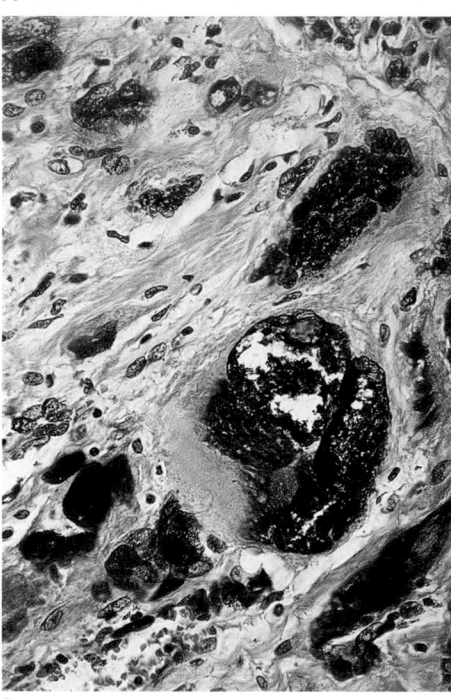

B

Fig. 19.174 A and **B**, Two views of bizarre leiomyoma. The size of some of the tumor cell nuclei makes them almost visible to the naked eye.

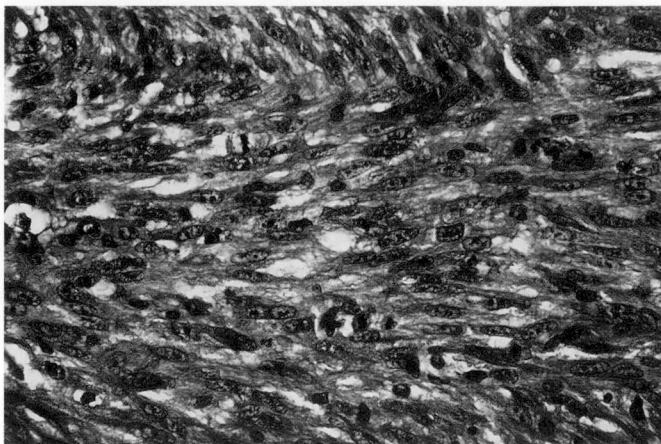

Fig. 19.175 Mitotically active leiomyoma. There is no pleomorphism or necrosis.

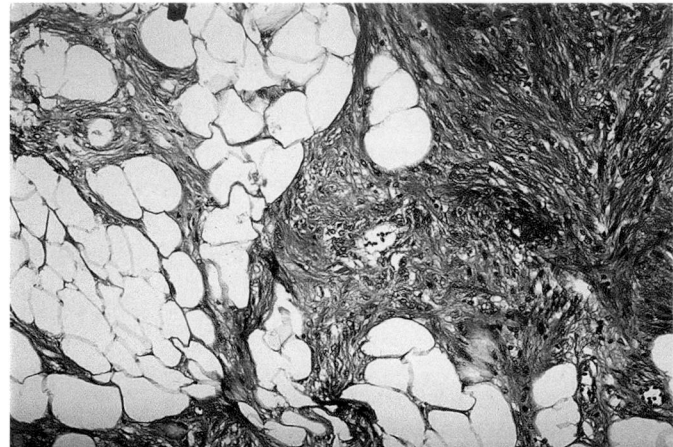

Fig. 19.176 Admixture of mature smooth muscle and adipose tissue in leiomyolipoma.

small myometrial tumors exhibiting this alteration. Ultrastructural study left no doubt as to the smooth muscle nature of the tumors on one hand, and the presence of lysosome-like granular cell changes on the other.

Leiomyolipoma (lipoleiomyoma) contains an admixture of smooth muscle and mature adipose tissue[671,690,693] (Fig. 19.176). It is believed that some of these tumors and the even rarer **lipomas** result from adipose metaplasia in leiomyomas.[690,697] A further variation on the theme is the **adenolipoleiomyoma**, the histogenesis of which is obscure.[677]

Palisaded leiomyoma is characterized by a degree of nuclear palisading such as to simulate a neurilemoma.[654]

Epithelioid (clear cell) leiomyoma (benign leiomyoblastoma) is partially or totally composed of rounded or polygonal cells, its appearance being similar to that of its more common counterpart in the gastrointestinal tract (Fig. 19.177). However, in contrast with the latter (which has been subsumed in the GIST concept) it is negative for CD117. Mixtures of epithelioid, clear cell, and plexiform patterns occur frequently enough to suggest that they represent variants of a single entity.[670,675] A transition to typical smooth muscle is sometimes observed. Ultrastructural studies have also provided support for the smooth muscle derivation of this peculiar neoplasm, as well as for several other types of myometrial tumors of unusual appearance.[659,679,680,702] Morphologically, similar tumors occur in the round ligament.[647]

A very interesting problem is posed by the occurrence of uterine tumors with a morphologic appearance consistent with epithelioid leiomyomas but accompanied by prominent hyalinization and featuring HMB-45 immunoreactivity.[681,700] It is not yet clear whether they should be regarded as a variant of epithelioid leiomyomas or as members of the epithelioid angiomyolipoma/PEComa family.

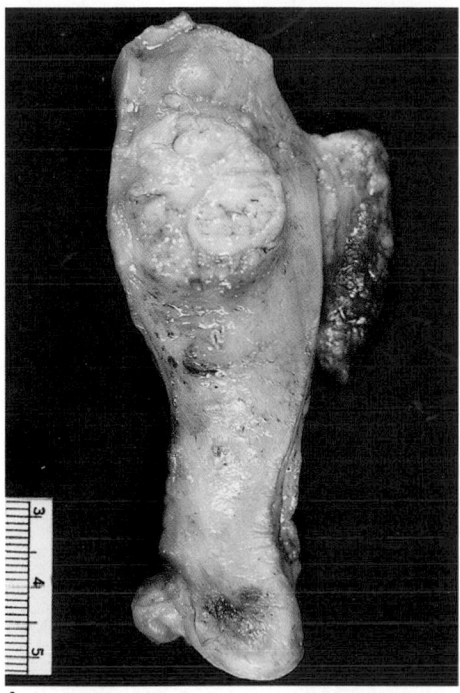

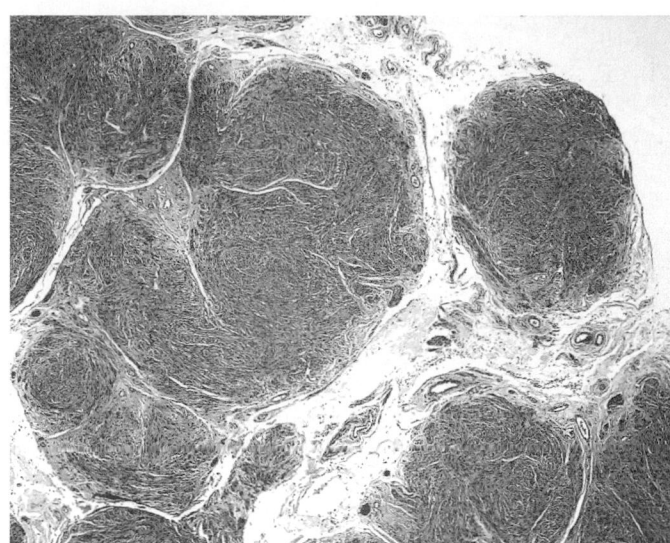

Fig. 19.178 Micronodular microscopic appearance of uterine leiomyoma having the gross appearance of so-called "cotyledonoid dissecting type."

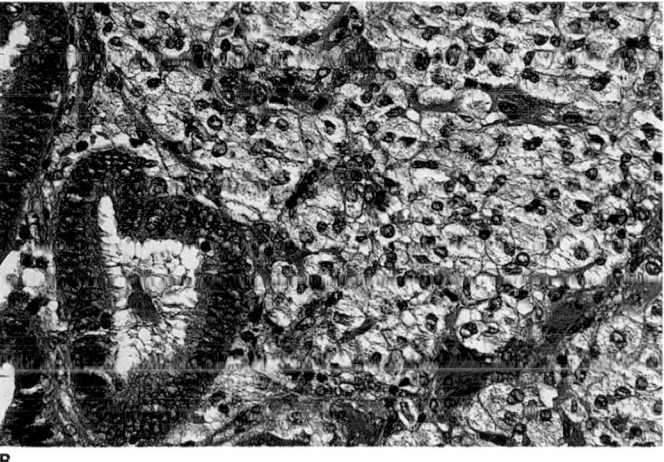

Fig. 19.177 Clear cell leiomyoma (benign leiomyoblastoma): A, gross appearance; B, microscopic appearance. The tumor cells have a round shape and an artifactually clear cytoplasm.

Cotyledonoid dissecting leiomyoma is so designated because its gross appearance resembles that of placental tissue. The tumor is exophytic, bulky, and extends from the uterine wall into the broad ligament and pelvic cavity.[652,696] Microscopically, the appearance is that of a leiomyoma with extensive degenerative changes (Fig. 19.178). Despite its dissecting pattern, it lacks vascular invasion and is of benign nature. Variations exist of leiomyomas that are cotyledonoid but not dissecting,[695] and dissecting but not cotyledonoid.[665,694] Believe it or not, there is also a cotyledonoid hydropic intravenous leiomyomatosis.[673]

Parasitic leiomyoma is the term given to the uterine leiomyoma that has become separate from the uterus and has acquired vascular connections with the omentum, pelvic wall, or other intra-abdominal sites, such as the cecal wall. The low-lying retroperitoneal smooth muscle tumors occurring in females and behaving in a benign fashion probably belong to this category, in the sense of being composed of myometrium-type smooth muscle, whether they actually arise from the myometrial wall or not.[649]

Leiomyoma with skeletal muscle differentiation has been reported as an exceptional event.[664,678]

Diffuse leiomyomatosis is the term given to involvement of almost the entire myometrium by innumerable, ill-defined leiomyomas, many of microscopic size.[655,682] A clonality analysis done in a case of this condition supports the interpretation that these minute leiomyomas are independent tumors.[648] This extremely rare condition should be distinguished from the nebulous *primary myometrial hypertrophy* or *myometrial hyperplasia*, defined as a uterus weighing over 120 g in the absence of any mass-like myometrial lesion.[658,676]

Intravenous leiomyomatosis is an extremely rare condition characterized by the growth of mature smooth muscle inside the lumen of uterine and pelvic veins[668,686] (Fig. 19.179). It is often associated with typical uterine leiomyomas, and it may arise from them.[685] The clinical and gross features are similar to those of the form of endometrial stromal sarcoma, but grossly apparent involvement of veins is more prominent. At the microscopic level, intravenous leiomyomatosis is composed of elongated smooth muscle cells, whereas endometrial stromal sarcoma is made up of round or oval endometrial stromal cells. The two processes may well be histogenetically related in view of the already discussed occurrence of occasional hybrids (combined muscle–stromal tumors) and the close kinship between the endometrial stroma and the myometrial smooth muscle. Mitotic figures are

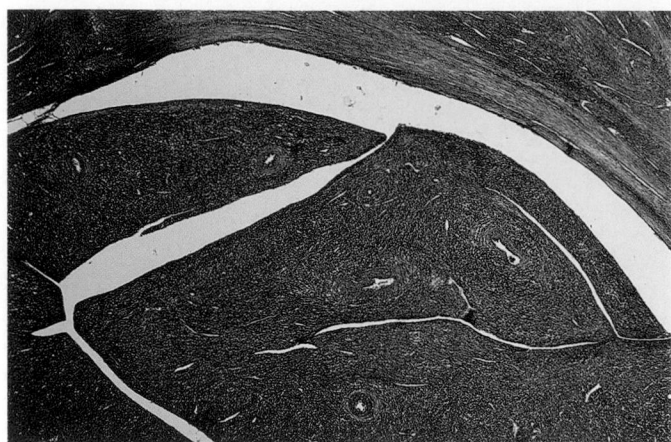

Fig. 19.179 Large plugs of mature smooth muscle filling the vascular lumina in intravenous leiomyomatosis.

rare or absent. The vessel permeation often extends to vessels in the broad ligament and in uterine and iliac veins; from there, it can proceed along the vena cava and even reach the right atrium.[651] However, distant metastases are exceptionally rare, and the long-term prognosis is excellent.[683] Cases have been described in which the microscopic appearance of the intravenous masses was that of epithelioid (clear cell) leiomyomas[650] (Fig. 19.180).

Benign metastasizing leiomyoma is the name given to the uterine tumor having the typical features of a leiomyoma (sometimes on the cellular side but invariably lacking coagulative necrosis, increased mitotic activity, and significant atypia) which is accompanied by nodules in the lung, regional lymph nodes, or other sites having a similar appearance and presumably representing metastases from it.[646,698] The extrauterine nodules may be just as bland-looking as the original uterine tumor or show features of leiomyosarcoma or smooth muscle tumor of uncertain, unknown or undetermined malignant potential (STUMP).[661] The interval between hysterectomy and the appearance of the lung nodules is, on average, 15 years. The nodules tend to be multiple,

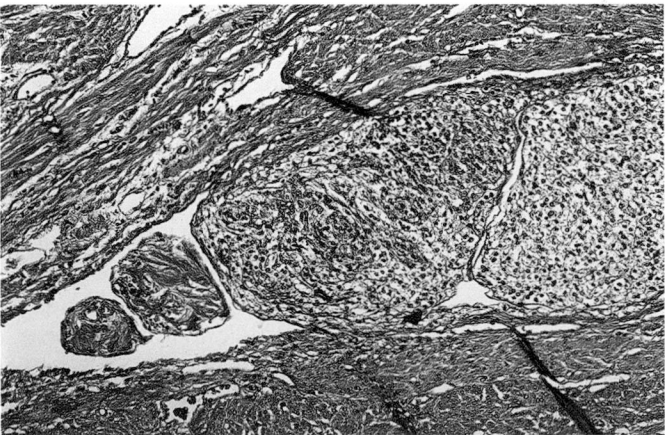

Fig. 19.180 Intravenous leiomyomatosis composed of clear smooth muscle cells.

and they have an average size of approximately 2 cm. The patients tend to be younger than those with conventional leiomyosarcoma, and the clinical course is much more indolent, with a median survival of 94 months after the excision of the "metastases."[674] Some of these occurrences may be explained on the basis of inadequate sampling of the original tumor, but the fact that in many instances the extrauterine foci have a microscopic appearance that is just as bland suggests that this cannot be the explanation for the entire category. Parenthetically, the similarities with ordinary leiomyomas also apply to their hormone receptor profile (high) and proliferative activity (low), the only difference being perhaps their tendency to overexpress p53[672,674] and the apparently frequent deletion of the long arm of chromosomes 19 and 22.[686a] Another possibility that has been advanced is that the extrauterine foci represent independent neoplasms.[653] However, the fact that they have been found to be clonally related speaks in favor of metastasis from a uterine neoplasm.[699]

Although this occurrence is unsettling, it is entirely credible. Other examples of tumors that generally behave in a benign fashion but once in a great while result in metastases having the same "benign" appearance certainly exist, benign mixed tumor of the salivary gland being a prime example. We simply have to accept the fact that tumors do not need to have the conventional morphologic attributes of malignancy to be able to metastasize. As to whether the particular neoplasm discussed in this section should be called a metastasizing leiomyoma or a low-grade leiomyosarcoma mimicking a leiomyoma depends on whether one wishes to designate tumors according to their morphology (in which case it would be a leiomyoma) or their behavior (in which case it would be a leiomyosarcoma). In this regard, it may be opportune to quote here Julian Huxley—the famous biologist, zoologist, humanist, and popular writer—who, in his lecture on "Biological aspects of cancer," given at the Sloan-Kettering Institute in 1955, stated when discussing the policy for designating lesions solely on the basis of their morphology: "This seems a regrettable example of specialist scholasticism. Cancer (malignancy) must be defined operatively in terms of what the tumor cells do, not what they look like; otherwise the term ceases to have biological meaning."[669]

One is also reminded of the comment made by Allen Graham, surgeon/pathologist at the Cleveland Clinic, as far back as 1924 in an analogous context involving the thyroid gland, when reflecting on "the academically irreconcilable conflict between a purely morphological and a biological interpretation of the term *carcinoma*," and when concluding that "terms such as *metastasizing adenoma*…are confusing, misleading, inaccurate, serve no useful purpose, and should be eliminated."[667] Eighty years have gone by and the "irreconcilable conflict" remains.

Leiomyosarcoma

Clinical and gross features

Leiomyosarcomas occur in an older average age group than leiomyomas (median age, 54 years), although they can also occur in younger patients.[703a] Some of the epidemiologic findings in patients with leiomyosarcoma parallel those from studies in endometrial carcinoma and suggest a role for unopposed estrogen stimulation.[704] The time-honored assumption that most leiomyosarcomas arise from preexisting leiomyomas is probably incorrect, as indicated by the fact that in one large series 67% of the leiomyosarcomas were solitary.[705] Some leiomyosarcomas are grossly similar to ordinary leiomyomas, but the majority are soft or fleshy, with necrotic or hemorrhagic areas and signs of invasiveness[703] (Fig. 19.181).

Microscopic features

Microscopically, typical leiomyosarcomas are hypercellular, with nuclear atypia and pleomorphism, mitotically

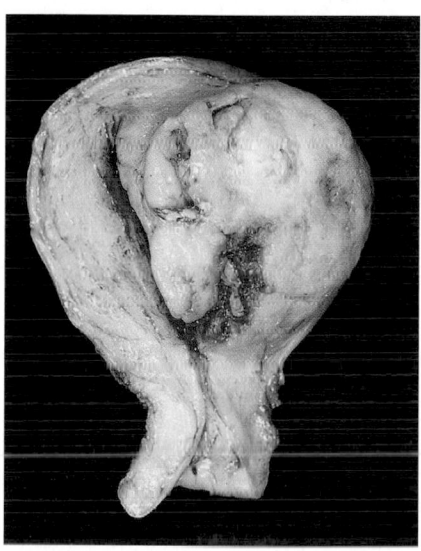

Fig. 19.181 Leiomyosarcoma resulting in a large intramural and submucous mass. There are foci of hemorrhage and necrosis.

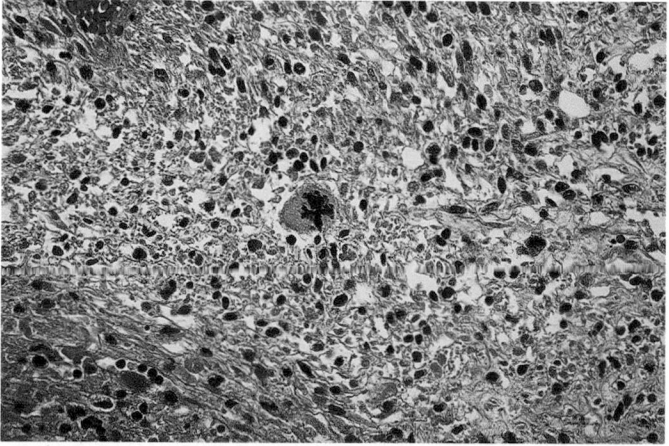

Fig. 19.182 Leiomyosarcoma showing hypercellularity, pleomorphism, atypical mitoses, and necrosis.

active (with some of the mitoses being atypical), and with areas of necrosis (Fig. 19.182). Alas, not all leiomyosarcomas will exhibit simultaneously all of these features, whereas some leiomyomas can display one or several of them.[706] The relative importance of these criteria for the differential diagnosis between leiomyoma and leiomyosarcoma is the subject of a special section below.

Electron microscopic, immunohistochemical, and molecular genetic features

Ultrastructurally and immunohistochemically, the features of leiomyosarcoma are those of smooth muscle cells.[707,710] There is consistent immunoreactivity for smooth and common muscle actin, desmin, calponin, h-caldesmon, and vimentin.[717] There is also common reactivity for low-molecular-weight keratin (as identified with CAM 5.2) and EMA,[708] a feature that may lead to a mistaken interpretation, particularly if the tumor cells have an epithelioid appearance.[716] Estrogen and progesterone receptors are expressed, although with a lesser degree of intensity than in leiomyomas.[709a,711,718] Another molecule consistently expressed by these tumors is oxytocin receptor, in a fashion similar to that seen in leiomyomas and in contrast with endometrial stromal tumors.[709b] It has been claimed that leiomyosarcomas are accompanied by loss of the cell adhesion molecule CD44, which is present in normal myometrium and in leiomyomas.[714] The immunohistochemical profile of uterine leiomyosarcomas is somewhat different from that of extrauterine leiomyosarcomas (except for those in the pelvic region), probably due at least in part to the estrogen dependency of the former.[715]

At the molecular genetic level, and in contrast to leiomyoma, there is common overexpression of p53.[712,718] There is also frequent overexpression of the c-*myc* oncogene, but this is also a feature of half of the leiomyomas.[709] Cyclins A and E (particularly the latter) are expressed at a much higher level in leiomyosarcomas than in leiomyomas.[713]

Leiomyosarcoma variants

Epithelioid (clear cell) leiomyosarcoma (malignant leiomyoblastoma) resembles microscopically the gastrointestinal tumors that used to carry this designation, most of which are currently included in the GIST category.[719,722,724] In contrast to the latter, they are usually negative for CD117. The main differential diagnosis is with their benign counterpart, i.e., epithelioid (clear cell) leiomyoma. General criteria apply (see below), such as larger size, infiltrating margins, mitotic activity, and presence of necrosis, and also absence of hyalinization.[719,722,724] The differential diagnosis also includes endometrial stromal tumors and metastatic carcinoma.[725]

Myxoid leiomyosarcoma can arise in the uterine wall, broad ligament, and other pelvic sites.[721] Grossly, it has a gelatinous appearance and deceptively well circumscribed borders. Microscopically, however, it is invasive.

The stroma is highly myxoid and the tumor cells are arranged as bundles of typical smooth muscle cells alternating with nondescript mesenchymal cells (Fig. 19.183). The main differential diagnosis (an important one) is with leiomyoma with hydropic degeneration (see p. 1604). In the past, it was frequent to see myxoid leiomyosarcomas underdiagnosed as leiomyomas; at present, the reverse is more likely to occur. Regarding this differential, it is important to point out that the mitotic count criteria used for the usual leiomyosarcoma (see below) do not apply, in the sense that myxoid leiomyosarcomas tend to recur and metastasize whether mitoses are scanty (which is the usual situation) or numerous.[721,723]

Leiomyosarcoma with osteoclast-like giant cells occurs more frequently in the uterus than in any of the other places where malignant smooth muscle tumors can develop (Fig. 19.184). The smooth muscle nature of the tumor cells—as confirmed immunohistochemically—

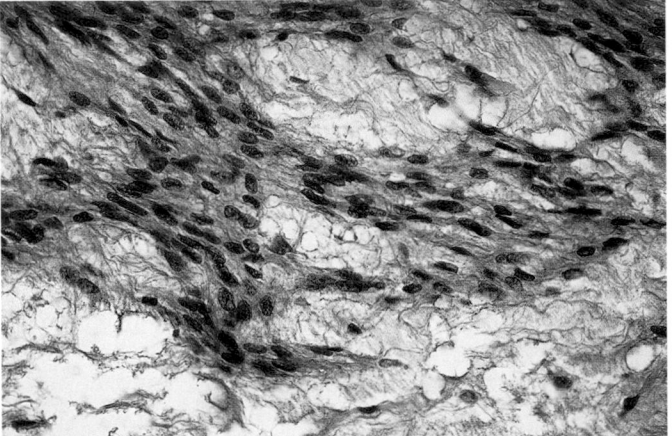

Fig. 19.183 Uterine myxoid leiomyosarcoma (slide courtesy of Dr. Robert E Scully, Boston).

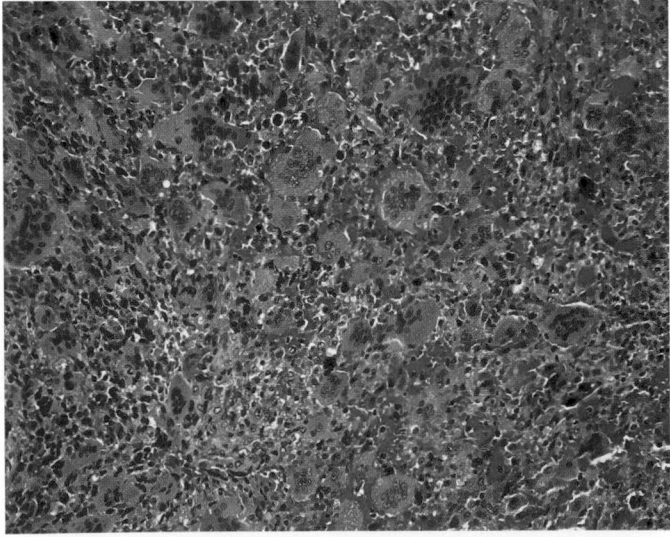

Fig. 19.184 Malignant giant cell tumor of uterus. This is regarded as a variant of leiomyosarcoma with osteoclast-like giant cells.

distinguishes this entity from so-called "malignant giant cell tumor."[726]

Intravenous leiomyosarcomatosis, an exceptionally rare condition, can be viewed as the malignant counterpart of intravenous leiomyomatosis.[720]

Spread, metastases, treatment, and prognosis

Uterine leiomyosarcoma usually spreads within the pelvis and in the form of distant metastases to the lung, bone, and other sites.[729] Lymph node metastases are exceptional. The standard treatment is total abdominal hysterectomy with bilateral salpingo-oophorectomy. Prognostic factors include the following:

1 *Tumor stage.* Extension outside the confines of the uterus is a finding of ominous prognosis.[731] In one series of 20 patients in whom this occurred, there were no survivors beyond 29 months.[727]
2 *Microscopic grade.* No consistent correlation has been found between survival and the histologic grade of the tumor. Specifically, the grading system used for sarcomas of the somatic soft tissue is not applicable.[730]
3 *DNA ploidy.* There is some evidence that the DNA ploidy pattern as determined by flow cytometry may be of prognostic significance.[728,732]

Prediction of behavior in uterine smooth muscle tumors

The majority of uterine smooth muscle tumors are readily classifiable into benign or malignant.[741,750] There are some lesions, however, for which that placement is very difficult, sometimes excruciatingly so. The morphologic reasons for this, which at the same time represent the main criteria upon which to base a decision, are the following:

1 *Necrosis.* Two patterns of necrosis have been identified in smooth muscle tumors, respectively named coagulative and hyalin (hyaline). In the former there is an abrupt transition between the necrotic and the viable cells. On low power, the typical appearance is that of a cuff of preserved tumor cells around large vessels surrounded by large expanses of necrotic tumor. On high power, two of the classical morphologic forms of nuclear necrosis (pyknosis and karyorrhexis) are evident. In hyaline necrosis, there is a distinct zonal pattern reminiscent of an evolving infarct: a center of "bland" necrosis (i.e., one in which nuclear debris are difficult to see), a periphery of granulation tissue, and a layer of hyalinized collagen in between. Coagulative necrosis, as above defined, is currently regarded as the most important prognostic predictor in these tumors. Because of the very fact that necrosis (or, rather, a particular type of necrosis) has acquired such a well-deserved significance in this area, it may be worthwhile to discuss it in some detail, beginning with the somewhat questionable nature of the terms

chosen, as emerges from the scholarly review on cell death by Majno and Joris.[742] In it, the authors point out that the term coagulation necrosis was first introduced by Conheim in 1877, influenced by the work of Weigert, for the lesion that we call today white infarct, under the mistaken notion that the process was due to a combination of necrosis and a coagulum of fibrin. Therefore, if the term coagulation (or coagulative) necrosis were to be used at all it should be as a synonym for white (anemic) infarct, not in opposition to it. As for "hyaline" necrosis, it is not much better, since "hyaline" refers to any homogeneous eosinophilic material, whether extracellular or intracellular (as in Mallory's alcoholic hyaline). Furthermore, in the situation in question, it is applied to the collagen that is deposited at the granulation tissue front of an infarct and is, therefore, dependent upon the stage of the latter. In fact, it would seem that the key morphologic difference between the two forms of necrosis is that the first shows prominent hematoxyphilic nuclear debris (karyorrhectic and pyknotic nuclei) whereas in the second the appearance is more homogeneous ("bland") because the nuclear remnants are difficult to see (karyolysis). It has been suggested that the name of the former be changed to "tumor cell necrosis,"[737] but this is not much of an improvement, since in both types it is largely the tumor cell that is undergoing necrosis.

Semantics aside, the observation made by Bell et al.[734] is of the greatest diagnostic significance and may turn out to have a sound biological basis, since karyorrhectic and pyknotic nuclei are generally a feature of death by apoptosis, whereas karyolytic nuclei are a feature of ischemic and other forms of accidental death (what Majno calls death by murder or oncosis).[742]

2 *Mitotic activity.* This remains another important criterion despite the somewhat inaccurate fashion in which it is measured, in terms of lack of standardization and poor reproducibility,[736,746,747] in the sense of being influenced by the thickness of the slide, microscope magnification factor, size of tumor cells, proportion of tumor cells to stroma, and observer criteria.[735] Regarding the latter, a common mistake among neophytes is to count the pyknotic nuclei often seen scattered around in smooth muscle tumors (whether from lymphocytes, mast cells, or smooth muscle cells) as mitotic figures. Another theoretical source of variation is the interval between excision and fixation, but this seems not to be important. The best way to eliminate most of these sources of inaccuracy would be to express the number of mitoses as a percentage of the tumor cell population, as has routinely been done when counting thymidine-labeled nuclei. We are in the process of developing a computer program for that purpose. When using current methodology, some practical measures can be taken to improve accuracy. One is to scan the sections for the most active area, do the mitotic count in 10 consecutive fields in that area, and repeat the procedure a minimum of four times. Another obvious measure is to sample the tumor adequately. Kempson[736] recommends a total of at least 10 sections or one section for each centimeter of diameter, whichever is greater. The section should have a real thickness as close as possible to the 5 μm indicated in the microtome setting. "High power field" (HPF) usually means the combination of a 10× eyepiece and a 40× objective. If the operator is using a 15× eyepiece and/or a 63× objective, adjustments should be made. The criteria for identifying mitotic figures should be strict. The members of the Multicenter Morphometric Mammary Carcinoma Project proposed the following[749]:

1 The nuclear membrane must be absent, so cells must have passed the prophase.
2 Clear, hairy extensions of nuclear material (condensed chromosomes) must be present, either clotted (beginning metaphase), in a plane (metaphase/anaphase), or in separate clots (telophase). Regular extensions with an empty central zone favor a nonmitosis.
3 Two parallel, clearly separate chromosome clots are to be counted as if they are separate mitoses, however obvious it is that only one mitotic figure is concerned. This is in view of future automated mitotic figure recognition with image analysis.

3 *Atypia.* This refers to the combination of pleomorphism (meaning marked differences in size and shape) and nuclear hyperchromasia, and it should be already evident on low-power examination. It is classified as focal or extensive, and graded (acknowledging the subjectivity of the exercise) as mild, moderate, or severe.
4 *Cellularity.* The term is self-explanatory, and the determination just as subjective. This is one of the least important parameters in this exercise.
5 *Tumor borders,* i.e., the relationship of the tumor with the surrounding myometrium.

The evaluation of these criteria, alone and in combination, allows a fairly accurate *but not infallible* prediction of tumor behavior. The points worth stressing are the following:

1 The weight of the morphologic factors is coagulative necrosis, high mitotic activity, pleomorphism, and cellularity, in this order of significance.
2 Tumors that are hypercellular but lack the other criteria are to be regarded as benign cellular leiomyomas (see p. 1605).
3 Tumors with atypia (even if marked and diffuse) should not be regarded as malignant if they lack coagulative necrosis and mitotic activity. Rather, they belong to the category variously called *atypical, bizarre,*

symplasmic, or *pleomorphic* if the change is focal, and to a *borderline category* if it is extensive.

4 Tumors with increased mitotic activity (up to 15 mitoses per 10 HPF) but lacking coagulative necrosis and atypia are to be regarded as *mitotically active leiomyomas* (see p. 1605).

5 Tumors with coagulative necrosis and diffuse atypia and/or increased mitotic activity (>10 per 10 HPF) should be regarded as leiomyosarcomas.

6 Tumors with coagulative necrosis but neither atypia nor increased mitotic activity should be placed in a *"borderline"* category (see below).

7 Tumors with diffuse moderate-to-severe atypia *and* more than 10 mitoses per 10 HPF should be called leiomyosarcoma even if they lack coagulative necrosis.

These recommendations are primarily based on the careful and painstaking work done by Richard Kempson and the changing members of this team (Bari, Hendrikson, Zaloudek, Bell, Longacre, and others) over a 35-year period.[734,737,738,739,741] This is shown in a simplified form for the benefit of the reader in Table 19.2, the arrangement being slightly different from that presented in the original articles. Another difference is the fact that the category "smooth muscle tumor of uncertain unknown or undetermined malignant potential (STUMP)" has been retained because it was felt that it best expresses the fact that in some uterine smooth muscle tumors it is simply impossible with current tools to predict their behavior with certainty. The best proof of this statement is the existence of a tumor type having *none* of the mor-

phologic features that identify it as a leiomyosarcoma but which spreads to distant organs (benign metastasizing leiomyoma, see p. 1608). In our opinion, one would serve the patient and the clinician better (and would also be closer to expressing the truth) by doing away with the traditional binary classification of these tumors into benign and malignant, i.e., leiomyoma versus leiomyosarcoma (which is improved only slightly by the addition of a borderline category), and by switching to a nomenclature that would simply identify these neoplasms as smooth muscle tumors, followed by an estimation (ideally expressed in percentages) of the probability of the tumor recurring or metastasizing, based on a careful evaluation of all the parameters discussed in this section and any others that may be found of help in this regard. Until and unless such a radical change in nosology takes place, and as long as we subject ourselves to the current manicheist approach, the above recommendations will have to do.

Two additional comments are in order. These considerations have been devised for the conventional type of uterine smooth muscle tumor, and cannot be applied unchanged to the variants. For instance, myxoid leiomyosarcoma is to be diagnosed as such even if in most cases it lacks coagulative necrosis, increased mitotic activity, and severe atypia.

The other comment applies to the hope that the abundant information that is being obtained regarding the phenotypic and genotypic features of these tumors will provide assistance to the pathologist in terms of an accurate prognostic assessment and a precise therapeutic recommendation.[740] Some claims are already being made

Table 19.2 Criteria and diagnostic terms for uterine smooth muscle tumors (freely adapted from the work of Richard Kempson MD, and his co-workers)

Coagulative necrosis	Mitotic count per 10 HPF	Atypia		Diagnosis
Present	Greater than 10	Moderate to severe (focal or diffuse)		Leiomyosarcoma
		None to mild		Leiomyosarcoma
	Equal or less than 10	Moderate to severe (focal or diffuse)		Leiomyosarcoma
		None to mild		STUMP (1)
Absent	Greater than 10	Moderate to severe	Diffuse	Leiomyosarcoma
			Focal	STUMP (2)
		None to mild		Mitotically active leiomyoma (up to 15 mitoses/10 HPF are allowed)
	Equal or less than 10	Moderate to severe	Diffuse	STUMP (3)
			Focal	Leiomyoma (4)
		None to mild		Leiomyoma

(1) Of the three tumors here placed in the STUMP category, this is the one most likely to behave in a malignant fashion. Actually, it is regarded as a probable leiomyosarcoma in Kempson's scheme. The alternative possibility of an infarction in a leiomyoma due to torsion or other factors should be considered.

(2) In Kempson's scheme, this is designated as STUMP if the mitotic activity is higher than 15.

(3) This is referred to as "atypical leiomyoma with low risk of recurrence" in Kempson's scheme.

(4) This is designated as "leiomyoma with limited experience" in Kempson's scheme.

along these lines, in the sense that the following features are usually present in leiomyosarcomas but rare or absent in leiomyomas: loss of heterozygosity for chromosome 10,[744] presence of galectin-3 and its binding site,[745] low levels of estrogen and progesterone receptors,[751] loss of CD44,[743] and lack of gamma smooth muscle isoactin gene expression.[748]

As exciting as all these propositions are, it is fair to say that the decision whether to place a uterine smooth muscle tumor into a given prognostic category—no matter how designated—remains for now largely dependent on the time-honored morphologic criteria (or, as someone coarsely put it, on "the physical appearance of [the] tissue specimens").[733]

Other tumors and tumorlike conditions

Postoperative spindle cell nodules similar to those occurring in the vagina have been observed in the endometrium.[759]

Extramedullary hematopoiesis can occur in the endometrium in the absence of any hematologic disorder or systemic disease.[799]

Adenomatoid tumors identical to those more commonly seen in the fallopian tube are sometimes found in the uterine wall, usually beneath the serosa and close to the cornua.[786,807] Exceptionally, they will be apparent in a curetting specimen. These tumors are usually small (mean diameter, 2 cm) and characterized microscopically by adenoid, angiomatoid, solid, and cystic patterns occurring singly or in combination[790,793] (Fig. 19.185). The most cystic examples can simulate lymphangiomas. They are often accompanied by smooth muscle hypertrophy and can be confused with leiomyomas. Their

mesothelial nature has been established on the basis of ultrastructural and immunohistochemical findings[789,797,802,803] and is also supported by its occasional coexistence with other lesions of reputed mesothelial derivation, such as benign multicystic mesothelioma.[755]

Arteriovenous fistula in the wall of the uterus may produce large pulsating masses. The vascular connections are demonstrable by angiography.[779]

Benign mesenchymal tumors other than those already described are practically nonexistent. *Lipomas* may result, at least in some instances, from adipose metaplasia of leiomyomas.[792,794] Cases have been reported of *lymphangiomyoma(tosis)* (some associated with tuberous sclerosis)[770,775] and related *HMB-45-positive epithelioid tumors* in the PEComa family.[795,809] The nosologic position of these tumors with regard to epithelioid leiomyoma is discussed on p. 1606.

Sarcomas of types other than those already described can arise in the uterus. They include *chondrosarcoma,*[758] *osteosarcoma,*[763] *rhabdomyosarcoma,*[788,791] *angiosarcoma,*[782,796] *malignant fibrous histiocytoma,*[757] *malignant mesenchymoma* (one arising in a leiomyoma),[762] *alveolar soft part sarcoma,*[769] and *Ewing's sarcoma/PNET*[761,772] (Fig. 19.186). A case of the latter contained areas of cartilaginous metaplasia[767] and another was associated with an endometrial adenocarcinoma.[798] Some of these sarcomas have developed following radiation therapy for cervical carcinoma or other malignancies.[784] Some of the angiosarcomas have been of epithelioid type, immunoreactive for keratin, and apparently arising within leiomyomas[804] (Fig. 19.187).

Before making a diagnosis of uterine sarcoma (particularly if the tumor is very pleomorphic and/or with

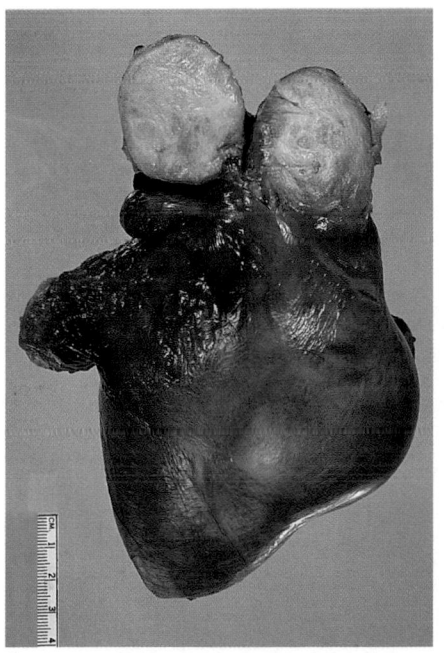

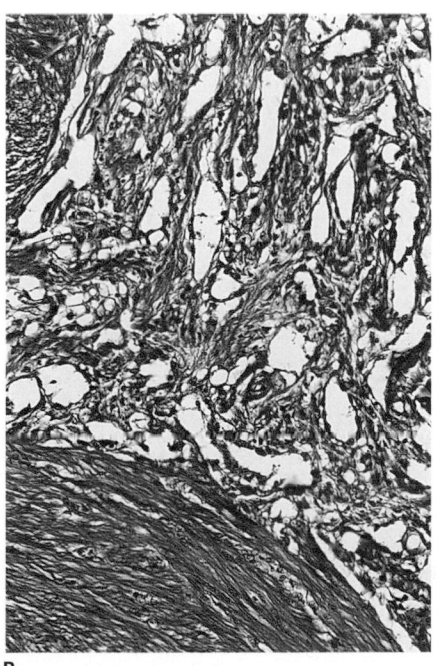

Fig. 19.185 A and **B,** Adenomatoid tumor of uterus. **A,** Gross appearance. The location at one of the cornua is characteristic. **B,** Microscopic appearance showing tubular formations lined by flattened mesothelial cells.

A

B

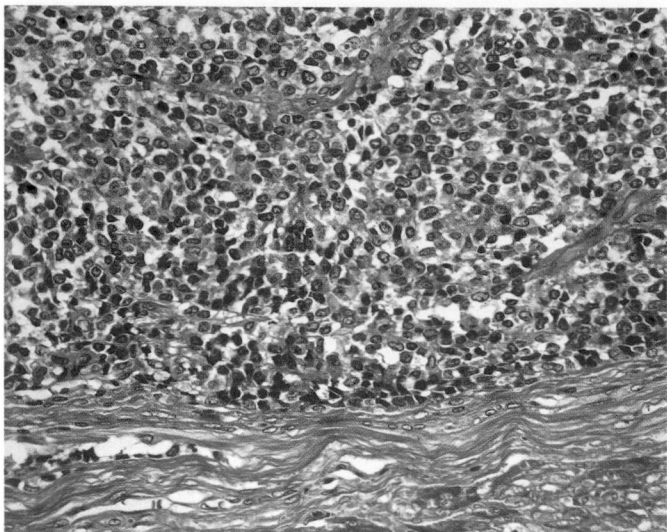

Fig. 19.186 Ewing's sarcoma/PNET presenting as a uterine mass, a most unusual occurrence.

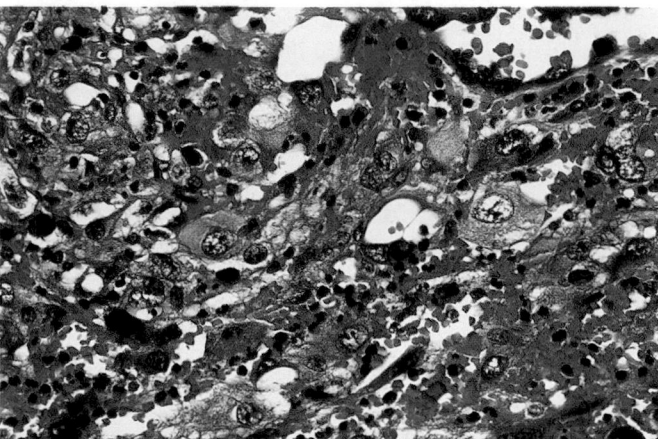

Fig. 19.187 Epithelioid angiosarcoma arising within an uterine leiomyosarcoma.

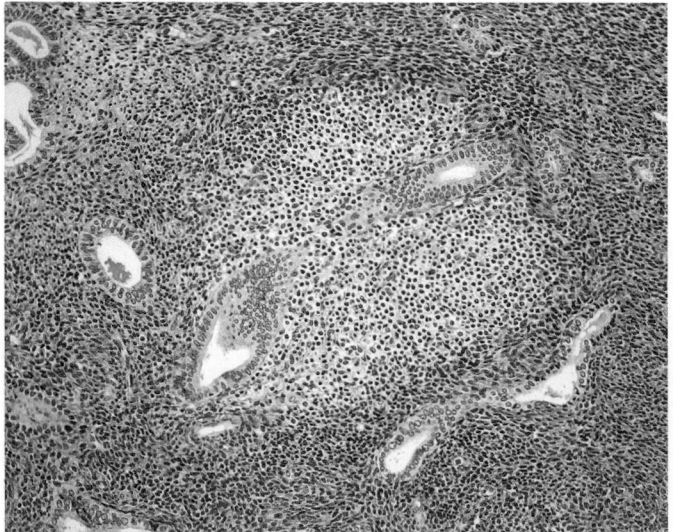

Fig. 19.188 Low-grade marginal zone-type malignant lymphoma involving uterine mucosa.

heterologous elements), the more likely possibility of an MMMT with predominance of the sarcoma-like component should be ruled out with thorough sampling.[764]

Malignant lymphomas can present initially in the endometrium, myometrium, or both.[766,771,810] The patients typically present with bleeding and a subepithelial mass. Most tumors are of diffuse large B-cell type.[753,810] Cases of low-grade B-cell lymphoma,[808] (Fig. 19.188) T-cell lymphoma,[780] Hodgkin's lymphoma,[774] and angiotropic lymphoma[760] with primary uterine involvement have also been described. Malignant lymphomas should be distinguished from florid but reactive immunoproliferative conditions involving the endometrium[811] and from *inflammatory pseudotumor*.[768] In these benign conditions, the large lymphoid cells are usually accompanied by plasma cells, small lymphocytes, and/or neutrophils.[765] **Granulocytic sarcomas** and **plasmacytoma/myeloma** can also involve the uterus, occasionally as the first manifestation of the disease.[771,787,800]

Other exceptionally rare primary uterine tumors include **Brenner tumor**[754] (microscopically identical to its ovarian counterpart and sometimes having a polypoid configuration),[752] **extrarenal Wilms' tumor**,[785] **glioma**,[812] **carcinoid tumor**,[756] **paraganglioma**[813] (including a pigmented variant[805]), and **yolk sac (endodermal sinus) tumor**.[777]

Metastatic carcinoma from extrapelvic sites may cause uterine bleeding as the presenting symptom. The breast, gastrointestinal tract, kidney, and skin (melanoma) are the most frequent primary sites.[778,781,801] The myometrium is more often involved than the endometrium, (Fig. 19.189) and sometimes the leiomyomas present contain metastatic tumor; however, it is not rare for the malignancy to be present in material from endometrial curettings, especially in cases of lobular carcinoma of the breast,[806] and also with neuroendocrine carcinomas and other neoplasms.[776] Exceptionally, a well-differentiated mucinous neoplasm of the appendix

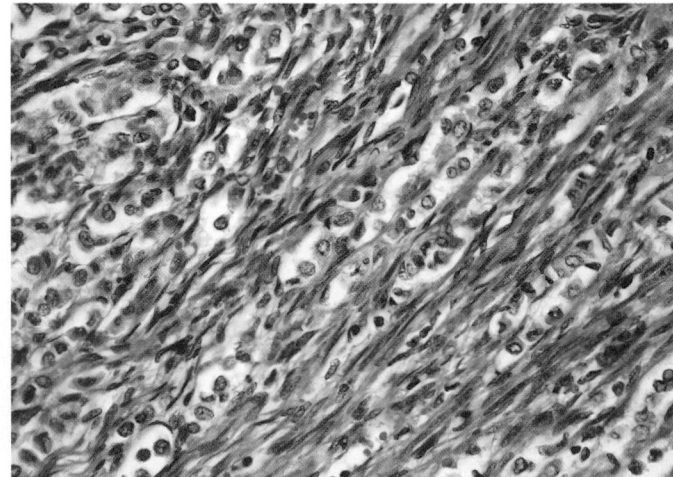

Fig. 19.189 Lobular breast carcinoma metastatic to myometrium. Note the Indian file pattern of growth.

will coat the endometrial surface in a pseudomyxomatous fashion.[783] On occasion, the metastatic breast lobular carcinoma is seen involving a tamoxifen-associated endometrial polyp.[773]

References

Normal anatomy

1 Arias-Stella J. Atypical endometrial changes produced by chorionic tissue. Hum Pathol 1972, **3**: 450–453.

2 Arias-Stella J Jr, Arias-Velasquez A, Arias-Stella J. Normal and abnormal mitoses in the atypical endometrial change associated with chorionic tissue effect. Am J Surg Pathol 1994, **18**: 694–701.

3 Azzopardi JC, Zayid I. Synthetic progestogen-oestrogen therapy and uterine changes. J Clin Pathol 1967, **20**: 731–738.

4 Banks ER, Mills SE, Frierson HF Jr. Uterine intravascular menstrual endometrium simulating malignancy. Am J Surg Pathol 1991, **15**: 407–412.

5 Clement PB, Scully RE. Idiopathic postmenopausal decidual reaction of the endometrium. A clinicopathologic analysis of four cases. Int J Gynecol Pathol 1988, **7**: 152–161.

6 Dallenbach-Hellweg G, Poulsen HE. Atlas of endometrial histopathology, ed. 2. Berlin, 1996, Springer, p. 225.

7 Ehrmann RL. Histologic dating of the endometrium. J Reprod Med 1969, **3**: 179–200.

8 Ferenczy A, Bertrand G, Gelfand MM. Proliferation kinetics of human endometrium during the normal menstrual cycle. Am J Obstet Gynecol 1979, **133**: 859–867.

9 Hendrickson MR, Kempson RL. Normal histology of the uterus and fallopian tubes. In Sternberg S (ed.): Histology for Pathologists, ed. 2. Philadelphia, 1997, Lippincott-Raven Publishers, pp. 879–928.

10 Hertig, AT. Gestational hyperplasia of the endometrium. A morphologic correlation of ova, endometrium, and corpora lutea during early pregnancy. Lab Invest 1964, **13**: 1153–1191.

11 Huettner PC, Gersell DJ. Arias-Stella reaction in nonpregnant women. A clinicopathologic study of nine cases. Int Gynecol Pathol 1994, **13**: 241–247.

12 Mazur MT, Hendrickson MR, Kempson RL. Optically clear nuclei. An alteration of endometrial epithelium in the presence of trophoblast. Am J Surg Pathol 1983, **7**: 415–423.

13 Merchant S, Malpica A, Deavers MT, Czapar C, Gershenson D, Silva EG. Vessels within vessels in the myometrium. Am J Surg Pathol 2002, **26**: 232–236.

14 Norris HJ, Hertig AT, Abell MR. The uterus. Baltimore, 1973, Williams & Wilkins.

15 Noyes RW. Uniformity of secretory endometrium. Study of multiple sections from 100 uteri removed at operation. Fertil Steril 1956, **7**: 103–109.

16 Noyes RW, Haman JO. Accuracy of endometrial dating. Fertil Steril 1954, **4**: 504–517.

17 Noyes RW, Hertig AT, Rock J. Dating the endometrial biopsy. Fertil Steril 1950, **1**: 3–25.

18 Poropatich C, Rojas M, Silverberg SG. Polymorphonuclear leukocytes in the endometrium during the normal menstrual cycle. Int J Gynecol Pathol 1987, **6**: 230–234.

19 Sahin AA, Silva EG, Landon G, Ordonez NG, Gershenson DM. Endometrial tissue in myometrial vessels not associated with menstruation. Int J Gynecol Pathol 1989, **8**: 139–146.

20 Sickel JZ, di Sant' Agnese PA. Anomalous immunostaining of "optically clear" nuclei in gestational endometrium. A potential pitfall in the diagnosis of pregnancy-related herpesvirus infection. Arch Pathol Lab Med 1994, **118**: 831–833.

21 Yokoyama S, Kashima K, Inoue S, Daa T, Nakayama I, Moriuchi A. Biotin-containing intranuclear inclusions in endometrial glands during gestation and puerperium. Am J Clin Pathol 1993, **99**: 13–17.

Curettage and biopsy

22 Baitlon D, Hadley JO. Endometrial biopsy. Pathologic findings in 3600 biopsies from selected patients. Am J Clin Pathol 1975, **63**: 9–15.

23 Carmichael DE. Asherman's syndrome. Obstet Gynecol 1970, **36**: 933–928.

24 Chambers JT, Chambers SK. Endometrial sampling. When? Where? Why? With what? Clin Obstet Gynecol 1992, **35**: 28–39.

25 Dijkhuizen FP, Mol BW, Brolmann HA, Heintz AP. The accuracy of endometrial sampling in the diagnosis of patients with endometrial carcinoma and hyperplasia: a meta-analysis. Cancer 2000, **89**: 1765–1772.

26 Foix A, Bruno RO, Davison T, Lema B. The pathology of postcurettage intrauterine adhesions. Am J Obstet Gynecol 1966, **96**: 1027–1033.

27 Hofmeister FJ, Vondrak B, Barbo DM. The value of the endometrial biopsy. A study of 14,655 office endometrial biopsies. Am J Obstet Gynecol 1966, **95**: 91–98.

28 Kahler VL, Creasy RK, Morris JA. Value of the endometrial biopsy. Obstet Gynecol 1969, **34**: 91–95.

29 Lampe B, Kürzl R, Hantschmann P. Reliability of tumor typing of endometrial carcinoma in prehysterectomy curettage. Int J Gynecol Pathol 1995, **14**: 2–6.

30 McLennan CE. Endometrial regeneration after curettage. Am J Obstet Gynecol 1969, **104**: 185–194.

31 Mitchard J, Hirschowitz L. Concordance of FIGO grade of endometrial adenocarcinomas in biopsy and hysterectomy specimens. Histopathology 2003, **42**: 372–378.

Effects of hormone administration
Estrogen therapy

32 Antunes CM, Strolley PD, Rosenshein NB, Davies JL, Tonascia JA, Brown C, Burnett L, Rutledge A, Pokempner M, Garcia R. Endometrial cancer and estrogen use. Report of a large case-control study. N Engl J Med 1979, **300**: 9–13.

33 Deligdisch L. Hormonal pathology of the endometrium. Mod Pathol 2000, **13**: 285–294.

34 Gordon J, Reagan JW, Finkle WD, Ziel HK. Estrogen and endometrial carcinoma. An independent pathology review supporting original risk estimate. N Engl J Med 1977, **297**: 570–571.

35 Silverberg SG, Mullen D, Faraci JA, Makowski EL, Miller A, Finch JL, Sutherland JV. Endometrial carcinoma. Clinical-pathologic comparison of cases in post-menopausal women receiving and not receiving exogenous estrogens. Cancer 1980, **45**: 3018–3026.

36 Smith DC, Prentice R, Thompson DJ, Herrmann WL. Association of exogenous estrogen and endometrial carcinoma. N Engl J Med 1975, **293**: 1164–1166.

37 Studd JWW, Thom MH, Paterson MEL, Wade-Evans T. The prevention and treatment of endometrial pathology in postmenopausal women receiving exogenous estrogens. In Pasetto N, Paoletti R, Ambrus JL (eds): The menopause and postmenopause. Lancaster, 1980, MTP Press, pp. 127–139.

38 Whitehead MI, King RJB, McQueen J, Campbell S. Endometrial histology and biochemistry in climacteric women during oestrogen and oestrogen/progestogen therapy. J R Soc Med 1979, **72**: 322–327.

39 Whitehead MI, Townsend PT, Pryse-Davies J, Ryder TA, King RJB. Effects of estrogens and progestins on the biochemistry and morphology of the post-menopausal endometrium. N Engl J Med 1981, **305**: 1599–1605.

40 Wright TC, Holinka CF, Ferenczy A, Gatsonis CA, Mutter GL, Nicosia S, Richart RM. Estradiol-induced hyperplasia in

endometrial biopsies from women on hormone replacement therapy. Am J Surg Pathol 2002, **26:** 1269–1275.

41 Ziel HK, Finkle WD. Increased risk of endometrial carcinoma among users of conjugated estrogens. N Engl J Med 1975, **293:** 1167–1170.

Progestational agents

42 Azzopardi JG, Zayid I. Synthetic progestogen-oestrogen therapy and uterine changes. J Clin Pathol 1967, **20:** 731–738.

43 Cohen CJ, Deppe G. Endometrial carcinoma and oral contraceptive agents. Obstet Gynecol 1977, **49:** 390–392.

44 Deligdisch L. Effects of hormone therapy on the endometrium. Mod Pathol 1993, **6:** 94–106.

45 Irey NS, Manion WC, Taylor HB. Vascular lesions in women taking oral contraceptives. Arch Pathol 1970, **89:** 1–8.

46 Maqueo M, Becerra C, Munguia H, Goldzieher JW. Endometrial histology and vaginal cytology during oral contraception with sequential estrogen and progestin. Am J Obstet Gynecol 1964, **90:** 396–400.

47 Ober WB. Synthetic progestogen-oestrogen preparations and endometrial morphology. J Clin Pathol 1966, **19:** 138–147.

48 Ober WB. Effects of oral and intrauterine administration of contraceptives on the uterus. Hum Pathol 1977, **8:** 513–527.

49 Rice-Wray E, Aranda-Rosell A, Maqueo M, Goldzieher JW. Comparison of the long-term endometrial effects of synthetic progestins used in fertility control. Am J Obstet Gynecol 1963, **87:** 429–433.

50 Sartwell PE, Masi AT, Arthes FG, Greene GR, Smith HE. Thromboembolism and oral contraceptives. An epidemiological case-control study. Am J Epidemiol 1969, **90:** 365–380.

51 Silverberg SG, Makowski EL. Endometrial carcinoma in young women taking oral contraceptive agents. Obstet Gynecol 1975, **46:** 503–506.

52 Silverberg SG, Makowski EL, Roche WD. Endometrial carcinoma in women under 40 years of age. Comparison of cases in oral contraceptive users and non-users. Cancer 1977, **39:** 592–598.

53 Vessey MP, Doll R. Investigation of relation between use of oral contraceptives and thromboembolic disease. A further report. Br Med J 1969, **2:** 651–657.

Tamoxifen

54 Barakat RR, Goóewski TA, Almadrones L, Saigo PE, Venkatram E, Hudis C, Hoskins WJ. Effect of adjuvant tamoxifen on the endometrium in women with breast cancer: a prospective study using office endometrial biopsy. J Clin Oncol 2000, **18:** 3459–3463.

55 Carcangiu ML. Uterine pathology in tamoxifen-treated patients with breast cancer. Anat Pathol 1998, **2:** 53–70.

56 Hachisuga T, Hideshima T, Kawarabayashi T, Eguchi F, Emoto M, Shirakusa T. Expression of steroid receptors, Ki-67, and epidermal growth factor receptor in tamoxifen-treated endometrium. Int J Gynecol Pathol 1999, **18:** 297–303.

57 Ismail SM. Endometrial pathology associated with prolonged tamoxifen therapy: a review. Adv Anat Pathol 1996, **3:** 266–271.

58 Kennedy MM, Baigrie CF, Manek S. Tamoxifen and the endometrium: review of 102 cases and comparison with HRT-related and non-HRT related endometrial pathology. Int J Gynecol Pathol 1999, **18:** 130–137.

59 Seidman JD, Kurman RJ. Tamoxifen and the endometrium. Int J Gynecol Pathol 1999, **18:** 293–296.

59a Wilder JD, Shahin S, Khattar N, Wilder DM, Yin J, Rushing RS, Beaven R, Kaetzel C, van Nagell Jr, Kryscio RJ, Lele SM. Tamoxifen-associated malignant endometrial tumors: pathologic features and expression of hormone receptors estrogen-alpha, estrogen-beta, and progesterone: a case controlled study (Abstract). Mod Pathol 2003, **16:** 214a.

Endometritis

60 Almoujahed MO, Briski LE, Prysak M, Johnson LB, Khatib R. Uterine granulomas. Clinical and pathologic features. Am J Clin Pathol 2002, **117:** 771–775.

61 Ashworth MT, Moss CI, Kenyon WE. Granulomatous endometritis following hysteroscopic resection of the endometrium. Histopathology 1991, **18:** 185–187.

62 Bayer-Garner IB, Korourian S. Plasma cells in chronic endometritis are easily identified when stained with syndecan-1. Mod Pathol 2001, **14:** 877–879.

63 Bell DA, Mondschein M, Scully RE. Giant cell arteritis of the female genital tract. A report of three cases. Am J Surg Pathol 1986, **10:** 696–701.

64 Bennett AE, Rathore S, Rhatigan RM. Focal necrotizing endometritis: a clinicopathologic study of 15 cases. Int J Gynecol Pathol 2002, **18:** 220–225.

65 Bhagavan BS, Gupta PK. Genital actinomyosis and intrauterine contraceptive devices. Cytopathologic diagnosis and clinical significance. Hum Pathol 1978, **9:** 567–578.

66 Bhagavan BS, Ruffier J, Shinn B. Pseudoactinomycotic radiate granules in the lower female genital tract. Relationship to the Splendore-Hoeppli phenomenon. Hum Pathol 1982, **13:** 898–904.

67 Buckley CH, Fox H. Histiocytic endometritis. Histopathology 1980, **4:** 105–110.

68 Burkman R, Schlesselman S, McCaffrey L, Gupta PK, Spence M. The relationship of genital tract *Actinomyces* and the development of pelvic inflammatory disease. Am J Obstet Gynecol 1982, **143:** 585–589.

69 Bylund DJ, Nanfro JJ, Marsh WL. Coccidioidomycosis of the female genital tract. Arch Pathol Lab Med 1986, **110:** 232–235.

70 Corfman PA, Segal SJ. Biologic effects of intrauterine devices. Am J Obstet Gynecol 1968, **100:** 448–459.

71 Crum CP, Egawa K, Fenoglio CM, Richart RM. Chronic endometritis. The role of immunohistochemistry in the detection of plasma cells. Am J Obstet Gynecol 1983, **147:** 812–815.

72 Dehner LP, Askin FB. Cytomegalovirus endometritis. Obstet Gynecol 1975, **45:** 211–214.

73 Di Carlo FJ Jr, Di Carlo JP, Robboy SJ, Lyons MM. Sarcoidosis of the uterus. Arch Pathol Lab Med 1989, **113:** 941–943.

74 Francke ML, Mihaescu A, Chaubert P. Isolated necrotizing arteritis of the female genital tract: a clinicopathologic and immunohistochemical study of 11 cases. Int J Gynecol Pathol 1998, **17:** 193–200.

75 Frank TS, Himebaugh KS, Wilson MD. Granulomatous endometritis associated with histologically occult cytomegalovirus in a healthy patient. Am J Surg Pathol 1992, **16:** 716–720.

76 Ganesan R, Ferryman SR, Meier L, Rollason TP. Vasculitis of the female genital tract with clinicopathologic correlation: a study of 46 cases with follow-up. Int J Gynecol Pathol 2000, **19:** 258–265.

77 Govan ADT. Tuberculous endometritis. J Pathol Bacteriol 1962, **83:** 363–372.

78 Gupta PK. Intrauterine contraceptive devices. Vaginal cytology, pathologic changes and clinical implications. Acta Cytol (Baltimore) 1982, **26:** 571–613.

79 Hart WR, Prins RP, Tsai JC. Isolated coccidioidomycosis of the uterus. Hum Pathol 1976, **7:** 235–239.

80 Ho K-L. Sarcoidosis of the uterus. Hum Pathol 1978, **10:** 219–222.

81 Ismail SM. Follicular myometritis. A previously undescribed component of pelvic inflammatory disease. Histopathology 1990, **16:** 91–93.

82 Kim KR, Lee YH, Ro JY. Nodular histocytic hyperplasia of the endometrium. Int J Gyncol Pathol 2002, **21:** 141–146.

83 Kiviat NB, Wolner-Hanssen P, Eschenbach DA, Wasserheit JN, Paavonen JA, Bell TA, Critchlow CW, Stamm WE, Moore DE, Holmes KK. Endometrial histopathology in patients with culture-

proved upper genital tract infection and laparoscopically diagnosed acute salpingitis. Am J Surg Pathol 1990, **14:** 167–175.

84 Leong AS, Vinyuvat S, Leong FW, Suthipintawong C. Anti-CD38 and VS38 antibodies for the detection of plasma cells in the diagnosis of chronic endometritis. Appl Immunohistochem 1997, **5:** 189–193.

85 Lombard CM, Moore MH, Seifer DB. Diagnosis of systemic polyarteritis nodosa following total abdominal hysterectomy and bilateral salpingo-oophorectomy. A case report. Int J Gynecol Pathol 1986, **5:** 63–68.

86 Molnar JJ, Poliak A. Recurrent endometrial malakoplakia. Am J Clin Pathol 1983, **80:** 762–764.

87 Müller-Holzner E, Ruth NR, Abfalter E, Schröcksnadel H, Dapunt O, Martin-Sances L, Nogales FF. IUD-associated pelvic actinomycosis. A report of five cases. Int J Gynecol Pathol 1995, **14:** 70–74.

88 Ober WB, Sobrero AJ, Kurman R, Gold S. Endometrial morphology and polyethylene intrauterine devices. A study of 200 endometrial biopsies. Obstet Gynecol 1968, **32:** 782–793.

89 Paavonen J, Aine R, Teisala K, Heinonen PK, Punnonen R. Comparison of endometrial biopsy and peritoneal fluid cytologic testing with laparoscopy in the diagnosis of acute pelvic inflammatory disease. Am J Obstet Gynecol 1985, **151:** 645–650.

90 Paavonen J, Kiviat N, Brunham RC, Stevens CE, Kuo C-C, Stamm WE, Miettinen A, Soules M, Eschenbach DA, Holmes KK. Prevalence and manifestations of endometritis among women with cervicitis. Am J Obstet Gynecol 1985, **152:** 280–286.

91 Paukku M, Puolakkainen M, Paavonen T, Paavonen J. Plasma cell endometritis is associated with chlamydia trachomatois infection. Am J Clin Pathol 1999, **112:** 211–215.

92 Poropatich C, Rojas M, Silverberg SG. Polymorphonuclear leukocytes in the endometrium during the normal menstrual cycle. Int J Gynecol Pathol 1987, **6:** 230–234.

93 Risse EKJ, Beerthuizen RJCM, Vooijs GP. Cytologic and histologic findings in women using an IUD. Obstet Gynecol 1981, **58:** 569–573.

94 Rotterdam H. Chronic endometritis. A clinicopathologic study. Pathol Annu 1978, **13**(Pt 2): 209–231.

95 Russack V, Lammers RJ. Xanthogranulomatous endometritis. Report of six cases and a proposed mechanism of development. Arch Pathol Lab Med 1990, **114:** 929–932.

96 Schmidt WA. IUDs, inflammation, and infection. Assessment after two decades of IUD use. Hum Pathol 1982, **13:** 878–881.

97 Sen DK, Fox H. The lymphoid tissue of the endometrium. Gynaecologia (Basel) 1967, **163:** 371–378.

98 Shintaku M, Sasaki M, Baba Y. Ceroid-containing histiocytic granuloma of the endometrium. Histopathology 1991, **18:** 169–172.

99 Silverberg SG, Haukkamaa M, Arko H, Nilsson CG, Luukkainen T. Endometrial morphology during long-term use of levonorgestrel-releasing intrauterine devices. Int J Gynecol Pathol 1986, **5:** 235–241.

100 Silvernagel SW, Harshbarger KE, Shevlin DW. Postoperative granulomas of the endometrium: histological features after endometrial ablation. Ann Diagn Pathol 1999, **1:** 82–90.

101 Stern RA, Svoboda-Newman SM, Frank TS. Analysis of chronic endometritis for chlamydia trachomatis by polymerase chain reaction. Hum Pathol 1996, **27:** 1085–1088.

102 Taylor ES, McMillan JH, Greer BE, Droegemueller W, Thompson HE. The intrauterine device and tubo-ovarian abscess. Am J Obstet Gynecol 1975, **123:** 338–347.

103 Venkataseshan VS, Woo TH. Diffuse viral papillomatosis (condyloma) of the uterine cavity. Int J Gynecol Pathol 1985, **4:** 370–377.

104 Westrom L, Bengtsson LP, Mardh P. The risk of pelvic inflammatory disease in women using intrauterine contraceptive devices as compared to non-users. Lancet 1976, **2:** 221–224.

105 Whiteley PF, Hamlett JD. Pyometra – a reappraisal. Am J Obstet Gynecol 1971, **109:** 108–112.

106 Winkler B, Reumann W, Mitao M, Gallo L, Richart RM, Crum CP. Chlamydial endometritis. A histological and immunohistochemical analysis. Am J Surg Pathol 1984, **8:** 771–778.

Metaplasia

107 Abell MR. Endometrial biopsy. Normal and abnormal diagnostic characteristics. In Gold JJ (ed.): Gynecologic endocrinology. New York, 1975, Harper & Row, pp. 156–190.

108 Bhatia NN, Hoshiko MG. Uterine osseous metaplasia. Obstet Gynecol 1982, **60:** 256–259.

109 Bird CC, Willis RA. The production of smooth muscle by the endometrial stroma of the adult human uterus. J Pathol Bacteriol 1965, **90:** 75–81.

110 Blaustein A. Morular metaplasia misdiagnosed as adenoacanthoma in young women with polycystic ovarian disease. Am J Surg Pathol 1982, **6:** 223–228.

111 Bomze EJ, Friedman NB. Squamous metaplasia and adenoacanthosis of the endometrium. Obstet Gynecol 1967, **30:** 619–625.

112 Crum CP, Richart RM, Fenoglio CM. Adenoacanthosis of the endometrium. A clinicopathologic study in premenopausal women. Am J Surg Pathol 1981, **5:** 15–20.

113 Demopoulos RI, Greco MA. Mucinous metaplasia of the endometrium. Ultrastructural and histochemical characteristics. Int J Gynecol Pathol 1983, **1:** 383–390.

114 Dutra FR. Intraglandular morules of the endometrium. Am J Clin Pathol 1959, **31:** 60–65.

115 Gersell DJ. Endometrial papillary syncytial change. Another perspective. Am J Clin Pathol 1993, **99:** 656–657.

116 Hendrickson MR, Kempson RL. Surgical pathology of the uterine corpus. In Bennington JL (ed.): Major problems in pathology, vol. 12. Philadelphia, 1980, W.B. Saunders.

117 Hendrickson MR, Kempson RL. Endometrial epithelial metaplasias. Proliferations frequently misdiagnosed as adenocarcinoma. Report of 89 cases and proposed classification. Am J Surg Pathol 1980, **4:** 525–542.

118 Kaku T, Silverberg SG, Tsukamoto N, Tsuruchi N, Kamura T, Saito T, Nakano H. Association of endometrial epithelial metaplasias with endometrial carcinoma and hyperplasia in Japanese and American women. Int J Gynecol Pathol 1993, **12:** 297–300.

119 Miranda MC, Mazur MT. Endometrial squamous metaplasia. An unusual response to progestin therapy of hyperplasia. Arch Pathol Lab Med 1995, **119:** 458–460.

120 Nucci MR, Prasad CJ, Crum CP, Mutter GL. Mucinous endometrial epithelial proliferations: a morphologic spectrum of changes with diverse clinical significance. Mod Pathol 2000, **12:** 1137–1142.

121 Quddus MR, Sung CJ, Zheng W, Lauchlan SC. P53 immunoreactivity in endometrial metaplasia with dysfunctional uterine bleeding. Histopathology 1999, **35:** 44–49.

122 Rorat E, Wallach RC. Papillary metaplasia of the endometrium. Clinical and histopathologic considerations. Obstet Gynecol 1984, **64:** 90S–92S.

123 Roth E, Taylor HB. Heterotopic cartilage in the uterus. Obstet Gynecol 1966, **27:** 838–844.

124 Salm R. Mucin production of the normal and abnormal endometrium. Arch Pathol 1962, **73:** 30–39.

125 Schueller EF. Ciliated epithelia of the human uterine mucosa. Obstet Gynecol 1968, **31:** 215–223.

126 Silver SA, Cheung AN, Tavassoli FA. Oncocytic metaplasia and carcinoma of the endometrium: an immunohistochemical and ultrastructural study. Int J Gynecol Pathol 1999, **18:** 12–19.

127 Tyagi SP, Saxena K, Rizvi R, Langley FA. Foetal remnants in the

uterus and their relation to other uterine heterotopia. Histopathology 1979, **3**: 339–345.

128 Wells M, Tiltman A. Intestinal metaplasia of the endometrium. Histopathology 1989, **15**: 431–433.

129 Zaman SS, Mazur MT. Endometrial papillary syncytial change. A nonspecific alteration associated with active breakdown. Am J Clin Pathol 1993, **99**: 741–745.

Adenomyosis and endometriosis

130 Ahmed AA, Swan RW, Owen A, Kraus FT, Patrick F. Uterus-like mass arising in broad ligament: a metaplasia or mullerian duct anomaly? Int J Gynecol Pathol 1998, **16**: 279–281.

131 Ahn GH, Scully RE. Clear cell carcinoma of the inguinal region arising from endometriosis. Cancer 1991, **67**: 116–120.

132 Barbieri RL. Etiology and epidemiology of endometriosis. Am J Obstet Gynecol 1990, **162**: 565–567.

133 Bergqvist A, Ljungberg O, Myhre E. Human endometrium and endometriotic tissue obtained simultaneously. A comparative histological study. Int J Gynecol Pathol 1984, **3**: 135–145.

133a Black M, Ali R, Stringer A, Deavers MT, Malpica A, Silva EG. Uterine adenomyosis, complete and incomplete (Abstract). Mod Pathol 2003, **16**: 182a.

134 Brooks JJ, Wheeler JE. Malignancy arising in extragonadal endometriosis. A case report and summary of the world literature. Cancer 1977, **40**: 3065–3073.

135 Chumas JC, Thanning L, Mann WJ. Malignant mixed müllerian tumor arising in extragenital endometriosis. Report of a case and review of the literature. Gynecol Oncol 1986, **23**: 227–233.

136 Clement PB. Pathology of endometriosis. Pathol Annu 1990, **25**(Pt 1): 245–295.

137 Clement PB, Granai CO, Young RH, Scully RE. Endometriosis with myxoid change. A case simulating pseudomyxoma peritonei. Am J Surg Pathol 1994, **18**: 849–853.

138 Clement PB, Young RH. Florid cystic endosalpingiosis with tumor-like manifestations: a report of four cases including the first reported cases of transmural endosalpingiosis of the uterus. Am J Surg Pathol 1999, **23**: 166–175.

138a Clement PB, Young RH. Two previously unemphasized features of endometriosis: micronodular stromal endometriosis and endometriosis with stromal elastosis. Int J Surg Pathol 2001, **8**: 223–227.

139 Emge LA. The elusive adenomyosis of the uterus. Its historical past and its present stage of recognition. Am J Obstet Gynecol 1962, **83**: 1541–1563.

140 Ferguson BR, Bennington JL, Haber SL. Histochemistry of mucosubstances and histology of mixed müllerian pelvic lymph node glandular inclusions. Evidence for histogenesis by müllerian metaplasia of coelomic epithelium. Obstet Gynecol 1969, **33**: 617–625.

141 Fukunaga M. Smooth muscle metaplasia in ovarian endometriosis. Histopathology 2000, **36**: 348–352.

142 Fukunaga M, Ushigome S. Epithelial metaplastic changes in ovarian endometriosis. Mod Pathol 1998, **11**: 784–788.

143 Goldblum JR, Clement PB, Hart WR. Adenosarcomamyosis with sparse glands. A potential mimic of low-grade endometrial stromal. Am J Clin Pathol 1995, **103**: 218–223.

144 Hall JB, Young RH, Nelson JH. The prognostic significance of adenomyosis in endometrial carcinoma. Gynecol Oncol 1984, **17**: 32–40.

145 Heaps JM, Nieberg RK, Berek JS. Malignant neoplasms arising in endometriosis. Obstet Gynecol 1990, **75**: 1023–1028.

146 Jung WY, Shin BK, Kim I. Uterine adenomyoma with uterus-like features: a report of two cases. Int J Surg Pathol 2002, **10**: 163–166.

147 Karp LA, Czernobilsky B. Glandular inclusions in pelvic and abdominal paraaortic lymph nodes. Am J Clin Pathol 1969, **52**: 212–218.

148 Leiman G. Carcinoma ex endometriosis: the jury is still out. Adv Anat Pathol 1996, **3**: 362–366.

149 Li SF, Nakayama K, Masuzawa H, Fujii S. The number of proliferating cell nuclear antigen positive cells in endometriotic lesions differs from that in the endometrium. Analysis of PCNA positive cells during the menstrual cycle and in post-menopause. Virchows Arch [A] 1993, **423**: 257–263.

150 Lu PY, Ory SJ. Endometriosis. Current management. Mayo Clin Proc 1995, **70**: 453–463.

151 Mai KT, Yazdi HM, Perkins DG, Parks W. Development of endometriosis from embryonic duct remnants. Hum Pathol 1998, **29**: 319–322.

152 Marcoux S, Maheux R, Berube S. Laparoscopic surgery in infertile women with minimal or mild endometriosis. Canadian Collaborative Group on Endometriosis. N Engl J Med 1997, **337**: 217–222.

153 Mathur BBL, Shah BS, Bhende YM. Adenomyosis uteri. Am J Obstet Gynecol 1962, **84**: 1820–1829.

154 McCluggage WG, Bryson C, Lamki H, Boyle DD. Benign, borderline, and malignant endometrioid neoplasia arising in endometriosis in association with tamoxifen therapy. Int J Gynecol Pathol 2000, **19**: 276–279.

155 McCluggage WG, Desai V, Manek S. Tamoxifen associated postmenopausal adenomyosis exhibits stromal fibrosis, glandular dilatation and epithelial metaplasia. Histopathology 2000, **37**: 340–346.

156 Molitor JJ. Adenomyosis. A clinical and pathological appraisal. Am J Obstet Gynecol 1971, **110**: 275–284.

157 Mostoufizadeh M, Scully RE. Malignant tumors arising in endometriosis. Clin Obstet Gynecol 1980, **23**: 951–963.

158 Nagai Y, Kishimoto T, Nikaido T, Nishihara K, Matsumoto T, Suzuki C, Ogishima T, Kuwahara Y, Hurukata Y, Mizunuma M, Nakata Y, Ishikura H. Squamous predominance in mixed-epithelial papillary cystadenomas of borderline malignancy of Mullerian type arising in endometriotic cysts: a study of four cases. Am J Surg Pathol 2003, **27**: 242–247.

159 Nakayama K, Masuzawa H, Li SF, Yoshikawa F, Toki T, Nikaido T, Silverberg SG, Fujii S. Immunohistochemical analysis of the peritoneum adjacent to endometriotic lesions using antibodies for Ber-EP4 antigen, estrogen receptors, and progesterone receptors. Implication of peritoneal metaplasia in the pathogenesis of endometriosis. Int J Gynecol Pathol 1994, **13**: 348–358.

160 Nothnick WB, Fan F, Iczkowski KA, Ashwell R, Thomas P, Tawfik OW. CD44s expression is reduced in endometriotic lesions compared to eutopic endometrium in women with endometriosis. Int J Gynecol Pathol 2001, **20**: 140–146.

161 Nuovo M, Bayani E, Gerold T, Leong M, Mir R. Endometrioid cystadenofibroma developing in juxtahepatic endometriosis: a case report. Int J Surg Pathol 1998, **6**: 109–112.

162 Olive DL, Schwartz LB. Endometriosis. N Engl J Med 1993, **328**: 1759–1769.

163 Prade M, Spatz A, Bentledy R, Duvillard P, Bognel C, Robboy SJ. Borderline and malignant serous tumor arising in pelvic lymph nodes. Evidence of origin in benign glandular inclusions. Int J Gynecol Pathol 1995, **14**: 87–91.

164 Roth LM. Endometriosis with perineural involvement. Am J Clin Pathol 1973, **59**: 807–809.

165 Seidman JD. Prognostic importance of hyperplasia and atypia in endometriosis. Int J Gynecol Pathol 1996, **15**: 1–9.

166 Seidman JD, Kjerulff KH. Pathologic findings from the Maryland Women's Health Study: practice patterns in the diagnosis of adenomyosis. Int J Gynecol Pathol 1997, **15**: 217–221.

167 Sinkre P, Hoang MP, Albores-Saavedra J. Mullerianosis of inguinal lymph nodes: report of a case. Int J Gynecol Pathol 2002, **21**: 60–64.

168 Slavin RE, Krum R, Van Dinh T. Endometriosis-associated intestinal tumors: a clinical and pathologic study of 6 cases and

review of the literature. Hum Pathol 2000, **31**: 456–463.

169 Steck WD, Helwig EB. Cutaneous endometriosis. JAMA 1965, **191**: 167–170.

170 Stern RC, Dash R, Bentley RC, Snyder MJ, Haney AF, Robboy SJ. Malignancy in endometriosis: frequency and comparison of ovarian and extraovarian types. Int J Gynecol Pathol 2001, **20**: 133–139.

171 Tamura M, Fukaya T, Murakami T, Uehara S, Yajima A. Analysis of clonality in human endometriotic cysts based on evaluation of X chromosome inactivation in archival formalin-fixed, paraffin-embedded tissue. Lab Invest 1998, **78**: 213–218.

172 Toki T, Horiuchi A, Li SF, Nakayama K, Silverberg SG, Fujii S. Proliferative activity of postmenopausal endometriosis: a histopathologic and immunocytochemical study. Int J Gynecol Pathol 1996, **15**: 45–53.

173 Winkelman J, Robinson R. Adenocarcinoma of endometrium involving adenomyosis. Report of an unusual case and review of the literature. Cancer 1966, **19**: 901–908.

Dysfunctional uterine bleeding and hyperplasia

174 Abell MR. Adenocarcinoma (gland-cell carcinoma) in situ of endometrium. Pathol Res Pract 1982, **174**: 221–236.

175 Ambros RA. Simple hyperplasia of the endometrium: an evaluation of proliferative activity by Ki-67 immunostaining. Int J Gynecol Pathol 2000, **19**: 206–211.

176 Ausems EWMA, van der Kamp J-K, Baak JPA. Nuclear morphometry in the determination of the prognosis of marked atypical endometrial hyperplasia. Int J Gynecol Pathol 1985, **4**: 180–185.

177 Baak JPA, Kurver PHJ, Diegenbach PC, Delemarre JFM, Brekelmans ECM, Nieuwlaat JE. Discrimination of hyperplasia and carcinoma of the endometrium by quantitative microscopy – a feasibility study. Histopathology 1981, **5**: 61–68.

178 Baak JP, Wisse-Brekelmans EC, Fleege JC, van der Putten HW, Bezemer PD. Assessment of the risk on endometrial cancer in hyperplasia, by means of morphological and morphometrical features. Pathol Res Pract 1992, **188**: 856–859.

179 Baloglu H, Cannizzaro LA, Jones J, Koss LG. Atypical endometrial hyperplasia shares genomic abnormalities with endometrioid carcinoma by comparative genomic hybridisation. Hum Pathol 2001, **32**: 615–622.

180 Bell CD, Ostrezega E. The significance of secretory features and coincident hyperplastic changes in endometrial biopsy specimens. Hum Pathol 1987, **18**: 830–838.

181 Bergeron C, Nogales FF, Masseroli M, Abeler V, Duvillard P, Muller-Holzner E, Pickartz H, Wells M. A multicentric European study testing the reproductivity of the WHO classification of endometrial hyperplasia with a proposal of a simplified working classification for biopsy and curettage specimens. Am J Surg Pathol 1999, **23**: 1102–1108.

182 Beutler HK, Dockerty MB, Randall L. Precancerous lesions of the endometrium. Am J Obstet Gynecol 1963, **86**: 433–443.

183 Campbell PE, Barter RA. The significance of atypical endometrial hyperplasia. J Obstet Gynaecol Br Commonw 1961, **68**: 668–672.

184 Castelbaum AJ, Wheeler J, Coutifaris CB, Mastroianni L Jr, Lessey BA. Timing of the endometrial biopsy may be critical for the accurate diagnosis of luteal phase deficiency. Fertil Steril 1994, **61**: 443–447.

185 Choo YC, Mak KC, Hsu C, Wong TS, Ma HK. Postmenopausal uterine bleeding of nonorganic cause. Obstet Gynecol 1985, **66**: 225–228.

186 Dallenbach-Hellweg G. The endometrium of infertility. Pathol Res Pract 1984, **178**: 527–537.

187 Dallenbach-Hellweg G. Histopathology of the endometrium (English translation by FD Dallenbach), ed. 3. New York, 1985, Springer-Verlag.

188 Dietel M. The histological diagnosis of endometrial hyperplasia: is there a need to simplify? Virchows Arch 2001, **439**: 604–608.

189 Feichter GE, Hoffken H, Heep J, Haag D, Heberling D, Brandt H, Rummel H, Goerttler KL. DNA-flow-cytometric measurements on the normal, atrophic, hyperplastic and neoplastic human endometrium. Virchows Arch [A] 1982, **398**: 53–65.

190 Fenoglio CM, Crum CP, Ferenczy A. Endometrial hyperplasia and carcinoma. Are ultrastructural, biochemical and immunocytochemical studies useful in distinguishing between them? Pathol Res Pract 1982, **174**: 257–284.

191 Fox H, Buckley CH. The endometrial hyperplasias and their relationship to endometrial neoplasia. Histopathology 1982, **6**: 493–510.

192 Gillam JS. Study of the inadequate secretion phase endometrium. Fertil Steril 1955, **6**: 18–36.

193 Gordon MD, Ireland K. Pathology of hyperplasia and carcinoma of the endometrium. Semin Oncol 1994, **21**: 64–70.

194 Gore H, Hertig AT. Carcinoma in situ of the endometrium. Am J Obstet Gynecol 1966, **94**: 135–155.

195 Greenblatt RB, Hammond DO, Clark SL. Membranous dysmenorrhea. Studies in etiology and treatment. Am J Obstet Gynecol 1954, **68**: 835–844.

196 Gusberg SB, Kaplan AL. Precursors of corpus cancer. IV. Adenomatous hyperplasia as stage 0 carcinoma of the endometrium. Am J Obstet Gynecol 1963, **87**: 662–667.

197 Hendrickson MR, Kempson RL. Surgical pathology of the uterine corpus. In Bennington JL (ed.): Major problems in pathology, vol. 12. Philadelphia, 1980, W.B. Saunders, pp. 285–318.

198 Hendrickson MR, Ross JC, Kempson RL. Toward the development of morphologic criteria for well-differentiated adenocarcinoma of the endometrium. Am J Surg Pathol 1983, **7**: 819–838.

199 Kurman RJ, Norris HJ. Evaluation of criteria for distinguishing atypical endometrial hyperplasia from well-differentiated carcinoma. Cancer 1982, **49**: 2547–2559.

200 Kurman RJ, Norris HJ. Endometrium. In Henson DE, Albores-Saavedra J (eds): The pathology of incipient neoplasia. Philadelphia, 1986, W.B. Saunders, pp. 265–277.

201 Lee KR, Scully RE. Complex endometrial hyperplasia and carcinoma in adolescents and young women 15 to 20 years of age. A report of 10 cases. Int J Gynecol Pathol 1989, **8**: 201–213.

202 McElin TW, Bird CC, Reeves BD, Scott RC. Diagnostic dilation and curettage. A 20-year survey. Obstet Gynecol 1969, **33**: 807–812.

203 McLennan CE, Rydell AH. Extent of endometrial shedding during normal menstruation. Obstet Gynecol 1965, **26**: 605–621.

204 Meyer WC, Malkasian GD, Dockerty MB, Decker DG. Postmenopausal bleeding from atrophic endometrium. Obstet Gynecol 1971, **38**: 731–738.

205 Michael H, Kotylo PA, Mohr M, Roth LM. DNA ploidy, cell cycle kinetics, and low versus high grade atypia in endometrial hyperplasia. Am J Clin Pathol 1996, **106**: 22–28.

206 Moszkowski E, Woodruff JD, Jones GES. The inadequate luteal phase. Am J Obstet Gynecol 1962, **83**: 363–372.

207 Mutter GL. Endometrial intraepithelial neoplasia (EIN): will it bring order to chaos? The Endometrial Collaborative Group. Gynecol Oncol 2000, **76**: 287–290.

208 Mutter GL. Histopathology of genetically defined endometrial precancers. Int J Gynecol Pathol 2001, **19**: 301–309.

209 Mutter GL, Nogales F, Kurman R, Silverberg S, Tavassoli F. Endometrial cancer. In Tavassoli FA, Stratton MR (eds): WHO classification of tumors: pathology and genetics, tumors of the breast and female genital organs. Lyon, 2002, IARC Press.

210 Norris HJ, Becker RL, Mikel UV. A comparative morphometric and cytophotometric study of endometrial hyperplasia, atypical hyperplasia, and endometrial carcinoma. Hum Pathol 1989, **20**: 219–223.

211 Norris HJ, Tavassoli FA, Kurman RJ. Endometrial hyperplasia and carcinoma. Diagnostic considerations. Am J Surg Pathol 1983, **7:** 839–847.

212 Noyes RW. The underdeveloped secretory endometrium. Am J Obstet Gynecol 1962, **83:** 363–372.

213 Pacheco JC, Kempers RD. Etiology of postmenopausal bleeding. Obstet Gynecol 1968, **32:** 40–46.

214 Picoff RC, Luginbuhl WH. Fibrin in the endometrial stroma. Its relation to uterine bleeding. Am J Obstet Gynecol 1964, **88:** 642–646.

215 Silverberg SG. Hyperplasia and carcinoma of the endometrium. Semin Diagn Pathol 1988, **5:** 135–153.

216 Silverberg SG. Problems in the differential diagnosis of endometrial hyperplasia and carcinoma. Mod Pathol 2000, **13:** 309–327.

217 Skov BG, Broholm H, Engel U, Franzmann MB, Nielsen AL, Lauritzen AF, Skov T. Comparison of the reproducibility of the WHO classifications of 1975 and 1994 of endometrial hyperplasia. Int J Gynecol Pathol 1997, **16:** 33–37.

218 Söderström K-O. Lectin binding to human endometrial hyperplasias and adenocarcinoma. Int J Gynecol Pathol 1987, **6:** 356–365.

219 Sommers SC. Defining the pathology of endometrial hyperplasia, dysplasia and carcinoma. Pathol Res Pract 1982, **174:** 175–197.

220 Stewart CJ, Campbell-Brown M, Critchley HO, Farquharson MA. Endometrial apoptosis in patients with dysfunctional uterine bleeding. Histopathology 1999, **34:** 99–105.

221 Tavassoli F, Kraus FT. Endometrial lesions in uteri resected for atypical endometrial hyperplasia. Am J Clin Pathol 1978, **70:** 770–779.

222 Thornburgh I, Anderson MC. The endometrial deficient secretory phase. Histopathology 1997, **30:** 11–15.

223 Vellios F. Endometrial hyperplasias, precursors of endometrial carcinoma. Pathol Annu 1972, **7:** 201–229.

224 Welch WR, Scully RE. Precancerous lesions of the endometrium. Hum Pathol 1977, **8:** 503–512.

225 Winkler B, Alvarez S, Richart RM, Crum CP. Pitfalls in the diagnosis of endometrial neoplasia. Obstet Gynecol 1984, **64:** 185–194.

226 Zaino RJ. Endometrial hyperplasia: is it time for a quantum leap to a new classification? Int J Gynecol Pathol 2001, **19:** 314–321.

Relationship with carcinoma

227 Baak JP, Wisse-Brekelmans EC, Fleege JC, van der Putten HW, Bezemer PD. Assessment of the risk on endometrial cancer in hyperplasia, by means of morphological and morphometrical features. Pathol Res Pract 1992, **188:** 856–859.

228 Chamlian LD, Taylor HB. Endometrial hyperplasia in young women. Obstet Gynecol 1970, **36:** 659–666.

229 Dietel M. The histological diagnosis of endometrial hyperplasia: is there a need to simplify? Virchows Arch 2001, **439:** 604–608.

230 Gal D. Hormonal therapy for lesions of the endometrium. Semin Oncol 1986, **13:** 33–36.

231 Gusberg SB, Kaplan AL. Precursors of corpus cancer. IV. Adenomatous hyperplasia as stage 0 carcinoma of the endometrium. Am J Obstet Gynecol 1963, **87:** 662–667.

232 Henson DE, Albores-Saavedra J. Pathology of incipient neoplasia, ed. 3. New York, 2001, Oxford University Press, p. 839.

233 Hertig AT, Sommers SC. Genesis of endometrial carcinoma. I. Study of prior biopsies. Cancer 1949, **2:** 946–956.

234 Kurman RJ, Kaminski PF, Norris HJ. The behavior of endometrial hyperplasia. A long-term study of "untreated" hyperplasia in 170 patients. Cancer 1985, **56:** 403–412.

235 McBride JM. Pre-menopausal cystic hyperplasia and endometrial carcinoma. J Obstet Gynaecol Br Emp 1959, **66:** 288–296.

236 Scully RE. Definition of precursors in gynecologic cancer. Cancer 1981, **48:** 531–537.

237 Silverberg SG. Hyperplasia and carcinoma of the endometrium. Semin Diagn Pathol 1988, **5:** 135–153.

238 Sivridis E, Giatromanolaki A. Prognostic aspects on endometrial hyperplasia and neoplasia. Virchows Arch 2001, **439:** 118–126.

239 Steiner G, Kistner RW, Craig JM. Histological effects of progestins on hyperplasia and carcinoma in situ of the endometrium – further observations. Metabolism 1965, **14:** 356–386.

240 Tavassoli F, Kraus FT. Endometrial lesions in uteri resected for atypical endometrial hyperplasia. Am J Clin Pathol 1978, **70:** 770–779.

241 Vellios F. Endometrial hyperplasias, precursors of endometrial carcinoma. Pathol Annu 1972, **7:** 201–229.

Tumors

Endometrial polyps

242 Clement PB, Young RH. Atypical polypoid adenomyoma of the uterus associated with Turner's syndrome. A report of three cases, including a review of "estrogen-associated" endometrial neoplasms and neoplasms associated with Turner's syndrome. Int J Gynecol Pathol 1987, **6:** 104–113.

243 Corley D, Rowe J, Curtis MT, Hogan WM, Noumoff JS, Livolsi VA. Postmenopausal bleeding from unusual endometrial polyps in women on chronic tamoxifen therapy. Obstet Gynecol 1992, **79:** 111–116.

244 Creagh TM, Krausz T, Flanagan AM. Atypical stromal cells in a hyperplastic endometrial polyp. Histopathology 1995, **27:** 386–387.

245 Duggan MA, Rowlands C, Kneafsey PD, Nation JG, Stuart GCE. Uterine atypical polypoid adenomyoma and ovarian endometrioid carcinoma. Metastatic disease or dual primaries? Int J Gynecol Pathol 1995, **14:** 81–86.

246 Fukunaga M, Endo Y, Ushigome S, Ishikawa E. Atypical polypoid adenomyomas of the uterus. Histopathology 1995, **27:** 35–42.

247 Gilks CB, Clement PB, Hart WR, Young RH. Uterine adenomyomas excluding atypical polypoid adenomyomas and adenomyomas of endocervical type: a clinicopathologic study of 30 cases of an underemphasized lesion that may cause diagnostic problems with brief consideration of adenomyomas of other female genital tract sites. Int J Gynecol Pathol 2000, **19:** 195–205.

247a Hachisuga T, Miyakawa T, Tsujioka H, Horiuchi S, Emoto M, Kawarabayashi T. K-*ras* mutation in tamoxifen-related endometrial polyps. Cancer 2003, **98:** 1890–1897.

248 Hattab EM, Allam-Nandyala P, Rhatigan RM. The stromal component of large endometrial polyps. Int J Gynecol Pathol 1999, **18:** 332–337.

249 Kennedy MM, Baigrie CF, Manek S. Tamoxifen and the endometrium: review of 102 cases and comparison with HRT-related and non-HRT related endometrial pathology. Int J Gynecol Pathol 1999, **18:** 130–137.

250 Lehman MB, Hart WR. Simple and complex hyperplastic papillary proliferations of the endometrium: a clinicopathologic study of nine cases of apparently localized papillary lesions with fibrovascular stromal cores and epithelial metaplasia. Am J Surg Pathol 2001, **25:** 1347–1354.

251 Longacre TA, Chung MH, Rouse RV, Hendrickson MR. Atypical polypoid adenomyofibromas (atypical polypoid adenomyomas) of the uterus: a clinicopathologic study of 55 cases. Am J Surg Pathol 1996, **20:** 1–20.

252 Mazur MT. Atypical polypoid adenomyomas of the endometrium. Am J Surg Pathol 1981, **5:** 473–482.

252a McCluggage WG, Sumathi VP, McManus DT. Uterine serous carcinoma and endometrial intraepithelial carcinoma arising in endometrial polyps: report of 5 cases, including 2 associated with tamoxifen therapy. Hum Pathol 2003, **34:** 939–943.

253 Mittal KR, Peng XC, Wallach RC, Demopoulos RI. Coexistent atypical polypoid adenomyoma and endometrial adenocarcinoma. Hum Pathol 1995, **26**: 574–575.

254 Mittal K, Schwartz L, Goswami S, Demopoulos R. Estrogen and progesterone receptor expression in endometrial polyps. Int J Gynecol Pathol 1996, **15**: 345–347.

254a Ota S, Catasus L, Matius-Guiu X, Bussaglia E, Lagarda H, Pons C, Munoz J, Kamura T, Prat J. Molecular pathology of atypical polypoid adenomyoma of the uterus. Hum Pathol 2003, **34**: 784–788.

255 Schlesinger C, Kamoi S, Ascher SM, Kendell M, Lage JM, Silverberg SG. Endometrial polyps: a comparison study of patients receiving tamoxifen with two control groups. Int J Gynecol Pathol 1998, **17**: 302–311.

256 Staros EB, Shilkitus WF. Atypical polypoid adenomyoma with carcinomatous transformation. A case report. Surg Pathol 1991, **4**: 157–166.

257 Tai LH, Tavassoli FA. Endometrial polyps with atypical (bizarre) stromal cells. Am J Surg Pathol 2002, **26**: 505–509.

258 Young RH, Treger T, Scully RE. Atypical polypoid adenomyoma of the uterus. A report of 27 cases. Am J Clin Pathol 1986, **86**: 139–145.

Endometrial carcinoma

General and clinical features

259 Beckner ME, Mori T, Silverberg SG. Endometrial carcinoma. Nontumor factors in prognosis. Int J Gynecol Pathol 1985, **4**: 131–145.

260 Clement PB, Young RH. Atypical polypoid adenomyoma of the uterus associated with Turner's syndrome. A report of three cases, including a review of "estrogen-associated" endometrial neoplasms and neoplasms associated with Turner's syndrome. Int J Gynecol Pathol 1987, **6**: 104–113.

261 Dallenbach Hellweg G, Hahn U. Mucinous and clear cell adenocarcinomas of the endometrium in patients receiving antiestrogens (tamoxifen) and gestagens. Int J Gynecol Pathol 1995, **14**: 7–15.

262 Deligdisch L, Cohen CJ. Histologic correlates and virulence implications of endometrial carcinoma associated with adenomatous hyperplasia. Cancer 1985, **56**: 1452–1455.

263 Deligdisch L, Kalir T, Cohen CJ, de Latour M, Le Bouedec G, Penault-Llorca F. Endometrial histopathology in 700 patients treated with tamoxifen for breast cancer. Gynecol Oncol 2000, **78**: 181–186.

264 Fechner RE, Kaufman RH. Endometrial adenocarcinoma in Stein-Leventhal syndrome. Cancer 1974, **34**: 444–452.

265 Fisher B, Costantino JP, Redmond CK, Fisher ER, Wickerham DL, Cronin WM. Endometrial cancer in tamoxifen-treated breast cancer patients. Findings from the National Surgical Adjuvant Breast and Bowel Project (NSABP) B-14. J Natl Cancer Inst 1994, **86**: 527–537.

266 Geisler HE, Huber CP, Rogers S. Carcinoma of the endometrium in premenopausal women. Am J Obstet Gynecol 1969, **104**: 657–663.

267 Gusberg SB. The changing nature of endometrial cancer. N Engl J Med 1980, **302**: 709–732.

268 Kaufman RH, Abbott JP, Wall JA. The endometrium before and after wedge resection of the ovaries in the Stein-Leventhal syndrome. Am J Obstet Gynecol 1959, **77**: 1271–1285.

269 McCarty KS Jr, Barton TK, Peete CH Jr, Creasman WT. Gonadal dysgenesis with adenocarcinoma of the endometrium. An electron microscopic and steroid receptor analyses with a review of the literature. Cancer 1978, **42**: 512–520.

270 Magriples U, Naftolin F, Schwartz PE, Carcangiu ML. High-grade endometrial carcinoma in tamoxifen-treated breast cancer patients. J Clin Oncol 1993, **11**: 485–490.

271 Parkash V, Carcangiu ML. Uterine papillary serous carcinoma after radiation therapy for carcinoma of the cervix. Cancer 1992, **69**: 496–501.

272 Robboy SJ, Miller AW III, Kurman RJ. The pathologic features and behavior of endometrial carcinoma associated with exogenous estrogen administration. Pathol Res Pract 1982, **174**: 237–256.

273 Rodriguez J, Hart WR. Endometrial cancers occurring 10 or more years after pelvic irradiation for carcinoma. Int J Gynecol Pathol 1982, **1**: 135–144.

274 Rose PG. Endometrial carcinoma. N Engl J Med 1996, **335**: 640–649.

275 Schammel DP, Mittal KR, Kaplan K, Deligdisch L, Tavassoli FA. Endometrial adenocarcinoma associated with intrauterine pregnancy: a report of five cases and a review of the literature. Int J Gynecol Pathol 1998, **17**: 327–335.

276 Shapiro S, Kelly JP, Rosenberg L, Kaufman DW, Helmrich SP, Rosenshein NB, Lewis JL, Knapp RC, Stolley PD, Schottenfeld D. Risk of localized and widespread endometrial cancer in relation to recent and discontinued use of conjugated estrogens. N Engl J Med 1985, **313**: 969–972.

277 Silva EG, Tornos CS, Follen-Mitchell M. Malignant neoplasms of the uterine corpus in patients treated for breast carcinoma. The effects of tamoxifen. Int J Gynecol Pathol 1994, **13**: 248–258.

278 Spiegel GW. Endometrial carcinoma in situ in postmenopausal women. Am J Surg Pathol 1995, **19**: 417–432.

279 Voigt LF, Weiss NS. Epidemiology of endometrial cancer. Cancer Treat Res 1989, **49**: 1–21.

Pathologic features

280 Ambros RA, Ballouk F, Malfetano JH, Ross JS. Significance of papillary (villoglandular) differentiation in endometrioid carcinoma of the uterus. Am J Surg Pathol 1994, **18**: 569–575.

281 Chen JL, Trost DC, Wilkinson EJ. Endometrial papillary adenocarcinomas. Two clinicopathological types. Int J Gynecol Pathol 1985, **4**: 279–288.

282 Clement PB. Pathology of the uterine corpus. Hum Pathol 1991, **22**: 776–791.

283 Clement PB, Young RH. Endometrioid carcinomas of the uterine corpus: a review of its pathology with emphasis on recent advances and problematic aspects. Adv Anat Pathol 2002, **9**: 145–184.

284 Esteller M, Garcia A, Martinez-Palones JM, Xercavins J, Reventos J. Clinicopathologic features and genetic alterations in endometrioid carcinoma of the uterus with villoglandular differentiation. Am J Clin Pathol 1999, **111**: 336–342.

285 Fanning J, Alvarez PM, Tsukada Y, Piver MS. Cervical implantation metastasis by endometrial adenocarcinoma. Cancer 1991, **68**: 1335–1339.

286 Frauenhoffer EE, Zaino RJ, Wolff TV, Whitney CE. Value of endocervical curettage in the staging of endometrial carcinoma. Int J Gynecol Pathol 1987, **6**: 195–202.

287 Gospel C. Ultrastructure of endometrial carcinoma. Review of fourteen cases. Cancer 1971, **28**: 745–754.

288 Hachisuga T, Fukuda K, Iwasaka T, Hirakawa T, Kawarabayashi T, Tsuneyoshi M. Endometrial adenocarcinomas of the uterine corpus in women younger than 50 years of age can be divided into two distinct clinical and pathologic entities based on anatomic location. Cancer 2001, **92**: 2578–2584.

289 Hall JB, Young RH, Nelson JH. The prognostic significance of adenomyosis in endometrial carcinoma. Gynecol Oncol 1984, **17**: 32–40.

290 Isaacson PG, Pilot LM Jr, Gooselaw JG. Foam cells in the stroma in carcinoma of the endometrium. Obstet Gynecol 1964, **23**: 9–11.

291 Jacques SM, Lawrence WD. Endometrial adenocarcinoma with variable-level myometrial involvement limited to adenomyosis. A clinicopathologic study of 23 cases. Gynecol Oncol 1990, **37**: 401–407.

292 Jacques SM, Qureshi F, Lawrence WD. Surface epithelial changes in endometrial adenocarcinoma. Diagnostic pitfalls in curettage specimens. Int J Gynecol Pathol 1995, **14**: 191–197.

293 Jacques SM, Qureshi F, Ramirez NC, Malviya VK, Lawrence WD. Tumors of uterine isthmus: clinicopathologic features and immunohistochemical characterization of p53 expression and hormone receptors. Int J Gynecol Pathol 1997, **16**: 38–44.

294 Kadar NRD, Kohorn EI, LiVolsi VA, Kapp DS. Histologic variants of cervical involvement by endometrial carcinoma. Obstet Gynecol 1982, **59**: 85–93.

295 Landry D, Mai KT, Senterman MK, Perkins DG, Yazdi HM, Veinot JP, Thomas J. Endometrioid adenocarcinoma of the uterus with a minimal deviation invasive pattern. Histopathology 2002, **42**: 77–82.

296 Larson DM, Copeland LJ, Gallagher HS, Gershenson DM, Freedman RS, Wharton JT, Kline RC. Nature of cervical involvement in endometrial carcinoma. Cancer 1987, **59**: 959–962.

297 Lax SF, Kurman RJ, Pizer ES, Wu L, Ronnett BM. A binary architectural grading system for uterine endometrial endometrioid carcinoma has superior reproducibility compared with FIGO grading and identifies subsets of advance-stage tumors with favourable and unfavourable prognosis. Am J Surg Pathol 2000, **24**: 1201–1208.

298 Longacre TA, Chung MH, Jensen DN, Hendrickson MR. Proposed criteria for the diagnosis of well-differentiated endometrial carcinoma. A diagnostic test for myoinvasion. Am J Surg Pathol 1995, **19**: 371–406.

299 Longacre TA, Hendrickson MR. Diffusely infiltrative endometrial adenocarcinoma: an adenoma malignum pattern of myoinvasion. Am J Surg Pathol 1999, **23**: 69–78.

300 Murray SK, Young RH, Scully RE. Uterine endometrioid carcinoma with small nonvillous papillae: an analysis of 26 cases of a favourable-prognosis tumor to be distinguished from serous carcinoma. Int J Surg Pathol 2001, **8**: 279–289.

301 Nascimento AF, Hirsch MS, Cviko A, Quade BJ, Nucci MR. The role of CD10 staining in distinguishing invasive endometrial adenocarcinoma from adenocarcinoma involving adenomyosis. Mod Pathol 2003, **16**: 22–27.

302 Risberg B, Grontoft O, Westholm B. Origin of carcinoma in secretory endometrium – a study using a whole-organ sectioning technique. Gynecol Oncol 1983, **15**: 32–41.

303 Salm R. Macrophages in endometrial lesions. J Pathol Bacteriol 1962, **83**: 405–409.

304 Silver SA, Sherman ME. Morphologic and immunophenotypic characterization of foam cells in endometrial lesions. Int J Gynecol Pathol 1998, **17**: 140–145.

304a Srodon M, Klein WM, Kurman RJ. CD10 immunostaining does not distinguish endometrial carcinoma invading myometrium from carcinoma involving adenomyosis. Am J Surg Pathol 2003, **27**: 786–789.

305 Zaino RJ, Kurman RJ, Brunetto VL, Morrow CP, Bentley RC, Cappellari JO, Bitterman P. Villoglandular adenocarcinoma of the endometrium: a clinicopathologic study of 61 cases: a gynecologic oncology group study. Am J Surg Pathol 1998, **22**: 1379–1385.

306 Zaino RJ, Kurman RJ, Diana KL, Morrow CP. The utility of the revised International Federation of Gynecology and Obstetrics histologic grading of endometrial adenocarcinoma using a defined nuclear grading system. A Gynecologic Oncology Group study. Cancer 1995, **75**: 81–86.

Variants and other microscopic types

307 Abeler V, Kjorstad KE. Endometrial squamous cell carcinoma. Report of three cases and review of the literature. Gynecol Oncol 1990, **36**: 321–326.

308 Abeler VM, Kjorstad KE, Nesland JM. Undifferentiated carcinoma of the endometrium. A histopathologic and clinical study of 31 cases. Cancer 1991, **68**: 98–105.

309 Aguirre P, Scully RE, Wolfe HJ, DeLellis RA. Endometrial carcinoma with argyrophil cells. A histochemical and immunohistochemical analysis. Hum Pathol 1984, **15**: 210–217.

310 Alberhasky RC, Connelly PJ, Christopherson WM. Carcinoma of the endometrium. IV. Mixed adenosquamous carcinoma. A clinical-pathological study of 68 cases with long-term follow-up. Am J Clin Pathol 1982, **77**: 655–664.

311 Bannatyne P, Russell P, Wills EJ. Argyrophilia and endometrial carcinoma. Int J Gynecol Pathol 1983, **2**: 235–254.

312 Carcangiu ML, Chambers JT. Uterine papillary serous carcinoma. A study on 108 cases with emphasis on the prognostic significance of associated endometrioid carcinoma, absence of invasion, and concomitant ovarian carcinoma. Gynecol Oncol 1992, **47**: 298–305.

313 Carcangiu ML, Chambers JT. Early pathologic stage clear cell carcinoma and uterine papillary serous carcinoma of the endometrium. Comparison of clinicopathologic features and survival. Int J Gynecol Pathol 1995, **14**: 30–38.

314 Carcangiu ML, Tan LK, Chambers JT. Stage 1A uterine serous carcinoma: a study of 13 cases. Am J Surg Pathol 1998, **21**: 1507–1514.

315 Christopherson WM, Alberhasky RC, Connelly PJ. Carcinoma of the endometrium. I. A clinicopathologic study of clear cell carcinoma and secretory carcinoma. Cancer 1982, **49**: 1511–1523.

316 Christopherson WM, Alberhasky RC, Connelly PJ. Glassy cell carcinoma of the endometrium. Hum Pathol 1982, **13**: 418–421.

317 Deligdisch L, Gil J, Heller D, Cohen CJ. Two types of endometrial papillary neoplasm. A morphometric study. Pathol Res Pract 1992, **188**: 473–477.

318 Eichhorn JH, Young RH, Clement PB. Sertoliform endometrial adenocarcinoma: a study of four cases. Int J Gynecol Pathol 1996, **15**: 119–126.

319 Fechner RE. Endometrium with pattern of mesonephroma. Report of a case. Obstet Gynecol 1968, **31**: 485–490.

320 Fukunaga M, Ushigome S. Transitional cell carcinoma of the endometrium. Histopathology 1998, **32**: 284–286.

321 Gaertner EM, Farley JH, Taylor RR, Silver SA. Collision of uterine rhaboid tumor and endometrial adenocarcinoma: a case report and review of the literature. Int J Gynecol Pathol 1999, **18**: 396–401.

322 Gitsch G, Friedlander ML, Wain GV, Hacker NF. Uterine papillary serous carcinoma. A clinical study. Cancer 1995, **75**: 2239–2243.

323 Hachisuga T, Sugimori H, Kaku T, Matsukuma K, Tsukamoto N, Nakano H. Glassy cell carcinoma of the endometrium. Gynecol Oncol 1990, **36**: 134–138.

324 Haqqani MT, Fox H. Adenosquamous carcinoma of the endometrium. J Clin Pathol 1976, **29**: 959–966.

325 Hendrickson MR, Kempson RL. Ciliated carcinoma – a variant of endometrial adenocarcinoma. A report of 10 cases. Int J Gynecol Pathol 1983, **2**: 1–12.

326 Hendrickson M, Ross J, Eifel P, Martinez A, Kempson R. Uterine papillary serous carcinoma. A highly malignant form of endometrial adenocarcinoma. Am J Surg Pathol 1982, **6**: 93–108.

327 Hopkin ID, Harlow RA, Stevens PJ. Squamous carcinoma of the body of the uterus. Br J Cancer 1970, **24**: 71–76.

328 Hoshida Y, Nagakawa T, Mano S, Taguchi K, Aozasa K. Hepatoid adenocarcinoma of the endometrium associated with alpha-fetoprotein production. Int J Gynecol Pathol 1997, **15**: 266–269.

329 Huntsman DG, Clement PB, Gilks CB, Scully RE. Small-cell carcinoma of the endometrium. A clinicopathological study of sixteen cases. Am J Surg Pathol 1994, **18**: 364–375.

330 Iezzoni GC, Mills SE. Nonneoplastic endometrial signet-ring cells. Vacuolated decidual cells and stromal histiocytes

mimicking adenocarcinoma. Am J Clin Pathol 2001, **115:** 249–255.

331 Inoue M, DeLellis RA, Scully RE. Immunohistochemical demonstration of chromogranin in endometrial carcinomas with argyrophil cells. Hum Pathol 1986, **17:** 841–847.

332 Jeffers MD, McDonald GS, McGuinness EP. Primary squamous cell carcinoma of the endometrium. Histopathology 1991, **19:** 177–179.

333 Jeffrey JF, Krepart GV, Lotocki RJ. Papillary serous adenocarcinoma of the endometrium. Obstet Gynecol 1986, **67:** 670–674.

334 Jones MA, Young RH, Scully RE. Endometrial adenocarcinoma with a component of giant cell carcinoma. Int J Gynecol Pathol 1991, **10:** 260–270.

335 Kalir T, Seijo L, Deligdisch L, Cohen C. Endometrial adenocarcinoma with choriocarcinomatous differentiation in an elderly virginal woman. Int J Gynecol Pathol 1995, **14:** 266–269.

336 Kuebler DL, Nikrui N, Bell DA. Cytologic features of endometrial papillary serous carcinoma. Acta Cytol 1989, **33:** 120–126.

337 Kurman RJ, Scully RE. Clear cell carcinoma of the endometrium. An analysis of 21 cases. Cancer 1976, **37:** 872–882.

338 Lax SF, Pizer ES, Ronnett BM, Kurman RJ. Clear cell carcinoma of the endometrium is characterized by a distinctive profile of p53, Ki-67, estrogen, and progesterone receptor expression. Hum Pathol 1998, **29:** 551–558.

339 Lininger RA, Ashfaq F, Albores-Saavedra J, Tavassoli FA. Transitional cell carcinoma of the endometrium and endometrial carcinoma with transitional cell differentiation. Cancer 1997, **79:** 1933–1943.

340 McCluggage WG, Roberts N, Bharucha H. Enteric differentiation in endometrial adenocarcinomas. A mucin histochemical study. Int J Gynecol Pathol 1995, **14:** 255–260.

341 Malpica A, Tornos C, Burke TW, Silva EG. Low-stage clear-cell carcinoma of the endometrium. Am J Surg Pathol 1995, **19:** 769–774.

342 Matias-Guiu X, Lerma E, Prat J. Clear cell tumors of the female genital tract. Semin Diagn Pathol 1998, **14:** 233–239.

343 Melhem MF, Tobon H. Mucinous adenocarcinoma of the endometrium. A clinico-pathological review of 18 cases. Int J Gynecol Pathol 1987, **6:** 347–355.

344 Mooney EE, Robboy SJ, Hammond CB, Berchuck A, Bentley RC. Signet-ring cell carcinoma of the endometrium: a primary tumor masquerading as a metastasis. Int J Gynecol Pathol 1997, **16:** 169–172.

345 Ng ABP. Mixed carcinoma of the endometrium. Am J Obstet Gynecol 1968, **102:** 506–515.

346 Ng ABP, Reagan JW, Storassli JP, Wentz WB. Mixed adenosquamous carcinoma of the endometrium. Am J Clin Pathol 1973, **59:** 765–781.

347 Ordi J, Nogales FF, Palacin A, Marquez M, Pahisa J, Vanrell JA, Cardesa A. Mesonephric adenocarcinoma of the uterine corpus: CD10 expression as evidence of mesonephric differentiation. Am J Surg Pathol 2001, **25:** 1540–1545.

348 Parkash V, Carcangiu ML. Uterine papillary serous carcinoma after radiation therapy for carcinoma of the cervix. Cancer 1992, **69:** 496–501.

348a Parkash V, Carcangiu ML. Endometrioid endometrial adenocarcinoma with psammoma bodies. Am J Surg Pathol 1997, **21:** 399–406.

349 Paz RA, Frigerio B, Sundblad AS, Eusebi V. Small-cell (oat cell) carcinoma of the endometrium. Arch Pathol Lab Med 1985, **109:** 270–272.

350 Peison B, Benisch B, Fox H. Invasive keratinising squamous cell carcinoma of the endometrium as extension of invasive cervical squamous cell carcinoma. Int J Surg Pathol 1997, **4:** 189–192.

351 Pesce C, Merino MJ, Chambers JT, Nogales F. Endometrial carcinoma with trophoblastic differentiation. An aggressive form of uterine cancer. Cancer 1991, **68:** 1799–1802.

352 Pitman MB, Young RH, Clement PB, Dickersin GR, Scully RE. Endometrioid carcinoma of the ovary and endometrium, oxyphilic cell type. A report of nine cases. Int J Gynecol Pathol 1994, **13:** 290–301.

353 Rorat E, Ferenczy A, Richart RM. The ultrastructure of clear cell adenocarcinoma of endometrium. Cancer 1974, **33:** 880–887.

354 Ross JC, Eifel PJ, Cox RS, Kempson RL, Hendrickson MR. Primary mucinous adenocarcinoma of the endometrium. A clinicopathologic and histochemical study. Am J Surg Pathol 1983, **7:** 715–729.

355 Roth LM. Clear-cell adenocarcinoma of the female genital tract. A light and electron microscopic study. Cancer 1974, **33:** 990–1001.

356 Ryder DE. Verrucous carcinoma of the endometrium – a unique neoplasm with long survival. Obstet Gynecol 1982, **59:** 78S–80S.

357 Salazar OM, DePapp EW, Bonfiglio TA, Feldstein ML, Rubin P, Rudolph JH. Adenosquamous carcinoma of the endometrium. An entity with an inherent poor prognosis? Cancer 1977, **40:** 119–130.

358 Sherman ME, Bitterman P, Rosenshein NB, Delgado G, Kurman RJ. Uterine serous carcinoma. A morphologically diverse neoplasm with unifying clinicopathologic features. Am J Surg Pathol 1992, **16:** 600–610.

359 Silva EG, Jenkins R. Serous carcinoma in endometrial polyps. Mod Pathol 1990, **3:** 120–128.

360 Silverberg SG, DeGiorgi LS. Clear cell carcinoma of the endometrium. Cancer 1973, **31:** 1127–1140.

361 Sivridis E, Buckley CH, Fox H. Argyrophil cells in normal, hyperplastic, and neoplastic endometrium. J Clin Pathol 1984, **37:** 378–381.

362 Sorvari TE. A histochemical study of epithelial mucosubstances in endometrial and cervical adenocarcinomas. With reference to normal endometrium and cervical mucosa. Acta Pathol Microbiol Scand 1969, **207**(Suppl): 56–60.

363 Tobon H, Watkins GJ. Secretory adenocarcinoma of the endometrium. Int J Gynecol Pathol 1985, **4:** 328–335.

364 Usadi RS, Bentley RC. Endometrioid carcinoma of the endometrium with sertoliform differentiation. Int J Gynecol Pathol 1995, **14:** 360–364.

364a Vang R, Tavassoli FA. Proliferative mucinous lesions of the endometrium: analysis of existing criteria for diagnosing carcinoma in biopsies and curettings. Int J Surg Pathol 2003, **11:** 261–270.

365 Vang R, Whitaker BP, Farhood AI, Silva EG, Ro RJ, Deavers MT. Immunohistochemical analysis of clear cell carcinoma of the gynecologic tract. Int J Gynecol Pathol 2001, **20:** 252–259.

366 van Hoeven KH, Hudock JA, Woodruff JM, Suhrland MJ. Small cell neuroendocrine carcinoma of the endometrium. Int J Gynecol Pathol 1995, **14:** 21–29.

367 Vargas MP, Merino MJ. Lymphoepitheliomalike carcinoma: an usual variant of endometrial cancer; a report of two cases. Int J Gynecol Pathol 1998, **17:** 272–276.

368 Warhol MJ, Rice RH, Pinkus GS, Robboy SJ. Evaluation of squamous epithelium in adenoacanthoma and adenosquamous carcinoma of the endometrium. Immunoperoxidase analysis of involucrin and keratin localization. Int J Gynecol Pathol 1984, **3:** 82–91.

369 Wheeler DT, Bell KA, Kurman RJ, Sherman ME. Minimal uterine serous carcinoma: diagnosis and clinicopathologic correlation. Am J Surg Pathol 2000, **24:** 797–806.

370 Yamamoto Y, Izumi K, Otsuka H, Kishi Y, Mimura T, Okitsu O. Primary squamous cell carcinoma of the endometrium. A case report and a suggestion of new histogenesis. Int J Gynecol Pathol 1995, **14:** 75–80.

371 Yamashina M, Kobara TY. Primary squamous cell carcinoma with its spindle cell variant in the endometrium. A case report and review of literature. Cancer 1986, **57:** 340–345.

372 Young RH, Scully RE. Uterine carcinomas simulating

microglandular hyperplasia. A report of six cases. Am J Surg Pathol 1994, **16**: 1092–1097.

373 Zaino RJ, Kurman RJ. Squamous differentiation in carcinoma of the endometrium. A critical appraisal of adenoacanthoma and adenosquamous carcinoma. Semin Diagn Pathol 1988, **5**: 154–171.

374 Zaino RJ, Kurman R, Herbold D, Gliedman J, Bundy BN, Voet R, Advani H. The significance of squamous differentiation in endometrial carcinoma. Data from a Gynecologic Oncology Group study. Cancer 1991, **68**: 2293–2302.

375 Zaloudek C, Hayashi GM, Ryan IP, Powell CB, Miller TR. Microglandular adenocarcinoma of the endometrium: a form of mucinous adenocarcinoma that may be confused with microglandular hyperplasia of the cervix. Int J Gynecol Pathol 1997, **16**: 52–59.

Cytology

376 Bibbo M, Shanklin DR, Wied L. Endometrial cytology on jet wash material. J Reprod Med 1972, **8**: 90–96.

377 Burk JR, Lehman HF, Wolf FS. Inadequacy of Papanicolaou smears in the detection of endometrial cancer. N Engl J Med 1974, **291**: 191–192.

378 Christopherson WM, Mendez WM, Ahuja EM, Lundin FE, Parker JE. Cervix cancer control in Louisville, Kentucky. Cancer 1970, **26**: 29–38.

379 Gusberg SB, Milano C. Detection of endometrial carcinoma and its precursors. Cancer 1981, **47**: 1173–1175.

380 Hibbard LT, Schwinn CP. Diagnosis of endometrial jet washings. Am J Obstet Gynecol 1971, **111**: 1039–1042.

381 Isaacs JH, Wilmoite RW. Aspiration cytology of the endometrium. Office and hospital sampling procedures. Am J Obstet Gynecol 1974, **118**: 679–687.

382 Ng ABP, Reagan JW, Hawliczek CT, Wentz BW. Significance of endometrial cells in the detection of endometrial carcinoma and its precursors. Acta Cytol (Baltimore) 1974, **18**: 356–361.

383 Reagan JW. Can screening for endometrial cancer be justified? [editorial]. Acta Cytol (Baltimore) 1980, **24**: 87–89.

384 Reagan JW. Cytologic aspects of endometrial neoplasia. Acta Cytol 1980, **24**: 488–489.

385 Reagan JW, Ng ABP. The cells of uterine adenocarcinoma. Baltimore, 1965, Williams & Wilkins.

386 Rodrigues MA, Rubin A, Koss LG, Harris J. Evaluation of endometrial jet wash technique (Gravlee) in 303 patients in a community hospital. Obstet Gynecol 1974, **43**: 392–399.

387 Vuopala S. Diagnostic accuracy and clinical applicability of cytological and histological methods for investigating endometrial carcinoma. Acta Obstet Gynecol Scand 1977, **70**(Suppl): 1–72.

Histochemical and immunohistochemical features

388 Brustein S, Fruchter R, Greene GL, Pertschuk LP. Immunocytochemical assay of progesterone receptors in paraffin-embedded specimens of endometrial carcinoma and hyperplasia. A preliminary evaluation. Mod Pathol 1989, **2**: 449–455.

389 Carcangiu ML, Chambers JT, Voynick IM, Pirro M, Schwartz PE. Immunohistochemical evaluation of estrogen and progesterone receptor content in 183 patients with endometrial carcinoma. Part I. Clinical and histologic correlations. Am J Clin Pathol 1990, **94**: 247–254.

390 Dabbs DJ, Geisinger KR, Norris HT. Intermediate filaments in endometrial and endocervical carcinomas. The diagnostic utility of vimentin patterns. Am J Surg Pathol 1986, **10**: 568–576.

391 Dabbs DJ, Sturtz K, Zaino RJ. The immunohistochemical discrimination of endometrioid adenocarcinomas. Hum Pathol 1996, **27**: 172–177.

392 Demopoulos RI, Mesia AF, Mittal K, Vamvakas E. Immunohistochemical comparison of uterine papillary serous and papillary endometrioid carcinoma: clues to pathogenesis. Int J Gynecol Pathol 2002, **18**: 233–237.

393 Elmore LW, Domson K, Moore BS, Kornstein M, Burks RT. Expression of c-kit (CD117) in benign and malignant human endometrial epithelium. Arch Pathol Lab Med 2001, **125**: 146–151.

394 Geisinger KR, Marshall RB, Kute TE, Homesley HD. Correlation of female sex steroid hormone receptors with histologic and ultrastructural differentiation in adenocarcinoma of the endometrium. Cancer 1986, **58**: 1506–1517.

395 Goldstein NS, Uzieblo A. WT1 immunoreactivity in uterine papillary serous carcinomas is different from ovarian serous carcinomas. Am J Clin Pathol 2002, **117**: 541–545.

396 Kounelis S, Kapranos N, Kouri E, Coppola D, Papadaki H, Jones MW. Immunohistochemical profile of endometrial adenocarcinoma: a study of 61 cases and review of the literature. Mod Pathol 2000, **13**: 379–388.

397 Lax SF, Pizer ES, Ronnett BM, Kurman RJ. Comparison of estrogen and progesterone receptor, Ki-67, and p53 immunoreactivity in uterine endometrioid carcinoma and endometrioid carcinoma with squamous, mucinous, secretory, and ciliated cell differentiaton. Hum Pathol 1998, **29**: 924–931.

398 Moll R, Levy R, Czernobilsky B, Hohlweg-Majert P, Dallenbach-Hellweg G, Franke WW. Cytokeratins of normal epithelia and some neoplasms of the female genital tract. Lab Invest 1983, **49**: 599–610.

399 Moll R, Pitz S, Levy R, Weikel W, Franke WW, Czernobilsky B. Complexity of expression of intermediate filament proteins, including glial filament protein, in endometrial and ovarian adenocarcinomas. Hum Pathol 1991, **22**: 989–1001.

400 Podczaski E, Kaminski PF, Zaino R. CA 125 and CA 19–9 immunolocalization in normal, hyperplastic, and carcinomatous endometrium. Cancer 1993, **71**: 2551–2556.

401 Puts JJG, Moesker O, Aldeweireldt J, Vooijs GP, Ramaekers FCS. Application of antibodies to intermediate filament proteins in simple and complex tumors of the female genital tract. Int J Gynecol Pathol 1987, **6**: 257–274.

402 Rolitsky CD, Theil KS, McGaughy VR, Copeland LJ, Niemann TH. HER-2/neu amplification and overexpression in endometrial carcinoma. Int J Gynecol Pathol 1999, **18**: 138–143.

403 Schlosshauer PW, Ellenson LH, Soslow RA. Beta-catenin and E-cadherin expression patterns in high-grade endometrial carcinoma are associated with histological subtype. Mod Pathol 2002, **15**: 1032–1037.

404 Takeda A, Matsuyama M, Kuzuya K, Chihara T, Ariyoshi Y, Suchi T, Kato K. Secretory component and IgA in endometrial adenocarcinomas. An immunohistochemical study. Acta Pathol Jpn 1983, **33**: 725–732.

405 Ueda G, Yamasaki M, Inoue M, Tanaka Y, Inoue Y, Nishino T, Ogawa M. Immunohistochemical demonstration of amylase in endometrial carcinomas. Int J Gynecol Pathol 1986, **5**: 47–51.

406 Ueda S, Tsubura A, Izumi H, Sasaki M, Morii S. Immunohistochemical studies on carcinoembryonic antigen in adenocarcinomas of the uterus. Acta Pathol Jpn 1983, **33**: 59–69.

407 Wang BY, Kalir T, Sabo E, Sherman DE, Cohen C, Burstein DE. Immunohistochemical staining of GLUT1 in benign, hyperplastic, and malignant endometrial epithelia. Cancer 2000, **88**: 2774–2781.

407a Zhang PJ, Williams E, Pasha T, Acs G. WTI is expressed in serous, but not in endometrioid, clear cell or mucinous carcinomas of the peritoneum, fallopian tube, ovaries and endometrium (Abstract). Mod Pathol 2003, **16**: 216a.

Molecular genetic features

408 Ali IU. Gatekeeper for endometrium: the PTEN tumor suppressor gene. J Nat Cancer Inst 2000, **92**: 861–863.

409 Bonatz G, Frahm SO, Klapper W, Helfenstein A, Heidorn K, Jonat W, Krupp G, Parwaresch R, Rudolph P. High telomerase activity

is associated with cell cycle deregulation and rapid progression in endometrioid adenocarcinoma of the uterus. Hum Pathol 2001, **32:** 605–614.

410 Burton JL, Wells M. Recent advances in the histopathology and molecular pathology of carcinoma of the endometrium. Histopathology 1998, **33:** 297–303.

411 Bussaglia E, del Rio E, Matias-Guiu X, Prat J. PTEN mutations in endometrial carcinomas: a molecular and clinicopathologic analysis of 38 cases. Hum Pathol 2000, **31:** 312–317.

412 Cao QJ, Einstein MH, Anderson PS, Runowicz CD, Balan R, Jones JG. Expression of COX-2, Ki-67, cyclin D1, and P21 in endometrioid carcinomas. Int J Gynecol Pathol 2002, **21:** 147–154.

413 Fernando SSE, Wu X, Perera LS. P53 Overexpression and steroid hormone receptor status in endometrial carcinoma. Int J Surg Pathol 2000, **8:** 213–222.

414 Hendrick Ellenson L. The molecular biology of endometrial tumorigenesis: does it have a message? Int J Gynecol Pathol 2000, **19:** 314–321.

415 Koshiyama M, Konishi I, Wang DP, Mandai M, Komatsu T, Yamamoto S, Nanbu K, Naito MF, Mori T. Immunohistochemical analysis of p53 protein over-expression in endometrial carcinomas. Inverse correlation with sex steroid receptor status. Virchows Arch [A] 1993, **423:** 265–271.

416 Koul A, Willen R, Bendhal PO, Nilbert M, Borg A. Distinct sites of gene alterations in endometrial carcinoma implicate alternate modes of tumorigenesis. Cancer 2002, **94:** 2369–2379.

416a Lovecchio M, Maiorano E, Vacca RA, Loverro G, Fanelli M, Resta L, Stefanelli S, Selvaggi L, Marra E, Perlino E. _1C integrin expression in human endometrial proliferative diseases. Am J Pathol 2003, **163:** 2453–2553.

417 Machin P, Catasus L, Pons C, Munoz J, Matias-Guiu X, Prat J. CTNNB1 mutations and beta-catenin expression in endometrial carcinoma. Hum Pathol 2002, **33:** 206–212.

418 Matias-Guiu X, Catasus L, Bussaglia E, Lagarda H, Garcia A, Pons C, Munoz J, Arguelles R, Machin P, Prat J. Molecular pathology of endometrial hyperplasia and carcinoma. Hum Pathol 2001, **32:** 569–577.

419 Palazzo JP, Mercer WE, Kovatich AJ, McHugh M. Immunohistochemical localization of p21 (waf1/cip1) in normal, hyperplastic, and neoplastic uterine tissues. Hum Pathol 1997, **28:** 60–66.

420 Ronnett BM, Burks RT, Cho KR, Hedrick L. DCC genetic alterations and expression in endometrial carcinoma. Mod Pathol 1997, **10:** 38–46.

421 Sasano H, Comeford J, Wilkinson DS, Schwartz A, Garrett CT. Serous papillary adenocarcinoma of the endometrium. Analysis of proto-oncogene amplification, flow cytometry, estrogen and progesterone receptors, and immunohistochemistry. Cancer 1990, **65:** 1545–1551.

422 Sherman ME. Theories of endometrial carcinogenesis: a multidisciplinary approach. Mod Pathol 2000, **13:** 295–308.

423 Susini T, Massi D, Paglierani M, Masciullo V, Scambia G, Giordano A, Amunni G, Massi G, Taddei GL. Expression of the retinoblastoma-related gene Rb2/p130 is downregulated in atypical endometrial hyperplasia and adenocarcinoma. Hum Pathol 2001, **32:** 360–367.

424 Tashiro H, Lax SF, Gaudin PB, Isacson C, Cho KR, Hedrick L. Microsatellite instability is uncommon in uterine serous carcinoma. Am J Pathol 1997, **150:** 75–79.

425 Tritz D, Pieretti M, Turner S, Powell D. Loss of heterozygosity in usual and special variant carcinomas of the endometrium. Hum Pathol 1997, **28:** 607–612.

426 Watanabe Y, Nakajima H, Nozaki K, Ueda H, Obata K, Hoshiai H, Noda K. Clinicopathologic and immunohistochemical features and microsatellite status of endometrial cancer of the uterine isthmus. Int J Gynecol Pathol 2001, **20:** 368–373.

Spread and metastases

427 Baergen RN, Warren CD, Isaacson C, Ellenson LH. Early uterine serous carcinoma: clonal origin of extrauterine disease. Int J Gynecol Pathol 2001, **20:** 214–219.

428 Boronow RC, Morrow CP, Creasman WT, Disaia PJ, Silverberg SG, Miller A, Blessing JA. Surgical staging in endometrial cancer. Clinical-pathologic findings of a prospective study. Obstet Gynecol 1984, **63:** 825–832.

429 Chen KTK, Kostich ND, Rosai J. Peritoneal foreign body granulomas to keratin in uterine adenoacanthoma. Arch Pathol Lab Med 1978, **102:** 174–177.

430 Creasman WI, Morrow CP, Bundy BN, Homesley HD, Graham JE, Heller PB: Surgical pathologic spread patterns of endometrial cancer. Cancer 1987, **60:** 2035–2041.

431 Kim KR, Scully RE. Peritoneal keratin granulomas with carcinomas of endometrium and ovary and atypical polypoid adenomyoma of endometrium. A clinicopathological analysis of 22 cases. Am J Surg Pathol 1990, **14:** 925–932.

432 Kupryjanczyk J, Thor AD, Beauchamp R, Poremba C, Scully RE, Yandell DW. Ovarian, peritoneal, and endometrial serous carcinoma: clonal origin of multifocal disease. Mod Pathol 1996, **9:** 166–173.

433 Schink JC, Rademaker AW, Miller DS, Lurain JR. Tumor size in endometrial cancer. Cancer 1991, **67:** 2791–2794.

434 Soslow RA, Pirog E, Isaacson C. Endometrial intraepithelial carcinoma with associated peritoneal carcinomatosis. Am J Surg Pathol 2000, **24:** 726–732.

434a Tambouret R, Clement PB, Young RH. Endometrial endometrioid adenocarcinoma with a deceptive pattern of spread to the uterine cervix. A manifestation of stage IIB endometrial carcinoma liable to be misinterpreted as an independent carcinoma or a benign lesion. Am J Surg Pathol 2003, **27:** 1080–1088.

434b Yan Z, Parkash V, Zheng W, Schwartz P, Costa J, Hui P. Minimal uterine serous carcinoma with extrauterine tumor of identical morphology: a study of 13 cases (Abstract). Mod Pathol 2003, **16:** 216a.

435 Young RH, Johnston WH. Serous adenocarcinoma of the uterus metastatic to the urinary bladder mimicking primary bladder neoplasia. A report of a case. Am J Surg Pathol 1990, **14:** 877–880.

Coexistent uterine and ovarian carcinoma

436 Emmert-Buck MR, Chuaqui R, Zhuang Z, Nogales F, Liotta LA, Merino MJ. Molecular analysis of synchronous uterine and ovarian endometrioid tumors. Int J Gynecol Pathol 1997, **16:** 143–148.

437 Fujii H, Matsumoto T, Yoshida M, Furugen Y, Takagaki T, Iwabuchi K, Nakata Y, Takagi Y, Moriya Y, Ohtsuji N, Ohtsuji M, Hirose S, Shirai T. Genetics of synchronous uterine and ovarian endometrioid carcinoma: combined analyses of loss of heterozygosity, PTEN mutations, and microsatellite instability. Hum Pathol 2002, **33:** 421–428.

438 Fujita M, Endomoto T, Wada H, Inoue M, Okudaira Y, Shroyer KR. Application of clonal analysis. Differential diagnosis for synchronous primary ovarian and endometrial cancers and metastatic cancer. Am J Clin Pathol 1996, **105:** 350–359.

439 Prat J, Matias-Guiu X, Barreto J. Simultaneous carcinoma involving the endometrium and the ovary. A clinicopathologic, immunohistochemical, and DNA flow cytometric study of 18 cases. Cancer 1991, **68:** 2455–2459.

440 Press MF. Are synchronous uterine and ovarian carcinomas independent primary tumors? Adv Anat Pathol 1997, **4:** 370–372.

Treatment

441 Aalders JG, Abeler V, Kolstad P. Recurrent adenocarcinoma of the endometrium. A clinical and histopathological study of 379 patients. Gynecol Oncol 1984, **17:** 85–103.

442 Baekelandt M. Hormonal treatment of endometrial carcinoma. Expert Rev Anticancer Ther 2002, **2**: 106–112.

443 Frank AH, Tseng PC, Haffty BG, Papadopoulos DP, Kacinski BM, Dowling SW, Carcangiu ML, Kohorn EI, Chambers JT, Chambers SK, et al. Adjuvant whole-abdominal radiation therapy in uterine papillary serous carcinoma. Cancer 1991, **68**: 1516–1519.

444 Kim YB, Holschneider CH, Ghosh K, Nieberg RK, Montz FJ. Progestin alone as primary treatment of endometrial carcinoma in premenopausal women: report of seven cases and review of the literature. Cancer 1997, **79**: 320–327.

445 Levine DA, Hoskins WJ. Update in the management of endometrial cancer. Cancer J 2002, **8**: S31–S40.

446 Lim P, Al Kushi A, Gilks B, Wong F, Aquino-Parsons C. Early stage uterine papillary serous carcinoma of the endometrium: effect of adjuvant whole abdominal radiotherapy and pathologic parameters and outcome. Cancer 2001, **91**: 752–757.

447 Price FV, Chambers SK, Carcangiu ML, Kohorn EI, Schwartz PE, Chambers JT. Intravenous cisplatin, doxorubicin, and cyclophosphamide in the treatment of uterine papillary serous carcinoma (UPSC). Gynecol Oncol 1993, **51**: 383–389.

447a Ricci R, Komminoth P, Bannwart F, Torhorst J, Wight E, Heitz PU, Caduff RF. PTEN as a molecular marker to distinguish metastatic from primary synchronous endometrioid carcinomas of the ovary and uterus. Diagn Mol Pathol 2003, **12**: 71–78.

448 Sears JD, Greven KM, Hoen HM, Randall ME. Prognostic factors and treatment outcome for patients with locally recurrent endometrial cancer. Cancer 1994, **74**: 1303–1308.

449 Silverberg SG, DeGiorgi LS. Histopathologic analysis of preoperative radiation therapy in endometrial carcinoma. Am J Obstet Gynecol 1974, **119**: 698–704.

450 Sonoda Y. Optimal therapy and management of endometrial cancer. Expert Rev Anticancer Ther 2003, **3**: 37–47.

451 Tewari KS, DiSaia PJ. Radiation therapy for gynecologic cancer. J Obstet Gynaecol Res 2003, **28**: 123–140.

452 Trope C, Kristensen GB, Abeler VM. Clear-cell and papillary serous cancer: treatment options. Best Pract Res Clin Obstet Gynaecol 2001, **15**: 433–446.

Prognosis

453 Alektiar KM, McKee A, Lin O, Vankatraman E, Zelefsky MJ, Mychalczak BR, McKee B, Hiskins WJ, Barakat RR. The significance of the amount of myometrial invasion in patients with stage IB endometrial carcinoma. Cancer 2002, **95**: 316–321.

454 Ambros RA, Kurman RJ. Combined assessment of vascular and myometrial invasion as a model to predict prognosis in stage I endometrioid adenocarcinoma of the uterine corpus. Cancer 1992, **69**: 1424–1431.

455 Ambros RA, Kurman RJ. Identification of patients with stage I uterine endometrioid adenocarcinoma at high risk of recurrence by DNA ploidy, myometrial invasion, and vascular invasion. Gynecol Oncol 1992, **45**: 235–239.

456 Ambros RA, Vigna PA, Figge J, Kallakury BV, Mastrangelo A, Eastman AY, Malfetano J, Figge HL, Ross JS. Observations on tumor and metastatic suppressor gene status in endometrial carcinoma with particular emphasis on p53. Cancer 1994, **73**: 1686–1692.

457 Ayhan A, Taskiran C, Yuce K, Kucukali T. The prognostic value of nuclear grading and the revised FIGO grading of endometrial adenocarcinoma. Int J Gynecol Pathol 2002, **22**: 71–74.

458 Beckner ME, Mori T, Silverberg SG. Endometrial carcinoma. Nontumor factors in prognosis. Int J Gynecol Pathol 1985, **4**: 131–145.

459 Benevolo M, Mariani L, Vocaturo G, Vasselli S, Natali PG, Mottolese M. Independent prognostic value of peritoneal immunocytodiagnosis in endometrial carcinoma. Am J Surg Pathol 2000, **24**: 241–247.

460 Bonatz G, Luttes J, Hamann S, Mettler L, Jonat W, Parwaresch R. Immunohistochemical assessment of p170 provides prognostic information in endometrial carcinoma. Histopathology 1999, **34**: 43–50.

461 Boronow RC. Advances in diagnosis, staging, and management of cervical and endometrial cancer, stages I and II. Cancer 1990, **65**: 648–659.

462 Boronow RC, Morrow CP, Creasman WT, DiSaia PJ, Silverberg SG, Miller A, Blessing JA. Surgical staging in endometrial cancer. Clinical-pathologic findings of a prospective study. Obstet Gynecol 1984, **63**: 825–832.

463 Britton LC, Wilson TO, Gaffey TA, Cha SS, Wieand HS, Podratz KC. DNA ploidy in endometrial carcinoma. Major objective prognostic factor. Mayo Clin Proc 1990, **65**: 643–650.

464 Chambers JT, Carcangiu ML, Voynick IM, Schwartz PE. Immunohistochemical evaluation of estrogen and progesterone receptor content in 183 patients with endometrial carcinoma. Part II. Correlation between biochemical and immunohistochemical methods and survival. Am J Clin Pathol 1990, **94**: 255–260.

465 Christopherson WM, Connelly PJ, Alberhasky RC. Carcinoma of the endometrium. V. An analysis of prognosticators in patients with favorable subtypes and stage I disease. Cancer 1983, **51**: 1705–1709.

466 Coppola D, Fu L, Nicosia SV, Kounelis S, Jones M. Prognostic significance of p53, bcl-2, vimentin, and S100 protein-positive Langerhans cells in endometrial carcinoma. Hum Pathol 1998, **29**: 455–462.

467 Creasman WT. Prognostic significance of hormone receptors in endometrial cancer. Cancer 1993, **71**: 1467–1470.

468 Fanning J, Alvarez PM, Tsukada Y, Piver MS. Prognostic significance of the extent of cervical involvement by endometrial cancer. Gynecol Oncol 1991, **40**: 46–47.

469 Gehrig PA, Van Le L, Olatidoye B, Geradts J. Estrogen receptor status, determined by immunohistochemistry, as a predictor of the recurrence of stage I endometrial carcinoma. Cancer 2000, **86**: 2083–2089.

470 Greven KM, Lanciano RM, Corn B, Case D, Randall ME. Pathologic stage III endometrial carcinoma. Prognostic factors and patterns of recurrence. Cancer 1993, **71**: 3697–3702.

471 Hachisuga T, Kaku T, Fukuda K, Eguchi F, Emoto M, Kamura T, Iwasaka T, Kawarabayashi T, Sugimori H, Mori M. The grading in lymphovascular space invasion in endometrial carcinoma. Cancer 2000, **86**: 2090–2097.

472 Hanson MB, Van Nagell JR, Powell DE, Donaldson ES, Gallion H, Merhige M, Pavlik EJ. The prognostic significance of lymph-vascular space invasion in stage I endometrial cancer. Cancer 1985, **55**: 1753–1757.

473 Hendrickson M, Ross J, Eifel PJ, Cox RS, Martinez A, Kempson R. Adenocarcinoma of the endometrium. Analysis of 256 cases with carcinoma limited to the uterine corpus. Pathology review and analysis of prognostic variables. Gynecol Oncol 1982, **13**: 373–392.

474 Hetzel DJ, Wilson TO, Keeney GL, Roche PC, Cha SS, Podratz KC. HER-2/neu expression. A major prognostic factor in endometrial cancer. Gynecol Oncol 1992, **47**: 179–185.

475 Homesley HD, Zaino R. Endometrial cancer. Prognostic factors. Semin Oncol 1994, **21**: 71–78.

476 Ikeda M, Watanabe Y, Nanjoh T, Noda K. Evaluation of DNA ploidy in endometrial cancer. Gynecol Oncol 1993, **50**: 25–29.

477 Inoue Y, Obata K, Abe K, Ohmura G, Doh K, Yoshioka T, Hoshiai H, Noda K. The prognostic significance of vascular invasion by endometrial carcinoma. Cancer 1996, **78**: 1447–1451.

478 Kaku T, Kamura T, Kinukawa N, Kobayashi H, Sakai K, Tsuruchi N, Saito T, Kawauchi S, Tsuneyoshi M, Nakano H. Angiogenesis in endometrial carcinoma. Cancer 1997, **80**: 741–747.

479 Kempson RL, Pokorny GE. Adenocarcinoma of the endometrium in women aged forty and younger. Cancer 1968, **21**: 650–662.

480 Larson DM, Copeland LJ, Gallagher HS, Gershenson DM,

Freedman RS, Wharton JT, Kline RC. Nature of cervical involvement in endometrial carcinoma. Cancer 1987, **59:** 959–962.

481 Lukes AS, Kohler MF, Pieper CF, Kerns BJ, Bentley R, Rodriguez GC, Soper JT, Clarke-Pearson DL, Bast RC Jr, Berchuck A. Multivariable analysis of DNA ploidy, p53, and HER-2/neu as prognostic factors in endometrial cancer. Cancer 1994, **73:** 2380–2385.

482 Malkasian GD Jr. Carcinoma of the endometrium. Effect of stage and grade on survival. Cancer 1978, **41:** 996–1001.

483 Mikuta JJ. International Federation of Gynecology and Obstetrics staging of endometrial cancer 1988. Cancer 1993, **71:** 1460–1463.

484 Ng ABP, Reagan JW. Incidence and prognosis of endometrial carcinoma by histologic grade and extent. Obstet Gynecol 1970, **35:** 437–443.

485 Niikura H, Sasano H, Matsunaga G, Watanabe K, Ito K, Sato S, Yajima A. Prognostic value of epidermal growth factor receptor expression in endometrioid endometrial carcinoma. Hum Pathol 1995, **26:** 892–896.

486 Nordstrom B, Strang P, Lindgren A, Bergstrom R, Tribukait B. Carcinoma of the endometrium: do the nuclear grade and DNA ploidy provide more prognostic information then do the FIGO and WHO classifications? Int J Gynecol Pathol 1997, **15:** 191–201.

487 Peiro G, Diebold J, Mayr D, Baretton GB, Kimming R, Schmidt M, Lohrs U. Prognostic relevance of hMLH1, hMSH2, and BAX protein expression in endometrial carcinoma. Mod Pathol 2001, **14:** 777–783.

488 Reinartz JJ, George E, Lindgren BR, Niehans GA. Expression of p53, transforming growth factor alpha, epidermal growth factor receptor, and c-erbB-2 in endometrial carcinoma and correlation with survival and known predictors of survival. Hum Pathol 1994, **25:** 1075–1083.

489 Robboy SJ, Miller AW III, Kurman RJ. The pathologic features and behavior of endometrial carcinoma associated with exogenous estrogen administration. Pathol Res Pract 1982, **174:** 237–256.

490 Sasano H, Watanabe K, Ito K, Sato S, Yajima A. New concepts in the diagnosis and prognosis of endometrial carcinoma. Pathol Annu 1995, **29(Pt 2):** 31–49.

491 Sidawy MK, Silverberg SG. Endometrial carcinoma. Pathologic factors of therapeutic and prognostic significance. Pathol Annu 1992, **27:** 153–185.

492 Stendahl U, Strang P, Wagenius G, Bergstrom R, Tribukait B. Prognostic significance of proliferation in endometrial adenocarcinomas. A multivariate analysis of clinical and flow cytometric variables. Int J Gynecol Pathol 1991, **10:** 271–284.

493 Susini T, Baldi F, Howard CM, Baldi A, Taddei G, Massi D, Rapi S, Savino L, Massi G, Giordano A. Expression of the retinoblastoma-related gene Rb2/p130 correlates with clinical outcome in endometrial cancer. J Clin Oncol 1998, **16:** 1085–1093.

494 Tobon H, Watkins GJ. Secretory adenocarcinoma of the endometrium. Int J Gynecol Pathol 1985, **4:** 328–335.

495 Tornos C, Silva EG, el-Naggar A, Burke TW. Aggressive stage I grade I endometrial carcinoma. Cancer 1992, **70:** 790–798.

496 Zaino RJ. Pathologic indicators of prognosis in endometrial adenocarcinoma. Selected aspects emphasizing the GOG experience. Gynecologic Oncology Group. Pathol Annu 1995, **30(Pt 1):** 1–28.

497 Zaino RJ, Davis AT, Ohlsson-Wilhelm BM, Brunetto VL. DNA content is an independent prognostic indicator in endometrial adenocarcinoma: a Gynaecologic Oncology Group study. Int J Gynecol Pathol 1998, **17:** 312–319.

498 Zaino RJ, Kurman RJ, Diana KL, Morrow CP. Pathologic models to predict outcome for women with endometrial adenocarcinoma: the importance of the distinction between surgical stage and clinical stage – a Gynaecologic Oncology Group study. Cancer 1996, **77:** 1115–1121.

499 Zaino RJ, Kurman R, Herbold D, Gliedman J, Bundy BN, Voet R,

Advani H. The significance of squamous differentiation in endometrial carcinoma. Data from a Gynecologic Oncology Group study. Cancer 1991, **68:** 2293–2302.

500 Zaino RJ, Silverberg SG, Norris HJ, Bundy BN, Morrow CP, Okagaki T. The prognostic value of nuclear versus architectural grading in endometrial adenocarcinoma. A Gynecologic Oncology Group study. Int J Gynecol Pathol 1994, **13:** 29–36.

Endometrial stromal tumors

501 Abrams J, Talcott J, Corson JM. Pulmonary metastases in patients with low-grade endometrial stromal sarcoma. Clinicopathologic findings with immunohistochemical characterization. Am J Surg Pathol 1989, **13:** 133–140.

502 Akhtar M, Kim PY, Young I. Ultrastructure of endometrial stromal sarcoma. Cancer 1975, **35:** 406–412.

503 Aubry MC, Myers JL, Colby TV, Leslie KO, Tazelaar HD. Endometrial stromal sarcoma metastatic to the lung: a detailed analysis of 16 patients. Am J Surg Pathol 2002, **26:** 440–449.

504 August CZ, Bauer KD, Lurain J, Murad T. Neoplasms of endometrial stroma. Histopathologic and flow cytometric analysis with clinical correlation. Hum Pathol 1989, **20:** 232–237.

505 Baker RJ, Hildebrandt RH, Rouse RV, Hendrickson MR, Longacre TA. Inhibin and CD99 (MIC2) expression in uterine stromal neoplasms with sex-cord-like elements. Hum Pathol 1999, **30:** 671–679.

506 Balaton AJ, Vuong PN, Vaury P, Baviera EE. Plexiform tumorlet of the uterus. Immunohistological evidence for a smooth muscle origin. Histopathology 1986, **10:** 749–754.

507 Chang KL, Crabtree GS, Lim-Tan SK, Kempson RL, Hendrickson MR. Primary uterine endometrial stromal neoplasms. A clinicopathologic study of 117 cases. Am J Surg Pathol 1994, **14:** 415–438.

508 Chu PG, Arber DA, Weiss LM, Chang KL. Utility of CD10 in distinguishing between endometrial stromal sarcoma and uterine smooth muscle tumors: an immunohistochemical comparison of 34 cases. Mod Pathol 2001, **14:** 465–471.

509 Clement PB, Scully RE. Uterine tumors resembling ovarian sex-cord tumors. A clinicopathologic analysis of fourteen cases. Am J Clin Pathol 1976, **66:** 512–525.

510 Clement PB, Scully RE. Endometrial stromal sarcomas of the uterus with extensive endometrioid glandular differentiation. A report of three cases that caused problems in differential diagnosis. Int J Gynecol Pathol 1992, **11:** 163–173.

511 De Fusco PA, Gaffey TA, Malkasian GD Jr, Long HJ, Cha SS. Endometrial stromal sarcoma. Review of Mayo Clinic experience, 1945–1980. Gynecol Oncol 1989, **35:** 8–14.

512 Devaney K, Tavassoli FA. Immunohistochemistry as a diagnostic aid in the interpretation of unusual mesenchymal tumors of the uterus. Mod Pathol 1991, **4:** 225–231.

513 Dickersin GR, Scully RE. Role of electron microscopy in metastatic endometrial stromal tumors. Ultrastruct Pathol 1993, **17:** 377–403.

514 Dionigi A, Oliva E, Clement PB, Young RH. Endometrial stromal nodules and endometrial stromal tumors with limited infiltration: a clinicopathologic study of 50 cases. Am J Surg Pathol 2002, **26:** 567–581.

515 el-Naggar AK, Abdul-Karim FW, Silva EG, McLemore D, Garnsey L. Uterine stromal neoplasms. A clinicopathologic and DNA flow cytometric correlation. Hum Pathol 1991, **22:** 897–903.

516 Evans HL. Endometrial stromal sarcoma and poorly differentiated endometrial sarcoma. Cancer 1982, **50:** 2170–2182.

517 Farhood AI, Abrams J. Immunohistochemistry of endometrial stromal sarcoma. Hum Pathol 1991, **22:** 224–230.

518 Fekete PS, Vellios F. The clinical and histologic spectrum of endometrial stromal neoplasms. A report of 41 cases. Int J Gynecol Pathol 1984, **3:** 198–212.

519 Fisher ER, Paulson JD, Gregorio RM. The myofibroblastic nature

of the uterine plexiform tumor. Arch Pathol Lab Med 1978, **102:** 477–480.

520 Franquemont DW, Frierson HF Jr, Mills SE. An immunohistochemical study of normal endometrial stroma and endometrial stromal neoplasms. Evidence for smooth muscle differentiation. Am J Surg Pathol 1991, **15:** 861–870.

521 Goodhue WW, Susin M, Kramer EE. Smooth muscle origin of uterine plexiform tumors. Ultrastructural and histochemical evidence. Arch Pathol 1974, **97:** 263–268.

522 Hitchcock CL, Norris HJ. Flow cytometric analysis of endometrial stromal sarcoma. Am J Clin Pathol 1992, **97:** 267–271.

523 Itoh T, Mochizuki M, Kumazaki S, Ishihara T, Fukayama M. Cystic pulmonary metastases of endometrial stromal sarcoma of the uterus, mimicking lymphangiomyomatosis: a case report with immunohistochemistry of HMB45. Pathol Int 1997, **47:** 725–729.

524 Kaminski PF, Tavassoli FA. Plexiform tumorlet. A clinical and pathologic study of 15 cases with ultrastructural observations. Int J Gynecol Pathol 1984, **3:** 124–134.

525 Katsanis WA, O'Connor DM, Gibb RK, Bendon RW. Endometrial stromal sarcoma involving the placenta. Ann Diagn Pathol 1999, **2:** 301–305.

526 Kempson RL, Hendrickson MR. Smooth muscle, endometrial stromal, and mixed Mullerian tumors of the uterus. Mod Pathol 2000, **13:** 328–342.

527 Kolda TF, Ro JY, Ordonez NG, Tornos C, Park YW, Hyman WJ, Ayala AG. Endometrial stromal sarcoma presenting as extrauterine metastases: a morphologic and immunohistochemical approach to diagnosis. Int J Surg Pathol 1997, **5:** 105–110.

528 Krishnamurthy S, Jungbluth AA, Busam KJ, Rosai J. Uterine tumors resembling ovarian sex-cord tumors have an immunophenotype consistent with true sex-cord differentiation. Am J Surg Pathol 1998, **22:** 1078–1082.

529 Lam KY, Khoo US, Cheung A. Collision of endometrioid carcinoma and stromal sarcoma of the uterus: a report of two cases. Int J Gynecol Pathol 1999, **18:** 77–81.

530 Larbig GG, Clemmer JJ, Koss LG, Foote FW. Plexiform tumorlets of endometrial stromal origin. Am J Clin Pathol 1965, **44:** 32–35.

531 Levine PH, Abou-Nassar S, Mittal K. Extrauterine low-grade endometrial stromal sarcoma with florid endometrioid glandular differentiation. Int J Gynecol Pathol 2001, **20:** 395–398.

532 Lillemoe TJ, Perrone T, Norris HJ, Dehner LP. Myogenous phenotype of epithelial-like areas in endometrial stromal sarcomas. Arch Pathol Lab Med 1991, **115:** 215–219.

533 Lloreta J, Prat J. Ultrastructure of an endometrial stromal nodule with skeletal muscle. Ultrastruct Pathol 1993, **17:** 405–410.

533a Loddenkemper C, Mechsner S, Foss H-D, Dallenbach FE, Anagnostopoulos I, Ebert AD, Stein H. Use of oxytocin receptor expression in distinguishing between uterine smooth muscle tumors and endometrial stromal sarcoma. Am J Surg Pathol 2003, **27:** 1458–1462.

534 McCluggage WG, Sumathi VP, Maxwell P. CD10 is a sensitive and diagnostically useful immunohistochemical marker of normal endometrial stroma and of endometrial stromal neoplasms. Histopathology 2001, **39:** 273–278.

535 Mazur MT, Askin FB. Endolymphatic stromal myosis. Unique presentation and ultrastructural study. Cancer 1978, **42:** 2661–2667.

536 Norris HJ, Taylor HB. Mesenchymal tumors of the uterus. I, A clinical and pathological study of 53 endometrial stromal tumors. Cancer 1966, **19:** 755–766.

537 Nucci MR, O'Connell JT, Heuttner PC, Cviko A, Sun D, Quade BJ. H-Caldesmon expression effectively distinguishes endometrial stromal tumors from uterine smooth muscle tumors. Am J Surg Pathol 2001, **25:** 455–463.

538 Oliva E, Clement PB, Young RH, Scully RE. Mixed endometrial stromal and smooth muscle tumors of the uterus: a clinicopathologic study of 15 cases. Am J Surg Pathol 1998, **22:** 997–1005.

539 Oliva E, Clement PB, Young RH. Endometrial stromal tumors: an update on a group of tumors with a protean phenotype. Adv Anat Pathol 2000, **7:** 257–281.

540 Oliva E, Clement PB, Young RH. Epithelioid endometrial and endometrioid stromal tumors: a report of four cases emphasising their distinction from epithelioid smooth muscle tumors and other oxyphilic uterine and extrauterine tumors. Int J Gynecol Pathol 2002, **21:** 48–55.

541 Oliva E, Young RH, Amin MB, Clement PB. An immunohistochemical analysis of endometrial stromal and smooth muscle tumors of the uterus: a study of 54 cases emphasizing the importance of using a panel because of overlap in immunoreactivity for individual antibodies. Am J Surg Pathol 2002, **26:** 403–412.

542 Oliva E, Young RH, Clement PB, Scully RE. Myxoid and fibrous endometrial stromal tumors of the uterus: a report of 10 cases. Int J Gynecol Pathol 1999, **18:** 310–319.

543 Rosai J, Lauren V. Ackerman and his man from Istanbul. Semin Diagn Pathol (in press).

544 Roth LM, Senteny GE. Stromomyoma of the uterus. Ultrastruct Pathol 1985, **9:** 137–143.

545 Rush DS, Tan J, Baergen RN, Soslow RA. h-Caldesmon, a novel smooth muscle-specific antibody, distinguishes between cellular leiomyoma and endometrial stromal sarcoma. Am J Surg Pathol 2001, **25:** 253–258.

546 Sabini G, Chumas JC, Mann WJ. Steroid hormone receptors in endometrial stromal sarcomas. A biochemical and immunohistochemical study. Am J Clin Pathol 1992, **97:** 381–386.

547 Shiraki M, Otis CN, Powell JL. Endometrial stromal sarcoma arising from ovarian and extraovarian endometriosis – report of two cases and review of the literature. Surg Pathol 1991, **4:** 333–343.

548 Suarez Vilela D, Izquierdo Garcia FM. Foam cells and histiocytes in endometrial stromal tumours. Histopathology 1998, **32:** 568–569.

549 Tang C-K, Toker C, Ances IG. Stromomyoma of the uterus. Cancer 1979, **43:** 308–316.

550 Tavassoli FA, Norris HJ. Mesenchymal tumours of the uterus. VII. A clinicopathological study of 60 endometrial stromal nodules. Histopathology 1981, **5:** 1–10.

551 Thatcher SS, Woodruff JD. Uterine stromatosis. A report of 33 cases. Obstet Gynecol 1982, **59:** 428–434.

552 Tsukamoto N, Kamura T, Matsukuma K, Imachi M, Uchino H, Saito T, Ono M. Endolymphatic stromal myosis. A case with positive estrogen and progesterone receptors and good response to progestins. Gynecol Oncol 1985, **20:** 120–128.

553 Ulbright TM, Kraus FT. Endometrial stromal tumors of extra-uterine tissue. Am J Clin Pathol 1981, **76:** 371–377.

554 Yilmaz A, Rush DS, Soslow RA. Endometrial stromal sarcomas with unusual histologic features: a report of 24 primary and metastatic tumors emphasizing fibroblastic and smooth muscle differentiation. Am J Surg Pathol 2002, **26:** 1142–1150.

555 Yoonessi M, Hart WR. Endometrial stromal sarcomas. Cancer 1977, **40:** 898–906.

Malignant mixed müllerian tumor (carcinosarcoma)

556 Amant F, Moerman P, Davel GH, De Vos R, Vergote I, Lindeque BG, de Jonge E. Uterine carcinosarcoma with melanocytic differentiation. Int J Gynecol Pathol 2001, **20:** 186–190.

557 Barwick KW, LiVolsi VA. Malignant mixed müllerian tumors of the uterus. Am J Surg Pathol 1979, **3:** 125–135.

558 Bitterman P, Chun B, Kurman RJ. The significance of epithelial

differentiation in mixed mesodermal tumors of the uterus. A clinicopathologic and immunohistochemical study. Am J Surg Pathol 1990, **4:** 317–328.

559 Chuang JT, Van Velden DJJ, Graham JB. Carcinosarcoma and mixed mesodermal tumor of the uterine corpus. Review of 49 cases. Obstet Gynecol 1970, **35:** 769–780.

560 Chumas JC, Mann WJ, Tseng L. Malignant mixed müllerian tumor of the endometrium in a young woman with polycystic ovaries. Cancer 1983, **52:** 1478–1481.

561 Costa MJ, Walls J. Epidermal growth factor receptor and c-erbB-2 oncoprotein expression in female genital tract carcinosarcomas (malignant mixed Mullerian tumors): clinicopathologic study of 82 cases. Cancer 1996, **77:** 533–542.

562 Costa MJ, Vogelsan J, Young LJ. p53 gene mutation in female genital tract carcinosarcomas (malignant mixed müllerian tumors). A clinicopathologic study of 74 cases. Mod Pathol 1994, **7:** 619 627.

563 de Brito PA, Silverberg SG, Orenstein JM. Carcinosarcoma (malignant mixed müllerian [mesodermal] tumor) of the female genital tract. Immunohistochemical and ultrastructural analysis of 28 cases. Hum Pathol 1993, **24:** 132–142.

564 Dellers EA, Valente PT, Edmonds PR, Balsara G. Extrauterine mixed mesodermal tumors. An immunohistochemical study. Arch Pathol Lab Med 1991, **115:** 918–920.

565 Donner LR. Uterine carcinosarcoma with complete sarcomatous overgrowth mimicking pure embryonal rhabdomyosarcoma. Int J Gynecol Pathol 2002, **22:** 89–91.

566 Doss LL, Llorens AS, Henriquez EM. Carcinosarcoma of the uterus. A 40-year experience from the state of Missouri. Gynecol Oncol 1984, **18:** 43–53.

567 Emoto M, Iwasaki H, Ishiguro M, Kikuchi M, Horiuchi S, Saito T, Tsukamoto N, Kawarabayashi T. Angiogenesis in carcinosarcomas of the uterus: differences in the microvessel density and expression of vascular endothelial growth factor between the epithelial and mesenchymal elements. Hum Pathol 1999, **30:** 1232 1241.

568 Fehr PE, Prem KA. Malignancy of the uterine corpus following irradiation therapy for squamous cell carcinoma of the cervix. Am J Obstet Gynecol 1974, **119:** 685–692.

569 Gagne E, Tetu B, Blondeau L, Raymond PE, Blais R. Morphologic prognostic factors of malignant mixed müllerian tumor of the uterus. A clinicopathologic study of 58 cases. Mod Pathol 1989, **2:** 433–438.

570 George E, Lillemoe TJ, Twiggs LB, Perrone T. Malignant mixed müllerian tumor versus high-grade endometrial carcinoma and aggressive variants of endometrial carcinoma. A comparative analysis of survival. Int J Gynecol Pathol 1995, **14:** 39–44.

571 George E, Manivel JC, Dehner LP, Wick MR. Malignant mixed müllerian tumors. An immunohistochemical study of 47 cases, with histogenetic considerations and clinical correlation. Hum Pathol 1991, **22:** 215–223.

572 Gersell DJ, Duncan DA, Fulling KH. Malignant mixed müllerian tumor of the uterus with neuroectodermal differentiation. Int J Gynecol Pathol 1989, **8:** 169–178.

573 Iwasa Y, Haga H, Konishi I, Kobashi Y, Higuchi K, Katsuyama E, Minamiguchi S, Yamabe H. Prognostic factors in uterine carcinosarcoma: a clinicopathologic study of 25 patients. Cancer 1998, **82:** 512–519.

574 Kohorn EI, Schwartz PE, Chambers JT, Peschel RE, Kapp DS, Merino M. Adjuvant therapy in mixed müllerian tumors of the uterus. Gynecol Oncol 1986, **23:** 212–221.

575 Kounelis S, Jones MW, Papadaki H, Bakker A, Swalsky P, Finkelstein SD. Carcinosarcomas (malignant mixed mullerian tumors) of the female genital tract: comparative molecular analysis of epithelial and mesenchymal components. Hum Pathol 1998, **29:** 82–87.

576 Krigman HR, Coogan AC, Marks JR. Simultaneous endometrial

malignant mixed mesodermal tumor and ovarian serous adenocarcinoma. Arch Pathol Lab Med 1995, **119:** 99–103.

577 Mayall P, Rutty K, Campbell F, Goddard H. p53 immunostaining suggests that uterine carcinosarcomas are monoclonal. Histopathology 1994, **24:** 211–214.

578 Meis JM, Lawrence WD. The immunohistochemical profile of malignant mixed müllerian tumor. Overlap with endometrial adenocarcinoma. Am J Clin Pathol 1990, **94:** 1–7.

579 Mikami Y, Hata S, Kiyokawa T, Minabe T. Expression of CD10 in malignant mullerian mixed tumors and adenosarcomas: an immunohistochemical study. Mod Pathol 2002, **15:** 923–930.

580 Mount SL, Lee KR, Taatjes DJ. Carcinosarcoma (malignant mixed müllerian tumor) of the uterus with a rhabdoid tumor component. An immunohistochemical, ultrastructural, and immunoelectron microscopic case study. Am J Clin Pathol 1995, **103:** 235–239.

581 Norris HJ, Roth E, Taylor HB. Mesenchymal tumors of the uterus. II. A clinical and pathologic study of 31 mixed mesodermal tumors. Obstet Gynecol 1966, **28:** 57–63.

582 Norris HJ, Taylor HB. Postirradiation sarcomas of the uterus. Obstet Gynecol 1965, **26:** 689–694.

583 Norris NJ, Taylor HB. Mesenchymal tumors of the uterus. III. A clinical and pathologic study of 31 carcinosarcomas. Cancer 1966, **19:** 1459–1465.

584 Press MF, Scully RE. Endometrial "sarcomas" complicating ovarian thecoma, polycystic ovarian disease and estrogen therapy. Gynecol Oncol 1985, **21:** 135–154.

585 Schaepman-van Geuns EJ. Mixed tumors and carcinosarcomas of the uterus evaluated five years after treatment. Cancer 1970, **25:** 72–77.

586 Shen DH, Khoo US, Xue WC, Ngan HY, Wang JL, Liu VW, Chan YK, Cheung AN. Primary peritoneal malignant mixed müllerian tumors: a clinicopathologic immunohistochemical, and genetic study. Cancer 2001, **91:** 1052–1060.

587 Shokeir MO, Noel SM, Clement PB. Malignant Müllerian mixed tumor of the uterus with a prominent alpha-fetoprotein-producing component of yolk sac tumor. Mod Pathol 1996, **9:** 647–651.

588 Silverberg SG, Major FJ, Blessing JA, Fetter B, Askin FB, Liao SY, Miller A. Carcinosarcoma (malignant mixed mesodermal tumor) of the uterus. A Gynecologic Oncology Group pathologic study of 203 cases. Int J Gynecol Pathol 1990, **9:** 1–19.

589 Spanos WJ, Peters LJ, Oswald MJ. Patterns of recurrence in malignant mixed müllerian tumor of the uterus. Cancer 1986, **57:** 155–159.

590 Spanos WJ, Wharton JT, Gomez L, Fletcher GH, Oswald MJ. Malignant mixed müllerian tumors of the uterus. Cancer 1984, **53:** 311–316.

591 Sreenan JJ, Hart WR. Carcinosarcomas of the female genital tract. A pathologic study of 29 metastatic tumors – further evidence for the dominant role of the epithelial component and the conversion theory of histogenesis. Am J Surg Pathol 1995, **19:** 666–674.

592 Varela-Duran J, Nochomovitz LE, Prem KA, Dehner LP. Postirradiation mixed müllerian tumors of the uterus. A comparative clinicopathologic study. Cancer 1980, **45:** 1625–1631.

593 Yamada SD, Burger RA, Brewster WR, Anton D, Kohler MF, Monk BJ. Pathologic variables and adjuvant therapy as predictor of recurrence and survival for patients with surgically evaluated carcinosarcoma of the uterus. Cancer 2000, **88:** 2782–2786.

594 Yorokoglu K, Aktas S, Gore O, Ozen E. Malignant mixed mullerian tumor of the uterus with prominent neuroectodermal differentiation: a case report. Int J Surg Pathol 1998, **6:** 155–158.

595 Yoshida Y, Kurokawa T, Fukuno N, Kishikawa Y, Kamitani N, Kotsuj F. Markers of apoptosis and angiogenesis indicate that carcinomatous components play an important role in the malignant behaviour of uterine carcinosarcoma. Hum Pathol 2001, **31:** 1448–1454.

Müllerian adenosarcoma and related tumors

596 Chen KTK. Rhabdomyosarcomatous uterine adenosarcoma. Int J Gynecol Pathol 1985, 4: 146–152.

597 Clement PB. Müllerian adenosarcomas of the uterus with sarcomatous overgrowth. A clinicopathological analysis of 10 cases. Am J Surg Pathol 1989, 13: 28–38.

598 Clement PB, Scully RE. Müllerian adenosarcoma of the uterus. A clinicopathologic analysis of ten cases of a distinctive type of müllerian mixed tumor. Cancer 1974, 34: 1138–1149.

599 Clement PB, Scully RE. Extrauterine mesodermal (müllerian) adenosarcoma. A clinicopathologic analysis of five cases. Am J Clin Pathol 1978, 69: 276–283.

600 Clement PB, Scully RE. Müllerian adenosarcomas of the uterus with sex cord-like elements. A clinicopathologic analysis of eight cases. Am J Clin Pathol 1989, 91: 664–672.

601 Clement PB, Scully RE. Müllerian adenosarcoma of the uterus. A clinicopathologic analysis of 100 cases with a review of the literature. Hum Pathol 1990, 21: 363–381.

602 Clement PB, Scully RE. Müllerian adenofibroma of the uterus with invasion of myometrium and pelvic veins. Int J Gynecol Pathol 1990, 9: 363–371.

603 Clement PB, Oliva E, Young RH. Mullerian adenosarcoma of the uterine corpus associated with tamoxifen therapy: a report of six cases and a review of tamoxifen-associated endometrial lesions. Int J Gynecol Pathol 1997, 15: 222–229.

604 Fehmian C, Jones J, Kress Y, Abadi M. Adenosarcoma of the uterus with extensive smooth muscle differentiation: ultrastructural study and review of the literature. Ultrastruct Pathol 1997, 21: 73–90.

605 Gloor E. Müllerian adenosarcoma of the uterus. Am J Surg Pathol 1979, 3: 203–209.

606 Grimalt M, Arguelles M, Ferenczy A. Papillary cyst-adenofibroma of endometrium. A histochemical and ultrastructural study. Cancer 1975, 36: 137–144.

607 Hirschfield L, Kahn LB, Chen S, Winkler B, Rosenberg S. Müllerian adenosarcoma with ovarian sex cord-like differentiation. A light and electron-microscopic study. Cancer 1986, 57: 1197–1200.

608 Horie Y, Ikawa S, Kadowaki K, Minagawa Y, Kigawa J, Terakawa N. Lipoadenofibroma of the uterine corpus. Report of a new variant of adenofibroma (benign müllerian mixed tumor). Arch Pathol Lab Med 1995, 119: 274–276.

609 Kaku T, Silverberg SG, Major FJ, Miller A, Fetter B, Brady MF. Adenosarcoma of the uterus. A Gynecologic Oncology Group clinicopathologic study of 31 cases. Int J Gynecol Pathol 1992, 11: 75–88.

610 Katzenstein AA, Askin FB, Feldman PS. Müllerian adenosarcoma of the uterus. An ultrastructural study of four cases. Cancer 1977, 40: 2233–2242.

611 Lack EE, Bitterman P, Sundeen JT. Müllerian adenosarcoma of the uterus with pure angiosarcoma. Case report. Hum Pathol 1991, 22: 1289–1291.

612 Miller KN, McClure SP. Papillary adenofibroma of the uterus. Report of a case involved by adenocarcinoma and review of the literature. Am J Clin Pathol 1992, 97: 806–809.

613 Peters WM, Wells MJ, Bryce FC. Müllerian clear cell carcinofibroma of the uterine corpus. Histopathology 1984, 8: 1069–1078.

614 Seidman JD, Wasserman CS, Aye LM, MacKoul PJ, O'Leary TJ. Cluster of uterine mullerian adenosarcoma in the Washington, DC metropolitan area with high incidence of sarcomatous overgrowth. Am J Surg Pathol 1999, 23: 809–814.

615 Silverberg SG. Adenomyomatosis of endometrium and endocervix. A hamartoma? Am J Clin Pathol 1975, 64: 192–199.

616 Valdez VA, Planas AT, Lopez VF, Goldberg M, Herrera NE. Adenosarcoma of uterus and ovary. A clinicopathologic study of two cases. Cancer 1979, 43: 1439–1447.

617 Vellios F, Ng ABP, Reagan JW. Papillary adenofibroma of the uterus. A benign mesodermal mixed tumor of müllerian origin. Am J Clin Pathol 1973, 60: 543–551.

618 Zaloudek CJ, Norris HJ. Adenofibroma and adenosarcoma of the uterus. A clinicopathologic study of 35 cases. Cancer 1981, 48: 354–366.

Leiomyoma

619 Bardsley V, Cooper P, Peat DS. Massive lymphocytic infiltration of uterine leiomyomas associated with GnRH agonist treatment. Histopathology 1998, 33: 80–82.

620 Brown JM, Malkasian GD Jr, Symmonds RE. Abdominal myomectomy. Am J Obstet Gynecol 1967, 99: 126–129.

621 Colgan TJ, Pendergast S, Le Blanc M. The histopathology of uterine leiomyomas following treatment with gonadotropin-releasing hormone analogues. Hum Pathol 1993, 24: 1073–1077.

622 Colgan TJ, Pron G, Mocarski EJM, Bennett JD, Asch MR, Common A. Pathologic features of uteri and leiomyomas following uterine artery embolization for leiomyomas. Am J Surg Pathol 2003, 27: 167–177.

623 Cramer SF, Patel A. The frequency of uterine leiomyomas. Am J Clin Pathol 1990, 94: 435–438.

624 Cramer SF, Horiszny J, Patel A, Sigrist S. The relation of fibrous degeneration to menopausal status in small uterine leiomyomas with evidence for postmenopausal origin of seeding myomas. Mod Pathol 1997, 9: 774–780.

625 Cramer SF, Marchetti C, Freedman J, Padela A. Relationships of myoma cell size and menopausal status in small uterine leiomyomas. Arch Pathol Lab Med 2000, 124: 1448–1453.

626 Demopoulus RI, Jones KY, Mittal KR, Vamvakas EC. Histology of leiomyomata in patients treated with leuprolide acetate. Int J Gynecol Pathol 1997, 16: 131–137.

627 Friedman AJ, Hoffman DI, Comite F, Browneller RW, Miller JD. Treatment of leiomyomata uteri with leuprolide acetate depot. A double-blind, placebo-controlled, multicenter study. The Leuprolide Study Group. Obstet Gynecol 1991, 77: 720–725.

628 Gutmann JN, Thornton KL, Diamond MP, Carcangiu ML. Evaluation of leuprolide acetate treatment on histopathology of uterine myomata. Fertil Steril 1994, 61: 622–626.

629 Hu J, Surti U. Subgroups of uterine leiomyomas based on cytogenetic analysis. Hum Pathol 1991, 22: 1009–1016.

630 Kalir T, Goldstein M, Dottino P, Brodman M, Gordon R, Deligdisch L, Wu H, Gil J. Morphometric and electron-microscopic analyses of the effects of gonadotropin-releasing hormone agonists on uterine leiomyomas. Arch Pathol Lab Med 1998, 122: 442–446.

631 Klotzbucher M, Wasserfall A, Fuhrmann U. Misexpresson of wild-type and truncated isoforms of the high-mobility group I proteins HMBI-C and HMGI(Y) in uterine leiomyomas. Am J Pathol 1999, 155: 1535–1542.

632 Konishi I, Fujii S, Ban C, Okuda Y, Okamura H, Tojo S. Ultrastructural study of minute uterine leiomyomas. Int J Gynecol Pathol 1983, 2: 113–120.

633 Laforga JB, Aranda FI. Uterine leiomyomas with T-cell infiltration associated with GnRH agonist goserelin. Histopathology 1999, 34: 471–472.

634 Lascano EF. Mast cells in human tumors. Cancer 1958, 11: 1110–1114.

635 Ligon AH, Morton CC. Genetics of uterine leiomyomata. Genes Chromosomes Cancer 2000, 28: 235–245.

636 McCluggage WG, Ellis PK, McClure N, Walker WJ, Jackson PA, Manek S. Pathologic features of uterine leiomyomas following uterine artery embolization. Int J Gynecol Pathol 2000, 19: 342–347.

637 Maluf HM, Gersell DJ. Uterine leiomyomas with high content of mast cells. Arch Pathol Lab Med 1994, 118: 712–714.

638 Mittal K, Popiolek D, Demopoulos RI. Uterine myxoid

leiomyosarcoma within a leiomyoma. Hum Pathol 2000, **31:** 398–400.

639 Nedwich A, Frumin A, Meranze DR. Erythrocytosis associated with uterine myomas. Am J Obstet Gynecol 1962, **84:** 174–178.

640 Nilbert M, Heim S, Mandahl N, Flodérus UM, Willén H, Mitelman F. Karyotypic rearrangements in 20 uterine leiomyomas. Cytogenet Cell Genet 1988, **49:** 300–304.

641 Orii A, Mori A, Zhai YL, Toki T, Nikaido T, Fujii S. Mast cells in smooth muscle tumors of the uterus. Int J Gynecol Pathol 1998, **17:** 336–342.

642 Parazzini F, La Vecchia C, Negri E, Cecchetti G, Fedele L. Epidemiologic characteristics of women with uterine fibroids. A case-control study. Obstet Gynecol 1988, **72:** 853–857.

643 Richards PA, Tiltman AJ. Anatomical variation of the oestrogen receptor in the non-neoplastic myometrium of fibromyomatous uteri. Virchows Arch 1996, **428:** 347–351.

644 Sreenan JJ, Prayson RA, Biscotti CV, Thornton MH, Easley KA, Hart WR. Histopathologic findings in 107 uterine leiomyomas treated with leuprolide acetate compared with 126 controls. Am J Surg Pathol 1996, **20:** 427–432.

645 Vu K, Greenspan DL, Wu TC, Zacur HA, Kurman RJ. Cellular proliferation, estrogen receptor, progesterone receptor, and bcl-2 expression in GnRH agonist-treated uterine leiomyomas. Hum Pathol 1998, **29:** 359–363.

Leiomyoma variants

646 Abell MR, Littler ER. Benign metastasizing uterine leiomyoma. Multiple lymph nodal metastases. Cancer 1975, **36:** 2206–2213.

647 Bakotic BW, Cabello-Inchausti B, Willis IH, Suster S. Clear-cell epithelioid leiomyoma of the round ligament. Mod Pathol 1999, **12:** 912–918.

648 Baschinsky DY, Isa A, Niemann TH, Prior TW, Lucas JG, Frankel WL. Diffuse leiomyomatosis of the uterus: a case report with clonality analysis. Hum Pathol 2000, **31:** 1429–1432.

649 Billings SD, Folpe AL, Weiss SW. Do leiomyomas of deep soft tissue exist? An analysis of highly differentiated smooth muscle tumors of deep soft tissue supporting two distinct subtypes. Am J Surg Pathol 2001, **25:** 1134–1142.

650 Brescia RJ, Tazelaar HD, Hobbs J, Miller AW. Intravascular lipoleiomyomatosis. A report of two cases. Hum Pathol 1989, **20:** 252–256.

651 Canzonieri V, D'Amore ES, Bartoloni G, Piazza M, Blandamura S, Carbone A. Leiomyomatosis with vascular invasion. A unified pathogenesis regarding leiomyoma with vascular microinvasion, benign metastasizing leiomyoma and intravenous leiomyomatosis. Virchows Arch 1994, **425:** 541–545.

652 Cheuk W, Chan JK, Liu JY. Cotyledonoid leiomyoma: a benign uterine tumor with alarming gross appearance. Arch Pathol Lab Med 2002, **126:** 210–213.

653 Cho KR, Woodruff JD, Epstein JI. Leiomyoma of the uterus with multiple extrauterine smooth muscle tumors: a case report suggesting multifocal origin. Hum Pathol 1989, **20:** 80–82.

654 Clement PB. The pathology of uterine smooth muscle tumors and mixed endometrial stromal-smooth muscle tumors: a selective review with emphasis on recent advances. Int J Gynecol Pathol 2000, **19:** 39–55.

655 Clement PB, Young RH. Diffuse leiomyomatosis of the uterus. A report of four cases. Int J Gynecol Pathol 1987, **6:** 322–330.

656 Clement PB, Young RH, Scully RE. Diffuse, perinodular, and other patterns of hydropic degeneration within and adjacent to uterine leiomyomas. Problems in differential diagnosis. Am J Surg Pathol 1992, **16:** 26–32.

657 Coad JE, Sulaiman RA, Das K, Staley N. Perinodular hydropic degeneration of a uterine leiomyoma: a diagnostic challenge. Hum Pathol 1997, **28:** 249–251.

658 Cramer SF, Patel A. Myometrial hyperplasia. Proposed criteria for a discrete morphological entity. Mod Pathol 1995, **8:** 71–77.

658a Dal Cin P, Christacos N, Morton CC, Quade BJ. Cellular leiomyoma: a genetically distinct entity among benign uterine tumors (Abstract). Mod Pathol 2003, **16:** 187a.

659 Dickersin GR, Selig MK, Park YN. The many faces of smooth muscle neoplasms in a gynecological sampling: an ultrastructural study. Ultrastruct Pathol 1997, **21:** 109–134.

660 Downes KA, Hart WR. Bizarre leiomyomas of the uterus: a comprehensive pathologic study of 24 cases with long-term follow-up. Am J Surg Pathol 1997, **21:** 1261–1270.

661 Esteban JM, Allen WM, Schaerf RH. Benign metastasising leiomyoma of the uterus: histologic and immunohistochemical characterization of primary and metastatic lesions. Arch Pathol Lab Med 1999, **123:** 960–962.

662 Fechner RE. Atypical leiomyomas and synthetic progestin therapy. Am J Clin Pathol 1968, **49:** 697–703.

663 Ferry JA, Harris NL, Scully RE. Uterine leiomyomas with lymphoid infiltration simulating lymphoma. A report of seven cases. Int J Gynecol Pathol 1989, **8:** 263–270.

664 Fornelli A, Pasquinelli G, Eusebi V. Leiomyoma of the uterus showing skeletal muscle differentiation: a case report. Hum Pathol 1999, **30:** 356–359.

665 Fukunaga M, Ushigome S. Dissecting leiomyoma of the uterus with extrauterine extension. Histopathology 1998, **32:** 160–164.

666 Gilks CB, Taylor GP, Clement PB. Inflammatory pseudotumor of the uterus. Int J Gynecol Pathol 1987, **6:** 275–286.

667 Graham A. Malignant epithelial tumors of the thyroid; with special reference to invasion of blood vessels. Surg Gynecol Obstet 1924, **39:** 781–790.

668 Harper RS, Scully RE. Intravenous leiomyomatosis of the uterus. Am J Clin Pathol 1965, **4:** 45–51.

669 Huxley J. Biological aspects of cancer. New York, 1958, Harcourt, Brace, p.14.

670 Hyde KE, Geisinger KR, Marshall RB, Jones TL. The clear-cell variant of uterine epithelioid leiomyoma. An immunohistologic and ultrastructural study. Arch Pathol Lab Med 1989, **113:** 551–553.

671 Jacobs DS, Cohen H, Johnson JS. Lipoleiomyomas of the uterus. Am J Clin Pathol 1965, **44:** 45–51.

672 Jautzke G, Muller-Ruchholtz E, Thalmann U. Immunohistological detection of estrogen and progesterone receptors in multiple and well differentiated leiomyomatous lung tumors in women with uterine leiomyomas (so-called benign metastasising leiomyomas). A report on 5 cases. Pathol Res Pract 1997, **192:** 215–223.

673 Jordan LB, Al-Nafussi A, Beattie G. Cotyledonoid hydropic intravenous leiomyomatosis: a new variant leiomyoma. Histopathology 2002, **40:** 245–252.

674 Kayser K, Zink S, Schneider T, Dienemann H, Andre S, Kaltner H, Schuring MP, Zick Y, Gabius HJ. Benign metastasising leiomyoma of the uterus: documentation of clinical, immunohistochemical and lectin-histochemical data of ten cases. Virchows Arch 2000, **437:** 284–292.

675 Kurman RJ, Norris HJ. Mesenchymal tumors of the uterus. VI. Epithelioid smooth muscle tumors including leiomyoblastoma and clear-cell leiomyoma. A clinical and pathologic analysis of 26 cases. Cancer 1976, **37:** 1853–1865.

676 Lemis PL, Lee ABH, Easler RE. Myometrial hypertrophy. A clinical pathologic study and review of the literature. Am J Obstet Gynecol 1962, **84:** 1032–1041.

677 McCluggage WG, Hamal P, Traub AI, Walsh MY. Uterine adenolipoleimioma: a rare hamartomatous lesion. Int J Gynecol Pathol 2000, **19:** 183–185.

678 Martin-Reay DG, Christ ML, La Pata RE. Uterine leiomyoma with skeletal-muscle differentiation. Report of a case. Am J Clin Pathol 1991, **96:** 344–347.

679 Mazur MT. Clear cell leiomyoma (leiomyoblastoma) of the uterus. Ultrastructural observations. Ultrastruct Pathol 1986, **10:** 249–255.

680 Mazur MT, Kraus FT. Histogenesis of morphologic variations in tumors of the uterine wall. Am J Surg Pathol 1980, **4**: 59–74.

680a McClean G, McCluggage WG. Unusual morphologic features of uterine leiomyomas treated with gonadotropin-releasing hormone agonists: massive lymphoid infiltration and vasculitis. Int J Surg Pathol 2003, **11**: 339–344.

681 Michal M, Zamecnik M. Hyalinized uterine mesenchymal neoplasms with HMB-45-positive epithelioid cells: epithelioid leiomyomas or angiomyolipomas? Report of four cases. Int J Surg Pathol 2000, **8**: 323–328.

682 Mulvany NJ, Ostör AG, Ross I. Diffuse leiomyomatosis of the uterus. Histopathology 1995, **27**: 175–179.

683 Mulvany NJ, Slavin JL, Ostor AG, Fortune DW. Intravenous leiomyomatosis of the uterus. A clinicopathologic study of 22 cases. Int J Gynecol Pathol 1994, **13**: 1–9.

684 Myles JL, Hart HR. Apoplectic leiomyomas of the uterus. Am J Surg Pathol 1985, **9**: 798–805.

685 Nogales FF, Novano N, Martinez de Victoria JM, Contreras F, Redondo C, Herraiz MA, Seco MA, Velasco A. Uterine intravascular leiomyomatosis. An update and report of seven cases. Int J Gynecol Pathol 1987, **6**: 331–339.

686 Norris HJ, Parmley T. Mesenchymal tumors of the uterus. V. Intravenous leiomyomatosis. A clinical and pathologic study of 14 cases. Cancer 1975, **36**: 2164–2178.

686a Nucci MR, Dal Cin P, Fletcher CDM, Fletcher JA. Unique cytogenetic profile is so-called benign metastasizing leiomyoma: evidence of a distinct clinicopathologic entity (Abstract). Mod Pathol 2003, **16**: 202a–203a.

687 O'Connor DM, Norris HJ. Mitotically active leiomyomas of the uterus. Hum Pathol 1990, **21**: 223–227.

688 Oliva E, Young RH, Clement PB, Bhan AK, Scully RE. Cellular benign mesenchymal tumors of the uterus. A comparative morphologic and immunohistochemical analysis of 33 highly cellular leiomyomas and six endometrial stromal nodules, two frequently confused tumors. Am J Surg Pathol 1995, **19**: 769–774.

689 Persaud V, Arjoon PD. Uterine leiomyoma. Incidence of degenerative change and a correlation of associated symptoms. Obstet Gynecol 1970, **35**: 432–436.

690 Pounder DJ. Fatty tumours of the uterus. J Clin Pathol 1982, **35**: 1380–1383.

691 Prakash S, Scully RE. Sarcoma-like pseudopregnancy. Changes in uterine leiomyomas. Report of a case resulting from prolonged norethindrone therapy. Obstet Gynecol 1964, **24**: 106–110.

692 Prayson RA, Hart WR. Mitotically active leiomyomas of the uterus. Am J Clin Pathol 1992, **97**: 14–20.

693 Resta L, Maiorano E, Piscitelli D, Botticella MA. Lipomatous tumors of the uterus. Clinico-pathological features of 10 cases with immunocytochemical study of histogenesis. Pathol Res Pract 1994, **190**: 378–383.

694 Roth LM, Reed RJ. Dissecting leiomyomas of the uterus other than cotyledonoid dissecting leiomyomas: a report of eight cases. Am J Surg Pathol 1999, **23**: 1032–1039.

695 Roth LM, Reed RJ. Cotyledonoid leiomyoma of the uterus: report of a case. Int J Gynecol Pathol 2000, **19**: 272–275.

696 Roth LM, Reed RJ, Sternberg WH. Cotyledonoid dissecting leiomyoma of the uterus: the Sternberg tumor. Am J Surg Pathol 1996, **20**: 1455–1461.

697 Shintaku M. Lipoleiomyomatous tumors of the uterus: a heterogeneous group? Histopathological study of five cases. Pathol Int 1997, **46**: 498–502.

698 Tench WD, Dail D, Gmelich JT, Matani N. Benign metastasizing leiomyomas. A review of 21 cases (abstract). Lab Invest 1978, **38**: 367.

699 Tietze L, Gunther K, Horbe A, Pawlik C, Klosterhalfen B, Handt S, Merkelbach-Bruse S. Benign metastasising leiomyoma: a cytogenetically balanced but clonal disease. Hum Pathol 2000, **31**: 126–128.

700 Vang R, Kempson RL. Perivascular epithelioid cell tumor ('PE Coma') of the uterus: a subset of HMB-45 positive epithelioid mesenchymal neoplasms with an uncertain relationship to pure smooth muscle tumors. Am J Surg Pathol 2001, **26**: 1–13.

701 Vang R, Medeiros LJ, Samoszuk M, Deavers MT. Uterine leiomyomas with eosinophils: a clinicopathologic study of 3 cases. Int J Gynecol Pathol 2001, **20**: 239–243.

702 Watanabe K, Ogura G, Suzuki T. Leiomyoblastoma of the uterus: an immunohistochemical and electron microscopic study of distinctive tumors with immature smooth muscle cell differentiation mimicking fetal uterine myocytes. Histopathology 2001, **42**: 379–386.

Leiomyosarcoma
Clinical and gross features

703 Christopherson WM, Williamson EO, Gray LA. Leiomyosarcoma of the uterus. Cancer 1972, **29**: 70–75.

703a McNeese CC, Silva EG, Deavers MT, Malpica A. Uterine leiomyosarcoma in patients under 45 years of age: a clinicopathologic study of 46 cases (Abstract). Mod Pathol 2003, **16**: 200a–201a.

704 Schwartz SM, Weiss NS, Daling JR, Gammon MD, Liff JM, Watt J, Lynch CF, Newcomb PA, Armstrong BK, Thompson WD. Exogenous sex hormone use, correlates of endogenous hormone levels, and the incidence of histologic types of sarcoma of the uterus. Cancer 1996, **77**: 717–724.

705 Taylor HB, Norris HJ. Mesenchymal tumors of the uterus. IV. Diagnosis and prognosis of leiomyosarcomas. Arch Pathol 1966, **82**: 40–44.

Microscopic features

706 Downes KA, Hart WR. Bizarre leiomyomas of the uterus: a comprehensive pathologic study of 24 cases with long-term follow-up. Am J Surg Pathol 1997, **21**: 1261–1270.

Electron microscopic, immunohistochemical, and molecular genetic features

707 Dickersin GR, Selig MK, Park YN. The many faces of smooth muscle neoplasms in a gynaecological sampling: an ultrastructural study. Ultrastruct Pathol 1997, **21**: 109–134.

708 Iwata J, Fletcher CM. Immunohistochemical detection of cytokeratin and epithelial membrane antigen in leiomyosarcoma: a systematic study of 100 cases. Pathol Int 2000, **50**: 7–14.

709 Jeffers MD, Richmond JA, Macaulay EM. Overexpression of the c-myc protooncogene occurs frequently in uterine sarcomas. Mod Pathol 1995, **8**: 701–704.

709a Kelley TW, Borden E, Patel R, Prok A, Goldblum JR. Estrogen and progesterone receptor expression in uterine and extra-uterine leiomyosarcoma: an immunohistochemical study (Abstract). Mod Pathol 2003, **16**: 15a.

709b Loddenkemper C, Mechsner S, Foss H-D, Dallenbach FE, Anagnostopoulos I, Ebert AD, Stein H. Use of oxytocin receptor expression in distinguishing between uterine smooth muscle tumors and endometrial stromal sarcoma. Am J Surg Pathol 2003, **27**: 1458–1462.

710 Marshall RJ, Braye SG. Alpha-1-antitrypsin, alpha-1-antichymotrypsin, actin, and myosin in uterine sarcomas. Int J Gynecol Pathol 1985, **4**: 346–354.

711 Mittal K, Iovine RI. MIB-1 (Ki-67), p53, estrogen receptor, and progesterone receptor expression in uterine smooth muscle tumors. Hum Pathol 2001, **32**: 984–987.

712 Niemann TH, Raab SS, Lenel JC, Rodgers JR, Robinson RA. p53 protein over-expression in smooth muscle tumors of the uterus. Hum Pathol 1995, **26**: 375–379.

713 Noguchi T, Dobashi Y, Minehara H, Itoman M, Kameya T. Involvement of cyclins in cell proliferation and their clinical implications in soft tissue smooth muscle tumors. Am J Pathol 2000, **156**: 2135–2147.

714 Poncelet C, Walker F, Modelenat P, Bringuier AF, Scoazec JY, Feldmann G, Darai E. Expression of CD44 standard and isoforms V3 and V6 in uterine smooth muscle tumors: a possible diagnostic tool for the diagnosis of leiomyosarcoma. Hum Pathol 2001, **32**: 1190–1196.

715 Rao UN, Finkelstein SD, Jones MW. Comparative immunohistochemical and molecular analysis of uterine and extrauterine leiomyosarcomas. Mod Pathol 1999, **12**: 1001–1009.

716 Rizeq MN, van de Rijn M, Hendrickson MR, Rouse RV. A comparative immunohistochemical study of uterine smooth muscle neoplasms with emphasis on the epithelioid variant. Hum Pathol 1994, **25**: 671–677.

717 Watanabe K, Tajino T, Sekiguchi M, Suzuki T. h-caldesmon as a specific marker for smooth muscle tumors. Comparison with other smooth muscle markers in bone tumors. Am J Clin Pathol 2000, **113**: 663–668.

718 Zhai YL, Kobayashi Y, Mori A, Orii A, Nikaido T, Konishi I, Fujii S. Expression of steroid receptors, Ki-67, and p53 in uterine leiomyosarcoma. Int J Gynecol Pathol 1999, **18**: 20–28.

Leiomyosarcoma variants

719 Buscema J, Carpenter SE, Rosenshein NB, Woodruff JD. Epithelioid leiomyosarcoma of the uterus. Cancer 1986, **7**: 1192–1196.

720 Coard KC, Fletcher HM. Leiomyosarcoma of the uterus with a florid intravascular component ("intravenous leiomyosarcomatosis"). Int J Gynecol Pathol 2002, **21**: 182–185.

721 King E, Dickersin GR, Scully RE. Myxoid leiomyosarcoma of the uterus. Am J Surg Pathol 1982, **6**: 589–598.

722 Kurman RJ, Norris HJ. Mesenchymal tumors of the uterus. VI. Epithelioid smooth muscle tumors including leiomyoblastoma and clear cell leiomyoma. A clinical and pathologic analysis of 26 cases. Cancer 1976, **37**: 1853–1865.

723 Pounder DJ, Iyer PV. Uterine leiomyosarcoma with myxoid stroma. Arch Pathol Lab Med 1985, **109**: 762–764.

724 Prayson RA, Goldblum JR, Hart WR. Epithelioid smooth-muscle tumors of the uterus: a clinicopathologic study of 18 patients. Am J Surg Pathol 1997, **21**: 383–391.

725 Seidman JD, Yetter RA, Papadimitriou JC. Epithelioid component of uterine leiomyosarcoma simulating metastatic carcinoma. Arch Pathol Lab Med 1992, **116**: 287–290.

726 Watanabe K, Hiraki H, Ohishi M, Mashiko K, Saginoya H, Suzuki T. Uterine leiomyosarcoma with osteoclast-like giant cells. Histopathological and cytological observations. Pathol Int 1997, **46**: 656–660.

Spread, metastases, treatment, and prognosis

727 Bartsich EG, Bowe ET, Moore JG. Leiomyosarcoma of the uterus. A 50-year review of 42 cases. Obstet Gynecol 1968, **32**: 101–106.

728 Jeffers MD, Oakes SJ, Richmond JA, Macauley EM. Proliferation, ploidy and prognosis in uterine smooth muscle tumours. Histopathology 1997, **29**: 217–223.

729 Lucas DR, Kolodziej P, Gross ML, Mott MP, Budev H, Zalupski MM, Ryan JR. Metastatic uterine leiomyosarcoma to bone: a clinicopathologic study. Int J Surg Pathol 1997, **4**: 159–168.

730 Pautier P, Genestie C, Rey A, Morice P, Roche B, Lhommé C, Haie-Meder C, Duvillard P. Analysis of clinicopathologic prognostic factors for 157 uterine sarcomas and evaluation of a grading score validated for soft tissue sarcoma. Cancer 2000, **88**: 1425–1431.

731 Salazar OM, Bonfiglio TA, Patten SF, Keller BE, Feldstein M, Dunne ME, Rudolph J. Uterine sarcomas. Natural history, treatment and prognosis. Cancer 1978, **42**: 1152–1160.

732 Tsushima K, Stanhope CR, Gaffey TA, Lieber MM. Uterine leiomyosarcomas and benign smooth muscle tumors. Usefulness of nuclear DNA patterns studied by flow cytometry. Mayo Clin Proc 1988, **63**: 248–255.

Prediction of behavior in uterine smooth muscle tumors

733 Anonymous: MSKCC people. In: Center News, Memorial Sloan-Kettering Cancer Centre, New York. April 2001, p. 12.

734 Bell SW, Kempson RL, Hendrickson MR. Problematic uterine smooth muscle neoplasms. A clinicopathologic study of 213 cases. Am J Surg Pathol 1994, **18**: 535–558.

735 Donhuijsen K. Mitosis counts. Reproducibility and significance in grading of malignancy. Hum Pathol 1986, **17**: 1122–1125.

736 Editorials. Mitosis counting – I. (Scully RE et al) Mitosis counting – II. (Kempson RL) Mitosis counting – III. (Norris HJ) Hum Pathol 1976, **7**: 481–484.

737 Hart WR. Problematic uterine smooth muscle neoplasms. Am J Surg Pathol 1997, **21**: 252–255.

738 Kempson RL, Bari W. Uterine sarcomas. Classification, diagnosis, and prognosis. Hum Pathol 1970, **1**: 331–349.

739 Kempson RL, Hendrickson MR. Smooth muscle, endometrial stromal, and mixed Mullerian tumors of the uterus. Mod Pathol 2000, **13**: 328–342.

740 Layfield LJ, Liu K, Dodge R, Barsky SH. Uterine smooth muscle tumors: utility of classification by proliferation, ploidy, and prognostic markers versus traditional histopathology. Arch Pathol Lab Med 2000, **124**: 221–227.

741 Longacre TA, Hendrickson MR, Kempson RL. Predicting clinical outcome for uterine smooth muscle neoplasms with a reasonable degree of certainty. Adv Anat Pathol 1997, **4**: 95–104.

742 Majno G, Joris I. Apoptosis, oncosis, and necrosis. Am J Pathol 1995, **146**: 3–15.

743 Poncelet C, Walker F, Modelenat P, Bringuier AF, Scoazec JY, Feldman G, Darai E. Expression of CD44 standard and isoforms V3 and V6 in uterine smooth muscle tumors: a possible diagnostic tool for the diagnosis of leiomyosarcoma. Hum Pathol 2001, **32**: 1190–1196.

744 Quade BJ, Pinto AP, Howard DR, Petters III WA, Crum CP. Frequent loss of heterozygosity for chromosome 10 in uterine leiomyosarcoma in contrast to leiomyoma. Am J Pathol 1999, **154**: 945–950.

745 Schwarz G, Remmelink M, Decaestecker C, Gielen I, Budel V, Burchert M, Darro F, Danguy A, Gabius HJ, Salmon I, Kiss R. Galectin fingerprinting in tumor diagnosis. Differential expression of galectin-3 and galectin-3 binding sites, but not galectin-1, in benign vs malignant uterine smooth muscle tumors. Am J Clin Pathol 1999, **111**: 623–631.

746 Silverberg SG. Reproducibility of the mitosis count in the histologic diagnosis of smooth muscle tumors of the uterus. Hum Pathol 1976, **7**: 451–454.

747 Thunnissen FBJM, Ambergen AW, Koss M, Travis WD, O'Leary TJ, Ellis IO. Mitotic counting in surgical pathology: sampling bias, heterogeneity and statistical uncertainty. Histopathology 2001, **39**: 1–8.

748 Trzyna W, McHugh M, McCue P, McHugh KM. Molecular determination of the malignant potential of smooth muscle neoplasms. Cancer 1997, **80**: 211–217.

749 van Diest PJ, Baak JP, Matze-Cok P, Wisse-Brekelmans EC, van Galen CM, Kurver PH, Bellot SM, Fijnheer J, van Gorp LH, Kwee WS, et al. Reproducibility of mitosis counting in 2,469 breast cancer specimens; results from the Multicenter Morphometric Mammary Carcinoma Project. Hum Pathol 1992, **23**: 603–607.

750 Wilkinson N, Rollason TP. Recent advances in the pathology of smooth muscle tumors of the uterus. Histopathology 2001, **39**: 331–341.

751 Zhai YL, Kobayashi Y, Mori A, Orii A, Nikaido T, Konishi I, Fujii S. Expression of steroid receptors, Ki-67, and p53 in uterine leiomyosarcoma. Int J Gynecol Pathol 1999, **18**: 20–28.

Other tumors and tumorlike conditions

752 Angeles-Angeles A, Gutierrez-Villalobos LG, Lome-Maldonado C, Jimenez-Moreno A. Polypoid brenner tumor of the uterus. Int J Gynecol Pathol 2002, **21**: 86–87.

753 Aozasa K, Saeki K, Ohsawa M, Horiuchi K, Mishima K, Tsujimoto M. Malignant lymphoma of the uterus. Report of seven cases with immunohistochemical study. Cancer 1993, **72:** 1959–1964.

754 Arhelger RB, Bocian JJ. Brenner tumor of the uterus. Cancer 1976, **38:** 1741–1743.

755 Chan JKC, Fong MH. Composite multicystic mesothelioma and adenomatoid tumour of the uterus: different morphological manifestations of the same process? Histopathology 1997, **29:** 375–377.

756 Chetty R, Clark SP, Bhathal PS. Carcinoid tumor of the uterine corpus. Virchows Arch A Pathol Anat Histopathol 1993, **422:** 93–95.

757 Chou S-T, Fortune D, Beischer NA, McLeish G, Castles LA, McKelvie BA, Planner RS. Primary malignant fibrous histiocytoma of the uterus – ultrastructural and immunocytochemical studies of two cases. Pathology 1985, **17:** 36–40.

758 Clement PB. Chondrosarcoma of the uterus. Report of a case and review of the literature. Hum Pathol 1978, **9:** 726–732.

759 Clement PB. Postoperative spindle-cell nodule of the endometrium. Arch Pathol Lab Med 1988, **112:** 566–568.

760 Davey DD, Munn R, Smith LW, Cibull ML. Angiotrophic lymphoma. Presentation in uterine vessels with cytogenetic studies. Arch Pathol Lab Med 1990, **114:** 879–882.

761 Daya D, Lukka H, Clement PB. Primitive neuroectodermal tumors of the uterus. A report of four cases. Hum Pathol 1992, **23:** 1120–1129.

762 den Bakker MA, Hegt VN, Sleddens HB, Nuijten AS, Dinjens WN. Malignant mesenchymona of the uterus, arising in a leiomyoma. Histopathology 2002, **40:** 65–70.

763 De Young B, Bitterman P, Lack EE. Primary osteosarcoma of the uterus. Report of a case with immunohistochemical study. Mod Pathol 1992, **5:** 212–215.

764 Donner LR. Uterine carcinosarcoma with complete sarcomatous overgrowth mimicking pure embryonal rhabdomyosarcoma. Int J Gynecol Pathol 2002, **22:** 89–91.

765 Ferry JA, Young RH. Malignant lymphoma, pseudolymphoma, and hematopoietic disorders of the female genital tract. Pathol Annu 1991, **26:** 227–263.

766 Ferry JA, Young RH. Malignant lymphoma of the genitourinary tract. Curr Diagn Pathol 1997, **4:** 145–169.

767 Fraggetta F, Magro G, Vasquez E. Primitive neuroectodermal tumor of the uterus with focal cartilaginous differentiation. Histopathology 1997, **30:** 483–485.

768 Gilks CB, Taylor GP, Clement PB. Inflammatory pseudotumor of the uterus. Int J Gynecol Pathol 1987, **6:** 275–286.

769 Gray GF, Glick AD, Kurtin PJ, Jones HW III. Alveolar soft part sarcoma of the uterus. Hum Pathol 1986, **17:** 297–300.

770 Gyure KA, Hart WR, Kennedy AW. Lymphangiomyomatosis of the uterus associated with tuberous sclerosis and malignant neoplasia of the female genital tract. A report of two cases. Int J Gynecol Pathol 1995, **14:** 344–351.

771 Harris NL, Scully RE. Malignant lymphoma and granulocytic sarcoma of the uterus and vagina. Cancer 1984, **53:** 2530–2545.

772 Hendrickson MR, Scheithauer BW. Primitive neuroectodermal tumor of the endometrium. Report of two cases, one with electron microscopic observations. Int J Gynecol Pathol 1986, **5:** 249–259.

773 Houghton JP, Ioffe OB, Silverberg SG, McGrady B, McCluggage WG. Metastatic breast lobular carcinoma involving tamoxifen-associated endometrial polyps: report of two cases and review of tamoxifen-associated polypoid uterine lesions. Mod Pathol 2003, **16:** 395–398.

774 Hung LHY, Kurtz DM. Hodgkin's disease of the endometrium. Arch Pathol Lab Med 1985, **109:** 952–953.

775 Jameson CF. Angiomyoma of the uterus in a patient with tuberous sclerosis. Histopathology 1990, **16:** 202–203.

776 Jordan CD, Andrews SJ, Memoli VA. Well-differentiated pulmonary neuroendocrine carcinoma metastatic to the endometrium: a case report. Mod Pathol 1997, **9:** 1066–1070.

777 Joseph MG, Fellows FG, Hearn SA. Primary endodermal sinus tumor of the endometrium. A clinicopathologic, immunocytochemical, and ultrastructural study. Cancer 1990, **65:** 297–302.

778 Kumar NB, Hart WR. Metastases to the uterine corpus from extragenital cancers. Cancer 1982, **50:** 2163–2169.

779 Liggins GC. Uterine arteriovenous fistula. Obstet Gynecol 1964, **23:** 214–217.

780 Masunaga A, Abe M, Tsuji E, Suzuki U, Ohgida T, Toyama M, Nakamura H, Mori S, Sugawara I, Itoyama S. Primary uterine T-cell lymphoma. Int J Gynecol Pathol 1998, **17:** 376–379.

781 Mazur MT, Hsueh S, Gersell DJ. Metastases to the female genital tract. Cancer 1984, **53:** 1978–1984.

782 Milne DS, Hinshaw K, Malcolm AJ, Hilton P. Primary angiosarcoma of the uterus. A case report. Histopathology 1994, **16:** 203–205.

783 Moore WF, Bentley RC, Kim KR, Olatidoye B, Gray SR, Robboy SJ. Goblet-cell mucinous epithelium lining the endometrium and endocervix: evidence of a metastasis from an appendiceal primary tumor through the use of cytokeratin-7 and -20 immunostains. Int J Gynecol Pathol 1998, **17:** 363–367.

784 Morrel B, Mulder AF, Chadha S, Tjokrowardojo AJ, Wijnen JA. Angiosarcoma of the uterus following radiotherapy for squamous cell carcinoma of the cervix. Eur J Obstet Gynecol Reprod Biol 1993, **49:** 193–197.

785 Muc RS, Grayson W, Grobbelaar JJ. Adult extrarenal Wilms tumor occurring in the uterus. Arch Pathol Lab Med 2001, **125:** 1081–1083.

786 Nogales FF, Isaac A, Hardisson D, Bosincu L, Palacios J, Ordi J, Mendoza E, Manzarbetia F, Olivera H, O'Valle F, Krasevic M, Marquez M. Adenomatoid tumors of the uterus: an analysis of 60 cases. Int J Gynecol Pathol 2002, **21:** 34–40.

787 Oliva E, Ferry JA, Young RH, Prat J, Srigley JR, Scully RE. Granulocytic sarcoma of the female genital tract: a clinicopathologic study of 11 cases. Am J Surg Pathol 1997, **21:** 1156–1165.

788 Ordi J, Stamatakos MD, Tavassoli FA. Pure pleomorphic rhabdomyosarcomas of the uterus. Int J Gynecol Pathol 1998, **16:** 369–377.

789 Otis CN. Uterine adenomatoid tumors: immunohistochemical characteristics with emphasis on Ber-EP4 immunoreactivity and distinction from adenocarcinoma. Int J Gynecol Pathol 1996, **15:** 146–151.

790 Palacios J, Suarez Manrique A, Ruiz Villaespesa A, Burgos Lizaldez E, Gamallo Amat C. Cystic adenomatoid tumor of the uterus. Int J Gynecol Pathol 1991, **10:** 296–301.

791 Podczaski E, Sees J, Kaminski P, Sorosky J, Larson JE, De Geest K, Zaino RJ, Mortel R. Rhabdomyosarcoma of the uterus in a postmenopausal patient. Gynecol Oncol 1990, **37:** 439–442.

792 Pounder DJ. Fatty tumours of the uterus. J Clin Pathol 1982, **35:** 1380–1383.

793 Quigley JC, Hart WR. Adenomatoid tumors of the uterus. Am J Clin Pathol 1981, **76:** 627–635.

794 Resta L, Maiorano E, Piscitelli D, Botticella MA. Lipomatous tumors of the uterus. Clinico-pathological features of 10 cases with immunocytochemical study of histogenesis. Pathol Res Pract 1994, **190:** 378–383.

795 Ruco LP, Pilozzi E, Wedard BM, Marzullo A, D'Andrea V, de Antoni E, Silvestrini G, Bonetti F. Epithelioid lymphangioleiomyomatosis-like tumour of the uterus in a patient without tuberous sclerosis: a lesion mimicking epithelioid leiomyosarcoma. Histopathology 1998, **33:** 91–93.

796 Schammel DP, Tavassoli FA. Uterine angiosarcomas:

a morphologic and immunohistochemcial study of four cases. Am J Surg Pathol 1998, **22:** 246–250.

797   Shintaku M, Sasaki M, Honda T. Thrombomodulin immunoreactivity in adenomatoid tumour of the uterus. Histopathology 1997, **28:** 375–377.

798   Sinkre P, Albores-Saavedra J, Miller DS, Copeland LJ, Hameed A. Endometrial endometrioid carcinomas associated with Ewing sarcoma/peripheral primitive neuroectodermal tumor. Int J Gynecol Pathol 2000, **19:** 127–132.

799   Sirgi KE, Swanson PE, Gersell DJ. Extramedullary hematopoiesis in the endometrium. Report of four cases and review of the literature. Am J Clin Pathol 1994, **101:** 643–646.

800   Smith NL, Baird DB, Strausbauch PH. Endometrial involvement by multiple myeloma. Int J Gynecol Pathol 1997, **16:** 173–175.

801   Stemmermann GN. Extrapelvic carcinoma metastatic to the uterus. Am J Obstet Gynecol 1961, **82:** 1261–1266.

802   Stephenson TJ, Mill PM. Adenomatoid tumours. An immunohistochemical and ultrastructural appraisal of their histogenesis. J Pathol 1986, **148:** 327–335.

803   Suzuki T, Yoshida Y, Kaku T, Kikuchi K, Mori M. Adenomatoid tumor of the uterus. Ultrastructural, histochemical, and immunohistochemical analysis. Arch Pathol Lab Med 1985, **109:** 1049–1051.

804   Tallini G, Price FV, Carcangiu ML. Epithelioid angiosarcoma arising in uterine leiomyomas. Am J Clin Pathol 1993, **100:** 514–518.

805   Tavassoli FA. Melanotic paraganglioma of the uterus. Cancer 1986, **58:** 942–948.

806   Taxy JB, Trujillo YP. Breast cancer metastatic to the uterus. Clinical manifestations of a rare event. Arch Pathol Lab Med 1994, **118:** 819–821.

807   Tiltman AJ. Adenomatoid tumours of the uterus. Histopathology 1980, **4:** 437–443.

808   van de Rijn M, Kamel OW, Chang PP, Lee A, Warnke RA, Salhany KE. Primary low-grade endometrial B-cell lymphoma. Am J Surg Pathol 1997, **21:** 187–194.

809   Vang R, Kempson RL. Perivascular epithelioid cell tumor ('PEComa') of the uterus: a subset of HMB-45 positive epithelioid mesenchymal neoplasms with an uncertain relationship to pure smooth muscle tumors. Am J Surg Pathol 2001, **26:** 1–13.

810   Vang R, Medeiros LJ, Ha CS, Deavers S. Non-Hodgkin's lymphoma involving the uterus: a clinicopathologic analysis of 26 cases. Mod Pathol 2000, **13:** 19–28.

811   Young RH, Harris NL, Scully RE. Lymphoma-like lesions of the lower female genital tract. A report of 16 cases. Int J Gynecol Pathol 1985, **4:** 289–299.

812   Young RH, Kleinman GM, Scully RE. Glioma of the uterus. Am J Surg Pathol 1981, **5:** 695–699.

813   Young TW, Thrasher TV. Nonchromaffin paraganglioma of the uterus. Arch Pathol Lab Med 1982, **106:** 608–609.

Fallopian tube (including broad and round ligaments)

Normal anatomy

The **fallopian tube** or salpinx is a tubular hollow structure measuring 11 to 12 cm in length that runs throughout the apex of the broad ligament and spans the distance between the uterine cornus and the ovary. It is divided into four segments: intramural (inside the uterine wall), isthmus (2 to 3 cm, thick-walled), ampulla (a thin-walled expanded area), and infundibulum (a trumpet-shaped ending that opens into the peritoneal cavity through the ostium and is fringed by the fimbriae). One of the latter structures, known as the ovarian fimbria, attaches the tube to the ovary.

The inner aspect of the tube is lined by mucosa arranged in the shape of longitudinal, branching folds (known as plicae), which merge with the fimbriae. There is good correlation between the microscopic features of this mucosa and its salpingoscopic appearance.[4] Microscopically, the epithelium is composed of three distinct cell types: secretory, ciliated, and intercalated (peg).[3] Amylase is secreted by the epithelium, and its presence can be demonstrated immunohistochemically.[1] The tubal epithelium also expresses the follicle stimulating hormone (FSH) receptor, similarly to the surface epithelium of the ovary.[8] Endocrine cells have been found only exceptionally. A low degree of proliferative activity takes place normally in the tubal epithelium, apparently not synchronized with the menstrual cycle. At the time of menstruation, as well as a few days post partum, the tubal mucosa may be normally infiltrated by neutrophils, probably as a reaction to blood and necrotic debris ("physiologic salpingitis"). It is accompanied by negative cultures and should not be confused with a bacterial salpingitis.[6,7]

The muscular wall (myosalpinx) is composed of an inner circular layer and an outer longitudinal layer; the isthmus near the uterotubal junction also possesses an inner longitudinal layer.

The lymphatics of the fallopian tube leave the tubal wall within the mesosalpinx, where they join efferent lymphatics from the ovary and uterus and follow the ovarian vessels to terminate in the aortic lymph nodes. Other lymphatics course within the broad ligament and drain into the interiliac nodes; a separate lymphatic channel from the ampulla of the tube follows the broad ligament to terminate in the superior gluteal lymph nodes.

The **broad ligament** is the peritoneal fold that supports the uterus on either side. This structure and the adjacent areas contain a variety of tubular structures related to the müllerian and wolffian systems that may give rise to grossly evident cysts.[5] Most of these are lined by müllerian-type epithelium and have been variously referred to—depending on their specific location and presumed histogenesis—as parovarian cyst, paratubal cyst (hydatid of Morgagni), subserosal müllerian cyst, Kobelt's cyst (appendix vesiculosa), paroöphoron cyst, epoöphoron cyst, and rete ovarii cyst[2] (see p. 1656). Walthard cell nests, which can also be cystic, are of a different (probably mesothelial) nature; they are discussed on p. 1650.

The **round ligament** is a fibrous cord attached to the superior lateral border of the uterus that passes over the external iliac vessels and the inguinal ligament to leave the abdominal cavity through the deep inguinal ring. From there, it follows the inguinal canal to anchor itself in the labium majus. It serves to orient the uterus because its insertion is *anterior* to that of the fallopian tube.

Inflammation

Bacterial infection of the fallopian tube is a common disease, and its incidence keeps increasing. It may follow invasive procedures (such as curettage or the insertion of intrauterine devices), and it commonly accompanies endometriosis,[26] but in most cases it is due to an ascending infection, often sexually transmitted[28] (Fig. 19.190). The inflammation may result in fusion of tubal plicae and obliteration of the ostium (Fig. 19.191A). Obstruction of the fimbriated end and, less commonly, of the intramural or isthmic portion leads to infertility.[15] Microscopically, the trapped epithelial spaces produce a complicated gland-like pattern that can simulate malignancy[10] (Fig. 19.191B).

The lumen is often distended and filled with secretions or pus (**pyosalpinx**) (Fig. 19.192). Massive intraluminal hemorrhage may lead to the formation of

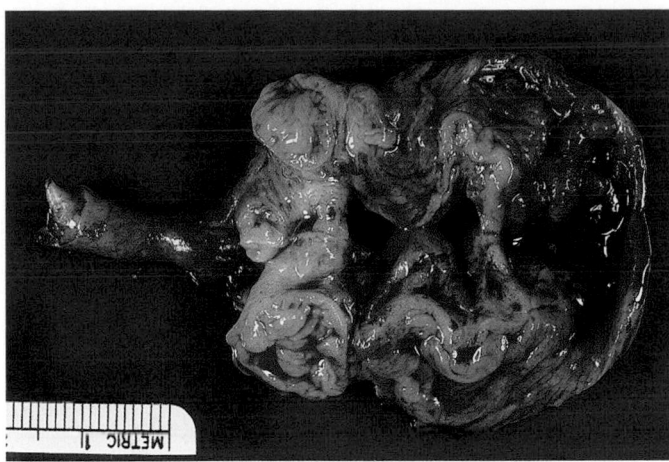

Fig. 19.190 Gross appearance of chronic salpingitis with superimposed acute changes.

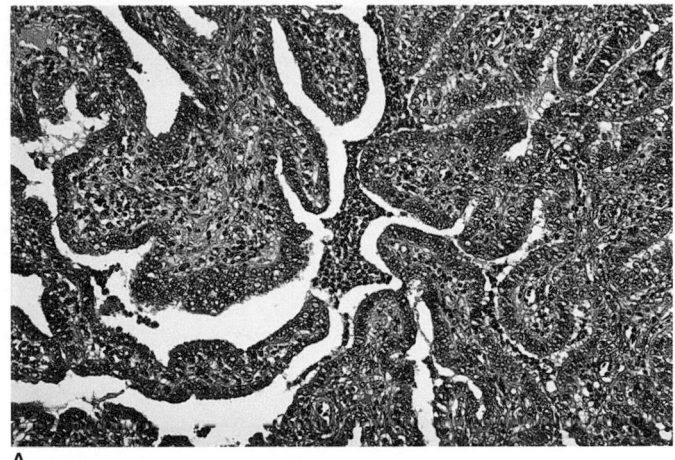

A

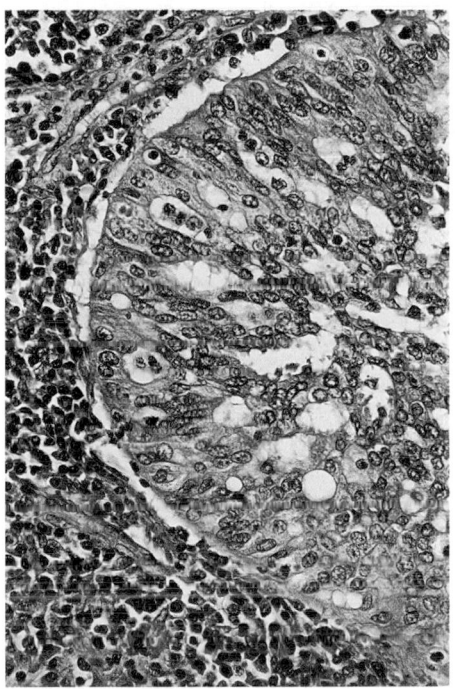

B

Fig. 19.191 Chronic salpingitis: **A**, blunting of villi due to heavy inflammatory infiltrate; **B**, marked secondary reactive hyperplasia of the mucosa, which may simulate a malignant process.

hematosalpinx, a rare condition that needs to be distinguished from the much more common form secondary to ruptured tubal pregnancy. In chronic inflammatory cases, the tubal wall is markedly fibrotic, and serosal adhesions are prominent. The inflammatory exudate often spreads to the ovary, resulting in the formation of a **tubo-ovarian abscess** and obliteration of the pelvic anatomic relationships (Fig. 19.193). The rupture of such an abscess may lead to localized or generalized peritonitis and requires prompt surgical intervention.[21,24] **Hydrosalpinx** is generally regarded as the end stage of a purulent salpingitis in which pus has been reabsorbed and replaced by a transudate of plasma.[11] The external gross appearance has been likened to that of a retort (Fig. 19.194). Exceptionally, the involvement is limited to the intramural portion of the tube. The wall is thin and fibrotic, with atrophy or even disappearance of the smooth muscle wall. The epithelium is flat and focally absent.

Pelvic inflammatory disease (PID) is the generic term used for inflammatory processes of this region in which the fallopian tube is the epicenter and presumably the source of the inflammation.[20,23,30] Eschenbach et al.[14] recovered *Neisseria gonorrhoeae* from 91 of 204 cases of acute PID in patients with cervical gonococcal infections. Chlamydial infection is also common, accounting for over 20% and perhaps as many as half of the cases.[29,31] This etiology should be suspected in cases of chronic salpingitis accompanied by marked lymphofollicular hyperplasia.[29] Polymicrobial tuboperitoneal infection (resulting from *Bacteroides fragilis*, peptostreptococci, peptococci, and other organisms) is responsible for most others. In established tubo-ovarian abscesses, the most common agents recovered are coliform organisms. *N. gonorrhoeae* was isolated only once in a series of 93 case studies by Mickal et al.[21] This finding, however, does not rule out its role as a possible initiating factor before superinfection has occurred, in view of the fact that isolation of *N. gonorrhoeae* is inversely proportional to the number of episodes of salpingitis.[27]

Tuberculosis of the tube develops by the hematogenous route. Most patients are young, and infertility is common.[19,26] In advanced cases, both tubes are replaced by caseous tuberculous masses (Fig. 19.195). There is often extreme adenomatous proliferation of the tubal mucosa in association with granulomatous inflammation, and this may lead to a mistaken diagnosis of carcinoma. The endometrium is concomitantly involved in approximately 80% of cases.[22]

Granulomatous inflammation of the tubes can also be produced by *Schistosoma*, *Oxyuris vermicularis*, *Actinomyces*, *Coccidioides immitis*, and other organisms.[13]

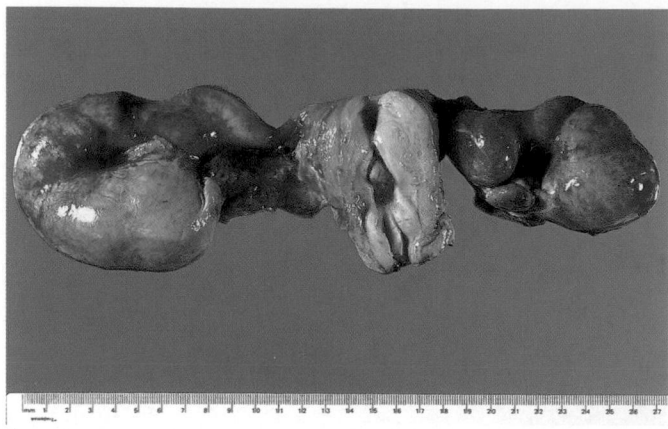

A

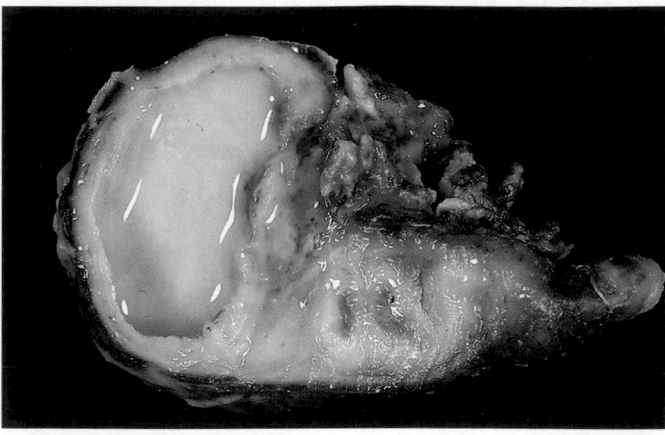

Fig. 19.192 A and **B**, Outer aspect and cut surface of pyosalpinx. (**A**, Courtesy of Dr. RA Cooke, Brisbane, Australia; from Cooke RA, Stewart B: Colour Atlas of Anatomical Pathology. Edinburgh, Churchill Livingstone, 2004; **B**, Courtesy of Dr Pedro J Grases Galofrè; from Grases Galofrè PJ: Patologia ginecològica. Bases para el diagnòstico morfològico, Barcelona, Masson, 2002)

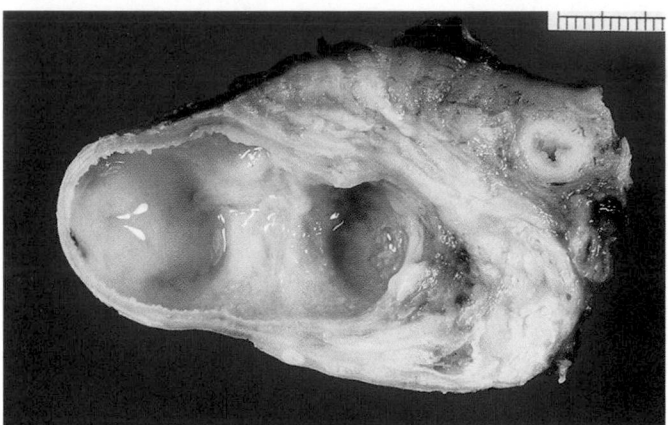

Fig. 19.193 Fusion of fallopian tube and ovary into a tubo-ovarian abscess.

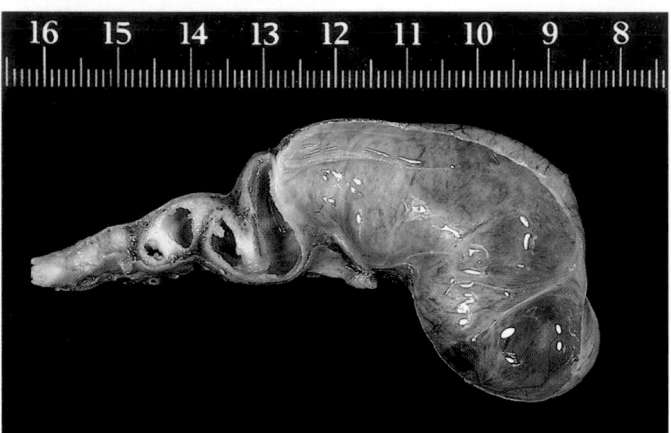

Fig. 19.194 Gross appearance of hydrosalpinx showing the typical retort-type appearance. (Courtesy of Dr Pedro J Grases Galofrè; from Grases Galofrè PJ: Patologia ginecològica. Bases para el diagnòstico morfològico, Barcelona, Masson, 2002)

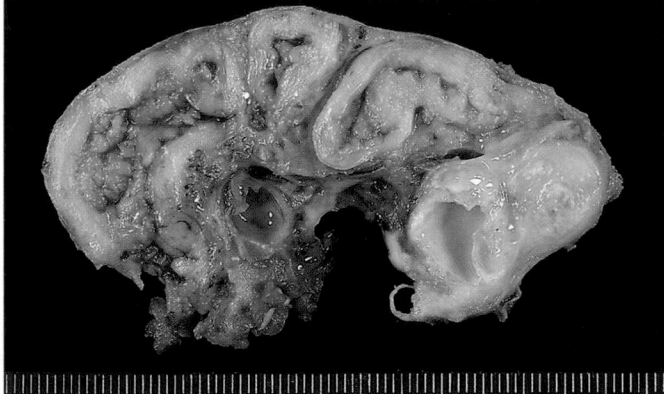

Fig. 19.195 Large caseating nodules in tuberculous salpingitis. (Courtesy of Dr Pedro J Grases Galofrè; from Grases Galofrè PJ: Patologia ginecològica. Bases para el diagnòstico morfològico, Barcelona, Masson, 2002.)

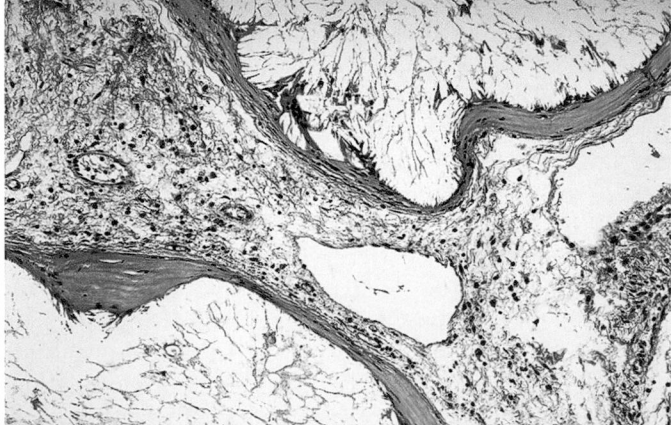

Fig. 19.196 Granulomatous reaction to contrast material injected into the fallopian tube.

Sarcoidosis and *Crohn's disease* may be accompanied by tubal involvement.

Foreign bodies introduced for diagnostic or therapeutic measures can induce a bizarre granulomatous response (Fig. 19.196). Reaction to *Lipiodol* following the Rubin test may be so proliferative as to resemble a neoplasm. The push of a uterine sound may drive lubricant into the tube, causing *lipoid granulomas*.[12]

Xanthogranulomatous (pseudoxanthomatous) salpingitis is characterized by an expansion of the tubal

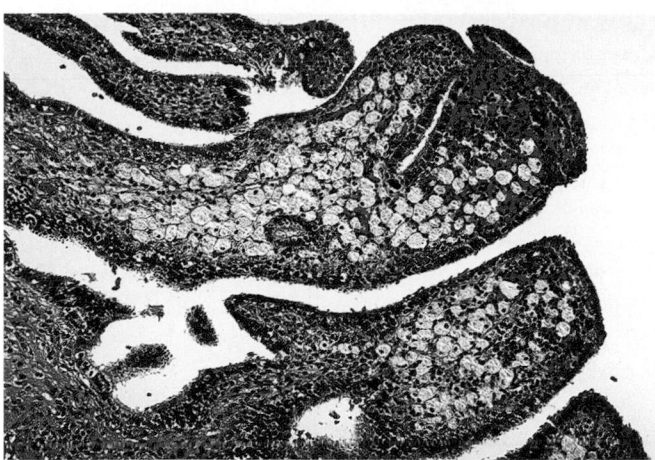

Fig. 19.197 Xanthogranulomatous salpingitis.

plicae by an infiltrate of foamy histiocytes (Fig. 19.197). Some cases may be due to endometriosis, and, therefore, the term "salpingitis" may be inaccurate.[17] Accordingly, some authors refer to it as *pseudoxanthomatous salpingiosis*.[25]

Giant cell arteritis is occasionally found in the tubes, ovary, and uterus of postmenopausal patients, either as an isolated finding (most frequently) or as a manifestation of a generalized immune-mediated disease.[9,18]

Torsion

Torsion of the fallopian tube and ovary is usually secondary to inflammation or tumor, but occasionally it develops in a previously normal organ, the appearance at surgery being that of a hemorrhagic infarct. This phenomenon can occur in adults[33] as well as in infants and children.[32,34] In children, torsion of the normal adnexa is about a third as common as torsion of an ovarian cyst or tumor. If the operation (which can be carried out laparoscopically) is done early enough, untwisting of the adnexa may lead to full recovery. Nonoperated cases may resolve spontaneously or result in a necrotic and calcified mass, which may later detach from the uterus. It has been suggested that this complication, when occurring in previously normal adnexa, is due to the fact that the infundibulopelvic ligament extends along the edge of the ovarian ligament so that the tube and ovary hang on a very narrow stalk.

Tubal pregnancy

The incidence of tubal pregnancy (eccyesis) has increased markedly in recent times.[48] It is often the consequence of chronic salpingitis, which leads to inflammatory destruction of the lining folds and retention of the ovum.[41] Congenital tubal abnormalities,

functional tubal disturbances, and salpingitis isthmica nodosa are responsible for a minority of the cases.[41,44] A history of infertility is associated with an increased risk of tubal pregnancy,[53] whereas induced abortion has no apparent effect on a woman's risk of tubal pregnancy in subsequent pregnancies.[42] High levels of trophinin, tastin, and bystin (three molecules thought to be involved in human embryo implantation) are expressed at high levels in trophoblast and fallopian tube epithelia in cases of tubal pregnancy, a fact of possible pathogenetic significance.[45a]

In tubal pregnancy the gestational sac is completely made up of tubal tissue, with no participation from the ovarian or intraligamentary tissues. Following implantation of the ovum in the tubal epithelium (usually in the ampullo-isthmic or midtubal portion), chorionic villi and extravillous (intermediate) trophoblasts can grow predominantly intraluminally[51] or penetrate deeply into the wall, just as they do in the uterus,[41,49] except that the wall here is much thinner. Trophoblastic invasion of muscle and vessels is a common finding of no clinical significance. Hydropic changes and polar trophoblastic proliferation can occur; they should not be overdiagnosed as hydatidiform mole.[37] Changes resembling atherosclerosis may be seen in tubal arteries at the site of implantation, analogous to those occurring in the uterus in orthotopic pregnancy.[36] The fallopian tube epithelium may undergo clear cell hyperplasia.[52] Although a few tubal pregnancies have gone to term,[39] the usual outcome is abortion. The maternal vessels rupture into the gestational sac and cause hematosalpinx (Fig. 19.198). In the presence of a large hematosalpinx, it may be difficult to identify the products of gestation; numerous blocks *from the intratubal blood clot* should be taken for this purpose. Tubal rupture can occur (usually near the end of the second month) because of destruction of the tubal wall by the invading trophoblast, and this may result in severe intra-abdominal hemorrhage. This rupture may result in a brisk reac-

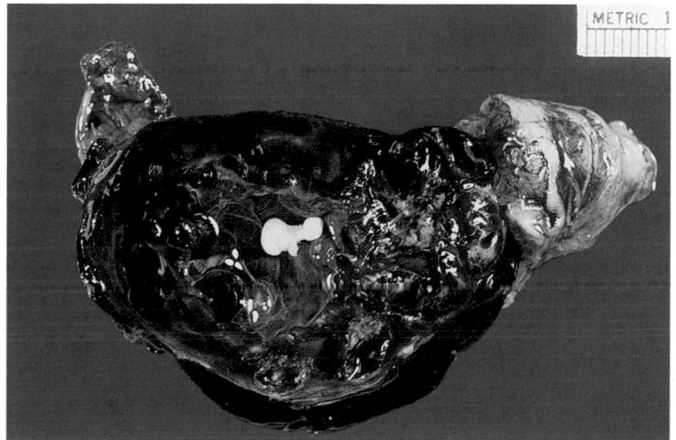

Fig. 19.198 Ruptured tubal pregnancy with marked hemorrhage (hematosalpinx). The tiny embryo is identifiable in the center of the clot.

tive proliferation of the mesothelium, with formation of papillae and psammoma bodies. These changes should be recognized as reactive and not misinterpreted as metastases or implants from an ovarian serous neoplasm. The necrotic trophoblastic tissue may be retained for a long time and appear as hyalinized ghost outlines of chorionic villi.[43] On occasion, the appearance of these retained tissues corresponds to that of so-called *placental site nodule*, as described in the uterine corpus.[38,46]

The usual treatment for tubal pregnancy is salpingectomy, which in most instances can be done laparoscopically.[40,45] It is possible to conserve the homolateral ovary in approximately 80% of cases. Segmental tubal resection may be appropriate in selected cases; some of these individuals may develop recurrent tubal pregnancy, which is more related to the preexisting disease than to the operation.[50] Conservative laparoscopic procedures for tubal ectopic pregnancy can result in extratubal trophoblastic implants accompanied by persistent beta-hCG postoperative serum titers.[39a]

Uterine curettings in the presence of a *viable* tubal pregnancy show gestational hyperplasia, sometimes associated with the Arias-Stella reaction. The key feature in the differential diagnosis between ectopic pregnancy and missed or incomplete abortion is the absence of fetal parts, chorionic villi, or trophoblastic cells in the latter (except for the extraordinarily rare occurrence of simultaneous intrauterine and ectopic pregnancy). Enlarged hyalinized spiral arteries and a fibrinoid matrix are not seen in the endometrium in cases of ectopic pregnancy, and, therefore, their presence is a strong indicator of intrauterine implantation.[47]

When trophoblastic elements are not obvious in routinely stained sections from the curettings, further search can be made with immunocytochemical stains for hCG, human placental lactogen (hPL), and keratin.[35,47] If none are found and a tubal mass is present, laparoscopy or laparotomy under the presumptive diagnosis of tubal pregnancy is indicated. Death of the embryo or fetus often results in expulsion of the endometrial decidual cast, regeneration of the epithelium, and reestablishment of the cyclic pattern. Therefore, the presence of a proliferative, secretory, or menstrual endometrium in a patient with an adnexal mass does not rule out the possibility of an ectopic pregnancy.

Other non-neoplastic processes

Walthard cell nests are small, glistening, round collections of flat to cuboidal cells with the appearance of transitional epithelium located on the tubal serosa,[68] sometimes accompanied by cystic changes. They are probably of mesothelial rather than müllerian or wolffian nature.[68] They should not be mistaken for serosal implants in patients with ovarian neoplasms.

Paratubal cysts, traditionally known as *hydatids of Morgagni*, are commonly seen as small round cysts attached by a pedicle to the fimbriated end of the tube. Their wall is paper-thin and their content is clear. Occasionally, they attain a large size and may undergo torsion.[69] Most are lined by tubal columnar epithelium containing both ciliated and secretory cells, sometimes projecting in a papillary fashion into the lumen and covered by a thin layer of smooth muscle.[56] Their appearance is consistent with origin from müllerian-type structures. Other paratubal cysts, lined by flat cells and surrounded by a thin fibrous wall, are regarded as of mesothelial origin.[65]

Endometriosis frequently involves the tube in the form of nodules located in the wall or serosa.[66] In this context, it should be mentioned that the most common manifestation of ectopic endometrium in the tube is focal replacement of tubal epithelium by uterine mucosa[63]; however, it is questionable whether this abnormality should be equated with conventional tubal endometriosis.

Cases have also been reported of the pathogenetically related *müllerianosis* (endometriosis plus endosalpingiosis plus endocervicosis) in the mesosalpinx.[60]

Endosalpingiosis is a term originally coined to describe the direct spread of tubal epithelium beyond the anatomical confines of the tube. Thus defined, its most common location is the ovarian surface close to the fimbria, suggesting that it may be secondary to extension of tubal epithelium over the inflammatory adhesions. Sometimes these changes are seen following surgical interventions, such as vaginal hysterectomy. Following the report of Burmeister et al.,[57] the term is more commonly used for a process of different pathogenesis, usually located in the peritoneum but also lymph node and other sites in the pelvis, probably representing a proliferative disorder of the mesothelium and subjacent tissue in which small cystic structures lined by an epithelium of tubal appearance form. Since this disorder is often associated with ovarian serous tumors, it is discussed in more detail in the next section of this chapter.

Decidual reaction of the tubal mucosa is a common finding in specimens of tubal ligation obtained at the time of cesarean section; it appears as small nodular collections of decidual cells covered by a flattened, sometimes inflamed epithelium (Fig. 19.199). Similar changes have been documented following hormonal therapy.[62]

Arias-Stella reaction can occur in the fallopian tube epithelium in association with either orthotopic or tubal pregnancy.[61]

Salpingitis isthmica nodosa is a usually bilateral lesion that presents grossly as a well-delimited nodular enlargement of the isthmic portion of the tube.[59] Microscopically, cystically dilated gland-like formations are seen surrounded by hypertrophic muscle (Fig. 19.200). Radiographic and tridimensional reconstructive studies have shown that the cystic formations are connected to the lumen of the tube. Although classically

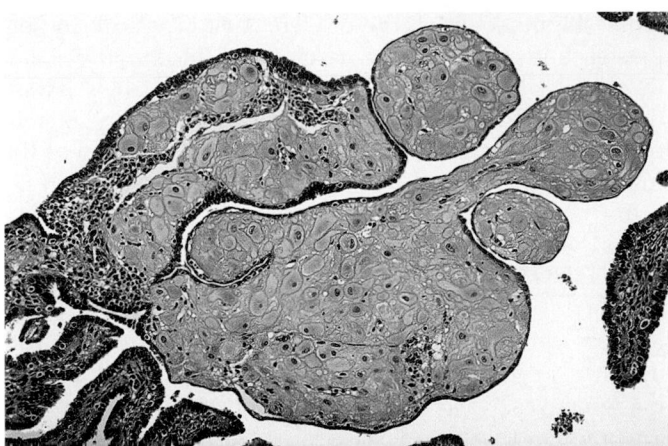

Fig. 19.199 Ectopic decidual reaction in the fallopian tube. This is a very common finding during pregnancy.

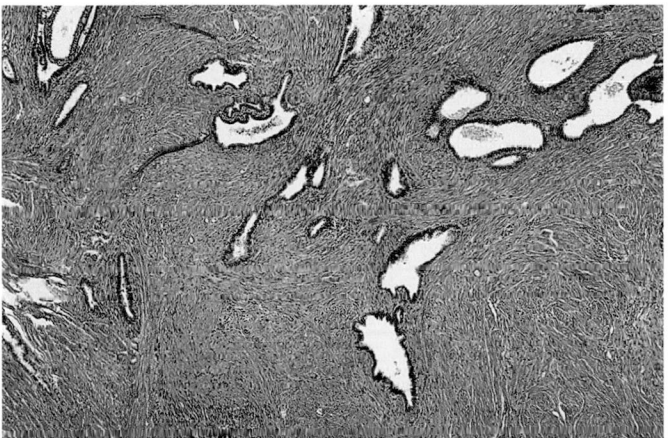

Fig. 19.200 Low-power view of salpingitis nodosa isthmica.

regarded as the result of inflammation (hence its name), convincing evidence has been presented that its pathogenesis is analogous to that of uterine adenomyosis.[55] It is accompanied by infertility in approximately one half of patients, and it may also lead to ectopic pregnancy.[44]

Tubal sterilization procedures lead to a sequence of morphologic alterations, which include proximal luminal dilatation, plical attenuation, chronic inflammation with pseudopolyp formation, and plical thickening in the distal segment.[7] The appearance varies depending on the length of time that has elapsed from the sterilization procedure.[67]

Metaplastic papillary tumor is a distinctive lesion characterized by eosinophilic and mucinous metaplasia of the mucosa resulting in a sharply outlined papillary configuration, occasionally encountered in tubes removed in the immediate postpartum period[54,64] (Fig. 19.201). Their behavior is benign. We favor the interpretation that this lesion is of non-neoplastic nature.

Transitional cell (urothelial) metaplasia has been observed; it has been hypothesized that it may represent the precursor lesion of the rare transitional cell carcinoma of the fallopian tube.[58]

Papillary endothelial hyperplasia can develop in adnexal vessels and simulate an angiosarcoma; as in other sites, it is the expression of organization and recanalization of thrombi.[64a]

Proliferative epithelial lesions

Proliferative epithelial lesions may be found during the microscopic examination of a specimen from tubal liga-

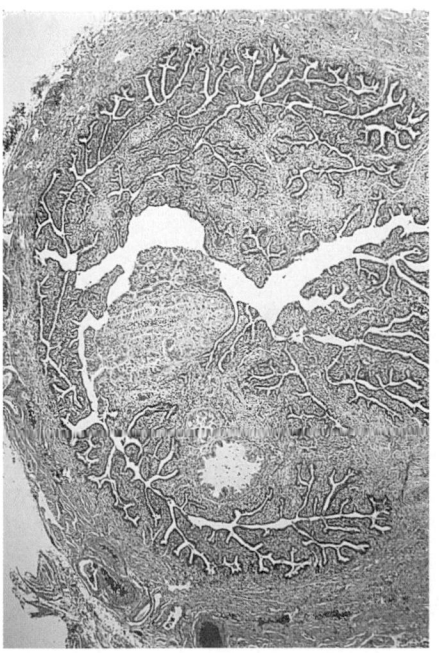

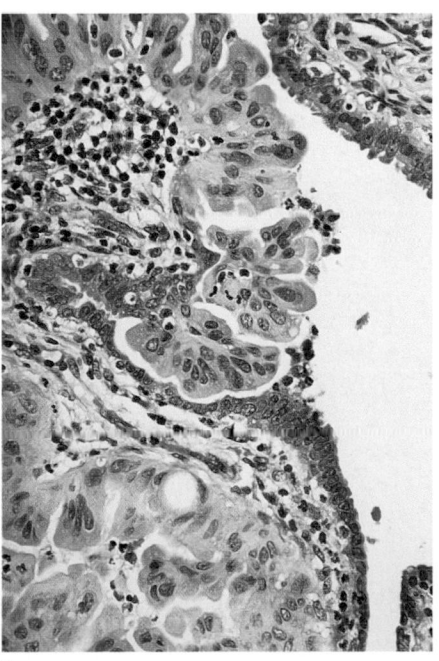

A

B

Fig. 19.201 A and **B,** So-called metaplastic papillary tumor of fallopian tube. This lesion, which occurred in a pregnant woman, is characterized by a papillary proliferation of acidophilic epithelium. This process is probably of non-neoplastic nature.

tion or salpingectomy. They may show one or more of the following features: nuclear crowding, stratification, loss of polarity, mild to moderate atypia, occasional mitoses, acidophilic metaplasia, and papillary formations[72,76,77] (Fig. 19.202). Mild degrees of this change are extremely common; in one study, they were found in 83% of all tubes examined.[79] More florid changes are usually seen in association with other lesions or circumstances, such as salpingitis, carriers of *BRCA1* mutations, exogenous or endogenous estrogen stimulation (including tamoxifen administration), and serous borderline tumors of the ovary.[71,74,75,78,79] The more severe forms of this process, which are rare, have been designated as *adenomatous hyperplasia*, *atypical hyperplasia*, and *carcinoma in situ*, and may be precursors of tubal carcinoma[73,76] (Fig. 19.203). The diagnosis of atypical hyperplasia requires the presence of moderate to severe nuclear atypia, and that of carcinoma in situ the presence of cells with "cytologically malignant nuclei" and abnormal mitotic figures.[79]

In a study of 26 women with *BRCA1/BRCA2* mutations who had undergone prophylactic oophorectomy with salpingectomy, there were two atypical hyperplasias and two in situ carcinomas in the tubes, an incidence which is clearly higher than in controls.[70] These findings suggest that ovarian surgical prophylaxis in these patients should be accompanied by removal of the tubes.

Carcinoma

Primary carcinoma of the fallopian tube is rare, accounting for approximately 1% of primary genital tract malignancies.[98] Most patients are postmenopausal, and the preoperative diagnosis is rarely correct. Nulliparity is common in this population. A growing number of cases are being reported in carriers of *BRCA1* and *BRCA2* mutations, leading some authors to recommend hysterectomy at the time of surgical prophylaxis.[82,94] The tumor may be bilateral, but more often the contralateral tube is either normal or the site of a hydrosalpinx. There is often a history and/or morphologic evidence of coexisting or preceding salpingitis, a fact of possible pathogenetic significance.[87] Atypical vaginal bleeding is the most common form of presentation.[89] The classical triad of the disease, represented by pain, vaginal discharge, and a palpable adnexal mass, occurs in less than half of cases. Cervicovaginal cytology is positive in only a minority of patients,[91] but an endometrial smear will reveal malignant cells in a high percentage of cases.[100] Grossly, the tube is enlarged and has fibrous adhesions, the outer appearance resembling that of chronic salpingitis. The fimbriated end of the tube may be open or closed, a fact of possible prognostic significance (see below) that should be noted in the report. Some tumors arise in the fimbriated portion of the organ and are, therefore, directly exposed to the peritoneal cavity even if they do not invade the tubal wall.[80] The cut surface shows a solid or papillary tumor filling the lumen (Fig. 19.204). Microscopically, all the major types of carcinomas known

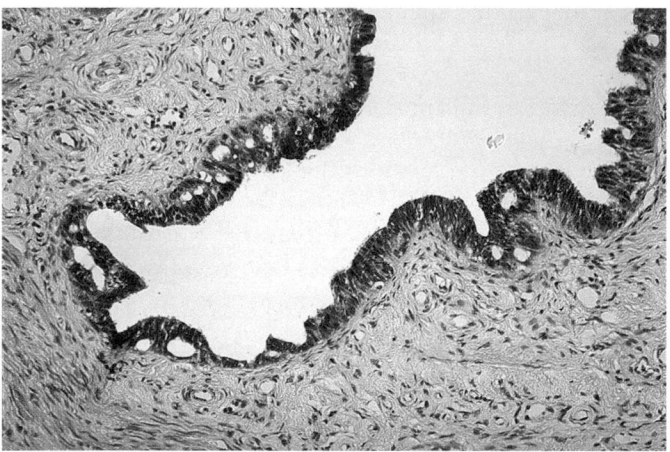

Fig. 19.202 Hyperplasia of the tubal epithelium in a patient with a borderline serous tumor of the homolateral ovary.

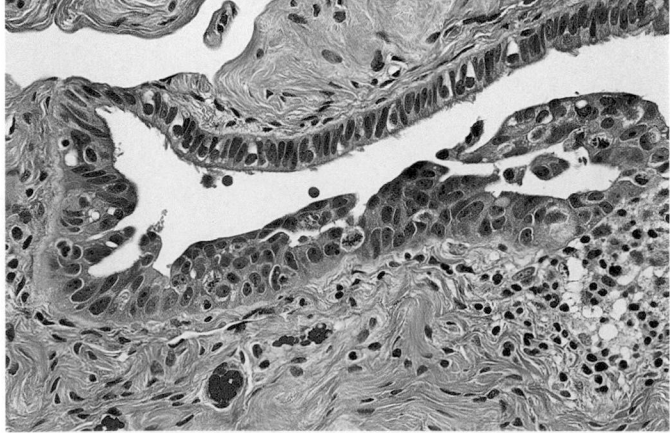

Fig. 19.203 Carcinoma in situ of the tubal epithelium. The ovary was uninvolved.

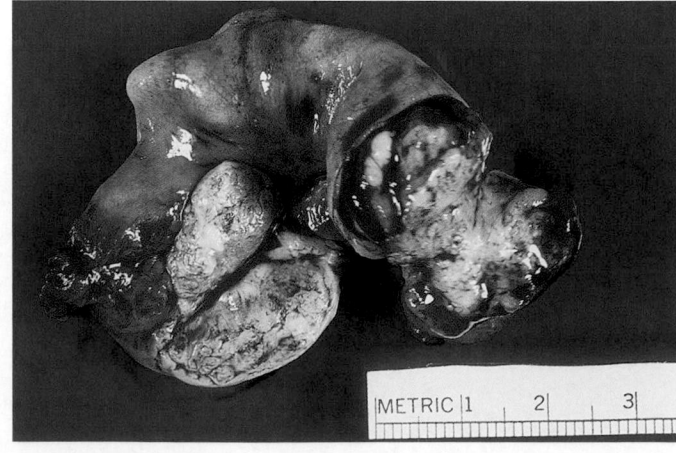

Fig. 19.204 Fallopian tube adenocarcinoma filling and distending the lumen of the organ.

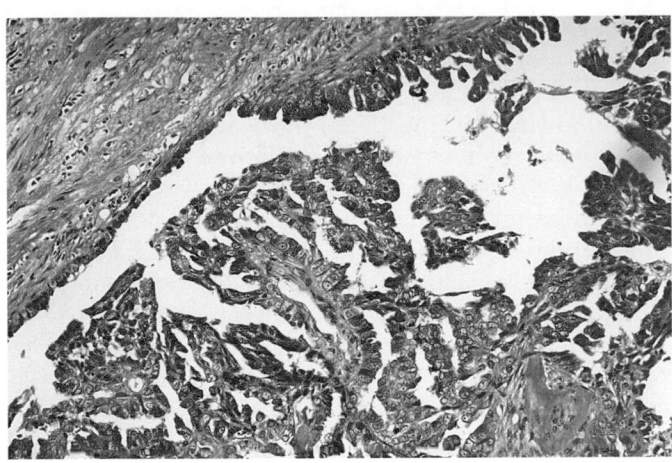

Fig. 19.205 High-power view showing the complex papillary architecture that is characteristic of adenocarcinomas of the fallopian tube.

to occur in the ovary (including their variants) have been reported in the tube. The most common type is papillary serous[101] (Fig. 19.205). Other types reported are endometrioid (including spindle cell, oxyphilic, adenoacanthomatous, adenosquamous and squamous types), mucinous, seromucinous, clear cell, and transitional cell.[28,81,84,86,90,93,102,103] The endometrioid carcinomas typically present as intraluminal masses and may simulate microscopically the so-called "female adnexal tumor of probable wolffian origin."[85] As in other sites in the female genital tract, serous carcinoma of the fallopian tube often expresses WT1.[103a]

The criteria for the diagnosis of primary tubal carcinoma should be very rigid because the frequency of this tumor is only a tenth of that of direct tubal extensions by uterine or ovarian carcinoma. By convention, a carcinoma extensively involving both endometrium and tube is classified as an endometrial tumor, and one extensively involving both ovary and tube is regarded as an ovarian neoplasm. In primary tubal carcinoma, the uterus and ovaries should appear largely normal on gross examination; the foci of malignancy in these organs, when present, should have the appearance of metastases or independent primaries by virtue of their size and distribution.[97]

The prognosis of tubal carcinoma depends more on staging than histologic grade.[81] The staging system currently used is adapted from the FIGO staging system for ovarian carcinoma.

Involvement of the tubal serosa, of the ovary or corpus uteri, or of other pelvic and abdominal structures is a common finding and indicates a poor prognosis.[83,99] Five-year survival rates are as high as 77% for stage I lesions, approximately 40% for stage II, and approximately 20% for stage III.[88,92,95–97] Absence of closure of the fimbriated end of the tube is another unfavorable prognostic sign.[81] Among stage I tumors, features of prognostic significance include the presence or absence of invasion of the tubal wall, depth of invasion when present, and the location of the tumor within the tube (fimbrial is worse than non-fimbrial).[80,81] The initial tumor recurrence is intra-abdominal in over 80% of cases, its pattern of spread mirroring that of ovarian carcinoma.

Borderline epithelial neoplasms have also been described in the fallopian tube. As in the ovary, they can be of serous, endometrioid, or mucinous type.[81,104]

Other tumors

Adenomatoid tumor is a benign, usually small lesion that may be found within the wall of the tube or beneath the uterine serosa near a cornu. The gross and microscopic features are identical to those of its epididymal counterpart (see Chapter 18). The ill-defined, seemingly infiltrating margins may lead to a mistaken diagnosis of carcinoma.[123] A marked degree of smooth muscle hyperplasia may be present and obscure the true nature of the lesion (Fig. 19.206). There is now agreement on the basis of ultrastructural and immunohistochemical findings that this entity is of mesothelial (rather than wolffian, müllerian, or endothelial) derivation and that it represents a unique variant of benign mesothelioma largely restricted to the genital region,[114,119] as originally postulated by Masson. However, the alternative should be considered of at least some of these lesions representing examples of nodular mesothelial hyperplasia of a reactive nature.

Papillary cystadenoma of the mesosalpinx has been seen in patients with von Hippel–Lindau disease.[106] Allelic deletions of the *VHL* gene have been detected in these cases.[121]

Mucinous lesions of the fallopian tubes comprise a wide variety of processes, which include mucinous metaplasia, mucinous cystadenoma and the already mentioned mucinous tumors of low malignant potential

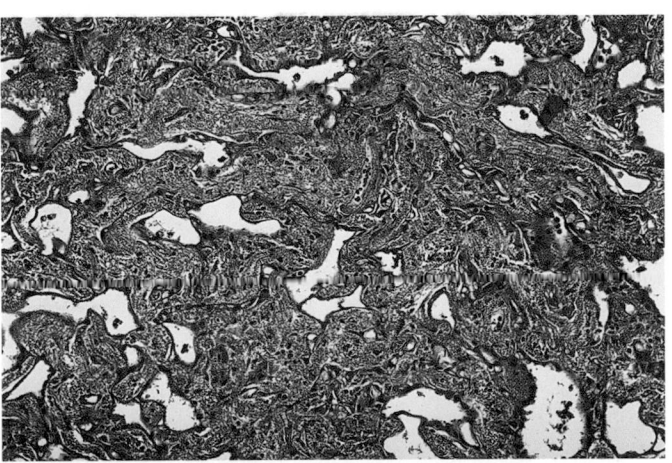

Fig. 19.206 Adenomatoid tumor accompanied by smooth muscle hyperplasia.

("borderline mucinous tumors") and mucinous adeno-carcinoma. Some of these lesions have occurred in patients with the Peutz–Jeghers syndrome, others in association with in situ or invasive adenocarcinoma of other portions of the female genital tract (such as endo-cervix) and still others in conjunction with mucinous neoplasms of the appendix.[112,120] It is possible that the latter are metastatic.

Approximately 50 cases of tubal **teratomas** have been published, all but one cystic and benign[110]; one of them contained a carcinoid tumor and another was entirely composed of mature thyroid tissue (struma salpingis).[109] Other benign tubal tumors, all very rare, are **leiomyoma, hemangioma, adenofibroma,**[80,113] **sex-cord tumor with annular tubules** (associated with endometriosis),[108] and **papilloma.**[107] The latter should be distinguished from the more common papillary hyperplasia associated with inflammation and hyperestrinism.

Malignant tumors other than carcinoma include **malignant mixed müllerian tumor**[105,111,115,117,123a] (some bilateral[122]) (Fig. 19.207), **leiomyosarcoma,** and **gesta-**tional choriocarcinoma.[118] All three tumor types resemble, grossly and microscopically, their more common uterine counterparts; tubal extension from the latter should always be considered in the differential diagnosis. Tubal involvement by **malignant lymphoma** is always the expression of systemic disease. **Secondary tubal invasion** by carcinoma of the ovary and uterus is a much more common event than primary tubal carcinoma. Most **metastases** to the tube also originate from genital organs, with very few exceptions[116] (Fig. 19.208).

Tumors and tumorlike conditions of broad and round ligaments

Cystic formations derived from müllerian or meso-nephric (wolffian) rests can be found in or around the broad ligament; they have been mentioned on p. 1640.

Female adnexal tumor of probable wolffian origin (wolffian adnexal tumor) is a distinctive lesion originally described in the broad ligament and subsequently also recognized in the ovary (see p. 1704). In its most typical form, it is seen within the leaves of the broad ligament or hanging on a pedicle from it or the fallopian tube. Grossly, it is predominantly solid. Microscopically, it is composed of epithelial cells growing in diffuse, trabecular, and tubular patterns (Fig. 19.209). Mitotic activity and capsular invasion may be present, but the prognosis is generally good.[132,135] As the name indicates, the tumor is thought to be of wolffian (mesonephric) derivation. Therefore, it could have been designated as mesonephric, but it was feared that such a terminology might have induced confusion with the many lesions in the female genital tract that in the past have been called mesonephric but which have no relation with the mesonephric system.

Other tumors and tumorlike conditions that can be found in the broad ligament unassociated with either

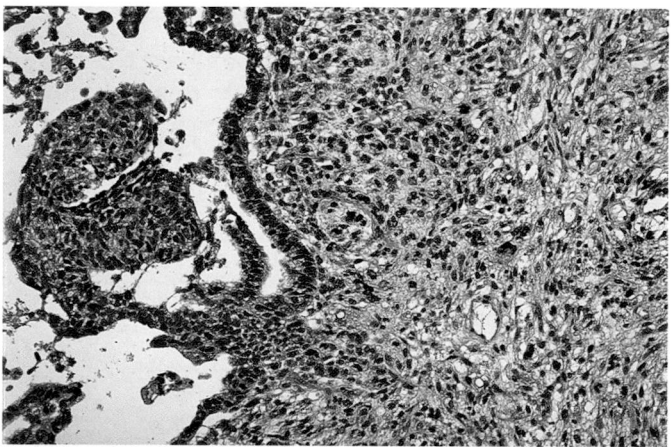

Fig. 19.207 Malignant mixed müllerian tumor of fallopian tube, showing the typical biphasic pattern.

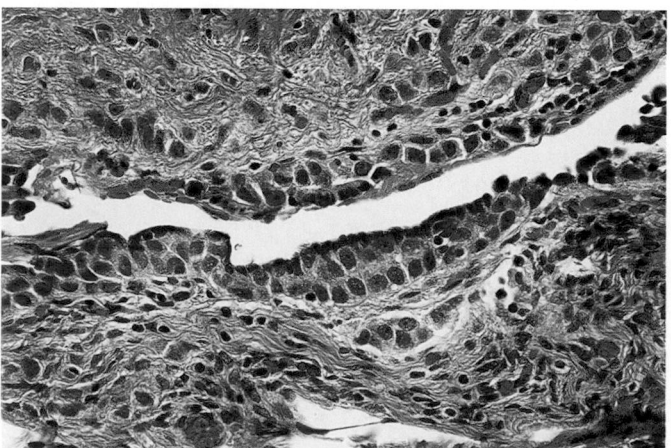

Fig. 19.208 Metastatic lobular carcinoma of breast growing beneath tubal epithelium.

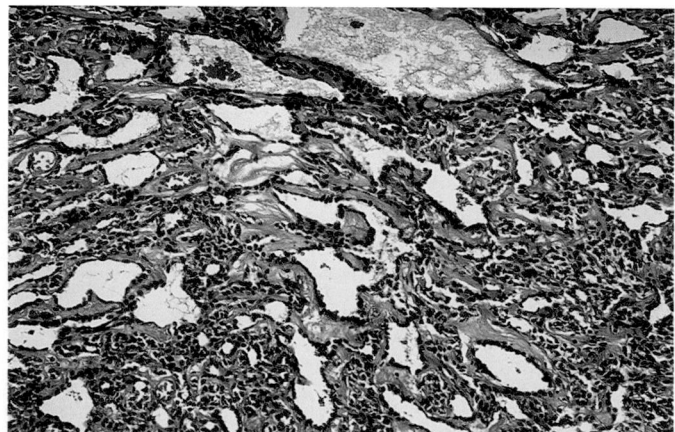

Fig. 19.209 Wolffian adnexal tumor of the broad ligament. The sieve-like low-power appearance is characteristic.

uterine or ovarian disease are endometriosis (including the possibly related condition known as uterus-like mass)[124]; borderline serous papillary tumors[126]; serous, endometrioid, clear cell, and mucinous carcinomas[125,127]; papillary cystadenomas and other neoplasms associated with von Hippel–Lindau disease[133,136]; ependymoma[129]; smooth muscle tumors; and other types of mesenchymal neoplasms. Some of the carcinomas of this region are thought to arise from foci of endometriosis.[127]

The **round ligament** is only rarely the site of primary disease. Striated muscle heteroplasia is an inconsequential incidental finding, thought to represent aberrant persistence of gubernacular rhabdomyoblasts.[131] Cases of leiomyomas (including the epithelioid variety), "fibromas," and benign mesenchymomas (angiomyolipomas) have been reported.[128,130,134]

References

Normal anatomy

1 Bruns DE, Mills SE, Savory J. Amylase in fallopian tube and serous ovarian neoplasms. Immunohistochemical localization. Arch Pathol Lab Med 1982, **106:** 17–20.

2 Gardner GH, Greene RR, Peckham B. Normal and cystic structures of the broad ligament. Am J Obstet Gynecol 1948, **55:** 917–939.

3 Hendrickson MR, Kempson RL. Normal histology of the uterus and fallopian tubes. In Sternberg S (ed.): Histology for pathologists, ed. 2. Philadelphia, 1997, Lippincott-Raven, pp. 879–928.

4 Hershlag A, Seifer DB, Carcangiu ML, Patton DL, Diamond MP, De Cherney AH. Salpingoscopy. Light microscopic and electron microscopic correlations (published erratum appears in Obstet Gynecol 1991 May; 77[5]: 809–10). Obstet Gynecol 1991, **77:** 399–405.

5 Hunt JL, Lynn AA. Histologic features of surgically removed fallopian tubes. Arch Pathol Lab Med 2002, **126:** 951–955.

6 Nassberg S, McKay DG, Hertig AT. Physiologic salpingitis. Am J Obstet Gynecol 1954, **67:** 130–137.

7 Rubin A, Czernobilsky B. Tubal ligation. A bacteriologic, histologic and clinical study. Obstet Gynecol 1970, **36:** 199–203.

8 Zheng W, Magid MS, Kramer EE, Chen YT. Follicle-stimulating hormone receptor is expressed in human ovarian surface epithelium and fallopian tube. Am J Pathol 1996, **148:** 47–53.

Inflammation

9 Bell DA, Mondschein M, Scully RE. Giant cell arteritis of the female genital tract. A report of three cases. Am J Surg Pathol 1986, **10:** 696–701.

10 Cheung ANY, Young RH, Scully RE. Pseudocarcinomatous hyperplasia of the fallopian tube associated with salpingitis. A report of 14 cases. Am J Surg Pathol 1994, **18:** 1125–1130.

11 David A, Garcia C-S, Czernobilsky B. Human hydrosalpinx. Histologic study and chemical composition of fluid. Am J Obstet Gynecol 1969, **105:** 400–411.

12 Elliott GB, Brody H, Elliott KA. Implications of "lipoid salpingitis." Fertil Steril 1965, **16:** 541–548.

13 Erthan Y, Zekioglu O, Ozdemir N, Sen S. Unilateral salpingitis due to enterobious vermicularis. Int J Gynecol Pathol 2000, **19:** 188–189.

14 Eschenbach DA, Buchanan TM, Pollock HM, Forsyth PS, Alexander ER, Lin JS, Wang SP, Wentworth BB, McCormack WM, Holmes KK. Polymicrobial etiology of acute pelvic inflammatory disease. N Engl J Med 1975, **29:** 166–171.

15 Fortier KJ, Haney AF. The pathologic spectrum of uterotubal junction obstruction. Obstet Gynecol 1985, **65:** 93–98.

16 Francis WAJ. Female genital tuberculosis. A review of 135 cases. J Obstet Gynaecol Br Commonw 1964, **71:** 418–428.

17 Furuya M, Murakami T, Sato O, Kikuchi K, Tanaka S, Shimizu M, Yoshiki T. Pseudoxanthomatous salpingitis of the fallopian tube: a report of four cases and a literature review. Int J Gynecol Pathol 2002, **21:** 56–59.

18 Ganesan R, Ferryman SR, Meier L, Rollason TP. Vasculitis of the female genital tract with clinicopathologic correlation: a study of 46 cases with follow-up. Int J Gynecol Pathol 2000, **19:** 258–265.

19 Henderson DN, Harkins JL, Stitt JF. Pelvic tuberculosis. Am J Obstet Gynecol 1966, **94:** 630–633.

20 McCormack WM. Pelvic inflammatory disease. N Engl J Med 1994, **330:** 115–119.

21 Mickal A, Sellmann AH, Beebe JL. Ruptured tuboovarian abscess. Am J Obstet Gynecol 1968, **100:** 432–436.

22 Nogales-Ortiz F, Tarancón I, Nogales FF Jr. The pathology of female genital tuberculosis. Obstet Gynecol 1979, **53:** 422–428.

23 Paavonen J. Pelvic inflammatory disease. From diagnosis to prevention. Dermatol Clin 1998, **16:** 747–756.

24 Pedowitz R, Bloomfield RD. Ruptured adnexal abscess (tuboovarian) with generalized peritonitis. Am J Obstet Gynecol 1964, **88:** 721–729.

25 Seidman JD, Oberer S, Bitterman P, Aisner SC. Pathogenesis of pseudoxanthomatous salpingiosis. Mod Pathol 1993, **6:** 53–55.

26 Seidman JD, Sherman ME, Bell KA, Katabuchi H, O'Leary TJ, Kurman RJ. Salpingitis, salpingoliths, and serous tumors of the ovaries: is there a connection? Int J Gynecol Pathol 2002, **21:** 101–107.

27 Sweet RL, Draper DL, Hadley WK. Etiology of acute salpingitis. Influence of episode number and duration of symptoms. Obstet Gynecol 1981, **58:** 62–68.

28 Thor AD, Young RH, Clement PB. Pathology of the fallopian tube, broad ligament, peritoneum, and pelvic soft tissues. Hum Pathol 1991, **22:** 856–867.

29 Wallace TM, Hart WR. Acute chlamydial salpingitis with ascites and adnexal mass simulating a malignant neoplasm. Int J Gynecol Pathol 1991, **10:** 394–401.

30 Washington AE, Aral SO, Wolner-Hanssen P, Grimes DA, Holmes KK. Assessing risk for pelvic inflammatory disease and its sequelae. JAMA 1991, **266:** 2581–2586.

31 Winkler B, Reumann W, Mitao M, Gallo L, Richart RM, Crum CP. Immunoperoxidase localization of chlamydial antigens in acute salpingitis. Am J Obstet Gynecol 1985, **152:** 275–278.

Torsion

32 Grosfeld JL. Torsion of normal ovary in the first two years of life. Am J Surg 1969, **117:** 726–727.

33 Hansen OH. Isolated torsion of the fallopian tube. Acta Obstet Gynecol Scand 1970, **49:** 3–6.

34 James DF, Barber HRK, Graber EA. Torsion of normal uterine adnexa in children. Report of three cases. Obstet Gynecol 1970, **35:** 226–230.

Tubal pregnancy

35 Angel E, Davis JR, Nagle RB. Immunohistochemical demonstration of placental hormones in the diagnosis of uterine versus ectopic pregnancy. Am J Clin Pathol 1985, **84:** 705–709.

36 Blaustein A, Shenker L. Vascular lesions of the uterine tube in ectopic pregnancy. Obstet Gynecol 1967, **30:** 551–555.

37 Burton JL, Lidbury EA, Gillespie AM, Tidy JA, Smith O, Lawry J, Hancock BW, Wells M. Over-diagnosis of hydatidiform mole in early tubal ectopic pregnancy. Histopathology 2001, **38:** 409–417.

38 Campello TR, Fittipaldi H, O'Valle F, Carvia RE, Nogales FF. Extrauterine (tubal) placental site nodule. Histopathology 1998, **32:** 562–565.

39 Chokroverty M, Caballes RL, Gear PE. An unruptured tubal pregnancy at term. Arch Pathol Lab Med 1986, **110**: 250–251.

39a Doss BJ, Jacques SM, Qureshi F, Ramirez NC, Lawrence WD. Extratubal secondary trophoblastic implants: clinicopathologic correlation and review of the literature. Hum Pathol 1998, **29**: 184–187.

40 Goldrath MH, Platt LD. Treatment of ectopic tubal pregnancies by laparoscopy. J Am Assoc Gynecol Laparosc 2002, **9**: 409–413.

41 Green LK, Kott ML. Histopathologic findings in ectopic tubal pregnancy. Int J Gynecol 1989, **8**: 255–262.

42 Holt VL, Daling JR, Voigt LF, McKnight B, Stergachis A, Chu J, Weiss NS. Induced abortion and the risk of subsequent ectopic pregnancy. Am J Public Health 1989, **79**: 1234–1238.

43 Jacques SM, Qureshi F, Ramirez NC, Lawrence WD. Retained trophoblastic tissue in fallopian tubes: a consequence of unsuspected ectopic pregnancies. Int J Gynecol Pathol 1998, **16**: 219–224.

44 Majmudar B, Henderson PH, Semple E. Salpingitis isthmica nodosa. A high-risk for tubal pregnancy. Obstet Gynecol 1983, **62**: 73–78.

45 Mohamed H, Maiti S, Phillips G. Laparoscopic management of ectopic pregnancy: a 5-year experience. J Obstet Gynaecol 2002, **22**: 411–414.

45a Nakyama J, Aoki D, Suga T, Akama TO, Ishizone S, Yamaguchi H, Imakawa K, Nadano D, Fazleabas AT, Katsuyama T, Nozawa S, Fukuda MN. Implantation-dependent expression of trophinin by maternal fallopian tube epithelia during tubal pregnancies: possible role of human chorionic gonadotrophin on ectopic pregnancy. Am J Pathol 2003, **163**: 2211–2219.

46 Nayar R, Snell J, Silverberg SG, Lage JM. Placental site nodule occurring in a fallopian tube. Hum Pathol 1997, **27**: 1243–1245.

47 O'Connor DM, Kurman RJ. Intermediate trophoblast in uterine curettings in the diagnosis of ectopic pregnancy. Obstet Gynecol 1988, **72**: 665–670.

48 Pauerstein CJ, Croxatto HB, Eddy CA, Ramzy I, Walters MD. Anatomy and pathology of tubal pregnancy. Obstet Gynecol 1986, **67**: 301–308.

49 Randall S, Buckley CH, Fox H. Placentation in the fallopian tube. Int J Gynecol Pathol 1987, **6**: 132–139.

50 Stock RJ. Histopathology of fallopian tubes with recurrent tubal pregnancy. Obstet Gynecol 1990, **75**: 9–14.

51 Stock RJ. Tubal pregnancy. Associated histopathology. Obstet Gynecol Clin North Am 1991, **18**: 73–94.

52 Tziortziotis DV, Bouros AC, Ziogas VS, Young RH. Clear cell hyperplasia of the fallopian tube epithelium associated with ectopic pregnancy: report of a case. Int J Gynecol Pathol 1997, **16**: 79–80.

53 Yang CP, Chow WH, Daling JR, Weiss NS, Moore DE. Does prior infertility increase the risk of tubal pregnancy? Fertil Steril 1987, **48**: 62–66.

Other non-neoplastic processes

54 Bartnik J, Powell WS, Moriber-Katz S, Amenta PS. Metaplastic papillary tumor of the fallopian tube. Case report, immunohistochemical features, and review of the literature. Arch Pathol Lab Med 1989, **113**: 545–547.

55 Benjamin CL, Beaver DC. Pathogenesis of salpingitis isthmica nodosa. Am J Clin Pathol 1951, **21**: 212–222.

56 Bransilver BR, Ferenczy A, Richart RM. Female genital tract remnants. An ultrastructural comparison of hydatid of Morgagni and mesonephric ducts and tubules. Arch Pathol 1973, **96**: 255–261.

57 Burmeister RE, Fechner RE, Franklin RR. Endosalpingiosis of the peritoneum. Obstet Gynecol 1969, **34**: 310–318.

58 Egan AJM, Russell P. Transitional (urothelial) cell metaplasia of the fallopian tube mucosa: morphological assessment of three cases. Int J Gynecol Pathol 1996, **15**: 72–76.

59 Jenkins CS, Williams SR, Schmidt GE. Salpingitis isthmica nodosa: a review of the literature, discussion of clinical significance, and consideration of patient management. Fertil Steril 1993, **60**: 599–607.

60 Lim S, Kim JY, Park K, Kim BR, Ahn G. Mullerianosis of the mesosalpinx: a case report. Int J Gynecol Pathol 2003, **22**: 209–212.

61 Milchgrub S, Sandstad J. Arias-Stella reaction in fallopian tube epithelium. A light and electron microscopic study with a review of the literature. Am J Clin Pathol 1991, **95**: 892–895.

62 Mills SE, Fechner RE. Stromal and epithelial changes in the fallopian tube following hormonal therapy. Hum Pathol 1980, **11**: 583–584.

63 Rubin IC, Lisa JR, Trinidad S. Further observations of ectopic endometrium of fallopian tube. Surg Gynecol Obstet 1956, **103**: 469–474.

64 Saffos RO, Rhatigan RM, Scully RE. Metaplastic papillary tumor of the fallopian tube – a distinctive lesion of pregnancy. Am J Clin Pathol 1980, **74**: 232–236.

64a Safneck Jr, Alguacil-Garcia A, Paraskevas M. Papillary endothelial hyperplasia of adnexal vasculature. Histopathology 1996, **28**: 157–162.

65 Samaha M, Woodruff JD. Paratubal cysts. Frequency, histogenesis, and associated clinical features. Obstet Gynecol 1985, **65**: 691–694.

66 Sheldon RS, Wilson RB, Dockerty MB. Serosal endometriosis of fallopian tubes. Am J Obstet Gynecol 1967, **99**: 882–884.

67 Stock RJ. Histopathologic changes in fallopian tubes subsequent to sterilization procedures. Int J Gynecol Pathol 1983, **2**: 13–27.

68 Teoh TB. The structure and development of Walthard nests. J Pathol Bacteriol 1953, **66**: 433–439.

69 Wittich AC. Hydatid of morgagni with torsion diagnosed during cesarean delivery. A case report. J Reprod Med 2002, **47**: 680–682.

Proliferative epithelial lesions

70 Carcangiu ML, Radice P, Manoukian S, Spatti G, Pensotti V, Crucianelli R, Gobbo M, Pasini B. Atypical epithelial proliferation in fallopian tubes from BCRA1 and BRC2 germ line mutation carriers at prophylactic oophorectomy. Int J Gynecol Pathol (in press).

71 Colgan TJ. Challenges in the early diagnosis and staging of fallopian-tube carcinomas associated with BRCA mutations. Int J Gynecol Pathol 2003, **22**: 109–120.

72 Moore SW, Enterline HT. Significance of proliferative epithelial lesions of the uterine tube. Obstet Gynecol 1975, **45**: 385–390.

73 Pickel H, Reich O, Tamussino K. Bilateral atypical hyperplasia of the fallopian tube associated with tamoxifen: a report of two cases. Int J Gynecol Pathol 1998, **17**: 284–285.

74 Piek JM, van Diest PJ, Zweemer RP, Jansen JW, Poort-Keesom RJ, Menko FH, Gille JJ, Jongsma AP, Pals G, Kenemans P, Verheijen RH. Dysplastic changes in prophylactically removed fallopian tubes of women predisposed to developing ovarian cancer. J Pathol 2001, **195**: 451–456.

75 Robey SS, Silva EG. Epithelial hyperplasia of the fallopian tube. Its association with serous borderline tumors of the ovary. Int J Gynecol Pathol 1989, **8**: 214–220.

76 Stern J, Buscema J, Parmley T, Woodruff JD, Rosenshein NB. Atypical epithelial proliferations in the fallopian tube. Am J Obstet Gynecol 1981, **140**: 309–312.

77 Woodruff JD, Pauerstein CJ. The fallopian tube. Structure, function, pathology, and management. Baltimore, 1969, Williams & Wilkins.

78 Yanai-Inbar I, Silverberg SG. Mucosal epithelial proliferation of the fallopian tube: prevalence, clinical associations, and optimal strategy for histopathologic assessment. Int J Gynecol Pathol 2000, **19**: 139–144.

79 Yanai-Inbar I, Siriaunkgul S, Silverberg SG. Mucosal epithelial proliferation of the fallopian tube. A particular association with

ovarian serous tumor of low malignant potential? Int J Gynecol Pathol 1995, **14**: 107–113.

Carcinoma

80 Alvarado-Cabrero I, Navani SS, Young RH, Scully RE. Tumors of the fimbriated end of the fallopian tube: a clinicopathologic analysis of 20 cases, including nine carcinomas. Int J Gynecol Pathol 1997, **16**: 189–196.

81 Alvarado-Cabrero I, Young RH, Vamvakas EC, Scully RE. Carcinoma of the fallopian tube: a clinicopathological study of 105 cases with observations on staging and prognostic factors. Gynecol Oncol 1999, **72**: 367–379.

82 Aziz S, Kuperstein G, Rosen B, Cole D, Nedelcu R, McLaughlin J, Narod SA. A genetic epidemiological study of carcinoma of the fallopian tube. Gynecol Oncol 2001, **80**: 341–345.

83 Baekelandt M, Jorunn Nesbakken A, Kristensen GB, Tropè CG, Abeler VM. Carcinoma of the fallopian tube. Cancer 2000, **89**: 2076–2084.

84 Cheung A, So K, Ngan H, Wong L. Primary squamous cell carcinoma of fallopian tube. Int J Gynecol Pathol 1994, **13**: 92–95.

85 Daya D, Young RH, Scully RE. Endometrioid carcinoma of the fallopian tube resembling an adnexal tumor of probable wolffian origin. A report of six cases. Int J Gynecol Pathol 1992, **11**: 122–130.

86 De la Torre FJ, Rojo F, Garcia A. Clear cells carcinoma of fallopian tubes associated with tubal endometriosis. Case report and review. Arch Gynecol Obstet 2002, **266**: 172–174.

87 Demopoulos RI, Aronov R, Mesia A. Clues to the pathogenesis of fallopian tube carcinoma: a morphological and immunohistochemical case control study. Int J Gynecol Pathol 2001, **20**: 128–132.

88 Eddy GL, Copeland LJ, Gershenson DM, Atkinson EN, Wharton JT, Rutledge FN. Fallopian tube carcinoma. Obstet Gynecol 1984, **64**: 546–552.

89 Hirai Y, Kaku S, Teshima H, Shimizu Y, Chen JT, Hamada T, Fujimoto I, Yamauchi K, Sakamoto A, Hasumi K, et al. Clinical study of primary carcinoma of the fallopian tube. Experience with 15 cases. Gynecol Oncol 1989, **34**: 20–26.

90 Koshiyama M, Konishi I, Yoshida M, Wang D-P, Mandal M, Mori T, Fuji S. Transitional cell carcinoma of the fallopian tube. A light and electron microscopic study. Int J Gynecol Pathol 1994, **13**: 175–180.

91 Lehto L. Cytology of the human fallopian tube. Acta Obstet Gynecol Scand 1963, **42**(Suppl 14): 1–95.

92 McMurray EH, Jacobs AJ, Perez CA, Camel HM, Kao M-S, Galakatos A. Carcinoma of the fallopian tube. Management and sites of failure. Cancer 1986, **58**: 2070–2075.

93 Navani SS, Alvarado-Cabrero I, Young RH, Scully RE. Endometrioid carcinoma of the fallopian tube: a clinicopathologic analysis of 26 cases. Gynecol Oncol 1996, **63**: 371–378.

94 Paley PJ, Swisher EM, Garcia RL, Agoff SN, Greer BE, Peters KL, Goff BA. Occult cancer of the fallopian tube in BRCA 1 germline mutation carriers at prophylactic oophorectomy: a case for recommending hysterectomy at surgical prophylaxis. Gynecol Oncol 2001, **80**: 176–180.

95 Podratz KC, Podczaski ES, Gaffey TA, O'Brien PC, Schray MF, Malkasian GD. Primary carcinoma of the fallopian tube. Am J Obstet Gynecol 1986, **154**: 1319–1326.

96 Roberts JA, Lifshitz S. Primary adenocarcinoma of the fallopian tube. Gynecol Oncol 1982, **13**: 301–308.

97 Rose PG, Piver MS, Tsukada Y. Fallopian tube cancer. The Roswell Park experience. Cancer 1990, **66**: 2661–2667.

98 Rosenblatt KA, Weiss NS, Schwartz SM. Incidence of malignant fallopian tube tumors. Gynecol Oncol 1989, **35**: 236–239.

99 Schiller HM, Silverberg SG. Staging and prognosis in primary carcinoma of the fallopian tube. Cancer 1971, **28**: 389–395.

100 Takashina T, Ito E, Kudo R. Cytologic diagnosis of primary tubal cancer. Acta Cytol (Baltimore) 1984, **29**: 367–372.

101 Talamo TS, Bender BL, Ellis LD, Scioscia EA. Adenocarcinoma of the fallopian tube. An ultrastructural study. Virchows Arch [A] 1982, **397**: 363–368.

102 Uehira K, Hashimoto H, Tsuneyoshi M, Enjoji M. Transitional cell carcinoma pattern in primary carcinoma of the fallopian tube. Cancer 1993, **72**: 2447–2456.

103 Voet RL, Lifshitz S. Primary clear cell adenocarcinoma of the fallopian tube. Light microscopic and ultrastructural findings. Int J Gynecol Pathol 1982, **1**: 292–298.

103a Zhang PJ, Williams E, Pasha T, Acs G. WTI is expressed in serous, but not in endometrioid, clear cell or mucinous carcinomas of the peritoneum, fallopian tube, ovaries and endometrium (Abstract). Mod Pathol 2003, **16**: 216a.

104 Zheng W, Wolf S, Kramer EE, Cox KA, Hoda SA. Borderline papillary serous tumor of the fallopian tube. Am J Surg Pathol 1996, **20**: 30–35.

Other tumors

105 Carlson J, Ackerman B, Wheeler J. Malignant mixed mullerian tumor of the fallopian tube. Cancer 1993, **71**: 187–192.

106 Gersell DJ, King TC. Papillary cystadenoma of the mesosalpinx in von Hippel Lindau disease. Am J Surg Pathol 1988, **12**: 145–149.

107 Gisser SD. Obstructing fallopian tube papilloma. Int J Gynecol Pathol 1986, **5**: 179–182.

108 Griffith LM, Carcangiu ML. Sex cord tumor with annular tubules associated with endometriosis of the fallopian tube. Am J Clin Pathol 1991, **96**: 259–262.

109 Hoda SA, Huvos AG. Struma salpingis associated with struma ovarii. Am J Surg Pathol 1993, **17**: 1187–1189.

110 Horn T, Jao W, Keh PC. Benign cystic teratoma of the fallopian tube (letter to the Editor). Arch Pathol Lab Med 1983, **107**: 48.

111 Imachi M, Tsukamoto N, Shigematsu T, Watanabe T, Uehira K, Amada S, Umezu T, Nakano H. Malignant mixed Mullerian tumor of the fallopian tube. Report of two cases and review of literature. Gynecol Oncol 1992, **47**: 114–124.

112 Jackson-York GL, Ramzy I. Synchronous papillary mucinous adenocarcinoma of the endocervix and fallopian tubes. Int J Gynecol Pathol 1991, **10**: 394–401.

113 Kanbour AI, Burgess F, Salazar H. Intramural adenofibroma of the fallopian tube. Light and electron microscopy. Cancer 1973, **31**: 1433–1439.

114 Mackay B, Bennington JL, Skoglund RW. The adenomatoid tumor. Fine structural evidence for a mesothelial origin. Cancer 1971, **27**: 109–115.

115 Manes JL, Taylor HB. Carcinosarcoma and mixed müllerian tumors of the fallopian tube. Report of four cases. Cancer 1976, **38**: 1687–1693.

116 Mazur MT, Hsueh S, Gersell DJ. Metastases to the female genital tract. Analysis of 325 cases. Cancer 1984, **53**: 1978–1984.

117 Muntz HG, Rutgers JL, Tarraza HM, Fuller AF Jr. Carcinosarcomas and mixed Mullerian tumors of the fallopian tube. Gynecol Oncol 1989, **34**: 109–115.

118 Riggs JA, Wainer AS, Hahn GA, Farell MD. Extrauterine tubal choriocarcinoma. Am J Obstet Gynecol 1964, **88**: 637–641.

119 Salazar H, Kanbour A, Burgess F. Ultrastructure and observations on the histogenesis of mesotheliomas "adenomatoid tumors" of the female genital tract. Cancer 1972, **29**: 141–152.

120 Seidman JD. Mucinous lesions of the fallopian tube. A report of seven cases. Am J Surg Pathol 1994, **18**: 1205–1212.

121 Shen T, Zhuang Z, Gersell DJ, Tavassoli FA. Allelic deletion of VHL gene detected in papillary tumors of the broad ligament, epididymis, and retroperitoneum in von Hippel-Lindau disease patients. Int J Surg Pathol 2001, **8**: 207–212.

122 van Dijk CM, Kooijman CD, van Lindert AC. Malignant mixed mullerian tumor of the fallopian tube. Histopathology 1990, **16**: 300–302.

123 Youngs LA, Taylor HB. Adenomatoid tumors of the uterus and fallopian tube. Am J Clin Pathol 1967, **48:** 537–545.

123a Li S, Zimmerman RL, LiVolsi VA. Mixed malignant germ cell tumor of the fallopian tube. Int J Gynecol Pathol 1999, **18:** 183–185.

Tumors and tumorlike conditions of broad and round ligaments

124 Ahmed AA, Swan RW, Owen A, Kraus FT, Patrick F. Uterus-like mass arising in the broad ligament: a metaplasia or mullerian duct anomaly? Int J Gynecol Pathol 1998, **16:** 279–281.

125 Altaras MM, Jaffe R, Corduba M, Holtzinger M, Bahary C. Primary paraovarian cystadenocarcinoma. Clinical and management aspects and literature review. Gynecol Oncol 1990, **38:** 268–272.

126 Aslani M, Ahn GH, Scully RE. Serous papillary cystadenoma of borderline malignancy of broad ligament. A report of 25 cases. Int J Gynecol Pathol 1988, **7:** 131–138.

127 Aslani M, Scully RE. Primary carcinoma of the broad ligament. Report of four cases and review of the literature. Cancer 1989, **64:** 1540–1545.

128 Bakotic BW, Cabello-Inchausti B, Willis IH, Suster S. Clear-cell epithelioid leiomyoma of the round ligament. Mod Pathol 1999, **12:** 912–918.

129 Bell DA, Woodruff JM, Scully RE. Ependymoma of the broad ligament. A report of two cases. Am J Surg Pathol 1984, **8:** 203–209.

130 Gardner GH, Greene RR, Peckham B. Tumors of the broad ligament. Am J Obstet Gynecol 1957, **73:** 536–555.

131 Honore LH, Manickavel V. Striated muscle heteroplasia in the uterine round ligament. A report of 30 cases. Arch Pathol Lab Med 1991, **115:** 223–225.

132 Kariminejad MH, Scully RE. Female adnexal tumor of probable wolffian origin. A distinctive pathologic entity. Cancer 1973, **31:** 671–677.

133 Korn WT, Schatzki SC, Di Sciullo AJ, Scully RE. Papillary cystadenoma of the broad ligament in von Hippel-Lindau disease. Am J Obstet Gynecol 1990, **163:** 596–598.

134 Nuovo MA, Nuovo GJ, Smith D, Lewis SH. Benign mesenchymoma of the round ligament. A report of two cases with immunohistochemistry. Am J Clin Pathol 1990, **93:** 421–424.

135 Rahilly MA, Williams AR, Krausz T, al Nafussi A. Female adnexal tumour of probable Wolffian origin. A clinicopathological and immunohistochemical study of three cases. Histopathology 1995, **26:** 69–74.

136 Werness BA, Guccion JG. Tumor of the broad ligament in von Hippel-Lindau disease of probable mullerian origin. Int J Gynecol Pathol 1998, **16:** 282–285.

Ovary

Normal anatomy

The ovaries are paired pelvic organs located on the sides of the uterus close to the lateral pelvic wall, behind the broad ligament and anterior to the rectum. They are connected to the broad ligament by the mesovarium (a double fold of peritoneum), to the uterine cornu by the ovarian (or utero-ovarian) ligament, and to the lateral pelvic wall by the infundibulopelvic (or suspensory) ligament. During the reproductive period, their average size is $4 \times 2 \times 1$ cm, and their average weight is 5 to 8 g; after menopause, they shrink to one half or less of this size.

The ovarian lymph vessels drain to large trunks that form a plexus at the hilus, from which they travel through the mesovarium to drain into the para-aortic nodes; others drain into the internal iliac, external iliac, interaortic, common iliac, and inguinal nodes.

The ovary is covered by a single layer of modified mesothelium variously known as *surface, celomic,* or *germinal epithelium.* This epithelium is immunoreactive for keratin, EMA, Ber-EP4, CA-125, desmoplakin, vimentin, estrogen and progesterone receptors, epidermal growth factor, and FSH.[3,13] The close embryologic and functional relationship of this structure with the lining epithelium of the müllerian ducts (i.e., the progenitor of the tubal, endometrial, and endocervical mucosa) probably explains the marked similarities among these tissues and the tumors arising from them. Indeed, the entire pelvic and lower abdominal mesothelium and the subjacent mesenchyme of females are referred to as the *secondary müllerian system.*

The *ovarian stroma* is divided into a cortical and a medullary region, but the boundaries between them are indistinct. It is composed mainly of spindle-shaped stromal cells resembling fibroblasts, typically arranged in whorls or a storiform pattern. The cells may contain cytoplasmic lipid and are surrounded by a dense network of reticulin fibers. Some of these cells have myoid ("myofibroblastic") features and exhibit immunoreactivity for smooth muscle actin and desmin.[4,8] Foci of smooth muscle hyperplasia may be found, most often in perimenopausal or postmenopausal women.[5] Other cells that may be found in the ovarian stroma are luteinized stromal cells (singly or in small nests, mainly in the medulla), so-called "enzymatically active" stromal cells, decidual cells, bundles of smooth muscle, nests of cells resembling endometrial stromal cells, mature fat cells, and neuroendocrine cells.[1,6]

The life cycle of the *ovarian follicle* includes primordial, maturing (primary, secondary, tertiary, and graafian), and atretic, together with corpora lutea and corpora albicantia for those that have reached full maturation. Primordial follicles contain germ cells that have originated from the yolk sac endoderm and migrated into the ovary, where they develop into oogonia and oocytes.[2] These remain arrested at the dictyate stage of mitotic prophase at the time of birth, entering an interphase period at the time of follicular maturation prior to ovulation. The maturing follicle is composed of the oocyte, the granulosa layer, and the two theca layers. *Granulosa cells* lack a reticulum around them and are immunoreactive for vimentin, keratin, and desmoplakin. They feature small rosettelike formations known as Call–Exner bodies, which contain at their center a deeply eosinophilic filamentous material consisting of excess basal lamina. Whether the granulosa cells derive from the ovarian stroma or from the *sex cords* (structures that first appear beneath the surface epithelium of the gonadal anlage and later converge toward the hilus of the gland) is still unresolved. The stroma-derived *theca cells* form an internal layer (which is typically luteinized) and an external layer (which is very cellular and can simulate a neoplastic process when cut tangentially). Internal theca cells are an important site of sex steroid production, as determined indirectly by the immunohistochemical detection of enzymes involved in steroid hormone biosynthesis.[9,10]

The mature *corpus luteum* is a 1.5 to 2.5 cm round yellow structure with lobulated outlines and a cystic center. Both the granulosa and the theca cells that form it show prominent luteinization. Morphologic criteria for the dating of the corpus luteum have been established.[11] The corpus luteum of pregnancy is characterized by its larger size, bright yellow color, prominent central cavity, and the presence of hyaline droplets and calcification.[2]

At the ovarian hilus, there are clusters of cells analogous to testicular Leydig cells known as *ovarian hilus cells*. They are closely associated with large hilar veins and lymph vessels and may form nodular protrusions within their lumina. They also exhibit an intimate relationship with the nonmedullated nerves of the region.[3,7] They may contain Reinke's crystalloids; lipids, and lipochrome pigment. Hyperplasia of these cells is found following the administration of chorionic gonadotropin, in pregnancy, and in the presence of choriocarcinoma.[3]

The *rete ovarii*, present in the ovarian hilus, represents the ovarian counterpart of the rete testis. It consists of a network of clefts, tubules, cysts, and papillae lined by an epithelium of variable height and surrounded by a cuff of spindle cell stroma. This epithelium is immunoreactive for keratin and CA-125.[12]

Walthard cell nests may be cystic or solid. They are located in the mesovarium, in the adjacent mesosalpinx, or within the ovarian hilus, and have a lining of urothelial appearance (sometimes mucin-producing) which is probably of mesothelial nature.

The previous description mainly pertains to the fully developed ovary in women of child-bearing age. The many modifications exhibited by the prepubertal and postmenopausal ovary are beyond the scope of this chapter. It should be mentioned, however, that prominent cystic follicles are normally seen during the first few months of life and at puberty, and that the shrunken postmenopausal ovary ("ovarium gyratum") has thick-walled medullary and hilar vessels (which should not be mistaken for hemangiomas). These atrophic ovaries may also contain clinically inconsequential granulomas and hyaline scars.[2]

The immunohistochemical profiles of the various cell components of the ovary are discussed in connection with the tumors of the respective structures.

Gonadal dysgenesis

Patients with gonadal dysgenesis have abnormally developed gonads and infantile sexual development. The conditions mentioned here are mainly those associated with an abnormal sex chromosome constitution, to be distinguished from those such as male and female pseudohermaphroditism, persistent müllerian duct syndrome (due to a defect in the müllerian inhibiting substance system), and end-organ defects.[25]

Sometimes, gonadal tissue is biopsied or removed in the course of evaluation of these malformations.[27,28]

Klinefelter's syndrome is usually characterized by the karyotype 47,XXY, and is further discussed in Chapter 18.

In patients with **gonadal dysgenesis**, either **"pure"** (with a 46,XX or 46,XY karyotype) or associated with the somatic features of **Turner's syndrome** (with a 45,XO karyotype), both gonads are represented by a streak of fibrous tissue that vaguely resembles ovarian stroma (Fig. 19.210).[18,29] These patients do not seem to have an increased incidence of gonadal tumors,[30] but various types of nongonadal neoplasms (such as atypical polypoid adenomyoma of uterus, leukemia, and soft tissue tumors) have been reported in patients with the syndrome.[15,22] Also, several cases of Turner's syndrome have been reported in association with endometrial adenocarcinoma; in some of these, prolonged estrogen therapy had been administered.[21]

In **mixed gonadal dysgenesis** (usually characterized by a 45,X/46,XY or 46,XY phenotype), one gonad is represented by a streak gonad or a streak testis and a contralateral testis (that is typically cryptorchid) or bilateral streak-testis.[14] Individuals with this condition are

Table 19.3 Disorders of sexual development*

Syndrome	Gonad	Ducts	External genitalia	Puberty	Barr	Chromosomes	FSH	17-KS	Estrogen	Remarks
								Hormones		
Klinefelter's	Testis with hyalinized sclerotic tubules and clumped Leydig cells	Male	Male	Normal penis with small testes; partial androgen lack	"True" are chromatin positive, a few are 2+ or 3+	All chromatin positive have 2 Xs and a Y in at least some cells. Chromatin negative are 46,XY	⇈	N or ↑	N	Affects 1:400 newborn males
Turner's	Streak gonad with whorled stroma	Female	Female	No pubertal development; rare cases show mild virilization	50% chromatin negative	Second sex chromosome missing or abnormal in some or all of the cells	⇈	↓	↓	1:7000 newborns, more common in abortuses; short stature
True hermaphrodite	Ovary and testis	All have uterus, most have tubes too, a few have vasa	Ambiguous but 80% favor the male	80% have gynecomastia, 50% menstruate	80% chromatin positive	60% are 46,XX in blood cells only; Y present in most of the others	N	N	N	
Mixed gonadal dysgenesis	Streak plus testis or tumor	Female; vas found occasionally	Vary from female (often with clitoromegaly) to male with hypospadias to normal male	Virilization, sometimes complete; breast development only with tumors	Chromatin negative	Almost all are mosaics including XO stem; many have Y-bearing stem as well	↑	N	?	
Dysgenetic male pseudohermaphroditism	Dysgenetic testis	Mixed male and/or female	Variably virilized	Rarely patients may be fertile	Chromatin negative	Some are XO/XY	↑	N	?	
Familial male pseudohermaphroditism that ranges from testicular feminization to	Immature infertile testis	No uterus, ± rudimentary vas	Female with short, blind vagina	Breasts develop but sexual hair is missing	Chromatin negative	46,XY	↑ or N	↑ or N	N	Sex-linked recessive or sex-limited autosomal dominant
Reifenstein's syndrome	Infertile testis	Male	Male with hypospadias ± cleft scrotum	Androgen lack is evident in incomplete virilization	Chromatin negative	46,XY	↑ or N	↑ or N	?	
Female pseudohermaphroditism 1. Congenital adrenal hyperplasia	Ovary	Female	Variably virilized	Amenorrhea with virilization	Chromatin positive	46,XX	N	⇈	N	Autosomal recessive
2. Nonadrenal	Ovary	Female	Variably virilized	Normal	Chromatin positive	46,XX	N	N	N	Consider maternal exposure to progestins or androgens

From Federman DD. Abnormal sexual development. A genetic and endocrine approach to differential diagnosis. Philadelphia, 1967, W.B. Saunders.
*The summaries under the several headings are necessarily brief; the text should be consulted for details, qualifications, and crucial exceptions.
↑ = Increased; ↑↑ = markedly increased; ↓ = decreased; N = normal.

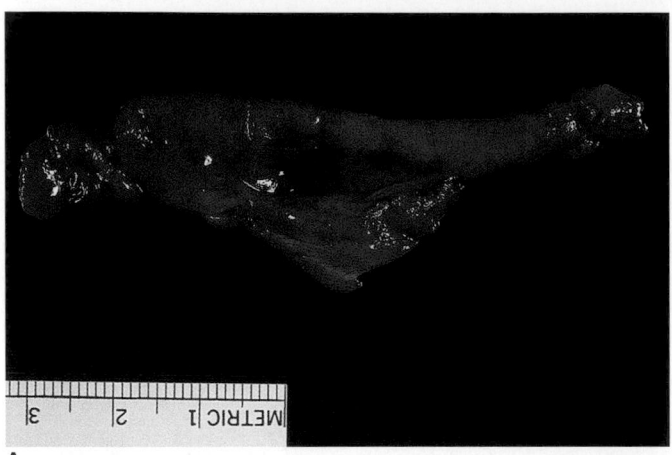

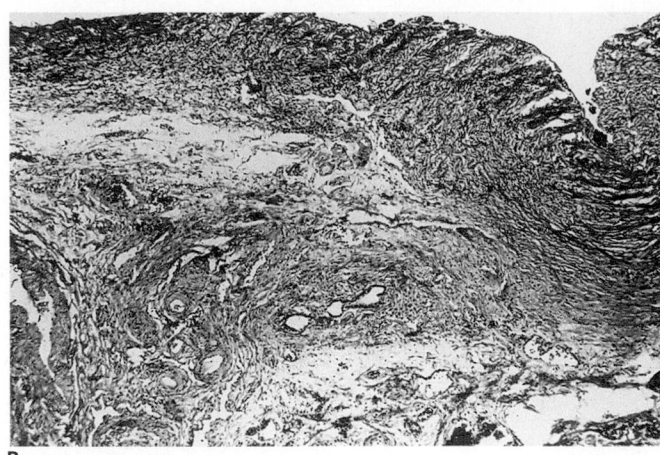

Fig. 19.210 Streak gonad in Turner's syndrome: **A**, gross appearance; **B**, microscopic appearance.

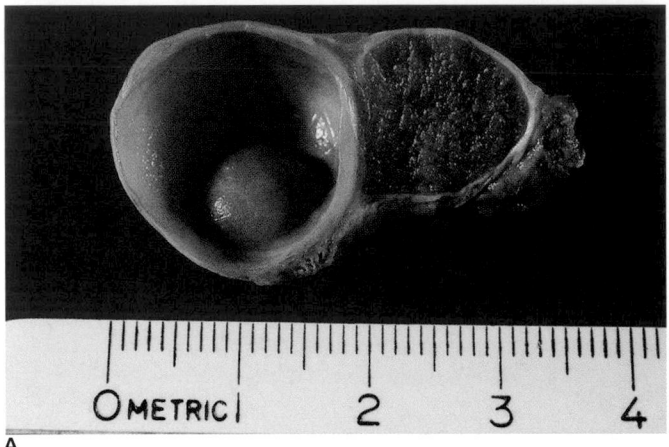

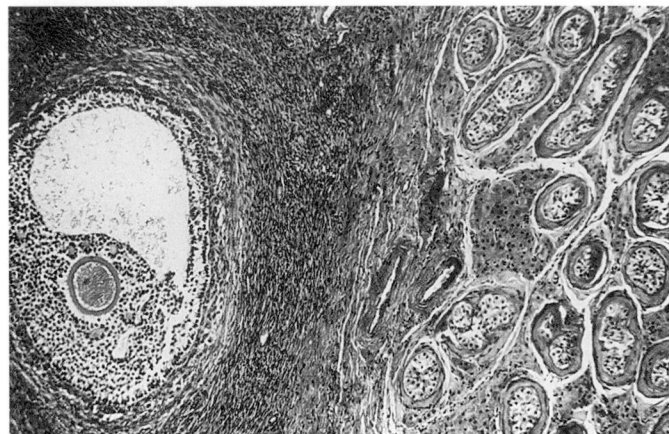

Fig. 19.211 A and **B**, Ovotestis in true hermaphroditism. **A**, Gross appearance. The testicular component is represented by the solid nodule, whereas the ovarian component has a largely cystic appearance. **B**, Microscopic appearance.

particularly prone to the development of gonadoblastomas, a complication prevented by early removal of the gonads[26] (see p. 1704). The tumors may totally obliterate the testicular elements and thus lead to an incorrect typing of the dysgenesis.

True hermaphrodites may have ovotestes containing both ova and immature seminiferous tubules or other combinations of ovary and testis[16,19,20] (Fig. 19.211). The most common karyotypes are 46,XX (60%), 46,XY (12%), and mosaic (28%). Multiple tumors can occur in these gonads.[24]

The familial syndrome of **testicular feminization** is the most common type of male pseudohermaphroditism. It occurs in individuals with a normal male chromosome constitution with an end-organ defect (androgen insensibility). It is characterized by the presence of several well-developed female secondary sex characteristics. These patients consult a gynecologist because of amenorrhea or sterility. They are found to have a vagina, no uterus, and bilateral cryptorchid testes. The latter often contain nodular masses of immature tubules that should not be confused with Sertoli–Leydig cell tumor[17,23] (Fig. 19.212). The syndrome is of further clinical importance because of the eventual occurrence of malignant tumors in the cryptorchid testes of approximately 9% of these

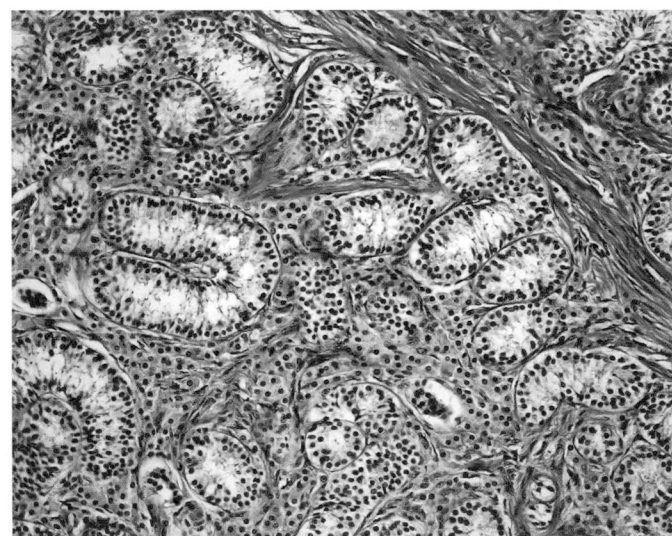

Fig. 19.212 Immature testicular tubules in testicular feminization syndrome.

patients. For this reason, the testes should be removed after puberty and supplemental estrogen therapy given. A classification of disorders of sexual development is presented in Table 19.3.

Cysts, stromal hyperplasia, and other non-neoplastic lesions

Ovarian diseases of surgical importance can be broadly divided into non-neoplastic cysts, inflammations, and neoplasms. Non-neoplastic cysts are unfortunately too commonly seen as surgical specimens. It has been said that if the ovaries were placed externally, their removal would be undertaken with more hesitation. The general surgeon exploring the abdomen may find a mildly cystic or nodular ovary in an otherwise normal abdominal cavity and remove it with the hope that a pathologic process will be found to justify the patient's symptoms and the surgery. More often than not, the microscopic diagnosis will be that of "cystic follicle" or "mature corpus luteum," but then it will be too late to replace the organ. Realizing that the ovary is normally a partially cystic structure and that the risk of carcinoma developing in these cystic structures is negligible should help avoid many of these excisions.

Inclusion cysts ("germinal inclusion cysts") are common in older women; they are generally small and multiple and have no clinical significance. Most of them probably arise from invaginations of the surface epithelium, with subsequent loss of the connection with the surface[35] (Fig. 19.213A). Microscopically, they are lined by a flattened, cuboidal, or columnar epithelium; tubal metaplasia is frequent (Fig. 19.213B). Psammoma bodies may be seen in their lumen or in the adjacent stroma.

Follicular cysts form by distention of developing or atretic follicles and usually do not exceed 10 cm in diameter (Fig. 19.214). It has been proposed that cystic follicular structures be designated as (normal) cystic follicles when measuring less than 2.5 cm and as follicular cysts when exceeding this diameter. The latter may occur at any age from infancy to menopause and are asymptomatic in the majority of cases. Occasionally, twisting of the pedicle occurs, with the resulting hemorrhagic infarct. In children, the cysts may be seen in conjunction with precocious puberty.[31,70] During reproductive life, they may be associated with endometrial hyperplasia and metrorrhagia.[57] The cyst fluid may contain estrogens.

The cyst wall is lined by theca with or without an inner granulosa layer (Fig. 19.215). The theca layer is frequently luteinized. The granulosa layer may be luteinized after puberty but not before. **Multiple luteinized follicular cysts** (theca-lutein cysts, hyperreactio luteinalis) are common in cases of hydatidiform mole and choriocarcinoma but also have been seen in twin pregnancies and, exceptionally, in uncomplicated single pregnancies[71] (Fig. 19.216). **Large solitary luteinized follicular cyst** is a rare lesion presenting during pregnancy and puerperium, unaccompanied by endocrine abnormalities. The median diameter of the cyst is 25 cm.[39]

Marked focal atypia is often seen in the luteinized cells of this lesion.[38]

Polycystic (sclerocystic) ovaries are characterized by multiple follicular cysts or cystic follicles with varying degrees of luteinization of the theca interna, covered by a dense fibrous capsule[68] (Fig. 19.217). Various clinical syn-

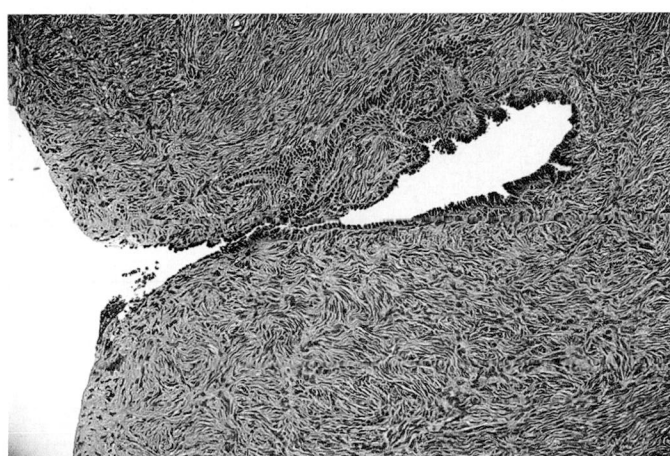

A

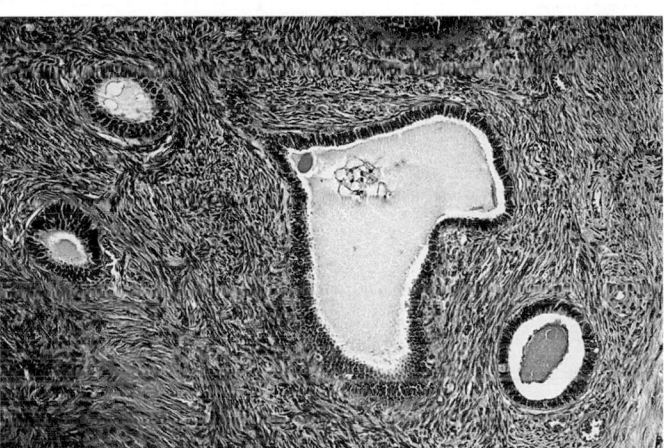

B

Fig. 19.213 A and **B**, Ovarian inclusion cysts. **A**, Cyst being formed through invagination of the surface epithelium. **B**, Multiple inclusion cysts within ovarian cortex. The lining is similar to that of the surface epithelium but tends to be taller and more prominent.

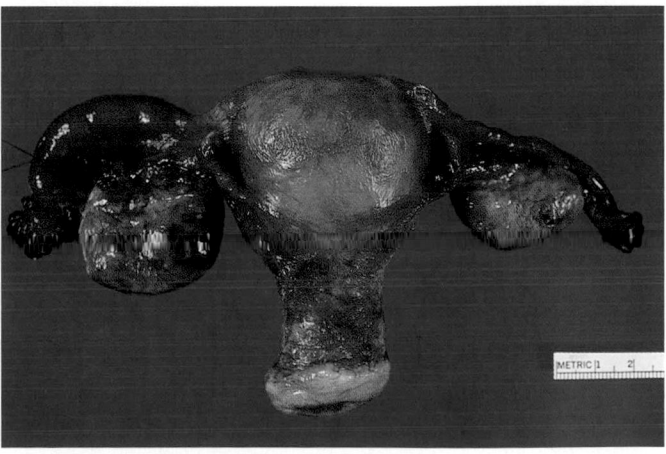

Fig. 19.214 Outer appearance of bilateral ovarian follicular cysts.

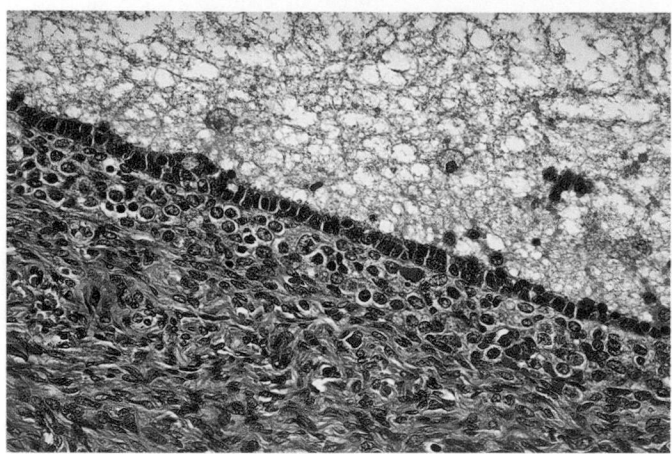

Fig. 19.215 Microscopic appearance of follicular cyst. A single layer of granulosa cells is resting on a thick theca layer.

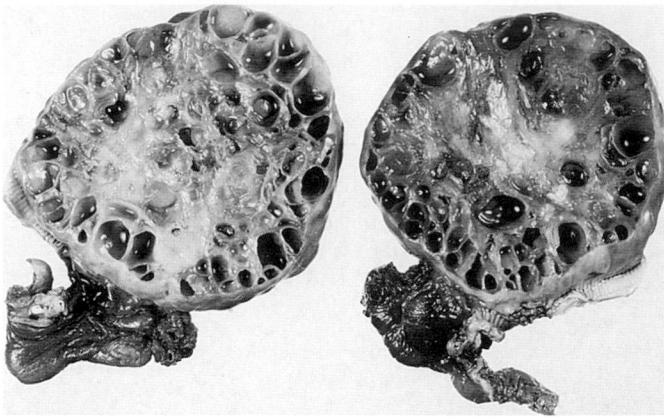

Fig. 19.216 Marked bilateral ovarian enlargement due to multiple theca–lutein cysts associated with normal pregnancy. The changes were misinterpreted as representing neoplasms and both ovaries were excised.

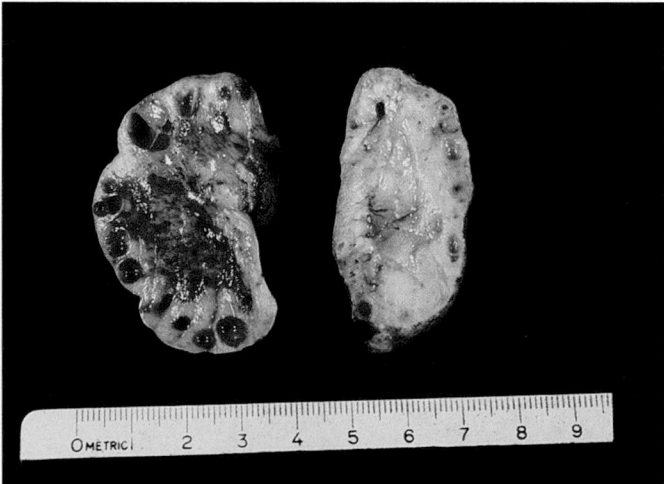

Fig. 19.217 Outer aspect and cut surface of ovary in a patient with Stein–Leventhal syndrome. Note the numerous follicular cysts beneath the ovarian surface and the absence of corpus luteum.

dromes may develop in patients with polycystic ovaries, including Stein–Leventhal syndrome (characterized by amenorrhea and sterility), so-called "metropathia hemorrhagica" (typically accompanied by endometrial hyperplasia), and frank virilism. These syndromes tend to overlap considerably, as do the pathologic findings.[45] The pathogenesis of Stein–Leventhal syndrome is poorly understood,[48,56] the issue being complicated by the fact that there is no consensus on its definition.[33] Some authors have proposed that it is a genetic disease, based on the occasional familial clustering and the apparently aberrant biochemical and molecular phenotype of the ovarian stromal cells in culture.[52] These patients have "masculinizing" pituitary and ovarian responses to stimulation by the specific gonadotropin-releasing hormone agonist nafarelin, suggesting that the regulation of the ovarian 17-hydroxylase and C-17,20-lyase activities is abnormal.[34] Dysregulation of 11β-hydroxysteroid dehydrogenase, causing increased oxidation of cortisol to cortisone, has also been documented.[64]

In general, the ovaries of patients with Stein–Leventhal syndrome have the features of polycystic ovaries just described. Corpora lutea and corpora albicantia are almost always absent. Residua of atretic follicles should not be misinterpreted as corpora albicantia. Rarely, typical polycystic ovaries associated with the clinical features of the Stein–Leventhal syndrome have been found associated with congenital adrenal hyperplasia and ovarian neoplasms.[53,55,73] Polycystic ovaries have also been observed in association with primary hypothyroidism.[54]

Most patients with Stein–Leventhal syndrome will respond favorably, with restoration of the menstrual cycle, to medical treatment with cortisone or clomiphene citrate.[56] Recently, metformin (an oral hypoglycemic agent) has been advocated because of the frequent association of polycystic ovaries with hyperinsulinemia.[32] Wedge resection of the ovary, regarded for many years as the standard therapy for this condition, is rarely if ever carried out nowadays. The endometrium of patients with Stein–Leventhal syndrome is usually hyperplastic, sometime markedly so. Exceptionally, an endometrial carcinoma develops against this background, the tumor being typically well-differentiated and superficial.[41,67]

Stromal hyperplasia is characterized by a diffuse or nodular proliferation of plump ovarian cortical stromal cells encroaching on the medulla.[36] Patchy luteinization of these cells may be present; when extensive, terms such as *(stromal) hyperthecosis, diffuse thecomatosis,* or *stromal luteinization* have been employed (Fig. 19.218). Stromal luteomas and thecomas may develop against this background (see p. 1695). Hyperthecosis may be associated with estrogenic or androgenic effects, obesity, hypertension, and an abnormal glucose tolerance test or even frank diabetes.[37] The onset of symptoms may be abrupt, thus simulating a virilizing ovarian tumor. Immuno-

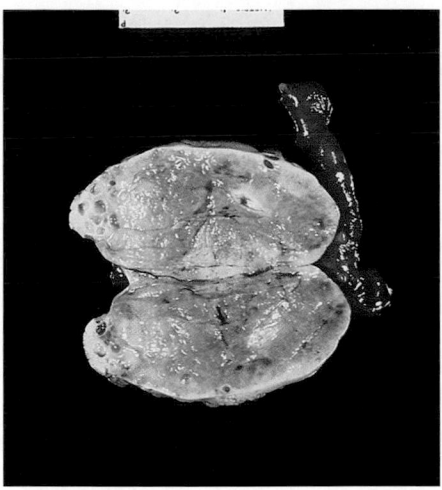

A

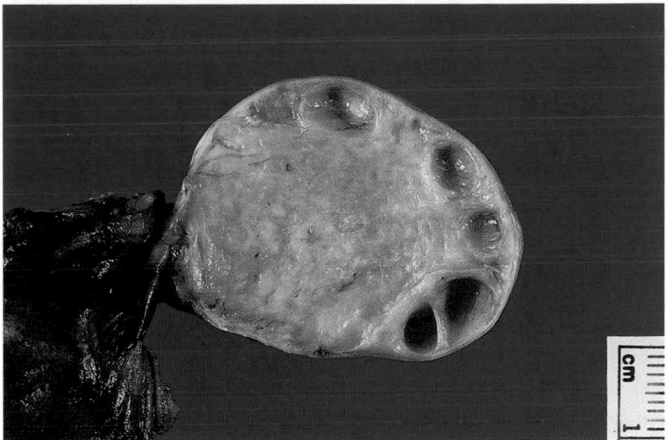

Fig. 19.219 Ovary showing a combination of multiple follicular cysts and stromal hyperplasia, providing support for a pathogenetic link between the two processes.

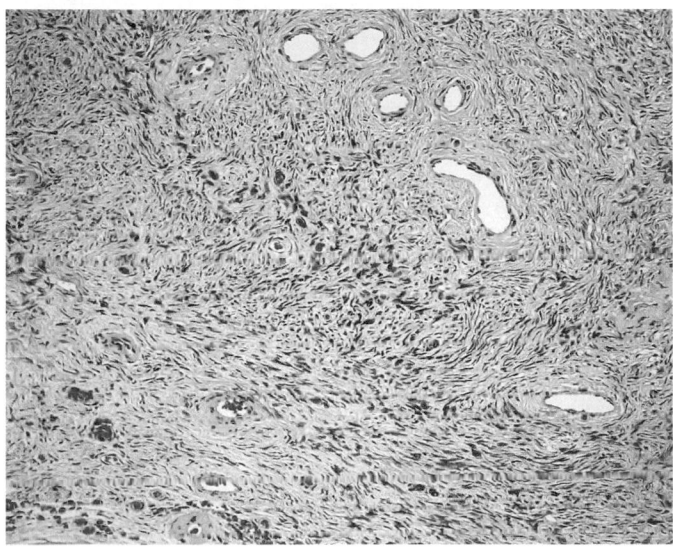

B

Fig. 19.218 A and B, Ovarian stromal hyperplasia. A, Gross appearance. The cut surface is solid and has a yellowish hue. B, Microscopic appearance. The ovarian stroma is hypercellular and slightly pleomorphic.

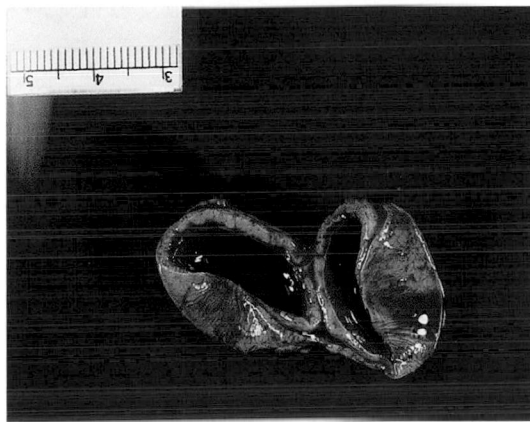

Fig. 19.220 Gross appearance of corpus luteum cyst. The luminal content is typically hemorrhagic.

histochemical studies have shown androgen production by the luteinized stromal cells, suggesting that estrogenic effects in these cases are mediated through peripheral aromatization of these androgens.[66]

The boundaries between polycystic disease and stromal hyperplasia are ill-defined[49,68] (Fig. 19.219). However, typical stromal hyperplasia lacks cysts and is usually more refractory to therapy.

Corpus luteum cysts are single and usually less than 6 cm in diameter. They may develop at the end of the menstrual cycle or may occur in pregnancy (Fig. 19.220). The cyst wall is composed of luteinized granulosa and theca cell layers. Hyaline bodies and foci of calcification may be found in the cysts associated with pregnancy. The fluid content is often bloody. If the cyst ruptures, hemorrhage into the peritoneal cavity occurs (sometimes over 500 ml), and an erroneous diagnosis of ruptured ectopic

pregnancy may be made.[46] It should be remembered that the corpus luteum is normally a cystic structure. The arbitrary diameter of 2.5 cm has been proposed to distinguish the (normal) cystic corpus luteum from a corpus luteum cyst, in a manner analogous to that employed for follicle-related cystic formations.

Ectopic decidual reaction can occur in the ovary during pregnancy and occasionally even in the absence of current or recent pregnancy. A functioning corpus luteum that has undergone destruction is present in most instances.[62]

So-called **luteomas of pregnancy** are yellow or orange solid nodules that may reach sizable proportions[38] (Fig. 19.221). They have been typically encountered during cesarean section in multiparous women. If left undisturbed, they will regress after delivery.[69] A mild degree of virilization can be present.[43,61] Microscopically, the lesions are composed of masses of uniform theca-lutein cells (Fig. 19.222). Occasionally, there is an associated granulosa cell proliferation.[63] Ultrastructurally, the proliferating cells exhibit abundant smooth endoplasmic

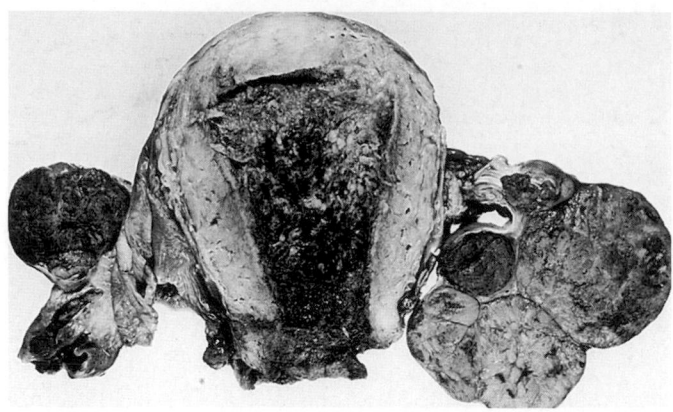

Fig. 19.221 Bilateral pregnancy luteomas in a 29-year-old woman that were discovered incidentally at the time of cesarean section performed for cord prolapse. The tumors bled excessively on manipulation by the surgeon and had to be removed.

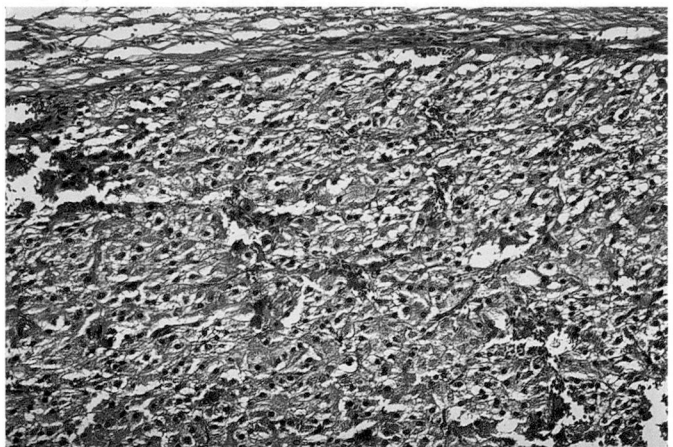

Fig. 19.222 Solid growth pattern of pregnancy luteoma.

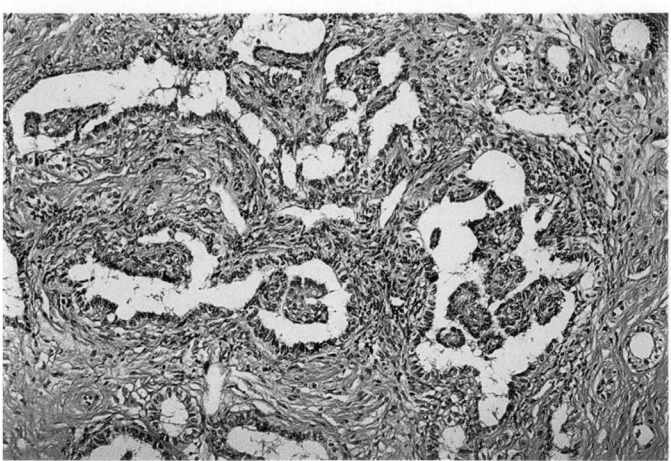

Fig. 19.223 Benign hyperplastic changes in rete ovarii. This alteration is of no clinical significance.

reticulum, dispersed Golgi apparatus, and tubular cristae in the mitochondria, in keeping with their function as steroid hormone-producing cells.[42] All of the reported lesions have been benign. It is reasonable to regard them as nodular hyperplasias of theca-lutein cells rather than true neoplasms.[61] If pregnancy luteoma is correctly identified by frozen section biopsy, no further surgery is necessary.

Developmental cysts derived from wolffian (mesonephric) and müllerian (paramesonephric) remnants are common in the region of the ovarian hilus. These are discussed on p. 1452. Suffice it to say here that, according to some authors, it is possible to distinguish these two types of tissues—and sometimes the cysts derived from them—on microscopic grounds.[44] Wolffian structures are lined by cuboidal, predominantly nonciliated epithelium resting on a well-developed basement membrane; müllerian formations are lined by generally taller, ciliated and nonciliated epithelium with larger nuclei and resting on an inconspicuous basement membrane. Both may have a smooth muscle coat. According to these criteria and some ultrastructural differences,[37]

hydatids of Morgagni (pedunculated cysts at the fimbriated end of the fallopian tube) are believed to be of müllerian origin, whereas most **parovarian** and **paratubal cysts** (in the tubo-ovarian ligament) and **Gartner's duct cysts** (in the vaginal wall) are thought to arise from wolffian remnants.

Cysts of the rete ovarii are characterized by a hilar position, an epithelial lining of variable height that is usually nonciliated, crevices along the inner surfaces, and a fibromuscular wall that often contains hyperplastic hilus cells.[65] The rete ovarii may also be the site of benign proliferative lesions that have been variously reported as adenomatous hyperplasia[47] and adenoma[60] (see p. 1650) (Fig. 19.223).

Epidermoid cysts, exceptionally rare, are thought to be related to Walthard cell nests, but some may well represent mature monodermal teratomas.[40,59,72] (see also p. 1689).

Amyloidosis can exceptionally present in the form of bilateral ovarian masses.[58]

Supernumerary ovaries are extremely rare.[50] Most of the reported cases have measured less than 1 cm. They should be distinguished from **accessory ovaries**, which are small portions of ovarian tissue situated near—and sometimes connected to—the normally placed ovary.[51]

Inflammation

Nonspecific inflammation of the ovary usually spreads from the endometrium and is practically always associated with tubal involvement. A large, loculated cystic mass filled with pus or secretion is often the result, the ovarian stroma forming part of the cystic wall (tubo-ovarian abscess or cyst). Exceptionally, a solid mass rich in foamy macrophages develops in longstanding cases ("xanthogranulomatous oophoritis").[77,83]

Granulomatous infections such as tuberculosis occur

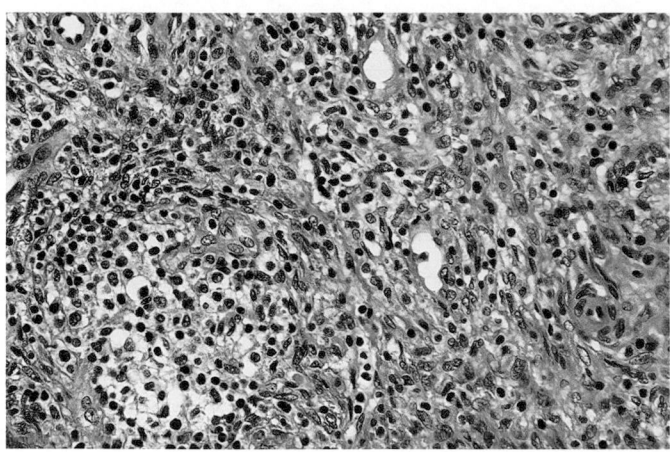

Fig. 19.224 Lymphocytic and plasmacytic infiltrate of ovary in oophoritis. This process is thought to have an autoimmune basis.

in the ovary. Invariably this is hematogenous in origin and often also involves the tube and endometrium. In time, the infection may subside and leave a large tubo-ovarian cystic mass. Other infectious agents responsible for granulomatous oophoritis are *Actinomyces* (particularly common after the introduction of intrauterine devices), *Schistosoma*, and *Enterobius vermicularis*. Rarely, *sarcoidosis* and *Crohn's disease* involve the ovary, the latter as a result of direct extension from the bowel. *Foreign body granulomas* can occur in the ovarian surface secondarily to talc, cornstarch, carbon pigment (at the site of fulguration surgery),[84] other foreign materials,[82] and keratin; the latter may originate from a ruptured ovarian cystic teratoma or may have spilled through the fallopian tube from an endometrial adenoacanthoma.[80] *Palisading granulomas* of unknown etiology have also been reported, most of them in patients with previous pelvic surgery.[78]

Autoimmune oophoritis is a poorly understood disorder characterized microscopically by lymphocytic and plasma cell infiltration in relation to developing follicles but not primordial follicles[76,85] (Fig. 19.224). It results in primary ovarian failure with either primary or secondary amenorrhea.[74] Many of the reported cases have been associated with adrenal failure (Addison's disease), hypothyroidism, or both conditions.[74,79]

Eosinophilic perifolliculitis is characterized by a predominantly eosinophilic infiltrate around the follicles; it is not clear how this rare disorder relates to autoimmune oophoritis.[81]

Giant cell arteritis occasionally involves the ovary of elderly women; it may occur as an isolated finding (most frequently) or as a component of generalized giant cell arteritis.[75]

Endometriosis

The ovary is the most common site of endometriosis, as defined by the presence of endometrial glands *and*

stroma outside the uterus (see p. 1401).[98] Several pathogenetic mechanisms have been suggested,[102] an interesting recent finding along these lines being the clonal nature of the epithelial cells in this condition.[95] Ovarian endometriosis is usually associated with infertility, and it remains active during the child-bearing years.[91,104] Pain associated with the menstrual cycle is the most common symptom; infrequently, the disease is complicated by massive ascites or perforation into the peritoneal cavity.[101] Grossly, it usually presents as small, slightly raised, blueberry-like spots on the ovarian surface, often accompanied by fibrous adhesions. In cases with extensive involvement, the entire ovary may be converted into a "chocolate cyst" as a result of repeated hemorrhages (Fig. 19.225). Microscopically, the typical lesions are composed of endometrial glands, endometrial stroma, and fresh and old (hemosiderin-containing) hemorrhagic foci (Fig. 19.226).[87] The endometrial stroma is responsible for the bleeding; it has cells with "naked nucleus" surrounded by reticulin and typical spiral arterioles, in conjunction with old and recent hemorrhage. Unfortunately, this diagnostic combination of findings is not always present. The more advanced the endometrial lesion, the more difficult the diagnosis and the greater the number of sections required to make it. Not infrequently, the repeated hemorrhages have totally destroyed the endometrial tissue, the cyst being lined by several layers of hemosiderin-laden macrophages. Under these circumstances, the most the pathologist can do is to report the case as a hemorrhagic cyst and comment that the changes are "consistent" with those of endometriosis. Sometimes, the lesion is entirely composed of *necrotic pseudoxanthomatous nodules*, to be distinguished from infectious granulomas and necrotic neoplasms[89] (Fig. 19.227). Other morphologic variations of endometriosis include the formation of Liesegang

Fig. 19.225 Inner surface of cyst in a case of ovarian endometriosis. The color is typically brown.

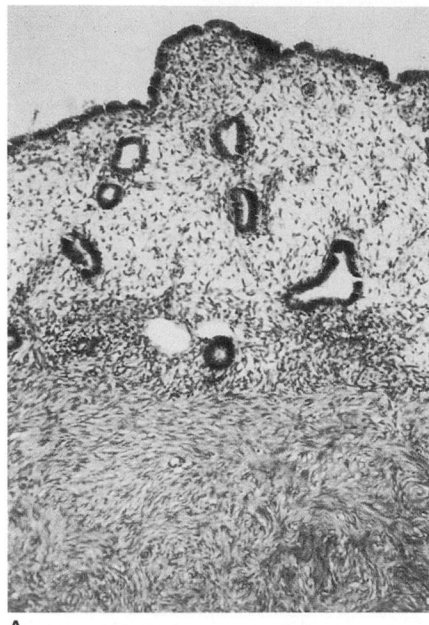

A

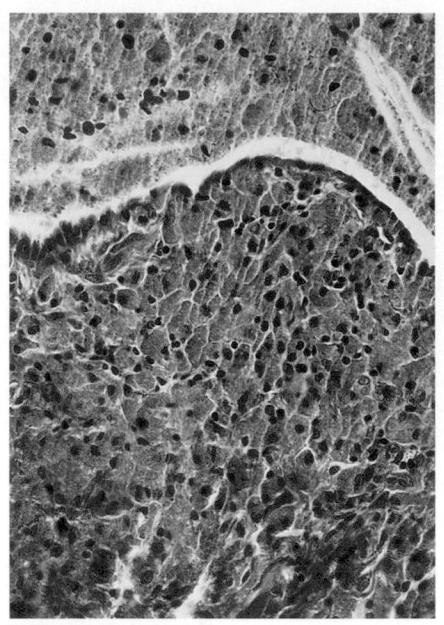

B

Fig. 19.226 A and **B**, Ovarian endometriosis. **A**, In this area endometrial tissue faithfully reproduces the appearance of normal endometrium, in terms of both glands and stroma. **B**, A more common appearance resulting from repeated hemorrhage and accumulation of hemosiderin-laden macrophages.

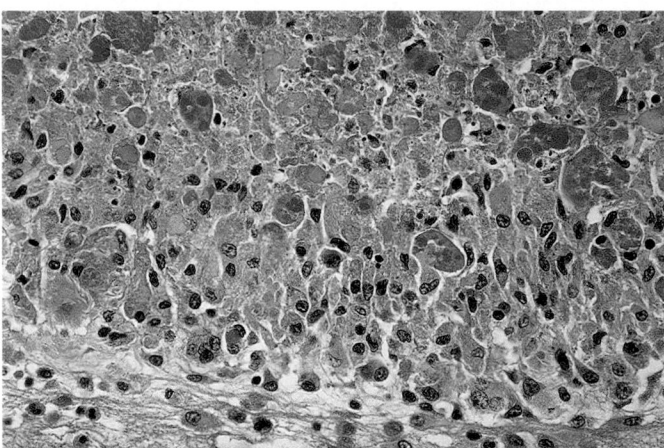

Fig. 19.227 Necrotic nodule surrounded by histiocytes in pelvic endometriosis.

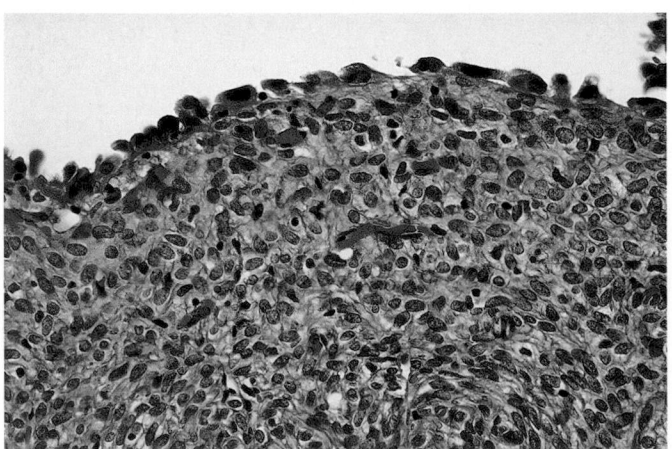

Fig. 19.228 Reactive changes in the lining of an ovarian endometriotic cyst. This change is sometimes referred to as "atypical endometriosis."

rings,[100] stromal elastosis,[88] and smooth muscle hyperplasia,[92] the latter sometimes resulting in the formation of uterus-like masses (see p. 1579).[99]

Ectopic endometrial tissue is subject to most of the influences that affect intrauterine endometrium. Consequently, it may be the site of reactive atypia (sometimes referred to as "atypical endometriosis"),[86,90,94,96] hyperplasia and metaplasia[93] (Fig. 19.228), and malignancy, of which endometrioid carcinoma is the most common form[103] (see p. 1667). Interestingly, p53 is absent in the epithelial cells of benign uncomplicated endometriotic cysts but present in about one half of the carcinomas arising from them as well as in the adjacent, morphologically non-neoplastic epithelium.[97]

Ovarian biopsy

Ovarian biopsy obtained by either laparotomy or surgical culdoscopy used to be carried out for the evaluation of selected patients with amenorrhea and sterility resulting from anovulation. The specimen, which roughly corresponded to about one fifth of the organ, was evaluated for the presence and quantity of follicles, evidence of ovulation (corpora lutea and albicantia), and the character of the stroma.[108,109]

Mori[105] attempted to correlate the morphologic findings in the ovarian biopsy with a series of endocrinologic analyses. He found that the ovaries of patients with hypergonadotropic ovarian failure contained no follicles, whereas in those of patients with normogonadotropic or hypogonadotropic ovarian failure, many developing follicles were present. The results were somewhat different in the series of 19 patients reported by Russell et al.,[107] all of whom had premature (before 35 years of age) hypergonadotropic ovarian failure. There were 14 cases classified as premature menopause, characterized by the absence of primordial follicles; three designated as "resistant ovary syndrome," having primordial follicles but little or no follicular development; and two cases of chronic—presumably autoimmune—oophoritis, characterized by a granulomatous reaction centered in the theca of the developing follicles.

Nowadays, ovarian biopsies are rarely if ever performed in women with premature ovarian failure and a normal karyotype. The reasons for this reluctance are the realization that they can provide misleading information (i.e., cases with no oocytes in the biopsy in which the patients eventually become pregnant) and the fact that affected patients generally require estrogen replacement regardless of the results of the biopsy.[106]

Tumors

Classification

The classification of ovarian tumors is primarily morphologic but is intended to reflect current concepts of embryogenesis and histogenesis of this complex organ.[110–116] Since many of these concepts are still controversial, it should be viewed as a working compromise, subject to changes and improvements. It is based on the premise that the ovary contains four major types of tissues, all of which can give rise to a variety of neoplasms:

1 Surface, celomic, or germinal epithelium
2 Germ cells
3 Sex cords
4 Ovarian stroma, specialized and nonspecific.

Surface epithelial tumors

Surface epithelial tumors, numerically the most important group of neoplasms, are thought to derive from the epithelium that normally lines the outer aspect of the ovary, variously referred to as *surface, celomic, or germinal*.[118] This epithelium is continuous with the mesothelium that covers the peritoneal cavity, representing a modification of it and sharing with it a common origin and many morphologic features.[119] Some authors have gone as far as suggesting that ovarian tumors arising from this structure should be regarded as mesotheliomas, a proposal that has not met with general acceptance, since clearcut histochemical, enzymatic, and biologic differences between ovarian surface epithelium and extraovarian peritoneal mesothelium exist.[120] Furthermore, ovarian epithelial tumors differ significantly as a group from peritoneal mesotheliomas on morphologic and behavioral grounds, these differences being highlighted by two rare but notable occurrences: the ovarian tumor with a bona fide mesotheliomatous appearance[117] and the existence of intra-abdominal extraovarian malignancies having more

resemblance to ovarian carcinomas than to peritoneal mesotheliomas (see p. 1676 and Chapter 26).

The ovarian surface epithelium, when involved in metaplastic or neoplastic conditions, often undergoes a "müllerian differentiation"; as a result, it may produce any of the adult structures formed by the müllerian ducts, including tubal, endometrial, and endocervical mucosa, singly or in combination.[122, 126] This plasticity is also evident at the immunohistochemical level.[128]

It has been suggested that the majority of surface tumors of the ovary arise not from the outer epithelium itself, but rather from the portion of this epithelium that has invaginated to produce surface epithelial glands and cysts. This is supported by some immunohistochemical similarities,[125] the overexpression of p53,[124] and the occasional finding of atypical proliferation (dysplasia) or carcinoma in situ in these structures.[123,127] Ovarian endometriosis may also give rise to these tumors, but this is probably true for only a small minority of them, even if they are of endometrioid type.

Surface epithelial ovarian tumors are classified according to the following parameters:

1 Cell type: serous, mucinous, endometrioid, etc.
2 Pattern of growth: cystic, solid, surface
3 Amount of fibrous stroma
4 Atypia and invasiveness: benign, borderline, and malignant.

Thorough sampling is essential to carry out these important determinations. It has been suggested that one block should be taken for every 1 to 2 cm of maximum tumor diameter.[121] The selection of the site of sampling is actually more important than the total number of blocks: solid foci, areas adjacent to the ovarian surface, and the base of the papillary formations need to be studied with particular care.

Serous tumors

Serous tumors make up about one fourth of all ovarian tumors. Most cases occur in adults. Approximately 30% to 50% are bilateral; molecular studies in these cases support the theory of a clonal origin.[187] Grossly, the better differentiated tumors consist of cystic masses, usually unilocular, containing a clear but sometimes viscous fluid (Fig. 19.229). Papillary formations are often present, most of them protruding into the cavity but some occasionally occur on the outer surface (Fig. 19.230). The more malignant tumors tend to be solid and invasive, with areas of necrosis and hemorrhage (Fig. 19.231).

Microscopically, cuboidal to columnar cells are seen lining the wall of the cysts and the papillae in the better differentiated tumors (Fig. 19.232). They are similar to normal tubal epithelium at both a light and electron microscopic level.[148] In approximately 30% of cases, calcific concretions with concentric laminations (psammoma

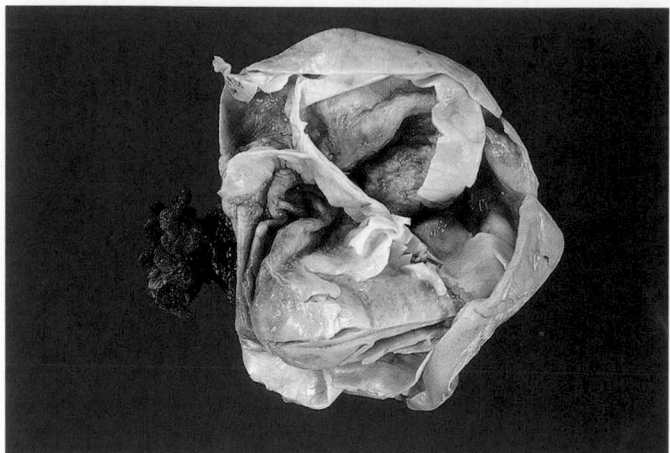

Fig. 19.229 Smooth outer and inner surfaces of the cystic formations in a case of ovarian serous cystadenoma.

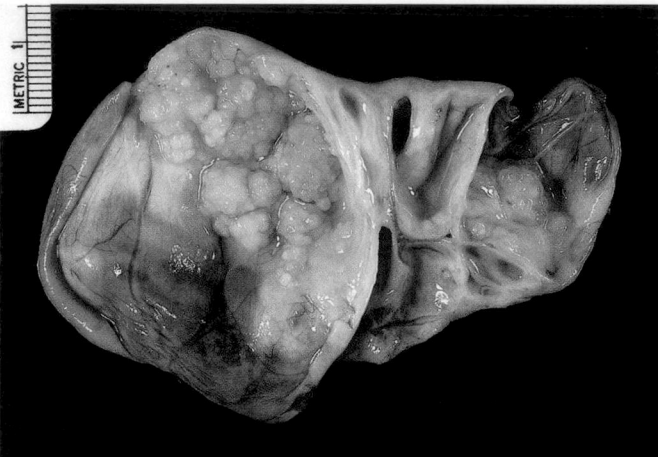

Fig. 19.230 Inner aspect of serous cystadenoma showing papillary structures protruding within.

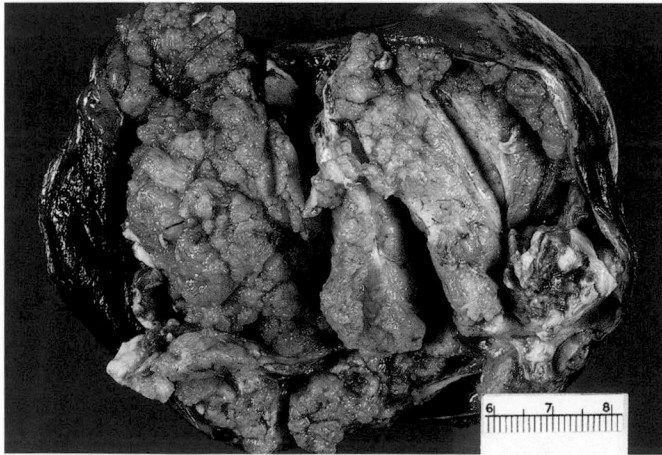

Fig. 19.231 Serous cystadenocarcinoma. The tumor is predominantly solid, with necrotic and hemorrhagic areas.

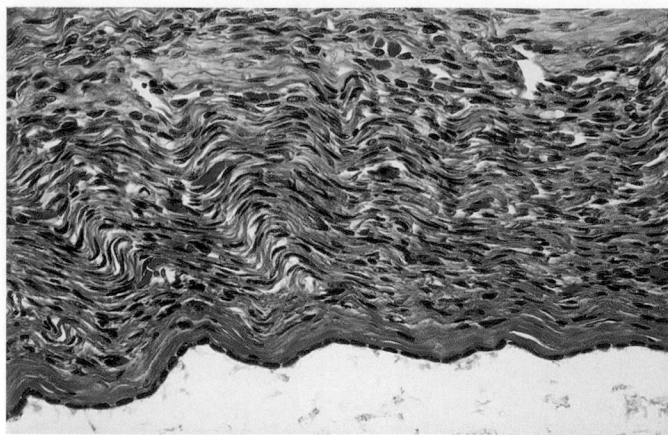

Fig. 19.232 Single layer of bland-looking epithelial cells lining one of the cystic structures of a serous cystadenoma.

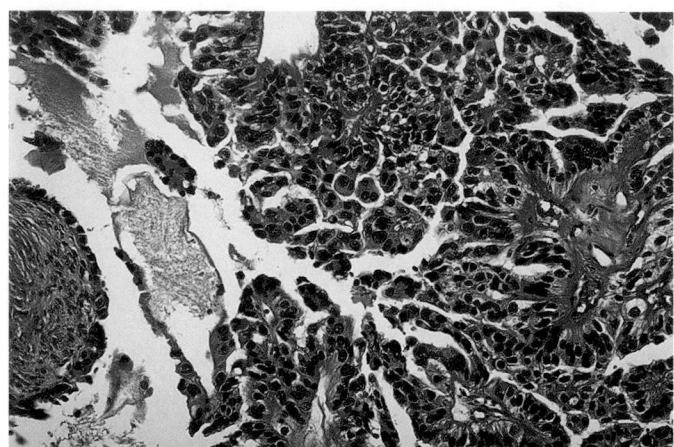

Fig. 19.233 Serous cyst adenocarcinoma. The tumor has a complex papillary architecture and a high nuclear grade.

bodies) are present. Ultrastructural studies suggest that the formation of these psammoma bodies is initiated intracellularly in association with autophagocytosis.[149]

A morphologic spectrum of proliferation exists in these tumors. At one end is the benign **serous cystadenoma**, in which the cysts and the papillae (if present, in which case the tumor is called serous papillary cystadenoma) are lined by a single layer of cells, without atypia, architectural complexity, or invasion (see Fig. 19.232). At the other end are the **serous adenocarcinoma**, **serous papillary adenocarcinoma**, and **serous papillary cystadenocarcinoma**, characterized by nuclear atypia, high mitotic activity, stratification, glandular complexity, branching papillary fronds, and *stromal invasion* (Fig. 19.233). In between are tumors showing some or all of the features associated with carcinoma but *lacking* definite stromal invasion, i.e., irregular or destructive stromal infiltration by small glands or sheets of cells[139,196] (Figs 19.234 and 19.235) (but see below). These tumors—known as **borderline, indeterminate, intermediate, of low malignant potential**, or **possibly malignant**—make up approximately 15% of all serous tumors.[146,188] It is important to separate them from the obviously invasive tumors because of their vastly better prognosis.[163] The outcome is even more favorable (as a matter of fact, no different from that of cystadenoma) when the "borderline" features are present only focally in an otherwise benign tumor ("cystadenomas with focally proliferative areas").[163] It should be pointed out that the decision as to whether an ovarian serous neoplasm is of malignant or borderline nature should be made purely on the basis of the morphologic features of the primary tumor, regardless of whether or not peritoneal lesions, lymph node metastases, or even lung deposits exist.[179,193] Allegedly, there are differences in nuclear features between these two tumor types that can be appreciated in a more consistent and reproducible fashion by the use of computerized interactive morphometric analysis.[157,167]

The additional proposal has been made that tumors should still be placed into the borderline category even if they show foci of stromal microinvasion, as long as they are otherwise typical of that category. The microinvasive

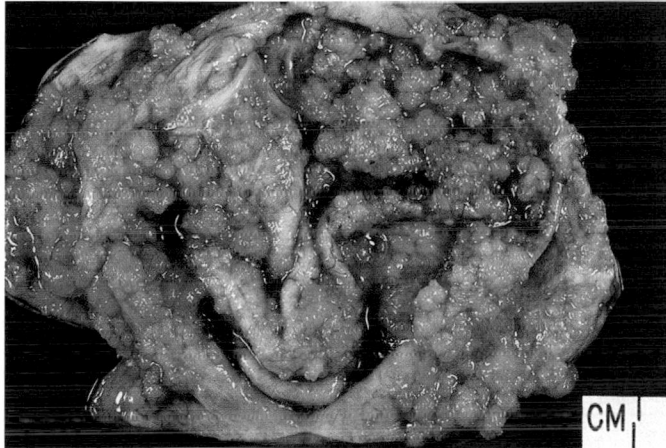

Fig. 19.234 Inner aspect of an ovarian borderline serous neoplasm. Numerous papillary projections facing the lumen can be appreciated.

foci appear as individual cells or clusters of cells with abundant eosinophilic cytoplasm ("eosinophilic metaplastic cells") or, less commonly, as small confluent nests with a cribriform pattern; these tumors have a prognosis similar to that of the usual noninvasive serous borderline tumor[131,175] (Fig. 19.236). This is a different phenomenon than the presence in a borderline tumor of focal areas having the typical appearance of serous carcinoma; the latter behave as aggressive neoplasms, with a prognosis similar to that of serous carcinoma.[164,168,190]

An interesting development has occurred in recent years concerning the serous cystadenoma–borderline tumor–(cyst)adenocarcinoma paradigm. It relates to the proposal by Kurman and his group of adding a fourth category to this scheme, which they have termed **micropapillary serous carcinoma** and placed in between the second and third existing categories.[133,185] These tumors are characterized by a filigree pattern of highly complex micropapillae arising from large bulbous papillary structures (Fig. 19.237). These micropapillae are covered by round to cuboidal cells with a high nucleocytoplasmic ratio, which can also be recognized on cytologic preparation.[130] Sometimes this is associated with a cribriform pattern. This proposal has generated a great deal of controversy, which seems to be centered on the choice of terms (i.e., regarding the lesion as a "carcinoma," which implies removing it from the borderline category) rather than on the morphologic observation itself, which rests on solid grounds,[150] and for which there is some molecular genetic backing.[192] To this writer, this saga is a perfect example of how a significant and clinically useful piece of information can suffer because of the world of semantic boundaries in which we move, in particular our dogged determination to divide tumors

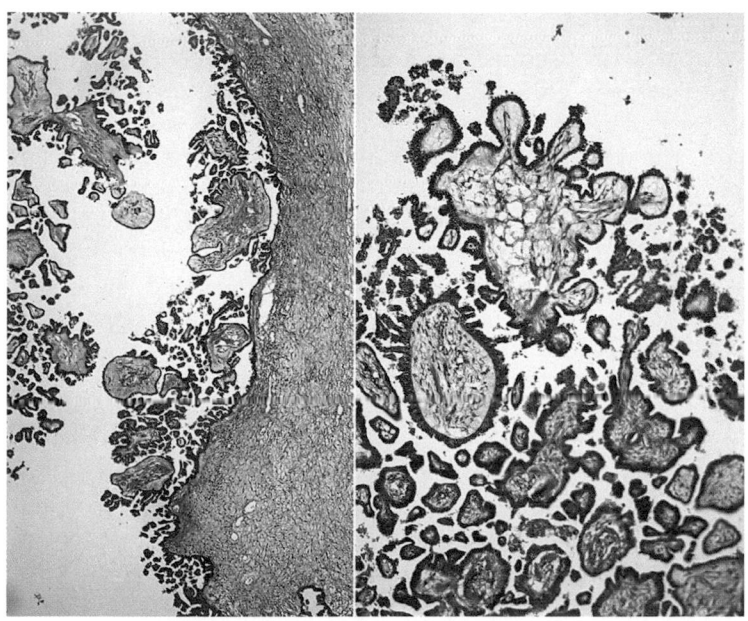

A   B

Fig. 19.235 Low- and medium-power appearance of ovarian borderline serous neoplasm. The growth is entirely exophytic.

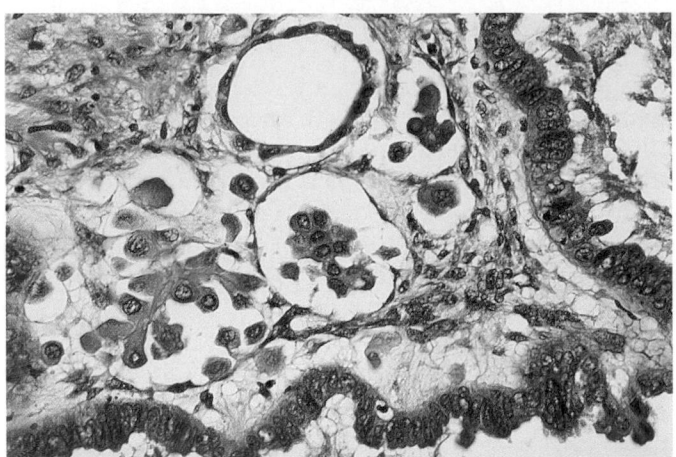

Fig. 19.236 Borderline serous neoplasm with foci of microinvasion represented by clusters of cells with abundant eosinophilic cytoplasm.

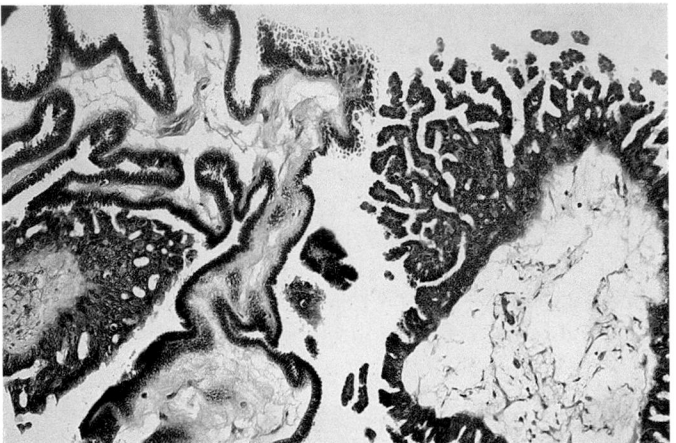

Fig. 19.237 Ovarian serous tumor with a micropapillary pattern of growth.

into benign and malignant categories. To put the matter in perspective, there was a time—not too long ago—when only two types of ovarian serous tumors were recognized: cystadenoma (benign) and (cyst)adenocarcinoma (malignant). Sometime in the 1950s, and after much discussion, a third category—that of borderline tumors—was added.[184] This meant progress, at the clinical level, because a group had been carved out that had a natural history of its own, different from that of the two previously recognized entities. It also meant progress at the conceptual level, because it sent the message that tumors do not have to be either benign or malignant but that there is a spectrum of behavior among them. Now we have the proposal to add yet another category, having a set of morphologic (and, most significantly, clinical) features that set it apart from the conventional borderline tumor on one hand and the serous carcinoma on the other. This, again, means progress, and Kurman's team ought to be complimented for the achievement. It is unfortunate that they felt the need to revert to classic ter-

minology to name their entity, which they regarded as the "malignant" type of borderline tumor, as opposed to the conventional borderline neoplasm, which they viewed as "benign."[186] As far as the biologic validity of their observation is concerned, there is immunohistochemical support for it in terms of p53 overexpression, and general agreement that Kurman's micropapillary serous tumor is associated with higher rates of recurrence of invasive carcinoma and (in some series) tumor deaths.[144,147,186,191] Another point worth making is that—prognostically speaking—The presence and type (noninvasive versus invasive) of peritoneal implants are more important than whether the primary ovarian tumor is of conventional or micropapillary type, and—if the latter—whether it is non-invasive or invasive.[169a,177,178,191a]

Going back to the general discussion of serous tumors, it ought to be mentioned that squamous metaplasia is exceptional in them, in contrast to endometrioid tumors; however, well-documented cases of this occurrence are on record.[197]

In some serous neoplasms, the fibroblastic stromal component is unduly prominent, appearing grossly as solid, white, nodular foci in an otherwise typical cystic neoplasm. These, too, can be separated into *benign* (**adenofibroma** and **cystadenofibroma**), *borderline*, and *malignant* (**adenofibrocarcinoma** and **cystadenofibrocarcinoma**) types[140, 141] (Fig. 19.238). The benign type occurs much more frequently than the others. The borderline category of this neoplasm is extremely rare; none of the reported cases have developed a recurrence following excision of the neoplasm.[161] Exceptionally, osseous metaplasia develops in these stroma-rich tumors.[132] In other instances, the stroma is partially luteinized and of a functioning nature.[200] An unexpected association has been found between benign and malignant ovarian adenofibromatous tumors and breast cancer and thyroid disorders.[189]

Other serous neoplasms grow exophytically on the surface of the ovary, with little if any involvement of the underlying organ, the normal shape of which is maintained. These are referred to as **surface papillomas** when benign, **borderline surface papillary tumors** when intermediate, and **serous surface papillary (adeno)carcinomas** when malignant. Most of the latter are bilateral, highly aggressive, and usually associated with peritoneal spread at the time of surgery[154,174,199] (Figs 19.239 and 19.240).

A somewhat different type of tumor predominantly involving the ovarian surface is so-called **serous psammocarcinoma**, a rare variant of serous carcinoma characterized by massive psammoma body formation and low-grade cytologic features (Fig. 19.241); the behavior of these tumors more closely resembles that of borderline serous tumors than of serous carcinomas.[151]

Immunohistochemically, the typical keratin profile of serous tumors is CK7+/CK20-.[136] They also express CK8,

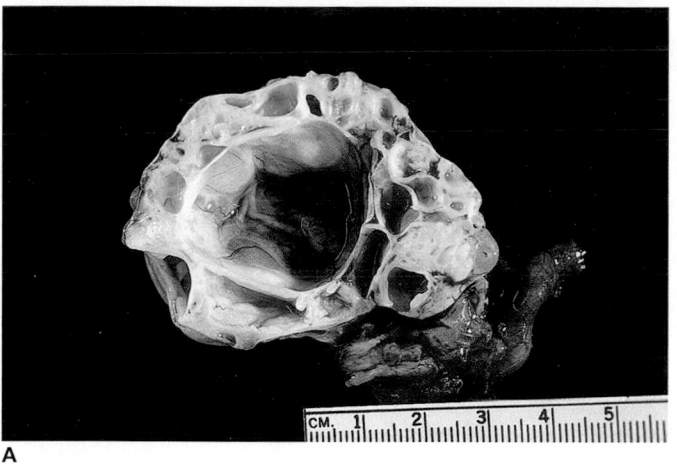

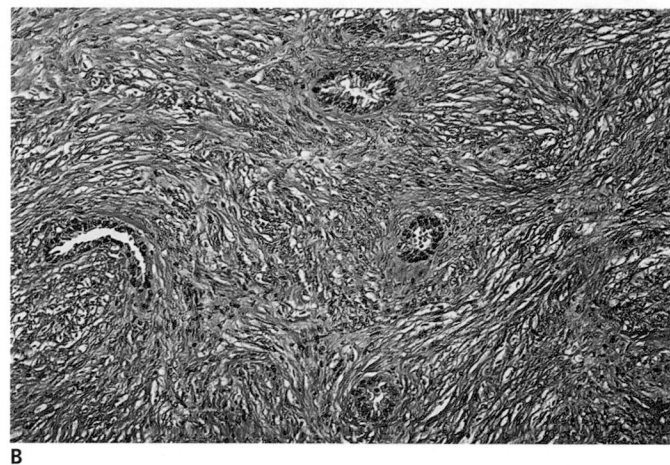

Fig. 19.238 Ovarian serous cystadenofibroma: **A**, gross appearance; **B**, microscopic appearance. The well-differentiated glands are embedded within a dense stroma.

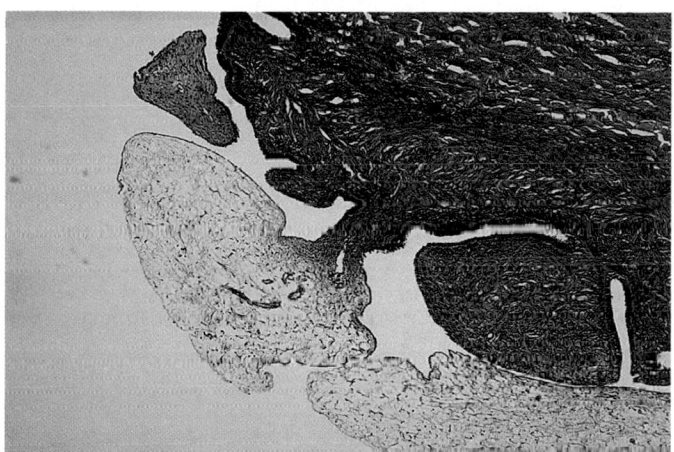

Fig. 19.239 Serous cystadenofibroma. The papillary structures protruding within the lumen have a prominent stromal component.

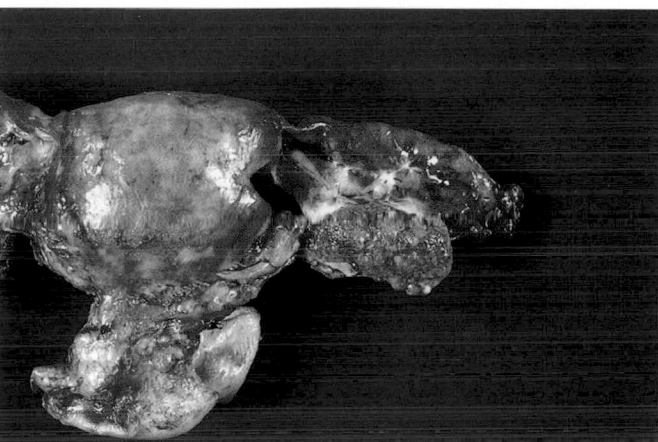

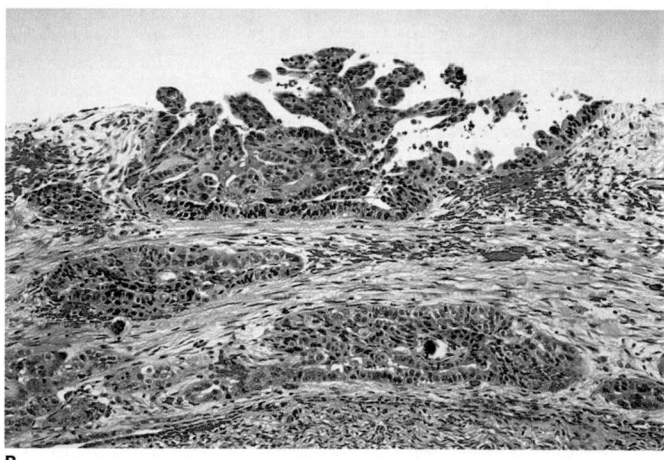

Fig. 19.240 A and **B**, Serous surface papillary carcinoma. **A**, Gross appearance. The ovary, which has a papillomatous outer surface, is only minimally enlarged. **B**, Microscopic appearance. There is hardly any infiltration of the stroma.

18, and 19, EMA, B72.3,[134,155,173] S-100 protein (particularly borderline tumors),[169] vimentin (erratically),[171] GFAP (occasionally),[173] HLA and Ia histocompatibility antigens[158] the β-subunit of hCG (in a minority of cases),[172] and receptors for estrogens, progesterone, and androgens (in over half the cases).[137,156]

WT-1 stains diffusely most ovarian serous carcinomas, as it does mesothelioma of peritoneum and other sites. It stains to a lesser extent ovarian endometrioid carcinoma, and is usually negative in ovarian mucinous carcinoma.[153,186] Significantly, it does not stain uterine papillary serous carcinoma.[152]

The expression of cadherins and catenins is said to be related to the degree of tumor differentiation, in the sense that it is higher in the carcinomas.[142,143] In addition, it has been claimed that mucinous tumors express N-cadherin whereas serous and endometrioid tumors do not.[176]

Serous tumors contain glycoconjugates that result in a pattern of lectin binding different from that of mucinous tumors.[182] Interestingly, one fourth of the serous and endometrioid tumors (but *not* the mucinous tumors) produce amylase, which can be demonstrated in the tumor cells (by immunohistochemistry), in the cyst fluid, and sometimes in the peripheral blood.[195,198]

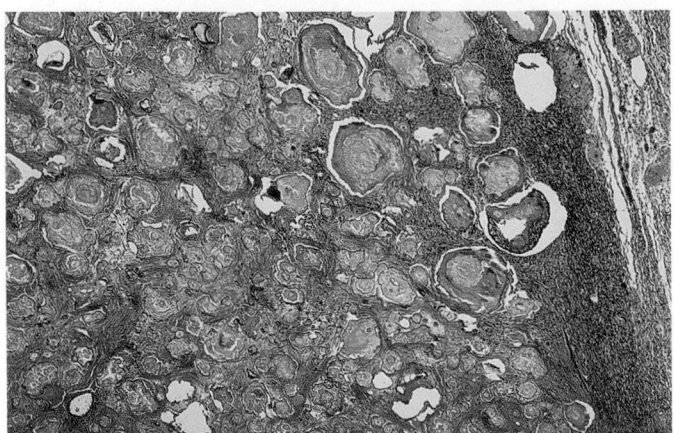

Fig. 19.241 So-called "serous carcinoma." Innumerable psammoma bodies are present, and the cellularity is very scanty.

Various monoclonal antibodies have been produced against epithelial (mainly serous) ovarian tumors, such as CA-125 and SMO47.[138,166,170]

Other markers that have been detected in ovarian serous tumors, some of them quite unexpectedly, include glycodelin (a glycoprotein with immunosuppressive and contraceptive properties),[160] osteopontin,[194] fibulin-1 (an extracellular matrix protein),[180] Coxsackie-adenovirus receptor,[165] retinoid acid receptor-α protein,[162] GLUT-1 (a facilitative glucose transporter, supposedly only in malignant tumors),[159] and MUC5AC.[129]

Important *negative* markers of serous tumors are CK20 and cytoplasmic CEA (in contrast to primary and metastatic mucinous tumors).[136,138]

A continuous basement membrane (as detected immunohistochemically with antibodies to laminin or type IV collagen) is present in benign cystadenomas and borderline tumors without microinvasion; disruption of this structure occurs in areas of microinvasion (in the borderline tumors) or frank invasion (in the cystadenocarcinomas).[135,145]

The stromal component of these tumors has been shown to express several molecules involved in steroid hormone metabolism, such as 17β-hydroxysteroid dehydrogenase (an estrogen-metabolizing enzyme) and adrenal-4-binding protein (a transcription factor that regulates the expression of steroidogenic enzymes.[181,183]

The molecular genetic abnormalities of these tumors are discussed on p. 1675.

Mucinous tumors

Mucinous neoplasms are less common than serous neoplasms and are bilateral in only 10% to 20% of cases. These bilateral tumors seem to be of clonal nature.[247] As in the case of their serous counterparts, ovarian mucinous tumors have been divided into *benign* (**mucinous cystadenoma**), *borderline*, and *malignant* (**mucinous adenocarcinoma** and **cystadenocarcinoma**). Grossly, they tend to grow larger than the serous types and are partially or completely cystic, often multiloculated. A fluid to viscous material of mucoid nature is present in the lumen (Figs 19.242 to 19.244). In the past, these tumors have been designated as *pseudomucinous* because the behavior of the luminal content toward acetic acid was allegedly different from that of "true" mucin; however, since the material secreted by the tumor cells has all the histochemical features of an epithelial mucosubstance, the designation of *mucinous* is wholly appropriate.[235]

Microscopically, ovarian mucinous tumors (particularly those of a borderline nature, see below) have been divided into two major types, a distinction that is not always easy (particularly with the carcinomas, in which it is rarely attempted), but which is backed by ultrastructural, histochemical, and immunohistochemical data.[227]

The first and most common type is referred to as *intestinal*, and is characterized by an epithelial lining with a "picket fence" appearance, goblet cells, Paneth cells, endocrine cells, the secretion of gastrointestinal and pancreatobiliary type mucin,[239] and the production of intestinal enzymes such as lipase, trypsin, amylase, and sucrase[240,244] (Fig. 19.245). The endocrine cells, which are more common in the borderline category, are argyrophil

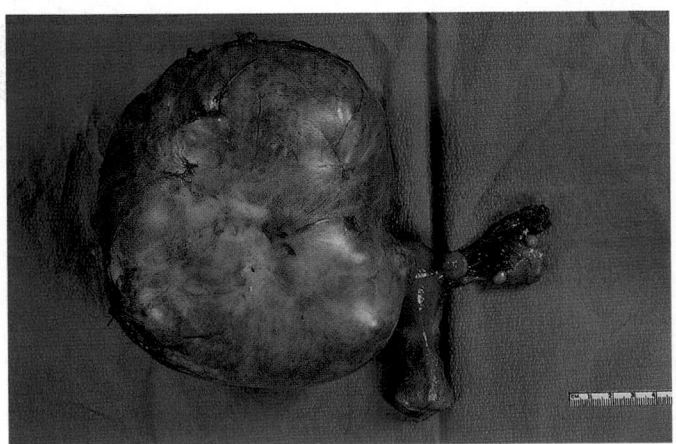

A

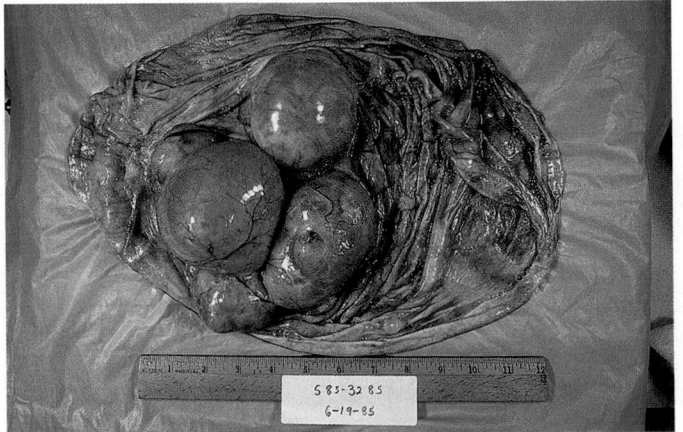

B

Fig. 19.242 A and **B,** Outer and inner aspect of mucinous cystadenoma.

and sometimes argentaffin.[218] 5-Hydroxytryptamine (serotonin), ACTH, gastrin, somatostatin, and other peptide hormones have been detected immunohistochemically in them.[201,223,237,242] There is usually no clinical

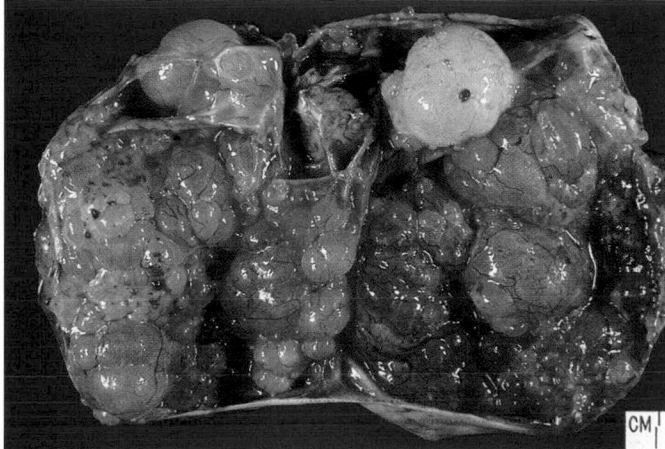

Fig. 19.243 Gross appearance of a mucinous ovarian neoplasm that had borderline features at the microscopic level.

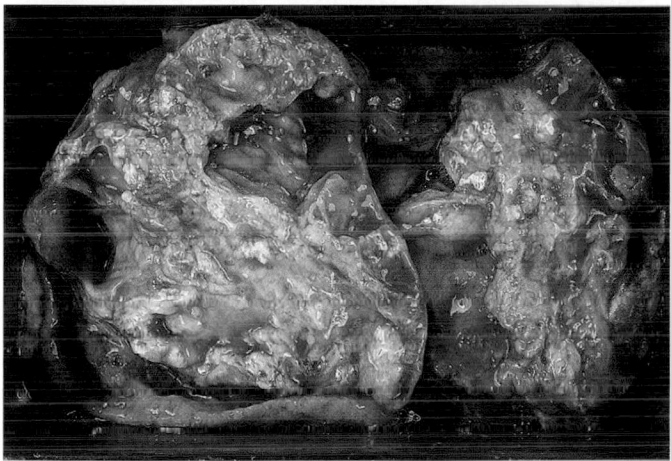

Fig. 19.244 Gross appearance of mucinous cystadenocarcinoma. The neoplasm is predominantly solid, but some mucin-containing cystic spaces can still be appreciated.

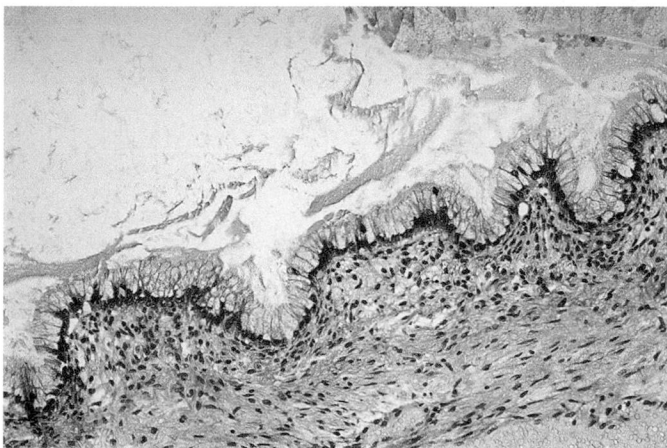

Fig. 19.245 Lining of mucinous cystadenoma. Goblet cells are evident. This subtype, which is by far the most common, is referred to as intestinal.

evidence of hormone excess, but cases associated with Zollinger–Ellison syndrome have been described.[205] The second type, referred to as *endocervical* or *müllerian*, is characterized by a lining of tall nonciliated cells with basally located nuclei and abundant intracellular mucin, which resembles endocervical epithelium both at the light and electron microscopic level (Fig. 19.246). Still others are mixed.[243] It has been pointed out that few if any of the endocervical-like tumors are pure, and it has additionally been suggested that they be combined with the mixed type tumors into a *seromucinous* category.[238]

Occasionally, mucinous tumors of the intestinal type have been found in association with carcinoid tumors in the same ovary.[233] On the basis of these findings, some authors (including the legendary Robert Meyer) have postulated a monodermal teratomatous derivation for these tumors; most evidence, however, favors a metaplastic origin from the surface epithelium.[210] Indeed, some tumors of the endocervical type have been found to coexist with endocervical adenocarcinoma,[222,249] and sometimes with endometriosis.[219] The stroma can be hypercellular, particularly in the area immediately beneath the neoplastic epithelium; on occasion, it may show signs of luteinization and be accompanied by hormonal manifestations.[214,224]

The *malignant* type of mucinous tumor is characterized by cell atypia, increased layering of cells, greater complexity of the glands and papillae (budding, bridging, appearance of solid foci), and areas of stromal invasion[213,248] (Fig. 19.247). Since the latter may be present in only a small area of the tumor, thorough sampling for microscopic examination is essential.

The existence and clinical significance of a *borderline* category in the mucinous tumors has proved more difficult to define than for their serous counterparts.[241] One of

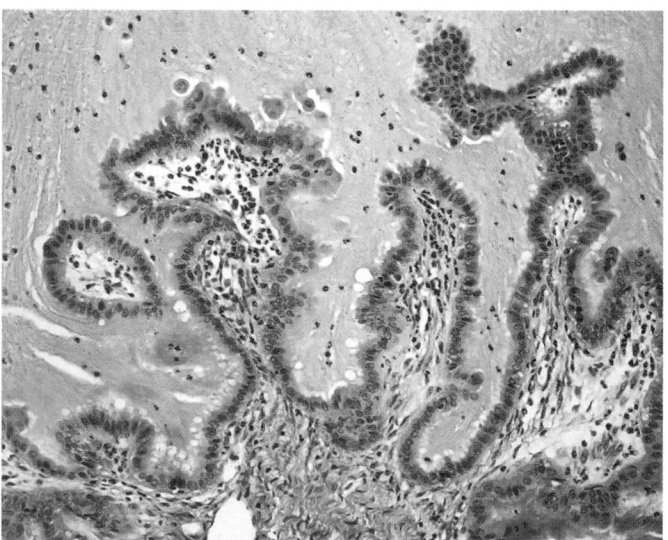

Fig. 19.246 In this instance, the lining of mucinous cystadenoma resembles endocervical epithelium.

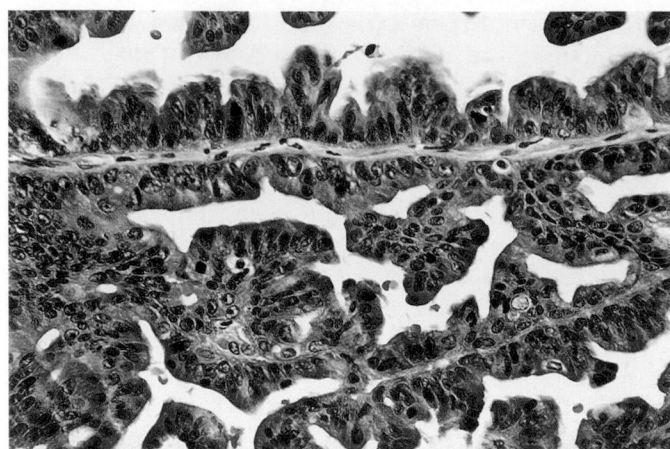

Fig. 19.247 Complex architecture and obvious nuclear atypia in mucinous cystadenocarcinoma.

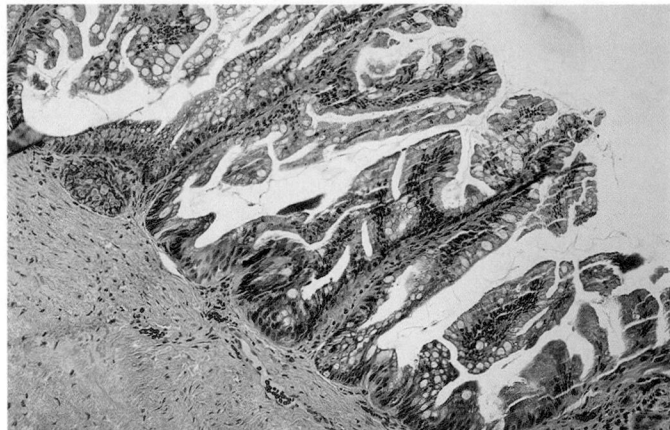

A

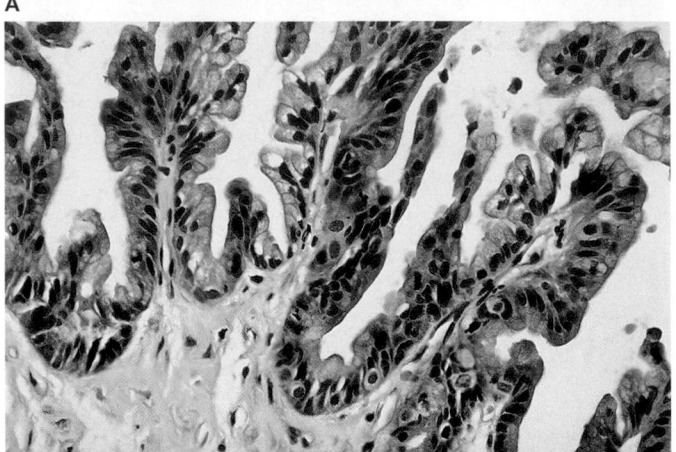

B

Fig. 19.248 A and **B**, Mucinous ovarian neoplasm of borderline type. It has been proposed that borderline tumors showing prominent atypia (**B**) be designated as focal intraepithelial carcinoma.

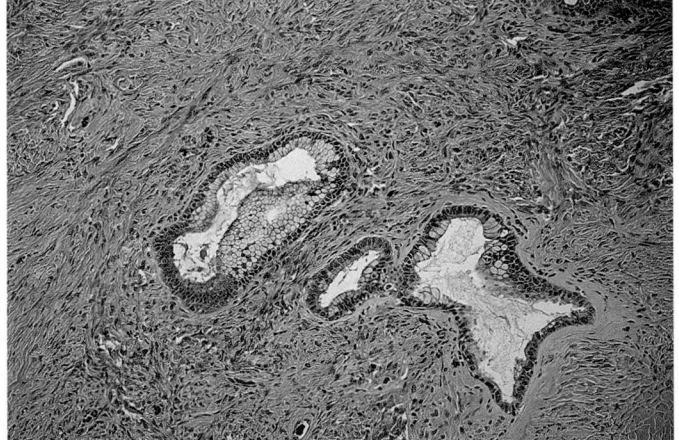

Fig. 19.249 Mucinous adenofibroma showing small glands lined by mucin-producing epithelial cells embedded in a dense fibrous stroma.

the problems is that stromal invasion is difficult to evaluate in cases with a complex interaction of glands and stroma. Hart and Norris[212] proposed the following rules for the distinction between borderline and malignant mucinous tumors: if there is unquestionable invasion, the tumor is classified as a carcinoma; if invasion is uncertain, the tumor is classified as borderline when the atypical epithelium is less than four cells in thickness and as carcinoma when it is four cells or greater. Some independent studies have confirmed the prognostic utility of this arbitrary and biologically questionable criterion,[207] but others have not.[246] Recently, the proposal has been made to subdivide the mucinous borderline tumors of intestinal type into those with epithelial atypia and those with focal intraepithelial carcinoma[220] (Fig. 19.248). Clinically, their outcome is usually equally favorable, but occasional patients in the latter group have experienced a fatal recurrence.[220,234] Likewise, mucinous carcinomas have been divided into expansile and infiltrative subtypes, some of the latter being microinvasive only.[220] Microinvasion is usually associated with an excellent prognosis.[217,220,228]

In a somewhat parallel proposal, it has been suggested that intestinal-type mucinous tumors be divided into conventional, atypical proliferative, and those with intraepithelial, microinvasive (<5 mm), and invasive (≥5 mm) carcinoma.[232]

There is a subgroup of mucinous tumors in which the stromal component is particularly prominent. These have been designated *mucinous adenofibroma* or *cystadenofibroma* if benign, and *mucinous adenocarcinofibroma* and *cystadenocarcinofibroma* if malignant (Fig. 19.249). The benign ones are sometimes misinterpreted as malignant and even as metastatic because of the irregularly shaped gland in a desmoplastic stroma,[204] or as microinvasive because of the presence of micronests of endocrine cells.[215]

Exceptionally, ovarian mucinous tumors have been found to contain foci of (1) *sarcoma-like nodules*, with a configuration and cytologic composition similar to those of giant cell tumor of soft parts,[230] characterized by a lack of reactivity for keratin[225]; (2) *sarcoma*, usually spindle-shaped, sometimes with heterologous features,[229,245] and also unreactive for keratin; and (3) *anaplastic carcinoma*, with pleomorphic round to spindle cells that are immunoreactive for keratin.[226,231] The distinction between the latter two lesions is very tenuous, both on microscopic and histogenetic grounds (as it is in the pancreas or thyroid under similar circumstances), and both are associated with a very poor prognosis. Actually, we favor the interpretation that the sarcoma-like nodules themselves are not a reactive phenomenon,[203] but rather are of neoplastic nature and related histogenetically to the other two processes, a possibility also expressed by others[209] and supported by occasional coexistence of these various lesions. However, it is important to consider the sarcoma-like nodules separately because of their excellent prognosis.[201,203,230,231] On occasion, the appearance of the mural nodule is that of a benign leiomyomatous growth.[221]

Immunohistochemically, the tumor cells of ovarian mucinous tumors express CEA (particularly if of intestinal type and/or malignant),[233] keratin, EMA (particularly if malignant),[208,211] MUC5AC (a gastrin mucin gene), and Dpc4 (a nuclear transcription factor inactivated in about half of pancreatic adenocarcinomas).[208,211,216] Regarding keratin expression, CK7 is always present, whereas CK20 is found in about half of cases.[206,216]

Mucinous cystadenocarcinomas tend to implant on and locally invade neighboring tissues such as the bowel, abdominal wall, and bladder. Metastases to distant areas are infrequent. Sometimes, mucinous tumors involving the ovary are accompanied by extensive deposits of intra-abdominal mucin (pseudomyxoma peritonei). The prevailing opinion at present is that the large majority of these tumors are metastatic to the ovary and peritoneal cavity from an appendiceal origin, and they are, therefore, discussed on p. 1707 and Chapter 11.

Endometrioid tumors

Endometrioid carcinoma comprises 10% to 25% of all primary ovarian carcinomas.[265] Coexistent endometriosis can be demonstrated in 10% to 20% of cases,[267] and some of the tumors can be seen actually arising from these endometriotic cysts. However, the identification of endometriosis is not a prerequisite for the diagnosis of endometrioid carcinoma, inasmuch as the majority of these tumors are thought to originate de novo from the ovarian surface epithelium. The occasional admixture of endometrioid with serous and/or mucinous patterns would seem to support this interpretation.

Grossly, endometrioid carcinoma may present as a cystic or solid mass (Fig. 19.250). The content tends to be hemorrhagic rather than serous or mucinous. Visible papillary formations are usually absent or inconspicuous. Microscopically, the tumors resemble greatly the appearance of the ordinary type of endometrial adenocarcinoma—hence their name[255,256] (Fig. 19.251). Most are well differentiated, with or without papillary formations. Half of the tumors have foci of squamous metaplasia, some of these

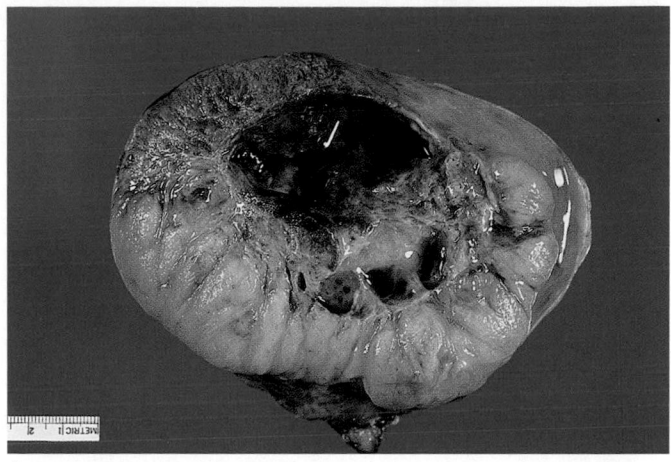

A

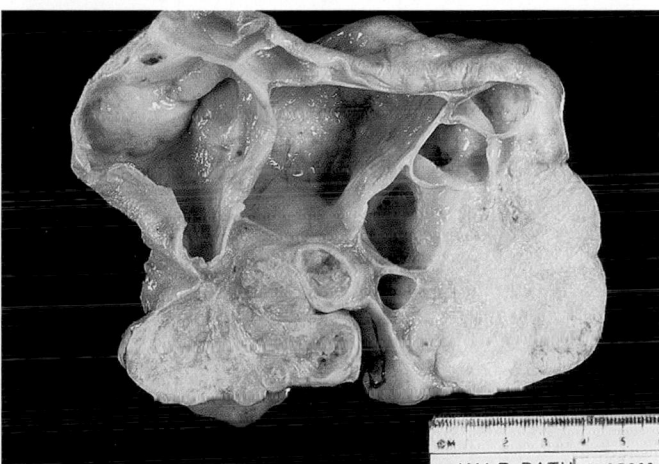

B

Fig. 19.250 A and **B**, Gross appearances of ovarian endometrioid carcinoma. Both tumors show a combination of solid and cystic appearances.

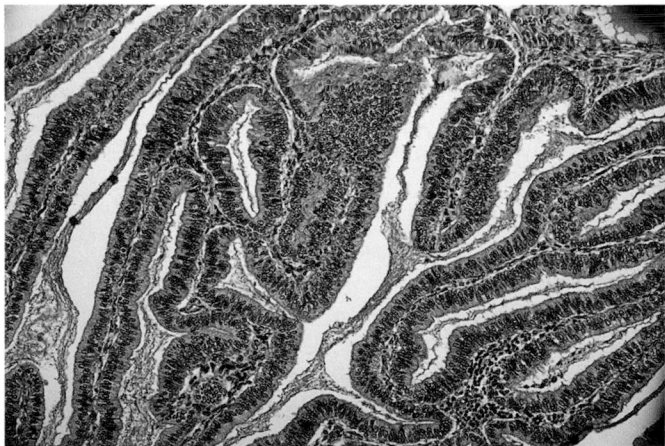

Fig. 19.251 Well-differentiated endometrioid carcinoma of ovary with focally villous architecture.

having been reported in the past as adenoacanthomas[263] (Fig. 19.252). In contrast to serous tumors, psammoma bodies are exceptional. Approximately 10% of endometrioid carcinomas have a component of non-neoplastic luteinized stromal cells.

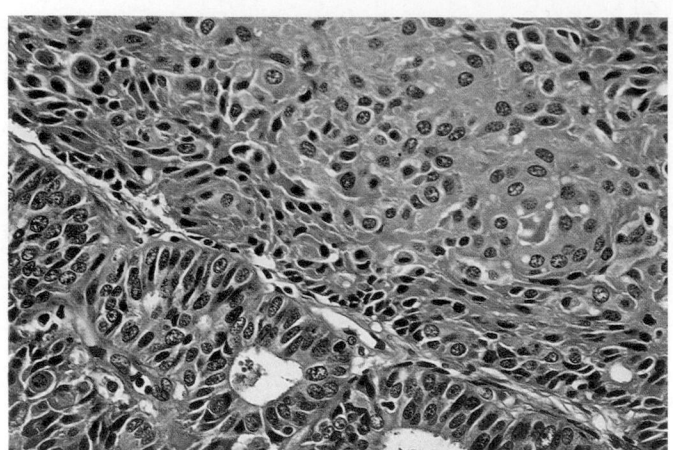

Fig. 19.252 Well-differentiated endometrioid ovarian carcinoma with extensive squamous metaplasia (so-called "adenoacanthoma").

As in uterine adenoacanthomas, the keratin produced by these ovarian neoplasms can result in the formation of peritoneal keratin granulomas.[262] It seems likely that at least some of the reported cases of primary **squamous cell carcinomas** of the ovary represent the extreme expression of this metaplastic tendency of endometrioid carcinoma.[266,276,279] Parenthetically, the other large category of ovarian squamous cell carcinoma is that associated with benign cystic teratomas (dermoid cysts).[271]

Histochemically, mucin may be found within the glandular lumina and in the apical border of the tumor cells but not in the cytoplasm. Scattered argyrophil cells are seen in almost half of cases.[278]

Immunohistochemically, the tumor cells are positive for keratin, EMA, and vimentin, whereas CEA is usually negative or weak.[257] There can also be positivity for CA19-9 and hPL.[254,260]

Ultrastructurally, the two most distinctive features (also shared with endometrial adenocarcinoma) are paranuclear collections of microfilaments and nucleoli with a "mesh basket" appearance.

At the molecular level, there are several differences with endometrioid carcinoma of the uterus despite their morphologic similarities, suggesting a different genetic pathway for their formation.[253] Mutations leading to β-catenin deregulation are found in nearly half of ovarian endometrioid adenocarcinomas.[283]

In some endometrioid carcinomas, the neoplastic glands are small and tubular or solid and elongated, simulating the pattern of sex cord–stromal tumors, particularly of Sertoli–Leydig cell type.[274,281] These are referred to either as sertoliform variants of endometrioid carcinoma or as endometrioid carcinoma resembling sex cord–stromal tumors.[270] Features that favor a diagnosis of endometrioid carcinoma in such cases are the older age of the patients, the usual absence of endocrine manifestations, and the occurrence elsewhere in the tumor of

larger tubular glands, foci of squamous metaplasia, luminal mucin accumulation, adenofibromatous components, immunoreactivity for keratin (including CK7), and negativity for inhibin.[250,259] Other morphologic variations of endometrioid carcinoma include presence of yolk sac elements,[268,275] tumors composed of ciliated cells,[258] tumors composed of oxyphilic (oncocytic) epithelium,[272,280] and tumors containing foci of collagenous spherulosis that simulate squamous metaplasia.[277] Endometrioid carcinomas containing yolk sac elements have also been described.[275] Other endometrioid carcinomas have been found to be composed of oxyphilic epithelium.[272]

Benign, atypical (proliferating), and borderline types of endometrioid ovarian tumors exist, in addition to the malignant ones.[251,252,261,273a] Most of these have a prominent stromal component and have been traditionally included with the adenofibromas or cystadenofibromas, depending on the degree of cystic change (Figs 19.253 and 19.254). Sometimes, benign and malignant areas coexist in the same case.[261,273] In the atypical category, the epithelial changes are equivalent to those of atypical endometrial hyperplasia; in the borderline category, they

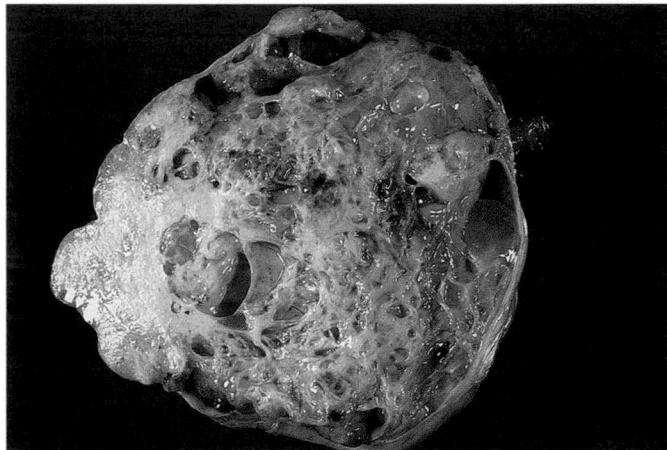

A

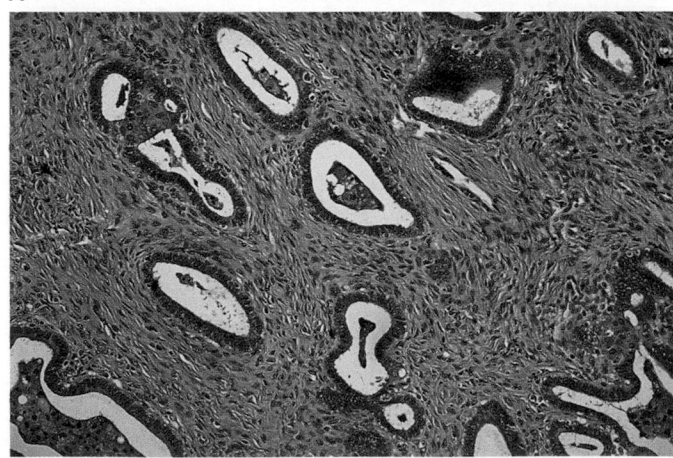

B

Fig. 19.253 A and **B,** Gross and microscopic appearance of endometrioid (cyst)adenofibroma.

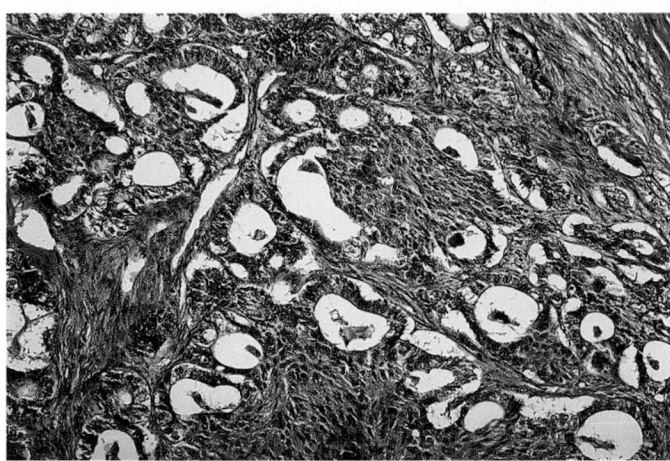

Fig. 19.254 Ovarian endometrioid neoplasm with borderline microscopic features mainly manifested by architectural complexity.

are akin to well-differentiated endometrial adenocarcinoma *without stromal invasion*.[251,269] Cytologic atypia and presence of microinvasion do not appear to affect the prognosis, in the sense that oophorectomy is generally curative for all of these forms.[252]

As a group, endometrioid carcinoma has a prognosis twice as good as that of serous or mucinous carcinoma.[264] However, this seems to be mainly a function of the fact that many of these tumors are stage I and well differentiated. When these various tumor types are evaluated stage for stage, the outcome is not significantly different.[255]

Some patients with endometrioid carcinoma of the ovary have either endometrial hyperplasia or a synchronous endometrial adenocarcinoma, often well differentiated and superficial and sometimes exhibiting squamous metaplasia (so-called "adenoacanthoma").[282] There is a wide disparity in the reported incidence of the latter occurrence (largely because of different diagnostic criteria), with most series ranging from 15% to 30%.[256,282] This is discussed further on p. 1679.

The most important differences among serous, mucinous, and endometrioid carcinomas are listed in Table 19.4.

Clear cell (mesonephroid) tumors

Clear cell (mesonephroid) adenocarcinoma is a distinctive ovarian tumor with a grossly spongy, often cystic appearance (Fig. 19.255), which microscopically can grow in tubular–cystic, papillary, and solid-sheet fashions[292,294] (Fig. 19.256). The cores of the papillae often exhibit prominent hyalinization (Fig. 19.257). Stroma-rich variants of this tumor are known as *clear cell adenocarcinofibroma* and *cystadenocarcinofibroma*.

The tumor cells are large. Some of the nuclei protrude into the lumina, resulting in a "hobnail" configuration (Fig. 19.258). Their cytoplasm is clear; it often contains glycogen, mucin, and fat, and it may exhibit PAS-positive, diastase-resistant hyaline globules, which are negative for α-fetoprotein.[289] In some of the tumor cells, the cytoplasm may appear oxyphilic rather than clear[280,303] (Fig. 19.259). Immunohistochemically, the tumor cells are always reactive for keratin (CK7, CK5/6, CAM 5.2, 34βE12), EMA, CEA, CD15 (Leu-M1), Ber-Ep4, vimentin, bcl-2, p53, and CA-125; variably reactive for estrogen and progesterone receptors, HER2/*neu* and α-fetoprotein (the latter not in relation to the hyaline bodies); and negative for CK20.[295,302,304] The hormone receptor pattern is peculiar in the sense that there is much greater expression of ER than PR, and that the former is exclusively of the beta rather than the alpha type.[287] A recently described additional marker of ovarian clear cell carcinoma is hepatocyte nuclear factor-1β, a transcription factor involved with liver differentiation.[301a]

At the molecular level, it has been claimed that clear cell carcinomas have an expression pattern of cell cycle regulatory molecules that is unique among ovarian adenocarcinomas.[301]

Clear cell adenocarcinoma was included in Schiller's original description of mesonephroma and regarded as of mesonephric rest derivation[298]; however, convincing evidence has been brought forward to indicate that it is of surface epithelial type and specifically related to endometrioid carcinoma, of which it should be regarded

Table 19.4 Differential characteristics of serous, mucinous, and endometrioid carcinomas

Characteristic	Serous	Mucinous	Endometrioid
Relative frequency	60–80%	5–15%	10–25%
Bilaterality	30–50%	10–20%	15–30%
Size	Moderate	Often huge	Moderate
Usual character of fluid	Clear	Slimy, viscous	Hemorrhagic
Coexistent endometrial hyperplasia or carcinoma	Exceptional	Exceptional	15–30%
Epithelium	Cuboidal	Columnar, with basally located nucleus	Columnar, with centrally located nucleus
Mucin	Only in luminal border	Often abundant, intracytoplasmic	Only in luminal border
Squamous metaplasia	Exceptional	Exceptional	50%
Cilia	Frequent	Absent	Rare
Psammoma bodies	30%	Exceptional	Exceptional

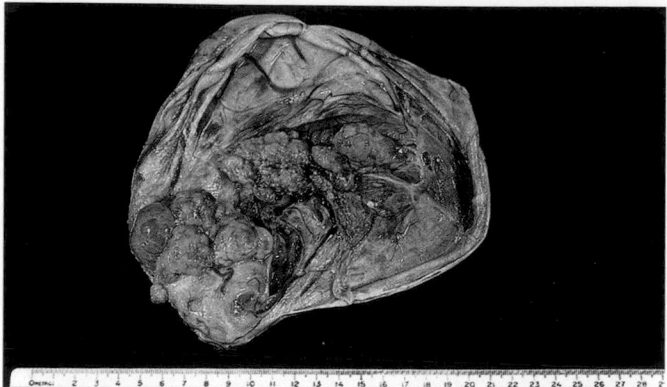

Fig. 19.255 Gross appearance of clear cell carcinoma of ovary. The tumor is predominantly cystic, but it contains several mural nodules.

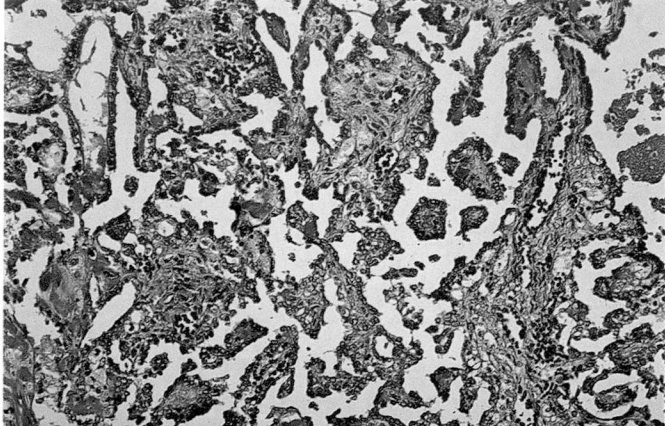

Fig. 19.256 A highly papillary configuration is seen in this low-power view of ovarian clear cell carcinoma.

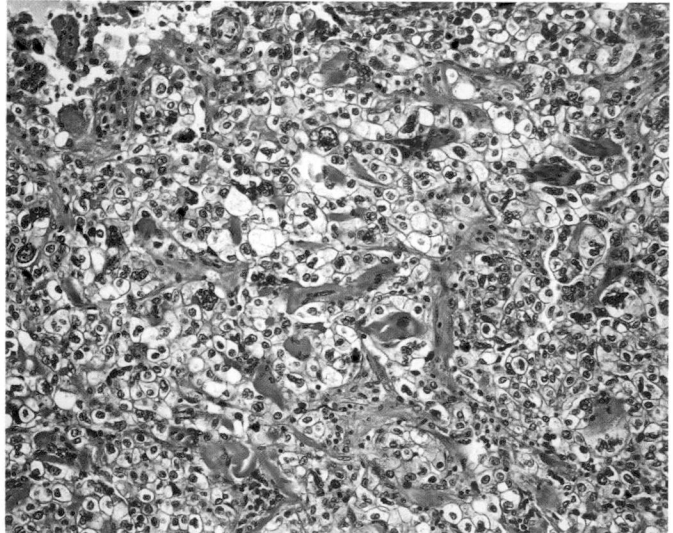

Fig. 19.257 Clear cell carcinoma of ovary showing short papillae with hyalinized cores lined by highly atypical cells.

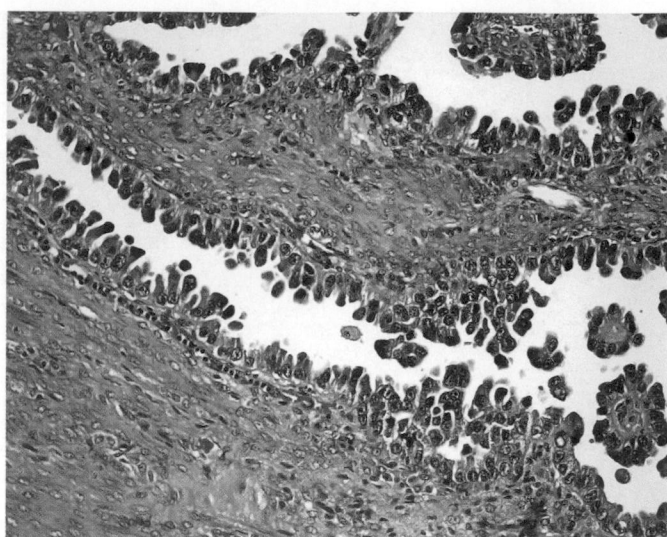

Fig. 19.258 Clear cell carcinoma of ovary. Note the high nuclear grade and the hobnail configuration.

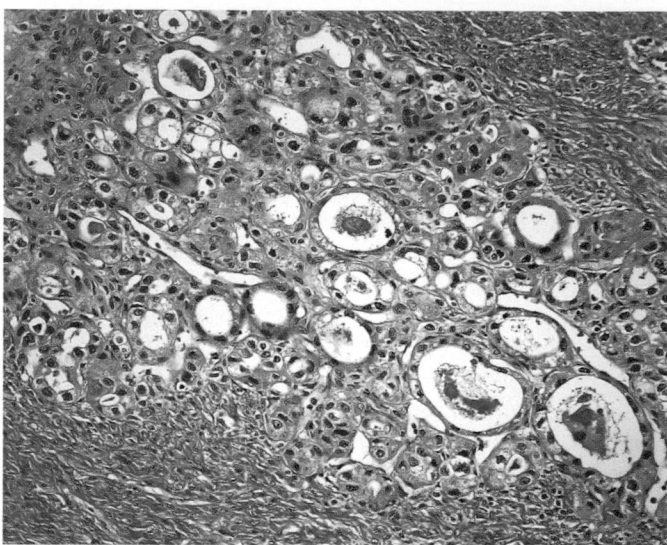

Fig. 19.259 Oxyphilic variant of clear cell carcinoma. Some of the tumor cells have a hybrid appearance.

as a variant.[299,300] This interpretation is supported by the high association with pelvic endometriosis, the origin in some cases from endometriotic cysts, the frequent admixture with typical endometrioid carcinoma, and the ultrastructural similarities with müllerian endometrioid epithelium.[284,299] At the electron microscopic level, the cytoplasmic clearing is seen to be largely due to the accumulation of glycogen,[290] and the hyalinization to the accumulation of basal lamina material.[291,293]

Patients with clear cell adenocarcinoma are usually in the fifth or sixth decades. The incidence of bilaterality is less than 10%, and the 5-year survival rate ranges from 37% to 47%.[285,286,296] Stage for stage, their prognosis is similar to that of patients with other epithelial ovarian carcinomas.[284,285,288]

Benign and **borderline** (low malignant potential) ovarian clear cell tumors are very rare. Their growth pattern may be that of a cystadenoma, an adenofibroma, or a cystadenofibroma. The borderline tumors are identified because of moderate to marked degrees of epithelial

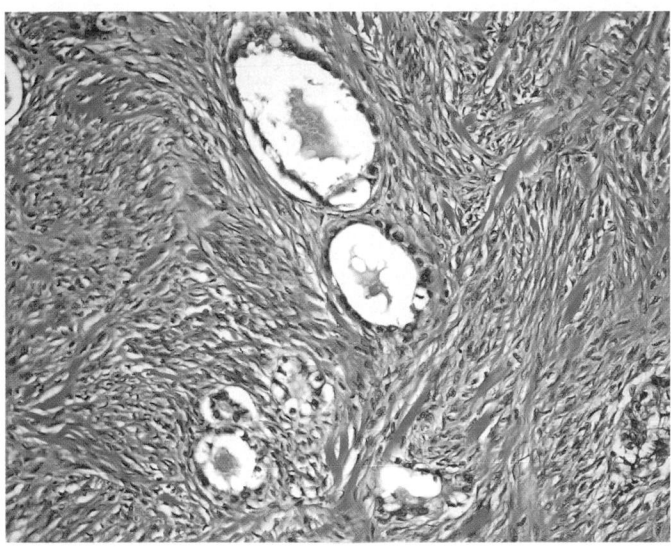

Fig. 19.260 Clear cell adenofibroma with mild to moderate nuclear atypia. These tumors are placed in a borderline or low malignant potential category.

proliferation and atypia in the absence of recognizable stromal invasion[297] (Fig. 19.260).

Brenner tumor and transitional cell carcinoma

Brenner tumors constitute between 1% and 2% of all ovarian neoplasms.[329] The average age at presentation is approximately 50 years, 71% of the patients being over 40 years of age. Some cases are accompanied by signs of hyperestrinism, such as uterine bleeding from endometrial hyperplasia in the postmenopausal woman.[313] The rate of growth is slow, and ascites is rare. Grossly, these tumors vary greatly in size; they are usually unilateral, firm, and white or yellowish white (Fig. 19.261). They closely resemble fibromas or thecomas, except for the frequent presence of small cystic areas filled with opaque, viscous, yellowish brown fluid. Microscopically, they consist of solid and cystic nests of epithelial cells resembling transitional epithelium (urothelium) surrounded by an abundant stromal component of dense, fibroblastic nature (Fig. 19.262). The epithelial cells have sharply defined outlines; those lining the cysts may be flattened, cuboidal, or columnar. The nuclei of the tumor cells are oval, with a small but distinct nucleolus and longitudinal grooves similar to those seen in granulosa cell tumors (Fig. 19.263). The cytoplasm is clear and immunoreactive for keratin, EMA, and CEA (the latter also present in the lumen of the cysts).[308] It may contain glycogen, mucin, and lipid.[313,324,328] The latter is found in larger amounts in the stromal cells in the cases accompanied by hyperestrinism. Scattered argyrophilic cells are present in about one third of cases; they are positive for chromogranin and 5-HT, have dense-core granules at the ultrastructural level, and are similar to those seen in normal urothelium.[305] Steroidogenic enzymes as detected immunohistochemically are usually absent.[325]

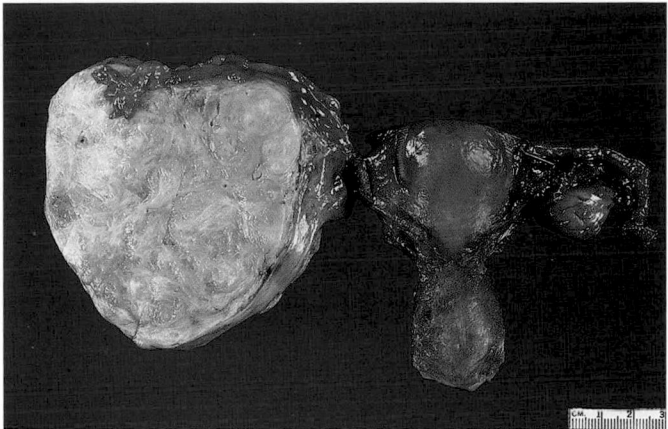

Fig. 19.261 Large Brenner tumor involving the right ovary. The gross appearance of this neoplasm is very similar to that of fibrothecoma.

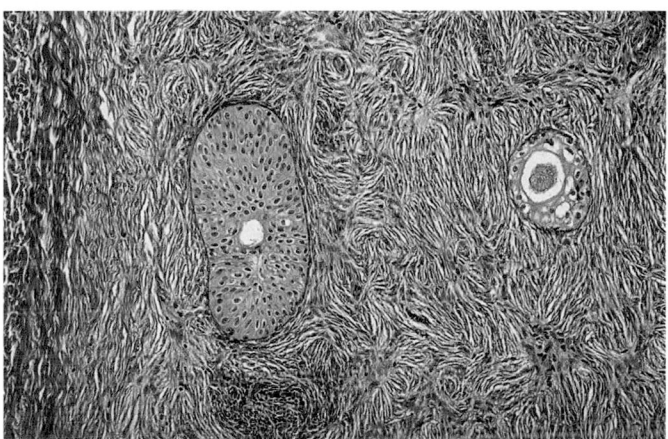

Fig. 19.262 Brenner tumor of ovary showing solid and cystic epithelial cells embedded within fibrous tissue.

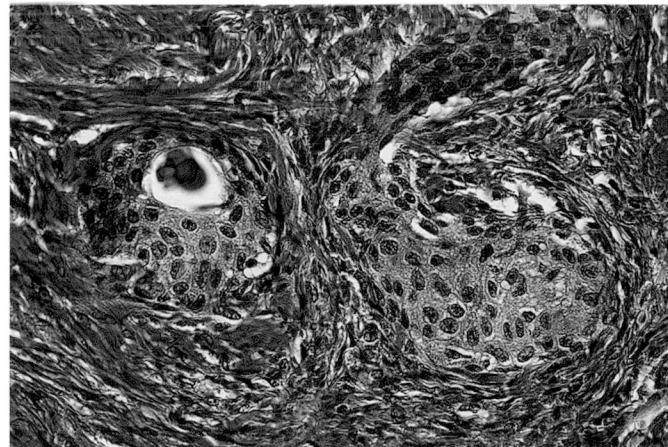

Fig. 19.263 The epithelial nests of Brenner tumor are composed of cells with oval nuclei, many of which exhibit longitudinal grooves.

Sometimes the cystic formations within the tumor are unduly prominent and accompanied by florid mucinous changes (a lesion analogous to cystitis glandularis); Roth et al.[321] refer to this pattern as *metaplastic* Brenner tumor as long as papillary fronds and nuclear atypia are absent.

If the latter two features are present (the pattern thus resembling that of a low-grade [grades I or II] transitional carcinoma of the urinary bladder), they designate it as a *proliferating* Brenner tumor[312,321] (Fig. 19.264). When this pattern is associated with a greater degree of atypia (equivalent to a grade III transitional cell carcinoma) but stromal invasion cannot be demonstrated, the terms *borderline* or *low malignant potential* have been suggested.[321] Typical, metaplastic, proliferating, and borderline Brenner tumors have been found to follow a benign clinical course after oophorectomy. The latter three types are sometimes grouped under the term *intermediate Brenner tumor*.[322] Cytologically malignant neoplasms associated with *stromal invasion* are referred to as *malignant Brenner tumors* (Fig. 19.265). Some of these cases have been bilat-

eral.[309,312,326] They are recognized mainly because of their association with a typical benign, metaplastic, proliferating, or borderline component.[320] The appearance may be that of a transitional cell, squamous, glandular, or undifferentiated carcinoma, or an admixture of these[320] (Fig. 19.266).

Austin and Norris[306] pointed out that malignant Brenner tumors with an associated benign component have a better prognosis than morphologically similar tumors in which such a component was absent. They refer to the latter as *transitional cell carcinomas* (non-Brenner type)[323] (Fig. 19.267). The claim that a transitional cell pattern in high-grade ovarian carcinoma is an indicator of favorable response to chemotherapy[319] has not been confirmed in other series, which have shown that—stage for stage—transitional cell carcinoma is not prognostically different from serous carcinoma.[307,311]

Brenner tumors can be seen in association with mucinous cystadenoma (Fig. 19.268) and, exceptionally, struma ovarii.[314] They have also been found to coexist with transitional cell tumors of the urinary bladder.[331,332] We have seen a case of benign Brenner tumor of the ovary associated with transitional cell carcinoma of the endometrium.

Most authors currently favor for Brenner tumor an origin from surface ovarian epithelium or the cysts derived from them, through a process of metaplasia.[327] The continuity that has been demonstrated between the epithelial nests of Brenner tumor and the ovarian surface supports this concept, which is currently preferred over the alternatives of an origin from Walthard cell nests (microscopically similar but usually located in the mesosalpinx rather than the ovary), granulosa cells, rete ovarii, or germ cells. Whether this metaplasia is truly along transitional cell (urothelial) lines remains controversial. Some authors have found no immunohistochemical similarities between bladder transitional cell tumors and either

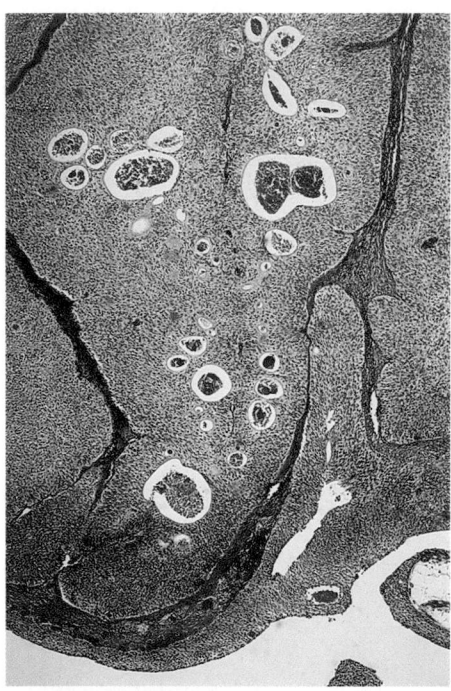

Fig. 19.264 Highly proliferating (borderline) Brenner tumor.

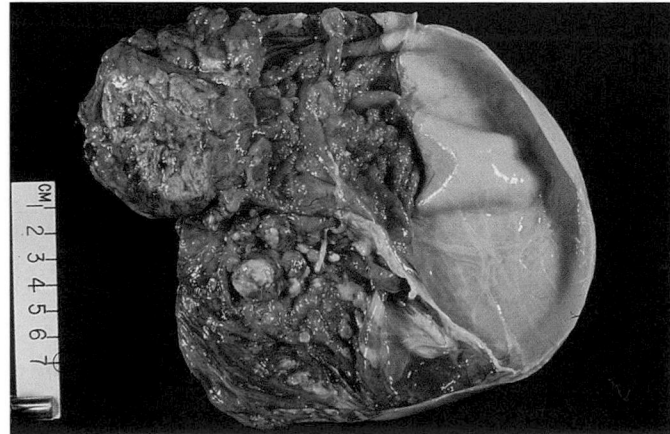

Fig. 19.265 Borderline Brenner tumor showing solid area with papillary formations, associated with a large cystic space.

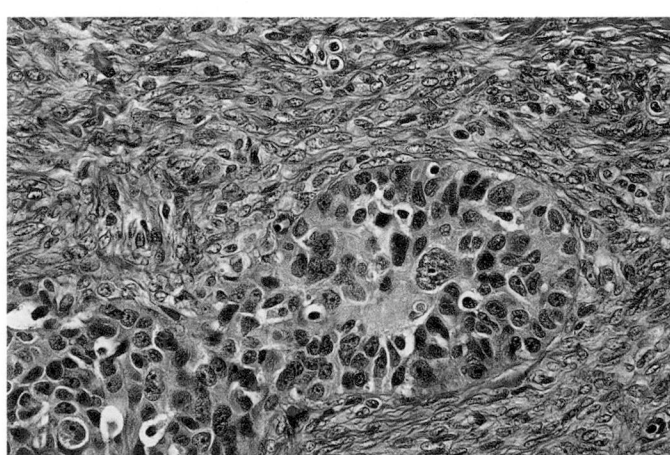

Fig. 19.266 Malignant Brenner tumor. The nuclear atypia is evident. Other areas of the tumor had the typical appearance of Brenner tumor.

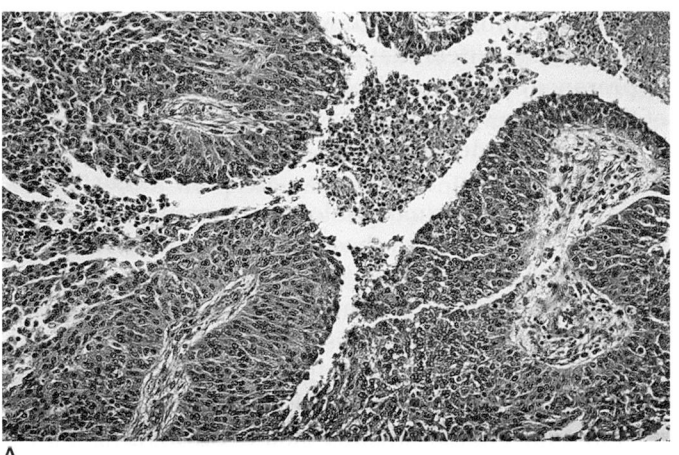
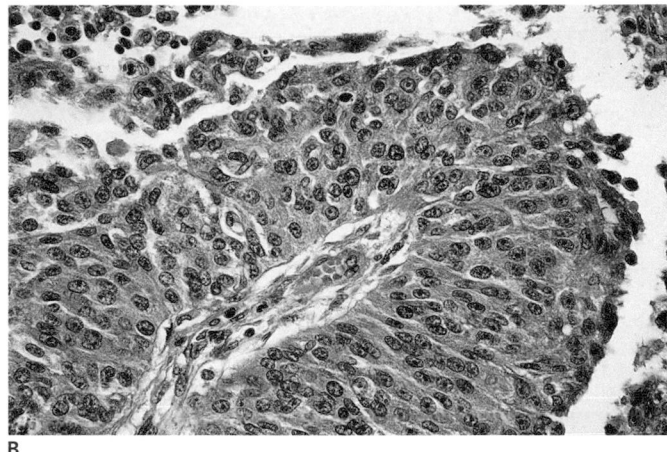

Fig. 19.267 A and **B**, Low- and high-power views of transitional cell carcinoma of ovary.

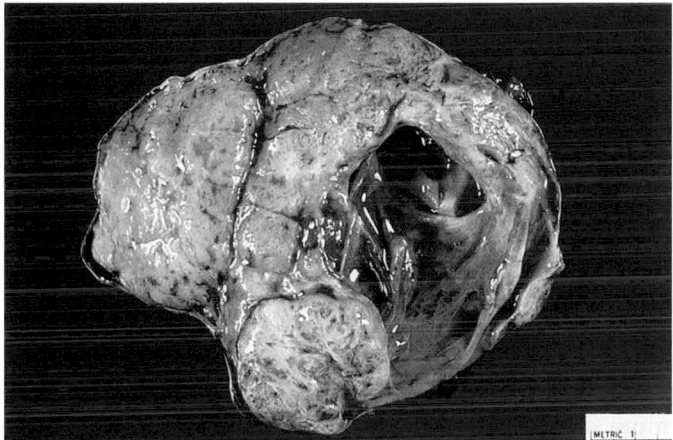

Fig. 19.268 Brenner tumor with typical solid appearance coexisting with mucinous cystadenoma. This is a well-recognized combination.

Brenner tumors or ovarian transitional cell carcinoma.[311a,316,317,330] Others have found an analogy by way of uroplakins and CK20, but surprisingly only in Brenner tumor and not in transitional cell carcinoma.[315,318]

Brenner tumors have exceptionally been seen to occur in accessory ovaries[310] or in other female genital tract sites, including vagina (see p. 1517 and p. 1614).

Malignant mixed müllerian tumor and müllerian adenosarcoma`

Malignant mixed müllerian tumor (MMMT) resembles grossly and microscopically in every respect its more common uterine counterpart (Fig. 19.269). Thus a *homologous* variety (with nonspecific malignant stroma; also called *carcinosarcoma*) and a *heterologous* variety (with malignant heterologous elements) occur.[340] The carcinomatous component may appear serous, endometrioid, squamous, or clear cell (mesonephroid). The sarcoma-like elements may have the appearance of chondrosarcoma (the most common), osteosarcoma, rhabdomyosarcoma, or angiosarcoma[346] (Fig. 19.270). Hyaline droplets containing α_1-antitrypsin are often present in the cytoplasm of the tumor cells.[339] Although some response to

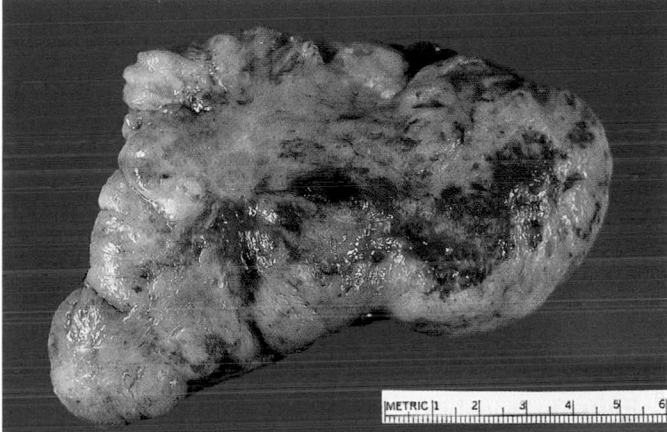
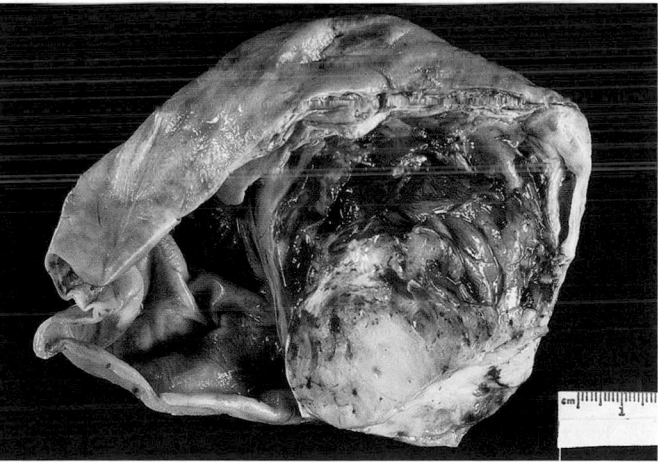

Fig. 19.269 A and **B**, Gross appearances of malignant mixed müllerian tumor of ovary. The neoplasms are large, variegated, solid and cystic, with hemorrhagic and necrotic areas.

chemotherapy has been noted,[347] the overall prognosis is extremely poor,[338] with some outstanding exceptions.[337] The most reliable prognostic criterion is the initial tumor stage.[333,334,335,345] Unfortunately, most tumors have already extended outside the ovary at the time of surgery.[343] The

12, and 8; gains in chromosomes 12 and 8; and rearrangements of 1, 3, 6, 11, and 19.[415,418,420] The loci most commonly affected are 19p+ (about half of the cases),[414] the short arm of chromosome 11,[409] and 17q (particularly with the serous tumors).[403] Trisomy 12 is sometimes the only chromosome abnormality found in benign and borderline serous tumors.[421]

Telomerase activity is found in virtually all carcinomas and borderline tumors but not in cystadenomas. Oncogenes reported to be amplified are HER2/*neu*, cyclin D1, cyclin A, *p21*, and *MDM2*.[397–402,405,413,417] In addition, EGFR and the M-CSF receptor are expressed along with the respective ligands (peptide growth factors) in some cases.[397,406,407]

Loss of *Dab2* (a candidate tumor suppressor gene) occurs in approximately 80% of ovarian carcinomas; it has also been detected in dysplastic lesions of the ovarian surface epithelium.[419]

Mutations of *p53* leading to overexpression of the protein product occur in approximately 30% of the cases overall, the prevalence being directly related to tumor grade and stage.[399,410,412] Mutations of k-*ras* are more common in mucinous than in serous or endometrioid carcinomas.[400,401] Among the serous tumors, they have been found by one group in about half of borderline serous tumors and micropapillary serous tumors with or without microinvasion, but not in high-grade conventional serous carcinomas, suggesting the existence of two different tumorigenic pathways.[416] Amplification and overexpression of the L-Myc proto-oncogene has recently been found to be a common feature of ovarian carcinoma.[418a]

Loss of heterozygosity at the *RB1* locus has been found in approximately 20% of cases; it is more common in the carcinomas than in the borderline tumors, and in the serous than the other types.[404]

Mutations of *DCC*, *BRCA1*, and *BRCA2* are rare in sporadic serous carcinomas.[408]

DNA ploidy analyses have shown that benign and borderline tumors are usually diploid, whereas a majority of the invasive carcinomas are aneuploid.[411]

Spread and metastases

The most common sites of involvement of ovarian serous carcinoma are the contralateral ovary, peritoneal cavity (further discussed in the next section), para-aortic and pelvic lymph nodes, and liver. With intra-abdominal spread, there are often ascites and involvement of the omentum.[429] Invasion of the intestinal wall may result in obstruction.[423] Ureteral involvement is usually associated with hydronephrosis. An umbilical metastasis ("sister Joseph's nodule") may be the first manifestation of the disease.[422,427] Lung and pleura are the most common sites of extra-abdominal spread.[425] Most lung metastases have a subpleural location. Metastases can also occur in unusual sites, such as the breast.[426]

The spread of borderline serous tumors is mainly in the form of invasive or noninvasive peritoneal implants (see below), but they can also involve lymph nodes of the neck and other sites, lung, and pleura.[424,428]

The sites of involvement of metastatic mucinous and endometrioid ovarian carcinoma are similar to those of the serous tumors, but there is less tendency to early and widespread peritoneal involvement.

Peritoneal lesions and the müllerian system

A variety of proliferative epithelial lesions involving the peritoneum have phenotypical features indicative of müllerian differentiation. Theoretically, they could develop through two different mechanisms: (1) spread from an ovarian (or, less commonly, endometrial or tubal source); (2) autochthonous origin from the so-called "secondary müllerian system," i.e., the pelvic and lower abdominal mesothelium and the subjacent mesenchyme of females. The two most important manifestations of this process are designated respectively as implants and endosalpingiosis, the assumption being that the first is an example of the former phenomenon, and the second of the latter.

Implants. One of the most common patterns of spread of ovarian carcinoma—particularly the serous type—is in the form of tumor deposits on the peritoneal surfaces (Fig. 19.272). Sites of early peritoneal spread are the lateral gutters and diaphragmatic surface (predominantly on the right side), omentum, and pelvic peritoneum, including the serosa of the uterine corpus and fallopian tube.[441] Involvement of abdominal viscera (bowel, liver, spleen) is generally by direct spread from the underlying peritoneum. There is a tendency for concentration of tumor nodules close to the primary tumor, so the pelvic peritoneum, sigmoid colon, cecum, and terminal ileum are most frequently involved. Sometimes, the entire peritoneal cavity is covered by implants measuring less than 1 cm in diameter and grossly simulating miliary tuberculosis.

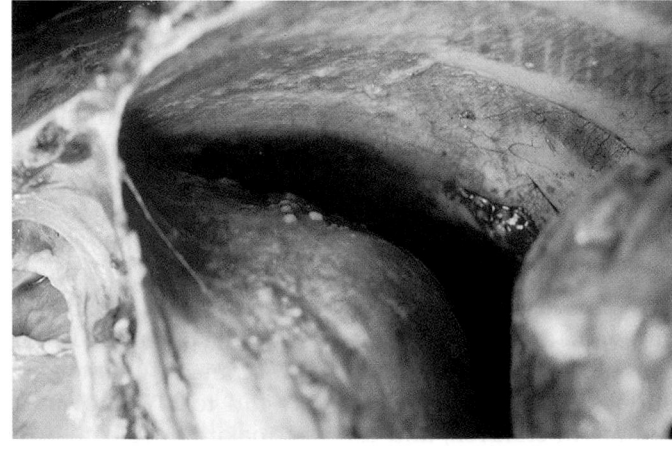

Fig. 19.272 Gross appearance of peritoneal implants from ovarian serous neoplasm.

which may or may not be correct. As a matter of fact, it has been suggested that most lesions designated endosalpingiosis of lymph nodes on morphologic grounds may be "bland-appearing" manifestations of metastatic tumor.[455] Molecular studies have provided conflicting results, in the sense of favoring multicentric origin in some instances and a clonal nature in others.[444,447,450,458]

Because of this pathogenetic uncertainty, which is however counterbalanced by the well-established prognostic significance of the various forms of peritoneal disease, it may be preferable to use a terminology that is pathogenetically noncommittal but which provides the clinician with clinically important information, on the basis of largely architectural criteria. Regardless of whether there is an ovarian component or not, or whether the disease being evaluated is on the peritoneal surface or in a lymph node, one should be able to recognize these main categories:

1 Lesions that are cytologically benign, noninvasive and nondesmoplastic. These include so-called "endosalpingiosis" and noninvasive nondesmoplastic ("epithelial") implants. Most of these patients do well and should be treated conservatively, but a small percentage will develop progressive disease.[443]

2 Lesions that lack nuclear atypia and stromal invasion, but which are associated with a prominent desmoplastic response ("desmoplastic" implants). These patients seem to do similarly to those in the first category.[443]

3 Lesions accompanied by "destructive" stromal invasion, whether they display nuclear atypia or not ("invasive" implants). These tend to behave in an aggressive fashion.[442]

4 Lesions lacking stromal invasion but exhibiting a micropapillary architecture and/or solid epithelial nests surrounded by clefts. This category is controversial, but the authors who proposed these criteria believe that the behavior of this lesion is as aggressive as those in the third category.[435]

Coexistence with uterine carcinoma

The simultaneous presence of carcinoma in the ovary and uterus is an uncommon but well-recognized event. The two tumors may have a similar appearance (usually endometrioid but sometimes papillary serous, clear cell, or mucinous) or be of different histologic types.[465] Theoretically, this phenomenon could be the result of (1) metastasis from an endometrial carcinoma into the ovary, (2) two independent primary tumors, or (3) metastasis from an ovarian carcinoma to the endometrium.[467] All three events probably occur, the third being by far the least common. A distinction between the first two possibilities is often difficult and may be impossible to make. The criteria used for this distinction and the information that has been recently obtained in this regard from appli-

cation of molecular genetic techniques are discussed under Uterus—corpus (see p. 1592). Briefly, ovarian metastasis from an endometrial tumor should be favored in the presence of multiplicity, bilaterality, and/or very small size of the ovarian tumor, involvement of the tubal lumen, and presence of deep myometrial invasion and/or vascular invasion in the uterine tumor.[465] Most neoplasms with an endometrioid appearance in both sites are probably independent neoplasms, and their prognosis is excellent; most of those with histologies other than endometrioid probably represent a single primary tumor with metastases, and their prognosis is correspondingly poor.[465,468]

Sometimes, the uterine tumor involves the cervix rather than the corpus; interestingly, a high proportion of these cervical tumors are of endometrioid type.[466] The lesion should be regarded as an ovarian metastasis from a cervical primary if there is bilateral ovarian involvement and extensive extracervical disease and if the microscopic type is one unusual for an ovarian primary (such as squamous cell carcinoma or small cell carcinoma).[469]

The association between ovarian and uterine neoplasms is also discussed in connection with the specific histologic types.

Cytology

The main role of diagnostic cytology in ovarian carcinoma is the identification of malignant cells in the peritoneal cavity. The value of peritoneal washing cytology to detect the microscopic spread of ovarian carcinoma has been acknowledged by the fact that the FIGO staging system incorporates the results of the washing in its scheme.[477] This technique is useful during the initial surgical staging and also in the course of second-look operations for the evaluation of therapy effect. Serous and endometrioid carcinomas are more often positive than carcinomas of other types, and high-grade tumors more than low-grade tumors.[476] Specifically, a high positive rate is related to advanced stage of disease, involvement of the ovarian surface, a moderate to large amount of fluid, and nonbloody serous ascites.[475]

Patients with positive fluids have a worse prognosis than others, but at least some of the difference is related to the stage of the disease; analysis of a large number of patients with stage I and II tumors is needed to determine the prognostic significance of a positive cytology independently of other prognostic factors.[473,476]

The interpretation of peritoneal washings can be made difficult by the admixture of reactive mesothelial cells and problems in distinguishing borderline from malignant tumors,[471] including those in the macropapillary category.[470,471,474]

Another potential use of cytology is in the aspiration of ovarian cysts; the procedure is fairly accurate but of limited practical value.[472]

eritoneal implants are present in 16% to 47% of borderline serous tumors and are associated with a mortality rate of 13% to 30%.[434] Although traditionally designated as "implants," it is possible and indeed likely that some arise in situ from the peritoneal mesothelium.[448] The large majority of ovarian borderline neoplasms associated with peritoneal implants have an exophytic pattern of growth on the ovarian surface, which provides them with direct contact with the peritoneal cavity.[459] The microscopic appearance of these implants is similar to that of the ovarian tumor and is, therefore, characterized by tufting, stratification, cytologic atypia, and psammoma bodies[432,451] (Fig. 19.273). They can be predominantly cystic or papillary. Some have been known to regress spontaneously, sometimes leaving a shower of psammoma bodies behind. Indeed, it has been suggested that salpingoliths (round calcific structures on the serosa of the fallopian tubes) may have a similar pathogenesis, at least in some instances.[460] Infiltration of underlying tissues and marked cytologic atypia are associated with a high probability of disease progression.[452] Accordingly, these implants have been divided into noninvasive and invasive. Noninvasive

implants are further subdivided into epithelial and desmoplastic. The epithelial implants may be exophytic or within invaginations beneath the peritoneal surface; they are characterized by a papillary pattern of growth, mild to moderate atypia, and lack of inflammation or stromal reaction. In desmoplastic noninvasive implants, the epithelial component is more irregular, the cells have a more abundant acidophilic cytoplasm, and—most importantly—there is inflammation (occasionally severe) and a brisk stromal reaction with a granulation tissue-like appearance (Fig. 19.274A). Invasive implants show haphazard "destructive" infiltration of the stroma (Fig. 19.274B). As a general rule, psammoma bodies are less numerous than in noninvasive implants. The nuclear atypia is not necessarily more pronounced (but see below).

Peritoneal implants should be distinguished from endosalpingiosis (as described later) and from florid mesothelial hyperplasia, of a type similar to that most commonly seen in hernia sacs and around ruptured tubal pregnancies.[438]

Occasionally, one or multiple peritoneal nodules with features of ovarian serous borderline or malignant

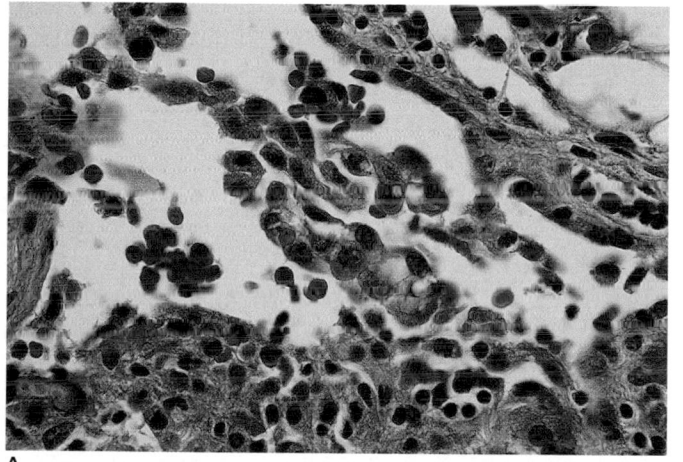
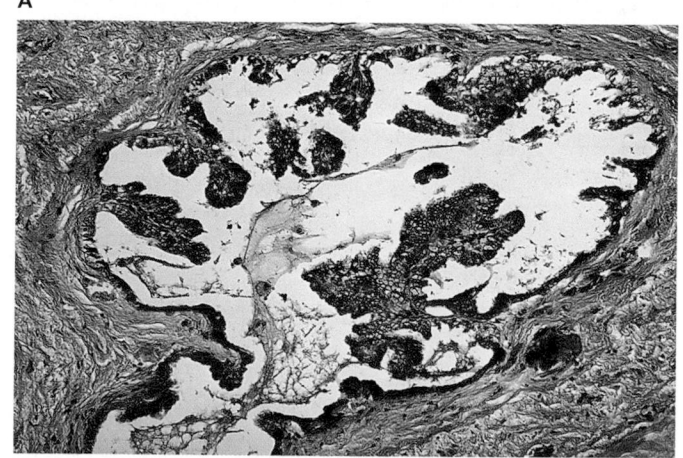

Fig. 19.273 A and **B**, Microscopic appearance of peritoneal implants of epithelial (noninvasive, nondesmoplastic) type.

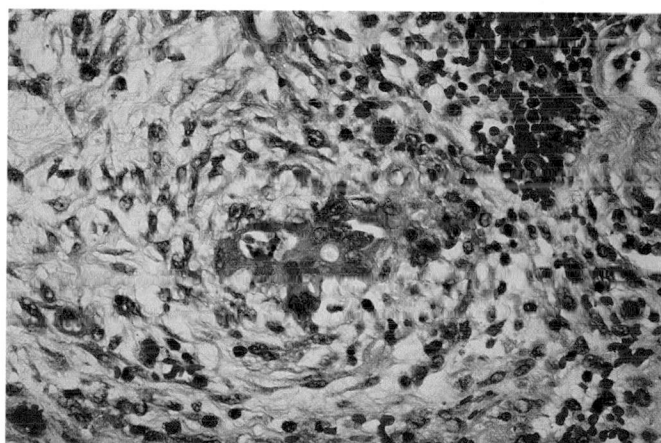
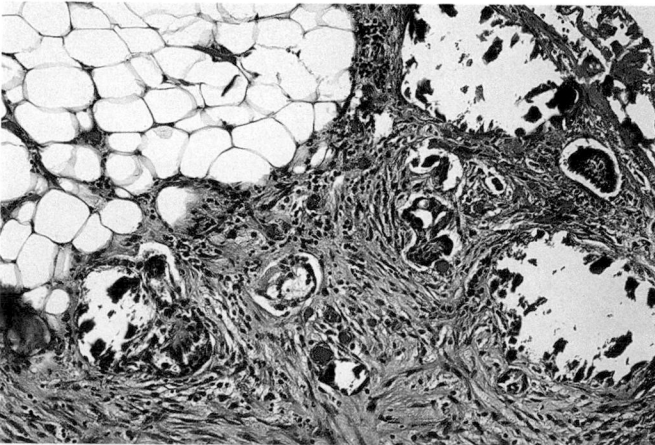

Fig. 19.274 Peritoneal implants of desmoplastic (**A**) and invasive (**B**) types.

tumors can be seen in the presence of minimal or no ovarian involvement. The malignant-appearing lesions have generally been regarded as ovarian carcinomas with widespread metastases if the ovary was affected, however focally and superficially (see discussion of serous surface papillary carcinomas on p. 1662), and as **extraovarian (peritoneal) papillary serous carcinomas** in the absence of ovarian abnormalities.[440,451,447] Their immunohistochemical and ultrastructural profile and their natural history are closer to ovarian serous carcinoma than to diffuse peritoneal mesothelioma[461,463]; they should, therefore, be viewed as *carcinomas* composed of cells analogous to those of the similarly named ovarian tumors. Notably, some of these tumors have developed after prophylactic oophorectomy in women with a family history of ovarian carcinoma.[456]

The immunohistochemical distinction between this tumor type and conventional peritoneal mesothelioma is not as sharp as it is between pleural mesothelioma and lung adenocarcinoma, and therefore the criteria employed in the latter instance are not necessarily applicable to the peritoneal situation. This predicament, which is not generally appreciated, has a very simple explanation: whereas in the thoracic cavity one is dealing with two totally unrelated tissue types (mesothelium and endodermally derived lung epithelium), in the abdomen one is dealing with a proliferation of mesothelial origin that in one instance manifests its potential to differentiate along müllerian lines. There are, however, some markers that are more likely to be positive in one or the other. Thus, B72.3, CEA, Ber-EP4, PLAP, and hormone receptors are more likely to be expressed by serous carcinoma, whereas calretinin, thrombomodulin, and CK5/6 are more likely to be seen in conventional mesothelioma.[431,437,445,446] Immunohistochemically, reactive mesothelial cells are more likely to be reactive for calretinin than implants, whereas the reverse is true for Ber-EP4, B72.3, and Leu-M1.[444a]

The **borderline tumors**, which have also been designated as *peritoneal serous micropapillomatosis of low malignant potential*,[436] have a natural history equivalent to that of their ovarian counterpart (i.e., characterized by a good long-term prognosis).[433,462] Morphologically, these tumors resemble the noninvasive implants of ovarian serous borderline tumors. Cases of primary peritoneal serous psammocarcinomas have also been reported, their morphology and natural history being equivalent in all regards to those of their ovarian counterparts.[462]

Before leaving the subject, one ought to mention the reverse situation, which is much more unusual, i.e., that of an ovarian-based tumor having the morphologic and immunohistochemical features of a conventional mesothelioma.[430,439]

Endosalpingiosis. The term *endosalpingiosis*, originally coined for an inflammatory condition of the fallopian tube characterized by attachment of the fimbria

to the ovarian surface followed by spread of the fallopian tube epithelium over the adjacent ovary (see p. 1636), is now applied to the presence beneath the peritoneal surface of glands and tubules (sometimes containing papillae and psammoma bodies), lined by cuboidal to low columnar cells, which are sometimes ciliated. Some resemble the endosalpingian mucosa, hence the name (Fig. 19.275). They are thought to be the result of müllerian differentiation or metaplasia of the celomic mesothelium. Endosalpingiosis is generally seen in association with ovarian serous tumors, usually of borderline type (alone or in conjunction with implants), but it may occur in the absence of ovarian abnormalities.[464] Exceptionally, it has been seen in association with lymphangioleiomyomatosis in retroperitoneal lymph nodes.[453] The vanishingly rare müllerian cysts that have been reported in the mesentery and retroperitoneum are probably related to endosalpingiosis.[449]

Implants or endosalpingiosis? The distinction between these two abnormalities is not always sharp morphologically, and the belief that the first represents a secondary deposit from an ovarian lesion whereas the second is primary at the site is simply an assumption,

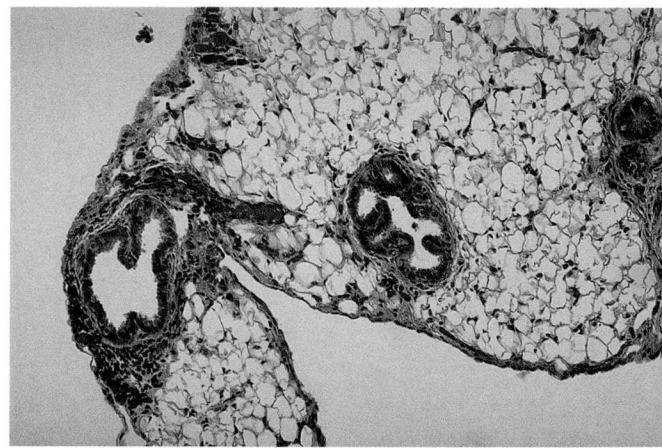

A

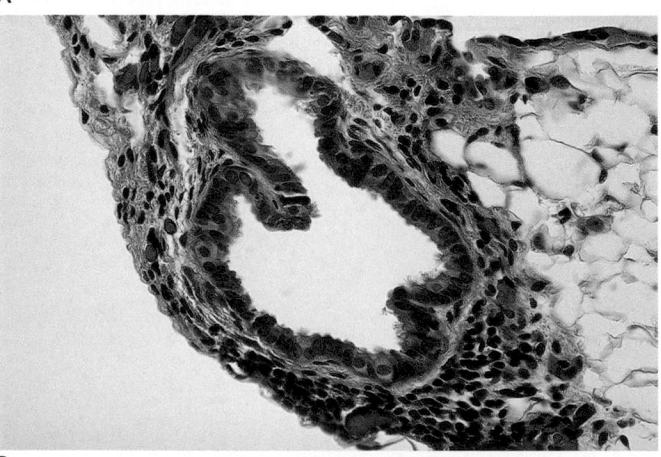

B
Fig. 19.275 A and B, Low- and high-power views of peritoneal endosalpingiosis.

Therapy

The primary form of therapy of surface epithelial tumors is surgical.[478,483,488] Benign tumors are cured by a conservative operation in the form of unilateral salpingo-oophorectomy. Although in the case of occasional small benign tumors (some surface papillomas and cystadenofibromas) the uninvolved portion of the ovary can be preserved, the majority require the excision of the entire gonad. Most borderline tumors in young females can also be treated conservatively with safety, the results following salpingo-oophorectomy being equivalent to those seen following more extensive procedures.[496] As a matter of fact, some cases have been treated with cystectomy only, the overall outcome being excellent; however, presence of tumor at the margin is a strong predictor of tumor recurrence.[486]

Carcinomas require bilateral salpingo-oophorectomy with total abdominal hysterectomy and omentectomy, with the possible exception of grade I mucinous cystadenocarcinoma, for which a conservative approach has been suggested by some authors in selected young patients.[497] The role of pelvic lymphadenectomy (as opposed to lymph node sampling) remains controversial.[480]

It is important to examine carefully the peritoneal cavity during the course of the operation and to biopsy selected sites to properly stage the disease for future therapy.[498] This surgical staging, which also applies to borderline tumors, should include sampling from pelvic and abdominal peritoneal surfaces, diaphragm, omentum, and lymph nodes (pelvic and para-aortic).[485,487] If ascitic fluid is present, it should be examined cytologically; if not, peritoneal washings should be taken.[479] Adjuvant therapy (radiation therapy and/or chemotherapy) is said to be particularly important for high-grade stage I tumors, for tumors accompanied by positive ascitic fluid, and for minimal stage III disease.[482,493,499]

In some institutions, "second-look" operations have been done as a standard procedure for patients with ovarian carcinomas treated with surgery and chemotherapy who are clinically free of disease, to determine prognosis and decide whether chemotherapy should be continued, discontinued, or changed. However, the practical value of this procedure is being increasingly questioned on the grounds that the subgroup of patients whose condition can be salvaged by a second-line therapy is small (approximately 8%) and that an effective salvage therapy still remains to be identified.[484,491]

The second-look operation includes direct visual inspection of the abdominal cavity, cytologic examination of peritoneal washings, and multiple biopsies of peritoneum, omentum, and lymph nodes. Residual tumor has been found pathologically in over 40% of patients in most series.[490,492,495] This tends to be found in the same site as the initial tumor.[494] The microscopic interpretation can be complicated by the presence of

mesothelial hyperplasia, psammoma bodies without accompanying epithelium, foreign body giant cell reaction, focal fibroblastic proliferation, fat necrosis, and other changes.[481] Immunohistochemical staining for CEA, CD15, and other markers can be helpful in the differential diagnosis.[489]

Prognosis

The overall prognosis of ovarian carcinoma remains poor, a direct result of its rapid growth rate and the lack of early symptoms. The overall survival rate is approximately 35% at 5 years, 28% at 10 years, and 15% at 25 years.[520] Factors known to influence prognosis are listed below:

1 *Age.* As a group, younger patients have a better outcome. This is at least partially due to the fact that there is a higher percentage of borderline, well-differentiated, and stage I tumors in this group.[501,541]

2 BRCA1 *mutations and family history.* It seems that the ovarian cancers developing in patients with *BRCA1* mutations have a significantly more favorable clinical course,[502,523,527] although the statement has been challenged.[514] In patients without *BRCA1* mutations, the prognosis is not significantly different whether there is a family history of breast cancer or not.[505]

3 Presence and extent of *tumor spread* beyond the ovary, as expressed by clinical staging. For the carcinomas (as opposed to the borderline tumors, see later section), this is the most important prognostic determinator.

4 *Ascites.* This clinical finding constitutes, by itself, an unfavorable prognostic sign.[500,508]

5 *Borderline tumors versus carcinomas.* This is a distinction of utmost significance for prognostic purposes.[525,532] The incidence of recurrence is nearly zero for borderline mucinous and endometrioid tumors and approximately 20% for borderline serous or seromucinous tumors.[503] The prognosis in borderline tumors is still very good even in the presence of involvement of the peritoneal cavity, microinvasion, or tumor recrudescence in the abdominal cavity. In one series, the survival was 99% for stage I tumor and an astonishing 92% for advanced stage disease.[518] Because of these figures, some authors have questioned whether it is justified to keep labeling these tumors as of low-grade malignant potential or even borderline.[518] The particular situation of micropapillary serous tumors within this scheme is discussed on p. 1678. The semantic controversy notwithstanding, there is agreement that this pattern is associated with a higher recurrence rate than the conventional borderline tumor.

6 *Tumor grade and type.* Among the carcinomas, tumor grade correlates closely with survival.[520,539,540] The problem is that the grading system has varied among published reports, and in some studies it has not

been specified at all.[521,536] Recently, Silverberg proposed a new system, modeled on the Nottingham grading scheme for breast carcinoma, designed to be applied to all invasive carcinomas of the ovary.[537] The preliminary results obtained with it are promising.[529] The microscopic type (serous, mucinous, endometrioid, or other) is of less significance in this regard, particularly among the lesser differentiated tumors.[520] However, as a group, endometrioid carcinomas do better when pure than when mixed with papillary serous or undifferentiated components.[542] Silverberg[537] made the important point that grading is less valuable than typing in predicting survival but better at predicting tumor responsiveness to chemotherapy and even as a guide as to which agents should be used. It follows that both grade and type should be specified in the pathology report.

7 *Psammoma bodies.* Serous tumors containing numerous such structures have a better prognosis,[538] the extreme example being psammocarcinoma, which does not behave significantly differently than a borderline tumor. This may be related to the fact that most of these tumors are well differentiated.

8 *Rupture of tumor capsule.* There is no convincing evidence that this occasional intraoperative complication has any influence on survival rates.[500,533]

9 *DNA ploidy.* DNA analysis with flow cytometry (using either fresh tissue or paraffin-embedded material) has proved a strong prognostic indicator among the ovarian carcinomas in the sense that aneuploid tumors belong to a higher grade and behave in a much more aggressive fashion than the diploid tumors.[510,511,526] Correlation has also been found between tumor DNA ploidy and response to chemotherapy.[504] The value of flow cytometry is very limited in the evaluation of borderline tumors.[507]

10 *CA-125.* This serum marker has been found of great value in the initial evaluation of these patients (particularly in stage II and beyond) and in the follow-up of recurrent disease.[528,534] It is believed to be an independent prognostic factor.[534]

11 *p53.* Overexpression of p53 has been claimed to be a marker of poor prognosis in most but not all studies.[509,513,519,535]

12 *Tumor angiogenesis.* Increased peritumoral vessel density is believed to be a marker of poor prognosis.[516,531]

13 *Intratumoral T cells.* It has been recently claimed that the presence of tumor-infiltrating T cells correlates with improved outcome in advanced ovarian cancer.[543]

14 *Other markers.* Overexpression of HER2/neu,[522] fatty acid synthase (OA-519),[512] nm23 (purported to be a metastasis suppressor gene),[530] P-glycoprotein (responsible for multidrug resistance),[515] various components of the cell cycle,[506,524] and CD24[517] have all been found to be associated with aggressive behavior in ovarian carcinoma, but their value as independent prognostic factors needs to be established.

Germ cell tumors

Germ cell tumors constitute approximately 20% of all ovarian neoplasms. Most of them are seen in children and young adults. Approximately 95% of these tumors are benign cystic teratomas; the younger the patient, the more likely the germ cell tumor will be malignant.[546,549]

In the sections that follow, the tumors are discussed as individual types; however, it should be recognized that a combination of various elements occurs in approximately 8% of cases. These are referred to as *mixed germ cell tumors*[545,548]; the most common combination is that of dysgerminoma with yolk sac tumor, but many others occur,[551] including some with a predominance of the polyembryoma component.[547]

One of the greatest achievements in oncology is represented by the therapy of malignant germ cell tumors. Chemotherapeutic regimens consisting of a combination of bleomycin, etoposide, and cisplatin have resulted in overall disease-free survival rates greater than 95%.[544,550]

Dysgerminoma

Dysgerminoma constitutes less than 1% of all ovarian tumors and approximately 5% of malignant ones.[557] Most patients are young. In Santesson's series of nearly 300 cases, 81% were under 30 years of age and 44% were under 20 years of age.[570] Dysgerminoma made up 6% of 188 childhood ovarian neoplasms collected by Abell et al.[552] Approximately 5% of dysgerminomas arise in abnormal gonads: pure or mixed gonadal dysgenesis (from a gonadoblastoma, see p. 1704) or testicular feminization (androgen insensitivity) syndrome. Exceptionally, the tumor is associated with hypercalcemia.[560]

Dysgerminoma is somewhat more common on the right side and is bilateral in 15% of cases.[570] It is often large (it may reach over 1000 g) and encapsulated, with a smooth, often convoluted surface (Fig. 19.276). The cut surface is solid and gray; foci of hemorrhage and necrosis can occur, but they are not as common or prominent as in other malignant germ cell tumors (Fig. 19.277). Microscopically, the tumor cells usually group themselves in well-defined nests separated by fibrous strands infiltrated by lymphocytes (most of which are of T-cell type[559]) (Fig. 19.278). Occasionally, a pseudotubular or cordlike arrangement may be seen (particularly at the tumor periphery), which may be quite confusing[554] (Fig. 19.279). Focal necrosis, hyaline changes in vessels, germinal centers, and granulomatous foci may be present. The individual tumor cells are uniform and have large nuclei, *one or more prominent elongated nucleoli*, and abundant clear to finely granular cytoplasm that contains glycogen and sometimes fine droplets of fat. The cell membrane is prominent.

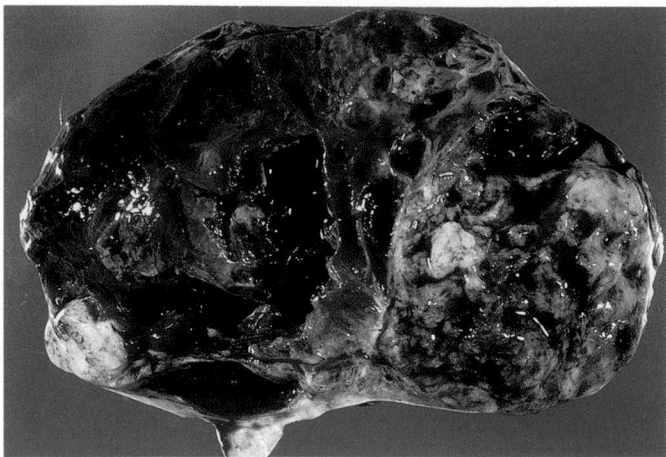

Fig. 19.282 Gross appearance of yolk sac tumor. The cut surface is remarkably heterogeneous due to extensive hemorrhage, necrosis, and cystic degeneration.

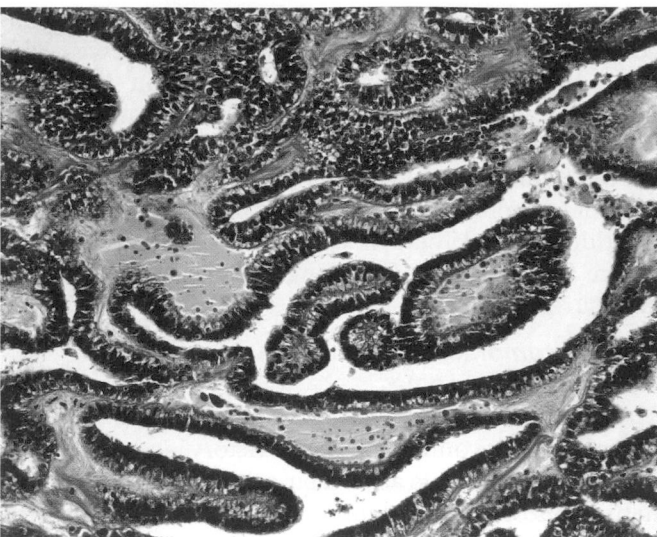

Fig. 19.284 Yolk sac tumor with endometrioid features.

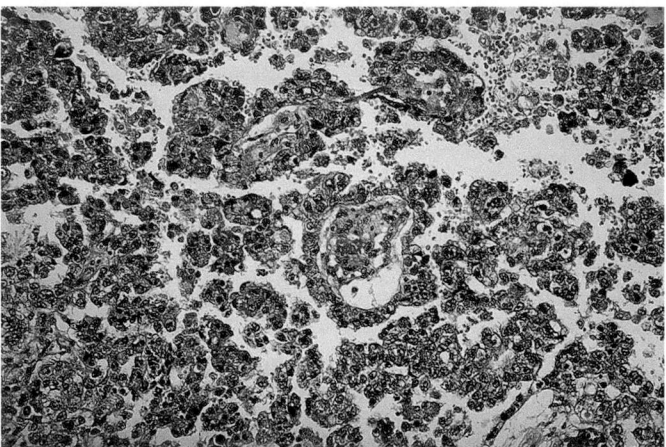

A

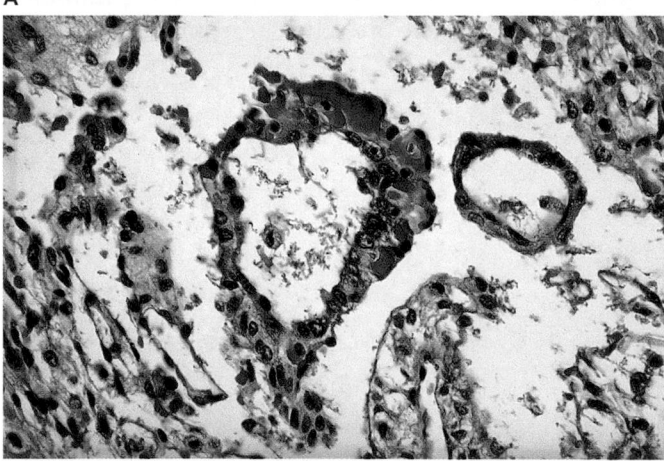

B

Fig. 19.283 A and **B**, Low- and high-power views of ovarian yolk sac tumor. Numerous hyaline globules are seen in the cytoplasm of the tumor cells lining the papillae (**B**).

formed by a loose meshwork lined by flat or cuboidal cells (Fig. 19.283), rounded or festooning pseudopapillary processes with central vessels (Schiller–Duval bodies), and solid "undifferentiated" areas. The mes-

enchyme-like component of these tumors has pluripotential properties; it usually presents in the form of spindle cells in a well-vascularized myxoid background, but it exhibits keratin immunoreactivity as a sign of early epithelial differentiation and may contain heterologous elements such as skeletal muscle.[589]

Intracytoplasmic and extracellular PAS-positive hyaline droplets are nearly always present. Their chemical composition is heterogeneous; they usually stain for α-fetoprotein, but they may also contain α_1-antitrypsin and basement membrane components (type IV collagen and laminin).[573] Yolk sac tumor also stains for pankeratin, but not for keratin 7 (in contrast with endometrioid and clear cell ovarian carcinoma) or WT-1 (in contrast with serous ovarian carcinoma).[597a] DNA ploidy studies have shown that yolk sac tumors are almost invariably aneuploid.[585]

A fourth of the yolk sac tumors have vesicular structures with eccentric constrictions surrounded by a dense spindle cell stroma; this has been referred to as a *polyvesicular vitelline pattern* and is said to be associated with a good prognosis when present in a pure form.[593] Others show a scattered hCG-positive syncytiotrophoblast component. Still others exhibit evidence of differentiation toward hepatic, intestinal, and parietal yolk sac structures[576] (Fig. 19.284). The latter are recognized by the presence of thick layers of intercellular basement membrane.[602] The *hepatoid* component, which can predominate almost to the exclusion of the others, is composed of masses, nests, and broad bands of large polyhedral cells with occasional glandular formations and numerous hyaline bodies. Their immunohistochemical profile is similar to that of hepatocellular carcinoma, including reactivity for α_1-antitrypsin and a canalicular pattern with polyclonal CEA.[578,597] These hepatoid yolk sac tumors are to be distinguished from *hepatoid ovarian carcinomas*, rare tumors of probable surface epithelial origin[581] (Fig. 19.285). In some yolk sac tumors, the presence of *glandular* formations may simulate the appearance of endometrioid carcinoma.[574]

Areas of luteinized stromal cells may be present and may sometimes be responsible for virilization.

Teilum's brilliant hypothesis that this tumor recapitulates normal yolk sac elements[601] has been amply confirmed by histochemical and ultrastructural studies,[591,592,594] including the recent detection of GATA-4, a transcription factor that regulates the differentiation and function of murine yolk sac endoderm.[599]

In the series of Kurman and Norris,[586] written less than 30 years ago, the actuarial survival at 3 years was only 13%; although 71% of the patients were thought to have stage I tumors, subclinical metastases were present in 84%. The introduction of multidrug chemotherapy has dramatically improved survival rates.[579] As usual, clinical stage is the most important prognostic indicator.[584,590] Serial determinations of serum α-fetoprotein are useful in monitoring the tumor course.[583,600]

Embryonal carcinoma also occurs in a young age group (median age, 15 years). In one series, 47% of the patients were prepubertal at the time of diagnosis, and 43% of them presented with precocious puberty.[587] Vaginal bleeding was recorded in 33%, amenorrhea in 7%, and hirsutism in 7%. Serum α-fetoprotein levels are often (but not always) elevated, whereas chorionic gonadotropin levels are invariably high, to a level that results in consistently positive pregnancy tests.

Grossly, the median diameter of these neoplasms is 17 cm. Their external surface is smooth and glistening, and their cut surface is predominantly solid and variegated, with extensive areas of necrosis and hemorrhage (Fig. 19.286). Microscopically, this tumor has a similar appearance to the embryonal carcinoma of the adult testis. As such, it is composed of solid sheets and nests of large primitive cells, occasionally forming papillae and abortive glandular structures (Fig. 19.286). Syncytiotrophoblast-like tumor cells are frequently seen scattered among the smaller cells; these are immunoreactive for hCG. In the Kurman and Norris series,[587] the prognosis was somewhat better than for yolk sac tumor, but current multidrug chemotherapeutic regimens have erased these differences.[572,577]

Embryonal carcinomas largely composed of embryoid bodies are referred to as *polyembryomas* (Fig. 19.287).

Choriocarcinoma

Most choriocarcinomas involving the ovary represent metastases from uterine tumors. The exceedingly rare primary ovarian choriocarcinomas can develop from an ovarian pregnancy (gestational type, which is the most common) or as a form of germ cell neoplasm (nongestational).[606] The latter can be pure or, more frequently, a component of a mixed germ cell tumor. It has also been seen in association with mature cystic teratoma of the contralateral ovary.[607] Microscopically, they show the typical admixture of syncytial and cytotrophoblastic elements in a necrotic and hemorrhagic background.

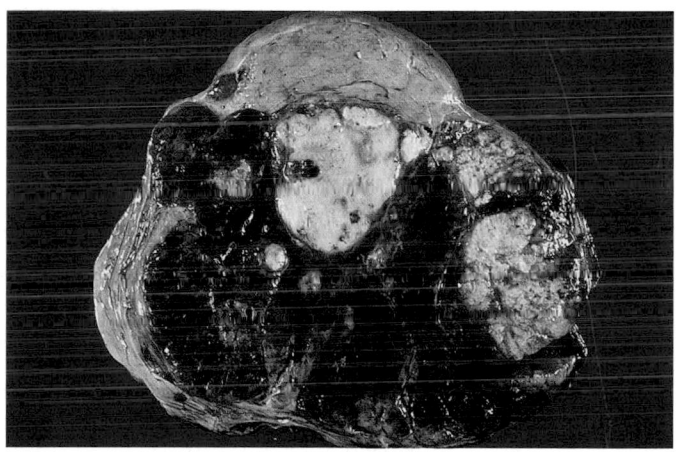

A

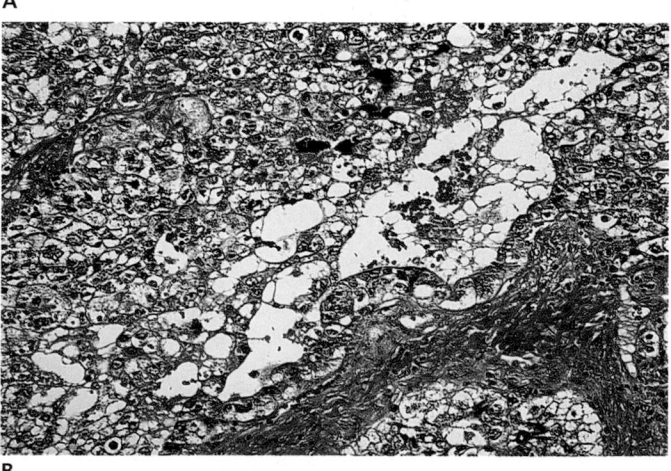

B

Fig. 19.286 A and **B**, Gross and microscopic appearance of embryonal carcinoma of ovary.

Fig. 19.285 Hepatoid carcinoma of ovary. This tumor, which greatly resembles hepatocellular carcinoma, should be distinguished from yolk sac tumor with hepatoid differentiation.

both the ovary and testis, as proposed many years ago by Gunnar Teilum.[742] Secondary changes, such as luteinization, may also develop. As a result, a wide array of tumor types may be seen, some of which do not fit easily into a rigid classification system. In general, a relationship exists between the morphologic appearance of the tumor and the presence and type of clinically evident hormonal activity.[738,739,741] However, there may be no demonstrable endocrine effects, and rare examples of hormonal effects opposite to those expected from the morphologic features also occur.[724,730] Along similar lines, there is general agreement between the cytoarchitectural features of the tumor and the presence of various steroid hormones, hormone precursors, and related enzymes, as demonstrated by immunohistochemical techniques.[722,740] However, it is important to emphasize that the classification of ovarian neoplasms is primarily based on their morphologic appearance, rather than on the presence or type of steroid hormones as determined immunohistochemically. The latter is plagued with so many conceptual and technical difficulties when evaluated in formalin-fixed, paraffin-embedded material (hormone loss from organic solvents, tissue diffusion of the lipid-soluble hormones, hormone-binding to receptors, etc.) as to make it unwise to classify an ovarian tumor as belonging to the sex cord–stromal category solely on this basis.

Recently, a number of immunohistochemical markers have become available that are of considerable assistance in the identification of these tumors.[732,743]

Inhibin has emerged as the most useful. The α-subunit of the molecule seems to have a greater degree of specificity than the βA-subunit.[721,726] It stains all types of sex cord–stromal tumors, the sex cordlike elements of other gynecologic neoplasms, and most trophoblastic tumors.[731,736] It is also useful for the identification of steroid hormone-secreting cells in the non-neoplastic stroma component of epithelial, germ cell, and other types of ovarian tumors.[729] It is also said to stain some carcinomas at other sites,[733] but this seems to be due at least in part to endogenous biotin.[727] It should be also pointed out that negativity for inhibin does not rule out a diagnosis of sex cord–stromal tumor (following the general rule that a negative stain never rules out anything).

Molecules functionally related to inhibin that also stain sex cord–stromal tumors are activin (a molecule biochemically similar to inhibin but with an opposite function, and composed of two βA-subunits), müllerian inhibiting substance (anti-müllerian hormone), and relaxin-like factor.[718,732,734,737]

Calretinin is more sensitive but less specific than inhibin, in the sense that it often stains sex cord–stromal tumors that are inhibin-negative, such as fibromas.[720,735] However, it also stains a good number of surface epithelial neoplasms.

A103, an antibody directed against the melanocytic marker Melan-A (Mart-1), has been found consistently to stain sex cord–stromal tumors and other types of steroid-producing cells, such as those of ovarian lipid cell tumor and adrenal cortical neoplasms.[719]

CD99 (O13; MIC2), a marker generally used for Ewing's sarcoma/PNET, also frequently (and somewhat unexpectedly) stains this family of neoplasms.[725,734]

Before going into the specific subtypes, WT-1, present in normal granulosa cells, is expressed by a majority of ovarian sex cord-stromal tumors.[722a] It ought to be mentioned that sex cord–stromal tumors of ovarian type are exceptionally encountered in extraovarian locations, such as the broad ligament.[728]

Granulosa cell tumor

Granulosa cell tumor is an ovarian neoplasm showing differentiation toward follicular granulosa cells. Whether it actually arises from granulosa cells in preexisting follicles or from the specialized ovarian stroma is debatable. Two distinct types exist, known respectively as adult and juvenile.

Adult granulosa cell tumor is usually diagnosed during child-bearing age, but it can occur after menopause and sometimes even before puberty. Three fourths of cases are associated with hyperestrinism; the excessive production of estrogens can lead to isosexual precocious puberty in children[763] and to metrorrhagia in adults, including postmenopausal patients.[753] Some of the cases are hormonally inactive at the clinical level, and a very few are androgenic.[748,769]

Grossly, adult granulosa cell tumors are usually encapsulated, with a smooth, lobulated outline and a predominantly solid cut surface (Fig. 19.301). The color is usually gray, but it may be yellow in areas of luteinization (Fig. 19.302). Cysts filled with straw-colored or mucoid fluid may be present (Fig. 19.303). Sometimes the cysts are so prominent as to simulate grossly the appearance of a cystadenoma (Fig. 19.304). Interestingly, a disproportionate number of androgenic granulosa cell tumors are large and cystic, either unilocular or multilocular.[769,772] The microscopic appearance of granulosa cell

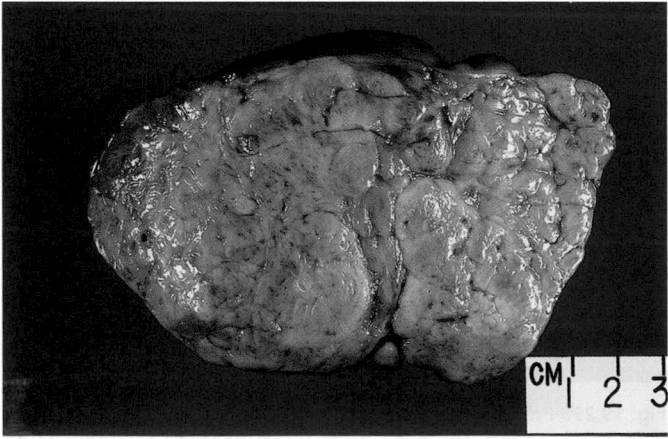

Fig. 19.301 Granulosa cell tumor with solid cut surface.

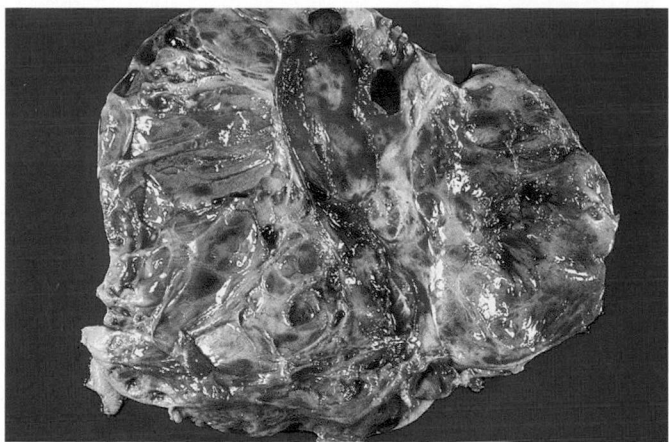

Fig. 19.302 Granulosa cell tumor showing admixture of solid and cystic areas.

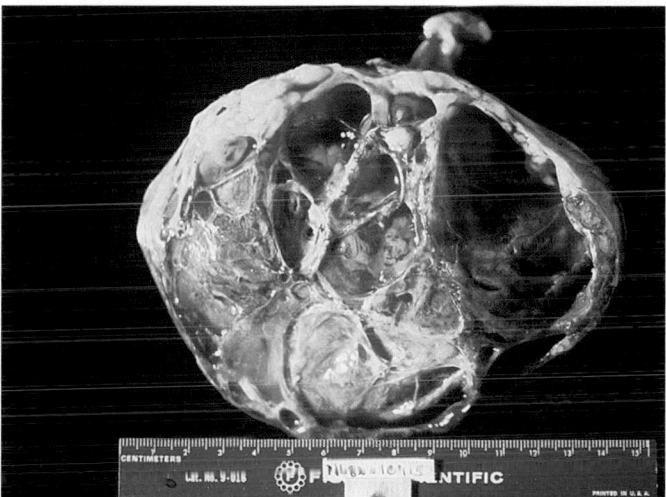

Fig. 19.303 Predominantly cystic granulosa cell tumor.

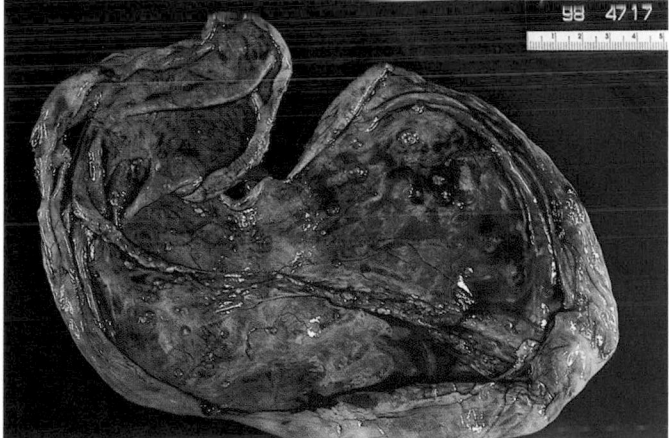

Fig. 19.304 Granulosa cell tumor with an entirely cystic gross appearance.

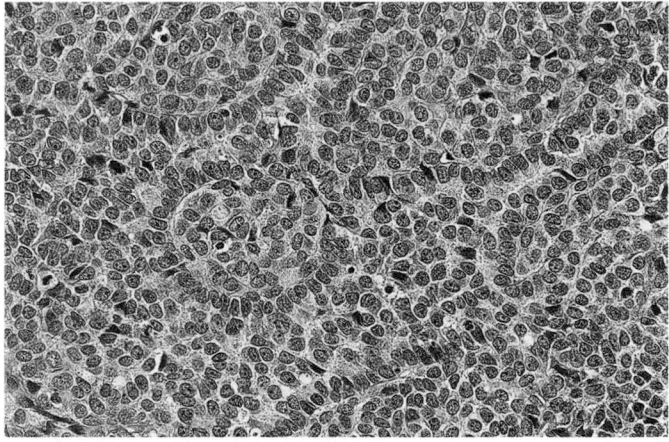

A

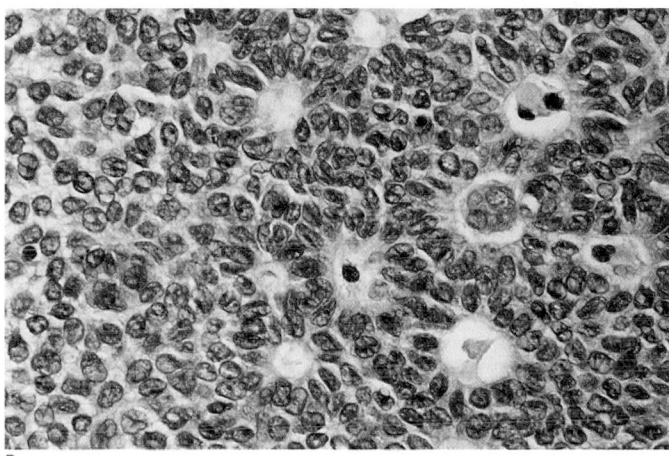

B

Fig. 19.305 A and **B,** Microscopic appearance of granulosa cell tumor. Call Exner bodies are seen in B.

19.305). A theca cell component may also be present. Focal luteinization of either the granulosa or the theca cell component may occur[786]; it is particularly prominent in those tumors associated with pregnancy, together with edema and disorderly arrangement.[785] An important diagnostic feature is the presence of folds or grooves in the nuclei, resulting in a "coffee-bean" appearance[771] (Fig. 19.306). Occasionally, bizarre nuclei and multinucleated giant cells (some of the "floret" type) are seen; this change is not a sign of malignancy *per se* but is rather of a degenerative nature.[788] Cases of granulosa cell tumor have been reported exhibiting hepatocytic differentiation.[746,770]

Traditionally, secretion of steroid hormones has been related to theca cells rather than granulosa cells, both in normal follicles and tumors; however, immunohistochemical studies have shown steroid production in both cell types, with a predominance of estradiol in the granulosa cells and progesterone in luteinized theca cells.[762] Other consistent immunohistochemical markers of granulosa cell tumors include vimentin, desmoplakin (desmosomal plaque protein), inhibin, follicle regulatory proteins, CD99 (O13; MIC2), and A103[752,753,764,765,767,774]

tumor is extremely variable, even within the same neoplasm. Patterns of growth include microfollicular (with Call–Exner bodies), macrofollicular, trabecular, insular, watered-silk, solid, and diffuse (sarcomatoid)[778] (Fig.

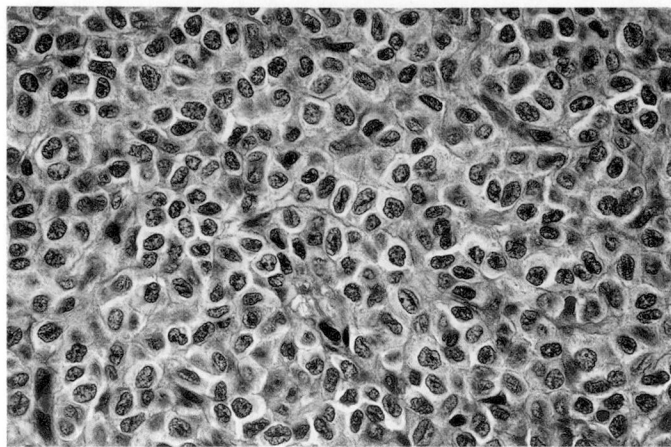

Fig. 19.306 Coffee-bean nuclei in adult type of ovarian granulosa cell tumor

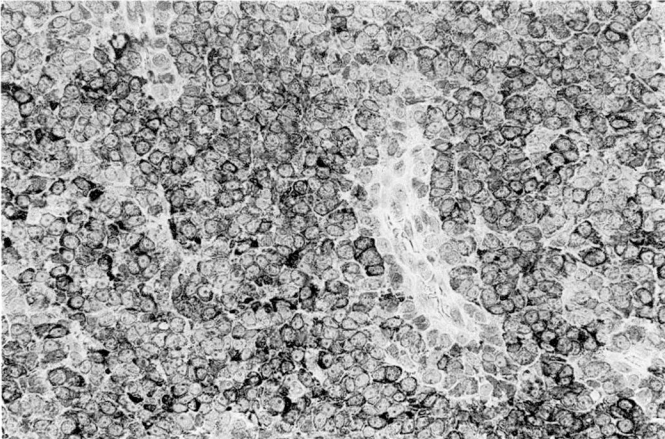

Fig. 19.307 Strong immunoreactivity for inhibin in granulosa cell tumor.

(Fig. 19.307). Keratin is present in one third to one half of cases; it has a typical dot-like distribution and consists mainly of CK8 and CK18 types.[751,773] Smooth muscle actin is seen in nearly all cases, but desmin less commonly so.[776] Approximately 50% of cases are reactive for S-100 protein, whereas none are immunoreactive for EMA.[751] The peptide hormone inhibin and follicle regulatory proteins, two substances normally produced by ovarian granulosa cells, have been found to be elevated in the serum of patients with granulosa cell tumor; inhibin has also been demonstrated immunohistochemically.[755] Curiously, granulosa cell tumors have also been found to be often immunoreactive for CD99 (O13; MIC2) a marker associated with Ewing's sarcoma/PNET (see Chapter 25).[764]

Ultrastructurally, the neoplastic granulosa cells have abundant intermediate filaments and specialized cell junctions, some of the latter having the appearance of typical desmosomes.[752] Cytogenetically, there is consistent trisomy for chromosome 12.[756,759] Strangely, in some cases with bizarre nuclei, the only foci showing trisomy 12 by FISH are those in which the bizarre nuclei are

present.[758] Other recurrent karyotypic aberrations of this tumor are trisomy 14 and monosomy 22.[766] Flow cytometry studies have shown that the large majority of adult granulosa cell tumors are diploid or near-diploid; there is no convincing evidence that DNA ploidy analysis has independent prognostic value.[749,754,760,779]

Juvenile granulosa cell tumor is diagnosed in nearly 80% of cases during the first two decades of life, most patients presenting with isosexual precocity (Fig. 19.308). A few cases have been associated with enchondromatosis (Ollier's disease)[781] or Maffucci's syndrome.[782] Typical morphologic features of this subtype include diffuse or macrofollicular patterns of growth (the former predominating), mucin-positive intrafollicular secretion, larger tumor cells with extensive luteinization, paucity of nuclear grooves, presence of a thecal component, nuclear atypia, and variable but often high mitotic activity[775,784,790] (Fig. 19.309). Like their adult counterpart, they show consistent trisomy for chromosome 12.[777]

DNA ploidy analysis has shown a greater percentage of aneuploidy in juvenile granulosa cell tumors than in the adult variety; however, the prognostic value of this determination still needs to be demonstrated.[761,780]

The differential diagnosis of granulosa cell tumor (particularly of the adult variety) includes poorly differentiated (predominantly solid) carcinoma of surface epithelial origin, carcinoid tumor, and the very rare tumors of endometrial stromal type[789] (see p. 1705). The nuclear features are of crucial importance in this regard. Some early series describing a poor prognosis for granulosa cell tumors are probably contaminated with solid ovarian carcinomas of surface origin. Strong and widespread positivity for keratin should point toward the direction of carcinoma in a controversial case, especially if this positivity is diffuse cytoplasmic rather than dot-like. The differential diagnosis also includes the *ovarian granulosa cell proliferations of pregnancy*; this change is usually microscopic, multiple, and associated with atretic follicles.[750]

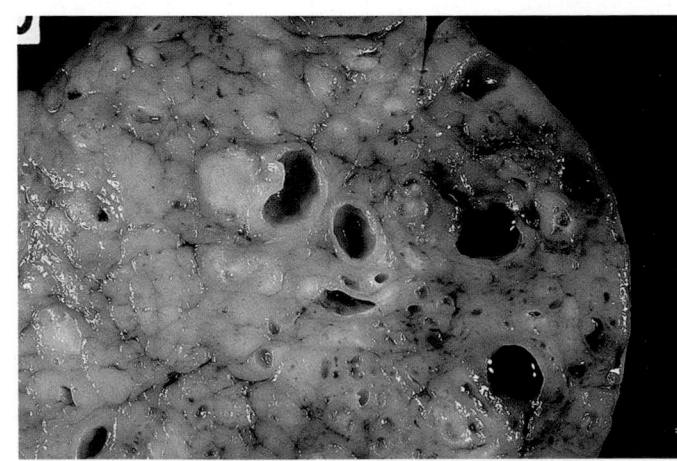

Fig. 19.308 Gross appearance of juvenile granulosa cell tumor.

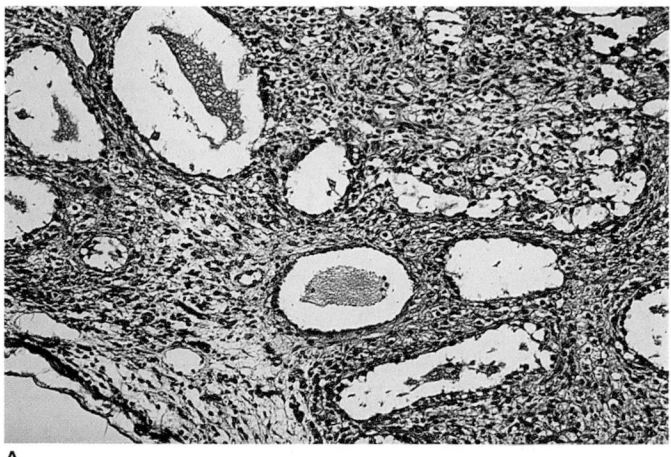 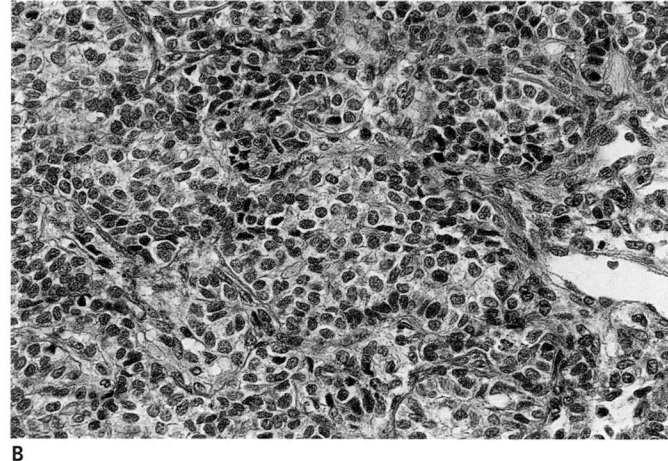

A

B

Fig. 19.309 A and **B**, Juvenile granulosa cell tumor. The follicle-like spaces seen on low-power examination (**A**) are a common feature of this neoplasm. On high power (**B**) the tumor cells are seen lack the coffee-bean nuclei seen in the adult type.

The prognosis of granulosa cell tumors is largely dependent upon the clinical staging.[768] It also depends on size, tumor rupture, and presence of nuclear atypia.[768,787] As a group, juvenile granulosa cell tumors behave more aggressively than their adult counterparts, and are more likely to produce distant metastases. The effect of the histologic pattern of the adult form on prognosis is not clear-cut. Some authors have claimed that tumors with follicular or trabecular patterns have a better prognosis than those with a sarcomatoid pattern, but most studies have failed to demonstrate a convincing relationship.[747] In the series of Norris and Taylor,[771] 12 of 187 patients had persistent tumor after surgery, and 10 died as a result. Most deaths occurred more than 5 years after the original diagnosis and treatment, indicating that 5-year survival figures are not accurate predictors of permanent cure.[757] The granulosa cell origin of a metastatic tumor should be suspected in the presence of a combination of microcystic and trabecular formations, especially if accompanied by Call–Exner bodies and grooved nuclei. Obviously, it is also essential to consider the possibility; otherwise, one is likely to confuse it with a transitional cell carcinoma or something else.[783]

Thecoma, fibroma, and related tumors

Fibroma and thecoma are closely related tumors, one often merging with the other, and therefore the term *fibrothecoma* is quite appropriate when referring to the entire group.

Thecoma presents after menopause in 65% of patients. It is usually unilateral and varies considerably in size. It has a well-defined capsule and a firm consistency. The cut surface is largely or entirely solid, but cysts may be present. It has a yellow color, an important feature in the differential diagnosis with fibroma (Fig. 19.310). Microscopically, it is composed of fascicles of spindle cells with centrally placed nuclei and a moderate amount of pale cytoplasm (Fig. 19.311). The intervening tissue may show considerable collagen deposition and focal hyaline plaque formation. The degree of cellularity varies considerably. Some tumors in young women are heavily calcified.[824]

With oil red O, the cells of thecoma show abundant intracytoplasmic neutral fat, and silver stains usually demonstrate reticulin fibers surrounding individual cells (as opposed to granulosa cell tumor, in which the reticulin surrounds clusters of cells). However, islands may occur in the thecoma that are devoid of reticulin, especially in areas of luteinization. Immunohistochemical localization of estradiol is usually limited to a small number of tumor cells.[797]

Thecomas may be associated with prominent stromal hyperplasia, particularly in postmenopausal patients. In

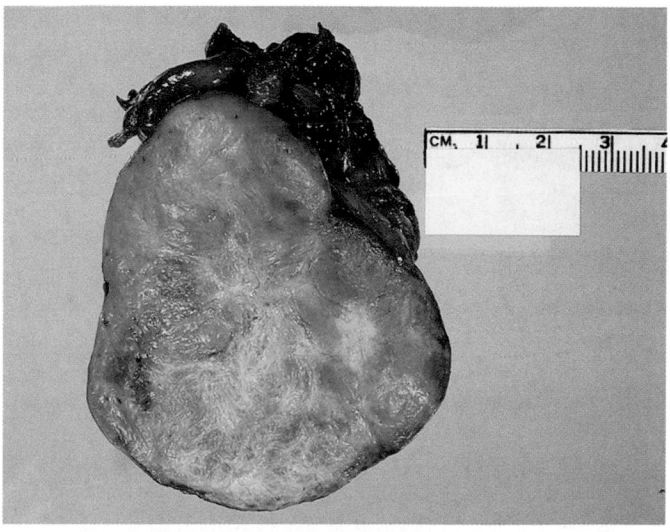

Fig. 19.310 Cut surface of thecoma showing a predominance of yellow areas alternating with whitish foci.

such cases, transitions may be seen from focal stromal hyperplasia through diffuse thecomatosis (hyperthecosis) to thecoma, suggesting a pathogenetic continuum. It is likely that the small tumors designated as **stromal**

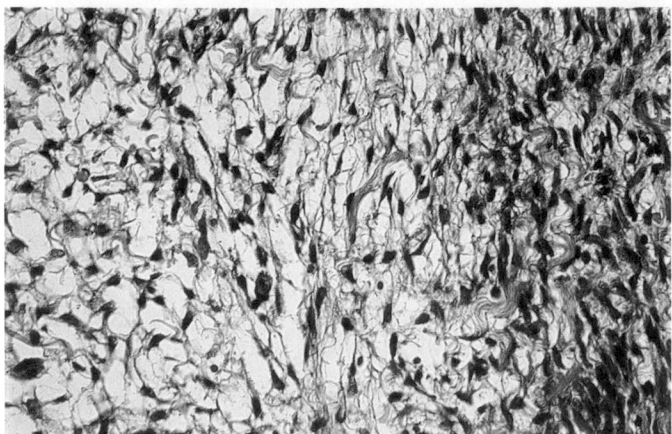

Fig. 19.311 Bland microscopic appearance of thecoma, with some variability in cellularity.

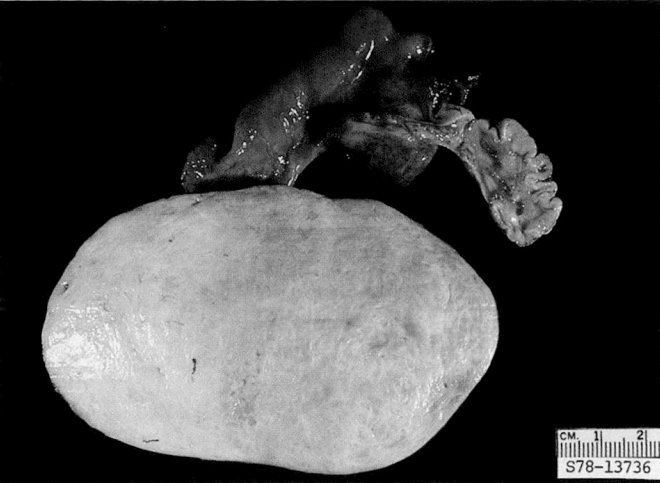

A

B

Fig. 19.312 A and B, Outer aspect and cut surface of ovarian fibroma. The white color contrasts with the yellow hue of thecoma (compare with Fig. 19.309).

luteomas[798,813] are yet another manifestation of this spectrum.

Sometimes, ovarian tumors otherwise typical of thecoma contain cells with the features of steroid hormone-secreting cells (lutein, Leydig, and adrenal cortical).[828] This tumor has generally been designated as **luteinized thecoma**,[810] whereas the terms *stromal–Leydig cell tumor* or *Leydig cell-containing thecoma* are reserved for the rare examples in which Reinke's crystalloids are identified in the cytoplasm of these cells.[815,816,828] These variants tend to occur in younger women and may have an androgenic rather than estrogenic effect on the host.

Thecomas are typically associated with estrogenic manifestations, although some (particularly those containing steroid cells, as just indicated) may be androgenic. They are nearly always benign, but a few malignant examples have been documented.[822] Some luteinized thecomas have been found to be associated with a peculiar form of *sclerosing peritonitis*.[792,799,823]

Fibromas are common ovarian tumors, usually unilateral, which occur almost invariably after puberty.[796] They are solid, lobulated, firm, uniformly white, and usually not accompanied by adhesions (Fig. 19.312). The average diameter is 6 cm. Myxoid changes may be seen, sometimes resulting in cystic degeneration. Grossly, fibromas need to be distinguished mainly from thecoma, Brenner tumor, and Krukenberg tumor.

Microscopically, fibromas are composed of closely packed spindle stromal cells arranged in a "feather-stitched" or storiform pattern (Fig. 19.313). Hyaline bands and edema may be present. Some fibromas occur in young women with the basal cell nevus (Gorlin's) syndrome; these are calcified, usually bilateral, and often multinodular.[808] Fibromas exhibiting a great deal of cellularity are referred to as *cellular fibromas* if the mitotic

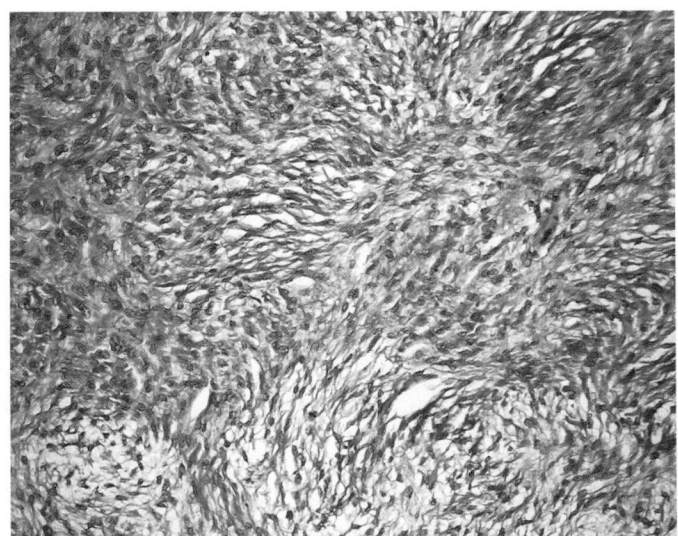

Fig. 19.313 Ovarian fibroma showing hypocellular appearance, bland nuclear features, and a suggestion of a storiform pattern of growth.

activity does not exceed 3 per 10 high-power fields; mitotically more active tumors are regarded as *fibrosarcomas*[807] (see p. 1705) (Figs 19.314 and 19.315). This is accompanied by a higher MIB-1 labeling index and allegedly by a different cytogenetic profile.[821] Some otherwise typical fibromas have a minor component of sex cord elements.[826]

Cytogenetically, both thecomas and fibromas have been found to exhibit trisomy of chromosome 12 in a minority of the tumor cells.[806,817]

Ovarian fibroma (especially if large) can be associated with ascites, sometimes in combination with right-sided pleural effusion (Meigs' syndrome).[812,824] This may lead to a mistaken impression of inoperable ovarian neoplasm, but removal of the tumor leads to the disappearance of these manifestations. The mechanism for the pleural effusion is said to be related to intrathoracic negative pressure and transdiaphragmatic passage of fluid through peritoneal "pores" or lymphatics. Meigs' syndrome can also occur in association with other ovarian tumors.[803]

Fibromas are benign, and oophorectomy is curative. Cellular fibromas may recur or be associated with peritoneal implants.[807]

Sclerosing stromal tumor is a benign ovarian neoplasm that shares many features with fibroma and thecoma. However, it occurs in a younger age group, has a less homogeneous gross appearance (Fig. 19.316), and is characterized microscopically by a lobular pattern of growth, interlobular fibrosis, marked vascularity, and the presence of a dual cell population: collagen-producing spindle cells and lipid-containing round or oval cells (Fig. 19.317). Some of the latter may have a signet ring appearance and thus simulate a Krukenberg tumor[791] (see also p. 1707). Endocrine manifestations are rarely present, and *ligandin* (a probable indicator of steroidogenesis) has been demonstrated immunohistochemically.[819] The tumor cells are also immunoreactive for smooth muscle actin and sometimes for desmin.[811,820] Evidence of differentiation along smooth muscle lines is also seen at the ultrastructural level.[814] Cytogenetically, this tumor shares the tendency for trisomy 12 that is also a feature of fibrothecomas.[801]

Massive edema of the ovary is probably not a neoplasm but is discussed here because of its gross similarities with fibroma. Most patients present with pain, abdominal mass, and/or menstrual irregularities; virilization, precocious puberty, and Meigs' syndrome have also been described.[802,809] Partial torsion of the meso-ovarium with interference in the venous and lym-

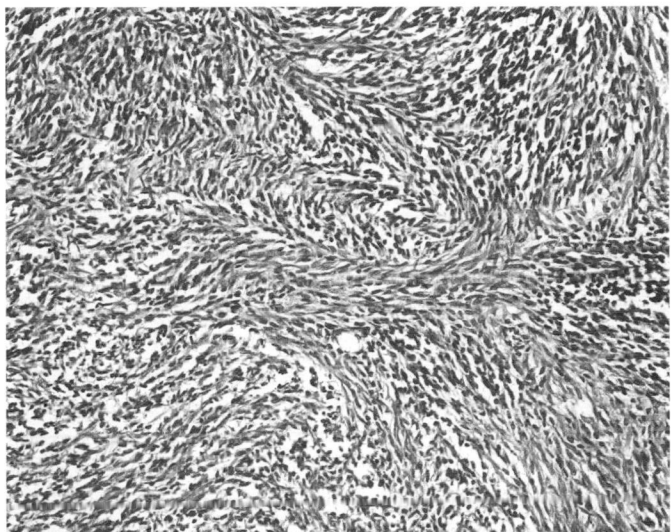

Fig. 19.314 Cellular fibroma. The tumor is hypercellular, but pleomorphism and mitotic activity are minimal.

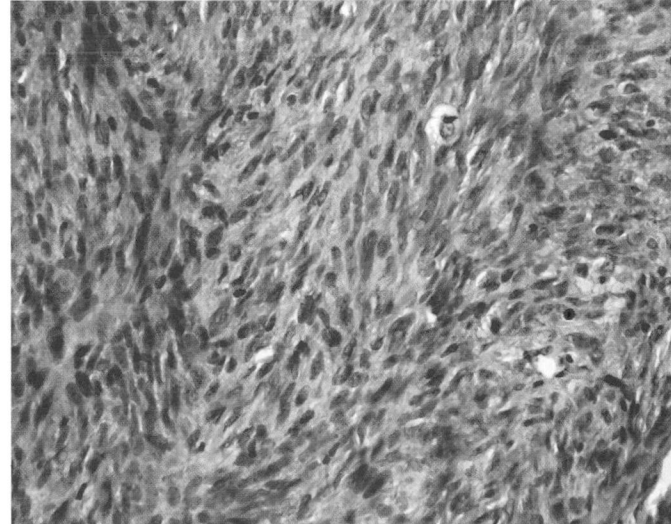

Fig. 19.315 Fibrosarcoma of ovary. Hypercellularity, nuclear hyperchromasia, and brisk mitotic activity are present. The latter is the most important feature in the differential diagnosis with cellular fibroma.

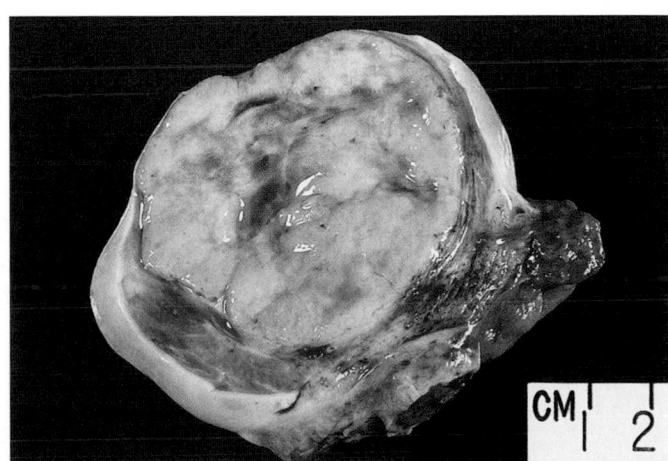

Fig. 19.316 Multinodular quality of cut surface of sclerosing stromal tumor.

phatic drainage has been suggested as the pathogenetic mechanism.[809] The cut surface has been described as watery (Fig. 19.318). Microscopically, there is marked edema of the stroma surrounding follicles and other

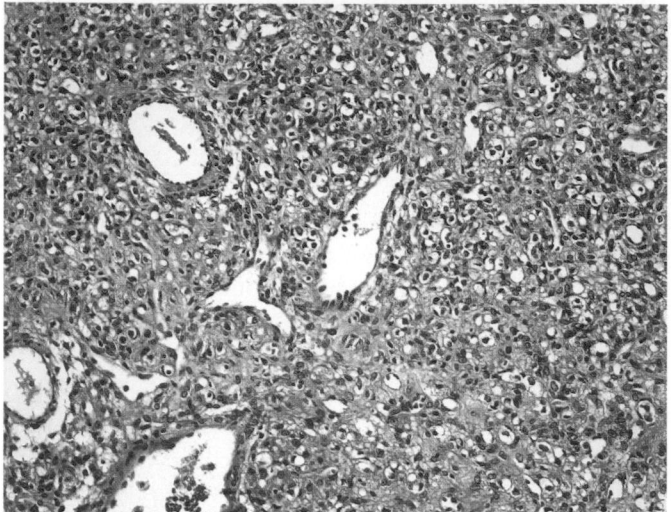

Fig. 19.317 Sclerosing stromal tumor of ovary. The hemangiopericytoma-like foci and the alternation of hypo- and hypercellular areas are important diagnostic clues.

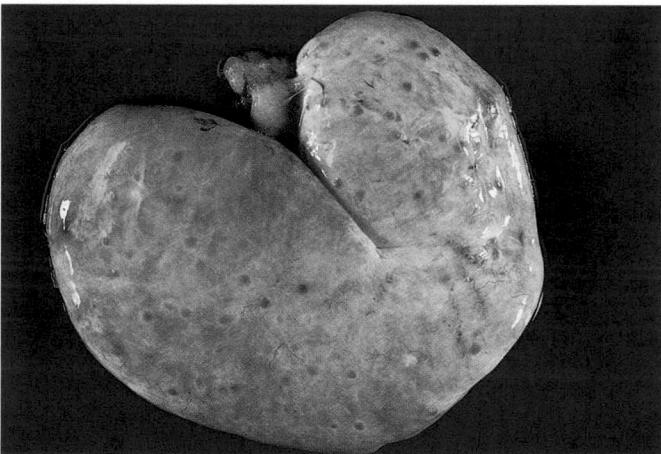

Fig. 19.318 Bulging cut surface of ovary involved by massive edema.

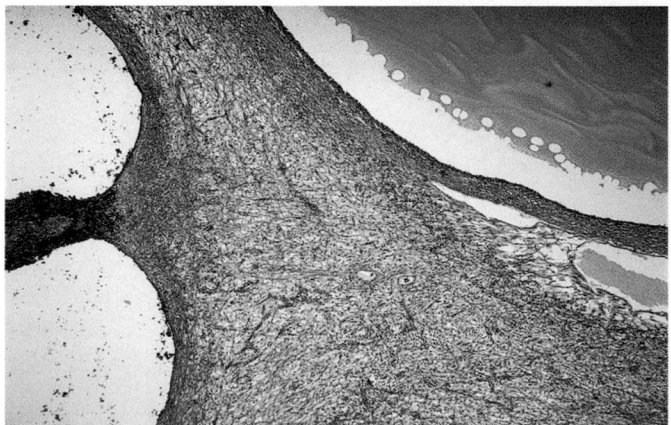

Fig. 19.319 Massive edema of ovary typically surrounding dilated follicles.

structures (Fig. 19.319).[805] Clusters of luteinized cells are often present.[800]

Fibromatosis is the term proposed by Young and Scully[827] for a disorder that they believe is possibly related to massive edema. The patients usually present because of menstrual irregularities. Grossly, the ovaries show a firm, white, cut surface. Microscopically, a diffuse proliferation of spindle cells separated by dense collagen is seen surrounding normal follicular structures. Luteinized cells may be present. The fact that some cases of massive ovarian edema are accompanied by small cellular foci of fibromatosis lends support to their interpretation. The term *fibromatosis*, although descriptively correct, should not be equated with the similarly named lesion of soft tissues, which under exceptional circumstances can involve the ovary.[804]

Myxoma of ovary presents as a solid and cystic mass, some of the cysts being occasionally filled with blood. Microscopically, scattered cells with fibroblastic/myofibroblastic features are seen in a well-vascularized myxoid background.[795,818] Some authors regard this as a distinct type of ovarian neoplasm, whereas others view it as part of the spectrum of differentiation in the fibrothecoma group.[793,794]

Endometrial abnormalities associated with granulosa cell tumor, thecoma, and related tumors

The endometrium of patients with granulosa cell tumors or thecomas exhibits various degrees of hyperplasia in about a fourth of cases,[831] even when the tumors are of minute size. In the remaining cases, the endometrium shows a normal proliferative or secretory pattern, and it may even be atrophic. Some of the hyperplasias are so florid as to closely resemble the appearance of an endometrial adenocarcinoma. This fact is at the heart of the controversy as to how often an endometrial adenocarcinoma occurs in the setting of these ovarian neoplasms. The quoted incidence varies from 3% to 21%,[829,831] this wide range strongly suggesting the lack of uniform diagnostic criteria. Some of the lesions are undoubtedly hyperplasias, proved by the fact that they have been found to regress following excision of the ovarian tumors. The bona fide carcinomas are nearly always well differentiated and superficial, and this explains the excellent prognosis associated with them. Cases of endometrial adenocarcinoma have also been reported in association with ovarian sclerosing stromal tumor.[830]

Rarely thecomas have been found to be associated with endometrial sarcomas of one type or another.[832]

Small cell carcinoma

There are two types of primary ovarian carcinoma composed of small cells, designated as hypercalcemic and pulmonary type, respectively.

Hypercalcemic-type small cell carcinoma, which is by far the most common, is a high-grade ovarian malignancy that may be confused with granulosa cell tumor.[835,846,848] It occurs in young females (average age, 23 years) and is nearly always bilateral. Some familial cases have been reported.[843] The tumor is associated with hypercalcemia in two thirds of cases, which disappears following removal of the tumor. Grossly, the tumor is large and solid, with areas of necrosis and hemorrhage (Fig. 19.320). Microscopically, a diffuse proliferation of small, closely packed cells of carcinomatous appearance with scant cytoplasm and small nuclei is seen (Fig. 19.321). Clusters of larger and more pleomorphic cells may be present, some of them resembling luteinized cells.[836] Cytoplasmic hyaline globules may also be seen. Tumors containing a large number of these cells have been referred to, tongue-in-cheek, as the large variant of small cell carcinoma. There may also be islands, cords, trabeculae, mucinous glands, and *follicle-like structures.* The latter are an important clue to the diagnosis.

The tumor cells may express keratin, vimentin, EMA, chromogranins and laminin, but not B72.3, S-100 protein, or inhibin.[833,844a,845,847] Immunoreactivity has apparently been found for human parathyroid hormone-related protein, but the correlation between the degree of staining and the serum calcium level is poor.[844] Ultrastructurally, the cells have a poorly differentiated appearance, with relatively abundant dilated rough endoplasmic reticulum and specialized cell junctions; neurosecretory-type granules are generally absent.[836,837] Most surprisingly, this tumor has been found to have a diploid DNA pattern.[838]

The prognosis is very poor because of frequent extra-ovarian spread. The histogenesis remains obscure, the messages provided by the various techniques being mixed. The keratin and EMA positivity, the negativity for inhibin, and the finding of k-*ras* mutations[845] suggest an epithelial origin[837]; the association with a paraneoplastic syndrome and the reported reactivity for chromogranin[833] point toward a neuroendocrine tumor; and the age distribution and presence of follicle-like formations are more in keeping with sex cord–stromal derivation.

Pulmonary-type small cell carcinoma resembles in all regards the homonymous lung tumor[840] (Fig. 19.322). It may be pure or associated with endometrioid carcinoma or other patterns. Immunohistochemically, there is reactivity for keratin, EMA, NSE, and (rarely) for chromogranin and Leu7. Ultrastructurally, neurosecretory-type granules can be identified.[837] In contrast to the hypercalcemic type, the DNA pattern is often aneuploid.[840] The prognosis is poor.

As in other organs, there are in the ovary high-grade neuroendocrine carcinomas that have a morphology other than the small cell carcinoma just described. Some of these have been described as **large cell neuroen-**

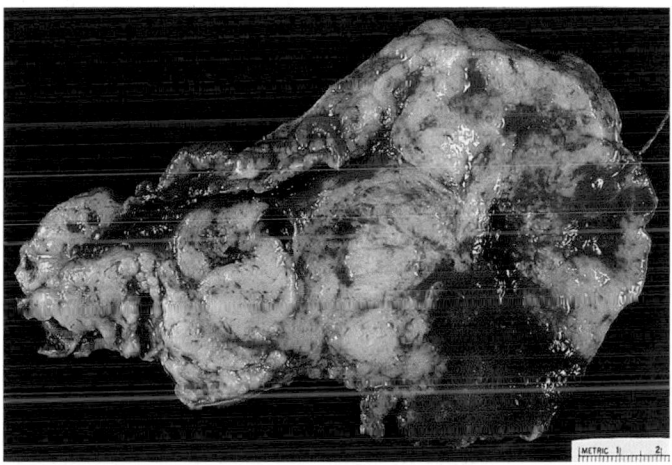

Fig. 19.320 Solid cut surface with hemorrhagic foci in ovarian small cell carcinoma of hypercalcemic type.

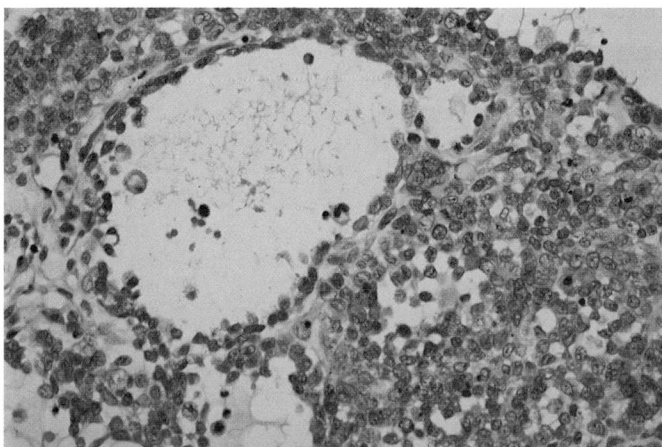

Fig. 19.321 Small cell carcinoma, hypercalcemic type. The presence of follicle-like formations is an important diagnostic feature.

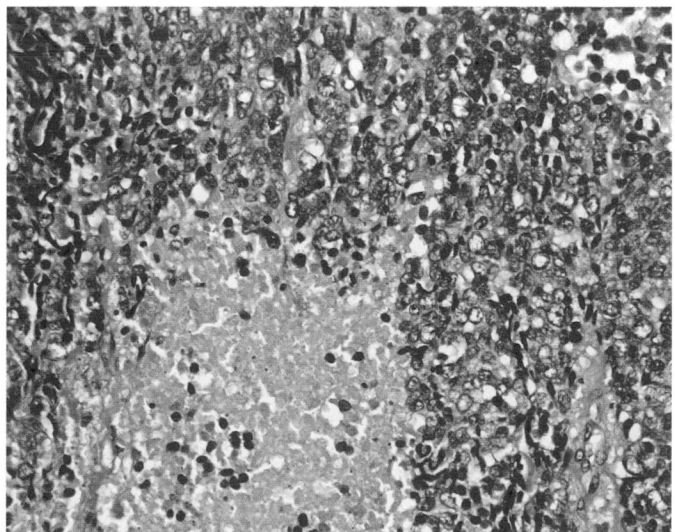

Fig. 19.322 Small cell carcinoma of pulmonary type. The sharply outlined foci of necrosis are a common feature of this tumor, which has a microscopic appearance very similar to its pulmonary counterpart.

Most Sertoli–Leydig cell tumors are seen in young patients (average age, 25 years) and are relatively rare after menopause. Some are diagnosed during pregnancy.[874] These tend to exhibit prominent intercellular edema.[873] Bilateral involvement is seen in less than 2% of cases. Cases have been reported in association with mature cystic teratoma.[869] Nearly half of the cases are accompanied by signs of androgen excess. This is manifested first by *defeminization* (amenorrhea, breast atrophy, loss of subcutaneous tissue deposits) and later by *masculinization* (clitoral hypertrophy, deepening of the voice, hirsutism). Usually prompt return of feminine characteristics follows excision of the tumor, but the manifestations of masculinization disappear more slowly. Urinary 17-ketosteroids are frequently normal, but elevations have been recorded. Tumor tissue incubated with progesterone or pregnenolone causes a synthesis of various hormones (androstenedione, 17-hydroxyprogesterone, testosterone), but the final aromatizing reaction to estrogens does not occur.[867,870]

Some Sertoli–Leydig cell tumors do not have demonstrable endocrine effect, whereas others are accompanied by secretion of estrogen or progesterone. The latter is often the case for pure Sertoli cell tumors.[872] It is opportune to mention again that the diagnosis of these neoplasms should be based on their morphologic appearance rather than on the nature of their hormonal manifestations; terms such as "feminizing mesenchymoma" should be avoided. Curiously, some cases of Sertoli–Leydig cell tumor have been associated with serum elevation of α-fetoprotein[850,862]; this marker has been detected immunohistochemically in areas of hepatocytic differentiation[875] and in the more conventional Leydig and Sertoli cell-like component.[855]

The prognosis of Sertoli–Leydig cell tumor, which is usually good, correlates with the stage and degree of differentiation of the tumor.[864,882] The overall incidence of clinical malignancy in one large series was 18%; all the well-differentiated tumors were benign, but 11% of those with intermediate differentiation, 59% of those with poor differentiation, and 19% of those with heterologous elements were malignant.[875] In one series of 28 cases of pure Sertoli cell tumor, there were two recurrences.[871] Conservative surgery is indicated in young women for Sertoli–Leydig cell tumors grossly confined to the ovary.[881,882]

Lipid (lipoid, steroid) cell tumor

A small group of ovarian tumors is composed entirely of cells with morphologic features indicative of steroid hormone secretion. These are manifested by an abundant eosinophilic or vacuolated cytoplasm that is often positive for fat stains and that, at the ultrastructural level, is shown to contain well-developed smooth endoplasmic reticulum and mitochondria with tubulovesicular cristae.[885] Normal steroid hormone-secreting cells can be

of lutein (thecal or stromal), Leydig (hilus), and adrenal cortical type.[887] Theoretically, these tumors could arise from any of these sources. In the few cases in which Reinke's crystalloids are found, the tumor can be categorized as Leydig or hilus cell tumor.[886,887,889] In a few others, an ectopic adrenal origin has been suggested on the basis of their hormonal profile (presence of Cushing's syndrome)[893] and the fact that adrenal cortical rests can be found in the hilus of the ovary and the broad ligament (although not within the adult ovary itself). In the majority of the cases, however, the exact origin of this tumor remains undecided; the descriptive terms **lipid, lipoid,** and—more recently—**steroid cell tumor** have therefore been proposed for the entire group, with the added designations *Leydig cell type* or *adrenal cortical type* whenever indicated.[892,893] None of these terms is ideal. "Lipid" and "lipoid" have been criticized on the grounds that the tumor cells may not always contain neutral fat, and the term "steroid cell" has been objected to because of the fact that nearly all of the sex cord–stromal tumors have the capability to secrete steroid hormones. In any event, any of these three designations is preferable to the old terms *luteoma, hypernephroma,* or *masculinovoblastoma.*

Enzymatic conversion studies performed on freshly excised tumors have demonstrated that a variety of androgenic hormones are produced by these tumors in vitro[890]; occasionally, large amounts of adrenal corticoids have been found.

Lipid cell tumors are usually unilateral and are composed of yellow or yellowish brown nodules separated by fibrous trabeculae (Fig. 19.331). Microscopically, they are characterized by masses of large rounded or polyhedral cells with the morphologic and ultrastructural features previously described for their normal counterparts (Fig. 19.332). Immunohistochemically, there is reactivity for vimentin in three fourths of cases, for keratin in one half, and for actin in about one third.[891] There is also consistent reactivity for inhibin, A103, and Mart-1.

Fig. 19.331 Cut surface of ovarian lipid cell tumor. The deep brown color is reminiscent of a renal or thyroid oncocytoma.

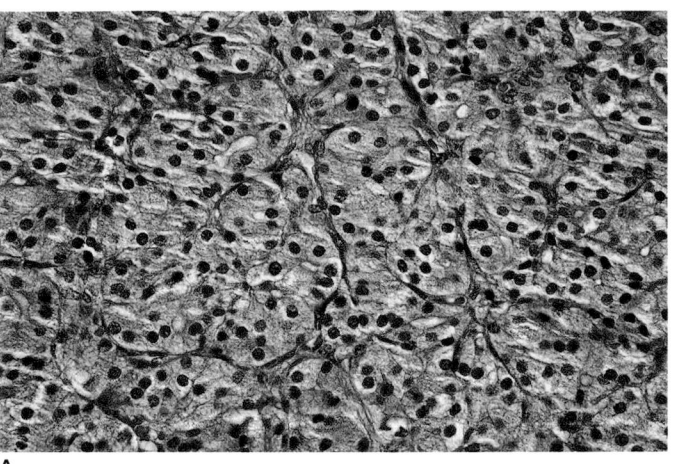

A B

Fig. 19.332 Two cases of lipid cell tumor showing acidophilic (**A**) and clear (**B**) appearances of the cytoplasmic of the tumor cells.

This neoplasm can occur at any age.[892] Most are associated with a virilizing syndrome (with defeminization and amenorrhea),[875] and—as already indicated—a few cases meet the criteria for Cushing's syndrome.[893] Some of the tumors are biologically inactive, at least at the clinical level, and others are associated with estrogenic or progestogenic manifestations. A few cases have been associated with endometrioid carcinoma.[884] The incidence of clinical malignancy is approximately 25%.[883,892] Malignant tumors tend to be larger (7 cm in diameter or greater), with foci of necrosis and hemorrhage, and to exhibit nuclear atypia and mitotic activity.[883,892] Tumors containing Reinke's crystalloids are almost invariably benign.[886,892] The malignant tumors can lead to peritoneal implants.[892]

Lipid cell tumors should be distinguished from lesions in which proliferation of steroid hormone-producing cells occurs as a secondary event. These include stromal luteoma (although the position of this lesion in the scheme of ovarian neoplasms remains controversial), luteinized granulosa cell tumor (particularly the juvenile type), fibrothecoma, stromal–Leydig cell tumor, and the non-neoplastic proliferation of steroid cells that may be seen at the periphery of other tumors, such as struma ovarii, strumal carcinoid, surface epithelial tumors, and metastatic carcinoma.[888]

Other types

Gynandroblastoma is the term used for the sex cord—stromal tumor composed of a mixture *in similar amounts* of clearly identifiable granulosa–theca cell and Sertoli–Leydig cell elements.[900] When thus defined, this entity is extremely rare, to the point that some authors doubt its existence. On occasion the granulosa cell component is of the juvenile rather than the adult type.[897,906] Reported cases of this entity have been accompanied by androgenic, estrogenic, or no hormonal effects.[907,908]

Sex cord tumor with annular tubules is a distinctive ovarian tumor that is associated in one third of the cases with the Peutz–Jeghers syndrome.[902,910,917] This lesion combines features suggestive of a granulosa cell tumor with a pattern of growth reminiscent of Sertoli cells.[895] Its morphologic hallmark is the presence of simple and complex annular tubules containing eosinophilic hyaline bodies, often calcified (Fig. 19.333). The appearance is similar to that of gonadoblastoma, from which it differs because of the clinical/genetic background and the presence of a germ cell component in the latter.

The ambiguous or biphasic nature of the tumor cells is also apparent on ultrastructural examination: features consistent with granulosa cell or nonspecialized ovarian stroma[898,903] alternate with features indicative of Sertoli cell differentiation, notably the presence of Charcot–Bottcher filaments.[894] Symptoms suggestive of hyperestrinism have been described in approximately 50% of cases. Tumors associated with the Peutz–Jeghers syndrome are typically multifocal, bilateral, small (or even microscopic), calcified, and usually benign, although exceptions occur.[905] Those unassociated with the syndrome are unilateral, often large, and clinically malignant in approximately 22% of cases.[901,918]

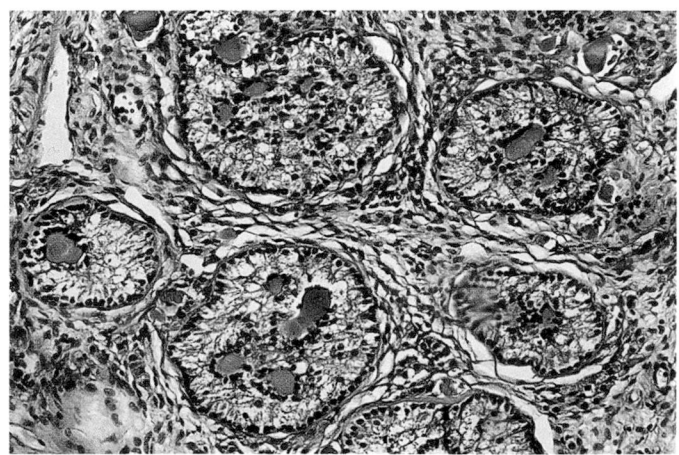

Fig. 19.333 Sex cord tumor with annular tubules. The patient was affected by Peutz–Jeghers syndrome.

4 Czernobilsky B, Shezen E, Lifschitz-Mercer B, Fogel M, Luzon A, Jacob N, Skalli O, Gabbiani G. Alpha smooth muscle actin (alpha-SM actin) in normal human ovaries, in ovarian stromal hyperplasia and in ovarian neoplasms. Virchows Arch [Cell Pathol] 1989, **57**: 55–61.

5 Doss BJ, Wanek SM, Jacques SM, Qureshi F, Ramirez NC, Lawrence WD. Ovarian smooth muscle metaplasia: an uncommon and possibly underrecognized entity. Int J Gynecol Pathol 1999, **18**: 58–62.

6 Fetissof F, Dubois MP, Heitz PU, Lansac J, Arbeille-Brassart B, Jobard P. Endocrine cells in the female genital tract. Int J Gynecol Pathol 1986, **5**: 75–87.

7 Laffargue P, Benkoël L, Laffargue F, Casanova P, Chamlian A. Ultrastructural and enzyme histochemical study of ovarian hilar cells in women and their relationships with sympathetic nerves. Hum Pathol 1978, **9**: 649–659.

8 Lastarria D, Sachdev RK, Babury RA, Yu HM, Nuovo GJ. Immunohistochemical analysis for desmin in normal and neoplastic ovarian stromal tissue. Arch Pathol Lab Med 1990, **114**: 502–505.

9 Sasano H, Sasano N. What's new in the localization of sex steroids in the human ovary and its tumors? Pathol Res Pract 1989, **185**: 942–948.

10 Sasano H, Okamoto M, Mason JI, Simpson ER, Mendelson CR, Sasano N, Silverberg SG. Immunolocalization of aromatase, 17 alpha-hydroxylase and side-chain cleavage cytochromes P-450 in the human ovary. J Reprod Fertil 1989, **85**: 163–169.

11 Visfeldt J, Starup J. Dating of the human corpus luteum of menstruation using histological parameters. Acta Pathol Microbiol Scand (A) 1974, **82**: 137–144.

12 Woolnough E, Russo L, Khan MS, Heatley MK. An immunohistochemical study of the rete ovarii and epoophoron. Pathology 2000, **32**: 77–83.

13 Zheng W, Magid MS, Kramer EE, Chen YT. Follicle-stimulating hormone receptor is expressed in human ovarian surface epithelium and fallopian tube. Am J Pathol 1996, **148**: 47–53.

Gonadal dysgenesis

14 Calabrese F, Valente M. Mixed gonadal dysgenesis: histological and ultrastructural finding in two cases. Int J Gynecol Pathol 1996, **15**: 270–277.

15 Clement PB, Young RH. Atypical polypoid adenomyoma of the uterus associated with Turner's syndrome. A report of three cases, including a review of "estrogen-associated" endometrial neoplasms and neoplasms associated with Turner's syndrome. Int J Gynecol Pathol 1987, **6**: 104–113.

16 Federman DD. Abnormal sexual development. A genetic and endocrine approach to differential diagnosis. Philadelphia, 1967, W.B. Saunders.

17 Ferenczy A, Richart RM. The fine structure of the gonads in the complete form of testicular feminization syndrome. Am J Obstet Gynecol 1972, **113**: 399–409.

18 Jones HW, Ferguson-Smith MA, Heller RH. The pathology and cytogenetics of gonadal agenesis. Am J Obstet Gynecol 1963, **87**: 578–600.

19 Jones HW, Ferguson-Smith MA, Heller RH. Pathologic and cytogenetic findings in true hermaphroditism. Report of 6 cases and review of 23 cases from the literature. Obstet Gynecol 1965, **25**: 435–447.

20 Kim KR, Kwon Y, Young Joung J, Kim KS, Ayala AG, Ro JY. True hermaphroditism and mixed gonadal dysgenesis in young children: a clinicopathologic study of 10 cases. Mod Pathol 2002, **15**: 1013–1019.

21 McCarty KS Jr, Barton TK, Peete CH Jr, Creasman WT. Gonadal dysgenesis with adenocarcinoma of the endometrium. An electron microscopic and steroid receptor analyses with a review of the literature. Cancer 1978, **42**: 512–520.

22 Males JL, Lain KC. Epithelioid sarcoma in XO/XX Turner's syndrome. Arch Pathol 1972, **94**: 214–216.

23 Neubecker RD, Theiss EA. Sertoli cell adenomas in patients with testicular feminization. Am J Clin Pathol 1962, **38**: 52–59.

24 Radhakrishnan S, Sivaraman L, Natarajan PS. True hermaphrodite with multiple gonadal neoplasms. Report of a case with cytogenetic study. Cancer 1978, **42**: 2726–2732.

25 Robboy SJ, Bentley RC, Russell P. Embryology of the female genital tract and disorders of abnormal sexual development. In Kurman RJ (ed.): Blaustein's Pathology of the female genital tract, ed. 5. New York, 2002, Springer-Verlag, pp. 3–36.

26 Robboy SJ, Miller T, Donahoe PK, Jahre C, Welch WR, Haseltine FP, Miller WA, Atkins L, Crawford JD. Dysgenesis of testicular and streak gonads in the syndrome of mixed gonadal dysgenesis. Perspective derived from a clinicopathologic analysis of twenty-one cases. Hum Pathol 1982, **13**: 700–716.

27 Rutgers JL. Advances in the pathology of intersex conditions. Hum Pathol 1991, **22**: 884–891.

28 Scully RE. Gonadal pathology of genetically determined diseases. Monogr Pathol 1991, **33**: 257–285.

29 Sohval AR. The syndrome of pure gonadal dysgenesis. Am J Med 1965, **38**: 615–625.

30 Taylor H, Barter RH, Jacobson CB. Neoplasms of dysgenetic gonads. Am J Obstet Gynecol 1966, **96**: 816–823.

Cysts, stromal hyperplasia, and other non-neoplastic lesions

31 Adelman S, Benson CD, Hertzler JH. Surgical lesions of the ovary in infancy and childhood. Surg Gynecol Obstet 1975, **141**: 219–222.

32 Awartani KA, Cheung AP. Metformin and polycystic ovary syndrome: a literature review. J Obstet Gynaecol Can 2002, **24**: 393–401.

33 Balen A, Michelmore K. What is polycystic ovary syndrome? Are national views important? Hum Reprod 2002, **17**: 2219–2227.

34 Barnes RB, Rosenfield RL, Burstein S, Ehrmann DA. Pituitary-ovarian responses to nafarelin testing in the polycystic ovary syndrome. N Engl J Med 1989, **320**: 559–565.

35 Blaustein A. Surface cells and inclusion cysts in fetal ovaries. Gynecol Oncol 1981, **12**: 222–233.

36 Boss JH, Scully RE, Wegner KH, Cohen RB. Structural variations in the adult ovary – clinical significance. Obstet Gynecol 1965, **25**: 747–764.

37 Bransilver BR, Ferenczy A, Richart RM. Female genital tract remnants. An ultrastructural comparison of hydatid of Morgagni and mesonephric ducts and tubules. Arch Pathol 1973, **96**: 255–261.

38 Clement PB. Tumor-like lesions of the ovary associated with pregnancy. Int J Gynecol Pathol 1993, **12**: 108–115.

39 Clement PB, Scully RE. Large solitary luteinized follicle cyst of pregnancy and puerperium. A clinicopathological analysis of eight cases. Am J Surg Pathol 1980, **4**: 431–438.

40 Fan LD, Zhang HY, Zhang XS. Ovarian epidermoid cyst: report of eight cases. Int J Gynecol Pathol 1996, **15**: 69–71.

41 Fechner RE, Kaufman RH. Endometrial adenocarcinoma in Stein-Leventhal syndrome. Cancer 1974, **34**: 444–452.

42 Garcia-Bunuel R, Brandes D. Luteoma of pregnancy. Ultrastructural features. Hum Pathol 1976, **7**: 205–214.

43 Garcia-Bunuel R, Berek JS, Woodruff JD. Luteomas of pregnancy. Obstet Gynecol 1975, **45**: 407–414.

44 Gardner GH, Greene RR, Peckham B. Normal and cystic structures of broad ligament. Am J Obstet Gynecol 1948, **55**: 917–939.

45 Goldzieher JW, Green JA. The polycystic ovary. I. Clinical and histologic features. J Clin Endocrinol 1962, **22**: 325–338.

46 Hallatt JG, Steele CH Jr, Snyder M. Ruptured corpus luteum

with hemoperitoneum. A study of 173 surgical cases. Am J Obstet Gynecol 1984, **149:** 5–9.

47 Heatley MK. Adenomatous hyperplasia of the rete ovarii. Histopathology 2000, **36:** 383–384.

48 Insler V, Lunenfeld B. Pathophysiology of polycystic ovarian disease. New insights. Hum Reprod 1991, **6:** 1025–1029.

49 Judd HL, Scully RE, Herbst AL, Yen SSC, Ingersol FM, Kliman B. Familial hyperthecosis. Comparison of endocrinologic and histologic findings with polycystic ovarian disease. Am J Obstet Gynecol 1973, **117:** 976–982.

50 Kamiyama K, Moromizato H, Toma T, Kinjo T, Iwamasa T. Two cases of supernumerary ovary: one with large fibroma with Meig's syndrome and the other with endometriosis and cystic change. Pathol Res Pract 2001, **197:** 847–851.

51 Lee B, Gore BZ. A case of supernumerary ovary. Obstet Gynecol 1984, **64:** 738–740.

52 Legro RS, Strauss JF. Molecular progress in infertility: polycystic ovary syndrome. Fertil Steril 2002, **78:** 569–576.

53 Leventhal ML. Functional and morphologic studies of the ovaries and suprarenal glands in the Stein-Leventhal syndrome. Am J Obstet Gynecol 1962, **84:** 154–164.

54 Lindsay AN, Voorhess ML, MacGillivray MH. Multicystic ovaries in primary hypothyroidism. Obstet Gynecol 1983, **61:** 433–437.

55 Lucis OJ, Hobkirk R, Hollenberg CH, MacDonald SA, Blahey P. Polycystic ovaries associated with congenital adrenal hyperplasia. Can Med Assoc J 1966, **94:** 1–7.

56 McKenna TJ. Pathogenesis and treatment of polycystic ovary syndrome. N Engl J Med 1988, **318:** 558–562.

57 Morris JM, Scully RE. Endocrine pathology of the ovary. St. Louis, 1958, C.V. Mosby.

58 Mount SL, Eltabbakh GH, Hardin NJ. Beta-2 microglobulin amyloidosis presenting as bilateral ovarian masses: a case report and review of the literature. Am J Surg Pathol 2001, **26:** 130–133.

59 Nogales FF, Silverberg SG. Epidermoid cysts of the ovary. A report of five cases with histogenetic considerations and ultrastructural findings. Am J Obstet Gynecol 1976, **124:** 523–528.

60 Nogales FF, Carvia RE, Donne C, Campello TR, Vidal M, Martin A. Adenomas of the rete ovarii. Hum Pathol 1998, **28:** 1428–1433.

61 Norris HJ, Taylor HB. Nodular theca-lutein hyperplasia of pregnancy (so-called "pregnancy luteoma"). Am J Clin Pathol 1967, **47:** 557–566.

62 Ober WB, Grady HG, Schoenbucher AK. Ectopic ovarian decidua without pregnancy. Am J Pathol 1957, **33:** 199–217.

63 Piana S, Nogales FF, Corrado S, Cardinale L, Gusolfino D, Rivasi F. Pregnancy luteoma with granulosa cell proliferation: an unusual hyperplastic lesion arising in pregnancy and mimicking an ovarian neoplasia. Pathol Res Pract 1999, **195:** 859–863.

64 Rodin A, Thakkar H, Taylor N, Clayton R. Hyperandrogenism in polycystic ovary syndrome. Evidence of dysregulation of 11β-hydroxysteroid dehydrogenase. N Engl J Med 1994, **330:** 460–465.

65 Rutgers JL, Scully RE. Cysts (cystadenomas) and tumors of the rete ovarii. Int J Gynecol Pathol 1988, **7:** 330–342.

66 Sasano H, Fukunaga M, Rojas M, Silverberg SG. Hyperthecosis of the ovary. Clinicopathologic study of 19 cases with immunohistochemical analysis of steroidogenic enzymes. Int J Gynecol Pathol 1989, **8:** 311–320.

67 Smyczek-Gargya B, Geppert M. Endometrial cancer associated with polycystic ovaries in young women. Pathol Res Pract 1992, **188:** 946–948.

68 Sommers SC. Polycystic ovaries revisited. In Fenoglio CM, Wolfe M (eds): Progress in surgical pathology. New York, 1980, Masson Publishing USA, pp. 221–232.

69 Sternberg WH, Barclay DL. Luteoma of pregnancy. Am J Obstet Gynecol 1966, **95:** 165–184.

70 Towne BH, Mahour GH, Woolley MM, Isaacs H. Ovarian cysts and tumors in infancy and childhood. J Pediatr Surg 1975, **10:** 311–320.

71 Wajda KJ, Lucas JG, Marsh WL Jr. Hyperreactio luteinalis. Benign disorder masquerading as an ovarian neoplasm. Arch Pathol Lab Med 1989, **113:** 921–925.

72 Young RH, Prat J, Scully RE. Epidermoid cyst of the ovary. A report of three cases with comments on histogenesis: Am J Clin Pathol 1980, **73:** 272–276.

73 Zourlas PA, Jones HW Jr. Stein-Leventhal syndrome with masculinizing ovarian tumors. Report of 3 cases. Obstet Gynecol 1969, **34:** 861–866.

Inflammation

74 Bannatyne P, Russell P, Shearman RP. Autoimmune oophoritis. A clinicopathologic assessment of 12 cases. Int J Gynecol Pathol 1990, **9:** 191–207.

75 Francke ML, Mihaescu A, Chaubert P. Isolated necrotizing of the female genital tract: a clinicopathologic and immunohistochemical study of 11 Cases. Int J Gynecol Pathol 1998, **17:** 193–200.

76 Gloor E, Hurlimann J. Autoimmune oophoritis. Am J Clin Pathol 1984, **81:** 105–109.

77 Gray Y, Libbey P. Xanthogranulomatous salpingitis and oophoritis: a case report and review of the literature. Arch Pathol Lab Med 2001, **125:** 260–263.

78 Herbold DR, Frable WJ, Kraus FT. Isolated noninfectious granulomas of the ovary. Int J Gynecol Pathol 1984, **2:** 380–391.

79 Irvine WJ, Barnes EW. Addison's disease and autoimmune ovarian failure. J Reprod Fertil 1974, **21**(Suppl): 1–31.

80 Kim KR, Scully RE. Peritoneal keratin granulomas with carcinomas of endometrium and ovary and atypical polypoid adenomyoma of endometrium: a clinicopathological analysis of 22 cases. Am J Surg Pathol 1990, **14:** 925–932.

81 Lewis I, Eosinophilic perifolliculitis. A variant of autoimmune oophoritis. Int J Gynecol Pathol 1993, **12:** 360–364.

82 Mostafa SAM, Bargeron CB, Flower RW, Rosenshein NB, Parmley TH, Woodruff JD. Foreign body granulomas in normal ovaries. Obstet Gynecol 1985, **66:** 701–702.

83 Pace EH, Voet RL, Melancon JT. Xanthogranulomatous oophoritis. An inflammatory pseudotumor of the ovary. Int J Gynecol Pathol 1984, **3:** 398–402.

84 Tatum ET, Beattie JF, Bryson K. Postoperative carbon pigment granuloma: a report of eight cases involving the ovary. Hum Pathol 1996, **27:** 1008–1011.

85 Tung KS, Teuscher C. Mechanisms of autoimmune disease in the testis and ovary. Hum Reprod Update 1995, **1:** 35–50.

Endometriosis

86 Ballouk F, Ross JS, Wolf BC. Ovarian endometriotic cysts. An analysis of cytologic atypia and DNA ploidy patterns. Am J Clin Pathol 1994, **102:** 415–419.

87 Clement PB. Pathology of endometriosis. Pathol Annu 1990, **25:** 245–295.

88 Clement PB, Young RH. Two previously unemphasized features of endometriosis: micronodular stromal endometriosis and endometriosis with stromal elastosis. Int J Surg Pathol 2001, **8:** 223–227.

89 Clement PB, Young RH, Scully RE. Necrotic pseudoxanthomatous nodules of ovary and peritoneum in endometriosis. Am J Surg Pathol 1988, **12:** 390–397.

90 Czernobilsky B, Morris WJ. A histologic study of ovarian endometriosis with emphasis on hyperplastic and atypical changes. Obstet Gynecol 1979, **53:** 318–323.

91 Devereux WP. Endometriosis. Long-term observation with

169a Longacre T, Tazelaar H, Kempson R, Hendrickson M. Serous tumors of low malignant potential: Stanford update. Mod Pathol 2003, **16**: 199a.

170 McCluggage WG, Maxwell P, Veenstra H, Fick CE, Laeng RH, Tiltman AJ. Monoclonal antibody SMO47 as an immunohistochemical marker of ovarian adenocarcinoma. Histopathology 2001, **38**: 542–549.

171 Miettinen M, Lehto V-P, Virtanen I. Expression of intermediate filaments in normal ovaries and ovarian epithelial, sex cord-stromal, and germinal tumors. Int J Gynecol Pathol 1983, **2**: 64–71.

172 Mohabeer J, Buckley CH, Fox H. An immunohistochemical study of the incidence and significance of human chorionic gonadotrophin synthesis by epithelial ovarian neoplasms. Gynecol Oncol 1983, **16**: 78–84.

173 Moll R, Pitz S, Levy R, Weikel W, Franke WW, Czernobilsky B. Complexity of expression of intermediate filament proteins, including glial filament protein, in endometrial and ovarian adenocarcinomas. Hum Pathol 1991, **22**: 989–1001.

174 Mulhollan TJ, Silva EG, Tornos C, Guerrieri C, Fromm GL, Gershenson D. Ovarian involvement by serous surface papillary carcinoma. Int J Gynecol Pathol 1994, **13**: 120–126.

175 Nayar R, Siriaunkgul S, Robbins KM, McGowan L, Ginzan S, Silverberg SG. Microinvasion of low malignant potential tumors of the ovary. Hum Pathol 1996, **27**: 521–527.

176 Peralta Soler A, Knudsen KA, Jaurand MC, Johnson KR, Wheelock MJ, Klein-Szanto AJ, Salazar H. The differential expression of n-cadherin and e-caderin distinguishes pleural mesotheliomas from lung adenocarcinomas. Hum Pathol 1996, **26**: 1363–1369.

177 Prat J. Ovarian tumors of borderline malignancy (tumors of low malignant potential): a critical appraisal. Adv Anat Pathol 1999, **6**: 247–274.

178 Prat J, de Nictolis M. Serous borderline tumors of the ovary: a long-term follow-up study of 137 cases, including 18 with a micropapillary pattern and 20 with microinvasion. Am J Surg Pathol 2002, **26**: 1111–1128.

179 Rice LW, Berkowitz RS, Mark SD, Yavner DL, Lage JM. Epithelial ovarian tumors of borderline malignancy. Gynecol Oncol 1990, **39**: 195–198.

180 Roger P, Pujol P, Lucas A, Baldet P, Rochefort H. Increased immunostaining of fibulin-1, an estrogen-regulated protein in the stroma of human ovarian epithelial tumors. Am J Pathol 1998, **153**: 1579–1588.

181 Sasano H, Kaga K, Sato S, Yajima A, Nagura H. Adrenal 4-binding protein in common epithelial and metastatic tumors of the ovary. Hum Pathol 1996, **27**: 595–598.

182 Sasano H, Saito Y, Nagura H, Kudo R, Rojas M, Silverberg SG. Lectin histochemistry in mucinous and serous ovarian neoplasms. Int J Gynecol 1991, **10**: 252–259.

183 Sasano H, Suzuki T, Niikura H, Kaga K, Sato S, Yajima A, Rainey WE, Nagura H. 17 Beta-hydroxysteroid dehydrogenase in common epithelial ovarian tumors. Mod Pathol 1996, **9**: 386–391.

184 Scully RE. One pathologist's reminiscences of the 20th century and random thoughts about the 21st: reflections at the millennium. Int J Surg Pathol 2002, **10**: 8–13.

185 Seidman JD, Kurman RJ. Subclassification of serous borderline tumors of the ovary into benign and malignant types: a clinicopathologic study of 65 advanced stage cases. Am J Surg Pathol 1996, **20**: 1331–1345.

186 Shimizu M, Toki T, Takagi Y, Konishi l, Fujii S. Immunohistochemical detection of the Wilms' tumor gene (WT1) in epithelial ovarian tumors. Int J Gynecol Pathol 2000, **19**: 158–163.

187 Sieben NL, Kolkman-Uljee SM, Flanagan AM, Le Cessie S, Cleton-Jansen AM, Cornelisse CJ, Fleuren GJ. Molecular genetic evidence for monoclonal origin of bilateral ovarian serous borderline tumors. Am J Pathol 2003, **162**: 1095–1101.

188 Silva EG, Kurman RJ, Russell P, Scully RE. Symposium: ovarian tumors of borderline malignancy. Int J Gynecol Pathol 1996, **15**: 281–307.

189 Silva EG, Tornos C, Malpica A, Deavers MT, Tortolero-Luna G, Gershenson DM. The association of benign and malignant ovarian adenofibromas with breast cancer and thyroid disorders. Int J Surg Pathol 2002, **10**: 33–39.

190 Silva EG, Tornos CS, Malpica A, Gershenson DM. Ovarian serous neoplasms of low malignant potential associated with focal areas of serous carcinoma. Mod Pathol 1997, **10**: 663–667.

191 Slomovitz BM, Caputo TA, Gretz HF, Economs K, Tortoriello DV, Schlosshauer PW, Baergen RN, Isacson C, Soslow RA. A comparative analysis of 57 serous borderline tumor with and without a non-invasive micropapillary component. Am J Surg Pathol 2002, **26**: 592–600.

191a Smith Sehdev AE, Sehdev PS, Kurman RJ. Noninvasive and invasive micropapillary (low-grade) serous carcinoma of the ovary. A clinicopathologic analysis of 135 cases. Am J Surg Pathol 2003, **27**: 725–736.

192 Staebler A, Heselmeyer-Haddad K, Bell K, Riopel M, Periman E, Ried T, Kurman RJ. Micropapillary serous carcinoma of the ovary has distinct patterns of chromosomal imbalances by comparative genomic hybridisation compared with atypical proliferative serous tumors and serous carcinomas. Hum Pathol 2002, **33**: 47–59.

193 Tan LK, Flynn SD, Carcangiu ML. Ovarian serous borderline tumors with lymph node involvement. Clinicopathologic and DNA content study of seven cases and review of the literature. Am J Surg Pathol 1994, **18**: 904–912.

194 Tiniakos DG, Yu H, Liapis H. Osteopontin expression in ovarian carcinomas and tumors of low malignant potential (LMP). Hum Pathol 1998, **29**: 1250–1254.

195 Ueda G, Yamasaki M, Inoue M, Tanaka Y, Abe Y, Ogawa M. Immunohistochemical study of amylase in common epithelial tumors of the ovary. Int J Gynecol Pathol 1985, **4**: 240–244.

196 Ulbright TM, Roth LM. Common epithelial tumors of the ovary. Proliferating and of low malignant potential. Semin Diagn Pathol 1985, **2**: 2–15.

197 Ulbright TM, Roth LM, Sutton GP. Papillary serous carcinoma of the ovary with squamous differentiation. Int J Gynecol Pathol 1990, **9**: 86–94.

198 Van Kley H, Cramer S, Bruns DE. Serous ovarian neoplastic amylase (SONA). A potentially useful marker for serous ovarian tumors. Cancer 1981, **48**: 1444–1449.

199 White PF, Merino MJ, Barwick KW. Serous surface papillary carcinoma of the ovary. A clinical, pathologic, ultrastructural, and immunohistochemical study of 11 cases. Pathol Annu 1985, **20**(Pt 1): 403–418.

200 Yasuda M, Itoh J, Hirasawa T, Hirazono K, Shinozuka T, Sasano H, Osamura RY. Serous borderline ovarian tumor with functioning stroma in a postmenopausal women: immunohistochemical analysis of steroidogenic pathway. Int J Gynecol Pathol 1998, **17**: 75–78.

Mucinous tumors

201 Aguirre P, Scully RE, Dayal Y, DeLellis RA. Mucinous tumors of the ovary with argyrophil cells. An immunohistochemical analysis. Am J Surg Pathol 1984, **8**: 345–356.

202 Baergen RN, Rutgers JL. Mural nodules in common epithelial tumors of the ovary. Int J Gynecol Pathol 1994, **13**: 62–72.

203 Baguè S, Rodriguez IM, Prat J. Sarcoma-like mural nodules in mucinous cystic tumors of the ovary revisited: a clinicopathologic analysis of 10 additional cases. Am J Surg Pathol 2002, **26**: 1467–1476.

204 Bell DA. Mucinous adenofibromas of the ovary. A report of 10

cases. Am J Surg Pathol 1991, **15**: 227–232.

205 Bhagavan BS, Slavin RE, Goldberg J, Rao RN. Ectopic gastrinoma and Zollinger-Ellison syndrome. Hum Pathol 1986, **17**: 584–592.

206 Cathro HP, Stoler MH. Expression of cytokeratins 7 and 20 in ovarian neoplasia. Am J Clin Pathol 2002, **117**: 944–951.

207 Chaitin BA, Gershenson DM, Evans HL. Mucinous tumors of the ovary. A clinicopathologic study of 70 cases. Cancer 1985, **55**: 1958–1962.

208 Charpin C, Bhan AK, Zurawski VR, Scully RE. Carcinoembryonic antigen (CEA) and carbohydrate determinant 19-9 (CA 19-9) localization in 121 primary and metastatic ovarian tumors. An immunohistochemical study with the use of monoclonal antibodies. Int J Gynecol Pathol 1982, **1**: 231–245.

209 Czernobilsky B, Dgani R, Roth LM. Ovarian mucinous cystadenocarcinoma with mural nodule of carcinomatous derivation. A light and electron microscopic study. Cancer 1983, **51**: 141–148.

210 Fenoglio CM, Ferenczy A, Richart RM. Mucinous tumors of the ovary. Ultrastructural studies of mucinous cystadenomas with histogenetic considerations. Cancer 1975, **36**: 1709–1722.

211 Griffin NR, Wells M. Immunolocalization of alpha-amylase in ovarian mucinous tumors. Int J Gynecol Pathol 1990, **9**: 41–46.

212 Hart WR, Norris HJ. Borderline and malignant mucinous tumors of the ovary. Cancer 1973, **31**: 1031–1045.

213 Hoerl HD, Hart WR. Primary ovarian mucinous cystadenocarcinomas: a clinicopathologic study of 49 cases with long-term follow-up. Am J Surg Pathol 1998, **22**: 1449–1462.

214 Ishikura H, Sasano H. Histopathologic and immunohistochemical study of steroidogenic cells in the stroma of ovarian tumors. Int J Gynecol Pathol 1998, **17**: 261–265.

215 Ishikura H, Shibata M, Yoshiki T. Endocrine cell micronests in an ovarian mucinous cystadenofibroma: a mimic of microinvasion. Int J Gynecol Pathol 1999, **18**: 392–395.

216 Ji H, Isacson C, Seidman JD, Kurman RJ, Ronnett BM. Cytokeratins 7 and 20, Dpc4, and MUC5AC in the distinction of metastatic mucinous carcinomas in the ovary from primary ovarian mucinous tumors: Dpc4 assists in identifying metastatic pancreatic carcinomas. Int J Gynecol Pathol 2002, **21**: 391–400.

217 Khunamornpong S, Russell P, Dalrymple JC. Proliferating (LMP) mucinous tumors of the ovaries with microinvasion: morphologic assessment of 13 Cases. Int J Gynecol Pathol 2002, **18**: 238–246.

218 Klemi PJ. Pathology of mucinous ovarian cystadenomas. I. Argyrophil and argentaffin cells and epithelial mucosubstances. Acta Pathol Microbiol Scand (A) 1978, **86**: 465–470.

219 Lee KR, Nucci MR. Ovarian mucinous and mixed epithelial carcinoma of mullerian (endocervical-like) type: A clinicopathologic analysis of four cases of an uncommon variant associated with endometriosis. Int J Gynecol Pathol 2002, **22**: 42–51.

220 Lee KR, Scully RE. Mucinous tumors of the ovary: a clinicopathologic study of 196 borderline tumors (of intestinal type) and carcinomas, including an evaluation of 11 cases with "pseudomyxoma peritonei". Am J Surg Pathol 2000, **24**: 1447–1464.

221 Lifschitz-Mercer B, Dgani R, Jacob N, Fogel M, Czernobilsky B. Ovarian mucinous cystadenoma with leiomyomatous mural nodule. Int J Gynecol Pathol 1990, **9**: 80–85.

222 LiVolsi VA, Merino MJ, Schwartz PE. Coexistent endocervical adenocarcinoma and mucinous adenocarcinoma of ovary. A clinicopathologic study of four cases. Int J Gynecol Pathol 1983, **1**: 391–402.

223 Louwerens JK, Schaberg A, Bosman FT. Neuroendocrine cells in cystic mucinous tumours of the ovary. Histopathology 1983, **7**: 389–398.

224 Matias-Guiu X, Prat J. Ovarian tumors with functioning stroma. An immunohistochemical study of 100 cases with human chorionic gonadotropin monoclonal and polyclonal antibodies. Cancer 1990, **65**: 2001–2005.

225 Matias-Guiu X, Aranda I, Prat J. Immunohistochemical study of sarcoma-like mural nodules in a mucinous cystadenocarcinoma of the ovary. Virchows Arch [A] 1991, **419**: 89–92.

226 Nichols GE, Mills SE, Ulbright TM, Czernobilsky B, Roth LM. Spindle cell mural nodules in cystic ovarian mucinous tumors. A clinicopathologic and immunohistochemical study of five cases. Am J Surg Pathol 1991, **15**: 1055–1062.

227 Nomura K, Aizawa S. Clinicopathologic and mucin histochemical analysis of 90 cases of ovarian mucinous borderline tumors of intestinal and mullerian types. Pathol Int 1997, **46**: 575–580.

228 Nomura K, Aizawa S. Noninvasive, microinvasive and invasive mucinous carcinomas of the ovary: a clinicopathologic analysis of 40 cases. Cancer 2000, **89**: 1541–1546.

229 Prat J, Scully RE. Sarcomas in ovarian mucinous tumors. A report of two cases. Cancer 1979, **44**: 1327–1331.

230 Prat J, Scully RE. Ovarian mucinous tumors with sarcoma-like nodules. A report of seven cases. Cancer 1979, **44**: 1332–1344.

231 Prat J, Young RH, Scully RE. Ovarian mucinous tumors with foci of anaplastic carcinoma. Cancer 1982, **50**: 300–304.

232 Riopel MA, Ronnett BM, Kurman RJ. Evaluation of diagnostic criteria and behavior of ovarian intestinal-type mucinous tumors: atypical proliferative (borderline) tumors and intraepithelial, microinvasive, invasive, and metastatic carcinoma. Am J Surg Pathol 1999, **23**: 617–635.

233 Robboy SJ. Insular carcinoid of ovary associated with malignant mucinous tumors. Cancer 1984, **54**: 2273–2276.

234 Rodriguez IM, Prat J. Mucinous tumors of the ovary: a clinicopathologic analysis of 75 borderline tumors (of intestinal type) and carcinomas. Am J Surg Pathol 2002, **26**: 139–152.

235 Rutgers JL, Baergen RN. Mucin histochemistry of ovarian borderline tumors of mucinous and mixed epithelial types. Mod Pathol 1994, **7**: 825–828.

236 Rutgers JL, Bell DA. Immunohistochemical characterization of ovarian borderline tumors of intestinal and mullerian types. Mod Pathol 1992, **5**: 367–371.

237 Sasaki E, Sasano N, Kimura N, Andoh N, Yajima A. Demonstration of neuroendocrine cells in ovarian mucinous tumors. Int J Gynecol Pathol 1989, **8**: 189–200.

238 Shappell HW, Riopel MA, Smith Sehdev AE, Ronnett BM, Kurman RJ. Diagnostic criteria and behavior of ovarian seromucinous (endocervical-type mucinous and mixed cell-type) tumors: atypical proliferative (borderline) tumors, intraepithelial, microinvasive, and invasive carcinomas. Am J Surg Pathol 2002, **26**: 1529–1541.

239 Shiohara S, Shiozawa T, Shimizu M, Toki T, Ishii K, Nikaido T, Fujii S. Histochemical analysis of estrogen and progesterone receptors and gastric-type mucin in mucinous ovarian tumors with reference to their pathogenesis. Cancer 1997, **80**: 908–916.

240 Shiozawa T, Tsukahara Y, Ishii K, Ota H, Nakayama J, Katsuyama T. Histochemical demonstration of gastrointestinal mucins in ovarian mucinous cystadenoma. Acta Pathol Jpn 1992, **42**: 104–110.

241 Siriaunkgul S, Robbins KM, McGowan L, Silverberg SG. Ovarian mucinous tumors of low malignant potential. A clinicopathologic study of 54 tumors of intestinal and Mullerian type. Int J Gynecol Pathol 1995, **14**: 198–208.

242 Sporrong B, Alumets J, Clase L, Falkmer S, Hakanson R, Ljungberg O, Sundler F. Neurohormonal peptide immunoreactive cells in mucinous cystadenomas and cystadenocarcinomas of the ovary. Virchows Arch [A] 1981, **392**: 271–280.

243 Szymanska K, Szamborski J, Miechowiecka N, Czerwinski W.

tissue in immature ovarian teratoma. Am J Surg Pathol 1980, **4:** 297–299.

627 Nogales FF, Ruiz Avila I, Concha A, del Moral E. Immature endodermal teratoma of the ovary. Embryologic correlations and immunohistochemistry. Hum Pathol 1993, **24:** 364–370.

628 Norris HJ, Zirkin HJ, Benson WL. Immature (malignant) teratoma of the ovary. A clinical and pathologic study of 58 cases. Cancer 1976, **37:** 2359–2372.

629 Notohara K, Hsueh CL, Awai M. Glial fibrillary acidic protein immunoreactivity of chondrocytes in immature and mature teratomas. Acta Pathol Jpn 1990, **40:** 335–342.

630 O'Connor DM, Norris HJ. The influence of grade on the outcome of stage I ovarian immature (malignant) teratomas and the reproducibility of grading. Int J Gynecol Pathol 1994, **13:** 283–289.

631 Ramdial PK, Bagratee JS. Membranous fat necrosis in mature cystic teratomas of the ovary. Int J Gynecol Pathol 1998, **17:** 120–122.

632 Schwartz PE, Merino MJ, LiVolsi VA. Immature ovarian teratomas. Maturation following chemotherapy. Am J Diagn Gynecol Obstet 1979, **1:** 361–366.

633 Steeper TA, Mukai K. Solid ovarian teratomas. An immunocytochemical study of thirteen cases with clinicopathologic correlation. Pathol Annu 1984, **19**(Pt 1): 81–92.

634 Yanai H, Matsuura H, Kawasaki M, Takada Y, Tabuchi Y, Yoshino T. Immature teratoma of the ovary with a minor rhabdomyosarcomatous component and fatal rhabdomyosarcomatous metastases: the first case in a child. Int J Gynecol Pathol 2002, **21:** 82–85.

Mature solid teratoma

635 Benirschke K, Easterday C, Abramson D. Malignant solid teratoma of the ovary. Report of three cases. Obstet Gynecol 1960, **15:** 512–521.

636 Peterson WF. Solid, histologically benign teratomas of the ovary. A report of four cases and review of the literature. Am J Obstet Gynecol 1956, **72:** 1094–1102.

637 Thurlbeck WM, Scully RE. Solid teratoma of the ovary. A clinicopathological analysis of 9 cases. Cancer 1960, **13:** 804–811.

Mature cystic teratoma

638 Ackerman LV. Autobiographical notes. In Rosai J (ed.): Guiding the surgeon's hand. Washington, D.C., 1997, The American Registry of Pathology/Armed Forces Institute of Pathology, p. 284.

639 Auer EA, Dockerty MB, Mayo CW. Ruptured dermoid cyst of the ovary simulating abdominal carcinomatosis. Mayo Clin Proc 1951, **26:** 489–497.

640 Blackwell WJ, Dockerty MB, Masson JC, Mussey RD. Dermoid cysts of the ovary. Their clinical and pathologic significance. Am J Obstet Gynecol 1946, **51:** 151–172.

641 Boman F, Vantyghem MC, Querleu D, Sasano H. Virilizing ovarian dermoid cyst with peripheral steroid cells: a case study with immunohistochemical study of steroidogenesis. Int J Gynecol Pathol 1999, **18:** 174–177.

642 Burg J, Kommoss F, Bittinger F, Moll R, Kirkpatrick CJ. Mature cystic teratoma of the ovary with struma and benign brenner tumor: a case report with immunohistochemical characterization. Int J Gynecol Pathol 2002, **21:** 74–77.

643 Calame J, Bosman FT, Schaberg A, Louwerens JWK. Immunocytochemical localization of neuroendocrine hormones and oncofetal antigens in ovarian teratomas. Int J Gynecol Pathol 1984, **3:** 92–100.

644 Cobo F, Pereira A, Nomdedeu B, Gallart T, Ordi J, Torne A, Monserrat E, Rozman C. Ovarian dermoid cyst-associated autoimmune hemolytic anemia. A case report with emphasis on pathogenic mechanisms. Am J Clin Pathol 1996, **105:** 567–571.

645 Czernobilsky B, Lifschitz-Mercer B, Luzon A, Jacob N, Ben-Hur H, Gorbacz S, Fogel M. Cytokeratin patterns in the epidermis of human ovarian mature cystic teratomas. Hum Pathol 1989, **20:** 185–192.

646 Dick HM, Honoré LH. Dental structures in benign ovarian cystic teratomas (dermoid cysts). A study of ten cases with a review of the literature. Oral Surg 1985, **60:** 299–307.

647 Ein SH, Darte JMM, Stephens CA. Cystic and solid ovarian tumors in children. A 44-year review. J Pediatr Surg 1970, **5:** 148–156.

648 Fortt RW, Mathie IK. Gliomatosis peritonei caused by ovarian teratoma. J Clin Pathol 1969, **22:** 348–353.

649 Harms D, Janig U, Gobel U. Gliomatosis peritonei in childhood and adolescence. Clinicopathological study of 13 cases including immunohistochemical findings. Pathol Res Pract 1989, **184:** 422–430.

650 Jaworski RC, Boable R, Greg J, Cocks P. Peritoneal "melanosis" associated with a ruptured ovarian dermoid cyst: report of a case with electron-probe energy dispersive X-ray analysis. Int J Gynecol Pathol 2001, **20:** 386–389.

651 Lewis MG. Melanin-pigmented components in ovarian teratomas in Ugandan Africans. J Pathol Bacteriol 1968, **95:** 405–409.

652 Linder D, McCaw BK, Hecht F. Parthenogenic origin of benign ovarian teratomas. N Engl J Med 1975, **292:** 63–66.

653 López-Beltrán A, Calañas AS, Jimena P, Escudero AL, Campello TR, Muñoz-Torres M, Escobar-Jiménez F, Carvia RE, Nogales FF. Virilizing mature ovarian cystic teratomas. Virchows Arch 1997, **431:** 149–151.

654 McKeel DW Jr, Askin FB. Ectopic hypophyseal hormonal cells in benign cystic teratoma of the ovary. Light microscopic histochemical dye staining and immunoperoxidase cytochemistry. Arch Pathol Lab Med 1978, **102:** 122–128.

655 McLachlin CM, Srigley JR. Prostatic tissue in mature cystic teratomas of the ovary. Am J Surg Pathol 1992, **16:** 780–784.

656 Miyake J, Ireland K. Ovarian mature teratoma with homunculus coexisting with an intrauterine pregnancy. Arch Pathol Lab Med 1986, **110:** 1192–1194.

657 Morimitsu Y, Nakashima O, Kage M, Kojiro M, Kawano K, Koga T. Coexistence of mature teratoma and thecoma in an ovary. A report of two cases. Acta Pathol Jpn 1991, **41:** 922–926.

658 Muretto P, Chilosi M, Rabitti C, Tommasoni S, Colato C. Biovularity and "coalescence of primary follicles" in ovaries with mature teratomas. Int J Surg Pathol 2001, **9:** 121–126.

659 Nielsen SNJ, Scheithauer BW, Gaffey TA. Gliomatosis peritonei. Cancer 1985, **56:** 2499–2503.

660 Payne D, Muss HB, Homesley HD, Jobson VW, Baird FG. Autoimmune hemolytic anemia and ovarian dermoid cysts. Case report and review of the literature. Cancer 1981, **48:** 721–724.

661 Rashad MH, Fathalla MF, Kerr MG. Sex chromatin and chromosome analysis in ovarian teratomas. Am J Obstet Gynecol 1966, **96:** 461–465.

662 Riley PA, Sutton PM. Why are ovarian teratomas benign whilst teratomas of the testis are malignant? Lancet 1975, **1:** 1360–1362.

663 Robboy SJ, Scully RE. Ovarian teratoma with glial implants on the peritoneum. An analysis of 12 cases. Hum Pathol 1970, **1:** 644–653.

664 Sahin AA, Ro JY, Chen J, Ayala AG. Spindle cell nodule and peptic ulcer arising in a fully developed gastric wall in a mature cystic teratoma. Arch Pathol Lab Med 1990, **114:** 529–531.

665 Truong LD, Jurco S III, McGavran MH. Gliomatosis peritonei. Report of two cases and review of literature. Am J Surg Pathol 1982, **6:** 443–449.

666 Vadmal M, Hadju SI. Prostatic tissue in benign cystic ovarian teratomas. Hum Pathol 1996, **27:** 428–429.

667 Vortmeyer AO, Devouassoux-Shisheboran M, Li G, Mohr V,

Tavassoli F, Zhuang Z. Microdissection-based analysis of mature ovarian teratoma. Am J Pathol 1999, **154**: 987–991.

668 Wheeler JE. Extraovarian teratoma with peritoneal gliomatosis. Hum Pathol 1978, **9**: 232–234.

669 Yanai-Inbar I, Scully RE. Relation of ovarian dermoid cysts and immature teratomas. An analysis of 350 cases of immature teratoma and 10 cases of dermoid cyst with microscopic foci of immature tissue. Int J Gynecol Pathol 1987, **6**: 203–212.

"Somatic-type" tumors developing in mature cystic teratoma

670 Chumas JC, Scully RE. Sebaceous tumors arising in ovarian dermoid cysts. Int J Gynecol Pathol 1991, **10**: 356–363.

671 Climie ARW, Heath LP. Malignant degeneration of benign cystic teratomas of the ovary. Review of the literature and report of a chondrosarcoma and carcinoid tumor. Cancer 1968, **22**: 824–832.

672 Davis GL. Malignant melanoma arising in mature ovarian cystic teratoma (dermoid cyst). Report of two cases and literature analysis. Int J Gynecol Pathol 1997, **15**: 356–362.

673 Devouassoux-Shisheboran M, Vortmeyer AO, Silver SA, Zhuang Z, Tavassoli FA. Teratomatous genotype detected in malignancies of a non-germ cell phenotype. Lab Invest 2000, **80**: 81–86.

674 Hirakawa T, Tsuneyoshi M, Enjoji M. Squamous cell carcinoma arising in mature cystic teratoma of the ovary. Clinicopathologic and topographic analysis. Am J Surg Pathol 1989, **13**: 397–405.

675 Hirschowitz L, Ansari A, Cahill DJ, Bamford DS, Love S. Central neurocytoma arising within a mature cystic teratoma of the ovary. Int J Gynecol Pathol 1997, **16**: 176–179.

676 Kanbour-Shakir A, Sawaday J, Kanbour AI, Kunschner A, Stock RJ. Primitive neuroectodermal tumor arising in an ovarian mature cystic teratoma. Immunohistochemical and electron microscopic studies. Int J Gynecol Pathol 1993, **12**: 270–275.

677 Kelley RR, Scully RE. Cancer developing in dermoid cysts of the ovary. Cancer 1961, **14**: 989–1000.

678 Kudo M. The nature of "blue nevus" in cystic teratomas of the ovary. An ultrastructural evidence for Schwann cell origin. Acta Pathol Jpn 1985, **35**: 693–698.

679 Madison JF, Cooper PH. A histiocytoid (epithelioid) vascular tumor of the ovary. Occurrence within a benign cystic teratoma. Mod Pathol 1989, **2**: 55–58.

680 Morimitsu Y, Nakashima O, Nakashima Y, Kojiro M, Shimokobe T. Apocrine adenocarcinoma arising in cystic teratoma of the ovary. Arch Pathol Lab Med 1993, **117**: 647–649.

681 Palmer PE, Bogojavlensky S, Bhan AK, Scully RE. Prolactinoma in wall of ovarian dermoid cyst with hyperprolactinemia. Obstet Gynecol 1990, **75**: 540–543.

682 Peterson WF. Malignant degeneration of benign cystic teratomas of the ovary. A collective review of the literature. Obstet Gynecol Survey 1957, **12**: 793–830.

683 Reid H, van der Walt JD, Fox H. Neuroblastoma arising in a mature cystic teratoma of the ovary. J Clin Pathol 1983, **36**: 68–73.

684 Ronnett BM, Seidman JD. Mucinous tumors arising in ovarian mature cystic teratomas. Am J Surg Pathol 2003, **27**: 650–657.

685 Shen DH, Khoo US, Xue WC, Cheung AN. Ovarian mature cystic teratoma with malignant transformation: an interphase cytogenetic study. Int J Gynecol Pathol 1998, **17**: 351–357.

686 Shimizu S, Kobayashi H, Suchi T, Torii Y, Narita K, Aoki S. Extramammary Paget's disease arising in mature cystic teratoma of the ovary. Am J Surg Pathol 1991, **15**: 1002–1006.

687 Silver SA, Tavassoli FA. Glomus tumor arising in a mature teratoma of the ovary: report of a case simulating a metastasis from cervical squamous carcinoma. Arch Pathol Lab Med 2000, **124**: 1373–1375.

688 Tsang P, Berman L, Kasznica J. Adnexal tumor and a pigmented nevoid lesion in a benign cystic ovarian teratoma. Arch Pathol Lab Med 1993, **117**: 846–847.

689 Ueda Y, Kimura A, Kawahara E, Kitagawa H, Nakanishi I. Malignant melanoma arising in a dermoid cyst of the ovary. Cancer 1991, **67**: 3141–3145.

690 Yadav A, Lellouch-Tubiana A, Fournet JC, Quazza JE, Kalifa C, Sainte-Rose C, Jaubert F. Glioblastoma multiforme in a mature ovarian teratoma with recurring brain tumors. Histopathology 1999, **35**: 170–173.

Epidermoid cyst

691 Young RH, Prat J, Scully RE. Epidermoid cyst of the ovary. A report of three cases with comments on histogenesis. Am J Clin Pathol 1980, **73**: 272–276.

Struma ovarii

692 Hasleton PS, Kelehan P, Wittaker JS, Turner L, Burslem RW. Benign and malignant struma ovarii. Arch Pathol Lab Med 1978, **102**: 180–184.

693 Ro JY, Sahin AA, el-Naggar AK, Ordonez NG, Mackay B, Llamas LL, Ayala AG. Intraluminal crystalloids in struma ovarii. Immunohistochemical, DNA flow cytometric, and ultrastructural study. Arch Pathol Lab Med 1991, **115**: 145–149.

694 Seifer DB, Weiss LM, Kempson RL. Malignant lymphoma arising within thyroid tissue in a mature cystic teratoma. Cancer 1986, **58**: 2459–2461.

695 Szyfelbein WM, Young RH, Scully RE. Cystic struma ovarii. A frequently unrecognized tumor. A report of 20 cases. Am J Surg Pathol 1994, **18**: 785–788.

696 Szyfelbein WM, Young RH, Scully RE. Struma ovarii simulating ovarian tumors of other types. A report of 30 cases. Am J Surg Pathol 1995, **19**: 21–29.

Carcinoid tumor and strumal carcinoid

697 Arhelger RB, Kelly B. Strumal carcinoid. Report of a case with electron microscopical observations. Arch Pathol 1974, **97**: 323–325.

698 Baker PM, Oliva E, Young RH, Talerman A, Scully RE. Ovarian mucinous carcinoids including some with a carcinomatous component: a report of 17 cases. Am J Surg Pathol 2001, **25**: 557–568.

699 Brunaud L, Antunes L, Sebbag H, Bresler L, Villemot JP, Boissel P. Ovarian strumal carcinoid tumor responsible for carcinoid heart disease. Eur J Obstet Gynecol Reprod Biol 2001, **98**: 124–126.

700 Czernobilsky B, Segal M, Dgani R. Primary ovarian carcinoid with marked heterogeneity of microscopic features. Cancer 1984, **54**: 585–589.

701 Dayal Y, Tashjian H Jr, Wolfe HJ. Immunocytochemical localization of calcitonin-producing cells in a strumal carcinoid with amyloid stroma. Cancer 1979, **43**: 1331–1338.

702 Hamazaki S, Okino T, Tsukayama C, Okada S. Expression of thyroid transcription factor-1 in strumal carcinoid and struma ovarii: an immunohistochemical study. Pathol Int 2002, **52**: 458–462.

703 Matias-Guiu X, Forteza J, Prat J. Mixed strumal and mucinous carcinoid tumor of the ovary. Int J Gynecol Pathol 1995, **14**: 179–183.

704 Motoyama T, Katayama Y, Watanabe H, Okazaki E, Shibuya H. Functioning ovarian carcinoids induce severe constipation. Cancer 1992, **70**: 513–518.

705 Robboy SJ, Norris HJ, Scully RE. Insular carcinoid primary in ovary – a clinicopathologic analysis of 48 cases. Cancer 1975, **36**: 406–420.

706 Robboy SJ, Scully RE. Strumal carcinoid of the ovary. An analysis of 50 cases of a distinctive tumor composed of thyroid tissue and carcinoid. Cancer 1980, **46**: 2019–2034.

707 Robboy SJ, Scully RE, Norris HJ. Carcinoid metastatic to ovary. A clinicopathologic analysis of 35 cases. Cancer 1974, 33: 798–811.

708 Robboy SJ, Scully RE, Norris HJ. Primary trabecular carcinoid of the ovary. Obstet Gynecol 1977, 49: 202–207.

709 Serratoni FT, Robboy SJ. Ultrastructure of primary and metastatic ovarian carcinoids. Analysis of 11 cases. Cancer 1975, 36: 157–160.

710 Shigeta H, Taga M, Kurogi K, Kitamura H, Motoyama T, Gorai I. Ovarian strumal carcinoid with severe constipation: immunohistochemical and mRNA analyses of peptide YY. Hum Pathol 1999, 30: 242–246.

711 Sidhu J, Sanchez RL. Prostatic acid tase in strumal carcinoids of the ovary. An immunohistochemical study. Cancer 1993, 72: 1673–1678.

712 Snyder RR, Tavassoli FA. Ovarian strumal carcinoid. Immunohistochemical, ultrastructural, and clinicopathologic observations. Int J Gynecol Pathol 1986, 3: 187–201.

713 Sporrong B, Falkmer S, Robboy SJ, Alumets J, Hakanson R, Ljungber O, Sundler F. Neurohormonal peptides in ovarian carcinoids. An immunohistochemical study of 81 primary carcinoids and of intraovarian metastases from six mid-gut carcinoids. Cancer 1982, 49: 68–74.

714 Stagno PA, Petras RE, Hart WR. Strumal carcinoids of the ovary. An immunohistologic and ultrastructural study. Arch Pathol Lab Med 1987, 111: 440–446.

715 Talerman A. Carcinoid tumors of the ovary. J Cancer Res Clin Oncol 1984, 107: 125–135.

716 Tamsen A, Mazur MT. Ovarian strumal carcinoid in association with multiple endocrine neoplasia, type IIA. Arch Pathol Lab Med 1992, 116: 200–203.

717 Ulbright TM, Roth LM, Ehrlich CE. Ovarian strumal carcinoid. An immunocytochemical and ultrastructural study of two cases. Am J Clin Pathol 1982, 77: 622–631.

Sex cord–stromal tumors

718 Bamberger AM, Ivell R, Balvers M, Kelp B, Bamberger CM, Riethdorf L, Loning T. Relaxin-like factor (RLF): a new specific marker for Leydig cells in the ovary. Int J Gynecol Pathol 1999, 18: 163–168.

719 Busam KJ, Iversen K, Coplan KA, Old LJ, Stockert E, Chen YT, McGregor D, Jungbluth A. Immunoreactivity for A103, and antibody to Melan-A (Mart-1), in adrenocortical and other steroid tumors. Am J Surg Pathol 1998, 22: 57–63.

720 Cao QJ, Jones JG, Li M. Expression of calretinin in human ovary, testis and ovarian sex cord-stromal tumors. Int J Gynecol Pathol 2001, 20: 346–352.

721 Choi YL, Kim HS, Ahn G. Immunoexpression of inhibin alfa subunit, inhibin/activin beta A subunit and CD99 in ovarian tumors. Arch Pathol Lab Med 2000, 124: 563–569.

722 Costa MJ, Morris R, Sasano H. Sex steroid biosynthesis enzymes in ovarian sex-cord stromal tumors. Int J Gynecol Pathol 1994, 13: 109–119.

722a Deavers MT, Malpica A, Liu J, Broaddus R, Silva EG. Ovarian sex cord-stromal tumors: an immunohistochemical study including a comparison of calretinin and inhibin. Mod Pathol 2003, 16: 584–580.

723 Fox H. Sex cord-stromal tumours of the ovary. J Pathol 1985, 145: 127–148.

724 Freeman DA. Steroid hormone-producing tumors of the adrenal, ovary, and testes. Endocrinol Metab Clin North Am 1991, 20: 751–766.

725 Gordon MD, Corles C, Renshaw AA, Beckstead J. CD99, Keratin, and vimentin staining of sex cord-stromal tumors, normal ovary, and testis. Mod Pathol 1998, 11: 769–773.

726 Iczkowski KA, Bostwick DG, Roche PC, Cheville JC. Inhibin A is a sensitive and specific marker for testicular sex cord-stromal tumors. Mod Pathol 1998, 11: 774–779.

727 Iezzoni JC, Mills SE, Pelkey TJ, Stoler MH. Inhibin is not an immunohistochemical marker for hepatocellular carcinoma. An example of the potential pitfall diagnostic immunohistochemistry caused by endogenous biotin. Am J Clin Pathol 1999, 111: 229–234.

728 Keitoku M, Konishi I, Nanbu K, Yamamoto S, Mandai M, Kataoka N, Oishi T, Mori T. Extraovarian sex cord-stromal tumor: case report and review of the literature. Int J Gynecol Pathol 1997, 16: 180–185.

729 Kommoss F, Oliva E, Bhan AK, Young RH, Scully RE. Inhibin expression in ovarian tumors and tumor-like lesions: an immunohistochemical study. Mod Pathol 1998, 11: 656–664.

730 Lobo RA. Ovarian hyperandrogenism and androgen-producing tumors. Endocrinol Metab Clin North Am 1991, 20: 773–805.

731 McCluggage WG. Value of inhibin staining in gynecological pathology. Int J Gynecol Pathol 2001, 20: 79–85.

732 McCluggage WG. Recent advances in immunohistochemistry in gynecological pathology. Histopathology 2002, 40: 309–326.

733 McCluggage WG, Maxwell P. Adenocarcinomas of various sites may exhibit immunoreactivity with anti-inhibin antibodies. Histopathology 1999, 35: 216–220.

734 Matias-Guiu X, Pons C, Prat J. Mullerian inhibiting substance, alpha-inhibin, and CD99 expression in sex cord stromal tumors and endometrioid ovarian carcinomas resembling sex cord-stromal tumors. Hum Pathol 1998, 29: 840–845.

735 Movahedi-Lankarani S, Kurman RJ. Carletinin, a more sensitive but less specific marker than alpha-inhibin for ovarian sex cord-stromal neoplasms: an immunohistochemical study of 215 cases. Am J Surg Pathol 2002, 26: 1477–1483.

736 Pelkey TJ, Frierson HF Jr, Mills SE, Stoler MH. Detection of the alpha-subunit of inhibin in trophoblastic neoplasia. Hum Pathol 1999, 30: 26–31.

737 Rey R, Sabourin JC, Venara M, Long WQ, Jaubert F, Zeller WP, Duvillard P, Chemes H, Bidart JM. Anti-Mullerian hormone is a specific marker of Sertoli-and granulosa-cell origin in gonadal tumors. Hum Pathol 2000, 31: 1202–1208.

738 Roth LM, Billings SD. Hormonally functional ovarian neoplasms. Endocrine Pathol 2002, 11: 1–17.

739 Sasano H. Functional pathology of human ovarian steroidogenesis. Normal cycling ovary and steroid-producing neoplasms. Endocr Pathol 1994, 5: 81–89.

740 Sasano H, Okamoto M, Mason JI, Simpson ER, Mendelson CR, Sasano N, Silverberg SG. Immunohistochemical studies of steroidogenic enzymes (aromatase, 17 alpha-hydroxylase and cholesterol side-chain cleavage cytochromes P-450) in sex cord-stromal tumors of the ovary. Hum Pathol 1989, 20: 452–457.

741 Tavassoli FA. Ovarian tumors with functioning manifestations. Endocr Pathol 1994, 5: 137–148.

742 Teilum G. Estrogen-producing Sertoli cell tumors (androblastoma tubular lipoides) of the human testis and ovary. Homologous ovarian and testicular tumors. J Clin Endocrinol 1949, 9: 301–318.

743 Yaziji H, Gown AM. Immunohistochemical analysis of gynecologic tumors. Int J Gynecol Pathol 2000, 20: 64–78.

744 Young RH, Scully RE. Ovarian sex cord-stromal tumors. Recent progress. Int J Gynecol Pathol 1982, 1: 101–123.

745 Young RH, Scully RE. Ovarian sex cord-stromal tumors. Problems in differential diagnosis. Pathol Annu 1988, 23(Pt 1): 273–296.

Granulosa cell tumor

746 Ahmed E, Young RH, Scully RE. Adult granulosa cell tumor of the ovary with foci of hepatic cell differentiation: a report of four cases and comparison with two cases of granulosa cell tumor with Leydig cells. Am J Surg Pathol 1999, 23: 1089–1093.

747 Bjorkholm E, Silfversward C. Prognostic factors in granulosa-cell tumors. Gynecol Oncol 1981, 11: 261–274.

748 Castro CY, Malpica A, Hearne RH, Silva EG, Castro CV. Androgenic adult granulosa cell tumor in a 13-year-old prepubertal patient: a case report and review of the literature. Int J Gynecol Pathol 2000, 19: 266–271.

749 Chadha S, Cornelisse CJ, Schaberg A. Flow cytometric DNA ploidy analysis of ovarian granulosa cell tumors. Gynecol Oncol 1990, 36: 240–245.

750 Clement PB, Young RH, Scully RE. Ovarian granulosa cell proliferations of pregnancy. A report of nine cases. Hum Pathol 1988, 19: 657–662.

751 Costa MJ, De Rose PB, Roth LM, Brescia RJ, Zaloudek CJ, Cohen C. Immunohistochemical phenotype of ovarian granulosa cell tumors. Absence of epithelial membrane antigen has diagnostic value. Hum Pathol 1994, 25: 60–66.

752 Czernobilsky B, Moll R, Leppien G, Schweikhart G, Franke WW. Desmosomal plaque-associated vimentin filaments in human ovarian granulosa cell tumors of various histologic patterns. Am J Pathol 1987, 126: 476–486.

753 Evans AT III, Gaffey TA, Malkasian GD Jr, Annegers JF. Clinicopathologic review of 118 granulosa and 82 theca cell tumors. Obstet Gynecol 1980, 55: 231–238.

754 Evans MP, Webb MJ, Gaffey TA, Katzmann JA, Suman VJ, Hu TC. DNA ploidy of ovarian granulosa cell tumors. Lack of correlation between DNA index or proliferative index and outcome in 40 patients. Cancer 1995, 75: 2295–2298.

755 Flemming P, Wellmann A, Maschjek H, Lang H, Georgii A. Monoclonal antibodies against inhibin represent key markers of adult granulosa cell tumors of the ovary even in their metastases. A report of three cases with late metastasis, being previously misinterpreted as hemangiopericytoma. Am J Surg Pathol 1995, 19: 927–933.

756 Fletcher JA, Gibas Z, Donovan K, Perez-Atayde A, Genest D, Morton CC, Lage JM. Ovarian granulosa-stromal cell tumors are characterized by trisomy 12. Am J Pathol 1991, 138: 515–520.

757 Fox H, Agrawal K, Langley FA. A clinicopathologic study of 92 cases of granulosa cell tumor of the ovary with special reference to the factors influencing prognosis. Cancer 1975, 35: 231–241.

758 Gaffey MJ, Frierson HF Jr, Iezzoni JC, Mills SE, Clement PB, Gersell DJ, Shashi V, von Kap-Herr C, Young RH. Ovarian granulosa cell tumors with bizarre nuclei: an immunohistochemical analysis with fluorescence in situ hybridization documenting trisomy 12 in bizarre component. Mod Pathol 1996, 9: 308–315.

759 Halperin D, Visscher DW, Wallis T, Lawrence WD. Evaluation of chromosome 12 copy number in ovarian granulosa cell tumors using interphase cytogenetics. Int J Gynecol Pathol 1995, 14: 319–323.

760 Hitchcock CL, Norris HJ, Khalifa MA, Wargotz ES. Flow cytometric analysis of granulosa tumors. Cancer 1989, 64: 2127–2132.

761 Jacoby AF, Young RH, Colvin RB, Flotte TJ, Preffer F, Scully RE, Swymer CM, Bell DA. DNA content in juvenile granulosa cell tumors of the ovary. A study of early-and advanced-stage disease. Gynecol Oncol 1992, 46: 97–103.

762 Kurman RJ, Goebelsmann U, Taylor CR. Steroid localization in granulosatheca tumors of the ovary. Cancer 1979, 43: 2377–2384.

763 Lack EE, Perez-Atayde AR, Murthy ASK, Goldstein DP, Crigler JF, Vawter GF. Granulosa theca cell tumors in premenarchal girls. A clinical and pathologic study of ten cases. Cancer 1981, 48: 1846–1854.

764 Loo KT, Leung AKF, Chan JKC. Immunohistochemical staining of ovarian granulosa cell tumours with MIC2 antibody. Histopathology 1995, 27: 388–390.

765 McCluggage WG, Maxwell P, Sloan JM. Immunohistochemical staining of ovarian granulosa cell tumors with monoclonal antibody against inhibin. Hum Pathol 1997, 28: 1034–1038.

766 Mayr D, Kaltz-Wittman C, Arbogast S, Amann G, Aust DE, Diebold J. Characteristic pattern of genetic aberrations in ovarian granulosa cell tumors. Mod Pathol 2002, 15: 951–957.

767 Miettinen M, Wahlstrom T, Virtanen I, Talerman A, Astengo-Osuna C. Cellular differentiation in ovarian sex cord-stromal and germ-cell tumors studied with antibodies to intermediate-filament proteins. Am J Surg Pathol 1985, 9: 640–651.

768 Miller BE, Barron BA, Wan JY, Delmore JE, Silva EG. Prognostic factors in adult granulosa cell tumor of the ovary. Cancer 1997, 79: 1951–1955.

769 Nakashima N, Young RH, Scully RE. Androgenic granulosa cell tumors of the ovary. A clinicopathologic analysis of 17 cases and review of the literature. Arch Pathol Lab Med 1984, 108: 786–791.

770 Nogales FF, Concha A, Plata C, Ruiz-Avila I. Granulosa cell tumor of the ovary with diffuse true hepatic differentiation simulating stromal luteinization. Am J Surg Pathol 1993, 17: 85–90.

771 Norris HJ, Taylor HB. Prognosis of granulosa-theca tumors of the ovary. Cancer 1968, 21: 255–263.

772 Norris HJ, Taylor HB. Virilization associated with cystic granulosa tumors. Obstet Gynecol 1969, 34: 629–635.

773 Otis CN, Powell JL, Barbuto D, Carcangiu ML. Intermediate filamentous proteins in adult granulosa cell tumors. An immunohistochemical study of 25 cases. Am J Surg Pathol 1992, 16: 962–968.

774 Rodgers KE, Marks JF, Ellefson DD, Yanagihara DL, Tonetta SA, Vasilev SA, Morrow CP, Montz FJ, di Zerega GS. Follicle regulatory protein. A novel marker for granulosa cell cancer patients. Gynecol Oncol 1990, 37: 381–387.

775 Roth LM, Nicholas TR, Ehrlich CE. Juvenile granulosa cell tumor. A clinicopathologic study of three cases with ultrastructural observations. Cancer 1979, 44: 2194–2205.

776 Santini D, Ceccarelli C, Leone O, Pasquinelli G, Piana S, Marabini A, Martinelli GN. Smooth muscle differentiation in normal human ovaries, ovarian stromal hyperplasia and ovarian granulosa-stromal cells tumors. Mod Pathol 1995, 8: 25–30.

777 Schofield DE, Fletcher JA. Trisomy 12 in pediatric granulosa-stromal cell tumors. Demonstration by a modified method of fluorescence in situ hybridization on paraffin-embedded material. Am J Pathol 1992, 141: 1265–1269.

778 Scully RE. Ovarian tumors. A review. Am J Pathol 1977, 87: 686–720.

779 Suh KS, Silverberg SG, Rhame JG, Wilkinson DS. Granulosa cell tumor of the ovary. Histopathologic and flow cytometric analysis with clinical correlation. Arch Pathol Lab Med 1990, 114: 496–501.

780 Swanson SA, Norris HJ, Kelsten ML, Wheeler JE. DNA content of juvenile granulosa tumors determined by flow cytometry. Int J Gynecol Pathol 1990, 9: 101–109.

781 Tamimi HK, Bolen JW. Enchondromatosis (Ollier's disease) and ovarian juvenile granulosa cell tumor. A case report and review of the literature. Cancer 1984, 53: 1605–1608.

782 Tanaka Y, Sasaki Y, Nishihira H, Izawa T, Nishi T. Ovarian juvenile granulosa cell tumor associated with Maffucci's syndrome. Am J Clin Pathol 1992, 97: 523–527.

783 Voytek TM, Ro JY, El-Naggar AK, Ordonez NG, Tornos C, Welch GR, Ayala AG. Metastatic ovarian granulosa cell tumor to urinary bladder mimicking primary transitional cell carcinoma: a case report with immunohistochemical, electron microscopic, DNA flow cytometry, and interphase cytogenetic studies. J Urol Pathol 1996, 4: 57–68.

784 Young RH, Dickersin GR, Scully RE. Juvenile granulosa cell tumor of the ovary. A clinicopathologic analysis of 125 cases. Am J Surg Pathol 1984, 8: 575–596.

785 Young RH, Dudley AG, Scully RE. Granulosa cell, Sertoli-Leydig cell, and unclassified sex cord-stromal tumors

associated with pregnancy. A clinico-pathological analysis of thirty-six cases. Gynecol Oncol 1984, **18**: 181–205.

786 Young RH, Oliva E, Scully RE. Luteinized adult granulosa cell tumors of the ovary. A report of four cases. Int J Gynecol Pathol 1994, **13**: 302–310.

787 Young RH, Scully RE. Ovarian sex cord-stromal tumors. Recent progress. Int J Gynecol Pathol 1982, **1**: 101–123.

788 Young RH, Scully RE. Ovarian sex cord-stromal tumors with bizarre nuclei. A clinicopathologic analysis of 17 cases. Int J-Gynecol Pathol 1983, **1**: 325–335.

789 Young RH, Scully RE. Ovarian sex cord-stromal tumors. Problems in differential diagnosis. Pathol Annu 1988, **23**(Pt 1): 237–296.

790 Zaloudek C, Norris HJ. Granulosa tumors of the ovary in children. A clinical and pathologic study of 32 cases. Am J Surg Pathol 1982, **6**: 513–522.

Thecoma, fibroma, and related tumors

791 Chalvardjian A, Scully RE. Sclerosing stromal tumors of the ovary. Cancer 1973, **31**: 664–670.

792 Clement PB, Young RH, Hanna W, Scully RE. Sclerosing peritonitis associated with luteinized thecomas of the ovary. A clinicopathological analysis of six cases. Am J Surg Pathol 1994, **18**: 1–13.

793 Costa MJ, Morris R, De Rose PB, Cohen C. Histologic and immunohistochemical evidence for considering ovarian myxoma as a variant of the thecomafibroma group of ovarian stromal tumors. Arch Pathol Lab Med 1993, **117**: 802–808.

794 Costa MJ, Thomas W, Majmudar B, Hewan-Lowe K. Ovarian myxoma. Ultrastructural and immunohistochemical findings. Ultrastruct Pathol 1992, **16**: 429–438.

795 Eichhorn JH, Scully RE. Ovarian myxoma. Clinicopathologic and immunocytologic analysis of five cases and a review of the literature. Int J Gynecol Pathol 1991, **10**: 156–169.

796 Fox H. Sex cord-stromal tumours of the ovary. J Pathol 1985, **145**: 127–148.

797 Gaffney EF, Majmudar B, Hewan-Lowe K. Ultrastructure and immunohistochemical localization of estradiol of three thecomas. Hum Pathol 1984, **15**: 153–160.

798 Hayes MC, Scully RE. Stromal luteoma of the ovary. A clinicopathological analysis of 25 cases. Int J Gynecol Pathol 1987, **6**: 313–321.

799 Iwasa Y, Minamiguchi S, Konishi I, Onodera H, Zhou J, Yamabe H. Sclerosing peritonitis associated with luteinized thecoma of the ovary. Pathol Int 1996, **46**: 510–514.

800 Kanbour AI, Salazar H, Tobon H. Massive ovarian edema. A non-neoplastic pelvic mass of young women. Arch Pathol Lab Med 1979, **103**: 42–45.

801 Kawauchi S, Tsuji T, Kaku T, Kamura T, Nakano H, Tsuneyoshi M. Sclerosing stromal tumor of the ovary: A clinicopathologic, immunohistochemical, ultrastructural, and cytogenetic analysis with special reference to its vasculature. Am J Surg Pathol 1998, **22**: 83–92.

802 Lacson AG, Alrabeeah A, Gillis DA, Salisbury S, Grantmyre EB. Secondary massive ovarian edema with Meigs' syndrome. Am J Clin Pathol 1989, **91**: 597–603.

803 Meigs JV. Pelvic tumors other than fibromas of the ovary with ascites and hydrothorax. Obstet Gynecol 1954, **3**: 471–486.

804 Nielsen GP, Young RH. Fibromatosis of soft tissue type involving the female genital tract: a report of two cases. Int J Gynecol Pathol 1998, **16**: 383–386.

805 Nogales FF, Martin-Sances L, Mendoza-Garcia E, Salamanca A, Gonzalez-Nunez MA, Pardo Mindan FJ. Massive ovarian oedema. Histopathology 1997, **28**: 229–234.

806 Persons DL, Hartmann LC, Herath JF, Keeney GL, Jenkins RB. Fluorescence in situ hybridization analysis of trisomy 12 in ovarian tumors. Am J Clin Pathol 1994, **102**: 775–779.

807 Prat J, Scully RE. Cellular fibromas and fibrosarcomas of the ovary. A comparative clinicopathologic analysis of seventeen cases. Cancer 1981, **47**: 2663–2670.

808 Raggio M, Kaplan AL, Harber JF. Recurrent ovarian fibromas with basal cell nevus syndrome (Gorlin syndrome). Obstet Gynecol 1983, **61**: 95S–96S.

809 Roth LM, Deaton RL, Sternberg WH. Massive ovarian edema. A clinicopathologic study of five cases including ultrastructural observations and review of the literature. Am J Surg Pathol 1979, **3**: 11–21.

810 Roth LM, Sternberg WH. Partly luteinized theca cell tumor of the ovary. Cancer 1983, **51**: 1697–1704.

811 Saitoh A, Tsutsumi Y, Osamura RY, Watanabe K. Sclerosing stromal tumor of the ovary. Immunohistochemical and electron-microscopic demonstration of smooth-muscle differentiation. Arch Pathol Lab Med 1989, **113**: 372–376.

812 Samanth KK, Black WC III. Benign ovarian stromal tumors associated with free peritoneal fluid. Am J Obstet Gynecol 1970, **107**: 538–545.

813 Scully RE. Stromal luteoma of the ovary. A distinctive type of lipoid-cell tumor. Cancer 1964, **17**: 769–778.

814 Shaw JA, Dabbs DJ, Geisinger KR. Sclerosing stromal tumor of the ovary. An ultrastructural and immunohistochemical analysis with histogenetic considerations. Ultrastruct Pathol 1992, **16**: 363–377.

815 Sternberg WH, Roth LM. Ovarian stromal tumors containing Leydig cells. I. Stromal-Leydig cell tumor and non-neoplastic transformation of ovarian stroma to Leydig cells. Cancer 1973, **32**: 940–951.

816 Takeuchi S, Ishihara N, Ohbyashi C, Itoh H, Maruo T. Stromal Leydig cell tumor of the ovary: case report and literature review. Int J Gynecol Pathol 1999, **18**: 178–182.

817 Taruscio D, Carcangiu ML, Ward DC. Detection of trisomy 12 on ovarian sex cord stromal tumors by fluorescence in situ hybridization. Diagn Mol Pathol 1993, **2**: 94–98.

818 Tetu B, Bonenfant JL. Ovarian myxoma. A study of two cases with long-term follow-up. Am J Clin Pathol 1991, **95**: 340–346.

819 Tiltman AJ. Sclerosing stromal tumor of the ovary. Demonstration of ligandin in three cases. Int J Gynecol Pathol 1985, **4**: 362–369.

820 Tiltman AJ, Haffajee Z. Sclerosing stromal tumors, thecomas, and fibromas of the ovary: an immunohistochemical profile. Int J Gynecol Pathol 2002, **18**: 254–258.

821 Tsuji T, Kawauchi S, Utsunomiya T, Nagata Y, Tsuneyoshi M. Fibrosarcoma versus cellular fibroma of the ovary: a comparative study of their proliferative activity and chromosome aberrations using MIB-1 immunostaining, DNA flow cytometry, and fluorescence in situ hybridisation. Am J Surg Pathol 1997, **21**: 52–59.

822 Waxman M, Vuletin JC, Urcuyo R, Belling CG. Ovarian low-grade stromal sarcoma with thecomatous features. A critical reappraisal of the so-called "malignant thecoma." Cancer 1979, **44**: 2206–2217.

823 Werness BA. Luteinized thecoma with sclerosing peritonitis. Arch Pathol Lab Med 1996, **120**: 303–306.

824 Young RH. Meigs' syndrome: Dr. Richard Cabot's hidden first American case. Int J Surg Pathol 2001, **8**: 165–168.

825 Young RH, Clement PB, Scully RE. Calcified thecomas in young women. A report of four cases. Int J Gynecol Pathol 1988, **7**: 343–350.

826 Young RH, Scully RE. Ovarian stromal tumors with minor sex-cord elements. A report of seven cases. Int J Gynecol Pathol 1983, **2**: 227–234.

827 Young RH, Scully RE. Fibromatosis and massive edema of the ovary, possibly related entities. A report of 14 cases of fibromatosis and 11 cases of massive edema. Int J Gynecol Pathol 1984, **3**: 153–178.

828 Zhang J, Young RH, Arseneau J, Scully RE. Ovarian stromal tumors containing lutein or Leydig cells (luteinized thecomas and stromal Leydig cell tumors). A clinicopathologic analysis of fifty cases. Int J Gynecol Pathol 1982, 1: 270–285.

Endometrial abnormalities associated with granulosa cell tumor, thecoma, and related tumors

829 Gusberg SB, Kardon P. Proliferative endometrial response to theca-granulosa cell tumors. Am J Obstet Gynecol 1971, 111: 633–643.

830 Katsube Y, Iwaoki Y, Silverberg SG, Fujiwara A. Sclerosing stromal tumor of the ovary associated with endometrial adenocarcinoma. A case report. Gynecol Oncol 1988, 29: 392–398.

831 Norris HJ, Taylor HB. Prognosis of granulosa-theca tumors of the ovary. Cancer 1968, 21: 255–263.

832 Press MF, Scully RE. Endometrial "sarcomas" complicating ovarian thecoma, polycystic ovarian disease and estrogen therapy. Gynecol Oncol 1985, 21: 135–154.

Small cell carcinoma

833 Aguirre P, Thor AD, Scully RE. Ovarian small cell carcinoma. Histogenetic considerations based on immunohistochemical and other findings. Am J Clin Pathol 1989, 92: 140–149.

834 Chen KTK. Composite large-cell neuroendocrine carcinoma and surface epithelial-stromal neoplasms of the ovary. Int J Surg Pathol 2000, 8: 169–174.

835 Dickersin GR, Kline IW, Scully RE. Small cell carcinoma of the ovary with hypercalcemia. A report of eleven cases. Cancer 1982, 49: 188–197.

836 Dickersin GR, Scully RE. An update on the electron microscopy of small cell carcinoma of the ovary with hypercalcemia. Ultrastruct Pathol 1993, 17: 411–422.

837 Dickersin GR, Scully RE. Ovarian small cell tumors: an electron microscopic review. Ultrastruct Pathol 1998, 22: 199–226.

838 Eichhorn JH, Bell DA, Young RH, Swymer CM, Flotte TJ, Preffer RI, Scully RE. DNA content and proliferative activity in ovarian small cell carcinomas of the hypercalcemic type. Implications for diagnosis, prognosis, and histogenesis. Am J Clin Pathol 1992, 98: 579–586.

839 Eichhorn JH, Lawrence WD, Young RH, Scully RE. Ovarian neuroendocrine carcinomas of non-small-cell type associated with surface epithelial adenocarcinomas: a study of five cases and review of the literature. Int J Gynecol Pathol 1997, 15: 303–314.

840 Eichhorn JH, Young RH, Scully RE. Primary ovarian small cell carcinoma of pulmonary type. A clinicopathologic, immunohistologic, and flow cytometric analysis of 11 cases. Am J Surg Pathol 1992, 16: 926–938.

841 Idei Y, Kitazawa S, Fujimori T, Ajiki T, Asaka K, Takeuchi S, Mochizuki M, Chiba T, Maeda S. Ovarian small cell carcinoma with K-ras mutation: a case report with genetic analysis. Hum Pathol 1996, 27: 77–79.

842 Jones K, Diaz JA, Donner LR. Neuroendocrine carcinoma arising in an ovarian mucinous cystadenoma. Int J Gynecol Pathol 1996, 15: 167–170.

843 Lamovec J, Bracko M, Cerar O. Familial occurrence of small-cell carcinoma of the ovary. Arch Pathol Lab Med 1995, 119: 551–554.

844 Matias-Guiu X, Prat J, Young RH, Capen CC, Rosol TJ, DeLellis RA, Scully RE. Human parathyroid hormone-related protein in ovarian small cell carcinoma. An immunohistochemical study. Cancer 1994, 73: 1878–1881.

844a Neto AG, Deavers MT, Silva EG, Malpica A. Immunohistochemical profile of ovarian small cell carcinoma (Abstract). Mod Pathol 2003, 16: 202a.

845 Riopel MA, Perlman EJ, Seidman JD, Kurman RJ, Sherman ME. Inhibin and epithelial membrane antigen immunohistochemistry assist in the diagnosis of sex cord-stromal tumors and provide clues to the histogenesis of hypercalcemic small cell carcinomas. Int J Gynecol Pathol 1998, 17: 46–53.

846 Scully RE. Small cell carcinoma of hypercalcemic type. Int J Gynecol Pathol 1993, 12: 148–152.

847 Ulbright TM, Roth LM, Stehman FB, Talerman A, Senekjian EK. Poorly differentiated (small cell) carcinoma of the ovary in young women. Evidence supporting a germ cell origin. Hum Pathol 1987, 18: 175–184.

848 Young RH, Oliva E, Scully RE. Small cell carcinoma of the ovary, hypercalcemic type. A clinicopathological analysis of 150 cases. Am J Surg Pathol 1994, 18: 1102–1116.

Sertoli–Leydig cell tumor

849 Aguirre P, Scully RE, DeLellis RA. Ovarian heterologous Sertoli-Leydig cell tumors with gastrointestinal-type epithelium. An immunohistochemical analysis. Arch Pathol Lab Med 1986, 110: 528–533.

850 Chadha S, Honnebier WJ, Schaberg A. Raised serum alphafetoprotein in Sertoli-Leydig cell tumor (androblastoma) of ovary. Report of two cases. Int J Gynecol Pathol 1987, 6: 82–88.

851 Costa MJ, Morris RJ, Wilson R, Judd R. Utility of immunohistochemistry in distinguishing ovarian Sertoli-stromal cell tumors from carcinosarcomas. Hum Pathol 1992, 23: 787–797.

852 Ferry JA, Young RH, Engel G, Scully RE. Oxyphilic Sertoli cell tumor of the ovary. A report of three cases, two in patients with the Peutz-Jeghers syndrome. Int J Gynecol Pathol 1994, 13: 259–266.

853 Fox H, Langley FA. Tumours of the ovary. London, 1976, Heinemann Medical Books, pp. 156–157.

854 Gagnon S, Tetu B, Silva EG, McCaughey WT. Frequency of alpha-fetoprotein production by Sertoli-Leydig cell tumors of the ovary. An immunohistochemical study of eight cases. Mod Pathol 1989, 2: 63–67.

855 Hittmair A, Zelger BG, Obrist P, Dirnhofer S. Ovarian Sertoli-Leydig cell tumor: a SRY gene-independent pathway of pseudomale gonadal differentiation. Hum Pathol 1997, 28: 1206–1210.

856 Jenson AB, Fechner RE. Ultrastructure of an intermediate Sertoli-Leydig cell tumor. A histogenetic misnomer. Lab Invest 1969, 21: 527–535.

857 Kurman RJ, Ganjei P, Nadji M. Contributions of immunocytochemistry to the diagnosis and study of ovarian neoplasms. Int J Gynecol Pathol 1984, 3: 3–26.

858 Meyer R. Tubuläre (testikuläre) und solide Foramen des Andreiblastoma ovarii und ihre Beziehung zur Vermännlickung. Beitr Pathol Anat 1930, 84: 485–520.

859 Mooney EE, Man YG, Bratthauer GL, Tavassoli FA. Evidence that Leydig cells in Sertoli-Leydig cell tumors have a reactive rather then a neoplastic profile. Cancer 2000, 86: 2312–2319.

860 Mooney EE, Nogales FF, Bergeron C, Tavassoli FA. Retiform Sertoli-Leydig cell tumors: clinical, morphological and immunohistochemical findings. Histopathology 2002, 41: 110–117.

861 Mooney EE, Nogales FF, Tavassoli FA. Hepatocytic differentiation in retiform Sertoli-Leydig cell tumors: distinguishing a heterologous element from Leydig cells. Hum Pathol 1999, 30: 611–617.

862 Motoyama I, Watanabe H, Gotoh A, Takeuchi S, Tanabe N, Nashimoto I. Ovarian Sertoli-Leydig cell tumor with elevated serum alpha-fetoprotein. Cancer 1989, 63: 2047–2053.

863 Prat J, Young RH, Scully RE. Ovarian Sertoli-Leydig cell tumors with heterologous elements. II. Cartilage and skeletal muscle.

1019 Young RH, Hart WR. Metastatic intestinal carcinomas simulating primary ovarian clear cell carcinoma and secretory endometrioid carcinoma: clinicopathologic and immunohistochemical study of five cases. Am J Surg Pathol 1998, **22:** 805–815.

1020 Young RH, Jackson A, Wells M. Ovarian metastasis from thyroid carcinoma 12 years after partial thyroidectomy mimicking struma ovarii. Report of a case. Int J Gynecol Pathol 1994, **13:** 181–185.

1021 Young RH, Scully RE. Ovarian metastases from cancer of the lung. Problems in interpretation – a report of seven cases. Gynecol Oncol 1985, **21:** 337–350.

1022 Young RH, Scully RE. Alveolar rhabdomyosarcoma metastatic to the ovary. A report of two cases and a discussion of the differential diagnosis of small cell malignant tumors of the ovary. Cancer 1989, **64:** 899–904.

1023 Young RH, Scully RE. Ovarian metastases from carcinoma of the gallbladder and extrahepatic bile ducts simulating primary tumors of the ovary. A report of six cases. Int J Gynecol Pathol 1990, **9:** 60–72.

1024 Young RH, Scully RE. Sarcomas metastatic to the ovary. A report of 21 cases. Int J Gynecol Pathol 1990, **9:** 231–252.

1025 Young RH, Scully RE. Malignant melanoma metastatic to the ovary. A clinicopathologic analysis of 20 cases. Am J Surg Pathol 1991, **15:** 849–860.

1026 Young RH, Scully RE. Metastatic tumors in the ovary. A problem-oriented approach and review of the recent literature. Semin Diagn Pathol 1991, **8:** 250–276.

1027 Zaloudek C, Miller TR, Stern JL. Desmoplastic small cell tumor of the ovary. A unique polyphenotypic tumor with an unfavorable prognosis. Int J Gynecol Pathol 1995, **14:** 260–265.

1028 Zukerberg LR, Young RH. Chordoma metastatic to the ovary. Arch Pathol Lab Med 1990, **114:** 208–210.

Pregnancy, trophoblastic disease, and placenta

Normal anatomy

The normal term *placenta* measures 15 to 20 cm in diameter and 1.5 to 3 cm in thickness and weighs 450 to 600 g. The main components are the umbilical cord, membranes (amnion and chorion), villous parenchyma, and maternal decidual tissue.[8,13]

The *umbilical cord* at term measures 55 to 65 cm in length.[21] It has an outer layer of amniotic epithelium, which becomes stratified at the fetal end. The bulk of the cord is made up of highly mucoid connective tissue known as Wharton's jelly. Embedded within its substance are the umbilical vessels, represented by two arteries and a single vein. The arteries have a double-layered muscular wall but no internal elastic lamina. The vein has a larger diameter and a thinner wall, consisting of a single layer of circular smooth muscle, and an internal elastic lamina. The umbilical cord may insert in the placenta in a central or eccentric fashion. Insertion at the margin is referred to as *battledore placenta*. Whereas it is easy to distinguish microscopically the arteries from the vein in the cord itself, this becomes difficult or impossible once those vessels branch into the chorionic plate.

The *placental membranes* consist of the amnion and chorion. The *amnion*, which represents the innermost covering of the amniotic cavity, is lined by a single layer of flat epithelial cells resting on a basement membrane.[5,23] Squamous metaplasia is common in them, especially near the insertion of the cord. The *chorion* is composed of a connective tissue membrane that carries the fetal vasculature. Its inner aspect is bounded by the outer layer of the amnion, and the outer aspect is associated with villi that sprout from the surface. The chorion associated with the membrane is referred to as *chorion laeve* and is distinguished from the *chorion frondosum* located in the placenta proper.[16,24] Some of the trophoblast located in the chorion laeve has a characteristic vacuolated appearance.[29]

The *trophoblastic villi* that arise from the trophoectoderm following formation of the blastocyst constitute the functional unit of the placenta. During the first trimester, they are composed of an outer syncytiotrophoblastic layer and an inner cytotrophoblastic layer, which surround a central mesenchymal core containing primitive fibroblasts and scattered macrophages (Hofbauer cells).

The *syncytiotrophoblast* is composed of multinucleated giant cells with abundant acidophilic cytoplasm that is strongly immunoreactive for hCG, keratin, hPL (variably, and depending on the gestational age), PLAP, pregnancy-specific β_1-glycoprotein (SP1), and inhibin.[10,26] They are negative for EMA, HNK1, and CD146 (Mel-CAM).[19] The *cytotrophoblast*, which is the progenitor of the syncytiotrophoblast, is made up of mononuclear cells with clear cytoplasm and a well-defined cell membrane, which are negative for all of the above markers except keratin. In the term placenta, the cytotrophoblast is inconspicuous, and the syncytiotrophoblast is clumped in the form of "syncytial knots."

The third trophoblastic type is represented by the *intermediate trophoblast*, also known as interstitial extravillous trophoblast and X cells.[14] This type is present in the villi and in the membranes but is particularly numerous in the extravillous region that forms the deepest structural component of the implantation site. The most distinctive immunohistochemical property of these cells is a strong reactivity for hPL. They are also positive for keratin, CD66a (CEACAM1), CD146 (Mel-CAM), HNK1 (only in the villi), EMA (only in the chorion), and HLA-G (a non-classical MHC class I antigen).[2,28] Recently, the proposal has been made that there are three subpopulations of intermediate trophoblastic cells with distinctive morphologic and immunohistochemical features: implantation site type, chorionic type, and villous type.[27] Trophoblastic cells have also been shown to produce and secrete parathyroid hormone-related protein, and this is also true for their neoplastic counterparts.[6] Villous trophoblast shows a membranous pattern of E-cadherin stain and a mixed membranous and granular pattern of β-catenin distribution.[18]

The villous vessels become apparent at 6 weeks. At about 8 weeks they contain only nucleated red blood cells, but by weeks 10 to 12 the percentage of nucleated cells has dropped to 10%, and after week 12 they are virtually absent.

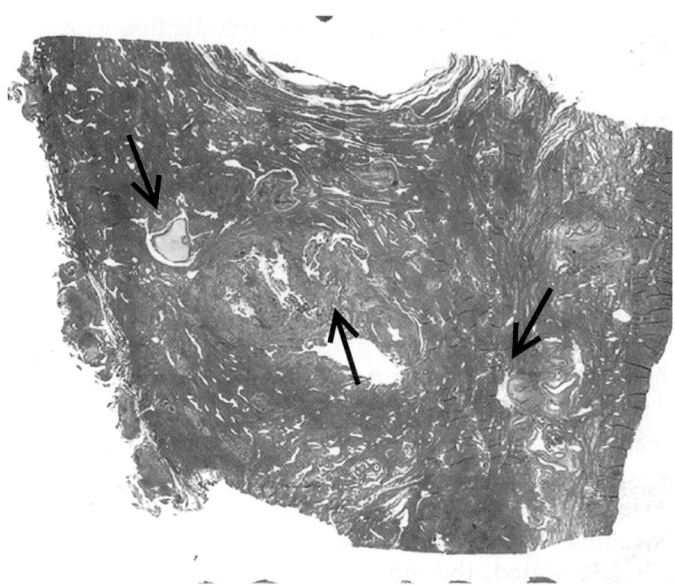

Fig. 19.358 Whole-mount view of invasive mole. Abnormal villi are seen permeating the thickened myometrium (arrows).

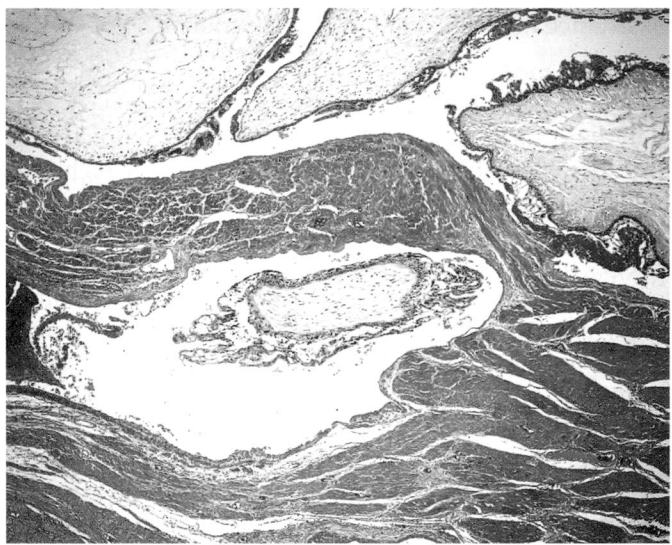

Fig. 19.359 Hydropic villi covered by proliferating trophoblast are seen permeating the myometrium in this invasive mole.

may occur. The vascular invasion may result in trophoblastic nodules in sites outside the uterus, such as the vagina, lung, brain, and spinal cord.[151,154] The lung nodules have a characteristic radiographic appearance[148,149]; they continue to produce hCG and have a similar tendency for hemorrhagic complications. The clinical manifestations depend on the site involved: a sizable mass in the lung may regress spontaneously without ever causing symptoms, whereas a deposit in the brain may produce fatal hemorrhage.[150,156] It should not escape the attention of the reader that an invasive mole has all of the biologic features of a malignant neoplasm except for the fact that it is self-limited. It invades the stroma, it produces tumor emboli, and it metastasizes distantly. This is probably telling us something very important about the neoplastic process, perhaps the fact that the program for the two cardinal properties that characterize it (invasion and metastases) are already present in the normal cell, and that the derepression of this mechanism may be the key to tumor formation.

To return to more pedestrian considerations, it should be mentioned that invasive mole is distinguished from the usual mole by its invasiveness and from choriocarcinoma by the presence of villi, which are also present in the "metastatic" foci. The degree of trophoblastic proliferation in invasive mole does not differ significantly from that of its ordinary counterpart. Patients with invasive mole are primarily treated with chemotherapy, but hysterectomy may be indicated in some circumstances.[153,155]

Choriocarcinoma

Choriocarcinoma, when untreated, is the most aggressive form of gestational trophoblastic disease. Most cases occur following a complete hydatidiform mole; consequently, this malignant tumor is more common in areas of the world in which hydatidiform mole is prevalent. It has been estimated that 1% to 2% of complete moles are followed by choriocarcinoma.[159]

Choriocarcinoma can also be preceded by a partial mole (a very unusual event), ectopic pregnancy, nonmolar intrauterine abortion, or term pregnancy.[160,186] In the latter instance, which is exceptionally rare, the tumor may appear as one or more masses in an otherwise normal placenta or develop following the delivery.[158,161,177] In addition, cases of "in situ" choriocarcinoma arising from the trophoblast of stem villi in the first trimester of pregnancy have been described.[170]

In cases of choriocarcinoma following abortion—whether molar or not—the latent period is almost always less than 1 year, although it can be considerably longer ("latent choriocarcinoma").[166] At the time of the diagnosis of the malignancy, the average age of the patient is 29 years. When reviewing the microscopic sections of a nonmolar abortion in women who subsequently developed choriocarcinoma, it is not unusual to find foci of increased trophoblastic proliferation. These foci, although not diagnostic of trophoblastic disease even in retrospect, suggest the existence of a precursor lesion.

Bagshawe et al.[157] have shown a striking relationship between the incidence and prognosis of choriocarcinoma and the ABO groups of both the woman and her husband. The highest risk is for women of group A married to men of the same group. The relative risk of the two extreme groups was 10.4:1. Women married to men of their own ABO group had the highest incidence of spontaneous regression of trophoblast after evacuation of a hydatidiform mole.

Grossly, choriocarcinoma characteristically forms soft, dark red, hemorrhagic, round nodular tumor masses (Fig. 19.360). Microscopically, the tumor is composed of clus-

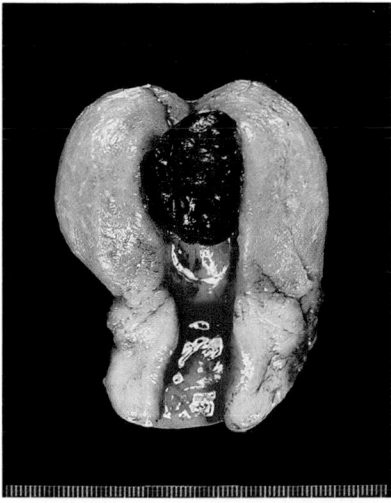

A

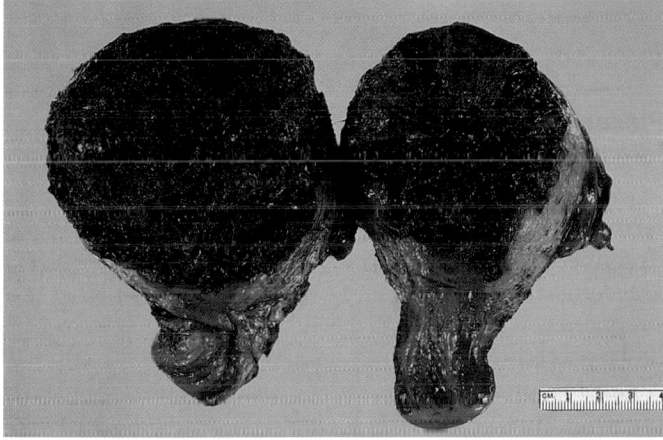

B

Fig. 19.360 Uterine choriocarcinoma showing typical highly hemorrhagic appearance.

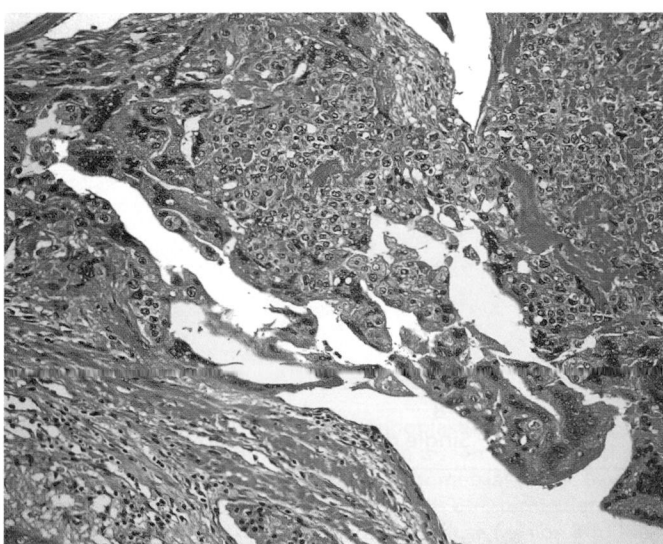

Fig. 19.361 Intimate admixture of syncytiotrophoblast and cytotrophoblast in choriocarcinoma.

ters of cytotrophoblast separated by streaming masses of syncytiotrophoblast, resulting in a characteristic dimorphic plexiform pattern[188] (Fig. 19.361). Hemorrhage and necrosis are usually present but have no real diagnostic significance, since they are also commonly found in spontaneous abortions. Villi are characteristically absent; as a matter of fact, their presence is said to rule out the diagnosis of choriocarcinoma no matter how atypical the trophoblastic cells may be.[167] The rationale for this criterion is hard to comprehend. After all, if such choriocarcinomas arise from complete moles, there should be a point in time at which both molar and choriocarcinomatous tissue are simultaneously present. Yet, there is no question that it represents a useful parameter at the practical level.

Immunohistochemically, choriocarcinoma cells are positive for hCG and keratin. There may also be reactivity for hPL, SP1, and CEA.[179]

Microscopic grading of choriocarcinoma is of little value. Some attempts at correlating various patterns of growth with prognosis have been recorded[165,184]; of these, the most convincing are those showing an improved prognosis in the presence of an intense inflammatory infiltrate at the interphase between tumor and stroma.[188,171,174,182]

The natural history of untreated choriocarcinoma is characterized by the development of early hematogenous metastases, the most common sites being the lung, brain, liver, kidney, and bowel.[173,181,189] They can be clinically solitary, may occur in the most unusual places, and often present with massive hemorrhage.[172] Interestingly, the fetus is rarely involved, even in cases of widespread metastatic disease.[189] Residual tumor in the uterus of patients dying of disseminated choriocarcinoma may be inconspicuous or altogether absent.[185]

Many of the morphologic changes seen in other organs in patients with choriocarcinoma are the result of increased secretion of hCG and other hormones by the tumor cells. These include hyperplasia of endocervical glands, decidual reaction (both endometrial and ectopic), Arias-Stella phenomenon, bilateral enlargement of the ovaries by theca-lutein cysts ("hyperreactio luteinalis"), and hyperplasia of mammary lobules. The detection of ovarian theca-lutein cysts long after a case of choriocarcinoma has been treated is usually a sign of persistent disease.[176] In the endometrial decidual reaction of patients with choriocarcinoma, the spiral arterioles fail to develop as they do in the normal cycle, the appearance of the mucosa being similar to that seen after the administration of progestogens.[185]

The evolution of the treatment of choriocarcinoma (and of gestational trophoblastic disease in general) is one of the greatest success stories in medical oncology.[187] When treated by surgery alone, the cure rate was only 40% for tumors apparently restricted to the uterus and less than 20% for those accompanied by metastases.[162] With the use of the chemotherapeutic agents methotrexate, actinomycin D, and chlorambucil (a combination

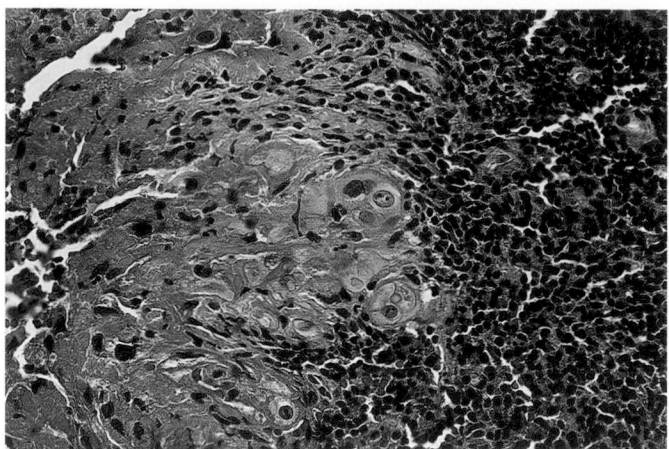

Fig. 19.363 Epithelioid trophoblastic tumor. The microscopic appearance closely simulates carcinoma of either squamous or glassy cell type.

(paternal) alleles not present in the adjacent normal uterine tissue.[218] It behaves as a malignant tumor, with metastases to lung and other sites.[219]

Tumorlike conditions of intermediate trophoblast

Presumably non-neoplastic proliferations of intermediate trophoblast that can create serious problems in the differential diagnosis with malignant trophoblastic tumors are exaggerated placental site reaction, placental site nodule, and placental site plaque.[224]

Exaggerated placental site reaction (EPSR) was called syncytial endometritis in the past, but this was a double misnomer since the lesion is not primarily of inflammatory nature and is not composed of syncytiotrophoblast. As the currently preferred name indicates, it is believed to be the result of excessive but otherwise normal infiltration of the implantation site by intermediate trophoblast (Fig. 19.364). Its distinction from placental

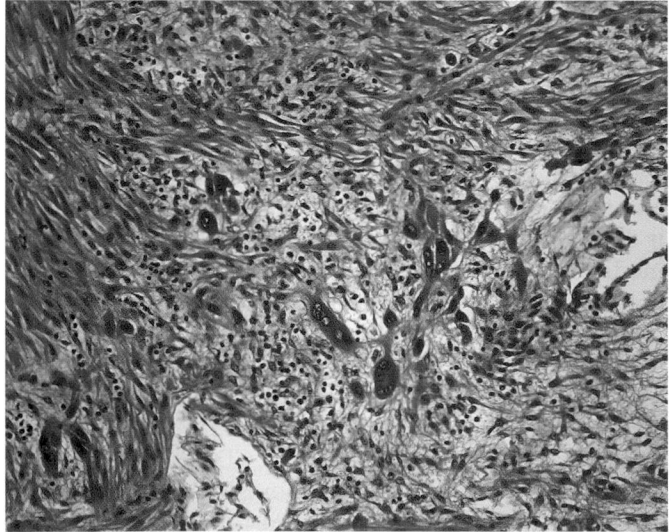

Fig. 19.364 Trophoblastic cells infiltrating the myometrium in a tumorlike fashion in exaggerated placental site reaction.

site implantation tumor can be difficult because the cytologic and immunohistochemical features are very similar. EPSR is to be favored when the lesion is microscopic in size, lacks mitotic activity, contains a hyaline material between the trophoblastic cells, and is admixed with decidua and villi.

Placental site nodules and plaques appear as single or multiple, mostly well-circumscribed, variably cellular round or flat lesions (nodules and plaques, respectively) that tend to be extensively hyalinized[222,226] (Fig. 19.365). Most cells have abundant amphophilic or acidophilic cytoplasm, irregularly shaped nuclei, and very scanty mitotic activity, but others have a glycogen-rich clear cytoplasm.[225] Mallory bodies (representing abnormal cytoplasmic aggregates of keratin filaments) may be present.[227] These nodules and plaques, which can also occur in the cervix, fallopian tube, and other sites,[220,221] are distinguished from placental site trophoblastic tumor because of their smaller size, better circumscription, extensive hyalinization, degenerative appearance, and paucity of mitotic activity.[223,228] It has been pointed out that placental site nodules and plaques closely resemble

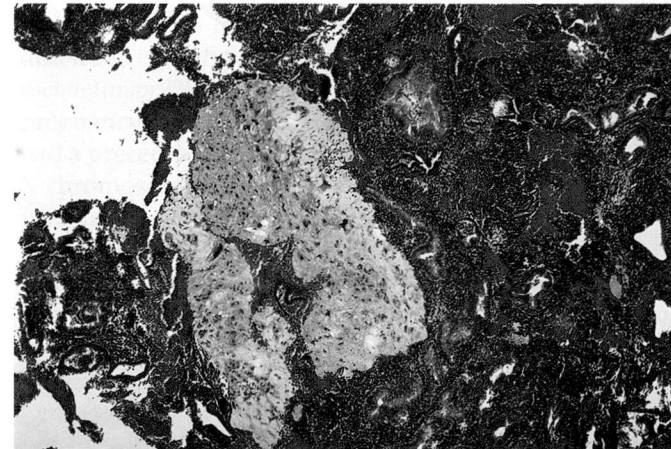

A

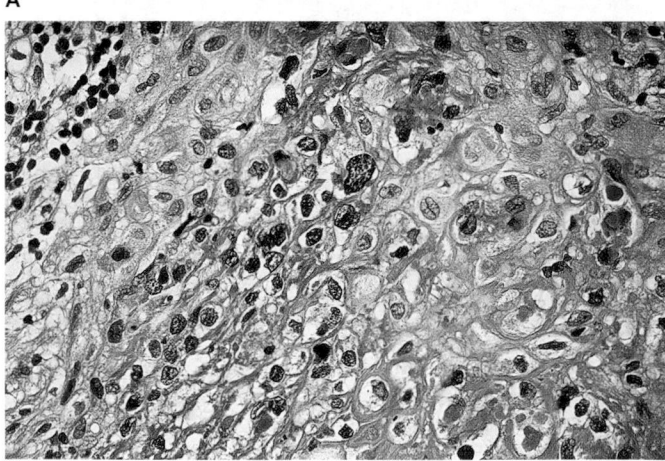

B

Fig. 19.365 A and B, Low- and medium-power appearance of placental site nodule. The appearance is vaguely chondroid and can be easily misinterpreted.

the intermediate trophoblast of the chorion laeve rather than that at the implantation site. As such, they are diffusely positive for PLAP but only focally positive or negative for hPL and CD146 (Mel-CAM).[225]

The differential diagnosis between placental site trophoblastic tumor and the non-neoplastic proliferations previously mentioned may not be always possible in a curettage specimen. In such cases, subsequent curettings and monitoring of serum levels of hCG and hPL become imperative.[213]

Non-neoplastic lesions of term placenta

Abnormally large placentas are frequently seen in association with polyhydramnios. They accompany conditions leading to fetal anemia or cardiac failure, such as erythroblastosis fetalis; infections, such as syphilis, toxoplasmosis, or cytomegalovirus; tumors of the placenta and fetus; or fetal renal vein thrombosis.[234,248,269] Histologically, these enlarged placentas retain immature features.

Abnormally small placentas are seen in prematurely born infants and in many growth-retarded ("small for dates") infants. Causes of the latter include maternal vascular disease and fetal malformations,[274,295] but many remain of undetermined etiology.

Placenta accreta refers to a condition in which placental villi adhere to the underlying myometrium, without an intervening layer of decidua[247,262,265] (Fig. 19.366). Morphologic subtypes of this condition are designated as *placenta increta* when the villi invade the myometrium and *placenta percreta* when the villous infiltration extends through the whole thickness of the myometrium.[273] Placenta percreta may result in spontaneous uterine rupture and fatal hemoperitoneum.[240] At the other extreme, mild (microscopic) forms of placenta accreta, which are not uncommon, are detected only through careful sampling of the placental basal plate.[240]

Placenta circummarginata and **placenta circumvallata** are two morphologic variants of extrachorial placenta (i.e., a placenta in which the chorionic plate is smaller than its basal plate). In placenta circummarginata, the transition from the membranous to the villous chorion is flat, whereas in placenta circumvallata the marginal membrane is folded or rolled back on itself. Wentworth[294] examined 895 placentas and found 25.5% to be circummarginate and 6.5% circumvallate. He considered these two malformations of no clinical significance. Others have reported an increased incidence of antepartum bleeding, particularly with circumvallation.[235]

Amnion nodosum is the result of fetal renal agenesis and is associated with oligohydramnios. It presents as small plaques on the amniotic surface, formed by squamous cells and fibrin. Ultrastructural and other studies

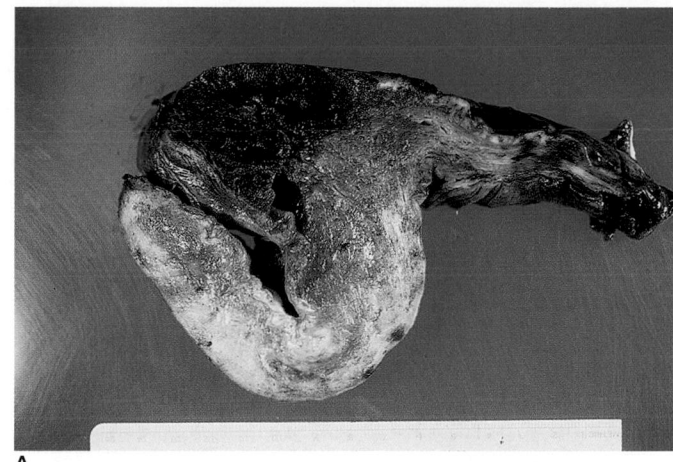

A

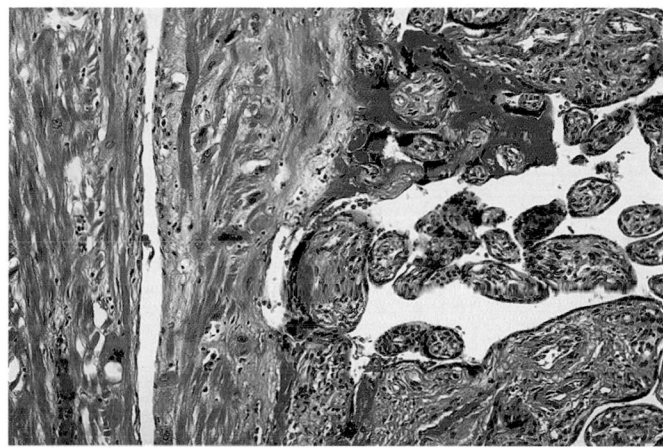

B

Fig. 19.366 A and B, Gross and microscopic appearance of placenta accreta. The penetration of the myometrium by chorionic villi is obvious at both levels.

suggest that amnion nodosum originates from the apposition of desquamated fetal skin elements on the amnion epithelium in the presence of oligohydramnios.[286]

Malformations of umbilical cord of clinical importance include *velamentous insertion* and the *absence of one umbilical artery*[262,265] (Fig. 19.367). The former is seen in 1% of all placentas and may result in massive fetal hemorrhage if located at the cervical opening. The latter, also present in approximately 1% of all cords, is associated with congenital abnormalities of the infant in 30% of cases.[239,255] The abnormalities may involve the cardiac, renal, skeletal, or other systems. There is also an increased incidence of prematurity (16.5%) and of small size for dates (34%).[239] The absence of one umbilical artery can be detected by gross inspection of the cross section of the cord, but it should always be confirmed microscopically.

Other malformations of the umbilical cord are represented by persistence of embryonic structures. The large majority of these are of no clinical significance and show no particular association with congenital malformations or perinatal complications. Most are located at the fetal end of the cord and are represented by *remnants of the*

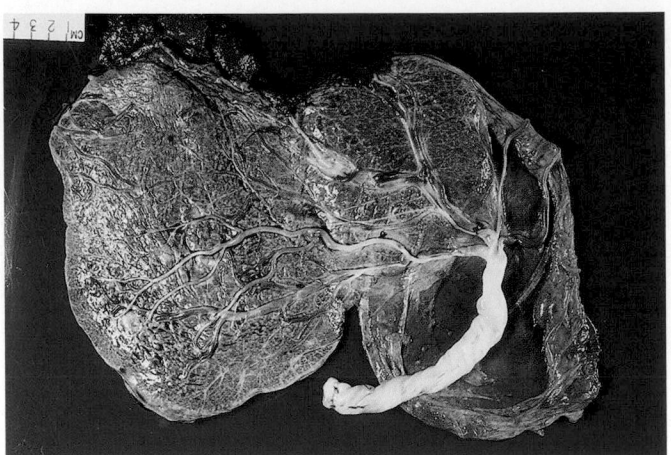

Fig. 19.367 Velamentous insertion of umbilical cord near an accessory placental lobe.

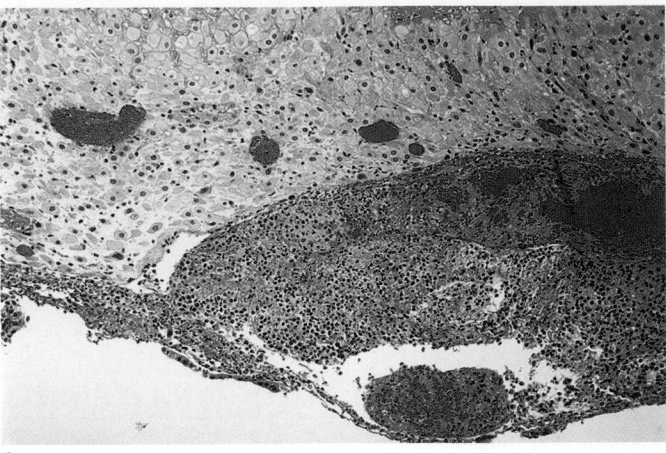

A

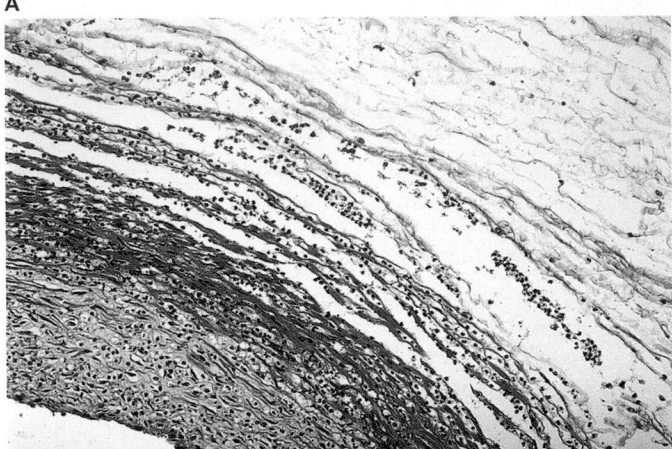

B

Fig. 19.368 A and **B**, Placental inflammation. The specimen shown in **A** shows a concentration of the inflammatory infiltrate on the placental maternal side, whereas the specimen depicted in **B** depicts inflammatory changes centered in umbilical vessels.

allantoic duct, omphalomesenteric duct, and *embryonic vessels*.[261]

Infection of the placenta is due most commonly to organisms that ascend from the maternal vaginal tract.[234,237] It shows a good correlation with prematurity and sepsis during the first 2 days of life.[282] Overall estimates of its frequency range from 5.4% to 24.4%.[249] It is manifested morphologically by an inflammatory infiltrate of predominantly neutrophilic nature that is contributed by both the maternal and fetal circulation. The former is primarily located in the peripheral membranes and chorionic plate, whereas the latter is concentrated in the umbilical and fetal surface vessels (Fig. 19.368). Grossly, the placental surface may appear cloudy and dull; however, in most cases the inflammation is detectable only microscopically. Infection may also reach the placenta through the maternal bloodstream, leading to inflammatory infiltrates within the villi.[232] These may be of acute, chronic, or granulomatous nature and may be associated with hemorrhagic vasculitis or vascular obliteration.[232,287] It should be mentioned here that fetal anoxia or meconium staining of the membranes *does not* result in inflammatory changes in the placenta.[271]

The most common cause of placental infection acquired from an ascending route is bacterial (including fusobacteria),[231] but other vaginal inhabitants such as *herpes virus* or *Candida* may be implicated.[281] Herpetic infection of placental tissues may be accompanied by necrotizing funisitis.[256] The diagnosis of herpetic infection can be confirmed by immunohistochemical stains or in situ hybridization.[289]

The organisms implicated in placentitis acquired through the hematogenous route are very numerous. They include cytomegalovirus (CMV), *Listeria*, rubella, syphilis, toxoplasmosis, tuberculosis, coccidioidomycosis, cryptococcosis, malaria, and even psittacosis[257,258,263,264,266,272,279] (Fig. 19.369). In CMV infection,

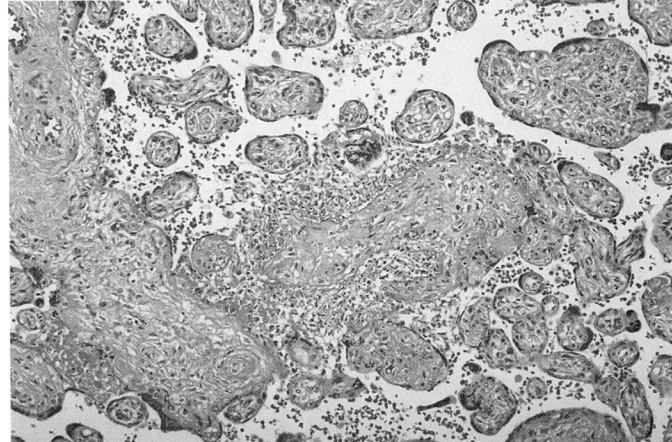

Fig. 19.369 Necrotizing villitis resulting from *Listeria* infection.

diagnostic viral inclusions are only rarely found.[276,290] However, immunohistochemical staining for CMV antigens is often positive, the infected cells being usually located in the villous stroma.[277] The diagnosis can also be made by detecting CMV genetic material by the PCR technique; these studies have shown that approximately

10% of cases of chronic villitis are caused by CMV infection.[278,285] In *syphilis*, the characteristic changes include vascular proliferation, acute or chronic villitis, and relative villous immaturity, manifested by enlarged hypercellular villi; in some instances, acute villitis is also present.[278,291,292] The diagnosis can be confirmed by performing PCR for *Treponema pallidum* DNA in the placental tissue.[251]

Placentas from HIV-infected patients do not have specific gross or microscopic alterations, although there is an increased incidence of chorioamnionitis in them.[288]

Chronic villitis is a nonspecific inflammatory process involving the villi that is morphologically similar to that seen in rubella but unaccompanied by serologic evidence of this infection.[232,283,284] The etiology of this condition, which may be associated with intrauterine growth retardation and occasional unexplained stillbirths, remains unknown; infection by unidentified organisms and abnormal immune reactions have been implicated.[236] It is found in 1% to 9% of all placentas, depending on the degree of sampling, diagnostic criteria, and patient population studied, and is sometimes seen in subsequent pregnancies of the same individual.[280]

Chronic villitis may be associated with **chronic chorioamnionitis**[253]; in some instances the latter may dominate the microscopic picture[254] (Fig. 19.370). The chorioamnionitis can be graded microscopically into mild, moderate, or severe; its frequency and severity are inversely related to gestational age at preterm birth.[230,259,275,297]

In **chronic intervillositis**, the inflammatory infiltrate is mainly histiocytic and predominantly located in the intervillous space; these rare cases have been found to be associated with poor fetal outcome.[238,259]

Acute funisitis, i.e., acute inflammation of the umbilical cord, is a sign of fetal inflammatory response, and therefore its detection is of some clinical importance. The inflammation begins as a discrete multifocal process that eventually coalesces; it is therefore recommended that a section be taken from each third of the umbilical cord.[267]

Microscopically, the key feature is umbilical vasculitis (Fig. 19.370). The association with fetal infection is stronger in preterm than in term placentas.[268] Autolysis of umbilical vascular smooth muscle following second trimester fetal death can simulate vasculitis, in that the necrotic cells may be confused with neutrophils.[252]

Placental infarct represents an area of villous necrosis secondary to local obstruction of the *maternal* uteroplacental circulation. Grossly, the fresh infarct is dark red and of firmer consistency than the surrounding tissue. Microscopically, it is characterized by crowding of villi, virtual obliteration of the intervillous space, and marked congestion of the villous vessels. When old, it appears grossly as a hard, white mass of granular appearance and microscopically as a mass of crowded "ghost" villi (Figs 19.372 and 19.373). True infarcts should be distinguished from hematomas, subchorionic fibrin plaques, foci of intervillous fibrin deposition, and intervillous laminated thrombi.[293] Wigglesworth[295] demonstrated by injection studies that infarcts and hematomas have a lobular distribution, thrombi occur in either the arterial or venous regions of the intervillous space, and perivillous fibrin deposits are predominantly venous lesions.

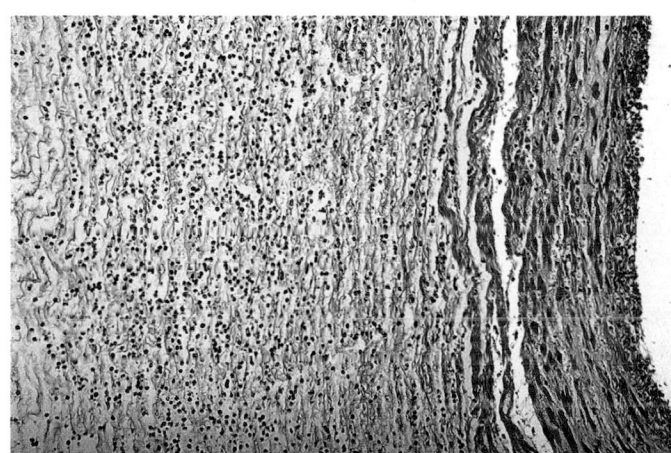

Fig. 19.371 Intense inflammatory infiltrate of the umbilical cord (funisitis).

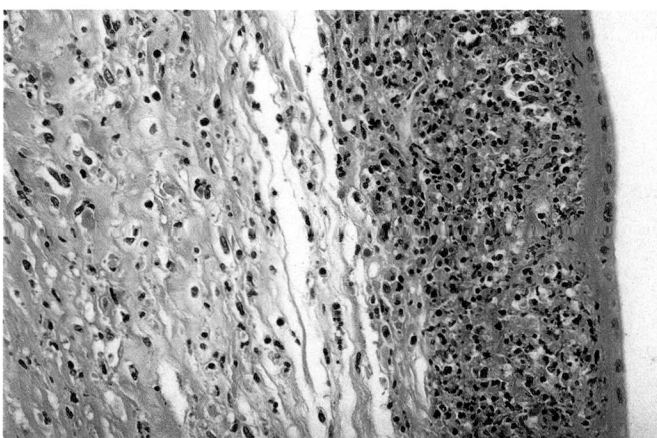

Fig. 19.370 Acute chorioamnionitis.

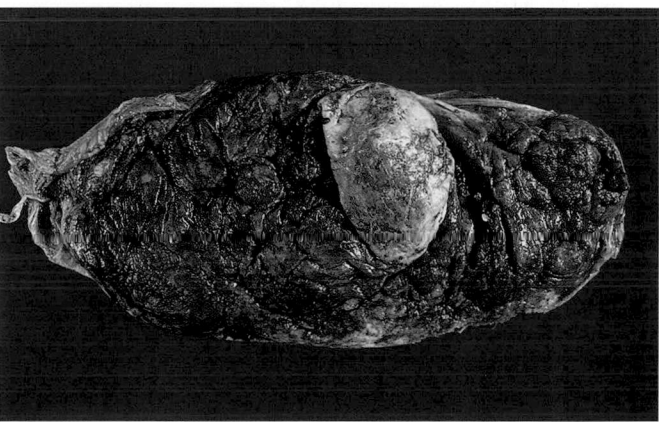

Fig. 19.372 Gross appearance of old placental infarct. The lesion is whitish and had a firm consistency.

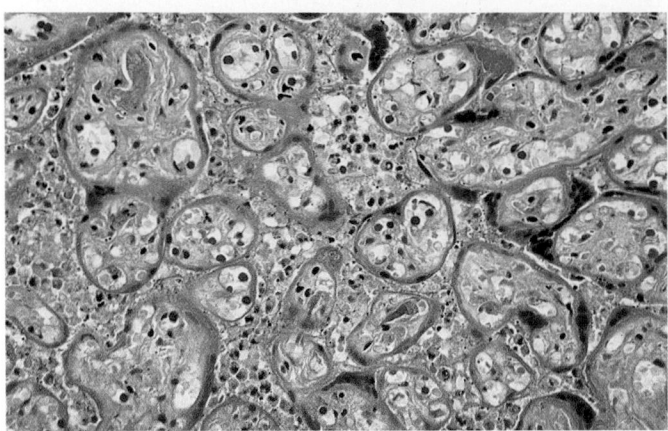

Fig. 19.373 Ghosts of chorionic villi in a longstanding placental infarct.

Minor degrees of infarction are seen in about 25% of placentas from uncomplicated term pregnancies and can, therefore, be regarded as an inconsequential phenomenon. A significant increase in the incidence and severity of infarcts in pregnancies has been found associated with preeclamptic toxemia, essential hypertension, Rh incompatibility, and nontoxic antepartum hemorrhage.[243] However, the fact that more than half of the placentas from pregnancies associated with preeclamptic toxemia show no infarcts indicates that the infarct per se is not necessarily the cause of the clinical manifestations of this disease. In most instances, the infarcts are the result of a retroplacental hematoma (abruptio placentae) or a thrombosed maternal vessel. Extensive placental infarcts are associated with a high incidence of neonatal asphyxia, low birth weight, and intrauterine death.[243]

Thrombosis of fetal arteries should be distinguished from placental infarcts (which, as already stated, are always secondary to occlusion of the maternal uteroplacental circulation).[271] The placental changes resulting from thrombosis of fetal arteries appear grossly as roughly triangular or hemispheric pale areas, otherwise indistinguishable from the surrounding normal placenta. They are better seen after formalin fixation. Microscopically, the villi are fibrosed and avascular, except for occasional small, thickened vessels. A thrombosed fetal artery is present at the apex of the lesion. Fox[242] found this lesion in 3.6% of 715 placentas examined. It was particularly frequent in diabetic women, and it did not seem to result in any deleterious effect on the fetus. It should be mentioned here that, in addition to fetal artery thrombosis, placentas of diabetic women often show an increased number of syncytial knots, fibrotic villi, Langhans cells, and foci of villous fibrinoid necrosis.[244-246]

Placental iron deposits are normal in the form of granular structures along the trophoblastic basement membrane; their presence in 7.5% or more of the villi is said to be abnormal and to be associated with fetal growth anomalies.[241]

Decidual vascular lesions of a necrotizing or inflammatory nature have been found in patients with lupus erythematosus.[229]

Sickle cell anemia can often be diagnosed by microscopic examination of the placenta, the deformation in the red blood cells developing as a result of the hypoxia created by the separation of the placenta from the uterine wall.[250]

Table 19.6 shows the correlation between morphologic changes in the placenta and a variety of clinical situations.

Placental site subinvolution may result in vaginal bleeding several weeks after delivery of the placenta, even in the absence of retained placental tissue. Curettage specimens from such cases contain large maternal vessels from the placental site partly filled with thrombi (Fig. 19.374). In the normal state, these thrombi become organized and remain as scars in the endometrium or adjacent myometrium. Some differences in deposition of immunoglobulins and complement factors have been detected immunohistochemically between subinvoluted and normal vessels. These have been interpreted as indicating that immunologic factors are necessary for the process of normal involution of uteroplacental arteries and that these may be deficient in subinvoluted vessels.[233]

Table 19.6 Correlation between morphologic changes in placenta and variety of clinical situations

	Normal pregnancy	Prolonged pregnancy	Premature onset of labor	Rh incompatibility	Diabetes	Essential hypertension	Toxemia
Infarct	±	±	±	±	+	++	++
Thrombosis of fetal arteries	±	+	±	±	++	±	±
Fibrinoid necrosis of villi	±	−	++	++	++	±	+
Immaturity of villi	±	±	±	++	++	±	±
Senescence of villi	±	++	±	±	±	±	+
Basement membrane thickening of villi	±	+	±	+	+	++	+++
Fibrosis of villi	±	+++	±	±	++	±	±

Based almost entirely on the gross and microscopic examination of placentas by Fox[242-248] and Fox and Langley.[249]

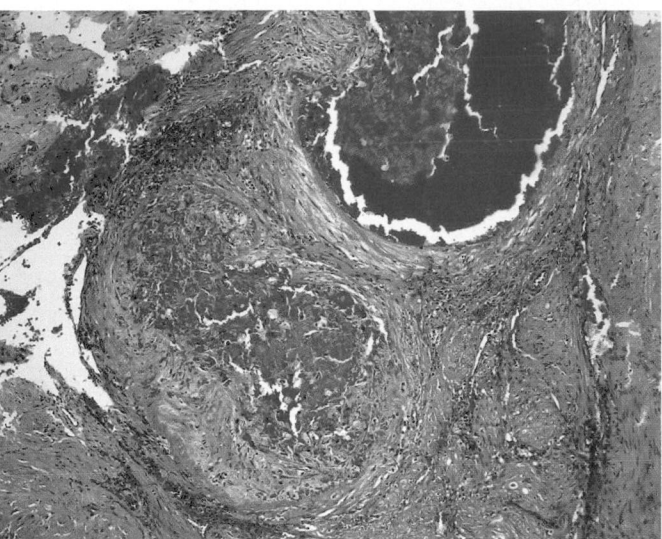

Fig. 19.374 Placental site subinvolution showing thick-walled vessels whose lumen is partially obliterated by organizing thrombi.

Tumors and tumorlike conditions of term placenta

Hemangiomas of placenta (chorangiomas) are found in approximately 1 of every 100 term specimens if a careful gross examination is performed.[308] Grossly, they are well circumscribed and purplish red. They may protrude on the fetal surface or be located entirely in the placental substance (Fig. 19.375). Microscopically, they are composed of a network of proliferating capillaries (Fig. 19.376). Mitoses may be present. Degenerative changes are common. Small hemangiomas (which represent the majority of the cases) are almost always asymptomatic, but the larger ones (more than 5 cm) may be associated with hydramnios, hemorrhage, premature delivery, premature placental separation, and placenta previa.[300] These manifestations may result in severe fetal distress

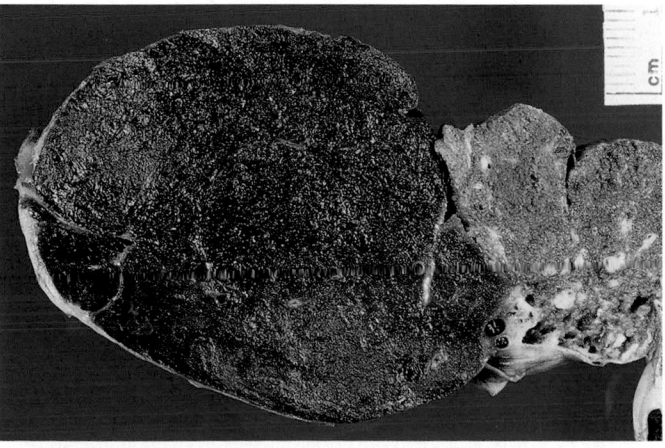

Fig. 19.375 Large placental hemangioma (chorangioma). The tumor is sharply circumscribed and of a deep red color.

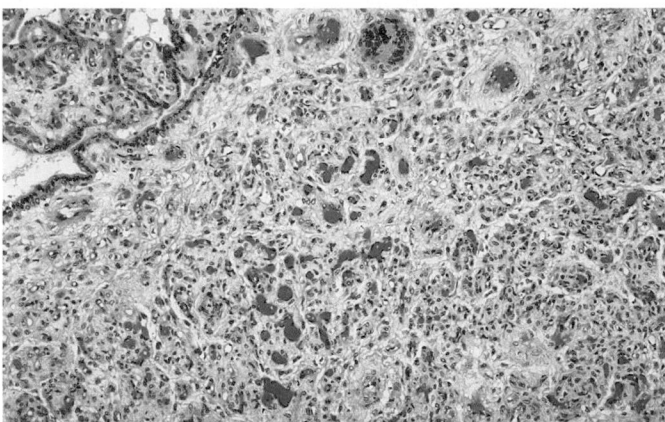

Fig. 19.376 Microscopic appearance of chorangioma. A complex network of capillaries distends the stroma of the placenta.

and intrauterine death. The left-to-right shunting of blood across the tumor may lead to transient congestive heart failure in the infant.[302] There is apparently no relationship between placental hemangioma and toxemia. A case of placental hemangioma has been seen in association with intraplacental choriocarcinoma.[299]

Immunohistochemically, the tumor cells show focal staining for cytokeratin 18, a finding that has suggested to the authors an origin from blood vessels of the chorionic plate and anchoring villi.[314]

Chorangiosis (villous vascular proliferation) is a condition characterized by an increase in the number of vascular channels per villus, and allegedly associated with neonatal morbidity and mortality.[298] **Chorangiomatosis** is as diffuse as chorangiosis but the vessels have a thicker wall containing actin-positive smooth muscle cells.[318]

Teratomas of the placenta are very rare; their typical location is between the amnion and chorion.[309,312,327]

Hepatocellular adenoma has been reported on several occasions.[303,311,328] An origin from displaced yolk sac elements with hepatocytic differentiation has been suggested.[304]

Heterotopic tissue such as adrenal cortex has also been described.[304]

Umbilical cord tumors are even less common than placental neoplasms. *Hemangiomas* occur, and may lead to nonimmune hydrops fetalis.[323] A few cases of *teratoma*[325] and *angiomyxoma*[329] have also been reported.

Direct extension of uterine tumors into the placenta has been reported in *leiomyoma* and *endometrial stromal sarcoma*.[307,310]

Metastatic tumors of maternal origin can lodge in the placenta and form distinct nodules. This phenomenon has been seen most often with malignant melanoma and malignant lymphoma/leukemia[301,313,317,320,321,324] but can also occur with carcinoma of lung and other organs.[305,322] Associated metastases to the fetus may or may not be present. Awareness of this dramatic event should not obscure the fact that in the large majority of pregnant women with widespread metastatic disease from any source the placenta and fetus are totally spared from the effects of the neoplasia.

An even stranger and rarer phenomenon is that of placental spread from congenital tumors in the fetus; this has been observed with leukemia and neuroblastoma.[315,319]

Giant pigmented nevi of the newborn can be accompanied by clusters of melanocytes in the placenta; this should not be taken as evidence that the tumor is malignant and that it has metastasized.[306,326]

Benign hemangioendothelioma has been seen to involve in a multicentric fashion the fetus and the placenta.[316]

References

Normal anatomy

1 Altshuler G. A conceptual approach to placental pathology and pregnancy outcome. Semin Diagn Pathol 1993, **10**: 204–221.

2 Bamberger AM, Sudhal S, Wagener C, Loning T. Expression pattern of the adhesion molecule CEACAM1 (C-CAM, CD66a, BGP) in gestational trophoblastic lesions. Int J Gynecol Pathol 2001, **20**: 160–165.

3 Benirschke K, Kaufmann P. Pathology of the human placenta. New York, 2000, Springer.

4 Bleisch VR. Diagnosis of monochorionic twin placentation. Am J Clin Pathol 1964, **42**: 277–284.

5 Danforth DM, Hull RW. The microscopic anatomy of the fetal membranes with particular reference to the detailed structure of the amnion. Am J Obstet Gynecol 1958, **75**: 536–550.

6 Deftos LJ, Burton DW, Brandt DW, Pinar H, Rubin LP. Neoplastic hormone – producing cells of the placenta produce and secrete parathyroid hormone – related protein. Studies by immunohistology, immunoassay, and polymerase chain reaction. Lab Invest 1994, **71**: 847–852.

7 Driscoll SG. Placental examination in a clinical setting. Arch Pathol Lab Med 1991, **115**: 668–671.

8 Fox H. Pathology of the placenta, ed. 2. London, 1997, W.B. Saunders.

9 Heatley MK, Maxwell P, Toner PG. The immunophenotype of human decidua and extra-uterine decidual reactions. Histopathology 1997, **29**: 437–442.

10 Horne CH, Rankin R, Bremner RD. Pregnancy-specific proteins as markers for gestational trophoblastic disease. Int J Gynecol Pathol 1984, **3**: 27–40.

11 Kämmerer U, Eggert AO, Kapp M, McLellan AD, Geijtenbeek TBH, Dietl J, van Kooyk Y, Kämpgen E. Unique appearance of proliferating antigen-presenting cell expressing DC-SIGN (CD209) in the deciduas of early human pregnancy. Am J Pathol 2003, **162**: 887–896.

12 Kaplan C. Placental pathology for the nineties. Pathol Annu 1993, **28**(Pt 1): 15–72.

13 Kingdom J, Jauniaux E, O'Brien PM, Royal College of Obstetricians and Gynaecologists Study Group. The placenta: basic science and clinical practice. London, 2000, RCOG Press.

14 Kurman RJ, Main CS, Chen H-C. Intermediate trophoblast. A distinctive form of trophoblast with specific morphological, biochemical and functional features. Placenta 1984, **5**: 349–370.

15 Langston C, Kaplan C, Macpherson T, Manci E, Peevy K, Clark B, Murtagh C, Cox S, Glen G. Practice guideline for examination of the placenta: developed by the placental pathology practice guideline development task force of the College of American Pathologists. Arch Pathol Lab Med 1997, **121**: 449–476.

16 Lewis SH, Benirschke K. Placenta. In Sternberg S (ed.): Histology for pathologists, ed. 2. Philadelphia, 1997, Lippincott-Raven, pp. 961–996.

17 Lewis SH, Perrin EV. Pathology of the placenta. New York, 1999, Churchill Livingstone.

18 Li HW, Cheung AN, Tsao SW, Cheung AL, O WS. Expression of E-cadherin and beta-catenin in trophoblastic tissue in normal and pathological pregnancies. Int J Gynecol Pathol 2002, **22**: 63–70.

19 McCluggage WG. Recent advances in immunohistochemistry in gynaecological pathology. Histopathology 2002, **40**: 309–326.

20 Macpherson T. Fact and fancy. What can we really tell from the placenta? Arch Pathol Lab Med 1991, **115**: 672–681.

21 Naeye RL. Umbilical cord length. Clinical significance. J Pediatr 1985, **107**: 278–281.

22 Naeye RL. Functionally important disorders of the placenta, umbilical cord, and fetal membranes. Hum Pathol 1987, **18**: 680–691.

23 Naeye RL. Disorders of the placenta, fetus, and neonate. Diagnosis and clinical significance. St. Louis, 1991, Mosby.

24 Novak RF. A brief review of the anatomy, histology, and ultrastructure of the full-term placenta. Arch Pathol Lab Med 1991, **115**: 654–659.

25 Sander CH. The surgical pathologist examines the placenta. Pathol Annu 1985, **20**(Pt 2): 235–288.

26 Shih IM, Kurman RJ. Immunohistochemical localization of inhibin-alpha in the placenta and gestational trophoblastic lesions. Int J Gynecol Pathol 1999, **18**: 144–150.

27 Shih IM, Seidman JD, Kurman RJ. Placental site nodule and characterization of distinctive type of intermediate trophoblast. Hum Pathol 1999, **30**: 687–694.

28 Singer G, Kurman RJ, McMaster MT, Shih IM. HLA-G immunoreactivity is specific for intermediate trophoblast in gestational trophoblastic disease and can serve as a useful marker in differential diagnosis. Am J Surg Pathol 2002, **26**: 914–920.

29 Yeh I-T, O'Connor DM, Kurman RJ. Vacuolated cytotrophoblast: a subpopulation of trophoblast in the chorion laeve. Placenta 1989, **10**: 429–438.

Abortion

30 Abaci F, Aterman K. Changes of the placenta and embryo in early spontaneous abortion. Am J Obstet Gynecol 1968, **102**: 252–263.

31 Al-Tamimi DM. Intermediate trophoblasts: their role in the diagnosis of intrauterine pregnancy. Int J Surg Pathol 1998, **6**: 11–16.

32 Berry CL. The examination of embryonic and fetal material in diagnostic histopathology laboratories. J Clin Pathol 1980, **33**: 317–326.

33 Cheville JC, Robinson RA, Benda JA. P53 expression in placentas with hydropic change and hydatidiform moles. Mod Pathol 1996, **9**: 392–396.

34 Clark RK, Damjanov I. Intermediate filaments of human trophoblast and choriocarcinoma cell lines. Virchows Arch [A] 1985, **407**: 203–208.

35 Clement PB, Young RH, Scully RE. Nontrophoblastic pathology of the female genital tract and peritoneum associated with pregnancy. Semin Diagn Pathol 1989, **6**: 372–406.

36 Conran RM, Hitchcock CL, Popek EJ, Norris HJ, Griffin JL, Geissel A, McCarthy WF. Diagnostic considerations in molar gestations. Hum Pathol 1993, **24**: 41–48.

37 Daya D, Sabet L. The use of cytokeratin as a sensitive and reliable marker for trophoblastic tissue. Am J Clin Pathol 1991, **95**: 137–141.

38 Fox H. Histological classification of tissue from spontaneous abortions. A valueless exercise? Histopathology 1993, **22**: 599–600.

39 Fox H, Herd ME, Harilal KR. Morphological changes in the placenta and decidua after induction of abortion by extra-amniotic prostaglandin. Histopathology 1978, **2**: 145–151.

40 Fukunaga M, Ushigome S, Fukunaga M. Spontaneous abortions and DNA ploidy. An application of flow cytometric DNA analysis in detection of non-diploidy in early abortions. Mod Pathol 1993, **6**: 619–624.

41 Genest DR, Roberts D, Boyd T Bieber FR. Fetoplacental histology as a predictor of karyotype. A controlled study of spontaneous first trimester abortions. Hum Pathol 1995, **26**: 201–209.

42 Gruber K, Gelven PL, Austin RM. Chorionic villi or trophoblastic tissue in uterine samples of four women with ectopic pregnancies. Int J Gynecol Pathol 1997, **16**: 28–32.

43 Hermonat PL, Kechelava S, Lowery CL, Korourian S. Trophoblasts are the preferential target for human papilloma virus infection in spontaneously aborted products of conception. Hum Pathol 1998, **29**: 170–174.

44 Hertig AT. Gestational hyperplasia of endometrium. A morphologic correlation of ova, endometrium, and corpora lutea during pregnancy. Lab Invest 1964, **13**: 1153–1191.

45 Horne CH, Rankin R, Bremner RD. Pregnancy-specific proteins as markers for gestational trophoblastic disease. Int J Gynecol Pathol 1984, **3**: 27–40.

46 Huettner PC, Gersell DJ. Arias-Stella reaction in nonpregnant women. A clinicopathologic study of nine cases. Int J Gynecol Pathol 1994, **13**: 241–247.

47 Inaba N, Ishige H, Ijichi M, Satoh N, Katoh T, Sekiya S, Shirotake S, Ohkawa R, Takamizawa H, Nitoh A, Renk T, Bohn H. Possible new markers in trophoblastic disease. Am J Obstet Gynecol 1982, **143**: 973–974.

48 Jauniaux E, Hustin J. Histological examination of first trimester spontaneous abortions. The impact of materno-embryonic interface features. Histopathology 1992, **21**: 409–414.

49 Kim YT, Cho NH, Ko JI, Yang WI, Kim JW, Choi EK, Lee SH. Expression of cyclin E in placenta with hydropic change and gestational trophoblastic diseases: implications for the malignant transformation of trophoblasts. Cancer 2000, **89**: 673–679.

50 Klatt EC. Pathologic examination of fetal specimens from dilation and evacuation procedures. Am J Clin Pathol 1995, **103**: 415–418.

51 Lindahl B, Ahlgren M. Identification of chorion villi in abortion specimens. Obstet Gynecol 1986, **67**: 79–81.

52 McFadden DE, Pantzer JT. Placental pathology of triploidy. Hum Pathol 1996, **27**: 1018–1020.

53 Nakamura Y, Moritsuka Y, Ohta Y, Itoh S, Haratake A, Kage M, Kawano K. S-100 protein in glands within decidua and cervical glands during early pregnancy. Hum Pathol 1989, **20**: 1204–1209.

54 Novak RW, Malone JM, Robinson HB. The role of the pathologist in the evaluation of first trimester abortions. Pathol Annu 1990, **25**(Pt 1): 297–311.

55 O'Connor DM, Kurman RJ. Intermediate trophoblast in uterine curettings in the diagnosis of ectopic pregnancy. Obstet Gynecol 1988, **72**: 665–670.

56 Oertel YC. The Arias-Stella reaction revisited. Arch Pathol Lab Med 1978, **102**: 651–654.

57 Ory SJ. Ectopic pregnancy: current evaluation and treatment. Mayo Clin Proc 1989, **64**: 874–877.

58 Paradinas FJ, Browne P, Fisher RA, Foskett M, Bagshawe KD, Newlands E. A clinical, histopathological and flow cytometric study of 149 complete moles, 146 partial moles and 107 non-molar hydropic abortions. Histopathology 1996, **28**: 101–110.

59 Poland BJ, Miller JR, Harris M, Livingston J. Spontaneous abortion. A study of 1961 women and their conceptuses. Acta Obstet Gynecol Scand 1981, **102**(Suppl).

60 Potter EL, Craig JM. Pathology of the fetus and the infant. London, 1976, Lloyd-Luke.

61 Redline RW, Hassold T, Zaragoza M. Determinants of villous trophoblastic hyperplasia in spontaneous abortions. Mod Pathol 1998, **11**: 762–768.

62 Redline RW, Zaragoza M, Hassold T. Prevalence of development and inflammatory lesions in nonmolar first trimester spontaneous abortions. Hum Pathol 1999, **30**: 93–100.

63 Rettig WJ, Cordon-Cardo C, Koulos JP, Lewis JL, Oettgen HF. Cell surface antigens of human trophoblast and choriocarcinoma defined by monoclonal antibodies. Int J Cancer 1985, **35**: 469–475.

64 Risch HA, Weiss NS, Clarke EA, Miller AB. Risk factors for spontaneous abortion and its recurrence. Am J Epidemiol 1988, **128**: 420–423.

65 Robb JA, Benirschke K, Barmeyer R. Intrauterine latent herpes simplex virus infection. I. Spontaneous abortion. Hum Pathol 1986, **17**: 1196–1209.

66 Rushton DI. Examination of products of conception from previable human pregnancies. J Clin Pathol 1981, **34**: 819–835.

67 Sasagawa M, Watanabe S, Ohmono Y, Honma S, Kanazawa K, Takeuchi S. Reactivity of two monoclonal antibodies (Troma 1 and CAM 5.2) on human tissue sections. Analysis of their usefulness as a histologic trophoblast marker in normal pregnancy and trophoblastic disease. Int J Gynecol Pathol 1986, **5**: 345–356.

68 Schammel DP, Bocklage T. p53, PCNA, and Ki-67 in hydropic molar and non-molar placentas: an immunohistochemical study. Int J Gynecol Pathol 1996, **15**: 158–166.

69 Strom J, Bewtra C, Monif GRG. Immunohistochemical localization of placental hormones as markers for differentiating uterine abortion vs ectopic pregnancy. Int J Surg Pathol 1993, **1**: 51–56.

70 Szulman AE. Examination of the early conceptus. Arch Pathol Lab Med 1991, **115**: 696–700.

71 Tyagi SP, Saxena K, Rizvi R, Langley FA. Foetal remnants in the uterus and their relation to other uterine heterotopia. Histopathology 1979, **3**: 339–345.

72 van Lijnschoten G, Arends IW, De La Fuente AA, Schouten HJ, Geraedts JP. Intra- and inter-observer variation in the interpretation of histological features suggesting chromosomal abnormality in early abortion specimens. Histopathology 1993, **22**: 25–29.

73 van Lijnschoten C, Arends JW, Leffers P, De La Fuente AA, Van Der Looij HJ, Geraedts JP. The value of histomorphological features of chorionic villi in early spontaneous abortion for the prediction of karyotype. Histopathology 1993, **22**: 557–563.

74 Wan SK, Lam PW, Pau MY, Chan JK. Multiclefted nuclei. A helpful feature for identification of intermediate trophoblastic cells in uterine curetting specimens. Am J Surg Pathol 1992, **16**: 1226–1232.

75 Wigglesworth JS. Perinatal pathology. Major problems in pathology, vol 15. Philadelphia, 1984, W.B. Saunders.

76 Wong SY, Ngan HY, Chan CC, Cheung AN. Apoptosis in gestational trophoblastic disease is correlated with clinical outcome and bcl-2 expression but not bax expression. Mod Pathol 1999, **12**: 1025–1033.

77 Zettergren L. Glial tissue in the uterus. Am J Pathol 1973, **71**: 419–426.

Gestational trophoblastic disease

78 Berkowitz RS, Goldstein DP. Chorionic tumors. N Engl J Med 1996, **335**: 1740–1748.

79 Chilosi M, Piazzola E, Lestani M, Benedetti A, Guasparri I, Granchelli G, Aldovini D, Leonardi E, Pizzolo G, Doglioni C, Menestrina F, Mariuzzi GM. Differential expression of p57kip2, a maternally imprinted cdk inhibitor, in normal human placenta and gestational trophoblastic disease. Lab Invest 1998, **78**: 269–276.

neoplasms. Morphologic correlates of therapeutic response. Am J Obstet Gynecol 1978, **130:** 801–806.

166 Dyke PC, Fink LM. Latent choriocarcinoma. Cancer 1967, **20:** 150–154.

167 Elston CW, Bagshawe KD. The diagnosis of trophoblastic tumours from uterine curettings. J Clin Pathol 1972, **25:** 111–118.

168 Elston CW, Bagshawe KD. Cellular reaction of trophoblastic tumors. Br J Cancer 1973, **28:** 245–255.

169 Fisher RA, Newlands ES, Jeffreys AJ, Boxer GM, Begent RH, Rustin GJ, Bagshawe KD. Gestational and nongestational trophoblastic tumors distinguished by DNA analysis. Cancer 1992, **69:** 839–845.

170 Fukunaga M, Nomura K, Ushigome S. Choriocarcinoma in situ of a first trimester: report of two cases indicating an origin of trophoblast of a stem villus. Virchows Arch 1996, **429:** 185–188.

171 Greenfield AW. Gestational trophoblastic disease. Prognostic variables and staging. Semin Oncol 1995, **22:** 142–148.

172 Heaton GE, Matthews TH, Christopherson WM. Malignant trophoblastic tumors with massive hemorrhage presenting as liver primary. A report of two cases. Am J Surg Pathol 1986, **10:** 342–347.

173 Ishizuka T, Tomoda Y, Kaseki S, Goto S, Hara T, Kobayashi T. Intracranial metastasis of choriocarcinoma. A clinicopathologic study. Cancer 1983, **52:** 1896–1903.

174 Ito H, Sekine T, Komuro N, Tanaka T, Yokoyama S, Hosokawa T. Histologic stromal reaction of the host with gestational choriocarcinoma and its relation to clinical stage classification and prognosis. Am J Obstet Gynecol 1981, **140:** 781–786.

175 Kaseki S. Prognosis and treatment of trophoblastic diseases. Excerpta Medica, 1980, International Congress Series no. **512:** 566–570.

176 Kohorn EI. Theca lutein ovarian cyst may be pathognomonic for trophoblastic neoplasia. Obstet Gynecol 1983, **62:** 80S–81S.

177 Lage J, Roberts DJ. Choriocarcinoma in a term placenta. Pathologic diagnosis of tumor in an asymptomatic patient with metastatic disease. Int J Gynecol Pathol 1993, **12:** 80–85.

178 Lewis J, Ketcham AS, Hertz R. Surgical intervention during chemotherapy of gestational trophoblastic neoplasms. Cancer 1966, **19:** 1517–1522.

179 Lind HM, Haghighi P. Carcinoembryonic antigen staining in choriocarcinoma. Am J Clin Pathol 1986, **86:** 538–540.

180 Lurain JR, Brewer JI, Torok EE, Halpern B. Gestational trophoblastic disease. Treatment results at the Brewer Trophoblastic Disease Center. Obstet Gynecol 1982, **60:** 354–360.

181 Mazur MT, Lurain JR, Brewer JI. Fatal gestational choriocarcinoma. Clinicopathologic study of patients treated at a trophoblastic disease center. Cancer 1982, **50:** 1833–1846.

182 Mogensen B, Olsen S. Cellular reaction to gestational choriocarcinoma and invasive mole. Acta Pathol Microbiol Scand (A) 1973, **81:** 453–456.

183 Mortakis AE, Braga CA. "Poor prognosis" metastatic gestational trophoblastic disease. The prognostic significance of the scoring system in predicting chemotherapy failures. Obstet Gynecol 1990, **76:** 272–277.

184 Nishikawa Y, Kaseki S, Tomoda Y, Ishizuka T, Asai Y, Susuki T, Ushijima H. Histopathologic classification of uterine choriocarcinoma. Cancer 1985, **55:** 1044–1051.

185 Ober WB, Edgcomb JH, Price EB Jr. The pathology of choriocarcinoma. Ann NY Acad Sci 1971, **172:** 299–321.

186 Olive DL, Lurain JR, Brewer JI. Choriocarcinoma associated with term gestation. Am J Obstet Gynecol 1984, **148:** 711–716.

187 Ostor A. "God's first cancer and man's first cure": milestones in gestational trophoblastic disease. Anat Pathol 1998, **1:** 165–178.

188 Redline RW, Abdul-Karim FW. Pathology of gestational trophoblastic disease. Semin Oncol 1995, **22:** 96–108.

189 Soper JT, Mutch DG, Chin N, Clarke-Pearson DL, Hammond CB.

Renal metastases of gestational trophoblastic disease. A report of eight cases. Obstet Gynecol 1988, **72:** 796–798.

190 Tsukamoto N, Matsumura M, Matsukuma K, Kamura T, Baba K. Choriocarcinoma in mother and fetus. Gynecol Oncol 1986, **24:** 113–119.

Placental site trophoblastic tumor and related lesions of intermediate trophoblast

191 Bamberger AM, Sudhal S, Wagener C, Loning T. Expression pattern of the adhesion molecule CEACAM1 (C-CAM, CD66a, BGP) in gestational trophoblastic lesions. Int J Gynecol Pathol 2001, **20:** 160–165.

192 Berger G, Verbaere J, Feroldi J. Placental site trophoblastic tumor of the uterus. An ultrastructural and immunohistochemical study. Ultrastruct Pathol 1984, **6:** 319–329.

193 Duncan DA, Mazur MT. Trophoblastic tumors. Ultrastructural comparison of choriocarcinoma and placental-site trophoblastic tumor. Hum Pathol 1989, **20:** 370–381.

194 Eckstein RP, Paradinas FJ, Bagshawe KD. Placental site trophoblastic tumour (trophoblastic pseudotumour). A study of four cases requiring hysterectomy including one fatal case. Histopathology 1982, **6:** 211–226.

195 Fukunaga M, Ushigome S. Metastasizing placental site trophoblastic tumor. An immunohistochemical and flow cytometric study of two cases. Am J Surg Pathol 1993, **17:** 1003–1010.

196 Gloor E, Dialdas J, Hurlimann J, Ribolzi J, Barrelet L. Placental site trophoblastic tumor (trophoblastic pseudotumor) of the uterus with metastases and fetal outcome. Clinial and autopsy observations of a case. Am J Surg Pathol 1983, **7:** 483–486.

197 Hui P, Parkash V, Perkins AS, Carcangiu ML. Pathogenesis of placental site trophoblastic tumor may require the presence of a paternally derived X chromosome. Lab Invest 2000, **80:** 965–972.

198 Kotylo PK, Michael H, Davis TE, Sutton GP, Mark PR, Roth LM. Flow cytometric DNA analysis of placental-site trophoblastic tumors. Int J Gynecol Pathol 1992, **11:** 245–252.

199 Kurman RJ. The morphology, biology, and pathology of intermediate trophoblast. A look back to the present. Hum Pathol 1991, **22:** 847–855.

200 Kurman RJ, Scully RE, Norris HJ. Trophoblastic pseudotumor of the uterus. An exaggerated form of "syncytial endometritis" simulating a malignant tumor. Cancer 1976, **38:** 1214–1226.

201 Kurman RJ, Young RH, Norris HJ, Main CS, Lawrence WD, Scully RE. Immunocytochemical localization of placental lactogen and chorionic gonadotropin in the normal placenta and trophoblastic tumors, with emphasis on intermediate trophoblast and the placental site trophoblastic tumor. Int J Gynecol Pathol 1984, **3:** 101–121.

202 Lathrop JC, Lauchlan S, Nayak R, Ambler M. Clinical characteristics of placental site trophoblastic tumor (PSTT). Gynecol Oncol 1988, **31:** 32–42.

203 Motoyama T, Ohta T, Ajioka Y, Watanabe H. Neoplastic and non-neoplastic intermediate trophoblasts. An immunohistochemical and ultrastructural study. Pathol Int 1994, **44:** 57–65.

204 Müller-Hocker J, Obernitz N, Johannes A, Löhrs U. p53 gene product and EFG-receptor are highly expressed in placental site trophoblastic tumor. Hum Pathol 1997, **28:** 1302–1306.

205 Orrell JM, Sanders DS. A particularly aggressive placental site trophoblastic tumour. Histopathology 1991, **18:** 559–561.

206 Rhoton-Vlasak A, Wagner JM, Rutgers JL, Baergen RN, Young RH, Roche PC, Plummer TB, Gleich GJ. Placental site trophoblastic tumor: human placental lactogen and pregnancy-associated major basic protein ad immunohistologic markers. Hum Pathol 1998, **29:** 280–288.

207 Scully RE, Young RH. Trophoblastic pseudotumor. A reappraisal. Am J Surg Pathol 1981, **5:** 75–76.

208 Shih IM, Kurman RJ. Ki-67 labeling index in the differential

diagnosis of exaggerated placental site, placental site trophoblastic tumor, and choriocarcinoma: a double immunohistochemical staining technique using Ki-67 and MEL-CAM antibodies. Hum Pathol 1998, **29:** 27–33.

209 Silva EG, Tornos C, Lage J, Ordonez NG, Morris M, Kavanagh J. Multiple nodules of intermediate trophoblast following hydatidiform moles. Int J Gynecol Pathol 1993, **12:** 324–332.

210 Singer G, Kurman RJ, McMaster MT, Shih IeM. HLA-G immunoreactivity is specific for intermediate trophoblast in gestational trophoblastic disease and can serve as a useful marker in differential diagnosis. Am J Surg Pathol 2002, **26:** 914–920.

211 Xue WC, Guan XY, Ngam HY, Shen DH, Khoo US, Cheung AN. Malignant placental site trophoblastic tumor: a cytogenetic study using comparative genomic hybridisation and chromosome in situ hybridisation. Cancer 2002, **94:** 2288–2294.

212 Yeh IT, O'Connor DM, Kurman RJ. Intermediate trophoblast. Further immunocytochemical characterization. Mod Pathol 1990, **3:** 282–287.

213 Young RH, Scully RE. Placental-site trophoblastic tumor. Current status. Clin Obstet Gynecol 1984, **27:** 248–258.

214 Young RH, Scully RE, McCluskey RT. A distinctive glomerular lesion complicating placental site trophoblastic tumor. Report of two cases. Hum Pathol 1985, **16:** 35–42.

Epithelioid trophoblastic tumor

215 Coulson LE, Kong CS, Zaloudek C. Epithelioid trophoblastic tumor of the uterus in postmenopausal women: a case report and review of the literature. Am J Surg Pathol 2000, **24:** 1558–1562.

216 Hamazaki S, Nakamoto S, Okino T, Tsukayama C, Mori M, Taguchi K, Okada S. Epithelioid trophoblastic tumor: morphological and immunohistochemical study of three lung lesions. Hum Pathol 1999, **30:** 1321–1327.

217 Mazur MT. Metastatic gestational choriocarcinoma. Unusual pathologic variant following therapy. Cancer 1989, **63:** 1370–1377.

218 Oldt RJ III, Kurman RJ, Shih IM. Molecular genetic analysis of placental site trophoblastic tumors and epithelioid trophoblastic tumors confirms their trophoblastic origin. Am J Pathol 2002, **161:** 1033–1037.

219 Shih IM, Kurman RJ. Epithelioid trophoblastic tumor: a neoplasm distinct from choriocarcinoma and placental site trophoblastic tumor simulating carcinoma. Am J Surg Pathol 1998, **22:** 1393–1403.

Tumorlike conditions of intermediate trophoblast

220 Campello TR, Fittipaldi H, O'Valle F, Carvia RE, Nogales FF. Extrauterine (tubal) placental site nodule. Histopathology 1998, **32:** 562–565.

221 El Hag IA, Ramesh K, Kollur SM, Salem M. Extrauterine placental site trophoblastic tumour in association with a lithopedion. Histopathology 2002, **41:** 446–449.

222 Huettner PC, Gersell DJ. Placental site nodules. A clinicopathologic study of 38 cases. Int J Gynecol Pathol 1994, **13:** 191–198.

223 Lee KC, Chan JK. Placental site nodule. Histopathology 1988, **16:** 193–195.

224 Shih IM, Kurman RJ. The pathology of intermediate trophoblastic tumors and tumor-like lesions. Int J Gynecol Pathol 2001, **20:** 31–47.

225 Shih IM, Seidman JD, Kurman RJ. Placental site nodule and characterization of distinctive type of intermediate trophoblast. Hum Pathol 1999, **30:** 687–694.

226 Shitabata PK, Rutgers JL. The placental site nodule. An immunohistochemical study. Hum Pathol 1994, **25:** 1295–1301.

227 Tsang WY, Chum NP, Tang SK, Tse CC, Chan JK. Mallory's bodies in placental site nodule. Arch Pathol Lab Med 1993, **117:** 547–550.

228 Young RH, Kurman RJ, Scully RE. Placental site nodules and

plaques. A clinicopathologic analysis of 20 cases. Am J Surg Pathol 1990, **14:** 1001–1009.

Non-neoplastic lesions of term placenta

229 Abramowsky CR, Vegas ME, Swinehart G, Gyves MT. Decidual vasculopathy of the placenta in lupus erythematosus. N Engl J Med 1980, **303:** 668–672.

230 Altshuler G. Role of the placenta in perinatal pathology (revisited). Pediatr Pathol Lab Med 1996, **16:** 207–233.

231 Altshuler G, Hyde S. Fusobacteria. An important cause of chorioamnionitis. Arch Pathol Lab Med 1985, **109:** 739–743.

232 Altshuler G, Russell P. The human placental villitides. A review of chronic intrauterine infection. Curr Top Pathol 1975, **60:** 63–112.

233 Andrew A, Bulmer JN, Morrison L, Wells M, Buckley CH. Subinvolution of the uteroplacental arteries. An immunohistochemical study. Int J Gynecol Pathol 1993, **12:** 28–33.

234 Benirschke K, Kaufmann P. Pathology of the human placenta. New York, 2000, Springer.

235 Benson RC, Fujikura T. Circumvallate and circummarginate placenta. Unimportant clinical entities. Obstet Gynecol 1969, **34:** 799–804.

236 Bjoro K Jr, Myhre E. The role of chronic nonspecific inflammatory lesions of the placenta in intrauterine growth retardation. Acta Pathol Microbiol Immunol Scand (A) 1984, **92:** 133–137.

237 Blanc WA. Pathways of fetal and early neonatal infection. Viral placentitis, bacterial and fungal chorioamnionitis. J Pediatr Surg 1961, **59:** 473–496.

238 Boyd TK, Redline RW. Chronic histiocytic intervillositis: a placental lesion associated with recurrent reproductive loss. Hum Pathol 2000, **31:** 1389–1396.

239 Bryan EM, Kohler HG. The missing umbilical artery. I. Prospective study based on a maternity unit. Arch Dis Child 1974, **49:** 844–852.

240 deRoux SJ, Prendergast NC, Adsay NV. Spontaneous uterine rupture with fatal hemoperitoneum due to placenta accreta percreta: a case report and review of the literature. Int J Gynecol Pathol 1999, **18:** 82–86.

241 Drachenberg CB, Papadimitriou JC. Placental iron deposits: significance in normal and abnormal pregnancies. Hum Pathol 1994, **25:** 379–385.

242 Fox H. Thrombosis of foetal arteries in the human placenta. J Obstet Gynaecol Br Commonw 1966, **73:** 961–965.

243 Fox H. The significance of placental infarction in perinatal morbidity and mortality. Biol Neonate 1967, **11:** 87–105.

244 Fox H. Fibrinoid necrosis of placental villi. J Obstet Gynaecol Br Commonw 1968, **75:** 448–452.

245 Fox H. Fibrosis of placental villi. J Pathol Bacteriol 1968, **95:** 573–579.

246 Fox H. Pathology of the placenta in maternal diabetes mellitus. Obstet Gynecol 1969, **34:** 792–798.

247 Fox H. Placenta accreta, 1945–1969. Obstet Gynecol Surv 1972, **27:** 475–490.

248 Fox H. Pathology of the placenta, ed. 2. London, 1997, W.B. Saunders.

249 Fox H, Langley FA. Leukocytic infiltration of the placenta and umbilical cord. A clinicopathologic study. Obstet Gynecol 1971, **37:** 451–458.

250 Fujikura T, Froehlich LA. Diagnosis of sickling by placental examination. Geographic differences in incidence. Am J Obstet Gynecol 1968, **100:** 1122–1124.

251 Genest DR, Choi-Hong SR, Tate JE, Qureshi F, Jacques SM, Crum C. Diagnosis of congenital syphilis from placental examination: comparison of histopathology, Steiner stain, and polymerase chain reaction for treponema pallidum DNA. Hum Pathol 1996, **27:** 366–372.

252 Genest DR, Granter S, Pinkus GS. Umbilical cord "pseudo-

vasculitis" following second trimester fetal death: a clinicopathologic and immunohistochemical study of 13 cases. Histopathology 1997, 30: 563–569.

253 Gersell DJ. Chronic villitis, chronic chorioamnionitis, and maternal floor infarction. Semin Diagn Pathol 1993, 10: 251–266.

254 Gersell DJ, Phillips NJ, Beckerman K. Chronic chorioamnionitis. A clinicopathologic study of 17 cases. Int J Gynecol Pathol 1991, 10: 217–229.

255 Heifetz SA. Single umbilical artery. A statistical analysis of 237 autopsy cases and review of the literature. Perspect Pediatr Pathol 1984, 8: 345–378.

256 Heifetz SA, Bauman M. Necrotizing funisitis and herpes simplex infection of placental and decidual tissues. Study of four cases. Hum Pathol 1994, 25: 715–722.

257 Hyde SR, Benirschke K. Gestational psittacosis: case report and literature review. Mod Pathol 1997, 10: 602–607.

258 Ismail MR, Ordi J, Menendez C, Ventura PJ, Aponte JJ, Kahigwa E, Hirt R, Cardesa A, Alonso PL. Placental pathology in malaria: a histological, immunohistochemical and quantitative study. Hum Pathol 2000, 31: 85–93.

259 Jacques SM, Qureshi F. Chronic intervillositis of the placenta. Arch Pathol Lab Med 1993, 117: 1032–1035.

260 Jacques SM, Qureshi F. Chronic chorioamnionitis: a clinicopathologic and immunohistochemical study. Hum Pathol 1999, 29: 1457–1461.

261 Jauniaux E, De Munter C, Vanesse M, Wilkin P, Hustin J. Embryonic remnants of the umbilical cord: morphologic and clinical aspects. Hum Pathol 1989, 20: 458–462.

262 Joshi VV. Handbook of placental pathology. New York, 1984, Igaku-Shoin.

263 Kaplan C. The placenta and viral infections. Semin Diagn Pathol 1993, 10: 232–250.

264 Kaplan C, Benirschke K, Tarzy B. Placental tuberculosis in early and late pregnancy. Am J Obstet Gynecol 1980, 137: 858–860.

265 Kaplan CG. Color atlas of gross placental pathology. New York, 1994, Igaku-Shoin.

266 Kida M, Abramowsky CR, Santoscoy C. Cryptococcosis of the placenta in a woman with acquired immunodeficiency syndrome. Hum Pathol 1989, 20: 920–921.

267 Kim CJ, Yoon BH, Kim M, Park JO, Cho SY, Chi JG. Histo-topographic distribution of acute inflammation of the human umbilical cord. Pathol Int 2001, 51: 861–865.

268 Kim CY, Yoon BH, Park SS, Kim MH, Chi JG. Acute funisitis of preterm but not term placentas is associated with severe fetal inflammatory response. Hum Pathol 2001, 32: 623–629.

269 Kingdom J, Jauniaux E, O'Brien PM, Royal College of Obstetricians and Gynaecologists Study Group. The placenta: basic science and clinical practice. London, 2000, RCOG Press.

270 Kraus FT. Placental thrombi and related problems. Semin Diagn Pathol 1993, 10: 275–283.

271 Lauweryns J, Bernat R, Lerut A, Detournay G. Intrauterine pneumonia. An experimental study. Biol Neonate 1978, 22: 301–318.

272 McCaffree MA, Altshuler G, Benirschke K. Placental coccidioidomycosis without fetal disease. Arch Pathol Lab Med 1978, 102: 512–514.

273 Morken NH, Henriksen H. Placenta percreta – two cases and review of the literature. Eur J Obstet Gynecol Reprod Biol 2001, 100: 112–115.

274 Morris ED. Placental insufficiency. Br Med Bull 1968, 24: 76–79.

275 Mostoufi-zadeh M, Driscoll SG, Biano SA, Kundsin RB. Placental evidence of cytomegalovirus infection of the fetus and neonate. Arch Pathol Lab Med 1984, 108: 403–406.

276 Mueller-Heubach E, Rubinstein DN, Schwarz SS. Histologic chorioamnionitis and preterm delivery in different patient populations. Obstet Gynecol 1990, 75: 622–626.

277 Muhlemann K, Miller RK, Metlay L, Menegus MA.

Cytomegalovirus infection of the human placenta: an immunocytochemical study. Hum Pathol 1992, 23: 1234–1237.

278 Nakamura Y, Sakuma S, Ohta Y, Kawano K, Hashimoto T. Detection of the human cytomegalovirus gene in placental chronic villitis by polymerase chain reaction. Hum Pathol 1994, 25: 815–818.

279 Qureshi F, Jacques SM, Reyes MP. Placental histopathology in syphilis. Hum Pathol 1993, 24: 779–784.

280 Redline RW, Abramowsky CR. Clinical and pathologic aspects of recurrent placental villitis. Hum Pathol 1985, 16: 727–731.

281 Robb JA, Benirschke K, Mannino F, Voland J. Intrauterine latent herpes simplex virus infection. II. Latent neonatal infection. Hum Pathol 1986, 17: 1210–1217.

282 Russell P. Inflammatory lesions of the human placenta. I. Clinical significance of acute chorioamnionitis. Am J Diagn Gynecol Obstet 1979, 1: 127–137.

283 Russell P. Inflammatory lesions of the human placenta. II. Villitis of unknown etiology in perspective. Am J Diagn Gynecol Obstet 1979, 1: 339–346.

284 Russell P, Atkinson K, Krishnan L. Recurrent reproductive failure due to severe placental villitis of unknown etiology. J Reprod Med 1980, 24: 93–98.

285 Saetta A, Agapitos E, Davaris PS. Determination of CMV placentitis. Diagnostic application of the polymerase chain reaction. Virchows Arch 1998, 432: 159–162.

286 Salazar H, Kanbour AI. Amnion nodosum. Ultrastructure and histopathogenesis. Arch Pathol 1974, 98: 39–46.

287 Sander CH, Stevens NG. Hemorrhagic endovasculitis of the placenta. An indepth morphologic appraisal with initial clinical and epidemiologic observations. Pathol Annu 1984, 19(Pt 1): 37–79.

288 Sander CM. What's new in placental pathology. Pathol Annu 1995, 30(Pt 1): 59–93.

289 Schwartz DA, Caldwell E. Herpes simplex virus infection of the placenta. The role of molecular pathology in the diagnosis of viral infection of placental-associated tissues. Arch Pathol Lab Med 1991, 115: 1141–1144.

290 Schwartz DA, Khan R, Stoll B. Characterization of the fetal inflammatory response to cytomegalovirus placentitis. An immunohistochemical study. Arch Pathol Lab Med 1992, 116: 21–27.

291 Schwartz DA, Larsen SA, Beck-Sague C, Fears M, Rice RJ. Pathology of the umbilical cord in congenital syphilis. Analysis of 25 specimens using histochemistry and immunofluorescent antibody to treponema pallidum. Hum Pathol 1995, 26: 784–791.

292 Walter P, Blot P, Ivanoff B. The placental lesions in congenital syphilis. A study of six cases. Virchows Arch [A] 1982, 397: 313–326.

293 Wentworth P. Placental infarction and toxemia of pregnancy. Am J Obstet Gynecol 1967, 99: 318–326.

294 Wentworth P. Circumvallate and circummarginate placentas. Their incidence and clinical significance. Am J Obstet Gynecol 1968, 102: 44–47.

295 Wigglesworth JS. Vascular anatomy of the human placenta and its significance for placental pathology. J Obstet Gynaecol Br Commonw 1969, 76: 979–989.

296 Younoszai MK, Haworth JC. Placental dimensions and relations in preterm, term, and growth-retarded infants. Am J Obstet Gynecol 1969, 103: 265–271.

297 Zlatnik FJ, Gellhaus TM, Benda JA, Koontz FP, Burmeister LF. Histologic chorioamnionitis, microbial infection, and prematurity. Obstet Gynecol 1990, 76: 355–359.

Tumors and tumorlike conditions of term placenta

298 Altshuler G. Chorangiosis. An important placental sign of neonatal morbidity and mortality. Arch Pathol Lab Med 1984, 108: 71–74.

299 Aonahata M, Masuzawa Y, Tsutsui Y. A case of intraplacental choriocarcinoma associated with placental hemangioma. Pathol Int 1999, 48: 897–901.

300 Asadourian LA, Taylor HB. Clinical significance of placental hemangiomas. Obstet Gynecol 1968, 31: 551–555.

301 Baergen RN, Johnson D, Moore T, Benirschke K. Maternal melanoma metastatic to the placenta: a case report and review of the literature. Arch Pathol lab Med 1997, 121: 508–511.

302 Cash JB, Powell DE. Placental chorioangioma. Presentation of a case with electron-microscopic and immunochemical studies. Am J Surg Pathol 1980, 4: 87–92.

303 Chen KTK, Ma CK, Kassel SH. Hepatocellular adenoma of the placenta. Am J Surg Pathol 1986, 10: 436–440.

304 Cox JN, Chavrier F. Heterotopic adrenocortical tissue within a placenta. Placenta 1980, 1: 131–133.

305 Delerive C, Locquet F, Mallart A, Janin A, Gosselin B. Placental metastasis from maternal bronchial oat cell carcinoma. Arch Pathol Lab Med 1989, 113: 556–558.

306 Demian SDE, Donnelly WH, Frias JL, Monif GRG. Placental lesions in congenital giant pigmented nevi. Am J Clin Pathol 1974, 61: 438–442.

307 Ernst LM, Hui P, Parkash V. Intraplacental smooth muscle tumor: a case report. Int J Gynecol Pathol 2001, 20: 284–288.

308 Fox H. Vascular tumors of the placenta. Obstet Gynecol Surv 1967, 22: 697–711.

309 Fox H. Pathology of the placenta, ed. 2. London, 1997, W.B. Saunders.

310 Katsanis WA, O'Connor DM, Gibb RK, Bendon RW. Endometrial stromal sarcoma involving the placenta. Ann Diagn Pathol 1999, 2: 301–305.

311 Khalifa MA, Gersell DJ, Hansen CH, Lage JM. Hepatic (hepatocellular) adenoma of the placenta: a study of four cases. Int J Gynecol Pathol 1998, 17: 241–244.

312 Kreczy A, Alge A, Menardi G, Gassner I, Gschwendtner A, Mikuz G. Teratoma of the umbilical cord. Case report with review of the literature. Arch Pathol Lab Med 1994, 118: 934–937.

313 Kurtin PJ, Gaffey TA, Habermann TM. Peripheral T-cell lymphoma involving the placenta. Cancer 1992, 70: 2963–2968.

314 Lifschitz-Mercer B, Fogel M, Kushnir I, Czernobilsky B. Chorangioma. A cytoskeletal profile. Int J Gynecol Pathol 1989, 8: 349–356.

315 Lynn AA, Parry SI, Morgan MA, Mennuti MT. Disseminated congenital neuroblastoma involving the placenta. Arch Pathol Lab Med 1997, 121: 741–744.

316 Marton T, Silhavy M, Csapó Z, Szendo B, Papp Z. Multifocal hemangioendothelioma of the fetus and placenta. Hum Pathol 1997, 28: 866–869.

317 Meguerian-Bedoyan Z, Lamant L, Hopfner C, Pulford K, Chittal S, Delsol G. Anaplastic large cell lymphoma of maternal origin involving the placenta: case report and literature survey. Am J Surg Pathol 1997, 21: 1236–1241.

318 Ogino S, Redline RW. Villous capillary lesions of the placenta: distinctions between choriangioma, chorangiomatosis, and choriangiosis. Hum Pathol 2000, 31: 945–954.

319 Perkins DG, Kopp CM, Haust MD. Placental infiltration in congenital neuroblastoma. A case study with ultrastructure. Histopathology 1980, 4: 383–389.

320 Potter JF, Schoeneman M. Metastasis of maternal cancer to the placenta and fetus. Cancer 1970, 25: 380–388.

321 Read EJ Jr, Platzer PB. Placental metastasis from maternal carcinoma of the lung. Obstet Gynecol 1981, 58: 387–391.

322 Schmitt FC, Zelandi Filho C, Bacchi MM, Castilho ED, Bacchi CE. Adenoid cystic carcinoma of trachea metastatic to the placenta. Hum Pathol 1989, 20: 193–195.

323 Seifer DB, Ferguson JE II, Behrens CM, Zemel S, Stevenson DK, Ross JC. Nonimmune hydrops fetalis in association with hemangioma of the umbilical cord. Obstet Gynecol 1985, 66: 283–286.

324 Sheikh SS, Khalifa MA, Marley EF, Bagg A, Lage JM. Acute monocytic leukaemia (FAB M5) involving the placenta associated with delivery of a healthy infant: case report and discussion. Int J Gynecol Pathol 1997, 15: 363–366.

325 Smith D, Majmudar B. Teratoma of the umbilical cord. Hum Pathol 1985, 16: 190–193.

326 Sotelo-Avila C, Graham M, Hanby DE, Rudolph AJ. Nevus cell aggregates in the placenta. A histochemical and electron microscopic study. Am J Clin Pathol 1988, 89: 395–400.

327 Unger JL. Placental teratoma. Am J Clin Pathol 1989, 92: 371–373.

328 Vesoulis Z, Agamanolis D. Benign hepatocellular tumor of the placenta. Am J Surg Pathol 1998, 22: 355–359.

329 Yavner DL, Redline RW. Angiomyxoma of the umbilical cord with massive cystic degeneration of Wharton's jelly. Arch Pathol Lab Med 1989, 113: 935–937.

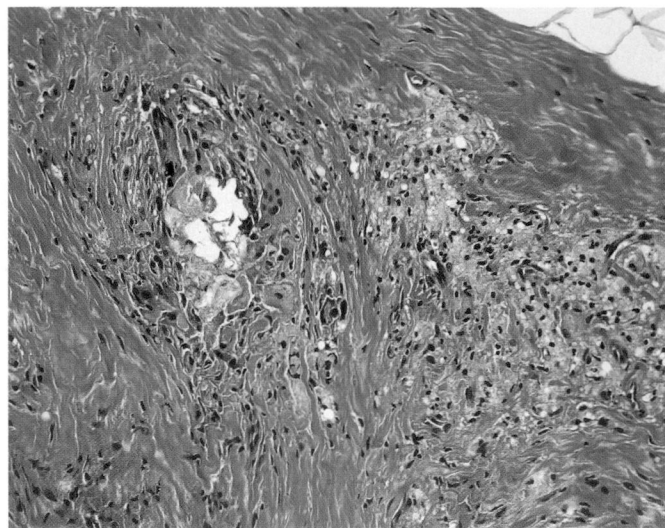

Fig. 20.7 Post-traumatic fat necrosis involving breast.

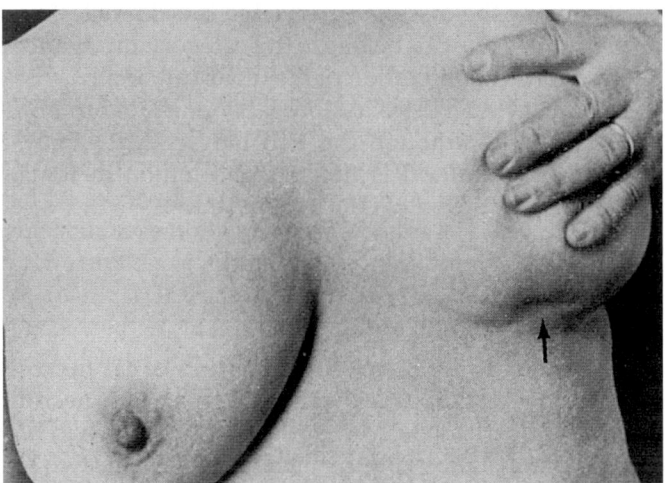

Fig. 20.8 Retraction of skin in a patient with fat necrosis (arrow), as seen in a photograph taken from a well-seasoned paper. (From Lee BJ, Adair F. Traumatic fat necrosis of the female breast and its differentiation from carcinoma. Ann Surg 1924, **80**: 670–691)

the deposition of hemoglobin-derived pigments. The microscopic diagnosis is usually easy, but the frozen section may cause some perplexity. A somewhat unorthodox clue to the diagnosis is the fact that a satisfactory frozen section is very difficult to obtain because this tissue is largely made up of liquefied fat.

Cases of mammary fat necrosis have also been reported following radiation therapy for breast carcinoma,[47] and as a local manifestation of Weber–Christian disease. Exceptionally, the fat necrosis acquires the morphologic features of the so-called "membranous type," particularly in post-radiation therapy cases.[48]

Other inflammatory diseases

Abscess of the breast usually results from rupture of mammary ducts, occurring most often during lactation but also independently from it.[58,59,82] It may be located deep within the parenchyma or in the periareolar region.[91] Microscopically, a central cavity filled with neutrophils and secretion is surrounded by inflamed and, eventually, fibrotic breast parenchyma, with obliteration of the lobular pattern. Clinically, a localized abscess may simulate carcinoma. Periareolar abscess associated with squamous metaplasia of lactiferous ducts is referred to as *Zuska's disease*.[84,91]

Lymphocytic mastitis is an unusual breast lesion of probable immune-mediated pathogenesis consisting microscopically of dense intralobular, perilobular, and perivascular lymphocytic infiltrates associated with lobular atrophy and sclerosis.[83] When the latter is intense, the term *sclerosing lymphocytic mastitis* has been employed[70] (Fig. 20.9). The lymphocytes are mainly of the B-cell type. Sometimes, the lymphocytic infiltrate is accompanied by a stromal infiltrate of epithelioid cells that can lead to a mistaken diagnosis of invasive carcinoma or granular cell tumor.[60] These cells appear to be of a fibroblastic or myofibroblastic nature.[52] Lymphocytic mastitis can result clinically in a palpable mass; most cases are seen in association with diabetes (hence the proposed synonym *diabetic mastopathy*[74,85,87]), but can also occur in the absence of this disorder.[52] On occasion, it has been associated with intraductal carcinoma.[57] It does not seem to be associated with an increased risk for lymphoma.[89]

Granulomatous mastitis (lobular granulomatous mastitis; granulomatous lobulitis) is a term that has been proposed for a granulomatous inflammatory process of the breast characterized by the presence of noncaseating granulomas, confined to breast lobules, in which no microorganisms are found; the suggestion has been made that the disease may be immunologically mediated and, therefore, analogous to granulomatous thyroiditis or granulomatous orchitis.[63,68]

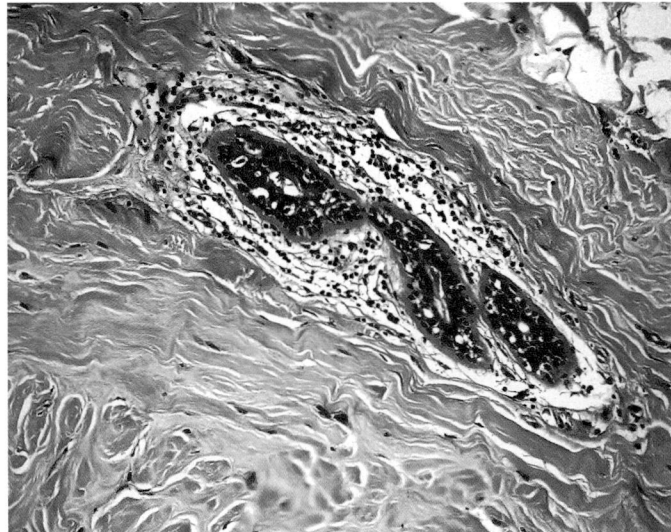

Fig. 20.9 Sclerosing lymphocytic mastitis in a diabetic woman. Some of the lymphocytes infiltrate the gland.

Tuberculosis of the breast may be secondary to either bloodstream dissemination or extension from an adjacent tuberculous process.[69] Grossly, multiple sinuses and areas of caseation necrosis occur. Microscopically, typical granulomas are identified in most cases. The lesion may be mistaken clinically for advanced breast carcinoma. The regional nodes are often involved; occasionally, these nodes are in an intramammary location.[51]

Actinomycosis, coccidioidomycosis, and **histoplasmosis** of the breast can cause necrotizing granulomatous masses and multiple sinus tracts.[54,78]

Sarcoidosis can begin in the breast and remain localized in this organ for long periods.[53,62] Alternatively, breast involvement may be a component of systemic disease.[71,77]

Foreign body reaction to the polyvinyl plastic or silicone that was used for mammoplasty in the 1960s sometimes resulted in tumorlike masses and sinus tracts[86] (Fig. 20.10).

Breast infarct can complicate a large variety of conditions, including intraductal papilloma, fibroadenoma, phylloides tumor, hyperplastic lobules during pregnancy, syphilis, and Wegener's granulomatosis.[66,72,80,90] It also has been reported in association with anticoagulant therapy,[76] postpartum abscess and gangrene, thrombophlebitis migrans disseminata, and mitral stenosis with heart failure.[81]

Mondor's disease is the eponymous term given to a peculiar thrombophlebitis involving the breast and contiguous thoracoabdominal wall.[61,73,79] The condition, which may simulate clinically a malignant neoplasm, often has a sudden onset and appears as a firm, slightly nodular cord beneath the skin. Ecchymosis may or may not be present. Microscopically, the process is one of phlebitis with thrombosis.[65] With time, the thrombus recanalizes completely. The condition is self-limited and practically never recurs. It may be related to mechanical injury, as suggested by the fact that in 8 of the 15 cases reported by Herrmann[64] the disease appeared a few months after radical mastectomy. A few cases have been found to be associated with untreated breast carcinoma.[55]

Rheumatoid nodules, periarteritis nodosa and the already mentioned **Wegener's granulomatosis** may present as single or multiple breast masses.[56,66,67,75,88]

Benign proliferative breast disease

Benign proliferative breast disease is an extremely complex and interrelated group of proliferative disorders of the breast parenchyma, most of which are probably not true neoplasms but, rather, hormone-induced hyperplastic processes. Some, like typical fibroadenoma, are recognized at a glance. Others raise the differential diagnosis of carcinoma at the clinical, gross, and microscopic level. Some of them are probably related to the development of malignancy but in a fashion that remains ill defined and highly controversial.

Fibroadenoma

Fibroadenoma is a common benign breast lesion typically occurring in patients between the ages of 20 and 35 years. It increases in size during pregnancy and tends to regress as the age of the patient increases. It is usually single, but in 20% of cases there are multiple lesions in the same breast or bilaterally.

Grossly, the usual fibroadenoma is a sharply demarcated, firm mass, usually no more than 3 cm in diameter. The cut surface is solid, grayish white, and bulging, with a whorl-like pattern and slit-like spaces. Necrosis is absent (Fig. 20.11).

Microscopically, fibroadenomas vary in appearance from case to case depending on the relative amounts of glandular and connective tissue and the configuration of the former (Fig. 20.12). They are labeled *intracanalicular* (a misnomer) when the connective tissue invaginates into the glandular spaces so that it appears to be within them, and *pericanalicular* when the regular round or oval glandular configuration of the glands is maintained. Often, both types of growth are seen in the same lesion. The distinction has no practical connotations. The tubules are composed of cuboidal or low columnar cells with round uniform nuclei resting on a myoepithelial cell layer. The stroma is usually made up of loose connective tissue rich in acid mucopolysaccharides, but it may be partially or totally composed of a dense fibrous type. The spindle cells are predominantly CD34-positive fibroblasts, admixed with scattered FXIIIa-positive

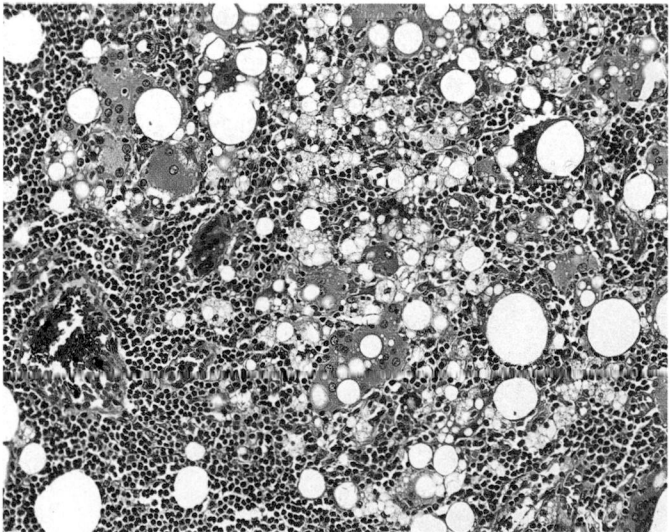

Fig. 20.10 Florid granulomatous reaction to silicone. Foamy macrophages, foreign body-type multinucleated giant cells, and lymphocytes are present.

dendrophages.[109,117] Elastic tissue is absent, in keeping with the presumed TDLU origin of the lesion. The cellularity of the stroma varies from case to case, but in any unduly hypercellular lesion the alternative diagnosis of phylloides tumor should be considered (see p. 1829).

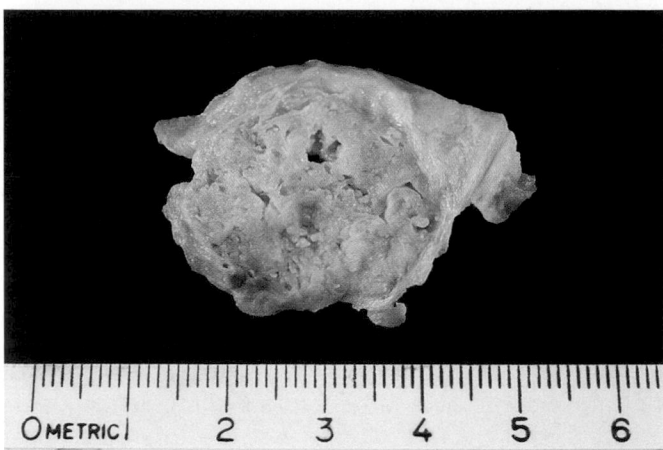

Fig. 20.11 Gross appearance of fibroadenoma. The lesion is sharply circumscribed and perfectly round, and it contains numerous slits.

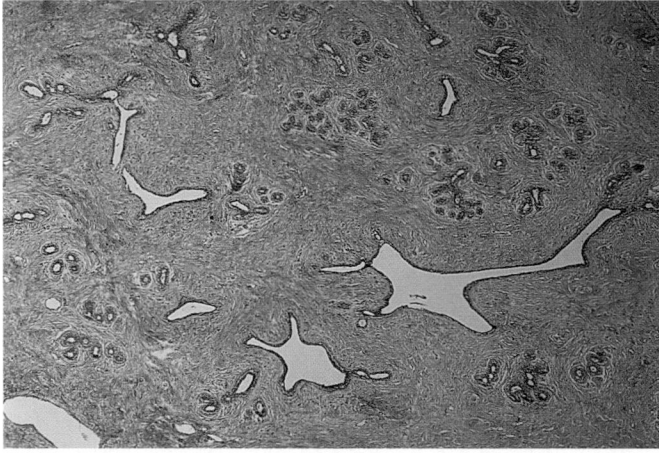

A

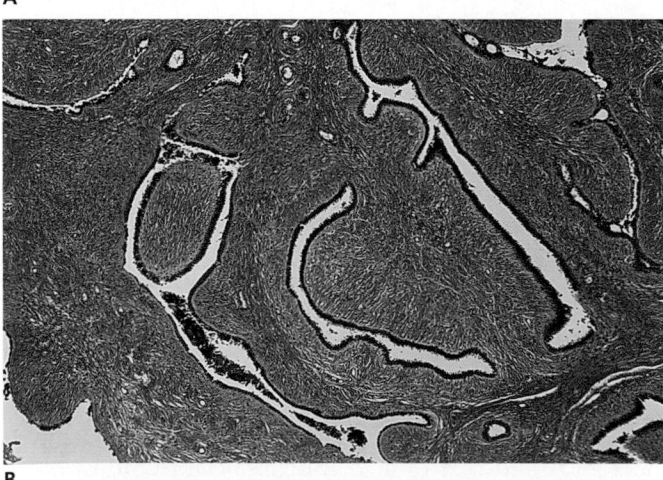

B

Fig. 20.12 Microscopic appearance of fibroadenoma. The tumor shown in **B** has a slightly hypercellular stroma but not to a degree that would justify a diagnosis of phyllodes tumor.

Morphologic variations in fibroadenoma are plentiful, some of more significance than others:

1 Hyalinization, calcification, and/or ossification of the stroma. These changes are more commonly seen in older patients and can be appreciated radiographically (Fig. 20.13).

2 Presence in the stroma of multinucleated giant cells of reactive nature, similar to those seen in polypoid lesions of nasal cavity and other sites.[94]

3 Presence in the stroma of mature adipose tissue, smooth muscle, or metaplastic cartilage.[104,110,116] Some of the lesions described as hamartoma or choristoma of the breast probably belong to this category[92,107,113] (see p. 1834).

4 Prominent myxoid changes. Most of these fibroadenomas are not otherwise different from the others. However, whenever multiple highly myxoid fibroadenomas are found, the possibility that they are a component of the syndrome that also includes endocrine hyperactivity, cardiac myxoma, cutaneous hyperpigmentation, and other abnormalities (Carney's complex) should be investigated. Other breast abnormalities that can be seen in the syndrome are lobular and nodular myxoid changes,[95] and ductal adenoma with tubular features (see p. 1773).

5 Peculiar fibrocellular stroma. Azzopardi[93] has pointed out the existence of a *fibroadenoma variant* in

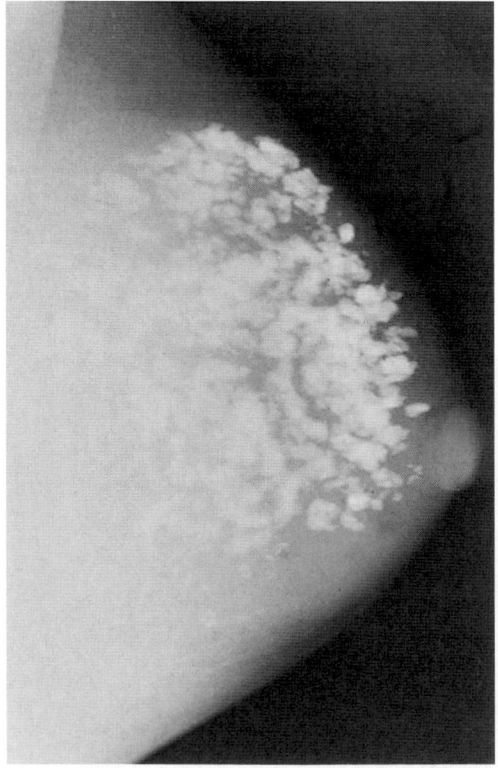

Fig. 20.13 Heavy, coarse calcification in a large breast fibroadenoma as seen in a mammogram.

which the stroma is simultaneously highly collagenous and cellular, has a somewhat laminated appearance, and is sometimes accompanied by a mononuclear infiltrate.

6 Hemorrhagic infarct. Fibroadenomas with this complication show grossly a bulging red appearance that can be quite perplexing. This complication is more likely to occur during pregnancy.

7 Ill-defined margins blending with a surrounding breast that shows the features of fibrocystic disease. This form, which has been designated *fibroadenomatosis* or *fibroadenomatoid hyperplasia*, shares the features of fibroadenoma and fibrocystic disease and suggests a pathogenetic link between the two.

8 Apocrine metaplasia. This change is found in approximately 15% of fibroadenomas.[93] In retrospect, it would seem that the change originally described as endocrine neoplasia in fibroadenoma[100] represents a morphologic variation on the theme of apocrine metaplasia; in the cases we have studied, the endocrine-like cells stained strongly for GCDFP-15 but were negative for chromogranin (Fig. 20.14).

9 Sclerosing adenosis. This occurs in less than 10% of cases.[93] Fibroadenomas with cysts, sclerosing adenosis, calcifications, or papillary apocrine changes are sometimes referred to as "complex."[99,106]

10 Squamous metaplasia. This is a rare finding; its presence in abundance should suggest the alternative possibility of phylloides tumor.

11 Lactational changes. These are manifested by an increase in the amount of cytoplasm in the epithelial cells, which appear vacuolated, and by dilatation of the glandular lumina by secretion.[111]

12 Young patient's, large tumor size, and hypercellularity. There is a reasonably distinct type of fibroadenoma that tends to occur in adolescents (often in blacks and sometimes involving both breasts), reach a large size (over 10 cm), and show hypercellularity of glands and/or stroma (Fig. 20.15).[98] These attributes can be found independently from each other, but there is clearly a link between them. A plethora of names exists to designate these lesions, depending on which feature predominates or which has impressed the writer the most. There are age-related terms, such as juvenile fibroadenoma[108,114]; size-related terms, such as giant or massive fibroadenoma; and cellularity-related terms, such as fetal or cellular fibroadenoma.[114] When the cellularity is mainly epithelial and very florid, they have also been called *fibroadenomas with atypical epithelial hyperplasia*[108]; when the stroma is prominent, they have been designated *fibroadenomas with stromal cellularity*.[102] It is easy to imagine the difficulty one may encounter in selecting a name for the fibroadenoma that at the same time is very large, is hypercellular, and occurs in an adolescent, not an infrequent occurrence. Of course, the choice of term is not very important. What matters is to recognize that the lesion is a fibroadenoma and not to confuse it with virginal hypertrophy or—more cogently—phylloides tumor. The epithelial hypercellularity can be dismissed as clinically inconsequential (unless it has

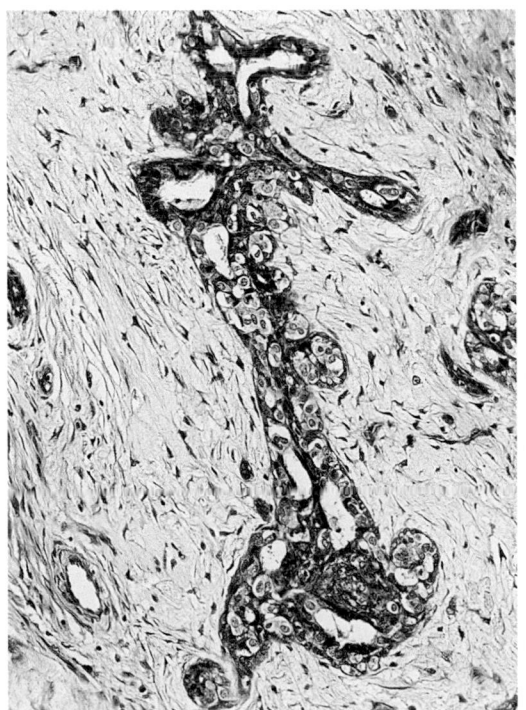
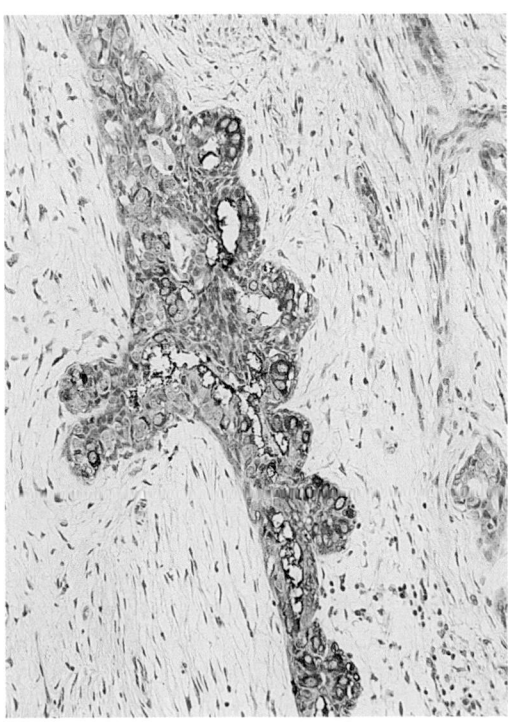

Fig. 20.14 A and **B**, Fibroadenoma with apocrine metaplasia. **A**, Hematoxylin–eosin section showing a prominent discontinuous layer of plump eosinophilic cells at the base of the gland. These should not be confused with neuroendocrine cells. **B**, Immunostain for GCDFP-15.

A   B

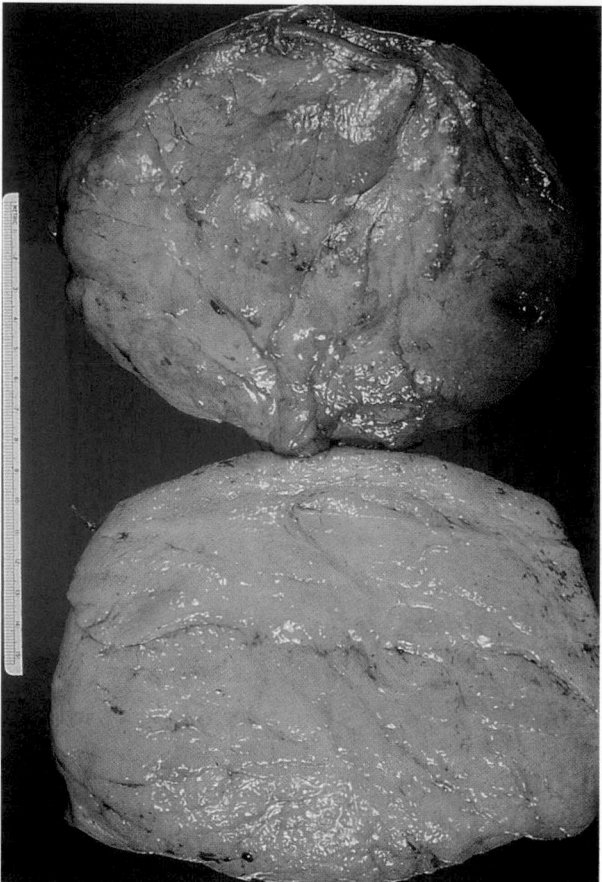

Fig. 20.15 Giant fibroadenoma occurring in an adolescent female.

the cytoarchitectural features of carcinoma). The stromal hypercellularity should be evaluated more carefully in terms of degree and atypicality; it is good to remember, however, that it is very rare for phylloides tumors to occur in young patients.

No differences have been found in the incidence, gross appearance, and microscopic configuration of fibroadenomas removed from patients taking oral contraceptives and those in control cases, except for the occasional formation of acini in the former.[101]

Ultrastructurally, the most interesting feature of fibroadenomas is the constant presence of a multilayered basal lamina around the epithelial and endothelial cells.[96,119] The stromal cells have features of fibroblasts.[115] Fibroadenomas contain progesterone receptors almost universally, and estrogen receptors in approximately one fourth of the cases.[118]

Cytogenetically, approximately 20% of fibroadenomas have been found to have clonal chromosome aberrations.[112] A lineage-restricted analysis has shown that these clonal aberrations are present in the stromal component, suggesting that fibroadenoma is a benign neoplasm of the specialized stroma of the breast with an accompanying epithelial component.[103] Rapidly growing

fibroadenomas in immunosuppressed individuals have been found to contain Epstein–Barr virus (EBV).[105]

A large-scale epidemiologic study has concluded that fibroadenoma represents a low long-term risk for breast carcinomas and that this risk is increased in women with complex fibroadenomas, ductal hyperplasias, or a family history of breast carcinoma.[99] This risk is not further increased if the fibroadenoma contains foci of atypical epithelial hyperplasia.[97]

Malignant transformation

Malignant changes in fibroadenomas are found in only 0.1% of cases.[120,124,125] They usually involve the epithelial component, and the large majority are in situ lesions[122,123,126] (Fig. 20.16). In some cases the malignant tumor is entirely within the confines of the fibroadenoma, but in others (see below) it involves the surrounding breast as well. The latter may simply represent extension into the fibroadenoma by a carcinoma originating elsewhere in the breast. In a series of 105 fibroadenomas containing carcinoma, 95% of the cases were in situ lesions, and lobular and ductal types occurred with equal frequency. Nine of ten fibroadenomas harboring an invasive carcinoma also contained carcinoma in situ (CIS), supporting the origin of the invasive component in the fibroadenoma. CIS within the fibroadenoma was associated with CIS in the surrounding breast in 21% of the cases. The prognosis for the entire group was excellent.[122]

Sarcomatous transformation of the stroma of a fibroadenoma is an even rarer phenomenon.[121] We have seen only one possible case in which a well-circumscribed small nodule had in some areas the appearance of an osteosarcoma, whereas in others it was composed of hyaline stroma enclosing slit-like glandular spaces, a configuration strongly reminiscent of an ancient fibroadenoma.

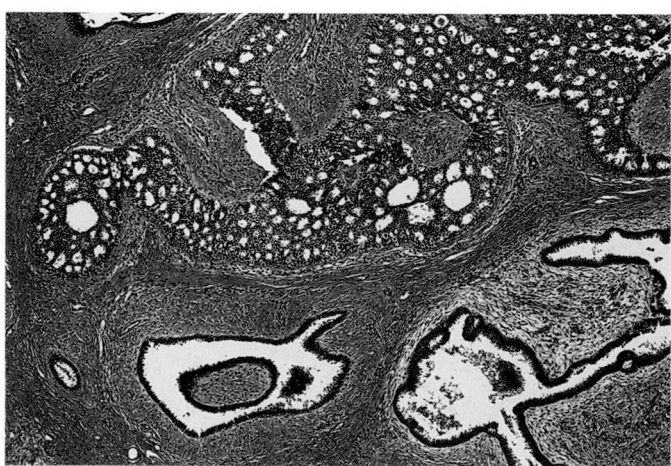

Fig. 20.16 Fibroadenoma with focal involvement by low-grade intraductal carcinoma.

Adenoma

Adenomas of the breast (exclusive of those having a salivary or sweat gland appearance and so-called "nipple adenoma," discussed on pp. 1827 and 1775, respectively) can be divided into the following categories.[129]

Tubular adenoma presents in young adults as a solitary, well-circumscribed, firm mass that is tan–yellow. Microscopically, a close packing of uniform small tubules lined by a single layer of epithelial cells and an attenuated layer of myoepithelial cells is seen; the stroma is characteristically sparse. Sometimes this pattern is seen combined with that of a fibroadenoma, suggesting that the two processes are closely related.[131] A type of *ductal adenoma with tubular features* has been found to be associated with Carney's syndrome. Microscopically, it presents as an encapsulated solid intraductal tumor composed of arrays of long, narrow tubules consisting of a dual population of epithelial and myoepithelial cells and a modest amount of fibrous tissue. Because of their complexity and cellularity, they can be mistaken for carcinoma.[128]

Lactating adenoma presents as a solitary or multiple freely movable breast mass during pregnancy or puerperium. The lesion is actually a localized focus of hyperplasia in the lactating breast, which may also develop in ectopic locations such as the axilla, chest wall, or vulva.[132] Grossly, the lesion is well circumscribed and lobulated. The cut surface is gray or tan, in contrast to the white color of fibroadenoma (Fig. 20.17). Necrotic changes are frequent.[130] Microscopically, proliferated glands are seen lined by actively secreting cuboidal cells (Fig. 20.18). This lesion should be distinguished from the

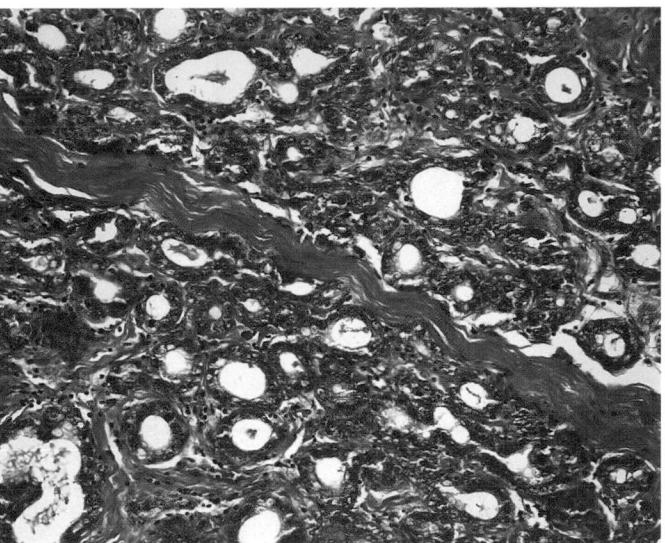

Fig. 20.18 So-called "lactating adenoma." The hyperplastic lobules show marked cytoplasmic vacuolization.

proliferative and secretory changes brought on by pregnancy in a preexisting fibroadenoma.[132]

Apocrine adenoma is a form of adenoma composed exclusively of apocrine cells. This exceptionally rare lesion should be distinguished from fibrocystic disease with focally prominent apocrine changes and from well-differentiated apocrine carcinoma.[127]

Intraductal papilloma

Intraductal papilloma of the breast occurs at an average age of 48 years. It can arise in large or small ducts; consequently, it can be identified grossly as a polypoid intraluminal mass or be found only on microscopic examination. The grossly visible papilloma can give rise to bloody nipple discharge and may be palpable in a subareolar location, but its diameter rarely exceeds 3 cm, a point of importance in the differential diagnosis with papillary carcinoma. The lesion is soft and fragile, and it may have areas of hemorrhage in it. The duct that contains the papilloma may be dilated (Fig. 20.19). Approximately 90% of cases are solitary. Multiple papillomas are seen in slightly younger patients, arise in smaller ducts, are usually not associated with nipple discharge, and are bilateral in one fourth of cases.

Microscopically, papillomas are complex, cellular, and often intricately arborescent (Fig. 20.20A). Features favoring benignancy in a papillary breast lesion are a well-developed stroma in the papillary folds, the presence of two cell types, normochromatic and often oval nuclei, scanty mitotic activity, the presence of apocrine metaplasia, and a lack of cribriform or trabecular patterns[139] (Fig. 20.20B). Necrosis is nearly always absent (but see below). The presence of a prominent myoepithelial cell

Fig. 20.17 Gross appearance of lactating adenoma. The mass has a distinct lobular configuration, yellowish color, and marked vascularization.

peripheral clefts, and the absence of a cribriform pattern. However, some minor differences between these lesions exist. One is secondary to the close interaction of the glandular epithelium of the mammary ducts and the squamous epithelium from the epidermis, resulting in formation of adenosquamous nests that may be incorrectly overinterpreted. The other difference is that otherwise typical nipple adenomas can exhibit small necrotic foci in the center of the proliferating ducts, a feature that in a more deeply located papillary/ductal hyperplastic lesion would be strongly suggestive of malignancy.[153]

A note of warning is in order. Just because an intraductal papillary lesion is located in or close to the nipple, it does not necessarily mean that it is a nipple adenoma and, therefore, benign. Intraductal papillary carcinomas and ordinary invasive ductal carcinomas can also occur in this location, some of them actually arising within a nipple adenoma.[149,150,153]

The treatment of uncomplicated nipple adenoma is local excision.[152,153]

Adenosis

The term adenosis can be applied to any hyperplastic process that primarily involves the glandular component of the breast; it should, therefore, be used with a qualifier in order to acquire a specific clinicopathologic connotation.

Blunt duct adenosis

In this very common alteration of the breast lobule, the involved components are lined by two cell types and show blunting of both the lateral outlines and the tips, hence the name originally proposed by Foote and Stewart in their epochal article.[156] There is an accompanying increase in the surrounding specialized connective tissue. Minor morphologic variations have been described as organoid, microcystic, and nonorganoid forms of the disease.[155] Blunt duct adenosis can be secondarily involved by duct hyperplasia.

Sclerosing adenosis

Sclerosing adenosis is the better known form of adenosis, mainly because of the high likelihood of it being misdiagnosed as carcinoma by the beginner. The average age of the patient is about 30 years. Grossly, it is small, has a disk-like and somewhat multinodular configuration, and cuts with increased resistance; in some cases, its overall gross appearance is quite reminiscent of invasive carcinoma.

Microscopically, the most important diagnostic feature of the lesion is its architecture as seen at very low magnification. The nodule retains a round or oval lobular configuration and is more cellular centrally than peripherally (Fig. 20.25). The elongated and compressed proliferating tubules are lined by two cell types that are themselves elongated along the tubular axis. The myoepithelial component predominates in some lesions and may even acquire spindle-shaped "myoid" features. Trabecular formations, pleomorphism, and necrosis are absent. The stroma is dense and may show foci of elastosis, although not as commonly as in radial scar or invasive carcinoma.

Morphologic variations of sclerosing adenosis that further complicate it are the very florid changes that accompany pregnancy, the presence of apocrine metaplasia (which is accompanied by nuclear and nucleolar enlargement), and the occasional occurrence of permeation of perineurial spaces[162] (Fig. 20.26) and the walls of veins[157] (Fig. 20.27).

The marked participation of myoepithelial cells in this process can be dramatically demonstrated with various immunohistochemical stains (smooth muscle actin, calponin, p63), and the presence of a basement membrane around the tubules with stains for laminin or type IV collagen.

The risk of subsequent invasive carcinoma in patients with sclerosing adenosis seems to be the same as for ordinary fibrocystic disease.[160] On rare occasions, the foci of sclerosing adenosis may be secondarily involved by lobular CIS[161] (Fig. 20.25D). In these cases, the distortion already present because of the sclerosing adenosis may result in a mistaken diagnosis of invasive lobular carcinoma. Fechner[159] pointed out that the differential diagnosis should be made at low power; the foci of sclerosing adenosis (with or without CIS) have dilated ductules peripherally and narrow ones centrally, whereas invasive lobular carcinoma has no overall organization. Immunohistochemical evaluation can be of assistance in the recognition of this complication.[158]

Nodular adenosis

Nodular adenosis combines features of blunt duct adenosis and sclerosing adenosis. The proliferating nodules are much more cellular than in blunt duct adenosis but better circumscribed than in sclerosing adenosis and without the fibrosis and distortion of the latter. Some authors regard nodular adenosis as the early nonsclerotic phase of sclerosing adenosis.

Adenosis tumor is simply a form of nodular or sclerosing adenosis of larger dimensions than usual, which therefore becomes palpable and more tumorlike clinically.[163] The term **florid adenosis** has been applied to lesions of nodular or sclerosing adenosis that are unduly cellular and proliferative. Neither of these two forms of adenosis represents a distinct entity.

Microglandular adenosis

Microglandular adenosis, also known as microglandular hyperplasia, is a rare form of adenosis in which small uni-

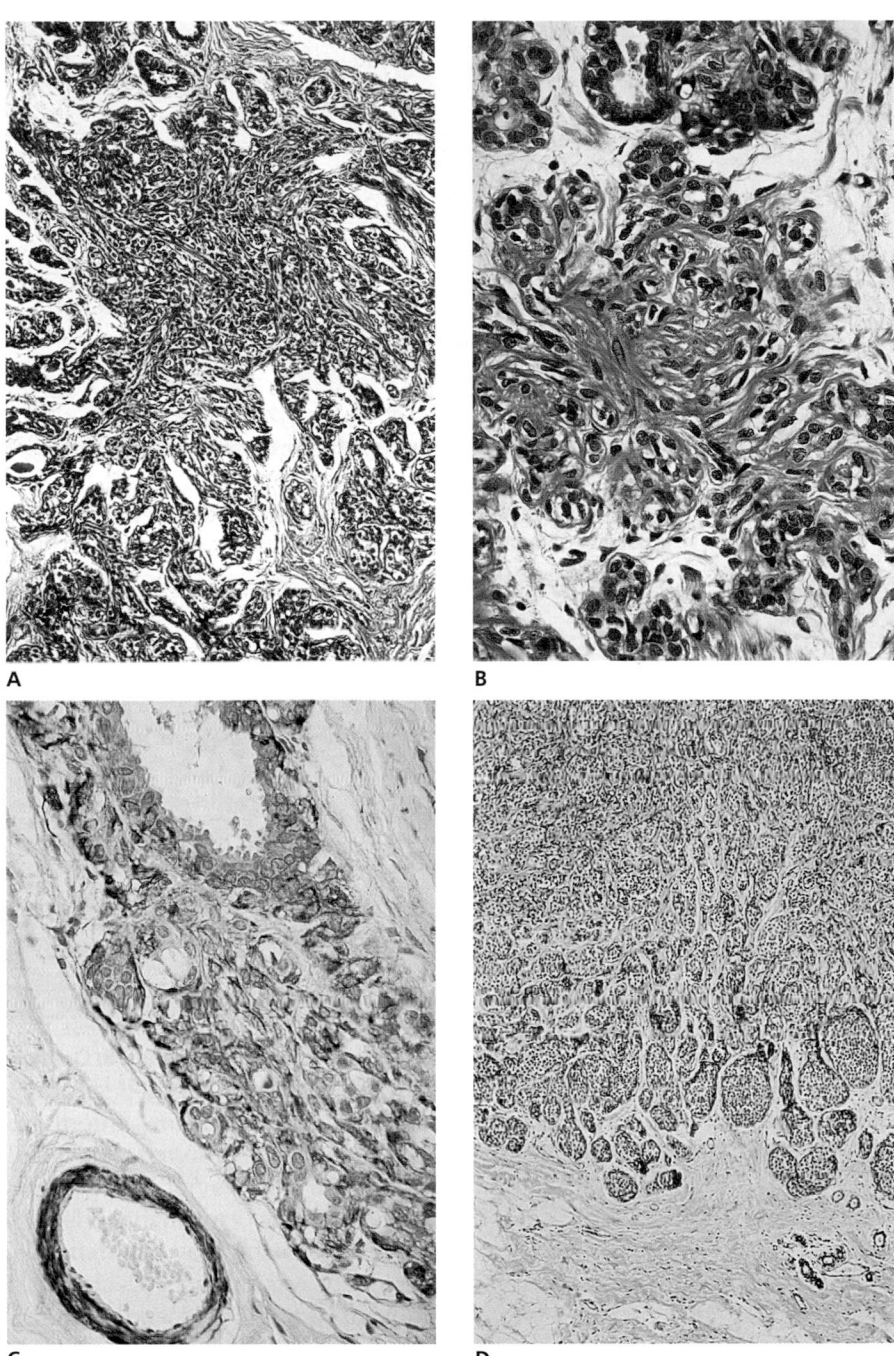

Fig. 20.25 A to **D**, Sclerosing adenosis. **A**, Low-power view. The lobular configuration of the lesion is obvious. **B**, Medium-power view. Note the spindle shape of the proliferating cells in the center of the lobule and the fibrillary quality of the cytoplasm, indicative of myoepithelial nature. **C**, Immunocytochemical stain for actin showing strong immunoreactivity in the myoepithelial cell component. **D**, Sclerosing adenosis with lobular carcinoma in situ. Note the regularity of the edge and absence of infiltrative features. (**D**, Courtesy of Dr. Robert E. Fechner, Charlottesville, VA)

form glands with open lumina containing an eosinophilic secretion are distributed in an irregular fashion within fibrous tissue or fat[164,174,178] (Fig. 20.28). There is no trabecular bar formation. The glands are lined by a single layer of small uniform cuboidal or flat cells with vacuolated or granular cytoplasm, lacking apocrine-type "snouts." In contrast to other forms of adenosis; the myoepithelial layer may be absent.[164,172] However, there is a thick basement membrane that can be well appreciated immunohistochemically and ultrastructurally.[178] The stroma may be hyalinized but is not cellular or elastotic. The main differential diagnosis of this lesion is with tubular carci-

noma.[164] Microglandular adenosis is an indolent condition and should be treated conservatively; however, enough cases have been reported in continuity with carcinoma to suggest that it may evolve into malignancy with a frequency greater than the other forms of adenosis described in this section.[168,170,175] Interestingly, a high percentage of these carcinomas in one series have been interpreted as being of the adenoid cystic type.[163a] Actually, this frequently occurring spatial relationship with an easily recognizable carcinoma, and the fact that microglandular adenosis is the only benign epithelial breast lesion devoid of myoepithelial cells, makes one

ance of the lining is indistinguishable from the lining of apocrine sweat glands. The individual cells have an abundant granular acidophilic cytoplasm, often containing supranuclear vacuoles and yellow–brown pigment, some of which contains iron. The apical portion of the cytoplasm shows the typical "apocrine snout." The nucleus is medium sized, and the nucleolus can be very prominent. Periodic acid–Schiff (PAS) stain shows a crescent of coarse glycolipid granules on the luminal side, and immunohistochemical stain for GCDFP-15 shows strong cytoplasmic reactivity.[194] Transitional or poorly developed phases of this process exist, which have been termed *partial* or *incomplete* apocrine metaplasia. In some of these cases, the apocrine metaplasia has atypical cytologic features and is accompanied by sclerosis. There is no evidence that patients with *atypical apocrine metaplasia* as thus defined are at an increased risk for the development of carcinoma.[184]

3 **Fibrosis.** This change is often present, but its degree varies markedly. It is probably an event secondary to the rupture of the cysts and it may proceed to hyalinization. The terms *fibrous disease* of the breast and *fibrous mastopathy* have been used by some authors to designate a breast condition in which the main change seems to be a more or less localized stromal fibrosis[196]; it is not clear whether this is related to fibrocystic disease or even whether it represents a distinct clinicopathologic entity, although the latter seems more likely.

4 **Calcification.** This is less common than in duct ectasia or carcinoma; it tends to have a coarse, highly irregular pattern. Chemically, it may be composed of calcium phosphate or calcium oxalate. On mammography, the latter is of an amorphous, low-to-medium density (in contrast to the medium-to-high density of calcium phosphate) and is nearly always associated with benign disease.[203] Calcium phosphate deposition is usually easily detectable on H&E sections and is highlighted by the von Kossa stain, which may be necessary to identify minute foci.[200] However, calcium oxalate crystals can be easily missed with these techniques; they are better seen with polarized lenses (because of their birefringent quality) or after silver nitrate–rubeanic acid with 5% acetic acid pretreatment.[201]

5 **Chronic inflammation.** This is another common but secondary feature of fibrocystic disease. It is not related to infection but rather to the rupture of cysts, with release of secretion in the stroma. Lymphocytes, plasma cells, and foamy histiocytes are the predominant elements. Fibrocystic disease with intense chronic inflammation should not be confused with mammary duct ectasia (see p. 1767).

6 **Epithelial hyperplasia.** This is the most important and troublesome component of fibrocystic disease

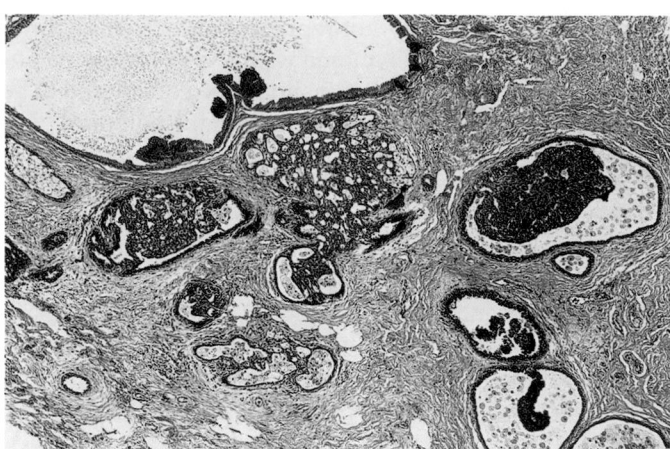

Fig. 20.30 Fibrocystic changes, including cystic dilatation, apocrine metaplasia, florid ductal hyperplasia, and fibrosis.

(Fig. 20.30). It is also the most significant because of its possible relationship to carcinoma and the fact that it is responsible for most difficulties in the differential diagnosis between fibrocystic disease and carcinoma. In most cases it is only of minimal degree, as confirmed by the fact that the degree of cell proliferation as measured by thymidine labeling is generally not significantly higher in fibrocystic disease than in the normal breast.[195] Epithelial hyperplasia is discussed in detail in the next section.

7 **Fibroadenomatoid change.** This is the least common abnormality seen as a component of fibrocystic disease. The stromal proliferation and slit-like epithelial formations result in a picture reminiscent of fibroadenoma but lacking the sharp circumscription of the latter (see p. 1769).

Ductal and lobular hyperplasia

Epithelial hyperplasia of **ductal** type, when florid, has been traditionally designated as papillomatosis, particularly in the United States. Azzopardi[204] has rightly objected to the term on grounds that in most instances the lesion does not form true papillae. He prefers the term epitheliosis, but this has not been widely accepted. Perhaps the more general term epithelial hyperplasia is the best compromise, followed by an indication of its degree: *mild* (when made up of three or four epithelial cells in thickness), *moderate to florid* (when more pronounced), and *atypical* (see following discussion). In the most proliferative cases, the entire lumen can be filled by the proliferation. Some forms of hyperplasia have true papillary qualities. The features that we have found most helpful in the identification of the benign nature of the proliferation are the following:

1 Nuclei that are oval (rather than round, except when cut transversely), normochromatic (rather than hyperchromatic), and with slight overlap;

small, single, indistinct nucleoli; scanty or no mitotic activity (Fig. 20.31).

2 Cytoplasm that is acidophilic and finely granular rather than pale and homogeneous.

3 Indistinct cytoplasmic borders, so that the nuclei seem to lie in a syncytial mass rather than within sharply outlined cell membranes.

4 Streaming effect, induced by the oval cells being vaguely arranged in parallel bundles (Fig. 20.32).

5 "Tufts" and "mounds" projecting into the lumen.

6 Presence of peripheral elongated clefts, bound on one side by a single layer of basally located cells and on the other by a solid intraluminal formation; sometimes this cleft spans almost the entirety of the circumference, with the retracted solid ball of epithelial cells hanging from the wall like the vascular tuft of a renal glomerulus (Fig. 20.33). The intratubular lumina of ductal hyperplasia tend to be irregular in size, shape (elongated rather than round), and location (predominating at the periphery) as opposed to regular in all three parameters as seen in the cribriform pattern of intraductal carcinoma.

7 Presence of irregularly shaped bridges connecting opposite portions of the wall. The cells in these bridges have oval nuclei arranged parallel to the long axis of the bridge (Fig. 20.34). Their appearance is very different from that seen in the rigid trabecular bars and Roman bridges of intraductal carcinoma.

8 Complete or incomplete apocrine metaplasia; cytoplasmic blebbing.

9 Presence of myoepithelial cells, whether scattered or as a continuous row, and clear, acidophilic, or elongated and smooth muscle-like ("myoid").

10 Presence of foamy macrophages, both in the lumen and intimately admixed with the proliferating epithelial cells.[206]

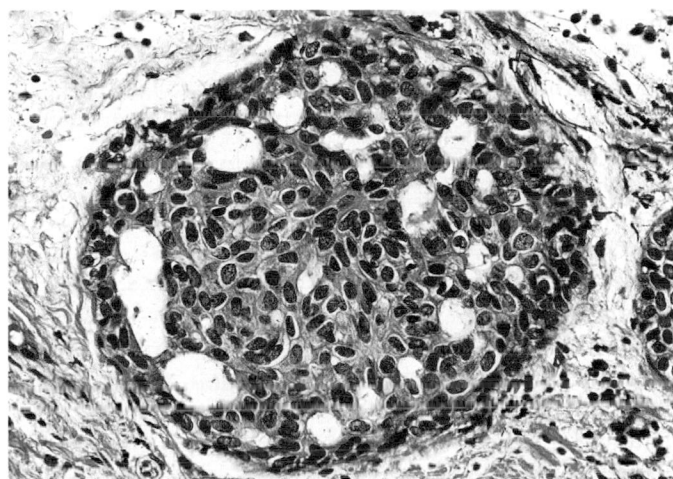

Fig. 20.31 Photomicrograph demonstrating florid ductal hyperplasia. There is no evidence of necrosis, and individual cells are well supported by their stroma. A prominent cleft has formed between a solid intraluminal proliferation and an outer epithelial row. This feature is usually indicative of a benign condition.

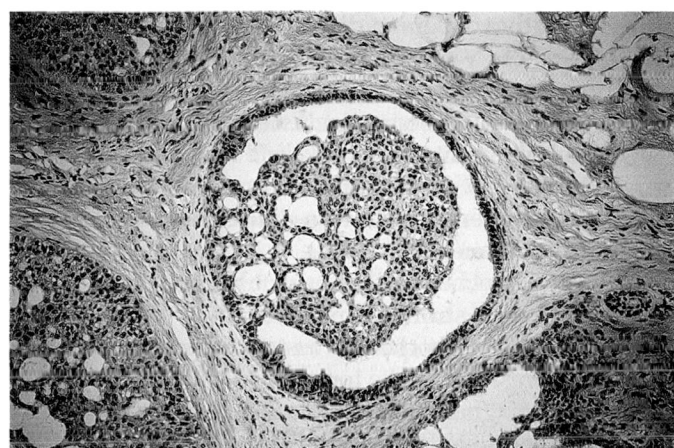

Fig. 20.33 Structure resembling a renal glomerulus in florid ductal hyperplasia.

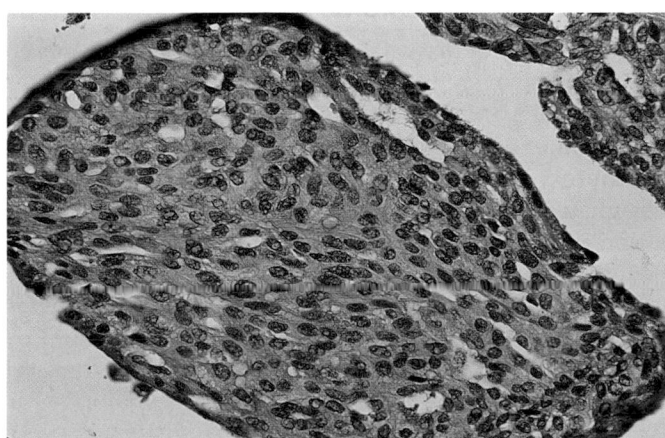

Fig. 20.32 Florid ductal hyperplasia. Note the oval shape of the nuclei and the parallel arrangement, resulting in a "streaming" effect.

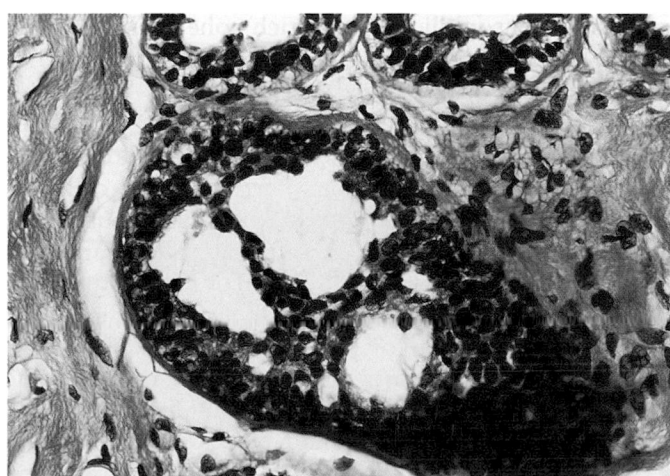

Fig. 20.34 Ductal hyperplasia showing irregularly shaped ridges connecting opposite portions of the wall. Note the fact that the oval nuclei are arranged parallel to the long axis of the ridge.

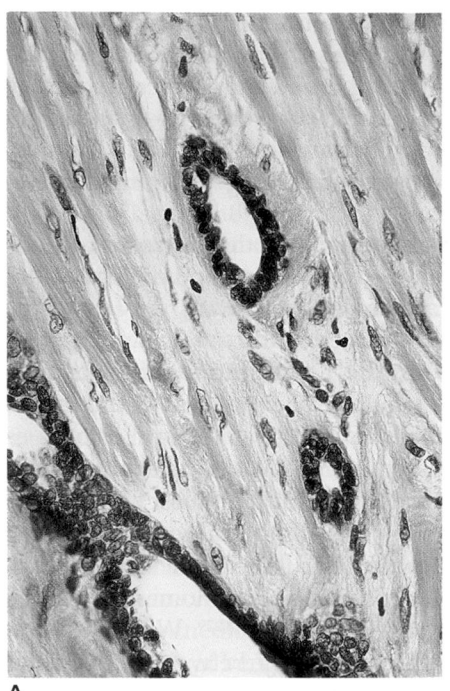
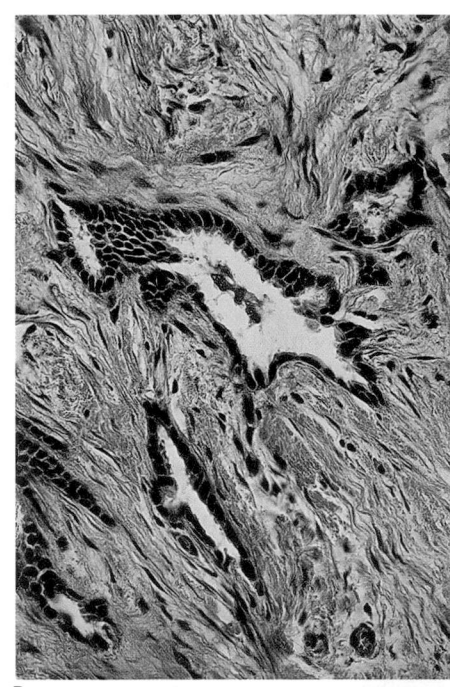

A **B**

Fig. 20.39 A, Benign ductular structures entrapped in radial scar. Note their regular contour and the hypocellular hyaline quality of the stroma. **B**, Tubular carcinoma shown for comparison. Note the angulated shape of the glands and the desmoplastic stroma.

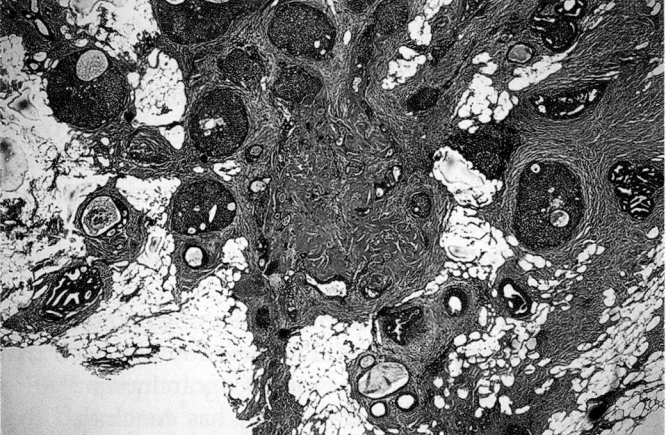
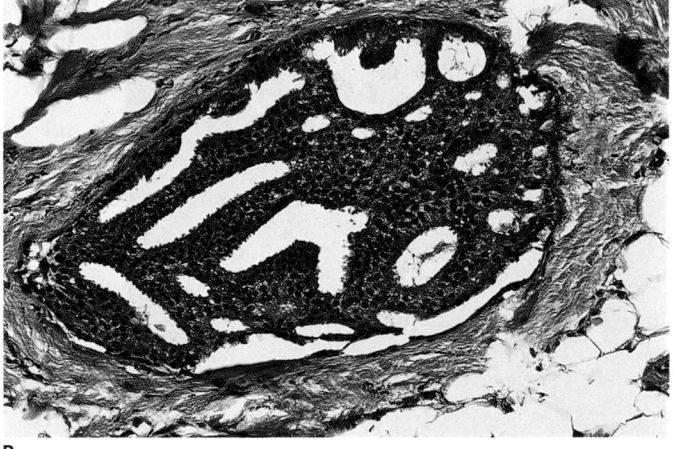

A **B**

Fig. 20.40 A and **B**, Radial scar with associated low-grade intraductal carcinoma.

is almost twice that of the women without scars, regardless of the histologic type of benign breast disease.[226] The accepted treatment of radial scar is conservative excision and follow-up.[219]

Atypical ductal and lobular hyperplasia

As already mentioned, there is a wide range in the degree of epithelial proliferation in fibrocystic disease. It has been postulated that there is a correlation between the degree of this proliferation and the likelihood of subsequent development of invasive carcinoma, and various attempts have been made to quantify both the degree of the change and the magnitude of the risk.[260] The most ambitious and successful attempts are those of the Page–Dupont team,[243,251,252] who have proposed the terms atypical ductal hyperplasia (ADH) and atypical lobular hyperplasia (ALH) for proliferative lesions in which

some but not all of the features of intraductal carcinoma or lobular CIS, respectively, are present (Figs 20.41 and 20.42). Using these criteria in a retrospective study, they diagnosed ADH and/or ALH in 3.6% of the cases and concluded that these patients had a risk of invasive breast carcinoma that was four to five times that of the general population (i.e., about half of that of ductal or lobular CIS). Largely on the basis of this study, a group convened by the College of American Pathologists[241] recommended grouping patients with "fibrocystic disease" in the following three categories:

I   No or mild hyperplasia: no increased risk for subsequent invasive carcinoma.

II Moderate or florid hyperplasia: 1.5 to 2 times the risk.

III Atypical ductal or lobular hyperplasia: 5 times the risk.

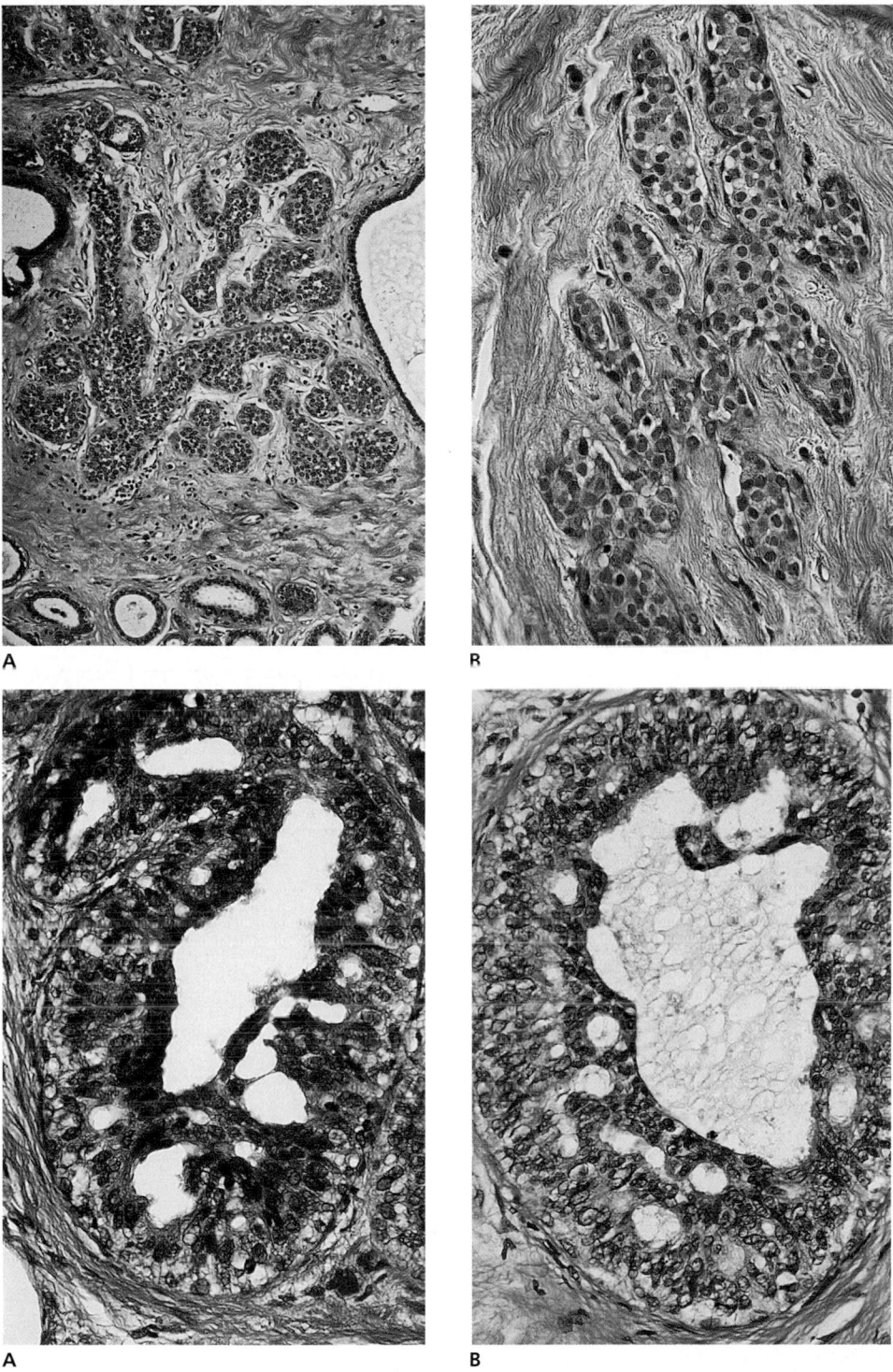

Fig. 20.41 A and **B**, Two different breast lesions diagnosed as atypical lobular hyperplasia by four experts in breast pathology. There is lobular enlargement and proliferation, but some lumina are preserved, and there is only minimal distention of individual units.

Fig. 20.42 A and **B**, Two different breast lesions diagnosed as atypical ductal hyperplasia by two experts in breast pathology. There is marked epithelial proliferation in structures of ductal type associated with atypia, but they were felt not to fulfill criteria for carcinoma in situ.

For completeness and comparison purposes, Page[250] added to this list the following category:

IV Ductal or lobular CIS: 8 to 10 times the risk.

This document was updated and refined in 1998.[244]

The Page–Dupont studies represent an extremely important contribution to the study of fibrocystic disease vis-à-vis breast carcinoma and have had a great impact on clinicians and pathologists. However, the terms ADH and ALH need to be defined in a more precise way, additional tests of inter- and intra-observer reproducibility need to be carried out, and the results obtained need to be confirmed in other populations. Several early studies have shown an unacceptably high level of observer variability in estimating the type and degree of epithelial hyperplasia,[237,238,255] although there is evidence that strict adherence to a standardized set of criteria will lead to more consistent results.[256]

The currently accepted definition of ADH is that of a lesion with cytologic (monomorphic cells with ovoid to rounded nuclei) and architectural (micropapillae, tufts, fronds, bridges, solid and cribriform patterns) features indistinguishable from those of low-grade DCIS, but (1) intimately admixed with usual ductal hyperplasia, and/or (2) showing only partial involvement of the TDLU. Quantitative requirements have been proposed (to measure <2 mm in aggregate or to be present in two spaces), but these have not been agreed upon[253,254,259] (Fig. 20.43).

A further variation on the theme is the lesion variously called *flat epithelial atypia*, low-grade (monomorphic) clinging carcinoma, atypical cystic lobules, and atypical columnar change.[240,245,247,249] This is characterized by replacement of the mature epithelial cells by a single or stratified layer of mildly atypical cells, accompanied by distension of the affected TDLUs (Fig. 20.44). Apical snouts can be prominent.[244a] Estrogen receptor alpha is usually strongly positive (especially in premenopausal women), and there is an increased expression of MIB-1.[242a] Its biologic significance is not very clear, but it is

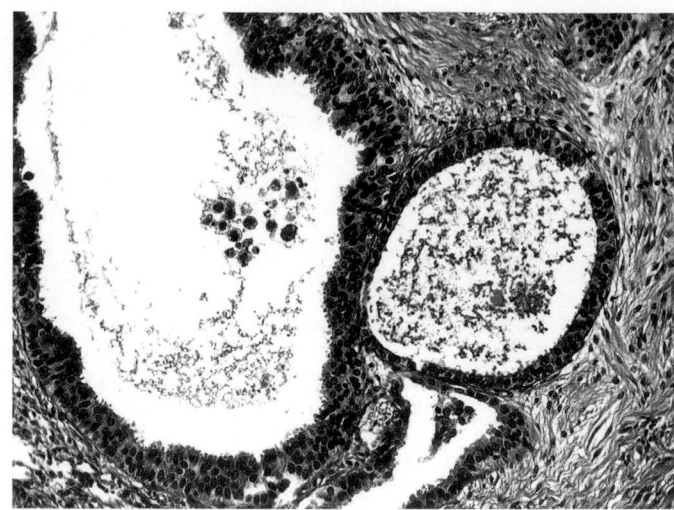

Fig. 20.44 Flat epithelial atypia. The spaces are dilated and lined by columnar epithelium showing scanty atypia.

generally thought to be similar to that of the conventional form of ADH (if one can call anything in this field "conventional").

Special techniques such as morphometry, DNA ploidy studies, immunohistochemical stains and genetic molecular tests have so far failed to establish a consistent separation between the various groups.[242,246,248]

Since an element of subjectivity in the microscopic interpretation persists and is unlikely to be completely eliminated, and in view of the fact that the current terminology suggests a sharper separation than that which the evidence seems to indicate, we proposed that consideration be given to adopting a terminology such as mammary intraepithelial neoplasia (MIN) of either ductal or lobular type, followed by a grading system[255] in accordance with the trends in many other sites, such as cervix, prostate (PIN), and gastrointestinal tract. Tavassoli and her group have enthusiastically accepted the idea and further developed it, according to the following scheme[239,257,258]:

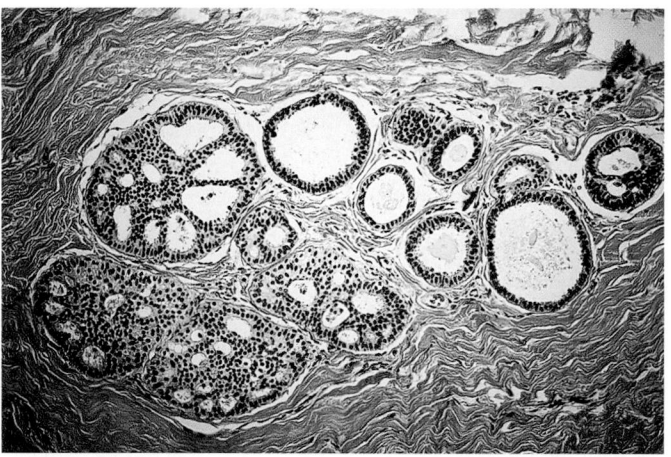

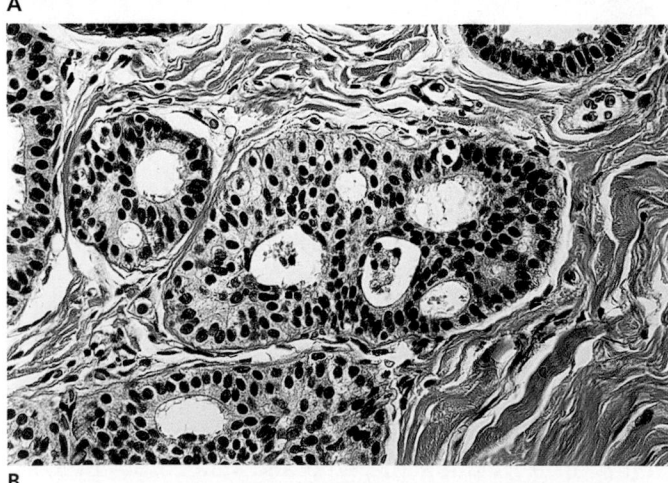

Fig. 20.43 A and **B,** Proliferative ductal lesion diagnosed as atypical ductal hyperplasia on account of the cytoarchitectural features and small size.

- Ductal intraepithelial neoplasia (DIN)
  - 1a (corresponding to usual ductal hyperplasia)
  - 1b (corresponding to flat epithelial atypia)
  - 1c (corresponding to ADH and small Grade I DCIS)
  - 2 (corresponding to larger Grade I DCIS and Grade II DCIS)
  - 3 (corresponding to Grade III DCIS)
- Lobular intraepithelial neoplasia (LIN), for the lesions in the ALH/lobular CIS spectrum (also subdivided into three categories: LIN1, LIN2, and LIN3)
- Mammary intraepithelial neoplasia (MIN), for the proliferative epithelial lesions not easily placed into either a ductal or a lobular category.

Tavassoli's proposal has obvious merits, and it is possible that a modified version of it will eventually be adopted. However, this is not likely to be any time soon. In all fairness, most of the arguments that have been raised against its adoption in its present format apply to other organ sites just as well, yet they have not prevented a terminology change taking place in those sites. There is one issue, however, that deserves serious consideration. The DIN numerical terminology above presented implies a continuum of changes, which may or may not exist. The alternative view, masterfully articulated by Azzopardi[236] and currently supported by many experts, is that proliferative breast disease can be divided into two distinct categories: the "usual" hyperplasia and the intraductal carcinoma. In this scheme, ADH and perhaps flat epithelial atypia are not the link or intermediate step between the two extremes but rather a "minor" form of intraductal carcinoma. If this were indeed the situation, linking these conditions in a graded system that presupposes a nosologic unity might be unwarranted and misleading.

This is the rationale behind the modification to the DIN scheme that was reluctantly agreed upon by the committee in charge of writing the section on Intraductal Proliferative lesions for the new edition of the WHO book on Tumors of the Breast and Female Genital Organs; The scheme that was finally adopted is the following:

Traditional terminology	DIN terminology
Usual ductal hyperplasia	(No DIN equivalent)
Flat epithelial atypia	DIN1A
Atypical ductal hyperplasia	DIN1B
DCIS grade I	DIN1C
DCIS grade II	DIN2
DCIS grade III	DIN3

This may well be a conceptual improvement over the original DIN scheme shown on the preceding page, but now people should be very careful when reading articles or pathology reports in which the DIN system has been used as to which of the two DIN systems the authors are referring to. Perhaps it may be prudent to wait for further developments (possibly coming from the molecular genetic field) before switching to one or the other of the DIN nomenclatures.

Relationship with carcinoma and treatment

A possible relationship between fibrocystic disease and breast carcinoma has been suggested over the years on the basis of the following evidence:

1   The time-honored observation that breasts excised for carcinoma usually also exhibit changes of fibrocystic disease[272] and that this fibrocystic disease seems to have a greater degree of epithelial proliferation than the one found in a population without carcinoma.[269]
2   The fact that retrospectively studied breast biopsies in patients who subsequently developed invasive carcinoma often show very florid and even atypical proliferative changes rather than the usual pattern of fibrocystic disease.[271,280]
3   The parallelism in the incidence of breast carcinoma and benign proliferative breast lesions in the various populations,[278] including the fact that kindreds sus-ceptible to breast carcinoma also inherit a predisposition to proliferative breast disease.[279]
4   The presence of karyotypic and molecular alterations in benign proliferative breast lesions that parallel those of breast carcinoma.[261,273,274,282,283]
5   The claim that patients with fibrocystic disease treated conservatively and subjected to long-term follow-up are found to develop invasive carcinoma at a higher rate than a control population.[264] Parenthetically, the breast carcinomas that develop in patients with a previous diagnosis of benign breast disease do not differ depending on the histologic category of the latter.[270]

A quantitative leap has been made by the realization that it is not the fibrocystic disease per se but rather the presence and type of proliferative epithelial disease that determines the risk for subsequent carcinoma and that this risk seems to range from one to five times that of the control population, as indicated in the section on atypical and ductal hyperplasia.[268,275] This fact, which has been confirmed in independent studies,[262,263,281] indicates that evaluation of epithelial hyperplasia is an important gauge in deciding on the best approach to these patients.[276] Naturally, several other factors need to be taken into consideration, including the length of time since the diagnosis of atypical hyperplasia was made.[265-267,277a] In general, a conservative approach to fibrocystic disease (i.e., local excision and follow-up) is amply justified.[277] However, extensive recurrent disease may justify the performance of a larger excision in selected circumstances, particularly if accompanied by atypical ductal hyperplasia, a strong family history of breast carcinoma, and/or the presence of germline BRCA1 or BRCA2 mutations.

Carcinoma

General features

Incidence

Breast carcinoma is the most common malignant tumor and the leading cause of carcinoma death in women, with more than 1,000,000 cases occurring worldwide annually.[287] In the United States, each year approximately 100,000 new cases are diagnosed and approximately 30,000 patients die from the disease. The incidence is high in North America and northern Europe (91.4 new cases per 100,000 women/year), intermediate in southern European and Latin American countries, and low in most Asian and African countries. In the United States, there has been a sharp increase in the detection of breast carcinoma, largely due to the widespread use of mammography.[289] Most of these cases have been localized, measuring less than 2 cm in diameter and/or in situ.[284] Until recently, this increase in the number of smaller (and presumably earlier) cases did not translate into an improved survival rate. As a matter of fact, the mortality rate for breast carcinoma changed very little from the 1930s to the early 1990s.[284] However, in some regions of the world (North America, western Europe, and Australia) breast cancer mortality is finally beginning to fall, presumably because of the combined action of earlier diagnosis and improved therapy.[285,288] Unfortunately, this is not true for countries such as Japan, Costa Rica, and Singapore, in which mortality continues to rise.[286]

Risk factors

Several risk factors for the development of breast carcinoma have been established, whereas many others remain questionable.[290] It has been proposed that the common denominator for most of these factors is strong and/or prolonged estrogen stimulation operating on a genetically susceptible background.[305]

1 Country of birth. This has already been touched upon in the previous paragraph.
2 Family history. Women who have a first-degree relative with breast carcinoma have a risk two or three times that of the general population, a risk further increased if the relative was affected at an early age and/or had bilateral disease.[315] The aspects related to the discovery of the genes responsible for a predisposition to breast carcinoma are discussed in the next section.
3 Menstrual and reproductive history. Increased risk is correlated with early menarche, nulliparity, late age at first birth, and late menopause.[304,307] Breast carcinoma is rare in women who have been castrated; oophorectomy before 35 years of age reduces the risk to one third. Women who have their first child before the age of 18 years have only one third the risk of those whose first child is delayed until age 30.[317] A reduction in the risk of breast carcinoma among premenopausal women who have lactated has been documented, but no such effect was detected among postmenopausal women.[306] Breast carcinoma risk is increased in postmenopausal women with a hyperandrogenic plasma hormone profile.[302]
4 Fibrocystic disease and epithelial hyperplasia. The controversial relationship between these changes and breast carcinoma is discussed in the preceding section.
5 Exogenous estrogens. In some older series, there has been an overall risk increase (2.5-fold),[303,309] whereas in others an increased risk (2- to 9-fold) was observed only in patients with a previous diagnosis of fibrocystic disease.[301] More recently, a large cohort study and a large case-control study have provided strong evidence for a greater increase in breast cancer risk in women using hormone replacement therapy than in those using estrogens alone.[310,311] Even more recently, highly publicized studies have added to the growing body of evidence that recent long-term use of hormone replacement therapy is associated with an increased risk of breast carcinoma, particularly of the lobular type.[294,296] In December 2002, the hormone estrogen was declared a known human carcinogen by the National Toxicology Program.

6 Contraceptive agents. The various epidemiologic studies that have been done in this regard have shown no increased risk,[325] or at most a very low increase among young long-term users.[310,339] The tumors that have developed in this population have not differed qualitatively from those seen in control cases.[297,298]
7 Ionizing radiation. An increased risk of breast carcinoma has been documented with exposure to ionizing radiation, particularly if this exposure occurred at the time of breast development [299,300,313,314]
8 Breast augmentation. Breast carcinomas (mainly of in situ types) are sometimes detected in women who have undergone augmentation mammoplasty.[295] However, the re-analysis of a previously published linkage study has shown that the incidence of breast carcinoma in that cohort was neither higher nor lower than that among the general population.[291,293]
9 Others. A peculiar association between breast carcinoma and meningioma has been repeatedly noted.[292] Even more peculiar is that fact that sometimes the breast carcinoma is found to metastasize within the meningioma. Patients with ataxia–telangiectasia syndrome and with Cowden's syndrome have an excess risk of breast cancer.[312,316]

Genetic predisposition

An epochal event in the study of breast carcinoma was the discovery of two genes which, when affected by a germline mutation, are responsible for approximately two thirds of familial breast carcinomas, or roughly 5% of all cases.[327] These are *BRCA1*, located on chromosome 17q, and *BRCA2*, located on chromosome 13q12-13.[321,322,330] *BRCA1* alterations also predispose to carcinoma of ovary and possibly fallopian tube (see Chapter 19).[330a] Mutations of this gene are present in approximately 2% of Ashkenazi Jews; it has been estimated that the risk for breast carcinoma among carriers is approximately 56% by the age of 70 years.[329]

The product of *BRCA1* is a cell cycle-regulated phosphoprotein[328] that can be detected immunohistochemically.[325] Analysis of the breast carcinomas developing in carriers of *BRCA1* mutations has shown a higher percentage of tumors with medullary features, i.e., tumors that tend to be of high grade, mitotically very active, with a syncytial growth pattern, pushing margins, confluent necrosis, and negative estrogen receptor status.[319,320,324]

The finding of a positive test for the mutation can lead to an agonizing decision on the part of the affected individual, the main choices being close follow-up and prophylactic mastectomy.[323,326]

Location

The location of breast carcinoma is usually indicated in relation to the breast quadrants. Approximately 50% are in the upper outer quadrant, 15% in the upper inner quadrant, 10% in the lower outer quadrant, 5% in the lower inner quadrant, 17% in the central region (within 1 cm of the areola), and 3% are diffuse (massive or multifocal). The marked difference in the carcinoma frequency depending on the quadrant, surprising at first, becomes easily explainable when one realizes that it matches closely the amount of breast parenchyma in each quadrant.

Several studies have documented the peculiar fact that breast carcinoma is slightly more frequent in the left breast than in the right. In one recent series, the excess for the left side was 13%.[331]

Multicentricity

Multicentricity (as defined by presence of carcinoma in a breast quadrant other than the one containing the dominant mass) was detected by Fisher et al.[335] in 121 (13.4%) of 904 cases of invasive carcinomas; one third of the smaller foci were invasive and the rest were in situ. Multicentricity was more common in lobular than in ductal carcinomas. As expected, a higher incidence of multicentricity was reported in studies in which whole organ preparations were examined by radiography and light microscopy.[336] Theoretically, multiple breast carcinoma can result from either intramammary spread of a single lesion or from independent events.[333,334] It is probable that both mechanisms operate in the individual case, as suggested by clonal studies.[337,338,338a] If aggregate diameters are used, unifocal and multifocal carcinomas are similar with respect to the frequency of regional lymph node involvement,[332] but a recent study showed that multicentric tumors are associated with a lower survival rate than unicentric tumors of the same aggregate volume.[331a]

Bilaterality

The chance that a patient with invasive breast carcinoma will develop a carcinoma in the contralateral breast is about five times that of the general population, and it is even higher if there is a family history of breast carcinoma.[339,341,342] In cases of lobular carcinoma, the figure can be as high as 25% to 50%.

The use of adjuvant chemotherapy significantly decreases the risk of metachronous contralateral breast carcinoma.[340] It is doubtful whether a biopsy of the opposite breast should be taken routinely in patients with breast carcinoma; it seems more logical to limit this practice only to those patients in whom an abnormality is suspected on clinical or mammographic grounds or to those with types of carcinoma for which the incidence of bilaterality is particularly high.[343]

Diagnosis

Clinical examination

Clinical examination, particularly palpation, is the time-honored method for the detection and evaluation of breast disease. It remains an extremely useful and practical technique, whether carried out by the physician or by the patient herself. However, both its sensitivity and discriminatory power are limited. Only 60% of the tumors detected by mammography are palpable. The clinical impression is incorrect in approximately 15% of the cases thought to be benign and approximately 10% of those thought to be malignant. The clinical evaluation of axillary lymph nodes is also fraught with error. Nodes clinically thought to be positive will be found free of metastases microscopically in 15% of cases.

Mammography

The widespread use of mammography has radically changed the diagnostic approach to breast cancer.[345,347a,354] Extremely small tumors (1 to 2 mm) can be detected with this technique, which relies primarily on the presence of calcification. The incidence of calcification in breast carcinoma is approximately 50% to 60%, and the incidence in benign breast disease is 20%.[346,355] There are also important qualitative differences in the appearance of the calcification. Mammographic findings in the United States are now universally reported using the Breast Imaging Reporting and Data System (BI-RADS).[344]

It should be kept in mind that a negative mammogram does not rule out the possibility of the presence of carcinoma, since approximately 20% of palpable tumors are not detectable with this technique. The incidence of false positivity is in the neighborhood of 1%.

The proper handling of breast lesions detected by mammography requires close cooperation between radiologist, surgeon, and pathologist.[346,348,357,360] Once the radiologist identifies the abnormal area on mammography, he should provide the surgeon with a "map" showing the relative position of the suspicious area within the breast. Once the appropriate area is excised, the cephalad and lateral margins should be marked by sutures, and an x-ray study should be taken of the specimen. If no lesion is seen, the surgeon should obtain additional tissue. If the abnormal area is present in the specimen, this can be accurately located by slicing the specimen, identifying the slices with a lead number, taking another x-ray study, and selecting for frozen sections the slice (and the specific area within the slice) containing the abnormal area. The whole procedure takes no more than 15 minutes and is well worth the small delay. Otherwise, small carcinomas can be entirely missed.[352] The highest yield is obtained from histologic examination of the areas with radiographic calcification and a fibrous parenchyma.[356]

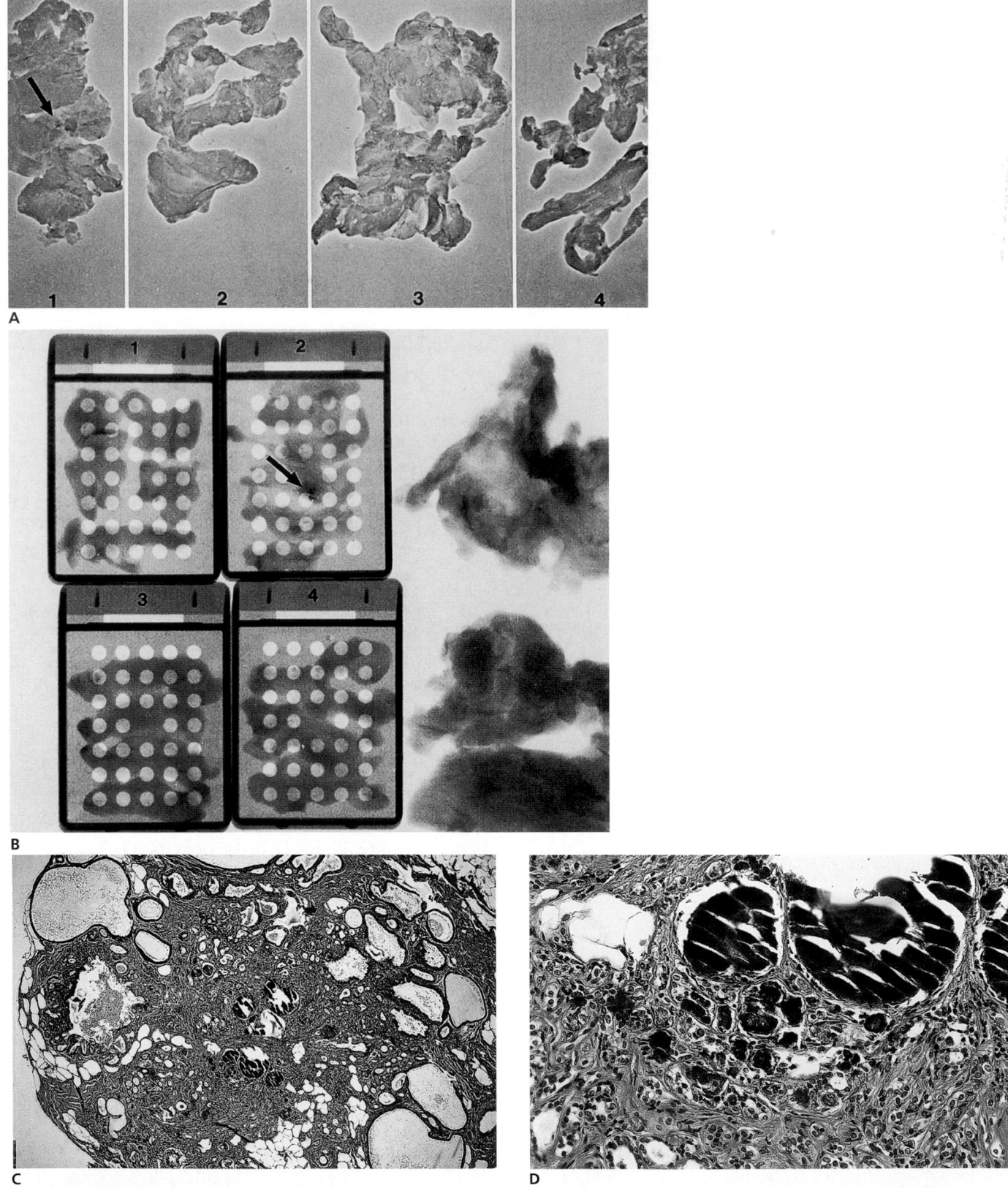

Fig. 20.45 A to **D**, Demonstration of the use of specimen radiography. All photographs were taken with Polaroid camera and film. A mammographically detected breast lesion was excised. **A**, The specimen was sliced into four portions and a radiograph taken. A pattern of calcification identical to that seen in original mammography was detected in slice 1 (arrow). **B**, The portion corresponding to this area of calcification was further divided into four fragments, and all four were embedded in paraffin. A radiograph of the cassettes shows that the suspicious area is in cassette 2 (arrow). The remainder of the slide (two fragments at right) shows no calcification. **C** and **D**, Low- and high-power views of the corresponding microscopic specimen.

X-ray studies can even be taken of the paraffin blocks to document the fact that the area seen in the mammogram has been embedded (Fig. 20.45). An important source of discrepancy between mammographic and microscopic findings is represented by calcium oxalate crystals, which are easily identified radiographically but easily missed on histologic examination.[350]

It should be obvious from the preceding comments that every attempt should be made to identify in the microscopic slide the area regarded by the radiologist as "suspicious" of carcinoma. However, if this is satisfactorily accomplished and the pathologist still fails to find carcinoma, neither he nor the radiologist should be overly surprised. Only 20% of the lesions labeled "suspicious" mammographically are malignant, and the large majority of these are carcinomas in situ. McDivitt[353] estimated that the chance of the pathologist finding an invasive carcinoma in a biopsy from a nonpalpable lesion that was interpreted "suspicious" by mammography is less than 2%. On the other hand, "nonpalpable" should not be viewed as synonymous with inconsequential. In a series of 558 patients with nonpalpable invasive carcinomas detected by mammography and subjected to axillary dissection, 27% had at least one positive node.[359]

Wolfe[361] has divided breasts into four groups on the basis of their mammographic appearance, which he believes correlates with the risk for development of carcinoma. This correlation might well exist, but it is perplexing that, if this is the case, no correlation seems to exist between these four patterns and the types of histologic alteration.[347]

The available information suggests that nuclear magnetic resonance is not likely to replace mammography as the imaging modality of choice, although contrast-enhanced techniques have rendered it more informative and potentially more useful.[358] It is said to be more sensitive for the detection of multicentric carcinoma.[351] Breast ultrasonography has emerged as a valuable examination tool, particularly for determining whether a mass lesion is cystic or solid.[349]

Where adopted for screening purposes, mammography is commonly done on a biennial basis from the age of 50 years onwards.

Cytology

The two methods that have been used to obtain cytologic material from breast lesions are aspiration of nipple secretion and aspiration of the lesion with a fine needle.

Nipple secretion aspiration cytology is, in our opinion, of limited use, whether for the diagnosis of a clinically or mammographically detectable breast lesion or for screening purposes. Some carcinomas will undoubtedly be found, but the number of false-positive results is so high as to render this technique of only marginal value. As a matter of fact, its use as a screening procedure may have a deleterious effect because a negative cytologic diagnosis may give a false sense of security and delay recognition of the carcinoma.

The situation with fine needle aspiration is quite different, as already shown in the early attempts at Memorial Sloan-Kettering Cancer Center in the 1930s (Fig. 20.46). There is no longer any question that in experienced hands the technique is highly reliable[363,370,375,380] (Fig. 20.47). The average sensitivity is approximately 87%, the specificity close to 100%, the predictive value of a positive diagnosis nearly 100%, and the predictive value of a negative diagnosis between 60% and 90%.[367,374,378,384,387] As expected, most benign lesions misinterpreted cytologically as possibly malignant belong to the fibrocystic disease category with marked epithelial proliferation.[365,369] The cytologic distinction between ADH and intraductal carcinoma has been attempted, both in mammographically detected lesions and to screen women with a family history of breast carcinoma.[362,373,381,383] Since the differential diagnosis between these two conditions is based not only on cytologic but also on architectural criteria as seen on tissue sections, it is not surprising to find that such attempts have not been very successful.[368,381] Along similar lines, it is generally not possible to distinguish between in situ and invasive ductal carcinoma on fine needle aspiration biopsy.[362]

The most significant variables in the accuracy of the procedure are size of the lesion and proficiency of the individual performing the aspiration.[364] Material from

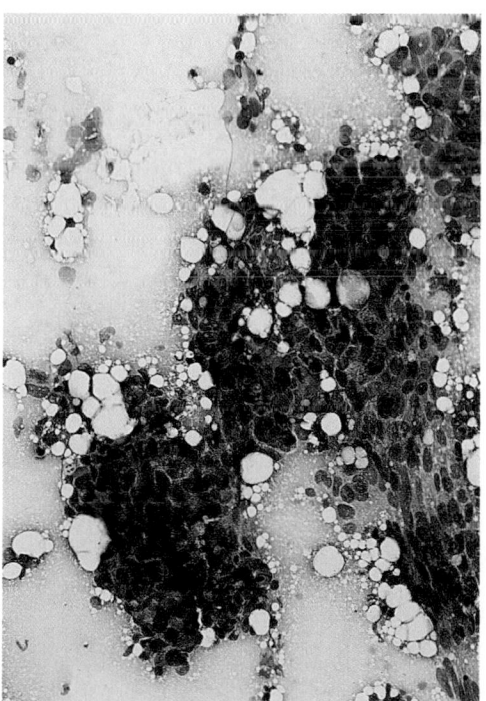

Fig. 20.46 Specimen from a fine needle aspiration (FNA) biopsy performed at Memorial Sloan-Kettering Cancer Center in 1935. This was diagnosed as breast carcinoma and followed by the performance of a mastectomy, which confirmed the cytologic interpretation. (Courtesy of Dr. Maureen Zakowski, Memorial Sloan-Kettering Cancer Center)

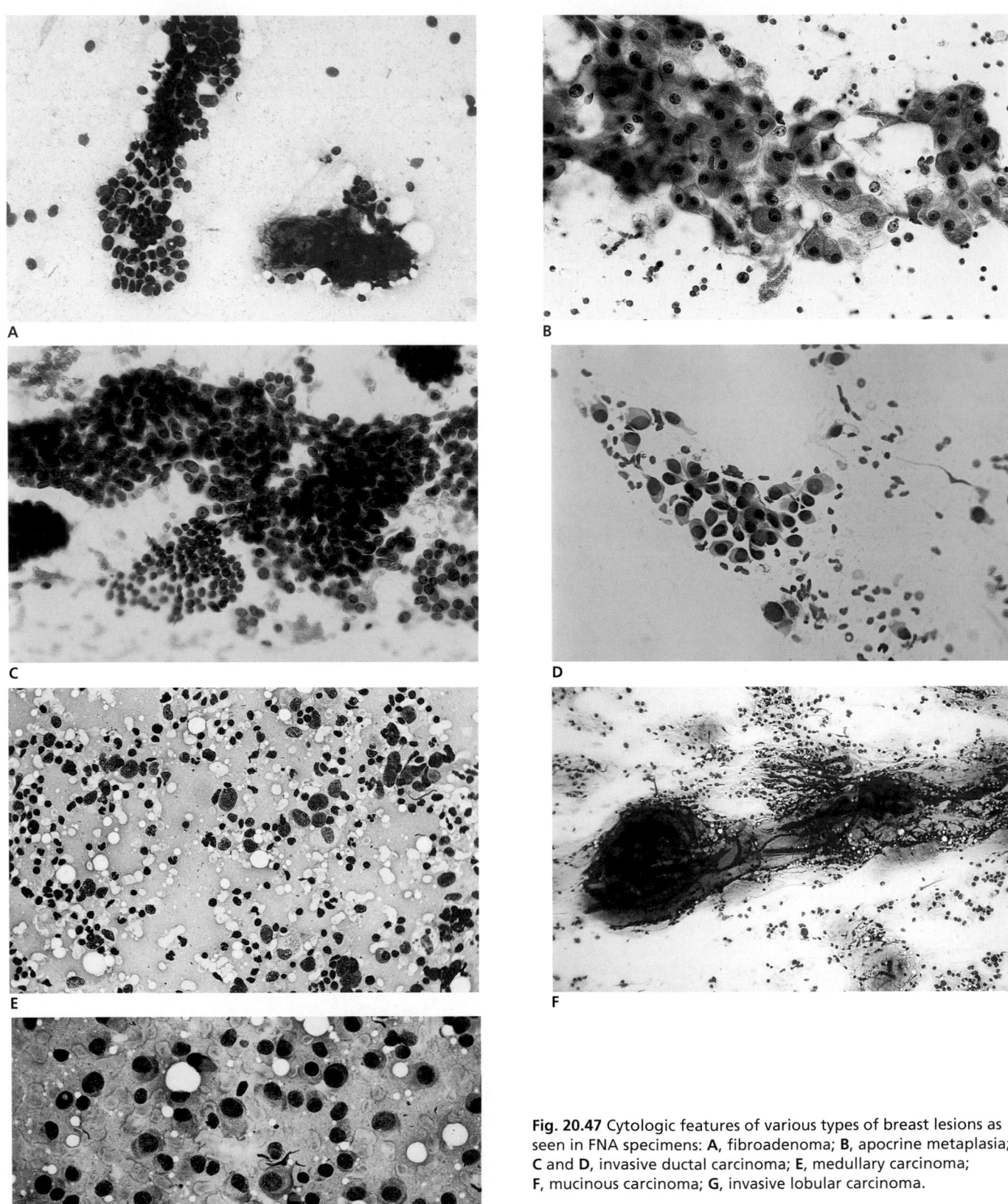

Fig. 20.47 Cytologic features of various types of breast lesions as seen in FNA specimens: **A**, fibroadenoma; **B**, apocrine metaplasia; **C** and **D**, invasive ductal carcinoma; **E**, medullary carcinoma; **F**, mucinous carcinoma; **G**, invasive lobular carcinoma.

fine needle aspiration is also suitable for hormone receptor determination,[376,379] kinetic studies,[377] and oncoprotein expression.[372]

Fine needle aspiration is less than ideal for some types of breast carcinoma. These include those associated with very extensive fibrosis, intraductal carcinoma, tubular and cribriform carcinoma, and, in general, the very small tumors. As Kline et al.[370] wisely pointed out, this technique should be used to supplement, and not to compete with, histologic examination. Most importantly, it should always be remembered that negative or inconclusive cytologic findings are not to be regarded as a definitive diagnosis if there is clinical suspicion of a malignant neoplasm.[366]

The performance of the fine needle aspiration procedures may lead to mechanical displacement of epithelium, hemorrhage, necrosis, and other changes.[371,385,386] The former is particularly troublesome, because it can mimic stromal and vascular invasion.[382,385] The frequency of this complication is probably related to the type of needle used and the skill of the operator.

Needle core biopsy

In recent years, the use of needle core biopsy for the nonoperative diagnosis of breast carcinoma has been generally favored over the alternative of fine needle aspiration,[395] some strong dissenters notwithstanding.[388] This is based on the fact that core biopsy allows evaluation of both cytologic *and* architectural features, that it may provide a definitive diagnosis of *invasive* carcinoma on one hand and a benign lesion (such as fibroadenoma) on the other, and that it allows for easier identification of microcalcifications. Furthermore, it reduces the number of inadequate samples and requires a lesser degree of diagnostic expertise. In order to obtain maximum information from the procedure, the pathologist should be provided with complete clinical information, including radiographic signs and the site of the biopsies. In cases with microcalcifications, the specimens should be x-rayed and submitted separately in case additional levels are needed.[389] The specimens should be fixed for a minimum of 6 hours and a minimum of three to five levels should be obtained initially, at least for the screen-detected cases, with additional levels and immunostains performed if necessary.[397]

A definite diagnosis on the basis of a core biopsy is possible in over 90% of cases. A reporting system has been recommended for these specimens, which takes into account the equivocal cases that will exist no matter how experienced and skillful the observer.[391a,401a] As a matter of fact, one should be a little concerned about the judgment of the pathologist who claims to be able to make an unequivocal diagnosis of benignancy or malignancy in every case. The categories, as currently used by the UK National Health Service Screening Programme[394] are the following:

- *Normal tissue/inadequate sample.* A comment as to the presence of normal breast tissue, microcalcification, and the adequacy of the sample should be made.
- *Benign lesions.* This applies to fibroadenoma, fibrocystic changes, sclerosing adenosis, usual ductal hyperplasia, some papillary lesions, and inflammatory changes.
- *Lesion of uncertain malignant potential.* To be used for conditions such as sclerosing ductal lesions (including radial scar), some papillary lesions, atypical ductal hyperplasia, and lobular neoplasia.
- *Suspicious of malignancy.* To be used for lesions that are suggestive but not entirely diagnostic of malignancy either because of scantiness of material or artifactual changes.
- *Malignant.* To be used when unequivocal changes of malignancy are present. Whenever possible, it should be stated whether the carcinoma is in situ or invasive. If in situ, the risk of finding invasive carcinoma in the excision specimen can be estimated from the microscopic features and amount of tumor present.[398]

All cases showing in situ or invasive carcinoma of either ductal or lobular type should undergo excision, and this also applies to cases diagnosed as ADH or "suspicious of malignancy."[399,401] The approach toward the other lesions (including negative biopsies and some cases of LCIS) should be personalized and requires experience, good judgment, and close interaction between the pathologist, the surgeon, and the radiologist.[393,396,400]

Well-known pitfalls of the needle core procedure include missing infiltrating lobular carcinoma (when made up of lymphocyte-like cells) and radiation-induced histiocytic proliferation (which may simulate residual carcinoma).[392]

Complications of the needle core procedure include hemorrhage, reactive spindle cell nodules, and epidermal inclusion cysts.[390,391] A different type of complication, already mentioned in connection with the fine needle aspiration procedure (but more likely with the core technique) is the mechanical displacement of tumor cells into the stroma or even inside the vessel lumina[402,403] (Fig. 20.48). It is doubtful whether the latter is of clinical significance.

Open biopsy and frozen section

Open biopsies from breast lesions are usually of excisional type when the tumor measures 2.5 cm or less and of incisional type for larger neoplasms. Performance of an open biopsy followed by frozen section and mastectomy if the diagnosis is carcinoma has been the standard approach for breast nodules for decades. The procedure is highly accurate; the false-positive rate is essentially zero, the false-negative rate is less than 1%, and the number of deferred diagnoses is less than 5%.[404,407] The greatest difficulties in frozen section are found with the evaluation of papillary proliferations, and it has therefore been routine policy to defer the diagnosis on these lesions until the permanent sections are available.

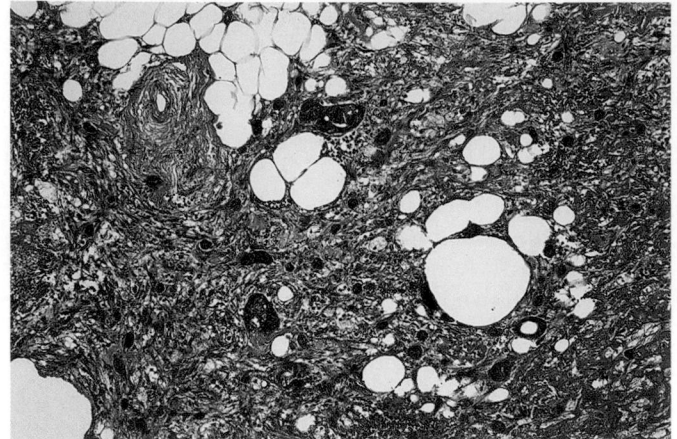

A

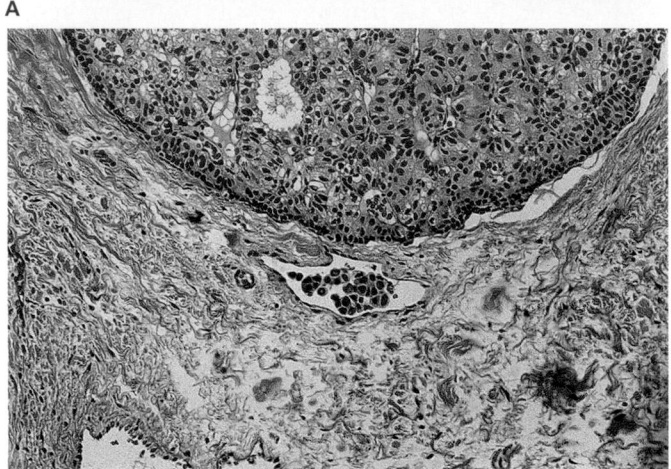

B

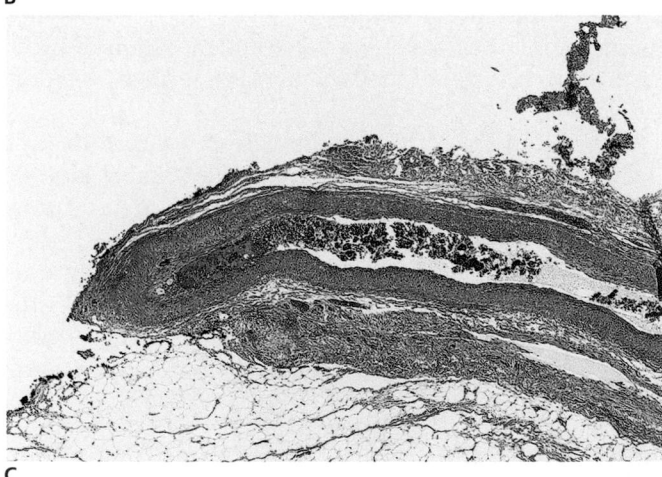

C

Fig. 20.48 Biopsy-induced artifactual changes: **A**, tumor cells along needle tract; **B**, tumor cells in lumen of lymph vessel; **C**, tumor cells in lumen of artery.

Much has changed in recent years concerning the indications for frozen section as a result of several factors: the wish to discuss with the patient the therapeutic options after the diagnosis has been made; the realization that a delay of days or weeks between biopsy and mastectomy does not affect prognosis; the increasing alternative use of needle core biopsy and fine needle aspiration biopsy; and the fact that an increasingly large number of cases

involve small, nonpalpable lesions. Indeed, the need for performing this time-honored procedure has been increasingly questioned, one of the most powerful reasons being that the final interpretation of the lesion may become difficult or even impossible if the entire specimen has been frozen.[408,412] The following recommendations have been made depending on the setting[406,407,409,410]:

1. A palpable mass, which usually measures over 1 cm in diameter, provides ample tissue for frozen section, permanent section, and hormone receptors. Therefore, not much harm results from doing the frozen section even if the medical indication is questionable.

2. A nonpalpable mass identified on a mammogram is often less than 1.0 cm in diameter. This *should not* be submitted for frozen section. If it turns out to be an invasive carcinoma, hormone receptor determinations can be done immunohistochemically on the paraffin-embedded material.

3. A biopsy carried out only for calcifications without a mass *should not* be frozen. Instead it should be examined by specimen radiography as already indicated (see p. 1789).

It should be added here that intraoperative cytologic examination can be very useful and that this procedure is used routinely by some authors in conjunction with (or instead of) the frozen section procedure. When interpreted by experienced individuals, the smears are as accurate as the frozen sections.[405]

Finally, frozen sections have been used effectively in evaluating reexcision lumpectomy margins.[411]

Microscopic types

The two key determinations to make in the morphologic study of breast carcinoma are (1) whether the tumor is confined to the epithelial component of the organ (in situ carcinoma) or has invaded the stroma (invasive carcinoma), and (2) whether it is of ductal or lobular type. The first criterion, whose prognostic significance far outweighs that of the second, is self-explanatory, but it may be appropriate to elaborate on the second. The term ductal carcinoma may be taken to imply that the tumor is either arising from or involving a duct, and an analogous assumption could be made about lobular carcinoma in relation to the lobule. The evidence obtained from the classic study of Wellings et al.[416] and several others indicates instead that both tumor types (and, for that matter, most benign proliferative breast diseases) arise from the same segment of the mammary gland (i.e., the TDLU). As far as location is concerned, it is certainly true that many ductal carcinomas preferentially involve structures with the appearance of ducts and that most lobular carcinomas preferentially involve lobules. However, numerous exceptions in both directions exist. It has been hypothesized that these cases represent—respectively—ductal carcinomas with secondary extension into lobules ("lobular cancerization"), or lobular carcinomas with secondary extension into ducts, but there is no convincing indication that this is indeed the case.[413–415] Be that as it may, it should be made clear that it is the type of tumor as defined by cytoarchitectural features that establishes its placement into one of these two categories rather than its precise location within the breast. Therefore, it may be more accurate and less confusing to refer to these tumors as ductal type and lobular type, respectively. For the sake of brevity and tradition, the conventional nomenclature of ductal and lobular will be used instead in this chapter.

In situ carcinoma

Ductal carcinoma in situ (DCIS)

Several morphologic variants of DCIS exist: papillary, comedocarcinoma, solid, cribriform, micropapillary, clinging, and cystic hypersecretory. Papillary carcinoma is a very distinct type, thought to arise from large ducts. The others, believed to originate in the TDLU (although often extending to larger ducts) have been traditionally divided into the high-grade comedocarcinoma (characterized by large pleomorphic cells associated with necrosis) and the low-grade solid/cribriform/micropapillary group (composed of smaller uniform cells unassociated with necrosis), with the "clinging" lesions being included in either of these two categories depending on their cytologic features.[418,423] In recent times, the trend has been to regard these tumors as part of a continuum and to divide them in a three-grade system largely on the basis of *cytologic* criteria. According to this scheme, classic comedocarcinoma becomes grade 3 DCIS, classic solid/cribriform/micropapillary lesions become grade 1 DCIS, and those showing intermediate cytologic features are reported as grade 2 DCIS. These criteria apply whether the proliferation is solid, cribriform, micropapillary, or flat (i.e., "clinging"). They also apply independently of the presence or absence of necrosis and/or calcification,[422] although there is a relationship between the presence and type of calcification and the type of CIS.[421] As many as six different grading systems have been proposed, representing minor variations on the theme[417,419,420,424,425] (Table 20.1). In one study, the highest reproducibility was obtained with Holland's classification.[426]

Comedocarcinoma

Comedocarcinoma may reach a relatively large size and become palpable. In one series, 28% were over 5 cm in diameter and another 33% were between 2 and 5 cm.[443] Over half of these tumors are centrally located, whereas this is true for less than 20% of invasive tumors.[441,455] The quoted incidence of multicentricity is approximately 33%,[431,438] and the incidence of bilaterality is 10%.[431]

Table 20.1 Assignment of points for mitotic counts according to the field area, using several microscopes

	Leitz Ortholux	Microscope Nikon Labophot	Leitz Diaplan
Objective	×25	×40	×40
Field diameter (mm)	0.59	0.44	0.63
Field area (mm²)	0.274	0.152	0.312
Mitotic count			
1 point	0–9	0–5	0–11
2 points	10–19	6–10	12–22
3 points	>20	>11	>23

Grossly, the tumor presents as a cluster of thick-walled ducts with normal breast parenchyma between them. When these ducts are compressed, plugs of necrotic tumor reminiscent grossly of those seen in comedones extrude from them, hence the name comedocarcinoma. If the duct walls are not thickened, the tumor may not be apparent grossly. Microscopically, the ducts show a solid growth of large pleomorphic tumor cells accompanied by generally abundant mitotic activity and lacking connective tissue support. Necrosis is always present and constitutes an important diagnostic sign, whether in the form of a large central focus or of individual tumor cells (Fig. 20.49). The mean diameter of the ducts containing necrosis is significantly larger than for those lacking this feature, suggesting the existence of a "hypoxic compartment" in these tumors.[442] Coarse calcification often supervenes in these necrotic areas, and this can be identified by mammography. Myoepithelial cells are usually absent in ducts involved by comedocarcinoma, but their presence in no way invalidates the diagnosis[434] (Fig. 20.50). The stroma around the involved ducts shows a characteristic concentric fibrosis accompanied by a mild-to-moderate mononuclear inflammatory reaction.

Tumors with the classical comedocarcinoma appearance (or the grade 3 DCIS of other classifications) are

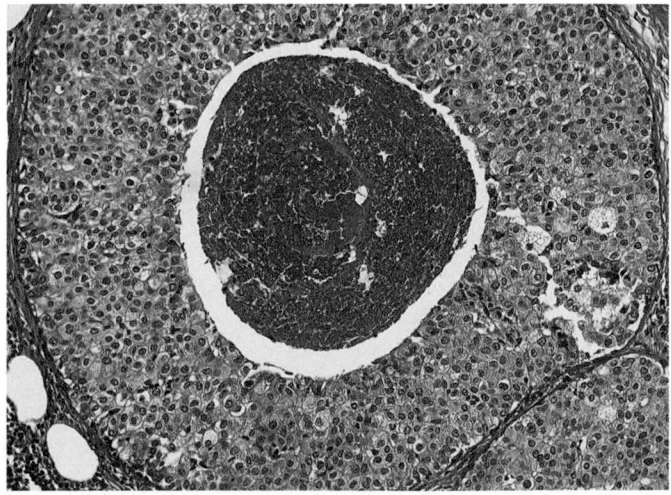

Fig. 20.49 In situ ductal carcinoma with comedo-type necrosis.

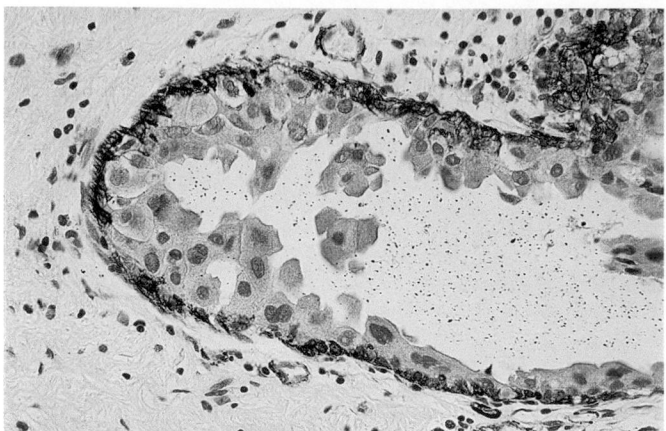

Fig. 20.50 Preservation of a myoepithelial cell layer in high-grade intraductal carcinoma. (Smooth muscle actin immunostain)

characterized by aneuploidy, negativity for hormone receptors, metallothionein expression, c-*erb*B-2 overexpression, presence of P-cadherin, and a high frequency of *p53* mutations.[427–430,435,437,439,440,446,448,449]

Once the diagnosis of comedocarcinoma has been established, two additional important determinations need to be made. The first is the degree of intraductal spread, which in some cases may be very extensive and even reach the nipple, resulting in Paget's disease.[444,445] The other is to search for areas of definite stromal invasion and, if these are present, to estimate the relative amounts of in situ and invasive components[453] (Fig. 20.51). The term *extensive intraductal carcinoma* (EIC) has been proposed for tumors in which the intraductal component comprises 25% or more of the area encompassed by the infiltrating tumor and is also present in the surrounding breast tissue.[452] Interestingly, no correlation exists between the size of the tumor and the degree of invasion present in it.[453] Lagios et al.[438] found occult foci of invasion in 21% of their cases. Even if no definite invasion is detected in the sections examined, the possibility always exists with comedocarcinoma—more than with any other form of DCIS—that a minute focus of invasion is present somewhere in the specimen.[432] This may explain the fact that some patients have axillary lymph node metastases in the absence of an identifiable invasive component.[438a,450] Another possible explanation is that the comedocarcinomatous areas themselves are actually invasive in a "pushing" fashion, as suggested by the large size they sometimes attain, the ultrastructural demonstration of basement membrane defects,[447] the prominent fibrosis associated with stromal metachromasia usually found around them,[451] and the fact that neural invasion has been exceptionally demonstrated in them.[436,454] Although we find this hypothesis appealing at the conceptual level, for practical purposes we would advise designating these tumors as invasive only when irregular ("destructive") infiltration of the stroma is detected in them. Rarely, these foci of invasion are accompanied by a granulomatous tissue response.[433]

(In situ) papillary carcinoma

Papillary carcinoma makes up only a small percentage of breast carcinomas. Grossly, it may present as a well-circumscribed mass, or it may ramify within several ducts to involve an entire breast segment. In the variant known as *intracystic papillary carcinoma*, the tumor appears as a mural nodule within a large cystic space supposedly representing a dilated duct[457,459] (Fig. 20.52). The microscopic criteria for the diagnosis must be strict, because most papillary breast lesions are benign. The most important differential features were listed in the classic study by Kraus and Neubecker[458] and further elaborated (and somewhat modified) by Azzopardi.[456] As a group, papillary carcinomas occur in an older age group and are larger than papillomas. Microscopically, features favoring carcinoma are (paradoxically) uniformity in size and shape of the epithelial cells (whether round, oval, or spindle, the latter arranged perpendicularly to the duct axis), presence of one cell type only (i.e., lack of myoepithelial cells), nuclear hyperchromasia and high nucleocytoplasmic ratio, high mitotic activity, lack of

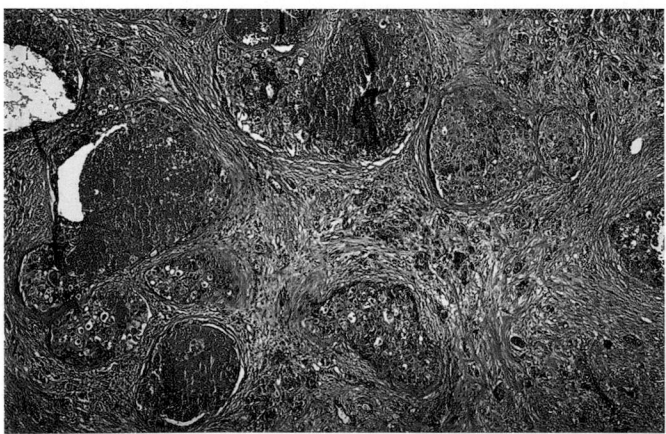

Fig. 20.51 Invasive ductal carcinoma associated with extensive intraductal carcinoma component.

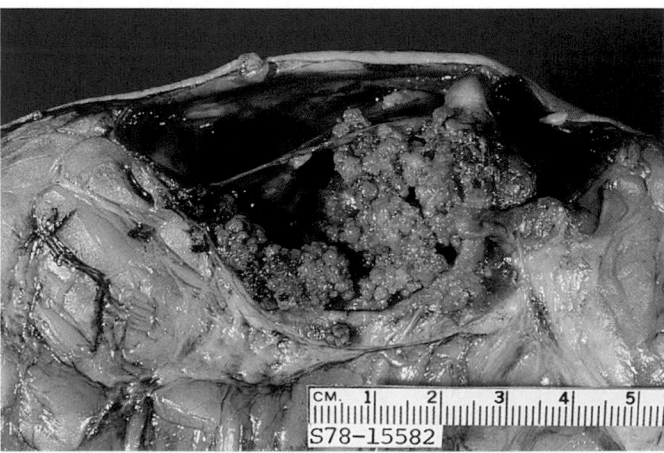

Fig. 20.52 Intracystic carcinoma of the breast. The papillary configuration of the tumor is already grossly evident.

apocrine metaplasia, cribriform and trabecular patterns, scanty or absent stroma, and lack of benign proliferative disease in the adjacent breast[456,458] (Fig. 20.53). It should be realized that no feature among those just listed is sufficient in itself to establish the distinction between papilloma and papillary carcinoma. The amount of stroma present could serve as an example of this fact; although scanty or nil in most papillary carcinomas, it may be bulky and well developed in others, prompting a mistaken diagnosis of benignancy (Fig. 20.54). Another diagnostic trap is provided by the presence of scattered large pale eosinophilic cells (known as clear or globoid cells) concentrated in the basilar portion, which can be mistaken for myoepithelial cells[458,460] (Fig. 20.55). In general, special techniques are not of great help in this differential diagnosis, except for those documenting the presence or absence of myoepithelial cells.[460]

It seems likely that most papillary carcinomas arise de novo. In some cases, however, there is convincing morphologic and immunohistochemical evidence for the carcinoma arising inside multiple papillomas.[461]

Papillary carcinoma with invasion is discussed on p. 1809.

A very unusual type of papillary carcinoma has been described composed of transitional-type epithelium, to be distinguished from the conventional papillary carcinoma and from adnexal-type tumors, such as eccrine acrospiroma (see p. 1827).

Other forms

In the *solid* form of DCIS, the glandular lumen is filled by the proliferation of medium-sized cells, which are larger than those of LCIS but smaller and more uniform than those of comedocarcinoma (Fig. 20.56). Azzopardi[463]

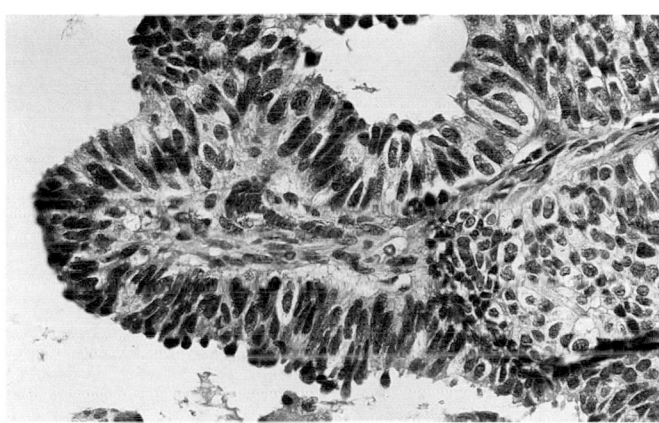

Fig. 20.53 High-power view of an in situ papillary carcinoma. Note the layering of cells, loss of nuclear polarity, marked hyperchromasia, and lack of a myoepithelial cell layer.

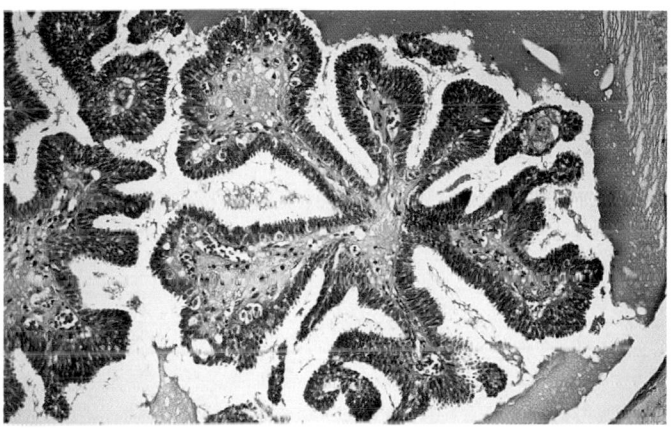

Fig. 20.54 In situ papillary carcinoma. The arborizing nature of this tumor and the stout fibrovascular core are not too different from those of a benign papilloma.

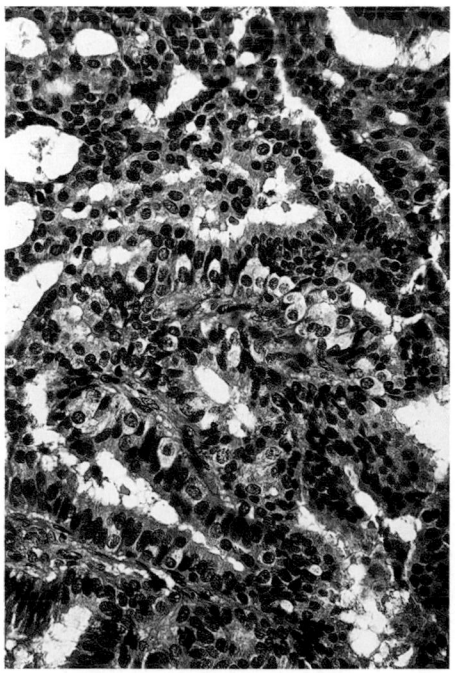

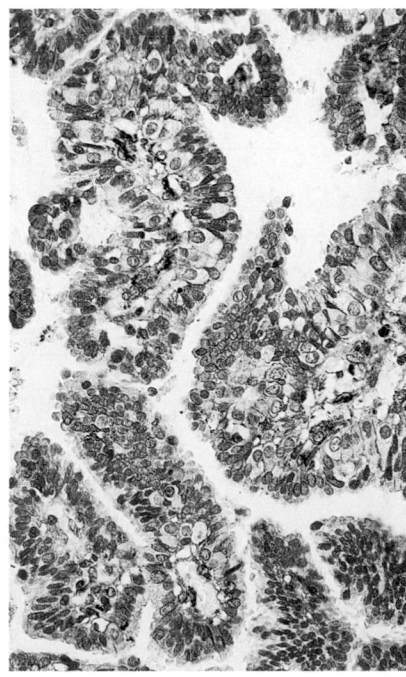

Fig. 20.55 A and B, Papillary carcinoma with so-called "globoid" or "clear cells." These cells, which are immunoreactive for GCDFP-15, should not be confused with myoepithelial cells. B, Negative immunostain for smooth muscle actin.

A   B

pointed out the sharp cell edges (as opposed to a "syncytial" quality) and the pallor of the cytoplasm (as opposed to prominent acidophilia) often exhibited by these cells. In the *cribriform* variety, round regular spaces are formed within the glands; the more regular these spaces are in terms of distribution, size, and shape, the more likely the lesion is to be malignant (Fig. 20.57). These spaces are often associated with two formations of similar pathogenesis, designated by Azzopardi[463] as trabecular bars and Roman bridges, respectively. Trabecular bars are rigid rows of cells with their long axes arranged more or less perpendicular (or at least not parallel) to the long axis of the bar; these should be distinguished from partial detachments of the duct lining (Fig. 20.58). Roman bridges are curvilinear trabecular bars connecting two portions of the epithelial lining. The cribriform pattern of DCIS should not be equated with that of adenoid cystic carcinoma (see p. 1827).

The *micropapillary* variety (more closely connected to the preceding types of DCIS than to conventional papillary carcinoma) shows elongated epithelial projections projecting into the glandular lumen; these lack connective tissue support, may have a space at the base, and often show a bulbous expansion at the tip (Fig. 20.59). This variant is more likely than others to involve multiple quadrants of the breast.[464]

Clinging carcinoma, the more controversial member of this family, shows one or two layers of malignant cells lining a glandular formation with a large empty lumen.[463] In the more easily recognizable (high-grade) forms, the tumor cells are large, highly atypical, and associated with individual cell necrosis, features which suggest a link with comedocarcinoma (Fig. 20.60). In other instances, the tumor cells are smaller and more regular; these have been interpreted as being related to the low-grade forms of intraductal carcinoma, particularly the micropapillary variety. Indeed, some authors refer to this as the "flat" variant of micropapillary in situ carcinoma.

The *cystic hypersecretory* form is a variation of DCIS characterized by cystic formations induced by the abundant secretory material present; although hardly a distinct entity, it deserves mention because of the ease with which it can be confused with a benign process.[470,476]

Adding to the complexity of the situation is the pattern traditionally known as *lobular cancerization*.[462,468] The term

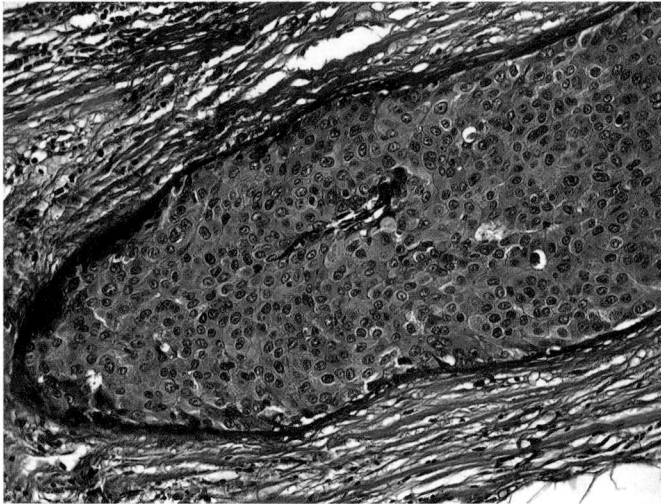

Fig. 20.56 Solid type of in situ ductal carcinoma. There is no necrosis.

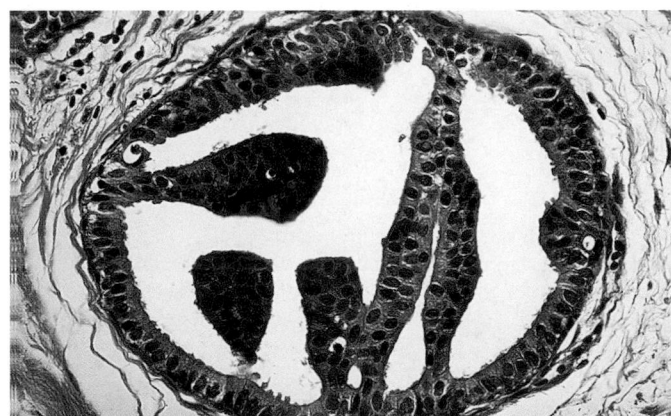

Fig. 20.58 Trabecular bars in intraductal carcinoma. Note the perpendicular arrangement of the nuclei in relation to the long axis of the bars.

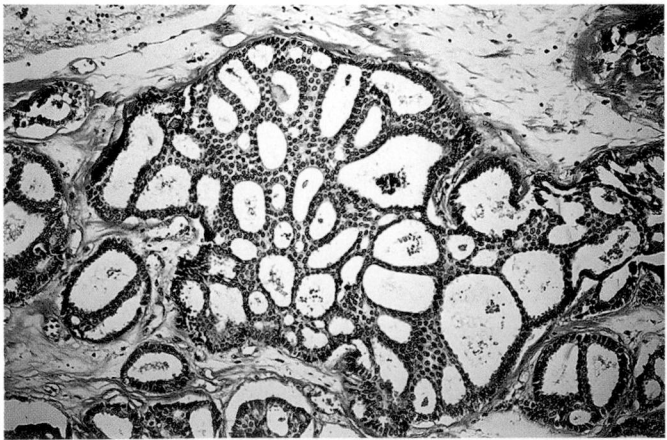

Fig. 20.57 Low-grade in situ ductal carcinoma of cribriform type.

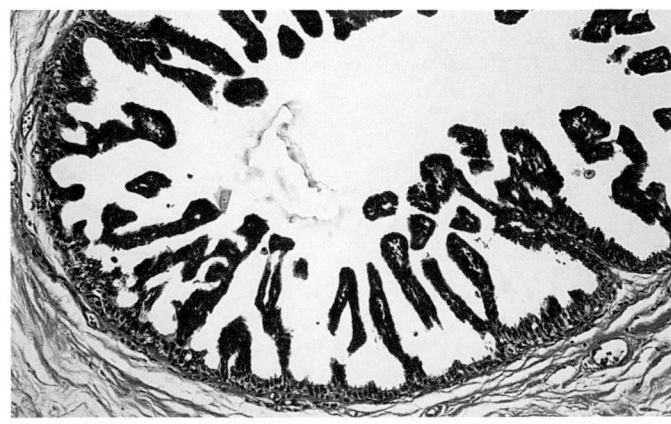

Fig. 20.59 Micropapillary carcinoma of breast. Some of the papillae lack a central fibrovascular core.

refers to the presence, in a structure easily identifiable as a lobule, of carcinoma with the cytoarchitectural features of DCIS (Fig. 20.61). The change was first described in connection with the high-grade (comedocarcinoma) form, but it was later realized that it could also be seen with the low-grade types. As the name indicates, the original assumption was that this represented a secondary extension into a lobule of a carcinoma of ductal origin, particularly when this was found associated with a conventional DCIS such as comedocarcinoma. The interpretation is probably erroneous. The available evidence suggests that this phenomenon represents instead a variation in the growth pattern of DCIS in which the structure involved is still easily recognizable as belonging to a lobule. Further evidence for the basic unity of these various manifestations comes from the occasional occurrence of DCIS and LCIS in the same TDLU.[475]

Rare additional morphologic variations of DCIS include cases with *signet ring cells*[469] (Fig. 20.62) with *apocrine-type cytology*,[171,173,477] and those with evidence of

endocrine differentiation.[466] The latter tumor, known as **endocrine DCIS (E-DCIS)**, is often accompanied by adjacent intraductal papillomas with pagetoid involvement by the carcinoma.[478] Key features for its recognition include the presence of endocrine-type festoons and rosettes, mucin deposition, bland-looking ovoid nuclei, and abundant granular eosinophilic cytoplasm (Fig. 20.63A). Necrosis is usually absent, and neuroendocrine

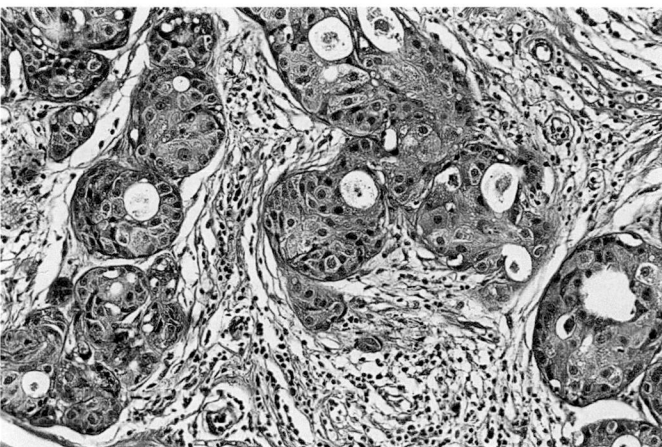

Fig. 20.62 Apocrine variant of in situ ductal carcinoma.

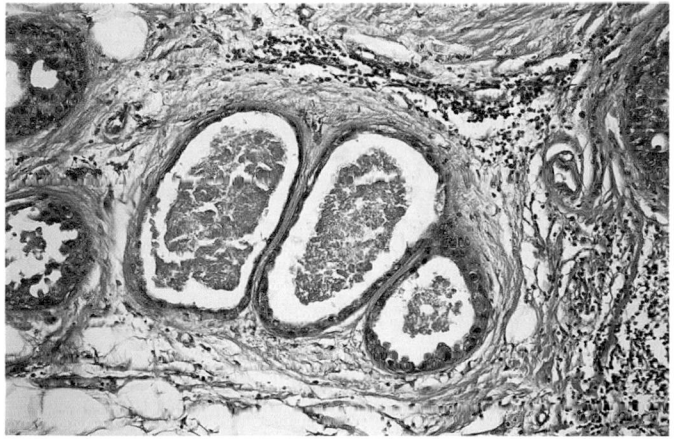

Fig. 20.60 Ductal carcinoma in situ of so-called "clinging type." One or two layers of atypical cells line dilated glandular structures containing granular intraluminal material in which ghosts of tumor cells are identified.

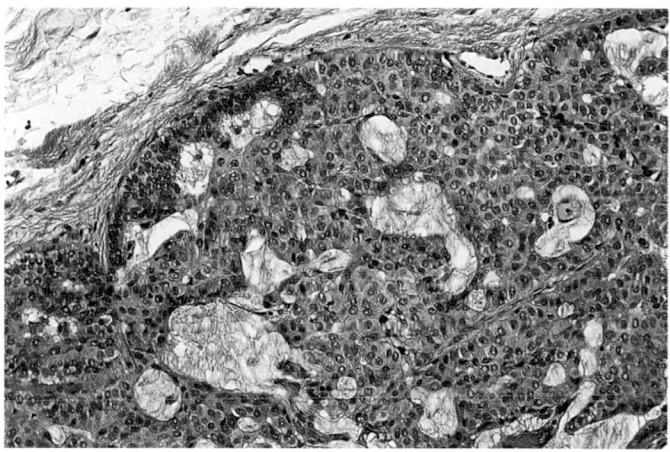

A

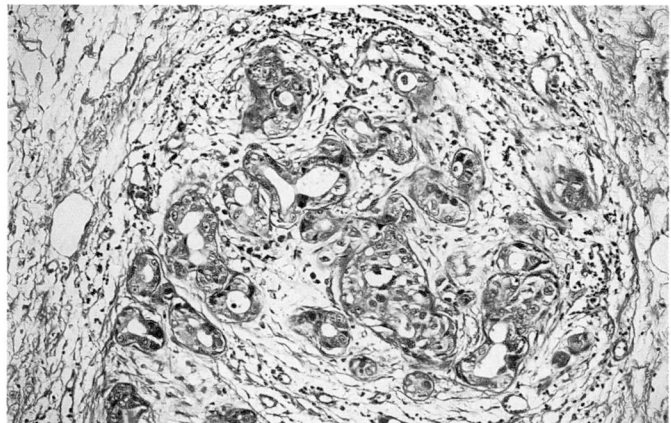

Fig. 20.61 So-called "lobular cancerization." The lobule is markedly expanded and composed of relatively large tumor cells with the appearance of ductal-type carcinoma. Typical ductal carcinoma was present elsewhere in the specimen.

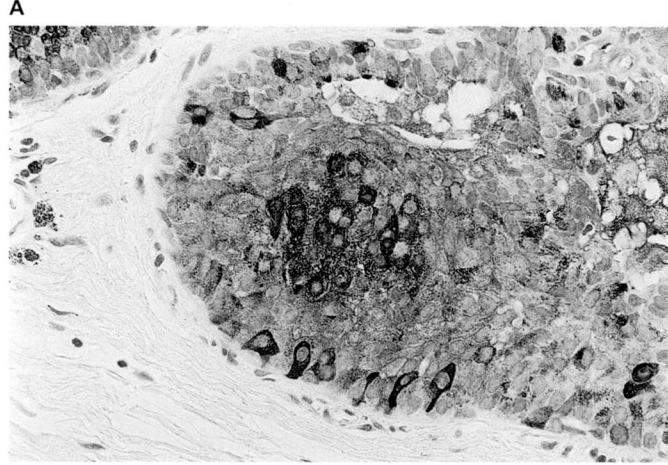

B

Fig. 20.63 Endocrine-type ductal carcinoma in situ: **A**, hematoxylin–eosin; **B**, chromogranin.

markers such as chromogranin and synaptophysin can be demonstrated[478] (Fig. 20.63B). Sometimes these tumors are accompanied by an invasive component, which is also of neuroendocrine type. This tumor is probably closely related to the lesion that has been described as *spindle cell DCIS*.[467]

A feature of diagnostic importance common to all forms of DCIS (although better developed in the comedocarcinoma type) is the appearance of the luminal content. The presence of nuclear debris, ghosts of dead cell outlines, granular and fragmented products, and inspissated densely stained material should raise suspicion and stimulate a thorough search for more diagnostic areas.[463]

Immunohistochemically, two important features of DCIS (particularly in relation to the differential diagnosis with LCIS) are the presence of E-cadherin and scantiness or absence of HMW keratin (as detected with 34βE12).[465] In addition, the high-grade form of DCIS also shows P-cadherin expression.[474]

The molecular genetic analyses that have been done so far in DCIS and ADH have given confusing and sometimes contradictory results. Suffice it to say that, on the whole, they suggest that genetic alterations may occur very early in breast tumorigenesis, prior to detectable morphologic changes, and that the interaction between epithelium and stroma may play an important role in tumor progression.[472]

Evolution

The assumed implication of the diagnosis of DCIS is that, if left untreated, the lesion will inevitably progress to an invasive carcinoma of similar morphologic features. This is a gross and inaccurate oversimplification of a very complex situation. These are some of the reasonably established facts:

1 The transformation to an invasive phenotype does not occur in all cases, at least during the normal life span of an individual.[489]

2 When such a transformation occurs, the process usually evolves over a period of years if not decades.[489]

3 There is a substantial difference in the frequency with which this phenomenon occurs depending on the type of DCIS: high for comedocarcinoma and low for all the others.[482,493] This can also be expressed by saying that the risk for the development of invasive carcinoma is directly proportional to the cytologic grade of the tumors.[486]

4 There is a definite relationship between the microscopic type of the DCIS and the invasive component, much more so than for LCIS; however, numerous exceptions occur.[484]

5 Not all invasive breast carcinomas go through the sequence just described; some (perhaps the majority) have a very short intraductal stage and become invasive long before being detectable by any technique. It is this very fact that takes some of the value away from

screening techniques such as mammography, which are much more likely to detect slow-growing carcinomas with a prolonged in situ stage.

The most informative data on which these conclusions are based derive from retrospective studies on DCIS that were treated by biopsy only.[481,485,488,491] In the series of Page et al.,[488] 7 of 25 patients with DCIS of non-comedocarcinoma type whose cases had been followed for over 3 years developed homolateral invasive breast carcinoma. In an earlier and smaller series by Betsill et al.,[479] invasive carcinoma had developed in 6 of the 10 patients for whom follow-up information was available. In a large series of patients treated with biopsy and local breast irradiation, it was found that comedo-type necrosis and uncertain/involved surgical margins were the best predictors of recurrence.[483,483a]

When mastectomy is done within 6 months after the identification of DCIS by biopsy, the incidence of invasive carcinoma in the mastectomy specimen was 6% in one series[490] and 18% in another.[480] Interestingly, residual DCIS was found in 60% of the specimens, a different quadrant being involved in 33% of them.[490] At present, the most common form of treatment of DCIS is local (breast-conserving) surgery with or without irradiation, but there are some patients for whom mastectomy is indicated.[487,492]

Lobular carcinoma in situ (LCIS)

Lobular CIS, also known as lobular neoplasia, has no distinguishing features on gross examination and is usually found incidentally in breasts removed for other reasons. It is multicentric in approximately 70% of cases[520] and bilateral in approximately 30% to 40%.[501] Most cases are found within 5 cm of the nipple from the skin surface in either the outer or inner upper quadrants.[511,512] Residual tumor foci are found in 60% of breasts removed following a diagnosis of LCIS made from a biopsy specimen.[514]

Microscopically, the lobules are distended and completely filled by relatively uniform, round, small-to-medium-sized cells with round and normochromatic (or only mildly hyperchromatic) nuclei. In the typical case, atypia, pleomorphism, mitotic activity, and necrosis are minimal or absent, and there is some lack of cohesiveness among the tumor cells[516,521] (Figs 20.64 and 20.65). Any of the following minor morphologic variations can occur, singly or in combination: moderate nuclear pleomorphism, larger nuclear size, appreciable mitotic activity, scattered signet ring cells (relatively common), apocrine changes (exceptional), focal necrosis, and variations in the shape of the involved lobules.[499,503,509,514] When the tumor cells are of medium to large size, with moderate to marked pleomorphism, occasional prominent nucleoli, and moderate to abundant cytoplasm, the lesion is referred to as *pleomorphic LCIS*.[518]

In LCIS, the neighboring terminal ducts often exhibit

proliferation of cells similar to those involving the lob-ules. These cells may form a continuous row beneath the secretory epithelium, a pattern that has been referred to as *mural* or *pagetoid* (Fig. 20.66); they can also grow in a solid, cribriform, or micropapillary fashion.[506,520]

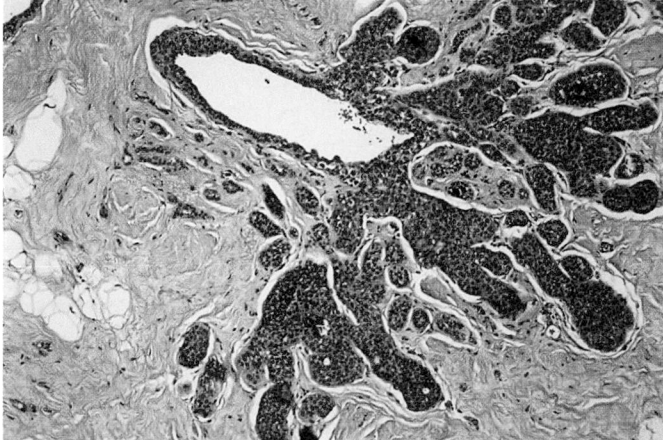

Fig. 20.64 Typical pattern of involvement of terminal duct–lobular unit by lobular carcinoma in situ.

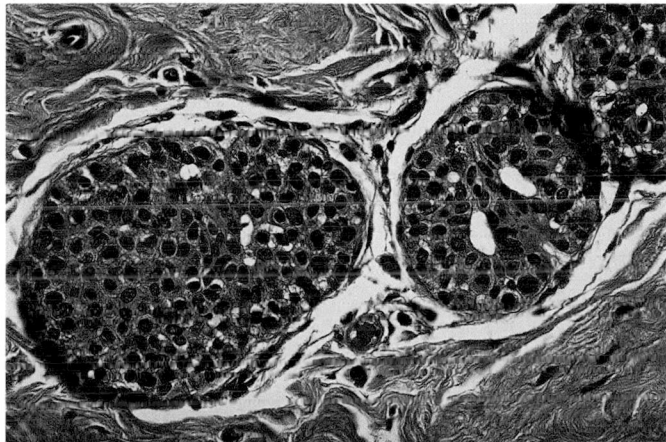

Fig. 20.65 Marked expansion of a lobular unit by lobular carcinoma in situ. A few small spaces are still present in the smaller focus.

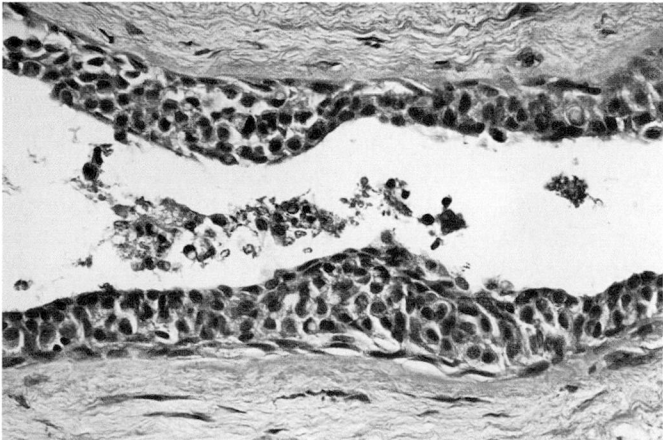

Fig. 20.66 Involvement of duct by lobular carcinoma in situ. In the presence of such change, a thorough search for typical areas of lobular involvement should be undertaken.

Occasionally, this change extends to larger (lactiferous) ducts, but Paget's disease practically never occurs.[515] The presence of these ductal changes is of histogenetic inter-est and sometimes the first clue for the existence of typical LCIS nearby, but it does not carry prognostic implications of its own.[496]

LCIS can also be found in fibroadenomas[508] and in foci of sclerosing adenosis[507] or collagenous spherulosis.[517] The diagnosis of LCIS (or whatever equivalent term one might like to use) should be made only in those cases in which the cellular proliferation has resulted in the for-mation of solid nests that have expanded the lobules, whereas the designation of lobular hyperplasia (pre-ceded by the qualifier "atypical") is to be given to those lesions accompanied by normal-sized lobules in which central lumina are still identifiable. LCIS should also be distinguished from DCIS, particularly the form tradi-tionally known as lobular cancerization and already discussed on p. 1795. The latter is identified by the fact that its cytoarchitectural features are those of one of the forms of DCIS, usually comedocarcinoma. When the lat-ter is the case, there is obvious cellular pleomorphism, atypical nuclear configuration, formation of small lumina, and necrosis.[495,505]

The only conventional special stains of some signifi-cance for the evaluation of LCIS are those for mucin, which show positivity in scattered tumor cells in about three fourths of cases.[497,499] Immunohistochemically, the tumor cells show positivity for keratin, EMA, and milk fat globule membrane antigen.[504] S-100 protein is demon-strable in 60% of cases.[502] Ultrastructural study or immunohistochemistry for any of the myoepithelial cell markers (see p. 1765) will show residual myoepithelial cells, which may lie flat on the basement membrane, perpendicular to it, or admixed with the tumor cells; the latter do not have myoepithelial features them-selves.[500,519] Laminin and collagen type IV can be demonstrated in the underlying basement membrane.

From the point of view of the differential diagnosis with DCIS, the two most important immunohistochemi-cal features of LCIS are the lack of reactivity for E-cadherin and the positivity for HMW keratin (as demonstrated with 34βE12), the latter often exhibiting a distinctive perinuclear pattern. By contrast, DCIS is con-sistently positive for E-cadherin and shows significantly reduced or absent HMW keratin.[494] As expected, the cases with hybrid or intermediate features also show hybrid immunohistochemical features, as manifested by either positivity or negativity for *both* markers.[498,510] The loss of E-cadherin in LCIS is due to gene mutations, which are, however, different from those of the invasive lobular component when present.[513]

Evolution

One of the most controversial aspects of breast pathology is the nature of LCIS, specifically in regard to the probability of development of invasive carcinoma following a biopsy diagnosis of LCIS without additional therapy. Although the figures obtained in the various reported series[522,525,527–531] are not exactly superimposable, it seems safe to conclude from them that (1) approximately 20% to 30% of patients will develop invasive carcinoma, a risk about 8 to 10 times higher than for a control population; (2) the risk seems greater in well-developed LCIS ("histologically flagrant") than in ALH ("histologically subtle"); (3) if the LCIS is well developed, the risk is about the same regardless of the amount of LCIS, or whether it is present in the classic form or as one of its morphologic variants; (4) this increased risk applies to both breasts, although it is greater on the side of the biopsy; (5) the invasive carcinoma may be of either lobular or ductal type; (6) the amount of LCIS or its morphologic variations bears little or no relation to the magnitude of the risk; and (7) if a patient with a biopsy diagnosis of LCIS is examined periodically, the chances of her dying as a result of breast carcinoma are minimal.

In relation to the cases of LCIS associated with invasive carcinomas of ductal type, careful review of the section will often reveal an additional component of DCIS.[526]

Most investigators agree that careful lifelong follow-up appears to be a safe and rational option for this lesion.[523–525] The performance of a simple mastectomy can be considered in the presence of a strong family history of carcinoma, extensive fibrocystic disease, or excessive apprehension on the part of the patient or if a prolonged follow-up evaluation cannot be assured.

Invasive carcinoma

Tumors included in this category are all those in which stromal invasion is detectable, whether an in situ component is identifiable or not and regardless of the relative proportion of the two components. In other words, it also includes so-called "microinvasive carcinoma" (see below). Like the in situ lesions, most of the invasive tumors can be divided into two major categories—ductal type and lobular type—acknowledging the existence of mixed and intermediate forms. It should be emphasized that the type of invasive carcinoma should be determined from its own appearance, rather than deduced from the type of in situ component present, if any, since there is not always correspondence between the two.

The classification of invasive breast carcinoma has evolved over a long period of time and, as a result, has had incorporated into it a wide range of criteria, such as cell type (as in apocrine carcinoma), type and amount of secretion (as in mucinous carcinoma), architectural features (as in papillary carcinoma), and pattern of spread (as in inflammatory carcinoma). Not surprisingly, this has resulted in a considerable degree of confusion.

Invasive ductal carcinoma

For purposes of discussion, invasive ductal carcinomas are here divided according to two major criteria: cytoarchitectural features and pattern of spread.

Cytoarchitectural variants

The morphologic variations on the theme of invasive ductal carcinoma are innumerable. Some of them are distinctive enough to deserve recognition as special types, especially when associated with a particular behavior. The others, which represent approximately 75% of all cases, are generically designated as invasive ductal carcinomas of classic, ordinary, or not-otherwise-specified (NOS) type.[532]

Classic (NOS) invasive ductal carcinoma. This lesion represents the prototypic expression of breast carcinoma, and it is the tumor type usually implied when the terms "breast carcinoma" or "breast cancer" are used without further qualification. The size, shape, consistency, and type of margins are highly variable; some of these factors depend on the relative amounts of tumor cells and stroma. Grossly, the typical case is firm and poorly circumscribed, cuts with a resistant gritty sensation, and shows a yellowish gray cut surface, with trabeculae radiating through the surrounding parenchyma into the fat, resulting in the notorious stellate or crab-like configuration from which the word "cancer" has originated (Fig. 20.67). Sometimes these strands are seen connecting with other tumor nodules located at some distance from the primary tumor. Areas of necrosis, hemorrhage, and cystic degeneration may be present, particularly in the larger neoplasms. The tumor may have invaded the overlying skin or the underlying fascia and pectoralis muscle. Tumors that are particularly hard because of the large amounts of stroma were traditionally referred to as "scirrhous carcinomas," a term no longer used. It is common for these neoplasms to exhibit "chalky streaks" on the cut surface, a feature caused not by necrosis as generally believed, but by duct elastosis[552] (see below; Fig. 20.68). When this occurs, the appearance of the lesion has an uncanny resemblance to an unripe pear, further accentuated by the consistency and the sensation one has while cutting it.

Other tumors are better delineated, softer, rounded, and lobulated. These have been variously designated as circumscribed, multinodular, or knobby carcinomas. In the past, they were also known as medullary carcinomas, a practice that should be avoided at all costs to avoid confusion with the specific variant of breast carcinoma bearing that name (see p. 1807).

Microscopically, the variations are also legion.[546] The tumor can grow in diffuse sheets, well-defined nests, cords, or as individual cells. Glandular/tubular differentiation may be well developed, barely detectable, or altogether absent. Parenthetically, this is the reason why the term adenocarcinoma is not advisable as a synonym for invasive ductal carcinoma (Fig. 20.69). The tumor

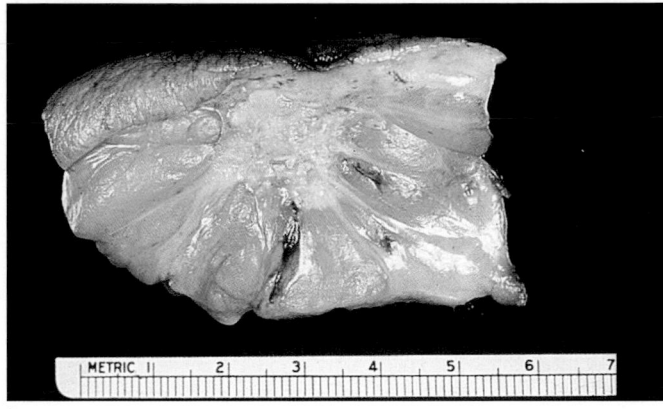

A **B**

Fig. 20.67 A and **B**, Typical gross appearance of invasive ductal carcinoma. Note the irregular (crab-like) shape of the tumor, white fibrous appearance, and chalky streaks. Retraction of the overlying skin is obvious in the specimen shown in **B**.

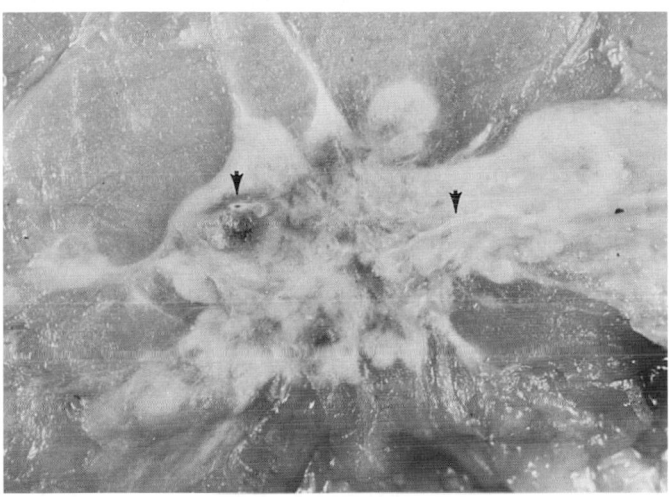
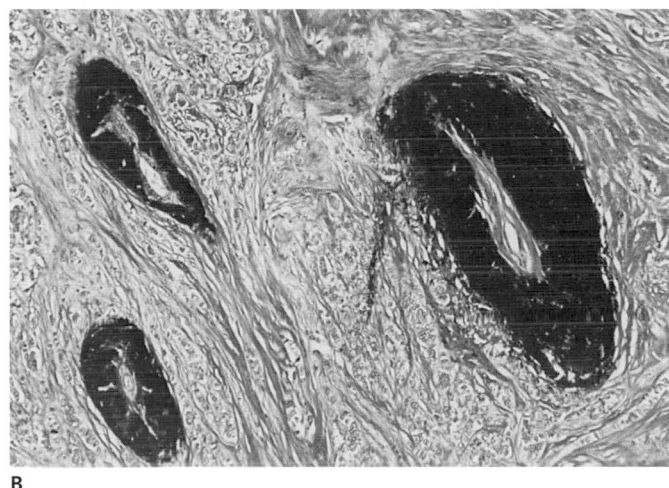

A **B**

Fig. 20.68 A, Gross appearance of typical invasive ductal carcinoma. "Chalky streaks" can be seen throughout the tumor. A central space can be identified in some of them (arrows). **B**, Elastic tissue stain of the lesion illustrated in **A** showing that "chalky streaks" correspond to a markedly thickened elastic layer in the wall of non-neoplastic ducts crossing the tumor. (**B**, Verhoeff–van Gieson)

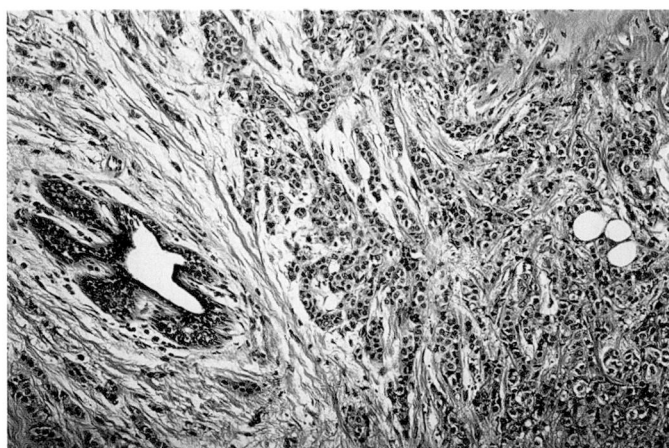

Fig. 20.69 Prototypical invasive ductal carcinoma.

cells vary in size and shape, but by definition they are larger and more pleomorphic than those of the classic form of invasive lobular carcinomas, their nuclei and nucleoli are more prominent, and mitotic figures are more numerous. Areas of necrosis occur in approxi-

mately 60% of cases.[547] Foci of squamous metaplasia, apocrine metaplasia, or clear cell changes may be seen. The amount of stroma ranges from none to abundant, and its appearance from densely fibrotic to cellular ("desmoplastic"). In cases with abundant stroma, it may be difficult to identify the tumor cells. Bulky masses of elastic tissue are present in approximately 90% of cases. As already indicated, this "elastosis," which can involve the wall of the ducts and the vessels (mainly veins), is responsible for the chalky streaks seen on gross examination.[533] Calcification can be detected in approximately 60% of cases, either as coarse or fine granules or, rarely, as psammoma bodies.[546] A mononuclear inflammatory infiltrate of variable intensity is usually present at the interphase between tumor and stroma. Granulomatous inflammation is rarely seen.[564]

Definite invasion of the perineurial spaces, lymph vessels, and blood vessels was found by Fisher et al.[546] in 28%, 33%, and 5% of cases, respectively. Lymph vessel invasion may be difficult to distinguish from artifactual tissue retraction. Features used to document the presence of lymphatic tumor emboli are the following: (1) the occurrence of the area in question outside the margin of the carcinoma, (2) the fact that the tumor emboli do not conform exactly to the space in which they lie, (3) the presence of an endothelial cell lining, and (4) the presence of blood vessels in the immediate vicinity.[569] If doubts persist, a stain with CD31, FLI-1, *Ulex europaeus* I lectin, FVIII-related antigen, or other endothelial cell markers might prove helpful[557,560,570] (Fig. 20.70). These reactions can even be carried out in the H&E-stained preparations after removing the coverslip and decolorizing the slide.[566]

The amount of mucin present in these tumors, as evaluated by Fisher et al.[546] in over 900 cases with the Alcian blue–PAS stain, was judged to be nil in 47% of cases, slight in 34%, moderate in 12%, and marked in 7%. In the same study, intracytoplasmic glycogen was found after PAS stain with diastase control in 62% of cases.[546] Focal argyrophilia was found in approximately 5% of cases.

Ultrastructurally, the tumor cells exhibit, in greater or lesser degree, features of glandular differentiation such as microvilli and terminal bars on their luminal side.[545] A particularly characteristic feature, although not as specific for breast carcinoma as originally suggested, is the presence of intracytoplasmic lumina bordered by microvilli.[535,571] These formations, when sufficiently large, appear as "bull's-eyes" at the light microscopic level, and are different from the formations seen in signet ring cells, which are intracytoplasmic vacuoles. Early claims that the ultrastructural features of some ductal carcinomas were indicative of myoepithelial cell origin remain controversial.[563] The desmoplastic stroma accompanying breast carcinomas is formed by cells having the ultrastructural features of fibroblasts and myofibroblasts.[565]

Immunohistochemically, the tumor cells show reactivity for low-molecular-weight keratin (particularly types 8, 18, and 19) and EMA.[553] Some of the tumors (particularly those with foci of squamous metaplasia) are also immunoreactive for HMW (epidermal-type) keratin.[573] In addition to EMA (which also stains carcinomas of most other sites), the cells of breast carcinoma are reactive for an apparently more organ-specific antigen obtained from milk fat globule membrane.[549] Close to 70% of cases are positive for lactalbumin, another marker almost entirely restricted to mammary epithelium.[542,556] CEA, B72.3, and BCA-225 are positive in the majority of cases.[555,558,567,568,572] Vimentin may also be expressed,[543] sometimes together with GFAP.[548] Breast carcinomas can be immunoreactive for S-100 protein, the proportion ranging from 10% to 45% in the various reported series[544,559]; this is a fact to remember in the differential diagnosis of metastatic tumors to axillary nodes, lest a breast carcinoma be mislabeled as metastatic melanoma. Even more treacherous is the fact that some cases may show an artifactual granular reactivity for HMB-45.[538] An increased expression of the bone matrix proteins osteonectin and osteopontin has been documented, with the added suggestion that this may play a role in the bone homing of breast carcinoma metastases.[536,550] The basement membrane components laminin and collagen IV show a discontinuous linear pattern or are altogether absent, in contrast to the continuous pattern they exhibit in the intraductal lesions.[541,574,576] An increased amount of type V collagen is found in the desmoplastic stroma.[534] Actin and related stains are negative, confirming the absence of myoepithelial cells around the tumor nests. A small number of carcinomas show focal reactivity for human chorionic gonadotrophin (hCG), SP-1 or other placental proteins,[554] chromogranin,[539] GCDFP-15,[561,575] or lactoferrin.[540]

Breast carcinomas have also shown an increased expression of T and Tn antigens (precursors to the MN blood group system), as detected by normal human sera[551] or peanut lectins.[537] In about half of cases they also express an antigen that is cross-reactive with a major glycoprotein of the mouse mammary tumor virus.[562]

Tubular carcinoma. Tubular carcinoma has also been designated as well-differentiated carcinoma, but the latter term is not advisable because it has also been used for other well-differentiated tumors with different patterns of growth. The average age of the patients is about 50 years.[594] Grossly, tubular carcinoma suggests malignancy by virtue of its poorly circumscribed margins and hard consistency. It is characteristically small, with a mean diameter of about 1 cm.[587,590] Microscopically, it simulates a benign condition (particularly radial scar and microglandular adenosis) because of the well-differentiated nature of the glands, absence of necrosis or mitoses, and

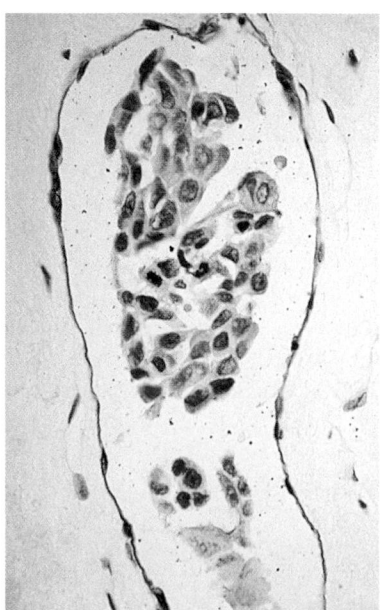

Fig. 20.70 Vascular invasion by breast carcinoma demonstrated by positivity of endothelial cells for *Ulex europaeus* lectin I.

scanty pleomorphism.[588] The clues to the diagnosis are the haphazard arrangement of the glands in the stroma with absence of any organoid configuration; frequent invasion of fat at the periphery of the lesion; cellular (but often also elastotic[593]) nature of the stroma; irregular and often angulated contours of the glands; open lumina with basophilic secretion; apocrine-type "snouts" in the apical cytoplasm; formation of trabecular bars; lack of a myoepithelial cell component (well appreciated in immunostained preparations); lack of basement membrane (well seen with an immunostain for type IV collagen); and occurrence in two thirds or more of the cases of typical intraductal carcinoma in ducts within or outside the lesion, nearly always of low-grade (micropapillary or cribriform) type[578,583,586,587,594] (Fig. 20.71).

Because of the marked degree of cellular differentiation, it is not unusual for these tumors to be underdiagnosed as fibroadenoma or some other benign process on fine needle aspiration (FNA) material.[579] They are better recognized in needle core preparations.

Ultrastructurally, the degree of ductal differentiation is striking, but myoepithelial cells and basement membrane are lacking.[582,584] A high incidence of multicentricity (56%), history of bilateral breast carcinoma (38%), and family history of breast carcinoma (40%) were found by Lagios et al.[585] in a series of 17 tubular carcinomas. At the genetic molecular level, tubular carcinoma shows several differences with invasive ductal carcinoma NOS.[595]

Metastases to axillary nodes occur in approximately 10% of cases,[578,580,587] and the prognosis is excellent.[581] In the series of McDivitt et al.,[587] only 4% of their 135 patients developed recurrent or metastatic disease during a mean follow-up period of 72 years. The recurrence rate after local excision is as high as 50%.[580]

Sometimes, a tubular carcinoma pattern is seen in association with an ordinary invasive ductal carcinoma. The prognosis of these "mixed" tumors is substantially worse than for pure tubular carcinoma,[577,580,589] although better than for the ordinary invasive ductal carcinoma, at least when the tubular component represents the dominant element.[577,580] It is likely that series of tubular carcinomas in which the incidence of nodal metastases is high include a high proportion of these "mixed" carcinomas.[591,592]

The tumor type known as tubulolobular carcinoma is discussed on p. 1817.

Cribriform carcinoma. Invasive cribriform carcinoma is a rare form of breast malignancy closely related to tubular carcinoma and sharing with it an excellent prognosis.[596,597] As the name indicates, the tumor has a cribriform appearance similar to that seen in the more common in situ counterpart, but it also exhibits stromal invasion (Fig. 20.72). This pattern is often seen in association with tubular formations, the relative proportion of the two elements determining the term used, according to the scheme proposed by Page et al.[596] The most important aspect of this concept is the realization that a breast carcinoma can be cribriform throughout yet invasive; we have seen examples of this tumor extensively invading the breast and beyond and being called in situ tumors simply because they had a cribriform pattern. Recently, the proposal has been made for the existence of yet another variation on the theme, in which the tumor has a similar invasive pattern and cytology but a solid configuration (*solid variant* of invasive cribriform carcinoma).[596a]

Mucinous carcinoma. Mucinous carcinoma, also known as mucoid, colloid, or gelatinous carcinoma, usually occurs in postmenopausal women.[600,610] Grossly, it is well circumscribed, crepitant to palpation, and formed by a currant jelly-like mass held together by delicate septa (Fig. 20.73). Foci of hemorrhage are frequent.

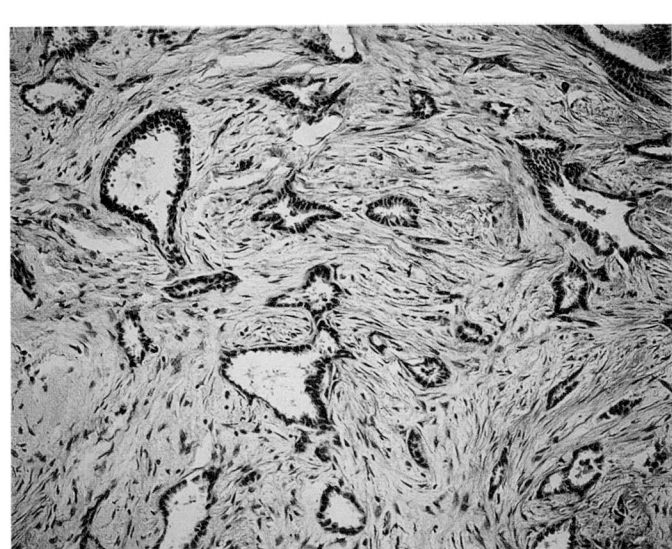

Fig. 20.71 Tubular carcinoma of breast. The angulated shape of the glands and the cellular stroma are characteristic of this lesion.

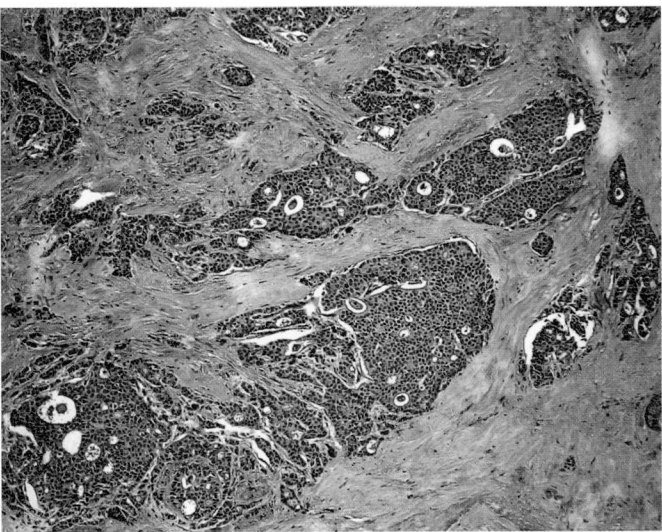

Fig. 20.72 Invasive cribriform carcinoma. Some of the nodules have a predominantly solid appearance.

Microscopically, the classic and often quoted description is that of small clusters of tumor cells "floating in a sea of mucin" (Fig. 20.74). These clusters may be solid or exhibit acinar formations. The mucin is almost entirely extracellular, and it may be of acid or neutral type.[621] Occasionally, mucinous carcinoma will consist almost entirely of

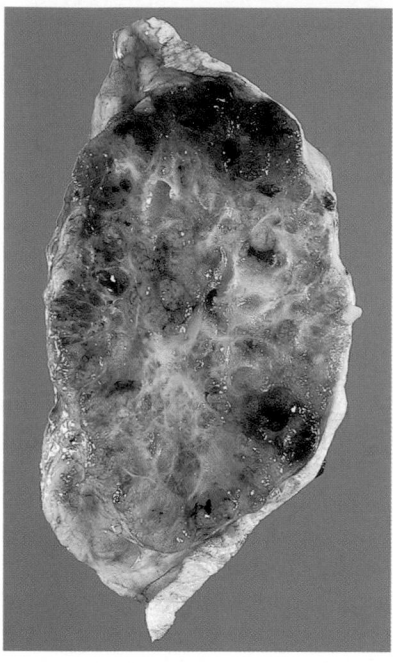

Fig. 20.73 Typical gelatinous gross appearance of pure mucinous carcinoma. Note the sharply circumscribed quality of the tumor. (Courtesy of Dr. RA Cooke, Brisbane, Australia; from Cooke RA, Stewart B: Colour Atlas of Anatomical Pathology. Edinburgh, Churchill Livingstone, 2004).

mucin, and a thorough sampling will be necessary to detect the neoplastic epithelium.[616] An easily recognizable in situ component is usually absent or inconspicuous (but see later section). Histochemically, the mucins secreted by this tumor are distinct *O*-acylated forms of sialomucins.[618] Immunohistochemically, there is strong MUC2 cytoplasmic immunoreactivity and decreased MUC1 immunoreactivity compared with ductal carcinoma NOS.[609,611]

Interestingly, about a fourth to nearly half of mucinous carcinomas show features consistent with endocrine differentiation, such as argyrophilia (Fig. 20.75), NSE immunoreactivity, and the presence of dense-core secretory granules by ultrastructural examination.[598,604,606,614] This unexpected finding has raised the possibility of a link between mucinous carcinoma and the breast neoplasm originally described as carcinoid tumor (see p. 1810).[604] Some authors have suggested the existence of two types of mucinous carcinoma on the basis of the presence or absence of endocrine differentiation, which they have designated as A and B, respectively.[598] Others have found that the variability of morphologic and ultrastructural features within these tumors precludes a sharp segregation,[601,603] or that such segregation has no influence on survival.[619]

It is important for prognostic reasons, and perhaps useful histogenetically, to restrict the term mucinous carcinoma to breast neoplasms exhibiting this feature throughout ("pure" mucinous carcinomas) and to exclude (1) the "impure" or "mixed" tumors in which the mucinous pattern is admixed with an ordinary invasive

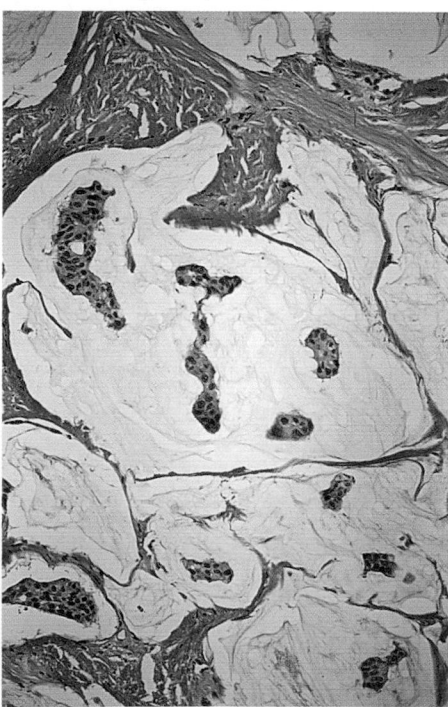

Fig. 20.74 Mucinous carcinoma of the breast. Clusters of well-differentiated tumor cells are seen floating in a sea of mucin.

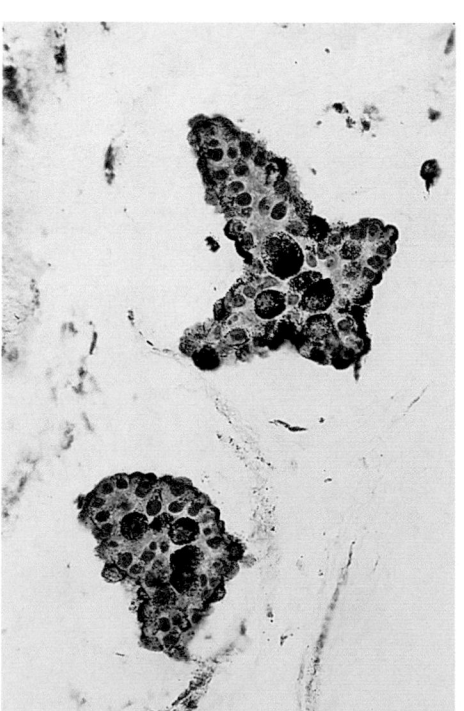

Fig. 20.75 Argyrophilic cells present in another case of mucinous carcinoma of the breast, indicative of neuroendocrine differentiation. (Sevier–Munger stain)

ductal carcinoma[612,620] (these having a prognosis analogous to the latter); and (2) signet ring carcinomas (see p. 1816), even if technically speaking these are also "mucinous" tumors). Along these lines, it should be pointed out that some degree of mucin production can be identified in over 60% of breast carcinomas. The distinctiveness of signet ring carcinoma resides in the fact that nearly all of it remains within the cell (possibly because of a blockage in secretion), and the uniqueness of mucinous carcinoma is that most of it is extracellular (see later section). In contrast to large bowel and other sites, a combination of these two patterns is very rare in the breast.

Pure mucinous carcinoma is associated with a very low incidence (2% to 4%) of nodal metastases.[602,610,613] The higher incidence reported in other series is probably attributable to the inclusion of "mixed" mucinous tumors. Consequently, the pure form of mucinous carcinoma carries an excellent short-term prognosis, particularly when the tumor measures less than 3 cm (or even less than 5 cm) in diameter.[600,610] However, it has been shown that deaths from this tumor can occur 12 years or more after therapy, indicating the need for long-term follow-up.[600,617] As already indicated, there seems to be no prognostic difference between the mucinous carcinomas with endocrine-like features and those without.[614]

Pure mucinous carcinoma is generally regarded as an invasive type of tumor. We would like to offer an alternative point of view, i.e., that this neoplasm is partially—and sometimes entirely—a form of in situ ductal carcinoma in which some component of the mucin secretion detaches the epithelium from the underlying stroma, breaks it up in strips and nests, and engulfs it (Fig. 20.76). This process may be facilitated by an "inversion of polarity" of the mucin secretion toward the base of the cell rather than the luminal border, as shown ultrastructurally, which is actually part of a field change.[597a,611] The implication is that it is the mucin, rather than the tumor cells, that is "invading" the stroma, in a fashion

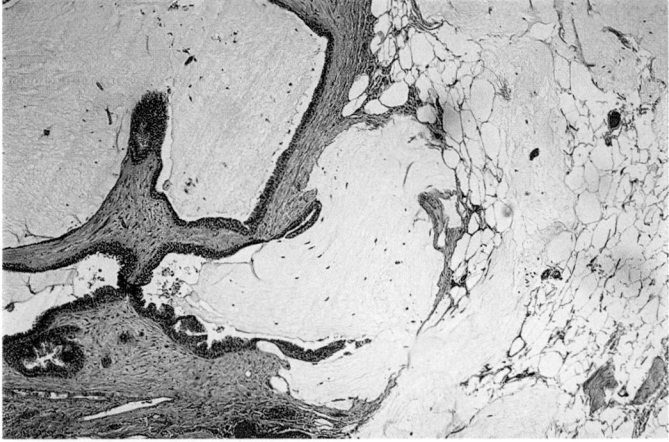

Fig. 20.76 Early form of mucin-producing low-grade carcinoma showing the mechanism of formation of the epithelial strips typically seen floating in the mucin.

analogous to that often seen in mucinous tumors of the appendix. This would explain not only the excellent prognosis of pure mucinous carcinoma but also the seemingly paradoxic fact that nearly all the mucin produced by this tumor is extracellular. Along these lines, it should be pointed out that not all mucin-containing breast nodules represent carcinomas.[599] Papillomas, papillary carcinomas, and ductal hyperplasia of either the florid or atypical type can also be accompanied by focal or sometimes abundant mucin secretion, which may accumulate in large extracellular pools.[608,615] Some of these lesions have been referred to as "mucocele-like tumors,"[616] but we feel that the term should be used in a descriptive rather than diagnostic sense. As in the appendix and other sites, the formation of a "mucocele" is nearly always the expression of mucin hyperproduction and extravasation by a proliferative epithelial process, which may be hyperplastic or neoplastic, benign or malignant, in situ or invasive.[605] The key determination is the nature of that process, rather than the spectacular, but relatively inconsequential, presence of the "mucocele." In practical terms, a thorough sampling is always mandatory.[615]

A further variation on the theme is represented by *mucinous cystadenocarcinoma*, an exceptionally rare tumor composed predominantly of tall columnar cells with abundant intracytoplasmic mucin and a multicystic gross quality similar to that of its ovarian counterpart.[607]

Medullary carcinoma. Medullary carcinoma usually appears in patients under 50 years of age and is said to be particularly common in Japanese women. It is also said to be particularly common in carriers of *BRCA1* mutations.[622,642] Grossly, it is well circumscribed and may become large; it can be mistaken clinically and grossly for a fibroadenoma, but it lacks the trabeculation or whorling of the latter. Its cut surface is solid, homogeneous, and gray, sometimes exhibiting small foci of necrosis (Fig. 20.77). Rare examples are partially or predominantly cystic.[631] Microscopically, the borders are always of the "pushing" type. The pattern of growth is diffuse, with minimal or no glandular differentiation or intraductal growth and absence of mucin secretion. The tumor cells are large and pleomorphic, with large nuclei and prominent nucleoli and numerous mitoses (some of them atypical). The cell borders are indistinct, giving the tumor a syncytial or sheet-like appearance somewhat reminiscent of a germ cell tumor of the embryonal carcinoma type. This is accentuated by the fact that the tumor cells located at the periphery of the clusters are more elongated and have a denser, more acidophilic cytoplasm, acquiring a vague resemblance to syncytiotrophoblast. Spindle cell metaplasia, bizarre tumor giant cells, extensive necrosis, and the absence of calcification are other common features.

A constant microscopic component is a prominent lymphoplasmacytic infiltrate at the periphery of the

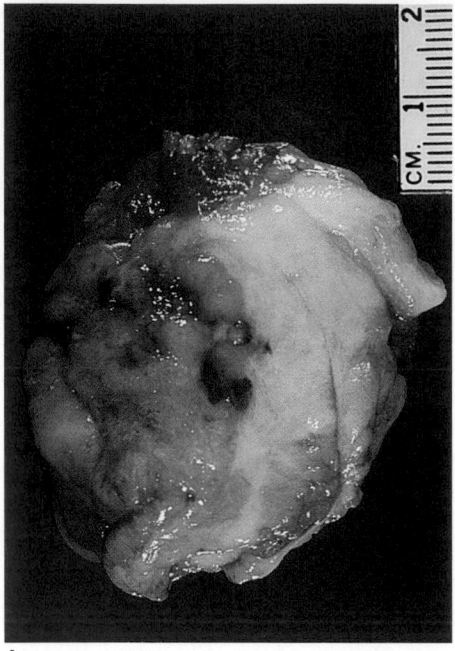

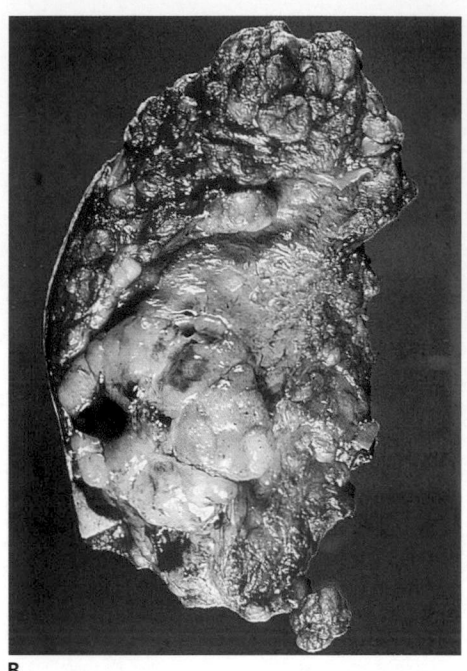

Fig. 20.77 A and **B**, Gross appearance of medullary carcinoma. Note the well-circumscribed character and fleshy appearance.

tumor, which is thought to represent a reaction of the host tissues to the neoplasm (Fig. 20.78). Most of the lymphocytes are of the peripheral T-cell type and similar to those seen in ordinary breast carcinoma, except for a possibly greater number of activated cytotoxic lymphocytes.[623,628,645] The plasma cells are of the IgA-producing type; some of the tumor cells also stain for IgA and for secretory component.[632] Ultrastructurally, the cells of medullary carcinoma do not seem to have distinctive features, despite early statements to the contrary.[630] Immunohistochemically, they share the markers of ordinary invasive ductal carcinoma but are more commonly positive for S-100 protein.[627] They are almost invariably negative for estrogen receptors[633] (see p. 1818).

The claim that medullary carcinomas lack keratin 19, in contrast to ordinary ductal carcinoma, has not been

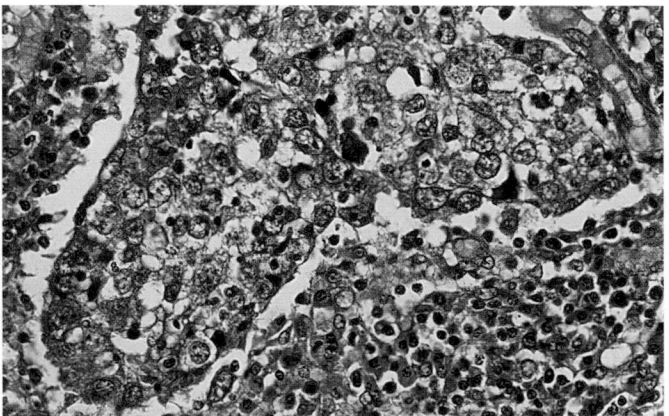

Fig. 20.78 Medullary carcinoma. The large tumor cells grow in a "syncytial" fashion and are sharply separated from the surrounding stroma, which is heavily infiltrated by lymphocytes and plasma cells.

substantiated.[626,643] An interesting feature of medullary carcinoma is the frequent expression of HLA-DR antigen, this being a possible reason for the prominent lymphocytic infiltration.[635,646]

Axillary lymph node metastases are common, but they are usually few in number and limited to the low axillary group. The prognosis for medullary carcinoma is better than for the ordinary invasive ductal carcinoma, a fact already apparent in the early reports on this tumor.[624,639] In the series of Ridolfi et al.,[640] the 10-year survival rate was 84%, as opposed to 63% for ordinary ductal carcinomas. The prognosis was particularly good for tumors that were smaller than 3 cm, and it remained better than for ductal carcinoma even when nodal metastases were present.

The terms *atypical medullary carcinoma* and *invasive ductal carcinoma with medullary features* have been used for tumors that depart somewhat from the foregoing definition, but the delineation of criteria for their recognition remains imprecise.[640,644] We have too often seen the term medullary carcinoma misused for highly cellular breast carcinomas that behaved in a very aggressive fashion, and we caution the reader to use this term only when all the pathologic features necessary for this diagnosis are present.[633,638] As a matter of fact, we and others wonder whether medullary carcinoma constitutes a bona fide subtype of breast carcinoma as currently defined.[625,629,641] We are particularly concerned about the lack of precise boundaries between it and the following tumors: the predominantly solid (undifferentiated) form of invasive ductal carcinoma; carcinoma with germ cell-like features, as also seen in the lung, the gastrointestinal tract, and other sites; and so-called "lymphoepithelioma-like carcinoma."[634] In regard to the latter, it should be noted that no evidence of EBV participation has been found in medullary carcinoma.[637] Also to be noted is the fact that microsatellite instability, a feature associated with carcinomas with a "medullary" morphology in large bowel and pancreas, is generally not present in medullary carcinoma of the breast.[636,637a]

Invasive papillary carcinoma. Most papillary carcinomas of the breast are entirely or predominantly in situ lesions; these are discussed on p. 1796. The invasive component of a papillary carcinoma may also be papillary or have the features of an ordinary ductal-type carcinoma; the prognosis is substantially better for the former. This tumor is said to occur more frequently among whites and postmenopausal women,[649] but, on the whole, it remains a very rare entity. Part of the problem may be that, although the recognition of an ordinary ductal-type carcinoma offers no difficulties, the documentation of invasion in tumors that maintain a well-differentiated pattern may not be as clear-cut. For instance, some of the cases reported as intracystic papillary carcinomas[647,650] may well represent invasive papillary carcinomas with a "pushing" pattern of growth. The distinctive features of these tumors can be appreciated on FNA specimens.[648,651]

Apocrine carcinoma. Apocrine carcinoma is a very rare form of breast malignancy (ranging from 1% to 4% of all cases), at least when defined as composed entirely or predominantly of apocrine-type epithelium.[652] The large tumor cells have an abundant acidophilic, somewhat granular cytoplasm, which may contain eosinophilic or golden brown granules that are strongly PAS positive. The nuclei are vesicular and nucleoli are prominent. Glandular differentiation is usually found, the luminal portion of the tumor having a characteristic bulbous expansion ("apocrine snout"). Some of these tumors present as mural nodules within a cyst lined by benign apocrine-type epithelium. Ultrastructurally, the cells of apocrine carcinoma show prominent mitochondria (some with abnormal cristae) and a variable number of large (400 to 600 nm) membrane-bound vesicles with dense homogeneous osmophilic cores.[656] Immunohistochemically, there is reactivity for GCDFP-15.[654] The gene coding for this marker is located on chromosome 7q and is identical to the gene of the prolactin-inducible protein (PIP); the expression of this gene in apocrine carcinoma has been demonstrated with in situ hybridization techniques.[655,657]

Since apocrine changes in the breast are usually indicative of benignancy (even when the cells exhibit prominent nucleolar enlargement), the diagnosis of apocrine carcinoma should be made only when the architectural features are clearly those of a malignant tumor. It is also important to limit the diagnosis of apocrine carcinoma to malignant tumors in which the apocrine change is widespread, in view of the fact that focal apocrine differentiation (as detected by GCDFP-15) can be detected in close to 10% of ordinary carcinomas.[654] Finally, it

should be noted that although apocrine carcinoma is usually a variant of either in situ or invasive ductal carcinoma, apocrine differentiation has also been described in in situ and invasive lobular carcinoma.[653] It has been shown that E-cadherin immunostaining distinguishes the ductal from the lobular lesions, as it does for their non-apocrine counterparts.[652a]

Juvenile (secretory) carcinoma. This rare form of breast carcinoma is seen primarily in children, but it can also occur in adults.[660,663,665] Grossly, it is well circumscribed and usually small (Fig. 20.79). The microscopic appearance is distinctive (Fig. 20.80). The margins are of the "pushing" type, and prominent hyalinization is often present in the central portion. The microscopic appearance is distinctive. Tubuloalveolar and focally papillary formations lined by cells with a vacuolated (sometimes hypernephroid) cytoplasm are seen forming lumina filled by an eosinophilic PAS-positive secretion.[662,664,665] Nucleoli may be prominent, but mitoses are very scanty. Ultrastructurally, the tumor cells contain numerous membrane-bound intracytoplasmic secretory vacuoles.[658]

Immunohistochemically, there is strong reactivity for α-lactalbumin and S-100 protein, accompanied by variable expression of GCDF-15 and CEA.[661] It has been hypothesized that there may be a histogenetic link between secretory carcinoma and the newly described acinic cell carcinoma of breast[659] (see p. 1828)

The overall prognosis is excellent, most series quoting a 5-year survival rate close to 100%.[662] Local recurrences and nodal metastases can develop, sometimes very late in the course of the disease.[660,664,665] Death resulting from disseminated tumor has been recorded only exceptionally.[665]

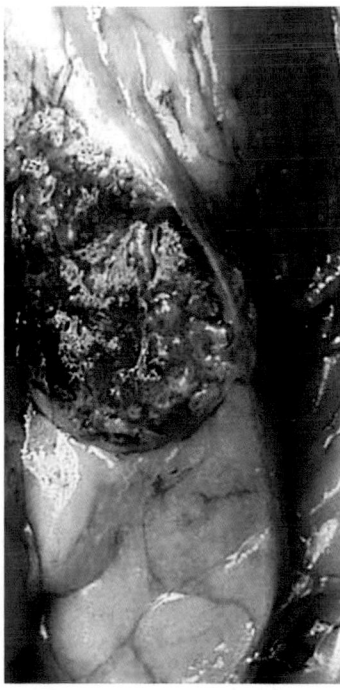

Fig. 20.79 Gross appearance of secretory carcinoma. The tumor is well circumscribed and shows a variegated cut surface.

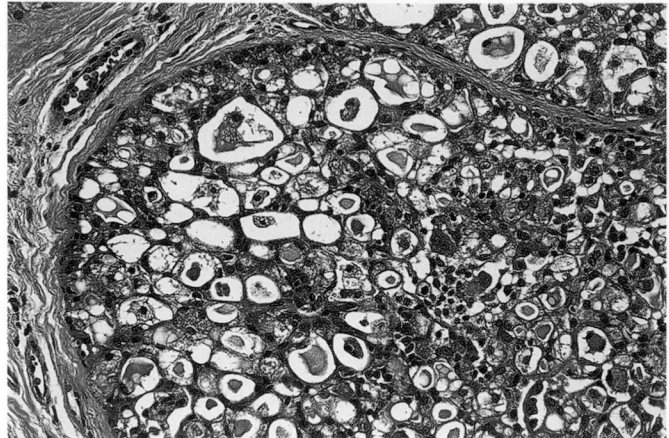

Fig. 20.80 Secretory carcinoma. The small uniform glands are filled by a secretory material.

Carcinomas with neuroendocrine features (including so-called "carcinoid tumor"). The term carcinoid tumor was originally proposed for a type of invasive ductal carcinoma exhibiting features consistent with endocrine differentiation.[673] In general, the clinical presentation is no different from that of the ordinary breast carcinoma. Specifically, none of the patients has had carcinoid syndrome, even in the presence of widespread disease. Multicentricity and bilaterality can occur.[673] There are no distinctive gross features.

Microscopically, the tumor cells are small, arranged in solid nests separated by fibrous tissue (Fig. 20.81). Ribbons and rosettelike formations may be seen. Mitoses are generally rare. The presence of an intraductal component and of mucin secretion has been detected in a minority of the cases.[673] The microscopic differential diagnosis includes lobular carcinoma and a metastasis to the breast of a carcinoid tumor located elsewhere.

The tumor cells of carcinoid tumor of the breast are argyrophilic but not argentaffin and are found to contain dense-core secretory granules of various types ultrastructurally[670,673] (Fig. 20.82).

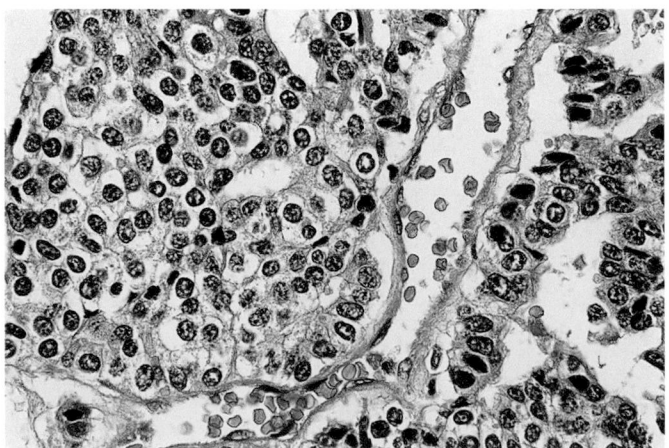

Fig. 20.81 Breast carcinoma with neuroendocrine differentiation (so-called "carcinoid tumor of breast").

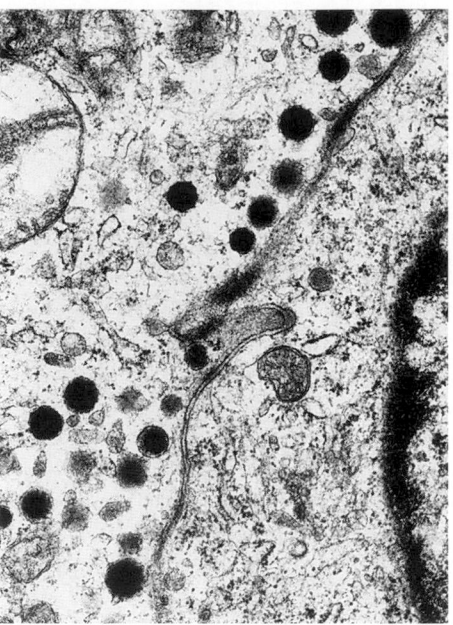

Fig. 20.82 Electron microscopic appearance of breast carcinoma with neuroendocrine differentiation. Primarily ectoplasmic dense-core neurosecretory type granules ranging in size from 140 to 225 nm are seen. (×29,400; courtesy of Dr. Robert A. Erlandson, Memorial Sloan-Kettering Cancer Center)

The nature of this neoplasm has been controversial from the very first description.[677,689] It has even been suggested that the argyrophilia and the dense-core secretory granules are not an indication of neuroendocrine differentiation at all but rather of lactalbumin secretion by the tumor cells.[671] To be sure, not all membrane-bound dense-core cytoplasmic granules are of neurosecretory type.[668] However, the immunohistochemical positivity that has been obtained for chromogranin, synaptophysin, and neuron-specific enolase,[669,682,692,693] and in some instances for specific hormone peptides,[681,687] would seem to verify that these tumors do indeed exhibit signs of endocrine differentiation (Fig. 20.83). Whether this justifies calling them carcinoid tumors is another matter. It seems to us that they are the example of a phenomenon similar to that described in practically all other organs (i.e., that of a carcinoma arising from primitive epithelial cells with the capacity to differentiate focally or extensively towards an endocrine line).[678] Such carcinomas otherwise resemble ordinary ductal-type carcinoma in most other ways: occasional presence of an in situ component, frequent positivity for estrogen receptors, pattern of metastases, expression of apocrine differentiation (especially in aged women), and outcome.[676a,679,683,686] Therefore, we like to view and designate this tumor as invasive ductal carcinoma with (neuro) endocrine differentiation or features, a term we prefer to the alternative designation argyrophilic carcinoma.[667,690] According to Azzopardi et al.,[667] this tumor constitutes approximately 5% of all breast carcinomas.

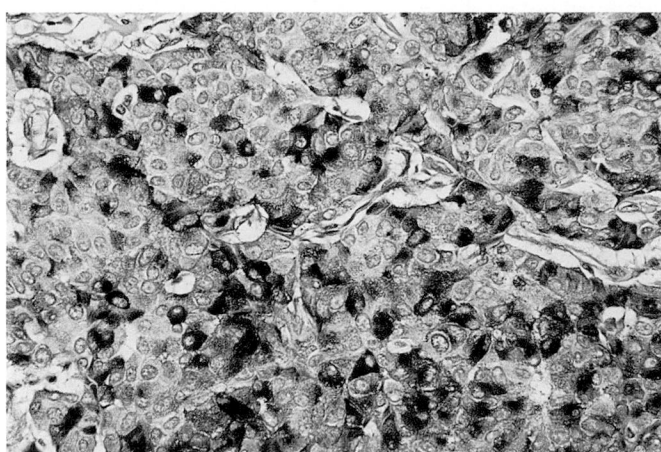

Fig. 20.83 Strong reactivity for chromogranin in breast carcinoma with neuroendocrine differentiation.

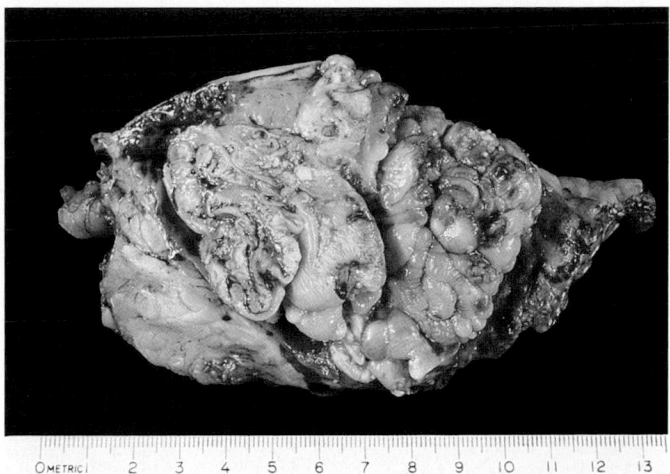

Fig. 20.84 Gross appearance of metaplastic carcinoma. A large, fleshy mass is seen protruding inside a cavity. Microscopically, this tumor showed an admixture of squamous and spindle elements.

It should be mentioned here that there are breast carcinomas of other morphologic patterns in which endocrine features have been found: the already mentioned mucinous carcinoma[674] (see p. 1806), small cell neuroendocrine carcinoma,[676,684,685,688] invasive ductal-type carcinomas of ordinary type,[680,690] and some types of in situ ductal carcinoma[672,678,691] (see p. 1799). Exceptionally, neuroendocrine carcinoma of either breast or nipple may have Merkel cell-like features.[666,675] Interestingly, carcinoid tumors of the conventional type are virtually nonexistent in the breast. We have seen only one case that had morphologic and histochemical features (argentaffinity) identical to those of classic (insular) carcinoid tumors of midgut derivation; remarkably, it was associated with the presence of argentaffin cells in the adjacent breast epithelium.

Metaplastic carcinoma. Metaplastic carcinoma is a generic term for breast carcinoma of ductal type in which the predominant component of the neoplasm has an appearance other than epithelial and glandular and more in keeping with another cell type. As such, the designation is too encompassing and imprecise and should not be used without a qualifier. It includes the following categories, which overlap considerably with each other:

1 A tumor equivalent to the one designated in other sites (notably the upper aerodigestive tract and lung) as *sarcomatoid carcinoma*, carcinoma with sarcoma-like stroma, and carcinosarcoma (Fig. 20.84). Grossly, it tends to be well circumscribed. Microscopically, the sarcoma-like component may resemble malignant fibrous histiocytoma, chondrosarcoma, osteosarcoma, rhabdomyosarcoma, angiosarcoma, or a combination of them.[696,697,703,705] There may be a gradual transition from carcinomatous to sarcoma-like elements, or the separation between them can be sharp.[702] When the latter is the case, the term *carcinosarcoma* tends to be used.[717,723] Tumors having overt carcinomas with direct transition to a cartilaginous and/or osseous matrix without an intervening spindle cell zone or osteoclastic giant cells have been referred to as "matrix producing carcinomas,"[722] but the distinction seems to be of little clinical value and dubious biologic significance.[700,708]

Immunohistochemically, the sarcoma-like elements of these tumors have usually acquired vimentin positivity and other features of a mesenchymal nature ("phenotypical switch") but occasionally still retain epithelial markers,[699,712] a fact best demonstrated by employing wide-spectrum keratin antibodies.[694]

As in other sites, molecular studies support the interpretation that the recognizable epithelial and the sarcoma-like components originate from the same stem cell.[719,720,726]

2 *Spindle cell carcinoma.* The overt carcinomatous component of these tumors, when present, may have invasive or in situ ductal features, and it may be entirely squamous.[721] The spindle cell component, which may be deceptively bland, forms abundant fibrocollagenous stroma with feathered, myxoid, angioid, and storiform patterns[725] (Fig. 20.85). The appearance may closely simulate that of a fibrosarcoma or even fibromatosis.[701,716] Areas of merging between the epithelial and the spindle component are common. The latter foci are usually immunoreactive for keratin.[709] Some of these arise in connection with a complex sclerosing lesion or so-called "adenomyoepithelioma," and contain some of the immunohistochemical markers of myoepithelial cells.[696a,698,701a,710,715] Whether to call them metaplastic carcinomas or malignant myoepitheliomas seems a matter of personal preference.[698a]

3 *Carcinoma with osteoclast-like giant cells.*[695,718,724] When these cells appear in conjunction with sarcoma-like elements, the tumor should be regarded as a variant of the first category listed. When they are seen in the stroma of what is otherwise a typical invasive ductal-type carcinoma lacking sarcomatoid foci, the tumor

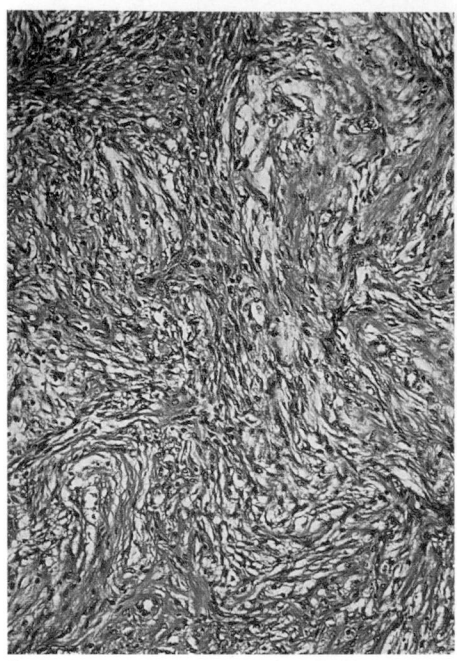 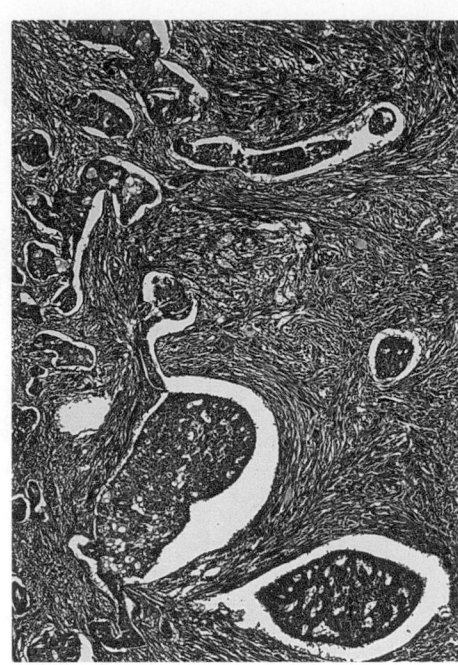

Fig. 20.85 A and **B**, Metaplastic carcinoma. The tumor shown in **A** exhibits a blending of the carcinomatous and sarcoma-like components, whereas that depicted in **B** has a biphasic ("carcinosarcomatous") appearance.

should be placed in a category of its own but closer to ordinary ductal carcinoma. All available evidence suggests that the osteoclast-like elements are of non-neoplastic histiocytic nature and that they form from fusion of mononuclear precursors.[704,706]

4 *Squamous cell carcinoma.* Although technically speaking this represents a form of tumor metaplasia, it differs so substantially from the others that we thought of discussing it separately (see next section).

5 *Others.* A single case of metaplastic carcinoma with melanocytic differentiation has been reported.[711] This is to be distinguished from the more common phenomenon of melanocytic colonization of carcinoma, and from the presence of lipofuscin granules that can simulate melanin.[713] The *pleomorphic carcinoma* is yet another variation of anaplastic breast carcinoma that can resemble sarcoma. This is regarded as a variant of ductal carcinoma and is, therefore, different from pleomorphic lobular carcinoma.[714]

The differential diagnosis of these tumor types (particularly the first two categories) includes phylloides tumor and primary breast sarcoma.

On the whole, the behavior of metaplastic carcinoma seems to be more aggressive than that of ordinary invasive ductal-type carcinoma.[696b,705,707] The differences in survival among the various subgroups are rather minor, although some authors have suggested a worse prognosis for the "carcinosarcoma" subgroup. Metastases tend to be hematogenous rather than to lymph nodes, in keeping with the sarcomatous phenotype.[696b,705] The size of the neoplasm at the time of initial excision is one of the best predictors of survival.[707]

Squamous cell carcinoma and related tumors. Squamous cell carcinoma is an extremely rare variant of breast tumor.[736] Tumors of cutaneous origin and those in which the squamous component is a portion of an otherwise typical phylloides tumor should be excluded. It is also important not to misinterpret the syncytial areas of medullary carcinoma or the partial apocrine changes sometimes seen in other tumors as representing squamous changes.

The gross appearance of squamous cell carcinoma differs little from that of the usual breast carcinomas, although sometimes a large central cyst filled with keratin can be identified. Microscopically, most cases seem to represent instances of squamous metaplasia in ductal carcinoma, indicating that squamous cell carcinoma could be viewed as a special type of metaplastic carcinoma.[734] This view is reinforced by the existence of so-called "spindle cell carcinoma," in which a well-differentiated squamous component merges with a prominent spindle cell sarcomatoid component[727,733] (see p. 1811). Occasionally, the tumor is accompanied by a prominent myxoid stroma.[732]

Two further variants are *acantholytic squamous cell carcinoma*, in which the lack of cohesiveness of tumor cells results in a pseudovascular or pseudoglandular appearance,[730] and *adenosquamous carcinoma*.[728,735,738] Some examples of the latter tumor type have been designated as mucoepidermoid carcinoma,[731] a term that should be avoided except for those tumors having cytoarchitectural features analogous to those of their salivary gland counterparts (see p. 1829).

It is difficult to ascertain the prognosis of squamous cell carcinoma in view of the differences in diagnostic criteria from series to series and the rarity of the disease. In the series of Wargotz et al.,[737] the 5-year disease-specific survival rate was 63%. On the whole, the behavior of this tumor does not seem to be substantially different from that of ordinary ductal-type invasive carcinoma.[727,729] This may not hold true for the acantholytic variant, which seems to be associated with a very aggressive course,[730] or for the low-grade adenosquamous carcinoma, which is said to have a favorable prognosis.[735]

Spread-related variants

Inflammatory carcinoma. The term inflammatory carcinoma was originally used in a clinical sense for a type of breast carcinoma in which the entire breast was reddened and warm, with widespread edema of the skin, thus simulating the appearance of mastitis. Pathologic studies in some of those cases revealed the lesion to be an undifferentiated carcinoma with widespread carcinomatosis of the dermal lymphatic vessels (Fig. 20.86). This led to the belief that an "inflammatory" clinical appearance always corresponded pathologically to dermal lymphatic permeation and vice versa. This assumption is not always correct. Patients may have inflammatory carcinoma clinically in the absence of dermal invasion; conversely, widespread permeation of dermal lymphatics can be seen in the absence of the clinical features of inflammatory carcinoma (so-called "occult" inflammatory carcinoma[745]). From a prognostic standpoint, the presence of dermal lymphatic permeation on microscopic examination is a sign of ominous prognosis, whether the clinical appearance is that of an inflammatory carcinoma or not.[710,742,743,745] The clinical recognition of this entity by an experienced observer is also reliable and associated with a poor prognosis, but ideally it should be accompanied by a skin biopsy showing dermal lymphatic involvement before the tumor is deemed inoperable.[744] Some authors

have recommended discarding the term inflammatory carcinoma altogether.[742] The choice of therapy for this neoplasm remains highly controversial.[739,741,746]

Paget's disease. Paget's disease is the name given to a crusted lesion of the nipple caused by breast carcinoma, as originally described by Sir James Paget in 1874.[763] It is accompanied in nearly all instances by an underlying breast carcinoma of in situ ductal type, with or without associated stromal invasion. In this regard, the presence of Paget's disease is only a secondary, albeit dramatic, feature of the tumor. The management and prognosis depend largely on the intraductal versus invasive nature of the underlying carcinoma and on the presence or absence of axillary lymph node involvement, rather than on the presence or appearance of the intraepithelial component in the nipple.[764]

Clinically, these weeping, eczema-like lesions are centered in the nipple (Fig. 20.87). Later they may involve the areola and surrounding epidermis, but they rarely extend more than a few centimeters. If a definite mass can be palpated beneath the diseased nipple, the underlying tumor will have an invasive component in over 90% of cases. Conversely, 66% of cases without a palpable mass are exclusively intraductal.[747]

Microscopically, large clear cells with atypical nuclei are seen within the epidermis, usually concentrated along the basal layer but also permeating the malpighian layer (Fig. 20.88). The cells can be isolated or in clusters, and sometimes they form small glandular structures. In rare instances they have an anaplastic appearance.[765] Occasionally, intracytoplasmic melanin granules are present, a feature that may result in a mistaken diagnosis of malignant melanoma; these granules have probably been transferred from neighboring melanocytes by the process of cytocrinia[748] (Fig. 20.89). This phenomenon should be distinguished from the exceptional type of carcinoma with melanocytic differentiation (see page 1812) and

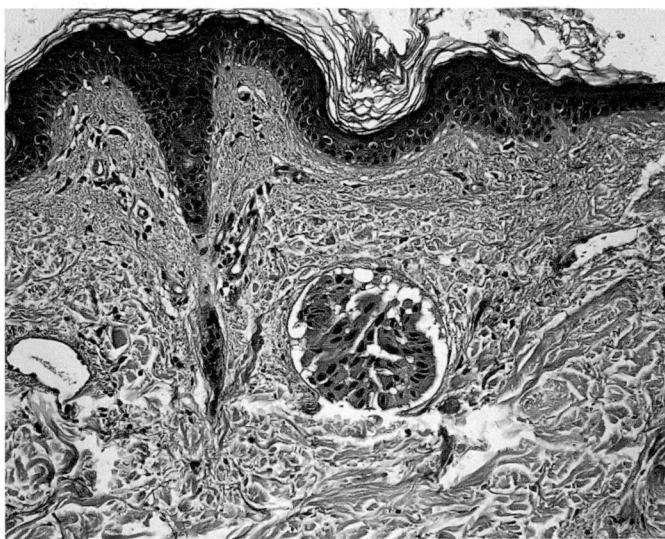

Fig. 20.86 Large tumor embolus in a dermal lymph vessel in a case with the clinical appearance of inflammatory carcinoma.

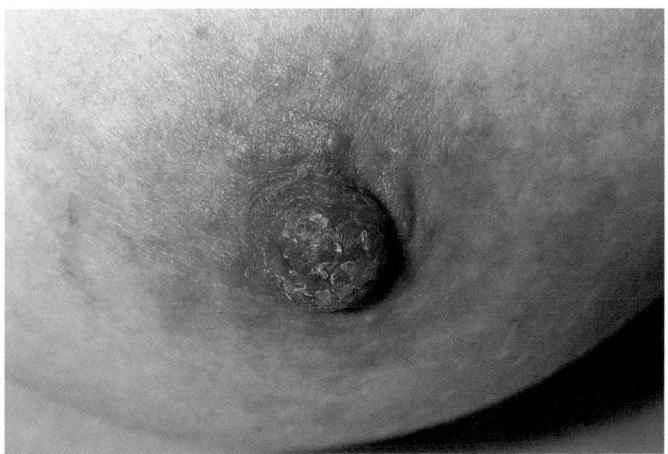

Fig. 20.87 Eczema-like hyperemic and eroded clinical appearance of Paget's disease. (Courtesy of Dr. RA Cooke, Brisbane, Australia; from Cooke RA, Stewart B: Colour Atlas of Anatomical Pathology. Edinburgh, Churchill Livingstone, 2004).

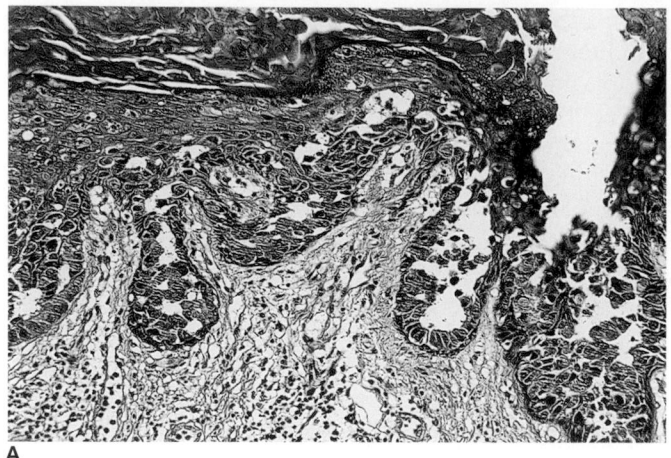 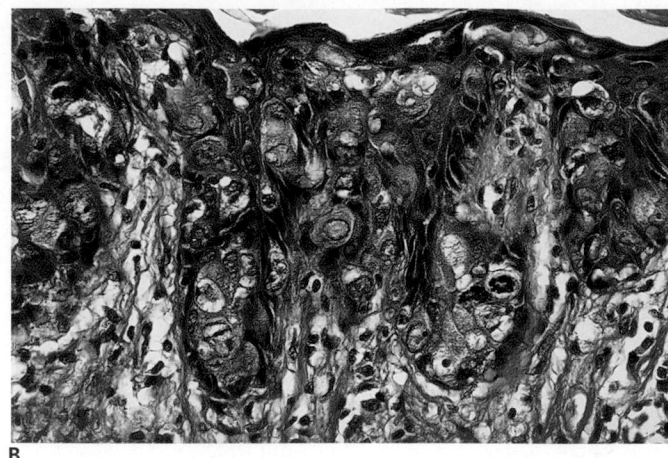

Fig. 20.88 A and **B**, Low- and high-power views of Paget's disease. The cleft-like separation between the tumor cells and the overlying squamous epithelium is characteristic.

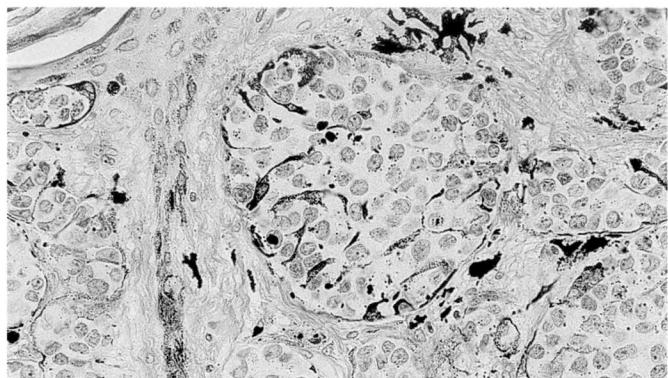

Fig. 20.89 Melanin colonization in breast carcinoma as seen with argentaffin stain. (Slide prepared by Dr. Pierre Masson, University of Montreal, and sent by him to Dr. Fred W. Stewart, Memorial Sloan-Kettering Cancer Center)

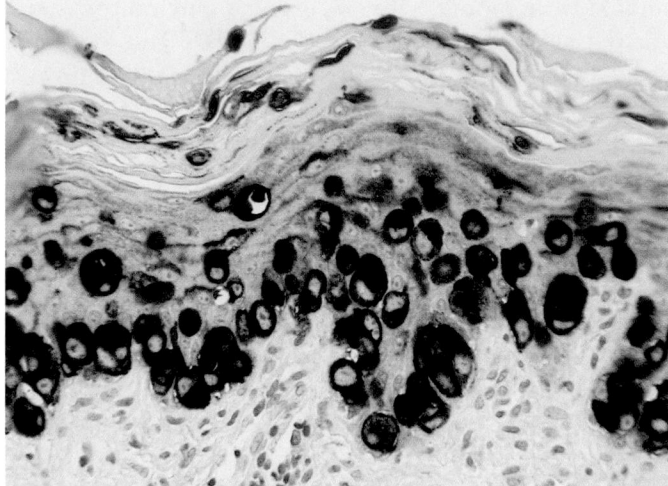

A

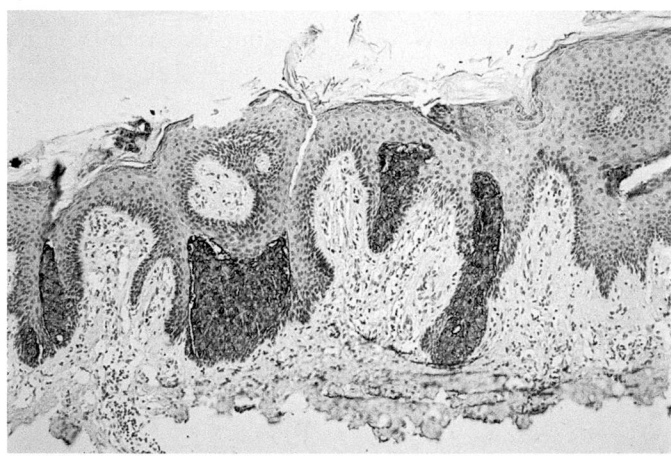

B

Fig. 20.90 Immunohistochemical demonstration of malignant intraepithelial cells in Paget's disease: **A**, EMA immunostain; **B**, HER2/*neu* immunostain.

from the carcinoma containing cytoplasmic lipofuscin granules mimicking melanin.[767]

The underlying breast carcinoma is practically always of ductal type and is composed of cells similar to those present within the nipple. If enough sections are taken, a connection between the carcinoma within the duct and the Paget's disease will be demonstrated in most instances. However, in some cases the underlying tumor is found 2 cm or more from the nipple.[764]

Mucin stains may or may not be positive, in contrast to their almost universal presence in extramammary Paget's disease.[761,767] Ultrastructurally, the tumor cells have microvilli and other features indicative of glandular differentiation.[766] Immunohistochemically, they show reactivity for EMA and the related milk fat globule membrane antigen, CEA (at least when using polyclonal antibodies), low-molecular-weight keratin (including CK7), HER2/*neu* and (in half of the cases) GCDFP-15[749,753,755,762,770] (Fig. 20.90). In general, they are negative for S-100 protein and involucrin.[762]

The main differential diagnosis is with Bowen's disease and malignant melanoma. Examples of these disorders located in the nipple have been reported,[771] and

there is no reason why they could not involve this structure. We can only say that, in our experience, whenever this differential diagnosis was considered for a lesion of the nipple (because of pigmentation, transepidermal

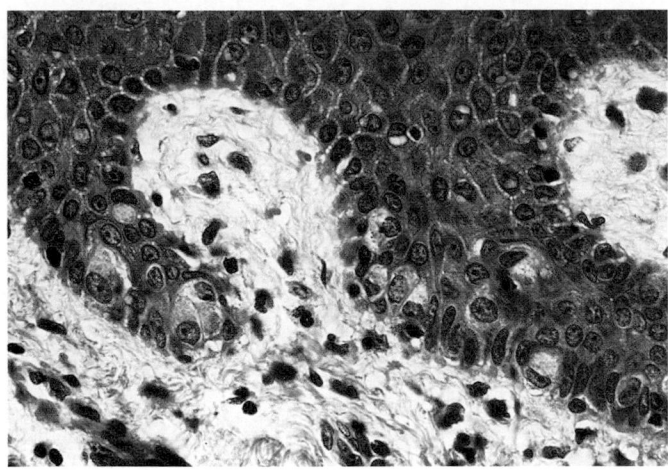

Fig. 20.91 Biopsy of nipple showing scattered clear cells in the basal layer ("Toker's cells"). These cells show a mild degree of nuclear atypia and were immunohistochemically similar to the cells of Paget's disease.

atypia, or any other reason), the definitive diagnosis invariably turned out to be Paget's disease.

The heated controversies in the past regarding the glandular versus keratinocytic versus melanocytic origin of Paget's disease have subsided. There can no longer be any doubt that Paget's cells exhibit glandular differentiation.[760] However, a point still unsettled is whether the Paget's cells in the nipple have migrated there from deeper ductal structures (possibly as a result of keratinocyte-induced chemotaxis[751]) or whether they represent an in situ malignant transformation either of the intraepidermal portion of the mammary ducts or of basally located multipotential epithelial cells capable of glandular differentiation.[756] The similarities in immunohistochemical profile and oncogene expression (such as c-*erb*B-2 or *ras*21) favor the former.[750,752,758,759,772] On the other hand, the existence of rare cases of Paget's disease without underlying ductal carcinoma or with very limited in situ carcinoma of the most distal lactiferous ducts suggests that, in some cases, the latter mechanism may be operating.[754,756] In this regard, the observation made by Toker[769] about the presence of clear cells in nipples without clinical evidence of Paget's disease and without microscopic evidence of breast carcinoma is of great interest. We have also observed these cells (although not nearly with that frequency) and found not only that they react immunohistochemically like Paget's cells[755] but also that they may exhibit mild nuclear atypical changes, suggesting the possibility of a dysplastic or "pre-Paget's" change[757] (Fig. 20.91). From a practical standpoint, these cells are distinguished from those of Paget's disease because of the lack of eczema-like changes clinically and the absence of clear-cut cytologic features of malignancy.

Invasive lobular carcinoma (ILC)

Classic type. In its most characteristic form, invasive lobular carcinoma (ILC) is characterized by the presence of small and relatively uniform tumor cells growing singly, in Indian file, and in a concentric ("pagetoid") fashion around lobules involved by in situ lobular neoplasia[774] (Figs 20.92 to 20.94). Most of the breast tumors designated in the past as small cell carcinomas belong to this category. Gland formation is not a feature of classic ILC. The stroma is usually abundant, is of dense fibrous type, and contains foci of periductal and perivenous elastosis in virtually every case. A lymphocytic infiltrate may be present, sometimes so intense as to obscure the neoplastic component.

It is currently accepted that the diagnosis of ILC can be made in the presence of these cytoarchitectural features

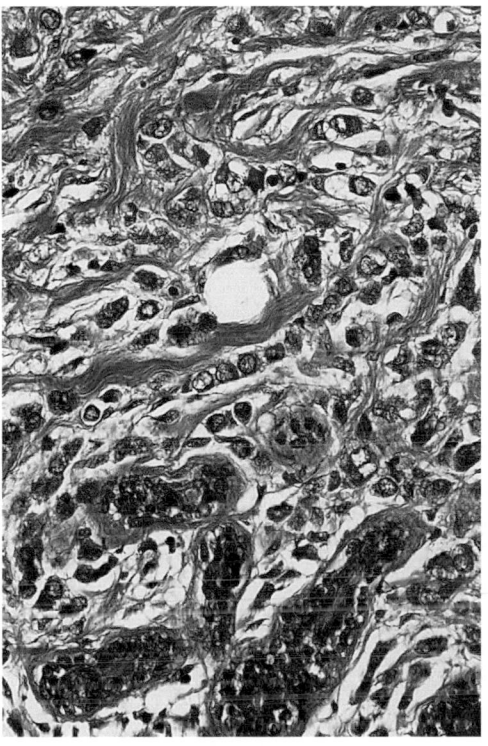

Fig. 20.92 Invasive lobular carcinoma. The tumor cells are small and uniform with round nuclei and grow in an Indian file fashion.

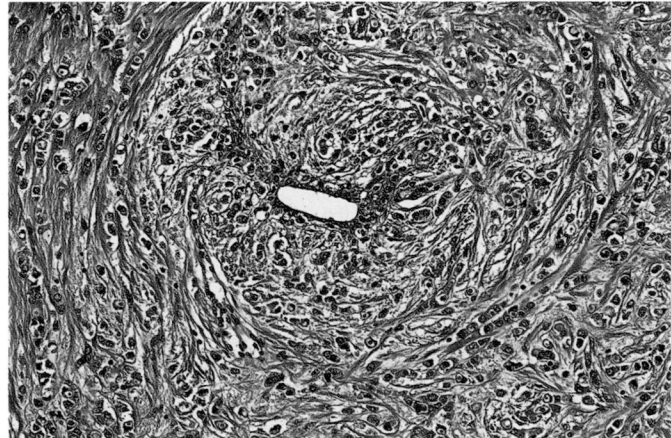

Fig. 20.93 Typical target-like growth of tumor cells around an uninvolved duct in invasive lobular carcinoma.

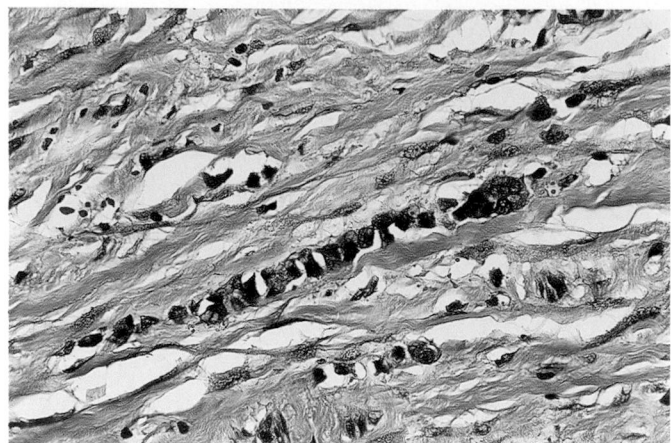

Fig. 20.94 Indian file pattern of growth of invasive lobular carcinoma.

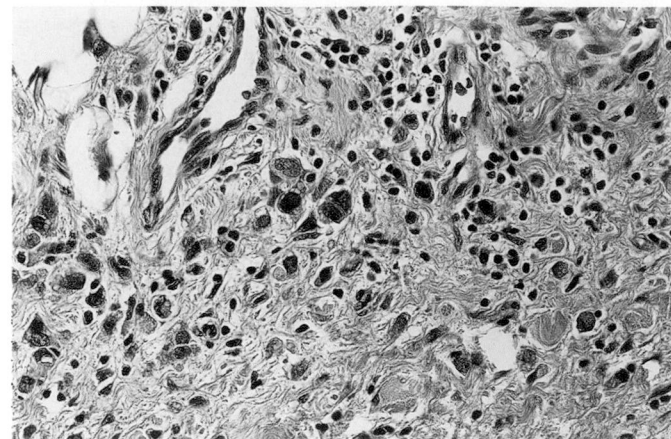

Fig. 20.95 Pleomorphic variant of invasive lobular carcinoma.

even if an in situ component is absent.[776,780] Conversely, an invasive tumor should not be called ILC simply because it is associated with in situ lobular neoplasia; rather, it should have the features of lobular carcinoma in the invasive component itself in order to deserve this designation.

The histochemical, ultrastructural, and immunohistochemical features of ILC are analogous to those described for its in situ counterpart. This includes the presence of HMW keratin, lack of accumulation of p53, and—most importantly—decrease or absence of E-cadherin.[773,775,777,778]

The main differential diagnosis of ILC is with IDC. The small size and uniformity of the cells and their lack of cohesiveness are the most important distinguishing features. It should be remarked, however, that in many cases the distinction is difficult and to a large extent subjective, as borne out by the fact that the incidence of ILC ranges from 0.7% to 20% in the published series.[779] Other entities that can be confused with ILC are carcinoma with neuroendocrine features and malignant lymphoma. The latter possibility arises more often when ILC metastasizes to axillary nodes and other sites, particularly the eyelid; we have seen several cases misdiagnosed as large cell malignant lymphoma or malignant histiocytosis because of their diffuse pattern of growth and the histiocyte-like appearance of the tumor cells. Reactions for keratin, EMA, CEA, LCA, and an old-fashioned mucicarmine stain should eliminate any problems not resolved by the examination of the routinely stained slides.

Pleomorphic lobular carcinoma. This form of invasive breast tumor has the pattern of growth of a classical breast carcinoma but exhibits a marked degree of nuclear pleomorphism and abundant cytoplasm[785] (Fig. 20.95). It also frequently shows apocrine differentiation, focal signet ring morphology, lack of hormone receptors, higher expression of p53 and HER2/*neu*, occasional expression of chromogranin, and lack of E-cadherin

staining (the latter in keeping with its lobular nature).[781–784]

Histiocytoid carcinoma. Histiocytoid carcinoma is characterized by a diffuse pattern of growth by tumor cells displaying abundant granular, foamy cytoplasm.[789,791] It may simulate the appearance of a granular cell tumor, hence the proposed synonym *myoblastoid carcinoma*.[786] This tumor type is currently viewed as a variant of invasive lobular carcinoma exhibiting apocrine differentiation, as evidenced by immunohistochemical reactivity for GCDFP-15 and the demonstration of mRNA for the related prolactin-inducible protein (PIP) by in situ hybridization.[786,793] In most cases E-cadherin is absent, as one would expect in a lobular carcinoma-type tumor, but other features are more suggestive of a link with ductal-type tumors.[788]

Histiocytoid carcinoma should also be distinguished from *lipid-rich carcinoma*. The latter is simply a form of breast carcinoma showing lipid accumulation in the cytoplasm of the tumor cells[787,790,792] (Fig. 20.96).

Signet ring carcinoma. Signet ring carcinoma is a type of breast carcinoma in which a significant number of

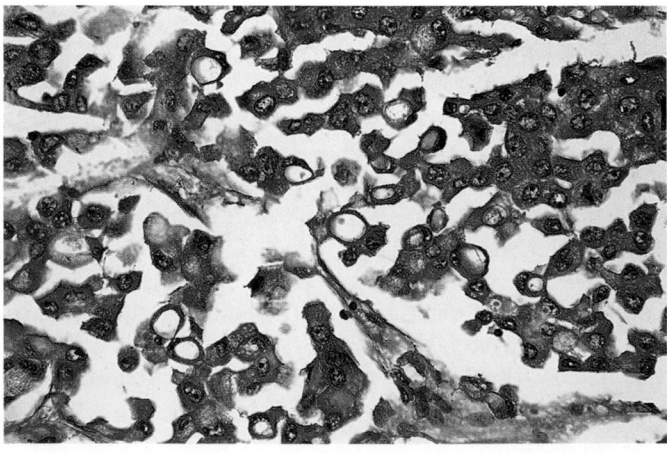

Fig. 20.96 Cytoplasmic vacuolization with nuclear displacement in breast carcinoma due to lipid accumulation.

tumor cells show intracytoplasmic mucin accumulation, resulting in the typical signet ring appearance[797] (Fig. 20.97). Unfortunately, the term "significant" is used differently by different people. Some will place a tumor into this category only if the majority of the cells have a signet ring morphology, whereas others would settle for a much smaller number.[794,796] In any event, it is important to sharply separate this tumor from mucinous carcinoma because of their vastly different prognoses, even if occasionally the two types have been found to coexist (see p. 1807).

Most cases of signet ring carcinoma show cytoarchitectural features (such as small cell size, uniformity, and dissociation) similar to those of classic ILC and sometimes coexist with it.[800] Furthermore, it is not rare for in situ or invasive lobular carcinoma to contain scattered signet ring cells.[801] For these reasons, most cases of signet ring carcinoma are regarded as variants of ILC.[799,802] Some, however, are probably more closely related to ductal carcinoma of either invasive[797] or in situ type.[795]

The signet ring morphology appears to be the result of deficiency in α-catenin, presumably due to mutations.[798] Ultrastructurally, it is manifested in its more extreme form by a large membrane-bound vacuole of varying, but usually low, electron density.[803] As already indicated, this is a different process from that of intracellular lumen formation, which is characterized ultrastructurally by a microvillus-coated cavity and which appears as a bull's-eye on light microscopic examination.

Tubulolobular carcinoma. This variant is characterized by the admixture of small tubular formations having a minute or undetectable lumen ("closed" or "almost closed" tubules) with cords of tumor cells growing in a lobular configuration similar to that of invasive lobular carcinoma.[804] Its immunohistochemical profile is intermediate between those of ductal and lobular carcinoma.[805a] It is associated with a higher incidence of multifocality and positive axillary nodes than pure tubular carcinoma.[805]

Other types. Some authors restrict their diagnosis of ILC to tumors having the features described for the classic type. Others have expanded considerably the concept and include in this category tumors that traditionally have been placed into the IDC category.[806,808,809] These include most of the tumors just described under the category of invasive lobular carcinoma "variants." Furthermore, cases having closely aggregated cells, solid pattern, trabecular pattern, loose alveolar pattern, and spindle cell chains have been accepted as ILC, *as long as the relatively bland and homogeneous cytologic appearance was maintained*. Perhaps the most distinctive of these forms is the alveolar variant, in which the tumor cells are arranged in sharply outlined groups separated by fibrous tissue sometimes containing osteoclast-like giant cells.[810,811]

The cytologic and/or architectural similarities between these various forms and classic ILC are undeniable. The problem, however, is that the more the concept of ILC is widened, and to some extent diluted, the less distinct the entity becomes and the less significant (or at least the less uniform) its clinical connotations are.[807]

Mixed ductal and lobular carcinoma

Biphasic carcinomas composed in part of a component with definite features of invasive ductal carcinoma and in part of a component with definite features of invasive lobular carcinoma do occur, but they are very rare. These

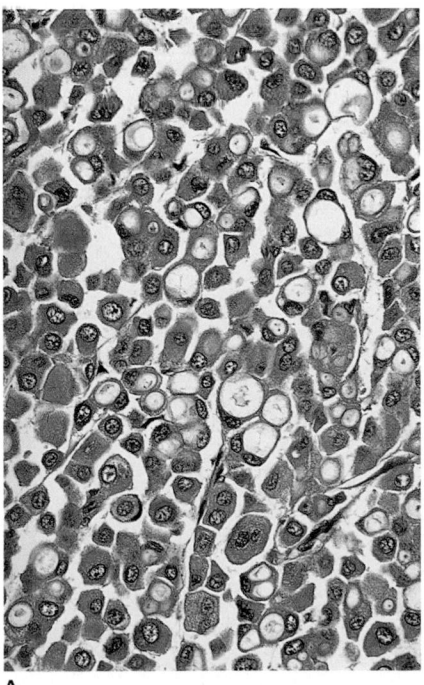 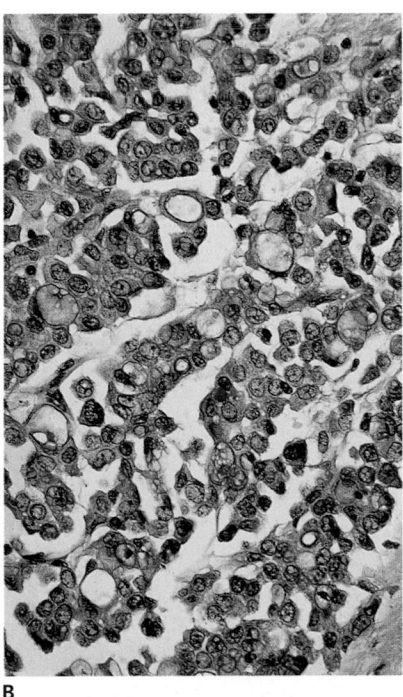

A   B

Fig. 20.97 A and **B**, Signet ring carcinoma of the breast, this is regarded as a variant of lobular carcinoma. **B**, Alcian blue–PAS stain.

tumors, of course, should be distinguished from the cases in which two separate neoplasms of different microscopic appearances are present in the same breast. They should also be distinguished from so-called tubu-lobular carcinoma, which has a reasonably distinct morphologic appearance (see page 1817).

Undetermined (unclassified) carcinoma

This category includes all cases of invasive carcinoma in which features of ductal or lobular type are not definite enough to place it into either category. Azzopardi[812] states that 3% to 4% of the invasive breast carcinomas belong to this category.

Microinvasive breast carcinoma

Once the concept of "microinvasive carcinoma" was entrenched in the gynecological literature, especially in connection with cervical squamous cell carcinoma, it was only natural that it would be proposed at other sites, including the breast, and the time has arrived. Alas, its application at this site is not as straightforward, one of the reasons being that the mammary epithelium is not separated from the stroma by a sharp, straight line as it is in the cervix.[818] Be that as it may, the proposal has been made to designate as microinvasive carcinoma any CIS of the breast showing one or more areas of stromal inva-sion not surpassing 1 mm in thickness.[815] Theoretically, it is applicable to both ductal and lobular lesions, but the term seems to be used more often to the former. It may be single or multiple, the mean number of foci being two.[817] Immunohistochemical evaluation with myoepithelial and basement membrane markers is useful for a confir-mation of the diagnosis.[815,819] Problems related to the definition criteria and clinical significance of this finding remain and need to be addressed.[814,818] On the whole, it would seem that patients with microinvasive carcinoma are at risk for nodal metastases[820] but that their survival rate is better than for patients with T1 invasive carci-noma.[816] Apparently, the risk for metastases is greater if the invasive component is in the form of cell clusters than in the form of a few isolated tumor cells.[813]

Hormone receptors

A crucial development in the evaluation of breast carci-noma has been the realization that the presence of hormone (estrogen and progesterone) receptors in the tumor tissue correlates well with response to hormone therapy and chemotherapy.[823,833] Traditionally, these hor-mone receptors were measured by the dextran-coated charcoal and sucrose gradient assay, but this has been replaced in nearly all centers by the immunohistochemi-cal method, on the grounds that it offers several important advantages (it does not require fresh tissue, it can be done with minute amounts of tumor, etc.), and

that the correlation between the two methods is very good[824,832,835,842,844] (Fig. 20.98). Several attempts have been made to semiquantitate this method by standardizing the technical procedure and reporting and by using the appropriate controls—a need that has been strongly emphasized.[821,838] Regarding the latter, Battifora's team has proposed a very innovative procedure for a control, which they refer to as the Quicgel method.[839] Although the idea is ingenious indeed (as we have been accus-tomed to expect from this group), it may be a little too complex to be widely adopted.

The two parameters evaluated in immunohistochemi-cal preparations of hormone receptors are the number of tumor cell nuclei stained and the intensity of the reac-tion. The first is expressed as a percentage of the entire tumor cell nuclei population, and the second is graded as negative, weak, moderate, and strong. The two parame-ters are sometimes combined into a scoring system, of which three major versions exist.[832,837] Although several sophisticated image analysis programs have been devised for this purpose,[822] in most laboratories these estimations are done visually.

Hormone receptors can also be evaluated in paraffin-embedded breast tissue by the in situ hybridization technique and by PCR.[829,831]

Not much correlation exists between the cytoarchitec-tural type of breast carcinoma and presence of hormone receptor protein[840]; specifically, no statistically significant difference has been found between ductal-type and lobu-lar-type tumors. However, most series have shown that most medullary carcinomas and intraductal carcinomas of the comedocarcinoma type are negative, whereas mucinous carcinomas have the highest rates of posi-tivity.[836,841] In DCIS, a predominance of large cells is the best morphologic predictor of estrogen receptor-negative status.[827]

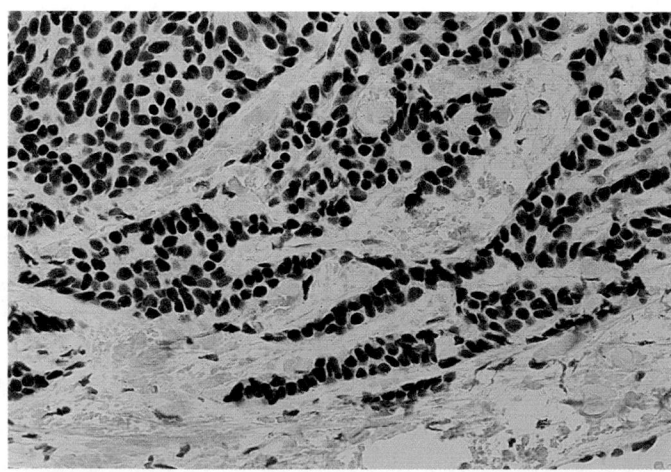

Fig. 20.98 Immunocytochemical stain for estrogen receptors in invasive breast carcinoma. The strong nuclear positivity in tumor cells is shown against a negative cytoplasmic and stromal background.

Generally, estrogen receptor concentrations are lower (and androgen receptor concentrations are greater) in tumors of premenopausal women than in those of post-menopausal women.[834,841] Fisher et al.[830] found the presence of estrogen receptors to be significantly associated with high nuclear and low histologic grades, absence of tumor necrosis, presence of marked tumor elastosis, and older patients' age groups. Hormone receptor positivity also correlates with bcl-2 immunoreactivity[861] and absence of *p53* mutations,[828] and it correlates inversely with the presence of epidermal growth factor receptors.[843]

It should be pointed out that most breast carcinoma cells also have receptors for androgens, and that these may be found in the absence of estrogen and progesterone receptors.[825] As a matter of fact, they seem to be more common in estrogen receptor-negative tumors.[820a]

HER2/*neu*

HER2/*neu* (c-*erb*B-2) is an oncogene that encodes a transmembrane glycoprotein with tyrosine kinase activity known as p185, which belongs to the family of epidermal growth factor receptors.[848,853] Its overexpression can be measured by immunohistochemistry or FISH (or its chromogenic equivalent),[854] and a good correlation exists between these methods[847,850,852] (Fig. 20.99). A heated controversy has been generated in recent years regarding the relative merits of the two methods, fueled by the availability of trastuzumab (Herceptin) as a therapeutic agent. Most workers in the field have concluded that the best approach from the point of view of cost effectiveness is to start with the immunohistochemical procedure, which is graded according to the scheme in Table 20.2.

If the results are either 3+ or 0, the determination can safely stop there, since the correlation with gene overexpression or lack of it, respectively, as measured by FISH, is nearly 100%. If the immunotest gives instead a result of

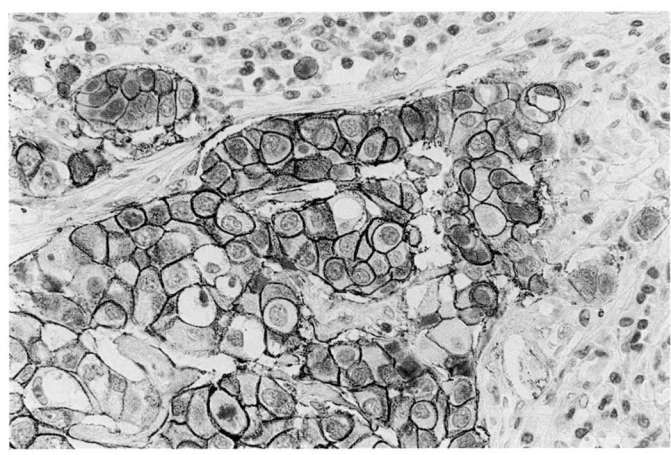

Fig. 20.99 Strong (3+) membrane immunoreactivity for HER2/*neu* in high-grade breast carcinoma.

1+ or 2+, the performance of FISH is recommended.

Overexpression of HER2/*neu* by either technique is a very good predictor of response to Herceptin, but not a very good predictor of response to chemotherapy or overall survival (see p. 1826).

In terms of relationship with tumor types, HER2/*neu* overexpression is found in nearly all cases of high-grade (comedo-type) DCIS, in 20% to 30% of invasive ductal carcinomas, and in a smaller percentage of invasive lobular carcinomas.[845,846,849,851]

Spread and metastases

Breast carcinoma spreads by direct invasion, by the lymphatic route, and by the blood vessel route.[888] Some of these metastases are already present at the time of diagnosis, and others become manifest clinically months, years, or decades after the initial therapy.[857]

Table 20.2 Grading of the immunohistochemical staining for HER2/*neu* overexpression

Staining pattern	Score	HER2/*neu* protein overexpression assessment
No staining is observed or membrane staining is observed in less than 10% of the tumor cells	0	Negative
A faint/barely perceptible membrane staining is detected in more than 10% of the tumor cells. The cells are only stained in part of their membrane	1+	Negative
A weak to moderate complete membrane staining is observed in more than 10% of the tumor cells	2+	Weakly positive
A strong complete membrane staining is observed in more than 10% of the tumor cells	3+	Strongly positive

Local invasion can occur in the breast parenchyma itself, nipple, skin, fascia, pectoralis muscle, or other structures of the chest wall. The invasion of the breast stroma can be by direct extension, via intramammary lymph vessels, and possibly via the tissue spaces present in foci of so-called "pseudoangiomatous stromal hyperplasia."[863] The degree of local invasion is generally greater in invasive lobular carcinoma and its variants, presumably aided by the lack of E-cadherin in the tumor cells.[870] The frequency of microscopic invasion in the breast outside the gross confines was evaluated by Rosen et al.[889] by performing a "local excision" with a 2-cm gross margin in specimens of radical mastectomy and studying microscopically the remainder of the breast. Of 18 mastectomies for carcinoma measuring less than 1 cm, residual invasive carcinoma was found in 11% and residual in situ carcinoma in an additional 22%. The importance of a thorough pathologic evaluation of local invasion in breast carcinoma is now greater because of the large number of conservative surgical procedures being performed.[860]

A somewhat related problem is that of microscopic involvement of the nipple by breast carcinoma, since this structure would obviously be left in the patient if a local excision of the lump were carried out. Nipple invasion has been found in 23% to 31% of all clinically detectable invasive carcinomas; the large majority are seen in tumors located less than 2.5 cm from the nipple.[876,884,894]

Local recurrence following mastectomy appears as superficial nodules in or near the surgical scar or as subcutaneous parasternal nodules. Their malignant nature should always be documented by biopsy because the condition can be closely simulated by foreign body granulomas and infectious processes. Although women with local recurrences have an increased risk of distant metastases,[869] these seem to represent partially independent events that occur at different times.[893]

Tumor recurrence following local excision often develops in the same breast segment, a fact that has led some authors to recommend a primary excision technique that removes en bloc the tumor mass and the associated duct system.[874]

The two lymph node stations typically involved with metastatic breast carcinoma are the axilla and the internal mammary region, with the supraclavicular area representing an extension of the former. It should be remembered that it is not too unusual to also find lymph nodes within the substance of the mammary gland ("intramammary lymph nodes").[890] Axillary node metastases are present in 40% to 50% of clinically detectable cases and are divided into levels according to their topographic relation with the insertion of the pectoralis minor muscle: low or proximal, medium, and high or distal. When extensive, they are clinically detectable, but the margin of error with clinical palpation is high. Careful dissection of the submitted nodes by the pathol-ogist is of extreme importance. The yield of nodes will increase if they are searched for after the axilla is cleared with an organic solvent,[875] but most workers have not found this necessary for a proper search.

Supraclavicular lymph node involvement is present in close to 20% of patients with axillary lymph node involvement but is almost zero in cases with negative axillae.[892]

The second major lymph node drainage area is to the internal mammary chain, which lies at the anterior ends of the intercostal spaces by the side of the internal thoracic artery. The overall incidence of metastatic involvement of this chain in clinically detectable breast carcinoma is approximately 22%.[865] It is less than 1% for tumors in the outer half of the breast and negative axillary nodes, approximately 20% for tumors in the inner half and negative axillary nodes, approximately 30% in tumors of the outer half and positive axillary nodes, and over 50% for tumors in the inner half and positive axillary nodes. Rarely, a metastatic lymph node will appear entirely necrotic and may simulate an infectious process; immunostains for keratin and EMA may be useful to detect the necrotic tumor cells.[891]

Distant metastases are seen most commonly in the skeletal system, lung and pleura, liver, ovary, adrenal gland, and central nervous system (including leptomeninges and eyes)[859,877,881] (Fig. 20.100). Carcinomatous meningitis is a particularly devastating pattern of spread.[873] Diffuse metastasis to spleen is very rare, but it can occur and cause idiopathic thrombocytopenic purpura.[862] Invasive lobular carcinoma (including the signet ring variant) has a particular tendency to metastasize to the abdominal cavity, particularly to the gastrointestinal tract, ovaries, and serosal surfaces[859a,867,880] (Fig. 20.101). A peculiar recipient for metastatic breast carcinoma is meningioma; over 30 cases have been reported.[882] Bone marrow examination (particularly biopsy) is very efficient in documenting systemic disease,[872,878] but the

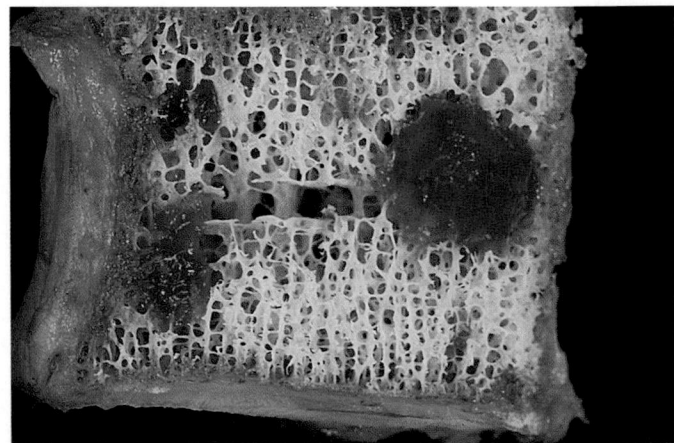

Fig. 20.100 Breast carcinoma metastatic to vertebra. The normal bone marrow has been flushed out by placing a thin slice of tissue under a strong jet of water.

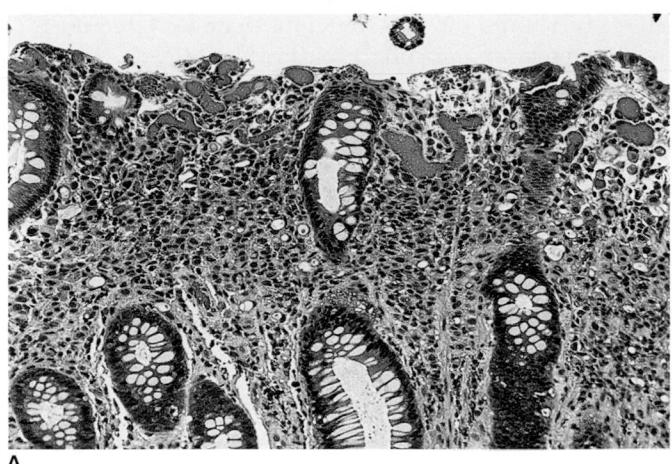 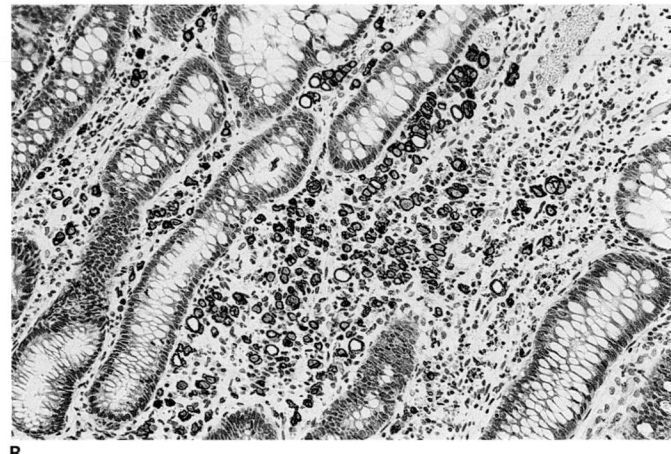

Fig. 20.101 **A** and **B**, Metastasis of mammary lobular carcinoma to lamina propria of large bowel mucosa. **B**, Keratin 7 immunostain.

incidence of positivity when both bone scan and x-ray studies are normal is too low (4%) to justify its routine use. Immunohistochemical techniques for various markers (particularly keratin) have been developed for the detection of occult breast carcinoma metastases in the bone marrow.[856,861,879,887] These are particularly useful in cases of lobular carcinoma, which can be easily missed in H&E-stained sections.[855] Recently, reverse transcriptase PCR assays for keratin 19,[864] MUC1,[885] and mammoglobin[868,871] have been employed in an attempt to detect occult breast carcinomas in bone marrow, lymph nodes, or peripheral blood.[886]

In the presence of metastatic deposits of unknown source, immunoreactivity for GCDF-15, lactalbumin, and hormone receptors strongly suggests a breast primary, especially when combined.[858,883]

The pattern of metastatic spread of breast carcinoma as evaluated by Fisher et al.[866] in a large randomized series of patients treated with various modalities brought them to the following conclusions: there is no orderly pattern of tumor dissemination; regional nodes are ineffective as barriers to tumor spread and, when positive, are more an indicator of a particular host–tumor relationship than the instigator of distant metastases; the bloodstream is of considerable importance in tumor dissemination; complex host–tumor interrelationships affect every facet of the disease; operable breast carcinoma is a systemic disease; and variations in local-regional therapy are unlikely to substantially affect survival.

Occult breast carcinoma

Sometimes a single enlarged axillary lymph node in an adult female is found to be involved by metastatic non-lymphoid tumor in the presence of a clinically and radiographically normal breast, with no evidence of tumor elsewhere.[897] When this situation arises, the diagnosis will be metastatic breast carcinoma or metastatic malignant melanoma in over 90% of cases. Making the

distinction between carcinoma and melanoma should be possible in nearly every case from the combination of morphologic features, immunohistochemical stains for keratin, CEA, vimentin, S-100 protein, HMB-45 and other markers, and (rarely needed at this point) electron microscopy. A note of caution is in order regarding the interpretation of S-100 protein stains, since this marker (originally thought to be very distinctive of melanoma in this situation) is now known to stain a high number of breast carcinomas (see p. 1804).

If this combined approach has shown that (1) the tumor is a carcinoma rather than a melanoma, (2) the appearance of this carcinoma is compatible with breast origin, and (3) there is no clinicoradiographic evidence of tumor elsewhere, then removal of the homolateral breast is justified even in the absence of clinical or mammographic abnormalities. A primary malignant tumor, which can be extremely small, will be found in most cases. This was true in 23 of 34 cases reviewed by Ashikari et al.[895] Two thirds of these tumors were less than 2 cm in diameter. Interestingly, the survival rates were the same whether or not a primary tumor was found in the breast, a fact confirmed by others.[896] In an updated series from the same institution, a primary tumor was found in 75% of cases and the disease-free survival rate was 60%.[898]

Occasionally, an occult carcinoma will be found on routine microscopic examination of a reduction mammoplasty specimen.[652a]

Sentinel lymph node

Since the appearance of the previous edition of this book, the technique of sentinel lymph node biopsy for the evaluation and management of breast carcinoma has gained enormous popularity, and one is curious to see how it will have fared by the time the next edition is written. At this point in time, it is fair to say that it shows great promise but has not yet become the standard of care.[906–908,910,911,915]

The procedure is based on the concept that if the sentinel node is negative, the other nodes of that group will also be negative in nearly all instances, whereas if it is positive, the chance that there will be additional metastases in that nodal group is about one third. The pathologic study of these nodes has put a lot of strain on the pathology laboratories, because in most instances the addition of this significant load has not been accompanied by a corresponding increase in resources. Many suggestions have been made regarding the proper technique for pathologic examination; some of the initial recommendations (which included intraoperative performance of immunohistochemistry) were so time-intensive and cost-prohibitive as to be practically unfeasible,[916,916a] as the authors of these recommendations have themselves acknowledged. At present, most workers accept that the study of the sentinel node that proves negative on frozen section should include at least three step sections stained with H&E plus at least one section immunostained for keratin.[903,905,912,914] Intraoperative performance of immunohistochemistry is technically feasible but hard to justify.[900] The immunostain of choice is a keratin cocktail, such as AE1/AE3[902] (Fig. 20.102). Whether molecular evaluation of these nodes will add clinically significant information remains to be seen.[913] Interestingly, it has been shown that a focal metastasis in a sentinel node is more likely to be located in the region of the inflow junction of the afferent lymph vessel than elsewhere.[904]

Pitfalls in the interpretation of these nodes include keratin-positive reticulum cells, mesothelial cell inclusions, ectopic breast tissue, traumatic displacement of breast epithelium induced by the biopsy procedure, and the ever present possibility of a "floater."[901,909] As a general rule, one should be very reluctant to make a diagnosis of metastatic carcinoma on the basis of keratin-positive cells that are not evident in the H&E preparations.

The prognostic significance of isolated tumor cells or even small clusters of cells in these nodes is yet to be determined.[899,916] It has been recommended that the term "micrometastases" be applied to a cluster of tumor cells not larger than 2 mm, and that the term "isolated tumor cells" be used for the presence of single cells interpreted as malignant.

Staging and grading

The most widely used clinical staging system for breast carcinoma is the one adopted by both the International Union against Cancer (UICC) and the American Joint Commission on Cancer Staging and End Results Reporting (AJC). It is based on the TNM system (T, tumor; N, nodes; M, metastases) and is shown in Appendix C.[917]

The microscopic grading of breast carcinoma is discussed in the section on Prognosis (p. 1825).

Therapy

The therapy of breast carcinoma includes surgery, radiation therapy, hormonal therapy, and chemotherapy (the latter sometimes combined with bone marrow transplantation), depending on the type and extent of the disease.[926]

Surgical therapy, traditionally synonymous with Halsted's radical mastectomy, now comprises a wide variety of options (some of them referred to as breast-conserving surgery), which include partial mastectomy (lumpectomy or segmentectomy), and total (simple) mastectomy.[928,930,936,947]

Radiation therapy is often employed as a postoperative adjunct (especially in connection with the more limited operations), sometimes as the primary treatment, and for the control of locally recurrent disease.[934,945]

When conservative surgery is employed, microscopic evaluation of the surgical margins becomes necessary.[948] Several studies have shown that patients with positive margins are more likely to develop local recurrence as well as distant failure.[922,935,940,943] For margin-negative cases, the likelihood of ipsilateral breast failure and distant metastases is related to the vicinity and amount of carcinoma near the margins.[926a] Surgical margins are more difficult to evaluate for intraductal tumors,[925,944] and their very utility in this circumstance has been questioned[946] (see also Chapter 2).

Breast implants used for reconstructive purposes usually develop a fibrous capsule around them[932] (Fig. 20.103). The inside surface of this capsule has a tendency to undergo *synovial metaplasia*, a process that has also

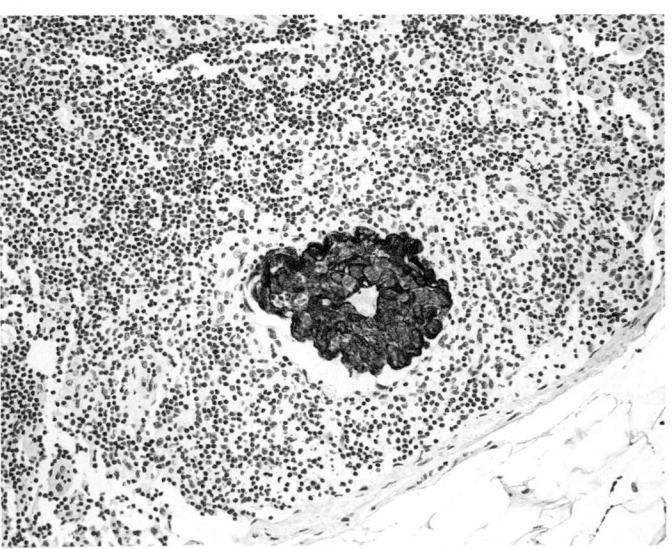

Fig. 20.102 Cluster of metastatic cells in sentinel lymph node highlighted with keratin stain.

Fig. 20.103 Breast implant (left) surrounded by a thick fibrous wall that has undergone heavy calcification (right).

been referred to as pseudoepithelization and that is microscopically very similar to "detritic synovitis."[924,927,929] Rarely, the capsule is surrounded by benign squamous epithelium.[931]

Systemic therapy is used for the palliative treatment of generalized disease.[949] Hormonal therapy, which has traditionally included the options of castration, adrenalectomy, and hypophysectomy, is now largely dependent on antiestrogen drugs. Of those, tamoxifen has emerged as the most important in the past 20 years, to the point of becoming the endocrine treatment of choice for all stages of estrogen receptor-positive breast cancer.[923,926,939]

Chemotherapy has had a significant impact on the survival of patients with metastatic breast carcinoma, the best results having been obtained with combination regimens.[918,919,938] In highly selected patients, this has been combined with autologous bone marrow transplantation, but the initially high hopes for this procedure have been somewhat dampened in recent years.[921,933,942] In addition, chemotherapy is currently used as an adjunct following local treatment with curative intent in patients with positive axillary nodes. The decision as to whether to give chemotherapy or hormonal therapy to node-negative patients is dependent upon a variety of clinical and pathologic parameters.[937,941] At present, five years of tamoxifen administration is the standard adjuvant endocrine therapy for early-stage, hormone-receptor-positive breast carcinoma.[926] Chemotherapy has also been used in combination with conservative surgery and radiation in patients with localized large (≥3 cm) tumors in order to avoid mastectomy.[920]

Effects of therapy on the tumor and on normal breast

Radiation therapy of breast carcinoma may result in bizarre nuclear changes, formation of giant tumor cells,

naked nuclei, and abnormal mitotic figures. Extensive tumor necrosis may develop, which is later surrounded by a thick fibrous wall. It is important to remember that morphologic viability is not necessarily equivalent to biologic viability (i.e., the capacity of the tumor cell to replicate). In the non-neoplastic breast, the most characteristic irradiation effect is atypia of epithelial cells in the terminal ductules, associated with lobular sclerosis and atrophy.[954,955] Cases of *pseudosclerodermatous panniculitis* after irradiation have been reported.[958]

Hormonal therapy of responsive tumors leads to prominent stromal fibrosis and hyalinization, an increase in the amount of elastic tissue, and degenerative changes in the tumor cells. The latter are manifested by cytoplasmic vacuolization, rupture of cell membranes, nuclear aberrations, and eventual necrosis. These changes may occur both in the primary tumor and in the metastases and can be very patchy: morphologically unaffected cells lying side by side with highly altered cells.

Chemotherapy can also induce striking morphologic changes in the tumor cells, including a degree of vacuolization such as to simulate histiocytes[950,953,956,957] (Fig. 20.104). It also results in atrophy of the TDLU, with

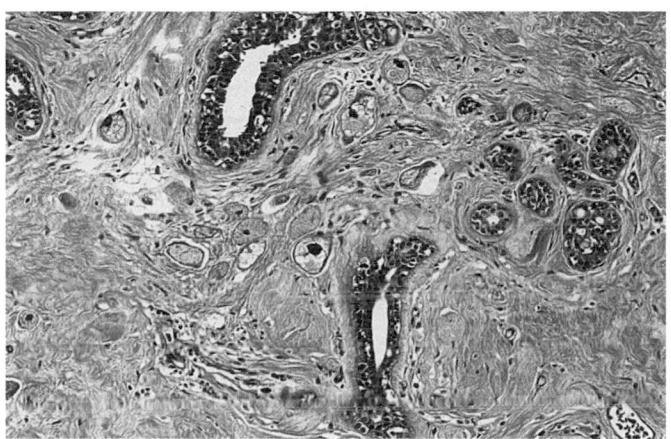

A

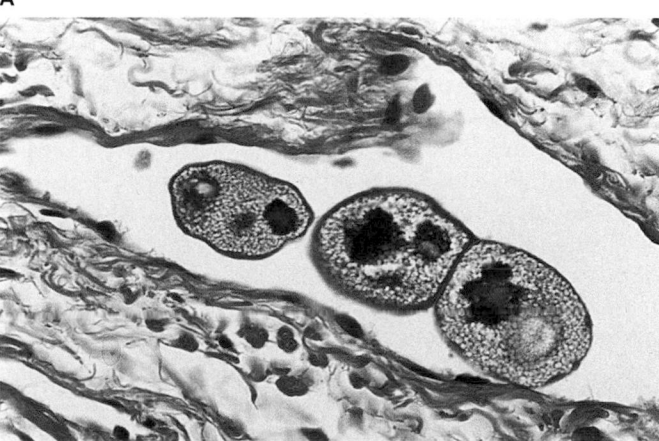

B

Fig. 20.104 A and **B**, Striking vacuolization of breast carcinoma cells induced by chemotherapy. The appearance simulates that of histiocytes. The tumor cells shown in **B** are located within a blood vessel. (Courtesy of Dr. Maria J. Merino, Bethesda, MD)

occasional atypia.[952] However, in most instances it does not affect the histologic grading of the carcinoma.[951] The microscopic features of the tumor correlate poorly with response to chemotherapy.[959]

Prognosis

The prognosis of breast carcinoma is related to a large variety of clinical and pathologic factors.[1007–1009,1013,1052,1057,1077,1093,1094,1119] These are listed not according to their relative importance but rather following the order in which they have been discussed in the preceding text.

1 **Patient's age.** Women who are younger than 50 years of age at the time of diagnosis have the best prognosis. Relative survival declines after the age of 50 years and is particularly low in older women.[962] As far as very young women (≤35 years of age) are concerned, some studies have shown a prognosis similar to that in older patients,[1078] whereas others have shown a significantly higher risk for recurrence and distant metastases.[1060] related to the fact that these patients tend to have higher grade tumor.[978,990]

2 *BRCA1* **status.** It would seem that the breast carcinomas developing in *BRCA1* mutation carriers are associated with a worse overall survival if they have not received adjuvant therapy.[1022,1076] No comparable data are yet available for carriers of *BRCA2* mutations.

3 **Pregnancy and oral contraceptives.** There is general agreement that carcinoma of the breast manifesting during pregnancy or lactation is generally an aggressive tumor with low expression of hormone receptors and high expression of Her2/*neu*,[1074a] and that it is associated with an overall poorer prognosis: the 5-year survival rate in most series ranging from 15% to 35%.[1067] However, it has been stated that this difference does not reach statistical significance when evaluated stage by stage.[1016,1068]

   No convincing evidence has been found that prior use of oral contraceptive agents has an effect on the evolution or survival of breast carcinoma.[1083]

4 **Early diagnosis.** The relative 5-, 8-, and 10-year survival rates for asymptomatic breast carcinomas detected in a large screening project (BCDDP) were 88%, 83%, and 79%, respectively.[1089] These figures are much higher than those for the clinically detectable carcinoma and relate to the fact that the tumors were small in most cases, were usually devoid of axillary metastases, and included a high percentage of microscopically favorable types.

5 **Presence or absence of invasiveness.** Needless to say, this is the single most important prognostic determinator in breast carcinoma. For all practical purposes, in situ carcinomas are 100% curable with mastectomy. In tumors of ductal type that have both an in situ and an invasive component, a relationship exists between the proportion of the invasive component and the probability of nodal metastases. The amount of in situ component correlates with the incidence of multicentricity and, indirectly, with the probability of occult invasion.[1042,1046] It should be noted, however, that sometimes in situ ductal malignancies of the comedocarcinoma type can be associated with metastases in the absence of detectable invasion (see p. 1796).

6 **Size.** The diameter of the primary tumor shows a good correlation with the incidence of nodal metastases and with survival rate.[988,1084] As a matter of fact—and despite earlier expressions of skepticism[1006]—this easily, quickly, and cheaply determined parameter has been found to be one of the strongest predictors of dissemination and rate of relapse in node-negative breast carcinomas.[1072] It should be noted that in tumors having both an in situ and an invasive component, the size of the latter is a better predictor than is the total tumor size.[1090] It has also been pointed out that size determination has a greater prognostic significance when measured microscopically than grossly.[961] Size is one of the two criteria for the definition of *minimal breast carcinoma*, which includes all in situ carcinomas regardless of size and invasive carcinomas of 1 cm or less in diameter. Saigo and Rosen[1087] studied 111 patients with invasive breast carcinoma of 1 cm or less in diameter associated with negative nodes who were treated with a minimum of a modified radical mastectomy and followed for at least 10 years: 75% were alive with no evidence of disease, 4% were alive with recurrent carcinoma, 6% had died of disease, and 15% had died of other causes.

7 **Site.** No relationship has been found in most studies between prognosis and the quadrant location of the primary tumor. However, in one recent large study it was found that medial location of the tumor was associated with a 50% risk of systemic relapse and tumor death when compared with lateral location.[1050] For a discussion on the relationship between tumor multicentricity and prognosis, see page 1789.

8 **Cytoarchitectural type.** There is no significant prognostic difference between ordinary invasive ductal and invasive lobular carcinoma. Morphologic variants of invasive ductal carcinoma with a more favorable prognosis are tubular carcinoma, cribriform carcinoma, medullary carcinoma (when strictly defined), pure mucinous carcinoma, papillary carcinoma, adenoid cystic carcinoma, and juvenile (secretory) carcinoma.[996,1039,1063a] A variant of lobular (and sometimes ductal) carcinoma associated with an extremely bad prognosis is signet ring carcinoma.

The prognosis of inflammatory carcinoma is also particularly ominous. Tumors that have been said to be more aggressive than ordinary ductal carcinoma but that actually show little difference in survival rates are squamous cell carcinoma, metaplastic carcinoma, and carcinomas with neuroendocrine features (including so-called "carcinoid tumor").[1056] The prognostic significance of these and other varieties is further discussed in the section on microscopic types.

9 **Microscopic grade.** The two most widely used systems over the years for the microscopic grading of breast carcinoma have been those of Bloom and Richardson[981] and Black,[980] the first based mainly on architectural features (extent of tubular formation) and the second on the degree of nuclear atypia. These are usually estimated by visual microscopic examination of routinely stained sections, although various attempts at quantitating these changes (particularly the nuclear aberrations) by computer-assisted analysis have been made.[968,969,1069,1104] Since both architecture and cytology have been found to correlate with prognosis, the sensible proposal has been made to use them in conjunction.[995,1045,1084] Elston has been the most vocal champion of this approach, which is usually referred to as the Nottingham modification of the Bloom–Richardson system and which also incorporates the evaluation of mitotic activity.[1002,1015] In this scheme, the grade is obtained by adding up the scores for tubule formation, nuclear pleomorphism, and mitotic count, each of which is given 1, 2, or 3 points. This results in a total score of between 3 and 9 points, which is translated into the final grade by the following formula: 3 to 5 points = Grade I; 6 to 7 points = Grade II; and 8 to 9 points = Grade III. The specific criteria for point assignments are described in the box and Table 20.1.

The utility of this and related grading systems has been convincingly and repeatedly proved[1013,1017,1027,1095] to the point that incorporation of this information into the routine pathology report is becoming a requirement.[1065] This is reinforced by the fact that an acceptable degree of interobserver reproducibility has been achieved.[993,1015,1075] The system was largely conceived for the invasive ductal carcinoma NOS, but it can also be applied to the special types of ductal carcinoma and to lobular carcinoma.[969a]

10 **Type of margins.** Tumors with "pushing" margins have a better prognosis than tumors with infiltrating margins. This applies not only to medullary carcinoma, but also to other types of well-circumscribed neoplasms.[989,1029,1040]

11 **Tumor necrosis.** Tumor necrosis is associated with an increased incidence of lymph node metastases and decreased survival rates,[975,989,1019,1054] particularly if very extensive.[1035] This feature is usually associated with tumors of high histologic grade.

Microscopic grading of breast carcinoma:
Nottingham Modification of the Bloom–Richardson system

Tubule formation
   1 point: Tubular formation in >75% of the tumor
   2 points: Tubular formation in 10 to 75% of the tumor
   3 points: Tubular formations in <10% of the tumor
   Note: For scoring tubule formations, the overall appearance of the tumor has to be taken into consideration.

Nuclear pleomorphism
   1 point: Nuclei with minimal variation in size and shape
   2 points: Nuclei with moderate variation in size and shape
   3 points: Nuclei with marked variation in size and shape
   Note: The tumor areas having cells with greatest atypia should be evaluated.

Mitotic count
   1, 2, or 3 points, according to Table 20.1
   Note: Mitotic figures are to be counted only at the periphery of the tumor. Counting should begin in the most mitotically active area; 10 high-power fields (APF) are to be counted in the same area (but not necessarily contiguous). The fields should be filled with as much tumor as possible; poorly preserved areas are to be avoided. Cells in the prophase should be ignored.

---

12 **Stromal reaction.** Surprisingly, it has been found that tumors with an absence of inflammatory reaction at the periphery have a lesser degree of nodal metastases and presumably a better prognosis.[1012] Obviously, these considerations do not apply to the specific case of medullary carcinoma.

13 **Microvessel density.** The interesting observation has recently been made that invasive breast carcinomas having a prominent vascular component in the surrounding stroma behave in a more aggressive fashion than the others.[1110–1112,1114] Accordingly, attempts have been made to quantitate the "density" of these vessels and to correlate this feature to other parameters, notably prognosis.[971] The original proponents of this approach have shown rather impressive results, and these have been corroborated by some independent observers.[984,997,1018] Others have failed to show significant correlations and have commented on the great difficulties encountered in estimating the surface or volume of the intricate vascular network that surrounds these tumors.[966,1064,1092] It should be added that microvessel density is a phenomenon independent from intratumoral endothelial cell proliferation,[1107] and that an increase in microvessel density has also been noted in intraductal carcinoma, particularly of the comedo type.[1024]

14 **Elastosis.** It has been claimed that breast carcinomas with no associated elastosis have a lower rate of response to endocrine therapy than those with gross elastosis.[1053] In terms of survival rate, no convincing differences have been found between tumors with and without elastosis.[983,1021]

15 **Keratin staining pattern.** In one study, carcinomas that expressed CK17 and CK5 had a worse clinical outcome than the others.[1101]

16 **CEA staining pattern.** This immunohistochemical feature has not been found to relate to prognosis.[1102]

17 **Vimentin staining pattern.** The claim has been made that vimentin expression is associated with poor prognosis in node-negative ductal carcinomas.[999]

18 **Cathepsin D.** Despite original claims to the contrary,[1097] assays for neither cathepsin D immunoreactivity in the tumor nor serum levels of this enzyme have proved to have independent prognostic value.[964,1000,1037,1043,1073,1086]

19 **HER2/*neu*.** As already stated, overexpression of this oncogene as determined either by immunohistochemistry or FISH is an excellent predictor of response to Herceptin but a weak predictor of response to chemotherapy.[1058] Although it identifies a subset of patients with poor prognosis, particularly when lymph node metastases are present,[974,1001,1026,1071] it correlates closely with tumor grade[1100] and loses much of its independent prognostic significance in multivariate analysis.[967,1080]

20 **p53 and nm23.** Accumulation of p53 protein (presumably as a result of gene mutation) and low expression of the nm23 protein have been said to correlate with reduced patient survival.[970,972,973,1030] However, the authors of a large study comprising 440 node-negative patients concluded that the immunohistochemical demonstration of p53 was not a reliable prognostic indicator in this population and that it was not associated with any major epidemiologic risk factor.[1079] This has been confirmed by others.[1074] It has also been shown that loss of heterozygosity for p53 is strongly associated with high histologic and nuclear grade.[1062]

21 **Bcl-2.** A relationship between Bcl-2 protein expression and long-term survival in breast carcinoma has been shown.[1031] Bcl-2 is also correlated with estrogen receptor status.[998,1036]

22 **Skin invasion.** Breast carcinomas in which invasion of the overlying skin has occurred are associated with a decreased survival rate.[1088] Invasion of dermal lymph vessels as a determinant of the "inflammatory carcinoma" picture is a particularly ominous prognostic sign.

23 **Nipple invasion.** Involvement of the nipple by carcinoma is associated with a higher incidence of axillary metastases.[1115]

24 **Lymphatic tumor emboli.** The presence of tumor emboli in lymphatic vessels within the breast is associated with an increased risk of tumor recurrence.[994,1059,1082]

25 **Blood vessel emboli.** This finding shows a high correlation with tumor size, histologic grade, tumor type, lymph node status, development of distant metastases, and poor prognosis.[985,1008,1047,1070]

26 **Paget's disease.** The presence or absence of Paget's disease in invasive ductal carcinoma is of no prognostic relevance per se.

27 **Estrogen receptors.** Several authors have concluded that patients with estrogen receptor-positive tumors—whether determined biochemically or immunohistochemically—have a longer disease-free survival than the others. However, the differences in long-term prognosis are minimal and perhaps not statistically significant.[960,986,1028]

28 **DNA ploidy.** Despite numerous studies evaluating DNA ploidy with flow cytometry, it is yet unclear whether this parameter adds *independent* information of therapeutic or prognostic value once the size of the tumor, microscopic grading, lymph node status, and hormone-receptor status have been taken into account.[965,977,1014,1038,1051,1098,1117]

29 **Cell proliferation.** This parameter, whether measured by the old-fashioned mitotic count,[979,997,1041,1044] by MIB-1 (Ki-67) or analogous immunostain,[1055,1085,1108,1113,1116] or by determination of S-phase fraction by flow cytometry,[1118] has emerged as a very important prognostic determinator.[1014,1063,1091,1109] As such, it has been incorporated into the combined grading scheme espoused by Elston (see paragraph 9). Actually, some view it as the most important component of that system.

30 **Cyclin D1.** Overexpression of this marker as detected by immunohistochemistry does not seem to carry independent prognostic connotations.[1105]

31 **Telomerase activity.** The level of this enzyme is associated with the proliferative index of breast carcinoma, but its measurement is not an independent predictor of survival.[987]

32 **Axillary lymph node metastases.** This is one of the most important prognostic parameters.[963,1032] Not only is there a sharp difference in survival rates between patients with positive and negative nodes, but the survival rate also depends on the level of axillary node involved (low, medium, or high),[976] the absolute number (fewer than four versus four or more),[1003,1010,1096] the amount of metastatic tumor,[1033,1081] the presence or absence of extranodal spread,[1011,1023,1048,1051] and the presence or absence of tumor cells in the efferent vessels.[991,1025] The prognostic significance of "micrometastases" and of "isolated tumor cells" (as applied currently to sentinel lymph nodes) remains to be determined.[992] For prognostic purposes, the best grouping seems to be the following: negative nodes, one to three positive nodes, and four or more positive nodes.

33 **Pattern of lymph node reaction.** It has been suggested that the microscopic appearance of the regional node (lymphoid response and/or sinus histiocytosis) is an indication of the type of host response to the tumor and that it relates to progno-

sis.[1099] The issue remains controversial; if there is indeed a correlation, it does not seem to be a statistically significant one.[1010,1012]

34 **Internal mammary lymph node metastases.** Survival in patients with involvement of this lymph node group is lower than in those without such involvement, especially if only patients with one to three positive axillary nodes are evaluated.[1061]

35 **Local recurrence.** This is a sign of ominous prognosis. In one series of 60 patients with ipsilateral chest wall recurrence and no detectable distant metastases, all patients eventually died of metastatic breast carcinoma.[1020]

36 **Type of therapy.** This is too complex and multifactorial an issue to be properly addressed here. Suffice to say that all available evidence suggests that the outcome in breast carcinoma depends more on the nature of the individual tumor than on the type of therapy performed. There is certainly a striking similarity in survival rates from different centers employing widely disparate therapeutic approaches.[1049] A complicating factor in evaluating therapeutic results is the marked individual variations in the natural life history of the disease, which renders imperative the use of carefully randomized studies. Most of these studies have shown no significant differences in survival among the various groups, which have included the following[1004,1005,1034]:

a For patients with clinically negative axillary nodes:
   Radical mastectomy versus total mastectomy with postoperative regional radiation
   Total mastectomy alone versus segmentectomy with postoperative regional radiation
b For patients with clinically positive axillary nodes:
   Radical mastectomy versus total mastectomy with postoperative regional radiation.

The results of 6 recently completed prospective randomized clinical trials have clearly demonstrated that the combination of breast conserving surgery and radiation therapy provides survival rates equivalent to those following mastectomy.[1087a]

Bloom et al.982 provided a good baseline on which to judge the effectiveness of therapy by showing that in a series of 250 untreated breast cancers, the 5-year survival rate after diagnosis was 18%.

37 **Gene expression profiling.** There are great hopes that evaluation of the expression of thousands of genes through microarray technology will allow a much sharper separation of prognostic groups than is currently possible.[1066,1103,1106]

Salivary and sweat gland-type tumors

(including myoepithelial tumors)

A small proportion of benign and malignant tumors of the breast have an appearance analogous to, or at least reminiscent of, that more commonly seen in salivary glands or sweat glands.[1173] This should not be too surprising, since the breast is a modified sweat gland and a close analogy exists between sweat gland tumors and salivary gland neoplasms. Some of the malignant tumors in this category share many of the features of ordinary breast carcinoma and could have been discussed in the preceding section. It was arbitrarily chosen to include them here because of the histogenetic link they seem to have (at least at the conceptual level) with benign tumors having an unmistakably salivary gland/sweat gland-type morphology.

The benign tumors in this category include **eccrine spiradenoma**,[1131] **syringomatous squamous tumors** (to be distinguished from low-grade mucoepidermoid carcinoma),[1143,1161,1171] **papillary syringocystadenoma**,[1163] **cylindroma**,[1138,1149a] **eccrine acrospiroma** (nodular hidradenoma),[1130] and **benign mixed tumor.** The latter, which is very rare in humans but relatively common in female dogs, has been interpreted by some as a variant of intraductal papilloma,[1161] but its appearance is quite similar to that of benign mixed tumor of salivary glands (pleomorphic adenoma) or of cutaneous sweat glands (chondroid syringoma)[1121,1124,1128] (Fig. 20.105). This tumor can arise in an otherwise normal breast, as single or multiple nodules against a background of ductal hyperplasia, or in association (probably coincidental) with breast carcinoma.[1149]

Adenoid cystic carcinoma is the most important member of the malignant category. It is important not to

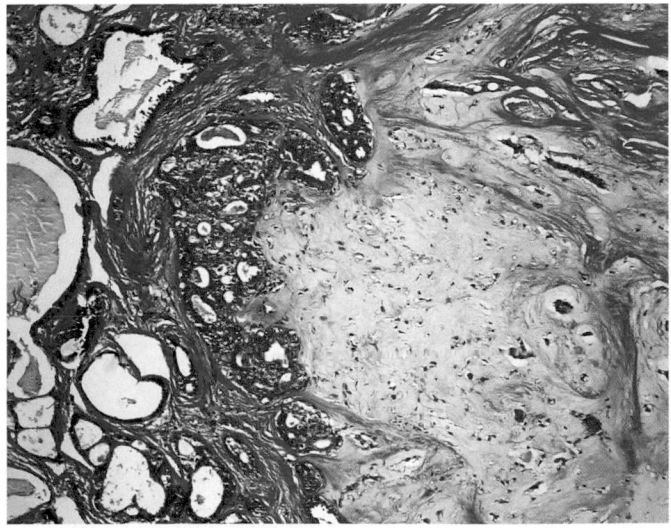

Fig. 20.105 Benign mixed tumor of breast. A prominent myxochondroid stroma is interspersed among the glandular structures.

confuse this very rare neoplasm with the much more common intraductal carcinoma with cribriform pattern (sometimes referred to as pseudoadenoid cystic carcinoma)[1139,1156] or with collagenous spherulosis (see p. 1782). True adenoid cystic carcinoma of the breast shows, as in the salivary glands, two types of cavity formation: true glandular lumina and the well-known eosinophilic "cylinders" containing eosinophilic basement membrane material and basophilic mucin[1144,1146] (Fig. 20.106). It may also show foci of sebaceous differentiation, indicating a potential to differentiate into skin adnexal structures.[1167] Perineural involvement may be present. As in the salivary gland, there are variants with a partially or predominantly solid pattern of growth.[1145,1159] Hormone receptors tend to be absent.[1169] Axillary lymph node metastases are extremely rare.[1153,1172] Some patients have developed local recurrence of pulmonary metastases many years after initial therapy,[1123,1153] but the prognosis for this tumor as a group is remarkably good.[1120] The relationship between microscopic grading and prognosis is controversial.[1145,1153,1159] As already mentioned (see p. 1777), some cases of adenoid cystic carcinoma are seen in association with microglandular adenosis.[1119a]

Acinic cell carcinoma is the newly added member of this family of tumors. As the name indicates, its appearance is highly reminiscent of the homologous tumor in the salivary glands. The similarities extend to the ultrastructural and immunohistochemical features.[1127,1154,1157]

Other malignant breast tumors that could be included in this category are **mucoepidermoid carcinoma** (see p. 1829), **apocrine carcinoma** (see p. 1809) and **oncocytic carcinoma**.[1126]

A more complicated issue is represented by the breast tumors of probable myoepithelial nature.[1136] First, it should be recognized that myoepithelial participation is an integral component of benign proliferative breast diseases (such as sclerosing adenosis, ductal hyperplasia, intraductal papilloma, and nipple adenoma) and that, in some instances, it dominates the histologic picture. Cases of sclerosing adenosis with great predominance of myoepithelial cells and presenting in the form of multifocal microscopic lesions have been designated as **myoepitheliosis**.[1166]

Second, myoepithelial cells are a normal constituent of the ducts and lobules, and therefore one might question whether these neoplasms should be regarded as of salivary or sweat gland type. They are discussed here because the morphologic variations they exhibit and classification problems they elicit are very similar to those they pose in the salivary glands (see Chapter 12). **Adenomyoepithelioma** is a small (average diameter: 1 cm), firm, well-circumscribed tumor microscopically composed of cells of polygonal shape and optically clear cytoplasm, arranged in nests that are sometimes centered by gland-forming epithelial cells.[1166] The patterns of growth may be spindle cell (myoid), tubular, or lobulated[1155,1166,1174] (Fig. 20.107). Interestingly, some of these lesions seem to arise on the basis of a peculiar form of adenosis designated as of adenomyoepithelial or apocrine type (see p. 1779). In the series of 18 adenomyoepitheliomas reported by Rosen,[1155] 2 developed local recurrences but there were no instances of metastatic spread. It seems likely that the cases formerly reported as clear cell hidradenoma[1134] belong to this category. **Malignant myoepithelioma (myoepithelial carcinoma)** is purely composed of myoepithelial cells and is

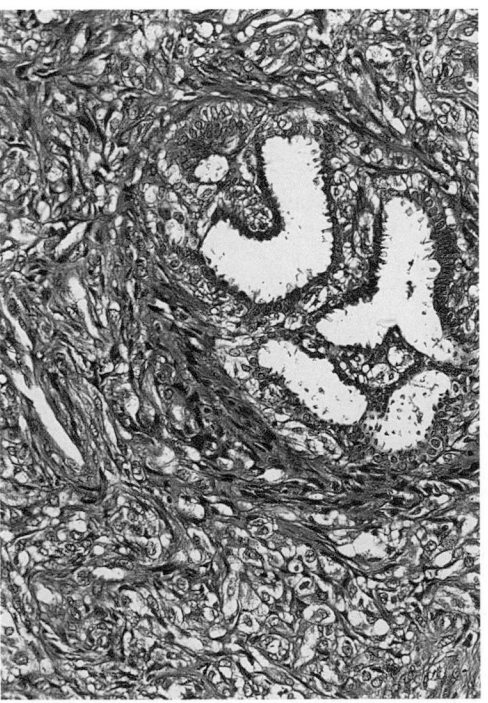

Fig. 20.107 Adenomyoepithelioma. In some areas there is a clear relationship between the secretory and the myoepithelial component (similar to that seen in adenomyoepitheliosis), but in others the spindle myoepithelial cells become the exclusive neoplastic element.

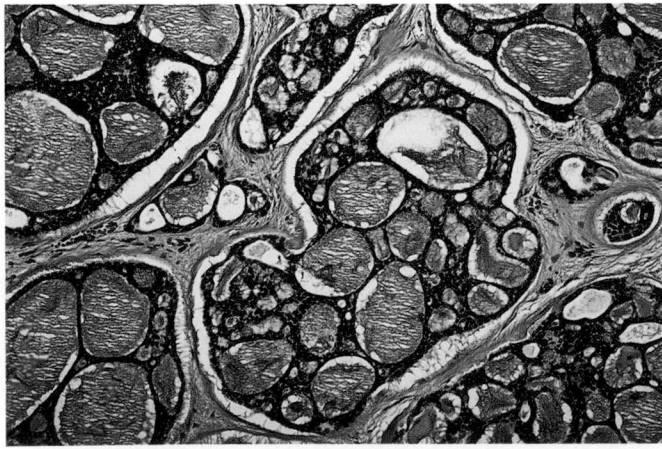

Fig. 20.106 Adenoid cystic carcinoma of breast. The appearance is similar to that of its more common homolog in salivary glands.

cytologically malignant.[1151,1166] Some of these carcinomas (which may be quite undifferentiated and sarcomatoid) arise on the basis of an adenomyoepithelioma, the latter providing the best clue for their recognition.[1125,1140a,1148,1160] Intraductal growth may be noted in them,[1165] and they may be multicentric.[1142]

The spindle cell (sarcomatoid) form of this tumor presents as a nonencapsulated cellular spindle cell tumor that grows in a fascicular pattern in the breast stroma.[1122,1147] Its light microscopic appearance resembles very much that of a mesenchymal neoplasm; support for the myoepithelial nature of the few reported cases is largely based on ultrastructural or immunohistochemical observations, and/or the existence of a preceding or coexisting adenomyoepithelioma.[1133,1152,1158] As already mentioned, there is a great deal of similarity between some of the spindle cell forms of metaplastic carcinomas and these spindle malignant myoepitheliomas.

Low-grade adenosquamous carcinoma is a well-differentiated tumor with dual glandular and squamous differentiation. Many of the reported cases have originated from an intraductal papillary tumor.[1132,1170] Local recurrence is common following conservative surgery, but nodal and distant metastases are exceptional.[1170] Whether this neoplasm and the related *low-grade mucoepidermoid carcinoma*[1150] are differentiations in the direction of salivary gland or sweat gland-type structures is not immediately obvious, but the occasional presence of low-grade adenosquamous foci in adenomyoepithelioma supports that interpretation.[1137]

Glycogen-rich (clear cell) carcinoma is composed of large clear cells, which are found to contain abundant glycogen.[1135,1140,1141,1162] The biphasic appearance of adenomyoepithelioma is not apparent. It is possible that some of these tumors are of myoepithelial or apocrine nature, but the evidence for either is not very compelling. These neoplasms are full-blown carcinomas, with a prognosis no better, and perhaps worse, than that of ordinary invasive ductal carcinoma.[1135,1168] Their differential diagnosis includes other breast tumors with clear cytoplasm, including the exceptional clear cell ("sugar") tumor[1129] (see p. 1836).

Stromal tumors and tumorlike conditions

Phylloides tumor

Phylloides tumor—the term currently preferred for the neoplasm named cystosarcoma phylloides by Johannes Müller in 1838[1184]—occurs in the same age group as breast carcinoma, the median age at the time of diagnosis being 45 years.[1177,1193] Very few of the patients are younger than 25 years of age, in striking contrast with the age distribution of fibroadenoma. However, phylloides tumor can certainly occur in young adults and even in adolescents,[1197] and, therefore, the diagnosis cannot be excluded on the basis of age. The interesting observation has been made that phylloides tumors are more common in Hispanics than in other ethnic groups, and that this risk is higher among those Hispanics born in Latin America than those born in the United States.[1177]

Grossly, the typical phylloides tumor is round, relatively well circumscribed, and firm. The nipple may be flattened, but the overlying skin is almost never attached. The cut surface is solid and gray–white and shows the cleft-like spaces that give the tumor its name (Fig. 20.108A). Areas of necrosis, cystic degeneration, and hemorrhage may be present (Fig. 20.108B). Rarely, the entire tumor undergoes hemorrhagic infarct. Many phylloides tumors are large and some reach huge dimensions, but others measure less than 5 cm in diameter. It follows, then, that the diagnosis of phylloides tumor can be neither made nor ruled out by size alone. A lesion with the microscopic appearance of fibroadenoma should still be diagnosed as such even if it reaches 10 cm or more in diameter (see p. 1771).

Microscopically, the two key features of phylloides tumor are stromal hypercellularity and the presence of benign glandular elements as an integral component of the neoplasm[1175] (Fig. 20.109). It is the amount and appearance of the stromal component that determines whether a breast neoplasm should be called a fibroadenoma or a phylloides tumor and, in the latter instance, what the chances are of the tumor behaving clinically in an aggressive fashion. Although a sharp distinction between benign and malignant forms of phylloides tumor is not always possible, sufficient information is available on the natural history of this neoplasm to allow a statement to be made about the likelihood of metastases and proper management on the basis of the pathologic features.

Tumors with the configuration of fibroadenomas having a cellular stroma without atypical features concentrated in the periductal areas are on the "benign" end of the spectrum; this stromal component has a fibroblastic appearance, with occasional admixture of mature adipose tissue foci. When the latter are prominent, the term *lipophylloides tumor* has been employed[1201] (Fig. 20.110). Cytologically, malignant phylloides tumors have marked nuclear atypia, numerous mitoses, and loss of the relationship between glands and stroma. An important diagnostic criterion of malignancy is overgrowth of the glands by the sarcomatous stroma so that low-power views of the tumor show only stroma without epithelial elements.[1186,1206] The neoplastic stromal component may be monomorphic or highly pleomorphic, and its appearance may be reminiscent of fibrosarcoma, malignant fibrous histiocytoma, or liposarcoma[1196]; metaplastic cartilage, bone, or, exceptionally,

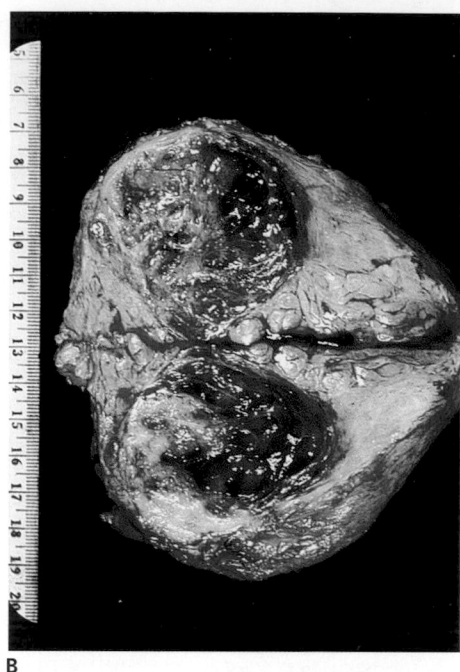

Fig. 20.108 A and **B**, Gross appearance of phylloides tumor. The tumor shown in **A** exhibits the typical appearance of the cut surface. The tumor illustrated in **B** has undergone extensive hemorrhagic infarct.

A

B

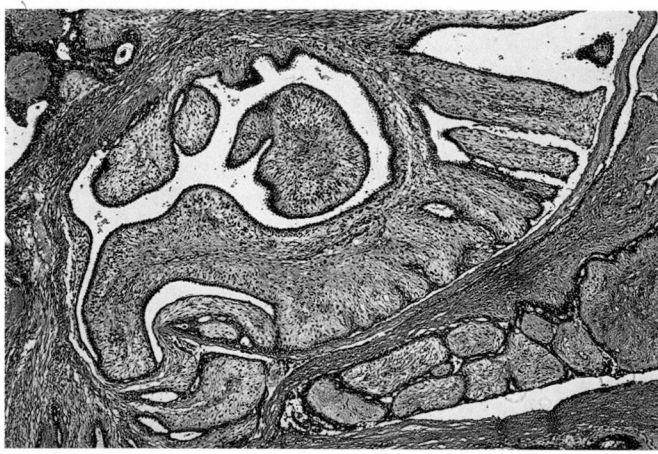
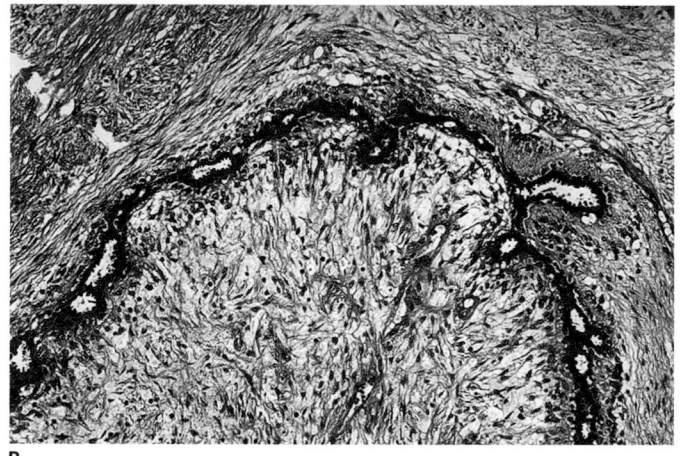

A

B

Fig. 20.109 A and **B**, Two views of low-grade phylloides tumor, showing cleft-like spaces and concentration of tumor cells beneath the epithelium.

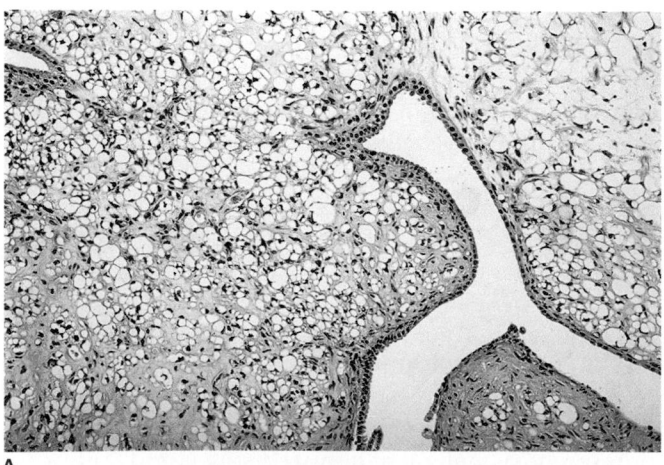
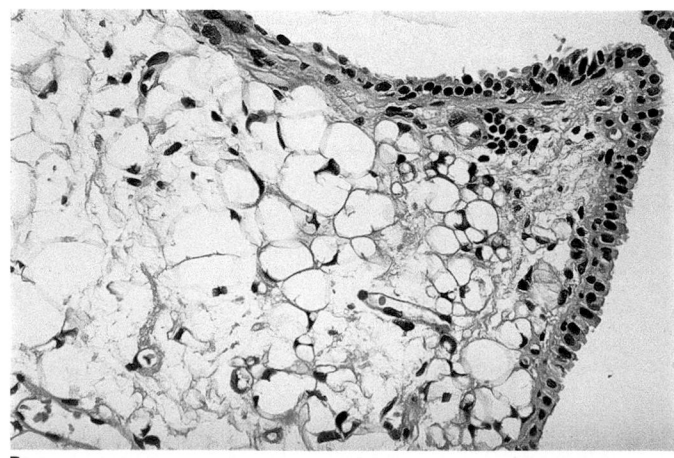

A

B

Fig. 20.110 A and **B**, Phylloides tumor with adipose tissue differentiation of the neoplastic stromal component.

skeletal muscle may be encountered.[1176,1202] Phylloides tumors with stromal elements other than fibromyxoid do worse than the others. Tumor necrosis is also associated with poor prognosis.[1181]

We view phylloides tumor as a tumor of the specialized mammary stroma with the capacity for epithelial induction.

The epithelial component, although probably not neoplastic, can have a markedly proliferative appearance, as it sometimes also does in fibroadenoma,[1193] a finding of no clinical significance. Very rarely, the features of carcinoma of either ductal or lobular type will be present in it.[1180,1188,1192,1193]

Ultrastructurally, the features of the tumor cells are largely those of fibroblasts, accompanied by focal myoid differentiation.[1198,1207] Immunohistochemically, there is frequent expression of CD34 and bcl-2, similar to other stromal tumors of the breast and in contrast to spindle cell (sarcomatoid) carcinomas, a feature of significance in the differential diagnosis.[1191] Progesterone receptors are present in nearly all cases and estrogen receptors in about one third, this profile being similar to that of fibroadenoma.[1205] The presence of these receptors seems to correlate with the microscopic grade of the tumor.[1203] There is overexpression of p53 in a variable number of histologically malignant and borderline cases, but very rarely in those with bland microscopic features.[1189,1204] Cytogenetically, phylloides tumors on the malignant side of the spectrum have a higher complexity of alterations than the others, with a tendency for a near-triploid stem line.[1182]

The behavior of the better-differentiated phylloides tumor is characterized by a tendency for local recurrence but an extreme rarity of distant metastases.[1187] If an enucleation has been done under the clinical impression of fibroadenoma, the patient can be safely followed for the possibility of recurrence. If the latter develops, or if this type of phylloides tumor is recognized at the time of initial surgery, local excision with a wide margin of normal tissue is the treatment of choice.[1179,1199] Recurrent phylloides tumor, which is the consequence of inadequate excision, may still be cured by wide local excision.[1190]

The cytologically malignant tumors are potentially metastasizing neoplasms, the incidence of metastases ranging from 3% to 12% in the various series. Deposits in the axillary nodes are exceptional. The most common sites of distant involvement are lung and bone, but the central nervous system also can be affected.[1185,1200] The metastases are of stromal elements only, although entrapping of normal structures in the lung may simulate a biphasic composition.

Wide local excision with an adequate margin of normal breast tissue is sufficient therapy for most cytologically malignant phylloides tumors[1199] but if there is any question of invasion of the fascia, the tumor should be removed together with the underlying muscle.

There is no need for removal of the axillary nodes, except for the exceptional instances in which they are clinically involved.

For the phylloides tumors that do not fall easily into one of these two extreme categories, the prognostic prediction and therapeutic recommendation have to be made on the basis of size, pushing versus peripheral margins, cellular atypia, and mitotic count.[1193,1195] There is some indication that DNA ploidy and S-phase fraction analysis may be useful adjuncts to the assessment of this tumor.[1183,1194]

The main differential diagnosis of the more malignant-looking phylloides tumors is with other types of sarcoma (largely depending on the presence or absence of a non-neoplastic epithelial component with the right architecture) and with sarcomatoid carcinoma (for which immunohistochemical evaluation may be helpful). The more benign-looking phylloides tumors need to be distinguished mainly from hypercellular fibroadenomas, acknowledging the fact that in some instances this may not be possible at a practical level or justified at a conceptual level. Along these lines, the neoplasm recently described as *periductal stromal tumor* could be viewed as being in between phylloides tumor and stromal sarcoma, in the sense that it contains epithelial structures like those of the former but lacks the phylloides architecture.[1178]

Vascular tumors

Angiosarcoma (malignant hemangioendothelioma) of the breast characteristically occurs in young women. Mammographically, it presents as a solitary mass that is usually uncalcified.[1216] Grossly, the tumor is soft, spongy, and hemorrhagic (Fig. 20.111). Microscopically, the diagnostic areas are characterized by anastomosing vascular channels lined by atypical endothelial cells (Fig. 20.112). The appearance may vary in the same tumor from that of a highly undifferentiated solid neoplasm to one that is extremely bland cytologically, to the point that some early cases were reported as metastasizing hemangiomas.[1230] However, close examination will usually reveal that even the better differentiated areas exhibit the telltale sign of angiosarcoma (i.e., freely anastomosing vascular channels) (Fig. 20.113). The tumor is thought to be of blood vessels rather than lymph vessels and is, therefore, also referred to as hemangiosarcoma. Occasionally, the tumor is of the epithelioid angiosarcoma type.[1217] Curiously, some cases of breast angiosarcoma have been found to contain estrogen receptors.[1210] The differential diagnosis of angiosarcoma includes metaplastic carcinoma (see p. 1811), the acantholytic variant of squamous cell carcinoma (see p. 1812), hemangioma (see following discussion), and pseudoangiomatous stromal hyperplasia (see p. 1836).

The overall prognosis of angiosarcoma is poor, with most patients developing metastases through the bloodstream.[1230] Donnell et al.[1212] have shown that a good correlation exists between microscopic grade and outcome. In their series, the 5-year disease-free survival was

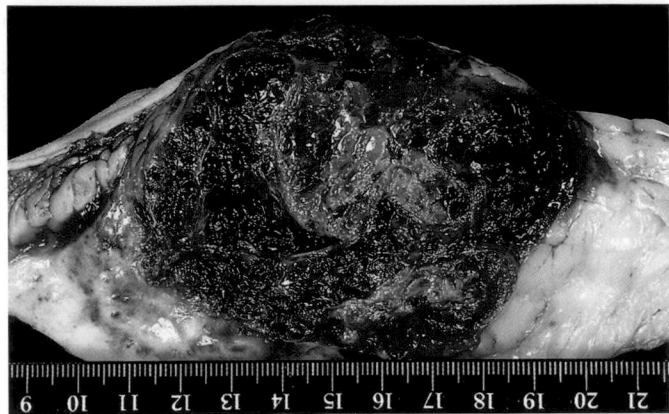

Fig. 20.111 Typical hemorrhagic gross appearance of angiosarcoma of breast. (Courtesy of Dr Pedro J Grases Galofrè; from Grases Galofrè PJ: Patologia ginecològic. Bases para el diagnòstico morfològico, Barcelona, Masson, 2002.)

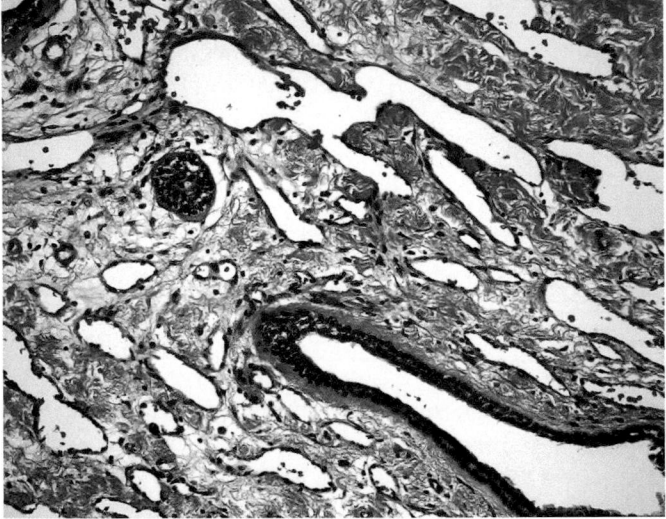

Fig. 20.112 Extremely well-differentiated angiosarcoma of breast.

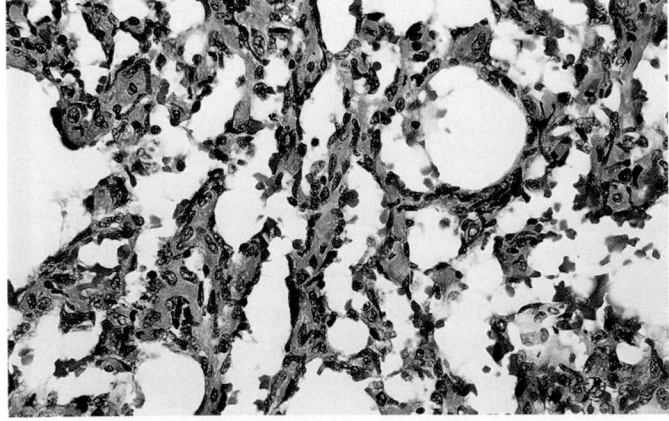

Fig. 20.113 Complex anastomosing vascular pattern in angiosarcoma of breast.

33%; 10 of their 13 patients with grade I lesions were alive and well. The relationship of grading with prognosis has been confirmed in other series.[1218,1225]

Lymphangiosarcoma can develop in the soft tissues of the upper extremity as a result of longstanding postmastectomy lymphedema (Stewart–Treves syndrome; see Chapter 25). Exceptionally, these tumors may develop in association with lymphedema resulting from segmental mastectomy.[1209] Following radiation therapy for carcinoma of the breast, the overlying skin can develop a variety of vascular proliferative lesions, which range from lymphangioma-like nodules to full-blown angiosarcomas[1213,1220,1221,1228] (see Chapter 4). In contrast to angiosarcoma of the Stewart–Treves type, the interval between the radiation and the development of the tumor is short and lymphedema is minimal or absent.[1209a] Exceptionally, this postradiation angiosarcoma is located in the breast itself.[1222]

The statement has often been made that nearly all vascular tumors of the breast are malignant. Although the bland microscopic appearance of some angiosarcomas cannot be overemphasized, it is also true that a number of perfectly benign vascular tumors can occur in this area. First of all, hemangiomas of various types that share the features of those seen elsewhere in the body can develop in the overlying skin and subcutaneous fat. The most likely to be overdiagnosed is angiolipoma, because sometimes it can be very cellular and the adipose tissue component can be inconspicuous.[1224,1231] The encapsulation and presence of hyaline thrombi in the vessels are important diagnostic clues (see Chapter 25).

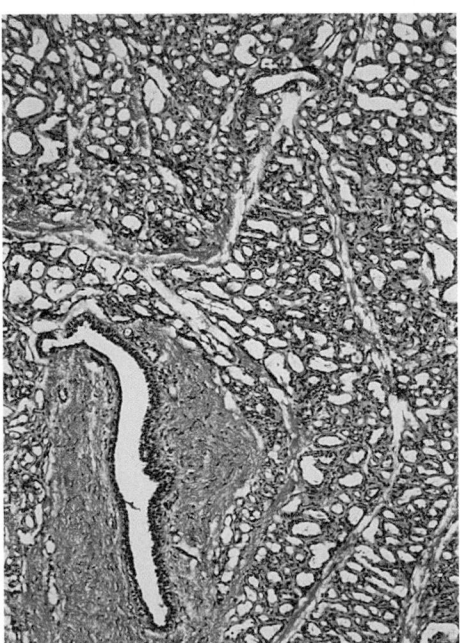

Fig. 20.114 Benign hemangioendothelioma of breast in a child. The appearance is identical to that of the homologous tumor seen more commonly in skin or salivary gland.

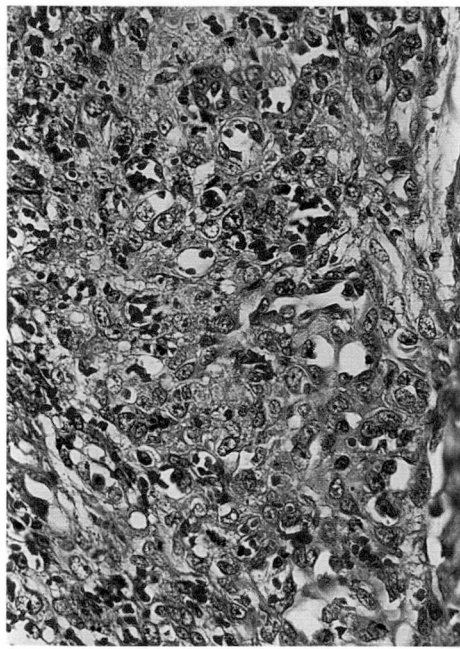

Fig. 20.115 Epithelioid (histiocytoid) hemangioma located within the breast substance. (Courtesy of Dr. Louis P. Dehner, St. Louis)

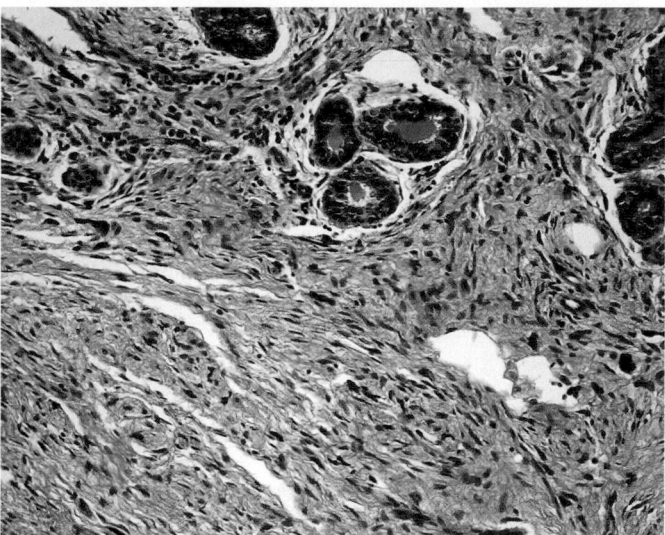

Fig. 20.116 Sarcoma of breast. The entrapped epithelial tissue lacks the features of a phylloides tumor.

Benign vascular breast tumors can also develop within the breast parenchyma.[1211] *Benign hemangioendothelioma* can occur in children, its microscopic appearance being similar to that of its more common cutaneous counterpart (Fig. 20.114). *Perilobular hemangioma* is usually detected only microscopically; it is characterized by dilated capillary vessels in a perilobular location, without anastomoses or cellular atypia.[1227] Autopsy studies have shown that it is a relatively common lesion, having been found in 11% of all breasts.[1215] Other *hemangiomas* are not located perilobularly; they also tend to be small but can reach a diameter of 2 cm.[1214] There are also *venous hemangiomas*.[1226] A few hemangiomas having a diffuse quality (although without anastomosing channels) have been referred to as *angiomatosis*.[1223] Other benign vascular tumors that can exceptionally involve the breast are *hemangiopericytoma*[1208,1219] and *cystic lymphangioma* (cystic hygroma).[1229] *Epithelioid hemangioma* and *Masson's hemangioma (papillary endothelial hyperplasia)* can also be located inside the breast parenchyma[1209b,1224] (Fig. 20.115).

Other malignant stromal tumors

Stromal sarcoma is the generic term given to malignant breast tumors thought to arise from the specialized stroma of this organ but lacking an epithelial component with a phylloides pattern[1235,1244] (Fig. 20.116). Grossly, the tumors appear solid, grayish white, and homogeneous. Necrosis may be present. Microscopically, most of them have the features of fibrosarcoma; focal osseous metapla-sia can occur. Infiltrative margins and severe atypia indicate a greater tendency for local recurrence and distant metastases.[1244]

Stromal tumors with an appearance equivalent to that of various types of sarcomas of somatic soft tissues exist.[1245] They include *liposarcoma*,[1233,1242] *leiomyosarcoma*,[1232,1236,1237,1241] *rhabdomyosarcoma* (but most such tumors are metastatic), *fibrosarcoma*,[1240] *malignant fibrous histiocytoma*,[1240] *chondrosarcoma*,[1234] *osteosarcoma*,[1239,1248] *follicular dendritic cell sarcoma*[1246] (including a myxoid variant[1238]), and *Ewing's sarcoma/PNET*.[1247] *Rhabdoid tumor* also occurs, but at least some of the cases are undifferentiated carcinomas with a rhabdoid phenotype.[1243]

Lymphoid tumors and tumorlike conditions

Malignant lymphoma can present as a primary mammary neoplasm or involve the breast as part of a systemic process.[1259,1270,1271] A few cases have been reported associated with (and perhaps arising from) lymphocytic lobulitis,[1269] and a case has been observed surrounding a silicone breast prosthesis.[1258] Grossly, the tumor is soft and grayish white. It is not accompanied by skin retraction or nipple discharge. For some peculiar reason, the right breast is affected more commonly than the left. Multiple nodules are sometimes encountered. The involvement is bilateral in one of every four patients. In adult patients, primary lymphomas of the breast are nearly always of non-Hodgkin's type and are usually composed of B cells,[1262,1266] only exceptional examples of T-cell lymphoma having been reported.[1251] They can be made up of either large or small cells[1250,1252] and most fit the category of MALT-type lymphomas[1254,1260,1264] (Fig.

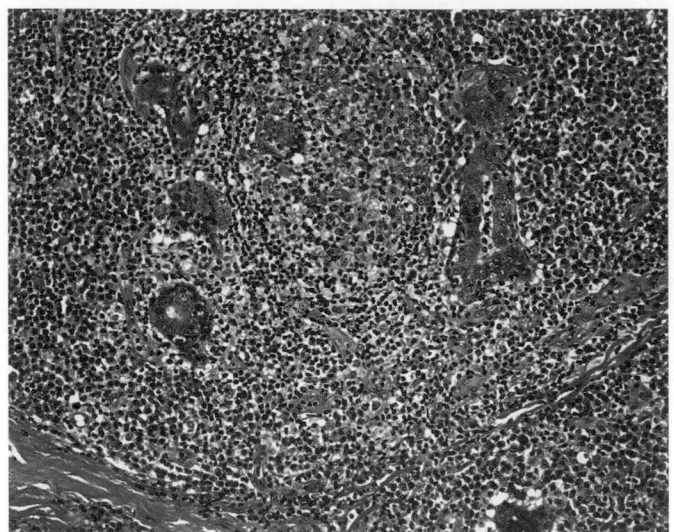

Fig. 20.117 MALT-type malignant lymphoma of breast. Some of the neoplastic lymphocytes infiltrate the glandular structures.

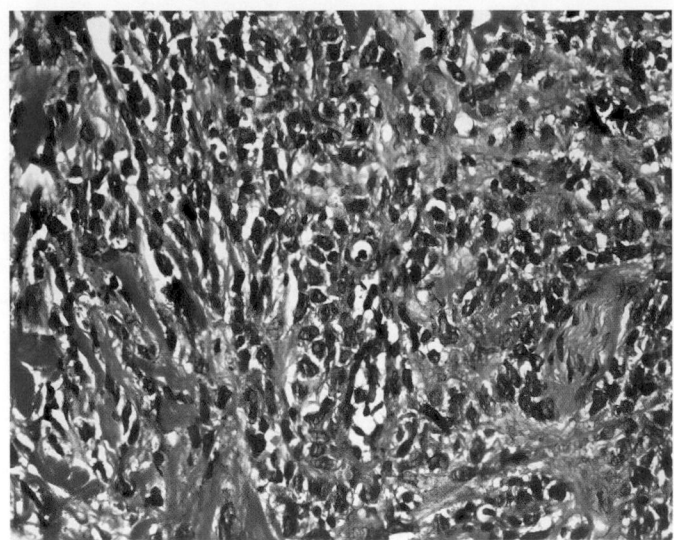

Fig. 20.118 Granulocytic sarcoma of breast. It is easy to misdiagnose this lesion as a large cell lymphoma.

20.117). This includes the tendency to surround and invade the wall and lumina of the epithelial structures, resulting in the so-called "lymphoepithelial lesion." Immunohistochemical studies have shown that nearly all of these cases lack evidence of marginal or mantle cell differentiation.[1252,1253] The targetoid pattern sometimes seen around the ducts may simulate the appearance of invasive lobular carcinoma; in such cases, stains for CD45, CD20, and keratin should solve the diagnostic dilemma. The survival of patients with breast lymphoma is related to stage and microscopic type.[1250,1257]

Pseudolymphoma has been described in the breast. As in other organs, its position in relation to MALT-type lymphoma has become fuzzy. Some cases seem clearly reactive on morphologic and immunohistochemical grounds, perhaps representing an exuberant local reaction to injury.[1261,1265,1267] Others, however, are composed of a monotonous small lymphocytic population and not easily separable from low-grade lymphomas. In some instances, the noncommittal diagnosis of *small lymphocytic proliferation* may be the best approach, followed by a recommendation for no further therapy if no systemic evidence of lymphoma is encountered.

Burkitt's lymphoma in some African children has resulted in involvement of the breast, with the formation of huge bilateral masses. Bilateral Burkitt-type lymphoma has also been seen in young women during pregnancy.[1253]

Hodgkin's lymphoma primary in the breast is exceptional. Most cases of Hodgkin's lymphoma involving the breast represent secondary involvement in stage IV disease.

Plasmacytoma has been seen presenting as a primary breast mass, sometimes associated with a serum monoclonal protein.[1263]

Myelocytic leukemia of either acute or chronic type can present as a localized mass ("granulocytic sarcoma") in the breast and be microscopically confused with large cell lymphoma[1256,1268] (Fig. 20.118). The most important clue to the diagnosis in H&E sections is the presence of eosinophilic myelocytes or metamyelocytes, identified by their round or slightly indented nucleus and bright eosinophilic cytoplasmic granules. The diagnosis can be confirmed by performing Leder's chloroacetate esterase stain or immunostains for CD117.

Myeloid metaplasia can exceptionally present in the form of a mass lesion in the breast in patients with idiopathic myelofibrosis.[1255]

Other primary tumors and tumorlike conditions

Basal cell carcinomas, **squamous cell carcinomas**, **keratinous cysts**, and **sweat gland tumors** may arise in the skin of the nipple or other sites in the breast, but they are not to be considered primary breast tumors.[1284,1295]

Hamartoma has already been mentioned (see p. 1770). The definition of this entity—if it is an entity at all—remains unsatisfactory. Its identification is said to depend on the combination of clinical, radiologic, and pathologic criteria.[1277,1285] Morphologically, lesions that have been thought to be hamartomas on mammography may exhibit a wide diversity of appearances, the common denominator being the admixture of epithelial and stromal elements, the latter including fat[1283,1289,1297,1304] (Figs 20.119 and 20.120). A reproducible morphologic or immunohistochemical distinction of this process from circumscribed fibrocystic disease and fibroadenoma has yet to be achieved.[1293] *Myoid hamartoma*[1282] (which can contain epithelioid cells[1290]) (Fig. 20.121) and *chondrolipoma* (a benign lesion composed of an admixture of fat, cartilage, and sometimes bone)[1298,1299,1301] are two other processes straddling the fence between malformation and benign neoplasia.

Granular cell tumor is important because of its ability to simulate grossly the appearance of invasive carci-

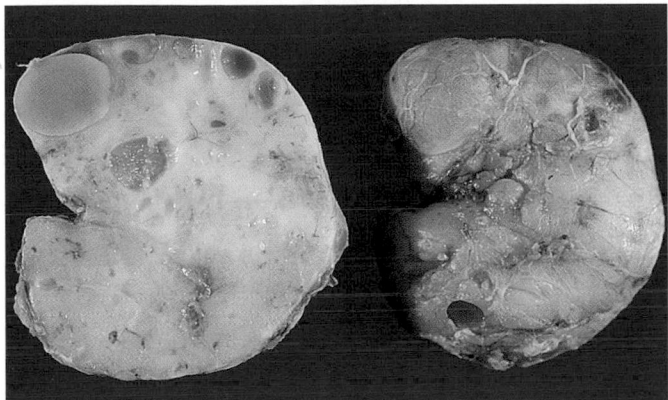

Fig. 20.119 Gross appearance of so-called "hamartoma of breast." There is a combination of cystic dilatation of ducts, fibrosis, and entrapment of adipose tissue. This lesion is more distinctive and impressive grossly than microscopically.

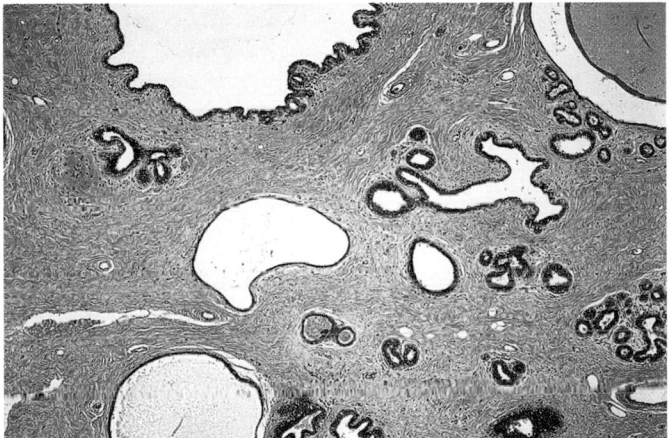

Fig. 20.120 Glandular epithelium and fibrous stroma with distorted arrangement in hamartoma of breast.

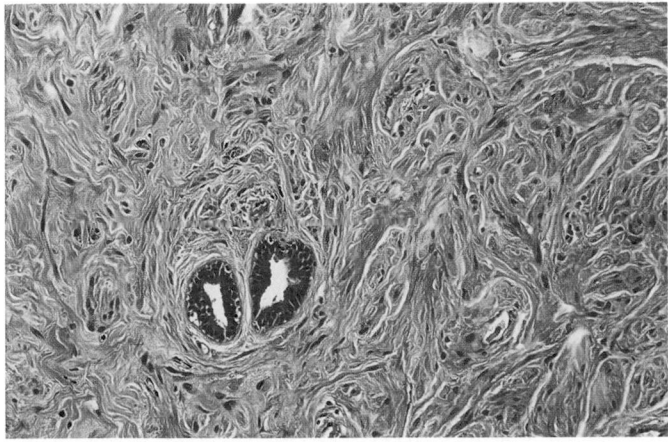

Fig. 20.121 So-called "myoid hamartoma of breast."

noma.[1280,1286,1296] It is usually small, but it may reach a size of 10 cm or more. On section, it is firm, homogeneous, and white or grayish yellow. As a rule, it is not attached to the overlying skin, but it may be fixed to the underlying fascia. The microscopic appearance is described in Chapter 25. The behavior is benign, and the treatment is local excision[1279] (see also below).

Myofibroblastoma is a benign mesenchymal tumor originally described in the male breast but also occurring in the female organ. This is described in detail on p. 1838.

Leiomyoma usually involves the nipple and is often painful[1303]; occasionally, it is seen within the breast substance.[1288] Some have been reported having epithelioid features and granular changes.[1308]

Benign peripheral nerve tumors of both schwannoma[1278] and perineurioma[1276] types have been described. Traumatic neuromas with granular cell changes have been described in mastectomy scars.[1311]

Nodular fasciitis is rarely seen within the breast, its appearance and behavior being similar to those of its more common soft tissue counterpart.

Fibromatosis (extra-abdominal desmoid tumor) can also be found within the substance of the breast (Fig. 20.122). It shares with its homolog in the somatic soft tissue a tendency for infiltration, local aggressiveness, and local recurrence.[1310] This is also true at the molecular level, in the sense that they have a similar spectrum of β-catenin and APC alterations.[1272]

Cases occurring during child-bearing age are, in general, more cellular than those seen after menopause,[1287] in the sense of being infiltrative, aggressive, and prone to local recurrence[1310]. A type of fibromatosis containing eosinophilic inclusions identical to those seen in infantile digital fibromatosis has been identified.[1305] Parenthetically, similar inclusions have been identified in the stromal component of fibroepithelial lesions having a phylloides tumor-like appearance.[1275,1294] Fibromatosis should be distinguished from the low-grade form of metaplastic carcinoma (see p. 1811).

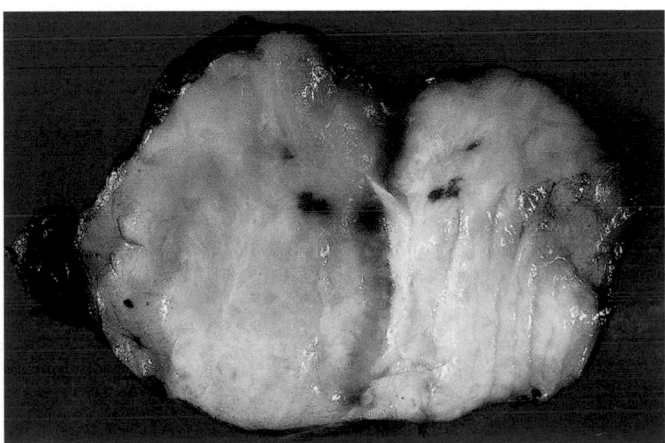

Fig. 20.122 Gross appearance of fibromatosis involving breast. The mass is solid and ill defined.

Clear cell ("sugar") tumor (a neoplasm of HMB45-positive epithelioid smooth muscle cells) has been reported in the breast.[1291]

Pseudoangiomatous stromal hyperplasia (PASH) is characterized by a proliferation of stromal spindle cells of fibroblastic/myofibroblastic nature associated with the formation of probably artifactual clefts that simulate vascular channels[1313] (Fig. 20.123). In the more cellular areas the pseudoangiomatous pattern may be absent.[1306] The spindle cells are immunoreactive for vimentin and CD34, and negative for FVIII-related antigen, *Ulex*, and CD31. In addition, they show intense positivity for progesterone receptors. The latter finding suggests that PASH represents a localized form of stromal overgrowth with a hormonal (primarily progestogenic) pathogenesis.[1273] It has been proposed that the stromal proliferation present in PASH is composed of CD34-positive cells similar to those seen in gynecomastoid lesions and in the stroma of fibroadenoma, and that there is a close relationship among these disorders.[1273a] As already indicated (p. 1820), breast carcinoma cells can grow along these pseudoangiomatous spaces.[1281]

Multinucleated giant cells of reactive appearance are sometimes found incidentally in the normal mammary stroma or in the stroma of fibroadenomas[1274,1309]; they are of no clinical significance and are probably analogous to those seen in non-neoplastic polypoid stromal lesions located beneath mucosal membranes, such as the nasal cavity, oral cavity, anus, and lower female genital tract[1309,1312] (Fig. 20.124).

Amyloidosis can appear as a solitary nodule within the breast parenchyma (so-called "amyloid tumor").[1300,1307]

Rosai–Dorfman disease (sinus histiocytosis with massive lymphadenopathy) can also present under exceptional circumstances as a breast mass.[1292]

Nodular mucinosis presents as a circumscribed area of myxoid stromal change in the breast.[1302] It should be distinguished from the various epithelial proliferative lesions resulting in a mucocele-like appearance (see p. 1807).

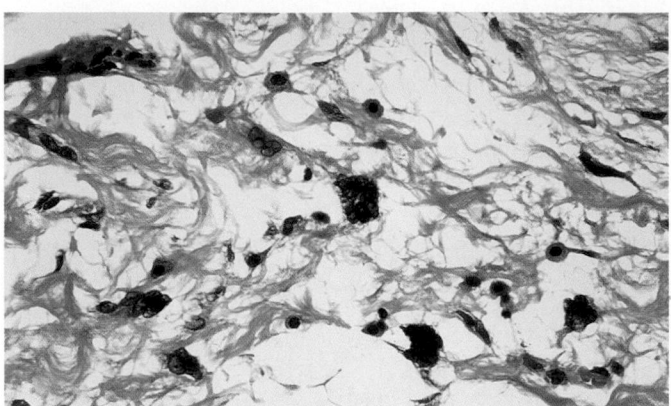

Fig. 20.124 Bizarre multinucleated cells in mammary stroma. This neoplastic change is analogous to that more often seen in the stroma of the upper aerodigestive tract and in the genital tract.

Metastatic tumors

Metastatic malignant tumors rarely affect the breast except in widely disseminated tumors.[1315] They typically appear as superficial, well-defined multinodular masses. Malignant melanoma and carcinoma of the lung, ovary, kidney, and stomach are the most common sources.[1317,1322] Most of the lung tumors are of the small cell neuroendocrine type. Metastases can also develop from better differentiated neuroendocrine tumors, such as bronchial carcinoid tumor, pancreatic endocrine tumor, and thyroid medullary carcinoma.[1318,1320,1321] One should not forget in this listing the metastases from contralateral breast carcinoma, which is not an infrequent finding in autopsy series.[1315] Azzopardi[1314] has made the interesting observation that presence of elastosis has not been documented in association with metastatic disease of the breast.

Metastatic carcinomas to the breast can simulate primary malignant tumors of this organ; exceptionally, they greatly mimic the appearance of DCIS.[316]

In children, the most common malignant tumor to metastasize to the breast (hematolymphoid malignancies excluded) is rhabdomyosarcoma, particularly of the alveolar type.[1319]

Breast diseases in children and adolescents

The most common breast "mass" for which clinical consultation is sought in this age group is actually not a pathologic condition at all but rather precocious, sometimes predominantly unilateral, breast development.[1323] Should such a "mass" be removed, no development of the breast will occur.[1331]

Fibroadenoma is the most common pathologic condition of the breast between puberty and 20 years of age, but it is exceptional before puberty.[1325]

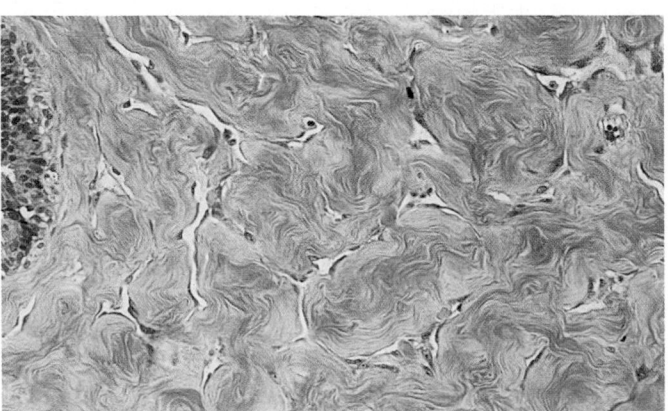

Fig. 20.123 Pseudoangiomatous stromal hyperplasia. Thin channels lined by spindle cells are seen scattered within a hyalinized stroma.

Virginal hypertrophy (gigantomastia; macromastia) may result in massive unilateral or bilateral enlargement.[1323] Microscopically, it is characterized by a combined proliferation of ducts and stroma with little, if any, lobular participation[1327] (Fig. 20.125).

Fibrocystic disease of the conventional type is practically never seen in this age group. However, highly proliferative epithelial lesions can develop. Some of them have the appearance of intraductal papillomas.[1326,1328] Others resemble duct hyperplasia (epitheliosis) of the adult breast, with or without associated sclerosis and ductular distortion.[1328] Wilson et al.[1333] studied 74 patients with a process they termed *papillary duct hyperplasia*, which they distinguish from the juvenile papillomatosis described later. They found that 28% of the patients had a family history for breast carcinoma but that none of them had developed carcinoma at the time of the last follow-up.

Juvenile papillomatosis (Swiss cheese disease) is a probably related but morphologically somewhat distinct form of ductal-type hyperplasia usually seen in young individuals (average age: 19 years) but occurring in a wide age range (10 to 44 years). Clinically, the localized, multinodular masses simulate the appearance of fibroadenoma. Grossly, the clustering of the cystic formations results in a cut surface appearance reminiscent of Swiss cheese—hence the alternative designation for this entity (Fig. 20.126). Microscopically, there is florid epithelial hyperplasia (sometimes with marked atypia and/or focal necrosis), cysts with or without apocrine metaplasia, duct stasis, and sclerosing adenosis[1326,1329] (Fig. 20.127). A family history of breast carcinoma is reported in 58% of cases, and 10% of the patients subsequently develop breast carcinoma.[1330,1332]

Carcinoma of the infantile breast is very rare. Most cases are of the so-called "juvenile (secretory) type" and are discussed on p. 1809. A few tumors have the appearance of ordinary invasive ductal carcinomas.

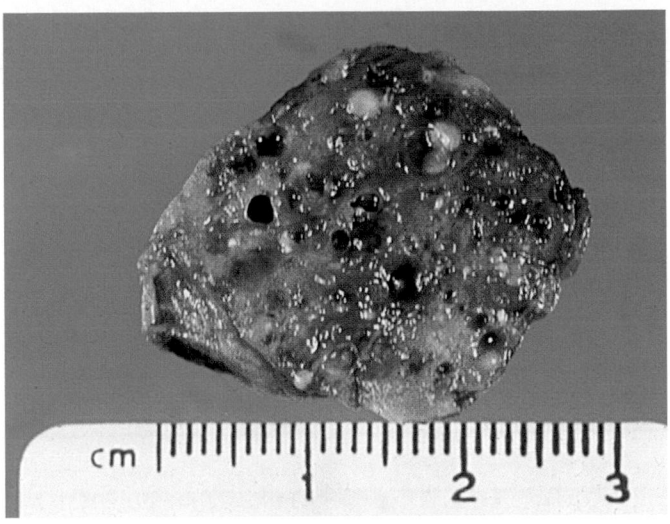

Fig. 20.126 Juvenile papillomatosis (Swiss cheese disease). The gross appearance is that of clustered cystic formations.

Fig. 20.127 Juvenile papillomatosis (Swiss cheese disease). Whole-mount view showing variously sized cystic formations, alternating with solid epithelial proliferations.

In the presence of a high-grade malignant round cell tumor of the breast in a child or adolescent, the possibility should be considered that it may be a solid variant of alveolar rhabdomyosarcoma, whether primary or metastatic.[1324]

Breast diseases in males

Gynecomastia

Gynecomastia is defined as the enlargement of the male breast resulting from hypertrophy and hyperplasia of both glandular and stromal components. It may result from numerous causes, which share a background of relative increase in estrogenic activity (whether endogenous or exogenous), decrease in androgenic activity, or both.[1335,1347] Development of gynecomastia before 25

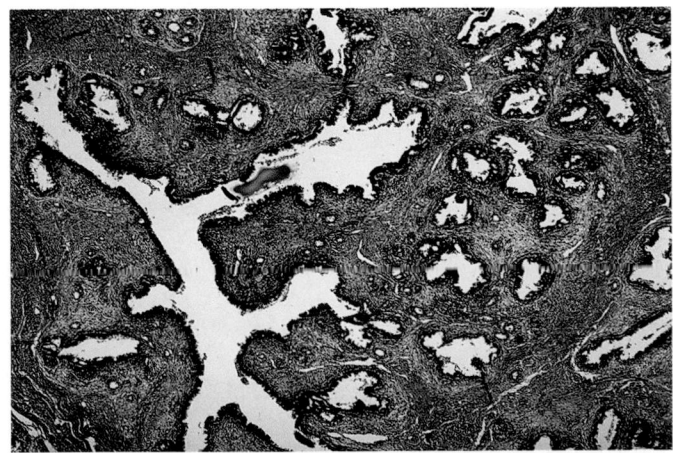

Fig. 20.125 So-called "virginal hypertrophy of breast," showing proliferative changes in epithelium and stroma.

years of age is usually related to hormonal pubertal changes, whereas development in later years may be caused by hormonally active tumors (Leydig cell tumor of testis, hCG-secreting germ cell tumors, lung carcinoma, or others), cirrhosis, or medications (digitalis, reserpine, Dilantin, and others).[1336] Cases have also been reported in type-1 neurofibromatosis.[1338] Clinical gynecomastia developing in diabetic patients may have the features of diabetic or lymphocytic mastitis, as seen in females[1342] (see p. 1768). Many cases remain idiopathic.

Clinically, gynecomastia is usually centered below the nipple, an important point in the differential diagnosis with carcinoma, which tends to be located eccentrically.[1335] It may be unilateral (at least at the clinical level, the left breast being more commonly involved than the right) or bilateral. It has been noted that pubertal and hormone-induced gynecomastias tend to be bilateral, whereas idiopathic and nonhormonal drug-induced gynecomastias are usually unilateral.[1345]

The gross appearance is characteristic. The mass is oval, disk shaped, of elastic consistency, and with well-circumscribed borders. Microscopically, the ducts show a variable and sometimes very prominent degree of epithelial hyperplasia and are surrounded by a prominent swollen stroma, which results in a typical "halo" effect[1345] (Fig. 20.128). This stroma contains large amounts of acid mucopolysaccharides (mainly hyaluronic acid) of a type similar to that seen in fibroadenoma of the female breast.[1339] There may be pseudoangiomatous stromal hyperplasia (PASH),[1337] and focal squamous metaplasia and formation of lobules may be observed.[1335,1340] Exceptionally, a population of clear or globoid cells immunoreactive for GCDFP-15 may be present.[1341]

The microscopic changes are related to the duration of the gynecomastia. Cases of short duration tend to have a prominent hyperplastic epithelial component and

stromal edema, whereas those of long duration have prominent stromal fibrosis.[1334] In rare cases, the intraductal epithelial hyperplasia is so extreme as to simulate carcinoma. In others, the proliferation has fibroadenoma-like qualities.[1344]

The possible relationship between gynecomastia and carcinoma is discussed in the next section.

The peculiar fact that, sometimes, changes morphologically similar to those of gynecomastia can be seen in the female breast has already been mentioned (see p. 1782).[1343,1346] Tongue-in-cheek, one could say that these are cases in which a female breast resembles a male breast that resembles a female breast.

Myofibroblastoma

Myofibroblastoma is the most commonly used term for a benign stromal neoplasm first described by Toker et al.[1361] as benign spindle cell tumor, and also known as myogenic stromal tumor.[1350] Originally thought to involve primarily the male breast, it is now known to occur in the female breast with a higher frequency, and is discussed in this section only on historical grounds.[1362]

Grossly, it is well circumscribed and usually small, although on occasion it can reach a large size.[1348,1349] Microscopically, uniform, bland-looking spindle cells are haphazardly arranged in fascicles separated by broad bands of hyalinized collagen (Fig. 20.129). The appearance is very reminiscent of both solitary fibrous tumor and spindle cell lipoma,[1351] the suggestion having been made that there is a close histogenetic link between these neoplasms.[1353,1354,1356]

Focally, there may be smooth muscle differentiation or cartilaginous metaplasia.[1352,1360] Ultrastructurally, the features are those of fibroblasts and myoid cells (i.e.,

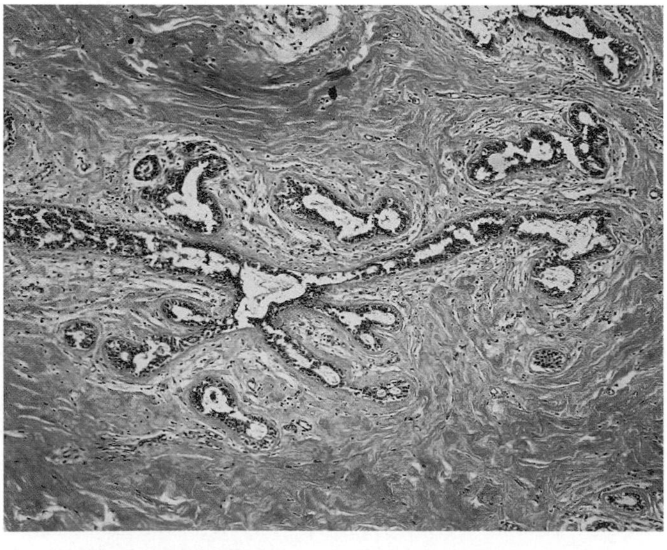

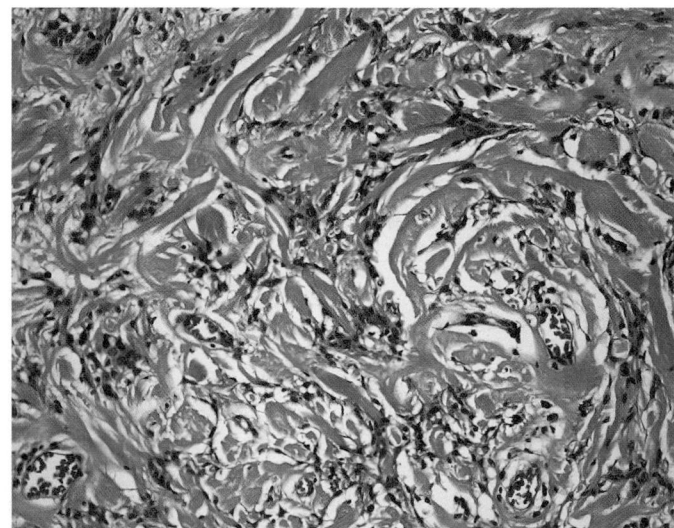

Fig. 20.128 Epithelial proliferation surrounded by a hypocellular myxoid halo in gynecomastia.

Fig. 20.129 Myofibroblastoma of male breast. The microscopic appearance is very reminiscent of solitary fibrous tumor.

myofibroblast-like), and immunoreactivity for desmin and caldesmon has been encountered in some cases.[1357,1362] Although estrogen and progesterone receptors are strongly expressed,[1355] the suggestion has been made that the lesion may be pathogenetically related to androgens.[1358]

A variation on the theme is represented by the epithelioid myofibroblastoma, cases of which have been reported against a background of gynecomastia.[1359]

Carcinoma

In the United States, only 1% of all breast carcinomas occur in males, but in some Arab countries the incidence rises to nearly 10%.[1370,1371] An increased incidence of breast carcinoma is seen in patients with Klinefelter's syndrome.[1386] Familial cases have also been recorded.[1369,1379] An important and not entirely resolved issue is that of the possible relationship between gynecomastia and breast carcinoma. In one series, microscopic changes consistent with gynecomastia were found in 40% of breast carcinoma cases.[1376] Furthermore, cases of primary breast carcinoma have occurred in patients with prostatic carcinoma treated with estrogens.[1382] Finally, countries in which the incidence of gynecomastia is high also have a high incidence of breast carcinoma. All these data would seem to point toward a pathogenetic link between the two entities.

Clinically, most breast carcinomas present in elderly individuals as breast nodules, with or without associated nipple abnormalities.[1364,1368] Nipple discharge in an adult male, especially if bloody, should arouse a strong suspicion of carcinoma. Skin involvement by fixation and Paget's disease are much more common in males. As in females, nipple involvement can simulate malignant melanoma.[1390]

Grossly and microscopically, carcinomas of the male breast are remarkably similar to those seen in females.[1370] As such, they can be in situ or invasive, and low grade or high grade,[1366,1377] but with a higher percentage of high-grade tumors.[1380] All of the microscopic types identified in the female breast have been encountered in males, including tumors with neuroendocrine features.[1383,1388] The least common of the major categories is invasive lobular carcinoma, only a few cases having been observed.[1372,1386,1387] Other very unusual types include adenomyoepithelioma[1391] and oncocytic carcinoma[1367] (Fig. 20.130).

The tumors can be identified by fine needle aspiration, the most important differential diagnosis using this modality being gynecomastia.[1365] The incidence of positivity for estrogen receptors is higher than in females.[1375,1380]

The overall survival rate is lower than for breast carcinoma,[1363,1374,1381,1385] but, as usual, the differences tend to

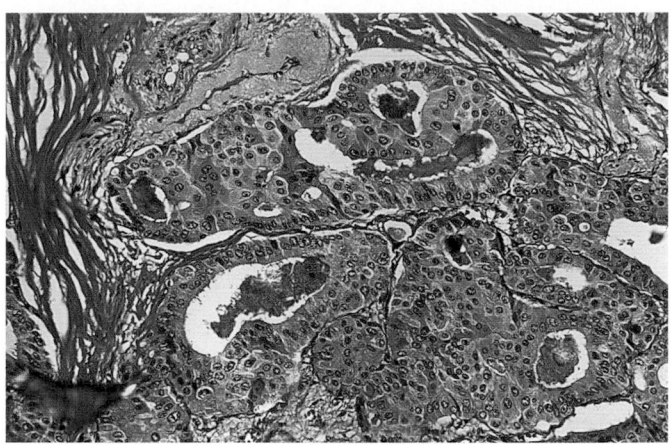

Fig. 20.130 Carcinoma of the male breast composed of well-differentiated tumor cells with abundant granular cytoplasm having oncocytic features.

disappear when the tumors are compared stage by stage.[1373,1394] Indeed, the prognosis of breast cancer in males, like that in females, is heavily influenced by clinical stage and microscopic grade.[1389,1392] It also correlates with mitotic activity, DNA ploidy, and p53 status.[1378,1384,1393]

Other lesions

Mammary duct ectasia[1405] and **sclerosing adenosis**[1397] can occur in the male breast. Fibrocystic disease, fibroadenoma, PASH, and phylloides tumor have also been reported but are vanishingly rare.[1395,1402]

Nipple adenoma and **intraductal papilloma** have been seen on several occasions, in one instance following estrogen therapy for prostatic carcinoma.[1400,1404,1406] There are also reports of **leiomyosarcoma** of the nipple[1401] and **neurofibromatosis** in a child whose condition simulated gynecomastia.[1403]

Metastatic carcinoma to the male breast usually originates from the prostate, is often bilateral, and is almost always seen following estrogen therapy.[1396] As such, it occurs against a background of gynecomastia. Some of these cases have been confused with primary breast carcinoma. Immunohistochemical stains for PSA and prostatic acid phosphatase are helpful in the differential diagnosis.[1399] The matter is complicated by the fact that the normal mammary duct epithelium of males and the hyperplastic epithelium of gynecomastia is often immunoreactive for PSA (but not for prostatic acid phosphatase). Male breast carcinoma is negative for both markers.[1398]

References

NORMAL ANATOMY

1 Anderson TJ. Normal breast: myths, realities, and prospects. Mod Pathol 1998, **11:** 115–119.

2 Azzopardi JG. Problems in breast pathology. In Bennington JL (consulting ed.): Major problems in pathology, vol. 11. Philadelphia, 1979, W.B. Saunders.

3 Barbareschi M, Pecciarini L, Cangi MG, Macri E, Rizzo A, Viale G, Doglioni C. p63, a p53 homologue, is a selective nuclear marker of myoepithelial cells of the human breast. Am J Surg Pathol 2001, 25: 1054–1060.

4 Barwick KW, Kashgarian M, Rosen PP. "Clear-cell" change within duct and lobular epithelium of the human breast. Pathol Annu 1982, 17: 319–328.

5 Battersby S, Anderson TJ. Histological changes in breast tissue that characterize recent pregnancy. Histopathology 1989, 15: 415–419.

6 Bocker W, Moll R, Poremba C, Holland R, Van Diest PJ, Dervan P, Burger H, Wai D, Diallo RI, Brandt B, Herbst H, Schmidt A, Lerch MM, Buchwallow IB. Common adult stem cells in the human breast give rise to glandular and myoepithelial cell lineages: a new cell biological concept. Lab Invest 2002, 82: 737–746.

7 Bussolati G, Gugliotta P, Sapino A, Eusebi V, Lloyd RV. Chromogranin reactive endocrine cells in argyrophilic carcinomas ("carcinoids") and normal tissue of the breast. Am J Pathol 1985, 120: 186–192.

8 Charpin C, Lissitzky JC, Jacquemier J, Lavaut MN, Kopp F, Pourreau-Schneider N, Martin PM, Toga M. Immunohistochemical detection of laminin in 98 human breast carcinomas. A light and electron microscopic study. Hum Pathol 1986, 17: 355–365.

9 Clayton F, Ordóñez NG, Hanssen GM, Hanssen H. Immunoperoxidase localization of lactalbumin in malignant breast neoplasms. Arch Pathol Lab Med 1982, 106: 268–270.

10 Cowan DF, Herbert TA. Involution of the breast in women aged 50 to 104 years. A histological study of 102 cases. Surg Pathol 1989, 2: 323–334.

11 Cunha GR. Role of mesenchymal-epithelial interactions in normal and abnormal development of the mammary gland and prostate. Cancer 1994, 74: 1030–1044.

12 Egan MJ, Newman J, Crocker J, Collard M. Immunohistochemical localization of S100 protein in benign and malignant conditions of the breast. Arch Pathol Lab Med 1987, 111: 28–31.

13 Farahmand S, Cowan DF. Elastosis in the normal aging breast. A histopathologic study of 140 cases. Arch Pathol Lab Med 1991, 115: 1241–1246.

14 Fechner RE. The surgical pathology of the reproductive system and breast during oral contraceptive therapy. Pathol Annu 1971, 6: 299–319.

15 Foschini MP, Scarpellini F, Grown AM, Eusebi V. Differential expression of myoepithelial markers in salivary, sweat and mammary glands. Int J Surg Pathol 2000, 8: 29–37.

16 Greenwalt DE, Johnson VG, Kuhajda FP, Eggleston JC, Mather IH. Localization of a membrane glycoprotein in benign fibrocystic disease and infiltrating duct carcinomas of the human breast with the use of a monoclonal antibody to guinea pig milk fat globule membrane. Am J Pathol 1985, 118: 351–359.

17 Joshi K, Ellis JTB, Hughes CM, Monaghan P, Neville AM. Cellular proliferation in the rat mammary gland during pregnancy and lactation. Lab Invest 1986, 54: 52–62.

18 Joshi K, Smith JA, Perusinghe N, Monoghan P. Cell proliferation in the human mammary epithelium. Differential contribution by epithelial and myoepithelial cells. Am J Pathol 1986, 124: 199–206.

19 Kiaer HW, Andersen JA. Focal pregnancy-like changes in the breast. Acta Pathol Microbiol Scand (A) 1977, 85: 931–941.

20 Larsen BL, Smith VR (eds). Lactation. A comprehensive treatise. New York, 1974, Academic Press.

21 Longacre TA, Bartow SA. A correlative morphologic study of human breast and endometrium in the menstrual cycle. Am J Surg Pathol 1986, 10: 382–393.

22 McCarty KS, Nath M. Breast. In Sternberg S (ed.): Histology for pathologists, ed. 2. Philadelphia, 1997, Lippincott-Raven, pp. 71–84.

23 Marucci G, Betts CM, Golouh R, Peterse JL, Foschini MP, Eusebi V. Toker cells are probably precursors of Paget cells carcinoma: a morphological and ultrastructural description. Virchows Arch 2002, 441: 117–123.

24 Monteagudo C, Merino MJ, San-Juan J, Liotta LA, Stetler-Stevenson WG. Immunohistochemical distribution of type IV collagenase in normal, benign, and malignant breast tissue. Am J Pathol 1990, 136: 585–592.

25 Ozzello L. Epithelial-stromal junction of normal and dysplastic mammary glands. Cancer 1970, 25: 586–600.

26 Ramakrishnan R, Khan SA, Badve S. Morphological changes in breast tissue with menstrual cycle. Mod Pathol 2002, 15: 1348–1356.

27 Reis-Filho JS, Milanezi F, Paredes J, Silva P, Pereira EM, Maeda SA, de Carvalho LV, Schmitt FC. Novel and classic myoepithelial/stem cell markers in metaplastic carcinomas of the breast. Appl Immunohistochem Mol Morphol 2003, 11: 1–8.

28 Rosen PP, Tench W. Lobules in the nipple. Frequency and significance for breast cancer treatment. Pathol Annu 1985, 20 (Pt 2): 317–322.

29 Rytina ER, Coady AT, Millis RR. Milk granuloma. An unusual appearance in lactational breast tissue. Histopathology 1990, 17: 466–468.

30 Satake T, Matsuyama M. Endocrine cells in a normal breast and non-cancerous breast lesion. Acta Pathol Jpn 1991, 41: 874–878.

31 Slavin JL, Billson VR, Ostor AG. Nodular breast lesions during pregnancy and lactation. Histopathology 1993, 22: 481–485.

32 Smith DM Jr, Peters TG, Donegan WL. Montgomery's areolar tubercle. A light microscopic study. Arch Pathol Lab Med 1982, 106: 60–63.

33 Tavassoli FA, Yeh IT. Lactational and clear cell changes of the breast in nonlactating, nonpregnant women. Am J Clin Pathol 1987, 87: 23–29.

34 Toker C. Clear cells of the nipple epidermis. Cancer 1970, 25: 601–610.

35 Tsubura A, Okada H, Senzaki H, Hatano T, Morii S. Keratin expression in the normal breast and in breast carcinoma. Histopathology 1991, 18: 517–522.

36 Vogel PM, Georgiade NG, Fetter BF, Vogel FS, McCarty KS Jr. The correlation of histologic changes in the human breast with the menstrual cycle. Am J Pathol 1981, 104: 23–34.

37 Wellings SR, Jensen HM, Marcum RG. An atlas of subgross pathology of the human breast with special reference to possible precancerous lesions. J Natl Cancer Inst 1975, 55: 231–273.

ECTOPIA

38 Edlow DW, Carter D. Heterotopic epithelium in axillary lymph nodes. Report of a case and review of the literature. Am J Clin Pathol 1973, 59: 666–673.

39 Jordan K, Laumann A, Conrad S, Medenica M. Axillary mass in a 20 year-old woman. Diagnosis: axillary accessory breast tissue. Arch Dermatol 2001, 137: 1367–1372.

40 O'Hara MF, Page DL. Adenomas of the breast and ectopic breast under lactational influences. Hum Pathol 1985, 16: 707–712.

41 Pfeifer JD, Barr RJ, Wick MR. Ectopic breast tissue and breast-like sweat gland metaplasias: an overlapping spectrum of lesions. J Cutan Pathol 1999, 26: 190–196.

42 Rosen PP, Tench W. Lobules in the nipple. Frequency and significance for breast cancer treatment. Pathol Annu 1985, 20 (Pt 2): 317–322.

43 Turner DR, Millis RR. Breast tissue inclusions in axillary lymph nodes. Histopathology 1980, **4:** 631–363.

INFLAMMATORY AND RELATED LESIONS
Mammary duct ectasia

44 Haagensen CD. Mammary-duct ectasia. A disease that may simulate carcinoma. Cancer 1951, **4:** 749–761.

45 Miller MA, Kottler SJ, Cohn LA, Johnson GC, Kreeger JM, Pace LV, Ramos-Vara JA, Turk JR, Turnquist SE. Mammary duct ectasia in dogs: 51 cases (1992–1999). J Am Vet Med Assoc 2001, **218:** 1303–1307.

46 Webb AJ. Mammary duct ectasia—periductal mastitis complex. Br J Surg 1995, **82:** 1300–1302.

Fat necrosis

47 Clarke D, Curtis JL, Martinez A, Fajardo L, Goffinet D. Fat necrosis of the breast simulating recurrent carcinoma after primary radiotherapy in the management of early stage breast carcinoma. Cancer 1983, **52:** 442–445.

48 Coyne JD, Parkinson D, Baildam AD. Membranous fat necrosis of the breast. Histopathology 1996, **28:** 61–64.

49 Dabbs DJ. Mammary ductal foam cells. Macrophage immunophenotype. Hum Pathol 1993, **24:** 977–981.

50 Kinoshita T, Yashiro N, Yoshigi J, Ihara N, Narita M. Fat necrosis of breast: a potential pitfall in breast MRI. Clin Imaging 2002, **26:** 250–253.

Other inflammatory diseases

51 Arnaout AH, Shousha S, Metaxas N, Husain OA. Intramammary tuberculous lymphadenitis. Histopathology 1990, **17:** 91–93.

52 Ashton MA, Lefkowitz M, Tavassoli FA. Epithelioid stromal cells in lymphocytic mastitis. A source of confusion with invasive carcinoma. Mod Pathol 1994, **7:** 49–54.

53 Banik S, Bishop PW, Ormerod LP, O'Brien TE. Sarcoidosis of the breast. J Clin Pathol 1986, **39:** 446–448.

54 Bocian JJ, Fahmy RN, Michas CA. A rare case of 'coccidioidoma' of the breast. Arch Pathol Lab Med 1991, **115:** 1064–1067.

55 Catania S, Zurrida S, Veronesi P, Galimberti V, Bono A, Pluchinotta A. Mondor's disease and breast cancer. Cancer 1992, **69:** 2267–2270.

56 Cooper NE. Rheumatoid nodule in the breast. Histopathology 1991, **19:** 193–194.

57 Coyne JD, Baildam AD, Asbury D. Lymphocytic mastopathy associated with ductal carcinoma in situ of the breast. Histopathology 1995, **26:** 579–580.

58 Dener C, Inan A. Breast abscesses in lactating women. World J Surg 2003, **27:** 130–133.

59 Eckland DA, Zeigler MG. Abscess in the nonlactating breast. Arch Surg 1973, **107:** 398–401.

60 Ely KA, Tse G, Simpson JF, Clarfeld R, Page DL. Diabetic mastopathy. A clinicopathologic review. Am J Clin Pathol 2000, **113:** 541–545.

61 Farrow JH. Thrombophlebitis of the superficial veins of the breast and anterior chest wall (Mondor's disease). Surg Gynecol Obstet 1955, **101:** 63–68.

62 Fitzgibbons PL, Smiley DF, Kern WH. Sarcoidosis presenting initially as breast mass. Report of two cases. Hum Pathol 1985, **16:** 851–852.

63 Fletcher A, Magrath IM, Riddell RH, Talbot IC. Granulomatous mastitis. A report of seven cases. J Clin Pathol 1982, **35:** 941–945.

64 Herrmann JB. Thrombophlebitis of breast and contiguous thoracicoabdominal wall (Mondor's disease). NY State J Med 1966, **66:** 3146–3152.

65 Johnson WC, Wallrich R, Helwig EB. Superficial thrombophlebitis of the chest wall. JAMA 1962, **180:** 103–108.

66 Jordan JM, Rowe WT, Allen NB. Wegener's granulomatosis involving the breast. Report of three cases and review of the literature. Am J Med 1987, **83:** 159–164.

67 Kariv R, Sidi Y, Gur H. Systemic vasculitis presenting as a tumorlike lesion. Four case reports and an analysis of 79 reported cases. Medicine (Baltimore) 2000, **79:** 349–359.

68 Kessler EI, Katzav JA. Lobular granulomatous mastitis. Surg Pathol 1990, **3:** 115–120.

69 Khanna R, Prasanna GV, Gupta P, Kumar M, Khanna S, Khanna A. Mammary tuberculosis: report on 52 cases. Postgrad Med J 2002, **78:** 422–424.

70 Lammie GA, Bobrow LG, Staunton MD, Levison DA, Page G, Millis RR. Sclerosing lymphocytic lobulitis of the breast. Evidence for an autoimmune pathogenesis. Histopathology 1991, **19:** 13–20.

71 Lower EE, Hawkins HH, Baughman RP. Breast disease in sarcoidosis. Sarcoidosis Vasc Diffuse Lung Dis 2001, **18:** 301–306.

72 Lucey JJ. Spontaneous infarction of the breast. J Clin Pathol 1975, **28:** 937–943.

73 Mayor M, Buron I, De Mora JC, Lazaro TE, Hernandez-Cano N, Rubio FA, Casado M. Mondor's disease. Int J Dermatol 2000, **39:** 922–925.

74 Morgan MC, Weaver MG, Crowe JP, Abdul-Karim FW. Diabetic mastopathy. A clinicopathologic study in palpable and nonpalpable breast lesions. Mod Pathol 1995, **8:** 349–354.

75 Ng WF, Chow LT, Lam PW. Localized polyarteritis nodosa of breast. Report of two cases and a review of the literature. Histopathology 1993, **23:** 535–539.

76 Nudelman HL, Kempson RL. Necrosis of the breast. A rare complication of anticoagulant therapy. Am J Surg 1966, **111:** 728–733.

77 Ojeda H, Sardi A, Totoonchie A. Sarcoidosis of the breast: implications for the general surgeon. Am Surg 2000, **66:** 1144–1148.

78 Osborne BM. Granulomatous mastitis caused by histoplasma and mimicking inflammatory breast carcinoma. Hum Pathol 1989, **20:** 47–52.

79 Pugh CM, DeWitty RL. Mondor's disease. J Natl Med Assoc 1996, **88:** 359–363.

80 Rickert RR, Rajan S. Localized breast infarcts associated with pregnancy. Arch Pathol 1974, **97:** 159–161.

81 Robitaille Y, Seemayer TA, Thelmo WL, Cumberlidge MC. Infarction of the mammary region mimicking carcinoma of the breast. Cancer 1974, **33:** 1183–1189.

82 Scholefield JH, Duncan JL, Rogers K. Review of a hospital experience of breast abscesses. Br J Surg 1987, **74:** 469–470.

83 Schwartz IS, Strauchen JA. Lymphocytic mastopathy. An autoimmune disease of the breast? Am J Clin Pathol 1990, **93:** 725–730.

84 Sebek B. Periareolar abscess associated with squamous metaplasia of lactiferous ducts (Zuska's disease). Lab Invest 1988, **58:** 83A.

85 Seidman JD, Schnaper LA, Phillips LE. Mastopathy in insulin-requiring diabetes mellitus. Hum Pathol 1994, **25:** 819–824.

86 Symmers W St C. Silicone mastitis in "topless" waitress and some other varieties of foreign-body mastitis. Br Med J 1968, **3:** 19–22.

87 Tomaszewski JE, Brooks JS, Hicks D, Livolsi VA. Diabetic mastopathy. A distinctive clinicopathologic entity. Hum Pathol 1992, **23:** 780–786.

88 Trueb RM, Scheidegger EP, Pericin M, Singh A, Hoffmann U, Sauva G, Burg G. Periarteritis nodosa presenting as a breast lesion: report of a case and review of the literature. Br J Dermatol 1999, **141:** 1117–1121.

89 Valdez R, Thorson J, Finn WG, Schnitzer B, Kleer CG. Lymphocytic mastitis and diabetic mastopathy: a molecular,

immunophenotypic, and clinicopathologic evaluation of 11 cases. Mod Pathol 2003, **16**: 223–228.

90 Vargas MP, Merino MJ. Infarcted myxoid fibroadenoma following fine-needle aspiration. Arch Pathol Lab Med 1996, **120**: 1069–1071.

91 Watt-Boolsen S, Rasmussen NR, Blichert-Toft M. Primary periareolar abscess in the nonlactating breast. Risk of recurrence. Am J Surg 1987, **153**: 571–573.

BENIGN PROLIFERATIVE BREAST DISEASE

Fibroadenoma

92 Arrigoni MG, Dockerty MB, Judd ES. The identification and treatment of mammary hamartoma. Surg Gynecol Obstet 1971, **133**: 577–582.

93 Azzopardi JG. Problems in breast pathology. In Bennington JL (consulting ed.): Major problems in pathology, vol. 11. Philadelphia, 1979, W.B. Saunders.

94 Berean K, Tron VA, Churg A, Clement PB. Mammary fibroadenoma with multinucleated stromal giant cells. Am J Surg Pathol 1986, **10**: 823–827.

95 Carney JA, Toorkey BC. Myxoid fibroadenoma and allied conditions (myxomatosis) of the breast. A heritable disorder with special associations including cardiac and cutaneous myxomas. Am J Surg Pathol 1991, **15**: 713–721.

96 Carstens PHB. Ultrastructure of human fibroadenoma. Arch Pathol 1974, **98**: 23–32.

97 Carter BA, Page DL, Schuyler P, Parl FF, Simpson JF, Jensen RA, Dupont WD. No elevation in long-term breast carcinoma risk for women with fibroadenomas that contain atypical hyperplasia. Cancer 2001, **92**: 30–36.

98 Dehner LP, Hill DA, Deschryver K. Pathology of the breast in children, adolescents, and young adults. Semin Diagn Pathol 1999, **16**: 235–247.

99 Dupont WD, Page DL, Parl FF, Vnencak-Jones CL, Plummer WD Jr, Rados MS, Schuyler PA. Long-term risk of breast cancer in women with fibroadenoma. N Engl J Med 1994, **331**: 10–15.

100 Eusebi V, Azzopardi JG. Lobular endocrine neoplasia in fibroadenoma of the breast. Histopathology 1980, **4**: 413–428.

101 Fechner RE. Fibroadenomas in patients receiving oral contraceptives. A clinical and pathologic study. Am J Clin Pathol 1970, **53**: 857–864.

102 Fekete P, Petrek J, Majmudar B, Someren A, Sandberg W. Fibroadenomas with stromal cellularity. A clinicopathologic study of 21 patients. Arch Pathol Lab Med 1987, **111**: 427–432.

103 Fletcher JA, Pinkus GS, Weidner N, Morton CC. Lineage-restricted clonality in biphasic solid tumors. Am J Pathol 1991, **138**: 1199–1207.

104 Goodman ZD, Taxy JB. Fibroadenomas of the breast with prominent smooth muscle. Am J Surg Pathol 1981, **5**: 99–101.

105 Kleer CG, Tseng MD, Gutsch DE, Rochford RA, Wu Z, Joynt LK, Helvie MA, Chang T, Van Golen KL, Merajver SD. Detection of Epstein-Barr virus in rapidly growing fibroadenomas of the breast in immunosuppressed hosts. Mod Pathol 2002, **15**: 759–764.

106 Kuijper A, Mommers EC, van der Wall E, van Diest PJ. Histopathology of fibroadenomas of the breast. Am J Clin Pathol 2001, **115**: 736–742.

107 Metcalf JS, Ellis B. Choristoma of the breast. Hum Pathol 1985, **16**: 739–740.

108 Mies C, Rosen PP. Juvenile fibroadenoma with atypical epithelial hyperplasia. Am J Surg Pathol 1987, **11**: 184–190.

109 Moore T, Lee AH. Expression of CD34 and bcl-2 in phyllodes tumors, fibroadenomas and spindle cell lesions of the breast. Histopathology 2001, **38**: 62–67.

110 Oberman HA, Nosanchuk HS, Finger JE. Periductal stromal tumors of breast with adipose metaplasia. Arch Surg 1969, **98**: 384–387.

111 O'Hara MF, Page DL. Adenomas of the breast and ectopic breast under lactational influences. Hum Pathol 1985, **16**: 707–712.

112 Petersson C, Pandis N, Rizou H, Mertens F, Dietrich CU, Adeyinka A, Idvall I, Bondeson L, Georgiou G, Ingvar C, Heim S, Mitelman F. Karyotypic abnormalities in fibroadenomas of the breast. Int J Cancer 1997, **70**: 282–286.

113 Petrik PK. Mammary hamartoma. Am J Surg Pathol 1987, **11**: 234–235.

114 Pike AM, Oberman HA. Juvenile (cellular) adenofibromas. A clinicopathologic study. Am J Surg Pathol 1985, **9**: 730–736.

115 Reddick RL, Shin TK, Sawhney D, Siegal GP. Stromal proliferations of the breast. An ultrastructural and immunohistochemical evaluation of cystosarcoma phylloides, juvenile fibroadenoma, and fibroadenoma. Hum Pathol 1987, **18**: 45–49.

116 Shimizu T, Ebihara Y, Serizawa H, Toyoda M, Hirota T. Histopathological study of stromal smooth muscle cells in fibroadenoma of the breast. Pathol Int 1996, **46**: 442–449.

117 Silverman JS, Tamsen A. Mammary fibroadenoma and some phylloides tumour stroma are composed of CD34+ fibroblasts and factor XIIIa+ dendrophages. Histopathology 1996, **29**: 411–419.

118 Umekita Y, Yoshida H. Immunohistochemical study of hormone receptor and hormone-regulated protein expression in phylloides tumour: comparison with fibroadenoma. Virchows Arch 1998, **433**: 311–314.

119 Yeh I-T, Francis DJ, Orenstein JM, Silverberg SG. Ultrastructure of cystosarcoma phylloides and fibroadenoma. A comparative study. Am J Clin Pathol 1985, **84**: 131–136.

Malignant transformation

120 Buzanowski-Konakry K, Harrison EG Jr, Payne WS. Lobular carcinoma arising in fibroadenoma of the breast. Cancer 1975, **35**: 450–456.

121 Curran RC, Dodge OG. Sarcoma of breast, with particular reference to its origin from fibroadenoma. J Clin Pathol 1962, **15**: 1–16.

122 Diaz NM, Palmer JO, McDivitt RW. Carcinoma arising within fibroadenomas of the breast. A clinicopathologic study of 105 patients. Am J Clin Pathol 1991, **95**: 614–622.

123 Fondo EY, Rosen PP, Fracchia AA, Urban JA. The problem of carcinoma developing in a fibroadenoma. Recent experience at Memorial Hospital. Cancer 1979, **43**: 563–567.

124 Goldman RC, Friedman NB. Carcinoma of the breast arising in fibroadenomas with emphasis on lobular carcinoma. A clinicopathologic study. Cancer 1969, **23**: 544–550.

125 McDivitt RW, Stewart FW, Farrow JH. Breast carcinoma arising in solitary fibroadenomas. Surg Gynecol Obstet 1967, **125**: 572–576.

126 Pick PW, Iossifides IA. Occurrence of breast carcinoma within a fibroadenoma. A review. Arch Pathol Lab Med 1984, **108**: 590–594.

Adenoma

127 Baddoura FK, Judd RL. Apocrine adenoma of the breast. Report of a case with investigation of lectin binding patterns in apocrine breast lesions. Mod Pathol 1990, **3**: 373–376.

128 Carney JA, Toorkey BC. Ductal adenoma of the breast with tubular features. A probable component of the complex of myxomas, spotty pigmentation, endocrine overactivity, and schwannomas. Am J Surg Pathol 1991, **15**: 722–731.

129 Hertel BF, Zaloudek C, Kempson RL. Breast adenomas. Cancer 1976, **37**: 2891–2905.

130 Le Gal Y. Adenomas of the breast. Relationship of adenofibromas to pregnancy and lactation. Am Surg 1961, **27**: 14–22.

131 Morris JA, Kelly JF. Multiple bilateral breast adenomata in identical adolescent Negro twins. Histopathology 1982, **6:** 539–547.

132 O'Hara MF, Page DL. Adenomas of the breast and ectopic breast under lactational influences. Hum Pathol 1985, **16:** 707–712.

Intraductal papilloma

133 Ali-Fehmi R, Carolin K, Wallis T, Visscher DW. Clinicopathologic analysis of breast lesions associated with multiple papillomas. Hum Pathol 2003, **34:** 234–239.

134 Azzopardi JG. Problems in breast pathology. In Bennington JL (consulting ed.): Major problems in pathology, vol. 11. Philadelphia, 1979, W.B. Saunders.

135 Azzopardi JG, Salm R. Ductal adenoma of the breast. A lesion which can mimic carcinoma. J Pathol 1984, **144:** 15–23.

136 Egan MJ, Newman J, Crocker J, Collard M. Immunohistochemical localization of S100 protein in benign and malignant conditions of the breast. Arch Pathol Lab Med 1987, **111:** 28–31.

137 Fenoglio C, Lattes R. Sclerosing papillary proliferations in the female breast. A benign lesion often mistaken for carcinoma. Cancer 1974, **33:** 691–700.

138 Jiao YF, Nakamura S, Oikawa T, Sugai T, Uesugi N. Sebaceous gland metaplasia in intraductal papilloma of the breast. Virchows Arch 2001, **438:** 505–508.

139 Kraus FT, Neubecker RD. The differential diagnosis of papillary tumors of the breast. Cancer 1962, **15:** 444–455.

140 Lammie GA, Millis RR. Ductal adenoma of the breast. A review of fifteen cases. Hum Pathol 1989, **20:** 903–908.

140a MacGrogan G, Tavassoli FA. Central atypical papillomas of the breast: a clinicopathological study of 199 cases. Virchows Arch 2003, **443:** 609–617.

141 Noguchi S, Motomura K, Inaji H, Imaoka S, Koyama H. Clonal analysis of solitary intraductal papilloma of the breast by means of polymerase chain reaction. Am J Pathol 1994, **144:** 1320–1325.

142 Page DL, Salhany KE, Jensen RA, Dupont WD. Subsequent breast carcinoma risk after biopsy with atypia in a breast papilloma. Cancer 1996, **78:** 258–266.

143 Papotti M, Eusebi V, Gugliotta P, Bussolati G. Immunohistochemical analysis of benign and malignant papillary lesions of the breast. Am J Surg Pathol 1983, **7:** 451–461.

144 Papotti M, Gugliotta P, Ghiringhello B, Bussolati G. Association of breast carcinoma and multiple intraductal papillomas. An histological and immunohistochemical investigation. Histopathology 1984, **8:** 963–975.

145 Raju U, Vertes D. Breast papillomas with atypical ductal hyperplasia: a clinicopathological study. Hum Pathol 1996, **27:** 1231–1238.

146 Raju UB, Lee MW, Zarbo RJ, Crissman JD. Papillary neoplasia of the breast. Immunohistochemically defined myoepithelial cells in the diagnosis of benign and malignant papillary breast neoplasms. Mod Pathol 1989, **2:** 569–576.

147 Rosen PP. Arthur Purdy Stout and papilloma of the breast. Comments on the occasion of his 100th birthday. Am J Surg Pathol 1986, **10**(Suppl 1). 100–107.

148 Sapino A, Botta G, Cassoni P, Papotti M, Bussolati G. Multiple papillomas of the breast: morphologic findings and clinical evolution. Anat Pathol 1996, **1:** 205–218.

Nipple adenoma

149 Bhagavan BS, Patchefsky A, Koss LG. Florid subareolar duct papillomatosis (nipple adenoma) and mammary carcinoma. Report of three cases. Hum Pathol 1973, **4:** 289–295.

150 Jones MW, Tavassoli FA. Coexistence of nipple duct adenoma and breast carcinoma. A clinicopathologic study of five cases and review of the literature. Mod Pathol 1995, **8:** 637–642.

151 Myers JL, Mazur MT, Urist MM, Peiper SC. Florid papillomatosis of the nipple. Immunohistochemical and flow cytometric analysis of two cases. Mod Pathol 1990, **3:** 288–293.

152 Perzin KH, Lattes R. Papillary adenoma of the nipple (florid papillomatosis, adenoma, adenomatosis). A clinicopathologic study. Cancer 1972, **29:** 996–1009.

153 Rosen PP, Caicco JA. Florid papillomatosis of the nipple. A study of 51 patients, including nine with mammary carcinoma. Am J Surg Pathol 1986, **10:** 87–101.

154 Taylor HB, Robertson AG. Adenomas of the nipple. Cancer 1966, **18:** 995–1002.

Adenosis
Blunt duct adenosis

155 Azzopardi JG. Problems in breast pathology. In Bennington JL (consulting ed.): Major problems in pathology, vol. 11. Philadelphia, 1979, W.B. Saunders.

156 Foote FW, Stewart FW. Comparative studies of cancerous vs. noncancerous breasts. Am Surg 1945, **121:** 6–79.

Sclerosing adenosis

157 Eusebi V, Azzopardi JG. Vascular infiltration in benign breast disease. J Pathol 1976, **118:** 9–16.

158 Eusebi V, Collina G, Bussolati G. Carcinoma in situ in sclerosing adenosis of the breast. An immunocytochemical study. Semin Diagn Pathol 1989, **6:** 146–152.

159 Fechner RE. Lobular carcinoma in situ in sclerosing adenosis. A potential source of confusion with invasive carcinoma. Am J Surg Pathol 1981, **5:** 233–239.

160 Jensen RA, Page DL, Dupont WD, Rogers LW. Invasive breast cancer risk in women with sclerosing adenosis. Cancer 1989, **64:** 1977–1983.

161 Oberman HA, Markey BA. Noninvasive carcinoma of the breast presenting in adenosis. Mod Pathol 1991, **4:** 31–35.

162 Taylor HB, Norris HJ. Epithelial invasion of nerves in benign diseases of the breast. Cancer 1967, **20:** 2245–2249.

Nodular adenosis

163 Nielsen BB. Adenosis tumour of the breast. A clinicopathological investigation of 27 cases. Histopathology 1987, **11:** 1259–1275.

Microglandular adenosis

163a Acs G, Simpson JF, Bleiweiss IJ, Hugh J, Reynolds C, Olson S, Page DL. Microglandular adenosis with transition into adenoid cystic carcinoma of the breast. Am J Surg Pathol 2003, **27:** 1052–1060.

164 Clement PB, Azzopardi JG. Microglandular adenosis of the breast. A lesion simulating tubular carcinoma. Histopathology 1983, **7:** 169–180.

165 Endoh Y, Tamura G, Katoh N, Motoyama T. Apocrine adenosis of the breast: clonal evidence of neoplasia. Histopathology 2001, **38:** 221–224.

166 Eusebi V, Casedei GP, Bussolati G, Azzopardi JG. Adenomyoepithelioma of the breast with a distinctive type of apocrine adenosis. Histopathology 1987, **11:** 305–315.

167 Eusebi V, Foschini MP, Betts CM, Gherardi G, Millis RR, Bussolati G, Azzopardi JG. Microglandular adenosis, apocrine adenosis, and tubular carcinoma of the breast. An immunohistochemical comparison. Am J Surg Pathol 1993, **17:** 99–109.

168 James B, Cranor M, Rosen PP. Carcinoma of the breast arising in microglandular adenosis. Am J Clin Pathol 1993, **100:** 507–513.

169 Kiaer H, Nielsen B, Paulsen S, Soresen IM, Dyreborg V, Blichert-Toft M. Adenomyoepithelial adenosis and low grade

malignant adenomyoepithelioma of the breast. Virchows Arch [A] 1984, **405:** 55–67.

170 Koenig C, Dadmanesh F, Bratthauer GL, Tavassoli FA. Carcinoma arising in microglandular adenosis: an immunohistochemical analysis of 20 intraepithelial and invasive neoplasms. Int J Surg Pathol 2000, **8:** 303–315.

171 Lee K, Chan JK, Gwi E. Tubular adenosis of the breast: a distinctive benign lesion mimicking invasive carcinoma. Am J Surg Pathol 1996, **20:** 46–54.

172 Millis RR, Eusebi V. Microglandular adenosis of the breast. Adv Anat Pathol 1995, **2:** 10–18.

173 Page DL, Simpson JF. What is apocrine adenosis, anyway? Histopathology 2001, **39:** 433–434.

174 Rosen PP. Microglandular adenosis. A benign lesion simulating invasive mammary carcinoma. Am J Surg Pathol 1983, **7:** 137–144.

175 Rosenblum MK, Purrazzella R, Rosen PP. Is microglandular adenosis a precancerous disease? A study of carcinoma arising therein. Am J Surg Pathol 1986, **10:** 237–245.

176 Seidman JD, Ashton M, Lefkowitz M. Atypical apocrine adenosis of the breast: a clinicopathologic study of 37 patients with 8.7 year follow-up. Cancer 1996, **77:** 2529–2537.

177 Simpson JF, Page DL, Dupont WD. Apocrine adenosis. A mimic of mammary carcinoma. Surg Pathol 1990, **3:** 289–299.

178 Tavassoli FA, Norris NJ. Microglandular adenosis of the breast. A clinicopathologic study of 11 cases with ultrastructural observations. Am J Surg Pathol 1983, **7:** 731–737.

179 Tsuda H, Mukai K, Fukutomi T, Hirohashi S. Malignant progression of adenomyoepithelial adenosis of the breast. Pathol Int 1994, **44:** 475–479.

Fibrocystic disease

180 Allen SS, Froberg DG. The effect of decreased caffeine consumption on benign proliferative breast disease. A randomized clinical trial. Surgery 1987, **101:** 720–730.

181 Angeli A, Bradlow HL, Dogliotti L (eds). Endocrinology of the breast. Basic and clinical aspects. Turin, Italy, September 19–22, 1984. Ann NY Acad Sci 1986, **464:** 1–640.

182 Azzopardi JG. Problems in breast pathology. In Bennington JL (consulting ed.): Major problems in pathology, vol. 11. Philadelphia, 1979, W.B. Saunders.

183 Bartow SA, Black WC, Waeckerlin RW, Mettler FA. Fibrocystic disease. A continuing enigma. Pathol Annu 1982, **17**(Pt 2): 93–111.

184 Carter DJ, Rosen PP. Atypical apocrine metaplasia in sclerosing lesions of the breast. A study of 51 patients. Mod Pathol 1991, **4:** 1–5.

185 Connolly JL, Schnitt SJ. Benign breast disease. Resolved and unresolved issues. Cancer 1993, **71:** 1187–1189.

186 Consensus Meeting, Oct 3 to 5, 1985, New York, Cancer Committee of the College of American Pathologists: Is 'fibrocystic disease' of the breast precancerous? Arch Pathol Lab Med 1986, **110:** 171–173.

187 Fechner RE. Fibrocystic disease in women receiving oral contraceptive hormones. Cancer 1970, **25:** 1332–1339.

188 Frantz VK, Pickren JW, Melcher GW, Auchincloss H Jr. Incidence of chronic cystic disease in so-called "normal breast." Cancer 1951, **4:** 762–783.

189 Golinger RC. Hormones and the pathophysiology of fibrocystic mastopathy. Surg Gynecol Obstet 1978, **146:** 273–285.

190 Hislop TG, Threlfall WJ. Oral contraceptives and benign breast disease. Am J Epidemiol 1984, **120:** 273–280.

191 LiVolsi VA, Stadel BV, Kelsey JL, Holford TR, White C. Fibrocystic breast disease in oral-contraceptive users. A histopathological evaluation of epithelial atypia. N Engl J Med 1978, **299:** 381–385.

192 Love SM, Gelman RS, Silen W. Fibrocystic "disease" of the breast. A nondisease? N Engl J Med 1982, **307:** 1010–1014.

193 Lubin F, Ron E, Wax Y, Black M, Funaro M, Shitrit A. A case-control study of caffeine and methylxanthines in benign breast disease. JAMA 1985, **253:** 2388–2392.

194 Mazoujian G, Pinkus GS, Davis S, Haagensen DE Jr. Immunohistochemistry of a gross cystic disease fluid protein (GCDFP-15) of the breast. A marker of apocrine epithelium and breast carcinomas with apocrine features. Am J Pathol 1983, **110:** 105–112.

195 Meyer JS, Connor RE. Cell proliferation in fibrocystic disease and post-menopausal breast ducts measured by thymidine labeling. Cancer 1982, **50:** 746–751.

196 Minkowitz S, Hedayati H, Hiller S, Gardner B. Fibrous mastopathy. A clinical histopathologic study. Cancer 1973, **32:** 913–916.

197 Ory H, Cole P, MacMahon B, Hoover R. Oral contraceptives and reduced risk of benign breast diseases. N Engl J Med 1976, **294:** 419–422.

198 Sandison AT. An autopsy study of the adult human breast. With special reference to proliferative epithelial changes of importance in the pathology of the breast. Natl Cancer Inst Monogr 1962, **8:** 1–145.

199 Schuerch C III, Rosen PP, Hirota T, Itabashi M, Yamamoto H, Kinne DW, Beattie EJ Jr. A pathologic study of benign breast disease in Tokyo and New York. Cancer 1982, **50:** 1899–1903.

200 Symonds DA. Use of the von Kossa stain in identifying occult calcifications in breast biopsies. Am J Clin Pathol 1990, **94:** 44–48.

201 Tornos C, Silva E, el-Naggar A, Pritzker KP. Calcium oxalate crystals in breast biopsies. The missing microcalcifications. Am J Surg Pathol 1990, **14:** 961–968.

202 Vorherr H. Fibrocystic breast disease. Pathophysiology, pathomorphology, clinical picture, and management. Am J Obstet Gynecol 1986, **154:** 161–179.

203 Winston JS, Yeh IT, Evers K, Friedman AK. Calcium oxalate is associated with benign breast tissue. Can we avoid biopsy? Am J Clin Pathol 1993, **100:** 488–492.

Ductal and lobular hyperplasia

204 Azzopardi JG. Problems in breast pathology. In Bennington JL (consulting ed.): Major problems in pathology, vol. 11. Philadelphia, 1979, W.B. Saunders.

205 Clement PB, Young RH, Azzopardi JG. Collagenous spherulosis of the breast. Am J Surg Pathol 1987, **11:** 411–417.

206 Damiani S, Cattani MG, Buonamici L, Eusebi V. Mammary foam cells. Characterization by immunohistochemistry and in situ hybridisation. Virchows Arch 1998, **432:** 433–440.

207 Eusebi V, Damiani S, Ellis IO, Azzopardi J, Rosai J. Breast tumor resembling the tall cell variant of papillary thyroid carcinoma: report of five cases. Am J Surg Pathol 2003; **27:** 1114–1118.

208 Grignon DJ, Ro JY, Mackay BN, Ordóñez NG, Ayala AG. Collagenous spherulosis of the breast. Immunohistochemical and ultrastructural studies. Am J Clin Pathol 1989, **91:** 386–392.

209 Guerry P, Erlandson RA, Rosen PP. Cystic hypersecretory hyperplasia and cystic hypersecretory duct carcinoma of the breast. Pathology, therapy, and follow-up of 39 patients. Cancer 1988, **61:** 1611–1620.

210 Maluf HM, Koerner FC, Dickersin GR. Collagenous spherulosis: and ultrastructural study. Ultrastruct Pathol 1998, **22:** 239–248.

211 Michal M, Skalova A. Collagenous spherulosis. A comment on its histogenesis. Pathol Res Pract 1990, **186:** 365–370.

212 Mooney EE, Kayani N, Tavassoli FA. Spherulosis of the breast. A spectrum of mucinous and collagenous lesions. Arch Pathol Lab Med 1999, **123:** 626–630.

213 Raju U, Crissman JD, Zarbo RJ, Gottlieb C. Epitheliosis of the breast. An immunohistochemical characterization and comparison to malignant intraductal proliferations of the breast. Am J Surg Pathol 1990, **14:** 939–947.

214 Sgroi D, Koerner FC. Involvement of collagenous spherulosis by lobular carcinoma in situ. Potential confusion with cribriform ductal carcinoma in situ. Am J Surg Pathol 1995, **19**: 1366–1370.

215 Tavassoli FA, Majeste RM, Snyder RC. Intranuclear helioid inclusions in mammary intraductal hyperplasias. Ultrastruct Pathol 1991, **15**: 267–279.

216 Tham K, Dupont WD, Page DL, Gray GF, Rogers LW. Micro-papillary hyperplasia with atypical features in female breasts, resembling gynecomastia. Prog Surg Pathol 1989, **10**: 101–110.

Sclerosing ductal lesions

217 Alvarado-Cabrero I, Tavassoli FA. Neoplastic and malignant lesions involving or arising in a radial scar: a clinicopathologic analysis of 17 cases. Breast J 2000, **6**: 96–102.

218 Andersen JA, Carter D, Linell F. A symposium on sclerosing duct lesions of the breast. Pathol Annu 1986, **21**(Pt 2): 144–179.

219 Andersen JA, Gram JB. Radial scar in the female breast. A long-term follow-up study of 32 cases. Cancer 1984, **53**: 2557–2560.

220 Consensus Meeting, Oct 3 to 5, 1985, New York, Cancer Committee of the College of American Pathologists: Is 'fibrocystic disease' of the breast precancerous? Arch Pathol Lab Med 1986, **110**: 171–173.

221 Davies JD. Hyperelastosis, obliteration and fibrous plaques in major ducts of the human breast. J Pathol 1973, **110**: 13–26.

222 Denley H, Pinder SE, Tan PH, Sim CS, Brown R, Barker T, Gearty J, Elston CW, Ellis IO. Metaplastic carcinoma of the breast arising within complex sclerosing lesion: a report of five cases. Histopathology 2000, **36**: 203–209.

223 Fenoglio C, Lattes R. Sclerosing papillary proliferations in the female breast. A benign lesion often mistaken for carcinoma. Cancer 1974, **33**: 691–700.

224 Fisher ER, Palekar AS, Kotwal N, Lipana N. A non-encapsulated sclerosing lesion of the breast. Am J Clin Pathol 1979, **71**: 240–246.

225 Gottlieb C, Raju U, Greenwald KA. Myoepithelial cells in the differential diagnosis of complex benign and malignant breast lesions. An immunohistochemical study. Mod Pathol 1990, **3**: 135–140.

226 Jacobs TW, Byrne C, Colditz G, Connolly JL, Schnitt SJ. Radial scars in benign breast-biopsy specimens and the risk of breast cancer. N Engl J Med 1999, **340**: 430–436.

227 Keen ME, Murad TM, Cohen MI, Matthies HJ. Benign breast lesions with malignant clinical and mammographic presentations. Hum Pathol 1985, **16**: 1147–1152.

228 Lele SM, Graves K, Galatica Z. Immunohistochemical detection of maspin is a useful adjunct in distinguishing radial sclerosing lesion from tubular carcinoma of the breast. Appl Immunohistochem Mol Morphol 2000, **8**: 32–36.

229 Linell F, Ljungberg O, Andersson I. Breast carcinoma. Aspects of early stages, progression and related problems. Acta Pathol Microbiol Scand [A] 1980, **272**(Suppl): 1–233.

229a Manfrin E, Reghellin D, Remo A, Canal F, Bonetti F. Radial scar and carcinoma of the breast (Abstract). Mod Pathol 2003, **16**: 40a.

230 Nielsen M, Christensen L, Andersen J. Radial scars in women with breast cancer. Cancer 1987, **59**: 1019–1025.

231 Nielsen M, Jensen J, Andersen JA. An autopsy study of radial scar in the female breast. Histopathology 1985, **9**: 287–295.

232 Rickert RR, Kalisher L, Hutter RVP. Indurative mastopathy. A benign sclerosing lesion of breast with elastosis which may simulate carcinoma. Cancer 1981, **47**: 561–571.

233 Sloane JP, Mayers MM. Carcinoma and atypical hyperplasia in radial scars and complex sclerosing lesions. Importance of lesion size and patient age. Histopathology 1993, **23**: 225–231.

234 Tremblay G, Buell RH, Seemayer TA. Elastosis in benign

235 sclerosing ductal proliferation of the female breast. Am J Surg Pathol 1977, **1**: 155–159.

235 Wellings SR, Alpers CE. Subgross pathologic features and incidence of radial scars in the breast. Hum Pathol 1984, **15**: 475–479.

Atypical ductal and lobular hyperplasia

236 Azzopardi JG. Problems in breast pathology. In Bennington JL (consulting ed.): Major problems in pathology, vol. 11. Philadelphia, 1979, W.B. Saunders.

237 Beck JS. Observer variability in reporting of breast lesions. J Clin Pathol 1985, **38**: 1358–1365.

238 Bodian CA, Perzin KH, Lattes R, Hoffmann P. Reproducibility and validity of pathologic classifications of benign breast disease and implications for clinical applications. Cancer 1993, **71**: 3908–3913.

239 Bratthauer GL, Tavassoli FA. Lobular intraepithelial neoplasia: previously unexplored aspects assessed in 775 cases and their clinical implications. Virchows Arch 2002, **440**: 134–138.

240 Brogi E, Oyama T, Koerner FC. Atypical cystic lobules in patients with lobular neoplasia. Int J Surg Pathol 2001, **9**: 201–206.

241 Consensus Meeting. Oct 3 to 5, 1985, New York, Cancer Committee of the College of American Pathologists: Is "fibrocystic disease" of the breast precancerous? Arch Pathol Lab Med 1986, **110**: 171–173.

242 Crissman JD, Visscher DW, Kubus J. Image cytophotometric DNA analysis of atypical hyperplasias and intraductal carcinomas of the breast. Arch Pathol Lab Med 1990, **114**: 1249–1253.

242a Dabbs DJ, Kessinger RL, McManus K, Johnson R. Biology of columnar cell lesions in core biopsies of breast (Abstract). Mod Pathol 2003, **16**: 26a.

243 Dupont WD, Page DL. Risk factors for breast cancer in women with proliferative breast disease. N Engl J Med 1985, **312**: 146–151.

244 Fitzgibbons PL, Henson DE, Hutter RV. Benign breast changes and the risk for subsequent breast cancer: an update of the 1985 consensus statement. Cancer Committee of the College of American Pathologists. Arch Pathol Lab Med 1998, **122**: 1053–1055.

244a Jhala D, Talley L, Chhieng D, Frost A. Presence of columnar alteration with prominent apical snouts and secretions and relation with biomarker expression in 200 breast cancer patients (Abstract). Mod Pathol 2003, **16**: 34a.

245 Fraser JL, Raza S, Chorny K, Connolly JL, Schnitt SJ. Columnar alteration with prominent apical snouts and secretions: a spectrum of changes frequently present in breast biopsies performed for microcalcifications. Am J Surg Pathol 1998, **22**: 1521–1527.

246 King EB, Chew KL, Hom JD, Duarte LA, Mayall B, Miller TR, Neuhaus JM, Wrensch MR, Petrakis NL. Characterization by image cytometry of duct epithelial proliferative disease of the breast. Mod Pathol 1991, **4**: 291–296.

247 Koerner FC, Oyama T, Maluf H. Morphological observations regarding the origins of atypical cystic lobules (low-grade clinging carcinoma of flat type). Virchows Arch 2001, **439**: 523–530.

248 Ohuchi N, Page DL, Merino MJ, Viglione MJ, Kufe DW, Schlom J. Expression of tumor-associated antigen (DF3) in atypical hyperplasias and in situ carcinomas of the human breast. JNCI 1987, **79**: 109–117.

249 Oyama T, Maluf H, Koerner F. Atypical cystic lobules: an early stage in the formation of low-grade ductal carcinoma in situ. Virchows Arch 1999, **435**: 413–421.

250 Page DL. Cancer risk assessment in benign breast biopsies. Hum Pathol 1986, **17**: 871–874.

251 Page DL, Dupont WD, Rogers LW, Rados MS. Atypical

hyperplastic lesions of the female breast. A long-term follow-up study. Cancer 1985, **55**: 2698–2708.

252 Page DL, Kidd TE, Dupont WD, Rogers LW. Lobular neoplasia of the breast (LN) has varying magnitudes of risk for subsequent invasive carcinoma (IBC) (abstract). Lab Invest 1988, **58**: 69A.

253 Page DL, Rogers LW. Combined histologic and cytologic criteria for the diagnosis of mammary atypical ductal hyperplasia. Hum Pathol 1992, **23**: 1095–1097.

254 Purcell CA, Norris HJ. Intraductal proliferations of the breast: a review of histologic criteria for atypical intraductal hyperplasia and ductal carcinoma in situ, including apocrine and papillary lesions. Ann Diagn Pathol 1998, **2**: 135–145.

255 Rosai J. Borderline epithelial lesions of the breast. Am J Surg Pathol 1991, **15**: 209–221.

256 Schnitt SJ, Connolly JL, Tavassoli FA, Fechner RE, Kempson RL, Gelman R, Page DL. Interobserver reproducibility in the diagnosis of ductal proliferative breast lesions using standardized criteria. Am J Surg Pathol 1992, **16**: 1133–1143.

257 Tavassoli FA. Ductal carcinoma in situ: introduction of the concept of ductal intraepithelial neoplasia. Mod Pathol 1998, **11**: 140–154.

258 Tavassoli FA, Hoefler H, Rosai J, Holland R, Ellis I, Schnitt S. Intraductal proliferative lesions. Pathology and genetics of tumours of the breast and female genital organs. Lyon IARC Press, 2003, pp. 14–20.

259 Tavassoli FA, Norris HJ. A comparison of the results of long-term follow-up for atypical intraductal hyperplasia and intraductal hyperplasia of the breast. Cancer 1990, **65**: 518–529.

260 Walker R. The pathology of "precancerous" breast disease. Pathol Annu 1995, **29**(Pt2): 75–97.

Relationship with carcinoma and treatment

261 Aubele MM, Cummings MC, Mattis AE, Zitzelsberger HF, Walch AK, Kremer M, Hofler H, Werner M. Accumulation of chromosomal imbalances from intraductal proliferative lesions to adjacent in situ and invasive ductal breast cancer. Diagn Mol Pathol 2000, **9**: 14–19.

262 Bianchi S, Palli D, Galli M, Zampi G. Benign breast disease and cancer risk. Crit Rev Oncol Hematol 1993, **15**: 221–242.

263 Bodian CA, Perzin KH, Lattes R, Hoffmann P, Abernathy TG. Prognostic significance of benign proliferative breast disease. Cancer 1993, **71**: 3896–3907.

264 Byrne C, Connolly JL, Colditz GA, Schnitt SJ. Biopsy confirmed benign breast disease, postmenopausal use of exogenous female hormones, and breast carcinoma risk. Cancer 2000, **89**: 2046–2052.

265 Connolly JL, Schnitt SJ. Benign breast disease. Resolved and unresolved issues. Cancer 1993, **71**: 1187–1189.

266 Dupont WD, Page DL. Relative risk of breast cancer varies with time since diagnosis of atypical hyperplasia. Hum Pathol 1989, **20**: 723–725.

267 Dupont WD, Page DL, Rogers LW, Parl FF. Influence of exogenous estrogens, proliferative breast disease, and other variables on breast cancer risk. Cancer 1989, **63**: 948–957.

268 Dupont WD, Parl FF, Hartmann WH, Brinton LA, Winfield AC, Worrell JA, Schuyler PA, Plummer WD. Breast cancer risk associated with proliferative breast disease and atypical hyperplasia. Cancer 1993, **71**: 1258–1265.

269 Frantz VK, Pickren JW, Melcher GW, Auchincloss H Jr. Incidence of chronic cystic disease in so-called "normal breast." Cancer 1951, **4**: 762–783.

270 Jacobs TW, Byrne C, Colditz G, Connolly JL, Schnitt SJ. Pathologic features of breast cancers in women with previous benign breast disease. Am J Clin Pathol 2001, **115**: 362–369.

271 Kern WH, Brooks RN. Atypical epithelial hyperplasia

associated with breast cancer and fibrocystic disease. Cancer 1969, **24**: 668–675.

272 McDivitt RW. Breast carcinoma. Hum Pathol 1978, **9**: 3–21.

273 Micale MA, Visscher DW, Gulino SE, Wolman SR. Chromosomal aneuploidy in proliferative breast disease. Hum Pathol 1994, **25**: 29–35.

274 Millikan R, Hulka B, Thor A, Zhang Y, Edgerton S, Zhang X, Pei H, He M, Wold L, Melton LJ, Ballard D, Conway K, Liu ET. p53 mutations in benign breast tissue. J Clin Oncol 1995, **13**: 2293–2300.

275 Page DL. Cancer risk assessment in benign breast biopsies. Hum Pathol 1986, **17**: 871–874.

276 Page DL, Dupont WD. Anatomic markers of human premalignancy and risk of breast cancer. Cancer 1990, **66**: 1326–1335.

277 Rosen PP. Proliferative breast "disease." An unresolved diagnostic dilemma. Cancer 1993, **71**: 3798–3807.

277a Schnitt SJ. Benign breast disease and breast cancer risk. Morphology and beyond. Am J Surg Pathol 2003, **27**: 836–841.

278 Schnitt SJ, Jimi A, Kojiro M. The increasing prevalence of benign proliferative breast lesions in Japanese women. Cancer 1993, **71**: 2528–2531.

279 Skolnick MH, Cannon-Albright LA, Goldgar DE, Ward JH, Marshall CJ. Schumann GB, Hogle H, McWhorter WP, Wright EC, Tran TD, et al. Inheritance of proliferative breast disease in breast cancer kindreds. Science 1990, **250**: 1715–1720.

280 Steinhoff NG, Black WC. Florid cystic disease preceding mammary cancer. Ann Surg 1970, **171**: 501–508.

281 Tavassoli FA, Norris HJ. A comparison of the results of long-term follow-up for atypical intraductal hyperplasia and intraductal hyperplasia of the breast. Cancer 1990, **65**: 518–529.

282 Washington C, Dalbegue F, Abreo F, Taubenberger JK, Lichy JH. Loss of heterozygosity in fibrocystic change of the breast: genetic relationship between proliferative lesions and associated carcinomas. Am J Pathol 2000, **157**: 323–329.

283 Younes M, Lebovitz RM, Bommer KE, Cagle PT, Morton D, Khan S, Laucirica R. p53 accumulation in benign breast biopsy specimens. Hum Pathol 1995, **26**: 155–158.

CARCINOMA
General features
Incidence

284 Garfinkel L, Boring CC, Heath CW Jr. Changing trends. An overview of breast cancer incidence and mortality. Cancer 1994, **74**: 222–227.

285 Jatoi I, Miller AB. Why is breast-cancer mortality declining? Lancet Oncol 2003, **4**: 251–254.

286 Parkin DM, Bray FI, Devesa SS. Cancer burden in the year 2000. The global picture. Eur J Cancer 2001, **37**: S4–66.

287 Parkin DM, Bray F, Ferlay J, Pisani P. Estimating the world cancer burden. Globocan 2000. Int J Cancer 2001, **94**: 153–156.

288 Peto R, Boreham J, Clarke M, Davies C, Beral V. UK and USA breast cancer deaths down 25% in year 2000 at ages 20–69 years. Lancet 2000, **355**: 1822.

289 Sondik EJ. Breast cancer trends. Incidence, mortality, and survival. Cancer 1994, **74**: 995–999.

Risk factors

290 Armstrong K, Eisen A, Weber B. Assessing the risk of breast cancer. N Engl J Med 2000, **342**: 564–571.

291 Berkel H, Birdsell DC, Jenkins H. Breast augmentation. A risk factor for breast cancer? N Engl J Med 1992, **326**: 1649–1653.

292 Bonito D, Giarelli L, Falconieri G, Bonifacio-Gori D, Tomasic G, Vielh P. Association of breast cancer and meningioma. Report of 12 new cases and review of the literature. Pathol Res Pract 1993, **189**: 399–404.

293 Bryant H, Brasher P. Breast implants and breast cancer. Reanalysis of a linkage study. N Engl J Med 1995, **332:** 1535–1539.

294 Chen CL, Weiss NS, Newcomb P, Barlow W, White E. Hormone replacement therapy in relation to breast cancer. JAMA 2002, **287:** 734–741.

295 Clark CP, Peters GN, O'Brien KM. Cancer in the augmented breast. Diagnosis and prognosis. Cancer 1993, **72:** 2170–2174.

296 Clemons M, Goss P. Estrogen and the risk of breast cancer. N Engl J Med 2001, **344:** 276–285.

297 Fechner RE. Breast cancer during oral contraceptive therapy. Cancer 1970, **26:** 1204–1211.

298 Fechner RE. The surgical pathology of the reproductive system and breast during oral contraceptive therapy. Pathol Annu 1971, **6:** 299–319.

299 Goss PE, Sierra S. Current perspectives on radiation-induced breast cancer. J Clin Oncol 1998, **16:** 338–347.

300 Hildreth NG, Shore RE, Hempelmann LH. Risk of breast cancer among women receiving radiation treatment in infancy for thymic enlargement. Lancet 1983, **2:** 273.

301 Hoover R, Gray LA Sr, Cole P, MacMahon B. Menopausal estrogens and breast cancer. N Engl J Med 1976, **295:** 401–405.

302 IARC. Hormonal contraception and post-menopausal hormonal therapy. IARC monographs on the evaluation of carcinogenic risks to humans, vol. 72. Lyon, 1998, IARC Press.

303 Kelsey JL, Gammon MD. The epidemiology of breast cancer. CA Cancer J Clin 1991, **41:** 146–165.

304 Kelsey JL, Gammon MD, John EM. Reproductive factors and breast cancer. Epidemiol Rev 1993, **15:** 36–47.

305 Moore DH, Moore DH II, Moore CT. Breast carcinoma etiological factors. Adv Cancer Res 1983, **40:** 189–253.

306 Newcomb PA, Storer BE, Longnecker MP, Mittendorf R, Greenberg ER, Clapp RW, Burke KP, Willett WC, MacMahon B. Lactation and a reduced risk of premenopausal breast cancer. N Engl J Med 1994, **330:** 81–87.

307 Pathak DR, Osuch JR, He J. Breast carcinoma etiology: current knowledge and new insight into the effects of reproductive and hormonal risk factors in black and white populations. Cancer 2000, **88:** 1230–1238.

308 Romieu I, Berlin JA, Colditz G. Oral contraceptives and breast cancer. Review and meta-analysis. Cancer 1990, **66:** 2253–2263.

309 Ross RK, Paganini-Hill A, Gerkins VR, Mack TM, Pfeffer R, Arthur M, Henderson BE. A case-control study of menopausal estrogen therapy and breast cancer. JAMA 1980, **243:** 1635–1639.

310 Ross RK, Paganini-Hill A, Wan PC, Pike MC. Effect of hormone replacement therapy on breast cancer risk estrogen versus estrogen plus progestin. J Natl Cancer Inst 2000, **92:** 328–332.

311 Schairer C, Lubin J, Troisi R, Sturgeon S, Brinton L, Hoover R. Menopausal estrogen and estrogen-progestin replacement therapy and breast cancer risk. JAMA 2000, **283:** 485–491.

312 Schrager CA, Schneider D, Gruener AC, Tsou HC, Peacocke M. Clinical and pathological features of breast disease in Cowden's syndrome: an underrecognized syndrome with an increased risk of breast cancer. Hum Pathol 1998, **29:** 47–53.

313 Shore RE, Hempelmann LH, Kowaluk E, Mansur PS, Pasternack BS, Albert RE, Haughie GE. Breast neoplasms in women treated with x-rays for acute postpartum mastitis. JNCI 1977, **59:** 813–822.

314 Simon N, Silverstone SM. Radiation as a cause of breast cancer. Bull NY Acad Sci 1976, **52:** 741–751.

315 Skolnick MH, Cannon-Albright LA. Genetic predisposition to breast cancer. Cancer 1992, **70:** 1747–1754.

316 Swift M, Morrell D, Massey RB, Chase CL. Incidence of cancer in 161 families affected by ataxia-telangiectasia. N Engl J Med 1991, **325:** 1831–1836.

317 Wang DY, Rubens RD, Allen DS, Millis RR, Bulbrook RD, Chaudary MA, Hayward JL. Influence of reproductive history of age at diagnosis of breast cancer and prognosis. Int J Cancer 1985, **36:** 427–432.

318 White E, Malone KE, Weiss NS, Daling JR. Breast cancer among young U.S. women in relation to oral contraceptive use. J Natl Cancer Inst 1994, **86:** 505–514.

Genetic predisposition

319 Adem C, Reynolds C, Soderberg CL, Slezak JM, McDonnel SK, Sebo TJ, Schaid DJ, Myers JL, Sellers TA, Hartmann LC, Jenkins RB. Pathologic characteristics of breast parenchyma in patients with hereditary breast carcinoma, including BRCA1 and BRCA2 mutations carriers. Cancer 2003, **97:** 1–11.

320 Armes JE, Egan AJ, Southey MC, Dite GS, McCredie MR, Giles GG, Hopper JL, Venter DJ. The histologic phenotypes of breast carcinoma occurring before age 40 years in women with and without BRCA1 or BRCA2 germline mutations: a population-based study. Cancer 1998, **83:** 2335–2345.

321 Blackwood MA, Weber BL. BRCA1 and BRCA2: from molecular genetics to clinical medicine. J Clin Oncol 1998, **16:** 1969–1977.

322 Futreal PA, Liu Q, Shattuck-Eidens D, Cochran C, Harshman K, Tavtigian S, Bennett LM, Haugen-Strano A, Swensen J, Miki Y, Eddington K, McClure M, Frye C, Weaver-Feldhaus J, Ding W, Gholami Z, Söderkvist P, Terry L, Jhanwar S, Berchuck A, Iglehart JD, Marks J, Ballinger DG, Barrett JC, Skolnick MH, Kamb A, Wiseman R. BRCA 1 mutations in primary breast and ovarian carcinomas. Science 1994, **266:** 120–122.

323 Hartmann LC, Schaid DJ, Woods JE, Crotty TP, Myers JL, Arnold PG, Petty PM, Sellers TA, Johnson JL, McDonnell SK, Frost MH, Jenkins RB. Efficacy of bilateral prophylactic mastectomy in women with a family history of breast cancer. N Engl J Med 1999, **340:** 77–84.

324 Lakhani Sr, Jacquemier J, Sloane JP, Gusterson BA, Anderson TJ, van de Vijver MJ, Farid LM, Venter D, Antoniou A, Storfer-Isser A, Smyth E, Steel CM, Haites N, Scott RJ, Goldgar D, Neuhausen S, Daly PA, Ormiston W, McManus R, Scherneck S, Ponder BA, Ford D, Peto J, Stoppa-Lyonet D, Easton DF, et al. Multifactorial analysis of differences between sporadic breast cancers and cancers involving BRCA1 and BRCA2 mutations. J Natl Cancer Inst 1998, **90:** 1138–1145.

325 Lee WY, Jin YT, Chang TW, Lin PW, Su IJ. Immunolocalization of BRCA1 protein in normal breast tissue and sporadic invasive ductal carcinomas: a correlation with other biological parameters. Histopathology 1999, **34:** 106–112.

326 Meijers-Heijboer H, van Geel B, van Putten WL, Henzen-Logmans SC, Seynaeve C, Menke-Pluymers MB, Bartels CC, Verhoog LC, van der Ouweland AM, Niermeijer MF, Brekelmans CT, Klijn JM. Breast cancer after prophylactic bilateral mastectomy in women with a BRCA1 or BRCA2 mutations. N Engl J Med 2001, **345:** 159–164.

327 Ponder B. Breast cancer genes. Searches begin and end (editorial). Nature 1994, **371:** 279.

328 Ruffner H, Verma IM. BRCA1 is a cell cycle-regulated nuclear phosphoprotein. Proc Natl Acad Sci U S A 1997, **94:** 7138–7143.

329 Struewing JP, Hartge P, Wacholder S, Baker SM, Berlin M, McAdams M, Timmerman MM, Brody LC, Tucker MA. The risk of cancer associated with specific mutations of BRCA1 and BRCA2 among Ashkenazi Jews. N Engl J Med 1997, **336:** 1401–1408.

330 Wooster R, Neuhausen Susan L, Mangion J, Quirk Y, Ford D, Collins N, Nguyen K, Seal S, Tran T, Averill D, Fields P, Marshall G, Narod S, Lenoir GM, Lynch H, Feunteun J, Devilee P, Cornelisse CJ, Menko FH, Daly PA, Ormiston W, McManus R, Pye C, Lewis CM, Cannon-Albright LA, Peto J, Ponder BAJ, Skolnick MH, Easton DF, Goldgar DE, Stratton MR. Localization of a breast cancer susceptibility gene, BRCA2, to chromosome 13q12–13. Science 1994, **265:** 2088–2090.

330a Guttmachet AE, Collins FS. Breast and ovarian cancer. N Engl J Med 2003, **348:** 2339–2347.

Location

331 Tulinius H, Sigvaldason H, Olafsdottir G. Left and right sided breast cancer. Pathol Res Pract 1990, **186:** 92–94.

Multicentricity

331a Andea AA, Bouwman D, Wallis T, Visscher DW. Correlation of tumor size with survival in multifocal breast carcinoma (Abstract). Mod Pathol 2003, **16:** 21a.

332 Andea AA, Wallis T, Newman LA, Bouwman D, Dey J, Visscher DW. Pathologic analysis of tumor size and lymph node status in multifocal/multicentric breast carcinoma. Cancer 2002, **94:** 1383–1390.

333 Dawson PJ. What is new in our understanding of multifocal breast cancer. Pathol Res Pract 1993, **189:** 111–116.

334 Dawson PJ, Baekey PA, Clark RA. Mechanisms of multifocal breast cancer. An immunocytochemical study. Hum Pathol 1995, **26:** 965–969.

335 Fisher ER, Gregorio R, Redmond C, Vellios F, Sommers SC, Fisher B. Pathologic findings from the National Surgical Adjuvant Breast Project (Protocol no. 4). I. Observations concerning the multicentricity of mammary cancer. Cancer 1975, **35:** 247–254.

336 Hutter RVP, Kim DU. The problem of multiple lesions of the breast. Cancer 1971, **28:** 1591–1607.

337 Middleton LP, Vlastos G, Mirza NQ, Eva S, Sahin AA. Multicentric mammary carcinoma: evidence of monoclonal proliferation. Cancer 2002, **94:** 1910–1916.

338 Noguchi S, Aihara T, Koyama H, Motomura K, Inaji H, Imaoka S. Discrimination between multicentric and multifocal carcinomas of the breast through clonal analysis. Cancer 1994, **74:** 872–877.

338a Volante M, Sapino A, Croce S, Bussolati G. Heterogeneous versus homogeneous genetic nature of multiple foci of in situ carcinoma of the breast. Hum Pathol 2003, **34:** 1163–1169.

Bilaterality

339 Anastassiades O, Iakovou E, Stavridou N, Gogas J, Karameris A. Multicentricity in breast cancer. A study of 366 cases. Am J Clin Pathol 1993, **99:** 238–243.

340 Broët P, de la Rochefordière A, Scholl SM, Fourquet A, Massen V, Durand J-C, Pouillart P, Asselain B. Contralateral breast cancer. Annual incidence and risk parameters. J Clin Oncol 1995, **13:** 1578–1583.

341 Dawson PJ. What is new in our understanding of multifocal breast cancer. Pathol Res Pract 1993, **189:** 111–116.

342 Heron DE, Komarnicky LT, Hyslop T, Schwartz GF, Mansfield CM. Bilateral breast carcinoma: risk factors and outcomes for patients with synchronous and metachronous disease. Cancer 2000, **88:** 2739–2750.

343 King RE, Terz JJ, Lawrence W Jr. Experience with opposite breast biopsy in patients with operable breast cancer. Cancer 1976, **37:** 43–45.

Diagnosis
Mammography

344 American College of Radiology. Breast imaging reporting and data system (BI-RADS), ed. 3. Reston, VA, 1998, American College of Radiology.

345 Bassett LW, Gambhir S. Breast imaging for the 1990s. Semin Oncol 1991, **18:** 80–86.

346 Charpin C, Bonnier P, Khouzami A, Andrac L, Habib M, Vacheret H, Lavaut MN, Piana L. Non palpable breast carcinomas. Histological and immunohistochemical studies of 160 cases. Pathol Res Pract 1993, **189:** 267–274.

347 Fisher ER, Palekar A, Kim WS, Redmond C. The histopathology of mammographic patterns. Am J Clin Pathol 1978, **69:** 421–426.

347a Fletcher SW, Elmore JG. Mammographic screening for breast cancer. N Engl J Med 2003, **348:** 1672–1680.

348 Gallager HS. Breast specimen radiography. Obligatory, adjuvant and investigative. Am J Clin Pathol 1975, **64:** 749–766.

349 Gisvold JJ. Imaging of the breast. Techniques and results. Mayo Clin Proc 1990, **65:** 56–66.

350 Gonzalez JE, Caldwell RG, Valaitis J. Calcium oxalate crystals in the breast. Pathology and significance. Am J Surg Pathol 1991, **15:** 586–591.

351 Kneeshaw PJ, Turnbull LW, Drew PJ. Current applications and future direction of MR mammography. Br J Cancer 2003, **88:** 4–10.

352 Koehl RH, Snyder RE, Hutter RVP, Foote FW Jr. The incidence and significance of calcifications within operative breast specimens. Am J Clin Pathol 1970, **53:** 3–14.

353 McDivitt RW. Breast carcinoma. Hum Pathol 1978, **9:** 3–21.

354 McLelland R. Screening mammography. Cancer 1991, **67:** 1129–1131.

355 Millis RR, Davis R, Stacey AJ. The detection and significance of calcification in the breasts. A radiological and pathological study. Br J Radiol 1976, **49:** 12–26.

356 Owings DV, Hann L, Schnitt SJ. How thoroughly should needle localization breast biopsies be sampled for microscopic examination? A prospective mammographic/pathologic correlative study. Am J Surg Pathol 1990, **14:** 578–583.

357 Rosen PP, Synder RE, Robbins G. Specimen radiography for nonpalpable breast lesions found by mammography. Procedures and results. Cancer 1974, **34:** 2028–2033.

358 Schnall MD. Breast MR imaging. Radiol Clin North Am 2003, **41:** 43–50.

359 Schwartz GF, Carter DL, Conant EF, Gannon FH, Finkel GC, Feig SA. Mammographically detected breast cancer. Nonpalpable is not a synonym for inconsequential. Cancer 1994, **73:** 1660–1665.

360 Stevens GM, Jamplis RW. Mammographically directed biopsy of nonpalpable breast lesions. Arch Surg 1971, **102:** 292–295.

361 Wolfe JN. Breast patterns as an index of risk for developing breast cancer. Am J Roentgenol 1976, **126:** 1130–1139.

Cytology

362 Abendroth CS, Wang HH, Ducatman BS. Comparative features of carcinoma in situ and atypical ductal hyperplasia of the breast on fine-needle aspiration biopsy specimens. Am J Clin Pathol 1991, **96:** 654–659.

363 Arisio R, Cuccorese C, Accinelli G, Mano MP, Bordon R, Fessia L. Role of fine-needle aspiration biopsy in breast lesions: analysis of a series of 4,110 cases. Diagn Cytopathol 1998, **18:** 462–467.

364 Barrows GH, Anderson TJ, Lamb JL, Dixon JM. Fine-needle aspiration of breast cancer. Relationship of clinical factors to cytology results in 689 primary malignancies. Cancer 1986, **58:** 1493–1498.

365 Dawson AE, Mulford DK, Sheils LA. The cytopathology of proliferative breast disease. Am J Clin Pathol 1995, **103:** 438–442.

366 Eisenberg AJ, Hajdu SI, Wilhelmus J, Melamed MR, Kinne D. Preoperative aspiration cytology of breast tumors. Acta Cytol (Baltimore) 1986, **30:** 135–146.

367 Frable WJ. Needle aspiration of the breast. Cancer 1984, **53:** 671–676.

368 Jeffrey PB, Ljung BM. Benign and malignant papillary lesions of the breast. A cytomorphologic study. Am J Clin Pathol 1994, **101:** 500–507.

369 Kline TS. Masquerades of malignancy. A review of 4,241 aspirates from the breast. Acta Cytol (Baltimore) 1981, **25:** 263–266.

370 Kline TS, Joshi LP, Neal HS. Fine-needle aspiration of the breast. Diagnoses and pitfalls. A review of 3545 cases. Cancer 1979, **44**: 1458–1464.

371 Lee KC, Chan JK, Ho LC. Histologic changes in the breast after fine-needle aspiration. Am J Surg Pathol 1994, **18**: 1039–1047.

372 Ljung BM, Chew K, Deng G, Matsumura K, Waldman F, Smith H. Fine needle aspiration techniques for the characterization of breast cancers. Cancer 1994, **74**: 1000–1005.

373 Marshall CJ, Schumann GB, Ward JH, Riding JM, Cannon-Albright L, Skolnick M. Cytologic identification of clinically occult proliferative breast disease in women with a family history of breast cancer. Am J Clin Pathol 1991, **95**: 157–165.

374 Norton LW, Davis JR, Wiens JL, Trego DC, Dunnington GL. Accuracy of aspiration cytology in detecting breast cancer. Surgery 1984, **96**: 806–811.

375 Oertel YC. Fine needle aspiration of the breast. Stoneham, MA, 1987, Butterworths.

376 Reiner A, Spona J, Reiner G, Schemper M, Kolb R, Kwasny W, Függer R, Jakesz R, Holzner JH. Estrogen receptor analysis on biopsies and fine-needle aspirates from human breast carcinoma. Correlation of biochemical and immunohistochemical methods using monoclonal antireceptor antibodies. Am J Pathol 1986, **125**: 443–449.

377 Remvikos Y, Magdelenat H, Zajdela A. DNA flow cytometry applied to fine needle sampling of human breast cancer. Cancer 1988, **61**: 1629–1634.

378 Rosenthal DL. Breast lesions diagnosed by fine needle aspiration. Pathol Res Pract 1986, **181**: 645–656.

379 Silfversward C, Gustafsson J-A, Gustafsson SA, Nordenskjold B, Wallgren A, Wrange O. Estrogen receptor analysis on fine needle aspirates and on histologic biopsies from human breast cancer. Eur J Cancer 1980, **16**: 1351–1357.

380 Sneige N, Singletary SE. Fine-needle aspiration of the breast. Diagnostic problems and approaches to surgical management. Pathol Annu 1994, **29**(Pt 1): 281–301.

381 Sneige N, Staerkel GA. Fine-needle aspiration cytology of ductal hyperplasia with and without atypia and ductal carcinoma in situ. Hum Pathol 1994, **25**: 485–492.

382 Tavassoli FA, Pestaner JP. Pseudoinvasion in intraductal carcinoma. Mod Pathol 1995, **8**: 380–383.

383 Thomas PA, Cangiarella J, Raab SS, Waisman J. Fine needle aspiration biopsy of proliferative breast disease. Mod Pathol 1995, **8**: 130–136.

384 Thomas PA, Vazquez MF, Waisman J. Comparison of fine needle aspiration and frozen section of palpable mammary lesions. Mod Pathol 1990, **3**: 570–574.

385 Youngson BJ, Cranor M, Rosen PP. Epithelial displacement in surgical breast specimens following needling procedures. Am J Surg Pathol 1994, **18**: 896–903.

386 Youngson BJ, Liberman L, Rosen PP. Displacement of carcinomatous epithelium in surgical breast specimens following stereotaxic core biopsy. Am J Clin Pathol **103**: 598–602.

387 Wanebo HJ, Feldman PS, Wilhelm MC, Covell JL, Binns RL. Fine needle aspiration cytology in lieu of open biopsy in management of primary breast cancer. Ann Surg 1984, **199**: 569–578.

Needle core biopsy

388 Ballo MS, Sneige N. Can core needle biopsy replace fine-needle aspiration cytology in the diagnosis of palpable breast carcinoma. A comparative study of 124 women. Cancer 1996, **78**: 773–777.

389 Chandrasoma PT. Microcalcification in the breast and the pathologist. Am J Surg Pathol 2002, **26**: 135–136.

390 Davies JD, Nonni A, D'Costa HF. Mammary epidermoid inclusion cysts after wide-core needle biopsies. Histopathology 1997, **31**: 549–551.

391 Gobbi H, Tse G, Page DL, Olson SJ, Jensen RA, Simpson JF. Reactive spindle cell nodules of the breast after core biopsy or fine needle aspiration. Am J Clin Pathol 2000, **113**: 288–294.

391a Hoda SA, Harigopal M, Harris GC, Pinder SE, Lee AHS, Ellis IO. Reporting needle core biopsies of breast carcinomas. Histopathology 2003, **43**: 84–90.

392 Hoda SA, Rosen PP. Practical considerations in the pathologic diagnosis of needle core biopsies of breast. Am J Clin Pathol 2002, **118**: 101–108.

393 Jacobs TW, Connolly JL, Schnitt SJ. Nonmalignant lesions in breast core needle biopsy: to excise or not to excise? Am J Surg Pathol 2002, **26**: 1095–1110.

394 Lee AH, Denley HE, Pinder SE, Ellis IO, Elston CW, Vujovic P, Macmillan RD, Evans AJ: for the Nottingham Breast Team. Excision biopsy findings of patients with breast needle core biopsies reported as suspicious of malignancy (B4) or lesion of uncertain malignant potential (B3). Histopathology 2003, **42**: 331–336.

395 Litherland JC. Should fine needle aspiration cytology in breast assessment be abandoned? Clin Radiol 2002, **57**: 81–84.

396 Middleton LP, Grant S, Stephens T, Stelling CB, Sniege N, Sahin AA. Lobular carcinoma in situ diagnosed by core needle biopsy: when should it be excised? Mod Pathol 2003, **16**: 120–129.

397 Renshaw AA. Adequate histologic sampling of breast core needle biopsies. Arch Pathol Lab Med 2001, **125**: 1055–1057.

398 Renshaw AA. Predicting invasion in the excision specimen from breast core needle biopsy specimens with only ductal carcinoma in situ. Arch Pathol Lab Med 2002, **126**: 39–41.

399 Renshaw AA, Cartagena N, Schenkman RH, Derhagopian RP, Gould EW. Atypical ductal hyperplasia in breast core needle biopsies. Correlation of size of the lesion, complete removal of the lesion, and the incidence of carcinoma in follow-up biopsies. Am J Clin Pathol 2001, **116**: 92–96.

400 Shah VI, Raju U, Chitale D, Deshpande V, Gregory N, Strand V. False-negative core needle biopsies of the breast: An analysis of clinical, radiologic, and pathologic findings in 27 consecutive cases of missed breast cancer. Cancer 2003, **97**: 1824–1831.

401 Shin SJ, Rosen PP. Excisional biopsy should be performed if lobular carcinoma in situ is seen on needle core biopsy. Arch Pathol Lab Med 2002, **126**: 697–701.

401a Shousha S. Issues in the intrepretation of breast core biopsies. Int J Surg Pathol 2003, **11**: 167–176.

402 Youngson BJ, Cranor M, Rosen PP. Epithelial displacement in surgical breast specimens following needling procedures. Am J Surg Pathol 1994, **18**: 896–903.

403 Youngson BJ, Liberman L, Rosen PP. Displacement of carcinomatous epithelium in surgical breast specimens following stereotaxic core biopsy. Am J Clin Pathol **103**: 598–602.

Open biopsy and frozen section

404 Bianchi S, Palli D, Ciatto S, Galli M, Giorgi D, Vezzosi V, Rosselli del Turco M, Cataliotti L, Cardona G, Zampi G. Accuracy and reliability of frozen section diagnosis in a series of 672 nonpalpable breast lesions. Am J Clin Pathol 1993, **103**: 199–205.

405 Esteban JM, Zaloudek C, Silverberg SG. Intraoperative diagnosis of breast lesions. Comparison of cytologic with frozen section technics. Am J Clin Pathol 1987, **88**: 681–688.

406 Fechner RE. Frozen section examination of breast biopsies. Practice parameter. Am J Clin Pathol 1995, **103**: 6–7.

407 Ferreiro JA, Gisvold JJ, Bostwick DG. Accuracy of frozen-section diagnosis of mammographically directed breast biopsies. Results of 1,490 consecutive cases. Am J Surg Pathol 1995, **19**: 1267–1271.

408 Niemann TH, Lucas JG, Marsh WL Jr. To freeze or not to freeze.

A comparison of methods for the handling of breast biopsies with no palpable abnormality. Am J Clin Pathol 1996, **106:** 225–228.

409 Oberman HA. A modest proposal (editorial). Am J Surg Pathol 1992, **16:** 69–70.

410 Recommendations of the Association of Directors of Anatomic and Surgical Pathology. Part I. Immediate management of mammographically detected breast lesions. Hum Pathol 1993, **24:** 689–690.

411 Sauter ER, Hoffman JP, Ottery FD, Kowalyshyn MJ, Litwin S, Eisenberg BL. Is frozen section analysis of reexcision lumpectomy margins worthwhile? Margin analysis in breast reexcisions. Cancer 1994, **73:** 2607–2612.

412 Speights VO Jr. Evaluation of frozen sections in grossly benign breast biopsies. Mod Pathol 1994, **7:** 762–765.

Microscopic types

413 Andersen JA. Invasive breast carcinoma with lobular involvement. Frequency and location of lobular carcinoma in situ. Acta Pathol Microbiol Scand (A) 1974, **82:** 719–729.

414 Ishige H, Komatsu T, Kondo Y, Sugano I, Horinaka E, Okui K. Lobular involvement in human breast carcinoma. Acta Pathol Jpn 1991, **41:** 227–232.

415 Kerner H, Lichtig C. Lobular cancerization: incidence and differential diagnosis with lobular carcinoma in situ of breast. Histopathology 1986, **10:** 621–629.

416 Wellings SR, Jensen HM, Marcum RG. An atlas of subgross pathology of the human breast with special reference to possible precancerous lesions. JNCI 1975, **55:** 231–273.

In situ carcinoma
Ductal carcinoma in situ (DCIS)

417 Badve S, A'Hern RP, Ward AM, Millis RR, Pinder SE, Ellis IO, Gusterson BA, Sloane P. Prediction of local recurrence of ductal carcinoma in situ of the breast using five histological classifications: a comparative study with long follow-up. Hum Pathol 1998, **29:** 915–923.

418 Bellamy CD, McDonald C, Salter DM, Chetty U, Anderson TJ. Noninvasive ductal carcinoma of the breast. The relevance of histologic categorization. Hum Pathol 1993, **24:** 16–23.

419 Douglas-Jones AG, Gupta SK, Attanoos RL, Morgan JM, Mansel RE. A critical appraisal of six modern classifications of ductal carcinoma in situ of the breast (DCIS): correlation with grade of associated invasive carcinoma. Histopathology 1996, **29:** 397–409.

420 Ellis IO, Pinder SE, Lee AH, Elston CW. A critical appraisal of existing classification systems of epithelial hyperplasia and in situ neoplasia of the breast with proposals for future methods of categorization: where are we going? Semin Diagn Pathol 1999, **16:** 202–208.

421 Holland R, Hendriks JH. Microcalcifications associated with ductal carcinoma in situ. Mammographic-pathologic correlation. Semin Diagn Pathol 1994, **11:** 181–192.

422 Holland R, Peterse JL, Millis RR, Eusebi V, Faverly D, van de Vijver MJ, Zafrani B. Ductal carcinoma in situ. A proposal for a new classification. Semin Diagn Pathol 1994, **11:** 167–180.

423 Lennington WJ, Jensen RA, Dalton LW, Page DL. Ductal carcinoma in situ of the breast. Heterogeneity of individual lesions. Cancer 1994, **73:** 118–124.

424 Shoker BS, Sloane JP. DCIS grading schemes and clinical implications. Histopathology 1999, **35:** 393–400.

425 Sloane JP, Amendoeira I, Apostolikas N, Bellocq JP, Bianchi S, Boecher W, Bussolati G, Coleman D, Connolly CE, Dervan P, Eusebi V, De Miguel C, Drijkoningen M, Elston CW, Faverley D, Gad A, Jacquemier J, Lacerda M, Martinez-Penuela J, Munt C, Peterse JL, Rank F, Sylvan M, Tsakraklides V, Zafrani B.

Consistency achieved by 23 European Pathologists in categorizing ductal carcinoma in situ of the breast using five classifications. European Commission Working Group on Breast Screening Pathology. Hum Pathol 1998, **29:** 1056–1062.

426 Wells WA, Carney PA, Eliassen MS, Grove MR, Tosteson AN. Pathologists' agreement with experts and reproducibility of breast ductal carcinoma-in-situ classification schemes. Am J Surg Pathol 2000, **24:** 651–659.

Comedocarcinoma

427 Bacus SS, Ruby SG, Weinberg DS, Chin D, Ortiz R, Bacus JW. HER-2/neu oncogene expression and proliferation in breast cancers. Am J Pathol 1990, **137:** 103–111.

428 Bhoola S, DeRose PB, Cohen C. Ductal carcinoma in situ of the breast: frequency of biomarkers according to histologic subtype. Appl Immunohistochem 1999, **7:** 108–115.

429 Bobrow LG, Happerfield LC, Gregory WM, Springall RD, Millis RR. The classification of ductal carcinoma in situ and its association with biological markers. Semin Diagn Pathol 1994, **11:** 199–207.

430 Bose S, Lesser ML, Norton L, Rosen PP. Immunophenotype of intraductal carcinoma. Arch Pathol Lab Med 1996, **120:** 81–85.

431 Brown PW, Silverman J, Owens E, Tabor DC, Terz JJ, Lawrence W Jr. Intraductal "noninfiltrating" carcinoma of the breast. Arch Surg 1976, **111:** 1063–1067.

432 Carter D, Smith RRL. Carcinoma in situ of the breast. Cancer 1977, **40:** 1189–1193.

433 Coyne J, Haboubi NY. Micro-invasive breast carcinoma with granulomatous stromal response. Histopathology 1992, **20:** 184–185.

434 Damiani S, Ludvikova M, Tomasic G, Bianchi S, Gown AM, Eusebi V. Myoepithelial cells and basal lamina in poorly differentiated in situ duct carcinoma of the breast. An immunocytochemical study. Virchows Arch 1999, **434:** 227–234.

435 Douglas-Jones AG, Schmid KW, Bier B, Horgan K, Lyons K, Dallimore ND, Moneypenny IJ, Jasani B. Metallothionein expression in duct carcinoma in situ of the breast. Hum Pathol 1995, **26:** 217–222.

436 Gobbi H, Jensen RA, Simpson JF, Olson SJ, Page DL. Atypical hyperplasia and ductal carcinoma in situ of the breast associated with perineural invasion. Hum Pathol 2001, **32:** 785–790.

437 Killeen JL, Namiki H. DNA analysis of ductal carcinoma in situ of the breast. A comparison with histologic features. Cancer 1991, **68:** 2602–2607.

438 Lagios MD, Westdahl PR, Margolin FR, Rose MR. Duct carcinoma in situ. Relationship of extent of noninvasive disease to the frequency of occult invasion, multicentricity, lymph node metastases, and short-term treatment failures. Cancer 1982, **50:** 1309–1314.

438a Lara JF, Young SM, Velilla RE, Santoro EJ, Templeton SF. The relevance of occult axillary micrometastasis in ductal carcinoma in situ. A clinicopathologic study with long-term follow-up. Cancer 2003, **98:** 2105–2113.

439 Leal CB, Schmitt FC, Bento MJ, Maia NC, Lopes CS. Ductal carcinoma in situ of the breast. Histologic categorization and its relationship to ploidy and immunohistochemical expression of hormone receptors, p53, and c-erbB-2 protein. Cancer 1995, **75:** 2123–2131.

440 Lodato RF, Maguire HC Jr, Greene MI, Weiner DB, Li Volsi VA. Immunohistochemical evaluation of c-erbB-2 oncogene expression in ductal carcinoma in situ and atypical ductal hyperplasia of the breast. Mod Pathol 1990, **3:** 449–454.

441 Mai KT, Yazdi HM, Burns BF, Perkins DG. Pattern of distribution of intraductal and infiltrating ductal carcinoma: a three-dimensional study using serial coronal giant sections of the breast. Hum Pathol 2000, **31:** 464–474.

442 Mayr NA, Staples JJ, Robinson RA, Vanmetre JE, Hussey DH. Morphometric studies in intraductal breast carcinoma using computerized image analysis. Cancer 1991, **67**: 2805–2812.

443 Millis RR, Thynne GSJ. In situ intraduct carcinoma of the breast. A long-term follow-up study. Br J Surg 1975, **62**: 957–962.

444 Moriya T, Silverberg SG. Intraductal carcinoma (ductal carcinoma in situ) of the breast. A comparison of pure noninvasive tumors with those including different proportions of infiltrating carcinoma. Cancer 1994, **74**: 2972–2978.

445 Ohuchi N, Furuta A, Mori S. Management of ductal carcinoma in situ with nipple discharge. Intraductal spreading of carcinoma is an unfavorable pathologic factor for breast-conserving surgery. Cancer 1994, **74**: 1294–1302.

446 O'Malley FP, Vnencak-Jones CL, Dupont WD, Parl F, Manning S, Page DL. p53 mutations are confined to the comedo type ductal carcinoma in situ of the breast. Immunohistochemical and sequencing data. Lab Invest 1994, **71**: 67–72.

447 Ozzello I, Sanpitak P. Epithelial-stromal junction of intraductal carcinoma of the breast. Cancer 1970, **26**: 1186–1198.

448 Paredes J, Milanezi F, Viegas L, Amendoeira I, Schmitt F. P-cadherin expression is associated with high-grade ductal carcinoma in situ of the breast. Virchows Arch 2002, **440**: 16–21.

449 Poller DN, Silverstein MJ, Galea M, Locker AP, Elston CW, Blamey RW, Ellis IO. Ideas in pathology. Ductal carcinoma in situ of the breast. A proposal for a new simplified histological classification association between cellular proliferation and c-erbB-2 protein expression. Mod Pathol 1994, **7**: 257–262.

450 Rosen PP. Axillary lymph node metastases in patients with occult noninvasive breast carcinoma. Cancer 1980, **46**: 1298–1306.

451 Sandstad E, Hartveit F. Stromal metachromasia. A marker for areas of incipient invasion in ductal carcinoma of the breast? Histopathology 1987, **11**: 73–80.

452 Schnitt SJ, Connolly JL, Khettry U, Mazoujian G, Brenner M, Silver B, Recht A, Beadle G, Harris JR. Pathologic findings on re-excision of the primary site in breast cancer patients considered for treatment by primary radiation therapy. Cancer 1987, **59**: 675–681.

453 Silverberg SG, Chitale AR. Assessment of significance of proportions of intraductal and infiltrating tumor growth in ductal carcinoma of the breast. Cancer 1973, **32**: 830–837.

454 Tsang WY, Chan JK. Neural invasion in intraductal carcinoma of the breast. Hum Pathol 1992, **23**: 202–204.

455 Westbrook KC, Gallager HS. Intraductal carcinoma of the breast. A comparative study. Am J Surg 1975, **130**: 667–670.

(In situ) papillary carcinoma

456 Azzopardi JG. Problems in breast pathology. In Bennington JL (consulting ed.): Major problems in pathology, vol. 11. Philadelphia, 1979, W.B. Saunders.

457 Carter D, Orr SL, Merino MJ. Intracystic papillary carcinoma of the breast. After mastectomy, radiotherapy or excisional biopsy alone. Cancer 1983, **52**: 14–19.

458 Kraus FT, Neubecker RD. The differential diagnosis of papillary tumors of the breast. Cancer 1962, **15**: 444–455.

459 Lefkowitz M, Lefkowitz W, Wargotz ES. Intraductal (intracystic) papillary carcinoma of the breast and its variants. A clinicopathological study of 77 cases. Hum Pathol 1994, **25**: 802–809.

460 Papotti M, Eusebi V, Gugliotta P, Bussolati G. Immunohistochemical analysis of benign and malignant papillary lesions of the breast. Am J Surg Pathol 1983, **7**: 451–461.

461 Papotti M, Gugliotta P, Ghiringhello B, Bussolati G. Association of breast carcinoma and multiple intraductal papillomas. An histological and immunohistochemical investigation. Histopathology 1984, **8**: 963–975.

Other forms

462 Andersen JA. Invasive breast carcinoma with lobular involvement. Frequency and location of lobular carcinoma in situ. Acta Pathol Microbiol Scand (A) 1974, **82**: 719–729.

463 Azzopardi JG. Problems in breast pathology. In Bennington JL (consulting ed.): Major problems in pathology, vol. 11. Philadelphia, 1979, W.B. Saunders.

464 Bellamy CO, McDonald C, Salter DM, Chetty U, Anderson TJ. Noninvasive ductal carcinoma of the breast. The relevance of histologic categorization. Hum Pathol 1993, **24**: 16–23.

465 Bratthauer GL, Moinfar F, Stamatakos MD, Mezzetti TP, Shekitka KM, Man YG, Tavassoli FA. Combined E-cadherin and high molecular weight cytokeratin immunoprofile differentiates lobular, ductal, and hybrid mammary intraepithelial neoplasias. Humpathol 2002, **33**: 620–627.

466 Cross AS, Azzopardi JG, Krausz T, Van Noorden S, Polak JM. A morphological and immunocytochemical study of a distinctive variant of ductal carcinoma in situ of the breast. Histopathology 1985, **9**: 21–37.

467 Farshid G, Moinfar F, Meredith DJ, Peiterse S, Tavassoli FA. Spindle cell ductal carcinoma in situ: an unusual variant of ductal intra-epithelial neoplasia that simulates ductal hyperplasia or a myoepithelial proliferation. Virchows Arch 2001, **439**: 70–77.

468 Fechner RE. Ductal carcinoma involving the lobule of the breast. A source of confusion with lobular carcinoma in situ. Cancer 1971, **28**: 274–281.

469 Fisher ER, Brown R. Intraductal signet ring carcinoma. A hitherto undescribed form of intraductal carcinoma of the breast. Cancer 1985, **55**: 2533–2537.

470 Guerry P, Erlandson RA, Rosen PP. Cystic hypersecretory hyperplasia and cystic hypersecretory duct carcinoma of the breast. Pathology, therapy, and follow-up of 39 patients. Cancer 1988, **61**: 1611–1620.

471 Leal C, Henrique R, Monteiro P, Lopes C, Bento MJ, De Sousa SP, Lopes P, Olson S, Silva MD, Page DL. Apocrine ductal carcinoma in situ of the breast: histologic classification and expression of biologic markers. Hum Pathol 2001, **32**: 487–493.

472 Lishman SC, Lakhani SR. Atypical lobular hyperplasia and lobular carcinoma in situ: surgical and molecular pathology. Histopathology 1999, **35**: 195–200.

473 O'Malley FP, Page DL, Nelson EH, Dupont WD. Ductal carcinoma in situ of the breast with apocrine cytology. Definition of a borderline category. Hum Pathol 1994, **25**: 164–168.

474 Paredes J, Milanezi F, Viegas L, Amendoeira I, Schmitt F. P-cadherin expression is associated with high-grade ductal carcinoma in situ of the breast. Virchows Arch 2002, **440**: 16–21.

475 Rosen PP. Coexistent lobular carcinoma in situ and intraductal carcinoma in a single lobular-duct unit. Am J Surg Pathol 1980, **4**: 241–246.

476 Rosen PP, Scott M. Cystic hypersecretory duct carcinoma of the breast. Am J Surg Pathol 1984, **8**: 31–41.

477 Tavassoli FA, Norris HJ. Intraductal apocrine carcinoma. A clinicopathologic study of 37 cases. Mod Pathol 1994, **7**: 813–818.

478 Tsang WY, Chan JK. Endocrine ductal carcinoma in situ (E-DCIS) of the breast: a form of low-grade DCIS with distinctive clinicopathologic and biologic characteristics. Am J Surg Pathol 1996, **20**: 921–943.

Evolution

479 Betsill WL, Rosen PP, Robbins GF. Intraductal carcinoma. Long term followup after treatment by biopsy only. JAMA 1978, **239**: 1863–1867.

480 Carter D, Smith RRL. Carcinoma in situ of the breast. Cancer 1977, **40**: 1189–1193.

481 Eusebi V, Feudale E, Foschini MP, Micheli A, Conti A, Riva C, Di Palma S, Rilke F. Long-term follow-up of in situ carcinoma of the breast. Semin Diagn Pathol 1994, 11: 220–235.

482 Eusebi V, Foschini MP, Cook MG, Berrino F, Azzopardi JG. Long-term follow-up of in situ carcinoma of the breast with special emphasis on clinging carcinoma. Semin Diagn Pathol 1989, 6: 165–173.

483 Fisher ER, Costantino J, Fisher B, Palekar AS, Redmond C, Mamounas E. for the National Surgical Adjuvant Breast and Bowel Project Collaborating Investigators: Pathologic findings from the national surgical adjuvant breast project (NSABP) protocol B-17. Intraductal carcinoma (ductal carcinoma in situ). Cancer 1995, 75: 1310–1319.

483a Jensen RA, Page DL. Ductal carcinoma in situ of the breast. Impact of pathology on therapeutic decisions. Am J Surg Pathol 2003, 27: 828–831.

484 Lampejo O, Barnes DM, Smith P, Millis RR. Evaluation of infiltrating ductal carcinomas with a DCIS component. Correlation of the histologic type of the in situ component with grade of the infiltrating component. Semin Diagn Pathol 1994, 11: 215–222.

485 McDivitt RW, Holleb AI, Foote FW. Prior breast disease in patients treated for papillary carcinoma. Arch Pathol 1968, 85: 117–124.

486 Moriya T, Silverberg SG. Intraductal carcinoma (ductal carcinoma in situ) of the breast. A comparison of pure noninvasive tumors with those including different proportions of infiltrating carcinoma. Cancer 1994, 74: 2972–2978.

487 Morrow M, Strom EA, Bassett LW, Dershaw DD, Fowble B, Harris JR, O'Malley F, Schnitt SJ, Singletary SE, Winchester DP; American College of Surgeons: College of American Pathologists.; Society of Surgical Oncology.; American College of Radiology. Standard for the management of ductal carcinoma in situ of the breast (DCIS). CA Cancer J Clin 2002, 52: 256–276.

488 Page DL, Dupont WD, Rogers LW, Landenberger M. Intraductal carcinoma of the breast. Follow-up after biopsy only. Cancer 1982, 49: 751–758.

489 Rosen PP, Braun DW Jr, Kinne DE. The clinical significance of pre-invasive breast carcinoma. Cancer 1980, 46: 919–925.

490 Rosen PP, Senie R, Schottenfeld D, Ashikari R. Noninvasive breast carcinoma. Ann Surg 1979, 189: 377–382.

491 Schnitt SJ, Silen W, Sadowsky NL, Connolly JL, Harris JR. Ductal carcinoma in situ (intraductal carcinoma) of the breast. N Engl J Med 1988, 318: 898–903.

492 Schwartz GF, Solin LJ, Olivotto IA, Ernster VL, Committee PI. [The consensus conference on the treatment of in situ ductal carcinoma of the breast, April 22–25, 1999]. Bull Cancer 2000, 6: 499–506.

493 Silverstein MJ, Waisman JR, Gamagami P, Gierson ED, Colburn WJ, Rosser RJ, Gordon PS, Lewinsky BS, Fingerhut A. Intraductal carcinoma of the breast (208 cases). Clinical factors influencing treatment choice. Cancer 1990, 66: 102–108.

Lobular carcinoma in situ (LCIS)

494 Acs G, Lawton TJ, Rebbeck TR, Li Volsi VA, Zhang PJ. Differential expression of E-cadherin in lobular and ductal neoplasms of the breast and its biologic and diagnostic implications. Am J Clin Pathol 2001, 115: 85–98.

495 Andersen JA. Invasive breast carcinoma with lobular involvement. Frequency and location of lobular carcinoma in situ. Acta Pathol Microbiol Scand (A) 1974, 82: 719–729.

496 Andersen JA. Lobular carcinoma in situ of the breast with ductal involvement. Frequency and possible influence on prognosis. Acta Pathol Microbiol Scand (A) 1974, 82: 655–662.

497 Andersen JA, Vendelboe ML. Cytoplasmic mucous globules in lobular carcinoma in situ. Diagnosis and prognosis. Am J Surg Pathol 1981, 5: 251–255.

498 Bratthauer GL, Moinfar F, Stamatakos MD, Mezzetti TP, Shekitka KM, Man YG, Tavassoli FA. Combined E-cadherin and high molecular weight cytokeratin immunoprofile differentiates lobular, ductal, and hybrid mammary intraepithelial neoplasias. Hum Pathol 2002, 33: 620–627.

499 Breslow A, Brancaccio ME. Intracellular mucin production by lobular breast carcinoma cells. Arch Pathol Lab Med 1976, 100: 620–621.

500 Bussolati G, Micca FB, Eusebi V, Betts CM. Myoepithelial cells in lobular carcinoma in situ of the breast. A parallel immunocytochemical and ultrastructural study. Ultrastruct Pathol 1981, 2: 219–230.

501 Carter D, Smith RRL. Carcinoma in situ of the breast. Cancer 1977, 40: 1189–1193.

502 Dwarakanath S, Lee AKC, DeLellis RA, Silverman ML, Frasca L, Wolfe HJ. S-100 protein positivity in breast carcinomas. A potential pitfall in diagnostic immunohistochemistry. Hum Pathol 1987, 18: 1144–1148.

503 Eusebi V, Betts C, Haagensen DE Jr, Gugliotta P, Bussolati G, Azzopardi JG. Apocrine differentiation in lobular carcinoma of the breast. A morphologic, immunologic, and ultrastructural study. Hum Pathol 1984, 15: 134–140.

504 Eusebi V, Pich A, Macchiorlatti E, Bussolati G. Morpho-functional differentiation in lobular carcinoma of the breast. Histopathology 1977, 1: 301–314.

505 Fechner RE. Ductal carcinoma involving the lobule of the breast. A source of confusion with lobular carcinoma in situ. Cancer 1971, 28: 274–281.

506 Fechner RE. Epithelial alterations in the extralobular ducts of breasts with lobular carcinoma. Arch Pathol 1972, 93: 164–171.

507 Fechner RE. Lobular carcinoma in situ in sclerosing adenosis. A potential source of confusion with invasive carcinoma. Am J Surg Pathol 1981, 5: 233–239.

508 Fondo EY, Rosen PP, Fracchia AA, Urban JA. The problem of carcinoma developing in a fibroadenoma. Recent experience at Memorial Hospital. Cancer 1979, 43: 563–567.

509 Haagensen CD, Lane N, Bodian C. Coexisting lobular neoplasia and carcinoma of the breast. Cancer 1983, 51: 1468–1482.

510 Jacobs TW, Pliss N, Kouria G, Schnitt SJ. Carcinomas in situ of the breast with indeterminate features: role of E-cadherin staining in categorization. Am J Surg Pathol 2001, 25: 229–236.

511 Lambird PA, Shelley WM. The spatial distribution of lobular in situ mammary carcinoma. Implications for size and site of breast biopsy. JAMA 1969, 210: 689–693.

512 Newman W. Lobular carcinoma of the female breast. Ann Surg 1966, 164: 305–314.

513 Rieger-Christ KM, Pezza JA, Dugan JM, Braasch JW, Hughes KS, Summerhayes IC. Disparate E-cadherin mutations in LCIS and associated invasive breast carcinomas. Mol Pathol 2001, 54: 91–97.

514 Rosen PP, Lieberman PH, Braun DW Jr, Kosloff C, Adair F. Lobular carcinoma in situ of the breast. Detailed analysis of 99 patients with average follow-up of 24 years. Am J Surg Pathol 1978, 2: 225–251.

515 Sahoo S, Green I, Rosen PP. Bilateral Paget disease of the nipple associated with lobular carcinoma in situ: application of immunohistochemistry to a rare finding. Arch Pathol Lab Med 2002, 126: 90–92.

516 Schnitt SJ, Morrow M. Lobular carcinoma in situ: current concepts and controversies. Semin Diagn Pathol 1999, 16: 209–223.

517 Sgroi D, Koerner FC. Involvement of collagenous spherulosis by lobular carcinoma in situ. Potential confusion with cribriform ductal carcinoma in situ. Am J Surg Pathol 1995, 19: 1366–1370.

518 Sneige N, Wang J, Baker BA, Krishnamurthy S, Middleton LP. Clinical, histopathologic, and biologic features of pleomorphic lobular (ductal-lobular) carcinoma in situ of the breast: a report of 24 cases. Mod Pathol 2002, **15:** 1044–1050.

519 Tobon H, Price HM. Lobular carcinoma in situ. Some ultrastructural observations. Cancer 1972, **39:** 1082–1091.

520 Warner NE. Lobular carcinoma of the breast. Cancer 1969, **23:** 840–846.

521 Wheeler JE, Enterline HT. Lobular carcinoma of the breast in situ and infiltrating. Pathol Annu 1976, **11:** 161–188.

Evolution

522 Andersen JA. Lobular carcinoma in situ. A long-term follow-up in 52 cases. Acta Pathol Microbiol Scand (A) 1974, **82:** 519–533.

523 Andersen JA. Lobular carcinoma in situ of the breast. An approach to rational treatment. Cancer 1977, **39:** 2597–2602.

524 Fisher ER, Costantino J, Fisher B, Palekar AS, Paik SM, Suarez CM, Wolmark N. Pathologic findings from the National Surgical Adjuvant Breast Project (NSABP) protocol B-17: five-year observations concerning lobular carcinoma in situ. Cancer 1996, **78:** 1403–1416.

525 Haagensen CD, Lane N, Lattes R, Bodian C. Lobular neoplasia (so-called lobular carcinoma in situ) of the breast. Cancer 1978, **42:** 737–769.

526 Maluf H, Koerner F. Lobular carcinoma in situ and infiltrating ductal carcinoma: frequent presence of DCIS as a precursor lesion. Int J Surg Pathol 2001, **9:** 127–131.

527 Ottesen GL, Graversen HP, Blichert-Toft M. Zedeler K, Andersen JA. Lobular carcinoma in situ of the female breast. Short-term results of a prospective nationwide study. The Danish Breast Cancer Cooperative Group. Am J Surg Pathol 1993, **17:** 14–21.

528 Page DL, Kidd TE Jr, Dupont WD, Simpson JF, Rogers LW. Lobular neoplasia of the breast. Higher risk for subsequent invasive cancer predicted by more extensive disease. Hum Pathol 1991, **22:** 1232–1239.

529 Rosen PP, Lieberman PH, Braun DW Jr, Kosloff C, Adair F. Lobular carcinoma in situ of the breast. Detailed analysis of 99 patients with average follow-up of 24 years. Am J Surg Pathol 1978, **2:** 225–251.

530 Wheeler JE, Enterline HT. Lobular carcinoma of the breast in situ and infiltrating. Pathol Annu 1976, **11:** 161–188.

531 Wheeler JE, Enterline HT, Roseman JM, Tomasulo JP, McIlraine CH, Fitts WT Jr, Kirshenbaum J. Lobular carcinoma in situ of the breast. Long-term follow-up. Cancer 1974, **34:** 554–563.

Invasive carcinoma
Invasive ductal carcinoma
Cytoarchitectural variants

532 Berg JW, Hutter RV. Breast cancer. Cancer 1995, **75:** 257–269.

Classic (NOS) invasive ductal carcinoma

533 Azzopardi JG, Laurini RN. Elastosis in breast cancer. Cancer 1974, **33:** 174–183.

534 Barsky SH, Grotendorst GR, Liotta LA. Increased content of type V collagen in desmoplasia of human breast carcinoma. Am J Pathol 1982, **108:** 276–283.

535 Battifora H. Intracytoplasmic lumina in breast carcinoma. A helpful histopathologic feature. Arch Pathol 1975, **99:** 614–617.

536 Bellahcène A, Castronovo V. Increased expression of osteonectin and osteopontin, two bone matrix proteins, in human breast cancer. Am J Pathol 1995, **146:** 95–100.

537 Bocker W, Klaubert A, Bahnsen J, Schweikhart G, Pollow K, Mitze M, Kreienberg R, Beck T, Stegner H-E. Peanut lectin histochemistry of 120 mammary carcinomas and its relation to tumor type, grading, staging, and receptor status. Virchows Arch [A] 1984, **403:** 149–161.

538 Bonetti F, Colombari R, Manfrin E, Zamboni G, Martignoni G, Mombello A, Chilosi M. Breast carcinoma with positive results for melanoma marker (HMB-45). HMB-45 immunoreactivity in normal and neoplastic breast. Am J Clin Pathol 1989, **92:** 491–495.

539 Bussolati G, Papotti M, Sapino A, Gugliotta P, Ghiringhello B, Azzopardi JG. Endocrine markers in argyrophilic carcinomas of the breast. Am J Surg Pathol 1987, **11:** 248–256.

540 Charpin C, Lachard A, Pourreau-Schneider N, Jacquemier J, Lavaut MN, Andonian C, Martin PM, Toga M. Localization of lactoferrin and nonspecific cross-reacting antigen in human breast carcinomas. An immunohistochemical study using the avidin-biotin-peroxidase complex method. Cancer 1985, **55:** 2612–2617.

541 Charpin C, Lissitzky JC, Jacquemier J, Lavaut MN, Kopp F, Pourreau-Schneider N, Martin PM, Toga M. Immunohistochemical detection of laminin in 98 human breast carcinomas. A light and electron microscopic study. Hum Pathol 1986, **17:** 355–365.

542 Clayton F, Ordóñez NG, Hanssen GM, Hanssen H. Immunoperoxidase localization of lactalbumin in malignant breast neoplasms. Arch Pathol Lab Med 1982, **106:** 268–270.

543 Domagala W, Wozniak L, Lasota J, Weber K, Osborn M. Vimentin is preferentially expressed in high-grade ductal and medullary, but not in lobular breast carcinomas. Am J Pathol 1990, **137:** 1059–1064.

544 Dwarakanath S, Lee AKC, DeLellis RA, Silverman ML, Frasca L, Wolfe HJ. S-100 protein positivity in breast carcinomas. A potential pitfall in diagnostic immunohistochemistry. Hum Pathol 1987, **18:** 1144–1148.

545 Fisher ER. Ultrastructure of the human breast and its disorders. Am J Clin Pathol 1976, **66:** 291–374.

546 Fisher ER, Gregorio RM, Fisher B, with the assistance of Redmond C, Vellios F, Sommers SC, and cooperating investigators. The pathology of invasive breast cancer. A syllabus derived from findings of the National Surgical Adjuvant Breast Project (Protocol No. 4). Cancer 1975, **36:** 1–85.

547 Fisher ER, Palekar AS, Gregorio RM, Redmond C, Fisher B. Pathological findings from the National Surgical Adjuvant Breast Project (Protocol No. 4). IV. Significance of tumor necrosis. Hum Pathol 1978, **9:** 523–530.

548 Gould VE, Koukoulis GK, Jansson DS, Nagle RB, Franke WW, Moll R. Coexpression patterns of vimentin and glial filament protein with cytokeratins in the normal, hyperplastic, and neoplastic breast. Am J Pathol 1990, **137:** 1143–1155.

549 Greenwalt DE, Johnson VG, Kuhajda FP, Eggleston JC, Mather IH. Localization of a membrane glycoprotein in benign fibrocystic disease and infiltrating duct carcinomas of the human breast with the use of a monoclonal antibody to guinea pig milk fat globule-membrane. Am J Pathol 1985, **118:** 351–359.

550 Hirota S, Ito A, Nagoshi J, Takeda M, Kurata A, Takatsuka Y, Kohri K, Nomura S, Kitamura Y. Expression of bone matrix protein messenger ribonucleic acids in human breast cancers. Possible involvement of osteopontin in development of calcifying foci. Lab Invest 1995, **72:** 64–69.

551 Howard DR, Taylor CR. A method for distinguishing benign from malignant breast lesions utilizing antibody present in normal human sera. Cancer 1979, **43:** 2279–2287.

552 Jackson JG, Orr JW. The ducts of carcinomatous breasts, with particular reference to connective-tissue changes. J Pathol Bacteriol 1957, **74:** 265–273.

553 Jarasch E-D, Nagle RB, Kaufmann M, Maurer C, Bocker WJ. Differential diagnosis of benign epithelial proliferations and carcinomas of the breast using antibodies to cytokeratins. Hum Pathol 1988, **19:** 276–289.

554 Kuhajda FP, Bohn H, Mendelsohn G. Pregnancy-specific beta-1

glycoprotein (SP-1) in breast carcinoma. Pathologic and clinical considerations. Cancer 1984, **54:** 1392–1396.

555 Kuhajda FP, Offutt LE, Mendelsohn G. The distribution of carcinoembryonic antigen in breast carcinoma. Diagnostic and prognostic implications. Cancer 1983, **52:** 1257–1264.

556 Lee AK, DeLellis RA, Rosen PP, Herbert-Stanton T, Tallberg K, Garcia C, Wolfe HJ. Alpha-lactalbumin as an immunohistochemical marker for metastatic breast carcinomas. Am J Surg Pathol 1984, **8:** 93–100.

557 Lee AKC, DeLellis RA, Wolfe HJ. Intramammary lymphatic invasion in breast carcinomas. Evaluation using ABH isoantigens as endothelial markers. Am J Surg Pathol 1986, **10:** 589–594.

558 Loy TS, Chapman RK, Diaz-Arias AA, Bulatao IS, Bickel JT. Distribution of BCA-225 in adenocarcinomas. An immunohistochemical study of 446 cases. Am J Clin Pathol 1991, **96:** 326–329.

559 Lunde S, Nesland JM, Holm R, Johannessen JV. Breast carcinomas with protein S-100 immunoreactivity. An immunocytochemical and ultrastructural study. Pathol Res Pract 1987, **182:** 627–631.

560 Martin SA, Perez-Reyes N, Mendelsohn G. Angioinvasion in breast carcinoma. An immunohistochemical study of factor VIII-related antigen. Cancer 1987, **59:** 1918–1922.

561 Mazoujian G, Bodian C, Haagensen DE Jr, Haagensen CD. Expression of GCDFP-15 in breast carcinomas. Relationship to pathologic and clinical factors. Cancer 1989, **63:** 2156–2161.

562 Mesa-Tejada R, Oster MW, Fenoglio CM, Magidson J, Spiegelman S. Diagnosis of primary breast carcinoma through immunohistochemical detection of antigen related to mouse mammary tumor virus in metastatic lesions. A report of two cases. Cancer 1982, **49:** 261–268.

563 Murad TM, Scharpelli DG. The ultrastructure of medullary and scirrhous mammary duct carcinoma. Am J Pathol 1967, **50:** 335–360.

564 Oberman HA. Invasive carcinoma of the breast with granulomatous response. Am J Clin Pathol 1987, **88:** 718–721.

565 Ohtani H, Sasano N. Myofibroblasts and myoepithelial cells in human breast carcinoma. An ultrastructural study. Virchows Arch [A] 1980, **385:** 247–261.

566 Ordóñez NG, Brooks T, Thompson S, Batsakis JG. Use of *Ulex europaeus* agglutinin I in the identification of lymphatic and blood vessel invasion in previously stained microscopic slides. Am J Surg Pathol 1987, **11:** 543–550.

567 Prey MU, Bedrossian CW, Masood S. The value of monoclonal antibody B72.3 for the diagnosis of breast carcinoma. Experience with the first commercially available source. Hum Pathol 1991, **22:** 598–602.

568 Robertson JF, Ellis IO, Bell J, Todd JH, Robins A, Elston CW, Blamey RW. Carcinoembryonic antigen immunocytochemistry in primary breast cancer. Cancer 1989, **64:** 1638–1645.

569 Rosen PP. Tumor emboli in intramammary lymphatics in breast carcinoma. Pathologic criteria for diagnosis and clinical significance. Pathol Annu 1983, **18**(Pt 2): 215–232.

570 Saigo PE, Rosen PP. The application of immunohistochemical stains to identify endothelial-lined channels in mammary carcinoma. Cancer 1987, **59:** 51–54.

571 Sobrinho-Simões M, Johannessen JV, Gould VE. The diagnostic significance of intracytoplasmic lumina in metastatic neoplasms. Ultrastruct Pathol 1981, **2:** 327–335.

572 Tavassoli FA, Jones MW, Majeste RM, Bratthauer GL, O'Leary TJ. Immunohistochemical staining with monoclonal Ab B72.3 in benign and malignant breast disease. Am J Surg Pathol 1990, **14:** 128–133.

573 Tsubura A, Okada H, Senzaki H, Hatano T, Morii S. Keratin expression in the normal breast and in breast carcinoma. Histopathology 1991, **18:** 517–522.

574 Wetzels RH, Holland R, van Haelst UJ, Lane EB, Leigh IM, Ramaekers FC. Detection of basement membrane components and basal cell keratin 14 in non-invasive and invasive carcinomas of the breast. Am J Pathol 1989, **134:** 571–579.

575 Wick MR, Lillemoe TJ, Copland GT, Swanson PE, Manivel JC, Kiang DT. Gross cystic disease fluid protein-15 as a marker for breast cancer. Immunohistochemical analysis of 690 human neoplasms and comparison with alpha-lactalbumin. Hum Pathol 1989, **20:** 281–287.

576 Willebrand D, Bosman FT, De Goeij AFPM. Patterns of basement membrane deposition in benign and malignant breast tumours. Histopathology 1986, **10:** 1231–1241.

Tubular carcinoma

577 Carstens PHB, Greenberg RA, Francis D, Lyon H. Tubular carcinoma of the breast. A long term follow-up. Histopathology 1985, **9:** 271–280.

578 Carstens PHB, Huvos AG, Foote FW Jr, Ashikari R. Tubular carcinoma of the breast. A clinicopathologic study of 35 cases. Am J Clin Pathol 1972, **58:** 231–238.

579 Dawson AE, Logan-Young W, Mulford DK. Aspiration cytology of tubular carcinoma. Diagnostic features with mammographic correlation. Am J Clin Pathol 1994, **101:** 488–492.

580 Deos PH, Norris HJ. Well-differentiated (tubular) carcinoma of the breast. A clinicopathologic study of 145 pure and mixed cases. Am J Clin Pathol 1982, **78:** 1–7.

581 Diab SG, Clark GM, Osborne CK, Libby A, Allred DC, Elledge RM. Tumor characteristics and clinical outcome of tubular and mucinous breast carcinomas. J Clin Oncol 1999, **17:** 1442–1448.

582 Erlandson RA, Carstens PHB. Ultrastructure of tubular carcinoma of the breast. Cancer 1972, **29:** 987–995.

583 Flotte TJ, Bell DA, Greco MA. Tubular carcinoma and sclerosing adenosis. The use of basal lamina as a differential feature. Am J Surg Pathol 1980, **4:** 75–77.

584 Jao W, Recant W, Swerdlow MA. Comparative ultrastructure of tubular carcinoma and sclerosing adenosis of the breast. Cancer 1976, **38:** 180–186.

585 Lagios MD, Rose MR, Margolin FR. Tubular carcinoma of the breast. Association with multicentricity, bilaterality, and family history of mammary carcinoma. Am J Clin Pathol 1980, **73:** 25–30.

586 Lele SM, Graves K, Galatica Z. Immunohistochemical detection of maspin is a useful adjunct in distinguishing radial sclerosing lesion from tubular carcinoma of the breast. Appl Immunohistochem Mol Morphol 2000, **8:** 32–36.

587 McDivitt RW, Boyce W, Gersell D. Tubular carcinoma of the breast. Clinical and pathological observations concerning 135 cases. Am J Surg Pathol 1982, **6:** 401–411.

588 Oberman HA, Fidler WJ Jr. Tubular carcinoma of the breast. Am J Surg Pathol 1979, **3:** 387–395.

589 Parl FF, Richardson LD. The histologic and biologic spectrum of tubular carcinoma of the breast. Hum Pathol 1983, **14:** 694–698.

590 Peters GN, Wolff M, Haagensen CD. Tubular carcinoma of the breast. Clinical pathologic correlations based on 100 cases. Ann Surg 1981, **193:** 138–149.

591 Stalsberg H, Hartmann WH. The delimitation of tubular carcinoma of the breast. Hum Pathol 2000, **31:** 601–607.

592 Taylor HB, Norris HJ. Well-differentiated carcinoma of the breast. Cancer 1970, **25:** 687–692.

593 Tremblay G. Elastosis in tubular carcinoma of the breast. Arch Pathol 1974, **98:** 302–307.

594 van Bogaert L-J. Clinicopathologic hallmarks of mammary tubular carcinoma. Hum Pathol 1982, **13:** 558–562.

595 Waldman FM, Hwang ES, Etzell J, Eng C, de Vries S,

Bennington J, Thor A. Genomic alterations in tubular breast carcinomas. Hum Pathol 2001, **32**: 222–226.

Cribriform carcinoma

596 Page DL, Dixon JM, Anderson TJ, Lee D, Stewart HJ. Invasive cribriform carcinoma of the breast. Histopathology 1983, **7**: 525–536.

596a Sanders ME, Page DL, Simpson JF, Edgerton ME, Jensen RA. Solid variant of cribriform carcinoma: a study of 24 cases (Abstract). Mod Pathol 2003, **16**: 45a.

597 Venable JG, Schwartz AM, Silverberg SG. Infiltrating cribriform carcinoma of the breast. A distinctive clinicopathologic entity. Hum Pathol 1990, **21**: 333–338.

Mucinous carcinoma

597a Adsay NV, Merati K, Nassar H, Shia J, Sarkar F, Pierson CR, Cheng JD, Visscher DW, Hruban RH, Klimstra DS. Pathogenesis of colloid (pure mucinous) carcinoma of exocrine organs. Coupling of gel-forming mucin (MUC2) production with altered cell polarity and abnormal cell-stroma interaction may be the key factor in the morphogenesis and idolent behaviour of colloid carcinoma in the breast and pancreas. Am J Surg Pathol 2003, **27**: 571–578.

598 Capella C, Eusebi V, Mann B, Azzopardi JG. Endocrine differentiation in mucoid carcinoma of the breast. Histopathology 1980, **4**: 613–630.

599 Chinyama CN, Davies JD. Mammary mucinous lesions: congeners, prevalence and important pathological associations. Histopathology 1996, **29**: 533–539.

600 Clayton F. Pure mucinous carcinomas of breast. Morphologic features and prognostic correlates. Hum Pathol 1986, **17**: 34–38.

601 Coady AT, Shousha S, Dawson PM, Moss M, James KR, Bull TB. Mucinous carcinoma of the breast. Further characterization of its three subtypes. Histopathology 1989, **15**: 617–626.

602 Diab SG, Clark GM, Osborne CK, Libby A, Allred DC, Elledge RM. Tumor characteristics and clinical outcome of tubular and mucinous breast carcinomas. J Clin Oncol 1999, **17**: 1442–1448.

603 Ferguson DJP, Anderson TJ, Wells CA, Battersby S. An ultrastructural study of mucoid carcinoma of the breast. Variability of cytoplasmic features. Histopathology 1986, **10**: 1219–1230.

604 Fisher ER, Palekar AS, NSABP collaborators. Solid and mucinous varieties of so-called mammary carcinoid tumors. Am J Clin Pathol 1979, **72**: 909–916.

605 Hamele-Bena D, Cranor ML, Rosen PP. Mammary mucocele-like lesions: benign and malignant. Am J Surg Pathol 1996, **20**: 1081–1085.

606 Hull MT, Warfel KA. Mucinous breast carcinomas with abundant intracytoplasmic mucin and neuroendocrine features. Light microscopic, immunohistochemical, and ultrastructural study. Ultrastruct Pathol 1987, **11**: 29–38.

607 Koenig C, Tavassoli FA. Mucinous cystadenocarcinoma of the breast. Am J Surg Pathol 1998, **22**: 698–703.

608 Komaki K, Sakamoto G, Sugano H, Kasumi F, Watanabe S, Nishi M, Morimoto T, Monden Y. The morphologic feature of mucus leakage appearing in low papillary carcinoma of the breast. Hum Pathol 1991, **22**: 231–236.

609 Matsukita S, Nomoto M, Kitajima S, Tanaka S, Goto M, Irimura T, Kim YS, Sato E, Yonezawa S. Expression of mucins (MUC1, MUC2, MUC5AC and MUC6) in mucinous carcinoma of the breast: comparison with invasive ductal carcinoma. Histopathology 2003, **42**: 26–36.

610 Norris HJ, Taylor HB. Prognosis of mucinous (gelatinous) carcinoma of the breast. Cancer 1965, **18**: 879–885.

611 O'Connell JT, Shao ZM, Drori E, Basbaum CB, Barsky SH. Altered mucin expression is a field change that accompanies mucinous (colloid) breast carcinoma histogenesis. Hum Pathol 1998, **29**: 1517–1523.

612 Rasmussen BB. Human mucinous breast carcinomas and their lymph node metastases. A histological review of 247 cases. Pathol Res Pract 1985, **180**: 377–382.

613 Rasmussen BB, Rose C, Christensen IB. Prognostic factors in primary mucinous breast carcinoma. Am J Clin Pathol 1987, **87**: 155–160.

614 Rasmussen BB, Rose C, Thorpe SM, Andersen KW, Hou-Jensen K. Argyrophilic cells in 202 human mucinous breast carcinomas. Relation to histopathologic and clinical factors. Am J Clin Pathol 1985, **84**: 737–740.

615 Ro JY, Sneige N, Sahin AA, Silva EG, del Junco GW, Ayala AG. Mucocele-like tumor of the breast associated with atypical ductal hyperplasia or mucinous carcinoma. A clinicopathologic study of seven cases. Arch Pathol Lab Med 1991, **115**: 137–140.

616 Rosen PP. Mucocele-like tumors of the breast. Am J Surg Pathol 1986, **10**: 464–469.

617 Rosen PP, Wang T-Y. Colloid carcinoma of the breast. Analysis of 64 patients with long-term follow-up (abstract). Am J Clin Pathol 1980, **73**: 304.

618 Saez C, Japon MA, Poveda MA, Segura DI. Mucinous (colloid) adenocarcinomas secrete distinct O-acylated forms of sialomucins: a histochemical study of gastric, colorectal and breast adenocarcinomas. Histopathology 2001, **39**: 554–560.

619 Scopsi L, Andreola S, Pilotti S, Bufalino R, Baldini MT, Testori A, Rilke F. Mucinous carcinoma of the breast. A clinicopathologic, histochemical, and immunocytochemical study with special reference to neuroendocrine differentiation. Am J Surg Pathol 1994, **18**: 702–711.

620 Toikkanen S, Kujari H. Pure and mixed mucinous carcinomas of the breast. A clinicopathologic analysis of 61 cases with long-term follow-up. Hum Pathol 1989, **20**: 758–764.

621 Walker RA. Mucoid carcinomas of the breast. A study using mucin histochemistry and peanut lectin. Histopathology 1982, **6**: 571–579.

Medullary carcinoma

622 Armes JE, Venter DJ. The pathology of inherited breast cancer. Pathology 2002, **34**: 309–314.

623 Ben-Ezra J, Sheibani K. Antigenic phenotype of the lymphocytic component of medullary carcinoma of the breast. Cancer 1987, **59**: 2037–2041.

624 Bloom HJG, Richardson WW, Fields JR. Host resistance and survival in carcinoma of breasts. A study of 104 cases of medullary carcinoma in a series of 1,411 cases of breast cancer followed for 20 years. Br Med J 1970, **3**: 181–188.

625 Crotty TB. Medullary carcinoma: it is a reproducible and prognostically significant type of mammary carcinoma? Adv Anat Pathol 1996, **3**: 179–184.

626 Dalal P, Shousha S. Keratin 19 in paraffin sections of medullary carcinoma and other benign and malignant breast lesions. Mod Pathol 1995, **8**: 413–416.

627 Dwarakanath S, Lee AKC, DeLellis RA, Silverman ML, Frasca L, Wolfe HJ. S-100 protein positivity in breast carcinomas. A potential pitfall in diagnostic immunohistochemistry. Hum Pathol 1987, **18**: 1144–1148.

628 Gaffey MJ, Frierson HF Jr, Mills SE, Boyd JC, Zarbo RJ, Simpson JF, Gross LK, Weiss LM. Medullary carcinoma of the breast. Identification of lymphocyte subpopulations and their significance. Mod Pathol 1993, **6**: 721–728.

629 Gaffey MJ, Mills SE, Frierson HF Jr, Zarbo RJ, Boyd JC, Simpson JF, Weiss LM. Medullary carcinoma of the breast. Interobserver variability in histopathologic diagnosis. Mod Pathol 1995, **8**: 31–38.

630 Harris M, Lessells AM. The ultrastructure of medullary, atypical medullary and non-medullary carcinomas of the breast. Histopathology 1986, **10**: 405–414.

631 Howell LP, Kline TS. Medullary carcinoma of the breast. An unusual cytologic finding in cyst fluid aspirates. Cancer 1990, **65**: 277–282.

632 Hsu S-M, Raine L, Nayak RN. Medullary carcinoma of breast. An immunohistochemical study of its lymphoid storma. Cancer 1981, **48**: 1368–1376.

633 Jensen ML, Kiaer H, Andersen J, Jensen V, Melsen F. Prognostic comparison of three classifications for medullary carcinomas of the breast. Histopathology 1997, **30**: 523–532.

634 Kumar S, Kumar D. Lymphoepithelioma-like carcinoma of the breast. Mod Pathol 1994, **7**: 129–131.

635 Lazzaro B, Anderson AE, Kajdacsy-Balla A, Hessner MJ. Antigenic characterization of medullary carcinoma of the breast: HLA-DR expression in lymph node positive cases. Appl Immunohistochem Mol Morphol 2001, **9**: 234–241.

636 Lee SC, Berg KD, Sherman ME, Griffin CA, Eshleman JR. Microsatellite instability is infrequent in medullary breast cancer. Am J Clin Pathol 2001, **115**: 823–827.

637 Lespagnard L, Cochaux P, Larsimont D, Degeyter M, Velu T, Heimann R. Absence of Epstein-Barr virus in medullary carcinoma of the breast as demonstrated by immunophenotyping, *in situ* hybridization and polymerase chain reaction. Am J Clin Pathol 1995, **103**: 449–452.

637a Osin P, Lu Y-J, Stone J, Crook T, Houlston RS, Gasco M, Gusterson BA, Shipley J. Distinct genetic and epigenetic changes in medullary breast cancer. Int J Surg Pathol 2003, **11**: 153–158.

638 Rapin V, Contesso G, Mouriesse H, Bertin F, LaCombe MJ, Piekarski JD, Travagli JP, Gadenne C, Friedman S. Medullary breast carcinoma. A reevaluation of 95 cases of breast cancer with inflammatory stroma. Cancer 1988, **61**: 2503–2510.

639 Richardson WW. Medullary carcinoma of the breast. A distinctive tumour type with a relatively good prognosis following radical mastectomy. Br J Cancer 1956, **10**: 415–423.

640 Ridolfi RL, Rosen PP, Port A, Kinne D, Miké V. Medullary carcinoma of the breast. A clinicopathologic study with 10 year follow-up. Cancer 1977, **40**: 1365–1385.

641 Rigaud C, Theobald S, Noel P, Badreddine J, Barlier C, Delobelle A, Gentile A, Jacquemier J, Maisongrosse V, Peffault de Latour M, et al. Medullary carcinoma of the breast. A multicenter study of its diagnostic consistency. Arch Pathol Lab Med 1993, **117**: 1005–1008.

642 Shousha S. Medullary carcinoma of the breast and BRCA1 mutation. Histopathology 2000, **37**: 182–185.

643 Tot T. The cytokeratin profile of medullary carcinoma of the breast. Histopathology 2000, **37**: 175–181.

644 Wargotz ES, Silverberg SG. Medullary carcinoma of the breast. A clinicopathologic study with appraisal of current diagnostic criteria (abstract). Lab Invest 1988, **58**: 100A.

645 Yakirevich E, Ben Izhak O, Rennert G, Kovacs ZG, Resnick MB. Cytotoxic phenotype of tumor infiltrating lymphocytes in medullary carcinoma of the breast. Mod Pathol 1999, **12**: 1050–1056.

646 Yazawa T, Kamma H, Ogata T. Frequent expression of HLA-DR antigen in medullary carcinoma of the breast. A possible reason for its prominent lymphocytic infiltration and favorable prognosis. Appl Immunohistochem 1993, **1**: 289–296.

Invasive papillary carcinoma

647 Carter D, Orr SL, Merino MJ. Intracystic papillary carcinoma of the breast. After mastectomy, radiotherapy or excisional biopsy alone. Cancer 1983, **52**: 14–19.

648 Corkill ME, Sneige N, Fanning T, el-Naggar A. Fine-needle aspiration cytology and flow cytometry of intracystic papillary carcinoma of breast. Am J Clin Pathol 1990, **94**: 673–680.

649 Fisher ER, Palekar AS, Redmond C, Barton B, Fisher B. Pathologic findings from the National Surgical Adjuvant Breast Project (Protocol No. 4). VI. Invasive papillary cancer. Am J Clin Pathol 1980, **73**: 313–322.

650 Leal C, Costa I, Fonseca D, Lopes P, Bento MJ, Lopes C. Intracystic (encysted) papillary carcinoma of the breast: a clinical, pathological, and immunohistochemical study. Hum Pathol 1998, **29**: 1097–1104.

651 Michael CW, Buschmann B. Can true papillary neoplasms of breast and their mimickers be accurately classified by cytology? Cancer Cytopathol 2002, **96**: 92–100.

Apocrine carcinoma

652 Abati AD, Kimmel M, Rosen PP. Apocrine mammary carcinoma. A clinicopathologic study of 72 cases. Am J Clin Pathol 1990, **94**: 371–377.

652a Chen X, Hoda SA, Rosen PP. E-Cadherin immunostain distinguishes apocrine ductal carcinoma from apocrine lobular carcinoma (Abstract). Mod Pathol 2003, **16**: 24a.

653 Eusebi V, Betts C, Haagensen DE Jr, Gugliotta P, Bussolati G, Azzopardi JG. Apocrine differentiation in lobular carcinoma of the breast. A morphologic, immunologic, and ultrastructural study. Hum Pathol 1984, **15**: 134–140.

654 Eusebi V, Millis RR, Cattani MG, Bussolati G, Azzopardi JG. Apocrine carcinoma of the breast. A morphologic and immunocytochemical study. Am J Pathol 1986, **123**: 532–541.

655 Losi L, Lorenzini R, Eusebi V, Bussolati G. Apocrine differentiation in invasive carcinoma of the breast. Comparison of monoclonal and polyclonal gross cystic disease fluid protein-15 antibodies with prolactin-inducible protein mRNA gene expression. Appl Immunohistochem 1995, **3**: 91–98.

656 Mossler JA, Barton TK, Brinkhous AD, McCarty KS, Moylan JA, McCarty KS Jr. Apocrine differentiation in human mammary carcinoma. Cancer 1980, **46**: 2463–2471.

657 Pagani A, Sapino A, Eusebi V, Bergnolo P, Bussolati G. PIP/GCDFP-15 gene expression and apocrine differentiation in carcinomas of the breast. Virchows Arch [A] 1994, **425**: 459–465.

Juvenile (secretory) carcinoma

658 Akhtar M, Robinson C, Ali MA, Godwin JT. Secretory carcinoma of the breast in adults. Light and electron microscopic study of three cases with review of the literature. Cancer 1983, **51**: 2245–2254.

659 Hirokawa M, Sugihara K, Sai T, Monobe Y, Kudo H, Sano N, Sano T. Secretory carcinoma of the breast: a tumor analogous to salivary gland acinic cell carcinoma? Histopathology 2002, **40**: 223–230.

660 Krausz T, Jenkins D, Grontoft O, Pollock DJ, Azzopardi JG. Secretory carcinoma of the breast in adults. Emphasis on late recurrence and metastasis. Histopathology 1989, **14**: 25–36.

661 Lamovec J, Bracko M. Secretory carcinoma of the breast. Light microscopical, immunohistochemical and flow cytometric study. Mod Pathol 1994, **7**: 475–479.

662 McDivitt RW, Stewart FW. Breast carcinoma in children. JAMA 1966, **195**: 388–390.

663 Oberman HA. Secretory carcinoma of the breast in adults. Am J Surg Pathol 1980, **4**: 465–470.

664 Rosen PP, Cranor ML. Secretory carcinoma of the breast. Arch Pathol Lab Med 1991, **115**: 141–144.

665 Tavassoli FA, Norris HJ. Secretory carcinoma of the breast. Cancer 1980, **45**: 2404–2413.

Carcinomas with neuroendocrine features (including "so-called carcinoid tumor")

666 Asioli S, Dorji T, Lorenzini P, Eusebi V. Primary neuroendocrine (Merkel cell) carcinoma of the nipple. Virchows Arch 2002, **440**: 4443–4454.

667 Azzopardi JG, Muretto P, Goddeeris P, Eusebi V, Lauweryns JM. "Carcinoid" tumours of the breast. The morphological

spectrum of argyrophil carcinomas. Histopathology 1982, **6:** 549–569.

668 Battersby S, Dely CJ, Hopkinson HE, Anderson TJ. The nature of breast dense core granules. Chromogranin reactivity. Histopathology 1992, **20:** 107–114.

669 Bussolati G, Papotti M, Sapino A, Gugliotta P, Ghiringhello B, Azzopardi JG. Endocrine markers in argyrophilic carcinomas of the breast. Am J Surg Pathol 1987, **11:** 248–256.

670 Capella C, Usellini L, Papotti M, Macri L, Finzi G, Eusebi V, Bussolati G. Ultrastructural features of neuroendocrine differentiated carcinomas of the breast. Ultrastruct Pathol 1990, **14:** 321–334.

671 Clayton F, Sibley RK, Ordóñez NG, Hanssen G. Argyrophilic breast carcinomas. Evidence of lactational differentiation. Am J Surg Pathol 1982, **6:** 323–333.

672 Cross AS, Azzopardi JG, Krausz T, Van Noorden S, Polak JM. A morphological and immunocytochemical study of a distinctive variant of ductal carcinomas in-situ of the breast. Histopathology 1985, **9:** 21–37.

673 Cubilla AL, Woodruff JM. Primary carcinoid tumor of the breast. A report of eight patients. Am J Surg Pathol 1977, **1:** 283–292.

674 Fisher ER, Palekar AS, NSABP Collaborators. Solid and mucinous varieties of so-called mammary carcinoid tumors. Am J Clin Pathol 1979, **72:** 909–916.

675 Fukunaga M. Neuroendocrine carcinoma of the breast with Merkel cell carcinoma-like features. Pathol Int 1998, **48:** 557–561.

676 Hoang MP, Maitra A, Gazdar AF, Albores-Saavedra J. Primary mammary small-cell carcinoma: a molecular analysis of 2 cases. Hum Pathol 2001, **32:** 753–757.

676a Makretsov N, Gilks B, Coldman AJ, Hayes M, Huntsman D. Tissue microarray analysis of neuroendocrine differentiation and its prognostic significance in breast cancer. Hum Pathol 2003, **34:** 1001–1008.

677 Maluf HM, Koerner FC. Carcinomas of the breast with endocrine differentiation. A review. Virchows Arch 1994, **425:** 449–457.

678 Maluf HM, Koerner FC. Solid papillary carcinoma of the breast. A form of intraductal carcinoma with endocrine differentiation frequently associated with mucinous carcinoma. Am J Surg Pathol 1995, **19:** 1237–1244.

679 Miremadi A, Pinder SE, Lee AH, Bell JA, Paish EC, Wencyk P, Elston CW, Nicholson RI, Blamey RW, Robertson JF, Ellis IO. Neuroendocrine differentiation and prognosis in breast adenocarcinoma. Histopathology 2002, **40:** 215–222.

680 Nesland JM, Holm R, Johannessen JV, Gould VE. Neurone specific enolase immunostaining in the diagnosis of breast carcinomas with neuroendocrine differentiation. Its usefulness and limitations. J Pathol 1986, **148:** 35–43.

681 Nesland JM, Memoli VA, Holm R, Gould VE, Johannessen JV. Breast carcinomas with neuroendocrine differentiation. Ultrastruct Pathol 1985, **8:** 225–240.

682 Pagani A, Papotti M, Hofler H, Weiler R, Winkler H, Bussolati G. Chromogranin A and B gene expression in carcinomas of the breast. Correlation of immunocytochemical, immunoblot, and hybridization analyses. Am J Pathol 1990, **136:** 319–327.

683 Papotti M, Macri L, Finzi G, Capella C, Eusebi V, Bussolati G. Neuroendocrine differentiation in carcinomas of the breast. A study of 51 cases. Semin Diagn Pathol 1989, **6:** 174–188.

684 Salmo EN, Connolly CE. Primary small cell carcinoma of the breast: report of a case and review of the literature. Histopathology 2001, **38:** 277–278.

685 Samli B, Celik S, Evrensel T, Orhan B, Tasdelen I. Primary neuroendocrine small cell carcinoma of the breast. Arch Pathol Lab Med 2000, **124:** 296–298.

686 Sapino A, Righi L, Cassoni P, Papotti M, Gugliotta P,

Bussolati G. Expression of apocrine differentiation markers in neuroendocrine breast carcinomas of aged women. Mod Pathol 2001, **14:** 768–776.

687 Scopsi L, Balslev E, Brunner N, Poulsen HS, Andersen J, Rank F, Larsson LI. Immunoreactive opioid peptides in human breast cancer. Am J Pathol 1989, **134:** 473–479.

688 Shin SJ, DeLellis RA, Ying L, Rosen PP. Small cell carcinoma of the breast: a clinicopathologic and immunohistochemical study of nine patients. Am J Surg Pathol 2000, **24:** 1231–1238.

689 Taxy JB, Tischler AS, Insalaco SJ, Battifora H. "Carcinoid" tumor of the breast. A variant of conventional breast cancer? Hum Pathol 1981, **12:** 170–179.

690 Toyoshima S. Mammary carcinoma with argyrophil cells. Cancer 1983, **52:** 2129–2138.

691 Tsang WY, Chan JK. Endocrine ductal carcinoma in situ (E-DCIS) of the breast: a form of low-grade DCIS with distinctive clinicopathologic and biologic characteristics. Am J Surg Pathol 1996, **20:** 921–943.

692 Uccini S, Monardo F, Paradiso P, Masciangelo R, Marzullo A, Ruco LP, Baroni CD. Synaptophysin in human breast carcinomas. Histopathology 1991, **18:** 271–273.

693 Wilander E, Påhlman S, Sällström J, Lindgren A. Neuron-specific enolase expression and neuroendocrine differentiation in carcinomas of the breast. Arch Pathol Lab Med 1987, **111:** 830–832.

Metaplastic carcinoma

694 Adem C, Reynolds C, Adlakha H, Roche PC, Nascimento AG. Wide spectrum screening keratin as a marker of metaplastic spindle cell carcinoma of the breast: an immunohistochemical study of 24 patients. Histopathology 2002, **40:** 556–562.

695 Agnantis NT, Rosen PP. Mammary carcinoma with osteoclast-like giant cells. A study of eight cases with follow-up data. Am J Clin Pathol 1979, **72:** 383–389.

696 Banerjee SS, Eyden BP, Wells S, McWilliam LJ, Harris M. Pseudoangiosarcomatous carcinoma. A clinicopathological study of seven cases. Histopathology 1992, **21:** 13–23.

696a Darsky SH, Shanmugasundaram G, Wu D. Metaplastic carcinoma, matrix-producing type (Matrix producing carcinomas) of the breast exhibit a myoepithelial histogenesis (Abstract). Mod Pathol 2003, **16:** 23a.

696b Carter MR, Lester S, Fletcher CDM. Metaplastic (spindle cell/sarcomatoid) carcinoma of the breast: analysis of 32 cases with evidence of aggressive behaviour (Abstract). Mod Pathol 2003, **16:** 24a.

697 Chhieng C, Cranor M, Lesser ME, Rosen PP. Metaplastic carcinoma of the breast with osteocartilaginous heterologous elements. Am J Surg Pathol 1998, **22:** 188–194.

698 Denley H, Pinder SE, Tan PH, Sim CS, Brown R, Barker T, Gearty J, Elston CW, Ellis IO. Metaplastic carcinoma of the breast arising within complex sclerosing lesion: a report of five cases. Histopathology 2000, **36:** 203–209.

698a Dunne B, Lee AHS, Pinder SE, Bell JA, Ellis IO. An immunohistochemcial study of metaplastic spindle cell carcinoma, phyllodes tumor and fibromatosis of the breast. Hum Pathol 2003, **34:** 1009–1015.

699 Eusebi V, Cattani MG, Ceccarelli C, Lamovec J. Sarcomatoid carcinomas of the breast. An immunohistochemical study of 14 cases. Progr Surg Pathol 1989, **10:** 83–100.

700 Foschini MP, Dina RE, Eusebi V. Sarcomatoid neoplasms of the breast. Proposed definitions for biphasic and monophasic sarcomatoid mammary carcinomas. Semin Diagn Pathol 1993, **10:** 128–136.

701 Gobbi H, Simpson JF, Borowsky A, Jensen RA, Page DL. Metaplastic breast tumors with a dominant fibromatosis-like phenotype have a high risk of local recurrence. Cancer 1999, **85:** 2170–2182.

701a Gobbi H, Simpson JF, Jensen RA, Olson SJ, Page DL. Metaplastic spindle cell breast tumors arising within papillomas, complex sclerosing lesions, and nipple adenomas. Mod Pathol 2003, **16**: 893–901.

702 Harris M, Persaud V. Carcinosarcoma of the breast. J Pathol 1974, **112**: 99–105.

703 Herrington CS, Tarin D, Buley I, Athanasou N. Osteosarcomatous differentiation in carcinoma of the breast. A case of "metaplastic" carcinoma with osteoclasts and osteoclast-like giant cells. Histopathology 1994, **24**: 282–285.

704 Holland R, van Haelst UJGM. Mammary carcinoma with osteoclast-like giant cells. Additional observations on six cases. Cancer 1984, **53**: 1963–1973.

705 Kaufman MW, Marti JR, Gallager HS, Hoehn JL. Carcinoma of the breast with pseudosarcomatous metaplasia. Cancer 1984, **53**: 1908–1917.

706 Nielsen BB, Kiaer HW. Carcinoma of the breast with stromal multinucleated giant cells. Histopathology 1985, **9**: 183–193.

707 Oberman HA. Metaplastic carcinoma of the breast. A clinicopathologic study of 29 patients. Am J Surg Pathol 1987, **11**: 918–929.

708 Pitts WC, Rojas VA, Gaffey MJ, Rouse RV, Esteban J, Frierson HF, Kempson RL, Weiss LM. Carcinomas with metaplasia and sarcomas of the breast. Am J Clin Pathol 1991, **95**: 623–632.

709 Raju GC, Wee A. Spindle cell carcinoma of the breast. Histopathology 1990, **16**: 497–499.

710 Reis-Filho JS, Milanezi F, Paredes J, Silva P, Pereira EM, Maeda SA, de Carvalho LV, Schmitt FC. Novel and classic myoepithelial/stem cell markers in metaplastic carcinomas of the breast. Appl Immunohistochem Mol Morphol 2003, **11**: 1–8.

711 Ruffolo EF, Koerner FC, Maluf HM. Metaplastic carcinoma of the breast with melanocytic differentiation. Mod Pathol 1997, **10**: 592–596.

712 Santeusanio G, Pascal RR, Bisceglia M, Costantino AM, Bosman C. Metaplastic breast carcinoma with epithelial phenotype of pseudosarcomatous components. Arch Pathol Lab Med 1988, **112**: 82–85.

713 Shin SJ, Kanomata N, Rosen PP. Mammary carcinoma with prominent cytoplasmic lipofuscin granules mimicking melanocytic differentiation. Histopathology 2000, **37**: 456–459.

714 Silver SA, Tavassoli FA. Pleomorphic carcinoma of the breast: clinicopathological analysis of 26 cases of an unusual high-grade phenotype of ductal carcinoma. Histopathology 2000, **36**: 505–514.

715 Simpson RH, Cope N, Skalova A, Michal M. Malignant adenomyoepithelioma of the breast with mixed osteogenic, spindle cell, and carcinomatous differentiation. Am J Surg Pathol 1998, **22**: 631–636.

716 Sneige N, Yaziji H, Mandavilli SR, Perez ER, Ordonez NG, Gown AM, Ayala A. Low-grade (fibromatosis-like) spindle cell carcinoma of the breast. Am J Surg Pathol 2001, **25**: 1009–1016.

717 Tavassoli FA. Classification of metaplastic carcinomas of the breast. Pathol Annu 1992, **27**(Pt 2): 89–119.

718 Tavassoli FA, Norris HJ. Breast carcinoma with osteoclastlike giant cells. Arch Pathol Lab Med 1986, **110**: 636–639.

719 Wada H, Enomoto T, Tsjuimoto M, Nomura T, Murata Y, Shroyer KR. Carcinosarcoma of the breast: molecular-biological study for analysis of histogenesis. Hum Pathol 1998, **29**: 1324–1328.

720 Wang X, Mori I, Tang W, Yang Q, Nakamura M, Nakamura K, Sato M, Sakurai T, Kennichi K. Metaplastic carcinoma of the breast: p53 analysis identified the same point mutation in the three histologic components. Mod Pathol 2001, **14**: 1183–1186.

721 Wargotz ES, Deos PH, Norris HJ. Metaplastic carcinomas of the breast. II. Spindle cell carcinoma. Hum Pathol 1989, **20**: 732–740.

722 Wargotz ES, Norris HJ. Metaplastic carcinomas of the breast. I. Matrix-producing carcinoma. Hum Pathol 1989, **20**: 628–635.

723 Wargotz ES, Norris HJ. Metaplastic carcinomas of the breast. III. Carcinosarcoma. Cancer 1989, **64**: 1490–1499.

724 Wargotz ES, Norris HJ. Metaplastic carcinoma of the breast. V. Metaplastic carcinoma with osteoclastic giant cells. Hum Pathol 1990, **21**: 1142–1150.

725 Weidner N. Malignant breast lesions that may mimic benign tumors. Semin Diagn Pathol 1995, **12**: 2–13.

726 Zhuang Z, Lininger RA, Man Y-G, Albuquerque A, Merino MJ, Tavassoli FA. Identical clonality of both components of mammary carcinosarcoma with differential loss of heterozygosity. Mod Pathol 1997, **10**: 354–362.

Squamous cell carcinoma and related tumors

727 Bauer TW, Rostock RA, Eggleston JC, Baral E. Spindle cell carcinoma of the breast. Four cases and review of the literature. Hum Pathol 1984, **15**: 147–152.

728 Drudis T, Arroyo C, Van Hoeven K, Cordon-Cardo C, Rosen PP. The pathology of low-grade adenosquamous carcinoma of the breast. An immunohistochemical study. Pathol Annu 1994, **29**(Pt 2): 181–197.

729 Eggers JW, Chesney TM. Squamous cell carcinoma of the breast. A clinicopathologic analysis of eight cases and review of the literature. Hum Pathol 1984, **15**: 526–531.

730 Eusebi V, Lamovec J, Cattani MG, Fedeli F, Millis RR. Acantholytic variant of squamous-cell carcinoma of the breast. Am J Surg Pathol 1986, **10**: 855–861.

731 Fisher ER, Palekar AS, Gregorio RM, Paulson JD. Mucoepidermoid and squamous cell carcinomas of breast with reference to squamous metaplasia and giant cell tumors. Am J Surg Pathol 1983, **7**: 15–27.

732 Foschini MP, Fulcheri E, Baraechini P, Ceccarelli C, Betts CM, Eusebi V. Squamous cell carcinoma with prominent myxoid stroma. Hum Pathol 1990, **21**: 859–865.

733 Gersell DJ, Katzenstein A-LA. Spindle cell carcinoma of the breast. A clinicopathologic and ultrastructural study. Hum Pathol 1981, **12**: 550–561.

734 Oberman HA. Metaplastic carcinoma of the breast. A clinicopathologic study of 29 patients. Am J Surg Pathol 1987, **11**: 918–929.

735 Rosen PP, Ernsberger D. Low-grade adenosquamous carcinoma. A variant of metaplastic mammary carcinoma. Am J Surg Pathol 1987, **11**: 351–358.

736 Toikkanen S. Primary squamous cell carcinoma of the breast. Cancer 1981, **48**: 1629–1632.

737 Wargotz ES, Norris HJ. Metaplastic carcinomas of the breast. IV. Squamous cell carcinoma of ductal origin. Cancer 1990, **65**: 272–276.

738 Woodard BH, Brinkhous AD, McCarty KS Sr, McCarty KS Jr. Adenosquamous differentiation in mammary carcinoma. An ultrastructural and steroid receptor study. Arch Pathol Lab Med 1980, **104**: 130–133.

Spread-related variants
Inflammatory carcinoma

739 Buzdar AU, Montague ED, Barker JL, Hortobagyi GN, Blumenschein GR. Management of inflammatory carcinoma of breast with combined modality approach. An update. Cancer 1981, **47**: 2537–2542.

740 Chang S, Parker SL, Pham T, Buzdar AU, Hursting SD. Inflammatory breast carcinoma incidence and survival: the surveillance, epidemiology, and end results program of the National Cancer Institute, 1975–1992. Cancer 1998, **82**: 2366–2372.

741 Chu AM, Wood WC, Doucette JA. Inflammatory breast carcinoma treated by radical radiotherapy. Cancer 1980, **45**: 2730–2737.

742 Ellis DL, Teitelbaum SL. Inflammatory carcinoma of the breast. A pathological definition. Cancer 1974, **33**: 1045–1047.

743 Fields JN, Kuske RR, Perez CA, Fineberg BB, Bartlett N. Prognostic factors in inflammatory breast cancer. Univariate and multivariate analysis. Cancer 1989, **63**: 1225–1232.

744 Lucas FV, Perez-Mesa C. Inflammatory carcinoma of the breast. Cancer 1978, **41**: 1595–1605.

745 Saltzstein SL. Clinically occult inflammatory carcinoma of the breast. Cancer 1974, **34**: 382–388.

746 Schafer P, Alberto P, Forni M, Obradovic D, Pipard G, Krauer F. Surgery as part of a combined modality approach for inflammatory breast carcinoma. Cancer 1987, **59**: 1063–1067.

Paget's disease

747 Ashikari R, Park K, Huvos AG, Urban JA. Paget's disease of the breast. Cancer 1970, **26**: 680–685.

748 Azzopardi JG, Eusebi V. Melanocyte colonization and pigmentation of breast carcinoma. Histopathology 1977, **1**: 21–30.

749 Bussolati G, Pich A. Mammary and extramammary Paget's disease. An immunocytochemical study. Am J Pathol 1975, **80**: 117–127.

750 Cohen C, Guarner J, De Rose PB. Mammary Paget's disease and associated carcinoma. An immunohistochemical study. Arch Pathol Lab Med 1993, **117**: 291–294.

751 de Potter CR, Eeckhout I, Schelfhout AM, Geerts ML, Roels HJ. Keratinocyte induced chemotaxis in the pathogenesis of Paget's disease of the breast. Histopathology 1994, **24**: 349–356.

752 Keatings L, Sinclair J, Wright C, Corbett IP, Watchorn C, Hennessy C, Angus B, Lennard T, Horne CH. c-erbB-2 oncoprotein expression in mammary and extramammary Paget's disease. An immunohistochemical study. Histopathology 1990, **17**: 243–247.

753 Kirkham N, Berry N, Jones DB, Taylor-Papadimitriou J. Paget's disease of the nipple. Immunohistochemical localization of milk fat globule membrane antigens. Cancer 1985, **55**: 1510–1512.

754 Lagios MD, Westdahl PR, Rose MR, Concannon S. Paget's disease of the nipple. Alternative management in cases without or with minimal extent of underlying breast carcinoma. Cancer 1984, **54**: 545–551.

755 Lundquist K, Kohler S, Rouse RV. Intraepidermal cytokeratin 7 expression is not restricted to Paget cells but is also seen in Toker cells and Merkel cells. Am J Surg Pathol 1999, **23**: 212–219.

756 Mai KT. Morphological evidence for field effect as a mechanism for tumour spread in mammary Paget's disease. Histopathology 1999, **35**: 567–576.

757 Marucci G, Betts CM, Golouh R, Peterse JL, Foschini MP, Eusebi V. Toker cells are probably precursors of Paget cell carcinoma: a morphological and ultrastructural description. Virchows Arch 2002, **441**: 117–123.

758 Meissner K, Riviere A, Haupt G, Loning T. Study of neu-protein expression in mammary Paget's disease with and without underlying breast carcinoma and in extramammary Paget's disease. Am J Pathol 1990, **137**: 1305–1309.

759 Mori O, Hachisuka H, Nakano S, Sasai Y, Shiku H. Expression of ras p21 in mammary and extramammary Paget's disease. Arch Pathol Lab Med 1990, **114**: 858–861.

760 Nagle RB, Lucas DO, McDaniel KM, Clark VA, Schmalzel GM. New evidence linking mammary and extramammary Paget cells to a common cell phenotype. Am J Clin Pathol 1985, **83**: 431–438.

761 Neubecker RD, Bradshaw RP. Mucin, melanin, and glycogen in Paget's disease of the breast. Am J Clin Pathol 1961, **36**: 40–53.

762 Ordóñez NG, Awalt H, Mackay B. Mammary and extramammary Paget's disease. An immunocytochemical and ultrastructural study. Cancer 1987, **59**: 1173–1183.

763 Paget J. On disease of the mammary areola preceding cancer of the mammary gland. St Barth Hosp Rep 1874, **10**: 87–89.

764 Paone JF, Baker RR. Pathogenesis and treatment of Paget's disease of the breast. Cancer 1981, **48**: 825–829.

765 Rayne SC, Santa Cruz DJ. Anaplastic Paget's disease. Am J Surg Pathol 1992, **16**: 1085–1091.

766 Sagebiel RW. Ultrastructural observations on epidermal cells in Paget's disease of the breast. Am J Pathol 1969, **57**: 49–64.

767 Shin SJ, Kanomata N, Rosen PP. Mammary carcinoma with prominent cytoplasmic lipofuscin granules mimicking melanocytic differentiation. Histopathology 2000, **37**: 456–459.

768 Sitakalin C, Ackerman AB. Mammary and extramammary Paget's disease. Am J Dermatopathol 1985, **7**: 335–340.

769 Toker C. Clear cells of the nipple epidermis. Cancer 1970, **25**: 601–610.

770 Vanstapel M-J, Gatter KC, DeWolf-Peeters C, Millard PR, Desmet VJ, Mason DY. Immunohistochemical study of mammary and extra-mammary Paget's disease. Histopathology 1984, **8**: 1013–1023.

771 Venkataseshan VS, Budd DC, Kim DU, Hutter RVP. Intraepidermal squamous carcinoma (Bowen's disease) of the nipple. Hum Pathol 1994, **25**: 1371–1374.

772 Wolber RA, Dupuis BA, Wick MR. Expression of c-erbB-2 oncoprotein in mammary and extramammary Paget's disease. Am J Clin Pathol 1991, **96**: 243–247.

Invasive lobular carcinoma (ILC)
Classic type

773 Acs G, Lawton TJ, Rebbeck TR, Li Volsi VA, Zhang PJ. Differential expression of E-cadherin in lobular and ductal neoplasms of the breast and its biologic and diagnostic implications. Am J Clin Pathol 2001, **115**: 85–98.

774 Di Costanzo D, Rosen PP, Gareen I, Franklin S, Lesser M. Prognosis in infiltrating lobular carcinoma. An analysis of "classical" and variant tumors. Am J Surg Pathol 1990, **14**: 12–23.

775 Domagala W, Harezga B, Szadowska A, Markiewski M, Weber K, Osborn M. Nuclear p53 protein accumulates preferentially in medullary and high-grade ductal but rarely in lobular breast carcinomas. Am J Pathol 1993, **142**: 669–674.

776 Fechner RE. Infiltrating lobular carcinoma without lobular carcinoma in situ. Cancer 1972, **29**: 1539–1545.

777 Goldstein NS, Bassi D, Watts JC, Layfield LJ, Yaziji H, Gown AM. E-cadherin reactivity of 95 non-invasive ductal and lobular lesions of the breast: implications for the interpretation of problematic lesions. Am J Clin Pathol 2001, **115**: 534–542.

778 Lehr H-A, Folpe A, Yaziji H, Kommoss F, Gown AM. Cytokeratin 8 immunostaining pattern and E-cadherin expression distinguish lobular from ductal breast carcinoma. Am J Clin Pathol 2000, **114**: 190–196.

779 Martinez V, Azzopardi JG. Invasive lobular carcinoma of the breast. Incidence and variants. Histopathology 1979, **3**: 467–488.

780 Silverstein MJ, Lewinsky BS, Waisman JR, Gierson ED, Colburn WJ, Senofsky GM, Gamagami P. Infiltrating lobular carcinoma. Is it different from infiltrating duct carcinoma? Cancer 1994, **73**: 1673–1677.

Pleomorphic lobular carcinoma

781 Frolik D, Caduff R, Varga Z. Pleomorphic lobular carcinoma of the breast: its cell kinetics, expression of oncogenes and tumour suppressor genes compared with invasive ductal carcinomas and classification infiltrating lobular carcinomas. Histopathology 2001, **39**: 503–513.

782 Middleton LP, Palacios DM, Bryant BR, Krebs P, Otis CN, Merino MJ. Pleomorphic lobular carcinoma: morphology, immunohistochemistry, and molecular analysis. Am J Surg Pathol 2000, **24**: 1650–1656.

breast cancer. Appl Immunohistochem Mol Morphol 2002, **10:** 40–46.

852 Smith KL, Robbins PD, Dawkins HJ, Papadimitriou JM, Redmond SL, Carrello S, Harvey JM, Sterrett GF. *c-erb*B-2 amplification in breast cancer. Detection in formalin-fixed, paraffin-embedded tissue by in situ hybridization. Hum Pathol 1994, **25:** 413–418.

853 Suo Z, Risberg B, Karlsson MG, Villman K, Skovlund E, Nesland JM. The expression of EGFR family ligands in breast carcinomas. Int J Surg Pathol 2002, **10:** 91–99.

854 Zhao J, Wu R, Au A, Marquez A, Yu Y, Shi Z. Determination of HER2 gene amplification by chromogenic in situ hybridization (CISH) in archival breast carcinoma. Mod Pathol 2002, **15:** 657–665.

Spread and metastases

855 Bitter MA, Fiorito D, Corkill ME, Huffer WE, Stemmer SM, Shpall EJ, Archer PG, Franklin WA. Bone marrow involvement by lobular carcinoma of the breast cannot be identified reliably by routine histological examination alone. Hum Pathol 1994, **25:** 781–788.

856 Braun S, Pantel K, Muller P, Janni W, Hepp F, Kentenich CR, Gastroph S, Wischnik A, Dimpfl T, Kindermann G, Riethmuller G, Schlimok G. Cytokeratin-positive cells in the bone marrow and survival of patients with stage I, II, or III breast cancer. N Engl J Med 2000, **342:** 525–533.

857 Brinkley D, Haybittle JL. The curability of breast cancer. Lancet 1975, **2:** 95–97.

858 Chaubert P, Hurlimann J. Mammary origin of metastases. Immunohistochemical determination. Arch Pathol Lab Med 1992, **116:** 1181–1188.

859 Cifuentes N, Pickren JW. Metastases from carcinoma of mammary gland. An autopsy study. J Surg Oncol 1979, **11:** 193–205.

859a Cohn M, Middleton L, Valero V, Sahin A. Gastrointestinal metastases of carcinoma of the breast (Abstract). Mod Pathol 2003, **16:** 26a.

860 Connolly JL, Schnitt SJ. Evaluation of breast biopsy specimens in patients considered for treatment by conservative surgery and radiation therapy for early breast cancer. Pathol Annu 1988, **23**(Pt 1): 1–23.

861 Cote RJ, Rosen PP, Hakes TB, Sedira M, Bazinet M, Kinne DW, Old LJ, Osborne MP. Monoclonal antibodies detect occult breast carcinoma metastases in the bone marrow of patients with early stage disease. Am J Surg Pathol 1988, **12:** 333–340.

862 Cummings OW, Mazur MT. Breast carcinoma diffusely metastatic to the spleen. A report of two cases presenting as idiopathic thrombocytopenic purpura. Am J Clin Pathol 1992, **97:** 484–489.

863 Damiani S, Peterse JL, Eusebi V. Malignant neoplasms infiltrating "pseudoangiomatous" stromal hyperplasia of the breast: an unrecognised pathway of tumour spread. Histopathology 2002, **41:** 208–215.

864 Datta YH, Adams PT, Drobyski WR, Ethier SP, Terry VH, Roth MS. Sensitive detection of occult breast cancer by the reverse-transcriptase polymerase chain reaction. J Clin Oncol 1994, **12:** 475–482.

865 Donegan WL. The influence of untreated internal mammary metastases upon the course of mammary cancer. Cancer 1977, **39:** 533–538.

866 Fisher B, Montague E, Redmond C, Barton B, Borland D, Fisher ER, Deutsch M, Schwarz G, Margolese R, Donegan W, Volk H, Honvolinka C, Gardner B, Cohn I Jr, Lesnick G, Cruz AB, Lawrence W, Nealon T, Butcher H, Lawton R. Comparison of radical mastectomy with alternative treatments for primary breast cancer. A first report of results from a prospective randomized clinical trial. Cancer 1977, **39:** 2827–2839.

867 Gagnon Y, Tetu B. Ovarian metastases of breast carcinoma. A clinicopathologic study of 59 cases. Cancer 1989, **64:** 892–898.

868 Gal S, Fidler C, Lo YM, Chin K, Moore J, Harris AL, Wainscoat JS. Detection of mammoglobin mRNA in the plasma of breast cancer patients. Ann NY Acad Sci 2001, **945:** 192–194.

869 Gilliland MD, Barton RM, Copeland EM III. The implications of local recurrence of breast cancer as the first site of therapeutic failure. Ann Surg 1983, **197:** 284–287.

870 Goldstein NS. Does the level of E-cadherin expression correlate with the primary breast carcinoma infiltration pattern and type of systemic metastases? Am J Clin Pathol 2002, **118:** 425–434.

871 Grunewald K, Haun M, Urbanek M, Fiegl M, Muller-Holzner E, Gunsilus E, Dunser M, Marth C, Gastl G. Mammaglobin gene expression: a superior marker of breast cancer cells in peripheral blood in comparison to epidermal-growth factor receptor and cytokeratin-19. Lab Invest 2000, **80:** 1071–1077.

872 Ingle JN, Tormey DC, Tan HK. The bone marrow examination in breast cancer. Diagnostic considerations and clinical usefulness. Cancer 1978, **41:** 670–674.

873 Jayson GC, Howell A, Harris M, Morgenstern G, Chang J, Ryder WD. Carcinomatous meningitis in patients with breast cancer. An aggressive disease variant. Cancer 1994, **74:** 3135–3141.

874 Johnson JE, Page DL, Winfield AC, Reynolds VH, Sawyers JL. Recurrent mammary carcinoma after local excision. A segmental problem. Cancer 1995, **75:** 1612–1618.

875 Koren R, Kyzer S, Paz A, Veltman V, Klein B, Gal R. Lymph node revealing solution: a new method for detection of minute axillary lymph nodes in breast cancer specimens. Am J Surg Pathol 1997, **21:** 1387–1390.

876 Lagios MD, Gates EA, Westdahl PR, Richards V, Alpert BS. A guide to the frequency of nipple involvement in breast cancer. A study of 149 consecutive mastectomies using a serial subgross and correlated radiographic technique. Am J Surg 1979, **138:** 135–142.

877 Lamovec J, Zidar A. Association of leptomeningeal carcinomatosis in carcinoma of the breast with infiltrating lobular carcinoma. An autopsy study. Arch Pathol Lab Med 1991, **115:** 507–510.

878 Landys K. Prognostic value of bone marrow biopsy in breast cancer. Cancer 1982, **49:** 513–518.

879 Lyda MH, Tetef M, Carter NH, Ikle D, Weiss LM, Arber DA. Keratin immunohistochemistry detects clinically significant metastasis in bone marrow biopsy specimens in women with lobular breast carcinoma. Am J Surg Pathol 2000, **24:** 1593–1599.

880 Merino MJ, LiVolsi VA. Signet ring carcinoma of the female breast. A clinicopathologic analysis of 24 cases. Cancer 1981, **48:** 1830–1837.

881 Merrill CF, Kaufman DI, Dimitrov NV. Breast cancer metastatic to the eye is a common entity. Cancer 1991, **68:** 623–627.

882 Miller RE. Breast cancer and meningioma. J Surg Oncol 1986, **31:** 182–183.

883 Monteagudo C, Merino MJ, La Porte N, Neumann RD. Value of gross cystic disease fluid protein-15 in distinguishing metastatic breast carcinomas among poorly differentiated neoplasms involving the ovary. Hum Pathol 1991, **22:** 368–372.

884 Morimoto T, Komaki K, Inui K, Umemoto A, Yamamoto H, Harada K, Inoue K. Involvement of nipple and areola in early breast cancer. Cancer 1985, **55:** 2459–2463.

885 Noguchi S, Aihara T, Nakamori S, Motomura K, Inaji H, Imaoka S, Koyama H. The detection of breast carcinoma micrometastases in axillary lymph nodes by means of reverse transcriptase-polymerase chain reaction. Cancer 1994, **74:** 1595–1600.

886 Ozbas S, Dafydd H, Purushotham AD. Bone marrow micrometastasis in breast cancer. Br J Surg 2003, **90:** 290–301.

887 Porro G, Menard S, Tagliabue E, Orefice S, Salvadori B,

Squicciarini P, Andreola S, Rilke F, Colnaghi MI. Monoclonal antibody detection of carcinoma cells in bone marrow biopsy specimens from breast cancer patients. Cancer 1988, **61**: 2407–2411.

888 Price JE. The biology of metastatic breast cancer. Cancer 1990, **66**: 1313–1320.

889 Rosen PP, Fracchia AA, Urban JA, Schattenfeld D, Robbins GF. "Residual" mammary carcinoma following simulated partial mastectomy. Cancer 1975, **35**: 739–747.

890 Schmidt WA, Boudoussquie AC, Vetto JT, Pommier RF, Alexander P, Thurmond A, Scanlan RM, Jones MK. Lymph nodes in the human female breast: a review of their detection and significance. Hum Pathol 2001, **32**: 178–187.

891 Sethi S, Carter D. Breast carcinoma associated with necrotic granulomas in axillary lymph nodes. Ann Diagn Pathol 1998, **2**: 370–376.

892 Veronesi U, Cascinelli N, Bufalino R, Morabito A, Greco M, Galluzzo D, Donne VD, DeLellis R, Piotti P, Sacchini V, Conti R, Clemente C. Risk of internal mammary lymph node metastases and its relevance on prognosis of breast cancer patients. Ann Surg 1983, **198**: 681–684.

893 Veronesi U, Marubini E, Del Vecchio M, Manzari A, Andreola S, Greco M, Luini A, Merson M, Saccozzi R, Rilke F, Salvadori B. Local recurrences and distant metastases after conservative breast cancer treatments: partly independent events. J Natl Cancer Inst 1995, **87**: 19–27.

894 Wertheim U, Ozzello L. Neoplastic involvement of nipple and skin flap in carcinoma of the breast. Am J Surg Pathol 1980, **4**: 543–549.

Occult breast carcinoma

895 Ashikari R, Rosen PP, Urban JA, Senoo T. Breast cancer presenting as an axillary mass. Ann Surg 1976, **183**: 415–417.

895a Ishag MT, Baschinsky DY, Beliava IV, Niemann TH, Marsh WL Jr. Pathologic findings in reduction mammaplasty specimens. Am J Clin Pathol 2003, **120**: 377–380.

896 Lloyd MS, Nash AG. "Occult" breast cancer. Ann R Coll Surg Engl 2001, **83**: 420–424.

897 Merson M, Andreola S, Galimberti V, Bufalino R, Marchini S, Veronesi U. Breast carcinoma presenting as axillary metastases without evidence of a primary tumor. Cancer 1992, **70**: 504–508.

898 Rosen PP, Kimmel M. Occult breast carcinoma presenting with axillary lymph node metastases. A follow-up study of 48 patients. Hum Pathol 1990, **21**: 518–523.

Sentinel lymph node

899 Allred DC, Elledge RM. Caution concerning micrometastatic breast carcinoma in sentinel lymph nodes. Cancer 1999, **86**: 905–907.

900 Beach RA, Lawson D, Waldrop SM, Cohen C. Rapid immunohistochemistry for cytokeratin in the intraoperative evaluation of sentinel lymph nodes for metastatic breast carcinoma. Appl Immunohistochem Mol Morphol 2003, **11**: 45–50.

901 Carter BA, Jensen RA, Simpson JF, Page DL. Benign transport of breast epithelium into axillary lymph nodes after biopsy. Am J Clin Pathol 2000, **113**: 259–265.

902 Cohen C, Alazraki N, Styblo T, Waldrop SM, Grant SF, Larsen T. Immunohistochemical evaluation of sentinel lymph nodes in breast carcinoma patients. Appl Immunohistochem Mol Morphol 2002, **10**: 296–303.

903 Creager AJ, Geisinger KR. Intraoperative evaluation of sentinel lymph nodes for breast carcinoma: current methodologies. Adv Anat Pathol 2002, **9**: 233–243.

904 Diaz LK, Hunt K, Ames F, Meric F, Kuerer H, Babiera G, Ross M, Singletary E, Middleton LP, Symmans WF, Kirshnamurthy S, Sahin A, Sneige N, Gilcrease MZ. Histologic localization of

905 Freneaux P, Nos C, Vincent-Salomon A, Genin P, Sigal-Zafrani B, Al Ghuzian A, Birolini MJ, Clough K, Sastre-Garau X. Histological detection of minimal metastatic involvement in axillary sentinel nodes: a rational basis for a sensitive methodology usable in daily practice. Mod Pathol 2002, **15**: 641–646.

906 Jani AB, Basu A, Heimann R, Hellman S. Sentinel lymph node versus axillary lymph node dissection for early-stage breast carcinoma: a comparison using a utility-adjusted number needed to treat analysis. Cancer 2003, **97**: 359–366.

907 Krag D, Weaver D, Ashikaga T, Moffat F, Klimberg VS, Shriver C, Feldman S, Kusminsky R, Gadd M, Kuhn J, Harlow S, Beitsch P. The sentinel node in breast: a multicenter validation study. N Engl J Med 1998, **339**: 941–946.

908 McMasters KM, Giuliano AE, Ross MI, Reintgen DS, Hunt KK, Byrd DR, Klimberg VS, Whitworth PW, Tafra LC, Edwards MJ. Sentinel-lymph-node biopsy for breast cancer – not yet the standard of care. N Engl J Med 1998, **339**: 990–995.

909 Maiorano E, Massarol GM, Pruneri G, Mastropasqua MG, Zurrida S, Orvieto E, Viale G. Ectopic breast tissue as a possible cause of false-positive axillary sentinel lymph node biopsies. Am J Surg Pathol 2003, **27**: 513–518.

910 Reintgen D, Giuliano R, Cox CE. Sentinel node biopsy in breast cancer: an overview. Breast J 2000, **6**: 299–305.

911 Schwartz GF, Giuliano AE, Veronesi U; Consensus Conference Committee. Proceedings of the consensus conference on the role of sentinel lymph node biopsy in carcinoma of the breast, April 19 to 22, 2001, Philadelphia, Pennsylvania. Hum Pathol 2002, **33**: 579–589.

912 Silverberg SG. Sentinel node processing: recommendations for pathologists. Am J Surg Pathol 2002, **26**: 383–385.

913 Taback B, Hashimoto K, Kuo CT, Chan A, Giuliano AE, Hoon DS. Molecular lymphatic mapping of the sentinel lymph node. Am J Pathol 2002, **161**: 1153–1161.

914 Turner RR, Ollila DW, Stern S, Giuliano AE. Optimal histopathologic examination of the sentinel lymph node for breast carcinoma staging. Am J Surg Pathol 1999, **23**: 263–267.

915 Veronesi U, Paganelli G, Viale G, Galimberti V, Luini A, Zurrida S, Robertson C, Sacchini V, Veronesi P, Orvieto E, de Cicco C, Intra M, Tosi G, Scarpa D. Sentinel lymph node biopsy and axillary dissection in breast cancer: results in a large series. J Natl Cancer Inst 1999, **91**: 368–373.

916 Viale G, Bosari S, Mazzarol G, Galimberti V, Luini A, Veronesi P, Paganelli G, Bedoni M, Orvieto E. Intraoperative examination of axillary sentinel lymph nodes in breast carcinoma patients. Cancer 1999, **85**: 2433–2438.

916a Weaver DL. Sentinel lymph nodes and breast carcinoma. Which micrometastases are clinically significant? Am J Surg Pathol 2003, **27**: 842–845.

Staging and grading

917 Kinne DW. Staging and follow-up of breast cancer patients. Cancer 1991, **67**: 1196–1198.

Therapy

918 Bonadonna G, Valagussa P, Brambilla C, Moliterni A, Zambetti M, Ferrari L. Adjuvant and neoadjuvant treatment of breast cancer with chemotherapy and/or endocrine therapy. Semin Oncol 1991, **18**: 515–524.

919 Bonadonna G, Valagussa P, Moliterni A, Zambetti M, Brambilla C. Adjuvant cyclophosphamide, methotrexate, and fluorouracil in node-positive breast cancer. The results of 20 years of follow-up. N Engl J Med 1995, **332**: 901–906.

920 Bonadonna G, Veronesi U, Brambilla C, Ferrari L, Luini A, Greco M, Bartoli C, Coopmans de Yoldi G, Zucali R, Rilke F, et

Relationship of necrosis and tumor border to lymph node metastases and 10-year survival in carcinoma of the breast. Am J Surg Pathol 1978, **2**: 39–46.

990 Chung M, Chang HR, Bland KI, Wanebo HJ. Younger women with breast carcinoma have a poorer prognosis than older women. Cancer 1996, **77**: 97–103.

991 Clemente CG, Boracchi P, Andreola S, Del Vecchio M, Veronesi P, Rilke FO. Peritumoral lymphatic invasion in patients with node-negative mammary duct carcinoma. Cancer 1992, **69**: 1396–1403.

992 Cummings MC, Walsh MD, Hohn BG, Bennett IC, Wright RG, McGuckin MA. Occult axillary lymph node metastases in breast cancer do matter: results of 10-year survival analysis. Am J Surg Pathol 2002, **26**: 1286–1295.

993 Dalton LW, Page DL, Dupont WD. Histologic grading of breast carcinoma. A reproducibility study. Cancer 1994, **73**: 2765–2770.

994 Davis BW, Gelber R, Goldhirsch A, Hartmann WH, Hollaway L, Russell I, Rudensta CM. Prognostic significance of peritumoral vessel invasion in clinical trials of adjuvant therapy for breast cancer with axillary lymph node metastasis. Hum Pathol 1985, **16**: 1212–1218.

995 Davis BW, Gelber RD, Goldhirsch A, Hartmann WH, Locher GW, Reed R, Golouh R, Save-Soderbergh J, Holloway L, Russell I, Rudenstam CM. Prognostic significance of tumor grade in clinical trials of adjuvant therapy for breast cancer with axillary lymph node metastasis. Cancer 1986, **58**: 2662–2670.

996 Dawson PJ, Ferguson DJ, Karrison T. The pathologic findings of breast cancer in patients surviving 25 years after radical mastectomy. Cancer 1982, **50**: 2131–2138.

997 de Jong JS, van Diest PJ, Baak JP. Hot spot microvessel density and the mitotic activity index are strong additional prognostic indicators in invasive breast cancer. Histopathology 2000, **36**: 306–312.

998 Doglioni C, Dei Tos AP, Laurino L, Chiarelli C, Barbareschi M, Viale G. The prevalence of BCL-w immunoreactivity in breast carcinomas and its clinicopathological correlates with particular reference to oestrogen receptor status. Virchows Arch 1994, **424**: 47–52.

999 Domagala W, Lasota J, Dukowicz A, Markiewski M, Striker G, Weber K, Osborn M. Vimentin expression appears to be associated with poor prognosis in node-negative ductal NOS breast carcinomas. Am J Pathol 1990, **137**: 1299–1304.

1000 Domagala W, Striker G, Szadowska A, Dukowicz A, Weber K, Osborn M. Cathepsin D in invasive ductal NOS breast carcinoma as defined by immunohistochemistry. No correlation with survival at 5 years. Am J Pathol 1992, **141**: 1003–1012.

1001 Ellis GK, Gown AM. New applications of monoclonal antibodies to the diagnosis and prognosis of breast cancer. Pathol Annu 1990, **25**(Pt 2): 193–235.

1002 Elston CW, Ellis IO. Pathological prognostic factors in breast cancer. I. The value of histological grades in breast cancer. Experience from a large study with long-term follow-up. Histopathology 1991, **19**: 403–410.

1003 Fisher B, Bauer M, Wickerham L, Redmond CK, Fisher ER. Relation of number of positive axillary nodes to the prognosis of patients with primary breast cancer. An NSABP update. Cancer 1983, **52**: 1551–1557.

1004 Fisher B, Montague E, Redmond C, Barton B, Borland D, Fisher ER, Deutsch M, Schwarz G, Margolese R, Donegan W, Volk H, Honvolinka C, Gardner B, Cohn I Jr, Lesnick G, Cruz AB, Lawrence W, Nealon T, Butcher H, Lawton R. Comparison of radical mastectomy with alternative treatments for primary breast cancer. A first report of result from a prospective randomized clinical trial. Cancer 1977, **39**: 2827–2839.

1005 Fisher B, Redmond C, Poisson R, Margolese R, Wolmark N, Wickerham L, Fisher E, Deutsch M, Caplan R, Pilch Y, et al. Eight-year results of a randomized clinical trial comparing total mastectomy and lumpectomy with or without irradiation in the treatment of breast cancer. N Engl J Med 1989, **320**: 822–828.

1006 Fisher B, Slack NH, Bross IDJ. Cancer of the breast. Size of neoplasm and prognosis. Cancer 1969, **24**: 1071–1080.

1007 Fisher ER, Anderson S, Redmond C, Fisher B. Pathologic findings from the National Surgical Adjuvant Breast Project protocol B-06. 10-year pathologic and clinical prognostic discriminants. Cancer 1993, **71**: 2507–2514.

1008 Fisher ER, Anderson S, Tan-Chiu E, Fisher B, Eaton L, Wolmark N. Fifteen-year prognostic discriminants for invasive breast carcinoma: National Surgical Adjuvant Breast and Bowel Project Protocol-06. Cancer 2001, **91**: 1679–1688.

1009 Fisher ER, Costantino J, Fisher B, Redmond C. Pathologic findings from the National Surgical Adjuvant Breast Project (Protocol 4). Discriminants for 15-year survival. National Surgical Adjuvant Breast and Bowel Project Investigators. Cancer 1993, **71**: 2141–2150.

1010 Fisher ER, Gregorio R, Redmond C, Dekker A, Fisher B. Pathologic findings from the National Surgical Adjuvant Breast Project (Protocol No. 4). II. The significance of regional node histology other than sinus histiocytosis in invasive mammary cancer. Am J Clin Pathol 1976, **65**: 21–30.

1011 Fisher ER, Gregorio RM, Redmond C, Kim WS, Fisher B. Pathologic findings from the National Surgical Adjuvant Breast Project (Protocol No. 4). III. The significance of extranodal extension of axillary metastases. Am J Clin Pathol 1976, **65**: 439–444.

1012 Fisher ER, Kotwal N, Hermann C, Fisher B. Types of tumor lymphoid response and sinus histiocytosis. Arch Pathol Lab Med 1983, **107**: 222–227.

1013 Fisher ER, Redmond C, Fisher B, Bass G. Pathologic findings from the National Surgical Adjuvant Breast and Bowel Projects (NSABP). Prognostic discriminants for 8-year survival for node-negative invasive breast cancer patients. Cancer 1990, **65**: 2121–2128.

1014 Frierson HF Jr. Ploidy analysis and S-phase fraction determination by flow cytometry of invasive adenocarcinomas of the breast. Am J Surg Pathol 1991, **15**: 358–367.

1015 Frierson HF Jr, Wolber RA, Berean KW, Franquemont DW, Gaffey MJ, Boyd JC, Wilbur DC. Interobserver reproducibility of the Nottingham modification of the Bloom and Richardson histologic grading scheme for infiltrating ductal carcinoma. Am J Clin Pathol 1995, **103**: 195–198.

1016 Gallenberg MM, Loprinzi CL. Breast cancer and pregnancy. Semin Oncol 1989, **16**: 369–376.

1017 Garne JP, Aspegren K, Linell F, Rank F, Ranstam J. Primary prognostic factors in invasive breast cancer with special reference to ductal carcinoma and histologic malignancy grade. Cancer 1994, **73**: 1438–1448.

1018 Gasparini G, Weidner N, Bevilacqua P, Maluta S, Dalla Palma P, Caffo O, Barbareschi M, Boracchi P, Marubini E, Pozza F. Tumor microvessel density, p53 expression, tumor size, and peritumoral lymphatic vessel invasion are relevant prognostic markers in node-negative breast carcinoma. J Clin Oncol 1994, **12**: 454–466.

1019 Gilchrist KW, Gray R, Fowble B, Tormey DC, Taylor SG 4th. Tumor necrosis is a prognostic predictor for early recurrence and death in lymph node-positive breast cancer. A 10-year follow-up study of 728 Eastern Cooperative Oncology Group patients. J Clin Oncol 1993, **11**: 1929–1935.

1020 Gilliland MD, Barton RM, Copeland EM III. The implications of local recurrence of breast cancer as the first site of therapeutic failure. Ann Surg 1983, **197**: 284–287.

1021 Glaubitz LC, Bowen JH, Cox EB, McCarty KS Jr. Elastosis in human breast cancer. Correlation with sex steroid receptors and comparison with clinical outcome. Arch Pathol Lab Med 1984, **108**: 27–30.

1022 Goffin JR, Chappuis PO, Begin LE, Wong N, Brunet JS, Hamel N, Paradis AJ, Boyd J, Foulkes WD. Impact of germline BRCA1 mutations and overexpression of p53 on prognosis and response to treatment following breast carcinoma: 10-year follow-up data. Cancer 2003, **97**: 527–536.

1023 Goldstein NS. The significance of extracapsular axillary lymph node extension by metastatic breast cancer. Int J Surg Pathol 1995, **3**: 65–66.

1024 Guidi AJ, Fischer L, Harris JR, Schnitt SJ. Microvessel density and distribution in ductal carcinoma in situ of the breast. J Natl Cancer Inst 1994, **86**: 614–619.

1025 Hartveit F, Skjaerven R, Maehle BO. Prognosis in breast cancer patients with tumour cells in the efferent vessels of their axillary nodes. Pathology 1983, **139**: 379–382.

1026 Heintz NH, Leslie KO, Rogers LA, Howard PL. Amplification of the c-erb B-2 oncogene and prognosis of breast adenocarcinoma. Arch Pathol Lab Med 1990, **114**: 160–163.

1027 Henson DE, Ries L, Freedman LS, Carriaga M. Relationship among outcome, stage of disease, and histologic grade for 22,616 cases of breast cancer. The basis for a prognostic index. Cancer 1991, **68**: 2142–2149.

1028 Hilf R, Feldstein ML, Gibson SL, Savlov ED. The relative importance of estrogen receptor analysis as a prognostic factor for recurrence or response to chemotherapy in women with breast cancer. Cancer 1980, **45**: 1993–2000.

1029 Hultborn KA, Tornberg B. Mammary carcinoma. The biologic character of mammary carcinoma studied in 517 cases by a new form of malignancy grading. Acta Radiol (Stockh) 1960, **196**: 1–143.

1030 Hurlimann J. Prognostic value of p53 protein expression in breast carcinomas. Pathol Res Pract 1993, **189**: 996–1003.

1031 Hurlimann J, Larrinaga B, Vala DLM: bcl-2 protein in invasive ductal breast carcinomas. Virchows Archiv 1995, **426**: 163–168.

1032 Hutter RVP. The influence of pathologic factors on breast cancer management. Cancer 1980, **46**: 961–976.

1033 Huvos AG, Hutter RVP, Berg JW. Significance of axillary macrometastases and micrometastases in mammary cancer. Ann Surg 1971, **173**: 44–46.

1034 Jacobson JA, Danforth DN, Cowan KH, d'Angelo T, Steinberg SM, Pierce L, Lippman ME, Lichter AS, Glatstein E, Okunieff P. Ten-year results of a comparison of conservation with mastectomy in the treatment of stage I and II breast cancer. N Engl J Med 1995, **332**: 907–911.

1035 Jimenez RE, Wallis T, Visscher DW. Centrally necrotizing carcinomas of the breast: a distinct histologic subtype with aggressive clinical behaviour. Am J Surg Pathol 2001, **25**: 331–337.

1036 Joensuu H, Pylkkanen L, Toikkanen S. Bcl-2 protein expression and long-term survival in breast cancer. Am J Pathol 1994, **145**: 1191–1198.

1037 Kandalaft PL, Chang KL, Ahn CW, Traweek ST, Mehta P, Battifora H. Prognostic significance of immunohistochemical analysis of cathepsin D in low stage breast cancer. Cancer 1993, **71**: 2756–2763.

1038 Keyhani-Rofagha S, O'Toole RV, Farrar WB, Sickle-Santanello B, De Cenzo J, Young D. Is DNA ploidy an independent prognostic indicator in infiltrative node-negative breast adenocarcinoma? Cancer 1990, **65**: 1577–1582.

1039 Kister SJ, Sommers SC, Haagensen CD, Cooley E. Re-evaluation of blood vessel invasion as a prognostic factor in carcinoma of the breast. Cancer 1966, **19**: 1213–1216.

1040 Kouchoukos NT, Ackerman LV, Butcher HR Jr. Prediction of axillary nodal metastases from the morphology of primary mammary carcinomas. A guide to operative therapy. Cancer 1967, **20**: 948–960.

1041 Kujari HP, Collan YUI, Atkin NB. Use of the mitotic counts for the prognosis and grading of breast cancer. Pathol Res Pract 1994, **190**: 593–599.

1042 Lagios MD, Westdahl PR, Margolin FR, Rose MR. Duct carcinoma in situ. Relationship of extent of noninvasive disease to the frequency of occult invasion, multicentricity, lymph node metastases, and short-term treatment failures. Cancer 1982, **50**: 1309–1314.

1043 Lah TT, Kalman E, Najjar D, Gorodetsky E, Brennan P, Somers R, Daskal I. Cells producing cathepsins D, B, and L in human breast carcinoma and their association with prognosis. Hum Pathol 2000, **31**: 149–160.

1044 Laroye GJ, Minkin S. The impact of mitotic index on predicting outcome in breast carcinoma. A comparison of different counting methods in patients with different lymph node status. Mod Pathol 1991, **4**: 456–460.

1045 Lash RH, Bauer TW, Hermann RE, Esselstyn CB. Partial mastectomy. Pathologic findings and prognosis. Hum Pathol 1986, **17**: 813–822.

1046 Lash RH, Bauer TW, Medendorp SV. Prognostic significance of the proportion of intraductal and infiltrating ductal carcinoma in women treated by partial mastectomy. Surg Pathol 1990, **3**: 47–58.

1047 Lee AKC, DeLellis RA, Silverman ML, Wolfe HJ. Lymphatic and blood vessel invasion in breast carcinoma. A useful prognostic indicator? Hum Pathol 1986, **17**: 984–987.

1048 Leonard C, Corkill M, Tompkin J, Zhen B, Waitz D, Norton L, Kinzie J. Are axillary recurrence and overall survival affected by axillary extranodal tumor extension in breast cancer? Implications for radiation therapy. J Clin Oncol 1995, **13**: 47–53.

1049 Lewison EF, Montague ACW, Kuller L. Breast cancer treated at The Johns Hopkins Hospital, 1951–1956. Review of international ten-year survival rates. Cancer 1966, **19**: 1359–1368.

1149a Nonaka D, Rosai J, Spagnola D, Fiaccavento S, Bisceglia M. Cylindroma of the breast of skin adnexal type: a study of four cases. (in press).

1050 Lohrisch C, Jackson J, Jones A, Mates D, Olivotto IA. Relationship between tumor location and relapse in 6781 women with early invasive breast cancer. J Clin Oncol 2000, **18**: 2828–2835.

1051 Mambo NC, Gallager HS. Carcinoma of the breast. The prognostic significance of extranodal extension of axillary disease. Cancer 1977, **39**: 2280–2285.

1052 Mansour EG, Ravdin PM, Dressler L. Prognostic factors in early breast carcinoma. Cancer 1994, **74**: 381–400.

1053 Masters JRW, Millis RR, King RJB, Rubens RD. Elastosis and response to endocrine therapy in human breast cancer. Br J Cancer 1979, **39**: 536–539.

1054 Mate TP, Carter D, Fischer DB, Hartman PV, McKhann C, Merino M, Prosnitz LR, Weissberg JB. A clinical and histopathologic analysis of the results of conservation surgery and radiation therapy in stage I and II breast carcinoma. Cancer 1986, **58**: 1995–2002.

1055 Mauri FA, Girlando S, Dalla Palma P, Buffa G, Perrone G, Doglioni C, Kreipe H, Barbareschi M. Ki-67 antibodies (Ki-S5, MIB-1, and Ki-67) in breast carcinomas. A brief quantitative comparison. Appl Immunohistochem 1994, **2**: 171–176.

1056 Miremadi A, Pinder SE, Lee AHS, Bell JA, Paish EC, Wencyk P, Elston CW, Nicholson RI, Blamey RW, Robertson JF, Ellis IO. Neuroendocrine differentiation and prognosis in breast adenocarcinoma. Histopathology 2002, **40**: 215–222.

1057 Mori I, Yang Q, Kukudo K. Predictive and prognostic markers for invasive breast cancer. Pathol Int 2002, **52**: 186–194.

1058 Muss HB, Thor AD, Berry DA, Kute T, Liu ET, Koerner F, Cirrincione CT, Budman DR, Wood WC, Barcos M, et al. c-erbB-2 expression and response to adjuvant therapy in women with node-positive early breast cancer. N Engl J Med 1994, **330**: 1260–1266.

1059 Nime FA, Rosen PP, Thaler HT, Ashikari R, Urban JA.

Prognostic significance of tumor emboli in intramammary lymphatics in patients with mammary carcinoma. Am J Surg Pathol 1977, **1**: 25–30.

1060 Nixon AJ, Neuberg D, Hayes DF, Gelman R, Connolly JL, Schnitt S, Abner A, Recht A, Vicini F, Harris JR. Relationship of patient age to pathologic features of the tumor and prognosis for patients with stage I or II breast cancer. J Clin Oncol 1994, **12**: 888–894.

1061 Noguchi M, Ohta N, Koyasaki N, Taniya T, Miyazaki I, Mizukami Y. Reappraisal of internal mammary node metastases as a prognostic factor in patients with breast cancer. Cancer 1991, **68**: 1918–1925.

1062 Otis CN, Krebs PA, Albuquerque A, Quezado MM, San Juan X, Sobel ME, Merino MJ. Loss of heterozygosity of p53, BRCA1, VHL, and estrogen receptor genes in breast carcinoma: correlation with related protein products and morphologic features. Int J Surg Pathol 2002, **10**: 237–245.

1063 Page DL. Prognosis and breast cancer. Recognition of lethal and favorable prognostic types. Am J Surg Pathol 1991, **15**: 334–349.

1063a Page DL. Special types of invasive breast cancer, with clinical implications. Am J Surg Pathol 2003, **27**: 832–835.

1064 Page DL, Dupont WD. Breast cancer angiogenesis. Through a narrow window. JNCI 1992, **84**: 1850–1851.

1065 Page DL, Ellis IO, Elston CW. Histologic grading of breast cancer. Let's do it (editorial). Am J Clin Pathol 1995, **103**: 123–124.

1066 Perou CM, Serlie T, Elsen MB, van de Rijn M, Jeffrey SS, Rees CA, Pollack JR, Ross DT, Johnsen H, Akslen LA, Fluge O, Pergamenschikov A, Williams C, Zhu SX, Lenning PE. Molecular portraits of human breast tumors. Nature 2000, **406**: 747–752.

1067 Peters MV. The effect of pregnancy on breast cancer. In Forrest APM, Kunkler PB (eds): Prognostic factors in breast carcinoma. Baltimore, 1968, Williams & Wilkins.

1068 Petrek JA, Dukoff R, Rogatko A. Prognosis of pregnancy-associated breast cancer. Cancer 1991, **67**: 869–872.

1069 Pienta KJ, Coffey DS. Correlation of nuclear morphometry with progression of breast cancer. Cancer 1991, **68**: 2012–2016.

1070 Pinder SE, Ellis IO, Galea M, O'Rouke S, Blamey RW, Elston CW. Pathological prognostic factors in breast cancer. III. Vascular invasion. Relationship with recurrence and survival in a large study with long-term follow-up. Histopathology 1994, **24**: 41–47.

1071 Press MF, Bernstein L, Thomas PA, Meisner LF, Zhou JY, Ma Y, Hung G, Robinson RA, Harris C, El-Naggar A, Slamon DJ, Phillips RN, Ross JS, Wolman SR, Flom KJ. HER-2/neu gene amplification characterized by fluorescence in situ hybridisation: poor prognosis in node-negative breast carcinomas. J Clin Oncol 1997, **15**: 2894–2904.

1072 Quiet CA, Ferguson DJ, Weichselbaum RR, Hellman S. Natural history of node-negative breast cancer. A study of 826 patients with long-term follow-up. J Clin Oncol 1995, **13**: 1144–1151.

1073 Ravdin PM, Tandon AK, Allred DC, Clark GM, Fuqua SA, Hilsenbeck SH, Chamness GC, Osborne CK. Cathepsin D by Western blotting and immunohistochemistry. Failure to confirm correlations with prognosis in node-negative breast cancer. J Clin Oncol 1994, **12**: 467–474.

1074 Reed W, Hannidal E, Boehler PJ, Gunderson S, Host H, Marthin J. The prognostic value of p53 and c-erb B-2 immunostaining is overrated for patients with lymph node negative breast carcinoma: a multivariate analysis of prognostic factors in 613 patients with a follow-up of 14-30 years. Cancer 2000, **88**: 804–813.

1074a Reed W, Sandstad B, Holm R, Nesland JM. The prognostic impact of hormone receptors and c-erbB-2 in pregnancy-associated breast cancer and their correlation with BRCA1 and cell cycle modulators. Int J Surg Pathol 2003, **11**: 485–488.

1075 Robbins P, Pinder S, de Klerk N, Dawkins H, Harvey J, Sterrett G, Ellis I, Elston C. Histological grading of breast carcinomas. A study of interobseryer agreement. Hum Pathol 1995, **26**: 873–879.

1076 Robson M. Are BRCA1- and BRCA2-associated breast cancers different? Prognosis of BRCA1-associated breast cancer. J Clin Oncol 2000, **18**: 113S–118S.

1077 Rosen PP, Groshen S, Kinne DW, Norton L. Factors influencing prognosis in node-negative breast carcinoma. Analysis of 767 T1N0M0/T2N0M0 patients with long-term follow-up. J Clin Oncol 1993, **11**: 2090–2100.

1078 Rosen PP, Lesser ML, Kinne DW, Beattie EJ. Breast carcinoma in women 35 years of age or younger. Ann Surg 1984, **199**: 133–142.

1079 Rosen PP, Lesser ML, Arroyo CD, Cranor M, Borgen P, Norton L. p53 in node-negative breast carcinoma. An immunohistochemical study of epidemiologic risk factors, histologic features, and prognosis. J Clin Oncol 1995, **13**: 821–830.

1080 Rosen PP, Lesser ML, Arroyo CD, Cranor M, Borgen P, Norton L. Immunohistochemical detection of HER2/neu in patients with axillary lymph node-negative breast carcinoma. A study of epidemiologic risk factors, histologic features, and prognosis. Cancer 1995, **75**: 1320–1326.

1081 Rosen PP, Saigo PE, Braun DW, Weathers E, Fracchia AA, Kinne DW. Axillary micro- and macrometastases in breast cancer. Prognostic significance of tumor size. Ann Surg 1981, **196**: 585–591.

1082 Roses DF, Bell DA, Flotte TJ, Taylor R, Ratech H, Dubin N. Pathologic predictors of recurrence in stage 1 (TINOMO) breast cancer. Am J Clin Pathol 1982, **78**: 817–820.

1083 Rosner D, Lane WW. Oral contraceptive use has no adverse effect on the prognosis of breast cancer. Cancer 1986, **57**: 591–596.

1084 Russo J, Frederick J, Ownby HE, Fine G, Hussain M, Kirckstein HI, Robbins TO, Rosenberg B. Predictors of recurrence and survival of patients with breast cancer. Am J Clin Pathol 1987, **88**: 123–131.

1085 Sahin AA, Ro J, Ro JY, Blick MB, el-Naggar AK, Ordonez NG, Fritsche HA, Smith TL, Hortobagyi GN, Ayala AG. Ki-67 immunostaining in node-negative stage I/II breast carcinoma. Significant correlation with prognosis. Cancer 1991, **68**: 549–557.

1086 Sahin AA, Sneige N, Ordonez NG, Singletary SE, Ro JY, El Naggar AK, Ayala AG. Immunohistochemical assessment of cathepsin D in stages I and II node-negative breast cancer. Appl Immunohistochem 1994, **2**: 15–21.

1087 Saigo P, Rosen PP. Prognostic factors in invasive mammary carcinomas 1.0 cm or less in diameter (abstract). Am J Clin Pathol 1980, **73**: 303–304.

1087a Schnitt SJ. Risk factors for local recurrence in patients with invasive breast cancer and negative surgical margins of excision: where are we and where are we going? Am J Clin Pathol 2003, **120**: 485–488.

1088 Sears HF, Janus C, Levy W, Hopson R, Creech R, Grotzinger P. Breast cancer without axillary metastases. Are there high-risk biologic subpopulations? Cancer 1982, **50**: 1820–1827.

1089 Seidman H, Gelb SK, Silverberg E, LaVerda N, Lubera JA. Survival experience in the breast cancer detection demonstration project. CA Cancer J Clin 1987, **37**: 258–290.

1090 Seidman JD, Schnaper LA, Aisner SC. Relationship of the size of the invasive component of the primary breast carcinoma to axillary lymph node metastasis. Cancer 1995, **75**: 65–71.

1091 Sigurdsson H, Baldetorp B, Borg A, Dalberg M, Ferno M, Killander D, Olsson H. Indicators of prognosis in node-negative breast cancer. N Engl J Med 1990, **322**: 1045–1053.

1092 Siitonen SM, Haapasalo HK, Rantala IS, Helin HJ, Isola JJ. Comparison of different immunohistochemical methods in the assessment of angiogenesis. Lack of prognostic value in a group of 77 selected node-negative breast carcinomas. Mod Pathol 1995, **8**: 745–752.

1093   Simpson J, Page D. Prognostic value of histopathology in the breast. Semin Oncol 1992, **19**: 254–262.

1094   Simpson JF, Page DL. Status of breast cancer prognostication based on histopathologic data. Am J Clin Pathol 1994, **102**: S3–S8.

1095   Simpson JF, Page DL. Cellular proliferation and prognosis in breast cancer. Statistical purity versus clinical utility. Hum Pathol 1994, **25**: 331–332.

1096   Smith JA III, Gamez-Araujo J, Gallager HS, White EC, McBride CM. Carcinoma of the breast. Analysis of total lymph node involvement versus level of metastasis. Cancer 1977, **39**: 527–532.

1097   Tandon AK, Clark GM, Chammness GC, Chirgwin JM, McGuire WL. Cathepsin D and prognosis in breast cancer. N Engl J Med 1990, **322**: 297–302.

1098   Toikkanen S, Joensuu H, Klemi P. Nuclear DNA content as a prognostic factor in T1-2N0 breast cancer. Am J Clin Pathol 1990, **93**: 471–479.

1099   Tsakraklides V, Olson P, Kersey JH, Good RA. Prognostic significance of the regional lymph node histology in cancer of the breast. Cancer 1974, **34**: 1259–1266.

1100   Tsuda H, Hirohashi S, Shimosato Y, Hirota T, Tsugane S, Watanabe S, Terada M, Yamamoto H. Correlation between histologic grade of malignancy and copy number of c-erbB-2 gene in breast carcinoma. A retrospective analysis of 176 cases. Cancer 1990, **65**: 1794–1800.

1101   van de Rijn M, Perou CM, Tibshirani R, Haas P, Kallioniemi O, Kononen J, Torhorst J, Sauter G, Zuber M, Kochli OR, Mross F, Dieterich H, Seitz R, Ross D, Botstein D, Brown P. Expression of cytokeratins 17 and 5 identifies a group of breast carcinomas with poor clinical outcome. Am J Pathol 2002, **161**: 1991–1996.

1102   van der Linden JC, Baak JPA, Lindeman J, Smeulders AWM, Meyer CJLM. Carcinoembryonic antigen expression and peanut agglutinin binding in primary breast cancer and lymph node metastases. Lack of correlation with clinical, histopathological, biochemical and morphometric features. Histopathology 1985, **9**: 1051–1059.

1103   van de Vijver MJ, He YD, van't Veer LJ, Dai H, Hart AA, Voskuil DW, Schreiber GJ, Peterse JL, Roberts C, Marton MJ, Parrish M, Atsma D, Witteveen A, Glas A, Delahaye L, van der Velde T, Bartelink H, Rodenhuis S, Rutgers ET, Friend SH, Bernards R. A gene-expression signature as a predictor of survival in breast cancer. N Engl J Med 2002, **347**: 1999–2009.

1104   van Diest PJ, Baak JP. The morphometric prognostic index is the strongest prognosticator in premenopausal lymph node-negative and lymph node-positive breast cancer patients. Hum Pathol 1991, **22**: 326–330.

1105   van Diest PJ, Michalides RJ, Jannink I, van der Valk P, Peterse HL, de Jong JS, Meijer CJ, Baak JP. Cyclin D1 expression in invasive breast cancer correlations and prognostic value. Am J Pathol 1997, **150**: 705–711.

1106   van't Veer LJ, Dal H, van de Vijver MJ, He YD, Hart AA, Mao M, Peterse HL, van der Kooy K, Marton MJ, Witteveen AT, Schreiber GJ, Kerkhoven RM, Roberts C, Linsley PS, Bernards R, Friend SH. Gene expression profiling predicts clinical outcome of breast cancer. Nature 2002, **415**: 530–536.

1107   Vartanian RK, Weidner N. Correlation of intratumoral endothelial cell proliferation with microvessel density (tumor angiogenesis) and tumor cell proliferation in breast carcinoma. Am J Pathol 1994, **144**: 1188–1194.

1108   Vielh P, Chevillard S, Mosseri V, Donatini B, Magdelenat H. Ki67 index and S-phase fraction in human breast carcinomas.

Comparison and correlations with prognostic factors. Am J Clin Pathol 1990, **94**: 681–686.

1109   Visscher DW, Zarbo RJ, Greenawald KA, Crissman JD. Prognostic significance of morphological parameters and flow cytometric DNA analysis in carcinoma of the breast. Pathol Annu 1990, **25**(Pt 1): 171–210.

1110   Weidner N. Tumor angiogenesis. Review of current applications in tumor prognostication. Semin Diagn Pathol 1993, **10**: 302–313.

1111   Weidner N. Intratumor microvessel density as a prognostic factor in cancer. Am J Pathol 1995 **147**: 9–19.

1112   Weidner N, Folkman J, Pozza F, Bevilacqua P, Allred EN, Moore DH, Meli S, Gasparini G. Tumor angiogenesis. A new significant and independent prognostic indicator in early-stage breast carcinoma. J Natl Cancer Inst 1992, **84**: 1875–1887.

1113   Weidner N, Moore DH, Vartanian R. Correlation of Ki-67 antigen expression with mitotic figure index and tumor grade in breast carcinomas using the novel "paraffin"-reactive MIB1 antibody. Hum Pathol 1994, **25**: 337–342.

1114   Weidner N, Semple JP, Welch WR, Folkman J. Tumor angiogenesis and metastasis – correlation in invasive breast carcinoma. N Engl J Med 1991, **324**: 1–8.

1115   Wertheim U, Ozzello L. Neoplastic involvement of nipple and skin flap in carcinoma of the breast. Am J Surg Pathol 1980, **4**: 543–549.

1116   Wintzer HO, Zipfel I, Schulte-Monting J, Hellerich U, von Kleist S. Ki-67 immunostaining in human breast tumors and its relationship to prognosis. Cancer 1991, **67**: 421–428.

1117   Witzig TE, Gonchoroff NJ, Therneau T, Gilbertson DT, Wold LE, Grant C, Grande J, Katzmann JA, Ahmann DL, Ingle JN. DNA content flow cytometry as a prognostic factor for node-positive breast cancer. The role of multiparameter ploidy analysis and specimen sonication. Cancer 1991, **68**: 1781–1788.

1118   Witzig TE, Ingle JN, Cha SS, Schaid DJ, Tabery RL, Wold LE, Grant C, Gonchoroff NJ, Katzmann JA. DNA ploidy and the percentage of cells in S-phase as prognostic factors for women with lymph node negative breast cancer. Cancer 1994, **74**: 1752–1761.

1119   Wold LE, Ingle JN, Pisansky TM, Johnson RE, Donohue JH. Prognostic factors for patients with carcinoma of the breast. Mayo Clin Proc 1995, **70**: 678–679.

SALIVARY AND SWEAT GLAND-TYPE TUMORS (INCLUDING MYOEPITHELIAL TUMORS)

1119a   Acs G, Simpson JF, Bleiweiss IJ, Hugh J, Reynolds C, Olson S, Page DL. Microglandular adenosis with transition into adenoid cystic carcinoma of the breast. Am J Surg Pathol 2003, **27**: 1052–1060.

1120   Arpino G, Clark GM, Mohsin S, Bardou VJ, Elledge RM. Adenoid cystic carcinoma of the breast: molecular markers, treatment, and clinical outcome. Cancer 2002, **94**: 2119–2127.

1121   Ballance WA, Ro JY, el-Naggar AK, Grignon DJ, Ayala AG, Romsdahl MG. Pleomorphic adenoma (benign mixed tumor) of the breast. An immunohistochemical, flow cytometric, and ultrastructural study and review of the literature. Am J Clin Pathol 1990, **93**: 795–801.

1122   Begin LR, Mitmaker B, Bahary J-P. Infiltrating myofibroblastoma of the breast. Surg Pathol 1989, **2**: 151–156.

1123   Cavanzo FJ, Taylor HB. Adenoid cystic carcinoma of the breast. An analysis of 21 cases. Cancer 1969, **24**: 740–745.

1124   Chen KT. Pleomorphic adenoma of the breast. Am J Clin Pathol 1990, **93**: 792–794.

1125   Chen PC, Chen CK, Nicastri AD, Wait RB. Myoepithelial carcinoma of the breast with distant metastasis and accompanied by adenomyoepitheliomas. Histopathology 1994, **24**: 543–548.

1126   Damiani S, Eusebi V, Losi L, d'Adda T, Rosai J. Oncocytic carcinoma (malignant oncocytoma) of the breast. Am J Surg Pathol 1998, **22**: 221–230.

1127 Damiani S, Pasquinelli G, Lamovec J, Peterse JL, Eusebi V. Acinic cell carcinoma of the breast: an immunohistochemical and ultrastructural study. Virchows Arch 2000, **437**: 74–81.

1128 Diaz NM, McDivitt RW, Wick MR. Pleomorphic adenoma of the breast. A clinicopathologic and immunohistochemical study of 10 cases. Hum Pathol 1991, **22**: 1206–1214.

1129 Dina R, Eusebi V. Clear cell tumors of the breast. Semin Diagn Pathol 1997, **14**: 175–182.

1130 Domoto H, Terahata S, Sato K, Tamai S. Nodular hidradenoma of the breast: report of two cases with literature review. Pathol Int 1998, **48**: 907–911.

1131 Draheim JH, Neubecker RD, Sprinz H. An unusual tumor of the breast resembling eccrine spiradenoma. Am J Clin Pathol 1959, **31**: 511–516.

1132 Drudis T, Arroyo C, Van Hoeven K, Cordon-Cardo C, Rosen PP. The pathology of low-grade adenosquamous carcinoma of the breast. An immunohistochemical study. Pathol Annu 1994, **29**(Pt 2): 181–197.

1133 Erlandson RA, Rosen PP. Infiltrating myoepithelioma of the breast. Am J Surg Pathol 1982, **6**: 785–793.

1134 Finck FM, Schwinn CP, Keasby LE. Clear cell hidradenoma of the breast. Cancer 1968, **22**: 125–135.

1135 Fisher ER, Tavares J, Bulatao IS, Sass R, Fisher B, collaborating NSABP investigators. Glycogen-rich, clear cell breast cancer. With comments concerning other clear cell variants. Hum Pathol 1985, **16**: 1085–1090.

1136 Foschini MP, Eusebi V. Carcinomas of the breast showing myoepithelial cell differentiation. A review of the literature. Virchows Arch 1998, **432**: 303–310.

1137 Foschini MP, Pizzicannella G, Peterse JL, Eusebi V. Adenomyoepithelioma of the breast associated with low-grade adenosquamous and sarcomatoid carcinomas. Virchows Archiv 1995, **427**: 243–250.

1138 Gokaslan ST, Carlile B, Dudak M, Albores-Saavedra J. Solitary cylindroma (dermal analog tumor) of the breast: a previously undescribed neoplasm at this site. Am J Surg Pathol 2001, **25**: 823–826.

1139 Harris M. Pseudoadenoid cystic carcinoma of the breast. Arch Pathol Lab Med 1977, **101**: 307–309.

1140 Hayes MMM, Seidman JD, Ashton MA. Glycogen-rich clear cell carcinoma of the breast. A clinicopathologic study of 21 cases. Am J Surg Pathol 1995, **19**: 904–911.

1140a Hermann ME, Bratthauer G, Stamatakos MD, Matusik J, Tavassoli FA. Malignancies arising in adenomyoepithelioma (AME) of breast: clinical outcome and immunohistochemical characterization (Abstract). Mod Pathol 2003, **16**: 33a.

1141 Hull MT, Warfel KA. Glycogen-rich clear cell carcinomas of the breast. A clinicopathologic and ultrastructural study. Am J Surg Pathol 1986, **10**: 553–559.

1142 Jolicoeur F, Seemayer TA, Gabbiani G, Robidouz A, Gaboury L, Oligny LL, Schurch W. Multifocal, nascent, and invasive myoepithelial carcinoma (malignant myoepithelioma) of the breast: an immunohistochemical and ultrastructural study. Int J Surg Pathol 2002, **10**: 281–291.

1143 Jones MW, Norris HJ, Snyder RC. Infiltrating syringomatous adenoma of the nipple. A clinical and pathological study of 11 cases. Am J Surg Pathol 1989, **13**: 197–201.

1144 Kasami M, Olson SJ, Simpson JF, Page DL. Maintenance of polarity and dual cell population in adenoid cystic carcinoma of the breast: an immunohistochemical study. Histopathology 1998, **32**: 232–238.

1145 Kleer CG, Oberman HA. Adenoid cystic carcinoma of the breast: value of histologic grading and proliferative activity. Am J Surg Pathol 1998, **22**: 569–575.

1146 Koss LG, Brannan CD, Ashikari R. Histologic and ultrastructural features of adenoid cystic carcinoma of the breast. Cancer 1970, **26**: 1271–1279.

1147 Maiorano E, Ricco R, Virgintino D, Lastilla G. Infiltrating myoepithelioma of the breast. Appl Immunohistochem 1994, **2**: 130–136.

1148 Michal M, Baumruk L, Burger J, Manhalova M. Adenomyoepithelioma of the breast with undifferentiated carcinoma component. Histopathology 1994, **24**: 274–276.

1149 Moran CA, Suster S, Carter D. Benign mixed tumors (pleomorphic adenomas) of the breast. Am J Surg Pathol 1990, **14**: 913–921.

1149a Nonaka D, Rosai J, Spagnola D, Fiaccavento S, Bisceglia M. Cylindroma of the breast of skin adnexal type: a study of four cases. (in press).

1150 Patchefsky AS, Frauenhoffer CM, Krall RA, Cooper HS. Low-grade mucoepidermoid carcinoma of the breast. Arch Pathol Lab Med 1979, **103**: 196–198.

1151 Pauwels C, De Potter C. Adenomyoepithelioma of the breast with features of malignancy. Histopathology 1994, **24**: 94–96.

1152 Reis-Filho JS, Milanezi F, Paredes J, Silva P, Periera EM, Maeda SA, De Carvalho LV, Schmitt FC. Novel and classic myoepithelial/stem cell markers in metaplastic carcinoma of the breast. Appl Immunohistochem Mol Morphol 2003, **11**: 1–8.

1153 Ro JY, Silva EG, Gallager HS. Adenoid cystic carcinoma of the breast. Hum Pathol 1987, **18**: 1276–1281.

1154 Roncaroli F, Lamovec J, Zidar A, Eusebi V. Acinic cell-like carcinoma of the breast. Virchows Arch 1996, **429**: 69–74.

1155 Rosen PP. Adenomyoepithelioma of the breast. Hum Pathol 1987, **18**: 1232–1237.

1156 Rosen PP. Adenoid cystic carcinoma of the breast. A morphologically heterogeneous neoplasm. Pathol Annu 1989, **24**(Pt 2): 237–254.

1157 Schmitt FC, Ribeiro CA, Alvarenga S, Lopes JM. Primary acinic-like carcinoma of the breast – a variant with good prognosis. Histopathology 2000, **36**: 286–289.

1158 Schürch W, Potvin C. Malignant myoepithelioma (myoepithelial carcinoma) of the breast. An ultrastructural and immunocytochemical study. Ultrastruct Pathol 1985, **8**: 1–11.

1159 Shin SJ, Rosen PP. Solid variant of mammary adenoid cystic carcinoma with basaloid features: a study of nine case. Am J Surg Pathol 2002, **26**: 413–420.

1160 Simpson RH, Cope H, Skalova A, Michal M. Malignant adenomyoepithelioma of the breast with mixed osteogenic, spindle cell, and carcinomatous differentiation. Am J Surg Pathol 1998, **22**: 631–636.

1161 Smith BH, Taylor HB. The occurrence of bone and cartilage in mammary tumors. Am J Clin Pathol 1969, **51**: 610–618.

1162 Storensen FB, Paulsen SM. Glycogen-rich clear cell carcinoma of the breast. A solid variant with mucus. A light microscopic, immunohistochemical and ultrastructural study of a case. Histopathology 1987, **11**: 857–869.

1163 Subramony C. Bilateral breast tumors resembling syringocystadenoma papilliferum. Am J Clin Pathol 1987, **87**: 656–659.

1164 Suster S, Moran CA, Hurt MA. Syringomatous squamous tumors of the breast. Cancer 1991, **67**: 2350–2355.

1165 Tamai M. Intraductal growth of malignant mammary myoepithelioma. Am J Surg Pathol 1992, **16**: 1116–1125.

1166 Tavassoli FA. Myoepithelial lesions of the breast. Myoepitheliosis, adenomyoepithelioma, and myoepithelial carcinoma. Am J Surg Pathol 1991, **15**: 554–568.

1167 Tavassoli FA, Norris HJ. Mammary adenoid cystic carcinoma with sebaceous differentiation. A morphologic study of the cell types. Arch Pathol Lab Med 1986, **110**: 1045–1053.

1168 Toikkanen S, Joensuu H. Glycogen-rich clear-cell carcinoma of the breast. A clinicopathologic and flow cytometric study. Hum Pathol 1991, **22**: 81–83.

1169 Trendell-Smith NJ, Peston D, Shousha S. Adenoid cystic carcinoma of the breast: a tumor commonly devoid of oestrogen receptors and related proteins. Histopathology 1999, **35**: 241–248.

1170 Van Hoeven KH, Drudis T, Cranor ML, Erlandson RA, Rosen PP. Low-grade adenosquamous carcinoma of the breast. A clinicopathologic study of 32 cases with ultrastructural analysis. Am J Surg Pathol 1993, 17: 248–258.

1171 Ward BE, Cooper PH, Subramony C. Syringomatous tumor of the nipple. Am J Clin Pathol 1989, 92: 692–696.

1172 Wells CA, Nicoll S, Ferguson DJP. Adenoid cystic carcinoma of the breast. A case with axillary lymph node metastasis. Histopathology 1986, 10: 415–424.

1173 Wick MR, Ockner DM, Mills SE, Ritter JH, Swanson PE. Homologous carcinomas in the breast, skin, and salivary glands. A histologic and immunohistochemical comparison of ductal mammary carcinoma, ductal sweat gland carcinoma, and salivary duct carcinoma. Am J Clin Pathol 1998, 109: 75–84.

1174 Zarbo RJ, Oberman HA. Cellular adenomyoepithelioma of the breast. Am J Surg Pathol 1983, 7: 863–870.

STROMAL TUMORS AND TUMORLIKE CONDITIONS
Phylloides tumor

1175 Azzopardi JG. Problems in breast pathology. In Bennington JL (consulting ed.): Major problems in pathology. Philadephia, 1979, W.B. Saunders.

1176 Barnes L, Pietruszka M. Rhabdomyosarcoma arising within a cystosarcoma phylloides. Case report and review of the literature. Am J Surg Pathol 1978, 2: 423–429.

1177 Bernstein L, Deapen D, Ross RK. The descriptive epidemiology of malignant cystosarcoma phylloides tumors of the breast. Cancer 1993, 71: 3020–3024.

1178 Burga AM, Tavassoli FA. Periductal stromal tumor: a rare lesion with low-grade sarcomatous behaviour. Am J Surg Pathol 2003, 27: 343–348.

1179 Chaney AW, Pollack A, Mcneese MD, Zagars GK, Pisters PW, Pollock RE, Hunt KK. Primary treatment of cystosarcoma phylloides of the breast. Cancer 2000, 89: 1502–1511.

1180 Christensen L, Nielsen M, Madsen PM. Cystosarcoma phylloides. A review of 19 cases with emphasis on the occurrence of associated breast carcinoma. Acta Pathol Microbiol Immunol Scand (A) 1986, 94: 35–41.

1181 Cohn-Cedermark G, Rutqvist LE, Rosendahl I, Silfversward C. Prognostic factors in cystosarcoma phylloides. A clinicopathologic study of 77 patients. Cancer 1991, 68: 2017–2022.

1182 Dietrich CU, Pandis N, Rizou H, Petersen C, Bardi G, Qvist H, Apostolikas N, Bohler PJ, Andersen JA, Idvall I, Mitelman F, Heim S. Cytogenetic findings in phylloides tumors of the breast: Karyotypic complexity differentiates between malignant and benign tumors. Hum Pathol 1997, 28: 1379–1382.

1183 el-Naggar AK, Ro JY, McLemore D, Garnsy L. DNA content and proliferative activity of cystosarcoma phylloides of the breast. Potential prognostic significance. Am J Clin Pathol 1990, 93: 480–485.

1184 Fiks A. Cystosarcoma phylloides of the mammary gland. Müller's tumor. For the 180th birthday of Johannes Müller. Virchows Arch [A] 1981, 392: 1–6.

1185 Grimes MM, Lattes R, Jaretzki A III. Cystosarcoma phylloides. Report of an unusual case, with death due to intraneural extension to the central nervous system. Cancer 1985, 56: 1691–1695.

1186 Hart WR, Bauer RC, Oberman HA. Cystosarcoma phylloides. A clinicopathologic study of twenty-six hypercellular periductal stromal tumors of the breast. Am J Clin Pathol 1978, 70: 211–216.

1187 Kleer CG, Giordano TJ, Braun T, Oberman H. Pathologic, immunohistochemical, and molecular features of benign and malignant phylloides tumor of the breast. Mod Pathol 2001, 14: 185–190.

1188 Knudsen PJT, Ostergaard J. Cystosarcoma phylloides with lobular and ductal carcinoma in situ. Arch Pathol Lab Med 1987, 111: 873–875.

1189 Millar EK, Beretov J, Marr P, Sarris M, Clarke RA, Kersley JH, Lee CS. Malignant phylloides tumours of the breast display increased stromal p53 protein expression. Histopathology 1999, 34: 491–496.

1190 Moffat CJC, Pinder SE, Dixon AR, Elston CW, Blarney RW, Ellis IO. Phylloides tumours of the breast. A clinicopathological review of thirty-two cases. Histopathology 1995, 27: 205–218.

1191 Moore T, Lee AH. Expression of CD34 and bcl-2 in phylloides tumors, fibroadenomas and spindle cell lesions of the breast. Histopathology 2001, 38: 62–67.

1192 Nishimura R, Hasebe T, Imoto S, Mukai K. Malignant phylloides tumour with a non-invasive ductal carcinoma component. Virchows Arch 1998, 432: 89–93.

1193 Norris HJ, Taylor HB. Relationship of histologic features to behavior of cystosarcoma phylloides. Analysis of ninety-four cases. Cancer 1967, 20: 2090–2099.

1194 Palko MJ, Wang SE, Shackney SE, Cottington EM, Levitt SB, Hartsock RJ. Flow cytometric S fraction as a predictor of clinical outcome in cystosarcoma phylloides. Arch Pathol Lab Med 1990, 114: 949–952.

1195 Pietruszka M, Barnes L. Cystosarcoma phylloides. A clinicopathologic analysis of 42 cases. Cancer 1978, 41: 1974–1983.

1196 Powell CM, Rosen PP. Adipose differentiation in cystosarcoma phylloides. A study of 14 cases. Am J Surg Pathol 1994, 18: 720–727.

1197 Rajan PB, Cranor ML, Rosen PP. Cystosarcoma phylloides in adolescent girls and young women: a study of 45 patients. Am J Surg Pathol 1998, 22: 64–69.

1198 Reddick RL, Shin TK, Sawhney D, Siegal GP. Stromal proliferations of the breast. An ultrastructural and immunohistochemical evaluation of cystosarcoma phylloides, juvenile fibroadenoma, and fibroadenoma. Hum Pathol 1987, 18: 45–49.

1199 Reinfuss M, Mitus J, Duda K, Stelmach A, Rys J, Smolak K. The treatment and prognosis of patients with phylloides tumor of the breast: an analysis of 170 cases. Cancer 1996, 77: 910–916.

1200 Rhodes RH, Frankel KA, Davis RL, Tatter D. Metastatic cystosarcoma phylloides. A report of 2 cases presenting with neurological symptoms. Cancer 1978, 41: 1179–1187.

1201 Rosen PP, Romain K, Liberman L. Mammary cystosarcoma with mature adipose stromal differentiation (lipophylloides tumor) arising in a lipomatous hamartoma. Arch Pathol Lab Med 1994, 118: 91–94.

1202 Silver SA, Tavassoli FA. Osteosarcomatous differentiation in phylloides tumors. Am J Surg Pathol 1999, 23: 815–821.

1203 Tse GM, Lee CS, Kung FY, Scolyer RA, Law BK, Lau TS, Putti TC. Hormonal receptors expression in epithelial cells of mammary phylloides tumors correlates with pathologic grade of the tumor. A multicenter study of 143 cases. Am J Clin Pathol 2002, 118: 522–526.

1204 Tse GM, Putti TC, Kung FY, Scolyer RA, Law BK, Lau TS, Lee CS. Increase p53 protein expression in malignant mammary phylloides tumors. Mod Pathol 2002, 15: 734–740.

1205 Umekita Y, Yoshida H. Immunohistochemical study of hormone receptor and hormone-regulated protein expression in phylloides tumour: comparison with fibroadenoma. Virchows Arch 1998, 433: 311–314.

1206 Ward RM, Evans HL. Cystosarcoma phylloides. A clinicopathologic study of 26 cases. Cancer 1986, 58: 2282–2289.

1207 Yeh I-T, Francis DJ, Orenstein JM, Silverberg SG. Ultrastructure of cystosarcoma phylloides and fibroadenoma. A comparative study. Am J Clin Pathol 1985, 84: 131–136.

Vascular tumors

1208 Arias Stella J Jr, Rosen PP. Hemangiopericytoma of the breast. Mod Pathol 1988, 2: 98–103.

1209   Benda JA, Al-Jurf AS, Benson AB III. Angiosarcoma of the breast following segmental mastectomy complicated by lymphedema. Am J clin Pathol 1987, **87**: 651–655.

1209a   Billings SD, McKenney JK, Folpe AL, Weiss SW. Post-radiation cutaneous angiosarcoma of the breast, and analysis of 26 cases (Abstract). Mod Pathol 2003, **16**: 88a.

1209b   Branton PA, Lininger R, Tavassoli FA. Papillary endothelial hyperplasia of the breast: the great impostor for angiosarcoma. A clinicopathologic review of 17 cases. Int J Surg Pathol 2003, **11**: 83–87.

1210   Brentani MM, Pacheco MM, Oshima CTF, Nagai MA, Lemos LB, Góes JCS. Steroid receptors in breast angiosarcoma. Cancer 1983, **51**: 2105–2111.

1211   Chen KTK. Rare variants of benign vascular tumors of the breast. Surg Pathol 1991, **4**: 309–316.

1212   Donnell RM, Rosen PP, Lieberman PH, Kaufman RJ, Kay S, Braun DW Jr, Kinne DW. Angiosarcoma and other vascular tumors of the breast. Pathologic analysis as a guide to prognosis. Am J Surg Pathol 1981, **5**: 629–642.

1213   Fineberg S, Rosen PP. Cutaneous angiosarcoma and atypical vascular lesions of the skin and breast after radiation therapy for breast carcinoma. Am J Clin Pathol 1994, **102**: 757–763.

1214   Jozefczyk MA, Rosen PP. Vascular tumors of the breast. II. Perilobular hemangiomas and hemangiomas. Am J Surg Pathol 1985, **9**: 491–503.

1215   Lesueur GC, Brown RW, Bhathal PS. Incidence of perilobular hemangioma in the female breast. Arch Pathol Lab Med 1983, **107**: 308–310.

1216   Liberman L, Dershaw DD, Kaufman RJ, Rosen PP. Angiosarcoma of the breast. Radiology 1992, **183**: 649–654.

1217   Macias-Martinez V, Murrieta-Tiburcio L, Molina-Cardenas H, Donimguez-Malagon H. Epithelioid angiosarcoma of the breast: clinicopathological, immunohistochemical and ultrastructural study of a case. Am J Surg Pathol 1997, **21**: 599–604.

1218   Merino MJ, Carter D, Berman M. Angiosarcoma of the breast. Am J Surg Pathol 1983, **7**: 53–60.

1219   Mittal KR, Gerald W, True LD. Hemangiopericytoma of the breast. Report of a case with ultrastructural and immunohistochemical findings. Hum Pathol 1986, **17**: 1181–1183.

1220   Monroe AT, Feigenberg SJ, Mendenhall NP. Angiosarcoma after breast-conserving therapy. Cancer 2003, **97**: 1832–40.

1221   Otis CN, Peschel R, McKhann C, Merino MJ, Duray PH. The rapid onset of cutaneous angiosarcoma after radiotherapy for breast carcinoma. Cancer 1986, **57**: 2130–2134.

1222   Parham DH, Fisher C. Angiosarcoma of the breast developing post radiotherapy. Histopathology 1997, **31**: 189–195.

1223   Rosen PP. Vascular tumors of the breast. III. Angiomatosis. Am J Surg Pathol 1985, **9**: 652–658.

1224   Rosen PP. Vascular tumors of the breast. V. Nonparenchymal hemangiomas of mammary subcutaneous tissues. Am J Surg Pathol 1985, **9**: 723–729.

1225   Rosen PP, Ernsberger DL. Grading mammary angiosarcoma. Prognostic study of 62 cases (abstract). Lab Invest 1988, **58**: 78A.

1226   Rosen PP, Jozefczyk MA, Boram LH. Vascular tumors of the breast. IV. The venous hemangioma. Am J Surg Pathol 1985, **9**: 659–665.

1227   Rosen PP, Ridolfi RL. The perilobular hemangioma. A benign microscopic vascular lesion of the breast. Am J Clin Pathol 1977, **68**: 21–23.

1228   Rosso R, Gianelli U, Carnevali L. Acquired progressive lymphangioma of the skin following radiotherapy for breast carcinoma. J Cutan Pathol 1995, **22**: 164–167.

1229   Sieber PR, Sharkey FE. Cystic hygroma of the breast. Arch Pathol Lab Med 1986, **110**: 353.

1230   Steingaszner LC, Enzinger FM, Taylor HB. Hemangiosarcoma of the breast. Cancer 1965, **18**: 352–361.

1231   Yu GH, Fishman SJ, Brooks JS. Cellular angiolipoma of the breast. Mod Pathol 1993, **6**: 497–499.

Other malignant stromal tumors

1232   Arista-Nasr J, Gonzalez-Gomez I, Angeles-Angeles A, Illanes-Baz E, Brandt-Brandt H, Larriva-Sahd J. Primary recurrent leiomyosarcoma of the breast. Case report with ultrastructural and immunohistochemical study and review of the literature. Am J Clin Pathol 1989, **92**: 500–505.

1233   Austin RM, Dupree WB. Liposarcoma of the breast. A clinicopathologic study of 20 cases. Hum Pathol 1986, **17**: 906–913.

1234   Beltaos E, Banerjee TK. Chondrosarcoma of the breast. Report of two cases. Am J Clin Pathol 1979, **71**: 345–349.

1235   Callery CD, Rosen PP, Kinne DW. Sarcoma of the breast. A study of 32 patients with reappraisal of classification and therapy. Ann Surg 1985, **201**: 527–532.

1236   Chen KTK, Kuo T-T, Hoffmann KD. Leiomyosarcoma of the breast. A case of long survival and late hepatic metastasis. Cancer 1981, **47**: 1883–1886.

1237   Falconieri G, della Libera D, Zanconati F, Bittesini L. Leiomyosarcoma of the female breast. Report of two new cases and a review of the literature. Am J Clin Pathol 1997, **108**: 19–25.

1238   Fisher C, Magnusson B, Hardarson S, Smith ME. Myxoid variant of follicular dendritic cell sarcoma arising in the breast. Ann Diagn Pathol 1999, **3**: 92–98.

1239   Going JJ, Lumsden AB, Anderson TJ. A classical osteogenic sarcoma of the breast. Histology, immunohistochemistry and ultrastructure. Histopathology 1986, **10**: 631–641.

1240   Jones MW, Norris HJ, Wargotz ES, Weiss SW. Fibrosarcoma-malignant fibrous histiocytoma of the breast. A clinicopathological study of 32 cases. Am J Surg Pathol 1992, **16**: 667–674.

1241   Kyriazis AP, Kyriazis AA. Primary rhabdomyosarcoma of the female breast: report of a case and review of the literature. Arch Pathol Lab Med 1998, **122**: 747–749.

1242   Mazaki T, Tanak T, Suenaga Y, Tomioka K, Takayama T. Liposarcoma of the breast: a case report and review of the literature. Int Surg 2002, **87**: 164–170.

1243   Mogotlane L, Chetty R. Infiltrating ductal carcinoma of the breast with rhabdoid phenotype. Int J Surg Pathol 2001, **9**: 237–239.

1244   Norris HJ, Taylor HB. Sarcomas and related mesenchymal tumors of the breast. Cancer 1968, **22**: 22–28.

1245   Pollard SG, Marks PV, Temple LN, Thompson HH. Breast sarcoma. A clinicopathologic review of 25 cases. Cancer 1990, **66**: 941–944.

1246   Pruneri G, Masullo M, Renne G, Taccagni G, Manzotti M, Luini A, Vaile G. Follicular dendritic cell sarcoma of the breast. Virchows Arch 2002, **441**: 194–199.

1247   Sezer O, Jugovic D, Blohmer JU, Turzynski A, Thiel G, Langelotz C, Possinger K, Kovar H. CD99 positivity and EWS-FLI1 gene rearrangement identify a breast tumor in 60-year-old patient with attributes of the Ewing family of neoplasms. Diagn Mol Pathol 1999, **8**: 120–124.

1248   Silver SA, Tavassoli FA. Primary osteogenic sarcoma of the breast: a clinicopathologic analysis of 50 cases. Am J Surg Pathol 1998, **22**: 925–933.

1249   Smith BH, Taylor HB. The occurrence of bone and cartilage in mammary tumors. Am J Clin Pathol 1969, **51**: 610–618.

LYMPHOID TUMORS AND TUMORLIKE CONDITIONS

1250   Abbondanzo SL, Seidman JD, Lefkowitz M, Tavassoli FA, Krishnan J. Primary diffuse large B-cell lymphoma of the breast. A clinicopathologic study of 31 cases. Pathol Res Pract 1996, **192**: 37–43.

1251   Aguilera NS, Tavassoli FA, Chu WS, Abbondonzo SL.

T-cell lymphoma presenting in the breast: a histologic, immunophenotypic and molecular genetic study of four cases. Mod Pathol 2000, **13**: 599–605.

1252 Arber DA, Simpson JF, Weiss LM, Rappaport H. Non-Hodgkin's lymphoma involving the breast. Am J Surg Pathol 1994, **18**: 288–295.

1253 Bobrow LG, Richards MA, Happerfield LC, Diss TC, Isaacson PG, Lammie GA, Millis RR. Breast lymphomas. A clinicopathologic review. Hum Pathol 1993, **24**: 274–278.

1254 Brogi E, Harris NL. Lymphomas of the breast: pathology and clinical behaviour. Semin Oncol 1999, **26**: 357–364.

1255 Brooks JJ, Krugman DT, Damjanov I. Myeloid metaplasia presenting as a breast mass. Am J Surg Pathol 1980, **4**: 281–285.

1256 Byrd JC, Edenfield WJ, Shields DJ, Dawson NA. Extramedullary myeloid cell tumors in acute nonlymphocytic leukemia. A clinical review. J Clin Oncol 1995, **13**: 1800–1816.

1257 Cohen PL, Brooks JJ. Lymphomas of the breast. A clinicopathologic and immunohistochemical study of primary and secondary cases. Cancer 1991, **67**: 1359–1369.

1258 Cook PD, Osborne BM, Connor RL, Strauss JF. Follicular lymphoma adjacent to foreign body granulomatous inflammation and fibrosis surrounding silicone breast prosthesis. Am J Surg Pathol 1995, **19**: 712–717.

1259 Domchek SM, Hecht JL, Fleming MD, Pinkus GS, Cannellos GP. Lymphomas of the breast: primary and secondary involvement. Cancer 2002, **94**: 6–13.

1260 Farinha P, Andre S, Cabecadas J, Soares J. High frequency of MALT lymphoma in a series of 14 cases of primary breast lymphoma. Appl Immunohistochem Mol Morphol 2002, **10**: 115–120.

1261 Fisher ER, Palekar AS, Paulson JD, Golinger R. Pseudolymphoma of breast. Cancer 1979, **44**: 258–263.

1262 Hugh JC, Jackson FI, Hanson J, Poppema S. Primary breast lymphoma. An immunohistologic study of 20 new cases. Cancer 1990, **66**: 2602–2611.

1263 Kirshenbaum G, Rhone DP. Solitary extramedullary plasmacytoma of the breast with serum monoclonal protein. A case report and review of the literature. Am J Clin Pathol 1985, **83**: 230–232.

1264 Koerner FC, Mattia AR. Mammary lymphoid tissue: a unique component of the mucosal immune system. Anat Pathol 1996, **1**: 53–67.

1265 Lin JJ, Farha GJ, Taylor RJ. Pseudolymphoma of the breast. I. In a study of 8,654 consecutive tylectomies and mastectomies. Cancer 1980, **45**: 973–978.

1266 Lin Y, Govindan R, Hess JL. Malignant hematopoietic breast tumors. Am J Clin Pathol 1997, **107**: 177–186.

1267 Oberman HA. Primary lymphoreticular neoplasms of the breast. Surg Gynecol Obstet 1966, **123**: 1047–1051.

1268 Pascoe HR. Tumors composed of immature granulocytes occurring in the breast in chronic granulocytic leukemia. Cancer 1970, **25**: 697–704.

1269 Rooney N, Snead D, Goodman S, Webb AJ. Primary breast lymphoma with skin involvement arising in lymphocytic lobulitis. Histopathology 1994, **24**: 81–84.

1270 Schouten JT, Weese JL, Carbone PP. Lymphoma of the breast. Ann Surg 1981, **194**: 749–753.

1271 Topalovski M, Crisan D, Mattson JC. Lymphoma of the breast: a clinicopathologic study of primary and secondary cases. Arch Pathol Lab Med 1999, **123**: 1208–1218.

OTHER PRIMARY TUMORS AND TUMORLIKE CONDITIONS

1272 Abraham SC, Reynolds C, Lee JH, Montgomery EA, Baisden BL, Krasinskas AM, Wu TT. Fibromatosis of the breast and mutations involving the APC/beta-catenin pathway. Hum Pathol 2002, **33**: 39–46.

1273 Anderson C, Ricci A Jr, Pedersen CA, Cartun RW. Immunocytochemical analysis of estrogen and progesterone receptors in benign stromal lesions of the breast. Evidence for hormonal etiology in pseudoangiomatous hyperplasia of mammary stroma. Am J Surg Pathol 1991, **15**: 145–149.

1273a Bansal I, Alassi O, Lee MW, Raju U. Stromal proliferations of the breast, a histologic continuum in fibroadenoma, pseudoangiomatous stromal hyperplasia and gynecomastoid lesions: an immunohistochemical study (Abstract). Mod Pathol 2003, **16**: 23a.

1274 Berean K, Tron VA, Churg A, Clement PB. Mammary fibroadenoma with multinucleated stromal giant cells. Am J Surg Pathol 1986, **10**: 823–827.

1275 Bittesini L, Dei Tos AP, Doglioni C, Della Libera D, Laurino L, Fletcher CD. Fibroepithelial tumor of the breast with digital fibroma-like inclusions in the stromal component. Case report with immunocytochemical and ultrastructural analysis. Am J Surg Pathol 1994, **18**: 296–301.

1276 Carneiro F, Brandao O, Correia AC, Sobrinho-Simoes M. Spindle cell tumor of the breast. Ultrastruct Pathol 1989, **13**: 593–598.

1277 Charpin C, Mathoulin MP, Andrac L, Barberis J, Boulat J, Sarradour B, Bonnier P, Piana L. Reappraisal of breast hamartomas. A morphological study of 41 cases. Pathol Res Pract 1994, **190**: 362–371.

1278 Cohen MB, Fisher PE. Schwann cell tumors of the breast and mammary region. Surg Pathol 1991, **4**: 47–56.

1279 Damiani S, Dina R, Eusebi V. Eosinophilic and granular cell tumors of the breast. Sem Diagn Pathol 1999, **16**: 117–125.

1280 Damiani S, Koerner FC, Dickersin GR, Cook MG, Eusebi V. Granular cell tumour of the breast. Virchows Arch [A] 1992, **420**: 219–226.

1281 Damiani S, Peterse JL, Eusebi V. Malignant neoplasms infiltrating "pseudoangiomatous" stromal hyperplasia of the breast: an unrecognised pathway of tumour spread. Histopathology 2002, **41**: 208–215.

1282 Daroca PJ Jr, Reed RJ, Love GL, Kraus SD. Myoid hamartomas of the breast. Hum Pathol 1985, **16**: 212–219.

1283 Davies JD, Kulka J, Mumford AD, Armstrong JS, Wells CA. Hamartomas of the breast. Six novel diagnostic features in three-dimensional thick sections. Histopathology 1994, **24**: 161–168.

1284 Davis AB, Patchefsky AS. Basal cell carcinoma of the nipple. Case report and review of the literature. Cancer 1977, **40**: 1780–1781.

1285 Daya D, Trus T, D'Souza TJ, Minuk T, Yemen B. Hamartoma of the breast, an underrecognized breast lesion. A clinicopathologic and radiographic study of 25 cases. Am J Clin Pathol 1995, **103**: 685–689.

1286 DeMay RM, Kay S. Granular cell tumor of the breast. Pathol Annu 1982, **19**(Pt 2): 121–148.

1287 Devouassoux-Shisheboran M, Schammel MD, Man YG, Tavassoli FA. Fibromatosis of the breast: age-correlated morphological features of 33 cases. Arch Pathol Lab Med 2000, **124**: 276–280.

1288 Diaz-Arias AA, Hurt MA, Loy TS, Seeger RM, Bickel JT. Leiomyoma of the breast. Hum Pathol 1989, **20**: 396–399.

1289 Fisher CJ, Hanby AM, Robinson L, Millis RR. Mammary hamartoma – a review of 35 cases. Histopathology 1992, **20**: 99–106.

1290 Garfein CF, Aulicino MR, Leytin A, Drossman S, Hermann G, Bleiweiss IJ. Epithelioid cells in myoid hamartoma of the breast: a potential diagnostic pitfall for core biopsies. Arch Pathol Lab Med 1996, **120**: 676–680.

1291 Govender D, Sabaratnam RM, Essa AS. Clear cell "sugar" tumor of the breast: another extrapulmonary site and review of the literature. Am J Surg Pathol 2002, **26**: 670–675.

1292 Green I, Dorfman RF, Rosai J. Breast involvement by extranodal Rosai-Dorfman Disease: report of seven cases. Am J Surg Pathol 1997, **21**: 664–668.

1293 Herbert M, Sandbank J, Liokumovich P, Yanai O, Pappo I, Karni T, Segal M. Breast hamartomas: clinicopathological and immunohistochemical studies of 24 cases. Histopathology 2002, **41**: 30–34.

1294 Hiraoka N, Mukai M, Hosoda Y, Hata J. Phylloides tumor of the breast containing the intracytoplasmic inclusion bodies identical with infantile digital fibromatosis. Am J Surg Pathol 1994, **18**: 506–511.

1295 Ilie B. Neoplasms in skin and subcutis over the breast, simulating breast neoplasms. Case reports and literature review. J Surg Oncol 1986, **31**: 191–198.

1296 Ingram DL, Mossler JA, Snowhite J, Leight GS, McCarty KS Jr. Granular cell tumors of the breast. Steroid receptor analysis and localization of carcinoembryonic antigen, myoglobin, and S100 protein. Arch Pathol Lab Med 1984, **108**: 897–901.

1297 Jones MW, Norris HJ, Wargotz ES. Hamartomas of the breast. Surg Gynecol Obstet 1991, **173**: 54–56.

1298 Kaplan L, Walts AE. Benign chondrolipomatous tumor of the human female breast. Arch Pathol Lab Med 1977, **101**: 149–151.

1299 Lugo M, Reyes JM, Putong PB. Benign chondrolipomatous tumors of the breast. Arch Pathol Lab Med 1982, **106**: 691–692.

1300 Luo JH, Rotterdam H. Primary amyloid tumor of the breast: a case report and review of the literature. Mod Pathol 1997, **10**: 735–738.

1301 Marsh WL Jr, Lucas JG, Olsen J. Chondrolipoma of the breast. Arch Pathol Lab Med 1989, **113**: 369–371.

1302 Michal M, Ludvikova M, Zamecnik M. Nodular mucinosis of the breast: report of three cases. Pathol Int 1998, **48**: 542–544.

1303 Nascimento AG, Karas M, Rosen PP, Caron AG. Leiomyoma of the nipple. Am J Surg Pathol 1979, **3**: 151–154.

1304 Oberman HA. Hamartomas and hamartoma variants of the breast. Semin Diagn Pathol 1989, **6**: 135–145.

1305 Pettinato G, Manivel JC, Gould EW, Albores-Saavedra J. Inclusion body fibromatosis of the breast. Two cases with immunohistochemical and ultrastructural findings. Am J Clin Pathol 1994, **101**: 714–718.

1306 Powell CM, Cranor ML, Rosen PP. Pseudoangiomatous stromal hyperplasia (PASH). A mammary stromal tumor with myofibroblastic differentiation. Am J Surg Pathol 1995, **19**: 270–277.

1307 Rocken C, Kronsbein H, Sletten K, Roessner A, Bassler R. Amyloidosis of the breast. Virchows Arch 2002, **440**: 527–535.

1308 Roncaroli F, Rossi R, Severi B, Martinelli GN, Eusebi V. Epithelioid leiomyoma of the breast with granular cell change. A case report. Hum Pathol 1993, **24**: 1260–1263.

1309 Rosen PP. Multinucleated mammary stromal giant cells. A benign lesion that simulates invasive carcinoma. Cancer 1979, **44**: 1305–1308.

1310 Rosen PP, Ernsberger D. Mammary fibromatosis. A benign spindle-cell tumor with significant risk for local recurrence. Cancer 1989, **63**: 1363–1369.

1311 Rosso R, Scelsi M, Carnevali L. Granular cell traumatic neuroma: a lesion occurring in mastectomy scars. Arch Pathol Lab Med 2000, **124**: 709–711.

1312 Ryska A, Reynolds C, Keeney GL. Benign tumors of the breast with multinucleated stromal giant cells. Immunohistochemical analysis of six cases and review of the literature. Virchows Arch 2001, **439**: 768–775.

1313 Vuitch MF, Rosen PP, Erlandson RA. Pseudoangiomatous hyperplasia of mammary stroma. Hum Pathol 1986, **17**: 185–191.

METASTATIC TUMORS

1314 Azzopardi JG. Problems in breast pathology. In Bennington JL (consulting ed.): Major problems in pathology, vol. 11. Philadelphia, 1979, W.B. Saunders.

1315 Di Bonito L, Luchi M, Giarelli L, Falconieri G, Viehl P. Metastatic tumors to the female breast. An autopsy study of 12 cases. Pathol Res Pract 1991, **187**: 432–436.

1316 Gupta D, Merino MJ, Farhood A, Middleton LP. Metastases to breast simulating ductal carcinoma in situ: report of two cases and review of the literature. Ann Diagn Pathol 2001, **4**: 15–20.

1317 Hajdu SI, Urban JA. Cancers metastatic to the breast. Cancer 1968, **22**: 1691–1696.

1318 Harrist TJ, Kalisher L. Breast metastasis. An unusual manifestation of a malignant carcinoid tumor. Cancer 1977, **40**: 3102–3106.

1319 Howarth CB, Caces JN, Pratt CB. Breast metastases in children with rhabdomyosarcoma. Cancer 1980, **46**: 2520–2524.

1320 Treilleux I, Freyer G, Tabone E, Chassagne-Clement C, Bremond A, Bailly C. Pancreatic neuroendocrine carcinoma metastatic to the breast as part of the multiple endocrine neoplasia type 1 syndrome. Endocr Pathol 1997, **8**: 251–258.

1321 Warner TFCS, Seo IS. Bronchial carcinoid appearing as a breast mass. Arch Pathol Lab Med 1980, **104**: 531–534.

1322 Yamasaki H, Saw D, Zdanowitz J, Faltz LL. Ovarian carcinoma metastasis to the breast case report and review of the literature. Am J Surg Pathol 1993, **17**: 193–197.

BREAST DISEASES IN CHILDREN AND ADOLESCENTS

1323 Bauer BS, Jones KM, Talbot CW. Mammary masses in the adolescent female. Surg Gynecol Obstet 1987, **165**: 63–65.

1324 Dehner LP, Hill DA, Deschryver K. Pathology of the breast in children, adolescents, and young adults. Semin Diagn Pathol 1999, **16**: 235–247.

1325 Farrow JH, Ashikari H. Breast lesions in young girls. Surg Clin North Am 1969, **49**: 261–269.

1326 Kiaer HW, Kiaer WW, Linell F, Jacobsen S. Extreme duct papillomatosis of the juvenile breast. Acta Pathol Microbiol Scand (A) 1979, **87**: 353–359.

1327 Pettinato G, Manivel JC, Kelly DR, Wold LE, Dehner LP. Lesions of the breast in children exclusive of typical fibroadenoma and gynecomastia. A clinipathologic study of 113 cases. Pathol Annu 1989, **24**(Pt 2): 296–328.

1328 Rosen PP. Papillary duct hyperplasia of the breast in children and young adults. Cancer 1985, **56**: 1611–1617.

1329 Rosen PP, Cantrell B, Mullen DL, DePalo A. Juvenile papillomatosis (Swiss cheese disease) of the breast. Am J Surg Pathol 1980, **4**: 3–12.

1330 Rosen PP, Kimmel M. Juvenile papillomatosis of the breast. A follow-up study of 41 patients having biopsies before 1979. Am J Clin Pathol 1990, **93**: 599–603.

1331 Steiner MW. Enlargement of the breast during childhood. Pediatr Clin North Am 1955, **2**: 575–593.

1332 Taffurelli M, Santini D, Martinelli G, Mazzoleni G, Rossati U, Giosa F, Grassigli A, Marrano D. Juvenile papillomatosis of the breast. A multidisciplinary study. Pathol Annu 1991, **26**(Pt 1): 25–35.

1333 Wilson M, Cranor ML, Rosen PP. Papillary duct hyperplasia of the breast in children and young women. Mod Pathol 1993, **6**: 570–574.

BREAST DISEASES IN MALES
Gynecomastia

1334 Andersen JA, Gram JB. Gynecomasty. Histological aspects in a surgical material. Acta Pathol Microbiol Immunol Scand (A) 1982, **90**: 185–190.

1335 Bannayan GA, Hajdu SI. Gynecomastia. Clinicopathologic

study of 351 cases. Am J Clin Pathol 1972, **57**: 431–437.

1336 Coen P, Kulin H, Ballantine T, Zaino R, Frauenhoffer E, Boal D, Inkster S, Brodie A, Santen R. An aromatase-producing sex-cord tumor resulting in prepubertal gynecomastia. N Engl J Med 1991, **324**: 317–322.

1337 Damiani S, Dina R, Eusebi V. Eosinophilic and granular cell tumors of the breast. Semin Diagn Pathol 1999, **16**: 117–125.

1338 Damiani S, Eusebi V. Gynecomastia in type-1 neurofibromatosis with features of pseudoangiomatous stromal hyperplasia with giant cells. Report of two cases. Virchows Arch 2001, **438**: 513–516.

1339 Fisher ER, Creed DL. Nature of the periductal stroma in gynecomastia. Lab Invest 1956, **5**: 267–275.

1340 Gottfried MR. Extensive squamous metaplasia in gynecomastia. Arch Pathol Lab Med 1986, **110**: 971–973.

1341 Guillou L, Gebhard S. Gynecomastia with unusual intraductal "clear cell" changes mimicking pagetoid ductal spread of lobular neoplasia. Path Res Pract 1995, **191**: 156–163.

1342 Hunfeld KP, Bassler R, Kronsbein H. "Diabetic mastopathy" in the male breast – a special type of gynecomastia. A comparative study of lymphocytic mastitis and gynecomastia. Pathol Res Pract 1997, **193**: 197–205.

1343 Kang Y, Wile M, Schinella R. Gynecomastia-like changes of the female breast: a clinicopathologic study of 4 cases. Arch Pathol Lab Med 2001, **125**: 505–509.

1344 Nielsen BB. Fibroadenomatoid hyperplasia of the male breast. Am J Surg Pathol 1990, **14**: 774–777.

1345 Sirtori C, Veronesi U. Gynecomastia. A review of 218 cases. Cancer 1957, **10**: 645–654.

1346 Umlas J. Gynecomastia-like lesions in the female breast. Arch Pathol Lab Med 2000, **124**: 844–847.

1347 Wilson JD, Aiman J, MacDonald PC. The pathogenesis of gynecomastia. Adv Intern Med 1980, **25**: 1–32.

Myofibroblastoma

1348 Ali S, Teichberg S, De Risi DC, Urmacher C. Giant myofibroblastoma of the male breast. Am J Surg Pathol 1994, **18**: 1170–1176.

1349 Al-Nafussi A. Spindle cell tumours of the breast: practical approach to diagnosis. Histopathology 1999, **35**: 1–13.

1350 Begin LR. Myogenic stromal tumor of the male breast (so-called myofibroblastoma). Ultrastruct Pathol 1991, **15**: 613–622.

1351 Damiani S, Miettinen M, Peterse JL, Eusebi V. Solitary fibrous tumour (myofibroblastoma) of the breast. Virchows Arch 1994, **425**: 89–92.

1352 Eyden BP, Shanks JH, Iochim E, Ali HH, Christensen L, Howat AJ. Myofibroblastoma of breast: evidence favouring smooth-muscle rather than myofibroblastic differentiation. Ultrastruct Pathol 1999, **23**: 249–258.

1353 McMenamin ME, DeSchryver K, Fletcher CD. Fibrous lesions of the breast: a review. Int J Surg Pathol 2000, **8**: 99–108.

1354 McMenamin ME, Fletcher CD. Mammary-type myofibroblastoma of soft tissue: a tumor closely related to spindle cell lipoma. Am J Surg Pathol 2001, **25**: 1022–1029.

1355 Magro G, Bisceglia M, Michal M. Expression of steroid hormone receptors, their regulated proteins, and bcl-2 protein in myofibroblastoma of the breast. Histopathology 2000, **36**: 515–521.

1356 Magro G, Bisceglia M, Michal M, Eusebi V. Spindle cell lipoma-like tumor, solitary fibrous tumor and myofibroblastoma of the breast: a clinico-pathological analysis of 13 cases in favour of a unifying histogenetic concept. Virchows Arch 2002, **440**: 249–260.

1357 Magro G, Gurrera A, Bisceglia M. H-caldesmon expression in myofibroblastoma of the breast: evidence supporting the distinction from leiomyoma. Histopathology 2003, **42**: 233–238.

1358 Morgan MB, Pitha JV. Myofibroblastoma of the breast revisited: an etiologic association with androgens? Hum Pathol 1998, **29**: 347–351.

1359 Reis-Filho JS, Faoro LN, Gasparetto EL, Totsugui JT, Schmitt FC. Mammary epithelioid myofibroblastoma arising in bilateral gynecomastia: case report with immunohistochemical profile. Int J Surg Pathol 2001, **9**: 331–334.

1360 Thomas TM, Myint A, Mak CK, Chan JK. Mammary myofibroblastoma with leiomyomatous differentiation. Am J Clin Pathol 1997, **107**: 52–55.

1361 Toker C, Tang C-K, Whitely JF, Berkheiser SW, Rachman R. Benign spindle cell breast tumor. Cancer 1981, **48**: 1615–1622.

1362 Wargotz ES, Weiss SW, Norris HJ. Myofibroblastoma of the breast. Sixteen cases of a distinctive benign mesenchymal tumor. Am J Surg Pathol 1987, **11**: 493–502.

Carcinoma

1363 Adami HO, Hakulinen T, Ewertz M, Tretli S, Holmberg L, Karjalainen S. The survival pattern in male breast cancer. An analysis of 1429 patients from the Nordic countries. Cancer 1989, **64**: 1177–1182.

1364 Bavafa S, Reyes CV, Choudhury AM. Male breast carcinoma. An updated experience at a Veterans Administration hospital and review of the literature. J Surg Oncol 1983, **24**: 41–45.

1365 Bhagat P, Kline TS. The male breast and malignant neoplasms. Diagnosis by aspiration biopsy cytology. Cancer 1990, **65**: 2338–2341.

1366 Camus MG, Joshi MG, Mackarem G, Lee AK, Rossi RL, Munson JL, Buyske J, Barbarisi LJ, Sanders LE, Hughes KS. Ductal carcinoma in situ of the male breast. Cancer 1994, **74**: 1289–1293.

1367 Costa MH, Silverberg SG. Oncocytic carcinoma of the male breast. Arch Pathol 1989, **113**: 1396–1398.

1368 Cunha F, Andre S, Soares J. Morphology of male breast carcinoma in the evaluation of prognosis. Pathol Res Pract 1990, **186**: 745–750.

1369 Demeter JG, Waterman NG, Verdi GD. Familial male breast carcinoma. Cancer 1990, **65**: 2342–2343.

1370 Donegan WL. Cancer of the breast in men. CA Cancer J Clin 1991, **41**: 339–354.

1371 El-Gazayerli M, Abdel-Aziz AS. On bilharziasis and male breast cancer in Egypt. A preliminary report and review of the literature. Br J Cancer 1963, **17**: 566–571.

1372 Giffler RF, Kay S. Small-cell carcinoma of the male mammary gland. A tumor resembling infiltrating lobular carcinoma. Am J Clin Pathol 1976, **66**: 715–722.

1373 Goss PE, Reid C, Pintilie M, Lim R, Miller N. Male breast carcinoma. A review of 229 patients who presented to the Princess Margaret Hospital during 40 years: 1955-1996. Cancer 1999, **85**: 629–639.

1374 Guinee VF, Olsson H, Moller T, Shallenberger RC, van den Blink JW, Peter Z, Durand M, Dische S, Cleton FJ, Zewuster R, et al. The prognosis of breast cancer in males. A report of 335 cases. Cancer 1993, **71**: 154–161.

1375 Hecht JR, Winchester DJ. Male breast cancer. Am J Clin Pathol 1994, **102**: S25–30.

1376 Heller KS, Rosen PP, Schottenfeld D, Ashikari R, Kinne DW. Male breast cancer. A clinicopathologic study of 97 cases. Ann Surg 1978, **188**: 60–65.

1377 Hittmair AP, Lininger RA, Tavassoli FA. Ductal carcinoma in situ (DCIS) in the male breast: a morphologic study of 84 cases of pure DCIS and 30 cases of DCIS associated with invasive carcinoma—A preliminary report. Cancer 1998, **83**: 2139–2149.

1378 Joshi MG, Lee AK, Loda M, Camus MG, Petersen C, Heatley GJ, Hughes KS. Male breast carcinoma: an evaluation of prognostic factors contributing to a poorer outcome. Cancer 1996, **77**: 490–498.

1379 Kozak FK, Hall JG, Baird PA. Familial breast cancer in males. A case report and review of the literature. Cancer 1986, **58:** 2736–2739.

1380 Muir D, Kanthan R, Kanthan SC. Male versus female breast cancers: a population-based comparative immunohistochemical analysis. Arch Pathol Lab Med 2003, **127:** 36–41.

1381 Norris HJ, Taylor HB. Carcinoma of the male breast. Cancer 1969, **23:** 1428–1435.

1382 O'Grady WP, McDivitt RW. Breast cancer in a man treated with diethylstilbestrol. Arch Pathol 1969, **88:** 162–165.

1383 Papotti M, Tanda F, Bussolati G, Pugno F, Bosincu L, Massareli G. Argyrophilic neuroendocrine carcinoma of the male breast. Ultrastruct Pathol 1993, **17:** 115–121.

1384 Pich A, Margaria E, Chiusa L, Ponti R, Geuna M. DNA ploidy and p53 expression correlate with survival and cell proliferative activity in male breast carcinoma. Hum Pathol 1996, **27:** 676–682.

1385 Ribeiro GG. Carcinoma of the male breast. A review of 200 cases. Br J Surg 1977, **64:** 381–383.

1386 Sanchez AG, Villanueva AG, Redondo C. Lobular carcinoma of the breast in a patient with Klinefelter's syndrome. A case with bilateral, synchronous, histologically different breast tumors. Cancer 1986, **57:** 1181–1183.

1387 San Miguel P, Sancho M, Enriquez JL, Fernandez J, Gonzalez-Palacios F. Lobular carcinoma of the male breast associated with the use of cimetidine. Virchows Arch 1997, **430:** 261–263.

1388 Scopsi L, Andreola S, Saccozzi R, Pilotti S, Boracchi P, Rosa P, Conti AR, Manzari A, Huttner WB, Rilke F. Argyrophilic carcinoma of the male breast. A neuroendocrine tumor containing predominantly chromogranin B (secretogranin I). Am J Surg Pathol 1991, **15:** 1063–1071.

1389 Spence RAJ, Mackenzie G, Anderson JR, Lyons AR, Bell M. Long-term survival following cancer of the male breast in Northern Ireland. A report of 81 cases. Cancer 1985, **55:** 648–652.

1390 Stretch JR, Denton KJ, Millard PR, Horak E. Paget's disease of the male breast clinically and histopathologically mimicking melanoma. Histopathology 1991, **19:** 470–472.

1391 Tamura G, Monma N, Suzuki Y, Satodate R, Abe H. Adenomyoepithelioma (myoepithelioma) of the breast in a male. Hum Pathol 1993, **24:** 678–681.

1392 Visfeldt J, Scheike O. Male breast cancer. I. Histologic typing and grading of 187 Danish cases. Cancer 1973, **32:** 985–990.

1393 Wang-Rodriguez J, Cross J, Gallagher S, Djahanban M, Armstrong JM, Wiedner N, Shapiro DH. Male breast carcinoma: correlation of ER, PR, Ki-67, Her2-Neu, and p53 with treatment and survival, a study of 65 cases. Mod Pathol 2002, **15:** 853–861.

1394 Wick MR, Sayadi H, Ritter JH, Hill DA, Reddy VB, Gattuso P. Low-stage carcinoma of the male breast. A histologic, immunohistochemical, and flow cytometric comparison with localized female breast carcinoma. Am J Clin Pathol 1999, **111:** 59–69.

Other lesions

1395 Badve S, Sloane JP. Pseudoangiomatous hyperplasia of male breast. Histopathology 1995, **26:** 463–466.

1396 Benson WR. Carcinoma of the prostate with metastases to breast and testis. Cancer 1957, **10:** 1235–1245.

1397 Bigotti G, Kasznica J. Sclerosing adenosis in the breast of a man with pulmonary oat cell carcinoma. Report of a case. Hum Pathol 1986, **17:** 861–863.

1398 Gatalica Z, Norris BA, Kovatich AJ. Immunohistochemical localization of prostatic-specific antigen in ductal epithelium of male breast: potential diagnostic pitfall in patients with gynecomastia. Appl Immunohistochem Mol Morphol 2000, **8:** 158–161.

1399 Green LK, Klima M. The use of immunohistochemistry in metastatic prostatic adenocarcinoma to the breast. Hum Pathol 1991, **22:** 242–246.

1400 Hassan MO, Gogate PA, Al-Kaisi N. Intraductal papilloma of the male breast. An ultrastructural and immunohistochemical study. Ultrastruct Pathol 1994, **18:** 601–610.

1401 Hernandez FJ. Leiomyosarcoma of male breast originating in the nipple. Am J Surg Pathol 1978, **2:** 299–304.

1402 Hilton DA, Jameson JS, Furness PN. A cellular fibroadenoma resembling a benign phylloides tumour in a young male with gynaecomastia. Histopathology 1991, **18:** 476–477.

1403 Lipper S, Willson CF, Copeland KC. Pseudogynecomastia due to neurofibromatosis. A light microscopic and ultrastructural study. Hum Pathol 1981, **12:** 755–779.

1404 Sara AS, Gottfried MR. Benign papilloma of the male breast following chronic phenothiazine therapy. Am J Clin Pathol 1987, **87:** 649–650.

1405 Tedeschi LG, McCarthy PE. Involutional mammary duct ectasia and periductal mastitis in a male. Hum Pathol 1974, **5:** 232–236.

1406 Waldo ED, Sidhu GS, Hu AW. Florid papillomatosis of the male nipple after diethylstilbestrol therapy. Arch Pathol 1975, **99:** 364–366.

21 Lymph nodes

Normal anatomy

The lymph node is one of the major anatomic components of the immune system.[1]

The three major regions of a lymph node are the cortex, paracortex, and medulla (Fig. 21.1A). The cortex is situated beneath the capsule and contains the largest number of follicles. The medulla, close to the hilum, is rich in lymph sinuses, arteries, and veins but contains only a minor lymphocytic component. Both cortex and medulla represent B zones and are therefore associated with humoral types of immune response.[4] The appearance of the follicles varies according to their state of activity. Primary follicles appear as round aggregates of lymphocytes; secondary follicles appear following antigenic stimulation and are characterized by the presence of germinal centers.[3] The cells present in these formations are B lymphocytes known as follicular center cells (centroblasts and centrocytes or small and large cleaved and noncleaved cells), macrophages, and follicular dendritic cells. The germinal center shows polarization toward the side of antigen stimulation and is surrounded by a mantle of small B lymphocytes[4] (Fig. 21.1B). Proliferated germinal centers are always indicative of humoral antibody production. Under conditions of intense antigenic stimulation, they also can appear within the medullary cords.[5]

The paracortex is the zone situated between the cortex and the medulla, which contains the mobile pool of T lymphocytes responsible for cell-mediated immune responses.[4] A characteristic feature is the presence of postcapillary venules, which are identifiable by their lining of high endothelial cells and the presence of lymphocytes in their walls. Another cell type present in the paracortex is the interdigitating dendritic cell. Expansion of the paracortex is indicative of a cell-mediated immunologic reaction. The number of lymphocytes within the lumen and wall of postcapillary venules gives a rough indication of the degree of lymphocyte recirculation.[2]

Afferent lymph vessels penetrate the nodal capsule to open into the marginal sinus; this communicates with an intricate intranodal sinus network that merges into efferent lymph vessels exiting the node at the hilum. The endothelial lining of the outer (subcapsular) side of the marginal sinus is nonphagocytic and similar to that of the afferent and efferent vessels; the lining of the

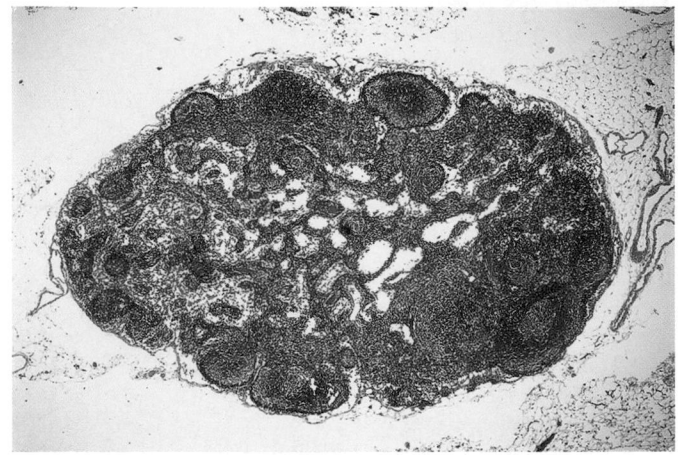

A

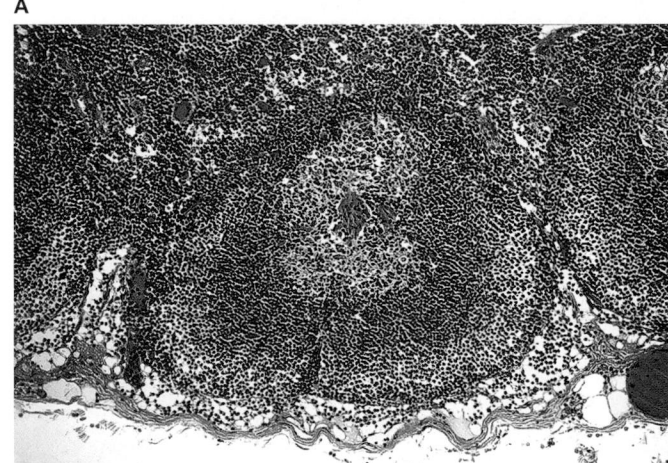

B

Fig. 21.1 A and **B**, Normal lymph node. **A**, The morphologic differences among the various nodal compartments are particularly evident in mesenteric lymph nodes, of which this is an example. **B**, Secondary lymphoid follicle with obvious polarity of the germinal center.

intranodal sinuses has strong phagocytic properties (littoral cells or sinus-lining histiocytes). The main arteries and veins pass through the hilum and radiate to the medulla, paracortex, and inner part of the cortex; other blood vessels penetrate the capsule to supply the superficial cortex and a small area surrounding the trabecula.

The morphologic and phenotypical features of the various populations of lymphoid cells and cells of the accessory immune system are discussed in the next sections and in connection with the respective proliferative pathologic changes affecting these populations.

Lymph node evaluation

The proper examination of a lymph node is a complicated task that may require the performance of a variety of specialized procedures depending on the nature of the case.

Biopsy

Selection of the lymph node to be biopsied is of great importance. Inguinal nodes are to be avoided whenever possible because of the high frequency of chronic inflammatory and fibrotic changes present in them. Axillary or cervical nodes are more likely to be informative in cases of generalized lymphadenopathy. Whenever possible, the largest lymph node in the region should be biopsied. Small superficial nodes may show only nonspecific hyperplasia, whereas a deeper node of the same group may show diagnostic features.

The surgeon biopsying intra-abdominal nodes or large cervical or axillary masses should have a frozen section performed to be certain that the tissue is representative—not to obtain a specific diagnosis at this point. This may save a second biopsy.

Adherence to a strict technique for the preparation of lymph nodes in the pathology laboratory is of paramount importance[6-8] (see Appendix E). The specimen should be received fresh in the laboratory immediately after excision, bisected as soon as it is received, and sampled for the appropriate studies. The portion to be embedded in paraffin (which should not exceed 3 mm in thickness) can be placed in 10% buffered formalin or, preferably, in B5 or analogous mercury-containing fixative. The alcohols and xylenes should be changed frequently. Sections should be cut with a sharp knife without distortion at 5 μm or less. As a routine procedure, initial examination of a preparation stained with hematoxylin–eosin is perfectly adequate, followed by whatever additional stains and special techniques the nature of the case may require (which may range from very many to none).[6,9,10]

A technique that complements the study of tissue sections and that is too often neglected is the examination of touch preparations from the cut surface of the fresh lymph node stained with Giemsa or Wright's solution (see Appendix E). This is particularly useful in the evaluation of lymphoma and leukemia. For instance, granulocytic leukemia can closely simulate large cell lymphoma in a hematoxylin–eosin-stained section, but an imprint will readily distinguish the two conditions.

Bacteriologic examination

If there is a possibility that the node contains an infectious process, an adequate sample of the biopsied lymph node must be sent directly for bacteriologic study or at least be placed in a sterile Petri dish in the refrigerator. If permanent sections show an inflammatory process, the material can then be retrieved and studied bacteriologically (see Appendix E).

Needle biopsy

Core needle biopsy is adequate for the diagnosis of metastatic carcinoma but is rarely used for the evaluation of primary lymphoid disorders.

Fine needle aspiration of lymph nodes is particularly useful for the documentation of metastatic carcinoma (Fig. 21.2). It is used most often in cervical lymph nodes[13] but also in other locations, including intra-abdominal and retroperitoneal regions.[11] The cytologic diagnosis of malignant lymphoma can be made in 50% to 75% of the cases, the accuracy being greatest in the high-grade lesions[12,14,15] (Fig. 21.2). The technique has been found most useful for the selection of a representative node for biopsy, for the diagnosis of recurrent lymphoma, for staging the extent of the disease, and for monitoring treatment.[17] Hemorrhage, necrosis, and myofibroblastic proliferation may develop along the needle tract; the latter should not be confused with Kaposi's sarcoma or other neoplasms.[16]

Electron microscopy

Ultrastructural examination of lymph nodes can be of use in some specific diseases, such as Langerhans' cell histiocytosis and various metastatic tumors. Its role in the evaluation of primary lymphoid disorders is very limited since the advent of immunocytochemical and genetic molecular techniques.[18,19]

Immunophenotyping

Phenotyping of lymphoid disorders has evolved into a highly complex field, as a result of the enormous cellular diversity within the immune system and the huge number (over 1000) of markers that have become available for this purpose.

Rosetting tests with coated or uncoated red blood cells and polyclonal antibodies, which were so useful for the early characterization of lymphomas, have been all but replaced by the use of monoclonal antibodies. These have received a multitude of designations, which are more dependent on the manufacturer's source than the features of the antibody.[20,21] Fortunately, an internationally agreed upon nomenclature (the CD system, which stands for cluster designation) has evolved, and this has allowed for better communication among the various laboratories.[22] Over 250 CD antigens have been identified; they are listed in detail at website <http://www.ncbi.nlm.nih.gov/prow/guide/45277084.htm> Many of these monoclonal antibodies are now applicable to paraffin sections (Table 21.1), whereas others can be employed only in fresh cells (from suspension, cytospin preparations, or frozen section) (Table 21.2). A detailed discussion of these tests is clearly outside the scope of this book.

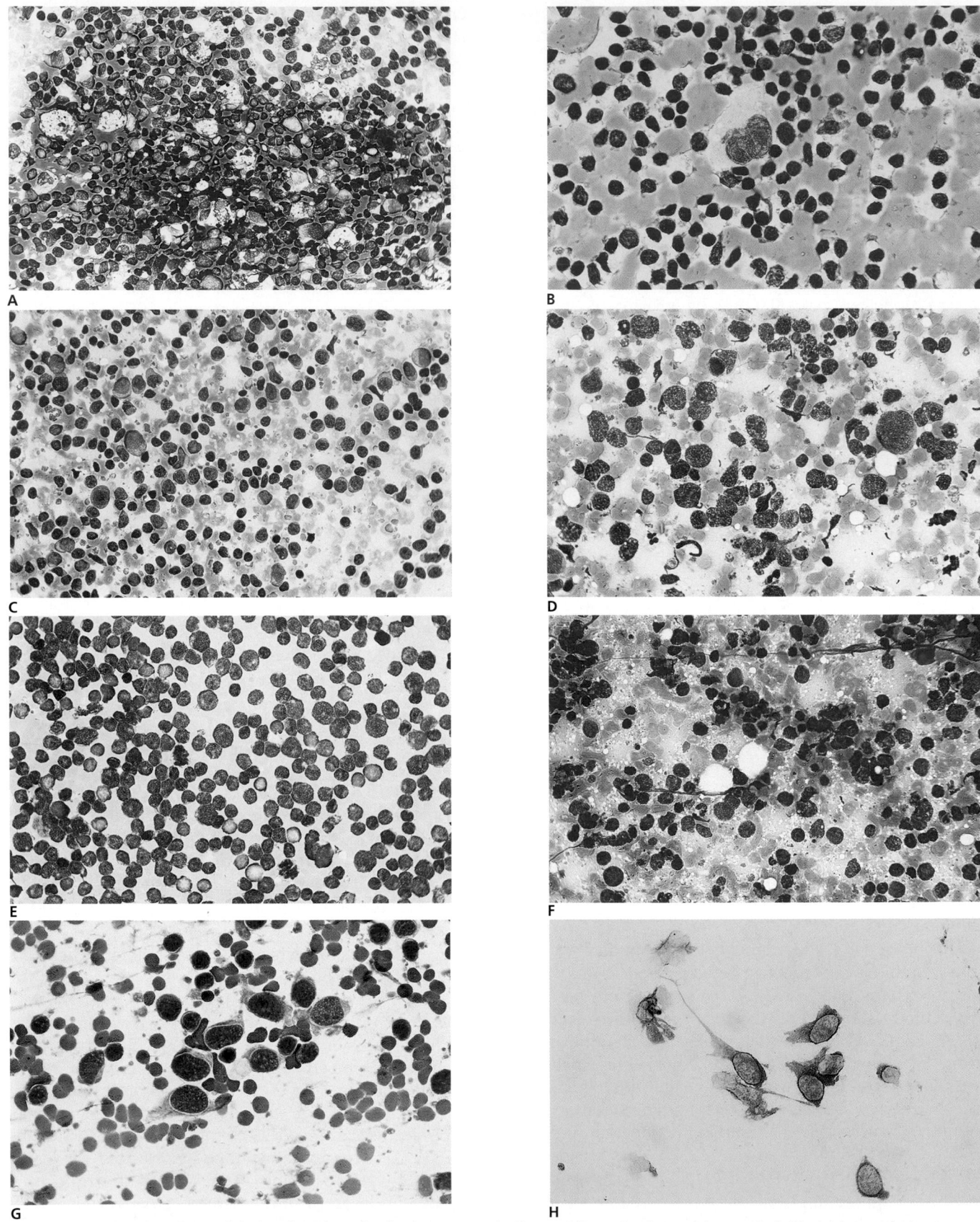

Fig. 21.2 A to **H**, Appearance of various lymph node diseases as seen in fine needle aspiration specimens: **A**, follicular hyperplasia; **B**, Hodgkin's lymphoma (Reed–Sternberg cell); **C**, small lymphocytic lymphoma/chronic lymphocytic leukemia; **D**, follicular lymphoma, large cleaved cell type; **E**, lymphoblastic lymphoma; **F**, metastatic pulmonary small cell carcinoma; **G**, metastatic alveolar rhabdomyosarcoma; **H**, same case as **G**, immunostained for desmin. (Courtesy of L. Alasio, Milan, Italy)

Table 21.1 Principal antibodies employed in immunohistochemical staining of paraffin tissue sections

CD antigen and/or antibody	Predominant normal cell reactivity	Reactivity in neoplasms	Comment/caution
Leukocytes			
CD45RB (PD7) Leukocyte common antigen*	B cells and most T cells, macrophages, myeloid cells	Most lymphomas and leukemias	Plasma cell neoplasms and Reed–Sternberg cells usually unreactive; some lymphoblastic and anaplastic large cell lymphomas unreactive
B lymphocytes			
Immunoglobulin (polyclonal)	B cells and plasma cells	B-cell and plasma cell neoplasms	Diffuse cytoplasmic staining for both light chains seen in macrophages, Reed–Sternberg cells, and degenerated cells (attributed to passive uptake); cytoplasmic Ig often detectable in paraffin sections; surface Ig often requires frozen tissue
CD79 (MB1/B29) (Ig associated)	B cells (B29 absent in plasma cells)	Most B lymphomas, B leukemias from pre-B-cell stage	Associated with antigen receptor (Ig) on B cells in a similar manner as CD3 on T cells; antibodies cross-react with all mammalian species tested
CD20 (L26)	B cells, sometimes macrophages	Most B-cell lymphomas, L&H cells in NLPHD, some Reed–Sternberg cells in ≈20% of classic Hodgkin's lymphoma, rare T-cell lymphomas	Does not work well in acid-decalcified tissues, particularly if Bouin fixed, (unless microwaved); plasma cell neoplasms usually unreactive, some thymomas may stain
CD45RA (4KB5, MB1)	B cells and subpopulation of T cells	Most B-cell lymphomas, few T-cell lymphomas, L&H cells in NLPHD, some myeloid leukemias	Plasma cell neoplasms usually unreactive
CDw75 (LN1)	B cells (mainly germinal center cells)	Many B-cell lymphomas, some T-cell lymphomas, L&H cells in NLPHD; Reed–Sternberg cells in classic Hodgkin's lymphoma (some cases)	Works better in mercuric chloride-containing fixatives
CD74 (LN2 and MB3)	B cells, interdigitating dendritic cells, some macrophages, Langerhans' cells	Many B-cell lymphomas, some T-cell lymphomas, Reed–Sternberg cells, many myeloid leukemias, Langerhans' cell histiocytosis	Works better in mercuric chloride-containing fixatives
MB2	B cells, some macrophages	Most B-cell lymphomas, some T-cell lymphomas, some myeloid leukemias	Plasma cell neoplasms unreactive, many nonhematolymphoid neoplasms reactive
T lymphocytes			
CD3 (polyclonal)	T cells	Many T-cell lymphomas	May require prolonged proteolytic digestion or wet heat pretreatment; may see nonspecific cytoplasmic staining in macrophages and plasma cells
βF1 (TCR beta chain)	T cells	Many T-cell lymphomas	Requires proteolytic digestion; more sensitive in frozen sections
CD43 (Leu-22, MTI, LIFT1)	T cells, plasma cells, some macrophages, granulocytes, erythroid cells, Langerhans' cells	Most T-cell lymphomas, 1/3 B-cell lymphomas, myeloid leukemias, many plasma cell neoplasms, Langerhans' cell histiocytosis	Can be exploited especially for diagnosis of small B-cell lymphoma/leukemia
CD45RO (UCHL1, A6, OPD4)	Major T-cell subset, some macrophages, granulocytes	Many T-cell lymphomas, few B-cell lymphomas, myeloid leukemias, some plasma cell neoplasms	May see nonspecific cytoplasmic staining
CD57 (Leu7, HNK1)	Subset of germinal center T cells, some natural killer cells	Few lymphoblastic lymphomas, some natural killer cell neoplasms	CD56 in frozen sections better marker for natural killer cells; IgM isotype may benefit from isotype-specific detection; subset of reactive T cells ring L&H cells in NLPHD

Table 21.1 *continued*

CD antigen and/or antibody	Predominant normal cell reactivity	Reactivity in neoplasms	Comment/caution
Hodgkin's lymphoma-associated			
CD15 (Leu-M1)	Granulocytes, some macrophages	Reed–Sternberg cells in most cases of classic Hodgkin's lymphoma, large cells in some B- and T-cell lymphomas, some myeloid leukemias	Many carcinomas reactive, CMV-infected cells reactive; IgM isotype may benefit from isotype-specific detection; L&H cells usually unreactive in paraffin sections
CD30 (BerH2)	Some activated B and T cells, some plasma cells	Reed–Sternberg cells in most cases of Hodgkin's lymphoma, most cases anaplastic large cell lymphomas, some B- and T-cell lymphomas, many plasma cell neoplasms; L&H cells usually unreactive in paraffin sections	Less sensitive in mercuric chloride-containing fixatives; embryonal carcinomas and few other nonhematolymphoid neoplasms reactive; cytoplasmic staining (nonspecific) of plasma cells may be abolished by prior wet heat treatment (such as microwave)
Accessory cells			
CD68-(KP 1)	Macrophages, myeloid cells	True histiocytic neoplasms, many myeloid leukemias, dot-like staining in some small cell B-lymphomas and leukemias, especially hairy cell leukemia, mastocytosis	Reactive in granular cell tumors, some melanomas, malignant fibrous histiocytomas, and renal cell carcinomas; PGM (CD68) does not stain myeloid cells
Lysozyme (polyclonal)	Macrophages, myeloid cells	True histiocytic lymphomas, myeloid leukemias	Reactive with many nonhematolymphoid neoplasms
S-100 protein (polyclonal/monoclonal)	Langerhans' cells, interdigitating (IDRC) and sometimes dendritic follicular cells	Langerhans' cell histiocytosis, IDRC tumors, rare T-cell lymphomas, true histiocytic lymphomas, myeloid leukemias, Rosai–Dorfman disease	Reactive with many nonhematolymphoid neoplasms
Mac-387	Macrophages, myeloid cells	True histiocytic lymphomas, myeloid leukemias	Reactive with some squamous cell carcinomas
Miscellaneous			
bcl-2	Nongerminal center B cells, most T cells, plasma cells	Overexpressed in most follicular lymphomas and some diffuse large B-cell lymphomas; also expressed in many other lymphomas and leukemias	Works best in B5 and Bouin 1-fixed tissues (unless microwaved); most useful in differentiating benign from malignant follicular lesions, i.e., non-neoplastic germinal center B cells unreactive
EBV-latent membrane protein (LMP-1)	EBV-infected cells	Reed–Sternberg cells in some cases of classic Hodgkin's lymphoma, i.e., those containing EBV DNA; most immunodeficiency-associated lymphomas	
Myeloperoxidase (polyclonal)	Myeloid cells	Myeloid leukemias	Most sensitive and specific marker for myeloid neoplasms
Epithelial membrane antigen	Plasma cells	In Hodgkin's lymphoma, mainly NLPHD type; plasma cell neoplasms, many anaplastic large cell lymphomas and some other B and T large cell lymphomas	Many epithelial tumors reactive

*CMV = Cytomegalovirus; EBV = Epstein–Barr virus; NLPHD = nodular lymphocyte predominance Hodgkin's lymphoma.

All of these markers produce cell membrane and/or Golgi staining except (1) CD74 (LN2): nuclear membrane staining; (2) S-100 protein: nuclear ± cytoplasmic staining; and (3) Mbw,CD68 (KP1), Mac-387, Ig, lysozyme, bcl-2m, and myeloperoxidase: diffuse cytoplasmic staining.

From Warnke RA, Weiss LM, Chan JKC, Cleary ML, Dorfman RF. Tumors of the lymph nodes and spleen. Atlas of tumor pathology, series 3, fascicle 14. Washington, D.C., 1995, Armed Forces Institute of Pathology.

Table 21.2 Principal antibodies employed in staining fresh cells in suspension or in cytospins and frozen sections

CD antigen or antibody	Predominant normal cell reactivity	Reactivity in neoplasms	Comment/caution
Leukocytes			
CD 45 (2D1, L3B12, T29/33)	Hematolymphoid cells	Nearly all lymphomas and leukemias	Some plasma cell neoplasms unreactive, few precursor cell neoplasms unreactive, some anaplastic large cell lymphomas unreactive
CD11A/18 (LFA-1α and β)	Hematolymphoid cells	Many lymphomas and leukemias	Many intermediate and high-grade B lineage lymphomas lack expression of the alpha and/or beta chain of LFA-1
B lymphocytes			
Immunoglobulins (Ig)	B cells (Ig staining of normal germinal center cells weak to absent)	Most B-cell lymphomas and leukemias, plasma cell neoplasms	Precursor B-cell lymphomas and leukemias do not express Ig except for cytoplasmic mu chains in pre-B-cell tumors; some follicular and diffuse large cell lymphomas of B-cell lineage lack expression; monoclonal anti-Ig reagents less sensitive than polyclonal reagents; detection of cytoplasmic Ig often better in fixed and processed tissues; neoplasms show Ig light chain expression restricted to either kappa or lambda chains
CD79 (MB1/B29) (Ig associated)	B cells (B29 absent in plasma cells)	Most B-cell lymphomas, B-cell leukemias from pre-B-cell stage	Associated with antigen receptor (Ig) on B cells in a similar manner as CD3 on T cells; antibodies cross react with all mammalian species tested
CD19 (B4, Leu-12)	B cells	More B cell lymphomas, and leukemias, few myeloid leukemias	Earliest expressed B-cell differentiation antigen; most plasma cell neoplasms unreactive
CD20 (B1, Leu-16, L26)	B cells	Most B-cell lymphomas, B-cell leukemias, Reed–Sternberg cells in some cases of classic Hodgkin's lymphoma	Most plasma cell neoplasms unreactive; cytoplasmic reactivity may be seen in macrophages
CD22 (Leu-14)	B cells	Most B-cell lymphomas, most B-cell leukemias	Expressed early in B-cell differentiation in the cytoplasm and arrives at the cell membrane at about the same time as Ig; may be undetectable on the surface in some chronic lymphocytic leukemias; most plasma cell neoplasms unreactive
CD24 (BA1)	B cells	Most B-cell lymphomas, most B cell leukemias	Most plasma cell neoplasms unreactive; granulocytes reactive; nonhematolymphoid neoplasms may be reactive
CD37	B cells	Most B-cell lymphomas, many B-cell leukemias, some T-cell lymphomas	Most plasma cell neoplasms unreactive; reactivity with subset of T-cell lymphomas may be useful in diagnosis
B-lymphocyte subsets			
CD10 (J5) (CALLA)	Precursor B cells, germinal center B cells	Many precursor B leukemias, some precursor T leukemias, many follicular lymphomas subset of the other	May be useful in separating follicular from other low-grade B-cell lymphomas; expressed by subset of myeloma; reactive with some non-hematolymphoid neoplasms, e.g., Ewing's sarcoma and malignant fibrous histiocytoma
CD21 (B2)	Mantle and marginal zone B cells, follicular dendritic cells	Most lymphomas of mantle and marginal zone B cells, follicular dendritic cell tumors	C3d (CR2) complement receptor; receptor for EBV
CD23	Mantle zone B cells, subset of follicular dendritic cells	CLL/small lymphocytic lymphoma often reactive; mantle cell lymphomas often unreactive	Low-affinity Fc receptor for IgE; upregulated by EBV infection
CD32	Mantle zone B cells, many macrophages, plasma cells	Most lymphomas of mantle zone B cells, subset of follicular and other B-cell lymphomas, myeloid leukemias, plasma cell neoplasms	Low-affinity Fc receptor for IgG; reactivity with many follicular lymphomas may be useful in diagnosis

Table 21.2 *continued*

CD antigen or antibody	Predominant normal cell reactivity	Reactivity in neoplasms	Comment/caution
B-lymphocyte subsets			
CD35 (TO5)	Mantle and marginal zone B cells, follicular dendritic cells, some macrophages	Most lymphomas of mantle and marginal zone B cells, follicular dendritic cell tumors	C3b (CR1) complement receptor
CD38 (OKT10, Leu-17)	Lymphoid progenitor cells, NK cells, plasma cells	Some B and T lymphomas, especially of progenitor cells, plasma cell neoplasms	One of few markers commonly expressed by plasma cell neoplasms
T lymphocytes			
CD2 (OKT11, Leu-5)	T cells, NK cells	Most T-cell lymphomas and leukemias, few myeloid leukemias	Sheep erythrocyte receptor
CD3 (OKT3, Leu-4)	T cells	Most T-cell lymphomas and leukemias	Associated with antigen receptor in a multimolecular complex; T-lymphoblastic lymphomas and leukemias more often show cytoplasmic rather than surface expression
CD5 (OKT1, Leu-1)	T cells, weak expression by small B-cell subset	Most T-cell lymphomas and leukemias, many diffuse small B-cell neoplasms	CD5-reactive B cells may be elevated in autoimmune disorders; expression of CD5 by many diffuse small B-cell neoplasms useful in diagnosis
CD7 (3A1, Leu-9)	Most T cells, NK cells	Many T-cell lymphomas and leukemias, some myeloid leukemias	Earliest expressed antigen in T-cell ontogeny and one of best T-cell markers for lymphoblastic neoplasms; most commonly deleted antigen in post-thymic T-cell malignancy, particularly mycosis fungoides
T-cell receptor beta chain (WT1, βF1)	T cells	Most T-cell lymphomas, leukemias	Some T-cell lymphomas, especially thymic ones, lack expression; few of the cases that lack expression show the alternative $\gamma\delta$ receptor
T-lymphocyte subsets			
CD1A (NA134, OKT6, Leu-3)	Cortical thymocytes, Langerhans' cells	Many thymic T-cell lymphomas and leukemias, Langerhans' cell histiocytosis	Reliable marker for many precursor T-cell neoplasms; thymomas are rich in CD1A-positive thymocytes
CD4 (OKT4, Leu-3)	Most helper/inducer T cells, class II MHC restricted T cells, many macrophages, many dendritic cells including follicular dendritic and Langerhans' cells	Many post-thymic T-cell lymphomas, often lacking or expressed together with CD8 on T-precursor neoplasms; many accessory cell neoplasms; some myeloid leukemias	HIV receptor generally predominates; reactive and neoplastic disorders may be one of myelomonocytic markers; expressed in some plasma cell neoplasms
CD8 (OKT8, Leu-2)	Most cytotoxic/suppressor T cells, class I MHC restricted, subset of NK cells splenic sinus lining cells	Minority of post-thymic T-cell lymphomas, often lacking or expressed together with CD4 on T-precursor neoplasms	Generally minority of T-subset neoplasms, but may predominate in early phase of some viral infections and in late phase of HIV infection
T-cell receptor delta chain	Few T cells	Few T-cell lymphomas and leukemias (predominantly thymic ones)	Reactive and neoplastic $\gamma\delta$ T cells generally lack expression of both CD4 and CD8
Myelomonocytic cells			
CD11c (Leu-M5)	Myelomonocytic cells	Hairy cell leukemia, monocytoid B-cell lymphoma, few small B-cell lymphomas/ leukemias, few T-cell lymphomas, some myeloid leukemias especially M4 and M5, Langerhans' cell histiocytosis	Sensitive but not totally specific marker for hairy cell leukemia or monocytoid B-cell lymphoma
CD13 (My7)	Myelomonocytic cells, many macrophages, interdigitating dendritic cells	Most myeloid leukemias from M1–M5, few B-lymphoblastic leukemias, rare T-lymphoblastic leukemias	Some nonhematolymphoid cells

Table 21.2 *continued*

CD antigen or antibody	Predominant normal cell reactivity	Reactivity in neoplasms	Comment/caution
Myelomonocytic cells—*continued*			
CD14 (Mo2, Leu-M3)	Monocytes and macrophages, dendritic cells, including follicular, interdigitating, and Langerhans' cells	Many M4 or M5 leukemias	My4 antibody but not others such as Leu-M3 reacts with some B-cell lymphomas and rare T-cell lymphomas
CD33 (My9)	Early myeloid cells and all monocytes	Most myeloid leukemias	B-cell and T-cell lymphomas unreactive
Natural killer cells			
CD16 (Leu-11)	NK cells, granulocytes	Many NK proliferative disorders	IgG Fc receptor III
CD56 (Leu-19, NKH1)	NK cells, few T cells	Many NK proliferative disorders, many nasal non-B-lymphomas, plasma cell neoplasms	Reactivity with neoplastic but not reactive plasma cells may be useful for diagnosis; reacts with neural and neuroendocrine cells and their neoplasms
Miscellaneous			
CD25 (TAG)	Activated T cells, B cells, and monocytes	Adult T-cell lymphoma/leukemia, hairy cell leukemia, most anaplastic large cell lymphomas, Reed–Sternberg cells in many cases of Hodgkin's lymphoma, some other B-cell and T-cell lymphomas	Low-affinity interleukin-2 receptor
CD34 (HPCA1)	Progenitor cells, endothelial cells	Some myeloid leukemias, some lymphoblastic leukemias	Useful in identifying some difficult-to-classify hematolymphoid neoplasms; useful for diagnosis of vascular tumors
Ki-67	Cells not in G0 phase of cell cycle (proliferating cells)	Cells not in G0 phase of cell cycle	General correlation with grade of lymphoma; most consistent correlation in lymphomas as is between high proliferation fraction and adverse survival in low-grade B-cell lymphoma; may be useful in differentiating proliferating tumor cells from nonproliferating host cells
TdT	Precursor cells in marrow, cortical thymocytes	Most lymphoblastic lymphomas and leukemias of a T- or B-lineage, some myeloid leukemias	Useful as marker of precursor cell lymphoma/leukemia

EBV = Epstein–Barr virus; HIV = human immunodeficiency virus; MHC = major histocompatibility complex; NK = natural killer.
From Warnke RA, Weiss LM, Chan JKC, Cleary ML, Dorfman RF. Tumors of the lymph nodes and spleen. Atlas of tumor pathology, series 3, fascicle 14. Washington, D.C., 1995, Armed Forces Institute of Pathology.

Cytogenetics and molecular genetics

Several nonrandom chromosomal translocations have been detected in malignant lymphoma (Table 21.3).[23,25,28–30] Remarkably, most of these translocations are associated with specific lymphoma subtypes even if exceptions occur. Many result from errors in the rearrangement of antigen receptor genes in progenitor B or T lymphocytes; they lead to deregulated expression of cellular oncogenes following their juxtaposition with antigen receptor genes. Probes for some of these oncogenes (such as *bcl-2, bcl-1, bcl-6,* and *myc*) may be used for molecular genetic studies. Because rearrangement of the *bcl-2* gene is the molecular marker of the t(14;18) chromosomal translocation, its detection by Southern blot

techniques can be used as a substitute for conventional cytogenetic analysis. The molecular genetic methods currently available to study lymphoid disease have evolved in a world of their own, which is quite remote from the modest aims of this book.[24,26,27]

Gene rearrangement analysis

Antigen receptor genes code for immunoglobulin and T-cell receptor protein molecules. B cells express immunoglobulins in both a membrane and soluble form, whereas T cells express T-cell receptors, which are membrane-bound molecules. These two kinds of molecules have significant functional and structural similarities and are involved in the specific recognition of antigens by lymphocytes.

Table 21.3 Recurrent chromosomal abnormalities in lymphomas

Chromosomal abnormality	Most frequent types of lymphoma	Antigen receptor gene	Oncogene
t(8;14)(q24;q32)	Small noncleaved cell lymphoma (Burkitt's and non-Burkitt's); some diffuse large cell lymphomas (B-cell type)	IgH	c-myc
t(2;8)(2p12;q24)		Igκ	c-myc
t(8;22)(q24;q11)		Igλ	c-myc
t(14;18)(q32;q21)	Follicular lymphoma, subset of large B-cell lymphomas	IgH	bcl-2
t(11;14)(q13;q32)	Mantle cell lymphoma	IgH	bcl-1 (PRAD 1)
t(3;v)(q27;v)*	Large cell lymphoma	IgH, Igκ, Igλ, others	bcl-6 (LAZ 3)
t(14;v)(q11;v)	Lymphoblastic lymphoma, adult T-cell leukemia/lymphoma	TCR α/TCRβ	Several
t(14;v)(q32;v)	Occasional small lymphocytic lymphoma, diffuse large cell lymphoma, others	IgH	bcl-3, unknown
t(7;v)(q35;v)	Lymphoblastic lymphoma (T-cell type)	TCRβ	Several
t(2;5)(p23;q35)	Anaplastic large cell lymphoma, others	NA†	NPM–ALK fusion gene

*Variable.
†NA = Not applicable.
From Warnke RA, Weiss LM, Chan JKC, Cleary ML, Dorfman RF. Tumors of the lymph nodes and spleen. Atlas of tumor pathology, series 3, fascicle 14. Washington, D.C., 1995, Armed Forces Institute of Pathology.

Both molecules are multisubunit glycoproteins. Each subunit can be divided roughly into two parts: a constant region and a variable region. Variable regions of two subunits collaborate to form highly specific antigen-binding sites. A given lymphocyte, throughout its lifetime, can express only one type of variable region for each of two (or in the case of T cells, at most three) antigen receptor subunits.

Genetic rearrangements that occur within the genes of these subunits determine which variable region is expressed for a given subunit (Fig. 21.3). During the lifetime of a lymphocyte, rearrangement generally occurs only once per allele or twice for a given gene, as there are two alleles for each gene. The rearrangement can be detected by Southern blot or polymerase chain reaction (PCR).[35] The Southern blot hybridization procedure is used to assess the size of rearranged fragments using a radiolabeled DNA hybridization probe specific for DNA sequences in or around the constant region. This procedure results in an autoradiogram in which a rearranged fragment can be identified as a dark band. In practice, detecting a rearrangement of antigen receptor DNA in a biopsy specimen requires that 1% or greater of the total number of cells within the specimen carry uniform rearrangements within their genome.

Three general types of applications of gene rearrangements to the diagnosis of lymphoid neoplasms exist: (1) for the differential diagnosis between benign and malignant lesions, (2) as markers for B- or T-cell derivation, and (3) as markers for the presence of multiple lymphocytic clones in a single patient (Tables 21.4 and 21.5).[32,34,36,37]

Table 21.4 Usual antigen receptor gene status in various lymphoproliferative lesions

Abnormality	IgH	Igκ	Igλ	TCRβ	TCRγ	TCRδ
Normal lymphoid tissue	G	G	G	G	Rp	Rp
Reactive lymphoid tissue	G	G	G	G	Rp	Rp
Lymphoid hyperplasia in a setting of immunodeficiency	G/R	Rp	G		Rp	Rp
B-cell lymphoma	R	R	G/R	G/R	G/Rp	G/Rp
T-cell lymphoma	G/R	G	G	R	R	R
Hodgkin's lymphoma	G/R	G	G	G	Rp	Rp
Hodgkin's lymphoma lymphocyte predominance	G	G	G	G	Rp	Rp

G = Germline band; R = rearranged band; Rp = polyclonal rearranged bands.
Some T-cell lymphomas may lack detectable TCP gene rearrangements. AILD-like T-cell lymphomas show a fairly high frequency of simultaneous IgH gene rearrangements (30% to 40%).
From Warnke RA, Weiss LM, Chan JKC, Cleary ML, Dorfman RF. Tumors of the lymph nodes and spleen. Atlas of tumor pathology, series 3, fascicle 14. Washington, D.C., 1995, Armed Forces Institute of Pathology.

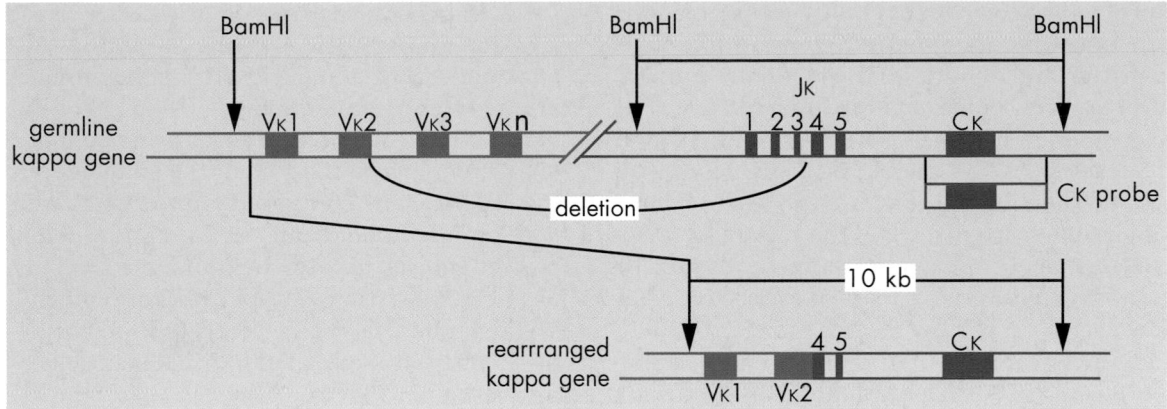

Fig. 21.3 Schematic representation of immunoglobulin gene rearrangement. The germline configuration of the kappa light chain gene (upper line) consists of numerous variable gene segments (V-kappa, 1–n), five joining gene segments (J-kappa, 1–5), and a single constant region gene segment (C-kappa). To assemble a functional light chain gene (lower line), select V and J segments are juxtaposed with each other by deletion of the intervening DNA. The deletion reconfigures restriction enzyme cutting sites upstream of J-kappa, changing the size of the *BamH1* fragment detected with a C-kappa hybridization probe (12 kb germline versus 10 kb rearranged in figure). (From Warnke RA, Weiss LM, Chan JKC, Cleary ML, Dorfman RF. Tumors of the lymph nodes and spleen. Atlas of tumor pathology, series 3, fascicle 14. Washington, D.C., 1995, Armed Forces Institute of Pathology)

Table 21.5 Commonly encountered gene rearrangement patterns and their interpretation

Antigen receptor gene status					
IgH	Igκ	Igλ	TCRβ	TCRγ	Most probable interpretation
R	R	G	G	G	B-cell neoplasms
R	R	R	G	G	B-cell neoplasms
G	G	G	R	R	T-cell neoplasm
R	G	G	R	R	T-cell neoplasm
G	G	G	G	G	No molecular support for lymphoma

R = Rearranged band; G = germline band.
From Warnke RA, Weiss LM, Chan JKC, Cleary ML, Dorfman RF. Tumors of the lymph nodes and spleen. Atlas of tumor pathology, series 3, fascicle 14. Washington, D.C., 1995, Armed Forces Institute of Pathology.

Application of these techniques to the primary diagnosis of malignancy assumes that clonal proliferations of lymphocytes are indicative of a neoplastic process, an assumption that remains controversial.[31] However, even if clonal antigen receptor gene rearrangements were not absolutely specific for neoplasia, they can still be confidently used for the staging or detection of relapse in lymphoid cases with established diagnosis.

Applications of antigen receptor gene rearrangements for determining the B- or T-cell derivation of a given tumor rely on the fact that rearrangements of these genes occur only in lymphoid tissues. Immunoglobulin gene rearrangements are largely limited to cells of B lineage, and T-cell receptor rearrangements are generally restricted to cells of T lineage, although exceptions occur. The technique can be adapted to fine needle aspiration material and to formalin-fixed, paraffin-embedded material.[33]

DNA ploidy studies

Examination of DNA ploidy by flow cytometry of cell suspensions from fluids or material from fine needle aspiration or from tissue sections has shown a good correlation with the microscopic grades of malignant lymphoma.[38,39,41] Whether it provides prognostic information above and beyond that obtainable from conventional morphology and immunophenotyping of the tumors remains controversial.[38,40]

Gene expression profiling

Some highly publicized studies have been recently published on the use of molecular profiling with the microchip technology to segregate diffuse large B-cell lymphomas into subtypes[42] and to predict survival after chemotherapy.[43] One hopes that more rigorous clinical and statistical evaluations than the ones carried out so far in these understandably rushed first efforts will validate their clinical utility.

Primary immunodeficiencies

The many varieties of primary immunodeficiencies can be broadly divided in three major categories according to the type of the immunologic deficit: humoral, cell-mediated, and due to defects in phagocytes and other cells of the accessory immune system.[44,50,51] The diagnosis of these disorders is based on a variety of laboratory tests, including qualitative and quantitative immunoglobulin determinations, delayed-type skin reactions, and in vitro stimulation of lymphocytes. Sometimes lymph nodes are biopsied to assess the amount and composition of the lymphoid tissue. In immune diseases of the humoral type, cortical reactive centers and medullary plasma cells are scanty or absent.[48] In diseases of cell-mediated immunity, the thickness of the paracortical area is greatly diminished.[48] When both humoral and cell-mediated types of immunities are defective, the lymphocyte and plasma cell content of the node is practically nil, the lymph node being reduced to a mass of connective tissue and blood vessels.[47]

Although rarely carried out at present, the procedure of injecting an antigen (such as diphtheria or tetanus toxoid) into the medial aspect of the thigh and biopsying the ipsilateral inguinal lymph node 5 to 7 days later has provided useful information about the capacity of the lymphoid tissue of these patients to react to an antigenic stimulus.[46]

The increased susceptibility of patients with primary immunodeficiencies to the development of malignant lymphoma is discussed on p. 1959.[45,49,52]

Patterns of hyperplasia

The various components of the lymph node react to various known and unknown stimuli by undergoing reactive changes, some being the expression of an inflammatory reaction and some being indicative of an immune response. The two are often present together. A similar microscopic picture may result from a variety of causes, but some agents produce a characteristic microscopic picture. When the hyperplastic change is very intense, the differential diagnosis with malignant lymphoma may become difficult[53,54,56] and may require the application of immunohistochemical, genetic, and molecular genetic methods.[55]

Although most lymph node reactions involve several compartments, it is useful to evaluate these compartments individually, not only because their presence and relative intensity correlates with various specific disorders (thus providing important etiologic clues), but also because each of them raises differential diagnostic problems with different types of malignant processes. From a topographic and functional standpoint, the major patterns of reactive lymphoid proliferations are follicular/nodular, interfollicular/paracortical, diffuse, sinusal, and mixed. These patterns also apply to the various types of malignant lymphoma (Table 21.6).[57]

Follicular hyperplasia

The criteria laid down in the classic article by Rappaport et al.[59] and further developed by Nathwani et al.[58] remain extremely useful and reliable to distinguish reactive follicular hyperplasia from follicular lymphoma (Table 21.7). In general, reactive follicles vary considerably in size and shape; their margins are sharply defined and surrounded by a mantle of small lymphocytes often arranged circumferentially with an onion-skin pattern and sometimes concentrating on one pole of the follicle (corresponding to the side of the antigenic stimulation); the follicles are composed of an admixture of small and large lymphoid cells with irregular (elongated and cleaved) nuclei; mitoses are numerous; and phagocytosis of nuclear debris by histiocytes is prominent. The lymphoid tissue present between the follicles is distinctly different from that of the follicles themselves (although this also may be true for follicular lymphoma); it is composed of a mixture of small lymphocytes, large lymphoid cells, prominent postcapillary venules, and sometimes a prominent component of mature plasma cells (Fig. 21.4).

It should be kept in mind that follicular hyperplasia may coexist in the same node with follicular lymphoma or other types of malignant lymphoma.[60]

The immunophenotypical differences between follicular hyperplasia and follicular lymphoma are discussed on p. 1937.

Progressively and regressively transformed germinal centers

Progressively transformed germinal centers are the morphologic expression of a distinct type of follicular hyperplasia. They usually are seen in conjunction with more typical reactive germinal centers and are often located more centrally within the node (Fig. 21.5).[64] They are large and contain numerous small lymphocytes, the borders are indistinct, and the interphase between the center of large lymphoid cells and the cuff of small lymphocytes is blurred. However, residual "starry sky" macrophages are present, together with scattered large lymphoid cells (cleaved and noncleaved) and occasional collections of epithelioid cells at the periphery.[68] There is an increased network of follicular dendritic cells, a larger number of mantle zone lymphocytes, and a relatively large number of T lymphocytes.[70] Evaluation of these features should allow the differential diagnosis between progressively transformed germinal centers and follicular lymphoma to be made with ease in most instances; however, cases exist in which this is extremely difficult on the basis of routinely stained sections.[66]

Progressively transformed germinal centers can occur as an isolated self-limited reactive process, particularly in young men.[62,67] However, they also show an interesting and still poorly understood relation with nodular lymphocyte predominance Hodgkin's lymphoma (NLPHL), which may manifest itself in three ways: they may precede the development of NLPHL, they may accompany NLPHL in involved nodes, or they may appear in the absence of NLPHL in recurrent post-therapy adenopathy[61,63,69] (see p. 1922). Indeed, the main

Table 21.6 Differential diagnosis based upon recognition of predominant pattern in lymph node at low magnification

Follicular/nodular	Interfollicular/paracortical	Diffuse	Sinus	Mixed/other
Non-neoplastic				
Reactive follicular hyperplasia	Immunoblastic proliferations	Immunoblastic proliferations	Sinus hyperplasia	Mixed hyperplasia
Explosive follicular hyperplasia (HIV)	Viral lymphadenitis (EBV, CMV, herpes)	Viral lymphadenitis (EBV, CMV, herpes)	Rosai–Dorfman disease	Dermatopathic lymphadenopathy
Progressive transformation of germinal centers	Post-vaccination lymphadenitis	Post-vaccination lymphadenitis	Lymphangiogram effect	Toxoplasmosis
Castleman's disease	Drug sensitivity, e.g., Dilantin	Drug sensitivity e.g., Dilantin	Whipple's disease	Cat-scratch disease
Rheumatoid lymphadenopathy			Vascular transformation of sinuses	Systemic lupus erythematosus
Luetic lymphadenitis			Hemophagocytic syndrome	Kawasaki's disease
Kimura's disease				Kikuchi's lymphadenitis
				Granulomatosis lymphadenitis
				Inflammatory pseudotumor
Uncertain if neoplastic				
Nodular lymphocyte predominance HD		Angioimmunoblastic lymphadenopathy	Langerhans' cell histiocytosis	Systemic Castleman's disease
Neoplastic				
Nodular sclerosing HD	Interfollicular HD	Mixed cellularity HD	Sinusoidal large cell lymphoma	Mucosa-associated lymphoid tissue lymphoma
Follicular lymphoma	T-zone lymphoma	Small cell B/T lymphoma/leukemia	Mastocytosis	Monocytoid B-cell lymphoma
Mantle cell lymphoma	Mixed cellularity HD	Large cell B/T lymphoma	Nonlymphoid leukemia	
Monocytoid B-cell lymphoma	Small cell B/T lymphoma/leukemia	Lymphoblastic lymphoma/leukemia	Histiocytic neoplasms	
CLL/SLL with proliferation centers	Large cell B/T lymphoma	Burkitt's lymphoma	Nonhematolymphoid neoplasms	
	Lymphoblastic lymphoma/leukemia	Plasmacytoma		
	Burkitt's lymphoma	Anaplastic large cell lymphoma		
	Plasmacytoma	Nonlymphoid leukemia		
	Nonlymphoid leukemia	Mastocytosis		
	Mastocytosis	Histiocytic neoplasms		
	Histiocytic neoplasms	Nonhematolymphoid neoplasms		
	Nonhematolymphoid neoplasms			

From Warnke RA, Weiss LM, Chan JKC, Cleary ML, Dorfman RF. Tumors of the lymph nodes and spleen. Atlas of tumor pathology, series 3, fascicle 14. Washington, D.C., 1995, Armed Forces Institute of Pathology.

differential diagnosis of progressively transformed germinal centers is with NLPHL, which should be suspected if T-cell rosettes are prominent. A thorough search for the atypical cells seen in this condition (see p. 1922) should therefore be undertaken.[65]

Regressively transformed germinal centers are small, practically devoid of lymphoid cells, and composed of follicular dendritic cells, vascular endothelial cells, and hyalinized PAS-positive intercellular material. These abnormal centers have an onion-skin appearance in low-power examination. Regressively transformed germinal centers are particularly prominent and numerous in Castleman's disease (see p. 1905). A peculiar form of regressive germinal centers with "follicular dendritic cells only" has been described in organ transplant recipients.[71]

Mantle/marginal zone hyperplasia

This pattern of hyperplasia, which blends with the lymphoid subtype of hyaline vascular Castleman's disease, is characterized by a monomorphic proliferation of small lymphoid cells with round nuclei and clear cytoplasm which may be arranged in a nodular, inverse follicular, and/or marginal zone pattern. The main differential

Table 21.7 Architectural and cytologic features of follicular lymphoma and of reactive follicular hyperplasia as described in a classic and still very pertinent article on the subject.

Follicular lymphoma	Reactive follicular hyperplasia
Architectural features	
Complete effacement of normal architecture	Preservation of nodal architecture
Even distribution of follicles throughout cortex and medulla	Follicles more prominent in cortical portion of lymph node
Slight or moderate variations in size and shape of follicles	Marked variations in size and shape of follicles with presence of elongated, angulated, and dumbbell-shaped forms
Fading of follicles	Sharply demarcated reaction centers
Massive infiltration of capsule and pericapsular fat with or without formation of neoplastic follicles outside capsule	No, or only moderate, infiltration of capsule and pericapsular fat tissue with inflammatory cells that may be arranged in perivascular focal aggregates (when associated with lymphadenitis)
Condensation of reticulin fibers at periphery of follicles	Little or no alteration of reticular framework
Cytologic features	
Follicles composed of neoplastic cells exhibiting cellular pleomorphism with nuclear irregularities	Centers of follicles (reaction centers) composed of lymphoid cells, histiocytes, and "reticulum cells," with few or no cellular and nuclear irregularities
Lack of phagocytosis	Active phagocytosis in reaction centers
Relative paucity of mitotic figures usually without significant difference in their number inside and outside the follicles; occurrence of atypical mitoses	Moderate to pronounced mitotic activity in reaction centers; rare or no mitoses outside reaction centers; no atypical mitoses
Similarity of cell type inside and outside follicles	Infiltration of tissue between reaction centers with inflammatory cells (when associated with lymphadenitis)

Slightly modified from Rappaport H, Winter WJ, Hicks EB. Follicular lymphoma. A re-evaluation of its position in the scheme of malignant lymphoma, based on a survey of 253 cases. Cancer 1956, **9**: 792–821.

diagnosis is with mantle cell lymphoma (p. 1943). Features in favor of benignancy are the lack of pericapsular infiltration, preservation of sinuses, scattered reactive follicles, and paracortical nodular hyperplasia.[72] Immunoglobulin gene rearrangement studies may be necessary to settle the issue.

Paracortical hyperplasia

Expansion of the paracortical (interfollicular) region can be nodular or diffuse. The nodular form is characteristic of dermatopathic lymphadenitis (see p. 1910) and of nodal reactions to malignancy.[73] The diffuse form is a feature of viral lymphadenitis (see p. 1902) and drug reactions (see p. 1910), and of immunoblastic proliferations in general (Fig. 21.6).

Sinus hyperplasia

The sinuses appear dilated and prominent in various disorders. The most common and least significant is *sinus hyperplasia* (sinus histiocytosis, sinus catarrh) seen in nodes draining infectious or neoplastic processes and characterized by an increased number of macrophages in the lumen (Fig. 21.7). Other reactive disorders involving primarily the sinuses are Rosai–Dorfman disease (RDD) (see p. 1911), Langerhans' cell histiocytosis (see p. 1913), Whipple's disease, vascular transformation of sinuses, and virus-associated hemophagocytic syndrome (see p. 1958).

Granulomatous inflammation

There is a large number of diseases that can result in granulomatous formations in lymph nodes. They include various types of infections, foreign body reactions, and secondary responses in lymph nodes draining carcinoma[74,79] or in patients with Hodgkin's lymphoma and other lymphomas, whether the node is involved by the malignancy or not.[75,76,78] Sometimes the appearance of the granulomas is such that a specific diagnosis can be strongly suggested on the basis of the hematoxylin–eosin-stained slide.[77] Features of importance in this regard are the presence and type of necrosis; presence, number, and size of Langerhans' giant cells; size, shape, and distribution of the granulomas; and type of associated changes in the intervening tissue. In most cases, however, a combination of clinical, morphologic, and bacteriologic data is necessary to determine the etiology of the granulomas. It is therefore important that any node suspected of harboring a granulomatous process be sampled for bacteriologic analysis in addition to being subjected to the standard microscopic examination.

Other cell types involved in nodal hyperplasia
Monocytoid B cells
Monocytoid B-cell hyperplasia is characterized by the filling of the sinuses by small lymphoid cells with round or angulated nuclei and clear cytoplasm, sometimes admixed with neutrophils (Fig. 21.8). A variant charac-

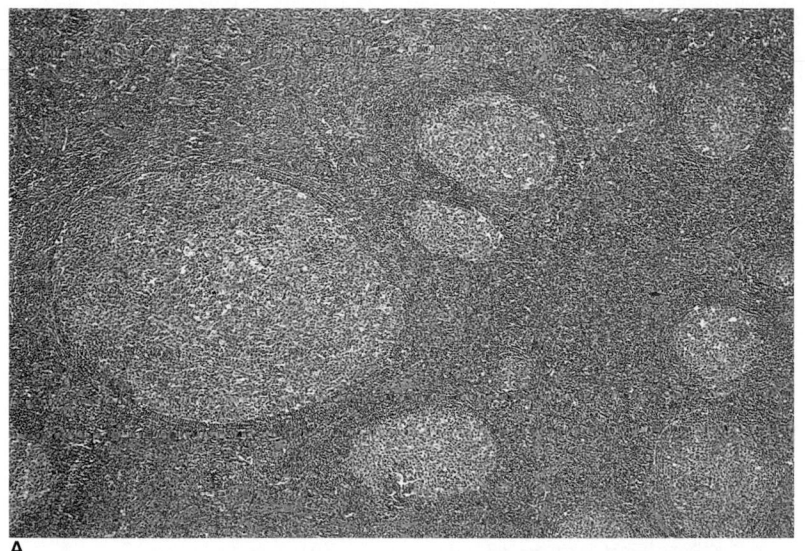

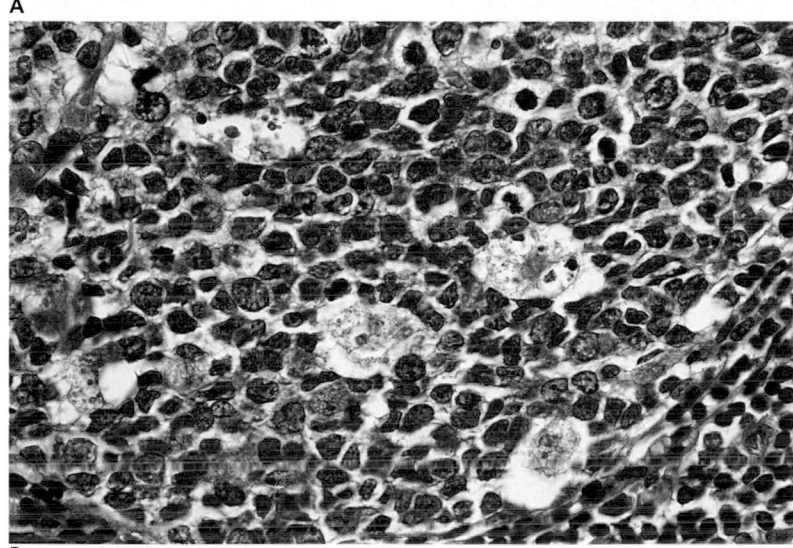

Fig. 21.4 A and **B**, Follicular hyperplasia. **A**, Low-power view showing marked differences in size of germinal centers, their well circumscribed character, and the fact that they are surrounded by a well-defined mantle. **B**, High-power view showing numerous "tingible body" macrophages.

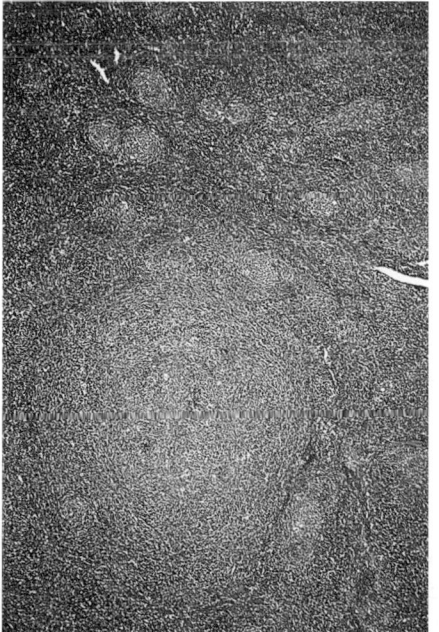

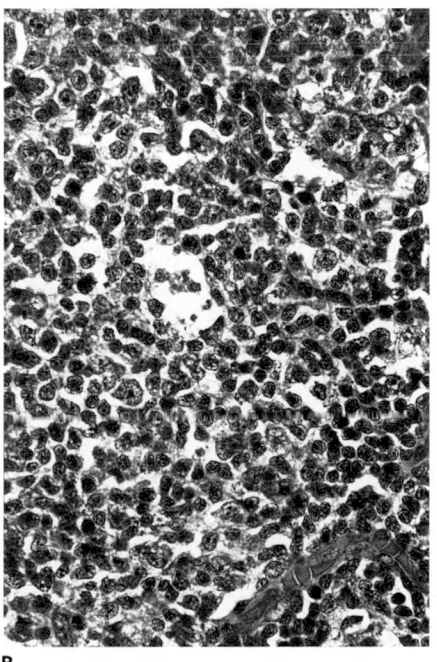

Fig. 21.5 A and **B**, Progressively transformed germinal centers. **A**, Low-power view showing that this formation is larger and less well defined than the adjacent hyperplastic follicles. **B**, High-power view showing cytologic composition not too dissimilar from that of ordinary hyperplastic follicles.

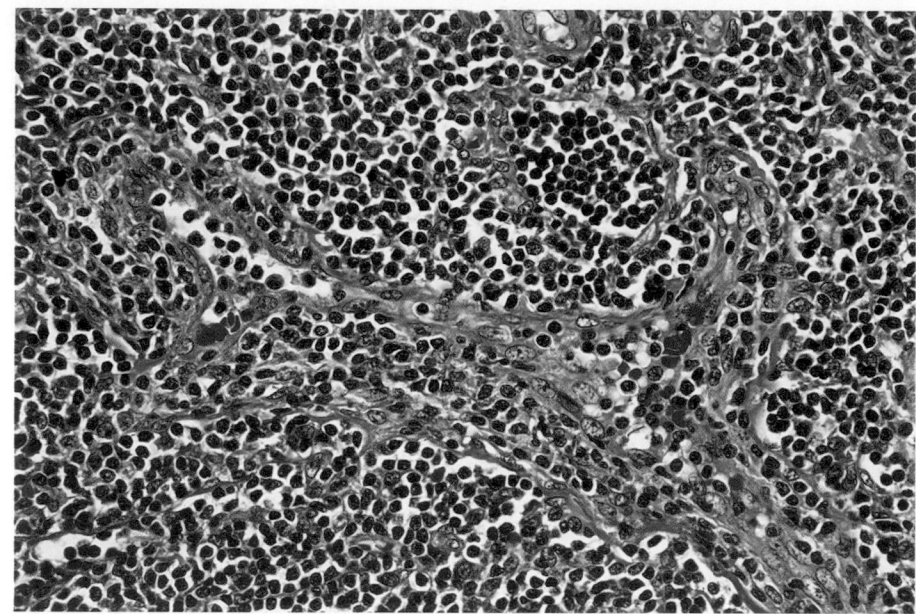

Fig. 21.6 Paracortical hyperplasia, identified by the prominence of postcapillary venules.

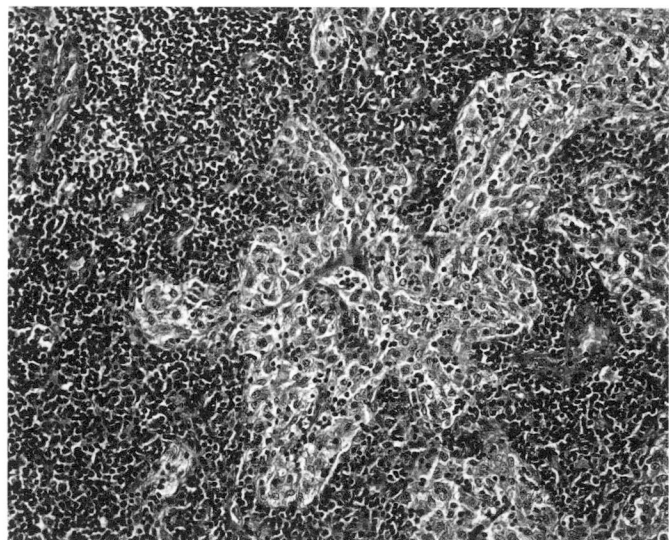

Fig. 21.7 Sinus hyperplasia. The cells present in the sinus represent an admixture of histiocytes and sinus lining cells.

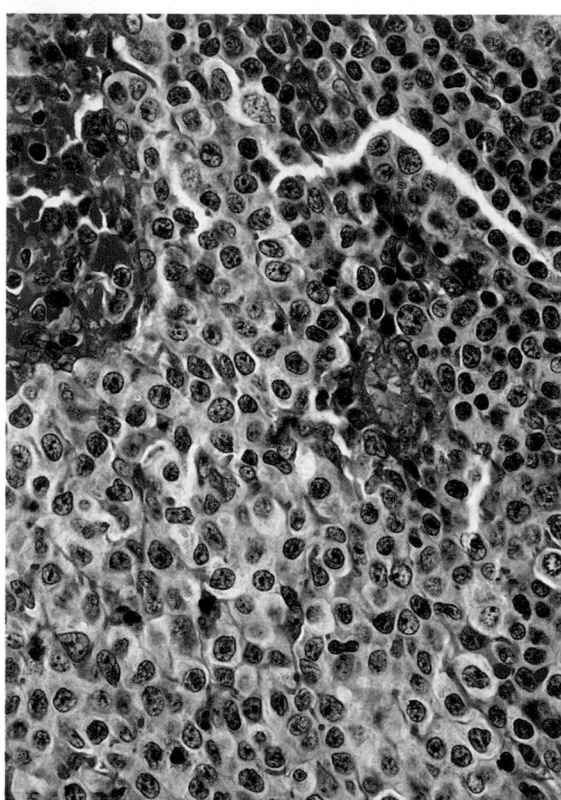

Fig. 21.8 Monocytoid B-cell hyperplasia. These cells are characterized by centrally located nuclei and clear appearance of the cytoplasm.

terized by the presence of a larger cell component has also been recognized.[83] It was originally described as immature sinus histiocytosis, but marker studies have shown that these monocytoid clear cells are of B-cell type.[84,86] This alteration occurs most frequently in toxoplasmosis, but it has also been seen in many other reactive disorders, such as cat-scratch disease,[81] infec-

tious mononucleosis, AIDS, and autoimmune disorders[80]; it may also accompany malignant lymphomas, including Hodgkin's lymphoma.[82] It should be distinguished from other nodal lesions featuring cells with clear cytoplasm (such as peripheral T-cell lymphomas, hairy cell leukemia, and mastocytosis) and also from a type of malignant lymphoma composed of cells with features of monocytoid B cells (nodal marginal zone B-cell lymphoma) (see p. 1945).[85]

Plasmacytoid monocytes

Clusters of cells with plasmacytoid cytoplasm, fine nuclear chromatin pattern, and small nucleoli are sometimes seen in a variety of reactive nodal lesions (Fig. 21.9). Pyknosis and "starry-sky" pattern may be present.[94] These cells were originally interpreted as T-associated plasma cells and later as a subtype of T cells, but more recent marker studies have shown that they belong to the macrophage/monocyte series. Accordingly, these cells have been renamed plasmacytoid monocytes.[87,91] They are particularly common in necrotizing lymphadenitis and Castleman's disease,[89,90] but they can also be seen in other lymphadenitides.[88] A variety of malignant lymphoma composed of plasmacytoid monocytes has also been described[92,93] (see p. 1957).

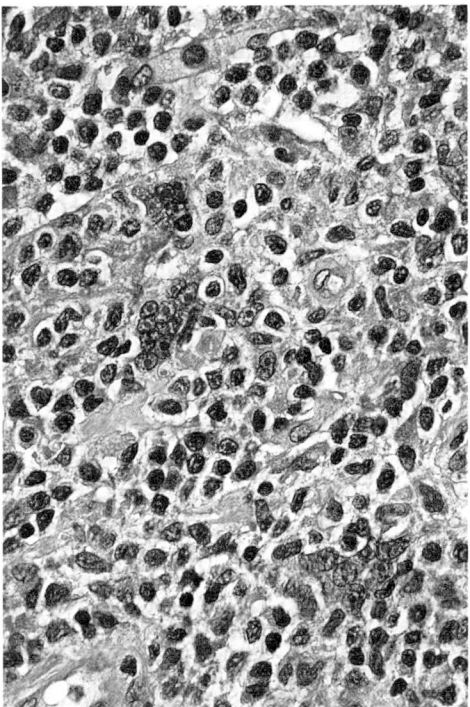

Fig. 21.10 So-called "polykaryocytes." These cells are characterized by numerous clustered nuclei.

Polykaryocytes

The term *polykaryocyte* is used for a type of multinucleated giant cells found in lymphoid tissues, of which the Warthin–Finkeldey giant cell of measles is the paradigm. These cells can be found in lymph nodes in association with a variety of reactive and neoplastic disorders. They measure 25 to 150 μm in diameter and have as many as 60 nuclei arranged in grapevine clusters.[95] Their cytoplasm is very scanty (Fig. 21.10). Although some studies suggested a T-cell phenotype, more recent evaluations are in keeping with the hypothesis that these cells are multinucleated forms of follicular dendritic cells, a possibility that fits much better their morphologic appearance.[96]

Inflammatory/hyperplastic diseases

Acute nonspecific lymphadenitis

The typical case of acute nonspecific lymphadenitis is rarely biopsied. Microscopically, the earliest change is sinus dilatation resulting from increased flow of lymph, followed by accumulation of neutrophils, vascular dilatation, and edema of the capsule. *Suppurative lymphadenitis* is a feature of staphylococcal infections, mesenteric lymphadenitis (see p. 1899), lymphogranuloma venereum (see p. 1900), and cat-scratch disease (see p. 1900). *Necrotizing features* may be seen in bubonic plague, tularemia, anthrax, typhoid fever, melioidosis,

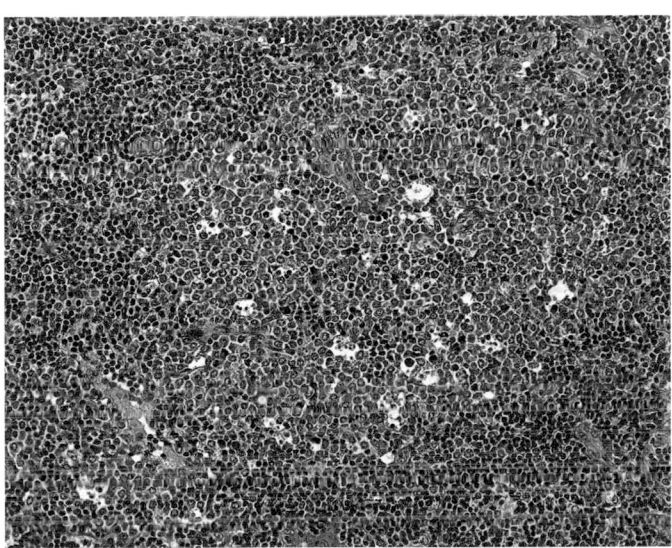

B

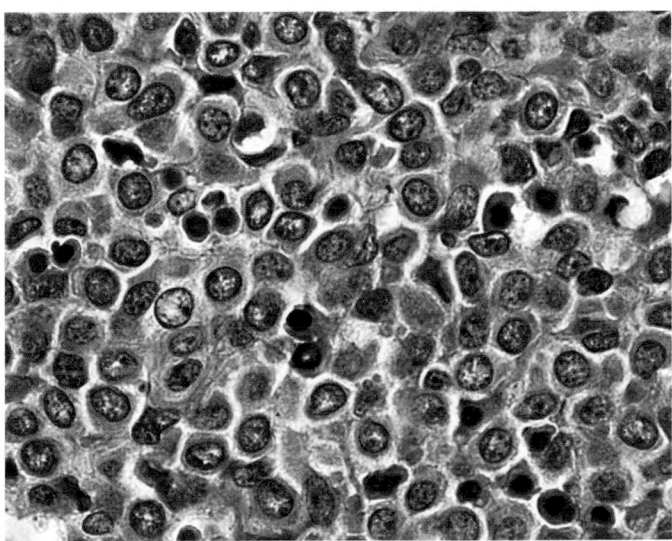

B

Fig. 21.9 Plasmacytoid monocytes as seen on low (**A**) and high power (**B**).

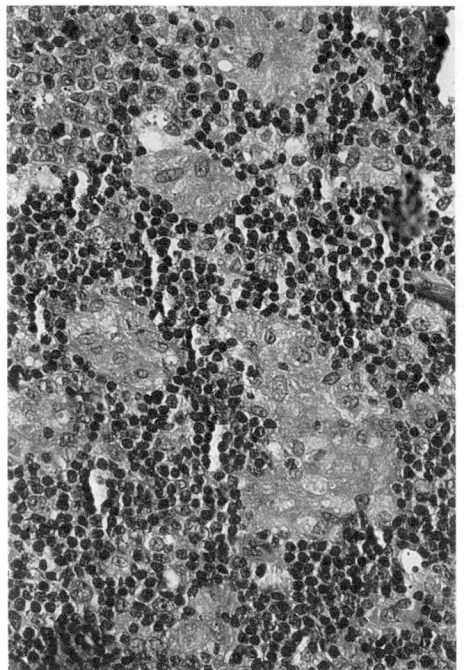

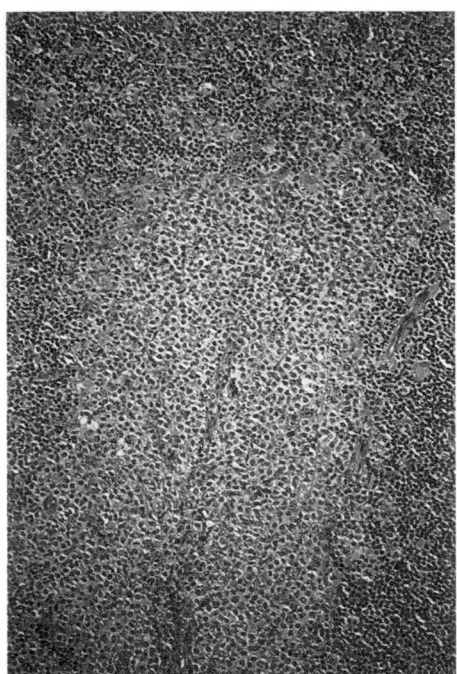

Fig. 21.17 A and **B**, Toxoplasmosis of lymph node. **A**, Small noncaseating granulomas composed of epithelioid cells are located at the periphery of a hyperplastic follicle. This picture is almost pathognomonic of this disease. **B**, An area of massive monocytoid B-cell hyperplasia.

The differential diagnosis of toxoplasmosis includes other infectious diseases and the lymphocyte predominance form of Hodgkin's lymphoma. In this regard, Miettinen et al.[168] have made the interesting point that occurrence of collections of epithelioid cells *within* germinal centers seems to be a nearly specific feature for toxoplasmosis.

Syphilis

Generalized lymphadenopathy is a common finding in secondary syphilis, whereas localized node enlargement can be seen in the primary and tertiary stages of the disease. In secondary syphilis, the changes are those of a florid follicular hyperplasia. In primary syphilis, the combination of changes may result in a mistaken diagnosis of malignant lymphoma. Most of the cases have presented as solitary inguinal lymphadenopathy.[173] There are capsular and pericapsular inflammation and extensive fibrosis, diffuse plasma cell infiltration, proliferation of blood vessels with endothelium swelling and inflammatory infiltration of their wall (phlebitis and endarteritis), and follicular hyperplasia[173] (Fig. 21.19). Rarely, noncaseating granulomas and abscesses are present. The morphologic features are not substantially different when occurring in HIV-infected patients[172] and can be identified in most cases by the Warthin–Starry or Levaditi stains or by immunofluorescence techniques applied to imprint preparations.[171] The organisms are most frequently found in the wall of blood vessels. Detection of *Treponema pallidum* is now also feasible in lymph node biopsies and fine needle aspirations by PCR and Southern blotting.[174]

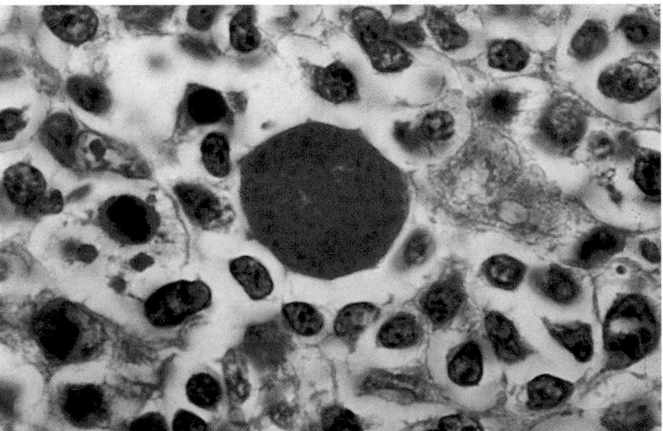

B

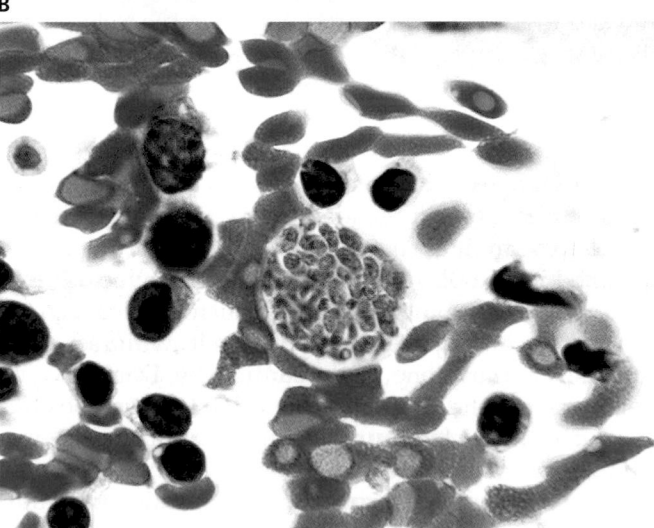

B

Fig. 21.18 *Toxoplasma* cyst as seen in a microscopic section (**A**) and a touch preparation (**B**). This is a very unusual finding in lymph nodes affected by the disease.

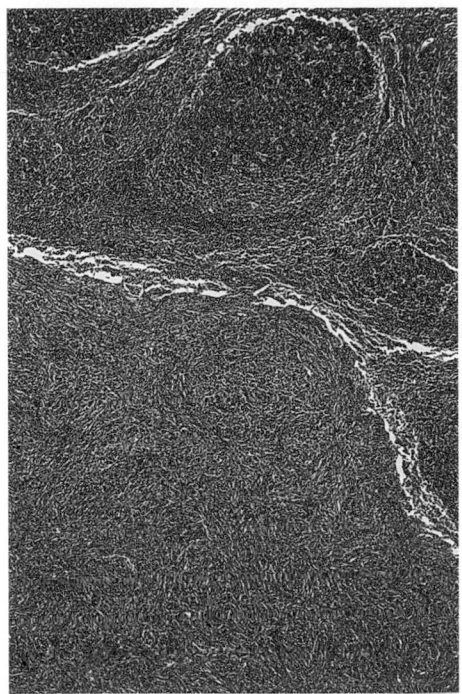
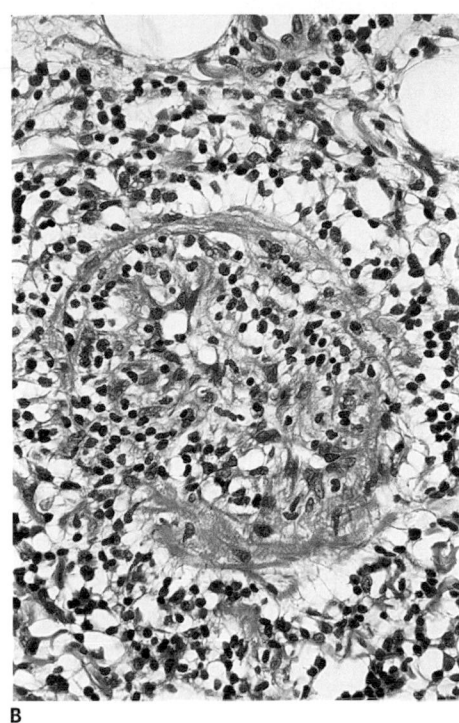

Fig. 21.19 A and **B**, Syphilis of lymph node. **A**, Follicular hyperplasia associated with striking pericapsular inflammation and fibrosis. **B**, The prominent vasculitis seen in this field is an important clue to the diagnosis.

Leprosy

Lymph nodes involved by the lepromatous type of leprosy have a very characteristic microscopic appearance. The main change is the progressive accumulation of large, pale, rounded histiocytes ("lepra" or "Virchow" cells), without granuloma formation and with minimal or no necrosis (Fig. 21.20). Wade–Fite and Fite–Faraco stains (modified Ziehl-Neelsen reactions) demonstrate packing of the cytoplasm by acid-fast organisms, which can also be demonstrated by a fluorescent method,[175] and with the PCR technique.[176]

Mesenteric lymphadenitis

Mesenteric (Masshoff's) lymphadenitis is produced by *Yersinia pseudotuberculosis* or *Yersinia enterocolitica*, two gram-negative polymorphic coccoid or ovoid motile organisms.[178–180,182] It is a benign, self-limited disease that can clinically simulate acute appendicitis. Micro-

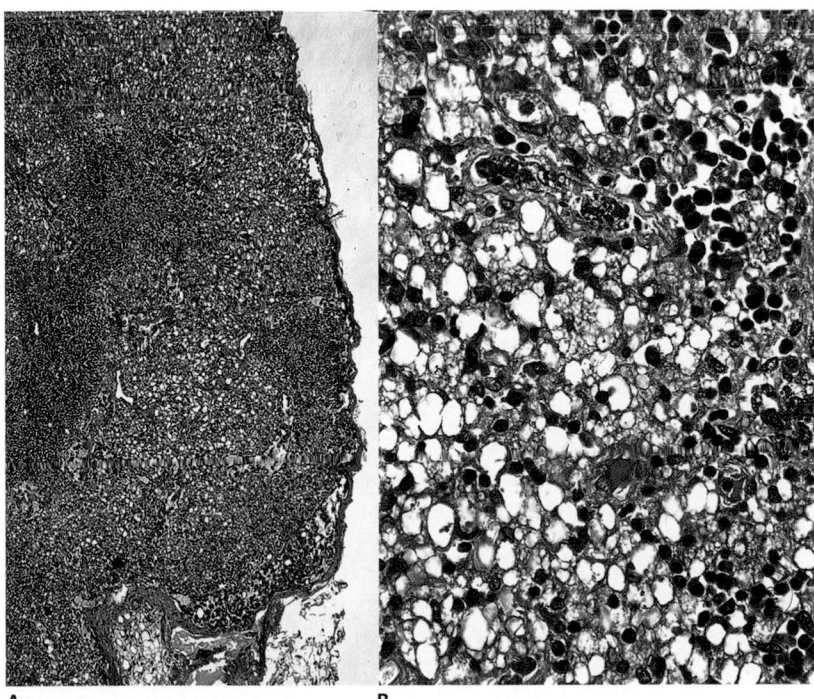

Fig. 21.20 Lymph node involvement by lepromatous leprosy. The sinuses are massively dilated as a result of the accumulation of foamy histiocytes.

scopically, there are capsular thickening and edema, increase of immunoblasts and plasma cells in the cortical and paracortical region, dilatation of sinuses with accumulation of large lymphocytes within, and germinal center hyperplasia.[177,183] In the lymphadenitis produced by *Yersinia pseudotuberculosis*, small granulomas and abscesses are commonly present, whereas this is unusual in infection caused by *Yersinia enterocolitica*.[183] These nodal changes are accompanied by inflammatory changes of the terminal ileum and cecum. Ideally, the diagnosis should be confirmed with cultures. Too often, the diagnosis of mesenteric lymphadenitis is made on normal or mildly hyperplastic nodes in an attempt to explain why a patient with the clinical picture of acute appendicitis has a normal appendix.

The organism can be identified with PCR techniques. Interestingly, pathogenetic Yersinia DNA has been detected in mesenteric lymph nodes in patients with Crohn's disease.[181]

Cat-scratch disease

Cat-scratch disease is characterized by a primary cutaneous lesion and enlargement of regional lymph nodes, usually axillary or cervical[185] (Fig. 21.21). The changes in the nodes vary with time. Early lesions have histiocytic proliferation and follicular hyperplasia, intermediate lesions have granulomatous changes, and late lesions have abscesses of various sizes[197] (Fig. 21.22). These abscesses are very suggestive of the diagnosis because of their pattern of central, sometimes stellate necrosis with neutrophils, surrounded by a palisading of histiocytes.[191] However, similar abscesses can be seen in lymphogranuloma venereum. Another common feature of lymph

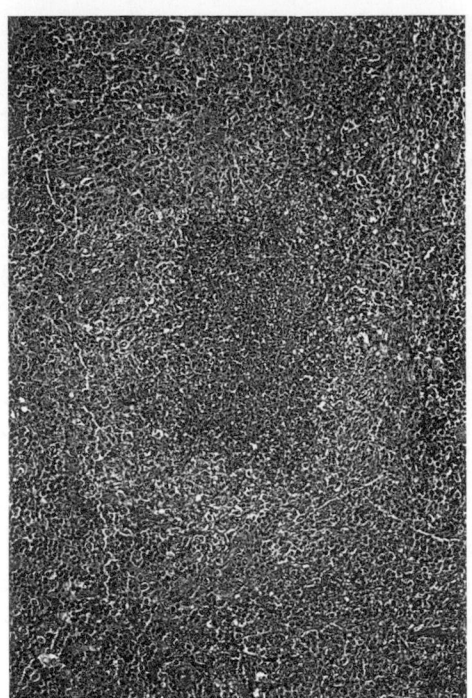

Fig. 21.22 An area of stellate necrosis in a proven case of cat-scratch disease.

nodes with cat-scratch disease is the packing of sinuses by monocytoid B cells, which, together with the follicular hyperplasia, may simulate toxoplasmosis.[190] However, clusters of perifollicular and intrafollicular epithelioid cells are absent.[187]

The primary lesion is a red papule in the skin at the site of inoculation, usually appearing between 7 and 12 days following contact. It may become pustular or crusted. Microscopically, there are foci of necrosis in the dermis surrounded by a mantle of histiocytes. Multinucleated giant cells, lymphocytes, and eosinophils are also present.[189]

The agent of cat-scratch disease is a coccobacillary pleomorphic extracellular bacterium that can be identified with the Warthin–Starry silver stain, particularly in those cases exhibiting extensive necrosis.[188,192,195] This organism, which has also been detected ultrastructurally,[193] was originally designated *Rochalimaea henselae* and has been renamed *Bartonella henselae*. The diagnosis can be confirmed by serology, immunofluorescence, or PCR.[184,194,196]

Rare complications of the disease include granulomatous conjunctivitis ("oculoglandular syndrome of Parinaud"), thrombocytopenic purpura, and central nervous system manifestations.[186]

Lymphogranuloma venereum

This sexually transmitted disease (not to be confused with granuloma inguinale) is caused by *Chlamydia trachomatis* organisms corresponding to serotypes L1, L2, and L3[199]: The initial lesion is a small (2 to 3 mm), painless

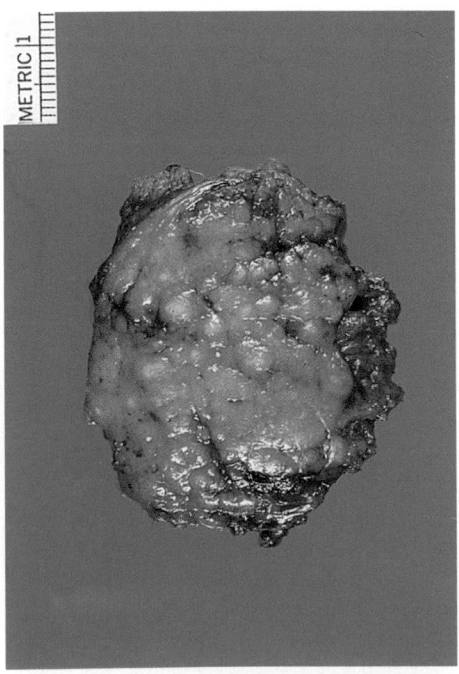

Fig. 21.21 Lymph node involved by cat-scratch disease.

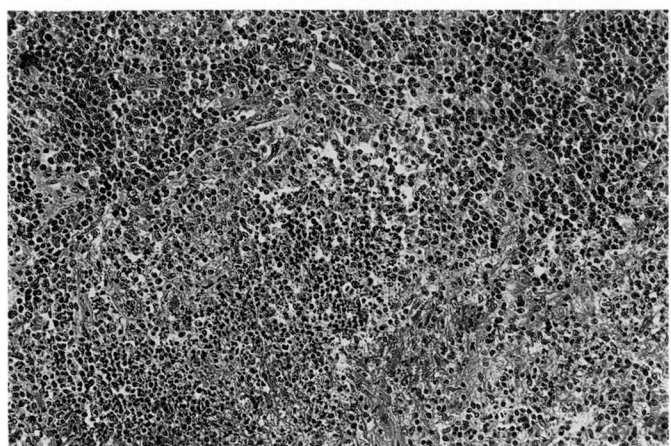

Fig. 21.23 Necrotizing granuloma in a lymph node affected by lymphogranuloma venereum.

genital vesicle or ulcer which often goes unnoticed and heals in a few days. This is followed by inguinal adenopathy, which can be very prominent. The earliest microscopic change in an affected node is represented by tiny necrotic foci infiltrated by neutrophils. These enlarge and coalesce to form the stellate abscess that is the most characteristic feature of this disease (Fig. 21.23). In later stages, epithelioid cells, scattered Langhans' giant cells, and fibroblasts are seen to line the walls. Confluence of these abscesses is common, and cutaneous sinus tracts may develop. The healing stage is represented by nodules with dense fibrous walls surrounding amorphous material.[201]

The microscopic picture just described is not pathognomonic of this disease. Similar changes can occur in cat-scratch disease, atypical mycobacteriosis, and tularemia. Therefore a presumptive diagnosis of lymphogranuloma venereum should be confirmed with the Frei test (a delayed hypersensitivity skin test using purified "lygranum" chlamydial antigen), complement fixation, immunofluorescent, or molecular testing.[198–200,202]

Tularemia

Tularemia is a bacterial disease produced by *Francisella tularensis*, an extremely virulent pathogen,[203,204,208] which has recently gained notoriety as a potential biowarfare agent.[209] In the ulcero-glandular form of the disease, prominent lymphadenopathy occurs; this predominates in the axillary region when mammalian vectors are involved and in cervical or inguinal regions with arthropod vectors.[205] A history of handling rabbits suggests the diagnosis in the first instance. The diagnosis is supported by a rise in hemagglutinin titers.[204,206]

Microscopically, the picture in the acute phase is that of an intense lymphadenitis with widespread necrosis. In the more chronic forms, there is a granulomatous reaction that in some cases may have a frankly tuberculoid appearance.[207]

Brucellosis

Brucellosis is caused by *Brucella abortus*, *melitensis*, or *suis*.[213] In the United States it has evolved from an occupational to a foodborne illness related to consumption of milk and cheese.[210] The most common clinical manifestations are fever, hepatomegaly, and splenomegaly.[211] Lymphadenopathy is uncommon and, when present, usually of modest dimensions. Microscopically, there may be nonspecific follicular hyperplasia and clusters of epithelioid histiocytes sometimes forming large non-caseating granulomas. This is accompanied by a polymorphic infiltrate containing eosinophils, plasma cells, and immunoblasts. When the latter are numerous, the microscopic picture may show a vague resemblance to Hodgkin's lymphoma.

A definitive diagnosis can only be made by recovery of the organism with bacteriologic or PCR techniques[212] or the detection of a high agglutination titer.[214]

AIDS-related lymphadenopathy

The lymph node abnormalities in AIDS patients can be of various types. They include mycobacterial and other opportunistic infections (some resulting in spindle cell pseudotumors),[224,232] Kaposi's sarcoma, malignant lymphomas of either Hodgkin's or non-Hodgkin's type, and *florid reactive hyperplasia*.[216,228] The latter change is the most common (Fig. 21.24). It may be accompanied by collections of monocytoid B cells in the sinuses, neutrophils, and features of dermatopathic lymphadenopathy. In many of the cases, the reactive germinal centers show a feature termed *follicle lysis*, characterized by invagination of mantle lymphocytes into the germinal centers. This is associated with disruption of these centers ("moth-eaten appearance") and a distinctive clustering of large follicular center cells,[217,234] resulting in an appearance that has been termed *explosive follicular hyperplasia*. Ultrastructurally, a prominence of follicular dendritic cells exhibiting alterations of their fine processes has been described[230]; it has been suggested also on the basis of immunohistochemically (fascin stain) that the AIDS virus preferentially infects these cells.[229,231] It has been suggested that the polykaryocytes (Warthin–Finkeldey cells) that are sometimes seen in HIV-infected nodes are a multinucleated form of follicular dendritic cell.[226] Immunohistochemically, positive stain for the HIV core protein P24 has been documented within the abnormal germinal centers.[225]

This combination of follicular changes is not pathognomonic of AIDS, but the possibility of this disease should be considered and investigated whenever they are found.

Some lymph nodes in AIDS patients may also show advanced lymphocyte depletion, with or without abnormal (regressively transformed) germinal centers.[217,230]

The interfollicular tissue may show prominent vascular proliferation, the resulting picture acquiring a vague

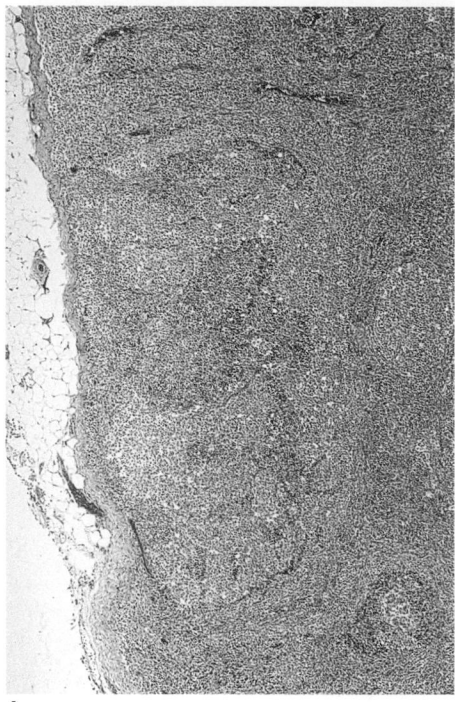 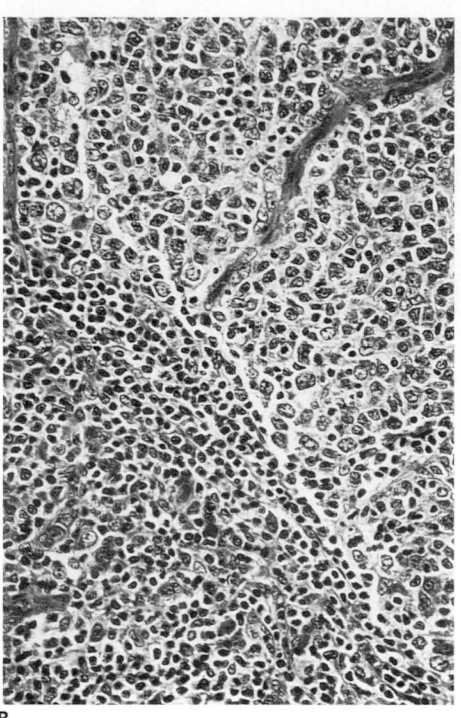

A   **B**

Fig. 21.24 Low-power (**A**) and high-power (**B**) microscopic views of AIDS-related lymphadenopathy. The depicted germinal center shows disruption of its architecture by intrusion of small lymphocytes from the mantle zone. This is a common but not pathognomonic feature of this disease.

resemblance to Castleman's disease. It is important to search in these areas and in the subcapsular region for the earliest signs of development of Kaposi's sarcoma.[222] These changes should be distinguished from those of vascular transformation of the sinuses (see p. 1969).

A rough relationship has been found among the pattern of nodal reaction, the cell suspension immunophenotypic data, and the patient's HIV status.[218,233]

The term *chronic lymphadenopathy syndrome* has been defined as an unexplained enlargement of nodes of at least 3 months' duration at two or more extrainguinal sites in an individual at risk for AIDS.[215] The microscopic picture is similar to that described previously.[223] Overall, up to a fourth of the patients have developed AIDS on follow-up, cachexia and weight loss being the clinical signs of this progression.[219,221]

The HIV-associated lymphoproliferative diseases of lymph nodes are discussed on p. 1959.

Infectious mononucleosis

The etiologic agent of classical infectious mononucleosis is the EBV,[227] but other agents may be involved in atypical cases.[220] It is rare for the pathologist to see a lymph node from a patient with a typical clinical picture because in most instances the presumptive clinical diagnosis is confirmed by examination of the peripheral blood and serologic evaluation without need of a lymph node biopsy. It is in the atypical case, presenting with lymphadenopathy without fever, sore throat, or splenomegaly, that the clinician will perform a lymph node biopsy to rule out the possibility of malignant lymphoma.

Microscopically, nodes and other lymphoid organs affected by infectious mononucleosis can be confused with malignant lymphoma because of the effacement of the architecture; infiltration of the trabecula, capsule, and perinodal fat; and the marked proliferation of immunoblasts, immature plasma cells, and mature plasma cells ("polymorphic B-cell hyperplasia") (Figs 21.25 and 21.26). These features are particularly prominent when the disease develops in transplant recipients or other immunosuppressed patients.[235] Necrosis may also be present; this is usually only focal but in immunodeficient children it may be massive.

Features of importance in the differential diagnosis with lymphoma include the predominantly sinusal distribution of the large lymphoid cells, follicular hyperplasia with marked mitotic activity and phagocytosis (these follicles being usually small), increase in the number of plasma cells, and vascular proliferation.[239] Another important feature is the fact that, although the nodal architecture may appear effaced, the sinusal pattern remains intact or even focally accentuated, a fact appreciated particularly well with reticulin stains. Another supposedly characteristic feature of this disease is the presence in the sinuses of clusters or "colonies" of lymphocytes in graduated sizes, from the small lymphocyte to the large lymphoid cell or immunoblast.[241] The latter cell usually has only one large vesicular nucleus with a thin nuclear membrane and one or two prominent amphophilic or basophilic nucleoli. A paranuclear "hof" is often seen. When binucleated, this cell may closely resemble a Reed–Sternberg cell and result in a mistaken diagnosis of Hodgkin's lymphoma[237,243] (Fig. 21.26).

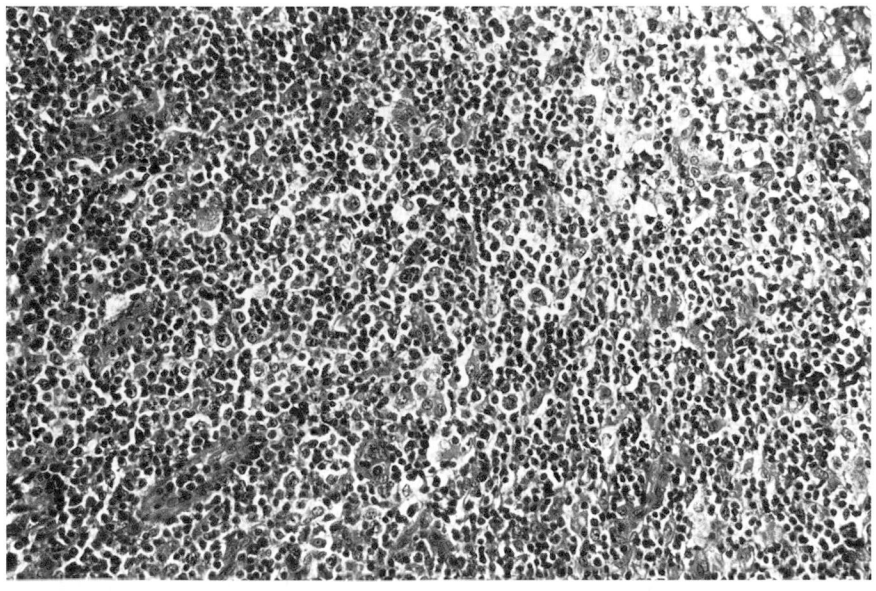

Fig. 21.25 Lymph node involved by infectious mononucleosis. There is a marked effacement of the architecture by a polymorphic lymphoid infiltrate.

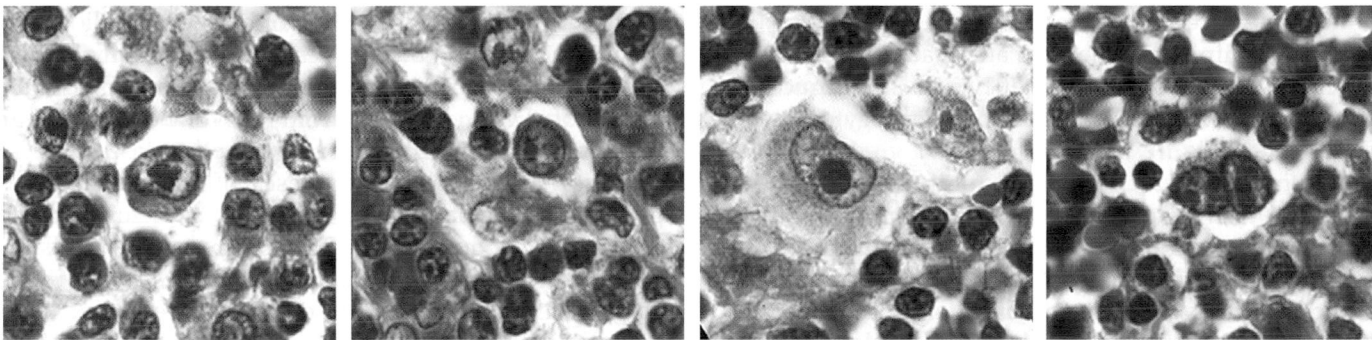

Fig. 21.26 Various types of immunoblasts seen in a lymph node involved by infectious mononucleosis. The binucleated form (shown in the fourth image) can simulate Reed–Sternberg cells. Note the basophilic character of the nucleus and the presence of a paranuclear hof.

Immunophenotyping evaluation should resolve the issue in most cases, despite the existence of an overlap that may be providing a pathogenetic insight into the nature and possible relationship of these two disorders.[238] The diagnosis of infectious mononucleosis can be confirmed by in situ hybridization techniques[236,240,242] (Fig. 21.27).

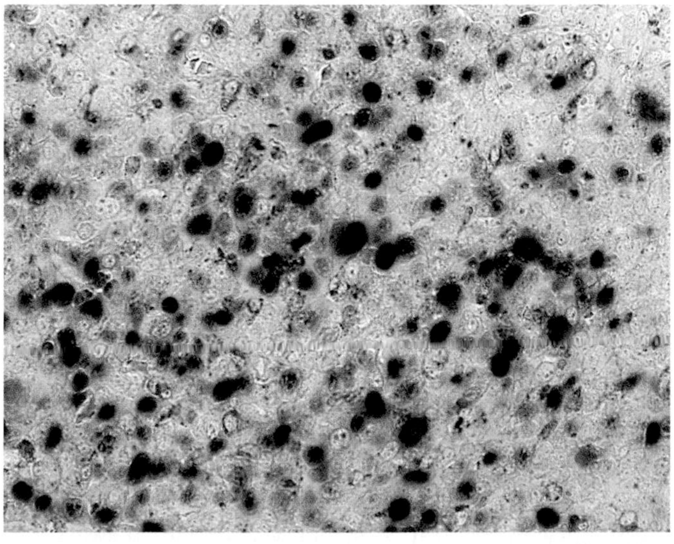

Other viral (including postvaccinial) lymphadenitides

Lymph nodes draining an area of the skin subjected to smallpox vaccination can enlarge and become painful. If removed and examined microscopically, they can be easily confused with lymphoma, especially if the history of vaccination is overlooked. Of 20 cases of postvaccinial lymphadenitis reported by Hartsock,[247] 13 were located in the supraclavicular region on the side of the vaccination. The largest node measured 6 cm in diameter. The interval between the vaccination and the biopsy varied between 1 week and 3 months.

Microscopically, the changes are those of a diffuse or nodular paracortical expansion, with mixed cellular proliferation, consisting of eosinophils, plasma cells, and a large number of immunoblasts. The alterations are accompanied by vascular and sinusal changes and focal discrete necrosis. The most important histologic feature of postvaccinal hyperplasia is the presence of numerous

Fig. 21.27 Demonstration of EBER antigen by in situ hybridization in a case of infectious mononucleosis.

marked expansion of the mantle zone and small, relatively inconspicuous germinal centers. This variant of Castleman's disease merges with the process designated as *mantle zone hyperplasia*, and it is the more likely to be confused with malignant lymphoma of either follicular or mantle cell type. Immunohistochemically, there is polyclonal immunoglobulin production by plasma cells, and large numbers of suppressor T cells are found in the interfollicular areas. An aberrant phenotype of Ki-B3-negative B lymphocytes has been detected in the mantle zone cells.[298] Strong positivity for FVIII-related antigen is seen in the endothelium of the interfollicular vessels, but only a weak and focal reaction for this marker is found in the hyalinized vessels located in the center of the follicles.[288]

The second major morphologic category of Castleman's disease is known as the *plasma cell type*.[289] It is characterized by a diffuse plasma cell proliferation in the interfollicular tissue, sometimes accompanied by numerous Russell bodies. The hyaline-vascular changes in the follicles are inconspicuous or absent; instead, one often encounters in the center of these follicles a deposition of an amorphous acidophilic material that probably contains fibrin and immune complexes. The overall appearance is reminiscent of that seen in the lymph nodes from patients with rheumatoid arthritis (Fig. 21.31). The abundant expression of interleukin-6 that has been detected in this condition is thought to be responsible for the marked plasma cell infiltration.[286]

From the point of view of clinical presentation, Castleman's disease has been divided into a solitary and a multicentric form. The *solitary form* presents as a mass located most commonly in the mediastinum but also described in the neck, lung, axilla, mesentery, broad ligament, retroperitoneum, soft tissues of the extremities, nasopharynx, meninges, and several other sites.[282] Grossly, it is round, well-circumscribed, with a solid gray cut surface, and can measure 15 cm or more in diameter (Fig. 21.32). Although this form by definition presents as a single mass, microscopic changes suggesting an early stage of the same process are sometimes seen in adjacent nodes. Microscopically, over 90% of the cases are of the hyaline-vascular type (including the lymphoid subtype), and the remainder are of the plasma cell type. The former is usually asymptomatic, whereas the plasma cell type is often associated with fever, anemia, elevated erythrosedimentation rate, hypergammaglobulinemia, and hypoalbuminemia. The disease reported in the Orient as idiopathic plasmacytic lymphadenopathy with polyclonal hypergammaglobulinemia is closely related to the plasma cell type of Castleman's disease but apparently not identical.[290] The treatment of solitary Castleman's disease is surgical excision, which has been found to result in rapid regression of the associated abnormalities whenever present.[272]

The *multicentric* or *systemic form* is nearly always of the plasma cell type,[296] although occasional examples of the hyaline vascular type (involving even the skin) are on record.[310] It presents with generalized lymphadenopathy and may also involve the spleen.[278,279,313] The clinical and laboratory features are similar to those of angioimmunoblastic lymphadenopathy. The etiology is unknown, the two main hypotheses (not mutually exclusive) being abnormal immune response and viral infection.[287]

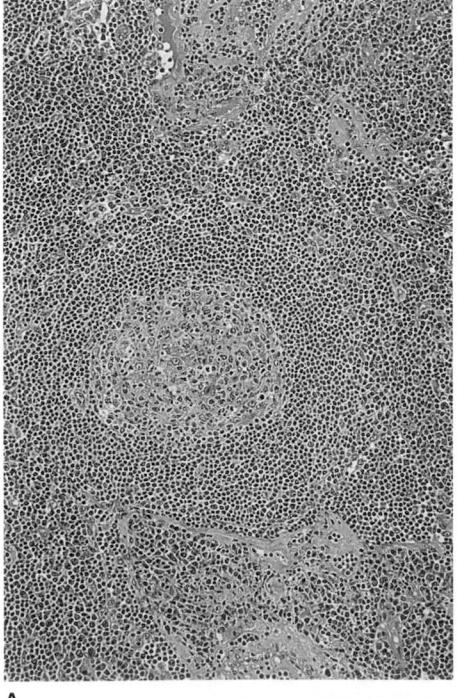

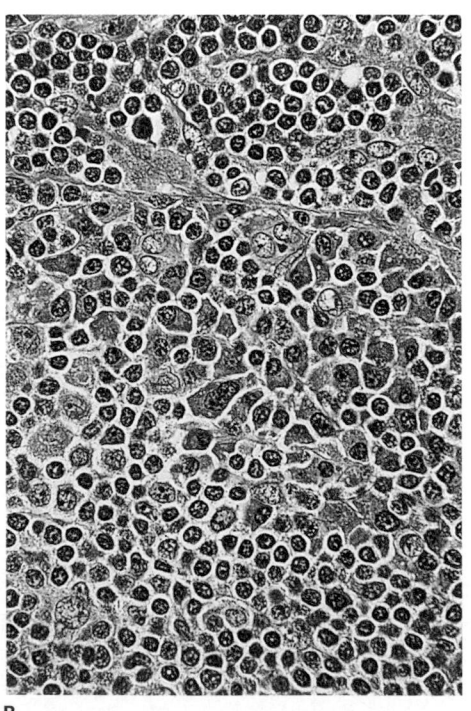

A

B

Fig. 21.31 A and **B**, Castleman's disease of plasma cell type. **A**, Low-power view showing follicular hyperplasia without vascular hyaline changes. **B**, High-power view of the interfollicular region showing a massive infiltration by plasma cells. Some of these plasma cells show multinucleation and mild nuclear atypia.

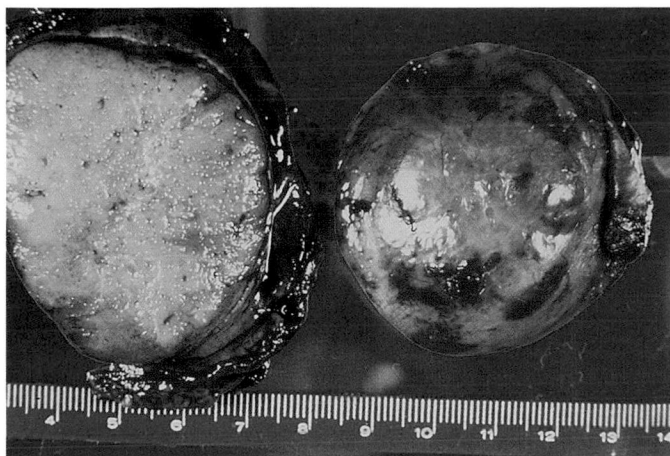

Fig. 21.32 Gross appearance of Castleman's disease of the hyaline vascular type.

Regarding the latter, a definite link has been documented between HHV-8 and a subset of multicentric Castleman's disease (this virus being also linked to Kaposi's sarcoma and primary effusion sarcoma).[271,304] Cases of HHV-8+ Castleman's disease are said to be characterized morphologically by dissolution of the lymphoid follicles.[270] It has been hypothesized that HHV-8 induces the changes of Castleman's disease through the production of interleukin-6.[285,297]

Sometimes multicentric Castleman's disease is seen in association with the POEMS syndrome, an acronymic designation for polyneuropathy, organomegaly, endocrinopathy, M-protein, and skin changes.[295,299] The latter include a distinctive vascular lesion known as glomeruloid hemangioma.[273] In other instances, Castleman's disease has been reported in association with amyloid deposits.[269,303]

The long-term prognosis of systemic Castleman's disease is poor; the disease tends to persist for months or years and to result sometimes in renal or pulmonary complications.[306] Furthermore, some of the patients have been found to have Kaposi's sarcoma, and others have developed large cell lymphomas of immunoblastic type. Evidence of clonal rearrangement for immunoglobulin and T-cell receptor genes has been found in cases of systemic Castleman's disease together with copies of the EBV genome, no such features having been detected in the solitary form of the disease.[283,284,302,307] This suggests that multicentric Castleman's disease is a disorder different from the classic localized type and one that may evolve into a clonal lymphoproliferation.

Some authors actually regard it as a lymphoproliferative process rather than a reactive/inflammatory condition.

An important theme of the hyaline vascular type of Castleman's disease is the active participation in it of a variety of nonlymphoid cellular components. One such component is the dendritic follicular cell, which is prominently present in the hyalinized nodules that characterize the disease and which is thought by some authors to be at the core of the pathogenesis of this disorder[301,309] (Fig. 21.33). These cells can become atypical ("dysplastic") both in the abnormal germinal centers and in the intervening tissue,[309] and can manifest cytogenetic and molecular evidence of clonality[275,305] (Fig. 21.34). Furthermore, they may result in the formation of full-blown dendritic follicular tumors (p. 1965).[274,292] Another type of proliferation involves the vascular and related contractile (myoid) elements that are present in the interfollicular tissue. Cases of Castleman's disease in which these elements are unduly prominent have been referred to as *stroma-rich*[276] (Fig. 21.35). Further proliferation of this component results in the formation of *angiomyoid proliferative lesions*,[292] and of lesions that have been referred to as *angiomatous hamartomas*[293] (Fig. 21.36), or *vascular neoplasms*, the latter sometimes having hemangiopericytoma-like features.[274] Finally, cases have been described of high-grade spindle cell sarcomas arising in Castleman's disease, which have been originally interpreted as of probable vascular nature because of the

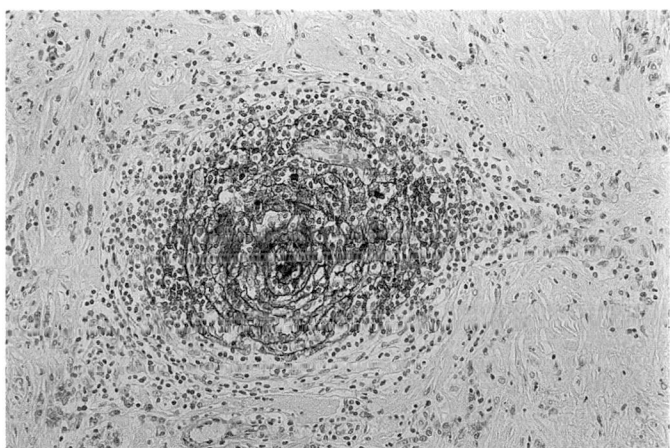

Fig. 21.33 Prominent network of CD21-positive dendritic follicular cells in the abnormal germinal center of Castleman's disease.

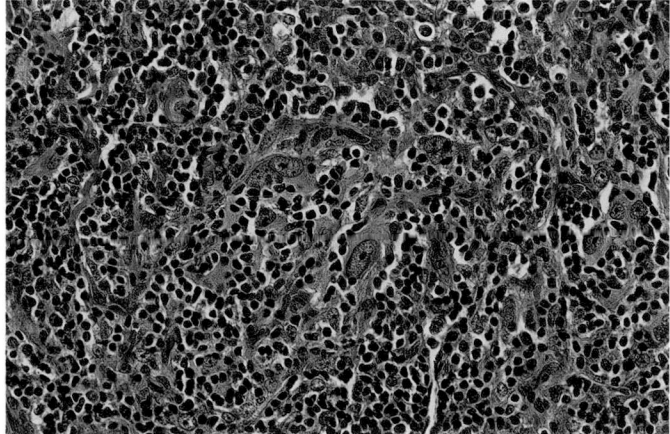

Fig. 21.34 "Dysplasia" of reticular/dendritic cells in Castleman's disease. These cells were immunoreactive for desmin.

consistently absent; what one may find instead are germinal centers composed of loose aggregates of pale histiocytes, rare immunoblasts, or large epithelioid cells; these are referred to as "burnt-out germinal centers" and can closely resemble the appearance of granulomas. Only occasionally one finds hyperplastic germinal centers of the conventional type.[335] There may also be a component of proliferating cells of dendritic/reticulum nature, some of them strongly positive for desmin.[325] An amorphous, eosinophilic PAS-positive intercellular material may be found scattered throughout the node. Extension of the infiltrate in the capsule and pericapsular tissue is common. Methyl green–pyronine stain shows that most of the large lymphoid cells are pyroninophilic, and immunoperoxidase stain reveals a polyclonal pattern of immunoglobulin production. Lymphoid cells positive for EBV are found in over 75% of the cases; most but not all of these cells are of B-cell nature.[334]

The nature of AILD has been controversial since the time of its first description and remains so today. It was originally regarded as a non-neoplastic hyperimmune proliferation of the B-cell system with an exaggerated transformation of lymphocytes into immunoblasts and plasma cells, possibly induced by a primary abnormality of the T cell system (such as a loss of suppressor T cells).[318,319,329] However, subsequent studies revealed the existence of cases having the AILD pattern but also exhibiting features suggesting the presence of a neoplastic lymphoid component. Thus Nathwani et al.[333] described cases of AILD characterized by the appearance of "clones" (clusters or islands) of tightly packed immunoblasts, followed by a diffuse replacement of the node by these elements (Fig. 21.39). Several Japanese groups described cases with the AILD pattern that also exhibited cytologic atypia in the small and large lymphoid cells (clear cells and/or convoluted cells).[337] In many of these cases, the existence of a clonal population of T lymphocytes was documented by molecular techniques.[331,339] Although these cases were initially interpreted as AILD-like T-cell lymphomas and an attempt was made to separate them from "true" AILD, it has become increasingly apparent that a sharp separation among these lesions is impossible. AILD should be viewed as an arbitrarily defined morphologic portion of a spectrum of atypical immunoproliferative disorders (also known as lymphogranulomatosis X in some circles)[327] that range from the probably reactive and reversible to the clearly neoplastic and aggressive. At present, the consensus is that the overwhelming majority of cases belong to this category and that they represent a subtype of peripheral T-cell lymphoma. It is further believed that this subtype is characterized by the expression of CD10.[316]

The issue is further complicated by the fact that some cases show a clonal population of B cells *in addition* to a clonal population of T cells.[321] The possible role of a viral agent in the genesis of this disorder has been repeatedly proposed but not yet conclusively demonstrated.[326,328,334]

From a practical standpoint, the presence of atypical lymphoid cells (whether immunoblastic "clones," clear cells, or small cells with convoluted nuclei) correlates with a more aggressive clinical course.[315,333] In retrospect, we believe that the cases that we described many years ago as "malignant histiocytosis with cutaneous involvement and eosinophilia"[330] belong to this general category as representatives of the more aggressive and neoplastic type. Similar cases have been described by others.[320]

Drug hypersensitivity

Antiepileptic drugs derived from hydantoin, such as diphenylhydantoin (Dilantin) and mephenytoin (Mesantoin), can result in a hypersensitivity reaction manifested by skin rash, fever, generalized lymphadenopathy (mainly cervical), and peripheral eosinophilia. The reaction, which is quite uncommon, tends to occur within the first few months of therapy. The changes disappear if the drug is discontinued. The nodal enlargement can occur in the absence of some of the other manifestations of the drug reaction.

Microscopically, partial effacement of the architecture by a polymorphic cellular infiltration is seen.[340] Histiocytes, immunoblasts, eosinophils, neutrophils, and plasma cells are all present. Some of the immunoblasts have atypical nuclear features, but Reed–Sternberg cells are absent. Foci of necrosis were noted in the classic article by Salzstein and Ackerman in which this condition was first described.[341] In some of the cases, the microscopic appearance is indistinguishable from that of AILD. The problem may simply be one of semantics, as one could interpret these cases as examples of the rare nonmalignant type of AILD induced by the anticonvulsant therapy.

Dermatopathic lymphadenitis

Dermatopathic lymphadenitis (lipomelanosis reticularis of Pautrier) is a form of nodal hyperplasia usually

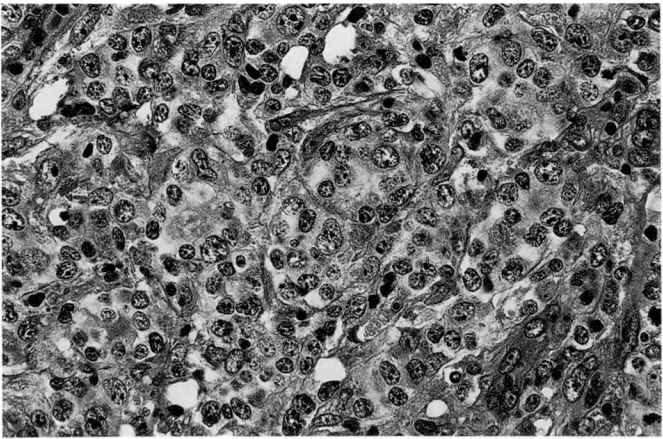

Fig. 21.39 Angioimmunoblastic lymphadenopathy with uniform proliferation of large lymphoid cells of neoplastic appearance.

secondary to a generalized dermatitis, particularly those with exfoliative features. Pathogenetically, it represents a T-cell response to skin antigens processed and presented by interdigitating dendritic cells. It may occur in any skin disorder in which itching and scratching are prominent; this includes inflammatory dermatoses such as psoriasis and neoplastic diseases such as mycosis fungoides. Rarely, the morphologic changes of dermatopathic lymphadenitis are seen in the absence of clinical skin disease.[344]

Grossly, the lymph node is enlarged, the cut surface bulging, and the color pale yellow. In florid cases, black linear areas are seen in the periphery, representing clumps of melanin pigment and simulating the appearance of malignant melanoma.

Microscopically, the nodal architecture is preserved. The main change is represented by a marked pale widening of the paracortical zone, which stands out prominently on low-power examination[346] (Fig. 21.40). Most of the large nonlymphoid cells occupying this area are thought to be of three types: histiocytes, Langerhans' cells, and interdigitating dendritic cells.[342,345] Many of the histiocytes contain phagocytosed melanin and neutral fat in their cytoplasm. Plasma cell infiltration and follicular hyperplasia are often present. A scattering of eosinophils also may be seen.

Nodes affected by dermatopathic lymphadenitis may be confused with Hodgkin's lymphoma, mycosis fungoides, monocytic leukemia, or Langerhans' cell histiocytosis. The differential diagnosis with mycosis fungoides is of particular concern because of the fact that mycosis fungoides is one of the cutaneous disorders that

can be associated with dermatopathic lymphadenitis.[343] Diagnostic assistance can be obtained from immunohistochemistry and molecular pathology. Dermatopathic lymph nodes *that are also involved by mycosis fungoides* may show loss of CD7 and CD62L expression, and sometimes also loss of the pan–T-cell markers CD5, CD3, and CD2.[348] At the molecular level, clonal rearrangements of T-cell receptor genes may be demonstrated.[347]

Rosai–Dorfman disease (sinus histiocytosis with massive lymphadenopathy)

Rosai–Dorfman disease (RDD), originally described as sinus histiocytosis with massive lymphadenopathy (SHML), presents in its most typical form as massive, painless, bilateral lymph node enlargement in the neck, associated with fever, leukocytosis, elevated erythrosedimentation rate, and polyclonal hypergammaglobulinemia.[359,381] Most cases occur during the first or second decade of life, but any age group can be affected. A few cases have affected two members of the same family.[370] There is a predisposition for the condition in blacks. Although the disease has a widespread geographic distribution and most of the reported cases have been from the United States and Western Europe, there is a disproportionally high number of cases from Africa and the Caribbean region.[359] Although the cervical region is by far the most common and most prominent site of involvement, other peripheral or central lymph node groups can be affected, with or without cervical disease.

Grossly, the nodes are matted together by prominent perinodal fibrosis. Their cut surface varies from gray to golden yellow, depending on the amount of fat present.

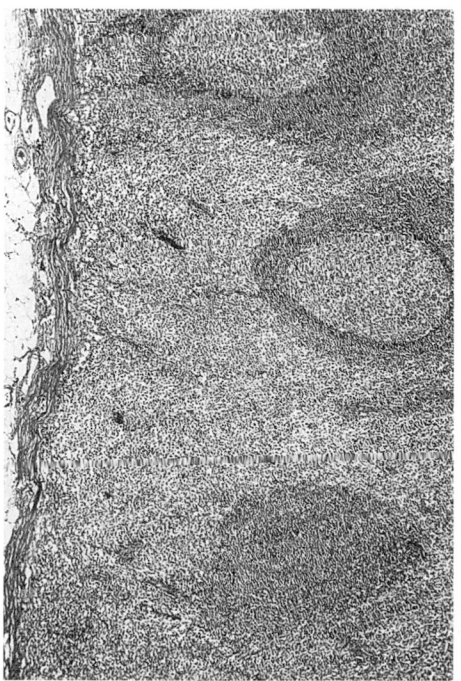

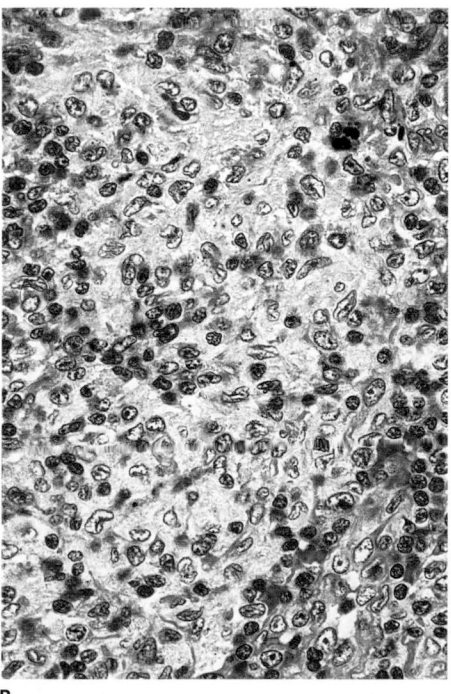

A   **B**

Fig. 21.40 A and **B**, Dermatopathic lymphadenitis. **A**, Massive expansion of the paracortical region, resulting in a wide, pale area between the capsule and the lymphoid follicles. **B**, High-power view of the paracortical region showing numerous cells with oval vesicular nuclei, which correspond to an admixture of interdigitating dendritic cells and Langerhans' cells.

Microscopically, there is a pronounced dilatation of the lymph sinuses, resulting in partial or complete architectural effacement (Fig. 21.41). These sinuses are occupied by lymphocytes, plasma cells, and—most notably—by numerous cells of histiocytic appearance with a large vesicular nucleus and abundant clear cytoplasm that may contain large amounts of neutral lipids. Many of these histiocytes have within their cytoplasm numerous intact lymphocytes, a feature that has been designated as emperipolesis or lymphocytophagocytosis. Although not specific, this is a constant feature of RDD (as least in the lymph node location) and is therefore of great diagnostic significance (Fig. 21.42). Sometimes other cell types are present within the cytoplasm of the histiocytes, such as plasma cells and red blood cells.

The intersinusal tissue exhibits a variable but sometimes impressive number of mature plasma cells, some of which may contain Russell's bodies. Capsular and pericapsular inflammation and fibrosis are common, but intranodal fibrosis is minimal or absent. In a minority of cases, small microabscesses or foci of necrosis are found within the dilated sinuses. Ultrastructurally, the histiocytes located in the sinuses have extensive pseudopodia and lack Birbeck's granules; viral particles or other evidence of infection is consistently lacking. The sinus histiocytes contain cytoplasmic fat (Fig. 21.43) and are strongly reactive for S-100 protein[372] (Fig. 21.44) but negative for CD1a; some of them are also positive for immunoglobulin, presumably phagocytosed from the surroundings. Their immunohistochemical profile (including the adhesion molecules pattern) suggests that they are monocytes that have been recently recruited from the circulation.[351,354,374,379] The plasma cells show a polyclonal pattern of immunoglobulin expression. The lymphocytes present are an admixture of B and T cells.

In over one fourth of the cases, RDD involves extranodal sites.[359] This usually occurs in the presence of massive lymphadenopathy, and the disease is therefore easily recognized. However, in some cases these extranodal manifestations represent the predominant or even exclusive manifestation of the disease. Practically all organ systems have been recorded as being the site of the disease. The most common are eyes and ocular adnexa

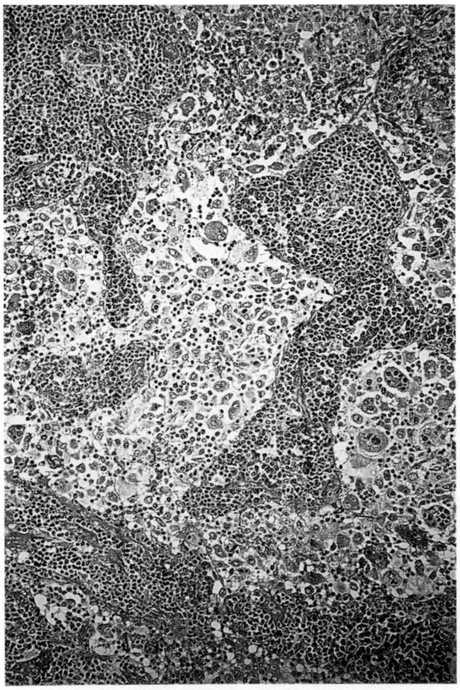

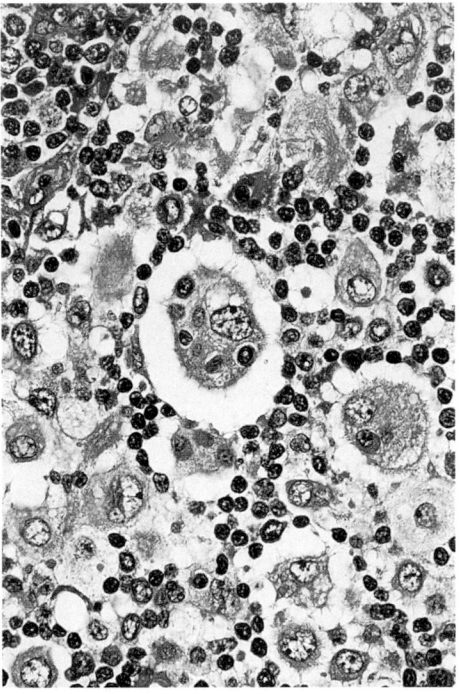

Fig. 21.42 Rosai–Dorfman disease. High-power view showing lymphocytophagocytosis by the sinus histiocytes.

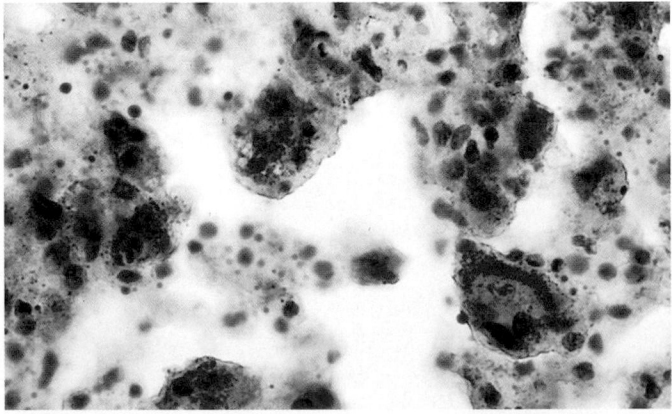

Fig. 21.43 Rosai–Dorfman disease. **A,** Oil red O stain showing abundant neutral lipid in the cytoplasm of the histiocytes.

Fig. 21.41 Rosai–Dorfman disease. Low-power view showing massive distension of the sinuses by the histiocytic infiltrate.

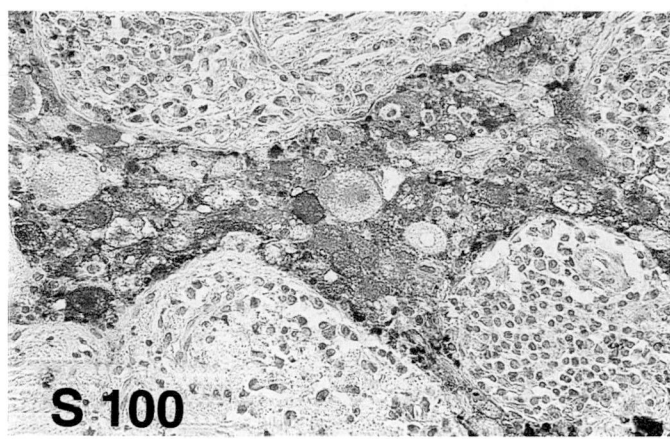

Fig. 21.44 Strong immunoreactivity of the sinus histiocytes for S-100 protein in Rosai Dorfman disease.

(especially orbit),[357] head and neck region,[388] upper respiratory tract,[356,366] skin and subcutaneous tissue,[352,373,384] skeletal system,[386] and central nervous system.[350,360,382] However, the disease has been reported in many other sites, including gastrointestinal tract,[365,375] salivary glands,[363] genitourinary tract, thyroid,[353] breast,[362] and uterine cervix.[374] In some instances, widespread nodal and extranodal dissemination is found.[391] Organs that stand out because of their almost universal sparing by the disorder are lung, spleen, and bone marrow (the latter exclusive of the focal bone lesions mentioned above). The histopathologic features of RDD in extranodal sites are similar to the nodal disease except for the fact that fibrosis tends to be more pronounced and lymphocytophagocytosis less conspicuous.

The etiology of RDD remains unknown, the two most likely possibilities (not mutually exclusive) being infection by a virus or some other microorganism and the manifestation of a subtle undefined immunologic defect. Despite some suggestive early data derived from serologic tests, the histiocytes of this disease are not infected by EBV.[385] HHV-6 has been detected in RDD tissues, but this organism is so commonly present in lymphoid tissue that the significance of this finding remains dubious.[367] Molecular studies done on involved tissue have failed to show evidence of clonality, in keeping with their presumed reactive nature.[369] This contrasts with the findings in at least some studies of Langerhans' cell histiocytosis, a disease that it otherwise resembles in many clinical, morphologic, and phenotypical aspects,[376,389,390] and with which it can coexist.[387] We have seen five cases of the latter occurrence. It has been suggested that stimulation of monocytes/macrophages via macrophage colony stimulating factor (M-CSF) leading to immune suppressive macrophages may be the main pathogenetic mechanism of RDD.[371]

RDD is relatively unaffected by therapy, although chemotherapy has proved effective in some cases.[364,378,383]

In many cases, RDD undergoes quick and complete spontaneous resolution. In others, it follows a protracted clinical course for years or decades. The latter is particularly true in cases with widespread extranodal involvement. In some instances the disease disappears, only to come back years later at another site. Some patients have died as a result of RDD, either because of extensive disease affecting vital organs or because of complications related to the immunologic abnormalities that may be present,[358,361] such as amyloidosis.[380]

The differential diagnosis of RDD includes nonspecific sinus hyperplasia (in which the cells lack emperipolesis and are S-100 protein-negative), Langerhans' cell histiocytosis (which are positive for both S-100 protein and CD1a), leprosy, and metastatic malignant melanoma. Perhaps the condition that resembles it most is the sinus histiocytosis induced by cobalt-chromium and titanium that can occur in pelvic lymph nodes after hip replacement.[349]

It should also be noted that focal RDD-like changes can sometimes be seen in lymph nodes involved by other processes, such as Hodgkin's[355] or non-Hodgkin's lymphoma.[368]

Langerhans' cell histiocytosis

The terms Langerhans' cell histiocytosis (LCH), Langerhans' cell granulomatosis, histiocytosis X, differentiated histiocytosis, and eosinophilic granuloma are applied to a specific, although remarkably variable, clinicopathologic entity characterized and defined by the proliferation of Langerhans' cells.[402,416,424] These cells are regarded as a distinct type of immune "accessory" cells that are involved in the capturing of some antigens and their presentation to the lymphoid cells. Contrary to a formerly held belief, these cells are not primarily phagocytic in nature. Their nuclei are highly characteristic: irregular, usually elongated, with prominent grooves and folds that traverse them in all directions. The cytoplasm is abundant and acidophilic, sometimes to the point that an embryonal rhabdomyosarcoma is simulated. Most Langerhans' cells are mononuclear, but occasional ones contain several nuclei while still maintaining the aforementioned nuclear and cytoplasmic features. Histochemically, they show weak acid phosphatase and nonspecific esterase activity but considerable leucyl-β-naphthylamidase activity and membrane-bound ATPase activity.[394] They are believed to develop from a lymphoid-committed precursor,[392] an hypothesis supported by the presence of an identical rearrangement of the immunoglobulin heavy chain gene in a case we studied which had both neoplastic Langerhans' cells and B lymphocytes.[418]

In paraffin sections, both Langerhans' cells and the cells of LCH are reactive for S-100 protein, vimentin, langerin, fascin (a dendritic cell marker), CD1a, CD74, and HLA-DR in most cases[408,429,430,436] (Fig. 21.45). They also

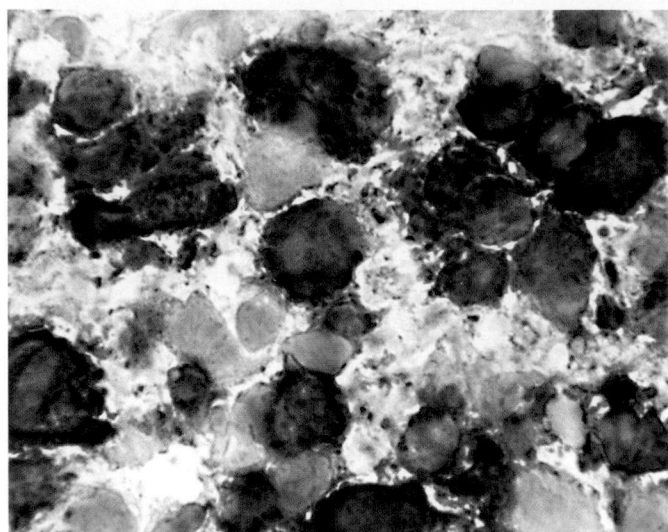

Fig. 21.45 Immunoreactivity of the cells of Langerhans' cell histiocytosis for langerin.

tend to be positive for peanut agglutinin lectin and the macrophage-associated antigens CD68, cathepsin D, and cathepsin E.[406,428,431] They generally do not express CD45RA, CD45RB, CDw75, α_1-antitrypsin, EMA, or CD15. The most useful of these formalin-resistant epitopes are S-100 protein and CD1a.[401]

In frozen sections, these cells are positive for CD45 but negative for CD45RA, CD4B, and CD45RD. In addition, they express CD1, CD4, CD11b, CD11c, CD14, CD16, CD25, CDw32, CD71, CD101, and HLA-A, -B, -C, and -DR, and they lack expression of most B- and T-cell markers.[398,426]

CD1 is the most useful marker in frozen sections in view of the fact that other histiocytic and dendritic/reticulum cells lack it. Interestingly, the cells of LCH—but not normal Langerhans' cells—may also be positive for cytoplasmic CD2 and CD3. At the molecular level, these cells show no rearrangement of the T-cell receptor gene.[444]

By electron microscopy, they contain a highly characteristic and apparently diagnostic organelle: the Birbeck's or Langerhans' granule. This is an elongated, zipperlike cytoplasmic structure of unknown function, sometimes continuous with the cell membrane.[420]

Scattered Langerhans' cells are normally present in the skin, lymph node, thymus, and other organs. Therefore the identification of a few cells with this feature in one of these sites is not necessarily indicative that the patient has LCH.[439] Rather, the infiltrate should have a sizable number of these cells before such a diagnosis is entertained. Conversely, the identification of Langerhans' cells is necessary for the diagnosis of LCH. There is already too much confusion in the literature stemming from the fact that cases have been given this label only because a widespread proliferation of histiocytes was associated with a compatible clinical picture.

LCH can present as solitary or multiple lesions in one organ system (bone being the most common: see Chapter 24) or as a disseminated disease.[425] Most patients are children or adolescents, but the disease can affect any age group, including the elderly.[404] The treatment, prognosis, and terminology used largely depend on the extent (staging) of the disease (see box) rather than microscopic features or pattern of DNA ploidy.[409,413,414,434] The term **Letterer–Siwe's disease** was used in the past for the systemic form occurring in infants, and **Hand–Schüller–Christian's disease** for the less widespread and more indolent type seen in older children and adults.[397] A self-healing, congenital form is known as **Hashimoto–Pritzker's disease**.[407]

Lymph node involvement can be seen as a component of the systemic form, or it may represent the initial and sometimes exclusive manifestation of the disease.[421,432,440] The microscopic appearance is characteristic. There is distention of the sinuses by an infiltrate of mononuclear and multinuclear Langerhans' cells, admixed with a variable number of eosinophils (Fig. 21.46); foci of necrosis are common, often surrounded by a rim of eosinophils (so-called "eosinophilic microabscesses"), and always confined to the sinuses.

Sometimes, incidental foci of LCH are seen in lymph

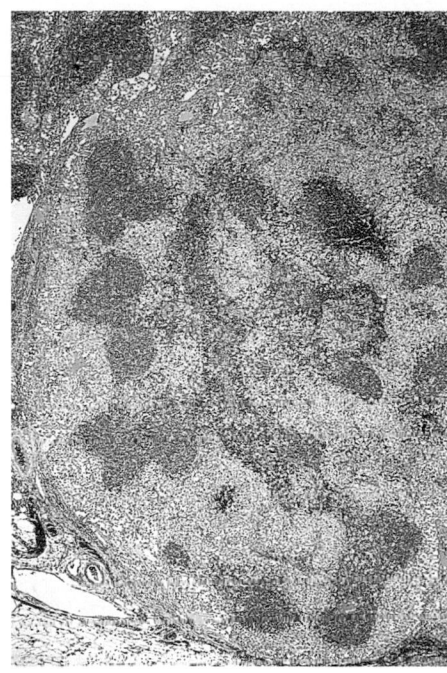
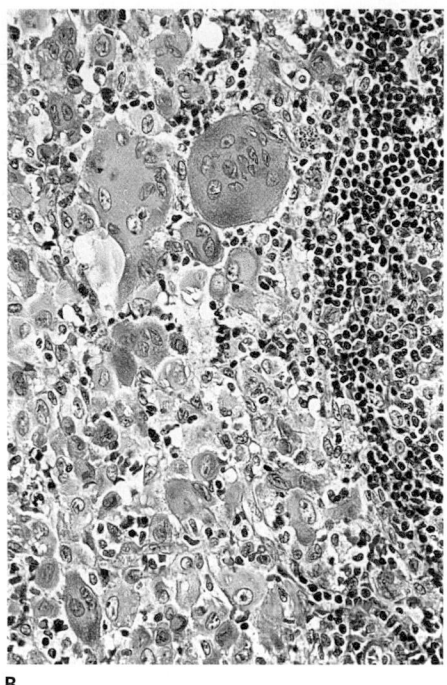

Fig. 21.46 A and **B**, Lymph node involvement by Langerhans' cell histiocytosis. **A**, The infiltrate has a predominantly sinusal distribution. **B**, High-power view showing mononuclear and multinucleated Langerhans' cells. There are also numerous eosinophils.

nodes involved by non-Hodgkin's lymphoma or Hodgkin's lymphoma, a sharp separation existing between the two processes.[400,412] In most of these cases, the Langerhans' cell proliferation is limited to the node and may represent a reaction to the lymphoma, but in others it is an expression of generalized LCH.[423] Follow-up studies have shown a broad spectrum of involvement, embracing all those syndromes that have been associated with LCH. However, the prognosis is usually excellent.

In addition to bone and lymph nodes, solitary LCH has been described in the lung, thymus, skin, central nervous system, and many other sites, including the stomach, liver, anus, female genital tract, and thyroid[393,403,405,410,419,427,438] (see respective chapters). Changes morphologically consistent with LCH have been seen in coexistence with RDD (see p. XXX) and in lymph nodes draining malignant melanoma or papillary thyroid carcinoma.[433,435]

The differential diagnosis of LCH is wide and to some extent influenced by the site of involvement. It includes RDD, parasitic infections, Kimura's disease, hypersensibility reactions, cat-scratch disease, Erdheim–Chester disease, and some types of malignant lymphomas, such as Hodgkin's lymphoma and peripheral T-cell lymphoma.[396] Erdheim–Chester disease is another "histiocytosis" of unknown etiology involving mainly the central nervous system, bones, and lung. The histiocytes in this condition are only focally S-100 protein-positive, are negative for CD1a, and lack Birbeck's granules.[411]

The etiology of LCH remains unknown. A viral cause has been suggested but not substantiated.[415,417] Molecular studies have shown evidence of clonality in some cases but not in others; localized pulmonary examples are particularly likely to be nonclonal.[441,443] The Langerhans' cells are affected by recurrent cytogenetic alterations,[422] and do not appear to be a particularly proliferative cell population.[399]

Exceptionally, a morphologically malignant process is seen in which the tumor cells have the ultrastructural and immunohistochemical features of Langerhans' cells.[395,442,437] This is to be regarded as Langerhans' cell sarcoma, and—as such—closely related to interdigitating reticulum cell sarcoma and other malignant tumors of the cells of the accessory immune system.

Kimura's disease

Kimura's disease is an inflammatory disorder of unknown etiology seen in an endemic form in the Orient[450] but also in other parts of the world, including the United States and Europe.[446] It usually presents as a mass lesion in the subcutaneous tissue of the head and neck region or the major salivary glands, often associated with regional lymphadenopathy. Sometimes lymph node enlargement is the only manifestation of the disease.

Microscopically, the involved nodes show marked hyperplasia of germinal centers, a few of which may be of the progressively transformed type. These germinal centers are often well vascularized and contain polykaryocytes, interstitial fibrosis, and deposition of a proteinaceous material. There is also extensive infiltration by mature eosinophils, with occasional formation of eosinophilic abscesses (Fig. 21.47). Hyalinized vessels are often seen in the paracortical region, and there is a variable degree of sinusal and paracortical sclerosis. An increase in the number of plasma cells and mast cells has

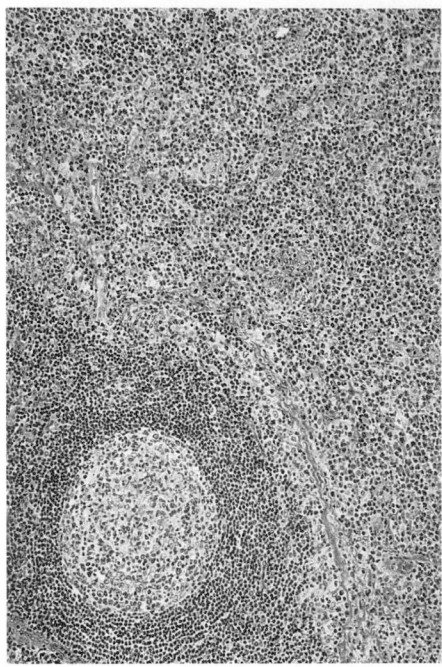

A

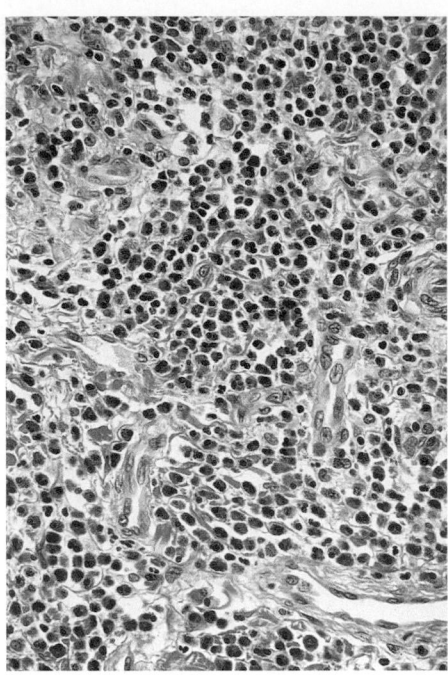

B

Fig. 21.47 Lymph node involvement by Kimura's disease. There is follicular hyperplasia and massive perinodal infiltration, which is predominantly composed of eosinophils. (Courtesy of Dr. T-T Kuo, Taipei, Taiwan)

been noted in the paracortex.[449] A surprising finding has been the presence of a clonal rearrangement of the TCR delta gene in a typical case of the disease.[447]

Despite early statements to the contrary, current evidence strongly suggests that Kimura's disease and the disease known to dermatologists as angiolymphoid hyperplasia with eosinophilia are different entities (see Chapter 4); specifically, the former disorder lacks the epithelioid (histiocytoid) endothelial cells that are the morphologic hallmark of the latter.[445,448,451,452]

Chronic granulomatous disease

Chronic granulomatous disease is the result of a genetically determined enzymatic defect of granulocytes and monocytes.[456,460] These cells ingest microorganisms but are unable to destroy them because of their inability to generate superoxide anion (O_2^-). This is due to a defect in any one of four components of NADPH oxidases, the enzyme responsible for the generation of the antimicrobial oxidants.[460] A pattern of Y-linked inheritance is seen in approximately 65% of the patients and results from mutations in the gene that encodes the g91-phox subunit of the cytochrome b558 component of the oxidase. The remaining 35% of patients inherit the disease in an autosomal recessive manner resulting from mutations in the genes that encode the other three oxidase components.[454,458,461] The traditional laboratory technique for the detection of the disease is the nitro blue tetrazolium test.[453]

The main clinical features are recurrent lymphadenitis, hepatosplenomegaly, skin rash, pulmonary infiltrates, anemia, leukocytosis, and hypergammaglobulinemia.[455,457,459] Microscopically, granulomas with necrotic purulent centers are seen in lymph nodes and

other organs. They closely simulate the appearance of cat-scratch disease and lymphogranuloma venereum. Collections of histiocytes containing a lipofuscin-like pigment are also commonly observed.

Lipophagic reactions

Accumulation of neutral lipid with formation of foamy macrophages (xanthoma cells) can be seen as an inconsequential secondary event in a variety of inflammatory and neoplastic conditions of lymph nodes, including Langerhans' cell histiocytosis, RDD, Erdheim–Chester disease, and Hodgkin's lymphoma. There are, in addition, conditions in which the **lipophagic granuloma** is the primary alteration. The lipophagic granuloma is defined as a collection of mononuclear and multinucleated giant cells, both of them exhibiting a cytoplasmic foamy appearance and lacking a significant participation of other cell types. By far the most common situation in which this occurs (so common as to be nearly universal, at least in Western countries), is represented by the incidental microscopic finding in periportal and mesenteric nodes in asymptomatic individuals, probably the result of mineral oil ingestion[466] (Fig. 21.48). Boitnott and Margolis[464] found this change in 78% of a series of forty-nine autopsied adults. Their chemical and histochemical studies showed that the oil droplets represent deposits of liquid-saturated hydrocarbons. Mineral oil is extensively used in the food processing industry, as a release agent and lubricant in capsules, tablets, bakery products, and dehydrated fruits and vegetables. Lipophagic granulomas of an extensive degree have been reported in association with long-term total parenteral nutrition therapy for short bowel syndrome.[467]

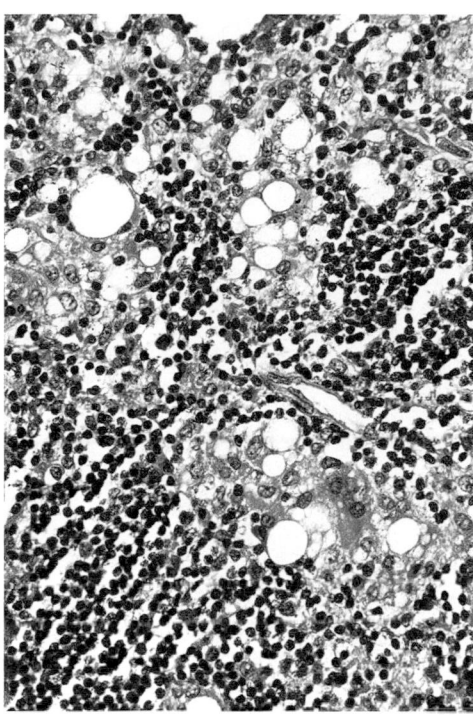

Fig. 21.48 Lymph node containing lipophagic granulomas. The change is manifested by the presence of mononuclear and multinucleated histiocytes located in the sinuses and containing large cytoplasmic vacuoles.

Whipple's disease can result in marked enlargement of mesenteric lymph nodes, with formation of numerous lipophagic granulomas. Collections of histiocytes containing a PAS-positive glycoprotein are also present.[465] Under oil immersion with electron microscopy, the characteristic bacillary bodies can be identified. Collections of PAS-positive histiocytes can also develop in peripheral nodes and may be the first clue to the diagnosis in a patient with gradual weight loss, weakness, and polyarthritis. Steatorrhea, the other classic symptom of the disease, may appear only in a later stage. In the presence of suggestive findings in routinely stained sections, confirmation of the diagnosis can now be obtained by the demonstration of the responsible organism (*Tropheryma whipplei*) by immunofluorescence or PCR.[462,463]

Lymphangiography induces a lipophagic granulomatous reaction that may persist for several months. The sinuses are markedly distended and lined by histiocytes, many of which are multinucleated. Eosinophils may be present in appreciable numbers in the medullary cords. This is preceded by a predominantly neutrophilic infiltration.[468]

Malignant lymphoma

Malignant lymphoma is the generic term given to tumors of the lymphoid system and specifically of lymphocytes and their precursor cells, whether of T, B, or null phenotypes. Although traditionally tumors presumed to be composed of histiocytes and other cells of the accessory immune system have also been included in the category of malignant lymphoma, it would seem more appropriate to regard them separately for both conceptual and practical reasons. Such tumors undoubtedly exist, and are discussed later in this chapter. One should be aware, however, that the large majority of tumors that were designated in the past as histiocytic lymphomas or reticulum cell sarcomas are in reality of lymphocytic nature and therefore true malignant lymphomas.

Although some overlapping exists, the term *malignant lymphoma* is reserved for those neoplastic processes that initially present as localized lesions and are characterized by the formation of gross tumor nodules. Conversely, neoplastic lymphoid proliferations that are systemic and diffuse from their inception are included among the leukemias (see Chapter 23).

The malignant lymphomas can be divided into two major categories: Hodgkin's lymphoma and all the others, which, for lack of a better term, are known collectively as non-Hodgkin's lymphomas.[469-473] Both groups are further subdivided into several more or less distinct subcategories.

Hodgkin's lymphoma

The disease originally described by Thomas Hodgkin in 1832 and which Samuel Wilks first proposed to be called Hodgkin's disease constitutes one of the richest chapters of history of oncologic pathology.[474,480,481,487] The original color illustrations have become icons,[476] and the original cases, still housed at the pathology museum of Guy's Hospital in London, have been "exhumed," studied microscopically and immunohistochemically, and the diagnosis has been confirmed after well over a century of fixation.[485] The interest in this enigmatic disease remains unabated, having been quoted as the paradigm for the emerging science of "molecular morphology."[488]

The conventional definition of Hodgkin's disease (a very ingrained term that the WHO Committee would like to see replaced by Hodgkin's lymphoma) is that of a type of malignant lymphoma in which Reed–Sternberg cells are present in a "characteristic background" of reactive inflammatory cells of various types, accompanied by fibrosis of a variable degree. Thus identification of typical Reed–Sternberg cells is necessary for the initial diagnosis of Hodgkin's lymphoma (except for NLPHL, see below). As far as the "characteristic background" or "appropriate milieu" is concerned, it is highly variable, but it lacks the monomorphic appearance of most other malignant lymphomas (again with the exception of NLPHL). Mature lymphocytes, eosinophils, plasma cells, and histiocytes may all be present in greater or lesser amount, depending on the microscopic type. Many of the Reed–Sternberg cells are surrounded by T lymphocytes arranged in a rosettelike fashion.

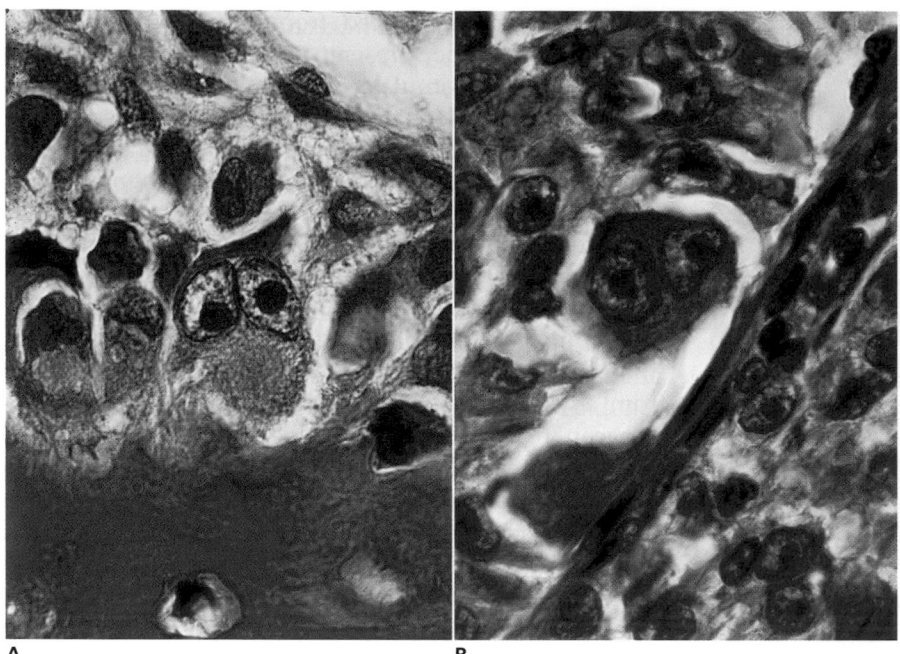

A   B

Fig. 21.53 Reed–Sternberg-like cells in malignant melanoma (**A**), and osteoblastoma (**B**).

Table 21.8 Major morphologic differences between the pleomorphic immunoblast (Reed–Sternberg-like cell) of infectious mononucleosis and the Reed–Sternberg cell of Hodgkin's lymphoma

Feature	Immunoblast	Reed–Sternberg cell
Nucleolus		
Stain pattern	Basophilic	Acidophilic
Contours	Irregular	Regular, with clear halo (inclusion-like)
Position	Adjacent to nuclear membrane	More centrally located
Cytoplasm		
Staining pattern	Usually amphophilic	Usually acidophilic
Pyroninophilia	Invariably strong	Variable
Paranuclear hof	Prominent	Inconspicuous
Surrounding cells	Mononuclear immunoblasts and plasmacytoid cells	Lymphocytes and histiocytes

Compiled from data in Dorfman RF, Warnke R. Lymphadenopathy simulating the malignant lymphomas. Hum Pathol 1974, **5:** 519–550.

possible progenitors, including B cells, T cells, histiocytes, follicular dendritic cells, and interdigitating dendritic cells.[511]

The immunocytochemical profile of the Reed–Sternberg cell is yet to be totally agreed upon because of the discrepancies among the various laboratories, which may be due to technical factors or to the heterogeneity of the disease, which sometimes manifests itself in sequential biopsies of the same case.[535,537] The most important findings in paraffin-embedded material have been the following:[492,494–496,498,500,503,505,508,512,522,528,529,540]

- CD15 (Leu-M1): This is expressed in over 80% of the cases; the pattern may be paranuclear (corresponding to the Golgi region), diffuse cytoplasmic, and/or corresponding to the cell membrane.

- CD30 (Ki-1): As recognized by the monoclonal antibody Be-Hz, this is found in approximately 90% of the cases (Fig. 21.54).
- CD45 (LCA): This is expressed in less than 10% of the cases.
- CD45 RO and CD43 (T-lineage-related antigens): These are expressed in less than 10% of the cases.
- CD20 (L26, B-lineage antigen): This is expressed in 10% to 20% of the cases.
- CD40 (a protein present in B cells and nerve growth factor receptor): This is expressed in approximately 70%.
- CD74: This is expressed in over 75%.
- Fascin: This is an actin-bundling protein which is normally expressed by dendritic cells.[502,525] This unexpected observation, coupled with the report of a

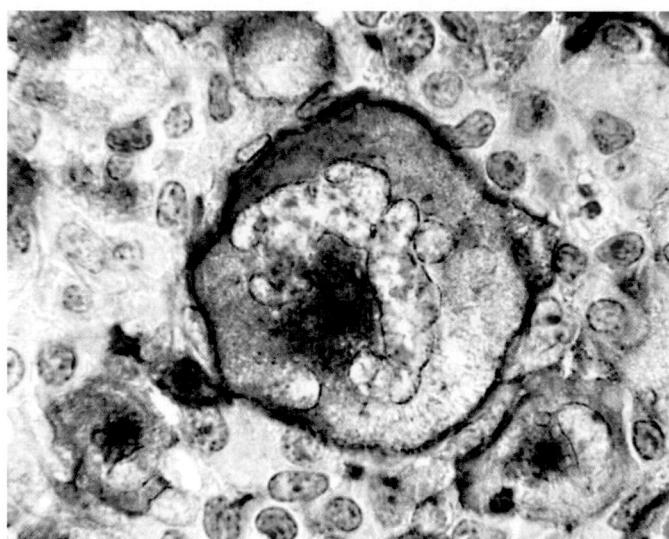

Fig. 21.54 Membrane and Golgi-type immunoreactivity for CD30 in a Reed–Sternberg cell. (Courtesy of Dr. Fabio Facchetti, Brescia, Italy).

subset of cases of Hodgkin's lymphoma in which the Reed–Sternberg cells stained for CD21 (another dendritic follicular cell marker) but not for any B-cell marker is intriguing and not exactly on line with the prevailing hypothesis about the nature of these cells.[519]

- Restin (an intermediate filament-associated protein): This is present in approximately 80%. The same is true for anaplastic large cell lymphoma but not for other types of non-Hodgkin's lymphoma.[500]
- Peanut agglutinin and *Bauhinia purpurea* lectins: They are expressed in over 60% of the cases, in contrast to their near universal absence in non-Hodgkin's lymphoma.
- Others, such as CD95 (a member of the superfamily that includes the nerve growth factor and tumor necrosis factors receptors) and its ligand,[520,527] the factor associated to TNFRs,[509] Fas ligand,[536] granzime B (a serine protease expressed by activated cytotoxic T cells and NK-cells),[523] and TARC (a lymphocyte-directed CC chemokine that attracts activated T-helper type 2 cells).[524]

In frozen sections, a large percentage of Reed–Sternberg cells have been found to exhibit reactivity for one or more pan–T cell or pan–B cell antigens, including the framework antigen of the T-cell receptor β chain. They also express polyclonal IgG (probably representing passive uptake via the Fc receptor), HLA-DR, CD25 (the interleukin-2 receptor), and CD71 (the transferrin receptor).

Molecular studies have also given rise to controversial results. Most cases of Hodgkin's lymphoma yield a germ-line configuration for immunoglobulin heavy and light chain genes and the β T-cell receptor genes, but this may simply result from a dilution factor by the non-neoplastic cells; indeed, some studies suggest that an increased number of Reed–Sternberg cells and their variants is associated with a detectable increase in clonal rearrangements of either gene.[499,504,513,516,539] In a remarkable experiment, Reed–Sternberg cells were isolated from 12 cases of "classic" Hodgkin's lymphoma (see next section) and found to have rearranged immunoglobulin variable-region heavy-chain (V_H) genes, indicating their origin from B cells. In half of the cases the population of Reed–Sternberg cells was polyclonal, and in the other half it was monoclonal or mixed.[507] Several other workers have provided additional evidence in favor of the interpretation that Reed–Sternberg cells derive from mature B cells at the germinal center stage of differentiation,[493,510,517,518] although some discordant hard-to-explain findings persist.[502,506]

The karyotype of these cells is generally hyperdiploid and with structural abnormalities, but no recurring chromosomal abnormalities have yet been detected.[526,532,533] Specifically, and in contrast with anaplastic large cell lymphoma, there is no t(2;59) translocation.[538]

Another controversial issue is the prevalence of t(14;18) in Hodgkin's lymphoma, the reported figures ranging from zero to over 30%; perhaps of significance in this regard is the fact that the bcl-2 protein (a hallmark of the 14;18 translocation) is never overexpressed, except in those exceptional instances of Hodgkin's lymphoma that arise in the setting of follicular lymphoma.[514,515,521,530]

Overexpression of the p53 product as detected immunohistochemically is common in Hodgkin's lymphoma, but it does not correlate with gene mutations, which are rare.[497,501]

Microscopic types

For many years, Jackson and Parker's classification of Hodgkin's lymphoma into granuloma, paragranuloma, and sarcoma variants[543] was widely used because of its reproducibility and clear-cut prognostic implications, the major objection being that too many of the cases (approximately 80%) fell into one of the categories—i.e., Hodgkin's granuloma. The concept of a sclerosing type of Hodgkin's lymphoma associated with a very good prognosis was first introduced by Smetana and Cohen in 1956[549] and was incorporated into a new classification proposed by Lukes et al.[544,545] In this scheme, six categories were included: lymphocytic and/or histiocytic (L&H) nodular, L&H diffuse, nodular sclerosis, mixed cellularity, diffuse fibrosis, and reticular. This classification, somewhat simplified and with some changes in nomenclature (not always for the better), was adopted by the Nomenclature Committee at the Rye Conference on Hodgkin's lymphoma.[546] This classification recognized four major types of Hodgkin's lymphoma: nodular sclerosis, lymphocyte predominance, lymphocyte depletion, and mixed cellularity. In the REAL/WHO scheme currently in use there has been a further reshuffling of the types into two major categories: the nodular subtype of

Table 21.9 Comparison between the different classifications of Hodgkin's lymphoma proposed over the years

Jackson and Parker (1947)[543]	Smetana and Cohen's modification (1956)[549]	Lukes (1963)[544]	Rve Conference (1966)[546]	WHO (2001)[558a]
Paragranuloma	Paragranuloma	Lymphocytic and histiocytic, diffuse	Lymphocyte predominance	Nodular lymphocyte predominant
		Lymphocytic and histiocytic, nodular		Classical
				Nodular sclerosis
	Nodular sclerosis	Nodular sclerosis	Nodular sclerosis	Lymphocyte-rich
Granuloma	Granuloma	Mixed cellularity	Mixed cellularity	Mixed cellularity
Sarcoma	Sarcoma	Diffuse fibrosis	Lymphocyte depletion	Lymphocyte-depleted
		Reticular		

lymphocyte predominance and the classical, the latter incorporating all other types of the Rye classification.[541,542,547,548] The relationships between these classifications is shown in Table 21.9.

Nodular lymphocyte predominance Hodgkin's lymphoma

In **nodular lymphocyte predominance** Hodgkin's lymphoma (NLPHL), the predominant cell is a small B lymphocyte, with or without an accompanying population of benign-appearing histiocytes.[572,578] Postcapillary venules with high endothelium may be prominent.[564,576] The lymph node architecture is partially or totally effaced, and the infiltrate has a variously well developed nodular pattern of growth.[571] The nodularity may be so pronounced as to simulate on low power the appearance of follicular lymphoma; however, the nodules of NLPHL are more irregular in size and staining quality, and the admixture of lymphocytes and epithelioid cells gives them a mottled appearance (Fig. 21.55). A rim of unin-volved or hyperplastic lymphoid tissue may be present. Progressively transformed germinal centers may be seen adjacent to the lesion.[557] Eosinophils, plasma cells, and foci of fibrosis are scanty or absent. Classic Reed–Sternberg cells are absent. One sees instead a variable but usually large number of a type of Reed–Sternberg cell (the L&H cell or "popcorn" cell) characterized by a folded, multilobed nucleus with smaller nucleoli. If numerous typical Reed–Sternberg cells are found in a node with a lymphocyte predominance background, the case probably belongs in the classic category (lymphocyte-rich). Occasionally, the L&H cells predominate at the margins of the nodules, creating a "wreath" around them. In others, they cluster in large confluent sheets resembling diffuse large cell lymphoma.

Poppema et al.[568–570] first proposed that cases of NLPHL (the L&H nodular type of the classification of Lukes et al.[561]) arise from B-cell regions of the node and specifically from progressively transformed germinal

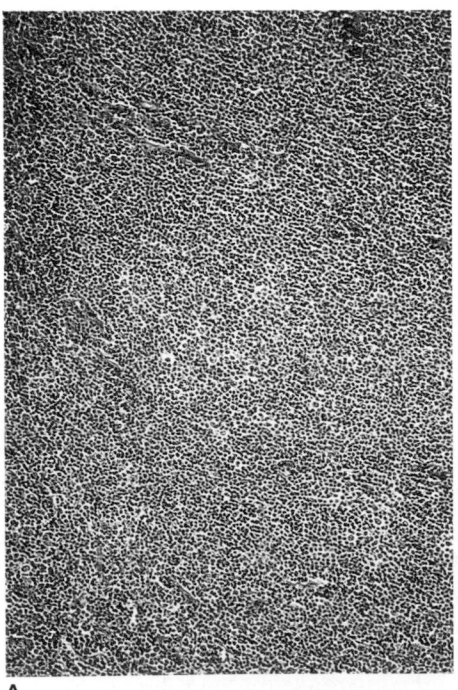

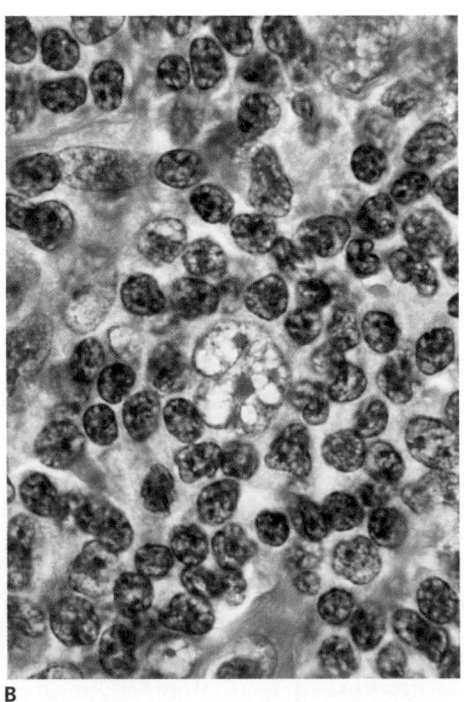

Fig. 21.55 A and **B,** Lymphocyte predominance Hodgkin's lymphoma. **A,** Low-power view showing a mottled appearance of the node. **B,** High-power view showing the lymphocytic and/or histiocytic (L&H) type of cell ("popcorn" cell) that is characteristic of this condition.

A

B

centers (see p. 1888). They supported their theory by showing that the L&H cell that is characteristic of this condition is of B-cell lineage, and this has been confirmed by many others.[552,553,555,559,565,566,570,573,579] L&H cells express the pan–B-cell markers CD19, CD20, CD22, CD74, CDw75, and CD45RA (Table 21.10). They are also positive for CD45RB (LCA) but consistently negative for T-cell markers. They may express CD30 or EMA, and

Table 21.10 Summary of various types of diffuse mixed cell lymphoma

Type	Lineage	Clinical features	Histologic features	Immunohistochemical features	Behavior
Follicular center cell type (diffuse centroblastic-centrocytic)	B	Adults, usually presenting with lymphadenopathy; may have known history of follicular lymphoma or arising de novo; disease often at high stage at presentation; extranodal involvement is common	Small cells with angulated (cleaved) or elongated nuclei, fairly condensed chromatin, and scanty cytoplasm; large cells with round or folded nuclei, vesicular chromatin, and multiple distinct nucleoli; neoplastic follicles should be absent; sclerosis common	Pan-B+; CD5–; CD10+/–; CD23+/–; may have irregular loose meshworks of follicular dendritic cells	No reliable data in literature on its behavior; some studies suggest that it is low-grade neoplasm, but prognosis is less favorable than for follicular lymphoma
Post-thymic T-cell lymphoma	T	Usually adults; nodal or extranodal presentation; disease often at high stage at presentation	Prominent high endothelial venules; continuous spectrum of small, medium-sized, and large lymphoid cells; nuclear irregularities, chromatin pattern often granular; clear cytoplasm commonly seen in some cells; may show rich component of inflammatory cells (such as eosinophils, histiocytes, and epithelioid cells)	Pan-T+ (often with loss of one or more pan-T antigens; usually CD4–, sometimes CD8+, CD4+CD8+ or CD4– CD8–)	Generally aggressive neoplasm
Lymphoplasmacytic/cytoid immunocytoma with increased blasts (polymorphic subtype)	B	Usually older adults; nodal or extranodal presentation; may have monoclonal gammopathy (20–40%); disease often disseminated at presentation; occasional cases may have circulating lymphoma cells	Small lymphocytes; lymphoplasmacytoid cells; plasma cells; immunoblasts; rare follicular center cells; Dutcher bodies (nuclear pseudoinclusions of immunoglobulin) may be found; specific lymphoma types should be excluded (e.g., follicular lymphoma, low-grade B-cell lymphoma of MALT)	Pan B+; CD5–; CD10–; CD23–; sIg +, cIg + (usually IgM type)	Low-grade neoplasm, but prognosis is worse than that of B-SLL/CLL or conventional LP immunocytoma; median survival 55 months; may rarely transform to diffuse large cell lymphoma
T-cell-rich large B-cell lymphoma	B	Older adults, usually presenting with lymphadenopathy; disease often disseminated at presentation	Small lymphocytes with round or irregular nuclei; scattered atypical large cells with round to folded nuclei, distinct nucleoli, and amphophilic cytoplasm; may show rich vascularity and component of inflammatory cells	Large atypical cells; pan-B+; small cells; pan-T+	Aggressive neoplasm; prognosis probably similar to conventional diffuse large cell lymphoma
Low-grade B-cell lymphoma of mucosa-associated lymphoid tissue (MALT)	B	Any age; tumor often localized to mucosal site and/or regional lymph nodes at presentation	Small lymphoid cells with round or irregular nuclei and pale to clear cytoplasm; scattered large blast cells with vesicular nuclei and distinct nucleoli; glandular invasion (lympho-epithelial lesions) common; plasma cells common	Pan-B+; CD5–; CD10–; CD23–	Low-grade neoplasm, with median survival of 8 years; may show late relapse locally or in other mucosal sites; may transform to diffuse large cell lymphoma

From Warnke RA, Weiss LM, Chan JKC, Cleary ML, Dorfman RF. Tumors of the lymph nodes and spleen. Atlas of tumor pathology, series 3, fascicle 14. Washington, D.C., 1995, Armed Forces Institute of Pathology.

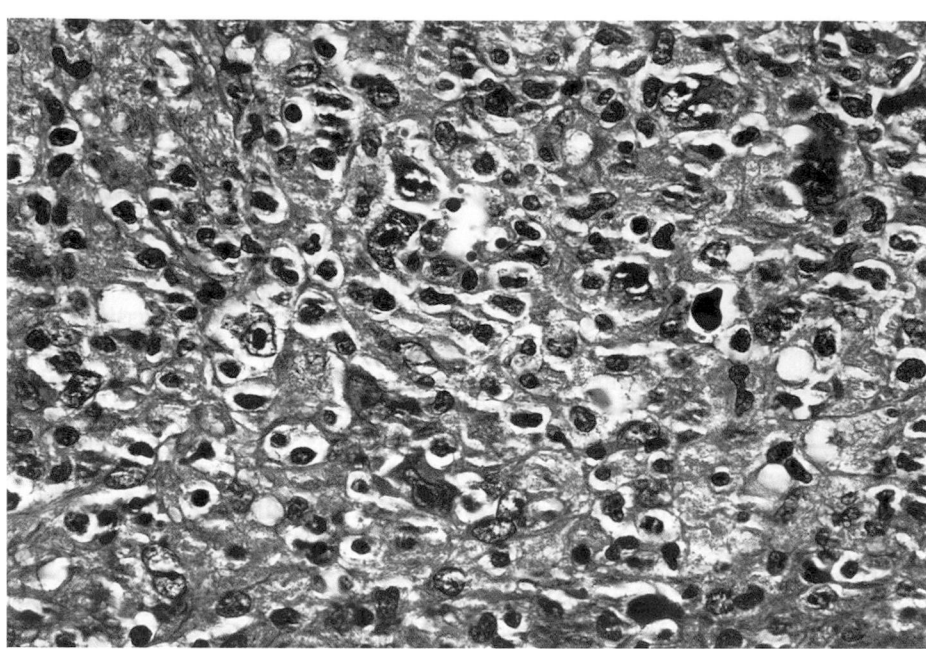

Fig. 21.60 Lymphocyte depletion type of Hodgkin's lymphoma. Numerous atypical cells are present in a densely fibrotic stroma. Lymphocytes are scanty.

"reticular" subtype of lymphocyte depletion Hodgkin's lymphoma needs to be distinguished from non-Hodgkin's lymphoma of large cell type (including the pleomorphic CD30+ type) and from the variant of nodular sclerosis Hodgkin's lymphoma with aggregates of lacunar cells.

The histologic subtypes of classical Hodgkin's lymphoma remain constant over long follow-up periods in most cases, particularly for the nodular sclerosis form.[589] In patients who had relapses in a site *not included* in the radiation field (and who have not received chemotherapy), the same histologic appearance was often maintained in the relapse biopsies.[581] When change occurs, it usually is toward a histologically more malignant form. It also should be remembered that patients with Hodgkin's lymphoma may develop non-Hodgkin's lymphoma or leukemia,[582,584] either spontaneously or as a result of therapy.

The microscopic typing of Hodgkin's lymphoma should always be made on examination of a biopsy obtained before the institution of treatment. Radiation therapy and chemotherapy result in focal necrosis, fibrosis, and profound nuclear aberrations – features that may render impossible a proper pathologic evaluation. These alterations may be seen in post-therapy biopsy material or at autopsy.[580]

The currently used terminology of Hodgkin's lymphoma is far from ideal, in the sense that there is very little relation between the names given and the microscopic picture observed. A case exhibiting lymphocyte predominance or mixed cellularity will be diagnosed as nodular sclerosis if bands of fibrous tissue are present. A case with marked predominance of lymphocytes will be categorized as mixed cellularity if there are numerous Reed–Sternberg cells. In lymphocyte depletion Hodgkin's lymphoma, lymphocytes are still the numerically more abundant cells, more so than in the mixed cellularity type.[586]

An interesting alternative approach was tried by Coppleson et al.[583] and consisted of evaluating individually the frequencies of the different cell types. They found that the presence of a large number of lymphocytes was associated with a good prognosis, whereas malignant and mononuclear cells and benign-appearing histiocytes independently influenced the prognosis adversely. Reed–Sternberg cells had no prognostic effect independent of the malignant mononuclear cells, and eosinophils and plasma cells had no prognostic value. However, these authors concluded that the Rye classification of Hodgkin's lymphoma (now substituted by the REAL/WHO scheme) furnished more prognostic information than any estimates of individual cell frequencies.

The differential diagnosis between Hodgkin's lymphoma and anaplastic large cell lymphoma is discussed on p. 1951.

Other microscopic features

There are some microscopic variations on the theme of Hodgkin's lymphoma worth mentioning, mainly because lack of knowledge of their occurrence may result in mistaken diagnoses. These mainly apply to classical Hodgkin's lymphoma and its subtype rather than NLPHL.

1 *Foamy macrophages.* Clumps of foamy macrophages resulting in a xanthogranulomatous appearance may be found, particularly in the nodular sclerosis form.[602]

2 *Eosinophils.* In some instances, the intensity of

eosinophilic infiltration is massive and accompanied by so-called "eosinophilic microabscesses." Such cases may be confused with Langerhans' cell histiocytosis, hypersensitivity reaction, or "allergic granulomatosis."

3 *Other inflammatory cells.* S-100 protein-positive dendritic cells,[590] mast cells,[592] and monocytoid B cells[596] may be very numerous.

4 *Focal interfollicular involvement.* In the early stages of the disease, only focal involvement of a lymph node may be encountered,[601] often restricted to the paracortical region between florid hyperplastic follicles; this pattern, which has been referred to as *interfollicular Hodgkin's lymphoma*, should not be regarded as a specific subtype.[593]

5 *Follicular involvement.* Sometimes the nodal involvement by Hodgkin's lymphoma is mainly in the germinal centers, the appearance being reminiscent of that of NLPHL.[595]

6 *Castleman's disease-like features.* Cases of Hodgkin's lymphoma may be accompanied or preceded by a plasmacytic infiltrate and abnormalities of germinal centers closely resembling those seen in Castleman's disease (see p. 1905).

7 *Fibrosis.* In cases of nodular sclerosis Hodgkin's lymphoma but sometimes also in other types, the amount of fibrosis can be such as to simulate the appearance of one of the inflammatory fibroscleroses (such as sclerosing mediastinitis or retroperitoneal fibrosis).

8 *Spindle cell proliferation.* In rare cases of Hodgkin's lymphoma, there is a proliferation of oval to spindle cells of such a degree as to simulate fibrosarcoma, malignant fibrous histiocytoma, or a follicular dendritic cell tumor; such lesions have been referred to as **fibrosarcomatous or fibroblastic Hodgkin's lymphoma.** Some of these spindle cells have a degree of nuclear atypia such as to indicate their neoplastic nature and relationship with Reed–Sternberg's and Hodgkin's cells; indeed, most of these lesions would be included in the grade II category of nodular sclerosis Hodgkin's lymphoma proposed by the British National Lymphoma Investigation Group (see p. 1925). Others are of a reactive nature and stromal derivation (i.e., made up of fibroblasts and myofibroblasts).[591]

9 *Noncaseating granulomas.* These formations are sometimes present in nodes and other organs involved by Hodgkin's lymphoma. Occasionally they are so numerous as to obscure the diagnostic features of the disease (Fig. 21.61). In other instances, these granulomas may be seen within otherwise uninvolved organs of patients with Hodgkin's lymphoma.[594] Their significance is unknown. Perhaps they represent an expression of delayed hypersensitivity. Some seen in the past were reactions to the contrast material used in lymphangiography.[597] Their presence does

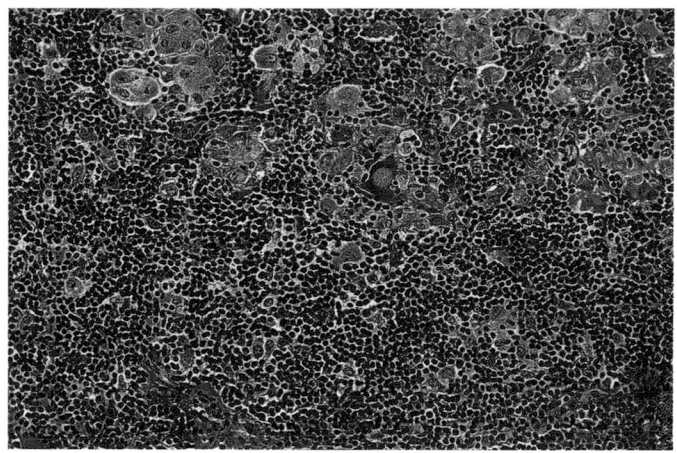

Fig. 21.61 Hodgkin's lymphoma accompanied by numerous sarcoid-like granulomas. The presence of this component can obscure the basic nature of the disease.

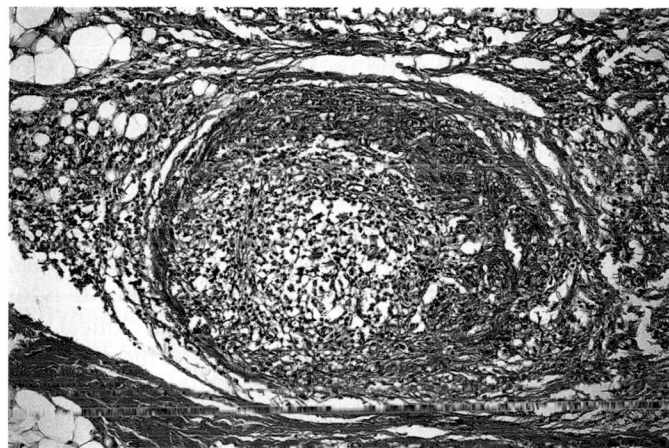

Fig. 21.62 Blood vessel invasion in Hodgkin's lymphoma.

not indicate involvement of that organ by Hodgkin's lymphoma and should therefore not influence the staging criteria. Actually, it has been suggested that, within a given stage, the presence of these granulomas is associated with a better prognosis.[599]

10 *Vascular invasion.* Blood vessel infiltration has been detected microscopically in 6% to 14% of the cases of Hodgkin's lymphoma by the use of elastic tissue stains[600] (Fig. 21.62). This finding is said to be associated with an increased incidence of extranodal organ involvement,[598] but the statement and the very validity of the observation have been questioned.

General and clinical features

Hodgkin's lymphoma comprises approximately 20% to 30% of all malignant lymphomas in the United States and Western Europe but a much lower percentage in Japan and other Oriental countries.[603] There is a wide range in age incidence, which varies according to geographic location. In the United States, there is a bimodal

spread in contiguity from a nodal site. For instance, direct extension from mediastinal nodes of lung or chest wall in nodular sclerosis Hodgkin's lymphoma does not result in an appreciable decrease in survival.[648]

6 *Laboratory findings.* Decreased hematocrit, elevated levels of lactate dehydrogenase, increased erythrosedimentation rate, increased β_2-microglobulin, and elevated serum levels of CD30 and soluble CD25 have all been claimed to have a negative impact on survival in high-stage patients.[643,646,649]

7 *Microscopic types.* Traditionally, NLPHL and nodular sclerosis have been the most favorable forms, mixed cellularity has been intermediate, and the lymphocyte depletion form has had the worst prognosis.[640,641] The long-term prognosis of NLPHL is so good that some authors have referred to it as "the benign form" of Hodgkin's lymphoma, and have even doubted that it represents a neoplastic process.[656] It should be said that this favorable prognosis is shared by the lymphocyte-rich form of classical Hodgkin's lymphoma.[642] A stark contrast is offered by lymphocyte depletion Hodgkin's lymphoma; in the series of Bearman et al.,[639] the median survival was 25.1 months, with only eight (21%) patients surviving 4 years or longer. In general, no prognostic differences have been found between the subtypes of nodular sclerosis or lymphocyte depletion[654]; however, the suggestion has been made that nodular sclerosis cases belonging to what the British have called grade II lesions (which include the so-called "syncytial variant" of other authors) are somewhat more aggressive[645] (see p. 1925).

It has been pointed out that at least some of the prognostic significance of the various microscopic types depends on the clinical stage, in view of the fact that a definite correlation between the two exists. Thus most NLPHL and nodular sclerosis cases are in stages I and II, whereas most lymphocyte depletion cases are in stages III and IV; however, until relatively recently the prognostic differences among microscopic types were maintained even within staging groups.[648] This is no longer the case. At present, only lymphocyte depletion histology carries an unfavorable significance, and in some series even this difference has been erased.[651]

8 *Noncaseating granulomas.* The presence of these formations may be associated with a slightly better prognosis within a given stage.[650]

9 *Follicular dendritic cells.* Cases with an extensive network of these cells in a follicle-like distribution are said to have a better prognosis than the others.[637,638]

10 *Epstein–Barr virus.* No differences in survival have been found between EBV-positive and EBV-negative cases.

11 *CD15.* It has been claimed that lack of expression of CD15 in cases of classical Hodgkin's lymphoma is an independent negative prognostic factor for relapses.[655]

Non-Hodgkin's lymphoma

The classification of non-Hodgkin's lymphoma that was most widely used until the early 1980s in the United States and many other countries was that proposed by Rappaport in 1966[676] (Table 21.11). This represented a slight modification of the classification that Gall and Rappaport had presented at a Seminar of the American Society of Clinical Pathologists held in New Orleans, Louisiana, in 1963. This, in turn, was based on the classification proposed by Gall and Mallory[664] as part of their comprehensive critical study of 618 lymphomas. Rappaport's classification was, of necessity, based entirely on morphologic grounds. Numerous independent clinicopathologic studies have shown its reproducibility, usefulness, and clinical relevance.[658] However, application of the remarkable advances in the fields of immunology, cytogenetics, and molecular pathology in the past 30 years to the study of lymphomas has shown that these can be viewed as clonal expansions of the normal anatomic and functional components of the immune system. Most of them have been studied using immunologic and molecular genetic markers and, as a result, have been "typed" as to their normal counterparts, from which presumably they arose. This "functional" approach, championed by Lukes[657,671] in this country and by Lennert in Germany, incorporated a number of entities and showed that a functional classification of lymphoma was possible to some extent on the basis of morphologic interpretation of routinely stained sections[669,670] (Table 21.11). Independent of this, aggressive clinical investigations coupled with staging laparotomies provided a wealth of new information on the sites of predilection and spread of the lymphomas according to type.[662,665,677] The results obtained with these investigations pointed to some inaccuracies and other deficiencies of Rappaport's classification and the need to revise it, taking into account all these new data.

Five new classifications were proposed,[661,668,672,673] which, needless to say, resulted in a confusing state of affairs for both pathologists and clinicians.

Because there was no clear-cut evidence that one classification was clearly superior to the others, the National Cancer Institute sponsored a retrospective study of 1175 cases of non-Hodgkin's lymphoma, which were classified according to the different categories by the investigators who proposed them, as well as by a panel of "control" pathologists.[674,675] Analysis of the data showed that all six classifications were successful in predicting the prognosis in a large number of lymphoma patients and that no classification appeared clearly superior to any other in this respect.[674] It also confirmed that lymphomas with a follicular pattern of growth (a feature consistently identified by all reviewers) had a more favorable prognosis than those with diffuse patterns within the same cytologic subtypes. This was true whether the nodularity was extensive or only partial. Finally, it confirmed the suspicion that within the "histiocytic lymphoma" category of Rappaport there was a variety of morphologically recognizable neoplasms with a somewhat different natural history. As a result of the analysis of these 1175 cases, the investigators involved in this study proposed a new classification ("Working Formulation") of non-Hodgkin's malignant lymphomas, based primarily on light microscopic differences, as seen in sections stained with hematoxylin–eosin, that showed a good correlation with survival. Ten major types plus a miscellaneous group were identified, and these were subdivided into three major prognostic groups that were

Table 21.11 Major classification schemes of non-Hodgkin's lymphoma

Rappaport	Lukes and Collins	Kiel
Nodular	Undefined cell type	Low-grade malignancy
Lymphocytic, well differentiated	T-cell type	Lymphocytic
Lymphocytic, poorly differentiated	Small lymphocytic	Chronic lymphocytic leukemia
Mixed (lymphocytic and histiocytic)	Sezary–mycosis fungoides (cerebriform)	Other
Histiocytic	Convoluted lymphocytic	Lymphoplasmacytoid
Diffuse	Immunoblastic sarcoma (T-cell)	Centrocytic
Lymphocytic, well differentiated	Small lymphocytic	Centroblastic-centrocytic
Without plasmacytoid features	B-cell type	Follicular, without sclerosis
With plasmacytoid features	Small lymphocytic	Follicular, with sclerosis
Lymphocytic, poorly differentiated	Plasmacytoid lymphocytic	Follicular and diffuse, without
Without plasmacytoid features	Follicular center cell*	sclerosis
With plasmacytoid features	Small cleaved	Follicular and diffuse, with sclerosis
Lymphoblastic	Large cleaved	Diffuse
Convoluted	Small noncleaved	Unclassified
Nonconvoluted	Large noncleaved	High-grade malignancy
Mixed (lymphocytic and histiocytic)	Immunoblastic sarcoma (B-cell)	Centroblastic
Histiocytic	Histiocytic	Lymphoblastic
Without sclerosis	Unclassified	Burkitt's type
With sclerosis	Composite	Convoluted cell type
Burkitt's tumor		Other (unclassified)
Undifferentiated		Immunoblastic
Unclassified		Unclassified
Composite		Unclassified
		Composite

International Formulation[675]

Low grade	Intermediate grade	High grade	Miscellaneous
ML,† small lymphocytic	ML, follicular, predominantly large cell	ML, large cell, immunoblastic	Composite
Consistent with chronic lymphocytic leukemia	With diffuse areas	Plasmacytoid	Mycosis fungoides
Plasmacytoid	With sclerosis	Clear cell	Histiocytic
ML, follicular, predominantly small cleaved cell	ML, diffuse, small cleaved cell	Polymorphous	Extramedullary plasmacytoma
With diffuse areas	With sclerosis	With epithelioid cell component	Unclassifiable
With sclerosis	ML, diffuse, mixed (small and large cell)	ML, lymphoblastic	Other
ML, follicular, mixed (small cleaved and large cell)	With sclerosis	Convoluted	
With diffuse areas	With epithelioid cell component	Nonconvoluted	
With sclerosis	ML, diffuse, large cell	ML, small noncleaved cell	
	Cleaved cell	Burkitt's	
	Noncleaved cell	With follicular areas	
	With sclerosis		

*Subdivided into (1) follicular, follicular and diffuse, and diffuse and (2) without sclerosis and with sclerosis.
†Malignant lymphoma.

REAL/WHO[667]

B-CELL NEOPLASMS

Precursor B-cell neoplasm
Precursor B lymphoblastic leukemia[1]/lymphoma[2]

Mature B-cell neoplasms
Chronic lymphocytic leukemia[1]/small lymphocytic lymphoma[2]
B-cell prolymphocytic leukemia
Lymphoplasmacytic lymphoma
Splenic marginal zone lymphoma
Hairy cell leukemia
Plasma cell myeloma
Solitary plasmacytoma of bone
Extraosseous plasmacytoma
Extranodal marginal zone B-cell lymphoma of mucosa-associated lymphoid tissue (MALT-lymphoma)
Nodal marginal zone B-cell lymphoma
Follicular lymphoma
Mantle cell lymphoma
Diffuse large B-cell lymphoma
Mediastinal (thymic) large B-cell lymphoma
Intravascular large B-cell lymphoma
Primary effusion lymphoma
Burkitt lymphoma[1]/leukemia[2]

B-cell proliferations of uncertain malignant potential
Lymphomatoid granulomatosis
Post-transplant lymphoproliferative disorder, polymorphic

T-CELL AND NK-CELL NEOPLASMS

Precursor T-cell neoplasms
Precursor T lymphoblastic leukemia[1]/lymphoma[2]
Blastic NK cell lymphoma**

Mature T-cell and NK-cell neoplasms
T-cell prolymphocytic leukemia
T-cell large granular lymphocytic leukemia
Aggressive NK cell leukemia
Adult T-cell leukemia/lymphoma
Extranodal NK/T cell lymphoma, nasal type
Enteropthy-type T-cell lymphoma
Hepatosplenic T-cell lymphoma
Subcutaneous panniculitis-like T-cell lymphoma
Mycosis fungoides
Sezary syndrome
Primary cutaneous anaplastic large cell lymphoma
Peripheral T-cell lymphoma, unspecified
Angioimmunoblastic T-cell lymphoma
Anaplastic large cell lymphoma

T-cell proliferation of uncertain malignant potential
Lymphomatoid papulosis

fication of Hodgkin's lymphoma had been seen as a compromise (not necessarily for the better) over the Lukes–Butler classification.[663] It was also pointed out from the very beginning that the Working Formulation did not take into account all the entities that had been recognized at that time. This, plus the continuing advances that have been made in the field, has led to additions and other substantial changes to the scheme.[674]

In the mid 1990s, an international group of hematopathologists prepared a list of lymphoid neoplasms that they felt could be recognized with available techniques and which appeared to be clinically distinctive.[660,666] The approach was strictly pragmatic, in the sense that the list included only those categories that appeared reasonably identifiable as such, without attempting to always relate them to normal stages of lymphoid differentiation. This attempt, to which the cute term REAL (Revised European American Lymphoma Classification) was given, has been the model upon which the new WHO classification of tumors of hematopoietic and lymphoid tissues is based.[667] The scheme and terminology recommended in the latter publication will be followed in the rest of the chapter, fully aware of the high probability that yet another classification will replace it by the time that the next edition of this book will be published.[659]

As one reflects upon this tortuous history and browses over the current scheme, one cannot help but smile when remembering the caustic comment of Rupert Willis in 1948 to the effect that "nowhere in pathology has a chaos of names so clouded clear concepts as in the subject of lymphoid tumors" and his criticism of the "artificial distinctions ... created by naming tumours merely according to the degree of differentiation attained by their cells."[678] What would he think, one wonders, if he were alive today?

Small lymphocytic lymphoma
Small lymphocytic lymphoma preferentially occurs in middle-aged and elderly individuals.[685,722] The symptoms are scanty, the evolution is prolonged, and the survival is very good. It is not unusual to find the disease incidentally in lymph node dissections done for carcinoma of one type or another.[735]

The architecture of the node in small lymphocytic lymphoma is massively and monotonously effaced by a population of small round lymphocytes with clumped chromatin, inconspicuous nucleoli, barely visible cytoplasm, and scanty mitotic activity (Figs 21.63 and 21.64).

The distribution of the disease is usually diffuse, but on occasions it is confined to the marginal zone, perifollicular, or interfollicular regions surrounding benign lymphoid follicles, the latter pattern being referred to as interfollicular small lymphocytic lymphoma.[692,697,701] Some cases show a propensity for invasion of the wall of

of favorable, intermediate, and unfavorable prognosis, respectively.

Although this classification gained some degree of acceptability, it was viewed by many as a compromise rather than a conceptual advance, just as the Rye classi-

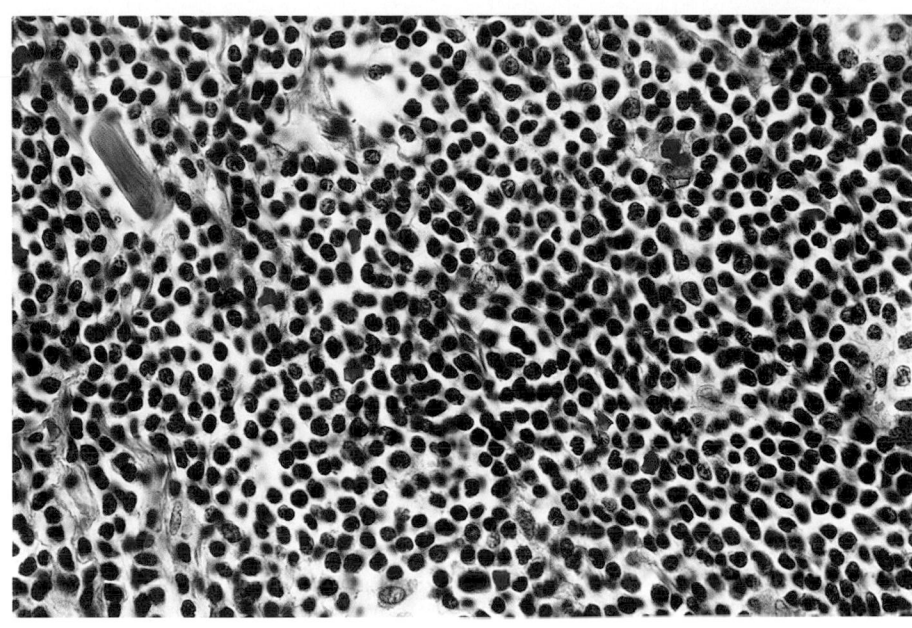

Fig. 21.63 Low-power view of small lymphocytic lymphoma. A monotonous proliferation of small lymphocytes effaces the architecture of the node.

veins.[714] Extranodal extension is seen in approximately a third of the cases.[733]

Cases of small lymphocytic lymphomas can be divided into three categories: (1) those with absolute lymphocytosis (i.e., chronic lymphocytic leukemia), (2) those associated with monoclonal gammopathy (50% of which have bone marrow involvement), and (3) those with neither; the latter are often accompanied by hypogammaglobulinemia.[685,687,703,718,723] There are no statistical differences in survival between these three groups and no appreciable morphologic differences between the first and the third groups.[684] In the cases associated with monoclonal gammopathy, some or most of the neoplastic lymphocytes may exhibit morphologic signs of plasmacytoid differentiation (as evidenced by oval shape, lateralization of the nucleus, appearance of a perinuclear halo, and pyroninophilia) and admixture of plasma cells. Effacement of the nodal architecture is generally not as complete as with the usual type. These cases are referred to as *small lymphocytic lymphoma with plasmacytic differentiation* and are discussed further in the section on lymphoma and dysproteinemia.

Immunohistochemically, small lymphocytic lymphomas are nearly always of B-cell type.[731] Monoclonal immunoglobulins, usually of the IgM type, are consistently found on their surface. They differ from the B

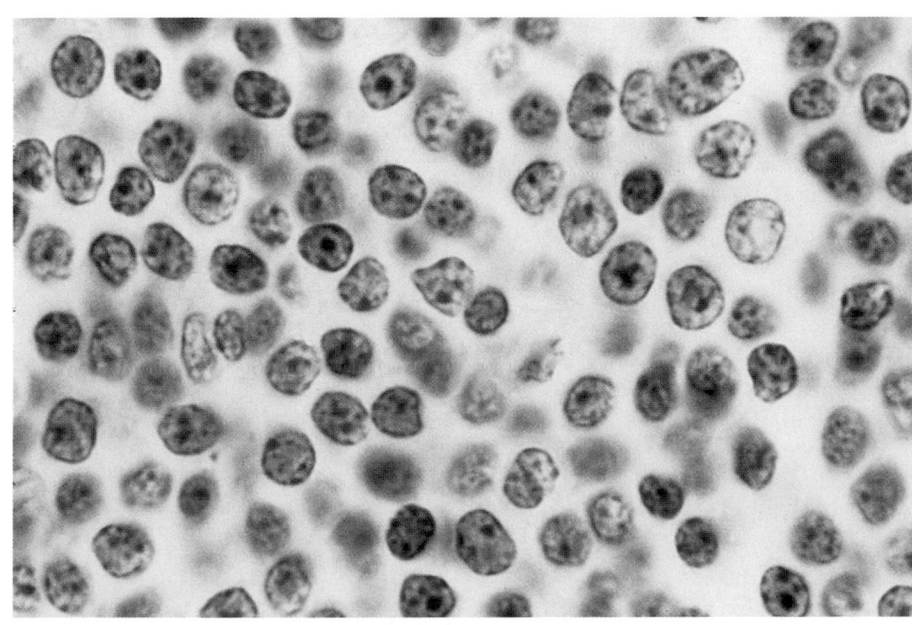

Fig. 21.64 High-power view of small lymphocytic lymphoma. The nuclear contours are regular, the chromatin is clumped, and nucleoli are inconspicuous.

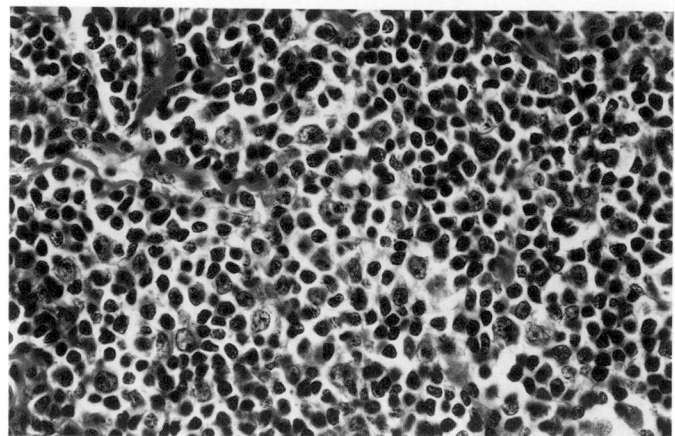

Fig. 21.65 So-called "growth center" in a lymph node involved by small lymphocytic lymphoma.

lymphocytes of follicular lymphoma in the intensity and appearance of the reaction (brighter and more clumped in the latter), as well as by their lesser content of complement receptors. They are usually reactive for the B-cell–related antigens CD5, CD23 (in contrast to mantle cell lymphoma),[695,712,732] and CD43. At the molecular level, Ig heavy and light chain genes are rearranged. Cytogenetically, trisomy 12 has been reported in one third of the cases (said to be associated with a poor prognosis), and abnormalities of 13q in up to one quarter (said to be associated with a good survival).[709] In a small number of cases of chronic lymphocytic leukemia, the lymphocytes have T- rather than B-cell markers and differ clinically and cytologically from the rest[690,717] (see Chapter 23). The cells are somewhat larger, have numerous azurophilic granules, and contain large amounts of acid phosphatase and β-glucuronidase.

Not infrequently, cases of small lymphocytic lymphoma with or without leukemia (but particularly the latter) show, in addition to the well-differentiated lymphocytes, an admixture of larger cells (prolymphocytes and paraimmunoblasts) with vesicular nuclei and prominent nucleoli, singly or in small aggregates that simulate germinal centers[694,723,727] (Fig. 21.65). These formations (known as proliferative centers, growth centers, or pseudofollicles) have an increased number of Ki-67-positive cells.[718] This feature, which is apparently of no prognostic significance,[683] should not lead to confusion with follicular lymphoma or NLPHL. As a matter of fact, the presence of these pseudofollicular formations and of prolymphocytes/paraimmunoblasts are features that corroborate the diagnosis of small lymphocytic lymphoma as opposed to conditions such as mantle cell lymphoma. It should be noted, however, that on occasion one sees cases of small lymphocytic lymphoma with typical Reed–Sternberg cells, suggesting a possible transformation to Hodgkin's lymphoma; it has been hypothesized that such a transformation may be mediated by the EBV.[721] A development of even greater clinical signifi-

cance is the transformation of a small lymphocytic lymphoma (or a chronic lymphocytic leukemia) into a "blastic," "histiocytic," or large cell neoplasm[682] (Figs 21.66 and 21.67). This occurrence, when developing in the background of chronic lymphocytic leukemia, has been traditionally known as *Richter's syndrome*[716,722a] and is accompanied by a precipitous decline in the clinical course. Fever, increasing lymphadenopathy, weight loss, and abdominal pain are frequent,[734] sometimes accompanied by hepatomegaly and splenomegaly. The earliest infiltrates may be detected in the lymph nodes or in the bone marrow.[699] Cell surface studies in these cases have shown that the large cells generally possess the same type of immunoglobulin heavy and light chain as the preexisting small lymphocytes, indicating that they represent dedifferentiation of the original tumor rather than a second neoplasm. However, exceptions to this rule have been reported, some of the pleomorphic cells having the immunocytochemical features of Reed–Sternberg cells.[688,730,736]

Lymphoma and dysproteinemia. In view of the fact that most malignant lymphomas arise from B lymphocytes (i.e., cells normally engaged in humoral immune responses) it is not surprising that in some of them the tumor cells express their potentialities by secreting immunoglobulins of one sort or another.[680,711] Ranging in between the typical malignant lymphoma without immunoglobulin abnormalities and the typical plasma cell myeloma with monoclonal peak and Bence Jones proteinuria, all types of morphologic and biochemical hybrids have been encountered.[686] Tumors have been described that secrete completely assembled immunoglobulins of the IgG, IgA, IgM, IgD, or IgE type (with or without concomitant production of isolated light chains), isolated light chains to the almost total exclusion of complete immunoglobulin molecules, and "heavy chains" (or, more accurately, Fc fragments) of IgG, IgM, or IgA

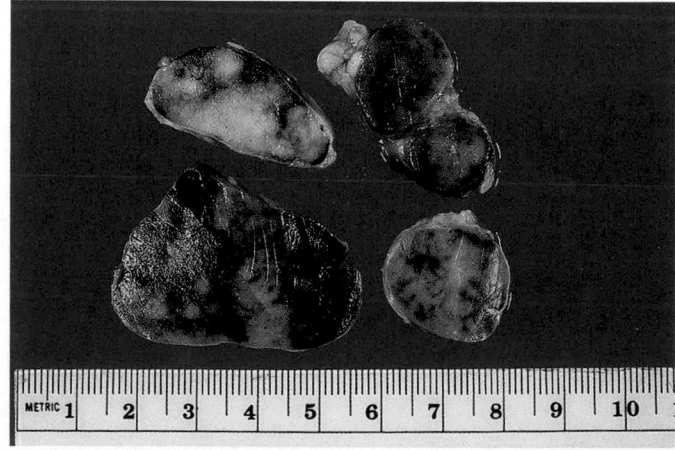

Fig. 21.66 Gross appearance of lymph nodes involved by chronic lymphocytic leukemia with anaplastic transformation (so-called "Richter's syndrome").

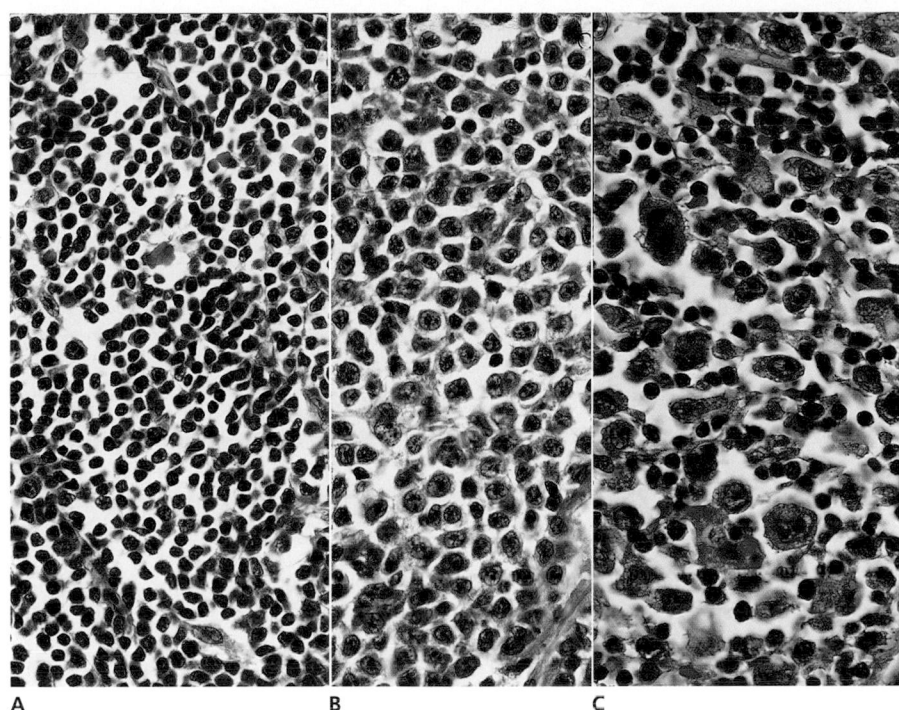

A   B   C

Fig. 21.67 Various morphologic types of lymph node involvement by chronic lymphocytic leukemia: **A**, monotonous infiltrate of small mature lymphocyte; **B**, somewhat immature forms, with slightly larger nuclei and more open chromatin; **C**, large pleomorphic tumor cells (so-called "Richter's syndrome").

specificity. Some of these immunoglobulins have the physicochemical properties of cryoglobulins and can result in necrotizing vasculitis.[689] This remarkably diverse expression of function has led to the introduction of such names as Waldenström's macroglobulinemia, light chain disease, α-chain disease, and Franklin's heavy chain disease and even to the proposal of grouping all immunoglobulin-secreting lymphoid and plasmacytic tumors under the term *immunocytoma*.[693,700,710]

This practice has led to considerable confusion as happens whenever morphologic and functional parameters are mixed in a common terminology. For instance, the serum picture of macroglobulinemia can be associated with a microscopic picture of small lymphocytic lymphoma, small lymphocytic lymphoma with plasmacytic differentiation, plasma cell myeloma, and large cell lymphoma.[715a] It is obvious that by giving a tissue diagnosis "consistent with macroglobulinemia," the pathologist is not rendering an accurate account of the situation. We believe that these neoplasms should be classified according to conventional morphologic criteria rather than by the biochemical findings in the patient's serum – i.e., a small lymphocytic lymphoma should be designated as such whether it produces macroglobulins, heavy chains, light chains, or no detectable globulins. Five main cytologic patterns are observed in these immunoglobulin-secreting neoplasms:

1 Malignant lymphomas of conventional appearance, usually of small lymphocytic type, indistinguishable from those not associated with immunoglobulin abnormalities.
2 Plasmacytomas, in which most of the tumor cells have

the characteristic light and electron microscopic features of plasma cells.
3 Tumors having the overall appearance of a malignant lymphoma of small lymphocytic type but in which a certain proportion of the tumor cells has undergone a plasmacytic differentiation, as evidenced light microscopically by lateralization of the nucleus, coarse chromatin clumping, appearance of a perinuclear clear halo, and/or increased basophilic cytoplasm and ultrastructurally by prominence of the Golgi apparatus and abundance of granular endoplasmic reticulum.[687,703]

Some of the tumor cells may be PAS positive. Immunoperoxidase stains will often show monoclonal immunoglobulin in the cytoplasm of the plasmacytoid cells much more frequently than in ordinary small lymphocytic lymphomas or chronic lymphocytic leukemias.[724,725] These tumors have been designated as small lymphocytic malignant lymphomas with plasmacytic differentiation, lymphoplasmacytoid lymphomas, or immunocytomas, lymphoplasmacytic type.[681] Their cell marker profile is similar to that of ordinary small lymphocytic lymphomas except for the presence of *cytoplasmic* immunoglobulin in some of the cells and a lesser percentage and degree of reactivity for CD5.[737] Intranuclear immunoglobulin inclusions (Butcher bodies) can also occur (Fig. 21.68).
4 Large cell lymphomas predominantly or exclusively composed of B-immunoblasts. These cases, once known as immunoblastic sarcomas, are better designated as large cell lymphoma, immunoblastic type.
5 Lymphomas composed of an admixture of immunoblasts, large plasmacytoid cells, and mature plasma

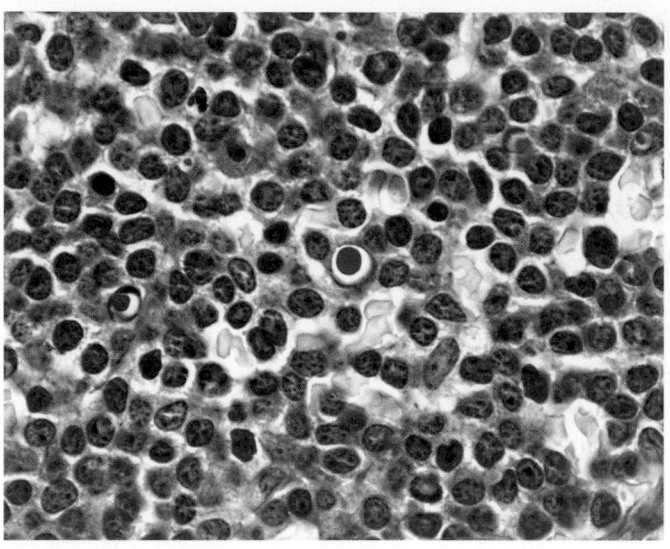
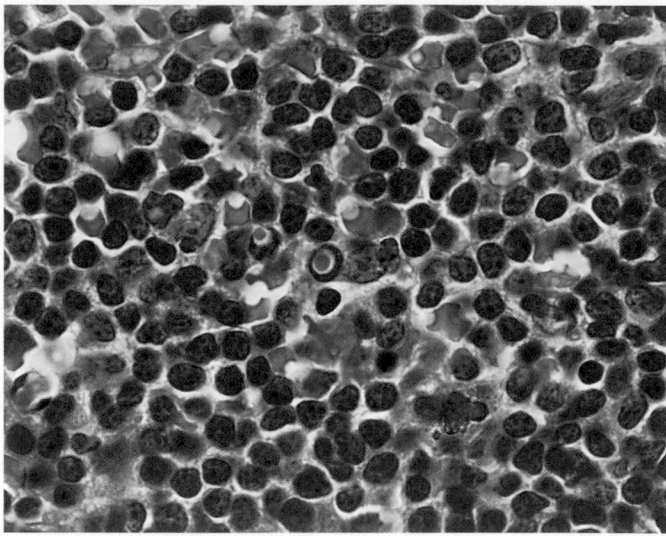

A   **B**

Fig. 21.68 Intranuclear immunoglobulin inclusions (Dutcher bodies) in a lymph node affected by lymphoplasmacytoid lymphoma as seen after hematoxylin–eosin (**A**) and PAS stains (**B**).

cells. These cases have sometimes been designated *pleomorphic immunocytomas* (Fig. 21.69). Some of the reported cases of primary plasmacytomas of lymph nodes[679,698] belong to this or to one or another of the previous categories. The term *plasmacytoma* of lymph nodes should be restricted to those rare cases having typical bone marrow involvement by plasmacytoma and/or cases in which nearly all of the malignant cells have plasmacytoid features, and in which a lymphocytic component is absent[715] (Fig. 21.70). Even under these circumstances the disease seems to be immunohistochemically different from other forms of extramedullary plasmacytomas, and almost never progresses to multiple myeloma.[719]

Attempts to correlate the microscopic appearance with the secretory activity of these tumors have been

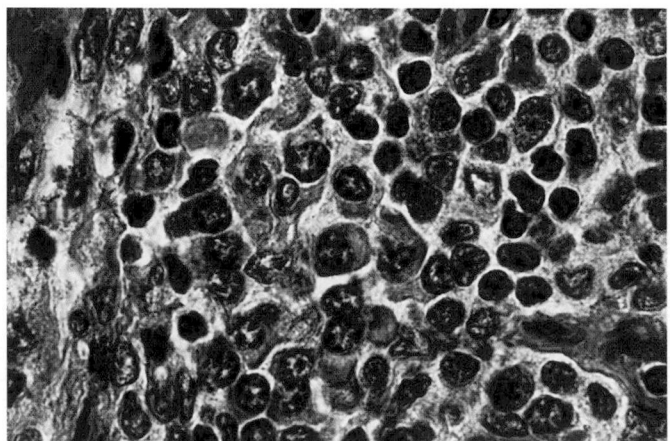

Fig. 21.69 Malignant lymphoma composed of lymphocytes and immature plasmacytoid forms (so-called "pleomorphic immunocytoma").

made by several authors. The results have been largely discouraging, although a few more or less distinctive patterns have emerged.[704,708] In general, tumors producing IgM globulin or "heavy chains" have the anatomic distribution and cytologic appearance of malignant lymphoma, whereas most of those secreting IgG globulin or a light chain are clinically and microscopically classifiable as plasma cell myeloma. Intranuclear and cytoplasmic inclusions are not specific for any type of immunoglobulin.[726] However, those composed of IgM or IgA are often PAS positive because of their high carbohydrate content, whereas those composed of IgG are not.[691,696] The immunoglobulin inclusions may appear as round eosinophilic bodies or crystals.[720] The former may be so abundant and prominent (perhaps resulting from a blockage in secretion) as to displace the nucleus laterally, creating a signet-ring effect.[707] A most peculiar variant on the theme is represented by the cases in which the immunoglobulin crystals are massively phagocytosed by histiocytes, resulting in an appearance that may simulate a variety of nonlymphoid diseases, including rhabdomyoma. This bizarre condition has been term *crystal-storing histiocytosis* but it truly represent a dysproteinemia-associated lymphoproliferative process akin to those described in this section. Examples have been reported in the soft tissue (particularly in the head and neck region), lung and other sites, and are discussed in the respective chapters.[702,705,706]

Tumors that have been reported as secreting IgA "heavy chains" have involved the gastrointestinal tract[729] or, much less commonly, the respiratory tract.[728] The former is discussed in Chapter XX. Production of IgM heavy chains, an exceptionally rare event, occurs in elderly patients who present with chronic lymphocytic leukemia.[713]

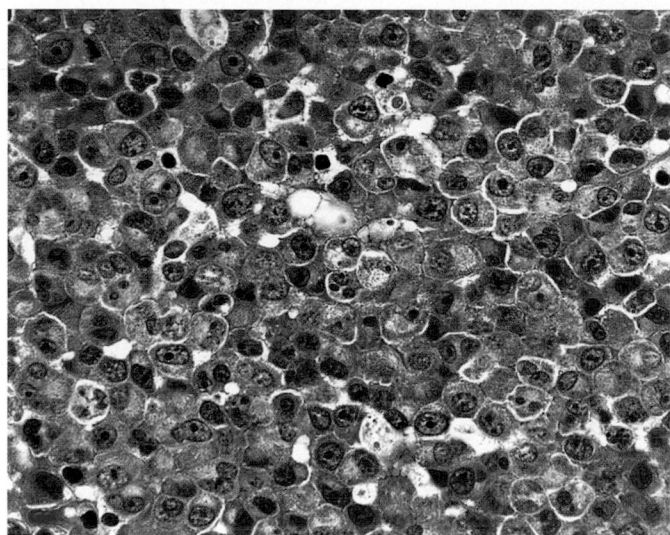

Fig. 21.70 Plasmacytoma of lymph node composed entirely of immature plasma cells (plasmablasts): **A**, hematoxylin–eosin; **A**, lambda immunostain.

Of all the anatomic types of malignant lymphoma, Hodgkin's lymphoma and follicular lymphoma are the least likely to be associated with immunoglobulin serum abnormalities. The more obvious the plasmacytic differentiation, the higher the chances of immunoglobulin alterations. However, it should be remembered that even fully differentiated plasma cell tumors may sometimes be associated with complete lack of detectable immunoglobulin production.

Follicular lymphoma

Follicular (nodular) lymphoma is a B-cell neoplasm that recapitulates the architectural and cytologic features of the normal secondary lymphoid follicle.[761] This tumor comprises up to 40% of all adult non-Hodgkin's lymphomas in the United States, but in other countries the relative incidence is much lower. Most cases occur in elderly individuals. It is very unusual under 20 years of age and relatively uncommon in blacks.[762] Most of the cases diagnosed in the past as follicular lymphomas in children actually represent NLPHL or reactive follicular hyperplasia. However, well-documented cases of follicular lymphoma in children are on record.[783,797]

Grossly and at low-power examination, the most distinctive feature of these tumors is the nodular pattern of growth (Figs 21.71 and 21.72). Rappaport et al.[785] have carefully outlined in a classic article the differential points between these neoplastic nodules and the reactive follicles of follicular hyperplasia (Figs 21.73 and 21.74) (see Table 21.10). With progression of the disease, this distinct nodularity becomes blurred, and eventually most of the proliferation acquires a diffuse pattern. The cytologic composition of the neoplastic nodules is characterized by a mixture in different proportions of small and large lymphoid cells, both of which resemble their normal follicular counterparts.[772] The small cells have

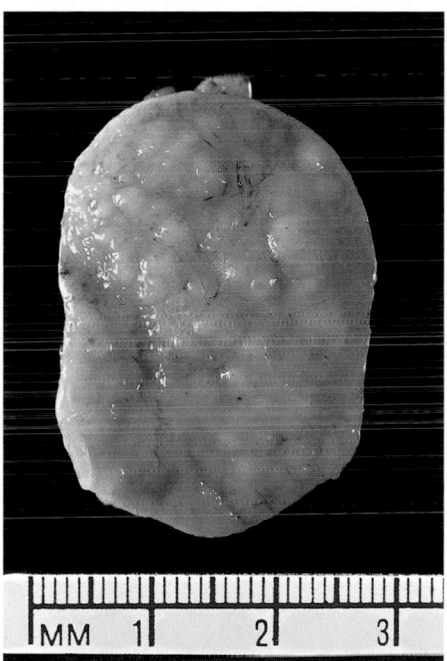

Fig. 21.71 Gross appearance of a lymph node affected by follicular lymphoma. The neoplastic nodules bulge onto the surface. (Courtesy of Dr. RA Cooke, Brisbane, Australia; from Cooke RA, Stewart B: Colour Atlas of Anatomical Pathology. Edinburgh, Churchill Livingstone, 2004).

scanty cytoplasm and an irregular, elongated cleaved nucleus with prominent indentations and infoldings; the size is similar or slightly larger than that of normal lymphocytes, the chromatin is coarse, and the nucleolus is inconspicuous (Fig. 21.75). These cells have been variously referred to as germinocytes, centrocytes, poorly differentiated lymphocytes, and small cleaved follicular center cells. The large cells are two or three times the size of normal lymphocytes; they have a distinct rim of

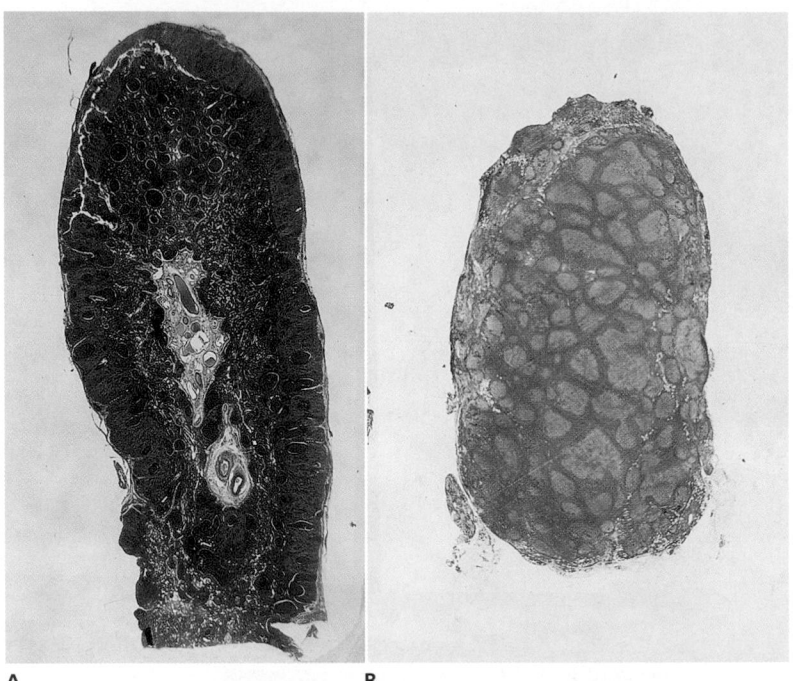

A   B

Fig. 21.72 Even distribution of neoplastic follicles in follicular lymphoma (**B**), as opposed to the predominantly cortical distribution typical of follicular hyperplasia (**A**).

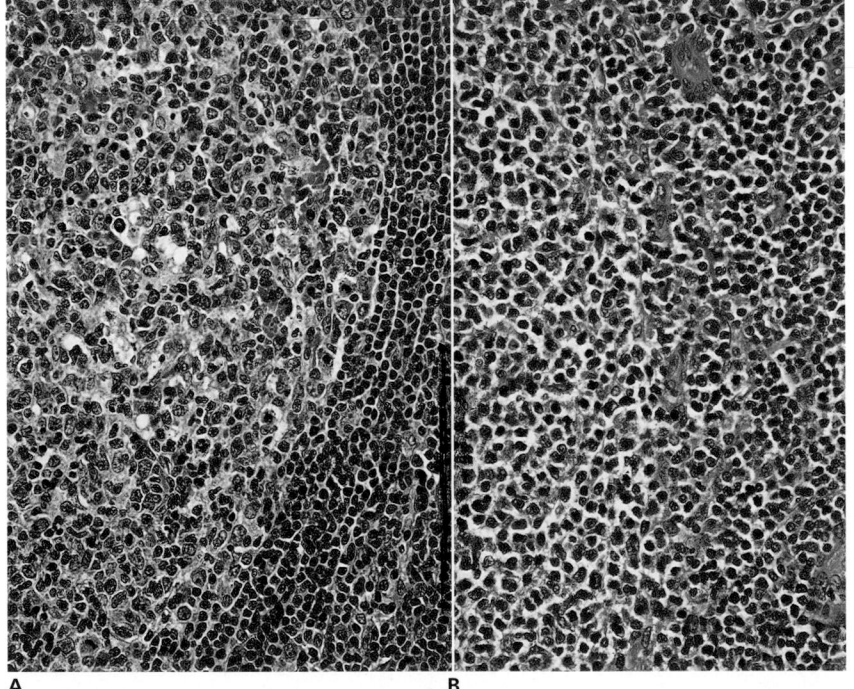

A   B

Fig. 21.73 Fuzzy edge of neoplastic nodule of follicular lymphoma (**B**), as opposed to sharp edge bound by the mantle zone in follicular hyperplasia (**A**).

cytoplasm and a vesicular nucleus with one or three nucleoli often adjacent to the nuclear membrane. These cells, which have a rapid turnover rate and probably represent the proliferating component of the tumor, have been designated over the years as germinoblasts, centroblasts, histiocytes, large (cleaved or noncleaved) follicular center cells, large lymphoid cells, and lymphoblasts. Some may be binucleated and simulate Reed–Sternberg cells.[775] It ought to be mentioned here that another type of large cell seen in follicular lymphoma is the non-neoplastic dendritic follicular cell, for

the very reason that the tumor involves lymphoid follicles; it is recognized because of its finely dispersed chromatin, the lack of identifiable cell boundaries, and the inconspicuousness of the nucleolus. In contrast to their counterparts in benign follicles, these cells show little or no immunoreactivity for fascin.[788]

Immunohistochemically, the follicles of follicular lymphoma (including all its variants) are composed of a monoclonal population of B cells admixed with a non-neoplastic population representing all the elements normally present in a normal germinal center, including

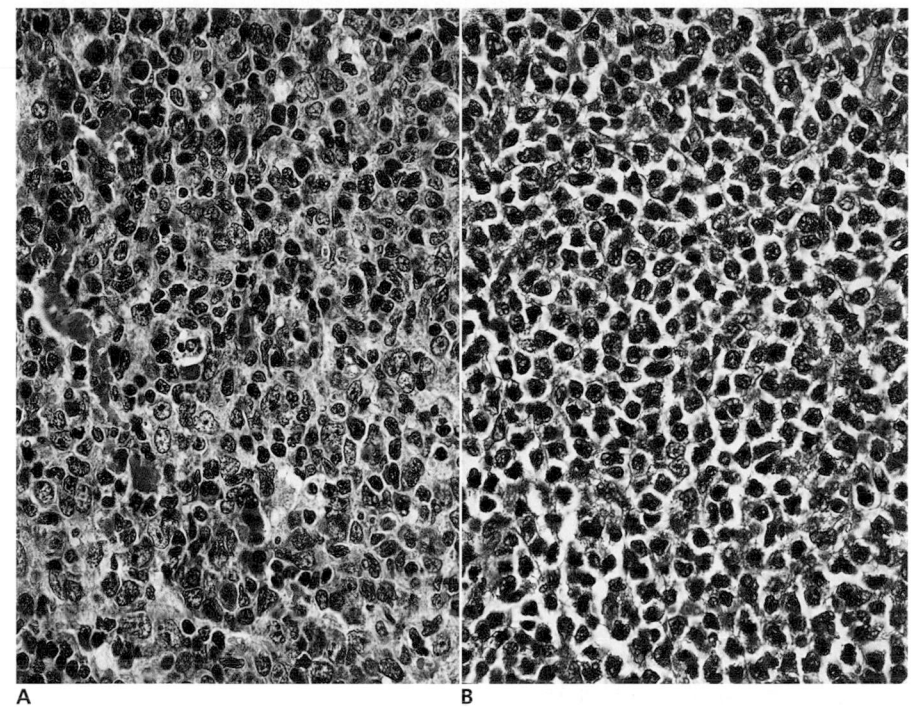

Fig. 21.74 Homogeneous population of small cleaved cells in follicular lymphoma (**B**), as opposed to the polymorphic composition seen in follicular hyperplasia, including the presence of tingible body macrophages (**A**).

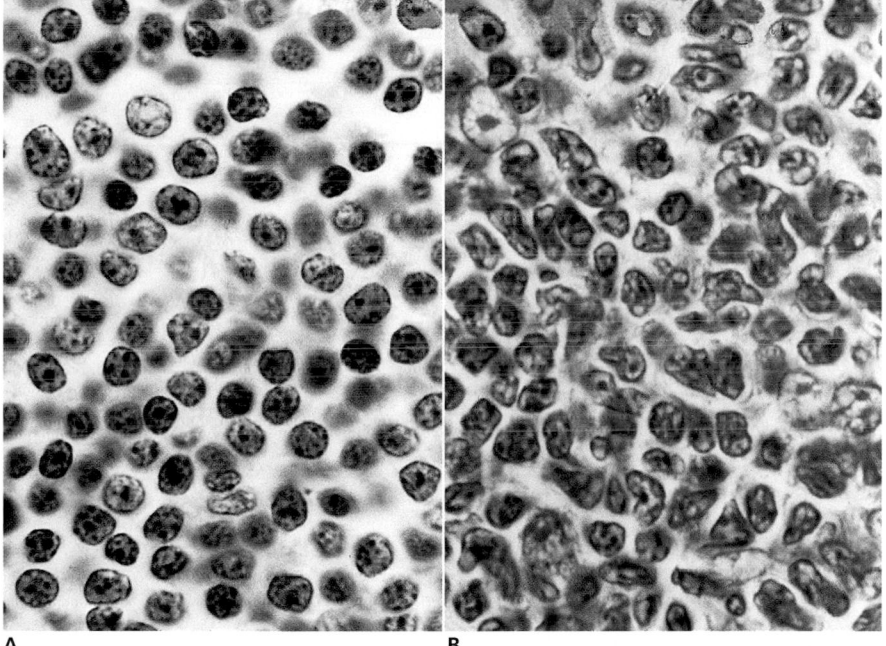

Fig. 21.75 Marked contrast between the cleaved cells of follicular lymphoma (**B**) and the regular mature lymphocytes of small lymphocytic lymphoma (**A**).

follicular center B cells, small T cells, macrophages, and follicular dendritic cells[790,793] (Figs 21.76 and 21.77). The tumor cells express pan B-antigens, such as CD19, CD20, CD22, and CD79a, in addition to HLA-DR, CDw75 (LN1), and CD74 (LN2). They also express surface and/or cytoplasmic immunoglobulins (usually of the IgM type) with light chain restriction and stain with monoclonal antibody MT2. CD10 (CALLA) has been detected in approximately 60% to 70% of the cases; CD5 and CD43 are usually negative.[798] The CD10 expression seen in most cases of follicular lymphoma has been used

for the differential diagnosis with follicular hyperplasia (in which it is nearly always weak or negative),[739,743] and as a probable indicator of follicle center origin if present in a diffuse large cell lymphoma.[766,774] Cytogenetically, over 85% of the cases have the t(14;18) (q32;q21) translocation. This results in the *bcl-2* gene being translocated from its normal position on chromosome 18 to chromosome 14, in juxtaposition with the J region of the immunoglobulin heavy chain gene.[752,760,779] The *bcl-2* gene product is an integral membrane protein located in the inner mitochondrial membrane, which function as a

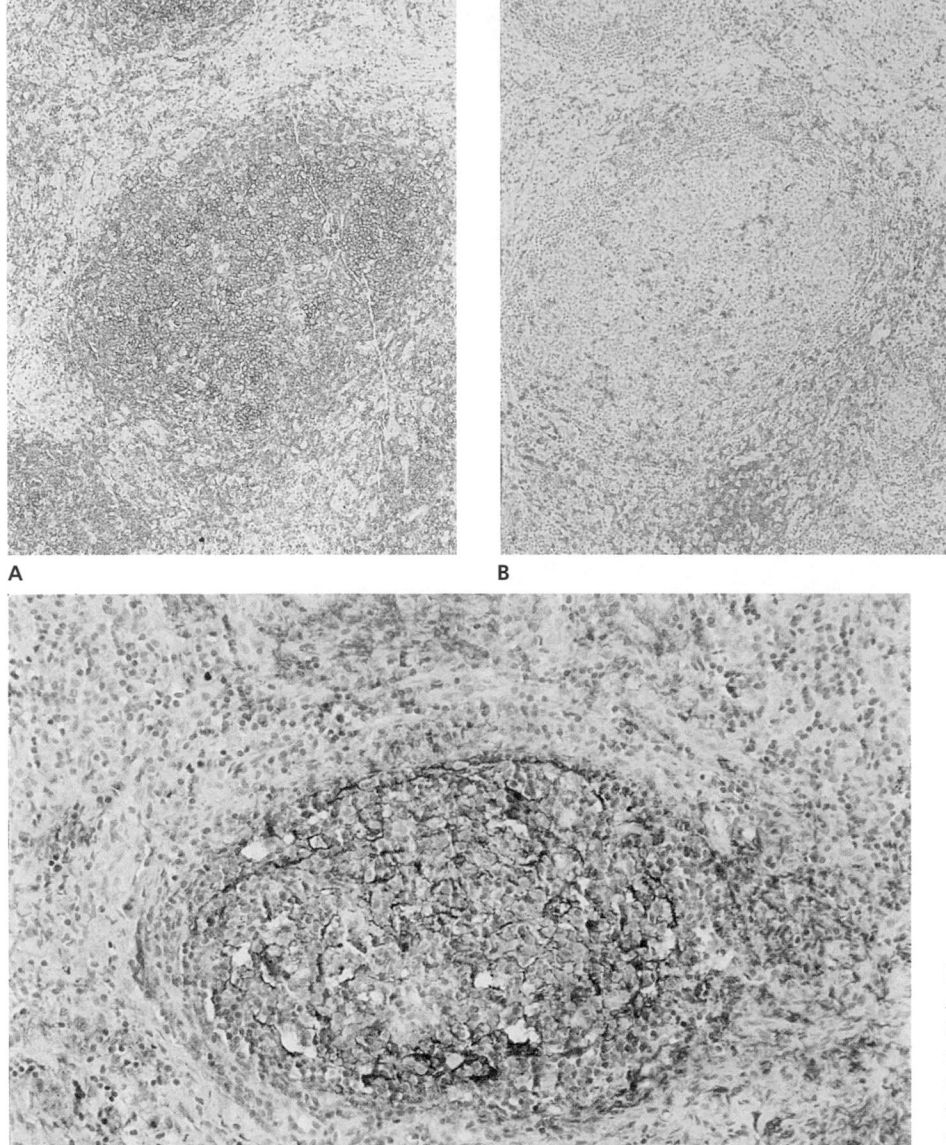

Fig. 21.76 A to C, Follicular lymphoma. A, CD20 stain decorates the neoplastic nodule and identifies the cells as of B-cell nature. B, CD3 stain shows a rim of non-neoplastic T cells around the follicles. C, CD21 stain shows a large number of dendritic follicular cells within the neoplastic follicle. (Courtesy of Dr. Glauco Frizzera, New York)

suppressor of apoptosis.[758,768] The *bcl-2* rearrangements can be identified by Southern blot and PCR techniques.[742,770] They can also be detected in the bone marrow and peripheral circulation, thus allowing for the monitoring of these patients for evidence of residual disease following therapy.[771,782] The bcl-2 protein can be identified immunohistochemically; it is present in approximately 85% of the follicular lymphomas while being absent in follicular hyperplasia.[756,793,795] Other types of translocations have been described in follicular lymphoma, such as t(8;14).[769] Rearrangement of *bcl-6* (located on chromosome 3q27) is seen in approximately 15% of the cases, and mutations of *bcl-6 5* are detected in 40% of the patients; the latter are said to be associated with a worse prognosis.[792] Immunohistochemically, expression of bcl-2 protein (which correlates poorly with 3q27 abnormalities) is present in nearly all cases of follicular

lymphoma.[791] Hence, it is useful for the differential diagnosis between follicular lymphoma and other low-grade lymphomas.[784]

Rearrangements of immunoglobulin heavy and light chain genes are present in virtually all cases of follicular lymphoma.

Depending on the relative proportion of small and large cells, follicular lymphomas are subdivided into three categories, respectively designated in the International Formulation as follows:

1 Predominantly small cleaved cells, when the population of large cells in the nodules is less than 20%
2 Mixed, small cleaved, and large cells, when the proportion of large cells is between 20% and 50%
3 Predominantly large cell, when the proportion of large cells is more than 50%

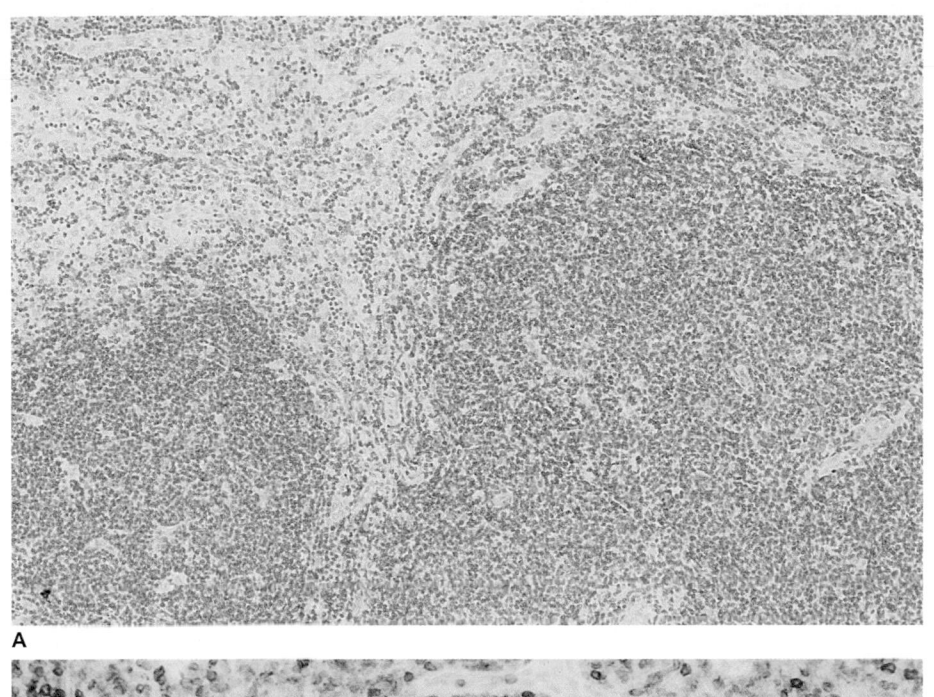

A

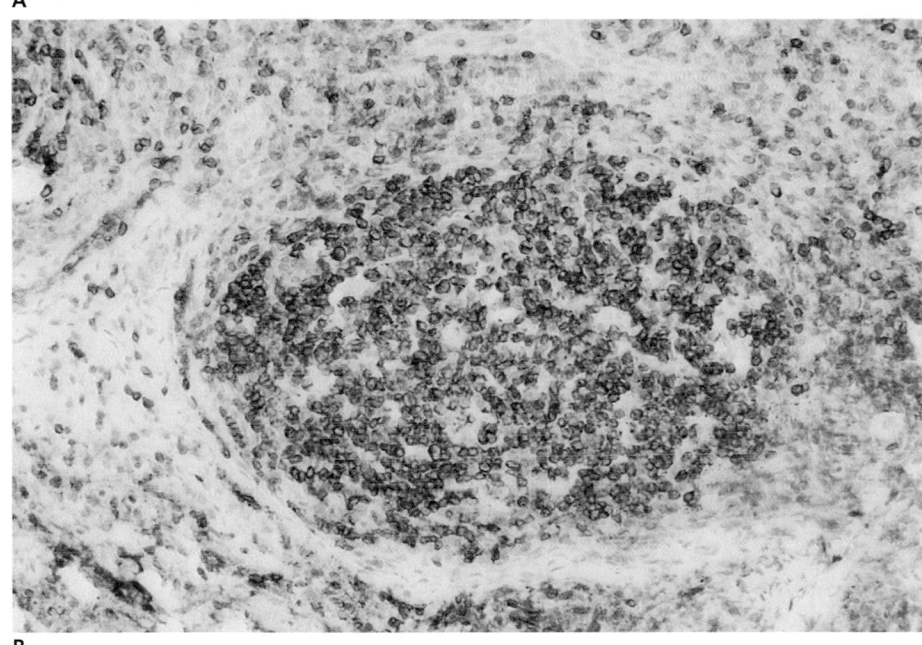

B

Fig. 21.77 Follicular lymphoma stained for MT2 (**A**) and bcl-2 (**B**). (Courtesy of Dr. Glauco Frizzera, New York)

A rare fourth category has been described, in which the neoplastic follicles are *entirely* composed of small lymphocytes.[748]

In the first category, which is the most common, mitotic activity is infrequent. Conversely, the appearance of large cells is often accompanied by a parallel increase in the number of mitoses.

Several important clinical differences exist between these groups, whether one uses this or a different terminology.[749,794] Patients in the first category are often asymptomatic, usually have generalized disease (often involving extranodal sites, such as the liver and bone marrow), and have a good prognosis, to the point that some authors advise against aggressive treatment for

them.[744,750,764,773,786,800] Tumors in the third category are more commonly localized at the time of presentation but run a more aggressive clinical course[759,762] and are more likely to lose their nodular pattern of growth and become diffuse. The prognosis of tumors in the second category is intermediate between these two but closer to the first. As a matter of fact, in an early series it was associated with an even longer survival.[741] Because of this fact, the first two categories are sometimes grouped under the term *low-grade follicular lymphoma*, the implication being that the predominantly large cell lymphoma is a high-grade tumor. Another morphologic parameter that has been evaluated in this tumor is the relative degree of nodularity. Warnke et al.[796] have shown that among the predominantly small cleaved cell and mixed lymphomas, the survival rate is similar in patients with purely nodular tumors and those with tumors of a nodular and diffuse pattern. However, in the predominantly large cell category, patients with tumors of both nodular and diffuse patterns have a worse prognosis than those with tumors of a pure nodular pattern.

The extranodal spread of follicular lymphoma is quite predictable. In the spleen, it tends to affect the B-derived lymphoid follicles located eccentrically in the white pulp. In the liver, the infiltrate is predominantly periportal. The bone marrow infiltrates tend to have a paratrabecular location. In the skin, there is an extensive dermal infiltrate without particular relation to vessels or adnexa.

In some cases of follicular lymphoma (particularly of the predominantly small cleaved cell type), malignant cells are found in the peripheral blood; hematologists refer to them by the inelegant term "buttock" cells because of their prominent nuclear cleft (Fig. 21.78). No prognostic significance has been assigned to this finding.

Specimens from subsequent biopsies or autopsy from patients with predominantly small cleaved cell lymphomas may show a similar microscopic appearance or a progression to a large cell type.[755,781] A more ominous development is represented by the occasional "blastic" or "blastoid" transformation of follicular lymphoma, in which the tumor cells acquire the morphologic features of markedly atypical cells; this is accompanied by a highly aggressive clinical course.[751,776] The resulting high-grade malignant tumor may have the morphologic and immunohistochemical features of a CD30+ anaplastic large cell lymphoma.[740]

Several morphologic variations in the theme of follicular lymphoma have been described. They include the following:

1 Presence of fine or coarse bands of fibrosis that accentuate even more the nodular character of the lesion but, in so doing, may induce confusion with carcinoma. This feature is more commonly seen in the large cell type[745]; it is particularly frequent in the retroperitoneum, but it also occurs in the cervical region, mediastinum, and other locations.

2 Presence of monocytoid B cell/marginal zone differentiation. In about 10% of follicular lymphomas, discrete foci of monocytoid B cells are seen, typically appearing on low power examination as a pale rim around the neoplastic follicles.[763,789] Molecular studies have shown a common clonal origin of the monocytoid B cells from follicle center cells.[738,799] Clinically, this feature is said to be associated with a shorter survival time.[777]

3 Deposition of proteinaceous material in the center of the nodules, similar to that seen in some reactive conditions, particularly the plasma cell variant of Castleman's disease (Fig. 21.79). The material is amorphous, acellular, brightly eosinophilic, and PAS positive.[749,787] Ultrastructurally, it is composed of membranous structures, membrane-bound vesicles, and electron-dense bodies.[749] It can appear both in predominantly small cleaved cell and mixed follicular lymphomas.[787]

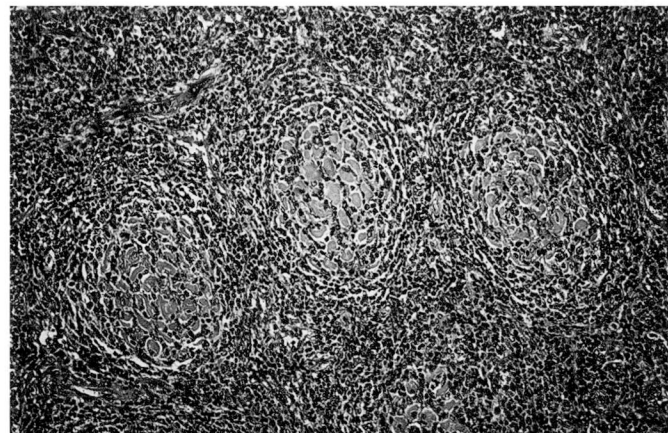

A

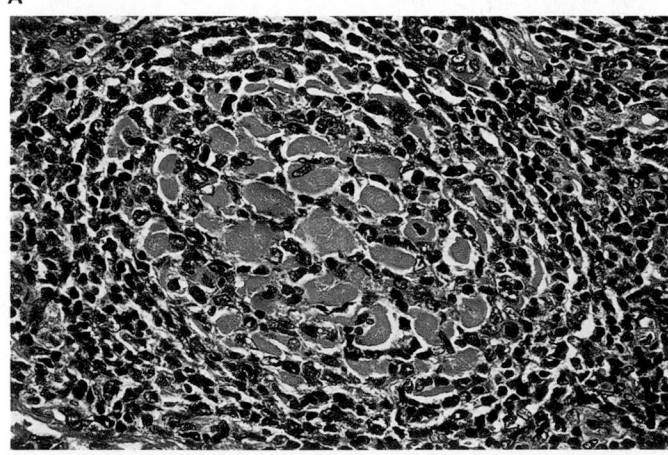

B

Fig. 21.79 Follicular lymphoma with deposition of proteinaceous material among the tumor cells. Ultrastructurally, some of this material was found to be within the cytoplasm of dendritic follicular cells.

Fig. 21.78 Blood smear from a patient with follicular lymphoma showing a so-called "notched nucleus cell" or "buttock cell."

4 Presence of large cytoplasmic eosinophilic globules—presumably immunoglobulins—that push the nucleus laterally and result in a signet ring effect[765] (Fig. 21.80).

5 Clear-cut plasmacytic differentiation in some or many of the neoplastic follicular center cells.[753,763]

6 Presence of cells with cerebriform nuclei (similar to those of T-cell lymphoma)[778] or multilobated nuclei.[747]

7 Permeation of the tumor follicles by small round lymphocytes of presumably mantle zone origin, the appearance simulating that of progressively transformed germinal center ("floral" variant)[757,780] (Fig. 21.81).

8 Presence of rosettes made up of cytoplasm and cytoplasmic processes of the lymphoid tumor cells and simulating the appearance of a neuroendocrine neoplasm (Fig. 21.82).[754]

9 Presence of hyaline vascular follicles similar to those seen in the vascular-hyaline type of Castleman's disease.

10 Inversion of the usual staining pattern as seen on low-power examination so that the neoplastic follicles appear darker than the surrounding lymphoid tissue. This pattern, which is referred to as the "reverse" or "inverse" variant of follicular lymphoma, carries no prognostic significance.[746]

11 Prominent epithelioid granulomatous response.[767]

Mantle cell lymphoma

Mantle cell lymphoma is a low-grade neoplasm also known as intermediate lymphocytic, mantle zone, centrocytic, and diffuse small cleaved cell lymphoma.[805,816,830] It comprises from 3% to 10% of all cases of non-Hodgkin's lymphoma. Like follicular lymphoma, it usually occurs in middle-aged and elderly individuals.[808,824] The low-power appearance is largely that of a diffuse lymphoma, although there may be a suggestion of nodularity accentuated by the occasional presence of small germinal center-like structures ("naked" germinal centers) (Fig. 21.83).[836] Most of the small lymphocytes are similar to those of small lymphocytic lymphoma, but others show slightly irregular and indented nuclear contours approaching those seen in small cleaved cell follicular lymphoma[834] (Fig. 21.84). In some cases, the tumor cells have larger nuclei with more dispersed

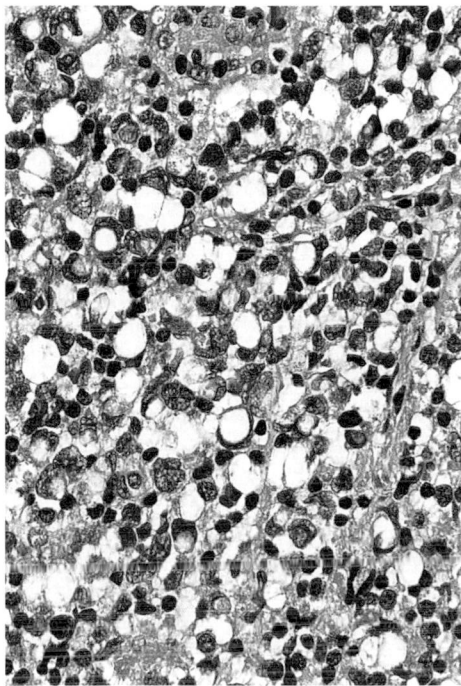

Fig. 21.80 Malignant lymphoma featuring signet ring changes in some of the tumor cells.

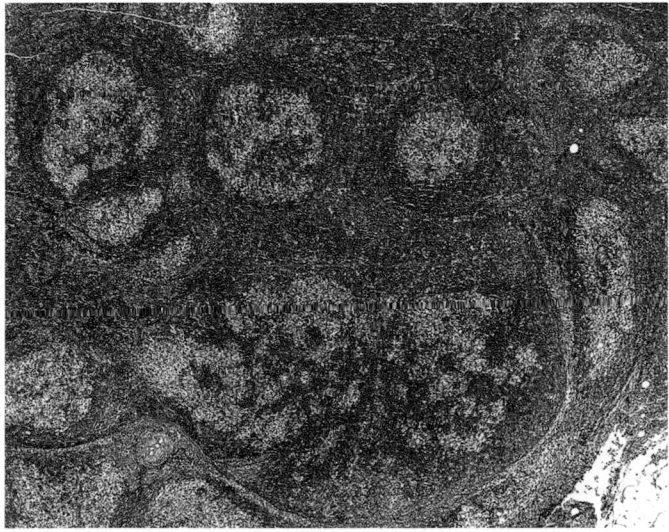

Fig. 21.81 So-called "floral variant" of follicular lymphoma.

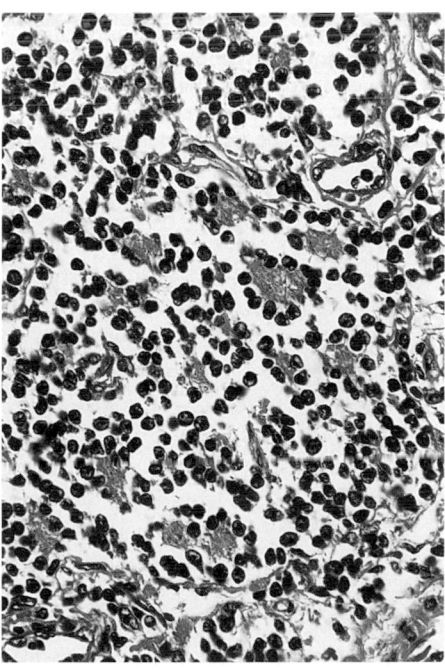

Fig. 21.82 Malignant lymphoma showing rosette formation by some of the lymphoid cells.

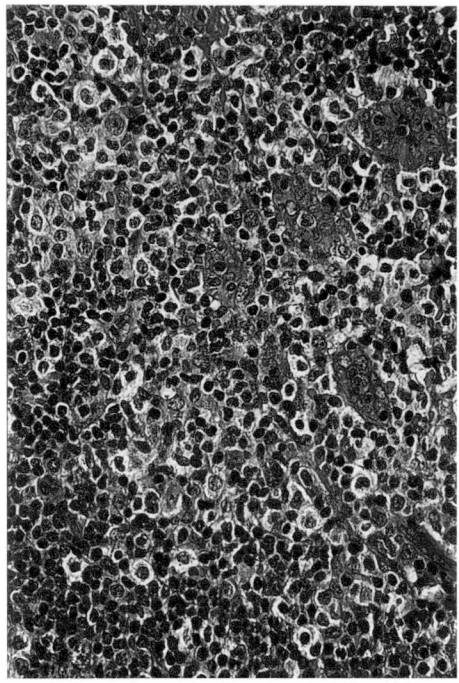

Fig. 21.88 Lymph node involvement by marginal zone B-cell lymphoma. This tumor also affected the thymus gland. (Courtesy of Dr. John Chan, Hong Kong)

believed that many of the extranodal processes described years ago as pseudolymphomas of the lung, stomach, skin, and other sites are examples of this process. Patients may suffer from autoimmune disorders such as Sjögren's disease and Hashimoto's thyroiditis.

Immunohistochemically, the cells of MALT-lymphoma are nearly always B cells expressing immunoglobulin light chain restriction. There are no specific cell marker differences that separate MALT lymphoma from the other low-grade B-cell lymphomas listed at the beginning of this section. However, as a group they are less likely to express CD5 and CD25 and more likely to express CD11C. At the molecular level, they show rearranged heavy and light immunoglobulin genes,[858] but there is no rearrangement of the *bcl-2* gene.[837] Trisomy 3 is a frequent, and some cases have been shown to have t/11;18) (q21;q21) translocation.[838,846,853,857]

3 *Splenic marginal zone lymphoma.* Several cases of lymphoma involving the marginal zone of the spleen have been reported, sometimes in association with bone marrow and peripheral blood involvement.[849,854] The disease is probably related if not identical to that reported under the term "splenic lymphoma with villous lymphocytes."

There appears to be considerable clinical, morphologic immunohistochemical overlap among the three entities just described.[843] Consequently, the proposal has been made that they represent a related family of neoplasms

showing morphologic evidence of differentiation into cells of marginal zone type.[852,856] These cells are thought to have the capacity to mature into both monocytoid B cells and plasma cells, and to display tissue-specific homing patterns. A corollary of this proposal is that the various clinical syndromes may be the result of the homing pattern of the specific neoplastic clone.[844] Accordingly, the recommendation has been made to use the term *marginal zone lymphoma* to encompass all tumors in this group and to subdivide them into extranodal, nodal, and splenic subtypes.

The proposal has been generally accepted, although it has been pointed out that important clinical and molecular genetic differences among the subgroups and even within a given subgroup exist.[839,839a,847] For instance, t(11;18) (q21;q21) seems to be found only in connection with the MALT type,[853] and trisomy 3 is very rare in the splenic form.[838] The nodal form of marginal zone B-cell lymphoma, which is the one that concerns us here, is a rare disease, comprising less than 2% of nodal lymphomas. The cytologic and architectural features correspond to those already described under the heading of monocytoid B-cell lymphoma. Transformation into a large cell lymphoma (and, exceptionally, even Hodgkin's lymphoma and anaplastic large cell lymphoma) can occur in any of the forms of marginal zone B-cell lymphoma, including that involving nodes.[840,851]

Diffuse mixed (small and large cell) lymphoma

Diffuse mixed lymphoma is not a specific lymphoma type but a heterogeneous category composed of lymphomas of various types that share a mixed composition of large and small lymphoid cells.[859–861] It includes (1) the diffuse mixed cell form of follicular lymphoma, (2) peripheral (post-thymic) T-cell lymphoma, (3) lymphoplasmacytic lymphoma with increased number of immunoblasts (also known as pleomorphic immunocytoma), (4) T-cell-rich large B-cell lymphoma, (5) some examples of marginal zone B-cell lymphoma with an admixture of large cells; and probably others. The differential diagnosis among these various entities is based on a combination of clinical, morphologic, and immunohistochemical criteria (Table 21.11).

Diffuse large B-cell lymphoma

Large B-cell lymphoma is the most complex and heterogeneous of all the non-Hodgkin's lymphomas.[895] The term replaces the old histiocytic lymphoma, which in turn replaced the older reticulum cell sarcoma. It is morphologically characterized by the large size of the cells, their vesicular nuclei with prominent nucleoli, and their relatively abundant cytoplasm. Only those with a known or presumed B-cell phenotype are discussed here (i.e., diffuse large B-cell lymphoma or DLBCL).

As a group, DLBCL occurs both in children and adults, but mostly in the latter.[896] In comparison with most other types of lymphoma, it has a greater tendency for extranodal presentation and for being localized at the time of presentation. The progression is rapid and the prognosis is poor if untreated, but excellent responses have been obtained with aggressive chemotherapy.[863,878] In more than half of the cases, the tumor is limited to one side of the diaphragm (40%, as opposed to 90% for follicular lymphoma).[867] Involvement of the bone marrow or liver is less common than in follicular or small lymphocytic lymphomas.[899] Approximately 40% of the cases present in extranodal sites, such as the digestive system, skin, and skeletal system.[867] When the liver or spleen is involved, it is usually in the form of scattered large tumor masses instead of the multiple smaller nodules or miliary type seen with the group of lymphomas composed of small lymphocytes. The involved nodes are usually markedly enlarged, homogeneous, individualized, and with little or no necrosis (Fig. 21.89).

Immunologic studies performed in large cell lymphomas have shown a significant heterogeneity.[864,903] This indicates that large cell lymphoma is not a specific entity like the others but rather a common denominator for all the highly anaplastic or "blastic" lymphomas, just as large cell undifferentiated carcinoma of the lung represents the end of the spectrum for all major microscopic types of pulmonary carcinoma.[891] Approximately 50% to 60% of the large cell lymphomas exhibit B-cell markers, 5% to 15% have T-cell markers, a few have features consistent with true histiocytes, and as many as a third of the cases have no markers at all ("null" lymphoma).[885] Gene rearrangement studies have shown that most tumors in the latter group are of B-cell nature.[868]

As already indicated, this section deals with the large cell lymphomas of known or presumed B-cell nature, which are the majority. Large cell lymphomas of T-cell type are discussed in p. 1950, and large cell tumors of documented or presumed histiocytic/reticulum/dendritic cell nature are dealt with on p. 1966.

Microscopically, the pattern of nodal involvement is by definition diffuse. However, it may be complete or partial, and on occasion it may be interfollicular or sinusal (see below). There is commonly extranodal extension, sometimes with accompanying sclerosis. Mitoses are numerous and a starry sky pattern may be present.

On cytologic grounds, a sharp separation used to be made between tumors composed of germinal center (large cleaved and noncleaved) cells and immunoblastic cells, but that distinction is not much stressed at present, one of the reasons being the poor intra- and interobserver reproducibility. Accordingly, some pathologists simply use the term diffuse large B-cell lymphoma without qualifiers. Others prefer to keep subclassifying them whenever possible into the types listed below, the first one being by far the most common.

Centroblastic. This is regarded as the diffuse counterpart of the nodular form of follicular lymphoma and is thought to be more aggressive.[902] It is composed of an admixture in varying proportions of cleaved and noncleaved large cells (Fig. 21.90). When the latter predominate, the distinction with the immunoblastic variant described below becomes particularly difficult. The subtle differences are the lighter-staining and less pyroninophilic cytoplasm, the more peripheral location of the nucleoli, the absence of plasmacytoid differentiation, the presence of scattered small and large cleaved cells, and the fact that a vaguely follicular residual pattern may still be present.[883]

Immunoblastic. In this form, the predominant tumor cell has the appearance of an immunoblast: large vesicular nucleus with prominent central nucleolus and thick nuclear membrane and deeply staining amphophilic and

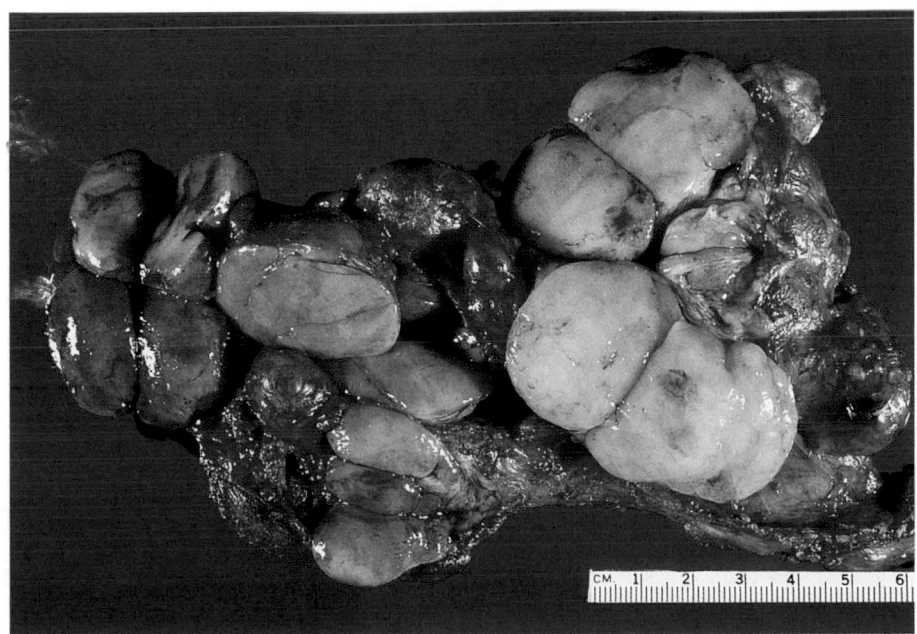

Fig. 21.89 Gross appearance of lymph nodes involved by non-Hodgkin's lymphoma of diffuse large B-cell type. The nodes are enlarged and show a homogeneous tan cut surface.

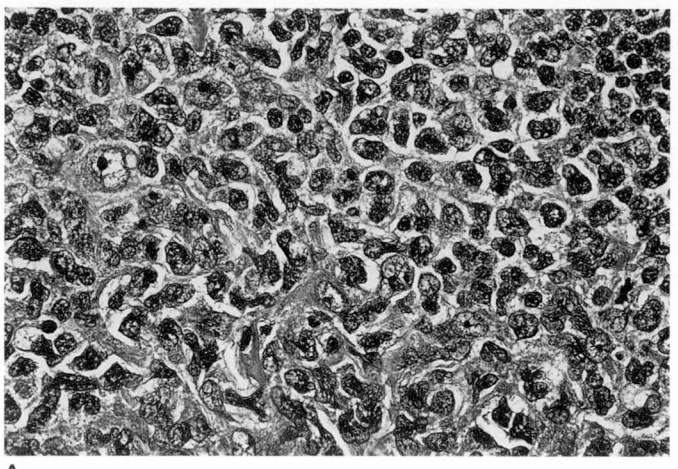 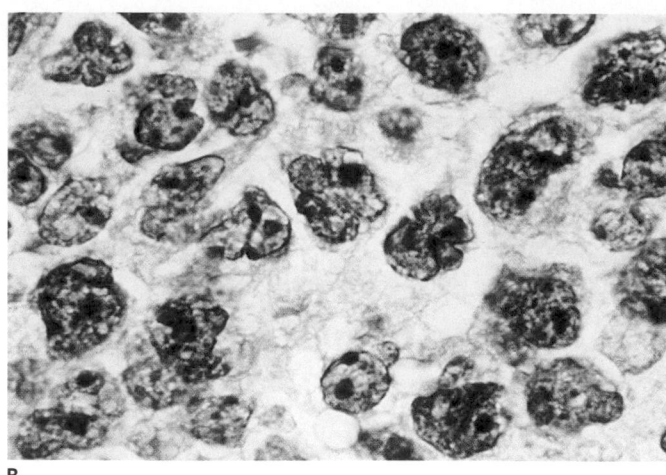

Fig. 21.90 Medium and high-power views of diffuse large B-cell lymphoma of large cleaved type.

pyroninophilic cytoplasm with a distinct nuclear hof (Fig. 21.91). Some of the cells are binucleated or multinucleated and simulate Reed–Sternberg cells, and others acquire plasmacytoid features (cartwheel chromatin, larger perinuclear hof). Immunoperoxidase staining often shows intracytoplasmic immunoglobulin. This is the most common type of lymphoma arising on the basis of natural immunodeficiency, immunosuppression, immunoproliferative states (such as angioimmunoblastic lymphadenopathy), and other immune-mediated diseases, such as Hashimoto's thyroiditis, Sjögren's disease, and lupus erythematosus.[880]

T-cell-rich. In this type, the neoplastic B cell population is overshadowed by a reactive population of T cells (Fig. 21.92). There may also be a population of histiocytes, this being the reason why in the WHO classification this variant is referred to as *T cell/histiocyte rich*.[881] The tumor cells may represent less than 10% of the entire cell population. The pattern of growth is predominantly diffuse and there may be a fine interstitial fibrosis. The main differential diagnosis is with NLPHL, with which it shares many phenotypical features,[894] and which

could be legitimately viewed as a special type of T-cell-rich B-cell lymphoma. As a matter of fact, some authors have questioned the validity of separating the two entities.[871] It would seem, though, that there are enough clinical, morphologic, and molecular genetic differences to keep them apart for the time being. To wit, T-cell-rich large B-cell lymphoma is clinically more aggressive,[874] has a different pattern of dendritic follicular cell staining,[873] and is said to have a different genetic pattern on comparative genomic hybridization.[875]

Anaplastic. This rare variant is characterized by the presence of large bizarre tumor cells, some resembling Reed–Sternberg cells, often growing in a cohesive pattern and/or sinusal pattern mimicking carcinoma. Despite the obvious morphologic similarities, this tumor is thought to be biologically unrelated to the anaplastic large cell lymphoma discussed on p. 1951.

At the molecular level, large B-cell lymphoma usually shows rearrangements of the immunoglobulin heavy and light chain genes. Rearrangements of *bcl-2* are found in 20% to 30% of the cases, suggesting a relationship with follicular lymphoma.[862] Approximately one third of

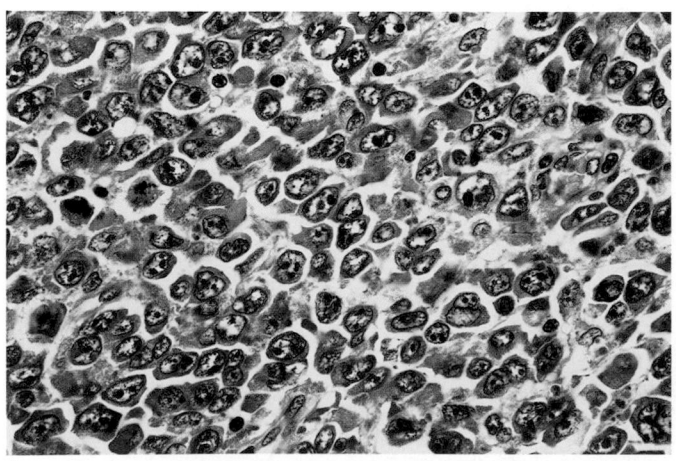 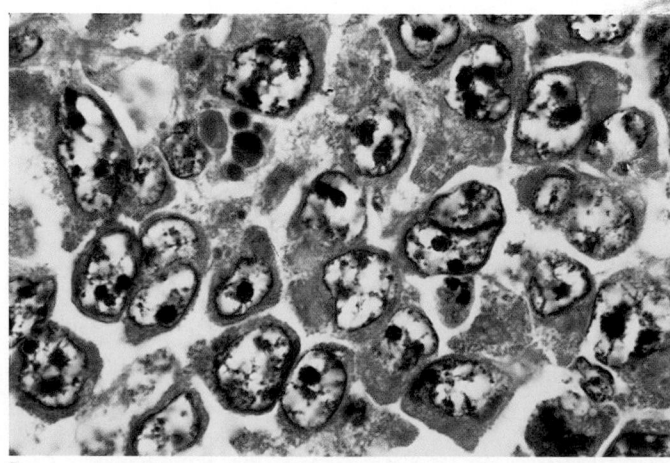

Fig. 21.91 Medium and high-power views of diffuse large B-cell lymphoma of immunoblastic type.

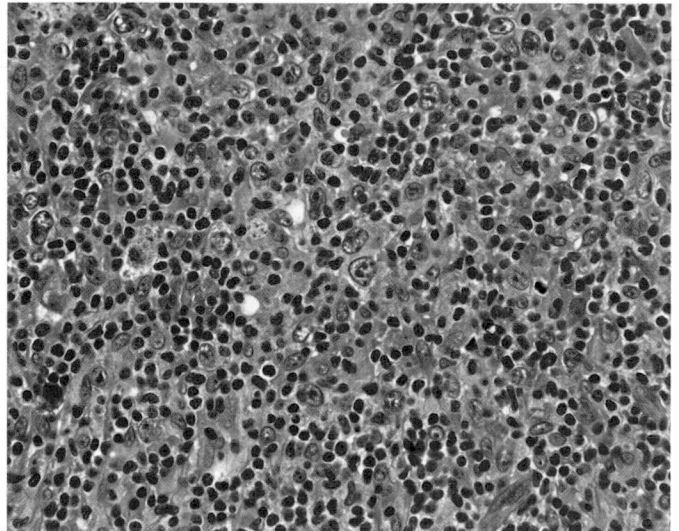

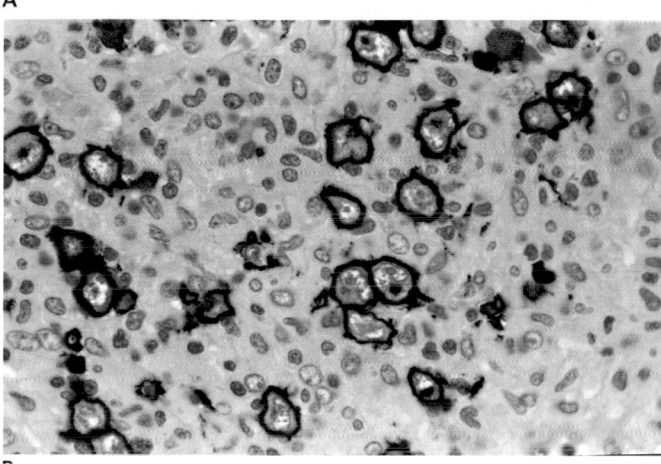

Fig. 21.92 T-cell-rich large B-cell lymphoma: **A**, hematoxylin–eosin; **B**, membrane and Golgi-type immunoreactivity for CD20 in the large tumor cells.

diffuse large lymphomas show rearrangements of *bcl-6*, this feature being more common at extranodal sites.[869,870,882,887,906] It is extremely rare for these lymphomas to show concomitant rearrangement of *bcl-2* and *bcl-6*, and there are no alterations in the T-cell receptor gene. Several cancer-related genes are involved with the large cell lymphomas, including *bcl-6*, which is affected in approximately 20% of the cases.[877]

Variants Numerous morphologic variations on the theme of large B-cell malignant lymphoma have been described, some of a cytologic and others of an architectural/topographic nature. Some of them relate to the lymphoma types described above and others do not. Most of these variations do not have an impact on therapy or prognosis, but they are important because they may result in a mistaken diagnosis. They include the following:

1 *Sclerosis*. Diffuse large cell lymphomas can undergo marked sclerosing changes, similar to those seen in

follicular lymphomas[865,892,893,900] (Fig. 21.93). This material is mainly composed of types I, III, and V collagen and fibronectin.[884] Sclerosis is a particularly common feature in mediastinal (thymic) large cell lymphomas (see Chapter 8).

2 *Spindling of tumor cells*. This phenomenon, which is probably related to the aforementioned fibrosis, seems to be more common in large cell lymphomas of mediastinum and bone, but it can be seen in any location, including lymph nodes.[901]

3 Presence of a *myxoid stroma* that can simulate the appearance of myxoid malignant fibrous histiocytoma or myxoid chondrosarcoma[876,898] (Fig. 21.94).

4 *Rosette formation*. This peculiar change, originally described in follicular lymphoma, has also been seen in large cell lymphoma. Ultrastructural studies have shown that the material in the center of the rosettes is made up of complex cell prolongations.[897]

5 *Filiform cell prolongations*. This phenomenon, which is probably related to that described in the previous paragraph, is appreciable in ultrastructural preparations and is similar to that sometimes seen in

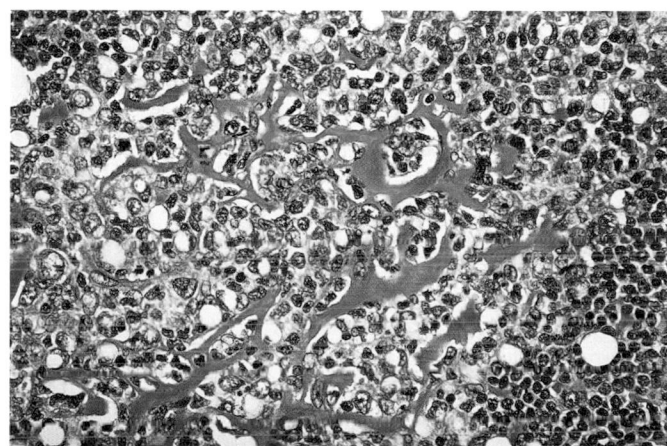

Fig. 21.93 Marked sclerosis and hyalinization in diffuse large B-cell lymphoma.

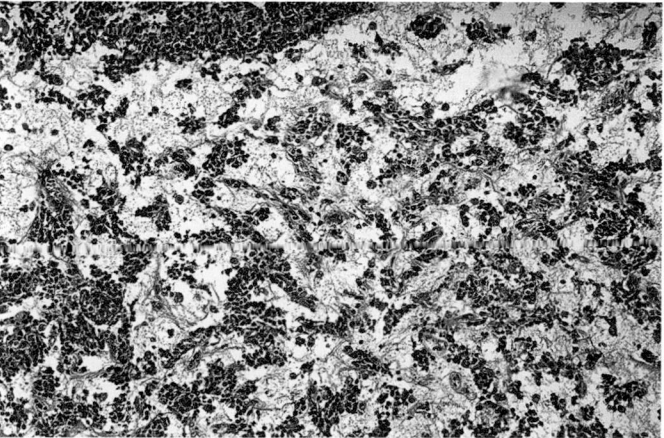

Fig. 21.94 Myxoid stromal change in diffuse large B-cell lymphoma. This is an exceptional occurrence.

carcinomas, mesotheliomas, and other neoplasms. Large cell lymphomas exhibiting this spectacular feature have been designated anemone cell, microvillous, filiform cell, villiform cell, and porcupine lymphomas.[866,889]

6 *Signet ring features.* This alteration, which is more common in follicular lymphoma, is rarely seen in large cell lymphoma and may simulate metastatic adenocarcinoma.[905]

7 *Sinusal pattern of spread*, in which the tumor cells are predominantly or entirely confined to the lymph node sinuses (and therefore to be referred as sinusal rather than sinusoidal) resulting in an appearance closely simulating that of metastatic carcinoma malignant melanoma, or anaplastic large cell lymphoma, or anaplastic large cell lymphoma[878,890] (Fig. 21.95A and B).

8 *Interfollicular pattern of growth.* This is more common in T-cell tumors but has also been described in B-cell neoplasms.[886]

9 *Nuclear multilobation.* Although originally thought to be a feature of T-cell tumors, this alteration is now known to be more common in B-cell neoplasms.[888,904]

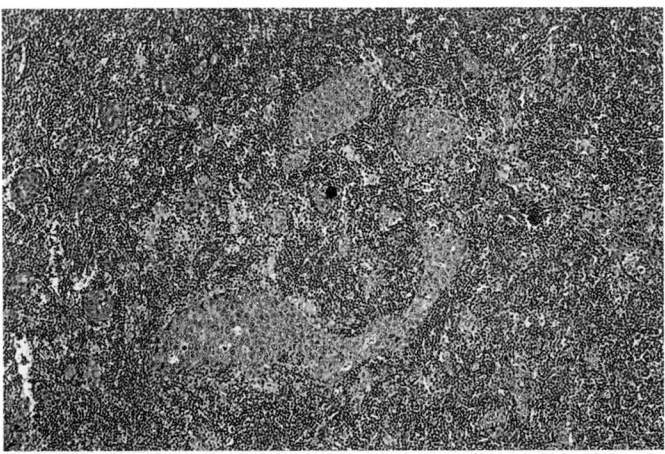

A

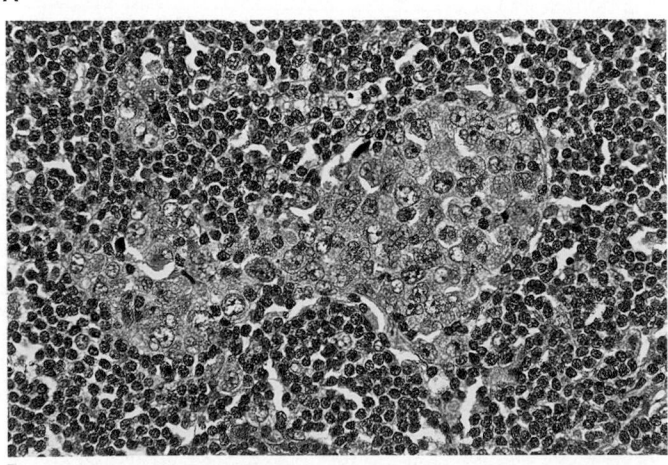

B

Fig. 21.95 Large B-cell lymphoma with a sinusal pattern of growth that simulates a metastatic tumor.

10 *Keratin positivity.* This phenotypic rather than morphologic variation ought to be mentioned here, with the added comment that it is exceptionally rare.[879]

Peripheral (post-thymic) T-cell lymphoma

Peripheral (post-thymic) T-cell lymphoma is the generic group given to a family of tumors composed of neoplastic lymphocytes with phenotypic and genotypic features of peripheral T cells.[909,928] This is an extremely heterogeneous group of lesions, many of them occurring primarily at extranodal sites, and which have received a myriad of designations. Most of them were identified as entities long before their peripheral T cell nature was ascertain. They include:

- *Mycosis fungoides* and *Sézary syndrome* (see Chapter 4);
- *NK/T-cell lymphoma, nasal type*, which includes most of the cases traditionally diagnosed as lethal midline granuloma[909a] (see Chapter 7);
- *Enteropathy-type T-cell lymphoma*, which includes most of the cases of intestinal lymphoma arising as a complication of celiac disease (see Chapter 11);
- *Hepatosplenic T-cell lymphoma* (see Chapters 13 and 22);
- *Subcutaneous panniculitis-like T-cell lymphoma* (see Chapter 4);
- Most if not all the cases described as *angioimmunoblastic lymphadenopathy*, which were already discussed in the section on reactive/inflammatory conditions (see p. 1908);
- The tumor type originally described by Lennert as malignant lymphoma with a constantly high number of epithelioid cells and variously known as: *Lennert's lymphoma* and *lymphoepithelioid lymphoma*.[908,915,919] It occurs in adults, it is often generalized (74% of the patients have stage IV disease at presentation), and the prognosis is poor.[913,925] Microscopically, there is effacement of the architecture by a lymphohistiocytic infiltrate, often accompanied by plasma cells and eosinophils and by proliferation of small vessels with plump endothelial cells. The polymorphic nature of the infiltrate and the occasional presence of Reed–Sternberg-like cells often elicits a mistaken diagnosis of Hodgkin's lymphoma. The key to the diagnosis resides in the atypical appearance of the small lymphocytes located between the reactive histiocytes (Fig. 21.96). In addition to Hodgkin's lymphoma, the differential diagnosis includes angioimmunoblastic lymphadenopathy. Some cases of Lennert's lymphoma have been seen to undergo a "blastic" transformation into a large cell lymphoma.[914]
- A subset of diffuse large cell lymphomas, including those described as T-cell immunoblastic sarcoma, T-cell lymphoma with multilobated nuclei,[921] erythrophagocytic T-cell lymphoma,[916] HTLV-1-related pleomorphic T-cell lymphoma (occurring in an endemic form in Japan),[918,926] T-zone lymphoma,[912] peripheral T-cell lymphoma with perifollicular growth pattern,[922]

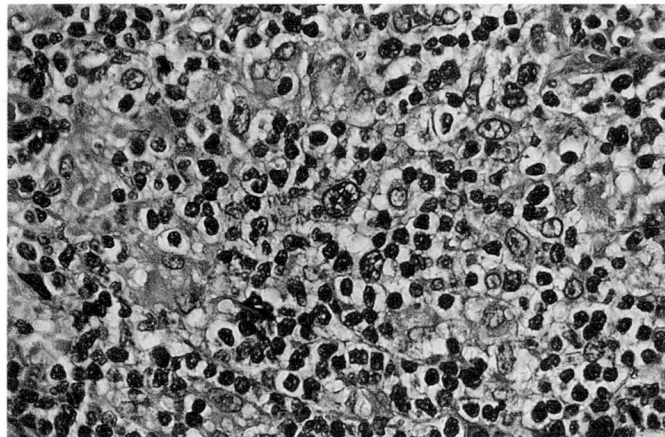

Fig. 21.96 Peripheral T-cell lymphoma with a high content of non-neoplastic histiocytes (so-called "Lennert's lymphoma").

and nodal CD8+ cytotoxic T-cell lymphoma[917] (Fig. 21.97).

- *Anaplastic large cell lymphoma* and its variants (see next section).

Immunohistochemically, all peripheral T-cell lymphomas show—by definition—the markers of the mature T cell.[907] In paraffin sections, they are positive for CD45RB in approximately 90% of the cases, and for the T-cell-associated markers CD45R0, CD43, and CD3 in a similar percentage. CD15 positivity is seen in 10% to 15% of the cases, but with a cytoplasmic granular quality that is generally different from that seen in Hodgkin's lymphoma.[923,930] In frozen sections, the tumor cells often show aberrant phenotypes, such as absence of CD2, CD3, CD5, and/or CD7. Most tumors express the α/β T-cell receptor, but aberrant absence of the β-f-1' antigen has been documented in one quarter of the cases.[920]

Most cases of peripheral T-cell lymphoma express a CD4+/CD8– mature helper phenotype; approximately 20% express a CD4–/CD8+ cytotoxic/suppressor pheno-type, with rare cases having CD4–/DC8– or CD4+/CD8+ phenotypes. The subset traditionally known as Lennert's lymphoma may also have either a helper or a cytotoxic phenotype.[931]

At the molecular level, most peripheral T-cell lymphomas exhibit clonal rearrangements of the β T-cell receptor gene, with a minority showing rearrangement of the γ or δ T-cell receptor genes.[911,929] The clonality of these tumors has also been shown through the demonstration of a single episomal configuration of the Epstein–Barr viral terminal repeat. Approximately 10% of peripheral T-cell lymphomas show clonal rearrangements of the immunoglobulin heavy chain gene in addition to clonal rearrangements of the β T-cell receptor gene.[924]

Karyotypically, the pattern is complex, but no consistent abnormality has yet been detected.

From an etiologic standpoint, evidence of a specific viral agent (HTLV-1) has been found for T-cell leukemia/lymphoma endemic to certain regions, such as Japan and the Caribbean.[927] Cases of T-cell lymphomas containing EB-viral DNA have been reported in the United States.[910] This is particularly true for the angiocentric lymphomas of upper respiratory tract (see Chapter 7).

Anaplastic large cell lymphoma

Anaplastic large cell lymphoma (ALCL, also known as Ki-1 lymphoma and pleomorphic histiocytoid lymphoma) occurs in all age groups, approximately 20% of the patients being under age 20 years.[933,952,970,971] Most cases arise de novo, but a few have been reported as engrafted on mycosis fungoides or Hodgkin's lymphoma or developing in HIV-infected patients.[996] Clinically, two types of presentation are recognized: a systemic form (which may affect nodes or extranodal sites, including skin) and a primary cutaneous form (without extracutaneous involvement at the time of

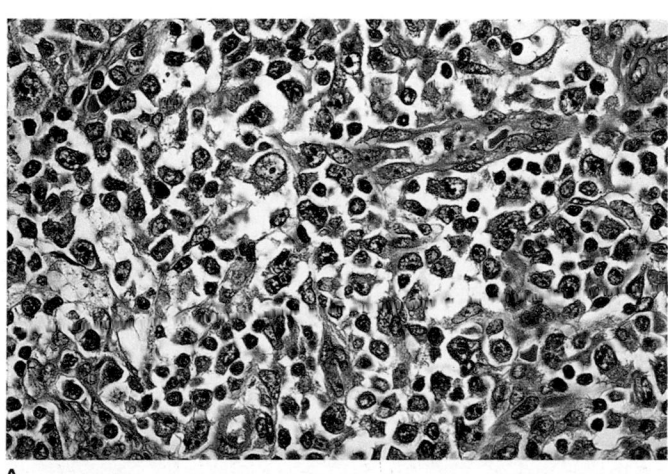 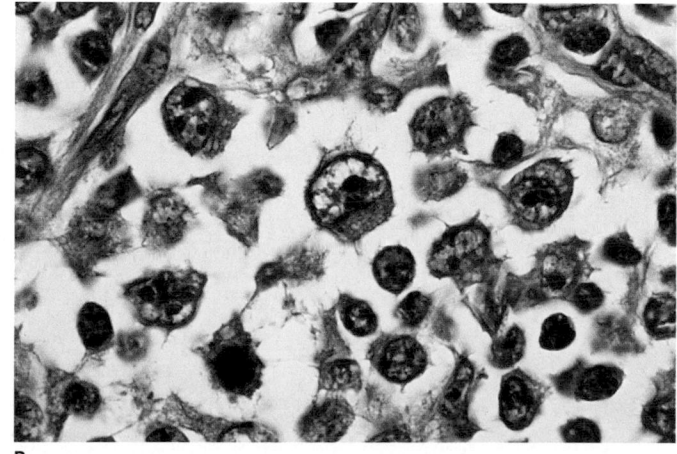

A   B

Fig. 21.97 Peripheral large T-cell lymphoma in a patient from Japan. Note the polymorphic appearance of the infiltrate and the prominent postcapillary venules.

presentation).[936,949,955] The systemic form can involve sites such as the bone marrow, bone, respiratory tract, and gastrointestinal tract.[950,998] It can occur in children or adults and is rather aggressive.[969,995,999] Exceptionally, it is accompanied by leukemic manifestations.[934] The cutaneous form occurs predominantly in adults and has an indolent course, with some of the individual lesions regressing spontaneously.[938,962] In retrospect, it should be acknowledged that the cases originally reported as *regressive atypical histiocytosis* and most of the cases diagnosed as malignant histiocytosis belong to this category[961,965,982,987] (see p. 1958 and Chapter 4).

Microscopically, the infiltrate has a polymorphic appearance, with a variable admixture of neutrophils, lymphocytes, histiocytes, and large highly atypical cells showing marked pleomorphism.[972] The nuclei of these cells are often horseshoe shaped and multiple, and nucleoli are prominent. Cells very similar to Reed–Sternberg cells may be seen. The cytoplasm is abundant and eosinophilic. It is characteristic for these tumor cells to form in a cohesive fashion and to involve preferentially the lymph node sinuses (Fig. 21.98). The undue prominence of the latter feature in some cases was one of the reasons for this lesion to be mistakenly placed in the category of malignant histiocytosis.

ALCL can simulate malignant melanoma, undifferentiated carcinoma, and various types of soft tissue sarcoma.[948]

Several morphologic variants of ALCL have been described.

1 *Small cell.* As the name indicates, this shows a predominant population of small to medium-sized cells. A very important clue is the presence of the characteristic large anaplastic cells around blood vessels.[947,973] Cases of the small cell variant have been seen to transform into the classic anaplastic large cell form.[968]

2 *Lymphohistiocytic.* The distinctiveness of this variant results from the presence of a large number of reactive (nonepithelioid) histiocytes (Fig. 21.99). Some of these histiocytes phagocytose red blood cells. As for the previous variant, an important diagnostic clue is the clustering of anaplastic tumor cells around vessels. Support for its inclusion into the ALCL umbrella is provided by the frequent finding of the NPM-ALK chimeric fusion protein.[989]

   Most cases have occurred in young patients and have presented with systemic symptoms and superficial lymphadenopathy.[988]

3 Other morphologic variations of ALCL which do not qualify as bona fide tumor variants are the neutrophil—and/or eosinophil—rich,[979,980] sarcomatoid,[948] giant cell,[959] signet ringlike,[958] and hypocellular.[951]

Immunohistochemically, the tumor cells of ALCL are by definition CD30+ (Ki-1) positive, both in frozen and in paraffin sections. The latter material requires the use of

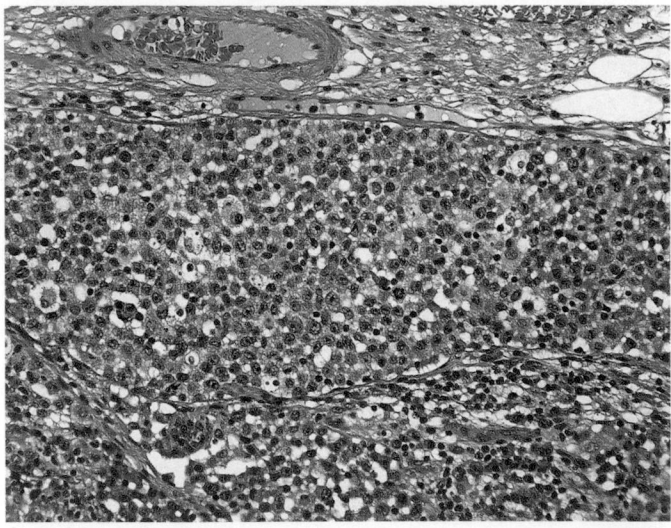

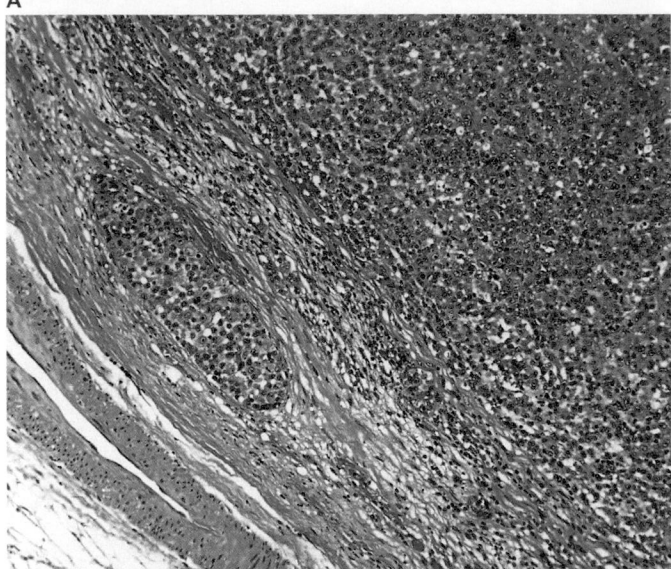

Fig. 21.98 Anaplastic large cell lymphoma: **A**, packing of the peripheral sinus; **B**, vascular involvement.

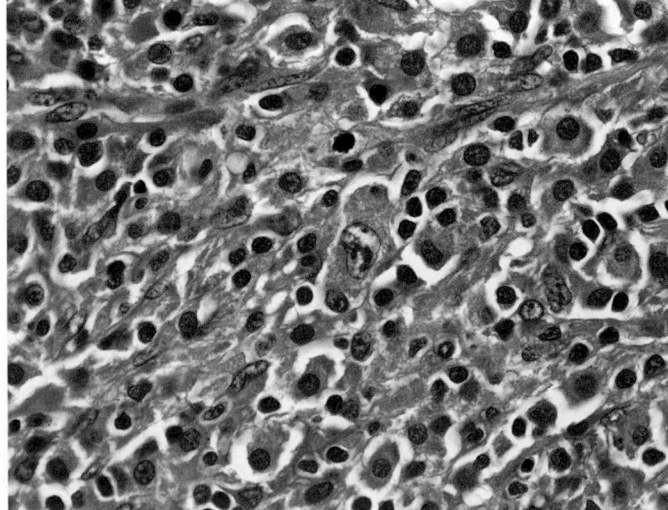

Fig. 21.99 So-called "lymphohistiocytic variant" of anaplastic large cell lymphoma.

monoclonal antibody BerH2[964] (Fig. 21.100). There is also consistent positivity for EMA, interleukin-2 receptor (particularly in the systemic cases),[956] clusterin (in a Golgi pattern), cadherins,[935,985] and galectin-3 (a β-galactoside-binding animal lectin).[974] Some histiocytic markers have also been detected (this being partially responsible for many of these cases having been thought at one time of being of histiocytic nature),[937,943,960,993] and there is occasional reactivity for keratin.[963]

Pan-lymphoid and some T-cell-related markers are found in approximately half of the cases, B-cell markers are absent or, rather, not allowed. In other words, if they are found in a lesion with the morphologic features of anaplastic large cell lymphoma, that lesion is taken out from that category and placed into that of an anaplastic variant of large B-cell lymphoma (see p. 1946).

At the molecular level, approximately half of the cases show rearrangement of one of the T-cell receptor genes.[966,986] Cytogenetically, 70% to 80% of the systemic cases show a t(2;5) (p23; q35) translocation:[939,940,945,981] This results in the juxtaposition of the nucleophosmin gene (which codes for a nucleolar phosphoprotein) on chromosome 5q35 with the "anaplastic lymphoma kinase" (*ALK*) gene (a novel tyrosine kinase gene) on chromosome 2p23[942,973] and the formation of the *NPM–ALK* chimeric gene.[975] The translocation can be detected by FISH or RT-PCR (also in paraffin-embedded tissue),[944] and the chimeric ALK protein (p80) that is expressed as a result of these genetic changes can be demonstrated immunohistochemically[946,984,990] (Fig. 21.101). The pattern can be predominantly nuclear, nuclear membrane (possibly centered in the nuclear pores), cytoplasmic, and/or membranous depending on the type of genetic aberration. However, it should be noted that not all cases of ALCL express this protein, particularly in the elderly. Also of importance is the fact that an increasing number of genetic and molecular "variants" of ALCL are being recognized in which the genetic aberration and the

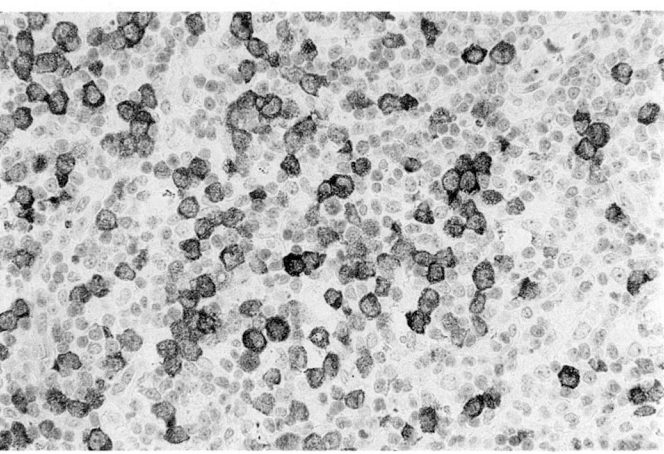

Fig. 21.101 ALK immunoreactivity in anaplastic large cell lymphoma.

resulting gene fusion are different from those described above.[959,967,991,997]

A complex and as yet not fully understood relationship seems to exist between ALCL and Hodgkin's lymphoma, to the point that some authors view these two diseases as part of a continuous spectrum.[953,977,992] It has also been suggested that ALCL represents the link between peripheral (post-thymic) T-cell lymphoma and Hodgkin's lymphoma. It had been stated that ALCL, in contrast to Hodgkin's lymphoma, usually lacks evidence of the EBV genome,[941,957,978,983] but this is not necessarily true, particularly in the ALK cases.[932,994]

Lymphoblastic lymphoma

Lymphoblastic lymphoma is seen primarily in children and adolescents, but it also occurs in adults.[1009,1011] It has a distinctive clinical presentation. In approximately half of the cases there is a mediastinal mass in the thymic region (the old Sternberg's sarcoma). The clinical course of the untreated disease is extremely aggressive, with rapid multisystem dissemination, leukemic blood picture, and death after a few months.[1005] Grossly, the tumor is whitish and soft and often exhibits foci of hemorrhage and necrosis. Microscopically, there is a diffuse and relatively monomorphic pattern of proliferation, broken only by a focal "starry sky" appearance in some of the cases. The tumor often extends outside the node or thymus to invade the adipose tissue in a diffuse fashion. Permeation of the wall of blood vessels in a targetoid fashion is another characteristic feature. The neoplastic cells have scanty cytoplasm and a nucleus that has a round contour (instead of the angulated shape typical of follicular lymphoma) but that shows, on close examination, the presence of delicate convolutions resulting from multiple small invaginations of the nuclear membrane (see Chapter 8). Oil-immersion examination of well-prepared, very thin sections is necessary to demonstrate this feature, which may be present in only a small percentage of the tumor cells or sometimes practically absent[1005]

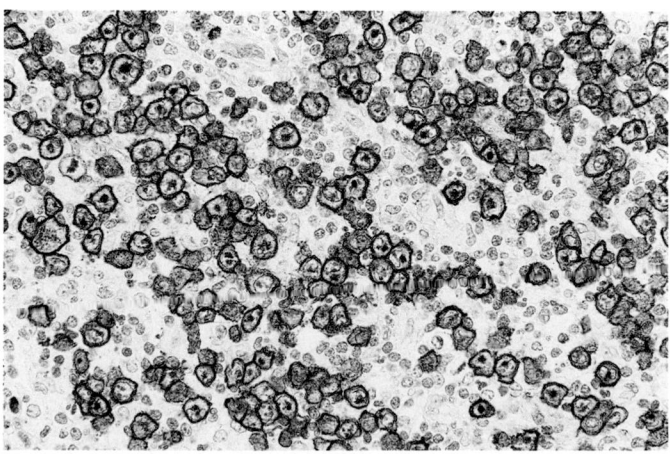

Fig. 21.100 Strong membranous and Golgi-type immunoreactivity for CD30 in anaplastic large cell lymphoma.

(Fig. 21.102). The chromatin is finely stippled, and nucleoli are inconspicuous. Mitotic activity is extremely high. These convoluted cells are similar to the cerebroid cells of mycosis fungoides-Sézary's syndrome (as one might assume from their similar names) but differ from the latter because the nuclear membrane is thinner, the chromatin more disperse, and the invaginations more delicate. Actually, the need for distinction between these two cell types is more theoretical than real because of the fact that the two diseases are vastly different in their clinical presentation.

An *atypical* or *large cell* variant of lymphoblastic lymphoma has been described, which is said to comprise approximately 10% of the cases.[1002]

Remnants of thymus often are found in the mediastinal mass, and this may lead to a mistaken diagnosis of thymoma; in this regard, it should be remembered that thymoma is very infrequent in children and that, when it occurs, it is characterized by a population of small or activated lymphocytes but not convoluted ones. When lymphoblastic lymphoma spreads to lymph nodes, it preferentially involves the paracortical (thymic-dependent) zone.

At the enzyme histochemical level, features of the cells of lymphoblastic lymphoma include the presence of acid phosphatase (focally strong in a paranuclear location, as in normal thymocytes), β-glucuronidase, α-naphthyl acetate esterase,[1010] and terminal deoxynucleotidyl transferase (TdT), a marker of thymocytes.[1001,1003] The latter can also be demonstrated immunohistochemically in paraffin-embedded material.[1006,1012]

Approximately 80% to 85% of lymphoblastic lymphomas show T-cell markers. Their phenotypes recapitulate those of the various stages of intrathymic T-cell differentiation, i.e., those of the precursor T lymphoblast, hence the choice of the WHO committee to designate this tumor as precursor T lymphoblastic lymphoma (and as precursor T lymphoblastic leukemia

when extensive marrow and peripheral blood involvement are present, an arbitrary distinction).[1008] In approximately 90% of the cases, these tumors express all of the pan-T-antigens, such as CD1, CD2, CD7, cytoplasmic CD3, and CD43. The latter two markers can be demonstrated in paraffin sections. Practically all cases express CD71 (the transferrin receptor antigen), 20% express HLA-DR, and 20% express markers of natural killer cells, such as CD16 and CD57. Positivity is also consistently encountered for CD99.

In approximately a third of the cases, translocations have been identified involving the alpha and delta T-cell receptor loci at 14q11.2, the beta locus at 7q35, and the gamma locus at 7p14–15 with a variety of partner genes (such as *MYC*, *TAL1*, *RBTN1*, *RBTN2*, and *HOX11*), leading to a dysregulation of transcription of the latter.

In approximately 15% to 20% of the cases of lymphoblastic lymphoma, the tumor cells express B-cell rather than T-cell markers, such as CD19, CD20, CD21, and CD24.[1013] These tumors are referred to as precursor B lymphoblastic lymphomas (or as precursor B lymphoblastic leukemia if accompanied by extensive bone marrow and peripheral blood involvement) in the WHO classification. These are predominantly extranodal tumors with low propensity for leukemic involvement.[1004] In keeping with their precursor nature, they may express cytoplasmic immunoglobulin but not surface immunoglobulin. Yet other lymphoblastic lymphomas lack both T-cell and B-cell features.[1003a]

The differential diagnosis of lymphoblastic lymphoma includes the already mentioned lymphoma when in a mediastinal location, Ewing sarcoma/PNET, Burkitt's lymphoma, and the blastoid variant of mantle cell lymphoma.[1000,1007,1014,1015]

Burkitt's lymphoma

Burkitt's lymphoma is a high-grade malignant lymphoma composed of germinal center B cells which can present in three clinical settings:

1 *Endemic.* This occurs in the Equatorial strip of Africa and is the most common form of childhood malignancy in this area. The patients characteristically present with jaw and orbital lesions. Involvement of the gastrointestinal tract, ovaries, kidney, and breast are also common;
2 *Sporadic.* This is seen throughout the world. It affects mainly children and adolescents, and has a greater tendency for involvement of the abdominal cavity than the endemic form;
3 *Immunodeficiency-associated.* This is seen primarily in association with HIV infection and it often occurs as the initial manifestation of the disease.[1023,1031]

In all three forms peripheral lymphadenopathy is rare and, when present, usually limited to a single group.[1016,1017] Bone marrow involvement is common in

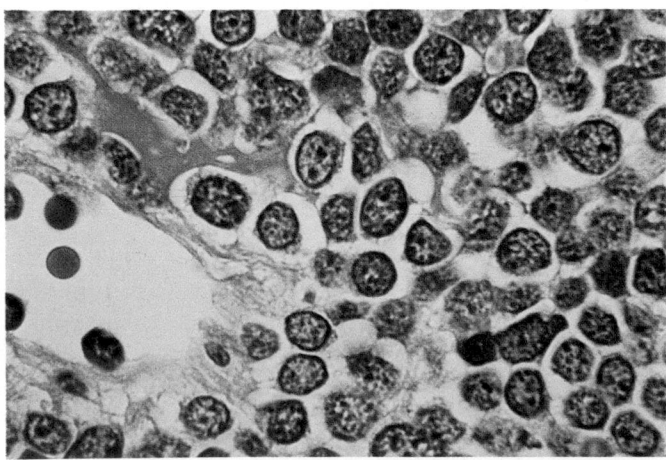

Fig. 21.102 Lymphoblastic lymphoma. In this example the nuclear convolutions are barely evident.

the late stage of the disease, but leukemic manifestations are very rare.[1029,1030]

Microscopically, the pattern of growth of Burkitt's lymphoma is usually diffuse, although early cases may show preferential involvement of germinal centers.[1028] The tumor cells are small (10 to 25 µm) and round. The nuclei are round or oval and have *several* prominent basophilic nucleoli. The chromatin is coarse and the nuclear membrane is rather thick. The cytoplasm is easily identifiable; it is amphophilic in hematoxylin–eosin-stained preparations and strongly pyroninophilic. Fat-containing small vacuoles are prominent; these are particularly well appreciated in touch preparations. Mitoses are numerous, and a prominent "starry sky" pattern is the rule, although by no means pathognomonic[1018] (Fig. 21.103). In well-fixed material, the cytoplasm of individual cells "squares off," forming acute angles in which the membranes of adjacent cells abut on each other. Ultrastructurally, the main features are abundant ribosomes, frequent lipid inclusions, lack of glycogen particles, and presence of nuclear pockets or projections[1019] (Fig. 21.104).

Two morphologic variants of Burkitt's lymphoma are recognized. In the form with *plasmacytoid differentiation*, which is more common in HIV-related cases, some tumor cells exhibit eccentric basophilic cytoplasm containing immunoglobulin and a single central nucleolus. In the *atypical* or *pleomorphic* form, the cell size is larger and a distinct pleomorphism is evident.[1026]

Most of the cells have a well-defined rim of cytoplasm; their nucleus contains a large, eosinophilic nucleolus. Binucleated and multinucleated cells are common. Phagocytosis of nuclear debris by reactive histiocytes is as common as in the classical form, resulting in a "starry sky" appearance. The pattern of growth is generally diffuse, but areas of minimal nodularity may be encountered. Clinically, gastrointestinal involvement is less common and bone marrow involvement more frequent than in the classic. The clinical course is said to be

more aggressive[1016,1017,1026] although the response to therapy is similar.[1032]

Immunohistochemically, it has been shown that virtually all cases of Burkitt's lymphoma are of B-cell lineage. They express immunoglobulins (predominantly IgM), invariably associated with heavy and light chain restriction.[1024] B-cell-specific antigens (such as CD19, CD20, and CD22) and B-cell-associated antigens (such as CD24 and HLA-DR) are present. Most cases also feature CD10. They are negative for the activation markers CD25 and CD30. In contrast to lymphoblastic lymphoma, they do not express TdT.

Cytogenetically, over 80% of Burkitt's lymphomas carry the t(8;14)(q23;q21) translocation,[1022] and practically all of the others carry a functionally analogous translocation.[1025] This results in the juxtaposition of the *myc* gene (located in 8q23) with one of the Ig heavy or light chain genes,[1021,1022] which in turn leads to a deregulation of *myc* gene expression and increased cell proliferation. In sporadic cases of Burkitt's lymphoma, the breakpoint shows a different distribution pattern, suggesting that the tumor develops at a later stage of B cell differentiation. There are also frequent mutations of the retinoblastoma-related gene *RB2/p130*, which may contribute to the increased rate of cell proliferation of this tumor.[1020] Burkitt's lymphomas (especially of the endemic form) harbor latent EBV genomes (Fig. 21.105). As a matter of fact, EBV was first discovered in a Burkitt's lymphoma cell line. These genomes have been found to be clonally homogeneous within the tumor, in keeping with their presence in the lymphoid cells *prior to* their clonal expansion.[1027]

Other non-Hodgkin's lymphomas

Types of non-Hodgkin's malignancies of the lymphoid system other than those already described include the following:

1 *Leukemias* and *myeloma* (see Chapter 23).
2 *Lymphomatoid granulomatosis* (see Chapter 7).
3 *Intravascular large B-cell lymphoma* (angiotropic lymphoma).[1037] This systemic malignant disease, originally regarded as a multicentric malignant transformation of endothelial cells and designated as malignant angioendotheliomatosis, is now known to be a type of malignant lymphoma with a remarkable tropism for blood vessels[1035] (see Chapter 4).
4 *Hairy cell leukemia*. This entity is fully discussed in Chapter 22. Suffice it to say here that the lymph nodes can be involved by the disease and that this involvement is characterized by diffuse infiltration of the subcapsular sinuses, cortex, and medullary cords by typical small mononuclear cells having nuclei slightly larger than those of lymphocytes, fine chromatin pattern, relatively abundant cytoplasm, and essentially no mitotic activity (Fig. 21.106). Despite the extensiveness

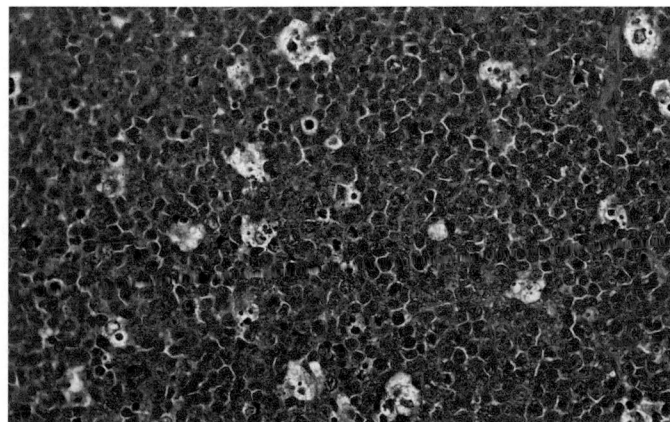

Fig. 21.103 Burkitt's lymphoma with characteristic starry sky appearance.

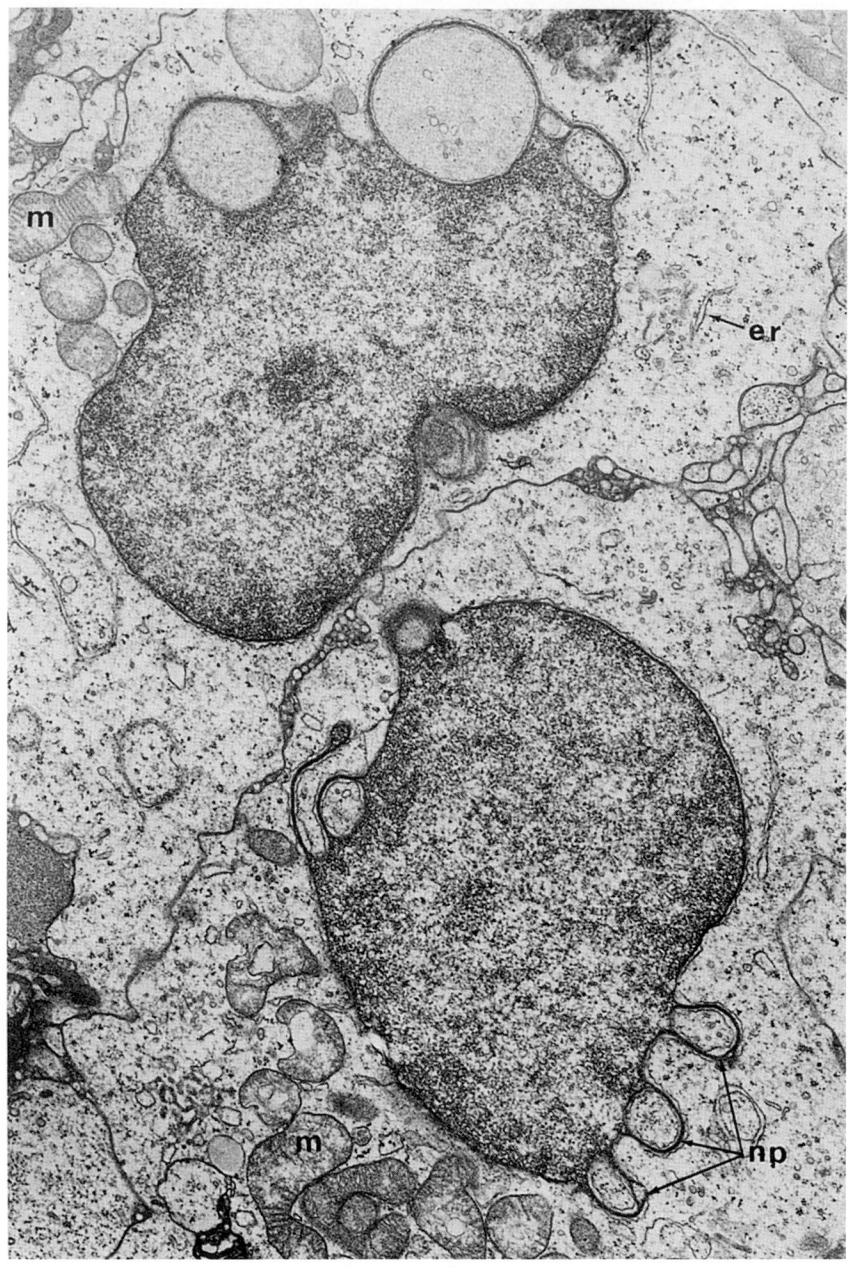

Fig. 21.104 These neoplastic cells from a patient with Burkitt's lymphoma have numerous peculiar, though not unique, nuclear projections (np), polar aggregation of mitochondria (m), sparse endoplasmic reticulum (er), and scattered ribosomes.

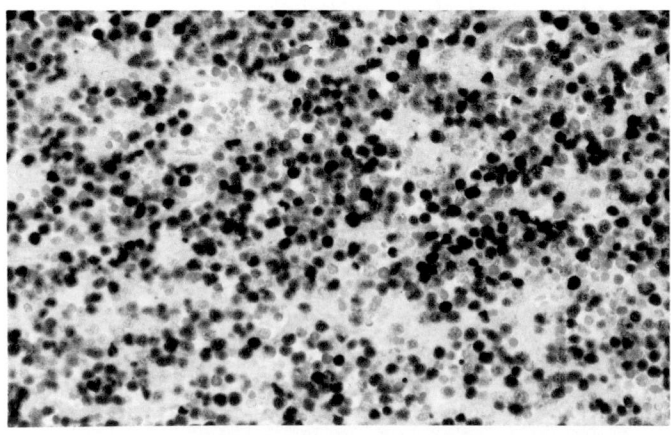

Fig. 21.105 Presence of EBV genome in Burkitt's lymphoma, as demonstrated with in situ hybridization for EBER.

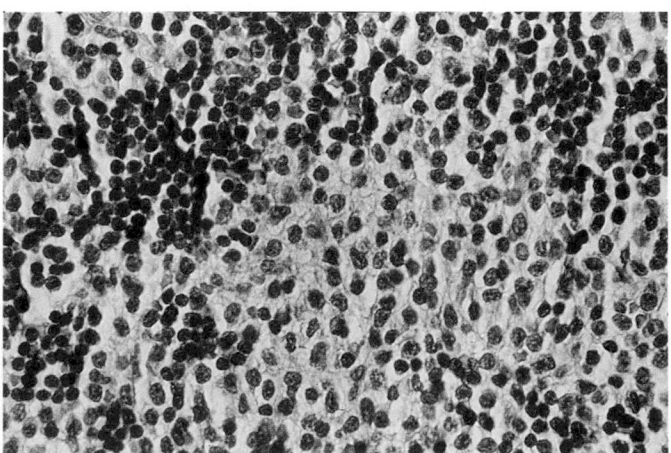

Fig. 21.106 Lymph node involvement by hairy cell leukemia.

of the infiltrate, the nodal architecture is partially preserved.[1033]

5 *Lymphoma of plasmacytoid monocytes.* These were formerly known as plasmacytoid T-cell lymphomas.[1034,1036]

6 *Mediastinal (thymic) large B-cell lymphoma* (see Chapter 8).

7 *Primary effusion lymphoma* (see Chapter 7).

8 The various types of primarily extranodal T-cell lymphomas listed on p. 1950.

Composite and discordant lymphomas

In general, there is constancy within the various types of malignant lymphoma, so that a patient with a certain type of lymphoma at a given site will have the same type at other sites and will maintain it during the entire evolution of the disease. However, on occasion one encounters two distinct types of lymphoma in the same patient, either sequentially or simultaneously, even in the same lymph node. The occurrence of two different and well-delineated varieties of lymphoma occurring in a single anatomic site or mass is known as *composite lymphoma*, and the occurrence of two different types of lymphoma at separate anatomic sites has been referred to as *discordant lymphoma*.[1042,1055] Some of these combinations may represent the occurrence of two unrelated neoplasms, either spontaneously or as a result of the therapy given for one of them. The majority, however, are probably the result of different biologic and morphologic manifestations of the same lesion, the more malignant one representing the morphologic expression of tumor progression.[1056,1064] Most of these examples of this pro-

gression are discussed in connection with the corresponding tumor types, but we thought it would be useful to list the most important manifestations of this phenomenon:

1 Low-grade B-cell lymphoma (small lymphocytic follicular, or TCRBCL that transforms into a diffuse large cell lymphoma.[1039,1043,1059a,1061,1063,1068]

2 Transformation of mantle cell lymphoma into a high grade tumor ("blastic transformation").[1057]

3 Low-grade T-cell lymphoma (such as mycosis fungoides) that transforms into a diffuse large cell lymphoma (see Chapter 4).[1040,1045,1048,1060,1065]

4 Combination of NLDHL and other lymphomas, particularly diffuse large cell lymphoma.[1047,1049–1051]

5 Combination of "classic" Hodgkin's lymphoma and large cell lymphoma of B-cell type (Fig. 21.107).[1044] We have seen this combination several times in the thymic region.[1044,1047,1052] The Hodgkin's lymphoma may coexist with, follow, or precede the non-Hodgkin's lymphoma.[1054,1066,1067]

6 Combination of "classic" Hodgkin's lymphoma and peripheral (post-thymic) T-cell lymphoma.[1041,1046,1052] Some of these tumors have expressed CD20.[1058]

7 Combination of "classic" Hodgkin's lymphoma and chronic lymphocytic leukemia.[1062]

8 Transformation of classical Hodgkin's lymphoma into anaplastic large cell lymphoma.[1059]

9 Malignant lymphomas with B- and T-cell neoplastic components.[1038]

10 Combination of small lymphocytic lymphoma and dendritic cell neoplasm.[1053]

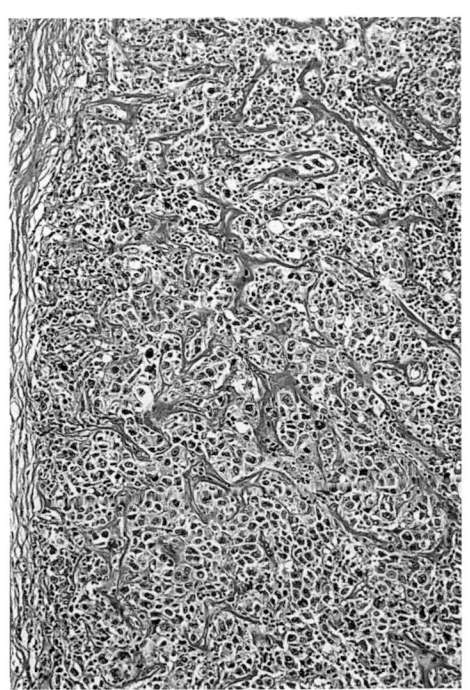 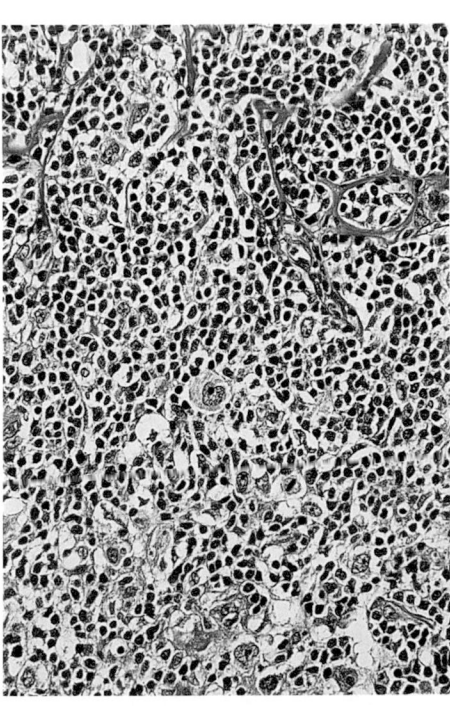

A **B**

Fig. 21.107 Composite lymphoma of mediastinum: **A** corresponds to large cell lymphoma with sclerosis (which had a B immunophenotype), and **B** corresponds to nodular sclerosis Hodgkin's lymphoma (which had the typical phenotype of Reed–Sternberg cells). (Slide contributed by Dr. Kiyoshi Mukai, Tokyo)

So-called "malignant histiocytosis"

Malignant histiocytosis is no longer regarded as a bona fide entity, but it was thought useful to discuss in a single section the various clinicopathologic conditions to which the term was applied (with or without a qualifier), with a mention of their place into the current nosologic scheme.

The term malignant histiocytosis was first proposed by Rappaport[1085] for a disease characterized by a systemic, neoplastic proliferation histologically resembling histiocytes and their precursors. Thus defined, the disease was found to affect any age group but with a predilection for children and young adults.[1089,1094] Fever, lymph node enlargement, and constitutional symptoms appeared early in the course of the disease. Hepatomegaly, splenomegaly, and skin involvement also were common.[1069,1087] In some patients, pulmonary symptoms dominated the clinical presentation.[1072] It was typical of the disease for the patient to be acutely ill when first seen by the physician. Common laboratory findings were anemia, leukopenia, and thrombocytopenia.[1091] There is also elevation of serum ferritin levels.[1074] Microscopically, the distinctive feature in the involved lymph nodes was said to be the proliferation of atypical cells with the appearance of histiocytes within the subcapsular or medullary sinuses and/or within the lymphoid parenchyma (Fig. 21.108). The degree of atypia varied greatly from case to case.[1092] The tumor cells were often found to surround lymphoid follicles in a concentric fashion. A variable number of cells within the infiltrate were seen to exhibit phagocytosis (especially of red blood cells), but it was noted that it was difficult to decide whether this phagocytosis was occurring in neoplastic cells or in accompanying reactive histiocytes. This feature was better demonstrated in bone marrow smears and touch preparations of lymph nodes than in tissue sections.[1090]

Most of the cases were rapidly progressive and fatal, two thirds of the patients dying within the first months after diagnosis.[1073,1084] At autopsy, widespread organ involvement was found, usually without formation of large tumor masses but rather growing diffusely in the interstitium.

The entity described by Scott and Robb-Smith[1088] as *histiocytic medullary reticulosis* needs to be discussed in this context.[1086,1087] This was originally described clinically as characterized by hepatosplenomegaly, jaundice, and rapidly fatal outcome and pathologically by prominent erythrophagocytosis by more or less atypical histiocytes. Probably some of these cases were of the same kind as the malignant histiocytosis as just described[1070]; as a matter of fact, some authors used the two terms synonymously.[1091] Other cases might have been examples of the virus-associated hemophagocytic syndrome[1082] (see Chapter 23). Along similar lines, it is possible that so-called "familial hemophagocytic reticulosis" is a viral infection occurring in a family with an immune defect that makes them susceptible to the virus.[1082,1083] Similarly, it is possible that some of the reported cases of lymphoma, leukemia, or myeloproliferative diseases terminating in histiocytic medullary reticulosis[1075,1078] represent overwhelming viral infections in a compromised host.

Some of the above considerations apply to the concept of malignant histiocytosis in a more global sense. The original definition of the disease was based on clinico-

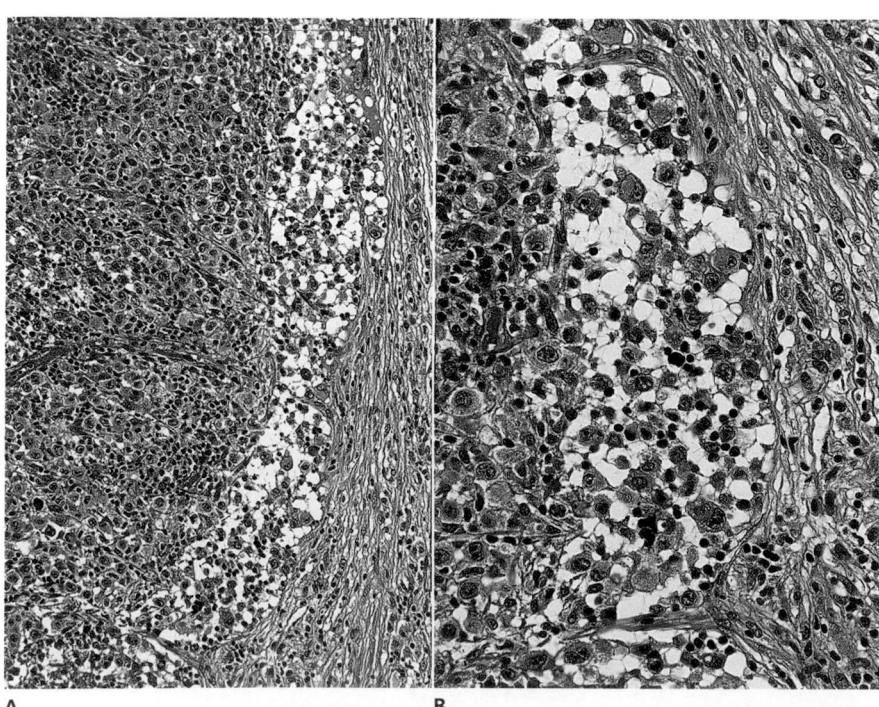

A   B

Fig. 21.108 Typical peripheral sinus involvement in the disease traditionally known as malignant histiocytosis. Most of these cases (including the one depicted here) proved to be anaplastic cell lymphomas.

morphologic criteria; subsequent enzyme histochemical, immunohistochemical, and ultrastructural studies claimed to have found support for the histiocytic nature of the cellular proliferation.[1077,1079,1080] However, cell marker and molecular analysis studies have shown that most cases are actually examples of lymphoma, usually anaplastic large cell (Ki-1 +) lymphoma or peripheral T-cell lymphoma[1071,1093] (with or without a hemophagocytic syndrome component). Malignant histiocytosis of the small bowel has been reinterpreted as a T-cell lymphoma (enteropathy-type, see Chapter 11). In view of these findings, the current view is that "malignant histiocytosis" is not a single disease entity and that effort should be made to classify each case according to current terminology based on a thorough immunohistochemical and molecular evaluation of the case.[1076]

Lymphoma in immunodeficiency states

An increase in the incidence of malignant lymphoma has been documented in most types of congenital and acquired immunodeficiency.[1113,1126,1134] Chronic antigenic stimulation—possibly by oncogenic viruses—and perhaps loss of antibody feedback inhibition of the lymphoid proliferation may account for the high rate of lymphoid malignancies.[1159] The EBV in particular has been repeatedly implicated.[1139]

1 *Primary immunodeficiencies.* Patients with genetically determined immune deficiencies have an increased incidence of malignant tumors, especially lymphomas.[1113,1132,1164] This includes ataxia–telangiectasia, Wiskott–Aldrich syndrome, X-linked lymphoproliferative syndrome, common variable immunodeficiency, and severe combined immunodeficiency syndrome.[1160]

   Patients with *ataxia–telangiectasia* and the *Wiskott–Aldrich syndrome* are particularly prone to this complication, approximately 10% of the reported patients having died from it.[1144] An interesting correlation exists between the type of immune deficiency and the type of lymphoma. In a series from the University of Minnesota, all the lymphomas arising in Wiskott–Aldrich syndrome were of non-Hodgkin's type (predominantly large B-cell lymphomas with immunoblastic features) presenting as localized extranodal masses, whereas those arising in patients with ataxia–telangiectasia were of both Hodgkin's and non-Hodgkin's types, with a more conventional organ distribution. Surprisingly for this age group, half of the cases of Hodgkin's lymphoma belonged to the lymphocyte depletion type. These cases are atypical in other regards, leading some authors to question whether they really belong to the Hodgkin's lymphoma category.[1168] Most of the non-Hodgkin's lymphomas in ataxia–telangiectasia were of the histologic types associated with the 14q+ chromosomal abnormality.[1118] Parenthetically, a gene for ataxia–telangiectasia (*ATM*) that codes a product similar to PI-3 kinase has been recently cloned.[1130,1161] Also, mutations of the *Jak-3* gene have been detected in severe combined immunodeficiency syndrome.[1141]

   The microscopic diagnosis of the lymphoma can be extremely difficult in early cases; sometimes, the only morphologic diagnosis of the lymphoma possible is that of an atypical lymphoproliferative process. The immunologic status of the patient is just as important a predictor of prognosis as the type of lymphoma that has developed.[1103]

   Several members of families affected by the *X-linked lymphoproliferative syndrome* (believed to result from an immunodeficiency to the EBV)[1151] have developed sporadic Burkitt's lymphoma, large B-cell lymphoma with immunoblastic features, fatal infectious mononucleosis, or "plasmacytoma."

2 *Organ transplant recipients.* The incidence of lymphoma is increased in recipients of all types of organ transplants as a direct or indirect result of the induced immunosuppression.[1152] In renal transplant recipients, this incidence is in the order of 4% to 6%.[1116] Skin tumors, malignant lymphomas, Kaposi's sarcoma, and cervical carcinoma are the most common neoplasms. The frequency of lymphoma has been estimated to be 350 times higher than in the age-matched general population.[1115,1135,1150] The incidence has been found to be particularly high in adult cardiac transplant patients treated with OKT-3-containing regimens.[1109,1167] In approximately half of the reported cases, the central nervous system is involved, compared with less than 1% in lymphoma patients in general. In 30% of the cases, the allograft is also involved.

   Microscopically, most of these lymphomas show marked cytologic polymorphism (small and large follicular center cells and immunoblasts), atypia of the immunoblasts, and extensive necrosis (Fig. 21.109).[1124]

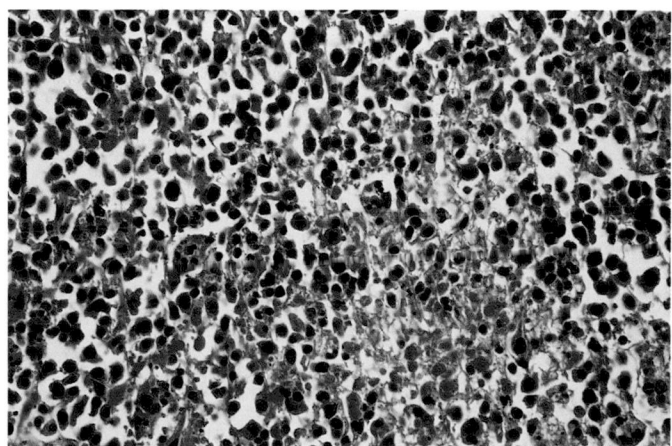

Fig. 21.109 Polymorphic lymphoproliferative process associated with necrosis in lymph node of a renal transplant patient. There was evidence of active EBV infection.

The initial infiltrate has polyclonal B cell features, in keeping with a reactive origin.[1122,1123] The development of lymphoma is signaled by the appearance of a monoclonal component with chromosomal aberrations.[1117] The term "polymorphic B-cell lymphoma" has been suggested for this tumor type. A transition has been observed from a polyclonal activation of B cells to an oligoclonal B cell proliferation and finally to a monoclonal B-cell lymphoma[1123,1164,1168] (Fig. 21.110). This separation is clinically relevant.[1108] Immunoglobulin rearrangement studies have shown the existence of a monoclonal population in early stages of the process, before the malignancy is recognizable morphologically.[1107,1109,1138] Virtually all cases of post-transplant lymphoproliferative disorders harbor EBV genomic DNA and RNA.[1153] In most cases, these genomes are clonal, indicating the presence of EBV in the progenitor B cell that originated the neoplastic population.[1148] In addition to this nearly constant latent activity, there is often also evidence of lytic activity by the virus[1143] sometimes in a recurrent pattern.[1172]

In contrast to HIV-associated lymphoma, *myc* rearrangements are uncommon in post-transplant lymphoma. A minority of these tumors have been found to be of T-cell type.[1120,1137] Cases have also been reported of post-transplant lymphomas having the morphologic and immunohistochemical features of Burkitt's lymphoma.[1120a]

Molecular studies have confirmed the recipient origin of the lymphoma in the transplanted patients.[1171]

The clinical course of post-transplant lymphoma/lymphoproliferative disease is usually very rapid.[1146,1154]

Treatment of post-transplant lymphoproliferative disorders consists of a combination of immunosuppression reduction and standard lymphoma therapy (chemotherapy and radiation).[1098]

3 *HIV.* Patients with HIV infection are at a high risk for developing malignant tumors, principally Kaposi's sarcoma and malignant lymphoma.[1102,1112,1119,1127,1133,1158,1170]

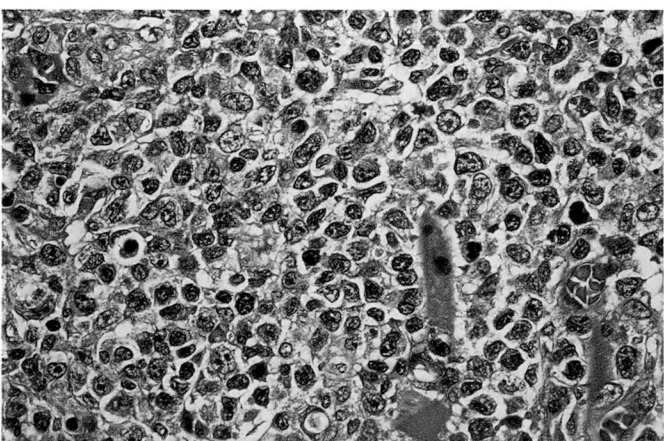

Fig. 21.110 Large B-cell lymphoma in a recipient of a renal transplant.

sometimes in combination.[1114a] It has been estimated that approximately 3% of AIDS patients develop non-Hodgkin's lymphoma, and that the risk of developing a lymphoma in this population is 60-fold greater than in the normal population. The incidence of lymphoma is highest in hemophiliacs and lowest in individuals born in the Caribbean or Africa who have acquired the disease by heterosexual contact. As a group, the age at diagnosis is younger than in the immune-competent operation.[1111] The majority of the cases present with multiple sites of extranodal involvement, with a high incidence of involvement of the gastrointestinal tract, central nervous system, bone marrow, liver, oral cavity, body cavities, and heart.[1104,1127] Practically all cases are of B-cell lineage and—as such—show clonal immunoglobulin gene rearrangements.[1108a,1112,1140] Morphologically, most cases are of Burkitt's or large B-cell type, the latter often showing immunoblastic/plasmacytoid features.[1106,1110,1155,1165] Cases have also been reported of peripheral T-cell lymphomas with a peculiar component of Touton-like giant cells,[1096] and others having the features of the polymorphic lymphoproliferative disorders seen more often in solid organ transplant recipient.[1145] Some of the lymphomas contain the HHV-8 virus and display anaplastic large cell features.[1131]

The molecular and cytogenetic features of Burkitt's lymphoma seen in the HIV-positive population are similar to those of sporadic Burkitt's lymphoma, especially in regard to rearrangements of the *myc* gene.[1105,1134] The *bcl-2* and T-cell receptor genes are unaffected. Evidence of EBV infection is often present.[1121,1136,1149]

The incidence of Hodgkin's lymphoma in HIV-infected patients does not seem to be unduly increased, but the disease presents several differences with that seen in the immunocompetent population.[1101] Almost all cases are clinical stage III or IV at presentation, with frequent involvement of unusual sites such as the liver and skin; spread often occurs in a noncontiguous fashion; there is a predominance of unfavorable histologic subtypes; Reed–Sternberg cells and (especially) their variants are more numerous and more atypical; there is an increased number of non-lymphoid stromal cells; and there is a much higher incidence of presence of the EBV genomes in Reed–Sternberg cells (reaching almost 100% in some series).[1097,1099,1125,1157,1169] It has been suggested that the immunomodulatory drugs that are given for these disorders may be pathogenetically involved with the development of these lymphomas.[1128] It has also been pointed out that the demographic, clinical, and prognostic features of Hodgkin's lymphoma developing in HIV-infected patients are nearly identical to those of HIV-related non-Hodgkin's lymphoma.[1158]

Sometimes, EBV+, B-cell lymphoproliferative disorders similar in all regards to those of immunocompromised individuals are seen in elderly individuals without overt immunodeficiencies of any type.[1147]

4 *Others.* Acquired diseases of the immune system in which an increased incidence of lymphoma has been recorded include rheumatoid arthritis,[1114,1129,1142] Sjögren's syndrome,[1162] Hashimoto's thyroiditis, and other autoimmune diseases.[1100] As already stated, it is possible that some or perhaps most of the latter represent early or preneoplastic stages of malignant lymphoma.

Cases of EBV+ lymphoproliferative disorders have also been seen in patients with low-grade B-cell neoplasms who had been treated with the immunosuppressive agent fludarabine.[1095]

Lymph node inclusions

Inclusions of various types of benign tissue can occur within lymph nodes. Lack of awareness of this phenomenon can lead to a mistaken diagnosis of metastatic carcinoma. These include the following:

1 *Salivary gland tissue.* This is an extremely common finding in high cervical nodes, to the point that it should be regarded as a normal event related to the embryology of the region[1177] (Fig. 21.111). Both ducts and acini are usually present. These inclusions may undergo neoplastic changes. Warthin's tumor is the most common type, but many other types have been reported, including benign mixed tumor, monomorphic adenoma, mucoepidermoid carcinoma, and acinic cell carcinoma (see Chapter 12).

2 *Squamous epithelium.* Microscopic cystic structures lined by well-differentiated squamous epithelium are sometimes seen in the upper cervical lesion. They are thought to represent an anomaly related to the aforementioned one, in the sense of being composed of

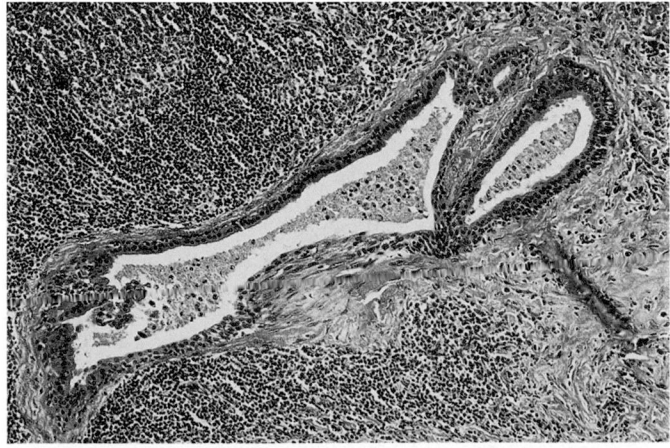

Fig. 21.111 Salivary gland inclusion composed of ductal structures in a high cervical lymph node. This is a very common occurrence.

branchial pouch derivatives. The term "benign lymphoepithelial cyst" is sometimes applied to them (see Chapter 12). We have hypothesized that these formations result from cystic dilatation of preexisting epithelial inclusions as the result of their stimulation by the lymphoid component that surrounds them, a pathogenesis that also applies to multilocular thymic cysts, other cystic structures of the head and neck region, and possibly to Warthin tumor itself (see Chapter 9). Similar formations have been described in peripancreatic lymph nodes.[1173] The obvious differential diagnosis is metastatic well-differentiated squamous cell carcinoma, which in the cervical region is notorious for its tendency to undergo marked cystic changes.[1188]

3 *Thyroid follicles.* These can be found in the capsular or subcapsular region of midcervical nodes in the absence of pathologic changes of the thyroid gland. The differential diagnosis with metastatic thyroid carcinoma can be very difficult (see Chapter 9).

4 *Decidual reaction.* During pregnancy, *decidual reaction* may occur within pelvic nodes and mimic metastatic carcinoma.[1178] The decidual reaction can occur in the stromal cells of endometriosis or in hormonally receptive cells of the region, in a fashion similar to that seen in peritoneal decidual reaction.

5 *Müllerian-type epithelium.* Glandular inclusions lined by cuboidal cells with a müllerian or coelomic appearance are commonly found in the capsule of the pelvic lymph nodes of females and sometimes within the node itself.[1184,1186] Their appearance and pathogenesis are similar to those of the peritoneal lesions generally known as endosalpingiosis (Fig. 21.112). Like the latter, these lymph node inclusions may be difficult to distinguish from metastases originating in low-grade ovarian neoplasms, since they may grow into the peripheral sinuses, form papillae, be accompanied by psammoma bodies, and even proliferate as small sheets of cells.[1180] Some authors have suggested that some of these "inclusions" are metastases actually from ovarian serous borderline tumors.[1189] Morphologically similar inclusions have been seen in the mediastinal nodes of males.[1185]

Nodal glandular inclusions of similar appearance but surrounded by endometrial-type stroma occur less frequently and represent *nodal endometriosis.* All of these müllerian-related nodal processes are discussed in more detail in Chapter 19.

6 *Nevus cells.* Clusters of normal-appearing nevus cells are occasionally found in the capsule of lymph nodes, without involvement of the nodal parenchyma (Fig. 21.113). Most of the reported cases have occurred in axillary lymph nodes.[1183] A related lesion is the *blue nevus* that has been reported in the lymph node capsule[1175] (Fig. 21.114). The morphologic features of these formations and their differential diagnosis with

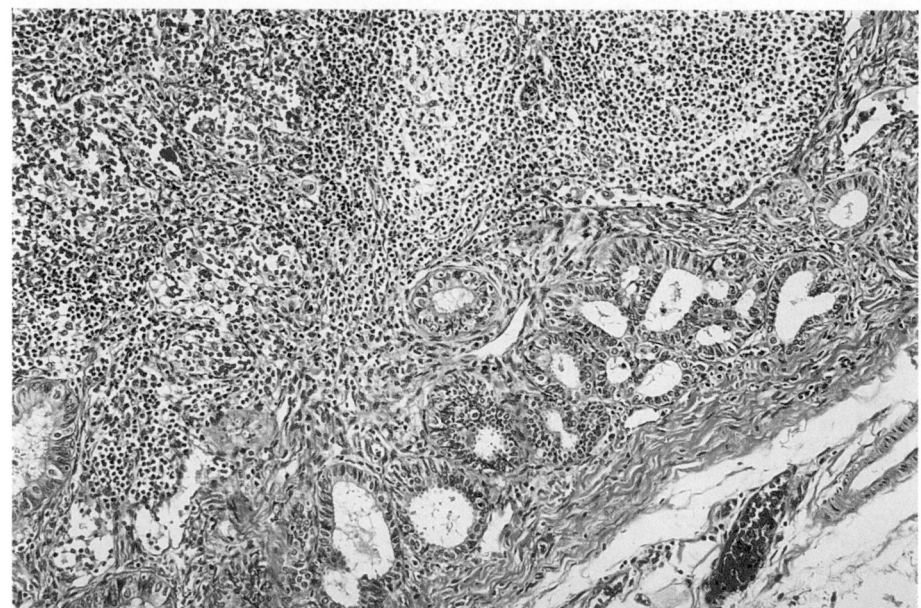

Fig. 21.112 Pelvic lymph node involved by endosalpingiosis. Glands lined by cuboidal cells with a müllerian appearance and lacking atypical figures are present in the capsule of the node.

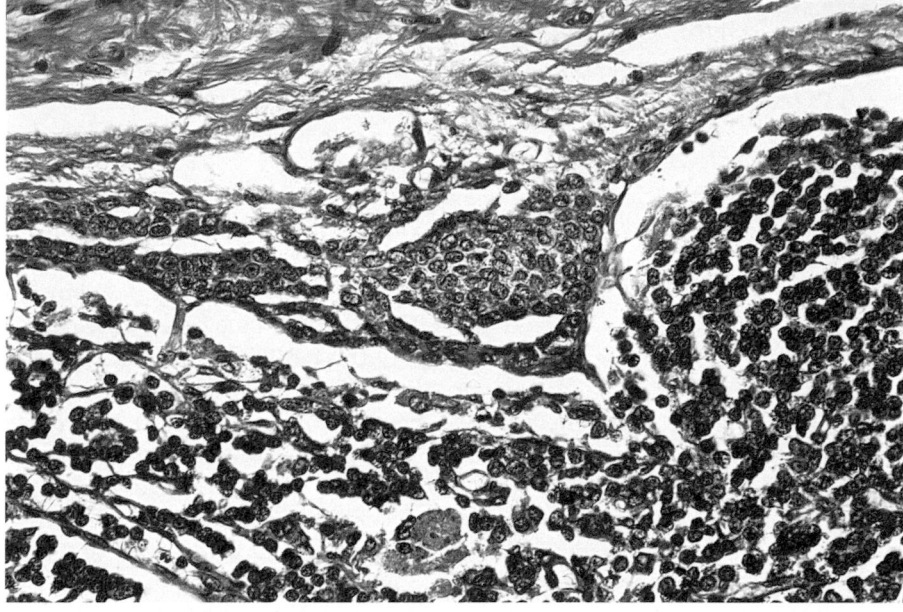

Fig. 21.113 Nevus cells in the capsule of an axillary lymph node. These inconsequential formations should not be mistaken for metastatic melanoma or metastatic carcinoma.

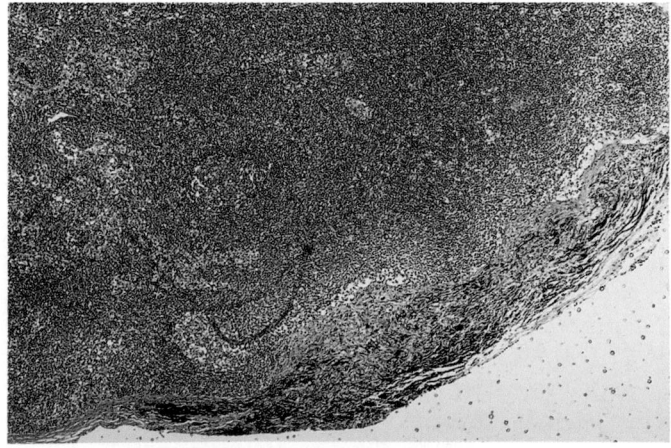

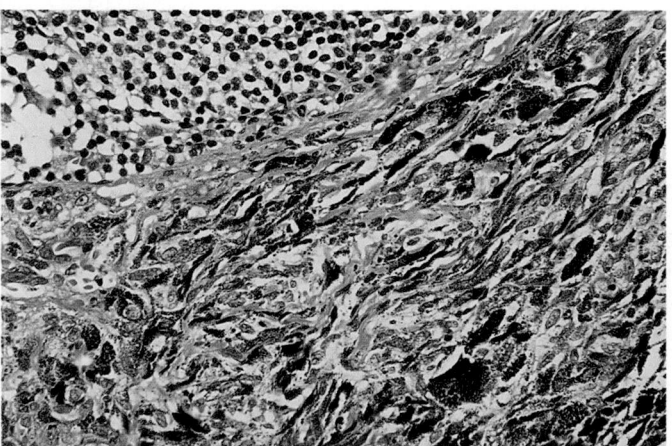

A

B

Fig. 21.114 Blue nevus involving lymph node capsule.

metastatic malignant melanoma are discussed in Chapter 4.

7 *Mesothelial cells*. Occasionally, mesothelial cells are found within lymph nodes in the apparent absence of a malignant mesothelioma.[1174,1176,1190] The obvious differential diagnosis is with metastatic malignant mesothelioma from an occult primary in the peritoneal cavity or pleura.[1191] The issue is discussed in more detail in Chapter 7.

8 *Breast tissue*. One of the most unusual forms of ectopia is represented by normal mammary lobules within axillary lymph nodes.[1179,1187,1192] A slightly more common occurrence is the presence in axillary nodes of tubules lined by a single layer of cuboidal cells (sometimes with a hobnail appearance), located in the nodal capsule or immediately beneath. These formations are similar to the müllerian-type epithelial inclusions in pelvic lymph nodes previously described. Since some of these cases occur in patients with breast carcinoma, the distinct possibility exists of mistaking them for metastatic tumor.[1181,1182] The issue is discussed in more detail in Chapter 20.

Other non-neoplastic lesions

Adipose metaplasia of lymph nodes, is very common. When extensive, it may lead to the formation of large masses, up to 10 cm or more in diameter. These nodes are sometimes referred to as *lipolymph nodes*; the external iliac and obturator groups are the sites most commonly involved.[1199]

Ectopic thymus sometimes seen in supraclavicular lymph node biopsies should be mentioned here for the sake of differential diagnosis even if it is not a lymph node lesion. The pathologist unaware of this occurrence might easily interpret the Hassall's corpuscles as islands of metastatic squamous cell carcinoma.

Vasculitis involving lymph nodes may be seen in a large number of disorders: polyarteritis nodosa (having necrotizing qualities and being rarely biopsied), Henoch–Schönlein purpura (leukocytoclastic, also rarely biopsied), Wegener's granulomatosis (sometimes accompanied by extensive infarct), systemic lupus erythematosus, drug hypersensitivity (see p. 1910), and mucocutaneous lymph node syndrome (see p. 1904). Some nodes otherwise showing the typical features of angioimmunoblastic lymphadenopathy may also show extensive vasculitis. One should also mention the obliterative vasculitis often seen in syphilitic lymphadenitis (see p. 1898).

Infarction of the lymph nodes presents with painful swelling, usually located in a superficial lymph node chain. Microscopically, there is extensive necrosis of medullary and cortical lymphoid cells, with marked reactive perinodal inflammation and a layer of granula-

tion tissue. A thin rim of viable subcapsular lymphoid tissue may be present.[1196] Thrombosis of veins within the substance and the hilum of the nodes has been suggested as the pathogenesis.[1196] Similar changes can be seen in mesenteric lymph nodes in patients with intestinal volvulus.[1200] Other cases are the result of embolism, arte-

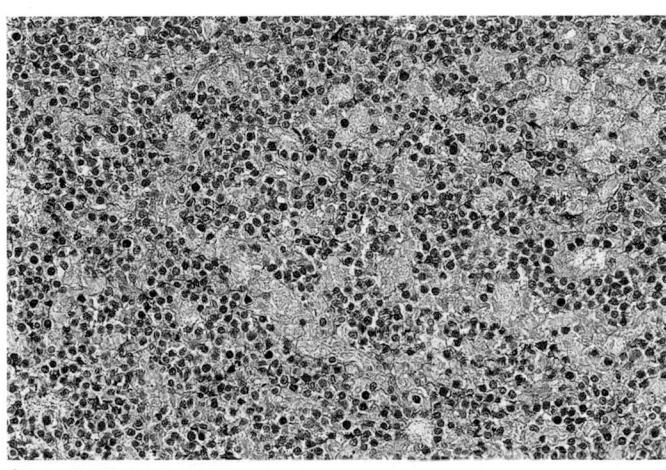

A

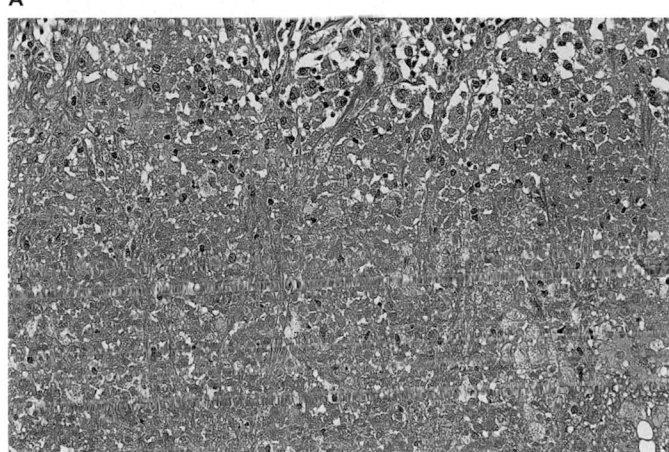

B

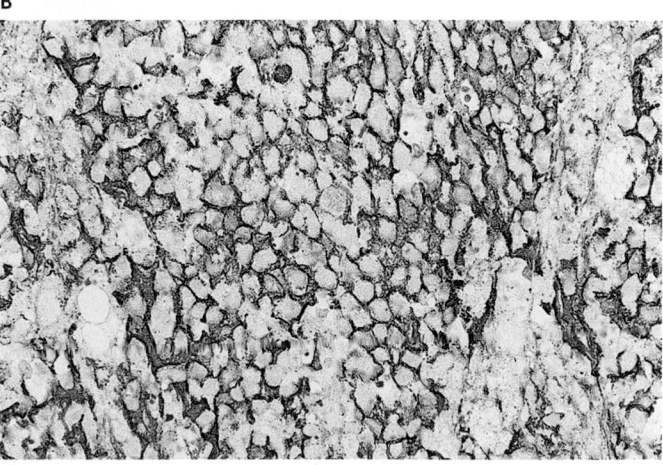

C

Fig. 21.115 A to C, Large B-cell lymphoma that has undergone massive infarct-type necrosis. **A,** The outlines of the tumor cells can still be discerned. **B,** A totally necrotic area, indistinguishable from that of a "benign" infarct. **C,** There is a remarkable degree of retained immunoreactivity for CD20 in the necrotic area.

rial occlusion in cases of polyarteritis nodosa and related disorders, or fine needle aspiration[1197,1202]; in these instances, the nodal infarct tends to have a segmental quality. The differential diagnosis of lymph node infarction includes necrotizing lymphadenitis (see p. 1894), mucocutaneous lymph node syndrome (see p. 1904), infectious mononucleosis[1198] necrotizing granulomatous inflammation, and necrotic malignant tumors. Two types of malignancies that have been occasionally found to undergo extensive and sometimes massive infarct-type necrosis when involving lymph nodes are malignant lymphoma[1195,1201] and metastatic malignant melanoma. Therefore thorough examination of the infarcted node, the extranodal region, and other nodes submitted is mandatory in order to exclude a concomitant or underlying malignancy[1201] (Fig. 21.115A,B). A thorough immunohistochemical study is also in order. We have often being amazed at the degree of preservation of the tumor cells reactivity in the face of extensive necrotic changes[1203,1205] (Fig. 21.115C). As a general rule, the possibility of an underlying malignancy should be suspected if the infarcted node is markedly enlarged.

Hyaline material sometimes accumulates in the stroma of lymph nodes. This finding is very frequent in those situated in the aorto-iliac region (Fig. 21.116). The material can undergo secondary calcification. Because of its homogeneous eosinophilic appearance, it can be confused with amyloid and has been referred to in the past

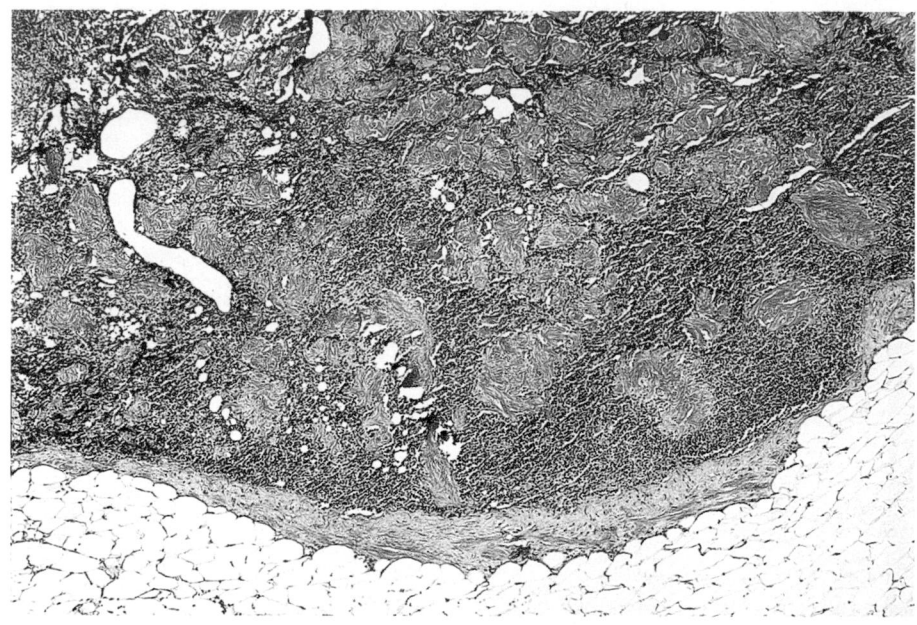

Fig. 21.116 Hyaline deposits in pelvic lymph node. This change is of no clinical significance.

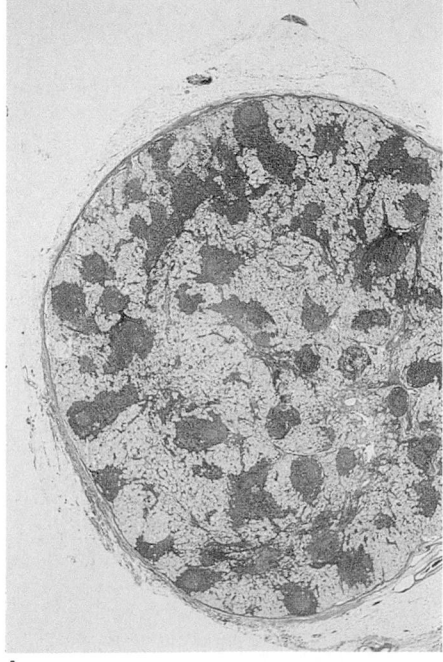

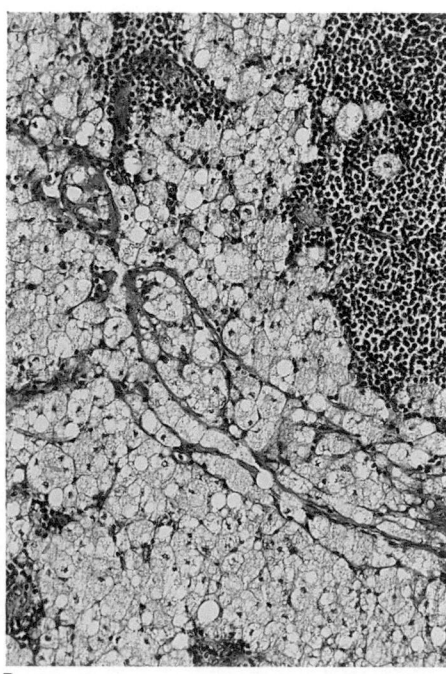

A **B**

Fig. 21.117 Low-power (**A**) and medium-power (**B**) appearances of silicone lymphadenitis. The sinuses are massively expanded by a histiocytic infiltrate, which simulates the appearance of Rosai–Dorfman disease (sinus histiocytosis with massive lymphadenopathy).

as para-amyloid. It should also be distinguished from the hyaline material deposited in nodes in cases of hemorrhagic spindle cell tumor with amianthoid fibers (see p. 1973). The presence of this hyaline material has no clinical significance.

Proteinaceous lymphadenopathy is the name given to a lymph node abnormality in which an eosinophilic extracellular material of proteinaceous nature is deposited in lymph nodes. This material simulates the appearance of amyloid but is histochemically and ultrastructurally distinct from it. The few patients that have been described with this obscure abnormality had hypergammaglobulinemia, and the hyaline material itself has been shown to contain precipitated immunoglobulin.[1194]

Foreign material of various types can accumulate in lymph nodes. One example is the *silicone lymphadenopathy* developing as a side effect of mammary augmentation produced by injection of liquid silicone or by placement of a bag-gel prosthesis. Microscopically, a nonbirefringent refractive material is present in the sinuses, together with variously sized vacuoles and multinucleated giant cells[1204] (Fig. 21.117).

A

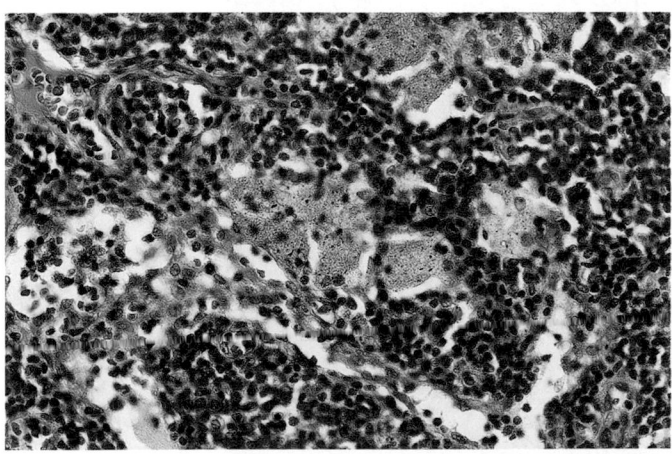

B

Fig. 21.118 Lymph node changes in a patient who had a prosthesis implanted in the joint drained by this node. A fine particulate black material can be appreciated in the high-power view. It is easy to dismiss this material as "dirt."

Another example is the already mentioned sinus histiocytosis of pelvic lymph nodes, which is induced by the cobalt-chromium and titanium contained in a hip prosthesis and which closely simulates the appearance of RDD[1193] (Fig. 21.118).

Tumors of the cells of the accessory immune system

The accessory immune system includes two major categories of cells: antigen-presenting cells (dendritic cells) and antigen-processing cells (macrophages).[1208,1220,1237,1262,1264,1266] The dendritic cells belong to the group of nonlymphoid elements classically designated by histologists and pathologists as reticulum cells, which have been divided into more or less well-defined subtypes on the basis of location, enzyme histochemical, ultrastructural, and immunohistochemical features. These are:

1 **Dendritic follicular cells.** These are associated with the B zones of the node and specifically with the germinal centers. Ultrastructurally, they have complex cell prolongations joined by complex desmosomes. Immunohistochemically, they exhibit reactivity for CD21, CD35, Ki-M4p, Ki-FDRC1p, CNA 42, fascin, Ki-M9, estrogen receptor α, epidermal growth factor receptor, and the low affinity nerve growth factor receptor.[1207,1215,1233,1242,1251,1255,1257a]

2 **Interdigitating dendritic cells.** These cells are associated with the T zones of the nodes. They also have complex cell prolongations that interdigitate with each other, but desmosomes are absent. Immunohistochemically, they are reactive for S-100 protein.[1229,1244]

3 **Langerhans' cells.** These are characterized by immunoreactivity to S-100 protein and CD1a, and the presence of Birbeck's granules at the ultrastructural level. They are closely related to the interdigitating cells.[1227] It has even been suggested that they represent two different morphofunctional manifestations of the same cell. Other closely related cells are veiled cells and dermal dendrocytes.

4 **Fibroblastic reticulum cells.** These are located in the capsule, hilus, and other stroma-rich areas of the node. They have a high content of alkaline phosphatase, exhibit filaments with focal condensations at the ultrastructural level, and probably correspond to the *myoid cells* described by others. A subset of these cells shows immunoreactivity for keratin.[1228] It is not clear whether these cells play a role in the immune reaction or whether they are structural supporting elements.

5 **Macrophages.** These cells are thought to be involved in the processing of antigens through the process of phagocytosis, hence the synonym of phagocytes. They are closely related to circulating monocytes. When the

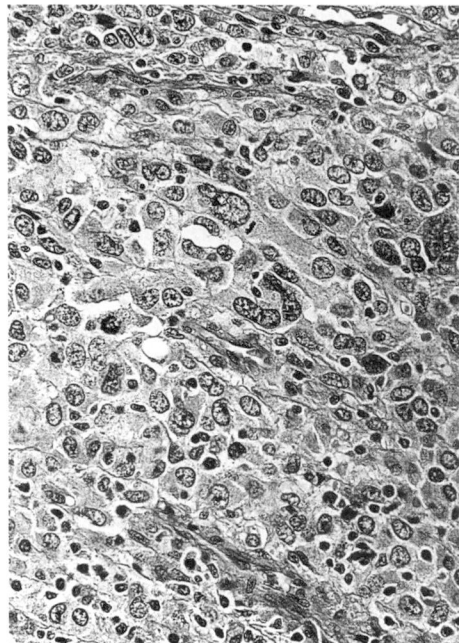

Fig. 21.122 Recurrent dendritic follicular cell tumor. There is a greater degree of pleomorphism than in the original neoplasm.

to be particularly aggressive.[1214] Recurrent and metastatic lesions may show increased atypia and pleomorphism.[1251]

Interdigitating dendritic cell tumor (interdigitating reticulum cell sarcoma) is even more unusual, or perhaps not as easily recognized.[1226] Most of the reported cases have arisen in lymph nodes,[1223,1228] but instances of extranodal involvement in sites such as skin, bowel, spleen, and testis have been recorded.[1236,1240,1241,1244] The microscopic appearance can be indistinguishable from that of dendritic follicular cell tumor, but there is more tendency to spindling and pleomorphism.[1263,1268] The diagnosis is dependent on the immunohistochemical profile, which unfortunately is not entirely specific. The tumor cells are

positive for CD45RB, S-100 protein, and the macrophage marker CD68 but are negative for CD21 and CD35. The behavior seems more aggressive than for the dendritic cell tumor.

Other reticulum/dendritic cell tumors. Other recently described tumors which may belong to this family are those thought to arise from fibroblastic reticulum cells (exhibiting immunoreactivity for vimentin, smooth muscle actin, and desmin),[1206] and those also exhibiting reactivity for low-molecular weight keratin[1212,1257b] (Fig. 21.123). The reticulum/dendritic cell nature of these tumors is supported by their ultrastructural features and already suggested by the scattering on non-neoplastic lymphocytes that is a constant feature of this tumor family. It is also possible that at least some of the "sarcomas" that have been described as a complication of Castleman's disease (above and beyond the already mentioned dendritic follicular cell tumors) may be of reticulum/dendritic cell nature.

True histiocytic lymphomas (sarcomas) in the sense of tumors of macrophages, i.e., the antigen-processing cells of the accessory immune system, remain rare and controversial.[1222,1252] The issue is complicated by the fact that—as already mentioned—the majority of neoplasms to which the term "histiocytic" was applied in the past (such as Rappaport's histiocytic lymphoma, malignant histiocytosis, and regressing atypical histiocytosis) have been shown to be of lymphocytic nature in the overwhelming majority of the cases. However, it would seem that tumors of true histiocytes do exist.[1239] Their presentation is highly variable, with a high proportion of extranodal involvement in sites such as the spleen, skin, bone, and particularly the gastrointestinal tract.[1219,1225,1245,1261] As in the case of the dendritic cell tumors, some "true histiocytic lymphomas" have been seen in combination with bona fide malignant lymphoma.[1256]

Microscopically, the tumor cells are large, with irregularly shaped nuclei and abundant, generally acidophilic

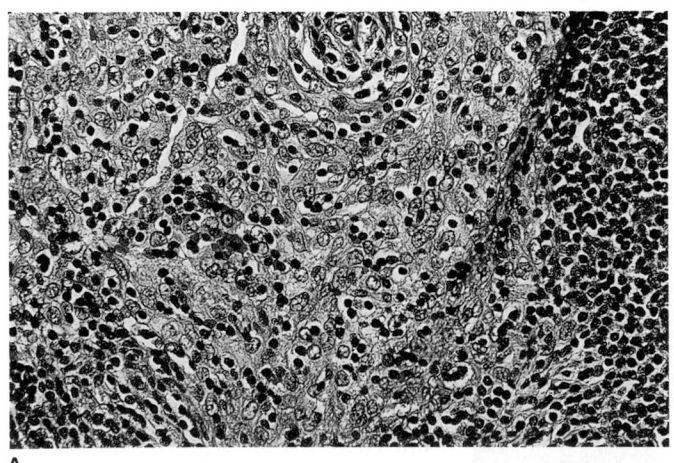

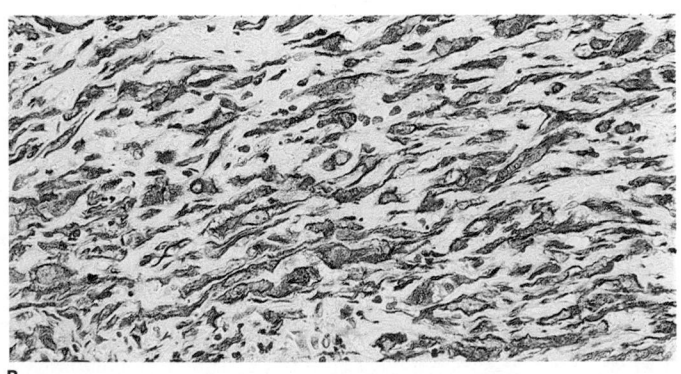

Fig. 21.123 Neoplasm interpreted as tumor of keratin-positive reticulum/dendritic cells: **A**, hematoxylin–eosin; **B**, immunostain for low-molecular-weight keratin (Cam5.2).

cytoplasm. Immunohistochemically, the tumor cells lack by definition B-cell- and T-cell-related markers and show reactivity for histiocytic markers, such as CD63, CD11c, CD13, CD14, CD15, CD32, CD33, Mac-387, and lysozyme.[1231,1235,1254] At the molecular level, some authors require the lack of rearrangement of immunoglobulin and T-cell receptor genes to retain a tumor in this category, whereas others accept the presence of such rearrangements.

Vascular tumors and tumorlike conditions

Hemangioma and **lymphangioma** involving nodes usually represent extension by contiguity of primary soft tissue lesions. However, rare cases of primary nodal hemangioma and lymphangioma have been described[1269,1280] (Fig. 21.124).

Epithelioid vascular neoplasms of lymph nodes include epithelioid hemangioma, epithelioid hemangioendothelioma, spindle and epithelioid hemangioendothelioma, and polymorphous hemangioendothelioma.[1271,1274,1287,1289]

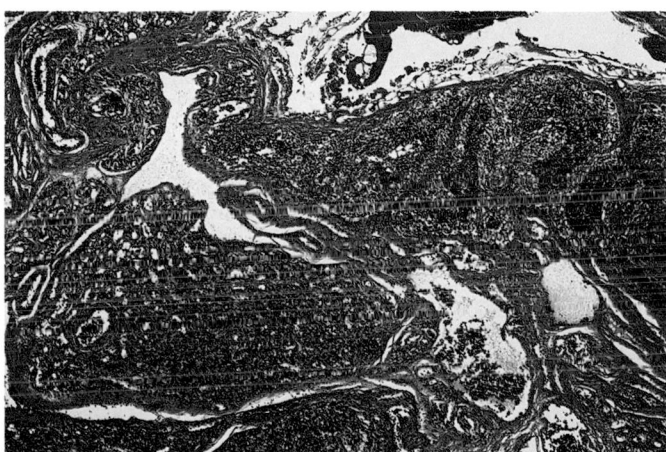

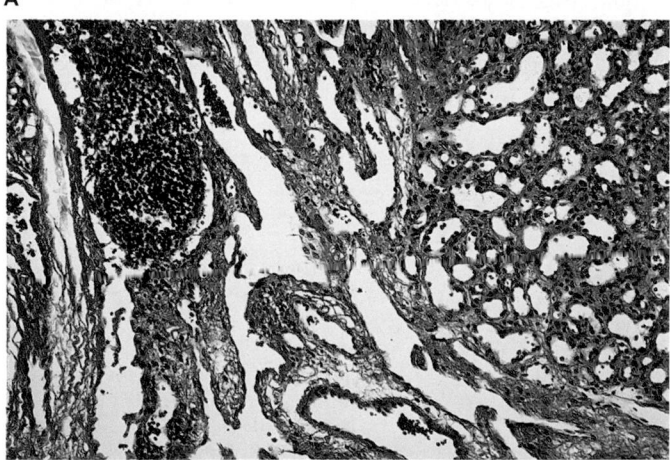

B

Fig. 21.124 Low- and medium-power view of nodal hemangioma.

The differential diagnosis includes (1) epithelioid hemangioma of soft tissue with a peripheral rim of germinal centers resulting in a nodelike appearance on low power (a much more common occurrence than true nodal epithelioid hemangioma),[1291] (2) Kimura's disease (an altogether different process lacking epithelioid endothelial cells (see p. 1915), and (3) bacillary angiomatosis.

Bacillary angiomatosis, which occurs almost exclusively in the setting of immunodeficiency (especially in patients with HIV infection) presents as multiple coalescent intranodal clusters of proliferating vessels. These vessels are lined by plump, somewhat epithelioid endothelial cells (hence the original term epithelioid angiomatosis for this condition). A feature of great diagnostic importance is the presence of abundant eosinophilic to amphophilic, amorphous, or granular material in the interstitium. When stained with the Warthin–Starry technique, this material is shown to be composed of aggregated bacillary organisms that are indistinguishable from those of cat-scratch disease. Another helpful feature is the presence of neutrophils, sometimes forming microabscesses.[1272,1275,1286]

Vascular transformation of the sinuses is characterized by a conversion of lymph node sinuses into a complex network of anastomosing endothelial-lined channels (Fig. 21.125).[1281] Fibrosis and reactive stromal changes are commonly present.[1285] *Nodal angiomatosis* probably refers to a more cellular form of the same condition[1277,1283] (Fig. 21.126). In the **nodular spindle-cell variant**, spindle-cell nodules composed of interlacing fascicles alternate with the vascular clefts.[1273] This variant is likely to be misdiagnosed as Kaposi's sarcoma. It is distinguished from the latter because it is confined to the

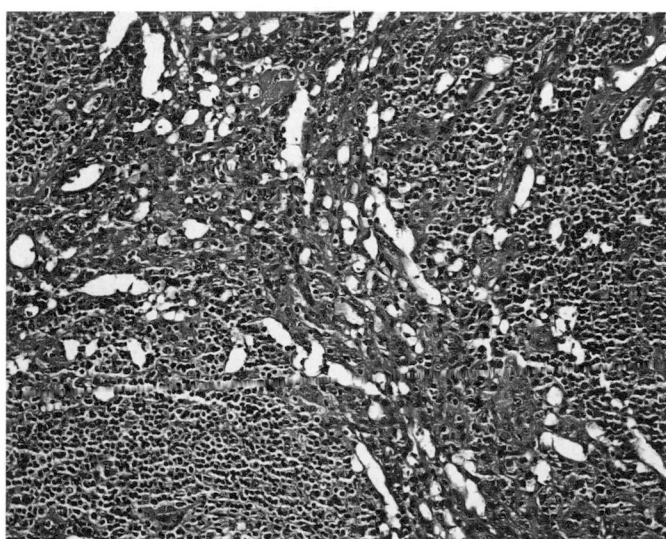

Fig. 21.125 Lymph node involvement by bacillary angiomatosis. An intense vascular proliferation featuring epithelioid endothelial cells is seen in the interfollicular region, accompanied by neutrophils and other inflammatory cells.

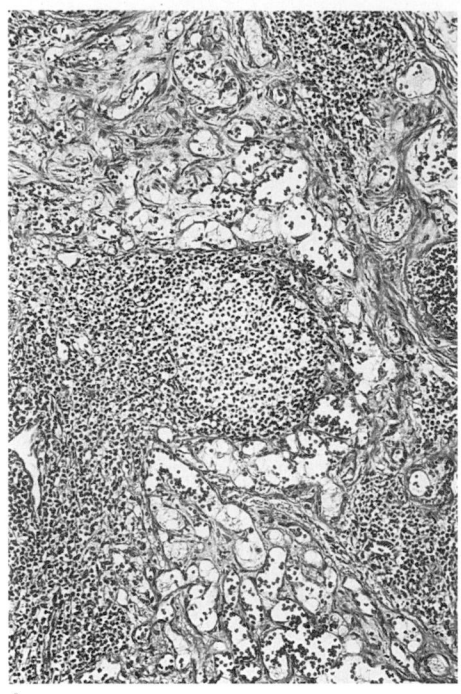 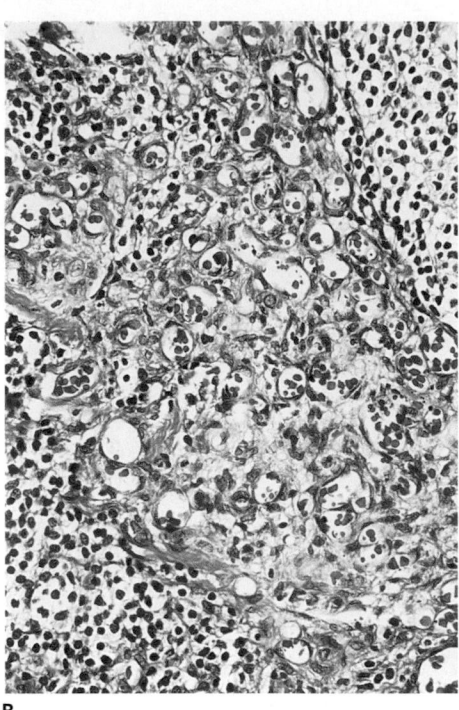

Fig. 21.126 Vascular transformation of lymph nodes. The process involves the sinuses, and it has a reactive appearance.

sinus (with sparing of the capsule and parenchyma), there is no cellular atypia, the fascicles blend with well-formed vascular channels, fibrosis is common, and PAS-positive hyaline globules are almost invariably absent. We have seen cases of this nodular spindle-cell variant in retroperitoneal lymph nodes draining renal cell carcinomas and have speculated about the possibility of its being the result of secretion of angiogenic factor by the carcinoma cells[1276,1282] (Fig. 21.127). Other cases of vascular transformation may result from proximal obstruction of the efferent vessels; indeed, the process

has been reproduced experimentally by complete occlusion of these vessels.[1288]

Kaposi's sarcoma of the lymph nodes may be associated with typical skin lesions or develop in their absence.[1284] The latter occurrence is seen mainly in African children, but it also occurs in adults affected by HIV-infection. Microscopically, the involved nodes show proliferation of spindle cells separated by slitlike spaces containing red blood cells (Fig. 21.128).[1270] The earliest changes are seen in the subcapsular and trabecular sinuses, but eventually there is involvement of the entire

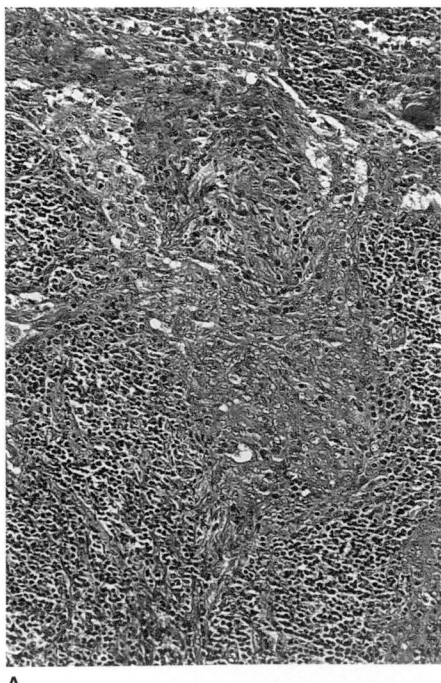 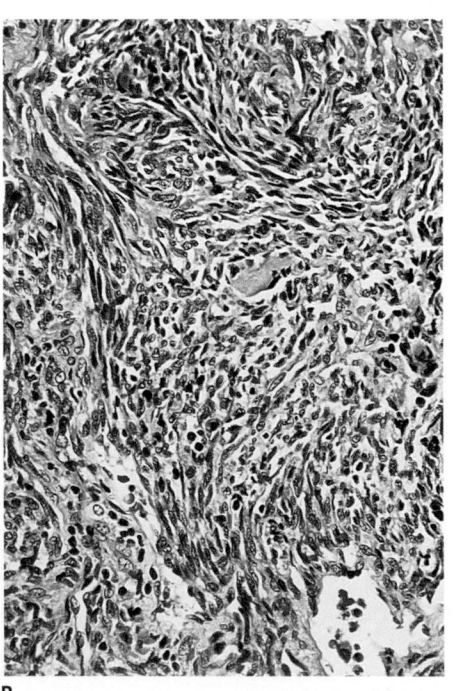

Fig. 21.127 Solid form of vascular transformation of lymph nodes. This process has also been designated as nodal angiomatosis. **A** shows the predominantly sinusal distribution of the lesions. The example shown in **B** occurred in a retroperitoneal lymph node in a patient with renal cell carcinoma.

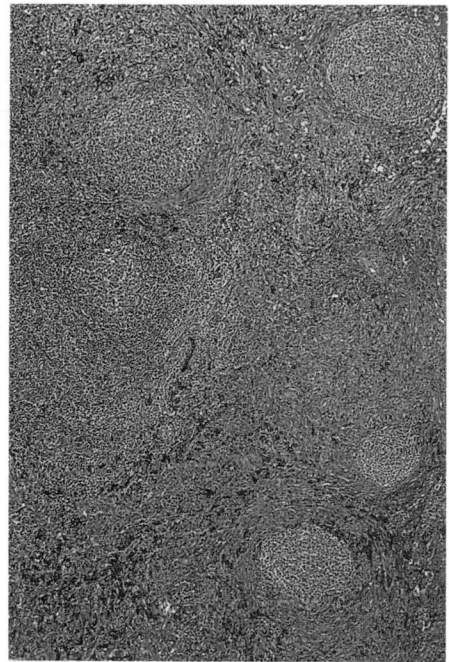

A

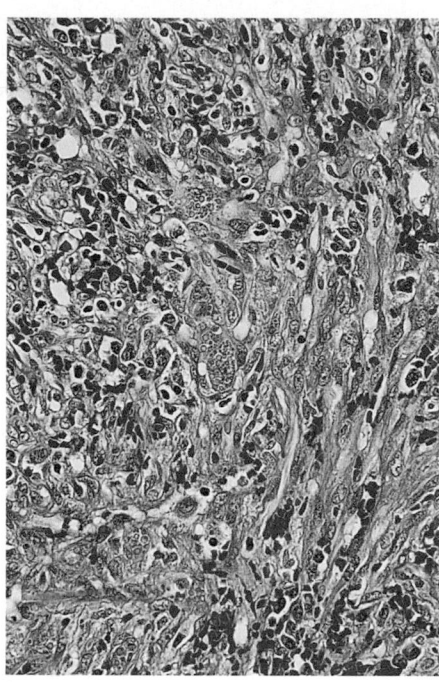

B

Fig. 21.128 Lymph node involvement by Kaposi's sarcoma. The infiltrate is predominantly sinusal and is characterized by a proliferation of spindle cells forming slits containing red blood cells.

node and extension into the perinodal tissues. Cytoplasmic and extracellular hyaline globules that are positive for PAS and PTAH are almost always present.[1279] Recognition of early nodal involvement by Kaposi's sarcoma is an extremely difficult task; often, only a diagnosis of "atypical vascular proliferation suggestive of early Kaposi's disease" can be made. In well-developed cases, the tumor may grow in a diffuse fashion or as discrete deposits. The spindle-cell lesion is often accompanied by a lymphoid proliferation with a prominent component of plasma cells and immunoblasts. Sometimes, this reactive lymphoid process acquires the features of Castleman's disease of the plasma cell type.[1278] In other instances, nodal Kaposi's sarcoma coexists with malignant lymphoma or leukemia.[1290]

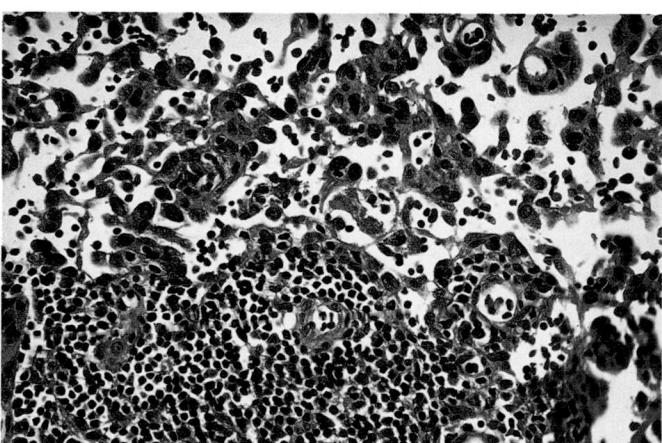

Fig. 21.129 Angiosarcoma of skin of scalp metastatic to a posterior cervical lymph node. The nodal lesion was the first manifestation of the disease.

If a lymph node is involved by a malignant tumor with the morphologic features of **angiosarcoma**, there is a high probability that the tumor is metastatic (Fig. 21.129).

Other primary tumors and tumorlike conditions

Mastocytosis of the diffuse (systemic) type often involves lymph nodes, resulting in a partial or complete effacement of the architecture by a monotonous proliferation of round or polygonal cells[1297,1315] (Fig. 21.130). Clues as to the nature of the proliferation include the regular contours of the round or oval nucleus, the clear or granular cytoplasm, the well-defined cell outlines, and the admixture of eosinophils. Special techniques that allow the identification of mast cells include Giemsa, metachromatic stains (i.e., toluidine blue, polychrome methylene blue), chloroacetate esterase (Leder), and immunohistochemical demonstration of tryptase, CD117, and the adhesion molecule CD44/HCAM (Fig. 21.131).[1291,1301,1308–1310,1316,1330]

It should be remembered that occasional mast cells are normally present in small number in lymph nodes. Their number is increased in some parasitoses, in Waldenström macroglobulinemia, and in several types of lymphadenitis, as documented in an early article by the Lennert's group.[1314]

Acute myeloid leukemia can first be seen in a lymph node biopsy and misdiagnosed as malignant lymphoma.[1318] Traditionally, the disease has been referred to as granulocytic sarcoma or chloroma when appearing as

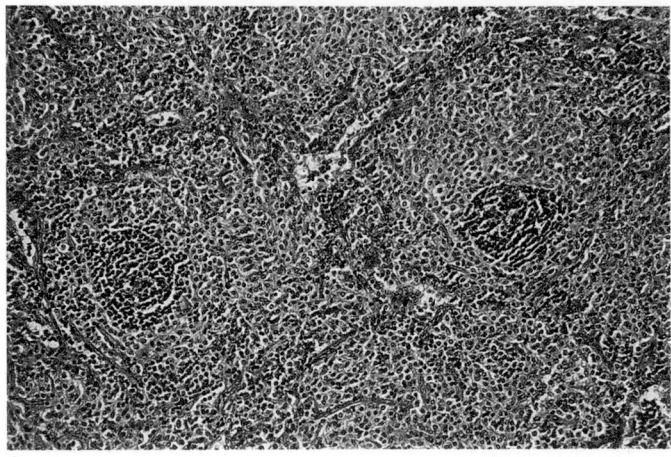
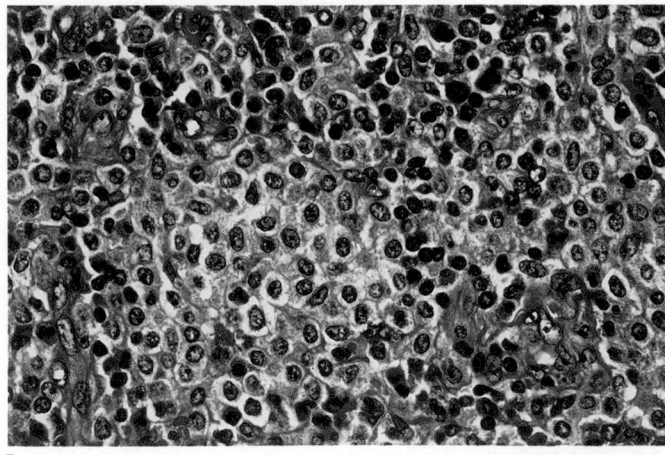

A

B

Fig. 21.130 Medium and high-power views of lymph node involvement in systemic mastocytosis. Note the perfectly round shape of the centrally located nuclei, the finely granular cytoplasm, and the well-defined cell membranes.

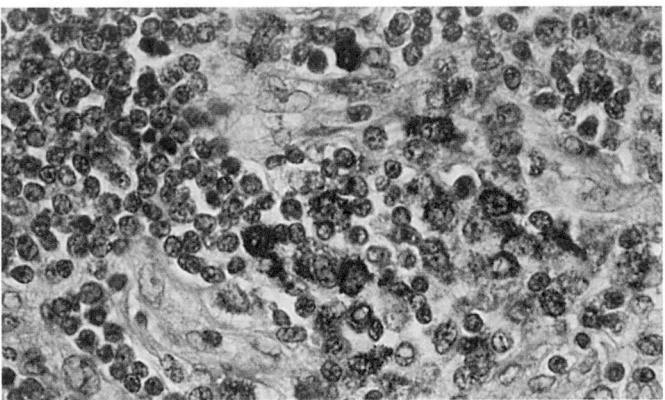

Fig. 21.131 Lymph node involved by systemic mastocytosis. The myeloid precursors stain an intense red color. (Leder's chloroacetate esterase)

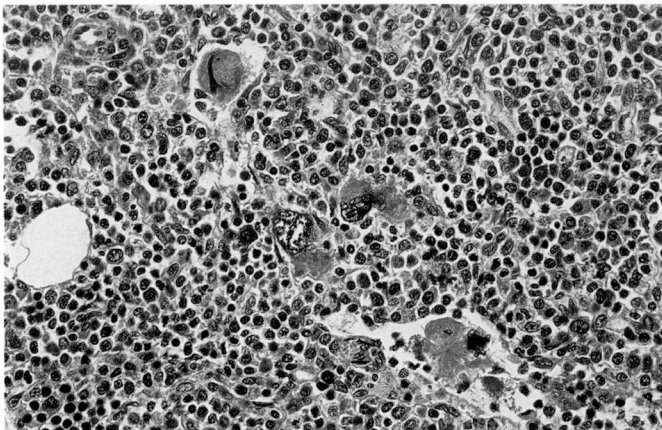

Fig. 21.132 Scattered megakaryocytes in lymph node involved by extramedullary hematopoiesis. These elements should not be confused with Reed–Sternberg cells or carcinoma cells.

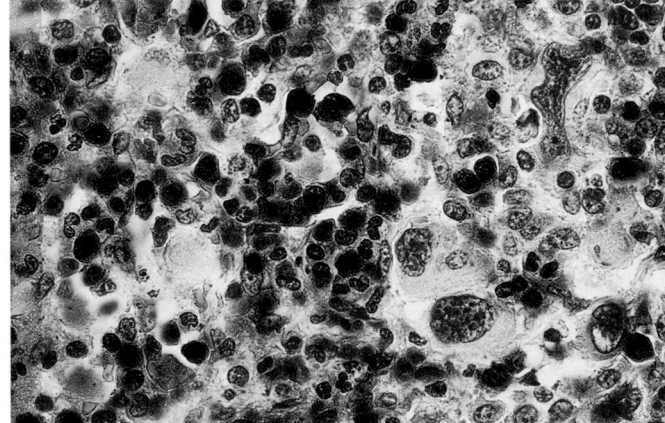

Fig. 21.133 Positivity with Leder's (chloroacetate esterase) stain in the myeloid precursors present in lymph node affected by extramedullary hematopoiesis.

a tumor mass in a lymph node or some other location outside the bone marrow. Clues to the diagnosis include a patchy or sinusal type of nodal involvement, sometimes associated with a single-file pattern of infiltration in the capsule; fine granularity of the cytoplasm; and presence of eosinophilic myelocytes. Immunohistochemically, there is reactivity for CD43, lysozyme, myeloperoxidase, CD99, and CD117.[1294,1323] Four phenotypic variants have been described.[1294] *Extramedullary hematopoiesis* accompanied by megakaryocytes can be confused with Hodgkin's lymphoma and other malignancies (Fig. 21.132). A Leder chloroacetate stain will reveal the immature myeloid forms (Fig. 21.133).

Smooth muscle proliferations of a primary nature can be seen within lymph nodes in the following situations:

1 *Smooth muscle proliferation in the hilum*. This is often accompanied by fibrosis and prominent vascularity.[1299] It is most common in the inguinal region and is of no clinical significance.

2 *Angiomyolipoma*. The most common location is the retroperitoneal region, usually in conjunction with a renal tumor of the same type (see Chapter 17).[1296] Immunoreactivity for HMB-45 and other melanocyte-related markers is a constant feature of this entity.

3 *Lymphangiomyomatosis.* This is seen exclusively in women, often in association with pulmonary involvement.[1300] Like the previous entity, with which it is histogenetically related, it exhibits immunoreactivity for HMB-45.

4 *Leiomyomatosis.* This has been reported mainly in intra-abdominal nodes, sometimes in association with uterine leiomyomas or leiomyomatosis peritonealis disseminata.[1307,1317]

5 *Angiomatous hamartoma.* This is a distinctive form of smooth muscle proliferation that seems to occur only in the inguinal region. It is characterized by a proliferation of thick-walled hilar blood vessels that sometimes extends into the nodal parenchyma.[1298]

6 *Intranodal leiomyoma.* Some of the reported cases have occurred in the setting of HIV infection.[1325]

Hemorrhagic spindle-cell tumor with amianthoid fibers (also known as palisaded myofibroblastoma) is a distinctive benign neoplasm that occurs preferentially in inguinal lymph nodes but that can involve other sites, such as the neck and mediastinum.[1295,1305,1306,1325,1328] The main microscopic features are the proliferation of bland-looking spindle cells, sometimes in a palisading fashion; extensive foci of recent and old hemorrhage; and giant rosettelike collections of collagen fibers (so-called "amianthoid fibers")[1320,1324,1327] (Fig. 21.134). The differential diagnosis includes Kaposi's sarcoma and intranodal schwannoma. Immunohistochemically, the spindle cells are reactive for vimentin and actin, particularly around the rosettelike formations. The staining qualities and ultrastructural features are more in favor of a smooth muscle than a myofibroblastic derivation.[1329] The

behavior has been benign in all reported cases, but there has been an occasional instance of recurrence.[1302]

Inflammatory pseudotumor of lymph nodes may be localized or affect several lymph node groups and may be accompanied by fever, anemia, elevated erythrosedimentation rate, and hypergammaglobulinemia.[1303,1304,1311,1312,1322] Microscopically, the process involves primarily the fibrous stroma of the node, with secondary spread into the lymphoid tissue and perinodal tissues. It is characterized by a storiform pattern of growth, vascular proliferation, and a polymorphic infiltrate composed of fibroblasts, plasma cells, immunoblasts, small lymphocytes, histiocytes, dendritic cells, and neutrophils (Fig. 21.135). Morphologic variations on this basic theme exist, which have been attributed to the stage of the disease at which the biopsy has been taken.[1321] Presence of the EBV genome has been documented in a minority of cases.

Inflammatory pseudotumor of lymph nodes (and spleen) seems to be a different entity than its homonym in the soft tissue, lung, and other sites. The latter group, which can follow an aggressive clinical course and which is accompanied by a balanced chromosomal translocation involving the *ALK* gene, is now regarded as a neoplastic process and has accordingly been renamed inflammatory myofibroblastic tumor. Conversely, the lymph node condition consistently lacks this genetic aberration and follows a generally favorable course, suggesting that it is truly an inflammatory/reactive process, perhaps related to the group of conditions generically known as inflammatory fibrosclerosis.[1313,1319] Consideration should also be given to the possibility of the actin- and desmin-positive spindle cells present in this

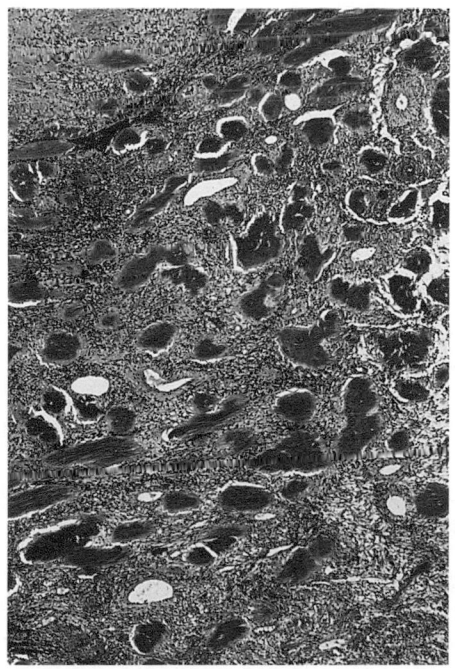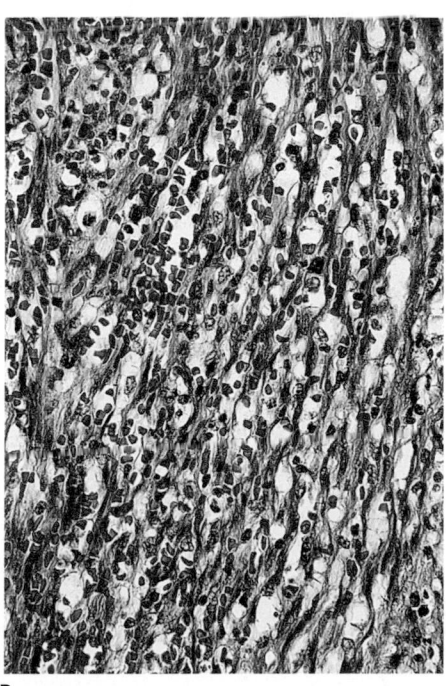

Fig. 21.134 A and **B**, Hemorrhagic spindle cell tumor with amianthoid fibers. **A**, Prominent deposition of "amianthoid" collagen throughout the tumor. **B**, The admixture of neoplastic spindle cells and extravasated red blood cells results in a Kaposi's sarcoma-like appearance.

A   B

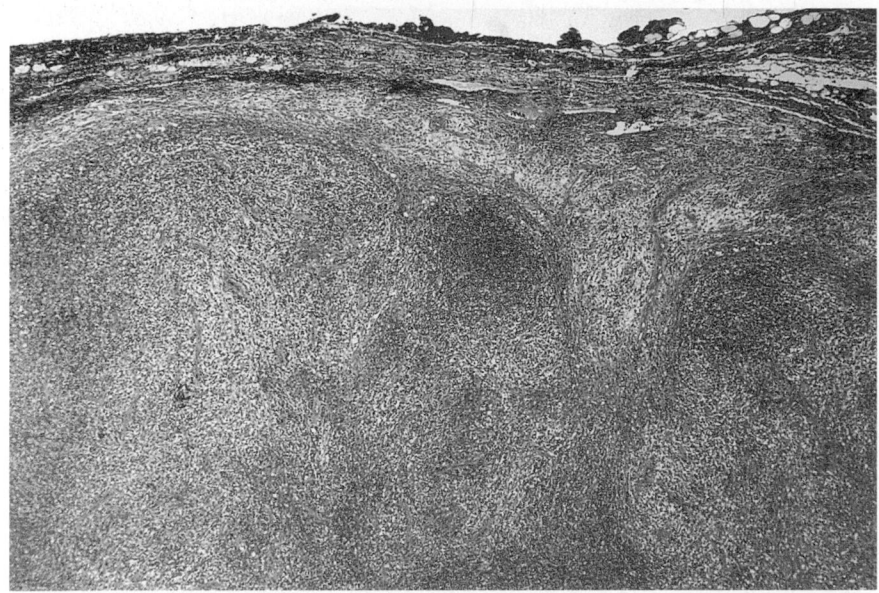

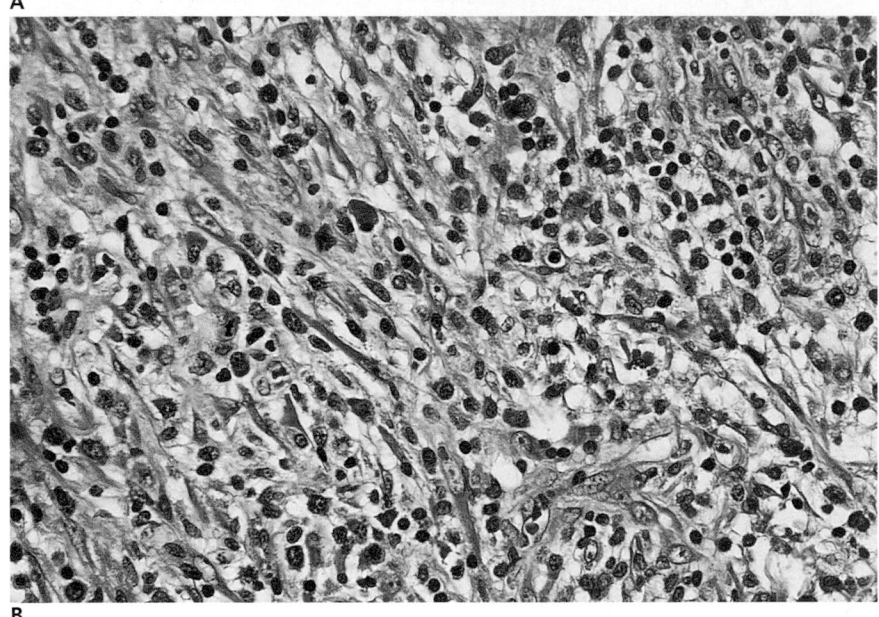

Fig. 21.135 A and **B**, Inflammatory pseudotumor of lymph node. **A**, Low-power appearance showing partial effacement of architecture and expansion of the sinusal and perinodal regions by a reactive proliferation. **B**, High-power view showing a polymorphic infiltrate composed of lymphocytes, plasma cells, and myofibroblasts.

disorder being of fibroblastic reticulum/dendritic cell rather than myofibroblastic type. Inflammatory pseudotumors of an altogether different type can result from *Mycobacterium avium intracellulare* infection in immunocompromised individuals (Fig. 21.136).

Anthracosis and **anthracosilicosis** can result in a pseudoneoplastic appearance because of the presence of a sometimes intense histiocytic proliferation with a focally storiform pattern of growth[1293] (Fig. 21.137).

Metastatic tumors

Lymph nodes are the most common site of metastatic malignancy, and sometimes constitute the first clinical manifestation of the disease.[1338,1344,1356] The task of the pathologist is to identify the presence of a malignant process in the node, to establish whether it is metastatic or not, and—if metastatic—to provide an estimate of its amount, microscopic type, and possible source. If malignant cells are identified within the efferent lymph vessels and/or extranodal adipose tissue, this should also be noted in the report because of the possible prognostic significance of these findings.

Any malignant tumor can give rise to lymph node metastases, but the incidence varies greatly depending on the tumor type. It is common with carcinomas, malignant melanomas, and germ cell tumors and rare with sarcomas and central nervous system tumors. It should also be noted that large cell lymphomas primary in an organ (such as stomach or thyroid) sometimes involve the regional nodes in a pattern consistent with metastatic spread (see also p. 1950).

An additional diagnosis to consider in a lymph node

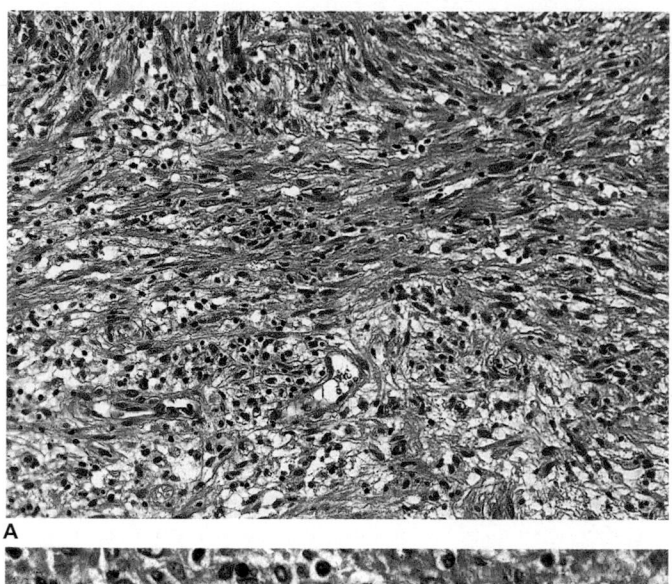

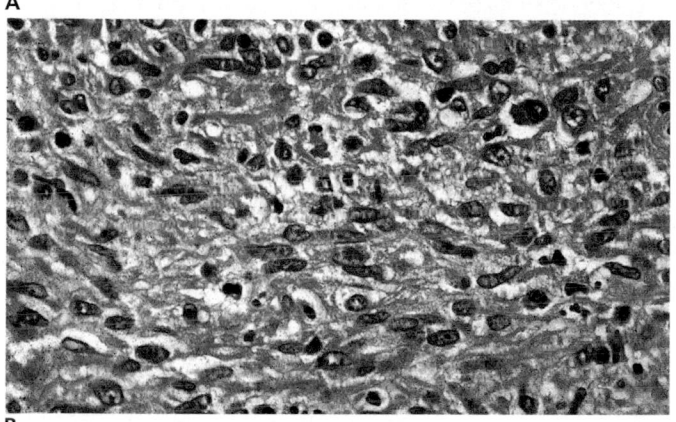

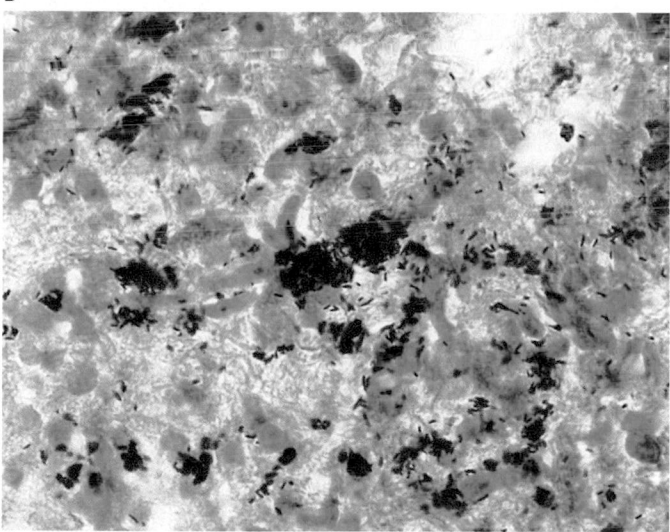

Fig. 21.136 Inflammatory pseudotumor of lymph node due to *Mycobacterium avium-intracellulare* infection in an HIV-infected patient: **A**, low-power view, showing spindle cell admixed with lymphocytes; **B**, high-power view; **C**, acid fast stain.

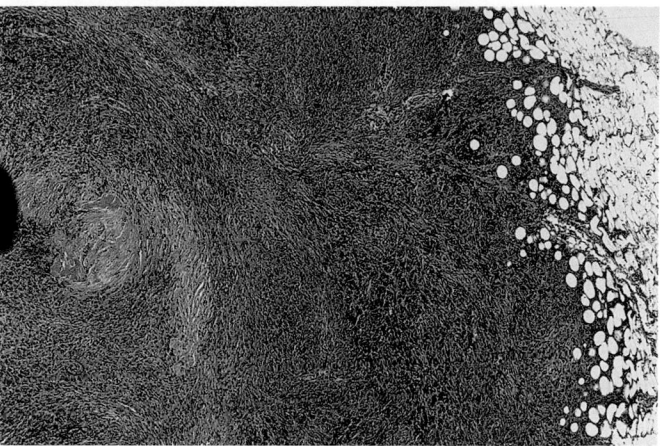

Fig. 21.137 Anthracosilicotic nodules in mediastinal lymph node. When florid, these changes may acquire pseudoneoplastic features.

tumors were located in the peritoneum rather than the pleura, regardless of the location of the nodes.[1350] The differential diagnosis includes reactive benign mesothelial cells in lymph nodes (see p. 1963) (Fig. 21.139A to C).

It is very rare for soft tissue sarcomas to present initially as a lymph node metastasis. The outstanding exception is alveolar rhabdomyosarcoma (particularly the solid variant), which can be confused with malignant lymphoma not only on morphologic grounds but also because it may involve several lymph node groups (so-called "lymphadenopathic form") (Fig. 21.140). Other sarcomas that have a greater than average tendency to metastasize to regional nodes are embryonal rhabdomyosarcoma, angiosarcoma, epithelioid sarcoma, and synovial sarcoma.

The differential diagnosis between metastatic undifferentiated carcinoma and diffuse large cell lymphoma in routine sections may be difficult or even impossible in some cases. Features favoring lymphoma are presence of focal nodularity within the tumor not induced by fibrosis and diffuse permeation of walls of veins (as opposed to tumor thrombi) and adipose tissue if an extranodal component is present. Features favoring metastatic tumor are focal nodal involvement, definite nesting, extensive necrosis, predominantly sinusal distribution, and solid tumor plugs in lymphatic vessels. The types of malignant lymphoma most likely to be misdiagnosed as metastatic carcinoma are anaplastic large cell lymphoma, large cell lymphoma with sclerosis resulting in prominent nesting, large cell lymphoma with a predominantly sinusal pattern of growth, nodular sclerosis Hodgkin's lymphoma with concentration of large mononuclear variants of Reed–Sternberg cells around areas of necrosis, and signet ring lymphoma. Yet another type is the composite lymphoma made up of follicular small cleaved and diffuse large cell components, the double error consisting in diagnosing the latter component as metastatic carcinoma and the former as follicular hyperplasia.

involvement by metastatic tumor is malignant mesothelioma (Fig. 21.138). We have seen several examples of this tumor type presenting initially with lymphadenopathy in the cervical or inguinal region; most of the primary

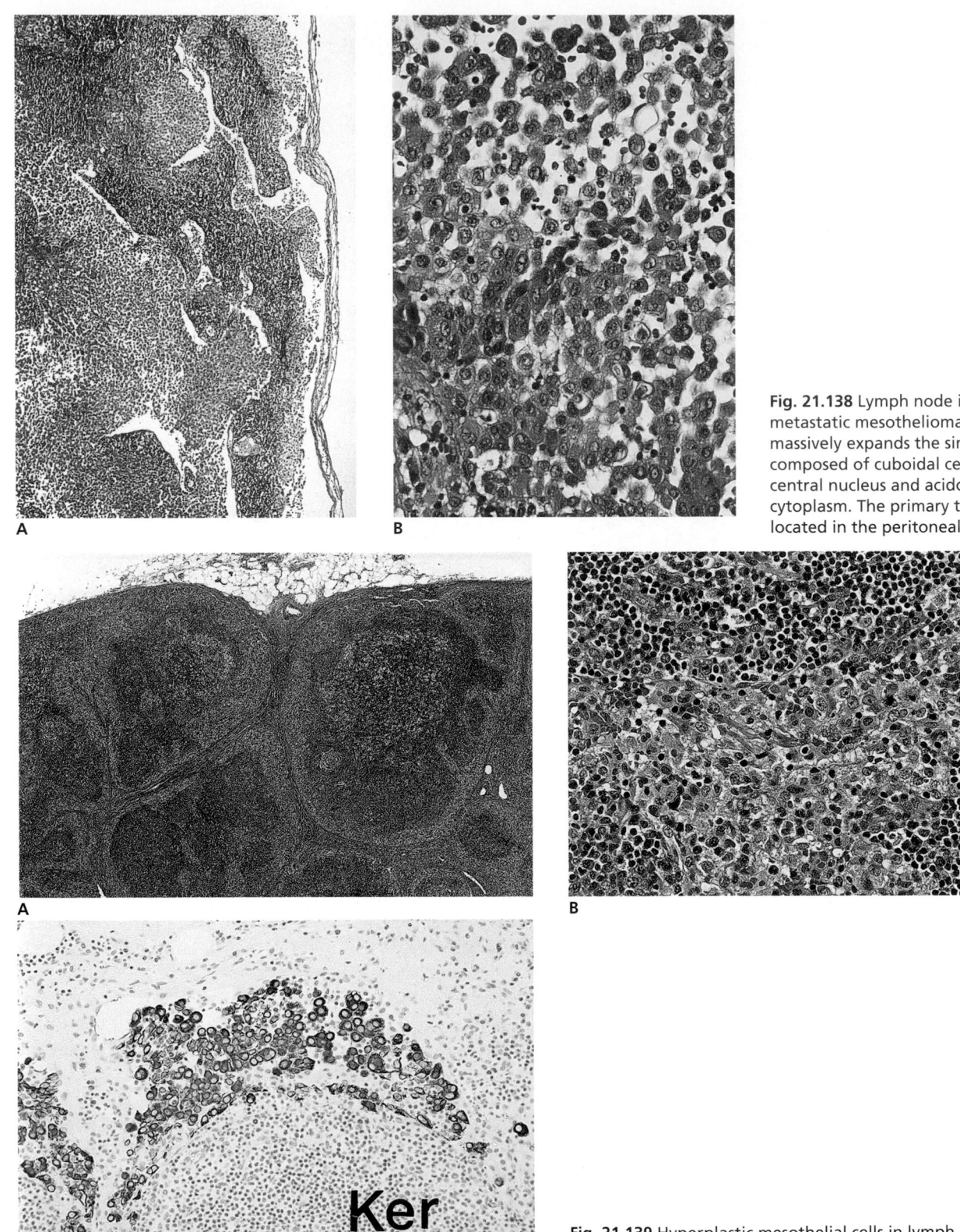

Fig. 21.138 Lymph node involved by metastatic mesothelioma. The tumor massively expands the sinuses and is composed of cuboidal cells with a central nucleus and acidophilic cytoplasm. The primary tumor was located in the peritoneal cavity.

Fig. 21.139 Hyperplastic mesothelial cells in lymph node: **A**, sinusal distribution; **B**, bland cytologic appearance; **C**, strong immunoreactivity for keratin.

The metastatic carcinomas that most closely simulate a malignant lymphoid process are nasopharyngeal lymphoepithelioma and lobular carcinoma of the breast (Figs 21.141 and 21.142). The first may masquerade clinically and pathologically as Hodgkin's lymphoma because of its common presentation in a young adult with painless unilateral cervical lymphadenopathy and the presence of a polymorphic population (including eosinophils) on

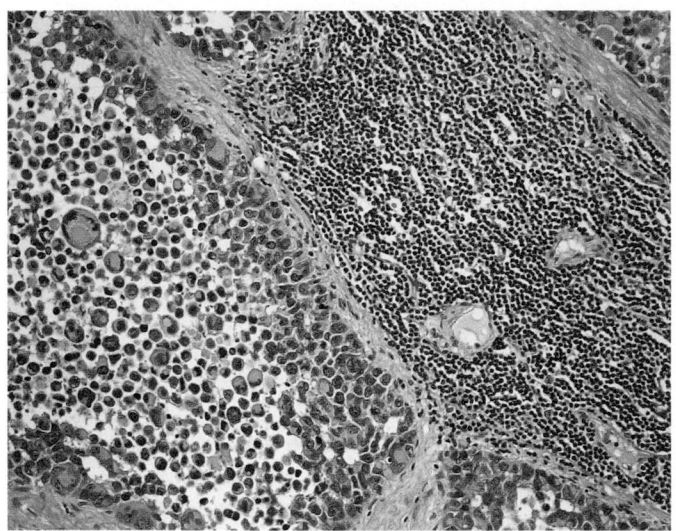

Fig. 21.140 Alveolar rhabdomyosarcoma metastatic to a lymph node. This is a relatively common occurrence in this tumor type and it may be the first clinical manifestation of the disease.

microscopic examination.[1341] The second may be confused with malignant lymphomas of one type or another. This is particularly true of the type composed of small uniform cells with only occasional signet ring formations, which can look remarkably lymphocyte-like (Fig. 21.143). Metastatic small cell neuroendocrine carcinoma from the lung or other sites can be difficult to distinguish from lymphoma; dense nuclear chromatin pattern, nuclear molding, focal areas of necrosis, and hematoxyphilic staining of vessel walls favor a diagnosis of small cell carcinoma. Somewhat similar considerations pertain to the diagnosis of metastatic Merkel cell tumor. Metastatic melanoma can closely simulate on cytologic grounds the appearance of large cell lymphoma and plasmacytoma. The balloon cell variety can closely mimic Rosai–Dorfman disease (Fig. 21.144). One should also not forget that metastases can develop in a node already involved by lymphoma or leukemia.

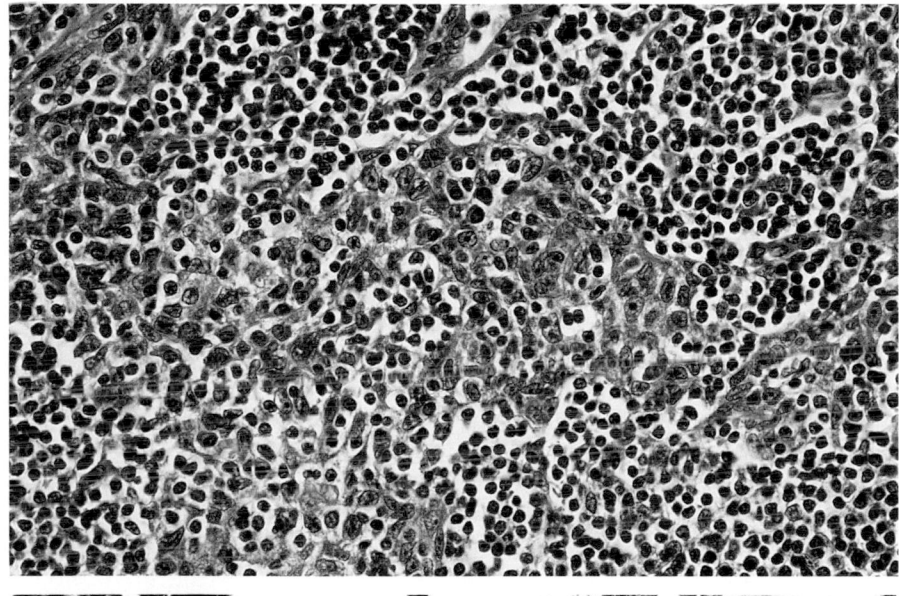

Fig. 21.141 Lymph node involved by metastatic lymphoepithelioma from the nasopharynx. The relatively diffuse pattern of the proliferation may result in a mistaken diagnosis of malignant lymphoma.

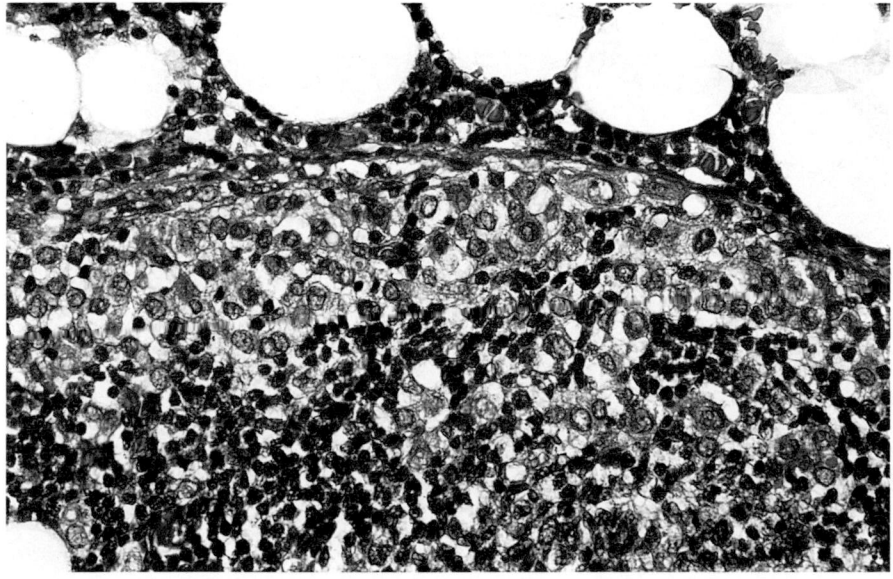

Fig. 21.142 Breast carcinoma of lobular type metastatic to the sinuses of a lymph node. The cytologic appearance may be confused with that of a malignant lymphoma.

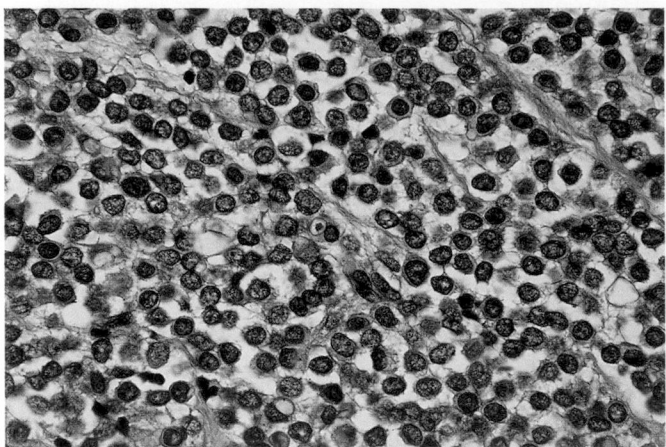
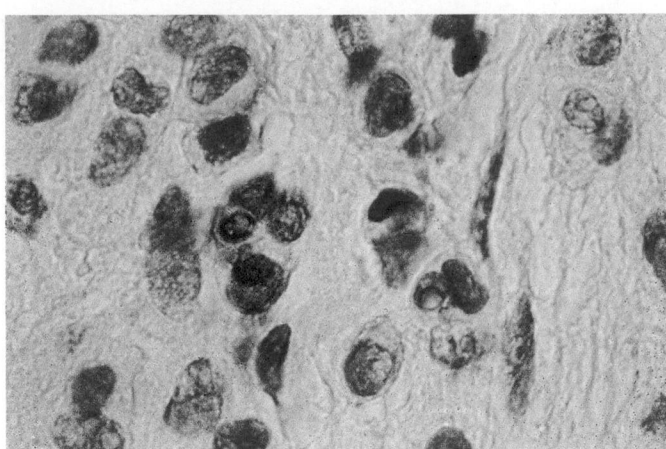

Fig. 21.143 A and **B**, Poorly differentiated adenocarcinoma with signet ring features initially misinterpreted as a malignant lymphoma. The mistake may have been partially induced by the fact that the tumor developed in a renal transplant recipient. **A**, Hematoxylin–eosin. **B**, Mucicarmine stain, showing a few droplets of intracytoplasmic mucin.

Among the conventional special stains, the two most likely to help in the differential diagnosis between metastatic carcinoma and lymphoma are PAS and mucin stains. In general, positivity for the latter will establish the diagnosis of adenocarcinoma. The presence of abundant glycogen and/or diastase-resistant mucosubstances in the cytoplasm of a large cell tumor on a PAS stain will also rule out, for all practical purposes, a diagnosis of lymphoma. We have found reticulin stains of only limited value in this differential diagnosis. Instead, touch preparations can be of great diagnostic utility by showing clumping of the tumor cells in carcinoma and the absence of clumping in lymphoma. Ultrastructural examination is also likely to be useful because it will usually demonstrate epithelial markers such as complex desmosomes, tonofibrils, and extracellular or intracellular glandular lumina.[1339] However, the special technique that is clearly the top choice for the efficient resolution of this problem is immunocytochemistry. The "basic kit" with which to approach an obviously malignant tumor involving a lymph node is CD45, keratin, and S-100 protein, as markers for lymphoid, epithelial, and melanocytic cells, respectively. A second line of reagents could include EMA, CEA, CD20, CD3, vimentin, and—depending on the circumstances—GCDFP-15 and lactalbumin (for breast), chromogranin (for endocrine tumors), and PSA/PAP (for prostate). When properly applied and interpreted, the performance of these reactions should solve all but a very small minority of cases.

Nodal metastases of squamous cell carcinoma have a particular tendency to undergo cystic changes. When these are prominent in a node located in the neck, a mistaken diagnosis of branchial cleft cyst may ensue (Figs 21.145 and 21.146).

It is just as important to mention some of the benign conditions of lymph nodes that can mistakenly be interpreted as metastatic carcinoma. They include hyperplastic mesothelial cells,[1331] megakaryocytes,[1345] signet-ring sinus histiocytosis,[1343] the related nodal muciphages and mucicarminophilic histiocytosis,[1337,1342] florid anthraco-

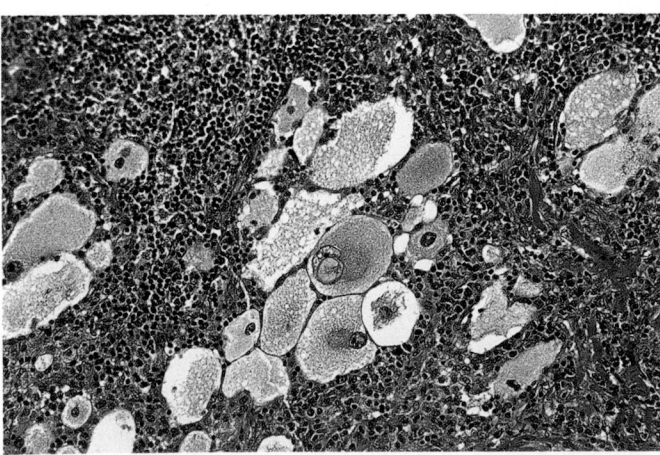

Fig. 21.144 Balloon cell melanoma metastic to a lymph node and simulating a histiocytic disorder.

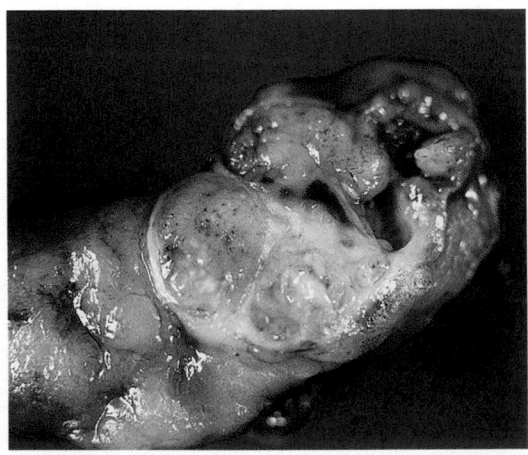

Fig. 21.145 Squamous cell carcinoma metastatic to lymph node. The tumor has undergone partial cystic transformation.

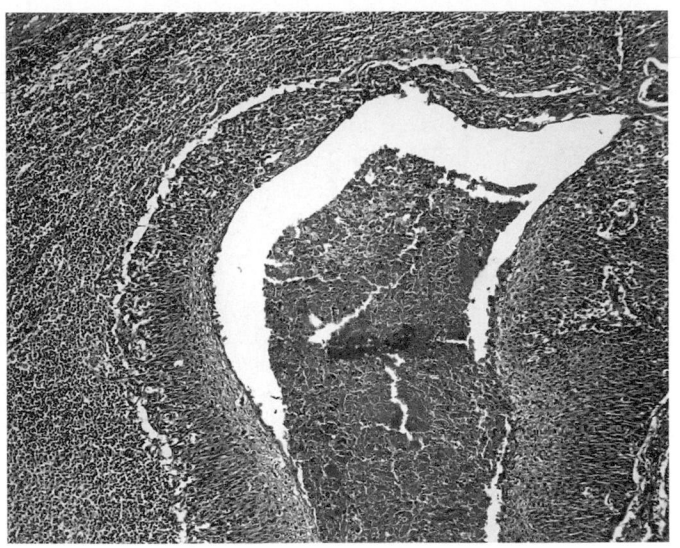
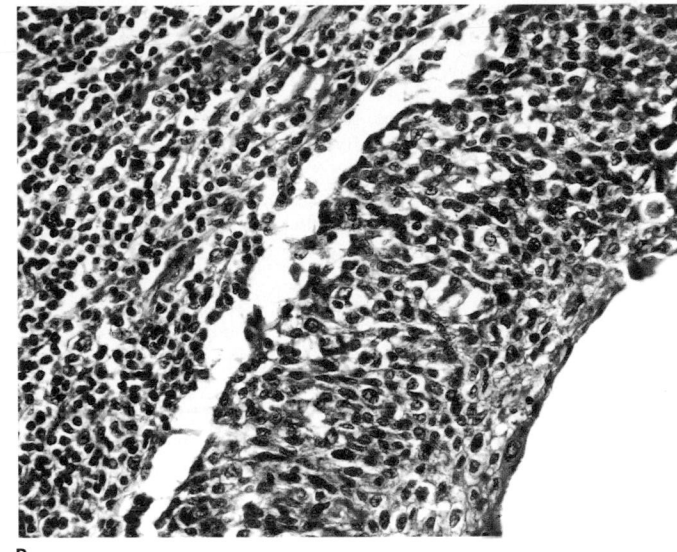

A   B

Fig. 21.146 A and **B**, Squamous cell carcinoma metastatic to cervical lymph node. **A**, Medium-power view, showing marked cystic change that may result in a mistaken diagnosis of branchial cleft cyst. **B**, High-power view showing malignant cytologic features involving the entire thickness of the epithelial strip.

sis/anthracosilicosis,[1332] and the various lymph node epithelial inclusions listed on p. 1961, without forgetting the banal germinal centers of hyperplastic follicles cut tangentially.

The location of a node involved by metastatic carcinoma gives important clues about the possible site of the primary. The large majority of tumors metastatic to *upper cervical* lymph nodes originate from the upper aerodigestive tract. Sites well known for harboring small, clinically undetectable primaries in the presence of cervical adenopathy are nasopharynx and retrotonsillar pillar.[1333,1346,1347] *Midcervical* nodes containing papillary carcinoma are usually examples of metastatic thyroid carcinoma, a possibility that becomes a virtual certainty in the presence of psammoma bodies. However, these papillary tumors may also originate from salivary gland, ovary, or thymus (see respective chapters). Squamous cell carcinomas in lymph nodes of this region usually arise in the upper aerodigestive tract, particularly pharynx and larynx.[1349] Most carcinomas metastatic to *supraclavicular* lymph nodes originate in the lung or breast. Other sources of metastases to this nodal group, particularly if located on the left side, are carcinoma of stomach, pancreas, prostate, and testis.[1346,1348] These reach the node through the terminal collecting lymphatic trunks. Supraclavicular nodes involved by intra-abdominal carcinomas are sometimes referred to as Virchow's or Troisier's nodes.[1334] The large majority of metastatic tumors in *axillary* nodes of adult females are breast carcinoma and malignant melanoma.[1336,1340] Lung carcinoma should also be considered, especially in older patients with a smoking history.[1335] *Inguinal* nodes are often the recipients of carcinomas from the external genital organs (usually evident on clinical examination) or malignant

melanomas of the lower extremities but only rarely from the internal abdominal organs (ovary, uterine cervix, anal canal) and even less commonly from the testis, unless direct extension to the scrotal skin has occurred.[1352]

References

Normal anatomy

1   Delves PJ, Roitt IM. The immune system. First of two parts. N Engl J Med 2000, **343**: 37–49.
2   Ioachim HL, Ratech H. Ioachim's Lymph node pathology, ed. 3. Philadelphia, 2002, Lippincott Williams & Wilkins.
3   Liu YJ, Zhang J, Lane PJ, Chan EY, MacLennan IC. Sites of specific B cell activation in primary and secondary responses to T-cell-dependent and T-cell-independent antigens. Eur J Immunol 1991, **21**: 2951–2962.
4   Stein H, Bonk A, Tolksdorf G, Lennert K, Rodt H, Gerdes J. Immunohistologic analysis of the organization of normal lymphoid tissue and non-Hodgkin's lymphomas. J Histochem Cytochem 1980, **28**: 746–760.
5   Szakal AK, Kosco MH, Tew JG. Microanatomy of lymphoid tissue during humoral immune responses. Structure function relationships. Annu Rev Immunol 1989, **7**: 91–109.

Lymph node evaluation
Biopsy

6   Banks PM. Technical factors in the preparation and evaluation of lymph node biopsies. In Knowles DM (ed.): Neoplastic hematopathology, ed. 2. Philadelphia, 2001, Lippincott Williams and Wilkins, pp. 467–482.
7   Banks PM, Long JC, Howard CA. Preparation of lymph node biopsy specimens. Hum Pathol 1979, **10**: 617–621.
8   Beard C, Nabers K, Bowling MC, Berard CW. Achieving technical excellence in lymph node specimens. An update. Lab Med 1985, **16**: 468–475.
9   Butler JJ. Non-neoplastic lesions of lymph nodes of man to be differentiated from lymphomas. NCI Monogr 1969, **32**: 233–255.
10 Weiss LM, Dorfman RF, Warnke RA. Lymph node work-up. In

Fenoglio-Preiser C (ed.): Advances in pathology, vol. 1. Chicago, 1988, Year Book Medical Publishers.

Needle biopsy

11 Cafferty LL, Katz RL, Ordonez NG, Carrasco CH, Cabanillas FR. Fine needle aspiration diagnosis of intraabdominal and retroperitoneal lymphomas by a morphologic and immunocytochemical approach. Cancer 1990, **65**: 72–77.

12 Frable WJ, Kardos TF. Fine needle aspiration biopsy. Applications in the diagnosis of lymphoproliferative diseases. Am J Surg Pathol 1988, **12**(Suppl 1): 62–72.

13 Kardos TF, Maygarden SJ, Blumberg AK, Wakely PE Jr, Frable WJ. Fine needle aspiration biopsy in the management of children and young adults with peripheral lymphadenopathy. Cancer 1989, **63**: 703–707.

14 Kern WH. Exfoliative and aspiration cytology of malignant lymphomas. Semin Diagn Pathol 1986, **3**: 211–218.

15 Pitts WC, Weiss LM. Fine needle aspiration biopsy of lymph nodes. Pathol Annu 1988, **23**(Pt 2): 329–360.

16 Tsang WY, Chan JK. Spectrum of morphologic changes in lymph nodes attributable to fine needle aspiration. Hum Pathol 1992, **23**: 562–565.

17 van Heerde P, Go DMDS, Koolman-Schellekens MA, Peterse JL. Cytodiagnosis of non-Hodgkin's lymphoma. A morphological analysis of 215 biopsy proven cases. Virchows Arch [A] 1984, **403**: 213–233.

Electron microscopy

18 Mackay B. Ultrastructural diagnosis of lymphomas and leukemias. Ultrastruct Pathol 1985, **9**: 209–214.

19 Peiper SC, Kahn LB. Ultrastructural comparison of Hodgkin's and non-Hodgkin's lymphomas. Histopathology 1982, **6**: 93–109.

Immunophenotyping

20 Chu PG, Chang KL, Arber DA, Weiss LM. Immunophenotyping of hematopoietic neoplasms. Semin Diagn Pathol 2000, **17**: 236–256.

21 Frizzera G, Wu D, Inghirami G. The usefulness of immunophenotypic and genotypic studies in the diagnosis and classification of hematopoietic and lymphoid neoplasms. An update. Am J Clin Pathol 1999, **111**: S13–S39.

22 Mason D, André P, Densussan A, Buckley C, Civin C, Clark E, De Haas M, Goyert S, Hadam M, Hart D, Horejsi V, Meuer S, Morrisey J, Schwartz-Albiez R, Shaw S, Simmons D, Ugussioni M, Van Der Schoot E, Vivier E, Zola H. CD antigens 2001. Mod Pathol 2002, **15**: 71–76.

Cytogenetics and molecular genetics

23 LeBeau M. The role of cytogenetics in the diagnosis and classification of hematopoietic neoplasms. In Knowles DM (ed.): Neoplastic hematopathology. Baltimore, 1992, Williams & Wilkins.

24 Medeioros LJ, Carr J. Overview of the role of molecular methods in the diagnosis of malignant lymphomas. Arch Pathol Lab Med 2000, **123**: 1189–1207.

25 Ngan BY, Chen-Levy Z, Weiss LM, Warnke RA, Cleary ML. Expression in non-Hodgkin's lymphoma of the bcl-2 protein associated with the t(14;18) chromosomal translocation. N Engl J Med 1988, **318**: 1638–1644.

26 Sen F, Vega F, Medeiros LJ. Molecular genetic methods in the diagnosis of hematologic neoplasms. Semin Diagn Pathol 2002, **19**: 72–93.

27 Staudt LM. Molecular diagnosis of the hematologic cancers. N Engl J Med 2003, **348**: 1777–1779.

28 Testa JR, Arthur DC. Cytogenetics of leukemia and lymphoma. In Wiernik PH (ed.): Contemporary issues in clinical oncology. Leukemias and lymphomas. New York, 1985, Churchill-Livingstone, pp. 155–182.

29 Weiss LM, Warnek RA, Sklar J. Cleary ML. Molecular analysis of the t(14;18) chromosomal translocation in malignant lymphomas. N Engl J Med 1987, **317**: 1185–1189.

30 Yunis JJ, Frizzera G, Olsen MM, McKenna J, Theologides A, Arnesen M. Multiple recurrent genomic defects in follicular lymphoma. A possible model for cancer. N Engl J Med 1987, **316**: 79–84.

Gene rearrangement analysis

31 Collins RD. Is clonality equivalent to malignancy: specifically, is immunoglobulin gene rearrangement diagnostic of malignant lymphoma? Hum Pathol 1997, **28**: 757–759.

32 Davis RE, Warnke RA, Dorfman RF, Cleary ML. Utility of molecular genetic analysis for the diagnosis of neoplasia in morphologically and immunophenotypically equivocal hematolymphoid lesions. Cancer 1991, **67**: 2890–2899.

33 Dubeau L, Weinberg K, Jones PA, Nichols PW. Studies on immunoglobulin gene rearrangement in formalin-fixed, paraffin-embedded pathology specimens. Am J Pathol 1988, **130**: 588–594.

34 Henni T, Gaulard P, Divine M, Le Couedic JP, Rocha D, Haioun C, Henni Z, Marolleau JP, Pinaudeau Y, Goossens M, et al. Comparison of genetic probe with immunophenotype analysis in lymphoproliferative disorders. A study of 87 cases. Blood 1988, **72**: 1937–1943.

35 Ilyas M, Jalal H, Linton C, Rooney N. The use of the polymerase chain reaction in the diagnosis of B-cell lymphomas from formalin-fixed paraffin-embedded tissue. Histopathology 1995, **26**: 333–338.

36 Kamat D, Laszewski MJ, Kemp JD, Goeken JA, Lutz CT, Platz CE, Dick FR. The diagnostic utility of immunophenotyping and immunogenotyping in the pathologic evaluation of lymphoid proliferations. Mod Pathol 1990, **3**: 105–112.

37 Medeiros LJ, Bagg A, Cossman J. Application of molecular genetics to the diagnosis of hematopoietic neoplasms. In Knowles DM (ed.): Neoplastic hematopathology. Baltimore, 1992, Williams & Wilkins.

DNA ploidy studies

38 Braylan RC. Flow-cytometric DNA analysis in the diagnosis and prognosis of lymphoma. Am J Clin Pathol 1993, **99**: 374–380.

39 Duque RE. Flow cytometric analysis of lymphomas and acute leukemias. Ann NY Acad Sci 1993, **677**: 309–325.

40 Duque RE, Andreeff M, Braylan RC, Diamond LW, Peiper SC. Consensus review of the clinical utility of DNA flow cytometry in neoplastic hematopathology. Cytometry 1993, **14**: 492–496.

41 Zander DS, Iturraspe JA, Everett ET, Massey JK, Braylan RC. Flow cytometry. In vitro assessment of its potential application for diagnosis and classification of lymphoid processes in cytologic preparations from fine needle aspirates. Am J Clin Pathol 1994, **101**: 577–586.

Gene expression profiling

42 Alizadeh AA, Eisen MB, Davis RE, Ma C, Lossos IS, Rosenwald A, Boldrick JC, Sabet H, Tran T, Yu X, Powell JI, Yang L, Marti GE, Moore T, Hudson J Jr, Lu L, Lewis DB, Tibshirani R, Sherlock G, Chan WC, Greiner TC, Weelsenburger DD, Armitage JO, Warnke R, Levy R, Wilson W, Grever MR, Byrd JC, Botstein D, Brown PO, Staudt LM. Distinct types of diffuse large B-cell lymphoma identified by gene expression profiling. Nature 2000, **403**: 503–511.

43 Rosenwald A, Wright G, Chan WC, Connors JM, Campo E, Fisher RI, Gascoyne RD, Müller-Hermelink K, Smeland EB, Staudt LM. The use of molecular profiling to predict survival after chemotherapy for diffuse large B-cell lymphoma. N Engl J Med 2002, **346**: 1937–1947.

Primary immunodeficiencies

44 Buckley RH. Primary immunodeficiency disease due to defects in lymphocytes. N Engl J Med 2000, **343:** 1313–1324.

45 Elenitoba-Johnson KS, Jaffe ES. Lymphoproliferative disorders associated with congenital immunodeficiencies. Semin Diagn Pathol 1997, **14:** 35–47.

46 Gitlin D, Janeway CA, Apt L, Craig JM. Agammaglobulinemia. In Lawrence H (ed.): Cellular and humoral aspects of hypersensitivity states. New York, 1959, Paul B Hoeber, pp. 375–441.

47 Heymer B, Niethammer D, Spanel R, Galle J, Kleihauer E, Haferkamp O. Pathomorphology of humoral, cellular and combined primary immunodeficiencies. Virchows Arch [A] 1977, **374:** 87–103.

48 Huber J, Zegers BJ, Schuurman IIJ. Pathology of congenital immunodeficiencies. Semin Diagn Pathol 1992, **9:** 31–62.

49 Knowles DM. Immunodeficiency-associated lymphoproliferative disorders. Mod Pathol 1999, **12:** 200–217.

50 Lekstrom-Himes JA, Gallin JI. Immunodeficiency disease caused by defects in phagocytes. N Engl J Med 2000, **343:** 1703–1714.

51 Rosen FS, Cooper MD, Wedgwood RJP. The primary immunodeficiencies. N Engl J Med 1995, **333:** 431–440.

52 Tinguely M, Vonlanthen R, Muller E, Dommann-Scherrer CC, Schneider J, Laissue JA, Borisch B. Hodgkin's disease like lymphoproliferative disorders in patients with different underlying immunodeficiency states. Mod Pathol 1998, **11:** 307–312.

Patterns of hyperplasia

53 Dorfman RF, Warnke R. Lymphadenopathy simulating the malignant lymphomas. Hum Pathol 1974, **5:** 519–550.

54 Ioachim HL, Ratech H. Ioachim's Lymph node pathology. Philadelphia, Lippincott Williams & Wilkins 2002, **3:** 624.

55 Swerdlow SH. Genetic and molecular genetic studies in the diagnosis of atypical lymphoid hyperplasias versus lymphoma. Elsevier, 2003, pp. 346–349.

56 Van Der Valk P, Meijer CJ. Reactive lymph nodes. Histology of Pathologists 1997, **2:** 651–674.

57 Warnke RA, Weiss LM, Chan JKC, Cleary ML, Dorfman RF. Tumors of the lymph nodes and spleen. Atlas of tumor pathology, 3rd series, fascicle 14. Washington, DC, 1995, Armed Forces Institute of Pathology.

Follicular hyperplasia

58 Nathwani BN, Winberg CD, Diamond LW, Bearman RM, Kim H. Morphologic criteria for the differentiation of follicular lymphoma from florid reactive hyperplasia. A study of 80 cases. Cancer 1981, **48:** 1794–1806.

59 Rappaport H, Winter WJ, Hicks EB. Follicular lymphoma. A reevaluation of its position in the scheme of malignant lymphoma, based on a survey of 253 cases. Cancer 1956, **9:** 792–821.

60 Ree HJ, Kadin ME, Kikuchi M, Ko YH, Go JH, Suzumiya J, Kim DS. Angioimmunoblastic lymphoma (AILD-type T-cell lymphoma) with hyperplasia germinal centers. Am J Surg Pathol 1998, **22:** 643–655.

Progressively and regressively transformed germinal centers

61 Burns BF, Colby TV, Dorfman RF. Differential diagnostic features of nodular L&H Hodgkin's disease, including progressive transformation of germinal centers. Am J Surg Pathol 1984, **8:** 253–261.

62 Ferry JA, Zukerberg LR, Harris NL. Florid progressive transformation of germinal centers. A syndrome affecting young men, without early progression to nodular lymphocyte predominance Hodgkin's disease. Am J Surg Pathol 1992, **16:** 252–258.

63 Hansmann ML, Fellbaum C, Hui PK, Moubayed P. Progressive transformation of germinal centers with and without association to Hodgkin's disease. Am J Clin Pathol 1990, **93:** 219–226.

64 Kojima M, Nakamura S, Motoori T, Itoh H, Shimizu K, Yamane N, Ohno Y, Ban S, Yoshida K, Hoshi K, Oyama T, Shimano S, Sugihara S, Sakata N, Masawa N. Progressive transformation of germinal centers: a clinicopathologic study of 42 Japanese patients. Int J Surg Pathol 2003, **11:** 101–107.

65 Nguyen PL, Ferry JA, Harris NL. Progressive transformation of germinal centers and nodular lymphocyte predominance Hodgkin's disease, a comparative immunohistochemical study. Am J Surg Pathol 1999, **23:** 27–33.

66 Osborne BM, Butler JJ. Follicular lymphoma mimicking progressive transformation of germinal centers. Am J Clin Pathol 1987, **88:** 264–269.

67 Osborne BM, Butler JJ, Gresik MV. Progressive transformation of germinal centers. Comparison of 23 pediatric patients to the adult population. Mod Pathol 1992, **5:** 135–140.

68 Poppema S, Kaiserling E, Lennert K. Hodgkin's disease with lymphocytic predominance, nodular type (nodular paragranuloma) and progressively transformed germinal centers. A cytohistological study. Histopathology 1979, **3:** 295–308.

69 Poppema S, Kaiserling E, Lennert K. Nodular paragranuloma and progressively transformed germinal centers. Ultrastructural and immunohistologic findings. Virchows Arch [Cell Pathol] 1979, **31:** 211–225.

70 Stein H, Gerdes J, Mason DY. The normal and malignant germinal centre. Clin Hematol 1982, **11:** 531–559.

71 Yamakawa M, Ikeda I, Masuda A, Enomoto H, Ando A, Kasajima T. An unusual regressive germinal center, the "FDC-only lymphoid follicle", in lymph nodes or organ transplant recipients. Am J Surg Pathol 1999, **23:** 536–545.

Mantle/marginal zone hyperplasia

72 Hunt JP, Chan JA, Samoszuk M, Brynes RK, Hernandez AM, Bass R, Weisenburger DD, Müller-Hermelink K, Nathwani BN. Hyperplasia of mantle/marginal zone B-cells with clear cytoplasm in peripheral lymph nodes. A clinicopathologic study of 35 cases. Am J Clin Pathol 2001, **116:** 550–559.

Paracortical hyperplasia

73 van den Oord JJ, de Wolf-Peeters C, Desmet VJ, Takahashi K, Ohtsuki Y, Akagi T. Nodular alteration of the paracortical area. An in situ immunohistochemical analysis of primary, secondary, and tertiary T-nodules. Am J Pathol 1985, **120:** 55–66.

Granulomatous inflammation

74 Gorton G, Linell F. Malignant tumours and sarcoid reactions in regional lymph nodes. Acta Radiol (Stockh) 1957, **47:** 381–392.

75 Hall PA, Kingston J, Stansfeld AG. Extensive necrosis in malignant lymphoma with granulomatous reaction mimicking tuberculosis. Histopathology 1988, **13:** 339–346.

76 Hollingsworth HC, Longo DL, Jaffe ES. Small noncleaved cell lymphoma associated with florid epithelioid granulomatous response. A clinicopathologic study of seven patients. Am J Surg Pathol 1993, **17:** 51–59.

77 Ioachim HL (ed.). Pathology of granulomas. New York, 1983, Raven Press.

78 Kadin ME, Donaldson SS, Dorfman RF. Isolated granulomas in Hodgkin's disease. N Engl J Med 1970, **283:** 859–861.

79 Nadel E, Ackerman LV. Lesions resembling Boeck's sarcoid. Am J Clin Pathol 1952, **20:** 952–957.

Other cell types involved in nodal hyperplasia
Monocytoid B cells

80 Aozasa K, Ohsawa M, Horiuchi K, Saeki K, Katayama S, Matsuzuka F, Yamamura T. The occurrence of monocytoid B lymphocytes in autoimmune disorders. Mod Pathol 1993, **6:** 121–124.

81 Kojima M, Hosomura Y, Itoh H, Johshita T, Ohno Y, Yoshida K, Asano S, Wakasa H, Nakamura S, Suchi T. Monocytoid B lymphocytes and epithelioid cell clusters in abscess-forming granulomatous lymphadenitis. With special reference to cat scratch disease. Acta Pathol Jpn 1991, **41:** 363–368.

82 Ohsawa M, Kanno H, Naka N, Aozasa K. Occurrence of monocytoid B lymphocytes in Hodgkin's disease. Mod Pathol 1994, **7:** 540–543.

83 Plank L, Hansmann ML, Fischer R. The cytological spectrum of the monocytoid B-cell reaction. Recognition of its large cell type. Histopathology 1993, **23:** 425–431.

84 Sheibani K, Fritz RM, Winberg CD, Burke JS, Rappaport H. "Monocytoid" cells in reactive follicular hyperplasia with and without multifocal histiocytic reactions. An immunohistochemical study of 21 cases including suspected cases of toxoplasmic lymphadenitis. Am J Clin Pathol 1984, **81:** 453–458.

85 Shin SS, Sheibani K. Monocytoid B-cell lymphoma. Am J Clin Pathol 1993, **99:** 421–425.

86 van den Oord JJ, de Wolf-Peeters C, De Vos R, Desmet VJ. Immature sinus histiocytosis. Light- and electron-microscopic features, immunologic phenotype, and relationship with marginal zone lymphocytes. Am J Pathol 1985, **118:** 266–277.

Plasmacytoid monocytes

87 Facchetti F, de Wolf-Peeters C, Mason DY, Pulford K, van den Oord JJ, Desmet VJ. Plasmacytoid T-cells. Immunohistochemical evidence for their monocyte/macrophage origin. Am J Pathol 1988, **133:** 15–21.

88 Facchetti F, de Wolf-Peeters C, de Vos R, van den Oord JJ, Pulford KA, Desmet VJ. Plasmacytoid monocytes (so-called plasmacytoid T-cells) in granulomatous lymphadenitis. Hum Pathol 1989, **20:** 588–593.

89 Facchetti F, de Wolf-Peeters C, van den Oord JJ, de Vos R, Desmet VJ. Plasmacytoid monocytes (so-called plasmacytoid T-cells) in Kikuchi's lymphadenitis. An immunohistologic study. Am J Clin Pathol 1989, **92:** 42–50.

90 Hansmann ML, Kikuchi M, Wacker HH, Radzun HJ, Nathwani BN, Hesse K, Parwaresch MR. Immunohistochemical monitoring of plasmacytoid cells in lymph node sections of Kikuchi-Fujimoto disease by a new panmacrophage antibody Ki-MIP. Hum Pathol 1992, **23:** 676–680.

91 Koo CH, Mason DY, Miller R, Ben-Ezra J, Sheibani K, Rappaport H. Additional evidence that "plasmacytoid T-cell lymphoma" associated with chronic myeloproliferative disorders is of macrophage/monocyte origin. Am J Clin Pathol 1990, **93:** 822–827.

92 Müller-Hermelink HK, Stein H, Steinmann G, Lennert K. Malignant lymphoma of plasmacytoid T-cells. Morphologic and immunologic studies characterizing a special type of T-cell. Am J Surg Pathol 1983, **7:** 849–862.

93 Prasthofer EF, Grizzle WE, Prchal JT, Grossi CE. Plasmacytoid T-cell lymphoma associated with chronic myeloproliferative disorder. Am J Surg Pathol 1985, **9:** 380–387.

94 Vollenweider R, Lennert K. Plasmacytoid T-cell clusters in nonspecific lymphadenitis. Virchows Arch [Cell Pathol] 1983, **44:** 1–14.

Polykaryocytes

95 Kjeldsberg CR, Kim H. Polykaryocytes resembling Warthin-Finkeldey giant cells in reactive and neoplastic lymphoid disorders. Hum Pathol 1981, **12:** 267–272.

96 Orenstein JM. The Warthin–Finkeldey-type giant T-cell in HIV infection, what is it? Ultrastruct Pathol 1998, **22:** 293–303.

Inflammatory/hyperplastic diseases
Necrotizing lymphadenitis

97 Chamulak GA, Brynes RK, Nathwani BN. Kikuchi-Fujimoto disease mimicking malignant lymphoma. Am J Surg Pathol 1990, **14:** 514–523.

98 Chan JKC, Saw D. Histiocytic necrotizing lymphadenitis (Kikuchi's disease). A clinicopathologic study of 9 cases. Pathology 1986, **18:** 22–28.

99 Chan JK, Luk SC, Ho PL. Stroma-rich Castleman's disease with superimposed Kikuchi's lymphadenitis-like changes. Int J Surg Pathol 1996-97, **4:** 197–202.

100 Chan JK, Wong KC, Ng CS. A fatal case of multicentric Kikuchi's histiocytic necrotizing lymphadenitis. Cancer 1989, **63:** 1856–1862.

101 Chiu CF, Chow KC, Lin TY, Tsai MH, Shih CM, Chen LM. Virus infection in patients with histiocytic necrotizing lymphadenitis in Taiwan, detection of Epstein virus, type 1 human T-cell lymphotropic virus, and parvovirus B19. Am J Clin Pathol 2000, **113:** 774–781.

102 Dorfman RF, Berry GJ. Kikuchi's histiocytic necrotizing lymphadenitis. An analysis of 108 cases with emphasis on differential diagnosis. Semin Diagn Pathol 1988, **5:** 329–345.

103 Eimoto T, Kikuchi M, Mitsui T. Histiocytic necrotizing lymphadenitis. An ultrastructural study in comparison with other types of lymphadenitis. Acta Pathol Jpn 1983, **33:** 863–879.

104 Facchetti F, de Wolf-Peeters C, van den Oord JJ, de Vos R, Desmet VJ. Plasmacytoid monocytes (so-called plasmacytoid T-cells) in Kikuchi's lymphadenitis. An immunohistologic study. Am J Clin Pathol 1989, **92:** 42–50.

105 Felgar RE, Furth EE, Wasik MA, Gluckman SJ, Salhany KE. Histiocytic necrotizing lymphadenitis (Kikuchi's disease): in situ end-labeling, immunohistochemical, and serologic evidence supporting cytotoxic lymphocyte-mediated apoptotic cell death. Mod Pathol 1997, **10:** 231–241.

106 Hollingsworth HC, Peiper SC, Weiss LM, Raffeld M, Jaffe ES. An investigation of the viral pathogenesis of Kikuchi-Fujimoto disease. Lack of evidence for Epstein–Barr virus or human herpesvirus type 6 as the causative agents. Arch Pathol Lab Med 1994, **118:** 134–140.

107 Huh J, Kang GH, Gong G, Kim SS, Ro JY, Kim CW. Kaposi's sarcoma-associated herpesvirus in Kikuchi's disease. Hum Pathol 1998, **29:** 1091–1096.

108 Kuo TT. Cutaneous manifestation of Kikuchi's histiocytic necrotizing lymphadenitis. Am J Surg Pathol 1990, **14:** 872–876.

109 Kuo TT. Kikuchi's disease (histiocytic necrotizing lymphadenitis). A clinicopathologic study of 79 cases with an analysis of histologic subtypes, immunohistology, and DNA ploidy. Am J Surg Pathol 1995, **19:** 798–809.

110 Lin HC, Su CY, Huang CC, Hwang CF, Chien CY. Kikuchi's disease: a review and analysis of 61 cases. Otolaryngol Head Neck Surg 2003, **128:** 650–653.

111 Menasce LP, Banerjee SS, Edmondson D, Harris M. Histiocytic necrotizing lymphadenitis (Kikuchi–Fujimoto disease): continuing diagnostic difficulties. Histopathology 1998, **33:** 248–254.

112 Pileri S, Kikuchi M, Lennert K. Histiocytic necrotizing lymphadenitis without granulocytic infiltration. Virchows Arch [A] 1982, **395:** 257–271.

113 Spies J, Foucar K, Thompson CT, LeBoit PE. The Histopathology of cutaneous lesions of Kikuchi's disease (necrotizing lymphadenitis): a report of five cases. Am J Surg Pathol 1999, **23:** 1040–1047.

114 Sumiyoshi Y, Kikuchi M, Ohshima K, Yoneda S, Kobari S, Takeshita M, Eizuru Y, Minamishima Y. Human herpesvirus-6

genomes in histiocytic necrotizing lymphadenitis (Kikuchi's disease) and other forms of lymphadenitis. Am J Clin Pathol 1993, **99**: 609–614.

115 Sumiyoshi Y, Kikuchi M, Takeshita M, Ohshima K, Masuda Y, Parwaresch MR. Immunohistologic studies of Kikuchi's disease. Hum Pathol 1993, **24**: 1114–1119.

116 Takakuwa T, Ohnuma S, Koike J, Hoshikawa M, Koizumi H. Involvement of cell-mediated killing in apoptosis in histiocytic necrotizing lymphadenitis (Kikuchi–Fujimoto disease). Histopathology 1996, **28**: 41–48.

117 Tsang WY, Chan JK. Fine needle aspiration cytologic diagnosis of Kikuchi's lymphadenitis. A report of 27 cases. Am J Clin Pathol 1994, **102**: 454–458.

118 Tsang WY, Chan JK, Ng CS. Kikuchi's lymphadenitis. A morphologic analysis of 75 cases with special reference to unusual features. Am J Surg Pathol 1994, **18**: 219–231.

119 Turner RR, Martin J, Dorfman RF. Necrotizing lymphadenitis. A study of 30 cases. Am J Surg Pathol 1983, **7**: 115–123.

120 Yoshino T, Mannami T, Ichimura K, Takenata K, Nose S, Yamadori I, Akagi T. Two cases of histiocytic necrotizing lymphadenitis (Kikuchi–Fujimoto's disease) following diffuse large B-cell lymphoma. Hum Pathol 2000, **31**: 1328–1331.

Chronic nonspecific lymphadenitis

121 Cozzutto C, Soave F. Xanthogranulomatous lymphadenitis. Virchows Arch [A] 1979, **385**: 103–108.

122 McCluggage WG, Walsh MY, Bharucha H. Anaplastic large cell malignant lymphoma with extensive eosinophilic or neutrophilic infiltration. Histopathology 1998, **32**: 110–115.

Tuberculosis

123 Ikonomopoulos JA, Gorgoulis VG, Zacharatos PV, Kanavaros P, Rassidakis A, Kittas C. Multiplex polymerase chain reaction for the detection of mycobacterial DNA in cases of tuberculosis and sarcoidosis. Mod Pathol 1999, **12**: 854–862.

124 Moore SW, Schneider JW, Schaaf HS. Diagnostic aspects of cervical lymphadenopathy in children in the developing world: a study of 1877 surgical specimens. Pediatr Surg Int 2003, **19**: 240–244.

Atypical mycobacteriosis

125 Kraus M, Benharroch D, Kaplan D, Sion-Vardy N, Leiberman A, Dima H, Shoham I, Fliss DM. Mycobacterial cervical lymphadenitis; this histological features of non-tuberculous mycobacterial infection. Histopathology 2000, **35**: 534–538.

126 Logani S, Lucas DR, Cheng JD, Iochim HL, Adsay NV. Spindle cell tumors associated with mycobacteria in lymph nodes of HIV-positive patients: 'Kaposi sarcoma with mycobacteria' and 'mycobacterial pseudotumor'. Am J Surg Pathol 1999, **23**: 656–661.

127 Mackellar A, Hilton HB, Masters PL. Mycobacterial lymphadenitis in childhood. Arch Dis Child 1967, **42**: 70–74.

128 Pinder SE, Colville A. Mycobacterial cervical lymphadenitis in children. Can histological assessment help differentiate infections caused by nontuberculous mycobacteria from *Mycobacterium tuberculosis*? Histopathology 1993, **22**: 59–64.

129 Reid JD, Wolinsky E. Histopathology of lymphadenitis caused by atypical mycobacteria. Am Rev Respir Dis 1969, **99**: 8–12.

130 Smith MB, Molina CP, Schnadig VJ, Boyars MC, Aronson JF. Pathologic features of mycobacterium kansasii infection in patients with acquired immunodeficiency syndrome. Arch Pathol Lab Med 2003, **127**: 554–557.

Sarcoidosis

131 Baughman RP, Lower EE, Du Bois RM. Sarcoidosis. Lancet 2003, **361**: 1111–1118.

132 Chilosi M, Menestrina F, Capelli P, Montagna L, Lestani M, Pizzolo G, Cipriani A, Agostini C, Trentin L, Zambello R, Semenzato G. Immunohistochemical analysis of sarcoid granulomas. Evaluation of Ki-67+ and interleukin-1+ cells. Am J Pathol 1988, **131**: 191–198.

133 Collison JM, Miller NR, Green WR. Involvement of orbital tissues by sarcoid. Am J Ophthalmol 1986, **102**: 302–307.

134 Cunningham JA. Sarcoidosis. Pathol Annu 1967, **2**: 31–46.

135 Cushard WG Jr, Simon AB, Caterbury JM, Reiss E. Parathyroid function in sarcoidosis. N Engl J Med 1972, **286**: 395–398.

136 Devaney K, Goodman ZD, Epstein MS, Zimmerman HJ, Ishak KG. Hepatic sarcoidosis. Clinicopathologic features in 100 patients. Am J Surg Pathol 1993, **17**: 1272–1280.

137 Devergne O, Emilie D, Peuchmaur M, Crevon MC, D'Agay MF, Galanaud P. Production of cytokines in sarcoid lymph nodes. Preferential expression of interleukin-1 β and interferon-gamma genes. Hum Pathol 1992, **23**: 317–323.

138 Du Bois RM, Goh N, McGrath D, Cullinan P. Is there a role for microorganisms in the pathogenesis of sarcoidosis? J Intern Med 2003, **253**: 4–17.

139 Fidler HM. Mycobacteria and sarcoidosis. Recent advances. Sarcoidosis 1994, **11**: 66–68.

140 Fink SD, Kremer JM. Cutaneous and musculoskeletal features, diagnostic modalities, and immunopathology in sarcoidosis. Curr Opin Rheumatol 1994, **6**: 78–81.

141 Gardner J, Kennedy HG, Hamblin A, Jones E. HLA associations in sarcoidosis. A study of two ethnic groups. Thorax 1984, **39**: 19–22.

142 Ghossein RA, Ross DG, Salomon RN, Rabson AR. A search for mycobacterial DNA in sarcoidosis using the polymerase chain reaction. Am J Clin Pathol 1994, **101**: 733–737.

143 Ikonomopoulos JA, Gorgoulis VG, Zacharatos PV, Kanavaros P, Rassidakis A, Kittas C. Multiplex polymerase chain reaction for the detection of mycobacterial DNA in cases of tuberculosis and sarcoidosis. Mod Pathol 1999, **12**: 854–862.

144 James DG, Williams WJ. Immunology of sarcoidosis. Am J Med 1982, **72**: 5–8.

145 Kim YC, Triffet M, Gibson LE. Foreign bodies in sarcoidosis. Am J Dermatopathol 2001, **22**: 408–412.

146 Kirkpatrick CJ, Curry A, Bisset DL. Light- and electron-microscopic studies on multinucleated giant cells in sarcoid granuloma. New aspects of asteroid and Schaumann bodies. Ultrastruct Pathol 1988, **12**: 581–597.

147 Li N, Bajoghli A, Kubba A, Bhawan J. Identification of mycobacterial DNA in cutaneous lesions of sarcoidosis. J Cutan Pathol 1999, **26**: 271–278.

148 Määtta KT. Histological study of mediastinal lymph nodes in clinical sarcoidosis. A report of 86 cases. Ann Acad Sci Fenn (Med.) 1968, **138**: 1–106.

149 Nethercott SE, Strawbridge WG. Identification of bacterial residues in sarcoid lesions. Lancet 1956, **2**: 1132.

150 Newman LS, Rose CS, Maier LA. Sarcoidosis. N Engl J Med 1997, **336**: 1224–1234.

151 Popper HH, Klemen H, Hoefler G, Winter E. Presence of mycobacterial DNA in sarcoidosis. Hum Pathol 1997, **28**: 796–800.

152 Reid JD, Andersen ME. Calcium oxalate in sarcoid granulomas. With particular reference to the small ovoid body and a note on the finding of dolomite. Am J Clin Pathol 1988, **90**: 545–558.

153 Roman J, Galis ZS. Sarcoidosis: a mysterious tale of inflammation, tissue remodelling, and matrix metalloproteinases. Hum Pathol 2003, **33**: 1155–1157.

154 Rosen Y, Vuletin JC, Pertschuk LP, Silverstein E. Sarcoidosis. From the pathologist's vantage point. Pathol Annu 1979, **14**(Pt 1): 405–439.

155 Sieracki JC, Fisher ER. The ceroid nature of the so-called "Hamazaki-Wesenberg bodies." Am J Clin Pathol 1973, **59**: 248–253.

156 Siltzbach LE. Geographic aspects of sarcoidosis. Trans NY Acad Sci 29(Series II): 1967, 364–374.

157 Tudway AJC. Yellow bodies in superficial and deep lymph nodes. J Clin Pathol 1979, **32**: 52–55.

158 Vanék J, Schwarz J. Demonstration of acid-fast rods in sarcoidosis. Am Rev Respir Dis 1970, **101**: 395–400.

159 Wesenberg W. Saurefeste, Spindelkorper Hamazaki bei Sarkoidose. Arch Klin Exp Med 1966, **227**: 101–112.

160 Winnacker JL, Becker KL, Friedlander M, Higgins GA, Moore CF. Sarcoidosis and hyperparathyroidism. Am J Med 1969, **46**: 305–312.

161 Zeimer HJ, Greenaway TM, Slavin J, Hards DK, Zhou H, Doery JCG, Hunter AN, Duffield A, Martin TJ, Grill V. Parathyroid-hormone-related protein in sarcoidosis. Am J Pathol 1998, **152**: 17–21.

Fungal infections

162 Brook I, Frazier EH. Microbiology of cervical lymphadenitis in adults. Acta Otolaryngol 1998, **118**: 443–446.

Toxoplasmosis

163 Bastien P. Molecular diagnosis of toxoplasmosis. Trans R Soc Trop Med Hyg 2002, **96**: S205–215.

164 Dorfman RF, Remington JS. Value of lymph-node biopsy in the diagnosis of acute acquired toxoplasmosis. N Engl J Med 1973, **289**: 878–881.

165 Frenkel JK. Toxoplasmosis. Mechanisms of infection, laboratory diagnosis and management. Curr Top Pathol 1971, **54**: 28–75.

166 Hill D, Dubey JP. *Toxoplasma gondii*: transmission, diagnosis and prevention. Clin Microbiol Infect 2002, **8**: 634–640.

167 McCabe RE, Brooks RG, Dorfman RF, Remington JS. Clinical spectrum in 107 cases of toxoplasmic lymphadenopathy. Rev Infect Dis 1987, **9**: 754–774.

168 Miettinen M, Franssila K. Malignant lymphoma simulating lymph node toxoplasmosis. Histopathology 1982, **6**: 129–140.

169 Saxen L, Saxen E, Tenhunen A. The significance of histological diagnosis in glandular toxoplasmosis. Acta Pathol Microbiol Scand 1962, **56**: 284–294.

170 Weiss LM, Chen YY, Berry GJ, Strickler JG, Dorfman RF, Warnke RA. Infrequent detection of *Toxoplasma gondii* genome in toxoplasmic lymphadenitis. A polymerase chain reaction study. Hum Pathol 1992, **23**: 154–158.

Syphilis

171 Choi YJ, Reiner L. Syphilitic lymphadenitis. Immunofluorescent identification of spirochetes from imprints. Am J Surg Pathol 1979, **3**: 553–555.

172 Farhi DC, Wells SJ, Siegel RJ. Syphilitic lymphadenopathy. Histology and human immunodeficiency virus status. Am J Clin Pathol 1999, **112**: 330–334.

173 Hartsock RJ, Halling W, King FM. Luetic lymphadenitis. A clinical and histologic study of 20 cases. Am J Clin Pathol 1970, **53**: 304–314.

174 Kouznetsov AV, Prinz JC. Molecular diagnosis of syphilis: the Schaudinn–Hoffmann lymph-node biopsy. Lancet 2002, **360**: 388–389.

Leprosy

175 Nayak SV, Shirvarudrapa AS, Mukkamil AS. Role of fluorescent microscopy in detecting mycobacterium leprae in tissue sections. Ann Diagn Pathol 2003, **7**: 78–81.

176 Rastogi N, Goh KS, Berchel M. Species-specific identification of mycobacterium leprae by PCR-restriction fragment length polymorphism analysis of the hsp65 gene. J Clin Microbiol 1999, **37**: 2016–2019.

Mesenteric lymphadenitis

177 Ahlqvist J, Ahvohen P, Rasanen JA, Wallgren GR. Enteric infection with *Yersinia enterocolitica*. Large pyroninophilic cell reaction in mesenteric lymph nodes associated with early production of specific antibodies. Acta Pathol Microbiol Scand (A) 1971, **79**: 109–122.

178 Cover TL, Aber RC. *Yersinia enterocolitica*. N Engl J Med 1989, **321**: 16–24.

179 Jansson E, Wallgren GR, Ahvenen P. *Y. enterocolitica* as a cause of acute mesenteric lymphadenitis. Acta Paediatr Scand 1968, **57**: 448–450.

180 Knapp W. Mesenteric adenitis due to Pasteurella pseudotubercolosis in young people. N Engl J Med 1958, **259**: 776–778.

181 Lamps LW, Madhsudhan KT, Havens JM, Greenson JK, Bronner MP, Chiles MC, Dean PJ, Scott MA. Pathogenic yersinia DNA is detected in bowel and mesenteric lymph nodes from patients from Crohn's disease. Am J Surg Pathol 2003, **27**: 220–227.

182 Nilthn B. Studies on *Yersinia enterocolitica* with special reference to bacterial diagnosis and occurrence in human enteric disease. Acta Pathol Microbiol Scand (Suppl) 1969, **206**: 1–48.

183 Schapers RFM, Reif R, Lennert K, Knapp W. Mesenteric lymphadenitis due to *Yersinia enterocolitica*. Virchows Arch [A] 1981, **390**: 127–138.

Cat-scratch disease

184 Adal KA, Cockerell CJ, Petri WA Jr. Cat scratch disease, bacillary angiomatosis, and other infections due to *Rochalimaea*. N Engl J Med 1994, **330**: 1509–1515.

185 Carithers HA. Cat-scratch disease. An overview based on a study of 1,200 patients. Am J Dis Child 1985, **139**: 1124–1133.

186 Carithers HA, Carithers CM, Edwards RO, Jr. Cat-scratch disease. Its natural history. JAMA 1969, **207**: 312–316.

187 Dorfman RF, Warnke R. Lymphadenopathy simulating the malignant lymphomas. Hum Pathol 1974, **5**: 519–550.

188 English CK, Wear DJ, Margileth AM, Lissner CR, Walsh GP. Cat-scratch disease. Isolation and culture of the bacterial agent. JAMA 1988, **259**: 1347–1352.

189 Johnson WT, Helwig EB. Cat-scratch disease. Histopathologic changes in the skin. Arch Dermatol 1969, **100**: 148–154.

190 Kojima M, Hosomura Y, Itoh H, Johshita T, Ohno Y, Yoshida K, Asano S, Wakasa H, Nakamura S, Suchi T. Monocytoid B lymphocytes and epithelioid cell clusters in abscess-forming granulomatous lymphadenitis. With special reference to cat scratch disease. Acta Pathol Jpn 1991, **41**: 363–368.

191 Kojima M, Nakamura S, Hosomura Y, Shimizu K, Kurabayashi Y, Itoh H, Yoshida K, Ohno Y, Kaneko A, Asano S, et al. Abscess-forming granulomatous lymphadenitis. Histological typing of suppurative granulomas and clinicopathological findings with special reference to cat scratch disease. Acta Pathol Jpn 1993, **43**: 11–17.

192 Miller-Catchpole R, Variakojis D, Vardiman JW, Loew JM, Carter J. Cat scratch disease. Identification of bacteria in seven cases of lymphadenitis. Am J Surg Pathol 1986, **10**: 276–281.

193 Osborne BM, Butler JJ, Mackay B. Ultrastructural observations in cat scratch disease. Am J Clin Pathol 1987, **87**: 739–744.

194 Scott MA, McCurley TL, Vnencak-Jones CL, Hager C, McCoy JA, Anderson B, Collins RD, Edwards KM. Cat-scratch disease, detection of *Bartonella henselae* DNA in archival biopsies from patients with clinically, serologically, and histologically defined disease. Am J Pathol 1997, 149: 2161–2167.

195 Wear DJ, Hadfield TL, Fisher FW, Schlagel CJ, King FM. Cat scratch disease. A bacterial infection. Science 1983, **221**: 1403–1405.

196 Windsor JJ. Cat-scratch disease: epidemiology, aetiology and treatment. Br J Biomed Sci 2001, **58**: 101–110.

197 Winship T. Pathologic changes in so-called cat-scratch fever. Review of findings in lymph nodes of 29 patients and cutaneous lesions in two patients. Am J Clin Pathol 1953, **23**: 1012–1018.

Lymphogranuloma venereum

198 Joseph AK, Rosen T. Laboratory techniques used in the diagnosis of chancroid, granuloma inguinale, and lymphogranuloma venereum. Dermatol Clin 1994, **12:** 1–8.

199 Mabey D, Peeling RW. Lymphogranloma venereum. Sex Transm Infect 2002, **78:** 90–92.

200 Mittal A, Sachdeva KG. Monoclonal antibody for the diagnosis of lymphogranuloma venereum. A preliminary report. Br J Biomed Sci 1993, **50:** 3–7.

201 Smith EB, Custer RP. The histopathology of lymphogranuloma venereum. J Urol 1950, **63:** 546–563.

202 Van Dyck E, Piot P. Laboratory techniques in the investigation of chancroid, lymphogranuloma venereum and donovanosis. Genitourin Med 1992, **68:** 130–133.

Tularemia

203 Ellis J, Oyston PC, Green M, Titball RW. Tularemia. Clin Microbiol Rev 2002, **15:** 631–646.

204 Evans ME, Gregory DW, Schaffner W, McGee ZA. Tularemia. A 30-year experience with 88 cases. Medicine (Baltimore) 1985, **64:** 251–267.

205 Ohara Y, Sato T, Fujita H, Ueno T, Homma M. Clinical manifestations of tularemia in Japan – analysis of 1,355 cases observed between 1924 and 1987. Infection 1991, **19:** 14–17.

206 Sato T, Fujita H, Ohara Y, Homma M. Microagglutination test for early and specific serodiagnosis of tularemia. J Clin Microbiol 1990, **28:** 2372–2374.

207 Sutinen S, Syrjala H. Histopathology of human lymph node tularemia caused by *Francisella tularensis* var *palaearctica*. Arch Pathol Lab Med 1986, **110:** 42–46.

208 Tarnvik A, Berglund L. Tularaemia. Eur Respir J 2003, **21:** 361–373.

209 Tjaden JA, Lazarus AA, Martin GJ. Bacteria as agents of biowarfare. How to proceed when the worst is suspected. Postgrad Med 2002, **112:** 67–70.

Brucellosis

210 Chomel BB, De Bess EE, Mangiamele DM, Reilly KF, Farver TB, Sun RK, Barrett LR. Changing trends in the epidemiology of human brucellosis in California from 1973 to 1992. A shift toward foodborne transmission. J Infect Dis 1994, **170:** 1216–1223.

211 Namiduru M, Gungor K, Dikensoy O, Baydar I, Ekinci E, Karaoglar, Bekir NA. Epidemiological, clinical and laboratory features of brucellosis a prospective evaluation of 120 adult patients. Int J Clin Pathol 2003, **57:** 20–24.

212 Nimri LF. Diagnosis of recent and relapsed cases of human brucellosis by PCR assay. BMC Infect Dis 2003, **3:** 5.

213 Trujillo IZ, Zavala AN, Caceres JG, Miranda CQ. Brucellosis. Infect Dis Clin North Am 1994, **8:** 225–241.

214 Weed LA, Dahlin DC. Bacteriologic examination of tissues removed for biopsy. Am J Clin Pathol 1950, **20:** 116–132.

AIDS-related lymphadenopathy

215 Abrams DI. Lymphadenopathy syndrome in male homosexuals. Adv Host Def Mechan 1985, **5:** 75–97.

216 Baroni CD, Uccini S. The lymphadenopathy of HIV infection. Am J Clin Pathol 1993, **99:** 397–401.

217 Burns BF, Wood GS, Dorfman RF. The varied histopathology of lymphadenopathy in the homosexual male. Am J Surg Pathol 1985, **9:** 287–297.

218 Chadburn A, Metroka C, Mouradian J. Progressive lymph node histology and its prognostic value in patients with acquired immunodeficiency syndrome and AIDS-related complex. Hum Pathol 1989, **20:** 579–587.

219 Fishbein DB, Kaplan JE, Spira TJ, Miller B, Schonberger LB, Pinsky PF, Getchell JP, Kalyanaraman VS, Braude JS.

Unexplained lymphadenopathy in homosexual men. A longitudinal study. JAMA 1985, **254:** 929–935.

220 Godshall SE, Kirchner JT. Infestious mononucleosis. Complexities of a common syndrome. Postgrad Med 2000, **107:** 175–186.

221 Groopman JE. Clinical symptomatology of the acquired immunodeficiency syndrome (AIDS) and related disorders. Prog Allergy 1986, **37:** 182–193.

222 Harris NL. Hypervascular follicular hyperplasia and Kaposi's sarcoma in patients at risk for AIDS. N Engl J Med 1984, **310:** 462–463.

223 Ioachim HL, Cronin W, Roy M, Maya M. Persistent lymphadenopathies in people at high risk for HIV infection. Clinicopathologic correlations and long-term follow-up in 79 cases. Am J Clin Pathol 1990, **93:** 208–218.

224 Logani S, Lucas DR, Cheng JD, Iochim HL, Adsay NV. Spindle cell tumors associated with mycobacteria in lymph nodes of HIV-positive patients: 'Kaposi sarcoma with mycobacteria' and 'mycobacterial pseudotumor'. Am J Surg Pathol 1999, **23:** 656–661.

225 O'Hara CJ, Groopman JE, Federman M. The ultrastructural and immunohistochemical demonstration of viral particles in lymph nodes from human immunodeficiency virus-related and nonhuman immunodeficiency virus-related lymphadenopathy syndromes. Hum Pathol 1988, **19:** 545–549.

226 Orenstein JM. The Warthin–Finkeldey-type giant T-cell in HIV infection, what is it? Ultrastruct Pathol 1998, **22:** 293–303.

227 Rickinson A. Epstein–Barr virus. Virus Res 2002, **82:** 109–113.

228 Said JW. AIDS-related lymphadenopathies. Semin Diagn Pathol 1988, **5:** 365–375.

229 Said JW, Pinkus JL, Yamashita J, Mishalani S, Matsumura F, Yamashiro S, Pinkus GS. The role of follicular and interdigitating dendritic cells in HIV-related lymphoid hyperplasia: localization of fascin. Mod Pathol 1997, **10:** 421–427.

230 Schuurman H-J, Kluin PM, Gmelig Meijling FHJ, Van Unnik JAM, Kater L. Lymphocyte status of lymph node and blood in acquired immunodeficiency syndrome (AIDS) and AIDS-related complex disease. J Pathol 1985, **147:** 269–280.

231 Tacchetti C, Favre A, Moresco L, Meszaros P, Luzzi P, Truini M, Rizzo F, Grossi CE, Ciccone E. HIV is trapped and masked in the cytoplasm of lymph node follicular dendritic cells. Am J Pathol 1997, **150:** 533–542.

232 Umlas J, Federman M, Crawford C, O'Hara CJ, Fitzgibbon JS, Modeste A. Spindle cell pseudotumor due to *Mycobacterium avium-intracellulare* in patients with acquired immunodeficiency syndrome (AIDS). Positive staining of mycobacteria for cytoskeleton filaments. Am J Surg Pathol 1991, **15:** 1181–1187.

233 Westermann CD, Hurtubise PE, Linnemann CC, Swerdlow SH. Comparison of histologic nodal reactive patterns, cell suspension immunophenotypic data, and HIV status. Mod Pathol 1990, **3:** 54–60.

234 Wood GS, Garcia CF, Dorfman RF, Warnke RA. The immunohistology of follicle lysis in lymph node biopsies from homosexual men. Blood 1985, **66:** 1092–1097.

Infectious mononucleosis

235 Frizzera G, Hanto DW, Gajl-Peczalska KJ, Rosai J, McKenna RW, Sibley RK, Holahan KP, Lindquist LL. Polymorphic diffuse B-cell hyperplasias and lymphomas in renal transplant recipients. Cancer Res 1981, **41:** 4262–4279.

236 Gulley ML. Molecular diagnosis of Epstein–Barr virus-related diseases. J Mol Diagn 2001, **3:** 1–10.

237 McMahon NJ, Gordon HW, Rosen RB. Reed–Sternberg cells in infectious mononucleosis. Am J Dis Child 1970, **120:** 148–150.

238 Reynolds DJ, Banks PM, Gulley ML. New characterization of infectious mononucleosis and a phenotypic comparison with Hodgkin's disease. Am J Pathol 1995, **146:** 379–388.

239 Salvador AH, Harrison EG, Kyle RA. Lymphadenopathy due to infectious mononucleosis. Its confusion with malignant lymphoma. Cancer 1971, **27**: 1029–1040.

240 Shin SS, Berry GJ, Weiss LM. Infectious mononucleosis. Diagnosis by in situ hybridization in two cases with atypical features. Am J Surg Pathol 1991, **15**: 625–631.

241 Sieracki JC, Fisher ER. Diagnostic problems involving nodal lymphomas. Pathol Annu 1970, **5**: 91–124.

242 Strickler JG, Fedeli F, Horwitz CA, Copenhaver CM, Frizzera G. Infectious mononucleosis in lymphoid tissue. Histopathology, in situ hybridization, and differential diagnosis. Arch Pathol Lab Med 1993, **117**: 269–278.

243 Tindle BH, Parker JW, Lukes RJ. "Reed–Sternberg cells" in infectious mononucleosis? Am J Clin Pathol 1972, **58**: 607–617.

Other viral (including postvaccinial) lymphadenitides

244 Audouin J, Le Tourneau A, Aubert J-P, Diebold J. Herpes simplex virus lymphadenitis mimicking tumoral relapse in a patient with Hodgkin's disease in remission. Virchows Arch [A] 1985, **408**: 313–321.

245 Dorfman RF, Herweg JC. Live, attenuated measles virus vaccine. Inguinal lymphadenopathy complicating administration. JAMA 1966, **198**: 320–321.

246 Gaffey MJ, Ben-Ezra JM, Weiss LM. Herpes simplex lymphadenitis. Am J Clin Pathol 1991, **95**: 709–714.

247 Hartsock RJ. Postvaccinial lymphadenitis. Hyperplasia of lymphoid tissue that simulates malignant lymphomas. Cancer 1968, **21**: 632–649.

248 Howat AJ, Campbell AR, Stewart DJ. Generalized lymphadenopathy due to herpes simplex virus type I. Histopathology 1991, **19**: 563–564.

249 Lapsley M, Kettle P, Sloan JM. Herpes simplex lymphadenitis. A case report and review of the published work. J Clin Pathol 1984, **37**: 1119–1122.

250 Miliauskas JR, Leong AS. Localized herpes simplex lymphadenitis. Report of three cases and review of the literature. Histopathology 1991, **19**: 355–360.

251 Tamaru J, Mikata A, Horie H, Itoh K, Asai T, Hondo R, Mori S. Herpes simplex lymphadenitis. Report of two cases with review of the literature. Am J Surg Pathol 1990, **14**: 571–577.

252 Witt MD, Torno MS, Sun N, Stein T. Herpes simplex virus lymphadenitis: case report and review of the literature. Clin Infect Dis 2002, **34**: 1–6.

Mucocutaneous lymph node syndrome

253 Beitz LO, Barron KS. Kawasaki syndrome. Curr Opin Dermatol 1995, 114–122.

254 Burns JC. Kawasaki disease: the mystery continues. Minerva Pediatr 2002, **54**: 287–294.

255 Giesker DW, Krause PJ, Pastuszak WT, Hine P, Forouhar FA. Lymph node biopsy for early diagnosis in Kawasaki disease. Am J Surg Pathol 1982, **6**: 493–501.

256 Marsh WL, Bishop JW, Koenig HM. Bone marrow and lymph node findings in a fatal case of Kawasaki's disease. Arch Pathol Lab Med 1980, **104**: 563–567.

257 Stamos JK, Corydon K, Donaldson J, Shulman ST. Lymphadenitis as the dominant manifestation of Kawasaki disease. Pediatrics 1994, **93**: 525–528.

Lupus erythematosus

257a Hu S, Kuo T-t, Hong H-S. Lupus lymphadenitis simulating Kikuchi's lymphadenitis in patients with systemic lupus erythematosus: a clinicopathological analysis of six cases and review of the literature. Pathol Int 2003, **53**: 221–226.

258 Kojima M, Nakamura S, Itoh H, Yoshida K, Asano S, Yamane N, Komatsumoto S, Ban S, Joshita T, Suchi T. Systemic lupus

erythematosus (SLE) lymphadenopathy presenting with histopathologic features of Castleman's disease, a clinicopathologic study of five cases. Pathol Res Pract 1997, **193**: 565–571.

259 Kojima M, Nakamura S, Morishita Y, Itoh H, Yoshida K, Ohno Y, Oyama T, Asano S, Joshita T, Mori S, Suchi T, Masawa N. Reactive follicular hyperplasia in the lymph node lesions from systemic lupus erythematosus patients: a clinicopathological and immunohistological study of 21 cases. Pathol Int 2000, **50**: 304–312.

260 Kubota K, Tamura J, Kurabayashi H, Yanagisawa T, Shirakura T, Mori S. Warthin-Finkeldey-like giant cells in a patient with systemic lupus erythematosus. Hum Pathol 1988, **19**: 1358–1359.

261 Medeiros LJ, Kaynor B, Harris NL. Lupus lymphadenitis. Report of a case with immunohistologic studies on frozen sections. Hum Pathol 1989, **20**: 295–299.

Rheumatoid arthritis

262 Kamel OW, van de Rijn M, Le Brun DP, Weiss LM, Warnke RA, Dorfman RF. Lymphoid neoplasms in patients with rheumatoid arthritis and dermatomyositis. Frequency of Epstein–Barr virus and other features associated with immunosuppression. Hum Pathol 1994, **25**: 638–643.

263 Kojima M, Hosomura Y, Itoh H, Johshita T, Yoshida K, Nakamura S, Suchi T. Reactive proliferative lesions in lymph nodes from rheumatoid arthritis patients. A clinicopathological and immunohistological study. Acta Pathol Jpn 1990, **40**: 249–254.

264 Kojima M, Nakamura S, Miyawaki S, Yashiro K, Oyama T, Itoh H, Sakata N, Sugihara S, Masawa N. Lymph node lesion in adult-onset Still's disease resembling peripheral T-cell lymphoma: a report of three cases. Int J Surg Pathol 2002, **10**: 197–202.

265 Nosanchuk JS, Schnitzer B. Follicular hyperplasia in lymph nodes from patients with rheumatoid arthritis. A clinicopathologic study. Cancer 1969, **24**: 343–354.

266 Robertson MDJ, Hart FD, White WF, Nuki G, Boardman PL. Rheumatoid lymphadenopathy. Ann Rheum Dis 1968, **27**: 253–260.

267 Rollins SD, Craig JP. Gold-associated lymphadenopathy in a patient with rheumatoid arthritis. Histologic and scanning electron microscopic features. Arch Pathol Lab Med 1991, **115**: 175–177.

Castleman's disease

268 Abdel-Reheim FA, Koss W, Rappaport ES, Arber DA. Coexistence of Hodgkin's disease and giant lymph node hyperplasia of the plasma-cell type (Castleman's disease). Arch Pathol Lab Med 196, **120**: 91–96.

269 Altiparmak MR, Pamuk GE, Pamuk ON, Dogusoy G. Secondary amyloidosis in Castleman's disease: review of the literature and report of a case. Ann Hematol 2002, **81**: 336–339.

270 Amin HM, Medeiros LJ, Manning JT, Jones D. Dissolution of the lymphoid follicle is a feature of the HHV8+ variant of plasma cell Castleman's disease. Am J Surg Pathol 2002, **27**: 91–100.

271 Ascoli V, Sirianni MC, Mezzaroma I, Mastroianni CM, Vullo V, Andreoni M, Narciso P, Scalzo CC, Nardi F, Pistilli A, Lo Coco F. Human herpesvirus-8 in lymphomatous and nonlymphomatous body cavity effusions developing in Kaposi's sarcoma and multicentric Castleman's disease. Ann Diagn Pathol 2000, **3**: 357–363.

272 Bowne WB, Lewis JJ, Filippa DA, Niesvizky R, Brooks AD, Burt ME, Brennan MF. The management of unicentric and multicentric Castleman's disease. A report of 16 cases and a review of the literature. Cancer 1999, **85**: 706–717.

273 Chan JK, Fletcher CD, Hicklin GA, Rosai J. Glomeruloid hemangioma. A distinctive cutaneous lesion of multicentric Castleman's disease associated with POEMS syndrome. Am J Surg Pathol 1990, **14**: 1036–1046.

274 Chan JK, Tsang WY, Ng CS. Follicular dendritic cell tumor and vascular neoplasm complicating hyaline-vascular Castleman's disease. Am J Surg Pathol 1994, **18**: 517–525.

275 Cokelaere K, Debiec-Rychter M, De Wolf-Peeters C, Hagemeijer A, Sciot R. Hyaline vascular Castleman's disease with HMGIC rearrangement in follicular dendritic cells: molecular evidence of mesenchymal tumorigenesis. Am J Surg Pathol 2002, **26**: 662–669.

276 Danon AD, Krishnan J, Frizzera G. Morpho-immunophenotypic diversity of Castleman's disease, hyaline-vascular type. With emphasis on a stroma-rich variant and a new pathogenetic hypothesis. Virchows Arch [A] 1993, **423**: 369–382.

277 Frizzera G. Castleman's disease and related disorders. Semin Diagn Pathol 1988, **5**: 346–364.

278 Frizzera G, Banks PM, Massarelli G, Rosai J. A systemic lymphoproliferative disorder with morphologic features of Castleman's disease. Pathological findings in 15 patients. Am J Surg Pathol 1983, **7**: 211–231.

279 Frizzera G, Peterson BA, Bayrd ED, Goldman A. A systemic lymphoproliferative disorder with morphologic features of Castleman's disease. Clinical findings and clinicopathologic correlations in 15 patients. J. Clin Oncol 1985, **3**: 1202–1216.

280 Gerald W, Kostianovsky M, Rosai J. Development of vascular neoplasia in Castleman's disease. Report of seven cases. Am J Surg Pathol 1990, **14**: 603–614.

281 Gould SJ, Diss T, Isaacson PG. Multicentric Castleman's disease in association with a solitary plasmacytoma. A case report. Histopathology 1990, **17**: 135–140.

282 Gulati P, Sun NC, Herman BK, Said JW, Cornford ME. Isolated leptomeningeal Castleman's disease with viral particles in the follicular dendritic cells. Arch Pathol Lab Med 1998, **122**: 1026–1029.

283 Hall PA, Donaghy M, Cotter FE, Stansfeld AG, Levison DA. An immunohistological and genotypic study of the plasma cell form of Castleman's disease. Histopathology 1989, **14**: 333–346.

284 Hanson CA, Frizzera G, Patton DF, Peterson BA, McClain KL, Gajl-Peczalska KJ, Kersey JH. Clonal rearrangement for immunoglobulin and T-cell receptor genes in systemic Castleman's disease. Association with Epstein–Barr virus. Am J Pathol 1988, **131**: 84–91.

285 Hengge UR, Ruzicka T, Tyring SK, Stuschke M, Roggendorf M, Schwartz RA, Seeber S. Update on Kaposi's sarcoma and other HHV-8 associated disease. Part 2: Pathogenesis, Castleman's disease, and pleural effusion lymphoma. Lancet Infect Dis 2002, **2**: 344–352.

286 Hsu SM, Waldron JA, Xie SS, Barlogie B. Expression of interleukin6 in Castleman's disease. Hum Pathol 1993, **24**: 833–839.

287 Isaacson PG. Commentary: Castleman's disease. Histopathology 1989, **14**: 429–432.

288 Jones EL, Crocker J, Gregory J, Guibarra M, Curran RC. Angiofollicular lymph node hyperplasia (Castleman's disease). An immunohistochemical and enzyme-histochemical study of the hyaline-vascular form of lesion. J Pathol 1984, **144**: 131–147.

289 Keller AR, Hochholzer L, Castleman, B. Hyaline-vascular and plasma-cell types of giant lymph node hyperplasia of mediastinum and other locations. Cancer 1972, **29**: 670–683.

290 Kojima M, Nakamura S, Shimizu K, Itoh H, Yamane Y, Murayama K, Tanaka H, Sugihara S, Shimano S, Sakata N, Masawa N. Clinical implication of idiopathic plasmacytic lymphadenopathy with polyclonal hypergammaglobulinemia. A report of 16 cases. Int J Surg Pathol(in press).

291 Larroche C, Cacoub P, Soulier J, Oksenhendler E, Chauvel JP, Piette JC, Raphael M. Castleman's disease and lymphoma: report of eight cases in HIV-negative patients and literature review. Am J Hematol 2002, **69**: 119–126.

292 Lin O, Frizzera G. Angiomyoid and follicular dendritic cell proliferative lesions in Castleman's disease of hyaline-vascular type: a study of 10 cases. Am J Surg Pathol 1997, **21**: 1295–1306.

293 Madero S, Oñate JM, Garzón A. Giant lymph node hyperplasia in an angiolipomatous mediastinal mass. Arch Pathol Lab Med 1986, **110**: 853–855.

294 Maheswaran PR, Ramsay AD, Norton AJ, Roche WR. Hodgkin's disease presenting with the histological features of Castleman's disease. Histopathology 1991, **18**: 249–253.

295 Mandler RN, Kerrigan DP, Smart J, Kuis W, Villiger P, Lotz M. Castleman's disease in POEMS syndrome with elevated interleukin-6. Cancer 1992, **69**: 2697–2703.

296 Menke DM, Camoriano JK, Banks PM. Angiofollicular lymph node hyperplasia. A comparison of unicentric, multicentric, hyaline vascular, and plasma cell types of disease by morphometric and clinical analysis. Mod Pathol 1992, **5**: 525–530.

297 Menke DM, Chadbum A, Cesarman E, Green E, Berenson J, Said J, Tiemann M, Parwaresch R, Thome SD. Analysis of the human herpesvirus 8(HHV-8) genome and HHV-8 vIL-6 expression in archival cases of Castleman disease at low risk for HIV infection. Am J Clin Pathol 2002, **117**: 268–275.

298 Menke DM, Tiemann M, Camoriano JK, Chang SF, Madan A, Chow M, Habermann TM, Parwaresch R. Diagnosis of Castleman's disease by identification of an immuno-phenotypically aberrant population of mantle zone B lymphocytes in paraffin-embedded lymph node biopsies. Am J Clin Pathol 1996, **105**: 268–276.

299 Munoz G, Geijo P, Moldenhauer F, Perez-Moro E, Razquin J, Piris MA. Plasmacellular Castleman's disease and POEMS syndrome. Histopathology 1990, **17**: 172–174.

300 Nagai K, Sato I, Shimoyama N. Pathohistological and immunohistochemical studies on Castleman's disease of the lymph node. Virchows Arch [A] 1986, **409**: 287–297.

301 Nguyen DT, Diamond LW, Hansmann ML, Alavaikko MJ, Schroder H, Fellbaum C, Fischer R. Castleman's disease. Differences in follicular dendritic network in the hyaline vascular and plasma cell variants. Histopathology 1994, **24**: 437–443.

302 Ohyashiki JH, Ohyashiki K, Kawakubo K, Serizawa H, Abe K, Mikata A, Toyama K. Molecular genetic, cytogenetic, and immunophenotypic analyses in Castleman's disease of the plasma cell type. Am J Clin Pathol 1994, **101**: 290–295.

303 Ordi J, Grau JM, Junque A, Nomdedeu B, Palacin A, Cardesa A. Secondary (AA) amyloidosis associated with Castleman's disease. Report of two cases and review of the literature. Am J Clin Pathol 1993, **100**: 394–397.

304 Parravicini C, Chandran B, Corbellino M, Berti E, Pauli M, Moore PS, Chang Y. Differential viral protein expression in Kaposi's sarcoma-associated herpesvirus-infected diseases. Kaposi's sarcoma, primary effusion lymphoma, and multicentric Castleman's disease. Am J Pathol 2000, **156**: 743–749.

305 Pauwels P, Dal Cin P, Vlasved LT, Aleva RM, van Erp WF, Jones D. A chromosomal abnormality in hyaline vascular Castleman's disease: evidence for clonal proliferation of dysplastic stromal cells. Am J Surg Pathol 2000, **24**: 882–888.

306 Peterson BA, Frizzera G. Multicentric Castleman's disease. Semin Oncol 1993, **20**: 636–647.

307 Radaszkiewicz T, Hansmann ML, Lennert K. Monoclonality and polyclonality of plasma cells in Castleman's disease of the plasma cell variant. Histopathology 1989, **14**: 11–24.

308 Rolon PG, Audouin J, Diebold J, Rolon PA, Gonzalez A. Multicentric angiofollicular lymph node hyperplasia associated

with a solitary osteolytic costal IgG lambda myeloma. POEMS syndrome in a South American (Paraguayan) patient. Pathol Res Pract 1989, **185:** 468–469.

309 Ruco LP, Gearing AJ, Pigott R, Pomponi D, Burgio VL, Cafolla A, Baiocchini A, Baroni CD. Expression of ICAM-1, VCAM-1 and ELAM-1 in angiofollicular lymph node hyperplasia (Castleman's disease). Evidence for dysplasia of follicular dendritic reticulum cells. Histopathology 1991, **19:** 523–528.

310 Skelton HG, Smith KJ. Extranodal multicentric Castleman's disease with cutaneous involvement. Mod Pathol 1998, **11:** 93–98.

311 Smir BN, Greiner TC, Weisenburger DD. Multicentric angiofollicular lymph node hyperplasia in children: a clinicopathologic study of eight patients. Mod Pathol 1997, **9:** 1135–1142.

312 Vasef M, Katzin WE, Mendelsohn G, Reydman M. Report of a case of localized Castleman's disease with progression to malignant lymphoma. Am J Clin Pathol 1992, **98:** 633–636.

313 Weisenburger DD, Nathwani BN, Winberg CD, Rappaport H. Multicentric angiofollicular lymph node hyperplasia. A clinicopathologic study of 16 cases. Hum Pathol 1985, **16:** 162–172.

314 Zarate-Osorno A, Medeiros LJ, Danon AD, Neiman RS. Hodgkin's disease with coexistent Castleman-like histologic features. A report of three cases. Arch Pathol Lab Med 1994, **118:** 270–274.

Angioimmunoblastic lymphadenopathy

315 Aozasa K, Ohsawa M, Fujita MQ, Kanayama Y, Tominaga N, Yonezawa T, Matsubuchi T, Hirata M, Uda H, Kanamaru A, et al. Angioimmunoblastic lymphadenopathy. Review of 44 patients with emphasis on prognostic behavior. Cancer 1989, **63:** 1625–1629.

316 Attygalle AD, Chuang SS, Diss TC, Isaacson PG, Du MQ, Dogan A. CD10 expression in nodal peripheral T-cell lymphomas: a feature specific to angioimmunoblastic T-cell lymphoma. Mod Pathol 2003, **16:** 225.

317 Bernengo MG, Levi L, Zina G. Skin lesions in angioimmunoblastic lymphadenopathy. Histological and immunological studies. Br J Dermatol 1981, **104:** 131–139.

318 Bluming AZ, Cohen HG, Saxon A. Angioimmunoblastic lymphadenopathy with dysproteinemia. A pathogenetic link between physiologic lymphoid proliferation and malignant lymphoma. Am J Med 1979, **67:** 421–428.

319 Cullen MH, Stansfeld AG, Oliver RTD, Lister TA, Malpas JS. Angioimmunoblastic lymphadenopathy. Report of ten cases and review of the literature. Q J Med 1979, **48:** 151–177.

320 Dargent JL, Jacobovitz D, Pradier O, Velu T, Martiat P, Delplace J, Neve P, Diebold J. A case of pleomorphic T-cell lymphoma with a high content of reactive histiocytes presented with hypereosinophilia. Pathol Res Pract 1995, **191:** 463–468.

321 Feller AC, Griesser H, Schilling CV, Wacker HH, Dallenbach F, Bartels H, Kuse R, Mak TW, Lennert K. Clonal gene rearrangement patterns correlate with immunophenotype and clinical parameters in patients with angioimmunoblastic lymphadenopathy. Am J Pathol 1988, **133:** 549–556.

322 Freter CE, Cossman J. Angioimmunoblastic lymphadenopathy with dysproteinemia. Semin Oncol 1993, **20:** 627–635.

323 Frizzera G, Moran EM, Rappaport H. Angio-immunoblastic lymphadenopathy with dysproteinaemia. Lancet 1974, **1:** 1070–1073.

324 Frizzera G, Moran EM, Rappaport H. Angio-immunoblastic lymphadenopathy. Diagnosis and clinical course. Am J Med 1975, **59:** 803–818.

325 Jones D, Jorgensen JL, Shasafaei A, Dorfman DM. Characteristic proliferations of reticular and dendritic cells in angioimmunoblastic lymphoma. Am J Surg Pathol 1998, **22:** 956–964.

326 Khan G, Norton AJ, Slavin G. Epstein–Barr virus in angioimmunoblastic T-cell lymphomas. Histopathology 1993, **22:** 145–149.

327 Knecht H, Schwarze E-W, Lennert K. Histological, immunohistological and autopsy findings in lymphogranulomatosis X (including angioimmunoblastic lymphadenopathy). Virchows Arch [A] 1985, **406:** 105–124.

328 Kon S, Sato T, Onodera K, Satoh M, Kikuchi K, Imai S, Osato T. Detection of Epstein–Barr virus DNA and EBV-determined nuclear antigen in angioimmunoblastic lymphadenopathy with dysproteinemia type T-cell lymphoma. Pathol Res Pract 1993, **189:** 1137–1144.

329 Kosmidis PA, Axelrod AR, Palacas C, Stahl M. Angioimmunoblastic lymphadenopathy. A T-cell deficiency. Cancer 1978, **42:** 447–452.

330 Liao DT, Rosai J, Daneshbod K. Malignant histiocytosis with cutaneous involvement and eosinophilia. Am J Clin Pathol 1972, **57:** 438–448.

331 Lorenzen J, Li G, Zhao-Hohn M, Wintzer C, Fischer R, Hansmann ML. Angioimmunoblastic lymphadenopathy type of T-cell lymphoma and angioimmunoblastic lymphadenopathy. A clinicopathological and molecular biological study of 13 Chinese patients using polymerase chain reaction and paraffin-embedded tissues. Virchows Arch 1994, **424:** 593–600.

332 Lukes RJ, Tindle BH. Immunoblastic lymphadenopathy. A hyperimmune entity resembling Hodgkin's disease. N Engl J Med 1975, **292:** 1–8.

333 Nathwani BN, Rappaport H, Moran EM, Pangalis GA, Kim H. Malignant lymphoma arising in angioimmunoblastic lymphadenopathy. Cancer 1978, **41:** 578–606.

334 Ohshima K, Takeo H, Kikuchi M, Kozuru M, Uike N, Masuda Y, Yoneda S, Takeshita M, Shibata T, Akamatsu M. Heterogeneity of Epstein–Barr virus infection in angioimmunoblastic lymphadenopathy type T-cell lymphoma. Histopathology 1994, **25:** 569–580.

335 Ree HJ, Kadin ME, Kikuchi M, Ko YH, Go JH, Suzumiya J, Kim DS. Angioimmunoblastic lymphoma (AILD-type T-cell lymphoma) with hyperplasia germinal centers. Am J Surg Pathol 1998, **22:** 643–655.

336 Seehafer JR, Goldberg NC, Dicken CH, Su WPD. Cutaneous manifestations of angioimmunoblastic lymphadenopathy. Arch Dermatol 1980, **116:** 41–45.

337 Shimoyama M, Minato K, Saito H, Takenaka T, Watanabe S, Nagatani T, Naruto M. Immunoblastic lymphadenopathy (IBL)-like T-cell lymphoma. Jpn J Clin Oncol 1979, **9**(Suppl 1): 347–356.

338 Smith JL, Hodges E, Quin CT, McCarthy KP, Wright DH. Frequent T- and B-cell oligoclones in histologically and immunophenotypically characterized angioimmunoblastic lymphadenopathy. Am J Pathol 2000, **156:** 661–669.

339 Weiss LM, Strickler JG, Dorfman RF, Horning SJ, Warnke RA, Sklar J. Clonal T-cell populations in angioimmunoblastic lymphadenopathy and angioimmunoblastic lymphadenopathylike lymphoma. Am J Pathol 1986, **122:** 392–398.

Drug hypersensitivity

340 Abbondanzo SL, Irey NS, Frizzera G. Dilantin-associated lymphadenopathy. Spectrum of histopathologic patterns. Am J Surg Pathol 1995, **19:** 675–686.

341 Saltzstein SL, Ackerman LV. Lymphadenopathy induced by anticonvulsant drugs clinically and pathologically mimicking malignant lymphomas. Cancer 1959, **12:** 164–182.

Dermatopathic lymphadenitis

342 Asano S, Muramatsu T, Kanno H, Wakasa H. Dermatopathic lymphadenopathy. Electronmicroscopic, enzyme-histochemical and immunohistochemical study. Acta Pathol Jpn 1987, **37:** 887–900.

343 Burke JS, Colby TV. Dermatopathic lymphadenopathy. Comparison of cases associated and unassociated with mycosis fungoides. Am J Surg Pathol 1981, **5:** 343–352.

344 Gould E, Porto R, Albores-Saavedra J, Ibe MJ. Dermatopathic lymphadenitis. The spectrum and significance of its morphologic features. Arch Pathol Lab Med 1988, **112:** 1145–1150.

345 Rausch E, Kaiserling E, Goos M. Langerhans cells and interdigitating reticulum cells in the thymus-dependent region in human dermatopathic lymphadenitis. Virchows Arch [Cell Pathol] 1977, **25:** 327–343.

346 Ree H, Fanger H. Paracortical alteration in lymphadenopathic and tumor-draining lymph nodes. Histologic study. Hum Pathol 1975, **6:** 363–372.

347 Weiss LM, Hu E, Wood GS, Moulds C, Cleary ML, Warnke R, Sklar J. Clonal rearrangements of T-cell receptor genes in mycosis fungoides and dermatopathic lymphadenopathy. N Engl J Med 1985, **313:** 539–544.

348 Weiss LM, Wood GS, Warnke RA. Immunophenotypic differences between dermatopathic lymphadenopathy and lymph node involvement in mycosis fungoides. Am J Pathol 1985, **120:** 179–185.

Rosai–Dorfman disease (sinus histiocytosis with massive lymphadenopathy)

349 Albores-Saavedra J, Vuitch F, Delgado R, Wiley E, Hagler H. Sinus histiocytosis of pelvic lymph nodes after hip replacement. A histiocytic proliferation induced by cobalt-chromium and titanium. Am J Surg Pathol 1994, **18:** 83–90.

350 Andriko JA, Morridon A, Colegial CH, Davis BJ, Jones RV. Rosai–Dorfman disease isolated to the central nervous system: a report of 11 cases. Mod Pathol 2001, **14:** 172–178.

351 Bonetti F, Chilosi M, Menestrina F, Scarpa A, Pelicci PG, Amorosi E, Fiore-Donati L, Knowles DM. Immunohistological analysis of Rosai–Dorfman histiocytosis. A disease of S-100 + CD1-histiocytes. Virchows Arch [A] 1987, **411:** 129–135.

352 Brenn T, Caloje E, Granter SR, Leonard N, Grayson W, Fletcher CD, McKee PH. Cutaneous Rosai–Dorfman disease is a distinct clinical entity. Am J Dermatopathol 2002, **24:** 385–391.

353 Cocker RS, Kang J, Kahn LB. Rosai–Dorfman disease. Report of a case presenting as a midline thyroid mass. Arch Pathol Lab Med 2003, **127:** e197–200.

354 Eisen RN, Buckley PJ, Rosai J. Immunophenotypic characterization of sinus histiocytosis with massive lymphadenopathy (Rosai–Dorfman disease). Semin Diagn Pathol 1990, **7:** 74–82.

355 Falk S, Stutte HJ, Frizzera G. Hodgkin's disease and sinus histiocytosis with massive lymphadenopathylike changes. Histopathology 1991, **19:** 221–224.

356 Foucar E, Rosai J, Dorfman RF. Sinus histiocytosis with massive lymphadenopathy. Ear, nose, and throat manifestations. Arch Otolaryngol 1978, **104:** 687–693.

357 Foucar E, Rosai J, Dorfman RF. The ophthalmologic manifestations of sinus histiocytosis with massive lymphadenopathy. Am J Ophthalmol 1979, **87:** 354–367.

358 Foucar E, Rosai J, Dorfman RF. Sinus histiocytosis with massive lymphadenopathy. An analysis of 14 deaths occurring in a patient registry. Cancer 1984, **54:** 1834–1840.

359 Foucar E, Rosai J, Dorfman R. Sinus histiocytosis with massive lymphadenopathy (Rosai–Dorfman disease). Review of the entity. Semin Diagn Pathol 1990, **7:** 19–73.

360 Foucar E, Rosai J, Dorfman RF, Brynes RK. The neurologic manifestations of sinus histiocytosis with massive lymphadenopathy. Neurology 1982, **32:** 365–371.

361 Foucar E, Rosai J, Dorfman RF, Eyman JM. Immunologic abnormalities and their significance in the pathogenesis of sinus histiocytosis with massive lymphadenopathy. Am J Clin Pathol 1984, **82:** 515–525.

362 Green I, Dorfman RF, Rosai J. Breast involvement by extranodal Rosai–Dorfman disease: report of seven cases. Am J Surg Pathol 1997, **21:** 664–668.

363 Juskevicius R, Finley JL. Rosai–Dorfman disease of the parotid gland: cytologic and histopathologic findings with immunohistochemical correlation. Arch Pathol Lab Med 2001, **125:** 1348–1350.

364 Komp DM. The treatment of sinus histiocytosis with massive lymphadenopathy (Rosai–Dorfman disease). Semin Diagn Pathol 1990, **7:** 83–86.

365 Lauwers GY, Perez-Atayde A, Dorfman RF, Rosai J. The digestive system manifestations of Rosai–Dorfman disease (sinus histiocytosis with massive lymphadenopathy): review of 11 cases. Hum Pathol 2000, **31:** 380–385.

366 Leighton SE, Gallimore AP. Extranodal sinus histiocytosis with massive lymphadenopathy affecting the subglottis and trachea. Histopathology 1994, **24:** 393–394.

367 Levine PH, Jahan N, Murari P, Manak M, Jaffe ES. Detection of human herpesvirus 6 in tissues involved by sinus histiocytosis with massive lymphadenopathy (Rosai–Dorfman disease). J Infect Dis 1992, **166:** 291–295.

368 Lu D, Estalilla OC, Manning JT, Medeiros LJ. Sinus histiocytosis with massive lymphadenopathy and malignant lymphoma involving the same lymph node: a report of four cases and review of the literature. Mod Pathol 2000, **13:** 414–419.

369 Marmaduke DP, Rosai J, Warnke R, Foucar K, Emmert-Buck MR, Liotta LA, Willman CL. Molecular assessment of clonality in sinus histiocytosis with massive lymphadenopathy (SHML). A reactive disorder of polyclonal histiocytes (abstract). Mod Pathol 1996, **9:** 117A (Abstract).

370 Marsh WL Jr, McCarrick JP, Harlan DM. Sinus histiocytosis with massive lymphadenopathy. Occurrence in identical twins with retroperitoneal disease. Arch Pathol Lab Med 1988, **112:** 298–301.

371 Middel P, Hemmerlein B, Fayyazi A, Kaboth U, Radzun HJ. Sinus histiocytosis with massive lymphadenopathy: evidence for its relationship to macrophages and for a cytokine-related disorder. Histopathology 2000, **35:** 525–533.

372 Miettinen M, Paljakka P, Haveri P, Saxén E. Sinus histiocytosis with massive lymphadenopathy. A nodal and extranodal proliferation of S-100 protein positive histiocytes? Am J Clin Pathol 1987, **88:** 270–277.

373 Montgomery EA, Meis JM, Frizzera G. Rosai–Dorfman disease of soft tissue. Am J Surg Pathol 1992, **16:** 122–129.

374 Murray J, Fox H. Rosai–Dorfman disease of the uterine cervix. Int J Gynecol Pathol 1991, **10:** 209–213.

375 Osborne BM, Hagemeister FB, Butler JJ. Extranodal gastrointestinal sinus histiocytosis with massive lymphadenopathy. Clinically presenting as a malignant tumor. Am J Surg Pathol 1981, **5:** 603–611.

376 Paulli M, Feller AC, Boveri E, Kindl S, Berti E, Rosso R, Merz H, Facchetti F, Gambini C, Bonetti F, et al. Cathepsin D and E co-expression in sinus histiocytosis with massive lymphadenopathy (Rosai–Dorfman disease) and Langerhans' cell histiocytosis. Further evidences of a phenotypic overlap between these histiocytic disorders. Virchows Arch 1994, **424:** 601–606.

377 Paulli M, Rosso R, Kindl S, Boveri E, Marocolo D, Chioda C, Agostini C, Magrini U, Facchetti F. Immunophenotypic characterization of the cell infiltrate in five cases of sinus

histiocytosis with massive lymphadenopathy (Rosai–Dorfman disease). Hum Pathol 1992, **23**: 647–654.

378 Pulsoni A, Anghel G, Falcucci P, Matera R, Pescarmona E, Ribersan M, Villiva N, Mandelli F. Treatment of sinus histiocytosis with massive lymphadenopathy (Rosai–Dorfman disease): report of a case and literature review. Am J Hematol 2002, **69**: 67–71.

379 Quaglino P, Tomasini C, Novelli M, Colonna S, Bernengo MG. Immunohistologic findings and adhesion molecule pattern in primary pure cutaneous Rosai–Dorfman disease with xanthomatous features. Am J Dermatopathol 1998, **20**: 393–398.

380 Rocken C, Wieker K, Grote H-J, Muller G, Franke A, Roessner A. Rosai–Dorfman disease and generalized AA amyloidosis: a case report. Hum Pathol 2000, **31**: 621–624.

381 Rosai J, Dorfman RF. Sinus histiocytosis with massive lymphadenopathy. A pseudolymphomatous benign disorder. Analysis of 34 cases. Cancer 1972, **30**: 1174–1188.

382 Song SK, Schwartz IS, Strauchen JA, Huang YP, Sachdev V, Daftary DR, Vas CJ. Meningeal nodules with features of extranodal sinus histiocytosis with massive lymphadenopathy. Am J Surg Pathol 1989, **13**: 406–412.

383 Suarez CR, Zeller WP, Silberman S, Rust G, Messmore H. Sinus histiocytosis with massive lymphadenopathy. Remission with chemotherapy. Am J Pediatr Hematol Oncol 1983, **5**: 235–241.

384 Thawerani H, Sanchez RL, Rosai J, Dorfman RF. The cutaneous manifestations of sinus histiocytosis with massive lymphadenopathy. Arch Dermatol 1978, **114**: 191–197.

385 Tsang WY, Yip TT, Chan JK. The Rosai–Dorfman disease histiocytes are not infected by Epstein–Barr virus. Histopathology 1994, **25**: 88–90.

386 Walker PD, Rosai J, Dorfman RF. The osseous manifestations of sinus histiocytosis with massive lymphadenopathy. Am J Clin Pathol 1981, **75**: 131–139.

387 Wang KH, Cheng CJ, Hu CH, Lee WR. Coexistence of localized Langerhans cell histiocytosis and cutaneous Rosai–Dorfman disease. Br J Dermatol 2002, **147**: 770–774.

388 Wenig BM, Abbondanzo SL, Childers EL, Kapadia SB, Heffner DR. Extranodal sinus histiocytosis with massive lymphadenopathy (Rosai–Dorfman disease) of the head and neck. Hum Pathol 1993, **24**: 483–492.

389 Willman CL, Busque L, Griffith BB, Favara BE, McClain KL, Duncan MH, Gilliland DG. Langerhans-cell histiocytosis (histiocytosis X). A clonal proliferative disease. N Engl J Med 1994, **331**: 154–160.

390 Woda BA, Sullivan JL. Reactive histiocytic disorders. Am J Clin Pathol 1993, **99**: 459–463.

391 Wright DH, Richards DB. Sinus histiocytosis with massive lymphadenopathy (Rosai–Dorfman disease). Report of a case with widespread nodal and extra nodal dissemination. Histopathology 1981, **5**: 697–709.

Langerhans' cell histiocytosis

392 Anjuère F, Del Hoyo GM, Martin P, Ardavin C. Langerhans' cell develop from a lymphoid-committed precursor. Blood 2000, **96**: 1633–1637.

393 Axiotis CA, Merino MJ, Duray PH. Langerhans cell histiocytosis of the female genital tract. Cancer 1991, **67**: 1650–1660.

394 Beckstead JH, Wood GS, Turner RR. Histiocytosis X cells and Langerhans cells. Enzyme histochemical and immunologic similarities. Hum Pathol 1984, **15**: 826–833.

395 Ben-Ezra J, Bailey A, Azumi N, Delsol G, Stroup R, Sheibani K, Rappaport H. Malignant histiocytosis X. A distinct clinicopathologic entity. Cancer 1991, **68**: 1050–1060.

396 Berg LC, Norelle A, Morgan WA, Washa DM. Cat-scratch disease simulating histiocytosis X. Hum Pathol 1998, **29**: 649–651.

397 Bingham EA, Bridges JM, Kelly AMT, Burrows D, Nevins NC. Letterer-Siwe disease. A study of thirteen cases over a 21-year period. Br J Dermatol 1982, **106**: 205–209.

398 Boulac A, Boullard ML, Geissmann F, Fraitag S, Andry P, Teillac D, Bensussan A, Revuz J, Boumsell L, Wechsler J, Bagot M. CD101 expression by Langerhan's cell histiocytosis cells. Histopathology 2000, **36**: 229–232.

399 Brabencova E, Tazi A, Lorenzato M, Bonay M, Kambouchner M, Emile JF, Hance AJ, Soler P. Langerhans' cells in Langerhan's cell granulomatosis are not actively proliferating cells. Am J Pathol 1998, **152**: 1143–1149.

400 Burns BF, Colby TV, Dorfman RF. Langerhans cell granulomatosis (histiocytosis X) associated with malignant lymphomas. Am J Surg Pathol 1983, **7**: 529–533.

401 Emile J-F, Wechsler J, Brousse N, Boulland ML, Cologon R, Freitag S, Voisin M-C, Gaulard P, Boumsell L, Zafrani E-S. Langerhans' cell histiocytosis. Definitive diagnosis with the use of monoclonal antibody O10 on routinely paraffin-embedded samples. Am J Surg Pathol 1995, **19**: 636–641.

402 Favara BE. Langerhans' cell histiocytosis pathobiology and pathogenesis. Semin Oncol 1991, **18**: 3–7.

403 Gilcrease MZ, Rajan B, Ostrowski ML, Ramzy I, Schwartz MR. Localized thymic Langerhan's cell histiocytosis and its relationship with myasthenia gravis: immunohistochemical, ultrastructural, and cytometric studies. Arch Pathol Lab Med 1997, **121**: 134–138.

404 Giona F, Caruso R, Testi AM, Moleti ML, Malagnino F, Martelli M, Ruco L, Giannetti GP, Annibali S, Mandell F. Langerhan's cell histiocytosis in adults: a clinical and therapeutic analysis of 11 patients from a single institution. Cancer 1997, **80**: 1786–1791.

405 Groisman GM, Rosh JR, Harpaz N. Langerhans cell histiocytosis of the stomach. A cause of granulomatous gastritis and gastric polyposis. Arch Pathol Lab Med 1994, **118**: 1232–1235.

406 Hage C, Willman CL, Favara BE, Isaacson PG. Langerhans' cell histiocytosis (histiocytosis X). Immunophenotype and growth fraction. Hum Pathol 1993, **24**: 840–845.

407 Hashimoto K, Griffin D, Kohsbaki M. Self-healing reticulohistiocytosis. A clinical, histologic, and ultrastructural study of the fourth case in the literature. Cancer 1982, **49**: 331–337.

408 Herzog KM, Tubbs RR. Langerhan's cell histiocytosis. Adv Anat Pathol 1999, 5: 347–358.

409 Howarth DM, Gilchrist GS, Mullan BP, Wiseman GA, Edmonson JH, Schomberg PJ. Langerhans cell histiocytosis: diagnosis, natural history, management and outcome. Cancer 1999, **85**: 2278–2290.

410 Kaplan KJ, Goodman ZD, Izhak KG. Liver involvement in Langerhan's cell histiocytosis: a study of nine cases. Mod Pathol 1999, **12**: 370–378.

411 Kenn W, Eck M, Allolio B, Jacob F, Illg A, Marx A, Müller-Hermelink HK, Hahn D. Erdheim–Chester disease: evidence for a disease entity different from Langerhan's cell histiocytosis? Three cases with detailed radiological and immunohistochemical analysis? Hum Pathol 2000, **31**: 734–739.

412 Kjedlsberg CR, Kim H. Eosinophilic granuloma as an incidental finding in malignant lymphoma. Arch Pathol Lab Med 1980, **104**: 137–140.

413 Komp DM. Concepts in staging and clinical studies for treatment of Langerhans' cell histiocytosis. Semin Oncol 1991, **18**: 18–23.

414 Lahey ME. Prognostic factors in histiocytosis X. Am J Pediatr Hematol/Oncol 1981, **3**: 57–65.

415 Leahy MA, Krejci SM, Friednash M, Stockert SS, Wilson H, Huff JC, Weston WL, Brice SL. Human herpesvirus 6 is present in lesions of Langerhans cell histiocytosis. J Invest Dermatol 1993, **101**: 642–645.

416 Lieberman PH, Jones CR, Steinman RM, Erlandson RA, Smith J, Gee T, Huvos A, Garin-Chesa P, Filippa DA, Urmacher C, Gangi MD, Sperber M. Langerhan's cell (eosinophilic) granulomatosis; a clinicopathologic study encompassing 50 years. Am J Surg Pathol 1996, **20**: 519–552.

417 McClain K, Jin H, Gresik V, Favara B. Langerhans cell histiocytosis. Lack of a viral etiology. Am J Hematol 1994, **47**: 16–20.

418 Magni M, Di Nocola M, Carlo-Stella C, Matteucci P, Lavazza C, Grisanti S, Bifulco C, Pilotti S, Papini D, Rosai J, Gianni AM. Identical rearrangement of immunoglobulin heavy chain gene in neoplastic Langerhan's cells and B-lymphocytes: evidence for a common precursor. Leuk Res 2002, **36**: 1131–1133.

419 Meehan SA, Smoller BR. Cutaneous Langerhans' cell histiocytosis of the genitalia in the elderly: a report of three cases. J Cutan Pathol 1998, **25**: 370–374.

420 Mierau GW, Favara BE, Brenman JM. Electron microscopy in histiocytosis X. Ultrastruct Pathol 1982, **3**: 137–142.

421 Motoi M, Helbron D, Kaiserling E, Lennert K. Eosinophilic granuloma of lymph nodes. A variant of histiocytosis X. Histopathology 1980, **4**: 585–606.

422 Murakami I, Gogusev J, Fournet JC, Glorion C, Jaubert F. Detection of molecular cytogenetic aberrations in Langerhans' cell histiocytosis of bone. Hum Pathol 2002, **33**: 555–560.

423 Neumann MP, Frizzera G. The coexistence of Langerhans' cell granulomatosis and malignant lymphoma may take different forms. Report of seven cases with a review of the literature. Hum Pathol 1986, **17**: 1060–1065.

424 Nezelof C, Basset F. From histiocytosis X to Langerhans' cell histiocytosis: a personal account. Int J Surg Pathol 2001, **9**: 137–146.

425 Ornvold K, Nielsen MH, Clausen N. Disseminated histiocytosis X. A clinical and immunohistochemical retrospective study. Acta Pathol Microbiol Immunol Scand (A) 1985, **93**: 311–316.

426 Ornvold K, Ralfkiaer E, Carstensen H. Immunohistochemical study of the abnormal cells in Langerhans cell histiocytosis (histiocytosis X). Virchows Arch [A] 1990, **416**: 403–410.

427 Otis CN, Fischer RA, Johnson N, Kelleher JF, Powell JL. Histiocytosis X of the vulva. A case report and review of the literature. Obstet Gynecol 1990, **75**: 555–558.

428 Paulli M, Feller AC, Boveri E, Kindl S, Berti E, Rosso R, Merz H, Facchetti F, Gambini C, Bonetti F, et al. Cathepsin D and E co-expression in sinus histiocytosis with massive lymphadenopathy (Rosai–Dorfman disease) and Langerhans' cell histiocytosis. Further evidences of a phenotypic overlap between these histiocytic disorders. Virchows Arch 1994, **424**: 601–606.

429 Pinkus GS, Lones MA, Matsumura F, Yamashiro S, Said JW, Pinkus JL. Langerhans cell histiocytosis. Immunohistochemical expression of fascin, a dendritic cell marker. Am J Clin Pathol 2002, **118**: 335–343.

430 Rabkin MS, Kjeldsberg CR, Wittwer CT, Marty J. A comparison study of two methods of peanut agglutinin staining with S100 immunostaining in 29 cases of histiocytosis X (Langerhans' cell histiocytosis). Arch Pathol Lab Med 1990, **114**: 511–515.

431 Ree HJ, Kadin ME. Peanut agglutinin. A useful marker for histiocytosis X and interdigitating reticulum cells. Cancer 1986, **57**: 282–287.

432 Reid H, Fox H, Whittaker JS. Eosinophilic granuloma of lymph nodes. Histopathology 1977, **1**: 31–37.

433 Richmond I, Eyden BP, Banerjee SS. Intranodal Langerhans' cell histiocytosis associated with malignant melanoma. Histopathology 1995, **26**: 380–382.

434 Risdall RJ, Dehner LP, Duray P, Kobrinsky N, Robison L, Nesbit ME Jr. Histiocytosis X (Langerhans' cell histiocytosis). Prognostic role of histopathology. Arch Pathol Lab Med 1983, **107**: 59–63.

435 Safali M, McCutcheon JM, Wright DH. Langerhans cell histiocytosis of lymph nodes: draining a papillary carcinoma of the thyroid. Histopathology 1997, **30**: 599–603.

436 Santamaria M, Llamas L, Ree HJ, Sheibani K, Ho YS, Su I-J, Hsu S-M. Expression of sialylated leu-M1 antigen in histiocytosis X. Am J Clin Pathol 1988, **89**: 211–219.

437 Terracciano L, Kocher T, Cathomas G, Bubendorf L, Lehmann FS. Langerhans' cell histicyotosis of the stomach with atypical morphological features. Pathol Int 1999, **49**: 553–556.

438 Thompson LD, Wenig BM, Adair CF, Smith BC, Heffess CS. Langerhan's cell histiocytosis of the thyroid: a series of seven cases and a review of the literature. Mod Pathol 1996, **9**: 145–149.

439 Vernon ML, Fountain L, Krebs HM, Barbosa LH, Fuccillo DA, Sever JL. Birbeck granules (Langerhans' cell granules) in human lymph nodes. Am J Clin Pathol 1973, **60**: 771–779.

440 Williams JW, Dorfman RF. Lymphadenopathy as the initial manifestation of histiocytosis X. Am J Surg Pathol 1979, **3**: 405–421.

441 Willman CL, Busque L, Griffith BB, Favara BE, McClain KL, Duncan MH, Gilliland DG. Langerhans'-cell histiocytosis (histiocytosis X) – a clonal proliferative disease. N Engl J Med 1994, **331**: 154–160.

442 Wood C, Wood GS, Deneau DG, Oseroff A, Beckstead JH, Malin J. Malignant histiocytosis X. Report of a rapidly fatal case in an elderly man. Cancer 1984, **54**: 347–352.

443 Yousem SA, Colby TV, Chen YY, Chen WG, Weiss LW. Pulmonary Langerhan's cell histiocytosis: molecular analysis of clonality. Am J Surg Pathol 2001, **25**: 630–636.

444 Yu RC, Chu AC. Lack of T-cell receptor gene rearrangements in cells involved in Langerhans' cell histiocytosis. Cancer 1995, **75**: 1162–1166.

Kimura's disease

445 Chan JK, Hui PK, Ng CS, Yuen NW, Kung IT, Gwi E. Epithelioid haemangioma (angiolymphoid hyperplasia with eosinophilia) and Kimura's disease in Chinese. Histopathology 1989, **15**: 557–574.

446 Chen H, Thompson LDR, Aguilera NS, Abbondanzo SL. Kimura disease: a clinicopathologic study of 21 cases. Am J Surg Pathol (in press).

447 Chim CS, Fung A, Shek TW, Liang R, Ho WK, Kwong YL. Analysis of clonality in Kimura's disease. Am J Surg Pathol 2002, **26**: 1083–1086.

448 Googe PB, Harris NL, Mihm MC Jr. Kimura's disease and angiolymphoid hyperplasia with eosinophilia. Two distinct histopathological entities. J Cutan Pathol 1987, **14**: 263–271.

449 Hui PK, Chan JK, Ng CS, Kung IT, Gwi E. Lymphadenopathy of Kimura's disease. Am J Surg Pathol 1989, **13**: 177–186.

450 Kung ITM, Gibson JB, Bannatyne PM. Kimura's disease. A clinico-pathologic study of 21 cases and its distinction form angiolymphoid hyperplasia with eosinophilia. Pathology 1984, **16**: 39–44.

451 Kuo TT, Shih LY, Chan HL. Kimura's disease. Involvement of regional lymph nodes and distinction from angiolymphoid hyperplasia with eosinophilia. Am J Surg Pathol 1988, **12**: 843–854.

452 Urabe A, Tsuneyoshi M, Enjoji M. Epithelioid hemangioma versus Kimura's disease. A comparative clinicopathologic study. Am J Surg Pathol 1987, **11**: 758–766.

Chronic granulomatous disease

453 Baehner RL, Nathan DG. Quantitative nitroblue tetrazolium test in chronic granulomatous disease. N Engl J Med 1968, **278**: 971–976.

454 Curnutte JT. Chronic granulomatous disease: The solving of a clinical riddle at the molecular level. Clin Immunol Immunopathol 1993, **67**: S2–15.

455 Johnston RB Jr. Clinical aspects of chronic granulomatous disease. Curr Opin Hematol 2001, **8**: 17–22.

456 Lakshman R, Finn A. Neutrophil disorders and their management. J Clin Pathol **54**: 7–19.

457 Lekstrom-Himes JA, Gallin JI. Immunodeficiency disease caused by defects in phagocytes. N Engl J Med 2000, **343**: 1703–1714.

458 Roos D. The genetic basis of chronic granulomatous disease. Immunol Rev 1994, **138**: 121–157.

459 Segal BH, Holland SM. Primary phagocytic disorders of childhood. Pediatr Clin North Am 2000, **47**: 1311–1338.

460 Segal BH, Leto TL, Gallin JL, Malech HL, Holland SM. Genetic, biochemical, and clinical features of chronic granulomatous disease. Medicine (Baltimore) 2000, **79**: 170–200.

461 Umeki S. Mechanisms for the activation/electron transfer of neutrophil NADPH-oxidase complex and molecular pathology of chronic granulomatous disease. Ann Hematol 1994, **68**: 267–277.

Lipophagic reactions

462 Alkan S, Beals TF, Schnitzer B. Primary diagnosis of Whipple disease manifesting as lymphadenopathy. Use of polymerase chain reaction for detection of *Tropheryma whippelii*. Am J Clin Pathol 2001, **116**: 899–904.

463 Baisden BL, Lepidi H, Raoult D, Argani P, Yardley JH, Dumler JS. Diagnosis of Whipple disease by immunohistochemical analysis. A sensitive and specific method for the detection of Tropheryma whipplei (the Whipple bacillus) in paraffin-embedded tissue. Am J Clin Pathol 2002, **118**: 742–748.

464 Boitnott JK, Margolis S. Mineral oil in human tissues. II. Oil droplets in lymph nodes of the porta hepatis. Bull Hopkins Hosp 1966, **118**: 414–422.

465 Fisher ER. Whipple's disease. Pathogenetic considerations. Electron microscopic and histochemical observations. JAMA 1962, **181**: 396–403.

466 Kelsall GR, Blackwell JB. The occurrence and significance of lipophage clusters in lymph nodes and spleen. Pathology 1969, **1**: 211–220.

467 Perez-Jaffe LA, Furth EE, Minda JM, Unger LD, Lawton TJ. Massive macrophage lipid accumulation presenting as hepatosplenomegaly and lymphadenopathy associated with long-term total parenteral nutrition therapy for short bowel syndrome. Hum Pathol 1998, **29**: 651–655.

468 Ravel R. Histopathology of lymph nodes after lymphangiography. Am J Clin Pathol 1966, **46**: 335–355.

Malignant lymphoma

469 Jaffe ES. Surgical pathology of the lymph nodes and related organs, ed. 2. Philadelphia, 1995, W.B. Saunders.

470 Jaffe ES, Harris NL, Stein H, Vardiman JW. Tumours of haematopoietic and lymphoid tissues. Pathology & Genetics, World Health Organization classification of tumours. Lyon, 2001, IARC Press.

471 Knowles DM. Molecular pathology of acquired immunodeficiency syndrome-related non-Hodgkin's lymphoma. Semin Diagn Pathol 1997, **14**: 67–82.

472 Lennert K, Feller AC. Histopathology of non-Hodgkin's lymphomas, ed. 2. New York, 1992, Springer-Verlag.

473 Warnke RA, Weiss LM, Chan JKC, Cleary ML, Dorfman RF. Tumors of the lymph nodes and spleen. Atlas of tumor pathology, 3rd series, fascicle 14. Washington, D.C., 1995, Armed Forces Institute of Pathology.

Hodgkin's lymphoma

474 Bonadonna G. Historical review of Hodgkin's disease. Br J Haematol 2000, **110**: 504–511.

475 Chang KL, Albujar PF, Chen YY, Johnson RM, Weiss LM. High prevalence of Epstein–Barr virus in the Reed–Sternberg cells of Hodgkin's disease occurring in Peru. Blood 1993, **81**: 496–501.

476 Dawson PJ. The original illustrations of Hodgkin's disease. Ann Diagn Pathol 2000, **3**: 386–393.

477 Gutensohn N, Cole P. Childhood social environment and Hodgkin's disease. N Engl J Med 1981, **304**: 135–140.

477a Hjalgrim H, Askling J, Rostgaard K, Hamilton-Dutoit S, Frisch M, Zhang J-S, Madsen M, Rosdahl N, Konradsen HB, Strom HH, Melbye M. Characteristics of Hodgkin's lymphoma after infectious mononucleosis. N Engl J Med 2003, **349**: 1324–1332.

478 Jaffett RF. Viruses and Hodgkin's disease. Ann Oncol 2002, **13**: 23–29.

479 Jarrett RF, Gallagher A, Jones DB, Alexander FE, Krajewski AS, Kelsey A, Adams J, Angus B, Gledhill S, Wright DH, et al. Detection of Epstein–Barr virus genomes in Hodgkin's disease. Relation to age. J Clin Pathol 1991, **44**: 844–848.

480 Kaplan HS. Hodgkin's disease. Cambridge 1980, **2**: 689.

481 Kass AM, Kass EH. Perfecting the world: the life and time of Dr Thomas Hogkin 1798–1866. Boston 1988, **1**: 642.

482 Mack TM, Cozen W, Shibata DK, Weiss LM, Nathwani BN, Hernandez AM, Taylor CR, Hamilton AS, Deapen DM, Rappaport EB. Concordance for Hodgkin's disease in identical twins suggesting genetic susceptibility to the young adult form of the disease. N Engl J Med 1995, **332**: 413–418.

483 Mueller N, Evans A, Harris NL, Comstock GW, Jellum E, Magnus K, Orentreich N, Polk BF, Vogelman J. Hodgkin's disease and Epstein–Barr virus. Altered antibody pattern before diagnosis. N Engl J Med 1989, **320**: 689–695.

484 Pallesen G, Hamilton-Dutoit SJ, Rowe M, Young LS. Expression of Epstein–Barr virus latent gene products in tumour cells of Hodgkin's disease. Lancet 1991, **337**: 320–322.

485 Poston RN. Positive Leu-M1 immunohistochemistry and diagnosis of the lymphoma cases described by Hodgkin's in 1832. AIMM 1999, **7**: 6–8.

486 Reynolds DJ, Banks PM, Gulley ML. New characterization of infectious mononucleosis and a phenotypic comparison with Hodgkin's disease. Am J Pathol 1995, **146**: 379–388.

487 Taylor CR, Riley CR. Evolving concepts of the nature of Hodgkin's disease: a history. Ann Diagn Pathol 2001a, **4**: 337–346.

488 Taylor CR, Riley CR. Molecular morphology of Hodgkin's lymphoma. Appl Immunohistochem Mol Morphol 2001b, **9**: 187–202.

489 Thomas RK, Re D, Zander T, Wolf J, Diehl V. Epidemiology and etiology of Hodgkin's lymphoma. Ann Oncol 2002, **13**: 147–152.

490 Weiss LM, Chang KL. Molecular biologic studies of Hodgkin's disease. Semin Diagn Pathol 1992, **9**: 272–278.

491 Weiss LM, Chen YY, Liu XF, Shibata D. Epstein–Barr virus and Hodgkin's disease. A correlative in situ hybridization and polymerase chain reaction study. Am J Pathol 1991, **139**: 1259–1265.

Reed–Sternberg cell

492 Agnarsson BA, Kadin ME. The immunophenotype of Reed–Sternberg cells. A study of 50 cases of Hodgkin's disease using fixed frozen tissues. Cancer 1989, **63**: 2083–2087.

493 Brauninger A, Hansmann ML, Strickler JG, Dummer R, Burg G, Rajewsky K, Kuppers R. Identification of common germinal-center B-cell precursors in two patients with both Hodgkin's disease and non-Hodgkin's lymphoma. New Engl J Med 1999, **340**: 1239–1247.

494 Carbone A, Gloghini A, Gruss H-J, Pinto A. CD40 antigen expression on Reed–Sternberg cells. A reliable diagnostic tool for Hodgkin's disease. Am J Pathol 1995, **146**: 780–781.

495 Casey TT, Olson SJ, Cousar JB, Collins RD. Immunophenotypes of Reed–Sternberg cells. A study of 19 cases of Hodgkin's disease in plastic-embedded sections. Blood 1989, **74**: 2624–2628.

496 Chang KL, Curtis CM, Momose H, Lopategui J, Weiss LM. Sensitivity and specificity of *Bauhinia purpurea* as a paraffin section marker for the Reed–Sternberg cells of Hodgkin's disease. Appl Immunohistochem 1993, **1**: 208–212.

497 Chen WG, Chen YY, Kamel OW, Koo CH, Weiss LM. P53 mutations in Hodgkin's disease. Lab Invest 1996, **75**: 519–527.

498 Chittal SM, Caveriviere P, Schwarting R, Gerdes J, Al Saati T, Rigal-Huguet F, Stein H, Delsol G. Monoclonal antibodies in the diagnosis of Hodgkin's disease. The search for a rational panel. Am J Surg Pathol 1988, **12**: 9–21.

499 Dallenbach FE, Stein H. Expression of T-cell-receptor β chain in Reed–Sternberg cells. Lancet 1989, **2**: 828–830.

500 Delabie J, Shipman R, Bruggen J, De Strooper B, van Leuven F, Tarcsay L, Cerletti N, Odink K, Diehl V, Bilbe G, et al. Expression of the novel intermediate filament-associated protein restin in Hodgkin's disease and anaplastic large-cell lymphoma. Blood 1992, **80**: 2891–2896.

501 Elenitoba-Johnson KS, Medeiros LJ, Khorsand J, King TC. P53 expression in Reed–Sternberg cells does not correlate with gene mutations in Hodgkin's disease. Am J Clin Pathol 1997, **106**: 728–738.

502 Fan G, Kotylo P, Neiman RS, Braziel RM. Comparison of fascin expression in anaplastic large cell lymphoma and Hodgkin's disease. Am J Clin Pathol 2003, **119**: 199–204.

503 Foss H-D, Hummel M, Gottstein S, Ziemann K, Falini B, Herbst H, Stein H. Frequent expression of IL-7 gene transcripts in tumor cells of classical Hodgkin's disease. Am J Pathol 1995, **146**: 33–39.

504 Griesser H, Feller AC, Mak TW, Lennert K. Clonal rearrangements of T-cell receptor and immunoglobulin genes and immunophenotypic antigen expression in different subclasses of Hodgkin's disease. Int J Cancer 1987, **40**: 157–160.

505 Hsu S-M, Yang K, Jaffe ES. Phenotypic expression of Hodgkin's and Reed–Sternberg cells in Hodgkin's disease. Am J Pathol 1985, **118**: 209–217.

506 Hsu PL, Xie SS, Hsu SM. Absence of T-cell- and B-cell-specific transcription factors TCF-1, GATA-3, and BSAP in Hodgkin's Reed Sternberg cells. Lab Invest 1997, **74**: 395–405.

507 Hummel M, Ziemann K, Lammert H, Pileri S, Sabattini E, Stein H. Hodgkin's disease with monoclonal and polyclonal populations of Reed–Sternberg cells. N Engl J Med 1995, **333**: 901–906.

508 Hyder DM, Schnitzer B. Utility of Leu M1 monoclonal antibody in the differential diagnosis of Hodgkin's disease. Arch Pathol Lab Med 1986, **110**: 416–419.

509 Izban KF, Ergin M, Martinez RL, Alkan S. Expression of the tumor necrosis factor receptor-associated factors (TRAFs)1 and 2 and is a characteristic feature of Hodgkin's and Reed–Sternberg cells. Mod Pathol 2000, **13**: 1324–1331.

510 Izban KF, Nawrocki JF, Alkan S, Hsi ED. Monoclonal IgH gene rearrangement in microdissected nodules from nodular sclerosis Hodgkin's disease. Am J Clin Pathol 1998, **110**: 599–606.

511 Kadin ME. A reappraisal of the Reed–Sternberg cell. A commentary. Blood Cells 1980, **6**: 525–532.

512 Kadin ME, Muramoto L, Said J. Expression of T-cell antigens on Reed–Sternberg cells in a subset of patients with nodular sclerosing and mixed cellularity Hodgkin's disease. Am J Pathol 1988, **130**: 345–353.

513 Knowles DM, Neri A, Pelicci PG, Burke JS, Wu A, Winberg CD, Sheibani K, Dalla-Favera R. Immunoglobulin and T-cell receptor β-chain gene rearrangement analysis of Hodgkin's disease. Implications for lineage determination and differential diagnosis. Proc Natl Acad Sci U S A 1986, **83**: 7942–7946.

514 Le Brun DP, Ngan BY, Weiss LM, Huie P, Warnke RA, Cleary ML. The bcl-2 oncogene in Hodgkin's disease arising in the setting of follicular non-Hodgkin's lymphoma. Blood 1994, **83**: 223–230.

515 Louie DC, Kant JA, Brooks JJ, Reed JC. Absence of t(14; 18) major and minor breakpoints and of Bcl-2 protein overproduction in Reed–Sternberg cells of Hodgkin's disease. Am J Pathol 1991, **139**: 1231–1237.

516 Manzanal AI, Santón A, Acevedo A, Aguilera B, Oliva H, Bellas C. Molecular analysis of the IgH gene in 212 cases of Hodgkin's disease: correlation of IgH clonality with the histologic and the immunocytochemical features. Mod Pathol 1997, **10**: 679–685.

517 Marafioti T, Hummel M, Foss HD, Laumen H, Korbiuhn P, Anagnostopoulos I, Lammert H, Demel G, Theil J, Wirth T, Stein H. Hodgkin's and Reed–Sternberg cell represent an expansion of a single clone originating from a germinal center B-cell with functional immunoglobulin gene rearrangements but defective immnoglobulin transcription. Blood 2000, **95**: 1443–1450.

518 Muschen M, Kuppers R, Spieker T, Brauninger A, Rajewsky K, Hansmann ML. Molecular single-cell analysis of Hodgkin's and Reed–Sternberg cells harbouring unmutated immunoglobulin variable region genes. Lab Invest 2001, **81**: 289–295.

519 Nakamura S, Nagahama M, Kagami Y, Yatabe Y, Takeuchi T, Kojima M, Motoori T, Suzuki R, Taji H, Ogura M, Mizoguchi Y, Okamoto M, Suzuki H, Oyama A, Seto M, Morishima Y, Koshikawa T, Takahashi T, Kurita S, Suchi T. Hodgkin's disease expressing follicular dendritic cell marker CD21 without any other B-cell marker; a clinicopathologic study of nine cases. Am J Surg Pathol 1999, **23**: 363–376.

520 Nguyen PL, Harris NL, Ritz J, Robertson MJ. Expression of CD95 antigen and bcl-2 protein in non-Hodgkin's lymphomas and Hodgkin's disease. Am J Pathol 1997, **148**: 847–853.

521 Nolte M, Werner M, Spann W, Schnabel B, von Wasielewski R, Wilkens L, Hubner K, Fischer R, Georgii A. The bcl/2/JH gene rearrangement is undetectable in Hodgkin's lymphomas. Results from the German Hodgkin trial. Virchows Arch 1995, **426**: 37–42.

522 O'Grady JT, Stewart S, Lowrey J, Howie SE, Krajewski AS. CD40 expression in Hodgkin's disease. Am J Pathol 1994, **144**: 21–26.

523 Oudejans JJ, Kummer JA, Jiwa M, Van Der Valk P, Ossenkoppele GJ, Kluin PM, Kluin-Nelemans JC, Meijer CJ. Granzyme B expression in Reed–Sternberg cells of Hodgkin's disease. Am J Pathol 1996, **148**: 233–240.

524 Peh SC, Kim LH, Poppema S. TARC, a CC chemokine, is frequently expressed in classic Hodgkin's lymphoma but not in NLP Hodgkin's lymphoma, T-cell-rich B-cel lymphoma, and most cases of anaplastic large cell lymphoma. Am J Surg Pathol 2001, **25**: 925–929.

525 Pinkus GS, Pinkus JL, Langhoff E, Matsumura F, Yamashiro S, Mosialos G, Said JW. Fascin, a sensitive new marker for Reed–Sternberg cells of Hodgkin's disease. Evidence for a dendritic or B-cell deriviation? Am J Pathol 1997, **150**: 543–562.

526 Poppema S, Kaleta J, Hepperle B. Chromosomal abnormalities in patients with Hodgkin's disease. Evidence for frequent involvement of the 14q chromosomal region but infrequent bcl-2 gene rearrangement in Reed–Sternberg cells. J Natl Cancer Inst 1992, **84**: 1789–1793.

527 Sakuma I, Yoshino T, Omonishi K, Nishiuchi R, Teramoto N, Yanai H, Kawahara K, Kubonishi I, Matsuo Y, Akagi T. CD95 ligand is expressed in Reed–Sternberg cells of Hodgkin's disease. Pathol Int 1999, **49**: 103–109.

528 Sarker AB, Akagi T, Jeon HJ, Miyake K, Murakami I, Yoshino T, Takahashi K, Nose S. *Bauhinia purpurea* – a new paraffin section marker for Reed–Sternberg cells of Hodgkin's disease. A comparison with Leu-M1 (CD15), LN2 (CD74), peanut agglutinin, and Ber-H2 (CD30). Am J Pathol 1992, **141**: 19–23.

529 Schmid C, Pan L, Diss T, Isaacson PG. Expression of B-cell

antigens by Hodgkin's and Reed–Sternberg cells. Am J Pathol 1991, **139:** 701–707.

530 Stetler-Stevenson M, Crush-Stanton S, Cossman J. Involvement of the bcl-2 gene in Hodgkin's disease. J Natl Cancer Inst 1990, **82:** 855–858.

531 Strum SB, Park JK, Rappaport H. Observation of cells resembling Sternberg-Reed cells in conditions other than Hodgkin's disease. Cancer 1977, **26:** 176–190.

532 Thangavelu M, Le Beau MM. Chromosomal abnormalities in Hodgkin's disease. Hematol Oncol Clin North Am 1989, **3:** 221–236.

533 Tilly H, Bastard C, Delastre T, Duval C, Bizet M, Lenormand B, Dauce JP, Monconduit M, Piguet H. Cytogenetic studies in untreated Hodgkin's disease. Blood 1991, **77:** 1298–1304.

534 Tindle BH, Parker JW, Lukes RJ. "Reed–Sternberg cells" in infectious mononucleosis? Am J Clin Pathol 1972, **58:** 607–617.

535 Vasef MA, Alsabeh R, Medeiros LJ, Weiss LM. Immunophenotype of Reed–Sternberg and Hodgkin's cells in sequential biopsy specimens of Hogkins disease. A paraffin-section immunohistochemical study using the heat induced epitope retrieval method. Am J Clin Pathol 1997, **108:** 54–59.

536 Verbeke CS, Wenthe U, Grobholz R, Zentgraf H. Fas ligand expression in Hodgkin's lymphoma. Am J Surg Pathol 2001, **25:** 388–394.

537 Watanabe K, Yamashita Y, Nakayama A, Hasegawa Y, Kojima H, Nagasawa T, Mori N. Varied B-cell immunophenotypes of Hodgkin/Reed–Sternberg cells in classic Hodgkin's disease. Histopathology 2000, **36:** 353–361.

538 Weber-Matthiesen K, Deerberg-Wittram J, Rosenwald A, Poetsch M, Grote W, Schlegelberger B. Translocation t(2.5) is not a primary event in Hodgkin's disease: simultaneous immunophenotyping and interphase cytogenetics. Am J Pathol 1996, **149:** 463–468.

539 Weiss LM, Strickler JG, Hu E, Warnke RA, Sklar J. Immunoglobulin gene rearrangements in Hodgkin's disease. Hum Pathol 1986, **17:** 1009–1014.

540 Zukerberg LR, Collins AB, Ferry JA, Harris NL. Coexpression of CD15 and CD20 by Reed–Sternberg cells in Hodgkin's disease. Am J Pathol 1991, **139:** 475–483.

Microscopic types

541 Harris NL. Hodgkin's disease: classification and differential diagnosis. Mod Pathol 1999, **12:** 159–175.

542 Jaffe ES, Harris NL, Stein H, Vardiman JW. Tumours of haematopoietic and lymphoid tissues. Pathology & Genetics, World Health Organization classification of tumours. Lyon, 2001, IARC Press.

543 Jackson H, Parker F. Hodgkin's disease. 1. General considerations. N Engl J Med 1944, **230:** 1–8.

544 Lukes RJ. Relationship of histologic features to clinical stages in Hodgkin's disease. Am J Roentgenol 1963, **90:** 944–955.

545 Lukes RJ, Butler JJ, Hicks EB. Natural history of Hodgkin's disease as related to its pathologic picture. Cancer 1966, **19:** 317–344.

546 Lukes RJ, Craver LF, Hall TC, Rappaport H, Ruben P. Report of Nomenclature Committee. Cancer Res 1966, **16:** 1311.

547 Mauch PM. Hodgkin's disease. Philadelphia 1999, Williams & Wilkins.

548 Pileri SA, Ascani S, Leoncini L, Sabattini E, Zinzani PL, Piccaluga P, Pileri A Jr, Giunti M, Falii B, Bolis GB, Stein H. Hodgkin's lymphoma: the pathologist's viewpoint. J Clin Pathol 2002, **55:** 162–176.

549 Smetana HF, Cohen BM. Mortality in relation to histologic type in Hodgkin's disease. Blood 1956, **11:** 211–224.

Nodular lymphocyte predominance Hodgkin's lymphoma

550 Brauninger A, Hansmann ML, Strickler JG, Dummer R, Burg G, Rajewsky K, Kuppers R. Identification of common germinal-center B-cell precursors in two patients with both Hodgkin's disease and non-Hodgkin's lymphoma. New Engl J Med 1999, **340:** 1239–1247.

551 Brauninger A, Küppers R, Strickler JG, Wacker HH, Rajewsky K, Hansmann ML. Hodgkin's and Reed–Sternberg cells in lymphocyte predominant Hodgkin's disease represent clonal populations of germinal center-derived tumor B-cells. Proc Natl Acad Sci U S A 1997, **94:** 9337–9342.

552 Chittal SM, Alard C, Rossi JF, al Saati T, Le Tourneau A, Diebold J, Delsol G. Further phenotypic evidence that nodular, lymphocyte-predominant Hodgkin's disease is a large B-cell lymphoma in evolution. Am J Surg Pathol 1990, **14:** 1024–1035.

553 Cibull ML, Stein H, Gatter KC, Mason DY. The expression of the CD3 antigen in Hodgkin's disease. Histopathology 1989, **15:** 599–605.

554 Colby TV, Hoppe RT, Warnke RA. Hodgkin's disease at autopsy. 1972–1977. Cancer 1981, **47:** 1852–1862.

555 Coles FB, Cartun RW, Pastuszak WT. Hodgkin's disease, lymphocyte-predominant type. Immunoreactivity with B-cell antibodies. Mod Pathol 1988, **1:** 274–278.

556 Delabie J, Greiner TC, Chan WC, Weisenberger DD. Concurrent lymphocyte predominance Hodgkin's disease and T-cell lymphoma: a report of three cases. Am J Surg Pathol 1997, **20:** 355–362.

556a Fan Z, Natkunam Y, Bair E, Tibshirani R, Warnke RA. Characterization of variant patterns of nodular lymphocyte predominant Hodgkin lymphoma with immunohistologic and clinical correlation. Am J Surg Pathol 2003, **27:** 1346–1356.

557 Ferry JA, Zukerberg LR, Harris NL. Florid progressive transformation of germinal centers. A syndrome affecting young men, without early progression to nodular lymphocyte predominance Hodgkin's disease. Am J Surg Pathol 1992, **16:** 252–258.

558 Gelb AB, Dorfman RF, Warnke RA. Coexistence of nodular lymphocyte predominance Hodgkin's disease and Hodgkin's disease of the usual type. Am J Surg Pathol 1993, **17:** 364–374.

558a Jaffe ES, Harris NL, Stein H, Vardiman JW. Tumours of haematopoietic and lymphoid tissues. World Health Organisation Classification of Tumours-Pathology and genetics, Lyon, IARC Press, 2001.

559 Kamel OW, Gelb AB, Shibuya RB, Warnke RA. Leu 7 (CD57) reactivity distinguishes nodular lymphocyte predominance Hodgkin's disease from nodular sclerosing Hodgkin's disease, T-cell-rich B-cell lymphoma and follicular lymphoma. Am J Pathol 1993, **142:** 541–546.

560 Khalidi HS, Lones MA, Zhou Y, Weiss LM, Medeiros LJ. Detection of Epstein–Barr virus in the L & H cells of nodular lymphocyte predominance Hodgkin's disease. Report of a case documented by immunohistochemical, in situ hybridization, and polymerase chain reaction methods. Am J Clin Pathol 1997, **108:** 687–692.

561 Lukes RJ, Butler JJ, Hicks EB. Natural history of Hodgkin's disease as related to its pathologic picture. Cancer 1966, **19:** 317–344.

562 Marafioti T, Hummel M, Anagnostopoulos I, Foss HD, Falini B, Delsol G, Isaacson PG, Pileri S, Stein H. Origin of nodular lymphocyte-predominant Hodgkin's disease from a clonal expansion of highly mutated germinal-center B-cells. N Engl J Med 1997, **337:** 453–458.

563 Mason DY, Banks PM, Chan J, Cleary ML, Delsol G, de Wolf Peeters C, Falini B, Gatter K, Grogan TM, Harris NL, et al. Nodular lymphocyte predominance Hodgkin's disease. A distinct clinicopathological entity (editorial). Am J Surg Pathol 1994, **18:** 526–530.

564 Möller P, Lennert K. On the angiostructure of lymph nodes in Hodgkin's disease. An immunohistochemical study using the

lectin I of *Ulex europaeus* as endothelial marker. Virchows Arch [A] 1984, **403**: 257–270.

565 Momose H, Chen YY, Ben-Ezra J, Weiss LM. Nodular lymphocyte-predominant Hodgkin's disease. Study of immunoglobulin light chain protein and mRNA expression. Hum Pathol 1992, **23**: 1115–1119.

566 Nicholas DS, Harris S, Wright DH. Lymphocyte predominance Hodgkin's disease – an immunohistochemical study. Histopathology 1990, **16**: 157–165.

567 Ohno T, Huang JZ, Wu G, Park KH, Weisenburger DD, Chan WC. The tumor cells in nodular lymphocyte-predominant Hodgkin's disease are clonally related to the large cell lymphoma occurring in the same individual. Direct demonstration by single cell analysis. Am J Clin Pathol 2001, **116**: 506–511.

568 Poppema S. Lymphocyte-predominance Hodgkin's disease. Semin Diagn Pathol 1992, **9**: 257–264.

569 Poppema S, Kaiserling E, Lennert K. Epidemiology of nodular paragranuloma (Hodgkin's disease with lymphocytic predominance, nodular). J Cancer Res Clin Oncol 1979, **95**: 57–63.

570 Poppema S, Kaiserling E, Lennert K. Hodgkin's disease with lymphocytic pre-dominance, nodular type (nodular paragranuloma) and progressively transformed germinal centers. A cytohistological study. Histopathology 1979, **3**: 295–308.

571 Regula DP Jr, Hoppe RT, Weiss LM. Nodular and diffuse types of lymphocyte predominance Hodgkin's disease. N Engl J Med 1988, **318**: 214–219.

572 Regula DP Jr, Weiss LM, Warnke RA, Dorfman RS. Lymphocyte predominance Hodgkin's disease. A reappraisal based upon histological and immunophenotypical findings in relapsing cases. Histopathology 1987, **11**: 1107–1120.

573 Ruprai AK, Pringle JH, Angel CA, Kind CN, Lauder I. Localization of immunoglobulin light chain mRNA expression in Hodgkin's disease by in situ hybridization. J Pathol 1991, **164**: 37–40.

574 Said JW, Sassoon AF, Shintaku IP, Kurtin PJ, Pinkus GS. Absence of bcl-2 major breakpoint region and JH gene rearrangement in lymphocyte predominance Hodgkin's disease. Results of Southern blot analysis and polymerase chain reaction. Am J Pathol 1991, **138**: 261–264.

575 Schmid C, Sargent C, Isaacson PG. L and H cells of nodular lymphocyte predominant Hodgkin's disease show immunoglobulin light-chain restriction. Am J Pathol 1991, **139**: 1281–1289.

576 Soderstrom N, Norberg B. Observations regarding the specific postcapillary venules of lymph nodes in malignant lymphomas. Acta Pathol Microbiol Scand (A) 1974, **82**: 71–79.

577 Stoler MH, Nichols GE, Symbula M, Weiss LM. Lymphocyte predominance Hodgkin's disease. Evidence for a k light chain-restricted monotypic B-cell neoplasm. Am J Pathol 1995, **146**: 810–818.

578 Trudel MA, Krikorian JG, Neiman RS. Lymphocyte predominance Hodgkin's disease. A clinicopathologic reassessment. Cancer 1987, **59**: 99–106.

579 Von Wasielewski R, Werner M, Fischer R, Hansmann ML, Hubner K, Hasenclever D, Franklin J, Sextro M, Diehl V, Georgii A. Lymphocyte-predominant Hodgkin's disease. An Immunohistochemical analysis of 208 reviewed Hodgkin's disease cases from the German Hodgkin's Study Group. Am J Pathol 1997b, **150**: 793–803.

Classical Hodgkin's lymphoma

580 Colby TV, Hoppe RT, Warnke RA. Hodgkin's disease at autopsy. 1972–1977. Cancer 1981, **47**: 1852–1862.

581 Colby TV, Warnke RA. The histology of the initial relapse of Hodgkin's disease. Cancer 1980, **45**: 289–292.

582 Coleman CN, Williams CJ, Flint A, Glatstein EJ, Rosenberg SA,

Kaplan HS. Hematologic neoplasia in patients treated for Hodgkin's disease. N Engl J Med 1977, **297**: 1249–1252.

583 Coppleson LW, Rappaport H, Strum SB, Rose J. Analysis of the Rye classification of Hodgkin's disease. The prognostic significance of cellular composition. J Natl Cancer Inst 1973, **51**: 379–390.

584 Krikorian JG, Burke JS, Rosenberg SA, Kaplan HS. Occurrence of non-Hodgkin's lymphoma after therapy for Hodgkin's disease. N Engl J Med 1979, **300**: 452–458.

585 MacLennan KA, Bennett MH, Tu A, Hudson BV, Easterling MJ, Hudson GV, Jelliffe AM. Relationship of histopathologic features to survival and relapse in nodular sclerosing Hodgkin's disease. A study of 1659 patients. Cancer 1989, **64**: 1686–1693.

586 Marshall AHE, Matilla A, Pollock DJ. A critique and case study of nodular sclerosing Hodgkin's disease. J Clin Pathol 1976, **29**: 923–930.

587 Seemayer TA, Lagace R, Schürch W. On the pathogenesis of sclerosis and nodularity in nodular sclerosing Hodgkin's disease. Virchows Arch [A] 1980, **385**: 283–291.

588 Strickler JG, Michie SA, Warnke RA, Dorfman RF. The "syncytial variant" of nodular sclerosing Hodgkin's disease. Am J Surg Pathol 1986, **10**: 470–477.

589 Strum SB, Rappaport H. Interrelations of the histologic types of Hodgkin's disease. Arch Pathol 1971, **91**: 127–134.

Other microscopic features

590 Alavaikko MJ, Hansmann ML, Nebendahl C, Parwaresch MR, Lennert K. Follicular dendritic cells in Hodgkin's disease. Am J Clin Pathol 1991, **95**: 194–200.

591 Colby TV, Hoppe RT, Warnke RA. Hodgkin's disease. A clinicopathologic study of 659 cases. Cancer 1982, **49**: 1848–1858.

592 Crocker J, Smith PJ. A quantitative study of mast cells in Hodgkin's disease. J Clin Pathol 1984, **37**: 519–522.

593 Doggett RS, Colby TV, Dorfman RF. Interfollicular Hodgkin's disease. Am J Surg Pathol 1983, **7**: 145–149.

594 Kadin ME, Donaldson SS, Dorfman RF. Isolated granulomas in Hodgkin's disease. N Engl J Med 1970, **283**: 859–861.

595 Kansal R, Singleton TP, Ross CW, Finn WG, Padmore RF, Schnitzer B. Follicular Hodgkin's lymphoma: a histopathologic study. Am J Clin Pathol 2002, **117**: 29–35.

596 Mohrmann RL, Nathwani BN, Brynes RK, Sheibani K. Hodgkin's disease occurring in monocytoid B-cell clusters. Am J Clin Pathol 1991, **95**: 802–808.

597 Pak HY, Friedman NB. Pseudosarcoid granulomas in Hodgkin's disease. Hum Pathol 1981, **12**: 832–837.

598 Rappaport H, Strum SB, Hutchison G, Allen LW. Clinical and biological significance of vascular invasion in Hodgkin's disease. Cancer Res 1971, **31**: 1794–1798.

599 Sacks EL, Donaldson SS, Gordon J, Dorfman RF. Epithelioid granulomas associated with Hodgkin's disease. Clinical correlations in 55 previously untreated patients. Cancer 1978, **41**: 562–567.

600 Strum SB, Hutchison GB, Park JK, Rappaport H. Further observations on the biologic significance of vascular invasion in Hodgkin's disease. Cancer 1971, **27**: 1–6.

601 Strum SB, Rappaport H. Significance of focal involvement of lymph nodes for the diagnosis and staging of Hodgkin's disease. Cancer 1970, **25**: 1314–1319.

602 Variakojis D, Strum SB, Rappaport H. The foamy macrophages in Hodgkin's disease. Arch Pathol 1971, **93**: 453–456.

General and clinical features

603 Akazaki K, Wakasa H. Frequency of lymphoreticular tumors and leukemias in Japan. J Natl Cancer Inst 1974, **52**: 339–343.

604 Bellas C, Santon A, Manzanal A, Campo E, Martin C, Acevedo A, Varona C, Forteza J, Morente M, Montalban C.

Pathological, immunological, and molecular features of Hodgkin's disease associated with HIV infection: comparison with ordinary Hodgkin's disease. Am J Surg Pathol 1996, **20**: 1520–1524.

605 Bodis S, Kraus MD, Pinkus G, Silver B, Kadin ME, Canellos GP, Shulman LN, Tarbell NJ, Mauch PM. Clinical presentation and outcome in lymphocyte-predominant Hodgkin's disease. J Clin Oncol 1997, **15**: 3060–3066.

606 Correa P, O'Conor GT. Epidemiologic patterns of Hodgkin's disease. Int J Cancer 1971, **8**: 192–201.

607 Cross RM. A clinicopathological study of nodular sclerosing Hodgkin's disease. J Clin Pathol 1968, **21**: 303–310.

608 Greer JP, Kinney MC, Cousar JB, Flexner JM, Dupont WD, Graber SE, Greco FA, Collins RD, Stein RS. Lymphocyte-depleted Hodgkin's disease. Clinicopathologic review of 25 patients. Am J Med 1986, **81**: 208–214.

609 Grufferman S, Delzell E. Epidemiology of Hodgkin's disease. Epidemiol Rev 1984, **6**: 76–106.

610 Levy R, Kaplan HS. Impaired lymphocyte function in untreated Hodgkin's disease. N Engl J Med 1974, **290**: 181–186.

611 Neiman RS. Current problems in the histopathologic diagnosis and classification of Hodgkin's disease. Pathol Annu 1978, **13**(Pt 2): 289–328.

612 Neiman RS, Rosen PJ, Lukes RJ. Lymphocyte-depletion Hodgkin's disease. A clinicopathologic entity. N Engl J Med 1973, **288**: 751–755.

613 Poppema S, Lennert K. Hodgkin's disease in childhood. Histopathologic classification in relation to age and sex. Cancer 1980, **45**: 1443–1447.

614 Siebert JD, Stuckey JH, Kurtin PJ, Banks PM. Extranodal lymphocyte predominance Hodgkin's disease. Clinical and pathologic features. Am J Clin Pathol 1995, **103**: 485–491.

615 Trotter MC, Cloud GA, Davis M, Sanford SP, Urist MM, Soong S-J, Halpern NB, Maddox WA, Balch CM. Predicting the risk of abdominal disease in Hodgkin's lymphoma. A multifactorial analysis of staging laparotomy results in 255 patients. Ann Surg 1985, **201**: 465–469.

616 Unger PD, Strauchen JA. Hodgkin's disease in AIDS complex patients. Report of four cases and tissue immunologic marker studies. Cancer 1986, **58**: 821–825.

617 White L, McCourt BA, Isaacs H, Siegel SE, Stowe SM, Higgins GR. Patterns of Hodgkin's disease at diagnosis in young children. Am J Pediatr Hematol Oncol 1983, **5**: 251–257.

Spread

618 Aisenberg AC. Malignant lymphoma. N Engl J Med 1973, **288**: 883–890, 935–941.

619 Glatstein E, Trueblood HW, Enright LP, Rosenberg SA, Kaplan HS. Surgical staging of abdominal involvement in unselected patients with Hodgkin's disease. Radiology 1970, **97**: 425–432.

620 Kadin ME, Glatstein E, Dorfman RF. Clinicopathologic studies of 117 untreated patients subjected to laparotomy for the staging of Hodgkin's disease. Cancer 1971, **27**: 1277–1294.

621 Kaplan HS. Contiguity and progression in Hodgkin's disease. Cancer Res 1971, **31**: 1811–1813.

622 Keller AR, Kaplan HS, Lukes RJ, Rappaport H. Correlation of histopathology with other prognostic indicators in Hodgkin's disease. Cancer 1968, **22**: 487–499.

623 Leslie KO, Colby TV. Hepatic parenchymal lymphoid aggregates in Hodgkin's disease. Hum Pathol 1984, **15**: 808–809.

Staging

624 Carbone PP, Kaplan HS, Musshoff K, Smithers DW, Tubiana M. Report of the committee on Hodgkin's disease staging classification. Cancer Res 1971, **31**: 1860–1861.

625 Hays DM, Ternberg JL, Chen TT, Sullivan MP, Fuller LM, Tefft M, Kung F, Gilchrist G, Fryer C, Heller RN, Wharam M, White L, Jenkins DL, Higgins G, Gehan EA. Complications related to 234 staging laparotomies performed in the Intergroup Hodgkin's Disease in Childhood Study. Surgery 1984, **96**: 471–478.

626 Lacher MJ. Routine staging laparotomy for patients with Hodgkin's disease is no longer necessary. Cancer Invest 1983, **1**: 93–99.

627 Lister TA, Crowther D, Sutcliffe SB, Glatstein E, Canellos GP, Young RC, Rosenberg SA, Coltman CA, Tubiana M. Report of a committee convened to discuss the evaluation and staging of patients with Hodgkin's disease. Cotswolds meeting. J Clin Oncol 1989, **7**: 1630–1636.

Treatment

628 Anderson JE, Litzow MR, Appelbaum FR, Schoch G, Fisher LD, Buckner CD, Petersen FB, Crawford SW, Press OW, Sanders JE, et al. Allogeneic, syngeneic, and autologous marrow transplantation for Hodgkin's disease. The 21-year Seattle experience. J Clin Oncol 1993, **11**: 2342–2350.

629 Colby TV, Hoppe RT, Warnke RA. Hodgkin's disease at autopsy. 1972–1977. Cancer 1981, **47**: 1852–1862.

630 Jones RJ, Piantadosi S, Mann RB, Ambinder RF, Seifter EJ, Vriesendorp HM, Abeloff MD, Burns WH, May WS, Rowley SD, et al. High-dose cytotoxic therapy and bone marrow transplantation for relapsed Hodgkin's disease. J Clin Oncol 1990, **8**: 527–537.

631 Rosenberg SA, Kaplan HS. The evolution and summary results of the Stanford randomized clinical trials of the management of Hodgkin's disease. 1962–1984. Int J Radiat Oncol Biol Phys 1985, **11**: 5–22.

632 Straus DJ. Strategies in the treatment of Hodgkin's disease. Semin Oncol 1985, **13**: 26–34.

633 Strum SB, Rappaport H. The persistence of Hodgkin's disease in long-term survivors. Am J Med 1971, **51**: 222–240.

634 Urba WJ, Longo DL. Hodgkin's disease. N Engl J Med 1992, **326**: 678–687.

635 Weissman LB, Corson JM, Neugut AI, Antman KH. Malignant mesothelioma following treatment for Hodgkin's disease. J Clin Oncol 1996, **14**: 2098–2100.

636 Wolden SL, Lamborn KR, Cleary SF, Tate DJ, Donaldson SS. Second cancers following pediatric Hodgkin's disease. J Clin Oncol 1998, **16**: 535–544.

Prognosis

637 Alavaikko MJ, Blanco G, Aine R, Lehtinen T, Fellbaum C, Taskinen PJ, Sarpola A, Hansmann ML. Follicular dendritic cells have prognostic relevance in Hodgkin's disease. Am J Clin Pathol 1994, **101**: 761–767.

638 Baur AS, Meuge-Moraw C, Michel G, Delacretaz F. Prognostic value of follicular dendritic cells in nodular sclerosing Hodgkin's disease. Histopathology 1998, **32**: 512–520.

639 Bearman RM, Pangalis GA, Rappaport H. Hodgkin's disease, lymphocyte depletion type. A clinicopathologic study of 39 patients. Cancer 1978, **41**: 293–302.

640 Butler JJ. Relationship of histologic findings to survival in Hodgkin's disease. Gann Monogr Cancer Res 1973, **15**: 275–286.

641 Colby TV, Hoppe RT, Warnke RA. Hodgkin's disease. A clinicopathologic study of 659 cases. Cancer 1981, **49**: 1848–1858.

642 Diehl V, Sextro M, Franklin J, Hansmann ML, Harris N, Jaffe E, Poppema S, Harris M, Franssila K, Van Krieken J, Marafioti T, Anagnostopoulos I, Stein H. Clinical presentation, course and prognostic factors in lymphocyte-predominant Hodgkin's disease and lymphocyte-rich classical Hodgkin's disease: report from the European Task Force on lymphoma project on lymphocyte-predominant Hodgkin's disease. J Clin Oncol 1999, **17**: 776–783.

643 Dimopoulos MA, Cabanillas F, Lee JJ, Swan F, Fuller L, Allen PK, Hagemeister FB. Prognostic role of serum β2-microglobulin in Hodgkin's disease. J Clin Oncol 1993, **11**: 1108–1111.

644 Eghbali H, Hoerni-Simon G, de Mascarel I, Durand M, Chauvergne J, Hoerni B. Hodgkin's disease in the elderly. A series of 30 patients aged older than 70 years. Cancer 1984, **53**: 2191–2193.

645 Ferry JA, Linggood RM, Convery KM, Efird JT, Eliseo R, Harris NL. Hodgkin disease, nodular sclerosis type. Implications of histologic subclassification. Cancer 1993, **71**: 457–463.

646 Gause A, Roschansky V, Tschiersch A, Smith K, Hasenclever D, Schmits R, Diehl V, Pfreundschuh M. Low serum interleukin-2 receptor levels correlate with a good prognosis in patients with Hodgkin's lymphoma. Ann Oncol 1991, **2**(Suppl): 43–47.

647 Kaplan HS. Hodgkin's disease, ed. 2. Cambridge, Mass, 1980, Harvard University Press.

648 Keller AR, Kaplan HS, Lukes RJ, Rappaport H. Correlation of histopathology with other prognostic indicators in Hodgkin's disease. Cancer 1968, **22**: 487–499.

649 Pizzolo G, Vinante F, Chilosi M, Dallenbach F, Josimovic-Alasevic O, Diamantstein T, Stein H. Serum levels of soluble CD30 molecule (Ki-1 antigen) in Hodgkin's disease. Relationship with disease activity and clinical stage. Br J Haematol 1990, **75**: 282–284.

650 Sacks EL, Donaldson SS, Gordon J, Dorfman RF. Epithelioid granulomas associated with Hodgkin's disease. Clinical correlations in 55 previously untreated patients. Cancer 1978, **41**: 562–567.

651 Shankar AG, Ashley S, Radford M, Barrett A, Wright D, Pinkerton CR. Does histology influence outcome in childhood Hodgkin's disease? Results from the United Kingdom Children's Cancer Study Group. J Clin Oncol 1997, **15**: 2622–2630.

652 Straus DJ, Gaynor JJ, Myers J, Merke DP, Caravelli J, Chapman D, Yahalom J, Clarkson BD. Prognostic factors among 185 adults with newly diagnosed advanced Hodgkin's disease treated with alternating potentially noncross-resistant chemotherapy and intermediate-dose radiation therapy. J Clin Oncol 1990, **8**: 1173–1186.

653 Torti FM, Portlock CS, Rosenberg SA, Kaplan HS. Extralymphatic Hodgkin's disease. Prognosis and response to therapy. Am J Med 1981, **70**: 487–492.

654 Trudel MA, Krikorian JG, Neiman RS. Lymphocyte predominance Hodgkin's disease. A clinicopathologic reassessment. Cancer 1987, **59**: 99–106.

655 Von Wasielewski R, Mengel M, Fischer R, Hansmann ML, Hübner K, Franklin J, Tesch H, Paulus U, Werner M, Diehl V, Georgii A. Classical Hodgkin's disease. Clinical impact of the immunophenotype. Am J Pathol 1997a, **151**: 1123–1130.

656 Wright CJE. Prospects of cure in lymphocyte-predominant Hodgkin's disease. Am J Clin Pathol 1977, **67**: 507–511.

Non-Hodgkin's lymphoma

657 Alavaikko M, Aine R. The Lukes and Collins classification on non-Hodgkin's lymphomas. 1. A histological reappraisal of 301 cases. Acta Pathol Microbiol Immunol Scand (A) 1982, **90**: 241–249.

658 Byrne GE Jr. Rappaport classification of non-Hodgkin's lymphoma. Histologic features and clinical significance. Cancer Treat Rep 1977, **61**: 935–944.

659 Chan JK. The new World Health Organisation classification of lymphomas: the past, the present and the future. Hematol Oncol 2001, **19**: 129–150.

660 Chan JKC, Banks PM, Cleary ML, Delsol G, De Wolf-Peeters C, Falini B, Gatter KC, Grogan TM, Harris NL, Isaacson PG, Jaffe ES, Knowles DM, Mason DY, Müller-Hermelink HK, Pileri SA, Piris MA, Ralfkiaer E, Stein H, Warnke RA. A revised European-American classification of lymphoid neoplasms proposed by the International Lymphoma Study Group. A summary version. Am J Clin Pathol 1995, **103**: 543–560.

661 Dorfman RF. Classification of the malignant lymphomas. Am J Surg Pathol 1977, **1**: 167–170.

662 Dorfman RF, Kim H. Relationship of histology to site in the non-Hodgkin's lymphomata. A study based on surgical staging procedures. Br J Cancer 1975, **31**: 217–220.

663 Ersboll J, Schultz HB, Hougaard P, Nissen NI, Hou-Jensen K. Comparison of the working formulation of non-Hodgkin's lymphoma with the Rappaport, Kiel, and Lukes & Collins classifications. Translational value and prognostic significance based on review of 658 patients treated at a single institution. Cancer 1985, **55**: 2442–2458.

664 Gall EA, Mallory TB. Malignant lymphoma. A clinicopathologic survey of 618 cases. Am J Pathol 1942, **18**: 381–429.

665 Goffinet DR, Warnke R, Dunnick NR, Castellino R, Glatstein E, Nelsen TS, Dorfman RF, Rosenberg SA, Kaplan AS. Clinical and surgical (laparotomy) evaluation of patients with non-Hodgkin's lymphomas. Cancer Treat Rep 1977, **61**: 981–992.

666 Harris NL, Jaffe ES, Stein H, Banks PM, Chan JK, Cleary ML, Delsol G, De Wolf-Peeters C, Falini B, Gatter KC, et al. A revised European-American classification of lymphoid neoplasms. A proposal from the International Lymphoma Study Group. Blood 1994, **84**: 1361–1392.

667 Jaffe ES, Harris NL, Stein H, Vardiman JW. Tumours of hematopoietic and lymphoid tissues, Pathology & Genetics, World Health Organization Classification of Tumours, Lyon IARC Press, 2001.

668 Lennert K. Classification of non-Hodgkin's lymphomas. In Lennert K, et al.: Malignant lymphomas other than Hodgkin's disease. Histology, cytology, ultrastructure, immunology. Berlin, 1978, Springer-Verlag, pt 3, 1978, pp. 83–110.

669 Lennert K, Collins RD, Lukes RJ. Concordance of the Kiel and Lukes-Collins classifications of non-Hodgkin's lymphomas. Histopathology 1983, **7**: 549–559.

670 Lukes RJ, Collins RD. Immunologic characterization of human malignant lymphomas. Cancer 1974, **34**: 1488–1503.

671 Lukes RJ, Parker JW, Taylor CR, Tindle BH, Cramer AD, Lincoln TL. Immunologic approach to non-Hodgkin lymphomas and related leukemias. Analysis of the results of multiparameter studies of 425 cases. Semin Hematol 1978, **15**: 322–351.

672 Nathwani BN. A critical analysis of the classifications of non-Hodgkin's lymphomas. Cancer 1979, **44**: 347–384.

673 Nathwani BN, Kim H, Rappaport H, Solomon J, Fox M. Non-Hodgkin's lymphomas. A clinicopathologic study comparing two classifications. Cancer 1978, **41**: 303–325.

674 NCI Non-Hodgkin's Classification Project Writing Committee. Classification of non-Hodgkin's lymphomas. Reproducibility of major classification systems. Cancer 1985, **55**: 91–95.

675 Non-Hodgkin's Lymphoma Pathologic Classification Project. National Cancer Institute sponsored study of classifications of non-Hodgkin's lymphoma. Summary and description of a working formulation for clinical usage. Cancer 1982, **49**: 2112–2135.

676 Rappaport H. Tumors of the hematopoietic system. In Atlas of tumor pathology, series 3, fascicle 8. Washington, D.C., 1966, Armed Forces Institute of Pathology.

677 Rosenberg SA, Dorfman RF, Kaplan HS. A summary of the results of a review of 405 patients with non-Hodgkin's lymphoma at Stanford University. Br J Cancer 1975, **31**: 168–173.

678 Willis R. The tumors of lymphoid tissue. In Wills R: Pathology of tumors. St. Louis, 1948, C.V. Mosby, pp. 760–761.

Small lymphocytic lymphoma

679 Addis BJ, Isaacson P, Billings JA. Plasmacytoma of lymph nodes. Cancer 1980, **46**: 340–346.

680 Alexanian R. Monoclonal gammopathy in lymphoma. Arch Intern Med 1975, **135**: 62–66.

681 Andriko JW, Swerdlow SH, Aguilera NI, Abbondanzo SL. Is lymphoplasmacytic lymphoma/immunocytoma a distinct entity? A clinicopathologic study of 20 cases. Am J Surg Pathol 2001, **25**: 742–751.

682 Armitage JO, Dick FR, Corder MP. Diffuse histiocytic lymphoma complicating chronic lymphocytic leukemia. Cancer 1978, **41**: 422–427.

683 Asplund SL, McKenna RW, Howard MS, Kroft SH. Immunophenotype does not correlate with lymph node histology in chronic lymphocytic leukemia/small lymphocytic lymphoma. Am J Surg Pathol 2002, **26**: 624–629.

684 Batata A, Shen B. Relationship between chronic lymphocytic leukemia and small lymphocytic lymphoma. A comparative study of membrane phenotypes in 270 cases. Cancer 1992, **70**: 625–632.

685 Ben-Ezra J, Burke JS, Swartz WG, Brownell MD, Brynes RK, Hill LR, Nathwani BN, Oken MM, Wolf BC, Woodruff R, et al. Small lymphocytic lymphoma. A clinicopathologic analysis of 268 cases. Blood 1989, **73**: 579–587.

686 Berger F, Felman P, Sonet A, Salles G, Bastion Y, Bryon PA, Coiffier B. Non-follicular small B-cell lymphomas. A heterogeneous group of patients with distinct clinical features and outcome. Blood 1994, **83**: 2829–2835.

687 Bonato M, Pittaluga S, Tierens A, Criel A, Verhoef G, Wlodarska I, Vantysel L, Michaux L, Vandekerckhove P, Van Den Berghe H, De Wolf-Peters C. Lymph node histology in typical and atypical chronic lymphocytic leukemia. Am J Surg Pathol 1998, **22**: 49–56.

688 Brecher M, Banks PM. Hodgkin's disease variant of Richter's syndrome. Report of eight cases. Am J Clin Pathol 1990, **93**: 333–339.

689 Brouet J-C, Clauvel J-P, Danon F, Klein M, Seligmann M. Biologic and clinical significance of cryoglobulins. A report of 86 cases. Am J Med 1974, **57**: 775–788.

690 Brouet J-C, Sasportes M, Flandrin G, Preud'Homme J-L, Seligmann M. Chronic lymphocytic leukaemia of T-cell origin. Immunological and clinical evaluation in eleven patients. Lancet 1975, **2**: 890–893.

691 Brunning RD, Parkin J. Intranuclear inclusions in plasma cells and lymphocytes from patients with monoclonal gammopathies. Am J Clin Pathol 1976, **66**: 10–21.

692 Carbone A, Pinto A, Gloghini A, Volpe R, Zagonel V. B-zone small lymphocytic lymphoma. A morphologic, immunophenotypic, and clinical study with comparison to "well-differentiated" lymphocytic disorders. Hum Pathol 1992, **23**: 438–448.

693 Cohen RJ, Bohannon RA, Wallterstein RO. Waldenstrom's macroglobulinemia. A study of ten cases. Am J Med 1966, **41**: 274.

694 Dick FR, Maca RD. The lymph node in chronic lymphocytic leukemia. Cancer 1978, **41**: 283–292.

695 Dorfman DM, Pinkus GS. Distinction between small lymphocytic and mantle cell lymphoma by immunoreactivity for CD23. Mod Pathol 1994, **7**: 326–331.

696 Dutcher TF, Fahey JL. The histopathology of the macroglobulinemia of Waldenstrom. J Natl Cancer Inst 1959, **22**: 887–917.

697 Ellison DJ, Nathwani BN, Cho SY, Martin SE. Interfollicular small lymphocytic lymphoma. The diagnostic significance of pseudofollicles. Hum Pathol 1989, **20**: 1108–1118.

698 Fishkin BG, Spiegelberg HL. Cervical lymph node metastasis as the first manifestation of localized extramedullary plasmacytoma. Cancer 1976, **38**: 1641–1644.

699 Foucar C, Rydell RE. Richter's syndrome in chronic lymphocytic leukemia. Cancer 1980, **46**: 118–134.

700 Franklin EC, Lowenstein J, Bigelow B, Meltzer M. Heavy chain disease. A new disorder of serum gamma-globulins. Report of the first case. Am J Med 1964, **37**: 332–350.

701 Gupta D, Lim MS, Medeiros LJ, Elenitoba-Johnson KS. Small lymphocytic lymphoma with perifollicular, marginal zone, or interfollicular distribution. Mod Pathol 2001, **13**: 1161–1166.

702 Harada M, Shimada M, Fukayama M, Kaneko T, Kitazume K, Weiss SW. Crystal-storing histiocytosis associated with lymphoplasmacytic lymphoma mimicking Weber–Christian disease: immunohistochemical, ultrastructural, and gene-rearrangement studies. Hum Pathol 1996, **27**: 84–87.

703 Harris NL, Bhan AK. B-cell neoplasms of the lymphocytic, lymphoplasmacytoid, and plasma cell types. Immunohistologic analysis and clinical correlation. Hum Pathol 1985, **16**: 829–837.

704 Harrison CV. The morphology of the lymph node in the macroglobulinaemia of Waldenstrom. J Clin Pathol 1972, **25**: 12–16.

705 Jones D, Bhatia VK, Krausz T, Pinkus GS. Crystal-storing histiocytosis: a disorder occurring in plasmacytic tumors expressing immunoglobulin kappa light chain. Hum Pathol 2000, **30**: 1441–1448.

706 Kapadia SB, Enzinger FM, Heffner DK, Hyams VJ, Frizzera G. Crystal-storing histiocytosis associated with lymphoplasmacytic neoplasms: report of three cases mimicking adult rhabdomyoma. Am J Surg Pathol 1993, **17**: 461–467.

707 Kim H, Dorfman RF, Rappaport H. Signet ring cell lymphoma. A rare morphologic and functional expression of nodular (follicular) lymphoma. Am J Surg Pathol 1978, **2**: 119–132.

708 Kim H, Heller P, Rappaport H. Monoclonal gammopathies associated with lymphoproliferative disorders. A morphologic study. Am J Clin Pathol 1973, **59**: 282–294.

709 Knuutila S, Elonen E, Teerenhovi L, Rossi L, Leskinen R, Bloomfield CD, de la Chapelle A. Trisomy 12 in B-cells of patients with B-cell chronic lymphocytic leukemia. N Engl J Med 1986, **314**: 865–869.

710 Kraus MD. Lymphoplasmacytic lymphoma/Waldenstrom macroglobulinemia. One disease of three? Am J Clin Pathol 2001, **116**: 799–801.

711 Krauss S, Sokal JE. Paraproteinemia in the lymphomas. Am J Med 1966, **40**: 400–413.

712 Kumar S, Green GA, Teruya-Feldstein J, Raffeld M, Jaffe ES. Use of CD23 (BU38) on paraffin sections in the diagnosis of small lymphocytic lymphoma and mantle cell lymphoma. Mod Pathol 1996, **9**: 925–929.

713 Lee SL, Rosner F, Ruberman W, Glasberg S. μ-Chain disease. Ann Intern Med 1971, **75**: 407–414.

714 Lennert K. Malignant lymphomas other than Hodgkin's disease. Histology. Cytology. Ultrastructure. Immunology. Berlin, 1978, Springer-Verlag.

715 Lin BT, Weiss LM. Primary plasmacytoma of lymph nodes. Hum Pathol 1997, **28**: 1083–1090.

715a Lin P, Bueso-Ramos C, Wilson CS, Mansoor A, Medeiros LJ. Waldenstrom macroglobulinemia involving extramedullary sites. Am J Surg Pathol 2003, **27**: 1104–1113.

716 Long JC, Aisenberg AC. Richter's syndrome. A terminal complication of chronic lymphocytic leukemia with distinct clinicopathologic features. Am J Clin Pathol 1975, **63**: 786–795.

717 McKenna RW, Parkin J, Kersey JH, Gajl-Peczalska KJ, Peterson L, Brunning RD. Chronic lymphoproliferative disorder with unusual clinical, morphologic, ultrastructural and membrane surface marker characteristics. Am J Med 1977, **62**: 588–596.

718 Medeiros LJ, Strickler JG, Picker LJ, Gelb AB, Weiss LM, Warnke RA. "Well-differentiated" lymphocytic neoplasms. Immunologic findings correlated with clinical presentation and morphologic features. Am J Pathol 1987, **129**: 523–535.

719 Menke DM, Horny HP, Griesser H, Tiemann M, Katzmann JA, Kaiserling E, Parwaresch R, Kyle RA. Primary lymph node

plasmacytomas (plasmacytic lymphomas). Am J Clin Pathol 2001, **115:** 119–126.

720 Mennemeyer R, Hammar SP, Cathey WJ. Malignant lymphoma with intracytoplasmic IgM crystalline inclusions. N Engl J Med 1974, **291:** 960–963.

721 Momose H, Jaffe ES, Shin SS, Chen YY, Weiss LM. Chronic lymphocytic leukemia/small lymphocytic lymphoma with Reed–Sternberg-like cells and possible transformation to Hodgkin's disease. Mediation by Epstein–Barr virus. Am J Surg Pathol 1992, **16:** 859–867.

722 Morrison WH, Hoppe RT, Weiss LM, Picozzi VJ Jr, Horning SJ. Small lymphocytic lymphoma. J Clin Oncol 1989, **7:** 598–606.

722a Nakamura N, Abe M. Richter syndrome in B-cell chronic lymphocytic leukaemia. Pathol Int 2003, **53:** 195–203.

723 Pangalis GA, Nathwani BN, Rappaport H. Malignant lymphoma, well differentiated lymphocytic. Its relationship with chronic lymphocytic leukemia and macroglobulinemia of Waldenström. Cancer 1977, **39:** 999–1010.

724 Pangalis GA, Nathwani BN, Rappaport H. Detection of cytoplasmic immunoglobulin in well-differentiated lymphoproliferative diseases by the immunoperoxidase method. Cancer 1980, **45:** 1334–1339.

725 Papadimitriou CS, Müller Hermelink U, Lennert K. Histologic and immunohistochemical findings in the differential diagnosis of chronic lymphocytic leukemia of B-cell type and lymphoplasmacytic/lymphoplasmacytoid lymphoma. Virchows Arch [A] 1979, **384:** 149–158.

726 Peters O, Thielemans C, Steenssens L, De Waele M, Hijmans W, Van Camp B. Intracellular inclusion bodies in 14 patients with B-cell lymphoproliferative disorders. J Clin Pathol 1984, **37:** 45–50.

727 Schmid C, Isaacson PG. Proliferation centres in B-cell malignant lymphoma, lymphocytic (BCLL). An immunophenotypic study. Histopathology 1994, **24:** 445–451.

728 Seligmann M. Immunochemical, clinical, and pathological features of a-chain disease. Arch Intern Med 1975, **135:** 78–82.

729 Seligmann M, Danon F, Hurez D, Mihaesco E, Preud'homme J-L. Alpha-chain disease. A new immunoglobulin abnormality. Science 1968, **162:** 1396–1397.

730 Sheibani K, Nathwani BN, Winberg CD, Scott EP, Teplitz RR, Rappaport H. Small lymphocytic lymphoma. Morphologic and immunologic progression. Am J Clin Pathol 1985, **84:** 237–243.

731 Spier CM, Grogan TM, Fielder K, Richter L, Rangel C. Immunophenotypes in "well-differentiated" lymphoproliferative disorders, with emphasis on small lymphocytic lymphoma. Hum Pathol 1986, **17:** 1126–1136.

732 Sundeen JT, Longo DL, Jaffe ES. CD5 expression in B-cell small lymphocytic malignancies. Correlations with clinical presentation and sites of disease. Am J Surg Pathol 1992, **16:** 130–137.

733 Swerdlow SH. Small B-cell lymphomas of the lymph nodes and spleen: practical insights to diagnosis and pathogenesis. Mod Pathol 1999, **12:** 125–140.

734 Trump DL, Mann RB, Phelps R, Roberts H, Conley CL. Richter's syndrome. Diffuse histiocytic lymphoma in patients with chronic lymphocytic leukemia. A report of five cases and review of the literature. Am J Med 1980, **68:** 539–548.

735 Weir EG, Epstein JI. Incidental small lymphocytic lymphoma/chronic lymphocytic leukemia in pelvic lymph nodes excised at radical prostatectomy. Arch Pathol Lab Med 2003, **127:** 567–570.

736 Williams J, Schned A, Cotelingam JD, Jaffe ES. Chronic lymphocytic leukemia with coexistent Hodgkin's disease. Implications for the origin of the Reed–Sternberg cell. Am J Surg Pathol 1991, **15:** 33–42.

737 Zukerberg LR, Medeiros LJ, Ferry JA, Harris NL. Diffuse low-grade B-cell lymphomas. Four clinically distinct subtypes defined by a combination of morphologic and immunophenotypic features. Am J Clin Pathol 1993, **100:** 373–385.

Follicular lymphoma

738 Abou-Elella A, Shafer MT, Wan XY, Velanker M, Weisenburger DD, Nathwani BN, Gascoyne RD, Greiner TC, Chan WC. Lymphomas with follicular and monocytoid B-cell components: evidence for a common clonal origin from follicle centre cells. Am J Clin Pathol 2000, **114:** 516–522.

739 Almasri NM, Iturraspe JA, Braylan RC. CD10 expression in follicular lymphoma and large cell lymphoma is different from that of reactive lymph node follicles. Arch Pathol Lab Med 1998, **122:** 539–544.

740 Alsabeh R, Medeiros LJ, Glackin C, Weiss LM. Transformation of follicular lymphoma into CD30-large cell lymphoma with anaplastic cytologic features. Am J Surg Pathol 1997, **21:** 528–536.

741 Anderson T, Bender RA, Fisher RI, DeVita VT, Chabner BA, Berard CW, Norton L, Young RC. Combination chemotherapy in non-Hodgkin's lymphoma. Results of long-term followup. Cancer Treat Rep 1977, **61:** 1057–1066.

742 Aster JC, Longtine JA. Detection of BCL2 rearrangements in follicular lymphoma. Am J Pathol 2002, **160:** 759–763.

743 Barcus ME, Karageorge LS, Veloso YL, Kornstein MJ. CD10 expression in follicular lymphoma versus reactive follicular hyperplasia: evaluation in paraffin-embedded tissue. Appl Immunohistochem Mol Morphol 2000, **8:** 253–266.

744 Bastion Y, Berger F, Bryon PA, Felman P, Ffreuch M, Coiffier B. Follicular lymphomas. Assessment of prognostic factors in 127 patients followed for 10 years. Ann Oncol 1991, **2:** 123–129.

745 Bennett MH. Sclerosis in non-Hodgkin's lymphomata. Br J Cancer 1975, **31:** 44–52.

746 Chan JK, Ng CS, Hui PK. An unusual morphological variant of follicular lymphoma. Report of two cases. Histopathology 1988, **12:** 649–658.

747 Chan JK, Ng CS, Tung S. Multilobated B-cell lymphoma, a variant of centroblastic lymphoma. Report of four cases. Histopathology 1986, **10:** 601–612.

748 Chang KL, Arber DA, Shibata D, Rappaport H, Weiss LM. Follicular small lymphocytic lymphoma. Am J Surg Pathol 1994, **18:** 999–1009.

749 Chittal SM, Caverivière P, Voigt J-J, Dumont J, Bénévent B, Fauré P, Bordessoule GD, Delsol G. Follicular lymphoma with abundant PAS-positive extracellular material. Immunohistochemical and ultrastructural observations. Am J Surg Pathol 1987, **11:** 618–624.

750 Coiffier B, Bastion Y, Berger F, Felman P, Bryon PA. Prognostic factors in follicular lymphomas. Semin Oncol 1993, **20:** 89–95.

751 Come SE, Jaffe ES, Anderson JC, Mann RB, Johnson BL, DeVita VT, Young RC. Non-Hodgkin's lymphomas in leukemic phase. Clinicopathologic correlations. Am J Med 1980, **69:** 667–674.

752 Crisan D, Anstett MJ. Bcl-2 gene rearrangements in follicular lymphomas. Lab Med 1993, **24:** 579–588.

753 Frizzera G, Anaya JS, Banks PM. Neoplastic plasma cells in follicular lymphomas. Clinical and pathologic findings in six cases. Virchows Arch [A] 1986, **409:** 149–162.

754 Frizzera G, Gajl-Peczalska K, Sibley RK, Rosai J, Cherwitz D, Hurd DD. Rosette formation in malignant lymphoma. Am J Pathol 1985, **119:** 351–356.

755 Garvin AJ, Simon RM, Osborne CK, Merrill J, Young RC, Berard CW. An autopsy study of histologic progression in non-Hodgkin's lymphomas. 192 cases from the National Cancer Institute. Cancer 1983, **52:** 393–398.

756 Gaulard P, d'Agay MF, Peuchmaur M, Brousse N, Gisselbrecht

Interdigitating reticulum cell sarcoma with unusual features. Ultrastruct Pathol 1991, **15**: 631–645.

1230 Han JH, Kim SH, Noh SH, Lee YC, Kim HG, Yang WI. Follicular dendritic cell sarcoma presenting as a submucosal tumor of the stomach. Arch Pathol Lab Med 2000, **124**: 1693–1696.

1231 Hanson CA, Jaszcz W, Kersey JH, Astorga MG, Peterson BA, Gajl-Peczalska KJ, Frizzera G. True histiocytic lymphoma. Histopathologic, immunophenotypic and genotypic analysis. Br J Haematol 1989, **73**: 187–198.

1232 Harvell JD, Fulton R, Jones CD, Terris DJ, Warnke RA. Composite dendritic cell neoplasm (NOS) and small lymphocytic lymphoma. Appl Immunohistochem Mol Morphol 2000, **8**: 322–328.

1233 Hollowood K, Pease C, Mackay AM, Fletcher CD. Sarcomatoid tumours of lymph nodes showing follicular dendritic cell differentiation. J Pathol 1991, **163**: 205–216.

1234 Hollowood K, Stamp G, Zouvani J, Fletcher CDM. Extranodal follicular dendritic cell sarcoma of the gastrointestinal tract. Morphologic, immunohistochemical and ultrastructural analysis of two cases. Am J Clin Pathol 1995, **103**: 90–97.

1235 Hsu SM, Ho YS, Hsu PL. Lymphomas of true histiocytic origin. Expression of different phenotypes in so-called true histiocytic lymphoma and malignant histiocytosis. Am J Pathol 1991, **138**: 1389–1404.

1236 Hui PK, Feller AC, Kaiserling E, Hesse G, Rodermund OE, Haneke E, Weber L, Lennert K. Skin tumor of T accessory cells (interdigitating reticulum cells) with high content of T lymphocytes. Am J Dermatopathol 1987, **9**: 129–137.

1237 Imal Y, Yamakawa M. Morphology, function and pathology of follicular dendritic cells. Pathol Int 1997, **46**: 807–833.

1238 Jones D, Amin M, Ordonez NG, Glassman AB, Hayes KJ, Medeiros LJ. Reticulum cell sarcoma of lymph node with mixed dendritic and fibroblastic features. Mod Pathol 2001, **14**: 1059–1067.

1239 Kamel O, Kell D, Gocke C, Warnke R. True histiocytic lymphoma. A study of 12 cases based on current definition (abstract). Mod Pathol 1994, **7**: 112A.

1240 Kawachi K, Nakatani Y, Inayama Y, Kawano N, Toda N, Misugi K. Interdigitating dendritic cell sarcoma of the spleen: report of a case with a review of the literature. Am J Surg Pathol 2002, **26**: 530–537.

1241 Luk IS, Shek TW, Tang VW, Ng WF. Interdigitating dendritic cell tumor of the testis: a novel testicular spindle cell neoplasm. Am J Surg Pathol 1999, **23**: 1141–1148.

1242 Maeda K, Matsuda M, Suzuki H, Saitoh HA. Immunohistochemical recognition of human follicular dendritic cells (FDCs) in routinely processed paraffin section. J Histochem Cytochem 2002, **50**: 1475–1486.

1243 Masuuaga A, Nakamura H, Katata T, Furubayashi T, Kanayama T, Yamada A, Shiroko Y, Itoyama S. Follicular dendritic cell tumor with histiocytic characteristics and fibroblastic antigen. Pathol Int 1997, **47**: 707–712.

1244 Miettinen M, Fletcher CD, Lasota J. True histiocytic lymphoma of small intestine. Analysis of two S-100 protein-positive cases with features of interdigitating reticulum cell sarcoma. Am J Clin Pathol 1993, **100**: 285–292.

1245 Milchgrub S, Kamel OW, Wiley E, Vuitch F, Cleary ML, Warnke RA. Malignant histiocytic neoplasms of the small intestine. Am J Surg Pathol 1992, **16**: 11–20.

1246 Monda L, Warnke R, Rosai J. A primary lymph node malignancy with features suggestive of dendritic reticulum cell differentiation. A report of 4 cases. Am J Pathol 1986, **122**: 562–572.

1247 Moriki T, Takahashi T, Wada M, Ueda S, Ichien M, Yamane T, Hara H. Follicular dendritic cell tumor of the mesentery. Pathol Res Pract 1998, **193**: 629–639.

1248 Nayler SJ, Verhaart MJ, Cooper K. Follicular dendritic cell tumor of the tonsil. Histopathology 1996, **28**: 89–92.

1249 Perez-Ordóñez B, Rosai J. Follicular dendritic cell tumor: review of the entity. Semin Diagn Pathol 1998, **15**: 144–154.

1250 Perez-Ordóñez B, Erlandson RA, Rosai J. Follicular dendritic cell tumor: report of 13 additional cases of a distinct entity. Am J Surg Pathol 1996, **20**: 944–955.

1251 Perez-Ordóñez B, Erlandson RA, Rosai J. Dendritic follicular cell tumor. Report of 13 additional cases of a distinctive entity. Am J Surg Pathol 1996, **20**: 944–955.

1252 Pileri SA, Grogan TM, Harris NL, Banks P, Campo E, Chan JK, Favera RD, Delsol G, De Wolf-Peeters C, Falini B, Gascoyne RD, Gaulard P, Gatter KC, Isaacson PG, Jaffe ES, Kluin P, Knowles DM, Mason DY, Mori S, Müller-Hermelink HK, Piris MA, Ralfkiaer E, Stein H, Su IJ, Warnke RA, Weiss LM. Tumors of histiocytes and accessory dendritic cells: an immunohistochemical approach to classification from the International Lymphoma Society Group based on 61 cases. Histopathology 2002, **41**: 1–29.

1253 Pruneri G, Masullo M, Renne G, Taccagni G, Manzotti M, Luini A, Viale G. Follicular dendritic cell sarcoma of the breast. Virchows Arch 2002, **441**: 194–199.

1254 Ralfkiaer E, Delsol G, O'Connor NT, Brandtzaeg P, Brousset P, Vejlsgaard GL, Mason DY. Malignant lymphomas of true histiocytic origin. A clinical, histological, immunophenotypic and genotypic study. J Pathol 1990, **160**: 9–17.

1255 Raymond I, Al Saati T, Tkaczuk J, Chittal S, Delsol G. CAN.42, a new monoclonal antibody directed against a fixative-resistant antigen of follicular dendritic reticulum cells. Am J Pathol 1998, **151**: 1577–1585.

1256 Rodilla CM, Acenero JF, Mayor LP, Carmona AA. True histiocytic lymphoma as a second neoplasm in a follicular centroblastic-centrocytic lymphoma. Pathol Res Pract 1997, **193**: 319–322.

1257 Saiz AD, Chan O, Strauchen JA. Follicular dendritic cell tumor in Castleman's disease: a report of two cases. Int J Surg Pathol 1997, **5**: 25–30.

1257a Sapino A, Cassoni P, Ferrero E, Bongiovanni M, Righi L, Fortunati N, Crafa P, Chiarle R, Bussolati G. Estrogen receptor alpha is a novel marker expressed by follicular dendritic cells in lymph nodes and tumor-associated lymphoid infiltrates. Am J Pathol 2003, **163**: 1313–1320.

1257b Schuerfeld K, Lazzi S, de Santi MM, Gozzetti A, Leoncini L, Pileri SA. Cytokeratin-positive intersititial cell neoplasm: a case report and classification issues. Histopathology 2003, **43**: 491–494.

1258 Selves J, Meggetto F, Brousset P, Voigt JJ, Pradere B, Grasset D, Icart J, Mariame B, Knecht H, Delsol G. Inflammatory pseudotumor of the liver: evidence for follicular dendritic reticulum cell proliferation associated with clonal Epstein–Barr virus. Am J Surg Pathol 1996, **20**: 747–753.

1259 Shah RN, Ozden O, Yeldandi A, Peterson LA, Rao S, Laskin WB. Follicular dendritic cell tumor presenting in the lung: a case report. Hum Pathol 2001, **32**: 745–749.

1260 Shek TW, Ho FC, Ng IO, Chan AC, Ma L, Srivastava G. Follicular dendritic cell tumor of the liver: evidence for Epstein–Barr virus-related clonal proliferation of follicular dendritic cells. Am J Surg Pathol 1997, **20**: 313–324.

1261 Soria C, Orradre JL, Garcia-Almagro D, Martinez B, Algara P, Piris MA. True histiocytic lymphoma (monocytic sarcoma). Am J Dermatopathol 1992, **14**: 511–517.

1261a Sun X, Chang K-C, Abruzzo LV, Lai R, Younes A, Jones D. Epidermal growth factor receptor expression in follicular dendritic cells: a shared feature of follicular dendritic cell sarcoma and Castleman's disease. Hum Pathol 2003, **34**: 835–840.

1262 Takahashi K, Naito M, Takeya M. Development and heterogeneity of macrophages and their related cells through their differentiation pathways. Pathol Int 1997, **46**: 473–485.

1263 van den Oord JJ, de Wolf-Peeters C, de Vos R, Thomas J, Desmet VJ. Sarcoma arising from interdigitating reticulum cells. Report of a case, studied with light and electron microscopy, and enzyme- and immunohistochemistry. Histopathology 1986, 10: 509–523.

1264 Wacker HH, Frahm SO, Heidebrecht HJ, Parwaresch R. Sinus-lining cells of lymph nodes recognized as a dendritic cell type by the new monoclonal antibody Ki-M9. Am J Pathol 1997, 151: 423–434.

1265 Weiss LM, Berry GJ, Dorfman RF, Banks P, Kaiserling E, Curtis J, Rosai J, Warnke RA. Spindle cell neoplasms of lymph nodes of probable reticulum cell lineage. True reticulum cell sarcoma? Am J Surg Pathol 1990, 14: 405–414.

1266 Wright-Browne V, McClain KL, Talpaz M, Ordonez N, Estrov Z. Physiology and pathophysiology of dendritic cells. Hum Pathol 1997, 28: 563–579.

1267 Yamakawa M, Andoh A, Masuda A, Miyauchi S, Kasajima T, Ohmori A, Oguma T, Takasaki K. Follicular dendritic cell sarcoma of the omentum. Virchows Arch 2002, 440: 660–663.

1268 Yamakawa M, Matsuda M, Imai Y, Arai S, Harada K, Sato T. Lymph node interdigitating cell sarcoma. A case report. Am J Clin Pathol 1992, 97: 139–146.

Vascular tumors and tumorlike conditions

1269 Almagro UA, Choi H, Rouse TM. Hemangioma in a lymph node. Arch Pathol Lab Med 1985, 109: 576–578.

1270 Bonzanini M, Togni R, Barabareschi M, Parenti A, Dalla Palma P. Primary Kaposi's sarcoma of intraparotid lymph node. Histopathology 1992, 21: 489–491.

1271 Chan JK, Frizzera G, Fletcher CD, Rosai J. Primary vascular tumors of lymph nodes other than Kaposi's sarcoma. Analysis of 39 cases and delineation of two new entities. Am J Surg Pathol 1992, 16: 335–350.

1272 Chan JK, Lewin KJ, Lombard CM, Teitelbaum S, Dorfman RF. Histopathology of bacillary angiomatosis of lymph node. Am J Surg Pathol 1991, 15: 430–437.

1273 Chan JK, Warnke RA, Dorfman R. Vascular transformation of sinuses in lymph nodes. A study of its morphological spectrum and distinction from Kaposi's sarcoma. Am J Surg Pathol 1991, 15: 732–743.

1274 Cho NH, Yang WI, Lee WJ. Spindle and epithelioid hemangioendothelioma of the inguinal lymph nodes. Histopathology 1997, 30: 595–598.

1275 Cockerell CJ, Whitlow MA, Webster GF, Friedman-Kien AE. Epithelioid angiomatosis. A distinct vascular disorder in patients with the acquired immunodeficiency syndrome or AIDS-related complex. Lancet 1987, 2: 654–656.

1276 Cook PD, Czerniak B, Chan JKC, Mackay B, Ordóñez NG, Ayala AG, Rosai J. Nodular spindle-cell vascular transformation of lymph nodes. A benign process occurring predominantly in retroperitoneal lymph nodes draining carcinomas that can simulate Kaposi's sarcoma or metastatic tumor. Am J Surg Pathol 1995, 19: 1010–1020.

1277 Fayemi AO, Toker C. Nodal angiomatosis. Arch Pathol 1975, 99: 170–172.

1278 Frizzera G, Banks PM, Massarelli G, Rosai J. A systemic lymphoproliferative disorder with morphologic features of Castleman's disease. Pathological findings in 15 patients. Am J Surg Pathol 1983, 7: 211–231.

1279 Fukunaga M, Silverberg SG. Hyaline globules in Kaposi's sarcoma. A light microscopic and immunohistochemical study. Mod Pathol 1991, 4: 187–190.

1280 Goldstein JED, Bartal N. Hemangioendothelioma of the lymph node. A case report. J Surg Oncol 1985, 23: 314–317.

1281 Haferkamp O, Rosenau W, Lennert K. Vascular transformation of lymph node sinuses due to venous obstruction. Arch Pathol Lab Med 1971, 92: 81–83.

1282 Le Jan S, Amy C, Cases A, Monnot C, Lamandé N, Favier J, Philippe J, Sibony M, Gasc J, Corvol P, Germain S. Angiopoietin-like 4 is a proangiogenic factor produced during ischemia and in convential renal cell carcinoma. Am J Pathol 2003, 162: 1521–1523.

1283 Lott MF, Davies JD. Lymph node hypervascularity. Haemangiomatoid lesions and pan-nodal vasodilatation. J Pathol 1983, 140: 209–219.

1284 O'Connell KM. Kaposi's sarcoma in lymph nodes. Histological study of lesions from 16 cases in Malawi. J Clin Pathol 1977, 30: 696–703.

1285 Ostrowski ML, Siddiqui T, Barnes RE, Howton MJ. Vascular transformation of lymph node sinuses. A process displaying a spectrum of histologic features. Arch Pathol Lab Med 1990, 114: 656–660.

1286 Perez-Piteira J, Ariza A, Mate JL, Ojanguren I, Navas-Palacios JJ. Bacillary angiomatosis. A gross mimicker of malignancy. Histopathology 1995, 26: 476–478.

1287 Silva EG, Phillips MJ, Langer B, Ordonez NG. Spindle and histiocytoid (epithelioid) hemangioendothelioma. Primary in lymph node. Am J Clin Pathol 1986, 85: 731–735.

1288 Steinmann G, Földi M, Racz P, Lennert K. Morphologic findings in lymph nodes after occlusion of their efferent lymphatic vessels and veins. Lab Invest 1982, 47: 43–50.

1289 Tsang WY, Chan JK, Dorfman RF, Rosai J. Vasoproliferative lesions of the lymph node. Pathol Annu 1994, 29(Pt 1): 63–133.

1290 Weshler Z, Leviatan A, Krasnokuki D, Kopolovitch J. Primary Kaposi's sarcoma in lymph nodes concurrent with chronic lymphatic leukemia. Am J Clin Pathol 1979, 71: 234–237.

1291 Wright DH, Padley NR, Judd MA. Angiolymphoid hyperplasia with eosinophilia simulating lymphadenopathy. Histopathology 1981, 5: 127–140.

Other primary tumors and tumorlike conditions

1292 Arber DA, Tamoyo R, Weiss LM. Paraffin section detection of the c-kit gene product (CD117) in human tissues: value in the diagnosis of mast cell disorders. Hum Pathol 1998, 29: 498–504.

1293 Argani P, Ghossein R, Rosai J. Anthracotic and anthracosilicotic spindle cell pseudotumors of mediastinal lymph nodes: report of five cases of a reactive lesion that simulates malignancy. Hum Pathol 1998, 29: 851–855.

1294 Audouin J, Comperat E, Le Tourneau A, Camilleri-Broët S, Adida C, Molina T, Diebold J. Myeloid sarcoma, clinical and morphological criteria useful for diagnosis. Int J Surg Pathol 2003, 11: 271–282.

1295 Barbareschi M, Mariscotti C, Ferrero S, Pignatiello U. Intranodal haemorrhagic spindle cell tumour. A benign Kaposi-like nodal tumour. Histopathology 1990, 17: 93–96.

1296 Brecher ME, Gill WB, Straus FH. Angiomyolipoma with regional lymph node involvement and long-term follow-up study. Hum Pathol 1986, 17: 962–963.

1297 Brunning RD, McKenna RW, Rosai J, Parkin JL, Risdall R. Systemic mastocytosis. Extracutaneous manifestations. Am J Surg Pathol 1983, 7: 425–438.

1298 Chan JK, Frizzera G, Fletcher CD, Rosai J. Primary vascular tumors of lymph nodes other than Kaposi's sarcoma. Analysis of 39 cases and delineation of two new entities. Am J Surg Pathol 1992, 16: 335–350.

1299 Channer JL, Davies JD. Smooth muscle proliferation in the hilum of superficial lymph nodes. Virchows Arch [A] 1985, 406: 261–270.

1300 Corrin B, Liebow AA, Friedman PJ. Pulmonary lymphangiomyomatosis. Am J Pathol 1975, 79: 348–382.

1301 Craig SS, DeBlois G, Schwartz LB. Mast cells in human keloid, small intestine, and lung by an immunoperoxidase technique using a murine monoclonal antibody against tryptase. Am J Pathol 1986, 124: 427–435.

1302 Creager AJ, Garwacki CP. Recurrent intranodal palisaded myofibroblastoma with metaplastic bone formation. Arch Pathol Lab Med 1999, 123: 433–436.

1303 Davis RE, Warnke RA, Dorfman RF. Inflammatory pseudotumor of lymph nodes. Additional observations and evidence for an inflammatory etiology. Am J Surg Pathol 1991, 15: 744–756.

1304 Facchetti F, De Wolf Peeters C, De Wever I, Frizzera G. Inflammatory pseudotumor of lymph nodes. Immunohistochemical evidence for its fibrohistiocytic nature. Am J Pathol 1990, 137: 281–289.

1305 Fletcher CD, Stirling RW. Intranodal myofibroblastoma presenting in the submandibular region. Evidence of a broader clinical and histological spectrum. Histopathology 1990, 16: 287–293.

1306 Hisaoka M, Hashiomoto H, Daimaru Y. Intranodal palisaded myofibroblastoma with so-called amianthoid fibers: a report of two cases with a review of the literature. Pathol Int 1998, 48: 307–312.

1307 Horie A, Ishii N, Matsumoto M, Hashizume Y, Kawakami M, Sato Y. Leiomyomatosis in the pelvic lymph node and peritoneum. Acta Pathol Jpn 1984, 34: 813–819.

1308 Horny HP, Menke DM, Kaiserling E. Neoplastic human tissue mast cells express the adhesion molecule CD44/HCAM. Virchows Arch 1996, 429: 91–94.

1309 Horny HP, Sillaber C, Menke D, Kaiserling E, Wehrmann M, Stehberger B, Chott A, Lechner K, Lennert K, Valent P. Diagnostic value of immunostaining for tryptase in patients with mastocytosis. Am J Surg Pathol 1998, 22: 1132–1140.

1310 Hudock J, Chatten J, Miettinen M. Immunohistochemical evaluation of myeloid leukemia infiltrates (granulocytic sarcomas) in formaldehyde-fixed, paraffin-embedded tissue. Am J Clin Pathol 1994, 102: 55–60.

1311 Kemper CA, Davis RE, Deresinski SC, Dorfmann RF. Inflammatory pseudotumor of intra-abdominal lymph nodes manifesting as recurrent fever of unknown origin. A case report. Am J Med 1991, 90: 519–523.

1312 Kojima M, Nakamura S, Shimizu K, Hosomura Y, Ohno Y, Itoh H, Yamane N, Yoshiba K, Masawa N. Inflammatory pseudotumor of lymph nodes: clinicopathologic and immunohistological study of 11 Japanese cases. Int J Surg Pathol 2001, 9: 207–214.

1313 Kutok JL, Pinkus GS, Dorfman DM, Fletcher CD. Inflammatory pseudotumor of lymph node and spleen: an entity biologically distinct from inflammatory myofibroblastic tumor. Hum Pathol 2002, 32: 1382–1387.

1314 Lennert K, Illert E. Die Häufigkeit der Gewebsmastzellen im Lymphknoten bei verschiedenen Erkrankungen. Frankf Z Pathol 1959, 70: 121–131.

1315 Lennert K, Parwaresch MR. Mast cells and mast cell neoplasia. A review. Histopathology 1979, 3: 349–365.

1316 Li WV, Kapadia SB, Sonmez-Alpan E, Swerdlow SH. Immunohistochemical characterization of mast cell disease in paraffin sections using tryptase, CD68, myeloperoxidase, lysozyme, and CD20 antibodies. Mod Pathol 1997, 9: 982–988.

1317 Mazzoleni G, Salerno A, Santini D, Marabini A, Martinelli G. Leiomyomatosis in pelvic lymph nodes. Histopathology 1992, 21: 588–589.

1318 Menasce LP, Banerjee SS, Beckett E, Harris M. Extra-medullary myeloid tumour (granulocytic sarcoma) is often misdiagnosed: a study of 26 cases. Histopathology 1999, 34: 391–398.

1319 Menke DM, Griesser H, Moder KG, Tefferi A, Luthra HS, Cohen MD, Colon-otero G, Lloyd RV. Lymphomas in patients with connective tissue disease: comparison of P53 protein expression and latent EBV infection in patients immunosuppressed and not immunosuppressed with methotrexate. Am J Clin Pathol 2000, 113: 212–218.

1320 Michal M, Chlumska A, Povysilova V. Intranodal "amianthoid" myofibroblastoma. Report of six cases immunohistochemical and electron microscopical study. Pathol Res Pract 1992, 188: 199–204.

1321 Moran CA, Suster S, Abbondanzo SL. Inflammatory pseudotumor of lymph nodes: a study of 25 cases with emphasis on morphological heterogeneity. Hum Pathol 1997, 28: 332–338.

1322 Perrone T, De Wolf-Peeters C, Frizzera G. Inflammatory pseudotumor of lymph nodes. A distinctive pattern of nodal reaction. Am J Surg Pathol 1988, 12: 351–361.

1323 Roth MJ, Medeiros LJ, Elenitoba-Johnson K, Kuchnio M, Jaffe ES, Stetler-Stevenson M. Extramedullary myeloid cell tumors. An immunohistochemical study of 29 cases using routinely fixed and processed paraffin-embedded tissue sections. Arch Pathol Lab Med 1995, 119: 790–798.

1324 Skalova A, Michal M, Chlumska A, Leivo I. Collagen composition and ultra-structure of the so-called amianthoid fibres in palisaded myofibroblastoma. Ultrastructural and immunohistochemical study. J Pathol 1992, 167: 335–340.

1325 Starasoler L, Vuitch F, Albores-Saavedra J. Intranodal leiomyoma. Another distinctive primary spindle cell neoplasm of lymph node. Am J Clin Pathol 1991, 95: 858–862.

1326 Suster S, Rosai J. Intranodal hemorrhagic spindle-cell tumor with "amianthoid" fibers. Report of six cases of a distinctive mesenchymal neoplasm of the inguinal region that simulates Kaposi's sarcoma. Am J Surg Pathol 1989, 13: 347–357.

1327 Tanda F, Massarelli G, Cossu A, Bosincu L, Cossu S, Ibba M. Primary spindle cell tumor of lymph node with "amianthoid" fibers. A histological, immunohistochemical and ultrastructural study. Ultrastruct Pathol 1993, 17: 195–205.

1328 Weiss SW, Gnepp DR, Bratthauer GL. Palisaded myofibroblastoma. A benign mesenchymal tumor of lymph node. Am J Surg Pathol 1989, 13: 341–346.

1329 White JET, Chan YF, Miller MV. Intranodal leiomyoma or myofibroblastoma. An identical lesion? Histopathology 1995, 26: 188–189.

1330 Yang F, Tran TA, Carlson JA, Hsi ED, Ross CW, Arber DA. Paraffin section immunophenotype of cutaneous and extracutaneous mast cell disease: comparison to other hematopoietic neoplasms. Am J Surg Pathol 2000, 24: 703–709.

Metastatic tumors

1331 Argani P, Ghossein R, Rosai J. Anthracotic and anthracosilicotic spindle cell pseudotumors of mediastinal lymph nodes: report of five cases of a reactive lesion that simulates malignancy. Hum Pathol 1998, 29: 851–855.

1332 Argani P, Rosai J. Hyperplastic mesothelial cells in lymph nodes: report of six cases of a benign process that can simulate metastatic involvement by mesothelioma or carcinoma. Hum Pathol 1998, 29: 339–346.

1333 Batsakis JG. The pathology of head and neck tumors. The occult primary and metastases to the head and neck, part 10. Head Neck Surg 1981, 3: 409–423.

1334 Cervin JR, Silverman JF, Loggie BW, Geisinger KR. Virchow's node revisited. Analysis with clinicopathologic correlation of 152 fine needle aspiration biopsies of supraclavicular lymph nodes. Arch Pathol Lab Med 1995, 119: 727–730.

1335 Clary CF, Michel RP, Wang N-S, Hanson RE. Metastatic carcinoma. The lung as the site for the clinically undiagnosed primary. Cancer 1983, 51: 362–366.

1336 Copeland EM, McBride CM. Axillary metastases from unknown primary sites. Ann Surg 1973, 178: 25–27.

1337 De Petris G, Siew S. Peritumoral and nodal muciphages. Am J Surg Pathol 1998, 22: 545–549.

1338 Didlolker MS, Fanous N, Elias EG, et al. Metastatic carcinomas from occult primary tumors. A study of 254 patients. Ann Surg 1977, 186: 628–630.

1339 Dvorak AM, Monahan RA. Metastatic adenocarcinoma of unknown primary site. Diagnostic electron microscopy to determine the site of tumor origin. Arch Pathol Lab Med 1982, **106**: 21–24.

1340 Feigenberg Z, Zer M, Dintsman M. Axillary metastases from an unknown primary source. Isr J Med Sci 1976, **12**: 1153–1158.

1341 Giffler RF, Gillespie JJ, Ayala AG, Newland JR. Lymphoepithelioma in cervical lymph nodes of children and young adults. Am J Surg Pathol 1977, **1**: 293–302.

1342 Groisman GM, Amar M, Weiner P, Zamir D. Mucicarminophilic histiocytosis (benign signet-ring cells) and hyperplastic mesothelial cells: two mimics of metastatic carcinoma within a single lymph node. Arch Pathol Lab Med 1998, **122**: 282–284.

1343 Guerrero-Medrano J, Delgado R, Albores-Saavedra J. Signet-ring sinus histiocytosis: a reactive disorder that mimics metastatic adenocarcinoma. Cancer 1997, **80**: 277–285.

1344 Haagensen CD, Feind CR, Herter FP, Slanetz CA Jr, Weinberg JA. The lymphatics in cancer. Philadelphia, 1972, W.B. Saunders.

1345 Hoda SA, Resetkova E, Yusuf Y, Cahan A, Rosen PP. Megakaryocytes mimicking metastatic breast carcinoma. Arch Pathol Lab Med 2002, **126**: 618–620.

1346 Lindbergh R. Distribution of cervical lymph node metastases from squamous cell carcinoma of the upper respiratory and digestive tracts. Cancer 1972, **29**: 1446–1449.

1347 Mancuso AA, Hanafee WN. Elusive head and neck carcinomas beneath intact mucosa. Laryngoscope 1983, **93**: 133–139.

1348 Markman M. Metastatic adenocarcinoma of unknown primary site. Analysis of 245 patients seen at the Johns Hopkins Hospital from 1965–1979. Med Pediatr Oncol 1982, **10**: 569–574.

1349 Silverman CL, Marks JE. Metastatic cancer of unknown origin. Epidermoid and undifferentiated carcinomas. Semin Oncol 1982, **9**: 435–441.

1350 Sussman J, Rosai J. Lymph node metastases as the initial manifestation of malignant mesothelioma. Report of six cases. Am J Surg Pathol 1990, **14**: 819–828.

1351 Willis RA. The spread of tumours in the human body, ed. 3. Stoneham, Mass, 1973, Butterworth.

1352 Zaren HA, Copeland EM. Inguinal node metastases. Cancer 1978, **41**: 919–923.

22 Spleen

Normal anatomy

The spleen performs a variety of functions, most of which have been correlated with specific anatomic compartments.[2,3a,3b,4,5,10] The most important are (1) hematopoiesis (erythrocytes, granulocytes, megakaryocytes, lymphocytes, and macrophages), (2) reservoir (storage or sequestration of platelets and other formed elements), (3) phagocytosis (removal of particulate matter, red blood cell destruction, pitting, and erythroclasis), and (4) immunity (trapping and processing of antigen, "homing" of lymphocytes, lymphocyte transformation and proliferation, and antibody production).[2,4] The first two functions are not important in normal adult humans.

Anatomically, the spleen is divided into two compartments—white pulp and red pulp—separated by an ill-defined interphase known as the marginal zone.[3,7,9,10] The white pulp is made up of T and B lymphocytes, the former located in the periarteriolar lymphoid sheath and the latter eccentrically to this sheath in the form of primary lymphoid follicles.[6] These lymphoid follicles contain germinal centers, particularly in children.[5]

The red pulp consists of a complex network of venous sinuses and the cords of Billroth. The ring fibers, which demarcate the cordal-sinusoidal relationships in the red pulp, are best appreciated with the PAS stain. The cords contain most of the splenic macrophages, which are responsible for the important phagocytic function of this organ. The sinuses are lined by a particular type of endothelial cell endowed with endothelial and histiocytic markers (known as littoral cell) and have a discontinuous wall, which allows traffic of blood cells between cords and sinuses.[1,8,11]

Biopsy and fine needle aspiration

Biopsy of the spleen is rarely attempted because of the possibility of hemorrhage and the preconceived notion that the biopsy will not be of diagnostic help. Obviously, the procedure should not be performed on patients with a bleeding tendency. A few authors have used it routinely, either with the Vim-Silverman–type needle to obtain a core of tissue or with a fine needle to obtain an aspirate.[13] These authors claim that morbidity is nil and that in some instances the technique results in a definitive diagnosis that is not easily obtainable by other means. A multicenter study in Italy on ultrasound-guided FNA of the spleen documented the high yield and low risk of the procedure.[12] The overall accuracy was 91%, and the incidence of major complications was less than 1%. Aspiration cytology and core needle biopsy gave similar diagnostic

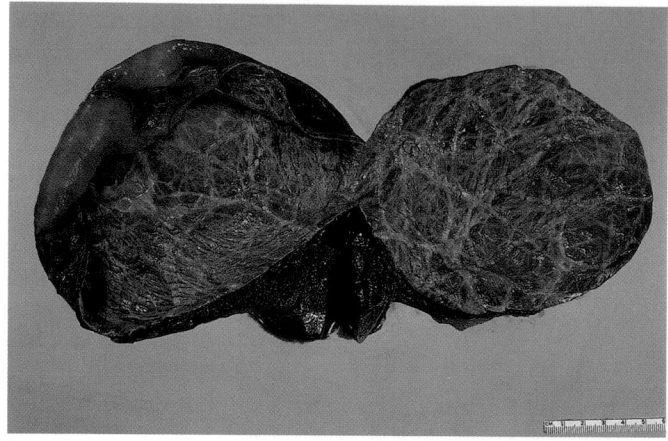

A

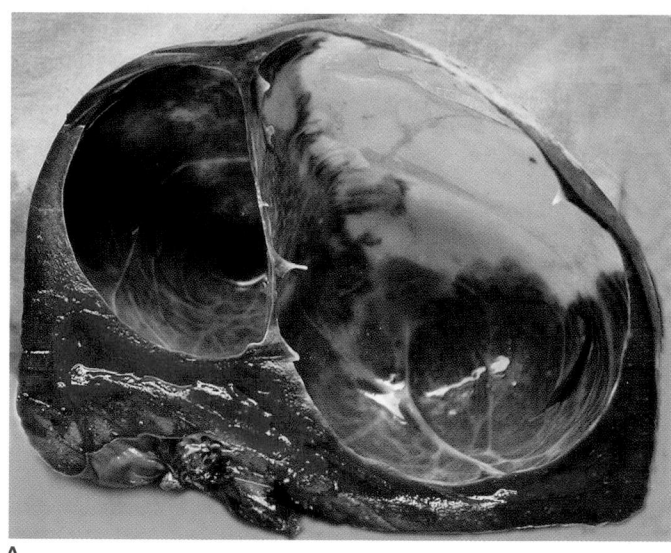

A

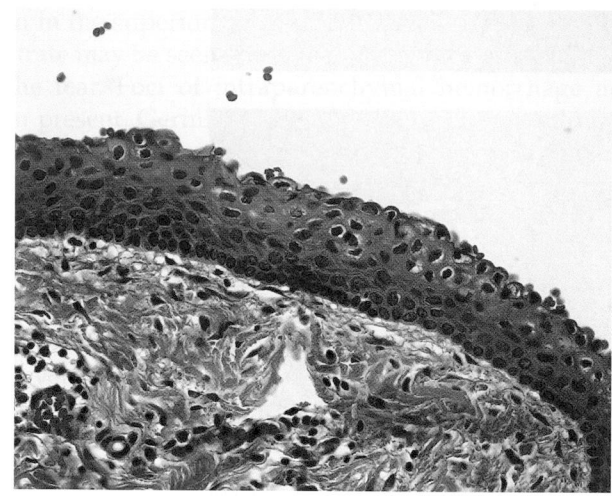

B

Fig. 22.3 A, Epithelial cyst. Grossly, it is very difficult, if not impossible, to distinguish this lesion from a pseudocyst. **B**, Squamous lining of the inner surface.

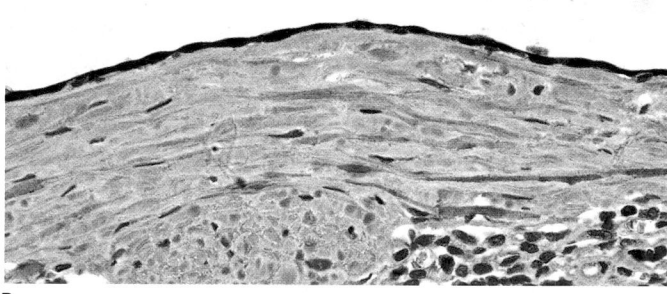

B

Fig. 22.4 Splenic cyst lined by mesothelial cells. **A**, Gross appearance. **B**, Immunoreactivity of the lining cells for calretinin.

Parasitic cysts resulting from Echinococcus infestation can involve the spleen (Fig. 22.5).

Inflammation

Reactive follicular hyperplasia of the spleen can be seen as an acute phenomenon in response to a systemic infection. Morphologically, it is often associated with variable degrees of congestion, diffuse immunoblastic and plasmacytic proliferation, and outpouring of neutrophils in the red pulp (so-called **septic spleen** or **acute septic splenitis**); measles and typhoid fever are the two better known etiologies. It also occurs in a chronic form in a large number of infectious disease—including AIDS[72,77]—and in immune-mediated diseases, such as idiopathic thrombocytopenic purpura, acquired hemolytic anemia, rheumatoid arthritis (including Felty's syndrome),[73] and the systemic form of Castleman's disease,[74,88] as well as in hemodialyzed patients.[82]

Diffuse lymphoid hyperplasia with production of immunoblasts and plasma cells can be the result of infection (particularly viral), graft rejection, or a component of

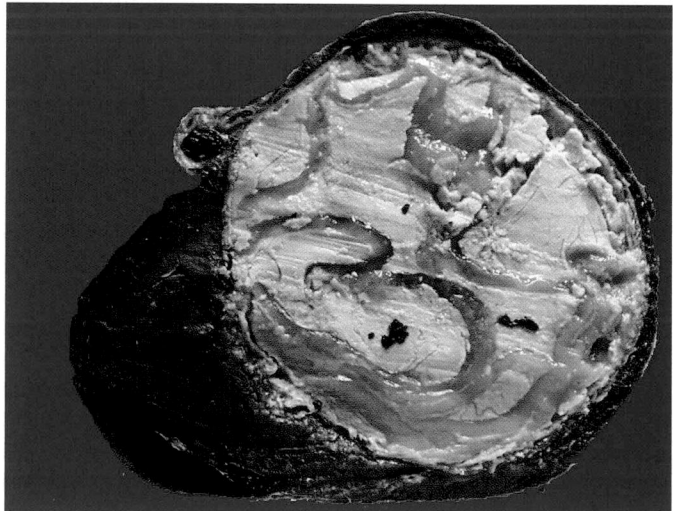

Fig. 22.5 Hydatidosis of spleen.

angioimmunoblastic lymphadenopathy (see Chapter 21). In infectious mononucleosis, the splenic involvement is mainly in the red pulp.

Bagshawe[66] compared the clinical and laboratory features of hypersplenism among forty-six patients with congestive splenomegaly and twenty-nine with reactive splenomegaly and found no significant differences between them. Massive splenomegaly of a reactive nature is commonly seen in inhabitants of several tropical countries, such as Zaire, Malagasy Republic, Nigeria, and New Guinea.[71] Spleens removed for this tropical splenomegaly syndrome are often extremely heavy (mean, 3270 g) and exhibit a uniform dark red, cut surface. Microscopically, there is marked dilatation of the sinuses and foci of extramedullary hematopoiesis but no significant fibrosis or hemosiderin deposition.[83] Signs of hypersplenism are the rule. Epidemiologic and therapeutic studies suggest a causal relationship with malaria.[83,85] In this regard, it is interesting that the cases of idiopathic splenomegaly reported by Banti in 1883[78] were from an area of central Italy that at the time was endemic for malaria (see p. 2026).

Abscess of the spleen, an extremely rare condition, can be the result of trauma or metastatic spread of infection from another site[69,70] (Fig. 22.6). Septic abscesses of the spleen secondary to subacute bacterial endocarditis may necessitate surgical intervention.[73]

Granulomatous inflammation is a relatively common finding in splenectomy specimens. The granulomas can be roughly divided into three major types: (1) large active granulomas containing epithelioid and Langhans' type of giant cells, with or without central necrosis; (2) small, widespread, sarcoid-like epithelioid granulomas with scanty giant cells and no necrosis (not to be equated with "epithelioid" germinal centers)[80]; and (3) old inactive granulomas, with fibrosis and calcification. A variant of the first type, characterized by extensive necrotizing changes, has been seen as a complication of leukemia in childhood.[87]

The third type of granuloma, which can be solitary or found scattered throughout the spleen, is particularly common in areas of endemic histoplasmosis.[89] We have evaluated twenty cases of splenectomy done for splenomegaly and/or hypersplenism in which the only major pathologic finding was the presence of active granulomas of either the first or second type.[79] All of the patients were adults. Fever, weight loss, hepatosplenomegaly, and the various manifestations of hypersplenism were the most common symptoms, and these were markedly ameliorated with splenectomy. The splenic granulomas were nearly always the expression of a generalized disease, which also often involved lymph nodes, liver, and bone marrow. Despite the performance of special stains and cultures, the etiology remained unknown in all but three cases. In these, the organisms identified were Histoplasma capsulatum, an atypical Mycobacterium, and Sporotrichum schenkii, respectively (Fig. 22.7). None of the patients developed malignant lymphoma on follow-up.

Sarcoid-like granulomas can be seen in the spleen of patients with Hodgkin's lymphoma[76] and, less commonly, non-Hodgkin's lymphoma or hairy cell leukemia,[67] with or without involvement of the spleen by tumor. In some cases of non-Hodgkin's lymphoma, the number of granulomas is such as to obscure the diagnosis of lymphoma if present.[88] It should be emphasized that the presence of splenic granulomas in patients with lymphoma is not an indication per se that the spleen is involved by tumor. Actually, some authors have suggested that in patients with Hodgkin's lymphoma, this finding is associated with an improved prognosis.[84] Neiman[81] found sarcoid-like granulomas in 24 of 412 splenectomy specimens; in addition to the conditions previously listed, he found them in chronic uremia and in a single case of IgA deficiency. He pointed out that in all

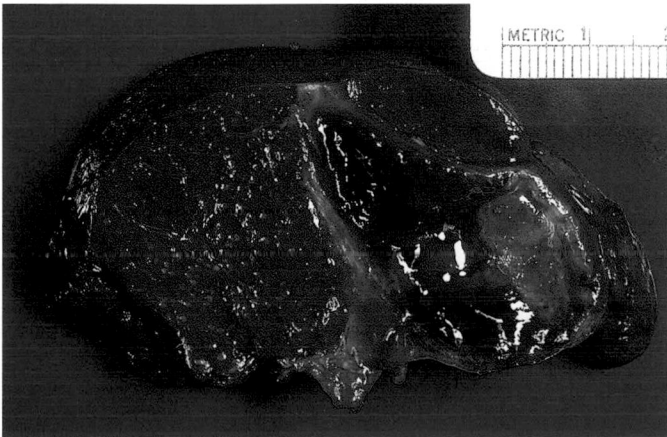

Fig. 22.6 Gross appearance of a thick-walled splenic abscess. The content is partially purulent and partially hemorrhagic.

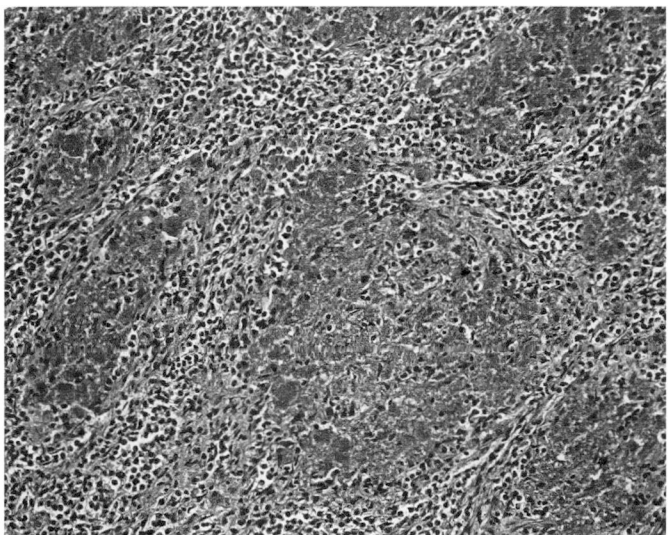

Fig. 22.7 Granulomas of spleen due to *M. avium* in an immunosuppressed patient.

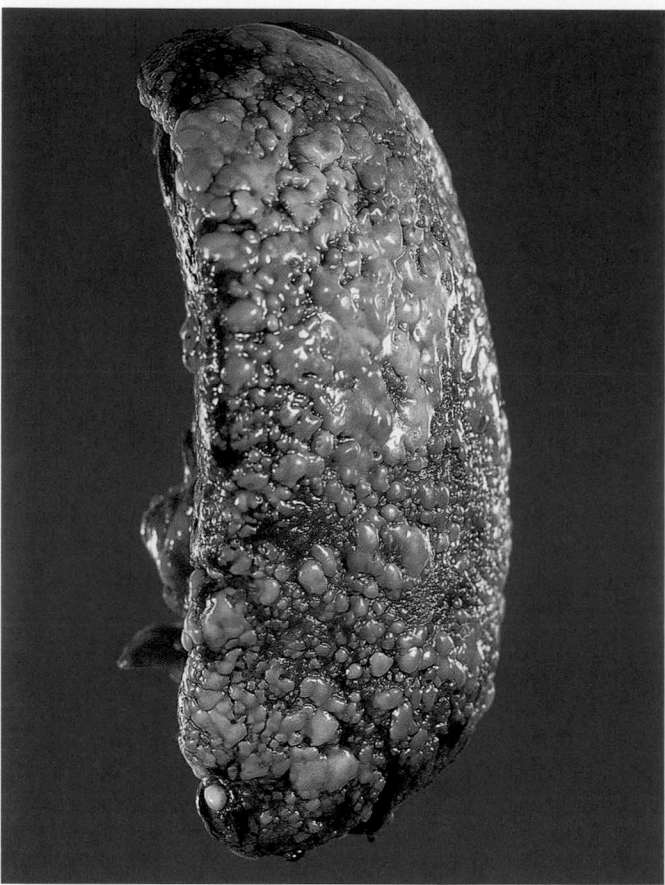

Fig. 22.8 Typical gross appearance of perisplenitis ("sugar-coated" or "snow-covered" spleen). (Courtesy of Dr. RA Cooke, Brisbane, Australia; from Cooke RA, Stewart B: Colour Atlas of Anatomical Pathology. Edinburgh, Churchill Livingstone, 2004).

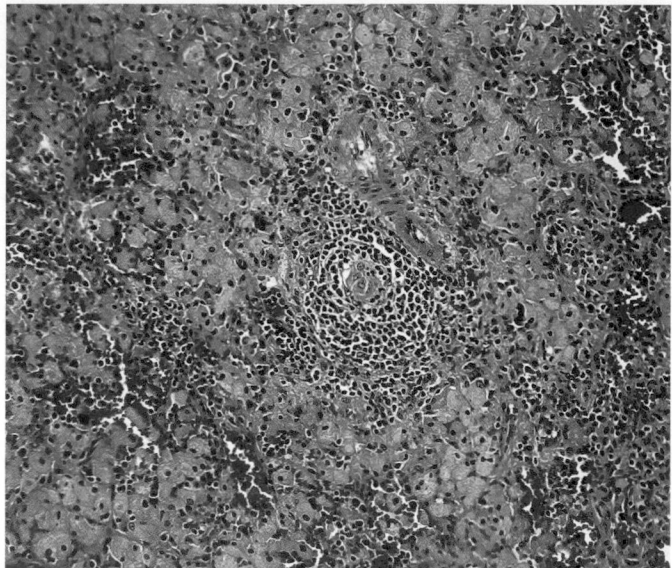

Fig. 22.9 Gaucher's disease of spleen. Macrophages with abundant pale acidophilic cytoplasm pack the red pulp.

cases the granulomas appeared to arise in the periarteriolar lymphoid sheath, suggesting that they are the result of abnormal or defective processing of antigen presented to the spleen. Granulomas have also been described in spleens affected by infectious mononucleosis.[86]

Perisplenitis presents as thick white fibrous plaques coating the surface. It is a common incidental finding at autopsy (Fig. 22.8).

Hypersplenism

Hypersplenism (dysplenism) is the generic term used for the group of disorders in which the removal of hematopoietic elements by the spleen increases to a pathologic degree.[90,92] Any of the cellular elements of the blood may be affected, singly or in combination. Thus neutropenia, thrombocytopenia, hemolytic anemia, or pancytopenia may all be present. In some conditions, such as spherocytic hemolytic anemia or idiopathic thrombocytopenic purpura, the basic abnormality resides in the blood elements themselves. In others, the hypersplenism results from widening of the splenic cords with an increase in macrophages and/or connective tissue fibers and premature destruction of the normal elements of the blood. Hypersplenism resulting

from this mechanism can be seen with congestive splenomegaly, Gaucher's disease (Fig. 22.9), malignant lymphoma, leukemia, Langerhans' cell histiocytosis, hemangioma, hamartoma, angiosarcoma, and practically any condition involving more or less diffusely the splenic parenchyma and particularly in the red pulp.[93]

A syndrome of hypersplenism developing in uremic hemodialyzed patients has also been recognized.[91] Splenectomy resulted in a marked improvement; a striking degree of lymphoid hyperplasia was found in the excised spleens.

Thrombocytopenic purpuras

Immune thrombocytopenic purpura (traditionally known as idiopathic thrombocytopenic purpura) is caused by the presence of an antiplatelet IgG, which is produced largely in the spleen.[99,106] Occasionally, thrombocytopenic purpura is seen as a manifestation of lupus erythematosus, viral infection, drug hypersensitivity,[101] chronic lymphocytic leukemia,[101] or Hodgkin's lymphoma.[108] The antibody-coated platelets have a short life span because they are rapidly removed by the cells of the reticuloendothelial system, particularly in the spleen and liver. There is some evidence that the number of antibody molecules bound to the platelets may determine the main site of removal. Heavily coated platelets are removed by the liver phagocytes, where as lightly coated platelets pass through the liver but are sequestered in the spleen.

Grossly, the spleen is of normal size or only mildly enlarged[103]; malpighian follicles may be prominent. Microscopically, there is formation of secondary follicles with well-developed germinal centers (containing the platelet antigen CD41),[104] prominence of histiocytes in the red pulp, dilatation of sinuses, variable numbers of perivascular plasma cells in the marginal zone, and infiltration with neutrophils of the red pulp.[98] Mild myeloid metaplasia, usually in the form of megakaryocytes, is present in most cases.[97,98,103] The germinal centers, which usually show phagocytosis of nuclear debris and periarterial fibrosis,[95] are no longer prominent in cases previously treated with steroids.[102]

Collections of foamy macrophages containing phospholipid deposits are present in the red pulp in some of the cases.[100,109] They are the result of phagocytosis of platelets and of incompletely degraded membrane derived phospholipids,[105,112] as supported by the fact that the platelet antigen CD41 has been detected immunohistochemically in them.[104] The phagocytosis of platelets by splenic histiocytes can be better appreciated in touch preparations. It should be noted that the presence of foamy macrophages in the spleen is not pathognomonic of this disorder (see p. 2026).

Splenectomy in idiopathic thrombocytopenic purpura is reserved for the patients unresponsive to steroid or immunosuppressive therapy.[96] It achieves sustained remission in 50% to 80% of the cases.[110] It is difficult to predict what effect the splenectomy will have in an individual case. However, Chang et al.[98] have shown that patients with prominent secondary follicles have a higher rate of antiplatelet antibody production and exhibit a better initial response, with a great increase in platelets postoperatively.

Thrombotic thrombocytic purpura may be accompanied by splenic enlargement.[107] The most important pathologic change is the presence of thrombi in arteries and arterioles without associated inflammation. Periodic acid-Schiff-positive hyaline subendothelial deposits are present. Other changes include hyperplasia of B cells and germinal centers, periarteriolar concentric fibrosis, hemosiderin-laden macrophages, hemophagocytosis, and extramedullary hematopoiesis.[111]

Hemolytic anemia

Congenital hemolytic anemia (hereditary spherocytosis) is a genetically determined disease in which the red blood cells acquire a spheric shape (spherocytes).[115] The abnormality lies in the cell membrane of the red blood cell. Consistent molecular alterations of spectrin and ankyrin have been detected, resulting in defects in the horizontal interactions that hold the membrane skeleton together, particularly the critical spectrin self-association reaction.[116,119,121,123] As a result, the erythrocytes lack the plasticity of normal red blood cells and become trapped in the interstices of the spleen.[124] The splenic function itself is normal.

Acquired hemolytic anemia can be caused by toxins (bacterial hemolysins), plasma lipid abnormalities, parasites that invade red blood cells, and most important, immune reactions that result in deposition of immune complexes on red blood cell membranes.[118] About one half of the cases of immune hemolytic anemias are unassociated with other significant pathologic abnormalities. The remaining cases are seen as a manifestation of a large variety of disease, such as various forms of acute and chronic leukemia, Hodgkin's lymphoma, sarcoidosis, lupus erythematosus, tuberculosis, and brucellosis. The Coombs test is the classic method to distinguish between the acquired (positive) and congenital (negative) types of hemolytic anemia. A positive Coombs test consists of agglutination of the patient's washed red blood cells following mixture with antihuman globulin rabbit serum.

Grossly, the spleen of both congenital and acquired hemolytic anemia is fairly firm and deep red, has a thin capsule and no grossly discernible malpighian follicles, and ranges in weight from 100 to 1000 g. In congenital hemolytic anemia, the splenic cords are congested, whereas the sinusoids appear relatively empty because of the presence of ghost red blood cells.[125] The lining cells of the sinuses are prominent, sometimes resulting in a glandlike appearance. Hemosiderin deposition and erythrophagocytosis are present in both conditions but are usually more pronounced in the acquired variety. Ultrastructural studies have shown that the splenic cords are not empty but rather contain red blood cells that have lost their electron density, thus corresponding to the red cell ghosts of light microscopy.[117]

In acquired hemolytic anemia, the congestion may predominate in the cords or sinuses or be equally prominent in both. A high correlation exists between spherocytosis and increased osmotic fragility on one hand and the degree of cord congestion on the other. Foci of extramedullary hematopoiesis may be present. Splenic infarcts are found in one fourth of the cases.[120]

Hereditary spherocytosis is the hematologic disease that most benefits from splenectomy.[122] The clinical cure rate is almost 100%, although the intrinsic red cell abnormality persists.[114] In acquired hemolytic anemia, splenectomy is usually reserved for cases that cannot be controlled by steroid or immunosuppressive therapy. A sustained remission rate is obtained in about 50% of the cases and an objective improvement is obtained, in an additional 25% of the cases. Studies of splenic sequestration using Cr[51]-tagged red cells give a rough estimation of the benefit to be expected from splenectomy.[113]

Congestive splenomegaly

Congestive splenomegaly is a direct consequence of portal hypertension. It may be caused by cirrhosis (by far the most common pathogenesis); thrombosis of hepatic veins (Budd-Chiari syndrome); thrombosis of the splenic veins; or occlusive thrombosis, cavernous transformation (recanalized thrombosis), sclerosis, or stenosis of the portal vein. Portal vein thrombosis may be the result of inflammation, trauma, or extrinsic pressure by inflammatory or neoplastic tissue.[126] Stenotic or sclerotic changes may be the result of extension into the main

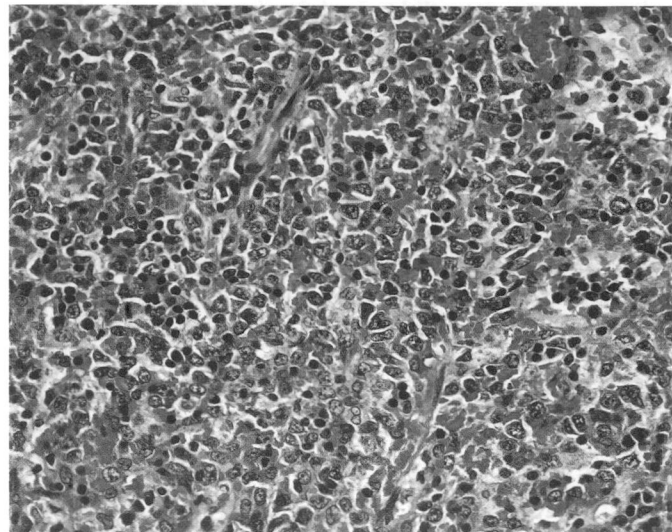

Fig. 22.13 Large B-cell lymphoma of spleen causing diffuse infiltration of the organ.

Secondary splenic involvement by tumor is particularly common in low-grade lymphomas, most of which are of B-cell type.[194] This includes small lymphocytic lymphoma, the closely related lymphoplasmacytoid lymphoma, mantle cell lymphoma, follicle center lymphoma (particularly of the small cell type), and marginal zone B-cell lymphoma. The latter is discussed below.

Splenic small lymphocytic lymphoma usually presents grossly as nodules measuring a few millimetres in diameter ("miliary" nodules) scattered throughout the organ. The low-power appearance is also distinctly nodular because of the preferential involvement of the white pulp.[172a] In this regard, it is important to point out that a nodular pattern of growth is common to several types of lymphoproliferative diseases of the spleen (including chronic lymphocytic leukemia) and that its presence should not be equated with a diagnosis of follicle center lymphoma[156] (Fig. 22.15).

In the early stages, the diagnosis of small lymphocytic lymphoma can be easily missed. Clues to the diagnosis in these cases include prominent enlargement and coalescence of follicles; presence of a marked expansion of their mantle zone; germinal centers that are absent, inconspicuous, or overrun by small cells; and presence of clusters of small lymphoid cells protruding beneath the endothelium of trabecular veins[167] (Figs 22.16 and 22.17). The only other condition in which we have seen the latter change in a prominent degree in an adult has been infectious mononucleosis. We have also seen the subendothelial space occupied by red cell precursors in infants with erythroblastosis fetalis and (together with granulocyte precursors) in adults with myelofibrosis. A helpful hint for the diagnosis of lymphoma is to carefully dissect and examine the lymph nodes in the splenic hilum, since they may show obvious lymphoma when the changes in the spleen are only equivocal.

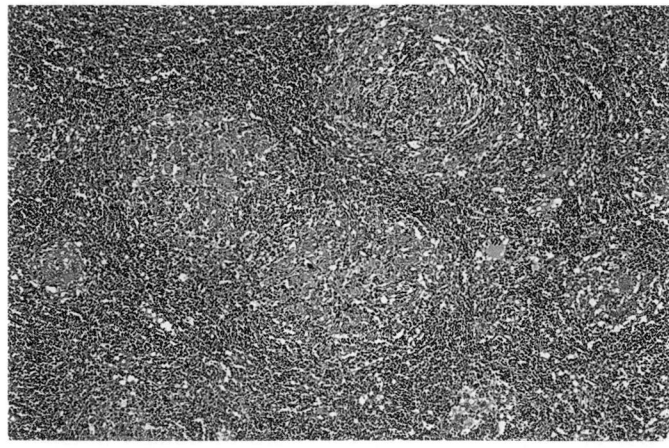

A

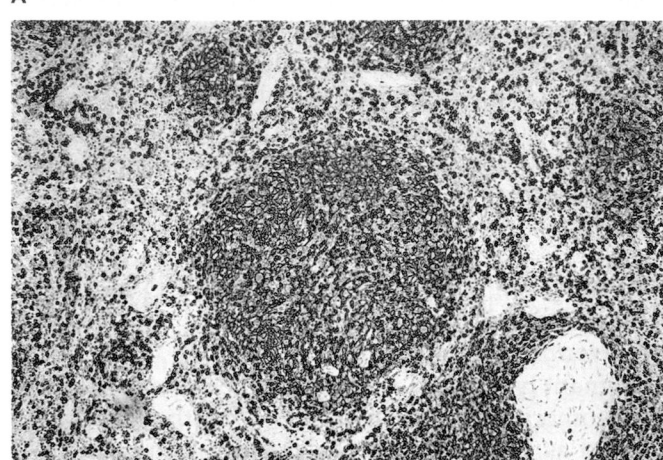

B

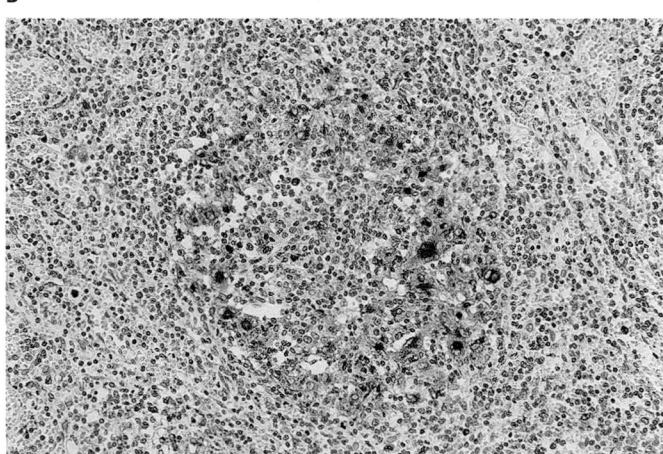

C

Fig. 22.14 Large T-cell lymphoma of spleen rich in reactive histiocytes. **A,** Low-power appearance. **B,** CD43 immunoreactivity of neoplastic T cells. **C,** Lysozyme positivity of reactive histiocytes.

An "entity" that exemplifies the difficulties sometimes encountered in the recognition of splenic small lymphocytic lymphoma is so-called idiopathic nontropical splenomegaly. Although originally regarded as a benign and probably reactive form of splenomegaly;[160] a follow-up study by the same group showed that half of these cases actually represented malignant lymphoma.[161]

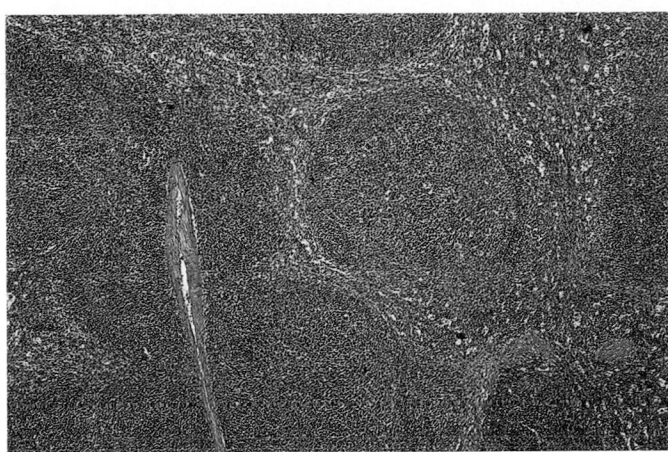

Fig. 22.15 Malignant lymphoma of spleen with a nodular pattern of growth, which in this organ is not limited to follicular lymphoma but can be seen in many types of Hodgkin's and non-Hodgkin's lymphoma.

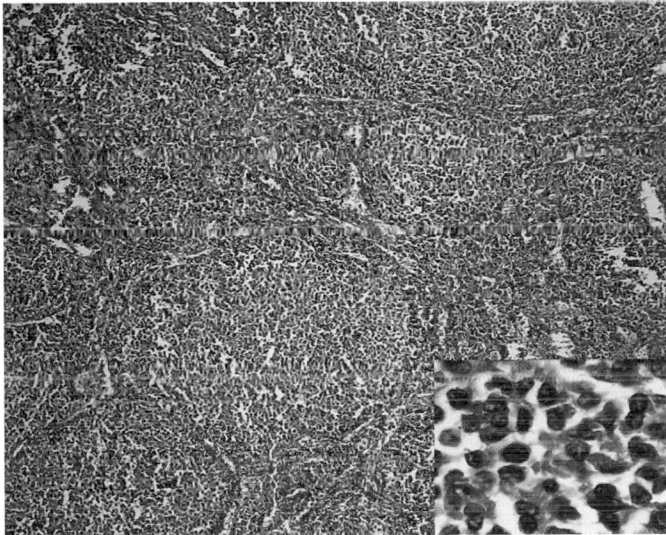

Fig. 22.16 Small lymphocytic lymphoma of spleen, so-called "paraimmunoblastic" type.

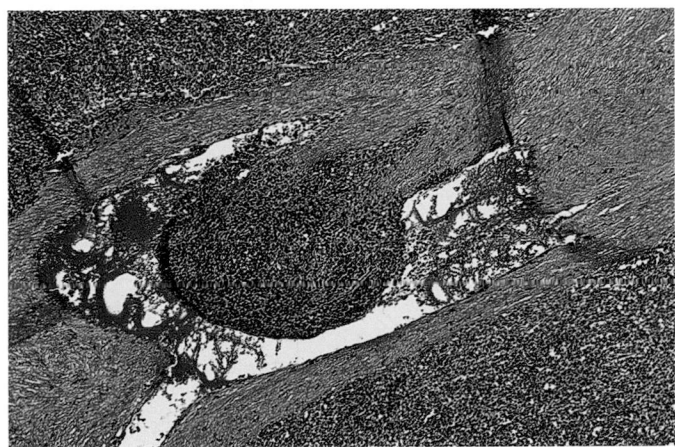

Fig. 22.17 Polypoid growth of malignant lymphoma cells beneath the endothelium of a trabecular vein. This is a useful diagnostic sign.

The treatment of malignant lymphoma involving exclusively or preferentially the spleen includes splenectomy, followed by chemotherapy.[183] The prognosis is directly related to the microscopic type and the clinical stage, in the sense that it is distinctly better for small lymphocytic tumors and for stage I and II disease.[152,170] Patients with localized splenic non-Hodgkin's lymphoma seem to have the same rate of survival as other Stage I non-Hodgkin's lymphoma patients.[173]

Two types of malignant lymphoma of the spleen that need to be singled out because of their distinctive features are marginal zone B-cell lymphoma and hepatosplenic gamma-delta T-cell lymphoma.

Marginal zone B-cell lymphoma (MZBCL) of the spleen usually presents with splenomegaly, anemia, and weight loss.[168,172,192] The bone marrow and liver are also involved in most cases. Grossly, the splenic involvement manifests itself through miliary expansion of the white pulp.

Histologically, there are nodular lymphoid infiltrates centered on preexistent germinal centers, which are barely visible.[161b] The tumor cells are small lymphocytes similar to mantle cells, with a component of larger cells with irregular nuclei and pale cytoplasm located towards the periphery of the nodules. Immunohistochemically, the cells express surface immunoglobulin (usually IgM) and bcl-2, but not CD5, CD10, CD23, CD11c or CD43.[182] There is no cyclin D1 protein expression.[190] Cytogenetically, there is frequent allelic loss of 7q31–32.[177] Somatic mutation analysis has shown that the tumor cells of MZBCL are memory B lymphocytes,[179] but other cases seem to be composed of naive marginal zone B cells.[154a]

The differential diagnosis of MZBCL includes mantle cell lymphoma[180,187] (Fig. 22.18), and follicle center

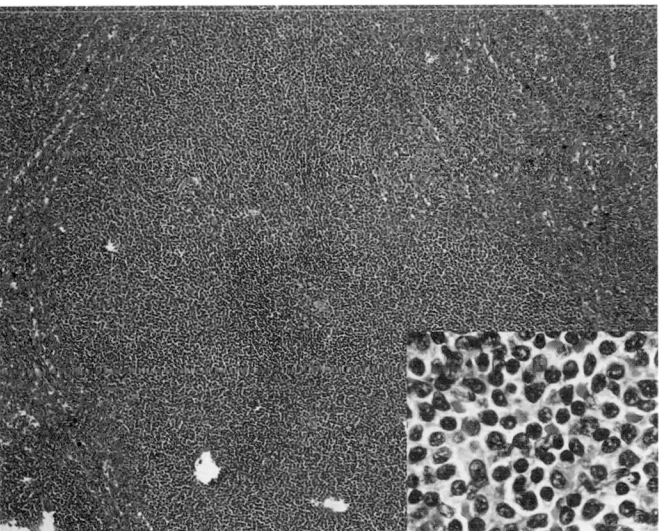

Fig. 22.18 Mantle cell lymphoma. Note the tiny residual germinal center. The inset shows the centrocyte-like appearance of the tumor cells.

lymphoma with preferential involvement of the marginal zone.[153]

Variants of NZBCL include cases with predominant red pulp involvement,[181] with plasmacytic differentiation,[195] with increased number of blasts and a more aggressive clinical course,[175] and with progression to large B-cell lymphoma.[158]

It has been suggested that MZBCL is the splenic equivalent of MALT lymphoma of other sites.[170,186,188,191] However, the overlap between these two entities is not complete, and is therefore better to keep them separate for the time being. Similar considerations apply to the splenic lymphoma with circulating lymphocytes originally described by Neimann's group,[178] which may be a leukemic variant of splenic marginal zone B-cell lymphoma[171] or represent a heterogeneous group of low-grade B-cell lymphomas.[184]

Hepatosplenic gamma-delta T-cell lymphoma seems to be a distinct clinical entity within the spectrum of peripheral T-cell lymphomas.[159,162,199] It typically presents with hepatosplenomegaly, fever and weight loss in young males, and carries a poor prognosis. Cases have been described in immunocompromised patients and in association with EBV.[166,185,200] Grossly, the spleen is usually very large, with a uniform cut surface in which the malpighian follicles cannot be identified. Microscopically, the neoplastic infiltration involves the cords and sinuses and is composed of medium-sized lymphoid cells with oval or folded nuclei, moderately condensed chromatin, and pale cytoplasm (Fig. 22.19). Tumor involvement of the liver and bone marrow is characterized by an intrasinusoidal distribution.[165]

The main differential diagnosis is with hairy cell leukaemia, from which it is distinguished by the absence of blood lakes and its different phenotype, which includes positivity for pan T cells and cytotoxic T cell and presence of the gamma-delta T-cell receptor.[189]

At the molecular level, there is usually clonal rearrangement of the gamma or delta chain of the T-cell receptor gene, and cytogenetically there is an isochromosome 7q.[166]

Hepatosplenic alpha beta T-cell lymphoma is a molecular variant of the splenic lymphoma just described which expresses TCR alpha-beta instead of gamma-delta chains. These are more common in women younger than 13 years or older than 50 years.[176]

Hodgkin's lymphoma

The spleen is the most common site of extranodal organ involvement by Hodgkin's lymphoma, but primary Hodgkin's lymphoma of the spleen is extremely rare, the morphologic features of Hodgkin's lymphoma in the spleen are discussed in Chapter 21. Grossly the involvement is in the form of one or multiple nodules, sometimes indistinguishable from those of large cell lymphoma (Fig. 22.20). Foci of involvement can be only a few millimetres in size, a fact which calls for a very meticulous gross inspection of the organ. The earliest lesions are located in the periarterial lymphoid sheath or marginal zones of the follicles. By far the most common type is nodular sclerosis, but others may be seen as well, including lymphocyte predominance[202] (Fig. 22.21). Some cases have initially presented with spontaneous splenic rupture.[201] As already mentioned, sarcoid-type granulomas can be seen in spleens of patients with Hodgkin's lymphoma and should not be construed by themselves as evidence of splenic involvement by the lymphoma.

Leukemias

Any type of leukemia can involve the spleen, the location being predominantly the red pulp for all types.[203,207] The earliest involvement is in the cords, with secondary spillage into the sinuses.

Chronic lymphocytic leukemia may appear grossly as a diffuse or miliary enlargement (Fig. 22.22). From a morphologic standpoint, it is not possible to distinguish it from small lymphocytic lymphoma.

Prolymphocytic leukemia shows a similar type of involvement, but the lymphocytes have nuclei that are larger, often indented, and with distinct nucleoli.[213] Massive splenomegaly is the predominant clinical finding.

Chronic myelocytic leukemia preferentially results grossly in a large, dark red, diffusely involved organ in which malpighian follicles are inconspicuous or absent. Infarcts are common. In rare cases, blastic transformation of chronic leukemia (known as Richter's syndrome in cases of chronic lymphocytic leukemia) is first seen in a splenectomy specimen.

Myelodysplasia (defined as a group of bone marrow disorders characterized by dysplastic changes in one or

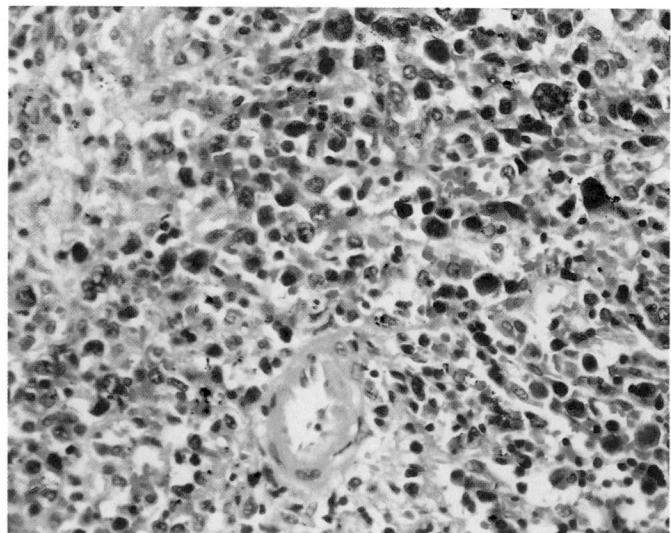

Fig. 22.19 Hepatosplenic T-cell lymphoma. Highly atypical lymphoid cells are present in a polymorphic background.

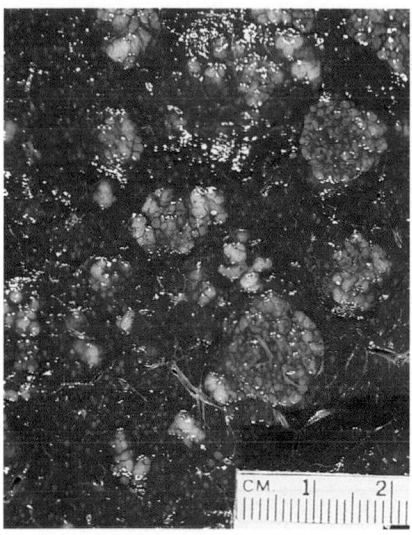

A

B

Fig. 22.20 A and B, Gross appearance of Hodgkin's lymphoma involving the spleen.

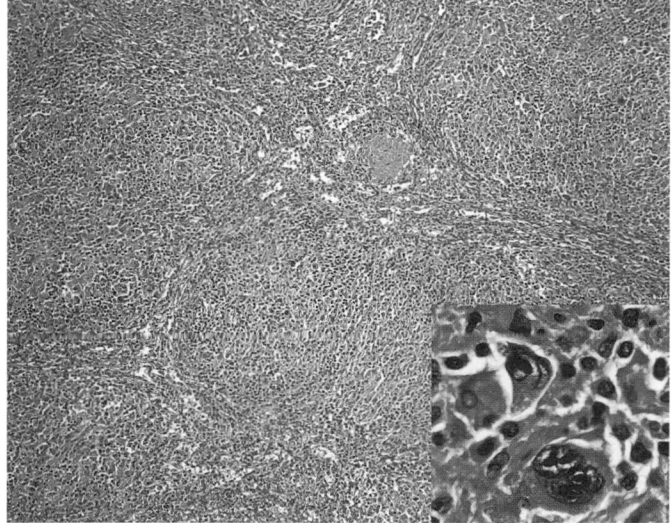

Fig. 22.21 Classic Hodgkin's lymphoma of spleen, nodular sclerosis subtype. The inset shows typical Reed-Sternberg cells.

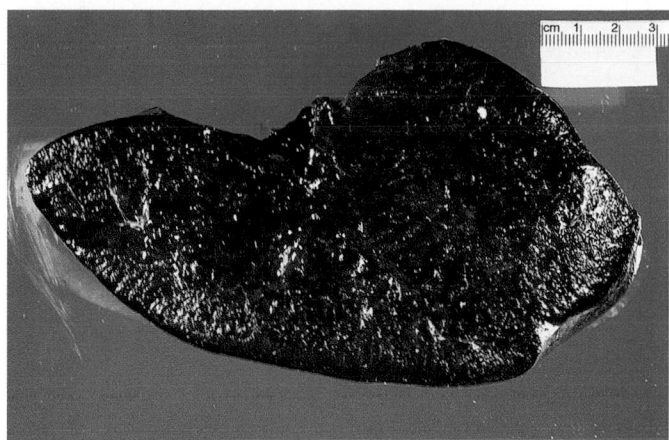

Fig. 22.22 The splenic involvement by chronic lymphocytic leukemia results in marked diffuse enlargement of the organ.

more myeloid cell lines, with or without concurrent increases in myeloblasts in the bone marrow and peripheral blood; see also Chapter 23) may be accompanied by several types of splenic abnormalities, including erythrophagocytosis, red pulp plasmacytosis, extramedullary hematopoiesis and clusters of monocytes, the latter allegedly correlating with an increased risk of disease progression.[212] Clinically, detectable splenomegaly is rare in this condition.

Hairy cell leukemia, formerly known as leukemic reticuloendotheliosis, is a specific subtype of B-cell malignancy[208]; it is further discussed in Chapter 23. Grossly the spleen shows diffuse and usually marked enlargement without formation of nodules, except in the very early stages of the disease (Fig. 22.23).[210] Microscopically, hairy cell leukemia is a disease of the red pulp, which shows diffuse infiltration by a monotonous population of small mononuclear cells with very scanty mitotic activity and practically no phagocytosis[204,215] (Fig. 22.24). The initial involvement occurs around the fibrous trabeculae. The nuclei of the hairy

Fig. 22.23 Gross appearance of hairy cell leukemia. Note the diffuse involvement, lack of nodularity, and dark red color.

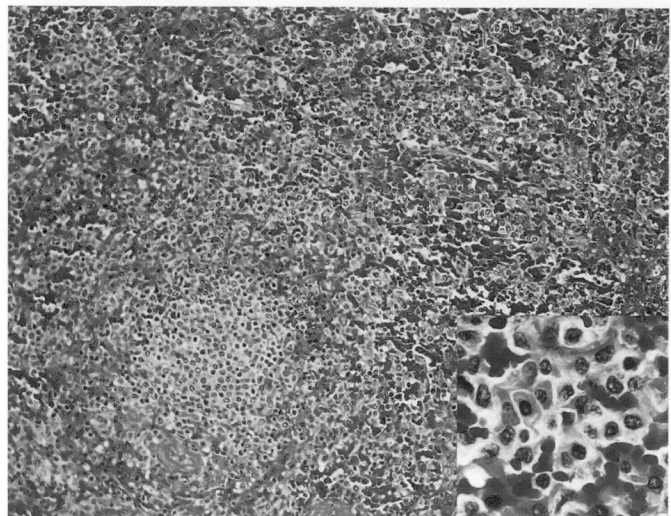

Fig. 22.24 Splenic involvement by hairy cell leukemia. The inset shows the bland monotonous appearance of the infiltrate.

cells are small, round, or oval, with irregular contours, occasional deep indentations ("coffee beans"), and inconspicuous nucleoli. Rarely, the nuclei have a multi-lobular appearance simulating those of T-cell lymphoma.[209] The cytoplasm is usually scanty, although in some cells it is moderate to abundant and lightly stained. Ultrastructurally, prominent cytoplasmic villous projections are evident.[205] The distinctive enzyme histochemical feature of the disease is the presence of tartrate-resistant acid phosphatase (isoenzyme 5); this enzyme can now be demonstrated immunohistochemically.[211] In addition to the above, the usual antigenic phenotype of hairy cells is CD45+, CD45RA+, CD20+, CDw75+, CD74+, LN3+, MB2+, CD45RO–, MT1–, CD15–, and CD30–.[218,219] The splenic vasculature is abnormal in the sense of showing an absolute increase in the volume, surface, and length of pulp arterial vessels, as well as enlargement of pulp cords and sinuses.[217] Pools of blood in the red pulp, lined by hairy cells and simulating dilated sinuses or even hemangiomas, are commonly seen and constitute an important diagnostic feature.[214] It has been suggested that this results from the hairy cells adhering to the sinus surface, producing endothelial cell injury and impeding the venous blood flow.[216] In what is perhaps the preceding stage of this process, some of the tumor cells are seen to aggregate in the subendothelial spaces of trabecular veins; sometimes this is the only recognizable site of involvement.[206]

The lymph nodes in the splenic hilum are often involved, the pattern of permeation being interfollicular.

Splenectomy is the treatment of choice, and long survivals are common.[220]

Myelofibrosis

Myelofibrosis (agnogenic myeloid metaplasia) is discussed in Chapter 23. Spleen involvement in the disease is the rule, the average weight being 2 kg.[224] Grossly, the spleen is diffusely dark red and moderately firm, with frequent areas of hemorrhage (Fig. 22.25). Microscopically, the diagnostic feature is the presence in the red pulp of all three hematopoietic cell lines: megakaryocytes, erythroid precursors, and granulocyte precursors. The latter are made evident with Leder's chloroacetate esterase stain (Fig. 22.26). The mega-

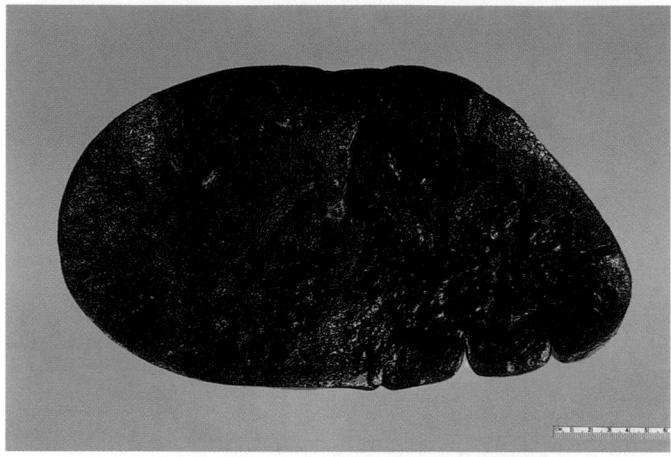

Fig. 22.25 Diffuse involvement of the spleen by myelofibrosis.

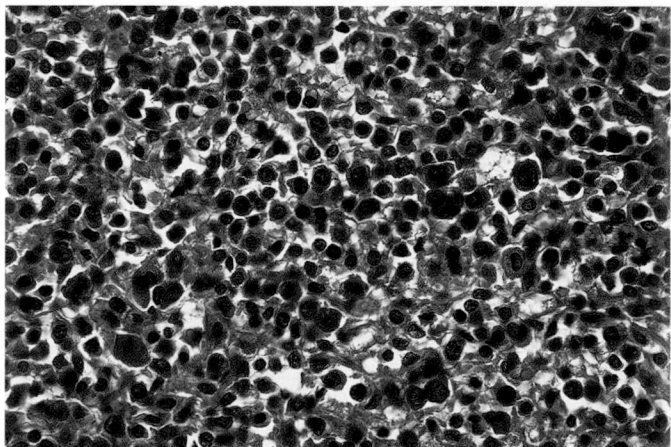

A

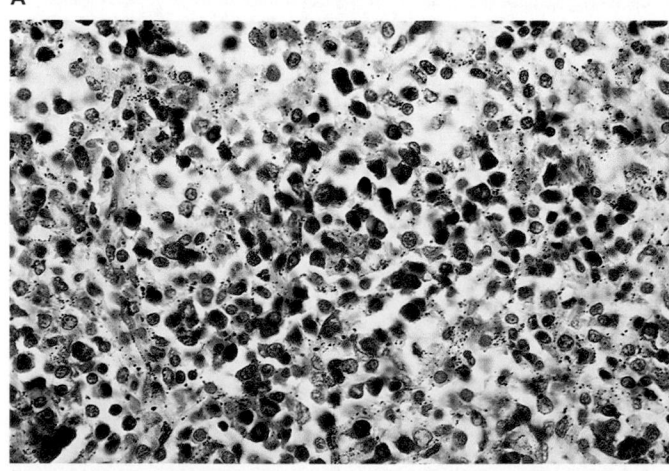

B

Fig. 22.26 Extramedullary hematopoiesis in spleen, as seen in H&E section (**A**) and with Leder acetate chloracetate stain (**B**).

karyocytes often have atypical nuclear features and can be confused with Reed-Sternberg cells; in contrast with the latter, their cytoplasm is strongly PAS positive.[222] They are immunohistochemically reactive for factor VIII-related antigen and negative for CD30 and Leu-M1.

It is believed that the hematopoietic cells present in the spleen result from filtration of circulating cells from the peripheral blood rather than arising de novo from splenic stem cells.[223,227]

Other splenic changes in myelofibrosis include congestion, hemosiderosis, and paucity of lymphoid follicles.[225,226]

Splenectomy is sometimes carried out for this disease, especially when hemolytic phenomena or thrombocytopenia is severe. The results are not spectacular, but in some cases a moderate improvement has been noted.

Splenic extramedullary hematopoiesis as seen in myelofibrosis should be distinguished from the rare myelolipomas occurring within or adjacent to the spleen.[221]

Mastocytosis

The general features of systemic mastocytosis are discussed in Chapter 23. The spleen is always involved, and the morphologic changes in it can be very confusing.[229] Grossly, ill-defined granuloma-like nodules having a fibrotic appearance are scattered throughout the organ. Microscopically, these highly fibrotic foci are often centered by a vessel, an important diagnostic clue.[229,232] The diagnosis depends on the identification of mast cells, which usually appear as small clusters embedded in fibrous tissue, accompanied by a variable number of eosinophils, lymphocytes, or histiocytes (Fig. 22.27). The nucleus is centrally located and of regular outline; the cytoplasm is light staining, with a variable degree of granularity; the cell borders tend to be sharply outlined. Confirmation of the diagnosis is obtained by staining the cytoplasmic granules with metachromatic dyes, with Leder's chloroacetate esterase reaction, or by the immunohistochemical demonstration of tryptase, chymase, carboxypeptidase, CD68, and CD117 (c-kit).[228–230,233] Conversely, mast cells are only weakly reactive for lysozyme and negative for myeloperoxidase and CD20.[231]

The lymph nodes in the splenic hilum are often involved; the diagnosis may be easier on them than on the spleen. The foci of involvement in the lymph nodes are usually perifollicular and may also show a perivascular distribution.

Other hematolymphoid conditions

Focal lymphoid hyperplasia can present in the spleen as a solitary nodule that may be confused grossly with lymphoma, especially if the splenectomy specimen has been obtained at staging laparotomy for that disease. Microscopically, the nodule is formed either by aggregates of reactive germinal centers or by a localized proliferation of lymphocytes, immunoblasts, and plasma cells.[235,236]

Langherhans' cell histiocytosis of the spleen is almost always the expression of systemic disease and is therefore rarely seen as a surgical specimen. The red pulp is preferentially affected.[234]

Castleman's disease can involve the spleen, although it rarely results in prominent splenomegaly. Most of the reported types have been of the plasma cell type,[239] but a

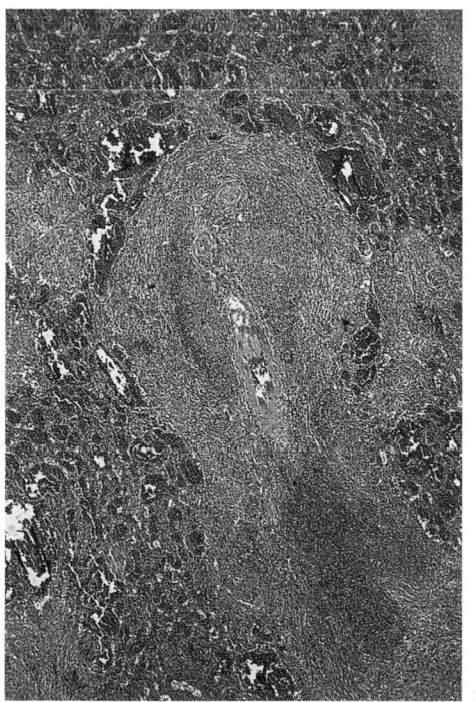

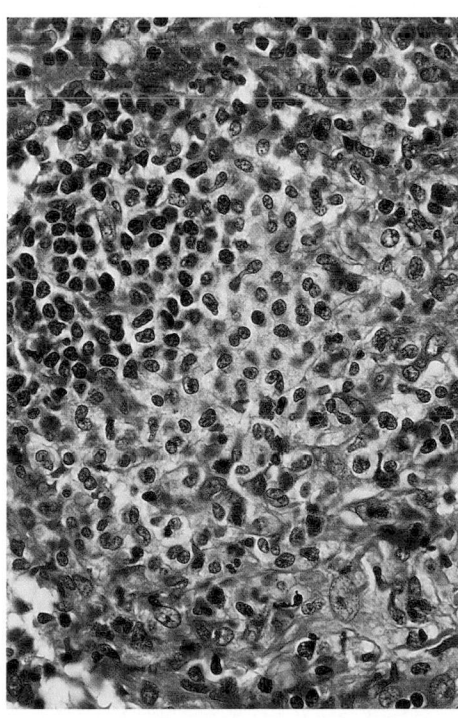

Fig. 22.27 Involvement of the spleen by systemic mastocytosis. **A,** Low-power view showing the perimalpighian and perivascular arrangement of the infiltrate. **B,** High-power view showing clusters of mast cells.

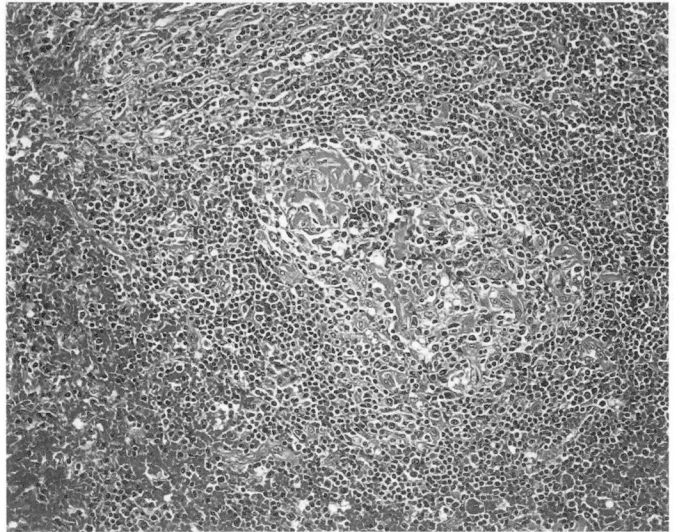

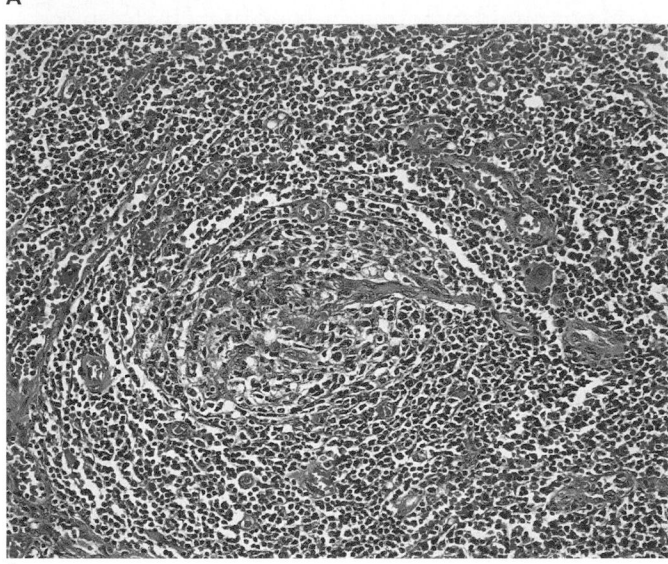

Fig. 22.28 Castleman's disease of hyaline-vascular type. **A**, Splenic involvement. **B**, Lymph node involvement in the same case.

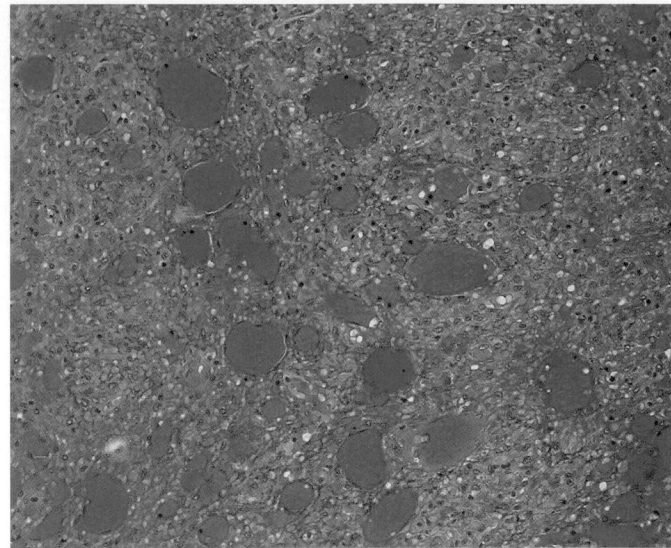

Fig. 22.29 Diffuse involvement of spleen by benign vascular tumor ("angiomatosis").

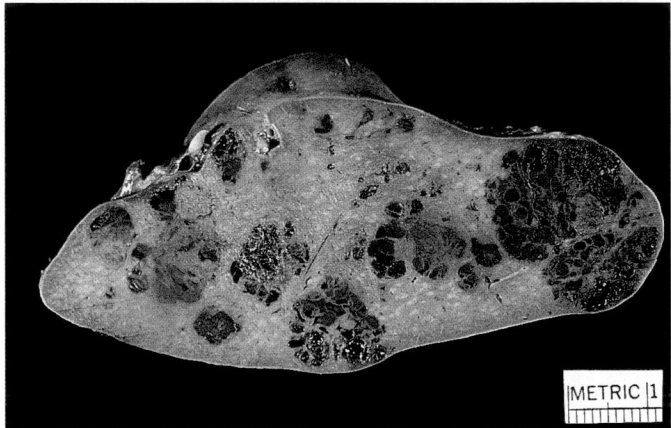

Fig. 22.30 Gross appearance of littoral cell angioma. Numerous hemorrhagic lesions with a lobular configuration are seen.

few instances of the hyaline-vascular type are also on record (Fig. 22.28).[237]

Wiskott-Aldrich syndrome, an x-linked hematologic disorder characterized by thrombocytopenia, eczema and immunodeficiency, is accompanied by a general depletion of the splenic white pulp, with significant reduction of the marginal zone thickness.[238]

Vascular tumors

Hemangioma is the most common primary tumor of the spleen.[241,249,254a] It is often of the cavernous variety. Most are under 2 cm in diameter and present as incidental findings. Rarely, they are large and/or multiple, and they may involve the entire spleen (angiomatoisis) (Fig. 22.29). They may be associated with hemangiomas of other sites (angiomatosis). The most common complication is rupture and bleeding.[252] Cases associated with

anemia, thrombocytopenia, and consumption coagulopathy (Kasabach–Merritt syndrome) have been reported.[247,262]

Littoral cell angioma varies in size from minute foci to large nodules almost completely replacing the splenic tissue (Fig. 22.30). Microscopically, it is composed of anastomosing vascular channels resembling splenic sinuses (Fig. 22.31). These channels have irregular lumina often featuring papillary projections and cystlike spaces. They are lined by tall endothelial cells which sometimes show hemophagocytosis. Immunohistochemically, the neoplastic cells express both endothelial (factor VIII) and histiocytic (KP-1, lysozyme) markers and occasionally also S-100 protein, mirroring the dual differentiation potential of the reticuloendothelial cells (littoral cells) lining the sinuses[248] (Fig. 22.32). However, their negativity for CD8 (not known at the time of the original report) has cast some doubts on their proposed littoral cell derivation.[241]

Multinodular hemangioma is a distinctive splenic vascular neoplasm having a striking multinodular quality that simulates the appearance of granulomas on low power examination (Fig. 22.33A). The individual vascular nodules, which have a vaguely lobulated architecture, are surrounded by a hyaline shell that stains strongly for FVIII-related antigen (Fig. 22.33B). The vessels within the nodules are markedly cellular and composed of an admixture of CD31-positive spindle and plump endothelial cells, actin-positive perithelial/smooth muscle cells, and CD68-positive histiocytes (Fig. 22.33C). The lesion is almost always solitary and the evolution is benign.

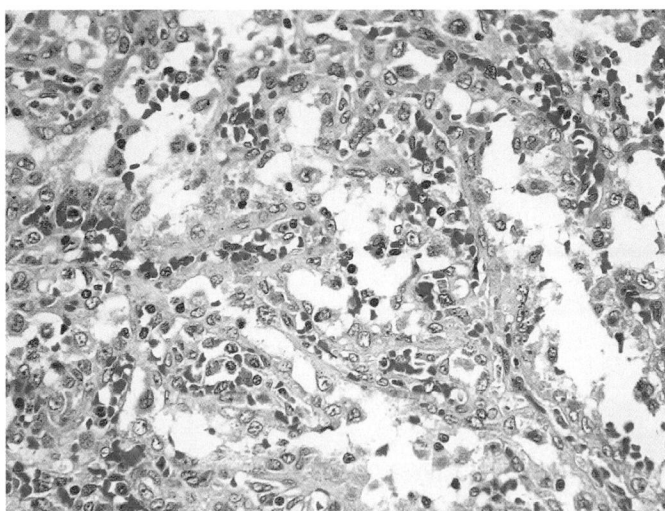

Fig. 22.31 Littoral cell angioma of spleen. The vascular spaces are lined by plump cells with the appearance of sinus lining ("littoral") cells.

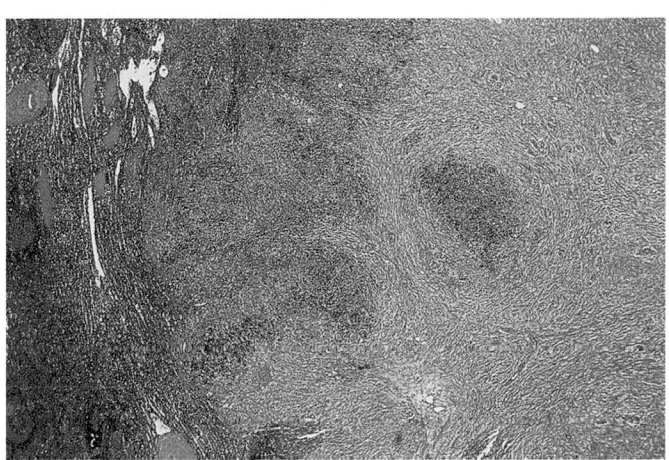

A

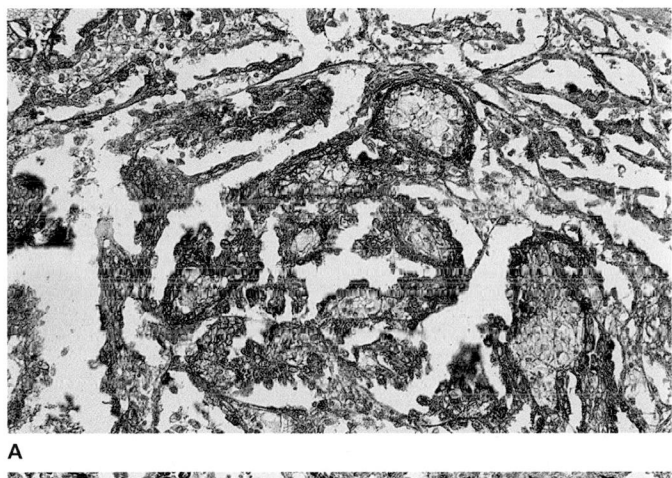

A

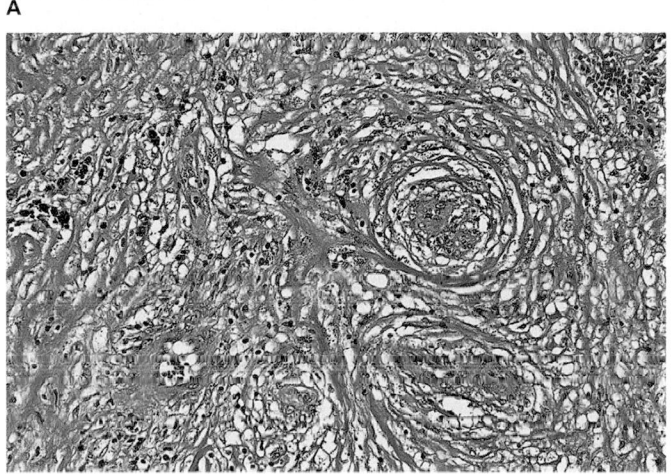

B

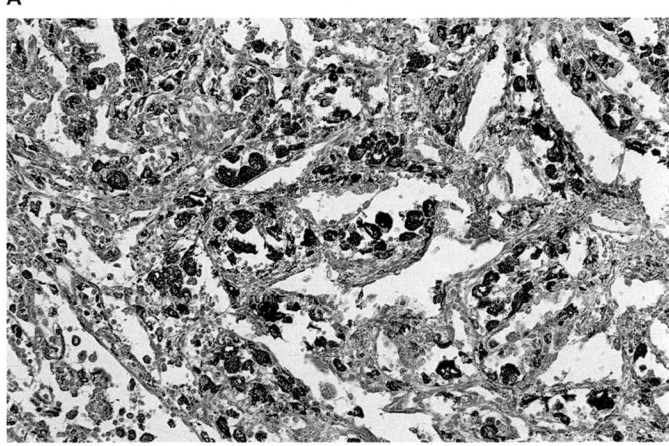

B

Fig. 22.32 Littoral cell angioma of spleen showing combined expression of endothelial and histiocytic markers. **A**, Factor VIII-related antigen. **B**, Lysozyme.

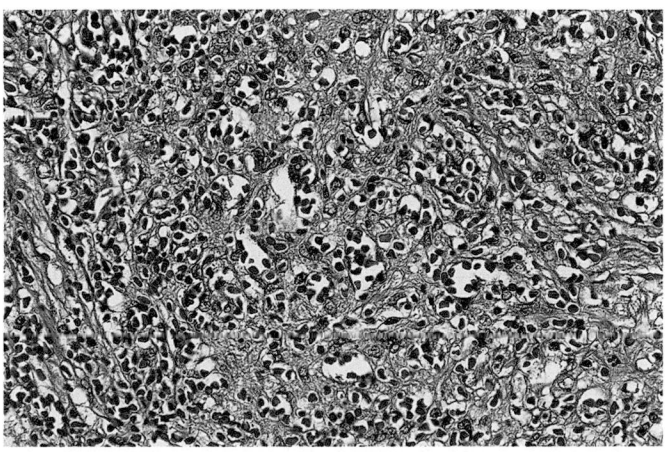

C

Fig. 22.33 Multinodular hemangioma of spleen. **A**, Low-power appearance showing a distinctly nodular architecture. **B**, Highly hyalinized area simulating an ancient granuloma. **C**, Cellular area of clearly angiomatous nature.

Other types of splenic hemangiomas include venous hemangioma, capillary hemangioma, benign (infantile) hemangioendothelioma[253] and diffuse sinusoidal hemangiomatosis (in which the entire spleen is permeated by blood vessel).[241,259]

Lymphangioma tends to be located in the subcapsular region but may involve the entire organ (diffuse lymphangiomatosis)[261] (Fig. 22.34). Most cases have been reported in children, sometimes in association with lymphangiomas in other organs.[250]

Hemangioendothelioma is the term that has been applied in the spleen (as in many other sites) in a somewhat loose fashion to vascular endothelial neoplasms that are either more cellular and/or are thought to be potentially more aggressive than hemangiomas but are not full-fledged angiosarcomas. Some of these tumors have been described as epithelioid (sometimes associated with functional hyposplenism),[244] some as epithelioid and spindle-cell,[264] and some as combining endothelial and myoid features.[252a,254] Some of these hemangioendotheliomas have been viewed as "borderline" (low-grade malignant) counterparts of littoral cell angiomas in view of the presence of combined endothelial and histiocytic markers.[243] As in other sites, it is probably wise never to use in the spleen the term hemangioendothelioma without a qualifier.

Angiosarcoma is the most common malignant primary nonlymphoid tumor of the spleen.[263] It may present as a well-defined hemorrhagic nodule or involve the spleen diffusely and may lead to spontaneous rupture of the organ[242,245] (Fig. 22.35). It may also be accompanied by microangiopathic anemia, thrombocytopenia, and consumption coagulopathy.[251] As in other sites, there are cases of angiosarcoma of spleen that have developed many years following the insertion of a foreign body (gauze sponge).[246] Microscopically, the pattern of growth of angiosarcoma may be solid, papillary, or characterized by the classic freely anastomosing vascular channels[256] (Fig. 22.36). Intracytoplasmic hyaline globules are common. Sometimes the tumor cells have an epitheliod appearance (epithelioid angiosarcoma).[246] Immunohistochemically, the tumor cells exhibit endothelial markers and often also histiocytic markers.[256] The latter finding supports the littoral cell nature of at least some angiosarcomas and demonstrates that this combined immunohistochemical staining pattern is not limited to a specific tumor type (littoral cell angioma) but rather shared by a spectrum of splenic vascular tumors.[241,258] The clinical course of splenic angiosarcoma is rapid and almost invariably fatal, with widespread metastases occurring frequently.[240,257,260]

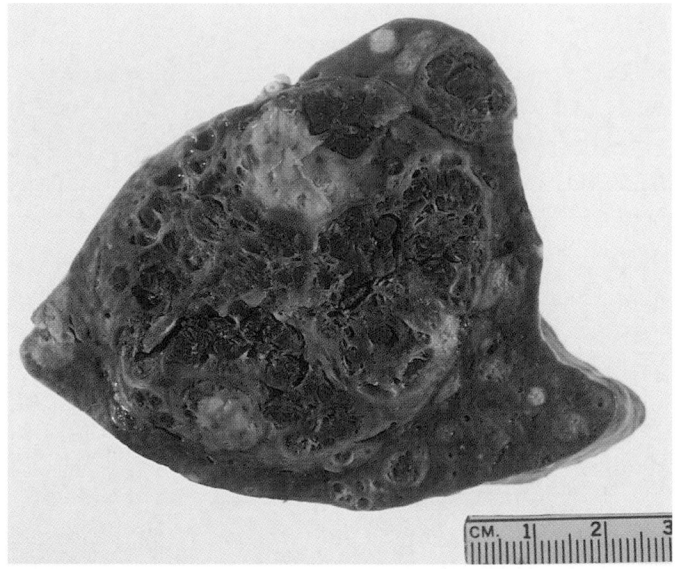

Fig. 22.35 Angiosarcoma of spleen. The tumor is markedly hemorrhagic and necrotic.

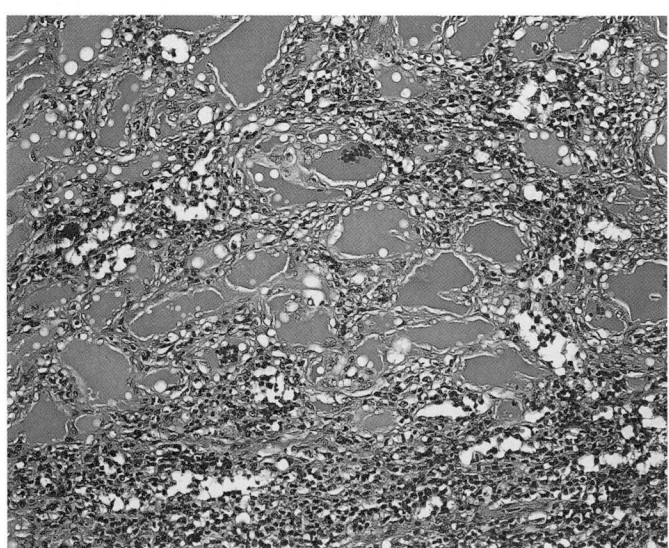

Fig. 22.34 Lymphangioma of spleen.

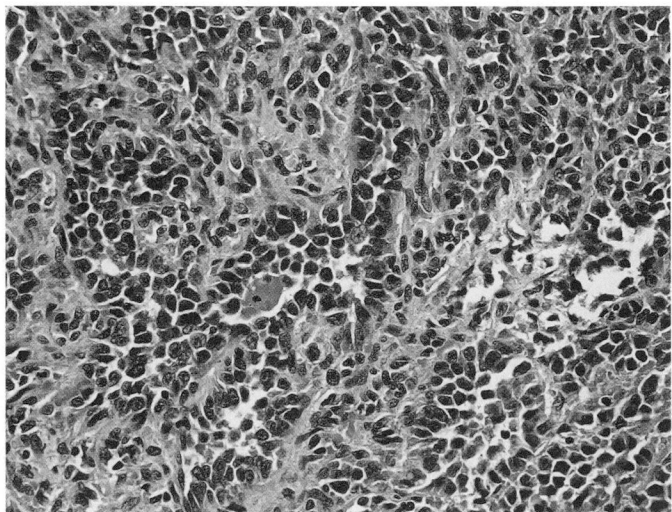

Fig. 22.36 Angiosarcoma of spleen. The tumor cells have markedly hyperchromatic nuclei that protrude into the vascular lumina.

Hemangiopericytoma is mentioned last in this listing of vascular splenic tumor because of its exceptional rarity[255] and the controversies that exist about its real nature.

Other primary tumors and tumorlike conditions

Hamartoma (splenadenoma or splenoma) is the term used for a nodular lesion of the spleen composed exclusively of red pulp elements[271a,277,281,286] (Fig. 22.37). It does not contain follicles or dendritic follicular cells, and fibrous trabeculae are scanty; foci of extramedullary hematopoiesis may be present.[268] This lesion may be large and accompanied by thrombocytopenia and other sign of hypersplenism.[278]

Inflammatory pseudotumor is a supposedly reactive tumor-like condition that may be encountered as an incidental finding at laparotomy or that may present as an asymptomatic splenic mass.[271a,274] Grossly, there is a great size range, with some lesions reaching up to 11 cm (Fig. 22.38). The lesions are usually solitary and may be multinodular.[283] Microscopically, there is a variable mixture of lymphocytes, plasma cells, eosinophils, histiocytes and spindle cells, the latter having an immunotype that has been interpreted as myofibroblastic, although we think that it is equally compatible (and pathogenetically more appealing) with the fibroblastic (myoid) subtype of dendritic/follicular cells (Fig. 22.39). The predominant pattern of growth may be sclerotic, xanthogranulomatous, or plasma cell granuloma-type.[266,279,283] Central coagulative necrosis is often present, usually in association with a neutrophilic infiltrate. Most of the small lymphocytes are of the T-cell type.[283] The evolution following splenectomy is benign.

The exact nature of this disorder is not clear. An analogy has been drawn between this lesion and inflammatory pseudotumor of soft tissue, a lesion now generally regarded as neoplastic and redesignated inflammatory myofibroblastic tumor.[275] However, whereas the latter is characterized by expression of ALK kinase and is unassociated with ABV, inflammatory pseudotumor of the spleen (like its homonym in the liver) is ALK-negative and often positive for EBV-encoded RNA with in situ hybridization tests.[272,275]

It should also be noted that splenic spindle cell pseudoneoplastic lesions can result from mycobacterial infection in immunocompromised patients.[282]

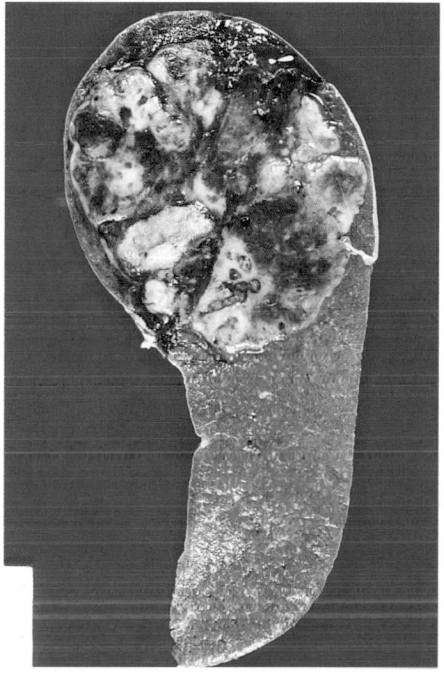

Fig. 22.38 Gross appearance of inflammatory pseudotumor of the spleen. The cut surface has a variegated color resulting from a combination of necrosis, hemorrhage, and cellular infiltration.

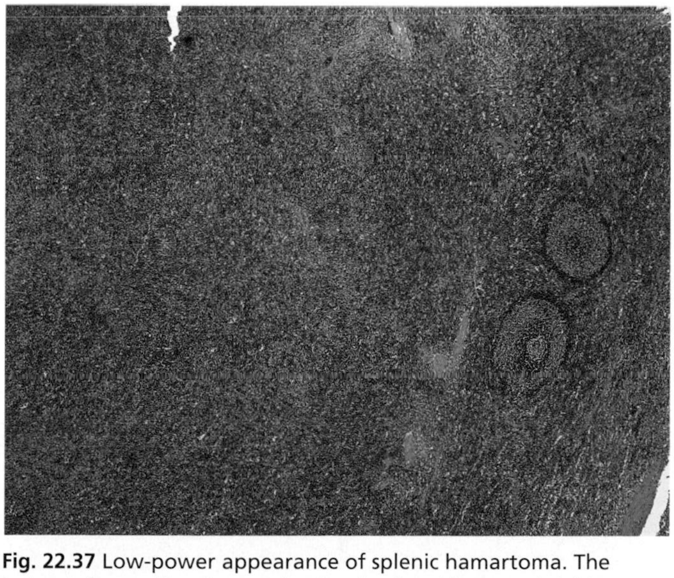

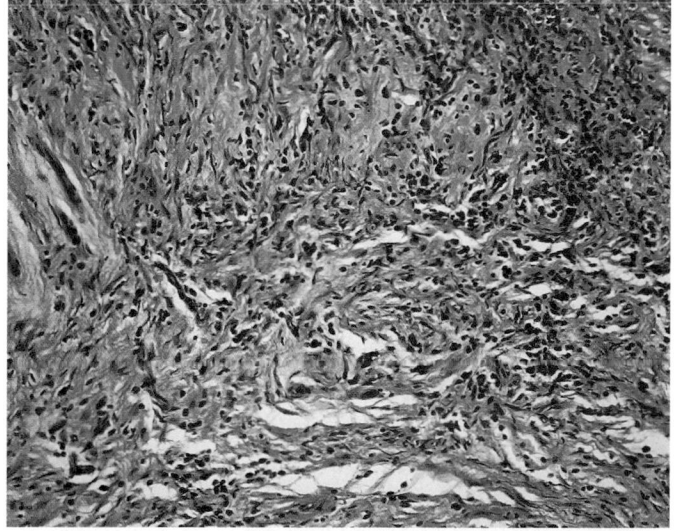

Fig. 22.37 Low-power appearance of splenic hamartoma. The lesion is formed by disorganized red pulp without malpighian follicles. Residual normal spleen is seen on the right.

Fig. 22.39 Inflammatory pseudotumor of spleen. Spindle cells of myofibroblastic appearance are admixed with various types of inflammatory cells.

Tumors of dendritic/reticulum cells may present as splenic tumors. Some have exhibited the phenotype of follicular dendritic cells,[276] whereas others have probably arisen from fibroblastic reticulum cells; the latter are distinguished from inflammatory pseudotumor (a sometimes very difficult task) by virtue of the predominance of the spindle cell component and with atypical features.[273a]

Along possibly related lines, cases with the morphologic features of malignant fibrous histiocytoma or large cell lymphoma have been reported in the spleen that had the phenotype of true histiocytes.[270,271,280,285]

Muscle tumors of the spleen include the EBV-related smooth muscle neoplasms seen in the context of AIDS (often occurring in children) and following renal transplantion,[265,273] and an exotic case of primary rhabdomyosarcoma.[269]

Lipoma has been reported as a solitary intrasplenic mass.[267]

Carcinosarcoma apparently primary in the spleen has been imaginatively interpreted as a probable extragenital type of malignant mixed müllerian tumor.[284]

Metastatic tumors

Metastatic carcinoma of the spleen is a very uncommon clinical problem[291] but a not too unusual finding at autopsy if a thorough examination of the organ is carried out.[287] Malignant melanoma and carcinoma of lung, breast, stomach, large bowel, pancreas and liver are the most common types found. Many others have been encountered, including ileal carcinoid[290,292] (Fig. 22.40). Grossly, splenic metastases can appear as solitary or diffuse nodules, involve the organ diffusely, or be limited to the splenic capsule.[292] Breast carcinoma diffusely

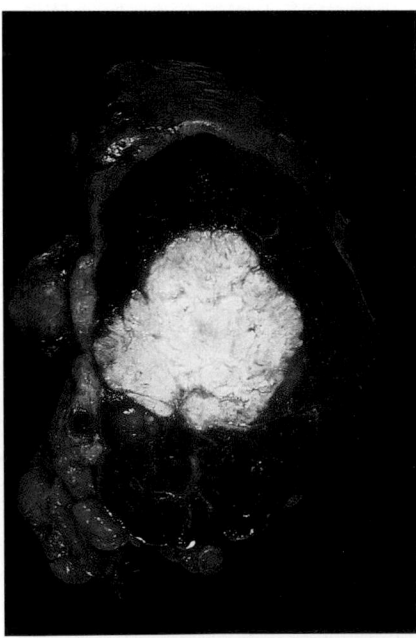

Fig. 22.40 Metastatic endometrial carcinoma to the spleen presenting as a single well-circumscribed nodule.

metastatic to the spleen may present as idiopathic thrombocytopenic purpura.[288] Occasionally, metastases in the spleen result in a nodular configuration that simulates follicular lymphoma on low-power examination.[289] The metastases can be superimposed on preexistent diseases of the spleen, such as hairy cell leukemia.[293]

References

Normal anatomy

1. Bishop MB, Lansing LS. The spleen. A correlative overview of normal and pathologic anatomy. Hum Pathol 1982, **13**: 334–342.
2. Enriquez P, Neiman RS. The pathology of the spleen. A functional approach. Chicago, 1976, American Society of Clinical Pathology.
3. Ham AW. The structure of the spleen. In Blaustein A (ed.): The spleen. New York, 1963, McGraw-Hill Book Co.
3a. Han J, van Krieken JM, te Velde J. Spleen. In Sternberg S (ed.): Histology for pathologists, ed. 2. Philadelphia, 1997, Lippincott-Raven Publishers, pp. 675–686.
3b. Kraus MD. Splenic histology and histopathology: an update. Semin Diagn Pathol 2003, **20**: 84–93.
4. Lennert K, Harms D (eds). Die Milz. Berlin, 1970, Springer-Verlag.
5. Millikin PD. The nodular white pulp of the human spleen. Arch Pathol 1969, **87**: 247–258.
6. van Krieken JHJM, te Velde J. Immunohistology of the human spleen. An inventory of the localization of lymphocyte subpopulations. Histopathology 1986, **10**: 285–294.
7. van Krieken JH, te Velde J. Normal histology of the human spleen. Am J Surg Pathol 1988, **12**: 777–785.
8. van Krieken JHJM, te Velde J, Hermans J, Welvaart K. The splenic red pulp. A histomorphometrical study in splenectomy specimens embedded in methylmethacrylate. Histopathology 1985, **9**: 401–416.
9. van Krieken JHJM, te Velde J, Kleiverda K, Leenheers-Binnendijk L, Van de Velde CJH. The human spleen. A histological study in splenectomy specimens embedded in methylmethacrylate. Histopathology 1985, **9**: 571–585.
10. Weiss L. The structure of the normal spleen. Semin Hematol 1965, **2**: 205–228.
11. Weiss L, Tavassoli M. Anatomical hazards to the passage of erythrocytes through the spleen. Semin Hematol 1970, **7**: 372–380.

Biopsy and fine needle aspiration

12. Civardi G, Vallisa D, Berte R, Giorgio A, Filice C, Caremani M, Caturelli E, Pompili M, De Sio I, Buscarini E, Cavanna L. Ultrasound-guided fine needle biopsy of the spleen: high clinical efficacy and low risk in a multicenter Italian study. Am J Hematol 2001, **67**: 93–99.
13. Soderström N. Cytologie der Milz in Punktaten. In Lennert K, Harms D (eds): Die Milz. Berlin, 1970, Springer-Verlag.
13a. Zeppa P, Picardi M, Marino G, Troncone G, Fulciniti F, Vetrani A, Rotoli B, Palombini L. Fine-needle aspiration biopsy and flow cytometry immunophenotyping of lymphoid and myeloproliferative disorders of the spleen. Cancer 2003, **99**: 118–27.

Rupture and splenectomy

14. Aldrete JS. Spontaneous rupture of the spleen in patients with infectious mononucleosis (editorial). Mayo Clin Proc 1992, **67**: 910–912.
15. Baack BR, Varsa EW, Burgdorf WH, Blaugrund AC. Splenosis. A report of subcutaneous involvement. Am J Dermatopathol 1990, **12**: 585–588.

16 Carr NJ, Turk EP. The histological features of splenosis. Histopathology 1992, **21:** 549–553.

17 Dalton ML Jr, Strange WH, Downs EA. Intrathoracic splenosis. Case report and review of the literature. Am Rev Respir Dis 1971, **103:** 827–830.

18 Debnath D, Valerio D. A traumatic rupture of the spleen in adults. J R Coll Surg Edinb 2002, **47:** 437–445.

19 Editorial. Infective hazards of splenectomy. Lancet 1976, **1:** 1167–1168.

20 Ellis EF, Smith RT. The role of the spleen in immunity. Pediatrics 1966, **37:** 111–119.

21 Farhi DC, Ashfaq R. Splenic pathology after traumatic injury. Am J Clin Pathol 1996, **105:** 474–478.

22 Fausel R, Sun NC, Klein S. Splenic rupture in a human immunodeficiency virus-infected patient with primary splenic lymphoma. Cancer 1990, **66:** 2414–2416.

23 Fleming CR, Dickson ER, Harrison EG Jr. Splenosis. Autotransplantation of splenic tissue. Am J Med 1976, **61:** 414–419.

24 Foster RP. Delayed haemorrhage from the ruptured spleen. Br J Surg 1970, **57:** 189–192.

25 Gabor S, Back F, Csiffary D. Peliosis lienis. Uncommon cause of rupture of the spleen. Pathol Res Pract 1992, **188:** 380–383.

26 Katkhouda N, Hurwitz MB, Rivera RT, Chandra M, Waldrep DJ, Gugenheim J, Mouiel J. Laparoscopic splenectomy: outcome and efficacy in 103 consecutive patients. Ann Surg 1998, **228:** 568–578.

27 Kraus MD, Fleming MD, Vonderheide RH. The spleen as a diagnostic specimen: a review of 10 years' experience at two tertiary care institutions. Cancer 2001, **91:** 2001–2009.

28 Kroft SH, Singleton TP, Dahiya M, Ross CW, Schnitzer B, Hsi ED. Ruptured spleens with expanded marginal zones do not reveal occult b-cell clones. Mod Pathol 1997, **10:** 1214–1220.

29 Kubosawa H, Konno A, Komatsu T, Ishige H, Kondo Y. Peliosis hepatis. An unusual case involving the spleen and lymph nodes. Acta Pathol Jpn 1989, **39:** 212–215.

30 Nordøy A. The spleenless state in man. In Lennert K, Harms D (eds): Die Milz. Berlin, 1970, Springer-Verlag.

31 O'Connor JV, Brown CC, Thomas JK, Williams J, Walsh E. Thoracic splenosis. Ann Thorac Surg 1998, **66:** 552–553.

32 Oliva E, Young RH. Paratesticular tumor-like lesions. Semin Diagn Pathol 2000, **17:** 340–358.

33 Orloff MJ, Peskin GW. Spontaneous rupture of the normal spleen. A surgical enigma. Int Abstr Surg 1958, **106:** 1–11.

34 Pedersen B, Videbaek A. On the late effects of removal of the normal spleen. A follow-up study of 40 persons. Acta Chir Scand 1966, **131:** 89–98.

35 Pratt DB, Andersen RC, Hitchcock CR. Splenic rupture. A review of 114 cases. Minn Med 1971, **54:** 177–184.

36 Rawsthorne GB, Cole TP, Kyle J. Spontaneous rupture of the spleen in infectious mononucleosis. Br J Surg 1970, **57:** 396–398.

37 Rickert CH, Maasjosthusmann U, Probst-Cousin S, August C, Gullotta F. A unique case of cerebral spleen. Am J Surg Pathol 1998, **22:** 894–896.

38 Sarda R, Sproat I, Kurtycz DF, Hafez R. Pulmonary parenchyma splenosis. Diagn Cytopathol 2001, **24:** 352–355.

39 Sherman R. Management of trauma to the spleen. Adv Surg 1984, **17:** 37–71.

40 Stites TB, Ultmann JE. Spontaneous rupture of the spleen in chronic lymphocytic leukemia. Cancer 1966, **19:** 1587–1590.

41 Traub A, Giebink GS, Smith C, Kuni CC, Brekke ML, Edlund D, Perry JF. Splenic reticuloendothelial function after splenectomy, spleen repair, and spleen autotransplantation. N Engl J Med 1987, **317:** 1559–1564.

Congenital anomalies

42 Cotelingam JD, Saito R. Hepatolienal fusion. Case report of an unusual lesion. Hum Pathol 1978, **9:** 234–236.

43 Esterly JR, Oppenheimer EH. Lymphangiectasis and other pulmonary lesions in the asplenia syndrome. Arch Pathol 1970, **90:** 553–560.

44 Gonzalez-Crussi F, Raibley S, Ballantine TVN, Grosfeld JL. Splenorenal fusion. Heterotopia simulating a renal neoplasm. Am J Dis Child 1977, **131:** 994–996.

45 Kevy SV, Tefft M, Vawter GF, Rosen FS. Hereditary splenic hypoplasia. Pediatrics 1968, **42:** 752–757.

46 Meneses MF, Ostrowski ML. Female splenic-gonadal fusion of the discontinuous type. Hum Pathol 1989, **20:** 486–488.

47 Oliva E, Young RH. Paratesticular tumor-like lesions. Semin Diagn Pathol 2000, **17:** 340–358.

48 Putschar WGJ, Manion WC. Congenital absence of the spleen and associated anomalies. Am J Pathol 1956, **26:** 429–470.

49 Putschar WGJ, Manion WC. Splenic-gonadal fusion. Cancer 1956, **32:** 15–34.

50 Rose V, Izukawa T, Moës CAF. Syndromes of asplenia and polysplenia. A review of cardiac and noncardiac malformations in 60 cases with special reference to diagnosis and prognosis. Br Heart J 1975, **37:** 840–852.

51 Vogel U, Negri G, Bultmann B. Ectopic prostatic tissue in the spleen. Virchows Arch 1996, **427:** 543–545.

52 Watson RJ. Splenogonadal fusion. Surgery 1968, **63:** 853–858.

Cysts

53 Arber DA, Strickler JG, Weiss LM. Splenic mesothelial cysts mimicking lymphangiomas. Am J Surg Pathol 1997, **21:** 334–338.

54 Blank E, Campbell JR. Epidermoid cysts of the spleen. Pediatrics 1973, **51:** 75–84.

55 Bürring K-F. Epithelial (true) splenic cysts. Pathogenesis of the mesothelial and so-called epidermoid cyst of the spleen. Am J Surg Pathol 1988, **12:** 275–281.

56 Du Plessis DG, Louw JA, Wranz PA. Mucinous epithelial cysts of the spleen associated with pseudomyxoma peritonea. Histopathology 1999, **35:** 551–557.

57 Fowler RH. Nonparasitic benign cystic tumors of the spleen. Surg Gynecol Obstet 1953, **96**(Suppl): 209–227.

58 Garvin DF, King FM. Cysts and nonlymphomatous tumors of the spleen. Pathol Annu 1981, **16**(Pt 1): 61–80.

59 Higaki K, Jimi A, Watanabe J, Kusaba A, Kojiro M. Epidermoid cyst of the spleen with CA 19-9 or carcinoembryonic antigen productions: a report of three cases. Am J Surg Pathol 1998, **22:** 704–708.

60 Lifschitz-Mercer B, Open M, Kushnir I, Czernobilsky B. Epidermoid cyst of the spleen. A cytokeratin profile with comparison to other squamous epithelia. Virchows Arch 1994, **424:** 213–216.

61 Morohoshi T, Hamamoto T, Kunimura T, Yoshida E, Kanda M, Funo K, Nagayama T, Maeda M, Araki S. Epidermoid cyst derived from an accessory spleen in the pancreas. A case report with literature survey. Acta Pathol Jpn 1991, **41:** 916–921.

62 Ough YD, Nash HR, Wood DA. Mesothelial cysts of the spleen with squamous metaplasia. Am J Clin Pathol 1981, **76:** 666–669.

63 Talerman A, Hart S. Epithelial cysts of the spleen. Br J Surg 1970, **57:** 201–204.

64 Tateyama H, Tada T, Murase T, Fujitake S, Eimoto T. Lymphoepithelial cyst and epidermoid cyst of the accessory spleen in the pancreas. Mod Pathol 1998, **11:** 1171–1177.

65 Tsakraklikes V, Hadley TW. Epidermoid cysts of the spleen. A report of five cases. Arch Pathol 1973, **96:** 251–254.

Inflammation

66 Bagshawe A. A comparative study of hypersplenism in reactive and congestive splenomegaly. Br J Haematol 1970, **19:** 729–737.

67 Bendix-Hansen K, Kristensen IB. Granulomas of spleen and liver in hairy cell leukaemia. Acta Pathol Microbiol Immunol Scand (A) 1984, **92:** 157–160.

68 Braylan RC, Long J, Jaffe ES, Greco FA, Orr SL, Berard CW. Malignant lymphoma obscured by concomitant extensive epithelioid granulomas. Report of three cases with similar clinicopathologic features. Cancer 1977, **39**: 1146–1155.

69 Briggs RD, Davidson AI, Fletcher BRG. Solitary abscesses of the spleen. J R Coll Surg Edinb 1977, **22**: 345–347.

70 Chun CH, Raff MJ, Contreras L, Varghese R, Waterman N, Daffner R, Melo JC. Splenic abscess. Medicine (Baltimore) 1980, **59**: 50–65.

71 Editorial. Tropical splenomegaly syndrome. Lancet 1976, **1**: 1058–1059.

72 Falk S, Muller H, Stutte HJ. The spleen in acquired immunodeficiency syndrome (AIDS). Pathol Res Pract 1988, **183**: 425–433.

73 Fishman D, Isenberg DA. Splenic involvement in rheumatic diseases. Semin Arthritis Rheum 1997, **27**: 141–155.

74 Gaba AR, Stein RS, Sweet DL, Variakojis D. Multicentric giant lymph node hyperplasia. Am J Clin Pathol 1978, **69**: 86–90.

75 Hermann RE, Deltaven KE, Hawk WA. Splenectomy for the diagnosis of splenomegaly. Ann Surg 1968, **168**: 896–900.

76 Kadin ME, Donaldson SS, Dorfman RF. Isolated granulomas in Hodgkin's disease. N Engl J Med 1970, **283**: 859–861.

77 Klatt EC, Meyer PR. Pathology of the spleen in the acquired immunodeficiency syndrome. Arch Pathol Lab Med 1987, **111**: 1050–1053.

78 Klemperer P. The pathologic anatomy of splenomegaly. Am J Clin Pathol 1936, **6**: 99–159.

79 Kuo T, Rosai J. Granulomatous inflammation in splenectomy specimens. Clinicopathologic study of 20 cases. Arch Pathol 1974, **98**: 261–268.

80 Millikin PD. Epithelioid germinal centers in the human spleen. Arch Pathol 1970, **89**: 314–320.

81 Neiman RS. Incidence and importance of splenic sarcoid-like granulomas. Arch Pathol 1977, **101**: 518–521.

82 Neiman RS, Bischel MD, Lukes RJ. Hypersplenism in the uremic hemodialyzed patient. Pathology and proposed pathophysiologic mechanisms. Am J Clin Pathol 1973, **60**: 502–511.

83 Pitney WR. The tropical splenomegaly syndrome. Trans R Soc Trop Med Hyg 1968, **62**: 717–728.

84 Sacks EL, Donaldson SS, Gordon J, Dorfman RF. Epithelioid granulomas asociated with Hodgkin's disease. Clinical conditions in 55 previously untreated patients. Cancer 1978, **41**: 562–567.

85 Sagoe AS. Tropical splenomegaly syndrome. Long-term proguanil therapy correlated with spleen size, serum IgM, and lymphocyte transformation. Br Med J 1970, **3**: 378–382.

86 Thomas DM, Akosa AB, Lampert IA. Granulomatous inflammation of the spleen in infectious mononucleosis. Histopathology 1990, **17**: 265–267.

87 Walker DA, Howat AJ, Shannon RS, Bouch DC, Lilleyman JS. Necrotizing granulomatous splenitis complicating leukemia in childhood. Cancer 1985, **56**: 371–373.

88 Weisenburger DD. Multicentric angiofollicular lymph node hyperplasia. Pathology of the spleen. Am J Surg Pathol 1988, **12**: 176–181.

89 Young JM, Bills RJ, Ulrich E. Discrete splenic calcification in necropsy material. Am J Pathol 1957, **33**: 189–197.

Hypersplenism

90 Bowdler AJ. Splenomegaly and hypersplenism. Clin Haematol 1983, **12**: 467–488.

91 Neiman RS, Bischel MD, Lukes RJ. Hypersplenism in the uremic hemodialyzed patient. Pathology and proposed pathophysiologic mechanisms. Am J Clin Pathol 1973, **60**: 502–511.

92 Peck-Radosavljevic M. Hypersplenism. Eur J Gastroenterol Hepatol 2001, **13**: 317–323.

93 Rappaport H. The pathologic anatomy of the splenic red pulp.
In Lennert K, Harms D (eds): Die Milz. Berlin, 1970, Springer-Verlag.

Thrombocytopenic purpuras

94 Baldini M. Idiopathic thrombocytopenic purpura. N Engl J Med 1966, **274**: 1245–1251, 1301–1306, 1360–1367.

95 Berendt HL, Mant MJ, Jewell LD. Periarterial fibrosis in the spleen in idiopathic thrombocytopenic purpura. Arch Pathol Lab Med 1986, **110**: 1152–1154.

96 Bowdler AJ. The role of the spleen and splenectomy in autoimmune hemolytic disease. Semin Hematol 1976, **13**: 335–348.

97 Bowman HE, Pettit VD, Caldwell FT, Smith EB. Morphology of the spleen in idiopathic thrombocytopenic purpura. Lab Invest 1955, **4**: 206–216.

98 Chang CS, Li CY, Cha SS. Chronic idiopathic thrombocytopenic purpura. Splenic pathologic features and their clinical correlation. Arch Pathol Lab Med 1993, **117**: 981–985.

99 Cines DB, Blanchette VA. Immune thrombocytopenic purpura. N Engl J Med 2002, **346**: 995–1008.

100 Cohn J, Tygstrup I. Foamy histiocytosis of the spleen in patients with chronic thrombocytopenia. Scand J Hematol 1976, **16**: 33–37.

101 Ebbe S, Wittels B, Dameshek W. Autoimmune thrombocytopenic purpura ("ITP" type) with chronic lymphocytic leukemia. Blood 1962, **19**: 23–27.

102 Hassan NMR, Neiman RS. The pathology of the spleen in steroid-treated immune thrombocytopenic purpura. Am J Clin Pathol 1985, **84**: 433–438.

103 Hayes MM, Jacobs P, Wood L, Dent DM. Splenic pathology in immune thrombocytopenia. J Clin Pathol 1985, **38**: 985–988.

104 Jiang DY, Li C-Y. Immunohistochemical study of the spleen in chronic immune thrombocytopenic purpura with special reference to hyperplastic follicles and foamy macrophages. Arch Pathol Lab Med 1995, **119**: 533–537.

105 Luk SC, Musclow E, Simon GT. Platelet phagocytosis in the spleen of patients with idiopathic thrombocytopenic purpura (ITP). Histopathology 1980, **4**: 127–136.

106 McMillan R. Chronic idiopathic thrombocytopenic purpura. N Engl J Med 1981, **304**: 1135–1147.

107 Moake JL. Thrombotic thrombocytopenic purpura: the systemic clumping "plague". Annu Rev Med 2002, **53**: 75–88.

108 Rudders RA, Aisenberg AC, Schiller AL. Hodgkin's disease presenting as "idiopathic" thrombocytopenic purpura. Cancer 1972, **30**: 220–230.

109 Saltzstein SL. Phospholipid accumulation in histiocytes of splenic pulp associated with thrombocytopenic purpura. Blood 1961, **18**: 73–88.

110 Sandler SG. The spleen and splenectomy in immune (idiopathic) thrombocytopenic purpura. Semin Hematol 2000, **37**(Suppl 1): 10–12.

111 Saracco SM, Farhi DC. Splenic pathology in thrombotic thrombocytopenic purpura. Am J Surg Pathol 1990, **14**: 223–229.

112 Tavasoli M, McMillan R. Structure of the spleen in idiopathic thrombocytopenic purpura. Am J Clin Pathol 1975, **64**: 180–191.

Hemolytic anemia

113 Amorosi EL. Hypersplenism. Semin Hematol 1965, **2**: 249–285.

114 Crosby WH. Splenectomy in hematologic disorders. N Engl J Med 1972, **286**: 1252–1254.

115 Jacob HS. The defective red blood cell in hereditary spherocytosis. Annu Rev Med 1969, **20**: 41–46.

116 Miraglia del Giudice E, Iolascon A, Pinto L, Nobili B, Perrotta S. Erythrocyte membrane protein alterations underlying clinical heterogeneity in hereditary spherocytosis. Br J Haematol 1994, **88**: 52–55.

117 Molnar Z, Rappaport H. Fine structure of the red pulp of the spleen in hereditary spherocytosis. Blood 1972, **39**: 81–98.

118 Pattern E. Immunohematologic diseases. JAMA 1987, **258:** 2945–2951.

119 Peters LL, Lux SE. Ankyrins. Structure and function in normal cells and hereditary spherocytes. Semin Hematol 1993, **30:** 85–118.

120 Rappaport H, Crosby WH. Autoimmune hemolytic anemia. II. Morphologic observations and clinicopathologic correlation. Am J Pathol 1957, **33:** 429–458.

121 Saad ST, Costa FF, Vicentim DL, Salles TS, Pranke PH. Red cell membrane protein abnormalities in hereditary spherocytosis in Brazil. Br J Haematol 1994, **88:** 295–299.

122 Sandusky WR, Leavell BS, Burton IB. Splenectomy. Indications and results in hematologic disorders. Ann Surg 1964, **159:** 695–710.

123 Tse WT, Lux SE. Red blood cell membrane disorders. Br J Haematol 1999, **104:** 2–13.

124 Weed RI. The importance of erythrocyte deformability. Am J Med 1970, **49:** 147–150.

125 Wiland OK, Smith EB. The morphology of the spleen in congenital hemolytic anemia (hereditary spherocytosis). Am J Clin Pathol 1956, **26:** 619–629.

Congestive splenomegaly

126 Bowder AJ. Splenomegaly and hypersplenism. Clin Haematol 1983, **12:** 467–488.

127 Ludwig J, Hashimoto E, Obata H, Baldus WP. Idiopathic portal hypertension. A histopathological study of 26 Japanese cases. Histopathology 1993, **22:** 227–234.

128 Okudaira M, Ohbu M, Okuda K. Idiopathic portal hypertension and its pathology. Semin Liver Dis 2002, **22:** 59–72.

129 Satterfield JV, Mulligan LV, Butcher HR Jr. Bleeding esophageal varices. Arch Surg 1965, **90:** 667–672.

130 Wanless IR, Bernier V. Fibrous thickening of the splenic capsule. A response to chronic splenic congestion. Arch Pathol Lab Med 1983, **107:** 595–599.

Other non-neoplastic disorders

131 Chen KTK, Flam MS, Workman RD. Amyloid tumor of the spleen. Am J Surg pathol 1987, **11:** 723–725.

132 Cruickshank B. Follicular (mineral oil) lipidosis. I. Epidemiologic studies of involvement of the spleen. Hum Pathol 1984, **15:** 724–730.

133 Cruickshank B, Thomas MJ. Mineral oil (follicular) lipidosis. II. Histologic studies of spleen, liver, lymph nodes, and bone marrow. Hum Pathol 1984, **15:** 731–737.

134 Dailey MO, Coleman CN, Fajardo LF. Splenic injury caused by therapeutic irradiation. Am J Surg Pathol 1981, **5:** 325–331.

135 Dawson PJ, Dawson G. Adult Niemann-Pick disease with sea-blue histiocytes in the spleen. Hum Pathol 1982, **13:** 1115–1120.

136 Diebold J, Audouin J. Peliosis of the spleen. Report of a case associated with chronic myelomonocytic leukemia, presenting with spontaneous splenic rupture. Am J Surg Pathol 1983, **7:** 197–204.

137 Gal AA, Mason JJ. Splenic involvement in Wegener's granulomatosis. Arch Pathol Lab Med 1996, **120:** 974–977.

138 Gupta PC, Chatterjea JB, Mukherjee AM, Chatterji A. Observations on the foam cell in thalassemia. Blood 1960, **16:** 1039–1044.

139 Lacson A, Berman LD, Neiman RS. Peliosis of the spleen. Am J Clin Pathol 1979, **71:** 586–590.

140 Liber A, Rose HG. Saturated hydrocarbons in follicular lipidosis of the spleen. Arch Pathol 1967, **83:** 116–122.

141 McCain M, Quinet R, Davis W, Serebro L, Zakem J, Nair P, Ishaq S. Splenic rupture as the presenting manifestation of vasculitis. Semin Arthritis Rheum 2002, **31:** 311–316.

142 Markowitz GS, Factor SM, Borczuk AC. Splenic para-amyloid material: a possible vasculopathy of the acquired immunodeficiency syndrome. Hum Pathol 1998, **29:** 371–376.

143 Parker AC, Bain AD, Brydon WG, Harkness RA, Smith AF, Smith II, Boyd DHA. Sea-blue histiocytosis associated with hyperlipidemia. J Clin Pathol 1976, **29:** 634–638.

144 Raghavan R, Alley S, Tawfik O, Webb P, Forster J, Uhl M. Splenic peliosis: a rare complication following liver transplantation. Dig Dis Sci 1999, **44:** 1128–1131.

145 Reidbord HR, Branimir LH, Fisher ER. Splenic lipidoses. Histochemical and ultrastructural differentiation with special reference to the syndrome of the sea-blue histiocyte. Arch Pathol 1972, **93:** 518–524.

146 Rentsch J, McColl G. Splenic infarction in Wegener's granulamatosis. J Rheumatol 2000, **27:** 1553–1555.

147 Rywlin AM, Lopez-Gomez A, Tachimes P, Pardo V. Ceroid histiocytosis of the spleen in hyperlipemia. Relationship to the syndrome of the sea-blue histiocyte. Am J Clin Pathol 1971, **56:** 572–579.

148 Silverstein MN, Ellefson RD, Ahern EJ. The syndrome of the sea-blue histiocyte. N Engl J Med 1970, **282:** 1–4.

149 Tada T, Wakabayashi T, Kishimoto H. Peliosis of the spleen. Am J Clin Pathol 1983, **79:** 708–713.

150 Wanless IR, Geddie WR. Mineral oil lipogranulomata in liver and spleen. A study of 465 autopsies. Arch Pathol Lab Med 1985, **109:** 283–286.

151 Warfel KA, Ellis GH. Peliosis of the spleen. Report of a case and review of the literature. Arch Pathol Lab Med 1982, **106:** 99–100.

Hematolymphoid tumors and tumorlike conditions

Non-Hodgkin's lymphoma

152 Ahmann DL, Kiely JM, Harrison EG Jr, Payne S. Malignant lymphoma of the spleen. Cancer 1966, **19:** 461–469.

153 Alkan S, Ross CW, Hanson CA, Schnitzer B. Follicular lymphoma with involvement of the splenic marginal zone: a pitfall in the differential diagnosis of splenic marginal zone cell lymphoma. Hum Pathol 1996, **27:** 503–506.

154 Arber DA, Strickler JG, Weiss LM. Splenic mesothelial cysts mimicking lymphangiomas. Am J Surg Pathol 1997, **21:** 334–338.

154a Bahler DW, Pindzola JA, Swerdlow SH. Splenic marginal zone lymphomas appear to originate from different B cell types. Am J Pathol 2002, **161:** 81–88.

155 Bellamy CO, Krajewski AS. Primary splenic large cell anaplastic lymphoma associated with HIV infection. Histopathology 1994, **24:** 481–483.

156 Burke JS. Surgical pathology of the spleen. An approach to the differential diagnosis of splenic lymphomas and leukemias. I. Diseases of the white pulp. Am J Surg Pathol 1981, **5:** 551–563.

157 Burke JS. Surgical pathology of the spleen. An approach to the differential diagnosis of splenic lymphomas and leukemias. II. Diseases of the red pulp. Am J Surg Pathol 1981, **5:** 681–694.

158 Camacho FI, Mollejo M, Mateo MS, Algara P, Navas C, Hernandez JM, Santoja C, Sole F, Sanchez-Beato M, Piris MA. Progression to large B-cell lymphoma in splenic marginal zone lymphoma: a description of a series of 12 cases. Am J Surg Pathol 2001, **25:** 1268–1276.

158a Chan JKC. Splenic involvement by peripheral T-cell and NK-cell neoplasms. Semin Diagn Pathol 2003, **20:** 105–120.

159 Chang KL, Arber DA. Hepatosplenic gamma-delta T-cell lymphoma—not just alphabet soup. Adv Anat Pathol 1998, **5:** 21–29.

160 Dacie JV, Brain MC, Harrison CV, Lewis SM, Worlledge SM. Non-tropical idiopathic splenomegaly (primary hypersplenism). A review of ten cases and their relationship to malignant lymphomas. Br J Haematol 1969, **17:** 317–333.

161 Dacie JV, Galton DAG, Gordon-Smith EC, Harrison CV. Non-tropical "idiopathic splenomegaly." A follow-up study of ten patients described in 1969. Br J Haematol 1978, **38:** 185–193.

23 Bone marrow

Richard D. Brunning

Biopsy procedure and processing of specimen

Trephine biopsy of the bone marrow has wide application in clinical medicine; its greatest utility is in the evaluation of patients with malignant lymphoma, acute leukemias, myeloproliferative disorders, myelodysplastic syndromes, metastatic tumor, granulomatous disorders, myelofibrosis, aplastic anemia, and plasma cell dyscrasias.[1,2,4–9] It also serves as the most reliable method for assessing marrow cellularity following the administration of antineoplastic drugs and in assessing the status of engraftment following bone marrow transplantation. Marrow biopsy is also utilized in the investigation of patients with infectious disease and metabolic disorders.

The trephine biopsy should be viewed as one component of the bone marrow specimen that ideally also includes smears and particle crush preparations from aspirated marrow and touch imprint preparations of the core biopsy specimen. In some instances, because of marrow fibrosis, the trephine biopsy specimen will be the only marrow tissue available for examination. Marrow biopsy can usually be done with relatively little discomfort to the patient and is accompanied by very low morbidity when performed by experienced individuals with the biopsy needles presently available.[12] The posterior superior iliac spines are the preferred sites. Bilateral trephine biopsies may be useful in the staging of patients with some types of lymphoma, granulomatous disorders, and metastatic tumor. This approach should be decided on an individual basis considering both the reason for the procedure and the impact of positive findings for therapy.[4,15,16] In general, severe thrombocytopenia is not a contraindication to marrow biopsy. Whenever a marrow biopsy is performed, careful attention should be directed to preventing hematoma formation by applying an adequate pressure bandage to the biopsy site following the procedure. Prior to performing a biopsy on a patient with a bleeding disorder or on anticoagulants, consultation should be obtained from a physician expert in coagulation disorders.

Considerable discussion has occurred about the relative merits of trephine biopsy of the bone marrow as opposed to sections of particles obtained by aspiration biopsy.[6,7,11,13] Particle sections are of limited value in marrow disorders that are accompanied by fibrosis; these frequently result in inadequately aspirated specimens.[1,2] In addition, assessment of cellularity, determination of the extent of marrow involvement by neoplastic processes, and the relationship of lesions to marrow structures such as bone trabeculae and vasculature can be accurately assessed only in trephine biopsies. Nevertheless, any particles obtained in a marrow aspirate should be processed for histologic examination.

Paraffin embedding is the preferred method for the routine processing of bone marrow biopsies, and the observations described in this chapter are based primarily on examination of specimens prepared in this manner.[10,15] Plastic embedding offers some advantages over the paraffin method, such as excellent cytology and the ability to perform numerous histochemical reactions. The use of plastic embedding has been facilitated by the introduction of resins such as glycol methacrylate.[3] However, plastic embedding techniques are more time-consuming than the processing of paraffin-embedded tissue, and with careful attention to technical detail, excellent results can be obtained with specimens processed in paraffin. Additionally, immunohistochemistry with a wide range of antibodies can now be performed with excellent results on most paraffin-embedded specimens.

Myelofibrosis is one of the more vexing problems in bone marrow histopathology because of the wide range of disorders that may cause marrow fibrosis and the usual difficulty in obtaining satisfactory aspirates for cytologic studies.[14] Although marrow fibrosis occurs as an idiopathic or primary disorder, it is usually a secondary phenomenon; the most common causes are metastatic tumor and malignant lymphoma. Fibrosis also occurs relatively frequently in the evolution of chronic myeloproliferative disorders, such as chronic myeloid leukemia and polycythemia vera. In general, fibrosis that occurs as a component of hematopoietic proliferations is characterized by the deposition of increased reticulin fibers; with metastatic tumors such as breast or prostate, there may be a severe desmoplastic reaction with collagenous fibrosis.

In those instances in which the etiology for the marrow fibrosis is not apparent, several techniques may be used in an attempt to determine the cause. Immunohistology, using paraffin-embedded specimens and the several antibodies described in the section on immunohistology, may be particularly helpful in identifying lymphoma or metastatic tumor; antibodies to myeloperoxidase, lysozyme or CD68, both KP-1 and PGM-1, are particularly useful for identifying cells of granulocytic or monocytic origin. An additional procedure that may be useful in hematopoietic disorders associated with marrow fibrosis is the preparation of particle crush preparations from trephine biopsy specimens. This approach may necessitate a second biopsy unless the problem of fibrosis is anticipated before the initial procedure. As soon as possible after the trephine specimen is obtained and before it is placed in a fixative, small portions of the biopsy are cut away with a sharp scalpel blade and used for particle crush preparations in the same manner as particles from aspirated specimens. These crush preparations can be used for routine stains, cytochemistry, and immunocytochemistry. Portions of the biopsy specimen obtained in this manner may also be used for cytogenetics, flow cytometry studies, routine electron microscopy and ultrastructural cytochemistry. However, electron microscopy is less frequently necessary because of the availability of immuno-histochemistry.

The use of special stains in bone marrow pathology should be determined following review of the routinely stained biopsy and the patient's clinical history.

Several instruments are available for the bone marrow trephine biopsy procedure. The most satisfactory from the standpoint of safety, ease of performance, and overall quality of specimen obtained is the Jamshidi-type biopsy needle; several such instruments, both reusable and disposable, are commercially available.[12] These instruments are produced in several sizes for both adult and pediatric patients. The 11-gauge needle is the most commonly used for routine procedures in adults and older children. The 8-gauge instruments are preferred by some for lymphoma staging procedures; this size may result in more postbiopsy discomfort. If difficulty is encountered with the 11-gauge needle in obtaining adequate specimens from patients with severe osteoporosis, an 8- or 9-gauge instrument should be used. Numerous modifications of the original instruments are available.

The importance of proper technique in performing the biopsy procedure cannot be overemphasized. Instructions for the use of the biopsy needles are included with the instruments, and some manufacturers provide audiovisual aids that illustrate proper technique. Accurate identification of body landmarks is crucial in obtaining satisfactory specimens; an improperly positioned needle may cause considerable discomfort to the patient and frequently yields an inadequate biopsy specimen. Individuals not acquainted with the biopsy technique are advised to familiarize themselves with the procedure on cadavers.

Optimally, the biopsy specimen should be at least 1.5 cm in length and should be free of distortion caused by crushing or other damage. Crush artifact and the deposition of fibrin in torn biopsies may render accurate interpretation difficult or impossible. In such instances the biopsy should be repeated. Aspiration through the biopsy needle prior to obtaining the trephine biopsy specimen should be discouraged because of the possibility of introducing hemorrhage or other artifact in the biopsy specimen.

Occasionally, in patients undergoing frequent repeat biopsies, a specimen may be obtained from a recently biopsied site. In these instances, the changes will reflect the stage of healing. The presence of granulation tissue in the biopsy may result in misinterpretation of cellularity. The appearance of the marrow biopsy may be inconsistent with the marrow smears, which show recovering or normal hematopoiesis (Fig. 23.1).

Imprint preparations should be routinely made from the biopsy specimen immediately after it is removed from the biopsy needle. These can be used for Romanowsky stains and special cytochemical and immunocytochemical procedures. Following the preparation of imprints, the specimen is placed in an appropriate fixative; the most satisfactory are B5 or 10% buffered neutral formalin.[15] Zenker's acetic acid gives excellent cytology but ablates several antigens which may be useful in evaluating neoplastic processes. In laboratories where bone marrow is processed with other tissues, buffered neutral formalin may be the preferred fixative. The other fixatives require special handling and are more suitable for laboratories dedicated to the pro-

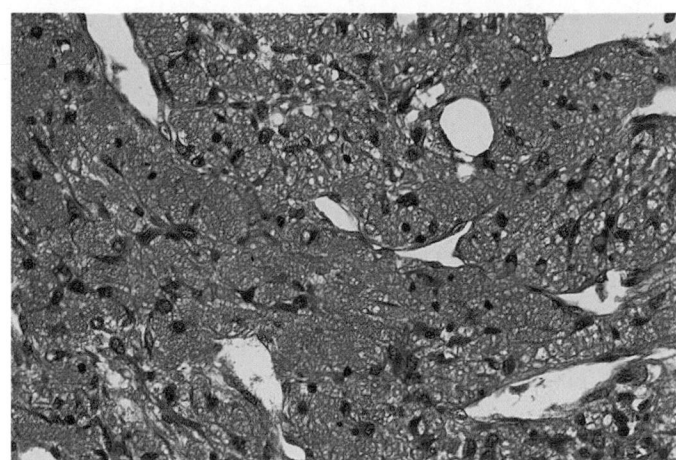

Fig. 23.1 Marrow biopsy obtained at site of a biopsy performed 14 days previously. The marrow space is replaced by granulation tissue.

cessing of hematopoietic tissue. In addition, because of environmental concerns and disposal problems, some institutions discourage the use of mercury-based fixative. As noted in the section on immunohistochemistry, reactivity with some antibodies may be ablated by some fixatives, and the choice of fixative may be determined by the reason for the biopsy. Following fixation for an appropriate period of time, the biopsy is decalcified. Several decalcification solutions are commercially available. Most biopsy specimens will be adequately decalcified following 45 to 60 minutes in a rapid decalcifying solution. Details of the processing methodology, including decalcification, have been published.[15]

The biopsies should be sectioned at 3 to 4 μm with a sharp knife that is checked frequently for the presence of defects. In those patients being evaluated for the extent of lymphomatous involvement, metastatic tumor, or granulomatous disease, the specimens should be completely sectioned and stepwise serial sections mounted for hematoxylin–eosin staining.[16] The remaining ribbon should be retained and stored in a manner that will facilitate the ready and accurate mounting of additional sections for special stains, immunocytochemical reactions, and molecular studies. Most of the stains used for other fixed tissues are also applicable to bone marrow sections. However, tissue processed with acid fixatives such as B5 and Zenker's or with acid decalcifiers will yield unsatisfactory results with the chloroacetate esterase stain.

Optimally, when interpreting the trephine biopsy, the pathologist should examine the trephine imprints, bone marrow aspirate, blood smears, and other pathology specimens. Knowledge of the patient's clinical history, hematology profile, immunoelectrophoretic studies, and radiographic findings may be of considerable importance and may greatly facilitate the interpretation of the biopsy specimen.

Immunohistology

As in other areas of pathology, immunohistology is an important resource in the evaluation of proliferative processes involving the marrow. The availability of antibodies reactive in paraffin-embedded tissue and the use of antigen retrieval have been of considerable importance in the application of immunohistology in bone marrow pathology. Although cryostat sections of marrow may be used for immunohistology, the procedure is difficult and is essentially limited to specialized laboratories.[29] In addition, cytologic preservation in cryostat sections is frequently of marginal quality.

Although decalcification with rapid acid decalcifiers may result in ablation of some antigens, an increasing number of antibodies to membrane antigens and cytoplasmic constituents are reactive in paraffin-embedded decalcified marrow biopsies and can be of considerable aid in identifying the lineage of immature cell populations in the marrow; these include antibodies to kappa and lambda light chains, leukocyte common antigen, myeloperoxidase, hemoglobin A, factor VIII, CD68, CD20 (L26), CD79a, CD3, CD45, CD34, TdT and tumor-related antigens and proliferation antigens[19,20,22,23,27-42] (Figs 23.2 to 23.10). Antibody to Pax 5, a B-cell transcription factor present in all stages of B-cell development up to the plasma cell, appears to have application in identifying a wide spectrum of B lymphocytes from precursor B to mature B cells.[39] The commercially available antibody is a monoclonal antibody BSAP, clone 24. It is reactive in both formalin and Zenker fixed tissue. Antibodies to kappa and lambda immunoglobulin light chains are particularly useful for determining the relative proportions of kappa- and lambda-containing cells in immunoproliferative disorders such as multiple myeloma.[33] Reactivity with these antibodies is generally restricted to processes in which the cells contain cytoplasmic immunoglobulin. The technique is not sufficiently sensitive to detect surface immunoglobulin on the lymphocytes in most lymphoproliferative diseases. Occasionally the lymphocytes in a B-cell lymphocytic lymphoma contain cytoplasmic immunoglobulin that may be detected by this method. The antibodies to lymphocyte antigens are useful in determining the B- or T-cell origin of the lymphoproliferative processes and the extent of marrow involvement (see Fig. 23.9). These antibodies are not determinants of clonality. Polyclonal antibody to myeloperoxidase is a specific and sensitive antibody for cells of neutrophil origin that reacts with the myeloblasts in acute myeloid leukemia[17,18,35] (see Fig. 23.5). Some studies however, have shown that in immunocytochemical reaction in paraffin-embedded tissue, monoclonal antibodies to myeloperoxidase are more specific. Several panels for the immunocytochemical characterization of acute leukemia have been described.[17,18,22,24,34]

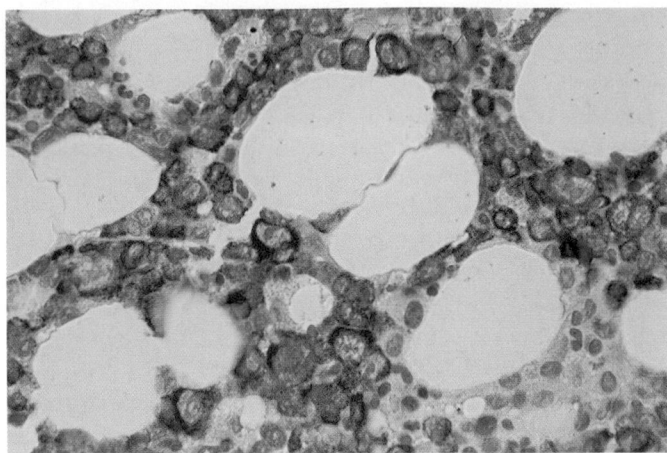

Fig. 23.2 Marrow biopsy from patient with multiple myeloma reacted with polyclonal antibody to lambda light chain; the blastic appearing plasma cells show intense cytoplasmic reaction. (Immunoperoxidase.)

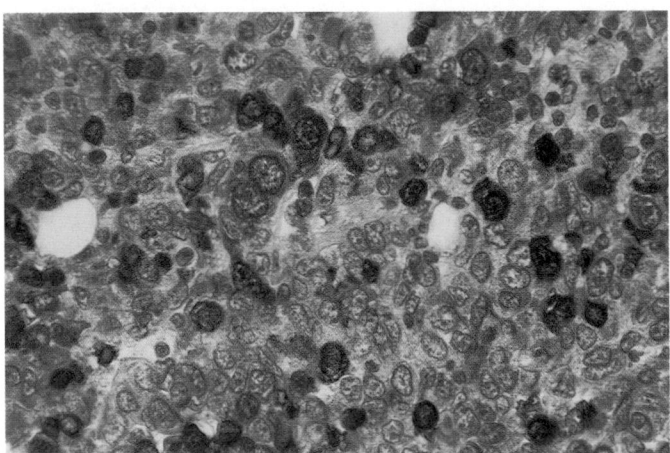

Fig. 23.3 Marrow from patient with erythroleukemia (AML-M6) reacted with antibody to hemoglobin A antibody; many of the erythroblasts show a positive cytoplasmic reaction. Intensity of reaction varies from very slight to marked. (Immunoperoxidase.)

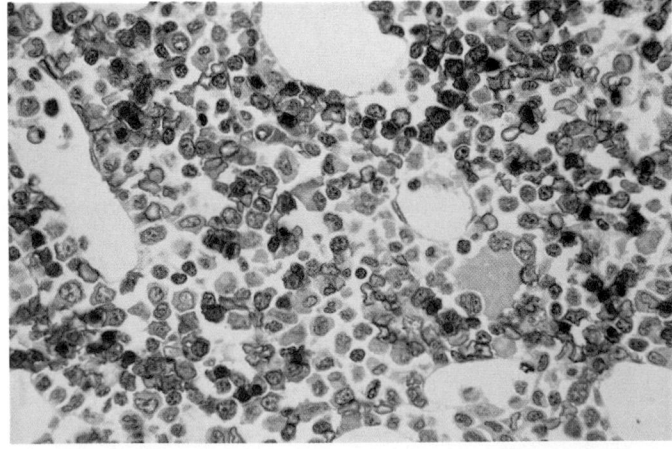

Fig. 23.4 Marrow biopsy from 2-year-old child with congenital neutropenia reacted with antibody to glycophorin A. There are numerous positive erythroid precursors at all stages of maturation. (Immunoperoxidase.)

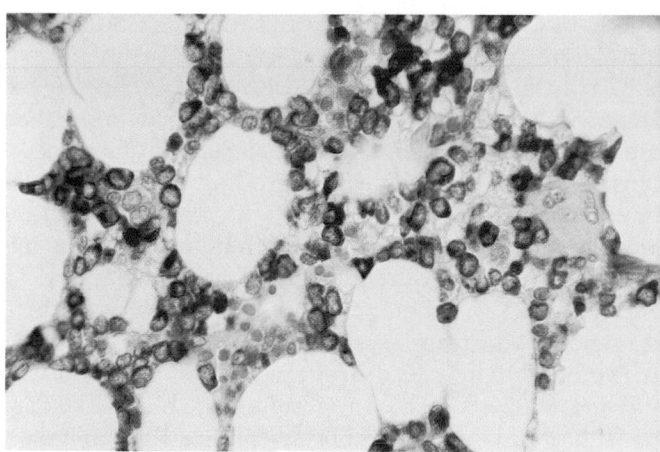

Fig. 23.5 Bone marrow biopsy from a patient with hypocellular acute myeloid leukemia reacted with polyclonal antibody to myeloperoxidase. The predominant myeloblasts and promyelocytes show intense cytoplasmic reactivity. (Immunoperoxidase.)

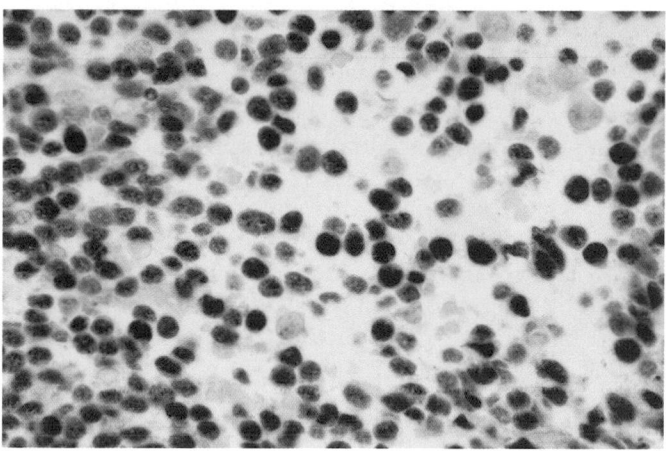

Fig. 23.8 Marrow biopsy from a child with precursor B acute lymphoblastic leukemia reacted with polyclonal antibody to TdT; the lymphoblasts show intense nuclear reactivity. (Immunoperoxidase.)

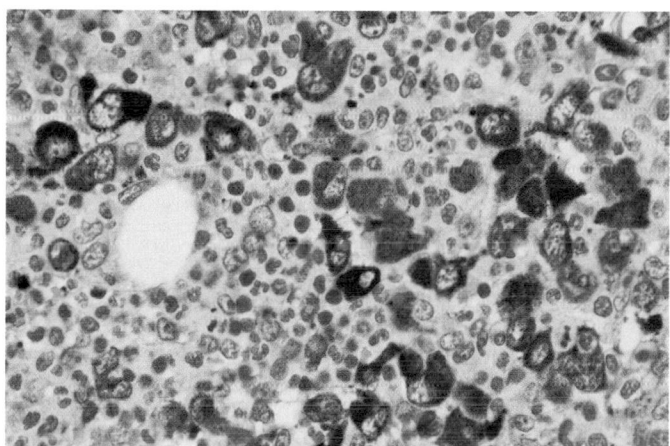

Fig. 23.6 Bone marrow biopsy from a patient with chronic myeloid leukemia in accelerated phase reacted with polyclonal antibody to factor VIIIa. There are numerous dysplastic megakaryocytes with hypolobated nuclei which show intense cytoplasmic reactivity. (Immunoperoxidase.)

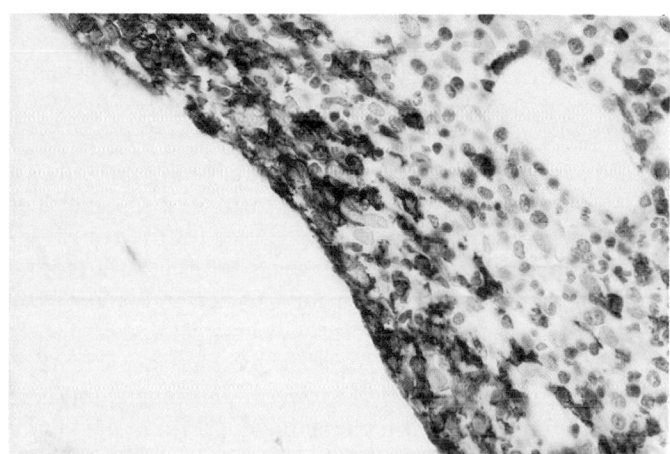

Fig. 23.9 Marrow biopsy from an adult male with recurrent follicular center cell lymphoma reacted with antibody to CD20 (L26). Numerous reacting lymphocytes are present in a paratrabecular location. (Immunoperoxidase.)

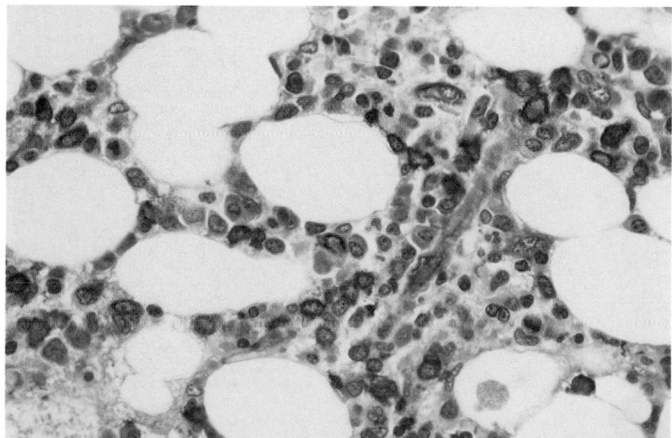

Fig. 23.7 Bone marrow biopsy from an adult male with therapy-related refractory anemia with excess blasts and hypocellular marrow reacted with antibody to CD34. The number of positive cells approximates the 18.5% blasts in the marrow smear. (Immunoperoxidase.)

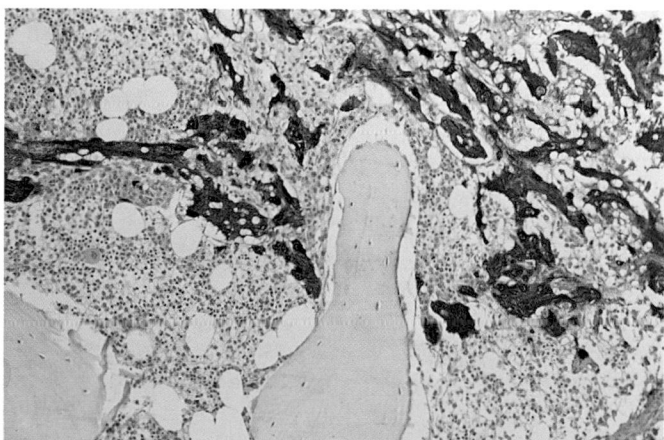

Fig. 23.10 Marrow biopsy from a child with neuroblastoma with ganglion differentiation reacted with antibody to neuron-specific enolase. The tumor cells are intensely reactive. (Immunoperoxidase.)

These generally include antibodies to CD68 (both PGM-1 and KP-1), myeloperoxidase, CD34, lysozyme, lymphocyte antibodies and TdT. Diagnostic kits for the avidin–biotin complex, peroxidase–antiperoxidase, and alkaline phosphatase– antialkaline phosphatase methods are commercially available.

It is important that the reactivity pattern of all antibodies be determined by each laboratory. The range of reactivity attributed to an antibody by the manufacturer should be confirmed with lesions of known antigenicity. The pattern of reactivity of the antibodies to lymphoid cells is generally based on studies of lymph nodes fixed in B5 or neutral buffered formalin. The same reactivity pattern may not be applicable to marrow biopsies fixed in Zenker's fixative or B5 and decalcified in a rapid acid decalcifier; L26, an excellent antibody to CD20, a pan B-cell antigen, works well in bone marrow biopsies fixed in B5 and decalcified with a rapid acid decalcifier, but may not react in Zenker fixed tissue decalcified in the same manner. The effects of decalcification on antibody reactivity should be determined by subjecting lymph node tissue to the same decalcification procedure employed for bone marrow biopsies.

B5 fixative generally yields superior lymphoid antigen and myeloid enzyme preservation in marrow biopsies and appears to be the fixative of choice for marrow biopsies performed for evaluation of lymphoproliferative and myeloproliferative disorders. As noted, Zenker's fixative, which results in superior cytomorphology, appears to hinder reactivity with some antibodies, including L26 (CD20) and antibody to common leukocyte antigen. Some antibodies that are particularly useful in the evaluation of bone marrow disorders appear to be equally reactive in Zenker and B5 fixed tissue decalcified in rapid acid decalcifiers; these include antibodies to kappa and lambda light chains, myeloperoxidase, lysozyme, hemoglobin A, and mast cell tryptase. Monoclonal antibody to glycophorin A on the erythrocyte membrane reacts in paraffin-embedded sections fixed in acidic formalin; megakaryocytes react with monoclonal antibody to CD61 (platelet glycoprotein IIIa) in biopsies fixed in acidic formalin.[21] Antibody to TdT works well with formalin-fixed tissue (see Fig. 23.8).

Enhancement techniques may be used to improve the reactivity of the various antibodies.[25,26]

This section is not intended to serve as a complete description of all of the antibodies available for bone marrow immunohistology; the individual antibodies that may be useful will be noted in the discussion of the various disease conditions.

Normocellular bone marrow

Assessment of marrow cellularity must take into account the age of the patient because the amount of hemato-poietic tissue in bone marrow from normal individuals varies with age.[43,43a] In the first decade, the mean marrow cellularity is 79%; the mean cellularity in the eighth decade is 29%. In the first three decades of life more than half of the marrow is composed of hematopoietic cells. During this period, there is a gradual decrease in the amount of hematopoietic tissue with an increase in fat cells. From the fourth to the seventh decade, there is relative stabilization of the number of hematopoietic cells (Figs 23.11, 23.12); beginning in the eighth decade, there is a renewed decrease.

The immediate subcortical area of the bone marrow may normally be more hypocellular than the deeper medullary areas. As a result, specimens that contain a substantial amount of subcortical marrow may be inadequate for estimating cellularity. In addition, the immediate paratrabecular areas may be preferentially hypocellular.

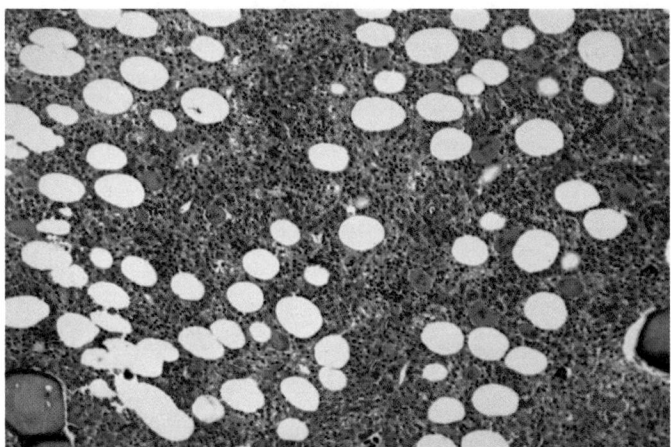

Fig. 23.11 Normocellular bone marrow from 42-year-old man obtained as part of evaluation as potential donor for bone marrow transplant. Hematopoietic cells and adipose tissue are present in approximately equal quantities.

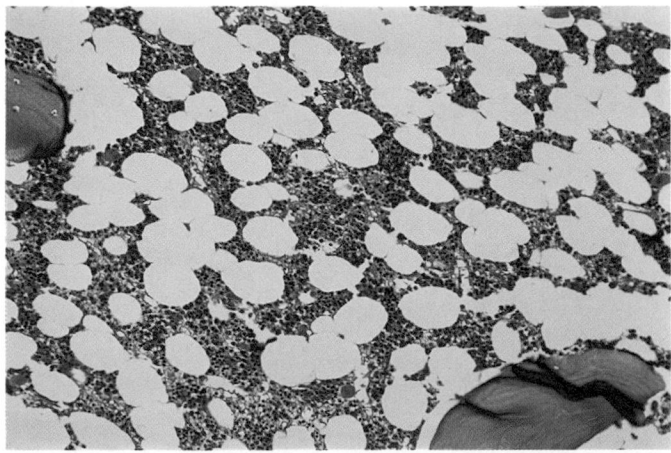

Fig. 23.12 Marrow biopsy from a 70-year-old male being evaluated for metastatic tumor. The marrow is approximately 30% to 35% cellular, normal for age. There was no evidence of tumor.

Alterations in cellularity

Aplastic anemia

Aplastic or hypoplastic marrow, referred to as aplastic anemia, occurs as both acquired and congenital forms. Acquired aplastic anemia may be idiopathic or result from known exposure to drugs, chemicals, viral infections, or ionizing radiation.[44,45,53–55,58] The pathophysiologic mechanism in the majority of cases of acquired aplastic anemia appears to be immune mediated.[66] Bone marrow aplasia also has been observed in paroxysmal nocturnal hemoglobinuria.[60] The term constitutional aplastic anemia is used collectively for all congenital forms of aplastic anemia, familial and nonfamilial, with and without associated malformations of body structures.[47] Fanconi's anemia is a syndrome of familial hypoplastic anemia occurring in the first decade of life that is associated with multiple organ malformations, including hypoplasia of the kidneys and absent or hypoplastic thumbs or radii.[47,50 52] An association of hypoplastic bone marrow and pancreatic dysfunction (Shwachman Diamond syndrome) is a rare disorder occurring in children.[63]

Selective aplasia or hypoplasia of the megakaryocytes associated with missing radii (TAR syndrome) is a rare disorder. An inherited autosomal dominant hematologic disorder associated with proximal fusion of the radius and ulna has been reported; the hematologic manifestations are somewhat variable and include adult onset of generalized bone marrow failure and amegakaryocytic thrombocytopenia presenting in childhood. The latter presentation has been associated with a mutation in homeobox genes *HOXA11*. The homeobox genes encode regulatory proteins that have a role in skeletal morphogenesis and hematopoiesis.[49,56,65]

In the most severe form of aplastic anemia, the intertrabecular marrow space is occupied predominantly by adipose tissue with scattered lymphocytes, plasma cells, tissue mast cells, and hemosiderin-laden macrophages (Fig. 23.13). In less severe processes, there is an increased amount of fat tissue and scattered small collections of erythroblasts, granulocytes, and megakaryocytes; in some instances, the decrease in megakaryocytes is disproportionate to other cell types. The blood findings in aplastic anemia are characterized by varying degrees of pancytopenia.

Uncommonly, the marrow biopsy in a patient with aplastic anemia contains aggregates of well-differentiated lymphocytes similar to the lesions that occur in a variety of immune disorders; these are described in this chapter as polymorphous lymphoid aggregates. Unusually large aggregates of benign T lymphocytes have been observed in aplastic marrows in patients with invasive malignant thymoma with an associated nonclonal T lymphocytosis in the blood (Fig. 23.14).[64]

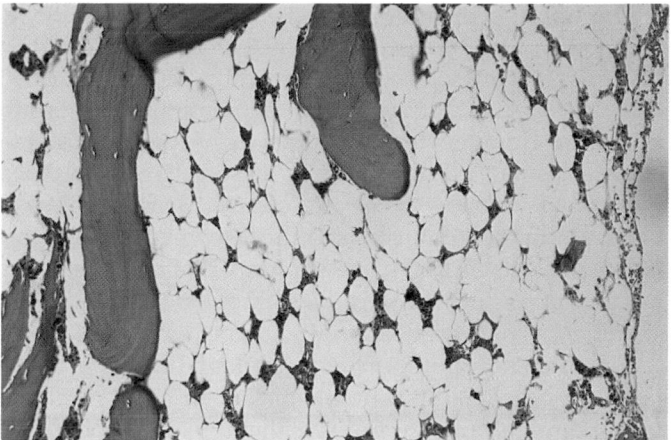

Fig. 23.13 Bone marrow section from a 7-year-old girl with idiopathic acquired aplastic anemia. Hematopoietic cells are almost totally absent. Sinuses and capillaries are prominent. Iron-laden macrophages reflecting increased iron stores from repeated red blood cell transfusions are present.

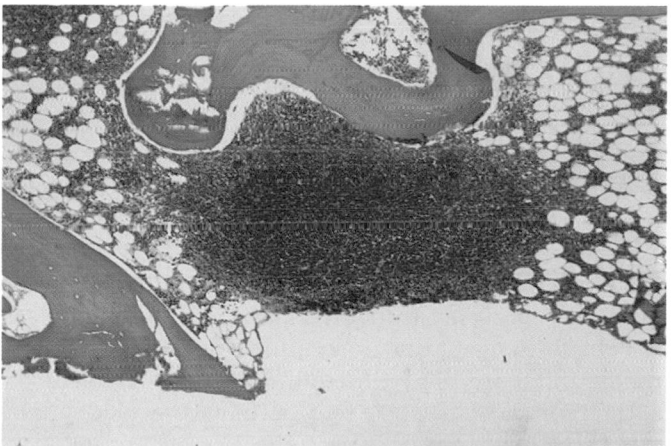

A

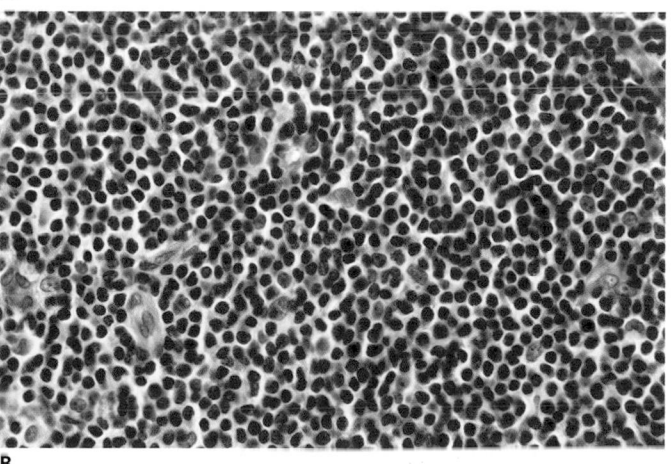

B

Fig. 23.14 A, Marrow biopsy from a 75-year-old male with invasive thymoma and nonclonal T-cell CD3+, CD4+, CD5+, CD8+ lymphocytosis. The markedly hypocellular marrow contains several large aggregates of small lymphocytes as illustrated; the predominant lymphocytes in the marrow specimen had the same phenotype as the blood and were nonclonal by molecular studies. The repeat marrow biopsy following thymectomy showed regression of the lymphocytic aggregates but persistence of hypoplasia. **B,** High magnification of specimen in **A.**

Inflammatory disorders

Granulomatous inflammation

The inflammatory diseases that are most readily identified in marrow biopsies are those associated with a granulomatous reaction; the etiologic bases include fungi, *Mycobacterium tuberculosis*, *Mycobacterium avium-intracellulare*, sarcoidosis, *Mycoplasma pneumoniae*, and viral infections such as infectious mononucleosis.[80,83–85,86,88,90–92,94–98] Granulomas may also be found in patients with Hodgkin's disease and non-Hodgkin's lymphomas with or without marrow involvement by the lymphoma.[81,87,96] Perivascular granulomas may be related to hypersensitivity states. In approximately 80% of the cases with bone marrow granulomas, no etiologic basis for the lesions is identified.[92]

Granulomas in the marrow are similar to those in other sites; the most commonly encountered are composed only of a collection of epithelioid histiocytes that may be surrounded by a rim of well-differentiated lymphocytes. The number may range from a single lesion to numerous and confluent granulomas (Figs 23.19 to 23.21). An unusual granulomatous lesion referred to as "doughnut" or ring granuloma, because of a central clear area or lumen, has been described in the bone marrow of some patients with Q fever.[83,91,95] The appearance of these lesions, which is similar to those in other organs, varies from what appear to be vascular structures or fat globules encircled by a rim of fibrinoid material, polymorphonuclear leukocytes, and monocytes to a collection of epithelioid histiocytes surrounding a clear space[91] (Fig. 23.20). In addition to Q fever, these lesions may be observed in marrows from patients with a variety of diseases, both neoplastic and non-neoplastic.[94] The vascular-associated granulomas observed in hypersensitivity states are similar in appearance.

Cells with prominent intranuclear inclusions may be found in granulomas in the marrow of patients with cytomegalovirus or other viral infection.[90]

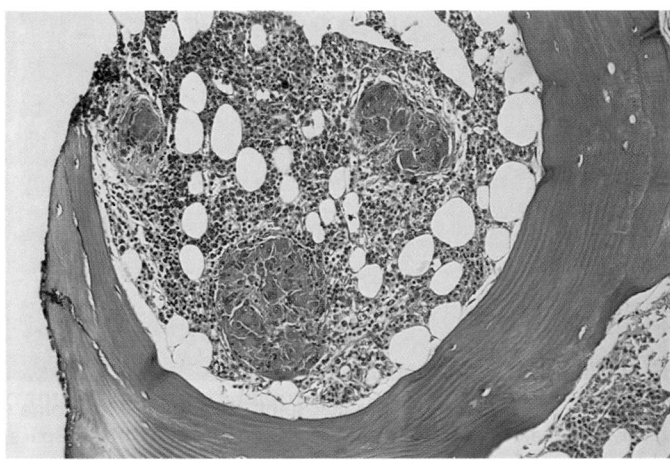

Fig. 23.19 Multiple noncaseating granulomas in marrow biopsy of a 33-year-old male admitted with marked hypercalcemia. Clinical diagnosis of sarcoidosis was established.

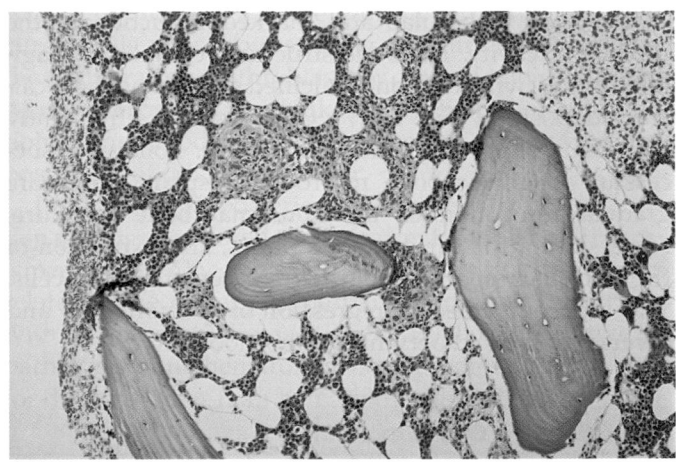

Fig. 23.20 Marrow biopsy with scattered granuloma-like lesions; many of the lesions had a central lumen and were interpreted as "doughnut" granulomas. No etiologic basis was identified.

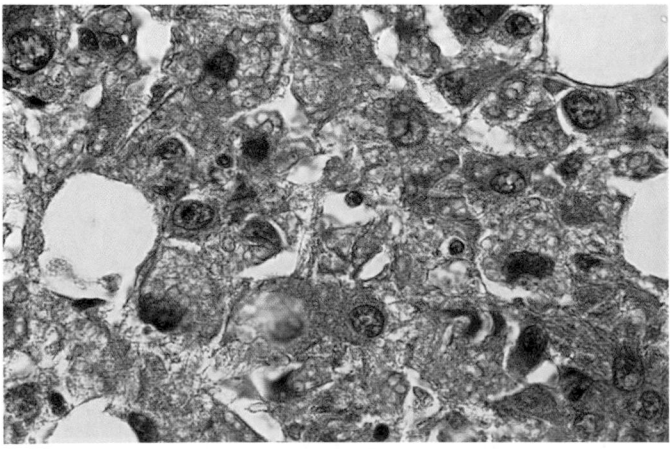

A

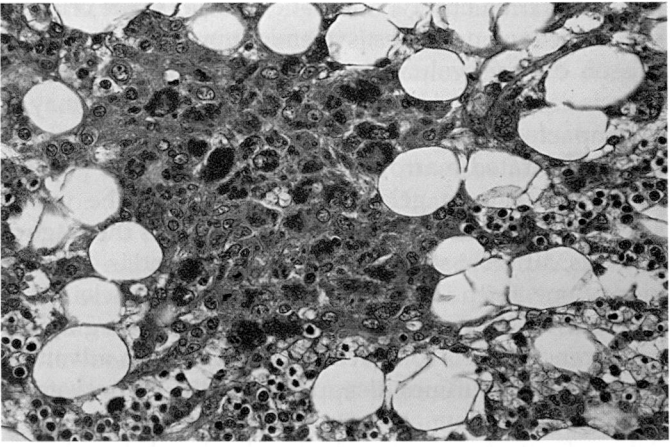

B

Fig. 23.21 Marrow biopsy from a patient with treated Hodgkin's disease. Numerous granulomas contain macrophages with numerous organisms **A** which were intensely PAS positive **B**. Culture studies were positive for histoplasmosis.

Acute parvovirus B19 infection may be associated with marked erythroblast hypoplasia and very immature giant erythroblasts; scattered erythroblasts may contain intranuclear inclusions[100] (Fig. 23.22). Recovery from the erythroid hypoplasia may be marked by a wave of regeneration with a large number of erythroblasts at an early stage of maturation, analogous to the proliferation of promyelocytes and myelocytes that occurs in agranulocytosis. Immunodeficient patients may develop a chronic parvovirus B19 infection; in these cases there may be an erythroid hyperplasia with numerous intranuclear inclusions in the erythroid precursors; the inclusions are most prominent in the basophilic and polychromatic stages of maturation (Fig. 23.22C). The parvovirus B19 relationship to the inclusions may be demonstrated with in situ hybridization studies.

As with other tissues, stains for acid-fast bacilli and fungi should be performed in all cases of marrow granulomas. Failure to detect acid-fast bacilli does not exclude infection with *M. tuberculosis*; organisms are found in approximately 25% of marrow specimens from patients with documented disease.[96] The need for culture of a portion of the bone marrow aspirate for acid-fast bacilli and fungi should be anticipated in all patients suspected of having a granulomatous disorder, particularly those

with AIDS or patients being investigated for a fever of undetermined etiology.[97]

Bone marrow biopsies performed on immunosuppressed patients should always be thoroughly examined for opportunistic infections (Figs 23.21, 23.23 to 23.25). Typical granuloma formation may not be present in the marrows of some patients with disseminated fungal or mycobacterial disease. Marrow biopsies from patients with AIDS may contain scattered macrophages with acid-fast bacilli in the absence of granuloma formation (Fig. 23.26). Uncommonly, *Pneumocystis carinii* may be observed in scattered macrophages in sections stained with periodic acid–Schiff or methenamine silver (Fig. 23.25). An increased number of macrophages with or without evident phagocytosis is sufficient reason to perform special stains for microorganisms.

The presence of infection-related granulomas in the bone marrow sections may occasionally be accompanied by macrophages containing microorganisms in the bone marrow smears or trephine imprints. The morphology of the organisms in these preparations is usually sufficient to establish a diagnosis.

Lipid granulomas, which have been reported to be the most frequent type of granuloma in bone marrow, are similar to those found in the liver, spleen, and lymph

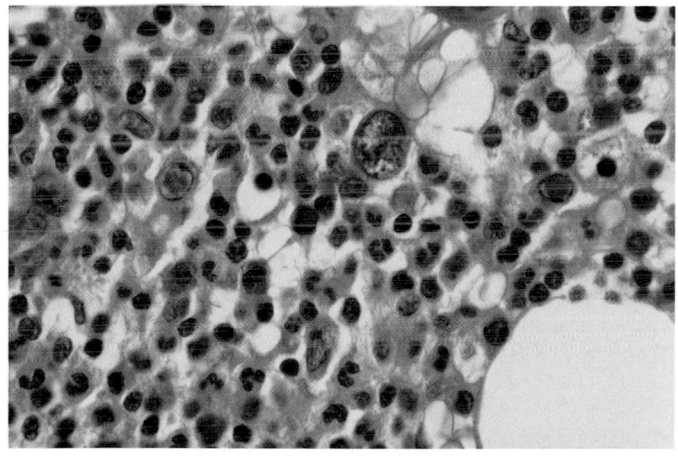

A

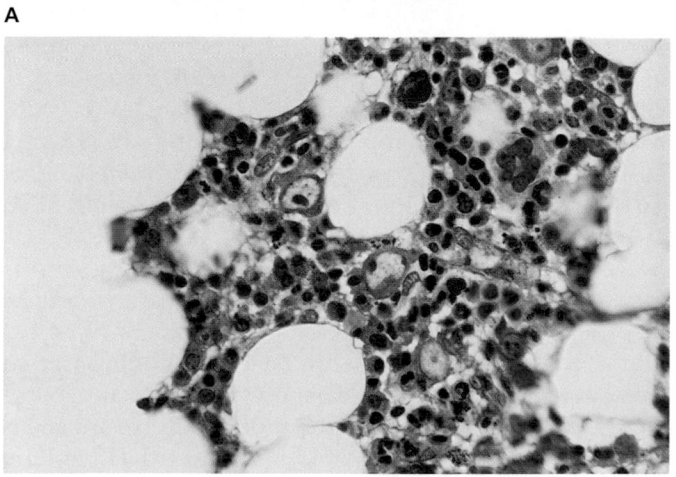

B

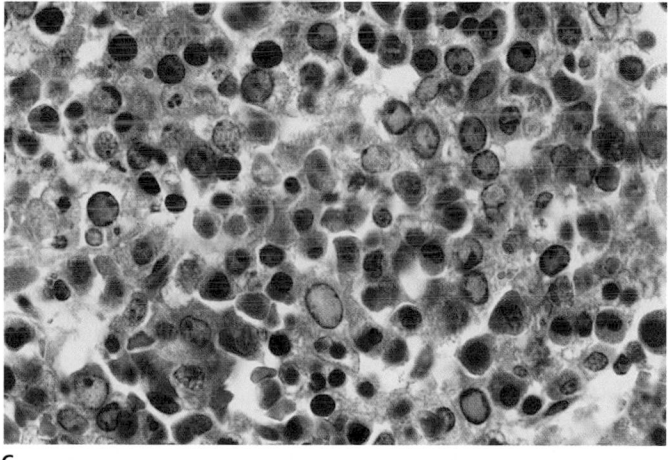

C

Fig. 23.22 A, Pre-transplant marrow biopsy from a 4-year-old child with Hunter syndrome (acid mucopolysaccharides, type II) and erythroid aplasia. Several cells that reacted with anti-hemoglobin A contained intranuclear inclusions. Giant erythroblasts were present in the marrow smear and biopsy as illustrated and the findings were interpreted as consistent with infection with parvovirus B19. **B,** Marrow biopsy from a 17-year-old being treated for metastatic medulloblastoma; occasional, very large erythroblasts with abundant cytoplasm and very prominent nucleoli were present. These cells and the overall marked erythroid hypoplasia are characteristic findings in parvovirus B19 infection. (Wright–Giemsa.) **C,** Marrow biopsy from an adult male with AIDS and concurrent parvovirus B19 infection. There are numerous erythroid precursors at all stages of maturation. Many of the more immature erythroblasts contain prominent intranuclear inclusions. (**C** contributed by Dr. Robert W. McKenna, Dallas, USA.)

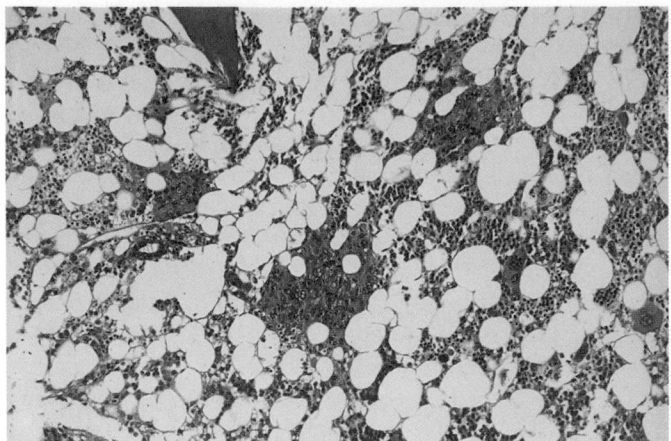

Fig. 23.23 Post-chemotherapy marrow biopsy from patient with marrow involvement by mantle cell lymphoma. Several granulomas containing microorganisms interpreted as cryptococcus are shown. The organisms were positive with Gomori's methenamine silver; culture studies were confirmatory of cryptococcus.

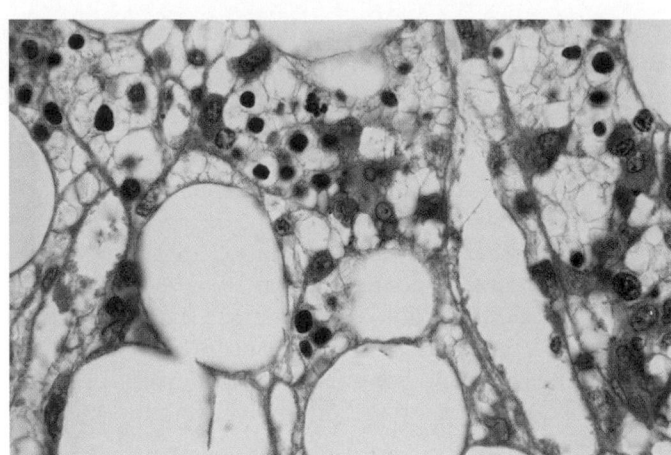

Fig. 23.25 Marrow from a patient with AIDS with scattered *Pneumocystis carinii* microorganisms occurring both singly and in small clusters. Microorganisms are not associated with any recognizable tissue response. (PAS.)

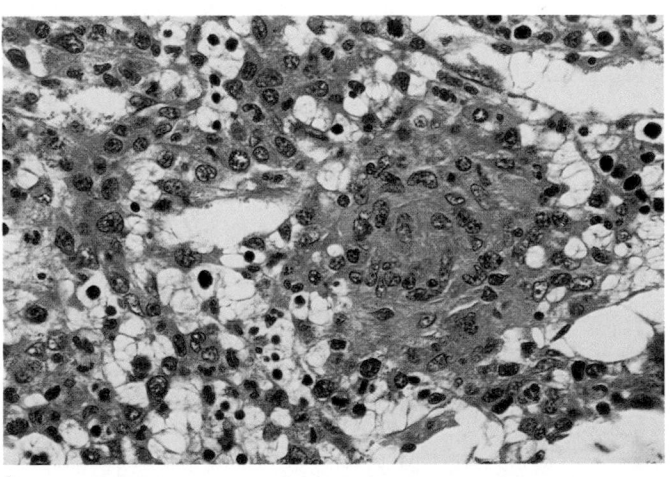

A

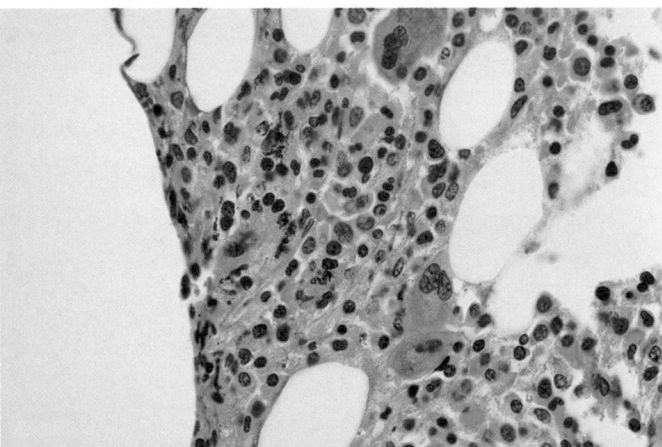

Fig. 23.26 Marrow biopsy from an AIDS patient. No granulomas were identified but numerous macrophages containing acid-fast bacilli were scattered throughout the marrow interstitium, some in perivascular locations as illustrated.

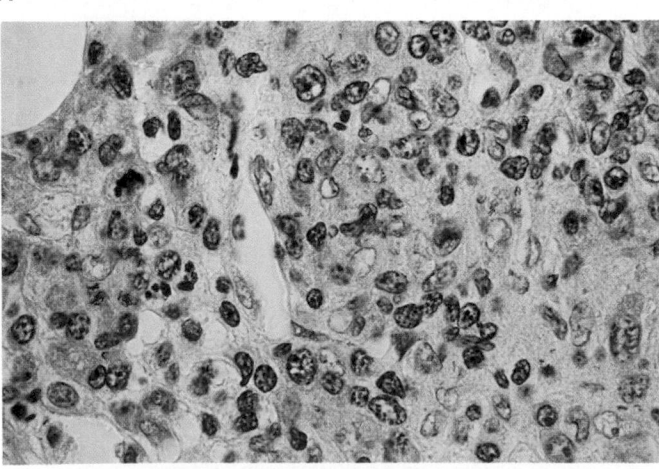

B

Fig. 23.24 A, Marrow biopsy from a patient with AIDS showing granuloma without evident necrosis. **B,** One of the granulomas in **A** showing numerous intracellular acid-fast bacilli. (**B** Fite.)

node.[82,93] These granulomas range from 0.2 to 0.8 μm in size and usually are associated with lymphocytic aggregates or sinusoids. The loosely spaced macrophages contain fat vacuoles of varying size. The lesions also contain admixed lymphocytes, plasma cells, and eosinophils; giant cells are found in approximately 5% of cases. Some of these granulomas resemble those found in sarcoidosis.

An unusual form of granulomatous reaction can be found in the bone marrow of patients with the genetic disorder of glyoxylate metabolism, primary hyperoxaluria.[89,99] This finding is secondary to the deposition of calcium oxalate crystals. The crystals, which have a slightly yellowish tinge, form a radial pattern, are encircled or engulfed by epithelioid and giant cells, and are doubly refractile with polarized light (Fig. 23.27).

Acquired immunodeficiency syndrome (AIDS)

Marrow biopsies from patients with AIDS have been generally reported to be hypercellular, although normocellular and hypocellular specimens may be observed; nonspecific findings include marrow damage, increased plasma cells, myelodysplasia, serous degeneration, lymphocytic infiltration, increased reticulin and "naked" megakaryocytic nuclei.[108,111,113,120–123] Opportunistic organisms including acid-fast bacilli and *P. carinii* and fungal organisms may be present, occasionally without granuloma formation (Figs 23.24 to 23.26).[104,109,110,114] Immune thrombocytopenia may be observed.[103,112,114,119]

As previously noted, persistent parvovirus B19 infection may be an important causative factor of anemia.[107] AIDS infected individuals may develop a persistent parvovirus B19 infection because of ineffective production of IgG parvovirus neutralizing antibodies.[106] This may result in a chronic anemia and erythroid hyperplasia with all stages of maturation. The erythroid precursors in these patients may show intranuclear inclusions primarily in the basophilic and polychromatic erythroblasts (Fig. 23.22C).

The marrow damage that may be present in AIDS patients is characterized principally by a loosely structured, hypocellular interstitium. Areas of fibrinoid necrosis may be present. The changes resemble those found in marrows from patients recovering from chemotherapy with myelotoxic agents and are distinct from serous degeneration, which usually occurs in severely malnourished individuals and which may also be present in marrow biopsies from patients with AIDS. Both of these alterations may be accompanied by an increase in plasma cells. Negative stains for microorganisms and absence of granulomas do not exclude the possibility of infection by microorganisms; a minority of patients with infection by *Mycobacterium avium* complex have demonstrable granulomas or acid-fast bacilli in their marrow biopsies. In addition, although infrequent, marrow with only mild nonspecific alterations may contain scattered macrophages with mycobacteria. These macrophages may resemble pseudo-Gaucher cells in hematoxylin–eosin stained specimens. Scattered macrophages containing *P. carinii* may also be present in a background of essentially normal appearing or only slightly altered marrow. As a result, it is considered prudent by some observers to routinely stain marrows from AIDS patients for acid-fast bacilli and fungi, regardless of the appearance of the marrow with routine stains.

Lymphocytic aggregates of varying size occur in the marrow of a relatively high percentage of patients with AIDS.[105,116] These are randomly distributed without any preferential paratrabecular distribution; in some cases the lesions appear to be preferentially perisinusoidal.

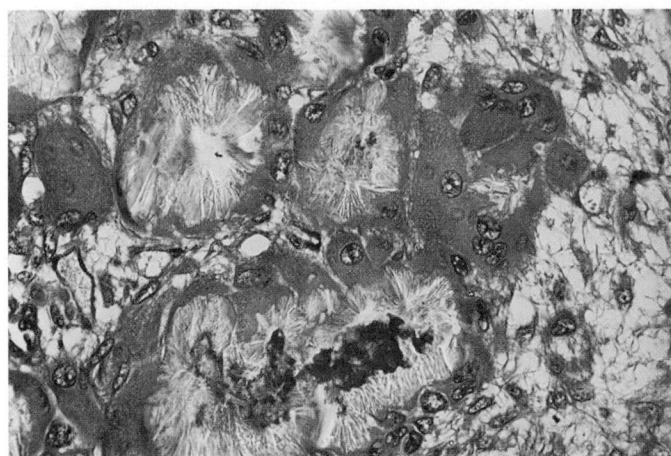

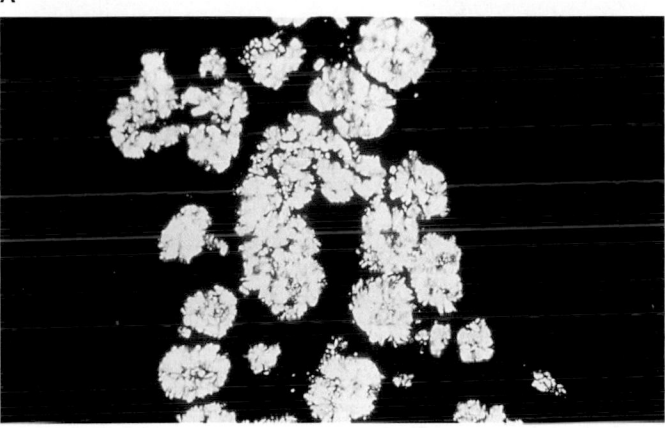

Fig. 23.27 A, Section of bone marrow trephine biopsy from a child with primary oxaluria. Calcium oxalate crystals in giant cells form a radial pattern. **B**, Calcium oxalate crystals are doubly refractile in polarized light.

Substantial portions of the marrow biopsy may be replaced by these lesions, which are similar to those found in the kidneys and other tissues.

Nonspecific inflammatory reactions

Nonspecific inflammatory alterations may be noted in the marrow from patients with a variety of systemic disorders, including acute infection, malignancy, connective tissue disease, and immune disorders, most notably AIDS. These alterations generally are characterized by changes in both the vascular structures and parenchyma. The terms tumor myelopathy and myelitis have been applied to the nonspecific marrow changes that are observed in a high percentage of patients with malignant lymphoma.[102] These changes include edema of the vessel walls, plasma cell and mast cell proliferations in the adventitia, protein deposits adjacent to the vessels, patchy edema, depressed erythropoiesis, and increased granulopoiesis and megakaryocytopoiesis. Acute necrosis of bone marrow tissue is reported in patients with tuberculosis and typhoid fever.[101]

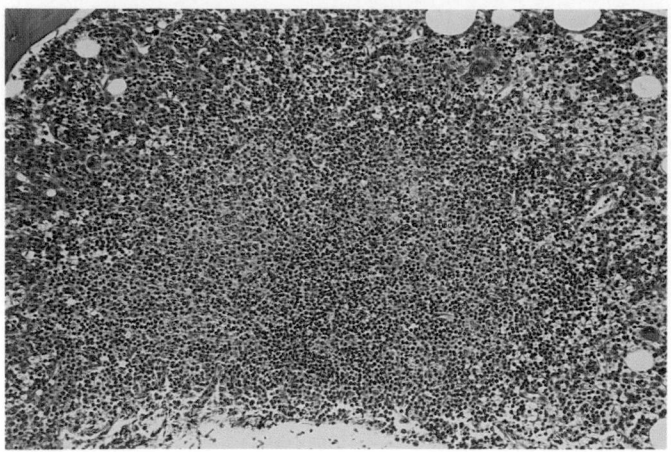
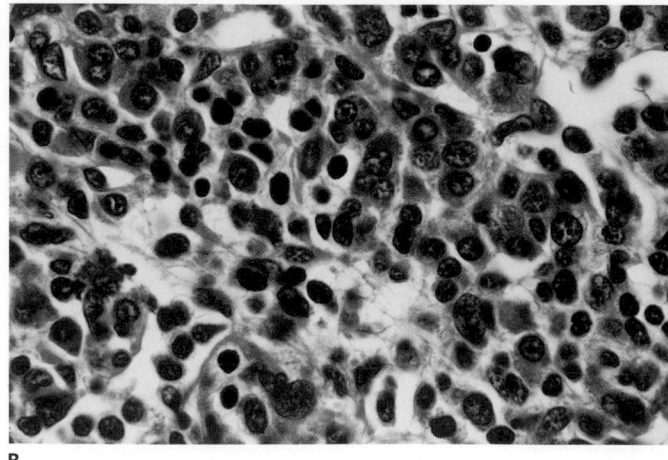

A **B**

Fig. 23.28 A, One of several lymphocytic–histiocytic aggregates in marrow biopsy from a patient with advanced AIDS. Acid-fast bacilli were also identified in this specimen. **B,** High magnification of specimen in **A** illustrating polycellular characteristics of the lesion.

They are composed primarily of small lymphocytes, some of which may have irregularly shaped nuclei. There are usually associated plasma cells, histiocytes, and increased vascular structures; eosinophils may be increased (Fig. 23.28). Occasional immunoblasts may be noted. This type of lymphocyte proliferation, polymorphous reactive lymphoid hyperplasia, is not unique to patients with AIDS and may be observed in marrow biopsies in a wide range of immunologic disorders. Because of the large size and cellular composition, these aggregates may be difficult to distinguish from the lesions of peripheral T-cell lymphoma; the latter lesions are frequently accompanied by numerous epithelioid histiocytes and scattered large transformed cells. In some instances, the distinction between the two processes based on morphologic criteria may not be possible.[116] Peripheral T-cell lymphoma in AIDS patients, however, is quite rare, and such a diagnosis should be established with considerable caution and only after review of all pathology specimens.[115] Molecular studies for T-cell receptor rearrangement may be necessary.

Occasionally, marrow specimens from patients with AIDS contain benign lymphoid follicles with germinal centers.

In addition to reactive lymphocytic lesions, the marrow biopsies from AIDS patients may exhibit a florid immunocytic reaction. In rare cases, this may be accompanied by a proliferation of immunoblasts and may resemble a neoplastic process because of the degree of replacement of marrow. The use of immunocytochemical reactions with anti-kappa and anti-lambda antibodies can be very useful in demonstrating the polyclonal nature of these lesions. In equivocal cases, immunoglobulin gene rearrangement studies may be necessary for determination of the biology of these processes.

Although it is important to recognize that marrow biopsies from patients with AIDS may show a variety of reactive lymphocytic proliferations, it is equally important to appreciate that these patients may develop a malignant lymphoma, of either non-Hodgkin's or Hodgkin's type, and the marrow biopsy may be the initial diagnostic specimen.[115,117] A single biopsy may contain both reactive lymphocytic lesions and malignant lymphoma. In suspected cases of Hodgkin's disease, adherence to established criteria for marrow involvement by Hodgkin's disease should be observed.

Patients with AIDS who are receiving zidovudine (AZT) may develop evidence of marrow suppression such as anemia and neutropenia. Marrow hypoplasia may be present.[118] Abnormal megakaryocytes with sparse cytoplasm, "naked" megakaryocyte nuclei, may be numerous; this finding is not specific for AIDS and may be present in other disorders, including the myeloproliferative diseases.

Leukemias and related disorders

Acute leukemia

The diagnosis and classification of the acute leukemias are optimally established from examination of Romanowsky-stained blood and bone marrow smears in conjunction with appropriate cytochemical techniques; this approach forms the basis for the World Health Organization (WHO) and French American British (FAB) Cooperative Group classifications.[125,129–132] Chromosome analysis also has an important role in the evaluation of cases of acute leukemia, primarily in regard to prognostic significance.[132,139] Although smears and imprint preparations are generally superior to sections in classifying the majority of cases of acute leukemia, there are some types of acute leukemia which are accompanied by fibrosis or with unusual morphologic patterns such as acute megakaryocytic leukemia with an associated t(1:11)(p13;q13) cytogenetic abnormality which occurs in infants in which the bone marrow sections are more informative than the bone marrow smears (Figs 23.29 to 23.31). In addition, as noted in the section on immuno-histology, the development of antibodies reactive in paraffin-embedded tissue, most notably anti-myeloper-oxidase and anti-lysozyme, has greatly enhanced the recognition of myeloid leukemia in trephine biopsy sections.[124,133,134,137]

In the majority of cases of acute leukemia, both myeloid and lymphoblastic, in children and adults, the marrow is markedly hypercellular because of the proliferation of leukemic cells, with replacement of normal hematopoietic cells. In a small minority of patients, particularly older individuals, acute myeloid leukemia and, rarely, acute lymphoblastic leukemia may present with a hypocellular marrow (i.e., hypoplastic or hypocellular acute leukemia).[126,127,135] The marrow biopsies in these patients may, on low magnification, suggest the diagnosis of aplastic anemia (Fig. 23.32). In contrast to aplastic anemia, in which the residual cells are well-differentiated lymphocytes and plasma cells, the cell population in the interstitium is principally blasts; some normal cells may be present but are markedly reduced. The diagnosis is confirmed by examination of blood and bone marrow smears and the use of appropriate immunocytochemical reactions, particularly anti-myeloperoxidase, anti-lysozyme, anti-CD117 (C-kit) and anti-CD34. In rare instances, acute lymphoblastic leukemia in children is preceded by an aplastic or hypocellular phase.

Myelofibrosis with a slight-to-moderate increase in reticulin fibers may be present in the initial or late stages of acute leukemia in a minority of cases; it may occur in both acute lymphoblastic and acute myeloid leukemia.[136] The presence of myelofibrosis in acute leukemia may result in difficult and inadequate marrow aspiration and an erroneous diagnosis of aplastic anemia if trephine

A

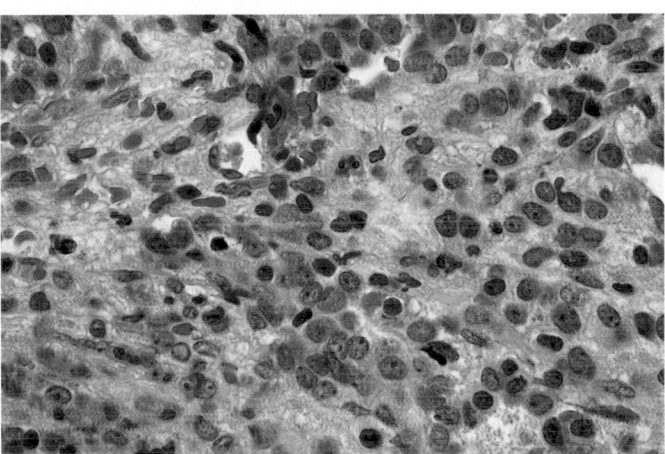

B

Fig. 23.30 A, Marrow biopsy from a 14-month-old child with acute megakaryoblastic leukemia with an associated t(1;22)(p13;q13) cytogenetic abnormality. The blasts frequently have a spindle shape and sometimes form intertwining bundles resembling metastatic tumor. **B,** High magnification of the specimen in **A** showing undifferentiated blasts.

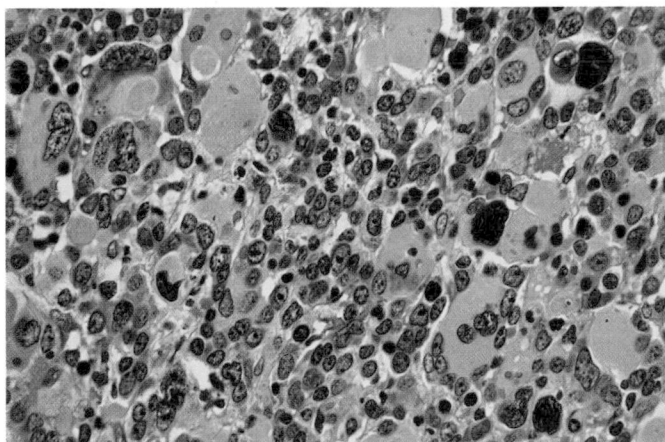

Fig. 23.29 Marrow from a patient with acute megakaryoblastic leukemia (AML-M7). The predominant cell population consists of blasts and numerous megakaryocytes at varying stages of maturation. Mature megakaryocytes have abundant cytoplasm that is uniformly eosinophilic.

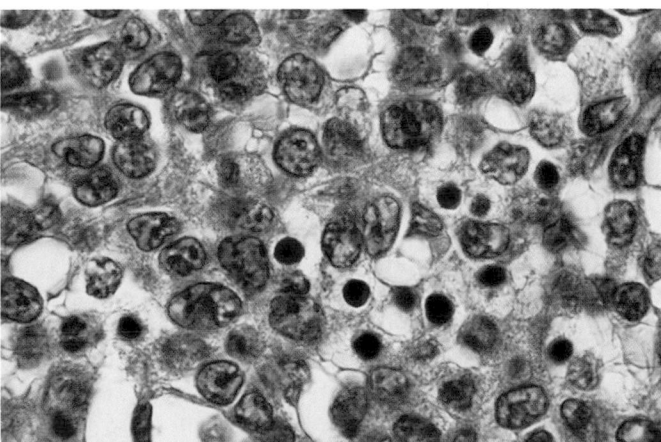

Fig. 23.31 Bone marrow biopsy from an adult female with a mediastinal mass and partial marrow involvement by precursor T-lymphoblastic lymphoma. In this area the lymphoblasts are the predominant cells; some of the lymphoblasts have convoluted nuclei. Scattered erythroid precursors are present.

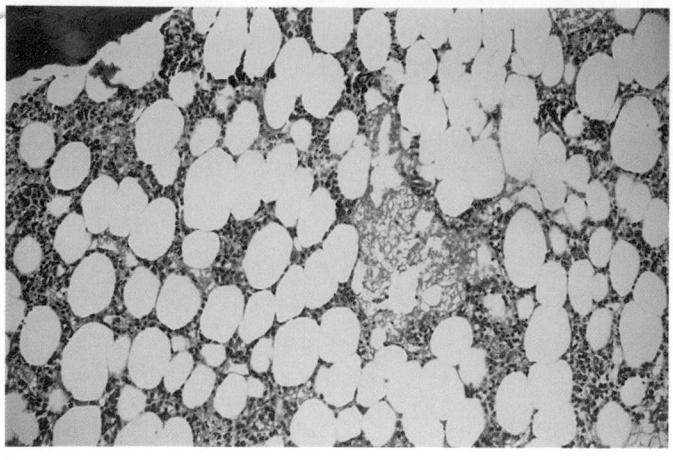
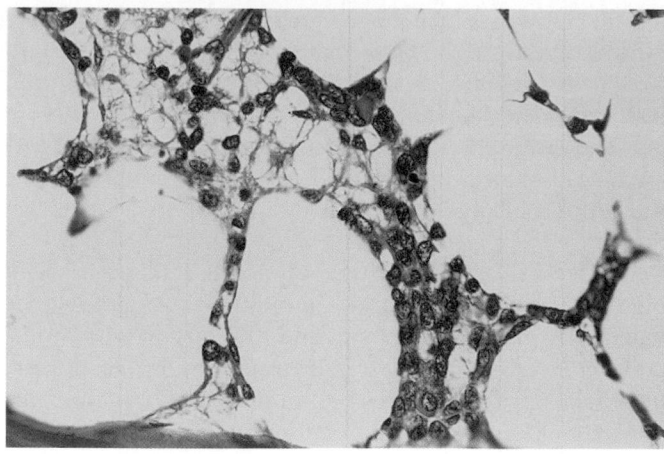

A   B

Fig. 23.32 A, Marrow section from a 67-year-old male with acute myeloid leukemia with markedly hypocellular marrow. **B,** Higher magnification of the same specimen showing numerous blast cells in the interstitium.

biopsy sections are not available. This emphasizes the importance of obtaining adequate marrow biopsies. The long-held view that difficult aspirations in acute leukemia are caused by "packed" marrows has little basis in fact. The vast majority of hypercellular marrows in acute leukemia are readily aspirated. If aspiration is difficult, it is probably a result of poor biopsy technique or an increase in reticulin fibers.

The trephine biopsy provides the only accurate assessment of marrow cellularity and is of considerable importance in monitoring changes following treatment for leukemia. The rapidity of development and degree of necrosis and aplasia following the institution of therapy will vary with the different chemotherapeutic agents or combination of agents used. In general, the sequence of histopathologic events is marked initially by nuclear karyorrhexis followed by karyolysis; the cells then disintegrate into a relatively uniform granular, eosinophilic debris. Subsequently the marrow shows a somewhat irregular, loosely structured appearance with scattered fat cells, vessels, stromal elements, and distended sinusoids (Fig. 23.33). Regeneration of fat cells is followed by regeneration of normal hematopoietic cells in the successfully treated patient. The erythroid cells are usually the first to recover and frequently manifest dyserythropoietic changes as the result of chemotherapeutic drugs.[128] The regeneration of the erythroid cells is followed in sequence by that of the granulocytes and megakaryocytes. This sequence may be altered with different drug regimens and the use of recombinant growth factors. The marrow from patients receiving recombinant granulocyte growth factor may show an early marked increase in neutrophil promyelocytes and myelocytes. In some patients, particularly in the pediatric age group, the post-chemotherapy marrow may contain numerous hematogones which may resemble lymphoblasts. These can usually be distinguished from the lymphoblasts by

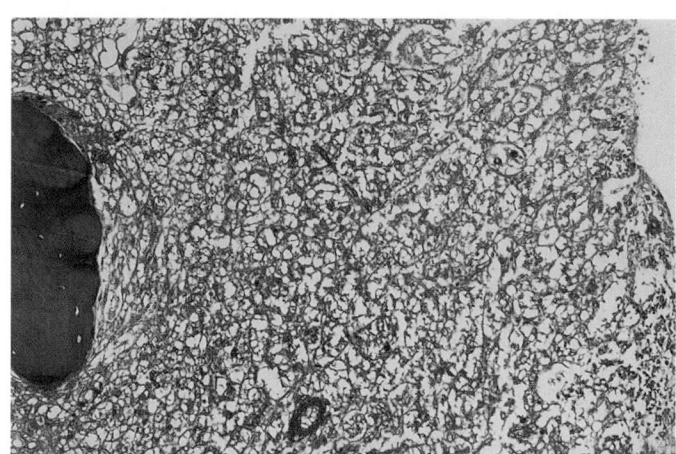

Fig. 23.33 Marrow biopsy 14 days after institution of therapy with daunorubicin and cytosine arabinoside for acute myeloid leukemia. Marrow is markedly hypocellular with dilated sinuses. Interstitial areas contain lightly eosinophilic, proteinaceous debris that represents residue of leukemic cell necrosis.

careful morphologic assessment and immunophenotypic characteristics.[138]

As noted, the course of events described in the preceding discussion is characteristic of effective therapy. In those patients in whom there has been partial or no response to treatment, the marrow will show varying numbers of leukemic cells. In the totally nonresponsive patient, the findings are essentially those of the pretreatment specimen; scattered isolated areas of necrosis may be present. In a partial response, the areas of residual leukemia will be intermixed with necrotic or regenerating normal marrow cells. In some patients, the areas of residual leukemia may be very small and difficult to distinguish from foci of regenerating normal cells, particularly early erythroblasts and promyelocytes. Careful comparison of suspicious foci with the cytologic pattern in the initial diagnostic biopsy should always be performed. Distinguishing foci of normal regenerative promyelocytes from the foci of leukemic promyelocytes in patients being treated for acute promyelocytic leukemia may be particularly troublesome. Normal promyelocyte regeneration is usually accentuated along the endosteal surface of the bone trabeculae and in perivascular locations. Acute promyelocytic leukemia in marrows with partial response may manifest as large or small focal lesions unrelated to bone trabeculae or vascular structures (Fig. 23.34). The cytoplasm of the leukemic promyelocyte may be more abundant than in normal promyelocytes.

In addition to assessment of the effects of chemotherapy, post-chemotherapy biopsy specimens should always be carefully evaluated for the presence of granulomas or other evidence of infection. In some instances, a focus of microorganisms may be present only as an area of nonspecific necrosis with a few histiocytes. These foci may be very difficult to recognize in a marrow biopsy showing cell necrosis as a result of chemotherapy. Any suspicious lesion should be studied with special stains. Proliferation of histiocytes, with and without hemophagocytosis, may be prominent in infected patients. The histiocytes are widely dispersed throughout the interstitium and in the sinusoids; in some patients this may be a very prominent feature.

Patients being monitored for the effects of chemotherapy will usually have sequential marrow biopsies at relatively short time intervals. If a specimen is from the area of a recent biopsy procedure, there may be evidence of granulation tissue and new bone formation (see Fig. 23.1). The biopsy repair site will usually be relatively well demarcated from the remainder of the biopsy specimen but at times may lead to difficulties in interpretation.

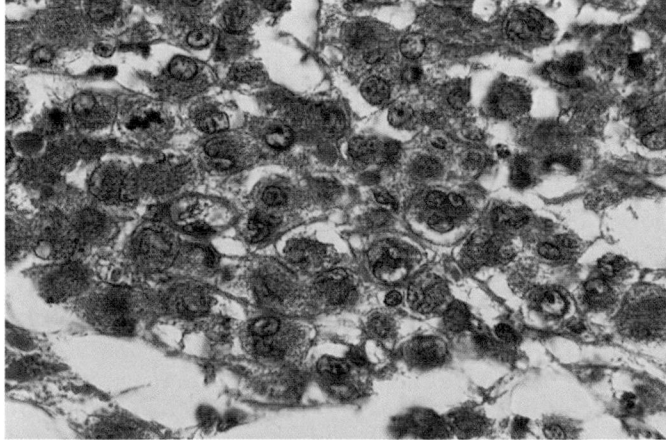

Fig. 23.34 Marrow biopsy from an adult woman with acute promyelocytic leukemia following two courses of chemotherapy which did not include *all trans*-retinoic acid. Large areas of marrow are replaced by leukemic promyelocytes.

Acute panmyelosis with myelofibrosis (acute myelofibrosis)

Although idiopathic myelofibrosis (agnogenic myeloid metaplasia) is usually a chronic disorder, an uncommon entity that is characterized by idiopathic marrow fibrosis and a rapid clinical course has been recognized. Several terms have been used for this process, including acute panmyelosis with myelofibrosis, acute myelofibrosis, acute myelosclerosis, malignant myelosclerosis, and acute myelodysplasia with myelofibrosis.[140–144] This entity is distinguished from chronic idiopathic myelofibrosis by abrupt onset, little or no red cell poikilocytosis, absence of or minimal splenomegaly, and a rapid clinical course. Cases of acute panmyelosis with myelofibrosis have also been reported as part of a spectrum of therapy-related leukemia occurring in patients previously treated with chemotherapy, primarily alkylating agents, and/or radiotherapy for a variety of tumors and occasionally benign conditions.[141]

In acute panmyelosis with myelofibrosis there is hyperplasia of all three myeloid cell lines: erythroblasts, granulocytes, and megakaryocytes (Fig. 23.35). The megakaryocytes, because of their size, developmental characteristics, and tendency to occur in clusters, may be particularly conspicuous; there may be considerable size variation from very small megakaryocytes with non-lobulated nuclei to large cells with bizarre nuclear shapes. The nuclear chromatin is usually finely stippled in contrast to the megakaryocytes in chronic idiopathic myelofibrosis in which the chromatin is more dense. Staining with anti factor VIII, anti CD41, CD61 and CD31 and PAS may be particularly useful in accentuating the megakaryocytes (Fig. 23.35C). The granulocytes and erythroid cells in acute myelofibrosis are predominantly immature, but some evidence of maturation is usually present. The more immature cells may be difficult to categorize in routinely stained sections. Giemsa-stained sections and sections immunocytochemically reacted with antibodies to myeloperoxidase, CD68 (KP-1 and PGM-1), lysozyme, and hemoglobin or glycophorin A may be of considerable help in distinguishing granulocytes, monocyte precursors and erythroblasts (see Figs 23.3 to 23.6). The reticulin stain in acute panmyelosis with myelofibrosis shows an increase in reticulin fibers; the fibers may be dense and confluent (Fig. 23.36). Stains for collagen are usually negative, although an occasional case may show collagen fibrosis.

The relationship of acute panmyelosis with myelofibrosis to acute megakaryoblastic leukemia has been the subject of considerable discussion, and some observers have equated the two disorders. Some cases of acute megakaryoblastic leukemia present with myelofibrosis; however, this is not an invariant finding, and myelofibrosis is not a feature of all cases of acute megakaryoblastic leukemia. Acute panmyelosis with

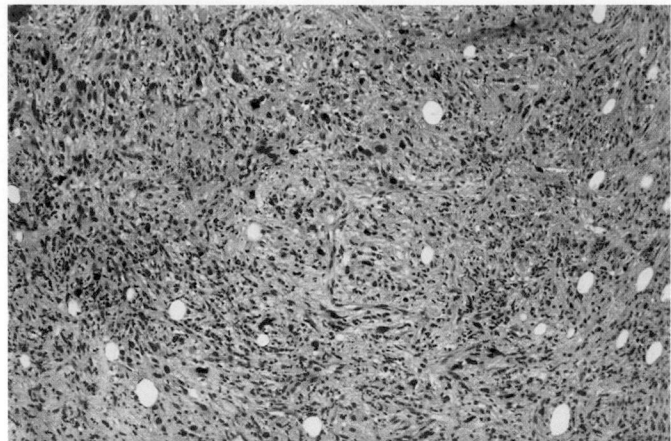

A

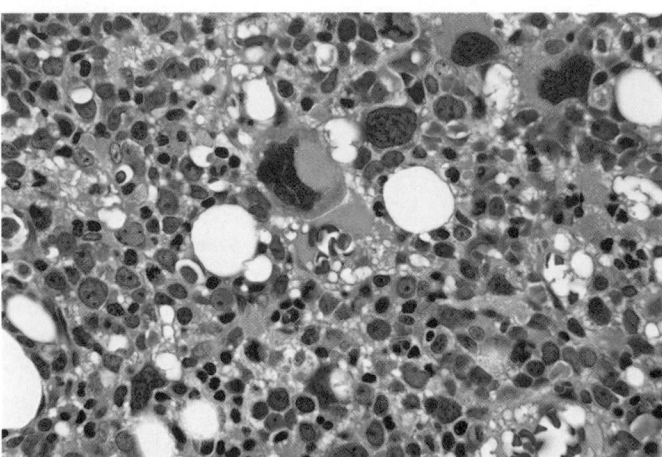

B

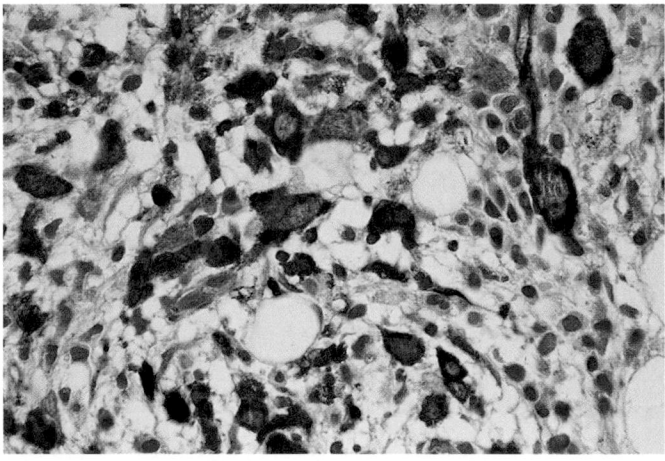

C

Fig. 23.35 **A**, Bone marrow biopsy from an adult male with acute panmyelosis with myelofibrosis. Marrow is markedly hypercellular as a result of panmyeloid hyperplasia. Megakaryocytes are numerous and vary markedly in size. **B**, High magnification of marrow biopsy from patient with acute panmyelosis with myelofibrosis. There is an increased number of blastic-appearing cells and markedly dysplastic megakaryocytes. **C**, High magnification of the specimen in **A** reacted with antibody to factor VIII. (**C**, Immunoperoxidase.) (**B** contributed by Dr. Attillio Orazi, Indianapolis, USA.)

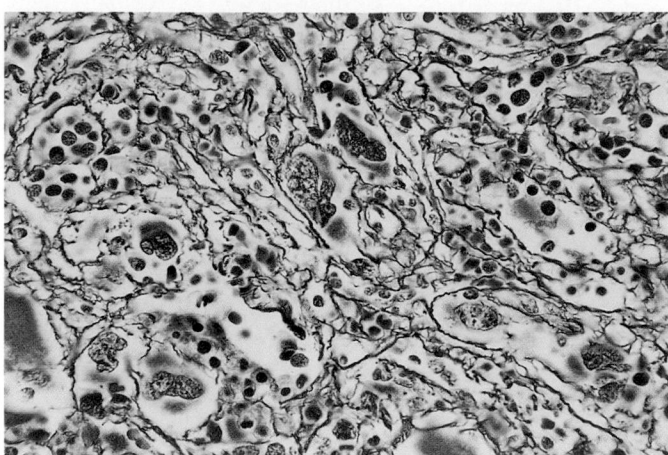

Fig. 23.36 Reticulin stain of biopsy from a case of acute panmyelosis with myelofibrosis showing a moderate to marked increase in coarse reticulin fibers. (Wilder reticulin stain.)

myelofibrosis is essentially a panmyeloid disorder, although in some instances the megakaryoblastic component may be the most obvious because of the prominent and bizarre features of the megakaryocytes. Acute panmyelosis with myelofibrosis is probably a type of acute myeloid leukemia with multilineage dysplasia in which myelofibrosis is a prominent feature.

Acute myelofibrosis is distinguished from other types of acute myeloid leukemia presenting with marrow fibrosis by the predominance of one cell line in most cases of acute leukemia and the essentially panmyeloid proliferation in acute myelofibrosis. This distinction between these entities, however, may not be possible in all instances and the therapeutic importance of the distinction is not completely clear.

The therapy-related acute panmyeloses have marrow findings that are generally similar to the de novo processes.

Myeloid sarcoma (granulocytic sarcoma)

Myeloid sarcoma is an unusual variant of myeloid malignancy in which there is an extramedullary tumor mass composed of myeloblasts or myeloblasts and more mature neutrophils.[147,150,153,154–156,159,160] The tumor may occur as an isolated finding or may be associated with acute myeloid leukemia, chronic myeloid leukemia, chronic idiopathic myelofibrosis, hypereosinophilic syndrome, and polycythemia vera.[145,146,149,156] An association of myeloid sarcoma and acute myeloid leukemia with the t(8;21) chromosome abnormality has been reported.[159] These tumors have also been associated with acute myeloid leukemia with abnormalities of chromosome 16. In earlier literature, the term chloroma was used for these lesions because of the green appearance of the freshly cut surface of the tumor. The green color, which is due to the presence of peroxidase in the leukemic cells, is not present in all tumors of this type, and the less specific designation of myeloid sarcoma is preferred. Although tumors of monocytes have not generally been classified with the myeloid sarcomas, they represent a similar process with a similar predilection to leukemic evolution, primarily acute monoblastic leukemia.[152,157]

The myeloid sarcomas are more frequent in children than adults and are most commonly associated with the subperiosteal bone structures; the most common sites are the skull, paranasal sinuses, sternum, ribs, vertebrae, and pelvis; lymph nodes and skin are also relatively frequently involved. Orbital masses leading to proptosis and spinal canal lesions resulting in neurologic manifestations are two of the clinical presentations associated with these tumors (Fig. 23.37). A high incidence of myeloid sarcomas involving the orbit has been reported in Turkish children with acute myelomonocytic leukemia.[148] Myeloid sarcomas may present as a mediastinal mass and clinically resemble a mediastinal lymphoma.[146]

A myeloid sarcoma may occur simultaneously with a typical blood and bone marrow pattern of acute myeloid leukemia or other type of myeloproliferative disorder or may antedate leukemia by many months or rarely years.[154] It may be the first evidence of relapse in a patient with acute myeloid leukemia on maintenance chemotherapy and may be the only evidence of recurrence. These tumors may also represent the initial manifestation of a blast crisis of chronic myeloid leukemia, and an isolated tumor mass or enlarged lymph node in a patient with chronic myeloid leukemia should be evaluated for this possibility, including cytogenetic studies for the Ph chromosome or molecular studies for evidence of the *bcr–abl* hybrid gene.[149,156]

Histologically, the tumor is composed of a relatively uniform population of immature cells and may be misdiagnosed as one of the poorly differentiated malignant lymphomas; this is particularly a problem with those lesions comprised predominantly of blasts. Occasionally, the presence of immature eosinophils and maturing neutrophils may indicate the true nature of the lesion. Attempts at histopathologic classification have generally resulted in three levels of differentiation: blastic, immature, and differentiated.[154,156] The blastic type is composed primarily of myeloblasts with little evidence of maturation to the promyelocyte stage (Fig. 23.38). The myeloblasts have a slight to moderate rim of basophilic cytoplasm, fine nuclear chromatin, and two to four nucleoli. Eosinophil myelocytes are not usually found with this degree of maturation. The immature type with an intermediate degree of differentiation contains principally myeloblasts and promyelocytes; eosinophil myelocytes are usually present. The differentiated type primarily consists of promyelocytes and later stages of maturation. Eosinophil myelocytes are most abundant in this type. Immunocytochemistry using antibodies to

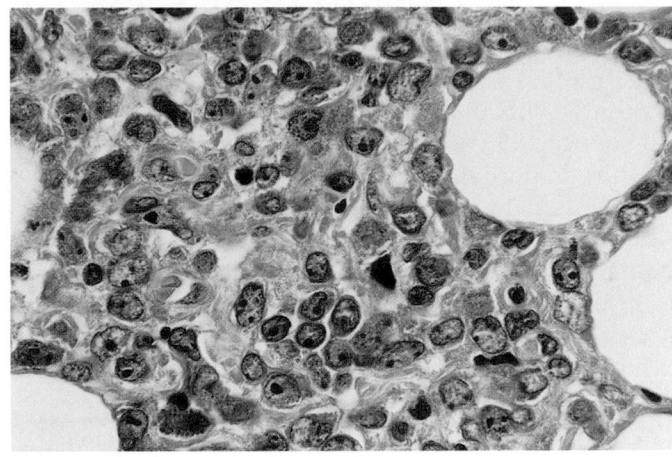

A

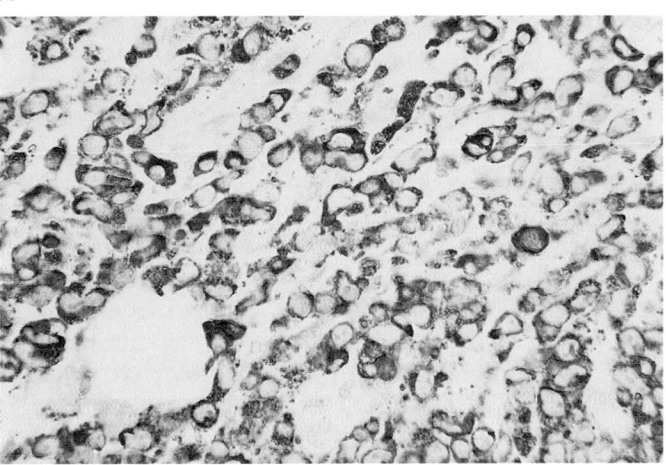

B

Fig. 23.37 **A**, Biopsy of orbital myeloid sarcoma from a 6-year-old child who presented with bilateral proptosis. Numerous blasts are present. Cytogenetic studies of this lesion showed t(8;21)(q22;q22) chromosome abnormality. Blood and marrow smears showed acute myeloblastic leukemia with maturation. **B**, The same specimen reacted with antibody to myeloperoxidase. Virtually all blasts are positive. (**B**, Immunoperoxidase.)

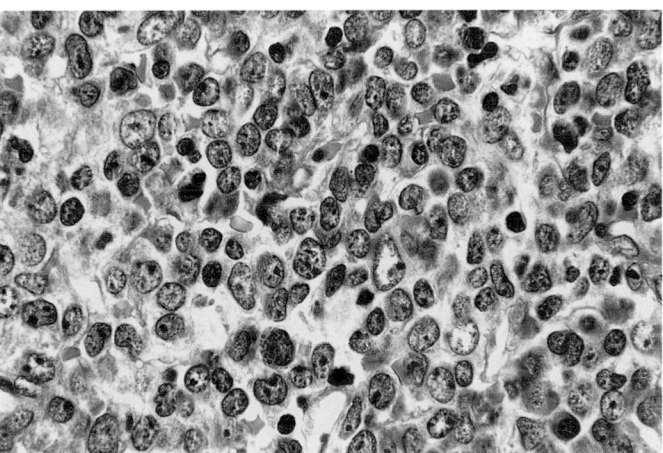

Fig. 23.38 Biopsy of a myeloid sarcoma from subcutaneous tissue of the chest wall of a 49-year-old man. The tumor is composed of poorly differentiated blast cells interpreted as myeloid sarcoma. There is essentially no evidence of differentiation. Blood and marrow showed no evidence of leukemia.

myeloperoxidase, lysozyme, CD68 (PG-M1) and CD117 (C-kit) are very useful in identification[158] (Fig. 23.37B). The naphthol ASD chloroacetate esterase reaction, which is positive only in neutrophils and mast cells, is also useful for the diagnosis of some of the lesions but the reaction is partially ablated by mercury based fixation and has largely been replaced by immunohistochemical reactions.[151] In the unusual myeloid lesions composed of immature erythroid cells or megakaryocytes antibodies to hemoglobin A, and glycophorin A for red blood cells and factor VIII, CD41, CD61 and CD31 for megakaryocytes may be used. Monocytic lesions react with antibodies to lysozyme and CD68 (KP-1 and PGM-1).

Imprint preparations of tumor masses may be particularly useful in identifying the myeloid nature of the cells. Auer rods may be found, and the myeloblasts may show intense staining with the myeloperoxidase cytochemical reaction.

Localized tumor masses occurring in the absence of blood or marrow involvement may respond to local radiation therapy. Eventually the process in the majority of patients will evolve into a form of acute myeloid leukemia or may be associated with additional tumor masses at other sites. The leukemic evolution may be characterized by a gradual increase in myeloblasts in the blood and marrow; frequently, blasts containing Auer rods are identified. Rarely the leukemic cells may be identified in body fluids due to the occurrence of myeloid sarcoma in one of these areas.

In 7 of 16 patients with isolated granulocytic sarcomas reported by Meis et al.,[154] the process did not show a leukemic evolution although 3 of the 7 patients developed granulocytic sarcomas at additional sites and died 2 to 8 months following initial presentation. The other 4 patients showed no evidence of recurrent disease from 3.5 to 16 years following presentation.

Unlike the myeloid sarcomas that occur in patients with established hematologic disorders, which are usually correctly diagnosed, the predominantly blastic myeloid sarcomas occurring as isolated lesions in the absence of some type of leukemia may be misdiagnosed as a malignant lymphoma or poorly differentiated tumor because of the lack of diagnostic features.[154] In lymph nodes involved by myeloid sarcoma, the germinal centers are frequently preserved; the infiltrate is usually present in the sinuses and occasionally in the paracortical and medullary areas. In other tissues, the cells usually display an infiltrative pattern with the overall architecture remaining intact. The presence of immature eosinophils or cells with lobulated nuclei should evoke suspicion of a myeloid sarcoma.

Myelodysplastic syndromes

The myelodysplastic syndromes are a heterogeneous group of myeloid disorders with varying potential for bone marrow failure and evolution to acute myeloid leukemia.[161–167,169] The myelodysplastic syndromes are basically disorders of ineffective myelopoiesis with hyperplastic marrows and cytopenias, frequently pancytopenia with or without an increase in blasts. In a minority of cases, the marrow is hypocellular. Seven major categories have been proposed in the World Health Organization classification of hematopoietic neoplasms: 1) refractory anemia; 2) idiopathic refractory sideroblastic anemia with unilineage dysplasia; 3) refractory cytopenia with multilineage dysplasia; 4) refractory anemia with excess blasts-1; 5) refractory anemia with excess blasts-2; 6) myelodysplastic syndrome, unclassified; and 7) the isolated 5q– syndrome. The classification is based primarily on examination of blood and bone marrow smears. However, marrow section specimens may add important information. Marrow sections in the 5q– syndrome may be particularly informative in demonstrating the megakaryocyte abnormalities characteristic of that disorder.

The WHO proposal also includes a new category of myeloid disorders, referred to as myelodysplastic/myeloproliferative diseases, for those myeloid processes which share features of both a myelodysplastic syndrome and a myeloproliferative process.[174] The category includes chronic myelomonocytic leukemia, juvenile myelomonocytic leukemia and atypical chronic myeloid leukemia.[175,176]

In some instances of myelodysplasia there is marrow hypocellularity which is characterized by the presence of a proteinaceous debris in the interstitium similar to the findings that occur in the marrow biopsies from patients on chemotherapy or with immune-related disorders such as AIDS. This type of change may be observed in marrow biopsies from children with a juvenile

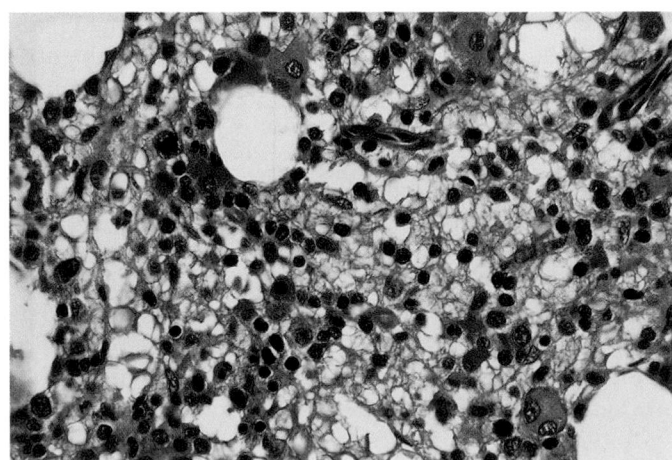

Fig. 23.39 Marrow biopsy from a 2-year-old child with myelodysplastic syndrome associated with isolated monosomy 7 cytogenetic abnormality. Marrow is moderately to markedly hypocellular for age with increased fat and prominent interstitial cell depletion. Small megakaryocytes with hypolobulated nuclei are present.

myelomonocytic leukemia associated with an isolated monosomy 7 cytogenetic abnormality (Fig. 23.39).

The cell population in biopsy specimens varies according to the subtype.[168] In sideroblastic anemia, there is generally a marked increase in erythroid precursors, with greatly increased iron accumulation in macrophages. In refractory anemia with excess blasts 1 and 2, the marrow is hypercellular in the majority of patients, with an increase in granulocytes and precursors. Chronic myelomonocytic leukemia is characterized by a hypercellular marrow with an increase in both monocytes and granulocytes. In any of these types of myelodysplastic syndrome, the marrow may be hypocellular in a minority of patients. This has been associated with an adverse prognosis in some studies.

Increased reticulin fibers may be observed in chronic myelomonocytic leukemia and refractory anemia with excess blasts, but is not usually a prominent feature.[170] In occasional patients there is a marked increase in reticulin fibers (Fig. 23.40). This has been associated with an adverse prognosis in some studies.

A finding referred to as abnormal localization of immature precursors (ALIP), characterized by aggregates (3 to 5 cells) and clusters (>5 cells) of myeloblasts and promyelocytes in central areas of the marrow tissue away from the endosteal surface of the bone trabeculae and vascular structures, has been described in the myelodysplastic syndromes[173] (Fig. 23.41); the finding of three or more in a bone marrow section has been reported to have predictive value for evolution to leukemia. Apoptosis may be a prominent feature in some cases (Fig. 23.42).

Although the precise classification of the myelodysplastic syndromes is based principally on the evaluation of blood and marrow smears, there are some forms of myelodysplastic syndromes in which the bone marrow biopsy findings are highly suggestive of a specific process. The de novo 5q– syndrome is a myelodysplastic syndrome occurring primarily in older women who present with a macrocytic anemia that is often severe, with normal to increased platelet counts and usually prolonged survival; the blast percentage in the marrow and blood is less than 5%.[164,171] The hematologic findings are in most cases those of refractory anemia. The marrow biopsy usually shows increased normal sized to slightly small megakaryocytes, many with hypolobulated nuclei (Fig. 23.43). Increased megakaryocytes may also be observed in association with abnormalities of chromosome 3 at bands q21 and q26. The megakaryocytes in cases with this association are abnormally small, many with hypolobulated nuclei.

Similar to the myeloid leukemias and myeloproliferative disorders, extramedullary myeloid sarcomas may occur in the course of a myelodysplastic syndrome (Fig. 23.44).

The therapy-related acute leukemias and myelodysplastic syndromes occur in patients who have been

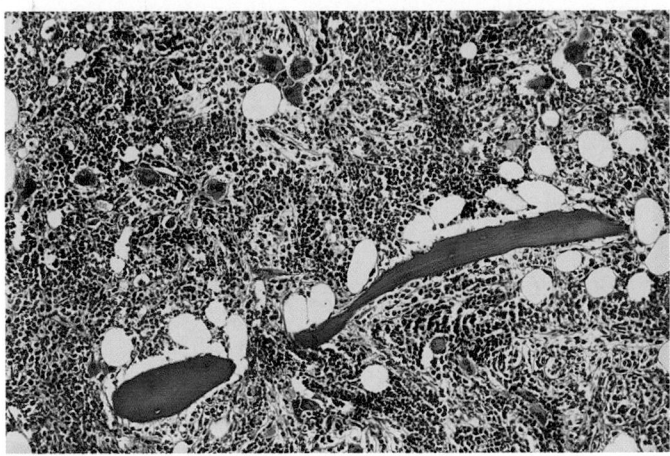

Fig. 23.40 Bone marrow biopsy from an adult male with refractory anemia with excess of blasts-2 (RAEB-2) based on presence of 18% marrow blasts and myeloblasts with Auer rods. There is marked fibrosis with numerous megakaryocytes.

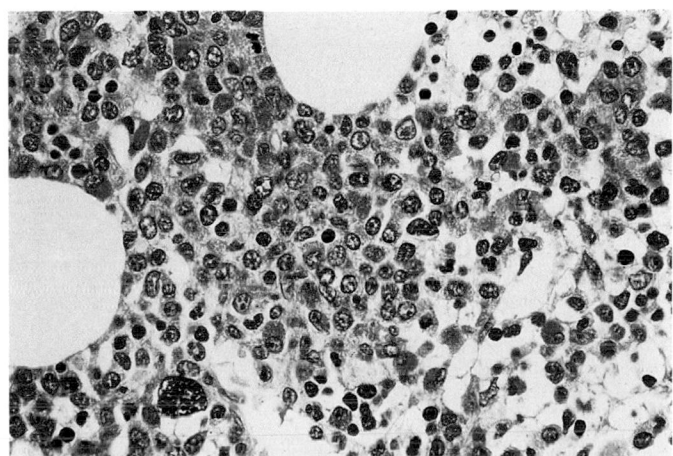

Fig. 23.41 Marrow biopsy from an adult with refractory anemia with excess blasts 2 (RAEB-2). Marrow is hypercellular. There are occasional foci of immature myeloid cells in the central marrow in nonparatrabecular and nonperivascular locations (ALIP).

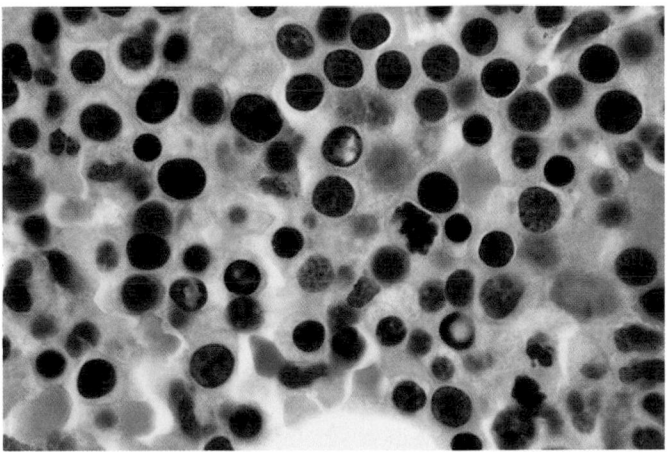

Fig. 23.42 Marrow from a patient with refractory anemia (RA) with marked erythroid hyperplasia and dyserythropoiesis. Several erythroid precursors with apoptotic nuclei are present.

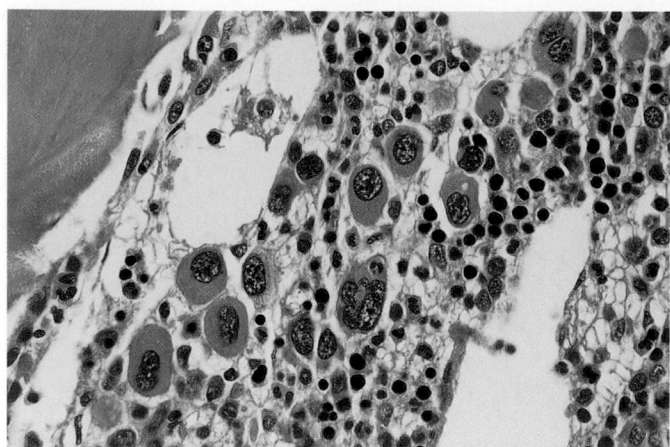

Fig. 23.43 Marrow biopsy from an adult woman with de novo myelodysplastic syndrome associated with an isolated 5q– (q21;q32) cytogenetic abnormality. There is an increase in megakaryocytes, many of which have hypolobulated nuclei. The majority of megakaryocytes are normal in size; small megakaryocytes are present.

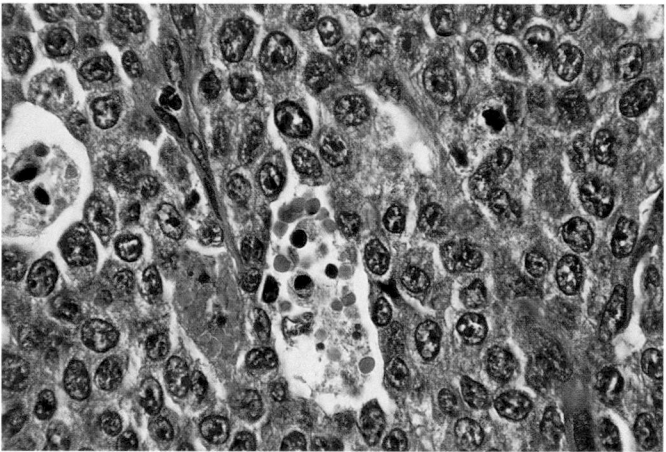

Fig. 23.44 Portion of a myeloid sarcoma presenting as a subcutaneous chest wall mass in an elderly woman with a 1-year history of chronic myelomonocytic leukemia with less than 5% blasts in marrow and blood. The mass consists of a relatively uniform population of blasts; scattered mitotic figures are present. Numerous tingible body macrophages impart a "starry sky" appearance to lesion. Many of the blasts reacted with antibody to myeloperoxidase and CD68 (KP-1). Blood and marrow examination at the time of appearance of the chest wall mass was essentially unchanged from the previous year, with less than 5% blasts.

treated with chemotherapy, radiation therapy or both for a variety of malignant and non-malignant conditions. Two major forms have been recognized: alkylating agent/radiation related type and topoisomerase II inhibitor related type.[167] The alkylating agent related type is generally a panmyelopathy which may or may not evolve to acute leukemia; in either instance it is a poor prognosis lesion with relatively short survival. The topoisomerase II related type usually presents as acute leukemia with specific cytogenetic abnormalities, particularly abnormalities involving chromosome 11q23. The bone marrow cellular-

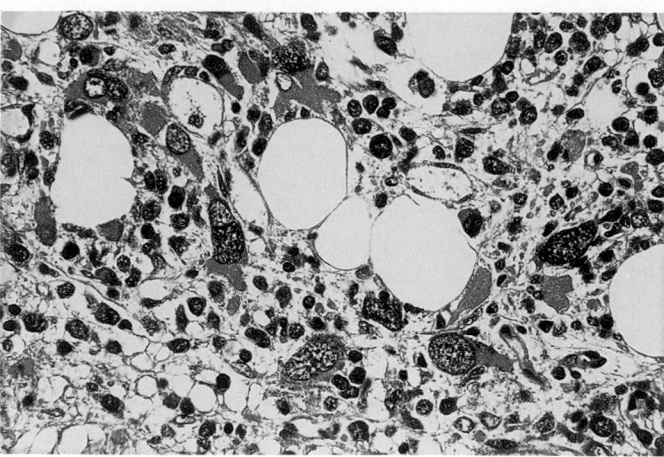

Fig. 23.45 Bone marrow biopsy from a patient with therapy-related myelodysplasia with myelofibrosis. There is predominance of neutrophils and megakaryocytes. Megakaryocytes show marked dysplasia.

ity in the therapy-related myelodysplastic syndromes related to alkylating agents is more variable than with the de novo myelodysplastic syndromes; in approximately 50% of patients the marrow is hypercellular; in 25% normocellular; and in 25% hypocellular.[162] In addition to changes characteristic of the myelodysplastic syndrome, the marrow specimen may show evidence of the initial lesion for which treatment was given. Megakaryocyte abnormalities may be particularly prominent in marrow biopsies[162] (Fig. 23.45). Reticulin fibrosis may be marked, and some of these cases have been described as acute myelodysplasia with myelofibrosis when there is a pronounced shift to immature cells.

Immunohistochemistry may be useful in evaluating the myelodysplastic syndromes. CD34 may be particularly useful in identifying precursor cells in cases of hypoplastic myelodysplastic syndromes that may resemble aplastic anemia.[172] However, the absence of CD34 reactivity does not exclude blasts since not all myeloblasts are CD34 positive. Anti-myeloperoxidase antibody and anti-lysozyme are useful for recognizing myeloblasts and monoblasts respectively. Anti-factor VIII, CD41, CD61 and CD31 may facilitate the recognition of small and abnormal megakaryocytes.

Chronic myeloid leukemia

Chronic myeloid leukemia is generally characterized by an elevated leukocyte count with basophilia, decreased neutrophil alkaline phosphatase, and the presence of the Philadelphia chromosome and/or molecular evidence of the bcr–abl hybrid gene in the hematopoietic cells.[181,188] The number of myeloblasts in the blood and marrow smears in the chronic phase does not usually exceed 5%. The trephine sections are markedly hypercellular, primarily because of an increase in granulocytes and megakaryocytes.[188] Macrophages resembling Gaucher cells, usually occurring singly, may be present in the bone marrow smears and sections; they are more prominent in perivascular locations.

The natural history of chronic myeloid leukemia includes a chronic phase of 3 to 4 years' duration followed by an accelerated phase that is characterized by a progressive increase in blast cells in the blood and/or marrow and increasing basophilia or myelofibrosis; the term blast transformation is used when the changes occur abruptly and the blasts exceed 20% in the blood or marrow[181,185,188] (Figs 23.46 to 23.48). Approximately 70% of blast crises are morphologically and immunophenotypically myeloid, and 30% are lymphocytic. The myeloid type may be characterized by proliferation of any of the myeloid cell lineages including myeloblasts, erythroblasts and megakaryoblasts. Immunohistochemical studies may be very useful in identifying the distribution and lineage of blast populations. In some patients, blast transformation may be initially manifest in bone marrow sections as large, irregular, focal collections of blasts. Extramedullary manifestation of blast crisis also occurs, and the diagnosis should be suspected in any patient with chronic myeloid leukemia who develops a tumor mass or lymphadenopathy.

The development of myelofibrosis in patients with chronic myeloid leukemia usually occurs late in the disease and has been associated with a more aggressive clinical course. Exceptions to this generalization have been reported and myelofibrosis may occur in the early stages of chronic myeloid leukemia with the same prognostic implications as when it occurs late in the disease.[178,179] The myelofibrosis in chronic myeloid leukemia is usually characterized by an increase in reticulin fibers; collagenous fibrosis is not common but may occasionally occur (Fig. 23.46). Reversal of myelofibrosis may occur following bone marrow transplantation.[184] A positive correlation between the degree of reticulin fibrosis and the number of CD61 positive megakaryocytes has been reported both pre and post allogeneic marrow transplant.[186]

Treatment with the tyrosine kinase inhibitor imatinib mesylate (Glivec) induces hematologic remission in a high percentage of patients with chronic myeloid leukemia in the chronic phase and accelerated phases of the disease.[177,180,182,183] The hematologic remission is accompanied by morphologic normalization or near normalization of the bone marrow in most cases. The normalization of the marrow may occur even with persistence of the Philadelphia chromosome, or evidence of the *abl–bcr* hybrid gene. The normalization of the marrow usually may lag behind remission of blood findings and may not be complete for several months.[177] Treatment with interferon usually results in a decrease in overall marrow cellularity and an increase in erythroid precursors. There may be a concurrent increase in megakaryocytes and reticulin fibers. Hydroxyurea therapy generally results in decrease in cellularity and no increase in megakaryocytes or reticulin fibers.[187]

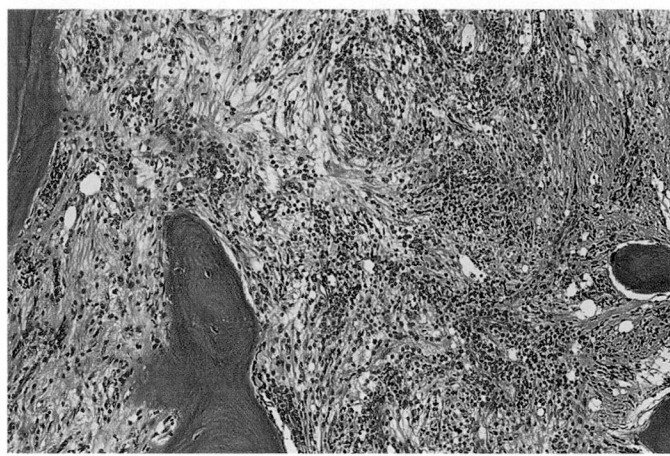

Fig. 23.46 Marrow biopsy from a patient in accelerated phase of chronic myeloid leukemia. There is marked reticulin fibrosis and small clusters of blasts.

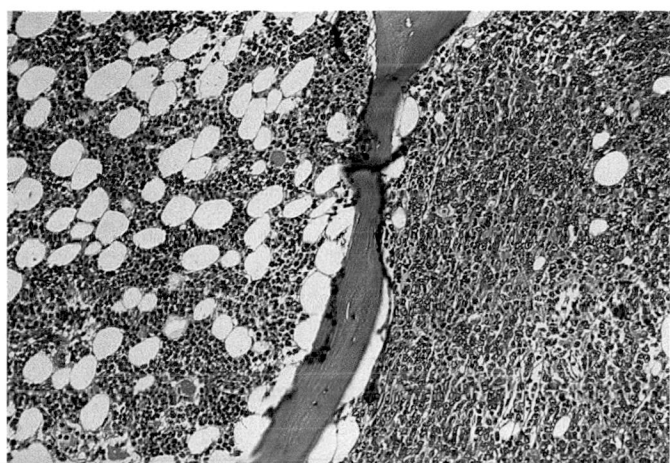

Fig. 23.47 Erythroblastic crisis of chronic myeloid leukemia. The marrow to the left of the bone trabecula shows the findings of treated chronic phase. The proliferation of primitive erythroblasts to the right of the bone represents a focus of blast transformation.

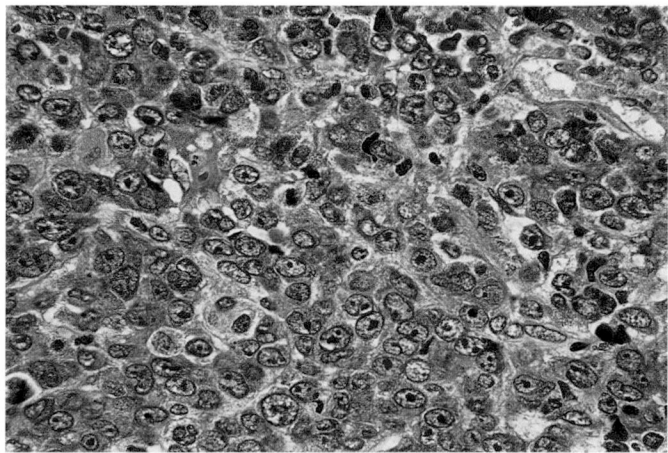

Fig. 23.48 High magnification of marrow biopsy from a patient with erythroblastic transformation of chronic myeloid leukemia. Cells are large with prominent nucleoli and basophilic cytoplasm.

Polycythemia vera

Polycythemia vera is classified with the myeloproliferative syndromes; the major diagnostic feature is an increased red cell mass, and there are usually splenomegaly and some degree of leukocytosis and thrombocytosis. The neutrophil alkaline phosphatase is elevated or at the upper range of normal in most patients. Precise criteria for the diagnosis have been established by the Polycythemia Vera Study Group; these have been modified slightly in the World Health Organization proposal for the classification of hematopoietic neoplasms.[197,203]

The bone marrow in polycythemia vera is usually markedly hypercellular.[189–191,201] However, this is not an invariant finding; 13% of the patients enrolled in the National Cancer Institute Polycythemia Vera Study had marrow biopsies with cellularity of less than 60%.[198] The cellularity of the marrows from patients in the study ranged from 37% to 100%, with a mean of 82%. The hypercellularity is due to panhyperplasia of myeloid cells, principally erythroid precursors and megakaryocytes; the megakaryocytes range in size from small to unusually large, frequently with hyperlobated nuclei and in clusters[189,199,201] (Fig. 23.49). The clusters may be accentuated in perisinusoidal and paratrabecular locations. Stains for iron usually show decreased or no hemosiderin deposits. A slight increase in reticulin fibers is present at the outset of the disease in 25% of cases; 11% of pretreatment biopsies show a marked increase in reticulin fibers.[189] The increase in reticulin corresponds, in general, to an increase in marrow cellularity.[190] An increase in reticulin fibers in pretreatment marrow biopsies is not necessarily indicative of the spent phase of the disease.

Immunohistochemical staining for the thrombopoietin receptor, c-mpl, on megakaryocytes may aid in

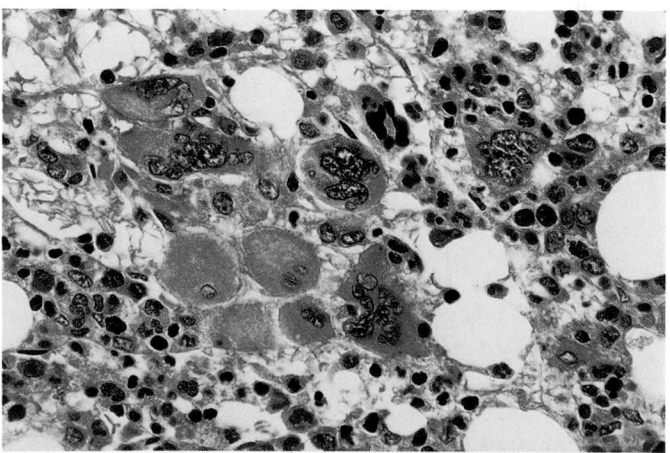

Fig. 23.49 Hyperplastic bone marrow from a patient with polycythemia vera. All cellular elements are increased. Megakaryocytes are prominent and show considerable variation in size; many are unusually large with hyperlobulated nuclei.

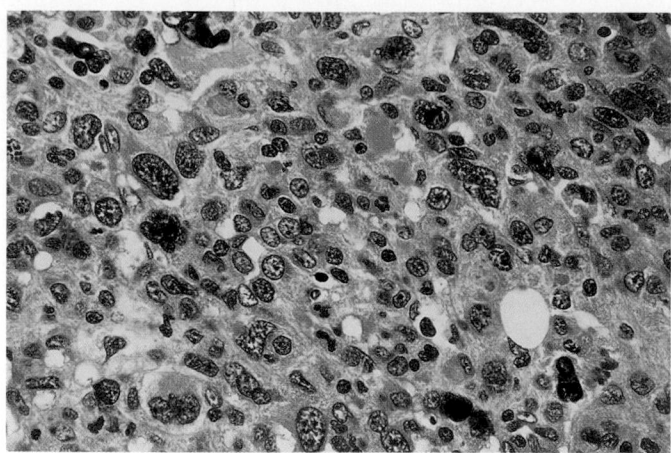

Fig. 23.50 Marrow biopsy from a patient in spent phase of polycythemia vera. Marrow is markedly hypercellular as a result of granulocytic and megakaryocytic hyperplasia. Megakaryocytes show dysplastic features.

distinguishing polycythemia vera from secondary erythrocytosis.[196,200] In contrast to normal controls and secondary erythrocytosis, which show moderate to strong staining intensity for c-mpl in the megakaryocytes, the megakaryocytes in polycythemia vera show weak staining or heterogeneous intensity with weak intensity in more than 20% of the megakaryocytes.

The evolution of polycythemia vera may be marked by a decrease in red cell mass and the development of myelofibrosis with a marked increase in reticulin fibers, collagenous fibrosis and abnormal megakaryocytes; the incidence of this complication, which is referred to as the "spent phase," varies from 9% to 20%[194,195,198,199,202] (Fig. 23.50). An additional complication in some patients is the occurrence of acute myeloid leukemia; the incidence is higher in patients treated with chemotherapy, P[32], or radiation as opposed to those treated only with phlebotomy.[190–193,195,202]

Essential thrombocythemia

Essential thrombocythemia is a myeloproliferative disorder that is closely related to polycythemia vera but lacks the essential diagnostic criteria of polycythemia vera, most notably an increase of red cell mass.[204,205,207] The principal findings relate to the increased megakaryocytes and thrombocytosis. The marrow is usually normocellular for age but may be hypercellular or hypocellular. The bone marrow findings are principally related to increased and large megakaryocytes with hyperlobulated nuclei (Fig. 23.51). The megakaryocytes occur singly and in clusters. The erythroid and granulocytic cell lines are usually normal. Reticulin is usually normal but may be slightly increased.

The distinction between essential thrombocytosis and secondary forms of thrombocytosis may be difficult from routine morphologic studies. Preliminary studies

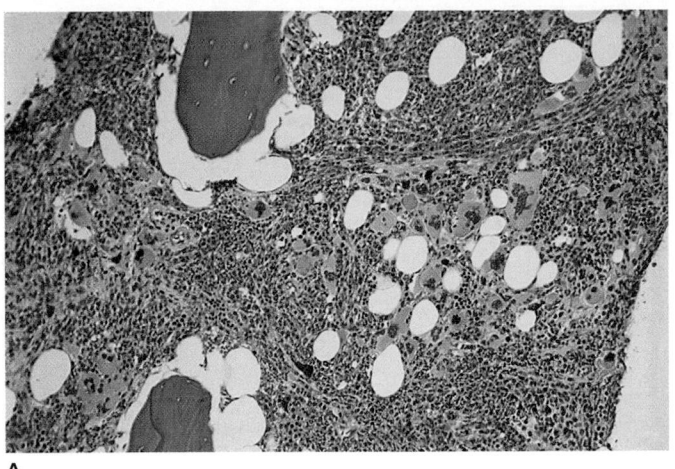 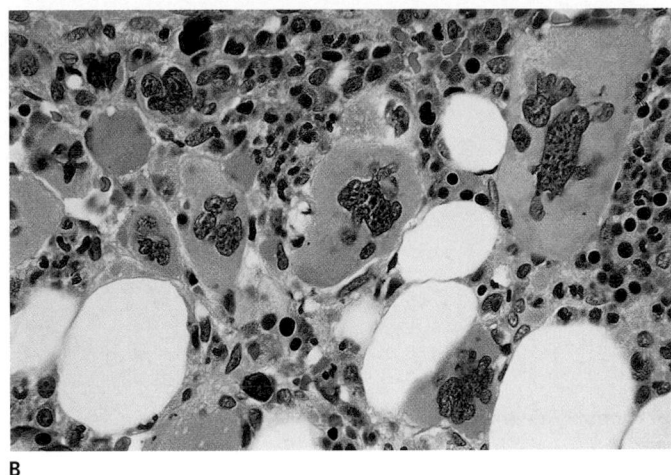

A   B

Fig. 23.51 A, Marrow biopsy from a patient with essential thrombocythemia. Marrow is hyperplastic with scattered clusters of large megakaryocytes. **B,** High magnification of specimen in **A** showing the very large megakaryocytes, some with hyperlobated nuclei.

assessing degree of megakaryocytic proliferation, angiogenesis as determined by CD34 expression, and c-mpl (thrombopoietin receptor) staining in the megakaryocytes have shown the utility of these factors in distinguishing essential thrombocythemia from secondary thrombocytosis; increased megakaryocyte proliferation, increased angiogenesis, and decreased c-mpl expression in megakaryocytes were found to be sensitive and specific indications of essential thrombocythemia.[206,208]

Essential thrombocythemia is an indolent disease in most patients with survival of 10–15 years. Transformation to acute myeloid leukemia occurs in less than 5% of patients and may be related to chemotherapy.

Chronic idiopathic myelofibrosis (agnogenic myeloid metaplasia)

Chronic idiopathic myelofibrosis (agnogenic myeloid metaplasia) is a clonal myeloproliferative disease of undetermined etiology characterized by myeloid cell proliferation and reactive fibrosis.[221,222] It occurs primarily in adults; the average age at diagnosis is approximately 60 years.[213,222,225,227] Rare cases have been reported in the pediatric population.[224] There is some degree of detectable hepatosplenomegaly caused by extramedullary hematopoiesis.

Chronic idiopathic myelofibrosis (CIM) may, at times, be confused with chronic myeloid leukemia or other types of chronic myeloproliferative disorders because of occasional similarities in the blood findings; the important differentiating clinical and laboratory findings have been described in detail.[222,223] The principal clinical and morphologic features have been described by the WHO.[222] The most important distinguishing biologic feature is the presence of the Philadelphia chromosome or molecular evidence of the *bcr–abl* hybrid gene in the hematopoietic cells in chronic myeloid leukemia and its absence in the cells from patients with chronic idiopathic

myelofibrosis. In addition, the neutrophil alkaline phosphatase is decreased in approximately 90% of the patients with chronic myeloid leukemia and is normal or increased in the majority of patients with idiopathic myelofibrosis. Marrow fibrosis in chronic myeloid leukemia is generally a late occurrence, and its onset usually heralds a more aggressive evolution, unlike idiopathic myelofibrosis in which marrow fibrosis is present to some extent from the inception and is generally associated with a more prolonged clinical course.[215,216]

Chronic idiopathic myelofibrosis is usually characterized by a progression from a prefibrotic stage to a fibrotic stage although biopsies from different sites have been reported to show substantial variation in the degree of fibrosis. Approximately 20–30% of patients with CIM present in the prefibrotic stage.[222] The marrow in this stage is hypercellular for age; there is an increase in abnormal megakaryocytes and granulocytes (Fig. 23.52). Erythroid precursors may be reduced. The megakaryocytes may form clusters adjacent to sinuses and bone trabeculae. The megakaryocytes vary in size and are frequently very large with abnormal clumping of the chromatin. There is no or minimal increase in reticulin fibers in the prefibrotic stage. Aggregates of well-differentiated lymphocytes may be present. The fibrotic stage is marked by variable degrees of reticulin and/or collagen fibrosis; the marrow varies from hypocellular to hypercellular. Expansion of the bone trabeculae may be present. The density of reticulin fibers may vary substantially in different areas of the biopsy. Sinusoids are usually increased in number and distended and contain hematopoietic cells. Megakaryocytes may be particularly prominent in the sinusoids (Fig. 23.53). In some cases, the marrow may be almost uniformly densely fibrotic with scattered foci of hematopoietic cells (Fig. 23.54). Scattered abnormal megakaryocytes may be the only recognizable hematopoietic cells.

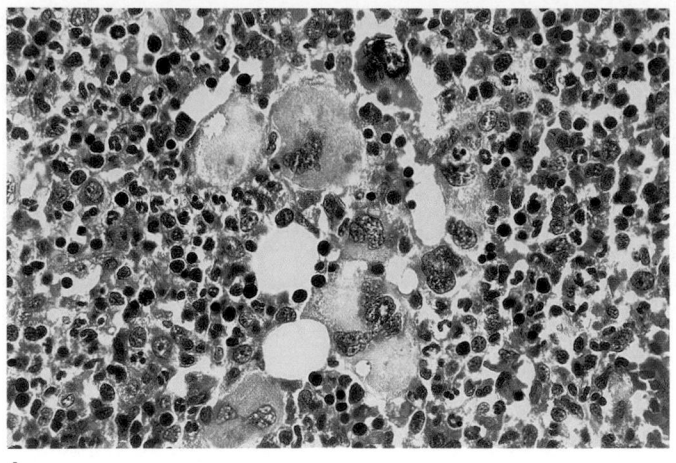
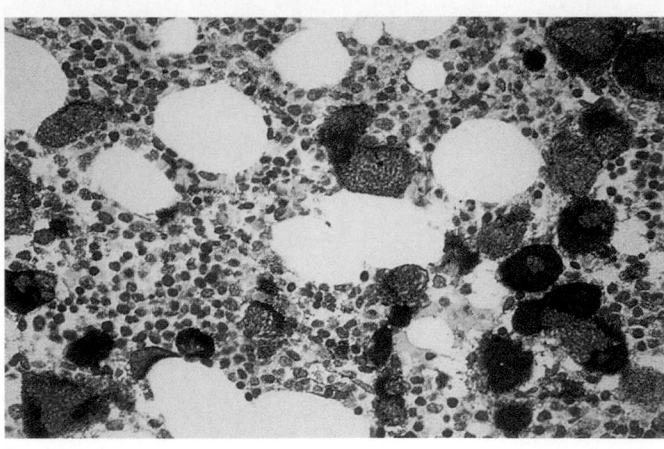

A **B**

Fig. 23.52 A, Marrow biopsy from the prefibrotic stage of chronic idiopathic myelofibrosis. There is a cluster of megakaryocytes which vary in size. Several are large with marked variation in nucleocytoplasmic ratio. **B,** Bone marrow section from prefibrotic stage of chronic idiopathic myelofibrosis reacted with antibody to CD61. This highlights the megakaryocytes, which vary in size from small to large. The nuclei show markedly abnormal chromatin clumping. (**B** contributed by Dr. J. Thiele, Cologne, FRG, and reproduced from World Health Organization Classification of Tumours, Pathology and Genetics, Tumours of Hematopoietic and Lymphoid Tissues, IARC, Lyon, 2001.)

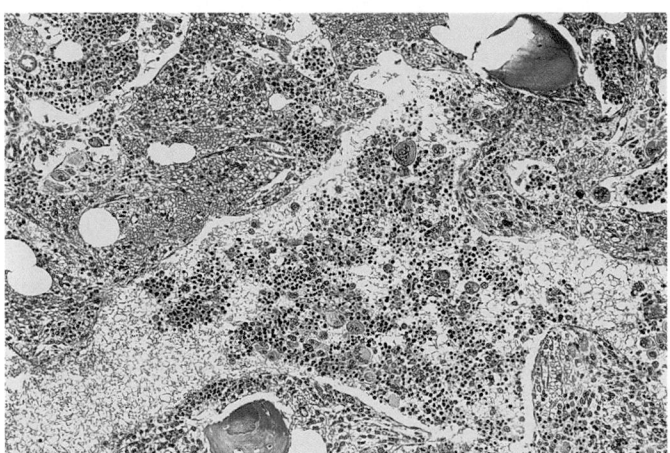
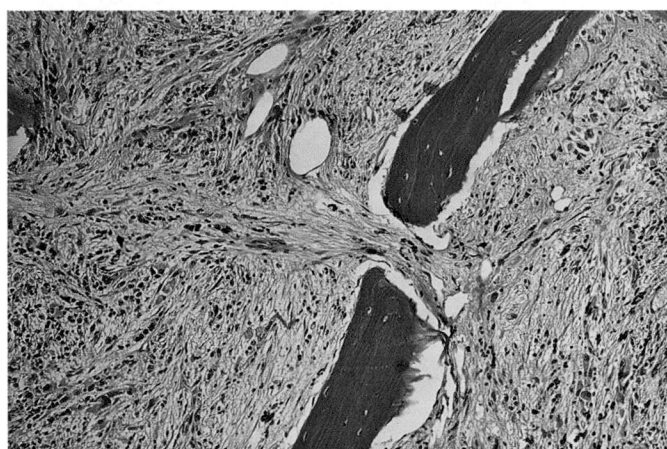

Fig. 23.53 Bone marrow biopsy from a patient with chronic idiopathic myelofibrosis showing prominent intrasinusoidal hematopoiesis. Predominant cells in the sinusoid are erythroid precursors and megakaryocytes.

Fig. 23.54 Trephine biopsy from an adult with a 7-year history of chronic idiopathic myelofibrosis (agnogenic myeloid metaplasia). There is extensive marrow fibrosis with marked reduction in hematopoietic tissue.

In approximately 40% of the patients with chronic idiopathic myelofibrosis, osteosclerotic changes can be demonstrated by radiographic examination, most notably in the bones of the axial skeleton and the proximal portions of the long bones.[226] The relative proportion of hematopoietic cells and fibrous tissue has been generally assumed to vary with the stage of disease, the amount of fibrous connective tissue progressively increasing, with the end stage characterized by marked marrow fibrosis and marked splenomegaly. Studies have been reported that show no correlation between extent of marrow fibrosis and duration of disease and spleen size.[228]

Increase in bone marrow microvascular density evaluated in sections stained with CD34 was found in a high percentage of cases of myelofibrosis with myeloid metaplasia.[218] The increase in microvascular density correlated significantly with spleen size and was a significant independent risk factor for survival. The degree of increased microvascular density was independent of reticulin fibrosis but correlated positively with hypercellularity and megakaryocyte clumping. Immunohistochemistry with CD105 (endoglin) in CIM is reported to show increased microvascular density and positive correlation with marrow fibrosis.[219]

The megakaryocytes in chronic myelofibrosis, including the prefibrotic phase, show strong expression of nuclear b-fibroblast growth factor (b-FGF) on immunohistochemical staining; an increase has also been observed in polycythemia vera and essential thrombocythemia. This contrasts with chronic myeloid leukemia and reactive increase in megakaryocytes in which the megakaryocytes show no or weak expression of b-FGF.[214]

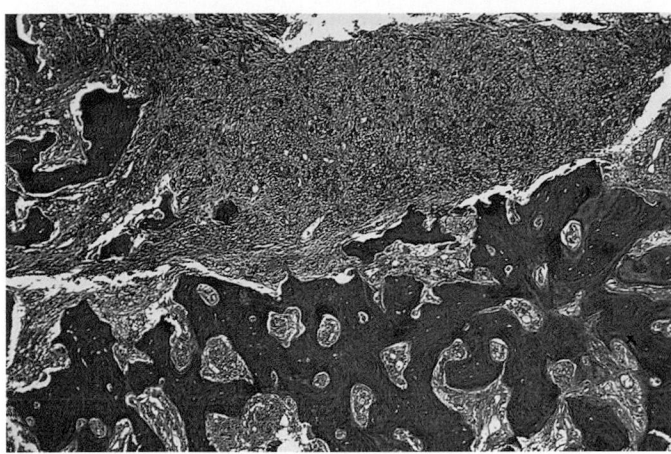

Fig. 23.55 Marrow biopsy from a patient with chronic idiopathic myelofibrosis shows extensive osteosclerosis and a cellular area comprised predominantly of blasts.

Similar to chronic myeloid leukemia, CIM may progress to an accelerated phase with increased blasts (Fig. 23.55). These may be present diffusely or uncommonly in focal aggregates. Myeloid sarcomas may occur in patients with long-standing chronic idiopathic myelofibrosis.[212] The lesions occur most frequently in the retroperitoneum, pelvis, mesentery, and pleura; lymph node and skin may also be involved. The tumors are usually composed primarily of hematopoietic cells with varying degrees of stromal reaction. The megakaryocytes may be particularly prominent because of their number and frequently bizarre appearance. Rarely, marked fibrosis may be present.

The majority of patients with chronic idiopathic myelofibrosis have a relatively long clinical course, with an estimated median survival of 3–5 years from the onset of disease. A minor population of patients with this disorder has a more rapid course with a median survival of approximately 2 years.[211,217,222] Amyloidosis has been reported as a concurrent condition.[209]

Marrow fibrosis may be an accompaniment of several disorders, both hematologic and nonhematologic, including autoimmune disorders, and a diagnosis of chronic idiopathic myelofibrosis should be based on firm diagnostic criteria.[210,220]

Chronic lymphocytic leukemia

Chronic lymphocytic leukemia (CLL) is essentially a B-cell disorder.[229,236,238,240,241,242] T-cell CLL is rare.[232] The diagnosis of B-cell CLL is usually established when there is a persistent absolute lymphocytosis in excess of 10,000, although the disease should be suspected in adults with a persistent absolute lymphocyte count exceeding 5000. Chronic lymphocytic leukemia is usually accompanied by some degree of lymphadenopathy and hepatosplenomegaly. The morphology of the proliferating lymphocytes in CLL and well-differentiated lymphocytic lymphoma is the same and the two disorders are considered by the WHO as different manifestations of the same process.[241,243] The distinction between these two closely related entities is based on arbitrary criteria; if the marrow shows a pattern of infiltration by small lymphocytes and the absolute lymphocyte count in the blood is less than 5×10^9/L, the diagnosis of well-differentiated lymphocytic lymphoma is more appropriate.

Clinical staging systems based on both laboratory and clinical features have been introduced: the higher the stage, the greater the tumor burden.[230,236,244] The system proposed by Rai et al. includes five stages: 0, lymphocytosis in blood and marrow; I, lymphocytosis and lymphadenopathy; II, lymphocytosis and hepatomegaly and/or splenomegaly; III, lymphocytosis and anemia; and IV, lymphocytosis and thrombocytopenia.[244] The system introduced by Binet has three stages: A) no anemia, no thrombocytopenia, fewer than three lymphoid areas enlarged (cervical, axillary and inguinal lymphadenopathy, spleen, liver); B) no anemia, no thrombocytopenia, more than three lymphoid areas involved; C) anemia (Hgb <10 g/dl) and/or platelet count <100 × 10^9/L.[230,236] The higher clinical stages are generally associated with a shorter survival compared to the lower clinical stages. High CD38 expression on the lymphocyte has been reported to be associated with a significantly shorter survival than cases lacking CD38 expression regardless of clinical stage. Two factors have been shown to have major prognostic impact on prognosis in CLL: the mutation status of the surface immunoglobulin variable region gene and the presence and type of genomic aberrations.[233,234] Patients in whom the leukemic cells have apparently traversed the germinal center and undergone somatic mutations of the immunoglobulin variable region gene have a significantly better prognosis than patients in whom the mutation has not occurred (pre-germinal center lymphocytes). There appears to be an inverse relationship in the majority of cases between expression of CD38 on the lymphocytes and the mutation status. However, this is not invariable, and determination of the mutation status should be performed.

The detection of genomic aberrations in the lymphocyte in CLL by fluorescent in situ hybridization has shown significant differences in survival patterns; patients with 17p13 and 11q22–23 deletions appear to have more advanced disease than patients with 12q trisomy, normal karyotype, and 13q14 deletion. Patients with 17p– have the shortest survival and patients with 13q– have the longest survival.[234]

p53 abnormalities in B-CLL have been associated with an excess of prolymphocytes and poor prognosis.[237]

Histopathologic staging of B-CLL is based on the pattern of involvement in bone marrow sections.[242,245] Five possible patterns are generally recognized: focal, diffuse, interstitial, focal and interstitial, and focal and diffuse (Fig. 23.56). The patients with focal, interstitial, or a combination of focal and interstitial involvement are predominantly in low clinical stages. The diffuse or focal and diffuse patterns generally occur in patients with advanced clinical stages. The diffuse pattern of marrow

involvement has been found to have adverse prognostic significance in several studies.[239,242,243,246]

Marrow biopsies from approximately 25% of patients with B-CLL demonstrate a slight increase in reticulin fibers.

In some patients with B-CLL, there is a dedifferentiation or transformation of the proliferating cell type; this usually occurs late in the course of the disease in approximately 5% of the patients and has been referred to as "prolymphocytoid" transformation.[235] This dedifferentiation is distinct from B prolymphocytic leukemia which is a de novo process with different morphologic features. In these patients, the marrow infiltration may contain foci of prolymphocytoid lymphocytes and paraimmunoblasts (Fig. 23.57). The prolymphocytoid lymphocytes have a moderate amount of basophilic to amphophilic cytoplasm, coarsely reticular nuclear chromatin, and relatively prominent single nucleoli. The paraimmunoblasts are larger, with more abundant cytoplasm, more dispersed nuclear chromatin, and frequently a single prominent eosinophilic nucleolus. These foci may be circumscribed by more well-differentiated lymphocytes and are similar to the immature foci or proliferation centers noted in the lymph nodes of some patients with this process[245] (Fig. 23.58). Difficulties may occur in distinguishing foci of transformation in CLL from poorly

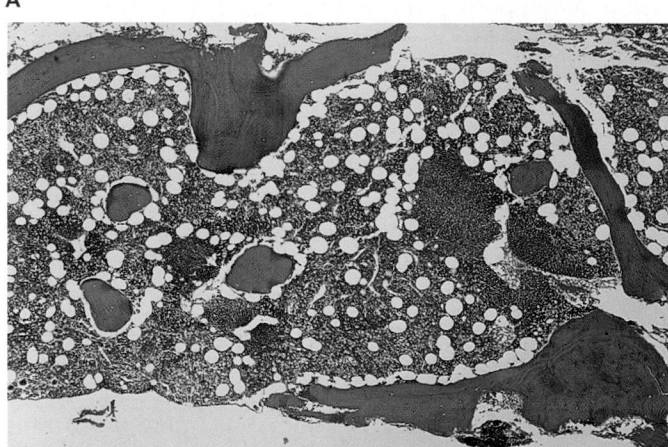

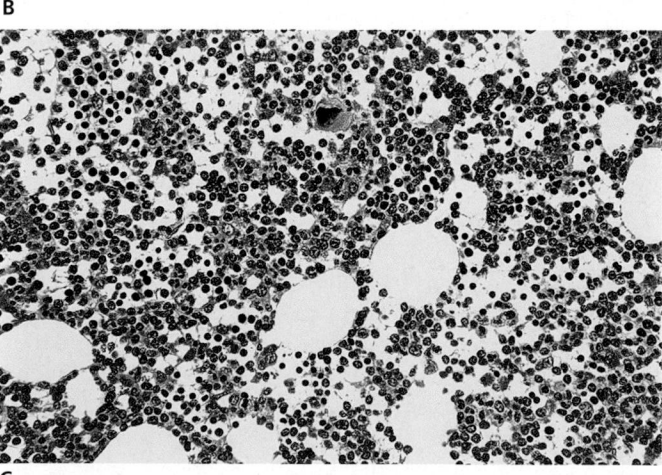

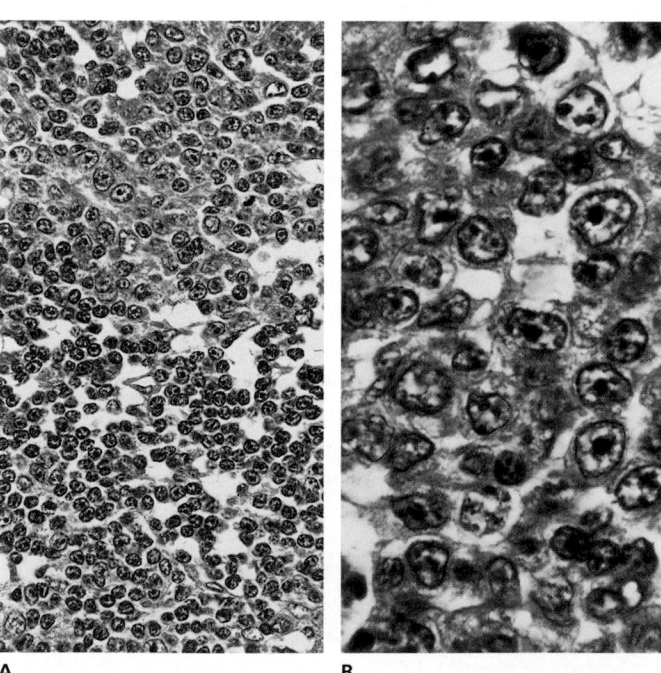

Fig. 23.56 **A**, Marrow biopsy from a patient with CLL showing diffuse pattern of involvement. The small lymphocytes completely replace normal marrow cells. **B**, Marrow biopsy from a patient with CLL with focal involvement. Leukemic cells occur in relatively well-demarcated foci, which are randomly distributed and surrounded by normal-appearing marrow. **C**, Marrow section from a patient with CLL illustrating an interstitial pattern of involvement; overall marrow architecture is preserved.

Fig. 23.57 **A**, Marrow biopsy from an adult female with a 4-year history of untreated B-cell chronic lymphocytic leukemia. There are two morphologic populations of lymphocytes; the lower portion of the figure on the left is predominantly small lymphocytes; the upper portion is predominantly prolymphocytoid lymphocytes and paraimmunoblasts. **B**, High magnification of the upper area of the specimen illustrating the prominent prolymphocytoid lymphocytes and paraimmunoblasts with very prominent, usually single, nucleoli.

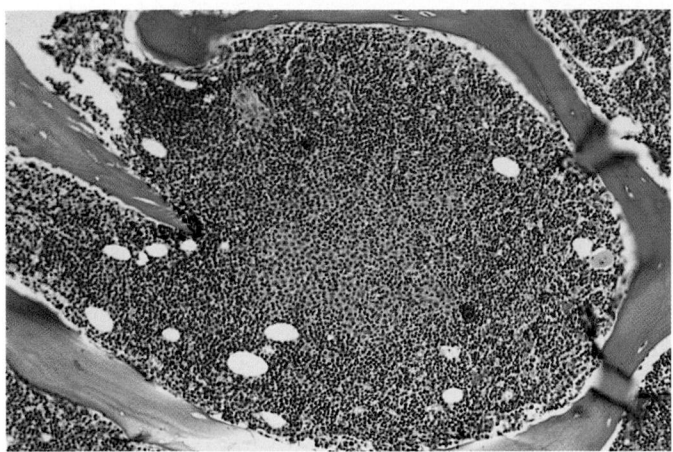

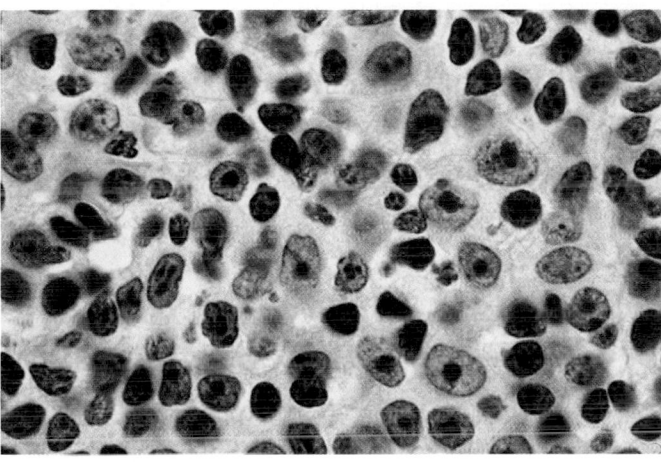

Fig. 23.58 A, Marrow biopsy illustrating a proliferation center in a patient with B-CLL. **B,** High magnification of the central portion of the proliferation center with prominent prolymphocytoid lymphocytes and paraimmunoblasts.

differentiated lymphocytic lymphoma. An important feature in CLL is the residual population of well-differentiated lymphocytes. In most instances, examination of the blood and marrow smears aids considerably in distinguishing these processes. Concurrence of CLL and other B-cell neoplasms including multiple myeloma and hairy cell leukemia has been reported.[231]

Richter's syndrome

Richter's syndrome is the occurrence of a pleomorphic lymphoma in a patient with a prior history of B-CLL[250,252,254,257,258,261,262] or another low-grade B-cell lymphoproliferative disorder such as plasmacytoid lymphoma. The reported incidence in B-CLL ranges from less than 1% to 10%.[262] The syndrome is usually characterized by an abrupt change in clinical course with the onset of fever, weight loss, localized adenopathy, dysglobulinemia, and histopathologic evidence of a pleomorphic lymphoma frequently containing multinucleated giant cells. A Hodgkin's type variant has been described.[248] The locus of the lymphomatous process is

not restricted to hematopoietic organs.[250] A high incidence of lytic bone lesions has been reported.[262] The bone marrow may be involved by the pleomorphic lymphoma; evidence of CLL and the supervening lymphoma may be present in the same biopsy specimen (Fig. 23.59). The blood smear usually shows no involvement by the pleomorphic cells and there may be lymphocytopenia. This transformation is marked by an aggressive clinical course and rapid deterioration. The term Richter transformation has been used to describe a somewhat broader spectrum of pathologic findings in patients with B-CLL who present with a similar clinical evolution.[253]

The biologic events resulting in Richter transformation are not completely understood, but a dedifferentiation or transformation of the well-differentiated lymphocyte has been suggested.[255,259] This theory is supported by evidence in some cases of similar surface markers including light chains on the cells of the original B-CLL lymphocytes and the malignant cells of the pleomorphic lymphoma.[249] However, instances in which the lymphocytes of the CLL and the cells of the pleomorphic lymphoma had dissimilar membrane light chain markers have also been described.[260]

Detection of trisomy 12 in a subpopulation of the neoplastic cells in cases of Richter transformation in which the pre-transformation specimens did not contain the cytogenetic finding has been suggested as evidence that the cytogenetic abnormality has a high frequency in Richter transformation but does not play a direct role in the event.[251]

Cases of non-Hodgkin's lymphoma, including Burkitt's lymphoma, occurring in patients with CLL in which genotypic studies show the same light chain rearrangement in the lymphoma cells as in the lymphocytes of the CLL, have been observed[256,261] (Fig. 23.60).

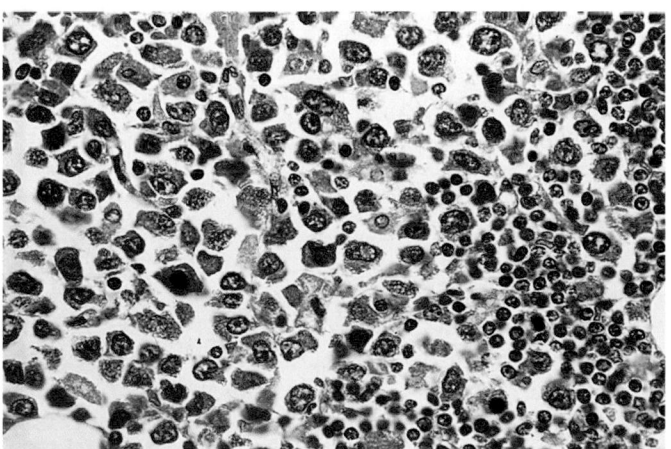

Fig. 23.59 Bone marrow trephine biopsy from a patient with a history of CLL who developed a pleomorphic lymphoma (B-immunoblastic lymphoma) and a clinical picture typical of Richter's syndrome. Biopsy contains two distinct cell populations, small lymphocytes, and large pleomorphic cells, some of which are multinucleated.

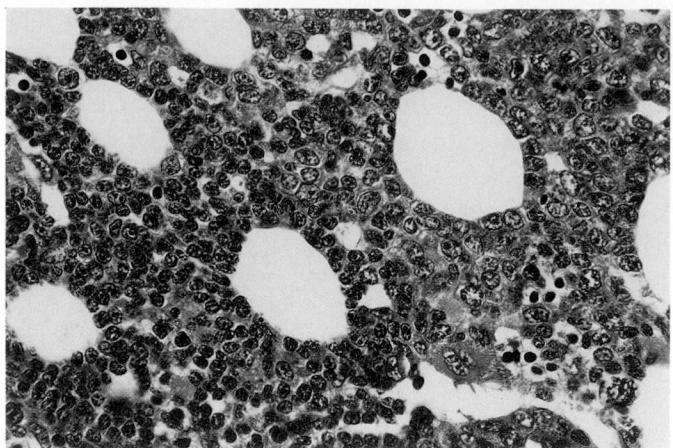

Fig. 23.60 Marrow biopsy from an adult male with a 9-year history of B-CLL. The patient had recent onset of fever, night sweats, myalgia, and axillary, cervical, and inguinal adenopathy prior to this biopsy. A population of small lymphocytes is at lower left. Burkitt's lymphoma cells predominate at upper right. Blood and marrow smears contained two lymphocyte populations: small well-differentiated lymphocytes and Burkitt's lymphoma cells. Cytogenetic studies of the marrow specimen showed t(8;22) (q24;q11) cytogenetic abnormality.

The occurrence of a diffuse histiocytic lymphoma in patients with a prior history of CLL who do not manifest the typical findings of Richter's syndrome has been reported.[247] In addition, true histiocytic proliferations with no apparent relationship to the B-lymphocyte system may rarely occur in patients with CLL.[263] The clinical course in these patients is very similar to that observed in Richter's syndrome.

Prolymphocytic leukemia

Prolymphocytic leukemia (PL), initially described by Galton et al.,[265] is a very rare disease that occurs primarily in older individuals and is characterized by a predominant proliferation of immature lymphocytes referred to as prolymphocytes. The disorder is distinct from chronic lymphocytic leukemia and prolymphocytoid transformation of CLL. Approximately 80% of the initially reported cases of this type of leukemia were of B-cell origin, the remainder of T-cell type.[266] The exact ratio of B- to T-cell prolymphocytic leukemia is difficult to determine because of the low frequency of both disorders. The lymphocyte count in PL of either B or T type is usually moderately to markedly increased; the number of prolymphocytes in the blood usually exceeds 55% of lymphocytes and may be more than 90%. The patients with B-cell PL usually have massive splenomegaly without prominent peripheral lymphadenopathy.[267,268] The prolymphocytes in B-PL are more uniform in appearance than the prolymphocytoid cells in prolymphocytoid transformation of B-CLL. In B-PL the prolymphocytes are medium to large in size, with a moderate amount of basophilic cytoplasm. There is usually a single promi-

nent nucleolus. The marrow infiltration is usually diffusely interstitial. Mitotic activity is reported as low, although cases with increased mitotic activity have been observed.[264,269] B-prolymphocytic leukemia is usually marked by an aggressive clinical course; occasionally patients have a prolonged survival. The leukemic phase of blastic variant of mantle cell lymphoma may be characterized by large lymphocytes with prominent nucleoli; it can be distinguished from prolymphocytic leukemia by cytogenetic and molecular studies for t(11;14)(q13;q32).

T-PL has a somewhat variable presentation and the leukocyte count may be only modestly elevated with a predominance of lymphocytes.[266] The lymphocytes may not have an unusually prominent nucleolus. Marrow infiltration may be modest with very substantial sparing of normal myeloid cells.

A very uncommon variant of B-CLL intermediate between typical B-CLL and B-PL and referred to as chronic lymphocytic leukemia/prolymphocytic leukemia has been described; it is distinguished by the presence of 11% to 55% prolymphocytoid lymphocytes in the blood.[267,268] Typical B-CLL has less than 11% prolymphocytes in the blood; B-PL is distinguished by more than 55% prolymphocytes. The degree of splenomegaly in patients with chronic lymphocytic leukemia/prolymphocytic leukemia is disproportionate to the degree of lymphadenopathy. Two major clinical patterns are described in this variant: one is characterized by a course similar to typical CLL and the other by a more rapidly progressive clinical evolution. The distinction of B-CLL/PL from prolymphocytoid transformation of B-CLL may be very difficult. Leukemic mantle cell lymphoma may resemble CLL/PL and it is important to exclude the possibility of leukemic mantle cell lymphoma when the findings suggest CLL/PL.

Hairy cell leukemia

Hairy cell leukemia is a chronic lymphoproliferative disorder of B-cell origin that is manifest primarily in blood, marrow, and spleen. There is a male predominance.[271,277,278,291,294] The age range is 20 to 80 years with a median of approximately 50 years. The patients generally have cytopenias or pancytopenia and splenomegaly without prominent peripheral lymphadenopathy; there is usually an associated monocytopenia. The majority of patients present with leukopenia and only occasional leukemic cells in the blood. Some 5% to 10% of patients have white blood cell counts exceeding 10×10^9/L; the hairy cells usually comprise the majority of the blood leukocytes in these patients.

The typical hairy cell measures 10 to 14 μm. The clear to lightly basophilic cytoplasm is variable in amount. The surface of the cell is marked by numerous delicate and broad projections; this finding is particularly striking in specimens examined by phase and electron microscopy.[283,296] Vacuoles and occasionally delicate azurophilic granules may be identified in the cytoplasm. The nucleus is oval, folded, or indented; the chromatin is coarsely reticular, and nucleoli are inconspicuous.

Aspiration biopsy of the marrow in patients with hairy cell leukemia is unsuccessful in 30% to 50% of cases because of increased reticulin fibrosis.[278,291] The pattern of marrow infiltration in trephine sections is virtually diagnostic in most patients.[272,273,275,293,298,299] The marrow in the majority of patients is hypercellular; in 10% to 15% of patients the involved marrow is hypocellular.[286] The involvement may be diffuse or partial; the diffuse type is more common (Fig. 23.61). Leukemic infiltrates in partial involvement are irregular in outline and poorly demarcated from the normal marrow cells. In the very early stages of the disease, partial involvement may take the form of relatively small, indistinctly outlined foci of leukemic cells. In formalin-fixed tissue, there is fre-quently a halo-like effect or clear area around the nucleus because of the abundant cytoplasm. The cell borders have an interlocking appearance. With some fixatives, such as Zenker's, the cytoplasm of the hairy cells is retracted with a resultant loosely structured appearance. The loosely structured appearance and widely spaced nuclei in hairy cell leukemia contrast with the marrow infiltrates in the lymphocytic lymphomas and CLL in which the nuclei of the cells are in close apposition. The nuclear chromatin of the hairy cells is relatively fine. Nucleoli are distinct but not usually prominent and mitotic figures are infrequent. In an occasional case, the hairy cells have a spindled or fusiform appearance and may resemble the marrow lesions in systemic mastocytosis (Fig. 23.62). A morphologic variant with hyperlobated nuclei resembling T-cell lymphoma has been described.[280] Marrow uninvolved by the leukemic process may be hypocellular or hypercellular. Morphologic subtypes of hairy cell leukemia based

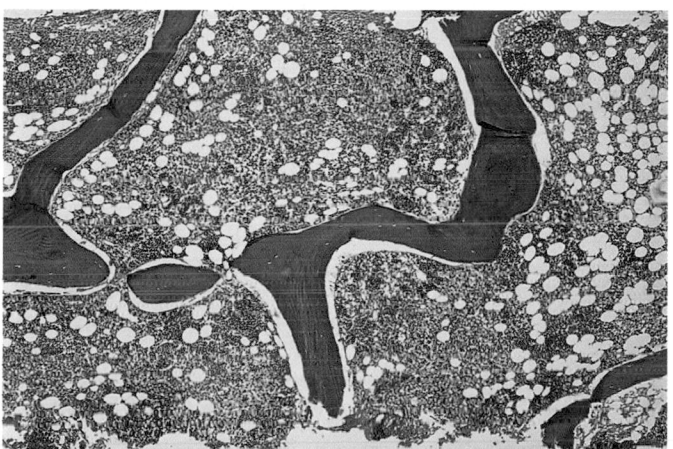
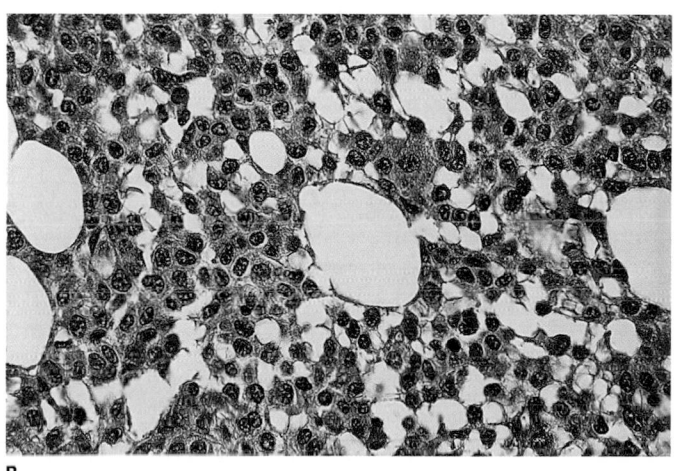

A   **B**

Fig. 23.61 A, Bone marrow section from a patient with extensive replacement by hairy cell leukemia; scattered foci of normal hematopoiesis are present. **B**, High magnification of specimen in **A**. Hairy cells are loosely spaced, in contrast to aggregates of lymphocytes in chronic lymphocytic leukemia and small lymphocyte lymphoma. Hairy cells have a relatively abundant lightly eosinophilic cytoplasm. Many of their nuclei are folded or irregular in outline. Nucleoli are inconspicuous and mitotic figures rare. The halo effect around nuclei, characteristic of formalin-fixed tissue, is not prominent in this specimen fixed with Zenker's.

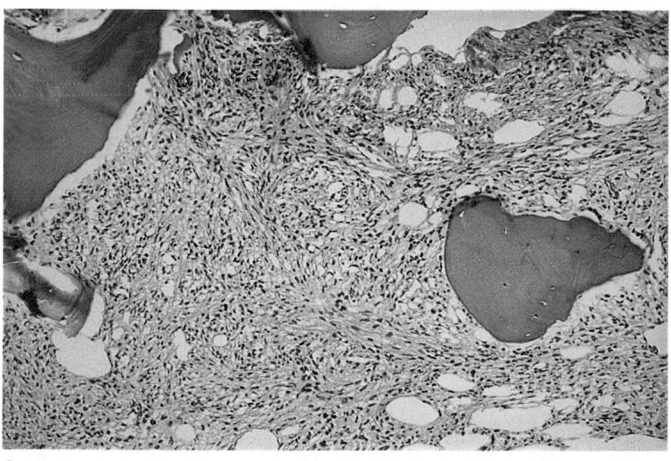
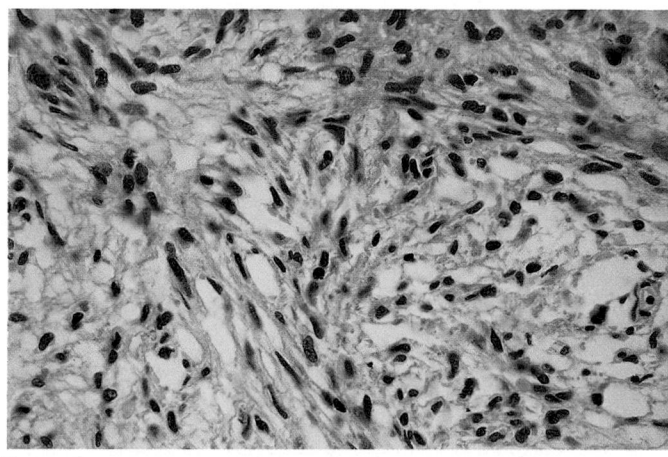

A   **B**

Fig. 23.62 A, Marrow biopsy from a patient with the stromal variant of hairy cell leukemia. **B**, High magnification of the biopsy in **A**. Many leukemia cells are elongated or spindle shaped.

on histopathology have been reported to have prognostic significance.[270] Normal-appearing mast cells may be increased.

Reticulin stain shows increased deposition of thickened reticulin fibers in the areas of the infiltrates; the reticulin fibers often appear to encircle individual cells. The reticulin fibers frequently extend into the adjacent normal-appearing marrow.

Hairy cells express light chain-restricted cytoplasmic and surface immunoglobulin and pan-B-cell antibodies, including CD19, CD20, CD22, DBA44, CD79a and PAX-5 but not CD79b[277,295]; CD20 (L26) and DBA44 are of considerable aid in evaluating the extent of the leukemic infiltrate and in assessing the effects of chemotherapy in paraffin-embedded biopsy sections[279] (Fig. 23.63). In addition, they express CD11c, which is also expressed on myeloid cells, CD25, interleukin-2 receptor, CD103 and HC2. They are negative for CD5, a T-cell antigen, and CD23, which are expressed on the lymphocytes in the majority of cases of B-cell chronic lymphocytic leukemia. In contrast to cases of B-CLL, follicular lymphoma and marginal zone lymphoma, hairy cells either do not express or only weakly express nuclear P27 kip, a cyclin-dependent kinase inhibitor, a characteristic also of mantle cell lymphoma.[284] Hairy cells also contain tartrate-resistant acid phosphatase (TRAP), which is a useful diagnostic feature of the disease.[282]

Rarely, hairy cell leukemia may focally involve the skeleton as a painful localized destructive lesion. This usually occurs in a patient with an established diagnosis; more rarely, hairy cell leukemia may present as a localized skeletal lesion as the initial and only manifestation of the disease.[276,281,285,287] These lesions occur principally in the upper portion of the femurs. Although the majority of these localized lesions are osteolytic, osteoblastic lesions may also occur. The localized lesions appear to respond to the purine analogs 2-deoxycoformycin and 2-deoxyadenosine and to radiation.

Treatment of hairy cell leukemia with the nucleoside analogs deoxycoformycin and 2-chlorodeoxyadenosine results in durable complete or partial remissions in the majority of cases.[292,294,297] The bone marrow biopsies from these patients generally show a return to normal marrow hematopoiesis. As noted, the recognition of residual leukemia is facilitated by the use of pan-B-cell monoclonal antibodies reactive in paraffin-embedded biopsies; anti-CD20 and DBA44 are particularly good antibodies for this purpose.[279] Treatment with the interferons frequently results in characteristic marrow changes with some evidence of residual leukemia.[290] Approximately 0.25% of cases of hairy cell leukemia develop abdominal lymphadenopathy as demonstrated by computed tomographic studies. The incidence is higher in patients who relapse after previously successful therapy or have long-standing disease. The development of abdominal adenopathy may be associated with resistant disease and with the appearance of large hairy cells in both the bone marrow and the enlarged lymph node. This constellation of clinical and morphologic findings has been interpreted as a type of transformation.[289]

Hairy cell leukemia variant

Hairy cell leukemia variant is a lymphoproliferative disorder usually presenting with a marked leukocytosis and lymphocytes with morphologic characteristics intermediate between hairy cells and prolymphocytes[271,274,288] (Fig. 23.64). The cells are large with basophilic cytoplasm with stellate projections and relatively prominent nucleoli. The disease is very rare and occurs primarily in older individuals. In contrast to

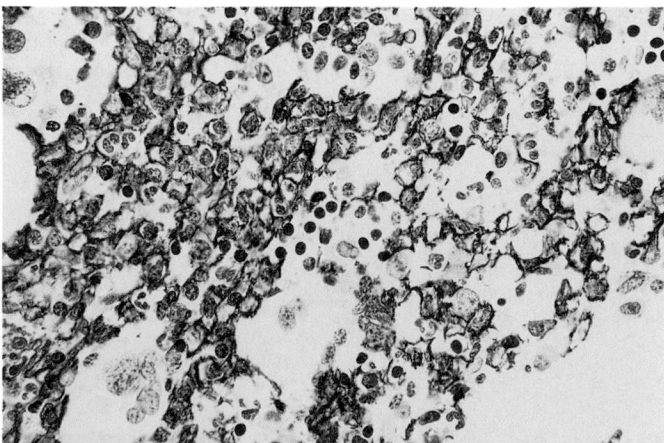

Fig. 23.63 Bone marrow biopsy from a patient with hairy cell leukemia reacted with antibody to CD20 (L26). Reactivity accentuates the leukemic infiltrate. Scattered normal myeloid cells, principally erythroid precursors, are present. (Immunoperoxidase.)

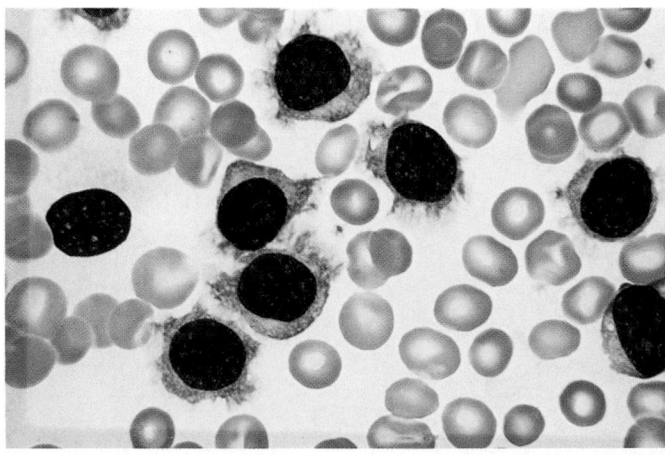

Fig. 23.64 Hairy cell leukemia variant. Several lymphoid cells in the blood smear of an adult male with markedly elevated leukocyte count. The hairy cell variant lymphocytes are large with a moderate amount of basophilic cytoplasm with stellate projections. The nuclei of several cells contain variably prominent nucleoli. (Wright–Giemsa.)

typical hairy cell leukemia, there is no associated neutropenia and monocytopenia. The cells may be TRAP positive. The cells usually express CD11c but are negative for CD25; they express CD103 in 60% of cases.[288] The marrow shows a diffuse interstitial pattern of infiltration similar to typical hairy cell leukemia. The pattern of splenic infiltration is similar to hairy cell leukemia, with a predominantly red pulp involvement. Hairy cell leukemia variant, unlike typical hairy cell leukemia, does not respond to the adenosine deaminase inhibitors 2-chorodeoxyadenosine and deoxycoformycin and has a shorter survival than typical hairy cell leukemia. Unlike typical hairy cell leukemia, the patients may not respond to treatment with interferons or nucleoside analogs.

Splenic lymphoma with villous lymphocytes

Splenic lymphoma with villous lymphocytes (SLVL) is a proliferation of small B lymphocytes with clinical and hematologic features that may resemble hairy cell leukemia.[300,305,308,309] The disease is more common in males; the mean age at presentation is 72 years. There is a slight to moderate lymphocytosis; the leukocyte count is less than $25 \times 10^9/L$ in the majority of patients. Anemia and thrombocytopenia are present in approximately 50% of cases. Most patients have marked splenomegaly and SLVL is generally viewed as a form of splenic marginal zone B-cell lymphoma.[300]

The lymphocytes in the blood have short villous projections that may have a polar distribution. Villi may not be present on all of the lymphoma cells and there may be considerable variation in the appearance of the cells. Some have a distinct but not prominent nucleolus (Fig. 23.65A). Plasmacytoid lymphocytes may be present.

The lymphocytes express moderate to intense surface immunoglobulin and pan-B-lymphocyte markers including CD19, CD22, and CD24.[307] In approximately half of the cases the lymphocytes express CD11c. The cells express CD5 and CD25 in 19% and 25% of cases, respectively. The cells may be TRAP positive. Approximately 50% to 60% of cases have a low IgM monoclonal gammopathy.[309] Chromosome 7q 21–32 deletion is found in approximately 40% of cases; trisomy 3 is present in 17% of cases.[305]

Virtually all patients with SLVL have some degree of marrow involvement. The degree and pattern of marrow involvement vary substantially; the pattern may be focal nonparatrabecular, focal paratrabecular, interstitial, diffuse or intrasinusoidal; there may be a predominance of one pattern in an individual case but mixed patterns are common[301,302,304,306] (Fig. 23.65B,C). The lymphoma cells may be predominantly small lymphocytes or an admixture of small lymphocytes and scattered large lymphocytes with relatively abundant cytoplasm, slightly dispersed chromatin, and variably prominent nucleoli. Mitotic figures are usually sparse. Some degree of plasma cell proliferation may be present. Occasionally,

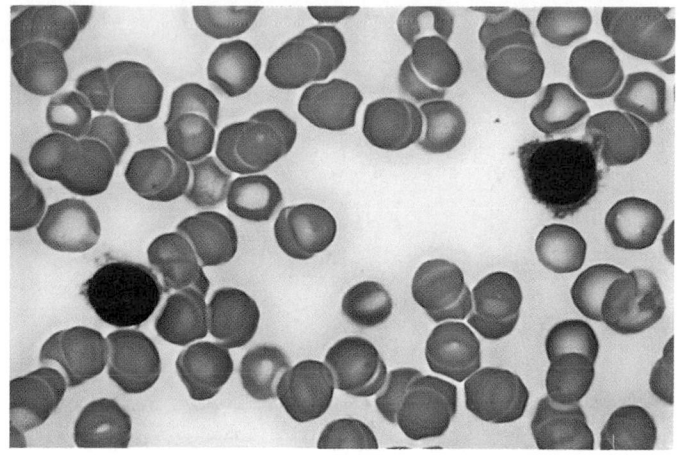

A

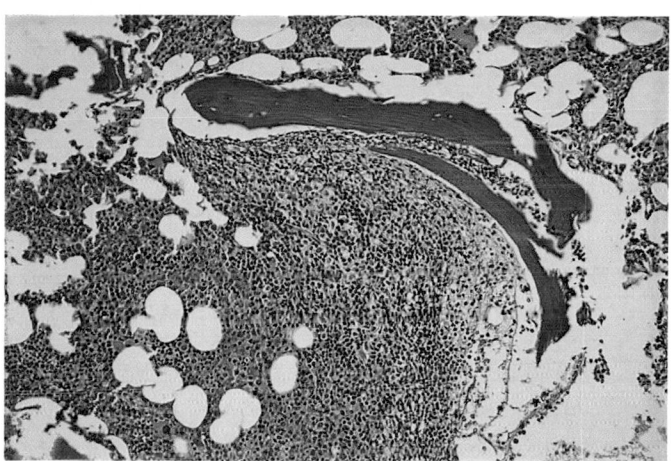

B

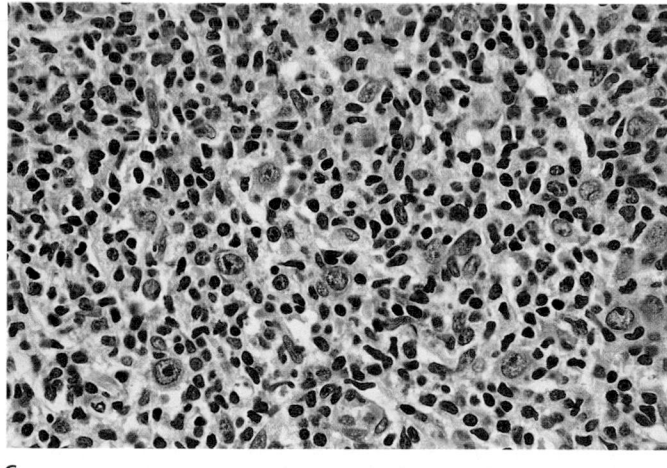

C

Fig. 23.65 A, Lymphocytes in blood smear from an adult male with splenic lymphoma with villous lymphocytes (SLVL). The cytoplasm of two of the lymphocytes has small villous projections. Nuclear chromatin is coarse. There are distinct but not prominent nucleoli. **B,** Bone marrow biopsy from a patient with SLVL showing a paratrabecular, poorly demarcated aggregate of lymphocytes. **C,** High magnification of a lesion from a patient with SLVL showing a predominant population of small lymphocytes with scattered large cells with abundant cytoplasm and prominent nucleoli. (**A,** Wright–Giemsa.)

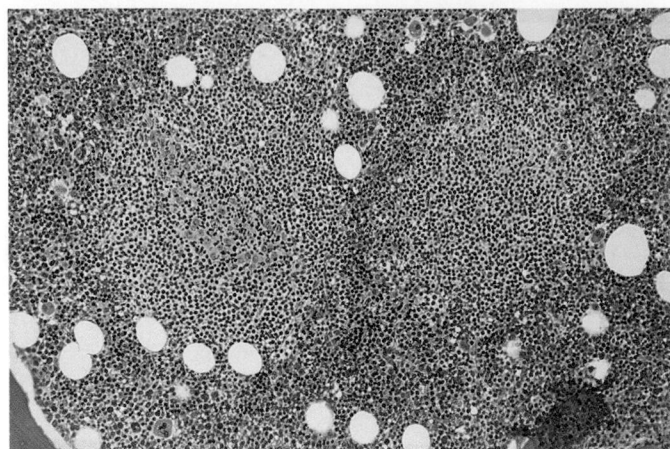

Fig. 23.66 Bone marrow biopsy from a patient with SLVL illustrating two well-circumscribed foci of lymphocytes. The lesion on the left contains a central area suggesting remnants of a germinal center with several centroblast-like cells.

foci of lymphoma with remnants of germinal centers may be found (Fig. 23.66).

The spleen shows primarily white pulp involvement with some involvement of the red pulp.[304]

Patients with splenic lymphoma with villous lymphocytes generally have a prolonged clinical course. Splenectomy is frequently beneficial in patients with severe anemia, neutropenia, and thrombocytopenia. Fludarabine therapy has been associated with remission.

A small number of patients with SLVL and concurrent hepatitis C infection have undergone remission of the lymphoma following treatment of the hepatitis C with interferon-α2b and disappearance of hepatitis C RNA; patients with SLVL not infected with hepatitis C did not respond to the same therapy.[303]

Non-Hodgkin's lymphoma

B-cell lymphoma

The incidence of marrow involvement in non-Hodgkin's lymphoma at the time of initial diagnosis varies with the different histopathologic subtypes; the incidence in aggregate for all types ranges from 40% to 55% in most of the larger studies of adults.[318] The incidence is higher in the low-grade lymphomas than in many of the high-grade lymphomas. Approximately 60% to 70% of the cases of follicular center cell lymphoma have marrow involvement at the time of initial diagnosis in contrast to 33% for T-immunoblastic lymphoma and 25% for B-immunoblastic lymphoma. Splenic marginal zone B-cell lymphoma is reported to have a very high incidence of involvement, approximately 80% to 90%; a similarly high incidence of involvement has been observed in mantle cell lymphoma.[314,315,340,341,348] Marrow involvement in MALT lymphoma was reported in approximately 20% of

cases in one study.[344] The incidence of marrow involvement in peripheral T-cell or node-based T-cell lymphoma varies from 30% to 70% in different series.[326,327,330] Blood involvement may occur with all types of lymphoma.[310,314,323,334,335,343]

The extent of lymphomatous infiltration varies considerably; it is less than 30% in more than half of cases with involvement.[323] In general, the small lymphocytic and follicular center cell lymphomas are characterized by substantial sparing of normal bone marrow.

The pattern of marrow involvement may be diffuse, focal paratrabecular, focal nonparatrabecular, interstitial, intrasinusoidal, and rarely intravascular (Figs 23.67 to 23.74); uncommonly, marrow lesions of follicular lymphoma are characterized by recapitulation of the neoplastic follicle as found in the lymph node[311,316,321,323,324,337,339,345] (Figs 23.70, 23.71). The diffuse and focal nonparatrabecular patterns may occur with all types of lymphoma of both B- and T-cell type. The focal paratrabecular pattern occurs principally but not

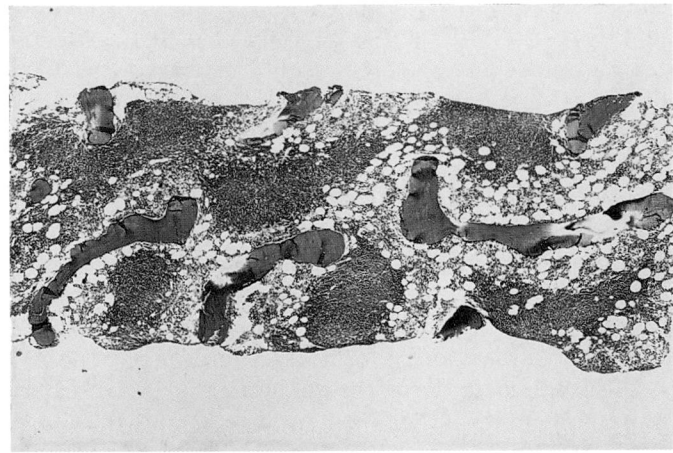

Fig. 23.67 Several focal aggregates of lymphocytes in marrow in a patient with small lymphocytic lymphoma. Foci of lymphocytes vary in size and have irregular, poorly circumscribed outlines.

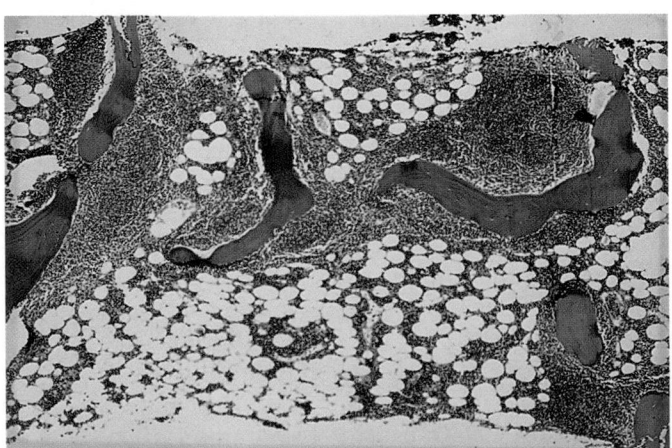

Fig. 23.68 Bone marrow section from a patient with follicular center cell lymphoma illustrating the prominent paratrabecular distribution of the infiltrate.

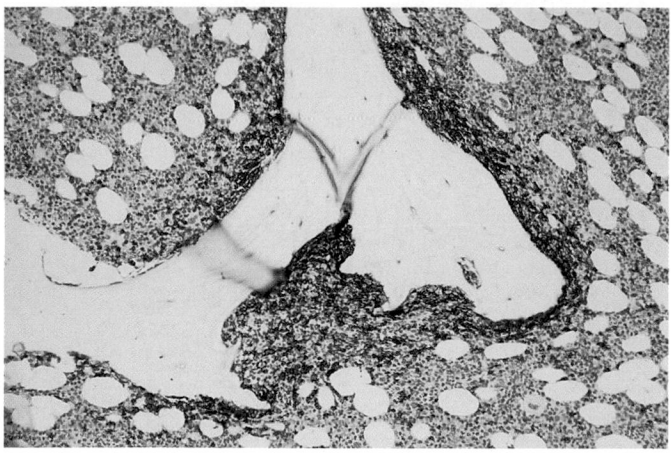

Fig. 23.69 Marrow from a patient with marrow involvement by follicular center cell lymphoma with prominent paratrabecular involvement reacted with antibody to CD20(L26). The infiltrate is accentuated by CD20 antibody. (Immunoperoxidase.)

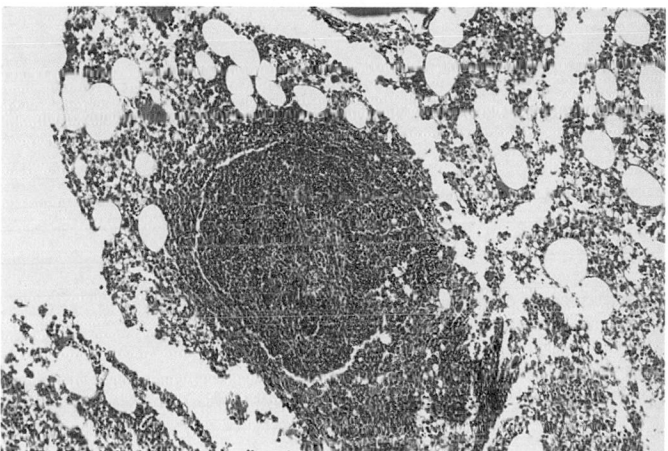

Fig. 23.70 Marrow biopsy from a patient with follicular center cell lymphoma with focal paratrabecular and nonparatrabecular involvement. A few of the nonparatrabecular foci, as illustrated, recapitulate neoplastic follicles. Amorphous eosinophilic proteinaceous debris is deposited in the central portion of the lesion.

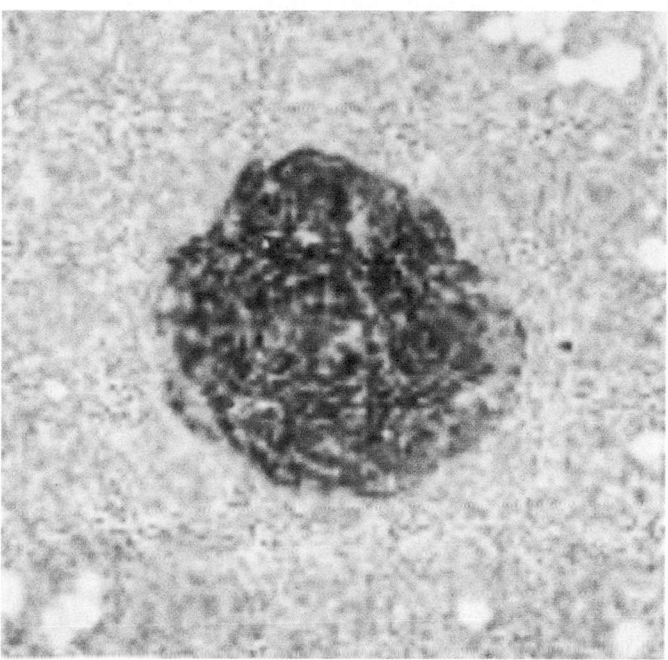

Fig. 23.71 Neoplastic follicle in marrow reacted with antibodies to CD21 and bcl-2. The dendritic cells express CD21 and the lymphocytes express CD20. (Immunoperoxidase.) (Reproduced from Am J Clin Pathol ©2002 American Society for Clinical Pathology. Reprinted with permission.)

exclusively in the follicular center cell lymphomas; follicular lymphomas may also involve the marrow in a focal nonparatrabecular pattern. The marrow biopsies from patients with mantle cell lymphoma and splenic marginal zone B-cell lymphoma may also show both focal paratrabecular and nonparatrabecular lesions.[346] The infiltrate in an occasional case of mantle cell lymphoma and splenic marginal zone B-cell lymphoma may contain remnants of benign germinal centers (Fig. 23.72B).[349] Splenic marginal zone B-cell lymphoma and hepatosplenic gamma/delta T-cell lymphoma may occur principally in an intrasinusoidal pattern[329] (Fig. 23.74).

The interstitial pattern of involvement, in which the lymphoma cells infiltrate the interstitium of the marrow with preservation of the overall marrow architecture with some sparing of normal hematopoiesis, may occur with all types of non-Hodgkin's lymphoma. The bone marrow in this type of involvement may be deceptively normal in appearance at low magnification and emphasizes the importance of examination of marrow biopsies at high magnification when evaluating for lymphoma involvement (Fig. 23.73). This pattern of infiltration may be present at the time of initial diagnosis or in patients who have received chemotherapy. Interstitial involvement in the more aggressive lymphomas may be accompanied by considerable depletion of normal hematopoietic cells.

The intrasinusoidal pattern of involvement may be particularly difficult to identify in routinely stained sections even in well-prepared specimens. The use of immunohistochemistry has been particularly important in recognizing this type of lesion, which appears to occur most frequently with splenic marginal zone B-cell lymphoma and gamma/delta T-cell lymphoma, in which it may be the predominant pattern of involvement (Fig. 23.74). It may be observed in other types of lymphoma, usually combined with other patterns.[329]

The follicular pattern of follicular lymphoma as observed in lymph nodes is uncommonly recapitulated in the marrow lesions (Fig. 23.70). Occasionally foci of transformation in B-CLL may mimic follicle formation (see Fig. 23.58). As noted, benign germinal centers may be found in occasional cases of mantle cell lymphoma and splenic marginal zone B-cell lymphoma[349] (Fig. 23.72). In some marrow lesions of follicular lymphoma,

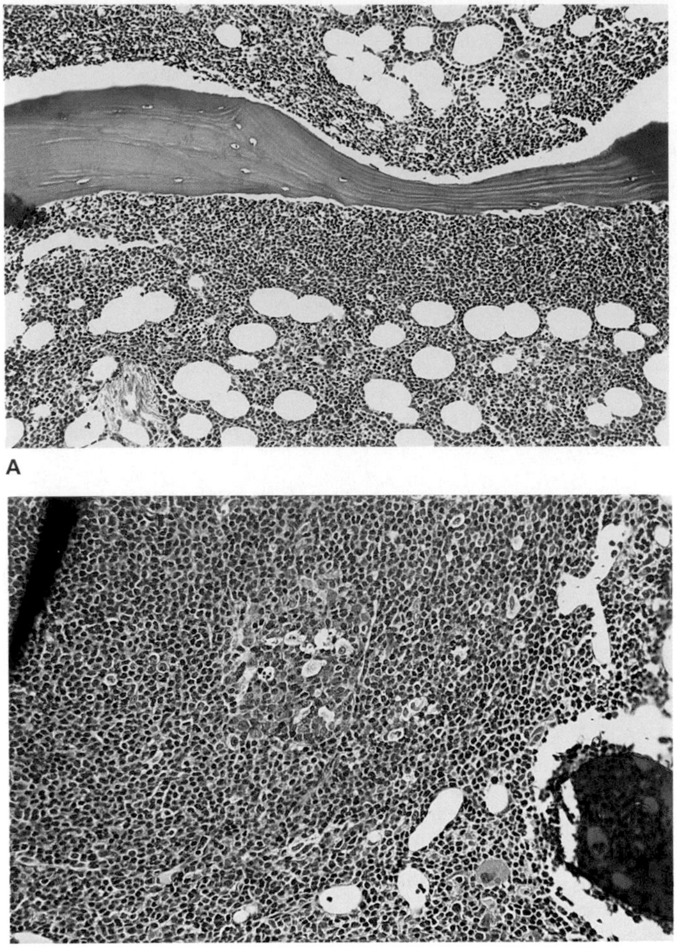

Fig. 23.72 A, Bone marrow biopsy from an adult male with extensive blood and marrow involvement by mantle cell lymphoma. Lymphoma cells expressed pan-B-cell markers, CD5, and intense surface immunoglobulin. In some areas, lymphoma marginates along the bone trabecula. **B,** Focus of marrow involvement from the same biopsy showing structure with remnants of germinal center including dendritic histiocytes.

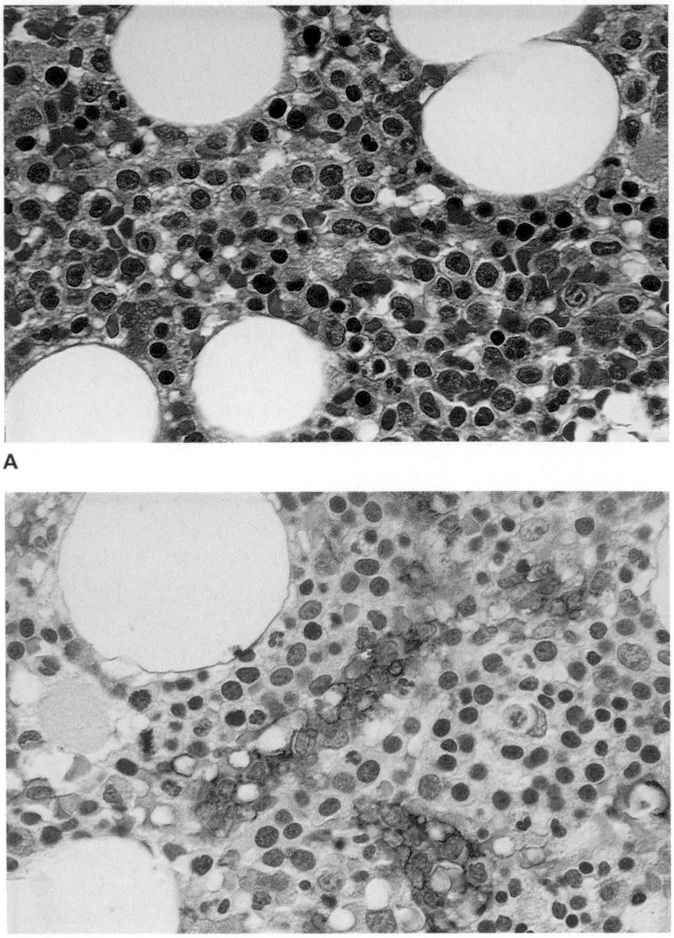

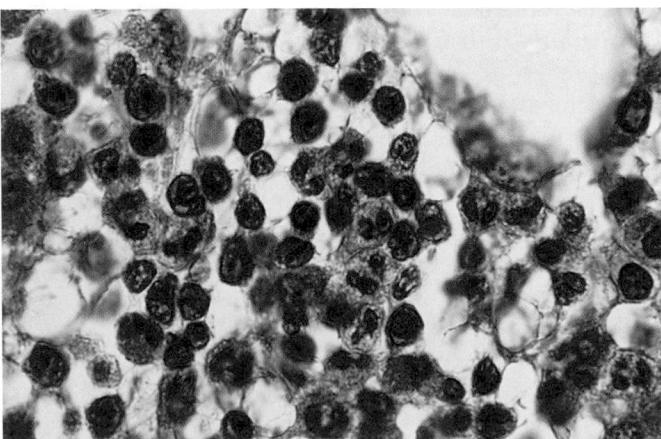

Fig. 23.73 High magnification of a marrow biopsy from a patient being treated for follicular center cell lymphoma. There is an infiltration of the interstitium by a population of small lymphocytes, several of which have irregular and cleaved nuclei.

Fig. 23.74 A, Bone marrow biopsy from a patient with splenic marginal zone B-cell lymphoma showing a preferential intrasinusoidal localization of the lymphoma cells. **B,** The same specimen as **A** reacted with antibody to CD20(L26) illustrating the preferential intrasinusoidal location of lymphoma cells. (**B,** Immunoperoxidase.)

the margins of the lymphomatous focus may be composed of transforming cells, imparting a somewhat reverse germinal center character to the lesion. In addition, the paratrabecular lesions may show a zoning phenomenon with a less differentiated population of cells immediately adjacent to the endosteal surface.

The cytopathology of the lesions in the marrow sections usually parallels the cytologic characteristics in the lymph node; this is particularly true for the T-cell lymphomas and Burkitt's lymphoma.[312,319] In approximately 20% to 25% of lymphomas, predominantly follicular, there may be discordance between the predominant cell type in the lymph node and the predominant cell type in the marrow.[315,322,324,342] In these cases, the marrow lesions usually consist of small cleaved cells, and the lymph node findings are a mixed or large cell type; the converse occurs but is less frequent. Those patients with diffuse large cell in the lymph node and small cleaved cells in the bone marrow usually have a high rate of complete remission and a high rate of 5-year survival compared to patients with large cells in the lymph node and bone marrow who have a low rate of complete remission with low 5-year survival.[342] In either instance, the cytologic characteristics in both sites are usually those of follicular center cell lymphoma. Molecular studies of microdissected lesions in 21 cases of discordant lymphoma have shown the same clone in the lymph node and marrow lesions in 44% of the specimens.[333] In 2 cases different clones were identified and in 4 cases the marrow lesions were polyclonal. These studies emphasize the importance of critical evaluation of lesions in post-therapy marrow; it cannot be assumed that all lymphocytic infiltrates are residual lymphomas. This caveat is particularly important in those instances where there is discordant morphology following antibody therapy.

Immunohistochemistry with an appropriate panel of antibodies has an important role in the evaluation of marrow biopsies in patients with lymphoma. It has utility in defining the cell type, extent of involvement, and detection of residual disease following therapy.[320,332]

In post-chemotherapy specimens, paratrabecular lesions may have a loosely structured hypocellular appearance.[338] It is important to evaluate these lesions with immunohistochemistry to determine if the lymphocytes are of the same lineage as in the pretreatment specimen.

Similar to the findings in lymph nodes, lymphomas of predominantly small lymphocytes in the marrow, B-cell chronic lymphocytic leukemia or B small lymphocytic lymphoma, may show foci of transformation. In occasional cases of follicular cell lymphoma, transformed cells resembling Reed–Sternberg cells or Reed–Sternberg mononuclear variants may be present[336] (Fig. 23.75).

There is no relationship between a diffuse or follicular pattern in the lymph node and the presence of focal or diffuse lesions in the marrow. Cases in which the lymph node has a diffuse pattern of involvement such as small lymphocytic lymphoma or chronic lymphocytic leukemia may manifest as focal lesions in the marrow. Cases with a follicular pattern in the lymph node may manifest as diffuse marrow involvement. Only rarely is the follicular pattern recapitulated in the marrow.[345]

Unusual variants of non-Hodgkin's lymphoma involving marrow may lead to diagnostic problems because of the unusual morphology of the lymphoma cells or because of an accompanying proliferation of reactive cells. In anaplastic large cell lymphoma, the lymphoma cells may by virtue of size and nuclear irregularity mimic megakaryocytes. The problem is accentuated when the foci of lymphoma are small and indistinctly demarcated from the surrounding normal marrow tissue or when the lymphoma cells are intermingled with normal marrow cells. In cases of the small cell variant of anaplastic large cell lymphoma, the marrow infiltration may be scattered in the interstitium and difficult to recognize amongst the normal myeloid cells.[330] Appropriate antibody studies including CD30, CD45, platelet factor VIII and CD61 are important in clarifying the origin of the abnormal cells.[325,330] The lymphoma cells in histiocyte-rich B-cell lymphoma and T-cell-rich B-cell lymphoma may be partially obscured by the nonmalignant cell proliferation.[317] In T-cell-rich B-cell lymphoma, antibody studies may accentuate the problem because of the large number of lymphocytes reacting with antibodies to T cells; demonstration of light chain restriction by flow cytometry or genotype studies for immunoglobulin gene arrangement may be necessary to establish clonal B-cell lineage. In histiocyte-rich B-cell lymphoma, reactions with antibodies to B lymphocytes such as CD20 and histiocytes (CD68) are useful in delineating the two cell populations (Fig. 23.76). The blastic variant of mantle cell lymphoma may resemble acute lymphoblastic leukemia. Reactions for TdT and cyclin D1 will help to distinguish those two processes.[347]

Post-transplant lymphoma of B-cell type does not commonly involve the marrow; when it does, the degree of infiltrate varies considerably.[328,331] Immunohistochemical reactions for B-cell origin and EBER studies may be very helpful in establishing the diagnosis (Fig. 23.77).

Granulomas may be found in all types of lymphomas in the marrow, with and without marrow involvement.[313]

T-cell lymphomas/leukemias

Peripheral T-cell lymphoma, unspecified

Peripheral T-cell lymphoma (PTCL) has such unusual features in bone marrow biopsies as to warrant separate consideration.[350,352,353] This type of lymphoma is characterized by a high incidence of marrow involvement at the time of initial diagnosis, up to 60% to 70% in some

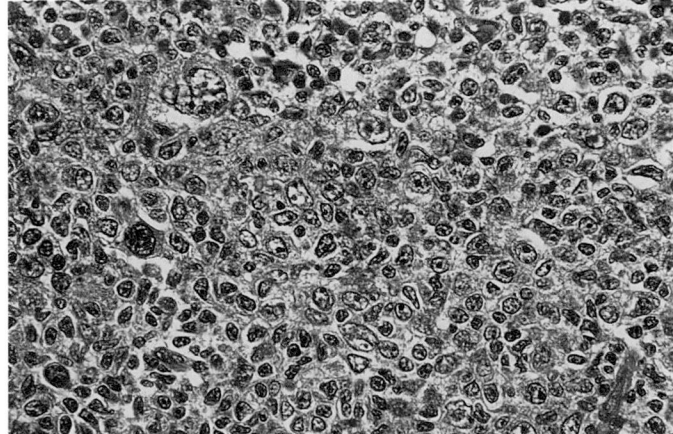

Fig. 23.75 Bone marrow section from a patient with a 6-year history of follicular center cell lymphoma. Cells resembling Reed–Sternberg cells and mononuclear variants are present.

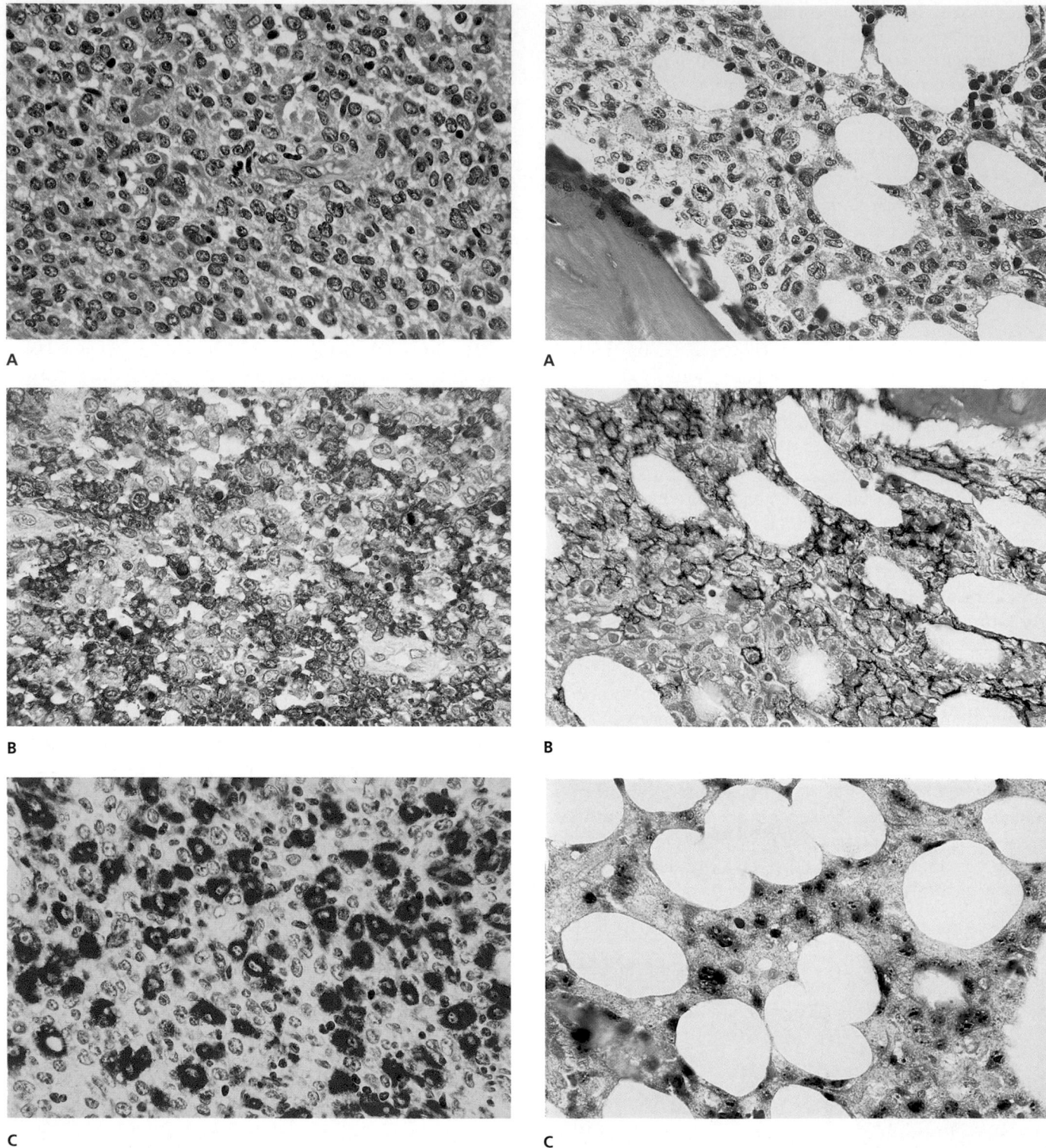

Fig. 23.76 A, Marrow from a patient with histiocyte-rich B-cell lymphoma. Histiocytes predominate in this area. **B**, The specimen in **A** reacted with antibody to CD20. The numerous lymphocytes are reactive, contrasting with the negative histiocytes. **C**, The marrow biopsy in **A** reacted with antibody to CD68 (KP-1). The numerous positively reacting histiocytes in this area contrast with the negatively reacting lymphoma cells. (**B** and **C**, Immunoperoxidase.)

Fig. 23.77 Post-transplant B-cell lymphoma. **A**,The lymphoma cells extensively infiltrate the marrow interstitium in this area; some residual myelopoiesis is present. **B**, The same specimen as **A** reacted with antibody to CD20; large lymphoma cells are positive. **C**, Numerous lymphoma cells are EBER positive. (**B**, Immunoperoxidase; **C**, EBER.)

studies. The marrow lesions are diffuse in approximately 60% of involved cases and focal in 40%.[352] The focal lesions are usually randomly distributed in contrast to the preferential paratrabecular involvement in follicular center cell lymphomas; occasional cases present with a focal nonparatrabecular and paratrabecular pattern. The infiltrates vary substantially in size and are usually irregular in configuration with poorly demarcated margins; in many instances the lesions appear to extend almost imperceptibly into adjacent normal marrow (Fig. 23.78). The diffuse lesions are characterized by complete intertrabecular replacement of marrow; in some instances the entire biopsy specimen is replaced (Fig. 23.79). Increased reticulin fibers are present in the area of lymphomatous involvement and frequently extend into the adjacent normal-appearing marrow.

The predominant cytologic pattern in the marrow lesions usually corresponds to the pattern in lymph node or other tissue biopsies and can generally be categorized into one of three primary histopathologic types: small lymphocytic, mixed cell, and large cell/immunoblastic. The mixed cell type is the most frequently encountered. In some instances there is a relatively distinct demarcation between large and small cells. Large lymphoid cells with abundant amphophilic cytoplasm and prominent eosinophilic nucleoli, resembling Reed–Sternberg cells and mononuclear Reed–Sternberg variants, may be present. The small- and medium-sized lymphocytes have nuclei with condensed chromatin which vary from regular to irregular in outline. The mixed cell and large cell/immunoblastic types usually have an associated polycellular infiltrate consisting of histiocytes, plasma cells, eosinophils, and neutrophils. Epithelioid histiocytes are frequently noted either in focal clusters or scattered throughout the lesions. The focal collections frequently have a granulomatous appearance. Increased vascularity may be a prominent feature; the vascular component is primarily an endothelial cell proliferation with straight-lined channels. Immunohistochemical reactions are useful in identifying the lymphoma cells.

The differential diagnosis of PTCL in marrow includes Hodgkin's disease, systemic mastocytosis, and polymorphous reactive lymphoid hyperplasia.[350,352] The most difficult problem relates to the last lesion, which may be present in marrow specimens from patients with a wide variety of immunologic disorders, including AIDS. Polymorphous reactive lymphoid hyperplasia has many histopathologic features similar to PTCL, including a heterogeneous population of lymphocytes with intermixed plasma cells, immunoblasts, eosinophils, endothelial cells, and epithelioid histiocytes. Distinction between the focal lesions of PTCL and the polymorphous reactive lymphoid lesions may not be possible solely on morphologic features. Markedly atypical cells with prominent nucleoli are more compatible with lymphoma. The size of

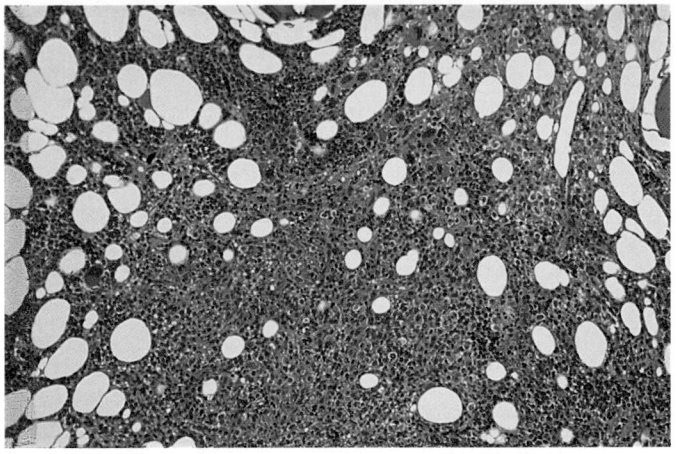

A

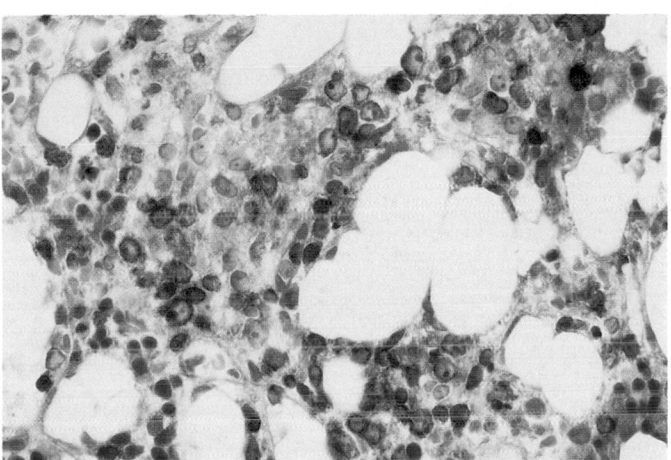

B

Fig. 23.78 **A,** Marrow section from a patient with partial involvement by peripheral T-cell lymphoma. The lymphoma population is poorly demarcated and infiltrates the interstitium with some preservation of normal architecture. **B,** Margin of the lesion in **A** reacted with antibody to CD3. Numerous large lymphocytes, some with prominent nucleoli, are positive. (**B,** Immunoperoxidase.)

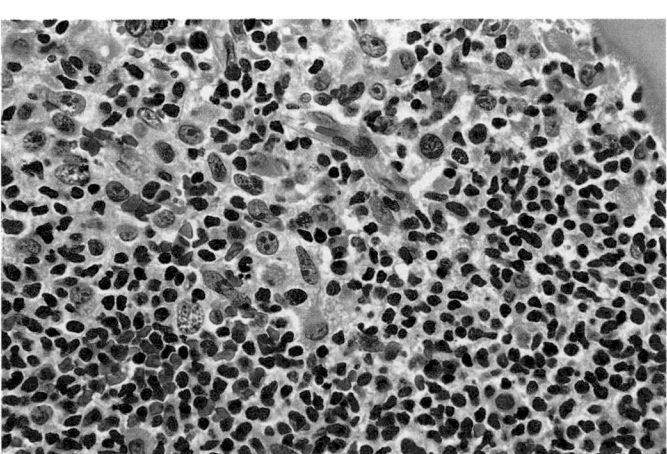

Fig. 23.79 Marrow biopsy from a patient with PTCL, showing extensive diffuse marrow involvement. The predominant cell population consists of small lymphocytes with a focus of large lymphocytes that have prominent nucleoli.

the lesions is not always a reliable distinguishing feature; reactive lesions may show extensive marrow replacement, particularly in patients with AIDS. The lesions of PTCL may be relatively small.

Hodgkin's disease in the marrow may appear similar to the lesions of PTCL. The presence of classic Reed–Sternberg cells and the lack of atypia in the lymphocyte population is evidence of Hodgkin's disease. Multinucleated immunoblasts resembling Reed–Sternberg cells may be present in PTCL; in these instances, review of lymph nodes and other tissue biopsies and immunologic studies are critical in distinguishing PTCL from Hodgkin's disease.

The lesions of systemic mastocytosis may be distinguished from PTCL by the reactivity of mast cells with antibody to mast cell tryptase.

Genotypic studies to determine T-cell clonality are an important advance in distinguishing PTCL in marrow biopsies or other tissues from the disorders considered in the differential diagnosis. Clonal rearrangement of one of the T-cell receptors is substantial evidence of a malignant process. The determination of clonality may be made on fresh aspirate or trephine biopsy specimens and fixed, paraffin-embedded tissue.[351]

Adult T-cell leukemia/lymphoma
Adult T-cell leukemia/lymphoma is an unusual form of post-thymic lymphoma occurring primarily in Japan; it is associated with the human retrovirus HTLV-1.[354,356] The highest incidence of this disease is in the Kyushu region of Japan; other endemic areas include the Caribbean basin and parts of western Africa. Sporadic cases are observed in other areas of the world. Blood and marrow involvement occurs in a substantial number of patients. Hypercalcemia is present in 28% of patients at diagnosis and in 50% of patients at some time during the course of the disease. The vast majority of patients with hypercalcemia show marrow involvement by lymphoma and evidence of increased osteoclastic activity and bone resorption.[355] However, increased osteoclastic activity may be present in the absence of marrow involvement by the lymphoma (Fig. 23.80).

Sézary syndrome
Sézary syndrome is a lymphoproliferative disorder of T-helper lymphocytes related to mycosis fungoides and characterized by erythroderma and abnormal lymphoid cells in the blood.[357,359–362] The leukocyte count may be normal or markedly elevated with a high percentage of Sézary cells. The Sézary cells, as observed in Romanowsky-stained blood smears, have distinctive features. The nucleus frequently has an unusual configuration that has been characterized as cerebriform (Fig. 23.81A). Cytoplasmic vacuoles, which stain positively with the PAS reaction, may be present in a perinuclear location. Large and small cell variants have been described.[357] Ultrastructurally, the cells show marked

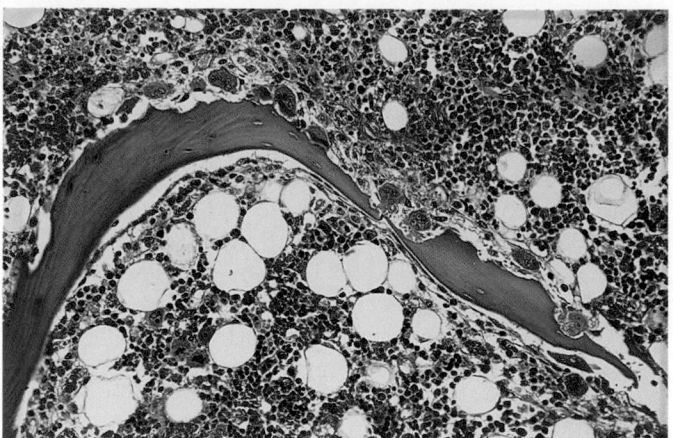

Fig. 23.80 Marrow biopsy from a patient with adult T-cell leukemia and hypercalcemia. Marked osteoclastic activity with bone resorption is present.

nuclear convolutions[358,362] (Fig. 23.81B). The bone marrow sections in the majority of patients appear normal; scattered Sézary cells may randomly infiltrate the interstitium. Marked marrow infiltration with replacement of normal hematopoietic cells is very uncommon. Rarely, small aggregates of Sézary cells may be observed.[357]

Large granulated T-cell lymphocytic leukemia
Large granulated T-cell lymphocytic leukemia is an uncommon form of T-cell leukemia which usually presents with a modest lymphocytosis and frequently severe neutropenia. Approximately 50% of patients have splenomegaly but lymphadenopathy is uncommon. Rheumatoid factor and hypergammaglobulinemia are present in a subset of patients. The lymphocytes in the blood are medium to large with relatively abundant cytoplasm which contains coarse azurophilic granules. The lymphocytes characteristically express CD3 and CD8 and are CD4 negative; CD11b, CD56, and CD57 are variably present. Similar lymphocytes may be present in reactive processes and the defining factor for a diagnosis of leukemia is T-cell receptor rearrangement, usually TCR β; occasional patients have rearrangement of TCR γ.

The marrow involvement, which is usually interstitial, may be very difficult to recognize in routine sections; reactivity with antibody to CD8 is particularly useful in identifying the infiltrates[363] (Fig. 23.82). Occasional aggregates of lymphocytes may be present and they usually contain an admixture of T and B cells. The splenic infiltration is principally in the red pulp.

Angioimmunoblastic T-cell lymphoma
The reported incidence of marrow involvement in this lesion, originally described as angioimmunoblastic lymphadenopathy, is 50% to 70%.[364,365,367] The blood may show several abnormalities including reactive lymphocytes, immunoblasts and eosinophilia.[368,369]

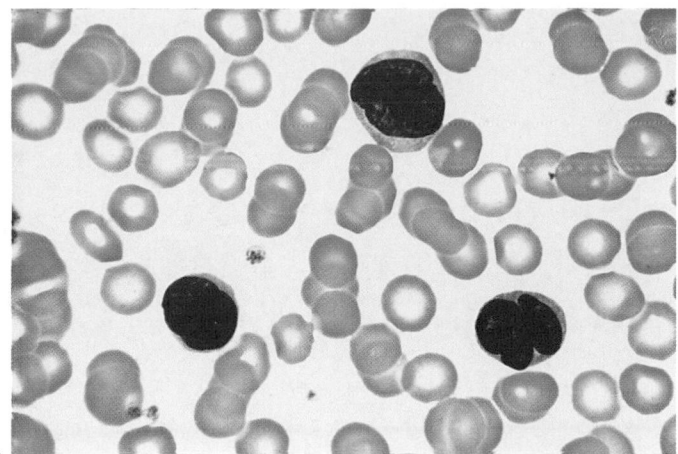

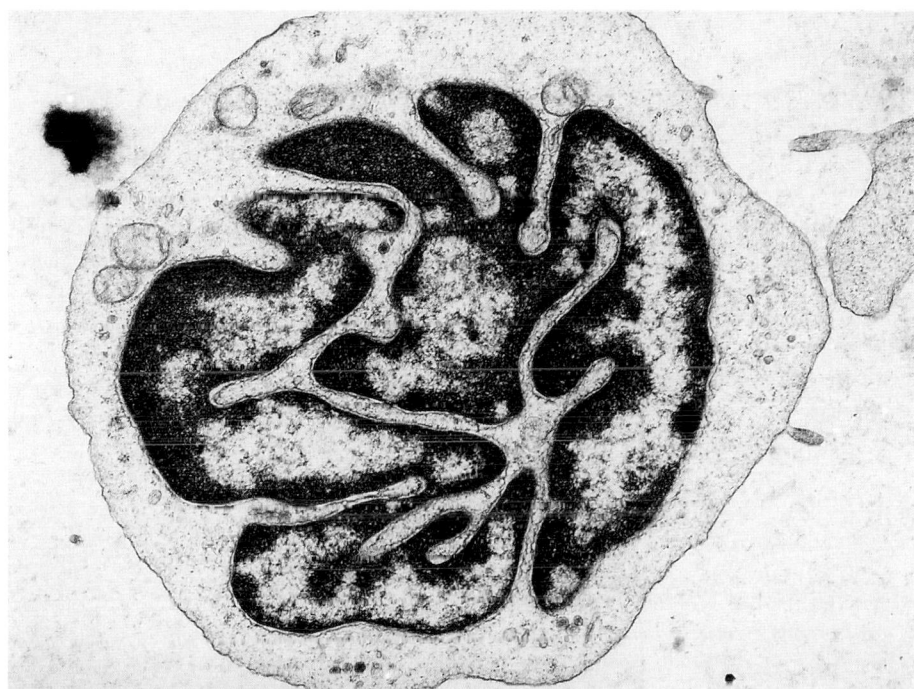

Fig. 23.81 A, Three Sézary cells in blood smear. The nucleus in the larger cell in the upper field has delicate folds imparting a "cerebriform" appearance. The two smaller cells in the lower field have a more condensed chromatin and markedly lobulated nuclei. **B**, Ultrastructure of a Sézary cell; extreme convolution of the nucleus is a characteristic feature (**B**, Uranyl acetate–lead citrate; ×22,000.)

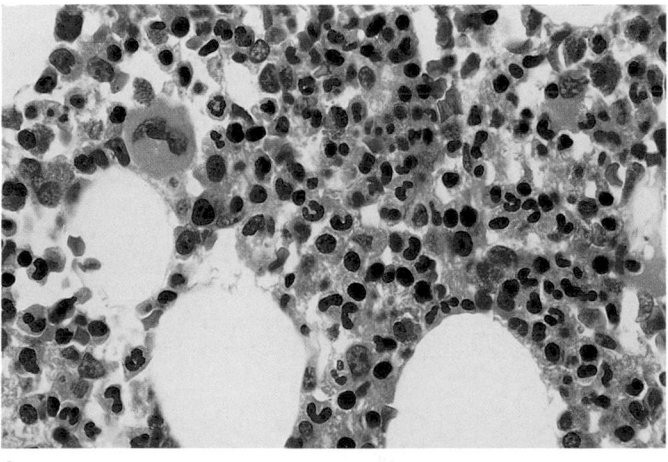

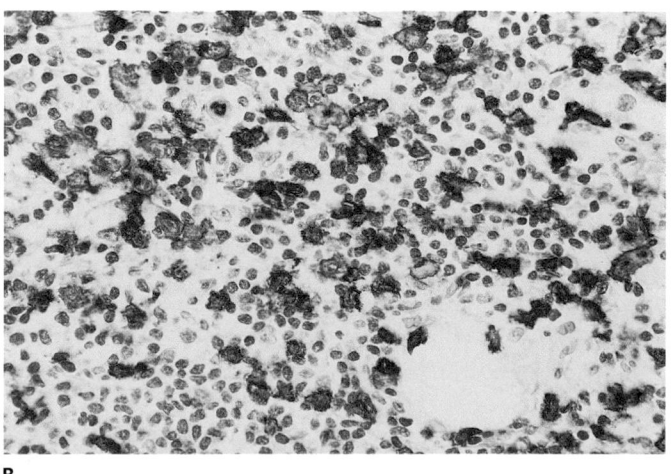

Fig. 23.82 A, Bone marrow biopsy from an adult female with large granulated T-cell lymphocytic leukemia. The leukemic lymphocytes are interspersed in the interstitium. **B**, Specimen in **A** reacted with antibody to CD8. There are numerous CD8 positive cells in the interstitium. (**B**, Immunoperoxidase.)

The bone marrow lesions may be diffuse or focal; focal involvement is more common.[366] The margins of the focal lesions are usually somewhat indistinct, with poor demarcation from the surrounding hematopoietic tissue. In some cases, confluent multifocal lesions replace extensive areas of normal marrow. The lesions of angioimmunoblastic T-cell lymphoma are somewhat loosely structured and contain varying proportions of lymphocytes, immunoblasts, plasma cells, and histiocytes; neutrophils and eosinophils are also present (Fig. 23.83). Vascular proliferation, endothelial cells, and fibroblasts are frequently identified. Stains for reticulin show a marked increase in reticulin fibers in the involved areas. Collections of epithelioid histiocytes, imparting a granulomatoid appearance to some of the lesions, are reported. The amorphous PAS-positive material found in lymph node biopsies is less frequently encountered in bone marrow lesions. Immunocytochemical reactions with antibodies to kappa and lambda light chains show a polyclonal proliferation of immunoblasts and plasma cells. The uninvolved marrow is frequently hypercellular. The hypercellularity may be a result of pan- hyperplasia or principally erythroid hyperplasia. The bone marrow and blood smears may contain varying numbers of immunocytes at varying stages of development, including immunoblasts and mature plasma cells. Reactive lymphocytes and eosinophilia may be observed.

The significance of marrow involvement in regard to clinical outcome is unclear. Some, but not all, studies have indicated that patients with marrow involvement have a shorter survival than patients without marrow involvement.[364,369]

Hepatosplenic T-cell lymphoma, post-transplant T-cell lymphoma, and aggressive NK-cell lymphoma

Several uncommon types of T-cell lymphomas and NK-cell lymphomas have been reported in which the marrow is commonly involved. They include hepatosplenic T-cell lymphoma, post-transplant T-cell lymphoma, and aggressive NK-cell lymphoma. These are of relatively rare occurrence and it is difficult to generalize about patterns of involvement.

Hepatosplenic T-cell lymphoma may be marked by an intrasinusoidal pattern but may also show subtle interstitial involvement without the characteristic intrasinusoidal pattern[373–375,377,379] (Fig. 23.84). The lymphoma cells may have blastic features. Immuno-histochemistry is very important in identifying the extent of disease. Cytogenetic studies usually show isochromosome 7, which is frequently associated with trisomy 8 and other abnormalities.[370,372,376]

Post-transplant T-cell lymphoma may be characterized by focal or extensive interstitial involvement (Fig. 23.85). The use of immunohistochemistry may be extraordinarily important in identifying the presence, extent and nature of these lesions since they may be overlooked

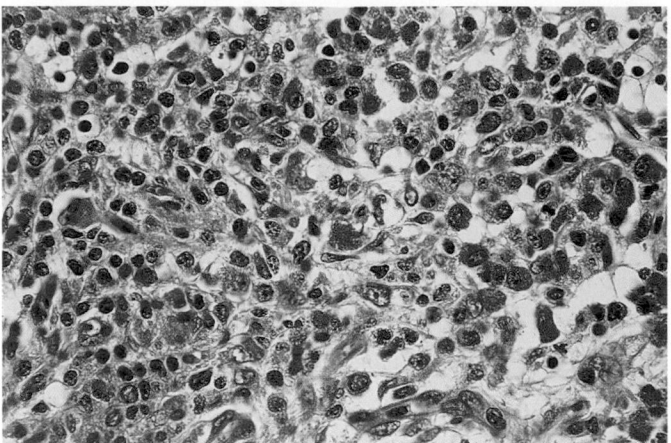

Fig. 23.83 Bone marrow biopsy from a patient with lymph node diagnosis of angioimmunoblastic T-cell lymphoma. Marrow is diffusely involved by the process with a heterogeneous cell population.

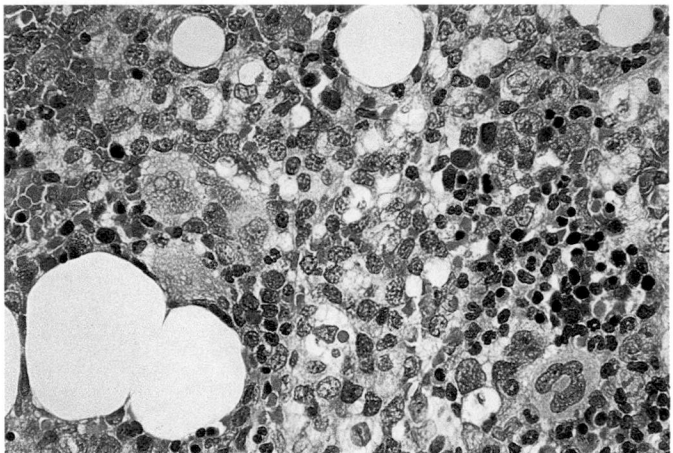

A

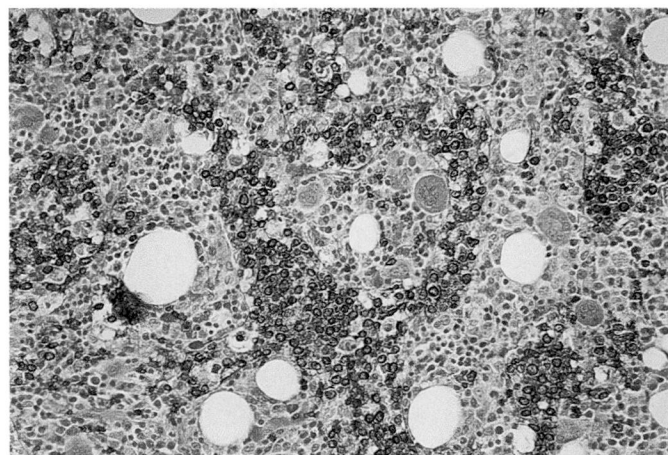

B

Fig. 23.84 **A**, Hypercellular marrow with involvement by hepatosplenic gamma delta T-cell lymphoma. The lymphoma cells expand the sinusoids. **B**, Specimen in **A** reacted with antibody to CD3, which highlights the intrasinusoidal localization of the lymphoma cells. (**B**, Immunoperoxidase.) (Slides contributed by Dr. Elaine Jaffe, Bethesda, USA.)

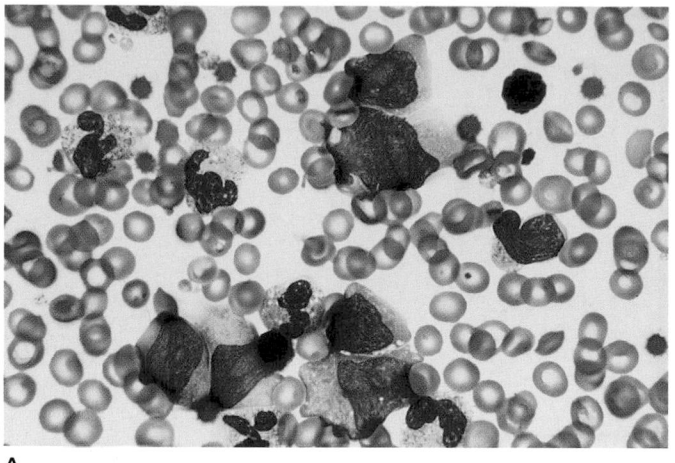
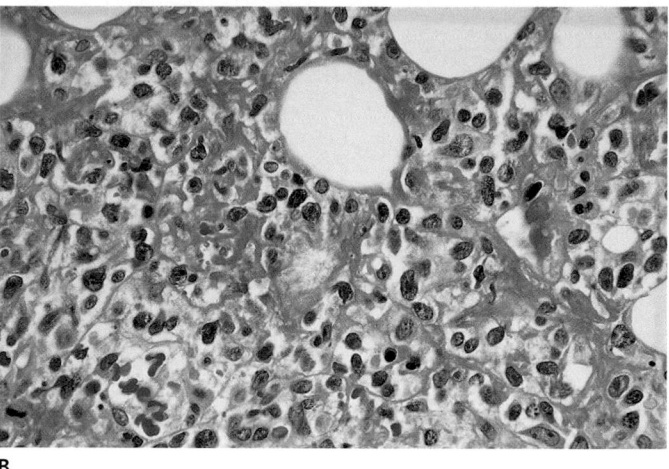

A   B

Fig. 23.85 Post-transplant T-cell lymphoma. **A,** Bone marrow smear from a 40-year-old female, 28 and 8 years following renal transplantation. The lymphoma cells, which expressed CD2 and CD3, are large with abundant cytoplasm and very prominent nucleoli. **B,** High magnification of marrow section showing extensive interstitial involvement by noncohesive lymphoma cells. There is substantial depletion of normal hematopoiesis with cellular debris.

in suboptimally prepared specimens. Examination of cytologic preparations, immunophenotyping, cytogenetics, and molecular studies may be important in classifying these lymphomas.

Aggressive NK-cell leukemia is a rare type of leukemia/lymphoma; it occurs most frequently in Asian teenagers and young adults.[371,372,378] This disorder may represent the leukemic counterpart of extranodal NK/T-cell lymphoma, nasal type.[372] Bone marrow involvement in the nasal type of NK-cell lymphoma at diagnosis is uncommon.[380] The blood, marrow, liver and spleen are commonly involved. The leukemia/lymphoma cells are large with ample and pale to slightly basophilic cytoplasm, which may contain fine or coarse azurophilic granules (Fig. 23.86A). The bone marrow infiltrates in biopsy sections may be diffuse, focal, or minimally inter-

stitial. The leukemic cells appear monotonous with regularly shaped nuclei, coarse chromatin, and small nucleoli (Fig. 23.86B). The disease generally follows an aggressive clinical course as the name implies.

Anaplastic large cell lymphoma

The majority of cases of anaplastic large cell lymphoma are of T-cell type. The marrow may show massive involvement or the cells may be almost imperceptibly scattered among the normal hematopoietic cells. The interstitium in the cases with marrow involvement may be very loosely structured with cell depletion (see Fig. 23.87). The cases with lymphoma cells scattered among the normal hematopoietic cells may be overlooked in routinely stained sections. In one series of 42 cases, 17% showed evidence of marrow involvement on routine

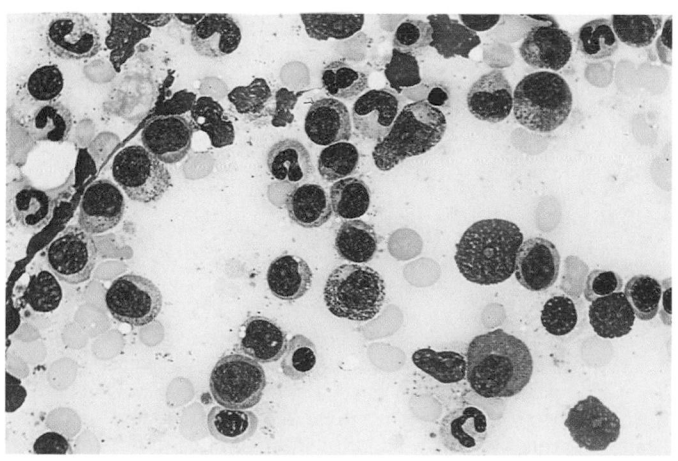
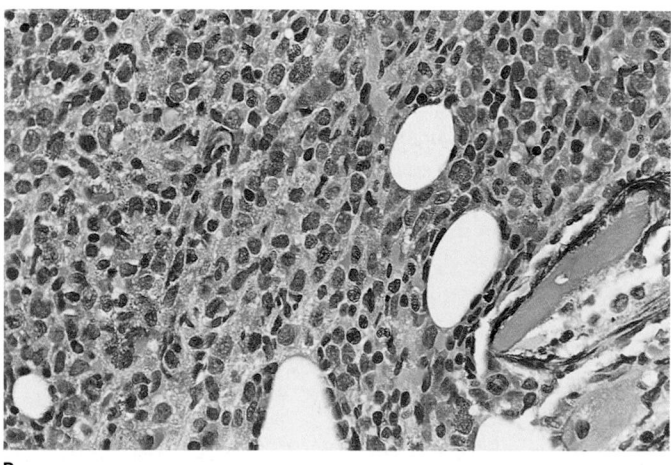

A   B

Fig. 23.86 Aggressive NK-cell leukemia. **A,** Bone marrow smear from a patient with aggressive NK-cell leukemia. The lymphoma cells have relatively abundant cytoplasm containing numerous coarse azurophilic granules; the lymphoma cells are distinguished from neutrophil myelocytes by the lack of specific granules. **B,** Marrow biopsy from the patient in **A** showing extensive replacement. The lymphoma cells are relatively uniform in appearance with round nuclei and abundant cytoplasm. (Slides contributed by Dr. John K.C. Chan, Hong Kong.)

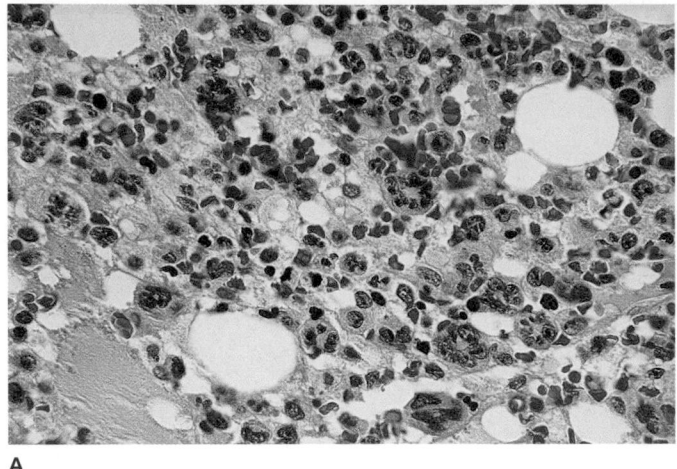

A

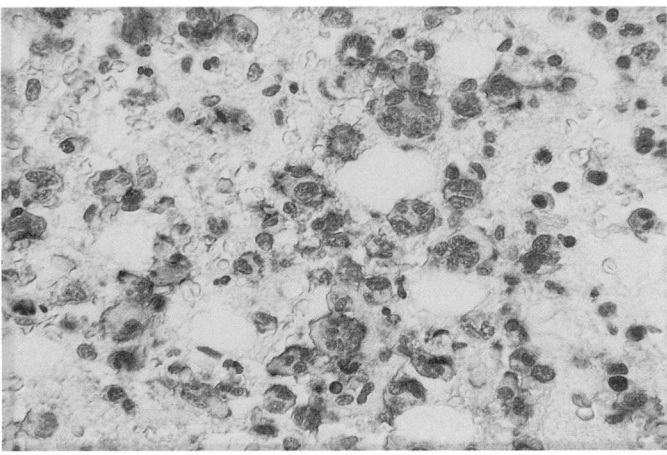

B

Fig. 23.87 A, Area of marrow biopsy from a patient with anaplastic large cell lymphoma, T-cell type. The lymphoma cells are intermixed with normal marrow cells. **B,** Specimen in **A** reacted with antibody to CD30. The lymphoma cells are positive. (**B,** Immunoperoxidase.)

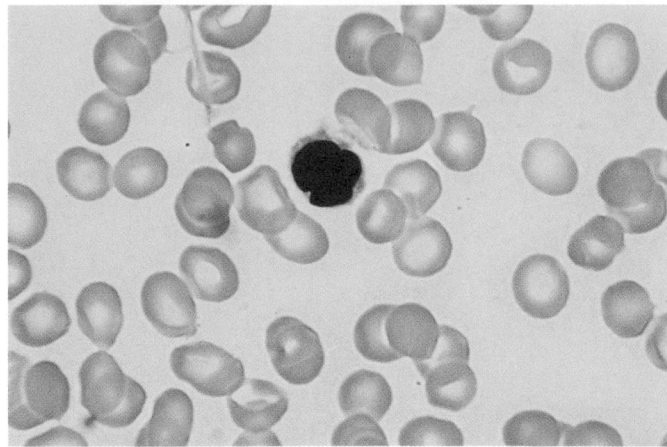

A

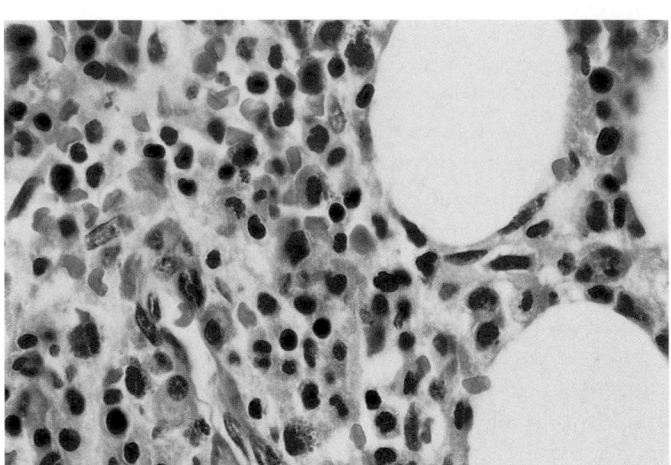

B

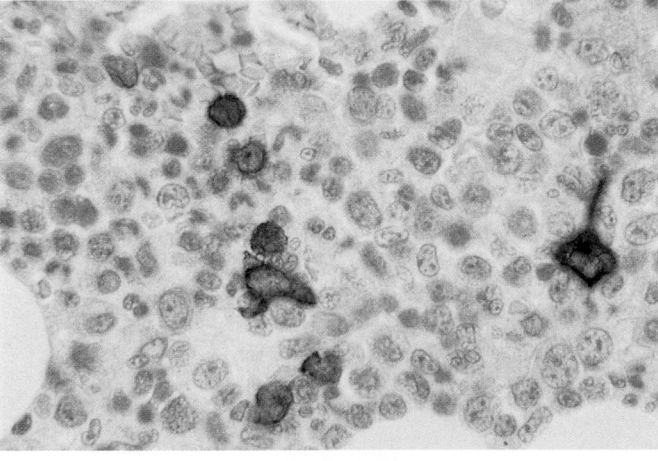

C

Fig. 23.88 A, Lymphoma cell in blood smear from a 17-year-old male with small cell variant of anaplastic large cell lymphoma with associated t(2;5)(p23;p35). The cell has a convoluted nucleus. **B,** Bone marrow section from the same patient. The few lymphoma cells are scattered in the interstitium and difficult to recognize in this H&E stain. **C,** The same specimen as **B** reacted with antibody to CD30, which highlights the small and large lymphoma cells. (**C,** Immunoperoxidase.)

sections. Following immunohistochemical staining with antibodies to CD30 and EMA, 23% of the previously classified negative biopsies were reclassified as positive[381] (Fig. 23.87B).

The small cell variant has a high incidence of marrow involvement when evaluated by routine morphology and immunohistochemistry[382] (Fig. 23.88). The degree of marrow involvement may be difficult to appreciate in routinely stained sections; similar to the large cell type, immunohistochemistry is important (Fig. 23.88B).

Lymphoma/leukemia

There are lymphomas involving marrow and frequently blood that may present terminology problems because of their close relationship to leukemic processes: these include small B-lymphocytic lymphoma, Burkitt's lymphoma, lymphoblastic lymphoma, and adult T-cell leukemia/lymphoma. The designation of these processes as leukemia or lymphoma may be arbitrary.

Small lymphocytic lymphoma represents a proliferation of well-differentiated lymphocytes and is considered to be the tissue counterpart of CLL.[395,400,403,404,407] It is characterized by a proliferation of small lymphocytes in lymph nodes and bone marrow without the requisite blood findings of CLL. The distinction from CLL is generally based on the number of lymphocytes in the blood: if there is an absolute monoclonal B-cell lymphocytosis of more than 5000/µl, the diagnosis of CLL is preferred; if the absolute B-lymphocyte count is less than 5000 µl, the term small lymphocyte lymphoma is used.[398] The immunophenotypic characteristics of the lymphocytes in B-cell CLL and B-cell small lymphocytic lymphoma (SLL) are the same and the pattern of marrow involvement is similar: diffuse, focal, interstitial, or a combination of these patterns.[398,400,403] In SLL the focal pattern is the most common, whereas in CLL the pattern is usually interstitial, mixed interstitial and focal, or diffuse. SLL may progress to blood involvement, but the magnitude of the leukocytosis does not usually reach the levels observed in CLL.

Burkitt's lymphoma presents with marrow involvement in 15% to 30% of patients.[383,388,391,393,402] In the WHO classification of hematopoietic tumors, the FAB designation of acute lymphoblastic leukemia L3 has been replaced by the term Burkitt lymphoma/leukemia, reflecting the fundamental identities of these two different manifestations of the same process.[385,392] Burkitt leukemia is frequently associated with Burkitt's lymphoma involving the ileocecal region of the small bowel with a t(8;14)(q24;q32) or variant chromosome translocation, (t(2;8)(q11;q24), t(8;22)(q24;q11) and is terminal deoxynucleotidyl transferase (TdT) negative.[383,391,392] The diagnostic terminology used in these cases should reflect the status of the marrow and blood. If tumor cells are present in the blood and the marrow is diffusely replaced, Burkitt leukemia is an appropriate designation. If few or no tumor cells are present in the blood and the marrow is partially involved with substantial sparing of normal hematopoiesis, a diagnosis of lymphoma is more appropriate. The therapeutic approach in these two situations is the same. Marrow involvement in Burkitt's lymphoma is usually characterized by diffuse infiltration of the interstitium with some preservation of adipose tissue although small focal lesions may occur. The "starry sky" appearance characteristic of lymph nodes in Burkitt's lymphoma is infrequently present in bone marrow biopsies. In contrast to the majority of cases of B-cell precursor ALL in which mitotic figures are sparse, there is prominent mitotic activity in Burkitt's lymphoma/leukemia.

Lymphoblastic lymphoma is of precursor T-cell origin in approximately 80% of cases and B-cell precursor type in 20%. Precursor T-cell acute lymphoblastic leukemia has a high incidence of mediastinal mass, occurs in young adults, more frequently in males, and has a predilection for early blood and marrow involvement[384,386,387,397] (see Fig. 23.31). Similar to the lymphoblasts in T-cell ALL, the lymphoma cells in T-lymphoblastic lymphoma are TdT positive. The blood and marrow may be involved at the time of initial diagnosis and the designation of a case as T-lymphoblastic lymphoma or T-cell ALL is arbitrary. The presence of extramedullary tumor masses and evidence of sparing of marrow function as indicated by a normal platelet count, hemoglobin levels greater than 10 g/dl, and a normal number of neutrophils in the blood are more compatible with a diagnosis of lymphoma with marrow involvement as opposed to ALL. The Children's Cancer Study Group proposed distinguishing leukemia from lymphoblastic lymphoma on the basis of the percentage of lymphoblasts in the marrow.[401] If there are less than 25% lymphoblasts the case is classified as lymphoma; if there are more than 25% lymphoblasts the case is classified as leukemia. In the cases of lymphoma, there may be substantial residual normal marrow with the lymphoma cells diffusely scattered in the interstitium. In other instances the marrow is completely replaced. In T-cell ALL, the marrow is diffusely replaced. In both lymphoblastic lymphoma and T-cell ALL, mitotic activity is usually prominent. The therapeutic approach in these two fundamentally similar processes is the same. B lymphoblastic lymphoma appears to have low propensity for blood and marrow involvement.[397,398a]

Other types of lymphoma with marrow involvement may present with blood involvement. Approximately 40% of the cases of follicular center cell lymphoma with lymphoma in the marrow have lymphoma cells in the blood.[399] In some instances, the count may be very high and resemble CLL. The distinction is based on the presence of lymphocytes with cleaved nuclei and the characteristic pattern of focal paratrabecular involvement in small cleaved cell lymphoma. Expression of CD5 and weak surface immunoglobulin on the lymphocytes supports a diagnosis of CLL; lack of CD5 and expression of CD10 and intense surface immunoglobulin are more compatible with small cleaved cell lymphoma.[394,398,407] The lymph node findings are definitive.

Mantle cell lymphoma may present with marked involvement of the marrow and blood; leukocyte counts of 270×10^9/L have been reported.[405,406] The blood findings may resemble CLL, CLL/PL, PLL and small cleaved cell lymphoma. The lymphoma cells may be quite pleomorphic with variation in size, nucleocytoplasmic ratio, degree of nuclear irregularity, and prominence of nucleoli (Fig. 23.89). The lymphocytes express pan-B-cell antigens, CD5, and strong surface immunoglobulin. The lymphocytes usually do not express CD23 or CD10. The bone marrow involvement may be diffuse or focal; the focal involvement may be paratrabecular or nonparatrabecular. Rarely, naked germinal centers may be observed in the marrow lesions. The lymphoma cells express bcl-1,

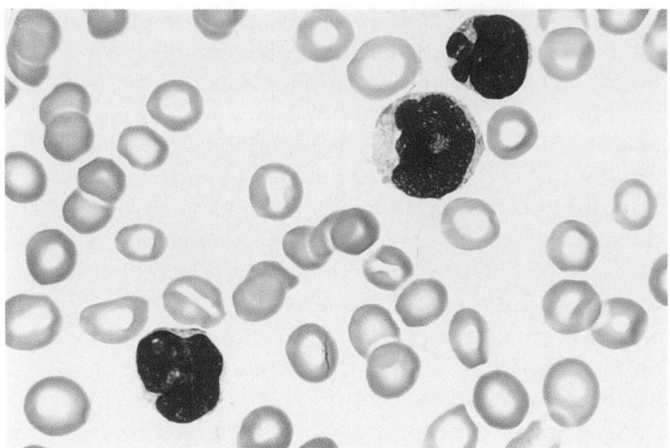

Fig. 23.89 Blood smear from an adult male with leukemia mantle cell lymphoma. The lymphoma cells vary considerably in size, nuclear lobulation, and degree of chromatin clumping. The large cell with a prominent nucleolus resembles a prolymphocyte. The smear is from the same patient as the specimen illustrated in Fig. 23.72.

cyclin D1, and in approximately 50% to 60% of cases show a t(11;14)(q13;q32) chromosome abnormality.

Aggressive NK-cell leukemia is a rare form of leukemia occurring more frequently in Asians than Caucasians, mostly young individuals, and might be the leukemic counterpart of extranodal NK/T-cell lymphoma, nasal type.[389,390,396] The blood is frequently involved; the white blood cell count ranges from low to markedly elevated. The number of leukemia/lymphoma cells may be low in the leukopenic cases to markedly elevated in patients with marked leukocytosis. The leukemic cells often appear monotonous with round or irregular nuclei with condensed chromatin and small nucleoli[390] (Fig. 23.86). The cells may resemble large granulated lymphocytes but the nuclear chromatin appears more dispersed and nucleoli are more prominent. In some cases, the cells resemble monoblasts. The marrow involvement may be diffuse, focal, or a subtle interstitial infiltration. There may be associated hemophagocytic histiocytes. Most cases are EBV positive in a clonal episomal form.[389,390]

The evaluation of blood and marrow samples from patients whose disease is being staged for lymphoma has been advanced substantially by antibodies reactive in paraffin-embedded tissue and genotypic and cytogenetic studies. Antibody studies provide objective evidence of extent of disease, and the genotypic and cytogenetic studies may provide evidence of clonality and cell lineage in equivocal cases.

Benign lymphocytic aggregates

Benign lymphocytic aggregates occur relatively frequently in bone marrow trephine and particle sections. The incidence in biopsy specimens varies from 3% to 47%.[410,411,413] The reported incidence in autopsy specimens is 26% to 62%. The incidence appears to increase with age and is higher in females than males. The aggregates occur in patients with a wide range of disorders, and the number and size in individual specimens vary considerably. Although lesions up to 1000 μm have been reported, the majority of aggregates are relatively small and well circumscribed.[414] Unusually large aggregates may occur in the marrows of patients with diseases related to the immune system such as AIDS and rheumatoid arthritis. Large and numerous lymphoid aggregates, sometimes with germinal center formation, may be observed in the marrow of patients receiving immunotherapy. These lesions may occasionally be paratrabecular (Fig. 23.90). The biologic significance of marrow lymphocytic aggregates in the majority of patients is unknown.[409]

The morphologic distinction between benign lymphocytic aggregates and malignant lymphoma, small lymphocytic type, in marrow biopsies from adults may be very difficult. Although general guidelines for making this distinction have been proposed, it is important to recognize that exceptions to these generalizations occur with distressing frequency.[414a]

Benign aggregates are usually few in number, well circumscribed, loosely structured, and contain histiocytes and plasma cells and frequently mast cells in addition to lymphocytes. The lymphocytes are usually small with generally round nuclei that have condensed chromatin and inconspicuous or no evident nucleoli. Occasional nuclei may have irregular outlines. Vascular structures are frequently present. Lymphoid follicles are uncommon in lymphocytic lesions in the marrow but when present are usually but not always evidence of a benign process. As previously noted, germinal centers may be observed in marrow lesions of mantle cell lymphoma and splenic marginal zone B-cell lymphoma. A

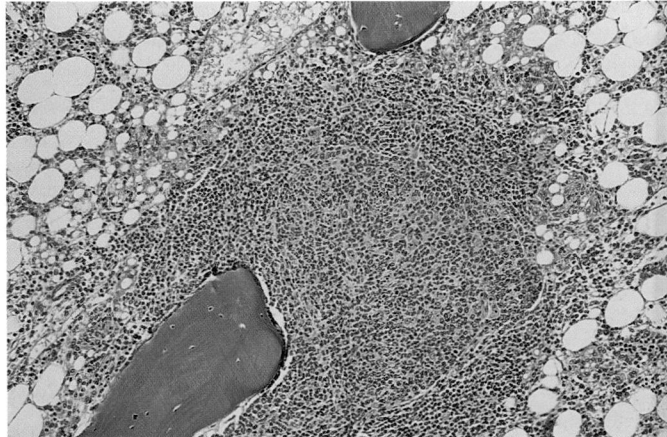

Fig. 23.90 Paratrabecular germinal center formation in marrow of a patient receiving interleukin-2 therapy for metastatic melanoma. Several vacuolated macrophages are present at the margin of the lesion.

preferential paratrabecular margination of a lymphoid infiltrate is evidence for a diagnosis of lymphoma. A random distribution of lymphoid aggregates with an occasional aggregate juxtaposed to a trabecula has no diagnostic specificity, since this pattern may occur with benign or malignant lesions. In occasional cases of follicular lymphoma, the follicular pattern in the lymph node is recapitulated in marrow lesions.

A particularly difficult diagnostic problem is the lymphocytic lesion referred to as polymorphous reactive lymphoid hyperplasia (see Fig. 23.28). These lymphoid aggregates are usually focal, poorly circumscribed, and randomly distributed. The lymphocytes are generally well differentiated; the nuclei of some and sometimes of many of the lymphocytes may be irregular. The infiltrate may be predominantly lymphocytes or have associated populations of plasma cells, immunoblasts, eosinophils, endothelial cells, phagocytic histiocytes, and epithelioid histiocytes. This lesion may occur in the marrow in any age group and is frequently associated with immune disorders such as immune cytopenias, collagen vascular disease, and, most notably, AIDS. The aggregates may be very large and in certain instances be virtually indistinguishable from the lesions of PTCL. Lesions of this type in marrow specimens from patients with AIDS are almost invariably reactive. In other instances in which the clinical or other tissue findings are equivocal, immunophenotypic or genotypic studies for clonality may be necessary.

It is important to recognize that benign lymphocytic aggregates may be present in marrow of patients with a prior diagnosis of marrow involvement by lymphoma; lymphoid aggregates in marrow specimens following chemotherapy should be evaluated as critically as those in the initial staging marrow biopsy. Marrow involvement by lymphoma in a patient with no other manifestation of the disease is very uncommon, and the diagnosis in such a situation should be approached with considerable caution and only if supporting immunophenotypic or genotypic evidence of a clonal process is present.

Marrow biopsies containing lymphocytic aggregates from patients treated with rituximab therapy for lymphoma should be carefully evaluated with immunohistochemistry to ascertain if the lymphocytes express the same antigens as the lymphoma cells which were present in the pretreatment specimen. Some loosely structured lesions, both randomly distributed and in paratrabecular locations, may be composed of reactive T cells rather than the B-cell lymphoma; this phenomenon is probably related to the therapeutic effects of the antibody (Fig. 23.91).

The application of antibodies that react with lymphocytes in paraffin-embedded, decalcified specimens may aid in distinguishing benign from malignant lymphocytic aggregates; as noted, this may be particularly

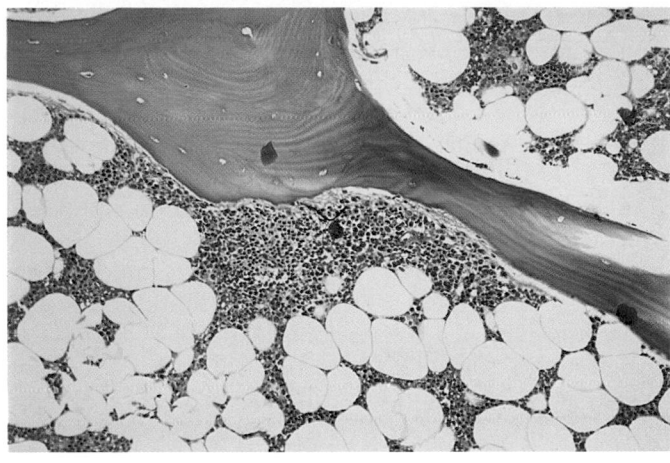

A

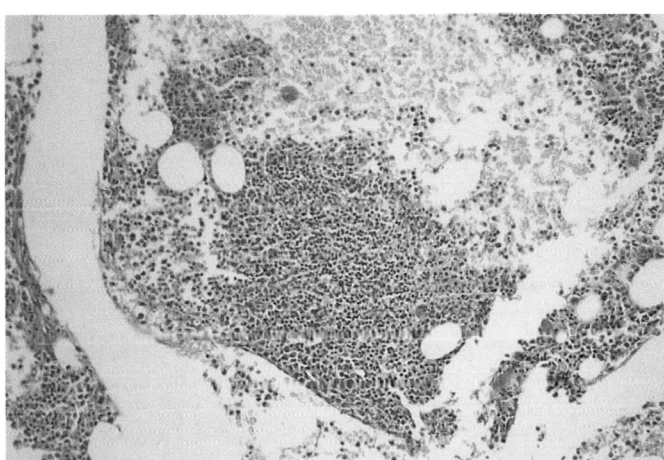

B

C

Fig. 23.91 Post rituximab therapy. A, One of several paratrabecular and nonparatrabecular lymphocytic aggregates in bone marrow biopsy following rituximab therapy. B, Same specimen as A reacted with antibody to CD20; the lymphocytes are nonreactive. Similar results were found with antibody to CD79a. C, Same specimen as A and B reacted with antibody to CD3. Most of the lymphocytes are intensely reactive. Similar results were found in other lymphocytic aggregates. (B and C, Immunoperoxidase.)

critical after chemotherapy or therapy with monoclonal antibodies.[408,412] However, antibodies to B lymphocytes and T lymphocytes do not provide information about clonality. Antibodies to kappa and lambda light chains which may impart evidence of clonality are not sufficiently sensitive in most instances to identify surface immunoglobulins in lymphomas in paraffin embedded biopsies. The presence of a mixed reactivity pattern (i.e., lymphocyte populations expressing both T and B surface antigens) in marrow lesions has been found to be more consistent with reactive lesions. A panel of antibodies, including CD10, bcl-2, CD5, and CD20, has been suggested as useful in distinguishing benign or atypical lymphocytic aggregates in the marrow from lymphoma; most benign aggregates do not express CD10 and CD23. There are exceptions to all generalizations, and caution should be exercised in the interpretation of immunocytochemical reactivity. Careful analysis of both lymph node and bone marrow specimens with the same panel of antibodies is necessary in evaluating marrow biopsies for lymphoma. Genotypic studies should be performed in those instances in which the marrow findings are indeterminate, and a therapeutic decision is contingent on the presence or absence of marrow involvement. Even with this approach, difficulties in distinguishing benign from malignant lesions persist and continued observation is the most prudent course in some patients.

Hodgkin's lymphoma

The incidence of marrow involvement in Hodgkin's lymphoma varies with the histopathologic type: it is approximately 10% in classical Hodgkin's mixed cellularity type and approximately 1% in lymphocyte predominant Hodgkin's and lymphocyte rich classical Hodgkin's disease.[427,428] Nodular sclerosis has an incidence of approximately 3%.[416,422,428] The overall incidence of bone marrow involvement in patients with stage IV disease is reported to be 32% and varies with the histologic subtype: 3% of lymphocyte predominant, 37% nodular sclerosis, 49% mixed cellularity, and 10% unclassified type.[422] The prognosis for patients with stage IV disease does not appear to be adversely affected by bone marrow involvement.

The lymphocyte depletion type of Hodgkin's lymphoma, which has a high incidence of marrow involvement, approximately 50%, is an uncommon form of Hodgkin's lymphoma.[418,423] Because the clinical presentation in some patients with lymphocyte depletion type disease is characterized by little or no peripheral lymphadenopathy, the initial diagnostic specimen may be the bone marrow biopsy.

The detection of marrow involvement appears in part to be related to the amount of tissue available for examination. Marrow involvement in most instances results from widely disseminated disease, is significantly associated with B symptoms, bulky disease, involvement of lymph nodes both above and below the diaphragm, and is negatively correlated with a large mediastinal mass.[422] Approximately 40% to 50% of patients with AIDS who develop Hodgkin's lymphoma have marrow involvement; the marrow may be the initial diagnostic specimen and the only site of involvement in this situation.[425]

The histopathologic classification of Hodgkin's lymphoma should not be based on examination of involved bone marrow because of different manifestations of the disease in lymph node and bone marrow tissue. Fibrosis is a common finding in Hodgkin's lesions in the marrow and is not limited to nodular sclerosis and lymphocyte depletion types.

Definitive histopathologic criteria for the diagnosis of marrow involvement in Hodgkin's lymphoma include typical Reed–Sternberg cells in a cellular background characteristic of Hodgkin's lymphoma or mononuclear Reed–Sternberg variants in a cellular background typical of Hodgkin's lymphoma if typical Reed–Sternberg cells are identified in other specimens[417,420,426] (Fig. 23.92). The presence of atypical cells lacking the features of Reed–Sternberg cells or mononuclear variants in a characteristic Hodgkin's environment in a patient with histopathologically proven disease should be considered highly suspicious for involvement. Foci of fibrosis in the absence of Reed–Sternberg cells or mononuclear variants in a patient with an established diagnosis of Hodgkin's lymphoma is not in itself sufficient evidence for a definitive diagnosis of marrow involvement but should be viewed as suspicious. In these latter two instances repeat biopsies should be performed.

Hodgkin's lesions in marrow may be diffuse or focal; the extent of involvement ranges from a single, small lesion to complete replacement of multiple biopsy specimens. Diffuse involvement is found in approximately 70% to 80% of positive marrow biopsies; the Hodgkin's

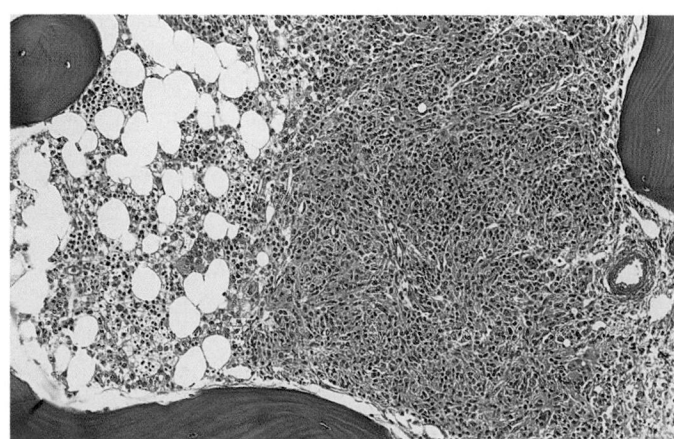

Fig. 23.92 Bone marrow biopsy from a patient with mixed cellularity Hodgkin's lymphoma. There is extensive involvement in this area of the biopsy.

tissue in these cases replaces the entire area between trabeculae.[424] Focal lesions are variable in size and may be surrounded by normal hematopoietic tissue or scattered in a hypocellular background (Fig. 23.93); the latter pattern is more frequent following chemotherapy. The focal lesions tend to be polycellular, with a predominant population of small lymphocytes with admixed neutrophils, eosinophils, plasma cells, histiocytes, Reed–Sternberg cells, and mononuclear variants. The diffuse lesions may manifest in several patterns. In the majority of cases, the Hodgkin's tissue is hypercellular with a population of cells characteristic of mixed cellularity Hodgkin's lymphoma in the lymph node (Fig. 23.92). In some patients the marrow shows extensive hypocellularity characterized by a generally loose, sparsely cellular connective tissue with scattered, variably sized hypercellular areas containing lymphocytes, histiocytes, Reed–Sternberg cells, and mononuclear variants. Areas of necrosis may be present and are more common in post-therapy specimens than at initial diagnosis (Fig. 23.94). Varying degrees of fibrosis may be present. In some cases, entire biopsy spec-

imens show replacement by dense fibrous connective tissue with few identifiable lymphocytes or histiocytes (Fig. 23.95). In others, scattered islands of cells are interspersed among the collagen fibers: some of these cells show features suggestive of Hodgkin's cells, others are too distorted for accurate identification. In some instances the Hodgkin's lesions are very hypercellular with a predominant population of Reed–Sternberg cells or mononuclear variants. Various combinations of these patterns may be present in the same biopsy specimen or in different specimens from the same patient. Necrosis and hypocellularity are more common in marrow from treated patients than untreated patients. In marrow involvement with lymphocyte depletion Hodgkin's lymphoma, a typical consolidated lesion characterized by an inflammatory cellular infiltrate accompanied by a distinct amorphous deposition of eosinophilic background substance and Reed–Sternberg cells has been described.[418]

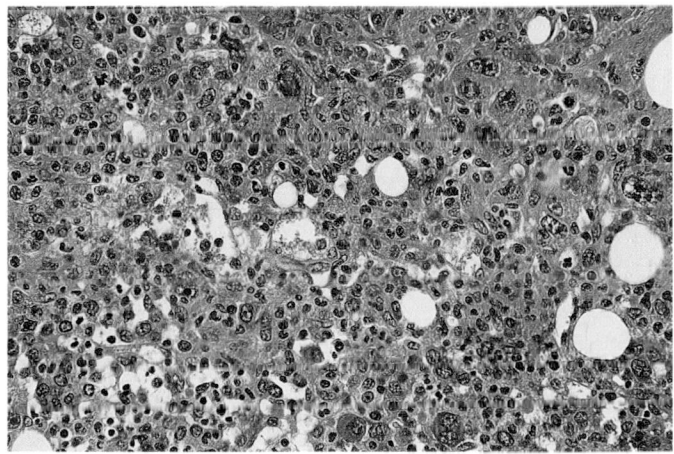

Fig. 23.93 Marrow with several scattered foci of Hodgkin's lymphoma. The lesions, which contain several Reed–Sternberg cells, are indistinctly demarcated from normal marrow.

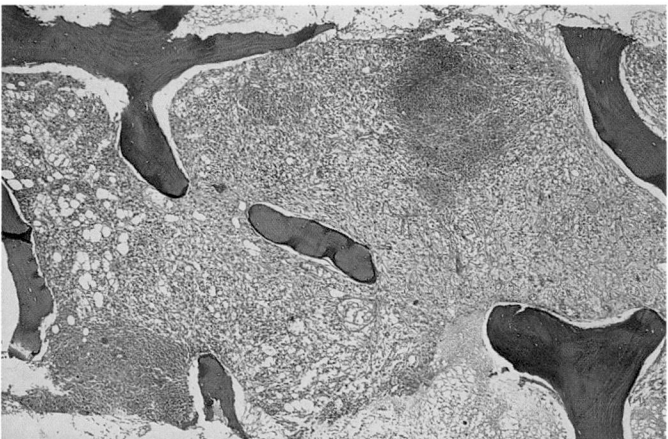

Fig. 23.94 Two foci of Hodgkin's lymphoma in a large area of necrotic debris in a post-treatment marrow specimen.

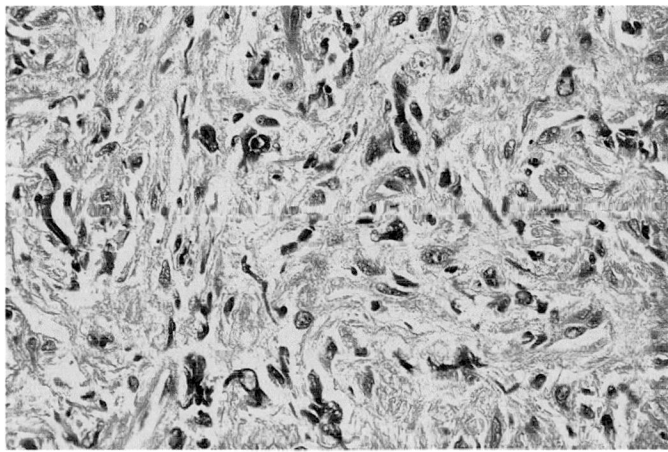

A

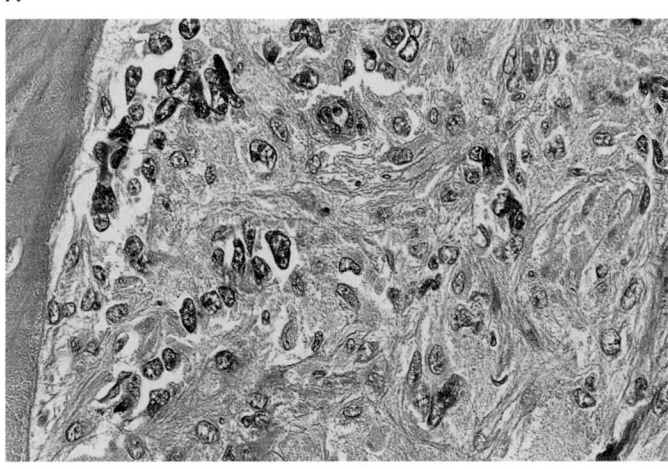

B

Fig. 23.95 A, Marrow biopsy from a patient with Hodgkin's lymphoma. The marrow space is completely replaced by dense fibrous connective tissue. Numerous vascular structures and small foci of distorted cells resembling Reed–Sternberg cells and mononuclear variants are present. B, Same specimen as A showing several focal collections of cells that resemble distorted Reed–Sternberg cells and mononuclear variants.

The presence of Reed–Sternberg cells or mononuclear variants is of critical importance to the recognition of Hodgkin's disease in marrow, and a definitive diagnosis should not be established without their identification in the appropriate cellular milieu. Several serial sections of the marrow biopsies may have to be examined before satisfactory Reed–Sternberg cells or mononuclear variants are detected. It is important not to misinterpret megakaryocytes as forms of Reed–Sternberg cells; this problem can be avoided by strict adherence to the principle of identifying Reed–Sternberg cells or variants only in the appropriate cellular background. Reed–Sternberg-like cells may be observed in marrow specimens with involvement by follicular center cell lymphoma, PTCL, and anaplastic large cell lymphoma (see Fig. 23.75); the clinical history, membrane surface marker studies, and characteristic tissue changes of Hodgkin's lymphoma should aid in distinguishing these disorders.[421] In some instances, genotypic studies may be necessary.

Uninvolved areas of marrow in specimens with involvement by Hodgkin's lymphoma may be hypercellular, normocellular, or hypocellular.[429] Nonspecific alterations, including stromal damage, inflammatory cell infiltration, and disturbed hematopoiesis, may be present.[415] These alterations may occur singly or in combination.

Similar to spleen, liver, and lymph nodes, benign granulomatous lesions may be present in bone marrow sections in patients with Hodgkin's lymphoma.[424] The marrow is the least likely organ in this group to contain the granulomas, but their presence may lead to diagnostic difficulty. The lack of typical Reed–Sternberg cells or mononuclear variants is an important feature in distinguishing these lesions from Hodgkin's lymphoma. The presence of granulomas does not constitute evidence of involvement. Granulomas in post-therapy patients should always be evaluated for the possibility of an infectious agent.[419,424] Benign lymphocytic aggregates may also be present.

Rarely, a patient whose disease is being staged for marrow involvement by Hodgkin's lymphoma has a concurrent parvovirus B19 infection. The presence of very large erythroid precursors in the smears or sections may result in confusion with Reed–Sternberg cells and consideration of marrow Hodgkin's lymphoma (see Fig. 23.22B). The lack of a characteristic cellular environment and the usually marked erythroid hypoplasia are strong evidence of parvovirus B19 infection. Serologic or molecular studies for parvovirus B19 should be performed in suspected cases.

Histiocytic disorders

Malignant histiocytosis

Malignant histiocytosis is a rare disease that uncommonly involves marrow. As a result, any comments about the characteristics of these lesions in the marrow are based on limited observations. The histocytic tumors are defined in the 2001 *WHO Classification of Hematopoietic Tumors* as "histiocytic and dendritic cell neoplasms derived from phagocytic and accessory cells which have major roles in the processing and presentation of antigens to lymphocytes."[431,438] The changing concept of "malignant histiocytosis" and the recognition that many of the lesions previously classified under this term represent other disorders mean that prior descriptions of marrow involvement in malignant histiocytosis are no longer valid.[430,432–437] Generalizations about patterns of marrow involvement must be qualified because of the rare occurrence of the disorder and the even more rare occurrence of marrow involvement. If the morphologic characteristics of a marrow lesion suggest a histiocytic disorder, appropriate cytochemical, immunologic, cytogenetic, and molecular studies should be performed. The diagnosis is essentially one of exclusion. Other poorly differentiated neoplasms of the hematopoietic system may have morphologic features that have been associated with malignant histiocytosis.[439] Cell marker studies for B- and T-cell lineage should be performed to exclude poorly differentiated lymphomas. Poorly differentiated carcinomas and plasmablastic tumors must also be excluded. Since the macrophage is derived from the monocyte system it may be difficult in some instances to distinguish between what is termed malignant histiocytosis and what is monoblastic/monocytic leukemia. The use of one or other of these terms may be arbitrary based on the constellation of clinical and morphologic findings.

In marrow biopsies, the infiltration by malignant histiocytes may be focal or diffuse (Fig. 23.96). Bone marrow involvement may be extremely difficult to recognize in sections that contain only scattered malignant cells. In smear preparations, the cells occur singly or in small groups scattered among the normal hematopoietic cells or, because of their large size, at the edges of the smears. The malignant histiocytes vary in size; cells up to 40 to 50 μm or larger may be found. The cytoplasm is usually abundant, with evidence of pseudopod formation and fragmentation; it is variably basophilic, occasionally with numerous small, sharply defined vacuoles in some cells. Very small azurophilic granules may be present in the cytoplasm of some of the larger cells. Occasional malignant histiocytes show evidence of phagocytosis; prominent hemophagocytosis is a relatively uncommon finding in unequivocally malignant-appearing cells. The nucleus may be round or contorted; the larger cells generally have more contorted nuclei. The chromatin is coarsely reticular. Nucleoli may be very prominent or inconspicuous. Stains for nonspecific esterase and acid phosphatase are positive. The demonstration of nonspecific esterase reactivity in poorly differentiated cells however is not sufficient to establish a diagnosis of malignant histiocytosis since this enzyme may be present in other poorly

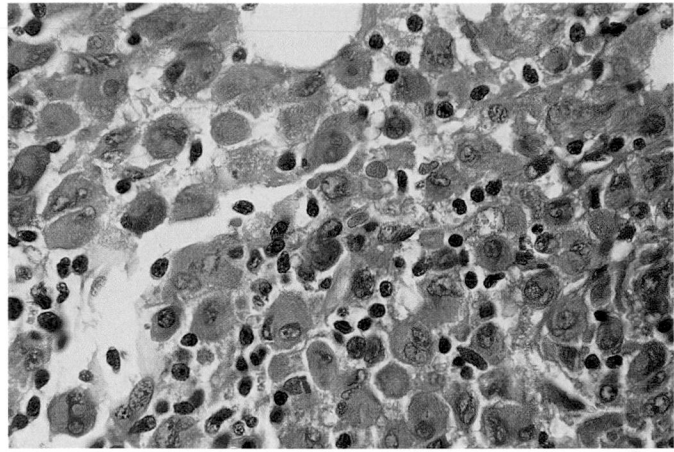

A

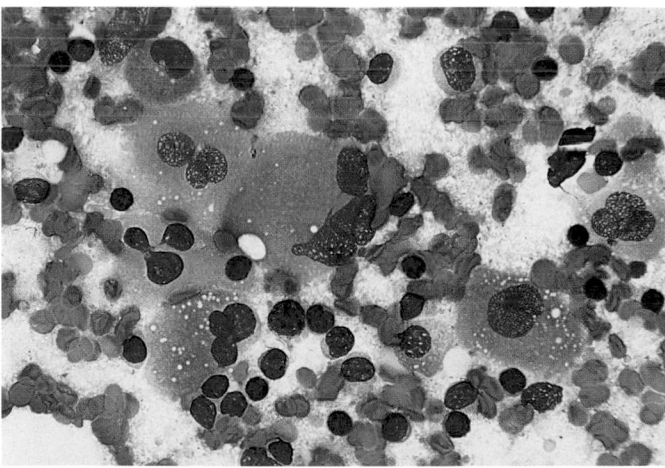

B

C

Fig. 23.96 A, Marrow biopsy from an adult female with marrow involvement by a histiocytic proliferation with an associated clonal t(9;11)(p21;q23) cytogenetic abnormality. The histiocytes have a somewhat bland appearance with abundant cytoplasm. **B**, The biopsy in **A** reacted with antibody to CD68 (KP-1). **C**, Smear from the specimen in **A** and **B** showing several histiocytes, most of which have lobated nuclei and abundant cytoplasm. (**B**, Immunoperoxidase.)

differentiated malignant cells. The malignant histiocyte should be reactive with antibodies to lysozyme, CD68 (KP-1 and PGM-1) and nonreactive to antibodies to T and B lymphocytes (Fig. 23.96B). There may be some degree of reactivity with antibody to S-100 protein. The proliferation of the malignant histiocytes may be accompanied by a proliferation of benign-appearing histiocytes with abundant cytoplasm and prominent hemophagocytosis; this probably results from cytokine stimulation related to the malignant cell proliferation.

Hemophagocytic syndromes

The hemophagocytic syndromes are a group of disorders with the unifying features of a proliferation of phagocytic histiocytes that may be present in all hematopoietic organs. These processes usually have systemic manifestations and may be accompanied by a fulminant clinical course and high mortality. Because of the multiorgan involvement and the associated high mortality, these disorders frequently have been interpreted as cases of malignant histiocytosis. The hemophagocytic syndromes appear to be an epiphenomenon that is triggered by a variety of causes including, but not limited to, viral infections (particularly Epstein–Barr virus—EBV) and some T-cell and B-cell lymphomas.[440,445,449,450,453,455–462,464–470] Viruses associated with this disorder include cytomegalovirus, Epstein–Barr virus, adenovirus, and parvovirus B19.[444,460,462] The process has been observed with bacterial infections and the protozoan infection, *Babesia microti*.[469] Patients with immune deficiency, either hereditary or acquired, appear to be at increased risk for this problem.[448]

The hemophagocytic syndromes frequently have an abrupt onset. Evidence of multisystem disease is usually present, particularly in patients with viral infections.[451,460] A high percentage of patients have coagulation abnormalities. There are usually cytopenias, frequently pancytopenia. The marrow smears contain numerous histiocytes, many showing evidence of phagocytosis of erythrocytes and precursors, platelets, and granulocytes. There is frequently an accompanying depression of erythroid precursors, granulocyte precursors, or both; megakaryocytes may be normal or increased in number. In biopsy sections, the increased histiocytes are dispersed throughout the interstitium and sinuses; occasional clusters may be present (Fig. 23.97). The evidence of phagocytic activity may be less prominent in sections compared with smear preparations (Fig. 23.98). In addition to the histiocytic proliferation, granulomas may be noted, and areas of cellular necrosis are frequently present. The bone marrow findings may change substantially over a period of days, with fluctuations in the number of granulocyte and erythroid precursors and megakaryocytes. Lymph nodes may show a marked increase in histiocytes in the sinusoidal spaces; evidence of hemophagocytosis may be much less marked than in the bone marrow or there may be marked erythrophagocytosis. The spleen may be

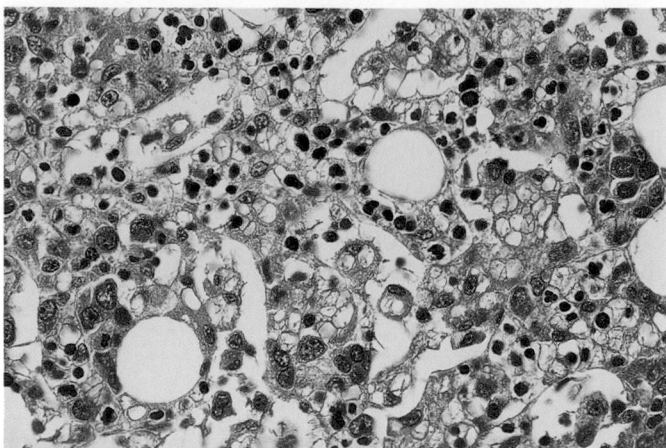

Fig. 23.97 Marrow biopsy from an adult male who developed hemophagocytic syndrome associated with bacterial infection. Numerous histiocytes, some showing hemophagocytosis, are present in sinusoids and interstitium.

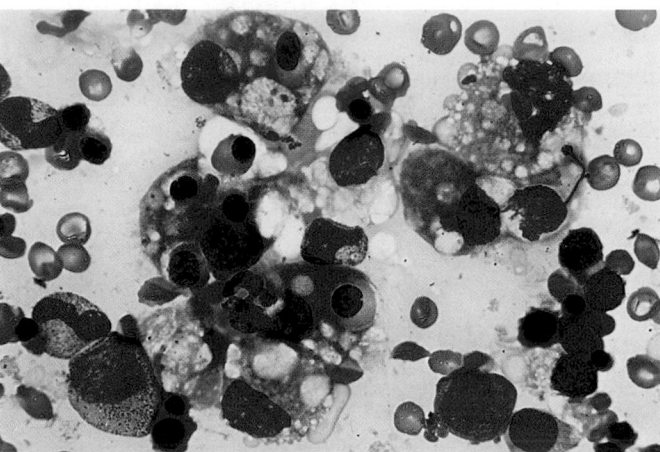

Fig. 23.98 Bone marrow smear from a lupus erythematosus patient with virus-associated hemophagocytic syndrome. Numerous macrophages with ingested red blood cells and erythroblasts are present. (Wright–Giemsa.)

markedly enlarged with prominent histiocytic infiltration in the red pulp. Areas of nonsuppurative necrosis have been observed in lymph nodes and spleen.[458]

The mechanism of macrophage activation in the hemophagocytic syndromes is not completely understood but appears to be related to the release of chemokines and cytokines including macrophage inflammatory protein-1 alpha and interferon gamma.[454] The phenomenon appears to be preceded in some patients by proliferation of activated or neoplastic Epstein–Barr virus-infected T lymphocytes that produce tumor necrosis factor-alpha.

The Epstein–Barr virus or T-cell related hemophagocytic syndromes may be difficult to distinguish morphologically from familial hemophagocytic lymphocytic histiocytosis. The latter disorder appears to be related to mutation of the perforin gene and diminished perforin in cytotoxic T cells and T/NK cells.[452,463] This

contrasts with the normal levels of perforin in the cytotoxic cells in patients with the secondary hemophagocytic syndromes.

The clinicopathologic features of virus-associated hemophagocytic syndrome (VAHS) have been reported in 80% of a group of patients with fatal infectious mononucleosis.[456] The VAHS phase was preceded by features of a viral-like illness. Sequential changes were present in the marrows of these patients; initially there was infiltration by atypical lymphoid cells with areas of necrosis, followed by depletion of normal hematopoietic cells and histiocytic activation with prominent hemophagocytosis; the end stage was marked by marrow aplasia. A similar sequence of histopathologic changes was found in the lymph nodes, spleen, and thymus gland.

Hemophagocytic histiocytosis has been reported as a terminal event in patients with T-cell lymphomas and T/NK-cell lymphomas; uncommonly it is associated with B-cell lymphoma.[445,449] The pathologic findings are similar to those in VAHS. The production of macrophage-activating cytokines by the malignant cells has been suggested as a causative mechanism of the histiocyte proliferation. The hemophagocytic syndrome may be associated with other types of lymphoma including anaplastic large cell lymphoma with an associated t(2;5) chromosome abnormality.[443]

The distinction between the hemophagocytic syndrome and "malignant histiocytosis" may be difficult because of similarities in clinical presentation.[441,442,446,450] The cells in the hemophagocytic syndrome are morphologically distinct; they have a low nucleocytoplasmic ratio and abundant lightly staining cytoplasm containing large vacuoles of varying sizes and phagocytosed cells or cellular products. Nucleoli, when present, are not prominent, and mitotic figures are rare. Although the hemophagocytic histiocyte proliferation may coexist with "malignant histiocytosis" or a malignant lymphoma, there is no evidence of a transition from the obviously malignant cells to the benign histiocytes.

Serologic studies for viral infection in patients with the picture of a hemophagocytic syndrome may not be reliable because impaired immune function may preclude a detectable antibody response. In these cases, molecular hybridization studies may be useful in documenting an EBV or parvovirus B19 infection.[447,450] In addition to studies for a viral infection, it is important that patients with a hemophagocytic process be carefully evaluated for immune suppression and non-Hodgkin's lymphoma. Patients with a hemophagocytic syndrome with both an EBV infection and a malignant lymphoproliferative lesion may be observed.

Langerhans' cell histiocytosis

Marrow involvement in Langerhans' cell histiocytosis (histiocytosis X) is uncommon and usually associated with the multisystem multifocal form of the disease (Letterer–Siwe disease).[472] The marrow lesions may be focal and small and barely perceptible or confluent and extensive replacing large areas of a biopsy (Fig. 23.99).[471] The small lesions may have a granulomatous appearance. Similar to the lesions in other organs, the Langerhans' cells have a low nucleocytoplasmic ratio; the nuclei are grooved, folded or lobated with dispersed chromatin and inconspicuous nucleoli. Hemosiderin and lipofuscin-like granules may be present in the cytoplasm. The lesions may be relatively monocellular or polycellular with admixed histiocytes, multinucleate giant cells, lymphocytes, plasma cells, eosinophils and neutrophils. Stains for reticulin show an increased number of reticulin fibers. Immunohistochemical reactions for S-100 protein and CD1a highlight the Langerhans' cell infiltrate. However, with some fixatives and decalcifying agents, the reaction with antibody to CD1a may be suboptimal in bone marrow biopsies. The cells are variably reactive for CD68 (KP-1), lysozyme and nonspecific esterase. In smear preparations and touch imprints, the Langerhans' cell has abundant cytoplasm which frequently contains particulate green–blue debris (Fig. 23.99C). Characteristic Birbeck granules are observed on ultrastructural examination.

Plasma cell dyscrasias

The plasma cell dyscrasias are proliferations of immunosecretory cells generally associated with perturbation of serum immunoglobulins. This group of diseases includes the plasma cell proliferations and lymphoplasmacytic lymphoma. The WHO classification of plasma cell neoplasms is shown in Table 23.1.[473]

Table 23.1 Plasma cell neoplasms[473]

Plasma cell myeloma
  Variants:
    Non-secretory myeloma
    Indolent myeloma
    Smoldering myeloma
    Plasma cell leukemia
Plasmacytoma
    Solitary plasmacytoma of bone
    Extramedullary plasmacytoma
Immunoglobulin deposition disease
Primary amyloidosis
Systemic light and heavy chain deposition disease
Osteosclerotic myeloma (POEMS syndrome)
Heavy chain disease (HCD)
    Gamma HCD
    Mu HCD
    Alpha HCD

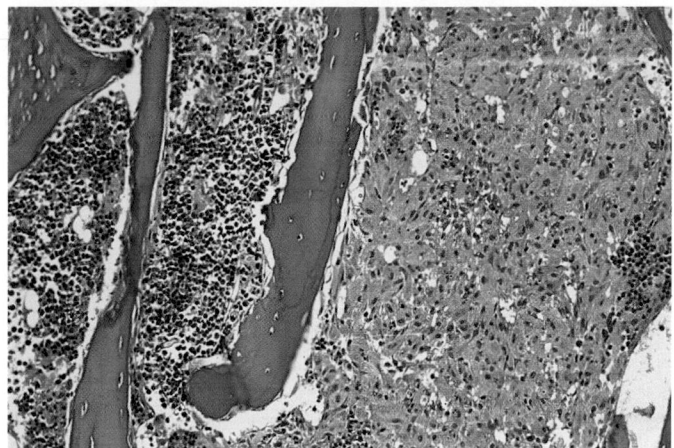

A

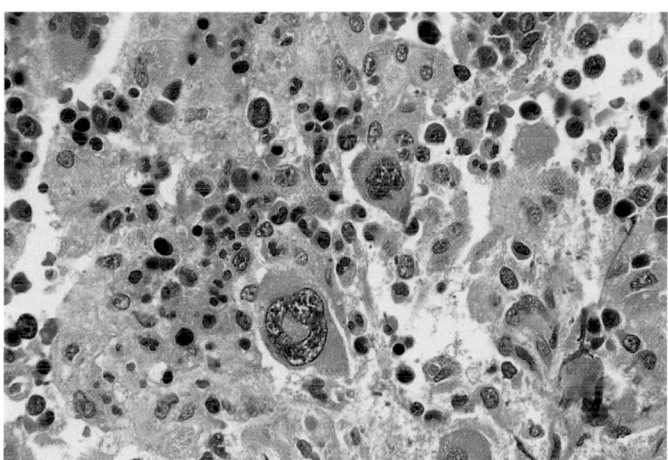

B

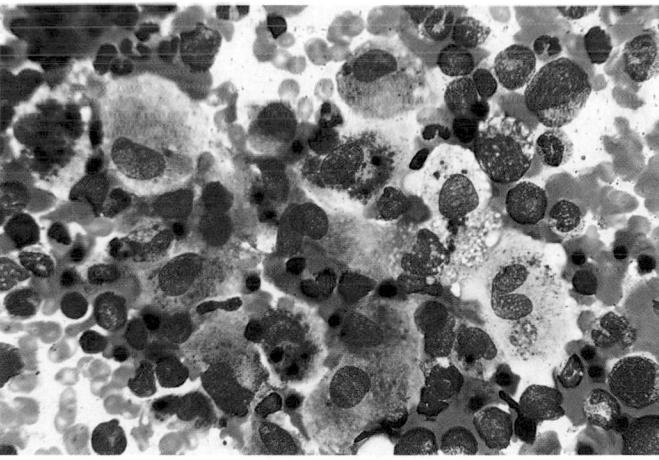

C

Fig. 23.99 A, Marrow biopsy from a child with Langerhans' cell histiocytosis showing extensive replacement. **B,** High magnification of the lesion in **A** showing giant cells and several histiocytes. Some residual myeloid cells are present. **C,** Bone marrow smear from the case illustrated in **A** and **B**. The Langerhans' cells are very large with abundant cytoplasm; several histiocytes contain nonspecific debris and occasionally red blood cells.

Table 23.2 Criteria for diagnosis of plasma cell myeloma[473]

Major criteria
1. Marrow plasmacytosis ≥30%
2. Plasmacytoma on biopsy
3. M component
    Serum IgG ≥3.5 g/dl; IgA ≥2 g/dl
    Urine ≥1 g/24 hours of Bence Jones protein

Minor criteria
1. Marrow plasmacytosis of 10–30%
2. M component present but less than in major criteria
3. Lytic bone lesions
4. Reduced normal serum immunoglobulins (<50% of normal)

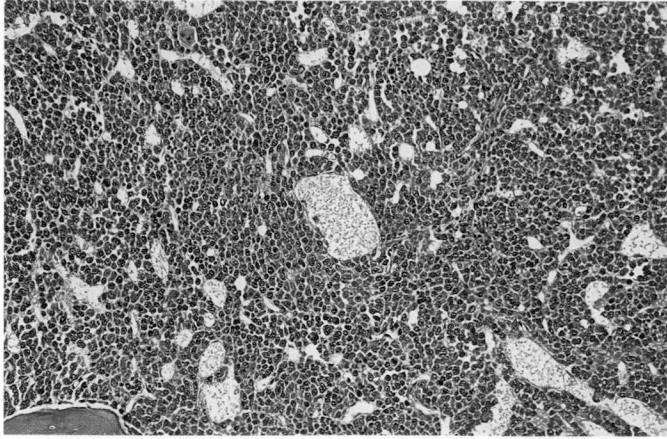

A

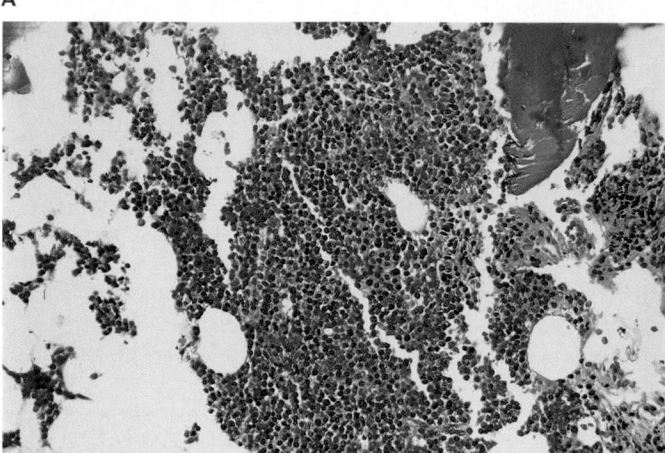

B

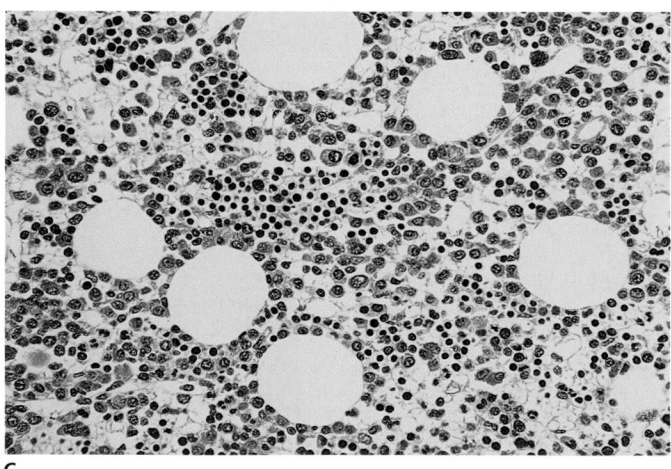

C

Fig. 23.100 A, Marrow biopsy from a patient with multiple myeloma with extensive diffuse replacement by myeloma cells. **B,** Marrow biopsy with a large focus of myeloma cells. **C,** Marrow biopsy showing essentially normal marrow architecture and interstitial infiltration by myeloma cells.

The prototype disorder for this group of diseases is plasma cell myeloma, of which the clinical syndrome is multiple myeloma. Monoclonal gammopathy of undetermined significance (MGUS) is viewed as a precursor lesion.

The criteria for diagnosis of plasma cell myeloma are listed in Table 23.2.[473]

The diagnosis requires a minimum of one major and one minor criterion, or three minor criteria which must include 1 and 2.[561]

Plasma cell myeloma

Plasma cell myeloma is a neoplastic proliferation of plasma cells accompanied by the production of a monoclonal immunoglobulin detectable in the serum, urine, or both.[475] The peak incidence is in the seventh decade; the disease is slightly more frequent in males than females. Osteolytic lesions in the skull, ribs, sternum, vertebrae, and pelvis are usually present; in rare cases, x-ray films reveal osteosclerotic lesions.

Marrow involvement in myeloma may be patchy, and the percentage of plasma cells may vary in aspirates and biopsies from different sites. In trephine sections, the distribution of plasma cells may be focal, interstitial, diffuse, or a combination of these patterns[477,479,482,508] (Fig. 23.100). There is variability in the appearance of the plasma cells in different cases from very immature plasma cells with a blastlike appearance to pleomorphic cells to mature-appearing plasma cells[476,480,488,492] (Fig. 23.101). Nucleoli may be very prominent in some of the more immature types, and binucleate cells resembling Reed–Sternberg cells may be found. Nuclear and cytoplasmic inclusions of varying types may be noted; these are usually related to immunoglobulin production (Fig. 23.102). The marrow in approximately 10% to 20% of cases shows an associated fibrosis[481,498] (Fig. 23.103).

Several approaches to the staging of myeloma have been introduced: these have included the correlation of myeloma cell mass with presenting laboratory findings, including hemoglobin, monoclonal immunoglobulin, and calcium levels and the presence of osteolytic bone lesions.[483,484,489,494] The serum β_2-microglobulin level and the plasma cell labeling index have been found to be significant prognostic factors.[478,485,490,491] β_2-Microglobulin levels above 4 ng/uL and plasma cell labeling index greater than 0.4% are associated with a shorter survival

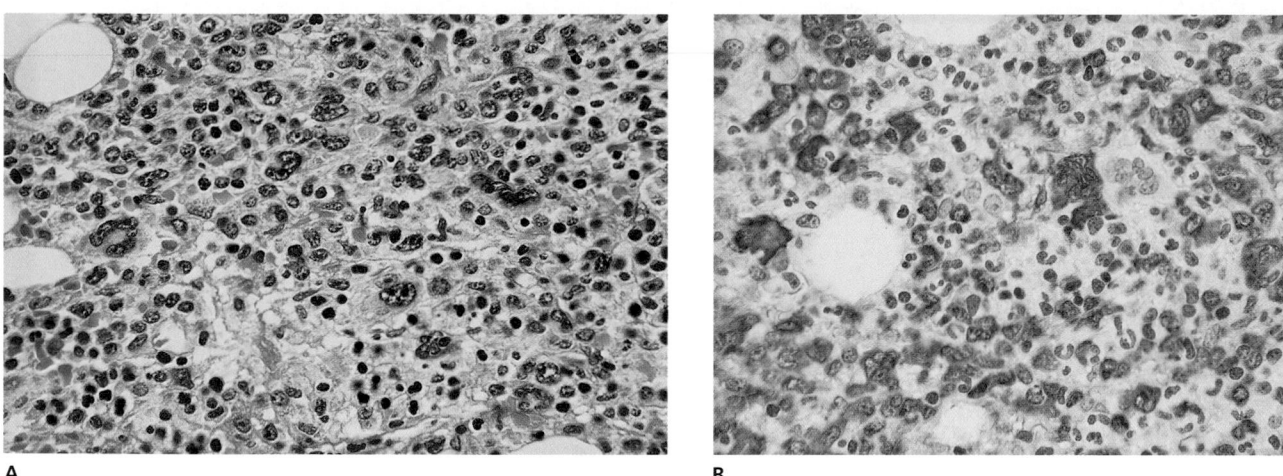

Fig. 23.101 A, Marrow from a patient with anaplastic myeloma; many of the plasma cells are large with lobulated nuclei. **B,** Specimen in **A** reacted with antibody to lambda light chains. The plasma cells show intense cytoplasmic reactivity. Numerous nonreactive residual myeloid cells are present. (**B,** Immunoperoxidase.)

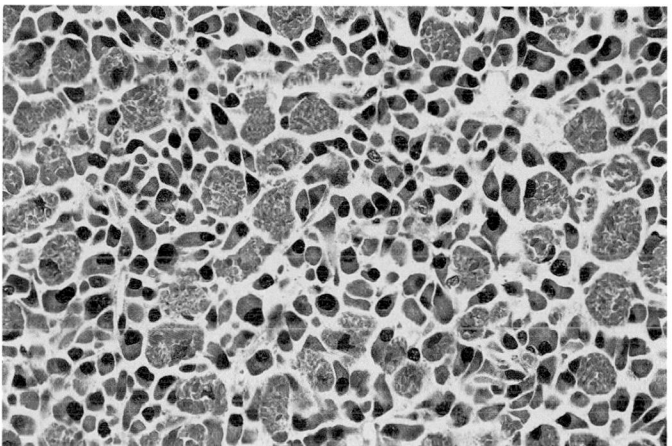

Fig. 23.102 Marrow biopsy from a 63-year-old patient with multiple myeloma with hypogammaglobulinemia and kappa light chain Bence Jones proteinuria. The cytoplasm of myeloma cells is distended by numerous, frequently confluent eosinophilic inclusions.

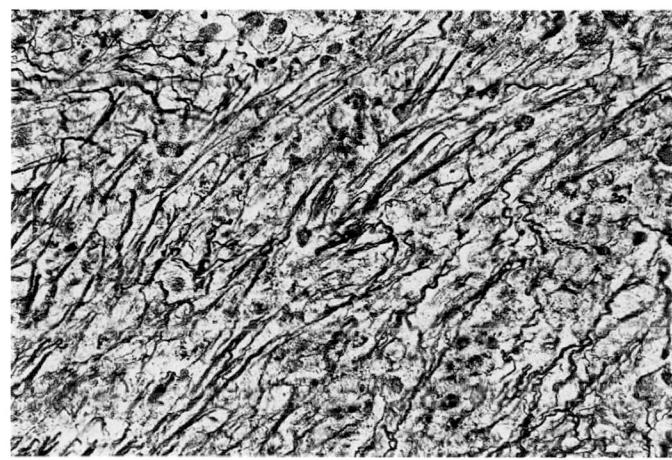

Fig. 23.103 Marrow biopsy from a patient with plasma cell myeloma and marked reticulin fibrosis.

than β_2-microglobulin levels less than 1 ng/µl and labeling index of 0. Chromosome abnormalities including deletions of 13q14, 17p13, as detected by interphase fluorescent in situ hybridization (FISH) have been associated with poor response to conventional induction therapy and short median overall survival.[497] Monosomy or a deletion of chromosome 13, as detected by FISH, in conjunction with β_2-microglobulin levels greater than or equal to 2.5 mg/L have been shown to be adverse prognostic factors in patients treated with high dose chromotherapy.[485] Recurrent translocations involving chromosome 14q32 as detected by FISH have also shown correlation with survival in patients receiving intensive chemotherapy; t(4;14) has been associated with short event-free survival and overall survival. In the same study, t(11;14) was associated with a longer overall survival time when compared to patients in whom the finding was not present.[499]

Hypodiploidy (pseudodiploid, hypodiploid, near tetraploid) has also been shown to be an adverse prognostic factor.[504]

Similar to mantle cell lymphoma with t(11;14)(q13;q32), the nuclei of the myeloma cells in patients with this translocation are cyclin D1 positive.[487,495]

Histopathologic staging of myeloma in bone marrow biopsies based on cytologic features of the myeloma cells and the degree of plasma cell infiltration has been shown to have prognostic significance.[476] The more mature type of plasma cell myeloma, plasmacytic, and less than 20% marrow replacement are favorable prognostic factors. The more immature or poorly differentiated the myeloma cells, i.e., plasmablastic, and the more extensive the marrow involvement (>50% replacement), the more unfavorable the prognosis. An anaplastic evolution of myeloma may occur, and some of these cases have the histopathologic features of immunoblastic lymphoma.[486]

Studies comparing anaplastic myeloma with B-immunoblastic lymphoma have demonstrated clinical and immunologic differences.[506,507] The plasma cells in anaplastic myeloma are usually of the IgG or IgA heavy chain class in contrast to B-immunoblastic lymphoma in which the cells are IgM. The cells in immunoblastic lymphoma usually express pan-B-cell antigens; the plasma cells in approximately 80% of cases of myeloma do not express pan-B-cell antigens. Exceptions to these generalizations occur. All clinical and laboratory findings should be considered. Histopathologic staging of myeloma in the marrow, using an approach similar to that used for CLL, has shown good correlation between pattern of marrow involvement and clinical stage; a diffuse pattern of involvement is usually associated with a more advanced clinical stage.[508] In some patients, the pattern of marrow involvement may be somewhat inconsistent from biopsy to biopsy, and focal involvement may be associated with an advanced clinical stage. Immunohistologic studies on paraffin-embedded biopsy specimens utilizing antibodies to kappa and lambda light chains are very useful in identifying myeloma cells, determining monoclonality and the extent of marrow involvement.[500–502,509]

As noted, the myeloma cells in patients with an associated t(11;14)(q13;q32) translocation are usually cyclin D1 positive; a substantial number of these cases are reported as having lymphoplasmacytoid morphology and extensive marrow infiltration.[487,495]

In rare cases, a patient with the clinical, radiographic, and histopathologic features of multiple myeloma will have no evidence of monoclonal immunoglobulin production in the serum or urine. These cases have been referred to as "nonsecretory" myeloma.[474,503,505] Considerable caution should be exercised in the use of this term, since striking reactive plasmacytosis may be observed with nonmalignant conditions, including liver disease, connective tissue disorders, chronic granulomatous disorders, hypersensitivity states, and drug-related agranulocytosis.[496] When a nonsecretory myeloma is suspected, the monoclonal nature of the proliferating plasma cells should be confirmed by immunoperoxidase or immunofluorescent techniques that will demonstrate kappa or lambda light chain restriction.[493,500,509] An increase in reactive plasma cells will be characterized by a relatively balanced population of kappa- and lambda-containing cells.

Plasma cell leukemia

The term plasma cell leukemia is applied to those processes in which a patient presents with a plasma cell proliferation in the blood; the plasma cells exceed 20% of the blood leukocytes, or the absolute plasma cell count exceeds 20 × 10⁹/L[510–512] (Fig. 23.104). The term should be reserved for cases with this finding at initial presentation. The marrow in plasma cell leukemia usually shows

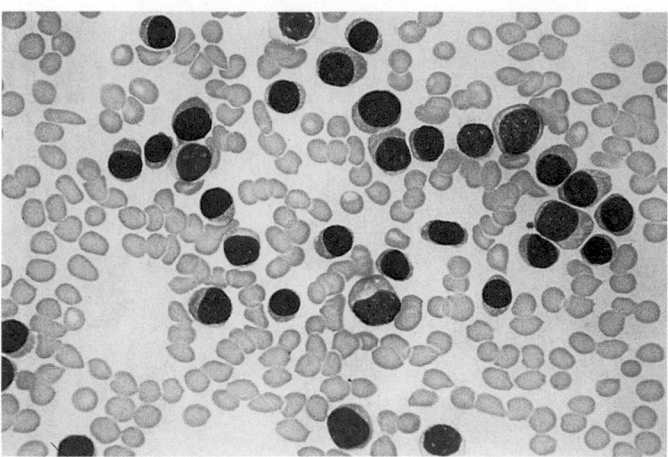

Fig. 23.104 Blood smear from a 47-year-old woman with leukocytosis of 24.0 ×10⁹/L and 90% plasma cells. Many of the plasma cells have "lymphoid" features. There was a serum IgG kappa monoclonal protein. (Wright–Giemsa.) (Reproduced from the Atlas of Tumor Pathology, Third Series, Fascicle 9, Tumors of the Bone Marrow. Brunning RD and McKenna RW, Armed Forces Institute of Pathology, Washington, D.C., 1994.)

diffuse and extensive replacement of normal hematopoietic cells by the plasma cells. In some cases, the myeloma cells have a lymphoid appearance. Patients with plasma cell leukemia have a higher incidence of organomegaly than those with other forms of myeloma, and the disease is usually associated with an unfavorable prognosis.

Multiple myeloma or amyloidosis may occur in patients with the adult Fanconi's syndrome; the renal abnormalities may precede the overt manifestations of the plasma cell dyscrasia by several years. Bence Jones proteinuria of kappa light chain type is a common finding. A high percentage of the patients with this variant of myeloma manifest crystalline inclusions in the cytoplasm of the proliferating plasma cells and renal tubular cells.[513]

Osteosclerotic myeloma (POEMS syndrome)

Osteosclerotic myeloma is a form of plasma cell dyscrasia characterized by sclerotic bone lesions and progressive demyelinating polyneuropathy.[515–518,520] The bone marrow aspirate usually contains less than 10% plasma cells. The plasma cell proliferation is usually evident as a plasmacytoma in the sclerotic lesions or in lymph nodes (Fig. 23.105A). The marrow from areas uninvolved by the sclerotic process may show typical myeloma cell infiltration. The megakaryocytes may be increased and large with hyperlobulated nuclei (Fig. 23.105C). The involved lymph nodes may show angiofollicular hyperplasia with a parafollicular infiltration of monoclonal plasma cells.[514] A high percentage of patients with osteosclerotic myeloma have multiorgan involvement, including polyneuropathy, organomegaly, endocrinopathy, and skin changes, the so-called "POEMS syndrome".[519] Approximately 75% of patients have a thrombocytosis. Polycythemia and leukocytosis

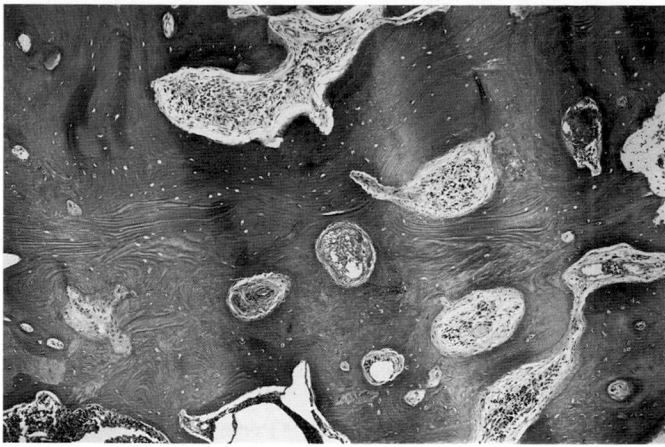

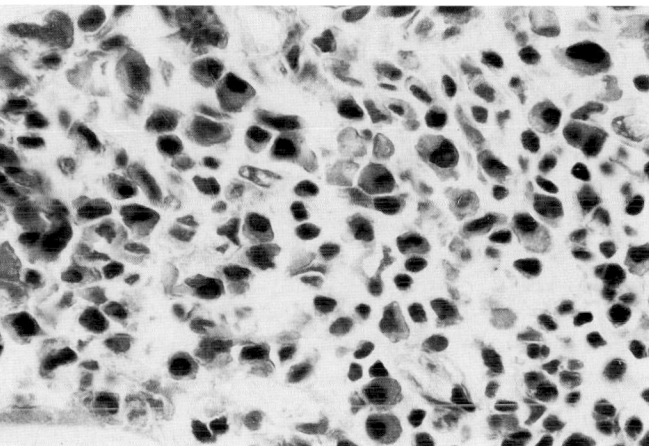

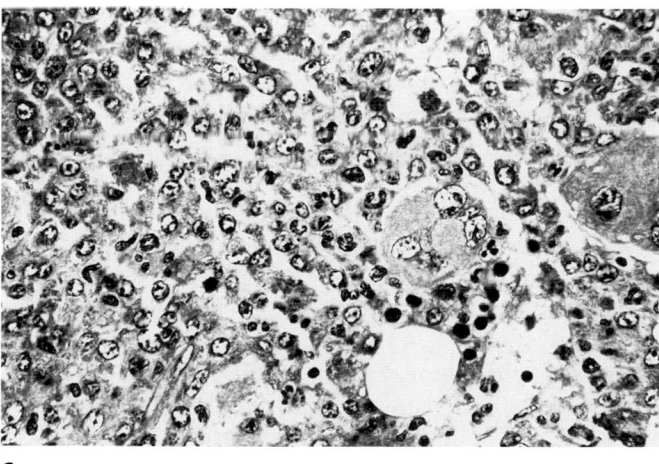

Fig. 23.105 **A**, An osteosclerotic bone lesion from a patient with osteosclerotic myeloma. **B**, High magnification of the marrow in the specimen in **A**. This area shows a large number of plasma cells that were lambda light chain restricted on immunohistochemical study. **C**, Marrow biopsy from a nonsclerotic area from a patient with osteosclerotic myeloma with POEMS syndrome. There was a thrombocytosis. The marrow in this area shows an infiltration by immature plasma cells. There was also an increase in large megakaryocytes, two of which are at right.

are present in about one third of cases. There is usually a low level of monoclonal protein of IgG or IgA class, with a predominance of lambda light chain type.

The median age of onset is 51 years compared with 64 years for typical myeloma; median survival is 97 months in contrast with 30 to 35 months for typical myeloma. The disease appears to be more common in Japan than in the United States or Europe.

An association of giant lymph node hyperplasia with osteoblastic bone lesions and the POEMS syndrome has been reported.[514,515]

Monoclonal gammopathy of undetermined significance

Approximately 1% to 2% of individuals over the age of 50 and 2% to 3% of patients over age 65 have a serum monoclonal gammopathy without other evidence of a plasma cell dyscrasia.[524,525] The monoclonal protein in these individuals is usually less than 3 g/dl and there is usually no or minimal Bence Jones protein in the urine. There is no associated hypercalcemia, anemia, renal impairment, or radiologic evidence of bone lesions.[523] The bone marrow in these patients may be entirely normal or may manifest a slight increase in mature-appearing plasma cells; the increase is less than 5%. Some of these cases represent incipient myeloma or another type of plasma cell dyscrasia or lymphoproliferative disorder; others continue for several years without undergoing an obvious neoplastic evolution. The term monoclonal gammopathy of undetermined significance (MGUS) has been applied to this constellation of findings.[524,525] If the morphologic findings are suspicious for but not diagnostic of myeloma, the patient should be followed with marrow examination and repeat protein electrophoresis at 6-month intervals. An increase in the number of abnormal plasma cells or light chain-restricted plasma cells and an increase in the amount of monoclonal immunoglobulin suggest a neoplastic process.[521] A stable immunoglobulin level and plasma cell percentage are more reflective of a benign monoclonal gammopathy. The plasma cell labeling index as described by Greipp and Kyle has been useful in distinguishing monoclonal gammopathy of undetermined significance and smoldering myeloma from overt multiple myeloma.[523] The diagnostic accuracy of a plasma cell labeling index of greater than 0.4 in distinguishing myeloma from MGUS and smoldering myeloma was 83%. The accuracy is increased when combined with the percentage of marrow plasma cells. Approximately 25% to 30% of patients with monoclonal gammopathy of undetermined significance eventually develop a plasma cell dyscrasia or related process; the interval to occurrence ranges up to 29 years.[524] Factors predicting transformation have varied in different studies: percentage of marrow plasma cells greater than or equal to 5%, Bence Jones proteinuria, and paraprotein isotype at initial presentation have been found to have some value. Bone marrow angiogenesis is reported to increase progressively in those patients who manifest progression of monoclonal gammopathy of undetermined significance to overt myeloma; median microvessel density correlated with the bone marrow plasma cell labeling index and the percentage of marrow plasma cells.[528] In a large series of patients with MGUS, the only independent risk factors for progression to an overt myeloma or related plasma cell dyscrasia was concentration of the serum monoclonal protein at diagnosis and the type of monoclonal protein. The risk for progression to myeloma or a related disorder at 10 years was 6% for an initial monoclonal protein of 0.5 g/dl or less compared to 34% for an initial monoclonal protein of 3.0 g/dl. Monoclonal proteins of IgM or IgA type had a higher risk of progression than an IgG paraprotein.[526] Several genomic abnormalities including monosomy 13, t(4;14)(p16.3;q32) and t(14;16)(q32;q23) have been found in MGUS: no obvious clinical or biologic correlations have been established. Similar cytogenetic findings are present in overt myeloma.[522]

Immunocytochemistry on paraffin-embedded specimens using antibodies to kappa and lambda light chains can be a very important approach to the study of myeloma and related disorders.[527] The primary use of the technique in this group of diseases is to determine the relative proportion of kappa- or lambda-reacting cells; a predominant population of plasma cells reacting with a single light chain antibody is evidence for a monoclonal proliferation (see Fig. 23.2). A balanced proliferation of kappa- and lambda-reacting plasma cells usually indicates a benign process. A light chain ratio determined by dividing the number of positively reacting plasma cells for the predominant light chain by the number of positively reacting cells for the other light chain has been proposed as an aid in the distinction of myeloma from monoclonal gammopathy of undetermined significance or a reactive increase in plasma cells.[527] Patients with overt myeloma generally have values above 16; patients with monoclonal gammopathy of undetermined significance or a reactive process have values less than 16. These results should not be viewed in isolation but should be combined with the plasma cell labeling index.

Plasmacytoma

A solitary plasmacytoma, in contrast to the disseminated proliferation of plasma cells in multiple myeloma, is a single focus of plasma cells occurring in either bone or soft tissue.[529–543] Solitary plasmacytomas are more frequent in males than females and have a peak incidence in the sixth decade, slightly earlier than multiple myeloma. Plasmacytomas are generally divided into two broad groups based on location: plasmacytoma of bone and extramedullary or soft tissue plasmacytoma. The recommended diagnostic criteria for solitary plasmacytoma of bone are shown in Table 23.3.[532]

Evidence for different biologic behavior of these two

Table 23.3 Criteria for diagnosis of solitary plasmacytoma[533]

- Single area of bone destruction due to clonal plasma cells
- Normal marrow without clonal disease
- Normal results on a radiologic skeletal survey and magnetic resonance imaging of the spine, pelvis, proximal femurs, and humeri.
- No anemia, hypercalcemia or renal impairment attributable to myeloma
- No or low serum or urinary level of monoclonal protein and preserved levels of uninvolved immunoglobulins

The criteria for a soft tissue plasmacytoma are essentially similar.

types has been reported: plasmacytoma of bone has been reported to have a greater predilection to progress to multiple myeloma than soft tissue plasmacytoma. Other studies have shown no significant difference between these two locations and the incidence of evolution to myeloma.[536] The solitary plasmacytoma of bone may occur in both flat and long bones; the most common site is the axial skeleton, particularly a vertebra.[530,535–537] Soft tissue extension from bone lesions may occur. The majority of plasmacytomas of bone show osteolytic change on radiologic examination, although osteolytic/osteoblastic lesions may occur.[543] The most frequent sites of extramedullary or soft tissue plasmacytomas are the nasal fossa, maxillary sinus, and nasopharynx.[535,536] Extension into adjacent bone tissue may occur, and multiple lesions may be present.

On microscopic examination the plasmacytoma is frequently very vascular with a minimal stromal component and consists of sheets of plasma cells of varying degrees of differentiation[536] (Fig. 23.106). The plasmacytic nature of the proliferating cells is readily recognized in the better-differentiated lesions. In plasmacytomas with a predominant population of more immature cells with a dispersed nuclear chromatin and single prominent nucleolus, there usually is a minor population of more differentiated plasma cells. Amyloid may be present and was noted in 25% of the lesions in one series.[536]

Immunocytochemical study with antibodies to kappa and lambda light chains is an important approach to the evaluation of a suspected plasmacytoma. A kappa or lambda light chain-restricted population confirms a diagnosis of plasmacytoma (Fig. 23.106B). There is a predominance of IgG heavy chain type in solitary plasmacytoma of bone and IgA heavy chain type in plasmacytomas from the upper respiratory tract.

Patients with an apparent solitary plasmacytoma should be carefully evaluated for the presence of disseminated disease; studies should include bilateral iliac crest bone marrow biopsies, radiologic skeletal survey, magnetic resonance imaging of the spine, pelvis, humeri and

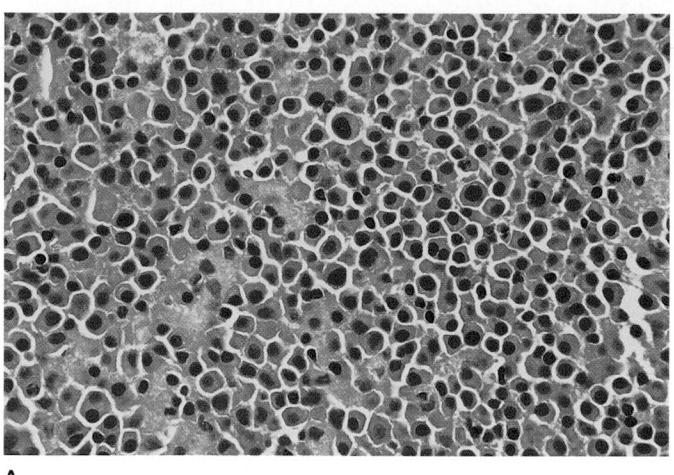
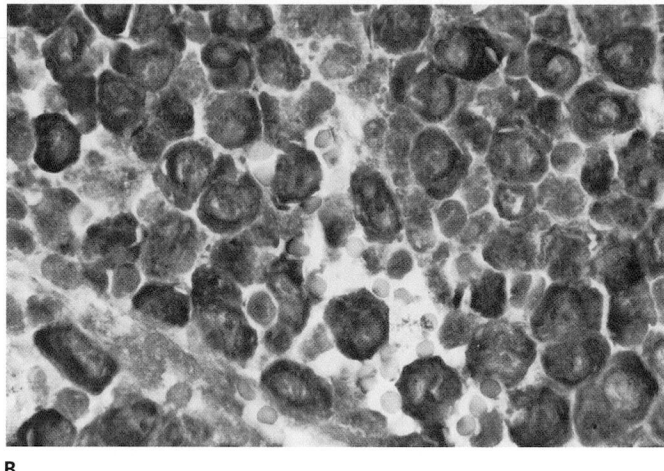

Fig. 23.106 A, Extramedullary plasmacytoma from the region of the nasopharynx. **B,** Plasmacytoma reacted with antibody to kappa light chains. The plasma cells show intense cytoplasmic reactivity. (**B,** Immunoperoxidase.)

femurs, immunoelectrophoretic examination of the serum and urine, and β_2-microglobulin assay. The patient with a solitary plasmacytoma usually has a normal hemoglobin level and no hypercalcemia. Approximately 50% of patients have a monoclonal protein in the serum and/or urine; the level almost invariably is less than 2 g/dl, and the nonmonoclonal immunoglobulins are normal in contrast to multiple myeloma, in which they are generally decreased. A marked reduction or disappearance of the monoclonal immunoglobulin will usually occur following tumoricidal radiation; the maximum reduction may not occur for several years.[536] Persistence of the monoclonal protein for more than one year after radiotherapy of the plasmacytoma has been identified as an adverse prognostic factor.[541]

Bone marrow biopsies performed on patients with a solitary plasmacytoma should be studied immunohistochemically with anti-kappa and anti-lambda antibodies to exclude the presence of a light chain-restricted population of plasma cells. Serum β_2-microglobulin levels should also be evaluated. The diagnosis of a solitary plasmacytoma should be made only if all studies for disseminated disease are negative.

Approximately 35% of patients with a solitary plasmacytoma who receive treatment, including radiation, chemotherapy, and surgical excision, will eventually develop multiple myeloma; this evolution may occur up to 12 years following initial diagnosis.[536] The presence of nuclear immaturity with prominent nucleoli appears to have some positive predictive value for the development of multiple myeloma. However, the presence of a monoclonal protein in serum, urine, or both does not predict the development of disseminated disease. Plasmacytomas of non-IgG immunoglobulin class have been reported to have a higher predilection for systemic spread than IgG-producing tumors. Local recurrence of the lesion is uncommon.

The differential diagnosis of a plasmacytoma includes plasma cell granuloma, plasmacytoid lymphoma, and large cell lymphoma of immunoblastic type. The plasma cell granuloma shows a balanced proliferation of kappa- and lambda-reacting cells on immunocytochemical evaluation. The plasmacytoid lymphoma comprises a mixture of lymphocytes and plasma cells. Some of the large cell lymphomas, particularly the B-immunoblastic lymphoma, may be difficult to distinguish from a plasmacytoma. The immunoblastic lymphoma will usually involve lymph nodes in contrast to a plasmacytoma. Immunophenotypic studies of plasmacytoma and immunoblastic lymphoma using a panel of monoclonal antibodies have shown significant immunophenotypic differences between these two processes.[540] The immunoblastic lymphomas have cytoplasmic IgM heavy chain and express pan-B-cell surface antigens such as CD19 and CD20. The plasmacytomas contain IgA or IgG heavy chain and are generally negative for pan-B-surface antigens; approximately 20% of plasmacytomas and myelomas are positive with pan-B-cell antibodies.

Lymphoplasmacytic lymphoma (Waldenström's macroglobulinemia)

In 1944, Waldenström described a clinical syndrome characterized by hyperglobulinemia, increased serum viscosity, and a proliferation of lymphocytes in hematopoietic tissue as well as other organs.[553] The clinical syndrome is referred to as Waldenström's macroglobulinemia in recognition of the original description and identification of the globulin as a macroglobulin in the majority of patients. The median age of onset is 60 years and there is a slight male predominance. Hepatosplenomegaly, lymphadenopathy, and neurologic abnormalities are frequent findings; anemia and hyperviscosity are commonly noted laboratory abnormalities.[544,553] The lymphoproliferative process associated with this syndrome usually involves the small B lymphocyte or the small B lymphocyte and plasmacytoid lymphocyte, i.e., lymphoplasmacytic lymphoma in the WHO classification.[544,548,549] Although commonly used to describe the histopathologic lesion occurring in patients with this syndrome, the term Waldenström's macroglobulinemia should be reserved for those patients with the clinical findings associated with an IgM paraproteinemia and lymphoplasmacytic lymphoma. Cases of lymphoplasmacytic lymphoma may also be associated with paraprotein of IgG and IgA type.[552] Some cases of lymphoplasmacytic lymphoma have no associated serum gammopathy.[544] IgM gammopathy may be associated with lymphomas other than plasmacytoid and has been reported in cases of multiple myeloma.[551]

The peripheral blood shows a leukemic picture in approximately 30% of cases; the predominant cells are small lymphocytes or a mixture of small lymphocytes and plasmacytoid lymphocytes. A similar population of cells predominates in the bone marrow[547,549,550] (Fig. 23.107). Mature plasma cells, tissue mast cells, and histiocytes may also be increased. In some cases, plasma cells may predominate. In marrow sections, the infiltrate may be focal or diffuse; the focal lesions may be preferentially paratrabecular or nonparatrabecular. Marrow involvement may be very extensive with a marked decrease in normal hematopoietic cells. Intranuclear inclusions, frequently referred to as Dutcher bodies, may be observed in some of the lymphocytes and plasma cells[547]; these inclusions, which are variably PAS positive, may be observed in other lymphomas, multiple myeloma, and reactive proliferations, and are not diagnostic of lymphoplasmacytic lymphoma.[545] In some cases of plasmacytoid lymphoma, the plasma cells and plasmacytoid lymphocytes contain abundant cytoplasmic inclusions. These inclusions may be numerous, and some of these cells resemble histiocytes; the inclusions are usually intensely PAS positive (Fig. 23.108). Plasma cells with similar inclusions may occasionally predominate in multiple myeloma. Like other small lymphocytic lymphomas, the lymphoplasmacytic lymphoma associated with Waldenström's macroglobulinemia may terminate with a clinicopathologic picture of Richter's syndrome.[546]

Heavy chain disease

The heavy chain diseases are clinical syndromes that are associated with the production of heavy chain fragments of the immunoglobulin molecule.[554–559] Gamma-chain disease has more of the features of a malignant lymphoma, lymphoplasmacytic type, than of multiple myeloma. The median age for this disease is 61 years, but it has been reported in individuals younger than 20.[558] Weakness, fatigue, fever, and lymphadenopathy are common symptoms; hepatomegaly, splenomegaly, and peripheral lymphadenopathy are each present in slightly more than half of the cases. There are frequently

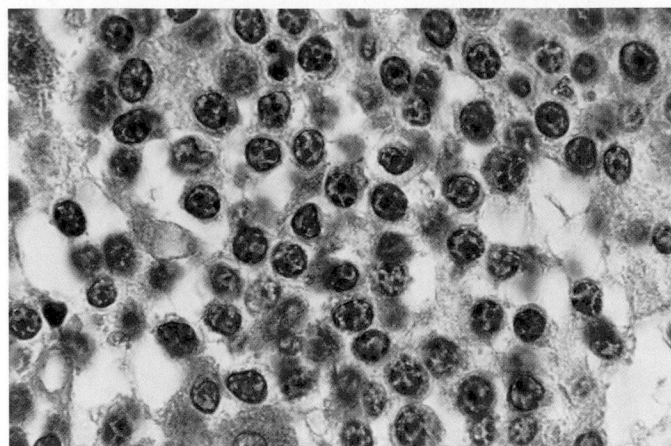

Fig. 23.107 Marrow from a patient with lymphoplasmacytic lymphoma and associated IgM gammopathy. The predominant lymphocytes have nuclei with very clumped chromatin and a slight to moderate amount of cytoplasm. Some lymphocytes contain small cytoplasmic and intranuclear inclusions. There is an increased number of tissue mast cells.

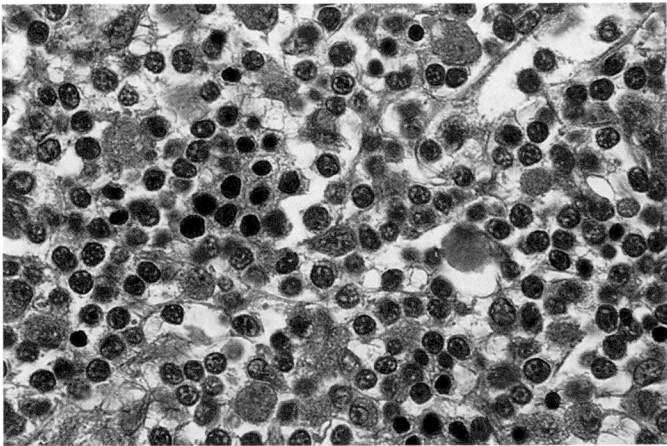

A

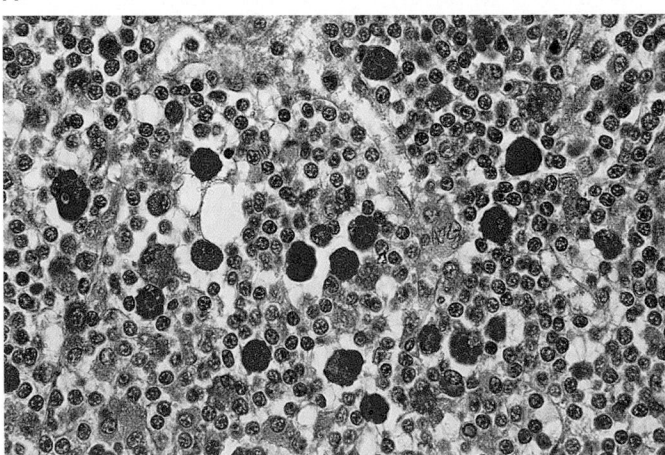

B

Fig. 23.108 A, Marrow section from a patient with lymphoplasmacytic lymphoma associated with serum IgM monoclonal gammopathy. Marrow is replaced by an infiltrate of lymphocytes and plasma cells; many of the plasma cells contain numerous cytoplasmic inclusions. Some lymphocytes contain prominent intranuclear inclusions (Dutcher bodies). **B,** Specimen illustrated in **A** reacted with PAS stain. Inclusions in plasma cells are strongly positive.

anemia, leukopenia, and thrombocytopenia. Atypical lymphocytes and plasma cells may be found in the peripheral blood. The bone marrow is usually abnormal and shows an increase in lymphocytes, plasma cells, or both. Occasionally the marrow is normal. There may be an accompanying eosinophilia. Most of the reported cases of mu-chain disease have had long histories of CLL.[555,557] The marrow in several of the reported cases contained vacuolated plasma cells. Alpha-chain disease is associated with extranodal marginal zone B-cell lymphoma (MALToma); the marrow is not usually involved. The occurrence of tumors composed of undifferentiated lymphoid cells in patients with heavy chain disease has been reported.[557,560]

Amyloidosis

Bone marrow biopsies in patients with systemic amyloidosis are performed to detect evidence of the disease and to ascertain the number of plasma cells and whether there is a light chain predominant population of plasma cells. In a large single institution study of 474 patients with primary systemic amyloidosis, 56% of marrow biopsies were positive; abdominal fat aspirate was positive in 80%.[567] One or both sites were positive in 89% of patients. In rare cases, amyloid may be detected in marrow biopsies from patients without any clinical evidence of disease.

Primary systemic amyloidosis is associated with another form of plasma cell dyscrasia in approximately 35% of patients; the two most common disorders are multiple myeloma and monoclonal gammopathy of undetermined significance.[563,565,568] The distinction between primary amyloidosis with or without associated myeloma can be difficult and is usually based on a constellation of clinical and morphologic findings. The majority of patients with concurrent myeloma and primary systemic amyloidosis have more than 10% marrow plasma cells which show either lambda or kappa light chain predominance demonstrated by flow cytometric or immunohistochemical studies.

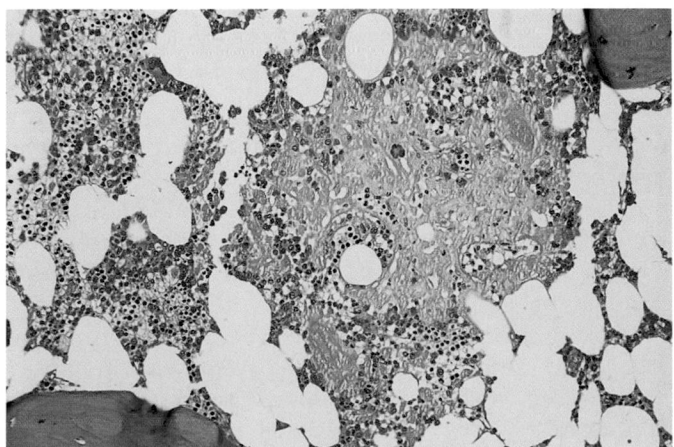

Fig. 23.109 Marrow with amyloid accumulation from a 50-year-old woman with primary amyloidosis.

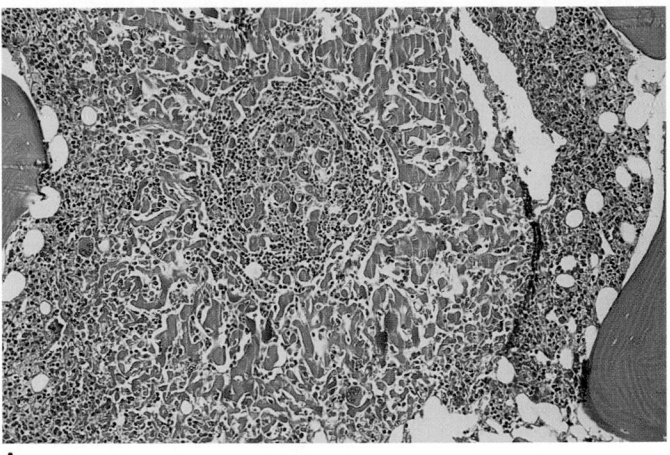

A

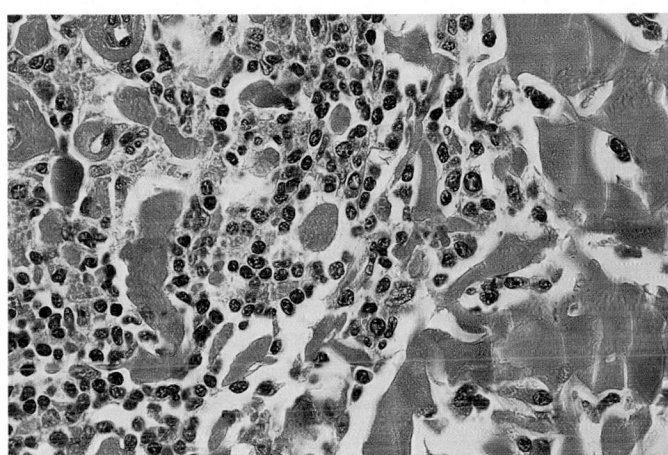

B

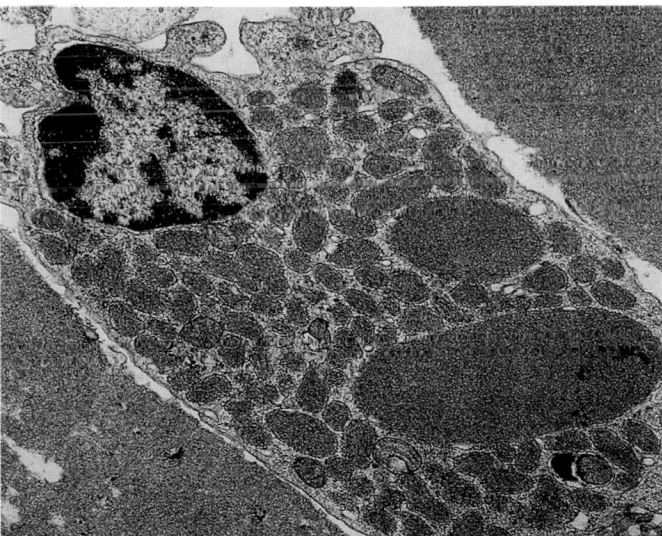

C

Fig. 23.110 Proteinaceous myelopathy. **A,** Marrow biopsy from a 25-year-old female with a 10-year history of lupus erythematosus. There is extensive intercellular accumulation of an amorphous eosinophilic substance resembling amyloid but lacking the histochemical and ultrastructural findings of amyloid. There is an associated proliferation of plasma cells and small lymphocytes. The plasma cells consisted of both kappa and lambda light chain positive populations. **B,** High magnification of the specimen in **A. C,** Ultrastructure of the intracellular and extracellular material. There was complete regression of the finding following high dose steroid and vinblastine therapy.

Marrow involvement may manifest either as small focal lesions or as extensive marrow replacement.[570] Early involvement is characterized by focal deposits of amyloid in the medullary vessels; these range from small deposits in the media to large accumulations that greatly expand the vessel walls, resulting in narrowing of the lumen. With more extensive involvement, the accumulation of amyloid is present in the perivascular tissue and marrow substance (Fig. 23.109). Congo red staining should be performed to confirm the diagnosis.

Very rarely a proteinaceous deposition resembling amyloid but lacking the histochemical and electron microscopic characteristics of amyloid, similar to the findings in proteinaceous lymphadenopathy, may occur in the marrow in association with immune disorders (Fig. 23.110). The origin of the proteinaceous substance appears to be immunoglobulin or portions of the immunoglobulin molecule produced by cells of the immune system, and the findings have been referred to as immune deposition disease.[561,562,564,569]

Systemic polyclonal B-immunoblastic proliferation

A florid polyclonal proliferation of B immunoblasts accompanied by a polyclonal hypergammaglobulinemia may occur in patients with a variety of immune disorders and involve blood, bone marrow, and lymph nodes.[571,572,574,575] The leukocyte count may be elevated with a high percentage of B immunoblasts, cells with intensely basophilic cytoplasm, relatively coarse nuclear chromatin, and distinct nucleoli. There frequently is some evidence of maturation of these cells to plasma cells. The bone marrow may show extensive infiltration and may resemble lymphoma or plasmablastic myeloma with immunoblasts, plasma cells, and intermediate forms (Fig. 23.111). Lymph nodes may show a similar infiltrate, with complete effacement of the normal architecture. Immunologic studies are critical in the evaluation of these lesions. The polyclonal nature of the infiltrate is demonstrated with immunocytochemical reactions that show essentially a balanced population of kappa- and lambda-reacting cells[573-575] (Fig. 23.111B,C).

The biology of this process is not completely clear; in some patients it appears to represent an acute immune reaction, and it has been observed in patients with laboratory findings of acute lupus erythematosus. It may in some instances be analogous to the polymorphous lymphoid lesions observed in transplant patients. There may be dramatic regression following steroid therapy.[574,575]

Systemic mastocytosis

Systemic mastocytosis is a relatively rare disorder characterized by mast cell proliferation in several organs. It

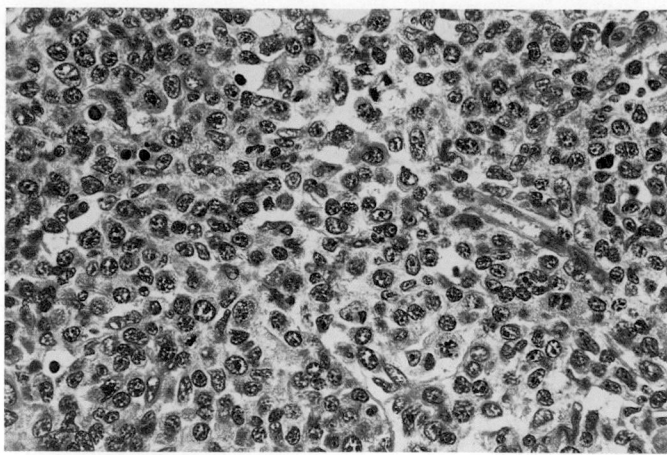

A

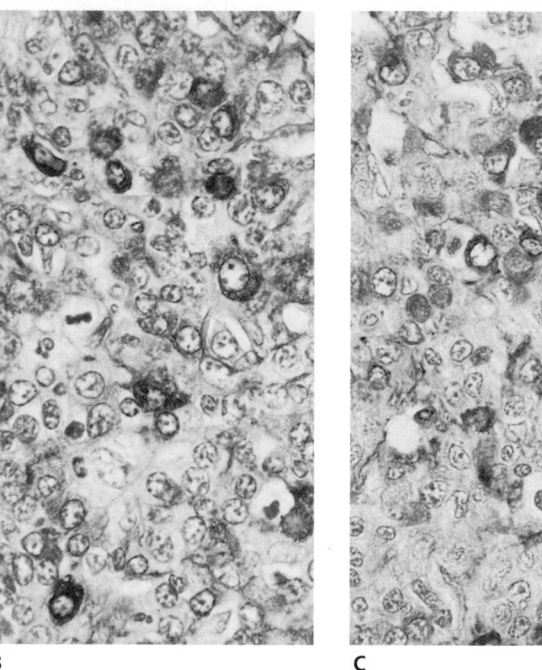

B   C

Fig. 23.111 A, Marrow biopsy from a 28-year-old woman with an autoimmune disorder characterized by extensive infiltration of marrow by plasma cells, lymphocytes and immunoblasts.
B, C, Specimen in **A** reacted with anti-kappa (**B**) and anti-lambda (**C**) antibodies using peroxidase–antiperoxidase– immunoperoxidase technique. There is balanced reactivity for kappa- and lambda-reacting cells. (**B** and **C,** Immunoperoxidase.)

usually occurs in combination with urticaria pigmentosa but may present in patients without cutaneous involvement.[576,577] The median age for patients presenting with systemic mastocytosis with urticaria pigmentosa is 45 years, the median age for patients with systemic mastocytosis presenting without urticaria pigmentosa is around 75 years.[576,594] The clinical symptoms are varied and include diarrhea, weakness, fractures, weight loss, arthralgia, flushing episodes, and bronchospasm.[576,589,593,594] An occasional patient may experience anaphylactoid shock. Splenomegaly may be present. Osteoblastic, osteolytic, or concurrent osteoblastic–osteolytic lesions may be found on radiologic examination; generalized osteoporosis may also occur (Fig. 23.112).

The blood findings may include eosinophilia, anemia, leukocytosis, or leukopenia, thrombocytopenia, and pancytopenia.[582]

The proposed World Health Organization classification of mastocytosis, based principally on a consensus classification published in 2001, is shown in Table 23.4.[595,596]

The bone marrow is the most frequent site of noncutaneous involvement in systemic mastocytosis; lesions may be found as a result of a specific search or may be detected in a biopsy performed for some purpose unrelated to suspected mastocytosis. In the latter instance, when there is no clinical suspicion of the disease, the lesions may be overlooked or misinterpreted because of the difficulty in identifying mast cells in routine sections and because of the changes inherent in the mast cells in

this disease; the cells are frequently large, spindled, or have lobulated nuclei and decreased granules that may be much smaller than normal mast cell granules.[581,590] Smears obtained by bone marrow aspirate may suggest the diagnosis of mastocytosis if large numbers of atypical mast cells are present; however, up to 7% mast cells have been reported in aspirate preparations in patients without mast cell disease.[588] An increase in mast cells may also be observed in lymphocytic and lymphoplasmacytic lymphomas and hairy cell leukemia.[599] A marked increase in mast cells in the marrow has been observed following the administration of stem cell growth factor. Because systemic mastocytosis may be associated with marked fibrosis, mast cells may not be readily aspirated.

The 2001 *WHO classification of hematopoietic tumours* proposes one major and four minor criteria for the diagnosis of systemic mastocytosis (Table 23.5).[596]

The mast cell lesions in bone marrow sections may be focal or diffuse. Focal lesions are more common and may be paratrabecular, perivascular, or randomly distributed.[576,578,585,598] The paratrabecular lesions frequently are marked by a margination of the infiltrate along the endosteal surface of the bone structure or juxtaposition of a lesion to a bone spicule. The perivascular lesions may be associated with prominent medial and adventitial hypertrophy and collagen fibrosis.

The focal lesions are variable in appearance but generally can be classified into two primary types based on cell

Table 23.4 WHO classification of mastocytosis[595,596]

Cutaneous mastocytosis
Indolent systemic mastocytosis
Systemic mastocytosis with associated clonal hematologic disorder
Aggressive systemic mastocytosis
Mast cell leukemia
Mast cell sarcoma
Extracutaneous mastocytoma

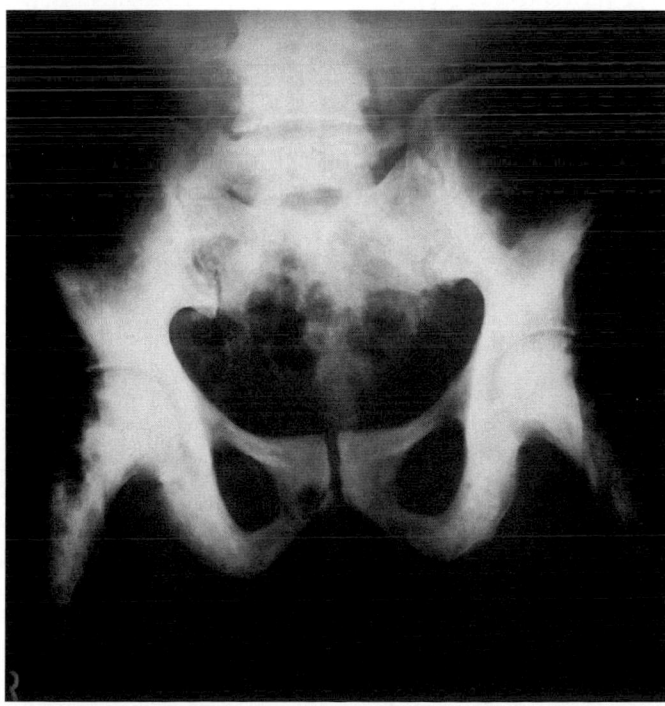

Fig. 23.112 Radiograph of pelvis and upper femurs from a patient with systemic mastocytosis; both osteosclerotic and osteolytic changes are prominent.

Table 23.5 Major and minor criteria for diagnosis of systemic mastocytosis[595,596]

A. Major criterion:
Multifocal dense infiltrates of mast cells (≥15 mast cells in aggregates detected in sections of bone marrow and/or other extracutaneous organs and confirmed by tryptase immunohistochemistry.
B. Minor criteria:
1. In biopsy section of bone marrow or other extracutaneous organs, more than 25% of the mast cells in the infiltrate are spindle shaped or have atypical morphology, or, of all the mast cells in bone marrow smears, more than 25% are immature or atypical mast cells.
2. Detection of *KIT* point mutations at codon 816 in specimens of bone marrow, blood or other extracutaneous organ.
3. Mast cells in bone marrow, blood or other extracutaneous organs that co-express CD117 with CD2 and/or CD25.
4. Serum total tryptase ≥20 ng/ml unless there is an associated clonal myeloid disorder, in which case this parameter is invalid.

The diagnosis of systemic mastocytosis may be made if the major and one minor criteria are present, or if three of the minor criteria are present.

composition: polycellular and monocellular. Both types may be observed in the same specimen. The polycellular lesions are characterized by mast cells, lymphocytes, histiocytes, eosinophils, neutrophils, fibroblasts, and endothelial cells in varying proportions; the eosinophils are frequently more numerous at the margins of the lesion. In some cases the different cell types appear to be randomly distributed; in others, the mast cells occur in a central aggregate and are surrounded by well-differentiated lymphocytes, or the mast cells encircle a focus of lymphocytes (Fig. 23.113). The mast cells in these lesions are frequently atypical and characterized by spindle shape and abundant eosinophilic cytoplasm with very fine granules. In the monomorphic lesions, the cellular composition is predominantly mast cells with only scattered lymphocytes and eosinophils (Fig. 23.114). The mast cells in these lesions may appear as intertwining bundles and vary in shape from round in cross section to spindle shaped in longitudinal cut. The cytoplasm is pale

to lightly eosinophilic. The nuclei are round or oval; occasionally the nuclei have a monocytoid configuration. Nucleoli are inconspicuous, and mitotic figures are rare. Some of these lesions may resemble aggregates of histiocytes or granulomas. The marrow exclusive of the mast cell lesions is usually hypercellular or normocellular with a granulocytic hyperplasia.[576,583,589] The diffuse lesions are characterized by the same cell types as the focal lesions. Changes in the bone trabeculae may be present; both widening and erosion of the trabeculae may be observed. Rarely, evidence of new bone formation may be present (Fig. 23.115). Reticulin stains show varying degrees of reticulin fibrosis.

There is an increased incidence of myeloproliferative disorders in patients with systemic mastocytosis: this is recognized in the WHO classification. The spectrum of disorders includes acute leukemia, myelodysplastic

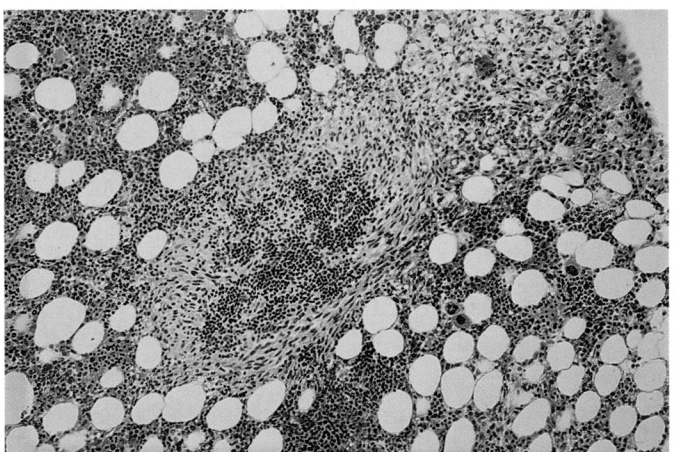

Fig. 23.113 Lesion in bone marrow from a patient with systemic mastocytosis and no evidence of urticaria pigmentosa. A central focus of well-differentiated lymphocytes is surrounded by lighter-staining mast cells.

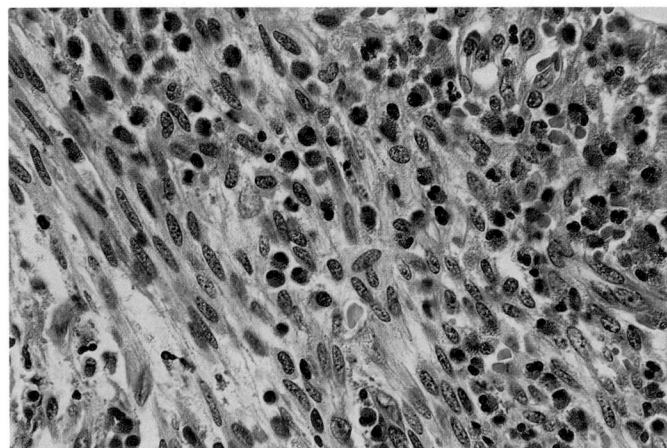

Fig. 23.114 High magnification of a marrow lesion in systemic mastocytosis. The mast cells have a spindle appearance. There are numerous interspersed eosinophils.

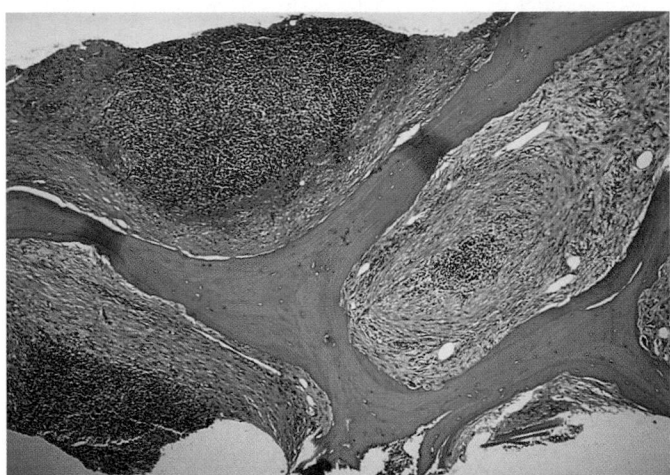

A

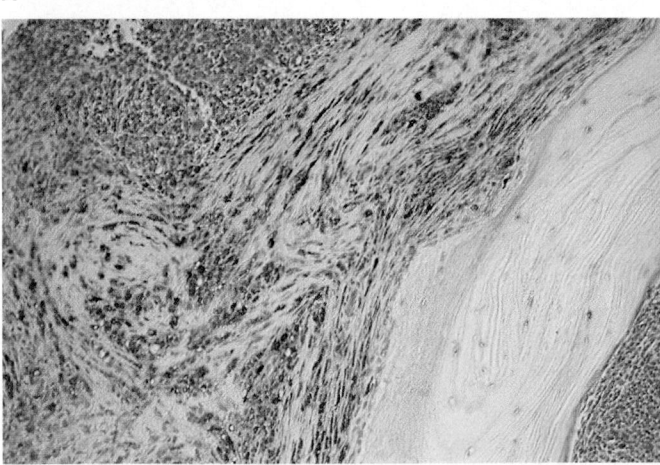

B

Fig. 23.115 **A**, Marrow biopsy from an adult male with systemic mastocytosis associated with a myeloproliferative disorder and no evidence of urticaria pigmentosa. There is extensive paratrabecular fibrosis and widening of bone trabeculae. The intervening marrow is markedly hypercellular, principally due to myeloid hyperplasia. Radiographic studies showed diffuse osteoblastic changes. **B**, Mast cell tryptase stain of the lesion in **A** showing numerous reactive cells.

syndromes, and chronic myeloproliferative disorders[580] (Fig. 23.116). Philadelphia chromosome positive chronic myeloid leukemia, however, is rarely encountered. The chronic myeloproliferative disorder occurring with systemic mastocytosis has more the features of a chronic myelomonocytic leukemia or an unclassified chronic myeloproliferative disorder. Caution should be exercised in the diagnosis of a concurrent myeloproliferative process in patients with mastocytosis as it is possible that marked myeloid hyperplasia may occur as the result of cytokines produced by the mast cell proliferation.

A highly specific antibody to human mast cell tryptase that may be used on decalcified and B5-fixed paraffin-embedded specimens is very useful for identification of mast cell lesions[597] (Fig. 23.116B). Other antibodies that react with mast cells include antibodies to α-antitrypsin, α-antichymotrypsin, CD68, and CD117 (c-kit).[579,584,600]

Because the mast cells in mastocytosis may be very atypical and possess very abundant cytoplasm without evident granules or have a fibroblastic appearance, there may be considerable difficulty in recognizing the true nature of the cells. Mast cell granules react with both toluidine blue and Giemsa stains. The granules are metachromatic and appear reddish purple. Considerable variability in degree of positivity and number of positive granules may be observed among different cells. The reactivity of the granules can be enhanced in decalcified tissue by treatment of the sections with potassium permanganate followed by oxalic acid before the staining procedure.[578] Zenker's and B5 fixatives, however, may interfere with reactivity with both Giemsa and toluidine blue stains. Mast cells also react with chloroacetate esterase in formalin-fixed tissue decalcified with EDTA; this stain may not work satisfactorily in specimens decalcified in rapid acid decalcifier or biopsy specimens processed with acid fixatives such as Zenker's or B5. The metachromatic and chloroacetate reactions have been largely supplemented by immunohistochemical studies.

The differential diagnosis of mast cell lesions in the marrow includes angioimmunoblastic such as T-cell lymphoma, Hodgkin's disease, chronic idiopathic myelofibrosis and granulomatous inflammation. The eosinophilic fibrohistiocytic lesion described by Rywlin and colleagues has many of the histopathologic characteristics of mastocytosis lesions and in most instances is a form of mast cell disease.[586,587,592] The primary distinction of mastocytosis from the other disorders is based on the immunohistochemical demonstration of mast cells with antibody to mast cell tryptase. Mast cells may be increased in lymphocytic and lymphoplasmacytic lymphomas and hairy cell leukemia in marrow biopsies but are diffusely scattered among the lymphoma cells and do not form mass lesions.[599]

Occasional patients with systemic mastocytosis may present with marked eosinophilia mimicking the hypereosinophilic syndrome with cardiac and central nervous system findings. Marrow examination should clarify the diagnosis.

The treatment of systemic mast cell tissue has generally been unsatisfactory with most antineoplastic agents. Cladribine (2-chlorodoxyudenosine) has been successful in some initial studies.[591]

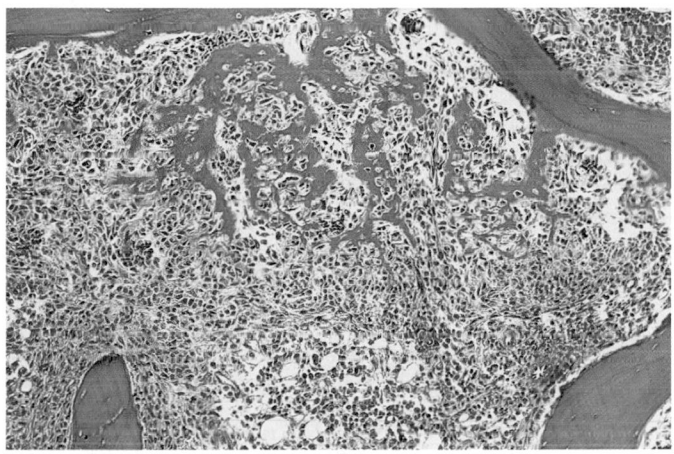

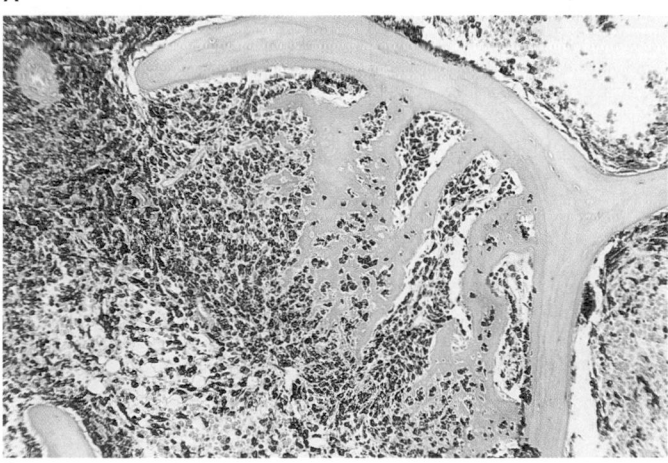

Fig. 23.116 A, Bone marrow biopsy from a patient with concurrent acute myeloblastic leukemia and systemic mastocytosis. Mast cell infiltration in this area of biopsy was associated with new bone formation. No other areas in bilateral biopsies show this finding. This was the patient's first marrow biopsy. **B,** Specimen in **A** reacted with antibody to mast cell tryptase. (**B**, Immunoperoxidase.)

Metastatic tumors

Bone marrow biopsies are used frequently for the staging of patients with histologically documented malignancies; they also may be performed on patients with suspected malignancy in an attempt to obtain material for a histologic diagnosis.[607,611,623,624,629,632] The tumors most frequently detected in bone marrow biopsies in adults are carcinoma of the breast, prostate, lung, stomach, colon, kidney, and thyroid gland. The bone marrow biopsy is widely used for staging small cell carcinoma of the lung.[601,603,609,614–623] Sarcomas have a relatively low incidence of marrow metastasis in adults.[605] In the pediatric age group, neuroblastoma is the most common metastatic lesion, followed by rhabdomyosarcoma, Ewing's sarcoma, and retinoblastoma.[613,626,630] Wilms' tumor metastatic to marrow is extremely uncommon.

In smears, tumor cells frequently, but not invariably, occur in clusters. This may be an important diagnostic feature because tumors of hematopoietic origin generally do not occur in cohesive aggregates. In marrows with extensive involvement, both clusters and individual cells may be present. In some small cell tumors the individual cells may resemble malignant lymphoid cells. In trephine sections, metastatic tumor may occur as small focal lesions surrounded by normal hematopoietic cells, or it may replace virtually the entire specimen. In focal lesions or those occupying only a portion of the biopsy, the tumor foci may be sharply demarcated from the adjacent hematopoietic tissue or may be associated with an irregularly shaped area of fibrosis (Figs 23.117, 23.118). Many tumors, most notably breast and prostate, may be associated with a marked desmoplastic reaction, and attempts at aspiration may be unsuccessful. These tumors also may be accompanied by marked osteosclerosis (Figs 23.119, 23.120). In the unusual occurrence of a metastatic sarcoma in the marrow, the lesion may resemble primary myelofibrosis.

In the majority of cases of metastatic tumor in marrow smears and aspirates, the tumor cells have characteristics that clearly distinguish them from normal hematopoietic cells. This distinction is aided by the frequent desmoplastic reaction that accompanies some of the tumors that most commonly metastasize to the marrow. In some instances the metastatic tumor cells may have features suggesting a hematopoietic origin, particularly megakaryocytes. This may be a particular problem with some cases of rhabdomyosarcoma in which the tumor cells may react with antibodies to platelet glycoproteins (Fig. 23.121). Antibody studies for actin and desmin and

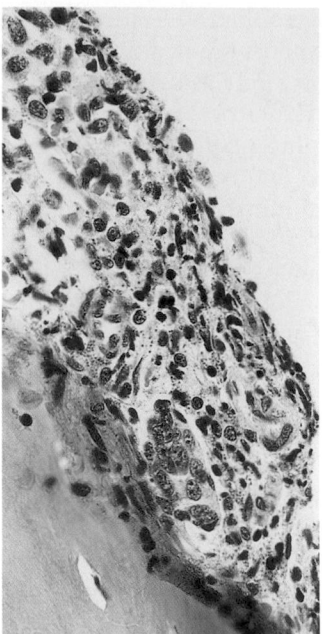

A

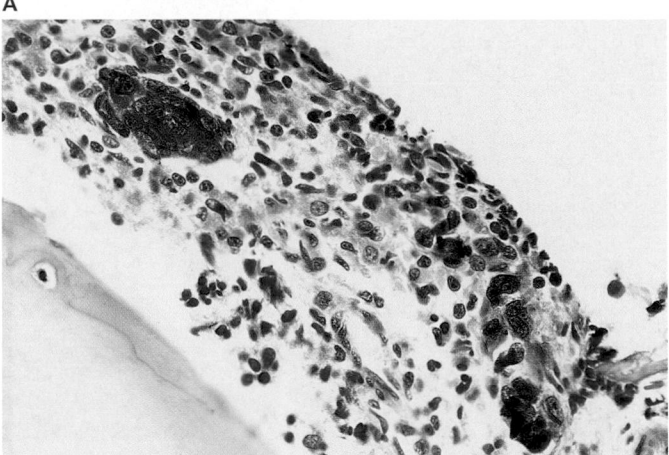

B

Fig. 23.118 A, Marrow biopsy from a child with metastatic neuroblastoma with small focal lesions. B, Specimen reacted with antibody to neuron-specific enolase. Small clusters of reactive cells are present. This was the only involved area in the biopsy. (B, Immunoperoxidase.)

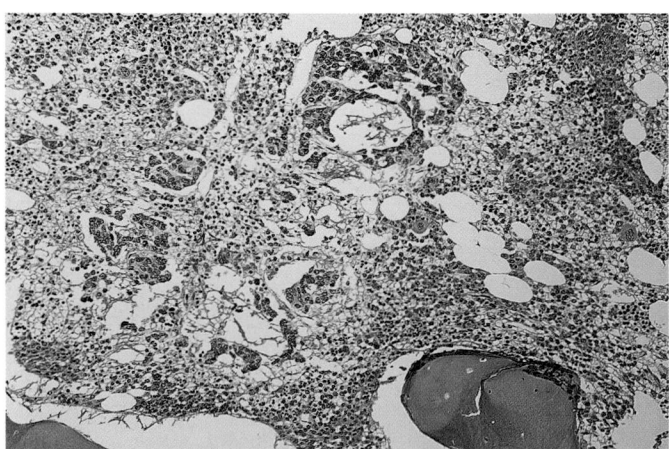

Fig. 23.117 Marrow biopsy from a child with metastatic neuroblastoma. Several foci of tumor are present.

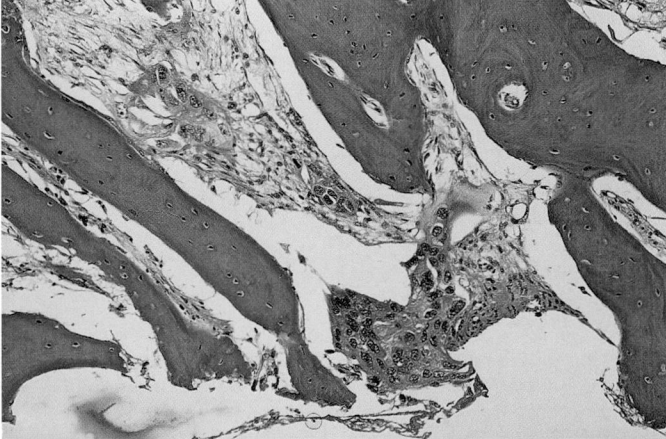

Fig. 23.119 Marrow from a patient with metastatic carcinoma of breast with osteosclerotic reaction and foci of tumor cells.

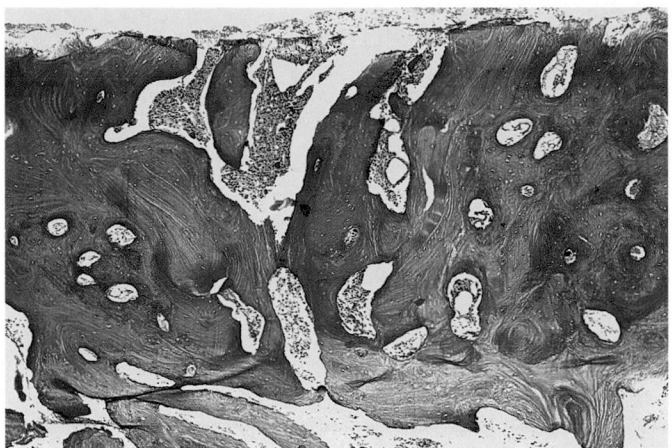

Fig. 23.120 Marrow biopsy from a patient with metastatic carcinoma of prostate with a marked osteoblastic lesion.

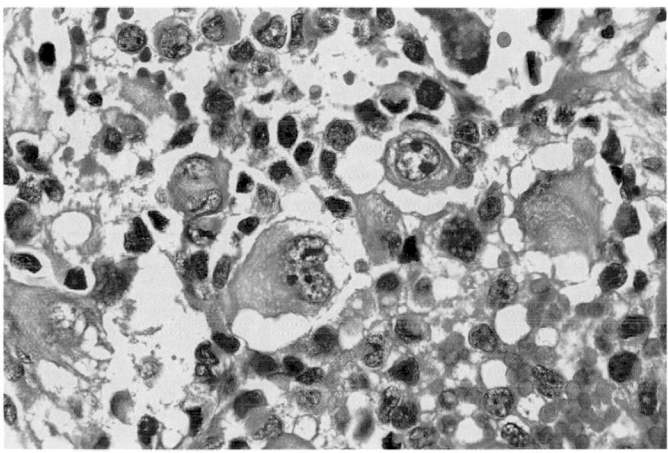

A

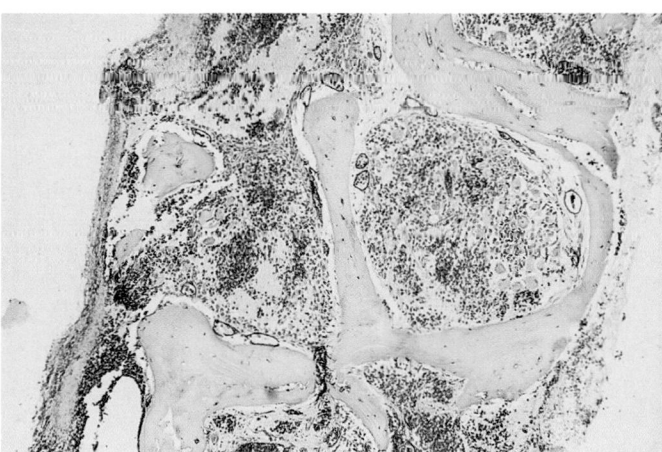

B

Fig. 23.121 A, Bone marrow biopsy from a 17-year-old male with partial replacement of marrow by a pleomorphic population of cells, some of which are large with very abundant cytoplasm. Larger cells have one or two nuclei with distinct and frequently prominent nucleoli. The majority of the cells reacted with antibodies to actin (**B**) and desmin; chromosome studies of the cells showed a t(2;13) (q35;q14) abnormality, a characteristic cytogenetic finding in alveolar rhabdomyosarcoma.

cytogenetic studies may be useful in recognizing this tumor (Fig. 23.121B).

The approach to determining the site of origin of a metastatic tumor in a patient without a known primary lesion should be the same as for determining metastatic lesions in other sites. Immunocytochemical techniques may be particularly useful both for determining the possible site of origin and for detecting small lesions.[622,624] Antibodies to the common leukocyte antigen are useful in distinguishing a malignant lymphoma from metastatic carcinoma or sarcoma. As with other tissue, it is important to use a panel of antibodies that has the capacity to recognize all reasonable possibilities. In instances in which small foci are identified with the immunocytochemical reaction, the tumor should be found in adjacent sections stained with hematoxylin and eosin. Electron microscopic studies may provide definitive evidence of cell origin in some cases.

Detection of micrometastasis from lung and breast carcinoma in bone marrow is increased with the use of immunologic markers applied to smears prepared from Ficoll Hypaque-separated specimens of bone marrow aspirate.[610,612,625] Molecular techniques for the identification of markers increase the detection level of micrometastasis.[602]

Special note is made here of neuroblastoma because the bone marrow biopsy may serve as the primary diagnostic specimen in patients with neuroblastoma if the aspirate or trephine biopsy specimen contains unequivocal tumor cells and there is significantly increased serum or urinary catecholamines or metabolites.[604,606,628] Because the detection rate increases with multiple biopsies, two aspirates and one trephine biopsy specimen from each posterior iliac crest are recommended for assessment of marrow involvement. Patients with stage 4S disease have less than 10% involvement; if there is more than 10%, the disease is stage 4.[606]

Tumor cells may be detected in bone marrow smears, particle sections, trephine imprints, or trephine biopsies. The relative merits of these various techniques for detecting tumor have been the subject of considerable discussion. The yield of positive results has increased with the performance of multiple trephine biopsies. Metastatic neuroblastoma in marrow sections may show varying degrees of differentiation. Following therapy, the lesions may show marked differentiation to ganglion cells (Fig. 23.122).

Immunologic markers may be used for the identification of neuroblastoma cells; antibodies to neuron-specific enolase, synaptophysin, and chromogranin have been recommended by the Second International Neuroblastoma Staging System Conference.[606] Immunocytologic quantification of neuroblastoma cells in bone marrow and blood at diagnosis and in marrow during induction therapy can identify patients with very high risk disease.[631]

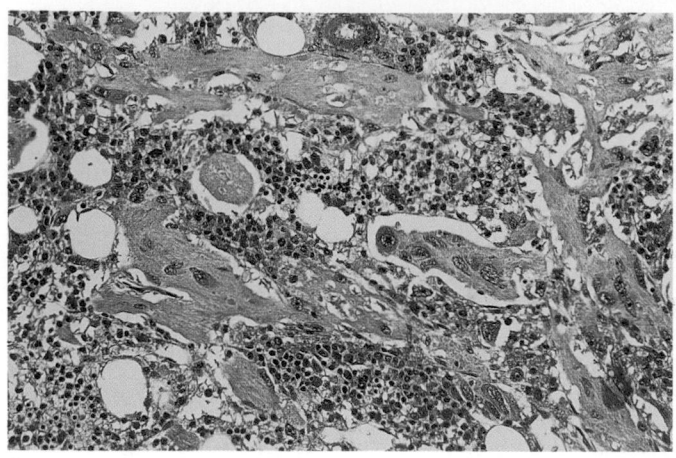
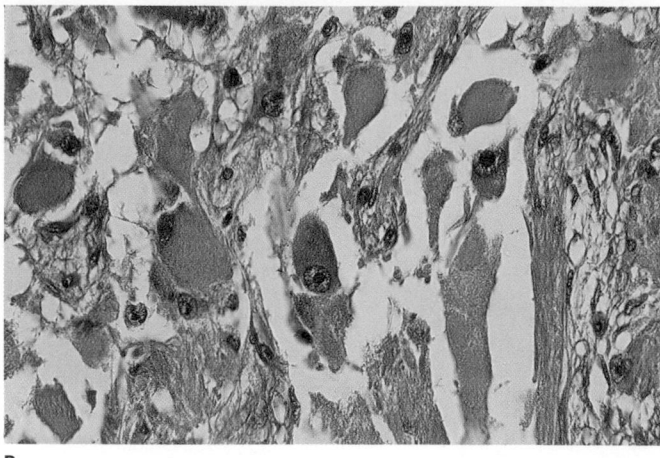

A   **B**

Fig. 23.122 **A**, Marrow biopsy from a child with metastatic neuroblastoma with ganglion differentiation. **B**, High magnification of the specimen in **A** showing marked variability in size of the tumor cells. In contrast to megakaryocytes, some tumor cells contain single, very prominent, nuclei. (See Fig. 23.10, which is the same specimen reacted with antibody to neuron-specific enolase.)

GD2 synthetase is a molecular marker for detecting metastatic neuroblastoma.[627] Immunostaining of marrow aspirates with anti-G (D2) monoclonal antibodies increases the detection rate of neuroblastoma cells in marrows with particularly low numbers of tumor cells.[608]

Lipid storage diseases

Gaucher's disease

Gaucher's disease is an autosomal recessive sphingolipid storage disorder resulting from the accumulation of glucosylceramide (glucocerebroside) in organs and tissues as a result of a deficiency in lysosomal β-glycosidase (glucocerebrosidase) which is encoded by a gene on chromosome 1.[633,634,636,640] It occurs in three forms: type I, chronic non-neuronopathic (adult) type; type II, acute neuronopathic type; and type III, subacute neuronopathic (juvenile) type.

The characteristic diagnostic morphologic feature of the disorder is the presence of Gaucher cells in the bone marrow, spleen, liver, and lymph nodes and other organs.

In the bone marrow sections, Gaucher cells may be found in small focal accumulations or may replace large portions of a biopsy. There is an associated increase in reticulin fibers. In imprint and smear preparations, the Gaucher cell is large, 30 to 100 μm in diameter, and has one or more centrally or eccentrically located nuclei.[635,639] The cytoplasm has a characteristic fibrillary or striated pattern and is pale blue–gray in color. In sections stained with H & E, the cytoplasm is slightly eosinophilic; a fibrillary pattern may be very prominent (Fig. 23.123). The Gaucher cells are variably and often intensely positive with the PAS reaction. The cells also stain positively for iron in older children and adults. Cells similar to

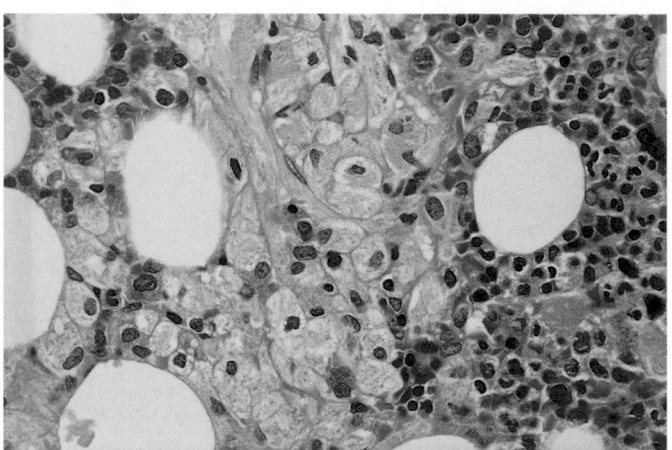

Fig. 23.123 Bone marrow section from an adult with type I chronic non-neuronopathic Gaucher's disease. The cytoplasm of many Gaucher cells has a fibrillary or granular appearance. Nuclei are small and usually eccentric in location.

Gaucher cells, pseudo-Gaucher cells, may be found in the marrow of some patients with chronic myelogenous leukemia,[637,638,641] type II congenital dyserythropoietic anemia,[645] and thalassemia.[646]

A monoclonal gammopathy may be present in patients with chronic Gaucher's disease and may be associated with a marrow plasmacytosis.[642] The coincidence of multiple myeloma, plasmacytoid lymphoma, and Gaucher's disease has been reported.[644]

Treatment of patients with Type 1 (adult type) Gaucher's disease with recombinant β-glucocerebrosidase (imiglucerase) results in a decrease in the relative volume of bone replaced by Gaucher cells and an increase in hematopoietic and fat cells and a decreased cortical bone structure. The decrease in amount of marrow replaced by Gaucher cells is the result of a decrease in both the number and size of Gaucher cells.[643]

Niemann–Pick disease

Niemann–Pick disease comprises a group of autosomal recessive sphingomyelin–cholesterol lipidoses characterized by organomegaly and the accumulation of sphingomyelin and other lipids throughout the body as a result of a deficiency of lysosomal acid sphingomyelinase.[647–652] The gene encoding acid sphingomyelinase in humans has mapped to chromosome 11 bands p 15.1–15.4. Three major clinical types are recognized: an acute neuronopathic form (A); a chronic form without nervous system involvement (B); and a chronic neuronopathic form (C).[650,651] The foam cell, as seen in the bone marrow in Niemann–Pick disease types A and B, does not have diagnostic specificity and may be found in other disorders of lipid metabolism such as hypercholesterolemia and Tangier disease.[648] In Romanowsky-stained smears, the cell measures 20 to 50 μm; the cytoplasm is filled with clear vacuoles of varying size.[648,649] In sections, the cells are randomly scattered singly and in aggregates; the cytoplasm of the Niemann–Pick cell is marked by confluent clear vacuoles of varying size. The cells may be difficult to appreciate because of the very light-staining cytoplasm. The nucleus is randomly located (Fig. 23.124). The vacuoles are PAS negative and positive with lipid stains.

Niemann–Pick disease type C is a panethnic autosomal recessive lipidosis with linkage to chromosome 18.[650] The basic defect involves a unique error in cellular trafficking of exogenous cholesterol that is associated with a lysosomal accumulation of unesterified cholesterol; the disease is distinct from the sphingomyelin lipidoses, Niemann–Pick disease types A and B. Foam cells or sea-blue histiocytes may be present in the marrow; these however are not distinctive and may be observed in several different lipidoses.

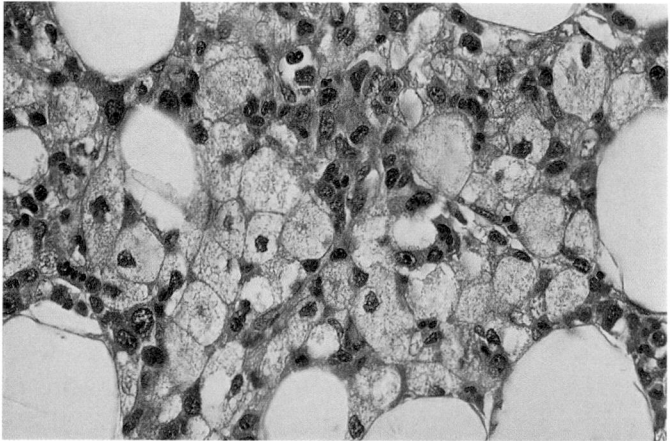

Fig. 23.124 Biopsy from a 14-month-old child with Niemann–Pick disease. Focal accumulations of foam cells are present. The cytoplasm of the foam cells is clear, with the suggestion of numerous confluent vacuoles.

Fabry's disease

Fabry's disease is an X-linked recessive inborn error of glycosphingolipid metabolism caused by deficient activity of α-galactosidase.[654] The characteristic storage cells in bone marrow specimens in this disease are filled with small globular inclusions that stain blue in Romanowsky-stained smears and are lightly eosinophilic in sections stained with H & E.[653,654] The cytoplasmic substance reacts intensely with the PAS and Sudan black B stains.

Sea-blue histiocyte syndrome

The macrophages of the sea-blue histiocyte syndrome[655,657,658] contain a substance that stains blue in Romanowsky-stained smears and yellow to tan in sections stained with H & E. Positive reactions occur with the PAS and Sudan black B stains. In some instances, the substance appears to be ceroid; in others the material has not been well characterized. Macrophages containing blue pigment may be observed in several unrelated disorders and lack diagnostic specificity. This cell type has also been reported in some cases of Niemann–Pick disease. The sea-blue histiocytes may resemble the macrophages in Whipple's disease, which may rarely be detected in marrow specimens.[656]

Bone marrow transplantation

Bone marrow transplantation is being increasingly used as a therapeutic approach in patients with primary bone marrow disease.[659] The objective of bone marrow transplantation is reconstitution of normal hematopoiesis in marrows that are aplastic; the aplasia may be the result of aplastic anemia or the marrow is rendered aplastic with chemotherapy and radiation in the preparative regimen employed prior to marrow transplantation for various neoplastic processes or, less commonly, inherited disorders.

The source of the marrow graft may be the patient's own marrow that has been harvested prior to the preparatory regimen (autologous) or from another individual (allogeneic), or peripheral blood stem cells. Autologous marrow in some cases is "purged" with chemotherapeutic agents and/or monoclonal antibodies to eradicate malignant cells. Umbilical cord blood cells are also being used.

Bone marrow transplant involves preparing the patient for transplant with a regimen utilizing chemotherapy with or without total body irradiation therapy. The preparative regimen has two purposes: to immunosuppress the patient and to eradicate malignant cells that may be present in the recipient. For patients with severe aplastic anemia, cyclophosphamide alone or cyclophosphamide plus antithymocyte globulin or cyclophosphamide plus total lymphoid irradiation has been utilized most commonly and now provides long-term success rates of over 80% in matched sibling donor patients. For patients with leukemia, regimens including chemotherapy and total body irradiation have most commonly been used; the combination of busulfan and cyclophosphamide has been successful in the preparation of patients with acute myeloid leukemia.

The major complications associated with bone marrow transplantation involve infection in the severely immunosuppressed host, graft rejection, and graft-versus-host disease.[663] Recurrent disease is also a cause of failure in patients with malignant diseases. Infection continues to be a major cause of peritransplant morbidity and, in some cases, mortality. The use of better antibiotics and growth factors to accelerate white blood cell production has decreased but not eliminated infectious complications. Graft rejection is an infrequent complication of matched sibling donor transplant; however, it is a significant complication in patients undergoing unrelated donor transplant, especially for diseases such as aplastic anemia. Certain methods of graft-versus-host disease prophylaxis, specifically T-cell depletion, may be associated with an increased risk of graft rejection.

The rate of engraftment following bone marrow transplantation is influenced by several factors, and although some generalizations can be made about reconstitution of hematopoiesis, there are frequent exceptions.[660–664] The amount of marrow damage incurred prior to the transplant from chemotherapy and radiation used for treatment of the disease for which the transplant is necessary may influence the success rate. Autologous marrow specimens that have been purged with antibodies or chemotherapeutic agents may reconstitute less quickly than allogeneic marrow grafts. The disease for which the transplant was performed may recur early in the transplant period.

Marrow biopsies are not usually performed in the first 7 days following transplantation. However, the marrow biopsies performed during this period show marked hypocellularity with hemorrhage and proteinaceous debris. Scattered fat cells and macrophages are present. The findings are similar to those in patients treated with myelotoxic agents for acute leukemia.[660–662,664] At 7 to 14 days, adipose tissue is reconstituted. The appearance of the marrow in the second to third week is variable; there may be evidence of hematopoiesis, or the marrow may be markedly hypocellular (Figs 23.125, 23.126). The initial stages of engraftment are usually characterized by foci of hematopoietic cells scattered throughout the adipose tissue in what appears to be a random distribution. These foci initially are usually unilineage and composed of tight clusters of erythroid precursors followed by aggregates of promyelocytes and myelocytes (Fig. 23.125B). Blasts are not increased. There is no preferential paratrabecular distribution of the promyelocyte and

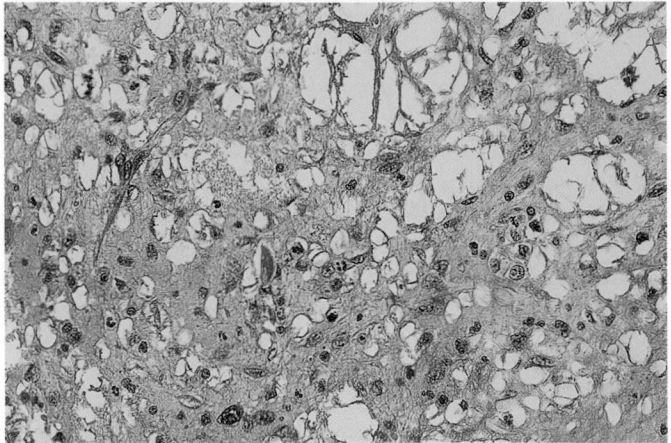

A

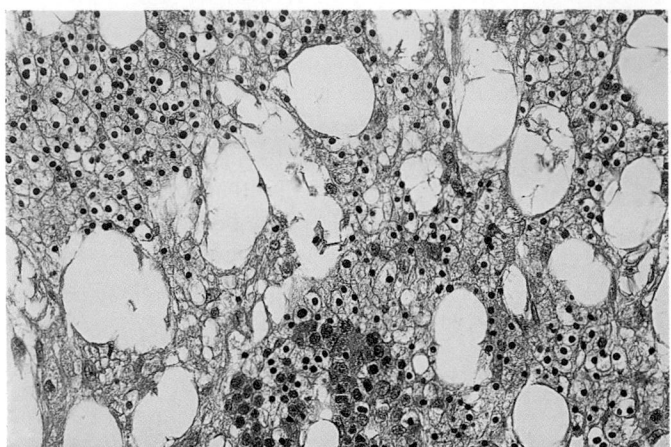

B

Fig. 23.125 A, Marrow biopsy 4 days post allogeneic marrow transplant for blast crisis of chronic myeloid leukemia. The marrow is markedly hypocellular with scattered cells and abundant interstitial proteinaceous debris. B, Marrow biopsy from the patient illustrated in A 28 days post transplant. Evidence of engraftment is characterized principally by erythroid precursors at a late stage of maturation and foci of more immature forms. There was no evidence of a t(9;22) cytogenetic abnormality in either biopsy.

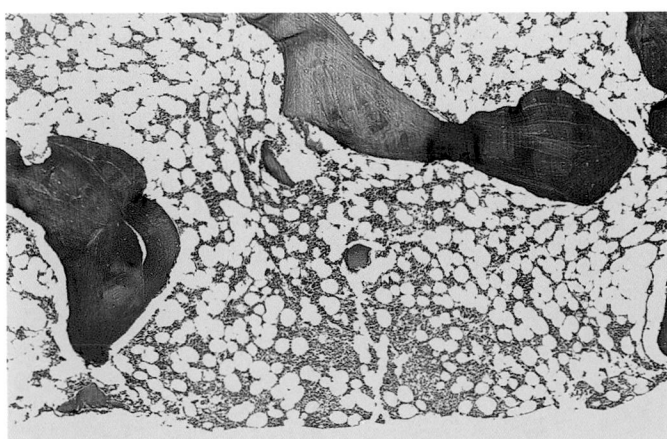

Fig. 23.126 Marrow biopsy from a 7-year-old child 14 days post allogeneic bone marrow transplant for aplastic anemia. The marrow is moderately to markedly hypocellular. Subsequent biopsies showed failure of engraftment.

myelocyte islands in this period. Megakaryocytes are usually sparse. Following this stage there is progressive spreading of the hematopoietic cells throughout the interstitium and gradual regression of adipose tissue; the foci of hematopoiesis at this stage of recovery are usually multilineage, although predominantly monolineage proliferation may persist (Figs 23.127, 23.128). Megakaryocyte reconstitution may lag behind the granulocytic and erythroid cells for prolonged periods. In some patients, megakaryocytes appear early in the engraftment period and may form small aggregates. There may be considerable variability in the amount of hematopoietic tissue in different areas of a large biopsy specimen; clot sections, small specimens, or fragmented specimens may be misleading.

There may be a marked shift to promyelocytes and myelocytes early in the post-transplant period; this is accentuated by the administration of recombinant granulocyte growth factor (Fig. 23.129). This shift to immaturity is not usually accompanied by an increase in blasts. During this period, patients frequently receive a large number of drugs, some of which may be associated with agranulocytosis. This factor should be considered in patients who manifest prolonged neutropenia with a morphologic appearance of "maturation arrest" of neutrophils in the marrow specimen.

Granulomas occur with greater frequency in post-transplant marrows than in marrows from other groups of patients; these granulomas usually consist of only a small collection of epithelioid histiocytes. In some cases, giant cells are present. Phagocytic histiocytes may be increased and diffusely scattered throughout the marrow. The histiocytes may manifest marked phagocytic activity; this finding warrants evaluation for an infectious process.

The rate of growth of the graft varies substantially in the first 3 to 4 weeks. In some cases the marrow may remain hypocellular for many months or years; in other cases one of the major myeloid cell lines remains depressed (Figs 23.130, 23.131). Remission of myelofibrosis and osteosclerosis may occur (Fig. 23.132).

Loss of graft is reflected by decreasing marrow cellularity and progressive cytopenias. This may occur gradually or abruptly. In some instances, there is a dissociation between the blood counts and marrow cellularity, with very hypocellular marrows and normal blood counts or normocellular marrows and blood cytopenias. Marrow sampling may be the basis of the discrepancy when normal blood counts occur with hypocellular marrow. There are no specific marrow findings reflecting graft-versus-host disease.

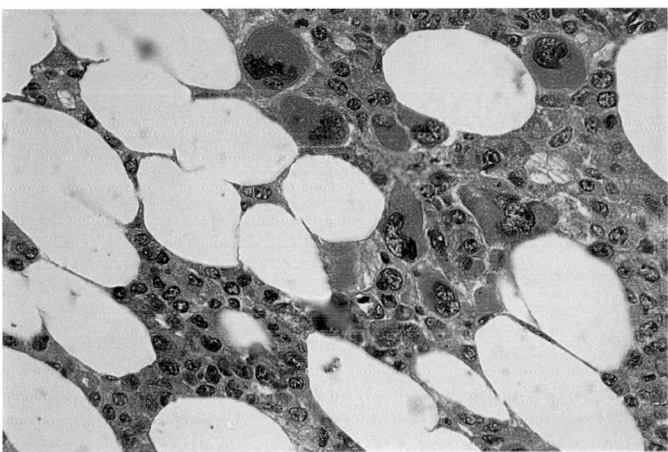

Fig. 23.127 Marrow from an adult male 18 days post unrelated marrow transplant for acute myeloid leukemia. The marrow is markedly hypocellular with scattered clusters of normal-appearing megakaryocytes; there is no evidence of leukemia.

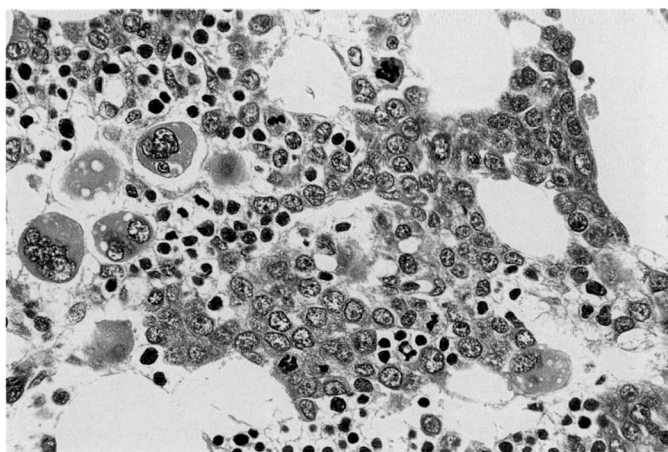

Fig. 23.128 Marrow from an adult female 21 days post autologous marrow transplant for chronic myeloid leukemia illustrating a focus of erythroid precursors at an early stage of maturation in an overall hypocellular marrow. Erythroid precursors at a late stage of maturation are located in the surrounding interstitium; there are several normal-appearing megakaryocytes.

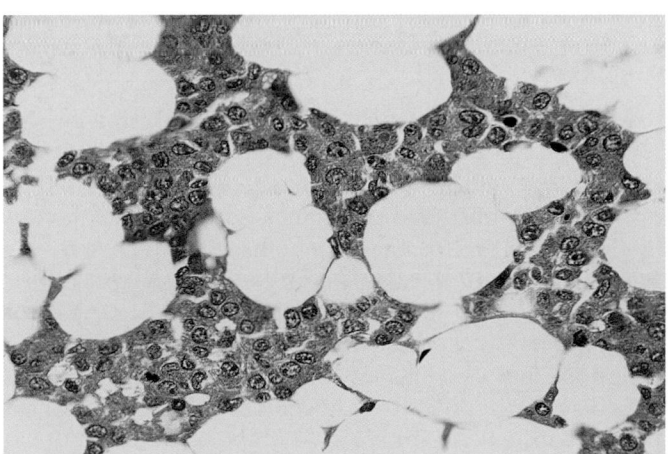

Fig. 23.129 Marrow biopsy 20 days post allogeneic sibling transplant for chronic myeloid leukemia; three days prior to the biopsy the patient received granulocyte colony stimulating factor for marked neutropenia. The cells in the interstitium are neutrophil precursors at the promyelocyte–myelocyte stage of maturation, a characteristic early effect of growth factor stimulation.

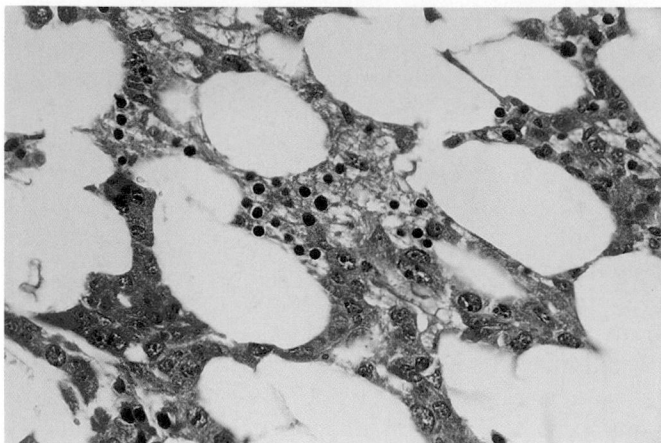

Fig. 23.130 Marrow biopsy from an 11-year-old child 100 days following unrelated donor marrow transplant for chronic myeloid leukemia. The marrow is moderately to markedly hypocellular with erythroid and granulocyte precursors and only rare megakaryocytes.

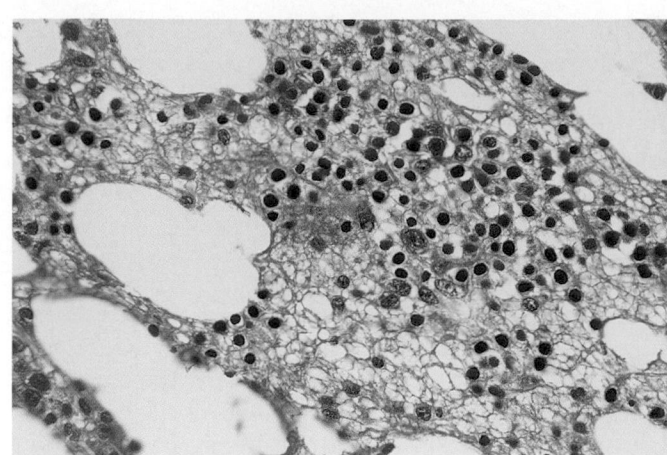

Fig. 23.131 Marrow biopsy from an adult 8 months following autologous marrow transplant for chronic myeloid leukemia. The marrow is markedly hypocellular with markedly decreased granulocytes and megakaryocytes. The interstitium is markedly depleted with principally late stage erythroid precursors.

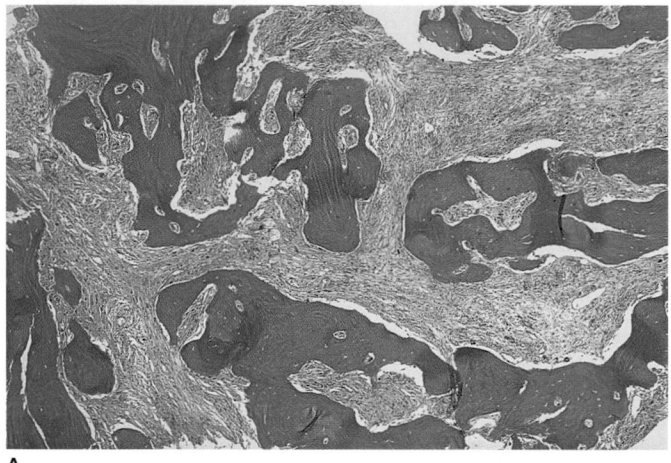

A

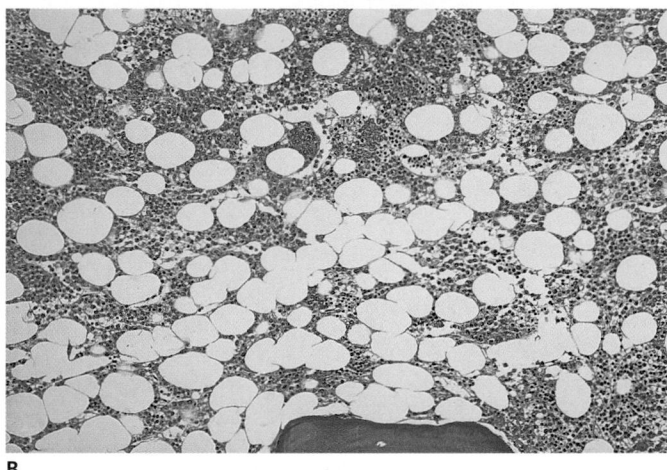

B

Fig. 23.132 A, Marrow biopsy with marked osteosclerosis from a 32-year-old patient with Philadelphia chromosome-positive chronic myeloid leukemia immediately prior to marrow transplant. **B,** Marrow biopsy from the patient illustrated in **A** 5 months post allogeneic marrow transplant. There is complete resolution of the osteosclerosis. The cytogenetics from this specimen were normal.

Marrow transplants in patients with leukemia present the additional problem of recognition of recurrent disease. Cytogenetics, membrane surface markers, and molecular studies are very important adjuncts to morphology in the evaluation of these patients. Fluorescent in situ hybridization studies using probes for the X and Y chromosomes may be used to determine graft and host cell populations in gender-mismatched transplants. This technique may also be used to identify recurrent leukemic cells in instances in which a specific cytogenetic defect has been identified and for which a probe is available.

References

Biopsy procedure and processing of specimen

1 Bain BJ. Bone marrow aspiration. J Clin Pathol 2001, **54:** 657–663.
2 Bain BJ. Bone marrow trephine biopsy. J Clin Pathol 2001, **54:** 737–742.
3 Brinn NT, Pickett JP. Glycol methacrylate for routine, special stains, histochemistry, enzyme histochemistry and immunohistochemistry. A simplified method for surgical biopsy tissue. J Histotechnol 1979, **2:** 125–130.
4 Brunning RD, Bloomfield CD, McKenna RW, Peterson L. Bilateral trephine bone marrow biopsies in lymphoma and other neoplastic diseases. Ann Intern Med 1975, **82:** 365–366.
5 Burkhardt R, Frisch B, Bartl R. Bone biopsy in haematological disorders. J Clin Pathol 1982, **35:** 257–284.
6 Contreras E, Ellis LD, Lee RE. Value of the bone marrow biopsy in the diagnosis of metastatic carcinoma. Cancer 1972, **29:** 778–783.
7 Dee JW, Valdivieso M, Drewinko B. Comparison of the efficacies of closed trephine needle biopsy, aspirated paraffin-embedded clot section, and smear preparation in the diagnosis of bone marrow involvement by lymphoma. Am J Clin Pathol 1976, **65:** 183–194.
8 Ellman L. Bone marrow biopsy in the evaluation of lymphoma, carcinoma, and granulomatous disorders. Am J Med 1976, **60:** 1–7.
9 Garrett TJ, Gee TS, Leiberman PH, McKenzie S, Clarkson BD. The

role of bone marrow aspiration and biopsy in detecting marrow involvement by non-hematologic malignancies. Cancer 1976, 38: 2401–2403.

10 Gatter KC, Heryet A, Brown DC, Mason DY. Is it necessary to embed bone marrow biopsies in plastic for haematological diagnosis? Histopathology 1987, 11: 1–7.

11 Gruppo RA, Lampkin BC, Granger S. Bone marrow cellularity determination. Comparison of the biopsy, aspirate and buffy coat. Blood 1977, 49: 29–31.

12 Jamshidi K, Swaim WR. Bone marrow biopsy with unaltered architecture: A new biopsy device. J Lab Clin Med 1971, 77: 335–342.

13 Liao KT. The superiority of histologic sections of aspirated bone marrow in malignant lymphomas. Cancer 1971, 27: 618–628.

14 McCarthy DM. Annotation, fibrosis of the bone marrow: content and causes. Br J Haematol 1985, 59: 1–7.

15 Peterson LC, Brunning RD. Bone marrow specimen processing. In Knowles DM (ed): Neoplastic hematopathology, ed. 2. Philadelphia, 2001, Lippincott, Williams & Wilkins, pp. 1391–1406.

16 Wang J, Weiss LM, Chang KL, Slovak ML, Gaal K, Forman SJ, Arber DA. Diagnostic utility of bilateral bone marrow examination, significance of morphologic and ancillary technique study in malignancy. Cancer 2002, 94: 1522–1531.

Immunohistology

17 Arber DA, Jenkins KA. Paraffin section immunophenotyping of acute leukemias in bone marrow specimens. Am J Clin Pathol 1996, 106: 462–468.

18 Arber DA, Snyder DS, Fine M, Dagis A, Niland J, Slovak ML. Myeloperoxidase immunoreactivity in adult lymphoblastic leukemia. Am J Clin Pathol 2001, 116: 25–33.

19 Bluth RF, Casey TT, McCurley TL. Differentiation of reactive from neoplastic small-cell lymphoid aggregates in paraffin-embedded marrow particle preparations using L-26 (CD20) and UCHL-1 (CD45RO) monoclonal antibodies. Am J Clin Pathol 1993, 99: 150–156.

20 Brown DC, Gatter KC. Monoclonal antibody Ki-67: its use in histopatholoy. Histopathology 1990, 17: 489–503.

21 Brown DC, Gatter KC. The bone marrow trephine biopsy: a review of normal histology. Histopathology 1993, 22: 411–422.

22 Chuang SS, Li CY. Useful panel of antibodies for the classification of acute leukemia by immunohistochemical methods in bone marrow trephine biopsy specimens. Am J Clin Pathol 1997, 107: 410–418.

23 Dhillon AP, Rode J, Leathem A. Neuron specific enolase. An aid to the diagnosis of melanoma and neuroblastoma. Histopathology 1982, 5: 81–92.

24 Dunphy C, Polski JM, Evans HL, Gardner LJ. Evaluation of bone marrow specimens with acute myelogenous leukemia for CD34, CD15, CD117 and myeloperoxidase. Arch Pathol Lab Med 2001, 125: 1063–1069.

25 Erber WN, Gibbs TA, Ivey JG. Antigen retrieval by microwave oven heating for immunohistochemical analysis of bone marrow trephine biopsies. Pathology 1996, 28: 45–50.

26 Erber WN, Willis JI, Hoffman GJ. An enhanced immunocytochemical method for staining bone marrow trephine sections. J Clin Pathol 1997, 50: 389–393.

27 Horny HP, Wehrmann M, Griesser H, Tiemann M, Bültmann B, Kaiserling E. Investigation of bone marrow lymphocyte subsets in normal, reactive, and neoplastic states, using paraffin-embedded biopsy specimens. Am J Clin Pathol 1993, 99: 142–149.

28 Kremer M, Dirnhofer S, Nickl A, Hoefler H, Quintanilla-Martinez L, Fend F. p27kip1 immunostaining for the differential diagnosis of small B-cell neoplasms in trephine bone marrow biopsies. Mod Pathol 2001, 14: 1022–1029.

29 Kronland R, Grogan T, Spier C, Wirt D, Rangel C, Richter L, Durie B, Greenberg B, Miller T, Jones S. Immunotopographic

assessment of lymphoid and plasma cell malignancies in the bone marrow. Hum Pathol 1985, 16: 1247–1254.

30 Kubic VL, Brunning RD. Immunohistochemical evaluation of neoplasms in bone marrow biopsies using monoclonal antibodies reactive in paraffin embedded tissue. Mod Pathol 1989, 2: 618–629.

31 Mason DY, Comans-Bitter WM, Cordell JL, Verhoeven MAJ, von Dongen JJM. Antibody L26 recognizes an intracellular epitope on the B cell associated CD20 antigen. Am J Pathol 1990, 136: 1215–1222.

32 Norton AJ, Isaacson PG. Monoclonal antibody L26: an antibody that is reactive with normal and neoplastic B lymphocytes in routinely fixed and paraffin wax embedded tissues. J Clin Pathol 1987, 40: 1405–1412.

33 Peterson LC, Brown BA, Crosson JT, Mladenovic J. Application of the immunoperoxidase technic to bone marrow trephine biopsies in the classification of patients with monoclonal gammopathies. Am J Clin Pathol 1986, 85: 688–693.

34 Pileri SA, Ascani S, Milani M, Visani G, Piccioli M, Orcioni GF, Poggi S, Sabattini E, Santini D, Falini B. Acute leukemia immunophenotyping in bone marrow routine sections. Br J Haematol 1999, 105: 394–401.

35 Pinkus GS, Pinkus JL. Myeloperoxidase. A specific marker for myeloid cells in paraffin sections. Mod Pathol 1991, 4: 733–741.

36 Poje EJ, Soori GS, Weisenburger DS. Systemic polyclonal B-immunoblastic proliferation with marked peripheral blood and bone marrow plasmacytosis. Am J Clin Pathol 1992, 98: 222–226.

37 Poppema S, Hollema H, Visser L, Vos H. Monoclonal antibodies (MT1, MT2, MB1, MB3) reactive with leukocytes subsets in paraffin-embedded tissue sections. Am J Pathol 1987, 127: 418–429.

38 Seshi B, True L, Carter D, Rosai J. Immunohistochemical characterization of a set of monoclonal antibodies to human neuron-specific enolase. Am J Pathol 1988, 131: 258–269.

39 Torlakovic E, Torlakovic G, Nguyen PI, Brunning RD, Delabie J. The value of anti-Pax-5 immunostaining in routinely fixed and paraffin embedded sections: a novel pan pre-B and B-cell marker. Am J Surg Pathol 2002, 26: 1343–1350.

40 Tsang WYW, Chan JKC, Ng CS, Pau MY. Utility of a paraffin section reactive CD56 antibody (123C3) for characterization and diagnosis of lymphoma. Am J Surg Pathol 1996, 20: 202–210.

41 Walls AF, Jones DB, Williams JH, Church MK, Holgate ST. Immunohistochemical identification of mast cells in formaldehyde-fixed tissue using monoclonal antibodies specific for tryptase. J Clin Pathol 1990, 162: 119–126.

42 Zutter M, Hockenbery D, Silverman GA, Korsmeyer SJ. Immunolocalization of the bcl-2 protein within hematopoietic neoplasms. Blood 1991, 78: 1062–1068.

Normocellular bone marrow

43 Hartsock RJ, Smith EB, Petty CS. Normal variations with aging of the amount of hematopoietic tissue in bone marrow from the anterior iliac crest. Am J Clin Pathol 1965, 43: 326–331.

43a Wickramasinghe SN. Bone marrow. In: Sternberg S (ed.). Histopathology for Pathologists 1997, 2e. Lippincott–Raven Publishers pp. 707–744.

Alterations in cellularity
Aplastic anemia

44 Ajlouni K, Doeblin T. The syndrome of hepatitis and aplastic anemia. Br J Haematol 1974, 27: 345–355.

45 Alter BP, Potter NU, Li FP. Classification and aetiology of the aplastic anemias. Clin Haematol 1978, 7: 431–465.

46 Crook TW, Rogers BB, McFarland RD, Kroft SH, Maretto P, Herandez JA, Latimer MJ, McKenna RW. Unusual bone marrow manifestations of parvovirus B19 infection in immunocompromised patients. Human Pathol 2000, 31: 161–168.

47 Dawson JP. Congenital pancytopenia associated with multiple congenital anomalies (Fanconi type). Review of the literature and report of a 20-year-old female with a 10-year follow-up and apparently good response to splenectomy. Pediatrics 1955, 15: 325–333.

48 Dessypris EN. The biology of pure red cell aplasia. Semin Hematol 1991, 28: 275–284.

49 Dokal I, Ganly P, Riceberg I, Marsh J, Steed A, Kendra J, Drysdale C, Hows C. Late onset bone marrow failure associated with proximal fusion of radius and ulna: a new syndrome. Br J Haematol 1989, 71: 277–289.

50 Estren S, Dameshek W. Familial hypoplastic anemia of childhood. Am J Dis Child 1947, 73: 671–687.

51 Evans DI. Congenital defects of the marrow stem cell. Bailliere's Clin Haematol 1989, 2: 162–190.

52 Gordon-Smith EC, Rutherford TR. Fanconi anaemia—constitutional, familial aplastic anaemia. Bailliere's Clin Haematol 1989, 2: 139–153.

53 Goswitz FA, Andrews GA, Kniseley RM. Effects of local irradiation (Co60 teletherapy) on the peripheral blood and bone marrow. Blood 1963, 21: 605–619.

54 Haak HL, Hartgrink-Groeneveld CA, Eernisse JG, Speck B, Van Rood JJ. Acquired aplastic anemia in adults. Acta Haematol 1977, 58: 257–277.

55 Kurtzman G, Young N. Viruses and bone marrow failure. Bailliere's Clin Haematol 1989, 2: 51–67.

56 Mark M, Rijli FM, Chambon P. Homeobox gene in embryogenesis and pathogenesis. Pediatr Res 1997, 42: 421–429.

57 Naeim F, Smith GS, Gale RP. Morphologic aspects of bone marrow transplantation in patients with aplastic anemia. Hum Pathol 1978, 9: 295–308.

58 Nissen C. The pathophysiology of aplastic anemia. Semin Hematol 1991, 28: 313–318.

59 Orazi A, Albitar M, Heerema NA, Haskins NS, Neiman RS. Hypoplastic myelodysplastic syndrome can be distinguished from acquired aplastic anemia by CD34 and PCNA immunostaining of bone marrow biopsy specimens. Am J Clin Pathol 1997, 107: 268–274.

60 Rosse WF. Paroxysmal nocturnal hemoglobinuria in aplastic anemia. Clin Haematol 1978, 7: 541–553.

61 Saarinen UM, Chorba TL, Tattersall P, Young NS, Anderson LJ, Palmer E, Coccia PF. Human parvovirus B-19 induced epidemic acute red cell aplasia in patients with hereditary hemolytic anemia. Blood 1986, 67: 1411–1417.

62 Sale GE, Marmont BS. Marrow mast cell counts do not predict bone marrow graft rejection. Hum Pathol 1980, 12: 605–608.

63 Shwachman H, Diamond LK, Oski FA, Khaw KT. The syndrome of pancreatic insufficiency and bone marrow dysfunction. J Pediatr 1964, 65: 645–663.

64 Smith GP, Perkins SL, Segal GH, Kjeldsberg CR. T-cell lymphocytosis associated with invasive thymomas. Am J Clin Pathol 1994, 102: 447–453.

65 Thompson AA, Nguyen LT. Amegakaryocytic thrombocytopenia and radio-ulnar synostosis are associated with HOX A11 mutation. Nat Genet 2000, 26: 397–398.

66 Young NS, Maciejewski J. The pathophysiology of aplastic anemia. N Engl J Med 1997, 336: 1365–1372.

Gelatinous transformation (serous degeneration)

67 Abella E, Feliu E, Granada I, Milla F, Oriol A, Ribera JM, Sanchez-Planell L, Berga LL, Reverter JC, Rozman C. Bone marrow changes in anorexia nervosa are correlated with the amount of weight loss and not with other clinical findings. Am J Clin Pathol 2002, 118: 582–588.

68 Bohm J. Gelatinous transformation of the bone marrow; the spectrum of underlying disease. Am J Surg Pathol 2000, 24: 56–65.

69 Seaman JP, Kjeldsberg CR, Linker A. Gelatinous transformation of the bone marrow. Hum Pathol 1978, 9: 685–692.

Osteopetrosis

70 Gerritsen EJ, Vossen JM, Van Loo IHG, Hermans J, Helfrich MH, Griscelli C, Fischer A. Autosomal recessive osteopetrosis: variability of findings at diagnosis and during the natural course. Pediatrics 1994, 93: 247–253.

71 Gerritsen JA, Vossen JM, Fasth A, Friedrich W, Morgan G, Padmos A, Vellodi A, Porras O, O'Meara A, Porta F, Bordigoni P, Cant A, Hermans J, Griscell C, Fischer A. Bone marrow transplantation for autosomal recessive osteopetrosis. A report from the Working Party on Inborn Errors of the European Bone Marrow Transplantation Group. J Pediatr 1994, 125: 896–902.

72 Coccia PF, Krivit W, Cervenka J, Clawson C, Kersey JH, Nesbit ME, Ramsay NK, Warkentin PI, Teitelbaum SL, Kahn AJ, Brown DM. Successful bone marrow transplantation for infantile malignant osteopetrosis. N Engl J Med 1980, 302: 701–708.

Bone marrow necrosis

73 Brown CH. Bone marrow necrosis. A study of seventy cases. Johns Hopkins Med J 1972, 131: 189–203.

74 Goodall HB. Atypical changes in the bone marrow in acute infections. In Clark WJ, Howard EB, Hackett PL (eds): Myeloproliferative disorder of animal and man. Oak Ridge, Tennessee, 1970, United States Energy Commission, pp. 314–339.

75 Kahlstron SC, Burton CC, Phemister DB. Infarction of bones in caisson disease. Surg Gynecol Obstet 1939, 68: 129–146.

76 Kundel DW, Brecher G, Bodey GP, Brittin GM. Reticulin fibrosis and bone infarction in acute leukemia. Implications for prognosis. Blood 1964, 23: 526–544.

77 Niebrugge DJ, Benjamin DR. Bone marrow necrosis preceding acute lymphoblastic leukemia in childhood. Cancer 1983, 52: 2162–2164.

78 Pui CH, Stass S, Green A. Bone marrow necrosis in children with malignant disease. Cancer 1985, 56: 1522–1525.

79 Smith RR, Spivak JL. Marrow cell necrosis in anorexia nervosa and in voluntary starvation. Br J Haematol 1985, 60: 525–530.

Inflammatory disorders
Granulomatous inflammation

80 Browne PM, Sharma OP, Salkin D. Bone marrow sarcoidosis. JAMA 1978, 240: 2654–2655.

81 Choe JK, Hyun BH, Salazar GH, Ashton JK, Sung C. Epithelioid granulomas of the bone marrow in non-Hodgkin's lymphoproliferative malignancies. Am J Clin Pathol 1983, 80: 19–24.

82 Cruikshank B, Thomas MJ. Mineral oil (follicular) lipidosis. II. Histologic studies of spleen, liver, lymph nodes, and bone marrow. Hum Pathol 1984, 15: 731–737.

83 Delsol G, Pellegrin M, Familiades J, Auvergnat JC. Bone marrow lesions in Q fever. Blood 1978, 52: 637–638.

84 Diebold J, Molina T, Camilleri-Broet S, Le Tourneau A, Audouin J. Bone marrow manifestations of infection and systemic diseases observed in bone marrow trephine biopsy review. Histopathology 2000, 37: 199–211.

85 Farhi DC, Mason UG, Horsburgh CR Jr. The bone marrow in disseminated Mycobacterium avium-intracellulare infection. Am J Clin Pathol 1985, 83: 463–468.

86 Hussong J, Peterson LR, Warren JR, Peterson LC. Detecting disseminated mycobacterium avium complex infections in HIV-positive patients, the usefulness of bone marrow trephine biopsy specimens, aspirate cultures, and blood cultures. Am J Clin Pathol 1998, 110: 806–809.

87 Kadin ME, Donaldson SS, Dorfman RF. Isolated granulomas in Hodgkin's disease. N Engl J Med 1970, 283: 859–861.

88 Kilby JM, Marques MB, Jaye DL, Tabereaux MB, Reddy VB, Waites KB. The yield of bone marrow biopsy and culture compared with blood culture in the evaluation of HIV-infected patients for mycobacterial and fungal infections. Am J Med 1998, **104**: 123–128.

89 McKenna RW, Dehner LP. Oxalosis. An unusual cause of myelophthisis in childhood. Am J Clin Pathol 1976, **66**: 991–997.

90 Nosanchuk JS. Bone marrow granulomas with acute cytomegalovirus infection. Arch Pathol Lab Med 1984, **108**: 93–94.

91 Okun DB, Sun NC, Tanaka KR. Bone marrow granulomas in Q fever. Am J Clin Pathol 1979, **71**: 117–121.

92 Pease GL. Granulomatous lesions in bone marrow. Blood 1956, **11**: 720–734.

93 Rywlin AM, Ortega R. Lipid granulomas of the bone marrow. Am J Clin Pathol 1972, **57**: 457–462.

94 Rywlin AM. A pathologist's view of the bone marrow. J Fla Med Assoc 1980, **67**: 121–124.

95 Srigley JR, Vellend H, Palmer N, Phillips MJ, Geddie WR, Van Nostrand AW, Edwards VD. Q-fever. The liver and bone marrow pathology. Am J Surg Pathol 1985, **9**: 752–758.

96 Swerdlow SH, Collins RD. Marrow granulomas. In Ioachim HE (ed): Pathology of granulomas. New York, 1983, Raven Press, pp. 125–150.

97 Volk EE, Miller ML, Kirkley BA, Washington JA. The diagnostic usefulness of bone marrow cultures in patients with fever of unknown origin. Am J Clin Pathol 1998, **110**: 150–153.

98 White RM, Johnston CL. Granulomatous bone marrow disease in Virginia. Study of 50 cases. Va Med 1985, **112**: 316–319.

99 Williams HE, Smith LH Jr. Primary hyperoxaluria. In Stanbury JB, Wyngaarden JB, Fredrickson DS, Goldstein JL, Brown MS (eds): The metabolic basis of inherited disease. New York, 1983, McGraw-Hill Book Co., pp. 204–228.

100 Young N. Hematologic and hematopoietic consequences of B19 parvovirus infection. Semin Hematol 1988, **25**: 159–172.

Nonspecific inflammatory reactions

101 Custer RP. An atlas of the blood and bone marrow. Philadelphia, 1974, W.B. Saunders.

102 Georgii A, Vykoupil KF. Unspecific mesenchymal reaction in bone marrow in patients with Hodgkin's disease. Recent Results Cancer Res 1974, **46**: 39–44.

Acquired immunodeficiency syndrome (AIDS)

103 Abrams DI, Kirpov DD, Goedert JJ, Sarngadharan MG, Gallo RC, Volberding PA. Antibodies to human T lymphotropic virus type III and development of the acquired immunodeficiency syndrome in homosexual men presenting with immune thrombocytopenia. Ann Intern Med 1986, **104**: 47–50.

104 Brynes RK, Ewing EP Jr, Joshi VV, Chan WC. The histopathology of HIV infection: an overview. Prog AIDS Pathol 1989, **1**: 1–28.

105 Castella A, Croxson TS, Mildvan D, Witt DH, Zalusky R. The bone marrow in AIDS. A histologic, hematologic, and microbiologic study. Am J Clin Pathol 1985, **84**: 425–432.

106 Crook TW, Rogers BB, McFarland RD, Kroft SH, Muretto P, Herandez JA, Latimer MJ, McKenna RW. Unusual bone marrow manifestations of parvovirus B19 infection in immunocompromised patients. Hum Pathol 2000, **31**: 161–168.

107 Frickhofen N, Abkowitz JL, Safford M, Berry M, Antunez-de-Mayolo J, Astrow A, Cohen R, Halperin I, King L, Mintzer D, Cohen B, Young NS. Persistent B19 parvovirus infection in patients infected with human immunodeficiency virus type 1 (HIV-1). A treatable cause of anemia in AIDS. Ann Intern Med 1990, **113**: 926–933.

108 Geller SA, Muller R, Greenberg ML, Siegal FP. Acquired immunodeficiency syndrome. Distinctive features of bone marrow biopsies. Arch Pathol Lab Med 1985, **109**: 138–141.

109 Hussong J, Peterson LR, Warren JR, Peterson LC. Detecting disseminated mycobacterium avium complex infections in HIV-positive patients. The usefulness of bone marrow trephine biopsy specimens, aspirate cultures, and blood cultures. Am J Clin Pathol 1998, **110**: 806–809.

110 Ioachim HL, Dorsett B, Cronin W, Maya M, Wahl S. Acquired immunodeficiency syndrome-associated lymphomas: clinical, pathologic, immunologic, and viral characteristics of 111 cases. Hum Pathol 1991, **22**: 659–673.

111 Karcher DS, Frost AR. The bone marrow in human immunodeficiency virus (HIV)-related disease. Morphology and clinical correlation. Am J Clin Pathol 1991, **95**: 63–71.

112 Morris L, Distenfeld A, Amorosi E, Karpatkin S. Autoimmune thrombocytopenic purpura in homosexual men. Ann Intern Med 1982, **96**: 714–717.

113 Namiki TS, Boone DC, Meyer PR. A comparison of bone marrow findings in patients with acquired immunodeficiency syndrome (AIDS) and AIDS related conditions. Hematol Oncol 1987, **5**: 99–106.

114 Nichols L, Florentine B, Lewis W, Sattler F, Rarrick MU, Brynes RK. Bone marrow examination for the diagnosis of mycobacterial and fungal infections in the acquired immunodeficiency syndrome. Arch Pathol Lab Med 1991, **115**: 1125–1132.

115 Nasr SA, Brynes RK, Garrison CP, Chan WC. Peripheral T-cell lymphoma in a patient with acquired immunodeficiency syndrome. Cancer 1988, **61**: 947–951.

116 Osborne BM, Guarda LA, Butler JJ. Bone marrow biopsies in patients with the acquired immunodeficiency syndrome. Hum Pathol 1984, **15**: 1048–1053.

117 Ponzoni M, Fumagalli L, Ross G, Freschi M, Re A, Vigano MG, Guidaboni M, Dolcetti R, McKenna RW, Facchetti F. Isolated bone marrow manifestation of HIV-associated Hodgkin lymphoma. Mod Pathol 2002, **15**: 1273–1278.

118 Richman DD, Fischi MA, Grieco MH, Gottlieb MS, Volberding PA, Laskin OL, Leedom JM, Groopman JE, Mildvan D, Hirsch MS, Jackson GG, Durack DT, Nusinoff-Lehrman S, and the AZT Collaborative Working Group. The efficacy of azidothymidine (AZT) in the treatment of patients with AIDS and AIDS related complex. A double-blind, placebo-controlled trial. N Engl J Med 1987, **317**: 192–197.

119 Savona S, Nardi MA, Lennette ET, Karpatkin S. Thrombocytopenic purpura in narcotics addicts. Ann Intern Med 1985, **102**: 737–741.

120 Schneider DR, Picker LJ. Myelodysplasia in the acquired immune deficiency syndrome. Am J Clin Pathol 1985, **84**: 144–152.

121 Spivak JL, Bender BS, Quinn TC. Hematologic abnormalities in the acquired immune deficiency syndrome. Am J Med 1984, **77**: 224–228.

122 Treacy M, Lai L, Costello C, Clark A. Peripheral blood and bone marrow abnormalities in patients with HIV and related disease. Br J Haematol 1987, **65**: 289–294.

123 Zon LI, Arkin C, Groopman JE. Haematologic manifestations of the human immune deficiency virus (HIV). Br J Haematol 1987, **66**: 251–256.

Leukemias and related disorders
Acute leukemia

124 Arber DA, Jenkins KA. Paraffin section immunophenotyping of acute leukemias in bone marrow specimens. Am J Clin Pathol 1996, **106**: 462–468.

125 Bennett JM, Catovsky D, Daniel MT, Sultan C, Flandrin G, Galton DAG, Gralnick HR. Proposals for the classification of the acute leukaemias. French-American-British (FAB) co-operative group. Br J Haematol 1976, **33**: 451–458.

126 Berdeaux DH, Glasser L, Serokmann R, Moon T, Durie BG. Hypoplastic acute leukemia. Review of 70 cases with multivariate regression analysis. Hematol Oncol 1986, **4**: 291–305.

127 Breatnach F, Chessells JM, Greaves MF. The aplastic presentation of childhood leukaemia. A feature of common-ALL. Br J Haematol 1981, **49**: 387–393.

128 Brunning R. The effects of leukemia and lymphoma therapy on hematopoietic cells. Am J Med Technol 1973, **39:** 165–174.

129 Brunning RD. Acute myeloid leukemias. In Knowles DM (ed): Neoplastic hematopathology, ed. 2. Philadelphia, 2001, Lippincott, Williams & Wilkins, pp. 1667–1716.

130 Brunning RD, Borowitz M, Matutes E, Head D, Flandrin G, Swerdlow SH, Bennett JM. Precursor B lymphoblastic leukemia/lymphoblastic lymphoma. Precursor B-cell acute lymphoblastic leukemia. In Jaffe ES, Harris NL, Stein H, Vardiman JW (eds): World Health Organization Classification of Tumors. Pathology and genetics of tumours of haematopoietic and lymphoid tissues. Lyon, 2001, IARC Press, pp. 111–114.

131 Brunning RD, Borowitz M, Matutes E, Head D, Flandrin G, Swerdlow SH, Bennett JM. Precursor T lymphoblastic leukemia/lymphoblastic lymphoma. Precursor T-cell acute lymphoblastic leukemia. In Jaffe ES, Harris NL, Stein H, Vardiman JW (eds): World Health Organization Classification of Tumors. Pathology and genetics of tumours of haematopoietic and lymphoid tissues. Lyon, 2001, IARC Press, pp. 115–117.

132 Brunning RD, Matutes E, Harris NL, Flandrin G, Vardiman JW, Bennett J, Head D. Acute myeloid leukemia: Introduction. In Jaffe ES, Harris NL, Stein H, Vardiman JW (eds): World Health Organization Classification of Tumors. Pathology and genetics of tumours of haematopoietic and lymphoid tissues. Lyon, 2001, IARC Press, pp. 77–80.

133 Chuang SS, Li CY. Useful panel of antibodies for the classification of acute leukemia by immunohistochemical methods in bone marrow trephine biopsy specimens. Am J Clin Pathol 1997, **107:** 410–418.

134 Dunphy CH, Polski JM, Evans HL, Gardner LJ. Evaluation of bone marrow specimens with acute myelogenous leukemia for CD34, CD15, CD117, and myeloperoxidase. Comparison of flow cytometric and enzyme cytochemical versus immunohistochemical techniques. Arch Pathol Lab Med 2001, **125:** 1063–1069.

135 Howe RB, Bloomfield CD, McKenna RW. Hypocellular acute leukemia. Am J Med 1982, **72:** 391–395.

136 Manoharan A, Horsley R, Pitney WR. The reticulin content of bone marrow in acute leukaemia in adults. Br J Haematol 1979, **43:** 185–190.

137 Pileri SA, Ascani S, Milani M, Visani G, Piccioli M, Orcioni GF, Poggi S, Sabattini E, Santini D, Falini B. Acute leukemia immunophenotyping in bone marrow routine sections. Br J Haematol 1999, **105:** 394–401.

138 Rimsza LM, Larson RS, Winter SS, Foucar K, Chong YY, Garner KW, Leith CP. Benign hematogone-rich lymphoid proliferations can be distinguished from B-lineage acute lymphoblastic leukemia by integration of morphology, immunophenotype, adhesion molecule expression, and architectural features. Am J Clin Pathol 2000, **114:** 66–75.

139 Yunis JJ, Brunning RD. Prognostic significance of chromosomal abnormalities in acute leukaemias and myelodysplastic syndromes. Clin Haematol 1986, **15:** 597–620.

Acute panmyelosis with myelofibrosis (acute myelofibrosis)

140 Bain B, Catovsky D, O'Brien M, Prentice HG, Lawlor E, Kumaran TO, McCann SR, Matutes E, Galton DA. Megakaryoblastic leukemia presenting as acute myelofibrosis. A study of four cases with the platelet-peroxidase reaction. Blood 1981, **58:** 206–213.

141 Bearman RM, Pangalis GA, Rappaport H. Acute (malignant) myelosclerosis. Cancer 1979, **43:** 279–293.

142 Brunning RD, Matutes E, Harris NL, Flandrin G, Vardiman JW, Bennett J, Head D, Harris NL. Acute myeloid leukemia not otherwise categorized. In Jaffe ES, Harris NL, Stein H, Vardiman JW (eds): World Health Organization Classification of Tumors. Pathology and genetics of tumours of haematopoietic and lymphoid tissues. Lyon, 2001, IARC Press, pp. 103, 104.

143 Hruban RH, Kuhajda FP, Mann RB. Acute myelofibrosis. Immunohistochemical study of four cases and comparison with acute megakaryoblastic leukemia. Am J Clin Pathol 1987, **88:** 578–588.

144 Sultan C, Sigaux F, Imbert M, Reyes F. Acute myelodysplasia with myelofibrosis. A report of eight cases. Br J Haematol 1981, **49:** 11–16.

Myeloid sarcoma (granulocytic sarcoma)

145 Beckman EN, Oehrle JS. Fibrous hematopoietic tumors arising in agnogenic myeloid metaplasia. Hum Pathol 1982, **13:** 804–810.

146 Brunning R, McKenna RW. Tumors of the hematopoietic system. Atlas of tumor pathology, series 3, fascicle 29. Washington D.C., 1994, Armed Forces Institute of Pathology, pp. 93–100.

147 Brunning RD, Matutes E, Harris NL, Flandrin G, Vardiman JW, Bennett J, Head D, Harris NL. Acute myeloid leukemia not otherwise categorized. In Jaffe ES, Harris NL, Stein H, Vardiman JW (eds): World Health Organization Classification of Tumors. Pathology and genetics of tumours of haematopoietic and lymphoid tissues. Lyon, 2001, IARC Press, pp. 104, 105.

148 Cavdar AO, Arcasoy A, Babacan E, Gözdasoglu S, Topuz Ü, Fraumeni JF. Ocular granulocytic sarcoma (chloroma) with acute myelomonocytic leukemia in Turkish children. Cancer 1978, **41:** 1606–1609.

149 Garfinkel LS, Bennett DE. Extramedullary myeloblastic transformation in chronic myelocytic leukemia simulating a coexistent malignant lymphoma. Am J Clin Pathol 1969, **51:** 638–645.

150 Gralnick HR, Dittmar K. Development of myeloblastoma with massive breast and ovarian involvement during remission in acute leukemia. Cancer 1969, **24:** 746–749.

151 Leder LD. The selective enzymochemical demonstration of neutrophilic myeloid cells and tissue mast cells in paraffin sections. Klin Wochenschr 1964, **42:** 553.

152 McKenna RW, Bloomfield CD, Dick F, Nesbit ME, Brunning RD. Acute monoblastic leukemia. Diagnosis and treatment of ten cases. Blood 1975, **46:** 481–494.

153 Mason TE, Damaree R, Margolis CI. Granulocytic sarcoma (chloroma) two years preceding myelogenous leukemia. Cancer 1973, **31:** 423–432.

154 Meis JM, Butler JJ, Osborne BM, Manning JT. Granulocytic sarcoma in non-leukemic patients. Cancer 1986, **58:** 2697–2709.

155 Muller S, Sangster G, Crocker J, Nar P, Burnett D, Brown G, Leyland MJ. An immunohistochemical and clinicopathological study of granulocytic sarcoma ('chloroma'). Hematol Oncol 1986, **4:** 101–112.

156 Neiman RS, Barcos M, Berard C, Bonner H, Mann R, Rydell RE, Bennett JM. Granulocytic sarcoma. A clinicopathologic study of 61 biopsied cases. Cancer 1981, **48:** 1426–1437.

157 Peterson LC, Dehner L, Brunning RD. Extramedullary masses as presenting features of acute monoblastic leukemia. Am J Clin Pathol 1980, **75:** 140–148.

158 Pinkus GS, Pinkus JL. Myeloperoxidase. A specific marker for myeloid cells in paraffin sections. Mod Pathol 1991, **4:** 733–741.

159 Tallman MS, Hakimian D, Shaw JM, Lissner GS, Russell EJ, Variakojis D. Granulocytic sarcoma is associated with the 8;21 translocation in acute myeloid leukemia. J Clin Oncol 1993, **11:** 690–697.

160 Wiernik PH, Serpick AA. Granulocytic sarcoma (chloroma). Blood 1970, **35:** 361–369.

Myelodysplastic syndromes

161 Bennett JM, Catovsky D, Daniel MT, Flandrin G, Galton DA, Gralnick HR, Sultan C. Proposals for the classification of the myelodysplastic syndromes. Br J Haematol 1982, **51:** 189–199.

162 Brunning RD. Myelodysplastic syndromes. In Knowles DM (ed): Neoplastic hematopathology, ed. 2. Philadelphia, 2001, Lippincott, Williams & Wilkins, pp. 1717–1745.

163 Brunning RD, Bennett JM, Flandrin G, Matutes E, Head D, Vardiman JW, Harris NL. Myelodysplastic syndromes: Introduction. In Jaffe ES, Harris NL, Stein H, Vardiman JW (eds): World Health Organization Classification of Tumors. Pathology and genetics of tumours of haematopoietic and lymphoid tissues. Lyon, 2001, IARC Press, pp. 63–67.

164 Brunning RD, Bennett JM, Flandrin G, Matutes E, Head D, Vardiman JW, Harris NL. Myelodysplastic syndrome associated with isolated del(5q) chromosome abnormality (5q– syndrome). In Jaffe ES, Harris NL, Stein H, Vardiman JW (eds): World Health Organization Classification of Tumors. Pathology and genetics of tumours of haematopoietic and lymphoid tissues. Lyon, 2001, IARC Press, p. 73.

165 Brunning RD, Bennett JM, Flandrin G, Matutes E, Head D, Vardiman JW, Harris NL. Refractory anemia with excess blasts. In Jaffe ES, Harris NL, Stein H, Vardiman JW (eds): World Health Organization Classification of Tumors. Pathology and genetics of tumours of haematopoietic and lymphoid tissues. Lyon, 2001, IARC Press, p. 71.

166 Brunning RD, Bennett JM, Flandrin G, Matutes E, Head D, Vardiman JW, Harris NL. Refractory cytopenia with multilineage dysplasia. In Jaffe ES, Harris NL, Stein H, Vardiman JW (eds): World Health Organization Classification of Tumors. Pathology and genetics of tumours of haematopoietic and lymphoid tissues. Lyon, 2001, IARC Press, p. 70.

167 Brunning RD, Matutes E, Flandrin G, Vardiman JW, Bennett J, Head D, Harris NL. Acute myeloid leukaemia and myelodysplastic syndromes, therapy related. In Jaffe ES, Harris NL, Stein H, Vardiman JW (eds): World Health Organization Classification of Tumors. Pathology and genetics of tumours of haematopoietic and lymphoid tissues. Lyon, 2001, IARC Press, pp. 89–91.

168 Delacretaz F, Schmidt PM, Piguet D, Bachmann F, Costa J. Histopathology of myelodysplastic syndromes. The FAB classification (proposals) applied to bone marrow biopsy. Am J Clin Pathol 1987, 87: 180–186.

169 List AF, Garewal HS, Sandberg AA. The myelodysplastic syndromes, biology and implications for management. J Clin Oncol 1990, 8: 1424–1441.

170 Maschek H, Georgii A, Kaloutal V, et al. Myelofibrosis in primary myelodysplastic syndromes. A retrospective study of 352 patients. Eur J Haematol 1992, 48: 208–214.

171 Mathew P, Tefferi A, Dewald GW, Goldberg SL, Hoagland HC, Noel P. The 5q- syndrome. A single institution study of 43 consecutive cases. Blood 1993, 81: 1040–1045.

172 Orazi A, Albitar M, Heerema NA, Haskins NS, Neiman RS. Hypoplastic myelodysplastic syndrome can be distinguished from acquired aplastic anemia by CD34 and PCNA immunostaining of bone marrow biopsy specimens. Am J Clin Pathol 1997, 107: 268–274.

173 Tricot G, Vlietnick R, Boogaerts MA, Hendrickx B, De Wolf-Peeters C, Van den Berghe H, Verwilghen RL. Prognostic factors in the myelodysplastic syndromes. Importance of initial data on peripheral blood counts, bone marrow, cytology, trephine biopsy and chromosomal analysis. Br J Haematol 1985, 60: 19–32.

174 Vardiman JW. Myelodysplastic/myeloproliferative diseases: introduction. In Jaffe ES, Harris NL, Stein H, Vardiman JW (eds): World Health Organization Classification of Tumors. Pathology and genetics of tumours of haematopoietic and lymphoid tissues. Lyon, 2001, IARC Press, pp. 17–19.

175 Vardiman JW, Pierre R, Bain B, Bennett JM, Imbert M, Brunning RD, Flandrin G. Chronic myelomonocytic leukaemia. In Jaffe ES, Harris NL, Stein H, Vardiman JW (eds): World Health Organization Classification of Tumors. Pathology and genetics of tumours of haematopoietic and lymphoid tissues. Lyon, 2001, IARC Press, pp. 47, 48.

176 Vardiman JW, Pierre R, Imbert M, Bain B, Brunning RD, Flandrin G. Juvenile myelomonocytic leukaemia. In Jaffe ES, Harris NL, Stein H, Vardiman JW (eds): World Health Organization Classification of Tumors. Pathology and genetics of tumours of haematopoietic and lymphoid tissues. Lyon, 2001, IARC Press, pp. 55–57.

Chronic myeloid leukemia

177 Braziel RM, Launder TM, Druker BJ, Olson SB, Magenis RE, Mauro MJ, Sawyers CL, Paquette RL, O'Dwyer ME. Hematopathologic and cytogenetic findings on imatinib mesylate-treated chronic myelogenous leukemia patients: 14 months' experience. Blood 2002, 100: 435–441.

178 Clough V, Geary CG, Hashmi K, Davson J, Knowlson T. Myelofibrosis in chronic granulocytic leukaemia. Br J Haematol 1979, 42: 515–526.

179 Dekmezian R, Kantarjian HM, Keating MJ, Talpaz M, McCredie KB, Freireich EJ. The relevance of reticulin stain-measured fibrosis at diagnosis in chronic myelogenous leukemia. Cancer 1987, 59: 1739–1743.

180 Kantarjian HM, Cortes JE, O'Brien S, Giles F, Garcia-Manero G, Faderl S, Thomas D, Jeha S, Rios MB, Letvak L, Buchinski K, Arlinghaus R, Talpaz M. Imatinib mesylate therapy in newly-diagnosed patients with Philadelphia chromosome-positive chronic myelogenous leukemia; high incidence of early complete and major cytogenetic responses. Blood 2002, 101: 97–100.

181 Kantarjian HM, Deisseroth A, Kurzrock R, Estrov Z, Talpaz M. Chronic myelogenous leukemia. A concise update. Blood 1993, 82: 691–703.

182 Kantarjian H, Sawyers C, Hochhaus A, Guilhot F, Schiffer C, Gumbucorti-Passerini C, Niederwieser D, Rosta D, Capdeville R, Zoellner U, Talpus M, Drucker B. Hematologic and cytogenetic responses to imatinib mesylate in chronic myelogenous leukemia. N Engl J Med 2002, 346: 645–652.

183 Lugli A, Ebnother M, Tichelli A, Gratwohl A, Zimpfer A, Cogliatti S, Linn M, Dirnhofer S. Bone marrow morphology in CML patients during treatment with STI571 (Glivec): evidence of complete morphological remission and correlation to hematologic and cytogenetic response. J Clin Pathol 2002, 55: A6.

184 McGlave PB, Brunning RD, Hurd DD, Kim TH. Reversal of severe bone marrow fibrosis and osteosclerosis following allogenic bone marrow transplantation for chronic granulocytic leukaemia. Br J Haematol 1982, 52: 189–194.

185 Muehleck SD, McKenna RW, Arthur DC, Parkin JL, Brunning RD. Transformation of chronic myelogenous leukemia. Clinical, morphologic and cytogenetic features. Am J Clin Pathol 1984, 82: 1–14.

186 Thiele J, Kvasnicka NM, Beelen DW, Flucke U, Spoer C, Paperno S, Leder LD, Schaefer UW. Megakaryopoiesis and myelofibrosis in chronic leukemia after allogeneic bone marrow transplantation: an immunohistochemical study of 127 patients. Mod Pathol 2000, 14: 129–138.

187 Thiele J, Kvasnicka HM, Schmitt-Graeff A, Bundschuh S, Biermann T, Roessler G, Wasmus M, Diehl V, Zankovich R, Schaefer HE. Effects of chemotherapy (busulfan-hydroxyurea) and interferon-alfa on bone marrow morphologic features in chronic myelogenous leukemia: histochemical and morphometric study on sequential bone marrow biopsy specimens with special emphasis on dynamic features. Am J Clin Pathol 2000, 114: 57–65.

188 Vardiman JW, Pierre R, Thiele J, Imbert M, Brunning RD. Chronic myelogenous leukemia. In Jaffe ES, Harris NL, Stein H, Vardiman JW (eds): World Health Organization Classification of Tumors. Pathology and genetics of tumours of haematopoietic and lymphoid tissues. Lyon, 2001, IARC Press, pp. 20–26.

Polycythemia vera

189 Ellis JT, Peterson P, Geller SA, Rappaport H. Studies of the bone marrow in polycythemia vera and the evolution of myelofibrosis

and second hematologic malignancies. Semin Hematol 1986, **12:** 144–155.

190   Ellis JT, Silver RT, Coleman M, Geller SA. The bone marrow in polycythaemia vera. Semin Hematol 1975, **12:** 433–444.

191   Klein H. Morphology of the hematopoietic tissues. In Klein H (ed.): Polycythemia, theory and management. Springfield, Ill., 1973, Charles Thomas, pp. 201–208.

192   Landaw SA. Acute leukemia in polycythemia vera. Semin Hematol 1986, **23:** 156–165.

193   Lawrence JH, Winchell HS, Donald WG. Leukemia in polycythemia vera. Relationship to splenic myeloid metaplasia and therapeutic radiation dose. Ann Intern Med 1969, **70:** 763–771.

194   Lazslo J. Myeloproliferative disorders (MPD). Myelofibrosis, myelosclerosis, extramedullary hematopoiesis, undifferentiated MPD and hemorrhagic thrombocythemia. Semin Hematol 1975, **12:** 409–432.

195   Modan B, Lilienfield AM. Polycythemia vera and leukemia. The role of radiation treatment. Medicine (Baltimore) 1965, **44:** 305–344.

196   Moliterno AR, Hankins WD, Spivak JL. Impaired expression of the thrombopoietin receptor by platelets from patients with polycythemic vera. N Engl J Med 1998, **338:** 572–680.

197   Pierre R, Imbert M, Thiele J, Vardiman JW, Brunning RD, Flandrin G. Polycythaemia vera. In Jaffe ES, Harris NL, Stein H, Vardiman JW (eds): World Health Organization Classification of Tumors. Pathology and genetics of tumours of haematopoietic and lymphoid tissues. Lyon, 2001, IARC Press, pp. 32–34.

198   Roberts BE, Miles DW, Woods CG. Polycythaemia vera and myelosclerosis. A bone marrow study. Br J Haematol 1969, **16:** 75–85.

199   Silverstein MN. The evolution into and the treatment of late stage polycythemia vera. Semin Hematol 1976, **13:** 79–84.

200   Tefferi A, Yoon S-Y, Li CY. Immunohistochemical staining for megakaryocyte c-mpl may complement morphologic distinction between polycythemia vera and secondary erythrocytosis. Blood 2000, **96:** 771–772.

201   Vykoupil KF, Thiele J, Stangel W, Krmpotic E, Georgii A. Polycythemia vera. I. Histopathology, ultrastructure and cytogenetics of the bone marrow in comparison with secondary polycythemia. Virchows Arch [A] 1980, **389:** 307–324.

202   Vykoupil KF, Thiele J, Stangel W, Krmpotic E, Georgii A. Polycythemia vera. II. Transgression towards leukemia with special emphasis on histological differential diagnosis, cytogenetics and survival. Virchows Arch [A] 1980, **389:** 325–341.

203   Wasserman LR. The management of polycythaemia vera. Br J Haematol 1971, **21:** 371–376.

Essential thrombocythemia

204   Buss DH, O'Connor ML, Woodruff RD, Richards II F, Brockschmidt JK. Bone marrow and peripheral blood findings in patients with extreme thrombocytosis. A report of 63 cases. Arch Pathol Lab Med 1991, **115:** 475–480.

205   Imbert M, Pierre R, Thiele J, Vardiman JW, Brunning RD, Flandrin G. Essential thrombocythaemia. In Jaffe ES, Harris NL, Stein H, Vardiman JW (eds): World Health Organization Classification of Tumors. Pathology and genetics of tumours of haematopoietic and lymphoid tissues. Lyon, 2001, IARC Press, pp. 39–41.

206   Mesa RA, Hanson CA, Li CY, Yoon S-Y, Rajkumar SV, Schroeder G, Tefferi A. Diagnostic and prognostic value of bone marrow angiogenesis and megakaryocyte c-mpl expression in essential thrombocythemia. Blood 2002, **99:** 4131–4137.

207   Murphy S, Iland H, Rosenthal D, Laszlo J. Essential thrombocythemia. An interim report from the Polycythemia Vera Study Group. Semin Hematol 1986, **23:** 177–182.

208   Pierconti F, Teofili L, Maggiano N, Vianeli N, Ascani S, Pileri S, Leone G, De Stefano V. The megakaryocyte pattern of expression of C-MPL in essential thrombocythemia correlates with thrombotic risk. J Clin Pathol 2002, **55**(suppl): A7.

Chronic idiopathic myelofibrosis (agnogenic myeloid metaplasia)

209   Akikusa B, Komatsu T, Kondo Y, Yokota T, Uchino F, Yonemitsu H. Amyloidosis complicating idiopathic myelofibrosis. Arch Pathol Lab Med 1987, **111:** 525–529.

210   Bass RD, Pullarkat V, Feinstein DI, Kaul A, Winberg CD, Brynes RK. Pathology of autoimmune myelofibrosis. A report of three cases and a review of the literature. Am J Clin Pathol 2001, **116:** 211–216.

211   Bearman RM, Pangalis GA, Rappaport H. Acute ("malignant") myelosclerosis. Cancer 1979, **43:** 279–293.

212   Beckman EN, Oehrle JS. Fibrous hematopoietic tumors arising in agnogenic myeloid metaplasia. Hum Pathol 1982, **13:** 804–810.

213   Block M, Burkhardt R, Chelloul N, Demmler K, Duhamel G, Georgii A, Kirsten WH, Lennert K, Nezelof C, Te Velde J. Myelofibrosis-osteosclerosis syndrome. Pathology and morphology. Adv Biosci 1975, **16:** 219–240.

214   Bock O, Schlue J, Lehmann U, von Wasielewski R, Langer F, Kreipe H. Megakaryocytes from chronic myeloproliferative disorders show enhanced nuclear bFGB expression. Blood 2002, **100:** 2274–2275.

215   Burston J, Pinniger JL. The reticulin content of bone marrow in haematological disorders. Br J Haematol 1963, **9:** 172–184.

216   Georgii A, Buesche G, Kreft A. The histopathology of chronic myeloproliferative diseases. Baillere's Clin Hematol 1998, **11:** 721–749.

217   Lubin J, Rozen S, Rwylin AM. Malignant myelosclerosis. Arch Intern Med 1976, **136:** 141–145.

218   Mesa RA, Hanson CA, Rajkuman V, Schroeder G, Tefferi A. Evaluation and clinical correlations of bone marrow angiogenesis in myelofibrosis with myeloid metaplasia. Blood 2000, **96:** 3374–3380.

219   Ponzoni M, Shendrik U, Ferreri AJM, Pruneri G, Saruida P, Bertolini F, Urazi A. Endoglin (CD105)-positive vessels are increased in chronic idiopathic myelofibrosis. J Clin Pathol 2002, **55**(suppl 1): A7.

220   Rondeau E, Solal-Celigny P, Dhermy D, Vroclans M, Brousse N, Bernard JF, Boivin P. Immune disorders in agnogenic myeloid metaplasia. Relations to myelofibrosis. Br J Haematol 1983, **53:** 467–475.

221   Tefferi A. Myelofibrosis with myeloid metaplasia. N Engl J Med 2000, **342:** 1255–1265.

222   Thiele J, Pierre R, Imbert M, Vardiman JW, Brunning RD, Flandrin G. Chronic idiopathic myelofibrosis. In Jaffe ES, Harris NL, Stein H, Vardiman JW (eds): World Health Organization Classification of Tumors. Pathology and genetics of tumours of haematopoietic and lymphoid tissues. Lyon, 2001, IARC Press, pp. 35–38.

223   Thiele J, Zankovich R, Steinberg T, Fischer R, Diehl V. Agnogenic myeloid metaplasia (AMM). Correlation of bone marrow lesions with laboratory data. A longitudinal clinicopathological study on 114 patients. Hematol Oncol 1989, **7:** 327–343.

224   Tobin MS, Tan C, Argano SAP. Myelofibrosis in pediatric age group. N Y State J Med 1969, **69:** 1080–1083.

225   Varki A, Lottenberg R, Griffith R, Reinhard E. The syndrome of idiopathic myelofibrosis. A clinicopathologic review with emphasis on the prognostic variables predicting survival. Medicine (Baltimore) 1983, **62:** 353–371.

226   Ward HP, Block MH. The natural history of agnogenic myeloid metaplasia (AMM) and a critical evaluation of its relationship with the myeloproliferative syndrome. Medicine (Baltimore) 1971, **50:** 357–420.

227   Weinstein IM. Idiopathic myelofibrosis. Historical review, diagnosis, and management. Blood Rev 1991, **5:** 98–104.

228 Wolf BC, Neiman RS. Myelofibrosis with myeloid metaplasia: pathophysiologic implications of the correlation between bone marrow changes and progression of splenomegaly. Blood 1985, **65**: 803–809.

Chronic lymphocytic leukemia

229 Bennett JM, Catovsky D, Daniel M-T, Flandrin G, Galton DAG, Gralnick HR, Sultan C. Proposals for the classification of chronic (mature) B and T lymphoid leukaemias. J Clin Pathol 1989, **42**: 567–584.

230 Binet L, Catovsky D, Chandra P, Dighiero G, Montserrat E, Rai KR, Sawitsky A. Chronic lymphocytic leukaemia. Proposals for a revised prognostic staging system. Br J Haematol 1981, **48**: 365–367.

231 Brouet JC, Fermand JP, Laurent G, Grange MJ, Chevalier A, Jacquillat C, Seligmann M. The association of chronic lymphocytic leukaemia and multiple myeloma. A study of eleven patients. Br J Haematol 1985, **59**: 55–66.

232 Brouet JC, Flandrin G, Sasportes M, Preud'Homme JL, Seligmann M. Chronic lymphocytic leukemia of T-cell origin. Lancet 1975, **2**: 890–893.

233 Damle RN, Wasil T, Fais F, Ghiotto F, Valetto A, Allen SL, Buchbinder A, Budman D, Dittman K, Kolitz J, Lichtman SM, Schulman P, Vinciguerra VP, Rai KP, Ferrarini M, Chiorazzi N. Ig V mutation status and CD38 expression as novel prognostic indicators in chronic lymphocytic leukemia. Blood 1999, **94**: 1840–1847.

234 Dohmer H, Stilgenbauer S, Benner A, Leupolt E, Krober A, Bullinger L, Dohner K, Bentz M, Lichter P. Genomic alternations and survival in chronic lymphocytic leukemia. N Engl J Med 2000, **343**: 1910–1916.

235 Enno A, Catovsky D, O'Brien M, Cherchi M, Kumaran TO, Galton DA. "Prolymphocytoid" transformation of chronic lymphocytic leukaemia. Br J Haematol 1979, **41**: 9–18.

236 International Workshop on Chronic Lymphocytic Leukemia. Chronic lymphocytic leukemia. Recommendations for diagnosis, staging, and response criteria. Ann Intern Med 1989, **110**: 236–238.

237 Lens D, Dyer MJ, Garcia-Marco JM, De Schouwer PJJC, Hamoudi RA, Jones D, Farahat N, Matutes E, Catovsky D. p53 abnormalities in CLL are associated with excess of prolymphocytes and poor prognosis. Br J Haematol 1997, **99**: 848–857.

238 Litz CE, Brunning RD. Chronic lymphoproliferative disorders. Classification and prognosis. Bailliere's Clin Haematol 1993, **6**: 767–783.

239 Montserrat E, Marques-Pereira JP, Gallart T, Rozman C. Bone marrow histopathologic patterns and immunologic findings in B chronic lymphocytic leukemia. Cancer 1984, **54**: 447–451.

240 Montserrat E, Rozman CR. Chronic lymphocytic leukemia. Prognostic factors and natural history. Bailliere's Clin Haematol 1993, **6**: 849–866.

241 Muller-Hermelink HK, Catovsky D, Montserrat E, Harris NL. Chronic lymphocytic leukaemia/small lymphocytic lymphoma. In Jaffe ES, Harris NL, Stein H, Vardiman JW (eds): World Health Organization Classification of Tumors. Pathology and genetics of tumours of haematopoietic and lymphoid tissues. Lyon, 2001, IARC Press, pp. 127–130.

242 Pangalis GA, Roussou PA, Kittas C, Kokkinou S, Fessas P. B-chronic lymphocytic leukemia. Prognostic implication of bone marrow histology in 120 patients experience from a single hematology unit. Cancer 1987, **59**: 767–771.

243 Pangalis GA, Roussou PA, Kittas C, Mitsoulis-Mentzikoff C, Matsouka-Alexandris P, Anagnostopoulos N, Rombos I, Fessas P. Patterns of bone marrow involvement in chronic lymphocytic leukemia and small lymphocytic (well-differentiated) non-Hodgkin's lymphoma. Its clinical significance in relation to their differential diagnosis and prognosis. Cancer 1984, **54**: 702–708.

244 Rai KR, Sawitsky A, Cronkite EP, Chanana AD, Levy RN, Pasternack BS. Clinical staging of chronic lymphocytic leukemia. Blood 1975, **46**: 219–234.

245 Rausig A. Lymphocytic leukemia and malignant lymphoma in the adult. Acta Med Scand 1976, **595**(Suppl): 1–270.

246 Rozman C, Hernandez-Nieto L, Montserrat E, Brugues R. Prognostic significance of bone marrow patterns in chronic lymphocytic leukaemia. Br J Haematol 1981, **47**: 529–537.

Richter's syndrome

247 Armitage JO, Dick FR, Corder M. Diffuse histiocytic lymphoma complicating chronic lymphocytic leukemia. Cancer 1978, **41**: 422–427.

248 Brecher M, Banks P. Hodgkin's disease variant of Richter's syndrome. Am J Clin Pathol 1990, **93**: 333–339.

249 Brouet JC, Preud'Homme JL, Seligmann M, Bernard J. Blast cells with monoclonal surface immunoglobulin in two cases of acute blast crisis supervening on chronic lymphocytic leukemia. Br Med J 1973, **4**: 23–24.

250 Brousse N, Solal-Celigny P, Herrara A, Breil P, Molas G, Flejou JF, Boivin P, Potet F. Gastrointestinal Richter's syndrome. Hum Pathol 1985, **16**: 854–857.

251 Brynes RK, McCourty A, Sun NCJ, Koo CH. Trisomy 12 in Richter's transformation of chronic lymphocytic leukemia. Am J Clin Pathol 1995, **104**: 199–203.

252 Case record of the Massachusetts General Hospital (Case 6–1978). N Engl J Med 1978, **298**: 387–396.

253 Foucar K, Rydell RE. Richter's syndrome in chronic lymphocytic leukemia. Cancer 1980, **46**: 118–134.

254 Goldstein J, Baden J. Richter's syndrome. South Med J 1977, **70**: 1381–1382.

255 Kroft SH. Lymphoma transformation. Genetic relatedness, stealth lymphomas, and the final frontier. Am J Clin Pathol 2001, **116**: 811–814.

256 Litz CE, Arthur DC, Gajl-Peczalska KJ, Rausch D, Copenhaver C, Coad JE, Brunning RD. Transformation of chronic lymphocytic leukemia to small non-cleaved cell lymphoma. A cytogenetic, immunological, and molecular study. Leukemia 1991, **5**: 972–978.

257 Long JC, Aisenberg AC. Richter's syndrome. A terminal complication of chronic lymphocytic leukemia with distinct clinicopathologic features. Am J Clin Pathol 1975, **63**: 786–795.

258 Richter MN. Generalized reticular cell sarcoma of lymph nodes associated with lymphatic leukemia. Am J Pathol 1928, **4**: 285–292.

259 Seligmann M, Preud'Homme JL, Brouet JC. Membrane markers in human lymphoid malignancies. Clinicopathologic correlations and insights into the differentiation of normal and neoplastic cells. In Clarkson B, Marks P, Till JR (eds): Differentiation of normal and neoplastic cells. Cold Spring Harbor, NY, 1978, Cold Spring Harbor Laboratory, pp. 859–876.

260 Splinter TA, Noorloos BV, Van Heerde P. CLL and diffuse histiocytic lymphoma in one patient. Clonal proliferation of two different cells. Scand J Haematol 1978, **20**: 29–36.

261 Traweek ST, Liu J, Johnson RM, Winberg CD, Rappaport H. High-grade transformation of chronic lymphocytic leukemia and low-grade non-Hodgkin's lymphoma. Genotypic confirmation of clonal identity. Am J Clin Pathol 1993, **100**: 519–526.

262 Trump DL, Mann RB, Phelps R, Roberts H, Conley CL. Richter's syndrome: diffuse histiocytic lymphoma in patients with chronic lymphocytic leukemia. Am J Med 1980, **68**: 539–548.

263 Wick MR, Li C-Y, Ludwig J, Levitt R, Pierre RV. Malignant histiocytosis as a terminal condition in chronic lymphocyte leukemia. Mayo Clin Proc 1980, **55**: 108–112.

Prolymphocytic leukemia

264 Bearman RM, Pangalis GA, Rappaport H. Prolymphocytic leukemia: clinical, histological, and cytochemical observations. Cancer 1978, **42**: 2360–2372.

265 Galton DA, Goldman JM, Wiltshaw E, Catovsky D, Henry K, Goldenberg GJ. Prolymphocytic leukaemia. Br J Haematol 1974, **27**: 7–23.

266 Matutes E, Brito-Babapulle V, Swansbury J, Ellis J, Morilla R, Deardon C, Sempere A, Catovsky D. Clinical and laboratory features of 78 cases of T-prolymphocytic leukemia. Blood 1991, **78**: 3269–3274.

267 Melo JV, Catovsky D, Galton DA. The relationship between chronic lymphocytic leukaemia and prolymphocytic leukaemia. I. Clinical and laboratory features of 300 patients and characterization of an intermediate group. Br J Haematol 1986, **63**: 377–387.

268 Melo JV, Catovsky D, Galton DAG. The relationship between chronic lymphocytic leukaemia and prolymphocytic leukaemia. II. Patterns of evolution of "prolymphocytoid" transformation. Br J Haematol 1986, **64**: 77–86.

269 Owens MR, Strauchen JA, Rowe JM, Bennett JM. Prolymphocytic leukemia: histologic features in atypical cases. Hematol Oncol 1984, **2**: 249–257.

Hairy cell leukemia, hairy cell leukemia variant

270 Bartl R, Frisch B, Hill W, Burkhardt R, Sommerfiled W, Sund M. Bone marrow histology in hairy cell leukemia. Identification of subtypes and their prognostic significance. Am J Clin Pathol 1983, **79**: 531–545.

271 Bennett JM, Catovsky D, Daniel M-T, Flandrin G, Galton DAG, Gralnick HR, Sultan C. Proposals for the classification of chronic (mature) B and T lymphoid leukemias. J Clin Pathol 1989, **42**: 567–584.

272 Burke JS. The value of the bone marrow biopsy in the diagnosis of hairy cell leukemia. Am J Clin Pathol 1978, **70**: 876–884.

273 Burke JS, Byrne GE Jr, Rappaport H. Hairy cell leukemia (leukemic reticuloendotheliosis). I. A clinical pathologic study of 21 patients. Cancer 1974, **33**: 1399–1410.

274 Catovsky D, O'Brien M, Melo JV, Wardle J, Brozovic M. Hairy cell leukemia (HCL) variant. An intermediate disease between HCL and B prolymphocytic leukemia. Semin Oncol 1984, **11**: 362–369.

275 Chang KL, Stroup R, Weiss LM. Hairy cell leukemia. Current status. Am J Clin Pathol 1992, **97**: 719–738.

276 Demanes DJ, Lane N, Beckstead JH. Bone involvement in hairy cell leukemia. Cancer 1982, **49**: 1697–1701.

277 Foucar K, Catovsky D. Hairy cell leukemia. In Jaffe ES, Harris NL, Stein H, Vardiman JW (eds): World Health Organization Classification of Tumors. Pathology and genetics of tumours of haematopoietic and lymphoid tissues. Lyon, 2001, IARC Press, pp. 138–141.

278 Golomb HM, Catovsky D, Golde DW. Hairy cell leukemia: a clinical review based on 71 cases. Ann Intern Med 1978, **89**: 677–683.

279 Hakimian D, Tallman MS, Kiley C, Peterson L. Detection of minimal residual disease by immunostaining of bone marrow biopsies after 2-chlorodeoxyadenosine for hairy cell leukemia. Blood 1993, **82**: 1798–1802.

280 Hanson CA, Ward PC, Schnitzer B. A multilobular variant of hairy cell leukemia with morphologic similarities to T-cell lymphoma. Am J Surg Pathol 1989, **13**: 671–679.

281 Herold CJ, Wittlich GR, Schwarzinger I, Haller J, Chott A, Mostbeck G, Hajek PC. Skeletal involvement in hairy cell leukemia. Skeletal Radiol 1988, **17**: 171–175.

282 Hoyer JD, Li CY, Yam LT, Hanson CA, Kurtin PJ. Immunohistochemical demonstration of acid phosphatase isoenzyme 5(tartrate-resistant) in paraffin sections of hairy cell leukemia and other hematologic disorders. Am J Clin Pathol 1997, **108**: 308–315.

283 Katayama I, Schneider GB. Further ultrastructural characterization of hairy cells of leukemic reticuloendotheliosis. Am J Pathol 1977, **86**: 163–182.

284 Kremer M, Dirnhofer S, Nickl A, Hoefler H, Quintanilla-Martinez L, Fend F. p27(kip1) immunostaining for the differential diagnosis of small b-cell neoplasms in trephine bone marrow biopsies. Mod Pathol 2001, **14**: 1022–1029.

285 Lal A, Tallman MS, Soble MB, Golubovich I, Peterson L. Hairy cell leukemia presenting as localized skeletal involvement. Leuk Lymphoma 2003, **43**: 2207–2211.

286 Lee WMF, Beckstead JH. Hairy cell leukemia with bone marrow hypoplasia. Cancer 1982, **50**: 2207–2210.

287 Lembersky BC, Ratain MJ, Golomb H. Skeletal complications in hairy cell leukemia: diagnosis and therapy. J Clin Oncol 1988, **6**: 1280–1284.

288 Matutes E, Wotherspoon A, Brito-Babapulle V, Catovsky D. The natural history and clinico-pathological features of the variant form of hairy cell leukemia. Leukemia 2001, **15**: 184–186.

289 Mercieca J, Matutes E, Moskovic E, MacLennan K, Matthey F, Costello C, Behrens J, Basu S, Roath S, Fairhead S. Massive abdominal lymphadenopathy in hairy cell leukaemia: a report of 12 cases. Br J Haematol 1992, **82**: 547–554.

290 Naeim F, Jacobs AD. Bone marrow changes in patients with hairy cell leukemia treated by recombinant alpha 2-interferon. Hum Pathol 1985, **16**: 1200–1205.

291 Paoletti M, Bitter MA, Vardiman JW. Hairy cell leukemia. Morphologic, cytochemical, and immunologic features. Clin Lab Med 1988, **8**: 179–195.

292 Piro LD, Carrera CJ, Carson DA, Beutler E. Lasting remissions in hairy cell leukemia induced by a single infusion of 2-chlorodeoxyadenosine. N Engl J Med 1990, **322**: 1117–1121.

293 Pittaluga S, Tierans A, Dodoo YL, Delabie J, De Wolf-Peeters C. How reliable is histologic examination of bone marrow trephine biopsy specimens for the staging of non-Hodgkin lymphoma? A study of hairy cell leukemia and mantle cell lymphoma involvement of the bone marrow trephine specimen by histologic, immunohistochemical, and polymerase chain reaction techniques. Am J Clin Pathol 1999, **111**: 179–184.

294 Platanias LC, Golomb H. Hairy cell leukaemia. Bailliere's Clin Haematol 1993, **6**: 887–898.

295 Robbins BA, Ellison DJ, Spinosa JC, Carey CA, Lukes RJ, Poppema S, Savan A, Piro LD. Diagnostic application of two-color flow cytometry in 161 cases of hairy cell leukemia. Blood 1993, **82**: 1277–1287.

296 Schnitzer B, Kass L. Hairy cell leukemia. Clinicopathologic and ultrastructural study. Am J Clin Pathol 1974, **61**: 176–187.

297 Spiers AD, Moore D, Cassileth PA, Harrington DP, Cummings FJ, Neimann RS, Bennett JM, O'Connell MJ. Remissions in hairy cell leukemia with Pentostatin (2' deoxycoformycin). N Engl J Med 1987, **316**: 825–830.

298 Turner A, Kjeldsberg CR. Hairy cell leukemia: a review. Medicine (Baltimore) 1978, **57**: 477–499.

299 Vykoupil KF, Thiele J, Georgii A. Hairy cell leukemia. Bone marrow findings in 24 patients. Virchows Arch [A] 1976, **370**: 273–289.

Splenic lymphoma with villous lymphocytes

300 Catovsky D, Matutes E. Splenic lymphoma with villous lymphocytes/splenic marginal zone lymphoma. Semin Hematol 1999, **36**: 148–154.

301 Franco V, Florena AM, Campesi G. Intrasinusoidal bone marrow infiltration: a possible hallmark of splenic lymphoma. Histopathology 1996, **29**: 571–575.

302 Franco V, Florena A-M, Stella M, Rizzo A, Iannitto E, Quintini G, Campesi G. Splenectomy influences bone marrow infiltration in patients with splenic marginal zone cell lymphoma with or without villous lymphocytes. Cancer 2000, **91**: 294–301.

303 Hermine O, Lefrere F, Bronowicki J-P, Mariette X, Jondeau K, Eclache-Sandreau V, Delmas B, Valensi F, Cacoub P, Brechet C, Varet B, Troussand X. Regression of splenic lymphoma with

villous lymphocytes after treatment of hepatitis C infection. N Engl J Med 2002, **347**: 89–94.

304 Isaacson PG, Matutes E, Burke M, Catovsky D. The histopathology of splenic lymphoma with villous lymphocytes. Blood 1994, **84**: 3828–3834.

305 Isaacson PG, Piris M, Catovsky D, Swerdlow S, Montserrat E, Berger F, Muller-Hermelink HK, Nathwani B, Harris NL. Splenic marginal zone lymphoma. In Jaffe ES, Harris NL, Stein H, Vardiman JW (eds): World Health Organization Classification of Tumors. Pathology and genetics of tumours of haematopoietic and lymphoid tissues. Lyon, 2001, IARC Press, pp. 135–137.

306 Kent SA, Variakojis D, Peterson LC. Comparative study of marginal zone lymphoma involving bone marrow. Am J Clin Pathol 2002, **117**: 698–708.

307 Matutes E, Morilla R, Dwusu-Ankomah K, Houlihan A, Catovsky D. The immunophenotype of splenic lymphoma with villous lymphocytes and its relevance to the differential diagnosis with other B-cell disorders. Blood 1993, **83**: 1558–1562.

308 Melo JV, Hegde U, Parreira A, Thompson I, Lampert IA, Catovsky D. Splenic B cell lymphoma with circulating villous lymphocytes. Differential diagnosis of B cell leukaemias with large spleens. J Clin Pathol 1987, **40**: 642–651.

309 Oscier D, Matutes E, Gardiner S, Glyde S, Mould S, Brito-Babapulle V, Ellis J, Catovsky D. Cytogenetic studies in splenic lymphoma with villous lymphocytes. Br J Haematol 1993, **85**: 487–491.

Non-Hodgkin lymphoma
B-cell lymphoma

310 Bain B, Matutes E, Robinson D, Lampert IA, Brito-Babapulle V, Morilla R, Catovsky D. Leukaemia as a manifestation of large cell lymphoma. Br J Haematol 1991, **77**: 301–310.

311 Bartl R, Frisch B, Burkhardt R, Kettner G, Mahl G, Fateh-Moghadam A, Sund M. Assessment of bone marrow histology in the malignant lymphoma (non-Hodgkin's): correlation with clinical factors for diagnosis, prognosis, classification and staging. Br J Haematol 1982, **51**: 511–530.

312 Bartl R, Hansmann ML, Frisch B, Burkhardt R. Comparative histology of malignant lymphomas in lymph node and bone marrow. Br J Haematol 1988, **69**: 229–237.

313 Choe JK, Hyun BH, Salazar GH, Ashton JK, Sung C. Epithelioid granulomas of the bone marrow in non-Hodgkin's lymphoproliferative malignancies. Am J Clin Pathol 1983, **80**: 19–24.

314 Cohen PL, Kurtin PJ, Donovan KA, Hanson CA. Bone marrow and peripheral blood involvement in mantle cell lymphoma. Br J Haematol 1998, **101**: 302–310.

315 Conlan MG, Bast M, Armitage JO, Weisenburger DD for the Nebraska Lymphoma Study Group. Bone marrow involvement by non-Hodgkin's lymphoma: the clinical significance of morphologic discordance between the lymph node and bone marrow. J Clin Oncol 1990, **8**: 1163–1172.

316 Crotty RPL, Smith BR, Tallini G. Morphologic, immunophenotypic, and molecular evaluation of bone marrow involvement in non-Hodgkin's lymphoma. Diagn Mol Pathol 1998, **7**: 90–95.

317 Delabie J, Vandenberghe E, Kennes C, Verhoef G, Foschini MP, Stul M, Cassiman JJ, De Wolf-Peeters C. Histiocyte rich B-cell lymphoma. A distinct clinicopathologic entity possibly related to lymphocyte predominant Hodgkin's disease, paragranuloma type. Am J Surg Pathol 1992, **16**: 37–48.

318 Dick F, Bloomfield CD, Brunning RD. Incidence, cytology, and histopathology of non-Hodgkin's lymphomas in the bone marrow. Cancer 1974, **33**: 1382–1398.

319 Diebold J, Jaffe ES, Raphael M, Warnke RA. Burkitt lymphoma. In Jaffe ES, Harris NL, Stein H, Vardiman JW (eds): World Health Organization Classification of Tumors. Pathology and genetics of tumours of haematopoietic and lymphoid tissues. Lyon, 2001, IARC Press, pp. 181–184.

320 Douglas VK, Gordon LI, Goolsby CL, White CA, Peterson LC. Lymphoid aggregates in bone marrow mimic residual lymphoma after rituximab therapy for non-Hodgkin lymphoma. Am J Clin Pathol 1999, **112**: 844–853.

321 Estabilla OC, Kou CH, Byrnes RK, Medeiros LJ. Intravascular large B-cell lymphoma. Am J Clin Pathol 1999, **112**: 248–255.

322 Fisher DE, Jacobson JO, Ault KA, Harris NL. Diffuse large cell lymphoma with discordant bone marrow histology. Clinical features and biologic implications. Cancer 1989, **64**: 1879–1887.

323 Foucar K, McKenna RW, Frizzera G, Brunning RD. Incidence and patterns of bone marrow and blood involvement by lymphoma in relationship to the Lukes-Collins classification. Blood 1979, **54**: 1417–1422.

324 Foucar K, McKenna RW, Frizzera G, Brunning RD. Bone marrow and blood involvement by lymphoma in relationship to the Lukes-Collins classification. Cancer 1982, **49**: 888–897.

325 Fraga M, Brousset P, Schlaifer D, Payen C, Robert A, Rubie H, Huguet-Rigl F, Delsol G. Bone marrow involvement in anaplastic large cell lymphoma. Immunohistochemical detection of minimal disease and its prognostic significance. Am J Clin Pathol 1995, **103**: 82–89.

326 Gaulard P, Kanavaros P, Farcet JP, Rocha FD, Haioun C, Divine M, Reyes F, Zafrani ES. Bone marrow histologic and immunohistochemical findings in peripheral T-cell lymphoma. A study of 38 cases. Hum Pathol 1991, **22**: 331–338.

327 Hanson CA, Brunning RD, Gajl-Peczalska KJ, Frizzera G, McKenna RW. Bone marrow manifestation of peripheral T-cell lymphoma. A study of 30 cases. Am J Clin Pathol 1986, **86**: 449–460.

328 Harris NL, Swerdlow SH, Frizzera G, Knowles DM. Post-transplant lymphoproliferative disorders. In Jaffe ES, Harris NL, Stein H, Vardiman JW (eds): World Health Organization Classification of Tumors. Pathology and genetics of tumours of haematopoietic and lymphoid tissues. Lyon, 2001, IARC Press, pp. 264–271.

329 Kent SA, Variakojis D, Peterson LC. Comparative study of marginal zone lymphoma involving bone marrow. Am J Clin Pathol 2002, **117**: 698–708.

330 Kinney MC, Collins RD, Greer JP, Whitlock JA, Sioutes N, Kadin ME. A small-cell-predominant variant of primary Ki-1 (CD30)+ T-cell lymphoma. Am J Surg Pathol 1993, **17**: 859–968.

331 Koeppen H, Newell K, Baunoch DA, Vardiman JW. Morphologic bone marrow changes in patients with post-transplantation lymphoproliferative disorders. Am J Surg Pathol 1998, **22**: 208–214.

332 Kremer M, Dirnhofer S, Nickl A, Hoefler H, Quintanilla-Martinez L, Fend F. p27(kip1) immunostaining for the differential diagnosis of small B-cell neoplasms in trephine bone marrow biopsies. Mod Pathol 2001, **14**: 1022–1029.

333 Kremer M, Spitzer M, Mandl-Weber S, Stecker K, Quintanilla-Martinez L, Fend F. Discordant bone marrow involvement in diffuse large B-cell lymphoma; molecular analysis of microdissected bone marrow infiltrates reveals a heterogeneous group of disorders. J Clin Pathol 2002, **55**(suppl 1): A5.

334 Litz CE, Brunning RD. Chronic lymphoproliferative disorders. Classification and diagnosis. Bailliere's Clin Haematol 1993, **6**: 767–789.

335 McKenna RW, Bloomfield CD, Brunning RD. Nodular lymphoma. Bone marrow and blood manifestations. Cancer 1975, **36**: 428–440.

336 McKenna RW, Brunning RD. Reed-Sternberg-like cells in nodular lymphoma involving the bone marrow. Am J Clin Pathol 1975, **63**: 779–785.

337 McKenna RW, Hernandez JA. Bone marrow in malignant lymphoma. Hematol Oncol Clin North Am 1988, **2**: 617–619.

338 Osborne BM, Butler JJ. Hypocellular paratrabecular foci of treated small cleaved cell lymphoma in bone marrow biopsies. Am J Surg Pathol 1989, 13: 382–388.

339 Perry DA, Bast MA, Armitage JO, Weisenburger DD. Diffuse intermediate lymphocyte lymphoma. A clinicopathologic study and comparison with small lymphocytic lymphoma and small cleaved cell lymphoma. Cancer 1990, 66: 1995–2000.

340 Pittaluga S, Tierans A, Dodoo YL, Delabie J, DeWolf-Peeters C. How reliable is histologic examination of bone marrow trephine biopsy specimens for the staging of non-Hodgkin lymphoma? A study of hairy cell leukemia and mantle cell lymphoma involvement of the bone marrow trephine specimen by histologic, immunohistochemical, and polymerase chain reaction techniques. Am J Clin Pathol 1999, 111: 179–184.

341 Pittaluga S, Verhoef G, Criel A, Maes A, Maes A, Nuyts J, Boogaerts M, DeWolf-Peeters C. Prognostic significance of bone marrow trephine and peripheral blood smears in 55 patients with mantle cell lymphoma. Leuk Lymphoma 1996, 21: 115–125.

342 Robertson LE, Redman JR, Butler JJ, Osborne BM, Velasquez WS, McLaughlin P, Swan F, Rodriguez MA, Hagemeister FB, Fuller LM. Discordant bone marrow involvement in diffuse large-cell lymphoma. A distinct clinical-pathologic entity associated with a continuous risk of relapse. J Clin Oncol 1991, 9: 236–242.

343 Schlette E, Lai R, Onciu M, Doherty D, Bueso-Ramos C, Medeiros LJ. Leukemic mantle cell lymphoma: clinical and pathologic spectrum of twenty-three cases. Mod Pathol 2001, 14: 1133–1140.

344 Thieblemont C, Berger F, Dumontet C, Moullet I, Bouafia F, Felman P, Salles G, Coiffer B. Mucosa-associated lymphoid tissue lymphoma is a disseminated disease in one-third of 158 patients analyzed. Blood 2000, 95: 802–806.

345 Torlakovic B, Torlakovic G, Brunning RD. Follicular pattern of bone marrow involvement by follicular lymphoma. Am J Clin Pathol 2002, 118: 780–786.

346 Van Huyen JPD, Molina T, Delmer A, Audouin J, LeTuourneau A, Zihoun R, Bernadou A, Diebold J. Splenic marginal zone lymphoma with or without plasmacytic differentiation. Am J Surg Pathol 2000, 24: 1581–1592.

347 Vasef MA, Medeiros LJ, Coo C, McCourty A, Brynes RK. Cyclin D1 immunohistochemical staining is useful in distinguishing mantle cell lymphoma from other low-grade B-cell neoplasms. Am J Clin Pathol 2000, 108: 302–307.

348 Wasman J, Rosenthal NS, Farhi DC. Mantle cell lymphoma. Morphologic findings in bone marrow involvement. Am J Clin Pathol 1996, 106: 196–200.

349 Weir EG, Borowitz MJ, Racke FR. Germinal centers in bone marrow specimens are associated with marginal zone lymphoma. Mod Pathol 2001, 14: 182A.

T-cell lymphomas/leukemias
Peripheral T-cell lymphoma, unspecified

350 Gaulard P, Kanavaros P, Farcet JP, Rocha FD, Haioun C, Divine M, Reyes F, Zafrani ES. Bone marrow histologic and immunohistochemical findings in peripheral T-cell lymphoma. A study of 38 cases. Hum Pathol 1991, 22: 331–338.

351 Gebhard S, Benhatter J, Bricod C, Meuge-Moraw C, Delacratez F. Polymerase chain reaction in the diagnosis of T-cell lymphoma in paraffin embedded bone marrow biopsies: a comparative study. Histopathology 2001, 38: 37–44.

352 Hanson CA, Brunning RD, Gajl-Peczalska KJ, Frizzera G, McKenna RW. Bone marrow manifestation of peripheral T cell lymphoma. Am J Clin Pathol 1986, 86: 449–460.

353 Jaffe ES. Pathologic and clinical spectrum of post-thymic T-cell malignancies. Cancer Invest 1984, 2: 413–426.

Adult T-cell leukemia/lymphoma

354 Kikuchi M, Jaffe ES, Ralfkiaer E. Adult T-cell leukemia/lymphoma. In Jaffe ES, Harris NL, Stein H, Vardiman JW (eds): World Health Organization Classification of Tumors. Pathology and genetics of tumours of haematopoietic and lymphoid tissues. Lyon, 2001, IARC Press, pp. 200–203.

355 Kiyokawa T, Yamaguchi K, Takeya M, Takahashi K, Watanabe T, Matsumoto T, Lee SY, Takatsuki K. Hypercalcemia and osteoclast proliferation in adult T-cell leukemia. Cancer 1987, 59: 1187–1191.

356 Yamaguchi K, Takatsuki K. Adult T cell leukaemia lymphoma. Bailliere's Clin Haematol 1993, 6: 899–915.

Sézary syndrome

357 Flandrin G, Brouet J. The Sézary cell: cytologic, cytochemical and immunologic studies. Mayo Clin Proc 1974, 49: 575–583.

358 Lutzner MA, Jordan HW. The ultrastructure of an abnormal cell in Sézary's syndrome. Blood 1968, 31: 719–726.

359 Ralfkiaer E, Jaffe ES. Sezary syndrome. In Jaffe ES, Harris NL, Stein H, Vardiman JW (eds): World Health Organization Classification of Tumors. Pathology and genetics of tumours of haematopoietic and lymphoid tissues. Lyon, 2001, IARC Press, pp. 219–220.

360 Taswell HF, Winkelman RK. Sézary syndrome. A malignant reticulemic erythroderma. JAMA 1961, 177: 465–472.

361 Variakojis D, Rosas-Uribe A, Rappaport H. Mycosis fungoides. Pathologic findings in staging laparotomies. Cancer 1974, 33: 1589–1600.

362 Zucker-Franklin D, Melton JW, Quagliata F. Ultrastructural, immunologic and functional studies on Sézary cells: a neoplastic variant of thymus derived (T) lymphocytes. Proc Natl Acad Sci USA 1974, 71: 1877–1881.

Large granulated T-cell lymphocytic leukemia

363 Morice WG, Kurtin PJ, Tefferi A, Hanson CA. Distinct bone marrow findings in T-cell granular lymphocytic leukemia revealed by paraffin section immunoperoxidase stains for CD8, TIA-1, granzyme B. Blood 2002, 99: 268–274.

Angioimmunoblastic T-cell lymphoma

364 Frizzera G, Moran EM, Rappaport H. Angio-immunoblastic lymphadenopathy with dysproteinaemia. Lancet 1974, 1: 1070–1073.

365 Frizzera G, Moran EM, Rappaport H. Angio-immunoblastic lymphadenopathy. Diagnosis and clinical course. Am J Med 1975, 59: 803–818.

366 Ghani AM, Krause JR. Bone marrow biopsy findings in angioimmunoblastic lymphadenopathy. Br J Haematol 1985, 61: 203–231.

367 Lukes RJ, Tindle BH. Immunoblastic lymphadenopathy. A hyperimmune entity resembling Hodgkin's disease. N Engl J Med 1975, 292: 1–8.

368 Pangalis GA, Moran EM, Rappaport H. Blood and bone marrow findings in angio-immunoblastic lymphadenopathy. Blood 1978, 51: 71–83.

369 Schnaidt U, Vykoupil KF, Thiele J, Georgii A. Angioimmunoblastic lymphadenopathy. Histopathology of bone marrow involvement. Virchows Arch [A] 1980, 389: 369–380.

Hepatosplenic T-cell lymphoma, post-transplant T-cell lymphoma, and aggressive NK-cell lymphoma

370 Alonsozana ELC, Stamberg J, Kumar D, Jaffe ES, Medeiros LJ, Frantz C, Schiffer CA, O'Connell BA, Kerman S, Stass SA, Abruzzo LV. Isochromosome 7q: the primary cytogenetic abnormality in hepatosplenic gamma delta T cell lymphoma. Leukemia 1997, 11: 1367–1372.

371 Chan JKC, Sin C, Wong KF, Ng CS, Tsang WY, Chan CH, Cheung MM, Lau WH. Nonnasal lymphoma expressing the natural killer cell marker CD56: a clinicopathologic study of 49 cases of an uncommon aggressive neoplasm. Blood 1997, 89: 4501–4513.

372 Chan JKC, Wong KF, Jaffe ES, Ralfkiaer E. Aggressive NK-cell leukaemia. In Jaffe ES, Harris NL, Stein H, Vardiman JW (eds): World Health Organization Classification of Tumors. Pathology and genetics of tumours of haematopoietic and lymphoid tissues. Lyon, 2001, IARC Press, pp. 198–200.

373 de Wolf-Peeters C, Achten R. Gamma/delta T-cell lymphomas: a homogeneous entity? Histopathology 2000, 36: 294–305.

374 Jaffe E, Ralfkiaer E. Hepatosplenic T-cell lymphoma. In Jaffe ES, Harris NL, Stein H, Vardiman JW (eds): World Health Organization Classification of Tumors. Pathology and genetics of tumours of haematopoietic and lymphoid tissues. Lyon, 2001, IARC Press, pp. 210–211.

375 Jaffe ES. Pathologic and clinical spectrum of post-thymic T-cell malignancies. Cancer Invest 1984, 2: 413–426.

376 Jonveaux P, Daniel MT, Martel V, Maarek O, Berger R. Isochromosome 7q and trisomy 8 are consistent primary non-random chromosome abnormalities associated with hepatosplenic T gamma/delta lymphoma. Leukemia 1996, 10: 1453–1455.

377 Macon WR, Levy NB, Kurtin PJ, Salhany KE, Elkhalifa MY, Casey TT, Craig FE, Vnencak-Jones CL, Gulley ML, Park JP, Cousar JB. Hepatosplenic αβ T-cell lymphomas: a report of 14 cases and comparison with hepatosplenic gamma delta T-cell lymphomas. Am J Surg Pathol 2001, 25: 285–296.

378 Shaw PH, Cohn SL, Morgan ER, Kovarik P, Haut PR, Kletzel M, Murphy SB. Natural killer cell lymphoma: report of two pediatric cases, therapeutic options and review of the literature. Cancer 2001, 91: 642–646.

379 Vega F, Medeiros LJ, Buesa-Ramos C, Jones D, Lai R, Luthra R, Abruzzo LV. Hepatosplenic gamma/delta T-cell lymphoma in bone marrow. A sinusoidal neoplasm with blastic cytologic features. Am J Clin Pathol 2001, 116: 410–419.

380 Wong KF, Chan JK, Cheung MMC, So JC. Bone marrow involvement by nasal NK cell lymphoma at diagnosis is uncommon. Am J Clin Pathol 2001, 115: 226–270.

Anaplastic large cell lymphoma

381 Fraga M, Brousset P, Schlaifer D, Payen C, Robert A, Rubie H, Huguet Rigal F, Delsol G. Bone marrow involvement in anaplastic large cell lymphoma. Immunohistochemical detection of minimal disease and its prognostic significance. Am J Clin Pathol 1995, 103: 82–89.

382 Kinney MC, Collins RD, Greer JP, Whitlock JA, Sioutos N, Kadin ME. A small-cell-predominant variant of primary Ki-1 (CD30)+ T-cell lymphoma. Am J Surg Pathol 1993, 17: 859–868.

Lymphoma/leukemia

383 Banks PM, Arseneau JC, Gralnick HR, Canellos GP, DeVita VT, Berard CW. American Burkitt's lymphoma. A clinicopathologic study of 30 cases II. Pathologic correlations. Am J Med 1975, 58: 322–329.

384 Barcos MP, Lukes RJ. Malignant lymphomas of convoluted lymphocytes. A new entity of possible T-cell type. In Sinks LR, Godden JO (eds): Conflicts in childhood cancer. An evaluation of current management, vol. 4. New York, 1975, Alan R. Liss, pp. 147–178.

385 Bennett JM, Catovsky D, Daniet MT, Flandrin G, Galton DA, Gralnick HR, Sultan C. Proposals for the classification of the acute leukaemias. Br J Haematol 1976, 33: 451–458.

386 Brunning RD, Borowitz M, Matutes E, Head D, Flandrin G, Swerdlow SH, Bennett JM. Precursor B lymphoblastic leukaemia/lymphoblastic lymphoma (precursor B-cell acute lymphoblastic leukaemia). In Jaffe ES, Harris NL, Stein H, Vardiman JW (eds): World Health Organization Classification of Tumors. Pathology and genetics of tumours of haematopoietic and lymphoid tissues. Lyon, 2001, IARC Press, pp. 111–114.

387 Brunning RD, Borowitz M, Matutes E, Head D, Flandrin G, Swerdlow SH, Bennett JM. Precursor T lymphoblastic leukaemia/lymphoblastic lymphoma (precursor T-cell acute lymphoblastic leukemia). In Jaffe ES, Harris NL, Stein H, Vardiman JW (eds): World Health Organization Classification of Tumors. Pathology and genetics of tumours of haematopoietic and lymphoid tissues. Lyon, 2001, IARC Press, pp. 115–117.

388 Brunning RD, McKenna RW, Bloomfield CD, Coccia P, Gajl-Peczalska KJ. Bone marrow involvement in Burkitt's lymphoma. Cancer 1977, 40: 1771–1779.

389 Chan JKC, Sin VC, Wong KF, Ng CAS, Tsang WYW, Chan CH, Cheung MMC, Lau WH. Nonnasal lymphoma expressing the natural killer cell marker CD56: a clinicopathologic study of 49 cases of an uncommon aggressive neoplasm. Blood 1997, 89: 4501–4513.

390 Chan JKC, Wong KF, Jaffe ES, Ralfkiaer E. Aggressive NK-cell leukaemia. In Jaffe ES, Harris NL, Stein H, Vardiman JW (eds): World Health Organization Classification of Tumors. Pathology and genetics of tumours of haematopoietic and lymphoid tissues. Lyon, 2001, IARC Press, pp. 198–200.

391 Dayton VD, Arthur DC, Gajl-Peczalsak KJ, Brunning R. L3 acute lymphoblastic leukaemia. Comparison with small noncleaved cell lymphoma involving the bone marrow. Am J Clin Pathol 1994, 101: 130–139.

392 Diebold J, Jaffe ES, Raphael M, Warnke R. Burkitt lymphoma. In Jaffe ES, Harris NL, Stein H, Vardiman JW (eds): World Health Organization Classification of Tumors. Pathology and genetics of tumours of haematopoietic and lymphoid tissues. Lyon, 2001, IARC Press, pp. 181–184.

393 Dorfman RF. Childhood lymphosarcoma in St. Louis, Missouri, clinically and histologically resembling Burkitt's tumor. Cancer 1965, 18: 418–430.

394 Foon KA, Todd RF. Immunologic classification of leukemia and lymphoma. Blood 1986, 68: 1–31.

395 Harris NL, Bhan AK. B-cell neoplasms of the lymphocytic, lymphoplasmacytoid, and plasma cell types: immunohistologic analysis and clinical correlation. Hum Pathol 1985, 16: 829–837.

396 Imamura N, Kusunoki Y, Kawa-Ha K, Yumura K, Hara J, Oda K, Abe K, Dohy H, Inada T, Kajihara H. Aggressive natural killer cell leukaemia/lymphoma: report of four cases and review of the literature. Br J Haematol 1990, 75: 49–59.

397 Lin P, Jones O, Dorfman DM, Medeiros LJ. Precursor B-cell lymphoblastic lymphoma: a predominantly extranodal tumor with low propensity for leukemic involvement. Am J Surg Pathol 2000, 24: 1480–1490.

398 Litz CE, Brunning RD. Chronic lymphoproliferative disorders: classification and diagnosis. Bailliere's Clin Haematol 1993, 6: 767–783.

398a Maitra A, McKenna RW, Weinberg AG, Scheider NR, Kroft SH. Precursor B-cell lymphoblastic lymphoma. A study of nine cases lacking blood and bone marrow involvement and review of the literature. Am J Clin Pathol 2001, 115: 868–875.

399 McKenna RW, Bloomfield CD, Brunning RD. Nodular lymphoma: bone marrow and blood manifestations. Cancer 1975, 36: 428–440.

400 Muller-Hermelink HK, Catovsky D, Montserret E, Harris NL. Chronic lymphocytic leukaemia/small lymphocytic lymphoma. In Jaffe ES, Harris NL, Stein H, Vardiman JW (eds): World Health Organization Classification of Tumors. Pathology and genetics of tumours of haematopoietic and lymphoid tissues. Lyon, 2001, IARC Press, pp. 127–130.

401 Murphy SB, Hustu HO. A randomized trial of combined modality theory of childhood non-Hodgkin's lymphoma. Cancer 1980, 45: 630–637.

402 O'Connor GT, Rappaport H, Smith EB. Childhood lymphoma resembling "Burkitt tumor" in the United States. Cancer 1978, 18: 411–417.

403 Pangalis GA, Nathwanti BN, Rappaport H. Malignant lymphoma, well-differentiated lymphocytic: its relationship with chronic lymphocytic leukemia and macroglobulinemia of Waldenström. Cancer 1977, 39: 999–1010.

404 Pangalis GA, Roussou PA, Kittas C, Mitsoulis-Mentzikoff C, Matsouka-Alexandridis P, Anagnostopoulos N, Rombos I, Fessas P. Patterns of bone marrow involvement in chronic lymphocytic leukemia and small lymphocytic (well-differentiated) non-Hodgkin's lymphoma. Its clinical significance in relation to their differential diagnosis and prognosis. Cancer 1984, 54: 702–708.

405 De Oliveira MS, Jaffe ES, Catovsky D. Leukaemic phase of mantle zone (intermediate) lymphoma: its characterization in 11 cases. J Clin Pathol 1989, 42: 962–972.

406 Schlette E, Lai R, Onciu M, Doherty D, Bueso-Ramos C, Medeiros LJ. Leukemic mantle cell lymphoma: clinical and pathologic spectrum of twenty-three cases. Mod Pathol 2001, 14: 1133–1140.

407 Zukerberg LR, Medeiros LJ, Ferry JA, Harris NL. Diffuse low-grade B-cell lymphomas. Four clinically distinct subtypes defined by a combination of morphologic and immunophenotypic features. Am J Clin Pathol 1993, 100: 373–385.

Benign lymphocytic aggregates

408 Bluth RF, Casey TT, McCurley TL. Differentiation of reactive from neoplastic small-cell lymphoid aggregates in paraffin-embedded marrow particle preparations using L-26 (CD20) and UCHL-1 (CD45RO) monoclonal antibodies. Am J Clin Pathol 1993, 99: 150–156.

409 Faulkner-Jones BE, Howie AJ, Boughton BJ, Franklin IM. Lymphoid aggregates in bone marrow: study of eventual outcome. J Clin Pathol 1988, 41: 768.

410 Hashimoto H, Hashimoto N. The occurrence of lymph nodules in human bone marrow with particular reference to their number. Kyushu J Med Sci 1963, 14: 343–354.

411 Hashimoto M, Higuchi M, Saito T. Lymph nodules in human bone marrow. Acta Pathol Jpn 1957, 7: 33–52.

412 Horny HP, Wehrmann M, Grisser H, Tiemann M, Bultmann B, Kaiserling E. Investigation of bone marrow lymphocyte subsets in normal, reactive, and neoplastic states, using paraffin-embedded biopsy specimens. Am J Clin Pathol 1993, 99: 142–149.

413 Maeda K, Hyun BH, Rebuck JW. Lymphoid follicles in bone marrow aspirates. Am J Clin Pathol 1977, 67: 41–48.

414 Rywlin AM, Ortega RS, Dominguez CJ. Lymphoid nodules of bone marrow: normal and abnormal. Blood 1974, 43: 389–400.

414a Thiele J, Zirbes TK, Kvasnicka HM, Fischer R. Focal lymphoid aggregates (nodules) in bone marrow biopsies: differentiation between hyperplasia and malignant lymphoma–a practical guideline. J Clin Pathol 1999, 52: 294–300.

Hodgkin's lymphoma

415 Bartl R, Frisch B, Burkhardt R, Huhn D, Pappenberger R. Assessment of bone marrow histology in Hodgkin's disease: correlation with clinical factors. Br J Haematol 1982, 51: 345–360.

416 Diehl V, Sextro M, Franklin J, Hansmann M-L, Harris N, Jaffe E, Poppema S, Harris M, Franssila K, van Kriecken J, Marafioti T, Anagnostopoulos I, Stein H. Clinical presentation, course, and prognostic factors in lymphocyte-predominant Hodgkin's disease: report from the European task force on Lymphoma Project on Lymphocyte-Predominant Hodgkin's disease. J Clin Oncol 1999, 17: 776–783.

417 Dorfman RF. In discussion of Lukes RJ: Criteria for involvement of lymph node, bone marrow, spleen, and liver in Hodgkin's disease. Cancer Res 1971, 31: 1768–1769.

418 Kinney MC, Greer JP, Stein RS, Collins RD, Cousar JB. Lymphocyte-depletion Hodgkin's disease. Histopathologic diagnosis of marrow involvement. Am J Surg Pathol 1986, 10: 219–226.

419 Koene-Bogman J. Granulomas and the diagnosis of Hodgkin's disease. N Engl J Med 1978, 299: 533.

420 Lukes RJ. Criteria for involvement of lymph node, bone marrow, spleen and liver in Hodgkin's disease. Cancer Res 1971, 31: 1755–1767.

421 McKenna RW, Brunning RD. Reed–Sternberg-like cells in nodular lymphoma involving the bone marrow. Am J Clin Pathol 1975, 63: 779–785.

422 Munker R, Hasenclever D, Brosteanu O, Hiller E, Diehl V. Bone marrow involvement in Hodgkin's disease: an analysis of 135 consecutive cases. J Clin Oncol 1995, 13: 403–409.

423 Neiman RS, Rosen PJ, Lukes RJ. Lymphocyte-depletion Hodgkin's disease. A clinicopathologic entity. N Engl J Med 1973, 288: 751–755.

424 O'Carroll DI, McKenna RW, Brunning RD. Bone marrow manifestations of Hodgkin's disease. Cancer 1976, 38: 1717–1728.

425 Ponzoni M, Fumagalli L, Ross G, Freschi M, Re A, Vigano MG, Guidaboni M, Dolcetti R, McKenna RW, Facchetti F. Isolated bone marrow involvement in human immunodeficiency virus-associated Hodgkin lymphoma. Mod Pathol 2002, 15: 1273–1278.

426 Rappaport H, Berard CW, Butler JJ, Dorfman RF, Lukes RJ, Thomas LB. Report of the Committee of Histopathological Criteria contributing to staging of Hodgkin's disease. Cancer Res 1971, 31: 1864–1865.

427 Siebert JD, Stuckey JH, Kurtin PJ, Banks PM. Extranodal lymphocyte predominance Hodgkin's disease. Clinical and pathologic features. Am J Clin Pathol 1995, 103: 485–491.

428 Stein H, Delsol G, Pileri S, Said J, Mann R, Poppema S, Jaffe ES, Swerdlow SH. Classical Hodgkin lymphoma. In Jaffe ES, Harris NL, Stein H, Vardiman JW (eds): World Health Organization Classification of Tumors. Pathology and genetics of tumours of haematopoietic and lymphoid tissues. Lyon, 2001, IARC Press, pp. 244–253.

429 Te Velde J, Den Ottolander GJ, Spaander PJ, Van den Berg C, Hartgrink-Groeneveld CA. The bone marrow in Hodgkin's disease: the non-involved marrow. Histopathology 1978, 2: 31–46.

Histiocytic disorders

Malignant histiocytosis

430 Copie-Bergman C, Wotherspoon AC, Norton AJ, Diss TC, Isaacson PG. True histiocytic lymphoma: a morphologic, immunohistochemical, and molecular genetic study of 13 cases. Am J Surg Pathol 1998, 22: 1386–1392.

431 Jaffe ES. Histocytic and dendritic cell neoplasms: introduction. In Jaffe ES, Harris NL, Stein H, Vardiman JW (eds): World Health Organization Classification of Tumors. Pathology and genetics of tumours of haematopoietic and lymphoid tissues. Lyon, 2001, IARC Press, pp. 275–277.

432 Lampert IA, Catovsky D, Bergier N. Malignant histiocytosis: a clinico-pathological study of 12 cases. Br J Haematol 1978, 40: 65–77.

433 Rappaport H. Tumors of the hematopoietic system. In Atlas of tumor pathology, series 3, fascicle 8. Washington D.C., 2001, Armed Forces Institute of Pathology.

434 Rousseau-Merck MF, Jaubert E, Nezelof C. Malignant histiocytosis in childhood. Hum Pathol 1985, 16: 321.

435 Van Heerde P, Feltkamp CA, Hart AA, Somers R. Malignant histiocytosis and related tumors. A clinicopathologic study of 42 cases using cytological, histochemical, and ultrastructural parameters. Hematol Oncol 1984, 2: 13–32.

436 Warnke RA, Kim H, Dorfman RF. Malignant histiocytosis (histiocytic medullary reticulosis) I. Clinicopathologic study of 29 cases. Cancer 1975, 35: 215–230.

437 Weiss LM, Azzi R, Dorfman RF, Warnke RA. Sinusoidal hematolymphoid malignancy ("malignant histiocytosis") presenting as atypical sinusoidal proliferation. A study of nine cases. Cancer 1986, 58: 1681–1688.

438 Weiss LM, Grogan TM, Muller-Hermelink KH, Stein H, Pura T, Favara B, Pauli M, Foller SC. Histocytic sarcoma. In Jaffe ES,

Harris NL, Stein H, Vardiman JW (eds): World Health Organization Classification of Tumors. Pathology and genetics of tumours of haematopoietic and lymphoid tissues. Lyon, 2001, IARC Press, pp. 278–279.

439 Wilson MS, Weiss LM, Gatter KC, Mason DY, Dorfman RF, Warnke RA. Malignant histiocytosis. A reassessment of cases previously reported in 1975 based on paraffin section immunophenotyping studies. Cancer 1990, 66: 530–536.

Hemophagocytic syndromes

440 Allory Y, Challine D, Haioun C, Copie-Bergman C, Delfau-Larue M-H, Boucher E, Charlotte F, Fabre A, Michel M, Gaulard P. Bone marrow involvement in lymphomas with hemophagocytic syndrome at presentation. A clinicopathologic study of 11 patients in a western institution. Am J Surg Pathol 2001, 25: 865–874.

441 Ashby MA, Williams CJ, Buchanan RB, Bleehen NM, Arno J. Mediastinal germ cell tumor associated with malignant histiocytosis and high rubella titres. Hematol Oncol 1986, 4: 183–194.

442 Chen R-L, Su I-J, Lin K-H, Lee S-H, Lin D-T, Chuu W-M, Lin K-S, Huang L-M, Lee C-Y. Fulminant childhood hemophagocytic syndrome mimicking histiocytic medullary reticulosis. Am J Clin Pathol 1991, 96: 171–176.

443 Chott A, Kaserer K, Augustin I, Vesely M, Heinz R, Oehlinger W, Hanck H, Radaszkiewicz T. Ki-1 positive large cell lymphoma. A clinicopathologic study of 41 cases. Am J Surg Pathol 1990, 14: 439–448.

444 Daum GS, Sullivan JL, Ansell J, Mulder C, Woda BA. Virus-associated hemophagocytic syndrome. Identification of an immunoproliferative precursor lesion. Hum Pathol 1987, 18: 1071–1074.

445 Falini B, Pileri S, De Solas I, Martelli MF, Mason DY, Delsol G, Gatter KC, Fagioli M. Peripheral T-cell lymphoma associated with hemophagocytic syndrome. Blood 1990, 75: 434–444.

446 Frizzera G. The clinico-pathological expressions of Epstein-Barr virus infection in lymphoid tissues. Virchows Arch [Cell Pathol] 1987, 53: 1–12.

447 Gaffey MJ, Frierson HF, Medeiros LJ, Weiss LM. The relationship of Epstein-Barr virus (sporadic) and familial hemophagocytic syndrome and secondary (lymphoma-related) hemophagocytosis. An in situ hybridization study. Hum Pathol 1993, 24: 657–667.

448 Henter JI, Elinder G, Ost A. Diagnostic guidelines for hemophagocytic lymphohistiocytosis. Semin Oncol 1991, 18: 29–33.

449 Jaffe ES, Costa J, Fauci AS, Cossman J, Tsosos M. Malignant lymphoma and erythrophagocytosis simulating malignant histiocytosis. Am J Med 1983, 75: 741–749.

450 Kikuta H, Sakiyama Y, Matsumoto S, Ohishi T, Nakano T, Nagashima T, Oka T, Hironaka T, Hirai K. Fatal Epstein-Barr virus-associated hemophagocytic syndrome. Blood 1993, 82: 3259–3264.

451 Kimura H, Hoshino Y, Kanegane H, Tsuge I, Okamura T, Kawa K, Morishima T. Clinical and virologic characteristics of chronic active Epstein-Barr virus infections. Blood 2001, 98: 280–286.

452 Kogawa K, Lee SM, Villanueva J, Marmer D, Sumegi J, Filipovich AH. Perforin expression in cytotoxic lymphocytes from patients with hemophagocytic lymphohistiocytosis and their family members. Blood 2002, 99: 61–66.

453 Lampert IA, Catovsky D, Bernier M. Malignant histiocytosis. A clinicopathological study of 12 cases. Br J Haematol 1978, 40: 65–77.

454 Lay J-D, Tsao C-J, Chen J-Y, Kadin M, Su I-J. Upregulation of tumor necrosis factor-α gene by Epstein-Barr virus and activation of macrophages in Epstein-Barr virus-infected T cells in the pathogenesis of hemophagocytic syndrome. J Clin Invest 1997, 100: 1969–1979.

455 Look AT, Naegele RF, Callihan T, Herrod HG, Henle W. Fatal Epstein-Barr virus infections in a child with acute lymphoblastic leukemia in remission. Cancer Res 1981, 41: 4280–4283.

456 Mroczek EC, Weisenburger DD, Grierson HL, Markin R, Purtilo DT. Fatal infectious mononucleosis and virus-associated hemophagocytic syndrome. Arch Pathol Lab Med 1987, 111: 530–535.

457 Reiner AP, Spivak JL. Hematophagocytic histiocytosis. A report of 23 new patients and a review of the literature. Medicine (Baltimore) 1988, 67: 349–368.

458 Reisman RP, Greco MA. Virus-associated hemophagocytic syndrome due to Epstein-Barr virus. Hum Pathol 1984, 15: 290–293.

459 Risdall RJ, Brunning RD, Hernandez JI, Gordon DH. Bacteria-associated hemophagocytic syndrome. Cancer 1984, 54: 2968–2972.

460 Risdall RJ, McKenna RW, Nesbit ME, Krivit W, Balfour HH, Simmons RL, Brunning RD. Virus associated hemophagocytic syndrome. Hum Pathol 1981, 12: 395–398.

461 Shimazaki C, Inaba T, Shimura K, Okamoto A, Takahashi R, Hirai H, Sudo Y, Ashihara E, Adachi Y, Murakami S, Saigo K, Fugita N, Nakagawa M. B-cell lymphoma associated with hemophagocytic syndrome: a clinical, immunological and cytogenetic study. Br J Haematol 1999, 104: 672–679.

462 Shirono K, Tsuda H. Parvovirus B19-associated hemophagocytic syndrome in healthy adults. Br J Haematol 1995, 89: 923–926.

463 Stepp SE, Dufourcq-Lagelouse R, LeDeist F, Bhawan S, Certain S, Mathew PA, Henter J-I, Bennett M, Fisher A, de Saint Basile G, Kumar V. Perforin gene defect in familial hemophagocytic lymphohistiocytosis. Science 1999, 286: 1957–1959.

464 Stroup RM, Burke JS, Sheibani K, Ben-Ezra J, Brownell M, Winberg CD. Splenic involvement by aggressive malignant lymphomas of B-cell and T-cell types. A morphologic and immunophenotypic study. Cancer 1992, 69: 413–420.

465 Su I-J, Wang C-H, Cheng A-L, Chen R-L. Hemophagocytic syndrome in Epstein-Barr virus associated T-lymphoproliferative disorders: disease spectrum, pathogenesis and management. Leuk Lymphoma 1995, 19: 401–406.

466 Sullivan JL, Woda BA, Herrod HG, Koh G, Rivara FP, Mulder C. Epstein-Barr virus-associated hemophagocytic syndrome. Virological and immunopathological studies. Blood 1985, 65: 1097–1104.

467 Takeshita M, Kikuchi M, Ohshima K, Nibu K, Suzumiya J, Hisano S, Migamoto Y, Okamura T. Bone marrow findings in malignant lymphoma with concurrent hemophagocytic syndrome. Leuk Lymphoma 1992, 12: 79–89.

468 Teruya-Feldstein J, Setsuda J, Yao X, Kingma DW, Straus S, Tosato G, Jaffe ES. MIP-1 alpha expression in tissues from patients with hemophagocytic syndrome. Lab Invest 1999, 79: 1583–1590.

469 Woda BA, Sullivan JL. Reactive histiocytic disorders. Am J Clin Pathol 1993, 99: 459–463.

470 Wong KF, Chan JKC, Ng CS, Chu YC, Lam PWY, Yuen HL. Anaplastic large cell Ki-1 lymphoma involving bone marrow: marrow findings and association with reactive hemophagocytosis. Am J Hematol 1991, 37: 112–119.

Langerhans' cell histiocytosis (histiocytosis X)

471 McClain K, Ramsay NKC, Robison L, Sundberg RD, Nesbit M Jr. Bone marrow involvement in histiocytosis X. Med Pediatr Oncol 1983, 11: 167–171.

472 Weiss LM, Grogan TM, Muller-Hermelink KH, Stein H, Pura T, Favara B, Pauli M, Foller SC. Langerhans cell histiocytosis. In Jaffe ES, Harris NL, Stein H, Vardiman JW (eds): World Health Organization Classification of Tumors. Pathology and genetics of tumours of haematopoietic and lymphoid tissues. Lyon, 2001, IARC Press, pp. 280–282.

Plasma cell dyscrasias

473 Grogan TM, Van Camp B, Kyle RA, Muller-Hermelink H-K, Harris NL. Plasma cell neoplasms. In Jaffe ES, Harris NL, Stein H, Vardiman JW (eds): World Health Organization Classification of Tumors. Pathology and genetics of tumours of haematopoietic and lymphoid tissues. Lyon, 2001, IARC Press, pp. 142–156.

Plasma cell myeloma

474 Azar HA, Zaino EC, Pham TD, Yannopoulos K. Non-secretory plasma cell myeloma. Observations on seven cases with electron microscopic studies. Am J Clin Pathol 1972, 58: 618–629.

475 Barlogie B, Epstein J, Selvanayagam P, Alexanian R. Plasma cell-myeloma. New biologic insights and advances in therapy. Blood 1989, 73: 865–879.

476 Bartl R, Frisch B, Burkhardt R, Fateh-Moghadam A, Mahl G, Gierster P, Sund M, Kettner G. Bone marrow histology in myeloma: its importance in diagnosis, prognosis, classification and staging. Br J Haematol 1982, 51: 361–375.

477 Bartl R, Frisch B, Fateh-Moghadam A, Kettner G, Jaeger K, Sommerfeld W. Histologic classification and staging of multiple myeloma. A retrospective study of 674 cases. Am J Clin Pathol 1987, 87: 342–355.

478 Bataille R, Durie BGM, Grenier J. Serum beta2 microglobulin and survival duration in multiple myeloma. A simple reliable marker for staging. Br J Haematol 1983, 55: 439–447.

479 Carbone A, Volpe R, Manconi R, Poletti A, Tirelli U, Monfardini S. Bone marrow pattern and clinical staging in multiple myeloma. Br J Haematol 1987, 65: 502.

480 Carter A, Hocherman I, Linn S, Cohen Y, Tatarsky I. Prognostic significance of plasma cell morphology in multiple myeloma. Cancer 1987, 60: 1060–1065.

481 Case record of the Massachusetts General Hospital; Case 4–1992. N Engl J Med 1992, 326: 255–263.

482 Cavo M, Baccarani M, Gobbi M, Lipizer A, Tura S. Prognostic value of bone marrow plasma cell infiltration in stage I multiple myeloma. Br J Haematol 1983, 55: 683–690.

483 Durie BG. Staging and kinetics of multiple myeloma. Semin Oncol 1986, 13: 300–309.

484 Durie BGM, Salmon SE, Moon TE. Pretreatment tumor mass, cell kinetics, and prognosis in multiple myeloma. Blood 1980, 55: 364–372.

485 Facon T, Avet-Loiseau H, Guillerm G, Moreau P, Genevieve F, Zandeck M, Lai J-L, Leleu X, Jouet J-P, Bauters F, Harousseau J-L, Bataille R, Mary J-Y. Chromosome 13 abnormalities identified by FISH analysis and serum B2-microglobulin produce a powerful myeloma staging system for patients receiving high-dose therapy. Blood 2001, 97: 1566–1571.

486 Falini B, DeSolas I, Levine AM, Parker JW, Lukes RJ, Taylor CR. Emergence of B-immunoblastic sarcoma in patients with multiple myeloma. A clinico-pathologic study of 10 cases. Blood 1982, 59: 923–933.

487 Fonseca R, Blood EA, Oken MM, Kyle RA, Dewald GW, Bailey RJ, Van Weir SA, Henderson KJ, Hoyer JD, Harrington D, Kay NE, Van Ness B, Greipp PR. Myeloma and the t(11;14)(q13;q32); evidence for a biologically defined unique subset of patients. Blood 2002, 99: 3735–3741.

488 Fritz E, Ludwig H, Kundi M. Prognostic relevance of cellular morphology in multiple myeloma. Blood 1984, 63: 1072–1079.

489 Gassmann W, Pralle H, Haferlach T, Pandurevic S, Graubner M, Schmitz N, Loffler H. Staging systems for multiple myeloma. A comparison. Br J Haematol 1985, 59: 703–711.

490 Gertz MA, Kyle RA, Greipp PR. The plasma cell labeling index; a valuable tool in primary systemic amyloidosis. Blood 1989, 74: 1108–1111.

491 Greipp PR, Katzmann JA, O'Fallon WM, Kyle RA. Impact of pretreatment β2 microglobulin levels on survival in patients with multiple myeloma. Blood 1985, 66: 188a.

492 Greipp PR, Raymond NM, Kyle RA, O'Fallon WM. Multiple myeloma. Significance of plasmablastic subtype in morphological classification. Blood 1985, 65: 305–310.

493 Greipp PR, Witzig TE, Gonchoroff NJ, Haberman TM, Katzmann JA, O'Fallon WM, Kyle RA. Immunofluorescence labeling indices in myeloma and related monoclonal gammopathies. Mayo Clin Proc 1987, 62: 969–977.

494 Greipp PR. Advances in the diagnosis and management of myeloma. Semin Hematol 1992, 29: 24–45.

495 Hoyer JD, Hanson CA, Fonseca R, Greipp PR, Dewald G, Kurtin PJ. The (11,14)(q13;q32) translocation in multiple myeloma. Am J Clin Pathol 2000, 113: 831–837.

496 Hyun BK, Kwa D, Gabaldon H, Ashton JK. Reactive plasmacytic lesions of the bone marrow. Am J Clin Pathol 1976, 65: 921–928.

497 Konigsberg R, Zojer N, Ackermann J, Kromer E, Kittler H, Fritz E, Kaufmann H, Nosslinger T, Riedl L, Gisslinger H, Jager U, Simonitsch I, Heinz R, Ludwig H, Huber H, Drach J. Predictive role of interphase cytogenetics for survival of patients with multiple myeloma. J Clin Oncol 2000, 18: 804–812.

498 Krzyzaniak RL, Buss DH, Cooper R, Wells HB. Marrow fibrosis and multiple myeloma. Am J Clin Pathol 1988, 89: 63–68.

499 Moreau P, Facon T, Leleu X, Morineau N, Huyghe P, Harousseau JL, Bataille R, Avet-Loiseau H. Recurrent 14q32 translocations determine the prognosis of multiple myeloma, especially in patients receiving intensive chemotherapy. Blood 2002, 100: 1579–1583.

500 Peterson LC, Brown BA, Crosson JT, Mladenovic J. Application of the immunoperoxidase technic to bone marrow trephine biopsies in the classification of patients with monoclonal gammopathies. Am J Clin Pathol 1986, 85: 688–693.

501 Petruch UR, Horny HP, Kaiserling E. Frequent expression of haemopoietic and non-haemopoietic antigens by neoplastic plasma cells. An immunohistochemical study using formalin-fixed, paraffin-embedded tissue. Histopathology 1992, 20: 35–40.

502 Pileri S, Poggi S, Baglioni P, Montanari M, Sabattini E, Galieni P, Tazzari PL, Gobbi M, Cavo M, Falini B. Histology and immunohistology of bone marrow biopsy in multiple myeloma. Eur J Haematol 1989, 43: 52–59.

503 Preud'Homme JL, Hurez D, Danon F, Brouet JC, Seligmann M. Intracytoplasmic and surface-bound immunoglobulins in "nonsecretory" and Bence-Jones myeloma. Clin Exp Immunol 1976, 25: 428–436.

504 Smadja NV, Bastard C, Brigaudeau C, Leroux D, Fruchart C. Hypodiploidy is a major prognostic factor in multiple myeloma. Blood 2001, 98: 2229–2238.

505 Smith DB, Harris M, Gowland E, Chang J, Scargge JH. Non-secretory multiple myeloma. A report of 13 cases with a review of the literature. Hematol Oncol 1986, 4: 307–313.

506 Strand WR, Banks PM, Kyle RA. Anaplastic plasma cell myeloma and immunoblastic lymphoma. Clinical, pathologic, and immunologic comparison. Am J Med 1984, 76: 861–867.

507 Strickler JG, Audeh MW, Copenhaver CM, Warnke RA. Immunophenotypic differences between plasmacytoma/multiple myeloma and immunoblastic lymphoma. Cancer 1988, 61: 1782–1786.

508 Supkanichnant S, Cousar JB, Leelasiri A, Graber SE, Greer JP, Collins RD. Diagnostic criteria and histologic grading in multiple myeloma. Histologic and immunohistologic analysis of 176 cases with clinical correlation. Hum Pathol 1994, 25: 308–318.

509 Thiry A, Delvenne P, Fontaine MA, Bonvier J. Comparison of bone marrow sections, smears, and immunohistological staining for immunoglobulin light chains in the diagnosis of benign and malignant plasma cell proliferations. Histopathology 1993, 22: 423–428.

Plasma cell leukemia

510 Garcia-Sanz R, Orfao A, Gonzales M, Tabernero MD, Blade J, Moro MJ, Fernandez-Caluo J, Sanz MA, Perez-Simon JA, Rasilo

A, San Miguel JF. Primary plasma cell leukemia: clinical immunophenotypic, DNA ploidy, and cytogenetic characteristics. Blood 1999, **93:** 1032–1037.

511 Kosmo MA, Gale RP. Plasma cell leukemia. Semin Hematol 1987, **24:** 202–208.

512 Kyle RA, Maldonado JE, Baryd ED. Plasma cell leukemia. Report on 17 cases. Arch Intern Med 1974, **133:** 813–818.

513 Maldonado J, Velosa JA, Kyle RA, Wagoner RD, Holley KE, Salassa RM. Fanconi syndrome in adults. A manifestation of a latent form of myeloma. Am J Med 1974, **58:** 354–364.

Osteosclerotic myeloma (POEMS syndrome)

514 Bitter MA, Komaiko W, Franklin WA. Giant lymph node hyperplasia with osteoblastic bone lesions and the POEMS (Takatsuki's) syndrome. Cancer 1985, **56:** 188–194.

515 Case record of the Massachusetts General Hospital; Case 39–1992. N Engl J Med 1992, **327:** 1014–1021.

516 Diego Miralles G, O'Fallon JR, Talley NJ. Plasma-cell dyscrasia with polyneuropathy. The spectrum of POEMS syndrome. N Engl J Med 1992, **327:** 1919–1923.

517 Imawari M, Akatsuka N, Beppu H, Suzuki H, Ishibashi M. Syndrome of plasma cell dyscrasia, polyneuropathy, and endocrine disturbances. Ann Intern Med 1974, **81:** 490–493.

518 Miralles GD, O'Fallon JR, Talley NJ. Plasma-cell dyscrasia with polyneuropathy. The spectrum of POEMS syndrome. N Engl J Med 1992, **327:** 1919–1923.

519 Soubrier MJ, Dubost J-J, Sauvezie BJH. POEMS syndrome. A study of 25 cases and a review of the literature. Am J Med 1994, **97:** 543–553.

520 Takatsuki K, Sanada I. Plasma cell dyscrasia with polyneuropathy and endocrine disorder. Clinical and laboratory features of 109 reported cases. Jpn J Clin Oncol 1983, **13:** 543–556.

Monoclonal gammopathy of undetermined significance

521 Cesana C, Klersy C, Barbarano L, Nosari AM, Crugnola M, Pungolino E, Gargantini L, Granata S, Valentini M, Morra E. Prognostic factors for malignant transformation in monoclonal gammopathy of undetermined significance and smoldering multiple myeloma. J Clin Oncol 2002, **20:** 1625–1634.

522 Fonseca R, Bailey RJ, Ahmann GJ, Rajkumar SV, Hoyer JD, Lust JA, Kyle RA, Gertz MA, Greipp PR, Dewald GW. Genomic abnormalities in monoclonal gammopathy of undetermined significance. Blood 2002, **100:** 1417–1424.

523 Greipp PR, Kyle RA. Clinical, morphological and cell kinetic differences among multiple myeloma, monoclonal gammopathy of undetermined significance, and smoldering multiple myeloma. Blood 1983, **62:** 166–171.

524 Kyle RA. "Benign" monoclonal gammopathy. After 20–35 years of follow-up. Mayo Clin Proc 1993, **68:** 26–36.

525 Kyle RA, Lust JA. Monoclonal gammopathies of undetermined significance. Semin Hematol 1989, **26:** 176–200.

526 Kyle RA, Therneau TM, Rajkumar SV, Offord JR, Larson DR, Plevak MF, Melton LJ III. A long-term study of prognosis in monoclonal gammopathy of undetermined significance. N Engl J Med 2002, **346:** 564–569.

527 Peterson LC, Brown BA, Crosson JT, Mladenovic J. Application of the immunoperoxidase technic to bone marrow trephine biopsies in the classification of patients with monoclonal gammopathies. Am J Clin Pathol 1986, **85:** 688–693.

528 Rajkumar SV, Mesa RA, Fonseca R, Schroeder G, Plevak MF, Dispenzieri A, Lacy MQ, Lust JA, Witzig TE, Gertz MA, Kyle RA, Russell SJ, Greipp PR. Bone marrow angiogenesis in 400 patients with monoclonal gammopathy of undetermined significance, multiple myeloma, and primary amyloidosis. Clin Cancer Res 2002, **8:** 2210–2216.

Plasmacytoma

529 Alexanian R. Localized and indolent myeloma. Blood 1980, **56:** 521–525.

530 Alexiou C, Kau RJ, Dietzfelbinger H, Kremer M, Spiess JC, Schratzenstaller B, Arnold W. Extramedullary plasmacytoma. Tumor occurrence and therapeutic concepts. Cancer 1999, **85:** 2305–2315.

531 Corwin J, Lindberg RD. Solitary plasmacytoma of bone vs. extramedullary plasmacytoma and their relationship to multiple myeloma. Cancer 1979, **43:** 1007–1013.

532 Dimopoulos MA, Moulopoulos LA, Maniatis A, Alexanian R. Solitary plasmacytoma of bone and asymptomatic multiple myeloma. Blood 2000, **96:** 2037–2044.

533 Galieni P, Cavo M, Avvisati G, Pulsoni A, Falbo R, Bonnelli MA, Russo D, Petrucci MT, Bucalossi A, Tura S. Solitary plasmacytoma of bone and extramedullary plasmacytoma: two different entities? Ann Oncol 1995, **6:** 687–691.

534 Holland J, Trenkner DA, Wasserman TH, Fineberg B. Plasmacytoma. Treatment results and conversion to myeloma. Cancer 1992, **69:** 1513–1517.

535 Kotner LM, Wang CC. Plasmacytoma of the upper air and food passages. Cancer 1972, **30:** 414–418.

536 Meis JM, Butler JJ, Osborne BM, Ordonez NG. Solitary plasmacytomas of bone and extramedullary plasmacytomas. A clinicopathologic and immunohistochemical study. Cancer 1987, **59:** 1475–1485.

537 Meyer JE, Schulz MD. "Solitary" myeloma of bone. A review of 12 cases. Cancer 1974, **34:** 438–440.

538 Mill WB, Griffith R. The role of radiation therapy in the management of plasma cell tumors. Cancer 1980, **45:** 647–652.

539 Peterson LC, Brown BA, Crosson JT, Mladenovic J. Application of the immunoperoxidase technic to bone marrow trephine biopsies in the classification of patients with monoclonal gammopathies. Am J Clin Pathol 1986, **85:** 688–693.

540 Strickler JG, Audeh MW, Copenhaver CM, Warnke RA. Immunophenotypic differences between plasmacytoma/multiple myeloma and immunoblastic lymphoma. Cancer 1988, **61:** 1782–1786.

541 Wilder RB, Ha CS, Cox JD, Weber D, Delasalle K, Alexanian R. Persistence of myeloma protein for more than one year after radiotherapy is an adverse prognostic factor in solitary plasmacytoma of bone. Cancer 2002, **94:** 1532–1537.

542 Wiltshaw E. The natural history of extramedullary plasmacytoma and its relation to solitary myeloma of bone and myelomatosis. Medicine (Baltimore) 1976, **55:** 217–238.

543 Woodruff RK, Whittle JM, Malpas JS. Solitary plasmacytoma. Extramedullary soft tissue plasmacytoma. Cancer 1979, **43:** 2340–2343.

Lymphoplasmacytic lymphoma (Waldenström's macroglobulinemia)

544 Berger F, Isaacson P, Piris M, Harris NL, Muller-Hermelink HK, Nathwani BN, Swerdlow SH. Lymphoplasmacytic lymphoma/Waldenström macroglobulinemia. In Jaffe ES, Harris NL, Stein H, Vardiman JW (eds): World Health Organization Classification of Tumors. Pathology and genetics of tumours of haematopoietic and lymphoid tissues. Lyon, 2001, IARC Press, pp. 132–134.

545 Brittin G, Tanaka Y, Brecher G. Intranuclear inclusions in multiple myeloma and macroglobulinemia. Blood 1963, **21:** 335–351.

546 Case records of the Massachusetts General Hospital (Case 6–1978). N Engl J Med 1978, **298:** 387–396.

547 Dutcher TF, Fahey JL. The histopathology of the macroglobulinemia of Waldenström. J Natl Cancer Inst U S A 1959, **22:** 887–917.

548 Non-Hodgkin's Lymphoma Classification Project. National Cancer Institute Sponsored Study of Classification of Non-

Hodgkin's Lymphomas. Summary and description of working formulations for clinical usage. Cancer 1982, **49:** 2112–2135.

549 Pangalis GA, Nathwani BN, Rappaport H. Malignant lymphoma, well differentiated lymphocytic. Its relationship with chronic lymphocytic leukemia and macroglobulinemia of Waldenström. Cancer 1977, **39:** 999–1010.

550 Rywlin AW, Civantos F, Ortega RS, Dominguez CJ. Bone marrow histology in monoclonal macroglobulinemia. Am J Clin Pathol 1975, **63:** 769–778.

551 Tubbs RR, Hoffman GC, Deodhar SD, Hewlett JS. IgM monoclonal gammopathy. Histopathologic and clinical spectrum. Cleve Clin Q 1976, **43:** 217–235.

552 Tursz T, Brouet J, Flandrin G, Danon F, Clauvel JP, Seligmann M. Clinical and pathologic features of Waldenstrom's macroglobulinemia in seven patients with serum monoclonal IgG or IgA. Am J Med 1977, **63:** 499–502.

553 Waldenström J. Incipient myelomatosis or "essential" hypergammaglobulinemia with fibrinogenopenia. A new syndrome. Acta Med Scand 1944, **117:** 216–247.

Heavy chain disease

554 Frangione B, Franklin EC. Heavy chain diseases. Clinical features and molecular significance of the disordered immunoglobulin structure. Semin Hematol 1973, **10:** 53–64.

555 Franklin EC. Mu-chain disease. Arch Intern Med 1975, **135:** 71–72.

556 Grogen TM, Van Camp B, Kyle RA, Muller-Hermelink H-K, Harris NL. Heavy chain diseases. In Jaffe ES, Harris NL, Stein H, Vardiman JW (eds): World Health Organization Classification of Tumors. Pathology and genetics of tumours of haematopoietic and lymphoid tissues. Lyon, 2001, IARC Press, pp. 154–156.

557 Jonsson V, Videbaek A, Axelsen NH, Harboe M. Mu-chain disease in a case of chronic lymphocytic leukemia and malignant histocytoma. I. Clinical aspects. Scand J Haematol 1976, **16:** 209–217.

558 Kyle RA, Greipp PR, Banks PM. The diverse picture of gamma heavy-chain disease. Report of seven cases and review of literature. Mayo Clin Proc 1981, **56:** 439–451.

559 Seligmann M, Preud'Homme JL, Brouet JC. Membrane markers in human lymphoid malignancies. Clinicopathological correlations and insights into the differentiation of normal and neoplastic cells. In Clarkson B, Marks P, Till JR (eds): Differentiation of normal and neoplastic hematopoietic cells. Cold Spring Harbor, NY, 1978, Cold Spring Harbor Laboratory, pp. 859–876.

560 Seligmann M. Immunochemical, clinical, and pathologic features of alpha-chain disease. Arch Intern Med 1975, **135:** 78–82.

Amyloidosis

561 Banerjee D, Mills DM, Hearn SA, Meek M, Turner KL. Proteinaceous lymphadenopathy due to monoclonal nonamyloid immunoglobulin deposit disease. Arch Pathol Lab Med 1990, **114:** 34–39.

562 Buxbaum JN, Chuba JV, Hellman GC, Solomon A, Gallo GR. Monoclonal immunoglobulin deposition disease: light chain and light and heavy chain deposition diseases and their relation to light chain amyloidosis. Clinical features, immunopathology and molecular analysis. Ann Intern Med 1990, **112:** 455–464.

563 Falk RH, Comenzo RL, Skinner M. The systemic amyloidoses. N Engl J Med 1997, **337:** 898–909.

564 Feiner HD. Pathology of dysproteinemia: Light chain amyloidosis, non-amyloid immunoglobulin deposition disease, cryoglobulinemia syndromes, and macroglobulinemia of Waldenstrom. Hum Pathol 1988, **19:** 1255–1272.

565 Gertz MA, Greipp PR, Kyle RA. Classification of amyloidosis by the detection of clonal excess of plasma cells in the bone marrow. J Lab Clin Med 1991, **118:** 33–39.

566 Gertz MA, Kyle RA. Primary systemic amyloidosis. A diagnostic primer. Mayo Clin Proc 1989, **64:** 1505–1519.

567 Kyle RA, Gertz M. Primary systemic amyloidosis. Clinical and laboratory features in 474 cases. Semin Hematol 1995, **32:** 45–59.

568 Kyle RA, Greipp PR. Amyloidosis (AL). Clinical and laboratory features in 229 cases. Mayo Clin Proc 1983, **58:** 665–683.

569 Osborne BM, Butler JJ, Mackay B. Proteinaceous lymphadenopathy with hypergammaglobulinemia. Am J Surg Pathol 1979, **3:** 137–145.

570 Wolf BC, Kumar A, Vera JC, Nieman RS. Bone marrow morphology and immunology in systemic amyloidosis. Am J Clin Pathol 1986, **86:** 84–88.

Systemic polyclonal B-immunoblastic proliferation

571 Hanto DW, Frizzera G, Purtilo DT, Sakamoto K, Sullivan JL, Saemundsen AK, Klein G, Simmons RL, Najarian JS. Clinical spectrum of lymphoproliferative disorders in renal transplant recipients and evidence for the role of Epstein-Barr virus. Cancer Res 1981, **41:** 4253–4261.

572 Koo CH, Nathwant BN, Winberg CD, Hill LR, Rappaport H. Atypical lymphoplasmacytic and immunoblastic proliferation in lymph nodes of patients with autoimmune disease (autoimmune disease-associated lymphadenopathy). Medicine (Baltimore) 1984, **63:** 274–290.

573 Peterson LC, Brown BA, Crosson JT, Mladenovic J. Application of the immunoperoxidase technique to bone marrow trephine biopsies in the classification of patients with monoclonal gammopathies. Am J Clin Pathol 1986, **85:** 688–693.

574 Peterson LC, Kueck B, Arthur DC, Dedeker K, Brunning RD. Systemic polyclonal immunoblastic proliferations. Cancer 1988, **61:** 1350–1358.

575 Poje EJ, Soori GS, Weisenburger DD. Systemic polyclonal B-immunoblastic proliferation with marked peripheral blood and bone marrow plasmacytosis. Am J Clin Pathol 1992, **98:** 222–226.

Systemic mastocytosis

576 Brunning RD, McKenna RW, Rosai J, Parkin JL, Risdall R. Systemic mastocytosis. Am J Surg Pathol 1983, **7:** 425–438.

577 Czarentski BM, Kolde G, Schoemann A, Urbanitz S, Urbanitz D. Bone marrow findings in adult patients with urticaria pigmentosa. J Am Acad Dermatol 1980, **18:** 45–51.

578 Horny HP, Parwaresch MR, Lennert K. Bone marrow findings in systemic mastocytosis. Hum Pathol 1985, **16:** 808–814.

579 Horny HP, Reimann O, Kaiserling E. Immunoreactivity of normal and neoplastic tissue mast cells. Am J Clin Pathol 1988, **89:** 335–340.

580 Horny HP, Ruck M, Wehrmann M, Kaiserling E. Blood findings in generalized mastocytosis. Evidence of frequent simultaneous occurrence of myeloproliferative disorders. Br J Haematol 1990, **76:** 186–193.

581 Johnstone JM. The appearance and significance of tissue mast cells in human bone marrow. J Clin Pathol 1954, **7:** 275–280.

582 Lawrence JB, Friedman BS, Travis WD, Chinchilli VM, Metcalfe DD, Gralnick HR. Hematologic manifestations of systemic mast cell disease. A prospective study of laboratory and morphologic features and their relation to prognosis. Am J Med 1991, **91:** 612–624.

583 Lennert K, Parwaresch MR. Mast cells and mast cell neoplasia. A review. Histopathology 1979, **3:** 349–365.

584 Natkunam Y, Rouse RV. Utility of paraffin section immunohistochemistry for c-kit (CD117) in the differential diagnosis of systemic mast cell disease involving the bone marrow. Am J Surg Pathol 2000, **24:** 81–99.

585 Rappaport H. Tumors of the hematopoietic system. In Atlas of tumor pathology. Atlas of tumor pathology, series 3, fascicle 8. Washington D.C., 2001, Armed Forces Institute of Pathology, pp. 336–344.

586 Rywlin AM. Mastocytic eosinophilic fibrohistiocytic lesion of the bone marrow. Hematology 1982, **24:** 1–4.

587 Rywlin AM, Hoffman EP, Ortega RS. Eosinophilic fibrohistiocytic lesion of bone marrow. Distinctive new morphologic finding, probably related to drug hypersensitivity. Blood 1972, **40:** 464–472.

588 Sagher F, Even-Paz Z. Mastocytosis and the mast cell. Chicago, 1967, Year Book Medical Publishers.

589 Scully RE, Mark EJ, McNeely BU. Case records of the Massachusetts General Hospital. N Engl J Med 1986, **315:** 816–824.

590 Stevens EC, Rosenthal NS. Bone marrow mast cell morphologic features and hematopoietic dyspoiesis in systemic mast cell disease. Am J Clin Pathol 2001, **116:** 177–182.

591 Tefferi A, Li C-Y, Butterfield JH, Hoagland HC. Treatment of systemic mast cell disease with cladribine. N Engl J Med 2001, **344:** 307–308.

592 Te Velde J, Vismans FJFE, Leenheers-Binnendijk L, Vos CJ, Smeenk D, Bijvoet OLM. The eosinophilic fibrohistiocytic lesion of the bone marrow. A mastocellular lesion in bone disease. Virchows Arch [A] 1978, **337:** 277–284.

593 Tharp MD. The spectrum of mastocytosis. Am J Med Sci 1985, **289:** 117–132.

594 Travis W, Li C-Y, Bergstralh E, Yam LT, Swee RG. Systemic mast cell disease. Analysis of 58 cases and literature review. Medicine (Baltimore) 1988, **67:** 345–368.

595 Valent P, Horny HO, Escribano L, Longley BJ, Li CY, Schwartz LB, Marone G, Nunez R, Akin C, Sotlar K, Sperr WR, Wolff K, Brunning RD, Parwaresch MR, Austen KF, Lennert K, Metcalfe DD, Vardiman JW, Bennett JM. Diagnostic criteria and classification of mastocytosis: a consensus proposal. Leuk Res 2001, **25:** 603–625.

596 Valent P, Horny H-P, Li CY, Longly BJ, Metcalfe DD, Parwaresch R-M, Bennett JM. Mastocytosis. In Jaffe ES, Harris NL, Stein H, Vardiman JW (eds): World Health Organization Classification of Tumors. Pathology and genetics of tumours of haematopoietic and lymphoid tissues. Lyon, 2001, IARC Press, pp. 293–302.

597 Walls AF, Jones DB, Williams JH, Church MK, Holgate ST. Immunohistochemical identification of mast cells in formalin-fixed tissue using monoclonal antibodies specific for tryptase. J Clin Pathol 1990, **162:** 119–126.

598 Webb TA, Li C-Y, Yam LT. Systemic mast cell disease. A clinical and hematopathologic study of 26 cases. Cancer 1982, **49:** 927–938.

599 Wilkins BS, Buchan SL, Webster J, Jones DB. Tryptase-positive mast cells accompany lymphocytic as well as lymphoplasmacytic lymphoma infiltrates in bone marrow biopsies. Histopathology 2001, **39:** 150–155.

600 Yang F, Tran TA, Carlson JA, Hsi ES, Ross CW, Arber DA. Paraffin section immunophenotype of cutaneous and extracutaneous mast cell disease. Comparison to other hematopoietic neoplasms. Am J Surg Pathol 2000, **24:** 703–709.

Metastatic tumors

601 Anner RM, Drewinko B. Frequency and significance of bone marrow involvement by metastatic solid tumors. Cancer 1977, **39:** 1337–1344.

602 Ballestrero A, Coviello DA, Garuti A, Nencioni A, Fama A, Rocco I, Bertorelli R, Gonella R, Patrone F. Reverse transcriptase polymerase chain reaction of the Maspin gene in the detection of bone marrow breast carcinoma cell contamination. Cancer 1992, **92:** 2030–2035.

603 Bezwoda WR, Lewis D, Livini N. Bone marrow involvement in anaplastic small cell lung cancer. Cancer 1986, **58:** 1762–1765.

604 Bostrom BB, Nesbitt ME, Brunning RD. The value of bone marrow biopsy in the diagnosis of metastatic neuroblastoma. Am J Pediatr Hematol Oncol 1985, **7:** 301–305.

605 Bramwell VHC, Littley MB, Chang J, Crowther D. Bone marrow involvement in adult soft tissue sarcoma. Eur J Cancer Clin Oncol 1982, **18:** 1099–1106.

606 Brodeur GM, Pritchard J, Berthold F, Carlsen NLT, Castel V, Castleberry RP, De Bernardi B, Evans AE, Favrot M, Hedborg F. Revisions of the international criteria for neuroblastoma diagnosis, staging, and response to treatment. J Clin Oncol 1993, **11:** 1466–1477.

607 Ceci G, Franciosi V, Passalacqua R, Di Blasio B, Boni C, Lottici R, De Lisi V, Nizzoli R, Guazzi A, Cocconi G. The value of bone marrow biopsy in breast cancer at the time of first relapse. A prospective study. Cancer 1988, **61:** 1041–1045.

608 Cheung NK, Heller G, Kushner BH, Liu C, Cheung IY. Detection of metastatic neuroblastoma in bone marrow: when is routine histology insensitive? J Clin Oncol 1997, **15:** 2807–2817.

609 Clamon GH, Edwards WR, Hamous JE, Scupham RK. Patterns of bone marrow involvement with small cell lung cancer. Cancer 1984, **54:** 100–102.

610 Cote RJ, Rosen PP, Hakes TB, Sedira M, Bazinet M, Kinne DW, Old LJ, Osborne MP. Monoclonal antibodies detect occult breast carcinoma metastases in the bone marrow of patients with early stage disease. Am J Surg Pathol 1988, **12:** 333–340.

611 Cote RJ, Rosen PP, Lesser ML, Old LJ, Osborne MP. Prediction of early relapse in patients with operable breast cancer by detection of occult bone marrow micrometastases. J Clin Oncol 1991, **9:** 1749–1756.

612 Diel IJ, Kaufmann M, Goerner R, Costa SD, Kaul S, Bastert G. Detection of tumor cells in bone marrow of patients with primary breast cancer. A prognostic factor for distant metastasis. J Clin Oncol 1992, **10:** 1534–1539.

613 Finklestein JZ, Ekert H, Isaacs H, Higgins G. Bone marrow metastases in children with solid tumors. Am J Dis Child 1976, **119:** 49–52.

614 Hansen HH, Muggia FM, Selawry OS. Bone-marrow examination in 100 consecutive patients with bronchogenic carcinoma. Lancet 1971, **2:** 443–445.

615 Hirsch F, Hansen HH, Dombernowsky P, Hainau B. Bone-marrow examination in the staging of small-cell anaplastic carcinoma of the lung with special reference to subtyping. Cancer 1977, **39:** 2563–2567.

616 Ingle JN, Tormey DC, Tan HK. The bone marrow examination in breast cancer. Diagnostic considerations and clinical usefulness. Cancer 1978, **41:** 670–674.

617 Kelly BW, Morris JF, Harwood BP, Bruya TE. Methods and prognostic value of bone marrow examination in small cell carcinoma of the lung. Cancer 1984, **53:** 99–102.

618 Kristjansen PEG, Osterlind K, Hansen M. Detection of bone marrow relapse in patients with small cell carcinoma of the lung. Cancer 1986, **58:** 2538–2541.

619 Landys K. Prognostic value of bone marrow biopsy in breast cancer. Cancer 1982, **49:** 513–518.

620 Lawrence JB, Eleff M, Behm FG, Johnston CL Jr. Bone marrow examination in small cell carcinoma of the lung. Comparison of trephine biopsy with aspiration. Cancer 1984, **53:** 2188–2190.

621 Levitan N, Byrne RE, Bromer RH, Faling LJ, Caslowitz P, Pattern DH, Hong WK. The value of the bone scan and bone marrow biopsy in staging small cell lung cancer. Cancer 1985, **56:** 652–654.

622 Lyda MH, Tetef M, Carter N, Ikle D, Weiss L, Arber DA. Keratin immunohistochemistry detects clinically significant metastases in bone marrow biopsy specimens in women with lobular breast carcinoma. Am J Surg Pathol 2000, **24:** 1593–1599.

623 Mead GM, Williams CJ, Thompson J, Smith AG, Whitehouse JMA. Bone marrow examination in small cell carcinoma of the bronchus. An unnecessary procedure? Hematol Oncol 1985, **3:** 159–163.

624 Meinhausen J, Choritz H, Georgii A. Frequency of skeletal metastases as revealed by routinely taken bone marrow biopsies. Virchows Arch [A] 1980, **389:** 409–417.

625 Pantel K, Izbicki JR, Angtswurm M, Braun S, Passlick B, Karg O, Thetter O, Riethmuller G. Immunocytological detection of bone

marrow micrometastasis in operable non-small cell lung cancer. Cancer Res 1993, **53:** 1027–1031.

626 Penchansky L. Bone marrow biopsy in the metastatic work-up of solid tumors in children. Cancer 1984, **54:** 1447–1448.

627 Lo Piccolo MSL, Cheung NK, Cheung IY. GD2 synthase: a new molecular marker for detecting neuroblastoma. Cancer 2001, **92:** 924–931.

628 Reid MM, Hamilton PJ. Histology of neuroblastoma involving bone marrow. The problem of detecting residual tumour after initiation of chemotherapy. Br J Haematol 1988, **69:** 487–490.

629 Ridell B, Landys K. Incidence and histopathology of metastases of mammary carcinoma in biopsies from the posterior iliac crest. Cancer 1979, **44:** 1782–1788.

630 Ruymann FB, Newton WA, Ragab AH, Donaldson MH, Foulkes M. Bone marrow metastases at diagnosis in children and adolescents with rhabdomyosarcoma. A report from the Intergroup Rhabdomyosarcoma Study. Cancer 1984, **53:** 368–373.

631 Seeger RC, Reynolds CP, Gallego R, Strum DO, Gerbing RB, Matthay KK. Quantitative tumor cell content of bone marrow and blood as a prediction of outcome in stage IV neuroblastoma: a children's cancer group study. J Clin Oncol 2000, **18:** 4067–4076.

632 Singh G, Krause JR, Breitfeld V. Bone marrow examination for metastatic tumor, aspiration and biopsy. Cancer 1977, **40:** 2317–2321.

Lipid storage diseases
Gaucher's disease

633 Barranger JA, Ginns BI. Glucosylceramide lipidoses: Gaucher disease. In Scriver CR, Beaudet AL, Sly WS, Valle E (eds): The metabolic basis of inherited disease, ed. 6. New York, 1989, McGraw-Hill Book Co., pp. 1655–1676.

634 Brady RO, Barranger JA. Glucosyl ceramide lipidosis. Gaucher's disease. In Stanbury JB, Wyngaarden JB, Fredrickson DS, Goldstein JL, Brown MS (eds): The metabolic basis of inherited disease. New York, 1983, McGraw-Hill Book Co., pp. 842–856.

635 Brunning RD. Morphologic alterations in nucleated blood and marrow cells in genetic disorders. Hum Pathol 1970, **1:** 99–124.

636 Butler F, Grabowski GA. Gaucher disease. In Scriver CR, Beaudet AL, Sly WS, Valle D (eds): The metabolic and molecular basis of inherited disease, ed. 8. Vol. II. New York, 2001, Mulencer Hill, pp. 3635–3668.

637 Dosik H, Rosner F, Sawitsky A. Acquired lipidosis. Gaucher-like cells and "blue cells" in chronic granulocytic leukemia. Semin Hematol 1972, **9:** 309–316.

638 Gerdes J, Marathe RL, Bloodworth JMB, MacKinney AA. Gaucher cells in chronic granulocytic leukemia. Arch Pathol 1969, **88:** 194–198.

639 Hansen HG, Graucob E. Hematologic cytology of storage disease. New York, 1985, Springer-Verlarg.

640 Imcerti C. Gaucher disease: an overview. Semin Hematol 1995, **32**(suppl): 3–9.

641 Kattlove HE, Williams JC, Gaynor E, Spivack M, Bradley RM, Brady R. Gaucher cells in chronic myelocytic leukemia. An acquired abnormality. Blood 1969, **33:** 379–390.

642 Pratt PW, Estren S, Kochwa S. Immunoglobulin abnormalities in Gaucher's disease. Report of 16 cases. Blood 1968, **31:** 633–640.

643 Rudzki Z, Okon K, Machaczka M, Rucinska M, Papla B, Skotnicki AB. Bone marrow histology in Gaucher disease treated with imuglucerase. J Clin Pathol 2002, **55**(suppl): A8.

644 Ruestow PC, Levinson DJ, Catchatourian R, Sreekanth S, Cohen H, Rosenfeld S. Coexistence of IgA myeloma and Gaucher's disease. Arch Intern Med 1980, **140:** 1115–1116.

645 Van Dorpe A, Broeckaert-Van Orshoven A, Desmet V, Verwilghen RL. Gaucher-like cells and congenital dyserythropoietic anaemia, type II (HEMPAS). Br J Haematol 1973, **25:** 165–170.

646 Zaino EC, Rossi MB, Pham TD, Azar H. Gaucher's cells in thalassemia. Blood 1971, **38:** 457–462.

Niemann–Pick disease

647 Brady RO. Sphingomyelin lipidoses: Niemann-Pick disease. In Stanbury JB, Wyngaarden JB, Fredrickson DS, Goldstein JL, Brown MS (eds): The metabolic basis of inherited disease. New York, 1983, McGraw-Hill Book Co., pp. 831–841.

648 Brunning RD. Morphologic alterations in nucleated blood and marrow cells in genetic disorders. Hum Pathol 1970, **1:** 99–124.

649 Hansen HG, Graucob E. Hematologic cytology of storage disease. New York, 1985, Springer-Verlag.

650 Patterson MC, Vanier MT, Suzuki K, Morris JA, Carsteu E, Neufeld EB, Blanchette-Mackie JE, Pentcheu DG. Niemann-Pick disease type C. A lipid trafficking disorder. In Scriver CR, Beaudet AL, Sly WS, Valle D (eds): The metabolic and molecular basis of inherited disease, ed. 8. Vol. II. New York, 2001, Mulencer Hill, pp. 3611–3634.

651 Schuchman EH, Desnick RJ. Niemann-Pick disease types A and B. Acid sphingomyelinase deficiencies. In Scriver CR, Beaudet AL, Sly WS, Valle D (eds): The metabolic and molecular basis of inherited disease, ed. 8. Vol. II. New York, 2001, Mulencer Hill, pp. 3589–3610.

652 Spence MW, Calahan JW. Sphingomyelin-cholesterol lipidoses. The Niemann-Pick group of diseases. In Scriver CR, Beaudet AL, Sly WS, Valle D (eds): The metabolic basis of inherited disease, ed. 6. New York, 1989, McGraw-Hill Book Co., pp. 1655–1676.

Fabry's disease

653 Brunning RD. Morphologic alterations in nucleated blood and marrow cells in genetic disorders. Hum Pathol 1970, **1:** 99–124.

654 Desnick RJ, Sweeley CC. Fabry's disease. α-Galactosidase deficiency. In Stanbury JB, Wyngaarden JB, Frederickson DS, Goldstein JL, Brown MS (eds): The metabolic basis of inherited disease. New York, 1983, McGraw-Hill Book Co., pp. 906–944.

Sea-blue histiocyte syndrome

655 Hansen HG, Graucob E. Hematologic cytology of storage disease. New York, 1985, Springer-Verlag.

656 Rausing A. Bone marrow biopsy in diagnosis of Whipple's disease. Acta Med Scand 1973, **193:** 5–8.

657 Silverstein MN, Ellefson RD, Ahern EF. The syndrome of the syndrome of the sea-blue histiocyte. N Engl J Med 1970, **282:** 1–4.

658 Silverstein MN, Ellefson RD. The syndrome of the sea-blue histiocyte. Semin Hematol 1972, **9:** 293–307.

Bone marrow transplantation

659 Forman SJ, Blume KG, Thomas ED (eds): Bone marrow transplantation. Boston, 1994, Blackwell Scientific Publications.

660 Hurwitz N. Bone marrow changes following chemotherapy and/or bone marrow transplantation. Curr Diagn Pathol 1997, **4:** 196–200.

661 Naeim F, Smith GS, Gale RP. Morphologic aspects of bone marrow transplantation in patients with aplastic anemia. Hum Pathol 1978, **9:** 295–308.

662 Sale GB, Buckner CD. Pathology of bone marrow in transplant recipients. Hematol Oncol Clin North Am 1988, **2:** 735–756.

663 Sloane JP, Norton J. The pathology of bone marrow transplantation. Histopathology 1993, **22:** 201–209.

664 Van Den Berg H, Kluin PhM, Zwaan FE, Vossen JM. Histopathology of bone marrow reconstitution after allogenic bone marrow transplantation. Histopathology 1989, **15:** 363–373.

24 Bone and joints

Bone

Normal anatomy

Adult bones are classified according to their shape into long (such as femur), flat (such as pelvis), and short (such as bones of hand and feet). Long bones (and some short bones such as metacarpal bones) are divided topographically into three regions: diaphysis, epiphysis, and metaphysis. The diaphysis is the shaft. The epiphysis is at both ends of the bone and is partially covered by articular cartilage. The metaphysis is at the junction of the diaphysis and epiphysis. In the growing bone, it begins at the epiphyseal plate (epiphyseal disk, physis). This is the place where endochondral ossification takes place, a process by which longitudinal, regularly spaced columns of vascularized cartilage are replaced by bone.[9,17] When the bone has reached its adult length, this process ends, and the epiphysis "closes" by becoming totally ossified. The time of closure of the epiphysis differs in various bones and in the sexes. The epiphyseal plate is very important in bone pathology because it is by far the most common site of occurrence of most primary bone tumors. In addition, whether the epiphysis is closed or open influences the extension of pathologic processes, in the sense that cartilage is often at least a partial barrier to spreading osteosarcoma. If the epiphysis is closed and cartilage is no longer present, this area is more easily invaded.[6]

Bones are also classified according to their embryologic development. The two main categories are *membranous* (such as the skull), if formed de novo from primitive connective tissue, and *endochondral* (such as long bones), if their formation is preceded by a cartilaginous anlage.[3]

On cross section, mature bones are seen formed by an outer *compact layer* (cortex, cortical bone, compact bone) and a central *spongy region* (spongiosa, medulla, cancellous bone). Compact bone contains vascular channels, which are divided into two types on the basis of their orientation and their relation to the lamellar structure of the surrounding bone: longitudinal (haversian canals) and transverse/oblique (Volkmann's canals). Except for the region of the articular cartilage, the cortex is surrounded by the *periosteum*, which consists of an outer fibrous layer and an inner cellular (cambium) layer of osteoprogenitor cells (fibroblasts and osteoblasts). It contains nerve filaments that carry proprioceptive and sensory impulses; small nerve filaments also may pass with the nutrient vessels into the medullary canal. Coarse bundles of collagenous fibers penetrating the outer compact layer from the outer layer of the periosteum are called Sharpey's fibers or perforating fibers.[17]

The periosteum may become detached and elevated from the bone in pathologic processes such as trauma, infection, and primary or secondary malignant tumors. Whenever this happens, new bone formation between the elevated periosteum and the bone will occur. This appears by radiographic examination as fine spicules placed perpendicular to the long axis of the bone. This finding is often considered a manifestation of a primary malignant neoplasm, particularly osteosarcoma and Ewing's sarcoma. However, periosteal bone proliferation also can occur in syphilis, tuberculosis, metastatic carcinoma, and subperiosteal hematoma. In some lesions, such as plasma cell myeloma, the periosteum may be destroyed or encroached upon so that no radiographic changes occur.

An understanding of the blood supply of bone helps to explain the spread and limitation of infection, the healing of fractures, and the involvement of bone by primary or secondary neoplasms. The metaphysis is mainly supplied by end arteries that enter from the diaphysis and terminate at the level of the epiphyseal plate. The epiphyses receive their blood supply from a network of widely anastomosing vessels. The diaphyseal cortex is supplied by vessels that enter through Volkmann's canals and communicate with the haversian system. A nutrient artery enters the medullary canal at about the center of the diaphysis, divides, and extends both distally and proximally. The metabolic exchange of calcium and phosphorus occurs primarily in the metaphysis.

Osteoblasts are bone-producing cells derived from marrow-residing mesenchymal cells. They have a plump appearance and often exhibit a perinuclear halo resulting from a prominent Golgi zone that gives them a resemblance to plasma cells. They have a high cytoplasmic content of alkaline phosphatase. Ultrastructurally, they resemble fibroblasts by virtue of a well-developed rough endoplasmic reticulum and Golgi apparatus. Indeed, osteoblasts are regarded as a specialized ("sophisticated") form of fibroblast.[5] Once these are incorporated into the bone matrix and housed in lacunae, they are referred to as osteocytes.

Osteoclasts are multinucleated giant cells involved in bone resorption.[19] As such, they often are found in shallow concavities in the surface of bone called Howship's lacunae. Osteoclasts arise from mononuclear monocyte–macrophage precursors.[20] Osteoclasts contain abundant tartrate-resistant acid phosphatase, respond to osteotropic hormones, and contract under the influence of calcitonin. They express osteoclast-specific antigens (detected by monoclonal antibodies 13c2 and 23c6) and various matrix metalloproteinases[15]; they are instead unreactive for T-cell antigens, most myeloid antigens, and mature macrophage antigens.[12]

Ultrastructurally, the cytoplasm of osteoclasts has a very large number of mitochondria and scanty lysosomes; a ruffled edge is present in the area of the cell membrane that is in the process of bone resorption.

Osteoid is the unmineralized organic precursor matrix of bone. It is composed of a mixture of collagen (mainly type I), acid mucopolysaccharides, and noncollagen proteins.[10] These include osteopontin,[14,18] osteocalcin,[16] and bone morphogenetic protein.[21] The latter is thought to play a critical role in initiating the process that begins with cartilage resorption and ends with bone formation.[22] Osteoid is not a homogeneous mass but rather shows a constant, patterned sequence of maturation and organization.[7] It has acidophilic properties in hematoxylin–eosin-stained sections, and it may be difficult to distinguish from hyalinized collagen.

Bone is formed through mineralization of the organic matrix of the osteoid.[8] Extracellular matrix vesicles are present at or near the mineralization front and constitute the initial site of hydroxyapatite mineral deposition.[2] In *woven bone* (fiber bone), there is a haphazard arrangement of collagen fibers within the matrix, which is best appreciated with reticulum stains or under polarized light. Formation of woven bone is the key criterion for the diagnosis of fibrous dysplasia, but it also appears in any condition associated with accelerated bone turnover, such as the callus of a healing fracture and osteitis fibrosa cystica. The difference resides in the fact that in the latter group the woven bone eventually becomes lamellar bone, whereas in fibrous dysplasia it does not. *Lamellar bone* is characterized by concentric parallel lamellae, as seen with examination under polarizing lenses.

Normal skeletal growth results from a balance between the processes of bone matrix synthesis and resorption, these activities being regulated by systemic and local factors.[1,3,13] Of these, transforming growth factor beta activity is particularly important for bone matrix production.[4] Vitamin D and parathyroid hormone also play an important role.[11] Molecules thought to regulate the growth plate thickness and bone length through their action on chondrocytes during endochondral ossification are fibroblast growth factor receptor-3, parathyroid hormone-related protein, and tartrate-resistant acid phosphatase.[3] Some proteins seem to act as negative regulators of bone cell function, e.g. osteoprotegerin in osteoclasts, and osteocalcin, bone sialoprotein, and 5-lipoxygenase in osteoblasts.[3]

Bone necrosis can be recognized by the staining quality of the dead bone, which is a deeper blue than normal bone. Lacunar cells are absent, and the margins of the bone are ragged (Fig. 24.1). The presence of osteoclasts on these margins indicates that the necrotic bone is already being reabsorbed.

Bone production can be recognized by the presence of well-stained small spicules of bone with cells in their lacunae and a prominent row of osteoblasts along their margins. New bone formation can be found in a variety of physiologic and pathologic processes, such as a healing fracture, Paget's disease, metaplastic ossification, myositis ossificans, and osteitis fibrosa cystica.

Bone resorption (destruction) can be recognized by the presence of numerous osteoclasts in the bone margins and in Howship's lacunae. It can involve necrotic bone, as indicated above, or viable bone, as in osteitis fibrosa cystica.

Metabolic bone diseases

A thorough discussion of metabolic bone diseases is outside the scope of this chapter. Some metabolic bone diseases will be mentioned briefly, but for a detailed discussion the reader is referred to the books, monographs, and excellent articles that have been written on the subject.[23,24,27,29,32,39–41,43,44]

Osteoporosis refers to a decreased mass of normally mineralized bone.[34a,46] It develops when an individual is unable to repair and maintain the mass of bone tissue that has been acquired throughout growth and maturation.[36] Quantitative microradiographic studies have shown that the main difference between the bone in most forms of osteoporosis and normal bone is an increase in the amount of resorption, bone formation levels being generally normal.[33] Osteoporosis occurs frequently after menopause, presumably because of estrogen deficiency.[30] The causes of osteoporosis are multiple.[35] Fluoride consumption has been shown to be important in its prevention.[26,37]

A good biopsy specimen from the iliac crest will show changes that correspond well with those in the spine.[25] Routine radiographic examination of the spine is not reliable, since the changes have to be advanced before they can be seen. Studies made at autopsy by Caldwell[28] have helped to clarify some issues. For instance, he showed that vertebral biconcavity is not a reliable index of osteoporosis, as commonly believed.

The treatment of osteoporosis is based on medications that slow down bone resorption by inhibiting the formation or activity of osteoclasts, and on those that promote bone formation, such as growth factors and hormones.[38]

Osteomalacia (comparable to rickets in a young person in whom the epiphyses are not yet closed) refers to the accumulation of unmineralized bone matrix resulting from a diminished rate of mineralization. It may be secondary to a wide spectrum of congenital and acquired metabolic abnormalities that result in sufficient decrease in serum calcium, phosphorus, or both to impair mineralization of the skeleton and epiphyseal growth.[34] Some cases have been seen as a complication of bone and soft tissue neoplasms (see Chapter 25). Osteomalacia changes can be demonstrated in adequate biopsies from long bones and iliac crests with preparation of nondecalcified specimens and examination with bright-field and phase-

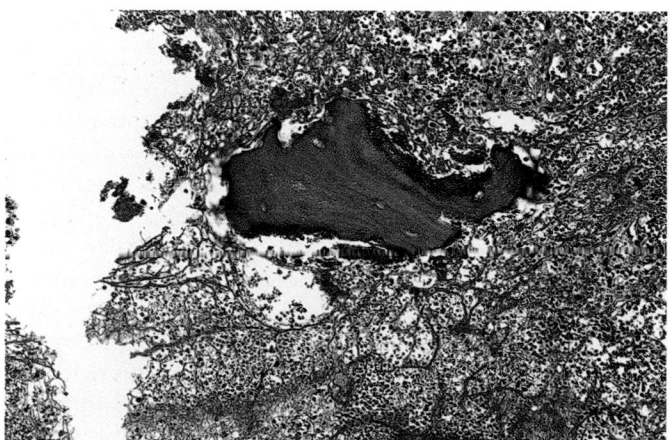

Fig. 24.1 The necrotic nature of this bone fragment is recognized because of the ragged basophilic edges and the empty lacunae.

contrast microscopes and with the use of fluorescent tetracycline markers.[31]

Sophisticated methods of investigating these metabolic bone processes have been devised, but many of them are difficult to implement in the routine pathology laboratory.[42,45]

Fractures

Fractures are breaks in the continuity of bone, usually with severance of periosteum, blood vessels, and sometimes muscles. The speed of return of bone to a normal state following fracture depends on factors such as the age and nutrition of the patient, severity of the fracture, vascularity of the area, and type of treatment. Fractures may fail to heal because of improper immobilization, complete devascularization of the fractured bone segments, persistent infection, and interposition of soft tissue between the ends of the bone.

Following a fracture, a hematoma forms between the two severed ends of bone. Organization of this hematoma begins with the ingrowth of young capillaries. After about 3 days, the devitalized bone fragments begin to be reabsorbed. Intramembranous bone growth makes its appearance from the inner layer of the periosteum, both proximal and distal to the fracture site. The newly formed trabeculae begin to calcify as the cartilage is replaced by bone. This process on each side of the fracture meets at the fracture site to form the primary callus. This is later reabsorbed and replaced by the secondary callus, which is made up of mature lamellar bone. The new bone is laid down predominantly along lines of stress. The formation and persistence of cartilage largely depend on mechanical factors.[49]

With early proper reduction of the fracture, adequate blood supply, no infection, and normal metabolism, the fracture heals rapidly with little visible callus. Exuberant callus usually means slow fracture healing. In children, even with prominent angulation or deformity, the bone remodels itself to an astonishing degree. For this reason, open reduction and internal fixation of fractures in children are seldom justified. Shortening of a long bone resulting from overriding of fragments will nearly always correct itself in children by overgrowth of bone.

The formation of exuberant cartilage and disorderly membranous bone in rapidly forming primary callus results in a bewildering microscopic pattern that may be confused with osteosarcoma. This phenomenon is particularly luxuriant in osteogenesis imperfecta.[50]

When a noncorrosive nail is driven into a bone to immobilize a fracture, it eventually becomes completely isolated from the bone substance.[47] The nail is separated from the medullary cavity by fibrous tissue that is continuous with the periosteum. Compact-type bone forms adjacent to the fibrous tissue. At a later stage, this becomes continuous with the original bone cortex. No foreign body giant cell reaction is observed.[48]

Osteomyelitis

Bacterial osteomyelitis may be caused by a large variety of microorganisms. About 70% to 90% of the cases are due to coagulase-positive staphylococci[65] (Fig. 24.2A). Other organisms involved are *Klebsiella*, *Aerobacter*, *Proteus*, *Pseudomonas*, streptococcus, pneumococcus, gonococcus, meningococcus, *Brucella*, and *Salmonella*.[61,67] The latter organism is often involved in the osteomyelitis that affects individuals with abnormal hemoglobin, particularly sickle cell disease.[54]

Osteomyelitis may be due to local or exogenous causes (such as compound fractures)[52] or may develop through the hematogenous route. The latter occurs most often in patients under 20 years of age and involves the bones of the lower extremity in about 75% of cases. It can be acute, subacute, or chronic, these designations referring to the duration of the disease rather than the microscopic composition of the inflammatory infiltrate. A form of osteomyelitis characterized by recurrent multifocal involvement in children, sometimes associated with palmoplantar pustulosis, has been described; bacterial cultures are negative and the etiology is unknown.[59]

Subacute and chronic osteomyelitis can closely simulate clinically and radiographically a malignant bone tumor (particularly Ewing's sarcoma, malignant lymphoma, and osteosarcoma) by virtue of the combination of destructive and regenerative bone changes[53] (Fig. 24.2B). Hematogenous pyogenic vertebral osteomyelitis is frequently under-diagnosed radiographically because of the subtle nature of the disease.[58] A variant of osteomyelitis characterized by very extensive regenerative bone changes is referred to as Garre's osteomyelitis, sclerosing osteomyelitis, or periostitis ossificans. This form is particularly common in the jaw-bone.[57]

The morphologic changes in osteomyelitis are conditioned by the age of the patient, bone involved (particularly in regard to its blood supply), virulence of the organism, and resistance of the host.[64] In the infant under 1 year of age, permanent epiphyseal damage and joint infection occur, but there is little damage to the metaphysis or diaphysis. In children over 1 year of age the reverse is true, in the sense that cortical metaphyseal involvement is extensive, whereas permanent damage to cartilage and joints is rare. From its center in the metaphysis, the infection permeates the cortex through the vessels of Volkmann's canals and may spread along the medullary canal to the rest of the bone. If pus accumulates beneath the periosteum, perforation through it usually takes place. The dead bone (sequestrum) is later surrounded by new bone laid down by the cambium layer of the periosteum (involucrum), and this may

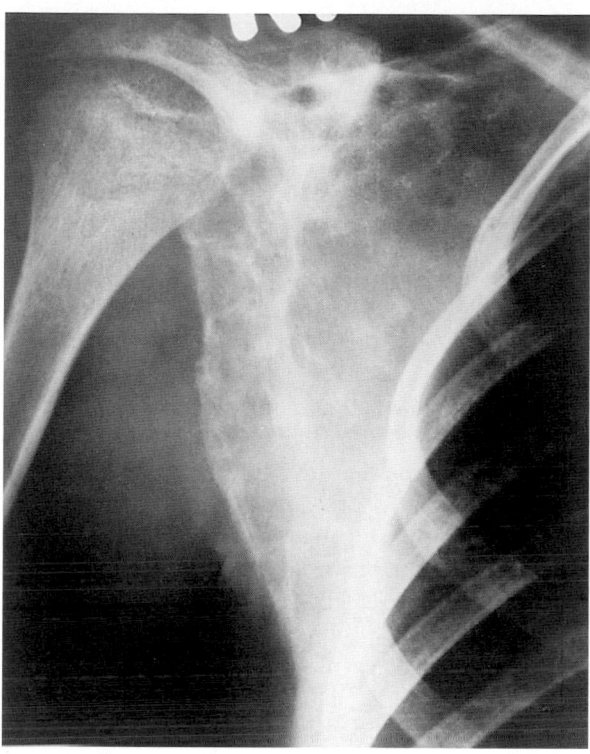
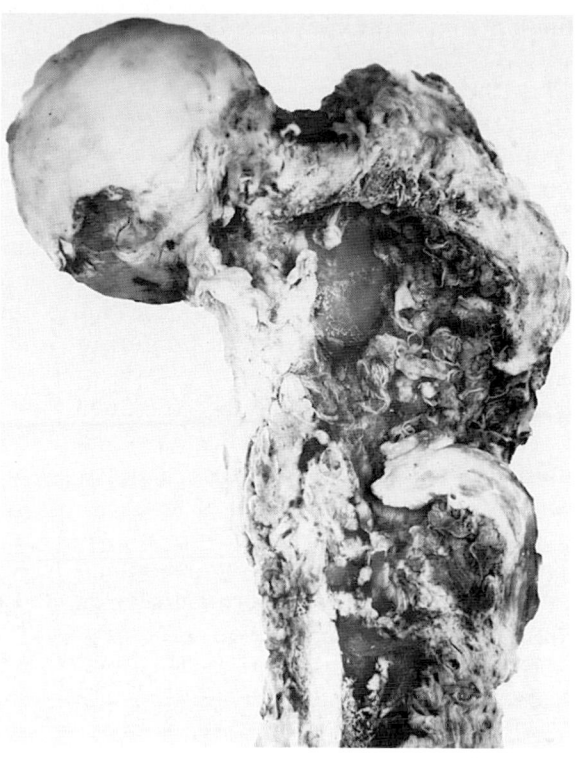

A B

Fig. 24.2 A, Extensive involvement of scapula by osteomyelitis of staphylococcal origin in an 8-year-old child. This was apparently the only bone involved. **B,** Osteomyelitis of upper femur with massive bone destruction and reactive sclerosis. (**A,** Courtesy of Dr. P Flynn, Redding, CA)

eventually extend around the entire bone (Figs 24.3 and 24.4).

Chronic osteomyelitis persists as long as infected dead bone remains. The dead bone is surrounded by granulation tissue that attacks the sequestrum, making it pitted on the surface next to the marrow cavity. The cortical surface remains smooth. Surgical removal of the sequestrum at the proper time usually allows the osteomyelitis to heal. However, the osteomyelitis may recur many years later if bacteria remain within the scar.

In the adult, there is again a high incidence of joint

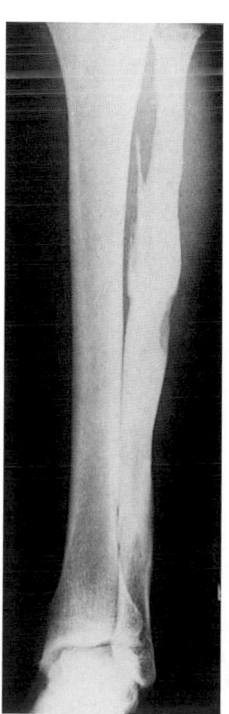

Fig. 24.3 Chronic osteomyelitis of fibula. Note dense, irregular bone.

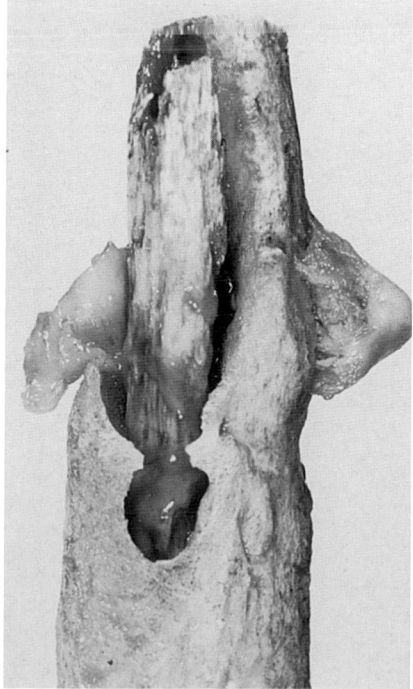

Fig. 24.4 Resected fibula showing dense outer involucrum surrounding loosened sequestrum with its pitted surface.

infection, but this time in association with involvement of extensive portions of bone.

Microscopically, the changes of osteomyelitis are represented by an admixture of inflammatory cells (including neutrophils, lymphocytes, and plasma cells), fibrosis, bone necrosis, and new bone formation. When the plasma cell population is particularly prominent, the disease has been designated as *plasma cell osteomyelitis*,[68] and when foamy macrophages are abundant, it has been called *xanthogranulomatous osteomyelitis*.[55] Chronic osteomyelitis may be accompanied by prominent periosteal bone proliferation (Fig. 24.5).

Osteomyelitic sinuses in the adult may become lined by epithelium that extends deeply in the bone and becomes discontinuous with the cutaneous surface. Despite apparent healing of the overlying skin, large epidermal inclusion cysts can slowly develop in the underlying bone. These are filled with keratin-containing debris similar to those present in epidermal inclusion cysts of the skin. Rarely, after a long period, squamous cell carcinoma develops within these sinuses. This complication is heralded by the appearance of pain and increasingly malodorous discharge.[56,60]

Tuberculous osteomyelitis as a hematogenous infection is usually seen in young adults or children. The bones most often infected are the vertebrae, pelvis, knee, ankle, elbow, and wrist. The areas usually involved are the metaphysis, epiphysis, and synovium.[51]

There has been considerable controversy as to which of these areas is the one first involved. Metaphyseal infection is more common in children, and epiphyseal infection is more common in adults, but with progression of the disease, all zones become affected. Tuberculous granulation tissue forming in the synovia destroys the synovial attachments. The cartilage, no longer nourished from the synovia, undergoes progressive destruction, allowing the inflammation to extend into the epiphysis and finally into the metaphyseal area. If the process begins in the epiphysis, the tuberculous granulation tissue quickly extends into the adjacent joint. When the process begins in the metaphyseal area, extension into the joint may be heralded by the development of fluid in it.

Cutaneous sinuses may occur in advanced tuberculosis. These sinuses allow entry of secondary bacterial infection that modifies the pathologic changes. When the tuberculous process begins to heal, fusion of the joint may be associated with complete or partial denudation of cartilage and "kissing sequestra." Sequestra are cortical in pyogenic processes, but in tuberculous osteomyelitis they are cancellous.

Fungal infections of bone include blastomycosis, actinomycosis, histoplasmosis, and coccidioidomycosis.[62,63]

Tertiary syphilis may involve the bone and cause both osseous destruction and production, often in association with conspicuous periosteal bone proliferation (Fig. 24.6). The necrotic, well-defined defects are mainly cortical and periosteal and are surrounded by sclerotic bone. They may occur in the vertebrae, flat bones of the hands and feet, and diaphysis of long tubular bones. The radiographic diagnosis is usually apparent if multiple x-ray studies of the bones are taken, but it may be difficult in single or isolated lesions, some of which closely resemble

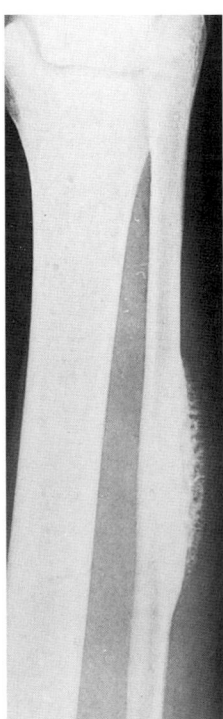

Fig. 24.5 Prominent periosteal bone proliferation in chronic osteomyelitis.

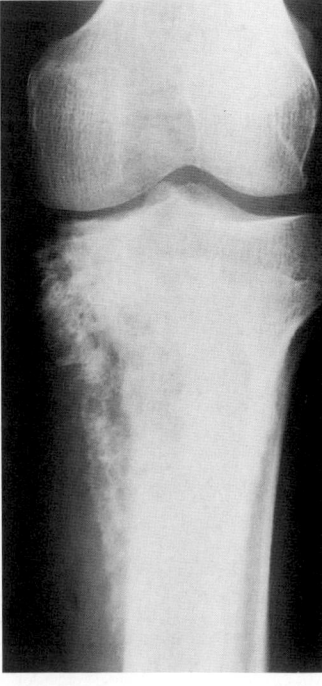

Fig. 24.6 Gummatous involvement of tibia in a 45-year-old woman. (Courtesy of Dr. RJ Reed, New Orleans)

the appearance of osteosarcoma. Biopsy will show a granulomatous process associated with bone destruction and production.

Malakoplakia of bone has been described. As in the bladder and other sites, it probably represents an unusual host reaction to bacterial infection.[66]

Bone necrosis

Infarct

Bone infarct can be the result of a large number of etiologic factors. Radiographically, the changes depend on the age of the lesion and the degree of repair. During the first 1 or 2 weeks, no abnormalities are detected on a plain x-ray. Resorption of the dead bone results in areas of decreased density, whereas new bone formation growing in apposition to dead trabeculae ("creeping apposition") leads to an increase in bone density. The process of reossification is often irregular, and the combination of incomplete resorption of dead bone and focal deposition of new bone results in a mottled and irregular radiographic appearance (Fig. 24.7).

An increased incidence of primary malignant bone tumors has been seen in association with large infarcts of long bones. Most of the reported cases have occurred in the medulla of the femur or tibia of male adults and have been diagnosed as malignant fibrous histiocytoma, osteosarcoma, fibrosarcoma, or angiosarcoma.[69–73]

Aseptic (avascular) bone necrosis

Aseptic bone necrosis (avascular necrosis, osteonecrosis) is a common abnormality that has been reported in practically every secondary epiphysis and in many primary epiphyses[76] (Fig. 24.8). Many of these sites have been described separately and given eponymic designations such as Osgood–Schlatter disease (for necrosis of the tibial tuberosity) and Legg–Calvé–Perthes disease (for necrosis of the upper femoral epiphysis).

The pathogenetic mechanism is thought to be interruption of the blood supply induced in most cases by a mechanical disruption, such as fracture or dislocation,[74,78] but sometimes by thrombosis induced by sickle cell disease.[75] The responsible injury seems to be a single event, inasmuch as extension of the osteonecrosis once developed is an extremely rare event.[77]

The initial necrosis of epiphyseal bone is followed by hyperemia of the surrounding tissues. The epiphyseal cartilage may or may not remain viable. The dead bone gradually undergoes resorption by a mechanism of "creeping substitution." This is a slow process that may take months or even years and that results in a dense

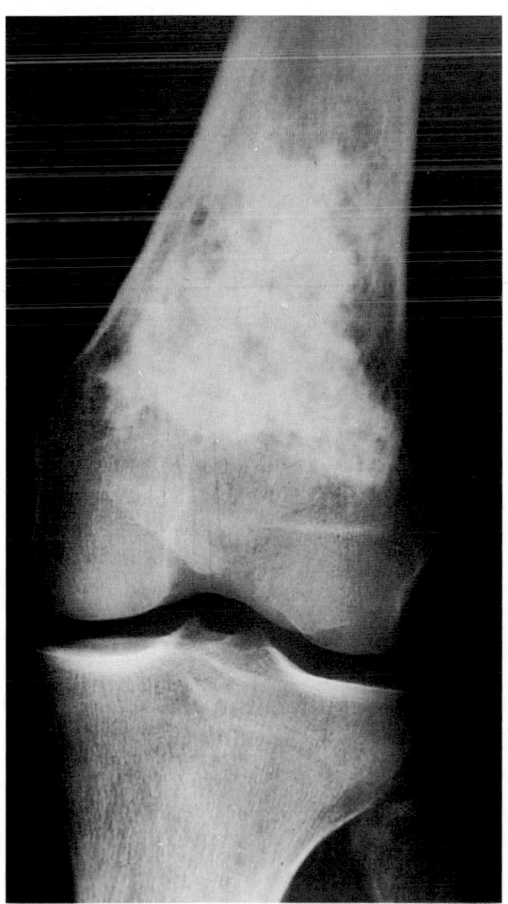

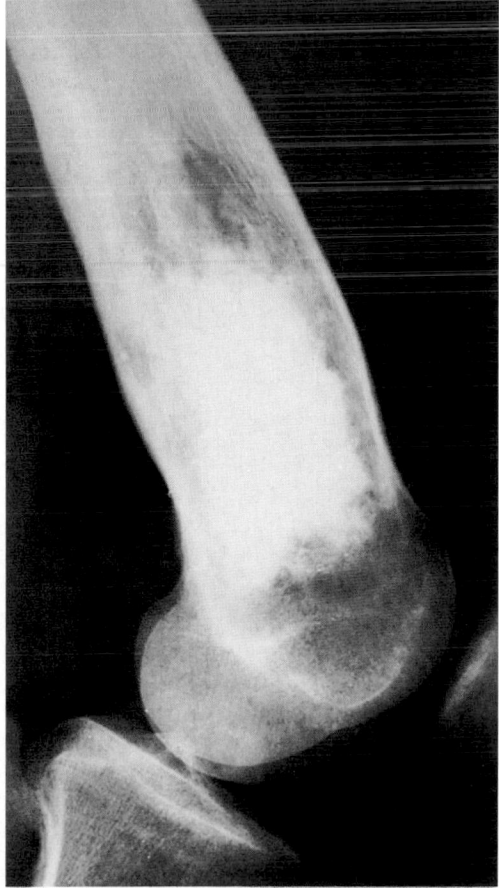

A B

Fig. 24.7 Large diaphysometaphyseal bone infarct of femur. The irregular area of increased radiodensity is indicative of new bone production superimposed on necrosis. (Courtesy of Dr. H Danziger, Welland, Ontario, Canada)

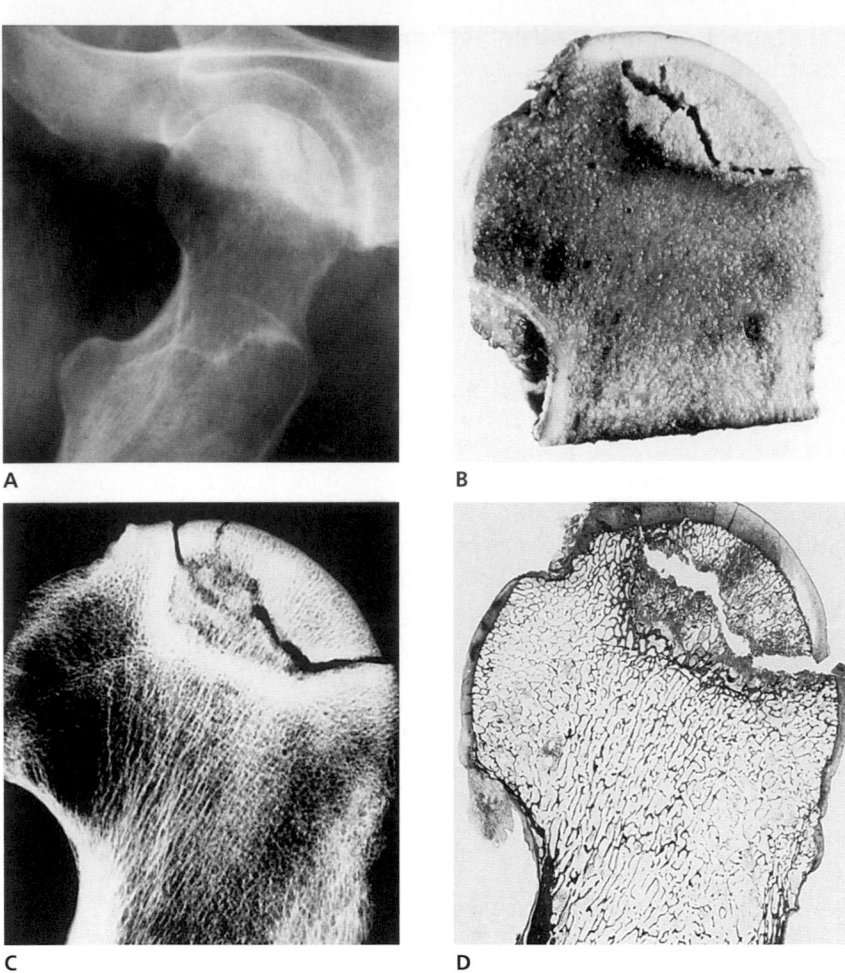

A

B

C

D

Fig. 24.8 A to D, Aseptic necrosis of femoral head with superimposed fracture. **A**, Radiograph. **B**, Cross section of excised specimen. **C**, Radiograph of a slice of the same specimen, emphasizing peripheral eburnation. **D**, The whole-mount specimen shows a well-delimited focus of necrosis.

radiographic appearance, particularly well appreciated in lesions of the femoral neck.[74] Microscopically, it is typical to see osteoclastic activity on one side of the dead trabeculae and osteoblastic activity on the other. The newly formed bone, which is of soft consistency, may flatten because of pressure, resulting in degenerative joint disease.

Osteochondritis dissecans

Osteochondritis dissecans results from a small area of necrosis involving the articular cartilage and subchondral bone that totally or partially separates from the adjacent structures. The etiology is uncertain but is probably related to trauma in most of the cases.[79] It occurs most frequently on the lateral aspect of the medial femoral condyle, near the intercondylar notch (Fig. 24.9). Microscopically, a portion of articular cartilage is always present, often exhibiting secondary calcification; in addition, a fragment of subchondral bone is found in approximately half of the cases.[79] If this osteochondromatous body remains attached to the joint surface or synovium, both components remain viable. If, instead, it becomes completely detached, its osseous portion dies, but the cartilage remains alive, apparently through nutrients obtained from the synovial fluid.

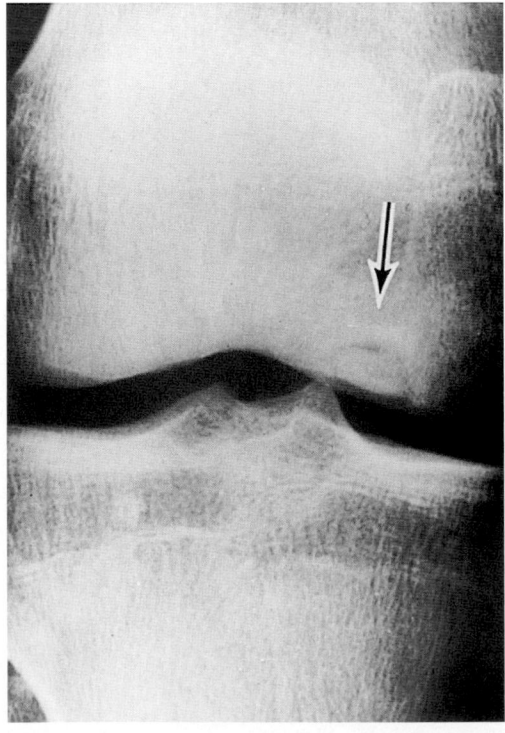

Fig. 24.9 Sharply delimited area of osteochondritis dissecans of medial condyle (arrow). This was easily enucleated.

Patients with bilateral symmetric involvement and cases with familial incidence have been described.

Radiation necrosis

Damage to the underlying bone can be a major complication of radiation therapy, whether alone or combined with chemotherapy.[80] Radiation changes resulting in serious complications have been reported in the jaw, ribs, pelvis, spine, humerus, and other bones.[81] The changes usually occur within 3 years of the therapy. Microscopically, these changes consist of necrotic bone, fibrosis of the bone marrow, and neovascularization. Irregular, heavily staining cement lines may develop and lead to confusion with Paget's disease.

Paget's disease

About 90% of the patients with Paget's disease are over 55 years of age. The disease is rare before the age of 40 years and uncommon between the ages of 40 and 55 years, although several cases of precocious onset are on record.[87] It affects men slightly more often than women (4:3). It has a very peculiar geographic distribution. The highest incidence is in England, Australia, and the Western European plain.[82,88] In an often quoted autopsy series from England, about one of every thirty patients over 40 years of age had Paget's disease.[83] The most common sites are the lumbosacral spine, pelvis, and skull. It may also occur in the femur, tibia, clavicle (Fig. 24.10), radius, ulna, fibula, and jaws,[96] but it is extremely rare in the ribs.

The disease is usually polyostotic and accompanied by serum elevations of alkaline phosphatase levels. However, it can also appear as a monostotic process in a long bone, jaw, or vertebra (Fig. 24.11). In such cases, the alkaline phosphatase levels may be normal.

The etiology of Paget's disease is unknown; the suggestion that it might be of viral origin has been raised by

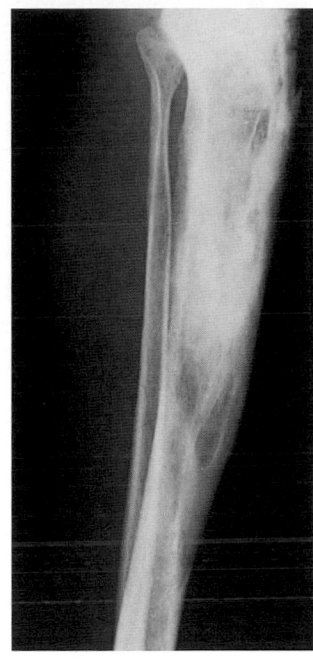

Fig. 24.11 Monostotic Paget's disease of tibia with bone destruction and bone formation. The nature of the process was obscure until biopsy.

the consistent finding of nuclear inclusions resembling viral nucleocapsids of the measles type in the lesional osteoclasts.[86,93,94]

The initial lesion is osteoclastic and therefore lytic (osteoporosis circumscripta)[84,85] (Fig. 24.12A). Abnormal hyperplasia soon follows, as evidenced by the deposition of primitive coarse-fibered bone in discontinuous trabeculae, which in turn is replaced by thick trabeculae with a disjointed lamellar pattern (Figs 24.12B and 24.13). This evolution in the morphogenesis of the disease can be better appreciated with reticulin stains than with the use of polarized light. The disorganization in the structure of the lamellar bone leads to the formation of *cement lines*. These are caused by the abrupt interruptions and changes in direction of bone lamellae and fibers resulting from resorption and regeneration of masses of bone during the course of the disease and represent the key to the diagnosis of Paget's disease. However, they are not specific for it; there are many pathologic processes that involve active reparative change accompanied by new bone formation with cement lines. These include irradiation effect, chronic osteomyelitis, reactive bone surrounding metastatic cancer, and polyostotic fibrous dysplasia. In general, the cement lines seen in these conditions are more orderly and structurally better oriented than those of Paget's disease.

Two important complications of Paget's disease are fractures and development of bone tumors. The fractures are usually of the transverse type.[90] Patients who are immobilized because of long bone fractures may undergo rapid dissolution of bone substance.[92]

The overall incidence of bone sarcoma in Paget's disease is relatively low if one considers the worldwide prevalence of the latter disorder.[83] Osteosarcoma is the

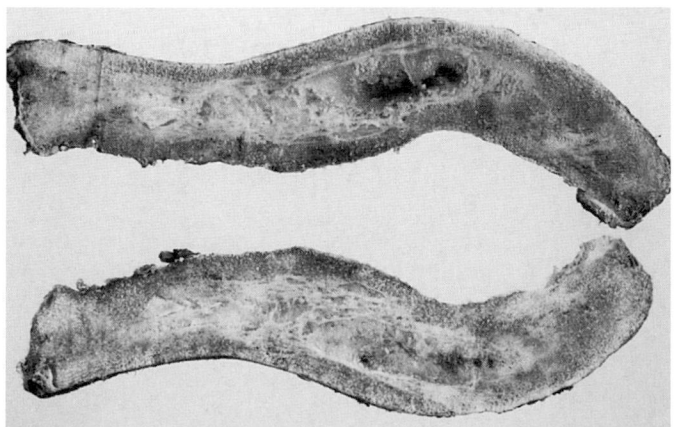

Fig. 24.10 Extensive Paget's disease of clavicle in a 60-year-old man. Note distortion and changes in cortex.

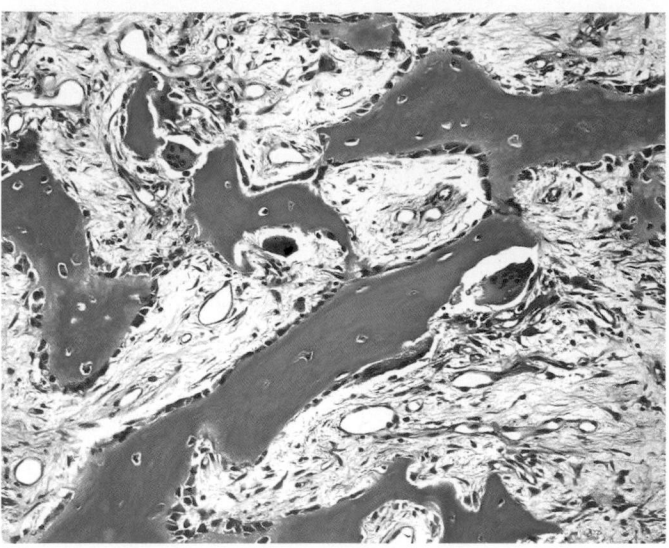
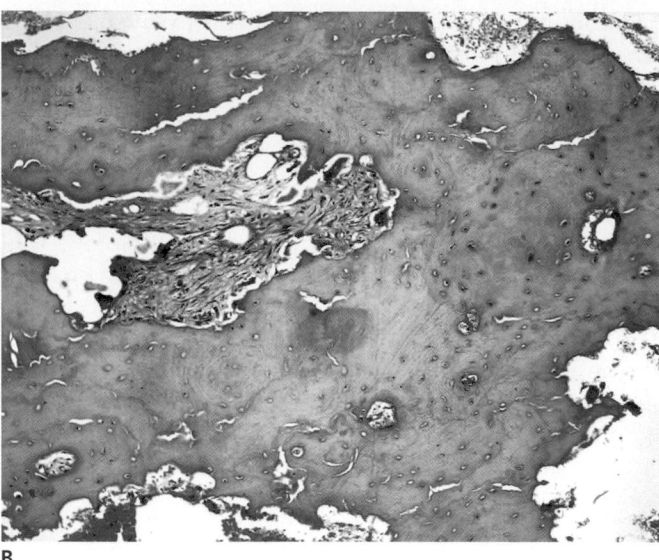

A

B

Fig. 24.12 A and **B**, Paget's disease. **A**, Early changes. There is prominent osteoclastic activity, resulting in bone resorption. **B**, A well-established case, with thick, irregularly shaped bone trabeculae.

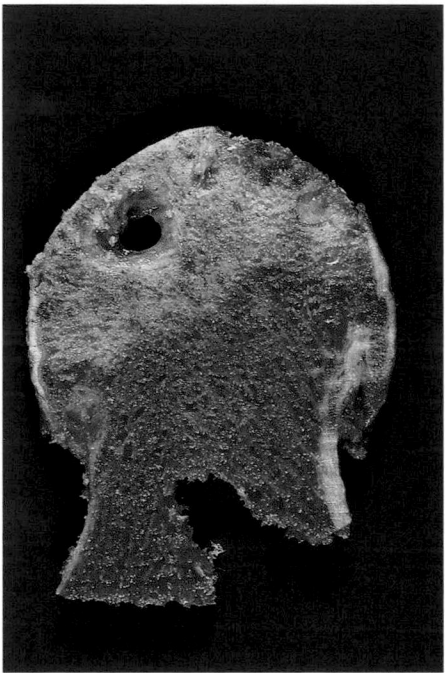

Fig. 24.13 Paget's disease of femoral head, accompanied by degenerative joint disease.

most common type, but chondrosarcoma, fibrosarcoma, and giant cell tumors have also been observed.[89,95] Instances of familial or geographic clustering of this complication have been seen. The most common locations of sarcomas arising in Paget's disease are the femur, humerus, pelvis, tibia, and skull. Osteosarcoma should be distinguished from the periosteal (juxtacortical) bone masses that can be seen as an exaggerated expression of the basic pathologic process of Paget's disease.[91]

Osteopetrosis

Osteopetrosis (Albers–Schönberg's disease, marble-bone disease) is a family of genetically-determined disorders resulting from a defect in bone remodeling secondary to malfunction of osteoclasts. The latter is due to the knock-out of genes required for osteoclast formation (*M-CSF, C-Fos, PU.1, NF-KappaB*) and those required for osteoclast activity (*c-Src, MitF, ATP6i*).[97,101] Microscopically, the disorder is characterized by persistence in the marrow cavity of unresorbed osteocartilaginous matrix.[97,100] The disease has been reversed by bone marrow transplantation[98] and has been successfully treated with recombinant human interferon gamma.[99]

Tumors

Classification and distribution

The terminology and classification of bone tumors and tumorlike lesions we use are largely those recommended by the WHO International Reference Center for the Histological Definition and Classification of Bone Tumours,[105] slightly modified to accommodate some new concepts and entities.[105]

In the WHO classification, most neoplasms are classified as either benign or malignant. Although a sharp separation between these two categories is feasible in most of them, some neoplasms (such as giant cell tumors and some well-differentiated cartilaginous tumors) exhibit borderline or intermediate characteristics. Most malignant bone tumors arise de novo, but there is a small number of benign bone lesions that predispose the patient to the development of skeletal malignancies;

these include Paget's disease, chondromatosis, osteo-chondromatosis, fibrous dysplasia, and osteofibrous dysplasia.[102]

Tumors of the skeletal system are relatively constant in their pattern of presentation.[103] The five basic parameters of importance in this regard are the age of the patient, bone involved, specific area within the bone (epiphysis, metaphysis, or diaphysis; cortex, medulla, or periosteum), radiographic appearance, and microscopic appearance. The pathologist should be fully aware of the first four before trying to evaluate the fifth.[104] Otherwise, serious mistakes may occur. Table 24.1 should help in providing a quick orientation for the pathologist confronted with a bone neoplasm.

Bone-forming tumors

Osteoma

Osteoma is seen almost exclusively in the flat bones of the skull and face. It may protrude inside a paranasal sinus (particularly the frontal and ethmoid) and block the normal drainage from these sinuses. Microscopically, it is composed of dense, mature, predominantly lamellar bone. This lesion is benign and probably not a true neoplasm. Some cases may represent end stages of fibrous dysplasia or related fibro-osseous lesions. Patients with Gardner's syndrome (intestinal polyposis and soft tissue tumors) may have multiple osteomas and other abnormalities.[107] Occasionally, osteomas involve bones other than skull and face. Most of these have a parosteal location and need to be distinguished from parosteal osteosarcoma.[106]

Osteoid osteoma and osteoblastoma

Osteoid osteoma is a benign bone neoplasm that is found more frequently in patients between 10 and 30 years of age, and that exhibits a 2:1 male–female ratio.[130] Intense pain is the most prominent symptom; this is often sharply localized and unaccompanied by clinical or laboratory evidence of infection. Vertebral lesions may be associated with scoliosis.[129]

Osteoid osteoma has been reported in practically every bone but occurs most frequently in the femur, tibia, humerus, bones of the hands and feet, vertebrae, and fibula.[122] Lesions of long bones are usually metaphyseal, but they may be epiphyseal and even juxta- or intra-articular.[110,121] Most are centered in the cortex (85%), but they may also occur in the spongiosa (13%) or subperiosteal region (2%).[131] Vertebral lesions usually affect the pedicle or the arch.[124]

Radiographically, the typical finding is a radiolucent central nidus that is seldom larger than 1.5 cm and that may or not contain a dense center (Fig. 24.14). This nidus is surrounded by a peripheral sclerotic reaction that may extend for several centimeters along both sides of the cortex and that may lead to a mistaken radiographic diagnosis of Garre's osteomyelitis (Fig. 24.15).

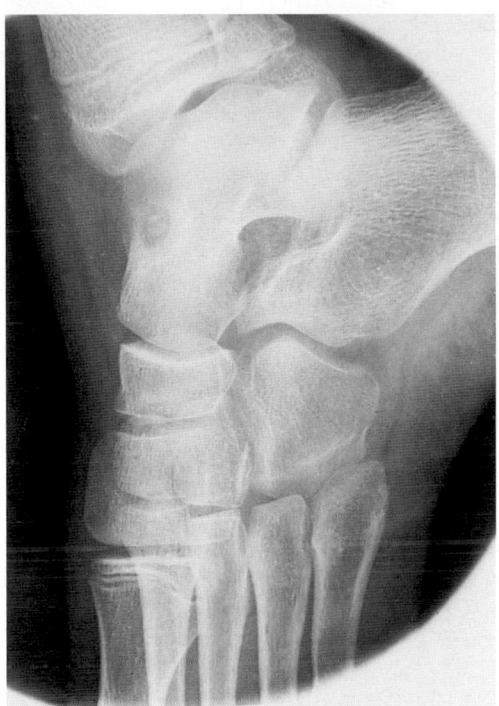

Fig. 24.14 Osteoid osteoma of talus. Note the small central osteolytic nidus surrounded by dense bone.

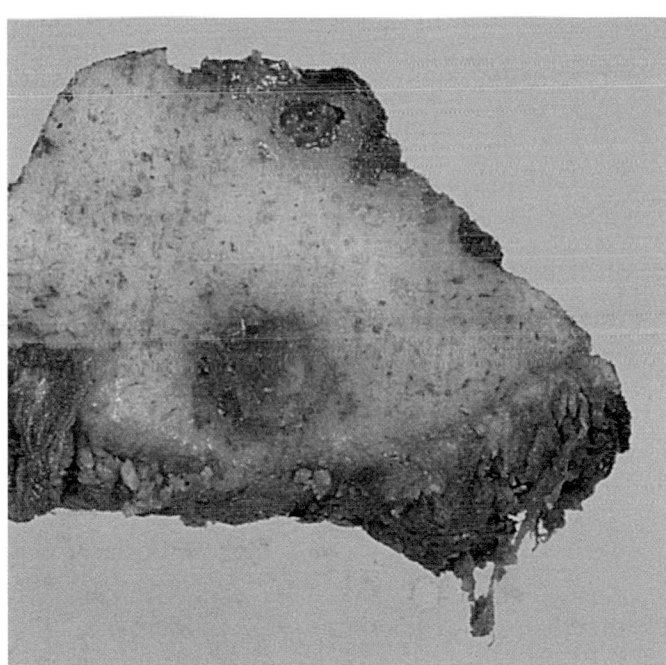

Fig. 24.15 Gross appearance of osteoid osteoma. The small, reddish central nidus is surrounded by a thick layer of sclerotic bone.

Microscopically, the sharply delineated central nidus is composed of more or less calcified osteoid lined by plump osteoblasts and growing within highly vascularized connective tissue, without evidence of inflammation (Figs 24.16 and 24.17). The appearance is so characteristic

Table 24.1 Usual age and sex of patient and location and behavior of most common primary bone tumors and tumorlike lesions*

Tumor or tumorlike lesion	Age (yr)	Sex (M:F)	Bones more commonly affected (in order of frequency)	Usual location within long bone	Behavior
Osteoma	40–50	2:1	Skull and facial bones	—	Benign
Osteoid osteoma	10–30	2:1	Femur, tibia, humerus, hands and feet, vertebrae, fibula	Cortex of metaphysis	Benign
Osteoblastoma	10–30	2:1	Vertebrae, tibia, femur, humerus, pelvis, ribs	Medulla of metaphysis	Benign
Osteosarcoma	10–25	3:2	Femur, tibia, humerus, pelvis, jaw, fibula	Medulla of metaphysis	Malignant; 20% 5-yr survival rate
Juxtacortical (parosteal) osteosarcoma	30–60	1:1	Femur, tibia, humerus	Juxtacortical area of metaphysis	Malignant; 80% 5-yr survival rate
Chondroma	10–40	1:1	Hands and feet, ribs, femur, humerus	Medulla of diaphysis	Benign
Osteochondroma	10–30	1:1	Femur, tibia, humerus, pelvis	Cortex of metaphysis	Benign
Chondroblastoma	10–25	2:1	Femur, humerus, tibia, feet, pelvis, scapula	Epiphysis, adjacent to cartilage plate	Practically always benign
Chondromyxoid fibroma	10–25	1:1	Tibia, femur, feet, pelvis	Metaphysis	Benign
Chondrosarcoma	30–60	3:1	Pelvis, ribs, femur, humerus, vertebrae	Central—medulla of diaphysis; peripheral—cortex or periosteum of metaphysis	Malignant; 5-yr survival rate—low grade, 78%; moderate grade, 53%; high grade, 22%
Mesenchymal chondrosarcoma	20–60	1:1	Ribs, skull and jaw, vertebrae, pelvis, soft tissues	Medulla or cortex of diaphysis	Malignant; extremely poor prognosis
Giant cell tumor	20–40	4:5	Femur, tibia, radius	Epiphysis and metaphysis	Potentially malignant; 50% recur; 10% metastasize
Ewing's sarcoma/PNET	5–20	1:2	Femur, pelvis, tibia, humerus, ribs, fibula	Medulla of diaphysis or metaphysis	Highly malignant; 20–30% 5-yr survival rate in recent series
Malignant lymphoma, large cell, and mixed cell types	30–60	1:1	Femur, pelvis, vertebrae, tibia, humerus, jaw, skull, ribs	Medulla of diaphysis or metaphysis	Malignant; 22–50% 5-yr survival rate
Plasma cell myeloma	40–60	2:1	Vertebrae, pelvis, ribs, sternum, skull	Medulla of diaphysis, metaphysis, or epiphysis	Malignant; diffuse form uniformly fatal, localized form often controlled with radiation therapy
Hemangioma	20–50	1:1	Skull, vertebrae, jaw	Medulla	Benign
Desmoplastic fibroma	20–30	1:1	Humerus, tibia, pelvis, jaw, femur, scapula	Metaphysis	Benign
Fibrosarcoma	20–60	1:1	Femur, tibia, jaw, humerus	Medulla of metaphysis	Malignant; 28% 5-yr survival rate
Chordoma	40–60	2:1	Sacrococcygeal, spheno-occipital, cervical vertebrae	—	Malignant; slow course; locally invasive; 48% distant metastases
Solitary bone cyst	10–20	3:1	Humerus, femur	Medulla of metaphysis	Benign
Aneurysmal bone cyst	10–20	1:1	Vertebrae, flat bones, femur, tibia	Metaphysis	Benign, sometimes secondary to another bone lesion
Metaphyseal fibrous defect	10–20	1:1	Tibia, femur, fibula	Metaphysis	Benign
Fibrous dysplasia	10–30	3:2	Ribs, femur, tibia, jaw, skull	Medulla of diaphysis or metaphysis	Locally aggressive; rarely complicated by sarcoma
Langerhans' cell histiocytosis	5–15	3:2	Skull, jaw, humerus, rib, femur	Metaphysis or diaphysis	Benign

*It should be emphasized that these data correspond to the typical case and they should not be taken in an absolute sense. Isolated exceptions to practically every one of these statements have occurred.

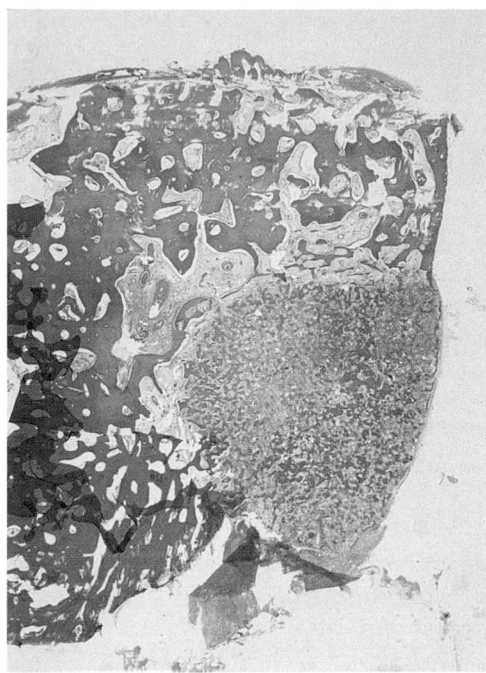

Fig. 24.16 Low power microscopic view showing a wedge-shaped nidus protruding slightly above the surface and surrounded by sclerotic bone.

that the lesion can still be diagnosed when removed piecemeal. Surrounding the nidus, there is a variably thick layer of dense bone.

The pain associated with osteoid osteoma is characteristically more intense at night, relieved by nonsteroidal anti-inflammatory drugs such as aspirin, and eliminated by the excision of the lesion. It has been attributed by some authors to the effect on nerves and vessels of osteoblast-produced prostaglandin E2, which is typically present in large amounts in these lesions.[120,134] Others believe that the pain is simply related to the presence of entrapped and proliferating nerves within and particularly around the nidus.[119,128]

Preoperative localization with CT scan and intraoperative monitoring of the location and resection with radioscintigraphy have markedly reduced the recurrence rate.[120,125] The nidus can also be demonstrated by administering tetracycline preoperatively and examining the lesion under ultraviolet light at operation.[109]

Osteoblastoma (benign osteoblastoma, giant osteoid osteoma) is a tumor closely related to osteoid osteoma both microscopically and ultrastructurally[115,133] (Fig. 24.18). It is distinguished from the latter by the larger size of the nidus, the absence or inconspicuousness of a surrounding area of reactive bone formation, and the lack of intense pain.[117] A cartilaginous matrix is present in some cases.[112] Most cases arise in the spongiosa of the bone, but cortical and subperiosteal forms also occur.[131] The majority of the cases are located in the spine or major bones of the lower extremity.[122,126] Osteomalacia can be seen as a complication.[135]

The differential diagnosis between osteoblastoma and osteosarcoma can be extremely difficult because the latter may be very well differentiated and the former is sometimes accompanied by the presence of scattered bizarre tumor cells probably of a degenerative nature,[113,116] or may be composed of large epithelioid cells accompanied by telangiectatic features.[108] As is the case in many other bone tumors, the radiographic pattern is of great assistance in this differential diagnosis. However, in some cases of osteoblastoma, the radiographic picture suggests a malignant neoplasm.[123,126]

Aggressive osteoblastoma and related lesions. Some lesions with the radiographic and architectural features

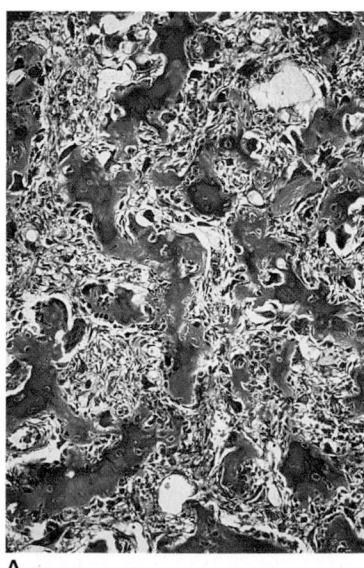
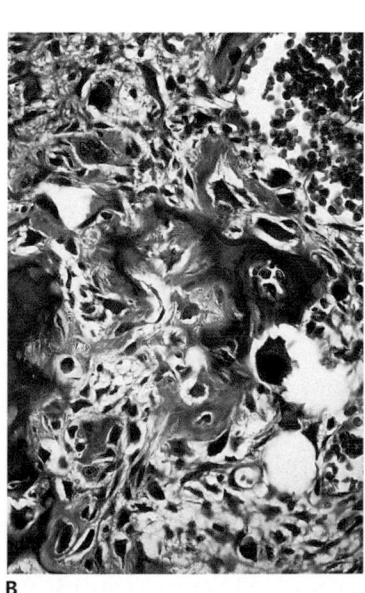

A   B

Fig. 24.17 Medium-power (**A**) and high-power (**B**) microscopic views of osteoid osteoma. There is exuberant new osteoid and bone formation by plump osteoblasts. The stroma is cellular and well vascularized.

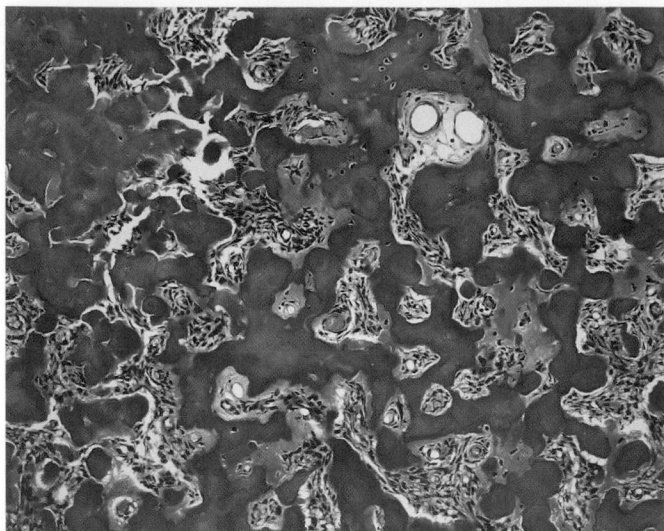

Fig. 24.18 Microscopic appearance of recurrent osteoblastoma. The appearance is similar to that of osteoid osteoma.

of osteoblastoma show atypical cytologic features that correlate with a tendency for local recurrence. These tumors have been designated as aggressive osteoblastomas. According to Dorfman and Weiss,[118] they are distinguished microscopically from the ordinary osteoblastomas because of the presence of wider or more irregular trabecula, by the focal lack of a trabecular pattern of the osteoid proliferation, and—most of all—by the fact that the osteoid trabeculae are bordered by epithelioid-appearing osteoblasts. They are distinguished from conventional osteosarcomas because of a low mitotic rate and the absence of the following features: lace-like osteoid, permeation of surrounding intertrabecular spaces, and atypical mitoses. The entity of aggressive osteoblastoma merges with—and may indeed be identical to—tumors described as malignant osteoblastoma,[132] osteosarcoma resembling osteoblastoma,[113] and osteoblastoma-like osteosarcoma,[111] some of which have metastasized. To complicate the issue further, there are several reported cases of supposedly ordinary osteoblastomas that have undergone malignant transformation toward osteosarcomas.[114,118]

Osteosarcoma

Generalities. Osteosarcoma is the most frequent primary malignant bone tumor, exclusive of hematopoietic malignancy.[172] It usually occurs in patients between 10 and 25 years of age and is exceptionally rare in preschool children.[201] Another peak age incidence occurs after 40, in association with other disorders (see the following discussion). There is a slight male predominance (1.5:1).

Predisposing factors. Most osteosarcomas arise de novo, but others arise within the context of a preexisting condition:

1 Paget's disease. A high number of osteosarcomas developing in patients over the age of 40 are located in bones affected by Paget's disease[188] (see p. 2145).

2 Radiation exposure. One of the classic cases of human carcinogenesis occurred in a group of factory workers in Illinois who developed osteosarcomas after moistening brushes in their mouths when applying radium paint to create luminous numerals on watches.[213,231] Some cases of osteosarcoma have also been reported years after Thorotrast administration.[251] Many others have been seen, in both adults and children, as a complication of external radiation therapy.[269] The average latency period ranges from 10 to 15 years in the various reported series.[193,272]

3 Chemotherapy. Children treated with alkylating agents for retinoblastoma and other malignancies have an increased risk of osteosarcoma.[262] The genetic factor probably plays an important contributory role.

4 Preexisting benign bone lesions. These include fibrous dysplasia, osteochondromatosis, and chondromatosis[252] (see respective sections).

5 Foreign bodies. A few but well-documented cases of osteosarcoma have been reported arising at the site of a total hip replacement or at sites of other orthopedic implants.[198,229]

6 Trauma. Isolated trauma, no matter how intense, does not cause osteosarcoma or other bone tumors.[179] If it did, one would expect to find an increased incidence of bone tumors after fractures, various orthopedic procedures, or other severe injuries. Trauma usually only calls attention to an already present advanced bone tumor.

Location. Most osteosarcomas arising de novo are located in the metaphyseal area of the long bones, particularly the lower end of the femur, the upper end of the tibia, and the upper end of the humerus.[162] A few cases arise in the diaphyses and an even smaller number in the epiphyses. Less commonly, osteosarcomas are found in flat bones (such as craniofacial bones, pelvis, and scapula),[180,199] spine,[225] and short bones.[222] Occasionally, osteosarcomas are multicentric, in either a synchronous or a metachronous fashion: most of these multicentric cases occur in children and tend to be densely sclerotic radiographically and extremely aggressive.[227] Germ-line and somatic mutations of *p53* have been found in some of these cases.[194]

The large majority of osteosarcomas arise within the medullary cavity, from which they extend into the cortex; only occasionally will they begin within the cortex itself[270]—when they do, they seem to have a predilection for the diaphysis.[204]

Gross appearance and spread. The gross appearance of the cut surface of an osteosarcoma varies a great deal, depending on the relative amounts of bone, cartilage, cellular stroma, and vessels (Figs 24.19 and 24.20). The range extends from bony hard to cystic, friable, and

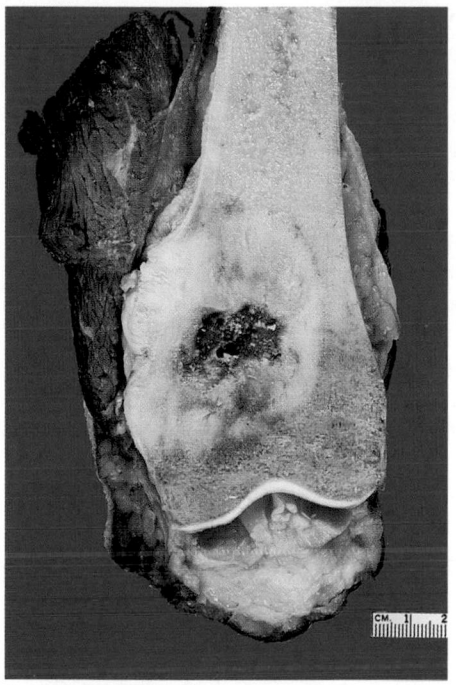
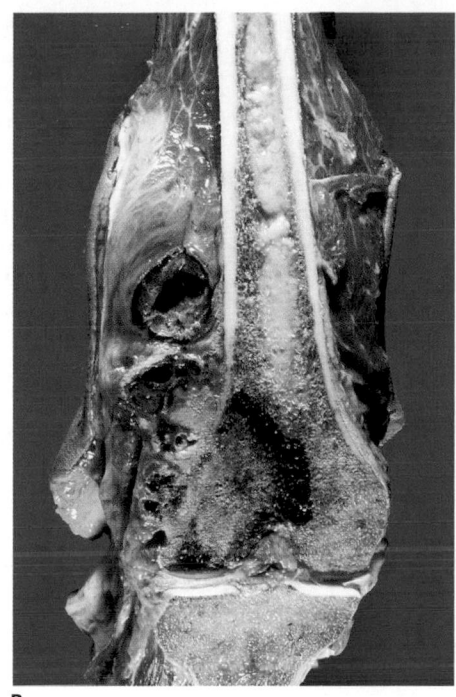

Fig. 24.19 A and **B**, Gross appearances of osteosarcoma of femur. In both instances the tumor is located at the classic metaphyseal site. The tumor shown in **A** is largely restricted to bone, whereas that illustrated in **B** is accompanied by massive soft tissue extension.

A

B

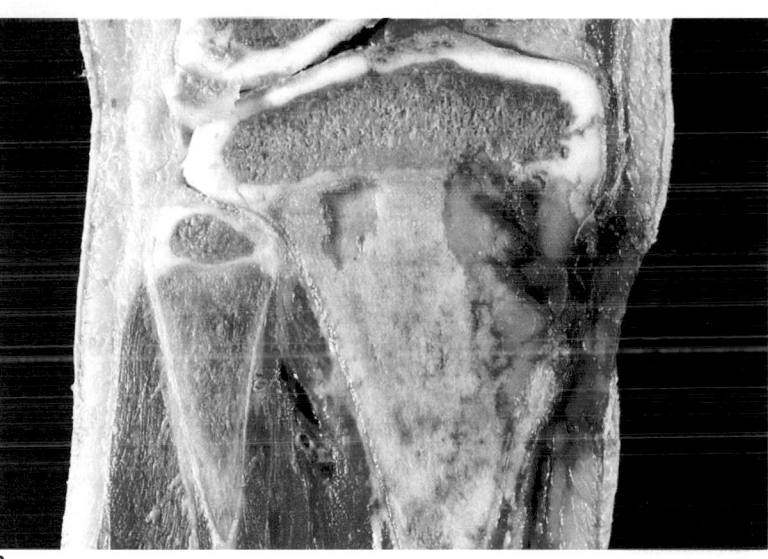

A   B

Fig. 24.20 A and **B**, Other gross appearances of osteosarcoma. **A**, Tumor extensively involving spine and producing a large soft tissue mass. **B**, This tumor of the upper tibial metaphysis is being temporarily restrained by the cartilage of the epiphyseal line. The hemorrhagic area represents the biopsy site.

hemorrhagic. From its usual origin in the metaphysis of a long bone, the tumor may:

1 Spread along the marrow cavity.
2 Invade the adjacent cortex.
3 Elevate or perforate the periosteum. In the latter circumstance, a radiographic sign known as Codman's triangle develops. The two long sides of this triangle are formed by the elevated periosteum and the underlying bone; the space within them is mainly occupied by reactive new bone, arranged perpendicular to the bone surface, but it may also contain malignant tumor.

This radiographic sign, although useful, is not specific for osteosarcoma or even for a malignant tumor; it can be produced by any lesion that elevates the periosteum, including hematoma.
4 Extend into the soft tissues. It may even reach beneath the skin, although cutaneous ulceration is very rare.
5 Extend into the epiphysis. This happens frequently after the epiphysis is closed, but it may also be seen when the epiphyseal growth line is still present.[249]
6 Extend into the joint space. This invasion occurs when the tumor extends under the capsule insertion to involve the margin of the articular cartilage. In the

knee, the tumor may extend across or around the osseous–tendinous junction of the cruciate ligaments into the joint space.[250]

7 Form satellite nodules independent from the main tumor mass proximal to the primary lesion, either in the same bone or transarticularly (Fig. 24.21). These have been called "skip" metastases[173] and may be responsible for an increased incidence of local recurrences and subsequent metastases.[209]

8 Metastasize through the bloodstream to distant sites, particularly the lung. In an autopsy series of fifty-four cases, the four main sites of metastases were lung (98%), other bones (37%), pleura (33%), and heart (20%).[266] Conversely, metastases to regional lymph nodes are so rare that they should be disregarded for purposes of therapy. On occasion, the lung metastases present in the form of extensive intraluminal tumor growth in the pulmonary arteries.[271]

Microscopic features. Microscopically, osteosarcoma may destroy the preexisting bone trabeculae or grow around them in an appositional fashion (Fig. 24.22). The key feature for the diagnosis is the detection, somewhere in the tumor, of osteoid and/or bone (calcified osteoid) produced directly by the tumor cells without interposition of cartilage (Fig. 24.23). Osteoid is recognized by its eosinophilic-staining quality, its glassy appearance, irregular contours, and the fact that it is surrounded by a rim of osteoblasts. It may be very difficult to distinguish osteoid from hyalinized collagen; a homogeneous rather than fibrillary appearance, beginning punctate calcifica-

tion, and a plump appearance of the cells around it are more in keeping with osteoid. A different but highly characteristic type of tumor bone is characterized by thin tubular anastomosing "microtrabeculae," which are very basophilic and vaguely reminiscent of the appearance of fungal hyphae (Fig. 24.24).

These osteoblastic areas are often mixed with fibroblastic and chondroblastic foci, the relative proportions among these three components varying a great deal from case to case. Depending on which component predominates, osteosarcomas have been divided into osteoblastic, fibroblastic, and chondroblastic, but there seems to be no prognostic significance to this division. The important fact to remember is that a malignant bone tumor should be designated as osteosarcoma whenever osteoid is seen unconnected with cartilage and being formed directly from the tumor cells, no matter how much neoplastic cartilage (with or without endochondral ossification) or fibrous tissue is present elsewhere.

Morphologic variations in osteosarcoma are plentiful.[163,244,283] The osteoid may be sparse or massive,

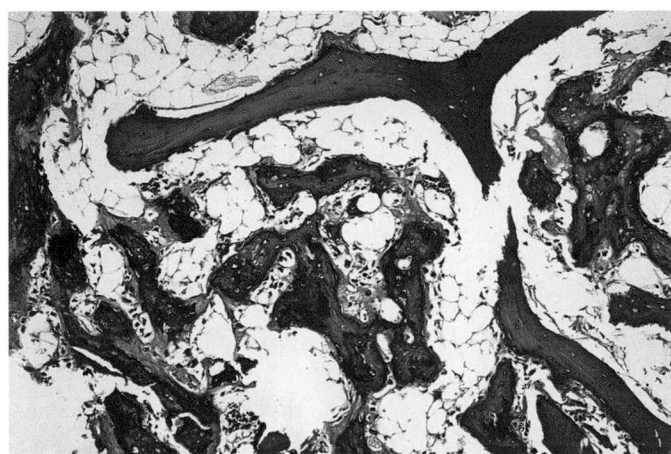

Fig. 24.22 Osteosarcoma. The malignant bone is more basophilic and has more irregular borders than the preexisting bone trabeculae.

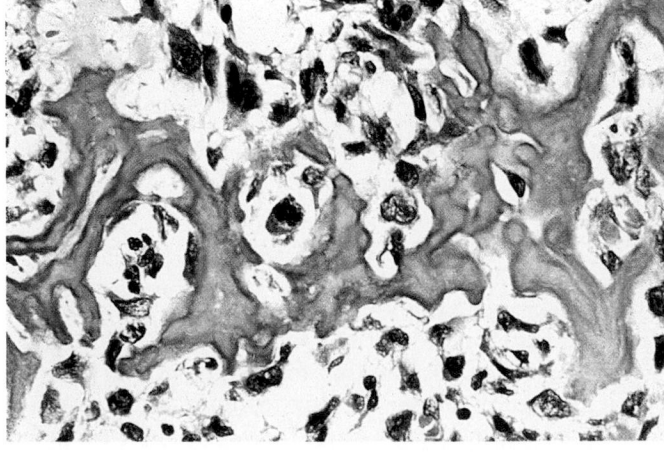

Fig. 24.23 Malignant bone formation by the tumor cells of osteosarcoma without interposition of cartilage.

Fig. 24.21 So-called "skip metastasis" located in the upper half of the femur. The primary tumor was located in the lower metaphysis of the same bone.

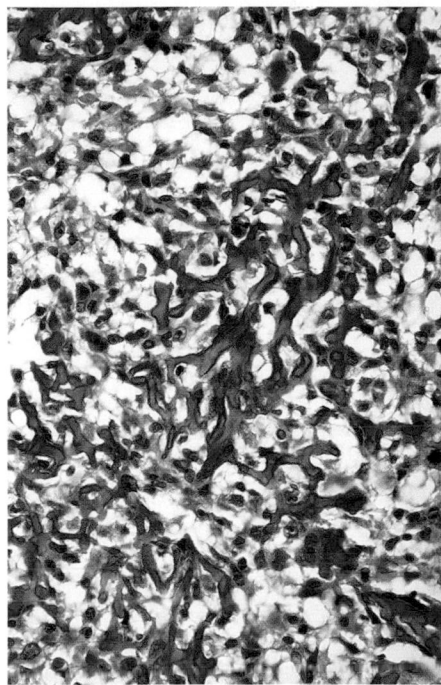

Fig. 24.24 Microscopic appearance of osteosarcoma showing characteristic basophilic thin trabeculae of neoplastic bone with an appearance that is reminiscent of fungal hyphae.

surrounded by pleomorphic bizarre cells or relatively acellular, irregularly shaped, or with a rosettelike configuration (the latter allegedly being a more aggressive variant).[220] The tumor cells may grow in diffuse, nesting, or pseudopapillary arrangements. The vessels may be scanty or numerous, sometimes with a dilated or hemangiopericytomatous appearance. The tumor cells may be spindle, oval, or round, and their size may range from small to giant; exceptionally, they have a distinctly epithelial-like appearance.[164,186,202,280] Osteoclast-like multinucleated giant cells are present in one fourth of the cases and may dominate the picture focally (so-called giant cell-rich osteosarcoma); the cartilage may be immature, mineralized, or highly myxoid. In the latter instance, the tumor may simulate a chondromyxoid fibroma.[160]

Depending on which one of the previously mentioned microscopic patterns happens to be present, the differential diagnosis of osteosarcoma may include a remarkably high number of benign and malignant lesions, such as fracture callus, myositis ossificans, fibrous dysplasia, osteoblastoma, fibrosarcoma, chondrosarcoma, giant cell tumor, malignant lymphoma, and metastatic carcinoma.[283] Exuberant fracture callus is particularly likely to be misdiagnosed as osteosarcoma by the unwary, with disastrous consequences for the patient. This callus may be secondary to a pathologic fracture in a benign lesion such as a metaphyseal fibrous defect or aneurysmal bone cyst, in a metastatic carcinoma, or in osteogenesis imperfecta (where it may be particularly exuberant).[145,197]

Myositis ossificans is a reactive lesion pathogenetically closely related to fracture callus and may induce similar diagnostic problems (see p. 2194).

Other entities that need to be considered in the differential diagnosis are discussed in connection with the osteosarcoma variants described in the following section.

Histochemical, immunohistochemical, and electron microscopic features. Osteosarcoma cells usually exhibit strong alkaline phosphatase activity, regardless of their appearance (osteoblastic or fibroblastic), a feature of diagnostic value.[257,279] Ultrastructurally, the better differentiated tumor cells resemble normal osteoblasts in their abundance of dilated cisternae of granular endoplasmic reticulum and sparse mitochondria.[178,212,245,254,275] Other cells present are osteocytes, chondroblasts, undifferentiated cells, and myofibroblasts.[237,255,256] The matrix is formed of nonperiodic fibrils, scattered collagen fibers, and focal calcium deposits of hydroxyapatite crystals.[181]

Immunohistochemically, the cells of osteosarcoma consistently express vimentin. In some cases they are also positive for smooth muscle actin and desmin (suggesting myofibroblastic or myoid differentiation) and exceptionally for keratin and EMA.[178,185,196,260] S-100 protein is always present in foci of chondroid differentiation, but it may also be seen in osteoblastic areas.[185]

Proteins specifically associated with bone metabolism—osteonectin, osteocalcin, osteopontin bone morphogenetic protein, and bone GLA protein—have been identified immunohistochemically in the cells of osteosarcoma and may be of utility in the differential diagnosis of this tumor.[151,174,195,242,259,281,282] Type I collagen is consistently found in the extracellular material; in addition, type II collagen is present in chondroid foci, and type IV collagen may also be encountered.[206]

Molecular genetic features:

- The most common cytogenetic abnormalities detected in osteosarcoma involve chromosomes 1, 2, 6, 12, and 17.[226,234,238a]
- Mutations of *p53* have been found in about 20% of osteosarcomas.[208,215,223,233]
- Interestingly, the *Gsalpha* gene mutation consistently found in fibrous dysplasia is generally absent in low-grade central osteosarcoma, pointing to a different pathogenesis for each of the two processes and providing a tool for their differential diagnosis.[232]

Microscopic variants and special types. In addition to the wide range in morphologic appearance already described in osteosarcoma, there are some cases in which the cytoarchitectural characteristics depart enough from the norm to justify recognition as a special category. It should be realized that these variations may be present only focally and that they may occur in combination; their main importance rests on their ability to simulate other bone processes microscopically and also on the fact that some of them carry distinctive prognostic connotations:

1 *Telangiectatic*. Blood-filled cystic formations are prominent, resulting in an appearance similar to that of aneurysmal bone cyst radiographically and pathologically, although the arteriographic pattern is usually different (Fig. 24.25). Pathologic fractures are very frequent.[191] The lesion is identified as osteosarcoma through the detection of malignant stroma in the septa that separate the bloody cysts[150] (Fig. 24.26). Telangiectatic osteosarcoma has been found to be associated with a more aggressive course than the conventional variety in one large series[214] but not in two others.[150,191]

2 *Small cell*. The small size and uniformity of the tumor cells and their diffuse pattern of growth closely simulate the appearance of Ewing's sarcoma and malignant lymphoma.[216,228] In some cases, these cells are spindle rather than round.[140] Focal production of osteoid (sometimes mixed with cartilage) by these small cells is the distinguishing feature.[151,248] Areas of cartilage formation can also be present.[140] In contrast to Ewing's sarcoma/primitive (or peripheral) neuroectodermal tumor, most cases of small cell osteosarcoma lack immunoreactivity for CD99.[168] There are no pathognomonic ultrastructural features, and it is difficult to distinguish small cell osteosarcoma from Ewing's sarcoma at this level when osteoid is not present in the sample.[169]

3 *Fibrohistiocytic*. The appearance in most areas is indistinguishable from that of malignant fibrous histiocytoma, especially in the areas of soft tissue extension and in the distant metastases; however, tumor osteoid is focally present.

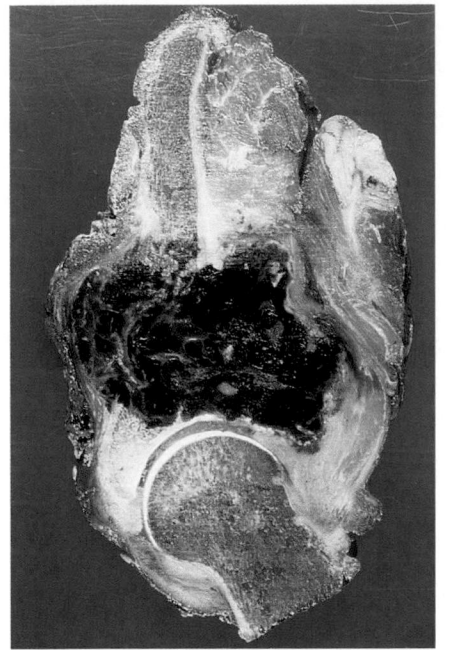

A   B

Fig. 24.25 Gross appearances of telangiectatic osteosarcoma.

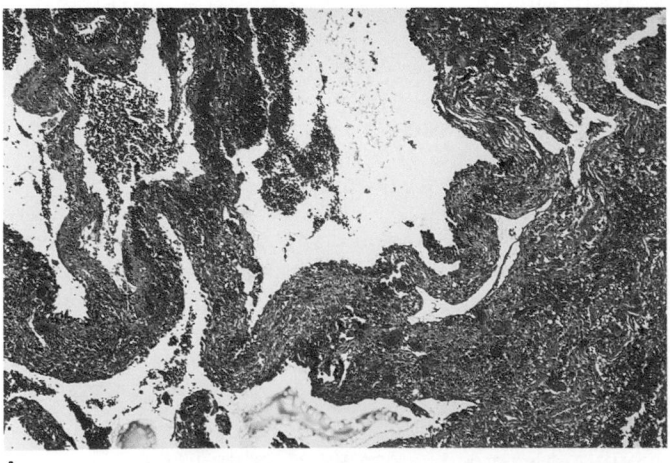
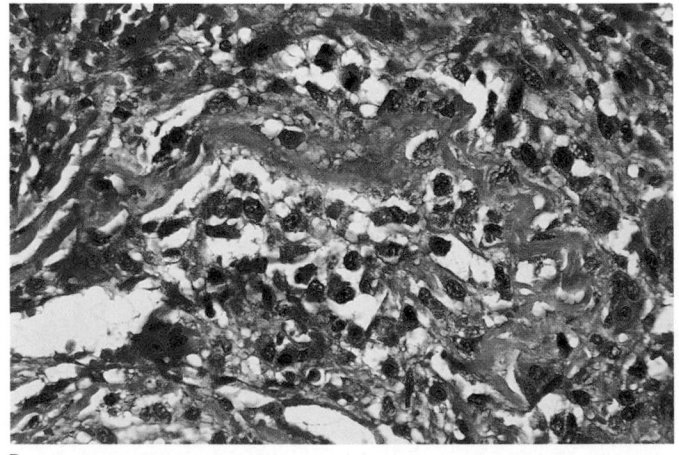

A   B

Fig. 24.26 A and **B**, Microscopic appearance of telangiectatic osteosarcoma. **A**, The low-power architecture closely simulates the appearance of an aneurysmal bone cyst. **B**, Malignant osteoid is present in the septa.

4 *Anaplastic.* The tumor is so bizarre and undifferentiated as to raise the possibility of any type of pleomorphic sarcoma or metastatic carcinoma. Once again, the key to the diagnosis is the identification of tumor osteoid.

5 *Well-differentiated (low-grade) intramedullary (intraosseous)* (Fig. 24.27). This tumor is microscopically so bland looking as to be often underdiagnosed as a benign lesion, particularly fibrous dysplasia.[265] Other cases resemble histologically parosteal osteosarcoma.[149] Most patients are adults, the femur and tibia being the most commonly affected sites. Exceptionally, the small phalangeal bones are affected.[258] Spindle cells with minimal atypia and scanty mitoses are seen mixed with abundant osteoid. Recurrences are common, but metastases are very rare (unless the tumor converts in the recurrence into a conventional high-grade osteosarcoma), i.e., undergoes "dedifferentiation."[203,219] In contrast to fibrous dysplasia, this tumor shows radiographic evidence of cortical destruction.[203] Microscopically, atypia is minimal but still present. This feature and the invasive growth pattern are helpful in distinguishing this tumor from fibrous dysplasia.[203]

Other variants of osteosarcoma are defined on the basis of topographic, clinical, or radiographic features, or a combination of them:

1 *Juxtacortical (parosteal) osteosarcoma.* This infrequent variant occurs in a slightly older age group than the conventional variety.[263] It usually arises in a juxtacortical position in the metaphyses of long bones (usually the posterior aspect of the lower femoral shaft) and grows very slowly, some cases having a life history of up to 15 years. Eventually, it forms a large lobulated mass with a tendency to encircle the bone (Figs 24.28 and 24.29). Later in its evolution, it may penetrate into the medullary cavity, a feature associated with a higher microscopic grade and decreased survival.[159] Satellite nodules may be present. Rare cases have been described at other sites, such as the mandible and

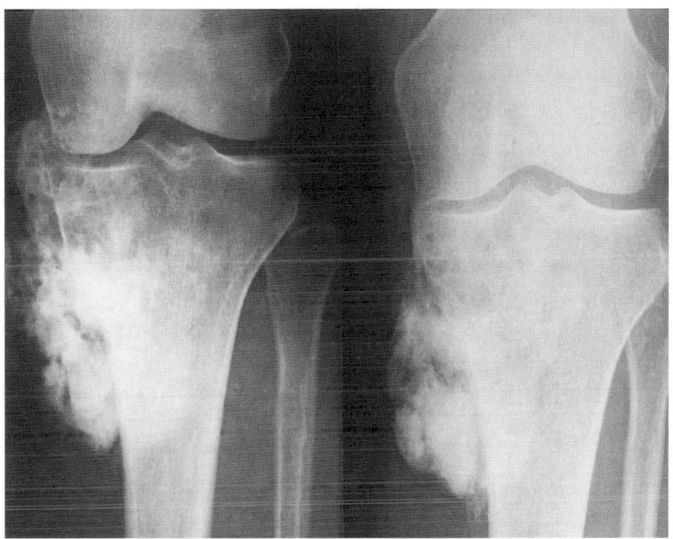

Fig. 24.28 Juxtacortical osteosarcoma occurring in a 40-year-old woman. Note the large extracortical component.

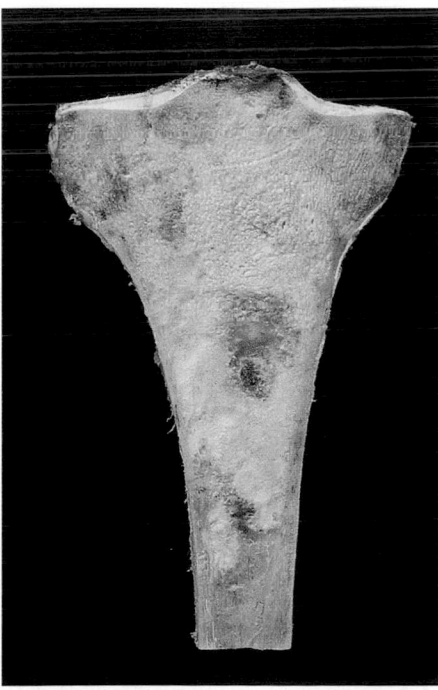

Fig. 24.27 Gross appearance of intraosseous well-differentiated osteosarcoma of tibia. (Courtesy of Dr. Juan Jose Segura, San José, Costa Rica)

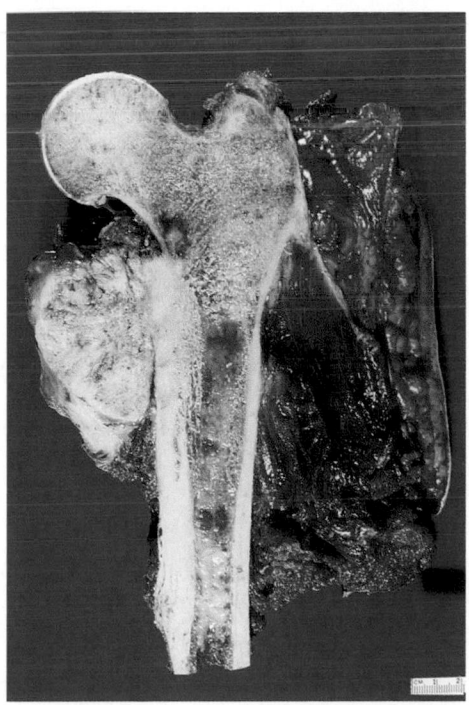

Fig. 24.29 Juxtacortical osteosarcoma of upper femur. There is only minimal involvement of the cortex.

small bones of the hand.[268] The radiographic appearance is highly characteristic.[267] Microscopically, there is a disorderly pattern of well-formed bone, osteoid, occasional cartilage, and a highly fibrous spindle-cell stroma (Fig. 24.30). The cytologic signs of malignancy in the fibrous stroma are often subtle, thus accounting for the great frequency of misdiagnoses made in this tumor.[171] Exceptionally, the tumor is rich in osteoclast-like giant cells.[243] The most important differential diagnosis is with myositis ossificans, which is distinguished mainly on the basis of its orderly pattern of maturation (see p. 2194). The prognosis for juxtacortical osteosarcoma is very good, even with segmental excision. It should be emphasized that not all osteosarcomas located juxtacortically belong to this variety. Those having morphologic features equivalent to those of the conventional intramedullary osteosarcoma are referred to as high-grade surface osteosarcomas and behave as aggressively as the former.[175,221,277] This is also true for the conventional intramedullary osteosarcoma with periosteal spread. Sometimes, features of a high-grade osteosarcoma are seen focally in what is otherwise a typical juxtacortical osteosarcoma, either initially or—more commonly—following repeated tumor recurrences; this phenomenon, which is referred to as "dedifferentiation," is associated with a markedly decreased survival rate.[136,246,263,278]

2 *Periosteal osteosarcoma.* This tumor type, which is very different from juxtacortical (parosteal) osteosarcoma despite the similarities in the misleading terminology chosen, grows on the surface of long bones.[264] Most of the reported cases have been located in the upper tibial shaft or femur and have presented as small lucent lesions on the bone surface, accompanied by bone spicules arranged perpendicular to the shaft. Exceptionally, they have been found in the small

bones of digits.[170] The lesions are limited to the cortex and only rarely invade the medullary cavity[167,183] (Fig. 24.31). Microscopically, the tumors are relatively high-grade osteosarcomas, with a prominent cartilaginous component (Fig. 24.32). The prognosis is better than for conventional osteosarcoma.[264] This entity is closely related to the one discussed on p. 2165 under the term juxtacortical (periosteal) chondrosarcoma, but some minor differences in location, microscopic grade, and behavior between the two have been described.

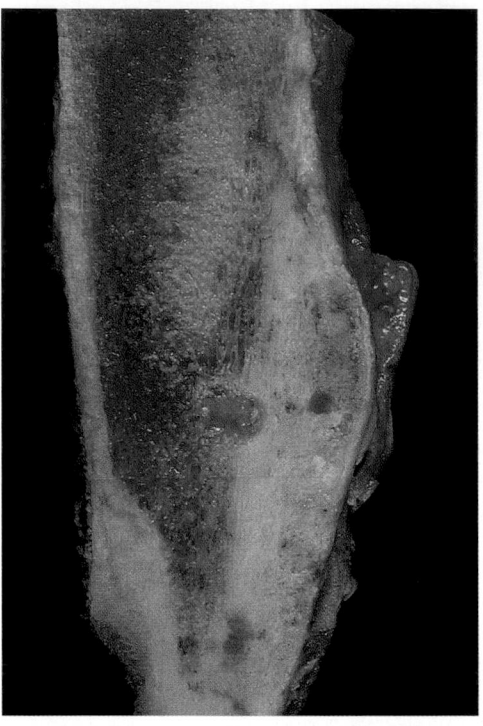

Fig. 24.31 Periosteal osteosarcoma. The white shining appearance is due to the high content of cartilage.

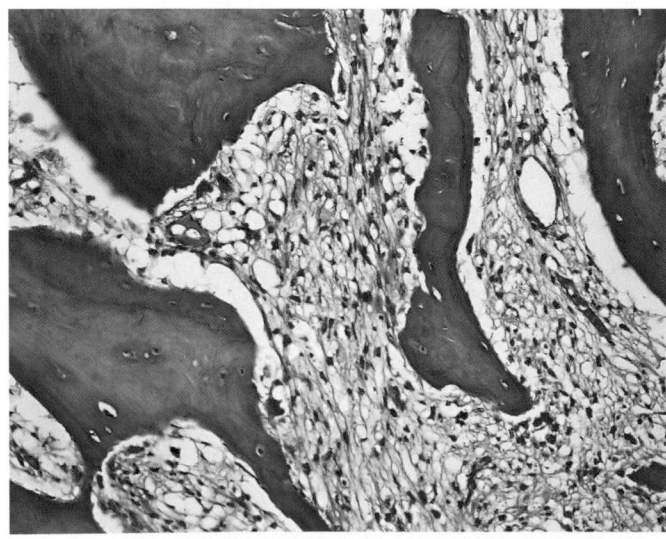

Fig. 24.30 Juxtacortical osteosarcoma. Moderately atypical spindle tumor cells grow between irregularly shaped bone trabeculae.

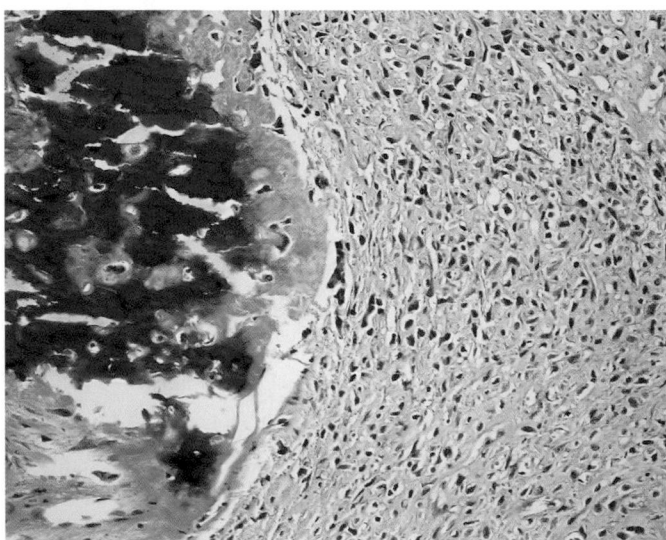

Fig. 24.32 Microscopic appearance of periosteal chondrosarcoma. There is a predominance of myxochondroid areas.

3 *Osteosarcoma of the jaw.* Gnathic osteosarcoma is distinctive enough to be treated separately from the rest.[161] Patients affected are slightly older (average age, 34 years), and most lesions show a prominent chondroblastic component. The most common sites of involvement are the body of the mandible and the alveolar ridge of the maxilla. The prognosis is relatively good.[161]

4 *Osteosarcoma in Paget's disease.* Nearly all the cases of Paget's disease complicated by osteosarcoma are of the polyostotic type. The tumors themselves are often multicentric. The most common locations are the pelvis, humerus, femur, tibia, and skull.[189,192,274] According to Schajowicz et al.,[240] these osteosarcomas are characterized microscopically by a large number of osteoclasts alternating with atypical osteoblasts. The prognosis is extremely poor.[189,274]

Diagnosis. Although most osteosarcomas have a very characteristic radiographic appearance, there is sufficient overlap with other malignant bone tumors and with benign conditions to make imperative a pathologic diagnosis before instituting definitive therapy. Depending on the size and location of the tumor and the skill and experience of the diagnostic team, the choice of procedure may be open biopsy, needle biopsy, fine needle aspiration, or frozen section.[177]

When performing an open biopsy, an attempt should be made to include tumor and adjacent non-neoplastic tissue; excessive trauma should be avoided, and the biopsy incision should be so placed that it will be entirely removed by the subsequent surgical excision.[211] There is no evidence that the performance of an incisional biopsy affects survival in these patients.[155]

Needle biopsy in experienced hands is extremely reliable and is of particular use in locations that are difficult to reach by open biopsy, such as the vertebral column.[139,166,239] Fine needle aspiration has also been used extensively with very good results.[153,273]

Laboratory tests are of no great value in the diagnosis of osteosarcoma. The only abnormality detected with some frequency is elevation of serum alkaline phosphatase, but this is merely an expression of bone production and, as such, is nonspecific. It can also be elevated in hyperparathyroidism, Paget's disease, and metastatic carcinoma from the breast or prostate. Conversely, it is apt to be negative in a predominantly osteolytic osteosarcoma.

Therapy. Formerly, the therapy of osteosarcoma of the extremities has usually consisted of amputation or disarticulation, depending on the location of the tumor. At present, more limited forms of surgery (limb-sparing procedures) have been coupled with other therapeutic modalities, particularly preoperative and postoperative neoadjuvant chemotherapy.[143,156,157,235] The preoperative chemotherapy can be administered systemically or intra-arterially.[196,276]

Microscopic studies of the tumor successfully treated with chemotherapy show extensive areas of necrosis and hemorrhage[138]; sites where viable tumor is more likely to persist are the soft tissue, cortex and subcortex, ligaments, and areas in contact with cartilage.[230] These morphologic changes correlate well with functional bone imaging, which therefore provides an accurate presurgical assessment of tumor response.[253] The presence of extensive tumor necrosis following chemotherapy constitutes a good prognostic sign[236] (see next section).

Surgical removal of metastatic nodules of osteosarcoma in the lungs prolongs survival in selected patients.[142,148,241]

Prognosis. The overall prognosis for osteosarcoma has significantly improved. For many years, the 5-year survival rate fluctuated very little from the figure of 20% in most series. Lately, many reports listing 5-year disease-free rates of 70% or more have appeared[182,205]; it is not clear how much of this apparent improvement is due to change in treatment (particularly the administration of multidrug chemotherapy following surgery), as opposed to a better selection of surgical candidates through more detailed radiographic studies.[184,238] When making these calculations, it is important to exclude cases of chondrosarcoma or fibrosarcoma, both of which carry a better prognosis than osteosarcoma.

Factors to be considered in regard to prognosis of osteosarcoma are the following:

1 *Age, sex, or pregnancy.* No apparent prognostic differences have been related to any of these parameters.[158,162,190]

2 *Presence of Paget's disease.* These tumors are usually highly malignant; most of the reported cases have proved fatal.[189,274]

3 *History of prior irradiation.* Radiation-induced osteosarcomas do not behave significantly differently from those arising de novo; in one large series, the 5-year survival rate was 28%.[137]

4 *Specific bone involved.* Osteosarcomas of the jaw and distal extremities (below the elbows and knees) have a better prognosis than the others.[162,218] With osteosarcoma of the jaw, survival figures of over 80% have been achieved with current surgical modalities. In contrast, osteosarcomas of other craniofacial bones and vertebrae (many of which arise within the context of Paget's disease) have a very poor prognosis.[146,192,217,247]

5 *Multifocal osteosarcoma.* This form is almost uniformly fatal.[227]

6 *Osteoblastic, chondroblastic, and fibroblastic types.* Some authors have claimed a better prognosis for the fibroblastic type, but the difference is so small as to be of no statistical significance. The chondroblastic type of osteosarcoma is said to be less responsive to chemotherapy than the osteoblastic or fibroblastic types.[141]

7 *Microscopic grading.* There is no definite relationship with prognosis[162,218] once the osteosarcoma variants are excluded.

8 *Parosteal and periosteal osteosarcoma.* As already indicated, both of these variants are associated with an improved prognosis, particularly the former.

9 *Microscopic variants.* Telangiectatic osteosarcoma has a worse prognosis (at least in one series), and well-differentiated intramedullary osteosarcoma has a better prognosis than conventional osteosarcoma. Small cell osteosarcoma has a prognosis that is the same or slightly worse than conventional osteosarcoma.[140,151]

10 *Serum elevation of alkaline phosphatase.* Tumors associated with serum elevations of this enzyme have been found to have an increased metastatic rate.[207]

11 *Postchemotherapy tumor necrosis.* It has been shown by several independent studies that the amount of tumor necrosis following chemotherapy is directly related to survival rate.[152,236] As a matter of fact, this feature has emerged as the single most important prognostic parameter in conventional osteosarcoma of extremities with no evidence of distant metastases at presentation.[165]

12 *Aneuploidy.* Alteration of DNA ploidy as measured by flow cytometry is correlated with the microscopic grade of the tumor and may prove of prognostic value.[187,210] The technique may also be of help in the differential diagnosis, since most osteosarcomas are hyperploid or aneuploid, whereas the vast majority of benign bone tumors are diploid; however, periosteal and well-differentiated osteosarcomas are also usually diploid.[147]

13 *Heat shock protein.* The claim has been advanced that expression of heat shock protein 72 correlates with good response to neoadjuvant chemotherapy in osteosarcomas.[261]

14 *RB gene.* Loss of heterozygosity of the *RB* gene is a poor prognostic factor.[176]

15 *HER2/neu expression.* The expression of this surface protein has been said to correlate with poor prognosis.[224] However, this claim has not been substantiated by other authors.[200]

16 *P-glycoprotein.* A widespread pattern of P-glycoprotein expression in tumor cells at the time of diagnosis is associated with an increased rate of systemic relapse.[144]

Cartilage-forming tumors

Chondroma

Chondroma is a common benign cartilaginous tumor that occurs most frequently in the small bones of the hands and feet, particularly the proximal phalanges. **Enchondromas** begin in the spongiosa of the diaphysis (enchondromas), from which they expand and thin the cortex. Chondromas of the thumb and terminal pha-langes are distinctly uncommon. About 30% of chondromas are multiple.[297]

Multiple enchondromas having a predominantly unilateral distribution are referred to as *Ollier's disease*. The association of multiple enchondromas with soft tissue hemangiomas (including spindle cell hemangioendotheliomas) is known as *Maffucci's syndrome*[291] (Fig. 24.33). In both conditions, there is a significant risk of malignant transformation, usually in the form of chondrosarcoma,[285,289,292,296] sometimes developing in multiple bones.[288] Ollier's disease is also associated with ovarian sex cord-stromal tumors.[298]

Enchondromas of the ribs and long bones are distinctly unusual. A variant of the latter, presenting in the metaphysis of long bones, is characterized by massive calcification within the neoplasm (calcifying enchondroma)[290] (Fig. 24.34).

Juxtacortical (periosteal) chondromas are much less common than enchondromas; they arise from the periosteal region of a long bone or a small bone of the hand or foot.[284] They characteristically erode and induce sclerosis of the contiguous cortex (Fig. 24.35). Radiographically, juxtacortical chondromas are smaller and better marginated than their malignant counterpart[294] (see p. 2165). Recurrence may follow incomplete excision.[295]

Microscopically, chondromas are composed of mature lobules of hyaline cartilage (Fig. 24.36). Foci of myxoid degeneration, calcification, and endochondral ossification are common. Juxtacortical chondroma tends to be more cellular than its medullary counterpart and may contain occasional plump or double nuclei.[284]

Although not strictly a chondroma, the peculiar chest wall lesion of infancy known as **cartilaginous and vascular hamartoma (mesenchymoma)** is discussed here because of its benign nature and predominant cartilaginous composition.[286,287,293] These chondroid areas, which often exhibit endochondral ossification, are mixed with spindle areas with an aneurysmal bone cyst-like appearance. Most of the cases are already present at birth, and the behavior is benign.

Osteochondroma

Osteochondroma is the most frequent benign bone tumor. It is usually asymptomatic, but it may lead to deformity or interfere with the function of adjacent structures such as tendons and blood vessels.[305] It may also undergo spontaneous regression.[304] The most common locations are the metaphyses of the lower femur, upper tibia, upper humerus, and pelvis. The radiographic appearance of osteochondroma is very characteristic; one of the most typical features is the fact that the lesions, when located in metaphyses of long bones, grow out in a direction opposite to the adjacent joint.

The average age of the patient at onset is approximately 10 years; in the large majority of the cases, the tumor appears before the patient is 20 years old.

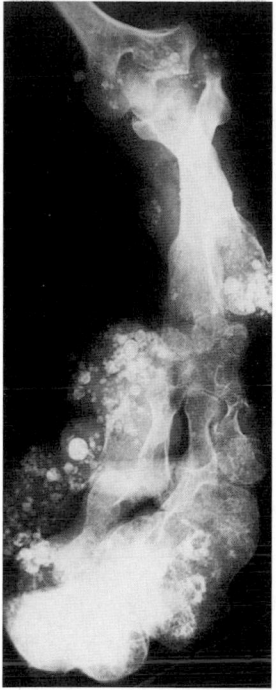
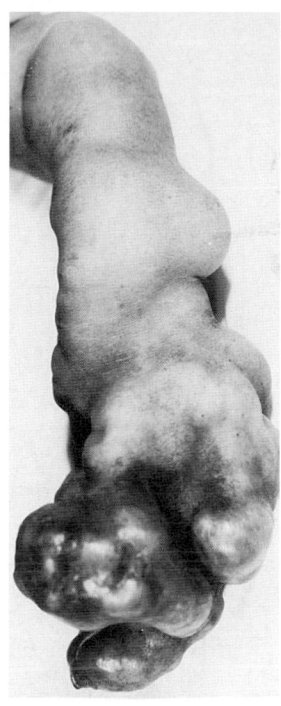

A

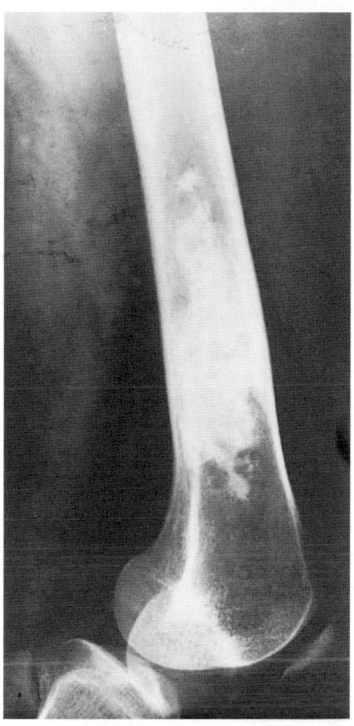

Fig. 24.34 Large asymptomatic enchondroma of femur in a 42-year-old woman. The tumor is extensively calcified.

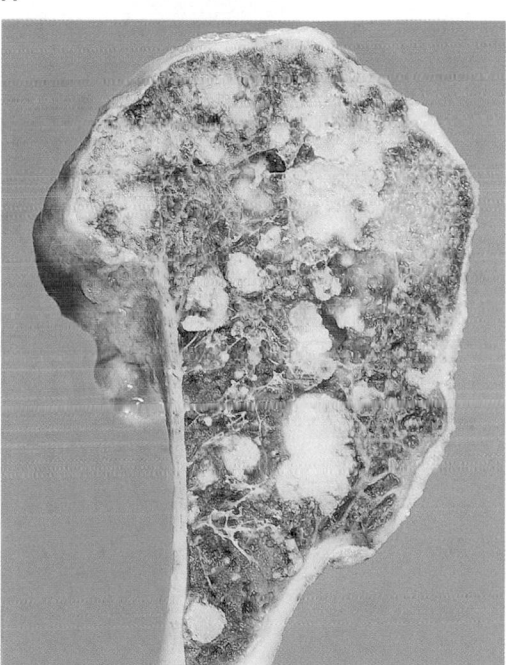

B

Fig. 24.33 A, Arm of a patient affected by Maffucci's syndrome. Innumerable chondromas are seen concentrated in the distal aspect of the extremity. The patient developed chondrosarcoma in the innominate bone, with pulmonary metastases. **B** Gross appearance of head of humerus affected by multiple chondromas in a patient with Ollier's disease. (**A**, Courtesy of Dr. O Urteaga A, Lima, Peru; **B**, Courtesy of Dr. RA Cooke, Brisbane, Australia; from Cooke RA, Stewart B: Colour Atlas of Anatomical Pathology. Edinburgh, Churchill Livingstone, 2004.)

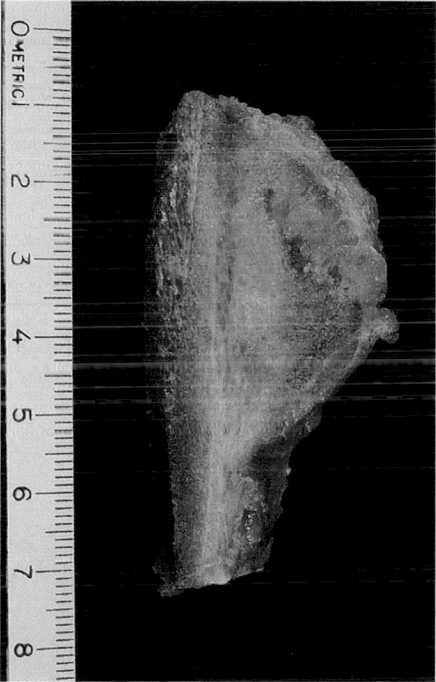

Fig. 24.35 Gross appearance of juxtacortical chondroma. The tumor produces a semispherical expansion of the involved bone.

The average greatest diameter is approximately 4 cm, but the tumors may reach sizes of 10 cm or more. The smaller tumors are sessile, whereas the larger ones tend to be pedunculated. Characteristically, there is a cap of cartilage covered by a fibrous membrane, which is continuous with the periosteum of the adjacent bone. This cap is usually lobulated in the large lesions (Figs 24.37 and 24.38). Its average thickness is about 0.6 cm; it is rare for it to exceed 1 cm. Microscopically, the cells resemble those of normal hyaline cartilage. Eosinophilic, PAS-positive inclusions may be seen in the cytoplasm.[304,307] The bulk of the lesion is made up of mature bone trabeculae located beneath the cartilaginous cap and containing normal bone marrow. At the interphase between cartilage and bone, there is active endochondral ossification. In older lesions, the cap thins out and may disappear altogether. A bursa may develop around the head of a longstanding osteochondroma; in turn, this bursa may develop complications such as osteocartilaginous loose bodies, synovial chondrometaplasia, and—exceptionally—chondrosarcoma.[308]

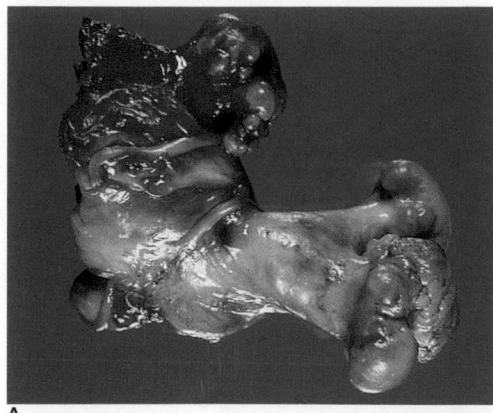

A

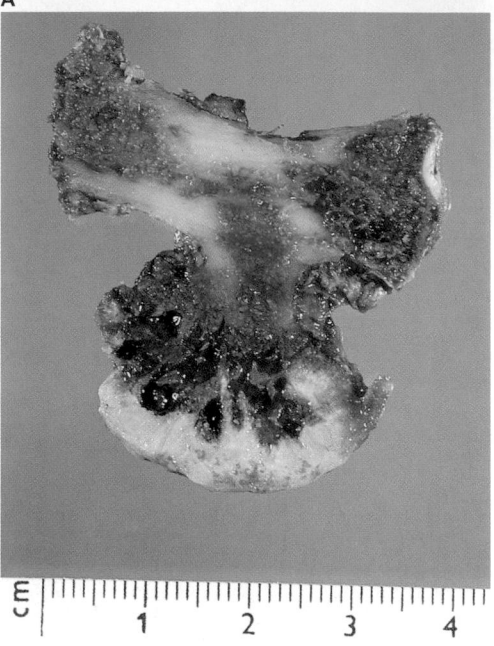

B

Fig. 24.37 A, Large osteochondroma of femur with a bilobed appearance. **B** Cut surface of osteochondroma of rib. Note the thick cartilaginous cup. (Courtesy of Dr. RA Cooke, Brisbane, Australia; from Cooke RA, Stewart B: Colour Atlas of Anatomical Pathology. Edinburgh, Churchill Livingstone, 2004)

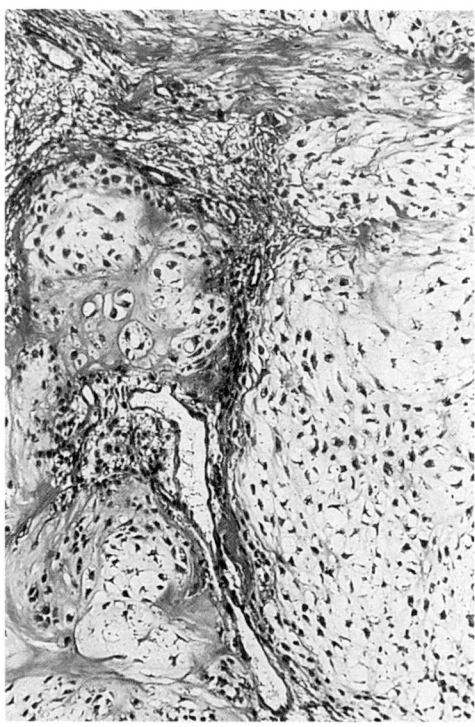

Fig. 24.36 Enchondroma of phalanx. The tumor has a typical lobulated appearance.

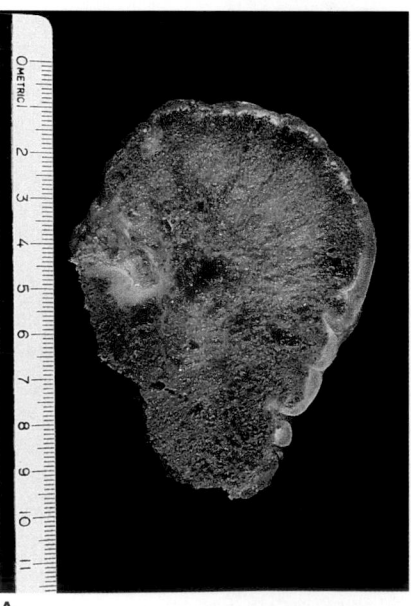

A

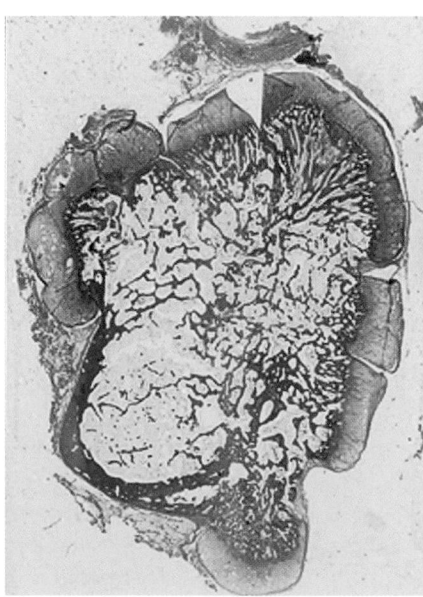

B

Fig. 24.38 Gross and whole-mount appearance of osteochondroma. Mature bone is covered by a well-differentiated cartilaginous cap.

The gross and microscopic appearance of a single lesion of the familial condition known as **osteochondromatosis** (multiple cartilaginous exostoses, Ehrenfried's hereditary deforming chondrodysplasia, diaphyseal aclasis) cannot be distinguished from solitary osteochondroma.[314] A very small proportion of the solitary tumors evolve into chondrosarcomas, but the incidence reaches 10% in the cases with multiple lesions.[313] The progression from osteochondroma to chondrosarcoma is associated with upregulation of PTHrP and bcl-2 expression.[300] Cytogenetically, clonal karyotypic abnormalities have been found in both sporadic and hereditary osteochondromas, most often involving chromosomal loci 8q24.1 and 11p11-12 (EXT2).[301]

Osteochondroma should be distinguished from the **bizarre parosteal osteochondromatous proliferation (Nora's lesion)**, which may occur in the bones of the hands and feet[306,312] and occasionally in long bones[299]; these lesions are radiographically distinctive but can simulate chondrosarcoma microscopically because of the presence of enlarged, bizarre, and binucleated chondrocytes.[310,312]

Subungual exostosis (Dupuytren's exostosis) is usually located on the great toe. It is thought to represent a different entity from osteochondromas but is also composed of a proliferating cartilaginous cap that merges into mature trabecular bone at its base. These exostoses may recur but are invariably benign.[309,311]

Osteochondromyxoma is a recently described congenital neoplasm associated with lentigines and other extraskeletal disorders; the syndrome seems to represent a variation of the Carney's complex.[302]

Chondroblastoma

Chondroblastoma occurs predominantly in males under 20 years of age, and it can be quite painful.[334] It usually arises in the epiphyseal end of long bones before the epiphyseal cartilage has disappeared, particularly in the distal end of the femur, proximal end of the humerus, and proximal end of the tibia[334] (Fig. 24.39).

Radiographically, the tumor usually is fairly well delimited and contains areas of rarefaction (Fig. 24.40). From the epiphysis it may extend into the metaphyseal area or the articular cavity. Occasionally, it is found entirely in a metaphyseal location or in a small bone.[315]

Microscopically, this lesion may be confusing because of its extreme cellularity and variability.[318a] The occasional scattered collections of giant cells may lead to an erroneous diagnosis of giant cell tumor (Fig. 24.41). The basic tumor cell is an embryonic chondroblast with only a limited capacity for the production of a cartilaginous matrix. The shape of this cell is usually polyhedral, although spindle elements can also be present. The cell membrane appears thick and sharply defined. The nuclei vary in shape from round to indented and lobulated; some resemble those of Langerhans' cells[325] (Fig. 24.42).

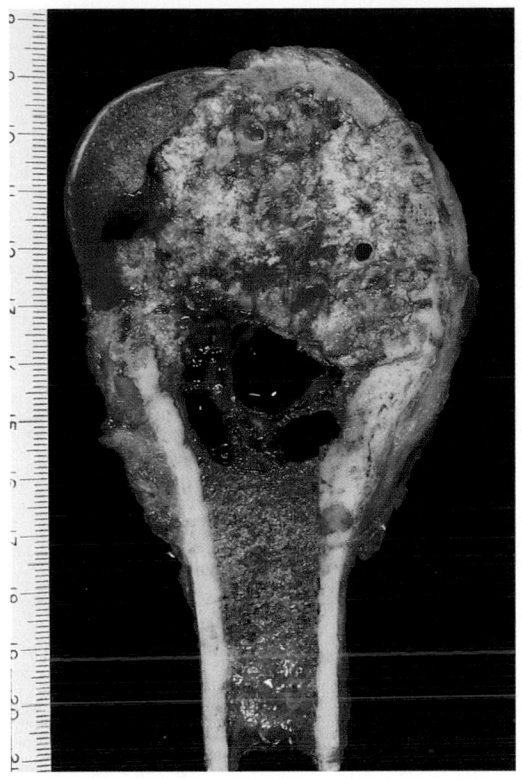

Fig. 24.39 Gross appearance of chondroblastoma of upper end of the humerus, associated with aneurysmal bone cyst-like changes.

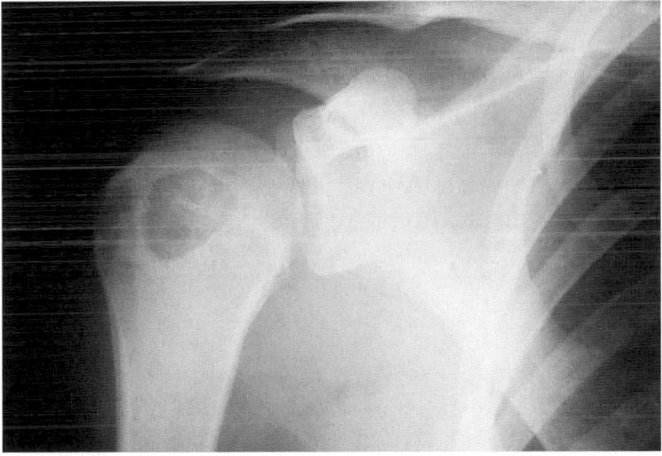

Fig. 24.40 Typical sharply delineated lytic appearance of chondroblastoma of humeral head.

Mitoses are exceptional. Intracytoplasmic glycogen granules are present, sometimes in large numbers. Reticulin fibers surround each individual cell. Recurrent lesions may show some degree of atypia, a feature that should not be interpreted as a sign of malignant change. A distinctive microscopic change is the presence of small zones of focal calcification. These zones range from a network of thin lines ("chicken wire") to obvious deposits surrounded by giant cells.

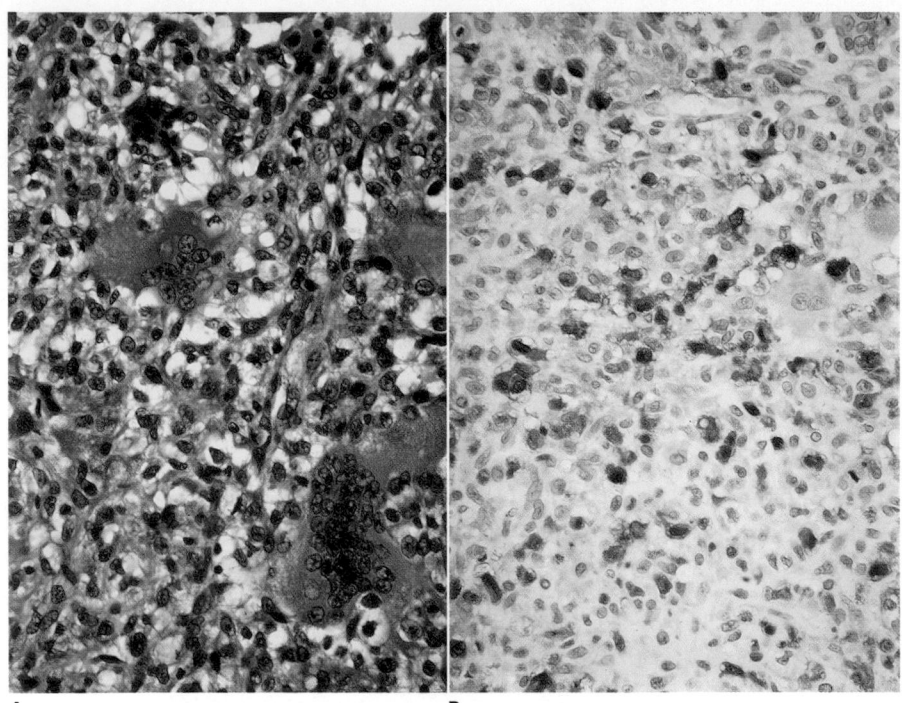

Fig. 24.41 A and **B**, Chondroblastoma. **A**, Small tumor cells of round shape are accompanied by scattered osteoclasts. **B**, Immunoreactivity for S-100 protein in the neoplastic component.

In approximately one fourth of the cases, areas resembling aneurysmal bone cyst are seen engrafted on the primary bone lesion[334] (see Fig. 24.39). In patients with recurrent lesions, the incidence of this phenomenon rises to 50%.

By electron microscopy, the cells of chondroblastoma closely resemble normal epiphyseal cartilage cells grown in tissue culture.[335,337] They often have a prominent "fibrous lamina" lying against the inner aspect of the nuclear membrane, resulting in the membrane thickening seen by light microscopy.[321] Cytoplasmic glycogen is usually abundant. Proteoglycans and calcium have been demonstrated by ultrastructural cytochemistry in the extracellular matrix.[326] Immunohistochemically, the cells of osteoblastoma coexpress vimentin and S-100 protein

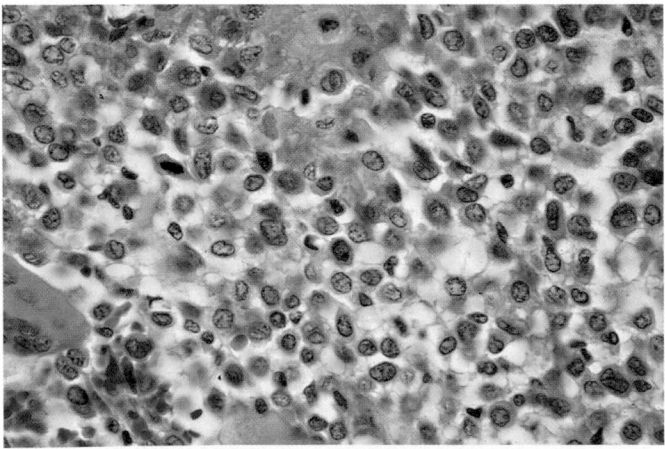

Fig. 24.42 Histiocyte-like appearance of the nuclei of chondroblastoma cells.

(Fig. 24.41B). They may also be immunoreactive for neuron-specific enolase, muscle-specific actin, and low-molecular-weight keratins.[330,333]

The histogenesis of chondroblastoma has been controversial. It has been variously regarded as a "chondromatous" variant of giant cell tumor, as arising from histiocytic or "reticuloendothelial cells," and as a truly cartilaginous neoplasm. The frequent areas of calcification, the occasional foci of well-developed cartilaginous stroma, the histochemical and ultrastructural profile, and the immunohistochemical positivity for S-100 protein all point toward a cartilaginous nature.[317,320,325–328]

The diagnosis is possible on the basis of fine needle aspiration material, which in a typical case will consist of neoplastic chondroblasts, multinucleated osteoclast-like giant cells, and chondroid matrix fragments.[319] Curettement with bone grafting, which is the preferred treatment, provides local control in over 80% of the cases.[318] Local recurrences can be treated similarly.[336]

Several cases of chondroblastoma, microscopically indistinguishable from the rest, have behaved locally in an aggressive fashion, invading the soft tissues and developing tumor thrombi in lymph channels. Most of these aggressive tumors were located in the pelvis.[331] A few others have given rise to distant metastases, usually to the lungs.[316,322,324,329] In nearly all of the reported cases of this phenomenon, the metastases have occurred after surgical manipulation of the primary tumor.[323,324,332]

Chondromyxoid fibroma and related tumors
Chondromyxoid fibroma of bone is an unusual benign tumor of cartilaginous origin.[345,354] It usually occurs in a long bone of a young adult, but it has also been reported

in the small bones of the hands and feet, pelvis, vertebrae, and skull base; in the latter location there is a risk of it being misdiagnosed as chordoma or chondrosarcoma.[343]

Radiographically, it is sharply defined and may attain a large size (Fig. 24.43). Grossly, it is solid and yellowish white or tan, replaces bone, and thins the cortex (Fig. 24.44). Microscopically, it comprises hypocellular lobules with a myxochondroid appearance, separated by intersecting bands of highly cellular tissue composed of fibroblast-like spindle cells and osteoclasts[341] (Fig. 24.45).

The occasional presence of large pleomorphic cells may result in an erroneous diagnosis of chondrosarcoma.[338,352,355] However, mitotic figures are exceptional. Some tumors show a combination of the features of chondroblastoma and chondromyxoid fibroma.[340]

Immunohistochemical reactivity for S-100 protein is the rule, in keeping with its presumed cartilaginous nature,[339] but there are also cells with myofibroblastic and myochondroblastic features.[350] The intercellular matrix is primarily of a cartilaginous nature but it exhibits significant differences from that present in any other cartilaginous neoplasm.[353]

Cytogenetically, recurrent anomalies of 6q25 have been found.[351] The most characteristic of these consist of the pericentrometric inversion inv(6)(p25q23).[342]

Local recurrence follows curettage of chondromyxoid fibroma in about 25% of the cases, sometimes after an interval as long as 30 years.[344] Because of this, en bloc excision is recommended whenever possible. Soft tissue extension or implantation may occur,[346,355] but distant metastases have not been reported.

Fibromyxoma is microscopically similar to chondromyxoid fibroma but lacks cartilaginous areas and tends to occur in older individuals.[347,348]

Myxoma of long bones is characterized by an expansile radiographic appearance, distal location, benign behavior, and microscopic appearance similar to soft tissue myxoma.[349]

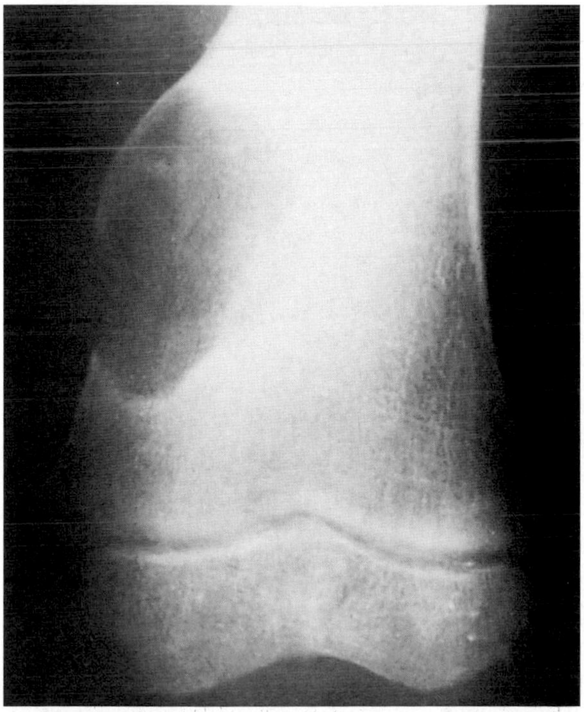

Fig. 24.44 Chondromyxoid fibroma of proximal femur extending into soft tissue. This rare event should not be regarded as evidence of malignancy.

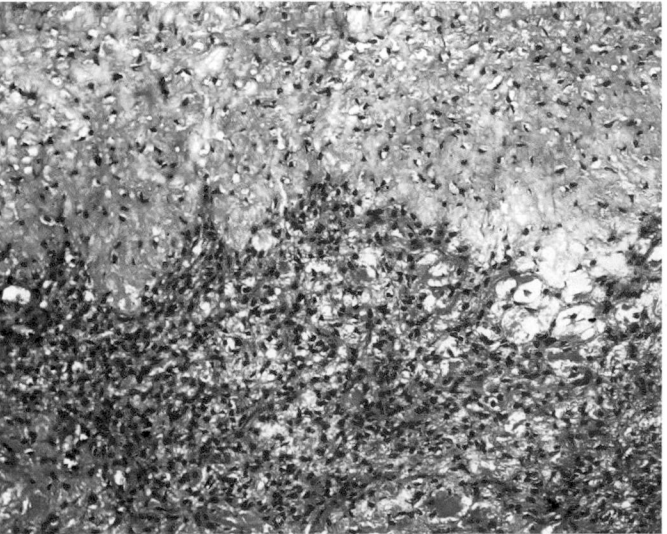

Fig. 24.43 Sharply delimited chondromyxoid fibroma of lower femoral metaphysis in a young boy.

Fig. 24.45 Chondromyxoid fibroma. The tumor has a lobulated appearance, in which myxochondroid islands alternate with more cellular foci.

Chondrosarcoma

Chondrosarcoma, a malignant tumor of cartilage-forming tissues, is divided into two major categories on the basis of microscopic criteria: conventional chondrosarcoma and chondrosarcoma variants. Each of these categories comprises several distinct types, some defined on microscopic grounds and others on the basis of location within the affected bone.

Conventional chondrosarcoma. The majority of the patients with conventional chondrosarcoma are between 30 and 60 years of age. Chondrosarcoma in childhood is distinctly uncommon[371,406] and tends more often to be located in the extremities than its adult counterpart[375]; most malignant bone tumors in this age group exhibiting cartilage formation are actually osteosarcomas with a predominant cartilaginous component.

Chondrosarcomas are divided according to location into central, peripheral, and juxtacortical (periosteal) forms.[362] **Central chondrosarcomas** are located in the medullary cavity, usually of a flat or long bone [360] (Figs 24.46). Radiographically, they present a rather characteristic picture of an osteolytic lesion with splotchy

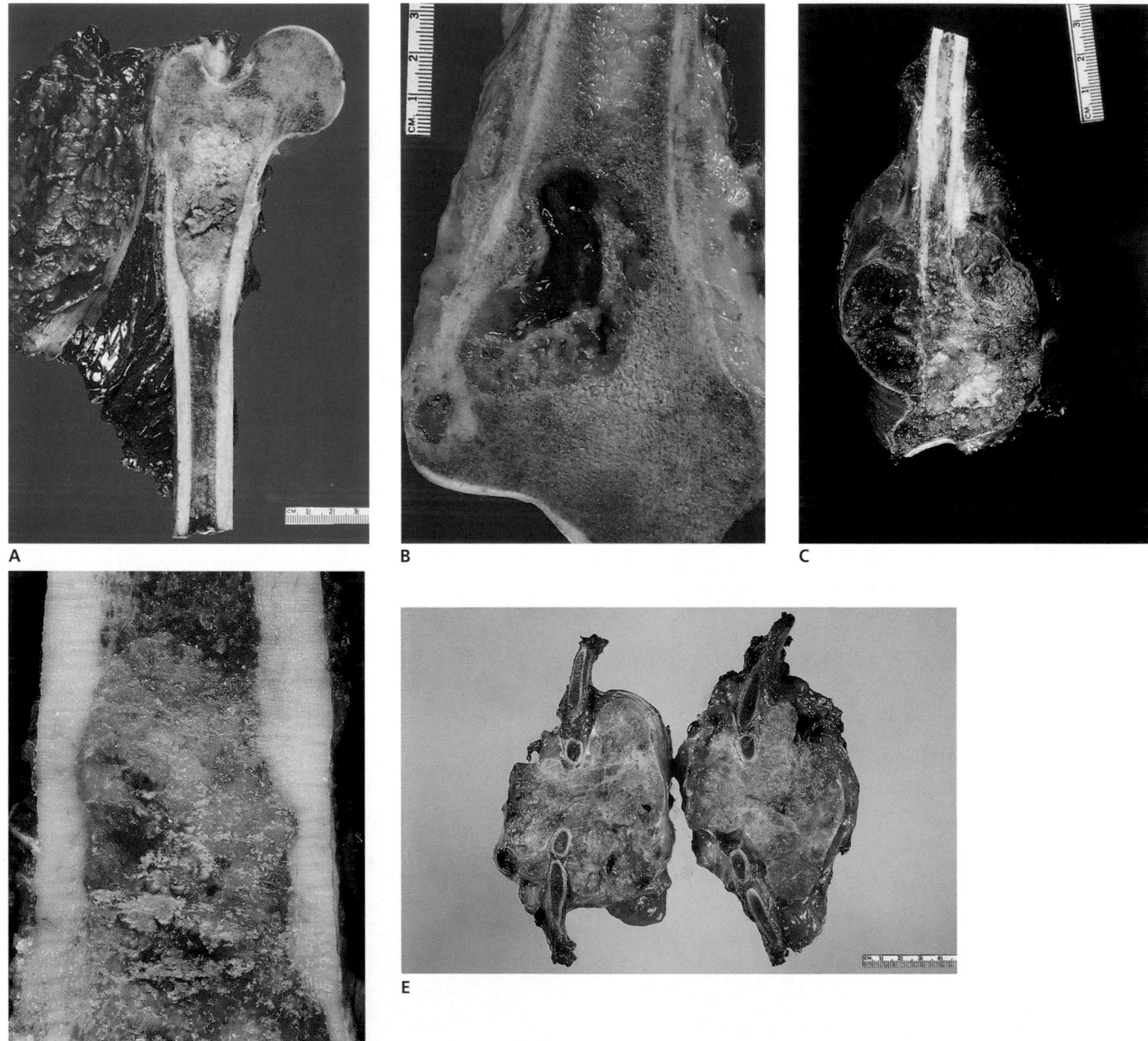

A

B

C

D

E

Fig. 24.46 Gross appearances of central chondrosarcoma: **A** to **D**, all of these tumors were located in the femur, the single most common site of occurrence; **E**, chondrosarcoma of rib, resulting in massive expansion of the bone.

calcification (Fig. 24.47). Ill-defined margins, fusiform thickening of the shaft, and perforation of the cortex are three important diagnostic signs.[357] In advanced stages, they may break through the cortex but only rarely grow beyond the periosteum. The pelvic bones, ribs (usually at the costochondral junction), and shoulder girdle are the most common locations. Chondrosarcomas of the small bones of the hands and feet are exceptional but have

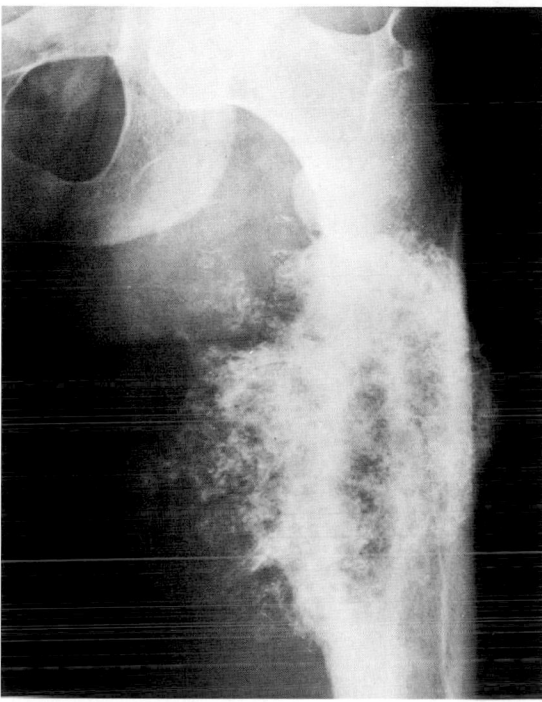

Fig. 24.47 Typical chondrosarcoma of femur showing splotchy calcification and extensive cortical destruction.

been described by several authors, particularly in the os calcis.[361,366,381,391,395] Chondrosarcoma can also involve the bones of the skull, especially the temporal bone and base of the skull, where the differential diagnosis includes chordoma, meningioma, and glomus jugulare tumor.[364,397]

Peripheral chondrosarcomas may arise de novo or from the cartilaginous cap of a preexisting osteochondroma (Fig. 24.48). Osteochondromatosis is particularly prone to this complication, as already indicated. In the 212 cases of chondrosarcoma reported by Dahlin and Henderson,[365] 19 apparently arose from osteochondroma. The risk of malignant transformation in a solitary osteochondroma is believed to be between 1% and 2%. The signs of malignancy in an osteochondroma include increased growth during adolescence, a diameter over 8 cm, and a cartilaginous cap that is irregular and thicker than 3 cm. Radiographically, peripheral chondrosarcomas present as large tumors, with a heavily calcified center surrounded by a lesser denser periphery with splotchy calcification (Fig. 24.49). Malignant change should be suspected radiographically in an osteochondroma if the cartilage cap has irregular margins or if there are lucent zones within the lesion.[372]

Juxtacortical (periosteal) chondrosarcoma involves the shaft of a long bone (most often the femur) and is characterized by a cartilaginous lobular pattern with areas of spotty calcification and endochondral ossification.[400] This tumor is closely related to the entity reported as periosteal osteosarcoma (see p. 2155). However, some minor differences in location, microscopic grade, and behavior between the two have been described.[359]

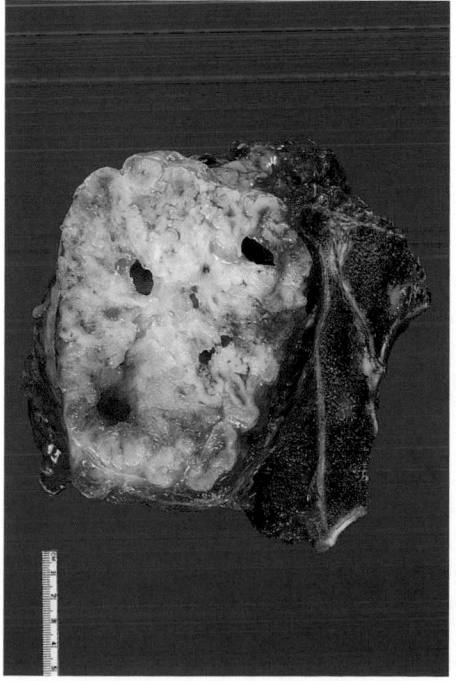

A

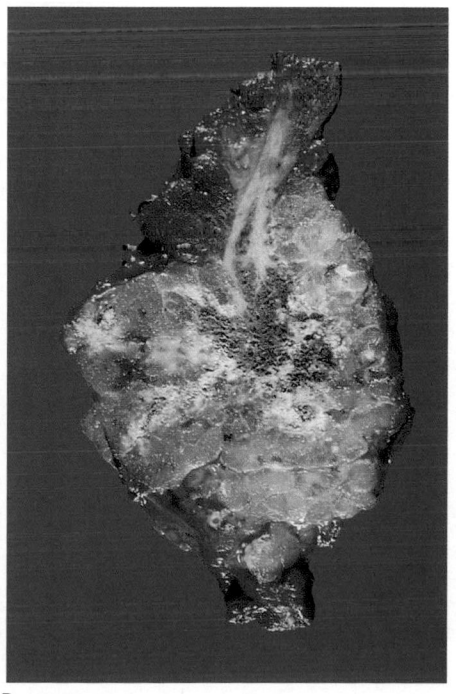

B

Fig. 24.48 A and **B**, Gross appearances of chondrosarcoma. **A**, Peripheral chondrosarcoma of femur resulting in a huge exophytic mass. **B**, Large expansile chondrosarcoma of sternum. (**A**, Courtesy of Dr. Juan Jose Segura, San José, Costa Rica)

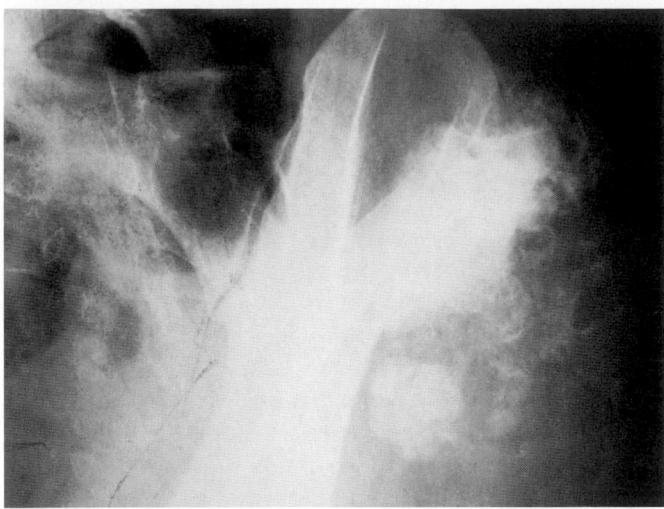

Fig. 24.49 Typical radiographic appearance of peripheral chondrosarcoma of innominate bone. (Courtesy of Dr. WT Hill, Houston)

Microscopically, conventional chondrosarcomas of central, peripheral, or juxtacortical types show a remarkably wide range of differentiation, the common denominator being the production of a cartilaginous matrix and the lack of direct bone formation by the tumor cells. This range in differentiation is the basis for the grading of these tumors into well, moderately, and poorly differentiated. The differential diagnosis between well-differentiated chondrosarcoma and chondroma rests on a combination of radiographic, architectural, and cytologic features[401] (Fig. 24.50). In well-differentiated chondrosarcoma, the nuclei are plump and hyperchromatic; there may be two or more nuclei per cell and two or more cells per lacuna (Fig. 24.51). Mirra et al.[389] have emphasized permeation of the bone marrow with trapping of host lamellar bone on all sides in well-differentiated chondrosarcoma as an important sign in the differential diagnosis with chondroma. Both the nuclear and architectural abnormalities of chondrosarcoma are often better seen at

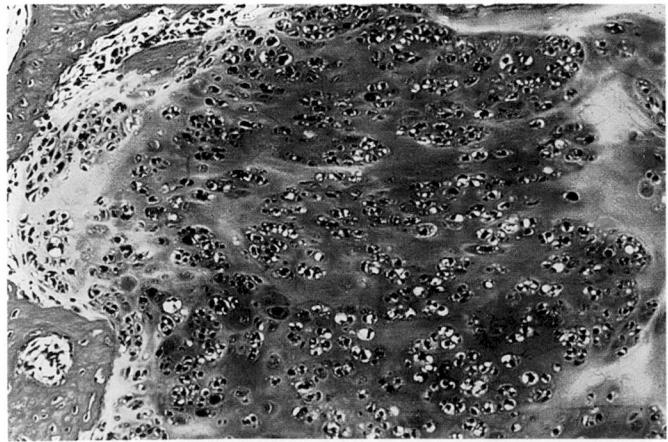

Fig. 24.50 Well-differentiated chondrosarcoma. The tumor has a distinctly lobulated quality.

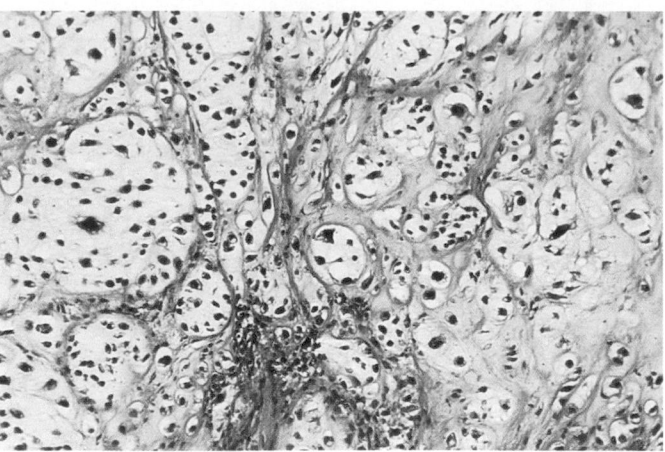

Fig. 24.51 Microscopic appearance of well-differentiated chondrosarcoma. The tumor retains a lobulated appearance, but nuclear atypicality is obvious.

the growing edge of the tumor. Correlation of the microscopic features with the clinical and especially the radiographic findings is essential. Large tumors of the long bones or ribs or those that begin to grow rapidly over adolescence and reach a size of 8 cm or more are almost invariably malignant.[386] Minor degrees of atypia in the cartilaginous cells under these circumstances justify a diagnosis of chondrosarcoma, whereas similar or even greater atypical changes in cartilaginous tumors of the hands and feet, osteochondromas, synovial osteochondromatosis, and soft tissue neoplasms are much less significant. It also should be noted that the minor atypical changes on which the diagnosis of malignancy are based are often focal, a point to remember when examining a small sample of a cartilaginous neoplasm.

Chondrosarcoma is distinguished from osteosarcoma by the lack of direct osteoid or bone formation by the tumor cells. Bone can be present in a bona fide chondrosarcoma, but this is non-neoplastic and probably originates from reabsorption of the tumor cartilage by a mechanism of endochondral ossification.

Histochemically, well-differentiated chondrosarcomas have a staining reaction similar to that of adult cartilage, whereas poorly differentiated tumors resemble fetal cartilage.[376] Biochemically, a marked variability in composition has been observed.[384,385] Ultrastructurally, the cells of well-differentiated tumors show cytoplasmic accumulation of glycogen, lipid droplets, and dilated cisternae of granular endoplasmic reticulum.[368] Immunohistochemically, there is reactivity for S-100 protein[390,392] (Fig. 24.52).

Cytogenetically, there is considerable heterogeneity among chondrosarcomas but also evidence that some of the karyotypic anomalies are not random.[382,383,397a]

Amplification of the c-*myc* oncogene and expression of Her2/neu, c-Fos and c-jun genes the c-*erb*B-2 oncogene have been detected in chondrosarcomas.[363,370,405] Overexpression of p53 is limited to the high-grade (poorly differentiated) types.[367,394,404]

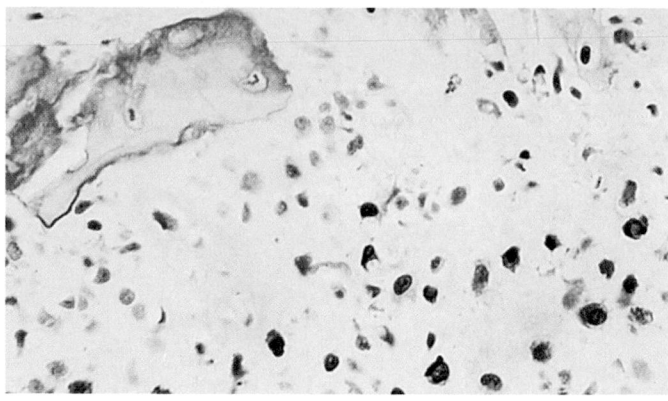

Fig. 24.52 Chondrosarcoma of bone. There is both cytoplasmic and nuclear staining for S-100 protein.

Soft tissue implantation following biopsy is a well-known complication of chondrosarcoma. Therefore if a large cartilaginous tumor is so located that the biopsy site cannot be entirely excised, the initial excision should be complete. If an extremely large tumor involves the pelvic bone, wide block excision or even hemipelvectomy is justified without prior histologic diagnosis. Chondrosarcomas of the rib should be excised en bloc with the adjacent uninvolved ribs and pleura.[387,388,393] Well-differentiated chondrosarcomas of the extremities are amenable to conservative therapy in the form of segmental resection.[403]

In contrast to osteosarcoma, microscopic grading of chondrosarcomas, whether done by a combination of cytoarchitectural features[369] or by nuclear grade alone,[378] is of value in predicting the final outcome. In the series reported by McKenna et al.,[388] the 5-year survival rates were 78%, 53%, and 22% for low-, moderate-, and high-grade tumors, respectively. In three more recent series,

the overall survival figures were generally better, but the differences between the three grades were still obvious.[369,373,374,396,398] Recurrences often are of a higher microscopic grade than the original tumor.[379] Equally important prognostically is the adequacy of initial therapy.[358,373,402] Preliminary results with flow cytometry suggest that determination of DNA ploidy may be an important prognostic determinator.[356,377,380] An association between 6q13-21 chromosome aberrations and locally aggressive behavior has been described.[399] High-grade chondrosarcomas metastasize early, particularly to the lungs. Lymph node metastases are practically nonexistent.

Chondrosarcoma variants

Clear cell chondrosarcoma. Clear cell chondrosarcoma is characterized by tumor cells with an abundant clear or ground glass cytoplasm and sharply defined borders, often interspersed with small trabeculae of woven bone.[411,412] It may be confused with chondroblastoma and may actually represent its malignant counterpart[413] (Fig. 24.53). Ultrastructurally, it shows chondroid cells in various stages of differentiation[409] and, immunohistochemically, exhibits immunoreactivity for S-100 protein and collagens types II and X (but not I).[407,412,413] Most patients are older than those affected by chondroblastoma.[408] Radiographically, the lesion is usually entirely lytic, slightly expansile, and sharply marginated.[408] Most of the cases have involved the proximal end of the femur or humerus, and the behavior has been that of a low-grade malignancy. However—and like conventional chondrosarcoma—it can undergo dedifferentiation.[410]

Myxoid chondrosarcoma (chordoid sarcoma). This variant of chondrosarcoma can occur in bone but is much more common in the soft tissues (see Chapter 25).[416,418] It is

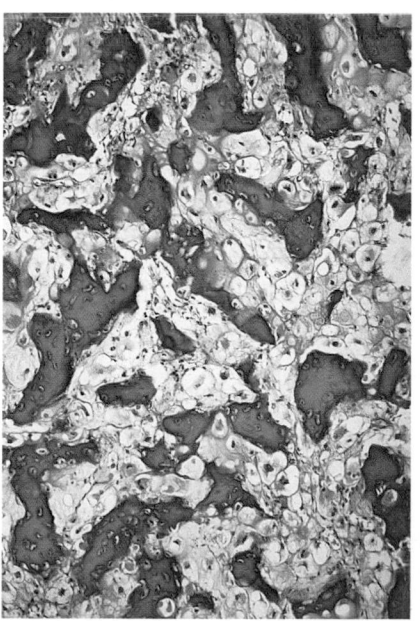

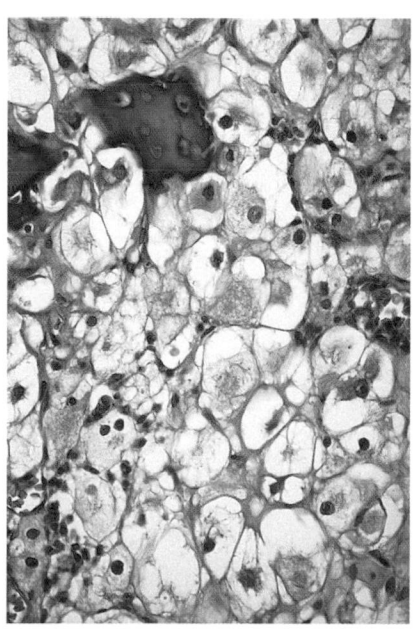

A   B

Fig. 24.53 A and **B**, Clear cell chondrosarcoma. **A,** Low-power appearance showing numerous bone trabeculae that may result in a mistaken diagnosis of osteosarcoma. **B,** High-power view showing plump and vacuolated appearance of the tumor cells. S-100 protein was strongly immunoreactive.

morphologically reminiscent of chordoma because of the rows of cuboidal cells separated by a myxoid background.[419] It reacts immunohistochemically for S-100 protein and vimentin but, in contrast to chordoma, is negative for keratin.[420] Ultrastructurally, it is closer in appearance to conventional chondrosarcoma than to chordoma.[421] Whether the tumor reported by Dabska[417] as **parachordoma** is also histogenetically related to myxoid chondrosarcoma remains to be determined.[422]

Dedifferentiated chondrosarcoma. The term dedifferentiated chondrosarcoma refers to the presence of a poorly differentiated sarcomatous component at the periphery of an otherwise typical low-grade chondrosarcoma.[427,432] The chondrosarcoma is usually of the central type, but it can also be peripheral[425,435] (Fig. 24.54). The dedifferentiation can be found in the initial lesion but occurs more often in specimens from recurrent tumor. The microscopic appearance of this component may be that of rhabdomyosarcoma, fibrosarcoma, osteosarcoma, or pleomorphic sarcoma with MFH-like features (Fig. 24.55).[430,436] As such, it is phenotypically different from the preexisting chondrosarcoma. Accordingly, these areas may acquire immunohistochemical positivity for alpha-1-antichymotrypsin, actin, desmin, myoglobin, and exceptionally even keratin.[428,438] In some cases, however, there is some ultrastructural and immunohistochemical (S-100 protein) preservation of the cartilaginous character of the tumor in the anaplastic portion.[423,429] Simultaneous cytogenetic and immunophenotyping studies indicate that both the differentiated and the "dedifferentiated" components originate from a common primitive mes-

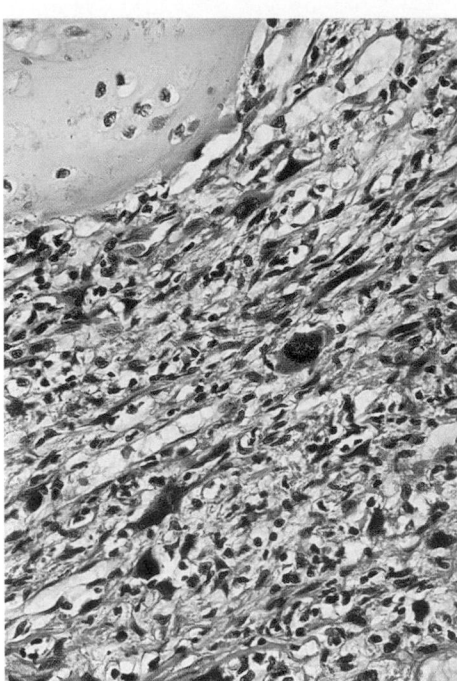

Fig. 24.55 Microscopic appearance of dedifferentiated chondrosarcoma. The edge of an island of well-differentiated cartilage (upper left) is surrounded by highly pleomorphic sarcoma containing tumor giant cells.

enchymal cell progenitor, and that the term "dedifferentiated" may be an inaccurate designation.[424,426] At the molecular level, the process of anaplastic transformation is accompanied by overexpression of *p53* and H-*ras* mutation.[437]

Regardless of terminology, the development of this component in chondrosarcoma is accompanied by a marked acceleration of the clinical course and a decidedly worsened prognosis.[431,433,434] The overall 5-year survival rate is quoted at 10% but in the pelvis it is in the neighbourhood of 35%.[424a]

Mesenchymal chondrosarcoma. Mesenchymal chondrosarcoma is a specific variant of chondrosarcoma characterized microscopically by a dimorphic pattern in which areas of well-differentiated cartilage alternate with undifferentiated stroma[439,441,449,450] (Fig. 24.56). The boundaries between the two components are usually abrupt. The undifferentiated element is composed of small cells and can be confused with malignant lymphoma, hemangiopericytoma, and Ewing's sarcoma. It should be noted that despite the apparently undifferentiated nature of this component at both the light and electron microscopic level, pleomorphism and mitotic activity are inconspicuous.[450,451] Immunohistochemically, the small cell component is positive for vimentin, CD99, and Leu7 but not for S-100 protein[444]; the latter is found instead in the chondroid areas.[458] There is also nuclear immunoreactivity for Sox9, a master regulator of chondrogenesis.[452a]

Most patients are in the second or third decade of life. The radiographic appearance resembles that of conven-

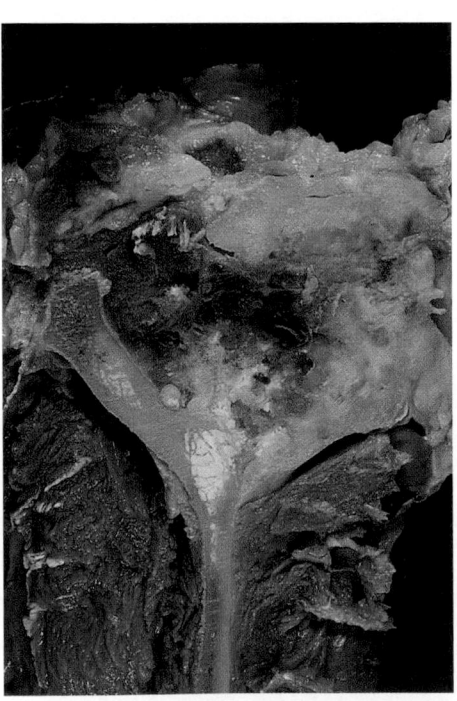

Fig. 24.54 Gross appearance of dedifferentiated chondrosarcoma of pelvic bone.

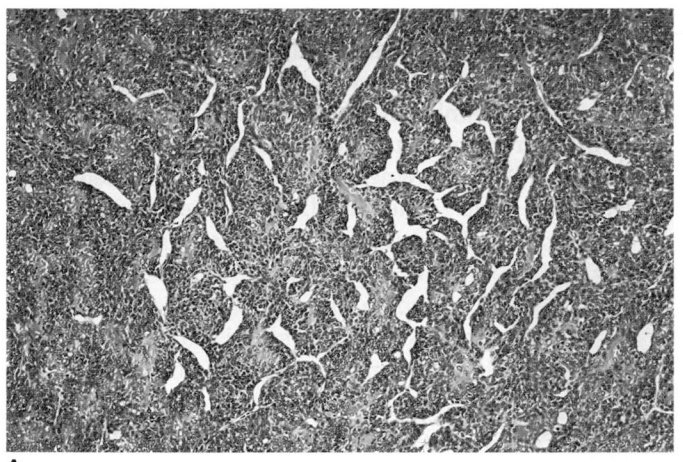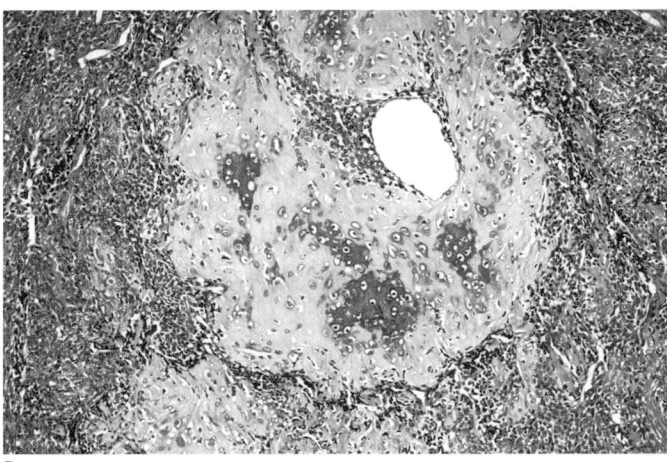

A　　　　　　　　　　　　　　　　　　　　　　　　　　**B**

Fig. 24.56 Mesenchymal chondrosarcoma: **A** illustrates a cellular, hemangiopericytoma-like component; **B** shows an island of well-differentiated cartilage in the center.

tional chondrosarcomas. The bones most commonly affected are the jaw, pelvis, femur, ribs, and spine.[449] A high percentage of these neoplasms involve extraosseous structures, such as the orbit, paraspinal region, meninges, or soft tissues of the extremities.[443,445] The prognosis is generally poor, although there is great variability in the clinical course.[446,450]

It has been proposed that mesenchymal chondrosarcoma represents a neoplastic caricature of embryonal endochondral osteogenesis.[440] Jacobson[447] postulated that mesenchymal chondrosarcoma is one morphologic type of the bone tumor that he proposes to call *polyhistioma*. He defines it as a malignant neoplasm whose basic cells are small and round, like those of Ewing's sarcoma, but that differentiate into various mesenchymal structures, such as bone and cartilage, and sometimes even into epithelial tissues. Additional case reports have confirmed the existence of multipotential bone tumors composed of a mixture of mesenchymal (chondrosarcoma) and epithelial (squamous cell carcinoma) elements.[442,448]

Giant cell tumor

Giant cell tumor (osteoclastoma) is usually seen in patients over 20 years of age.[462] It is more common in women than in men and seems to occur more frequently in Oriental than in Western countries.[505]

The classic location is the epiphysis of a long bone, from which it may spread into the metaphyseal area, break through the cortex, invade intermuscular septa, or even cross a joint space. The sites most commonly affected (in order of frequency) are the lower end of the femur, the upper end of the tibia, and the lower end of the radius.[462] It also occurs in the humerus, fibula, and skull, particularly the sphenoid bone.[458,465,511] Occasionally, a giant cell tumor will be seen in a child[490] and/or in a metaphyseal or diaphyseal location.[467] Involvement of the bones of the hands and feet, jaw, and vertebrae (other than sacrum) is distinctly unusual. Although giant cell tumor has been documented at these sites,[459,498,510] the occurrence of a giant cell-containing lesion in any of these locations should suggest an alternative diagnosis. Multicentricity has been reported, particularly in young patients and in the small bones of hands and feet[471a] (see p. 2171).

Radiographically, the typical appearance of a giant cell tumor is that of an entirely lytic, expansile lesion in the epiphysis, usually without peripheral bone sclerosis, or periosteal reaction (Fig. 24.57).

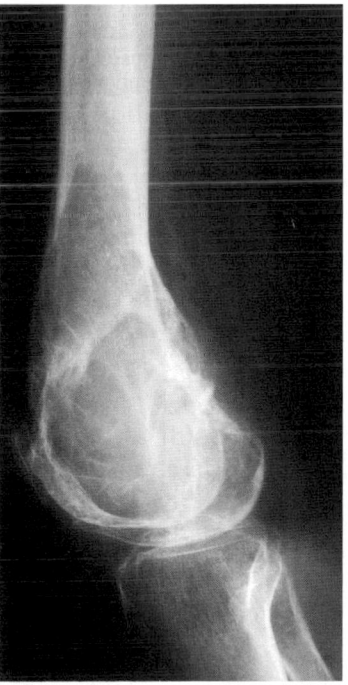

Fig. 24.57 Typical radiograph of giant cell tumor of distal end of femur involving epiphysis and metaphyseal area. The lesion was resected surgically. (From Sissons HA. Malignant tumors of bone and cartilage. In Raven RW (ed.): Cancer, vol. 2. London, 1958, Butterworth)

of clinical malignancy (expressed by uncontrollable local recurrence or metastases) has been in the range of 10%.[463] The type of initial surgical removal is the most significant factor in recurrence; in one large series, the recurrence rate was 34% following curettage and 7% following wide resection.[480] A good relation also exists between surgical stage and prognosis[491]; in one series all cases of metastasizing giant cell tumor were deemed to be stage III lesions, with interruption of the cortex and soft tissue extension.[457]

It is also of interest that nearly all cases of metastases of giant cell tumor have occurred after a surgical intervention to the primary tumor, suggesting the possibility of mechanical disruption with access to the bloodstream. However, no relationship has been found between the presence of giant cells in blood vessels and prognosis. Microscopic grading of giant cell tumors is not of great value except for the obviously sarcomatous (grade III) lesions.[496] Indeed, some of these metastases have occurred in tumors with an entirely benign microscopic appearance (1% to 2% of all cases), and the metastases themselves may have a very innocuous look[493]; those developing in the lung, which are by far the most common, are often surrounded by a rim of mature bone. It should be mentioned here that grade III lesions are those characterized by the combination of pleomorphism, marked nuclear atypia, and high mitotic activity in the neoplastic mononuclear component, often accompanied by necrosis; exceptionally, bizarre (symplasmic) nuclear forms are seen in the absence of the other features, and these should not be labeled as malignant.[475]

Nonrandom chromosomal abnormalities have been found in giant cell tumors, particularly in the form of telomeric fusions[502]; these seem to be more common in the clinically more aggressive neoplasms.[461]

DNA ploidy analysis of giant cell tumors has not yet been shown to have prognostic value above and beyond that provided by the more conventional parameters.[469,474,497]

Similarly, no statistically significant relationship seems to exist between prognosis and either proliferation index or vascular density.[504] Instead, it has been claimed that tumors overexpressing p53 have a higher potential for recurrence and metastases.[479] As a matter of fact, the suggestion has been made that molecular abnormalities of p53 and H-ras underlie the process of malignant transformation in these tumors.[487]

Malignant giant cell tumor

As already mentioned, all giant cell tumors of bone should be regarded as potentially low-grade malignancies because of their tendency to recur and their occasional capacity to metastasize regardless of histologic appearance. A contentious issue is the existence of a cytologically malignant giant cell tumor (i.e., a lesion that retains the clinical, topographic, and general microscopic features of giant cell tumor but that exhibits clear-cut evidence of malignancy in the mononuclear stromal component). As such, it is equivalent to a grade III giant cell tumor. It represents a most unusual process, part of the reason being the conceptual and practical difficulties in separating it from other malignant tumors, particularly so-called giant cell-rich osteosarcoma (when osteoid production is present) and malignant fibrous histiocytoma (when osteoid production is absent).

On occasion, a typical benign-appearing giant cell tumor is seen in combination with but sharply segregated from a high-grade sarcoma. This phenomenon has been referred to as dedifferentiation, in analogy to the situation occurring more commonly with chondrosarcoma and chordoma.[482] In other instances a high-grade sarcoma is seen developing at the site of a previously treated giant cell tumor[456a] (Fig. 24.62).

Marrow tumors

Ewing's sarcoma/primitive neuroectodermal tumor

Ewing's sarcoma, traditionally regarded as an undifferentiated type of bone sarcoma of children, has now been linked with the neoplasm originally described in the soft tissues as primitive (or peripheral) neuroectodermal tumor (PNET), and the term Ewing's sarcoma/PNET (ES/PNET) is currently favored for this tumor family.[523] The best evidence for the pathogenetic unity of these processes is provided by the nearly universal presence of the genetic aberration to be described below.[534,535,541,552,567,583,597,600a] It has been commented that the bone tumors tend to be more undifferentiated (and therefore more in keeping with the original definition of James Ewing), whereas their soft tissue counterparts tend to show better evidence of neuroectodermal differentiation.[598,609] However, the overlap is considerable, as reflected by terms such as extraskeletal Ewing's sarcoma on one hand and PNET of bone on the other.[529,558,605,619,620] The link is also supported by the fact that neural differentiation can be induced in conventional Ewing's sarcoma of bone by agents such as dibutyril cyclic AMP, and retinoic acid[586] and that it can become very evident in post-therapy specimens.[529a] This unitary concept has also embraced the malignant small round cell tumor of the thoraco-pulmonary region (so-called Askin tumor), which is now regarded as an example of ES/PNET located in the chest wall.[519]

It should be made clear that this unitary concept does not include neuroblastoma and related tumors of the sympathetic nervous system, which lack the molecular aberrations of ES/PNET.[518]

Clinical features. ES/PNET of bone is usually seen in patients between the ages of 5 and 20 years,[564,626] with only a minority of the cases presenting in infancy or adulthood.[546,569,576,622] Clinically the tumor may simulate osteomyelitis because of pain, fever, and leukocytosis. It occurs most often in long bones (femur, tibia, humerus,

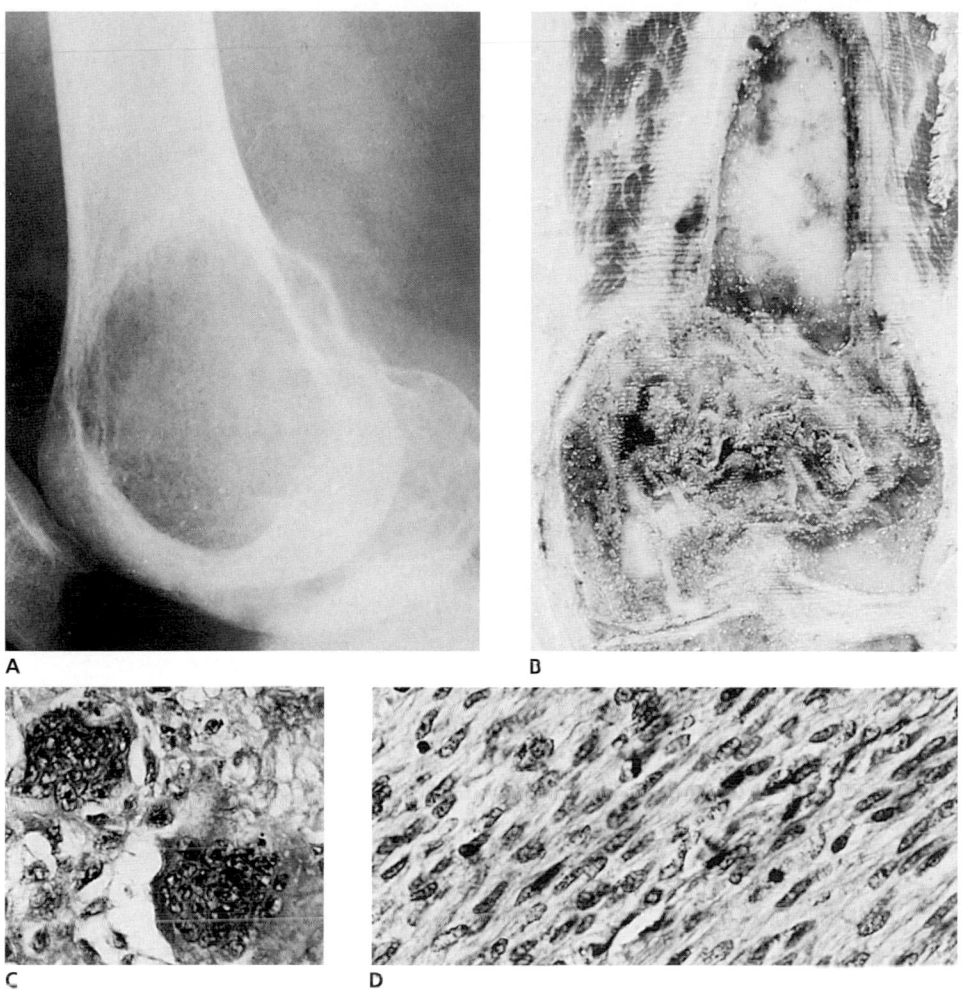

Fig. 24.62 A, Giant cell tumor of distal end of femur. The lesion was curetted and replaced with bone chips. **B,** The giant cell tumor shown in **A** recurred, necessitating amputation. Gross specimen demonstrates bone chips still in place with tumor replacing femur. Review of original sections showed benign giant cell tumor, but re-cuts of curetted material demonstrated malignant stroma. **C,** Original section of curettings referred to in **B** showing areas of rather innocuous-appearing stroma with typical multinucleated giant cells. These changes were called benign. **D,** Later tissue section of malignant giant cell tumor referred to in **B** and **C** that has the appearance of fibrosarcoma. There was no evidence of osteoid formation. The patient died of pulmonary metastases.

and fibula) and in bones of the pelvis, rib, vertebra, mandible, and clavicle.[560,610,616] It generally arises in the medullary canal of the shaft (hence its traditional inclusion among the "marrow tumors"), from which it permeates the cortex and invades the soft tissues (Fig. 24.63). Rarely, it is predominantly periosteal in location.[522] As already indicated, tumors with the appearance of ES/PNET can present clinically as a soft tissue neoplasm with a normal appearance of the underlying bone on plain x-ray films. However, CT scans, MRI, and microscopic examination of these cases may reveal that the tumor arose in the medullary canal and that it has diffusely permeated the marrow spaces to extend outside the bone without destroying a significant amount of bone trabeculae, thus remaining undetectable by conventional radiography. This possibility should always be kept in mind before making a diagnosis of primary extraskeletal ES/PNET (see Chapter 25).[562]

Following the reassessment of ES/PNET on the basis of its distinct molecular alterations, it has become apparent that, in addition to bone and soft tissue, the lesion can occur in a wide variety of sites, including skin and viscera[557,587]; these are discussed in the respective chapters.

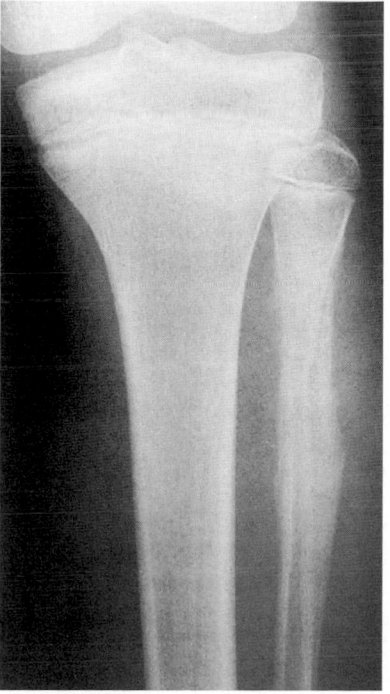

Fig. 24.63 Ewing's sarcoma of fibula. Growth is ill defined and accompanied by a prominent periosteal reaction.

The typical radiographic changes in bone associated with ES/PNET are cortical thickening and widening of the medullary canal. With progress of the lesion, reactive periosteal bone may be deposited in layers parallel to the cortex (onion-skin appearance) or at right angles to it (sun-ray appearance) (Fig. 24.64).

Microscopic features. Microscopically, ES/PNET consists of solid sheets of cells divided into irregular masses by fibrous strands (Fig. 24.65). Individual cells are small and uniform. The cell outlines are indistinct, resulting in a "syncytial" appearance. The nuclei are round, with frequent indentations, small nucleoli, and variable but usually brisk mitotic activity (Fig. 24.66). There is a well-developed vascular network. Some of the tumor cells may arrange themselves around the vessels in a pseudorosette fashion. Exceptionally, a few true rosettes (without central lumen) are formed, these having provided some of the earlier evidence for a neuroepithelial differentiation in these neoplasms.[561] Necrosis is common and may dominate the microscopic picture. Some tumors are composed of larger and more pleomorphic cells exhibiting conspicuous nucleoli (so-called large cell or atypical variant).[582] Other tumors display an organoid pattern characterized by bicellular strands of tissue separated by a "filmy" vascular stroma, referred to as the "filigree pattern."[563]

The morphologic features of the ES/PNET cells can be recognized on cytologic examination, which represents an important diagnostic tool, both in bone and in soft tissue lesions[555] (Fig. 24.67).

The differential diagnosis of ES/PNET includes practically all other "small round cell tumors," particularly lymphoblastic lymphoma, desmoplastic small cell tumor, and embryonal/alveolar rhabdomyosarcoma.[574,577] The immunohistochemical and molecular genetic features (described below) are very useful and sometimes indispensable for this task.

A most peculiar morphologic variation in the theme is the lesion combining features of ES/PNET and adamantinoma, and variously called adamantinoma-like Ewing's sarcoma and Ewing's sarcoma-like adamantinoma.[524,549] The fact that these cases display the 11;22 translocation would seem to indicate that they represent

Fig. 24.64 Gross appearance of Ewing's sarcoma. It has a typical ill-defined quality, with extensive involvement of medulla and cortex associated with elevation of periosteum.

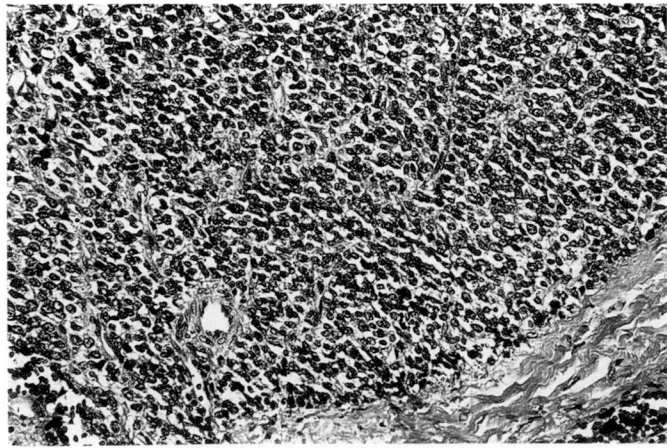

Fig. 24.65 Diffuse pattern of growth and monotonous cytologic appearance in Ewing's sarcoma/PNET.

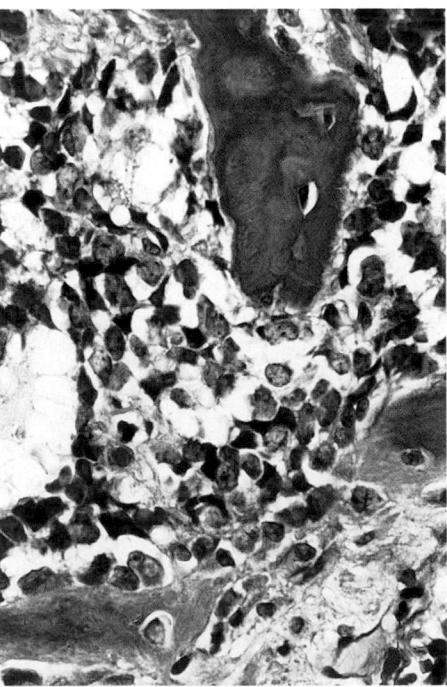

Fig. 24.66 Microscopic appearance of Ewing's sarcoma/PNET. Uniform cells with darkly staining nuclei and very scanty cytoplasm infiltrate the marrow spaces around bone trabeculae.

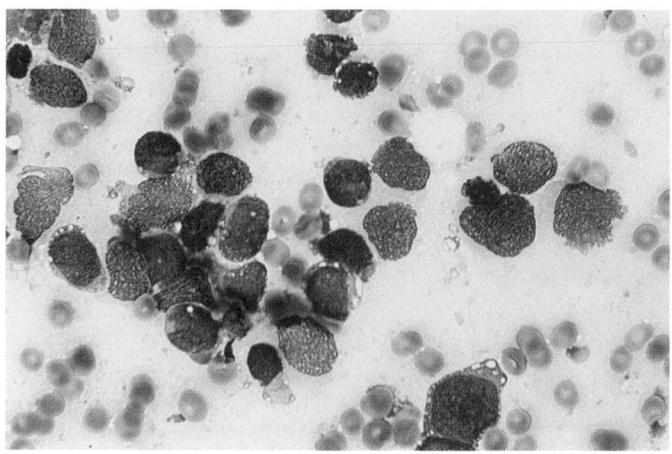

Fig. 24.67 Cytologic appearance of Ewing's sarcoma/PNET as seen in a fine needle aspiration specimen.

a subtype of ES/PNET resembling adamantinoma rather than the reverse.[525]

Histochemical, electron microscopic, and immunohistochemical features. The cells of ES/PNET usually contain large amounts of cytoplasmic glycogen, as demonstrated by a PAS stain with diastase control or by electron microscopy (Figs 24.68 and 24.69). Traditionally, this has represented an important feature for the differential diagnosis with other small round cell tumors.[602] However, it is far from being specific. Some cases of this entity show little or no glycogen (at least in routine formalin-fixed and paraffin-embedded preparations), whereas sizable amounts of this substance can be found in metastatic neuroblastoma and malignant lymphoma occasionally, and in embryonal rhabdomyosarcoma commonly.[618,627]

Ultrastructurally, the cells of ES/PNET show a rather primitive appearance. Occasionally, a few dense core granules will be found, either in the cytoplasm or in cell prolongations.[571,575,614]

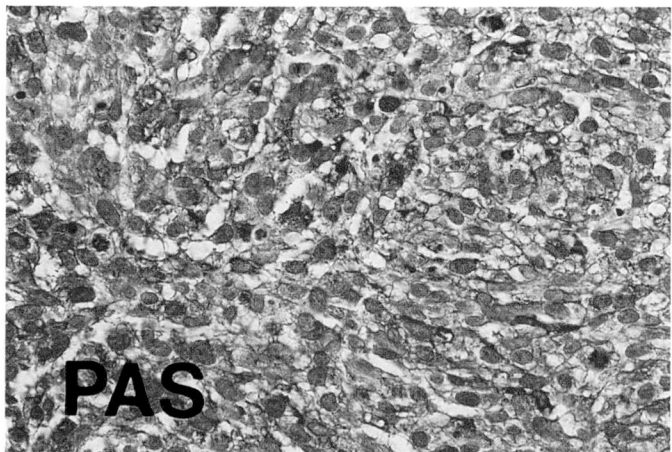

Fig. 24.68 PAS stain in Ewing's sarcoma/PNET showing large amounts of cytoplasmic glycogen. The material was entirely removed by diastase treatment.

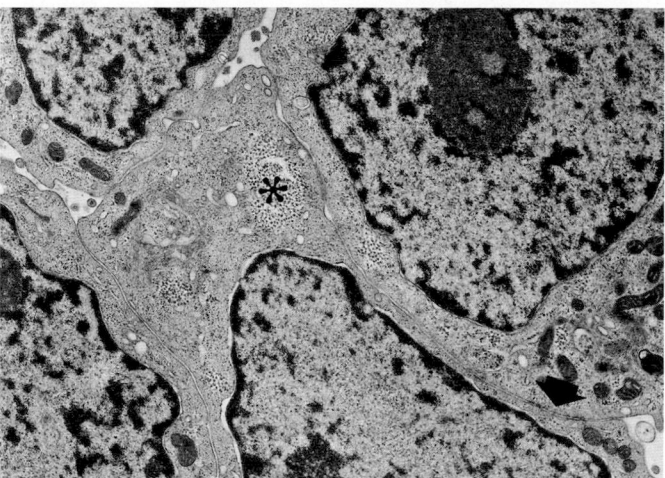

Fig. 24.69 Electron microscopic appearance of Ewing's sarcoma/PNET. Undifferentiated tumor cells with multiple small foci of cytoplasmic glycogen (asterisk) are joined by two rudimentary cell junctions (arrow). (×12,000; courtesy of Dr. Robert A. Erlandson, Memorial Sloan-Kettering Cancer Center)

Immunohistochemically, there is the expected consistent positivity for vimentin. In addition, there is frequent reactivity for low-molecular-weight keratin, a fact not yet widely appreciated.[530,537,554,621] Furthermore, positivity has been described for neuron-specific enolase, protein gene product 9.5, Leu7, and neurofilaments, these reactions again providing evidence for neuroepithelial differentiation.[528,570,573,579,580,594,608] The latter has also been evidenced by the demonstration of chromogranin mRNA by RT-PCR.[590] The expression of some of these neural (including glial) markers seems to be related to the type of gene fusion described in the following section.[515]

CD99 (O13; HBA71; p30/32; MIC2) is a cell membrane protein coded by a gene located on the short arms of the X and Y chromosomes that is consistently expressed by the cells of ES/PNET (Fig. 24.70).[516,595,606] It is, however, not pathognomonic for this family of tumors, inasmuch as expression of this marker has also been documented in embryonal rhabdomyosarcoma, other soft tissue sarcomas, and lymphoblastic lymphoma.[543,544,559,592,613,624] The EWS–FLI1 fusion described in the following section results in the expression of the FLI1 protein, which can be detected at the immunohistochemical level; it should be noted, however, that there are several cell types—such as endothelial cells—that express this protein under normal conditions.[547,572]

Desmosome-associated proteins are demonstrable immunohistochemically in the areas of cell junctions, but neural cell adhesion molecules are not.[550] Various types of collagen are found in the extracellular matrix.[601]

Molecular genetic features. Over 95% of the cases of ES/PNET show on cytogenetic examination the reciprocal translocation 11;22 (q24;q12), which results in the fusion of the *EWS* (Ewing's sarcoma) gene with the *FLI*

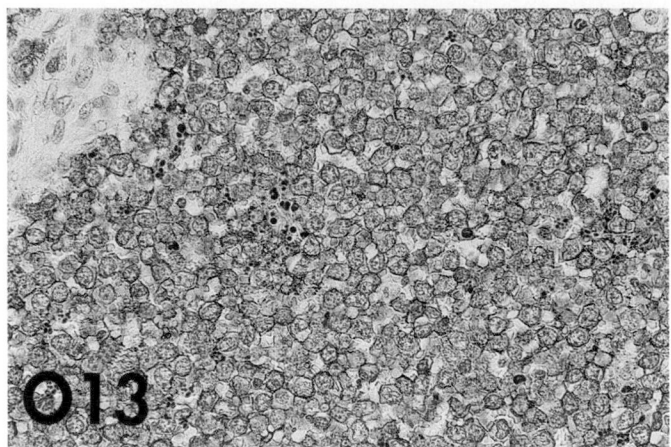

Fig. 24.70 CD99(013) stain in Ewing's sarcoma/ PNET. All of the tumor cells show strong membrane immunoreactivity for this marker.

or *ERG* genes.[534,536,539,552,568] The most common fusion is the one that results in "in frame linking" of *EWS* exon 7 with *FLI* exon 6. These translocations, which are detectable by RT-PCR, can be used for the primary diagnosis and for the detection of metastatic or residual disease in tissue or body fluids, including peripheral blood.[540,545,607,611,612,625] Regarding tissue samples, some success has been reported with formalin-fixed paraffin-embedded material,[514] but fresh tissue is clearly preferable for consistent results. The *EWS* rearrangement has also been detected by the FISH technique in fresh frozen sections and paraffin sections.[566,581] Apparently there are no phenotypic differences among cases of ES/PNET associated with *EWS–FLI1* and those associated with *EWS–ERG*.[553]

It needs to be noted that therapy-induced neural differentiation in Ewing's sarcoma may result in lack of expression of EWS–FLI1.[565]

The fact that there is a remarkable correlation between this gene fusion and ES/PNET is undeniable; whether it can be regarded as pathognomonic of the entity remains controversial. Suffice it to say that a few cases have been reported in which the ES/PNET transcript was found in tumors having phenotypic features of other tumor types.[617]

Additional chromosomal aberrations exist in ES/PNET, such as deletion of INK4A in a third of the cases.[622] ES/PNET has also been found to express the *secretogranin II* and *cholestokinin* genes, although rarely to a degree such as to make their respective products demonstrable with immunohistochemical techniques.[548,589]

Another gene that has been found to be activated in ES/PNET is *TRK*, this phenomenon being supposedly associated with neural differentiation.[585]

Spread and metastases. The metastatic spread of ES/PNET is to the lungs and pleura, other bones (particularly the skull), central nervous system, and (rarely) regional lymph nodes. About 25% of the patients have multiple bone and/or visceral lesions at the time of presentation.[527,551]

Treatment. The treatment of ES/PNET represents one of the success stories of medical oncology. In the past, surgical excision (including amputation) and radiation therapy resulted in a 5-year survival rate of less than 10%, and the pathologist was warned to question a previous diagnosis of Ewing's sarcoma in a long-term survivor.[584] The combination of high-dose irradiation and multidrug chemotherapy—sometimes combined with limited surgery—has dramatically changed the picture.[521,596,599] Local control is achieved in over 85% of the cases, and the actuarial 5-year disease-free survival is 75%. Parenthetically, it should be noted that therapy may result in increased pleomorphism and the appearance of bizarre giant cells.[615] Radiographic evidence of effective treatment consists of reconstitution of the cortical pattern, "periostitis," and regression of the extraosseous soft tissue mass if one was present; any localized lysis at the primary site should be regarded as suspicious for recurrence.[542]

Prognosis. Prognostic factors related to ES/PNET are listed below.

1 *Osseous versus extraosseous location.* The claim has been made that classical Ewing's sarcoma of bone has a better prognosis than PNET of soft tissue.[526,556,604]

2 *Soft tissue extension.* Direct extension of an osseous Ewing's sarcoma into soft tissues is a bad prognostic sign.[578]

3 *Metastases.* Not surprisingly, presence of metastases at presentation is a poor prognostic sign, particularly if these metastases are in the skeletal system rather than the lung.[531]

4 *Surgical margins.* Although surgery plays a role in the treatment of ES/PNET, the prognostic importance of the status of the surgical margins has diminished considerably with current chemotherapeutic regimes.[588]

5 *Therapy-induced necrosis.* As for osteosarcoma, there is a close relationship between presence and amount of tumor necrosis following chemotherapy and outcome. It has been recommended that the changes be graded as follows: I, gross viable tumor; II, microscopic viable tumor; III, no viable tumor cells.[520,593,600]

6 *Microscopic features.* A filigree microscopic pattern is said to represent an unfavorable prognostic indicator, at least with the therapy used at the time that the observation was made.[563]

7 *Neural differentiation.* The claim was originally made that presence of neural (neuroepithelial, neuroectodermal) differentiation in ES/PNET was associated with a poor outcome, but more recent series have failed to find a statistically significant difference.[591]

8 *Type of gene fusion transcript.* The claim has been made that patients with the most common type of gene fusion (*EWS* exon 7 linked in frame with exon 6 of *FLI1*) are less likely to metastasize and have a better prognosis than patients having any other type of fusion.[534,628] This may be related to the fact that tumors with *EWS–FLI1*-type fusion seem to have a lower proliferation rate.[533]

9 *p53.* Overexpression of p53 seems to define a small subset of cases with a markedly unfavorable outcome.[517,532]

10 *c-myc.* In one study, c-myc amplification has been found to be a marker of poor prognosis.[603]

11 *INK4A.* The suggestion has been advanced that deletion of this gene may identify a subgroup of patients with poor prognosis.[623]

12 *DNA content.* DNA content, as determined by flow cytometry or cytophotometry, seems to correlate with prognosis, in that patients with diploid tumors do better than those with aneuploid ones.[538]

Malignant lymphoma and related lesions

Malignant lymphomas can involve the skeletal system primarily or as a manifestation of systemic disease.[631,611]

Large cell lymphoma primary of bone is more common in adults than children, 60% of the cases occurring in patients over the age of 30 years. There is no sex predilection.

Grossly, most cases involve the diaphysis or metaphysis of a long bone or the vertebrae, producing patchy cortical and medullary destruction.[661a] This is associated with minimal to moderate periosteal reaction, usually of the lamellated type. The tumor, which is pinkish gray and granular, frequently extends into the soft tissues and invades the muscle.

Radiographically, a combination of bone production and bone destruction often involves a wide area of a long bone[637] (Fig. 24.71). This pattern is very suggestive of the diagnosis, but osteosarcoma and chronic osteomyelitis may closely simulate it.

Microscopically, the appearance is similar to that of large cell lymphomas in nodal and other extranodal sites.[633,637,656,661] Some cases are accompanied by prominent fibrosis. Traditionally, the main source of diagnostic difficulty has resided in their distinction from Ewing's sarcoma.[643,646,660] The cells of malignant lymphoma are larger, and their nuclei are somewhat pleomorphic, with many indented, multilobulated, or horseshoe-shaped forms. They usually have prominent nucleoli, unlike the fine nucleoli of Ewing's sarcoma (Fig. 24.72). Cytoplasmic outlines of large cell lymphoma are well defined, whereas those of Ewing's tumor are indistinct. The cytoplasm is more abundant and often eosinophilic. Reticulin fibers occur between individual cells and groups of cells, whereas in Ewing's sarcoma they are mainly restricted to perivascular areas. Ultrastructurally,

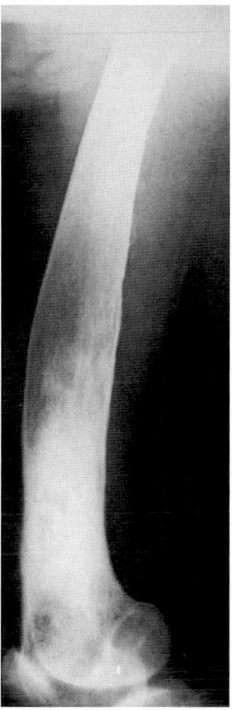

Fig. 24.71 Malignant lymphoma involving lower end of femur demonstrating bone destruction and bone production. Such lesions are often erroneously diagnosed as chronic osteomyelitis.

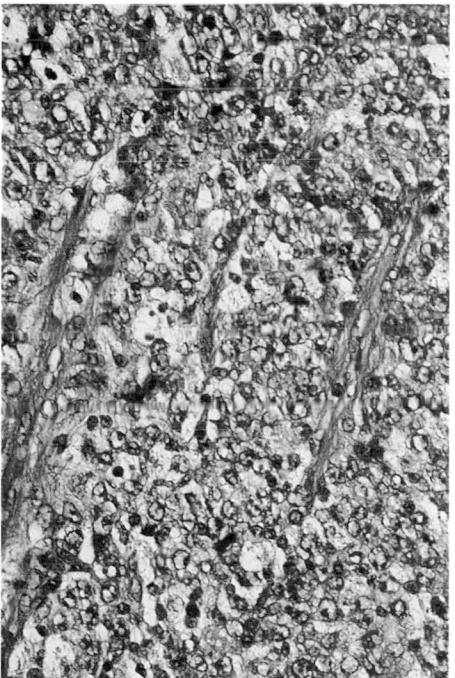

Fig. 24.72 Malignant lymphoma of bone. The tumor is of large cell type and is associated with some fibrosis.

the features are analogous to those of nodal and other extranodal lymphomas.[647] Immunohistochemically, there is positivity for CD45 and—in the large majority of the cases—for B-cell markers.[639,654,655] bcl-2 is expressed in approximately 70% of the cases.[637a]

The 5-year survival rate for localized large B-cell lymphomas of bone has ranged from 30% to 60% in most series.[632] The stage of the disease is the single most important prognostic determinator,[651] but there is also a definite relation with cell type.[638] Tumors expressing antigens associated with germinal centers are said to behave better than the others.[637a] The workup of these patients should include skeletal survey and bone marrow examination. The treatment usually consists of a combination of irradiation therapy and chemotherapy.[630]

Hodgkin's lymphoma produces radiographically detectable bone lesions in approximately 15% of the patients. The involvement is multifocal in about 60% of the cases, the most frequent sites being vertebrae, pelvis, ribs, sternum, and femur.[642] The osseous lesions of Hodgkin's lymphoma are often asymptomatic and in half of the cases are not demonstrable radiographically. When they become apparent in the x-ray film, the foci may be osteolytic, mixed, or purely osteoblastic. The latter appearance is particularly common in vertebrae. Exceptionally, Hodgkin's lymphoma will present initially as a bone mass,[636] with or without associated involvement of the adjacent soft tissues.[629,636,650,652] Osteonecrosis of the femoral or humeral head can occur as a complication of therapy for Hodgkin's lymphoma or non-Hodgkin's lymphoma.[657]

Anaplastic large cell lymphoma exhibiting CD30, EMA, and granzyme B immunoreactivity and either a null or a T-cell phenotype occurs as a primary bone lesion and needs to be distinguished mainly from Hodgkin's lymphoma.[635,641,649] The outcome is poor.

Burkitt's lymphoma, as originally reported from Africa, typically presented with massive jawbone involvement. It can also result in tumor masses in the long bones and pelvis.[640]

Lymphoblastic lymphoma of precursor B-cell type can present as a solitary bone tumor and simulate Ewing's sarcoma.[645,652] Immunohistochemically, the tumor cells are positive for TdT, CD43, CD99, CD79a, and (inconstantly) for CD20.

Acute leukemia of childhood is associated with radiographic abnormalities in the skeletal system in 70% to 90% of the cases.[648,659] In the large majority of instances, the changes are widespread and therefore unlikely to be confused with a primary bone neoplasm.[658] In contrast, destructive bone lesions are extremely rare in the chronic leukemias. Chabner et al.[634] reported six cases in a series of 205 patients with chronic granulocytic leukemia. In three of the patients, the bone lesion appeared at the time of blastic transformation.

Plasma cell myeloma and **plasmacytoma** are discussed in Chapter 23. Amyloidoma of bone is regarded as a manifestation of a plasma cell neoplasm and is also addressed in the chapter dealing with bone marrow.[653]

Vascular tumors

Hemangiomas of bone are often seen in the vertebrae as an incidental post mortem finding. In a classic autopsy study by Töpfer,[686] hemangiomas were detected in 11.9% of 2154 cases. They were multiple in 34% of the cases. These lesions should probably be regarded as vascular malformations rather than true neoplasms.

The most common locations of clinically significant osseous hemangiomas are skull, vertebrae, and jawbones.[688,691] Hemangiomas in the long bones are extremely rare. When a lesion involves the flat bones (particularly the skull), sunburst trabeculation occurs because of elevation of the periosteum. Grossly, the cut section of these tumors often has a currant jelly appearance. Microscopically, there is a thick-walled lattice-like pattern of endothelial-lined cavernous spaces filled with blood (Fig. 24.73).

Multiple hemangiomas are mainly seen in children and are associated in about half of the cases with cutaneous, soft tissue, or visceral hemangiomas.[684] Hemangiomas of the sacrum in infants are often accompanied by a variety of congenital abnormalities.[666]

Massive osteolysis (Gorham's disease) is probably not a vascular neoplasm but is included in this discussion because of its microscopic similarities with skeletal angiomatosis. It has a destructive character that the latter lacks. It results in reabsorption of a whole bone or several bones and the filling of the residual spaces by a heavily vascularized fibrous tissue.[667,668]

Lymphangiomas of bone are exceptional.[670] Most cases are multiple and associated with soft tissue tumors of similar appearance; variations on the theme have been termed *cystic angiomatosis* and *hamartomatous hemolymphangiomatosis*.[682]

Glomus tumor of the subungual soft tissues may erode the underlying bone. Much rarer is the occurrence of a purely intraosseous glomus tumor involving the terminal phalanx.[675]

Hemangiopericytoma can present as a primary bone lesion, the most common location being the pelvis[683,693] (Fig. 24.74). Benign and malignant forms have been described. The differential diagnosis includes metastatic

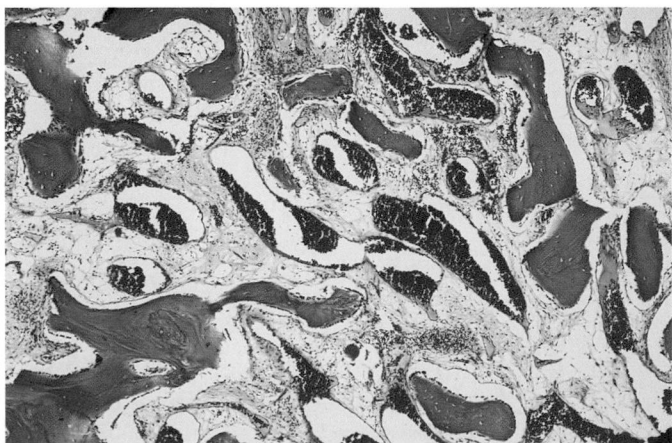

Fig. 24.73 Cavernous hemangioma of bone. Large dilated vessels with thin walls expand marrow spaces and elicit some new bone formation in surrounding trabeculae.

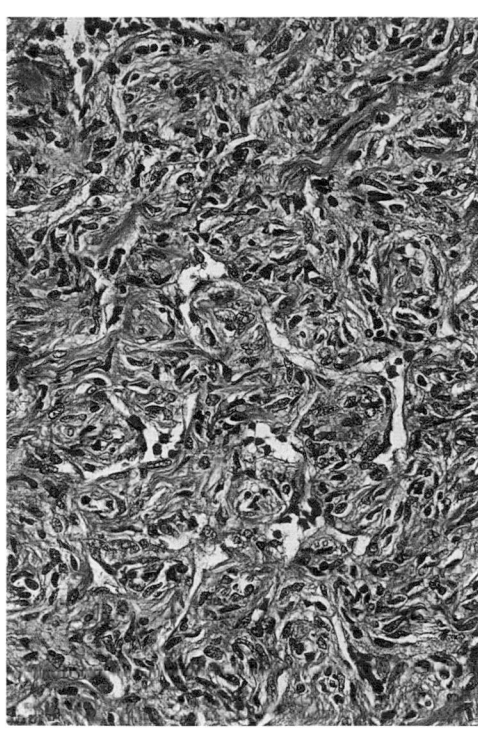

Fig. 24.74 Primary hemangiopericytoma of bone. The appearance is similar to that of the more common soft tissue lesion.

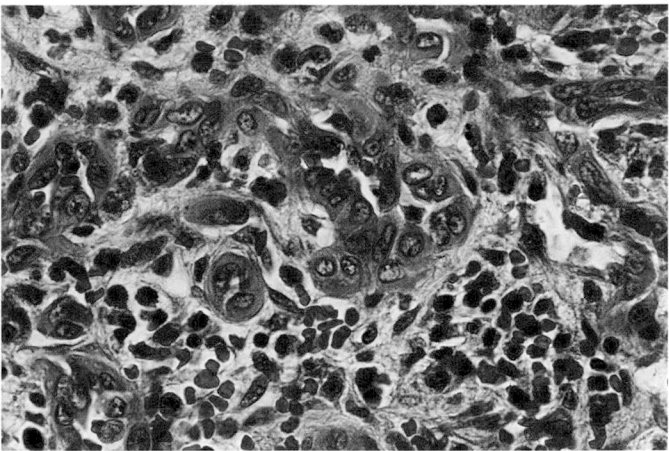

Fig. 24.75 Epithelioid hemangioendothelioma. The tumor cells have a plump appearance and acidophilic cytoplasm. The stroma contains an inflammatory infiltrate rich in eosinophils.

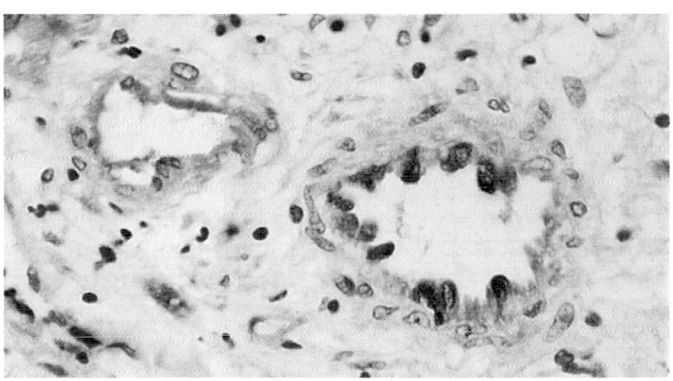

Fig. 24.76 Epithelioid hemangioendothelioma of bone (FVIII-related antigen).

hemangiopericytoma of meninges, which is actually more common than primary hemangiopericytoma of bone.

Phosphaturic mesenchymal tumor is discussed here because it usually exhibits microscopically areas with a hemangiopericytoma like appearance, combined with foci of giant cells.[677] There is also osteoid production and poorly developed cartilaginous areas. These peculiar tumors of bone or soft tissue cause osteomalacia or rickets through the production of a renal phosphaturic substance that depletes total body phosphates by reducing tubular reabsorption of phosphate.[663] This substance is said to be fibroblastic growth factor 23.[669a] Their behavior is usually benign.[690]

Epithelioid hemangioendothelioma of bone is the most common and distinctive member of the family of epithelioid (histiocytoid) vascular neoplasms, originally embraced in the histiocytoid hemangioma concept.[672,681] It is a borderline type of vascular neoplasm characterized microscopically by the presence of epithelial- or histiocyte-like endothelial cells with abundant acidophilic and often vacuolated cytoplasm, large vesicular nucleus (sometimes with prominent grooves), modest atypia, scanty mitotic activity, inconspicuous or absent anastomosing channels, recent and old hemorrhage, and an inconstant but sometimes prominent inflammatory component rich in eosinophils (Figs 24.75 and 24.76). A myxoid stroma is prominent in some cases and may produce confusion with a cartilaginous neoplasm.[676] Many of the tumors classified as grade I (and perhaps grade II)

hemangioendotheliomas of bone in some series[664,680] belong in this category.

In this regard, it should be emphasized that a range of cytologic atypia exists among epithelioid vascular tumors of bone. Those showing only a modest degree of atypia fit better the category of epithelioid hemangioendothelioma described above and are the most numerous. Those showing little or no atypia could be termed epithelioid hemangiomas (although controversy persists about the use of this term)[665a,673,678] whereas those exhibiting marked atypia (often accompanied by mitotic activity and necrosis) are better designated as epithelioid angiosarcomas (see later discussion). It should also be noted that the epithelioid features may be admixed with spindle cell forms in all three subtypes, whether one regards these combined forms as distinct tumor entities[671] or simply as morphologic variations of a continuous spectrum, as we prefer to.

Immunohistochemically, the cells of epithelioid vascular neoplasms display endothelial cell markers, such as factor VIII, CD31, and CD34. However, these antigens can be poorly expressed and/or coexist with epithelial markers such as keratin.[689]

Occasionally, fibrosarcoma can present as a multicentric process involving numerous bones.[709] Before this diagnosis is made, the possibility of metastatic sarcomatoid carcinoma (particularly from the kidney) should be ruled out.

Malignant fibrous histiocytoma having a morphologic appearance analogous to that of the more common soft tissue sarcoma bearing that name occurs in bone[711,716,720,722,726] (Fig. 24.83). Many of the reported cases have been located in long bones or the jaw.[695,711] Close to 30% of these tumors arise in bone infarcts,[706,710] around foreign bodies,[697,718] following irradiation,[713] in Paget's disease, or as expression of "dedifferentiation" or anaplastic transformation in chondrosarcoma, chordoma, or giant cell tumor.[698,721] The mean age at the time of presentation is 40 years.[711] The morphologic, ultrastructural, and immunohistochemical features of most tumor cells correspond to those of fibroblasts and myofibroblasts.[719,728]

The histogenesis and differential diagnosis of this tumor when involving bone are just as controversial as for its more common soft tissue counterpart, if not more so. As Dahlin et al.[705] have pointed out, areas indistin-

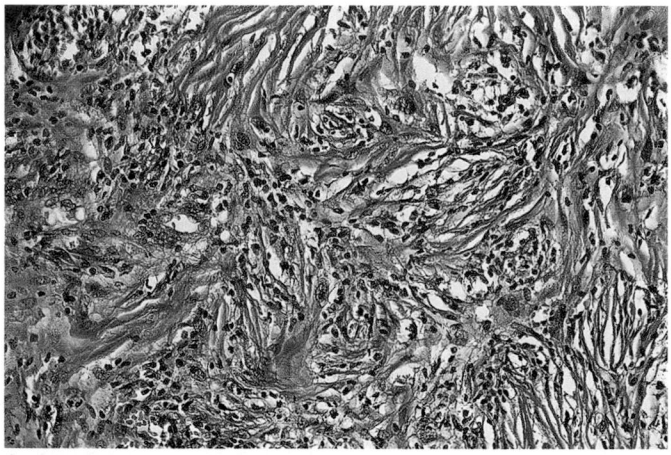

A

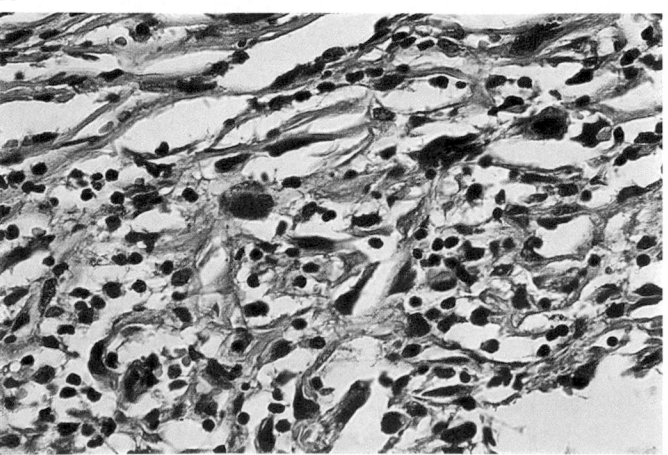

B

Fig. 24.83 So-called 'malignant fibrous histiocytoma of bone': **A**, storiform area; **B**, pleomorphic area.

guishable from those of malignant fibrous histiocytoma can be found in otherwise typical examples of osteosarcoma or chondrosarcoma. Only when thorough sampling of the tumor reveals no areas suggestive of any of these lesions may a diagnosis of malignant fibrous histiocytoma of bone be justified. Even under these circumstances, it is not clear whether this is a real entity or simply a pleomorphic, poorly differentiated sarcoma. The latter possibility would explain why the overall prognosis is so poor, at least in some series.[702,726] In one series, tumors with marked desmoplasia had a worse prognosis (5-year survival rate of 20%) than those with a prominent chronic inflammatory infiltrate (5-year survival rate of 78%).[730]

Muscle tumors

Malignant smooth muscle tumors of bone are very rare, and **leiomyomas** are virtually nonexistent. Most of the reported cases of **leiomyosarcoma** have occurred in the jaw and in long bones, particularly the femur.[731,732,733,736,743] The ultrastructural and immunohistochemical features are analogous to those of its soft tissue counterpart.[733,735] Specifically, the tumor cells are immunoreactive for common and smooth muscle actin, desmin, and h-caldesmon and they are enveloped by type IV collagen.[744] They may also be positive for keratin and S-100 protein.[734,745] Ultrastructurally, cytoplasmic microfilaments with focal densities are found.[740] Exceptional cases have been of the epithelioid variety (leiomyoblastoma).[738]

Isolated examples of primary **rhabdomyosarcomas** of bone are on record.[737,741] Some have been of the pleomorphic type and others had embryonal features.[739,742]

Adipose tissue tumors

Lipoma of bone is a very rare tumor. The few reported cases have occurred in adults and have presented radiographically as sharply outlined lytic lesions.[750] Microscopically, they are composed of mature adipose tissue devoid of hematopoietic elements; dystrophic calcification, fat necrosis, and hemorrhage may be present.[746,747]

Liposarcoma of bone is even more exceptional.[748,749] It is likely that many of the cases reported as such in the past would be reclassified today in other categories.

Chordoma and other notochordal lesions

The notochord is a phylogenetic structure representing a primitive spine which in higher organisms is replaced by the vertebrae and sacrum. Remnants of the notochord are found in humans within the vertebral bodies and intervertebral discs and, more rarely, in the presacral soft tissues.[772,780,791,797]

Ecchordosis physaliphora is a grossly visible notochordal remnant found incidentally at autopsy as a discrete gelatinous nodule attached to the clivus or overlying the anterior surface of the pons.[796]

Giant notochordal hamartoma is an extremely rare exaggerated form of the same process located within the vertebral bodies and which can be easily overdiagnosed as chordoma, from which it is distinguished by a combination of clinical, radiographic, and microscopic features.[774a,781]

Chordoma is more frequent in the fifth and sixth decades but occurs in all ages and in both sexes. Chordomas grow slowly, the duration of the symptoms before diagnosis usually being over 5 years. About 50% arise in the sacrococcygeal area, 35% in the spheno-occipital area, and the remainder along the cervico-thoraco-lumbar ("mobile") spine.[754,766] The sacrococcygeal tumors are more common in the fifth and sixth decades of life, whereas many of the spheno-occipital neoplasms occur in children and adolescents.[760,767a,806] In the former, a portion of the sacrum is seen destroyed by an osteolytic or rarely an osteoblastic process (Fig. 24.84). If the tumor encroaches on the spine, symptoms of spinal cord compression arise. The retroperitoneal space is often involved by direct extension. The tumor may grow large enough to narrow the lumen of the large bowel, impinge on the bladder, or invade the skin by direct extension.[763] It can be felt as a firm extrarectal mass. Spheno-occipital chordomas may present with a nasal, paranasal, or nasopharyngeal mass; multiple cranial nerve involvement; and destruction of bone.[756,792] Exceptionally, they may lead to fatal acute pontocerebellar hemorrhage.[762]

Grossly, chordoma is gelatinous and soft and contains areas of hemorrhage (Fig. 24.85). Microscopically, it closely resembles normal notochord tissue in its different stages of development. It grows in cell cords and lobules separated by a variable but usually extensive amount of mucoid intercellular tissue (Fig. 24.86). Some of the tumor cells (known as physaliferous) are extremely large, with

vacuolated cytoplasm and prominent vesicular nucleus; some of the cytoplasmic vacuoles contain glycogen, presumably in the process of being broken down.[775] Other tumor cells are small, with inconspicuous nuclei and no visible nucleoli. Mitotic figures are generally scanty or

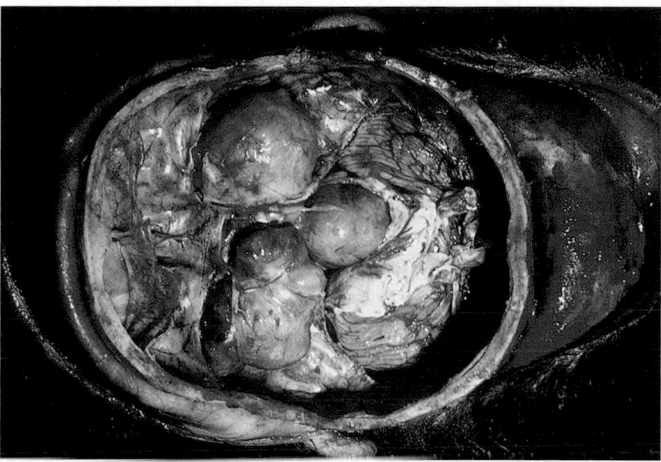

A

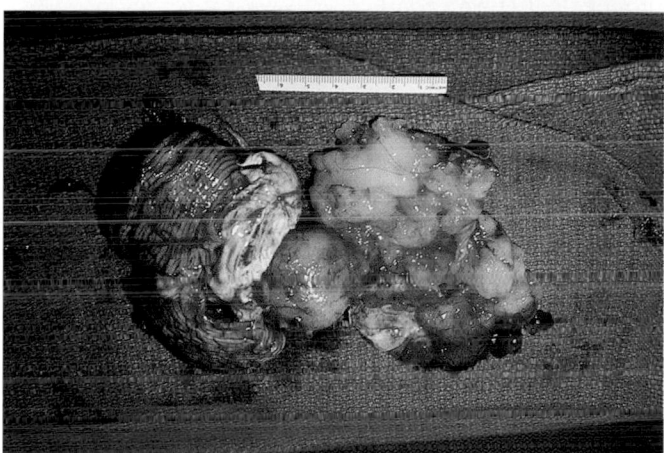

B

Fig. 24.85 A and **B**, Chordoma of spheno-occipital region as seen at autopsy. The gelatinous appearance of the tumor is well appreciated in **B**.

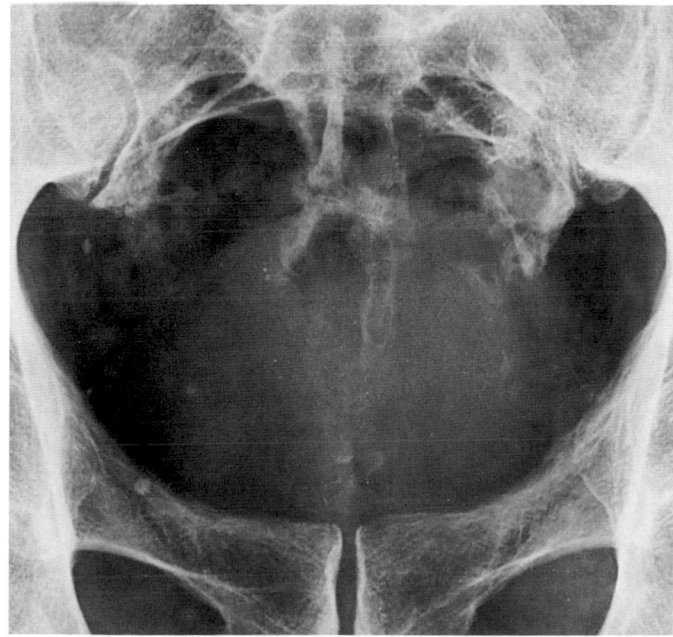

Fig. 24.84 Osteolytic destruction of sacrum by chordoma.

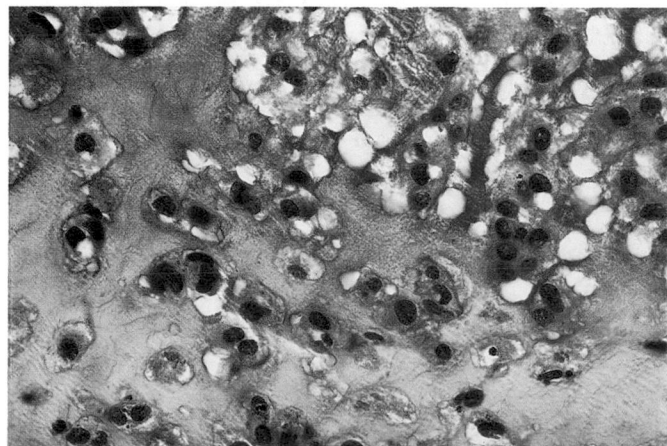

Fig. 24.86 Microscopic appearance of chordoma. The bubbly appearance of the myxoid stroma is evident.

absent. Areas of cartilage and bone may be present.[705] In some areas, the tumor may simulate carcinoma, particularly of renal cell origin. The microscopic differential diagnosis also includes chondrosarcoma, signet cell adenocarcinoma of the rectum, and myxopapillary ependymoma. Ultrastructurally, chordoma cells may contain peculiar mitochondrial–endoplasmic reticulum complexes, as well as parallel bundles of crisscrossing microtubules within the granular endoplasmic reticulum, two interesting albeit nonspecific features[761,771,798] (Fig. 24.87). They also have desmosomes, in keeping with their epithelial nature.[794] Immunohistochemically, chordoma shows reactivity for S-100 protein, keratin, epithelial membrane antigen, HBME-1, cathepsin K, and E-cadherin,[751,759,764,777,779,783,786,788,795] but only rarely for CEA[751] (Fig. 24.88). Among the keratins, those regularly expressed are CK8, CK19, and (less consistently) CK5; they are instead usually negative for CK7 and CK20.[788,785] Microtubule-associated (Tau) proteins are also commonly expressed.[769] GFA reactivity is commonly encountered with the use of polyclonal antibodies, less so with their monoclonal counterparts.[804] Strong 5-nucleotidase positivity has been found in the cell membrane of the tumor cells, another feature of potential diagnostic utility.[755] The lectin-binding pattern of chordoma closely recapitulates that of the human fetal notochord.[773] The extracellular material contains collagen of nearly all types (I, II, III, IV, V, and VI); laminin is also present, as evidence of basement membrane deposition.[799]

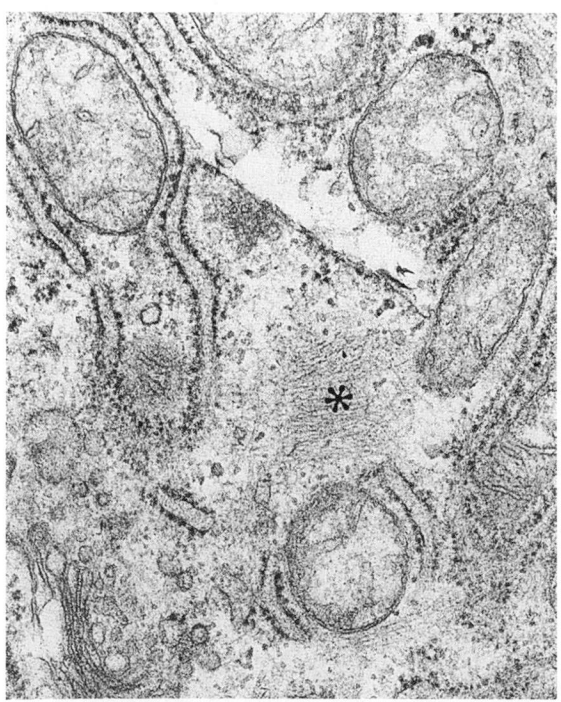

Fig. 24.87 Electron microscopic appearance of chordoma of sacrum. Mitochondria surrounded by cisternae of rough endoplasmic reticulum and aggregates of cytokeratin filaments (asterisk) are illustrated. (Courtesy of Dr. Robert A. Erlandson, Memorial Sloan-Kettering Cancer Center)

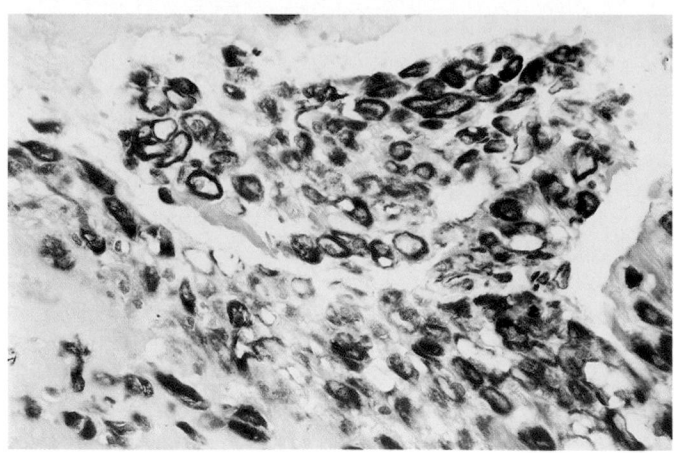

Fig. 24.88 Strong immunoreactivity of chordoma for keratin. This tumor was also positive for S-100 protein.

The characteristic physaliferous cells of chordoma can be identified in material from fine needle aspiration, which is also amenable to histochemical and immunohistochemical evaluation.[802]

The natural history of chordoma is characterized by repeated episodes of local recurrence and an often fatal outcome. Recurrences may develop 10 years or longer after the initial therapy.[752] Distant metastases are also late in the evolution of the disease.[757] In one series, the frequency of metastatic disease was 43%.[767] The most common sites are the skin (where they can simulate a sweat gland tumor) and bone, but they can occur in many other places, including the ovary.[763,808]

Treatment is in the form of surgical excision, radiation therapy, or a combination of both modalities.[787,789,791,807] The recurrence rate is very high following surgery, particularly when the tumor is entered during the procedure.[772] Adverse prognostic factors are represented by large tumor size, positive surgical margins, tumor necrosis, and high proliferative activity.[753,774,776,784]

Foci of high-grade spindle cell and/or pleomorphic sarcoma can be present in conjunction with areas of typical chordoma, either in the primary tumor or in the recurrences.[768] This phenomenon is analogous to that of "dedifferentiated" chondrosarcoma and carries an equally ominous prognostic significance.[778,801] The high-grade foci exhibit a high proliferative index and have an aneuploid–hyperploid pattern on flow cytometry, in stark contrast to that of the conventional chordomatous component.[768] Indeed, some of the prognostic factors noted above relate to the presence of these high-grade foci.

Chondroid chordoma is a controversial tumor entity, originally defined as a chordoma with prominent cartilaginous foci.[766] It occurs most often in the spheno-occipital region, but it may also be seen in the sacro-coccygeal area.[758] The overall prognosis is better than that of conventional chordoma, although the differences in recent series are not as pronounced as in previous work.[782]

Ultrastructurally and immunohistochemically, the tumor seems to share features of chordoma and chondrosarcoma.[800] Immunohistochemically, most authors have found reactivity for S-100 protein, keratin, and—less commonly—EMA and CEA.[770,782,790,793,794,803,805] Although the two extreme suggestions have been made that this tumor is a chondrosarcoma with no relation to chondroma[803] or a chordoma with no cartilaginous features,[770] most evidence suggests that both components are present.

Adamantinoma of long bones

Adamantinoma of long bones characteristically involves the tibia but has been reported in other long bones, such as the femur, ulna, and fibula.[817,820] Occasionally, adamantinoma of the tibia is seen also involving the adjacent fibula.[825] It may be located in the shaft or in the metaphyseal area of the bone.[810]

Radiographically, it presents as single or multiple lytic areas in the cortex or medulla, surrounded by marked sclerosis. Grossly, it is poorly defined and may extend into the overlying soft tissues.

Microscopically, several patterns of growth have been described. The most common consists of solid nests of basaloid cells with palisading at the periphery and sometimes a stellate configuration in the center. Less frequent forms have been described as spindle, squamoid, and tubular; the latter simulates closely the appearance of a vascular neoplasm[810] (Fig. 24.89). Electron microscopic and immunohistochemical studies have confirmed the epithelial nature of the tumor cells[816,821–823,827] (Figs 24.90 and 24.91). The keratins expressed by adamantinoma are mainly 14 and 19, with lesser representation of keratins 5, 17, 7, and 13.[813] In contrast to other bone and soft tissue tumors with epithelial phenotypes—such as synovial

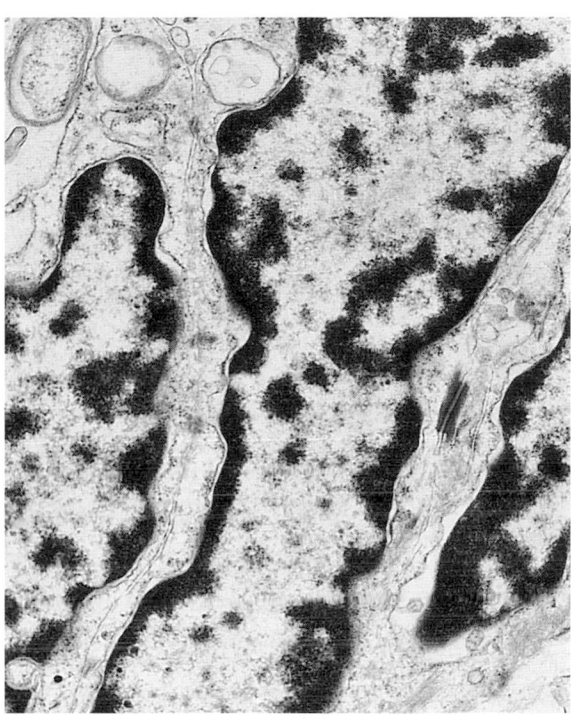

Fig. 24.90 Electron microscopic appearance of adamantinoma of tibia showing spindle-shaped epithelial tumor cells joined by desmosomes. (×15,600; courtesy of Dr. Robert A Erlandson, Memorial Sloan-Kettering Cancer Center)

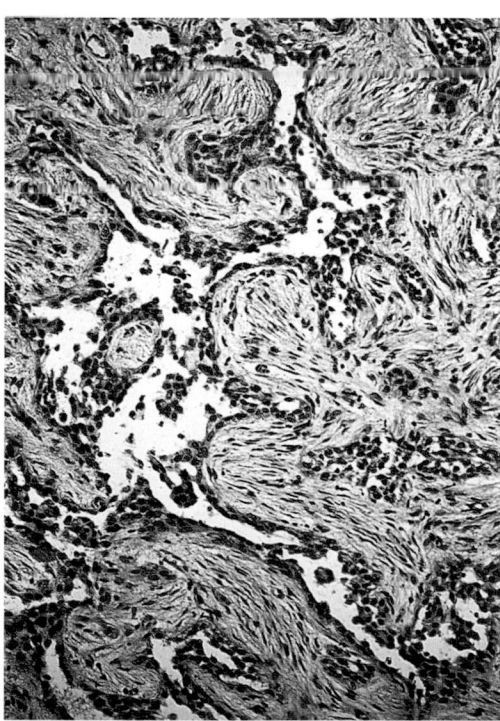

Fig. 24.89 Adamantinoma of tibia. Lack of cohesiveness of tumor cells in some of the islands results in a pseudovascular appearance.

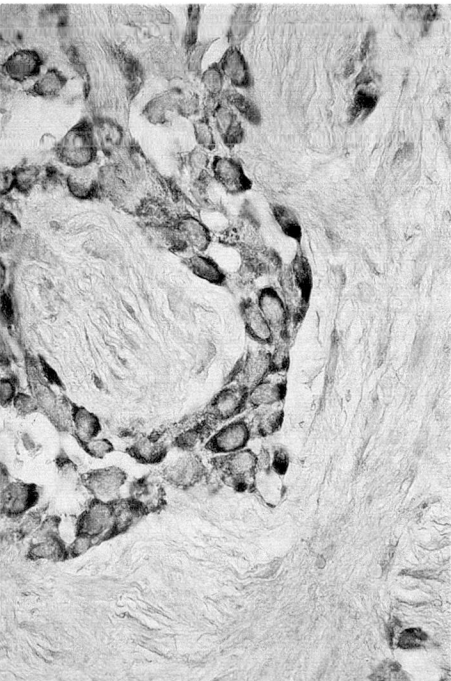

Fig. 24.91 Immunoreactivity for keratin in the tumor cells of adamantinoma of tibia.

sarcoma, chordoma, and epithelioid sarcoma—it lacks immunoreactivity for keratins 8 and 18.[813]

On occasion adamantinoma is accompanied by osteofibrous dysplasia, the relative proportions of the two lesions varying greatly from case to case.[811,824,826] Of great interest is the fact that the spindle cells of the dysplastic component are also immunoreactive for keratin, suggesting a common histogenesis.[809,818]

The histogenesis of this tumor remains controversial. Now that the presence of epithelial differentiation has been proved beyond doubt, the two favored possibilities are origin from intraosseous epithelial rests, possibly of skin adnexal type,[812] or epithelial metaplasia in a primary mesenchymal process, the latter being suggested by the above mentioned immunoreactivity for keratin, the distribution pattern of the extracellular matrix components, and the type of cytogenetic abnormalities present.[814,815,818] It is of interest that morphologically identical tumors can occur in the soft tissues of the pretibial area in the absence of bone involvement.[819] The odd tumor type combining features of adamantinoma and Ewing's sarcoma (variously called adamantinoma-like Ewing's sarcoma and Ewing-like adamantinoma) is discussed on p. 2174.

Adamantinoma of bone is a low-grade malignant tumor characterized by a tendency for local recurrence and the occasional development of lymph node and distant metastases, particularly to lung.[817] En bloc excision and amputation are the therapeutic choices, depending on the circumstances of the case.[817]

Peripheral nerve tumors

Schwannoma rarely presents as an intraosseous mass.[829,831] A strong predilection for the mandible has been noted, and origin from the mandibular nerve sometimes has been demonstrated.[835] Schwannomas of the sacrum can reach huge dimensions and present as retrorectal masses; they may simulate a malignant tumor on radiographic grounds (particularly chordoma) and present great technical difficulties for their surgical removal.[834] A few of the reported cases of intraosseous schwannoma have been of the *melanotic* variety.[833]

Recklinghausen's disease often results in several types of skeletal abnormalities (such as scoliosis, bowing, pseudoarthrosis, and other disorders of growth)[832] and may be accompanied by malignant bone tumors such as fibrosarcoma or malignant fibrous histiocytoma[830]; however, intraosseous neurofibromas are extremely rare.

Malignant peripheral nerve sheath tumor has been rarely seen in bone in patients with or without Recklinghausen's disease; several of the cases have involved jawbones.[828]

Xanthoma

Xanthoma of bone presents in patients over the age of 20 years and has a male:female ratio of 2:1. It is almost always solitary, and the flat bones (pelvis, ribs, skull) are the most frequent sites. Radiographically, it presents as a well-defined, sometimes expansile lytic lesion, often with a sclerotic margin. Microscopically, an admixture of foamy cells, multinucleated giant cells, cholesterol clefts, and fibrosis is seen. The differential diagnosis includes Rosai–Dorfman's disease and secondary xanthomatous changes in other bone lesions, such as Langerhans' cell histiocytosis and fibrous/post-traumatic dysplasia.[836]

Fibrocartilaginous mesenchymoma

Fibrocartilaginous mesenchymoma is a term that has been applied to a rare benign condition affecting the metaphysis of long bones (particularly the fibula) and characterized microscopically by an admixture of spindle cells, bone trabeculae, and islands of cartilage. Some of the cartilage is in the form of structures resembling epiphyseal plates. The condition is also known as subperiosteal fibrocartilaginous pseudotumor of long bones and focal fibrocartilaginous dysplasia.[838] Recurrences may supervene, but metastases have not been reported.[837]

Others

Other types of mesenchymal neoplasms that have exceptionally presented as primary bone lesions include *clear cell sarcoma (malignant melanoma of soft part type)*,[845] *alveolar soft part sarcoma*,[842] *dendritic reticulum cell tumor*,[841] *desmoplastic small cell tumor*,[839] *malignant mesenchymoma*,[843,844] and *monotypic epithelioid angiomyolipoma (PEComa)*.[840]

Metastatic tumors

Metastatic tumors are the most frequent of all malignant neoplasms of bone[862] (Fig. 24.92). Since in most cases the lesions are multiple and the presence of a tumor elsewhere is known, the diagnosis is obvious. However, solitary metastases from occult primaries can be confused with primary bone tumors. More than 80% of all bone metastases originate in the breast, lung, prostate, thyroid, or kidney. These metastases can be accompanied by visceral deposits or represent the only apparent site of dissemination.[865] Soft tissue sarcomas rarely metastasize to the skeletal system,[856] the outstanding exception being embryonal rhabdomyosarcoma of the soft tissues in children.[847]

About 70% of bone metastases affect the axial skeleton (cranium, ribs, spine, sacrum), and the remaining involve the appendicular skeleton (long bones) or both compartments. In all bones, metastases are preferentially situated in red bone marrow.[846] When located in long bones, the area usually involved is the metaphysis.

Metastatic bone lesions are usually osteolytic but may be osteoblastic or mixed. Tumors with a tendency to produce pure osteoblastic metastases are prostatic carcinoma, carcinoid tumor and other neuroendocrine neoplasms, and—less commonly—breast carcinoma.[848,863] The mechanism is thought to be the production of bone

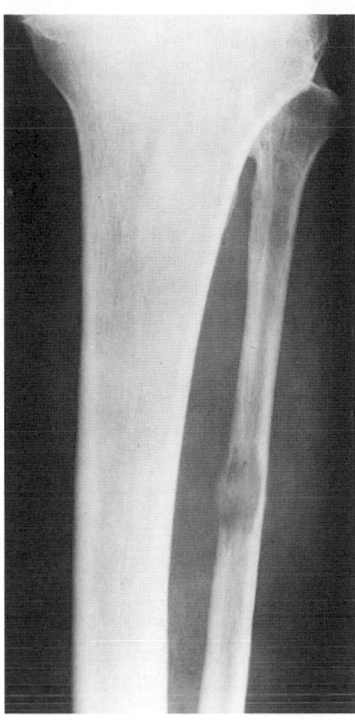

Fig. 24.92 Ill-defined lytic lesion in midshaft of fibula produced by metastasis of lung carcinoma.

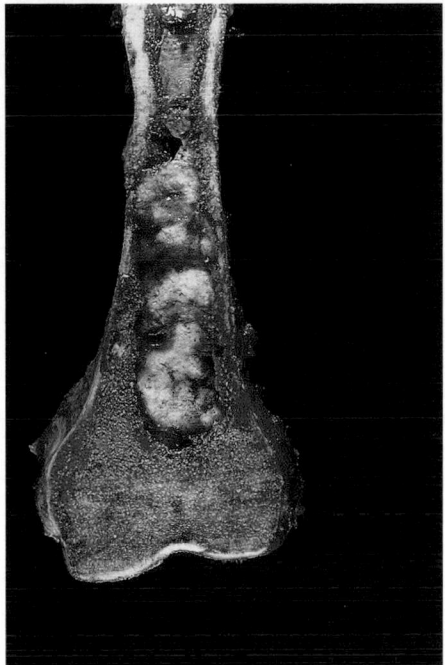

A

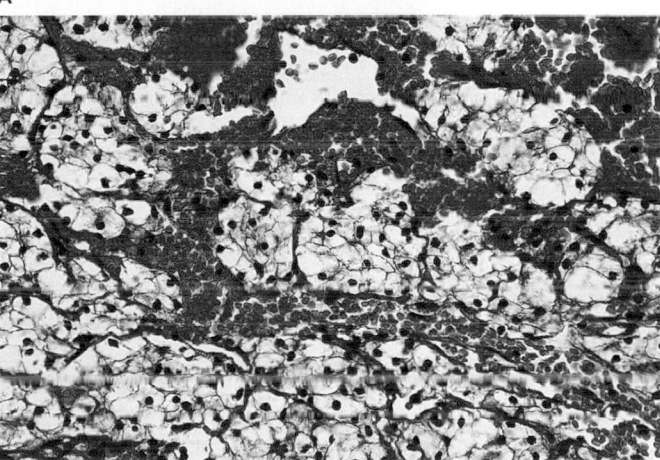

B

Fig. 24.93 A, Gross appearance of femur with medullary involvement by metastatic renal cell carcinoma. B, Microscopic appearance. The optically clear appearance of the cytoplasm and the extensive hemorrhage are characteristic features.

growth factors by the tumor cells, such as TGF-beta, fibroblast growth factor, and bone morphogenetic proteins.[851,858] If the osteoblastic bone metastases of prostatic carcinoma are extensive, they can be accompanied by osteomalacia, possibly because the organism cannot satisfy the high calcium demand for new bone formation.[849]

The bone or bones involved and the character of the changes seen radiographically are helpful in predicting the site of the primary neoplasm. Thyroid carcinoma usually metastasizes to the bones of the shoulder girdle, skull, ribs, and sternum. Carcinoma of the kidney tends to involve the skull, sternum, flat bones of the pelvis, femur, and scapula[853] (Fig. 24.93). Bone metastases peripheral to the knees or elbows are rare, but they certainly occur, as distally as the terminal phalanges.[854,857,864]

Periosteal bone proliferation may rarely accompany a metastatic lesion.[859] This is more likely to occur in certain sclerosing lesions such as those of the prostate. Exuberant new bone formation can also occur because of a pathologic fracture associated with metastatic carcinoma and lead to diagnostic confusion with osteosarcoma[855] (Fig. 24.94). Metastatic malignant tumors—including carcinoma and melanoma—can be accompanied by a prominent population of osteoclasts and simulate a giant cell tumor.[850] A soft tissue component may be present, particularly in bone metastases from the sternum or spine; sometimes, a pulsating mass will form as a result. Any tumor metastatic to bone, if extensive enough, may lead to hypercalcemia and elevation of serum acid phosphatase.

The mechanism of bone resorption is thought to

be related to the transformation of tumor-infiltrating macrophages into osteoclasts.[861] Tumor-produced PTH-related protein is thought to be a mediator of the osteolytic process. In turn, the production of this protein is said to be stimulated by the secretion of TGF-beta by the tumor cells.[852]

Most metastatic bone lesions cause pain. Treatment is for its relief and to prevent fracture of weight-bearing bones. Localized radiation therapy is highly effective, inducing partial or complete relief of pain in over 80% of the cases. When a pathologic fracture supervenes, internal fixation and radiation therapy provide the best results.[860] Palliative measures such as estrogen therapy and/or orchiectomy may afford relief in patients with

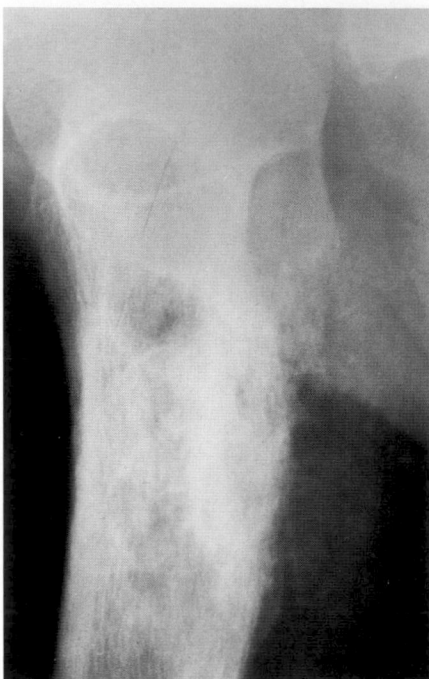

Fig. 24.94 Metastatic carcinoma in femur, with extensive callus formation, which simulated osteosarcoma both radiographically and microscopically. The primary tumor was probably in lung.

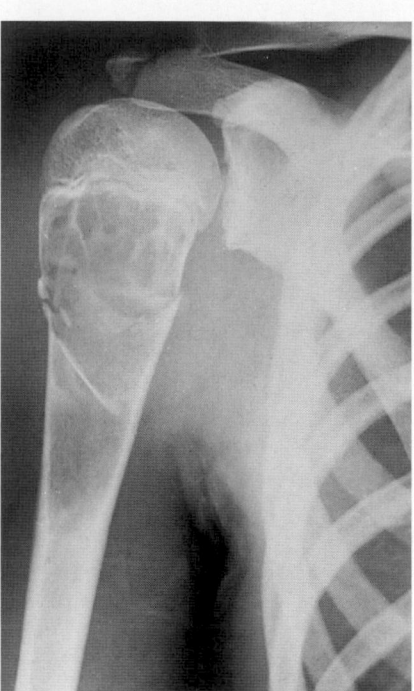

Fig. 24.95 Typical solitary bone cyst of upper end of humerus abutting against epiphyseal plate in a 13-year-old boy.

disseminated metastases from carcinoma of the prostate. The pain of metastatic carcinoma from the breast or prostate is commonly relieved by testosterone, with occasional striking objective improvement in the condition of the bone. Hormonal therapy with estrogens or tamoxifen, or ovarian ablation provides pain relief in 25% to 50% of patients with metastatic breast cancer. Strontium-89 and hormonal manipulation have proved equally successful for pain relief in prostatic carcinoma. In a few instances, a single metastatic focus, particularly from the thyroid or kidney, may be excised with benefit.

Tumorlike lesions

Solitary bone cyst

Solitary (unicameral) bone cysts usually occur in long bones, most often in the upper portion of the shaft of the humerus and femur (Fig. 24.95). They also may be seen in short bones, particularly the calcaneus.[869] Most cases are seen in males, and almost all occur in patients under 20 years of age.

These lesions usually are advanced when first seen. Most are centered in the metaphysis and their natural evolution is to migrate away from the epiphyseal line. The cortex is thinned, but periosteal bone proliferation does not take place except in areas of fracture. Bones affected by these lesions often fracture, usually in the proximal portion of the cystic area.

The cyst contains a clear or yellow fluid and is lined by a smooth fibrous membrane that may be brown (Fig.

24.96). The fluid may be hemorrhagic if a previous fracture has occurred. Microscopically, well-vascularized connective tissue, hemosiderin (often within macrophages), and cholesterol clefts are frequent. The bone surrounding the cyst may have a dense quality, with irregular cement lines.[866,868]

The diagnosis may be difficult in the presence of reparative changes following fracture, in recurrent lesions after bone grafting, and when articular cartilage is included in the curettings, but it becomes clear if the history and the x-ray films are available.

It is believed that this lesion arises on the basis of a local disorder of development and bone growth. A synovial origin has been suggested as an alternative pathogenesis.[868]

The treatment of choice is curettement and replacement of the cyst with bone chips. The results of therapy correlate well with the cyst "activity" as determined by its location. Good results are obtained when the cyst has migrated away from the epiphyseal line, but recurrences often develop when it has not.[869]

Aneurysmal bone cyst

Aneurysmal bone cyst is seen usually in patients between 10 and 20 years of age[877,897] and is slightly more common in females.[884] It occurs mainly in the vertebrae and flat bones but can also arise in the shaft of long bones.[874,892] Multiple involvement is frequent in the vertebral lesions. Exceptionally, a lesion with the features of an osseous aneurysmal bone cyst is seen in a soft tissue location and even within the wall of a major artery.[889,890,895]

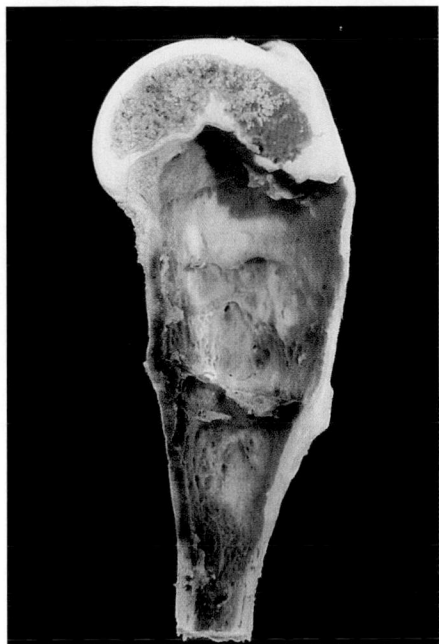

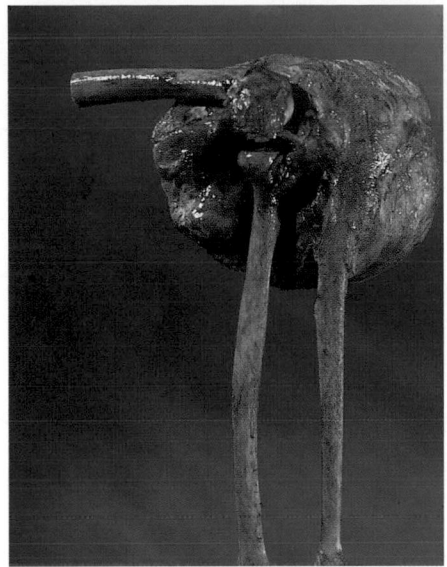

A

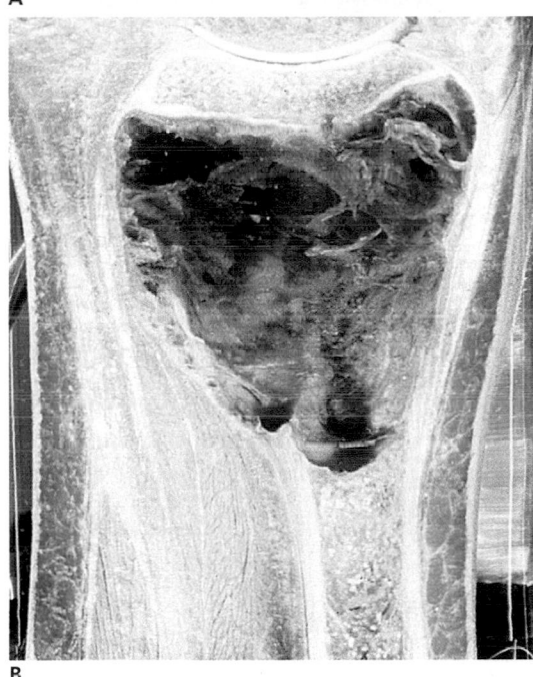

B

Fig. 24.96 A and **B**, Gross appearances of solitary bone cyst.
A, A large lesion located in the upper metaphysis of the humerus.
B, A triangular lesion located in the upper end of the tibia.
There has been secondary hemorrhage, leading to an appearance
not too dissimilar to that of an aneurysmal bone cyst.

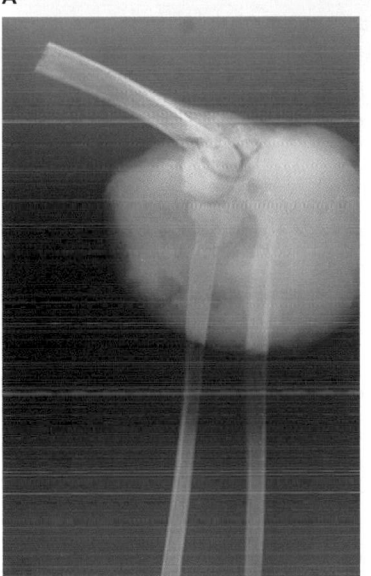

B

Fig. 24.97 Gross (**A**) and radiographic (**B**) appearances of large
aneurysmal bone cyst of ulna. (Courtesy of Dr. Juan Jose Segura,
San José, Costa Rica)

Radiographically, aneurysmal bone cyst shows eccentric expansion of the bone, with erosion and destruction of the cortex and a small peripheral area of periosteal new bone formation (Fig. 24.97). Grossly, it forms a spongy hemorrhagic mass covered by a thin shell of reactive bone, which may extend into the soft tissue. Microscopically, large spaces filled with blood are seen. They do not have an endothelial lining but are rather delimited by cells with the morphologic, ultrastructural, and immunohistochemical features of fibroblasts, myofibroblasts, and histiocytes.[870,871] These cells also occupy the septa that separate the cysts.[871] A row of osteoclasts is often seen immediately beneath the surface (Figs 24.98 and 24.99). The septa also contain blood vessels and foci of osteoid and bone. An additional feature of great diagnostic significance is the deposition of a peculiar degenerated calcifying fibromyxoid tissue.[896]

The differential diagnosis includes solitary bone cyst, giant cell tumor, hemangioma, telangiectatic osteosarcoma, and—especially for the lesions located in the jaw—giant cell reparative granuloma.

The pathogenesis of aneurysmal bone cyst remains elusive. In a few cases, the lesion is preceded by trauma

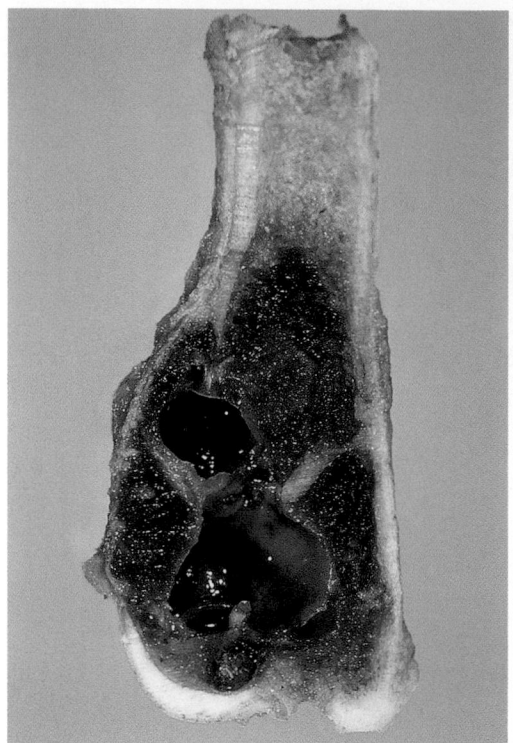

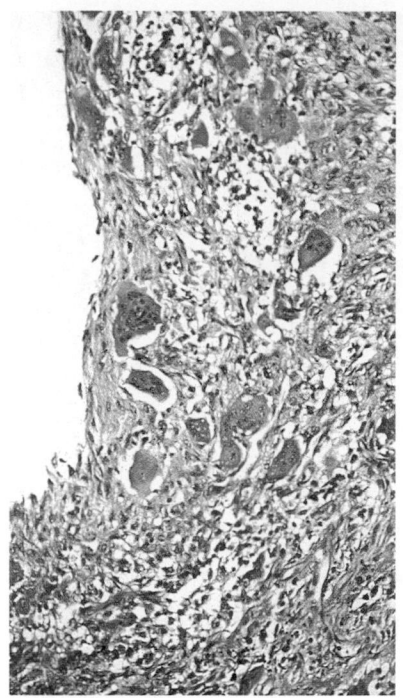

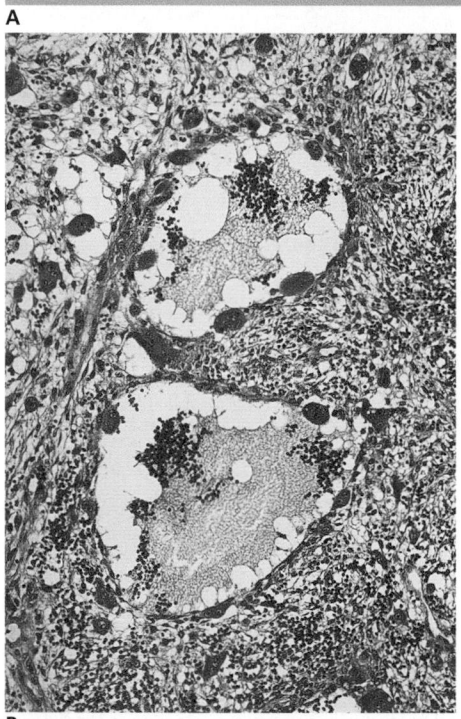

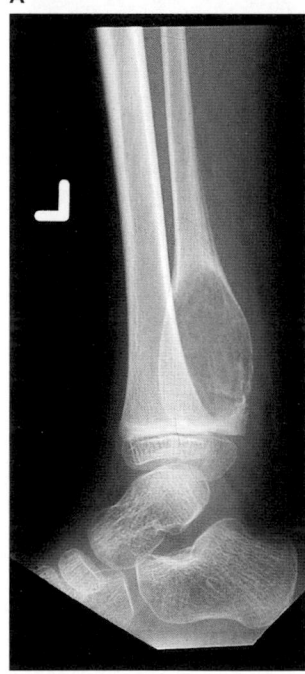

Fig. 24.99 Microscopic (**A**) and radiographic (**B**) appearances of aneurysmal bone cyst of lower end of fibula.

Fig. 24.98 A and **B,** Aneurysmal bone cyst of lower end of ulna. **A,** The large blood-filled cavities expand the metaphysis. **B,** Microscopic appearance, showing two cavities lined by osteoclast-like multinucleated giant cells. The intervening stroma is cellular but contains no neoplastic osteoid. (**A,** Courtesy of Dr. RA Cooke, Brisbane, Australia; from Cooke RA, Stewart B: Colour Atlas of Anatomical Pathology. Edinburgh, Churchill Livingstone, 2004.)

with fracture or subperiosteal hematoma.[876] In others, it seems to arise in some preexisting bone lesion as a result of changed hemodynamics.[873,880,885] Areas grossly and microscopically indistinguishable from aneurysmal bone cyst can occur in chondroblastoma, giant cell tumor, fibrous dysplasia, nonossifying fibroma, osteoblastoma, chondrosarcoma, and in the vascular and cartilaginous hamartoma of the chest wall in infants.[886] However, in most aneurysmal bone cysts, an underlying lesion is not encountered.[875,896] Naturally, this might be the result of sampling or the fact that the aneurysmal bone cyst destroyed all evidence of the preexisting lesion. It has been suggested that insulin-like growth factor-1, which has been consistently found in this lesion, may play a role in its pathogenesis.[883] The fact that nonrandom cytogenetic aberrations have been found in this lesion (involving chromosome segments 17p11-13 and/or 19q22), irrespective of subtype, suggests that at least some aneurysmal bone cysts are true neoplasms.[894]

Recurrence supervenes in approximately one fourth of the cases treated by curettage alone because of incompleteness of surgical excision.[891,897] En bloc resection or curettage with bone grafting affords better results.[881] It has been claimed that lesions containing fibromyxoid areas and immature osteoid are more likely to recur.[879a]

A few cases of reasonably convincing malignant transformation of aneurysmal bone cyst into osteosarcoma have been described; this exceptionally rare phenomenon should be distinguished from telangiectatic osteosarcoma and osteosarcoma with aneurysmal cyst-like areas.[882]

Sometimes lesions with the features of aneurysmal bone cysts are seen in association with solid areas composed of an admixture of fibrous tissue, new bone formation, and osteoclasts. In other instances, solid areas with this mixed appearance are seen in the absence of typical aneurysmal bone cyst features. Depending on the location of the lesion, variation in microscopic appearance, and the pathologist's bias, these lesions have been variously referred to as *giant cell reaction, (extragnathic) giant cell reparative granuloma, giant cell containing fibrous lesion,* and *solid variant of aneurysmal bone cyst.*[878,879,887,888,893,898,899] Locations include the small bones of the hand and feet, vertebrae, sacrum, and—less commonly—long bones. In the latter locations, they tend to have a metaphysical location[872] (Fig. 24.100). Determining whether these lesions

are reactive or neoplastic and establishing their exact place in the classification of bone diseases remain to be accomplished.

Other cysts

Ganglion cysts morphologically indistinguishable from those commonly seen in the periarticular soft tissue are occasionally found in an intraosseous location, always close to a joint space[901,902] (Fig. 24.101).

The cyst is surrounded by a zone of condensed bone, is often multiloculated, and has a gelatinous content and a wall of attenuated fibrous tissue. The bones of the ankle, particularly the tibia, are those most commonly affected.[903] Intraosseous ganglia need to be distinguished from solitary bone cysts and the periarticular cysts seen in association with degenerative joint diseases.

Subpubic cartilaginous cyst is the name given to a fibrocartilaginous mass with extensive degenerative cystic changes that has been observed in the proximity of the symphysis pubis.[900]

Metaphyseal fibrous defect (nonossifying fibroma)

Metaphyseal fibrous defects are distinctive lesions of bone that occur in adolescents, most often in long tubular bones, particularly the upper or lower tibia or the lower femur.[907] They are eccentric, sharply delimited lesions not too distant from the epiphysis and sometimes accompanied by epiphyseal disorders (Fig. 24.102). When loose

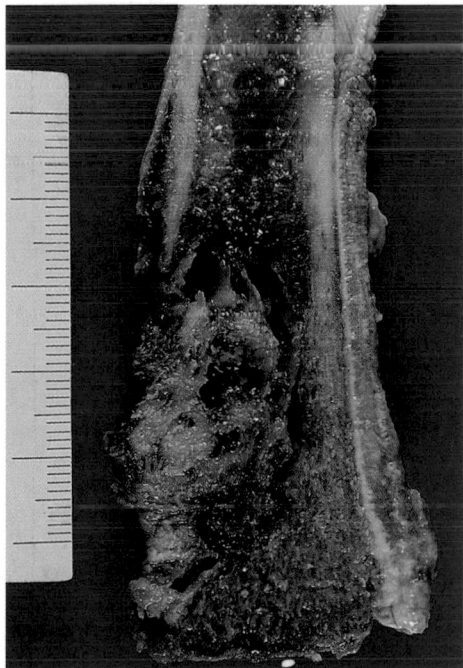

Fig. 24.100 Gross appearance of so-called "solid variant" of aneurysmal bone cyst. A few hemorrhagic cystic areas are present at the periphery.

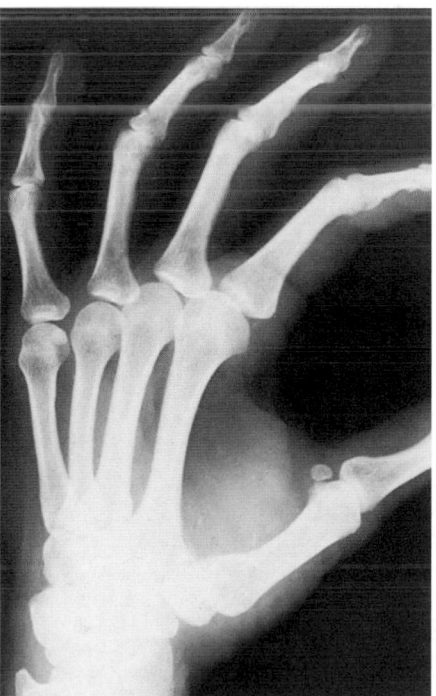

Fig. 24.101 Intraosseous ganglion cyst involving base of first metacarpal. It was associated with a larger ganglion of adjacent soft tissue, which is also apparent in the radiograph. (Courtesy of Dr. G Davis, St. Louis)

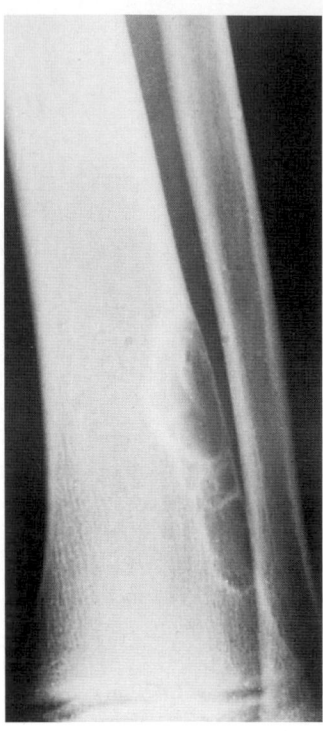

Fig. 24.102 Metaphyseal fibrous defect of lower end of tibia. Note its sharp delineation and sclerotic margins.

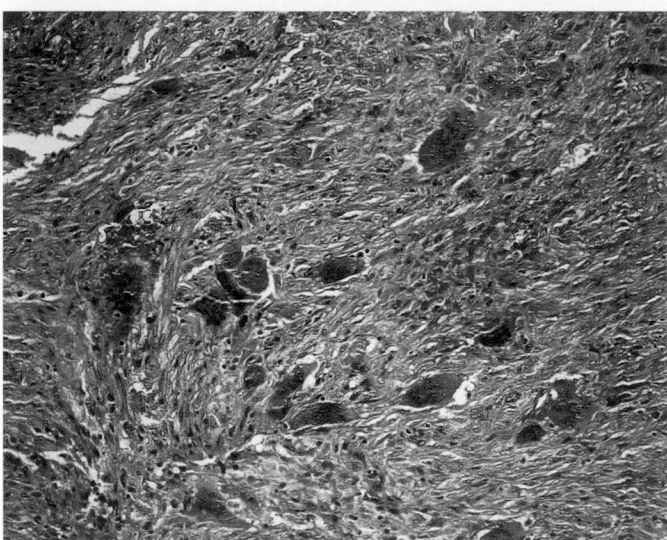

Fig. 24.104 Metaphyseal fibrous defect. The predominant element is a spindle cell of fibroblastic appearance. There are also irregularly scattered osteoclasts.

and associated with an intramedullary component, they have been designated as nonossifying or nonosteogenic fibromas (Fig. 24.103). There has been a longstanding and still unresolved controversy regarding whether these lesions are neoplastic or whether they represent developmental aberration at the epiphyseal plate.

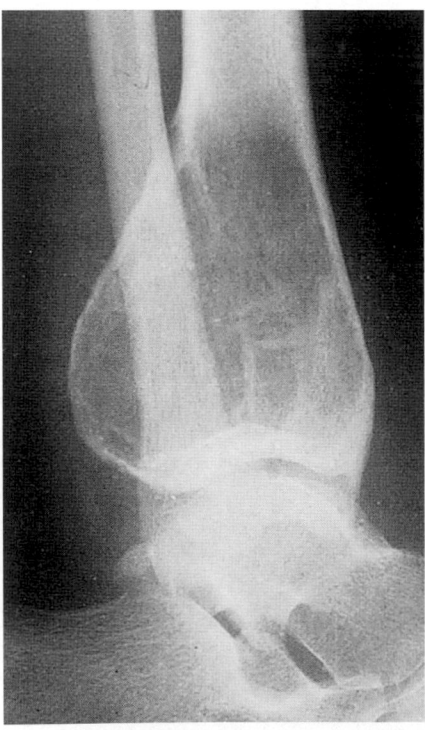

Fig. 24.103 Large metaphyseal fibrous defect expanding lower tibial metaphysis. Lesions of this size are sometimes called nonossifying fibroma.

Grossly, the lesion is granular and brown or dark red. Microscopically, it consists of cellular masses of fibrous tissue often arranged in a storiform pattern (Figs 24.104 and 24.105). Scattered osteoclasts and collections of foamy and hemosiderin-laden macrophages are frequent. The microscopic appearance is very reminiscent of a benign fibrous histiocytoma and is designated as such by some authors, especially when it occurs in adult patients in places other than metaphyses of long bones.[905] Exceptionally, bizarre nuclear features are present, which are not necessarily indicative of a malignant nature.[906]

Clinically, there are few or no symptoms except pain. The lesion is usually found incidentally on x-ray examination. Fractures can occur through the thinned cortex.[904]

Fibrous dysplasia and related lesions

Fibrous dysplasia is a non-neoplastic condition that can present in two forms: monostotic and polyostotic. The monostotic variety is usually seen in older children and young adults and most commonly affects the rib, femur, and tibia.[916] The less common polyostotic type is characterized by a unilateral distribution and is usually associated with endocrine dysfunction, precocious puberty in female individuals, and areas of cutaneous hyperpigmentation (Albright's syndrome). This syndrome is the result of a somatic mutation of the c-*fos* oncogene in affected tissues that results in the activation of the signal-transduction pathway that generates cyclic AMP.[912,921,929,934] The mutation of the alpha subunit of signal-transducing G proteins (Gsalpha) can be detected in paraffin-embedded material.[932]

Radiographs of these lesions in the rib show a fusiform, expanded mass with thinning of the cortex. In the tibia, a lobulated, sharply delimited lesion of the shaft is formed (Fig. 24.106). This lesion may have a

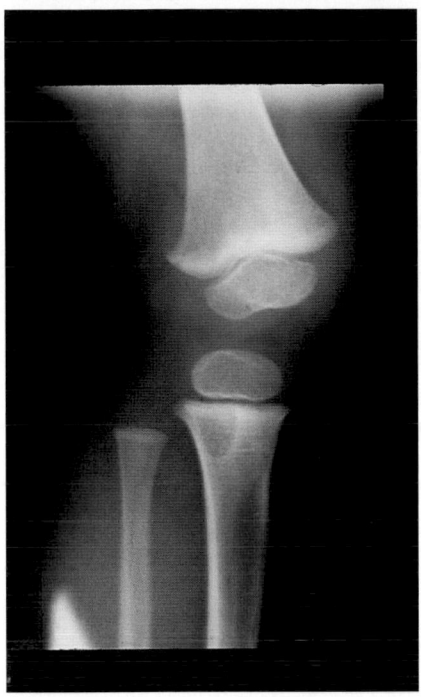

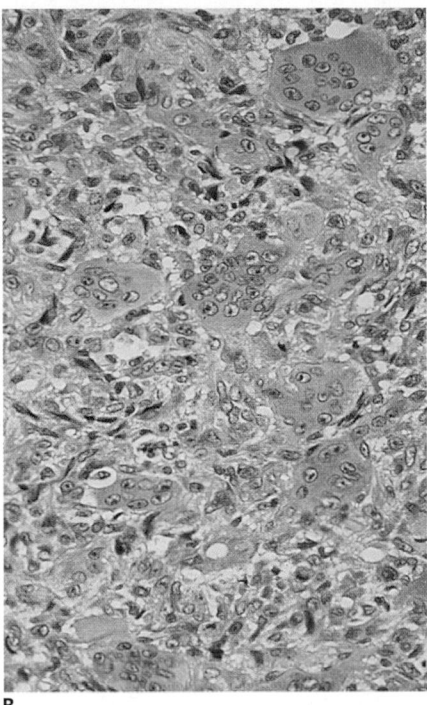

A   B

Fig. 24.105 Radiographic (**A**) and microscopic (**B**) appearances of metaphyseal fibrous defect involving the upper metaphysis of the tibia.

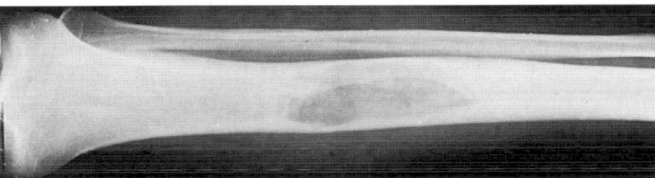

Fig. 24.106 Fibrous dysplasia of tibia forming a sharply delimited lesion.

multilocular appearance because of endosteal cortical scalloping. Comparable lesions in membranous bone, particularly in the maxilla or the mandible, may show an overgrowth of dense bone. Occasionally the lesion protrudes far beyond the normal bone contour ("fibrous dysplasia protuberans").[913]

Grossly, the tissue cuts with a gritty consistency and is grayish yellow (Fig. 24.107). The cortical bone often is thinned and expanded.

Microscopically, narrow, curved, and misshaped bone trabeculae, often having a characteristic fishhook configuration, are interspersed with fibrous tissue of variable cellularity[928] (Fig. 24.108). The coarse fiber ("woven") bone present in this condition does not transform into lamellar bone, suggesting that fibrous dysplasia represents a maturation defect so that the process of bone formation is arrested at an early stage resembling membranous ossification. Rows of cuboidal appositional osteoblasts do not appear on the surface of the trabeculae except as a pattern of reaction following local trauma. Silver stains are helpful in showing this failure of maturation. Ultrastructurally, the immature woven bone trabeculae are lined by abnormal osteoblasts with a fibroblast-like appearance.[915]

Fig. 24.107 Gross appearance of fibrous dysplasia of the rib. The lesion forms a fusiform, expanded mass that is grayish white.

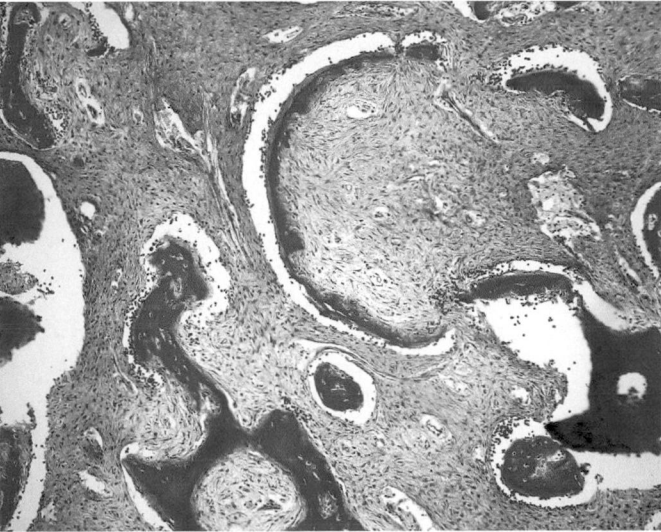

Fig. 24.108 Typical low-power appearance of fibrous dysplasia.

If a lesion of fibrous dysplasia is biopsied over a period of years, maturation is still absent. This fundamental histologic abnormality makes it possible to distinguish fibrous dysplasia from other lesions. In some instances, however, particularly in femoral lesions, the differential diagnosis becomes nearly impossible.[927]

Occasionally, lesions of fibrous dysplasia show calcified spherules similar to those seen in cementifying fibromas.[926,935,937] Other cases show highly cellular areas that may be diagnosed incorrectly as sarcoma. Focal areas of hyaline cartilage and cystic areas may also be present. The former are more common in the polyostotic variety and can dominate the microscopic picture to such a degree that a mistaken diagnosis of a cartilaginous tumor can be made.[925] The transition of normal to abnormal bone is often abrupt. This is helpful in distinguishing it radiographically from osteitis fibrosa cystica resulting from hyperparathyroidism.

It has been suggested that some rib lesions resembling fibrous dysplasia but showing progressive maturation of the bone toward the periphery are secondary to trauma ("post-traumatic dysplasia or lesion").[919,922] Some of these lesions are bilateral and strikingly symmetrical.[914]

Fibrous dysplasia may be accompanied by intramuscular myxoma of the same extremity.[908] In addition, fibrous dysplasia of either monostotic or polyostotic type can be complicated by the development of a primary bone sarcoma, particularly osteosarcoma[917] but also chondrosarcoma and malignant fibrous histiocytoma.[918,930]

Resection cures fibrous dysplasia in bones such as the rib. Curettement is adequate in long bones such as the tibia. In the maxilla, where some deformity may exist, partial removal of the lesion is all that is necessary.

Osteofibrous dysplasia (fibro-osseous dysplasia, ossifying fibroma; Campanacci's lesion) is distinguished microscopically from fibrous dysplasia by the osteoblastic rimming of the bone trabeculae and the presence of lamellar bone and radiographically by its cortical rather than medullary location and its greater tendency to recur[910,911,920] (Fig. 24.109). The tibia and fibula are the bones usually affected, the lesions usually being eccentrically located.[910,923]

Clonal chromosomal abnormalities have been identified in this lesion, suggesting a neoplastic nature.[909] Immunohistochemically, reactivity for keratin neurofibromin, S-100 protein, and Leu 7 are commonly found in osteofibrous dysplasia, in contrast to fibrous dysplasia[924,933,936] (Fig. 24.110). A peculiar and as yet unexplained relationship exists between osteofibrous dysplasia and adamantinoma of long bones (see p. 2185). In contrast to fibrous dysplasia, there are no activating mutations of Gsalpha, suggesting that the two disorders are not pathogenetically related, despite their morphologic and some phenotypic similarities.[931,932]

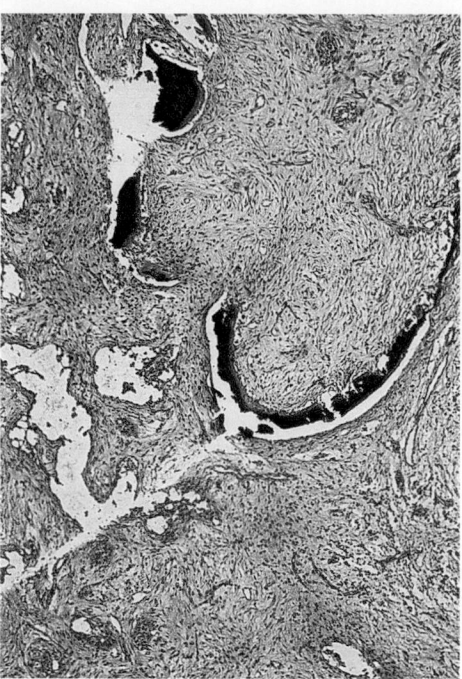

Fig. 24.109 Osteofibrous dysplasia. The low-power view is similar to that of fibrous dysplasia, but on high power there was osteoblastic rimming of the bone trabeculae.

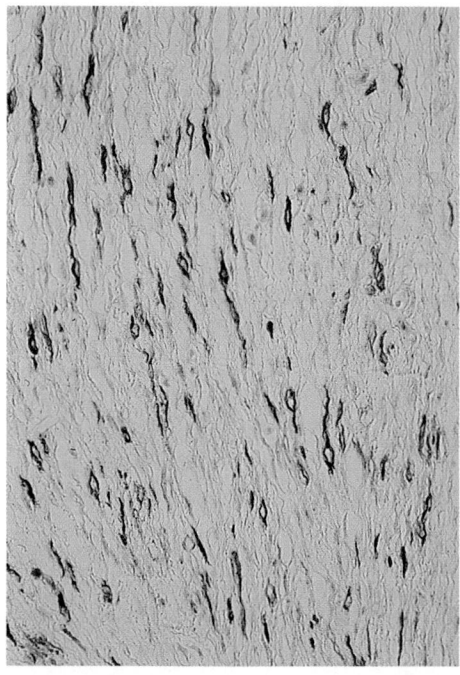

Fig. 24.110 Immunoreactivity of spindle cells of osteofibrous dysplasia for keratin. This does not occur in fibrous dysplasia.

Myositis ossificans

Localized myositis ossificans is a reactive condition that is sometimes mistaken microscopically for osteosarcoma.[938,939a,945] The term is inaccurate because the muscle may not be involved, and inflammation is virtually absent. A history of trauma is obtained in only half of the patients. The most common locations are the flexor muscles of the upper arm (especially the brachialis anticus), the quadriceps femoris, the adductor muscles of the thigh, the gluteal muscles, and the soft tissues of the hand. Radiographic studies show periosteal reaction and faint soft tissue calcification within 3 to 6 weeks of the injury; these are gradually replaced by mature heterotopic bone by 10 to 12 weeks (Fig. 24.111). Arteriography done during the active stage of the disease shows numerous fine vessels followed by a dense, poorly defined stain in the mass.[946]

Microscopically, there is a highly cellular stroma associated with new bone and, less commonly, cartilage formation. In an early lesion, the centrally placed areas

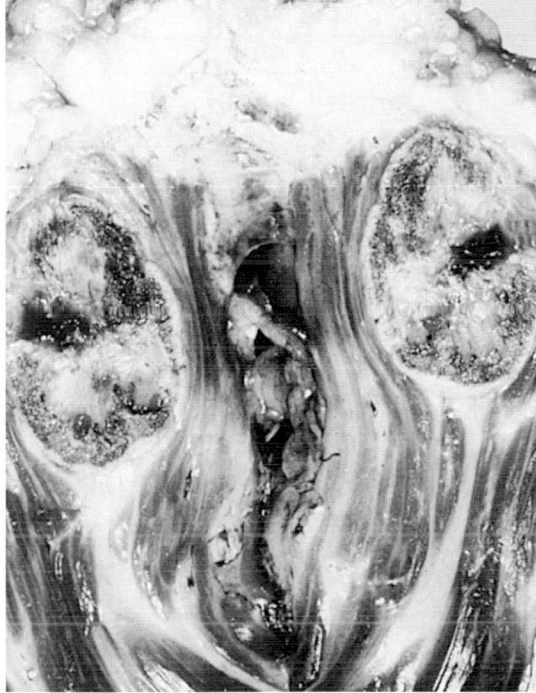

A

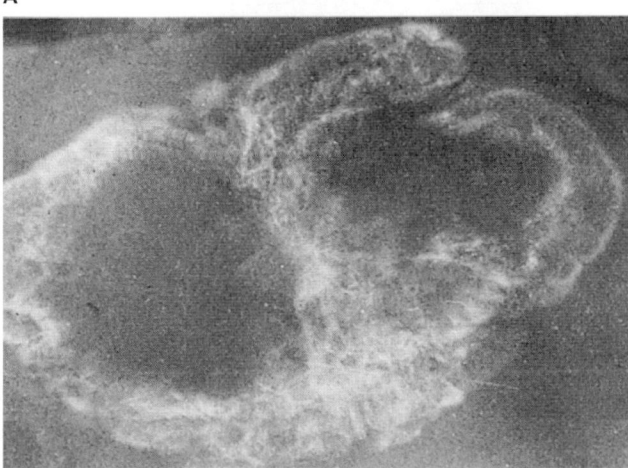

B
Fig. 24.111 A, Well-defined myositis ossificans occurring in muscle. **B,** Same lesion, illustrating bone formation in periphery. (From Ackerman LV. Extraosseous localized nonneoplastic bone and cartilage formation [so-called myositis ossificans]. J Bone Joint Surg 1958, **40A:** 279–298)

may be very difficult to distinguish from osteosarcoma because of their extreme cellularity. As the process evolves, osteoid appears in an orderly pattern at the periphery of this mass and subsequently matures into well-developed bone. Several microscopic subtypes have been described, which correspond to different stages of the process.[945] The most important diagnostic feature is provided by the maturation pattern ("zonal phenomenon"), characterized by a central cellular area, an intermediate zone of osteoid formation, and a peripheral shell of highly organized bone[938] (Figs 24.112 and 24.113). Ultrastructurally, cells with features of myofibroblasts are prominent, as is also the case with other reactive conditions of mesenchymal tissues.[942]

The most important differential diagnosis is with extraosseous osteosarcoma and juxtacortical osteosarcoma. In the former condition, there should be greater cytologic atypia, and the zonal phenomenon does not occur (see Chapter 25). It is doubtful whether myositis ossificans ever develops into osteosarcoma. It is likely that many of the reported cases of this complication actually represent misdiagnosed instances of juxtacortical or extraosseous osteosarcoma.

A reactive lesion histologically and pathogenetically probably related to myositis ossificans has been reported in the small bones of the hand as *florid reactive periostitis*, *parosteal fasciitis*, *fibro-osseous tumor of the digits*, and other descriptive terms.[939,939a,940,944] Localized myositis ossificans also needs to be distinguished from multicentric myositis ossificans, also known as *progressive osseous heteroplasia*, which results from mutations of the *GNAS1* gene.[941,943]

Fig. 24.112 Schematic representation of zonal phenomenon in myositis ossificans. (From Ackerman LV. Extraosseous localized nonneoplastic bone and cartilage formation [so-called myositis ossificans]. J Bone Joint Surg 1958, **40A:** 279–298)

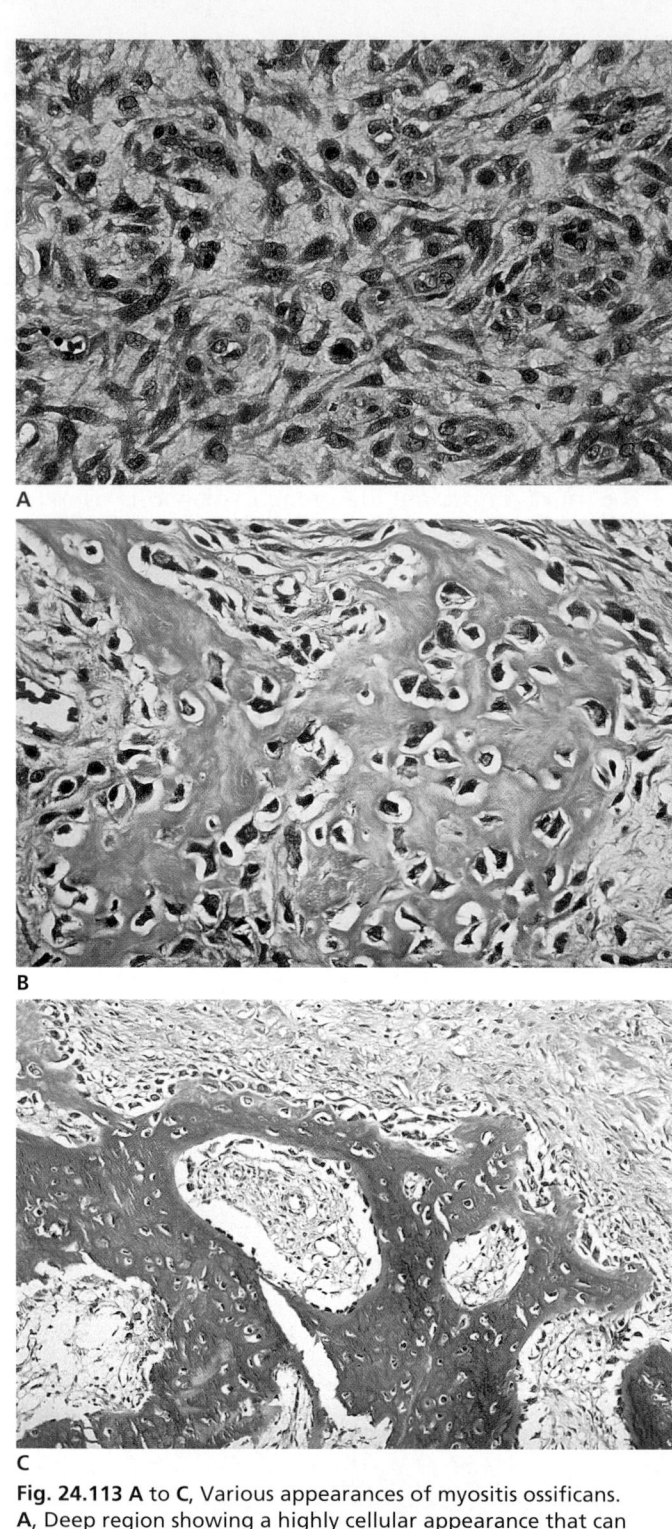

Fig. 24.113 A to **C**, Various appearances of myositis ossificans. **A**, Deep region showing a highly cellular appearance that can simulate a soft tissue sarcoma. **B**, Midportion showing osteoid formation by plump osteoblasts. **C**, Peripheral portion showing a shell of well-formed bone.

Langerhans' cell histiocytosis

The unifying feature of the group of conditions designated as Langerhans' cell histiocytosis (histiocytosis X, eosinophilic granuloma) is an infiltration by a cell of the accessory immune system known as Langerhans' cell.

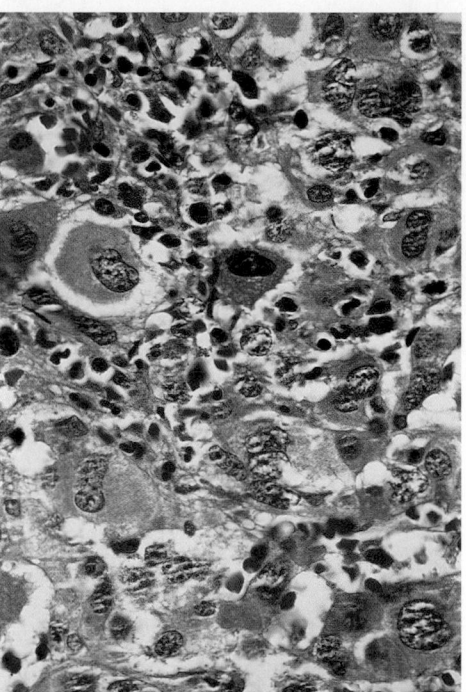

Fig. 24.114 Langerhans' cell histiocytosis. Polymorphic appearance resulting from an admixture of Langerhans' cells, nonspecific histiocytes, lymphocytes, and eosinophils. There is a mild atypia in the Langerhans' cells that can simulate a malignant process.

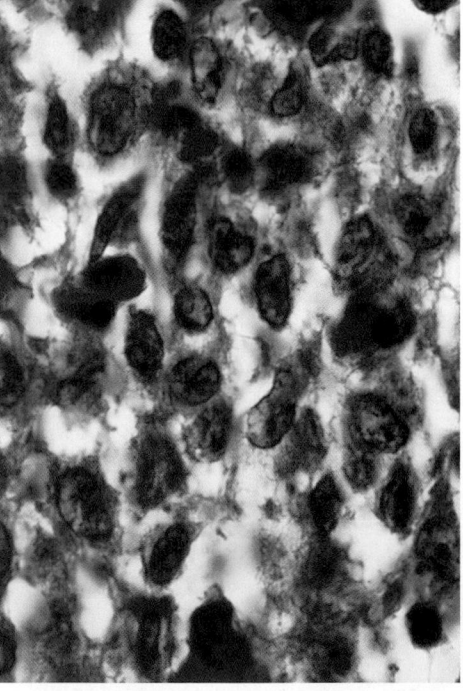

Fig. 24.115 High-power view showing elongated nuclei with occasional longitudinal grooves in the Langerhans' cells.

This is accompanied by a variable admixture of eosinophils, giant cells, neutrophils, foamy cells, and areas of fibrosis (Fig. 24.114). Langerhans' cells have a characteristic morphologic appearance (Fig. 24.115). Their nuclei often are lobulated or indented, sometimes with a longitudinal groove; their cytoplasm is, for the most part, distinctly acidophilic. A specific intracytoplasmic organelle, known as Langerhans' or Birbeck's granule, is regularly present on electron microscopic examination (Fig. 24.116).

Langerhans' cell histiocytosis of bone can be divided into three major categories on the basis of type and extent of the organ involvement:

1 Solitary bone involvement
2 Multiple bone involvement (with or without skin involvement)
3 Multiple organ involvement (bone, liver, spleen, and others)

The cases with solitary bone involvement, which represent the most common variety, have been traditionally referred to as eosinophilic granuloma.[949] Young adults are most commonly affected.[950] Any bone can be involved, with the possible exception of the hands and feet. The most common sites are the cranial vault, jaw, humerus, rib, and femur (Fig. 24.117). Radiographically, they present as an osteolytic lesion often in the metaphyseal area of long bones, sometimes associated with periosteal bone proliferation. They can be confused radiographically with metastatic carcinoma (Fig. 24.118) or Ewing's sarcoma (Fig. 24.119). After fracture, this process may extend into adjacent soft tissues. Recurrences may develop in soft tissue after surgery. These lesions may spontaneously regress. They are extremely radiosensitive and can be cured with small amounts of radiation. The long-term prognosis is excellent.[947] It is exceptional for these patients to develop other bone lesions or involvement of other organs.

Cases of multiple bone involvement have been traditionally designated as multiple or polyostotic eosinophilic granulomas.[948] Depending on the location, the bony infiltration may result in proptosis, diabetes insipidus, chronic otitis media, or a combination of these conditions. The eponym of Hand–Schüller–Christian

disease has been applied to this variety. Since the circumstances on which this designation is based are fortuitous and erratic, it would probably be better to drop the term entirely. This form is characterized by a prolonged clinical course, often marked by alternating episodes of regressions and recrudescences. The eventual outcome is favorable in most cases.

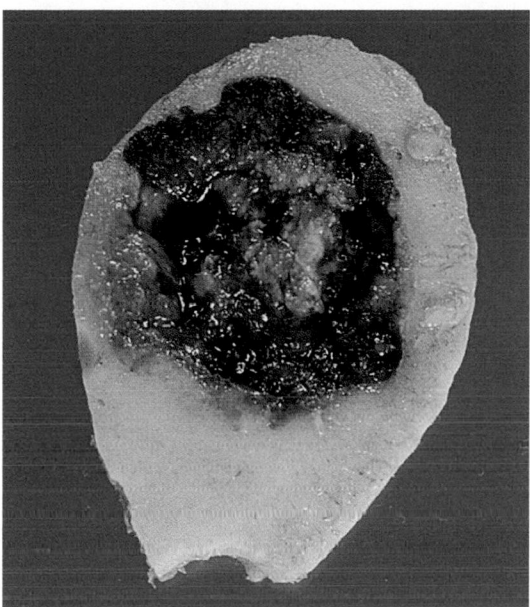

Fig. 24.117 Gross appearance of Langerhans' cell histiocytosis of skull. A sharply circumscribed, dark brown lesion is seen. (Courtesy of Dr. J. Segura, San José, Costa Rica)

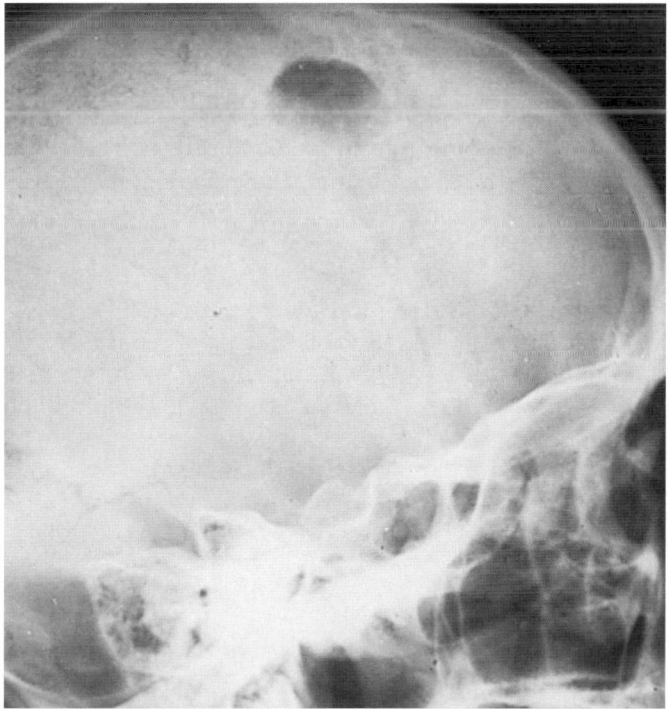

Fig. 24.118 Osteolytic lesion of skull in a 25-year-old woman. Radiographically, the lesion was thought to be metastatic carcinoma but proved to be a solitary lesion of Langerhans' cell histiocytosis.

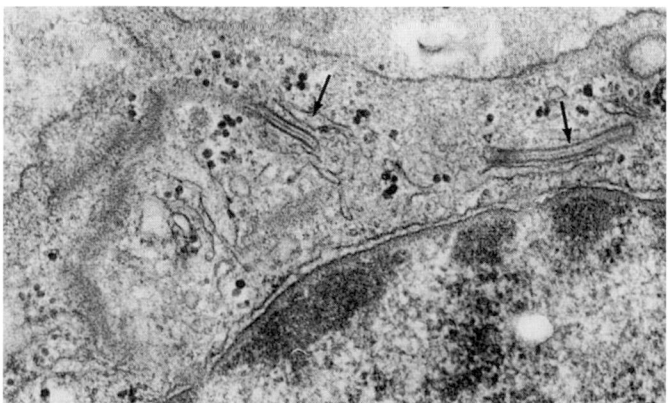

Fig. 24.116 This cell from Langerhans' cell histiocytosis of bone contains several Birbeck's granules (arrows). This is a constant feature of Langerhans' cells in this group of diseases.

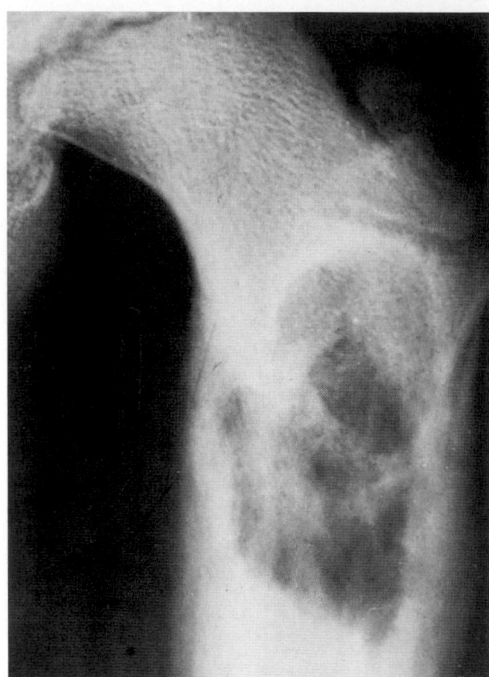

Fig. 24.119 Osteolytic lesion of femur in a 12-year-old boy. This was thought to be Ewing's sarcoma but proved microscopically to be Langerhans' cell histiocytosis.

This type of Langerhans' cell histiocytosis blends imperceptibly with the form having multiple organ involvement. Following the skeletal system, the skin and the lungs are the two most common sites affected. It is difficult to predict the outcome of the disease in a particular case, but there are several parameters that can be used as guidelines. Poor prognostic factors are young age (under 18 months) at the time of diagnosis, hepatomegaly, anemia and/or thrombocytopenia, bone marrow involvement, and hemorrhagic skin lesions. Features not associated with a poor prognosis are seborrhea-like skin lesions, diabetes insipidus, and pulmonary lesions.[952] Microscopically, it is very difficult to separate the aggressive from the more indolent forms. In a typical case of the former, the infiltrate is more monomorphic, with more mitoses and necrosis and fewer giant cells and eosinophils than in a typical case of the latter,[951] but in our experience the overlap has been too great to rely on these features alone.

The differential diagnosis of Langerhans' cell histiocytosis of bone at the microscopic level includes osteomyelitis and the osseous manifestations of Rosai–Dorfman's disease.[953]

Other histiocytic lesions

Rosai–Dorfman's disease (sinus histiocytosis with massive lymphadenopathy) can involve the skeletal system either as a manifestation of multisystem disease or—less commonly—as a mass limited to this site. The morphologic features are similar to those seen at other extranodal sites, in the sense that secondary xanthoma-tous changes and fibrosis are common. These features, plus the paucity of emperipolesis, can render its recognition difficult.

Erdheim–Chester disease is a lipid-storing histiocytosis of non-Langerhans' cell type which may be restricted to the bones or involve multiple organ systems, including lung and central nervous system. The foamy histiocytes that accumulate in this disease are CD68+ and CD1a−. The disease may be accompanied by extensive necrosis.[957] In the lung the involvement is primarily septal, a fact of diagnostic significance both radiographically and morphologically. As in the case of Langerhans' cell histiocytosis, there is controversy as to whether the disease is reactive or neoplastic.[954–956]

Joints and related structures

Normal anatomy

Joints that permit free movements of the bone, referred to as *diarthroses*, are covered by hyaline cartilage and enclosed in a joint capsule. This capsule is composed of an outer fibrous layer of dense connective tissues, which is continuous with the periosteum of the bones, and an inner synovial layer.[958] The latter, also referred to as *synovial membrane*, contains fibroblast-like cells (synoviocytes, type B cells)[961] and macrophages of presumed bone marrow derivation (type A cells). Synoviocytes secrete collagen and proteoglycan and have a highly characteristic phenotype that includes the strong expression of vascular cell adhesion molecule-1 (VCAM-1)[960] and of the antigen detected by Mab67,[959] as well as high activity of the enzyme uridine diphosphoglucose dehydrogenase. Synoviocytes are immunoreactive for vimentin but not for keratin or other epithelial markers.

A layer of loose connective tissue or adipose tissue is present in some regions of the joint between the synovial and the fibrous layers, resulting in the formation of folds or "villi," which protrude into the joint cavity. In old age, these villi may contain islands of cartilage.

Tendons are composed of closely packed parallel type I collagen fibers. They are surrounded by a layer of connective tissue known as the *tendon sheath*. In long tendons, this sheath is composed of an inner layer adjacent to the collagen and an outer layer that is loosely bound to the tissues surrounding the tendon. The space between these two layers is somewhat reminiscent of a joint cavity.

Non-neoplastic diseases

Ganglia and cystic meniscus

Ganglia occur around joints and—less commonly— around tendon sheaths. They are annoying deformities that may cause pain, weakness, partial disability of the joint, and bone changes. Ganglia located in the popliteal space can result in pain or foot drop because of compression of the common peroneal nerve.[964] Individuals overusing the wrist and fingers (pianists, computer operators) are prone to this condition. A history of injury preceding ganglion formation may exist.

Ganglia develop by myxoid degeneration and cystic softening of the connective tissue of the joint capsule or tendon sheath. The theory of a rent in the synovial membrane of a joint leading to the collection of synovial fluid and the formation of a false capsule can seldom be substantiated.

The most common location of ganglia is on the dorsal carpal area of the hand, where the cystic lesion pushes its way toward the surface between the tendons of the extensor indicis proprius and the extensor carpi radialis (Figs 24.120 and 24.121). The second most frequent location is the volar surface of the wrist, superficial and medial to the radial artery. Ganglia also arise on the volar surfaces of the fingers just distal to the metacarpophalangeal joints, in the dorsum of the foot, around the ankle and knee, and in the various articular and ligamentous areas of the spine. Intraosseous ganglia are discussed on p. 2192. Ganglia are not lined by synovia and do not communicate with the joint cavity, two features distinguishing them from Baker's cysts (see later section) (Fig. 24.122).

A lesion microscopically similar to soft tissue ganglion may occur in the menisci of the knee and is referred to simply as *cystic meniscus*. The most common site is the peripheral portion of the middle third of the lateral meniscus.[962,963] It may remain confined to the meniscus or extend extracapsularly. A traumatic etiology is favored.

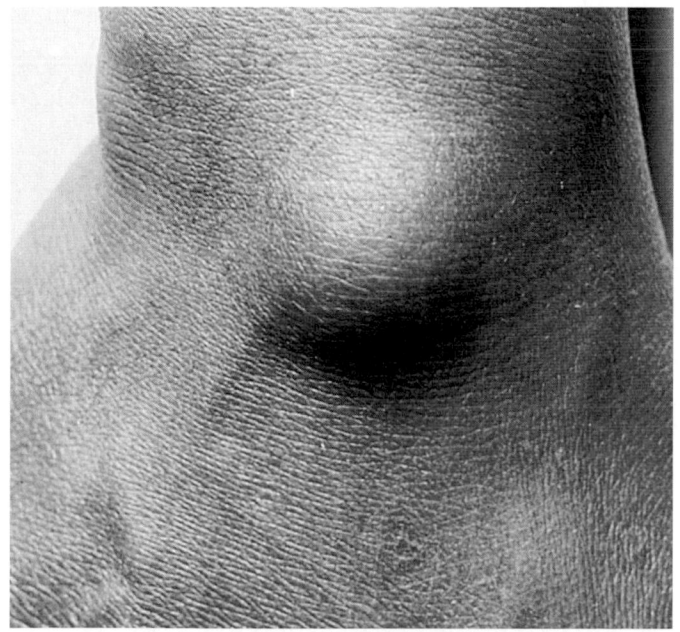

Fig. 24.120 Typical location and appearance of ganglion.

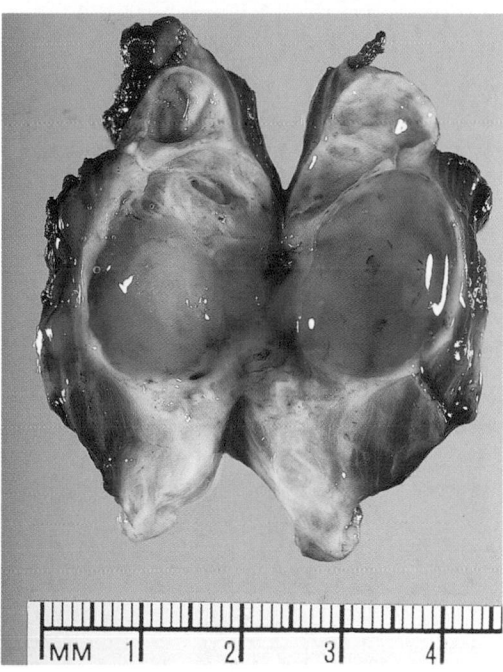

Fig. 24.121 Gross appearance of ganglion cyst. (Courtesy of Dr. RA Cooke, Brisbane, Australia; from Cooke RA, Stewart B: Colour Atlas of Anatomical Pathology. Edinburgh, Churchill Livingstone, 2004.)

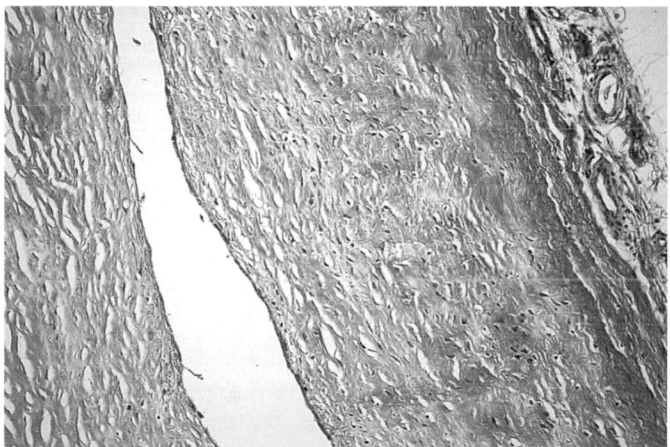

Fig. 24.122 Microscopic appearance of ganglion. The wall is composed of dense fibrous tissue, and there is no synovial lining.

Bursae and Baker's cyst

Bursae are found where muscles, tendons, and skin glide over bony prominences. They are subject to all the diseases that occur in large joint spaces. Inflammation may be associated with the formation of cysts, fluid, and loose bodies (Fig. 24.123). The incomplete removal of loose bodies may be followed by the disappearance of the remaining ones from the bursa.

A related lesion is *subdeltoid bursitis* associated with *calcareous tendonitis*. This entity is primarily a degeneration of a tendon or muscle in the rotator cuff of the shoulder followed by deposition of calcium in necrotic collagenous tissue. This calcific material stimulates a secondary inflammatory reaction.[965]

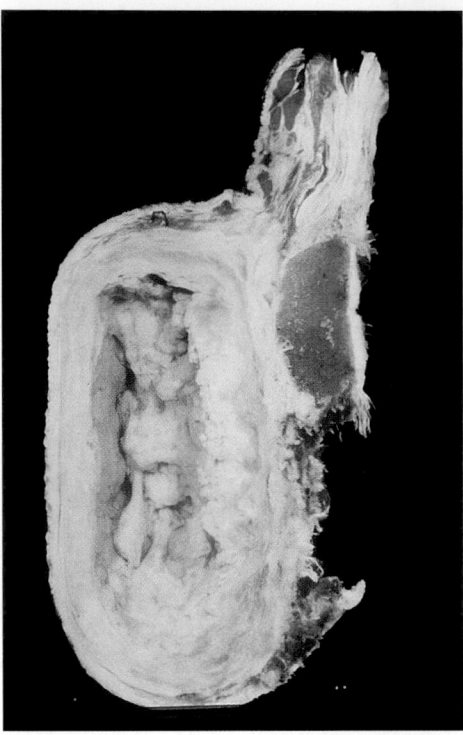

Fig. 24.123 Gross appearance of prepatellar bursa with chronic inflammation.

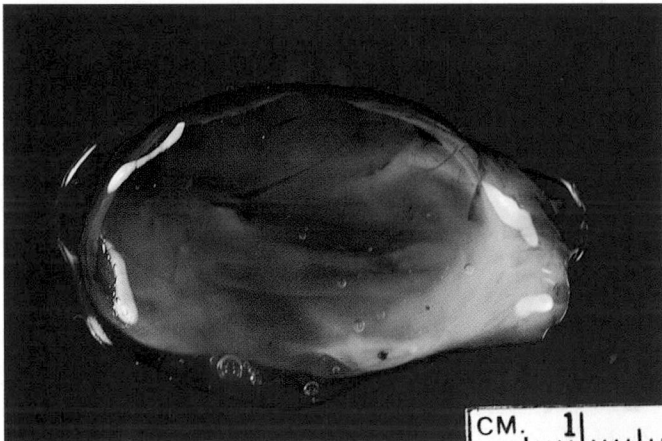

Fig. 24.124 Gross appearance of Baker's cyst.

Baker's cyst occurs in the popliteal space from herniation of the synovial membrane through the posterior part of the capsule or from escape of joint fluid through normal anatomic connections of the knee joint with the semimembraneous bursa (Fig. 24.124). The cyst is lined by true synovium and may have cartilage in its wall. Any joint disease leading to increased intra-articular pressure, such as degenerative joint disease, neuropathic arthropathy, and rheumatoid arthritis, may result in the formation of Baker's cyst.[966]

Carpal tunnel syndrome

The carpal tunnel is the space between the flexor retinaculum or transverse carpal ligament and the carpal bones.

The medial nerve courses through this tunnel and its compression in this location by a variety of causes produces the symptoms of carpal tunnel syndrome.[968–970] These include bony deformity following trauma, masses within the canal (i.e., hemangiomas, lipomas, ganglia), rheumatoid arthritis, and amyloidosis.[967] Often, no specific etiology can be demonstrated.

Arthritis

Synovial biopsy

Needle biopsy of the synovium, particularly of the knee joint, is of aid in the assessment of synovial inflammatory conditions[972,973,977] (Fig. 24.125). The procedure is safe, simple, and easily repeated. It is indicated for inflammatory joint diseases when the etiology remains in doubt, particularly when only one joint is affected. Examination of the synovial fluid should always be performed before biopsy. It is possible to diagnose tuberculosis and other specific granulomatous lesions by this method.[971–977] Other diagnosable diseases are pigmented villonodular synovitis, amyloidosis, Whipple's disease, hemochromatosis, metastatic disease, and gout. A heavy neutrophilic infiltrate is highly characteristic of infectious arthritis, although it also may be seen in Behçet's disease and familial Mediterranean fever. Unfortunately, the histologic findings in the most common rheumatic diseases are often nonspecific[971]; however, the combination of prominent lymphoid follicles and marked hyperplasia of synovial cells is highly suggestive of rheumatoid arthritis. By the use of a small-caliber synovial biopsy needle (Parker–Pearson technique), Schumacher and Kulka[975] were able to obtain sufficient synovial tissue for diagnosis in 92% of the 109 joint biopsies they performed. Histologic examination proved to be of direct diagnostic value in 38 cases.

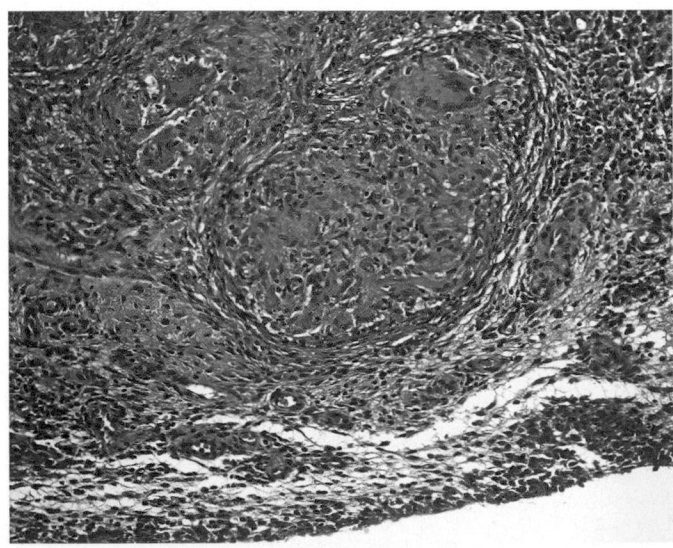

Fig. 24.125 Synovitis with non-necrotizing granulomas consistent with sarcoidosis.

Degenerative joint disease (osteoarthritis)

The term osteoarthritis is inaccurate because this type of joint disease is degenerative and not inflammatory.[982] The pathologic changes are related directly to age and are conditioned by use and occupation of the patient. These morphologic changes have been beautifully described in the classical works of Collins,[980] Hirsch et al.,[986] and Bauer and Bennett.[979]

The earliest change is an even degeneration of the hyaline cartilage of the articular surface, first detected as a fibrillation of the cartilaginous matrix at a right angle to the surface, and eventually resulting in a papillary appearance and sometimes in the freeing of fragments of cartilage. This leads to thinning of cartilage and compensatory overgrowth of the apposite joint surface. Once the articular cartilage disappears, the two bony surfaces are brought into contact, with progressive thickening of the trabeculae ("eburnation") (Figs 24.126 and 24.127). There is also increased activity of the perichondrium at the periphery of the joint, with formation of so-called Heberden's nodes. The synovial membrane may remain normal or undergo thickening, with formation of papillary metaplastic masses of cartilage, bone, or adipose tissue. Detachment of these masses gives rise to intra-articular loose bodies known as rice bodies.

In some cases of severe osteoarthritis there are foci of subchondral acute inflammation resembling osteomyelitis, but these are probably of a non-infectious nature.[991]

It should be emphasized that the changes of degenerative joint disease are centered in the cartilage, a type of tissue notorious for its poor capacity for repair.[984,996] These changes are more prominent on the joint surface exposed to friction, weight bearing, or movement, but they also occur in areas of the joint not subject to these mechanical forces.[985] The mechanical attrition of the cartilage is preceded by a loss of chondroitin sulfate matrix. Loss of cartilage thickness leads to narrowing of the joint space and loss of stability of the chondro-osseous junction. The osteophytes seen at the margins of osteoarthritic joints progress through discrete stages of cartilage differentiation that can be followed with collagen type-specific probes.[970] The cartilage degradation in osteoarthritis is believed to be mediated by cytokines, in particular IL-1.[995]

Some degree of synovial hyperplasia with hyperemia and lymphocytic infiltration can be seen in advanced stages of the disease, especially in the hip; these changes should not be confused with rheumatoid arthritis.

A secondary change sometimes seen in the osteoarthritic head of a femur is the presence of cysts located close to the surface. These are surrounded by dense bone and contain fluid or loose connective tissue[985,988,989,994] (Fig. 24.128). Other secondary features of the disease are

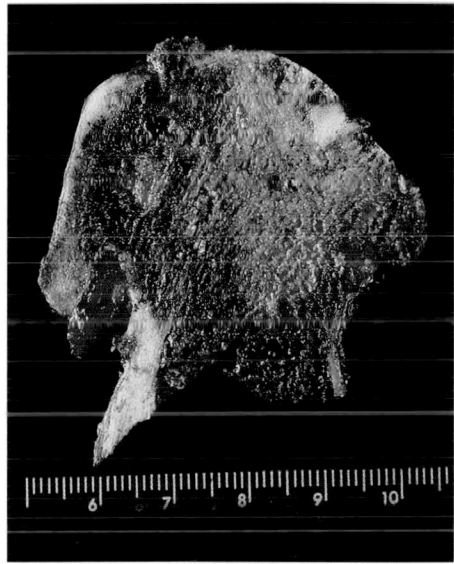

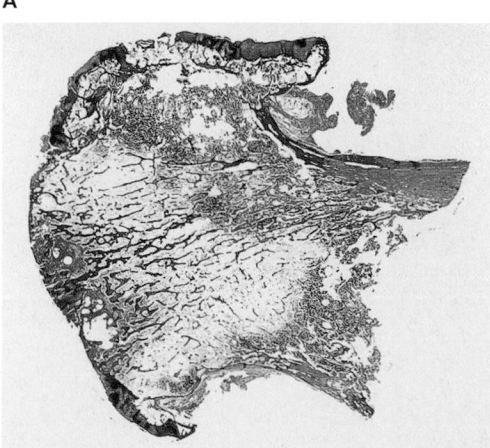

Fig. 24.126 Advanced osteoarthritis of femoral head: **A**, gross appearance, showing near-total disappearance of articular cartilage; **B**, whole mount of the same case.

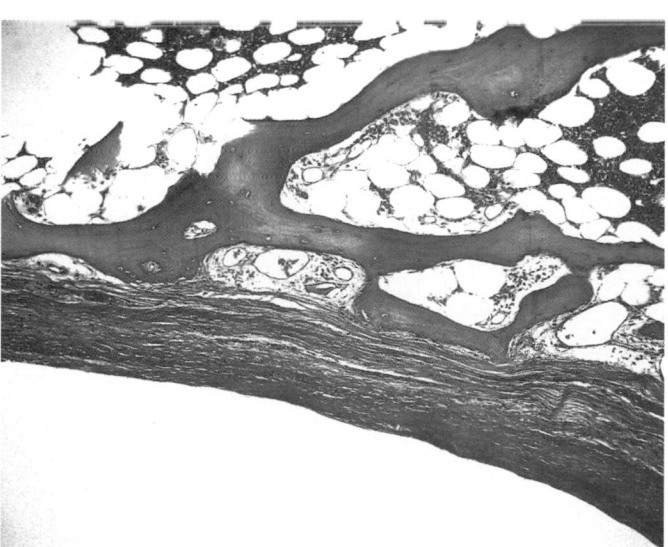

Fig. 24.127 Osteoarthritis. The articular cartilage has been replaced by a thin layer of fibrous tissue.

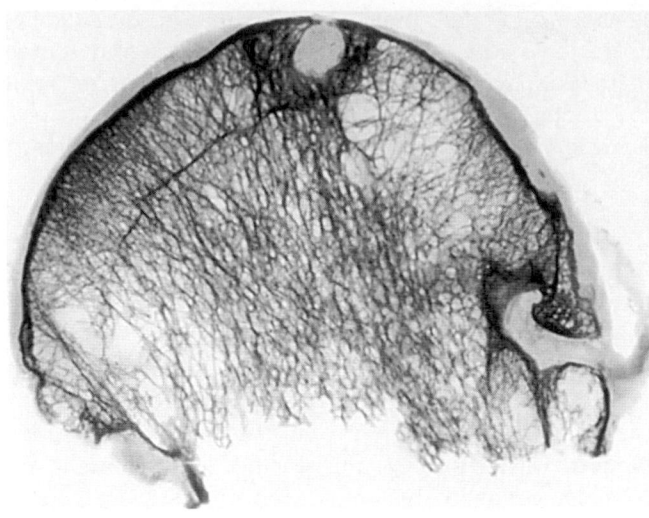

Fig. 24.128 Specimen radiograph of femoral head with osteoarthrosis. Note irregular thinning of articular cartilage and formation of a subchondral cyst surrounded by sclerotized bone.

represented by changes in the capsular and synovial nerves.[981,993]

Neuropathic arthropathy (Charcot's joint) is a particularly destructive variant of degenerative joint disease (Fig. 24.129). The process is usually slowly progressive, although on rare occasions it may have an extremely rapid evolution.[990] Particles of dead bone and cartilage often are seen in large amounts embedded in the synovial membrane.[987] However, they are not specific for this condition.

Chondromalacia patellae is the name given to a condition of obscure etiology characterized by softening, fibrillation, fissuring, and erosion of the articular cartilage of the patella.[992] Microscopically, the changes are indistinguishable from those of degenerative joint disease.[983]

Rheumatoid arthritis

Rheumatoid arthritis is an immune-complex disease that manifests as a chronic polyarticular arthritis. It is mostly seen in women during the second and third decades of life.[1020] The joints of the feet and hands are nearly always involved. Other joints frequently affected are the elbows, knees, wrists, ankles, hips, spine, and temporomandibular articulations.

Lysosomes and interleukins are mediators of the inflammatory reaction seen in this disease and in other joint diseases.[997,1005,1025] Basic fibroblastic growth factor may play a role in synovial hyperplasia and joint destruction.[1017] The etiology of rheumatoid arthritis is unknown, but a viral participation has long been suspected on the basis of epidemiologic, morphologic, and immunohistologic findings.[1024] The HLA linkage and the autoantibody production observed in most patients support an autoimmune element in this disease.[1023]

The earliest morphologic changes occur in the synovial membrane. Hyperemia of the synovium is followed by proliferation of the synovial lining cells and infiltration by plasma cells and lymphocytes[1011] (Fig. 24.130). Lymphoid follicles are often present.[1009] The small synovial blood vessels are lined by plump endothelial cells, and fibrin deposits often are seen close to the synovial lining or within the stroma. Two additional microscopic features, which are also nonspecific, include the presence of synovial giant cells and bone and

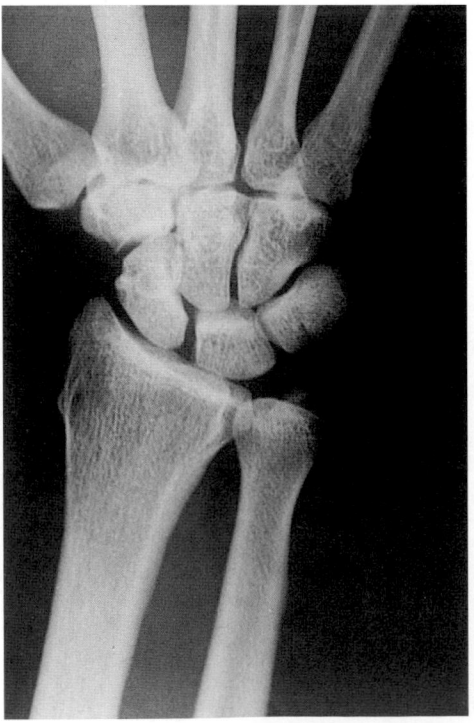

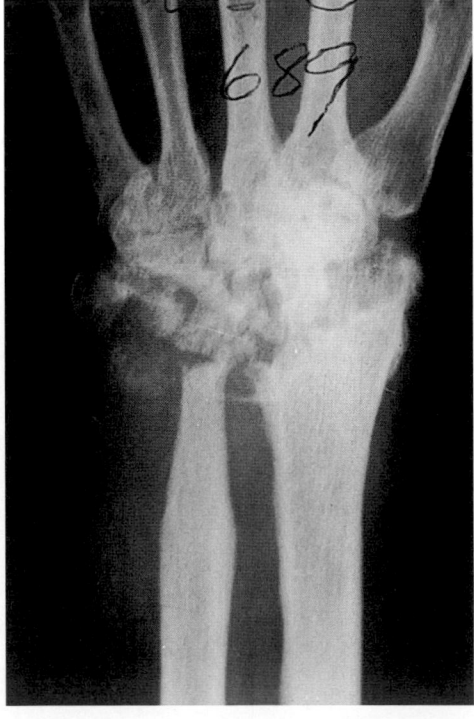

Fig. 24.129 Neuropathic changes in wrist secondary to syringomyelia.

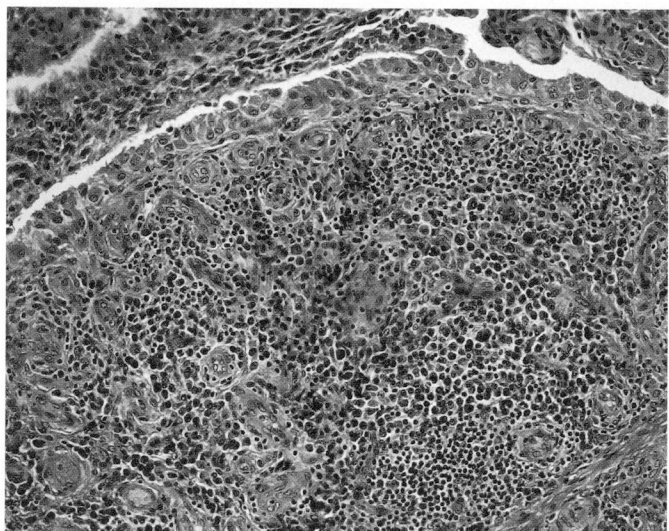

Fig. 24.130 Synovial hyperplasia and heavy lymphoplasmacytic infiltrate in rheumatoid arthritis.

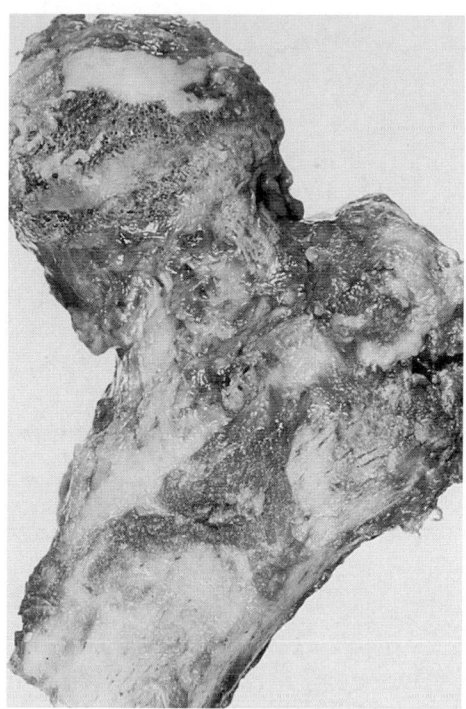

Fig. 24.131 Advanced rheumatoid arthritis involving femur. There is prominent proliferation of synovium and almost complete destruction of overlying articular cartilage.

cartilage fragments within the actual synovial membrane.[1015] They need to be distinguished from multinucleated plasma cells, foreign body cells, and Touton giant cells that can also occur in joints with rheumatoid arthritis. These synovial giant cells tend to be present in patients with active, seropositive disease, but there is no correlation with the serologic titer.[1003] Bhan and Roy[1000] found them in seropositive and in seronegative cases, as well as in tuberculosis, traumatic arthritis, and villonodular synovitis. The cartilage and bone fragments tend to occur in joints with advanced disease. They appear to arise as a result of the erosive destructive process of the articular surface and can be distinguished by virtue of their position and clear demarcation from the metaplastic cartilage and bone that sometimes arises from synovial cells. They also have been seen in synovial membranes of osteoarthritis, osteochondritis dissecans, chondromalacia patellae, and particularly in neuropathic joints.[1008,1015]

In the second phase, granulation tissue grows into the subchondral marrow of the bone. Osteoporosis occurs early and may result in spontaneous fractures of long bones (particularly the femoral neck) and the pelvis.[1022] Prominent pannus is formed over the articular cartilage (Fig. 24.131). Cartilage and even bone form in this pannus. The granulation tissue of the subchondral area and the pannus within the joint attack the cartilage.[1001] Its destruction may be followed by fibrous ankylosis and eventually bony ankylosis. Increased articular pressure may lead to bursting of the joint capsule and acute joint rupture,[1002] bone cysts ("rheumatoid geodes"),[1016] or herniation of the capsule into the soft tissues.[1010] The bone cysts are radiographically similar to those seen in association with degenerative joint disease, but in rheumatoid arthritis they contain granulation tissue instead of fluid or myxoid material. The microscopic changes of rheuma-

toid arthritis correlate well with the radiographic findings, but not too closely with the clinical findings.[1013]

Tenosynovitis and "rheumatoid nodules" are the two most common extra-articular manifestations of rheumatoid arthritis.[1006,1007] Rheumatoid nodules, which are seen in approximately 20% of the patients, occur most often in tendons and tendon sheaths and periarticular subcutaneous tissue but also have been seen in the heart and large vessels, lung and pleura, kidney, meninges, and synovial membrane itself.[1018] Microscopically, they are composed of a necrotic center impregnated with fibrin, surrounded by a predominantly histiocytic inflammatory reaction often arranged in a palisading fashion (Fig. 24.132). They are not specific to rheumatoid arthritis. Nodules morphologically indistinguishable can occur in rheumatic fever, in systemic lupus erythematosus, and in children in the absence of any apparent disease.[998,1004] Berardinelli et al.[999] followed ten cases of the latter and found rheumatoid factor 2 to 16 years after the appearance of the nodules. Rheumatoid nodules also need to be distinguished from suture granulomas from previous surgical procedures.[1012]

Sokoloff et al.[1021] found nonnecrotizing arteritis in 10% of patients with rheumatoid arthritis. Necrotizing arteritis has also been described.[1014,1019] Polyneuritis can be observed.

The pulmonary manifestations of rheumatoid arthritis have been discussed in Chapter 7 and the lymph node changes in Chapter 21.

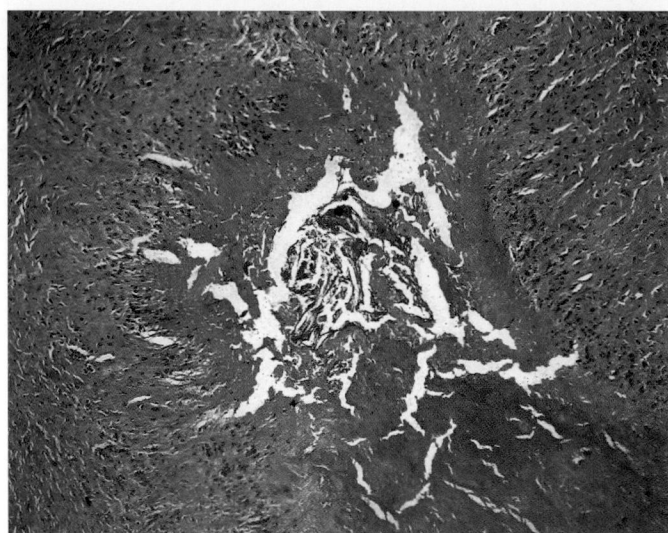

Fig. 24.132 Rheumatoid nodule with early cystic change of the "necrobiotic" center. Note the peripheral palisading of histiocytes.

Amyloidosis is a significant complication of the disease. As a matter of fact, in the United States, rheumatoid arthritis has displaced tuberculosis as the most common underlying disorder associated with amyloid deposition.

Infectious arthritis

Bacterial, fungal, and parasitic infections can reach the joints either by hematogenous spread or by contiguous extension from a neighboring osteomyelitis (Fig. 24.133). A form of infectious arthritis that has risen dramatically in recognition and frequency in recent years is *Lyme disease*, an arthropod-transmitted spirochetosis that also involves skin, heart, and nervous system.[1026,1028,1029,1031] The microscopic changes in the synovium are those of a nonspecific chronic synovitis, but the spirochete can occasionally be detected with the Liederle stain.[1027]

Fig. 24.133 Tuberculous bursitis with innumerable "rice bodies." The latter are mainly composed of fibrin and have no diagnostic significance. (Courtesy of Dr. EF Lascano, Buenos Aires)

Spirochetal antigens have also been demonstrated ultra-structurally in cases of chronic Lyme disease.[1030]

Gout and pseudogout

About 2% to 5% of chronic joint disease is caused by gout. The metatarsophalangeal joints are often the first to be involved, but other joints of the hands and feet are also frequently involved. The disease may also involve the joints of the long bones (Fig. 24.134A).

Calcification and even ossification of tophi occur frequently.[1035] The urate deposits progressively destroy the cartilage and may cause osteolytic, irregular destruction of subchondral bone. These deposits may extend out from a joint into the soft tissue and cause destruction of the ligaments. This destruction eventually leads to subcutaneous deposits that may erode through the skin. The microscopic pattern of gout is unmistakable. Fixation in alcohol is important for the preservation of sodium urate monohydrate deposits that appear as needle-shaped, doubly refractile crystals. The deGalantha stain is particularly suited for their demonstration. Even if alcohol fixation is not done, the appearance of tophi is usually diagnostic because of the typical granulomatous response that they elicit (Fig. 24.134B). Furthermore, the negative birefringence of these crystals can still be demonstrated after staining with nonaqueous alcoholic eosin.[1033,1037] Histiocytes and foreign body giant cells predominate in the infiltrate. Palisading of the histiocytes sometimes occurs and may be a source of confusion with rheumatoid nodules.

Gout should also be distinguished from *chondrocalcinosis* (pseudogout syndrome), a rare condition in which the symptoms result from diffuse deposition of calcium pyrophosphate crystals in the articular cartilage.[1032,1034,1036] Many of these cases involve the temporomandibular joint and are discussed further in Chapter 6.

Intervertebral disk prolapse

Material curetted from an intervertebral disk because of prolapse is a very common surgical specimen. Features such as fibrillation, cluttering of chondrocytes, and granular change are generally regarded as indicators of degeneration related to prolapse.[1038] Weidner et al.[1039] found instead that the feature that better correlated with prolapse was neovascularization occurring at the edges of the fibrocartilaginous fragments.

Other articular and periarticular diseases

Hemophilia is characterized by the accumulation of hemosiderin-laden macrophages in the synovium. In contrast to pigmented villonodular synovitis (PVNS), there are few if any foamy macrophages or spindle cells. The morphologic features of hemophilic arthropathy are those of a degenerative rather than an inflammatory process.[1050]

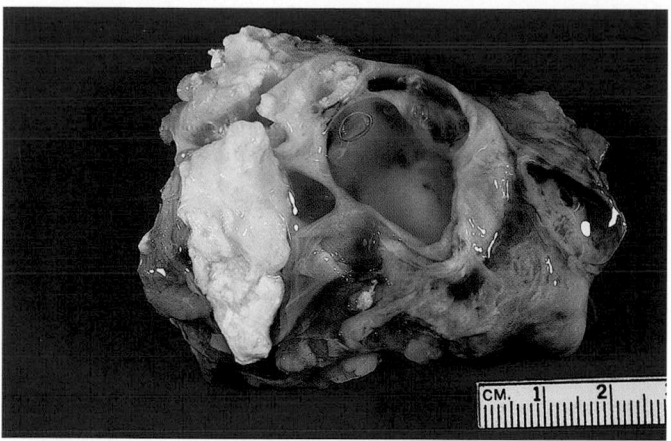

Amyloid can deposit in the synovium, articular cartilage, menisci, periarticular tissue, and intervertebral disk in old age, apparently unrelated to osteoarthritis and in the absence of systemic amyloidosis.[1040,1041,1045,1046,1051] Heavier amounts can be seen as an expression of primary amyloidosis or multiple myeloma.[1047] Amyloidosis is one of the causes of the carpal tunnel syndrome[1043,1044] (see p. 2200). The amyloid material usually consists of transthyretin (AF/ASCI, prealbumin).[1046]

SAPHO is a peculiar syndrome of unknown etiology in which synovitis is seen in combination with acne, pustulosis, hyperostosis, and osteitis.[1048]

Tumors and tumorlike conditions

Tendosynovial giant cell tumor

Tendosynovial giant cell tumor (TSGCT, nodular tendosynovitis, fibrous histiocytoma of tendon sheath, xanthogranuloma, benign synovioma) is a common lesion that occurs more frequently in women than men, usually appearing in young and middle-aged persons. Most cases are distributed between the wrist and fingertips and between the ankle and toe tips. It is more often proximal than distal on both the hands and feet and occurs most frequently on their flexor surfaces. Other sites can be affected, including the vertebral column.[1056a]

Grossly, it presents as a single mass usually measuring 1 to 3 cm in diameter. It has a fairly well-defined capsule, may be somewhat lobulated, and varies in color from whitish gray to yellowish brown (Fig. 24.135). The so-called diffuse form tends to have a larger size and infiltrative margins.[1056,1061]

Microscopically, this lesion contains closely packed medium-sized polyhedral cells with a variable admixture of giant cells containing fat and hemosiderin (Fig. 24.136). Cells in zones of active proliferation may show mitotic figures. Focal zones of hyalinization constitute the more quiescent areas. Sometimes, the whole lesion adopts a hypocellular fibrohyalinized appearance. We suspect that the cases reported as *tendon sheath fibromas* are histogenetically related to TSGCT.[1054,1058] Their location, clinical presentation, and recurrence rate are certainly comparable. Ultrastructural and immunohistochemical studies of TSGCT have shown cells with the features of synovial cells admixed with fibroblastic elements, histiocytes, and lymphocytes.[1052,1059,1062] The multinucleated giant cells have the phenotypic features of osteoclasts.[1055]

The great cellularity of this tumor, its variable pattern, and the presence of mitotic figures may lead to an erroneous diagnosis of sarcoma. However, these tumors are nearly always benign. They may erode contiguous bone by pressure. If incompletely removed, they may recur locally.

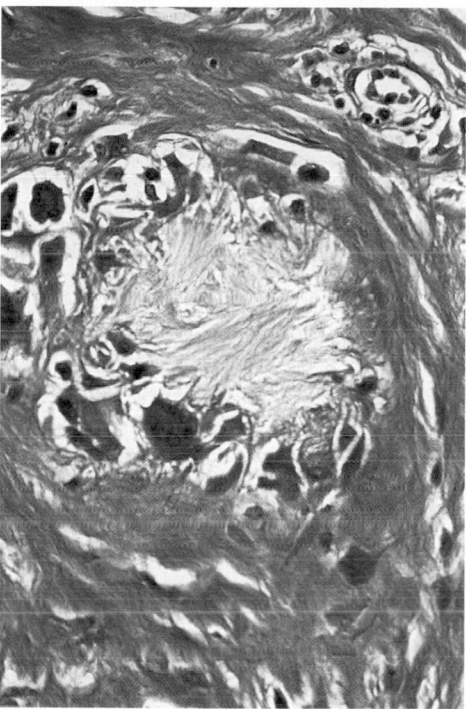

Fig. 24.134 A and **B**, Gout. **A**, Gross appearance of large gouty deposit in the posterior knee. **B**, A lesion of periarticular gout showing a foreign body-type giant cell reaction to the deposited crystals. The crystalline nature of this material is not obvious in this formalin-fixed specimen.

Scleroderma (progressive systemic sclerosis) is often accompanied by arthralgia or arthritis, and sometimes these dominate the clinical picture. The main microscopic changes in the synovial membrane are superficial deposition of fibrin, mild mononuclear infiltrate, minimal hyperplasia of synovial lining cells, proliferation of collagen fibers, and focal obliteration of small vessels.[1049]

Lupus erythematosus may be accompanied by microscopic changes in the synovium which are indistinguishable from those of rheumatoid arthritis. As a rule, however, there is a more intense surface fibrin deposition and a lesser degree of proliferation of synovial cells.[1042]

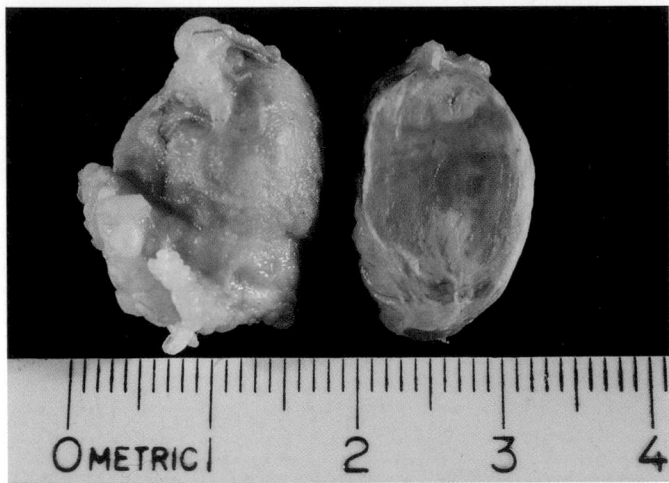

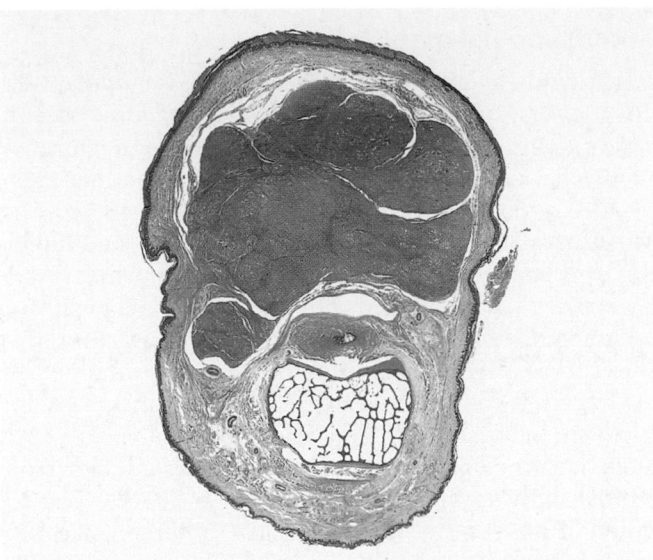

B

Fig. 24.135 A, Gross appearance of tendosynovial giant cell tumor. The lesion is small, well circumscribed, solid, and with a brownish cast. **B**, Whole-mount appearance of a lesion located in the finger. Note the lobulated quality.

The nature of this lesion is still controversial: Jaffe et al.[1057] considered it a reactive process—hence the name of nodular tenosynovitis. Most authors currently regard it as neoplastic, a hypothesis supported by the presence in this lesion of clonal chromosomal aberrations.[1060]

A very rare malignant counterpart of this lesion has been described. Features that should suggest malignancy are a high number of mitotic figures, marked nuclear hyperchromasia, and lack or paucity of multinucleated giant cells.[1053,1063] The main differential diagnosis of TSGCT is epithelioid sarcoma. The presence of granuloma-like formations, necrosis, invasiveness, epithelioid features, and keratin immunoreactivity favors the latter.

Pigmented villonodular synovitis and bursitis

PVNS is believed to be closely related to TSGCT, to the point that the diffuse type of the latter is also known as extra-articular PVNS.[1074]

PVNS tends to occur in young adults.[1068,1069] Although the knee joint is the usual site, the process may also involve the ankle, hip, shoulder, or even elbow joint.[1070] Usually only one articulation is affected, instances of bilateral disease being exceptional. Occasionally, the lesion may penetrate within the underlying bone.[1073]

The process may be focal or diffuse. When diffuse, it is made up of brownish–yellow spongy tissue. Its appearance depends on the content of hemosiderin pigment. Large amounts of tissue often are present, and complete removal may be impossible (Fig. 24.137). Microscopically, the cellular component is similar to that of TSGCT, but in addition there are papillary projections made up of foamy cells and hemosiderin-containing phagocytes (Fig. 24.138). Large clefts and pseudoglandular or alveolar spaces lined by synovial cells are also present.[1075] The histiocytic nature of the predominant cell type is supported by their immunohistochemical profile.[1075a]

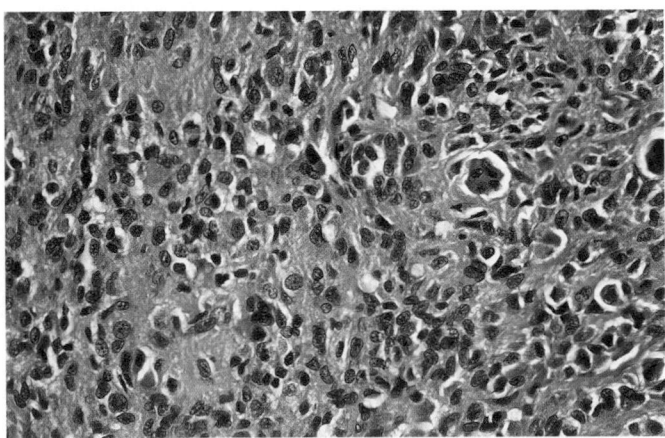

Fig. 24.136 Microscopic appearance of tendosynovial giant cell tumor. A polymorphic infiltrate of small histiocytes and multinucleated giant cells is embedded in dense fibrous tissue.

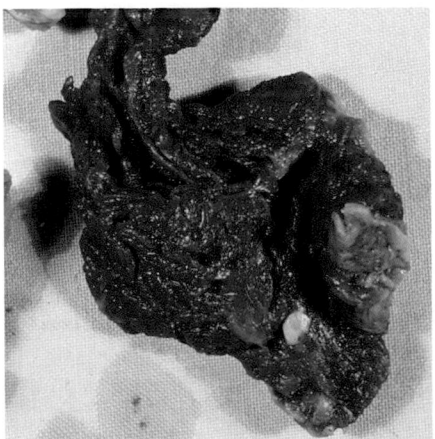

Fig. 24.137 Gross appearance of pigmented villonodular synovitis of knee joint. The lesion has a characteristic dark brown color resulting from extensive hemosiderin deposition. (Courtesy of Dr. Jack Uecker, St. Paul, MN)

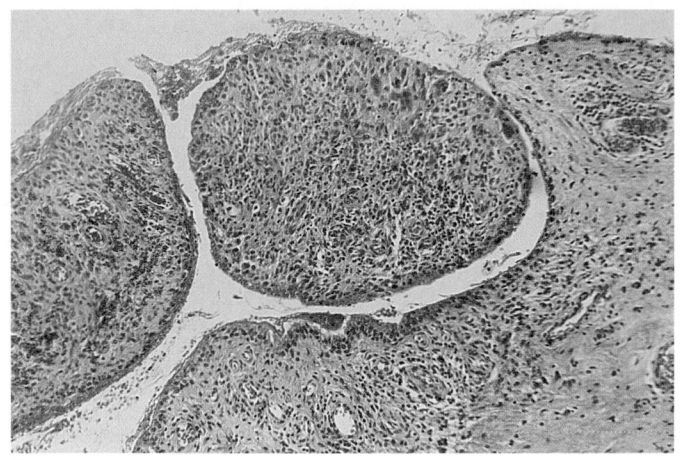
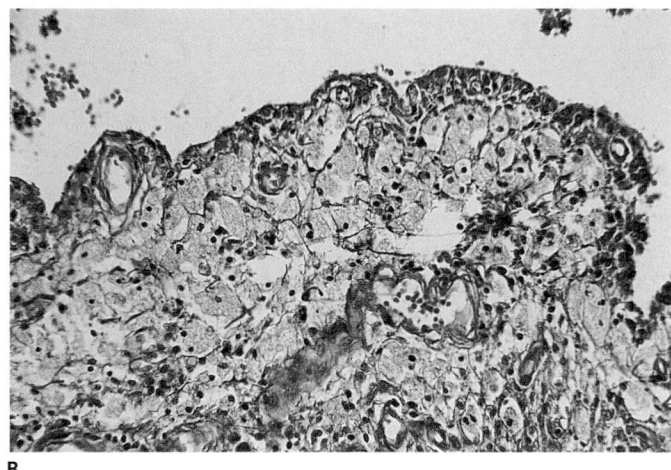

A

B

Fig. 24.138 A and **B**, Microscopic appearance of pigmented villonodular synovitis. **A**, Low-power view showing the villous appearance of the proliferation and hyperplastic synovium. **B**, High-power view. In this area, foamy cells predominate. In others, there were large collections of hemosiderin-laden macrophages.

The capacity of this lesion to result in bone cyst formation and late cartilage and bone loss has been attributed to the production of metalloproteinases such as collagenase and stromelysin.[1066] Clonal chromosomal aberrations similar to those of TSGCT have been found in PVNS, supporting a pathogenetic link between the two conditions and the neoplastic nature of both.[1071,1072]

This disease can be treated by excision. It may recur locally because complete removal is often impossible.[1064] If it recurs locally, radiation therapy may be helpful. As for TSGCT, isolated examples of malignant PVNS have been described.[1065,1067,1074]

Synovial osteochondromatosis and chondrosarcoma

Synovial osteochondromatosis (synovial chondrometaplasia) is characterized by the formation of osteocartilaginous bodies in the synovial membrane.[1076] This condition most often is monoarticular, affecting the knee or hip and communicating bursae. It is aggravated by infection and trauma. Sometimes a similar condition is seen in the soft tissue adjacent to but not communicating with the joint.[1084] This is referred to as tenosynovial or extra-articular chondromatosis.[1078a] The etiology is unknown, but the presence of clonal chromosomal aberrations suggests that it represents a neoplastic condition.[1083]

Grossly, the osteocartilaginous bodies may remain confined to the synovium or be extruded within the joint cavity. They usually are partially calcified (Fig. 24.139). Innumerable small bodies can be seen grossly in the resected lesion (Figs 24.140 and 24.141). A single nodule beneath thinned synovium contains hyaline cartilage and at times bone. The disease seems to follow this sequence:

(1) active intrasynovial disease with no loose bodies,
(2) intrasynovial proliferation and free loose bodies, and

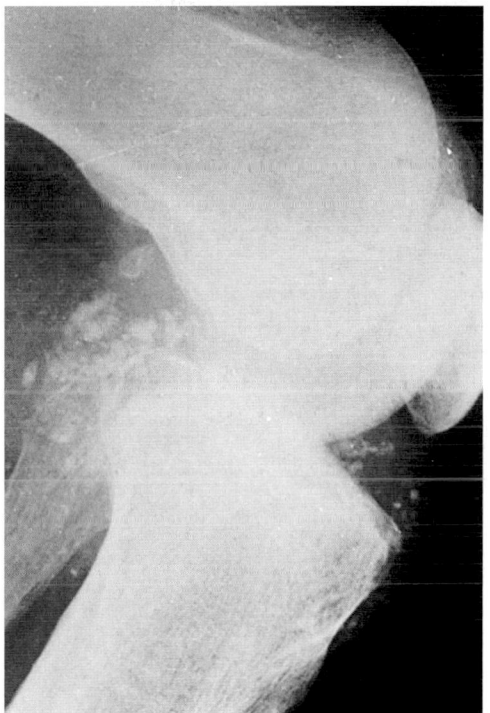

Fig. 24.139 Synovial osteochondromatosis. Nodules can be seen clearly in the joint space.

(3) multiple free osteochondral bodies with no demonstrable intrasynovial disease.[1081]

To make a diagnosis of synovial osteochondromatosis, one should find cartilaginous or osteocartilaginous bodies attached to the synovial membrane in addition to those free in the joint spaces. The latter also can occur in degenerative joint disease, neuropathic arthropathy, and osteochondritis dissecans, in which case the process is referred to as *secondary synovial chondrometaplasia*.[1085] Microscopically, the chondrocytes of primary synovial osteochondromatosis may show some degree of atypia

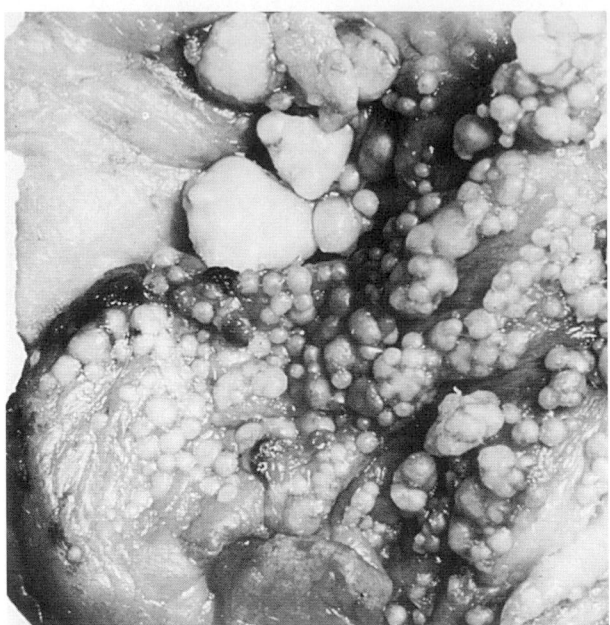

Fig. 24.140 Extensive involvement of synovium of knee joint by osteochondromatosis.

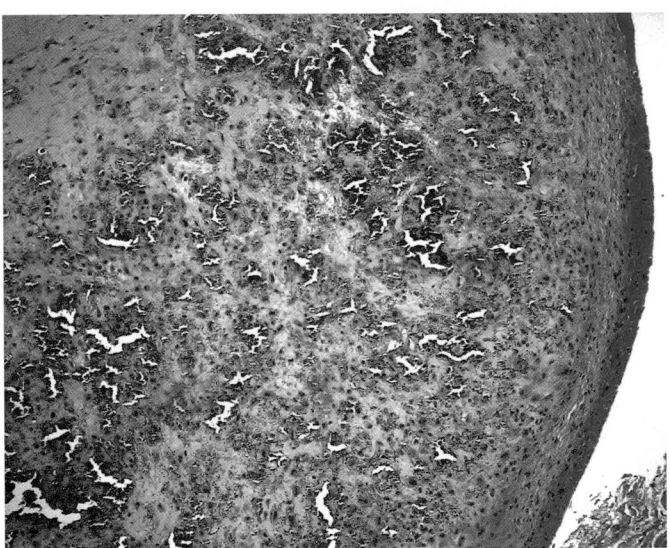

Fig. 24.141 Microscopic appearance of one of the nodules of synovial osteochondromatosis. The lesion has undergone focal calcification, as is usually the case.

and even binucleated forms, but this does not necessarily indicate malignancy.[1082] Local recrudescence after treatment may supervene. Rare cases of malignant transformation have been reported that should be distinguished from the condition described below.[1078]

Synovial chondrosarcoma is an exceptionally rare entity that closely resembles synovial chondromatosis radiographically and grossly[1077,1080] (Fig. 24.142). The distinction, which may be quite difficult, is based on the presence in the chondrosarcoma of obvious cytologic features of malignancy in the chondrocytes.[1080]

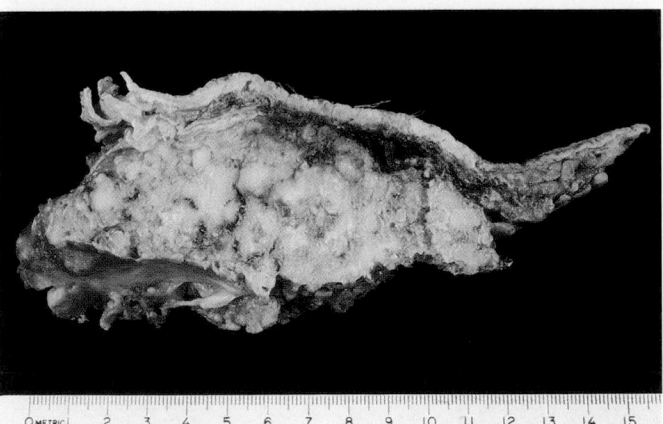

Fig. 24.142 Gross appearance of synovial chondrosarcoma. The lesion has a more expansile quality than the usual synovial osteochondromatosis.

Other tumors

Most tumors involving the joint space represent direct extension from neoplasms initially located in the adjacent bones.

The only primary tumor of the joints that is seen with any frequency in addition to those already mentioned is **synovial hemangioma**. Most patients are young adults, and there is a predominance for the male sex. The knee is the most common site, followed by the elbow and finger. In most cases the tumor is confined to the intra-articular synovium, but sometimes it is located in a bursa adjacent to a joint. The most common microscopic pattern is cavernous hemangioma, followed by lobular capillary hemangioma, arteriovenous hemangioma, and venous hemangioma.[1086]

Isolated cases of *intra-articular hemangiopericytoma*, *intracapsular chondroma*, *synovial sarcoma*, *epithelioid sarcoma*, arthroplasty-associated *malignant fibrous histiocytoma*, and *malignant lymphoma* around joints involved by rheumatoid arthritis have been reported.[1087–1090]

References

BONE
Normal anatomy

1 Alliston T, Derynck D. Interfering with bone remodelling. Nature 2002, **416**: 686–687.

2 Anderson HC. Mechanism of mineral formation in bone. Lab Invest 1989, **60**: 320–330.

3 Boyce BF, Hughes DE, Wright KR, Xing L, Dai A. Recent advances in bone biology provide insight into the pathogenesis of bone disease. Lab Invest 1999, **79**: 83–94.

4 Centrella M, McCarthy TL, Canalis E. Skeletal tissue and transforming growth factor beta. FASEB J 1988, **2**: 3066–3073.

5 Ducy P, Schinke T, Karsenty G. The osteoblast: a sophisticated fibroblast under central surveillance. Science 2000, **289**: 1501–1504.

6 Enneking WF, Kagan A. Transepiphyseal extension of osteosarcoma. Incidence, mechanism, and implications. Cancer 1978, **41**: 1526–1537.

7 Fornasier VL. Osteoid. An ultrastructural study. Hum Pathol 1977, **8**: 243–254.

8 Glimcher MJ. Mechanism of calcification. Role of collagen fibrils and collagen–phosphoprotein complexes *in vitro* and *in vivo*. Anat Rec 1989, **224**: 139–153.

9 Gurley MA, Roth SI. Bone. In Sternberg SS (ed.): Histology for pathologists. New York, 1992. Raven Press, Ltd.

10 Heinegard D, Oldberg A. Structure and biology of cartilage and bone matrix non-collagenous macromolecules. FASEB J 1989, **3**: 2042–2051.

11 Huffer WE. Morphology and biochemistry of bone remodeling. Possible control by vitamin D, parathyroid hormone, and other substances. Lab Invest 1988, **59**: 418–442.

12 Kukita T, McManus LM, Miller M, Civin C, Roodman GD. Osteoclast-like cells formed in long-term human bone marrow cultures express a similar surface phenotype as authentic osteoclasts. Lab Invest 1989, **60**: 532–538.

13 Marks SJ Jr, Popoff SN. Bone cell biology. The regulation of development, structure, and function in the skeleton. Am J Anat 1988, **83**: 1–44.

14 Noda M, Vogel RL, Craig AM, Prahl J, De Luca HF, Denhardt DT. Identification of a DNA sequence responsible for binding of the 1,25-dihydroxyvitamin D3 receptor and 1.25-dihydroxyvitamin D3 enhancement of mouse secreted phosphoprotein 1 (SPP-1 or osteopontin) gene expression. Proc Natl Acad Sci USA 1990, **87**: 9995–9999.

15 Okada Y, Naka K, Kawamura K, Matsumoto T, Nakanishi I, Fujimoto N, Sato H, Seiki M. Localization of matrix metalloproteinase 9 (92 Kilodalton gelatinase/type IV collagenase = gelatinase B) in osteoclasts. Implications for bone resorption. Lab Invest 1995, **72**: 311–322.

16 Owen TA, Bortell R, Yocum SA, Smock SL, Zhang M, Abate C, Shalhoub V, Aronin N, Wright KL, van Wijnen AJ, et al. Coordinate occupancy of AP-1 sites in the vitamin D-responsive and CCAAT box elements by Fos–Jun in the osteo calcin gene: Model for phenotype suppression of transcription. Proc Natl Acad Sci USA 1990, **87**: 9990–9994.

17 Porter GA, Gurley M, Roth SI. In Sternberg S (ed.): Histology for pathologists. Philadelphia, 1997, Lippincott–Raven Publishers, pp. 85–106.

18 Reinholt FP, Hultenby K, Oldberg A, Heinegard D. Osteopontin. A possible anchor of osteoclasts to bone. Proc Natl Acad Sci USA 1990, **87**: 4473–4475.

19 Teitelbaum SL. Bone resorption by osteoclasts. Science 2000, **289**: 1504–1508.

20 Udagawa N, Takahashi N, Akatsu T, Tanaka H, Sasaki T, Nishihara T, Koga T, Martin TJ, Suda T. Origin of osteoclasts. Mature monocytes and macrophages are capable of differentiating into osteoclasts under a suitable microenvironment prepared by bone marrow-derived stromal cells. Proc Natl Acad Sci USA 1990, **87**: 7260–7264.

21 Wozney JM, Rosen V, Celeste AJ, Mitsock LM, Whitters MJ, Kriz RW, Hewick RM, Wang EA. Novel regulators of bone formation. Molecular clones and activities. Science 1988, **242**: 1528–1534.

22 Zheng MH, Wood DJ, Papadimitriou JM. What's new in the role of cytokines on osteoblast proliferation and differentiation? Pathol Res Pract 1992, **188**: 1104–1121.

Metabolic bone diseases

23 Avioli LV, Krane SM (eds). Metabolic bone disease, vol. I. New York, 1977, Academic Press, Inc.

24 Avioli LV, Teitelbaum SL. The renal osteodystrophies. In Brenner BM, Rector FC (eds): The kidney. Philadelphia, 1976, WB Saunders Co, pp. 1542–1591.

25 Becks JS, Nordin BEC. Histological assessment of osteoporosis by iliac crest biopsy. J Pathol Bacteriol 1960, **80**: 391–397.

26 Bernstein DS, Sadowsky N, Hegsted DM, Guri CD, Stare FJ.

Prevalence of osteoporosis in high- and low-fluoride areas in North Dakota. JAMA 1966, **198**: 499–504.

27 Bullough PG. Atlas of orthopedic pathology, ed 2. St. Louis, 1992, Mosby.

28 Caldwell RA. Observations on the incidence, aetiology and pathology of senile osteoporosis. J Clin Pathol 1962, **15**: 421–431.

29 Coe FL, Favus MJ (eds). Disorders of bone and mineral metabolism. New York, 1992, Raven Press.

30 Davis ME, Strandjord NM, Lanzl LH. Estrogens and the aging process. JAMA 1966, **196**: 219–224.

31 Fallon MD, Teitelbaum SL. The interpretation of fluorescent tetracycline markers in the diagnosis of metabolic bone diseases. Hum Pathol 1982, **13**: 416–417.

32 Falvo KA, Bullough PG. Osteogenesis imperfecta. A histometric analysis. J Bone Joint Surg (Am) 1973, **55**: 275–286.

33 Jowsey J, Kelly PJ, Riggs BL, Bianco AJ Jr. Scholz DA, Gershon-Cohen J. Quantitative microradiographic studies of normal and osteoporotic bone. J Bone Joint Surg (Am) 1965, **47**: 785–806.

34 Mankin HJ. Rickets, osteomalacia, and renal osteodystrophy. Part II. J Bone Joint Surg (Am) 1974, **56**: 352–386.

34a Orwoll ES, Bliziotes M. Osteoporosis: pathophysiology and clinical management. N Engl J Med 23003, **348**: 2269–2270.

35 Raisz LG. Local and systemic factors in the pathogenesis of osteoporosis. N Engl J Med 1988, **318**: 818–828.

36 Riggs BL, Melton LJ III. Involutional osteoporosis. N Engl J Med 1986, **314**: 1676–1686.

37 Riggs BL, Melton LJ. The prevention and treatment of osteoporosis. N Engl J Med 1992, **327**: 620–627.

38 Rodan GA, Martin TJ. Therapeutic approaches to bone disease. Science 2000, **289**: 1508–1514.

39 Sillence DO, Horton WA, Rimoin DL. Morphologic studies in the skeletal dysplasias. A review. Am J Pathol 1979, **96**: 811–870.

40 Stevenson JC (ed.). New techniques in metabolic bone diseases. London, 1990, Wright.

41 Teitelbaum SL. Metabolic and other nontumorous disorders of the bone. In Kissane JM (ed.): Anderson's pathology, ed. 8. St. Louis, 1985, The CV Mosby Co, pp. 1705–1777.

42 Teitelbaum SL. Renal osteodystrophy. Hum Pathol 1984, **15**: 306–323.

43 Teitelbaum SL, Bullough PG. The pathophysiology of bone and joint disease. Am J Pathol 1979, **96**: 283–354.

44 Teitelbaum SL, Nichols SH. Tetracycline based morphometric analysis of trabecular bone kinetics. In Meunier P (ed.): Bone histomorphometry. Second International Workshop on Bone Morphology. Lyon, France, 1976, Armour Co, pp. 311–319.

45 Vigorita VJ. The bone biopsy protocol for evaluating osteoporosis and osteomalacia. Am J Surg Pathol 1984, **8**: 925–930.

46 Vigorita VJ. Osteoporosis. A diagnosable disorder? Pathol Annu 1988, **23**(Pt 2): 185–212.

Fractures

47 Collins DH. Structural changes around nails and screws in human bones. J Pathol Bacteriol 1953, **65**: 109–121.

48 Collins DH. Tissue changes in human femurs containing plastic appliances. J Bone Joint Surg (Br) 1954, **36**: 458–563.

49 Mindell ER, Rodbard S, Kwasman BG. Chrondrogenesis in bone repair. A study of the healing fracture callus in the rat. Clin Orthop 1971, **79**: 187–196.

50 Schwarz E. Hypercallosis in osteogenesis imperfecta. Am J Roentgenol Radium Ther Nucl Med 1961, **85**: 645–648.

Osteomyelitis

51 Berney S, Goldstein M, Bishko F. Clinical and diagnostic features of tuberculous arthritis. Am J Med 1972, **53**: 36–42.

52 Bohm E, Josten C. What's new in exogenous osteomyelitis? Pathol Res Pract 1992, **188**: 254–258.

53 Cabanela ME, Sim FH, Beabout JW, Dahlin DC. Osteomyelitis

appearing as neoplasms. A diagnostic problem. Arch Surg 1974, **109:** 68–72.

54 Chambers JB, Forsythe DA, Bertrand SL, Iwinski HJ, Steflik DE. Retrospective review of osteoarticular infections in a pediatric sickle cell age group. J Pediatr Orthop 2000, **20:** 682–685.

55 Cozzutto C. Xanthogranulomatous osteomyelitis. Arch Pathol Lab Med 1984, **108:** 973–976.

56 Farrow R, Cureton RJR. Carcinomatous invasion of bone in osteomyelitis. Br J Surg 1962, **50:** 107–109.

57 Felsberg GJ, Gore RL, Schweitzer ME, Jui V. Sclerosing osteomyelitis of Garre (periostitis ossificans). Oral Surg Oral Med Oral Pathol 1990, **70:** 117–120.

58 Garcia A Jr, Grantham SA. Hematogenous pyogenic vertebral osteomyelitis. J Bone Joint Surg (Am) 1960, **42:** 429–436.

59 Girschick HJ, Huppertz HI, Harmsen D, Krauspe R, Muller-Hermelink HK, Papadopoulos T. Chronic recurrent multifocal osteomyelitis in children: diagnostic value of histopathology and microbial testing. Hum Pathol 1999, **30:** 59–65.

60 Johnson LL, Kempson RL. Epidermoid carcinoma in chronic osteomyelitis. Diagnostic problems and management. J Bone Joint Surg (Am) 1965, **47:** 133–145.

61 Lewis P, Sutter VL, Finegold M. Bone infections involving anaerobic bacteria. Medicine (Baltimore) 1978, **57:** 279–305.

62 Moore RM, Green NE. Blastomycosis of bone. A report of six cases. J Bone Joint Surg (Am) 1982, **64:** 1097–1101.

63 Schwarz J. What's new in mycotic bone and joint diseases? Pathol Res Pract 1984, **178:** 617–634.

64 Trueta J. The three types of acute haematogenous osteomyelitis. J Bone Joint Surg (Br) 1959, **41:** 671–680.

65 Waldvogel FA, Vasey H. Osteomyelitis. The past decade. N Engl J Med 1980, **300:** 360–370.

66 Weisenburger DD, Vinh TN, Levinson B. Malakoplakia of bone. An unusual cause of pathologic fracture in an immunosuppressed patient. Clin Orthop 1985, **201:** 106–110.

67 Wu P-C, Khin N-M, Pang S-W. Salmonella osteomyelitis. An important differential diagnosis of granulomatous osteomyelitis. Am J Surg Pathol 1985, **9:** 531–537.

68 Yasuma T, Nakajima Y. Clinicopathological study on plasma cell osteomyelitis. Acta Pathol Jpn 1981, **31:** 835–844.

Bone necrosis

Infarct

69 Cerilli LA, Fechner RE. Angiosarcoma arising in a bone infarct. Ann Diagn Pathol 1999, **3:** 370–373.

70 Desai P, Perino G, Present D, Steiner GC. Sarcoma in association with bone infarcts: report of five cases. Arch Pathol Lab Med 1996, **120:** 482–489.

71 Galli SJ, Weintraub HP, Proppe KH. Malignant fibrous histiocytoma and pleomorphic sarcoma in association with medullary bone infarcts. Cancer 1978, **41:** 607–619.

72 Mirra JM, Bullough PG, Marcove RC, Jacobs B, Huvos AG. Malignant fibrous histiocytoma and osteosarcoma in association with bone infarcts. Report of four cases, two in caisson workers. J Bone Joint Surg (Am) 1974, **56:** 932–940.

73 Torres FX, Kyriakos M. Bone infarct-associated osteosarcoma. Cancer 1992, **70:** 2418–2430.

Aseptic (avascular) bone necrosis

74 Bohr H, Larsen EJ. On necrosis of the femoral head after fracture of the neck of the femur. J Bone Joint Surg (Br) 1965, **47:** 330–338.

75 Golding JSR, Maciver JF, Went LN. The bone changes in sickle-cell anaemia and its genetic variants. J Bone Joint Surg (Br) 1959, **41:** 711–718.

76 Mankin HJ. Nontraumatic necrosis of bone (osteonecrosis). N Engl J Med 1992, **326:** 1473–1479.

77 Yamamoto T, DiCarlo EF, Bullough PG. The prevalence and clinicopathological appearance of extension of osteonecrosis in the femoral head. J Bone Joint Surg (Br) 1999, **81:** 328–332.

78 Yamamoto T, Yamaguchi T, Lee KB, Bullough PG. A clinicopathologic study of osteonecrosis in the osteoarthritic hip. Osteoarthritis Cartilage 2000, **8:** 303–308.

Osteochondritis dissecans

79 Milgram JW. Radiological and pathological manifestations of osteochondritis of the distal femur. A study of 50 cases. Radiology 1978, **126:** 305–311.

Radiation necrosis

80 Dzik-Jurasz AS, Brooker S, Husband JE, Tait D. What is the prevalence of symptomatic or asymptomatic femoral head osteonecrosis in patients previously treated with chemoradiation? A magnetic resonance study of anal cancer patients. Clin Oncol 2001, **13:** 130–134.

81 Sengupta S, Prathap K. Radiation necrosis of the humerus. A report of three cases. Acta Radiol 1973, **12:** 313–320.

Paget's disease

82 Barry HC. Paget's disease of bone. Edinburgh, 1969, E & S Livingstone, Ltd.

83 Collins DH. Paget's disease of bone. Incidence and subclinical forms. Lancet 1956, **2:** 51–57.

84 Collins DH, Winn JM. Focal Paget's disease of the skull (osteoporosis circumscripta). J Pathol Bacteriol 1955, **69:** 1–9.

85 Eisman JA, Martin TJ. Osteolytic Paget's disease. Recognition and risks of biopsy. J Bone Joint Surg (Am) 1986, **68:** 112–117.

86 Fallon MD, Schwamm HA. Paget's disease of bone. An update on the pathogenesis, pathophysiology, and treatment of osteitis deformans. Pathol Annu 1989, **24**(Pt 1): 115–159.

87 Greenspan A, Norman A, Sterling AP. Precocious onset of Paget's disease – a report of three cases and review of the literature. J Can Assoc Radiol 1977, **28:** 69–72.

88 Hadjipavlou AG, Gaitanis IN, Kontakis GM. Paget's disease of the bone and its management. J Bone Joint Surg (Br) 2002, **84:** 160–169.

89 Hadjipavlou A, Lander P, Srolovitz H, Enker IP. Malignant transformation in Paget disease of bone. Cancer 1992, **70:** 2802–2808.

90 Lake ME. The pathology of fracture in Paget's disease. Aust NZ J Surg 1958, **27:** 307–312.

91 Lamovec J, Rener M, Spiler M. Pseudosarcoma in Paget's disease of bone. Ann Diagn Pathol 1999, **3:** 99–103.

92 Melton LJ 3rd., Tiegs RD, Atkinson EJ, O'Fallon WM. Fracture risk among patients with Paget's disease: a population-based cohort study. J Bone Miner Res 2000, **15:** 2123–2128.

93 Mii Y, Miyauchi Y, Honoki K, Morishita T, Miura S, Aoki M, Tamai S, Tsunoda S, Nishitani M, Sakaki T. Electron microscopic evidence of a viral nature for osteoclast inclusions in Paget's disease of bone. Virchows Arch Pathol 1994, **424:** 99–104.

94 Mills BG, Singer FR. Nuclear inclusions in Paget's disease of bone. Science 1976, **194:** 201–202.

95 Price CHG, Goldie W. Paget's sarcoma of bone. A study of 80 cases from the Bristol and the Leeds bone tumour registries. J Bone Joint Surg (Br) 1969, **51:** 205–224.

96 Smith BJ, Eveson JW. Paget's disease of bone with particular reference to dentistry. J Oral Pathol 1981, **10:** 233–247.

Osteopetrosis

97 Boyce BF, Hughes DE, Wright KR, Xing L, Dai A. Recent advances in bone biology provide insight into the pathogenesis of bone disease. Lab Invest 1999, **79:** 83–94.

98 Coccia PF, Krivit W, Cervenka J, Clawson C, Kersey JH, Kim TH, Nesbit ME, Ramsay MKC, Warkentin PI, Teitelbaum SL, Kahn AJ, Brown DM. Successful bone marrow transplantation for

infantile malignant osteopetrosis. N Engl J Med 1980, **302:** 701–708.

99 Key LL Jr, Rodriguiz RM, Willi SM, Wright NM, Hatcher HC, Eyre DR, Cure JK, Griffin PP, Ries WL. Long-term treatment of osteopetrosis with recombinant human interferon gamma. N Engl J Med 1995, **332:** 1594–1599.

100 Milgram JW, Murali J. Osteopetrosis. A morphological study of twenty-one cases. J Bone Joint Surg (Am) 1982, **64:** 912–919.

101 Taranta A, Migliaccio S, Recchia I, Caniglia M, Luciani M, De Rossi G, Dionisi-Vici C, Pinto RM, Francalanci P, Boldrini R, Lanino E, Dini G, Morreale G, Ralston SH, Villa A, Vezzoni P, Del Principe D, Cassiani F, Palumbo G, Teti A. Genotype-phenotype relationship in human *ATP6i*-dependent autosomal recessive osteoporosis. Am J Pathol 2003, **162:** 57–68.

Tumors

Classification and distribution

102 Dorfman HD. Malignant transformation of benign bone lesions. In Proceedings of the Seventh National Cancer Conference, vol 7. Philadelphia, 1973, JB Lippincott Co, pp. 901–913.

103 Dorfman HD, Czerniak B. Bone Cancers. Cancer 1995, **75:** 203–210.

104 Hudson TM. Radiologic-pathologic correlation of musculoskeletal lesions. Baltimore, 1987, Williams & Wilkins.

105 Schajowiz F, Sissons HA, Sobin LH. The World Health Organization's histologic classification of bone tumors. A commentary on the second edition. Cancer 1995, **75:** 1208–1214.

Bone-forming tumors

Osteoma

106 Bertoni F, Unni KK, Beabout JW, Sim FH. Parosteal osteoma of bones other than of the skull and face. Cancer 1995, **75:** 2466–2473.

107 Chang CHJ, Piatt ED, Thomas KE, Watne AL. Bone abnormalities in Gardner's syndrome. Am J Roentgenol Radium Ther Nucl Med 1968, **103:** 645–652.

Osteoid osteoma and osteoblastoma

108 Angervall L, Persson S, Stenman G, Kindblom LG. Large cell, epithelioid, telangiectatic osteoblastoma: a unique pseudosarcomatous variant of osteoblastoma. Hum Pathol 1999, **30:** 1254–1259.

109 Ayala AG, Murray JA, Erling MA, Raymond AK. Osteoid-osteoma. Intraoperative tetracycline-fluorescence demonstration of the nidus. J Bone Joint Surg (Am) 1986, **68:** 747–751.

110 Bauer TW, Zehr RJ, Belhobek GH, Marks KE. Juxta-articular osteoid osteoma. Am J Surg Pathol 1991, **15:** 381–387.

111 Bertoni F, Bacchini P, Donati D, Martini A, Picci P, Campanacci M. Osteoblastoma-like osteosarcoma. The Rizzoli Institute experience. Mod Pathol 1993, **6:** 707–716.

112 Bertoni F, Unni KK, Lucas DR, McLeod RA. Osteoblastoma with cartilaginous matrix. An unusual morphologic presentation in 18 cases. Am J Surg Pathol 1993, **17:** 69–74.

113 Bertoni F, Unni KK, McLeod RA, Dahlin DC. Osteosarcoma resembling osteoblastoma. Cancer 1985, **55:** 416–426.

114 Beyer WF, Kühn H. Can an osteoblastoma become malignant? Virchows Arch [A] 1985, **408:** 297–305.

115 Byers PD. Solitary benign osteoblastic lesions of bone – osteoid osteoma and benign osteoblastoma. Cancer 1968, **22:** 43–57.

116 Cheung FMF, Wu WC, Lam CK, Fu YK. Diagnostic criteria for pseudomalignant osteoblastoma. Histopathology 1997, **31:** 196–200.

117 Della Rocca C, Huvos AG. Osteoblastoma: varied histological presentations with a benign clinical course: an analysis of 55 cases. Am J Surg Pathol 1996, **20:** 841–850.

118 Dorfman HD, Weiss SW. Borderline osteoblastic tumors.

Problems in the differential diagnosis of aggressive osteoblastoma and low-grade osteosarcoma. Semin Diagn Pathol 1984, **1:** 215–234.

119 Hasegawa T, Hirose T, Sakamoto R, Seki K, Ikata T, Hizawa K. Mechanism of pain in osteoid osteomas. An immunohistochemical study. Histopathology 1993, **22:** 487–491.

120 Healey JH, Ghalman B. Osteoid osteoma and osteoblastoma. Current concepts and recent advances. Clin Orthop 1986, **204:** 76–85.

121 Kawaguchi Y, Sato C, Hasegawa T, Oka S, Kuwahara H, Norimatsu H. Intraarticular osteoid osteoma associated with synovitis: a possible role of cyclooxygenase-2 expression by osteoblasts in the nidus. Mod Pathol 2000, **13:** 1086–1091.

122 Loizaga JM, Calvo M, Lopez Barea F, Martinez Tello FJ, Perez Villanueva J. Osteoblastoma and osteoid osteoma. Clinical and morphological features of 162 cases. Pathol Res Pract 1993, **189:** 33–41.

123 Lucas DR, Unni KK, McLeod RA, O'Connor MI, Sim FH. Osteoblastoma. Clinicopathologic study of 306 cases. Hum Pathol 1994, **25:** 117–134.

124 MacLennan DI, Wilson FC Jr. Osteoid osteoma of the spine. A review of the literature and report of six new cases. J Bone Joint Surg (Am) 1967, **49:** 111–121.

125 Marcove RC, Heelan RT, Huvos AG, Healey J, Lindeque BG. Osteoid osteoma. Diagnosis, localization, and treatment. Clin Orthop 1991, **267:** 197–201.

126 Marsh BW, Bonfiglio M, Brady LP, Enneking WF. Benign osteoblastoma. Range of manifestations. J Bone Joint Surg (Am) 1975, **57:** 1–9.

127 McLeod RA, Dahlin DC, Beabout JW. The spectrum of osteoblastoma. Am J Roentgenol 1976, **126:** 321–335.

128 O'Connell JX, Nanthakumar SS, Nielsen GP, Rosenberg AE. Osteoid osteoma: the uniquely innervated bone tumor. Mod Pathol 1998, **11:** 175–180.

129 Pettine KA, Klassen RA. Osteoid-osteoma and osteoblastoma of the spine. J Bone Joint Surg (Am) 1986, **68:** 354–361.

130 Rigault P, Mouterde P, Padovani JP, Jaubert F, Guyonvarch G. Ostéome ostéoïde chez l'enfant. A propos de 29 cas. Rev Chir Orthop 1975, **61:** 627–646.

131 Schajowicz F, Lemos C. Osteoid osteoma and osteoblastoma. Acta Orthop Scand 1970, **41:** 272–291.

132 Schajowicz F, Lemos C. Malignant osteoblastoma. J Bone Joint Surg 1976, **58:** 202–211.

133 Steiner GC. Ultrastructure of osteoid osteoma. Hum Pathol 1976, **7:** 309–325.

134 Wold LE, Pritchard DJ, Bergert J, Wilson DM. Prostaglandin synthesis by osteoid osteoma and osteoblastoma. Mod Pathol 1988, **1:** 129–131.

135 Yoshikawa S, Nakamura T, Takagi M, Imamura T, Okano K, Sasaki S. Benign osteoblastoma as a cause of osteomalacia. A report of two cases. J Bone Joint Surg (Br) 1977, **59:** 279–286.

Osteosarcoma

136 Ahuja SC, Villacin AB, Smith J, Bullough PG, Huvos AG, Marcove RC. Juxtacortical (parosteal) osteogenic sarcoma. Histologic grading and prognosis. J Bone Joint Surg (Am) 1977, **59:** 632–647.

137 Arlen M, Higinbotham NL, Huvos AG, Marcove RC, Miller T, Shah IC. Radiation-induced sarcoma of bone. Cancer 1971, **28:** 1087–1099.

138 Ayala AG, Raymond AK, Jaffe N. The pathologist's role in the diagnosis and treatment of osteosarcoma in children. Hum Pathol 1984, **15:** 258–266.

139 Ayala AG, Raymond AK, Ro JY, Carrasco CH, Fanning CV, Murray JA. Needle biopsy of primary bone lesions. M.D. Anderson experience. Pathol Annu 1989, **24**(Pt 1): 219–251.

140 Ayala AG, Ro JY, Raymond AK, Jaffe N, Chawla S, Carrasco H,

Link M, Jimenez J, Edeiken J, Wallace S, et al. Small cell osteosarcoma. A clinico pathologic study of 27 cases. Cancer 1989, **64**: 2162–2173.

141 Bacci G, Ferrari S, Delepine N, Bertoni F, Picci P, Mercuri M, Bacchini P, Brach Del Prever A, Tienghi A, Comandone A, Campanacci M. Predictive factors of histologic response to primary chemotherapy in osteosarcoma of the extremity: study of 272 patients preoperatively treated with high-dose methotrexate, doxorubicin, and cisplatin. J Clin Oncol 1998, **16**: 658–663.

142 Bacci G, Mercuri M, Briccola A, Ferrari S, Bertoni F, Donati D, Monti C, Zanoni A, Forni C, Manfrini M. Osteogenic sarcoma of the extremity with detectable lung metastases at presentation: results of treatment of 23 patients with chemotherapy followed by simultaneous resection and metastatic lesions. Cancer 1997, **79**: 245–254.

143 Bacci G, Picci P, Ruggieri P, Mercuri M, Avella M, Capanna R, Brach Del Prever A, Mancini A, Gherlinzoni F, Padovani G, et al. Primary chemotherapy and delayed surgery (neoadjuvant chemotherapy) for osteosarcoma of the extremities. The Istituto Rizzoli Experience in 127 patients treated preoperatively with intravenous methotrexate (high versus moderate doses) and intraarterial cisplatin. Cancer 1990, **65**: 2539–2553.

144 Baldini N, Scotlandi K, Serra M, Picci P, Bacci G, Sottili S, Campanacci M. P-glycoprotein expression in osteosarcoma: a basis for risk-adapted adjuvant chemotherapy. J Orthop Res 1999, **17**: 629–632.

145 Banta JV, Schreiber RR, Kulik WJ. Hyperplastic callus formation in osteogenesis imperfecta simulating osteosarcoma. J Bone Joint Surg (Am) 1971, **53**: 115–122.

146 Barwick KW, Huvos AG, Smith J. Primary osteogenic sarcoma of the vertebral column. A clinicopathologic correlation of ten patients. Cancer 1980, **46**: 595–604.

147 Bauer HC, Kreicbergs A, Silversward C, Tribukait B. DNA analysis in the differential diagnosis of osteosarcoma. Cancer 1988, **61**: 2532–2540.

148 Belli L, Scholl S, Livartowski A, Ashby M, Palangie T, Levasseur P, Pouillart P. Resection of pulmonary metastases in osteosarcoma. A retrospective analysis of 44 patients. Cancer 1989, **63**: 2546–2550.

149 Bertoni F, Bacchii P, Fabbri N, Mercuri M, Picci P, Ruggieri P, Campanacci M. Osteosarcoma. Low-grade intraosseous-type osteosarcoma, histologically resembling parosteal osteosarcoma, fibrous dysplasia, and desmoplastic fibroma. Cancer 1993, **71**: 338–345.

150 Bertoni F, Pignatti G, Bachini P, Picci P, Bacci G, Campanacci M. Telangiectatic or hemorrhagic osteosarcoma of bone. A clinicopathologic study of 41 patients at the Rizzoli Institute. Progr Surg Pathol 1989, **10**: 63–82.

151 Bertoni F, Present D, Bacchini P, Pignatti G, Picci P, Campanacci M. The Istituto Rizzoli experience with small cell osteosarcoma. Cancer 1989, **64**: 2591–2599.

152 Bjornsson J, Inwards CY, Wold LE, Sim FH, Taylor WF. Prognostic significance of spontaneous tumour necrosis in osteosarcoma. Virchows Arch [A] 1993, **423**: 195–199.

153 Bommer KK, Ramzy I, Mody D. Fine-needle aspiration biopsy in the diagnosis and management of bone lesions: a study of 450 cases. Cancer 1997, **81**: 148–156.

154 Bosse A, Vollmer E, Bocker W, Roessner A, Wuisman P, Jones D, Fisher LW. The impact of osteonectin for differential diagnosis of bone tumors. An immunohistochemical approach. Pathol Res Pract 1990, **186**: 651–657.

155 Broström L-A, Harris MA, Simon MA, Cooperman DR, Nilsonne U. The effect of biopsy on survival of patients with osteosarcoma. J Bone Joint Surg (Br) 1979, **61**: 209–212.

156 Burgers JM, van Glabbeke M, Busson A, Cohen P, Mazabraud AR, Abbatucci JS, Kalifa C, Tubiana M, Lemerle JS, Voute PA, et al. Osteosarcoma of the limbs. Report of the EORTC-SIOP 03 trial 20781 investigating the value of adjuvant treatment with chemotherapy and/or prophylactic lung irradiation. Cancer 1988, **61**: 1024–1031.

157 Campanacci M, Bacci G, Gertoni F, Picci P, Minutillo A, Franceschi C. The treatment of osteosacoma of the extremities. Twenty years' experience at the Istituto Ortopedico Rizzoli. Cancer 1981, **48**: 1569–1581.

158 Campanacci M, Cervellati G. Osteosarcoma. A review of 345 cases. Ital J Orthop Traumatol 1975, **1**: 5–22.

159 Campanacci M, Picci P, Gherlinzoni F, Guerra A, Bertoni F, Neff JR. Parosteal osteosarcoma. J Bone Joint Surg (Br) 1984, **66**: 313–321.

160 Chow LT, Lin J, Yip KM, Kumta SM, Ahuja AT, King WW, Lee JC. Chondromyxoid fibroma-like osteosarcoma: a distinct variant of low-grade osteosarcoma. Histopathology 1996, **29**: 429–436.

161 Clark JL, Unni KK, Dahlin DC, Devine KD. Osteosarcoma of the jaw. Cancer 1983, **51**: 2311–2316.

162 Dahlin DC, Coventry MB. Osteogenic sarcoma. A study of 600 cases. J Bone Joint Surg (Am) 1967, **49**: 101–110.

163 Dahlin DC, Unni KK. Osteosarcoma of bone and its important recognizable varieties. Am J Surg Pathol 1977, **1**: 61–72.

164 Dardick I, Schatz J, Colgan T. Osteogenic sarcoma with epithelial differentiation. Ultrastruct Pathol 1992, **16**: 463–474.

165 Davis AM, Bell RS, Goodwin PJ. Prognosic factors in osteosarcoma. A critical review. J Clin Oncol 1994, **12**: 423–431.

166 deSantos LA, Murray JA, Ayala AG. The value of percutaneous needle biopsy in the management of primary bone tumors. Cancer 1979, **43**: 735–744.

167 deSantos LA, Murray JA, Finklestein JB, Spjut HJ, Ayala AG. The radiographic spectrum of periosteal osteosarcoma. Radiology 1978, **127**: 123–129.

168 Devaney K, Vinh TN, Sweet DE. Small cell osteosarcoma of bone. An immunohistochemical study with differential diagnostic considerations. Hum Pathol 1993, **24**: 1211–1225.

169 Dickersin GR, Rosenberg AE. The ultrastructure of small-cell osteosarcoma, with a review of the light microscopy and differential diagnosis. Hum Pathol 1991, **22**: 267–275.

170 Dominguez-Malagon H, Ro JY, Ayala AG. Periosteal osteosarcoma of the digits: a case report. Int J Surg Pathol 1996, **4**: 55–59.

171 Edeiken J, Farrell C, Ackerman LV, Spjut HJ. Parosteal sarcoma. Am J Roentgenol Radium Ther Nucl Med 1971, **111**: 579–583.

172 Enneking WF (ed). Osteosarcoma. Symposium. Clin Orthop 1975, **111**: 1–104.

173 Enneking WF, Kagan A. "Skip" metastases in osteosarcoma. Cancer 1975, **36**: 2192–2205.

174 Fanburg JC, Rosenberg AE, Weaver DL, Leslie KO, Mann KG, Taatjes DJ, Tracy RP. Osteocalcin and osteonectin immunoreactivity in the diagnosis of osteosarcoma. Am J Clin Pathol 1997, **108**: 464–473.

175 Farr GH, Huvos AG. Juxtacortical osteogenic sarcoma. J Bone Joint Surg (Am) 1972, **51**: 1205–1216.

176 Feugeas O, Guriec N, Babin-Boilletot A, Marcellin L, Simon P, Babin S, Thyss A, Hofman P, Terrier P, Kalifa C, Brunat-Mentigny M, Patricot LM, Oberling F. Loss of heterozyosity of the RB gene is a poor prognostic factor in patients with osteosarcoma. J Clin Oncol 1996, **14**: 467–472.

177 Fechner RE, Huvos AG, Mirra JM, Spjut HJ, Unni KK. A symposium on the pathology of bone tumors. Pathol Annu 1984, **9**(Pt 1): 125–194.

178 Franchi A, Comin CE, Santucci M. Submicroscopic and immunohistochemical profile of surface osteosarcomas. Ultrastruct Pathol 1999, **23**: 233–240.

179 Frentzel-Beyme R, Wagner G. Malignant bone tumours. Status of aetiological knowledge and needs of epidemiologicaI research. Arch Orthop Trauma Surg 1979, **94**: 81–89.

180 Gadwal SR, Gannon FH, Fanburg-Smith JC, Becoskie EM,

Thompson LD. Primary osteosarcoma of the head and neck in pediatric patients: a clinicopathologic study of 22 cases with review of the literature. Cancer 2001, **91**: 598–605.

181 Garbe LR, Monges GM, Pellegrin EM, Payan HL. Ultrastructural study of osteosarcomas. Hum Pathol 1981, **12**: 891–896.

182 Glasser DB, Lane JM, Huvos AG, Marcove RC, Rosen G. Survival, prognosis, and therapeutic response in osteogenic sarcoma. The Memorial Hospital experience. Cancer 1992, **69**: 698–708.

183 Hall RB, Robinson LH, Malawar MM, Dunham WK. Periosteal osteosarcoma. Cancer 1985, **55**: 165–171.

184 Harvei S, Solheim O. The prognosis in osteosarcoma. Norwegian national data. Cancer 1981, **48**: 1719–1723.

185 Hasegawa T, Hirose T, Kudo E, Hizawa K, Usui M, Ishii S. Immunophenotypic heterogeneity in osteosarcomas. Hum Pathol 1991, **22**: 583–590.

186 Hasegawa T, Shibata T, Hirose T, Seki K, Hizawa K. Osteosarcoma with epithelioid features. An immunohistochemical study. Arch Pathol Lab Med 1993, **117**: 295–298.

187 Hiddemann W, Roessner A, Wörmann B, Mellin W, Klockenkemper B, Bösing T, Büchner T, Grundmann E. Tumor heterogeneity in osteosarcoma as identified by flow cytometry. Cancer 1987, **59**: 324–328.

188 Huvos AG. Osteogenic sarcoma of bones and soft tissues in older persons. A clinicopathologic analysis of 117 patients older than 60 years. Cancer 1986, **57**: 1442–1449.

189 Huvos AG, Butler A, Bretsky SS. Osteogenic sarcoma associated with Paget's disease of bone. A clinicopathologic study of 65 patients. Cancer 1983, **52**: 1489–1495.

190 Huvos AG, Butler A, Bretsky SS. Osteogenic sarcoma in pregnant women. Prognosis, therapeutic implications, and literature review. Cancer 1985, **56**: 2326–2331.

191 Huvos AG, Rosen G, Bretsky SS, Butler A. Telangiectatic osteogenic sarcoma. A clinicopathologic study of 124 patients. Cancer 1982, **49**: 1679–1689.

192 Huvos AG, Sundaresan N, Bretsky SS, Butler A. Osteogenic sarcoma of the skull. A clinicopathologic study of 19 patients. Cancer 1985, **56**: 1214–1221.

193 Huvos AG, Woodard HQ, Cahan WG, Higinbotham NL, Stewart FW, Butler A, Bretsky SS. Postradiation osteogenic sarcoma of bone and soft tissues. A clinicopathologic study of 66 patients. Cancer 1985, **55**: 1244–1255.

194 Iavarone A, Matthay KK, Steinkirchner TM, Israel MA. Germ-line and somatic p53 gene mutations in multifocal osteogenic sarcoma. Proc Natl Acad Sci USA 1992, **89**: 4207–4209.

195 Iwasaki R, Yamamuro T, Kotoura Y, Okumura H, Kasai R, Nakashima Y. Immunohistochemical study of bone GLA protein in primary bone tumors. Cancer 1992, **70**: 619–624.

196 Jaffe N, Raymond AK, Ayala A, Carrasco CH, Wallace S, Robertson R, Griffiths M, Wang YM. Effect of cumulative courses of intraarterial cisdiamminedichloroplatin-II on the primary tumor in osteosarcoma. Cancer 1989, **63**: 63–67.

197 Kahn LB, Wood FW, Ackerman LV. Fracture callus associated with benign and malignant bone lesions and mimicking osteosarcoma. Am J Clin Pathol 1969, **52**: 14–24.

198 Keel SB, Jaffe KA, Petur Nielsen G, Rosenberg AE. Orthopaedic implant-related sarcoma: a study of twelve cases. Mod Pathol 2001, **14**: 969–977.

199 Kellie SJ, Pratt CB, Parham DM, Fleming ID, Meyer WH, Rao BN. Sarcomas (other than Ewing's) of flat bones in children and adolescents. A clinicopathologic study. Cancer 1990, **65**: 1011–1016.

200 Kilpatrick SE, Geisinger KE, King TS, Sciarrotta J, Ward WG, Gold SH, Bos GD. Clinicopathologic analysis of HER-2neu immunoexpression among various histologic subtypes and grades of osteosarcoma. Mod Pathol 2001, **14**: 1277–1283.

201 Kozakewich H, Perez-Atayde AR, Goorin AM, Wilkinson RH, Gebhardt MC, Vawter GF. Osteosarcoma in young children. Cancer 1991, **67**: 638–642.

202 Kramer K, Hicks DG, Palis J, Rosier RN, Oppenheimer J, Fallon MD, Cohen HJ. Epithelioid osteosarcoma of bone. Immunocytochemical evidence suggesting divergent epithelial and mesenchymal differentiation in a primary osseous neoplasm. Cancer 1993, **71**: 2977–2982.

203 Kurt AM, Unni KK, McLeod RA, Pritchard DJ. Low-grade intraosseous osteosarcoma. Cancer 1990, **65**: 1418–1428.

204 Kyriakos M. Intracortical osteosarcoma. Cancer 1980, **56**: 2525–2533.

205 Lane JM, Hurson B, Boland PJ, Glasser DB. Osteogenic sarcoma. Clin Orthop 1986, **204**: 93–110.

206 Lanzer WL, Liotta LA, Yee C, Azar HA, Costa J. Synthesis of pro-collagen type II by a xenotransplanted human chondroblastic osteosarcoma. Am J Pathol 1981, **104**: 217–226.

207 Levine AM, Resenberg SA. Alkaline phosphatase levels in osteosarcoma tissue are related to prognosis. Cancer 1979, **44**: 2291–2293.

208 Lonardo F, Ueda T, Huvos AG, Healey J, Ladanyi M. p53 and MDM2 alterations in osteosarcomas: correlation with clinicopathologic features and proliferative rate. Cancer 1997, **79**: 1541–1547.

209 Malawer MM, Dunham WK. Skip metastases in osteosarcoma. Recent experience. J Surg Oncol 1983, **22**: 236–245.

210 Mankin HJ, Conner JF, Schiller AL, Perlmutter N, Alho A, McGuire M. Grading of bone tumors by analysis of nuclear DNA content using flow cytometry. J Bone Joint Surg (Am) 1985, **67**: 404–413.

211 Mankin HJ, Lange TA, Spanier SS. The hazards of biopsy in patients with malignant primary bone and soft-tissue tumors. J Bone Joint Surg (Am) 1982, **64**: 1121–1127.

212 Martínez-Tello FJ, Navas-Palacios JJ. The ultrastructure of conventional, parosteal, and periosteal osteosarcomas. Cancer 1982, **50**: 949–961.

213 Martland HS, Humphries RE. Osteogenic sarcoma in dial painters using luminous paint. Arch Pathol 1929, **7**: 406–417.

214 Matsuno T, Unni KK, McLeod RA, Dahlin DC. Telangiectatic osteogenic sarcoma. Cancer 1976, **38**: 2538–2547.

215 Naka T, Iwamoto Y, Shinohara N, Chuman H, Tsuneyoshi M. p53 accumulation in malignant bone tumors: an immunohistochemical analysis of 217 cases. Int J Surg Pathol 1997, **5**: 1–10.

216 Nakajima H, Sim FH, Bond JR, Unni KK. Small cell osteosarcoma of bone: review of 72 cases. Cancer 1997, **79**: 2095–2106.

217 Nora FE, Unni KK, Pritchard DJ, Dahlin DC. Osteosarcoma of extragnathic craniofacial bones. Mayo Clin Proc 1983, **58**: 268–272.

218 O'Hara JM, Hutter RVP, Foote FW Jr, Miller T, Woodward HQ. An analysis of 30 patients surviving longer than ten years after treatment for osteogenic sarcoma. J Bone Joint Surg (Am) 1968, **50**: 335–354.

219 Ogose A, Hotta T, Emura I, Imaizumi S, Takeda M, Yamamura S. Repeated dedifferentiation of low-grade intraosseous osteosarcoma. Hum Pathol 2000, **31**: 615–618.

220 Okada K, Hasegawa T, Yokoyama R. Rossette-forming epithelioid osteosarcoma: a histologic subtype with highly aggressive clinical behaviour. Hum Pathol 2001, **32**: 726–733.

221 Okada K, Unni KK, Swee RG, Sim FH. High grade surface osteosarcoma: a clinicopathologic study of 46 cases. Cancer 1999, **85**: 1044–1054.

222 Okada K, Wold LE, Beabout JW, Shives TC. Osteosarcoma of the hand. A clinicopathologic study of 12 cases. Cancer 1993, **72**: 719–725.

223 Oliveira P, Nogueira M, Pinto A, Almeida MO. Analysis of p53 expression in osteosarcoma of the jaw: correlation with

clinicopathologic and DNA ploidy findings. Hum Pathol 1997, **28**: 1361–1365.

224 Onda M, Matsuda S, Higaki S, Lijima T, Fukushima J, Yokokura A, Kojima T, Horiuchi H, Kurokawa T, Yamamoto T. ErB-2 expression is correlated with poor prognosis for patients with osteosarcoma. Cancer 1996, **77**: 71–78.

225 Ozaki T, Flege S, Liljenqvist U, Hillman A, Delling G, Salzer-Kuntschik M, Jurgens H, Kotz R, Winkelmann W, Bielack SS. Osteosarcoma of the spine: experience of the cooperative osteosarcoma study group. Cancer 2002, **94**: 1069–1077.

226 Ozisik YY, Meloni AM, Peier A, Altungoz O, Spanier SS, Zalupski MM, Leong SP, Sandberg AA. Cytogenetic findings in 19 malignant bone tumors. Cancer 1994, **74**: 2268–2275.

227 Parham DM, Prat CB, Parvey LS, Webber BL, Champion J. Childhood multifocal osteosarcoma. Clinicopathologic and radiologic correlates. Cancer 1985, **55**: 2653–2658.

228 Park S-H, Kim I. Small cell osteogenic sarcoma of the ribs: cytological, immunohistochemical and ultrastructural study with literature review. Ultrastruct Pathol 1999, **23**: 133–140.

229 Penman HG, Ring PA. Osteosarcoma in association with total hip replacement. J Bone Joint Surg (Br) 1984, **66**: 632–634.

230 Picci P, Bacci G, Campanacci M, Gasparini M, Pilotti S, Cerasoli S, Bertoni F, Guerra A, Capanna R, Albisinni U, Galletti S, Gherlinzoni F, Calderoni P, Sudanese A, Baldini N, Bernini M, Jaffe N. Histologic evaluation of necrosis in osteosarcoma induced by chemotherapy. Regional mapping of viable and nonviable tumor. Cancer 1985, **56**: 1515–1521.

231 Polednak AP. Bone cancer among female radium dial workers. Latency periods and incidence rates by time after exposure. Brief communication. J Natl Cancer Inst 1978, **60**: 77–82.

232 Pollandt K, Engels C, Kaiser E, Werner M, Delling G. Gsalpha gene mutations in monostotic fibrous dysplasia of bone and fibrous dysplasia-like-low-grade central osteosarcoma. Virchows Arch 2001, **439**: 170–175.

233 Radig K, Schneider-Stock R, Haeckel C, Neumann W, Roessner A. p53 gene mutations in osteosarcomas of low-grade malignancy. Hum Pathol 1998, **29**: 1310–1316.

234 Ragland BD, Bell WC, Lopez RR, Siegal GP. Cytogenetics and molecular biology of osteosarcoma. Lab Invest 2002, **82**: 365–373.

235 Rao BN, Champion JE, Pratt CB, Carnesale P, Dilawari R, Fleming I, Green A, Austin B, Wrenn E, Kumar M. Limb salvage procedures for children with osteosarcoma. An alternative to amputation. J Pediatr Surg 1983, **18**: 901–908.

236 Raymond AK, Chawla SP, Carrasco CH, Ayala AG, Fanning CV, Grice B, Armen T, Plager C, Papadopoulos NEJ, Edeiken J, Wallace S, Jaffe N, Murray JA, Benjamin RS. Osteosarcoma chemotherapy effect. A prognostic factor. Semin Diagn Pathol 1987, **4**: 212–236.

237 Reddick RL, Michelitch HJ, Levine AM, Triche TJ. Osteogenic sarcoma. A study of the ultrastructure. Cancer 1980, **45**: 64–71.

238 Rosen G, Marcove RC, Caparros B, Nirenberg A, Kosloff C, Huvos AG. Primary osteogenic sarcoma. The rationale for preoperative chemotherapy and delayed surgery. Cancer 1979, **43**: 2163–2177.

238a Sandberg AA. Cytogenetics and molecular genetics of bone and soft-tissue tumors. Am J Med Genet 2002, **115**: 189–193.

239 Schajowicz F, Derqui JC. Puncture biopsy in lesions of the locomotor system. Review of results in 4,050 cases, including 941 vertebral punctures. Cancer 1968, **21**: 531–548.

240 Schajowicz F, Santini Araujo E, Berenstein M. Sarcoma complicating Paget's disease of bone. A clinicopathological study of 62 cases. J Bone Joint Surg (Br) 1983, **65**: 299–307.

241 Schaller RT Jr, Haas J, Schaller J, Morgan A, Bleyer A. Improved survival in children with osteosarcoma following resection of pulmonary metastases. J Pediatr Surg 1982, **17**: 546–550.

242 Schulz A, Jundt G, Berghäuser K-H, Gehron-Robey P, Termine JD. Immunohistochemical study of osteonectin in various types of osteosarcoma. Am J Pathol 1988, **132**: 233–238.

243 Sciot R, Samson I, Dal Cin P, Lateur L, Van Damme B, Van Den Berghe H, Desmet V. Giant cell rich parosteal osteosarcoma. Histopathology 1995, **27**: 51–55.

244 Scranton PE, DeCicco FA, Totten RS, Yunis EJ. Prognostic factors in osteosarcoma. A review of 20 years' experience at the University of Pittsburgh Health Center Hospitals. Cancer 1975, **36**: 2179–2191.

245 Shapiro F. Ultrastructural observations on osteosarcoma tissue. A study of 10 cases. Ultrastruct Pathol 1983, **4**: 151–161.

246 Sheth DS, Yasko AW, Raymond AK, Ayala AG, Carrasco CH, Benjamin RS, Jaffe N, Murray JA. Conventional and dedifferentiated parosteal osteosarcoma: diagnosis, treatment, and outcome. Cancer 1996, **78**: 2136–2145.

247 Shives TC, Dahlin DC, Sim FH, Pritchard DJ, Earle JD. Osteosarcoma of the spine. J Bone Joint Surg (Am) 1986, **68**: 660–668.

248 Sim FH, Unni KK, Beabout JW, Dahlin DC. Osteosarcoma with small cells simulating Ewing's tumor. J Bone Joint Surg (Am) 1979, **62**: 207–215.

249 Simon MA, Bos GD. Epiphyseal extension of metaphyseal osteosarcoma in skeletally immature individuals. J Bone Joint Surg (Am) 1980, **62**: 195–204.

250 Simon MA, Hecht JD. Invasion of joints by primary bone sarcomas in adults. Cancer 1982, **50**: 1649–1655.

251 Sindelar WF, Costa J, Ketcham AS. Osteosarcoma associated with Thorotrast administration. Cancer 1978, **42**: 2604–2609.

252 Smith GD, Chalmers J, McQueen MM. Osteosarcoma arising in relation to an enchondroma. A report of three cases. J Bone Joint Surg (Br) 1986, **68**: 315–319.

253 Sommer H-J, Knop J, Heise U, Winkler K, Delling G. Histomorphometric changes of osteosarcoma after chemotherapy. Correlation with 99mTC methylene diphosphonate functional imaging. Cancer 1987, **59**: 252–258.

254 Stark A, Aparisi T, Ericsson JLE. Human osteogenic sarcoma. Fine structure of the osteoblastic type. Ultrastruct Pathol 1983, **4**: 311–329.

255 Stark A, Aparisi T, Ericsson JLE. Human osteogenic sarcoma. Fine structure of the chondroblastic type. Ultrastruct Pathol 1984, **6**: 51–67.

256 Stark A, Aparisi T, Ericsson JLE. Human osteogenic sarcoma. Fine structure of the fibroblastic type. Ultrastruct Pathol 1984, **7**: 301–319.

257 Stark A, Aparisi T, Ericsson JLE. Human osteogenic sarcoma. Fine structural localization of alkaline phosphatase. Ultrastruct Pathol 1985, **8**: 143–154.

258 Sugano I, Tajima Y, Ishida Y, Nagao K, Saga N, Ohno T, Miyakawa E. Phalangeal intraosseous well-differentiated osteosarcoma of the hand. Virchows Arch 1997, **430**: 185–189.

259 Sulzbacher I, Birner P, Trieb K, Lang S, Chott A. Expression of osteopontin and vascular endothelial growth factor in benign and malignant bone tumors. Virchows Arch 2002, **441**: 345–349.

260 Swanson PE, Dehner LP, Sirgi KE, Wick MR. Cytokeratin immunoreactivity in malignant tumors of bone and soft tissue. A reappraisal of cytokeratin as a reliable marker in diagnostic immunohistochemistry. Appl Immunohistochem 1994, **2**: 103–112.

261 Trieb K, Lechleitner T, Lang S, Windhager R, Kotz R, Dirnhofer S. Heat shock protein 72 expression in osteosarcomas correlates with good response to neoadjuvant chemotherapy. Hum Pathol 1998, **29**: 1050–1055.

262 Tucker MA, Dángio GJ, Boice JD Jr, Strong LC, Li FP, Stovall M, Stone BJ, Green DM, Lombardi F, Newton W, Hoover RN, Fraumeni JF Jr. Bone sarcomas linked to radiotherapy and chemotherapy in children. N Engl J Med 1987, **317**: 588–593.

263 Unni KK, Dahlin DC, Beabout JW, Ivins JC. Parosteal osteogenic sarcoma. Cancer 1976, **37**: 2466–2475.

264 Unni KK, Dahlin DC, Beabout JW. Periosteal osteogenic sarcoma. Cancer 1976, **37**: 2476–2485.

265 Unni KK, Dahlin DC, McLeod RA, Pritchard DJ. Intraosseous well-differentiated osteosarcoma. Cancer 1977, **40**: 1337–1347.

266 Uribe-Botero G, Russell WO, Sutow WW, Martin RG. Primary osteosarcoma of bone. A clinicopathologic investigation of 243 cases, with necropsy studies in 54. Am J Clin Pathol 1977, **67**: 427–435.

267 Van der Heul RO, Von Ronnen JR. Juxtacortical osteosarcoma. Diagnosis, differential diagnosis, treatment, and an analysis of eighty cases. J Bone Joint Surg (Am) 1967, **49**: 415–439.

268 van der Walt JD, Ryan JF. Parosteal osteogenic sarcoma of the hand. Histopathology 1990, **16**: 75–78.

269 Varela-Duran J, Dehner LP. Postirradiation osteosarcoma in childhood. A clinicopathologic study of three cases and review of the literature. Am J Pediatr Hematol Oncol 1980, **2**: 263–271.

270 Vigorita VJ, Jones JK, Ghelman B, Marcove RC. Intracortical osteosarcoma. Am J Surg Pathol 1984, **8**: 65–71.

271 Wakasa K, Sakurai M, Uchida A, Yoshikawa H, Maeda A. Massive pulmonary tumor emboli in osteosarcoma. Occult and fatal complication. Cancer 1990, **66**: 583–586.

272 Weatherby RP, Dahlin DC, Ivins JC. Postradiation sarcoma of bone. Review of 78 Mayo Clinic cases. Mayo Clin Proc 1981, **56**: 294–306.

273 White VA, Fanning CV, Ayala AG, Raymond AK, Carrasco CH, Murray JA. Osteosarcoma and the role of fine needle aspiration. A study of 51 cases. Cancer 1988, **62**: 1238–1246.

274 Wick MR, Siegal GP, Unni KK, McLeod RA, Greditzer HG III. Sarcomas of bone complicating osteitis deformans (Paget's disease). Fifty years' experience. Am J Surg Pathol 1981, **5**: 47–59.

275 Williams AH, Schwinn CP, Parker JW. The ultrastructure of osteosarcoma. A review of twenty cases. Cancer 1976, **37**: 1293–1301.

276 Winkler K, Bielack S, Delling G, Salzer-Kuntschik M, Kotz R, Greenshaw C, Jurgens H, Ritter J, Kusnierz-Glaz C, Erttmann R, et al. Effect of intraarterial versus intravenous cisplatin in addition to systemic doxorubicin, high-dose methotrexate, and ifosfamide on histologic tumor response in osteosarcoma (study COSS-86). Cancer 1990, **66**: 1703–1710.

277 Wold LE, Unni KK, Beabout JW, Pritchard DJ. High-grade surface osteosarcomas. Am J Surg Pathol 1984, **8**: 181–186.

278 Wold LE, Unni KK, Beabout JW, Sim FH, Dahlin DC. Dedifferentiated parosteal osteosarcoma. J Bone Joint Surg (Am) 1984, **66**: 53–59.

279 Yoshida H, Adachi H, Hamada Y, Aki T, Yumoto T, Morimoto K, Orido T. Osteosarcoma. Ultrastructural and immunohistochemical studies on alkaline phosphatase-positive tumor cells constituting a variety of histologic types. Acta Pathol Jpn 1988, **38**: 325–338.

280 Yoshida H, Yumoto T, Adachi H, Minamizaki T, Maeda N, Furuse K. Osteosarcoma with prominent epithelioid features. Acta Pathol Jpn 1989, **39**: 439–445.

281 Yoshikawa H, Rettig WJ, Takaoka K, Alderman E, Rup B, Rosen V, Wozney JM, Lane JM, Huvos AG, Garin-Chesa P. Expression of bone morphogenetic proteins in human osteosarcoma. Immunohistochemical detection with monoclonal antibody. Cancer 1994, **73**: 85–91.

282 Yoshikawa H, Rettig WJ, Lane JM, Takaoka K, Alderman E, Rup B, Rosen V, Healey JH, Huvos AG, Garin-Chesa P. Immunohistochemical detection of bone morphogenetic proteins in bone and soft-tissue sarcomas. Cancer 1994, **74**: 842–847.

283 Yunis EJ, Barnes L. The histologic diversity of osteosarcoma. Pathol Annu 1986, **21**(Pt 1): 121–141.

Cartilage-forming tumors

Chondroma

284 Boriani S, Bacchini P, Bertoni F, Campanacci M. Periosteal chondroma. A review of twenty cases. J Bone Joint Surg (Am) 1983, **65**: 205–212.

285 Bovee JV, van Roggen JF, Cleton-Jansen AM, Taminiau AH, van der Woude HJ, Hogendoom PCW. Malignant progression in multiple enchondromatosis (Ollier's disease): an autopsy-based molecular genetic study. Hum Pathol 2000, **31**: 1299–1303.

286 Brand T, Hatch EI, Schaller RT, Stevenson JK, Arensman Rm, Schwartz MC. Surgical management of the infant with mesenchymal hamartoma of the chest wall. J Pediatr Surg 1986, **21**: 556–558.

287 Campbell AN, Wagget J, Mott MG. Benign mesenchymoma of the chest wall in infancy. J Surg Oncol 1982, **21**: 267–270.

288 Cannon SR, Sweetnam DR. Multiple chondrosarcomas in dyschondroplasia (Ollier's disease). Cancer 1985, **55**: 836–840.

289 Cowan WK. Malignant change and multiple metastases in Ollier's disease. J Clin Pathol 1965, **18**: 650–653.

290 Laurence W, Franklin EL. Calcifying enchondroma of long bones. J Bone Joint Surg (Br) 1953, **35**: 224–228.

291 Lewis RJ, Ketcham AS. Maffucci's syndrome. Functional and neoplastic significance. Case report and review of the literature. J Bone Joint Surg (Am) 1973, **55**: 1465–1479.

292 Liu J, Hudkins PG, Swee RG, Unni KK. Bone sarcomas associated with Ollier's disease. Cancer 1987, **59**: 1376–1385.

293 McCarthy EF, Dorfman HD. Vascular and cartilaginous hamartoma of the ribs in infancy with secondary aneurysmal bone cyst formation. Am J Surg Pathol 1980, **4**: 247–253.

294 Nojima T, Unni KK, McLeod RA, Pritchard DJ. Periosteal chondroma and periosteal chondrosarcoma. Am J Surg Pathol 1985, **9**: 666–677.

295 Nosanchuk JS, Kaufer H. Recurrent periosteal chondroma. Report of two cases and a review of the literature. J Bone Joint Surg (Am) 1969, **51**: 375–380.

296 Sun T-C, Swee RG, Shives TC, Unni KK. Chondrosarcoma in Maffucci's syndrome. J Bone Joint Surg (Am) 1985, **67**: 1214–1215.

297 Takigawa K. Chondroma of the bones of the hand. J Bone Joint Surg (Am) 1971, **53**: 1591–1600.

298 Tamimi HK, Bolen JW. Enchondromatosis (Ollier's disease) and ovarian juvenile granulosa cell tumor. A case report and review of the literature. Cancer 1984, **53**: 1605–1608.

Osteochondroma

299 Abramovici L, Steiner GC. Bizarre parosteal osteochondromatous proliferation (Nora's lesion): a retrospective study of 12 cases, 2 arising in long bones. Hum Pathol 2002, **33**: 1205–1210.

300 Bovee JV, van den Broek LJ, Cleton Jansen AM, Hogendoorn PC. Up-regulation of PTHrP and Bcl-2 expression characterizes the progression of osteochondroma towards peripheral chondrosarcoma and is a late event in central chondrosarcoma. Lab Invest 2000, **80**: 1925–1934.

301 Bridge AJ, Nelson M, Orndal C, Bhatia P, Neff JR. Clonal karyotypic abnormalities of the hereditary multiple exostoses chromosomal loci 8q24.1(EX1) and 11p11-12(EXT2) in patients with sporadic and hereditary osteochondromas. Cancer 1998, **82**: 1657–1663.

302 Carney JA, Boccon-Gibod L, Jarka DE, Tanaka Y, Swee RG, Unni KK, Stratakis CA. Osteochondromyxoma of bone: a congenital tumor associated with lentigines and other unusual disorders. Am J Surg Pathol 2001, **25**: 164–176.

303 Copeland RL, Meehan PL, Morrissy RT. Spontaneous regression of osteochondromas. Two case reports. J Bone Joint Surg (Am) 1985, **67**: 971–973.

304 del Rosario AD, Bui HX, Singh J, Ginsburg R, Ross JS. Intracytoplasmic eosinophilic hyaline globules in cartilaginous

neoplasms. A surgical, pathological, ultrastructural, and electron probe x-ray microanalytic study. Hum Pathol 1994, **25:** 1283–1289.

305 Han SK, Henein HG, Novin N, Giargiana FA Jr. An unusual arterial complication seen with a solitary osteochondroma. Am Surg 1977, **43:** 471–472.

306 Horiguchi H, Sakane M, Matsui M, Wadano Y. Bizarre parosteal osteochondromatous proliferation (Nora's lesion) of the foot. Pathol Int 2001, **51:** 816–823.

307 Hwang W-S, McQueen D, Monson RC, Reed MH. The significance of cytoplasmic chondrocyte inclusions in multiple osteochondromatosis, solitary osteochondromas, and chondrodysplasias. Am J Clin Pathol 1982, **78:** 89–91.

308 Josefczyk MA, Huvos AG, Smith J, Urmacher C. Bursa formation in secondary chondrosarcoma with intrabursal chondrosarcomatosis. Am J Surg Pathol 1985, **9:** 309–314.

309 Landon GC, Johnson KA, Dahlin DC. Subungual exostoses. J Bone Joint Surg (Am) 1979, **61:** 256–259.

310 Meneses MF, Unni KK, Swee RG. Bizarre parosteal osteochondromatous proliferation of bone (Nora's lesion). Am J Surg Pathol 1993, **17:** 691–697.

311 Miller-Breslow A, Dorfman HD. Dupuytren's (subungual) exostosis. Am J Surg Pathol 1988, **12:** 368–378.

312 Nora FE, Dahlin DC, Beaubout JW. Bizarre parosteal osteochondromatous proliferations of the hands and feet. Am J Surg Pathol 1983, **7:** 245–250.

313 Ochsner PE. Zum problem der neoplastischen Entartung bei multiplen kartilaginären Exostosen. Z Orthop 1978, **116:** 369–378.

314 Unni KK, Dahlin DC. Premalignant tumors and conditions of bone. Am J Surg Pathol 1979, **3:** 47–60.

Chondroblastoma

315 Aronsohn RS, Hart WR, Martel W. Metaphyseal chondroblastoma of bone. Am J Roentgenol 1976, **127:** 686–688.

316 Birch PJ, Buchanan R, Golding P, Pringle JAS. Chondroblastoma of the rib with widespread bone metastases. Histopathology 1994, **25:** 583–585.

317 Brecher ME, Simon MA. Chondroblastoma. An immunohistochemical study. Hum Pathol 1988, **19:** 1043–1047.

318 Coleman SS. Benign chondroblastoma with recurrent soft-tissue and intra-articular lesions. J Bone Joint Surg (Am) 1966, **48:** 1554–1560.

318a De Silva MV, Reid R. Chondroblastoma: varied histologic appearance, potential diagnostic pitfalls, and clinicopathologic features associated with local recurrence. Ann Diagn Pathol 2003, **7:** 205–213.

319 Fanning CV, Sneige NS, Carrasco CH, Ayala AG, Murray JA, Raymond AK. Fine needle aspiration cytology of chondroblastoma of bone. Cancer 1990, **65:** 1847–1863.

320 Hicks DG, Krasinskas AM, Sickel JZ, Hughes SS, Puzas JE, Moynas R, Rosier RN. Chondroblastoma. In situ hybridization and immunohistochemical evidence supporting a cartilaginous origin. Int J Surg Pathol 1994, **1:** 155–162.

321 Huvos AG, Marcove RC, Erlandson RA, Mike V. Chondroblastoma of bone. A clinico-pathologic and electron microscopic study. Cancer 1972, **29:** 760–771.

322 Kahn LB, Wood FM, Ackerman LV. Malignant chondroblastoma. Report of two cases and review of the literature. Arch Pathol 1969, **88:** 371–376.

323 Kunze E, Graewe TH, Peitsch E. Histology and biology of metastatic chondroblastoma. Report of a case with a review of the literature. Pathol Res Pract 1987, **182:** 113–120.

324 Kyriakos M, Land VJ, Penning HL, Parker SG. Metastatic chondroblastoma. Report of a fatal case with a review of the literature on atypical, aggressive, and malignant chondroblastoma. Cancer 1985, **55:** 1770–1789.

325 Levine GD, Bensch KG. Chondroblastoma – the nature of the basic cell. A study by means of histochemistry, tissue culture, electron microscopy, and autoradiography. Cancer 1972, **29:** 1546–1562.

326 Mii Y, Miyauchi Y, Honoki K, Morishita T, Miura S, Aoki M, Tamai S. Ultrastructural cytochemical demonstration of proteoglycans and calcium in the extracellular matrix of chondroblastomas. Hum Pathol 1994, **25:** 1290–1294.

327 Monda L, Wick MR. S-100 protein immunostaining in the differential diagnosis of chondroblastoma. Hum Pathol 1985, **16:** 287–293.

328 Nakamura Y, Becker LE, Marks A. S-100 protein in tumors of cartilage and bone. An immunohistochemical study. Cancer 1983, **58:** 1820–1824.

329 Posl M, Werner M, Amling M, Ritzel H, Delling G. Malignant transformation of chondroblastoma. Histopathology 1996, **29:** 477–480.

330 Povysil C, Tomanova R, Matejovsky Z. Muscle-specific actin expression in chondroblastomas. Hum Pathol 1997, **28:** 316–320.

331 Reyes CV, Kathuria S. Recurrent and aggressive chondroblastoma of the pelvis with late malignant neoplastic changes. Am J Surg Pathol 1979, **3:** 449–455.

332 Schajowicz F, Gallardo H. Epiphysial chondroblastoma of bone. A clinicopathological study of sixty-nine cases. J Bone Joint Surg (Br) 1970, **52:** 205–226.

333 Semmelink HJ, Pruszczynski M, Wiersma-van Tilburg A, Smedts F, Ramaekers FC. Cytokeratin expression in chondroblastomas. Histopathology 1990, **16:** 257–263.

334 Springfield DS, Capanna R, Gherlinzoni F, Picci P, Campanacci M. Chondroblastoma. A review of seventy cases. J Bone Joint Surg (Am) 1985, **67:** 748–754.

335 Steiner GC. Ultrastructure of benign cartilaginous tumors of intraosseous origin. Hum Pathol 1979, **10:** 71–86.

336 Turcotte RE, Kurt AM, Sim FH, Unni KK, McLeod RA. Chondroblastoma. Hum Pathol 1993, **24:** 944–949.

337 Welsh RA, Meyer AT. A histogenetic study of chondroblastoma. Cancer 1964, **17:** 578–589.

Chondromyxoid fibroma and related tumors

338 Bahk WJ, Mirra JM, Sohn KR, Shin DS. Pseudoanaplastic chondromyxoid fibroma. Ann Diagn Pathol 1998, **2:** 241–246.

339 Bleiweiss IJ, Klein MJ. Chondromyxoid fibroma. Report of six cases with immunohistochemical studies. Mod Pathol 1990, **3:** 664–666.

340 Dahlin DC. Chondromyxoid fibroma of bone, with emphasis on its morphological relationship to benign chondroblastoma. Cancer 1956, **9:** 195–203.

341 Gherlinzoni F, Rock M, Picci P. Chondromyxoid fibroma. The experience at the Istituto Ortopedico Rizzoli. J Bone Joint Surg (Am) 1983, **65:** 198–204.

342 Granter SR, Renshaw AA, Kozakewich HP, Fletcher JA. The pericentromeric inversion, inv (6)(p25q13), is a novel diagnostic marker in chondromyxoid fibroma. Mod Pathol 1998, **11:** 1071–1074.

343 Keel SB, Bhan AK, Liebsch NJ, Rosenberg AE. Chondromyxoid fibroma of the skull base: a tumor which may be confused with chordoma and chondrosarcoma: a report of three cases and review of the literature. Am J Surg Pathol 1997, **21:** 577–582.

344 Kikuchi F, Dorfman HD, Kane PB. Recurrent chondromyxoid fibroma of the thoracic spine 30 years after primary excision: case report and review of the literature. Int J Surg Pathol 2001, **9:** 323–330.

345 Kreicbergs A, Lönnquist PA, Willems J. Chondromyxoid fibroma. A review of the literature and a report on our own experience. Acta Pathol Microbiol Immunol Scand (A) 1985, **93:** 189–197.

346 Kyriakos M. Soft tissue implantation of chondromyxoid fibroma. Am J Surg Pathol 1979, **3:** 363–372.

347 Marcove RC, Kambolis C, Bullough PG, Jaffe HL. Fibromyxoma of bone. Cancer 1964, **17:** 1209–1213.

348 Marcove RC, Lindeque BG, Huvos AG. Fibromyxoma of the bone. Surg Gynecol Obstet 1989, **169**: 115–118.

349 McClure DK, Dahlin DC. Myxoma of bone. Report of three cases. Mayo Clin Proc 1977, **52**: 249–253.

350 Nielsen GP, Keel SB, Dickersin GR, Selig MK, Bhan AK, Rosenberg AE. Chondromyxoid fibroma: a tumor showing myofibroblastic, myochondroblastic, and chondrocytic differentiation. Mod Pathol 1999, **12**: 514–517.

351 Safar A, Nelson M, Neff JR, Maale GE, Bayani J, Squire J, Bridge JA. Recurrent anomalies of 6q25 in chondromyxoid fibroma. Hum Pathol 2000, **31**: 306–311.

352 Schajowicz F, Gallardo H. Chondromyxoid fibroma (fibromyxoid chondroma) of bone. A clinico-pathological study of thirty-two cases. J Bone Joint Surg (Br) 1971, **53**: 198–216.

353 Soder S, Inwards C, Muller S, Kirchner T, Aigner T. Cell biology and matrix biochemistry of chondromyxoid fibroma. Am J Clin Pathol 2001, **116**: 271–277.

354 Wu CT, Inwards CY, O'Laughlin S, Rock MG, Beabout JW, Unni KK. Chondromyxoid fibroma of bone: a clinicopathologic review of 27 cases. Hum Pathol 1998, **29**: 438–446.

355 Zillmer DA, Dorfman HD. Chondromyxoid fibroma of bone. Thirty-six cases with clinicopathologic correlation. Hum Pathol 1989, **20**: 952–964.

Chondrosarcoma

356 Alho A, Connor JF, Mankin HJ, Schiller AL, Campbell CJ. Assessment of malignancy of cartilage tumors using flow cytometry. A preliminary report. J Bone Joint Surg (Am) 1983, **65**: 779–785.

357 Barnes R, Catto M. Chondrosarcoma of bone. J Bone Joint Surg (Br) 1966, **48**: 729–764.

358 Bergh P, Gunterberg B, Meis-Kindblom JM, Kindblom LG. Prognostic factors and outcome of pelvic, sacral, and spinal chondrosarcomas: a center-based study of 69 cases. Cancer 2001, **91**: 1201–1212.

359 Bertoni F, Boriani S, Laus M, Campanacci M. Periosteal chondrosarcoma and periosteal osteosarcoma. Two distinct entities. J Bone Joint Surg (Br) 1982, **64**: 370–376.

360 Bjornsson J, McLeod RA, Unni KK, Ilstrup DM, Pritchard DJ. Primary chondrosarcoma of long bones and limb girdles. Cancer 1998, **83**: 2105–2119.

361 Bovee JV, van Der Heul RO, Taminiau AH, Hogendoom PC. Chondrosarcoma of the phalanx: a locally aggressive lesion with minimal metastatic potential: a report of 35 cases and a review of the literature. Cancer 1999, **86**: 1724–1732.

362 Campanacci M, Guernelli N, Leonessa C, Boni A. Chondrosarcoma. A study of 133 cases, 80 with long term follow up. Ital J Orthop Traumatol 1975, **1**: 387–414.

363 Castresana J, Barrios C, Gomez L, Kreichergs A. Amplification of the c-*myc* proto-oncogene in human chondrosarcoma. Diagn Mol Pathol 1992, **1**: 235–238.

364 Coltrera MD, Googe PB, Harrist TJ, Hyams VJ, Schiller AL, Goodman ML. Chondrosarcoma of the temporal bone. Diagnosis and treatment of 13 cases and review of the literature. Cancer 1986, **58**: 2689–2696.

365 Dahlin DC, Henderson ED. Chondrosarcoma, a surgical and pathological problem. J Bone Joint Surg (Am) 1956, **38**: 1025–1038.

366 Dahlin DC, Salvador AH. Chondrosarcomas of bones of the hands and feet. A study of 30 cases. Cancer 1974, **34**: 755–760.

367 Dobashi Y, Sugimura H, Sato A, Hirabayashi T, Kanda H, Kitagawa T, Kawaguchi N, Imamura T, Machinami R. Possible association of p53 overexpression and mutation with high-grade chondrosarcoma. Diagn Mol Pathol 1993, **2**: 257–263.

368 Erlandson RA, Huvos AG. Chondrosarcoma. A light and electron microscopic study. Cancer 1974, **34**: 1642–1652.

369 Evans HL, Ayala AG, Romsdahl MM. Prognostic factors in chondrosarcoma of bone. A clinicopathologic analysis with emphasis on histologic grading. Cancer 1977, **40**: 818–831.

370 Franchi A, Calzolari A, Zampi G. Immunohistochemical detection of c-fos and c-jun expression in osseous and cartilaginous tumours of the skeleton. Virchows Arch 1998, **432**: 515–519.

371 Gadwal SR, Fanburg-Smith JC, Gannon FH, Thompson LD. Primary chondrosarcoma of the head and neck in pediatric patients: a clinicopathologic study of 14 cases and review of the literature. Cancer 2000, **88**: 2181–2188.

372 Garrison RC, Unni KK, McLeod RA, Pritchard DJ, Dahlin DC. Chondrosarcoma arising in osteochondroma. Cancer 1982, **49**: 1890–1897.

373 Gitelis S, Bertoni F, Picci P, Campanacci M. Chondrosarcoma of bone. The experience at the Istituto Ortopedico Rizzoli. J Bone Joint Surg (Am) 1981, **63**: 1248–1257.

374 Healey JH, Lane JM. Chondrosarcoma. Clin Orthop 1986, **204**: 119–129.

375 Huvos AG, Marcove RC. Chondrosarcoma in the young. A clinicopathologic analysis of 790 patients younger than 21 years of age. Am J Surg Pathol 1987, **11**: 930–942.

376 Kindblom L, Angervall L. Histochemical characterization of mucosubstances in bone and soft tissue tumors. Cancer 1975, **36**: 985–994.

377 Kreicbergs A, Boquist L, Borssén B, Larsson S-E. Prognostic factors in chondrosarcoma. A comparative study of cellular DNA content and clinicopathologic features. Cancer 1982, **50**: 577–583.

378 Kreicbergs A, Slezak E, Söderberg G. The prognostic significance of different histomorphologic features in chondrosarcoma. Virchows Arch [A] 1981, **390**: 1–10.

379 Kristensen IB, Sunde LM, Jensen OM. Chondrosarcoma. Increasing grade of malignancy in local recurrence. Acta Pathol Microbiol Immunol Scand (A) 1986, **94**: 73–77.

380 Kusuzaki K, Murata H, Takeshita H, Hirata M, Hashiguchi S, Tsuji Y, Nakamura S, Ashihara T, Hirasawa Y. Usefulness of cytofluorometric DNA ploidy analysis in distinguishing benign cartilaginous tumors from chondrosarcomas. Mod Pathol 1999, **12**: 863–872.

381 Lansche WE, Spjut HJ. Chondrosarcoma of the small bones of the hand. J Bone Joint Surg (Am) 1958, **40**: 1139–1149.

382 Larramendy ML, Mandahl N, Mertens F, Blomqfist C, Kivioja AH, Karaharju E, Valle J, Bohling T, Tarkkanen M, Rydholm A, Akerman M, Bauer HC, Anttila JP, Elomaa I, Knuutila S. Clinical significance of genetic imbalances revealed by comparative genomic hybridization in chondrosarcomas. Hum Pathol 1999, **30**: 1247–1253.

383 Mandahl N, Heim S, Arheden K, Rydholm A, Willen H, Mitelman F. Chromosomal rearrangements in chondromatous tumors. Cancer 1990, **65**: 242–248.

384 Mankin HJ, Cantley KP, Lippiello L, Schiller AL, Campbell CJ. The biology of human chondrosarcoma. I. Description of the cases, grading, and biochemical analyses. J Bone Joint Surg (Am) 1980, **62**: 160–176.

385 Mankin HJ, Cantley KP, Schiller AL, Lippiello L. The biology of human chondrosarcoma. II. Variation in chemical composition among types and subtypes of benign and malignant cartilage tumors. J Bone Joint Surg (Am) 1980, **62**: 176–188.

386 Marcove RC, Huvos AG. Cartilaginous tumors of the ribs. Cancer 1971, **27**: 794–801.

387 McAfee MK, Pairolero PC, Bergstralh EJ, Piehler JM, Unni KK, McLeod RA, Bernatz PE, Payne WS. Chondrosarcoma of the chest wall. Factors affecting survival. Ann Thorac Surg 1985, **40**: 535–541.

388 McKenna RJ, Schwinn CP, Soong KY, Higinbotham NL. Sarcomata of the osteogenic series (osteosarcoma, fibrosarcoma, chondrosarcoma, parosteal osteogenic sarcoma, and sarcomata arising in abnormal bone). J Bone Joint Surg (Am) 1966, **48**: 1–26.

389 Mirra JM, Gold R, Downs J, Eckardt JJ. A new histologic approach to the differentiation of enchondroma and chondrosarcoma of the bones. A clinicopathologic analysis of 51 cases. Clin Orthop 1985, 201: 214–237.

390 Nakamura Y, Becker LE, Marks A. S-100 protein in tumors of cartilage and bone. An immunohistochemical study. Cancer 1983, 58: 1820–1824.

391 Ogose A, Unni KK, Swee RG, May GK, Rowland CM, Sim FH. Chondrosarcoma of small bones of the hands and feet. Cancer 1997, 80: 50–59.

392 Okajima K, Honda I, Kitagawa T. Imunohistochemical distribution of S-100 protein in tumors and tumorlike lesions of bone and cartilage. Cancer 1988, 61: 792–799.

393 O'Neal LW, Ackerman LV. Cartilaginous tumors of ribs and sternum. J Thorac Surg 1951, 21: 71–108.

394 Oshiro Y, Chaturvedi V, Hayden D, Nazeer T, Johnson M, Johnston DA, Ordonez NG, Ayala AG, Czerniak B. Altered p53 is associated with aggressive behaviour of chondrosarcoma: a long term follow-up study. Cancer 1998, 83: 2324–2334.

395 Ostrowski ML, Spjut HJ. Lesions of the bones of the hands and feet. Am J Surg Pathol 1997, 21: 676–690.

396 Pritchard DJ, Lunke RJ, Taylor WF, Dahlin DC, Medley BE. Chondrosarcoma. A clinicopathologic and statistical analysis. Cancer 1980, 45: 149–157.

397 Rosenberg AE, Neilsen GP, Keel SB, Renard LG, Fitzek MM, Munzenrider JE, Liebsch NJ. Chondrosarcoma of the base of the skull: a clinicopathologic study of 200 cases with emphasis on its distinction from chordoma. Am J Surg Pathol 1999, 23: 1370–1378.

397a Sandberg AA, Bridge JA. Updates on the cytogenetics and molecular genetics of bone soft tissue tumors: chondrosarcoma and other cartilaginous neoplasms. Cancer Genet Cytogenet 2003, 143: 1–31.

398 Sanerkin NG, Gallagher P. A review of the behaviour of chondrosarcoma of bone. J Bone Joint Surg (Br) 1979, 61: 395–400.

399 Sawyer JR, Swanson CM, Lukacs JL, Nicholas RW, North PE, Thomas JR. Evidence of an association between 6q13-21 chromosome aberrations and locally aggressive behavior in patients with cartilage tumors. Cancer 1998, 82: 474–483.

400 Schajowicz F. Juxtacortical chondrosarcoma. J Bone Joint Surg (Br) 1977, 59: 473–480.

401 Schiller AL. Diagnosis of borderline cartilage lesions of bone. Semin Diagn Pathol 1985, 2: 42–62.

402 Sheth DS, Yasko AW, Johnson ME, Ayala AG, Murray JA, Romsdahl MM. Chondrosarcoma of the pelvis: prognostic factors for 67 patients treated with definitive surgery. Cancer 1996, 78: 745–750.

403 Smith WS, Simon MA. Segmental resection for chondrosarcoma. J Bone Joint Surg (Am) 1975, 57: 1097–1103.

404 Terek RM, Healey JH, Garin-Chesa P, Mak S, Huvos A, Albino AP. p53 mutations in chondrosarcoma. Diagn Mol Pathol 1998, 7: 51–56.

405 Wrba F, Gullick WJ, Fertl H, Amann G, Salzer-Kuntschik M. Immunohistochemical detection of the c-erbB-2 proto-oncogene product in normal, benign and malignant cartilage tissues. Histopathology 1989, 15: 71–76.

406 Young CL, Sim FH, Unni KK, McLeod RA. Chondrosarcoma of bone in children. Cancer 1990, 66: 1641–1648.

Chondrosarcoma variants
Clear cell chondrosarcoma

407 Aigner T, Dertinger S, Belke J, Kirchner T. Chondrocytic cell differentiation in clear cell chondrosarcoma. Hum Pathol 1996, 27: 1301–1305.

408 Bjornsson J, Unni KK, Dahlin DC, Beabout JW, Sim FH. Clear cell chondrosarcoma of bone. Observations in 47 cases. Am J Surg Pathol 1984, 8: 223–230.

409 Faraggiana T, Sender B, Glicksman P. Light- and electron-microscopic study of clear cell chondrosarcoma. Am J Clin Pathol 1981, 75: 117–121.

410 Kalil RK, Inwards CY, Unni KK, Bertoni F, Bacchini P, Wenger DE, Sim FH. Dedifferentiated clear cell chondrosarcoma. Am J Surg Pathol 2000, 24: 1079–1086.

411 Masui F, Ushigome S, Fujii K. Clear cell chondrosarcoma: pathological and immunohistochemical study 1999, 34: 447–452.

412 Swanson PE. Clear cell tumors of bone. Semin Diagn Pathol 1998, 14: 281–291.

413 Unni KK, Dahlin DC, Beabout JW, Sim FH. Chondrosarcoma. Clear-cell variant. A report of sixteen cases. J Bone Joint Surg (Am) 1976, 58: 676–683.

414 Wang LT, Liu TC. Clear cell chondrosarcoma of bone. A report of three cases with immunohistochemical and affinity histochemical observations. Pathol Res Pract 1993, 189: 411–415.

415 Weiss A-PC, Dorfman HD. S-100 protein in human cartilage lesions. J Bone Joint Surg (Am) 1986, 68: 521–526.

Myxoid chondrosarcoma (chordoid sarcoma)

416 Antonescu CR, Argani P, Erlandson RA, Healey JH, Ladanyi M, Huvos AG. Skeletal and extraskeletal myxoid chondrosarcoma: a comparative clinicopathologic, ultrastructural, and molecular study. Cancer 1998, 83: 1504–1521.

417 Dabska M. Parachordoma. A new clinicopathologic entity. Cancer 1977, 40: 1586–1592.

418 Kilpatrick SE, Inwards CY, Fletcher CD, Smith MA, Gitelis S. Myxoid chondrosarcoma (chordoid sarcoma) of bone: a report of two cases and review of the literature. Cancer 1997, 79: 1903–1910.

419 Martin RF, Melnick PJ, Warner NE, Terry R, Bullock WK, Schwinn CP. Chordoid sarcoma. Am J Clin Pathol 1972, 59: 623–635.

420 Miettinen M, Lehto V-P, Dahl D, Virtanen I. Differential diagnosis of chordoma, chondroid, and ependymal tumors as aided by anti-intermediate filament antibodies. Am J Pathol 1983, 112: 160–169.

421 Pardo-Mindan FJ, Guillen FJ, Villas C, Vazquez JJ. A comparative ultrastructural study of chondrosarcoma, chordoid sarcoma, and chordoma. Cancer 1981, 47: 2611–2619.

422 Shin HJ, Mackay B, Ichinose H, Ayala AG, Romsdahl MM. Parachordoma Ultrastruct Pathol 1994, 18: 249–256.

Dedifferentiated chondrosarcoma

423 Abenoza P, Neumann MP, Manivel JC, Wick MR. Dedifferentiated chondrosarcoma. An ultrastructural study of two cases, with immunocytochemical correlations. Ultrastruct Pathol 1986, 10: 529–538.

424 Aigner T, Dertinger S, Neureiter D, Kirchner T. De-differentiated chondrosarcoma is not a 'de-differentiated' chondrosarcoma. Histopathology 1998, 33: 11–19.

424a Bertoni F, El Ghoneimy A, Bacchini P, Inwards CY, Donati D. Dedifferentiated chondrosarcoma of the pelvis. A report of the clinicopathologic features of fourteen cases treated at the Istituto Rizzoli (Abstract). Mod Pathol 2003, 16: 9a.

425 Bertoni F, Present D, Bacchini P, Picci P, Pignatti G, Gherlinzoni F, Campanacci M. Dedifferentiated peripheral chondrosarcomas. A report of seven cases. Cancer 1989, 63: 2054–2059.

426 Bridge JA, De Boer J, Travis J, Johansson SL, Elmberger G, Noel SM, Neff JR. Simultaneous interphase cytogenetic analysis and fluorescence immunophenotyping of dedifferentiated chondrosarcoma. Implications for histopathogenesis. Am J Pathol 1994, 144: 215–220.

427 Dahlin DC, Beabout JW. Dedifferentiation of low-grade chondrosarcomas. Cancer 1971, 28: 461–466.

428 Dervan PA, O'Loughlin J, Hurson BJ. Dedifferentiated chondrosarcoma with muscle and cytokeratin differentiation in the anaplastic component. Histopathology 1988, 12: 517–526.

429 Jaworski RC. Dedifferentiated chondrosarcoma. An ultrastructural study. Cancer 1984, **53:** 2674–2678.

430 Johnson S, Tetu B, Ayala AG, Chawla SP. Chondrosarcoma with additional mesenchymal component (dedifferentiated chondrosarcoma). I. A clinicopathologic study of 26 cases. Cancer 1986, **58:** 278–286.

431 McCarthy EF, Dorfman HD. Chondrosarcoma of bone with dedifferentiation. A study of eighteen cases. Hum Pathol 1982, **13:** 36–40.

432 McFarland GB, McKinley LM, Reed RJ. Dedifferentiation of low-grade chondrosarcomas. Clin Orthop 1977, **122:** 157–164.

433 Meis JM. "Dedifferentiation" in bone and soft-tissue tumors. A histological indicator of tumor progression. Pathol Annu 1991, **26**(Pt 1)**:** 37–62.

434 Mirra JM, Marcove RC. Fibrosarcomatous dedifferentiation of primary and secondary chondrosarcoma. Review of five cases. J Bone Joint Surg (Am) 1974, **56:** 285–296.

435 Mitchel A, Rudan JR, Fenton PV. Juxtacortical dedifferentiated chondrosarcoma from a primary periosteal chondrosarcoma. Mod Pathol 1996, **9:** 279–283.

436 Reith JD, Bauer TW, Fischler DF, Joyce MJ, Marks KE. Dedifferentiated chondrosarcoma with rhabdomyosarcomatous differentiation. Am J Surg Pathol 1996, **20:** 293–298.

437 Sakamoto A, Oda Y, Adachi T, Oshiro Y, Tamiya S, Tanaka K, Matsuda S, Iwamoto Y, Tsuneyoshi M. H-ras oncogene mutation in dedifferentiated chondrosarcoma: polymerase chain reaction-restriction fragment length polymorphism analysis. Mod Pathol 2001, **14:** 343–349.

438 Tetu B, Ordóñez NG, Ayala AG, Mackay B: Chondrosarcoma with additional mesenchymal component (dedifferentiated chondrosarcoma). II. An immunohistochemical and electron microscopic study. Cancer 1986, **58:** 287–298.

Mesenchymal chondrosarcoma

439 Bertoni F, Picci P, Bacchini P, Capanna R, Innao V, Bacci G, Campanacci M. Mesenchymal chondrosarcoma of bone and soft tissues. Cancer 1983, **52:** 533–541.

440 Dabska M, Huvos AG. Mesenchymal chondrosarcoma in the young. A clinicopathologic study of 19 patients with explanation of histogenesis. Virchows Arch [A] 1983, **399:** 89–104.

441 Dowlig EA. Mesenchymal chondrosarcoma. J Bone Joint Surg (Am) 1964, **46:** 747–754.

442 Frydman CP, Klein MJ, Abdelwahab IF, Zwass A. Primitive multipotential primary sarcoma of bone. A case report and immunohistochemical study. Mod Pathol 1991, **4:** 768–772.

443 Goldman RL. "Mesenchymal" chondrosarcoma, a rare malignant chondroid tumor usually primary in bone. Report of a case arising in extraskeletal soft tissue. Cancer 1967, **20:** 1494–1498.

444 Granter SR, Renshaw AA, Fletcher CD, Bhan AK, Rosenberg AE. CD99 reactivity in mesenchymal chondrosarcoma. Hum Pathol 1996, **27:** 1273–1276.

445 Guccion JG, Font RL, Enzinger FM, Zimmerman LE. Extraskeletal mesenchymal chondrosarcoma. Arch Pathol 1973, **95:** 336–340.

446 Huvos AG, Rosen G, Dabska M, Marcove RC. Mesenchymal chondrosarcoma. A clinicopathologic analysis of 35 patients with emphasis on treatment. Cancer 1983, **51:** 1230–1237.

447 Jacobson SA. Polyhistioma. A malignant tumor of bone and extraskeletal tissues. Cancer 1977, **40:** 2116–2130.

448 Ling LL-L, Steiner GC. Primary multipotential malignant neoplasm of bone. Chondrosarcoma associated with squamous cell carcinoma. Hum Pathol 1986, **17:** 317–320.

449 Nakashima Y, Unni KK, Shives TC, Swee RG, Dahlin DC. Mesenchymal chondrosarcoma of bone and soft tissue. A review of 111 cases. Cancer 1986, **57:** 2444–2453.

450 Salvador AH, Beabout JW, Dahlin DC. Mesenchymal chondrosarcoma. Observations on 30 new cases. Cancer 1971, **28:** 605–615.

451 Steiner GC, Mirra JM, Bullough PG. Mesenchymal chondrosarcoma. A study of the ultrastructure. Cancer 1973, **32:** 926–939.

452 Swanson PE, Lillemoe TJ, Manivel JC, Wick MR. Mesenchymal chondrosarcoma. An immunohistochemical study. Arch Pathol Lab Med 1990, **114:** 943–948.

452a Wehrli BM, Huang W, De Cromrugghe B, Ayala AG, Czerniak B. Sox9, a master regulator of chondrogenesis, distinguishes mesenchymal chondrosarcoma from other small blue round cell tumors. Hum Pathol 2003, **34:** 263–269.

Giant cell tumor

453 Aparisi T. Giant cell tumor of bone. Acta Orthop Scand 1978, **173** (Suppl): 1–38.

454 Aparisi T, Arborgh B, Ericsson JLE. Giant cell tumor of bone. Virchows Arch [A] 1979, **381:** 159–178.

455 Aqel NM, Pringle JA, Horton MA. Cellular heterogeneity in giant cell tumour of bone (osteoclastoma). An immunohistological study of 16 cases. Histopathology 1988, **13:** 675–685.

456 Athanason NA, Bliss E, Gatter KC, Heryet A. An immunohistological study of giant-cell tumour of bone. Evidence for an osteoclast origin of the giant cells. J Pathol 1985, **147:** 153–158.

456a Bertoni F, Bacchini P, Staals EL. Malignancy in giant cell tumor of bone. Cancer 2003, **97:** 2520–2590.

457 Bertoni F, Present D, Enneking WF. Giant-cell tumor of bone with pulmonary metastases. J Bone Joint Surg (Am) 1985, **67:** 890–900.

458 Bertoni F, Unni KK, Beabout JW, Ebersold MJ. Giant cell tumor of the skull. Cancer 1992, **70:** 1124–1132.

459 Biscaglia R, Bacchini P, Bertoni F. Giant cell tumor of the bones of the hand and foot. Cancer 2000, **88:** 2022–2032.

460 Bouropoulou V, Kontogeorgos G, Manika Z. A histological and immunoenzymatic study on the histogenesis of "giant cell tumor of bones." Pathol Res Pract 1985, **180:** 61–67.

461 Bridge JA, Neff JR, Bhatia PS, Sanger WG, Murphey MD. Cytogenetic findings and biologic behavior of giant cell tumors of bone. Cancer 1990, **65:** 2697–2703.

462 Campanacci M, Giunti A, Olmi R. Giant-cell tumours of bone. A study of 209 cases with long-term follow-up in 130. Ital J Orthop Traumatol 1975, **1:** 249–277.

463 Dahlin DC, Cupps RE, Johnson EW Jr. Giant-cell tumor. A study of 195 cases. Cancer 1970, **25:** 1061–1070.

464 Eckardt JJ, Grogan TJ. Giant cell tumor of bone. Clin Orthop 1986, **204:** 45–58.

465 Emley WE. Giant cell tumor of the sphenoid bone. A case report and review of literature. Arch Otolaryngol 1971, **94:** 369–374.

466 Emura I, Inoue Y, Ohnishi Y, Morita T, Saito H, Tajima T. Histochemical, immunohistochemical and ultrastructural investigations of giant cell tumors of bone. Acta Pathol Jpn 1986, **36:** 691–702.

467 Fain JS, Unni KK, Beabout JW, Rock MG. Nonepiphyseal giant cell tumor of the long bones. Clinical, radiologic, and pathologic study. Cancer 1993, **71:** 3514–3519.

468 Fornasier VL, Flores L, Hastings D, Sharp T. Virus-like filamentous intranuclear inclusions in a giant-cell tumor, not associated with Paget's disease of bone. A case report. J Bone Joint Surg (Am) 1985, **67:** 333–336.

469 Fukunaga M, Nikaido T, Shimoda T, Ushigoma S, Nakamori K. A flow cytometric DNA analysis of giant cell tumors of bone including two cases with malignant transformation. Cancer 1992, **70:** 1886–1894.

470 Goldring SR, Schiller AL, Mankin HJ, Dayer J-M, Krane SM. Characterization of cells from human giant cell tumors of bone. Clin Orthop 1986, **204:** 59–75.

471 Hanaoka H, Friedman B, Mack RP. Ultrastructure and histogenesis of giant-cell tumor of bone. Cancer 1970, **25:** 1408–1423.

471a Hoch BL, Inwards C, Rosenberg AE. Multicentric giant cell tumor of bone: a clinicopathologic analysis of thirty cases (Abstract). Mod Pathol 2003, **16**: 13a–14a.

472 Huang L, Xu J, Wood DJ, Zheng MH. Gene expression of osteoprotegerin ligand, osteoprotegerin, and receptor activator of NF-kB in giant cell tumor of bone: possible involvement in tumor cell-induced osteoclast-like cell formation. Am J Pathol 2000, **156**: 761–767.

473 Kasahara K, Yamamuro T, Kasahara A. Giant-cell tumour of bone. Cytological studies. Br J Cancer 1979, **40**: 201–209.

474 Ladanyi M, Traganos F, Huvos AG. Benign metastasizing giant cell tumors of bone. A DNA flow cytometric study. Cancer 1989, **64**: 1521–1526.

475 Layfield LJ, Bentley RC, Mirra JM. Pseudoanaplastic giant cell tumor of bone. Arch Pathol Lab Med 1999, **123**: 163–166.

476 Liu TC, Ji ZM, Wang LT. Giant cell tumors of bone. An immunohistochemical study. Pathol Res Pract 1989, **185**: 448–453.

477 Mankin HJ, Fogelson FS, Thrasher AZ, Jaffer F. Massive resection and allograft transplantation in the treatment of malignant bone tumors. N Engl J Med 1976, **294**: 1247–1255.

478 Masui F, Ushigome S, Fujii K. Giant cell tumor of bone: an immunohistochemical comparative study. Pathol Int 1998, **48**: 355–361.

479 Masui F, Ushigome S, Fujii K. Giant cell tumor of bone: a clinicopathologic study of prognostic factors. Pathol Int 1998, **48**: 723–729.

480 McDonald DJ, Sim FH, McLeod RA, Dahlin DC. Giant-cell tumor of bone. J Bone Joint Surg (Am) 1986, **68**: 235–242.

481 Medeiros J, Beckstead J, Rosenberg A, Warnke R, Wood G. Giant cells and mononuclear cells of giant cell tumor of bone resemble histiocytes. Appl Immunohistochem 1993, **1**: 115–122.

482 Meis JM, Dorfman HD, Nathanson SD, Haggar AM, Wu KK. Primary malignant giant cell tumor of bone. "Dedifferentiated" giant cell tumor. Mod Pathol 1989, **2**: 541–546.

483 Metze K, Ciplea AG, Hettwer H, Barckhaus RH. Size dependent enzyme activities of multinucleated (osteoclastic) giant cells in bone tumors. Pathol Res Pract 1987, **182**: 214–221.

484 Mii Y, Miyauchi Y, Morishita T, Miura S, Honoki K, Aoki M, Tamai S. Osteoclast origin of giant cells in giant cell tumors of bone. Ultrastructural and cytochemical study of six cases. Ultrastruct Pathol 1991, **15**: 623–629.

485 Nascimento AG, Huvos AG, Marcove RC. Primary malignant giant cell tumor of bone. A study of eight cases and review of the literature. Cancer 1979, **44**: 1393–1402.

486 Negoescu A, Mandache E. The ultrastructure of nuclear inclusions in the giant-cell tumor of bone. Pathol Res Pract 1989, **184**: 410–417.

487 Oda Y, Sakamoto A, Saito T, Matsuda S, Tanaka K, Iwamoto Y, Tsuneyoshi M. Secondary malignant giant-cell tumour of bone: molecular abnormalities of p53 and H-ras gene correlated with malignant transformation. Histopathology 2001, **39**: 629–637.

488 Oliveira P, Perez E, Ortega A, Terual R, Gomes C, Moreno LF, Duenas A, De La Garza J, Melendez-Zajgla J, Maldonado V. Estrogen receptor expression in giant cell tumors of the bone. Hum Pathol 2002, **33**: 165–169.

489 Parrish FF. Allograft replacement of all or part of the end of a long bone following excision of a tumor. Report of twenty-one cases. J Bone Joint Surg (Am) 1973, **55**: 1–22.

490 Picci P, Manfrini M, Zucchi V, Gherlinzoni F, Rock M, Bertoni F, Neff JR. Giant-cell tumor of bone in skeletally immature patients. J Bone Joint Surg (Am) 1983, **65**: 486–490.

491 Present D, Bertoni F, Hudson T, Enneking WF. The correlation between the radiologic staging studies and histopathologic findings in aggressive stage 3 giant cell tumor of bone. Cancer 1986, **57**: 237–244.

492 Regezi JA, Zarbo RJ, Lloyd RV. Muramidase, α-1 antitrypsin, α-1 antichymotrypsin, and S-100 protein immunoreactivity in giant cell lesions. Cancer 1987, **59**: 64–68.

493 Rock MG, Pritchard DJ, Unni KK. Metastases from histologically benign giant-cell tumor of bone. J Bone Joint Surg (Am) 1984, **66**: 269–274.

494 Roessner A, Bassewitz DBv, Schlake W, Thorwesten G, Grundmann E. Biologic characterization of human bone tumors. III. Giant cell tumor of bone. A combined electron microscopical, histochemical, and autoradiographical study. Pathol Res Pract 1984, **178**: 431–440.

495 Roux S, Amazit L, Meduri G, Guiochon-Mantel A, Milgrom E, Mariette X. RANK (receptor activator of nuclear factor kappa B) and RANK ligand are expressed in giant cell tumors of bone. Am J Clin Pathol 2002, **117**: 210–216.

496 Sanerkin NG. Malignancy, aggressiveness, and recurrence in giant cell tumor of bone. Cancer 1980, **46**: 1641–1649.

497 Sara AS, Ayala AG, el-Naggar A, Ro JY, Raymond AK, Murray JA. Giant cell tumor of bone. A clinicopathologic and DNA flow cytometric analysis. Cancer 1990, **66**: 2186–2190.

498 Savini R, Gherlinzoni F, Morandi M, Neff JR, Picci P. Surgical treatment of giant-cell tumor of the spine. Istituto Ortopedico Rizzoli. J Bone Joint Surg (Am) 1983, **65**: 1283–1290.

499 Schajowicz F. Giant-cell tumors of bone (osteoclastoma). A pathological and histochemical study. J Bone Joint Surg (Am) 1961, **43**: 1–29.

500 Schajowicz F, Ubios AM, Santini Araujo E, Cabrini RL. Virus-like intranuclear inclusions in giant cell tumor of bone. Clin Orthop 1985, **201**: 247–250.

501 Schoedel KE, Greco MA, Stetler-Stevenson WG, Ohori NP, Goswami S, Present D, Steinger GC. Expression of metalloproteinases and tissue inhibitors of metalloproteinases in giant cell tumor of bone: an immunohistochemical study with clinical correlation. Hum Pathol 1996, **27**: 1144–1148.

502 Sciot R, Dal Cin P, Fletcher CD, Hernandez JM, Garcia JL, Samson I, Ramos L, Brys P, Van Damme B, Van den Berghe H. Inflammatory myofibroblastic tumor of bone: report of two cases with evidence of clonal chromosomal changes. Am J Surg Pathol 1997, **21**: 1166–1172.

503 Steiner GC, Ghosh L, Dorfman HD. Ultrastructure of giant cell tumors of bone. Hum Pathol 1972, **3**: 569–586.

504 Sulh MA, Greco MA, Jiang T, Goswami SB, Present D, Steiner G. Proliferation index and vascular density of giant cell tumors of bone: are they prognostic markers? Cancer 1996, **77**: 2044–2051.

505 Sung HW, Kuo DP, Shu WP, Chai YB, Liu CC, Li SM. Giant-cell tumor of bone. Analysis of two hundred and eight cases in Chinese patients. J Bone Joint Surg (Am) 1982, **64**: 755–761.

506 Sybrandy S, de la Fuente AA. Multiple giant tumour of bone. Report of a case. J Bone Joint Surg (Br) 1973, **55**: 350–356.

507 Teot LA, O'Keefe RJ, Rosier RN, O'Connell JX, Fox EJ, Hicks DG. Extraosseous primary and recurrent giant cell tumors: transforming growth factor-beta1 and -beta2 expression may explain metaplastic bone formation. Hum Pathol 1996, **27**: 625–632.

508 Ueda Y, Imai K, Tsuchiya H, Fujimoto N, Nakanishi I, Katsuda S, Seiki M, Okada Y. Matrix metalloproteinase 9 (gelatinise B) is expressed in multinucleated giant cells of human giant cell tumor of bone and is associated with vascular invasion. Am J Pathol 1996, **148**: 611–622.

509 Watanabe K, Tajino T, Kusakabe T, Saitoh A, Suzuki T. Giant cell tumor of bone: frequent actin immunoreactivity in stromal tumor cells. Pathol Int 1997, **47**: 680–684.

510 Wold LE, Swee RG. Giant cell tumor of the small bones of the hands and feet. Semin Diagn Pathol 1984, **1**: 173–184.

511 Wolfe JT III, Scheithauer BW, Dahlin DC. Giant-cell tumor of the sphenoid bone. Review of 10 cases. J Neurosurg 1983, **59**: 322–327.

511a Wülling M, Delling G, Kaiser E. The origin of the neoplastic stromal cell in giant cell tumor of bone. Hum Pathol 2003, **34**: 983–993.

512 Yoshida H, Akeho M, Yumoto T. Giant cell tumor of bone. Enzyme histochemical, biochemical and tissue culture studies. Virchows Arch [A] 1982, **395**: 319–330.

513 Zheng MH, Fan Y, Wysocki SJ, Lau AT, Robertson T, Beilharz M, Wood DJ, Papadimitriou JM. Gene expression of transforming growth factor-beta 1 and its type II receptor in giant cell tumors of bone. Possible involvement in osteoclast-like cell migration. Am J Pathol 1994, **145**: 1095–1104.

Marrow tumors

Ewing's sarcoma/primitive neuroectodermal tumor

514 Adams V, Hany MA, Schmid M, Hassam S, Briner J, Niggli FK. Detection of t(11;22)(q24;q12) translocation breakpoint in paraffin-embedded tissue of the Ewing's sarcoma family by nested reverse transcription-polymerase chain reaction. Diagn Mol Pathol 1996, **5**: 107–113.

515 Amann G, Zoubek A, Salzer-Kuntschik M, Windhager R, Kovar H. Relation of neuroglial marker expression and EWS gene fusion types in MIC2/CD99-positive tumors of the Ewing family. Hum Pathol 1999, **30**: 1058–1064.

516 Ambros IM, Ambros PF, Strehl S, Kovar H, Gadner H, Salzer-Kuntschik M. MIC2 is a specific marker for Ewing's sarcoma and peripheral primitive neuroectodermal tumors. Evidence for a common histogenesis of Ewing's sarcoma and peripheral primitive neuroectodermal tumors from MIC2 expression and specific chromosome aberration. Cancer 1991, **67**: 1886–1893.

517 Amir G, Issakov J, Meller I, Sucher E, Peyser A, Cohen IJ, Yaniv I, Arush MWB, Tavori U, Kollender Y, Ron N, Peylan-Ramu N. Expression of p53 gene product and cell proliferation marker Ki-67 in Ewing's sarcoma: correlation with clinical outcome. Hum Pathol 2002, **33**: 170–174.

518 Askin FB, Perlman EJ. Neuroblastoma and peripheral neuroectodermal tumors. Am J Clin Pathol 1998, **109**: S23–S30.

519 Askin FB, Rosai J, Sibley RK, Dehner LP, McAlister WH. Malignant small cell tumor of the thoracopulmonary region in childhood; a distinctive clinicopathologic entity of uncertain histogenesis. Cancer 1979, **43**: 2438–2451.

520 Bacci G, Mercuri M, Briccoli A, Ferrari S, Bertoni F, Donati D, Monti C, Zanoni A, Forni C, Manfrini M. Osteogenic sarcoma of the extremity with detectable lung metastases at presentation: results of treatment of 23 patients with chemotherapy followed by simultaneous resection and metastatic lesions. Cancer 1997, **79**: 245–254.

521 Bacci G, Toni A, Avella M, Manfrini M, Sudanese A, Ciaroni D, Boriani S, Emiliani E, Campanacci M. Long-term results in 144 localized Ewing's sarcoma patients treated with combined therapy. Cancer 1989, **63**: 1477–1486.

522 Bator SM, Bauer TW, Marks KE, Norris DG. Periosteal Ewing's sarcoma. Cancer 1986, **58**: 1781–1784.

523 Batsakis JG, El-Naggar AK. Ewing's sarcoma and primitive neuroectodermal tumors; cytogenetic cynosures seeking a common histogenesis. Adv Anat Pathol 1997, **4**: 207–220.

524 Bridge JA, Fidler ME, Neff JR, Degenhardt J, Wang M, Walker C, Dorfman HD, Baker KS, Seemayer TA. Adamantinoma-like Ewing's sarcoma: genomic confirmation, phenotypic drift. Am J Surg Pathol 1999, **23**: 159–165.

525 Bridge AJ, Nelson M, Orndal C, Bhatia P, Neff JR. Clonal karyotypic abnormalities of the hereditary multiple exostoses chromosomal loci 8q24.1(EX1) and 11p11-12(EXT2) in patients with sporadic and hereditary osteochondromas. Cancer 1998, **82**: 1657–1663.

526 Brinkhuis M, Winjnaendts LC, van der Linden JC, van Unnik AJ, Voute PA, Baak JP, Meijer CJ. Peripheral primitive neuroectodermal tumour and extraosseous Ewing's sarcoma; a histological, immunohistochemical and DNA flow cytometric study. Virchows Arch 1995, **425**: 611–616.

527 Cangir A, Vietti TJ, Gehan EA, Burgert EO Jr, Thomas P, Tefft M, Nesbit ME, Kissane J, Pritchard D. Ewing's sarcoma metastatic at diagnosis. Results and comparisons of two intergroup Ewing's sarcoma studies. Cancer 1990, **66**: 887–893.

528 Carter RL, al-Sams SZ, Corbett RP, Clinton S. A comparative study of immunohistochemical staining for neuron-specific enolase, protein gene product 9.5 and S-100 protein in neuroblastoma, Ewing's sarcoma and other round cell tumours in children. Histopathology 1990, **16**: 461–467.

529 Cavazzana AO, Miser JS, Jefferson J, Triche TJ. Experimental evidence for a neural origin of Ewing's sarcoma of bone. Am J Pathol 1987, **127**: 507–518.

529a Collini P, Mezzelani A, Modena P, Dagrada P, Tamborini E, Luksch R, Gronchi A, Navarria P, Sozzi G, Pilotti S. Evidence of neural differentiation in a case of post-therapy primitive neuroectodermal tumor/Ewing sarcoma of bone. Am J Surg Pathol 2003, **27**: 1161–1166.

530 Collini P, Sampietro G, Bertulli R, Casali PG, Luksch R, Mezzelani A, Sozzi G, Pilotti S. Cytokeratin immunoreactivity in 41 cases of ES/PNET confirmed by molecular diagnostic studies. Am J Surg Pathol 2001, **25**: 273–274.

531 Cotterill SJ, Ahrens S, Paulussen M, Jurgens HF, Voute PA, Gadner H, Craft AW. Pronostic factors in Ewing's tumor of bone: analysis of 975 patients from the European intergroup cooperative Ewing's sarcoma study group. J Clin Oncol 2000, **18**: 3108–3114.

532 de Alava E, Antonescu CR, Panizo A, Leung D, Meyers PA, Huvos AG, Pardo-Mindan FJ, Healey JH, Ladanyi M. Prognostic impact of p53 status in Ewing sarcoma. Cancer 2000, **89**: 783–792.

533 de Alava E, Panizo A, Antonescu CR, Huvos AG, Pardo-Mindan FJ, Barr FG, Ladanyi M. Associaton of EWS-FLI1 type 1 fusion with lower proliferative rate in Ewing's sarcoma. Am J Pathol 2000, **156**: 849–855.

534 de Alava E, Pardo J. Ewing tumor: tumor biology and clinical applications. Int J Surg Pathol 2001, **9**: 7–17.

535 Dehner LP. Primitive neuroectodermal tumor and Ewing's sarcoma. Am J Surg Pathol 1993, **17**: 1–13.

536 Delattre O, Zucman J, Melot T, Garau XS, Zucker JM, Lenoir GM, Ambros PF, Sheer D, Turc-Carel C, Triche TJ, et al. The Ewing family of tumors – a sub-group of small-round-cell tumors defined by specific chimeric transcripts. N Engl J Med 1994, **331**: 294–299.

537 Devoe K, Weidner N. Immunohistochemistry of small round-cell tumors. Semin Diagn Pathol 2000, **17**: 216–224.

538 Dierick AM, Langlois M, Van Oostveldt P, Roels H. The prognostic significance of the DNA content in Ewing's sarcoma. A retrospective cytophotometric and flow cytometric study. Histopathology 1993, **23**: 333–339.

539 Dockhorn-Dworniczak B, Schafer KL, Dantcheva R, Blasius S, Winkelmann W, Strehl S, Burdach S, van Valen F, Jurgens H, Bocker W. Diagnostic value of the molecular genetic detection of the t(11;22) translocation in Ewing's tumours. Virchows Arch 1994, **425**: 107–112.

540 Downing JR, Head DR, Parham DM, Douglass EC, Hulshof MG, Link MP, Motroni TA, Grier HE, Curcio-Brint AM, Shapiro DN. Detection of the (11;22) (q24;q12) translocation of Ewing's sarcoma and peripheral neuroectodermal tumor by reverse transcription polymerase chain reaction. Am J Pathol 1993, **143**: 1294–1300.

541 Editorial. Ewing's sarcoma and its congeners. An interim appraisal. Lancet 1992, **339**: 99–100.

542 Ehara S, Kattapuram SV, Egglin TK. Ewing's sarcoma. Radiographic pattern of healing and bony complications in patients with long-term survival. Cancer 1991, **68**: 1531–1535.

543 Fellinger EJ, Garin-Chesa P, Glasser DB, Huvos AG, Rettig WJ. Comparison of cell surface antigen HBA71 (p30/32MIC2), neuron-specific enolase, and vimentin in the

immunohistochemical analysis of Ewing's sarcoma of bone. Am J Surg Pathol 1992, **16**: 746–755.

544 Fellinger EJ, Garin-Chesa P, Triche TJ, Huvos AG, Rettig WJ. Immunohistochemical analysis of Ewing's sarcoma cell surface antigen p30/32MIC2. Am J Pathol 1991, **139**: 317–325.

545 Fidelia-Lambert MN, Zhuang Z, Tsokos M. Sensitive detection of rare Ewing's sarcoma cells in peripheral blood by reverse transcriptase polymerase chain reaction. Hum Pathol 1999, **30**: 78–80.

546 Fizazi K, Dohollou N, Blay J-Y, Guerin S, Le Cesne AL, Andre F, Pouillart P, Tursz T, Bui BB. Ewing's family of tumors in adults: multivariate analysis of survival and long-term results of multimodality therapy in 182 patients. J Clin Oncol 1998, **16**: 3736–3743.

547 Folpe AL, Hill CE, Parham DM, O'Shea PA, Weiss SW. Immunohistochemical detection of FLI-1 protein expression: a study of 132 round cell tumors with emphasis on CD99-positive mimics of Ewing's sarcoma/primitive neuroectodermal tumor. Am J Surg Pathol 2000, **24**: 1657–1662.

548 Friedman JM, Vitale M, Maimon J, Israel MA, Horowitz ME, Schneider BS. Expression of the cholecystokinin gene in pediatric tumors. Proc Natl Acad Sci USA 1992, **89**: 5819–5823.

549 Fukunaga M, Ushigome S. Periosteal Ewing-like adamantinoma. Virchows Arch 1998, **433**: 385–389.

550 Garin-Chesa P, Fellinger EJ, Huvos AG, Beresford HR, Melamed MR, Triche TJ, Rettig WJ. Immunohistochemical analysis of neural cell adhesion molecules. Differential expression in small round cell tumors of childhood and adolescence. Am J Pathol 1991, **139**: 275–286.

551 Gasparini M, Barni S, Lattuada A, Musumeci R, Bonadonna G, Fossati-Bellani F. Ten years experience with Ewing's sarcoma. Tumori 1977, **63**: 77–90.

552 Gerald WL. A practical approach to the differential diagnosis of small round cell tumors of infancy using recent scientific and technical advances. Int J Surg Pathol 2000, **8**: 87–97.

553 Ginsberg JP, de Alava E, Ladanyi M, Wexler LH, Kovar H, Paulussen M, Zoubek A, Dockhorn-Dworniczak B, Juergens H, Wunder JS, Andrulis IL, Malik R, Sorensen PH, Womer RB, Barr FG. EWS-FLI1 and EWS-ERG gene fusions are associated with similar clinical phenotypes in Ewing's sarcoma. J Clin Oncol 1999, **17**: 1809–1814.

554 Gu M, Antonescu CR, Guiter G, Huvos AG, Ladanyi M, Zakowski MF. Cytokeratin immunoreactivity in Ewing's sarcoma: prevalence in 50 cases confirmed by molecular studies. Am J Surg Pathol 2000, **24**: 410–416.

555 Guiter GE, Gamboni MM, Zakowski MF. The cytology of extraskeletal Ewing sarcoma. Cancer 1999, **87**: 141–148.

556 Hartman KR, Triche TJ, Kinsella TJ, Miser JS. Prognostic value of histopathology in Ewing's sarcoma. Long-term follow-up of distal extremity primary tumors. Cancer 1991, **67**: 163–171.

557 Hasegawa SL, Davison JM, Rutten A, Fletcher JA, Fletcher CD. Primary cutaneous Ewing's sarcoma: immunophenotypic and molecular cytogenetic evaluation of five cases. Am J Surg Pathol 1998, **22**: 310–318.

558 Hasegawa T, Hirose T, Kudo E, Hizawa K, Yamawaki S, Ishii S. Atypical primitive neuroectodermal tumors. Comparative light and electron microscopic and immunohistochemical studies on peripheral neuroepitheliomas and Ewing's sarcomas. Acta Pathol Jpn 1991, **41**: 444–454.

559 Hess E, Cohen C, DeRose PB, Yost BA, Costa MJ. Nonspecificity of p30/32MIC2 immunolocalization with the 013 monoclonal antibody in the diagnosis of Ewing's sarcoma: application of an algorithmic immunohistochemical analysis. Appl Immunohistochem 1997, **5**: 94–103.

560 Hoffmann C, Ahrens S, Dunst J, Hillmann A, Winkelmann W, Craft A, Gobel U, Rube C, Voute PA, Harms D, Jurgens H. Pelvic Ewing sarcoma: a retrospective analysis of 241 cases. Cancer 1999, **85**: 869–877.

561 Jaffe R, Santamaria M, Yunis EJ, Tannery NH, Agostini RM Jr, Medina J, Goodman M. The neuroectodermal tumor of bone. Am J Surg Pathol 1984, **8**: 885–898.

562 Kaspers GJ, Kamphorst W, van de Graaff M, van Alphen HA, Veerman AJ. Primary spinal epidural extraosseous Ewing's sarcoma. Cancer 1991, **68**: 648–654.

563 Kissane JM, Askin FB, Foulkes M, Stratton LB, Shirley SF. Ewing's sarcoma of bone. Clinicopathologic aspects of 303 cases from the Intergroup Ewing's Sarcoma Study. Hum Pathol 1983, **14**: 773–779.

564 Kissane JM, Askin FB, Nesbit M, Vietti T, Burgert EO Jr, Cangir A, Gehan EA, Perez CA, Pritchard DJ, Tefft M. Sarcomas of bone in childhood. Pathologic aspects. In Glicksmann A, Tefft M (eds): Bone and soft tissue sarcomas. J Natl Cancer Inst Monograph 1981, **56**: 29–41.

565 Knezevich SR, Hendson G, Mathers JA, Carpenter B, Lopez-Terrada D, Brown KL, Sorensen PH. Absence of detectable EWS.FLI1 expression after therapy-induced neural differentiation in Ewing sarcoma. Hum Pathol 1998, **29**: 289–294.

566 Kumar S, Pack S, Kumar D, Walker R, Quezado M, Zhuang Z, Meltzer P, Tsokos M. Detection of EWS-FLI-1 fusion in Ewing's sarcoma/peripheral primitive neuroectodermal tumor by fluorescence in situ hybridisation using formalin-fixed paraffin-embedded tissue. Hum Pathol 1999, **30**: 324–330.

567 Ladanyi M, Heinemann FS, Huvos AG, Rao PH, Chen QG, Jhanwar SC. Neural differentiation in small round cell tumors of bone and soft tissue with the translocation t(11;22)(q24;q12). An immunohistochemical study of 11 cases. Hum Pathol 1990, **21**: 1245–1251.

568 Ladanyi M, Lewis R, Garin-Chesa P, Rettig WJ, Huvos AG, Healey JH, Jhanwar SC. EWS rearrangement in Ewing's sarcoma and peripheral neuroectodermal tumor. Molecular detection and correlation with cytogenetic analysis and MIC2 expression. Diagn Mol Pathol 1993, **2**: 141–146.

569 Lawlor ER, Mathers JA, Bainbridge T, Horsman DE, Kawai A, Healey JH, Huvos AG, Bridge JA, Ladanyi M, Sorensen PH. Peripheral primitive neuroectodermal tumors in adults: documentation by molecular analysis. J Clin Oncol 1998, **16**: 1150–1157.

570 Leong A S-Y, Milios J. Small round cell tumors in childhood. Immunohistochemical studies in rhabdomyosarcoma, neuroblastoma, Ewing's sarcoma, and lymphoblastic lymphoma. Surg Pathol 1989, **2**: 5–18.

571 Llombart-Bosch A, Contesso G, Reydro-Olaya A. Histology, immunohistochemistry, and electron microscopy of small round cell tumors of bone. Semin Diagn Pathol 1996, **13**: 153–170.

572 Llombart-Bosch A, Navarro S. Immunohistochemical detection of EWS and FLI-1 proteins in Ewing sarcoma and primitive neuroectodermal tumors: comparative analysis with CD99(MIC-2) expression. Appl Immunohistochem Molecul Morphol 2001, **9**: 255–260.

573 Löning TH, Liebsch J, Delling G. Osteosarcomas and Ewing's sarcomas. Comparative immunocytochemical investigation of filamentous proteins and cell membrane determinants. Virchows Arch [A] 1985, **407**: 323–336.

574 Lucas DR, Kolodziej P, Gross ML, Mott MP, Budev H, Zalupski MM, Ryan JR. Metastatic uterine leiomyosarcoma to bone: a clinicopathologic study. Int J Surg Pathol 1996-1997, **4**: 159–168.

575 Mawad JK, Mackay B, Raymond AK, Ayala AG. Electron microscopy in the diagnosis of small round cell tumors of bone. Ultrastruct Pathol 1994, **18**: 263–268.

576 Maygarden SJ, Askin FB, Siegal GP, Gilula LA, Schoppe J, Foulkes M, Kissane JM, Nesbit M. Ewing sarcoma of bone in infants and toddlers. A clinicopathologic report from the Intergroup Ewing's Study. Cancer 1993, **71**: 2109–2118.

577 Meis-Kindblom JM, Stenman G, Kindblom LG. Differential diagnosis of small round cell tumors. Semin Diagn Pathol 1996, **13**: 213–241.

578 Mendenhall CM, Marcus RB Jr, Enneking WF, Springfield DS, Thar TL, Million RR. The prognostic significance of soft tissue extension in Ewing's sarcoma. Cancer 1983, **51**: 913–917.

579 Miettinen M, Lehto V-P, Virtanen I. Histogenesis of Ewing's sarcoma. An evaluation of intermediate filaments and endothelial cell markers. Virchows Arch [Cell Pathol] 1982, **41**: 277–284.

580 Moll R, Lee I, Gould VE, Berndt R, Roessner A, Franke WW. Immunocytochemical analysis of Ewing's tumors. Patterns of expression of intermediate filaments and desmosomal proteins indicate cell type heterogeneity and pluripotential differentiation. Am J Pathol 1987, **127**: 288–304.

581 Montforte-Munoz H, Lopez-Terrada D, Affendie H, Rowland JM, Triche TJ. Documentation of EWS gene rearrangements by fluorescence in-situ hybridization (FISH) in frozen sections of Ewing's sarcoma-peripheral primitive neuroectodermal tumor. Am J Surg Pathol 1999, **23**: 309–315.

582 Nascimento AG, Unni KK, Pritchard DJ, Cooper KL, Dahlin DC. A clinicopathologic study of 20 cases of large-cell (atypical) Ewing's sarcoma of bone. Am J Surg Pathol 1980, **4**: 29–36.

583 Navarro S, Cavazzana AO, Llombart-Bosch A, Triche TJ. Comparison of Ewing's sarcoma of bone and peripheral neuroepithelioma. An immunocytochemical and ultrastructural analysis of two primitive neuroectodermal neoplasms. Arch Pathol Lab Med 1994, **118**: 608–615.

584 Neff JR. Nonmetastatic Ewing's sarcoma of bone. The role of surgical therapy. Clin Orthop 1980, **204**: 111–118.

585 Nogueira E, Navarro S, Pellin A, Lombart-Bosch A. Activation of TRK genes in Ewing's sarcoma: trk a receptor expression linked to neural differentiation. Diagn Mol Pathol 1997, **6**: 10–16.

586 Noguera R, Triche TJ, Navarro S, Tsokos M, Llombart-Bosch A. Dynamic model of differentiation in Ewing's sarcoma cells. Comparative analysis of morphologic, immunocytochemical, and oncogene expression parameters. Lab Invest 1992, **66**: 143–151.

587 O'Sullivan MJ, Perlman EJ, Furman J, Humphrey PA, Dehner LP, Pfeifer JD. Visceral primitive peripheral neuroectodermal tumors: a clinicopathologic and molecular study. Hum Pathol 2001, **32**: 1109–1115.

588 Ozaki T, Hillmann A, Hoffmann C, Rube C, Blasius S, Dunst J, Jurgens H, Winkelmann W. Significance of surgical margin on the prognosis of patients with Ewing's sarcoma: a report from the Cooperative Ewing's Sarcoma Study. Cancer 1996, **78**: 892–900.

589 Pagani A, Fischer-Colbrie R, Sanfilippo B, Winkler H, Cerrato M, Bussolati G. Secretogranin II expression in Ewing's sarcomas and primitive neuroectodermal tumors. Diagn Mol Pathol 1992, **1**: 165–172.

590 Pagani A, Macri L, Rosolen A, Toffolatti L, Stella A, Bussolati G. Neuroendocrine differentiation in Ewing's sarcoma and primitive neuroectodermal tumors revealed by reverse transcriptase-polymerase chain reaction of chromogranin mRNA. Diagn Mol Pathol 1998, **7**: 36–43.

591 Parham DM, Hijazi Y, Sternberg SM, Meyer WH, Horowitz M, Tzen CY, Wexler LH, Tsokos M. Neuroectodermal differentiation in Ewing's sarcoma family of tumors does not predict tumor behaviour. Hum Pathol 1999, **30**: 911–918.

592 Perlman EJ, Dickman PS, Askin FB, Grier HE, Miser JS, Link MP. Ewing's sarcoma – routine diagnostic utilization of MIC2 analysis. A Pediatric Oncology Group/Children's Cancer Group Intergroup Study. Hum Pathol 1994, **25**: 304–307.

593 Picci P, Bohling T, Bacci G, Ferrari S, Sangiorgi L, Mercuri M, Ruggieri P, Manfrini M, Ferraro A, Casadei R, Benassi MS, Mancini AF, Rosito P, Cazzola A, Barbieri E, Tienghi A, Brach del Prever A, Comandone A, Bacchini P, Bertoni F. Chemotherapy-induced tumor necrosis as a prognostic factor in localized Ewing's sarcoma of the extremities. J Clin Oncol 1997, **15**: 1553–1559.

594 Pinto A, Grant LH, Hayes FA, Schell MJ, Parham DM. Immunohistochemical expression of neuron-specific enolase and Leu 7 in Ewing's sarcoma of bone. Cancer 1989, **64**: 1266–1273.

595 Ramani P, Rampling D, Link M. Immunocytochemical study of 12E7 in small round-cell tumours of childhood. An assessment of its sensitivity and specificity. Histopathology 1993, **23**: 557–561.

596 Razek A, Perez CA, Tefft M, Nesbit M, Vietti T, Burgert EO Jr, Kissane J, Pritchard DJ, Gehan EA. Intergroup Ewing's sarcoma study. Local control related to radiation dose, volume, and site of primary lesion in Ewing's sarcoma. Cancer 1980, **46**: 516–521.

597 Rettig WJ, Garin-Chesa P, Huvos AG. Ewing's sarcoma. New approaches to histogenesis and molecular plasticity. Lab Invest 1992, **66**: 133–137.

598 Roessner A, Jurgens H. Round cell tumours of bone. Pathol Res Pract 1993, **189**: 111–136.

599 Rosen G, Caparros B, Nirenberg A, Marcove RC, Huvos AG, Kosloff C, Lane J, Murphy ML. Ewing's sarcoma. Ten-year experience with adjuvant chemotherapy. Cancer 1981, **47**: 2204–2213.

600 Rosito P, Mancini AF, Rondelli R, Abate ME, Pession A, Bedei L, Bacci G, Picci P, Mercuri M, Ruggieri P, Frezza G, Campanacci M, Paolucci G. Italian cooperative study for the treatment of children and young adults with localized Ewing sarcoma of bone: a preliminary report of 6 years of experience. Cancer 1999, **86**: 421–428.

600a Sandberg AA, Bridge JA. Updates of cytogenetics and molecular genetics of bone and tissue tumors: Ewing sarcoma and peripheral primitive neuroectodermal tumors. Cancer Genet Cytogenet 2000, **123**: 1–26.

601 Scarpa S, Modesti A, Triche TJ. Extracellular matrix synthesis by undifferentiated childhood tumor cell lines. Am J Pathol 1987, **129**: 74–85.

602 Schajowicz F. Ewing's sarcoma and reticulum-cell sarcoma of bone. With special reference to the histochemical demonstration of glycogen as an aid to differential diagnosis. J Bone Joint Surg (Am) 1959, **41**: 349–356.

603 Scheurlen WG, Schwabe GC, Joos S, Mollenhauer J, Sorensen N, Kuhl J. Molecular analysis of childhood primitive neuroectodermal tumors defines markers associated with poor outcome. J Clin Oncol 1998, **16**: 2478–2485.

604 Schmidt D, Herrmann C, Jurgens H, Harms D. Malignant peripheral neuroectodermal tumor and its necessary distinction from Ewing's sarcoma. A report from the Kiel Pediatric Tumor Registry. Cancer 1991, **68**: 2251–2259.

605 Schmidt D, Mackay B, Ayala AG. Ewing's sarcoma with neuroblastoma-like features. Ultrastruct Pathol 1982, **3**: 143–151.

606 Scotlandi K, Serra M, Manara MC, Benini S, Sarti M, Maurici D, Lollini PL, Picci P, Bertoni F, Baldini N. Immunostaining of the p30/32MIC2 antigen and molecular detection of EWS rearrangements for the diagnosis of Ewing's sarcoma and peripheral neuroectodermal tumor. Hum Pathol 1996, **27**: 408–416.

607 Selleri L, Hermanson GG, Eubanks JH, Lewis KA, Evans GA. Molecular localization of the t(11;22)(q24;q12) translocation of Ewing sarcoma by chromosomal in situ suppression hybridization. Proc Natl Acad Sci USA 1991, **88**: 887–891.

608 Shanfeld RL, Edelman J, Willis JE, Tuason L, Goldblum JR. Immunohistochemical analysis of neural markers in peripheral primitive neuroectodermal tumors (pNET) without light microscopic evidence of neural differentiation. Appl Immunohistochem 1997, **5**: 78–86.

609 Shishikura A, Ushigome S, Shimoda T. Primitive neuroectodermal tumors of bone and soft tissue. Histological subclassification and clinicopathologic correlations. Acta Pathol Jpn 1993, **43**: 176–186.

610 Siegal GP, Oliver WR, Reinus WR, Gilula LA, Foulkes MA, Kissane JM, Askin FB. Primary Ewing's sarcoma involving the bones of the head and neck. Cancer 1987, **60**: 2829–2840.

611 Sorensen P, Liu X, Delattre O, Rowland J, Biggs C, Thomas G, Triche T. Reverse transcriptase PCR amplification of EWS/FL-1 fusion transcripts as a diagnostic test for peripheral primitive neuroectodermal tumors of childhood. Diagn Mol Pathol 1993, **2**: 147–157.

612 Stephenson CF, Bridge JA, Sandberg AA. Cytogenetic and pathologic aspects of Ewing's sarcoma and neuroectodermal tumors. Hum Pathol 1992, **23**: 1270–1277.

613 Stevenson AJ, Chatten J, Bertoni P, Miettinen M. CD99 (p30/32MIC) neuroectodermal/Ewing's sarcoma antigen as an immunohistochemical marker. Review of more than 600 tumors and the literature experience. Appl Immunohistochem 1994, **2**: 231–240.

614 Suh CH, Ordonez NG, Hicks J, Mackay B. Ultrastructure of the Ewing's sarcoma family of tumors. Ultrastruct Pathol 2002, **26**: 67–76.

615 Telles NC, Rabson AS, Pomeroy TC. Ewing's sarcoma. An autopsy study. Cancer 1978, **41**: 2321–2329.

616 Thomas PRM, Foulkes MA, Gilula LA, Burgert EO, Evans RG, Kissane J, Nesbit ME, Pritchard DJ, Tefft M, Vietti TJ. Primary Ewing's sarcoma of the ribs. A report from the Intergroup Ewing's Sarcoma Study. Cancer 1983, **51**: 1021–1027.

617 Thorner P, Squire J, Chilton-MacNeill S, Marrano P, Bayani J, Malkin D, Greenberg M, Lorenzana A, Zielenska M. Is the EWS/FLI-1 fusion transcript specific for Ewing sarcoma and peripheral primitive neuroectodermal tumor? A report of four cases showing this transcript in a wider range of tumor types. Am J Pathol 1996, **148**: 1125–1138.

618 Triche TJ, Ross WE. Glycogen-containing neuroblastoma with clinical and histopathologic features of Ewing's sarcoma. Cancer 1978, **41**: 1425–1432.

619 Tsuneyoshi M, Yokoyama R, Hashimoto H, Enjoji M. Comparative study of neuroectodermal tumor and Ewing's sarcoma of the bone. Histopathologic, immunohistochemical and ultrastructural features. Acta Pathol Jpn 1989, **39**: 573–581.

620 Ushigome S, Shimoda T, Takaki K, Nikaido T, Takakuwa T, Ishikawa E, Spjut HJ. Immunocytochemical and ultrastructural studies of the histogenesis of Ewing's sarcoma and putatively related tumors. Cancer 1989, **64**: 52–62.

621 Vakar-Lopez F, Ayala AG, Raymond AK, Czerniak B. Epithelial phenotype in Ewing's sarcoma/primitive neuroectodermal tumor. Int J Surg Pathol 2001, **8**: 59–65.

622 Verrill MW, Judson IR, Harmer CL, Fisher C, Thomas M, Wiltshaw E. Ewing's sarcoma and primitive neuroectodermal tumor in adults: are they different from Ewing's sarcoma and primitive neuroectodermal tumor in children? J Clin Oncol 1997, **15**: 2611–2621.

623 Wei G, Antonescu CR, de Alava E, Leung D, Huvos AG, Meyers PA, Healey JH, Ladanyi M. Prognostic impact of INK4A deletion in Ewing sarcoma. Cancer 2000, **89**: 793–799.

624 Weidner N, Tjoe J. Immunohistochemical profile of monoclonal antibody O13. Antibody that recognizes glycoprotein p30/32MIC2 and is useful in diagnosing Ewing's sarcoma and peripheral neuroepithelioma. Am J Surg Pathol 1994, **18**: 486–494.

625 West DC, Grier HE, Swallow MM, Demetri GD, Granowetter L, Sklar J. Detection of circulating tumor cells in patients with Ewing's sarcoma and peripheral primitive neuroectodermal tumor. J Clin Oncol 1997, **15**: 583–588.

626 Wilkins RM, Pritchard DJ, Burgert EO Jr, Unni KK. Ewing's sarcoma of bone. Experience with 140 patients. Cancer 1986, **58**: 2551–2555.

627 Yunis EJ, Agostini RM Jr, Walpusk JA, Hubbard JD. Glycogen in neuroblastomas. A light- and electron-microscopic study of 40 cases. Am J Surg Pathol 1979, **3**: 313–323.

628 Zoubek A, Dockhorn-Dworniczak B, Delattre O, Christiansen H, Niggli F, Gatterer-Menz I, Smith TL, Jurgens H, Gadner H, Kovar H. Does expression of different EWS chimeric transcripts define clinically distinct risk groups of Ewing tumor patients? J Clin Oncol 1996, **14**: 1245–1251.

Malignant lymphoma and related lesions

629 Abbondanzo SL, Devaney K. Hodgkin's disease involving bone and adjacent soft tissue in adults: a clinicopathologic and immunophenotypic study of seven cases. Int J Surg Pathol 1996, **3**: 147–154.

630 Baar J, Burkes RL, Bell R, Blackstein ME, Fernandes B, Langer F. Primary non-Hodgkin's lymphoma of bone. A clinicopathologic study. Cancer 1994, **73**: 1194–1199.

631 Baar J, Burkes RL, Gospodarowicz M. Primary non-Hodgkin's lymphoma of bone. Semin Oncol 1999, **26**: 270–275.

632 Bacci G, Jaffe N, Emiliani E, Van Horn J, Manfrini M, Picci P, Bertoni F, Gherlinzoni F, Campanacci M. Therapy for primary non-Hodgkin's lymphoma of bone and a comparison of results with Ewing's sarcoma. Ten years' experience at the Istituto Ortopedico Rizzoli. Cancer 1986, **57**: 1468–1472.

633 Boston HC, Dahlin DC, Ivins JC, Cupps RE. Malignant lymphoma (so-called reticulum cell sarcoma) of bone. Cancer 1974, **34**: 1131–1137.

634 Chabner BA, Haskell CM, Canellos GP. Destructive bone lesions in chronic granulocytic leukemia. Medicine (Baltimore) 1969, **48**: 401–410.

635 Chan JK, Ng CS, Hui PK, Leung WT, Sin VC, Lam TK, Chick KW, Lam WY. Anaplastic large cell Ki-1 lymphoma of bone. Cancer 1991, **68**: 2186–2191.

636 Chan K-W, Rosen G, Miller DR, Tan CTC. Hodgkin's disease in adolescents presenting as a primary bone lesion. A report of four cases and review of literature. Am J Pediatr Hematol Oncol 1982, **4**: 11–17.

637 Clayton F, Butler JJ, Ayala AG, Ro JY, Zornoza J. Non-Hodgkin's lymphoma in bone. Pathologic and radiologic features with clinical correlates. Cancer 1987, **60**: 2494–2501.

637a De Leval L, Braaten KM, Ancukiewicz M, Kiggundu E, Delaney T, Mankin HJ, Harris NL. Diffuse large B-cell lymphoma of bone. An analysis of differentiation-associated antigens with clinical correlation. Am J Surg Pathol 2003, **27**: 1269–1277.

638 Dosoretz DE, Raymond AK, Murphy GF, Doppke KP, Schiller AL, Wang CC, Suit HD. Primary lymphoma of bone. The relationship of morphologic diversity to clinical behavior. Cancer 1982, **50**: 1009–1014.

639 Falini B, Binazzi R, Pileri S, Mori A, Bertoni F, Canino S, Fagioli M, Minelli O, Ciani C, Pellicioli P. Large cell lymphoma of bone. A report of three cases of B-cell origin. Histopathology 1988, **12**: 177–190.

640 Fowles JV, Olweny CLM, Katongole-Mbidde E, Lukanga-Ndawula A, Owor R. Burkitt's lymphoma in the appendicular skeleton. J Bone Joint Surg (Br) 1983, **65**: 464–471.

641 Gianelli U, Patriarca C, Moro A, Ponzoni M, Giardini R, Massimino M, Alfano RM, Armiraglio E, Nuciforo P, Bosari S, Coggi G, Parafioriti A. Lymphomas of the bone: a pathological and clinical study of 54 cases. Int J Surg Pathol 2002, **10**: 257–266.

642 Horan FT. Bone involvement in Hodgkin's disease. Br J Surg 1969, **56**: 277–281.

643 Howat AJ, Thomas HUW, Waters KD, Campbell PE. Malignant lymphoma of bone in children. Cancer 1987, **59**: 335–339.

644 Huebner-Chan D, Fernandes B, Yang G, Lim MS. An immunophenotypic and molecular study of primary large B-cell lymphoma of the bone. Mod Pathol 2001, **14**: 1000–1007.

645 Iravani S, Singleton TP, Ross CW, Schnitzer B. Precursor B lymphoblastic lymphoma presenting as lytic bone lesions. Am J Clin Pathol 1999, **112**: 836–843.

646 Llombart-Bosch A, Blache R, Peydro-Olaya A. Round-cell

sarcomas of bone and their differential diagnosis (with particular emphasis on Ewing's sarcoma and reticulosarcoma). A study of 233 tumors with optical and electron microscopic techniques. Pathol Annu 1982, **17**(Pt 2): 113–145.

647 Mahoney JP, Alexander RW. Primary histiocytic lymphoma of bone. A light and ultrastructural study of four cases. Am J Surg Pathol 1980, **4**: 149–161.

648 Marsh WL Jr, Bylund DJ, Heath VC, Anderson MJ. Osteoarticular and pulmonary manifestations of acute leukemia. Case report and review of the literature. Cancer 1986, **57**: 385–390.

649 Nagasaka T, Nakamura S, Medeiros LJ, Juco J, Lai R. Anaplastic large cell lymphomas presented as bone lesions: a clinicopathologic study of six cases and review of the literature. Mod Pathol 2000, **13**: 1143–1149.

650 Ostrowski ML, Inwards CY, Strickler JG, Witzig TE, Wenger DE, Unni KK. Osseous Hodgkin Disease. Cancer 1999, **85**: 1166–1178.

651 Ostrowski ML, Unni KK, Banks PM, Shives TC, Evans RG, O'Connell MJ, Taylor WF. Malignant lymphoma of bone. Cancer 1986, **58**: 2646–2655.

652 Ozdemirli M, Mankin HJ, Aisenberg AC, Harris NL. Hodgkin's disease presenting as a solitary bone tumor: a report of four cases and a review of the literature. Cancer 1996, **77**: 79–88.

653 Pambuccian SE, Horyd ID, Cawte T, Huvos AG. Amyloidoma of bone, a plasma cell/plasmacytoid neoplasm: report of three cases and review of the literature. Am J Surg Pathol 1997, **21**: 179–186.

654 Pettit CK, Zukerberg LR, Gray MH, Ferry JA, Rosenberg AE, Harmon DC, Harris NL. Primary lymphoma of bone. A B-cell neoplasm with a high frequency of multilobated cells. Am J Surg Pathol 1990, **14**: 329–334.

655 Radaszkiewicz T, Hansmann ML. Primary high-grade malignant lymphomas of bone. Virchows Arch [A] 1988, **413**: 269–274.

656 Reimer RR, Chabner BA, Young RC, Reddick R, Johnson RE. Lymphoma presenting in bone. Results of histopathology, staging, and therapy. Ann Intern Med 1977, **87**: 50–55.

657 Rossleigh MA, Smith J, Straus DJ, Engel IA. Osteonecrosis in patients with malignant lymphoma. A review of 31 cases. Cancer 1986, **58**: 1112–1116.

658 Simmons CR, Harle TS, Singleton EB. The osseous manifestations of leukemia in children. Radiol Clin North Am 1968, **6**: 115–129.

659 Thomas LB, Forkner CE, Frei E, Besse BE, Stabenau JR. The skeletal lesions of acute leukemia. Cancer 1961, **14**: 608–621.

660 Triche TJ, Askin FB, Kissane JM. Neuroblastoma, Ewing's sarcoma, and the differential diagnosis of small-, round-, blue-cell tumors. In Finegold M (ed.): Pathology of neoplasia in children and adolescents, vol 18. Major Series in Pathology. Philadelphia, 1986, WB Saunders Co.

661 Vassallo J, Roessner A, Vollmer E, Grundmann E. Malignant lymphomas with primary bone manifestation. Pathol Res Pract 1987, **182**: 381–389.

661a Wu SL, McGregor DK, Medeiros LJ, Raymond AK, Deavers MT. Primary lymphoma of bone: a clinicopathologic study of 15 cases (Abstract). Mod Pathol 2003, **16**: 20a.

Vascular tumors

662 Bollinger BK, Laskin WB, Knight CB. Epithelioid hemangioendothelioma with multiple site involvement. Literature review and observations. Cancer 1994, **73**: 610–615.

663 Cai Q, Hodgson SF, Kao PC, Lennon VA, Klee GG, Zinsmiester AR, Kumar R. Brief report. Inhibition of renal phosphate transport by a tumor product in a patient with oncogenic osteomalacia. N Engl J Med 1994, **330**: 1645–1649.

664 Campanacci M, Boriani S, Giunti A. Hemangioendothelioma of bone. A study of 29 cases. Cancer 1980, **46**: 804–814.

664a Deshpande V, Rosenberg AE, O'Connell JX, Nielsen GP. Epithelioid angiosarcoma of the bone. A series of 10 cases. Am J Surg Pathol 2003, **27**: 709–716.

665 Dorfman HD, Steiner GC, Jaffe HL. Vascular tumors of bone. Hum Pathol 1971, **2**: 349–376.

665a Evans HL, Raymond K, Ayala AG. Vascular tumors of bone: a study of 17 cases other than ordinary hemangioma, with an evaluation of the relationship of hemangioendothelioma of bone to epithelioid hemangioma, epithelioid hemangioendothelioma, and high-grade angiosarcoma. Hum Pathol 2003, **34**: 680–689.

666 Goldberg NS, Hebert AA, Esterly NB. Sacral hemangiomas and multiple congenital abnormalities. Arch Dermatol 1986, **122**: 684–687.

667 Gorham LW, Stout AP. Massive osteolysis (acute spontaneous absorption of bone, phantom bone, disappearing bone). Its relation to hemangiomatosis. J Bone Joint Surg (Am) 1955, **37**: 985–1004.

668 Halliday DR, Dahlin DC, Pugh DG, Young HH. Massive osteolysis and angiomatosis. Radiology 1964, **82**: 627–644.

669 Hasegawa T, Fujii Y, Seki K, Yang P, Hirose T, Matsuzaki K, Sano T. Epithelioid angiosarcoma of the bone. Hum Pathol 1997, **28**: 985–989.

669a Jonsson KB, Zahradnik R, Larsson T, White KE, Sugimoto T, Imanishi Y, Yamamoto T, Hampson G, Koshiyama H, Ljunggren O, Oba K, Yang IM, Miyauchi A, Econs MJ, Lavigne J, Juppner H. Fibroblast growth factor 23 in oncogenic osteomalacia and X-linked hypophosphatemia. N Engl J Med 2003, **348**: 1656–1663.

670 Jumbelic M, Feuerstein IM, Dorfman HD. Solitary intraosseous lymphangioma. A case report. J Bone Joint Surg (Am) 1984, **66**: 1479–1480.

671 Keel SB, Rosenberg AE. Hemorrhagic epithelioid and spindle cell hemangioma: a newly recognized, unique vascular tumor of bone. Cancer 1999, **85**: 1966–1972.

672 Kleer CG, Unni KK, McLeod RA. Epithelioid hemangioendothelioma of bone. Am J Surg Pathol 1996, **20**: 1301–1311.

673 Lamovec J, Bracko M. Epithelioid hemangioma of small tubular bones: a report of three cases, two of them associated with pregnancy. Mod Pathol 1996, **9**: 821–827.

674 Larsson S-E, Lorentzon R, Boquist L. Malignant hemangioendothelioma of bone. J Bone Joint Surg (Am) 1975, **57**: 84–89.

675 Mackenzie DH. Intraosseous glomus tumors. Report of two cases. J Bone Joint Surg (Br) 1962, **44**: 648–651.

676 Mirra JM, Kameda N. Myxoid angioblastomatosis of bones. A case report of a rare, multifocal entity with light, ultramicroscopic, and immunopathologic correlation. Am J Surg Pathol 1985, **9**: 450–458.

677 Nuovo MA, Dorfman HD, Sun CC, Chalew SA. Tumor-induced osteomalacia and rickets. Am J Surg Pathol 1989, **13**: 588–599.

678 O'Connell JX, Kattapuram SV, Mankin HJ, Bhan AK, Rosenberg AE. Epithelioid hemangioma of bone. A tumor often mistaken for low-grade angiosarcoma or malignant hemangioendothelioma. Am J Surg Pathol 1993, **17**: 610–617.

679 Ose D, Vollmer R, Shelburne J, McComb R, Harrelson J. Histiocytoid hemangioma of the skin and scapula. A case report with electron microscopy and immunohistochemistry. Cancer 1983, **51**: 1656–1662.

680 Otis J, Hutter RVP, Foote FW Jr, Marcove RC, Stewart FW. Hemangioendothelioma of bone. Surg Gynecol Obstet 1968, **127**: 295–305.

681 Rosai J, Gold J, Landy R. The histiocytoid hemangiomas. A unifying concept embracing several previously described entities of skin, soft tissue, large vessels, bone, and heart. Hum Pathol 1979, **10**: 707–730.

682 Schajowicz F, Aiello CL, Francone MV, Giannini RE. Cystic angiomatosis (hamartomatous haemolymphangiomatosis) of bone. A clinicopathological study of three cases. J Bone Joint Surg (Br) 1978, **60**: 100–106.

683 Sellke FW, Laszewski MJ, Robinson RA, Davis R, Rossi NP.

chordomas in children and adolescents: a clinicopathologic analysis of 72 cases (Abstract). Mod Pathol 2003, **16:** 13a.

768 Hruban RH, May M, Marcove RC, Huvos AG. Lumbo-sacral chordoma with high-grade malignant cartilaginous and spindle cell components. Am J Surg Pathol 1990, **14:** 384–389.

769 Hu B, McPhaul L, Cornford M, Gaal K, Mirra J, French SW. Expression of Tau proteins and tubulin in extraskeletal myxoid chondrosarcoma, chordoma, and other chondroid tumors. Am J Clin Pathol 1999, **112:** 189–193.

770 Jeffrey PB, Biava CG, Davis RL. Chondroid chordoma. A hyalinized chordoma without cartilaginous differentiation. Am J Clin Pathol 1995, **103:** 271–279.

771 Jeffrey PB, Davis RL, Biava C, Rosenblum M. Microtubule aggregates in a clival chordoma. Arch Pathol Lab Med 1993, **117:** 1055–1057.

772 Kaiser TE, Pritchard DJ, Unni KK. Clinicopathologic study of sacrococcygeal chordoma. Cancer 1984, **54:** 2574–2578.

773 Kaneko Y, Iwaki T, Fukui M. Lectin histochemistry of human fetal notochord, ecchordosis physaliphora, and chordomas. Arch Pathol Lab Med 1992, **116:** 60–64.

774 Kilgore S, Prayson RA. Apoptotic and proliferative markers in chordomas: a study of 26 tumors. Ann Diagn Pathol 2002, **6:** 222–228.

774a Knapik JA, Vlasak R, Reith JD. Notochordal hamartoma and its necessary distinction from chordoma. Mod Pathol 2003, **16:** 15a.

775 Lam R. The nature of cytoplasmic vacuoles in chordoma cells. A correlative enzyme and electron microscopic histochemical study. Pathol Res Pract 1990, **186:** 642–650.

776 Matsuno A, Sasaki T, Nagashima T, Matsuura R, Tanaka H, Hirakawa M, Murakami M, Kirini T. Immunohistochemical examination of proliferative potentials and the expression of cell cycle-related proteins of intracranial chordomas. Hum Pathol 1997, **28:** 714–719.

777 Meis JM, Giraldo AA. Chordoma. An immunohistochemical study of 20 cases. Arch Pathol Lab Med 1988, **112:** 553–556.

778 Meis JM, Raymond AK, Evans HL, Charles RE, Giraldo AA. "Dedifferentiated" chordoma. A clinicopathologic and immunohistochemical study of three cases. Am J Surg Pathol 1987, **11:** 516–525.

779 Miettinen M. Chordoma. Antibodies to epithelial membrane antigen and carcinoembryonic antigen in differential diagnosis. Arch Pathol Lab Med 1984, **108:** 891–892.

780 Mindell ER. Current concepts review. Chordoma. J Bone Joint Surg (Am) 1981, **63:** 501–505.

781 Mirra JM, Brien EW. Giant notochordal hamartoma of intraosseous origin: a newly reported benign entity to be distinguished from chordoma. Report of two cases. Skeletal Radiol 2001, **30:** 698–709.

782 Mitchell A, Scheithauer BW, Unni KK, Forsyth PJ, Wold LE, McGivney DJ. Chordoma and chondroid neoplasms of the spheno-occiput. An immunohistochemical study of 41 cases with prognostic and nosologic implications. Cancer 1993, **72:** 2943–2949.

783 Mori K, Chano T, Kushima R, Huduka S, Okabe H. Expression of E-cadherin in chordomas: diagnostic marker and possible role of tumor cell affinity. Virchows Arch 2002, **440:** 123–127.

784 Naka T, Fukuda T, Chuman H, Iwamoto Y, Sugioka Y, Fukui M, Tsuneyoshi M. Proliferative activities in conventional chordoma: a clinicopathologic, DNA flow cytometric, and immunohistochemical analysis of 17 specimens with special reference to anaplastic chordoma showing a diffuse proliferation and nuclear atypia. Hum Pathol 1996, **27:** 381–388.

785 Naka T, Iwamoto Y, Shinohara N, Chuman H, Fukui M, Tsuneyoshi M. Cytokeratin subtyping in chordomas and the fetal notochord: an immunohistochemical analysis of aberrant expression. Mod Pathol 1997, **10:** 545–551.

786 Nakamura Y, Becker LE, Marks A. S 100 protein in human

787 O'Connell JX, Renard LG, Liebsch NJ, Efird JT, Munzenrider JE, Rosenberg AE. Base of skull chordoma. A correlative study of histologic and clinical features of 62 cases. Cancer 1994, **74:** 2261–2267.

788 O'Hara BJ, Paetau A, Miettinen M. Keratin subsets and monoclonal antibody HBME-1 in chordoma: immunohistochemical differential diagnosis between tumors simulating chordoma. Hum Pathol 1998, **29:** 119–126.

789 Pearlman AW, Friedman M. Radical radiation therapy of chordoma. Am J Roentgenol Radium Ther Nucl Med 1970, **108:** 333–341.

790 Persson S, Kindblom LG, Angervall L. Classical and chondroid chordoma. A light-microscopic, histochemical, ultrastructural and immunohistochemical analysis of the various cell types. Pathol Res Pract 1991, **187:** 828–838.

791 Rich TA, Schiller A, Suit HD, Mankin HJ. Clinical and pathologic review of 48 cases of chordoma. Cancer 1985, **56:** 182–187.

792 Richter HJ, Batsakis JG, Boles R. Chordomas. Nasopharyngeal presentation and atypical long survival. Ann Otol Rhinol Laryngol 1975, **84:** 327–332.

793 Rosenberg AE, Brown GA, Bhan AK, Lee JM. Chondroid chordoma – a variant of chordoma. A morphologic and immunohistochemical study. Am J Clin Pathol 1994, **101:** 36–41.

794 Rutherfoord GS, Davies AG. Chordomas – ultrastructure and immunohistochemistry. A report based on the examination of six cases. Histopathology 1987, **11:** 775–787.

795 Salisbury JR, Isaacson PG. Demonstration of cytokeratins and an epithelial membrane antigen in chordomas and human fetal notochord. Am J Surg Pathol 1985, **9:** 791–797.

796 Sarasa JL, Fortes J. Ecchordosis physaliphora. An immunohistochemical study of two cases. Histopathology 1991, **18:** 273–275.

797 Sundaresan N. Chordomas. Clin Orthop 1986, **204:** 135–142.

798 Ueda Y, Nakanishi I, Tsuchiya H, Tomita K. Microtubular aggregates in the rough endoplasmic reticulum of sacrococcygeal chordoma. Ultrastruct Pathol 1991, **15:** 77–82.

799 Ueda Y, Oda Y, Kawashima A, Tsuchiya H, Tomita K, Nakanishi I. Collagenous and basement membrane proteins of chordoma. Immunohistochemical analysis. Histopathology 1992, **21:** 345–352.

800 Valderrama E, Kahn LB, Lipper S, Marc J. Chondroid chordoma. Electron-microscopic study of two cases. Am J Surg Pathol 1983, **7:** 625–632.

801 Volpe R, Mazabraud A. A clinicopathologic review of 25 cases of chordoma (a pleomorphic and metastasizing neoplasm). Am J Surg Pathol 1983, **7:** 161–170.

802 Walaas L, Kindblom LG. Fine-needle aspiration biopsy in the preoperative diagnosis of chordoma. A study of 17 cases with application of electron microscopic, histochemical, and immunocytochemical examination. Hum Pathol 1991, **22:** 22–28.

803 Walker WP, Landas SK, Bromley CM, Sturm MT. Immunohistochemical distinction of classic and chondroid chordomas. Mod Pathol 1991, **4:** 661–666.

804 Wittchow R, Landas SK. Glial fibrillary acidic protein expression in pleomorphic adenoma, chordoma, and astrocytoma. A comparison of three antibodies. Arch Pathol Lab Med 1991, **115:** 1030–1033.

805 Wojno KJ, Hruban RH, Garin-Chesa P, Huvos AG. Chondroid chordomas and low-grade chondrosarcomas of the craniospinal axis. An immunohistochemical analysis of 17 cases. Am J Surg Pathol 1992, **16:** 1144–1152.

806 Wold LE, Laws ER Jr. Cranial chordomas in children and young adults. J Neurosurg 1983, **59:** 1043–1047.

807 Yonemoto T, Tatezaki SI, Takenouchi T, Ishii T, Satoh T, Moriya

chordoma and human and rabbit notochord. Arch Pathol Lab Med 1983, **107:** 118–120.

H. The surgical management of sacrococcygeal chordoma. Cancer 1999, **85**: 878–883.

808 Zukerberg LR, Young RH. Chordoma metastatic to the ovary. Arch Pathol Lab Med 1990, **114**: 208–210.

Adamantinoma of long bones

809 Benassi MS, Campanacci L, Gamberi G, Ferrari C, Picci P, Sangiorgi L, Campanacci M. Cytokeratin expression and distribution in adamantinoma of the long bones and osteofibrous dysplasia of tibia and fibula. An immunohistochemical study correlated to histogenesis. Histopathology 1994, **25**: 71–76.

810 Campanacci M, Giunti A, Bertoni F, Laus M, Gitelis S. Adamantinoma of the long bones. The experience at the Istituto Ortopedico Rizzoli. Am J Surg Pathol 1981, **5**: 533–542.

811 Czerniak B, Rojas-Corona RR, Dorfman HD. Morphologic diversity of long bone adamantinoma. The concept of differentiated (regressing) adamantinoma and its relationship to osteofibrous dysplasia. Cancer 1989, **64**: 2319–2334.

812 Eisenstein W, Pitcock JA. Adamantinoma of the tibia. An eccrine carcinoma. Arch Pathol Lab Med 1984, **108**: 246–250.

813 Hazelbag HM, Fleuren GJ, v.d.Broek LJ, Taminiau AH, Hogendoorn PC. Adamantinoma of the long bones. Keratin subclass immunoreactivity pattern with reference to its histogenesis. Am J Surg Pathol 1993, **17**: 1225–1233.

814 Hazelbag HM, Van den Broek LJ, Fleuren GJ, Taminiau AH, Hogendoorn PC. Distribution of extracellular matrix components in adamantinoma of long bones suggests fibrous-to-epithelial transformation. Hum Pathol 1997, **28**: 183–188.

815 Hazelbag HM, Wessels JW, Mollevangers P, van den Berg E, Molenaar WH, Hogendoorn PC. Cytogenetic analysis of adamantinoma of long bones: further indications for a common histogenesis with osteofibrous dysplasia. Cancer Genet Cytogenet 1997, **97**: 5–11.

816 Jundt G, Remberger K, Roessner A, Schulz A, Bohndorf K. Adamantinoma of long bones. A histopathological and immunohistochemical study of 23 cases. Pathol Res Pract 1995, **191**: 112–120.

817 Keeney GL, Unni KK, Beabout JW, Pritchard DJ. Adamantinoma of long bones. A clinicopathologic study of 85 cases. Cancer 1989, **64**: 730–737.

818 Kuruvilla G, Steiner GC. Osteofibrous dysplasia-like adamantinoma of bone: a report of five cases with immunohistochemical and ultrastructural studies. Hum Pathol 1998, **29**: 809–814.

819 Mills SE, Rosai J. Adamantinoma of the pretibial soft tissue. Clinicopathologic features, differential diagnosis, and possible relationship to intraosseous disease. J Clin Pathol 1985, **83**: 108–114.

820 Moon NF, Mori H. Adamantinoma of the appendicular skeleton—updated. Clin Orthop 1986, **204**: 215–237.

821 Perez-Atayde AR, Kozakewich HPW, Vawter GF. Adamantinoma of the tibia. An ultrastructural and immunohistochemical study. Cancer 1985, **55**: 1015–1023.

822 Rosai J. Adamantinoma of the tibia. Electron microscopic evidence of its epithelial origin. Am J Clin Pathol 1969, **51**: 786–792.

823 Rosai J, Pinkus GS. Immunohistochemical demonstration of epithelial differentiation in adamantinoma of the tibia. Am J Surg Pathol 1982, **6**: 427–434.

824 Ueda Y, Roessner A, Boose A, Edel G, Bocker W, Wuisman P. Juvenile intracortical adamantinoma of the tibia with predominant osteofibrous dysplasia-like features. Pathol Res Pract 1991, **187**: 1039–1043.

825 Unni KK, Dahlin DC, Beabout JW, Ivins JC. Adamantinomas of long bones. Cancer 1974, **34**: 1796–1805.

826 Weiss SW, Dorfman HD. Adamantinoma of long bone. An analysis of nine new cases with emphasis on metastasizing lesions and fibrous dysplasia-like changes. Hum Pathol 1977, **8**: 141–153.

827 Yoneyama T, Winter WG, Milsow L. Tibial adamantinoma. Its histogenesis from ultrastructural studies. Cancer 1977, **40**: 1138–1142.

Peripheral nerve tumors

828 Bullock MJ, Bedard YC, Bell RS, Kandel R. Intraosseous malignant peripheral nerve sheath tumor. Report of a case and review of the literature. Arch Pathol Lab Med 1995, **119**: 367–370.

829 De La Monte SM, Dorfman HD, Chandra R, Malawer M. Intraosseous schwannoma. Histologic features, ultrastructure, and review of the literature. Hum Pathol 1984, **15**: 551–558.

830 Ducatman BS, Scheithauer BW, Dahlin DC. Malignant bone tumors associated with neurofibromatosis. Mayo Clin Proc 1983, **58**: 578–582.

831 Fawcett KJ, Dahlin DC. Neurilemoma of bone. Am J Clin Pathol 1967, **47**: 759–766.

832 Hunt JC, Pugh DG. Skeletal lesions in neurofibromatosis. Radiology 1961, **76**: 1–19.

833 Myers JL, Bernreuter W, Dunham W. Melanotic schwannoma. Clinicopathologic, immunohistochemical, and ultrastructural features of a rare primary bone tumor. Am J Clin Pathol 1990, **93**: 424–429.

834 Turk PS, Peters N, Libbey NP, Wanebo HJ. Diagnosis and management of giant intrasacral schwannoma. Cancer 1992, **70**: 2650–2657.

835 Wirth WA, Bray CB. Intra-osseous neurilemoma. Case report and review of thirty-one cases from the literature. J Bone Joint Surg (Am) 1977, **59**: 252–255.

Xanthoma

836 Bertoni F, Unni KK, McLeod RA, Sim FH. Xanthoma of bone. Am J Clin Pathol 1988, **90**: 377–384.

Fibrocartilaginous mesenchymoma

837 Bulychova IV, Unni KK, Bertoni F, Beabout JW. Fibrocartilaginous mesenchymoma of bone. Am J Surg Pathol 1993, **17**: 830–836.

838 Kim CJ, Choi IH, Cho TJ, Chung CY, Chi JG. The histological spectrum of subperiosteal fibrocartilaginous pseudotumor of long bone (focal fibrocartilaginous dysplasia). Pathol Int 1999, **49**: 1000–1006.

Others

839 Adsay V, Cheng J, Athanasian E, Gerald W, Rosai J. Primary desmoplastic small cell tumor of soft tissues and bone of the hand. Am J Surg Pathol 1999, **23**: 1408–1413.

840 Insabato L, De Rosa G, Terracciano LM, Fazioli F, Di Santo F, Rosai J. Primary monotypic epithelioid angiomyolipoma of bone. Histopathology 2002, **40**: 286–290.

841 Jones D, Amin M, Ordonez NG, Glassman AB, Hayes KJ, Medeiros LJ. Reticulum cell sarcoma of lymph node with mixed dendritic and fibroblastic features. Mod Pathol 2001, **14**: 1059–1067.

842 Park YK, Unni KK, Kim YW, Han CS, Yang MH, Wenger DE, Sim FH, Lucas DR, Ryan JR, Nadim YA, Nojima T, Fletcher CD. Primary alveolar soft part sarcoma of bone. Histopathology 1999, **35**: 411–417.

843 Scheele PM Jr, Von Kuster LC, Krivchenia G. Primary malignant mesenchymoma of bone. Arch Pathol Lab Med 1990, **114**: 614–617.

844 Van Dorpe J, Sciot R, Samson I, De Vos R, Brys P, Van Damme B. Primary osteorhabdomyosarcoma (malignant mesenchymoma) of bone: a case report and review of the literature. Mod Pathol 1997, **10**: 1047–1053.

845 Yokoyama R, Mukai K, Hirota T, Beppu Y, Fukuma H. Primary

malignant melanoma (clear cell sarcoma) of bone: report of a case arising in the ulna. Cancer 1996, **77**: 2471–2475.

Metastatic tumors

846 Berrettoni BA, Carter JR. Mechanisms of cancer metastasis to bone. J Bone Joint Surg (Am) 1986, **68**: 308–312.

847 Caffey J, Andersen DH. Metastatic embryonal rhabdomyosarcoma in the growing skeleton. Clinical, radiographic, and microscopic features. Am J Dis Child 1958, **95**: 581–600.

848 Carlin BI, Andriole GL. The natural history, skeletal complications, and management of bone metastases in patients with prostate carcinoma. Cancer 2000, **88**: 2989–2994.

849 Charhon SA, Chapuy MC, Delvin EE, Valentin-Opran A, Edouard CM, Meunier PJ. Histomorphometric analysis of sclerotic bone metastases from prostatic carcinoma with special reference to osteomalacia. Cancer 1983, **51**: 918–924.

850 Daroca PJ Jr, Reed RJ, Martin PC. Metastatic amelanotic melanoma simulating giant-cell tumor of bone. Hum Pathol 1990, **21**: 978–980.

851 Goltzman D. Mechanisms of the development of osteoblastic metastases. Cancer 1997, **80**: 1581–1587.

852 Guise TA. Molecular mechanisms of ostelytic bone metastases. Cancer 2000, **88**: 2892–2898.

853 Gurney H, Larcos G, McKay M, Kefford R, Langlands A. Bone metastases in hypernephroma. Frequency of scapular involvement. Cancer 1989, **64**: 1429–1431.

854 Healey JH, Turnbull ADM, Miedema B, Lane JM. Acrometastases. A study of twenty-nine patients with osseous involvement of the hands and feet. J Bone Joint Surg (Am) 1986, **68**: 743–746.

855 Kahn LB, Wood FW, Ackerman LV. Fracture callus associated with benign and malignant bone lesions and mimicking osteosarcoma. Am J Clin Pathol 1969, **52**: 14–24.

856 Lucas DR, Kolodziej P, Gross ML, Mott MP, Budev H, Zalupski MM, Ryan JR. Metastatic uterine leiomyosarcoma to bone: a clinicopathologic study. Int J Surg Pathol 1996-1997, **4**: 159–168.

857 Morris DM, House HC. The significance of metastasis to the bones and soft tissues of the hand. J Surg Oncol 1985, **28**: 146–150.

858 Mundy GR. Mechanisms of bone metastasis. Cancer 1997, **80**: 1546–1556.

859 Norman A, Ulin R. A comparative study of periosteal new-bone response in metastatic bone tumors (solitary) and primary bone sarcomas. Radiology 1969, **92**: 705–708.

860 Perez CA, Bradfield JS, Morgan HC. Management of pathologic fractures. Cancer 1972, **29**: 1027–1037.

861 Quinn JM, Matsumura Y, Tarin D, McGee JO, Athanasou NA. Cellular and hormonal mechanisms associated with malignant bone resorption. Lab Invest 1994, **71**: 465–471.

862 Simon MA, Bartucci EJ. The search for the primary tumor in patients with skeletal metastases of unknown origin. Cancer 1986, **58**: 1088–1095.

863 Thomas BM. Three unusual carcinoid tumours, with particular reference to osteoblastic bone metastases. Clin Radiol 1968, **19**: 221–225.

864 Troncoso A, Ro JY, Grignon DJ, Han WS, Wexler H, von Eschenbach A, Ayala AG. Renal cell carcinoma with acrometastasis. Report of two cases and review of the literature. Mod Pathol 1991, **4**: 66–69.

865 Yamashita K, Ueda T, Komatsubara Y, Koyama H, Inaji H, Yonenobu K, Ono K. Breast cancer with bone-only metastases. Visceral metastases-free rate in relation to anatomic distribution of bone metastases. Cancer 1991, **68**: 634–637.

Tumorlike lesions

Solitary bone cyst

866 Amling M, Werner M, Posl M, Maas R, Korn U, Delling G. Calcifying solitary bone cyst. Morphologic aspects and differential diagnosis of sclerotic bone tumours. Virchows Arch 1995, **426**: 235–242.

867 Campanacci M, Capanna R, Picci P. Unicameral and aneurysmal bone cysts. Clin Orthop 1986, **204**: 25–36.

868 Mirra JM, Bernard GW, Bullough PG, Johnston W, Mink G. Cementum-like bone production in solitary bone cysts (so-called "cementoma" of long bones). Report of three cases. Electron microscopic observations supporting a synovial origin to the simple bone cyst. Clin Orthop 1978, **135**: 295–307.

869 Smith RW, Smith CF. Solitary unicameral bone cyst of the calcaneus. A review of twenty cases. J Bone Joint Surg (Am) 1974, **56**: 49–56.

Aneurysmal bone cyst

870 Aho HJ, Aho AJ, Einola S. Aneurysmal bone cyst. A study of ultrastructure and malignant transformation. Virchows Arch [A] 1982, **395**: 169–179.

871 Alles JU, Schulz A. Immunocytochemical markers (endothelial and histiocytic) and ultrastructure of primary aneurysmal bone cysts. Hum Pathol 1986, **17**: 39–45.

872 Bertoni F, Bacchini P, Capanna R, Ruggieri P, Biagini R, Ferruzzi A, Bettelli G, Picci P, Campanacci M. Solid variant of aneurysmal bone cyst. Cancer 1993, **71**: 729–734.

873 Buraczewski J, Dabska M. Pathogenesis of aneurysmal bone cyst. Relationship between the aneurysmal bone cyst and fibrous dysplasia of bone. Cancer 1971, **28**: 597–604.

874 Capanna R, Albisinni U, Picci P, Calderoni P, Campanacci M, Springfield DS. Aneurysmal bone cyst of the spine. J Bone Joint Surg (Am) 1985, **67**: 527–531.

875 Clough JR, Price CHG. Aneurysmal bone cyst. Pathogenesis and long term results of treatment. Clin Orthop 1973, **97**: 52–63.

876 Dabezies EJ, D'Ambrosia RD, Chuinard RG, Ferguson AB. Aneurysmal bone cyst after fracture. A report of three cases. J Bone Joint Surg (Am) 1982, **64**: 617–621.

877 Dabska M, Buraczewski J. Aneurysmal bone cyst. Pathology, clinical course and radiologic appearances. Cancer 1969, **23**: 371–389.

878 D'Alonzo RT, Pitcock JA, Milford LW. Giant cell reaction of bone. Report of two cases. J Bone Joint Surg (Am) 1972, **54**: 1267–1271.

879 Dehner LP, Risdall RJ, L'Heureux P. Giant cell-containing "fibrous" lesion of the sacrum. Am J Surg Pathol 1978, **2**: 55–70.

879a de Silva MV, Raby N, Reid R. Fibromyxoid areas and immature osteoid are associated with recurrence of primary aneurysmal bone cysts. Histopathology 203, **43**: 180–188.

880 Edling NPG. Is the aneurysmal bone cyst a true entity? Cancer 1965, **18**: 1127–1130.

881 Koskinen EVS, Visuri TI, Holmström T, Roukkula MA. Aneurysmal bone cyst. Evaluation of resection and of curettage in 20 cases. Clin Orthop 1976, **118**: 136–146.

882 Kyriakos M, Hardy D. Malignant transformation of aneurysmal bone cyst, with an analysis of the literature. Cancer 1991, **68**: 1770–1780.

883 Leithner A, Lang S, Windhager R, Leithner K, Karlic H, Kotz R, Haas OA. Expression of insulin-like growth factor-1 (IGF-1) in aneurysmal bone cyst. Mod Pathol 2001, **14**: 1100–1104.

884 Leithner A, Windhager R, Lang S, Haas OA, Kainberger F, Kotz R. Aneurysmal bone cyst. A population based epidemiologic study and literature review. Clin Orthop 1999, **363**: 176–179.

885 Levy WM, Miller AS, Bonakdarpour A, Aegerter E. Aneurysmal bone cyst secondary to other osseous lesions. Report of 57 cases. Am J Clin Pathol 1975, **63**: 1–8.

886 McCarthy EF, Dortman HD. Vascular and cartilaginous hamartoma of the ribs in infancy with secondary aneurysmal bone cyst formation. Am J Surg Pathol 1980, **4**: 247–253.

887 Oda Y, Tsuneyoshi M, Shinohara N. "Solid" variant of aneurysmal bone cyst (extragnathic giant cell reparative granuloma) in the axial skeleton and long bones. A study of its

morphologic spectrum and distinction from allied giant cell lesions. Cancer 1992, **70**: 2642–2649.

888 Panico L, Passeretti U, De Rosa N, D'Antonio A, De Rosa G. Giant cell reparative granuloma of the distal skeletal bones. A report of five cases with immunohistochemical findings. Virchows Arch 1994, **425**: 315–320.

889 Petrik PK, Findlay JM, Sherlock RA. Aneurysmal cyst, bone type, primary in an artery. Am J Surg Pathol 1993, **17**: 1062–1066.

890 Rodriguez-Peralto JL, Lopez-Barea F, Sanchez-Herrera S, Atienza M. Primary aneurysmal cyst of soft tissues (extraosseous aneurysmal cyst). Am J Surg Pathol 1994, **18**: 632–636.

891 Ruiter DJ, van Rijssel ThG, van der Velde EA. Aneurysmal bone cysts. A clinicopathological study of 105 cases. Cancer 1977, **39**: 2231–2239.

892 Sabanathan S, Chen K, Robertson CS, Salama FD. Aneurysmal bone cyst of the rib. Thorax 1984, **39**: 125–130.

893 Sanerkin NG, Mott MG, Roylance J. An unusual intraosseous lesion with fibroblastic, osteoclastic, osteoblastic, aneurysmal and fibromyxoid elements. "Solid" variant of aneurysmal bone cyst. Cancer 1983, **51**: 2278–2286.

894 Sciot R, Dorfman H, Brys P, Dal Cin P, De Wever I, Fletcher CD, Jonson K, Mandahl N, Mertens F, Mitelman F, Rosai J, Rydholm A, Samson I, Tallini G, Van den Berghe H, Vanni R, Willen H. Cytogenetic-morphologic correlations in aneurysmal bone cyst, giant cell tumor of bone and combined lesions. A report from the CHAMP study group. Mod Pathol 2000, **13**: 1206–1210.

895 Shannon P, Bedard Y, Bell R, Kandel R. Aneurysmal cyst of soft tissue. report of a case with serial magnetic resonance imaging and biopsy. Hum Pathol 1997, **28**: 255–257.

896 Tillman BP, Dahlin DC, Lipscomb PR, Stewart JR. Aneurysmal bone cyst. An analysis of 95 cases. Mayo Clin Proc 1968, **43**: 478–495.

897 Vergel De Dios AM, Bond JR, Shives TC, McLeod RA, Unni KK. Aneurysmal bone cyst. A clinicopathologic study of 238 cases. Cancer 1992, **69**: 2921–2931.

898 Wold LE, Dobyns JH, Swee RG, Dahlin DC. Giant cell reaction (giant cell reparative granuloma) of the small bones of the hands and feet. Am J Surg Pathol 1986, **10**: 491–496.

899 Yamaguchi T, Dorfman HD. Giant cell reparative granuloma. A comparative clinicopathologic study of lesions in gnathic and extragnathic sites. Int J Surg Pathol 2001, **9**: 189–200.

Other cysts

900 Alguacil-Garcia A, Littman CD. Subpubic cartilaginous cyst: report of two cases. Am J Surg Pathol 1996, **20**: 975–979.

901 Bauer TW, Dorfman, HD. Intraosseous ganglion. A clinicopathologic study of 11 cases. Am J Surg Pathol 1982, **6**: 207–213.

902 Schajowicz F, Sainz MC, Slullitel JA. Juxta-articular bone cysts (intra-osseous ganglia). J Bone Joint Surg (Br) 1979, **61**: 107–116.

903 Sim FH, Dahlin DC. Ganglion cysts of bone. Mayo Clin Proc 1971, **46**: 484–488.

Metaphyseal fibrous defect (nonossifying fibroma)

904 Arata MA, Peterson HA, Dahlin DC. Pathological fractures through non-ossifying fibromas. Review of the Mayo Clinic experience. J Bone Joint Surg (Am) 1981, **63**: 980–988.

905 Clarke BE, Xipell JM, Thomas DP. Benign fibrous histiocytoma of bone. Am J Surg Pathol 1985, **9**: 806–815.

906 Craver RD, Heinrich S, Mirra J. Fibrous cortical defect with bizarre nuclear features. Ann Diagn Pathol 1997, **1**: 26–30.

907 Cunningham JB, Ackerman LV. Metaphyseal fibrous defects. J Bone Joint Surg (Am) 1956, **38**: 797–808.

Fibrous dysplasia and related lesions

908 Aoki T, Kouho H, Hisaoka M, Hashimoto H, Nakata H, Sakai A. Intramuscular myxoma with fibrous dysplasia. A report of two cases with a review of the literature. Pathol Int 1995, **45**: 165–171.

909 Bridge JA, Dembinski A, De Boer J, Travis J, Neff JR. Clonal chromosomal abnormalities in osteofibrous dysplasia. Implications for histopathogenesis and its relationship with adamantinoma. Cancer 1994, **73**: 1746–1752.

910 Campanacci M, Laus M. Osteofibrous dysplasia of the tibia and fibula. J Bone Joint Surg (Am) 1981, **63**: 367–375.

911 Campbell CJ, Hawk T. A variant of fibrous dysplasia (osteofibrous dysplasia). J Bone Joint Surg (Am) 1982, **64**: 231–236.

912 Candeliere GA, Glorieux FH, Prud'homme J, St-Arnaud R. Increased expression of the *c-fos* proto-oncogene in bone from patients with fibrous dysplasia. N Engl J Med 1995, **332**: 1546–1551.

913 Dorfman HD, Ishida T, Tsuneyoshi M. Exophytic variant of fibrous dysplasia (fibrous dysplasia protuberans). Hum Pathol 1994, **25**: 1234–1237.

914 Gouldesbrough DR. Symmetrical fibro-osseous dysplasia of rib – evidence for a traumatic aetiology. Histopathology 1990, **17**: 267–270.

915 Greco MA, Steiner GC. Ultrastructure of fibrous dysplasia of bone. A study of its fibrous, osseous, and cartilaginous components. Ultrastruct Pathol 1986, **10**: 55–66.

916 Harris WH, Dudley HR, Barry RJ. The natural history of fibrous dysplasia. J Bone Joint Surg (Am) 1962, **44**: 207–233.

917 Huvos AG, Higinbotham NL, Miller TR. Bone sarcomas arising in fibrous dysplasia. J Bone Joint Surg (Am) 1972, **54**: 1047–1056.

918 Ishida T, Machinami R, Kojima T, Kikuchi F. Malignant fibrous histiocytoma and osteosarcoma in association with fibrous dysplasia of bone. Report of three cases. Pathol Res Pract 1992, **188**: 757–763.

919 Kandel RA, Pritzker KPH, Bedard YC. Symmetrical fibro-osseous dysplasia of rib – post-traumatic dysplasia? Histopathology 1981, **5**: 651–658.

920 Kempson RL. Ossifying fibroma of the long bones. Arch Pathol 1966, **82**: 218–233.

921 Marie PJ, De Pollak C, Chanson P, Lomri A. Increased proliferation of osteoblastic cells expressing the activating GS alpha mutation in monostotic and polyostotic fibrous dysplasia. Am J Pathol 1997, **150**: 1059–1069.

922 McDermott MB, Kyriakos M, Flanagan FL. Posttraumatic fibro-osseous lesion of rib. Hum Pathol 1999, **30**: 770–780.

923 Nakashima Y, Yamamuro T, Fujiwara Y, Kotoura Y, Mori E, Hamashima Y. Osteofibrous dysplasia (ossifying fibroma of long bones). A study of 12 cases. Cancer 1983, **52**: 909–914.

924 Park YK, Unni KK, McLeod RA, Pritchard DJ. Osteofibrous dysplasia. Clinico-pathologic study of 80 cases. Hum Pathol 1993, **24**: 1339–1347.

925 Pelzmann KS, Nagel DZ, Salyer WR. Polyostotic fibrous dysplasia and fibrochondrodysplasia. Skeletal Radiol 1980, **5**: 116–118.

926 Povysil C, Matejovsky Z. Fibro-osseous lesion with calcified spherules (cementifying fibromalike lesion) of the tibia. Ultrastruct Pathol 1993, **17**: 25–34.

927 Ragsdale BD. Polymorphic fibro-osseous lesions of bone. An almost site-specific diagnostic problem of the proximal femur. Hum Pathol 1993, **24**: 505–512.

928 Reed RJ. Fibrous dysplasia of bone. A review of 25 cases. Arch Pathol 1963, **75**: 480–495.

929 Riminucci M, Fisher LW, Shenker A, Spiegel AM, Bianco P, Robey PG. Fibrous dysplasia of bone in the McCune-Albright syndrome. Abnormalities in bone formation. Am J Pathol 1997, **151**: 1587–1600.

930 Ruggieri P, Sim FH, Bond JR, Unni KK. Malignancies in fibrous dysplasia. Cancer 1994, **73**: 1411–1424.

931 Sakamoto A, Oda Y, Iwamoto Y, Tsuneyoshi M. A comparative

study of fibrous dysplasia and osteofibrous dysplasia with regard to expression of c-fos and c-jun products and bone matrix proteins: a clinicopathologic review and immunohistochemical study of c-fos, c-jun type I collagen, osteonectin, osteopontin, and osteocalcin. Hum Pathol 1999, **30**: 1418–1426.

932 Sakamoto A, Oda Y, Iwamoto Y, Tsuneyoshi M. A comparative study of fibrous dysplasia and osteofibrous dysplasia with regard to Gsalfa mutation at the Arg 201 codon: polymerase chain reaction-restriction fragment length polymorphism analysis of paraffin-embedded tissue. J Mol Diagn 2000, **2**: 67–72.

933 Sakamoto A, Oda Y, Oshiro Y, Tamiya S, Iwamoto Y, Tsuneyoshi M. Immunoexpression of neurofibromin, S-100 protein, and leu-7 and mutation analysis of the NF1 gene at codon 1423 in osteofibrous dysplasia. Hum Pathol 2001, **32**: 1245–1251.

934 Schwindinger WF, Francomano CA, Levine MA. Identification of a mutation in the gene encoding the alpha subunit of the stimulatory G protein of adenylyl cyclase in McCune-Albright syndrome. Proc Natl Acad Sci USA 1992, **89**: 5152–5156.

935 Sissons HA, Steiner GC, Dorfman HD. Calcified spherules in fibro-osseous lesions of bone. Arch Pathol Lab Med 1993, **117**: 284–290.

936 Sweet DE, Vinh TN, Devaney K. Cortical osteofibrous dysplasia of long bone and its relationship to adamantinoma. A clinicopathologic study of 30 cases. Am J Surg Pathol 1992, **16**: 282–290.

937 Voytek TM, Ro JY, Edeiken J, Ayala AG. Fibrous dysplasia and cemento-ossifying fibroma. A histologic spectrum. Am J Surg Pathol 1995, **19**: 775–781.

Myositis ossificans

938 Ackerman LV. Extraosseous localized nonneoplastic bone and cartilage formation (so-called myositis ossificans). J Bone Joint Surg (Am) 1958, **40**: 279–298.

939 Craver RD, Correa-Gracian H, Heinrich S. Florid reactive periostitis. Hum Pathol 1997, **28**: 745–747.

939a de Silva MC, Reid R. Myositis ossificans and fibroosseous pseudotumor of digits : a clinicopathological review of 64 cases with emphasis on diagnostic pitfalls. Int J Surg Pathol 2003, **11**: 187–195.

940 Dupree WB, Enzinger FM. Fibro-osseous pseudotumor of the digits. Cancer 1986, **58**: 2103–2109.

941 Jüppner H. The genetic basis of progressive osseous heteroplasia. N Engl J Med 2002, **346**: 128–130.

942 Povysil C, Matejovsky Z. Ultrastructural evidence of myofibroblasts in pseudo-malignant myositis ossificans. Virchows Arch [A] 1979, **381**: 189–203.

943 Shore EM, Ahn J, Jan de Beur S. Paternally inherited inactivating mutations of the *GNAS1* gene in progressive osseous heteroplasia. N Engl J Med 2002, **346**: 99–106.

944 Spjut HJ, Dorfman HD. Florid reactive periostitis of the tubular bones of the hands and feet. Am J Surg Pathol 1981, **5**: 423–433.

945 Sumiyoshi K, Tsuneyoshi M, Enjoji M. Myositis ossificans. A clinicopathologic study of 21 cases. Acta Pathol Jpn 1985, **35**: 1109–1122.

946 Yaghmai I. Myositis ossificans. Diagnostic value of arteriography. AJR 1977, **128**: 811–816.

Langerhans' cell histiocytosis

947 Howarth DM, Gilchrist GS, Mullan BP, Wiseman GA, Edmonson JH, Schomberg PJ. Langerhans cell histiocytosis: diagnosis, natural history, management and outcome. Cancer 1999, **85**: 2278–2290.

948 Lieberman PH, Jones CR, Dargeon HWK, Begg CF. A reappraisal of eosinophilic granuloma of bone. Hand-Schüller-Christian syndrome and Letterer-Siwe syndrome. Medicine (Baltimore) 1969, **48**: 375–400.

949 Makley JT, Carter JR. Eosinophilic granuloma of bone. Clin Orthop 1986, **204**: 37–44.

950 McGavran MH, Spady HA. Eosinophilic granuloma of bone. A study of 28 cases. J Bone Joint Surg (Am) 1960, **42**: 979–992.

951 Newton WA, Hamoudi AB. Histiocytosis. A histologic classification with clinical correlation. Perspect Pediatr Pathol 1973, **1**: 251–283.

952 Nezelof C, Frileux-Herbet F, Cronier-Sachot J. Disseminated histiocytosis X. Analysis of prognostic factors based on a retrospective study of 50 cases. Cancer 1979, **44**: 1824–1838.

953 Walker PD, Rosai J, Dorfman RF. The osseous manifestations of sinus histiocytosis with massive lymphadenopathy. Am J Clin Pathol 1981, **75**: 131–139.

Other histiocytic lesions

954 Al-Quran S, Rieth J, Bradley J, Rimsza L. Erdheim-Chester disease: case report, PCR-based analysis of clonality, and review of literature. Mod Pathol 2002, **15**: 666–672.

955 Chetritt J, Paradis V, Dargere D, Adle-Biassette H, Maurage CA, Mussini JM, Vital A, Wechsler J, Bedossa P. Chester-Erdheim disease: a neoplastic disorder. Hum Pathol 1999, **30**: 1093–1096.

956 Kenn W, Eck M, Allolio B, Jacob F, Illg A, Marx A, Mueller-Hermelink HK, Hahn D. Erdheim-Chester disease: evidence for a disease entity different from Langerhans cell histiocytosis? Three cases with detailed radiological and immunohistochemical analysis. Hum Pathol 2000, **31**: 734–739.

957 Kim N-R, Ko Y-H, Choe YH, Lee H-G, Huh B, Ahn G-H. Erdheim-Chester disease with extensive marrow necrosis. A case report and literature review. Int J Surg Pathol 2001, **9**: 73–79.

JOINTS AND RELATED STRUCTURES
Normal anatomy

958 Bullough PG. Joints. In Sternberg S (ed.): History for Pathologists, ed. 2. Philadelphia, 1997, Lippincott-Raven Publishers, pp. 107–128.

959 Stevens CR, Map PI, Revell PA. A monoclonal antibody (Mab 67) marks type B synoviocytes. Rheumatol Int 1990, **10**: 103–106.

960 Wilkinson LS, Edwards JCW, Poston RN, Haskard DO. Expression of vascular cell adhesion molecule-1 in normal and inflamed synovium. Lab Invest 1993, **68**: 82–88.

961 Wilkinson LS, Pitsillides AA, Worrall JG, Edwards JCW. Light microscopic characterization of the fibroblast-like synovial intimal cell (synoviocyte). Arthritis Rheum 1992, **35**: 1179–1184.

Non-neoplastic diseases
Ganglia and cystic meniscus

962 Glasgow MM, Allen PW, Blakeway C. Arthroscopic treatment of cysts of the lateral meniscus. J Bone Joint Surg Br 1993, **75**: 299–302.

963 Romanini L, Calvisi V, Collodel M, Masciocchi C. Cystic degeneration of the lateral meniscus. Pathogenesis and diagnostic approach. Ital J Orthop Traumatol 1988, **14**: 493–500.

964 Stack RE, Bianco AH Jr, MacCarthy CS. Compression of the common peroneal nerve by ganglion cyst. Report of nine cases. J Bone Joint Surg (Am) 1965, **47**: 773–778.

Bursae and Baker's cyst

965 Pederson HE, Key JA. Pathology of calcareous tendinitis and subdeltoid bursitis. Arch Surg 1951, **62**: 50–63.

966 Wagner T, Abgarowicz T. Microscopic appearance of Baker's cyst in cases of rheumatoid arthritis. Rheumatologia 1970, **8**: 21–26.

Carpal tunnel syndrome

967 Bastian FO. Amyloidosis and the carpal tunnel syndrome. Am J Clin Pathol 1974, **61**: 711–717.

968 Entin MA. Carpal tunnel syndrome and its variants. Surg Clin North Am 1968, **48**: 1097–1112.

969 Phalen GS. The carpal-tunnel syndrome. Seventeen years'

experience in diagnosis and treatment of six hundred and fifty-four hands. J Bone Joint Surg (Am) 1966, **48:** 211–228.

970 Spinner RJ, Bachman JW, Amadio PC. The many faces of carpal tunnel syndrome. Mayo Clin Proc 1989, **64:** 829–836.

Arthritis

Synovial biopsy

971 Goldenberg DL, Cohen AS. Synovial membrane histopathology in the differential diagnosis of rheumatoid arthritis, gout, pseudogout, systemic lupus erythematosus, infectious arthritis and degenerative joint disease. Medicine 1978, **57:** 239–252.

972 O'Connell JX. Pathology of the synovium. Am J Clin Pathol 2000, **114:** 773–784.

973 Revell PA. The synovial biopsy. In Anthony PP, MacSween RNM (eds): Recent advances in histopathology, vol 13. Edinburgh, 1987, Churchill-Livingstone.

974 Rodnan GP, Yunis EJ, Totten RS. Experience with punch biopsy of synovium in the study of joint disease. Ann Intern Med 1960, **53:** 319–331.

975 Schumacher HR, Kulka JP. Needle biopsy of the synovial membrane. Experience with the Parker-Pearson technic. N Engl J Med 1972, **286:** 416–419.

976 Schwartz S, Cooper N. Synovial membrane punch biopsy. Arch Intern Med 1961, **108:** 400–406.

977 Soren A. Histodiagnosis and clinical correlation of rheumatoid and other synovitis. Philadelphia, 1978, JP Lippincott Co.

Degenerative joint disease (osteoarthritis)

978 Aigner T, Dietz U, Stöss H, Von der Mark K. Differential expression of collagen types I, II, III, and X in human osteophytes. Lab Invest 1995, **73:** 236–243.

979 Bennett GA, Waine H, Bauer W. Changes in the knee joint at various ages. New York, 1942, Commonwealth Fund.

980 Collins DH. The pathology of articular and spinal diseases. London, 1949, Edward Arnold & Co.

981 Di Francesco L, Sokoloff L. Lipochondral degeneration of capsular tissue in osteoarthritic hips. Am J Surg Pathol 1995, **19:** 278–283.

982 Gardner DL, Salter DM, Oates K. Advances in the microscopy of osteoarthritis. Microsc Res Tech 1997, **37:** 245–270.

983 Haliburton RA, Sullivan CR. The patella in degenerative joint disease. A clinicopathologic study. Arch Surg 1958, **77:** 677–683.

984 Hamerman D. The biology of osteoarthritis. N Engl J Med 1989, **320:** 1322–1330.

985 Harrison MHM, Schajowicz F, Tureta J. Osteoarthritis of the hip. A study of the nature and evolution of the disease. J Bone Joint Surg (Br) 1953, **35:** 598–626.

986 Hirsch C, Schajowicz F, Galante J. Structural changes in the cervical spine. A study on autopsy specimens in different age groups. Acta Orthop Scand (Suppl) 1967, **109:** 7–77.

987 Horwitz T. Bone and cartilage debris in the synovial membrane. Its significance in the early diagnosis of neuro-arthropathy. J Bone Joint Surg (Am) 1948, **30:** 579–588.

988 Jayson MI, Rubenstein D, Dixon AS. Intra-articular pressure and rheumatoid geodes (bone 'cysts'). Ann Rheum Dis 1970, **29:** 496–502.

989 Mankin HJ. The reaction of articular cartilage to injury and osteoarthritis. N Engl J Med 1974, **291:** 1285–1292, 1335–1340.

990 Norman A, Robbins H, Milgram JE. The acute neuropathic arthropathy. A rapid, severely disorganizing form of arthritis. Radiology 1968, **90:** 1159–1164.

991 O'Connell JX, Nielsen GP, Rosenberg AE. Subchondral acute inflammation in severe arthritis: a sterile osteomyelitis? Am J Surg Pathol 1999, **23:** 192–197.

992 Outerbridge RE. The etiology of chondromalacia patellae. J Bone Joint Surg (Br) 1961, **43:** 752–757.

993 Rabinowicz T, Jacqueline F. Pathology of the capsular and synovial hip nerves in chronic hip diseases. Pathol Res Pract 1990, **186:** 283–292.

994 Rhaney K, Lamb DW. The cysts of osteoarthritis of the hip. A radiological and pathological study. J Bone Joint Surg (Br) 1955, **37:** 663–675.

995 Sadouk M, Pelletier J-P, Tardif G, Klansa D, Cloutier J-M, Martel-Pelletier J. Human synovial fibroblasts coexpress IL-1 receptor Type I and Type II mRNA. The increased level of the IL-I receptor in osteoarthritic cells is related to an increased level of the Type I receptor. Lab Invest 1995, **74:** 347–355.

996 Sokoloff L. Pathology and pathogenesis of osteoarthritis. In McCarty DJ (ed.): Arthritis and applied conditions, ed. 9. Philadelphia, 1979, Lea & Febiger, pp. 1135–1153.

Rheumatoid arthritis

997 Baumann H, Kushner I. Production of interleukin-6 by synovial fibroblasts in rheumatoid arthritis. Am J Pathology 1998, **152:** 641–644.

998 Beatty EC Jr. Rheumatic-like nodules occurring in nonrheumatic children. Arch Pathol 1959, **68:** 154–159.

999 Berardinelli JL, Hyman CJ, Campbell EE, Fireman P. Presence of rheumatoid factor in ten children with isolated rheumatoid-like nodules. J Pediatr 1972, **81:** 751–757.

1000 Bhan AK, Roy S. Synovial giant cells in rheumatoid arthritis and other joint diseases. Ann Rheum Dis 1971, **30:** 294–298.

1001 Cooper NS. Pathology of rheumatoid arthritis. Med Clin North Am 1968, **52:** 607–621.

1002 Dixon AStJ, Grant C. Acute synovial rupture in rheumatoid arthritis. Clinical and experimental observations. Lancet 1964, **1:** 742–745.

1003 Grimley PM, Sokoloff L. Synovial giant cells in rheumatoid arthritis. Am J Pathol 1966, **49:** 931–954.

1004 Hahn BH, Yardley JH, Stevens MB. "Rheumatoid" nodules in systemic lupus erythematosus. Ann Intern Med 1970, **72:** 49–58.

1005 Harris ED Jr. Rheumatoid arthritis. Pathophysiology and implications for therapy. N Engl J Med 1990, **322:** 1277–1289.

1006 Hart FD. Rheumatoid arthritis. Extra-articular manifestations. Br Med J 1969, **3:** 131–136.

1007 Hart FD. Rheumatoid arthritis. Extra-articular manifestations. Part II. Br Med J 1970, **2:** 747–752.

1008 Horwitz T. Bone and cartilage debris in the synovial membrane. Its significance in the early diagnosis of neuro-arthropathy. J Bone Joint Surg (Am) 1948, **30:** 579–588.

1009 Imai Y, Sato T, Yamakava M, Kasajima T, Suda A, Watanabe Y. A morphological and immunohistochemical study of lymphoid germinal centers in synovial and lymph node tissues from rheumatoid arthritis patients with special reference to complement components and their receptors. Acta Pathol Jpn 1989, **39:** 127–134.

1010 Jayson MI, Dixon AS, Kates A, Pinder I, Coomes EN. Popliteal and calf cysts in rheumatoid arthritis. Treatment by anterior synovectomy. Ann Rheum Dis 1972, **31:** 9–15.

1011 Koizumi F, Matsuno H, Wakaki K, Ishii Y, Kurashige Y, Nasamura H. Synovitis in rheumatoid arthritis: scoring of characteristic histopathological features. Pathol Int 1999, **49:** 298–304.

1012 Marcus VA, Roy I, Sullivan JD, Sutton JR. Necrobiotic palisading suture granulomas involving bone and joint: report of two cases. Am J Surg Pathol 1997, **21:** 563–565.

1013 Matsuno H, Yodoh K, Nakazawa F, Koizumi F. Relationship between histological findings and clinical findings in rheumatoid arthritis. Pathol Int 2002, **52:** 527–533.

1014 Mongan ES, Cass FM, Jacox RF, Vaughan JH. A study of the relation of seronegative and seropositive rheumatoid arthritis to each other and to necrotizing vasculitis. Am J Med 1969, **47:** 23–25.

1015 Muirden KD. Giant cells, cartilage and bone fragments within rheumatoid synovial membrane. Clinicopathological correlations. Aust Ann Med 1970, **2:** 105–110.

1016 Palmer DG. Synovial cysts in rheumatoid disease. Ann Intern Med 1969, **70:** 61–68.

1017 Qu Z, Huang X-N, Almadi P, Andresevic J, Planck SR, Hart CE, Rosenbaum JT. Expression of basic fibroblast growth factor in synovial tissue from patients with rheumatoid arthritis and degenerative joint disease. Lab Invest 1995, **73:** 339–346.

1018 Roberts WC, Kehol JA, Carpenter DF, Golden A. Cardiac valvular lesions in rheumatoid arthritis. Arch Intern Med 1968, **122:** 141–146.

1019 Schmid FR, Cooper NS, Ziff M, McEwen C. Arteritis in rheumatoid arthritis. Am J Med 1961, **30:** 56–83.

1020 Sokoloff L. Pathology of rheumatoid arthritis and allied disorders. In McCarty DJ (ed.): Arthritis and applied conditions, ed 9. Philadelphia, 1979, Lea & Febiger, pp. 429–447.

1021 Sokoloff L, Wilen SL, Bunim JJ. Arthritis of striated muscle in rheumatoid arthritis. Am J Pathol 1951, **27:** 157–173.

1022 Taylor RT, Huskisson EC, Whitehouse GH, Hart FD. Spontaneous fractures of pelvis in rheumatoid arthritis. Br Med J 1971, **4:** 663–664.

1023 Winchester R. The molecular basis of susceptibility to rheumatoid arthritis. Adv Immunol 1994, **56:** 389–466.

1024 Ziegler B, Gay RE, Huang GQ, Fassbender HG, Gay S. Immunohistochemical localization of HTLV-I p19- and p24-related antigens in synovial joints of patients with rheumatoid arthritis. Am J Pathol 1989, **135:** 1–5.

1025 Zvaifer NJ. Rheumatoid arthritis. The multiple pathways to chronic synovitis (editorial). Lab Invest 1995, **73:** 307–310.

Infectious arthritis

1026 Baumgarten JM, Montiel NJ, Sinha AA. Lyme disease-part 1: epidemiology and etiology. Cutis 2002, **69:** 349–352.

1027 Johnston YE, Duray PH, Steere AC, Kashgarian M, Buza J, Malawista SE, Askenase PW. Lyme arthritis. Spirochetes found in synovial microangiopathic lesions. Am J Pathol 1985, **118:** 26–34.

1028 Meyerhoff J. Lyme disease. Am J Med 1983, **75:** 663–670.

1029 Montiel NJ, Baumgarten JM, Sinha AA. Lyme disease-part II: clinical features and treatment. Cutis 2002, **69:** 443–448.

1030 Nanagara R, Duray PH, Schumacher HR Jr. Ultrastructural demonstration of spirochetal antigens in synovial fluid and synovial membrane in chronic Lyme disease. Possible factors contributing to persistence of organisms. Hum Pathol 1996, **27:** 1025–1034.

1031 Steere AC. Lyme disease. N Engl J Med 1989, **321:** 586–596.

Gout and pseudogout

1032 Chaplin AJ. Calcium pyrophosphate. Histological characterization of crystals in pseudogout. Arch Pathol Lab Med 1976, **100:** 12–15.

1033 Darby AJ, Harness NF, Pritchard MS. Demonstration of urate crystals after formalin fixation. Histopathology 1998, **32:** 382–383.

1034 Ishida T, Dorfman HD, Bullough PG. Tophaceous pseudogout (tumoral calcium pyrophosphate dihydrate crystal deposition disease). Hum Pathol 1995, **26:** 587–593.

1035 Lichtenstein L, Scott HW, Levin MH. Pathologic changes in gout – survey of eleven necropsied cases. Am J Pathol 1956, **32:** 871–895.

1036 Moskowitz RW, Katz D. Chondrocalcinosis and chondrocalsynovitis (pseudogout syndrome). Analysis of 24 cases. Am J Med 1967, **43:** 322–334.

1037 Shidham V, Chivukula M, Basir Z, Shidham G. Evaluation of crystals in formalin fixed, paraffin-embedded tissue sections for the differential diagnosis of pseudogout, gout, and tumoral calcinosis. Mod Pathol 2001, **14:** 806–810.

Intervertebral disk prolapse

1038 Ford JL, Downes S. Cellularity of human annulus tissue: an investigation into the cellularity of tissue of different pathologies. Histopathology 2002, **41:** 531–537.

1039 Weidner N, Rice DT. Intervertebral disk material. Criteria for determining probable prolapse. Hum Pathol 1988, **19:** 406–410.

Other articular and periarticular diseases

1040 Athanasou NA, Sallie B. Localized deposition of amyloid in articular cartilage. Histopathology 1992, **20:** 41–46.

1041 Cary NRB. Clinicopathological importance of deposits of amyloid in the femoral head. J Clin Pathol 1985, **38:** 868–872.

1042 Goldenberg DL, Cohen AS. Synovial membrane histopathology in the differential diagnosis of rheumatoid arthritis, gout, pseudogout, systemic lupus erythematosus, infectious arthritis and degenerative joint disease. Medicine (Baltimore) 1978, **57:** 239–252.

1043 Kyle RA, Eilers SG, Linscheid RL, Gaffey TA. Amyloid localized to tenosynovium at carpal tunnel release. Natural history of 124 cases. Am J Clin Pathol 1989, **91:** 393–397.

1044 Kyle RA, Gertz MA, Linke RP. Amyloid localized to tenosynovium at carpal tunnel release. Immunohistochemical identification of amyloid type. Am J Clin Pathol 1992, **97:** 250–253.

1045 Ladefoged C, Merrild U, Jorgensen B. Amyloid deposits in surgically removed articular and periarticular tissue. Histopathology 1989, **15:** 289–296.

1046 Mihara S, Kawai S, Gondo T, Ishihara T. Intervertebral disc amyloidosis. Histochemical, immunohistochemical and ultrastructural observations. Histopathology 1994, **25:** 415–420.

1047 Pambuccian SE, Horyd ID, Cawte T, Huvos AG. Amyloidoma of bone, a plasma cell/plasmacytoid neoplasm: report of three cases and review of the literature. Am J Surg Pathol 1997, **21:** 179–186.

1048 Reith JD, Bauer TW, Schils JP. Osseous manifestations of SAPHO (synovitis, acne, pustolsis, hyperostosis, osteitis) syndrome. Am J Surg Pathol 1996, **20:** 1368–1377.

1049 Rodnan GP, Medsger TA. The rheumatic manifestations of progressive systemic sclerosis (scleroderma). Clin Orthop 1968, **57:** 81–93.

1050 Roosendaal G, van Rinsum AC, Vianen ME, van den Berg HM, Lafeber FPJG, Bijlsma JW. Haemophilic arthropathy resembles degenerative rather than inflammatory joint disease. Histopathology 1999, **34:** 144–153.

1051 Rumpelt HJ, Braun A, Spier R, Suren EG, Thies E. Localized amyloid in the menisci of the knee joint. Pathol Res Pract 1996, **192:** 547–551.

Tumors and tumorlike conditions
Tendosynovial giant cell tumor

1052 Alguacil-Garcia A, Unni KK, Goellner JR. Giant cell tumor of tendon sheath and pigmented villonodular synovitis. An ultrastructural study. Am J Clin Pathol 1978, **69:** 6–17.

1053 Bertoni F, Unni KK, Beabout JW, Sim FH. Malignant giant cell tumor of the tendon sheaths and joints (malignant pigmented villonodular synovitis). Am J Surg Pathol 1997, **21:** 153–163.

1054 Chung EB, Enzinger FM. Fibroma of tendon sheath. Cancer 1979, **44:** 1945–1954.

1055 Darling JM, Goldring SR, Harada Y, Handel ML, Glowacki J, Gravallese EM. Multinucleated cells in pigmented villondular synovitis and giant cell tumor of tendon sheath express features of osteoclasts. Am J Pathol 1997, **150:** 1383–1393.

1056 Ferrer J, Namiq A, Carda C, Lopez-Gines C, Tawfik O, Llombart-Bosch A. Diffuse type of giant-cell tumor of tendon sheath: an ultrastructural study of two cases with cytogenetic support. Ultrastruct Pathol 2002, **26**: 15–22.

1056a Furlong MA, Motamedi K, Laskin WB, Vinh TN, Murphey M, Sweet DE, Fetsch JF. Synovial-type giant cell tumors of the vertebral column: a clinicopathologic study of 15 cases, with a review of the literature and discussion of the differential diagnosis. Hum Pathol 2003, **34**: 670–679.

1057 Jaffe HL, Lichtenstein L, Sutro CJ. Pigmented villonodular synovitis, bursitis, and tenosynovitis. Arch Pathol 1941, **31**: 731–765.

1058 Maluf HM, DeYoung BR, Swanson PE, Wick MR. Fibroma and giant cell tumor of tendon sheath. A comparative histological and immunohistological study. Mod Pathol 1995, **8**: 155–159.

1059 O'Connel JX, Fanburg JC, Rosenberg AE. Giant cell tumor of tendon sheath and pigmented villonodular synovitis. Immunophenotype suggests a synovial cell origin. Hum Pathol 1995, **26**: 771–775.

1060 Sciot R, Rosai J, Dal Cin P, De Wever I, Fletcher CD, Mandahl N, Mertens F, Mitelman F, Rydholm A, Tallini G, van den Berghe H, Vanni R, Willen H. Analysis of 35 cases of localized and diffuse tenosynovial giant cell tumor: a report from the Chromosomes and Morphology (CHAMP) Study Group. Mod Pathol 1999, **12:** 576–579.

1061 Somerhausen NS, Fletcher CD. Diffuse-type giant cell tumor: clinicopathologic and immunohistochemical analysis of 50 cases with extraarticular disease. Am J Surg Pathol 2000, **24:** 479–492.

1062 Tashiro H, Iwasaki H, Kikuchi M, Ogata K, Okazaki M. Giant cell tumors of tendon sheath. A single and multiple local immunostaining analysis. Pathol Int 1995, **45**: 147–155.

1063 Ushijima M, Hashimoto H, Tsuneyoshi M, Enjoji M, Miyamoto Y, Okue A. Malignant giant cell tumor of tendon sheath. Report of a case. Acta Pathol Jpn 1985, **35**: 699–709.

Pigmented villonodular synovitis and bursitis

1064 Byers PD, Cotton RE, Deacon OW, Lowy M, Newman PH, Sissons HA, Thomson AD. The diagnosis and treatment of pigmented villonodular synovitis. J Bone Joint Surg (Br) 1968, **50**: 290–305.

1065 Choong PF, Willen H, Nilbert M, Mertens F, Mandahl N, Carlen B, Rydholm A. Pigmented villonodular synovitis. Monoclonality and metastasis – a case for neoplastic origin? Acta Orthop Scand 1998, **66**: 64–68.

1066 Darling JM, Glimcher LH, Shortkroff S, Albano B, Gravallese EM. Expression of metalloproteinases in pigmented villonodular synovitis. Hum Pathol 1994, **25**: 825–830.

1067 Layfield LJ, Meloni-Ehrig A, Liu K, Shepard R, Harrelson M. Malignant giant cell tumor of synovium (malignant pigmented villonodular synovitis). Arch Pathol Lab Med 2000, **124**: 1636–1641.

1068 Myers BW, Masi AT. Pigmented villonodular synovitis and tenosynovitis. A clinical epidemiologic study of 166 cases and literature review. Medicine 1980, **59**: 223–238.

1069 Nilsonne U, Moberger G. Pigmented villonodular synovitis of joints. Histological and clinical problems in diagnosis. Acta Orthop Scand 1969, **40**: 448–460.

1070 Rao AS, Vigorita VJ. Pigmented villonodular synovitis (giant-cell tumor of the tendon sheath and synovial membrane). A review of eighty-one cases. J Bone Joint Surg (Am) 1984, **66**: 76–94.

1071 Ray RA, Morton CC, Lipinski KK, Corson JM, Fletcher JA. Cytogenetic evidence of clonality in a case of pigmented villonodular synovitis. Cancer 1991, **67**: 121–125.

1072 Sciot R, Rosai J, Dal Cin P, De Wever I, Fletcher CD, Mandahl N, Mertens F, Mitelman F, Rydholm A, Tallini G, van den Berghe H, Vanni R, Willen H. Analysis of 35 cases of localized and diffuse tenosynovial giant cell tumor: a report from the Chromosomes and Morphology (CHAMP) Study Group. Mod Pathol 1999, **12**: 576–579.

1073 Scott FM. Bone lesions in pigmented villonodular synovitis. J Bone Joint Surg (Br) 1968, **50**: 306–311.

1074 Somerhausen NS, Fletcher CD. Diffuse-type giant cell tumor: clinicopathologic and immunohistochemical analysis of 50 cases with extraarticular disease. Am J Surg Pathol 2000, **24**: 479–492.

1075 Ushijima M, Hashimoto H, Tsuneyoshi M, Enjoji M. Pigmented villonodular synovitis. A clinicopathologic study of 52 cases. Acta Pathol Jpn 1986, **36**: 317–326.

1075a Yoshida W, Uzuki M, Kurose A, Yoshida M, Nishida J, Shimamura T, Sawai T. Cell characterization of mononuclear and giant cells constituting pigmented villonodular synovitis. Hum Pathol 2003, **34**: 65–73.

Synovial osteochondromatosis and chondrosarcoma

1076 Baunsgaard P, Nielsen BB. Primary synovial chondrometaplasia. Histologic variations in the structure of metaplastic nodules. Acta Pathol Microbiol Immunol Scand (A) 1984, **92**: 455–460.

1077 Bertoni F, Unni KK, Beabout JW, Sim FH. Chondrosarcomas of the synovium. Cancer 1991, **67**: 155–162.

1078 Davis RI, Hamilton A, Biggart JD. Primary synovial chondromatosis: a clinicopathologic review and assessment of malignant potential. Hum Pathol 1998, **29**: 683–688.

1078a Fetsch JF, Vinh TN, Remotti F, Walker EA, Murphey MD, Sweet DE. Tenosynovial (extraarticular) chondromatosis. An analysis of 37 cases of an underrecognized clinicopathologic entity with a strong predilection for the hands and feet and a high local recurrence rate. Am J Surg Pathol 2003, **27**: 1260–1268.

1079 Goldman RL, Lichtenstein L. Synovial chondrosarcoma. Cancer 1964, **12**: 1233–1240.

1080 King JW, Spjut HJ, Fechner RE, Vanderpool DW. Synovial chondrosarcoma of the knee joint. J Bone Joint Surg (Am) 1967, **49**: 1389–1396.

1081 Milgram JW. Synovial osteochondromatosis. A histopathological study of thirty cases. J Bone Joint Surg (Am) 1977, **59**: 792–801.

1082 Murphy FP, Dahlin DC, Sullivan CR. Articular synovial chondromatosis. J Bone Joint Surg (Am) 1962, **44**: 77–86.

1083 Sciot R, Dal Cin P, Bellemans J, Samson I, Van den Berghe H, Van Damme B. Synovial chondromatosis: clonal chromosome changes provide further evidence for a neoplastic disorder. Virchows Arch 1998, **433**: 189–191.

1084 Sviland L, Malcolm AJ. Synovial chondromatosis presenting as painless soft tissue mass. A report of 19 cases. Histopathology 1995, **27**: 275–279.

1085 Villacin AB, Brigham LN, Bullough PG. Primary and secondary synovial chondrometaplasia. Histopathologic and clinicoradiologic differences. Hum Pathol 1979, **10**: 439–451.

Other tumors

1086 Devaney K, Vinh TN, Sweet DE. Synovial hemangioma. A report of 20 cases with differential diagnostic considerations. Hum Pathol 1993, **24**: 737–745.

1087 Goodlad JR, Hollowood K, Smith MA, Chan JK, Fletcher CD. Primary juxtaarticular soft tissue lymphoma arising in the vicinity of inflamed joints in patients with rheumatoid arthritis. Histopathology 1999, **34**: 199–204.

1088 Ladefoged C, Jensen NK. Synovial haemangiopericytoma of the knee joint. Histopathology 1989, **15**: 635–637.

1089 Lucas DR, Miller PR, Mott MP, Kronick JL, Unni KK. Arthroplasty-associated malignant fibrous histiocytoma: two case reports. Histopathology 2001, **39**: 620–628.

1090 Rodriguez-Peralto JL, Lopez-Barea F, Gonzalez-Lopez J. Intracapsular chondroma of the knee: an unusual neoplasm. Int J Surg Pathol 1997, **5**: 49–54.

25 Soft tissues

Normal anatomy

Soft tissue is loosely defined as the complex of non-epithelial extraskeletal structures of the body exclusive of the supportive tissue of the various organs and the hematopoietic/lymphoid tissue. It is composed of fibrous (connective) tissue, adipose tissue, skeletal muscle, blood and lymph vessels, and peripheral nervous system. Most of the soft tissue is derived embryologically from mesoderm, with a neuroectodermal contribution corresponding to the peripheral nerves, and presumably to some of the soft tissues of the head and neck region.[8]

Fibrous tissue consists primarily of fibroblasts and an extracellular matrix that contains fibrillary structures (collagen and elastin) and nonfibrillary extracellular matrix ("ground substance"). Fibrous tissue is classified according to its texture into loose (most locations) and dense (tendons, aponeuroses, and ligaments). *Fibroblasts* are responsible for the production of the various extracellular materials, including the many types of collagen. Their shape varies from spindle (especially when stretched along bundles of collagen fibers) to stellate (in myxoid areas). Immunohistochemically, they are reactive for vimentin and focally for actin. *Fibrocytes* represent the quiescent stage of fibroblasts. *Myofibroblasts* are modified fibroblasts that show features intermediate between fibroblasts and smooth muscle cells.[22–24]

Adipose tissue is divided into two major types: *white fat*, mainly located in the subcutaneous tissue, mediastinum, abdomen, and retroperitoneum; and *brown fat*, which is concentrated in the interscapular region, neck, mediastinum, axillae, and retroperitoneum (especially perirenal region). Brown fat, whose main function is heat production, is much more conspicuous in infants and children. White fat consists of *lipocytes*. These are round or oval cells having most of the cytoplasm occupied by a single large lipid droplet that pushes the crescent-shaped nucleus to the periphery.[2] *Brown fat cells* are smaller, with an acidophilic multivacuolated cytoplasm and a centrally located nucleus showing fine indentations; mitochondria are numerous at the ultrastructural level.

Skeletal muscle is mainly derived from within myotomes (but also from mesectoderm in the head and neck region) through the formation of myoblasts and eventually of myotubes (muscle fibers). The most distinguishing feature of these fibers is the presence of myofibrils, which are composed of two types of microfilaments: thin (made of actin) and thick (made of myosin).[12] The periodic arrangement and interdigitation of thin and thick filaments results in the cross-banding seen at a light microscopic level. The I (isotropic) band is made only of thin filaments, the adjacent A (anisotropic) band is a zone of overlapping thin and thick filaments, and the H band is made up only of thick myofilaments. The I band is divided in its center by the Z line or disc, which is thought to serve as an attachment site for the *sarcomere* (that is, the repeating individual unit of the muscle fiber).

Blood vessels are divided into arterial and venous compartments joined by a network of capillaries. The several types of cells present in blood vessels are divided into two major types: endothelial cell (located toward the lumen) and a closely related group composed of pericytes, smooth muscle cells, and glomus cells (located toward the outside). Endothelial cells are usually recognized with ease by their shape and location, but both of these can be greatly altered in neoplastic conditions; therefore one has to rely on the presence of other features to identify them. Ultrastructurally, endothelial cells exhibit numerous pinocytotic vesicles, cytoplasmic microfilaments, specialized cell junctions, microvilli, continuous basal lamina, and—most important—the Weibel–Palade body, a membrane-bound organelle thought to be specific to this cell type[5] and shown to contain the von Willebrand factor.[31]

Immunohistochemically, endothelial cells exhibit reactivity for vimentin, factor VIII-related antigen (FVIII-RA), *Ulex europaeus* I lectin, CD31, CD34, endothelin, FLI-1, thrombomodulin, FKBP12 (a cytosolic binding protein that interacts with calcineurin), and basal lamina components.[1,4,6,7,10,11,13,15–17,20,21,25–28,30] Of these, CDE31 appears the most useful virtue of its sensitivity and specificity. FVIII-RA is also very specific (the only other positive cell type being the megakaryocyte), but the labile nature of this antigen and its tendency to diffuse out in the tissues limit its utility. FLI-1 (a nuclear transcription factor involved in the pathogenesis of Ewing's sarcoma/PNET) seems also extremely promising.[10] Use of monoclonal antibodies for other endothelial markers indicates that phenotypic diversity exists among these cells, a fact of potential diagnostic utility.[9,19,29]

Endothelial cells of normal lymph vessels show a much weaker staining for FVIII-RA than endothelial cells from blood vessels, but a similar degree of reactivity for *Ulex*,[4,14] and for thrombomodulin, which has been recently touted as the best marker for lymphatic endothelium.[1]

The cells of the pericyte–smooth muscle–glomus family are characterized ultrastructurally by cytoplasmic microfilaments exhibiting focal condensations, numerous pinocytotic vesicles, and a thick continuous basal lamina. Immunohistochemically, they show reactivity for actin, vimentin, and myosin; positivity for desmin is largely restricted to smooth muscle cells, and is not as strong as that exhibited by the "parenchymal" (non-blood vessel-related) cells. A novel marker of pericytes known as RGS5 has been identified through microarray analysis.[1a]

Peripheral nerves are formed by axons, Schwann's cells, perineurial cells, and fibroblasts.[18] Most of the fibroblasts are located in the *epineurium*, which is the outer sheath of fully developed nerves. They are immunoreactive for CD34.[13a] Each nerve fascicle is surrounded by the *perineurium*, a structure continuous with the pia arachnoid of the central nervous system; *perineurial cells* are immunoreactive for EMA and Glut-1 and negative for S-100 protein.[13a] *Schwann's cells* look somewhat similar to fibroblasts at the light microscopic level but are easily distinguished from them immunohistochemically because of their strong immunoreactivity for S-100 protein and ultrastructurally by an intimate relationship to axons (with the formation of mesoaxons) and the presence of a continuous basal lamina that coats the surface of the cell facing the endoneurium. Schwann's cells are of neuroectodermal derivation, whereas perineurial cells apparently originate from fibroblasts.[3]

Infections and hematomas

Soft tissue involvement by infectious processes usually is the result of direct extension from cutaneous, visceral, or osseous foci or the complication of trauma or surgery. Rarely, the process has a hematogenous source.

The severity of the inflammatory reaction and the type of tissue response observed pathologically depend on the type, dose, and virulence of the infecting organism; the resistance of the host tissues; the presence or absence of necrotic tissue, hematoma, or foreign body; and the anatomic features of the infected area.

Clinical types of infectious processes, such as hemolytic streptococcal gangrene, necrotizing fasciitis, and Melency's synergistic gangrene, must be diagnosed by clinical appearance and bacteriologic study. In **necrotizing fasciitis** the process is accompanied by severe systemic toxicity; it is usually caused by group A streptococci, but other bacteria may be involved.[34] All of the pyogenic and necrotizing infections result in acute inflammatory tissue reactions indistinguishable microscopically. **Granulomatous inflammations** of soft tissue include tuberculosis, atypical mycobacteriosis, actinomycosis, blastomycosis, coccidioidomycosis, sporotrichosis, and dirofilariasis.[32] A proper search for microorganisms should be made with special stains and cultures.

Hematoma, if deep and encysted, can simulate clinically and radiographically a malignant soft tissue tumor. They occur most commonly in and around the tensor fasciae latae and have been variously referred to as ancient hematoma, calcifying myonecrosis, chronic expanding hematoma, and post-traumatic cyst of soft tissues.[33]

Tumors

Classification

Soft tissue tumors constitute a large and heterogeneous group of neoplasms. This chapter deals primarily with tumors located in the somatic soft tissues; it excludes those arising from the soft tissues of the mediastinum, retroperitoneum, and visceral organs and those primarily involving the dermis, such as Kaposi's sarcoma or dermatofibrosarcoma protuberans.

Traditionally, soft tissue sarcomas have been classified according to a histogenetic concept (e.g., fibrosarcoma as a tumor arising from fibroblasts, osteosarcoma as a tumor arising from osteoblasts, and so on). However, morphologic, immunohistochemical, and data from experimental animals suggest that most if not all sarcomas arise from primitive multipotential mesenchymal cells, which in the course of neoplastic transformation undergo differentiation along one or more lines.[35] The acceptance of this alternative scheme does not require a change in terminology: A liposarcoma remains such but is now viewed not as a tumor arising from a lipoblast but as a tumor exhibiting lipoblastic differentiation. At a practical level, the importance of this classification based on histogenesis and/or differentiation is that it correlates with a variety of clinical parameters, such as location, pattern of growth, multiplicity, likelihood of recurrence, incidence and distribution of metastases, therapeutic response (such as the good response to ifosfamide-based regimes in synovial sarcoma and the greater resistance to chemotherapeutic agents in leiomyosarcoma), prognosis, and patient's age.[36]

Clinical features

A definite relationship exists between soft tissue tumor type and the age of presentation.[38,39] For instance, embryonal rhabdomyosarcoma is typically tumor of infants and children, synovial sarcoma mainly affects adolescents and young adults, and liposarcomas and malignant fibrous histiocytomas are usually seen in middle-aged and elderly patients. Some of the pediatric cases are congenital. It is interesting that congenital soft tissue tumors rarely behave malignantly, even if an aggressive behavior might have been expected from their microscopic appearance.[37]

Diagnosis and special techniques

For any large soft tissue tumor in which the possibility of malignancy exists, the proper initial diagnostic procedure is to obtain material through incisional biopsy or fine needle biopsy or aspiration. The latter technique is being used with increasing frequency in the United States, with rates of accuracy equivalent to those obtainable with frozen section.[49] After the tumor has been accurately classified, it can be treated properly. Incisional biopsy has not been shown to result in an increase of recurrence or metastases; on the contrary, when followed by adequate treatment, it is associated with a lower incidence of local recurrence than is primary excision of the sarcoma performed without prior biopsy.[50] At the time of the definitive surgery the area of the biopsy or aspiration should be excised in continuity with the tumor.

Performance of frozen sections is useful in determining the type of neoplasm, the degree of malignancy, and the adequacy of surgical margins.

Light microscopic evaluation of hematoxylin–eosin-stained sections remains the standard technique for the diagnosis of these tumors and is sufficient in the majority of the cases.[43] However, there are special techniques that have been successfully applied to increase diagnostic accuracy; these include conventional special stains, electron microscopy, immunohistochemistry, and cytogenetic/molecular methods. Examples of the first category are reticulin stain for vascular tumors and synovial sarcomas, periodic acid–Schiff for alveolar soft part sarcomas (for the demonstration of intracytoplasmic crystals), phosphotungstic acid–hematoxylin or Masson's trichrome for tumors of striated muscle, and mucin stains for synovial sarcomas and myxoid tumors in general.

Electron microscopy also can be very helpful.[44,57] Smooth and striated muscle cells, Schwann's cells, endothelial cells, glomus cells, and the cells of granular cell tumor and alveolar soft part sarcoma have distinctive ultrastructural features that often lead to a specific diagnosis.[42,53] These ultrastructural studies can also be performed on material obtained from fine needle aspiration.[47]

Enzyme histochemical determinations are of limited use. Alkaline phosphatase is particularly strong in osteosarcoma and vascular endothelial tumors, whereas acid phosphatase and nonspecific esterase are demonstrable in giant cell tumors and histiocytic tumors in general.[41]

Immunohistochemistry for tissue-related markers (such as smooth muscle actin or FVIII-related antigen) has proved of great value and is being extensively used to accurately classify these neoplasms: the specificity, sensitivity, and applicability of this technique to routinely processed material clearly render it the method of choice in most circumstances.[40,41b,51,55] The number of available markers is very large and continues to grow.[54] An area of particular expansion is that of the transcription factors, as exemplified by myogenin, WT-1, and FLI-1. These nuclear-based markers have a degree of sensitivity and specificity that in many cases surpasses those of the conventional markers located in the cytoplasm, cell membrane, or extracellular space.

The systematic use of cytogenetics has shown the existence of nonrandom chromosomal alterations (mainly translocations) in association with several types of soft tissue tumors.[45,46,48,52,55a,56] Furthermore, the molecular alterations (gene fusions) that result from these translocations are being characterized and have become a powerful tool for the study of these tumors, particularly those occurring in children[41a] (see Table 3.1, Chapter 3).

As in other fields of oncology, attempts are being made to classify soft tumors on the basis of their gene expression profile.[55b]

The specific applications of these various methods are described under the respective tumor types.

Grading and staging

Some degree of microscopic grading of soft tissue is already built into the conventional microscopic classification of these tumors. Thus dermatofibrosarcoma protuberans is by definition a low-grade neoplasm, whereas all alveolar rhabdomyosarcomas are high-grade tumors. In addition, several attempts have been made to establish some general guidelines for the grading of soft tissue sarcomas independent of their microscopic type.[58,61,71–74] The number of grades has varied in the different systems: two (low-grade and high-grade), three (I, II, and III, or low-grade, intermediate-grade, and high-grade), and four (I, II, III, and IV) grades have been recognized.

In a two-grade system, tumors are assigned to the low-grade category when their metastasizing potential is low (15% or less).[64,66] Understandably, many clinicians prefer such a system because it makes their therapeutic decision easier. Yet we believe that a three-grade system reflects better the morphologic and behavioral span of these neoplasms.

The criteria used have included degree of cellularity, pleomorphism, mitotic activity, and necrosis, and have been found to be of definite prognostic value for both adult and pediatric soft tissue tumors[61,70,71]; however, it is misleading to overemphasize grading that is independent of the specific microscopic type of the sarcoma and the circumstances in which it occurs, such as the patient's age or the depth and size of the tumor.[69] For instance, a congenital fibrosarcoma and a superficially located malignant fibrous histiocytoma may both be regarded as grade III tumors, yet their incidence of metastatic spread is extremely low; conversely, a deeply seated malignant peripheral nerve sheath tumor in a patient with Recklinghausen's disease may appear as a grade I tumor because of uniformity of proliferation and low mitotic count, yet it will usually behave in a very aggressive fashion. Additional difficulties relate to the inherently subjective nature of the evaluation, the sampling issue in biopsy material, and the confounding effect of preoperative therapy.[60] It is remarkable that, despite these severe limitations, microscopic grading (within the various histotypes and whenever applicable) remains one of the best prognostic indicators. The two grading schemes that have been most widely applied are those of the French Federation of Cancer Centers Sarcoma Groups and the NCI.[62,65] The results that have been obtained with these two methods are

French Federation of Cancer Centers Sarcoma Group grading system

Tumor differentiation

Score 1: Sarcomas closely resembling normal adult mesenchymal tissue. Examples: well differentiated liposarcomas and well-differentiated fibrosarcoma.

Score 2: Sarcomas for which the histological typing is certain. Examples: biphasic synovial sarcoma, alveolar soft-part sarcoma, myxoid liposarcoma.

Score 3: Embryonal sarcomas, undifferentiated sarcomas, and sarcomas of doubtful tumor type.

Mitosis count

The count is made at $g \times 400$ in 10 successive fields. This count is taken to establish the score:

Score 1: 0 to 9 mitoses per 10 fields

Score 2: 10 to 19 mitoses per 10 fields

Score 3: More than 20 mitoses per 10 fields

Tumor necrosis

Score 0: No necrosis on any examined slides

Score 1: Less than 50% tumor necrosis for all the examined tumor surface

Score 2: Tumor necrosis on more than half of the examined tumor surface

The three-grade system is set up as follows: Grade I is defined as a total of 2 or 3 when summing the scores obtained for each of the three histologic criteria; Grade II represents a total of 4 or 5; Grade III represents a total of 6, 7, or 8.

Enneking staging system for soft tissue sarcoma

Stage I:

| G1 | Without metastases | T1 |
| G1 | Without metastases | T2 |

Stage II:

| G2 | Without metastases | T1 |
| G2 | Without metastases | T2 |

Stage III:

| G1 or G2 | With metastases | T1 |
| G1 or G2 | With metastases | T2 |

roughly equivalent, but the French system seems to have a slight edge.[68] It is based on the evaluation of three separate parameters: tumor differentiation, mitotic rate, and amount of tumor necrosis, according to the following scheme.[62]

Two main staging systems for soft tissue sarcoma have been proposed. The one espoused by the American Joint Committee (AJC) is largely based on the TNM system, in that it uses the size of the primary tumor (T), the status of lymph nodes (N), the presence of distant metastases (M), and the tumor's histologic grade (G)[47] (see Appendix C).

In the Enneking system,[53] which is also applied to tumors of bone and which is better suited to lesions in

the extremities, soft tissue sarcomas are grouped according to anatomic settings (T1, intracompartmental, or T2, extracompartmental); grades (G1, low, and G2, high) and presence or absence of metastases, giving the scheme shown in the box.

Prognosis

The prognosis of soft tissue tumors depends on a variety of parameters, many of which are interrelated.

1 **Tumor size.** There is a definite relationship between tumor size and outcome. This is true for practically all tumor types in which this parameter has been analyzed.[88,90]

2 **Depth.** Superficially located tumors (dermis and subcutaneous tissue) have a much better prognosis than deep-seated lesions (intermuscular or intramuscular, retroperitoneal) of similar microscopic type.[81,87] The difference is largely due to the fact that superficial lesions tend to be considerably smaller at the time of excision.

3 **Location.** Tumors of the retroperitoneum do much worse than microscopically similar lesions located in the extremities. Among the latter, local recurrence has been found to be more frequent with those of the upper extremity than those of the lower extremity.[81]

4 **Microscopic type.** Some soft tissue neoplasms (such as atypical lipomatous tumors) are low-grade lesions with no capacity to metastasize, whereas other neoplasms of similar cell type (such as pleomorphic liposarcoma) are highly aggressive and prone to spread distantly.

5 **Surgical margins.** Not surprisingly, adequacy of surgical margins is statistically associated with local relapse.[76,80,85,81,89,93a] Parenthetically, local recurrence is of relatively minor importance in the development of distant metastases.[82,92]

6 **Microscopic grade.** As already indicated, a relationship has been found between various microscopic grading systems and outcome, which in some cases is directly related to the histotype but in others it is applied within a given histotype.

7 **Clinical stage.** As for most other tumors, this determination—which incorporates several of the previously mentioned parameters, as well as the presence or absence of metastases—is the most powerful prognostic determinator.

8 **DNA ploidy.** Several flow cytometric studies performed in soft tissue sarcomas of various microscopic types have shown—as expected—that DNA aneuploidy correlates with a higher microscopic grade, a higher rate of cell proliferation, and decreased survival rates.[75,86] However, it is doubtful whether DNA analysis is an independent prognostic factor when applied to soft tissue sarcomas that

have been segregated by microscopic type, anatomic site, stage, grade, margin status, and type of therapy.[78]

9 **Cell proliferation.** As already indicated, mitotic activity is incorporated into most grading schemes. Evaluation of proliferation markers such as MIB-1 and p105 has been shown to correlate with prognosis but—as for ploidy values—it remains to be seen whether it qualifies as an independent variable.[91,93]

10 **Genetic alterations.** It has been shown that soft tissue tumors exhibiting mutations of *p53* or altered expression of the retinoblastoma gene behave more aggressively than those lacking these changes,[77,79,83] but similar provisos apply. Along similar lines, claims have been made of a relationship between the type of gene fusion in the sarcomas associated with chromosomal translocations and prognosis (as in alveolar rhabdomyosarcoma and synovial sarcoma; these are discussed in the respective sections).

Therapy

Soft tissue tumors that are relatively small and/or clearly benign on clinical grounds (such as superficially located lipomas, schwannomas, hemangiomas, and tenosynovial giant cell tumors) can be removed directly, but in most others the excision should be preceded by an incisional or needle biopsy, or at least a fine needle aspiration. A few tumors (such as schwannomas) can be safely enucleated, but for most others—even if benign—a rim of uninvolved normal tissue should be excised in continuity with the neoplasm to prevent recurrence. Many soft tissue sarcomas, such as fibrosarcoma, myxoid liposarcoma, and leiomyosarcoma, may appear grossly encapsulated, but microscopic examination will often show tumor cells beyond the apparent capsule; therefore enucleation will usually fail. A wide local excision is particularly important for infiltrative lesions such as fibromatosis and dermatofibrosarcoma protuberans.

Full-fledged soft tissue sarcomas in children are currently treated, for the most part, by a combination of surgery, radiation therapy, and multidrug chemotherapy, with results that are vastly superior to those obtained in the prechemotherapy era.[100]

The treatment of high-grade soft tissue sarcomas in adults has undergone radical changes.[95,102,106] It has been thought for many years that amputation or disarticulation offered the best chances of cure for sarcomas involving an extremity. Contrariwise, many studies done during the past 30 years have shown that for several types of soft tissue sarcomas, a wide local excision offers as good a chance of survival as an amputation, especially if supplemented by other types of therapy.[98,108] Very good results along this line have been obtained by combining limited (even incomplete)

surgery with radical-dose radiation therapy (6300 to 7000 rad over 6½ to 7½ weeks).[103,104] Tumor histologic grade correlates well with the incidence of local recurrence and disease-free survival following this therapeutic modality.[103,104,107]

A controversial issue is the usefulness of adjuvant preoperative or postoperative chemotherapy for sarcomas of adult patients.[94,99,105] Results from a randomized study conducted at the National Cancer Institute strongly suggest that chemotherapy diminishes the likelihood of tumor recurrence, at least on a short-term basis, whether the sarcoma is located in the extremities, head and neck region, or trunk.[97,101]

Finally, surgical resection of pulmonary metastases has proved of value in 20% to 25% of the patients who develop this complication.[96]

Pathogenesis

Much has been written in the medical and legal literature on the possible relationship between trauma and soft tissue sarcoma, but no convincing evidence has been provided for a definite cause–effect relationship between the two.[117] Individuals subjected to repeated serious trauma (such as football players) do not have an increased incidence of soft tissue tumors. In the overwhelming majority of the cases in which a relation between tumor and trauma seems to exist, careful review of the evidence and doubling rates studies will show that the tumor antedated the trauma and that the latter simply called the attention of the patient to its presence (so-called "traumatic determinism").

The large majority of soft tissue sarcomas arise de novo rather than from malignant degeneration of preexisting benign tumors. Although the latter phenomenon may occur (as in neurofibromas), in most cases in which a given benign tumor is said to have become malignant, review of the original material will show that it was malignant from its inception. Conclusive evidence has accumulated that a variety of soft tissue sarcomas can arise as a complication of radiation therapy.[114,116] Malignant fibrous histiocytomas and soft tissue (extraskeletal) osteosarcomas are the most common types. The average latent period is approximately 10 years, and the prognosis is poor. Soft tissue sarcomas have also developed around foreign bodies, such as bullets, shrapnel, and surgically implanted material.[113] The latency period has varied from 2 years to over 50 years, and the most common microscopic types have been malignant fibrous histiocytoma and angiosarcoma.[111]

A possible association between exposure to phenoxy herbicides and development of soft tissue sarcoma has been suggested.[110,115,118] However, several case control studies have failed to show any significant association among the United States soldiers stationed in Vietnam and exposed to Agent Orange, a defoliant that contained dioxin as a contaminant.[109,112]

Tumors and tumorlike conditions of fibroblasts and myofibroblasts

Calcifying aponeurotic fibroma

Calcifying aponeurotic fibroma is a distinctive lesion originally described as juvenile aponeurotic fibroma, typically presenting as a soft tissue mass in the hand or wrist of a child or adolescent,[124] but sometimes also occurring in the proximal extremities or trunk.[121] At surgery, it may appear as a nodule or as an ill-defined infiltrating mass in the subcutaneous tissue or attached to a tendon (Fig. 25.1). Sometimes, foci of calcification may be detected on gross inspection.[120]

Microscopically, the lesion is characterized by a diffuse fibroblastic growth in which spotty calcification occurs (Fig. 25.2). Infiltration of fat and striated muscle is often seen at the periphery. Mitoses are scarce, and atypical cytologic features are absent. Scattered osteoclast-like giant cells are frequently seen. The cells inside and surrounding the calcified foci have a strong resemblance to chondrocytes. It is this feature that led some authors to postulate that this lesion is basically of cartilaginous origin and represents the cartilaginous analog of fibromatosis.[122,123,125] Immunohistochemically, the proliferating cells are reactive for vimentin, common and smooth muscle actin (sometimes), CD99, S-100 protein, and CD68.[121]

Calcifying aponeurotic fibroma can be confused with rheumatoid nodule, schwannoma, and fibromatosis. Local recurrence is common, especially in young children. However, distant metastases do not occur.[119]

Fibroma of tendon sheath

Fibroma of tendon sheath is a well-circumscribed, often lobulated tumor found attached to tendon or tendon

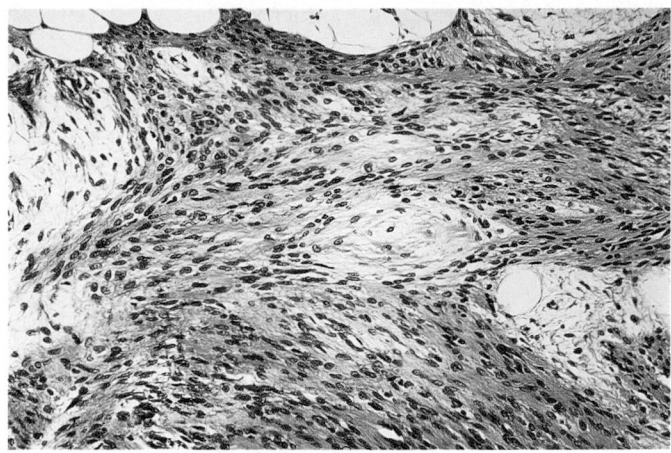

A

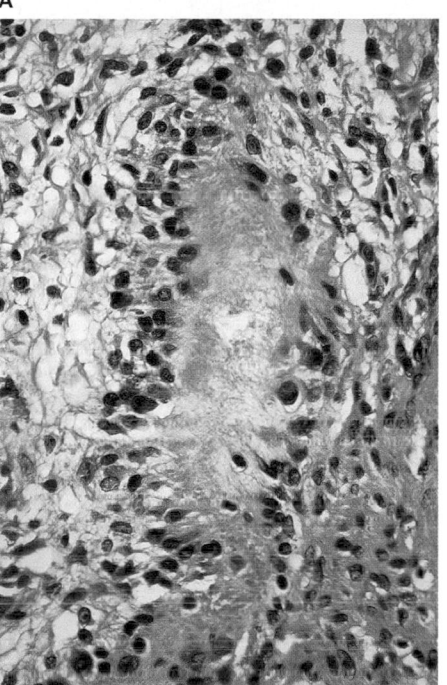

B

Fig. 25.2 A and B, Low- and high-power appearance of calcifying aponeurotic fibroma. The tumor cells arrange themselves in a palisading fashion around finely calcified material.

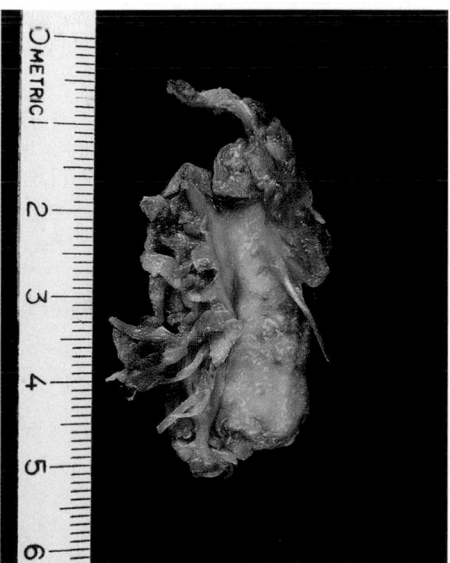

Fig. 25.1 Gross appearance of calcifying aponeurotic fibroma. The mass is unencapsulated and ill defined.

sheath. Microscopically, it is composed of dense fibrous tissue containing spindle and sometimes stellate mesenchymal cells (Fig. 25.3). Frequently, there are dilated or slit-like channels, some of them resembling tenosynovial spaces.[126,128,134] Occasionally, a component of bizarre tumor cells unaccompanied by mitoses is seen.[130] Ultrastructurally, most of the cells have features of myofibroblasts.[128] The behavior is benign. It is not clear whether this is a distinct entity or rather a heterogeneous process representing the end stage of lesions, such as tendosynovial giant cell tumor or nodular fasciitis.[131–133] We favor the latter interpretation. The translocation 2;11 has been found in one case, suggesting that at least some examples are of neoplastic nature.[127]

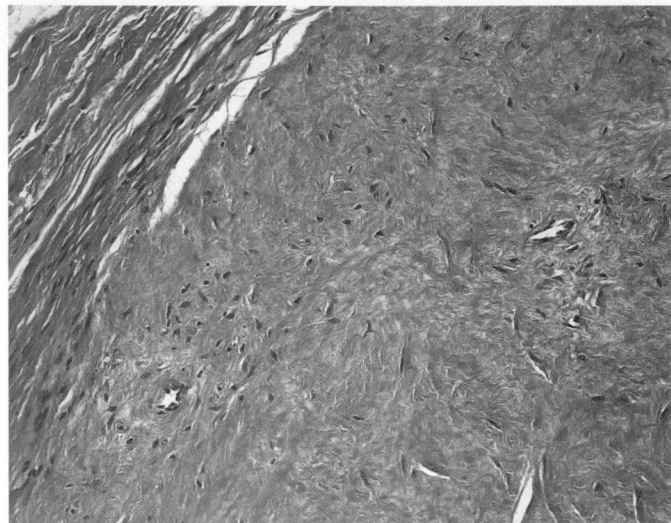

Fig. 25.3 Tendon sheath fibroma. The lesion is hypocellular and contains abundant collagen.

Other types of fibroma

Collagenous fibroma (desmoplastic fibroblastoma) is a benign lesion usually centered in the subcutaneous tissue and with a wide anatomic distribution. The most distinctive microscopic feature is the presence of stellate fibroblasts (together with ordinary spindle-shaped fibroblasts) separated by a collagenous matrix with or without myxoid features.[134a,138,139] This lesion, which is cured by a conservative excision, could be viewed as the skin and soft tissue equivalent of the generally polypoid lesions containing similar stellate cells that occur in various mucosa-lined sites, such as oral cavity, anus, and vulvovaginal region.

Nuchal-type fibroma is a benign lesion found in the posterior aspect of the neck and characterized microscopically by hypocellular bundles of thick collagen fibers, with entrapped adipose tissue and traumatic neuroma-like structures. A high percentage of the patients are diabetic.[137] This process is probably closely related to **nuchal fibrocartilaginous pseudotumor**, which is characteristically located in the deep soft tissue overlying the posterior aspect of the lower cervical vertebrae.[136] It is thought to be due to fibrocartilaginous metaplasia of the nuchal ligament, probably trauma-induced.

Superficial acral fibromyxoma is the name given to a soft tissue tumor with a predilection for the finger and toes and composed of spindle and stellate bland-looking tumor cells with a nondescript, storiform, or fascicular pattern of growth, embedded in a myxoid or collagenous stroma.[135]

Giant cell fibroblastoma

Giant cell fibroblastoma is a mesenchymal neoplasm occurring almost exclusively in children younger than 10 years of age,[142,149] but which is exceptionally also seen in adults. Most of these lesions are located in the superficial soft tissues of back or thigh. Microscopically, an ill-defined proliferation of fibroblasts is seen in a heavily collagenized and focally myxoid stroma. Typical features include the presence of multinucleated cells with a floret-like appearance, other types of atypical tumor cells, and the formation of cystic and sinusoidal structures lined by spindle and floret cells[144,150] (Fig. 25.4). Ultrastructurally and immunohistochemically, the cells have the features of primitive mesenchymal cells.[140] At the molecular level they are characterized by the gene fusion transcripts resulting from the balanced translocation t(17;22)(q22;q13).[149,151] Local recurrence is frequent, but distant metastases do not occur.[143,145]

The suggestion that giant cell fibroblastoma is related to dermatofibrosarcoma protuberans and that it may represent its infantile counterpart[150] has received strong support from the similarities of their ultrastructural, immunohistochemical, and molecular profiles[145,148] and the description of hybrid and combined cases, whether in the original lesion or in the recurrence.[141,146,147] In one such case the dermatofibrosarcoma component had pigmented features (Bednar's tumor).[152]

Nodular fasciitis and related lesions

Nodular fasciitis is the preferred designation for the condition originally designated as subcutaneous pseudosarcomatous fibromatosis.[170] It is a distinctive lesion and a very important one because of its ability to simulate a malignant process.[153,154,169,179,183] It can affect patients of all ages but is most prevalent in young adults, the peak age being 40 years.[167,183]

The most common locations are the upper extremities (particularly the flexor aspect of the forearms), trunk, and neck, but they have been described almost anywhere. Two important clinical features of nodular fasciitis are its history of rapid growth (usually a few weeks) and its small size. It usually extends above the fascia into the subcutis, but it may grow beneath it into skeletal muscle, remain within the fascia as a fusiform expansion of this structure, or be centered in the dermis[163,171,174,180] (Fig. 25.5). Like other soft tissue reactive conditions of fibrous tissue nature, it has infiltrative margins.

Microscopically, the lesion is characterized by a cellular spindle cell growth set in a loosely textured mucoid matrix (Figs 25.6 and 25.7). Vascular proliferation, lymphocytic infiltration, and extravasated red blood cells are also present. A feature of diagnostic significance is the presence of undulating wide bands of collagen lined on the sides by spindle cells, similar to those seen in keloid scars (Fig. 25.8). Storiform areas may be seen focally. Focal metaplastic bone formation may be present, establishing a link between nodular fasciitis and myositis ossificans.[157,158] The high cellularity of the

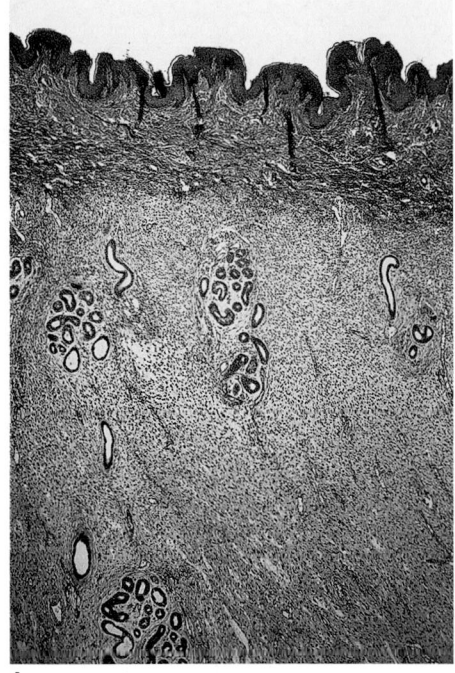

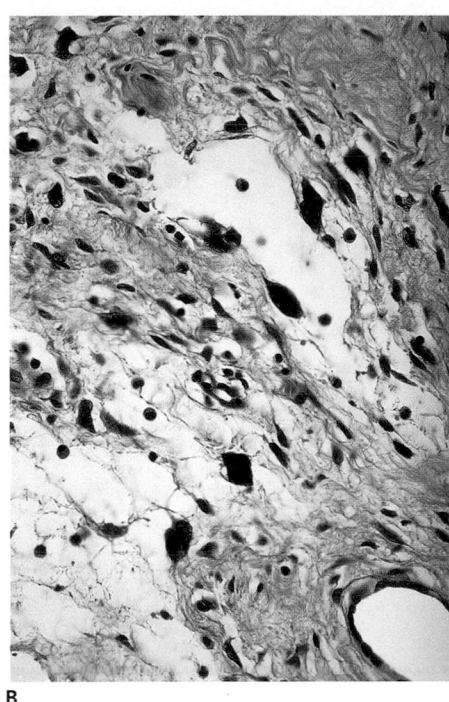

Fig. 25.4 A and **B,** Low- and high-power appearance of giant cell fibroblastoma. Some of the tumor cells line empty spaces that simulate vascular structures.

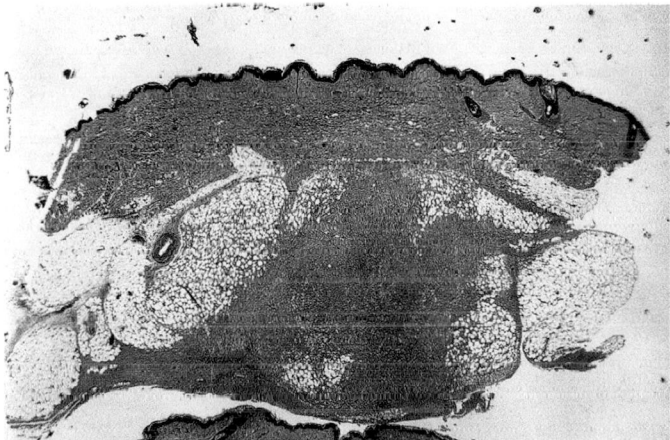

Fig. 25.5 Panoramic view of nodular fasciitis. The lesion is small, ill defined, and centered in the subcutaneous tissue.

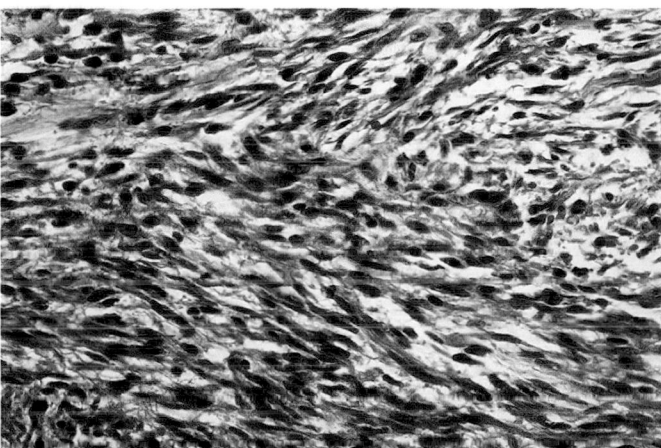

Fig. 25.6 A highly cellular example of nodular fasciitis.

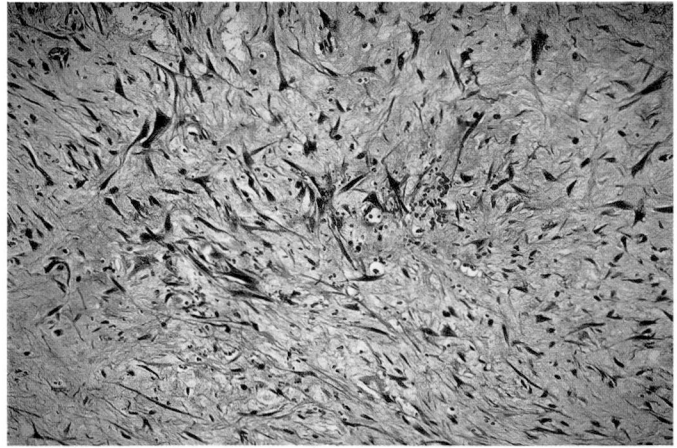

Fig. 25.7 Nodular fasciitis with marked myxoid features.

lesion and the presence of mitotic figures are responsible for the frequent confusion of this lesion with sarcoma. Small size, short duration, red blood cell extravasation, keloid-type collagen, and lack of markedly atypical cells are the main features favoring a diagnosis of nodular fasciitis. In other words, it is permissible for nodular fasciitis to be hypercellular, infiltrative, and mitotically active, but not to have cells with large atypical hyperchromatic nuclei.

Ultrastructurally and immunohistochemically, many of the proliferating spindle cells have features of myofibroblasts.[175,187] The DNA pattern is always diploid.[161] Follow-up studies of this entity have conclusively shown that it is perfectly benign.[167,169,179] Traditionally, it has been regarded as the prototypical pattern of mesenchymal

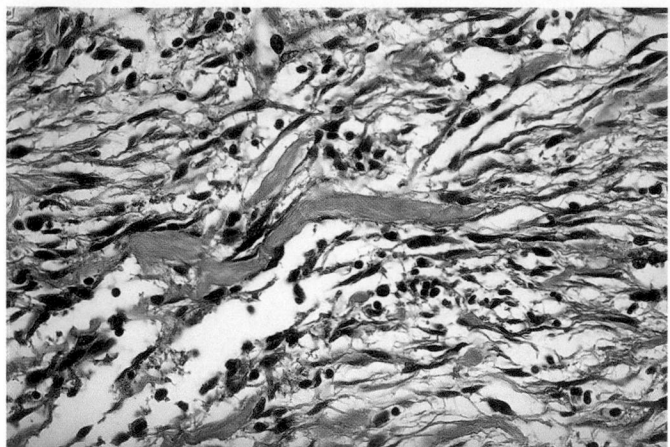

Fig. 25.8 Keloid-like collagen deposition in nodular fasciitis.

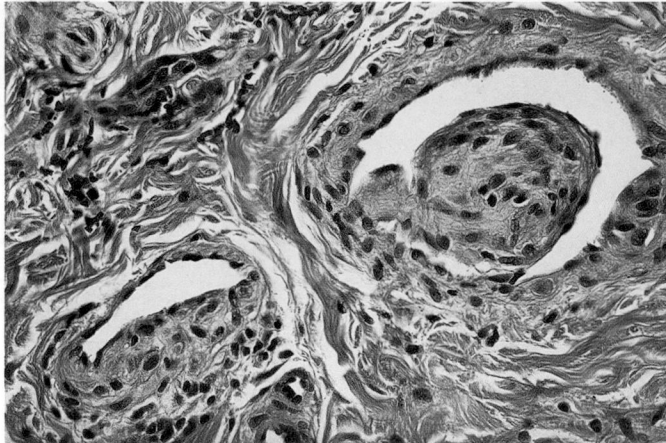

Fig. 25.9 Involvement of wall and lumen of blood vessels in nodular fasciitis.

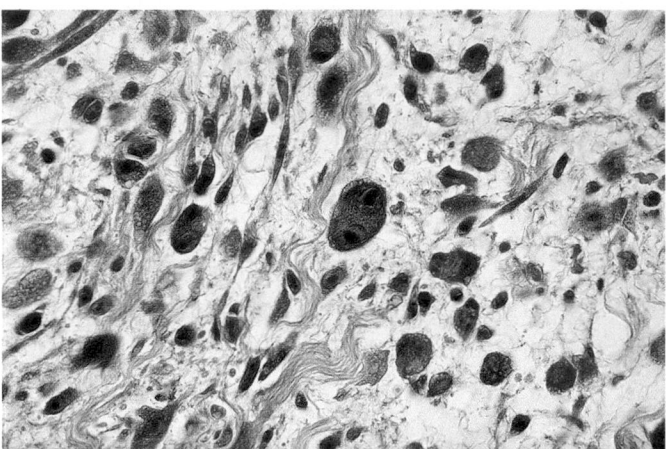

Fig. 25.10 Ganglion-like cells in proliferative fasciitis.

reaction to injury, but the recent finding of clonal chromosomal rearrangements has led some authors to favor the interpretation that it is a neoplastic process.[159] Perhaps it is, depending on how one defines a neoplasm, but benign it remains.

In addition to sarcoma, the differential diagnosis of nodular fasciitis includes the exuberant mesenchymal reactions that can accompany malignant tumors, particularly papillary thyroid carcinoma.[186]

Cranial fasciitis is a distinct variant of nodular fasciitis seen generally in children and sometimes in adults and characterized by involvement of the skull with erosion of the underlying cranium.[172]

Intravascular fasciitis is another morphologic variant of fasciitis in which involvement of the wall and lumen of the medium-sized veins and arteries occurs.[177,180,181] This is an exaggerated expression of a phenomenon seen frequently in ordinary nodular fasciitis and which constitutes a useful diagnostic sign, i.e., the fact that, at the periphery of the lesion, the walls of small to medium-sized vessels are involved by the reactive mesenchymal process (Fig. 25.9).

In *proliferative fasciitis* the location of the lesion, rapidity of growth, and self-limited nature are the same as those of nodular fasciitis, but the presence of large basophilic cells resembling ganglion cells indicates a link with proliferative myositis (see subsequent discussion) (Fig. 25.10). It usually affects adults, although it can also be seen in children.[173] It follows a benign clinical course.[155,182] As in the other conditions described in this section, myofibroblasts are the cells that predominate ultrastructurally.[156] It should be mentioned here that the presence in a soft tissue lesion of the ganglion-like cells mentioned above does not guarantee that the condition is of a reactive nature. Indeed, we have seen several cases of soft tissue sarcoma containing these cells that could be regarded as the malignant counterpart of proliferative fasciitis/myositis.

Nodular fasciitis and the variants described previously are characteristically located in the somatic soft tissues, but fasciitis-like lesions with a somewhat different morphologic appearance (even more sarcomatoid) can develop from the stromal tissue of a variety of organs, such as the bladder, prostate, vulva, vagina, and cervix (see respective chapters).

Proliferative myositis can be confused with sarcoma not only clinically and at surgery but also microscopically.[168] The skeletal muscles of the shoulder, thorax, and thigh are those most commonly affected. Most patients are over the age of 45 years, but it can also present in children.[173] Grossly, the lesion does not look like a sarcoma but rather like an ill-defined scar-like induration of the muscle (Fig. 25.11). Microscopically, a cellular proliferation rich in fibroblasts is seen surrounding individual fibers (Fig. 25.12). The hallmark of the lesion is the presence of very large basophilic cells with vesicular nuclei and very prominent nucleoli, resembling ganglion cells or rhabdomyoblasts (Fig. 25.13). Their appearance and immunohistochemical profile suggest a

Fig. 25.11 Gross appearance of proliferative myositis. There is an ill-defined whitish material in between the skeletal muscle fibers.

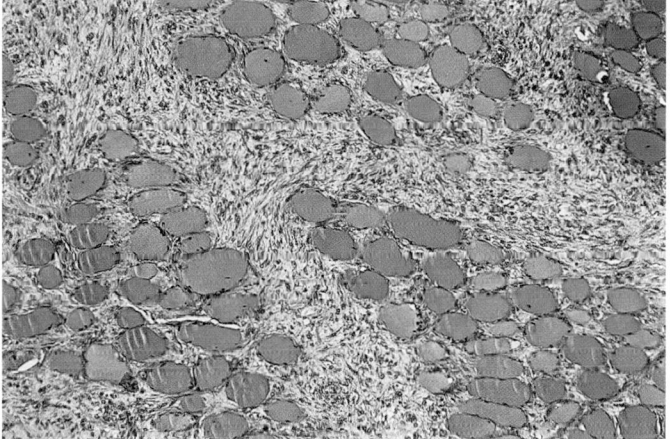

Fig. 25.12 Low-power appearance of proliferative myositis.

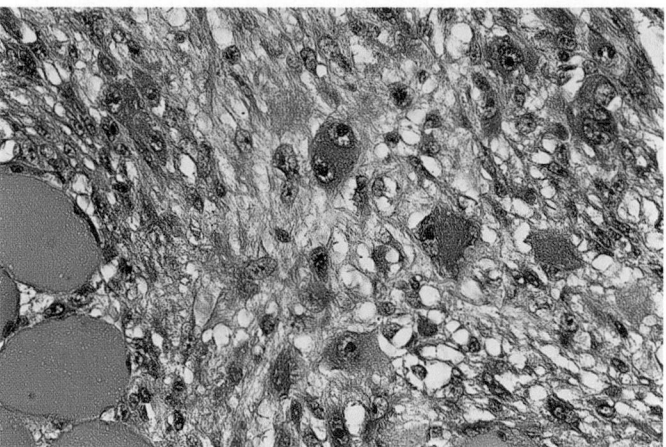

Fig. 25.13 On high power, the ganglion-like cells of proliferative myositis look similar to those of proliferative fasciitis (compare with Fig. 25.10).

myofibroblastic nature.[160] Conservative surgery is curative.[162]

Focal myositis is an altogether different inflammatory condition that affects children and adults. It typically evolves over a period of a few weeks as a localized, painful swelling of the soft tissues.[164,184] Most cases occur in the lower extremities. Both clinically and at surgery, the impression given is often of a neoplasm. Grossly, the lesion is pale and ill defined. Microscopically, degeneration and regeneration of muscle fibers are seen in association with interstitial inflammation and fibrosis. The inflammatory infiltrate is mainly composed of T lymphocytes, with few accompanying CD4+ cells.[185] The lesion is solitary and self-limited and should be distinguished from polymyositis. Enzyme histochemical and electron microscopic studies suggest that the disease may be the result of a denervation process.[165] Search for a viral agent has so far proved elusive.[185]

Other pseudoneoplastic myofibroblastic processes pathogenetically related to nodular fasciitis and representing an exaggerated reaction to injury include *proliferative funiculitis* (involving the spermatic cord and probably secondary to ischemia or torsion)[166] and *atypical decubital fibroplasia* (occurring primarily in physically debilitated or immobilized patients).[176] The latter condition merges with *ischemic fasciitis*, in which a central area of necrosis is seen surrounded by a ring of neoformed vessels and proliferating fibroblasts/myofibroblasts.[178]

Nodular fasciitis and the variants described previously are characteristically located in the somatic soft tissues, but fasciitis-like lesions with a somewhat different morphologic appearance (even more sarcomatoid) can develop from the stromal tissue of a variety of organs such as the bladder, prostate, vulva, vagina, and cervix (see respective chapters).

Myositis ossificans

Although myositis ossificans is located in the soft tissue and is pathogenetically and histologically linked to the previous entities, it is discussed in Chapter 24 because of its intimate relation to bone and periosteum.

Elastofibroma

Elastofibroma is a benign, poorly circumscribed tumor-like condition involving almost exclusively the subscapular region of elderly individuals, although isolated cases have been seen in the deltoid muscle, infraolecranon area, hip, thigh, and stomach.[190] Multicentric and familial cases have been described, suggesting the existence of a constitutional background.[198] There is often a history of hard manual labor. At surgery, the lesions usually are found at the apex of the scapula, beneath the rhomboid and latissimus dorsi muscles (Fig. 25.14). The right side is affected more commonly than the left. Bilaterality is frequent. A periosteal origin has been suggested.[196]

Microscopically, collagen bundles alternate with numerous acidophilic, refractive cylinders often containing a central dense core, both of which stain strongly

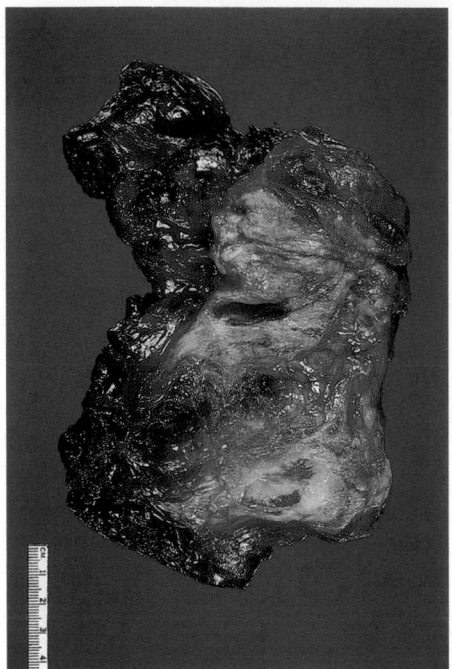

Fig. 25.14 Gross appearance of elastofibroma.

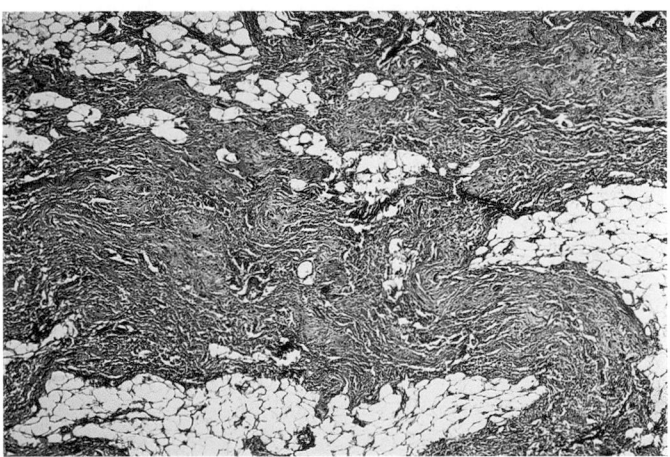

Fig. 25.15 On low power, dermatofibroma appears as an irregularly shaped fibrohyaline mass within adipose tissue.

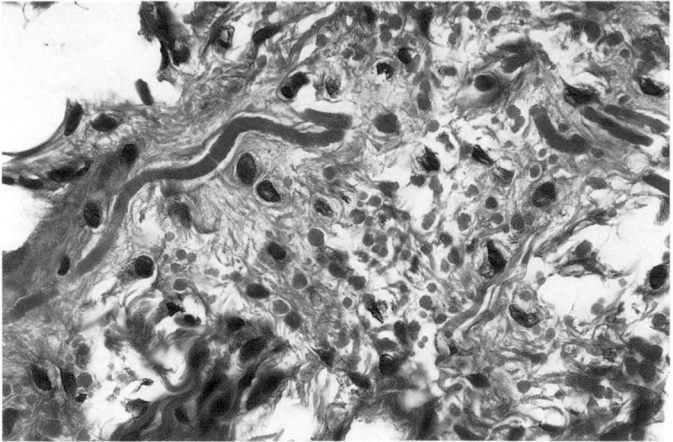

A

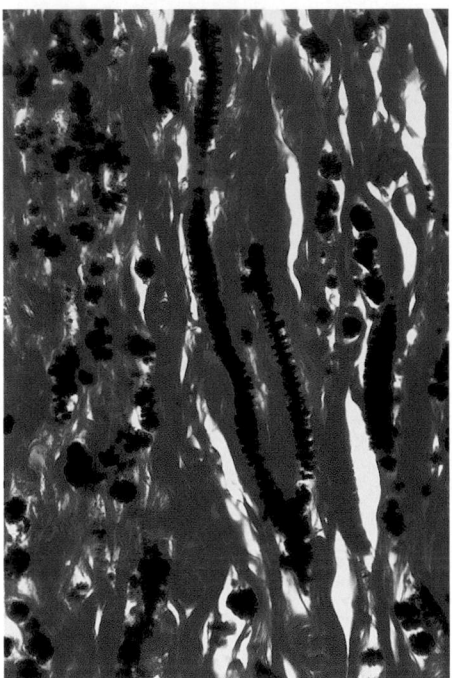

B

Fig. 25.16 A and **B**, High-power view of elastofibroma showing diagnostic rods of elastic tissue. (**B**, Elastic tissue stain)

with elastic stains (Figs 25.15 and 25.16). Ultrastructurally, the cylinders are made up of immature amorphous elastic tissue, whereas the central core contains mature fibers.[188,189,192,200] Elastase digestion fully removes this material.[188]

The biochemical composition is that of elastin but with a slightly different amino acid composition than normal elastic tissue.[194,199] The collagen deposited in the lesion is a mixture of types I, II, and III; the presence of type II collagen is perplexing because this is normally present only in articular cartilage and some ocular structures.[197] This lesion is not a true neoplasm but rather a reactive hyperplasia involving abnormal elastogenesis[191,193]; it would seem that the new material synthesized by the tumor cells is laid down around preexisting elastic fibers.[195]

Solitary fibrous tumor

This soft tissue neoplasm, formerly thought to be of mesothelial nature and limited to mesothelium-covered surfaces, is now known to be composed of a subset of fibroblast-like cells and to be quite ubiquitous. Curiously, the soft tissues of the extremities are among the rarest sites of occurrence of this entity; however, well-documented examples are on record.[201,207] As in other sites, both benign and malignant varieties exist. Microscopically, the alternation of hyper- and hypocellular areas, the deposition of dense keloid-type collagen, and the occurrence of hemangiopericytoma-like areas are the most distinguishing features. Occasionally the stroma is very myxoid.[202] In rare instances there is an associated component of mature adipose tissue, in which case the term *lipomatous hemangiopericytoma* has been used.[204,205] It seems likely that the tumor originally described as *giant cell angiofibroma*[203] is a giant cell-rich variant of solitary fibrous tumor.[206]

Fibromatosis

The generic term **fibromatosis** was originally proposed by Stout[277] for a group of related conditions having in common the following features:

1 Proliferation of well-differentiated fibroblasts (later shown to be mainly myofibroblasts)
2 Infiltrative pattern of growth
3 Presence of a variable (but usually abundant) amount of collagen between the proliferating cells
4 Lack of cytologic features of malignancy
5 Scanty or absent mitotic activity
6 Aggressive clinical behavior characterized by repeated local recurrences but lack of capacity to metastasize distantly.

Grossly, these lesions are often large, firm, and whitish, with ill-defined outlines and an irregularly whorled cut surface[208] (Figs 25.17 and 25.18). They often arise in a muscular fascia. Microscopically, most of the proliferating cells have features intermediate between those of fibroblasts and smooth muscle cells (i.e., of myofibroblasts) (Figs 25.19 and 25.20). This was first described in a classic ultrastructural study of palmar fibromatosis by Gabbiani and Majno.[238] The authors noted nuclear deformations of the type found in contracted cells (retrospectively identified by light microscopy as cross-banded nuclei) and a cytoplasmic fibrillary system similar to that seen in smooth muscle cells. They suggested that the proliferating fibroblasts had modulated toward a contractile cell—which they proposed to designate the myofibroblast—and that this was responsible for the contracture evident clinically. The myofibroblastic appearance of the cells of fibromatosis has been confirmed by many,[239,254] as has the fact that this cell type is implicated in a large number of reactive conditions as well as neoplasms of soft tissue.[227,229] In an ultrastructural study of fibromatosis, Welsh[282] described intracytoplasmic collagen formation, probably representing a disruption of collagen synthesis. This alteration is, however, nonspecific; it has also been detected in a variety of

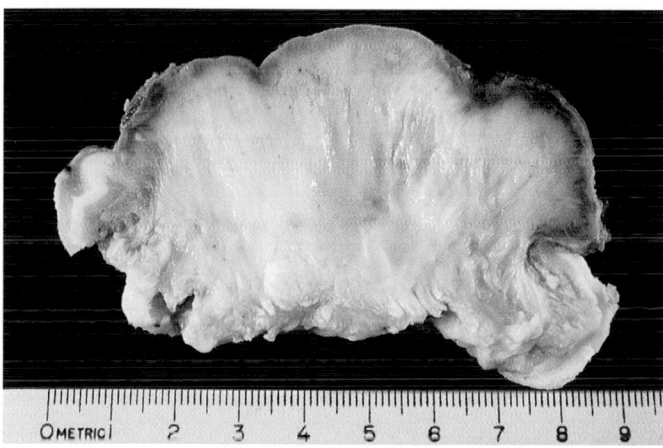

Fig. 25.17 Plantar fibromatosis. The tissue is whitish and unencapsulated, with an elastic consistency.

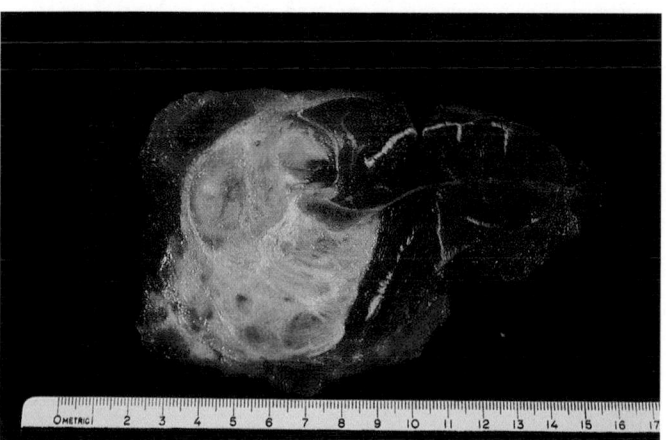

Fig. 25.18 Deep-seated fibromatosis embedded within major skeletal muscle.

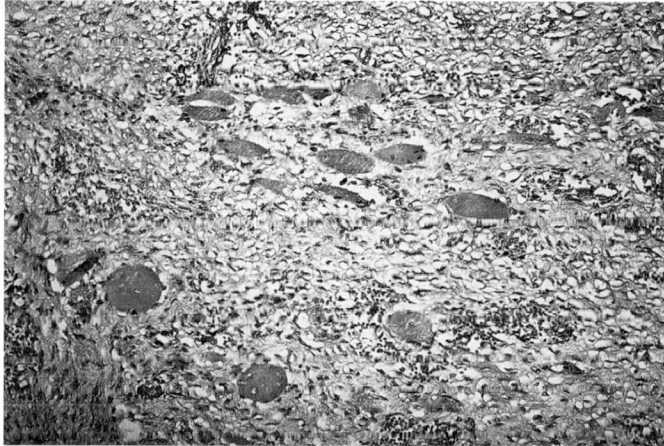

Fig. 25.19 The spindle cells of fibromatosis grow diffusely between skeletal muscle fibers.

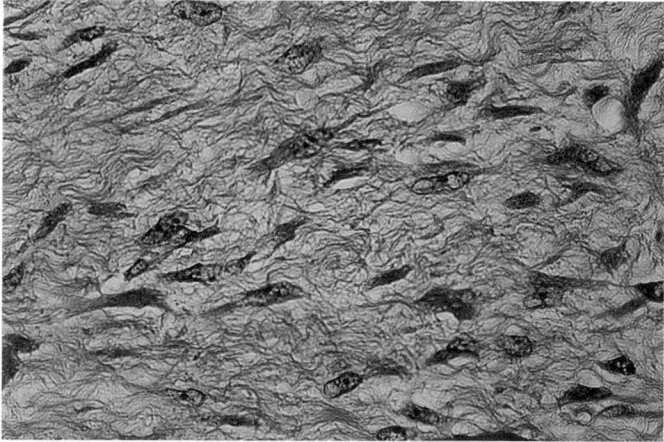

Fig. 25.20 On high power, the cells of fibromatosis have features consistent with myofibroblasts.

collagen-producing soft tissue sarcomas.[256] Clonal chromosomal aberrations are present in approximately half of the deep-seated fibromatoses but only in 10% of those located superficially. Trisomies 8 and 20 and loss of 5q material represent the recurring changes.[225] Another molecular difference between superficial and deep fibromatosis is the lack of β-catenin and *APC* gene mutations.[259]

Other light microscopic features commonly encountered in fibromatosis are a perivascular lymphocytic infiltrate located at the advancing edge of the lesion and thick-walled vessels sharply outlined from the surrounding tissue. Dystrophic calcification and metaplastic ossification have also been described.[236]

Some pathologists add the adjective *aggressive* to some forms of fibromatosis to emphasize the biologic behavior. We do not use the term, since we regard it as redundant; most deep-seated fibromatoses are potentially aggressive. Besides, there is little correlation between the cellularity or other microscopic features of these lesions and their biologic behavior.[285] Other authors have gone even further and have used *differentiated fibrosarcoma* as a synonym for the histologically more cellular or clinically more aggressive types of fibromatosis. We are opposed to this terminology because the designation of sarcoma endows this lesion in the mind of many surgeons with a metastasizing potential that it does not possess. Although we recognize the difficulties involved, we always attempt to make a distinction between fibromatosis and well-differentiated fibrosarcoma, reserving the latter term for tumors showing atypical cytologic features and/or a significant number of mitotic figures (more than one per high-power field). As Enzinger[230] remarked, it is usually not possible on the basis of the histologic examination to predict whether or not a fibromatosis will recur, but it is possible to predict whether a fibrous tumor is or is not capable of metastases.

Most soft tissue fibromatoses are in intimate contact with skeletal muscles—hence their designation as *musculoaponeurotic fibromatosis*.[231] This is preferable to the obsolete term *desmoid tumor*, traditionally used for a neoplasm of the abdominal wall appearing in women during or following pregnancy. In our experience, this lesion is almost as common in men and in other locations, such as the shoulder girdle, head and neck area, and thigh.[246,258,265] It can also occur in the mediastinum, retroperitoneum, abdominal cavity (see subsequent discussion), and breast.[218,219,270]

The treatment of choice is a prompt radical excision, including a wide margin of involved tissue. Sometimes this requires the removal of the entire muscle involved. The incidence of local recurrence is lower in fibromatoses of the abdominal wall than in those located elsewhere.[246] Some of the latter have recurred as many as five times or more. Only rarely, however, has local aggressiveness forced amputation. Actually, cessation of attempts to

excise persistent tissue locally may be followed by failure of the lesion to enlarge further. Because of this observation, some authors have advised against the reexcision of a recurrent lesion that does not appear to be growing.[267] Enzinger and Shiraki[231] analyzed 30 cases located in the shoulder girdle that had been followed for a minimum of 10 years. In 57% of the patients the tumor recurred one or more times. However, at the end of the follow-up period, *all patients* were living without any evidence of continuing tumor growth. A higher incidence of recurrence was seen in young individuals and in those patients with tumors of large size.

Radiation therapy may be effective in achieving local control. It has been used in the form of external radiation following conservative (and sometimes inadequate) surgery[252] and in the form of iridium implantation coupled with surgery for the treatment of recurrences.[287] Some cases of fibromatosis have also been successfully managed with endocrine therapy, such as tamoxifen.[275,283]

Juvenile fibromatosis is a term that has often been applied to examples of fibromatosis occurring in children and adolescents.[210,240,271] Except for their greater frequency in this age group and, in some specific instances, their greater propensity for local recurrence, there is very little either on clinical or microscopic grounds that differentiates fibromatosis in children from that occurring in other age groups.[222] There are, however, three variants of fibromatosis apparently restricted to childhood that present a distinctive clinicopathologic picture: fibromatosis colli (congenital torticollis), infantile digital fibromatosis, and infantile myofibromatosis.

Fibromatosis colli (congenital torticollis) is a type of fibromatosis affecting the lower third of the sternomastoid muscle and appearing at birth or shortly thereafter, sometimes bilaterally.[223] Fibromatosis colli is frequently associated with various congenital anomalies. Thus, Iwahara and Ikeda[248] found congenital (usually ipsilateral) dislocations of the hip in 14% of their patients. An association between complicated deliveries (particularly breech deliveries) and fibromatosis colli has been established. Although some instances of spontaneous disappearance have been recorded, this condition usually necessitates resection of the muscle. Microscopically, the cellularity of the fibrous tissue depends on the age of the process. This condition has been considered to be caused by birth injury, but there is rarely evidence of previous hemorrhage.[217]

Infantile digital fibromatosis is a form of fibromatosis usually restricted to childhood.[266] The typical location is on the exterior surface of the end phalanges of the fingers and toes, but it may also occur outside the digits and at sites such as the oral cavity and breast[262,264] (Fig. 25.21). The lesions are often multiple and either present at birth or appear during the first 2 years of life. However, morphologically identical lesions in adults are on record.[279]

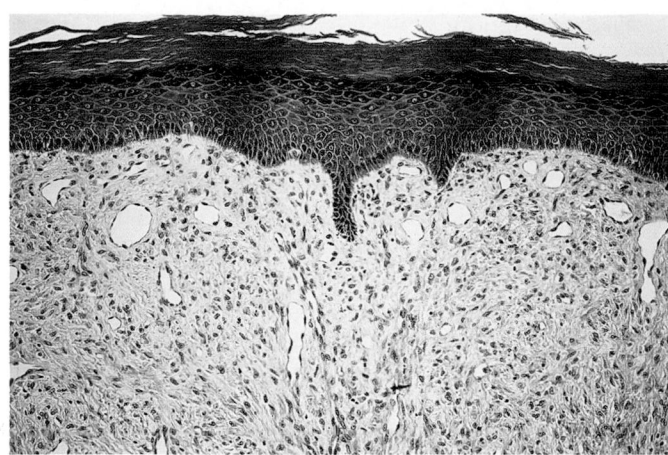

Fig. 25.21 Low-power view of infantile digital fibromatosis growing beneath a flattened epidermis.

The component cells are myofibroblasts.[214] A distinctive microscopic feature, generally not observed in other forms of fibromatosis, is the presence of peculiar eosinophilic cytoplasmic inclusions (Fig. 25.22). These have been examined ultrastructurally and found to be composed of compact masses of granules and filaments without a limiting membrane.[211,220] Their significance is obscure; their similarity with the "virus factories" seen in cells with certain viruses has been commented on, but they are currently thought to derive from cytoplasmic contractile proteins, probably actin.[232,244,249,260,261,286] This disease has a high tendency for local recurrence.[272]

Infantile myofibromatosis presents as solitary (myofibroma)[280] or multiple (myofibromatosis)[216,226,235] nodules

in the skin, soft tissues, or bone, either limited to these sites or associated with internal organ involvement.[212,243,269,273,280] A large majority of the cases occur before the age of 2 years, and approximately 60% are congenital.[221] However, this lesion can also occur in adults.[213,224,245] Solitary forms are more common in males, and multicentric forms are more common in females.[221] A familial incidence has been detected, and evidence for an autosomal dominant pattern of transmission has been obtained.[251] Microscopically, peripheral areas that resemble smooth muscle alternate with hemangiopericytoma-like areas and foci having a more typical fibroblastic configuration (Fig. 25.23). Central necrosis and intravascular growth may be present.[221] Ultrastructurally, the lesion is largely composed of myofibroblasts, hence its name[257]; however, a whole range of differentiation exists between fibroblasts and fully developed, desmin-positive smooth muscle cells.[234] Indeed, myofibromatosis seems to be a member of a family of tumors showing vessel-related myoid differentiation, which also includes

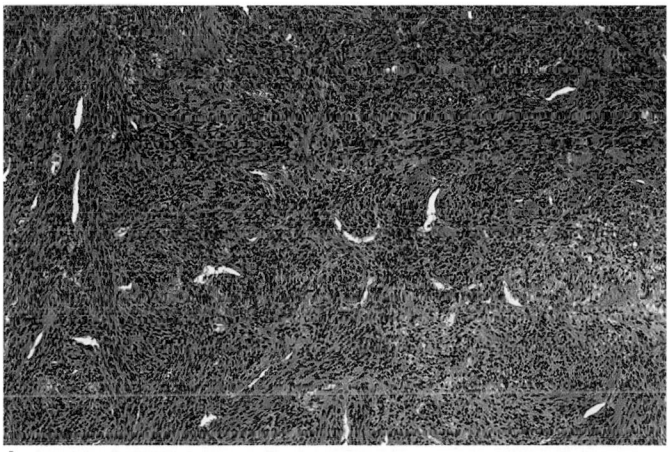

A

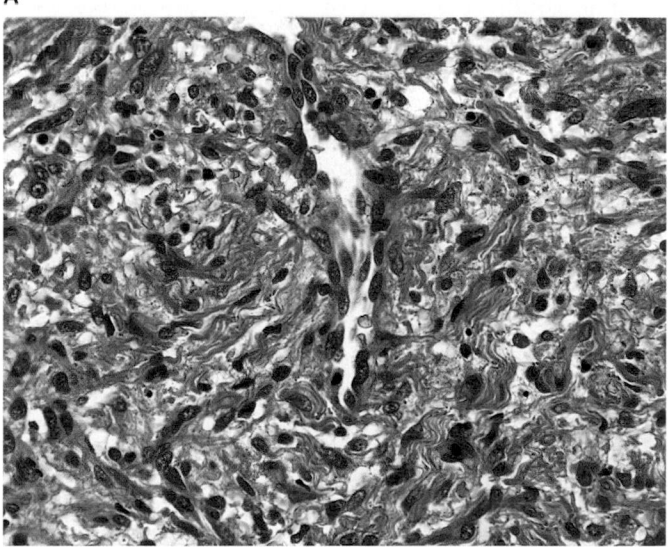

B

Fig. 25.23 A and **B**, Infantile myofibromatosis. The field shown in **A** contains hemangiopericytoma-like features. The higher power shown in **B** emphasizes the hypercellularity of the lesion.

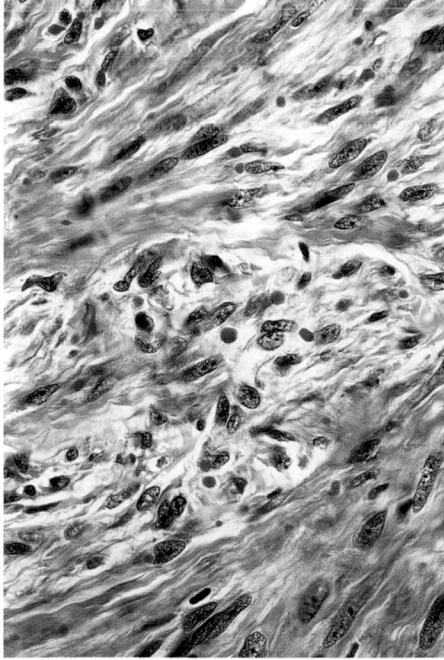

Fig. 25.22 On high power, the cells of infantile digital fibromatosis are seen to contain cytoplasmic hyaline globules.

glomangiopericytoma, myopericytoma, and hemangiopericytoma, particularly the infantile form of the latter (see p. 2290).[241] Infantile myofibromatosis can undergo spontaneous regression, allegedly through the mechanism of apoptosis.[237]

Lipofibromatosis is a minor variation on the theme of infantile fibromatosis, in which a spindle cell component of fibroblastic appearance (mainly located in septa and skeletal muscle) is admixed with mature adipose tissue.[233] It resembles fibrous hamartoma of infancy (see p. 2315), but for the lack of a primitive nodular fibromyxoid component; local recurrence is very common.[233]

Fibromatosis hyalinica multiplex (multiple juvenile hyaline fibromatosis, systemic hyalinosis) is a morphologically distinctive type of familial multiple fibromatosis affecting children but not present at birth,[247] probably resulting from an inborn error of metabolism and characterized microscopically by a conspicuous hyalinization of the connective tissue of the skin, oral cavity, articular capsule, and bone.[228] Multinucleated histiocytic giant cells can be present.[242] Ultrastructurally, the cells have the features of fibroblasts; numerous cisternae of endoplasmic reticulum are seen, many of which are dilated ("fibril-filled balls"). Entangled cytoplasmic tubules may also be present.[281,284]

Some forms of fibromatosis derive their names from their particular location.[208] **Penile fibromatosis** (Peyronie's disease) is discussed in Chapter 18. **Palmar fibromatosis** is also known as Dupuytren's contracture, and **plantar fibromatosis** as Ledderhose's disease.[250,255,263,274] These conditions occur predominantly in adults. Contracture of the fingers or toes is the leading clinical manifestation. The lesions can be multiple and bilateral and may coexist in the upper and lower extremities. The plantar form tends to be more localized than its palmar counterpart. Microscopically, they have been classified into three phases: proliferative, involutive, and residual.[279] During the proliferative phase, cellularity may be marked (especially for the plantar lesions), and this may lead to a mistaken diagnosis of fibrosarcoma. It is well to remember that fibrosarcoma of the palmar and plantar areas is exceptional[209] and that the differential diagnosis of a cellular spindle cell tumor of the sole is usually between fibromatosis, synovial sarcoma, malignant melanoma, and Kaposi's sarcoma.

Fibromatoses also have been classified according to the presumed inciting cause, such as **cicatricial fibromatosis** and **postirradiation fibromatosis**. The cicatricial form may follow accidental trauma or arise in the scar of surgical procedures. Postirradiation fibromatosis differs from the other forms by virtue of the common occurrence of bizarre cells with large hyperchromatic nuclei. This feature, which in the absence of radiation exposure would be strong evidence of malignancy, should be interpreted more conservatively under these circumstances.

The association of soft tissue tumors, usually of the fibromatosis type, with multiple colonic polyposis and occasionally multiple osteomas is known as **Gardner's syndrome**.[215,268,277] In this condition, the fibromatosis has a particular tendency to involve intra-abdominal structures, such as the omentum and mesentery,[218,219,253] and to manifest itself following a surgical procedure in the area. It is important not to misdiagnose intra-abdominal fibromatosis involving the intestinal wall (a not uncommon occurrence) as a gastrointestinal stromal tumor (GIST).[267a] Along these lines, it should be mentioned that —despite early statements to the contrary—fibromatosis seems to be a CD117-negative tumor, as opposed to bonafide GIST.[257a]

Fibrosarcoma

Fibrosarcomas are commonly tumors of adults, although they can occur in any age group and even be present as congenital neoplasms.[290,293,296,301] The latter are to be regarded as a special category (see below). Fibrosarcomas can arise from superficial and deep connective tissues such as fascia, tendon, periosteum, and scar; grow slowly or rapidly; and often appear well circumscribed[302] (Fig. 25.24). They usually are soft and cellular and may contain areas of necrosis and hemorrhage.

Microscopically, the well-differentiated tumors are easily recognized as fibroblastic (Fig. 25.25). The cells are arranged in fascicles that intersect each other at acute angles resulting in a herringbone appearance. The individual cells resemble fibroblasts, and a reticulin stain demonstrates abundant fibers *wrapped around each cell*.[304] The fibroblastic nature is more difficult to recognize in the undifferentiated tumors (Fig. 25.26). It should be remembered that many other soft tissue tumors, particularly synovial sarcoma, liposarcoma, malignant fibrous histiocytoma, and malignant peripheral nerve sheath tumor, often contain areas closely resembling fibrosarcoma. Only careful examination of different blocks of the tumor

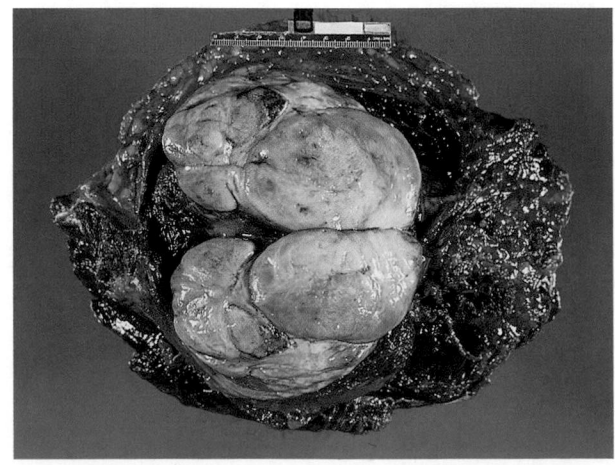

Fig. 25.24 Well-circumscribed fibrosarcoma growing within skeletal muscle.

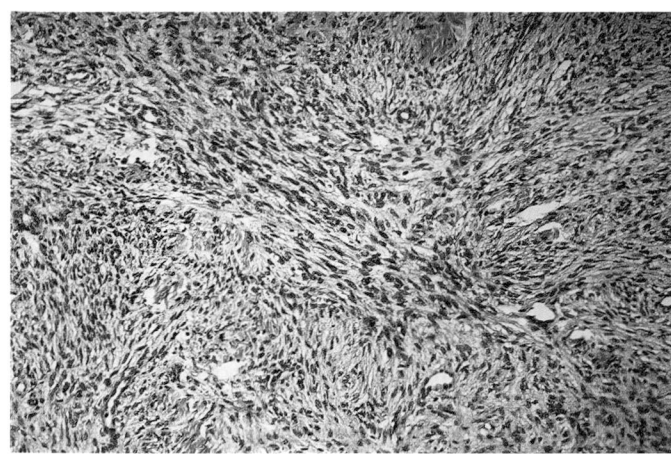

Fig. 25.25 Low-power appearance of well-differentiated fibrosarcoma. The tumor has a monotonous hypercellular look.

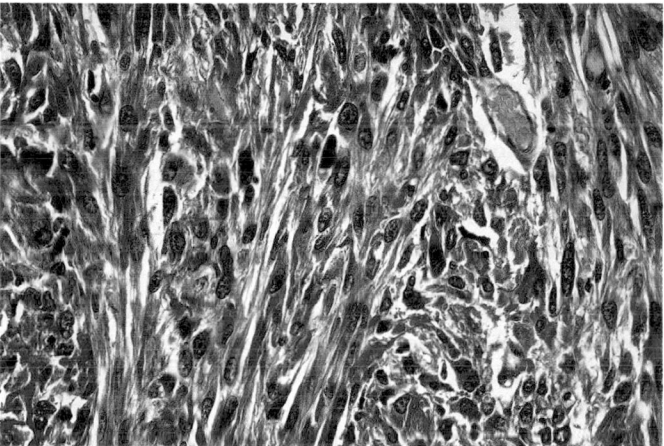

Fig. 25.26 Fibrosarcoma showing a moderate degree of nuclear pleomorphism.

will provide the correct diagnosis in these instances. Although a pleomorphic type of fibrosarcoma probably exists (see under "Malignant fibrous histiocytoma"), one should question the diagnosis of fibrosarcoma in the presence of a soft tissue sarcoma with numerous tumor giant cells. Ultrastructurally, most of the fibrosarcoma cells recapitulate the morphology of normal fibroblasts, whereas others have features of myofibroblasts.[291,294,305] Immunohistochemically, the prototypical fibrosarcoma should have reactivity for vimentin and type I collagen but not for smooth muscle markers, histiocytic markers, or basal lamina components.[295] The presence of focal immunoreactivity for smooth muscle actin, laminin, or collagen (not an unusual occurrence) should be taken to indicate incipient differentiation along myoid or possibly myofibroblastic lines.

As already indicated, another important differential diagnosis is with fibromatosis. The main light microscopic differences are discussed on p. 2250. With special techniques and allowing for some degree of overlap, fibrosarcoma is more likely than fibromatosis to have a high proliferative index, an aneuploid DNA pattern, and

p53 positivity.[298] In contrast to the fibromatoses, fibrosarcomas are capable of distant metastases. The survival rate in a recent large series was 41% at 5 years and 29% at 10 years.[307] Generally, the more superficial and differentiated the tumor, the better the prognosis. Increased mitotic activity and marked cellularity (as expressed by a grading system) are associated with an increased incidence of metastases.[307] In two large series,[299,306] fibrosarcomas in children under 5 years of age at the time of diagnosis were shown to have a high recurrence rate but an incidence of distant metastases of only 7% to 8%. Many of these belong to the category of congenital fibrosarcoma discussed below. Instead, fibrosarcomas occurring in children 10 years old or older have a metastatic rate close to that of adult patients (i.e., 50%).[303] The treatment of choice is radical excision. Postoperative radiation therapy should be considered if microscopic residual or positive margins are encountered. Since subclinical microscopic metastases are presumed to exist in many patients at the time of surgery, adjuvant chemotherapy has been recommended following the surgical excision of the tumor in high-grade lesions.[307]

Congenital fibrosarcoma is an extremely cellular tumor characterized by very rapid growth and the capability for extensive local invasion, but its metastatic rate is negligible[292] (Fig. 25.27). At the molecular level, it is characterized by the *ETV6–NTRK3* gene fusion (as detected by RT-PCR), resulting from the chromosomal translocation t(12;15)(p13;q25).[289,300a] This gene fusion is not present in the conditions that enter in the differential diagnosis with congenital fibrosarcoma, namely adult-type fibrosarcoma, infantile fibromatosis, and infantile myofibromatosis.

Sclerosing epithelioid fibrosarcoma is a variant of fibrosarcoma that simulates the appearance of infiltrating carcinoma[297,300] (Fig. 25.28). It is composed of small,

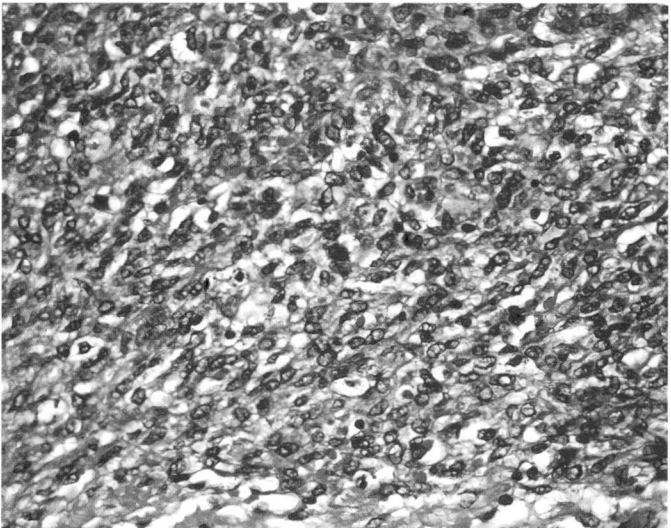

Fig. 25.27 Congenital fibrosarcoma. The tumor is extremely cellular and mitotically active.

repeated failures at local control.[349,442,452] The best example in this category is the tumor traditionally known as **dermatofibrosarcoma protuberans** and also discussed in Chapter 4.[324,333,354] It is typically centered in the dermis, but it can also occur in deeper soft tissues. This lesion is characterized microscopically by lack of circumscription; high cellularity; a relatively monomorphic appearance; nuclear hyperchromasia; moderate to high mitotic activity; lack or inconspicuousness of giant, foamy, or hemosiderin-laden cells; and—most of all—by the presence of what has been called a *storiform* pattern of growth (Fig. 25.31). This refers to a peculiar arrangement of the tumor cells around a central point, producing radiating "spokes" grouped at right angles to each other. Tridimensional reconstruction studies suggest that this structure develops at the periphery of adjacent proliferating cell groups.[400] This pattern can also be seen in benign fibrous histiocytomas as well as in tumors of totally unrelated types, such as thymoma. The collagen deposited in dermatofibrosarcoma appears as nonpolarizable thin strands, in contrast to that present in most dermatofibromas.[325] The histogenesis of this tumor remains controversial; the immunohistochemical profile is more in keeping with a fibroblastic than a fibrohistiocytic or neural derivation,[340,394] although the existence of a pigmented variant (Bednar's tumor, see below) suggests otherwise.

Virtually all cases of dermatofibrosarcoma protuberans have a translocation that involves chromosomes 17 and 22, resulting in fusion of the collagen type I α I (COL1A1) and platelet-derived growth factor β (PDGFβ) genes. They have also been shown to have a distinctive gene expression profile.[395a]

The main differential diagnosis is with deep-seated benign fibrous histiocytoma[379]; stains for CD34 (positive in dermatofibrosarcoma protuberans) and factor XIIIa (positive in benign fibrous histiocytoma of skin) are helpful in this regard.

As previously noted, a close link exists between dermatofibrosarcoma protuberans and giant cell fibroblastoma, which also applies to the genetic molecular alterations.[435a,444] Indeed, the latter is regarded by some as the juvenile variant of the former.[326] It should be noted, however, that classical forms of dermatofibrosarcoma can also be seen in the pediatric age group.[398]

Sometimes tumors with the typical appearance of dermatofibrosarcoma protuberans develop foci indistinguishable from fibrosarcoma, myofibrosarcoma, or malignant fibrous histiocytoma.[359,404,416,458] Significantly, there is usually a loss of CD34 immunoreactivity in these foci.[359] There is disagreement among the various series as to whether this development is accompanied by a more aggressive clinical course,[335,338] but most evidence suggests that it does.[404] In other instances the tumor progresses to a more pleomorphic (MFH-like) pattern.[417]

Pigmented dermatofibrosarcoma (Bednar's tumor) looks like the usual dermatofibrosarcoma protuberans

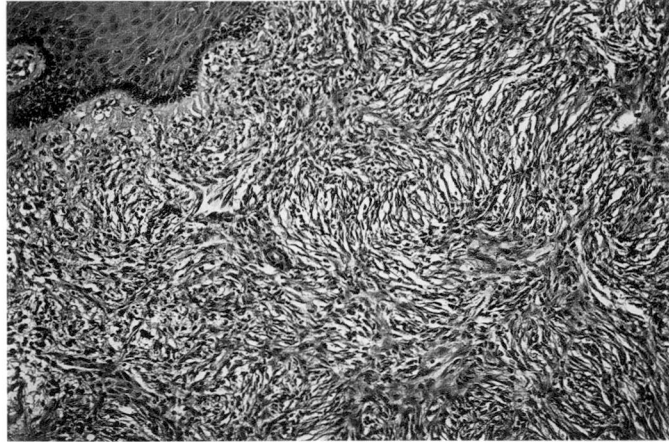

A

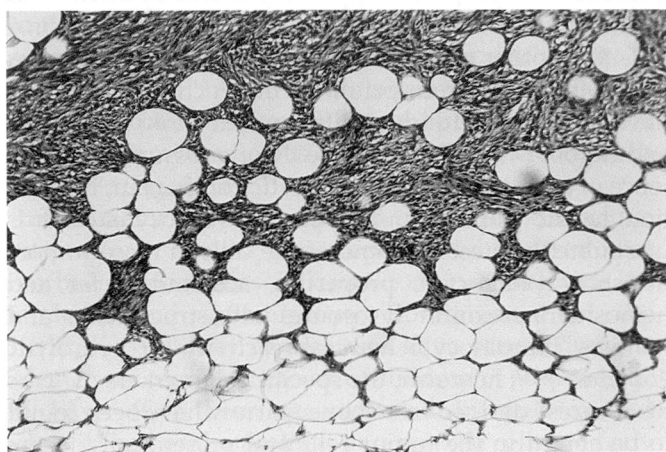

B

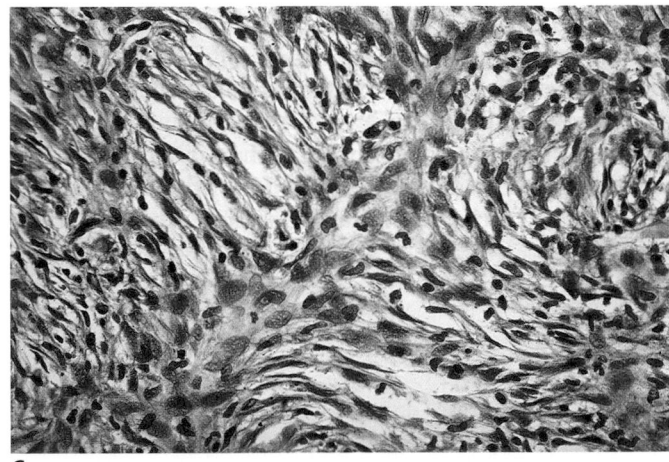

C

Fig. 25.31 Dermatofibrosarcoma protuberans: **A,** diffuse hypercellular growth in the dermis; **B,** typical pattern of infiltration of the subcutaneous fat; **C,** storiform pattern of growth.

except for the presence of a population of dendritic cells heavily loaded with melanin (Fig. 25.32); the occurrence of this variant is of interest because it raises the possibility of a peripheral nerve origin,[342,410] a possibility that others have also raised for the usual type of dermatofibrosarcoma protuberans.[364] The alternative possibility, that the melanin-containing dendritic cells are not

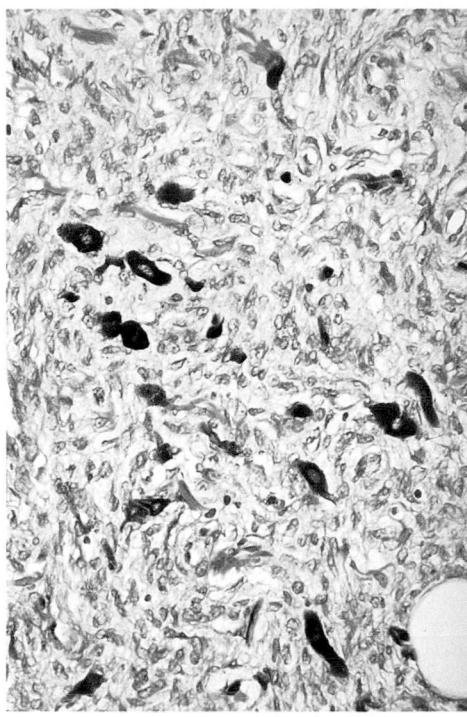

Fig. 25.32 Pigmented dermatofibrosarcoma protuberans (Bednar's tumor). Scattered, heavily pigmented cells are seen among the spindle neoplastic elements.

neoplastic but rather represent secondary melanocyte colonization, has been suggested.[339,355] A case with the Bednar's tumor pattern has been seen in the recurrence of a giant cell fibroblastoma, further supporting the relationship between these various neoplasms.[337]

Atypical fibroxanthoma is another tumor that can be placed in an intermediate or borderline category. It typically presents as a small nodule in the sun-exposed skin of elderly individuals.[384,387] Less commonly, it appears as a large mass in the trunk and limbs of younger patients.[357] Some cases develop in parts of the body previously subjected to radiation therapy.[425] The differential diagnosis includes spindle cell squamous cell carcinoma and spindle cell (desmoplastic) malignant melanoma. Immunohistochemical stains for S-100 protein and keratin are useful in this differential diagnosis.[388] The large majority of atypical fibroxanthomas are cured by local excision,[357,371] but a few cases accompanied by metastases are on record.[365] This tumor type is discussed in more detail in Chapter 4.

Malignant fibrous histiocytoma (MFH) and related tumors. This tumor, also known as fibroxanthosarcoma and fibrohistiocytic sarcoma, is listed in most recent series as the most common type of soft tissue sarcoma. Many tumors formerly designated pleomorphic rhabdomyosarcoma or pleomorphic liposarcoma were renamed MFH in the 1970s and 1980s. However, as already mentioned, serious doubts have been raised about the existence of MFH as a specific entity.[352] It may well be that this designation embraces sarcomas of various types

(particularly fibrosarcomas) having some common morphologic features, such as pleomorphism and a storiform pattern of growth.[408] In retrospect, the somewhat arbitrary assumption that fibrosarcomas are almost never pleomorphic is at least partially responsible for the almost epidemic proportions that MFH reached some years ago.

Several morphologic variants of MFH have been described. **Storiform-pleomorphic MFH** is the prototypic and most common member of this group.[402,403,439,453] Most cases occur in the deep soft tissues of extremities in adults, with a peak in the seventh decade, but cases have also been recorded in children[426,432,445] (Fig. 25.33). Some develop at the site of previous radiation therapy.[424] Still others have appeared around an infarct or a foreign body or at the site of a surgical scar.[372] Nearly half of them involve the deep fascia or the substance of a skeletal muscle.[383,454] Often they are quite large at the time of excision. As the name indicates, the presence of highly pleomorphic tumor cells and a storiform pattern of growth are the two most important microscopic features, even if the latter is not essential for the diagnosis[401,402] (Fig. 25.34). Sometimes the cytoplasm of the giant tumor cells is seen to contain numerous variably sized hyaline globules, thought to be related to apoptosis and lugubriously called *thanatosomes*.[421] Inflammatory elements, such as lymphocytes, plasma cells, and eosinophils, are usually mixed with the neoplastic cells. Metaplastic bone and cartilage formation may be present focally.[329] Ultrastructurally, MFH consists of a mixture of cells resembling fibroblasts, myofibroblasts, histiocytes, and primitive mesenchymal cells.[374,369,390,443,447] Peculiar intranuclear inclusions consisting of closely packed undulating fibrils have been found

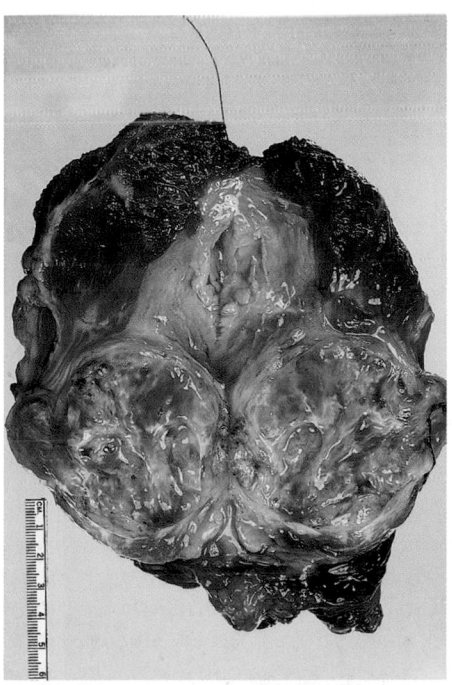

Fig. 25.33 Large malignant fibrous histiocytoma with areas of cystic change and necrosis.

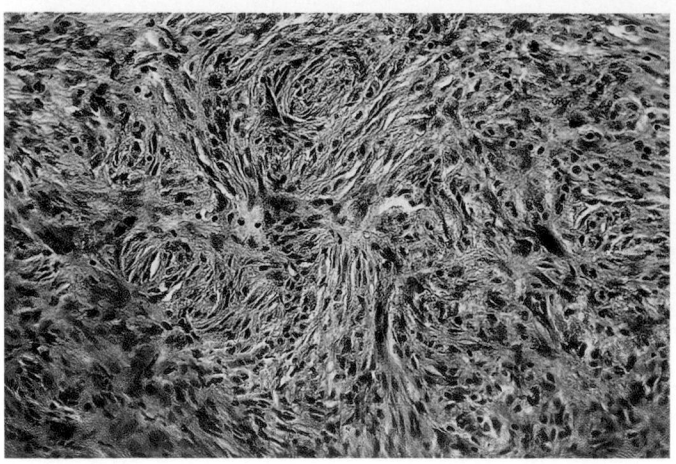
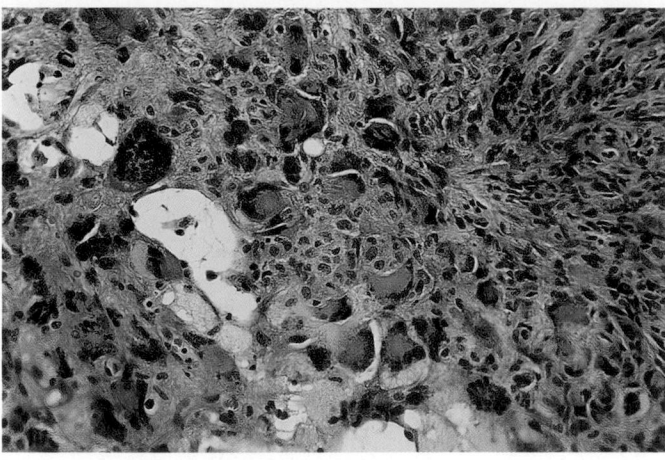

Fig. 25.34 Malignant fibrous histiocytoma of storiform–pleomorphic type: **A**, storiform pattern of growth; **B**, marked pleomorphism, with numerous multinucleated giant cells.

in some cases.[446] Immunohistochemically, there is usually reactivity for vimentin, α_1-antitrypsin, α_1-antichymotrypsin, KP-1 (CD68), factor XIIIa, ferritin, and the plasma proenzyme factor XIII, and sometimes also for actin, desmin, and lysozyme.[330,341,367,373,385,395,407,408,412,428,457] A variety of lysosomal enzymes have also been detected using standard enzyme histochemical techniques.[327,411] It should be remarked that none of these antigens are specific for histiocytes.[437] Some cases of MFH have also shown immunoreactivity for keratin.[368,396,431,433]

This tumor is prone to local recurrence and has the capacity to metastasize to distant sites, especially the lungs and regional lymph nodes.[439] The most important prognostic factors are size and depth of its location, two parameters that are closely related.[328,382,423,432,434] In the classic series of 200 cases reported by Weiss and Enzinger,[455] tumors that were small, were superficially located, or had a prominent inflammatory component (other than neutrophilic) metastasized only rarely.

Myxoid MFH is to be regarded as equivalent to **myxofibrosarcoma** the latter term being preferred at present.[322,386] Most of these tumors arise in the extremities of adults. They are usually attached to the fascia or within a major muscle, but they can also be very superficial.[396a] Grossly, they are mucoid and resemble myxoid liposarcomas (Fig. 25.35). Microscopically, the low-grade forms resemble liposarcoma by virtue of an abundant matrix of acid mucopolysaccharides, high vascularity, and the presence of cells resembling lipoblasts[362,405] (Fig. 25.36). They are identified by the presence elsewhere in the tumor of typical areas of MFH and the absence of true lipoblasts, which should contain neutral fat in the cytoplasmic vacuoles rather than acid mucopolysaccharides. Other features of differential value include the presence of a greater degree of pleomorphism in the myxoid areas and the fact that the vessels have a coarser quality. Some electron microscopic differences between the two have also been described.[391,448] The overall prognosis is better

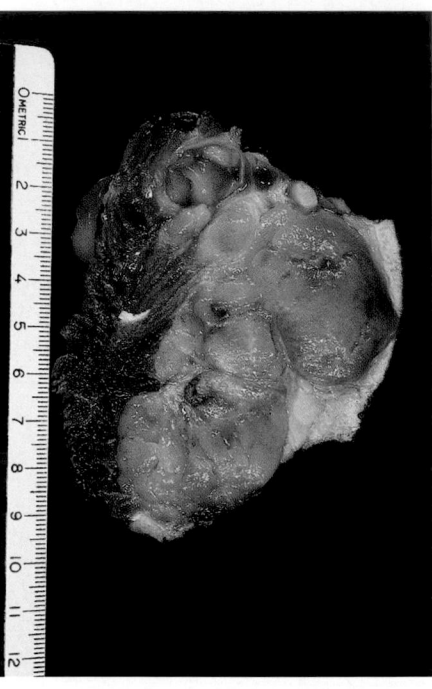

Fig. 25.35 Gross appearance of myxofibrosarcoma (myxoid MFH).

than for the conventional storiform-pleomorphic MFH.[455] Altered expression of cell cycle regulators (such as reduced expression of p21) is said to be a poor prognostic factor.[416a] There is a relationship between microscopic grade and prognosis, but even the lower grade tumors have a potential for recurrence.[370a]

Low-grade fibromyxoid sarcoma (Evans' tumor) is a soft tissue neoplasm characterized by alternating fibrous and myxoid areas, a focally whorled pattern of growth, low cellularity, and a bland appearance of the fibroblastic spindle cells[346,347] (Fig. 25.37). Areas of hypercellularity and necrosis may be present.[356] Both local recurrences and distant metastases have been common in the reported cases from a single source.[346,347,361] The main

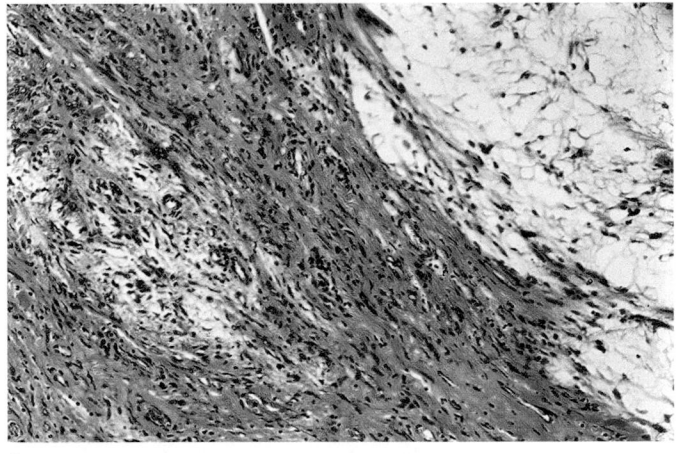

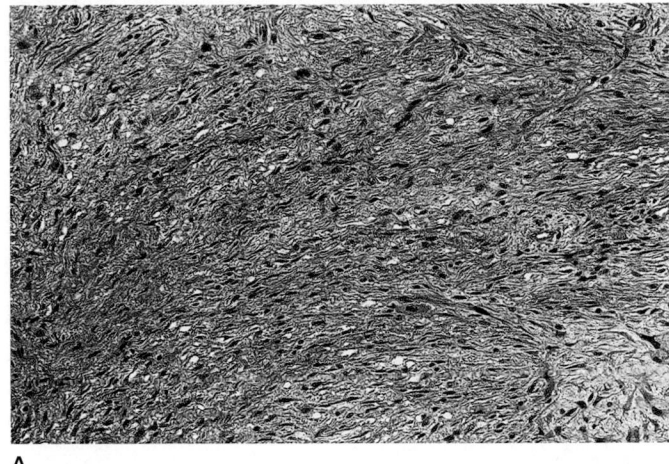

A

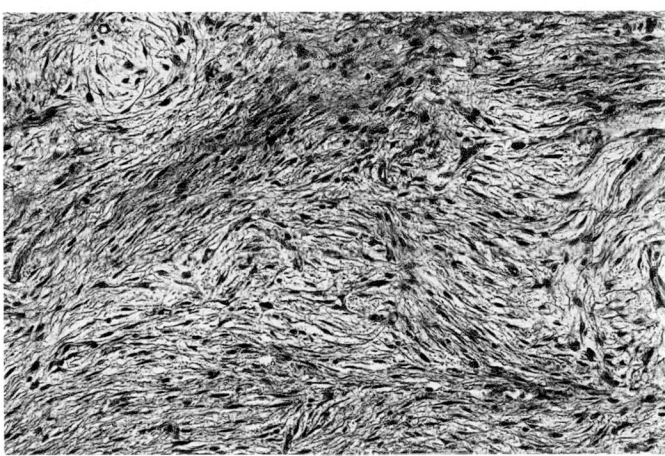

B

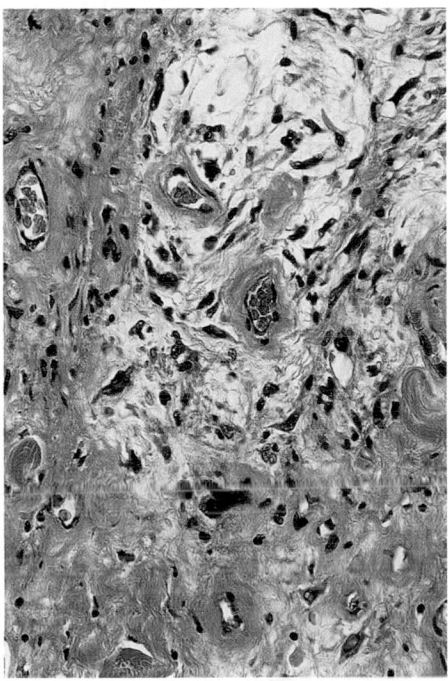

B

Fig. 25.37 A and B, Low- and high-power views of low-grade fibromyxoid sarcoma. There is very little pleomorphism. The fibrosis predominates over the myxoid change.

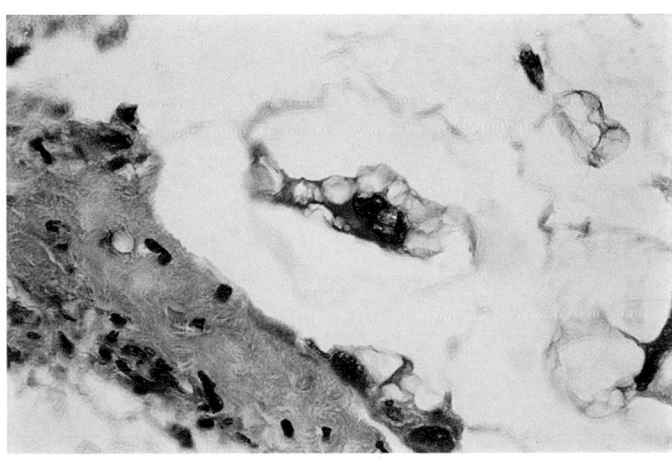

C

Fig. 25.36 Myxofibrosarcoma (myxoid MFH): **A**, alternation of cellular and myxoid areas; **B**, moderate pleomorphism of tumor cells; **C**, lipoblast-like tumor cells floating in myxoid material.

differential diagnosis is with myxofibrosarcoma. Low-grade fibromyxoid sarcoma is more fibrous and less myxoid, and the vascular network is less well developed.

It is now accepted that the neoplasm originally described as *hyalinizing spindle cell tumor with giant rosettes* is a morphologic variant of low-grade fibromyxoid sarcoma characterized by the presence of huge rosettelike formations made up of hyalinized collagen[392] (Fig. 25.38). The similarities also apply to the clinical behavior, including the capability for distant metastases.[356,418] These two tumor types also share the t(7;16)(q34;p11) translocation,[428a] and a variety of ultrastructural features.[356a]

Inflammatory myxohyaline tumor (acral myxoinflammatory fibroblastic sarcoma) is a low-grade malignant tumor usually found in the distal extremities that can simulate an inflammatory condition, Hodgkin's lymphoma, and various types of soft tissue sarcoma. Microscopically, it has an infiltrative multinodular quality and a polymorphic cellular composition in a hyaline or myxoid background (Fig. 25.39). There is a dense mononuclear inflammatory infiltrate containing scattered stromal cells of either epithelioid or spindle shape. Some of the latter are very large, with bizarre nuclei and prominent nucleoli, resulting in a resemblance to Reed–Sternberg cells or virus-infected cells.[399,409] The immunohistochemical profile, which is nonspecific, includes occasional focal

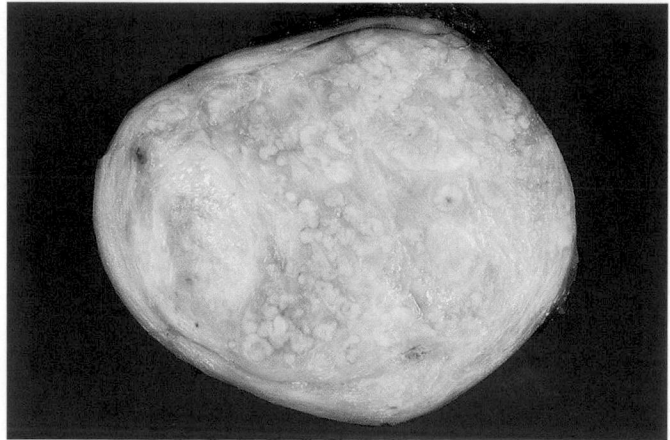

A

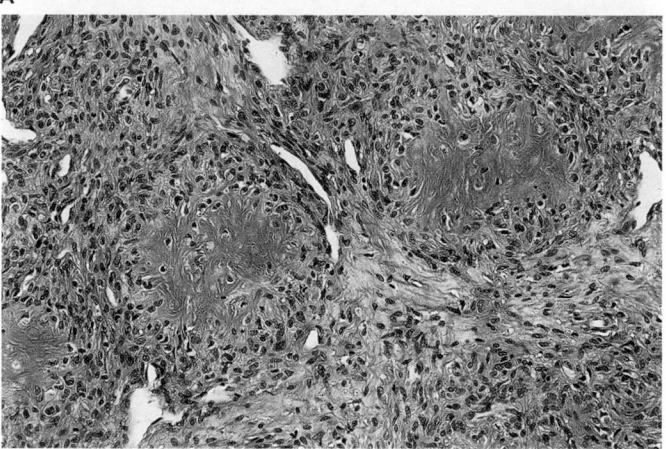

B

Fig. 25.38 Hyalinizing spindle cell tumor with giant rosettes: **A**, gross appearance of tumor located in anterior abdominal wall; **B**, giant rosettelike structures surrounded by tumor cells.

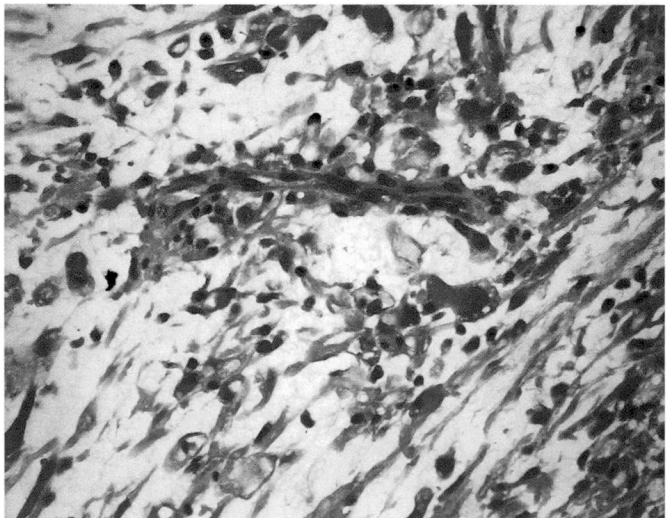

Fig. 25.39 Inflammatory myxohyaline tumor. Note the atypical cells with large nucleoli.

reactivity for keratin. Local recurrence is common, but distant metastases are exceptional.[435]

Plexiform fibrohistiocytic tumor occurs chiefly in children and young adults.[429] It usually presents as a small, slow-growing dermal or subcutaneous mass, often in an upper extremity. Microscopically, there is a multinodular or plexiform proliferation of fibroblast-like and histiocyte-like cells admixed with osteoclast-like giant cells[345] (Fig. 25.40). The immunohistochemical and ultrastructural features suggest a myofibroblastic derivation.[370] Local recurrence is very common, and a few cases have resulted in regional lymph node metastases.[345] We have seen several cases in which the typical appearance of this tumor type merged with a pattern highly reminiscent of neurothekeoma, suggesting a histogenetic link between the two entities.[377]

Inflammatory MFH is a tumor in which the neoplastic cells (some with a bland appearance and others that are bizarre and anaplastic) are mixed with, and even obscured by, an intense inflammatory infiltrate rich in neutrophils[389] (Fig. 25.41). Some of the tumor cells contain phagocytosed neutrophils in their cytoplasm. Storiform

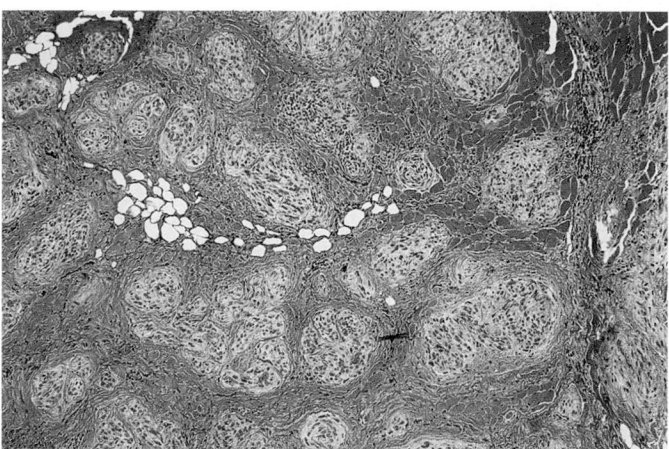

A

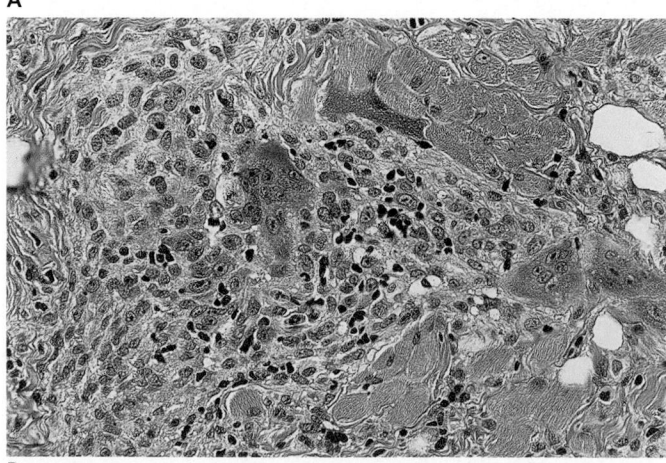

B

Fig. 25.40 A and **B**, Plexiform fibrohistiocytic tumor. **A**, Low-power view, showing nodular and plexiform pattern of growth. **B**, High-power view of one of the nodules, showing mononuclear tumor cells and scattered osteoclast-like giant cells.

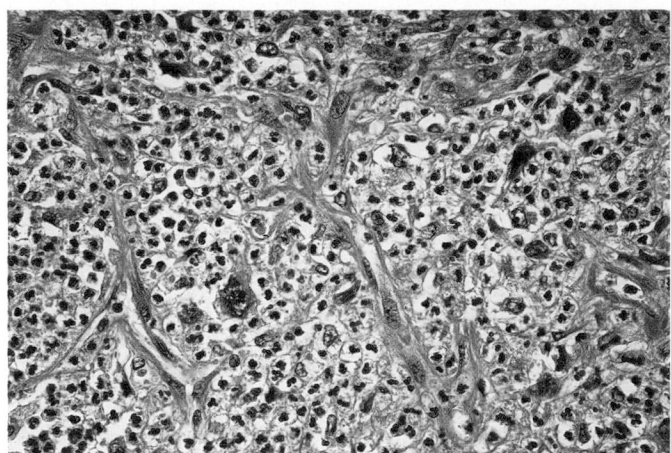

Fig. 25.41 So-called "inflammatory MFH." In this case the infiltrate is largely of neutrophilic nature.

pattern, collections of foamy cells, and areas of tissue necrosis are also consistently present. In all likelihood this is a pattern of growth rather than a specific tumor type, in the sense that the same microscopic appearance (i.e., intense neutrophilic infiltration in pleomorphic tumors associated with phagocytosis of neutrophils by the tumor cells) can be seen in otherwise typical liposarcomas, irradiated osteosarcomas, and metastatic carcinomas from various sites, such as lung, adrenal cortex, and kidney (Fig. 25.42). As a matter of fact, it would appear that most tumors with the inflammatory MFH pattern are dedifferentiated liposarcomas.[333a] Sometimes this tissue-inflammatory reaction is accompanied by a peripheral leukemoid reaction and eosinophilia.[451] In other instances the inflammatory infiltrate is predominantly composed of lymphocytes and plasma cells rather than neutrophils; in the case of liposarcomas, these tumors are referred to as lymphocyte-rich or inflammatory (see p. 2282).

Angiomatoid MFH usually appears in the extremities of children and young adults as a circumscribed, multinodular, or multicystic hemorrhagic mass[336,343,422] (Fig. 25.43). Occasional congenital examples have been

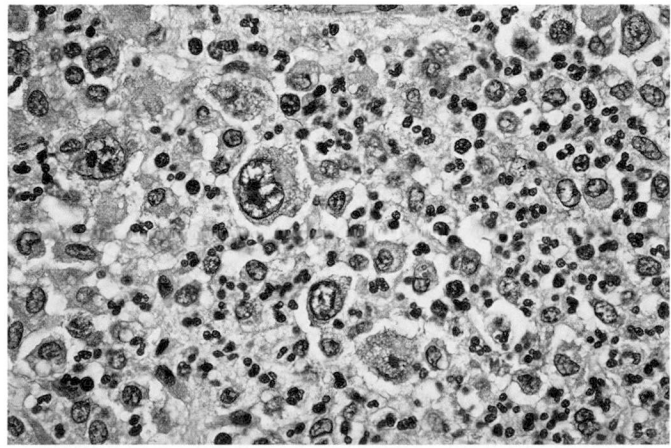

Fig. 25.42 Inflammatory MFH pattern in a case of lung carcinoma.

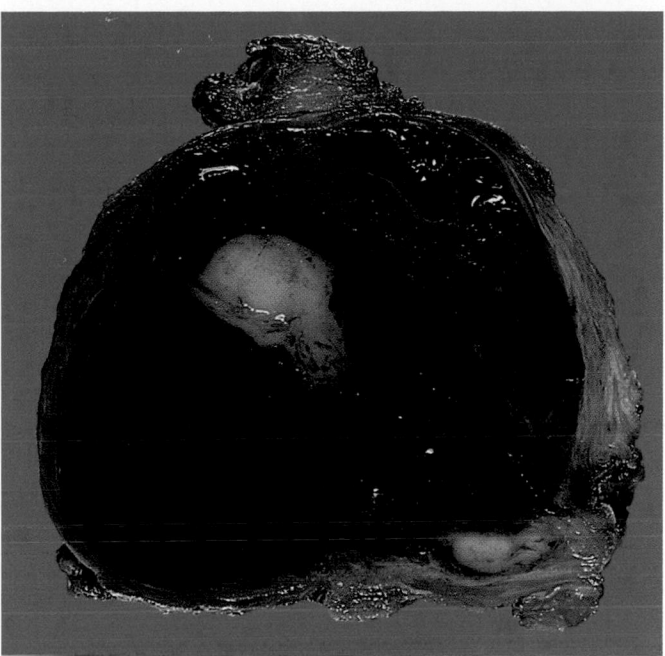

Fig. 25.43 Angiomatoid MFH. A small solid focus of white tumor is seen within a large hemorrhagic cyst. (Courtesy of Dr. Hector Rodriguez-Martinez, Mexico City)

described.[323] Microscopically, highly cellular foci are mixed with focal areas of hemorrhagic cyst-like spaces and large aggregates of chronic inflammatory cells. The latter are often arranged at the periphery of the tumor in the form of lymphoid follicles and may simulate the appearance of a lymph node (Fig. 25.44A,B).

Although this tumor was originally placed under the MFH umbrella on the basis of morphologic, immunohistochemical, and ultrastructural features,[438,446] several studies have provided evidence to suggest a vascular or myoid nature.[348,351,381,440] Also, immunoreactivity for desmin has been found in over half of the cases[351] (Fig. 25.44C). We favor the interpretation that angiomatoid MFH is a tumor of vessel-related myoid cells with associated inflammatory features. Indeed, we have seen several cases in which the typical features of this entity merged with those of an inflammation-free component having hemangiopericytoid/glomoid features (Fig. 25.45). We have also seen cases lacking the central hemorrhagic cavity, as if they were the "solid variant" of this tumor type (Fig. 25.46).

Angiomatoid MFH is a low-grade malignant tumor that has a tendency for local recurrence and that can also metastasize distantly.[336,343] It is important to recognize that perfectly benign dermal fibrous histiocytomas (so-called "dermatofibromas") also can be accompanied by hemorrhagic foci and that this does not endow them with any particular aggressive behavior[436] (see Chapter 4).

Most of the retroperitoneal and mediastinal lesions formerly called **xanthogranuloma**[415] are examples of fibrous histiocytomas (usually malignant), whereas

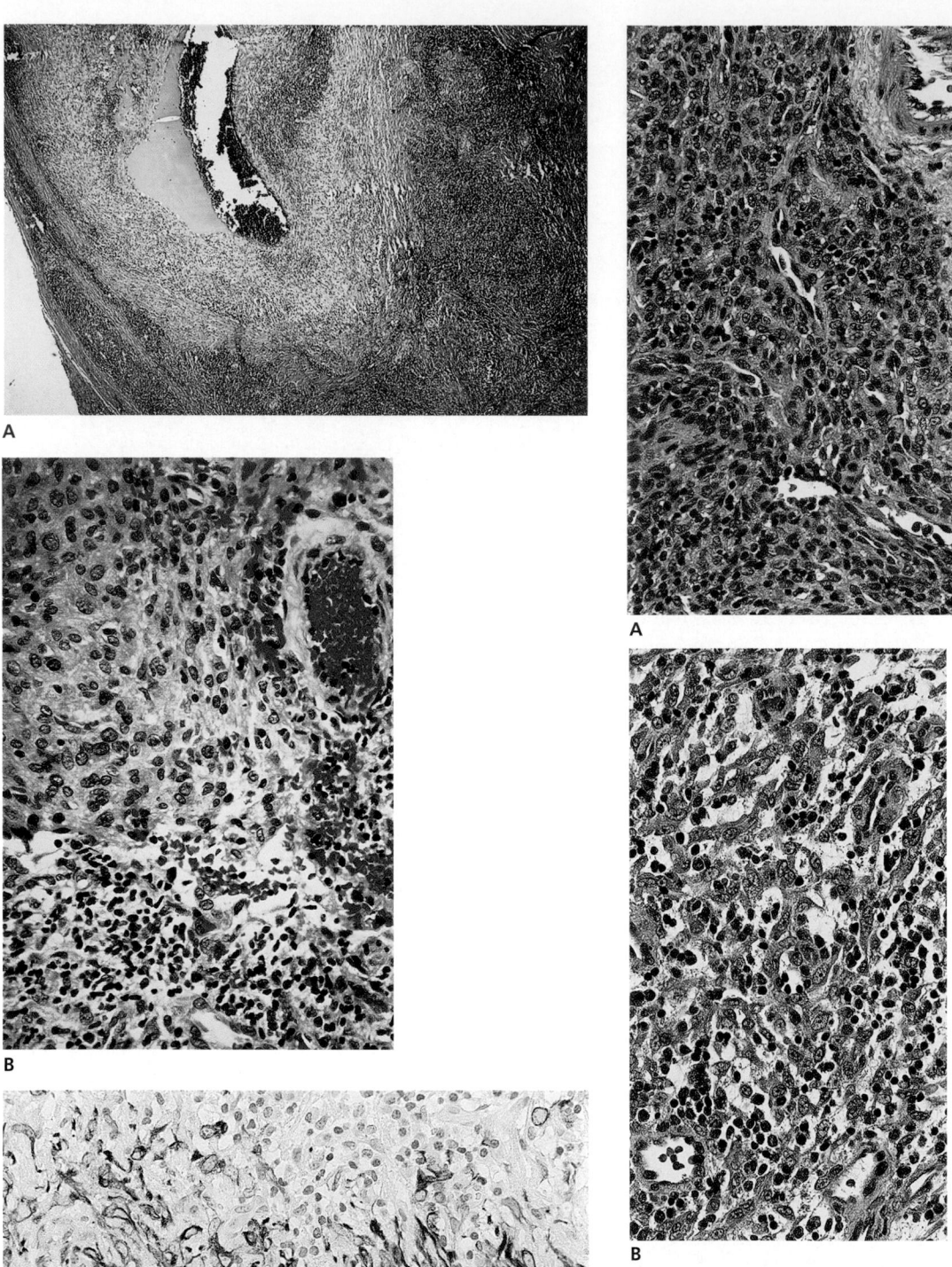

Fig. 25.44 A to **C**, Angiomatoid MFH. **A**, Low-power view showing a blood-filled space surrounded by a wall of tumor cells and a peripheral rim of lymphocytes. **B**, High-power view of the tumor cell component. **C**, Strong immunoreactivity for desmin.

Fig. 25.45 Angiomatoid MFH (**A**) blending with tumor tissue having a glomangiopericytoid appearance (**B**).

others probably represent idiopathic mediastinal or retroperitoneal inflammatory fibrosclerosis, malakoplakia, or Rosai–Dorfman disease[334] (see Chapter 21). We think therefore that the term xanthogranuloma should not be used as a specific diagnosis.

It has been suggested that epithelioid sarcoma and malignant giant cell tumor of soft parts also represent malignant tumors of histiocytes; however, until more definite evidence for this is obtained, it is preferable to

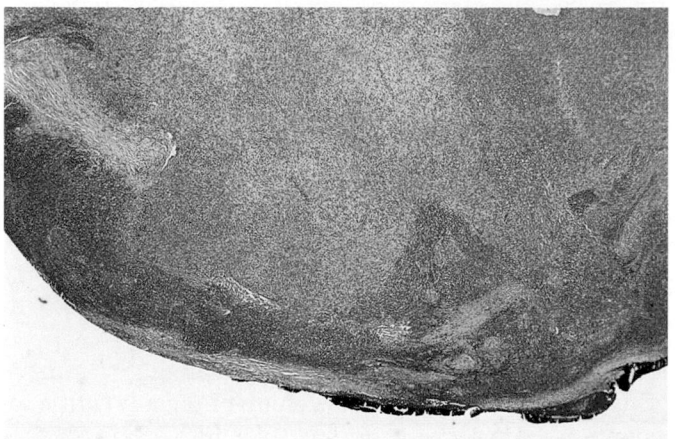
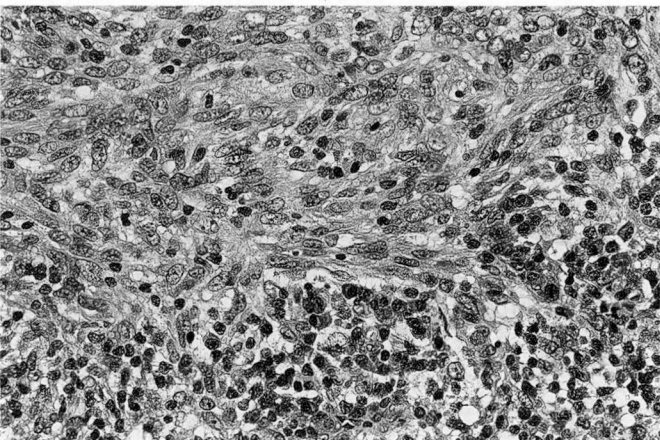

Fig. 25.46 A and **B**, Soft tissue tumor with an angiomatoid MFH pattern but lacking the central hemorrhagic area.

categorize them as tumors of uncertain cell type (see pp. 2321 and 2323, respectively).

The microscopic appearance of benign and malignant fibrous histiocytoma can be closely simulated by a number of benign and malignant conditions, including malakoplakia,[334] silica reaction,[456] histioid leprosy, and metastatic carcinoma (particularly from the kidney).

Tumors and tumorlike conditions of peripheral nerves

Proliferative lesions of peripheral nerves are divided into non-neoplastic (such as traumatic neuroma), benign tumors (such as schwannomas, neurofibromas, and perineuriomas), and malignant tumors, collectively designated as malignant peripheral nerve sheath tumors (MPNST). Despite the fact that these lesions may overlap and coexist with each other, it is important to make a distinction among them in view of their markedly different natural history. For a discussion on the features of schwannoma and neurofibroma in the mediastinum and retroperitoneal area, see Chapters 8 and 26, respectively.

Neuroma

The large majority of neuromas follow trauma—hence their designation as **traumatic neuromas**. When a peripheral nerve is severed or crushed, the proximal end regenerates, and if it fails to meet the distal end, a tangled mass of nerve fibers results. Microscopically, all the elements of a nerve can be recognized: axons, Schwann's cells, perineurial cells, and fibroblasts (Fig. 25.47). In addition, scar tissue is often present. Not surprisingly, this lesion may be exquisitely painful. Immunohistochemically, the Schwann's cells of traumatic neuroma show aberrant expression of the macrophage-associated antigens CD68 and Ki-M1-P, in keeping with the macrophagic properties that they are known to acquire under these circumstances.[463] **Amputation neuroma**, a term made popular during the First World War, is a type of traumatic neuroma in which the original trauma involves the loss of part or all of an extremity.

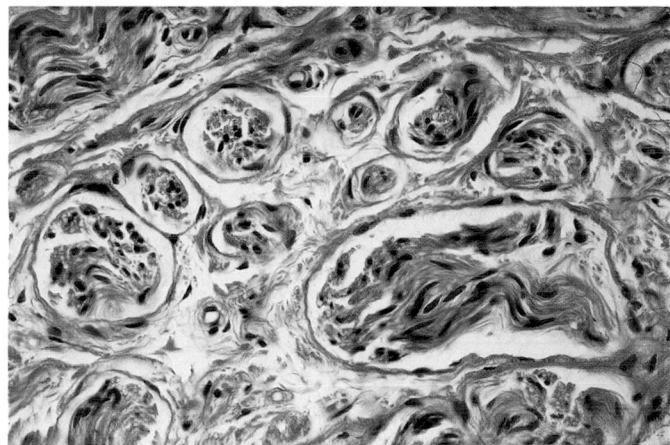

Fig. 25.47 Traumatic neuroma. The haphazardly distributed nerve trunks are surrounded by fibrous tissue.

Morton's neuroma (Morton's metatarsalgia) can be regarded as a subtype of traumatic neuroma caused by repeated mild trauma to the region.[462] Its typical location is the interdigital plantar nerve between the third and fourth toes. The lesion is more common in female adults. Microscopically, the affected nerve is markedly distorted. There is extensive perineurial fibrosis often arranged in a concentric fashion. The arterioles are thickened and sometimes occluded by thrombi.[464,465]

Palisaded encapsulated neuroma (solitary circumscribed neuroma) presents as a small, solitary, asymptomatic papule in the skin (see Chapter 4). Its most common location is the face of middle-aged individuals. Microscopically, the lesion is centered in the dermis (in contrast to schwannoma, which is rarely seen in this location) and is characterized by a proliferation of Schwann's cells and numerous axons located within a capsule derived from perineurium.[461] Immunohistochemically, the Schwann's cells are reactive for S-100 protein, the axons for neurofilaments, and the capsule for EMA, indicating the presence of perineurial cells.[459,460]

Schwannoma (neurilemoma)

Schwannoma (neurilemoma) is one of the few *truly encapsulated* neoplasms of the human body and is almost always solitary. Its most common locations are the flexor surfaces of the extremities, neck, mediastinum, retroperitoneum, posterior spinal roots, and cerebellopontine angle.[502] The nerve of origin often can be demonstrated in the periphery, flattened along the capsule but not penetrating the substance of the tumor (Fig. 25.48). Since this is a benign neoplasm that only rarely recurs locally, every attempt should be made to preserve the nerve, if this is of any clinical significance (e.g., facial nerve or vagus nerve).

Grossly, the larger schwannomas often contain cystic areas (Fig. 25.49). The microscopic appearance is distinctive. Two different patterns usually can be recognized, designated by Antoni as A and B. The type A areas, which in small tumors comprise almost their entirety, are quite cellular, composed of spindle cells often arranged in a palisading fashion or in an organoid arrangement (Verocay bodies) (Fig. 25.50).

In type B areas the tumor cells are separated by abundant edematous fluid that may form cystic spaces. Occasionally, isolated cells with bizarre hyperchromatic nuclei are observed[497]; they are particularly common in so-called *ancient schwannomas* and are of no particular significance[472] (Fig. 25.51). Mitoses are usually absent or extremely scanty. Blood vessels can be of such prominence as to simulate a vascular neoplasm (Fig. 25.52). By electron microscopy, they have been found to be of the fenestrated type, a rather surprising feature.[488] Thrombosis and hyaline thickening of the adventitia are common. Sometimes, large nodular masses of collagen with radiating edges are seen, a feature sometimes descriptively designated as "amianthoid" fibers or collagenous spherules. The majority of soft tissue tumors exhibiting these formations are of peripheral nerve sheath derivation,[471,505,506] but this does not apply to

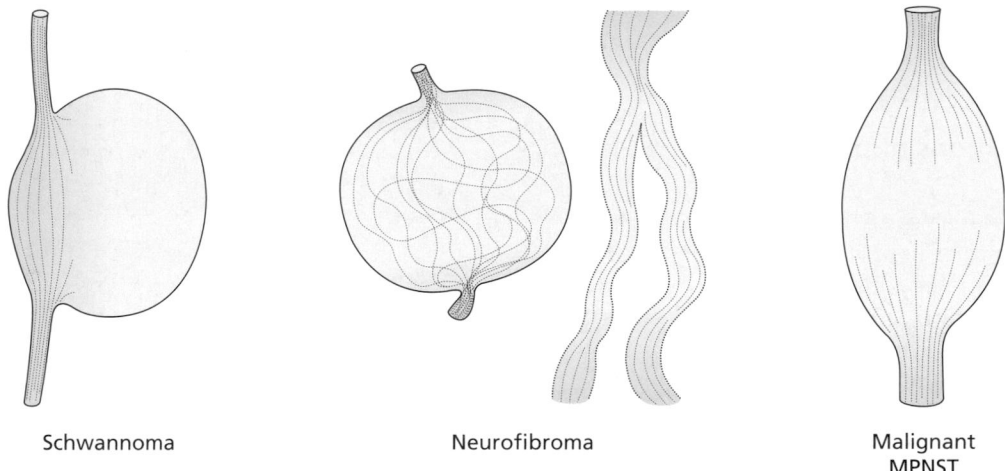

Schwannoma   Neurofibroma   Malignant MPNST

Fig. 25.48 Schematic drawing emphasizing the main differences between the three major types of peripheral nerve tumors. Note diameter of nerve involved and behavior of neurites (thin black lines) in relation to neoplasm.

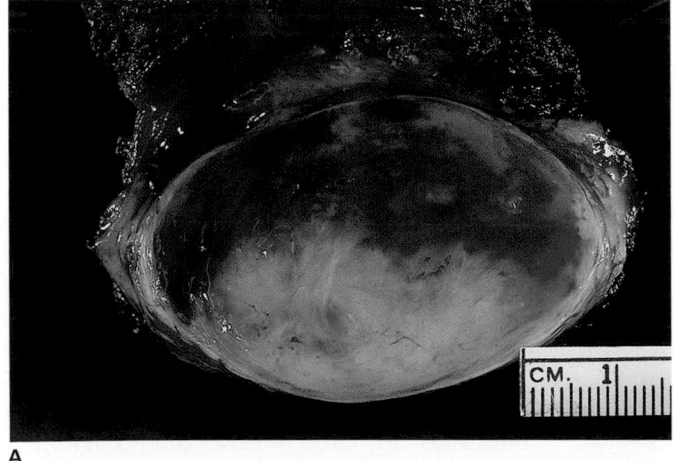

A

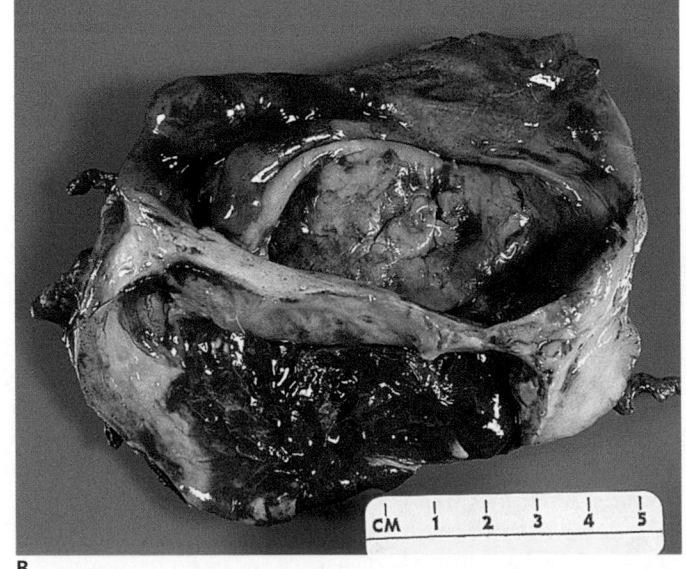

B

Fig. 25.49 A and **B**, Gross appearances of schwannoma. The tumor shown in **B** has undergone marked secondary cystic changes.

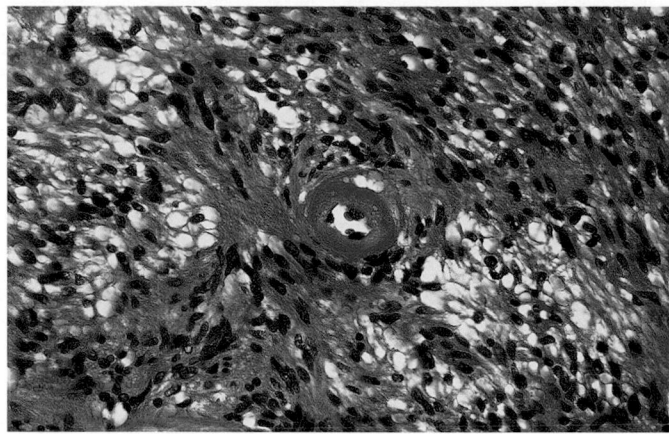

Fig. 25.50 Schwannoma with a suggestion of nuclear palisading and hyaline thickening of vessel walls.

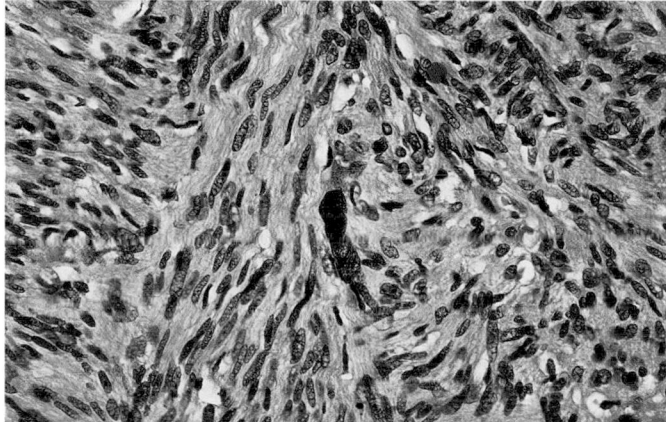

Fig. 25.51 Large hyperchromatic nuclei in schwannoma. This is not necessarily an indication of malignant change.

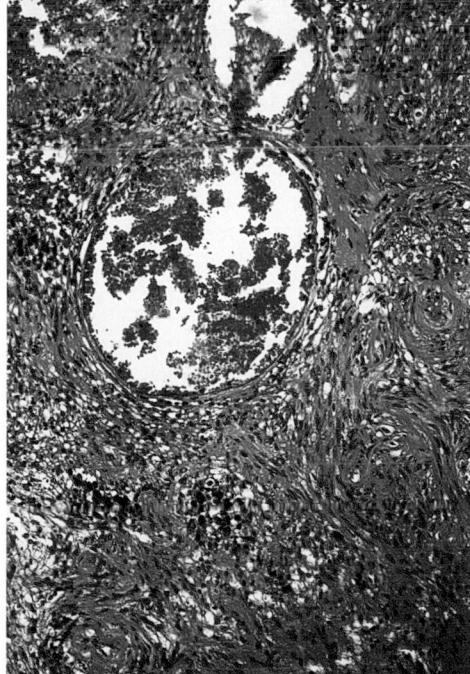

Fig. 25.52 Schwannoma showing large vascular spaces that may lead to confusion with a vascular neoplasm. Hemosiderin-laden macrophages are also present as evidence of previous hemorrhage.

lesions of lymph nodes containing similar structures (see Chapter 21).

Palisading of nuclei is not unique to schwannoma. It can also occur in leiomyoma, leiomyosarcoma, GIST, calcifying aponeurotic fibroma, and even in non-neoplastic smooth muscle (most commonly in the appendiceal wall). Axons are not present, except in the portion of the capsule where the nerve is attached. Collections of foamy macrophages are sometimes seen, especially in the larger neoplasms. More unusual is the presence of clusters of granular cell similar to those seen in granular cell tumors.[468] The rare occurrence of plexiform areas in schwannoma may cause them to be mistaken for neurofibroma.[478,493] Epithelioid areas can also be present, although much less commonly than in MPNST.[481,508] When these areas predominate, the tumor has been referred to as *benign epithelioid schwannoma*.[495] A few cases containing a glandular component have been described (*benign glandular schwannomas*)[466,503]; care should be exercised to rule out the possibility of sweat gland entrapment before making this diagnosis.

Rare schwannomas are found to contain melanin pigment.[507] When this feature is prominent and accompanied by psammoma body formation, the possibility of the tumor representing a psammomatous melanotic schwannoma should be considered[467] (see subsequent sections).

Exceptionally, otherwise typical schwannomas or those with epithelioid features have been found to contain foci of small, round hyperchromatic Schwann's cells with scanty cytoplasm, sometimes forming rosettes and simulating neuroblastoma.[475,483]

It is generally agreed that the neoplasm described in this section originates from Schwann's cells, hence the current preference for the term schwannoma for it.[477] By electron microscopy, the tumor cells have a continuous basal lamina; numerous, extremely thin cytoplasmic processes; aggregates of intracytoplasmic microfibrils; peculiar intracytoplasmic lamellar bodies; and extracellular long-spacing collagen[474,482,489,509] (Fig. 25.53). Parenthetically, the latter feature is not specific for peripheral nerve cell tumors.[476] Immunohistochemically, the tumor cells show immunoreactivity for S-100 protein, calcineurin, basal lamina components (such as laminin, type IV collagen, and merosin), vimentin, nerve growth factor receptor, lipocortin-1, and sometimes glial fibrillary acidic protein and KP-l (CD68)[473,482,484–486,490–492,494,496,498,499,501,504] (Fig. 25.54). Whether they also exhibit positivity for myelin markers—such as myelin basic protein and P2 protein—remains a disputed issue.[470] Keratin, desmoplakin, neurofilaments, and desmin are not expressed.[485]

Malignant transformation of schwannoma is—in contrast to neurofibroma—an exceptionally rare event. However, several indubitable cases are on record.[487,512] Interestingly, in most of them the malignant component has exhibited an epithelioid morphology.

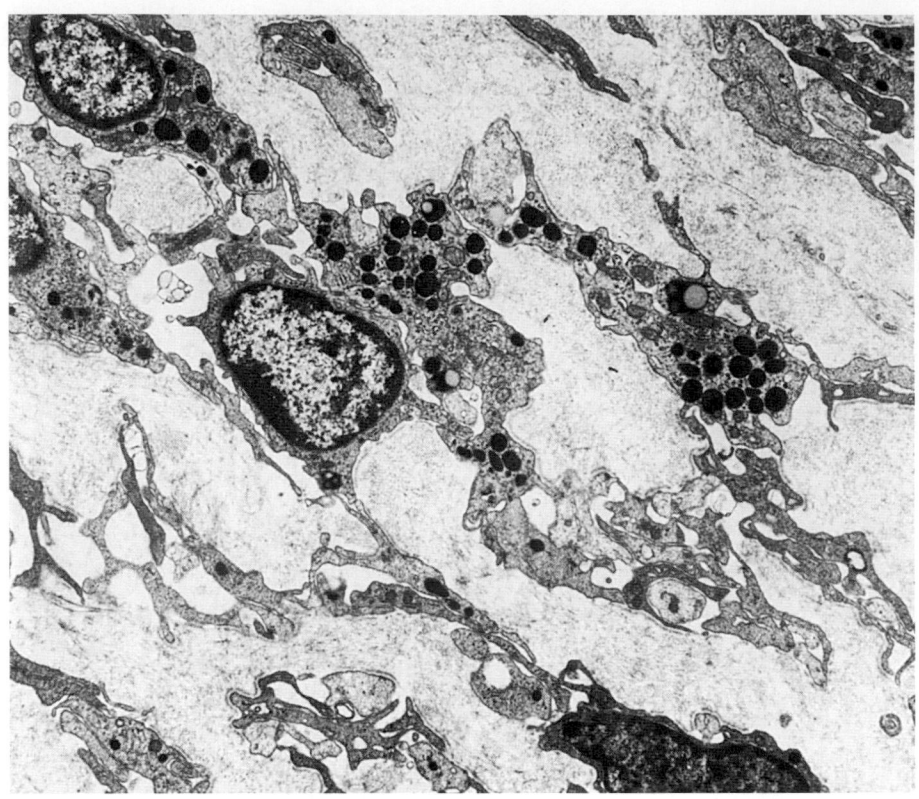

Fig. 25.53 Electron microscopic appearance of schwannoma of retroperitoneum. Elongated cells with processes are partially covered by basal lamina. Cells contain lipid of varied density.

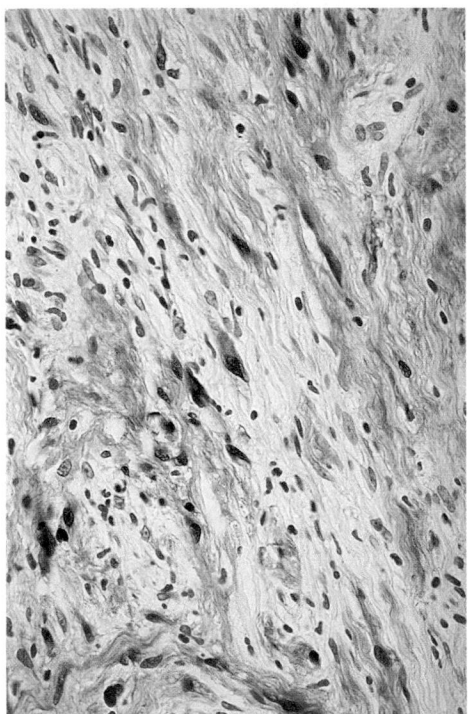

Fig. 25.54 S-100 protein immunoreactivity in schwannoma.

Cellular schwannoma is the term used for highly cellular schwannomas that are exclusively composed of Antoni A areas but lack Verocay bodies[479,511] (Fig. 25.55). These changes can be accompanied by nuclear atypia, mitotic activity, and focal necrosis. Most reported cases have been in the retroperitoneum, pelvis,

and mediastinum.[469,510] The differential diagnosis with a low-grade MPNST remains a difficult and controversial subject.

Psammomatous melanotic schwannoma is a distinctive type of peripheral nerve sheath tumor that occurs as a component of the Carney's syndrome.[467] Most arise from the spinal nerve roots.[480,499] As the name indicates, the tumor is characterized microscopically by the presence of melanin pigmentation and the deposition of psammoma bodies (Fig. 25.56). In contrast to all other types of schwannoma described in this section, the psammomatous melanotic variety is regarded as a low-grade malignancy because of its tendency for local recurrence and the fact that a few of the reported cases have metastasized.[467]

Neurofibroma

The gross, microscopic, and ultrastructural features of neurofibroma, as well as its natural history, are distinct from those of schwannoma.[560] The fact that in some instances the differential diagnosis may be difficult or that in isolated cases features of both lesions may coexist does not justify lumping them together.

The gross appearance of neurofibroma varies a great deal from lesion to lesion. As a rule, the tumors are not encapsulated and have a softer consistency than schwannoma (Fig. 25.57). The more superficial tumors appear as small, soft, pedunculated nodules protruding from the skin ("molluscum pendulum"). Deeper tumors grow larger. Tumors resulting in diffuse tortuous enlargement of peripheral nerves are designated as *plexiform neurofi-*

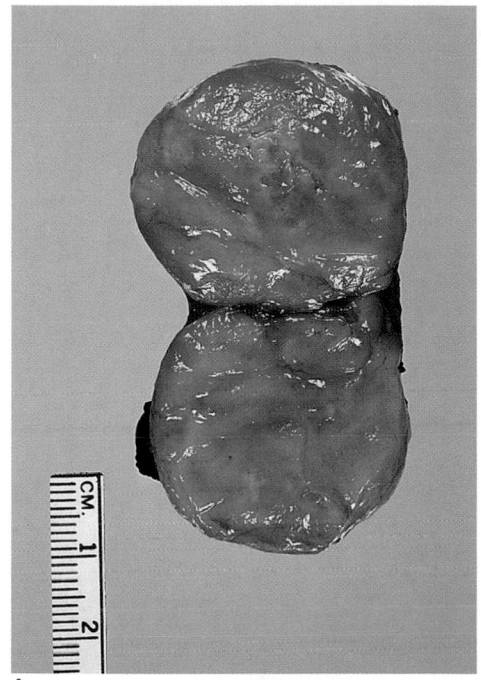

A

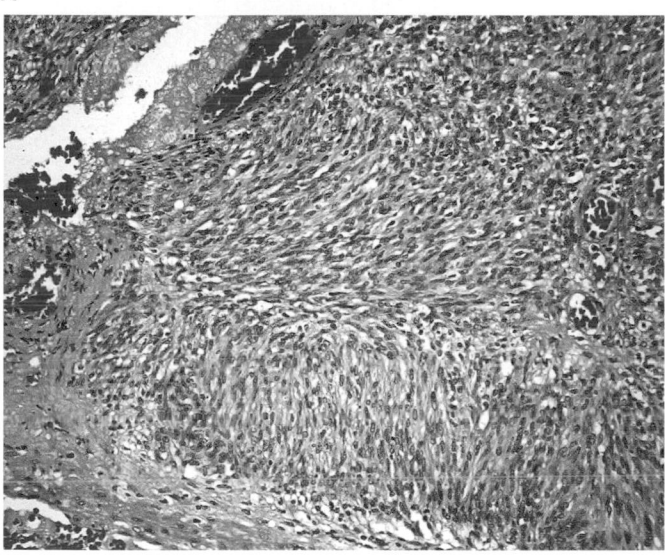

B

Fig. 25.55 Cellular schwannoma: **A**, gross appearance; **B**, microscopic appearance. The tumor has a homogeneous hypercellular quality.

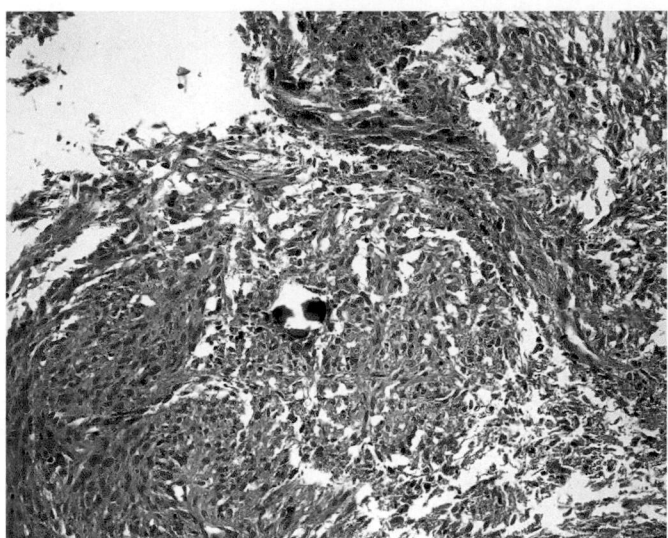

Fig. 25.56 Melanocytic psammomatous schwannoma in a patient with Carney's syndrome.

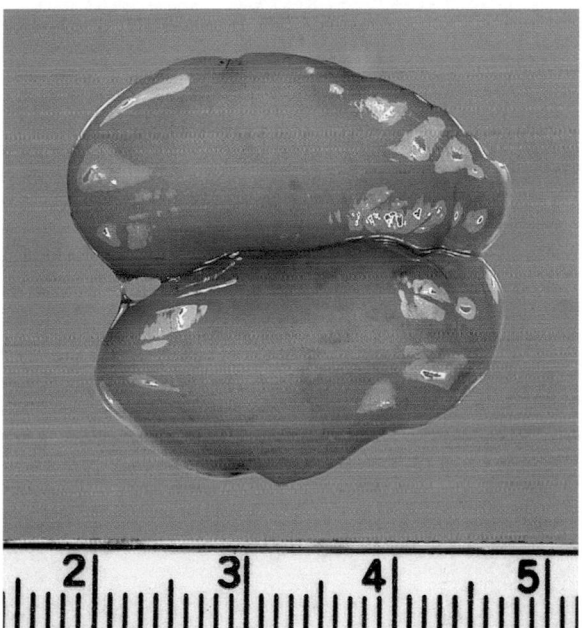

Fig. 25.57 Well-circumscribed neurofibroma of soft tissue. The tumor has a gelatinous appearance.

bromas and are usually seen in the context of type I neurofibromatosis[546] (Fig. 25.58). The diffuse involvement of the nerves may make a complete resection impossible. This particular form of neurofibroma is more commonly seen in the orbit, neck, back, and inguinal region.

Microscopically, neurofibromas are formed by a combined proliferation of all the elements of a peripheral nerve: axons, Schwann's cells, fibroblasts, and (in the plexiform type) perineurial cells (Fig. 25.59). Axons can be demonstrated by silver or acetylcholinesterase stains or by immunostaining for neuron-specific enolase, neurofilaments, or various neuropeptides.[539,563] Schwann's

cells usually represent the predominant cellular element. Most have markedly elongated nuclei, with a wavy, serpentine configuration and pointed ends (Fig. 25.60). Ultrastructurally, they are seen to enclose axons in plasmalemmal invaginations (mesaxons)[564] (Fig. 25.61). They are immunoreactive for S-100 protein and surrounded by basement membrane components.[521] A population of factor XIIIa-positive and CD34-positive cells is also present; the nature of these cells and their histogenetic relationship with normal nerve constituents is not clear.[561,566] EMA-positive perineurial cells are common in plexiform but not in ordinary neurofibromas.[562] Immunoreactivity for PGP 9.5 is the rule, but its degree of specificity in rela-

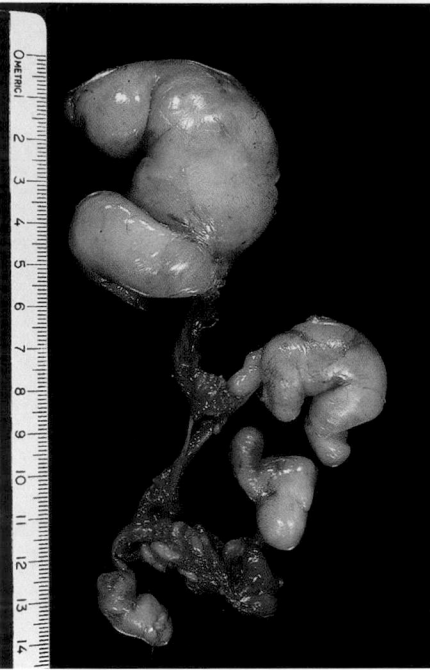

Fig. 25.58 Typical gross appearance of plexiform neurofibroma. This tumor variety is indicative of Recklinghausen's disease.

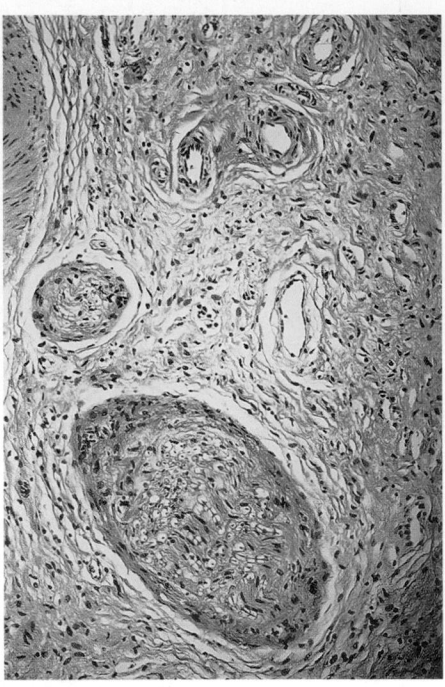

Fig. 25.59 Neurofibroma with plexiform features.

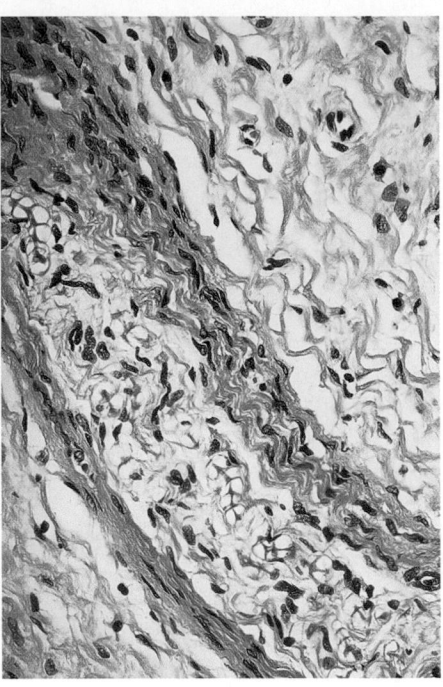

Fig. 25.60 The nuclei of the tumor cells of neurofibroma show a typical fascicular pattern of growth and serpentine shape.

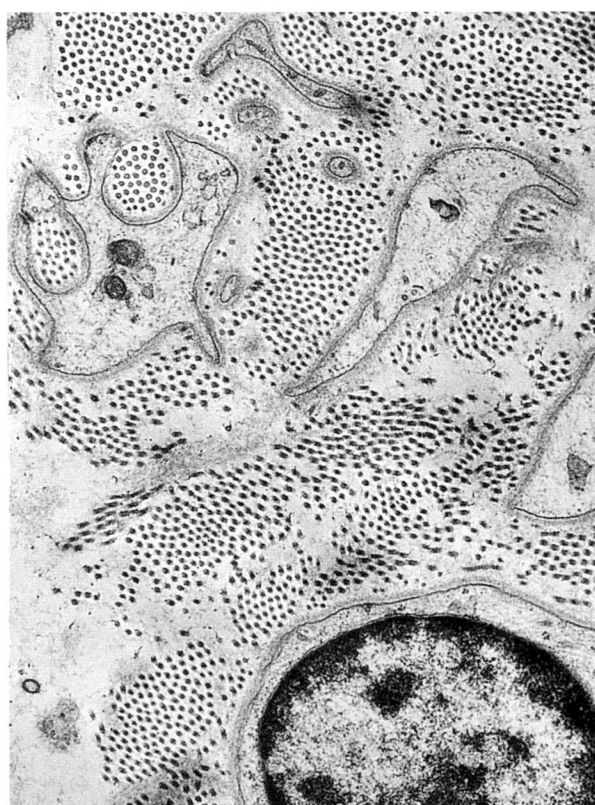

Fig. 25.61 Electron microscopic appearance of plexiform neurofibroma in a patient with Recklinghausen's neurofibromatosis. This area shows Schwann cell processes, one of which (upper left) is enveloping collagen fibrils. Note the continuous basal lamina. (×14,900; courtesy of Dr. Robert A. Erlandson, Memorial Sloan-Kettering Cancer Center)

tion to other nerve sheath tumors and other mesenchymal neoplasm is very low.[520a] The stroma contains a rich network of collagen fibers, among which almost all major types are represented (I, III, IV, V, and VI).[521,549,550] Mucinous changes in the stroma may be prominent and result in a mistaken diagnosis of myxoma or myxoid liposarcoma.[547] As with schwannomas, neurofibromas may exhibit scattered large hyperchromatic nuclei; these *neurofibromas with atypia* may also have increased cellularity but mitotic activity is scanty or absent, and the MIB-1 index is very low[541] (Fig. 25.62).

The stroma of neurofibromas often contains numerous mast cells.[537,552] Distorted organoid structures resembling Wagner–Meissner or Pacini's corpuscles are sometimes seen. Tumors in which these formations are particularly prominent have sometimes been designated as *tumors of tactile end organs*, and *pacinian neurofibromas*, respectively.[532,538,542,556] There is some question, however, as to whether the latter lesions are of neoplastic or hyperplastic nature.[526]

In contrast to schwannomas, Verocay bodies, palisading of nuclei, and hyaline thickening of the vessel wall are almost always absent in neurofibromas. Sometimes, otherwise typical neurofibromas are seen to contain melanin, a feature not unexpected in view of the embryologic relationship between Schwann's cells and melanocytes.[516,518] These *pigmented neurofibromas* should be differentiated from blue nevi and malignant melanomas.[524] Occasionally, an otherwise typical neurofibroma will show foci of skeletal muscle differentiation (*neuromuscular hamartoma*).[513,544] Some neurofibromas (as well as other

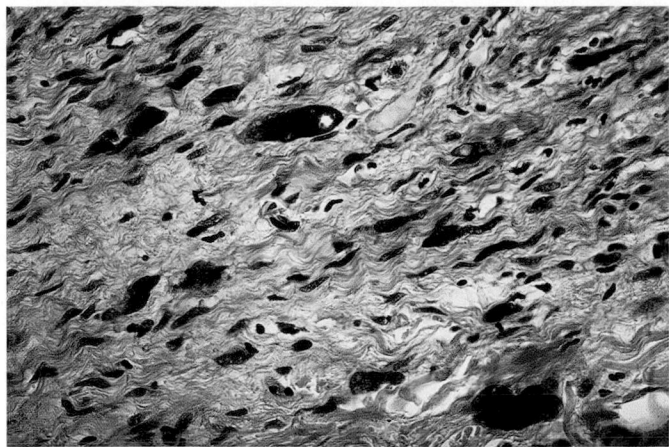

Fig. 25.62 Neurofibroma with large bizarre hyperchromatic nuclei.

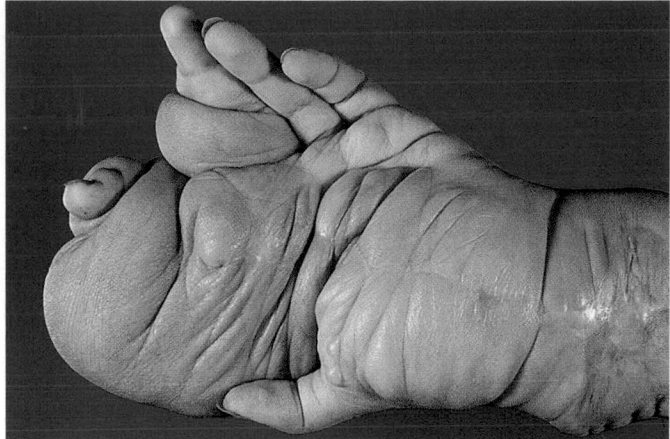

Fig. 25.63 Marked deformation of distal upper extremity by diffuse neurofibromatosis. This patient developed a malignant peripheral nerve sheath tumor.

types of benign and malignant peripheral nerve tumors) may be partially composed of granular cells, similar in all respects to those of granular cell tumor.[525] Still others—of somewhat disputed histogenesis—have a dendritic cell morphology and contain pseudorosettes.[548]

Malignant transformation of neurofibroma should be suspected in the presence of frequent mitoses, overly expressed cell proliferation markers, and the presence of p53 in many tumor cells.[540]

Neurofibromatosis (Recklinghausen's disease). Multiple neurofibromas represent the most important component of the genetically determined disorder known as neurofibromatosis or Recklinghausen's disease type I.[522,551] This is one of the most common autosomal dominant diseases in humans, the prevalence being 1 in 2500 to 3300. The responsible gene (*NF1*) is located near the centromere of chromosome 17[514,527,570] and encodes a ubiquitous protein known as neurofibromin, which is necessary for the correct negative regulation of *ras* proteins.[515,523,530,531] It has been shown that the tumors developing in this syndrome require a loss of *NF1* in the cells destined to become neoplastic, as well as heterozygosity in the non-neoplastic cells.[571] In neurofibromatosis type I, neurofibromas may occur in every conceivable site: axilla, thigh, buttock, deep-lying soft tissue, orbit, mediastinum, retroperitoneum, tongue, gastrointestinal tract, and many others.[553] Plexiform neurofibromas may result in massive enlargement of a limb or some other part of the body ("elephantiasis neuromatosa") (Fig. 25.63). In addition to neurofibromas, patients with type I Recklinghausen's disease often have many other associated lesions, the most common being the *café au lait spot*. This consists microscopically of an increase in the amount of melanin in the epidermal basal layer and is sometimes seen overlying a neurofibroma. It can be distinguished from the pigmented spots associated with Albright's syndrome by virtue of its distribution and smooth, delicate margins.[517] Solitary café au lait spots are common in normal individuals.

Only when they are present in a number of five or more can a significant association with neurofibromatosis be detected.[568] Other lesions sometimes seen in patients with Recklinghausen's disease include congenital malformations of various types,[533] megacolon, various types of vascular lesions,[543,555] fibrosing alveolitis,[565] schwannoma, lipoma, pheochromocytoma, neuroblastoma,[520,569] ganglioneuroma,[545] carcinoid tumor,[535] gastrointestinal stromal tumor,[528] and Wilms' tumor.[519,559] Increased serum levels of nerve growth factor have been detected in these patients.[557]

Type II (central) Recklinghausen's disease is genetically different from type I, resulting from an alteration of a gene located in chromosome 22.[554,567] It is characterized by the presence of a variety of neoplasms in the central nervous system, the most distinctive of which are bilateral acoustic schwannomas (see Chapter 28). Meningiomas, astrocytomas, and tumors of other types also occur.[536]

A small proportion of patients with type I neurofibromatosis develop MPNST. The incidence quoted ranges between 5% and 13%.[534,558] The malignant tumors arise almost always in *large* nerve trunks of the neck or extremities. For practical purposes, peripheral superficial neurofibromas never become malignant, and the only reasons for surgical removal are size and unsightliness. An increased incidence of nonlymphatic leukemia seems to exist in patients with type I Recklinghausen's disease.[529]

Perineurioma

Benign tumors of the peripheral nerve composed predominantly or exclusively of perineurial cells are now recognized.[587] Microscopically, they are composed of extremely elongated cells arranged in parallel bundles, the appearance being not too dissimilar from that of neurofibroma or pacinian neurofibroma (Fig. 25.64). Some cases have a storiform pattern of growth and may

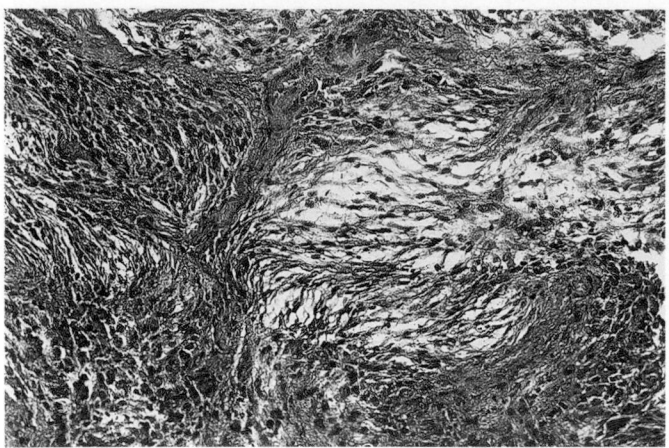 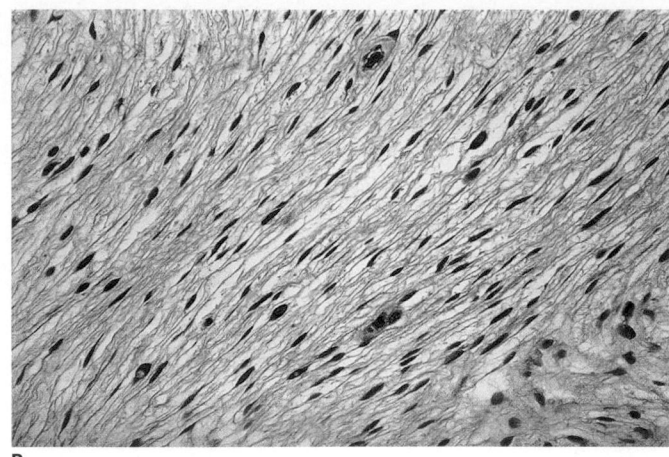

A **B**

Fig. 25.64 A and **B**, Two morphologic aspects of perineurioma. The tumor shown in **A** can simulate myxofibrosarcoma.

correspond to the former *storiform perineurial fibromas*.[582] The diagnosis of perineurioma should be suspected in myxoid lesions of soft tissue in which a storiform or fascicular pattern of growth is evident.[583,588] It has been argued whether so-called *localized hypertrophic neuropathy*[573,586] is a non-neoplastic condition or an intraneurial variant of perineurioma, but the documented presence of nonrandom chromosomal aberrations favors the latter.[578] Other recently recognized variants of this tumor include *sclerosing perineurioma*, which has a predilection for the fingers and palms of young adults,[576] and *reticular perineurioma*, with a predominant lace-like or reticular growth pattern composed of anastomosing cords of spindle cells.[579]

Ultrastructurally, perineurioma is characterized by nonbranching, thin cytoplasmic processes coated by an external lamina and joined at their ends by a tight junction, few organelles, actin and vimentin filaments, and numerous pinocytotic vesicles[575,581,583] (Fig. 25.65). Immunohistochemically, the tumor cells are positive for EMA and Glut-1 and negative for S-100 protein, recapitulating the profile of normal perineurial cells[572,579a,584,585] (Fig. 25.66). There is also frequent expression of claudin-1, a recently described tight junction-associated protein.[577] At the cytogenetic level, many cases show deletion of part or all of chromosome 22.[574,578] In addition, mutations of the *NF2* gene have been documented.[580]

Nerve sheath myxoma

This controversial benign tumor of peripheral nerves can occur in the skin, soft tissues, or an intraspinal location.[594] It has a gross and microscopic appearance reminiscent of myxoma, except for the presence of plumper, epithelial-like cells and a distinct fascicular or plexiform arrangement; the latter feature is sometimes so pronounced that some authors have suggested the less

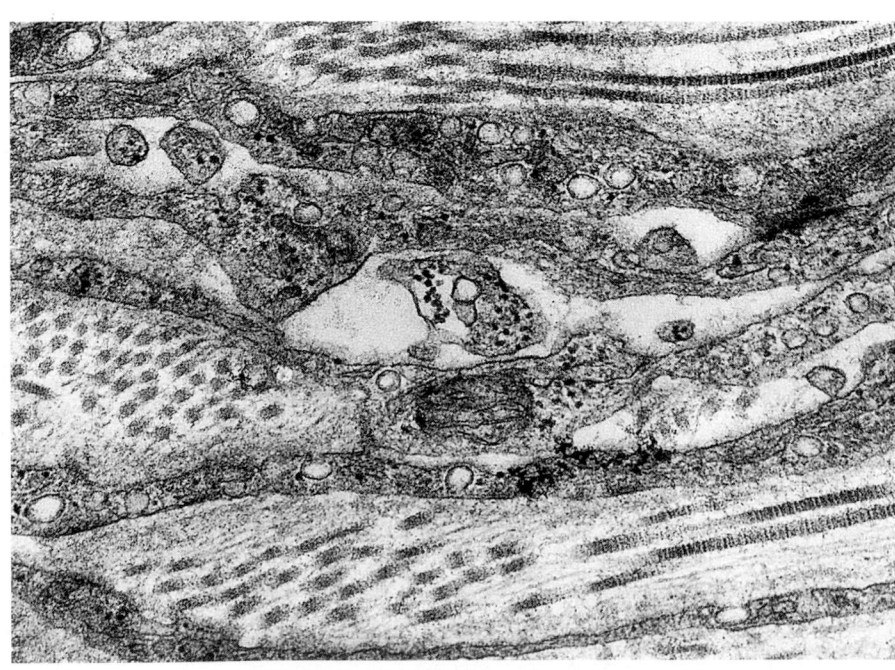

Fig. 25.65 Electron microscopic appearance of perineurioma. Thin perineurial cell cytoplasmic processes with prominent pinocytotic vesicles. The processes are coated by a continuous basal lamina. (×42,000; courtesy of Dr. Robert A. Erlandson, Memorial Sloan-Kettering Cancer Center)

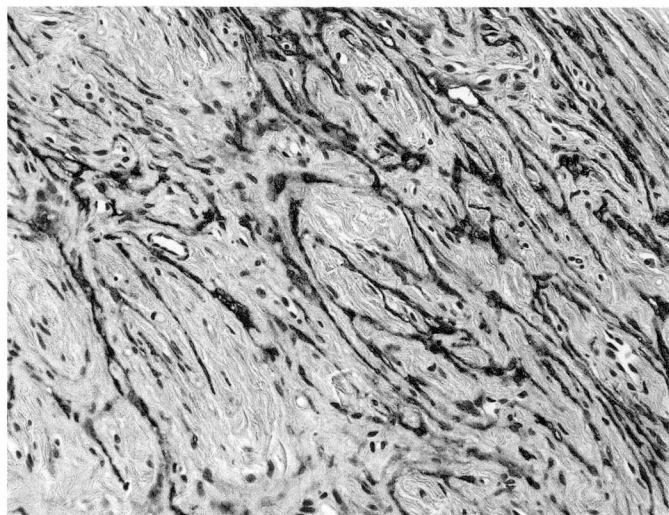

Fig. 25.66 EMA immunoreactivity in perineurioma.

committal designation of *plexiform myxoma*.[589,595] It seems likely that nerve sheath myxoma and the cutaneous tumor described as *neurothekeoma*[592] are closely related, if not identical (see Chapter 4) (Fig. 25.67). As mentioned in the previous section, the differential diagnosis includes perineurioma (which can show prominent myxoid features and a fascicular or storiform pattern of growth) and myxoid neurofibroma (which is immunoreactive for S-100 protein).[590,591,593]

Malignant peripheral nerve sheath tumor (MPNST)

Malignant peripheral nerve sheath tumor (MPNST) is the currently preferred term for the neoplasm also known over the years as *malignant schwannoma, neurogenic sarcoma*, and *neurofibrosarcoma*.[622] Approximately half of these tumors arise de novo, and the other half from nerves involved by neurofibromas as part of type I Recklinghausen's disease. Some have occurred in areas of previous irradiation,[615,646] and a few have originated from the Schwann's cell-like (satellite cell) component of ganglioneuroma.[598,619,621,649] The development of MPNST in Recklinghausen's disease

has been found to be associated with chromosome 17p deletions and *p53* gene mutations.[642]

Because of its difficult microscopic recognition, errors are often made, more often than not by diagnosing MPNST as some other type of soft tissue sarcoma. There are two circumstances in which the diagnosis of MPNST should be the primary consideration in the presence of a malignant tumor of soft tissues composed of spindle cells: (1) when the tumor develops in a patient with type I Recklinghausen's disease or (2) when the tumor is obviously arising within the anatomic compartment of a major nerve or in continuity with a neurofibroma.[608] In the absence of these circumstances the light microscopic diagnosis of MPNST is often only presumptive and dependent on a combination of features, none of which is diagnostic by itself. They include: serpentine shape of the tumor cells; arrangement in palisades or whorls; marked contrast between the deeply hyperchromatic nuclei and the pale cytoplasm ("punched-out nuclei"); perivascular concentration of tumor cells, with a plumper shape; epithelioid appearance of the endothelial cells of these vessels; presence of large gaping vascular spaces, resulting in a hemangiopericytoma-like appearance; and geographic areas of necrosis, with tumor palisading at the edges[625] (Figs 25.68 to 25.70). In most areas the appearance is that of an extremely cellular spindle cell neoplasm. Mitoses are usually abundant. Although most tumors are quite monomorphic (a feature they share with fibrosarcoma and monophasic synovial sarcoma), some can be extremely bizarre. At the light microscopic level the latter can simulate the appearance of a pleomorphic liposarcoma or malignant fibrous histiocytoma very closely and may be identified as neural only on ultrastructural examination.[627] Metaplastic tissues such as cartilage, bone, muscle, or blood vessels are present in approximately 15% of the cases[617,617,645] (Fig. 25.71). The most spectacular variant is characterized by the presence

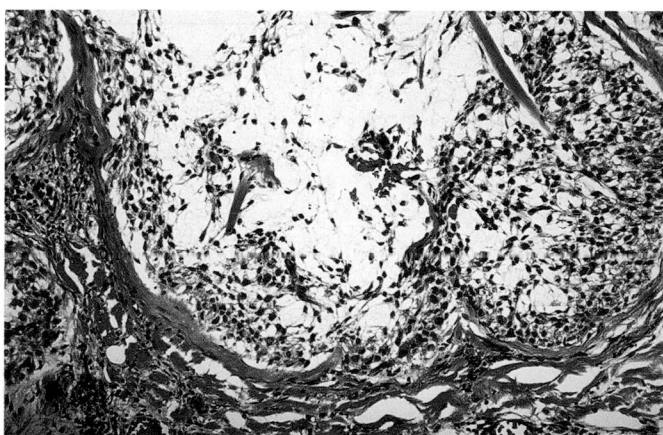

Fig. 25.67 Lobulated appearance of neurothekeoma. There is focal hypercellularity.

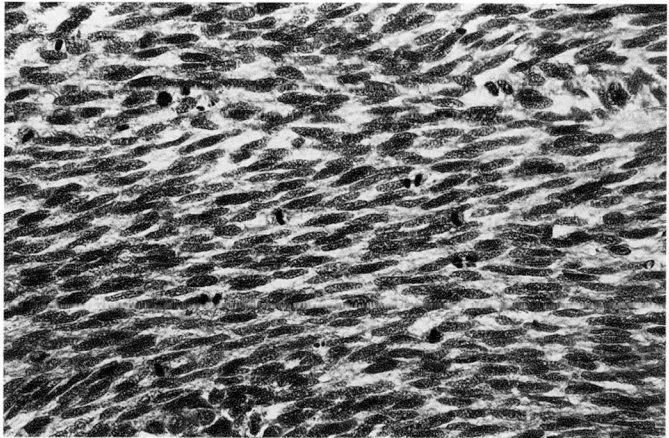

Fig. 25.68 Malignant peripheral nerve sheath tumor (MPNST). The marked hypercellularity and the high mitotic activity in the absence of significant pleomorphism are commonly seen in this tumor type.

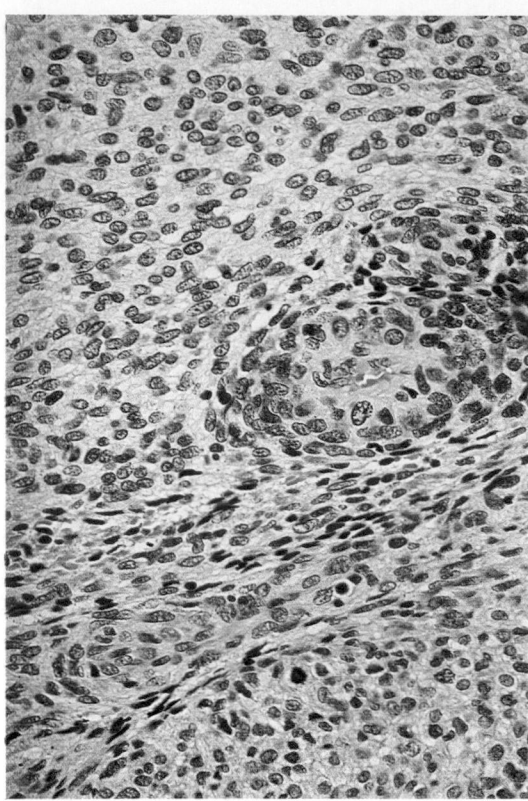

Fig.25.69 MPNST. The plump and almost epithelioid appearance of the cells surrounding the vessels is a common feature in this tumor type.

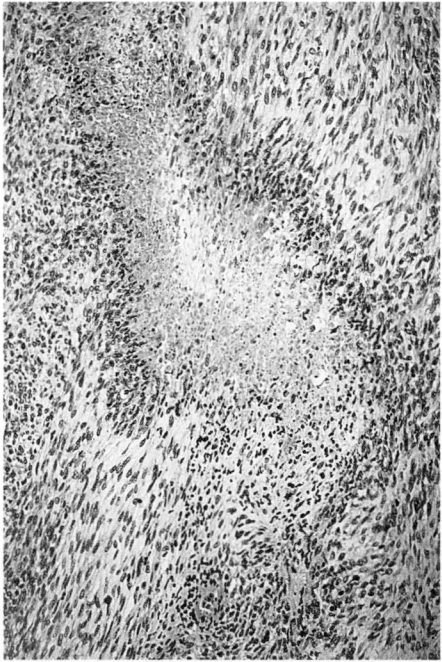

Fig. 25.70 MPNST. The area of necrosis with irregular borders and palisading at the edges is similar to that seen in glioblastoma multiforme of brain.

of well-developed skeletal muscle and has been dignified by the picturesque term *malignant triton tumor*[600,612,667] (Fig. 25.72). Areas of recognizable MPNST should be present to make such a diagnosis in these metaplastic

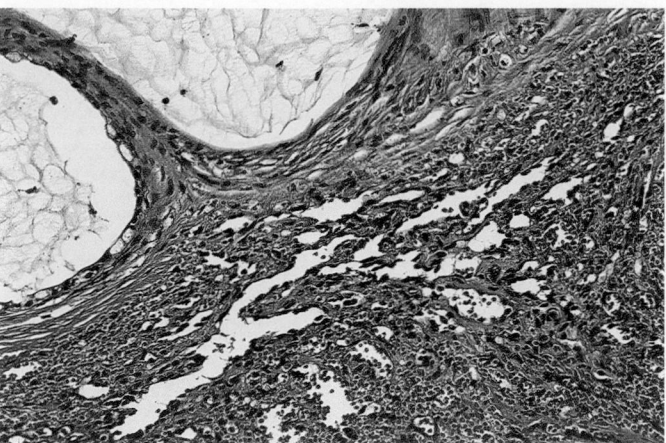

Fig. 25.71 MPNST with divergent differentiation into blood vessels and mucin-producing glands.

tumors; otherwise a diagnosis corresponding to the morphologic appearance of the tumor is appropriate, even if the patient has Recklinghausen's disease.[601,643] This applies, for instance, to *angiosarcoma* of peripheral nerves, of which several examples have been reported, including the *epithelioid* variety.[639]

In some MPNST, part or most of the tumor is composed of plump cells with polygonal acidophilic cytoplasm and an epithelioid-like appearance; these are designated as *epithelioid malignant MPNST*[596,613,635,644] (Figs 25.73 and 25.74). One such case exhibited squamous differentiation.[597] Epithelioid MPNST of the skin may be associated with HMB-45 immunoreactivity and be indistinguishable from some neurotropic/spindle cell/desmoplastic forms of malignant melanoma.[652,655] Interestingly, most of the MPNST that have arisen from malignant transformation of benign schwannomas have been of the epithelioid type.[648,650,669] Occasionally, MPNST show foci of *glandular differentiation*, with or without mucin production and with positivity for keratin, EMA, CEA, chromogranin, somatostatin, serotonin, and some peptide hormones[605,610,666,668]; it has been suggested that these formations represent foci of ependymal or neuroendocrine differentiation, but this view has been contested.[611,661] Glands, skeletal muscle and other tissues can coexist in the same tumor[651] (Fig. 25.71). In general, any peripheral nerve tumor should be suspected of being malignant if it contains epithelial glandular structures, no matter how well differentiated they are. Melanin can be present in the tumor cells, particularly if the tumor arises from spinal nerve roots; the distinction between melanocytic MPNST and primary malignant melanoma of nerves has little practical significance and may not be warranted from a conceptual standpoint.[634]

The belief that these MPNST generally originate in Schwann's cells is largely based on circumstantial evidence, the reasoning being that if these tumors represent the malignant counterpart of neurofibromas and the latter arise primarily from Schwann's cells, then the former also

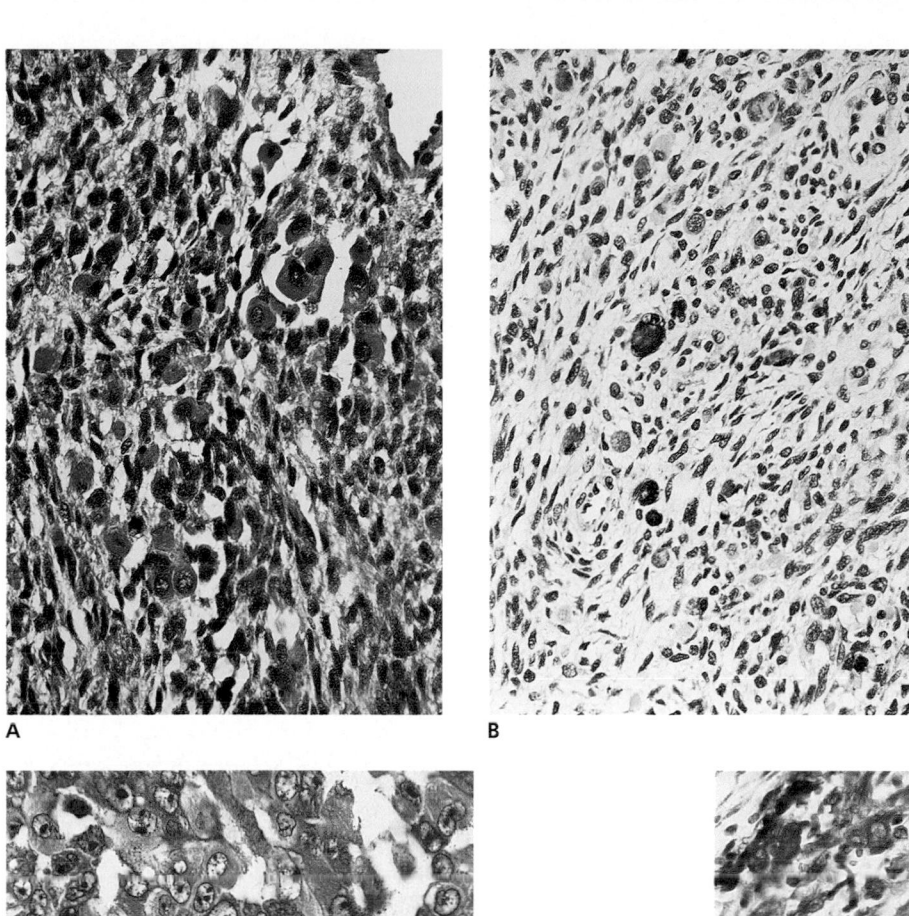

A   B

Fig. 25.72 A and **B**, MPNST with skeletal muscle differentiation (so-called "Triton tumor"). **B**, Positive immunostain for myoglobin.

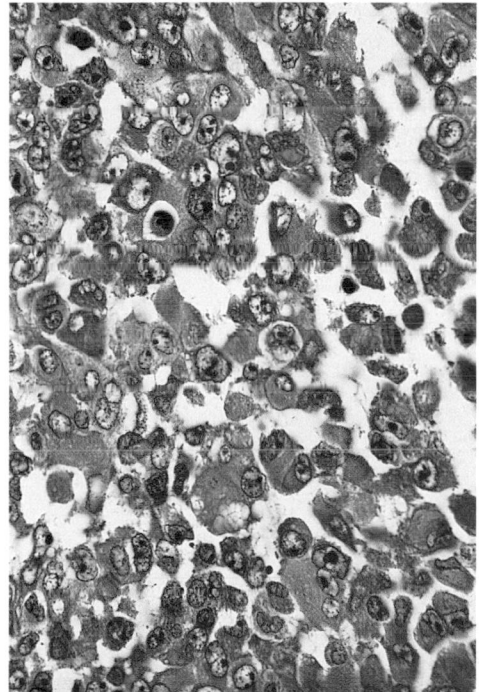

Fig. 25.73 MPNST of epithelioid type.

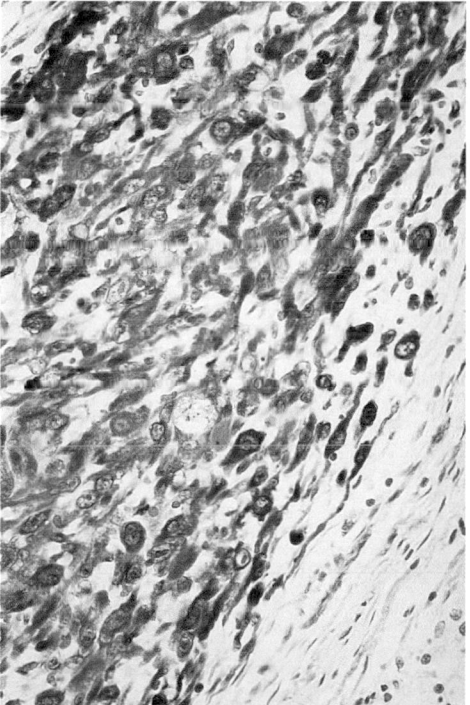

Fig. 25.74 Same case as Fig. 25.73 showing strong immunoreactivity for S-100 protein.

must have that origin. Some of the microscopic features just mentioned and tissue culture studies[654] favor this hypothesis, which is also supported by the electron microscope description of infoldings of the cell membrane with lamellar configuration, presence of discontinuous basal lamina material, conspicuous intercellular junctions, and occasional dense-core granules.[603,604,614,626,654,657,660] Further support comes from the fact that immunohistochemically the tumor cells show reactivity for Schwann's cell markers, such as S-100 protein and Leu7, in approximately half of the cases,[624,632,663,665] the former being particularly prominent in neurofibroma-like areas and in foci of melanocytic differentiation.[638] However, some MPNST show no discernible schwannian features at any level and may actually exhibit features suggestive of perineurial or fibroblastic nature.[618,628,629] Indeed, the existence of a *perineurial MPNST (malignant perineurioma)* has been supported on morphologic, immunohistochemical, and ultrastructural grounds.[630] Because of this fact, a histogenetically noncommittal term, such as MPNST, seems preferable to the time-honored malignant schwannoma. Regarding immunoreactivity to S-100 protein, it tends to be focal and not particularly strong, except in the epithelioid variant of this tumor[669b]; therefore, the presence of *strong and diffuse* immunoreactivity for S-100 protein in a malignant spindle cell tumor with morphologic features suggestive of MPNST should raise the possibility of the alternative diagnosis of malignant melanoma, particularly if the lesion is located in the skin or a lymph node[633] (Figs 25.75 and 25.76).

The large majority of MPNST arise in adults, but they have also been recorded in children.[640,641,647] The most common locations are the neck, forearm, lower leg, and buttock.[602,631] Grossly, the finding of a large mass producing fusiform enlargement of a major nerve, such as the sciatic nerve, is characteristic[658] (Fig. 25.77). Most MPNST are deep-seated, but they can occur in the subcutis or even in the skin.[607,620]

The clinical evolution is that of a highly malignant neoplasm, despite the relatively slow growth rate of some cases.[599,609,623,653,662] Local recurrence (often in the cut nerve ends) and distant metastases are frequent[609,664] (Fig. 25.78). In general, there is little correlation between microscopic grading and prognosis.[617,659] However, the *plexiform variant* of MPNST occurring in a superficial location in children has been associated with a better prognosis.[641] As a matter of fact, the lack of well-documented metastasizing examples of this entity has led some authors to question their placement into a malignant category.[669a] Semantics aside, the fact remains that these tumors have a high tendency for recurrence and may be very troublesome to treat, as we have had the opportunity to observe on several occasions.

Occasionally, malignant tumors are found in major peripheral nerves or elsewhere in the soft tissue, having

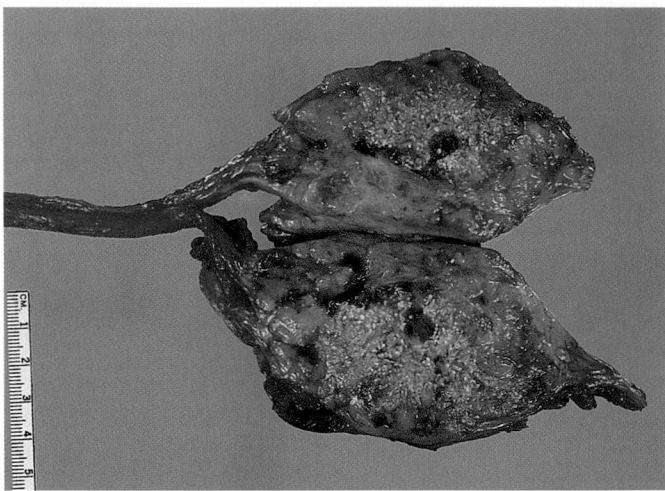

Fig. 25.77 MPNST producing a characteristic fusiform expansion of the sciatic nerve. Foci of necrosis and hemorrhage are present.

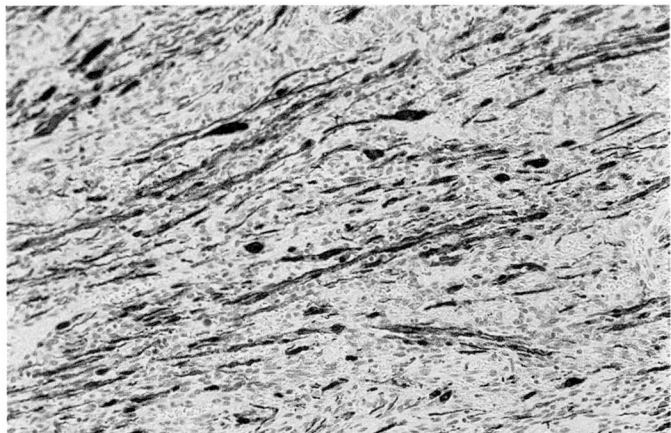

Fig. 25.75 Patchy and not particularly intense immunoreactivity for S-100 protein in MPNST.

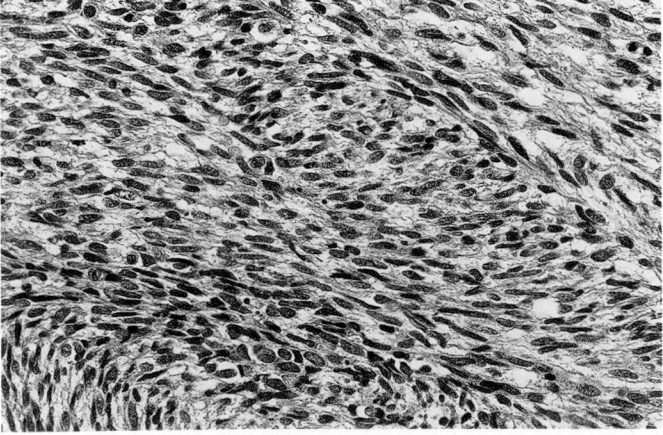

Fig. 25.76 The contrast between the dark hyperchromatic nuclei and the light cytoplasm is typical of MPNST.

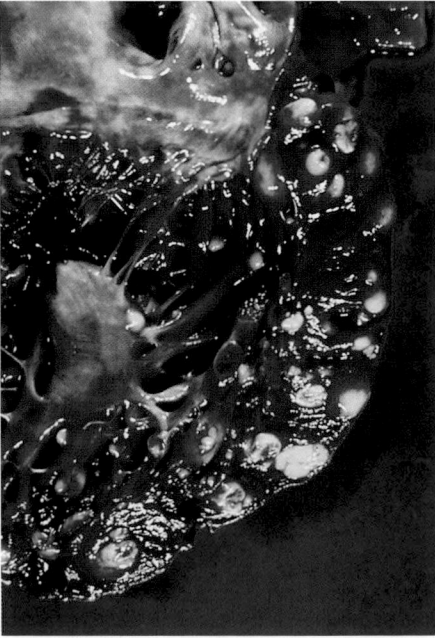

Fig. 25.78 Multiple tumor nodules in the heart in a case of widely metastatic MPNST.

a light and electron microscopic appearance suggestive of primitive neuroectodermal origin. Sometimes these features are seen together with areas of typical MPNST and sometimes in a pure form.[636,637] The latter form, known as peripheral neuroepithelioma, peripheral or adult neuroblastoma, or primitive neuroectodermal tumor (PNET), is discussed on p. 2324. The rare occurrence of neuroblastoma-like areas in benign schwannoma has already been mentioned (see p. 2265).

No consistent chromosomal abnormalities have been found in MPNST. A claim that a high proportion of these tumors are associated with the t(X;18) translocation that is typical of synovial sarcoma has not been substantiated by subsequent studies.[606,656]

Other tumors of peripheral nerves

In addition to benign and malignant tumors composed of the constitutive cells of peripheral nerves, these structures are occasionally involved in a selective fashion by mesenchymal or other neoplasms. Thus isolated cases of *hemangioma, fibrolipomatous hamartoma* (Fig. 25.79), *angiosarcoma*, and *malignant lymphoma* have been described.[670,672a,673] Some of these tumors have occurred in nerves affected by neurofibroma and/or in patients with type I Recklinghausen's disease.[672] Most of the lymphomas have been of B-cell type.[671]

Tumors of adipose tissue

Lipoma

Benign fatty tumors can arise in any location in which fat is normally present. The majority occur in the upper half of the body, particularly the trunk and neck, but they can develop in any other site, including the hand.[697] Most lipomas are subcutaneous, an important point in the differential diagnosis with liposarcomas, which are almost always deep-seated. However, lipomas can also occur in the deep soft tissues; these are subclassified into *intramuscular* (most common in the trunk) and *intermuscular* (most common in the anterior abdominal wall).[681] There are about 120 lipomas for every liposarcoma.[698] Most patients are in the fifth or sixth decade of life. Only rarely are children affected. Lipomas may be single or multiple. Multiple lipomas are more common in women; many are seen in a familial setting, and some occur in patients with neurofibromatosis or multiple endocrine neoplasia. In **diffuse lipomatosis**, massive enlargement of a limb may be seen as a result of diffuse proliferation of mature adipose tissue. In the familial variant of this process, lipomatosis has a symmetric distribution.[677]

Lipomas can grow to a large size; they are usually encapsulated when located in the superficial soft tissues but tend to be poorly circumscribed when arising in deeper structures.[684,691] Grossly, lipomas consist of bright yellow fat separated by fine fibrous trabeculae (Fig. 25.80). Microscopically, they are composed of mature adipose tissue with no cellular atypia.

Areas of fat necrosis, infarct, and calcification may be present. It is important not to confuse the histiocytes associated with fat necrosis with lipoblasts. The fact that they are often seen arranged in a circumferential fashion around a large lipid droplet (as is the case in fat necrosis at other sites) is a helpful diagnostic sign. Rarely, lipomas are seen to contain foci of mature metaplastic cartilage and bone.[689]

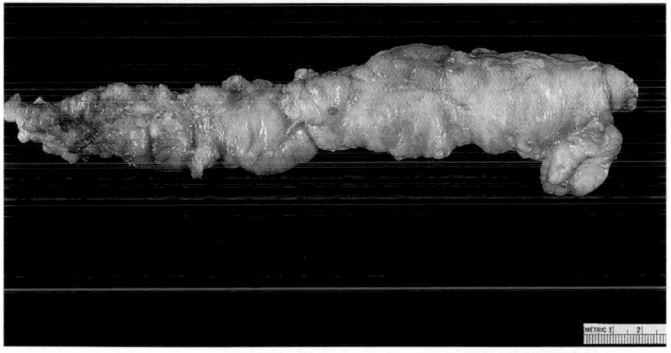

A

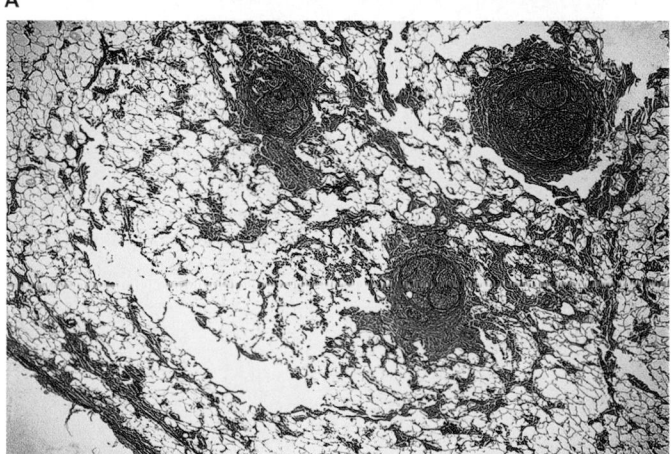

A

Fig. 25.79 A and **B,** Gross and microscopic appearance of fibrolipomatous hamartoma of nerve.

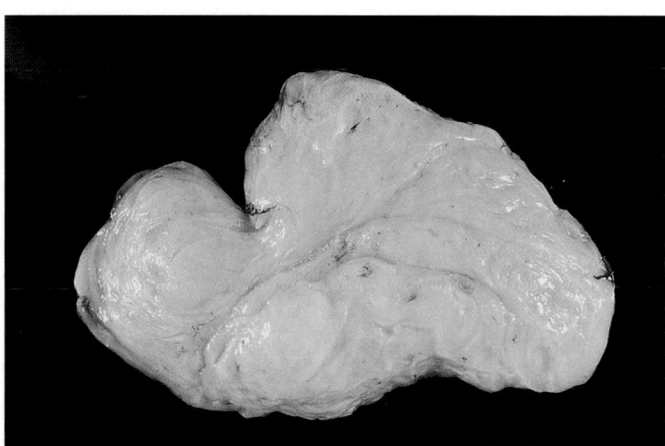

Fig. 25.80 Gross appearance of lipoma. Except for the circumscription, the appearance is indistinguishable from that of normal fat.

Ultrastructurally, only univacuolar mature adipocytes are present in typical lipomas.[690] Although the light microscopic and electron microscopic appearance of a lipoma does not differ significantly from that of normal adult fat, its lipid content as determined by biochemical extraction and the activity of lipoprotein lipase is different.[699,704]

Morphologic variations that lipomas may exhibit include the following:

1 **Fibrolipoma.** This is characterized by the presence of prominent bundles of *mature* fibrous tissue traversing the fatty lobules. It should not be equated with spindle cell lipoma (see later section).

2 **Myxolipoma.** This tumor features focally well-developed myxoid changes. It should not be overdiagnosed as myxoid liposarcoma.

3 **Chondroid lipoma.** This recently described variant is usually deep-seated (Fig. 25.81). It is characterized by a component of eosinophilic and vacuolated cells containing glycogen and lipid that resembles brown fat cells, lipoblasts, and chondroblasts[696] (Fig. 25.82). These cells are immunoreactive for vimentin, S-100 protein, and CD68; curiously, some are also positive for keratin.[692,696]

4 **Myolipoma.** This tumor is characterized by an admixture in variable proportions of mature adipose tissue and bundles of well-differentiated smooth muscle.[695]

5 **Spindle cell lipoma.** This is a benign fatty tumor characteristically located in the regions of the shoulder and posterior neck of adults, but it has also been found in many other locations, including the limbs, face, oral cavity, trunk, and anus.[683,700] It is composed of an admixture of mature lipocytes and uniform spindle cells set in a mucinous and fibrous background[679] (Fig. 25.83). Features that assist in distinguishing it from myxoid liposarcoma include the absence of lipoblasts and of a prominent plexiform vascular pattern, the presence of thick ("ropy") collagen bundles, and the great uniformity of the proliferating spindle cells. In

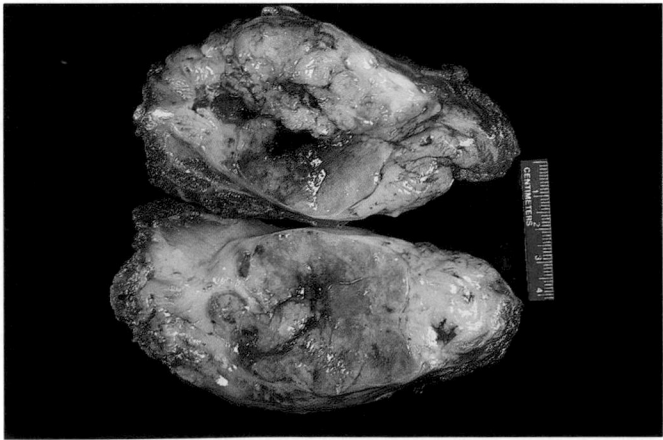

Fig. 25.81 Gross appearance of chondroid lipoma.

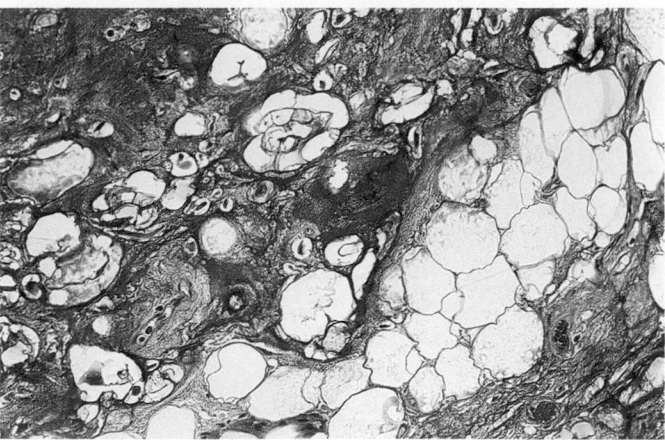

Fig. 25.82 Microscopic appearance of chondroid lipoma, showing admixture of mature fat and chondroid tissue.

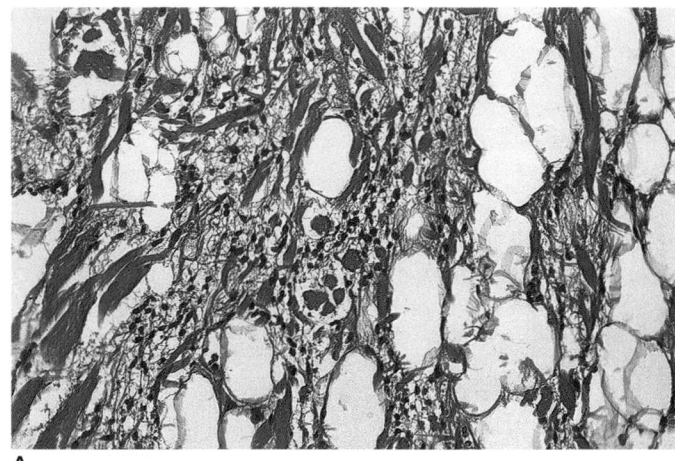

A

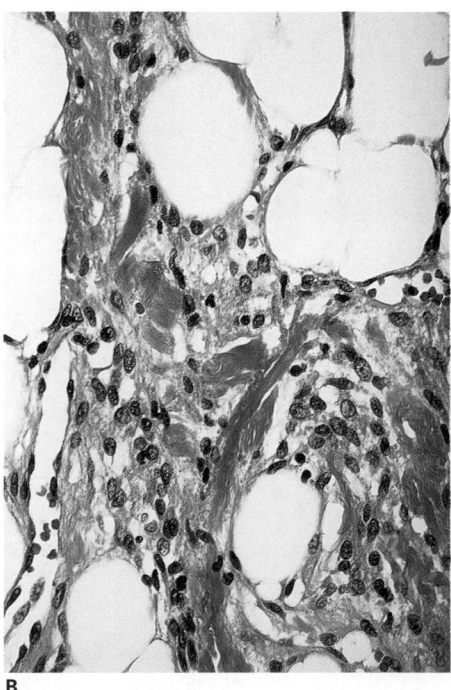

B

Fig. 25.83 Spindle cell lipoma. The oval to spindle cells are concentrated in the fibrous bands within lobules of mature adipose tissue.

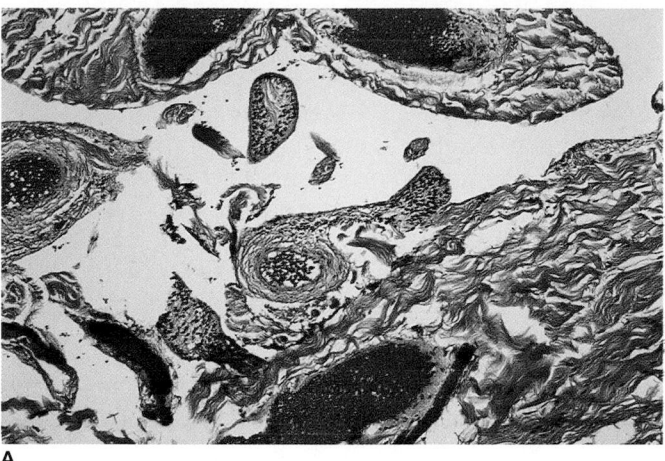
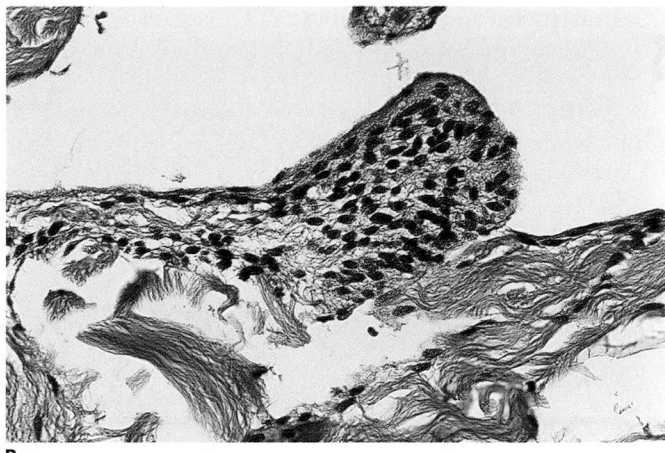

Fig. 25.84 A and **B,** Spindle cell lipoma with pseudoangiomatous appearance resulting from accumulation of tumor cells beneath artifactual tissue spaces.

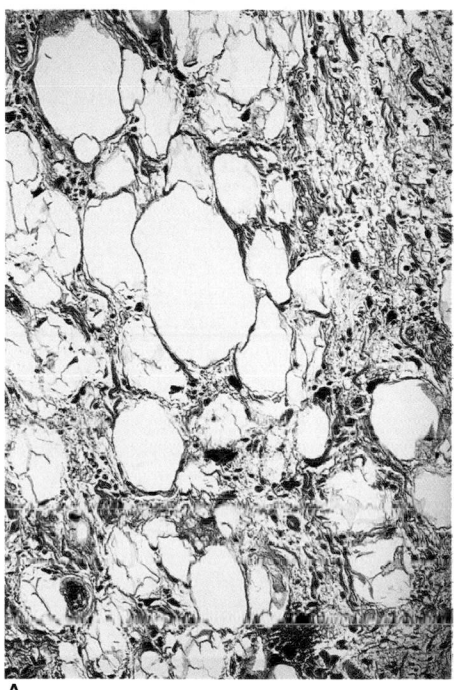
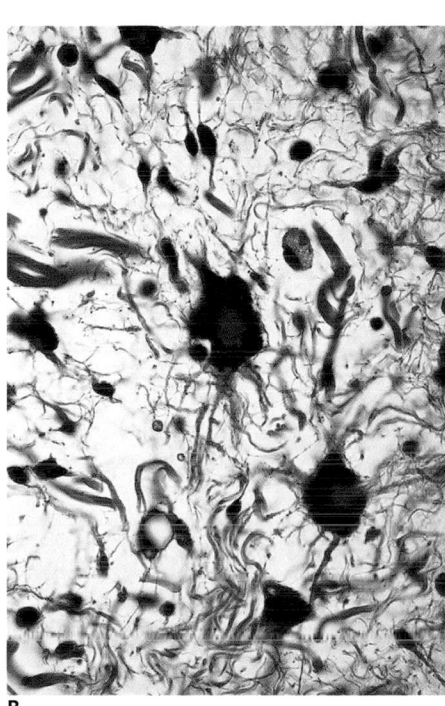

Fig. 25.85 A and **B,** Pleomorphic lipoma. The high-power view (**B**) highlights the floret cells.

some instances the appearance of irregular branching spaces with villiform projections results in a pseudoangiomatous appearance[685] (Fig. 25.84). Ultra-structurally, spindle cell lipomas are composed of a mixture of spindle mesenchymal cells and mature lipocytes.[675]

6 **Pleomorphic lipoma.** This is a lipoma containing hyperchromatic multinucleated ("floret-like") tumor cells within the fibrous septa traversing the neoplasm (Fig. 25.85). As for spindle cell lipoma, its most common location is the shoulder and posterior neck region.[703] We have also seen them in the dermis and beneath mucosal membranes. The most difficult differential diagnosis is with a sclerosing form of well-differentiated liposarcoma (atypical lipomatous tumor). The location of the lesion is an important clue,

and the proportion of floret-type giant cells and lipoblasts is the most important distinguishing feature at the microscopic level.[674]

7 **Angiolipoma.** These are well-circumscribed small tumors occurring shortly after puberty. They are often painful and characteristically multiple. They are located in the subcutis, most commonly on the trunk or extremities. Vascularity often is limited to a band of tissue on the periphery of the neoplasm (Fig. 25.86). Hyaline thrombi are common and constitute an important diagnostic sign[676] (Fig. 25.87). Angiolipomas in which the vascular component predominates (cellular angiolipomas) can be confused with Kaposi's sarcoma or angiosarcoma[688] (Fig. 25.88). The pain correlates well with the degree of vascularity.[687] The fact that angiolipomas lack chromosomal aberrations (like

hemangiomas and unlike lipomas) suggests that they are hemangiomas with fat rather than true mixed tumors.[702]

So-called *infiltrating angiolipomas* are unrelated to the lesion just described. They are probably not true mixed tumors but rather intramuscular large-vessel hemangiomas in which portions of the affected muscle tissue have been replaced by fat.[678]

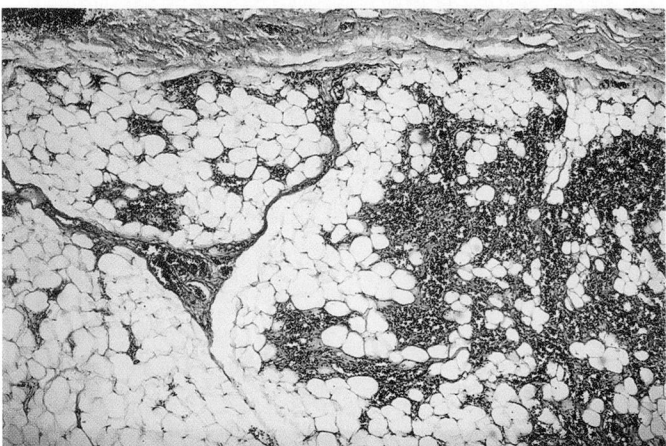

Fig. 25.86 Angiolipoma showing intimate admixture of blood vessels and mature adipose tissue.

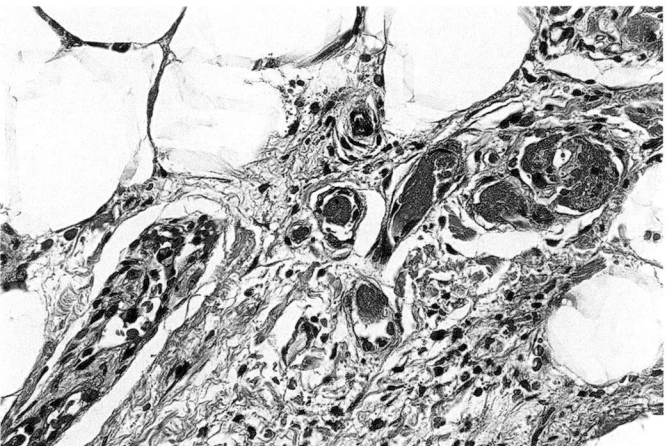

Fig. 25.87 Numerous hyaline thrombi in angiolipoma.

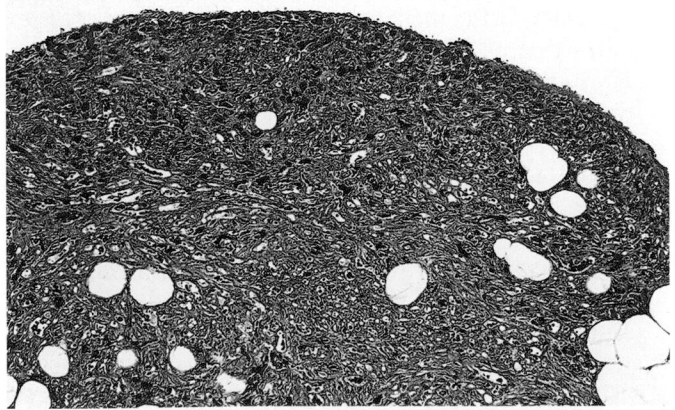

Fig. 25.88 Cellular angiolipoma. This benign tumor should not be confused with Kaposi's sarcoma.

Cytogenetically, 80% of solitary lipomas exhibit chromosomal aberrations affecting mainly 12q, 6p, and 13q.[680,701] In contrast with atypical lipomatous tumors, marker ring or giant chromosomes are extremely rare. Multiple lipomas usually exhibit a normal karyotype. Nearly all spindle cell and pleomorphic lipomas have aberrations of 16q, this finding supporting the close link between these two tumor types and the fact that they are distinct from atypical lipomatous tumors.[682,686,694]

The gene involved in chromosome region 12q15 of lipoma cells is known as *HMGI-C* and encodes an "architectural" transcription factor.[693]

Lipoblastoma/lipoblastomasis

Lipoblastoma/lipoblastomasis affects infants and young children (below the age of 5 years) almost exclusively.[708,710–713] It commonly involves the proximal portion of the lower and upper extremities. Grossly, the lesion is soft and lobulated (Fig. 25.89). It is subdivided into (benign) lipoblastoma (sometimes also designated as embryonal or fetal lipoma) when well circumscribed and lipoblastomatosis when deep-seated and ill defined. Microscopically, it closely resembles fetal fat.[707] It may be confused with myxoid liposarcoma because of the presence of lipoblasts, a plexiform vascular pattern, and an abundant myxoid stroma (Fig. 25.90). Its ultrastructural appearance is also very similar to that of myxoid liposarcoma.[705] It is distinguished from the latter by virtue of the young age of the patient, distinct lobulation, and absence of giant cells or pleomorphic nuclei.[706,711] Cytogenetically, lipoblastoma/lipoblastomasis is often associated with rearrangements of 8q.[709,712] The clinical course is benign. In the series of Chung and Enzinger,[706] the recurrence rate was 14% and was attributed to incomplete removal of the tumor.

Lipoblastomas that are not removed in infancy mature into lipomas, a clue to their primeval nature being the prominent fibrous septa that still divide them into distinct lobules[775a] (Fig. 25.91).

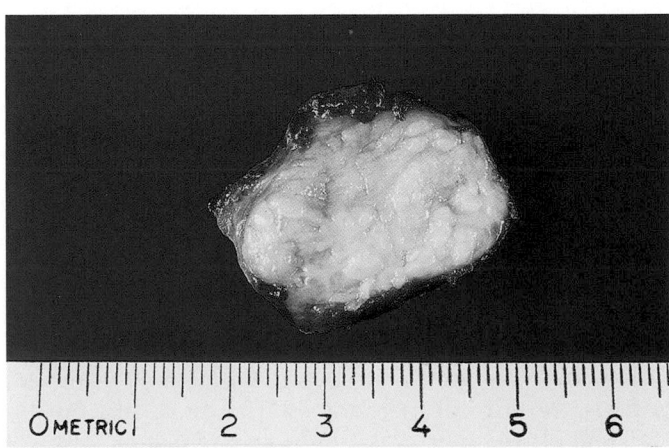

Fig. 25.89 Gross appearance of lipoblastoma. The tumor has a mucoid cut surface.

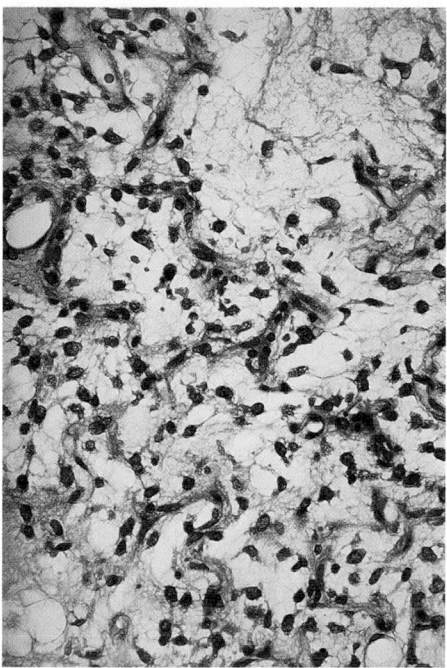

Fig. 25.90 Lipoblastoma. On high power, the appearance is reminiscent of myxoid liposarcoma.

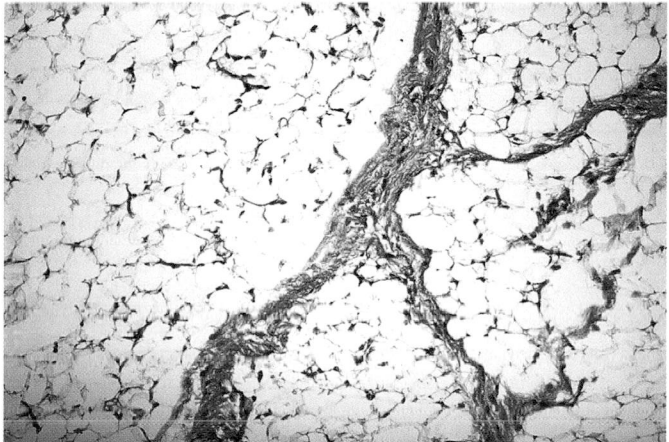

Fig. 25.91 "Mature" lipoblastoma. The lesion retains the lobulation that is characteristic of this tumor type.

Hibernoma

Hibernoma is a rare benign neoplasm occurring usually in the interscapular region, axilla, and thigh, but also in the mediastinum and retroperitoneum.[717,720] Its cut surface has a typical brown color, and its microscopic pattern is characteristic—an organoid arrangement of large cells with centrally located nucleus and a cytoplasm filled with many small vacuoles that stain for neutral fat (Figs 25.92 and 25.93). Cytogenetically, it is often associated with aberrations of 11q.[716,722]

This tumor has received its name because it resembles the brown fat of the hibernating glands of animals,[715] a similarity that is maintained at the electron microscopic level.[718,719,723] Interestingly, endocrine-like activity resembling that of adrenal cortical tissue has been detected in

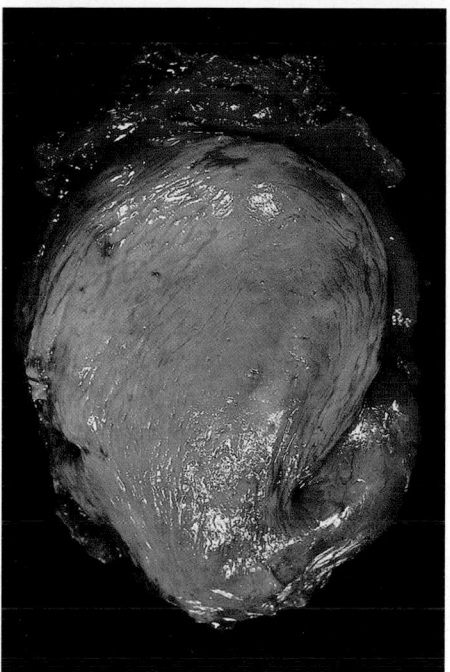

Fig. 25.92 Gross appearance of hibernoma exhibiting the typical light brown cut surface.

one case.[714] Sometimes the features of hibernoma are seen mixed with those of ordinary lipoma or of spindle cell lipoma (hybrid tumors) (Fig. 25.94). Other hibernomas are accompanied by a myxoid matrix.[717] Malignant soft tissue tumors in which many of the tumor cells have features of brown fat occur and are regarded as a morphologic variant of liposarcoma. Interestingly, hibernomas of the interscapular region develop regularly in transgenic mice containing the adipocyte-specific regulatory region from the adipocyte *P2* gene linked to the simian virus 40 transforming genes.[721]

Liposarcoma (including atypical lipomatous tumor)

Liposarcoma is the most frequent soft tissue sarcoma in adults.[741] Indubitable cases of liposarcoma have also been observed in adolescents and children.[734,760,766,777] However, most cases so diagnosed in this age group (particularly in the past) were in reality examples of lipoblastomatosis or giant cell fibroblastoma.[736]

Liposarcomas are usually large and occur most frequently in the lower extremities (popliteal fossa and medial thigh); retroperitoneal, perirenal, and mesenteric region; and shoulder area.[775] Their relative frequency at these various sites is greatly dependent on the tumor subtype. Although liposarcomas of the posterior neck, upper back and shoulder undoubtedly occur, it should be remembered that this is the classic site for lesions that can simulate liposarcoma, including spindle cell lipoma, pleomorphic lipoma, lipoblastoma/tosis, and hibernoma. Grossly, they are well circumscribed but not encapsulated.[782] Depending on the subtype, they may have a mucoid, slimy surface suggestive of myxoma, a bright

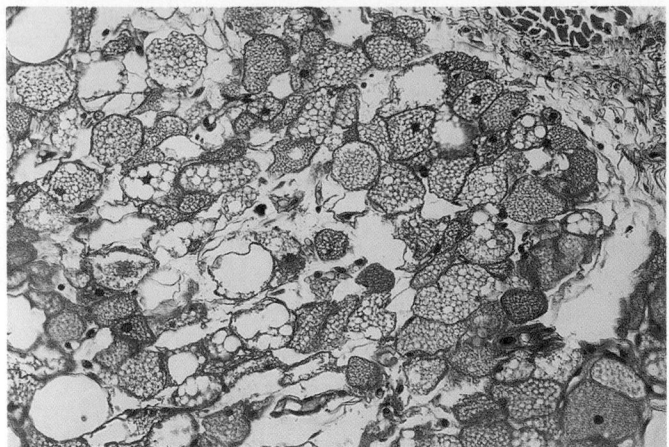

A

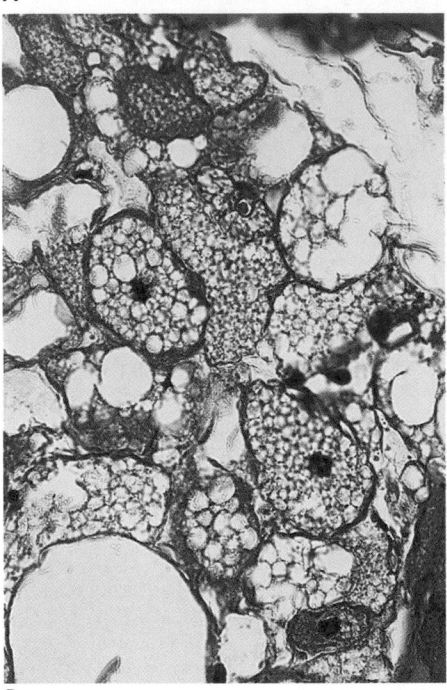

B

Fig. 25.93 A and **B,** Low- and high-power appearance of hibernoma. Note the central location of the indented nuclei.

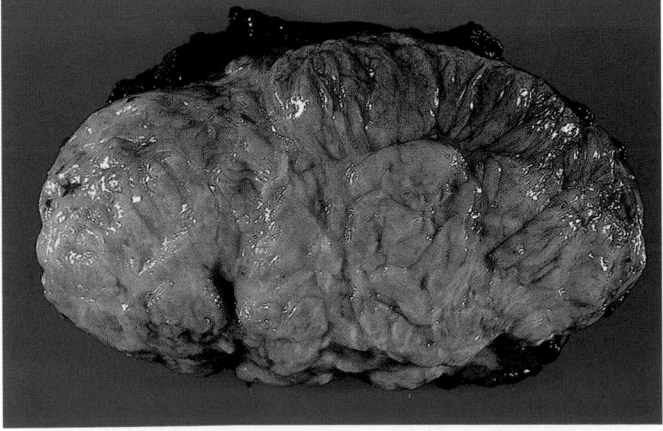

Fig. 25.94 Gross appearance of benign adipose tissue tumor that combines features of hibernoma and lipoma.

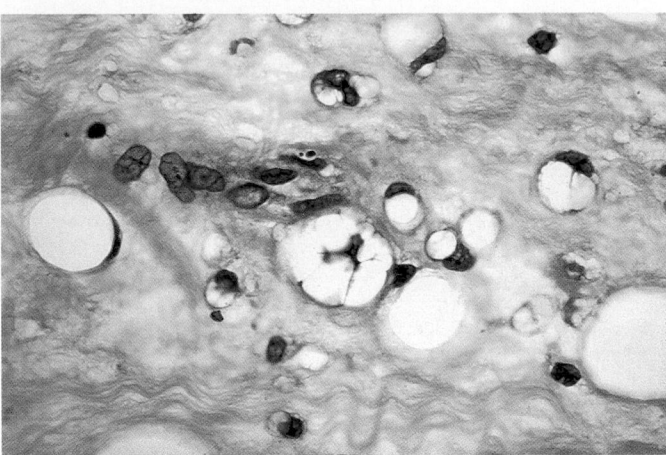

Fig. 25.95 Typical lipoblast from a case of metastatic liposarcoma, showing nuclear indentation by lipid-containing cytoplasmic vacuoles.

yellow appearance mimicking lipoma, or a surface resembling cerebral convolutions. Rarely, liposarcomas present as multicentric tumors[724,752] and/or are associated with independent benign multiple lipomas in the same patient.

The common morphologic denominator of liposarcoma is the *lipoblast*. This appears as a mononuclear or multinucleated cell with one or more cytoplasmic vacuoles that contain fat. The nucleus may be pushed aside by a single large vacuole, resulting in a signet ring configuration, or it may remain centrally located but exhibit small indentations by multiple small vacuoles, the appearance being similar to that of mature sebaceous cells or spongiocytes of adrenal cortex (Fig. 25.95). This highly characteristic scalloped nuclear appearance can also be appreciated in specimens obtained from fine needle aspiration.[785] In their classic article on the subject, Enzinger and Winslow[742] divided liposarcomas into four types: myxoid, round cell, well differentiated, and pleomorphic, acknowledging the existence of mixed forms.

Myxoid liposarcoma, which is the most common type of liposarcoma, shows a marked predilection for the lower extremities, particularly the thigh (Fig. 25.96). Microscopically, it has few or no mitotic figures and it is characterized by proliferating lipoblasts in different stages of differentiation, a prominent anastomosing capillary network, and a mucoid matrix rich in hyaluronidase-sensitive acid mucopolysaccharides[787] (Fig. 25.97). The presence of a delicate network of thin-walled vessels is an important feature in the differential diagnosis with myxoma and other myxoid tumors.[778] The mucoid extracellular material may accumulate in large pools, thus simulating a tumor of lymph vessel origin. Metaplastic cartilage is found in rare instances. Ultrastructurally, cells varying in appearance from primitive mesenchymal cells to typical multivacuolated and univacuolated lipoblasts are seen.[730,731,776] The abundant capillaries are intimately related to all of these various cell types in a manner analogous to that of developing fetal adipose tissue.[730,763,765]

Cytogenetically, myxoid liposarcoma is characterized by the reciprocal translocation t(12;16)(q13;p11), which results in the *TLS–CHOP* rearrangement.[727,784] *CHOP* is a gene involved in adipocyte differentiation.[726,738,749,753,781]

In the **round cell type** the tumor cells are small and

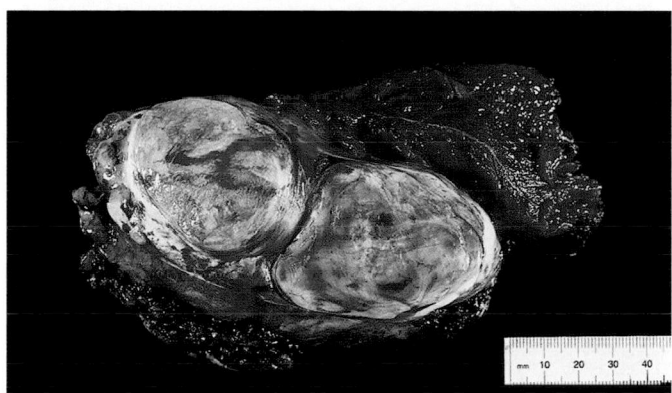

Fig. 25.96 Gross appearance of myxoid liposarcoma of thigh, characteristically located in the intermuscular spaces.

have a distinctly acidophilic cytoplasm (Fig. 25.98). The presence among them of scattered lipoblasts establishes the diagnosis. Mitoses are more common than in the myxoid form, whereas the vascular network is less prominent. Pseudoglandular arrangement of the tumor cells is frequent. Immunoreactivity for S-100 protein is a constant and diagnostically useful feature.[739]

It has become increasingly evident that round cell liposarcoma is not a specific subtype but rather a poorly differentiated form of myxoid liposarcoma, as supported by the presence of a common chromosomal translocation and gene fusion.[633,783] Actually, a whole range exists in the prevalence of round cells in myxoid liposarcoma, an increasing number of these cells indicating a greater degree of tumor aggressiveness, with the pure round cell liposarcoma representing the end of the spectrum.[761,779] Along these lines, a rare form of myxoid liposarcoma exists in which the poorly differentiated nature is manifested not through the presence of round cells but of spindle or pleomorphic elements.[783]

Atypical lipomatous tumor resembles ordinary lipoma grossly (Figs 25.99 and 25.100). It also resembles it

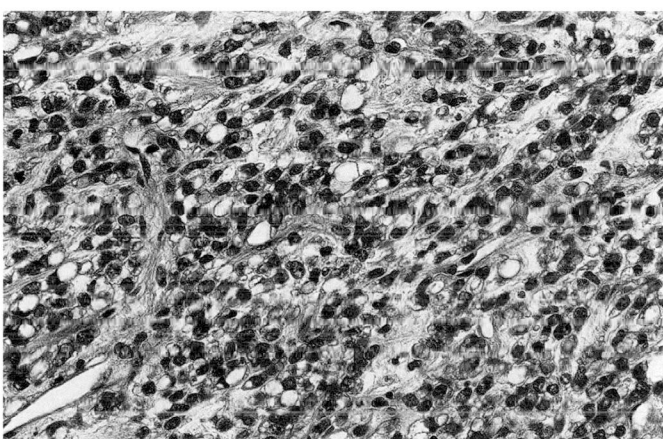

Fig. 25.98 Round cell liposarcoma. This tumor is to be viewed as a poorly differentiated form of myxoid liposarcoma.

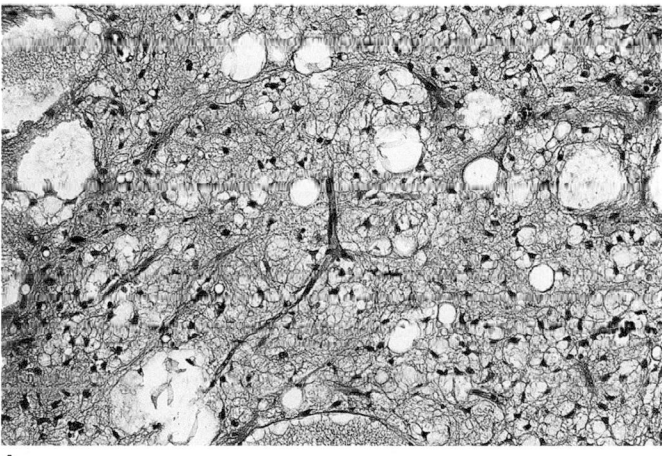

A

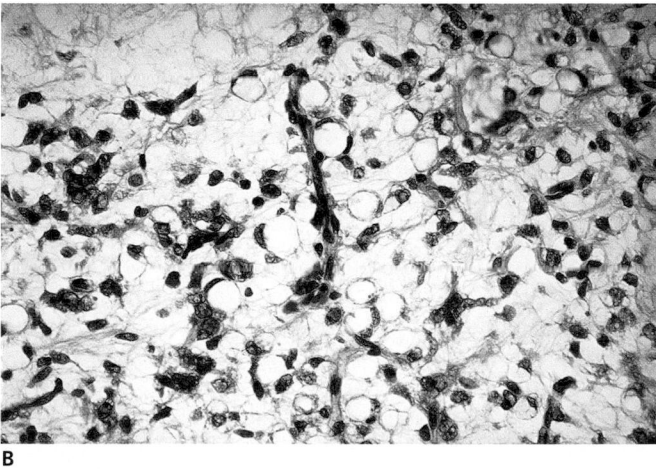

B

Fig. 25.97 A and **B**, Low- and high-power appearance of myxoid liposarcoma.

Fig. 25.99 Atypical lipomatous tumor. The neoplasm is well circumscribed and not very different from an ordinary lipoma.

Fig. 25.100 Gross appearance of a retroperitoneal atypical lipomatous tumor that microscopically combined features of the sclerosing and lipoma-like subtypes.

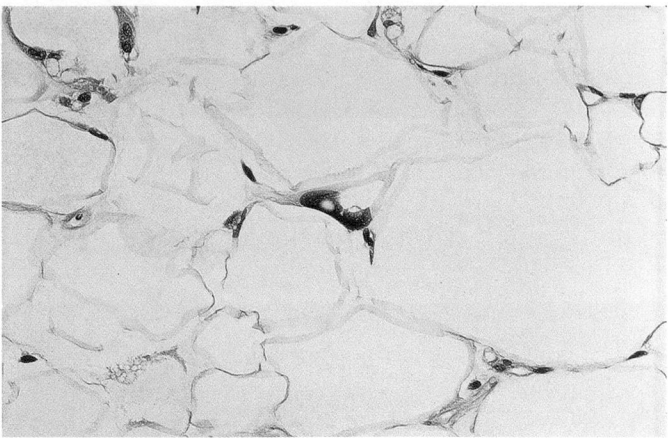

Fig. 25.102 Lipoma-like subtype of atypical lipomatous tumor. A single atypical cell with a nuclear vacuole ("Lochkern") is seen in the center of the field.

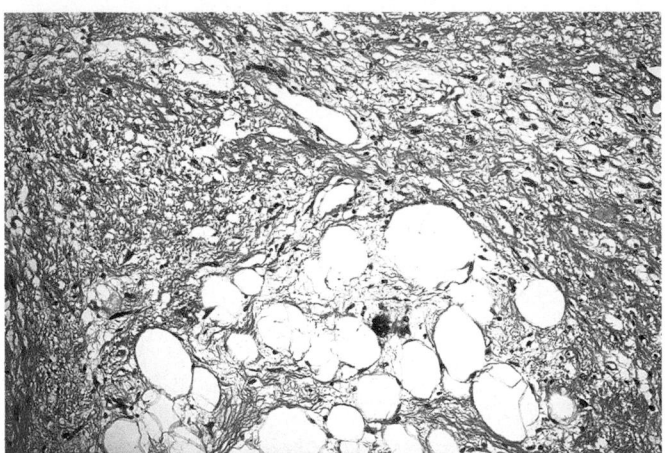

Fig. 25.101 Low-power microscopic view of an atypical lipomatous tumor with prominent sclerosing pattern. This corresponds to the well-differentiated liposarcoma, sclerosing type, of other classification schemes.

on low-power examination, but closer inspection shows scattered tumor cells with large, deep-staining nuclei. These atypical cells may concentrate on the fibrous strands that traverse the adipose tissue lobules (*sclerosing subtype*) (Fig. 25.101) or be scattered among the mature adipocytes (*lipoma-like subtype*) (Fig. 25.102). Some of the atypical cells have features of lipoblasts by virtue of the cytoplasmic vacuoles producing nuclear indentations, but most do not. Some of the nuclei have sharply outlined vacuoles ("Lochkern"), which at the ultrastructural level are seen to correspond to invaginations of the nuclear membrane, i.e., pseudoinclusions. It should be pointed out that occasional adipocytes with hyperchromatic and slightly enlarged nuclei containing pseudoinclusions can be seen in the non-neoplastic fat of somatic soft tissues and other sites, such as breast.

Atypical lipomatous tumor was included in the category of *well-differentiated liposarcoma* in the Enzinger–Winslow classification,[742] but the proposed switch in

terminology is justified by the fact that this is a non-metastasizing neoplasm (unless it were to undergo differentiation, see below).[729,733,744,747,762] The term *atypical lipoma* has been used by some authors as a synonym for atypical lipomatous tumor and by others for the tumors in this category showing only a minimal degree of atypia; it is probably better to avoid it. The behavior of atypical lipomatous tumors is substantially different depending on their location.[767] Those situated in the somatic soft tissues may recur, but these recurrences are controllable so that there are no tumor-related deaths; instead, those originating in the retroperitoneum have a very high incidence of recurrence (some of these recurrences having a "dedifferentiated" appearance, see subsequent discussion), and some of the patients die as a result. In view of these findings and based on pragmatic criteria, the proposal has been made to use the term *atypical lipoma* for the former and *well-differentiated liposarcoma* for the latter.[729] We prefer to designate the entire group as *atypical lipomatous tumor*, followed by a statement as to the predicted natural history based on the size and location of the mass.

Occasionally, smooth muscle bundles are seen in these neoplasms, a phenomenon akin to that already mentioned in connection with lipomas.[745] These tumors, which have been referred to as lipoleiomyosarcomas, should not be overinterpreted as dedifferentiated liposarcomas.[750] In other instances a heavy inflammatory infiltrate of either neutrophilic or lymphoplasmacytic nature is present, with some of the inflammatory cells being located within the cytoplasm of the giant tumor cells. Tumors with this appearance have been called *inflammatory liposarcoma* and *lymphocyte-rich liposarcoma*[728,764] (Fig. 25.103).

Spindle cell liposarcoma is an unusual and controversial variant of atypical lipomatous tumor characterized by a population of relatively bland spindle cells arrayed in fascicles and whorls, set in a variably myxoid stroma

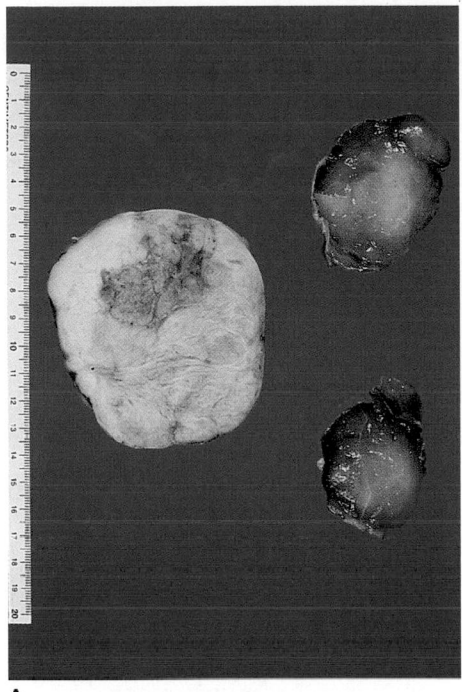

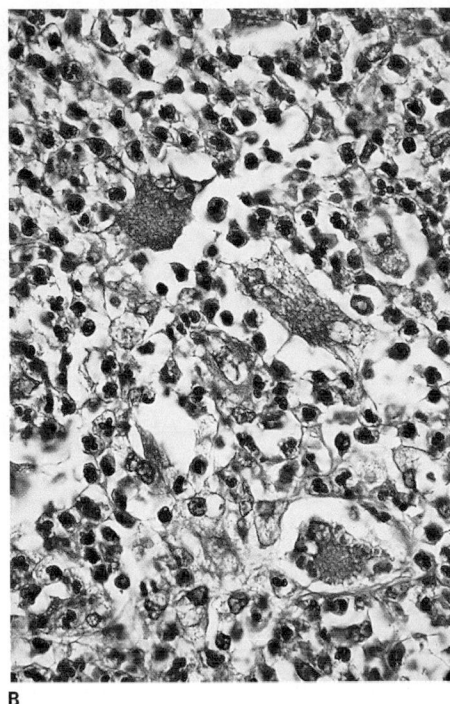

Fig. 25.103 A and **B,** Inflammatory liposarcoma. **A,** Gross appearance. The inflammatory liposarcoma is represented by the larger mass, whereas the others were atypical lipomatous tumors. All three masses were located in the retroperitoneum. **B,** Microscopic appearance showing highly pleomorphic tumor cells surrounded by numerous neutrophils. The appearance is that of so-called "inflammatory MFH." (Compare with Figs 25.41 and 25.42.)

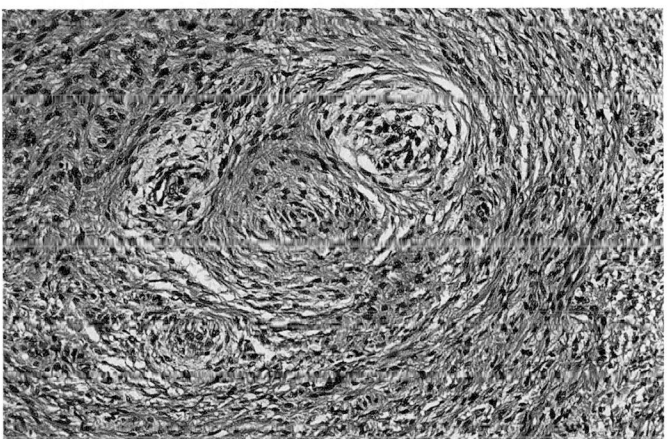

Fig. 25.104 So-called "spindle cell liposarcoma" exhibiting a whorling pattern of growth.

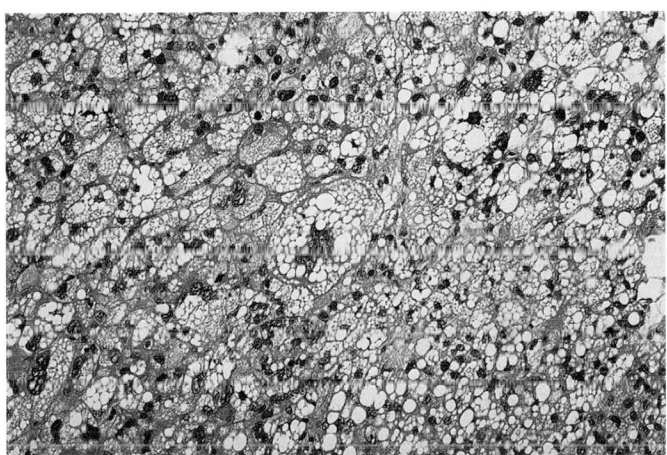

Fig. 25.105 Pleomorphic liposarcoma with numerous giant lipoblasts.

(Fig. 25.104). Most of the reported cases were located in the subcutaneous tissue of the shoulder girdle or upper limbs and therefore appeared different from the tumors that were described as fibroblastic or spindle cell liposarcomas in previous works.

Cytogenetically, close to 80% of the atypical lipomatous tumors (including the dedifferentiated examples) show marker ring and giant chromosomes, in stark contrast to lipomas of either ordinary or spindle/pleomorphic type.[749,775a] At the molecular level, atypical lipomatous tumors are characterized by alterations of the p53/mdm2 pathway, a feature that persists in the dedifferentiated examples described below.[725] Mdm2 protein expression, which can be detected immunohistochemically, correlates with 12q13-15 amplification.[737a]

Pleomorphic liposarcoma is a highly cellular, poorly differentiated neoplasm containing numerous tumor giant cells, some of them having the features of lipoblasts[740,772] (Fig. 25.105). The differential diagnosis includes malignant fibrous histiocytoma and pleomorphic rhabdomyosarcoma. In addition, an *epithelioid variant* of pleomorphic rhabdomyosarcoma has been described that simulates undifferentiated carcinoma, also because of its focal reactivity for keratin[759,770] (Fig. 25.106).

Dedifferentiated liposarcoma is the term used for the emergence of a nonlipogenic component within an atypical lipomatous tumor or, much more rarely, in myxoid liposarcoma.[769] The dedifferentiated component may already be present at the time of the original excision but is much more commonly seen in the recurrent or metasta-

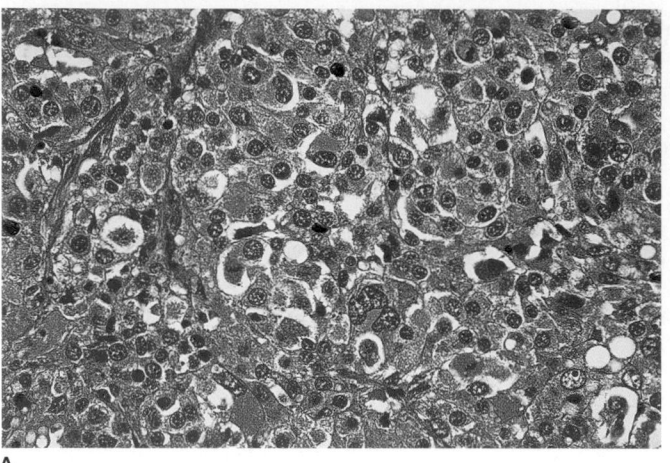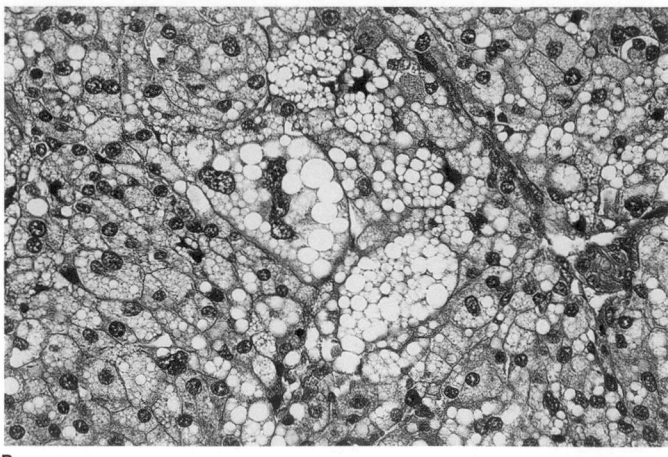

A   B

Fig. 25.106 A and **B**, Epithelioid variant of pleomorphic liposarcoma. The epithelioid features are better demonstrated in **A**, whereas the liposarcomatous nature of the tumor is better shown in **B**.

tic foci. It is much more common in retroperitoneal neoplasms, but it has also been documented in tumors of the extremities[768,729a] (Fig. 25.107). Microscopically, the dedifferentiated component is usually high grade, with an appearance reminiscent of fibrosarcoma or malignant fibrous histiocytoma, with or without myxoid features[743,757,780,784,786] (Fig. 25.108). Heterologous elements, such as blood vessels, skeletal muscle or cartilage may be present[746]; these foci, which are viewed as evidence of divergent differentiation, are accompanied by their respective immunohistochemical markers[756,773a] (Fig. 25.109). Occasionally, the dedifferentiated component appears in the form of a discontinuous micronodular pattern throughout the tumor.[768] In other cases, it exhibits a

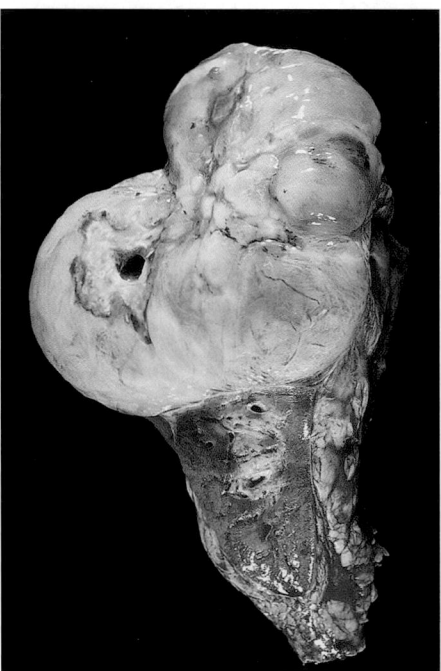

Fig. 25.107 Dedifferentiated liposarcoma of retroperitoneum abutting on the kidney, a common occurrence.

whorling pattern with a neural-like or meningothelial-like appearance associated with metaplastic bone formation.[748,771] The dedifferentiated component can also be low-grade, with a resemblance to fibromatosis or well-differentiated fibrosarcoma.[758] Tumor progression is accompanied by overexpression of p53.[754]

Histochemical and immunohistochemical features. Fat stains are of little help in the diagnosis of liposarcoma, since they can be almost absent in the pure round cell and pleomorphic forms, whereas they may be present in a host of nonlipogenic soft tissue neoplasms. S-100 protein is focally but consistently found immunohistochemically in the cells of both benign and malignant adipose tissue tumors.[737,755] Other markers usually found in this family of neoplasms are mdm2,[725] caveolin (also present in smooth muscle neoplasms),[731] and leptin (a cytokine-like peptide).[773]

Differential diagnosis. The benign lesions most commonly confused with liposarcoma are lipoblastoma/lipoblastomatosis, spindle cell and pleomorphic lipoma, myxoid, inflamed or necrotic lipoma, lipogranuloma (such as that resulting from injection of liquid silicone), and localized lipoatrophy (such as that seen at sites of insulin injections).[738a] We have been particularly impressed by the similarity to myxoid liposarcoma of lipomas that can be present in individuals who have subjected themselves to a drastic diet program. As a general rule, the diagnosis of liposarcoma should be questioned for any tumor seen in the pediatric age group or any tumor that is small, superficial, embedded within a major muscle, or located in the neck region. Although bona fide liposarcomas have been documented in all of these situations, the features of malignancy need to be assessed in a particularly critical fashion because of the high frequency with which benign lesions that simulate liposarcoma occur in these settings.

Treatment and prognosis. The primary treatment of all types of liposarcoma is surgical, inasmuch as radia-

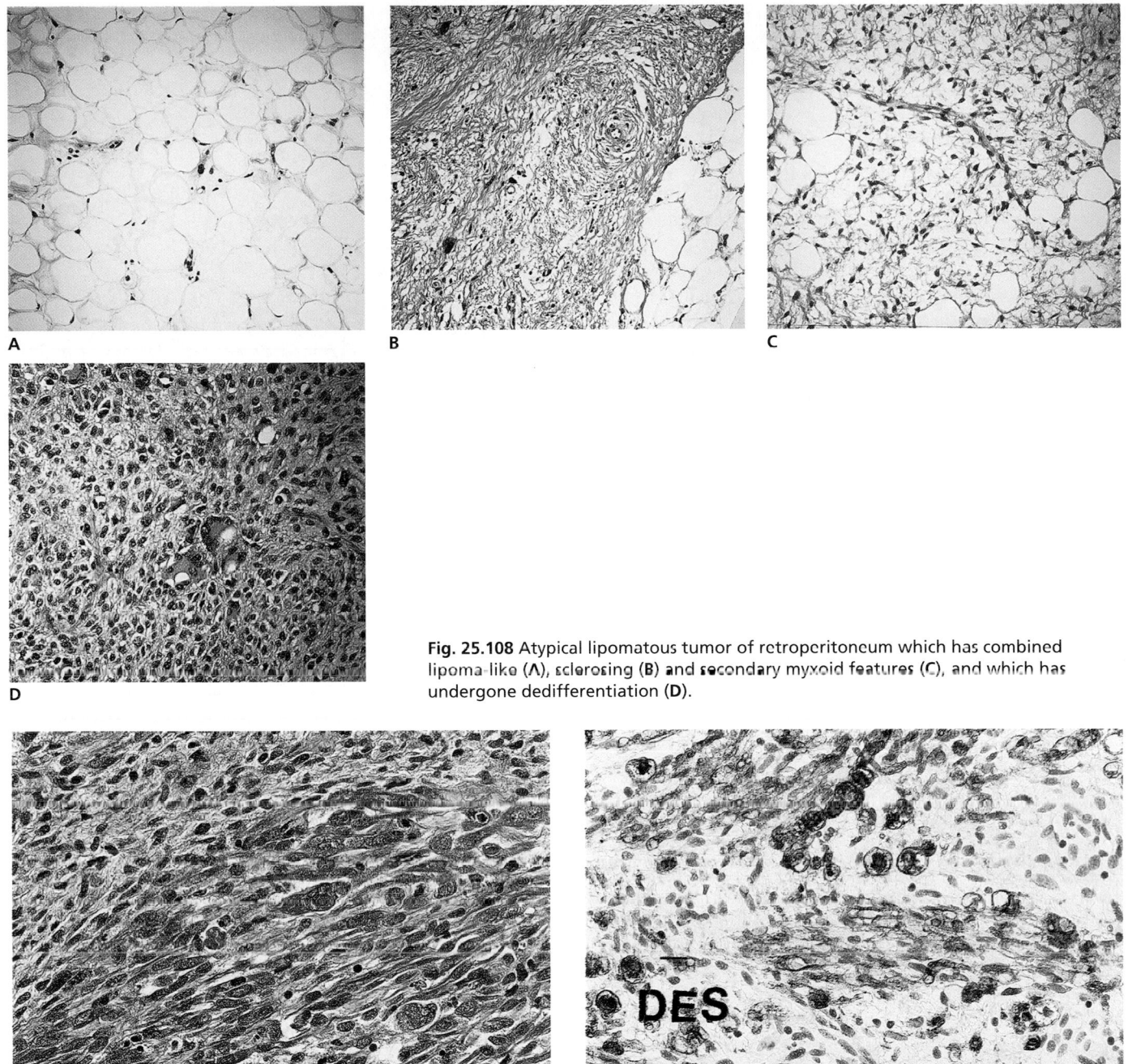

Fig. 25.108 Atypical lipomatous tumor of retroperitoneum which has combined lipoma-like (**A**), sclerosing (**B**) and secondary myxoid features (**C**), and which has undergone dedifferentiation (**D**).

Fig. 25.109 A and **B**, Dedifferentiated retroperitoneal liposarcoma with divergent differentiation toward skeletal muscle. **B**, Desmin immunostain.

tion therapy and chemotherapy are generally of only dubious value.

Tumor location, size, and histologic subtype are the most important prognostic indicators.[774] Both the pure myxoid liposarcomas and the atypical lipomatous tumors (particularly the latter) tend to recur locally rather than to metastasize.[735] By contrast, the pure round cell, pleomorphic, and dedifferentiated types often give rise to widespread metastases.[740,751] In the classic series of Enzinger and Winslow,[742] the 5-year survival rate of patients with myxoid and well-differentiated forms (atypical lipomatous tumors) exceeded 70%, whereas for the round cell pleomorphic varieties it was only 18%.

Tumors and tumorlike conditions of blood and lymph vessels

Hemangioma

Hemangiomas occupy a gray zone between hamartomatous malformations and true neoplasms. They are frequently designated and regarded as tumors because of their usually localized nature and mass effect. The fact that they consistently lack chromosomal alterations speaks against a true neoplastic nature. Although clearly benign, they can become very large and unsightly and can even be fatal if they affect vital structures. They almost never become malignant, although a few well-documented examples of this complication are on record. A high percentage occur in children, and many are already present at birth.[794,815] Over half of the cases are in the head and neck area; they can also occur in the trunk or extremities. Most hemangiomas are solitary; when multiple (with or without associated lesions in internal organs) or affecting a large segment of the body, the condition is known as *(multifocal) angiomatosis*.[806,818]

Hemangiomas have been classified according to their clinical appearance and the caliber of vessel involved. A close correlation exists between these two parameters.

Capillary hemangiomas are made up of small vessels of capillary caliber and can occur in any organ. The most distinctive and common variant of this type is known as *benign hemangioendothelioma* or *juvenile* or *hyperplastic hemangioma*. Its most common location is the skin, where it appears as an elevated nodule with an intense crimson color. Such a hemangioma is traditionally known to dermatologists as a *strawberry hemangioma*. It is usually present at birth or appears during the first month and enlarges rapidly during the first few months of life, only to stop growing when the child is approximately 6 months old. Subsequently, it becomes flaccid, pale blue, and covered with tiny wrinkles, and it eventually disappears completely.[798,812,814]

Other locations for this lesion include the salivary gland and breast. Microscopically, the lesion exhibits a vaguely lobular configuration on low-power examination (Fig. 25.110). Masses of closely packed spindle cells are seen with neoformed spaces that contain little blood (Fig. 25.111). Ultrastructurally and immunohistochemically, most of the cells are endothelial, but there is also a

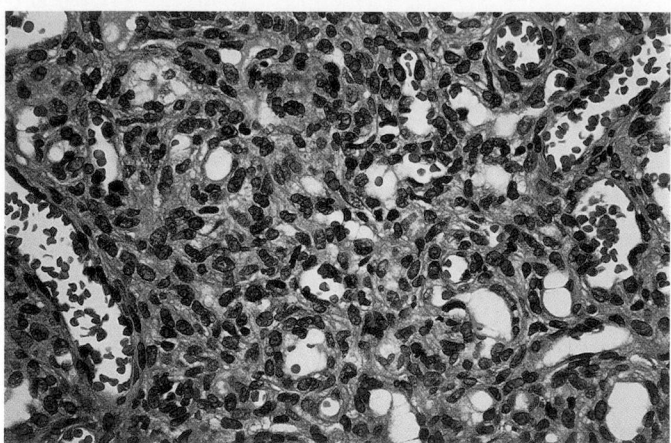

Fig. 25.111 The high cellularity and mitotic activity of juvenile hemangioendothelioma should not lead to an overdiagnosis of malignancy.

component of pericytes/smooth muscle cells and fibroblasts.[802,807,822,823,829] Mitotic figures are usually present and can be numerous. At the periphery, the tumor may be seen to invade subcutaneous tissue or skeletal muscle. Perineurial involvement has also been observed[792,816] (Fig. 25.112). Mast cells may be numerous.[796] Some benign hemangioendotheliomas have an appearance that closely simulates Kaposi's sarcoma. These tumors, which have been referred to as *Kaposi-like* or *kaposiform hemangioendotheliomas* are usually located in the retroperitoneum or deep soft tissue of the extremities and are often associated with thrombocytopenia and hemorrhage (Kasabach–Merritt syndrome).[795,801,824,830] Some of these cases have occurred in adult patients.[813] In contrast to Kaposi's sarcoma, they are not associated with HHV8.[812a] In contrast to the usual type of benign (juvenile) hemangioendothelioma, they are negative for Glut-1 and Lewis Y antigen.[812a] Involvement of regional nodes has been documented, but not distant metastases.[812a]

Cavernous hemangiomas are composed of larger vessels with cystically dilated lumina and thin walls. Those

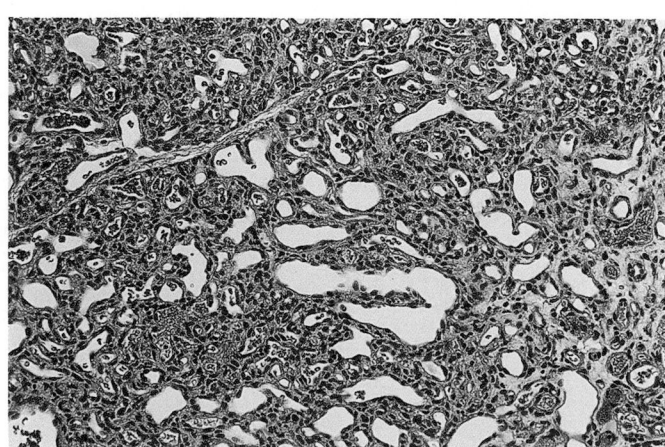

Fig. 25.110 Infantile hemangioendothelioma showing vaguely lobulated architecture.

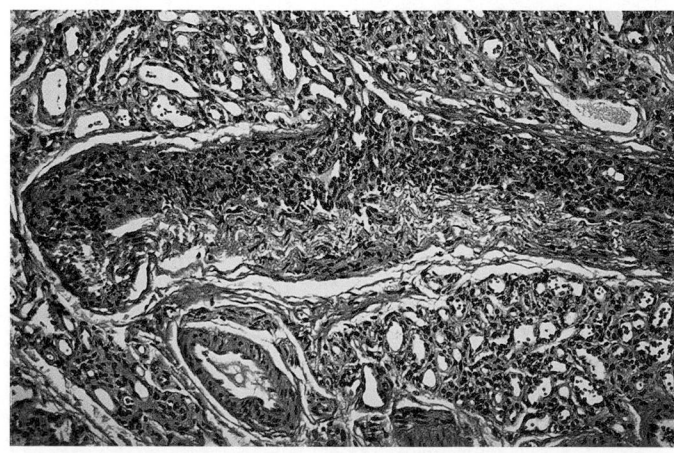

Fig. 25.112 Perineurial spread in juvenile hemangioendothelioma.

occurring in the skin are traditionally known as *port-wine nevus* or *nevus flammeus*. This lesion, which is present at birth, grows very slowly and in proportion to the growth of the patient; in time, it becomes nodular and soft. In contrast to the strawberry nevus, it does not regress spontaneously.[798] Large, deep cavernous hemangiomas may undergo thrombosis, ulceration, and infection (Fig. 25.113). The thrombi may be seen in various stages of organization and recanalization, the latter including papillary endothelial hyperplasia (Masson's lesion). They can also be associated with thrombocytopenia and with intravascular coagulation, which are corrected by removal of the tumor.[821,826] Cavernous hemangiomas containing dilated, interconnecting thin-walled channels with occasional pseudopapillary projections have been designated as *sinusoidal hemangiomas*[791] (Fig. 25.114).

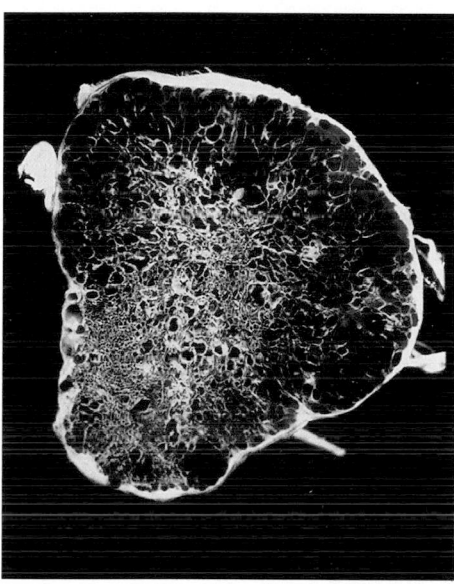

Fig. 25.113 Cavernous hemangioma of soft tissues of orbit.

Large-vessel hemangiomas may be composed of vessels with the structure of veins (*venous hemangiomas*) or a combination of veins and arteries (*racemose, cirsoid,* or *arteriovenous hemangiomas*).[808] The structure of the vessel wall is often abnormal and not easily identifiable as arterial or venous. They occur in the back, gluteal region, thigh, and other sites; sometimes an entire extremity is involved. The association of varicose veins, (dysplastic) cutaneous hemangiomas, and soft tissue and bone hypertrophy is known as *Klippel–Trenaunay syndrome*.[810,811] Venous hemangiomas of the feet have been seen in patients with Turner's syndrome.[827] Thrombosis and calcification are common in large-vessel hemangiomas; the latter can be large enough to be detectable radiographically.

Skeletal muscle (intramuscular) hemangiomas usually have a venous or cavernous microscopic appearance[790] (Fig. 25.115). In other cases, they are very cellular, with plump nuclei, mitotic figures, intraluminal papillary projections, and even infiltration of perineurial spaces.[789] It should be remembered that bona fide angiosarcomas of skeletal muscle are exceptionally rare.

Intravascular papillary endothelial hyperplasia (Masson's hemangioma or Masson's lesion) is probably not a true neoplasm but is discussed here because of its capacity to simulate microscopically benign and malignant vascular tumors.[793,809] First described by Masson in hemorrhoidal vessels as "vegetant intravascular hemangioendothelioma,"[793] it is currently thought to represent an exuberant organization and recanalization of a thrombus, an interpretation supported by immunohistochemical studies.[788] It can occur in previously normal vessels or in varices, hemorrhoids, hematomas, pyogenic

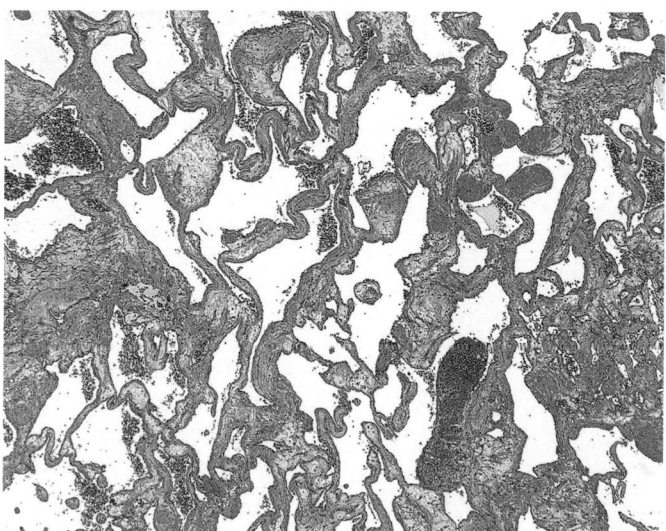

Fig. 25.114 Sinusoidal hemangioma. The vascular spaces are widely dilated.

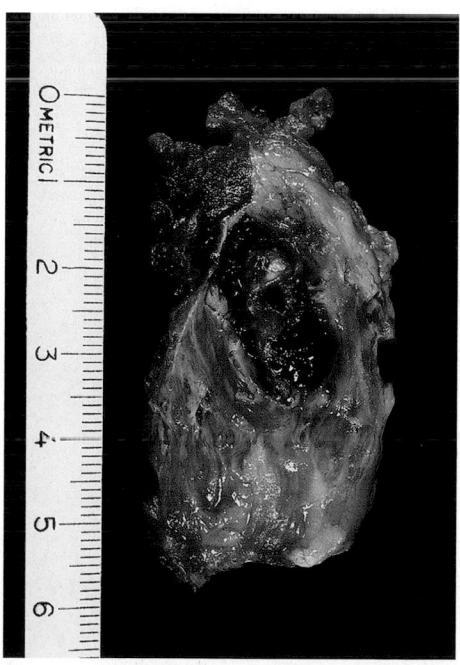

Fig. 25.115 Gross appearance of skeletal hemangioma.

granulomas, hemangiomas, and angiosarcomas.[809,817,819] The de novo ("pure") form is usually found in the extremities (particularly the fingers) and the head and neck region, whereas the type engrafted on a preexisting vascular disorder ("mixed") tends to be in the trunk.[804] It simulates angiosarcoma because of the presence of papillary formations, anastomosing vascular channels, and plump endothelial cells. It is identified because of the exclusively intravascular nature of the process; the lack of necrosis, bizarre cells, and atypical mitoses; the characteristically fibrinous and/or hyaline (deeply eosinophilic) appearance of the papillary stalks; and the frequent finding of residual organizing thrombi (Fig. 25.116).

Spindle cell hemangioma, a vascular tumor originally described as spindle cell hemangioendothelioma,[828] may present at any age, has a male predominance, occurs preferentially in the dermis and subcutaneous tissue of the distal extremities, and combines histologically the features of cavernous hemangioma and Kaposi's sarcoma[815a,820,825] (Fig. 25.117). The latter areas often have a component of epithelioid (histiocytoid) endothelial cells. The immunohistochemical features are those of endothelial cells.[801] Development of recurrences or new lesions is common, but metastases have been documented in only one case, following repeated recurrences and radiation therapy.[828] Some cases have occurred in patients with Maffucci's or Klippel–Trenaunay syndrome.[797,799] Variously described as a low-grade angiosarcoma[828] and a non-neoplastic lesion related to a vascular malformation,[799,805] it is currently classified as a benign endothelial neoplasm.

Hobnail hemangioma[803] is discussed in Chapter 4.

Glomus tumor

Glomus tumor, also known as *glomangioma*, originates in the neuromyoarterial glomus, a normal arteriovenous shunt abundantly supplied with nerve fibers and fulfilling a temperature-regulating function.[848] The classical location of the glomus tumor is the subungual region, but it can occur elsewhere in the skin, soft tissues (particularly in the flexor surface of the arms and about the knee), nerves, stomach (see Chapter 11), nasal cavity, and trachea.[834,835,841,848,853,855] It has also been reported in the sacrococcygeal region, arising from the coccygeal body (glomus coccygeum) and associated with coccydynia,[838] but there is some question as to whether this is a true neoplasm or simply a normal structure of this region.[832,833,851]

Subungual lesions are always supplied by numerous nerve fibers and are exquisitely painful, two features often absent in glomus tumors arising elsewhere. The tumor may erode the terminal phalanx or even present as an intraosseous lesion in this location.[845] Superficial lesions are well circumscribed. Glomus tumors in children tend to be multiple and of an infiltrative nature.[844] They may present clinically as varicosities of the lower extremities.

Microscopically, glomus tumors consist of blood vessels lined by normal endothelial cells and surrounded by a solid proliferation of round or cuboidal "epithelioid" cells with perfectly round nuclei and acidophilic cytoplasm (Fig. 25.118). As seen under an electron microscope, the tumor cells have features of smooth muscle rather than of pericytes.[857] Immunohistochemically, they manifest reactivity for myosin, vimentin, actin, and basal lamina components but not for desmin[836,837,847,850]

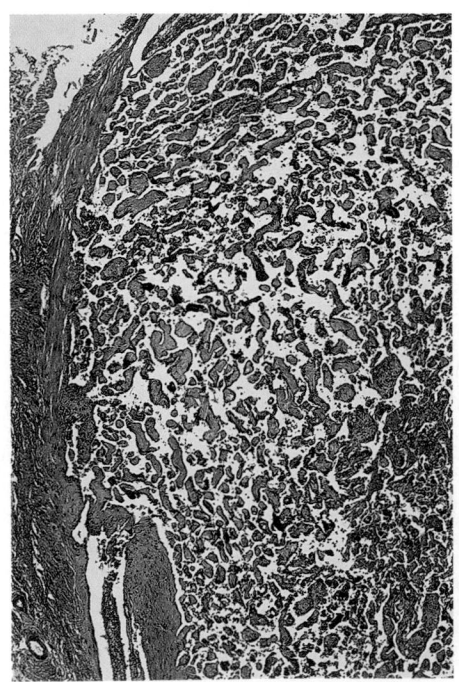 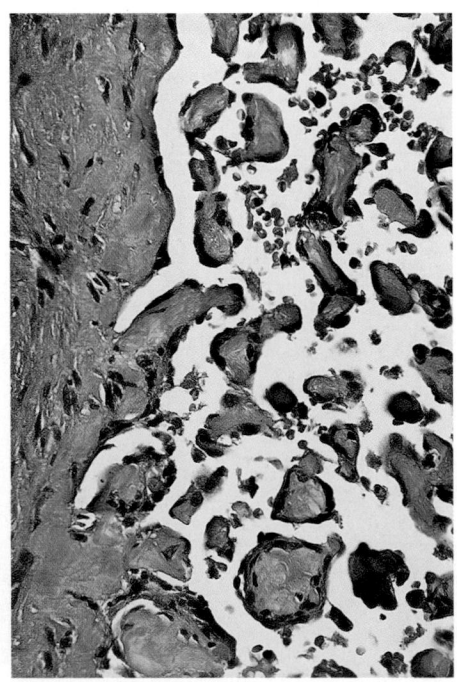

A   B

Fig. 25.116 A and **B**, Intravascular papillary endothelial hyperplasia. The confinement of the lesion to the vascular lumen and the hyaline core of the papillae are characteristic features.

(Fig. 25.119). Numerous substance P-containing nerve fibers have been detected among the glomus cells.[843]

Three microscopic types of glomus tumor have been recognized: *solid, angiomatous,* and *myxoid*[846,856] (Fig. 25.120). The solid type can be confused with sweat gland tumor, melanocytic nevus, or metastatic carcinoma.[842] This is particularly the case when the tumor cells are very epithelioid and/or grow in an Indian-file fashion.[852] The

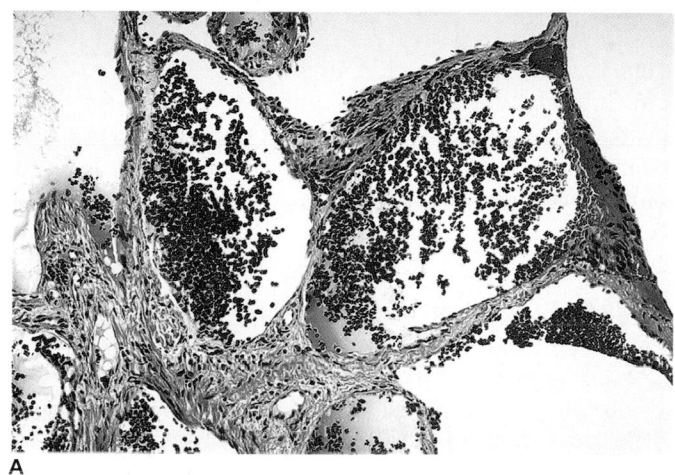

A

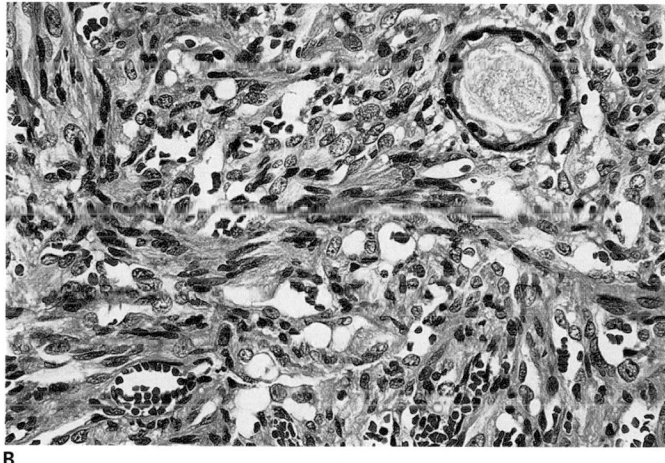

B

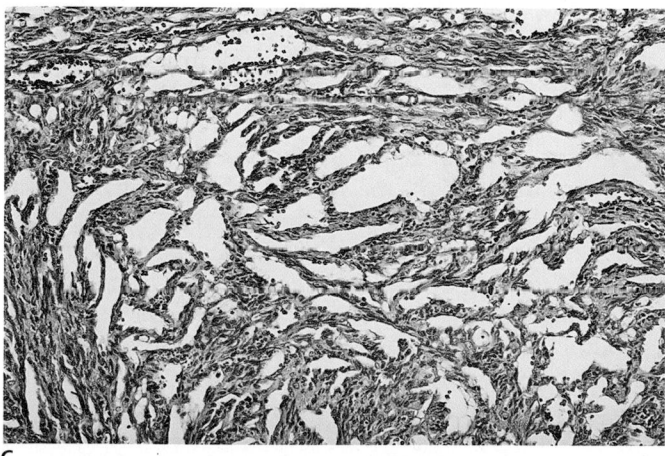

C

Fig. 25.117 Spindle cell hemangioendothelioma: **A,** cavernous hemangioma-like area; **B,** Kaposi's sarcoma-like area; **C,** characteristic "spongy" low-power appearance.

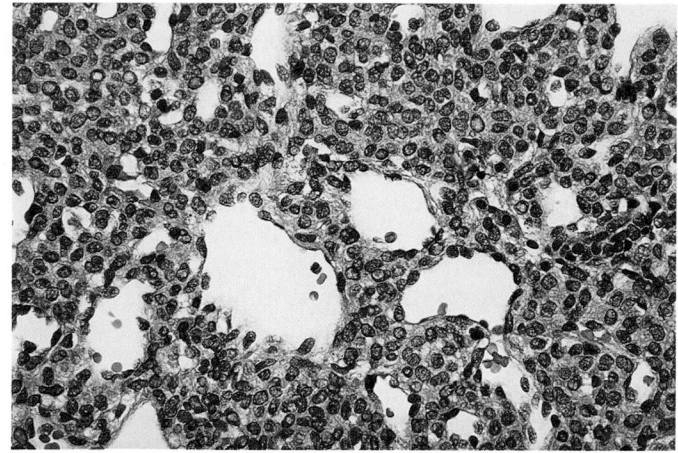

Fig. 25.118 Glomus tumor. The distribution of round glomus cells around the open vascular lumen is a key to the diagnosis.

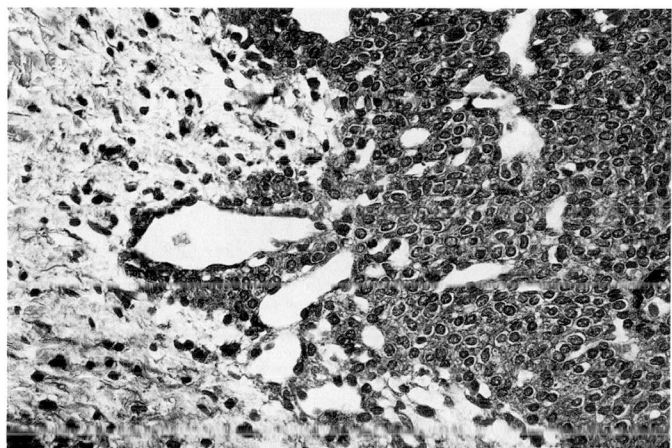

Fig. 25.119 Immunoreactivity for smooth muscle actin in glomus tumor.

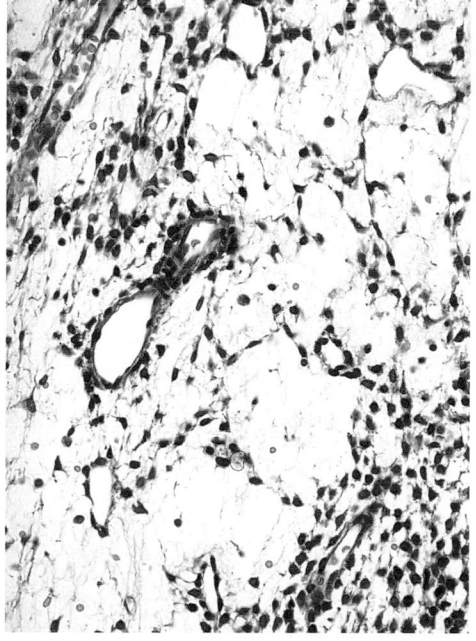

Fig. 25.120 Glomus tumor showing prominent secondary edematous changes.

angiomatous type can have a diffuse quality, in the sense of looking like an angiomatosis with an increased number of glomus cells in the vessel wall[839] (Fig. 25.121). An *oncocytic variant* of glomus tumor, in which the cytoplasm of the glomus cells is packed with mitochondria, has also been described.[854] Often the diagnostic relationship between tumor cells and blood vessels can be clearly seen only at the very periphery of the neoplasm. Mast cells are common (Fig. 25.122).

On rare occasions, glomus tumors behave in an aggressive fashion, with local recurrences and invasion of adjacent structures.[839,840] In other instances, lesions with the typical cytoarchitectural features of glomus tumor merge with a cytologically malignant tumor; these have been designated *glomangiosarcomas*.[831,840,849]

There are also examples of cytologically atypical glomus tumors. A proposal has recently been made to subclassify these as symplasmic, of uncertain malignant potential, and malignant.[839] The microscopic criteria used for the segregation are beyond the scope of this work: suffice it to say that those called malignant (the only ones

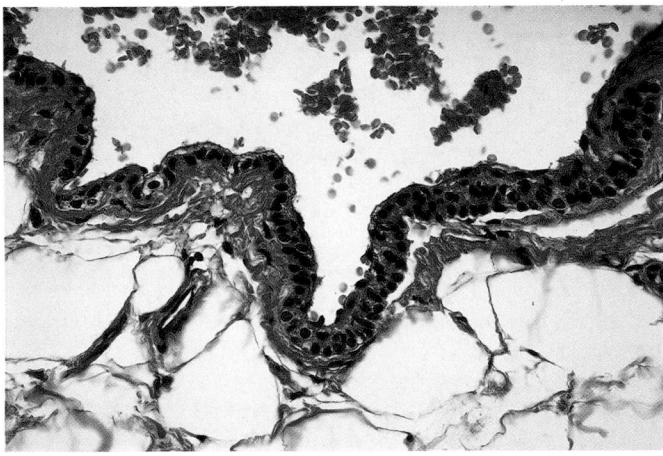

Fig. 25.121 Angiomatous type of glomus tumor. The appearance is somewhat similar to that of a cavernous hemangioma, but the dilated vessel contains a single layer of glomus cells.

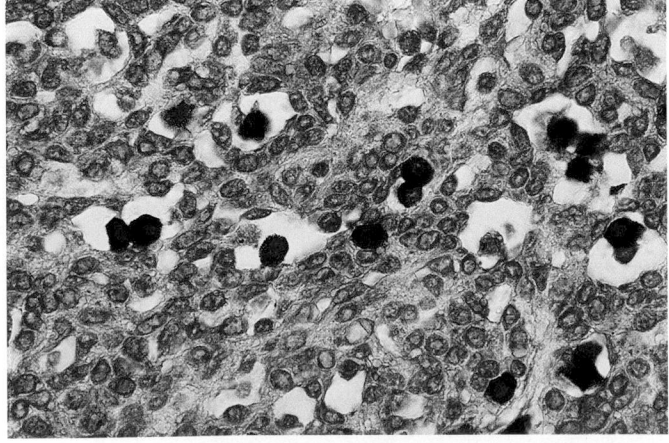

Fig. 25.122 Numerous mast cells in glomus tumor demonstrated with a metachromatic stain (toluidine blue).

to metastasize) were defined as glomus tumors with a deep location and a size of more than 2 cm, or atypical mitotic figures, or moderate to high nuclear grade and 5 or more mitoses per 50 high-power fields.[839] These malignant glomus tumors overlap considerably with the malignant myopericytomas mentioned in the next section.

Hemangiopericytoma

Stout originally defined hemangiopericytoma as a tumor of Zimmerman's pericytes.[865] The concept proved controversial from its inception and has been under heavy attack lately.[859] There is no question that the term has been abused and that a large variety of tumor types have been inappropriately placed under this rubric, as Stout himself decried.[866] At the same time, we believe that the concept is theoretically sound and that it could be rescued if the following considerations were accepted:

1 There is a family of tumor types composed of cells with pericytic features, which blend on one side with vascular smooth muscle cells and on the other with vascular glomus cells. Parenthetically, this was Stout's original contention, in that he considered hemangiopericytoma a less organoid type of glomus tumor. This tumor is usually found in the soft tissues of the extremities (usually distal), tends to have a multinodular pattern of growth, and can be multiple (Fig. 25.123). The most typical cases we have seen have presented as multinodular growths around the ankle of young adults.[861] Depending on some variations of their microscopic appearance along the pericytic/smooth muscle/glomus cell lines and in order to avoid the persisting confusion surrounding the generic term hemangiopericytoma, it has been recently proposed that this tumor be subdivided into (and renamed) glomangiopericytoma and adult myofibromatosis.[860] This is fine, as long as it is realized that this tumor complex comes as close as any to Stout's original concept of hemangiopericytoma. The natural history of these lesions is characterized by a tendency to local recurrence, not surprising in view of their multinodular pattern of growth. Metastasizing examples are also on record.[862]

2 The other large major category that Stout, in later papers and perhaps inappropriately, included into the category of hemangiopericytoma is that currently designated as solitary fibrous tumor, the main reason being the presence of branching vessels with a staghorn appearance[859a] (Fig. 25.124). Most of these tumors are found in the pleural space, peritoneal cavity (particularly pelvis), and orbit, but can occur in many other sites and can be benign or malignant. There is no evidence that the cells of this tumor are related to pericytes. These considerations also apply to myxoid hemangiopericytoma (Fig. 25.125) and to the tumor recently described as lipomatous hemangiopericytoma (which for all

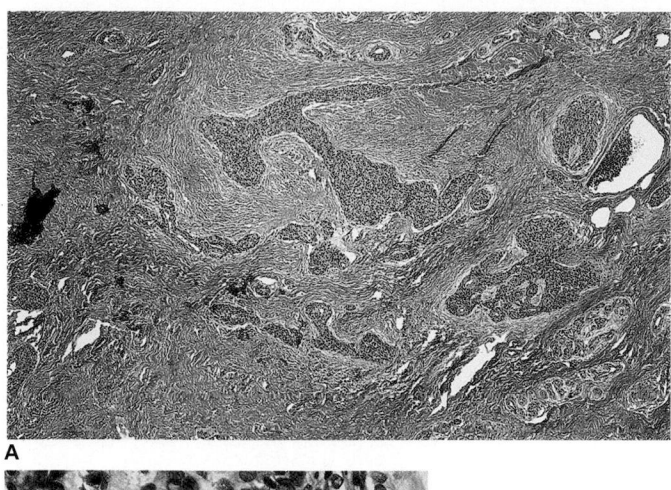

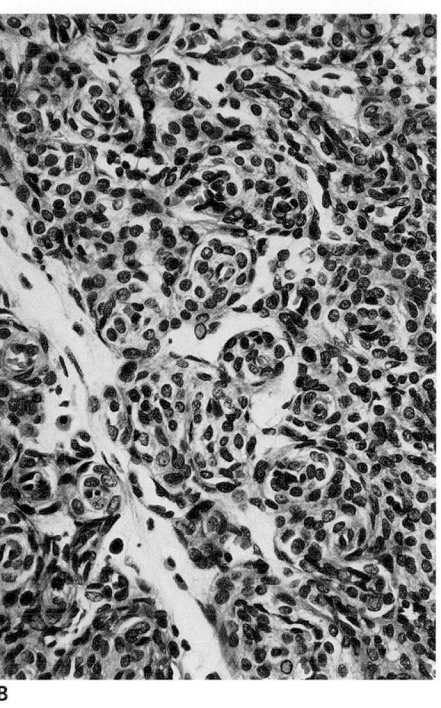

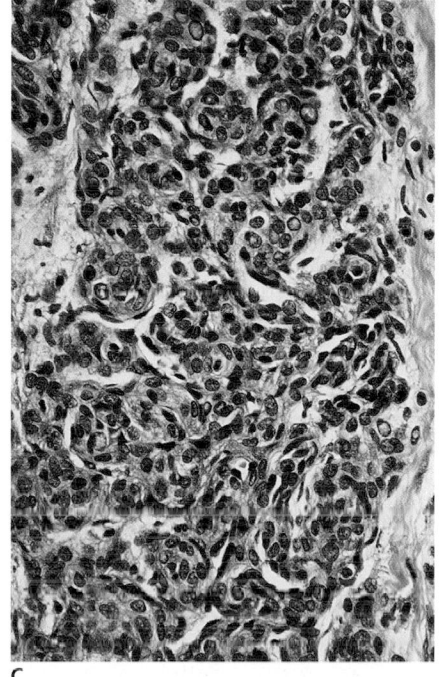

Fig. 25.123 A to **C**, Tumor of soft tissues of the ankle showing hybrid features between glomus tumor and hemangiopericytoma. **A**, Characteristic multinodular quality as seen on low power. **B** and **C**, High-power view showing a cytologic appearance intermediate between that of glomus cells and pericytes.

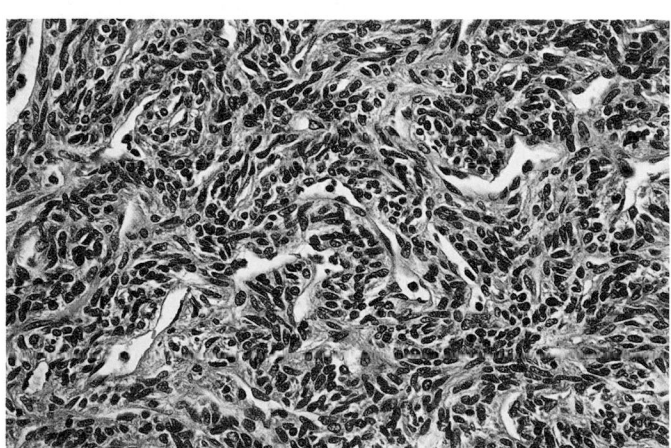

Fig. 25.124 This lesion, traditionally included among the hemangiopericytomas, is now regarded as a solitary fibrous tumor.

practical purposes can be considered a fat-containing solitary fibrous tumor),[864] and to most cases of so-called "angioblastic meningioma" (to be regarded as solitary fibrous tumor of the meninges, see Chapter 28).[858,863]

3 There are many other tumor types that can have a hemangiopericytoma-like pattern of growth similar to that described in the preceding paragraph, most but not all of them of malignant mesenchymal nature.[867] They include: synovial sarcoma (particularly the monophasic variant); malignant peripheral nerve sheath tumor (MPNST); mesenchymal chondrosarcoma (also containing areas of relatively mature cartilage), so-called "phosphaturic mesenchymal tumor" (in which the hemangiopericytoma-like areas are associated with osteoclast-like cells, cartilage, and other patterns, see p. 2327); infantile fibrosarcoma; and even thymoma (which will exhibit epithelial markers at the immunohistochemical and ultrastructural level) (Fig. 25.126).

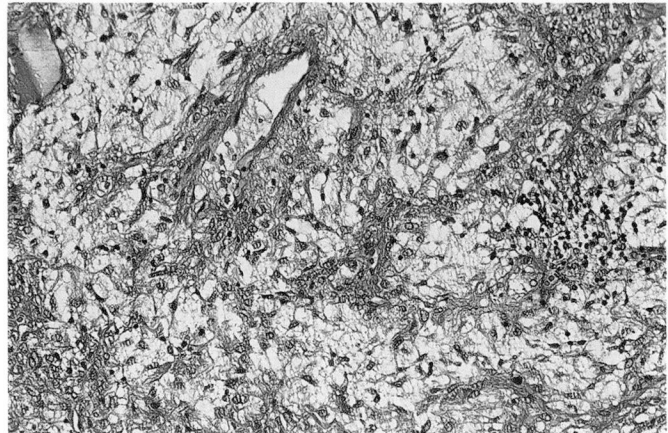

Fig. 25.125 So-called "myxoid hemangiopericytoma." This neoplasm should probably be viewed as a myxoid variant of solitary fibrous tumor.

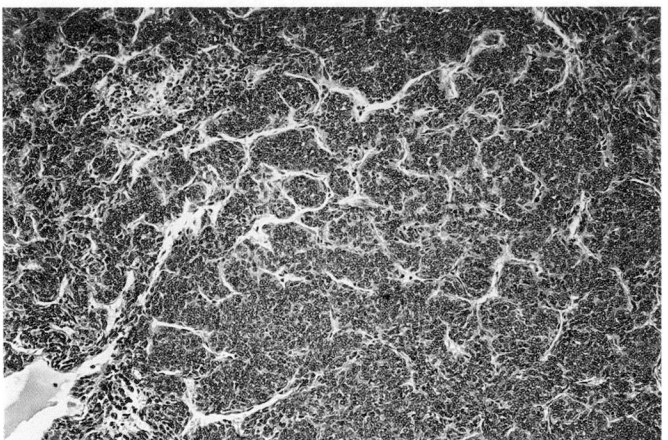

Fig. 25.126 Hemangiopericytoma-like pattern in thymoma.

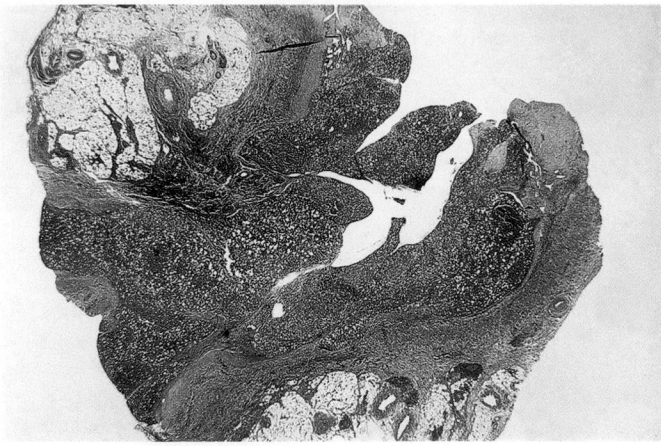

A

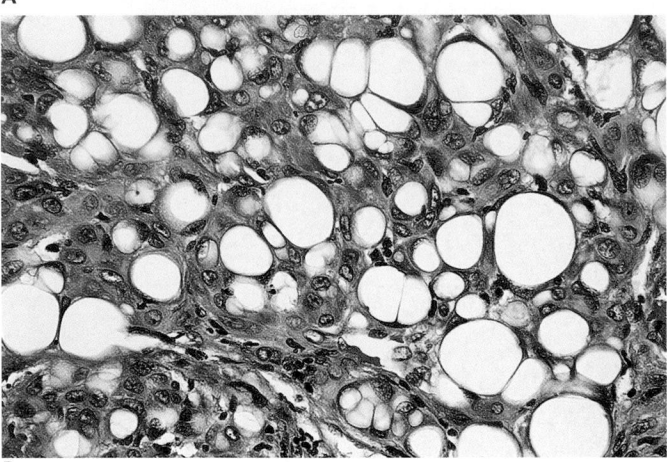

B

Fig. 25.127 A and **B**, Epithelioid hemangioendothelioma. **A**, The tumor partially fills the lumen of the femoral vein. **B**, Prominent cytoplasmic vacuolization is apparent on high-power examination of the same case.

Hemangioendothelioma

The term *hemangioendothelioma* has been used over the years both for benign and malignant vascular tumors composed of endothelial cells, and therefore it lacks specificity. Currently, its preferred use is for vascular tumors of an endothelial nature that occupy an *intermediate* position between the benign hemangioma and the full-blown angiosarcoma.[869] Because of the possibility of misunderstanding, it is better to always use the term with one of the qualifiers that follow.

Epithelioid hemangioendothelioma. This tumor is composed of a distinctive type of endothelial cells having an epithelial-like or histiocyte-like appearance. The cytoplasm is abundant and eosinophilic, often vacuolated. The nucleus is round, vesicular, and occasionally indented. Vascular lumina are present, most of them small; some are located intracellularly and are responsible for the cytoplasmic vacuolation (Fig. 25.127). Mitoses, pleomorphism, and necrosis are variable but usually scanty or absent. An inflammatory infiltrate is often present at the periphery; this may contain well-formed germinal centers and/or a large number of eosinophils.

The stroma may be scanty or have a prominent myxoid appearance. Osteoclast-like multinucleated giant cells may be present.[887] The endothelial nature of the tumor cells has been confirmed ultrastructurally and immunohistochemically.[870] The acidophilic staining quality of the cytoplasm is due to the presence of packed intermediate filaments of vimentin type.

Tumors with this set of morphologic features have been described in a large number of sites, including the skin, bone, lung, pleura, liver, peritoneum, and lymph nodes.[888] Those located in the soft tissue are seen in adults and often arise from the wall of a vein in an extremity.[869,885,886] They also occur in the head and neck area.[874] Local recurrences and distant metastases can develop, but the prognosis remains better than for angiosarcoma of either the conventional or epithelioid type (see below).[877,878]

Epithelioid hemangioendothelioma is one of several related proliferative lesions of endothelial cells having as a common denominator an epithelioid or histiocytoid morphology, often accompanied by immunoreactivity for keratin.[876] These were originally embraced under the generic category of *histiocytoid hemangioma*,[868,872,882] but it has become clear that lesions composed of epithelioid (histiocytoid) cells can be present in infectious processes (such as Peruvian verruca and bacillary angiomatosis), in the skin disorder of unknown pathogenesis traditionally known as angiolymphoid hyperplasia with eosinophilia (also designated as epithelioid hemangioma), in the low-grade neoplasm described here, and in the fully malignant epithelioid angiosarcoma (see next section).[875,883] Despite early statements to the contrary, Kimura's disease as seen in the Orient does not belong to this group.[884]

A morphologically distinct subtype of epithelioid hemangioendothelioma is characterized by a marked histologic resemblance to epithelioid sarcoma, to the point of having been named epithelioid sarcoma-like hemangioendothelioma.[871] One of the clues to the diagnosis is the presence of cytoplasmic vacuoles consistent with intracytoplasmic vascular lumen formation. Immunohistochemically, the tumor cells are reactive for keratin, vimentin, CD31, and FLI-1, but not CD34.[871] The existence of this tumor makes one wonder about the nature of classic epithelioid sarcoma, which could conceivably represent the extreme form of epithelioid transformation of an endothelial vascular neoplasm.

Malignant endovascular papillary angioendothelioma (Dabska's tumor; papillary intralymphatic angioendothelioma [PILA]). Malignant endovascular papillary angioendothelioma is an extremely rare but distinctive tumor usually seen in children but also reported in adults, located in the skin or soft tissues and characterized by papillary tufts that are lined by plump endothelial cells located within dilated vascular lumina, some of which have a glomeruloid configuration (Fig. 25.128). Many of the tumor cells have epithelioid or histiocytoid features, including cytoplasmic eosinophilia and vacuolation. The lesion has a uniformly good prognosis, although nodal metastases have occurred in a few instances.[873,874a,879,881]

Retiform hemangioendothelioma. See Chapter 4.

Composite hemangioendothelioma is the name that has been proposed for a vascular neoplasm showing various combinations of benign, low-grade malignant, and malignant components.[880] The two most common patterns are those of epithelioid and retiform hemangioendothelioma. This probably does not represent a specific entity but rather the manifestation of the fact that there is a great deal of overlap between the seemingly endless number of types and subtypes of vascular tumors that are being described.

Angiosarcoma

The term *angiosarcoma*, if used without adjectives or prefixes, refers to a malignant neoplasm arising from the *endothelial cells of blood vessels*, and is therefore synonymous with malignant hemangioendothelioma.[910,914] It is usually seen in adults, the most common sites being the skin, soft tissue, breast, bone, liver, and spleen. Some soft tissue angiosarcomas arise from major vessels, such as the inferior vena cava, pulmonary artery, or aorta.[889,903] These tend to have a very undifferentiated appearance and a solid pattern of growth,[915] to such an extent that they may not be identifiable as being of endothelial nature.[890,891] Accordingly, topographic terms such as intimal sarcoma, luminal sarcoma, and arterial/venous trunk sarcoma have been used for them.[895,903]

Angiosarcomas have been reported in previously irradiated fields,[894,907] around longstanding foreign bodies,[898,900] in arteriovenous fistulas[892] (including surgically constructed ones),[913] as a secondary somatic-type development in mediastinal or retroperitoneal germ cell tumors,[911] or arising within preexisting benign tumors, such as hemangioma/vascular malformation, neurofibroma, intramuscular lipoma, or leiomyoma.[893,906,908,916]

Grossly, angiosarcomas tend to be highly hemorrhagic and deeply invasive (Fig. 25.129). Their microscopic appearance ranges from a pattern so well differentiated as to simulate a benign hemangioma to

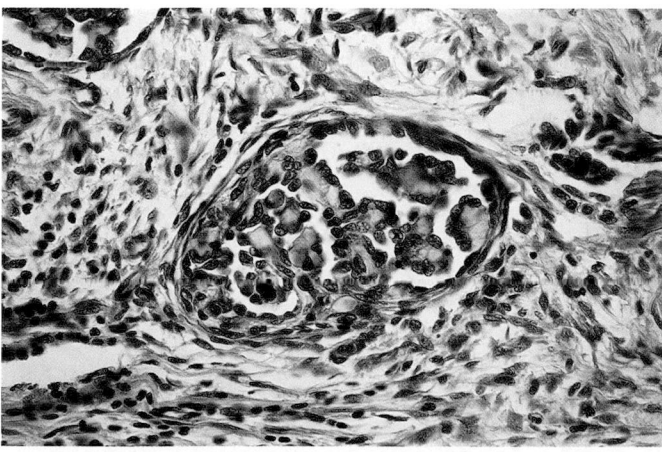

Fig. 25.128 Malignant endovascular papillary angioendothelioma (Dabska's tumor). The papillary configuration of the endothelial fronds can be appreciated.

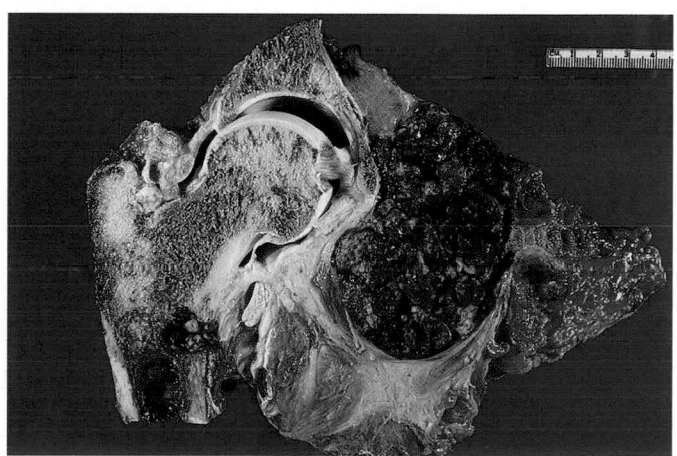

Fig. 25.129 Gross hemorrhagic appearance of angiosarcoma in the region of the hip.

one so undifferentiated and solid as to simulate carcinoma, malignant melanoma, or other types of sarcoma.[905] The diagnostic areas of angiosarcoma are represented by the freely anastomosing vascular channels lined by atypical endothelial cells (Fig. 25.130), a pattern that is accentuated by silver reticulin stains or immunostains for basement membrane components.[908] Clusters of reactive lymphocytes and clumps of hemosiderin are common.

Variations in the appearance of the neoplastic endothelial cells are great. Their shape ranges from very elongated to plump and epithelioid and their size from small to giant, with occasional development of multinucleated forms[896] (Fig. 25.131). The latter are sometimes seen to display prominent hyaline globules containing α_1-antitrypsin and α_1-antichymotrypsin.[912] In rare cases, foci of granular cells similar to those seen in granular cell tumors are present.[904] The predominantly epithelioid appearance of the neoplastic endothelial cells can also be seen in the primarily intraluminal ("intimal") tumors of large vessels.[899]

The differential diagnosis of angiosarcoma includes hemangioma for the better differentiated lesions, Kaposi's sarcoma for those with a predominantly spindle component, and carcinoma or amelanotic melanoma for the poorly differentiated types. Metastatic renal cell carcinoma, because of its high degree of vascularity, is particularly notorious for its ability to simulate angiosarcoma; in this regard, it should be kept in mind that clear tumor cells are not a feature of angiosarcoma.

Immunohistochemically and ultrastructurally, various endothelial markers can be demonstrated depending on the degree of differentiation[901] (Fig. 25.132); of these, CD31 is probably the most reliable. In the epithelioid variant of angiosarcoma, coexpression of keratin is common.[896]

A well-defined clinicopathologic form of angiosarcoma involves the head and neck region (particularly the scalp) of elderly individuals. It begins in the skin but often extends into the subcutis. The clinical course includes repeated local occurrences over a long period of time, followed in some cases by lymph node and pulmonary metastases.[897,902,908]

Neoplastic angioendotheliomatosis, once regarded as a form of multicentric angiosarcoma, is now viewed as a type of malignant lymphoma with a particular tropism for vascular lumina; this entity is discussed in Chapter 4.

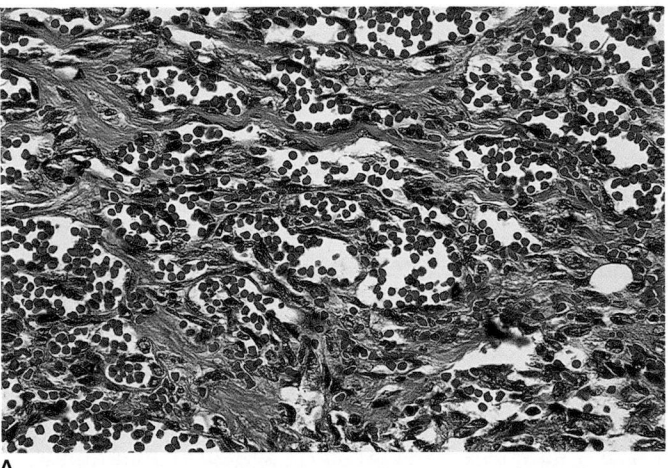

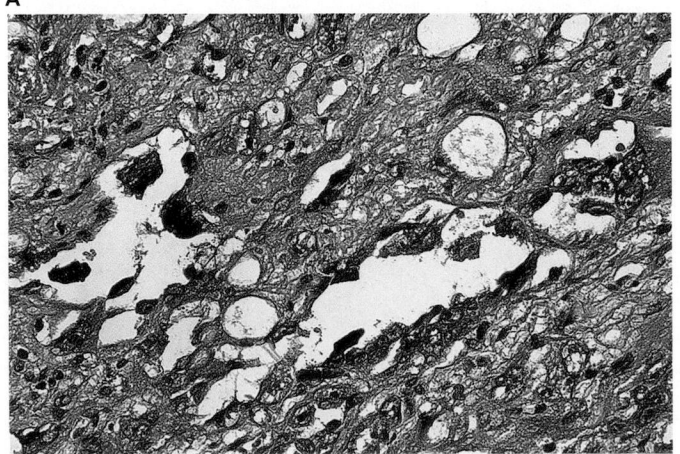

Fig. 25.130 A and **B**, Angiosarcoma of mediastinal soft tissues. **A**, Anastomosing vascular channels. **B**, On high power, the channels are seen to be lined by highly atypical endothelial cells.

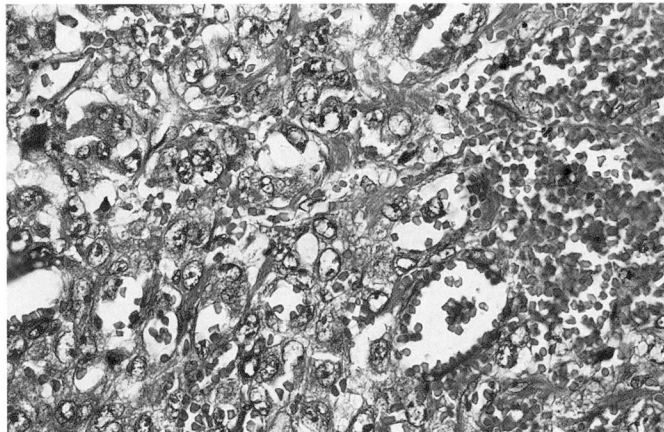

Fig. 25.131 Epithelioid angiosarcoma arising from the region of the seminal vesicle.

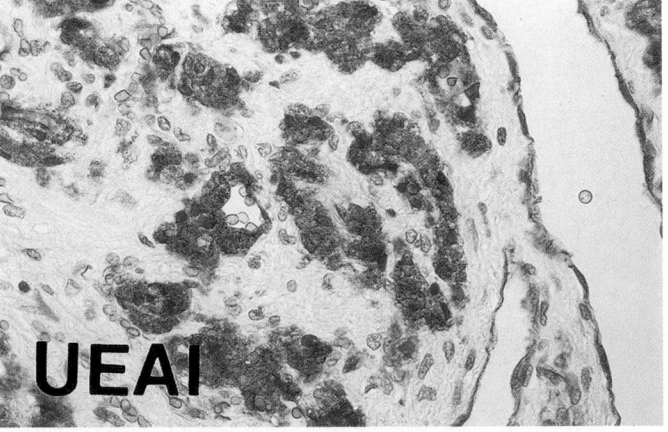

Fig. 25.132 *Ulex europaeus* lectin I reactivity in angiosarcoma.

Lymphangioma and lymphangiomyoma

Most **lymphangiomas** represent malformations rather than true neoplasms and are thought to result from failure of the lymphatic system to communicate with the venous system.[921] Three forms exist: *capillary, cavernous,* and *cystic* (Fig. 25.133). The capillary form occurs in the skin, whereas the cavernous variety prefers deep soft tissues. Cystic lymphangioma has been traditionally known as *hygroma.* Its most common presentation is in the form of a poorly defined soft tissue mass in the neck of children, usually situated posterior to the sternocleidomastoid muscle and sometimes extending into the mediastinum (Figs 25.134 and 25.135). Those developing

in utero often progress to hydrops and cause fetal death. Many of the fetuses have karyotypes consistent with Turner's syndrome[918,921] or other chromosomal abnormalities. Some lymphangiomas are diffuse and/or multicentric, the condition being designated as *lymphangiomatosis.* These cases may be limited to the soft tissues or be accompanied by osseous and/or visceral manifestations.[933] A preferred location is the thoracic cavity, with resulting chylous pleural effusion and/or chyloperi-cardium.[919] Other cases affect diffusely the extremities.[925]

Microscopically, lymphangioma consists of large lymphatic channels growing in loose connective tissue (Fig. 25.136). A few disorganized bundles of smooth muscle can be present in the wall of the larger channels. Focal areas of papillary endothelial proliferation similar to those described by Masson in blood vessels are sometimes found.[930] Large collections of lymphocytes may be present in the stroma and cause mistakes in

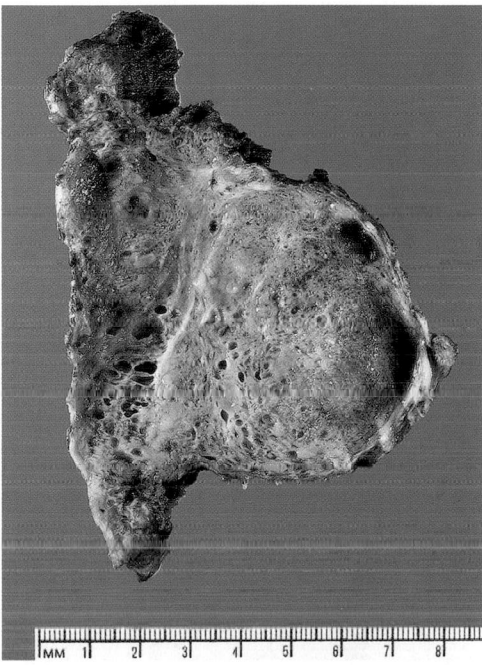

Fig. 25.133 Cavernous lymphangioma. (Courtesy of Dr. RA Cooke, Brisbane, Australia; from Cooke RA, Stewart B: Colour Atlas of Anatomical Pathology. Edinburgh, Churchill Livingstone, 2004).

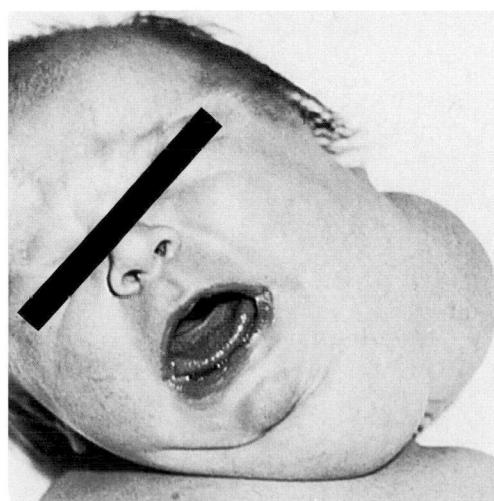

Fig. 25.134 Large cystic hygroma in an infant. (From Maxwell JH. Tumors of the face and neck in infancy and childhood. South Med J 1952, **45:** 292–299)

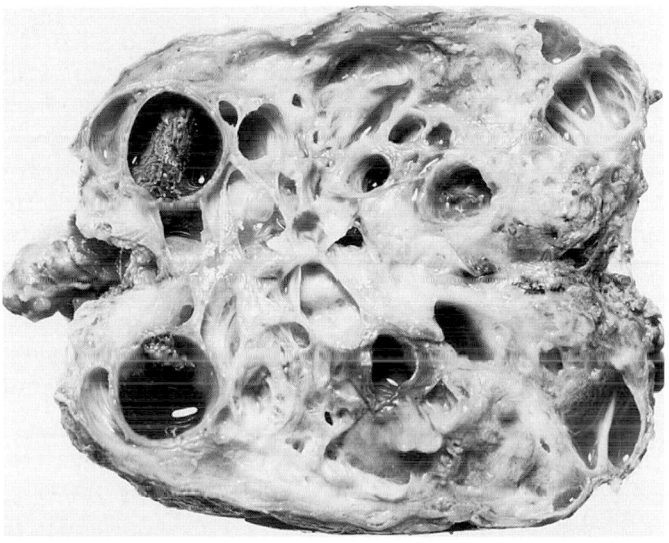

Fig. 25.135 Large cystic hygroma in the neck of an 18-month-old infant. The tumor extended into the superior portion of the mediastinum.

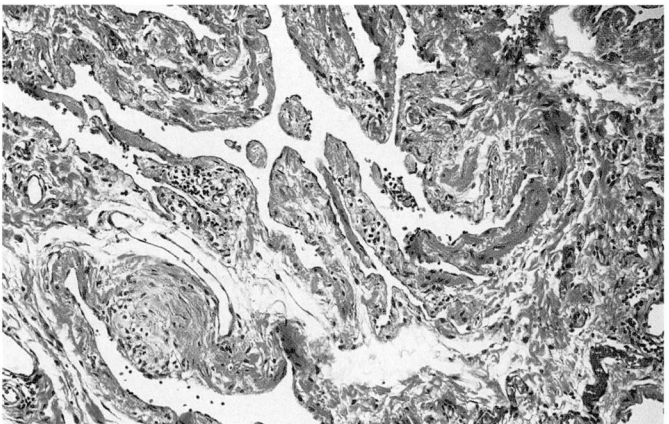

Fig. 25.136 Lymphangioma of soft tissue showing dilated spaces lined by flattened endothelium. A scattering of lymphocytes is present in the stroma.

interpretation. Lymphangioma practically never becomes malignant and is curable by excision.[927] The variant of cutaneous lymphangioma originally named acquired progressive lymphangioma and recently redesignated benign lymphangioendothelioma[928] is discussed in Chapter 4.

Lymphangiomyoma is the preferred term for a benign neoplasm seen exclusively in females and originally described as lymphangiopericytoma.[923,935] The localized form is restricted to the mediastinum and retroperitoneum. It is often seen in close association with the thoracic duct and its tributaries and it often results in chylothorax.[922] Chylous ascites and chyluria (secondary to ureteral wall involvement) may also be present. The diffuse form of the disease, known as *lymphangio(leio)myomatosis*, typically involves the lung[934] (see Chapter 7). Some cases of lymphangiomyoma/lymphangiomyomatosis are seen in patients with the tuberous sclerosis complex, indicating a pathogenetic link.[929]

Microscopically, there is a proliferation of intimately mingled lymph vessels and smooth muscle elements (Fig. 25.137). Immunohistochemically, the tumor cells (which are plumper and paler than those of ordinary leiomyomas) are reactive for actin, desmin, and HMB-45.[920] This profile (particularly the HMB-45 immunoreactivity) links these tumors with renal and extrarenal angiomyolipomas (including their epithelioid and monotypic variants), pulmonary clear cell ("sugar") tumor, the recently described clear cell myomelanocytic tumor of the thigh,[924] and other neoplasms into the continuously enlarging PEComa concept.

Although immunohistochemical evaluation of hormone receptors in lymphangiomyoma/lymphangiomyomatosis has resulted in conflicting findings,[926,932] good therapeutic results have been reported with progesterone therapy[931] or oophorectomy.[917]

Lymphangiosarcoma and related lesions

Lymphangiosarcoma is regarded as the lymph vessel counterpart of angiosarcoma, the latter term implying— when used without a qualifier—an origin from blood vessels. The cutaneous examples of lymphangiosarcoma, which are the most common, present clinically as bluish or purple elevations. They are often multiple, although in late stages they coalesce to form a large hemorrhagic mass (Fig. 25.138). Microscopically, they show a wide variation of patterns, ranging from solid undifferentiated areas that can simulate carcinoma to others so well differentiated as to be indistinguishable from lymphangioma or lymphangiectasia (Fig. 25.139). As in the case of (hem)angiosarcoma, the most typical areas are represented by freely anastomosing channels lined by atypical endothelial cells. Ultrastructural and immunohistochemical studies have documented the presence of endothelial markers, but have also shown that some of these tumors differentiate in the direction of blood vessels rather than lymph vessels.[936,942,943]

The behavior of full-blown lymphangiosarcoma is extremely malignant. In a series of 129 patients, only 11 survived over 5 years.[950]

Generally, the diagnosis of lymphangiosarcoma has been made in the presence of malignant vascular tumors

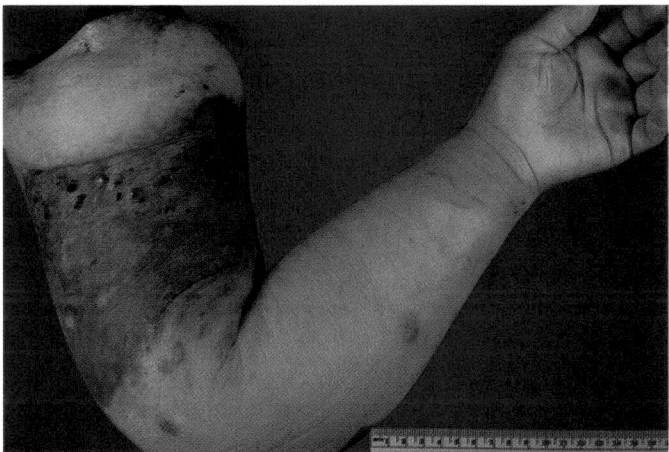

Fig. 25.138 Amputated upper extremity in a case of post-mastectomy lymphangiosarcoma.

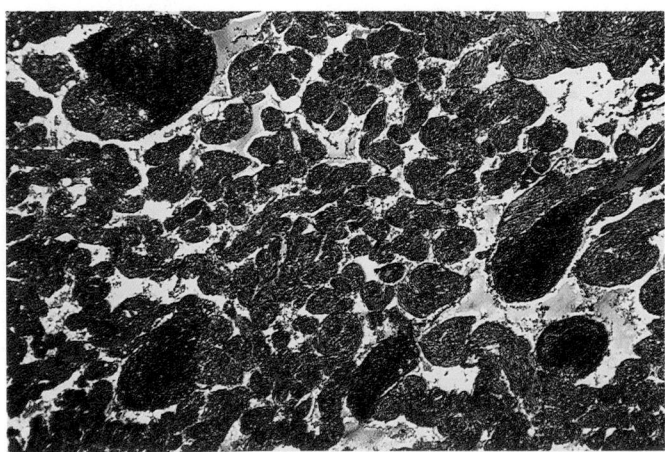

Fig. 25.137 Microscopic appearance of lymphangioma.

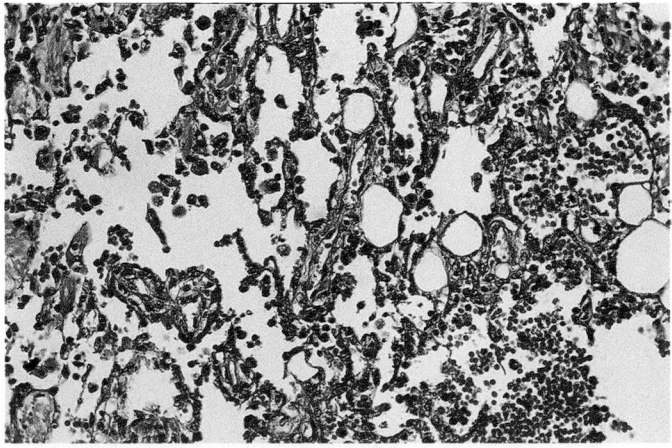

Fig. 25.139 Post-mastectomy lymphangiosarcoma showing an intricate network of neoplastic vessels.

superimposed on areas of chronic lymphedema, the prototypical example being the lymphangiosarcoma developing in patients who have had longstanding massive lymphedema after radical mastectomy for breast carcinoma (Stewart–Treves syndrome).[938,944,948,949] The average interval is approximately 10 years. A pathogenetically analogous situation is the lymphangiosarcoma developing secondarily to chronic lymphedema of the lower leg.[941,945] In these instances, it is extremely difficult to detect the early neoplastic changes in the lymphangiectatic vessels, and all the pathologist can do is to indicate the presence of "atypical vascular hyperplasia," which may be an indicator of early neoplasia or a preneoplastic process.

With the decrease in the number of radical mastectomies performed during the last few decades and the corresponding increase in the number of conservative breast operations followed by radiation, the pattern of breast carcinoma-associated vascular proliferative processes has changed. The malignant tumors developing under these circumstances have similar morphologic features, but the interval from the time of therapy is generally shorter, the tumor is in the skin overlying the breast rather than in the arm, and there is no accompanying lymphedema.[947] The matter is complicated by the fact that radiation therapy may also induce lymph vessel proliferations with the appearance of lymphangioma circumscriptum[937] or progressive acquired lymphangioma.[946] Furthermore, an increasingly large number of cases are being described of *atypical vascular lesions* in the skin of radiated breast.[939] These lesions are characterized by dermal vascular proliferation and associated inflammation, but not enough architectural or cytologic atypia to justify a diagnosis of malignancy. Time will tell whether these are entirely benign lesions of reactive nature or whether they are the forerunners of angiosarcoma. Our own experience suggests that in some cases the latter is true.

Tumors of smooth muscle

Leiomyoma

Several types of leiomyomas exist. **Cutaneous leiomyomas** located in the dermis (also discussed in Chapter 4) arise from arrectores pilorum muscles; they are characteristically superficial, small, multiple, and grouped.

Genital leiomyomas are solitary tumors that arise from smooth muscle bundles located in the superficial subcutaneous tissue of genital areas and structures that are topographically and functionally related to them, such as the nipple, areola, axilla, scrotum, penis, vulvar labia, and anal skin.[961]

Vascular leiomyomas (angioleiomyomas) arise from the smooth muscle of blood vessels. They occur more frequently in females and are usually located in the soft tissues of the lower limbs.[955,960,962] They constitute, together with traumatic neuroma, glomus tumor, eccrine

spiradenoma, and angiolipoma, the classic five spontaneously painful nodules of skin and soft tissues.[959]

Grossly, leiomyomas are yellow or yellowish pink, sharply circumscribed, and fairly firm (Fig. 25.140). Microscopically, they are made up of intersecting fascicles of smooth muscle cells encircling vascular lumina lined by normal endothelial cells (Fig. 25.141). The vascular organoid appearance resulting from this feature is marked, but the vascular elastic lamina is absent. Mitotic activity is absent, and there is no necrosis or hemorrhage. Foci of cartilaginous metaplasia may be present.[957] Islands of mature fat may be present in between the smooth muscle fibers. Tumors composed of smooth muscle and adipose tissue (*myolipoma*) are discussed on p. 2277. Occasionally, bizarre nuclear forms similar to those seen in uterine symplasmatic leiomyoma are encountered[952] (Fig. 25.142). Angioleiomyomas have been subdivided into capillary (solid), cavernous, and venous types[955]; as already indicated, transitional forms with glomus tumor and hemangiopericytoma also occur.

The pain often associated with vascular leiomyomas is thought to be mediated by the nerves present within the

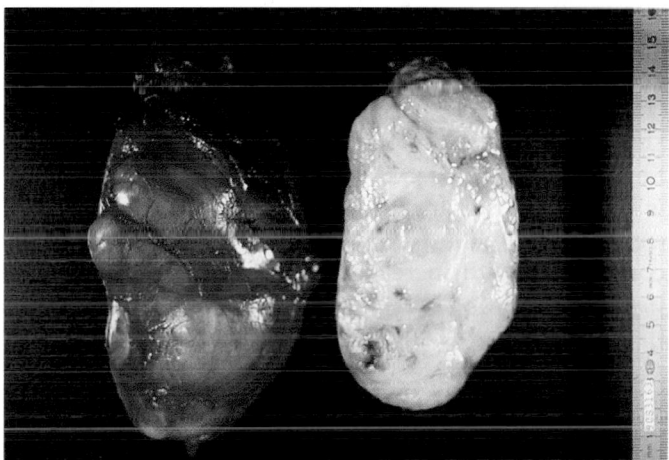

Fig. 25.140 Gross appearance of a soft tissue leiomyoma located in the leg of a child.

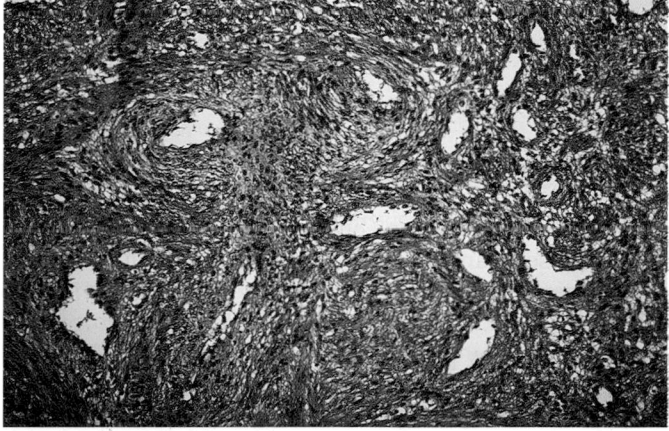

Fig. 25.141 Vascular leiomyoma. The neoplastic smooth muscle cells are clearly related to vessel walls.

demonstrated in well-differentiated tumors with PTAH. Reticulin stain shows wavy, undulating fibers between long lines of tumor cells, without individual cells being wrapped within. Immunohistochemically, both leiomyomas and well-differentiated leiomyosarcomas show reactivity for vimentin (particularly in those of vascular origin), actin, smooth muscle myosin, desmin, H-caldesmon, and basal lamina components, including laminin and type IV collagen[966,972,978,989,993,999,1005] (Fig. 25.147B). Surprisingly, normal and neoplastic smooth muscle cells have been found also to react for keratin and EMA; this feature seems to be particularly prominent in tumors of the female genital tract and large vessels[967,980,992,1003] (Fig. 25.149). Other markers that have been detected in smooth muscle tumors of soft tissues are estrogen receptors,[1007] caveolin (a member of the membrane-scaffolding proteins, also present in adipose tissue tumors),[964] and placental alkaline phosphatase (although not as frequently as in rhabdomyosarcomas).[976] Estrogen receptor protein has also been detected in some of these tumors, raising the possibility of hormonal responsiveness.[981a,1007] Cytogenetic analysis has shown a variety of chromosomal aberrations but no specific karyotypic marker; curiously, a relatively high number of these tumors show no detectable karyotypic abnormalities.[985a,989a,1000] Gene expression profiles of this tumor type are being developed.[995a]

The differential diagnosis between leiomyoma and leiomyosarcoma of the soft tissues depends on a combination of gross and microscopic features. High mitotic activity is virtually diagnostic of malignancy. A diagnosis of leiomyosarcoma should also be strongly suspected for tumors that are overly large, necrotic, or hemorrhagic, even if their mitotic count is low.[1001] Prognosis in leiomyosarcoma correlates primarily with tumor size and depth, two parameters that are closely related.[974,981] In one large series, 40% of the cutaneous leiomyosarcomas recurred, but none metastasized; among the subcutaneous tumors, one half recurred, and one third

resulted in metastases or tumor-related deaths.[974] Prognosis is even worse for the tumors located intramuscularly. Mitotic activity also correlates with prognosis[1008]; however, the fact remains that in many metastasizing leiomyosarcomas of soft tissue, there are less than ten mitoses per high-power field. It has been shown recently that the very presence of smooth muscle differentiation in pleomorphic spindle cell sarcomas of the extremities is an independent indicator of poor prognosis.[971a] Simple enucleation of the tumor virtually guarantees local recurrence. The majority of these tumors eventually give rise to distant metastases, sometimes 15 years or more after the original excision.

It should be noted that all the comments made above are intended for the smooth muscle tumors located in soft tissues and do not necessarily apply to those in the uterus or gastrointestinal tract.

Clear cell (epithelioid) smooth muscle tumors

Smooth muscle tumors of soft tissues may have a round cell (clear cell, epithelioid) configuration, in whole or in part, similar to that seen more often in mesenchymal tumors of the stomach and other intra-abdominal sites[1013] (Fig. 25.150). The term *bizarre leiomyoblastoma* has been used for this tumor type, which has benign and malignant forms. An intravascular variant has also been described.[1011] We prefer to designate these tumors as *leiomyomas* or *leiomyosarcomas clear cell (epithelioid) variant*, and classify them as benign or malignant by using similar criteria to those we apply for smooth muscle tumors

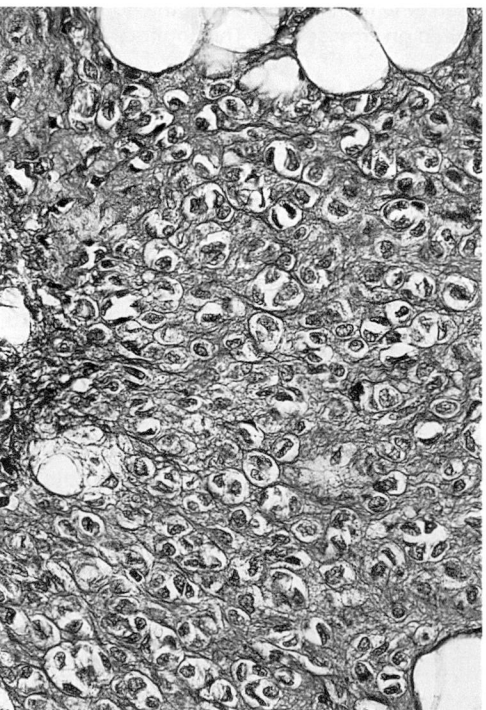

Fig. 25.150 Epithelioid smooth muscle tumor. The PAS stain highlights the thick basement membrane that surrounds individual tumor cells.

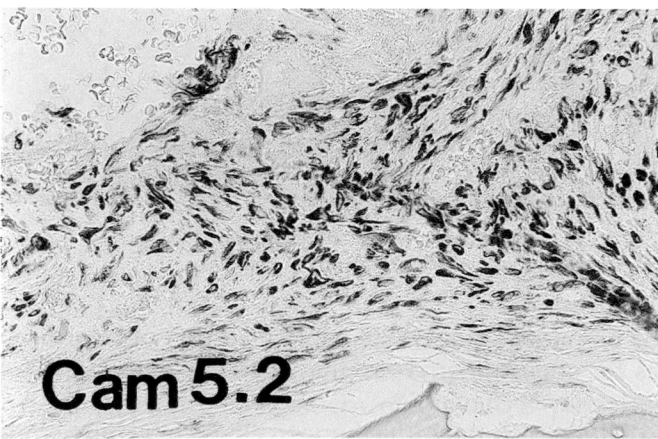

Fig. 25.149 Immunoreactivity for low-molecular-weight keratin (Cam 5.2) in leiomyosarcoma.

in general, although acknowledging the fact that this distinction can be extremely difficult to make in the individual case. Immunohistochemical or ultrastructural markers of smooth muscle differentiation tend to be expressed only focally and imperfectly in these tumors.[1012,1013]

The morphologic similarities that these tumors exhibit with the gastrointestinal stromal neoplasms currently known as GISTs suggests a possible histogenetic relationship and the need for an immunohistochemical and molecular study of these tumors.

Tumors of striated muscle

Rhabdomyoma

Bona fide soft tissue benign tumors of skeletal muscle origin are exceedingly rare.[1014,1016,1026] They can be divided into distinct subtypes, although some overlap exists.[1015,1024,1028,1029] Those known as the *adult* type are found almost exclusively in the oral cavity and its vicinity in adult patients. They can be multifocal and may recur locally.[1019,1027] Microscopically, the cells are well differentiated, large, rounded or polygonal, with abundant acidophilic cytoplasm containing variable amounts of lipid and glycogen. Some cells have features of "spider cells." Cross striations and intracytoplasmic rod-like ("jack straw") inclusions are frequent, and intranuclear inclusions may be seen. There is no mitotic activity or nuclear atypia. The differential diagnosis includes granular cell tumor, hibernoma, and the peculiar condition known as crystal-storing histiocytosis.[1020]

The *fetal* form of rhabdomyoma is seen almost exclusively in two locations: the head and neck area (particularly the retroauricular area) in children under 3 years of age and the vulvovaginal region of middle-aged women.[1017,1018,1021] The latter, also referred to as *genital rhabdomyoma*, is separated by some authors from the other fetal types. Microscopically, both forms are very cellular, formed by immature skeletal muscle fibers (some containing cross striations) and primitive mesenchymal cells (Fig. 25.151). Their development is equivalent to that of fetal skeletal muscle of 7 to 12 weeks gestation. Nuclear aberrations are absent, and mitoses are generally rare. The vulvovaginal cases tend to have a myxoid quality. Kapadia et al.[1021] have divided their cases of fetal rhabdomyoma into "classic" (having the above described features) and "intermediate." The latter were characterized by the presence of large, ganglion cell-like rhabdomyoblasts with vesicular nuclei and prominent nucleoli, interlacing ribbon- or strap-like rhabdomyoblasts with deeply acidophilic cytoplasm, fascicles simulating smooth muscle, plexiform patterns with infiltration of fat, and intimate relationship with peripheral nerves.

The main differential diagnosis of fetal rhabdomyoma is with well-differentiated rhabdomyosarcoma. The distinction can be very difficult because of the overlap of

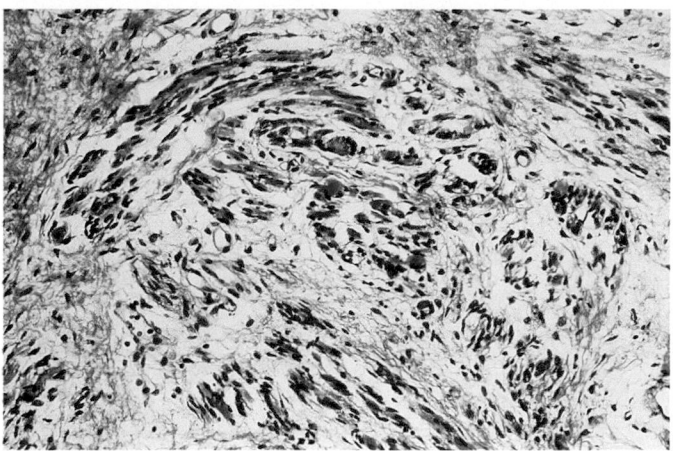

Fig. 25.151 Fetal rhabdomyoma. (Courtesy of Dr. Louis Dehner, St. Louis, MO)

many histologic features; nuclear atypia is said to be the most important distinguishing feature.[1021,1023]

The immunohistochemical features of rhabdomyoma (especially the adult type) recapitulate those of normal skeletal muscle cells[1022,1025]; the markers that these cells can exhibit are listed in the section on rhabdomyosarcoma. Ultrastructurally, hypertrophied Z-band material, thick and thin filaments, numerous mitochondria (some with abnormal configuration or with inclusions), intranuclear bodies, and cytoplasmic bodies have been observed.

It is likely that so-called "cardiac rhabdomyoma," seen in association with the tuberous sclerosis syndrome, is not a true neoplasm (see Chapter 27).

Rhabdomyosarcoma

There are three major categories of rhabdomyosarcoma: pleomorphic, embryonal, and alveolar,[1030,1077] as well as several minor subtypes.[1116]

Pleomorphic rhabdomyosarcoma, which constituted practically all the cases of rhabdomyosarcoma in the older literature, is actually the least common of the three categories. It arises in areas where myotome-derived skeletal muscle occurs and is therefore usually located in an extremity, especially the thigh.[1084,1094,1137] It occurs almost exclusively in adults, but isolated cases in children have been reported.[1068,1069] Grossly, it may be confined within fascial compartments and have the shape of the muscle from which it arises. Microscopically, the tumor is very pleomorphic, with numerous tumor giant cells[1129a] (Fig. 25.152). Making a differential diagnosis with liposarcoma and malignant fibrous histiocytoma is so difficult that a diagnosis of pleomorphic rhabdomyosarcoma should not be made unless there is incontrovertible evidence of skeletal muscle differentiation in the form of cross striations or through the demonstration of specific ultrastructural or immunohistochemical markers (see subsequent discussion). One should be very careful to avoid the following pitfalls: (1) entrapped non-neoplastic

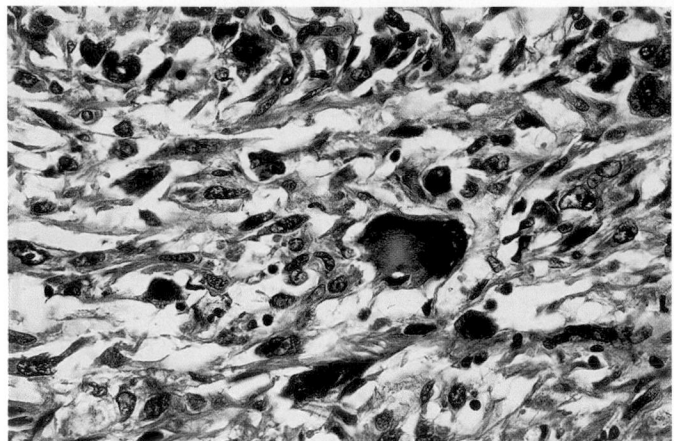

Fig. 25.152 Pleomorphic-type rhabdomyosarcoma. The tumor was immunoreactive for desmin and skeletal muscle actin.

skeletal muscle fibers; (2) release of myoglobin from necrotic muscle with subsequent nonspecific absorption by tumor cells, which thus become immunoreactive[1062]; and (3) presence of skeletal muscle differentiation in other malignant tumors.[1064] In regard to the latter event, it is somewhat ironic that the best evidence of skeletal muscle differentiation in malignant tumors is often found not in rhabdomyosarcoma per se but rather in tumors such as MPNST (see p. 2307), malignant thymoma (see Chapter 8), mixed müllerian tumor of the female genital tract (see Chapter 19), malignant germ cell tumors (particularly extragonadal ones), medulloblastoma (see Chapter 28), and Wilms' tumor (see Chapter 17).

When defined by the restrictive criteria listed previously, pleomorphic rhabdomyosarcoma becomes a very rare neoplasm[1105]; however, well-documented cases exist.[1049,1070] The behavior of pleomorphic rhabdomyosarcoma seems not to be substantially different from that of other pleomorphic sarcomas of soft tissue.

The other two types of rhabdomyosarcomas occur primarily in children and adolescents and actually constitute the most common form of soft tissue sarcoma in this age group.[1071,1139,1141] Sometimes these two types are grouped under the term "juvenile,"[1112] a potentially misleading practice considering the vast clinical, morphologic, molecular, and behavioral differences that exist between the two.

Embryonal rhabdomyosarcoma arises from unsegmented and undifferentiated mesoderm and is common in the head and neck region (particularly the orbit, nasopharynx, middle ear, and oral cavity), retroperitoneum, bile ducts, and urogenital tract.[1080,1098,1119] A smaller percentage occur in the extremities, and these are associated with a higher relapse rate and a lower survival rate.[1075,1136] A few occur initially within the thoracic cavity.[1046] Cases with primary presentation in the skin are also on record.[1127] The large majority occur in children between the ages of 3 and 12 years, but they can also be seen in younger patients[1120] and in adults.[1065a,1076,1095] Some cases have been associated with hypercalcemia or with elevated parathormone levels.[1058] Grossly, the tumor is poorly circumscribed, white, and soft. When growing beneath a mucosal membrane, such as the vagina, urinary bladder, or nasal cavity, it frequently forms large polypoid masses resembling a bunch of grapes—hence the name *sarcoma botryoides*. This is currently regarded as a variation in the pattern of growth of embryonal rhabdomyosarcoma and is referred to as the *botryoid subtype*. The appearance is quite similar to that of an allergic nasal polyp, and, as such, is deceptively benign.

Microscopically, the tumor cells are small and spindle shaped. Some have a deeply acidophilic cytoplasm (Fig. 25.153). A feature of diagnostic value is the presence of highly cellular areas usually surrounding blood vessels, alternating with parvicellular regions that have abundant mucoid intercellular material (Fig. 25.154). A highly characteristic feature of the polypoid ("botryoid") tumors is the presence of a dense zone of undifferentiated tumor cells immediately beneath the epithelium, a

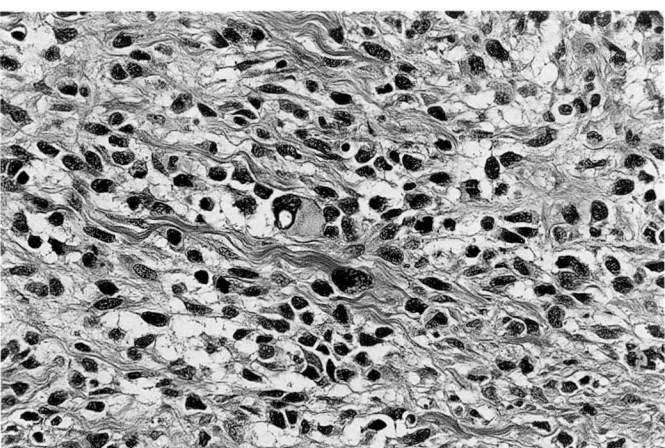

Fig. 25.153 Embryonal rhabdomyosarcoma. Most of the nuclei are oval; the cytoplasm is scanty and acidophilic.

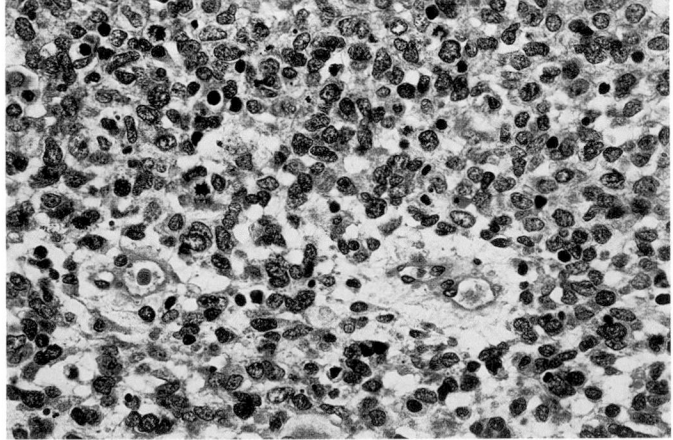

Fig. 25.154 Embryonal rhabdomyosarcoma composed predominantly of round cells. There is a perivascular pseudorosette around a blood vessel.

formation known as *Nicholson's cambium layer* (Fig. 25.155). Cross striations may or may not be present; in contrast to pleomorphic rhabdomyosarcoma in adults, their presence is not indispensable for the light microscopic diagnosis, as long as all the other features are present. Confirmation of the diagnosis, always desirable, can be obtained with ultrastructural and particularly the numerous immunohistochemical markers that are available (see the subsequent discussion).

Occasional tumors within the embryonal category have focally anaplastic features, with bizarre nuclear forms; these should not be classified as pleomorphic rhabdomyosarcomas but rather as pleomorphic subtypes of embryonal (and rarely alveolar) rhabdomyosarcoma[1088] (Fig. 25.156). It has been suggested that they are associated with a more aggressive clinical course, especially when the pleomorphic features are extensive[1072,1088]; conversely, well-differentiated tumors (with over 50% rhabdomyoblasts) are associated with an excellent response to chemotherapy.[1129] Tumors examined following multidrug chemotherapy tend to show a greater

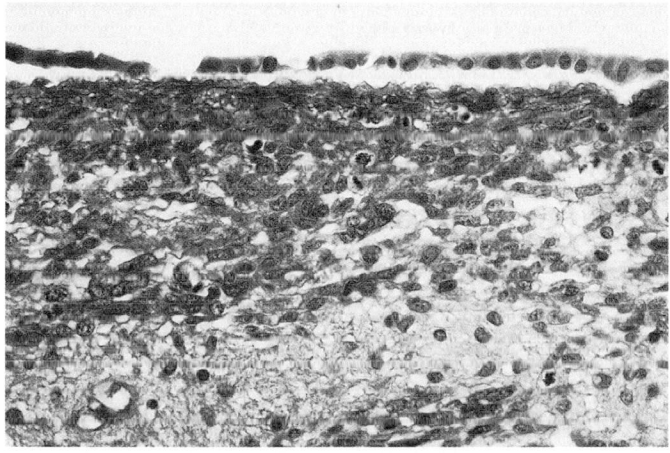

Fig. 25.155 Botryoid rhabdomyosarcoma of common bile duct showing a concentration of tumor cells immediately beneath the epithelium ("cambium layer").

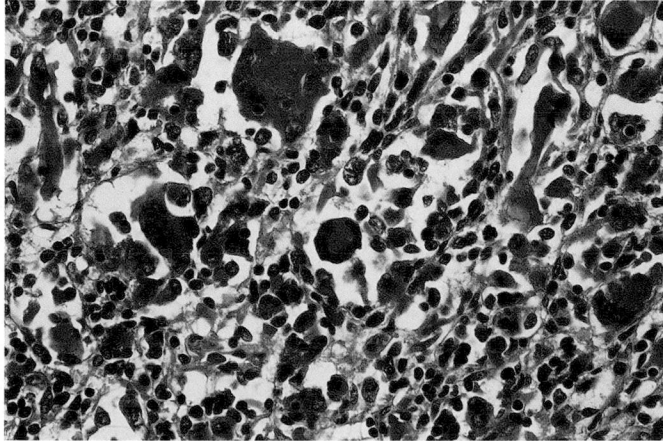

Fig. 25.156 Embryonal rhabdomyosarcoma with pleomorphic features in a child.

degree of differentiation than the pretherapy specimen, suggesting that the drugs have either induced maturation or resulted in a selection of the better differentiated components.[1047,1106]

The most common sites of metastatic involvement are the soft tissues, serosal surfaces, lung, bone marrow, and lymph nodes.[1042,1121,1125] Cases associated with diffuse bone marrow involvement may simulate acute leukemia.[1073] Rhabdomyosarcomas arising from genitourinary sites or extremities are particularly prone to metastasize to lymph nodes,[1092] whereas tumors originating in head and neck structures adjacent to meningeal surfaces have a high incidence of direct meningeal extension.

The prognosis of embryonal rhabdomyosarcoma has markedly improved following multimodality treatment with excision, radiation therapy, and multidrug chemotherapy.[1033,1066] Over 80% of children now survive when the disease is localized to the region of origin.[1099,1100] Age at diagnosis is an independent predictor of outcome.[1091]

A prognostically favorable variant of embryonal rhabdomyosarcoma is represented by the *spindle cell* type, which is composed of elongated spindle cells arranged in a fasciculated or storiform pattern.[1039] Most reported cases have been in males, and the most common locations have been the paratesticular area and the head and neck region.[1093] This entity bears some resemblance to the tumors described by Lundgren et al.[1097] as *infantile rhabdomyofibrosarcomas*, but it is not clear whether the two are identical. The latter microscopically simulated fibrosarcoma and were characterized by an aggressive clinical course.

Very rarely, accumulation of cytoplasmic glycogen or lipids in embryonal rhabdomyosarcoma results in a clear cell appearance that can simulate clear cell carcinoma.[1041,1148] Another morphologic variation is represented by tumor cells containing cytoplasmic globular inclusions composed of intermediate filaments and resulting in a rhabdoid appearance.[1087]

Occasionally, in infants and children, tumors with a location and appearance otherwise characteristic of embryonal rhabdomyosarcoma are seen to contain collections of cells exhibiting neuronal, melanocytic, and/or schwannian differentiation; these have been interpreted by some as originating from the migratory neural crest (ectomesenchyme) and designated as *ectomesenchymomas*.[1082,1083,1128] Others have been given the histogenetically less committal name of *gangliorhabdomyosarcoma*.[1086] Little is known about their natural history, which does not seem to differ much from that of the ordinary embryonal rhabdomyosarcoma.

Alveolar rhabdomyosarcoma may be related to the embryonal form and it is said to occasionally coexist with it; however, it should be regarded as a separate entity because it differs from the latter in several ways. For instance, it predominates in an older age group (10 to 25 years) and occurs more frequently in the extremities, the most common locations being forearms, arms, and perirectal and perineal regions (Fig. 25.157).

Microscopically, small, round, or oval tumor cells are seen separated in nests by connective tissue septa (Fig. 25.158). The tumor cells in contact with these fibrous strands remain firmly attached to them, but the others tend to detach because of a lack of cohesiveness, which results in a typical alveolar or pseudoglandular appearance. The deep acidophilia of the cytoplasm and the presence of occasional multinucleated giant cells are important diagnostic features[1132] (Fig. 25.159). Cases in which the alveolar pattern is poorly developed are referred to as the "solid" variant of alveolar rhabdomyosarcoma and are particularly difficult to diagnose.[1075a] Before identification of this entity,[1059,1123] many of these tumors were misdiagnosed as primary malignant lymphoma ("reticulum cell sarcoma") of the soft tissues. The comments made regarding cross striations and special studies for the diagnosis of embryonal rhabdomyosarcomas also apply for the alveolar type.

The prognosis of alveolar rhabdomyosarcoma is distinctly worse than for the embryonal variety, even with

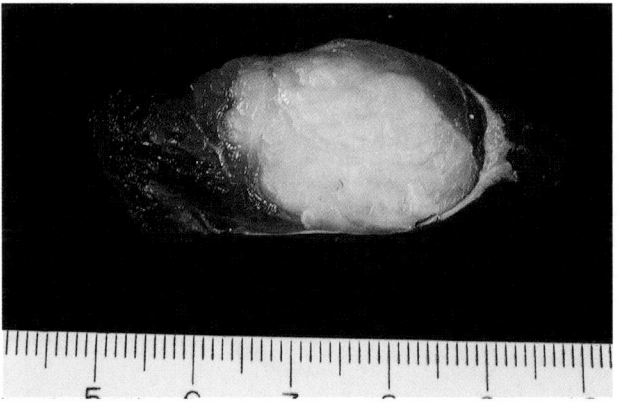

Fig. 25.157 Gross appearance of alveolar rhabdomyosarcoma. The tumor is embedded within skeletal muscle.

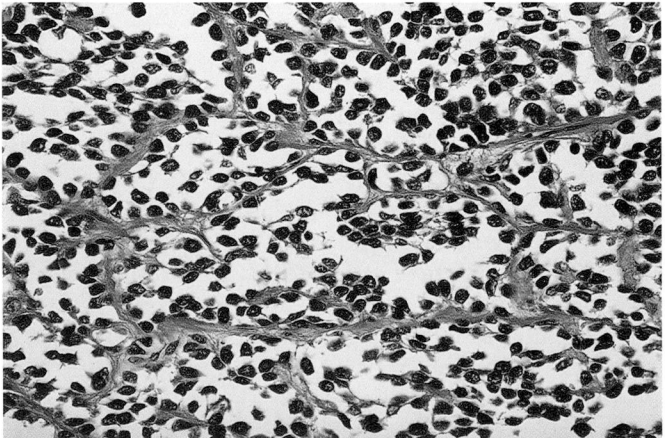

Fig. 25.158 Typical low-power appearance of alveolar rhabdomyosarcoma. Note the small size of the tumor cells.

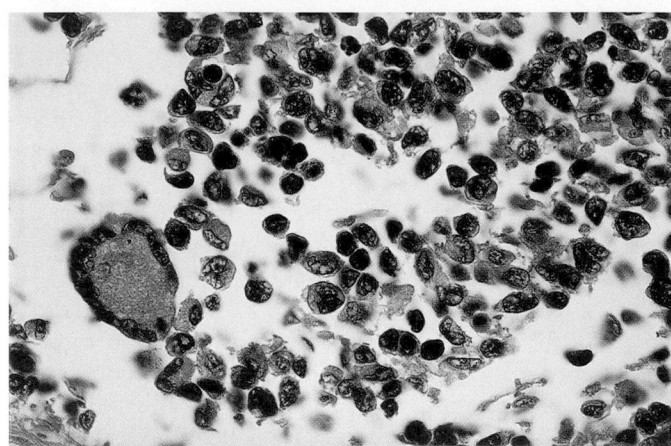

Fig. 25.159 On high power, this rhabdomyosarcoma shows a single multinucleated tumor giant cell among the mononuclear small cells, an important diagnostic clue.

the current multimodality therapies.[1074,1122,1133,1145] In the classic series reported by Enzinger[1060] (which antedates current therapeutic regimens), 92% of the patients had died from widespread metastasis within the first 4 years after diagnosis. The lung and regional lymph nodes are the most common metastatic sites. The ovary can also be involved.[1146] Peripheral lymph node involvement, sometimes in a multiple fashion, may be the first manifestation of the disease ("lymphadenopathic form"). A common site for occult primary alveolar rhabdomyosarcoma is the perirectal–perineal region. *Sclerosing rhabdomyosarcoma* refers to a type of rhabdomyosarcoma accompanied by such a prominent deposition of matrix material as to simulate an osteosarcoma or a chondrosarcoma.[1067] It is not clear whether this is a variety of either alveolar or embryonal rhabdomyosarcoma or a new distinct subtype.

Electron microscopic features. Ultrastructural examination may confirm a diagnosis of rhabdomyosarcoma through the identification of sarcomere-related structures, such as Z bands, thick and thin filaments in a hexagonal array, an A band containing thick filaments, and H and M bands, or leptomeric structures[1036,1061,1078,1096,1101,1108] (Fig. 25.160). There is a good correlation between the light and electron microscopic features of these tumors.[1131] Drawbacks of this technique are those related to sampling and the absence of these features in the poorly differentiated cells.[1035,1044] These facts, plus the availability of a large panel of relatively specific immunohistochemical (and, in the case of alveolar rhabdomyosarcoma, molecular) markers, has greatly diminished the diagnostic utility of electron microscopy in this field, the spectacular pictures sometimes obtained notwithstanding.

Histochemical and immunohistochemical features. Conventional special stains such as PTAH, Masson's trichrome, and silver impregnation technique are of only relative use in the diagnosis of rhabdomyosarcoma. They highlight the cross striations when these are already

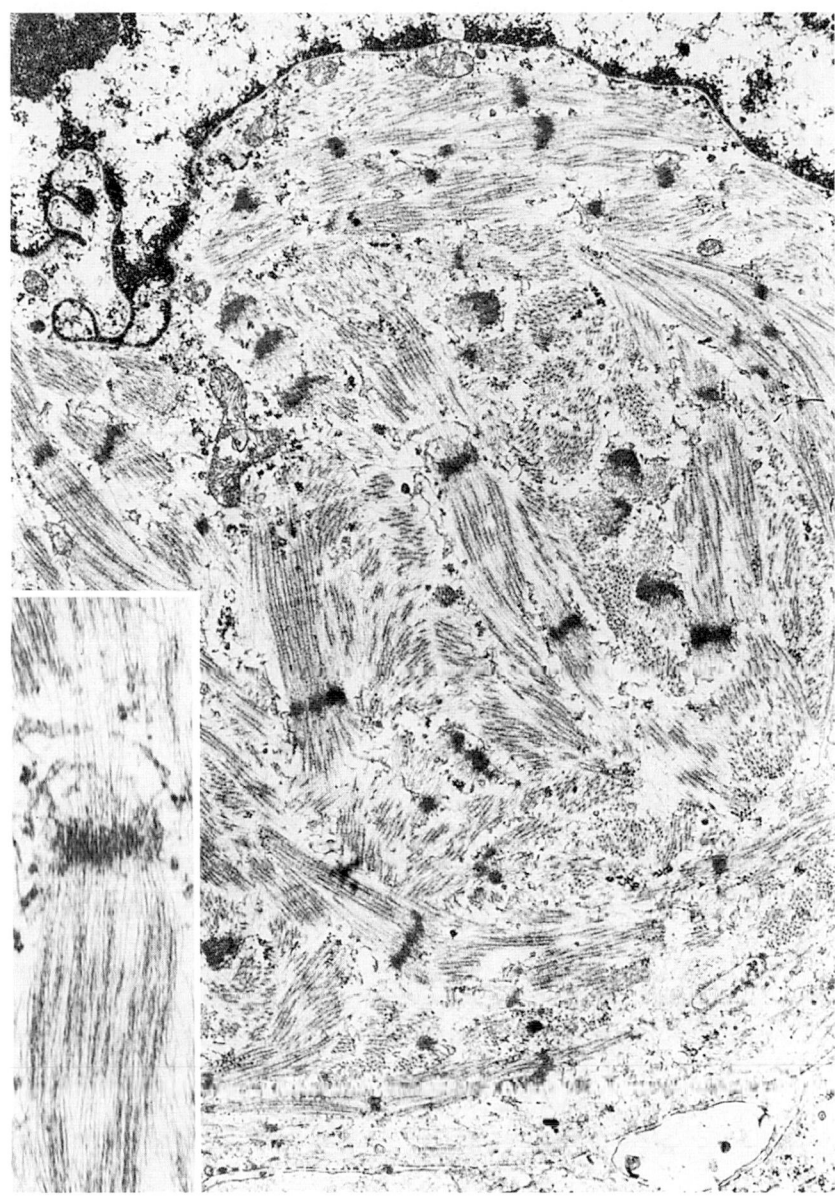

Fig. 25.160 Electron micrograph of embryonal rhabdomyosarcoma. The cytoplasm of tumor cells contains abortive cross striations, too small and haphazardly oriented to be visible with the light microscope. Inset shows a Z band and clearly visible double set of filaments. (×18,000; inset ×45,000; courtesy of Dr. B. Lane, New York)

appreciated in a good H&E preparation, but they only rarely detect them if they are not already apparent in the routine preparations.

Immunohistochemistry, on the contrary, has proved of great value. Hardly any other tumor type has been described for which the array of markers is as varied as for rhabdomyosarcoma, and the list continues to grow.[1031,1063,1081,1126,1130,1138,1140] There is a range of specificity and sensitivity among these markers and this translates into their relative practical utility. The most important follow:

1 **Myogenin.** The myogenin gene codes for a phospho-protein that induces skeletal muscle differentiation in mesenchymal cells.[1055,1143] The protein, which has a high degree of specificity,[1040,1090] can be demonstrated in the nuclei of the tumor cells in all types and virtually all cases of rhabdomyosarcoma, but it is expressed in a particularly strong and widespread fashion in the alveolar type[1053] (Fig. 25.161).

MyoD1 is a related nuclear protein with a similar degree of specificity, but—in contrast to myogenin—not well demonstrated in formalin-fixed paraffin-embedded material, and therefore of lesser diagnostic utility.[1043,1054] The MyoD1 protein present in these tumors binds DNA but it is relatively non-functional as a transcriptional activator, suggesting the lack of a factor needed for its activity.[1137]

2 **Desmin.** This intermediate filament is a specific indicator for muscle differentiation, but it is present in both smooth and striated muscle. In general, only tumors with round rhabdomyoblasts or strap cells show positivity for this marker.[1107]

3 **Sarcomeric actin.** Rhabdomyosarcomas consistently express sarcomeric actin, which represents one of the best markers for this tumor.[1050,1102,1110,1134] The

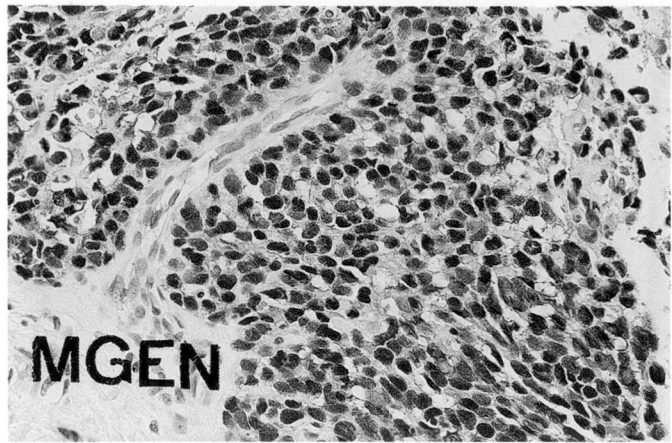

Fig. 25.161 Widespread nuclear immunoreactivity for myogenin in alveolar rhabdomyosarcoma.

interesting and surprising observation has been made that the specific sarcomeric actin expressed by these tumors is not of the alpha-skeletal muscle but the alpha-cardiac type.[1045] Rhabdomyosarcoma cells also express common muscle actin, but little or no smooth muscle actin.

4 **Myosin.** This marker has proved very effective for the identification of skeletal muscle differentiation.[1089,1138] Adult sarcomeric and fetal forms of myosin exist; expression of fetal heavy chain skeletal myosin, viewed as the expression of an oncofetal antigen, was found in one series in 81% of rhabdomyosarcomas.[1048,1049,1065]

5 **Myoglobin.** This protein appears to be specific for striated muscle differentiation, and it would therefore seem well suited for this purpose.[1034,1085,1109] Unfortunately, it is expressed only when the tumor cell has acquired a high degree of differentiation. It is therefore often negative in poorly differentiated tumors.[1038] One should also be careful of diffusion from neighboring injured skeletal muscle fibers.[1062]

6 **Tropomyosin α-actinin, titin, and Z protein.** These are constituent proteins of sarcomeric muscle and show a high degree of specificity. Unfortunately, most of them stain only well-differentiated cells in a minority of the tumors, a fact that greatly limits their diagnostic application.[1111,1114]

7 **Vimentin.** This antigen is consistently positive, particularly in the lesser differentiated tumors, but it lacks specificity as a skeletal muscle marker.[1107] It is the first marker to appear in the tumor cells, followed sequentially by actin, desmin, fast myosin, and myoglobin.[1037,1144]

8 **Enzymes.** These can be demonstrated immunohistochemically or through standard enzymatic histochemical techniques; most of the latter require fresh frozen tissue. They include *creatine kinase subunit M (muscle type*[1051]), myo(pho)sphorilase,

acetylcholinesterase, adenosine triphosphatase,[1142] and β-*enolase*.[1118,1124]

9 **CARP.** This cardiac ankyrin-related protein and its homolog *arpp* are expressed in all types of rhabdomyosarcoma, the expression patterns being different from those of muscle actin or desmin.[1079]

10 **Basal lamina components (type IV collagen, laminin).** No specificity can be ascribed to these markers, since they are also present in other types of mesenchymal cells and in epithelial cells.[1032]

11 **Antiskeletal muscle antibody from myasthenic patients.** The specific antigen against which this antibody is directed is not known, but it is clearly associated with the skeletal muscle fiber.[1113]

12 **Insulin-like growth factor II.** This has been found to be consistently expressed in rhabdomyosarcomas, in contrast to most other types of childhood malignancy.[1147]

13 **Other markers.** Rhabdomyosarcomas have been found to show focal immunoreactivity for keratin, neurofilaments, and S-100 protein.[1103]

This is a wide and somewhat confusing choice of options. In our institution, we have chosen the battery of myogenin, sarcomeric actin, and desmin for the routine investigation of these neoplasms.

Molecular genetic features. Alveolar rhabdomyosarcomas are consistently associated with the translocation t(2;13) or t(1;13), which results in the gene fusions *PAX3–FKHR* and *PAX7–FKHR*, respectively.[1056,1117,1135] These are not present in embryonal rhabdomyosarcomas, which lack a specific cytogenetic or molecular marker. In a recent study, it was concluded that alveolar rhabdomyosarcomas with *PAX3–FKHR* are associated with a more aggressive clinical course than those having *PAX7–FKHR*.[1135] *MYCN* amplification has been detected in close to half of the alveolar tumors but not in the embryonal types.[1057]

Most rhabdomyosarcomas have been shown to be aneuploid, in contrast to other types of childhood sarcomas.[1104] It has been suggested that DNA content is a predictor of outcome in some subsets of embryonal rhabdomyosarcoma.[1115]

Tumors of pluripotential mesenchyme

Stout[1156] coined the term **mesenchymoma** for tumors consisting of two or more mesenchymal elements in addition to fibrous tissue. Benign and malignant forms exist. The prototypical benign variant is composed of smooth muscle, fat, and blood vessels (angiomyolipoma). Cartilage may also be present in benign mesenchymoma, establishing a histogenetic link with the tumors described in the following section.[1151–1153] It is debatable whether benign mesenchymoma is of a neoplastic or hamartomatous nature.[1150] The malignant variant contains in the same neoplasm multiple varieties of soft tissue sarcomas, such as chondrosarcoma, liposarcoma, and leiomyosarcoma. The retroperitoneum and thigh are the most common sites.[1149] Nash and Stout[1154] reviewed 42 cases occurring in children, in 9 of which the tumor was present at birth. Most malignant mesenchymomas are high-grade neoplasms,[1149] but some cases have been characterized by a low-grade histology and an indolent clinical course.[1155]

Tumors of metaplastic mesenchyme

Soft tissue (extraskeletal) chondromas are seen most frequently in the soft tissues of the hands and feet of adults.[1181,1186] Grossly, they are lobulated, have a typical hyaline appearance, and are often calcified (Fig. 25.162). Some nuclear hyperchromasia may be present and should not be interpreted as evidence of malignancy.[1016,1199] Chondrosarcomas of the hands and feet exist, but they are exceptionally rare.[1168] The occasional presence of a cellular fibroblastic growth around the lobules may prompt confusion with calcifying aponeurotic fibroma. Also confusing is the fact that sometimes the cartilaginous cells have an acidophilic cytoplasm simulating that of a histiocyte and sometimes a vacuolated appearance reminiscent of a lipoblast (Fig. 25.163). A histologic variant with proliferation of osteoclast-like giant

cells and a chondroblastoma-like appearance has been described[1164,1165] (Fig. 25.164). Local recurrence is not infrequent.

Soft tissue (extraskeletal) chondrosarcoma, when used without a qualifier, refers to a soft tissue neoplasm generally composed of lobules of well-differentiated cartilage. In general, these tumors exhibit a less aggressive behavior than their skeletal counterparts.[1204,1208]

Myxoid chondrosarcoma is a specific type of soft tissue tumor which may have been incorrectly named, evidence accumulating to the effect that it is unrelated to cartilage. This tumor type rarely if ever occurs within bone.[1158,1200] Most of the reported cases have been in the extremities of adult patients,[1172,1192,1195] but they have also been reported in the trunk and/or in children[1178] (Fig. 25.165). Microscopically, there are strands and cords of relatively small cells with acidophilic cytoplasm that are occasionally vacuolated, embedded in an abundant myxoid matrix[1177,1205] (Fig. 25.166). Well-differentiated chondrocytes are absent. Glycogen is present in many of the tumor cells. Acid mucopolysaccharides are abundant in the stroma. In contrast with those present in myxoma

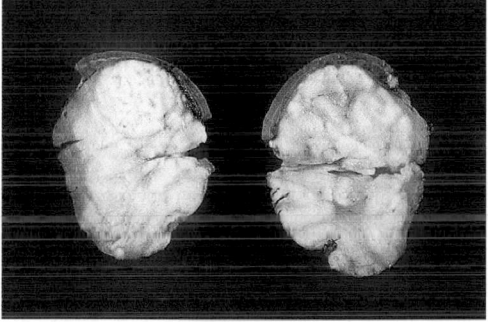

Fig. 25.162 Gross appearance of chondroma of soft tissues of hand. The tumor was partially calcified.

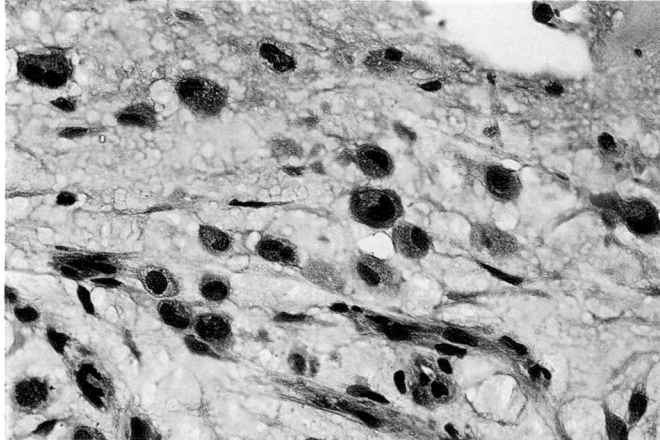

Fig. 25.163 The tumor cells of this soft tissue chondroma have a histiocyte-like quality, similar to that seen in chondroblastoma of bone.

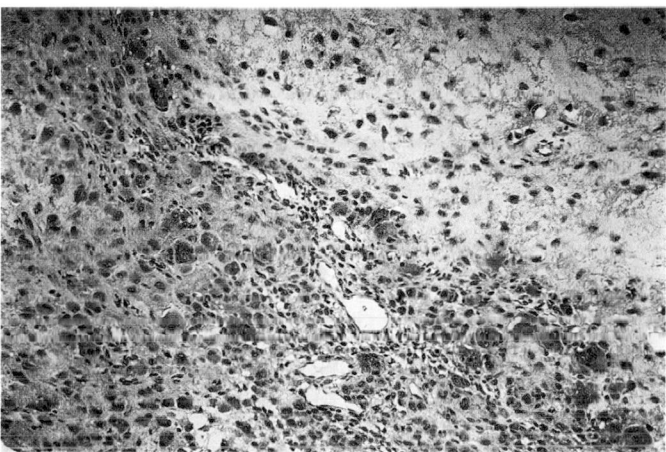

Fig. 25.164 Soft tissue chondroma with a hypercellular component having osteoclast-like giant cells and resembling chondromyxoid fibroma of bone.

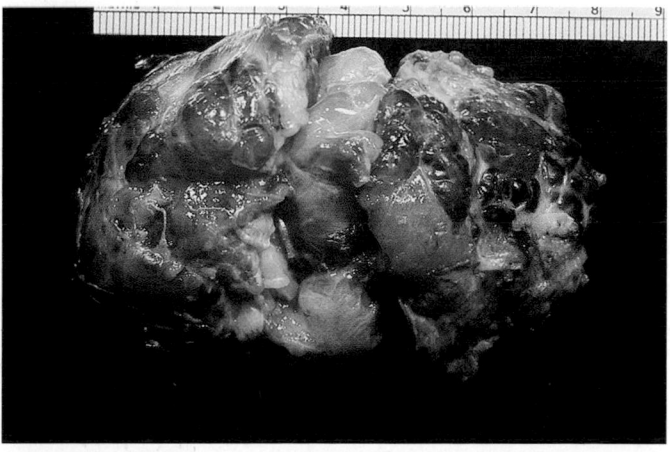

Fig. 25.165 Lobulated outer appearance of myxoid chondrosarcoma.

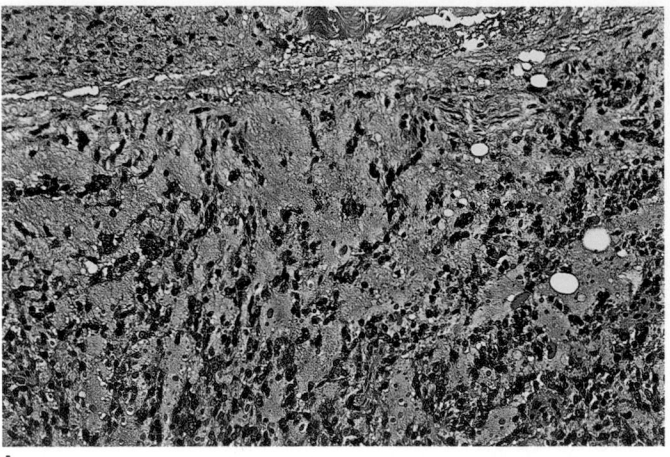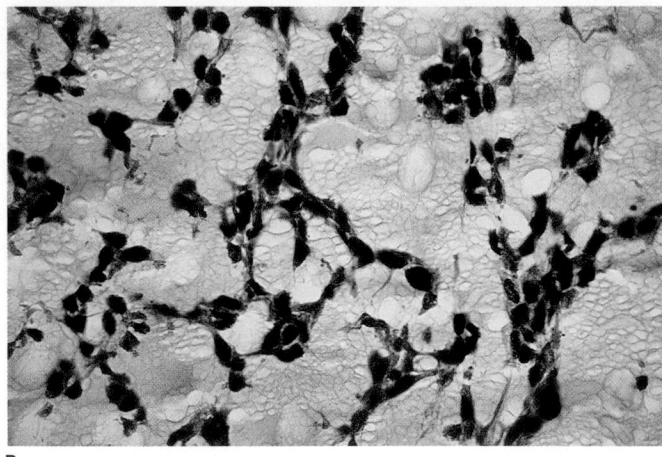

A   B

Fig. 25.166 Low- and high-power views of myxoid chondrosarcoma. Note the thin anastomosing strands of tumor cells surrounded by an abundant myxoid matrix. In contrast to myxoid liposarcoma, vascularity is scanty.

and myxoid liposarcoma, they are partially resistant to testicular hyaluronidase treatment because they are largely composed of chondroitin-4-sulfate, chondroitin-6-sulfate, and keratan sulfate. In some tumors, this myxochondroid stroma is scanty, and the diagnosis may consequently be missed.[1188,1198a] Rhabdoid features may be present; as usual, they portend an aggressive behavior.[1196] A high-grade form of myxoid chondrosarcoma has been described, characterized by the presence of numerous large epithelioid cells and a very aggressive behavior.[1187]

Ultrastructurally, the most conspicuous features of the cells of myxoid chondrosarcoma are a well-developed granular endoplasmic reticulum (sometimes containing peculiar parallel microtubules, a very distinctive feature

of this entity), abundant cytoplasmic filaments, and cytoplasmic glycogen.[1170,1191,1198,1205,1207] In addition, some tumor cells have been shown to contain microtubules and neuroendocrine-type granules.[1164,1176] Immunohistochemically, myxoid chondrosarcomas are only focally and erratically positive for S-100 protein, much less so than one would expect in a true cartilaginous neoplasm.[1171] We and others have found that a high proportion of the cases show focal immunoreactivity for neural/neuroendocrine markers, such as neuron-specific enolase, Leu7, synaptophysin, Hu (a marker of primitive neural/neuroendocrine cells) and Tau proteins (microtubule-associated proteins required for polymerization of tubulin), but not for keratin[1164,1171a,1175,1180] (Fig. 25.167). These surprising results, which are supported by

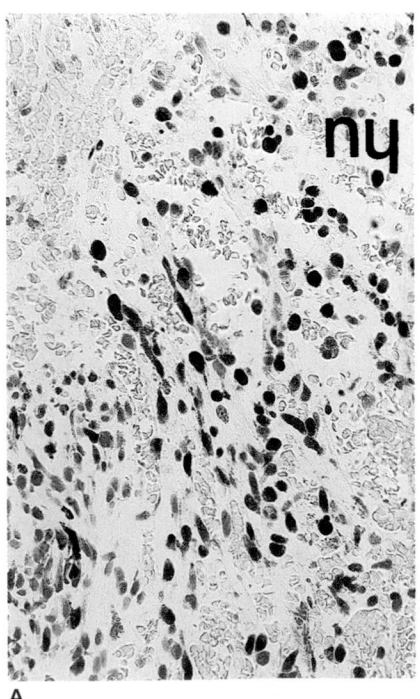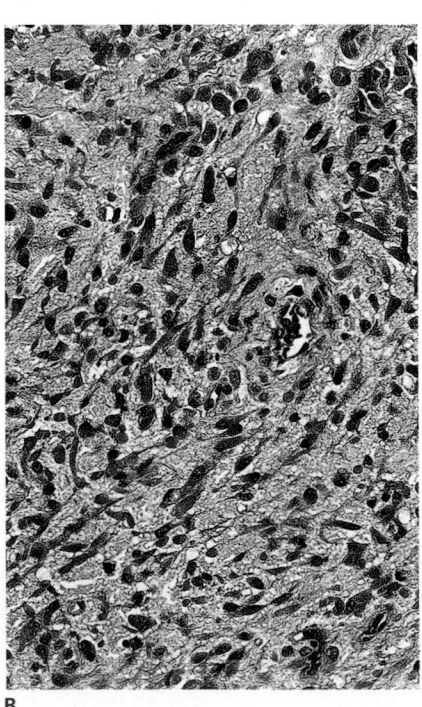

A   B

Fig. 25.167 A and **B**, Myxoid chondrosarcoma with immunohistochemical evidence of neuroendocrine differentiation. **B**, Hu immunostain showing nuclear reactivity.

microarray analyses,[1202a] suggest that this peculiar lesion may represent a primary myxoid neuroendocrine tumor of soft tissue.[1164]

Cytogenetically, myxoid chondrosarcoma is characterized by the chromosomal translocation t(9;22)(q22-31;q11-12),[1202] or t(9;17)(q22;q11) which result in the gene fusions *EWS–CHN* and *RBP56–CHN*, respectively.[1197]

Myxoid chondrosarcoma is an aggressive neoplasm that recurs locally and metastasizes distantly, particularly to the lungs[1185,1201]; in some instances, the lung metastasis is the first manifestation of the tumor.[1169]

It seems likely that cases reported as *chordoid sarcoma* or *chordoid tumor*[1162,1190,1206] belong to the same category as myxoid chondrosarcoma, whereas the cases published as *parachordomas* may be related to myoepitheliomas of soft tissue (see p. 2327).

Mesenchymal chondrosarcoma has been described in the orbit, dura, trunk, retroperitoneum, extremities, and kidney.[1160,1177,1189,1194,1209,1211] Like its counterpart in the bone, it is characterized microscopically by an alternating pattern of highly cellular undifferentiated small cells (often growing in a hemangiopericytomatous fashion) and islands of well-differentiated cartilage (Fig. 25.168) (see Chapter 24). Immunohistochemically, it may show a polyphenotypic profile, including expression of CD99 (in the small cell component), S-100 protein (in the cartilaginous component), and focal positivity for actin, desmin, and NSE.[1179] Despite the morphologic resemblance of the small cell component of mesenchymal chondrosarcoma to Ewing sarcoma/PNET, the chromosomal translocation associated with the latter is uniformly absent.[1183a] The prognosis is poor.[1194]

Soft tissue (extraskeletal) osteosarcoma is distinguished from chondrosarcoma by applying the same criteria used for skeletal tumors (i.e., the occurrence of osteoid and bone formation directly produced by the tumor cells, without interposition of cartilage)[1184] (Fig. 25.169). It usually occurs in the extremities of adults[1157,1174,1182,1203] (Fig. 25.170). A small proportion of these tumors arise following exposure to x-rays.[1183] As for their most common counterpart in the skeletal system, the predominant histologic pattern may be osteoblastic, chondroblastic, fibroblastic, MFH-like, telangiectatic, or well differentiated (the latter being analogous to parosteal osteosarcoma).[1159,1193,1210] The immunohistochemical profile is also analogous to that of skeletal osteosarcoma, including expression of osteocalcin and osteonectin.[1173] The prognosis is much worse than for chondrosarcoma, the overall mortality rate being over 60%.[1166] The most important differential diagnosis is with myositis ossificans (see Chapter 24).[1199] The presence of marked nuclear atypia and lack of differentiation ("zone phenomenon") are the most important identifying features. It should also be distinguished from other soft tissue tumors in which metaplastic bone is formed, such as fibrosarcoma, synovial sarcoma, and MFH.[1161]

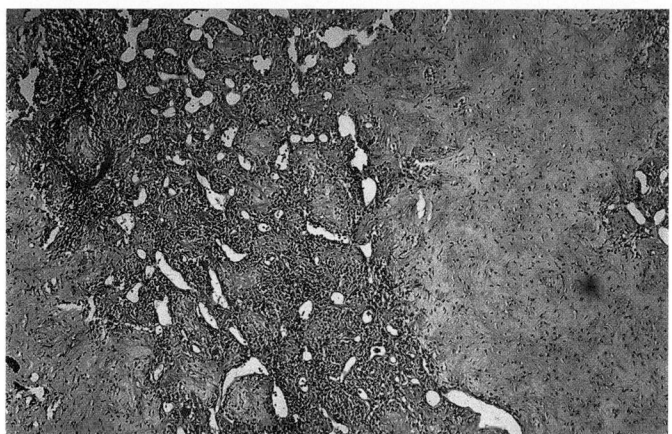

Fig. 25.168 Mesenchymal chondrosarcoma. Hypercellular areas with hemangiopericytoma-like features are admixed with islands of well-differentiated cartilage.

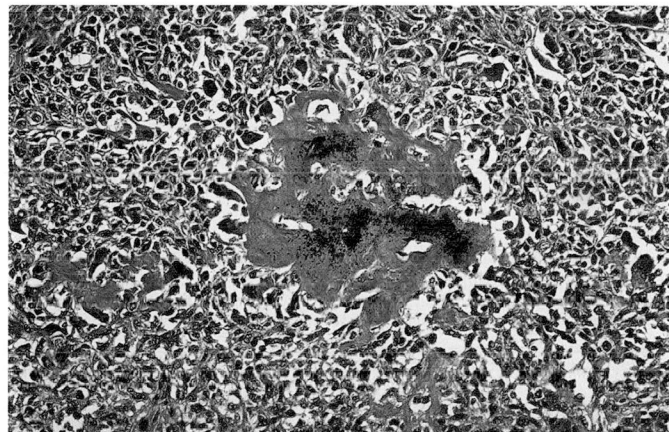

Fig. 25.169 Extraskeletal osteosarcoma with a central nidus of neoplastic bone.

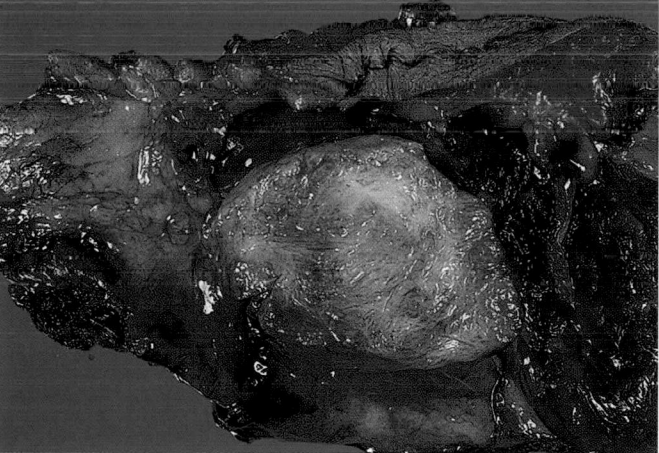

Fig. 25.170 Extraskeletal osteosarcoma. The neoplasm is embedded within skeletal muscle and is relatively well circumscribed.

Tumors resembling synovial tissue

Synovial sarcoma typically arises about the knee and ankle joints of children and young adults,[1228,1236,1241,1258,1264,1279] but it can also occur in older patients[1217a] (Fig. 25.171). It also occurs around other joints, such as shoulder and hip. It

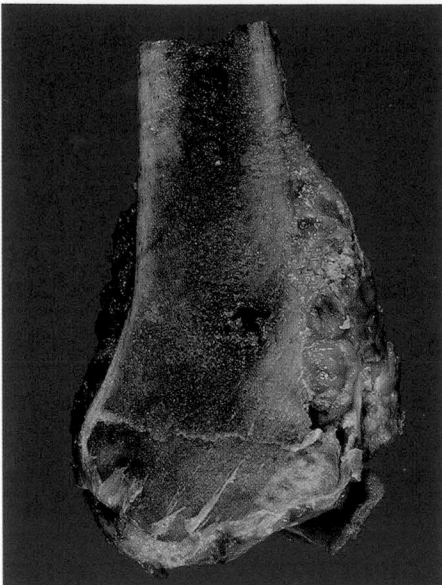

Fig. 25.171 Gross appearance of deep-seated synovial sarcoma involving periosteum of femur in an adolescent boy.

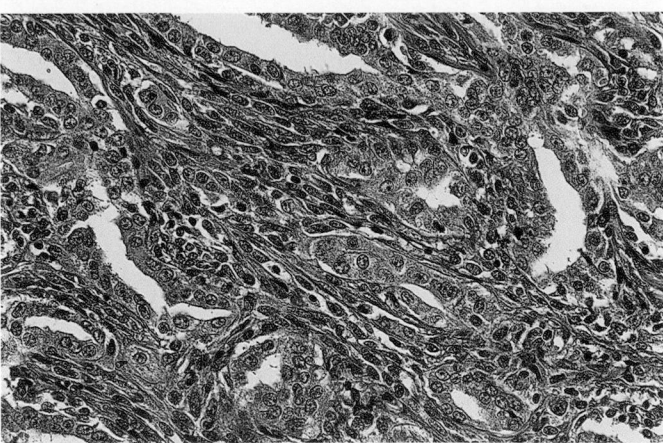

Fig. 25.172 Typical biphasic appearance of synovial sarcoma.

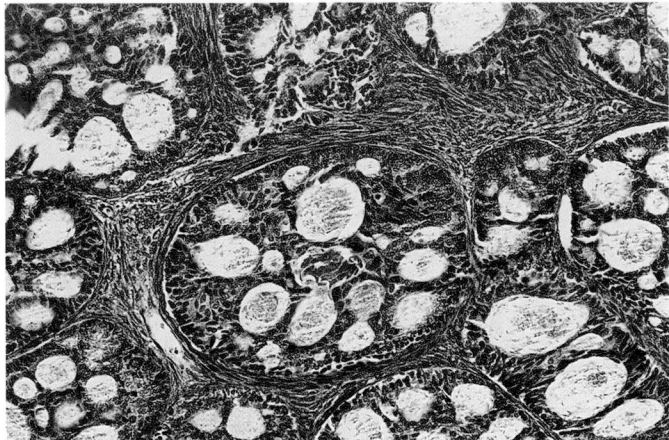

Fig. 25.173 Synovial sarcoma with an adenocarcinoma-like appearance of the epithelial component.

often grows close to the joints, tendon sheaths, and bursae, but it is extremely rare for it to invade the joint space and synovial membrane, with which it is probably unrelated. It can also be seen in many other soft tissue locations, including neck (particularly the retropharyngeal area),[1216,1268] anterior abdominal wall,[1226] retroperitoneum,[1273] mediastinum,[1283] blood vessels,[1254,1271] and nerves.[1261] Lately, it has become evident that the distribution of this tumor is even wider, with cases reported in the oral cavity,[1274] lung,[1285] and prostate.[1231]

Grossly, it tends to be well-circumscribed, firm, and grayish pink. Focal calcification is frequent and may be detected radiographically.[1282]

Microscopically, the classical form of synovial sarcoma is that of a *biphasic* tumor composed of sharply segregated epithelial and sarcomatous components (the terms being used descriptively and not histogenetically) (Figs 25.172 and 25.173). The epithelial areas usually appear in the forms of gland-like spaces lined by cuboidal (synovial-like) or columnar cells, but can also present as solid nests of large pale cells. It is exceptional for this component to exhibit squamous features.[1257]

The sarcomatous component is made up of spindle cells with a fibroblast-like appearance. It tends to be hypercellular but with a relatively monotonous appearance, plump nuclei, a focally whorled pattern, distinct lobulation or fasciculation, hemangiopericytoma-like areas, and a large number of mast cells (Fig. 25.174). Hyalinization, calcification, and osseous metaplasia can be present. When the calcification is particularly heavy, the term *calcifying synovial sarcoma* has been used[1282] (Fig. 25.175). The osteoid and bone formation can be extensive enough to obscure the true nature of the tumor.[1256] In other instances, the stroma may have a prominent myxoid quality.[1240]

Monophasic synovial sarcoma is composed of only one of the two components. In the large majority of cases, this applies to the spindle cell sarcomatous component, which is easily misdiagnosed as fibrosarcoma, hemangiopericytoma, or some other spindle cell neoplasm by the unwary[1249,1252] (Fig. 25.176). A search for epithelial-looking foci should be carried out in these situations, as well as a thorough immunohistochemical (and possibly molecular) evaluation (see below).

Theoretically, a monophasic form of synovial sarcoma composed only of the epithelial elements of the tumor should also exist. The fact that in some neoplasms the glandular elements are so prominent as to simulate a metastatic adenocarcinoma cannot be denied.[1237,1250] It has also been suggested that some of the reported cases of carcinoma of soft tissue and of epithelioid sarcoma are epithelial-rich forms of synovial sarcoma, the latter supposition being based on the occasional coexistence of the two tumors[1270] and their ultrastructural similarities.[1239,1244] However, the existence of a pure form of monophasic epithelial synovial sarcoma has yet to be convincingly demonstrated at the cytogenetic/molecular level.

A *poorly differentiated* form of synovial sarcoma is being

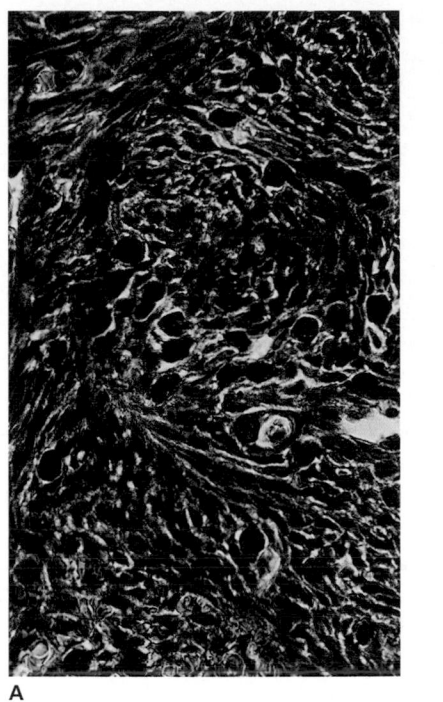 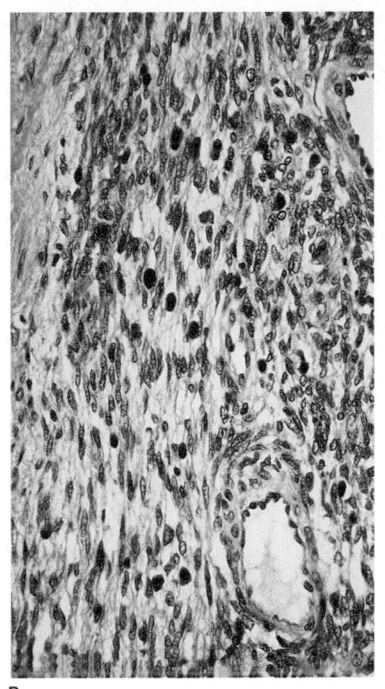

A   B

Fig. 25.174 A and **B**, Mast cells in monophasic synovial sarcoma, a useful diagnostic clue. **B**, Toluidine blue metachromatic stain.

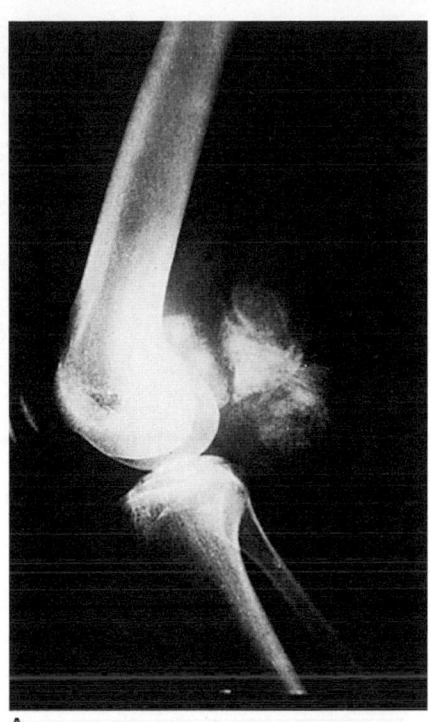

A

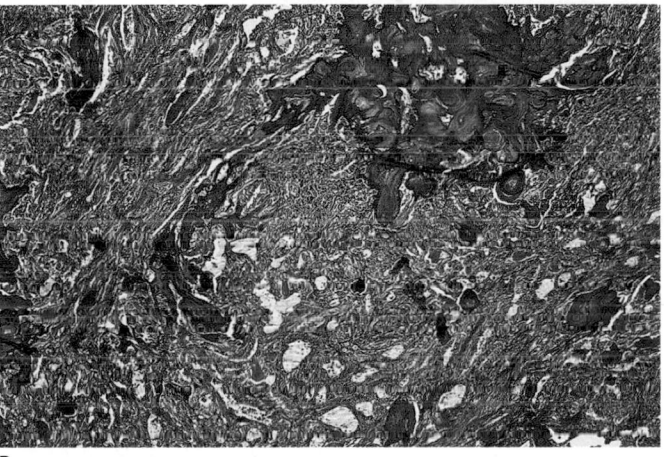

B

Fig. 25.175 A and **B**, Calcifying synovial sarcoma. **A**, Radiographic appearance of tumor located in popliteal space. **B**, Microscopic appearance. (**A** From Varela-Duran J, Enzinger FM. Calcifying synovial sarcoma. A clinicopathologic study of 32 cases. Cancer 1982, **50**: 345–352)

increasingly recognized, characterized by a greater degree of cellularity, atypia, and mitotic activity.[1222a,1230,1265] The tumor cells may be spindle, small, or large and clear.[1281] Here too, immunohistochemical and particularly cytogenetic/molecular confirmation (see below) becomes crucial.

In terms of special stains, the biphasic quality of the classic synovial sarcoma is highlighted by the reticulin preparations. Mucin stains reveal the presence of acid mucopolysaccharides (hyaluronic acid, chondroitin sulfate, heparitin sulfate) in the spindle cell areas and of PAS-positive, sialic acid-containing glycoproteins in the epithelial foci.[1260]

Ultrastructurally, the epithelial areas have features of true glandular epithelium; subtle features of epithelial differentiation are sometimes also found in the spindle cell component, such as intercellular spaces within processes and specialized cell junctions[1221–1224,1227,1232,1239,1246,1279] (Figs 25.177 and 25.178).

Immunohistochemically, there is strong reactivity for keratin in the epithelial areas and often in the spindle cells as well.[1212,1218,1245,1269] Since normal or reactive syn-

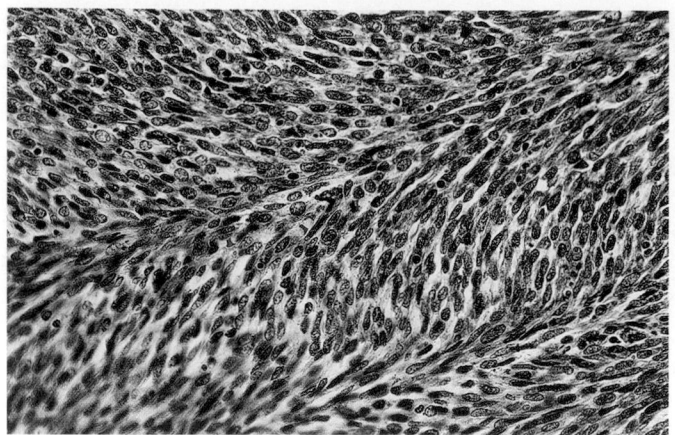

Fig. 25.176 Monophasic synovial sarcoma. The tumor is hypercellular but remarkably monomorphic.

ovial cells do not express keratin, the possibility has been raised that synovial sarcoma is not differentiating toward synovial structures, as traditionally believed, but toward true epithelium. The corollary of this theory is that the tumor should be viewed as a primary carcinoma (or carcinosarcoma) of soft tissue,[1233,1242,1255] whether arising from epithelial rests or—more likely—from mesenchymal tissues that have undergone epithelial metaplasia. Of importance in this regard is the fact that, whereas many types of soft tissue sarcoma (including epithelioid sarcoma) exhibit immunoreactivity for keratins 8 and 18, only synovial sarcoma shows positivity for keratins 7, 14, and 19, as well as for the desmosome-associated protein desmoplakin.[1251] Vimentin, EMA, CEA, calponin, HBME-1, and occasionally S-100 protein are also expressed by

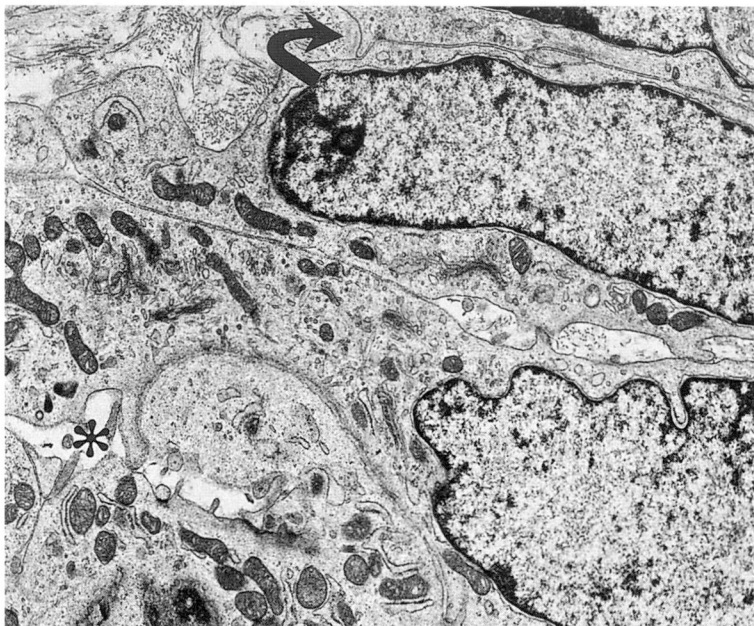

Fig. 25.177 Electron microscopic appearance of monophasic synovial sarcoma with spindle-shaped tumor cells. Note the rudimentary lumen with microvilli (asterisk) and the remnants of basal lamina (arrow). (×7700; courtesy of Dr. Robert A. Erlandson, Memorial Sloan-Kettering Cancer Center)

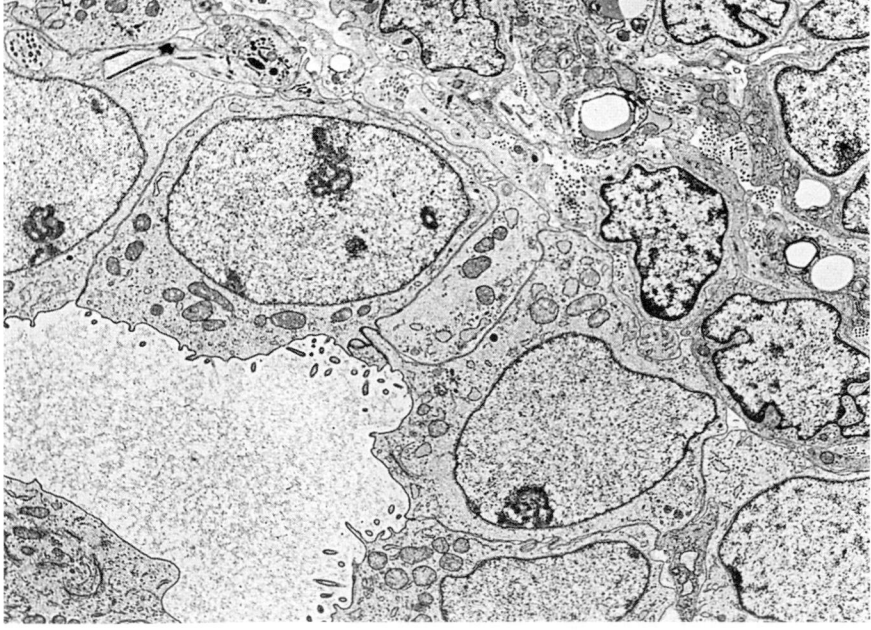

Fig. 25.178 Electron microscopic appearance of biphasic synovial sarcoma. There is a glandular formation of epithelioid tumor cells with sparse luminal microvilli (lower left). (×4300; courtesy of Dr. Robert A. Erlandson, Memorial Sloan-Kettering Cancer Center)

this tumor.[1212,1218,1228a,1229,1235,1242,1253,1263,1266] As a matter of fact, it is not rare to find monophasic synovial sarcomas that are focally reactive for EMA but not keratin. It has also been found that a significant number of cases of synovial sarcoma are immunoreactive for CD99, the marker characteristically associated with Ewing's sarcoma/PNET (see p. 2324),[1222] bcl-2,[1247] Her2/*neu*,[1261a] and MAGE-CT (a cancer testis antigen)[1213] (Fig. 25.179). Finally, it has been observed that synovial sarcomas may exhibit focal reactivity for calretinin (but not for WT1), a point of importance in the differential diagnosis with mesothelioma, a tumor which they may closely resemble.[1253]

Synovial sarcoma exhibits in over 90% of the cases the chromosomal translocation t(x:18)(p11.2;q11.2), which results in the fusion of the *SYT* gene on chromosome 18 with either *SSX1* (in two thirds of the cases) or *SSX2* (the other third) on chromosome X.[1269a] Other molecular variants exist. This highly specific molecular alteration can be detected with RT-PCR in fresh or paraffin-embedded material,[1215,1234] whereas the translocation can be identified with conventional cytogenetics or FISH.[1272,1259] Notably, a high degree of correlation exists between the type of gene fusion and the tumor subtype, in the sense that nearly all biphasic tumors carry the *SYT–SSX1* fusion, whereas most of those with *SYT–SSX2* are monophasic. There is instead no association between the fusion type and the immunohistochemical expression of epithelial markers.[1214]

Synovial sarcoma can recur locally and metastasize distantly, particularly to the lung and lymph nodes. The incidence of nodal metastases is in the range of 10% to 15% (i.e., much higher than that of most soft tissue sarcomas of adults). The preferred treatment is local excision, with wide margins of normal tissue, supplemented by a high dose of radiation therapy.[1277] Synovial sarcoma has been traditionally regarded as a tumor of ominous prognosis[1236]; in several series, however, the 5-year survival rate has approached 50%.[1219,1248,1280] The prognosis is even

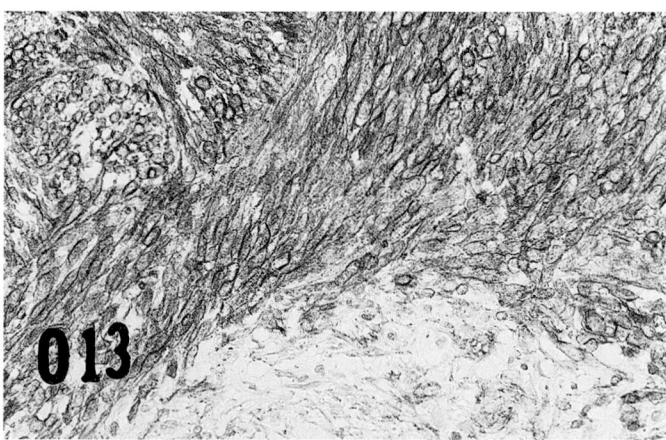

Fig. 25.179 Strong CD99 (O13) immunoreactivity in monophasic synovial sarcoma.

better for the synovial sarcomas associated with heavy calcification (calcifying synovial sarcoma), where the survival rate reaches the figure of 80%.[1282] The prognosis is also related to age (better in young patients), site (better for distal lesions),[1243,1278] size (better for tumors less than 5 cm in diameter),[1275,1276,1284] status of the surgical margins,[1275] mitotic activity (better for tumors having fewer than 15 mitoses per 10 high-power fields),[1217] necrosis (worse for tumors having tumor necrosis of more than 50%), rhabdoid cells (worse when present), microscopic grade (which takes into account some of parameters just listed), and DNA ploidy pattern (worse for aneuploid tumors).[1225,1262,1267] Early reports that the type of gene fusion showed a significant association with prognosis[1238] have not been confirmed in other series.[1233a]

Tumors of extragonadal germ cells

Soft tissue teratomas are more frequent in females and present either at birth or in early childhood.[1286] In some cases, there is an association with twinning or malformations. The most common locations, in descending order of frequency, are the sacrococcygeal area, head and neck, retroperitoneum, mediastinum, and central nervous system.[1287,1291,1294,1295] Taken as a whole, approximately three fourths are benign. However, there are important variations in the incidence of malignancy according to location, age, and sex.[1289,1290] Nearly all the teratomas presenting in the neck during infancy are benign, usually asymmetric, and massive; the rare teratomas of the neck presenting in adults have a high incidence of malignancy.[1288,1293]

The terminology and diagnostic criteria used in the evaluation of these lesions is the same as for those of gonadal origin (see Chapters 18 and 19). The benign form is often multicystic and contains a variety of well-differentiated tissues. The malignant types may have the appearance of teratocarcinoma, embryonal carcinoma, or yolk sac tumor. Immature neuroectodermal components are common; although they occasionally exhibit metastasizing capacity, their natural tendency is toward spontaneous maturation.[1292]

Tumors of neural tissue (other than peripheral nerves)

Pigmented neuroectodermal tumor of infancy

Pigmented neuroectodermal tumor of infancy, also known as melanotic progonoma and retinal anlage tumor, is a neurally derived neoplasm.[1297,1302] The classical location is the maxilla, but it also has been reported in the mandible, skull and other bones, mediastinum, soft tissues (thigh, forearm, cheek), and epididymis.[1298,1300,1302,1305,1307] Microscopically, most tumor cells are small and round, with the appearance of neuroblasts. As a result, this tumor may be misdiagnosed as neuroblastoma. The diagnostic feature is the presence of pseudoglandular or alveolar formations lined by a wall of larger cells containing abundant CNS-type (spiculated) melanin in their cytoplasm (Fig. 25.180). Rarely, a skeletal muscle component is present.[1303] Immunohistochemically, the large cells are strongly reactive for keratin and HMB-45 and less so for vimentin and NSE, whereas the small cells show only positivity for NSE. Both cell components are negative for S-100 protein.[1296,1303,1304,1306] Ultrastructurally, there are melanosomes at various stages of maturation in the large cells, and neurosecretory granules and cytoplasmic processes in the small cells.[1303]

The clinical course is usually benign. Most supposedly malignant varieties probably represent malignant teratomas with a pigmented neuroectodermal component. However, unquestionable recurrent and metastatic cases of pigmented neuroectodermal tumor of infancy have been seen.[129,1300,1303]

Other neural tumors

Meningiomas can present as a soft tissue mass at the base of the nose or scalp[1309] (see Chapters 4 and 7).

Myxopapillary ependymomas can appear as soft tissue masses over the sacrococcygeal area, unconnected with the spine or spinal cord structures[1308,1311] (Fig. 25.181). The clinical diagnosis is usually that of pilonidal cyst. Grossly, they are well circumscribed and can be shelled out easily. Their microscopic appearance is homologous to that of their more common counterpart in the filum terminale and cauda equina (see Chapter 28) (Fig. 25.182). Metastases have occurred in approximately one fifth of the cases.[1310]

Myxopapillary ependymomas should be distinguished from sacrococcygeal ependymal rests, which probably represent their precursors. These are small (less than 0.5 cm) nodules that are usually found incidentally in tissue from pilonidal sinuses and that consist of clusters of ependymal cells near the junction of dermis and subcutis.[1313]

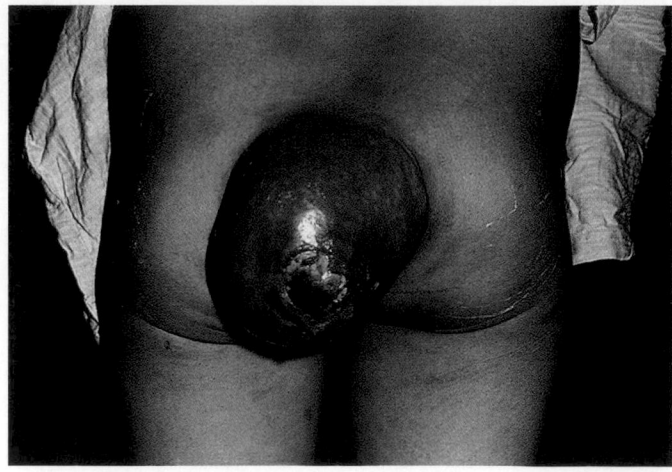

Fig. 25.181 Myxopapillary ependymoma of the sacrococcygeal region resulting in a huge protruding mass that is focally ulcerated. (Courtesy of Dr. Juan Jose Segura, San José, Costa Rica)

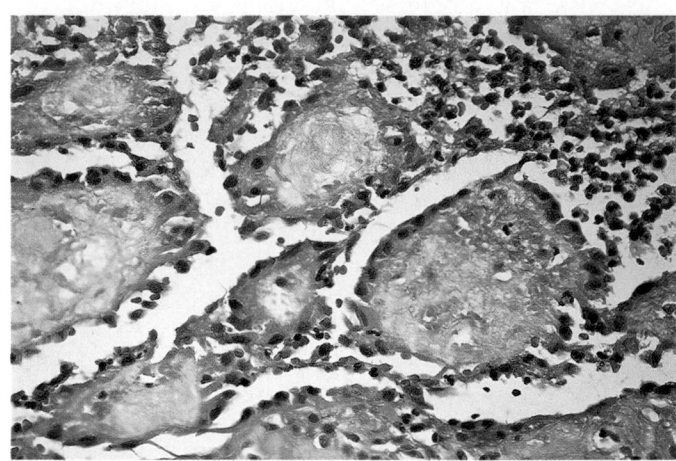

Fig. 25.182 Myxopapillary ependymoma involving soft tissues of buttock. The tumor papillae have an abundant hyalinized core.

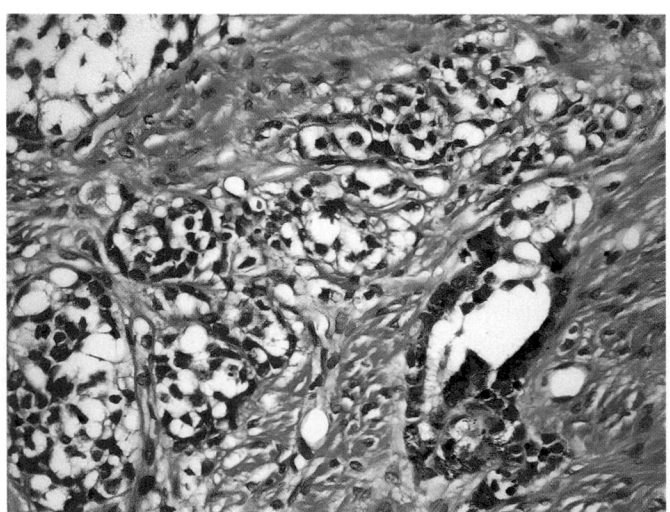

Fig. 25.180 Pigmented neuroectodermal tumor of infancy. Nests of neuroblast-like cells are adjacent to gland-like spaces lined by larger cells containing neural-type melanin.

Gliomas of soft tissue have been generally located at the root of the nose in infants, but they can occur in other sites such as orbit, scalp, chest wall, and gluteal region[1312]; they are probably not neoplasms but examples of heterotopic glial tissue[1314] (Fig. 25.183).

Primitive neuroectodermal tumors (PNET) are discussed on p. 2324.

Tumors of hematopoietic tissue

Malignant lymphomas may exceptionally manifest themselves as soft tissue masses, usually located in an extremity.[1322] This occurrence is more common with non-Hodgkin's lymphomas than with Hodgkin's lymphoma, but both of these major types occur.[1315,1321] Most cases are of B-cell derivation, but examples of peripheral T-cell lymphoma with primary involvement of soft tissues are on record.[1317,1320] Exceptionally, these lymphomas develop in areas of post-mastectomy lymphedema and are confused clinically with angiosarcoma.[1319]

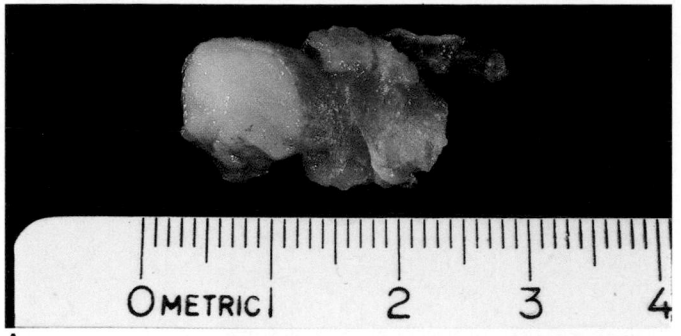

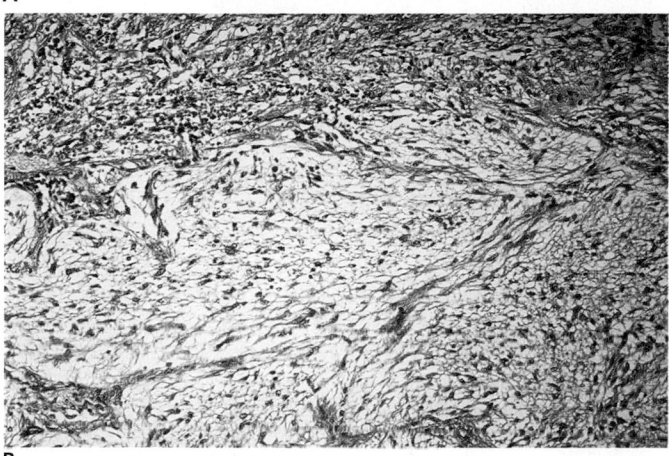

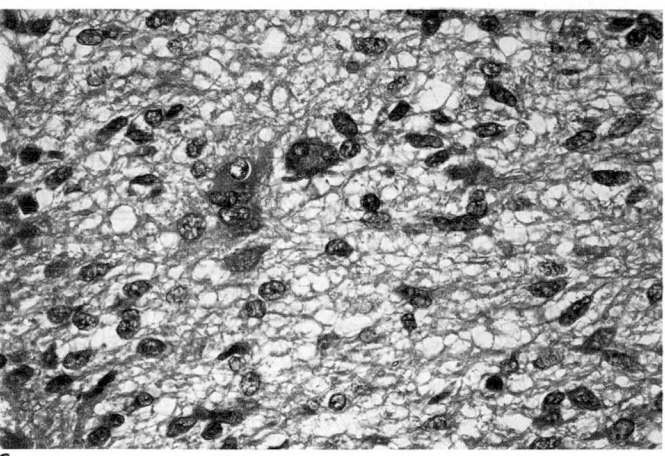

Fig. 25.183 Soft tissue "glioma" involving the orbit: **A**, gross appearance; **B**, low-power view; **C**, high-power view showing the glial fibrillary background and scattered multinucleated cells. This lesion is probably of malformative rather than neoplastic nature.

Plasmacytomas of soft tissue represent, for the most part, direct extension from underlying osseous foci.[1316] However, isolated soft tissue masses also can occur in the absence of bone involvement. They have a tendency to become disseminated.

Extramedullary hematopoiesis may present in the form of nodules in the mediastinum, retroperitoneum, or other soft tissue areas; they have been described in agnogenic myeloid metaplasia and congenital spherocytosis and in other types of anemia,[1318] and should be distinguished from myelolipoma (see Chapter 16).

Tumors of uncertain cell type

Fibrous hamartoma of infancy

Fibrous hamartoma of infancy is a tumorlike condition seen almost exclusively during the first 2 years of life and sometimes present at birth.[1323,1326] It predominates in boys, and the most common locations are the region of the shoulder, axilla, and upper arm. It is almost always solitary. Grossly, it is poorly circumscribed and composed of whitish tissue of fibrous appearance intermixed with islands of fat.

Microscopically, the distinctive feature of this lesion is an organoid pattern, three distinct types of tissue being present: (1) well-differentiated spindle cells of fibroblastic/myofibroblastic appearance accompanied by deposition of collagen; (2) mature adipose tissue, and (3) immature, cellular areas arranged in a whorl-like pattern and resembling primitive mesenchyme (Fig. 25.184). Positivity for vimentin occurs in both fibrous and immature areas, whereas reactivity for actin (and sometimes desmin) is found mainly in the spindle cell areas, suggesting the existence of a myofibroblastic component.[1324,1325,1327] Although there may be local recurrence, the clinical course is basically that of a benign disease.[1323]

Myxoma

Myxomas are rare neoplasms that have a mucoid, slimy gross appearance[1340] (Fig. 25.185). They almost always occur in adults and are more common in females.[1331] The diagnosis of myxoma in a child should be seriously questioned. A high proportion of myxomas arise within skeletal muscle, especially in the thigh region. The prognosis is excellent. In most of the reported series, there was not a single case of local recurrence.[1331,1333] Multiple intramuscular myxomas are nearly always seen in association with fibrous dysplasia of the bones of the same extremity.[1328,1334,1342] The presence of multiple myxomas in the skin, breast, or other locations should raise the possibility of Carney's syndrome, which also includes spotty cutaneous pigmentation, nodular pigmented adrenal disease, and other endocrine abnormalities.[1330] Another important location of myxoma is the juxta-articular region (juxta-articular myxoma), particularly in the knee.[1337]

Microscopically, a typical myxoma has a bland and hypocellular appearance throughout, mitotic activity is practically absent, and blood vessels are extremely scanty (Fig. 25.186), the latter feature having been well documented with angiographic and microangiographic studies. Focal aggregates of foamy histiocytes may be present; these contain neutral fat with the oil red O stain and should not be confused with the lipoblasts of myxoid liposarcoma.[1333]

Ultrastructurally, the principal cell of intramuscular myxoma resembles a fibroblast, with prominent granular endoplasmic reticulum, well-developed Golgi apparatus, and cytoplasmic filaments.[1332] Immunohistochemically,

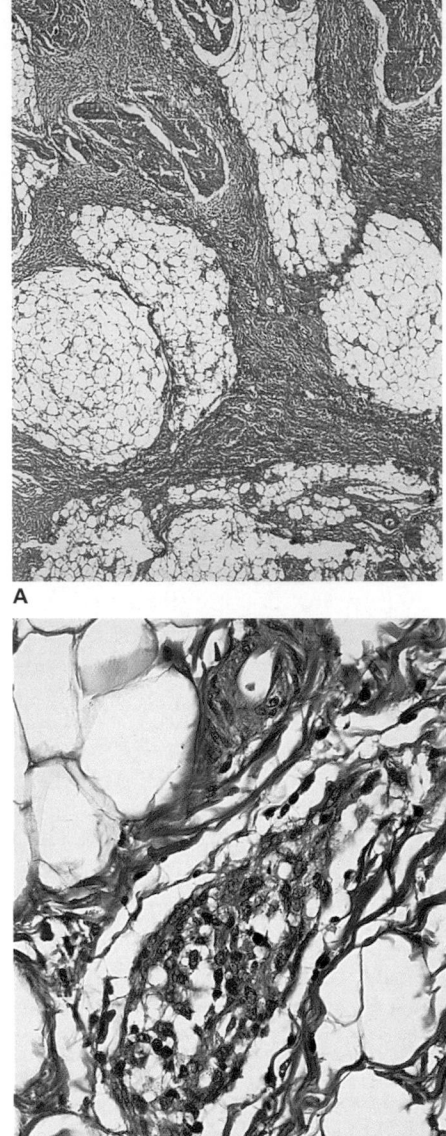

A

B

Fig. 25.184 A and **B**, Fibrous hamartoma of infancy. **A**, Low-power microscopic view showing an admixture of islands of mature adipose tissue and cellular fibrous foci. **B**, High-power view showing an oval cluster of plump mesenchymal cells.

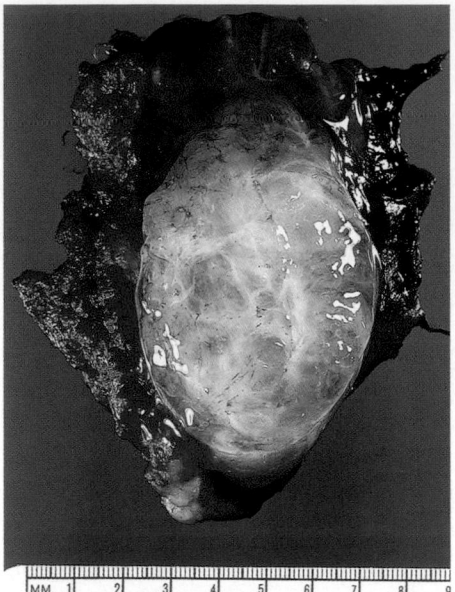

Fig. 25.185 Typical gross appearance of intramuscular myxoma. (Courtesy of Dr. RA Cooke, Brisbane, Australia; from Cooke RA, Stewart B: Colour Atlas of Anatomical Pathology. Edinburgh, Churchill Livingstone, 2004).

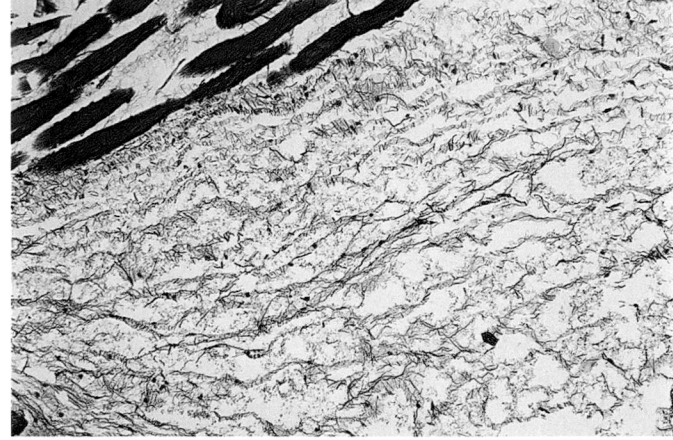

A

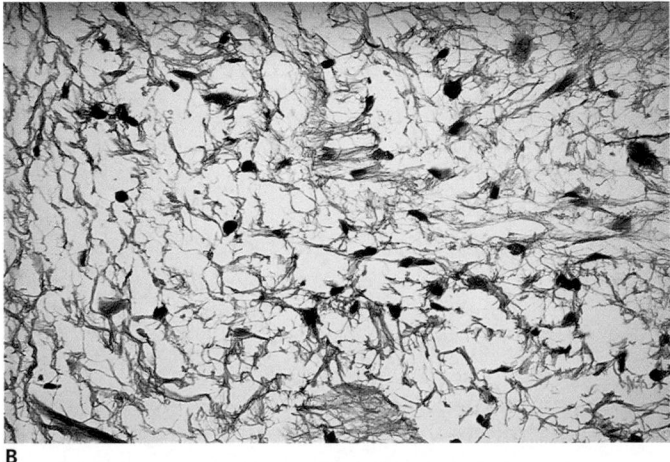

B

Fig. 25.186 A and **B**, Intramuscular myxoma. **A**, Note the hypocellular quality, lack of encapsulation, and intramuscular location. **B**, The high-power view highlights the lack of atypia and paucity of vessels.

myxoma shows no reactivity for S-100 protein, this constituting another difference from myxoid liposarcoma.[1333] Desmin is also absent, but vimentin is expressed.[1338] The myxoid material is entirely digestible by hyaluronidase.

The differential diagnosis of myxoma comprises two types of diseases. The first is a group of neoplasms in which myxoid change can be a prominent secondary feature, such as liposarcoma, myxofibrosarcoma, chondrosarcoma, leiomyosarcoma, embryonal rhabdomyosarcoma, neurofibroma, nerve sheath myxoma/neurothekeoma, and aggressive angiomyxoma.[1336] The latter occurs preferentially in the soft tissues of the female genital tract (see Chapter 19), but a counterpart located in the superficial soft tissue has been described.[1328,1329] If a myxoid tumor is hypercellular and hypervascular, the alternative possibility of low-grade myxofibrosarcoma should be considered. However, a *cellular variant* of myxoma has been described which is more cellular and more vascular than the ordinary type[1339,1341]; this tumor lacks the pleomorphism, nuclear atypia, and curvilinear vascular pattern of low-grade myxofibrosarcoma.[1341]

The second group of diseases from which myxoma should be distinguished is a variety of non-neoplastic disorders resulting in focal mucinous degeneration of the skin or soft tissues, such as nodular fasciitis, localized myxedema, mucous (myxoid) cyst, ganglion, follicular mucinosis (alopecia mucinosa), papular mucinosis, and cutaneous focal mucinosis.[1335]

Granular cell tumor

The classic location of granular cell tumor, classically known as granular cell myoblastoma, is the tongue. It has been seen, however, in innumerable other locations such as the skin, vulva, breast, larynx, bronchus, esophagus, stomach, appendix, rectum, anus, bile ducts, pancreas, urinary bladder, uterus, brain, pituitary gland, and soft tissue.[1347,1350,1352,1357,1358,1360,1367,1371,1383,1392] Multiplicity of lesions can be observed, particularly in black patients.[1371,1384] A few congenital examples have been reported, most of them located in the gingiva,[1351,1361,1364] but some exhibiting systemic involvement.[1379]

These tumors are usually small, although we have seen cases measuring up to 5 cm in diameter. They have a hard consistency and ill-defined margins (Fig. 25.187). This, together with the ulceration sometimes complicating the larger cutaneous tumors, explains why they are sometimes confused clinically and on gross inspection with a malignant neoplasm. Rarely, they have a polypoid shape.[1362] The individual cells are large and their cytoplasm is highly granular (Fig. 25.188). Most granules are small and regular. They alternate with larger round droplets having a homogeneous eosinophilic appearance and a stronger PAS positivity. If the tumor grows near an epithelial surface, in sites such as skin, vulva, or larynx, secondary epithelial hyperplasia occurs that may be incorrectly diagnosed as carcinoma[1388] (Fig. 25.189). Elastosis is often present in the stroma.[1366]

Histochemically, the cytoplasmic granules contain large amounts of hydrolytic enzymes (such as acid phosphatase), and they are consistently positive for Luxol fast blue.[1370] Ultrastructurally, they have the appearance of lysosomes. Other interesting electron microscopic findings are the presence of a second cell population with "angulated bodies" resulting in a Gaucher cell-like appearance[1346] and of replicated basal lamina material around the granular cells, the latter suggesting repeated cycles of cellular injury and repair.[1345] Immunohisto-

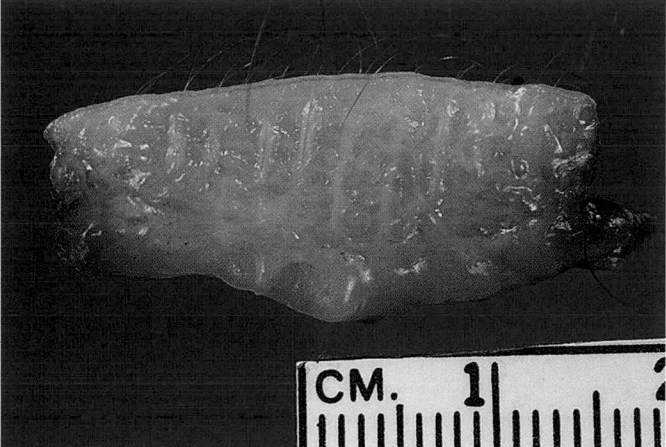

Fig. 25.187 Granular cell tumor of skin. There is an ill-defined permeation of the dermis by whitish tissue.

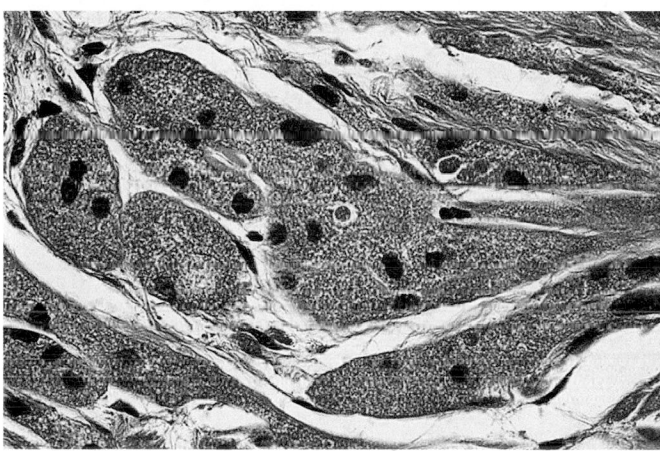

Fig. 25.188 Granular cell tumor. The cells contain innumerable fine cytoplasmic granules as well as scattered larger eosinophilic globules.

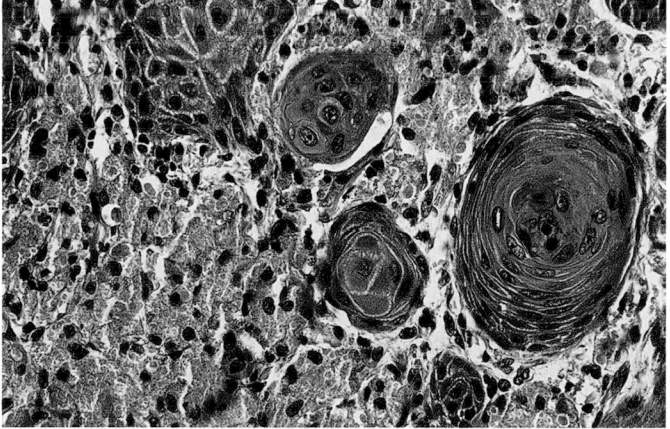

Fig. 25.189 Pseudoepitheliomatous hyperplasia in squamous epithelium overlying granular cell tumor.

chemically, positivity has been described (in at least some of the lesions) for S-100 protein, laminin, calretinin, the alpha subunit of inhibin HLA-DR, myelin basic protein, and CEA.[1354,1365,1372–1374,1377,1380] The presence of the latter two markers remains controversial[1349]; the apparent CEA reactivity may be caused by the presence of a cross-reacting antigen.[1364,1376] The expression of HLA-DR is thought to be related not to the cell of origin but rather to some common immunologic pathogenesis.[1381]

The large majority of the granular cell tumors pursue a benign clinical course. Most cases reported in the old literature as malignant granular cell myoblastomas are in reality examples of alveolar soft part sarcoma. However, there have been several well-documented cases of tumors with a light and electron microscopic appearance entirely consistent with that of granular cell tumor that have resulted in distant metastases.[1343,1359,1382,1389–1391] Features favoring malignancy in granular cell tumor (especially when seen in combination) are necrosis, high mitotic activity, spindling of tumor cells, vesicular nuclei with large nucleoli, and high MIB-1 values.[1353]

The histogenesis of this lesion is still being argued.[1378] Most writers on the subject favor a Schwann's cell origin, based on histochemical, immunohistochemical, and ultrastructural findings and on the occurrence of typical lesions, within nerves[1344,1346,1356,1385] (Fig. 25.190). However, in some lesions, there is no evidence of Schwann's cell participation.[1362] Furthermore, changes histochemically and ultrastructurally indistinguishable from those previously discussed have been documented in neoplastic and non-neoplastic smooth muscle cells and in tumoral ameloblasts.[1348,1375,1386] We therefore favor the view that granular cell tumor is not a specific entity but rather the expression of a degenerative change resulting in a cytoplasmic accumulation of lysosomes that can occur not only in Schwann's cells but also in a variety of other cell types, whether previously normal or forming part of a benign or a malignant neoplasm, such as MPNST, leiomyosarcoma, or angiosarcoma.[1355,1368,1369,1377] We favor making the diagnosis of granular cell tumor only when the entire lesion is granular and to designate the other cases according to their basic component, noting that focal granular changes are present.

Alveolar soft part sarcoma

Alveolar soft part sarcoma, a malignant soft tissue tumor designated in the past as malignant organoid granular cell myoblastoma and malignant nonchromaffin paraganglioma, involves most often the deep soft tissues of the thigh and leg.[1406] It has also been seen in the oral cavity and pharynx (including tongue), mediastinum (sometimes arising from the pulmonary vein), stomach, retroperitoneum, orbit, uterus, and vagina.[1397a,1399,1402,1419,1423,1425] We have also seen it inside the patella. Most patients are young females. Grossly, the tumors are well circumscribed, usually large, moderately firm, and gray or yellowish (Fig. 25.191). Areas of necrosis or hemorrhage are common in the larger neoplasms.

Microscopically, the tumor cells are separated by fibrous tissue into well-defined nests. Detachment of the central cells results in a typical alveolar pattern (Fig. 25.192). The individual cells are large and have vesicular nuclei, prominent nucleoli, and a granular cytoplasm.

Fig. 25.191 Alveolar soft part sarcoma. The tumor is multinodular, relatively well circumscribed, and embedded within skeletal muscle.

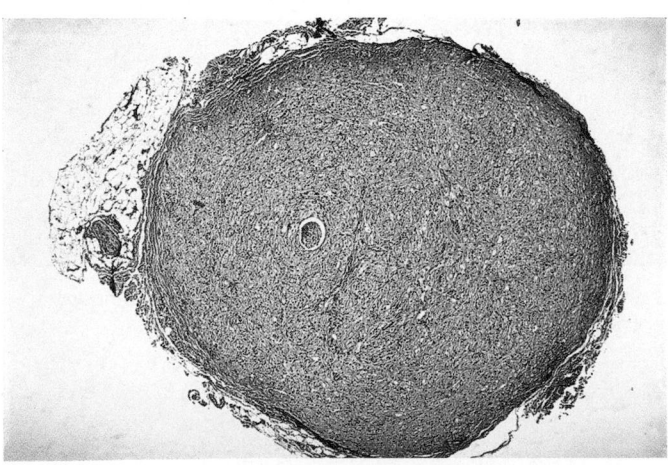

Fig. 25.190 Granular cell tumor growing concentrically within and around a nerve cut transversally.

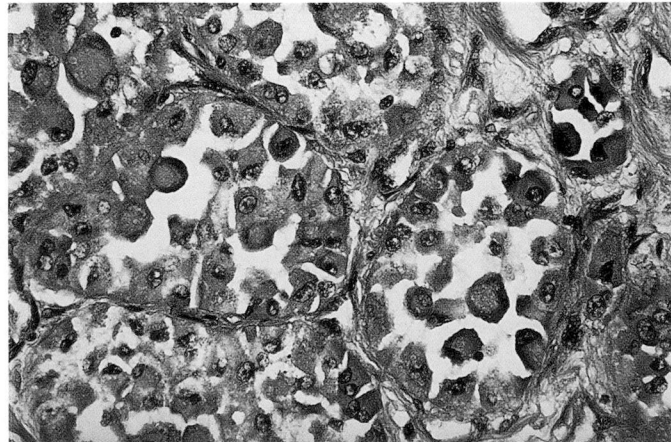

Fig. 25.192 Typical microscopic appearance of alveolar soft part sarcoma. Note the lack of mitoses.

Mitoses are exceptional. PAS stain sometimes demonstrates the presence of diastase-resistant intracytoplasmic needle-like structures (Fig. 25.193). These are seen by electron microscopy as membrane-bound crystals with a periodicity of 58 to 100 nm, sometimes arranged in a cross-grid pattern[1398] (Fig. 25.194). This feature is of great diagnostic value in lesions of controversial nature.[1422] Other ultrastructural features include numerous vesicles with an electron-dense content in the Golgi region (possibly representing the precursors of the crystals) and smooth tubular aggregates associated with plasmalemmal invaginations.[1415]

Alveolar soft part sarcomas occurring in children are often associated with a more solid pattern of growth, and

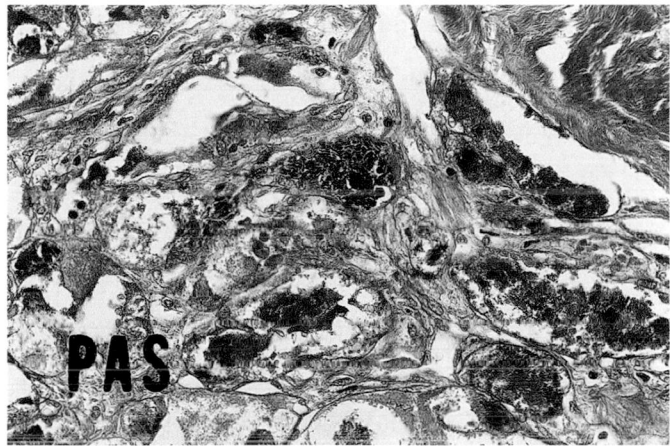

Fig. 25.193 PAS-positive cytoplasmic granules in alveolar soft part sarcoma, some having a crystalline appearance.

therefore tend to be misdiagnosed (Fig. 25.195). Conversely, the alveolar appearance of this entity can be closely simulated by other malignant neoplasms, notably malignant melanoma and renal cell carcinoma (Fig. 25.196).

Alveolar soft part sarcoma is highly malignant, despite its deceivingly slow and indolent clinical course. Vein invasion is common. Blood-borne metastases appear in the lungs and other organs as long as 30 years or more following excision of the primary tumor.[1407,1408] Not infrequently, a metastasis in the lung or in another organ is the first manifestation of the disease. There is a good correlation between tumor size and survival.[1397]

The histogenesis of this strange neoplasm has not yet been definitely established.[1394,1412] We believe there is no convincing evidence to support the theory that this tumor represents a malignant counterpart of granular cell tumor, that it arises from nonchromaffin paraganglia, or that it is related to renin-producing cells of blood vessel walls.[1398] Instead, a wealth of data has accumulated in recent years supporting the interpretation that alveolar soft part sarcoma is of myogenous derivation and that it represents a distinct variant of rhabdomyosarcoma.[1401] This includes the (admittedly inconsistent) immunohistochemical demonstration of smooth muscle and sarcomeric actin, desmin, Z-protein, fast myosin, β-enolase, and the MM isozyme of creatine kinase[1400,1403,1410,1411,1413,1414,1416,1417,1420] (Fig. 25.197); the demonstration of ATPase activity in the crystalline inclusions[1409]; the detection of similar membrane-bound cytoplasmic crystals in a normal human muscle spindle[1395];

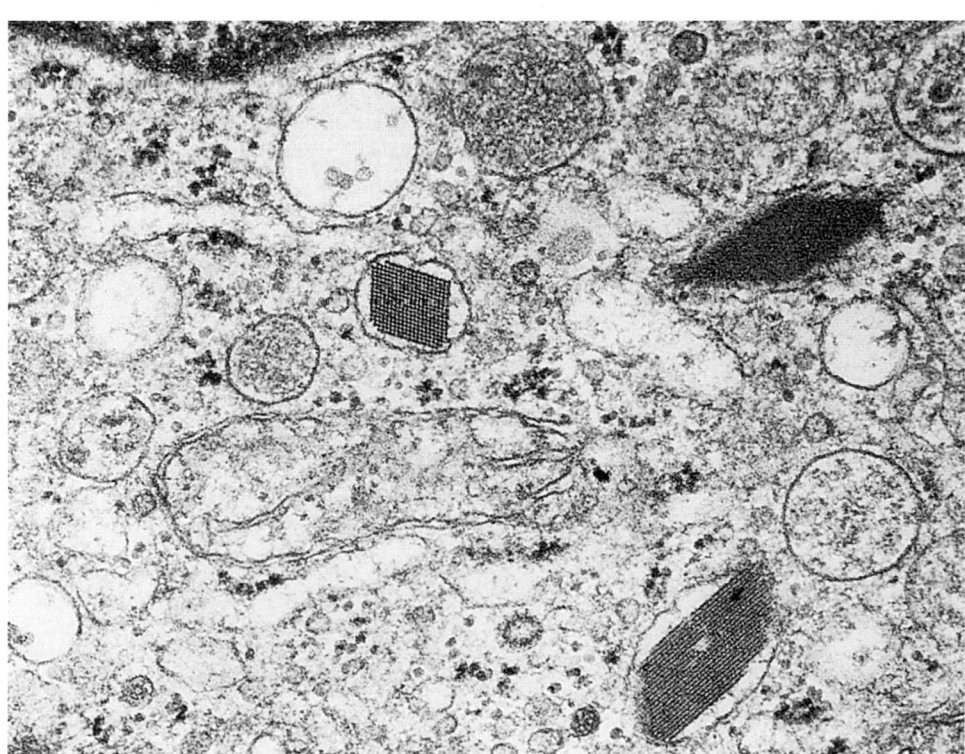

Fig. 25.194 Electron microscopic appearance of alveolar soft part sarcoma. Detailed view of characteristic crystalloid inclusions that demonstrate orderly 70 Å periodicity. Both linear and cross-hatched crystalloid patterns may be noted. (×70,000; courtesy of Dr. J. Sciubba, New Hyde Park, NY)

the presence of T-tubule-like structures at the ultrastructural level[1415]; and the (not independently confirmed) demonstration of MyoD1 protein, a nuclear phosphoprotein that is the product of a regulatory gene that controls the commitment of a cell to a myogenic lineage.[1421] However, we freely admit that the matter is far from set-

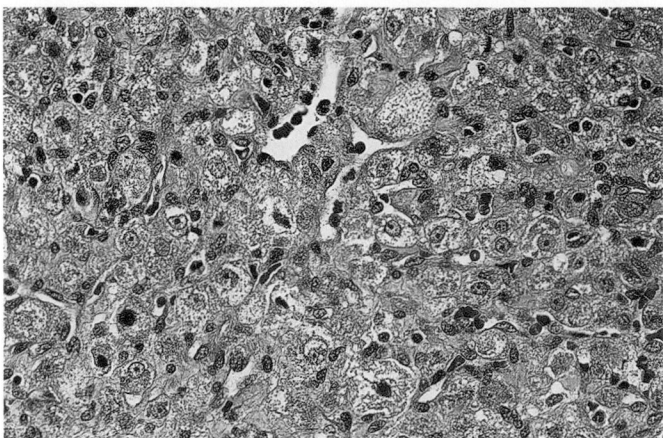

Fig. 25.195 Alveolar soft part sarcoma with a nesting pattern of growth and lack of alveolar formations. This variant, which is particularly common in children, is likely to be misdiagnosed.

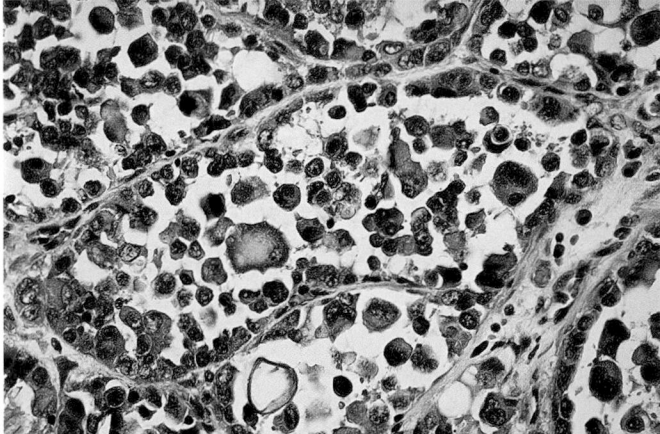

Fig. 25.196 Metastatic malignant melanoma closely simulating the appearance of alveolar soft part sarcoma.

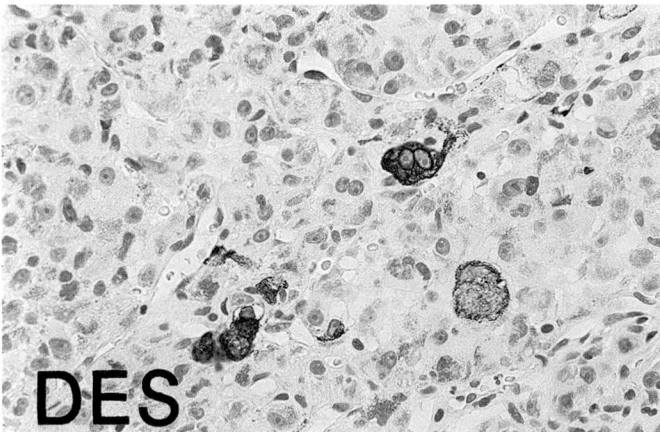

Fig. 25.197 Desmin immunoreactivity in scattered tumor cells of alveolar soft part sarcoma.

tled.[1424,1418] Along these lines, the demonstration that the precrystalline cytoplasmic granules of this tumor contain monocarboxylate transporter 1 and CD147[1404] is of interest but does not particularly contribute to the solution of the histogenetic riddle that surrounds this tumor.

At the cytogenetic level, alveolar soft part sarcoma has been found to be associated with the chromosomal unbalanced translocation der(17)t(X;17)(p11.2;q25), which results in the fusion of the *TFE3* transcription factor gene to the *ASPL* gene.[1405,1412,1421a] Interestingly, a similar but balanced translocation has been detected in a type of renal neoplasm which is probably epithelial but which bears some morphologic resemblance to alveolar soft part sarcoma (see also Chapter 17).[1333] The presence of aberrant nuclear expression of TFE3 can be demonstrated in these tumors by immunohistochemistry.[1393a]

Clear cell sarcoma of tendons and aponeuroses (malignant melanoma of soft parts)

This malignant tumor arises chiefly from large tendons and aponeuroses of the extremities.[1434,1436,1444] The feet are the most common site, but it has been described in several other sites, including the penis and the gastrointestinal tract.[1446,1449] Most of the patients are young adults.

Grossly, the tumors are firm, well circumscribed, and gray or white and are cut with a gritty sensation (Fig. 25.198). Microscopically, solid nests and fascicles of pale fusiform or cuboidal cells are present (Fig. 25.199). The nucleoli are large and deeply basophilic. Multinucleated giant cells are often seen. Abundant extracellular and intracellular iron is present. In many of the cases the tumor cells also contain cytoplasmic melanin,[1429,1432,1448] strongly suggesting that this neoplasm is of neuroectodermal derivation and that it represents a peculiar type of malignant melanoma of soft parts.[1428,1432,1442] In keeping with this interpretation is the fact that the tumor cells consistently exhibit immunoreactivity for S-100 protein, HMB-45, Leu7, NSE, and vimentin[1432,1437,1438,1447] and that

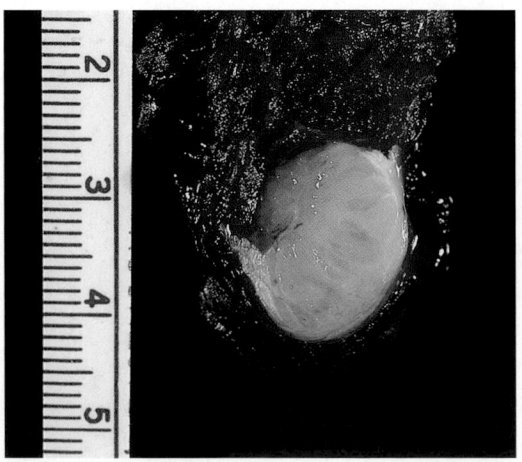

Fig. 25.198 Gross appearance of clear cell sarcoma (malignant melanoma of soft parts) located in the posterior thigh.

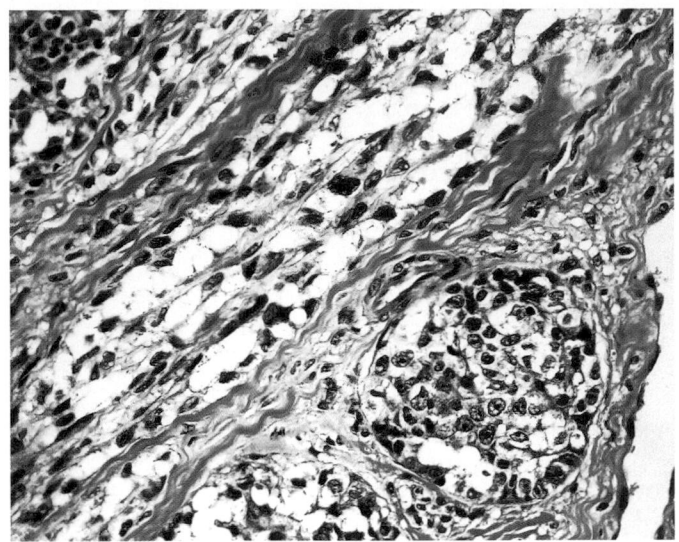

Fig. 25.199 Clear cell sarcoma of soft parts. Note the fascicular pattern of growth and the prominent nucleoli.

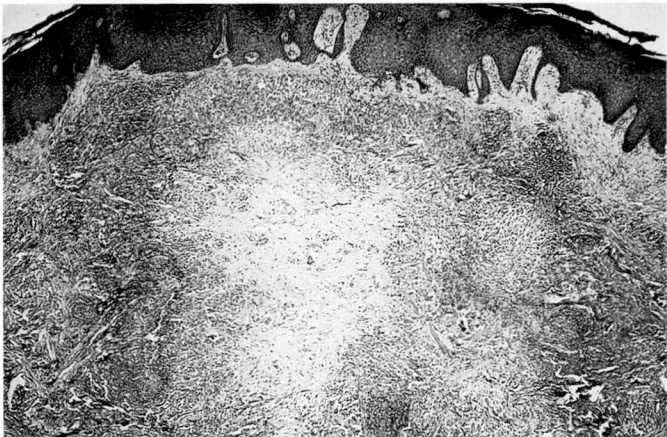

Fig. 25.200 The low-power appearance of this dermally located epithelioid sarcoma simulates a granuloma annulare or rheumatoid nodule.

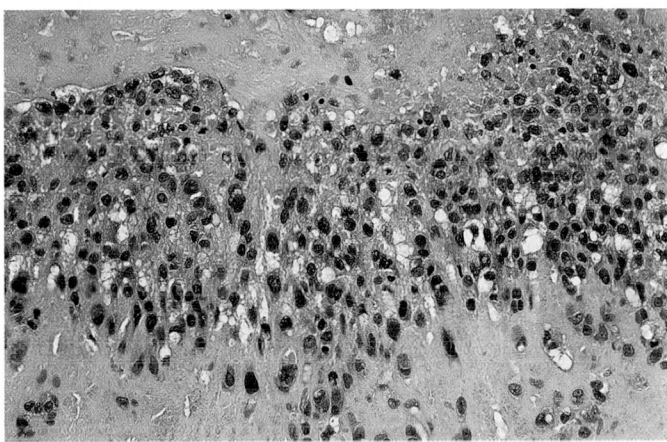

Fig. 25.201 Tightly clustered epithelioid tumor cells around the necrotic center in epithelioid sarcoma.

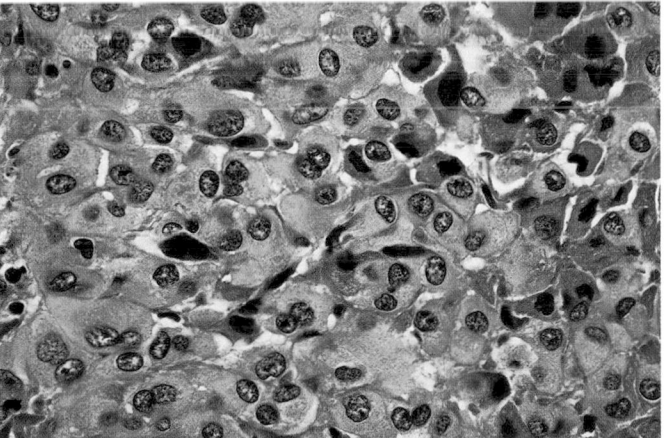

Fig. 25.202 Remarkable epithelioid quality of tumor cells in epithelioid sarcoma. Note the diffuse tissue eosinophilia.

ultrastructurally there are melanosomes plus features consistent with a neural derivation.[1430,1443] When compared with conventional melanoma of skin metastatic to soft tissue by DNA ploidy analysis, clear cell sarcoma is more likely to be diploid or to show a lesser degree of aneuploidy.[1435] Like conventional melanoma, the clear cell carcinoma type may exhibit immunoreactivity for keratin.[1441]

Clear cell sarcoma is associated with the chromosomal translocation t(12;22)(q13;q12),[1431,1444a] which results in the *EWS–ATF1* gene fusion and the expression of the melanocyte-specific splice form of the MIFT transcript.[1427]

The clinical course of clear cell sarcoma is characterized by slow but relentless progression with frequent local recurrences and eventual nodal and distant metastases.[1426,1433,1436] Large tumor size and necrosis are statistically significant predictors of poor prognosis.[1439,1440,1445]

Epithelioid sarcoma

Epithelioid sarcoma usually affects adolescents and young adults.[1458,1463] A few cases have been reported in patients with neurofibromatosis.[1475] The extremities are the most common location, particularly the hands and fingers. Several instances of vulvar involvement have also been recorded.[1480] The tumors tend to be superficially located and are sometimes centered in the reticular dermis. Others are found in the subcutis or deeper soft tissues, particularly fascial planes, aponeuroses, and tendon sheaths.[1476] The necrosis often seen in the center of the nodules and the epithelioid appearance of the tumor cells often results in a mistaken diagnosis of infectious granuloma or, more frequently, necrobiotic collagen granuloma[1476] (Fig. 25.200).

One of the most characteristic features is the striking acidophilia of the tumor tissue, which is due to the stain-ing characteristics of the cytoplasm and the extensive desmoplasia (Figs 25.201 and 25.202). Metaplastic elements such as bone and cartilage may be present.[1456] Sometimes, most of the tumor cells have a spindle shape and simulate a fibroma or a dermatofibrosarcoma

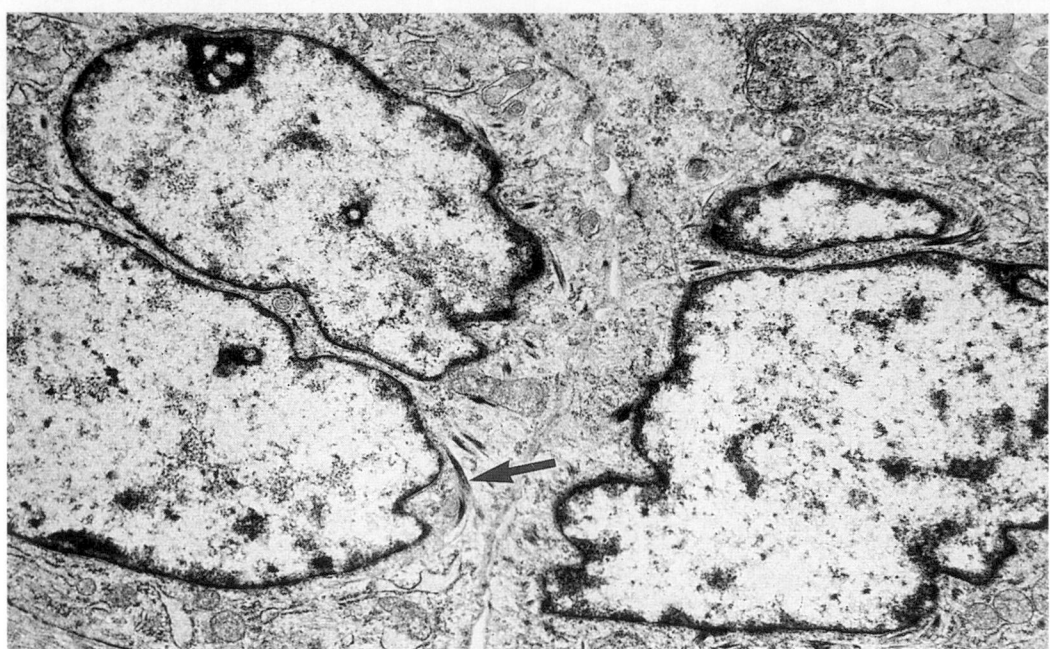

Fig. 25.203 Electron microscopic appearance of epithelioid sarcoma. Small tonofibrils (arrow) are present in the epithelioid tumor cells. (×11,100; courtesy of Dr. Robert A. Erlandson, Memorial Sloan-Kettering Cancer Center)

protuberans.[1469] Sometimes, epithelioid sarcomas of the soft tissue or vulva exhibit rhabdoid features; this is particularly common in the so-called "proximal type" (see below).[1470,1473]

Ultrastructurally, the tumor cells exhibit abundant intermediate filaments, desmosome-like cell junctions, and small intercellular spaces surrounded by filopodia or microvilli[1451,1461,1467,1471] (Fig. 25.203). Immunohistochemically, there is positivity for keratin, EMA, vimentin, CD34, tissue polypeptide antigen, and occasionally CEA[1454,1455,1457,1460,1465,1471] (Fig. 25.204). The coexpression of vimentin and keratin is thought to be characteristic of this tumor; however, vimentin-negative cases that still retain positivity for keratin and CD34 have been reported.[1450] Regarding keratin subtypes, Miettinen et al.[1467] found positivity for CK8 in 94% of the cases, CK19 in 72%, 34βEH12 in 48%, and CK7 in 22%. Keratin

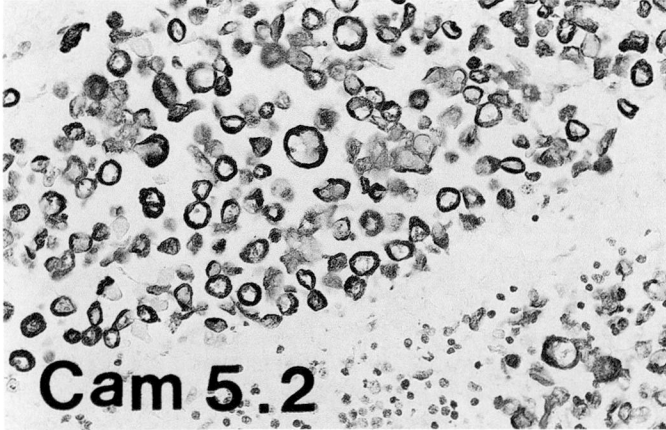

Fig. 25.204 Strong keratin immunoreactivity (Cam 5.2) in epithelioid sarcoma.

5/6 is usually negative or expressed only focally, in contrast to squamous cell carcinoma.[1464a]

The histogenesis of this tumor remains obscure. It clearly exhibits features of epithelial differentiation and therefore could be regarded as a form of carcinoma of soft tissue, together with synovial sarcoma and the exceptionally rare adamantinoma of soft tissues.[1468] Whether the epithelial features present in these tumors derive from metaplasia of mesenchymal elements remains to be determined. Another possibility, already mentioned in this chapter, is that epithelioid sarcoma is a peculiar form of epithelioid hemangioendothelioma.[1457a]

The tumor spreads to noncontiguous areas of skin, soft tissue, fascia, and bone, as well as by direct extension along fascial planes.[1452,1472] Local recurrence is the rule, although it may take years for this to develop. Lymph node metastases are relatively common and constitute an ominous prognostic sign.[1474] Metastases also occur in the lungs, other organs, and skin: for some peculiar reason, the scalp is a preferred site.[1480] Sometimes a lymph node metastasis is the first clinical manifestation of the disease.[1479] Excision plus radiation therapy achieves a low rate of local recurrence.[1477] A more aggressive clinical course is associated with a proximal or axial tumor location, increased size and depth, hemorrhage, mitotic figures, necrosis, rhabdoid features, and vascular invasion.[1453,1459] Some of these features may be seen in combination. Indeed, the proposal has been made for the existence of a *proximal type* of epithelioid sarcoma characterized by a proximal location (pelvis, perineal and pubic region, vulva, buttock), deep invasion, necrosis, and sometimes prominent rhabdoid features[1462,1464] (Fig. 25.205). The keratin profile of this variant is more restricted than that of conventional epithelioid sarcoma

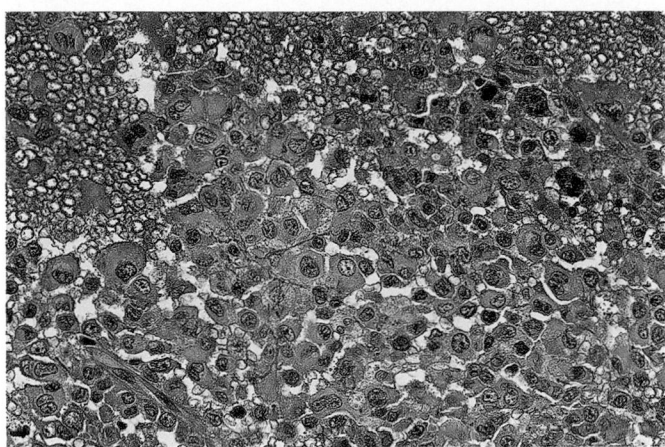

Fig. 25.205 So-called "proximal variant" of epithelioid sarcoma. Many of the tumor cells have a rhabdoid quality.

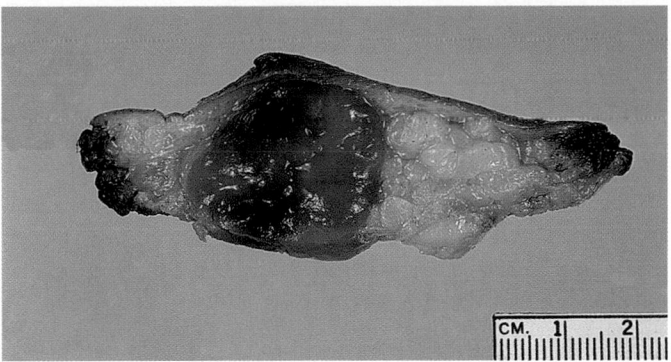

Fig. 25.206 Malignant giant cell tumor of soft parts. The tumor is relatively well circumscribed, bulges on the cut surface, and is focally hemorrhagic.

and more in keeping with rhabdoid tumors of other types.[1478] We believe this is a valid concept, but warn the pathologist always to consider the alternative possibility of undifferentiated carcinoma before making this diagnosis.

Giant cell tumor of soft parts

Giant cell tumor of soft parts is a rare neoplasm that mainly affects adults and the elderly and is usually located in the extremities. Most cases are located deeply, but a superficial variety in the subcutaneous tissue and fascia has also been described[1484] (Fig. 25.206). The tumor is composed of an admixture of osteoclast-like multinucleated giant cells and stromal cells[1481,1485,1489] (Fig. 25.207). The stromal cells are probably the only neoplastic component; some are elongated and fibroblast-like, whereas others are plump, resembling histiocytes. Some of the latter may be multinucleated but different from the osteoclast-like elements. The giant cells resemble osteoclasts not only light microscopically, but also ultrastructurally and in their content of hydrolytic enzymes, such as acid phosphatase (Fig. 25.208). Metaplastic bone may be present, usually in the form of peripheral shell, perhaps induced by secretion of transforming growth factor β-1 and β-2 by the tumor cells.[1490] The tumor has a characteristic multinodular configuration on low-power examination. Vascularity is pronounced, a fact also evident in angiographic studies.[1482] The overall appearance of the tumor is highly reminiscent of giant cell tumor of bones. The histogenesis is unclear.[1481,1485] In earlier schemes this tumor had been included as one of the histologic types of MFH,[1486] but this is no longer favored.

The behavior is dependent upon the location, size, and microscopic appearance. Low-grade (benign, of low malignant potential) and high-grade (malignant) forms have been separated from each other on the basis of the atypia, pleomorphism and mitotic activity of the mononuclear neoplastic component.[1483,1487,1488]

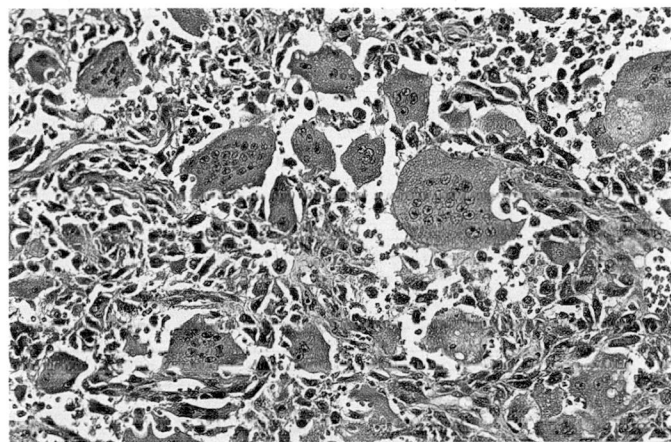

Fig. 25.207 Giant cell tumor of soft parts. The appearance is remarkably similar to that of giant cell tumor of bone.

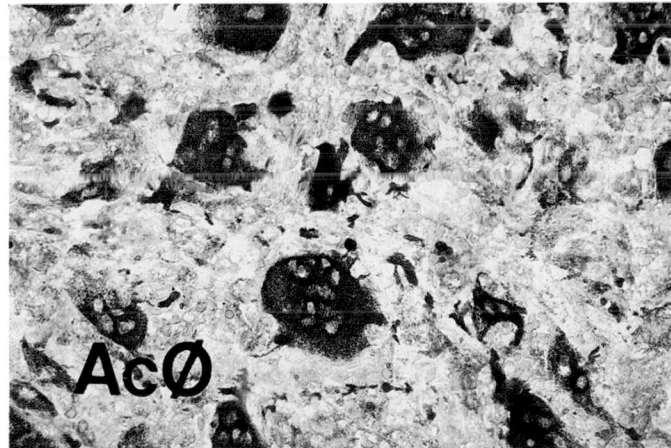

Fig. 25.208 Intense positivity for acid phosphatase in the multinucleated cells of giant cell tumor of soft tissues.

Ossifying fibromyxoid tumor

Ossifying fibromyxoid tumor is a soft tissue neoplasm which usually presents in adult patients as a small, painless, well-circumscribed mass in the subcutaneous tissue or muscle of the extremities.[1492] Microscopically, the tumor cells are typically arranged in a cord- or nest-like pattern within a myxoid matrix that blends with foci of fibrosis and osteoid formation. The low-power appearance is distinctive by virtue of lobulation and an incomplete shell of mature bone in the region corresponding to the tumor capsule[1492] (Fig. 25.209). The tumor cells are small and round, with scanty atypia and few mitoses (Fig. 25.210).

Immunohistochemically, there is widespread immunoreactivity for S-100 protein and vimentin, associated with focal reactivity for Leu7 and glial fibrillary acidic protein, and negativity for type II collagen. Ultrastructurally, there are complex cell processes and basement membrane deposition. This combination of features is more in keeping with a schwannian than a cartilaginous or other mesenchymal derivation.[1491,1494] However, the detection of desmin and smooth muscle by some authors suggests that a partial differentiation toward a smooth muscle phenotype may be taking place in these tumors.[1495,1496]

The behavior of this tumor is indolent, but local recurrences developed in a quarter of the cases reported by Enzinger et al.[1492] in whom follow-up information was available. Additional atypical and malignant cases have been reported.[1492a,1493]

Extraskeletal Ewing's sarcoma/PNET

Tumors morphologically indistinguishable from **Ewing's sarcoma** of the skeletal system can present as soft tissue masses. In some cases, they simply represent soft tissue extensions of tumor originating in the underlying bone. In others, bone involvement is absent, and these are regarded as primary Ewing's sarcomas of soft tissues.[1524,1527,1530] Most of the patients are adolescents or young adults, and the usual sites of involvement are the soft tissues of the lower extremity and paravertebral region.[1498] Like their skeletal counterpart, they are composed of uniform small, round, or oval cells containing cytoplasmic glycogen and sometimes arranged in a "peritheliomatous" pattern (Figs 25.211 and 25.212). Ultrastructurally, the cells are rather primitive, with abundant cytoplasmic glycogen, poorly developed cell junctions, and no evidence of neural differentiation.[1510,1514,1532,1539] The course is aggressive and distant metastases are common, particularly to lung and skeleton.

As already discussed in Chapter 24, Ewing's sarcoma of both osseous and extraosseous sites is currently regarded as merging imperceptibly with **primitive neurectodermal tumor** (PNET)[1515,1525,1537] and subsuming the clinicopathologic entity originally described as malignant small cell tumor of the thoracopulmonary region[1499,1502,1511,1520] (Fig. 25.213). The nosologic unity of Ewing's sarcoma/PNET is strongly supported by the existence of numerous intermediate forms,[1516,1527,1528,1540] the strong immunoreactivity for CD99 (O13; HBA71; 12E7; RFB-1),[1523] and—most important—the presence of a consistent chromosomal translocation (11:22;q24;q12),[1535] which leads to the fusion of the Ewing's sarcoma gene (*ESG*) in chromosome 22 to *FLI-1* or *ERG* gene in

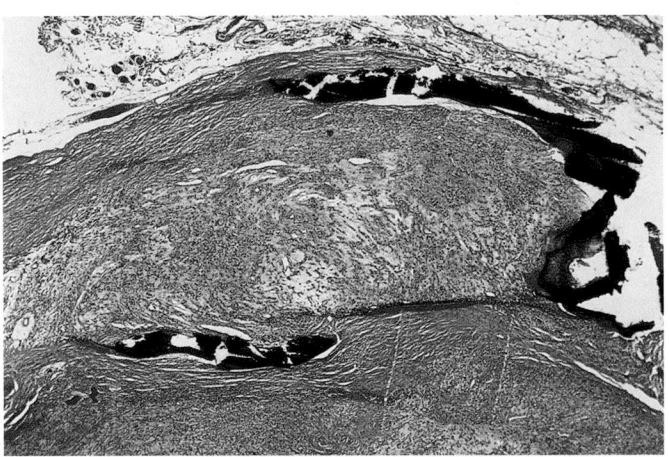

Fig. 25.209 Low-power view of ossifying fibromyxoid tumor. A shell of metaplastic bone partially surrounds the tumor periphery.

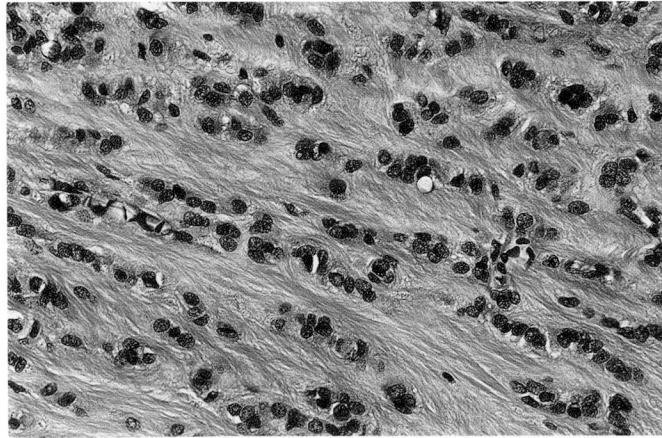

Fig. 25.210 On high power, the cells of ossifying fibromyxoid tumor are medium-sized, only moderately atypical, and embedded in a hyaline matrix.

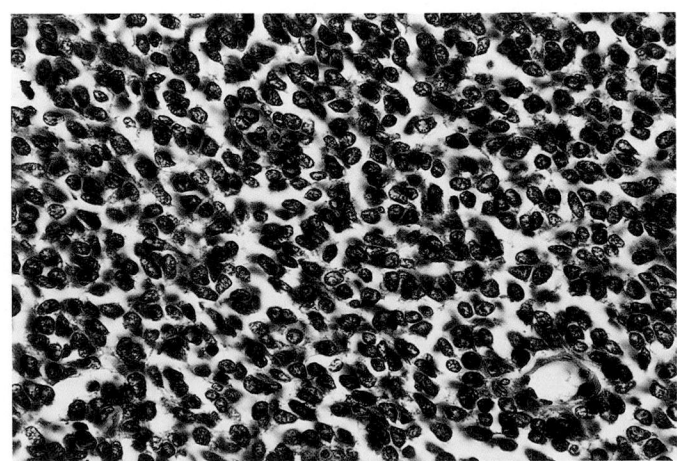

Fig. 25.211 Extraskeletal Ewing's sarcoma/PNET. The tumor is extremely cellular, with hardly any intervening stroma. Some tumor cells are attached to a vessel wall in a pseudorosette arrangement.

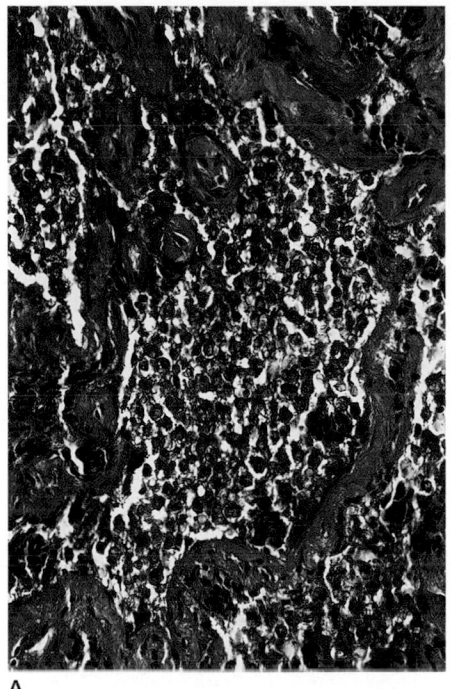
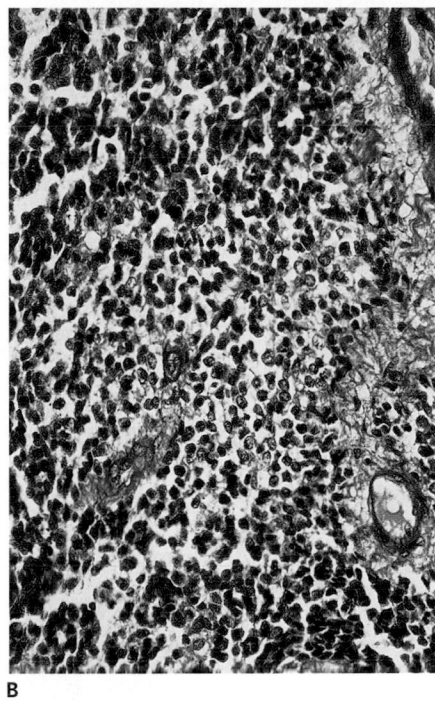

Fig. 25.212 Abundant cytoplasmic glycogen in the cells of Ewing's sarcoma/PNET, as shown with PAS stain (**A**) with diastase control (**B**).

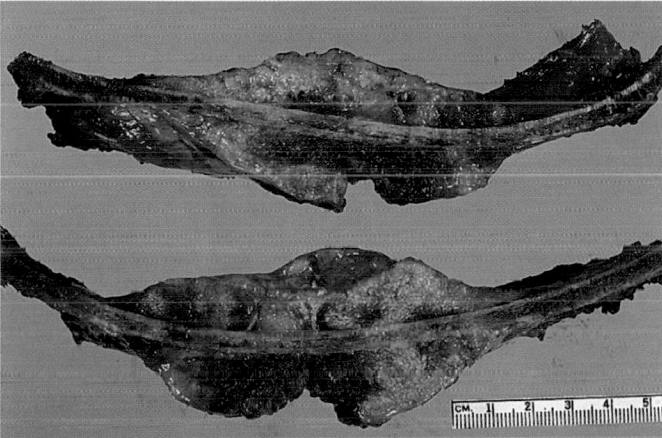

Fig. 25.213 Ewing's sarcoma/PNET of thoracopulmonary region. The tumor is present on both sides of the rib, but the bone was only minimally involved.

chromosome 11 and the production of a chimeric transcript.[1503,1504] This genetic alteration can be detected with RT-PCR or FISH in fresh or paraffin-embedded material.[1517]

CD99 recognizes a cell membrane protein of yet unknown function (p30/32 MIC 2; 013), which is the product of *MIC2*, a pseudoautosomal gene located on the short arm of the X and Y chromosomes.[1497,1507,1531] It is not specific for Ewing's sarcoma/PNET. Other markers that have been detected immunohistochemically in this family of tumors—some of them pointing toward a neuroepithelial line of differentiation—include neuron-specific enolase, synaptophysin, S-100 protein, PGP 9.5, secretogranin II, vimentin, and keratin.[1500,1512,1513,1518,1522] The keratin reactivity has been detected in close to a fifth

of the cases, and it may be quite extensive.[1501,1536] The 11;22 translocation, present in approximately 90% of the cases, can be detected by RT-PCR or chromosomal in situ suppression hybridization,[1506,1519,1526,1529] and the protein transcript can be identified with the recently produced anti-FLI-1 antibody.[1508]

The claim that tumors having easily detectable neuroepithelial markers have a more aggressive clinical course than the others[1515] has not been substantiated.[1523] Furthermore, most attempts to subdivide them on phenotypic grounds have been unsuccessful.[1521,1529] The fact remains that—statistically speaking—tumors located in bone are more likely to exhibit a more undifferentiated phenotype (in keeping with the original Ewing's sarcoma concept), whereas those located in soft tissues—including most thoracopulmonary examples—tend to display various degrees of neuroepithelial differentiation.[1520]

The differential diagnosis of Ewing's sarcoma/PNET of soft tissues includes embryonal and alveolar rhabdomyosarcoma (especially the solid variant of the latter), malignant lymphoma, desmoplastic small cell tumor, and so-called "rhabdoid tumor."[1505,1534] A combined morphologic, immunohistochemical and molecular approach will place most tumors into one or another of these categories, allowing for the existence of hybrid forms.[1409,1533]

Desmoplastic small cell tumor

Desmoplastic small cell tumor is typically located within the abdominal cavity (see Chapter 24), but has also been seen in the pleural cavity, CNS, and—more pertinently for the purposes of this chapter—in the soft tissues and bone of the hand.[1541]

Rhabdoid tumor

Rhabdoid tumor was originally described as a primary renal neoplasm (see Chapter 17), but examples of a morphologically similar neoplasm have been subsequently identified in many other sites, particularly soft tissues.[1551] Some of the cases have involved major nerves.[1530] Most patients are infants or children, but it can also occur in adults. Microscopically, solid sheets of cells are present with areas of compartmentalization. The most striking morphologic feature is the deeply and homogeneously acidophilic cytoplasm of the tumor cells (the result of packing by intermediate filaments), with occasional lateral displacement of the nucleus[1543] (Figs 25.214 and 25.215). Myxoid, pseudoalveolar, and hyalinized areas may be present.[1548] Immunohistochemically, there is positivity for vimentin and often for keratin and EMA but generally not for skeletal muscle markers or S-100 protein[1546] (Fig. 25.216). However, a great deal of phenotypical diversity has been recorded in these lesions,[1547,1550] including the common expression of neural/neuroendocrine markers.[1542]

Metastases occur early (to the lungs, liver, and lymph nodes), response to therapy is poor, and the clinical course is extremely aggressive.[1549,1551] Most evidence suggests that rhabdoid tumor of soft tissues is not a specific tumor entity but rather the expression of a "rhabdoid" phenotype that can develop in a wide variety of tumor types, including epithelioid sarcoma, synovial sarcoma, intra-abdominal desmoplastic small cell tumor, rhabdomyosarcoma, malignant melanoma, and various types of carcinoma.[1547,1552,1553] Of practical importance is the fact that the emergence of the rhabdoid phenotype is invariably associated with an aggressive and almost always lethal clinical course.[1542,1544]

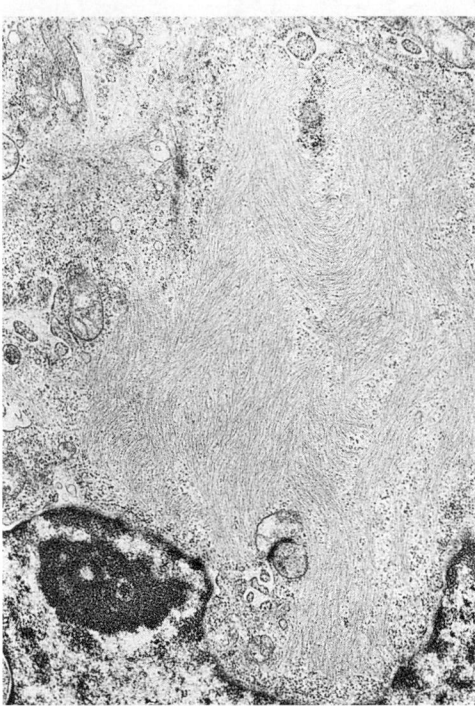

Fig. 25.215 Electron microscopic appearance of rhabdoid tumor of soft tissue. The cytoplasmic organelles of this rhabdoid cell are displaced by a large aggregate of intermediate filaments, immunohistochemically shown to be of vimentin type. (×15,000; courtesy of Dr. Robert A. Erlandson, Memorial Sloan-Kettering Cancer Center)

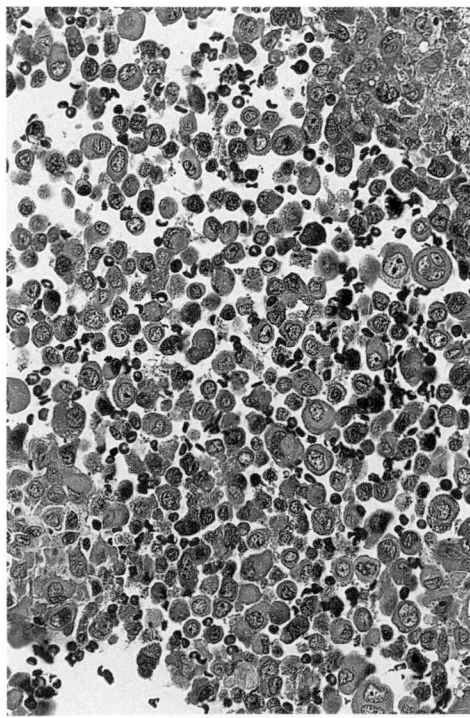

Fig. 25.214 Soft tissue tumor of the vulvar region with rhabdoid features. The tumor cells are small and round to oval, and their nuclei are displaced laterally.

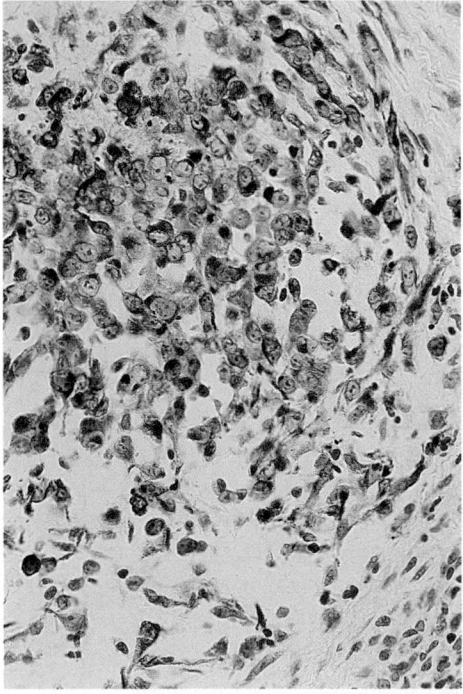

Fig. 25.216 Rhabdoid tumor immunostained for keratin. The reaction has a characteristic punctate quality.

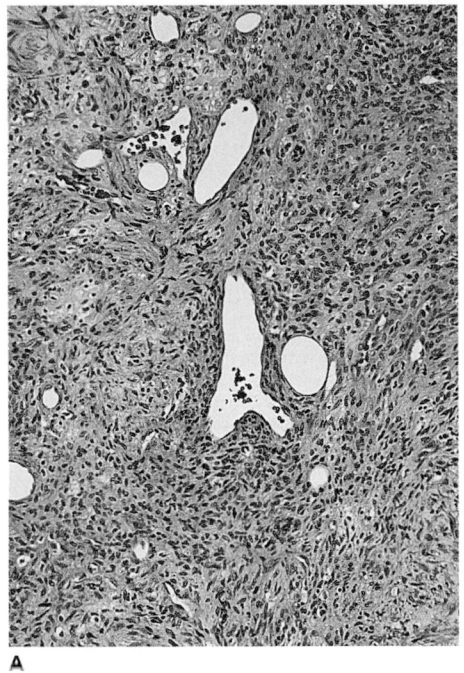
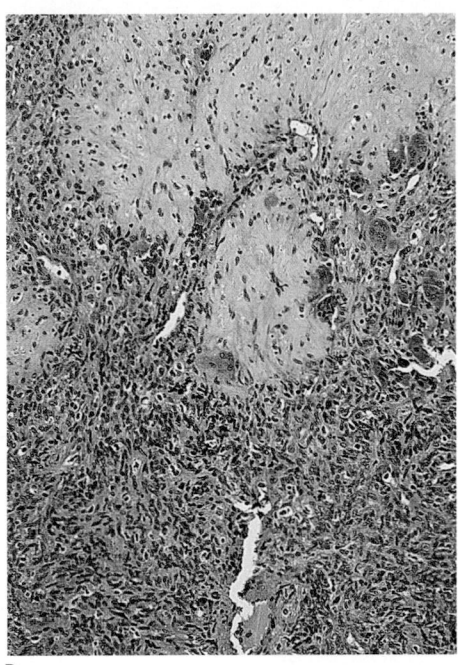

A   B

Fig. 25.217 A and **B**, Phosphaturic mesenchymal tumor. **A**, This area has a hemangiopericytoma-like quality. **B**, In this area from the same tumor, there is chondroid differentiation and a scattering of osteoclast-like giant cells.

Phosphaturic mesenchymal tumor

An interesting association has been reported between some tumors of soft tissue or bone and osteomalacia or rickets.[1557] The syndrome results from tumor production of a renal phosphaturic substance that depletes total-body phosphates by inhibiting tubular reabsorption of phosphate.[1554,1556] It is characterized biochemically by hypophosphatemia, renal phosphate wasting, and decreased serum 1,25-dihydroxy vitamin D3 levels.[1555] The soft tissue tumors associated with this complication have shown an admixture of microscopic features.[1557] In our experience the most characteristic feature has been the association of hemangiopericytoma-like areas and osteoclast-like giant cells, with or without foci of osseous and cartilaginous metaplasia. A "grungy" calcified matrix is said to be particularly distinctive[1554] (Fig. 25.217). The behavior has been generally benign,[1555,1557] but malignant examples are on record.[1554a]

Pleomorphic hyalinizing angiectatic tumor of soft parts

This recently described tumor type can simulate schwannoma by virtue of the angiectatic vasculature, the presence of hemosiderin-laden macrophages, and the occurrence of a spindle cell component with scattered bizarre nuclear forms but practically no mitotic activity (Fig. 25.218). Two diagnostic clues are represented by the nuclear pseudoinclusions and the fact that many of the bizarre cells are embedded within a fibrinous material surrounding the angiectatic vessels. CD34 is focally positive and S-100 protein is negative. Cytogenetically, supernumerary ring chromosomes have been found, linking this tumor with other low-grade mesenchymal malignancies, such as dermatofibrosarcoma protuber-

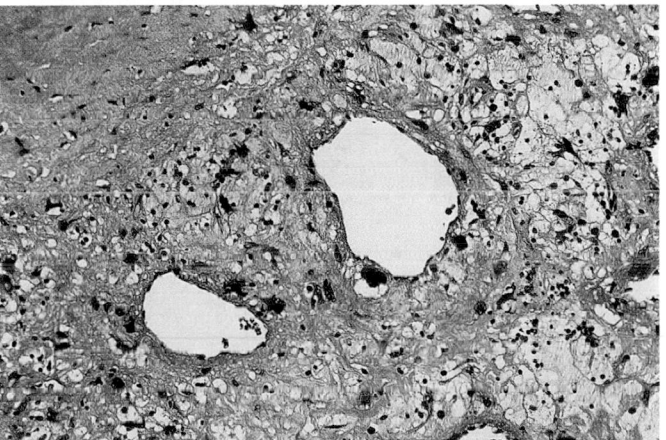

Fig. 25.218 Pleomorphic hyalinizing angiectatic tumor of soft parts. The pleomorphic tumor cells surround dilated vessels.

ans, parosteal osteosarcoma, and well-differentiated liposarcoma.[1557a] Local recurrences have been described but not distant metastases.[1558]

Myoepithelioma of soft tissue

The proposal has been made that there exists in the soft tissue a group of tumors showing differentiation toward myoepithelial cells presumably connected with skin adnexa, which can occur either in a pure form (myoepitheliomas) or in association with glandular structures (mixed tumors).[1560a,1562,1563] Microscopically, the myoepithelial component is present in the form of nests, cords, and ductules of epithelioid cells, and/or nests of spindle cells within a hyalinized or chondromyxoid stroma (Fig. 25.219A). Osteoid production and chondroid differentiation may be present. Immunohistochemically, there may be reactivity for keratin, S-100 protein, smooth muscle actin, desmin, GFAP, and EMA[1562] (Fig. 25.219B,C). These tumors have the capability for local recurrence and distant metastases.

It has further been suggested that the mysterious neoplasm originally reported by Dabska as *parachordoma*[1561,1564] may be part of this spectrum. Parachordoma has been typically described adjacent to tendons,

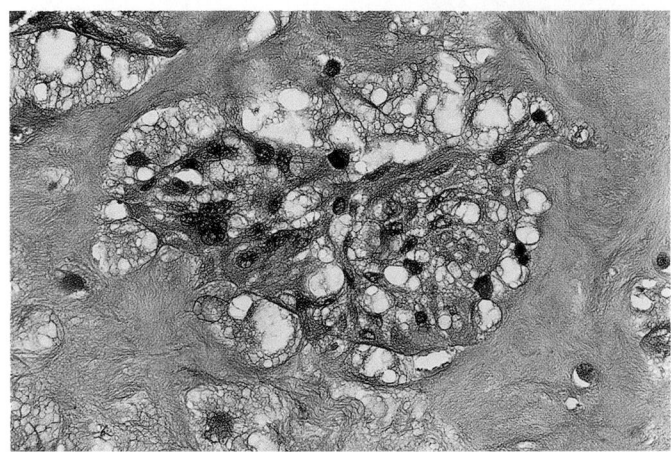

A

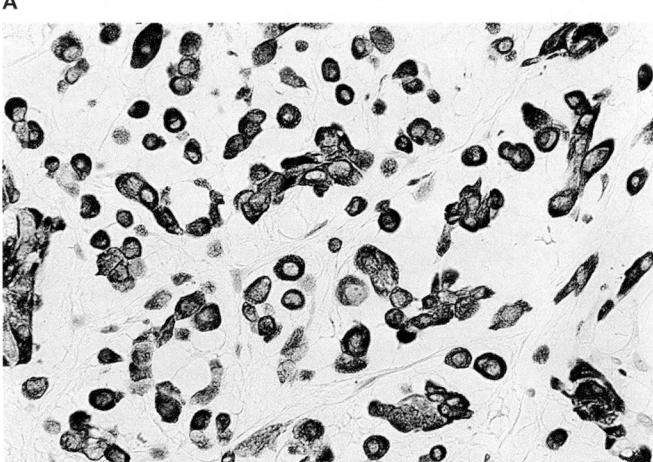

B

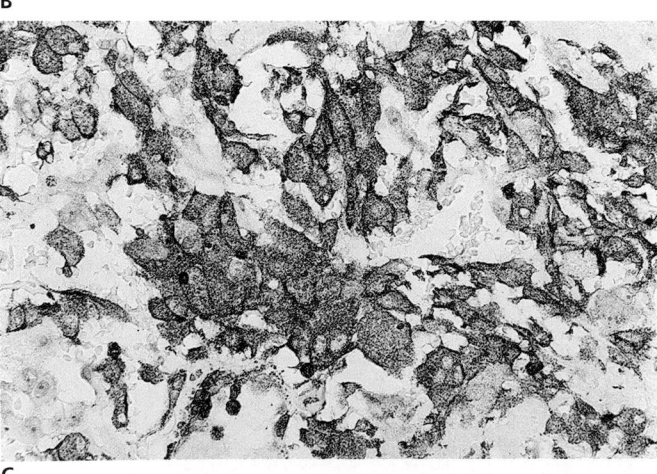

C

Fig. 25.219 A to **C,** Myoepithelioma of soft parts. The appearance is highly reminiscent of so-called "parachordoma." **B,** Keratin (Cam 5.2). **C,** Smooth muscle actin.

synovium, and osseous structures within extremities. Microscopically, well-circumscribed lobules composed of small cellular aggregates embedded within a hyalinized and chondroid matrix are present.[1559,1560] Some of the tumor cells are reminiscent of physaliphorous cells, hence the name.

Other tumors

Oncocytoma has been reported as a primary tumor of soft tissues, and we have seen a similar example.[1566] The appearance does not differ from that of oncocytomas at other sites, and the origin may be related to deeply seated skin adnexa.

Metastatic tumors

Skeletal muscle or other deep soft tissue metastases of carcinoma or melanoma occur, but only rarely do they represent the first clinical manifestation of the disease. Reported cases include metastases from carcinoma of the kidney, lung, breast, and large bowel[1567,1567a] (Fig. 25.220).

Other tumorlike conditions

Tumoral calcinosis is characterized by the formation of large, painless, calcified masses in the periarticular soft tissues, especially along extensor surfaces (Figs 25.221) and 25.222). The elbows and hips are the most common sites. Curiously, the knee is always spared.

The disease has a genetic basis. It is inherited as an autosomal dominant trait with variable clinical expressivity. The largest series have been reported from African countries.[1580] The serum calcium is usually normal, but there is hyperphosphatemia and elevated serum dihydroxyvitamin D levels.[1576] The disease may recur after excision.[1572]

Calcifying fibrous pseudotumor is a benign and probably non-neoplastic fibrous lesion characterized by the presence of abundant hyalinized collagen with psammomatous or dystrophic calcifications and a lymphoplasmacytic infiltrate (Fig. 25.223). Most patients are

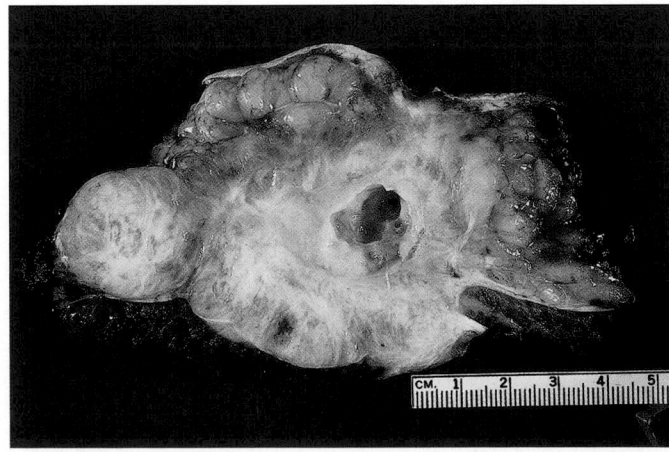

Fig. 25.220 Carcinoma of large bowel metastatic to soft tissues and skin.

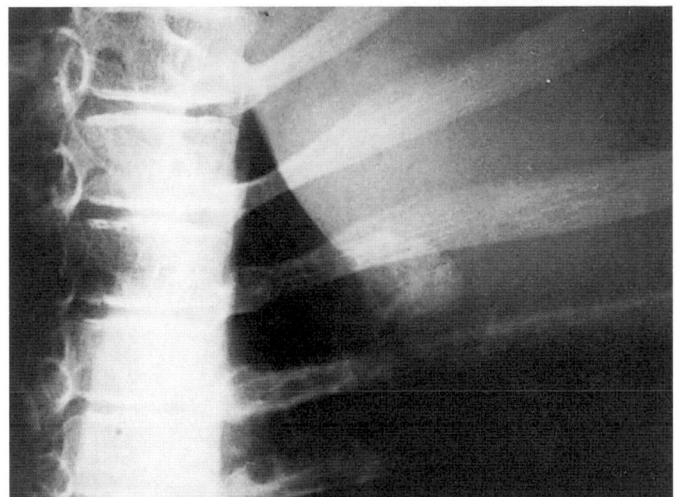

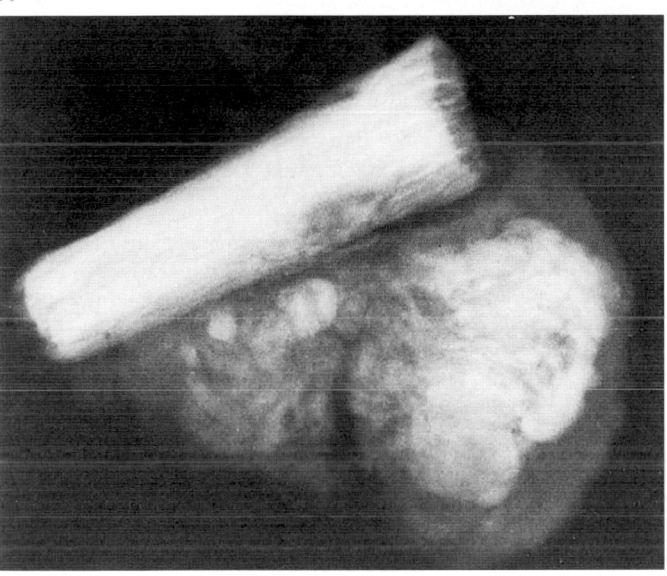

Fig. 25.221 A and **B**, Radiograph showing an area of tumoral calcinosis adjacent to a posterior rib in a 9-year-old child. **B**, Radiograph of excised specimen. Calcification is lobulated, splotchy, and independent of the eighth rib.

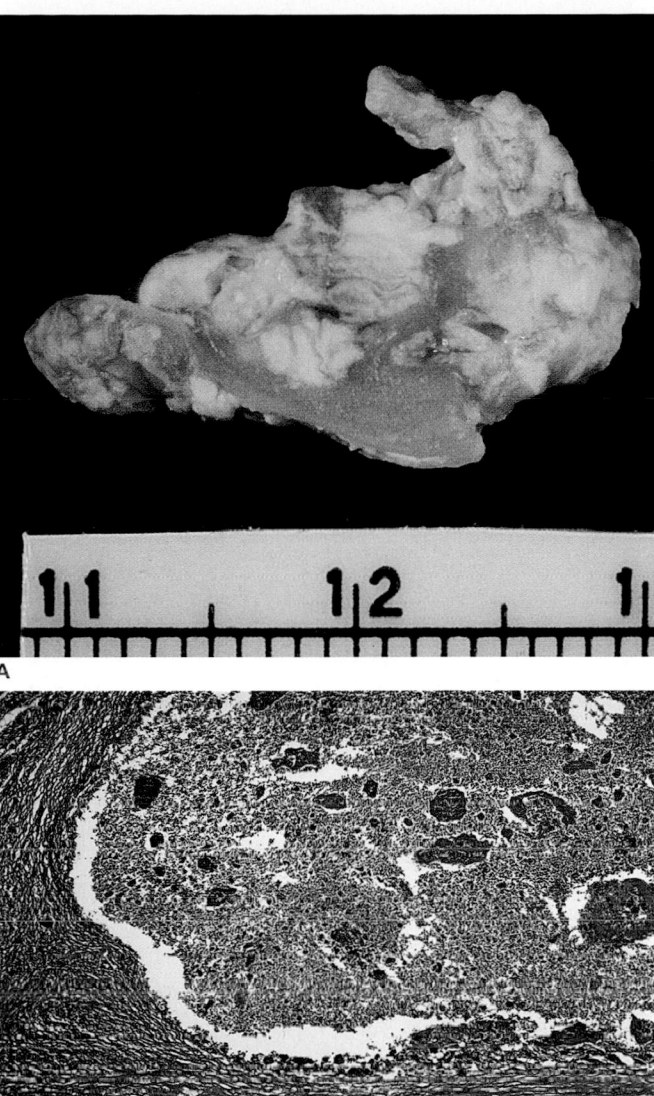

Fig. 25.222 Tumoral calcinosis. **A**, Gross appearance. The lesion is characteristically multinodular, and the material has a chalky quality. **B**, Microscopic appearance. Note the absence of cartilaginous features.

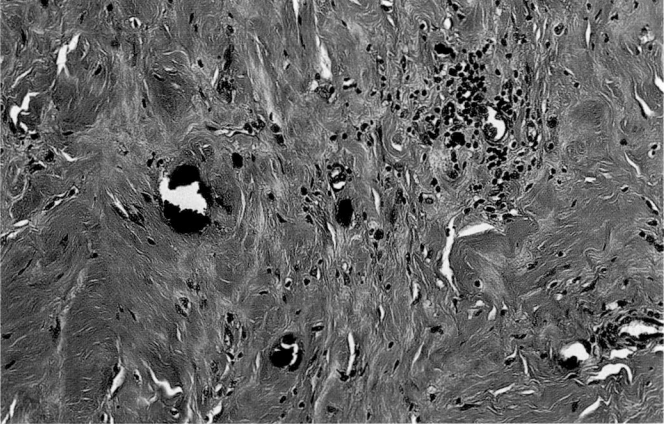

Fig. 25.223 Inflammatory calcifying pseudotumor. Round calcific concretions are seen against a fibrohyaline background containing scattered lymphocytes.

adolescents and young adults, and the behavior is benign.[1570]

There is immunoreactivity for CD34 in most cases, but not for ALK-1. The latter finding does not lend support to the suggestion that calcifying fibrous pseudotumor may represent a late stage of inflammatory myofibroblastic tumor.[1578]

Amyloid tumor (amyloidoma) can present as a localized mass in the soft tissues. The mediastinum and retroperitoneum are the most common locations. The amyloid may be of AL (more frequently) or AA type.[1574]

Aneurysmal (bone) cyst morphologically similar to that more commonly seen in the skeletal system can develop in the soft tissues.[1579,1581]

Rosai–Dorfman disease (sinus histiocytosis with massive lymphadenopathy) may present as a mass in the soft tissue, with or without associated lymph node involvement (Fig. 25.224). It is most commonly located in the extremities, but it can also occur in the trunk and head and neck region. As is also the case in other extranodal sites, emperipolesis is usually inconspicuous, and secondary collagen deposition is prominent.[1577]

Castleman's disease has been described in the form of a subcutaneous mass in a distal extremity.[1583]

Polyvinylpyrrolidone (PVP) granuloma is a tumor-like condition of skin or soft tissue that follows injections of drugs containing PVP.[1568,1573] The prominent myxoid features and focal cellularity may simulate a neoplastic process, particularly myxoid liposarcoma and signet ring carcinoma.[1575] PVP is localized in the cytoplasm of foamy histiocytes and multinucleated giant cells, many of which appear vacuolated. These cells are positive for mucicarmine, colloidal iron, GMS, Congo red, Sudan black B, and argentaffin stains[1575]; the presence of PVP can be detected by infrared spectrophotometry.[1573]

Bronchogenic cysts of skin and soft tissue are usually discovered at or seen after birth in male infants. The most common location is the suprasternal notch and manubrium sterni[1571]; despite their name, they are probably of branchial arch derivation (i.e., *branchiogenic*)[1569,1582] (see Chapter 4).

Fig. 25.224 Gross appearance of Rosai–Dorfman disease (sinus histiocytosis with massive lymphadenopathy) involving skin and soft tissues in the buttock region.

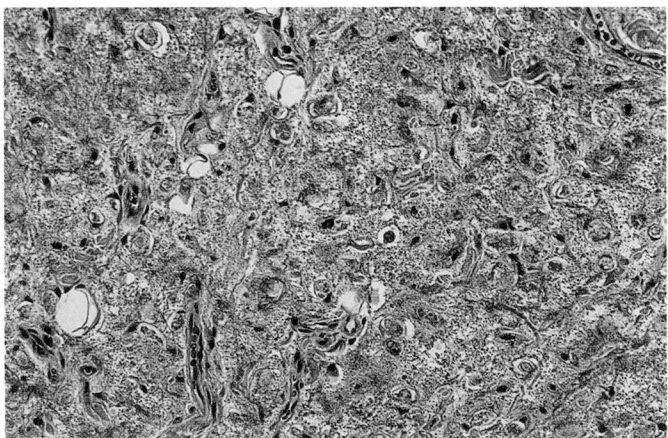

Fig. 25.225 So-called "mucicarminophilic histiocytosis." The highly myxoid quality of this lesion may induce confusion with a myxoid neoplasm.

References

Normal anatomy

1 Appleton MA, Attanoos RL, Jasani B. Thrombomodulin as a marker of vascular and lymphatic tumours. Histopathology 1997, **29**: 153–157.

1a Bondjers C, Kalén M, Hellström M, Scheidl SJ, Abramsson A, Renner O, Lindahl P, Cho H, Kehrl J, Betsholtz C. Transcription profiling of platelet-derived growth factor-B-deficient mouse embryos identifies RGS5 as a novel marker for pericytes and vascular smooth muscle cells. Am J Pathol 2003, **162**: 721–729.

2 Brooks JSJ, Perosio PM. Adipose tissue. In Sternberg S (ed.): Histology for pathologists, ed. 2. Philadelphia, 1997, Lippincott-Raven, pp. 167–196.

3 Bunge MB, Wood PM, Tynan LB, Bates ML, Sanes JR. Perineurium originates from fibroblasts. Demonstration in vitro with a retroviral marker. Science 1989, **243**: 229–231.

4 Burgdorf W, Mukai K, Rosai J. Immunohistochemical identification of factor VIII-related antigen in endothelial cells of cutaneous lesions of alleged vascular nature. Am J Clin Pathol 1981, **75**: 167–171.

5 Carstens PH. The Weibel-Palade body in the diagnosis of endothelial tumors. Ultrastruct Pathol 1981, **2**: 315–325.

6 Cohen PR, Rapini RP, Farhood AI. Expression of the human hematopoietic progenitor cell antigen CD34 in vascular and spindle cell tumors. J Cutan Pathol 1993, **20**: 15–20.

7 DeYoung BR, Swanson PE, Argenyi ZB, Ritter JH, Fitsgibbon JF, Stahl DJ, Hoover W, Wick MR. CD31 immunoreactivity in mesenchymal neoplasms of the skin and subcutis. Report of 145 cases and review of putative immunohistologic markers of endothelial differentiation. J Cutan Pathol 1995, **22**: 215–222.

8 Etchevers HC, Vincent C, Le Douarin NM, Couly GF. The cephalic neural crest provides pericytes and smooth muscle cells to all blood vessels of the face and forebrain. Development 2001, **128**: 1059–1068.

9 Fajardo LF. The complexity of endothelial cells. A review. Am J Clin Pathol 1989, **92**: 241–250.

10 Folpe AL, Chand Eric M, Goldblum JR, Wiess SW. Expression of Fli-1, a nuclear transcription factor, distinguishes vascular neoplasms from potential mimics. Am J Surg Pathol 2001, **25**: 1061–1066.

11 Gottlieb AI, Langille BL, Wong MK, Kim DW. Structure and function of the endothelial cytoskeleton. Lab Invest 1991, **65**: 123–137.

12 Heffner RR Jr. Skeletal muscle. In Sternberg S (ed.): Histology for pathologists, ed. 2. Philadelphia, 1997, Lippincott-Raven, pp. 197–222.

13 Higgins JPT, Montgomary K, Wang L, Domanay E, Warnke RA, Brooks JD, van de Rijn M. Expression of FKBP12 in benign and malignant vascular endothelium: an immunohistochemical study on conventional sections and tissue microarrays. Am J Surg Pathol 2002, **27**: 58–64.

13a Hirose T, Tani T, Shimada T, Ishizawa K, Shimada S, Sano T. Immunohistochemical demonstration of EMA/Glut1-positive perineurial cells and CD34-positive firoblastic cells in peripheral nerve sheath tumors. Mod Pathol 2003, **16**: 293–298.

14 Hultberg BM, Svanholm H. Immunohistochemical differentiation between lymphangiographically verified lymphatic vessels and blood vessels. Virchows Arch [A] 1989, **414**: 209–215.

15 Miettinen M, Holthofer H, Lehto V-P, Miettinen A, Virtanen I. *Ulex europaeus* I lectin as a marker for tumors derived from endothelial cells. Am J Clin Pathol 1983, **79**: 32–36.

16 Miettinen M, Lindenmayer AE, Chaubal A. Endothelial cell markers CD31, CD34, and BNH9 antibody to H- and Y-antigens. Evaluation of their specificity and sensitivity in the diagnosis of vascular tumors and comparison with von Willebrand factor. Mod Pathol 1994, **7**: 82–90.

17 Mukai K, Rosai J, Burgdorf W. Localization of factor VIII-related antigen in vascular endothelial cells using an immunoperoxidase method. Am J Surg Pathol 1980, **4**: 273–276.

18 Ortiz-Hidalgo C, Weller RO. Peripheral nervous system. In Sternberg S (ed.): Histology for pathologists, ed. 2. Philadelphia, 1997, Lippincott-Raven, pp. 285–314.

19 Page C, Rose M, Yacoub M, Pigott R. Antigenic heterogeneity of vascular endothelium. Am J Pathol 1992, **141**: 673–683.

20 Ramani P, Bradley NJ, Fletcher CD. QBEND/10, a new monoclonal antibody to endothelium. Assessment of its diagnostic utility in paraffin sections. Histopathology 1990, **17**: 237–242.

21 Rubanyi GM, Botelho LH. Endothelins. FASEB J 1991, **5**: 2713–2720.

22 Schmitt-Graff A, Desmouliere A, Gabbiani G. Heterogeneity of myofibroblast phenotypic features. An example of fibroblastic cell plasticity. Virchows Arch 1994, **425**: 3–24.

23 Schurch W, Seemayer TA, Gabbiani G. Myofibroblast. In Sternberg S (ed.): Histology for pathologists, ed. 2. Philadelphia, 1997, Lippincott-Raven, pp. 129–166.

24 Schurch W, Seemayer TA, Gabbiani G. The myofibroblast: a quarter century after its discovery. Am J Surg Pathol 1998, **22**: 141–147.

25 Stephenson TJ, Mills PM. Monoclonal antibodies to blood group isoantigens. An alternative marker to factor VIII-related antigen for benign and malignant vascular endothelial cells. J Pathol 1985, **147**: 139–148.

26 Suzuki Y, Hashimoto K, Crissman J, Kanzaki T, Nishiyama S. The value of blood group-specific lectin and endothelial associated antibodies in the diagnosis of vascular proliferations. J Cutan Pathol 1986, **13**: 408–419.

27 Tokunaga O, Fan J, Watanabe T, Kobayashi M, Kumazaki T, Mitsui Y. Endothelin. Immunohistologic localization in aorta and biosynthesis by cultured human aortic endothelial cells. Lab Invest 1992, **67**: 210–217.

28 Traweek ST, Kandalaft PL, Mehta P, Battifora H. The human hematopoietic progenitor cell antigen (CD34) in vascular neoplasia. Am J Clin Pathol 1991, **96**: 25–31.

29 Turner RR, Beckstead JH, Warnke RA, Wood GS. Endothelial cell phenotypic diversity. In situ demonstration of immunologic and enzymatic heterogeneity that correlates with specific morphologic subtypes. Am J Clin Pathol 1987, **87**: 569–575.

30 Voigt J, Gorguet B, Szekeres G, Saati T, Delsol G. Comparison of the reactivities of monoclonal antibodies QBEND10 (CD34) and BNH9 in vascular tumors. Appl Immunohistochem 1993, **1**: 51–57.

31 Warhol MJ, Sweet JM. The ultrastructural localization of von Willebrand factor in endothelial cells. Am J Pathol 1984, **117**: 310–315.

Infections and hematomas

32 Herzberg AJ, Boyd PR, Gutierrez Y. Subcutaneous dirofilariasis in Collier County, Florida, USA. Am J Surg Pathol 1995, **19**: 934–939.

33 Mentzel T, Goodlad JR, Smith MA, Fletcher CD. Ancient hematoma: an unifying concept for a post-traumatic lesion mimicking an aggressive soft tissue neoplasm. Mod Pathol 1997, **10**: 334–340.

34 Woo ML, Patrick WGD, Simon MTP, French GL. Necrotising fasciitis caused by *Vibrio vulnificus*. J Clin Pathol 1984, **37**: 1301–1304.

Tumors
Classification

35 Mills SE. Sometimes we don't look like our parents (editorial). Mod Pathol 1995, **8**: 347.

36 Ross J, Hendrickson MR, Kempson RL. The problem of the poorly differentiated sarcoma. Semin Oncol 1982, **9**: 467–483.

Clinical features

37 Kauffman SL, Stout AP. Congenital mesenchymal tumors. Cancer 1965, **18**: 460–476.

38 Rydholm A, Berg NO, Gullberg B, Thorngren K-G, Persson BM. Epidemiology of soft-tissue sarcoma in the locomotor system. A retrospective population-based study of the inter-relationships between clinical and morphologic variables. Acta Pathol Microbiol Immunol Scand (A) 1984, **92**: 363–374.

39 Soule EH, Mahour GH, Mills SD, Lynn HB. Soft-tissue sarcomas of infants and children. A clinicopathologic study of 135 cases. Mayo Clin Proc 1968, **43**: 313–326.

Diagnosis and special techniques

40 Altmannsberger M, Dirk T, Osborn M, Weber K. Immunohistochemistry of cytoskeletal filaments in the diagnosis of soft tissue tumors. Semin Diagn Pathol 1986, **3**: 306–316.

41 Bendix-Hansen K, Myhre-Jensen O. Enzyme histochemical investigations on bone and soft tissue tumours. Acta Pathol Microbiol Immunol Scand (A) 1985, **93**: 73–80.

41a Chang C-C, Shidham VB. Review. Molecular genetics of pediatric soft tissue tumors. Clinical application. J Mol Diagn 2003, **5**: 143–154.

41b Coindre JM. Review. Immunohistochemistry in the diagnosis of soft tissue tumours. Histopathology 2003, **43**: 1–16.

42 Dickersin GR. Embryonic ultrastructure as a guide in the diagnosis of tumors. Ultrastruct Pathol 1987, **11**: 609–652.

43 Enjoji M, Hashimoto H. Diagnosis of soft tissue sarcomas. Pathol Res Pract 1984, **178**: 215–226.

44 Fisher C. The value of electronmicroscopy and immunohistochemistry in the diagnosis of soft tissue sarcomas. A study of 200 cases. Histopathology 1990, **16**: 441–454.

45 Fletcher JA, Kozakewich HP, Hoffer FA, Lage JM, Weidner N, Tepper R, Pinkus GS, Morton CC, Corson JM. Diagnostic relevance of clonal cytogenetic aberrations in malignant soft-tissue tumors. N Engl J Med 1991, **324**: 436–442.

46 Goodlad JR, Fletcher CDM. Recent developments in soft tissue tumours. Histopathology 1995, **27**: 103–120.

47 Kindblom L-G, Walaas L, Widehn S. Ultrastructural studies in the preoperative cytologic diagnosis of soft tissue tumors. Semin Diagn Pathol 1986, **3**: 317–344.

48 Ladanyi M. The emerging molecular genetics of sarcoma translocations. Diagn Mol Pathol 1995, **4**: 162–173.

49 Layfield LJ, Anders KH, Glasgow BJ, Mirra JM. Fine-needle aspiration of primary soft-tissue lesions. Arch Pathol Lab Med 1986, **110**: 420–424.

50 Lieberman Z, Ackerman LV. Principles in management of soft tissue sarcomas. Surgery 1954, **35**: 350–365.

51 Miettinen M. Immunohistochemistry of soft-tissue tumors. Possibilities and limitations in surgical pathology. Pathol Annu 1990, **25**(Pt 1): 1–36.

52 Molenaar WM, De Jong B, Buist J, Idenburg VJ, Seruca R, Vos AM, Hoekstra HJ. Chromosomal analysis and the classification of soft tissue sarcomas. Lab Invest 1989, **60**: 266–274.

53 Nakanishi I, Katsuda S, Ooi A, Kajikawa K, Matsubara F. Diagnostic aspect of spindle cell sarcomas by electron microscopy. Acta Pathol Jpn 1983, **33**: 425–437.

54 Ordonez NG. Application of immunocytochemistry in the diagnosis of soft tissue sarcomas: a review and update. Adv Anat Pathol 1999, **5**: 67–85.

55 Parham DM. Immunohistochemistry of childhood sarcomas. Old and new markers. Mod Pathol 1993, **6**: 133–138.

55a Sandberg AA. Cytogenetics and molecular genetics of bone and soft-tissue tumors. Am J Med Genet 2002, **115**: 189–193.

55b Segal NH, Pavlidis P, Antonescu CR, Maki RG, Noble WS, DeSantis D, Woodruff JM, Lewis JJ, Brennan MF, Houghton AN, Cordon-Cardo C. Classification and subtype prediction of adult soft tissue sarcoma by functional genomics. Am J Pathol 2003, **163**: 691–700.

56 Sreekantaiah C, Ladanyi M, Rodriguez E, Chaganti RS. Chromosomal aberrations in soft tissue tumors. Relevance to diagnosis, classification, and molecular mechanisms. Am J Pathol 1994, **144**: 1121–1134.

57 van Haelst UJGM. General considerations on electron microscopy of tumors of soft tissues. Progr Surg Pathol 1980, **2**: 225–257.

Grading and staging

58 Angervall L, Kindblom L-G, Rydholm A, Stener B. The diagnosis and prognosis of soft tissue tumors. Semin Diagn Pathol 1986, **3**: 240–258.

59 Beahrs OH, Henson DE, Hutter RVP, Kennedy BJ. Manual for staging of cancer, ed. 4. Philadelphia, 1992, JB Lippincott Co.

60 Brown FM, Fletcher CD. Problems in grading soft tissue sarcomas. Am J Clin Pathol 2000, **114**: S82–S89.

61 Coindre JM, Nguyen BB, Bonichon F, de Mascarel I, Trojani M. Histopathologic grading in spindle cell soft tissue sarcomas. Cancer 1988, **61**: 2305–2309.

62 Coindre JM, Terrier P, Guillou L, Le Doussal V, Collin F, Ranchare D, Sastre X, Vilain MO, Bonichon F, N'Guyen Bui B. Predictive value of grade for metastasis development in the main histologic types of adult soft tissue sarcomas: a study of 1240 patients from the French Federation of Cancer Centers Sarcoma Group. Cancer 2001, **91**: 1914–1926.

63 Coindre JM, Trojani M, Contesso G, David M, Rouesse J, Bui NB, Bodaert A, De Mascarel I, De Mascarel A, Goussot J-F. Reproducibility of a histopathologic grading system for adult soft tissue sarcoma. Cancer 1986, **58**: 306–309.

64 Cooper JE, Allen PW. Low-grade sarcomas. Pathol Annu 1990, **25**(Pt 2): 1–18.

65 Costa J, Wesley RA, Glatstein E, Rosenberg SA. The grading of soft tissue sarcomas. Results of a clinicohistopathologic correlation in a series of 163 cases. Cancer 1984, **53**: 530–541.

66 Donohue JH, Collin C, Friedrich C, Godbold J, Hajdu SI, Brennan MF. Lowgrade soft tissue sarcomas of the extremities. Analysis of risk factors for metastasis. Cancer 1988, **62**: 184–193.

67 Enneking WF. Musculoskeletal tumor staging. 1988 update. Cancer Treat Res 1989, **44**: 39–49.

68 Guillou L, Coindre JM, Bonichon F, N'Guyen BB, Terrier P, Collin F, Vilain MO, Mandard AM, Le Doussai V, Leroux A, Jacquemier J, Duplay H, Sastre-Garau X, Costa J. Comparative study of the National Cancer Institute and French federation of cancer centres sarcoma group grading systems in a population of 410 adult patients with soft tissue sarcoma. J Clin Oncol 1997, **15**: 350–362.

69 Hashimoto H, Daimaru Y, Takeshita S, Tsuneyoshi M, Enjoji M. Prognostic significance of histologic parameters of soft tissue sarcomas. Cancer 1992, **70**: 2816–2822.

70 Heise HW, Myers MH, Russell WO, Suit HD, Enzinger FM, Edmonson JH, Cohen J, Martin RG, Miller WT, Hajdu SI. Recurrence-free survival time for surgically treated soft tissue sarcoma patients. Multivariate analysis of five prognostic factors. Cancer 1986, **57**: 172–177.

71 Myhre-Jensen O, Kaae S, Madsen EH, Sneppen O. Histopathological grading in soft-tissue tumours. Relation to survival in 261 surgically treated patients. Acta Pathol Microbiol Immunol Scand (A) 1983, **91**: 145–150.

72 Parham DM, Webber BL, Jenkins JJ III, Cantor AB, Maurer HM. Nonrhabdomyosarcomatous soft tissue sarcomas of childhood. Formulation of a simplified system for grading. Mod Pathol 1995, **8**: 705–710.

73 Russell WO, Cohen J, Enzinger F, Hajdu SI, Heise H, Martin RG, Meissner W, Miller WT, Schmidtz RL, Suit HD. A clinical and pathological staging system for soft tissue sarcomas. Cancer 1977, **40**: 1562–1570.

74 Trojani M, Contesso G, Coindre JM, Rouesse J, Bui NB, De Mascarel A, Goussot JF, David M, Bonichon F, Lagarde C. Soft-tissue sarcomas of adults. Study of pathological prognostic variables and definition of a histopathological grading system. Int J Cancer 1984, **33**: 37–42.

Prognosis

75 Agarwal V, Greenebaum E, Wersto R, Koss LG. DNA ploidy of spindle cell soft-tissue tumors and its relationship to histology and clinical outcome. Arch Pathol Lab Med 1991, **115**: 558–562.

76 Bell RS, O'Sullivan B, Liu FF, Powell J, Langer F, Fornasier VL, Cummings B, Miceli PN, Hawkins N, Quirt I, et al. The surgical margin in soft-tissue sarcoma. J Bone Joint Surg (Am) 1989, **71**: 370–375.

77 Cance WG, Brennan MF, Dudas ME, Huang CM, Cordon-Cardo C. Altered expression of the retinoblastoma gene product in human sarcomas. N Engl J Med 1990, **323**: 1457–1462.

78 Dreinhofer KE, Baldetorp B, Akerman M, Ferno M, Rydholm A, Gustafson P. DNA ploidy in soft tissue sarcoma: comparison of flow and image cytometry with clinical follow-up in 93 patients. Cytometry 2002, **50**: 19–24.

79 Drobnjak M, Latres E, Pollack D, Karpeh M, Dudas M, Woodruff JM, Brennan MF, Cordon-Cardo C. Prognostic implications of p53 nuclear overexpression and high proliferation index of Ki-67 in adult soft-tissue sarcomas. J Natl Cancer Inst 1994, **86**: 549–554.

80 Enneking WF, Maale GE. The effect of inadvertent tumor contamination of wounds during the surgical resection of musculoskeletal neoplasms. Cancer 1988, **62**: 1251–1256.

81 Gerrand CH, Bell RS, Wunder JS, Kandel RA, O'Sullivan B, Catton CN, Griffin AM, Davis AM. The influence of anatomic location on outcome in patients with soft tissue sarcoma of the extremity. Cancer 2003, **97**: 385–492.

82 Gustafson P, Rooser B, Rydholm A. Is local recurrence of minor importance for metastases in soft tissue sarcoma? Cancer 1991, **67**: 2083–2086.

83 Herbert SH, Corn BW, Solin LJ, Lanciano RM, Schultz DJ, McKenna WG, Coia LR. Limb-preserving treatment for soft tissue sarcomas of the extremities. The significance of surgical margins. Cancer 1993, **72**: 1230–1238.

84 Heslin MJ, Woodruff J, Brennan MF. Prognostic significance of a positive microscopic margin in high-risk extremity soft tissue sarcoma: implications for management. J Clin Oncol 1996, **14**: 473–478.

85 Kawai A, Noguchi M, Beppu Y, Yokoyama R, Mukai K, Hirohashi S, Inoue H, Fukuma H. Nuclear immunoreaction of p53 protein in soft tissue sarcomas. A possible prognostic factor. Cancer 1994, **73**: 2499–2505.

86 Kroese MC, Rutgers DH, Wils IS, van Unnik JA, Roholl PJ. The relevance of the DNA index and proliferation rate in the grading of benign and malignant soft tissue tumors. Cancer 1990, **65**: 1782–1788.

87 Le Doussal V, Coindre JM, Leroux A, Hacene K, Terrier P, Bui NB, Bonichon F, Collin F, Mandard AM, Contesso G. Prognostic factors for patients with localized primary malignant fibrous histioctyoma: a multicenter study of 216 patients and multivariate analysis. Cancer 1996, **77**: 1823–1830.

88 Rooser B, Attewell R, Berg NO, Rydholm A. Prognostication in soft tissue sarcoma. A model with four risk factors. Cancer 1988, **61**: 817–823.

89 Stojadinovic A, Leung DH, Hoos A, Jaques DP, Lewis JJ, Brennan M. Analysis of the prognostic significance of microscopic margin in 2084 localized primary adult soft tissue sarcomas. Ann Surg 2002, **235**: 424–434.

90 Stotter AT, A'Hern RP, Fisher C, Mott AF, Fallowfield ME, Westbury G. The influence of local recurrence of extremity soft tissue sarcoma on metastasis and survival. Cancer 1990, **65**: 1119–1129.

91 Swanson SA, Brooks JJ. Proliferation markers Ki-67 and p105 in soft-tissue lesions. Correlation with DNA flow cytometric characteristics. Am J Pathol 1990, **137**: 1491–1500.

92 Tanabe KK, Pollock RE, Ellis LM, Murphy A, Sherman N, Romsdahl MM. Influence of surgical margins on outcome in patients with preoperatively irradiated extremity soft tissue sarcomas. Cancer 1994, **73**: 1652–1659.

93 Ueda T, Aozasa K, Tsujimoto M, Ohsawa M, Uchida A, Aoki Y, Ono K, Matsumoto K. Prognostic significance of Ki-67 reactivity in soft tissue sarcomas. Cancer 1989, **63**: 1607–1611.

93a Zagars GK, Ballo MT, Pisters PWT, Pollock RE, Patel SR, Benjamin RS, Evans HL. Prognostic factors for patients with localized soft-tissue sarcoma treated with conservation surgery and radiation therapy. Cancer 2003, **97**: 2530–2543.

Therapy

94 Casper ES, Gaynor JJ, Harrison LB, Panicek DM, Hajdu SI, Brennan MF. Preoperative and postoperative adjuvant combination chemotherapy for adults with high grade soft tissue sarcoma. Cancer 1994, **73**: 1644–1651.

95 Editorial. Changes in treating soft-tissue sarcomas. Br Med J 1979, **2**: 562–563.

96 Eilber FR, Huth JF, Mirra J, Rosen G. Progress in the recognition and treatment of soft tissue sarcomas. Cancer 1990, **65**: 660–666.

97 Glenn J, Kinsella T, Glatstein E, Tepper J, Baker A, Sugarbaker P, Sindelar W, Roth J, Brennan M, Costa J, Seipp C, Wesley R, Young RC, Rosenberg SA. A randomized, prospective trial of adjuvant chemotherapy in adults with soft tissue sarcomas of the head and neck, breast and trunk. Cancer 1985, **55**: 1206–1214.

98 Karakousis CP, Emrich LJ, Rao U, Krishnamsetty RM. Feasibility of limb salvage and survival in soft tissue sarcomas. Cancer 1986, **57**: 484–491.

99 Mazanet R, Antman KH. Adjuvant therapy for sarcomas. Semin Oncol 1991, **18**: 603–612.

100 Nesbit ME Jr. Advances and management of solid tumors in children. Cancer 1990, **65**: 696–702.

101 Potter DA, Kinsella T, Glatstein E, Wesley R, White DE, Seipp CA, Chang AE, Lack EE, Costa J, Rosenberg SA. High-grade soft tissue sarcomas of the extremities. Cancer 1986, **58**: 190–205.

102 Singer S, Demetri GD, Baldini EH, Fletcher CD. Management of soft-tissue sarcomas: an overview and update. Lancet Oncol 2002, **1**: 75–85.

103 Suit HD, Russell WO, Martin RG. Sarcoma of soft tissue. Clinical and histopathologic parameters and response to treatment. Cancer 1975, **35**: 1478–1483.

104 Tepper JE. Role of radiation therapy in the management of patients with bone and soft tissue sarcomas. Semin Oncol 1989, **16**: 281–288.

105 Ueda T, Aozasa K, Tsujimoto M, Hamada H, Hayashi H, Ono K, Matsumoto K. Multivariate analysis for clinical prognostic factors in 163 patients with soft tissue sarcoma. Cancer 1988, **62**: 1444–1450.

106 Walker MJ, Wood DK, Briele HA, Greager JA, Patel M, Das Gupta TK. Soft tissue sarcomas of the distal extremities. Surgery 1986, **99**: 392–398.

107 Willett CG, Schiller AL, Suit HD, Mankin HJ, Rosenberg A. The histologic response of soft tissue sarcoma to radiation therapy. Cancer 1987, **60**: 1500–1504.

108 Yang JC, Rosenberg SA. Surgery for adult patients with soft tissue sarcomas. Semin Oncol 1989, **16**: 289–296.

Pathogenesis

109 Greenwald P, Kovasznay B, Collins DN, et al. Sarcoma of soft tissues after Vietnam service. J Natl Cancer Inst 1984, **73**: 1107–1109.

110 Hardell L, Eriksson M. The association between soft tissue sarcomas and exposure to phenoxyacetic acids. A new case-referent study. Cancer 1988, **62**: 652–656.

111 Jennings TA, Peterson L, Axiotis CA, Friedlaender GE, Cooke RA, Rosai J. Angiosarcoma associated with foreign body material. A report of three cases. Cancer 1988, **62**: 2436–2444.

112 Kang H, Enzinger FM, Breslin P, et al. Soft tissue sarcoma and military service in Vietnam. A case control study. J Natl Cancer Inst 1987, **79**: 693–699.

113 Keel SB, Jaffe KA, Nielsen G, Rosenberg AE. Orthopaedic implant-related sarcoma: a study of twelve cases. Mod Pathol 2001, **14**: 969–977.

114 Laskin WB, Silverman TA, Enzinger FM. Postradiation soft tissue sarcomas. An analysis of 53 cases. Cancer 1988, **62**: 2330–2340.

115 Lynge E, Storm HH, Jensen OM. The evaluation of trends in soft tissue sarcoma according to diagnostic criteria and consumption of phenoxyherbicides. Cancer 1987, **60**: 1896–1901.

116 Mark RJ, Bailet JW, Poen J, Tran LM, Calcaterra TC, Abemayor E, Fu YS, Parker RG. Postirradiation sarcoma of the head and neck. Cancer 1993, **72**: 887–893.

117 Monkman GR, Orwoll G, Ivins JC. Trauma and oncogenesis. Mayo Clin Proc 1974, **49**: 157–163.

118 Wingren G, Fredrikson M, Brage HN, Nordenskjold B, Axelson O. Soft tissue sarcoma and occupational exposures. Cancer 1990, **66**: 806–811.

Tumors and tumorlike conditions of fibroblasts and myofibroblasts

Calcifying aponeurotic fibroma

119 Allen PM, Enzinger FM. Juvenile aponeurotic fibroma. Cancer 1970, **26**: 857–867.

120 Chung EB. Pitfalls in diagnosing benign soft tissue tumors in infancy and childhood. Pathol Annu 1985, **20**(Pt 2): 323–386.

121 Fetsch JF, Miettinen M. Calcifying aponeurotic fibroma: a clinicopathologic study of 22 cases arising in uncommon sites. Hum Pathol 1998, **29**: 1504–1510.

122 Goldman RL. The cartilage analogue of fibromatosis (aponeurotic fibroma). Further observations based on 7 new cases. Cancer 1970, **26**: 1325–1331.

123 Iwasaki H, Kikuchi M, Eimoto T, Enjoji M, Yoh S, Sakurai H. Juvenile aponeurotic fibroma. An ultrastructural study. Ultrastruct Pathol 1983, **4**: 75–83.

124 Keasbey LE. Juvenile aponeurotic fibroma (calcifying fibroma). Cancer 1953, **6**: 338–346.

125 Lichtenstein L, Goldman RL. The cartilage analogue of fibromatosis. Cancer 1964, **17**: 810–816.

Fibroma of tendon sheath

126 Chung EB, Enzinger FM. Fibroma of tendon sheath. Cancer 1979, **44**: 1945–1954.

127 Dal Cin P, Sciot R, De Smet L, Van den Berghe H. Translocation 2;11 in a fibroma of tendon sheath. Histopathology 1998, **32**: 433–435.

128 Hashimoto H, Tsuneyoshi M, Daimaru Y, Ushijima M, Enjoji M. Fibroma of tendon sheath. A tumor of myofibroblasts.

A clinicopathologic study of 18 cases. Acta Pathol Jpn 1985, **35**: 1099–1107.

129 Humphreys S, McKee PH, Fletcher CDM. Fibroma of tendon sheath. A clinicopathologic study. J Cutan Pathol 1986, **13**: 331–338.

130 Lamovec J, Bracko M, Voncina D. Pleomorphic fibroma of tendon sheath. Am J Surg Pathol 1991, **15**: 1202–1205.

131 Maluf HM, De Young BR, Swanson PE, Wick MR. Fibroma and giant cell tumor of tendon sheath. A comparative histological and immunohistological study. Mod Pathol 1995, **8**: 155–159.

132 Pulitzer DR, Martin PC, Reed RJ. Fibroma of tendon sheath. A clinicopathologic study of 32 cases. Am J Surg Pathol 1989, **13**: 472–479.

133 Satti MB. Tendon sheath tumours. A pathological study of the relationship between giant cell tumour and fibroma of tendon sheath. Histopathology 1992, **20**: 213–220.

134 Smith PS, Pieterse AS, McClure J. Fibroma of tendon sheath. J Clin Pathol 1982, **35**: 842–848.

Other types of fibroma

134a Evans HL. Desmoplastic fibroblastoma. A report of seven cases. Am J Surg Pathol 1995, **19**: 1077–1081.

135 Fetsch JF, Laskin WB, Miettinen M. Superficial acral fibromyxoma: a clinicopathologic and immunohistochemical analysis of 37 cases of a distinctive soft tissue tumor with a predilection for the finger and toes. Hum Pathol 2001, **32**: 704–714.

136 Laskin WB, Fetsch JF, Miettinen M. Nuchal fibrocartilaginous pseudotumor: a clinicopathologic study of five cases and review of the literature. Mod Pathol 1999, **12**: 663–668.

137 Michal M, Fetsch JF, Hes O, Miettinen M. Nuchal-type fibroma. A clinicopathologic study of 52 cases. Cancer 1999, **85**: 156–163.

138 Miettinen M, Fetsch JF. Collagenous fibroma (desmoplastic fibroblastoma): a clinicopathologic analysis of 63 cases of a distinctive soft tissue lesion with stellate-shaped fibroblasts. Hum Pathol 1998, **29**: 676–682.

139 Nielsen GP, O'Connell JX, Dickersin GR, Rosenberg AE. Collagenous fibroma (desmoplastic fibroblastoma): a report of seven cases. Mod Pathol 1997, **9**: 781–785.

Giant cell fibroblastoma

140 Abdul-Karim FW, Evans HL, Silva EG. Giant cell fibroblastoma. A report of three cases. Am J Clin Pathol 1985, **83**: 165–170.

141 Alguacil-Garcia A. Giant cell fibroblastoma recurring as dermatofibrosarcoma protuberans. Am J Surg Pathol 1991, **15**: 798–801.

142 Chou P, Gonzalez-Crussi F, Mangkornkanok M. Giant cell fibroblastoma. Cancer 1989, **63**: 756–762.

143 Chung EB. Pitfalls in diagnosing benign soft tissue tumors in infancy and childhood. Pathol Annu 1985, **20**(Pt 2): 323–386.

144 Dymock RB, Allen PW, Stirling JW, Gilbert EF, Thornbery JM. Giant cell fibroblastoma. A distinctive, recurrent tumor of childhood. Am J Surg Pathol 1987, **11**: 263–271.

145 Fletcher CD. Giant cell fibroblastoma of soft tissue: A clinicopathological and immunohistochemical study. Histopathology 1988, **13**: 499–508.

146 Goldblum JR. Giant cell fibroblastoma: a report of three cases with histologic and immunohistochemical evidence of a relationship to dermatofibrosarcoma protuberans. Arch Pathol Lab Med 2002, **120**: 1052–1055.

147 Michal M, Zamecnik M. Giant cell fibroblastoma with a dermatofibrosarcoma protuberans component. Am J Dermatopathol 1992, **14**: 549–552.

148 Pinto A, Hwang W, Wong A, Seagram C. Giant cell fibroblastoma in childhood. Immunohistochemical and ultrastructural study. Mod Pathol 1992, **5**: 639–642.

149 Rubin BP, Fletcher JA, Fletcher CD. The histologic, genetic, and biological relationships between dermatofibrosarcoma protuberans and giant cell fibroblastoma: an unexpected story. Adv Anat Pathol 1997, **4**: 336–341.

150 Shmookler BM, Enzinger FM, Weiss SW. Giant cell fibroblastoma. A juvenile form of dermatofibrosarcoma protuberans. Cancer 1989, **64**: 2154–2161.

151 Terrier-Lacombe MJ, Guillou L, Maire G, Terrier P, Vince DR, de Saint Aubain Somerhausen N, Collin F, Pedeutour F, Coindre JM. Dermatofibrosarcoma protuberans, giant cell fibroblastoma, and hybrid lesions in children: clinicopathologic comparative analysis of 28 cases with molecular data – a study from the French Federation of Cancer Centres Sarcoma Group. Am J Surg Pathol 2002, **27**: 27–39.

152 Zamecnik M, Michal M. Giant-cell fibroblastoma with pigmented dermatofibrosarcoma protuberans component. Am J Surg Pathol 1994, **18**: 736–740.

Nodular fasciitis and related lesions

153 Allen PW. Nodular fasciitis. Pathology 1972, **4**: 9–26.

154 Bernstein KE, Lattes R. Nodular (pseudosarcomatous) fasciitis, a nonrecurrent lesion. Cancer 1982, **49**: 1668–1678.

155 Chung EB, Enzinger FM. Proliferative fasciitis. Cancer 1975, **36**: 1450–1458.

156 Craver JL, McDivitt RW. Proliferative fasciitis. Ultrastructural study of two cases. Arch Pathol Lab Med 1981, **105**: 542–545.

157 Dahl I, Angervall L. Pseudosarcomatous proliferative lesions of soft tissue with or without bone formation. Acta Pathol Microbiol Scand (A) 1977, **85**: 577–589.

158 Daroca PJ Jr, Pulitzer DR, LoCicero J III. Ossifying fasciitis. Arch Pathol Lab Med 1982, **106**: 682–685.

159 Donner LR, Silva T, Dobin SM. Clonal rearrangement of 15p11.2, 16p11.2, and 16p13.3 in a case of nodular fasciitis: additional evidence favoring nodular fasciitis as a benign neoplasm and not a reactive tumefaction. Cancer Genet Cytogenet 2002, **139**: 138–140.

160 el-Jabbour JN, Bennett MH, Burke MM, Lessells A, O'Halloran A. Proliferative myositis. An immunohistochemical and ultrastructural study. Am J Surg Pathol 1991, **15**: 654–659.

161 el-Jabbour JN, Wilson GD, Bennett MH, Burke MM, Davey AT, Eames K. Flow cytometric study of nodular fasciitis, proliferative fasciitis, and proliferative myositis. Hum Pathol 1991, **22**: 1146–1149.

162 Enzinger FM, Dulcey F. Proliferative myositis. Report of 33 cases. Cancer 1967, **20**: 2213–2223.

163 Goodlad JR, Fletcher CD. Intradermal variant of nodular "fasciitis." Histopathology 1990, **17**: 569–571.

164 Heffner RR Jr, Armbrustmacher VW, Earle KM. Focal myositis. Cancer 1977, **40**: 301–306.

165 Heffner RR Jr, Barron SA. Denervating changes in focal myositis, a benign inflammatory pseudotumor. Arch Pathol Lab Med 1980, **104**: 261–264.

166 Hollowood K, Fletcher CD. Pseudosarcomatous myofibroblastic proliferations of the spermatic cord ("proliferative funiculitis"). Histologic and immunohistochemical analysis of a distinctive entity. Am J Surg Pathol 1992, **16**: 448–454.

167 Hutter RVP, Stewart FW, Foote FW Jr. Fasciitis. A report of 70 cases with follow-up proving the benignity of the lesion. Cancer 1962, **15**: 992–1003.

168 Kern WH. Proliferative myositis. A pseudosarcomatous reaction to injury. Arch Pathol 1960, **69**: 209–216.

169 Kleinstiver BJ, Rodriguez HA. Nodular fasciitis. A study of 45 cases and review of the literature. J Bone Joint Surg (Am) 1968, **50**: 1204–1212.

170 Konwaler BE, Keasbey L, Kaplan L. Subcutaneous pseudosarcomatous fibromatosis (fasciitis). Report of 8 cases. Am J Clin Pathol 1955, **25**: 241–252.

171 Lai FM, Lam WY. Nodular fasciitis of the dermis. J Cutan Pathol 1993, 20: 66–69.

172 Lauer DH, Enzinger FM. Cranial fasciitis of childhood. Cancer 1980, 45: 401–406.

173 Meis JM, Enzinger FM. Proliferative fasciitis and myositis of childhood. Am J Surg Pathol 1992, 16: 364–372.

174 Meister P, Bückmann FW, Konrad E. Extent and level of fascial involvement in 100 cases with nodular fasciitis. Virchows Arch [A] 1978, 380: 177–185.

175 Montgomery EA, Meis JM. Nodular fasciitis. Its morphologic spectrum and immunohistochemical profile. Am J Surg Pathol 1991, 15: 942–948.

176 Montgomery EA, Meis JM, Mitchell MS, Enzinger FM. Atypical decubital fibroplasia. A distinctive fibroblastic pseudotumor occurring in debilitated patients. Am J Surg Pathol 1992, 16: 708–715.

177 Patchefsky AS, Enzinger FM. Intravascular fasciitis. A report of 17 cases. Am J Surg Pathol 1981, 5: 29–36.

178 Perosio PM, Weiss SW. Ischemic fasciitis. A juxta-skeletal fibroblastic proliferation with a predilection for elderly patients. Mod Pathol 1993, 6: 69–72.

179 Price EB Jr, Silliphant WM, Shuman R. Nodular fasciitis. A clinicopathologic analysis of 65 cases. Am J Clin Pathol 1961, 35: 122–136.

180 Price SK, Kahn LB, Saxe N. Dermal and intravascular fasciitis. Unusual variants of nodular fasciitis. Am J Dermatopathol 1993, 15: 539–543.

181 Samaratunga H, Searle J, O'Loughlin B. Intravascular fasciitis: a case report and review of the literature. Pathology 1996, 28: 8–11.

182 Sasano H, Yamaki H, Ohashi Y, Ohtsuki S, Nagura H. Proliferative fasciitis of the forearm: case report with immunohistochemical, ultrastructural and DNA ploidy study and review of the literature. Pathol Int 1998, 48: 486–490.

183 Shimuzu S, Hashimoto H, Enjoji M. Nodular fasciitis. An analysis of 250 patients. Pathology 1984, 16: 161–166.

184 Toti P, Catella AM, Benvenuti A. Focal myositis. A pseudotumoral lesion. Histopathology 1994, 24: 171–173.

185 Toti P, Ramano L, Villanova M, Zazzi M, Luzi P. Focal myositis: a polymerase chain reaction analysis for a viral etiology. Hum Pathol 1997, 28: 111–113.

186 Toti P, Tanganelli P, Schurfeld K, Stumpo M, Barbagli L, Vatti R, Luzi P. Scarring in papillary carcinoma of the thyroid: report of two cases with exuberant nodular fasciitis-like stroma. Histopathology 1999, 35: 418–422.

187 Wirman JA. Nodular fasciitis, a lesion of myofibroblasts. An ultrastructural study. Cancer 1976, 38: 2378–2389.

Elastofibroma

188 Banfield WG, Lee CK. Elastofibroma. An electron microscopic study. J Natl Cancer Inst 1968, 40: 1067–1077.

189 Dixon AY, Lee SH. An ultrastructural study of elastofibromas. Hum Pathol 1980, 11: 257–262.

190 Enjoji M, Sumiyoshi K, Sueyuski K. Elastofibromatous lesion of the stomach in a patient with elastofibroma dorsi. Am J Surg Pathol 1985, 9: 233–237.

191 Fukuda Y, Miyake H, Masuda Y, Masugi Y. Histogenesis of unique elastinophilic fibers of elastofibroma. Ultrastructural and immunohistochemical studies. Hum Pathol 1987, 18: 424–429.

192 Govoni E, Severi B, Laschi R, Lorenzini P, Ronchetti IP, Baccarani M. Elastofibroma. An in vivo model of abnormal neoelastogenesis. Ultrastruct Pathol 1988, 12: 327–339.

193 Järvi OH, Saxén AE, Hopsu-Havu VK, Wartiovaara JJ, Vaissalo VT. Elastofibroma. A degenerative pseudotumor. Cancer 1969, 23: 42–63.

194 Kahn HJ, Hanna WM. "Abberrant elastic" in elastofibroma. An immunohistochemical and ultrastructural study. Ultrastruct Pathol 1995, 19: 45–50.

195 Kindblom L-G, Spicer SS. Elastofibroma. A correlated light and electron microscopic study. Virchows Arch [A] 1982, 396: 127–140.

196 Kumaratilake JS, Krishnan R, Lomax-Smith J, Cleary EG. Elastofibroma. Disturbed elastic fibrillogenesis by periosteal-derived cells? An immunoelectron microscopic and in situ hybridization study. Hum Pathol 1991, 22: 1017–1029.

197 Madri JA, Dise CA, LiVolsi VA, Merino MJ, Bibro MC. Elastofibroma dorsi. An immunochemical study of collagen content. Hum Pathol 1981, 12: 186–190.

198 Nagamine N, Nohara Y, Ito E. Elastofibroma in Okinawa. A clinicopathologic study of 170 cases. Cancer 1982, 50: 1794–1805.

199 Nakamura Y, Okamoto K, Tanimura A, Kato M, Morimatsu M. Elastase digestion and biochemical analysis of the elastin from an elastofibroma. Cancer 1986, 58: 1070–1075.

200 Stemmermann GN, Stout AP. Elastofibroma dorsi. Am J Clin Pathol 1962, 37: 490–506.

Solitary fibrous tumor

201 Brunnemann RB, Ro JY, Ordonez NG, Mooney J, El-Naggar AK, Ayala AG. Extrapleural solitary fibrous tumor: a clinicopathologic study of 24 cases. Mod Pathol 1999, 12: 1034–1042.

202 De Saint Aubain Somerhausen N, Rubin BP, Fletcher CD. Myxoid solitary fibrous tumor: a study of seven cases with emphasis on differential diagnosis. Mod Pathol 1999, 12: 463–471.

203 Dei Tos AP, Seregard S, Calonje E, Chan JK, Fletcher CD. Giant cell angiofibroma. A distinctive orbital tumor in adults. Am J Surg Pathol 1995, 19: 1286–1293.

204 Folpe AL, Devaney K, Weiss SW. Lipomatous hemangiopericytoma: a rare variant of hemangiopericytoma that may be confused with liposarcoma. Am J Surg Pathol 1999, 23: 1201–1207.

205 Guillou L, Gebhard S, Coindre JM. Lipomatous hemangiopericytoma: a fat containing variant of solitary fibrous tumor? Clinicopathologic, immunohistochemical, and ultrastructural analysis of a series in favour of a unifying concept. Hum Pathol 2000, 31: 1108–1115.

206 Guillou L, Gebhard S, Coindre JM. Orbital and extraorbital giant cell angiofibroma: a giant cell-rich variant of solitary fibrous tumor? Clinicopathologic and immunohistochemical analysis of a series in favour of a unifying concept. Am J Surg Pathol 2000, 24: 971–979.

207 Nielsen GP, O'Connell JX, Dickersin GR, Rosenberg AE. Solitary fibrous tumor of soft tissue: a report of 15 cases, including 5 malignant examples with light microscopic, immunohistochemical, and ultrastructural data. Mod Pathol 1997, 10: 1028–1037.

Fibromatosis

208 Allen PW. The fibromatoses. A clinicopathologic classification based on 140 cases. Am J Surg Pathol 1977, 1: 255–270, 305–321.

209 Allen RA, Woolner LB, Ghormley RK. Soft-tissue tumors of the sole. With special reference to plantar fibromatosis. J Bone Joint Surg (Am) 1955, 37: 14–26.

210 Ayala AG, Ro JY, Goepfert H, Cangir A, Khorsand J, Flake G. Desmoid fibromatosis. A clinicopathologic study of 25 children. Semin Diagn Pathol 1986, 3: 138–150.

211 Battifora H, Hines JR. Recurrent digital fibromas of childhood. An electron microscope study. Cancer 1971, 27: 1530–1536.

212 Beatty EC Jr. Congenital generalized fibromatosis in infancy. Am J Dis Child 1962, 103: 620–624.

213 Beham A, Badve S, Suster S, Fletcher CD. Solitary myofibroma in adults. Clinicopathological analysis of a series. Histopathology 1993, 22: 335–341.

214 Bhawan J, Bacchetta C, Joris I, Majno G. A myofibroblastic tumor. Infantile digital fibroma (recurrent digital fibrous tumor of childhood). Am J Pathol 1979, 94: 19–28.

215 Bochetto JF, Raycroft JE, Delnnocentes LW. Multiple polyposis, exostosis, and soft tissue tumors. Surg Gynecol Obstet 1963, 117: 489–494.

216 Briselli MF, Soule EH, Gilchrist GS. Congenital fibromatosis. Report of 18 cases of solitary and 4 cases of multiple tumors. Mayo Clin Proc 1980, 55: 554–562.

217 Brown JB, McDowell F. Wry-neck facial distortion prevented by resection of fibrosed sternomastoid muscle in infancy and childhood. Ann Surg 1950, 131: 721–733.

218 Burke AP, Sobin LH, Shekitka KM. Mesenteric fibromatosis. A follow-up study. Arch Pathol Lab Med 1990, 114: 832–835.

219 Burke AP, Sobin LH, Shekitka KM, Federspiel BH, Helwig EB. Intraabdominal fibromatosis. A pathologic analysis of 130 tumors with comparison of clinical subgroups. Am J Surg Pathol 1990, 14: 335–341.

220 Burry AF, Kerr JFR, Pope JH. Recurring digital fibrous tumour of childhood. An electron microscopic and virological study. Pathology 1970, 2: 287–291.

221 Chung EB, Enzinger FM. Infantile myofibromatosis. Cancer 1981, 48: 1807–1818.

222 Cooper PH. Fibrous proliferations of infancy and childhood. J Cutan Pathol 1992, 19: 257–267.

223 Coventry MB, Harris LE, Bianco AJ, Bulbulian AH. Congenital muscular torticollis (wry neck). Postgrad Med 1960, 28: 383–392.

224 Daimaru Y, Hashimoto H, Enjoji M. Myofibromatosis in adults (adult counterpart of infantile myofibromatosis). Am J Surg Pathol 1989, 13: 859–865.

225 De Wever I, Dal Cin P, Fletcher CD, Mandahl N, Mertens F, Mitelman F, Rosai J, Rydholm A, Sciot R, Tallini G, Van Den Berghe H, Vanni R, Willen H. Cytogenetic, clinical and morphologic correlations in 78 cases of fibromatosis: a report from the CHAMP study group, chromosomes and morphology. Mod Pathol 2001, 13: 1080–1085.

226 Dimmick JE, Wood WS. Congenital multiple fibromatosis. Am J Dermatopathol 1983, 5: 289–295.

227 Dominguez-Malagon H. Proliferative disorders of myofibroblasts. Ultrastruct Pathol 1993, 17: 211–220.

228 Drescher E, Woyke S, Markiewicz C, Tegi S. Juvenile fibromatosis in siblings (fibromatosis hyalinica multiplex juvenilis). J Pediatr Surg 1967, 2: 427–430.

229 Editorial. The myofibroblast. Lancet 1978, 2: 1290–1291.

230 Enzinger FM. Histological typing of soft tissue tumours. International histological classification of tumours. No 3. Geneva, 1969, World Health Organization.

231 Enzinger FM, Shiraki M. Musculo-aponeurotic fibromatosis of the shoulder girdle (extra-abdominal desmoid). Analysis of 30 cases followed up for ten or more years. Cancer 1967, 20: 1131–1140.

232 Faraggiana T, Churg J, Strauss L. Ultrastructural histochemistry of infantile digital fibromatosis. Ultrastruct Pathol 1981, 2: 241–247.

233 Fetsch JF, Miettinen M, Laskin WB, Michal M, Enzinger FM. A clinicopathologic study of 45 pediatric soft tissue tumors with an admixture of adipose tissue and fibroblastic elements, and a proposal for classification as lipofibromatosis. Am J Surg Pathol 2000, 24: 1491–1500.

234 Fletcher CDM, Achu P, Van Noorden S, McKee PH. Infantile myofibromatosis. A light microscopic, histochemical and immunohistochemical study suggesting true smooth muscle differentiation. Histopathology 1987, 11: 245–258.

235 Fletcher CDM, Stirling RW, Smith MA, Pambakian H, McKee PH. Multicentric extra-abdominal "myofibromatosis." Report of a case with ultrastructural findings. Histopathology 1986, 10: 713–724.

236 Fromowitz FB, Hurst LC, Nathan J, Badalamente M. Infantile (desmoid type) fibromatosis with extensive ossification. Am J Surg Pathol 1987, 11: 66–75.

237 Fukasawa Y, Ishikura H, Takada A, Yokoyama S, Imamura M, Yoshiki T, Sato H. Massive apoptosis in infantile myofibromatosis. A putative mechanism of tumor regression. Am J Pathol 1994, 144: 480–485.

238 Gabbiani G, Majno G. Dupuytren's contracture. Fibroblast contraction? An ultrastructural study. Am J Pathol 1972, 66: 131–138.

239 Goellner JR, Soule EH. Desmoid tumors. An ultrastructural study of eight cases. Hum Pathol 1980, 11: 43–50.

240 Goslee L, Clermont V, Bernstein J, Woolley PW Jr. Superficial connective tissue tumors in early infancy. J Pediatr 1964, 65: 377–387.

241 Granter SR, Badizadegan K, Fletcher CD. Myofibromatosis in adults, glomangiopericytoma, and myopericytoma: a spectrum of tumors showing perivascular myoid differentiation. Am J Surg Pathol 1998, 22: 513–525.

242 Haleem A, Al-Hindi HN, Al-Juboury M, Al Husseini H, Al Ajlan A. Juvenile hyaline fibromatosis: morphologic, immunohistochemical, and ultrastructural study of three siblings. Am J Dermatopathol 2002, 24: 218–224.

243 Hasegawa T, Hirose T, Seki K, Hizawa K, Okada J, Nakanishi H. Solitary infantile myofibromatosis of bone. An immunohistochemical and ultrastructural study. Am J Surg Pathol 1993, 17: 308–313.

244 Hayashi T, Tsuda N, Chowdhury PR, Anami M, Kishikawa M, Iseki M, Kobayashi K. Infantile digital fibromatosis. A study of the development and regression of cytoplasmic inclusion bodies. Mod Pathol 1995, 8: 548–552.

245 Hogan SF, Salassa JR. Recurrent adult myofibromatosis. A case report. Am J Clin Pathol 1992, 97: 810–814.

246 Hunt RT, Morgan HC, Ackerman LV. Principles in the management of extra-abdominal desmoids. Cancer 1960, 13: 825–836.

247 Ishikawa H, Mori S. Systemic hyalinosis or fibromatosis hyalinica multiplex juvenilis as a congenital syndrome. A new entity based on the inborn error of the acid mucopolysaccharide metabolism in connective tissue cells? Acta Derm Venereol 1973, 53: 185–191.

248 Iwahara T, Ikeda A. On the ipsilateral involvement of congenital muscular torticollis and congenital dislocation of the hip. J Jpn Orthop Assoc 1962, 35: 1221–1226.

249 Iwasaki H, Kikuchi M, Ohtsuki I, Enjoji M, Suenaga N, Mori R. Infantile digital fibromatosis. Identification of actin filaments in cytoplasmic inclusions by heavy meromyosin binding. Cancer 1983, 52: 1653–1661.

250 Iwasaki H, Müller H, Stutte HJ, Brennscheidt U. Palmar fibromatosis (Dupuytren's contracture). Ultrastructural and enzyme histochemical studies of 43 cases. Virchows Arch [A] 1984, 405: 41–53.

251 Jennings TA, Duray PH, Collins FS, Sabetta J, Enzinger FM. Infantile myofibromatosis. Evidence for an autosomal-dominant disorder. Am J Surg Pathol 1984, 8: 529–538.

252 Kiel KD, Suit HD. Radiation therapy in the treatment of aggressive fibromatoses (desmoid tumors). Cancer 1984, 54: 2051–2055.

253 Kim D-H, Goldsmith HS, Quan SH, Huvos AG. Intraabdominal desmoid tumor. Cancer 1971, 27: 1041–1043.

254 Kiryu H, Tsuneyoshi M, Enjoji M. Myofibroblasts in fibromatoses. An electron microscopic study. Acta Pathol Jpn 1985, 35: 533–547.

255 Larsen RD, Posch JL. Dupuytren's contracture. With special reference to pathology. J Bone Joint Surg (Am) 1958, 40: 773–792.

256 Levine AM, Reddick R, Triche T. Intracellular collagen fibrils in human sarcomas. Lab Invest 1978, 39: 531–540.

257 Liew S-H, Haynes M. Localized form of congenital generalized fibromatosis. A report of 3 cases with myofibroblasts. Pathology 1981, 13: 257–266.

257a Lucas DR, Al-Abbadi M, Tabaczka P, Hamre MR, Weaver DW, Mott MP. c-kit expression in desmoid fibromatosis: comparative immunohistochemical of two commercial antibodies. (Abstract) Mod Pathol 2003, 16: 16a.

258 Masson JK, Soule EH. Desmoid tumors of head and neck. Am J Surg 1966, 112: 615–622.

259 Montgomery E, Lee JH, Abraham SC, Wu TT. Superficial fibromatoses are genetically distinct from deep fibromatoses. Mod Pathol 2001, 14: 695–701.

260 Mortimer G, Gibson AAM. Recurring digital fibroma. J Clin Pathol 1982, 35: 849–854.

261 Mukai M, Torikata C, Iri H, Hata J, Naito M, Shimoda T. Immunohistochemical identification of aggregated actin filaments in formalin-fixed, paraffin-embedded sections. I. A study of infantile digital fibromatosis by a new pretreatment. Am J Surg Pathol 1992, 16: 110–115.

262 Pettinato G, Manivel JC, Gould EW, Albores-Saavedra J. Inclusion body fibromatosis of the breast. Two cases with immunohistochemical and ultrastructural findings. Am J Clin Pathol 1994, 101: 714–718.

263 Pickren JW, Smith AG, Stevenson TW Jr, Stout AP. Fibromatosis of the plantar fascia. Cancer 1951, 4: 846–856.

264 Purdy LJ, Colby TV. Infantile digital fibromatosis occurring outside the digit. Am J Surg Pathol 1984, 8: 787–790.

265 Reitamo JJ, Hayry P, Nykyri E, Saxen AE. The desmoid tumor. Incidence, sex, age, and anatomical distribution in the Finnish population. Am J Clin Pathol 1982, 77: 665–681.

266 Reye RDK. Recurring digital fibrous tumors of childhood. Arch Pathol 1965, 80: 228–231.

267 Rock MG, Pritchard DJ, Reiman HM, Soule EH, Brewster RC. Extra-abdominal desmoid tumors. J Bone Joint Surg (Am) 1984, 66: 1369–1374.

267a Rodriquez JA, Guarda LA, Rosai J. Mesenteric fibromatosis with involvement of the gastrointestinal tract. A GIST simulator: a study of 25 cases. Am J Clin Pathol (In press).

268 Rodriguez-Bigas MA, Mahoney MC, Karakousis CP, Petrelli NJ. Desmoid tumors in patients with familial adenomatous polyposis. Cancer 1994, 74: 1270–1274.

269 Ruggli VL, Kim H-S, Hawkins E. Congenital generalized fibromatosis with visceral involvement. A case report. Cancer 1980, 45: 954–960.

270 Rosen PP, Ernsberger D. Mammary fibromatosis. A benign spindle cell tumor with significant risk for local recurrence. Cancer 1989, 63: 1363–1369.

271 Rosenberg HS, Stenback WA, Spjut HJ. The fibromatoses of infancy and childhood. Perspect Pediatr Pathol 1978, 4: 269–348.

272 Santa Cruz DJ, Reiner CB. Recurrent digital fibroma of childhood. J Cutan Pathol 1978, 5: 339–346.

273 Shnitka TK, Douglas MA, Horner RH. Congenital generalized fibromatosis. Cancer 1958, 11: 627–639.

274 Skoog T. Dupuytren's contracture. Pathogenesis and surgical treatment. Surg Clin North Am 1967, 47: 433–444.

275 Sportiello DJ, Hoogerland DL. A recurrent pelvic desmoid tumor successfully treated with tamoxifen. Cancer 1991, 67: 1443–1446.

276 Staley CJ. Gardner's syndrome. Simultaneous occurrence of polyposis coli, osteomatosis and soft tissue tumors. Arch Surg 1961, 82: 420–422.

277 Stout AP. Juvenile fibromatosis. Cancer 1954, 7: 953–978.

278 Ushijima M, Tsuneyoshi M, Enjoji M. Dupuytren type fibromatoses. A rare cause of neonatal intestinal obstruction. A clinicopathologic study of 62 cases. Acta Pathol Jpn 1984, 34: 991–1001.

279 Viale G, Doglioni C, Iuzzolino P, Bontempini L, Colombi R, Coggi G, Dell'Orto P. Infantile digital fibromatosis-like tumour (inclusion body fibromatosis) of adulthood. Report of two cases with ultrastructural and immunocyto-chemical findings. Histopathology 1988, 12: 415–424.

280 Walts AF, Asch M, Raj C. Solitary lesion of congenital fibromatosis. Am J Surg Pathol 1982, 6: 255–260.

281 Wang N-S, Knaack J. Fibromatosis hyalinica multiplex juvenilis. Ultrastruct Pathol 1979, 3: 153–160.

282 Welsh RA. Intracytoplasmic collagen formations in desmoid fibromatosis. Am J Pathol 1966, 49: 515–535.

283 Wilcken N, Tattersall MH. Endocrine therapy for desmoid tumors. Cancer 1991, 68: 1384–1388.

284 Woyke S, Domagala W, Olszewski W. Ultrastructure of a fibromatosis hyalinica multiplex juvenilis. Cancer 1970, 26: 1157–1168.

285 Yokoyama R, Tsuneyoshi M, Enjoji M, Shinohara N, Masuda S. Extra-abdominal desmoid tumors. Correlations between histologic features and biologic behavior. Surg Pathol 1989, 2: 29–42.

286 Yun K. Infantile digital fibromatosis. Immunohistochemical and ultrastructural observations of cytoplasmic inclusions. Cancer 1988, 61: 500–507.

287 Zelefsky MJ, Harrison LB, Shiu MH, Armstrong JG, Hajdu SI, Brennan MF. Combined surgical resection and iridium 192 implantation for locally advanced and recurrent desmoid tumors. Cancer 1991, 67: 380–384.

Fibrosarcoma

288 Antonescu CR, Rosenblum MK, Pereira P, Nascimento AG, Woodruff JM. Sclerosing epithelioid fibrosarcoma: a study of 16 cases and confirmation of a clinicopathologically distinct tumor. Am J Surg Pathol 2001, 25: 699–709.

289 Bourgeois J, Knezevich SR, Mathers JA, Sorensen PH. Molecular detection of the ETV6-NTRK3 gene fusion differentiates congenital fibrosarcoma from other childhood spindle cell tumors. Am J Surg Pathol 2000, 24: 937–946.

290 Chung EB, Enzinger FM. Infantile fibrosarcoma. Cancer 1976, 38: 729–739.

291 Chung AM, Kahn LB. Myofibroblasts and related cells in malignant fibrous and fibrohistiocytic tumors. Hum Pathol 1977, 8: 205–218.

292 Dehner LP, Askin FB. Tumors of fibrous tissue origin in childhood. A clinico-pathologic study of cutaneous and soft tissue neoplasms in 66 children. Cancer 1976, 38: 888–900.

293 Gonzalez-Crussi F, Wiederhold MD, Sotelo-Avila C. Congenital fibrosarcoma. Presence of a histiocytic component. Cancer 1980, 46: 77–86.

294 Guber S, Rudolph R. The myofibroblast. Surg Gynecol Obstet 1978, 146: 641–649.

295 Hall J, Tseng SCG, Timpl R, Hendrix MJC, Stern R. Collagen types in fibrosarcoma. Absence of type III collagen in reticulin. Hum Pathol 1985, 16: 439–446.

296 Iwasaki H, Enjoji M. Infantile and adult fibrosarcomas of the soft tissues. Acta Pathol Jpn 1979, 29: 377–388.

297 Meis-Kindblom JM, Kindblom L-G, Enzinger FM. Sclerosing epithelioid fibrosarcoma. A variant of fibrosarcoma simulating carcinoma. Am J Surg Pathol 1995, 19: 979–993.

298 Oshiro Y, Fukuda T, Tsuneyoshi M. Fibrosarcoma versus fibromatoses and cellular nodular fasciitis. A comparative study of their proliferative activity using proliferating cell nuclear antigen, DNA flow cytometry, and p53. Am J Surg Pathol 1994, 18: 712–719.

299 Pritchard DJ, Soule EH, Taylor WF, Ivins JC. Fibrosarcoma. A clinicopathologic and statistical study of 199 tumors of the soft tissues of the extremities and trunk. Cancer 1974, 33: 888–897.

300 Reid R, Barrett A, Hamblen DL. Sclerosing epithelioid fibrosarcoma. Histopathology 1997, 28: 451–455.

300a Sandberg AA, Bridge JA. Updates on the cytogenetics and molecular genetics of bone soft tissue tumors: congenital (infantile) fibrosarcoma and mesoblastic nephroma. Cancer Genet Cytogenet 2002, **132:** 1–13.

301 Schofield DE, Fletcher JA, Grier HE, Yunis EJ. Fibrosarcoma in infants and children. Application of new techniques. Am J Surg Pathol 1994, **18:** 14–24.

302 Scott SM, Reiman HM, Pritchard DJ, Ilstrup DM. Soft tissue fibrosarcoma. A clinicopathologic study of 132 cases. Cancer 1989, **64:** 925–931.

303 Soule EH, Pritchard DJ. Fibrosarcoma in infants and children. A review of 110 cases. Cancer 1977, **40:** 1711–1721.

304 Stout AP. Fibrosarcoma. The malignant tumor of fibroblasts. Cancer 1948, **1:** 30–63.

305 Stout AP. Fibrosarcoma in infants and children. Cancer 1962, **15:** 1028–1040.

306 van der Werf-Messing B, van Unnik JAM. Fibrosarcoma of the soft tissue. A clinicopathologic study. Cancer 1965, **18:** 1113–1123.

307 Weiss SW. Proliferative fibroblastic lesions. From hyperplasia to neoplasia. Am J Surg Pathol 1986, **10**(Suppl 1): 14–25.

Myofibroblastic tumors

308 Cessna MH, Zhou H, Sanger WG, Perkins SL, Tripp S, Pickering D, Daines C, Coffin CM. Expression of ALK1 and p80 in inflammatory myofibroblastic tumor and its mesenchymal mimics: a study of 135 cases. Mod Pathol 2002, **15:** 931–938.

309 Coffin CM, Watterson J, Priest JR, Dehner LP. Extrapulmonary inflammatory myofibroblastic tumor (inflammatory pseudotumor). A clinicopathologic and immunohistochemical study of 84 cases. Am J Surg Pathol 1995, **19:** 859–872.

310 Eyden BP, Banerjee SS, Harris M, Mene A. A study of spindle cell sarcomas showing myofibroblastic differentiation. Ultrastruct Pathol 1991, **15:** 367–378.

310a Fisher C, Goldblum JR, Montgomery E. Calponin and H-caldesmon in sarcomas of myofibroblasts. (Abstract) Mod Pathol 2003, **16:** 11A.

311 Herrera GA, Johnson WW, Lockard VG, Walker BL. Soft tissue myofibroblastomas. Mod Pathol 1991, **4:** 571–577.

312 Mackay B, Ordóñez NG, Salter JE Jr, Pollock RE. Myofibroblastoma of the axilla. Ultrastruct Pathol 1995, **19:** 265–268.

313 Meis JM, Enzinger FM. Inflammatory fibrosarcoma of the mesentery and retroperitoneum. A tumor closely simulating inflammatory pseudotumor. Am J Surg Pathol 1991, **15:** 1146–1156.

314 Meis-Kindblom JM, Kjellstram C, Kindblom LG. Inflammatory fibrosarcoma: update, reappraisal, and perspective on its place in the spectrum of inflammatory myofibroblastic tumors. Semin Diagn Pathol 1998, **15:** 133–143.

315 Mentzel T, Dry S, Katenkamp D, Fletcher CD. Low-grade myofibroblastic sarcoma: analysis of 18 cases in the spectrum of myofibroblastic tumors. Am J Surg Pathol 1998, **22:** 1228–1238.

316 Montgomery E, Goldblum JR, Fisher C. Myofibrosarcoma: a clinicopathologic study. Am J Surg Pathol 2001, **25:** 219–228.

317 O'Brien JE, Stout AP. Malignant fibrous xanthomas. Cancer 1964, **17:** 1445–1455.

318 Ramachandra S, Hollowood K, Bisceglia M, Fletcher CDM. Inflammatory pseudotumour of soft tissues. A clinicopathological and immunohistochemical analysis of 18 cases. Histopathology 1995, **27:** 313–323.

318a Rubin BP, Coffin CM, Fanburg-Smith JC. Inflammatory myofibroblastic tumors in adults. (Abstract) Mod Pathol 2003, **16:** 19A.

319 Schurch W. The myofibroblast in neoplasia. Curr Top Pathol 1999, **93:** 135–148.

320 Souid AK, Ziemba MC, Dubansky AS, Mazur M, Oliphant M, Thomas FD, Ratner M, Sadowitz PD. Inflammatory myofibroblastic tumor in children. Cancer 1993, **72:** 2042–2048.

320a Yamamoto H, Oda Y, Saito T, Sakamoto A, Miyajima K, Tamiya S, Tsuneyoshi M. p53 mutation and MDM2 amplification in inflammatory myofibroblastic tumours. Histopathology 2003, **42:** 431–439.

Fibrohistiocytic tumors

321 Alguacil-Garcia A, Unni KK, Goellner JR. Malignant fibrous histiocytoma. An ultrastructural study of six cases. Am J Clin Pathol 1978, **69:** 121–129.

322 Angervall L, Kindblom L-G, Merck C. Myxofibrosarcoma. A study of 30 cases. Acta Pathol Microbiol Scand (A) 1977, **85:** 127–140.

323 Argenyi ZB, Van Rybroek JJ, Kemp JD, Soper RT. Congenital angiomatoid malignant fibrous histiocytoma. A light-microscopic, immunopathologic, and electron-microscopic study. Am J Dermatopathol 1988, **10:** 59–67.

324 Barnes L, Coleman JA Jr, Johnson JT. Dermatofibrosarcoma protuberans of the head and neck. Arch Otolaryngol 1984, **110:** 398–404.

325 Barr RJ, Young EM, King DF. Non-polarized collagen in dermatofibrosarcoma protuberans. A useful diagnostic aid. J Cutan Pathol 1986, **13:** 339–346.

326 Beham A, Fletcher CD. Dermatofibrosarcoma protuberans with areas resembling giant cell fibroblastoma. Report of two cases. Histopathology 1990, **17:** 165–167.

327 Bendix-Hansen K, Myhre-Jensen O. Enzyme histochemical investigations on bone and soft tissue tumours. Acta Pathol Microbiol Immunol Scand (A) 1985, **93:** 73–80.

328 Bertoni F, Capanna R, Biagini P, Guerra A, Ruggieri P, Present D, Campanacci M. Malignant fibrous histiocytoma of soft tissue. An analysis of 78 cases located and deeply seated in the extremities. Cancer 1985, **56:** 356–367.

329 Bhagavan BS, Dorfman HD. The significance of bone and cartilage formation in malignant fibrous histiocytoma of soft tissue. Cancer 1982, **49:** 480–488.

330 Binder SW, Said JW, Shintaku IP, Pinkus GS. A histiocyte-specific marker in the diagnosis of malignant fibrous histiocytoma. Use of monoclonal antibody KP-1 (CD68). Am J Clin Pathol 1992, **97:** 759–763.

331 Black WC, McGavran MH, Graham P. Nodular subepidermal fibrosis. A clinical pathologic study emphasizing the frequency of clinical misdiagnoses. Arch Surg 1969, **98:** 296–300.

332 Brecher ME, Franklin WA. Absence of mononuclear phagocyte antigens in malignant fibrous histiocytoma. Am J Clin Pathol 1986, **86:** 344–348.

333 Burkhardt BR, Soule EH, Winkelman RK, Ivins JC. Dermatofibrosarcoma protuberans. Study of 56 cases. Am J Surg 1966, **111:** 638–644.

333a Coindre JM, Guillou L, Chibon F, Mariani O, Hostein I, Aurias A. Most inflammatory MFH (IMFH) are dedifferentiated liposarcomas (DDLS). Analysis of 7 IMFH and comparison to 8 DDLS with an IMFH component. (Abstract) Mod Pathol 2003, **16:** 10A.

334 Colby TV. Malakoplakia. Two unusual cases which presented diagnostic problems. Am J Surg Pathol 1978, **2:** 377–382.

335 Connelly JH, Evans HL. Dermatofibrosarcoma protuberans. A clinicopathologic review with emphasis on fibrosarcomatous areas. Am J Surg Pathol 1992, **16:** 921–925.

336 Costa MJ, Weiss SW. Angiomatoid malignant fibrous histiocytoma. A follow-up study of 108 cases with evaluation of possible histologic predictors of outcome. Am J Surg Pathol 1990, **14:** 1126–1132.

337 De Chadarevian JP, Coppola D, Billmire DF. Bednar tumor pattern in recurring giant cell fibroblastoma. Am J Clin Pathol 1993, **100:** 164–166.

338 Ding J, Hashimoto H, Enjoji M. Dermatofibrosarcoma protuberans with fibrosarcomatous areas. A clinicopathologic study of nine cases and a comparison with allied tumors. Cancer 1989, **64**: 721–729.

339 Ding JA, Hashimoto H, Sugimoto T, Tsuneyoshi M, Enjoji M. Bednar tumor (pigmented dermatofibrosarcoma protuberans). An analysis of six cases. Acta Pathol Jpn 1990, **40**: 744–754.

340 Dominguez-Malagon HR, Ordóñez NG, Mackay B. Dermatofibrosarcoma protuberans. Ultrastructural and immunocytochemical observations. Ultrastruct Pathol 1995, **19**: 281–290.

341 Du Boulay CE. Demonstration of alpha-1-antitrypsin and alpha-1-antichymotrypsin in fibrous histiocytomas using the immunoperoxidase technique. Am J Surg Pathol 1982, **6**: 559 564.

342 Dupree WB, Langloss JM, Weiss SW. Pigmented dermatofibrosarcoma protuberans (Bednar tumor). A pathologic, ultrastructural, and immunohistochemical study. Am J Surg Pathol 1985, **9**: 630–639.

343 Enzinger FM. Angiomatoid malignant fibrous histiocytoma. A distinct fibrohistiocytic tumor of children and young adults simulating a vascular neoplasm. Cancer 1979, **44**: 2147–2157.

344 Enzinger FM. Malignant fibrous histiocytoma 20 years after Stout. Am J Surg Pathol 1986, **10**(Suppl 1): 43–53.

345 Enzinger FM, Zhang RY. Plexiform fibrohistiocytic tumor presenting in children and young adults. An analysis of 65 cases. Am J Surg Pathol 1988, **12**: 818–826.

346 Evans HL. Low-grade fibromyxoid sarcoma. A report of two metastasizing neoplasms having a deceptively benign appearance. Am J Clin Pathol 1987, **88**: 615 619.

347 Evans HL. Low-grade fibromyxoid sarcoma. A report of 12 cases. Am J Surg Pathol 1993, **17**: 595–600.

348 Fanburg-Smith JC, Miettinen M. Angiomatoid "malignant" fibrous histiocytoma: a clinicopathologic study of 158 cases and further exploration of the myoid phenotype. Hum Pathol 1999, **30**: 1336–1343.

348a Fanburg-Smith JC, Rubin BP, Miettinen M. Deep juvenile xanthogranuloma. A study of 30 intramuscular and 19 subcutaneous cases. (Abstract) Mod Pathol 2003, **16**: 11A.

349 Fisher ER, Hellstrom HR. Dermatofibrosarcoma with metastases simulating Hodgkin's disease and reticulum cell sarcoma. Cancer 1966, **19**: 1165–1171.

350 Fisher ER, Vuzevski VD. Cytogenesis of the schwannoma (neurilemoma), neurofibroma, dermatofibroma, and dermatofibrosarcoma as revealed by electron microscopy. Am J Clin Pathol 1968, **49**: 141–154.

351 Fletcher CD. Angiomatoid "malignant fibrous histiocytoma." An immunohistochemical study indicative of myoid differentiation. Hum Pathol 1991, **22**: 563–568.

352 Fletcher CD. Pleomorphic malignant fibrous histiocytoma: fact or fiction?: a critical reappraisal based on 159 tumors diagnosed as pleomorphic sarcoma. Am J Surg Pathol 1992, **16**: 213–228.

353 Fletcher CDM. Benign fibrous histiocytoma of subcutaneous and deep soft tissue. A clinicopathologic analysis of 21 cases. Am J Surg Pathol 1990, **14**: 801–809.

354 Fletcher CDM, Evans BJ, MacArtney JC, Smith N, Wilson Jones E, McKee PH. Dermatofibrosarcoma protuberans. A clinicopathologic and immunohistochemical study with a review of the literature. Histopathology 1985, **9**: 921–938.

355 Fletcher CD, Theaker JM, Flanagan A, Krausz T. Pigmented dermatofibrosarcoma protuberans (Bednar tumour). Melanocytic colonization or neuroectodermal differentiation? A clinicopathological and immunohistochemical study. Histopathology 1988, **13**: 631–643.

356 Folpe AL, Lane KL, Paull G, Wiess SW. Low-grade fibromyxoid sarcoma and hyalinizing spindle cell tumor with giant rosettes: a clinicopathologic study of 73 cases supporting their identity

and assessing the impact of high-grade areas. Am J Surg Pathol 2000, **24**: 1353–1360.

356a Franchi A, Massi D, Santucci M. Hyalinizing spindle cell tumor with giant rosettes and low-grade fibromyxoid sarcoma: an immunohistochemical and ultrastructural comparative investigation. Ultrastruct Pathol 2003, **27**: 349–355.

357 Fretzin DF, Helwig EB. Atypical fibroxanthoma of the skin. A clinicopathologic study of 140 cases. Cancer 1973, **31**: 1541–1552.

358 Fu Y, Gabbiani G, Kaye GI, Lattes R. Malignant soft tissue tumors of probable histiocytic origin (malignant fibrous histiocytomas). General considerations and electron microscopic and tissue culture studies. Cancer 1975, **35**: 176–198.

359 Goldblum JR. CD34 positivity in fibrosarcomas which arise in dermatofibrosarcoma protuberans. Arch Pathol Lab Med 1995, **119**: 238–241.

360 Goldblum JR, Reith JD, Weiss SW. Sarcomas arising in dermatofibrosarcoma protuberans: a reappraisal of biologic behaviour in eighteen cases treated by wide local excision with extended clinical follow-up. Am J Surg Pathol 2000, **24**: 1125–1130.

361 Goodlad JR, Mentzel T, Fletcher CD. Low grade fibromyxoid sarcoma. Clinicopathological analysis of eleven new cases in support of a distinct entity. Histopathology 1995, **26**: 229–237.

362 Graadt van Roggen JF, Hogendoorn PC, Fletcher CD. Myxoid tumours of soft tissue. Histopathology 1999, **35**: 291–312.

363 Harris M. The ultrastructure of benign and malignant fibrous histiocytomas. Histopathology 1980, **4**: 29–44.

364 Hashimoto K, Brownstein MH, Jakobiec FA. Dermatofibrosarcoma protuberans. A tumor with perineural and endoneural features. Arch Dermatol 1974, **110**: 874–885.

365 Helwig EB, May D. Atypical fibroxanthoma of the skin with metastasis. Cancer 1986, **57**: 368 376.

366 Herrera GA, Reimann BE, Salinas JA. Malignant schwannomas presenting as malignant fibrous histiocytomas. Ultrastruct Pathol 1982, **3**: 253–261.

367 Hirose T, Kudo E, Hasegawa T, Abe J, Hizawa K. Expression of intermediate filaments in malignant fibrous histiocytomas. Hum Pathol 1989, **20**: 871–877.

368 Hirose T, Sano T, Abe J, Hizawa K, Hatakeyama S, Mori I. Malignant fibrous histiocytoma with epithelial differentiation? Ultrastruct Pathol 1988, **12**: 529–536.

369 Hoffman MA, Dickersin GR. Malignant fibrous histiocytoma. An ultrastructural study of 11 cases. Hum Pathol 1983, **14**: 913–922.

370 Hollowood K, Holley MP, Fletcher CD. Plexiform fibrohistiocytic tumour. Clinicopathological, immunohistochemical and ultrastructural analysis in favour of a myofibroblastic lesion. Histopathology 1991, **19**: 503–513.

370a Huang H-Y, Lal P, Qin J, Antonescu Cr. A comparison of 3 grading schemes to predict outcome of low grade myxofibrosarcoma (Abstract). Mod Pathol 2003, **16**: 14A.

371 Hudson AW, Winkelmann RK. Atypical fibroxanthomas of the skin. A reappraisal of 19 cases in which the original diagnosis was spindle cell squamous carcinoma. Cancer 1972, **29**: 413–422.

372 Inoshita T, Youngberg GA. Malignant fibrous histiocytoma arising in previous surgical sites. Report of two cases. Cancer 1984, **53**: 176–183.

373 Inoue A, Aozasa K, Tsujimoto M, Tamai M, Chatani F, Ueno H. Immunohistologic study on malignant fibrous histiocytoma. Acta Pathol Jpn 1984, **34**: 759–765.

374 Iwasaki H, Isayama T, Johnzaki H, Kikuchi M. Malignant fibrous histiocytoma. Evidence of perivascular mesenchymal cell origin. Immunocytochemical studies with monoclonal anti-MFH antibodies. Am J Pathol 1987, **128**: 528–537.

375 Iwasaki H, Isayama T, Ohjimi Y, Kikuchi M, Yoh S, Shinohara N, Yoshitake K, Ishiguro M, Kamada N, Enjoji M. Malignant

fibrous histiocytoma. A tumor of facultative histiocytes showing mesenchymal differentiation in cultured cell lines. Cancer 1992, **69**: 437–447.

376 Iwasaki H, Kikuchi M, Takii M, Enjoji M. Benign and malignant fibrous histiocytomas of the soft tissues. Functional characterization of the cultured cells. Cancer 1982, **50**: 520–530.

377 Jaffer S, Eusebi V, Rosai J. Neurothekeomas and plexiform fibrohistiocytic tumors: a relationship? Lab Invest 2000, **80**: 11A.

378 Janney CG, Hurt MA, Santa Cruz DJ. Deep juvenile xanthogranuloma. Subcutaneous and intramuscular forms. Am J Surg Pathol 1991, **15**: 150–159.

379 Kamino H, Jacobson M. Dermatofibroma extending into the subcutaneous tissue. Differential diagnosis from dermatofibrosarcoma protuberans. Am J Surg Pathol 1990, **14**: 1156–1164.

380 Kauffman SL, Stout AP. Histiocytic tumors (fibrous xanthoma and histiocytoma) in children. Cancer 1961, **14**: 469–482.

381 Kay S. Angiomatoid malignant fibrous histiocytoma. Report of two cases with ultrastructural observations of one case. Arch Pathol Lab Med 1985, **109**: 934–937.

382 Kearney MM, Soule EH, Ivins JC. Malignant fibrous histiocytoma. A retrospective study of 167 cases. Cancer 1980, **45**: 167–178.

383 Kempson RL, Kyriakos M. Fibroxanthosarcoma of the soft tissues. A type of malignant fibrous histiocytoma. Cancer 1972, **29**: 961–976.

384 Kempson RL, McGavran MH. Atypical fibroxanthoma of the skin. Cancer 1964, **17**: 1463–1471.

385 Kindblom L-G, Jacobsen GK, Jacobsen M. Immunohistochemical investigations of tumors of supposed fibroblastic-histiocytic origin. Hum Pathol 1982, **13**: 834–840.

386 Kindblom L-G, Merck C, Angervall L. The ultrastructure of myxofibrosarcoma. A study of 11 cases. Virchows Arch [A] 1979, **381**: 121–139.

387 Kroe DJ, Pitcock JA. Atypical fibroxanthoma of the skin. Report of ten cases. Am J Clin Pathol 1969, **51**: 487–492.

388 Kuwano H, Hashimoto H, Enjoji M. Atypical fibroxanthoma distinguishable from spindle cell carcinoma in sarcoma-like skin lesions. A clinicopathologic and immunohistochemical study of 21 cases. Cancer 1985, **55**: 172–180.

389 Kyriakos M, Kempson RL. Inflammatory fibrous histiocytoma. An aggressive and lethal lesion. Cancer 1976, **37**: 1584–1606.

390 Lagacé R. The ultrastructural spectrum of malignant fibrous histiocytoma. Ultrastruct Pathol 1987, **11**: 153–159.

391 Lagacé R, Delage C, Seemayer TA. Myxoid variant of malignant fibrous histiocytoma. Ultrastructural observations. Cancer 1979, **43**: 526–534.

392 Lane KL, Shannon RH, Weiss SW. Hyalinizing spindle cell tumor with giant rosettes: a distinctive tumor closely resembling low-grade fibromyxoid sarcoma. Am J Surg Pathol 1998, **21**: 1481–1488.

393 Lattes R. Malignant fibrous histiocytoma. A review article. Am J Surg Pathol 1982, **6**: 761–771.

394 Lautier R, Wolff HH, Jones RE. An immunohistochemical study of dermatofibrosarcoma protuberans supports its fibroblastic character and contradicts neuroectodermal or histiocytic components. Am J Dermatopathol 1990, **12**: 25–30.

395 Lawson CW, Fisher C, Gatter KC. An immunohistochemical study of differentiation in malignant fibrous histiocytoma. Histopathology 1987, **11**: 375–383.

395a Linn SC, West RB, Pollack JR, Zhu S, Hernandez-Boussard T, Nielsen TO, Rubin BP, Patel R, Goldblum JR, Siegmund D, Botstein D, Brown PO, Gilks BC, van de Rijn M. Gene expression patterns and gene copy number changes in dermatofibrosarcoma protuberans. Am J Pathol 2003, **163**: 2383–2395.

396 Litzky LA, Brooks JJ. Cytokeratin immunoreactivity in malignant fibrous histiocytoma and spindle cell tumors.

Comparison between frozen and paraffin-embedded tissues. Mod Pathol 1992, **5**: 30–34.

396a Mansoor A, White CR. Myxofibrosarcoma presenting in the skin: clinicopathological features and differential diagnosis with cutaneous myxoid neoplasms. Am J Dermatopathol 2003, **25**: 281–286.

397 Marshall-Taylor C, Fanburg-Smith JC. Hemosiderotic fibrohistiocytic lipomatous lesion: ten cases of a previously undescribed fatty lesion of foot/ankle. Mod Pathol 2001, **13**: 1192–1199.

398 McKee PH, Fletcher CD. Dermatofibrosarcoma protuberans presenting in infancy and childhood. J Cutan Pathol 1991, **18**: 241–246.

399 Meis-Kindblom JM, Kindblom LG. Acral myxoinflammatory fibroblastic sarcoma: a low-grade tumor of the hands and feet. Am J Surg Pathol 1998, **22**: 911–924.

400 Meister P, Höhne N, Konrad E, Eder M. Fibrous histiocytoma. An analysis of the storiform pattern. Virchows Arch [A] 1979, **383**: 31–41.

401 Meister P, Konrad E, Höhne N. Incidence and histological structure of the storiform pattern in benign and malignant fibrous histiocytomas. Virchows Arch [A] 1981, **393**: 93–101.

402 Meister P, Konrad E, Krauss F. Fibrous histiocytoma. A histological and statistical analysis of 155 cases. Pathol Res Pract 1978, **162**: 361–379.

403 Meister P, Konrad EA, Nothrath W, Eder M. Malignant fibrous histiocytoma. Histological patterns and cell types. Pathol Res Pract 1980, **168**: 193–212.

404 Mentzel T, Beham A, Katenkamp D, Dei Tos AP, Fletcher CD. Fibrosarcomatous ("high-grade") dermatofibrosarcoma protuberans: clinicopathologic and immunohistochemical study of a series of 41 cases with emphasis on prognostic significance. Am J Surg Pathol 1998, **22**: 576–587.

405 Mentzel T, Calonje E, Wadden C, Camplejohn RS, Beham A, Smith MA, Fletcher CD. Myxofibrosarcoma: a clinicopathologic analysis of 75 cases with emphasis on the low-grade variant. Am J Surg Pathol 1996, **20**: 391–405.

406 Michal M, Fanburg-Smith JC. Plexiform xanthomatous tumor: a report of 20 cases in 12 patients. Am J Surg Pathol 2002, **26**: 1302–1311.

407 Miettinen M, Lehto V-P, Badley RA, Virtanen I. Expression of intermediate filaments in soft tissue sarcomas. Int J Cancer 1982, **30**: 541–546.

408 Miettinen M, Soini Y. Malignant fibrous histiocytoma. Heterogeneous patterns of intermediate filament proteins by immunohistochemistry. Arch Pathol Lab Med 1989, **113**: 1363–1366.

409 Montgomery EA, Devaney KO, Giordano TJ, Weiss SW. Inflammatory myxohyaline tumor of distal extremities with virocyte or Reed–Sternberg-like cells: a distinctive lesion with features simulating inflammatory condition, Hodgkin's disease and various sarcomas. Mod Pathol 1998, **11**: 384–391.

410 Nakamura T, Ogata H, Katsuyama T. Pigmented dermatofibrosarcoma protuberans. Report of two cases as a variant of dermatofibrosarcoma protuberans with partial neural differentiation. Am J Dermatopathol 1987, **9**: 18–25.

411 Nakanishi S, Hizawa K. Enzyme histochemical observation of fibrohistiocytic tumors. Acta Pathol Jpn 1984, **34**: 1003–1016.

412 Nemes Z, Thomazy V. Factor XIIIa and the classic histiocytic makers in malignant fibrous histiocytoma. A comparative immunohistochemical study. Hum Pathol 1988, **19**: 822–829.

413 Niemi KM. The benign fibrohistiocytic tumours of the skin. Acta Derm Venereol (Stockh) 1970, **50**(Suppl 63): 1–66.

414 O'Brien JE, Stout AP. Malignant fibrous xanthomas. Cancer 1964, **17**: 1445–1455.

415 Oberling C. Retroperitoneal xanthogranuloma. Am J Cancer 1935, **23**: 477–489.

416 O'Connell JX, Trotter MJ. Fibrosarcomatous dermatofibrosarcoma protuberans with myofibroblastic differentiation: a histologically distinct variant. Mod Pathol 1996, **9:** 273–278.

416a Oda Y, Takahira T, Kawaguchi K, Yamamoto H, Tamiya S, Matsuda S, Tanaka K, Kinukawa N, Iwamoto Y, Tsuneyoshi M. Altered expression of cell cycle regulators in myxofibrosarcoma, with special emphasis on their prognostic implications. Hum Pathol 2003, **34:** 1035–1042.

417 O'Dowd J, Laidler P. Progression of dermatofibrosarcoma protuberans to malignant fibrous histiocytoma. Report of a case with implications for tumor histogenesis. Hum Pathol 1988, **19:** 368–370.

418 O'Sullivan MJ, Sirgi KE, Dehner LP. Low-grade fibrosarcoma (hyalinizing spindle cell tumor with giant rosettes) with pulmonary metastases at presentation: case report and review of the literature. Int J Surg Pathol 2002, **10:** 211–216.

419 Ozzello L, Hamels J. The histiocytic nature of dermatofibrosarcoma protuberans–tissue culture and electron microscopic study. Am J Clin Pathol 1976, **65:** 136–148.

420 Ozzello L, Stout AP, Murray MR. Cultural characteristics of malignant histiocytoma and fibrous xanthomas. Cancer 1963, **16:** 331–344.

421 Papadimitriou JC, Drachenberg CB, Brenner DS, Newkirk C, Trump BF, Silverberg SG. "Thanatosomes": a unifying morphogenetic concept for tumor hyaline globules related to apoptosis. Hum Pathol 2001, **31:** 1455–1465.

422 Pettinato G, Manivel JC, De Rosa G, Petrella G, Jaszcz W. Angiomatoid malignant fibrous histiocytoma. Cytologic, immunohistochemical, ultrastructural, and flow cytometric study of 20 cases. Mod Pathol 1990, **3:** 479–487.

423 Pezzi CM, Rawlings MS Jr, Esgro JJ, Pollock RE, Romsdahl MM. Prognostic factors in 227 patients with malignant fibrous histiocytoma. Cancer 1992, **69:** 2098–2103.

424 Pinkston JA, Sekine I. Postirradiation sarcoma (malignant fibrous histiocytoma) following cervix cancer. Cancer 1982, **49:** 434–438.

425 Rachmaninoff N, McDonald JR, Cook JC. Sarcoma-like tumors of the skin following irradiation. Am J Clin Pathol 1961, **36:** 427–437.

426 Raney RB, Allen A, O'Neill J, Handler SD, Uri A, Littman P. Malignant fibrous histiocytoma of soft tissue in childhood. Cancer 1986, **57:** 2198–2201.

427 Reed R. Histiocytes, fibrocytes, and facultative transformations. Am J Dermatopathol 1982, **4:** 253–262.

428 Reid MB, Gray C, Fear JD, Bird CC. Immunohistological demonstration of factors XIIIA and XIIIS in reactive and neoplastic fibroblastic and fibro-histiocytic lesions. Histopathology 1986, **10:** 1171–1178.

428a Reid R, De Silva C, Patterson L, Ryan E, Fisher C. Low-grade fibromyxoid sarcoma and hyalinizing spindle cell tumor with giant rosettes share a common t(7;16)(q34;p11) translocation. Am J Surg Pathol 2003, **27:** 1229–1236.

429 Remstein ED, Arndt CA, Nascimento AG. Plexiform fibrohistiocytic tumor: clinicopathologic analysis of 22 cases. Am J Surg Pathol 1999, **23:** 662–670.

430 Roholl PJ, Kleyne J, Van Unnik JAM. Characterization of tumor cells in malignant fibrous histiocytomas and other soft-tissue tumors, in comparison with malignant histiocytes. II. Immunoperoxidase study on cryostat sections. Am J Pathol 1985, **121:** 269–274.

431 Roholl PJ, Prinsen I, Rademakers LP, Hsu SM, van Unnik JA. Two cell lines with epithelial cell-like characteristics established from malignant fibrous histiocytomas. Cancer 1991, **68:** 1963–1972.

432 Rooser B, Willen H, Gustafson P, Alvegard TA, Rydholm A. Malignant fibrous histiocytoma of soft tissue. A population-based epidemiologic and prognostic study of 137 patients. Cancer 1991, **67:** 499–505.

433 Rosenberg AE, O'Connell JX, Dickersin GR, Bhan AK. Expression of epithelial markers in malignant fibrous histiocytoma of the musculoskeletal system. An immunohistochemical and electron microscopic study. Hum Pathol 1993, **24:** 284–293.

434 Rydholm A, Syk I. Malignant fibrous histiocytoma of soft tissue. Correlation between clinical variables and histologic malignancy grade. Cancer 1986, **57:** 2323–2324.

435 Sakaki M, Hirokawa M, Wakatsuki S, Sano T, Endo K, Fujii Y, Ikeda T, Kawaguchi S, Hirose T, Hasegawa T. Acral myxoinflammatory fibroblastic sarcoma: a report of five cases and review of the literature. Virchows Arch 2003, **442:** 25–30.

435a Sandberg AA, Bridge JA. Updates on the cytogenetics and molecular genetics of bone soft tissue tumors. Dermatofibrosarcoma protuberans and giant cell fibroblastoma. Cancer Genet Cytogenet 2003, **140:** 1–12.

436 Santa Cruz DJ, Kyriakos M. Aneurysmal ("angiomatoid") fibrous histiocytoma of the skin. Cancer 1981, **47:** 2053–2061.

437 Smith ME, Costa MJ, Weiss SW. Evaluation of CD68 and other histiocytic antigens in angiomatoid malignant fibrous histiocytoma. Am J Surg Pathol 1991, **15:** 757–763.

438 Soini Y, Miettinen M. Alpha-1-antitrypsin and lysozyme. Their limited significance in fibrohistiocytic tumors. Am J Clin Pathol 1989, **91:** 515–521.

439 Soule EH, Enriquez P. Atypical fibrous histiocytoma, malignant fibrous histiocytoma, malignant histiocytoma and epithelioid sarcoma. A comparative study of 65 tumors. Cancer 1972, **30:** 128–143.

440 Sun C-CJ, Toker C, Breitenecker R. An ultrastructural study of angiomatoid fibrous histiocytoma. Cancer 1982, **49:** 2103–2111.

441 Tamada S, Ackerman AB. Dermatofibroma with monster cells. Am J Dermatopathol 1987, **9:** 380–387.

442 Taylor HB, Helwig EB. Dermatofibrosarcoma protuberans. A study of 115 cases. Cancer 1962, **15:** 717–725.

443 Tavy JB, Battifora H. Malignant fibrous histiocytoma. An electron microscopic study. Cancer 1977, **40:** 254–267.

444 Terrier-Lacombe MJ, Guillou L, Maire G, Terrier P, Vince DR, De Saint Aubain Somerhausen N, Collin F, Pedeutour F, Coindre JM. Dermatofibrosarcoma protuberans, giant cell fibroblastoma, and hybrid lesions in children: clinicopathologic comparative analysis of 28 cases with molecular data – a study from the French Federation of Cancer Centres Sarcoma Group. Am J Surg Pathol 2002, **27:** 27–39.

445 Tracy T Jr, Neifield JP, DeMay RM, Salzberg AM. Malignant fibrous histiocytomas in children. J Pediatr Surg 1984, **19:** 81–83.

446 Tralka TS, Yee C, Triche TJ, Costa J. Unusual intranuclear inclusions in malignant fibrous histiocytoma. Presence in primary tumor, metastases, and xenografts. Ultrastruct Pathol 1982, **3:** 161–167.

447 Tsuneyoshi M, Enjoji M, Shinohara N. Malignant fibrous histiocytoma. An electron microscopic study of 17 cases. Virchows Arch [A] 1981, **392:** 135–145.

448 Tsuneyoshi M, Hashimoto H, Enjoji M. Myxoid malignant fibrous histiocytoma versus myxoid liposarcoma. A comparative ultrastructural study. Virchows Arch [A] 1983, **400:** 187–199.

449 Ushijima M, Hashimoto H, Tsuneyoshi M, Enjoji M. Giant cell tumor of the tendon sheath (nodular tenosynovitis). A study of 207 cases to compare the large joint group with the common digit group. Cancer 1986, **57:** 875–884.

450 Vernon-Roberts B. The macrophage. Cambridge, 1972, Cambridge University Press.

451 Vilanova JR, Burgos-Bretones J, Simon R, Rivera-Pomar JM. Leukaemoid reaction and eosinophilia in "inflammatory fibrous histiocytoma." Virchows Arch [A] 1980, **388:** 237–243.

452 Volpe E, Carbone A. Dermatofibrosarcoma protuberans metastatic to lymph nodes and showing a dominant histiocytic component. Am J Dermatopathol 1983, **5**: 327–334.

453 Weiss SW. Malignant fibrous histiocytoma. A reaffirmation. Am J Surg Pathol 1982, **6**: 773–784.

454 Weiss SW, Enzinger FM. Malignant fibrous histiocytoma. An analysis of 200 cases. Cancer 1978, **41**: 2250–2266.

455 Weiss SW, Enzinger FM. Myxoid variant of malignant fibrous histiocytoma. Cancer 1977, **39**: 1672–1685.

456 Weiss SW, Enzinger FM, Johnson FB. Silica reaction simulating fibrous histiocytoma. Cancer 1978, **42**: 2738–2743.

457 Wood GS, Beckstead JH, Turner RR, Hendrickson MR, Kempson RL, Warnke RA. Malignant fibrous histiocytoma tumor cells resemble fibroblasts. Am J Surg Pathol 1986, **10**: 323–335.

458 Wrotnowski U, Cooper PH, Shmookler BM. Fibrosarcomatous change in dermatofibrosarcoma protuberans. Am J Surg Pathol 1988, **12**: 287–293.

Tumors and tumorlike conditions of peripheral nerves

Neuroma

459 Albrecht S, Kahn HJ, From L. Palisaded encapsulated neuroma. An immunohistochemical study. Mod Pathol 1989, **2**: 403–406.

460 Argenyi ZB. Immunohistochemical characterization of palisaded, encapsulated neuroma. J Cutan Pathol 1990, **17**: 329–335.

461 Dakin MC, Leppard B, Theaker JM. The palisaded, encapsulated neuroma (solitary circumscribed neuroma). Histopathology 1992, **20**: 405–410.

462 Ha'Eri GB, Fornasier VL, Schatzker J. Morton's neuroma pathogenesis and ultrastructure. Clin Orthop 1979, **141**: 256–259.

463 Kaiserling E, Xiao JC, Ruck P, Horny HP. Aberrant expression of macrophage-associated antigens (CD68 and Ki-M1P) by Schwann cells in reactive and neoplastic neural tissue. Light- and electron-microscopic findings. Mod Pathol 1993, **6**: 463–468.

464 Reed RJ, Bliss BO. Morton's neuroma. Regressive and productive inter metatarsal elastofibrositis. Arch Pathol 1973, **95**: 123–129.

465 Scotti TM. The lesion of Morton's metatarsalgia (Morton's toe). Arch Pathol 1957, **63**: 91–102.

Schwannoma (neurilemoma)

466 Brooks JJ, Draffen RM. Benign glandular schwannoma. Arch Pathol Lab Med 1992, **116**: 192–195.

467 Carney JA. Psammomatous melanotic schwannoma. A distinctive, heritable tumor with special associations, including cardiac myxoma and the Cushing syndrome. Am J Surg Pathol 1990, **14**: 206–222.

468 Carpenter PM, Grafe MR, Varki NM. Granular cells in a cellular neurilemoma. Arch Pathol Lab Med 1992, **116**: 1083–1085.

469 Casadei GP, Scheithauer BW, Hirose T, Manfrini M, Van Houton C, Wood MB. Cellular schwannoma. A clinicopathologic, DNA flow cytometric, and proliferation marker study of 70 patients. Cancer 1995, **75**: 1109–1119.

470 Clark HB, Minesky JJ, Agrawal D, Agrawal HC. Myelin basic protein and P2 protein are not immunohistochemical markers for Schwann cell neoplasms. A comparative study using antisera to S-100, P2, and myelin basic proteins. Am J Pathol 1985, **121**: 96–101.

471 Connolly CE. "Crystalline" collagen production by an unusual benign soft tissue tumour ("amianthioma"). Histopathology 1981, **5**: 11–20.

472 Dahl I, Hagmar B, Idvall I. Benign solitary neurilemmoma (schwannoma). A correlative cytological and histological study of 28 cases. Acta Pathol Microbiol Immunol Scand (A) 1984, **92**: 91–101.

473 Dei Tos AP, Doglioni C, Laurino L, Fletcher CD. KP1 (CD68) expression in benign neural tumours. Further evidence of its low specificity as a histiocytic/myeloid marker. Histopathology 1993, **23**: 185–187.

474 Dickersin GR. The electron microscopic spectrum of nerve sheath tumors. Ultrastruct Pathol 1987, **11**: 103–146.

475 Fisher C, Chappell ME, Weiss SW. Neuroblastoma-like epithelioid schwannoma. Histopathology 1995, **26**: 193–194.

476 Fisher ER, Vuzevski VD. Cytogenesis of schwannoma (neurilemoma), neurofibroma, dermatofibroma and dermatofibrosarcoma as revealed by electron microscopy. Am J Clin Pathol 1968, **49**: 141–154.

477 Fletcher CD. Peripheral nerve sheath tumors. A clinicopathologic update. Pathol Annu 1990, **25**(Pt 1): 53–74.

478 Fletcher CDM, Davies SE. Benign plexiform (multinodular) schwannoma. A rare tumour unassociated with neurofibromatosis. Histopathology 1986, **10**: 971–980.

479 Fletcher CDM, Davies SE, McKee PH. Cellular schwannoma. A distinct pseudosarcomatous entity. Histopathology 1987, **11**: 21–35.

480 Font RL, Truong LD. Melanotic schwannoma of soft tissues. Electron-microscopic observations and review of literature. Am J Surg Pathol 1984, **8**: 129–138.

481 Franks AJ. Epithelioid neurilemmoma of the trigeminal nerve. An immunohistochemical and ultrastructural study. Histopathology 1985, **9**: 1339–1350.

482 Gay RE, Gay S, Jones RE Jr. Histological and immunohistological identification of collagens in basement membranes of Schwann cells of neurofibromas. Am J Dermatopathol 1983, **5**: 317–325.

483 Goldblum JR, Beals TF, Weiss SW. Neuroblastoma-like neurilemoma. Am J Surg Pathol 1994, **18**: 266–273.

484 Goto S, Matsukado Y, Mihara Y, Inoue N, Miyamoto E. An immunocytochemical demonstration of calcineurin in human nerve cell tumors. A comparison with neuron-specific enolase and glial fibrillary acidic protein. Cancer 1987, **60**: 2948–2957.

485 Gould VE, Moll R, Moll I, Lee I, Schwechheimer K, Franke WW. The intermediate filament complement of the spectrum of nerve sheath neoplasms. Lab Invest 1986, **55**: 463–474.

486 Gown AM, Thompson SJ, Bothwell M. Monoclonal antibody to nerve growth factor receptor. A new marker for nerve sheath tumors (abstract). Lab Invest 1988, **58**: 35A.

487 Hanada M, Tanaka T, Kanayama S, Takami M, Kimura M. Malignant transformation of intrathoracic ancient neurilemoma in a patient without von Recklinghausen's disease. Acta Pathol Jpn 1982, **32**: 527–536.

488 Hirano A, Dembitzer HM, Zimmerman HM. Fenestrated blood vessels in neurilemoma. Lab Invest 1972, **27**: 305–309.

489 Hwang WS, Benediktsson H. Lamellar bodies in benign and malignant schwannomas. Acta Pathol Microbiol Immunol Scand (A) 1982, **90**: 89–93.

490 Johnson MD, Glick AD, Davis BW. Immuno-histochemical evaluation of Leu7, myelin basic protein, S100-protein glial-fibrillary acidic-protein, and LN3 immunoreactivity in nerve sheath tumors and sarcomas. Arch Pathol Lab Med 1988, **112**: 155–160.

491 Johnson MD, Kamso-Pratt J, Pepinsky RB, Whetsell WO Jr. Lipocortin-I immunoreactivity in central and peripheral nervous system glial tumors. Hum Pathol 1989, **20**: 772–776.

492 Kahn HJ, Marks A, Thom H, Baumal R. Role of antibody to S 100 protein in diagnostic pathology. Am J Clin Pathol 1983, **79**: 341–347.

493 Kao GF, Laskin WB, Olsen TG. Solitary cutaneous plexiform neurilemmoma (schwannoma). A clinicopathologic, immunohistochemical, and ultrastructural study of 11 cases. Mod Pathol 1989, **2**: 20–26.

494 Kawahara E, Oda Y, Ooi A, Katsuda S, Nakanishi I, Umeda S. Expression of glial fibrillary acidic protein (GFAP) in peripheral nerve sheath tumors. A comparative study of immunoreactivity of GFAP, vimentin, S-100 protein, and neurofilament in 38 schwannomas and 18 neurofibromas. Am J Surg Pathol 1988, **12**: 115–120.

495 Kindblom LG, Meis-Kindblom JM, Havel G, Busch C. Benign epithelioid schwannoma. Am J Surg Pathol 1998, **22**: 762–770.

496 Leivo I, Engvall E, Laurila P, Miettinen M. Distribution of merosin, a laminin-related tissue-specific basement membrane protein, in human Schwann cell neoplasms. Lab Invest 1989, **61**: 426–432.

497 Lin BT, Weiss LM, Medeiros LJ. Neurofibroma and cellular neurofibroma with atypia: a report of 14 tumors. Am J Surg Pathol 1997, **21**: 1443–1449.

498 Memoli VA, Brown EF, Gould VE. Glial fibrillary acidic protein (GFAP). Immunoreactivity in peripheral nerve sheath tumors. Ultrastruct Pathol 1984, **7**: 269–275.

499 Mennemeyer RP, Hammar SP, Tytus JS, Hallman KO, Raisis JE, Bockus D. Melanotic schwannoma. Clinical and ultrastructural studies of three cases with evidence of intracellular melanin synthesis. Am J Surg Pathol 1979, **3**: 3–10.

500 Miettinen M. Melanotic schwannoma coexpression of vimentin and glial fibrillary acidic protein. Ultrastruct Pathol 1987, **11**: 39–46.

501 Miettinen M, Foidart J-M, Ekblom P. Immunohistochemical demonstration of laminin, the major glycoprotein of basement membranes, as an aid in the diagnosis of soft tissue tumors. Am J Clin Pathol 1983, **79**: 306–311.

502 Oberman HA, Sullenger G. Neurogenous tumors of the head and neck. Cancer 1967, **20**: 1992–2001.

503 Oda Y, Hashimoto H, Tsuneyoshi M, Iwata Y. Benign glandular peripheral nerve sheath tumor. Pathol Res Pract 1994, **190**: 466–473.

504 Ogawa K, Oguchi M, Yamabe H, Nakashima Y, Hamashima Y. Distribution of collagen type IV in soft tissue tumors. An immunohistochemical study. Cancer 1986, **58**: 269–277.

505 Orenstein JM. Amianthoid fibers in a synovial sarcoma and a malignant schwannoma. Ultrastruct Pathol 1983, **4**: 163–176.

506 Skelton HG III, Smith KJ, Lupton GP. Collagenous spherulosis in a schwannoma. Am J Dermatopathol 1994, **16**: 549–553.

507 Szpak CA, Shelburne J, Linder J, Klintworth GK. The presence of stage II melanosomes (premelanosomes) in neoplasms other than melanomas. Mod Pathol 1988, **1**: 35–43.

508 Taxy JB, Battifora H. Epithelioid schwannoma. Diagnosis by electron microscopy. Ultrastruct Pathol 1981, **2**: 19–24.

509 Waggener JD. Ultrastructure of benign peripheral nerve sheath tumors. Cancer 1966, **19**: 699–709.

510 White W, Shiu MH, Rosenblum MK, Erlandson RA, Woodruff JM. Cellular schwannoma. A clinicopathologic study of 57 patients and 58 tumors. Cancer 1990, **66**: 1266–1275.

511 Woodruff JM, Godwin TA, Erlandson RA, Susin M, Martini N. Cellular schwannoma. A variety of schwannoma sometimes mistaken for a malignant tumor. Am J Surg Pathol 1981, **5**: 733–744.

512 Yousem SA, Colby TV, Urich H. Malignant epithelioid schwannoma arising in a benign schwannoma. A case report. Cancer 1985, **55**: 2799–2803.

Neurofibroma

513 Azzopardi JG, Eusebi V, Tison V, Betts C. Neurofibroma with rhabdomyomatous differentiation. Benign "triton" tumour of the vagina. Histopathology 1983, **7**: 561–572.

514 Barker D, Wright E, Nguyen K, Cannon L, Fain P, Goldgar D, Bishop DT, Carey J, Baty B, Kivlin J, Willard H, Waye JS, Greig G, Leinwand L, Nakamura Y, O'Connell P, Leppert M, Lalouel J-M, White R, Skolnick M. Gene for von Recklinghausen neurofibromatosis is in the pericentromeric region of chromosome 17. Science 1987, **236**: 1100–1102.

515 Basu TN, Gutmann DH, Fletcher JA, Glover TW, Collins FS, Downward J. Aberrant regulation of *ras* proteins in malignant tumour cells from type I neurofibromatosis patients. Nature 1992, **356**: 713–715.

516 Bednár B. Storiform neurofibromas of skin, pigmented and nonpigmented. Cancer 1957, **10**: 368–376.

517 Benedict PH, Szabó G, Fitzpatrick TB, Sinesi SJ. Melanotic macules in Albright's syndrome and in neurofibromatosis. JAMA 1968, **205**: 618–626.

518 Bird CC, Willis RA. The histogenesis of pigmented neurofibromas. J Pathol 1969, **97**: 631–637.

519 Blatt J, Jaffe R, Deutsch M, Adkins JC. Neurofibromatosis and childhood tumors. Cancer 1986, **57**: 1225–1229.

520 Bolande RP, Towler WF. A possible relationship of neuroblastoma to von Recklinghausen's disease. Cancer 1970, **26**: 162–172.

520a Campbell LK, Thomas JR, Lamps LW, Smoller BR, Folpe AL. Protein gene product 9.5 (PGP 9.5) is not a specific marker of neural and nerve sheath tumors; an immunohistochemical study of 95 mesenchymal neoplasms. Mod Pathol 2003, **16**: 963–969.

521 Chanoki M, Ishii M, Fukai K, Kobayashi H, Hamada T, Muragaki Y, Ooshima A. Immunohistochemical localization of type I, III, IV, V, and VI collagens and laminin in neurofibroma and neurofibrosarcoma. Am J Dermatopathol 1991, **13**: 365–373.

522 Crowe FW, Schull WJ, Neel JV. Multiple neurofibromatosis. Springfield, Ill, 1956, Charles C Thomas, Publisher.

523 De Clue JE, Cohen BD, Lowy DR. Identification and characterization of the neurofibromatosis type I protein product. Proc Natl Acad Sci U S A 1991, **88**: 9914–9918.

524 Fetsch JF, Michal M, Miettinen M. Pigmented (melanotic) neurofibroma: a clinicopathologic and immunohistochemical analysis of 19 lesions from 17 patients. Am J Surg Pathol 2000, **24**: 331–343.

525 Finkel G, Lane B. Granular cell variant of neurofibromatosis. Ultrastructure of benign and malignant tumors. Hum Pathol 1982, **13**: 959–963.

526 Fletcher CD, Theaker JM. Digital pacinian neuroma. A distinctive hyperplastic lesion. Histopathology 1989, **15**: 249–256.

527 Fountain JW, Wallace MR, Bruce MA, Seizinger BR, Menon AG, Gusella JF, Michels VV, Schmidt MA, Dewald GW, Collins FS. Physical mapping of a translocation breakpoint in neurofibromatosis. Science 1989, **244**: 1085–1087.

528 Fuller CE, Williams GT. Gastrointestinal manifestations of type I neurofibromatosis (von Recklinghausen's disease). Histopathology 1991, **19**: 1–11.

529 Goerg C, Goerg K, Pflueger KH, Havemann K. Neurofibromatosis and acute monocytic leukemia in adults. Cancer 1989, **64**: 1717–1719.

530 Gutmann DH, Wood DL, Collins FS. Identification of the neurofibromatosis type I gene product. Proc Natl Acad Sci U S A 1991, **88**: 9658–9662.

531 Hermonen J, Hirvonen O, Ylä-Outinen H, Lakkakorpi J, Björkstrand A-S, Laurikainen L, Kallionen M, Oikarinen A, Peltonen S, Peltonen J. Neurofibromin. Expression by normal human keratinocytes *in vivo* and *in vitro* and in epidermal malignancies. Lab Invest 1995, **73**: 221–228.

532 Hill RP. Neuroma of Wagner-Meissner tactile corpuscles. Cancer 1951, **4**: 879–882.

533 Holt JF. Neurofibromatosis in children. Am J Roentgenol 1978, **130**: 651–658.

534 Hosoi K. Multiple neurofibromatosis (von Recklinghausen's disease), with special reference to malignant transformation. Arch Surg 1931, **22**: 258–281.

615 Ducatman BS, Scheithauer BW. Postirradiation neurofibrosarcoma. Cancer 1983, **51**: 1028–1033.

616 Ducatman BS, Scheithauer BW. Malignant peripheral nerve sheath tumors with divergent differentiation. Cancer 1984, **54**: 1049–1057.

617 Ducatman BS, Scheithauer BW, Piepgras DG, Reiman HM, Ilstrup DM. Malignant peripheral nerve sheath tumors. Cancer 1986, **57**: 2006–2021.

618 Fisher C, Carter RL, Ramachandra S, Thomas DM. Peripheral nerve sheath differentiation in malignant soft tissue tumours. An ultrastructural and immunohistochemical study. Histopathology 1992, **20**: 115–125.

619 Fletcher CD, Fernando IN, Braimbridge MV, McKee PH, Lyall JR. Malignant nerve sheath tumour arising in a ganglioneuroma. Histopathology 1988, **12**: 445–448.

620 George E, Swanson PE, Wick MR. Malignant peripheral nerve sheath tumors of the skin. Am J Dermatopathol 1989, **11**: 213–221.

621 Ghali VS, Gold JE, Vincent RA, Cosgrove JM. Malignant peripheral nerve sheath tumor arising spontaneously from retroperitoneal ganglioneuroma. A case report, review of the literature, and immunohistochemical study. Hum Pathol 1992, **23**: 72–75.

622 Ghosh BC, Ghosh L, Huvos AG, Fortner JG. Malignant schwannoma. A clinicopathologic study. Cancer 1973, **31**: 184–190.

623 Gore I. Primary malignant tumors of nerve. A report of eight cases. Cancer 1952, **5**: 278–296.

624 Gray MH, Rosenberg AE, Dickersin GR, Bhan AK. Glial fibrillary acidic protein and keratin expression by benign and malignant nerve sheath tumors. Hum Pathol 1989, **20**: 1089–1096.

625 Guccion JG, Enzinger FM. Malignant schwannoma associated with von Reck-linghausen's neurofibromatosis. Virchows Arch [A] 1979, **383**: 43–57.

626 Herrera GA, Pinto de Moraes H. Neurogenic sarcomas in patients with neurofibromatosis (von Recklinghausen's disease). Light, electron microscopy and immunohistochemistry study. Virchows Arch [A] 1984, **403**: 361–376.

627 Herrera GA, Reimann BE, Salinas JA. Malignant schwannomas presenting as malignant fibrous histiocytomas. Ultrastruct Pathol 1982, **3**: 253–261.

628 Hirose T, Hasegawa T, Kudo E, Seki K, Sano T, Hizawa K. Malignant peripheral nerve sheath tumors. An immunohistochemical study in relation to ultra structural features. Hum Pathol 1992, **23**: 865–870.

629 Hirose T, Sano T, Hizawa K. Heterogeneity of malignant schwannomas. Ultrastruct Pathol 1988, **12**: 107–116.

630 Hirose T, Scheithauer BW, Sano T. Perineurial malignant peripheral nerve sheath tumor (MPNST): a clinicopathologic, immunohistochemical, and ultrastructural study of seven cases. Am J Surg Pathol 1998, **22**: 1368–1378.

631 Hruban RH, Shiu MH, Senie RT, Woodruff JM. Malignant peripheral nerve sheath tumors of the buttock and lower extremity. A study of 43 cases. Cancer 1990, **66**: 1253–1265.

632 Johnson TL, Lee MW, Meis JM, Zarbo RJ, Crissman JD. Immunohistochemical characterization of malignant peripheral nerve sheath tumors. Surg Pathol 1994, **4**: 121–135.

633 King R, Busam K, Rosai J. Metastatic malignant melanoma resembling malignant peripheral nerve sheath tumor: report of 16 cases. Am J Surg Pathol 1999, **23**: 1499–1505.

634 Krausz T, Azzopardi JG, Pearse E. Malignant melanoma of the sympathetic chain. With a consideration of pigmented nerve sheath tumours. Histopathology 1984, **8**: 881–894.

635 Laskin WB, Weiss SW, Bratthauer GL. Epithelioid variant of malignant peripheral nerve sheath tumour (malignant epithelioid schwannoma). Am J Surg Pathol 1991, **15**: 1136–1145.

636 Lattes R. Peripheral neuroepithelioma. Proceedings of the 39th Annual Anatomic Pathology Slide Seminar of the American Society of Clinical Pathologists. Chicago, 1975, American Society of Clinical Pathology, pp. 49–52.

637 Mackay B, Luna MA, Butler JJ. Adult neuroblastoma. Electron microscopic observations in nine cases. Cancer 1976, **37**: 1334–1351.

638 Matsunou H, Shimoda T, Kakimoto S, Yamashita H, Ishikawa E, Mukai M. Histopathologic and immunohistochemical study of malignant tumors of peripheral nerve sheath (malignant schwannoma). Cancer 1985, **56**: 2269–2279.

639 McMenamin ME, Fletcher CD. Expanding the spectrum of malignant change in schwannomas: epithelioid malignant change, epithelioid malignant peripheral nerve sheath tumor, and epithelioid angiosarcoma: a study of 17 cases. Am J Surg Pathol 2000, **25**: 13–25.

640 Meis JM, Enzinger FM, Martz KL, Neal JA. Malignant peripheral nerve sheath tumors (malignant schwannomas) in children. Am J Surg Pathol 1992, **16**: 694–707.

641 Meis-Kindblom JM, Enzinger FM. Plexiform malignant peripheral nerve sheath tumor of infancy and childhood. Am J Surg Pathol 1994, **18**: 479–485.

642 Menon AG, Anderson KM, Riccardi VM, Chung RY, Whaley JM, Yandell DW, Farmer GE, Freiman RN, Lee JK, Li FP, et al. Chromosome 17p deletions and p53 gene mutations associated with the formation of malignant neurofibrosarcomas in von Recklinghausen neurofibromatosis. Proc Natl Acad Sci U S A 1990, **87**: 5435–5439.

643 Millstein DI, Tang C-K, Campbell EW Jr. Angiosarcoma developing in a patient with neurofibromatosis (von Recklinghausen's disease). Cancer 1981, **47**: 950–954.

644 Morgan KG, Gray C. Malignant epithelioid schwannoma of superficial soft tissue? A case report with immunohistology and electron microscopy. Histopathology 1985, **9**: 765–775.

645 Morphopoulos GD, Banrjee SS, Ali HH, Stewart M, Vasudev KS, Eyden BTP, Harris M. Malignant peripheral nerve sheath tumour with vascular differentiation: a report of four cases. Histopathology 1997, **28**: 401–410.

646 Newbould MJ, Wilkinson N, Mene A. Post-radiation malignant peripheral nerve sheath tumour. A report of two cases. Histopathology 1990, **17**: 263–265.

647 Raney B, Schnaufer L, Ziegler M, Chatten J, Littman P, Jarrett P. Treatment of children with neurogenic sarcoma. Experience at the Children's Hospital of Philadelphia, 1958–1984. Cancer 1987, **59**: 1–5.

648 Rasbridge SA, Browse NL, Tighe JR, Fletcher CD. Malignant nerve sheath tumour arising in a benign ancient schwannoma. Histopathology 1989, **14**: 525–528.

649 Ricci A Jr, Parham DM, Woodruff JM, Callihan T, Green A, Erlandson RA. Malignant peripheral nerve sheath tumors arising from ganglioneuromas. Am J Surg Pathol 1984, **8**: 19–29.

650 Robson DK, Ironside JW. Malignant peripheral nerve sheath tumour arising in a schwannoma. Histopathology 1990, **16**: 295–297.

651 Rose DS, Wilkins MJ, Birch R, Evans DJ. Malignant peripheral nerve sheath tumour with rhabdomyoblastic and glandular differentiation. Immunohistochemical features. Histopathology 1992, **21**: 287–290.

652 Shimizu S, Teraki Y, Ishiko A, Shimizu H, Harada T, Mukai M, Nishikawa T. Malignant epithelioid schwannoma of the skin showing partial HMB-45 positivity. Am J Dermatopathol 1993, **15**: 378–384.

653 Storm FK, Eilber FR, Mirra J, Morton DL. Neurofibrosarcoma. Cancer 1980, **45**: 126–129.

654 Stout AP. Discussion of case 5, Seventeenth Seminar of the American Society of Clinical Pathologists, Chicago, III, October, 1951.

655 Suster S, Amazon K, Rosen LB, Ollague JM. Malignant epithelioid schwannoma of the skin. A low-grade neurotropic malignant melanoma? Am J Dermatopathol 1989, **11**: 338–344.

656 Tamborini E, Agus V, Perrone F, Papini D, Romano R, Pasini B, Gronchi A, Colecchia M, Rosai J, Pierotti MA, Pilotti S. Lack of SYT-SSX fusion transcripts in malignant peripheral nerve sheath tumors on RT-PCR analysis of 34 archival cases. Lab Invest 2002, **82**: 609–618.

657 Taxy JB, Battifora H, Trujillo Y, Dorfman HD. Electron microscopy in the diagnosis of malignant schwannoma. Cancer 1981, **48**: 1381–1391.

658 Thomas JE, Piepgras DG, Scheithauer B, Onofrio BM, Shives TC. Neurogenic tumors of the sciatic nerve. Mayo Clin Proc 1983, **58**: 640–647.

659 Trojanowski JQ, Kleinman GM, Proppe KH. Malignant tumors of nerve sheath origin. Cancer 1980, **46**: 1202–1212.

660 Tsuneyoshi M, Enjoji M. Primary malignant peripheral nerve tumors (malignant schwannomas). A clinicopathologic and electron microscopic study. Acta Pathol Jpn 1979, **29**: 363–375.

661 Uri AK, Witzelben CL, Raney RB. Electron microscopy of glandular schwannoma. Cancer 1984, **53**: 493–497.

662 Wanebo JE, Malik JM, Vanden Berg SR, Wanebo HJ, Driesen N, Persing JA. Malignant peripheral nerve sheath tumors. A clinicopathologic study of 28 cases. Cancer 1993, **71**: 1247–1253.

663 Weiss SW, Langloss JM, Enzinger FM. Value of S-100 protein in the diagnosis of soft tissue tumors with particular reference to benign and malignant Schwann cell tumors. Lab Invest 1983, **49**: 299–308.

664 White HR Jr. Survival in malignant schwannoma. An 18-year study. Cancer 1971, **27**: 720–729.

665 Wick MR, Swanson PE, Scheithauer BW, Manivel JC. Malignant peripheral nerve sheath tumor. An immunohistochemical study of 62 cases. Am J Clin Pathol 1987, **87**: 425–433.

666 Woodruff JM. Peripheral nerve tumors showing glandular differentiation (glandular schwannomas). Cancer 1976, **37**: 2399–2413.

667 Woodruff JM, Chevnik NL, Smith MC, Millett WB, Foote FW. Peripheral nerve tumors with rhabdomyosarcomatous differentiation (malignant "triton" tumors). Cancer 1973, **32**: 426–439.

668 Woodruff JM, Christensen WN. Glandular peripheral nerve sheath tumors. Cancer 1993, **72**: 3618–3628.

669 Woodruff JM, Selig AM, Crowley K, Allen PW. Schwannoma (neurilemoma) with malignant transformation. A rare, distinctive peripheral nerve tumor. Am J Surg Pathol 1994, **18**: 882–895.

669a Woodruff JM, Scheithauer BW, Kurtkaya-Yapicier Ö, Raffel C, Amr SS, LaQuaglia MP, Antonescu CR. Congenital and childhood plexiform (multinodular) cellular schwannoma. A troublesome mimic of malignant peripheral nerve sheath tumor. Am J Surg Pathol 2003, **27**: 1321–1329.

669b Zhou H, Coffin CM, Perkins SL, Tripp SR, Liew M, Viskochil DH. Malignant peripheral nerve sheath tumor. A comparison of grade, immunophenotype, and cell cycle/growth. Activation marker expression in sporadic and neurofibromatosis 1-related lesions. Am J Surg Pathol 2003, **27**: 1337–1345.

Other tumors of peripheral nerves

670 Eusebi V, Bondi A, Cancellieri A, Canedi L, Frizzera G. Primary malignant lymphoma of sciatic nerve. Report of a case. Am J Surg Pathol 1990, **14**: 881–885.

671 Misdraji J, Ino Y, Louis DN, Rosenberg AE, Chiocca EA, Harris NL. Primary lymphoma of peripheral nerve: report of four cases. Am J Surg Pathol 2000, **24**: 1257–1265.

672 Radi MJ, Foucar E, Palmer CH, Gooding RA. Malignant lymphoma arising in a large congenital neurofibroma of the head and neck. Report of a case. Cancer 1988, **61**: 1667–1673.

672a Silverman TA, Enzinger FM. Fibrolipomatous hamartoma of nerve; a clinico-pathologic analysis of 26 cases. Am J Surg Pathol 1985, **9**: 7–14.

673 Vigna PA, Kusior MF, Collins MB, Ross JS. Peripheral nerve hemangioma. Potential for clinical aggressiveness. Arch Pathol Lab Med 1994, **118**: 1038–1041.

Tumors of adipose tissue

Lipoma

674 Azzopardi JG, Iocco J, Salm R. Pleomorphic lipoma. A tumour simulating liposarcoma. Histopathology 1983, **7**: 511–523.

675 Bolen JW, Thorning D. Spindle cell lipoma. A clinical, light- and electron-microscopic study. Am J Surg Pathol 1981, **5**: 435–441.

676 Dixon AY, McGregor DH, Lee SH. Angiolipomas. An ultrastructural and clinicopathological study. Hum Pathol 1981, **12**: 739–747.

677 Enzi G. Multiple symmetric lipomatosis. An updated clinical report. Medicine (Baltimore) 1984, **63**: 56–64.

678 Enzinger FM. Benign lipomatous tumors simulating a sarcoma. In M.D. Anderson Tumor Institute. Management of primary bone and soft tissue tumors. Chicago, 1977, Year Book Medical Publishers, pp. 11–24.

679 Enzinger FM, Harvey DA. Spindle cell lipoma. Cancer 1975, **36**: 1852–1859.

680 Fletcher CD, Akerman M, Dal Cin P, De Wever I, Mandahl N, Mertens F, Mitelman F, Rosai J, Rydholm A, Sciot R, Tallini G, Van Der Berghe H, Van de Ven W, Vanni R, Willen H. Correlation between clinicopathologic features and karyotype in lipomatous tumors. A report of 178 cases from the chromosomes and morphology (CHAMP) collaborative study group. Am J Pathol 1996, **148**: 623–630.

681 Fletcher CD, Martin-Bates E. Intramuscular and intermuscular lipoma: Neglected diagnoses. Histopathology 1988, **12**: 275–287.

682 Fletcher CD, Akerman M, Dal Cin P, De Wever I, Mandahl N, Mertens F, Mitelman F, Rosai J, Rydholm A, Sciot R, Tallini G, Van den Berghe H, Van de Ven W, Vanni R, Willen H. Correlation between clinicopathologic features and karyotype in lipomatous tumors. A report of 178 cases from the chromosomes and morphology (CHAMP) collaborative study group. Am J Pathol (in press).

683 Fletcher CDM, Martin-Bates E. Spindle cell lipoma. A clinicopathological study with some original observations. Histopathology 1987, **11**: 803–817.

684 Greenberg SD, Isensee C, Gonzalez-Angulo A, Wallace SA. Infiltrating lipomas of the thigh. Am J Clin Pathol 1963, **39**: 66–72.

685 Hawley IC, Krausz T, Evans DJ, Fletcher CD. Spindle cell lipoma – a pseudoangiomatous variant. Histopathology 1994, **24**: 565–569.

686 Heim S, Mandahl N, Rydholm A, Willen H, Mitelman F. Different karyotypic features characterize different clinico-pathologic subgroups of benign lipogenic tumors. Int J Cancer 1988, **42**: 863–867.

687 Howard WR, Helwig EB. Angiolipoma. Arch Dermatol 1960, **82**: 924–931.

688 Hunt SJ, Santa Cruz DJ, Barr RJ. Cellular angiolipoma. Am J Surg Pathol 1990, **14**: 75–81.

689 Katzer B. Histopathology of rare chondroosteoblastic metaplasis in benign lipomas. Pathol Res Pract 1989, **184**: 437–445.

690 Kin YH, Reiner L. Ultrastructure of lipoma. Cancer 1982, **50**: 102–106.

691 Kindblom L-G, Angervall L, Stener B, Wickbom I. Intermuscular and intramuscular lipomas and hibernomas. A clinical, roentgenologic, histologic, and prognostic study of 46 cases. Cancer 1974, **33**: 754–762.

692 Kindblom L-G, Meis-Kindblom JM. Chondroid lipoma. An

ultrastructural and immunohistochemical analysis with further observations regarding its differentiation. Hum Pathol 1995, **26:** 706–715.

693 Lovell-Badge R. Living with bad architecture. Nature 1995, **376:** 725–726.

694 Mandahl N, Heim S, Arheden K, Rydholm A, Willen H, Mitelman F. Three major cytogenetic subgroups can be identified among chromosomally abnormal solitary lipomas. Hum Genet 1988, **79:** 203–208.

695 Meis JM, Enzinger FM. Myolipoma of soft tissue. Am J Surg Pathol 1991, **15:** 121–125.

696 Meis JM, Enzinger FM. Chondroid lipoma. A unique tumor simulating liposarcoma and myxoid chondrosarcoma. Am J Surg Pathol 1993, **17:** 1103–1112.

697 Paarlberg D, Linscheid RL, Soule EH. Lipomas of the hand. Including a case of lipoblastomatosis in a child. Mayo Clin Proc 1972, **47:** 121–124.

698 Pack GT, Pierson JC. Liposarcoma. Surgery 1954, **36:** 687–712.

699 Popper H, Knipping G. A histochemical and biochemical study of a liposarcoma with several aspects on the development of fat synthesis. Pathol Res Pract 1981, **171:** 373–380.

700 Robb JA, Jones RA. Spindle cell lipoma in a perianal location. Hum Pathol 1982, **13:** 1052.

701 Rubin BP, Dal Cin P. The genetics of lipomatous tumors. Semin Diagn Pathol 2001, **18:** 286–293.

702 Sciot R, Akerman M, Dal Cin P, De Wever I, Fletcher CD, Mandahl N, Mertens F, Mitelman F, Rosai J, Rydholm A, Tallini F, Van den Berghe H, Vanni R, Willen H. Cytogenetic analysis of subcutaneous angiolipoma: further evidence supporting its difference from ordinary pure lipomas: a report of the CHAMP Study Group. Am J Surg Pathol 1997, **21:** 441–444.

703 Shmookler BM, Enzinger FM. Pleomorphic lipoma. A benign tumor simulating liposarcoma. A clinicopathologic analysis of 48 cases. Cancer 1981, **47:** 126–133.

704 Solvonuk PF, Taylor GP, Hancock R, Wood WS, Frohlich J. Correlation of morphologic and biochemical observations in human lipomas. Lab Invest 1984, **51:** 469–474.

Lipoblastoma/lipoblastomasis

705 Bolen JW, Thorning D. Benign lipoblastoma and myxoid liposarcoma. A comparative light- and electron-microscopic study. Am J Surg Pathol 1980, **4:** 163–174.

706 Chung EB, Enzinger FM. Benign lipoblastomatosis. An analysis of 35 cases. Cancer 1973, **32:** 482–492.

707 Coffin CM. Lipoblastoma. An embryonal tumor of soft tissue related to organogenesis. Semin Diagn Pathol 1994, **11:** 98–103.

708 Collins MH, Chatten J. Lipoblastoma/lipoblastomatosis: a clinicopathologic study of 25 tumors. Am J Surg Pathol 1997, **21:** 1131–1137.

709 Fletcher CD, Akerman M, Dal Cin P, De Wever I, Mandahl N, Mertens F, Mitelman F, Rosai J, Rydholm A, Sciot R, Tallini G, Van Der Berghe H, Van de Ven W, Vanni R, Willen H. Correlation between clinicopathologic features and karyotype in lipomatous tumors. A report of 178 cases from the chromosomes and morphology (CHAMP) collaborative study group. Am J Pathol 1996, **148:** 623–630.

710 Greco AMA, Garcia RL, Vuletin JC. Benign lipoblastomatosis. Ultrastructure and histogenesis. Cancer 1980, **45:** 511–515.

711 Mentzel T, Calonje E, Fletcher CD. Lipoblastoma and lipoblastomatosis. A clinicopathological study of 14 cases. Histopathology 1993, **23:** 527–533.

712 Rubin BP, Dal Cin P. The genetics of lipomatous tumors. Semin Diagn Pathol 2001, **18:** 286–293.

713 Vellios F, Baez MF, Schumacher HB. Lipoblastomatosis. A tumor of fetal fat different from hibernoma. Am J Pathol 1958, **34:** 1149–1155.

Hibernoma

714 Allegra SR, Gmuer C, O'Leary GP Jr. Endocrine activity in a large hibernoma. Hum Pathol 1983, **14:** 1044–1052.

715 Brines OA, Johnson MH. Hibernoma, a special fatty tumor. Report of a case. Am J Pathol 1949, **25:** 467–479.

716 Fletcher CD, Akerman M, Dal Cin P, De Wever I, Mandahl N, Mertens F, Mitelman F, Rosai J, Rydholm A, Sciot R, Tallini G, Van Der Berghe H, Van de Ven W, Vanni R, Willen H. Correlation between clinicopathologic features and karyotype in lipomatous tumors. A report of 178 cases from the chromosomes and morphology (CHAMP) collaborative study group. Am J Pathol 1996, **148:** 623–630.

717 Furlong MA, Fanburg-Smith JC, Miettinen M. The morphologic spectrum of hibernoma: a clinicopathologic study of 170 cases. Am J Surg Pathol 2001, **25:** 809–814.

718 Gaffney EF, Hargreaves HK, Semple E, Vellios F. Hibernoma. Distinctive light and electron microscopic features and relationship to brown adipose tissue. Hum Pathol 1983, **14:** 677–687.

719 Levine GD. Hibernoma. An electron microscopic study. Hum Pathol 1972, **3:** 351–359.

720 Rigor VU, Goldstone SE, Jones J, Bernstein R, Gold MS, Weiner S. Hibernoma. A case report and discussion of a rare tumor. Cancer 1986, **57:** 2207–2211.

721 Ross SR, Choy L, Graves RA, Fox N, Solevjeva V, Klaus S, Ricquier D, Spiegelman BM. Hibernoma formation in transgenic mice and isolation of a brown adipocyte cell line expressing the uncoupling protein gene. Proc Natl Acad Sci U S A 1992, **89:** 7561–7565.

722 Rubin BP, Dal Cin P. The genetics of lipomatous tumors. Semin Diagn Pathol 2001, **18:** 286–293.

723 Seemayer TA, Knaack J, Wang N, Ahmed MN. On the ultrastructure of hibernoma. Cancer 1975, **36:** 1785–1793.

Liposarcoma (including atypical lipomatous tumor)

724 Ackerman LV. Multiple primary liposarcomas. Am J Pathol 1944, **20:** 789–798.

725 Adachi T, Oda Y, Sakamoto A, Saito T, Tamiya S, Masuda K, Tsuneyoshi M. Immunoreactivity of p53, mdm2, and p21^WAF1 in dedifferentiated liposarcoma: special emphasis on the distinct immunophenotype of the well-differentiated component. Int J Surg Pathol 2001, **9:** 99–109.

726 Aman P, Ron D, Mandahl N, Fioretos T, Heim S, Arheden K, Willen H, Rydholm A, Mitelman F. Rearrangement of the transcription factor gene CHOP in myxoid liposarcomas with t(12: 16)(q13; p11). Genes Chromosom Cancer 1992, **5:** 278–285.

727 Antonescu CR, Elahi A, Humphrey M, Lui MY, Healey JH, Brennan MF, Woodruff JM, Jhanwar SC, Ladanyi M. Specificity of TLS-CHOP rearrangement for classic myxoid/round cell liposarcoma: absence in predominantly myxoid well-differentiated liposarcomas. J Mol Diagn 2001, **2:** 132–138.

728 Argani P, Facchetti F, Inghirami G, Rosai J. Lymphocyte-rich well-differentiated liposarcoma: report of nine cases. Am J Surg Pathol 1997, **21:** 884–895.

729 Azumi N, Curtis J, Kempson RL, Hendrickson MR. Atypical and malignant neoplasms showing lipomatous differentiation. A study of 111 cases. Am J Surg Pathol 1987, **11:** 161–183.

729a Barbashina V, Singer S, Antonescu CR. Dedifferentiated liposarcoma of the extremities. (Abstract) Mod Pathol 2003, **16:** 9A.

730 Battifora H, Nunez-Alonso C. Myxoid liposarcoma. Study of 10 cases. Ultrastruct Pathol 1980, **1:** 157–169.

731 Bayer-Garner I, Morgan M, Smoller BR. Caveolin expression is common among benign and malignant smooth muscle and adipocyte neoplasms. Mod Pathol 2002, **15:** 1–5.

732 Bolen JW, Thorning D. Liposarcomas. A histogenetic approach to the classification of adipose tissue neoplasms. Am J Surg Pathol 1984, **8:** 3–17.

733 Brooks JJ, Connor AM. Atypical lipoma of the extremities and peripheral soft tissues with dedifferentiation. Implications for management. Surg Pathol 1990, 3: 169–178.

734 Castleberry RP, Kelly DR, Wilson ER, Cain WS, Salter MR. Childhood liposarcoma. Report of a case and review of the literature. Cancer 1984, 54: 579–584.

735 Chang HR, Hajdu SI, Collin C, Brennan MF. The prognostic value of histologic subtypes in primary extremity liposarcoma. Cancer 1989, 64: 1514–1520.

736 Chung EB. Pitfalls in diagnosing benign soft tissue tumors in infancy and childhood. Pathol Annu 1985, 20(Pt 2): 323–386.

737 Cocchia D, Lauriola L, Stolfi VM, Tallini G, Michetti F. S-100 antigen labels neoplastic cells in liposarcoma and cartilaginous tumours. Virchows Arch [A] 1983, 402: 139–145.

737a Coindre JM, Pelmus M, Chibon F, Mariani O, Hostein I, Aurias A. Immunohistochemistry for Mdm2 and cdk4 in soft tissue sarcomas: analysis of a series of 322 cases and comparison to comparative genomic hybridization analysis. (Abstract) Mod Pathol 2003, 16: 10A.

738 Crozat A, Aman P, Mandahl N, Ron D. Fusion of CHOP to a novel RNA-binding protein in human myxoid liposarcoma. Nature 1993, 363: 640–644.

738a Dahl PR, Zalla MJ, Winkelmann RK. Localized involutional lipoatrophy: a clinicopathologic study of 16 patients. J Am Acad Dermatol 1996, 35: 523–528.

739 Dei Tos AP, Seregard S, Calonje E, Chan JK, Fletcher CD. Giant cell angiofibroma. A distinctive orbital tumor in adults. Am J Surg Pathol 1995, 19: 1286–1293.

740 Downes KA, Goldblum JR, Montgomery EA, Fisher C. Pleomorphic liposarcoma: a clinicopathologic analysis of 19 cases. Mod Pathol 2001, 14: 179–184.

741 Enterline HT, Culberson JD, Rochlin DB, Brady LW. Liposarcoma. A clinical and pathological study of 53 cases. Cancer 1960, 13: 932–950.

742 Enzinger FM, Winslow DJ. Liposarcoma. A study of 103 cases. Virchows Arch [A] 1962, 335: 367–388.

743 Evans HL. Liposarcoma. A study of 55 cases with a reassessment of its classification. Am J Surg Pathol 1979, 3: 507–523.

744 Evans HL. Liposarcomas and atypical lipomatous tumors. A study of 66 cases followed for a minimum of 10 years. Surg Pathol 1988, 1. 41–54.

745 Evans HL. Smooth muscle in atypical lipomatous tumors. A report of three cases. Am J Surg Pathol 1990, 14: 714–718.

746 Evans HL, Khurana KK, Kemp BL, Ayala AG. Heterologous elements in the dedifferentiated component of dedifferentiated liposarcoma. Am J Surg Pathol 1994, 18: 1150–1157.

747 Evans HL, Soule EH, Winkelmann RK. Atypical lipoma, atypical intramuscular lipoma, and well-differentiated retroperitoneal liposarcoma. A reappraisal of 30 cases formerly classified as well differentiated liposarcoma. Cancer 1979, 43: 574–584.

748 Fanburg-Smith JC, Miettinen M. Liposarcoma with meningothelial-like whorls: a study of 17 cases of a distinctive histological pattern associated with dedifferentiated liposarcoma. Histopathology 1999, 33: 414–424.

749 Fletcher CDM, Akerman M, Dal Cin P, De Wever I, Mandahl N, Mertens F, Mitelman F, Rosai J, Rydholm A, Sciot R, Tallini G, Van den Berghe H, Van de Ven W, Vanni R, Willen H. Correlation between clinicopathologic features and karyotype in lipomatous tumors. A report of 178 cases from the chromosomes and morphology (CHAMP) collaborative study group. Am J Pathol (in press).

750 Folpe AL, Weiss SW. Lipoleiomyosarcoma (well-differentiated liposarcoma with leiomyosarcomatous differentiation): a clinicopathologic study of nine cases including one with dedifferentiation. Am J Surg Pathol 2002, 26: 742–749.

751 Gebhard S, Coindre JM, Michels JM, Terrier P, Bertrand F, Trassard M, Taylor S, Chateau MC, Marques B, Picot V, Guillou L. Pleomorphic liposarcoma: clinicopathologic, immunohistochemical, and follow-up analysis of 63 cases: a study from the French Federation of Cancer Centers Sarcoma Group. Am J Surg Pathol 2002, 26: 601–616.

752 Georgiades DE, Alcalais CB, Karabela VG. Multicentric well-differentiated liposarcomas. A case report and a brief review of the literature. Cancer 1969, 24: 1091–1097.

753 Gibas Z, Miettinen M, Limon J, Nedoszytko B, Mrozek K, Roszkiewicz A, Rys J, Niezabitowski A, Debiec-Rychter M. Cytogenetic and immunohistochemical profile of myxoid liposarcoma. Am J Clin Pathol 1995, 103: 20–26.

754 Goldblum JR, Frank TS, Poy EL, Weiss SW. p53 mutations and tumor progression in well-differentiated liposarcoma and dermatofibrosarcoma protuberans. Int J Surg Pathol 1995, 3: 35–42.

755 Hashimoto H, Daimaru Y, Enjoji M. S-100 protein distribution in liposarcoma. An immunoperoxidase study with special reference to the distinction of liposarcoma from myxoid malignant fibrous histiocytoma. Virchows Arch [A] 1984, 405: 1–10.

756 Hashimoto H, Daimaru Y, Tsuneyoshi M, Enjoji M. Soft tissue sarcoma with additional anaplastic components. A clinicopathologic and immunohistochemical study of 27 cases. Cancer 1990, 66: 1578–1589.

757 Hashimoto H, Enjoji M. Liposarcoma. A clinicopathologic subtyping of 52 cases. Acta Pathol Jpn 1990, 32: 933–948.

758 Henricks WH, Chu YC, Goldblum JR, Weiss SW. Dedifferentiated liposarcoma: a clinicopathological analysis of 155 cases with a proposal for an expanded definition of dedifferentiation. Am J Surg Pathol 1997, 21: 271–281.

759 Huang HY, Antonescu CR. Epithelioid variant of pleomorphic liposarcoma: a comparative immunohistochemical and ultrastructural analysis of six cases with emphasis on overlapping features with epithelial malignancies. Ultrastruct Pathol 2002, 26: 299–308.

760 Kauffman SL, Stout AP. Lipoblastic tumors of children. Cancer 1959, 12: 912–923.

761 Kilpatrick SE, Doyon J, Choong PF, Sim FH, Nascimento AG. The clinicopathologic spectrum of myxoid and round cell liposarcoma: a study of 95 cases. Cancer 1996, 77: 1450–1458.

762 Kindblom L-G, Angervall L, Fassina AS. Atypical lipoma. Acta Pathol Microbiol Immunol Scand (A) 1982, 90: 27–36.

763 Kindblom L-G, Save-Soderbergh J. The ultrastructure of liposarcoma. A study of 10 cases. Acta Pathol Microbiol Scand (A) 1979, 87: 109–121.

764 Kraus MD, Guillou L, Fletcher CD. Well-differentiated inflammatory liposarcoma: an uncommon and easily overlooked variant of a common sarcoma. Am J Surg Pathol 1997, 21: 518–527.

765 Lagacé R, Jacob S, Seemayer TA. Myxoid liposarcoma. An electron microscopic study. Biological and histogenetic considerations. Virchows Arch [A] 1979, 384: 159–172.

766 La Quaglia MP, Spiro SA, Ghavimi F, Hajdu SI, Meyers P, Exelby PR. Liposarcoma in patients younger than or equal to 22 years of age. Cancer 1993, 72: 3114–3119.

767 Lucas DR, Nascimento AG, Sanjay BK, Rock MG. Well-differentiated liposarcoma. The Mayo Clinic experience with 58 cases. Am J Clin Pathol 1994, 102: 677–683.

768 McCormick D, Mentzel T, Beham A, Fletcher CD. Dedifferentiated liposarcoma. Clinicopathologic analysis of 32 cases suggesting a better prognostic subgroup among pleomorphic sarcomas. Am J Surg Pathol 1994, 18: 1213–1223.

769 Mentzel T, Fletcher CD. Dedifferentiated myxoid liposarcoma: a clinicopathological study suggesting a closer relationship

between myxoid and well-differentiated liposarcoma. Histopathology 1997, **30:** 457–463.

770 Miettinen M, Enzinger FM. Epithelioid variant of pleomorphic liposarcoma: a study of 12 cases of a distinctive variant of high-grade liposarcoma. Mod Pathol 1999, **12:** 722–728.

771 Nascimento AG, Kurtin PJ, Guillou L, Fletcher CD. Dedifferentiated liposarcoma: a report of nine cases with a peculiar neuralike whorling pattern associated with metaplastic bone formation. Am J Surg Pathol 1998, **22:** 945–955.

772 Oliveira AM, Nascimento AG. Pleomorphic liposarcoma. Semin Diagn Pathol 2001, **18:** 274–285.

773 Oliveira AM, Nascimento AG, Lloyd RV. Leptin and leptin receptor mRNA are widely expressed in tumors of adipocytic differentiation. Mod Pathol 2001, **14:** 549–555.

773a Panoussopoulos D, Theodoropoulos G, Lazaris AC, Papadimitriou K. Focal divergent chondrosarcomatous differentiation in a primary pleomorphic liposarcoma and expression of transforming growth factor β. Report of a case and review of the literature. Int J Surg Pathol 2004, **12:** 79–85.

774 Reitan JB, Kaalhus O, Brennhovd IO, Sager EM, Stenwig AE, Talle K. Prognostic factors in liposarcoma. Cancer 1985, **55:** 2482–2490.

775 Reszel PA, Soule EH, Coventry MB. Liposarcoma of extremities and limb girdles. Study of 222 cases. J Bone Joint Surg (Am) 1966, **48:** 229–244.

775a Rosai J, Akerman M, Dal Cin P, DeWever I, Fletcher CDM, Mandahl M, Mertens F, Mitelman F, Rydholm A, Sciot R, Tallini G, Van Den Berghe H, Van DeVen W, Vanni R, Willen H. Combined morphologic and karyotypic study of 59 atypical lipomatous tumors: evaluation of their relationship and differential diagnosis with other adipose tissue tumors. Am J Surg Pathol 1996, **20:** 1182–1189.

776 Rossouw DJ, Cinti S, Dickersin GR. Liposarcoma. An ultrastructural study of 15 cases. Am J Clin Pathol 1986, **85:** 649–667.

777 Schmookler BM, Enzinger FM. Liposarcoma occurring in children. An analysis of 17 cases and review of the literature. Cancer 1983, **52:** 567–574.

778 Siebert JD, Williams RP, Pulitzer DR. Myxoid liposarcoma with cartilaginous differentiation. Mod Pathol 1996, **9:** 249–252.

779 Smith TA, Easley KA, Goldblum JR. Myxoid/round cell liposarcoma of the extremities: a clinicopathologic study of 29 cases with particular attention to extent of round cell liposarcoma. Am J Surg Pathol 1996, **20:** 171–180.

780 Snover DC, Sumner HW, Dehner LP. Variability of histologic pattern in recurrent soft tissue sarcomas originally diagnosed as liposarcoma. Cancer 1982, **49:** 1005–1015.

781 Sreekantaiah C, Karakousis CP, Leong SP, Sandberg AA. Cytogenetic findings in liposarcoma correlate with histopathologic subtypes. Cancer 1992, **69:** 2484–2495.

782 Stout AP. Liposarcoma. The malignant tumor of lipoblasts. Ann Surg 1944, **119:** 86–197.

783 Tallini G, Akerman M, Dal Cin P, De Wever I, Fletcher CD, Mandahl N, Mertens F, Mitelman F, Rosai J, Rydholm A, Sciot R, Van Den Berghe H, Van Den Ven W, Vanni R, Willen H. Combined morphologic and karyotypic study of 28 myxoid liposarcomas: implications for a revised morphologic typing. A report of the CHAMP study group. Am J Surg Pathol 1996, **20:** 1047–1055.

784 Tallini G, Erlandson RA, Brennan MF, Woodruff JM. Divergent myosarcomatous differentiation in retroperitoneal liposarcoma. Am J Surg Pathol 1993, **17:** 546–556.

785 Walaas L, Kindblom L-G. Lipomatous tumors. A correlative cytologic and histologic study of 27 tumors examined by fine needle aspiration cytology. Hum Pathol 1985, **16:** 6–18.

786 Weiss SW, Rao VK. Well-differentiated liposarcoma (atypical lipoma) of deep soft tissue of the extremities, retroperitoneum, and miscellaneous sites. A follow-up study of 92 cases with analysis of the incidence of "dedifferentiation." Am J Surg Pathol 1992, **16:** 1051–1058.

787 Winslow DJ, Enzinger FM. Hyaluronidase-sensitive acid mucopolysaccharides in liposarcomas. Am J Pathol 1960, **37:** 497–505.

Tumors and tumorlike conditions of blood and lymph vessels

Hemangioma

788 Albrecht S, Kahn HJ. Immunohistochemistry of intravascular papillary endothelial hyperplasia. J Cutan Pathol 1990, **17:** 16–21.

789 Allen PW, Enzinger FM. Hemangioma of skeletal muscle. An analysis of 89 cases. Cancer 1972, **29:** 8–22.

790 Beham A, Fletcher CD. Intramuscular angioma. A clinicopathological analysis of 74 cases. Histopathology 1991, **18:** 53–59.

791 Calonje E, Fletcher CD. Sinusoidal hemangioma. A distinctive benign vascular neoplasm within the group of cavernous hemangiomas. Am J Surg Pathol 1991, **15:** 1130–1135.

792 Calonje E, Mentzel T, Fletcher CD. Pseudomalignant perineurial invasion in cellular ("infantile") capillary haemangiomas. Histopathology 1995, **26:** 159–164.

793 Clearkin KP, Enzinger FM. Intravascular papillary endothelial hyperplasia. Arch Pathol Lab Med 1976, **100:** 441–444.

794 Coffin CM, Dehner LP. Vascular tumors in children and adolescents. A clinicopathologic study of 228 tumors in 222 patients. Pathol Annu 1993, **28(Pt 1):** 97–120.

795 Dabashi Y, Eisen RN. Infantile hemangioendothelioma of the pelvis associated with Kasabach–Merritt syndrome. Pediatr Pathol 1990, **10:** 407–415.

796 Dethlefsen SM, Mulliken JB, Glowacki J. An ultrastructural study of mast cell interactions in hemangiomas. Ultrastruct Pathol 1986, **10:** 175–183.

797 Fanburg JC, Meis-Kindblom JM, Rosenberg AE. Multiple enchondromas associated with spindle cell hemangioendotheliomas. An overlooked variant of Maffucci's syndrome. Am J Surg Pathol 1995, **19:** 1029–1038.

798 Finn MC, Glowacki J, Mulliken JB. Congenital vascular lesions. Clinical application of a new classification. J Pediatr Surg 1983, **18:** 894–900.

799 Fletcher CD, Beham A, Schmid C. Spindle cell haemangioendothelioma. A clinicopathological and immunohistochemical study indicative of a non-neoplastic lesion. Histopathology 1991, **18:** 291–301.

800 Fukunaga M, Ushigome S, Ishikawa E. Kaposiform haemangioendothelioma associated with Kasabach–Merritt syndrome. Histopathology 1997, **28:** 281–284.

801 Fukunaga M, Ushigome S, Nikaido T, Ishikawa E, Nakamori K. Spindle cell hemangioendothelioma. An immunohistochemical and flow cytometric study of six cases. Pathol Int 1995, **45:** 589–595.

802 Gonzalez-Crussi F, Reyes-Mugica M. Cellular hemangiomas ("hemangioendotheliomas") in infants. Light microscopic, immunohistochemical, and ultrastructural observations. Am J Surg Pathol 1991, **15:** 769–778.

803 Guillou L, Calonje E, Speight P, Rosai J, Fletcher CD. Hobnail hemangioma: a pseudomalignant vascular lesion with a reappraisal of targetoid hemosiderotic hemangioma. Am J Surg Pathol 1999, **23:** 97–105.

804 Hashimoto H, Daimaru Y, Enjoji M. Intravascular papillary endothelial hyperplasia. A clinicopathologic study of 91 cases. Am J Dermatopathol 1983, **5:** 539–546.

805 Imayama S, Murakamai Y, Hashimoto H, Hori Y. Spindle cell hemangioendothelioma exhibits the ultrastructural features of reactive vascular proliferation rather than of angiosarcoma. Am J Clin Pathol 1992, **97:** 279–287.

806 Koblenzer PJ, Bukowski MJ. Angiomatosis (hamartomatous hem-lymphangiomatosis). Report of a case with diffuse involvement. Pediatrics 1961, **28**: 65–76.

807 Kojimahara M, Baba Y, Nakajima T. Ultrastructural study of hemangiomas. Acta Pathol Jpn 1987, **37**: 605–609.

808 Koutlas IG, Jessurun J. Arteriovenous hemangioma. A clinicopathological and immunohistochemical study. J Cutan Pathol 1994, **21**: 343–349.

809 Kuo T-T, Sayers CP, Rosai J. Masson's "vegetant intravascular hemangioen-dothelioma." A lesion often mistaken for angiosarcoma. Study of seventeen cases located in the skin and soft tissues. Cancer 1976, **38**: 1227–1236.

810 Lie JT. Pathology of angiodysplasia in Klippel-Trenaunay syndrome. Pathol Res Pract 1988, **183**: 747–755.

811 Lindenauer SM. The Klippel-Trenaunay syndrome. Varicosity, hypertrophy and hemangioma with no arteriovenous fistula. Ann Surg 1965, **162**: 303–314.

812 Lister WA. The natural history of strawberry nevi. Lancet 1938, **1**: 1429–1434.

812a Lyons LL, North PE, Stoler MH, Folpe AL, Weiss SW. Kaposiform hemangioendothelioma is histologically, immunohistocemically and biologically distinct from common (juvenile) hemangioma(JH): a bi-institutional analysis of 33 cases. (Abstract) Mod Pathol 2003, **16**: 16A–17A.

813 Mentzel T, Massoleni G, Dei Tos AP, Fletcher CD. Kaposiform hemangioendothelioma in adults. Clinicopathologic and immunohistochemical analysis of three cases. Am J Clin Pathol 1997, **108**: 450–455.

814 Modlin JJ. Capillary hemangiomas of the skin. Surgery 1955, **38**: 169–180.

815 Mulliken JB, Young AE. Vascular birthmarks. Hemangiomas and malformations. Philadelphia, 1988, W.B. Saunders.

815a Perkins P, Weiss SW. Spindle cell hemangioendothelioma: an analysis of 78 cases with reassessment of its pathogenesis and biologic behavior. Am J Surg Pathol 1996, **20**: 1196–1204.

816 Perrone T. Vessel-nerve intermingling in benign infantile hemangioendothelioma. Hum Pathol 1985, **16**: 198–200.

817 Pins MR, Rosenthal DI, Springfield DS, Rosenberg AE. Florid extravascular papillary endothelial hyperplasia (Masson's pseudoangiosarcoma) presenting as a soft-tissue sarcoma. Arch Pathol Lab Med 1993, **117**: 259–263.

818 Rao VK, Weiss SW. Angiomatosis of soft tissue. An analysis of the histologic features and clinical outcome in 51 cases. Am J Surg Pathol 1992, **16**: 764–771.

819 Salyer WR, Salyer DC. Intravascular angiomatosis. Development and distinction from angiosarcoma. Cancer 1975, **36**: 995–1004.

820 Scott GA, Rosai J. Spindle cell hemangioendothelioma. Report of seven additional cases of a recently described vascular neoplasm. Am J Dermatopathol 1988, **10**: 281–288.

821 Shim WKT. Hemangiomas of infancy complicated by thrombocytopenia. Am J Surg 1968, **116**: 896–906.

822 Smoller BR, Apfelberg DB. Infantile (juvenile) capillary hemangioma. A tumor of heterogeneous cellular elements. J Cutan Pathol 1993, **20**: 330–336.

823 Taxy JB, Gray SR. Cellular angiomas of infancy. An ultrastructural study of two cases. Cancer 1979, **43**: 2322–2331.

824 Tsang WY, Chan JK. Kaposi-like infantile hemangioendothelioma. A distinctive vascular neoplasm of the retroperitoneum. Am J Surg Pathol 1991, **15**: 982–989.

825 Tsang WY, Chan JK, Fletcher CD. Recently characterized vascular tumours of skin and soft tissues. Histopathology 1991, **19**: 489–501.

826 Weinblatt ME, Kahn E, Kochen JA. Hemangioendothelioma with intravascular coagulation and ischemic colitis. Cancer 1984, **54**: 2300–2304.

827 Weiss SW. Pedal hemangioma (venous malformation) occurring in Turner's syndrome. An additional manifestation of the syndrome. Hum Pathol 1988, **19**: 1015–1018.

828 Weiss SW, Enzinger FM. Spindle cell hemangioendothelioma. A low-grade angiosarcoma resembling a cavernous hemangioma and Kaposi's sarcoma. Am J Surg Pathol 1986, **10**: 521–530.

829 Yasunga C, Sueishi K, Ohgami H, Suita S, Kawanami T. Heterogenous expression of endothelial cell markers in infantile hemangioendothelioma. Immunohistochemical study of two solitary cases and one multiple one. Am J Clin Pathol 1989, **91**: 673–681.

830 Zukerberg LR, Nickoloff BJ, Weiss SW. Kaposiform hemangioendothelioma of infancy and childhood. An aggressive neoplasm associated with Kasabach–Merritt syndrome and lymphangiomatosis. Am J Surg Pathol 1993, **17**: 321–328.

Glomus tumor

831 Aiba M, Hirayama A, Kuramochi S. Glomangiosarcoma in a glomus tumor. An immunohistochemical and ultrastructural study. Cancer 1988, **61**: 1467–1471.

832 Albrecht S, Zbieranowski I. Incidental glomus coccygeum. When a normal structure looks like a tumor. Am J Surg Pathol 1990, **14**: 922–924.

833 Bell RS, Goodman SB, Fornasier VL. Coccygeal glomus tumors. A case of mistaken identity? J Bone Joint Surg (Am) 1982, **64**: 595–597.

834 Calonje E, Fletcher CDM. Cutaneous intraneural glomus tumor. Am J Dermatopathol 1995, **17**: 395–398.

835 Carroll RE, Berman AT. Glomus tumors of the hand. Review of the literature and report of 28 cases. J Bone Joint Surg (Am) 1972, **54**: 691–703.

836 Dervan PA, Tobbia IN, Casey M, O'Loughlin J, O'Brien M. Glomus tumours. An immunohistochemical profile of 11 cases. Histopathology 1989, **14**: 483–491.

837 Di Sant'Agnese PA, De Mesy Jensen KL. Thick (myosin) filaments in a glomus tumor. Am J Clin Pathol 1983, **79**: 130–134.

838 Duncan L, Halverson J, De Schryver-Kecskemeti K. Glomus tumor of the coccyx. A curable cause of coccygodynia. Arch Pathol Lab Med 1991, **115**: 78–80.

839 Folpe AL, Fanburg-Smith JC, Miettinen M, Weiss SW. Atypical and malignant glomus tumor. analysis of 52 cases, with a proposal for the reclassification of glomus tumor. Am J Surg Pathol 2000, **25**: 1–12.

840 Gould EW, Manivel JC, Albores-Saavedra J, Monforte H. Locally infiltrative glomus tumors and glomangiosarcomas. A clinical, ultrastructural, and immunohistochemical study. Cancer 1990, **65**: 310–318.

841 Ito H, Motohiro K, Nomura S, Tahara E. Glomus tumor of the trachea. Immunohistochemical and electron microscopic studies. Pathol Res Pract 1988, **183**: 778–784.

842 Kaye VM, Dehner LP. Cutaneous glomus tumor. A comparative immunohistochemical study with pseudoangiomatous intradermal melanocytic nevi. Am J Dermatopathol 1991, **13**: 2–6.

843 Kishimoto S, Nagatani H, Miyashita A, Kobayashi K. Immunohistochemical demonstration of substance P-containing nerve fibers in glomus tumors. Br J Dermatol 1985, **113**: 213–218.

844 Kohout E, Stout AR. The glomus tumor in children. Cancer 1961, **14**: 555–556.

845 Lattes R, Bull DC. A case of glomus tumor with primary involvement of bone. Ann Surg 1948, **127**: 187–191.

846 Masson P. Le glomus neuromyo-artériel des régions tactiles et ses tumeurs. Lyon Chir 1924, **21**: 259–280.

847 Miettinen M, Lehto V-P, Virtanen I. Glomus tumor cells. Evaluation of smooth muscle and endothelial cell properties. Virchows Arch [Cell Pathol] 1983, **43**: 139–149.

848 Murray MR, Stout AP. The glomus tumor. Investigations of its distribution and behavior, and the identity of its "epithelioid" cell. Am J Pathol 1942, **18**: 183–203.

849 Noer H, Krogdahl A. Glomangiosarcoma of the lower extremity. Histopathology 1991, **18**: 365–366.

850 Nuovo MA, Grimes MM, Knowles DM. Glomus tumors. A clinicopathologic and immunohistochemical analysis of forty cases. Surg Pathol 1990, **3**: 31–46.

851 Pambakian H, Smith MA. Glomus tumours of the coccygeal body associated with coccydynia. A preliminary report. J Bone Joint Surg (Br) 1981, **633**: 424–426.

852 Pulitzer DR, Martin PC, Reed RJ. Epithelioid glomus tumor. Hum Pathol 1995, **26**: 1022–1027.

853 Shugart RR, Soule EH, Johnson EW. Glomus tumor. Surg Gynecol Obstet 1963, **117**: 334–340.

854 Slater DN, Cotton DWK, Azzopardi JG. Oncocytic glomus tumour. A new variant. Histopathology 1987, **11**: 523–531.

855 Stout AP. Tumors of the neuromyoarterial glomus. Am J Cancer 1935, **24**: 255–272.

856 Tsuneyoshi M, Enjoji M. Glomus tumor. A clinicopathologic and electron microscopic study. Cancer 1982, **50**: 1601–1607.

857 Venkatachalam MA, Greally JG. Fine structure of glomus tumor. Similarity of glomus cells to smooth muscle. Cancer 1969, **23**: 1176–1184.

Hemangiopericytoma

858 D'Amore ES, Manivel JC, Sung JH. Soft-tissue and meningeal hemangiopericytomas. An immunohistochemical and ultrastructural study. Hum Pathol 1990, **21**: 414–423.

859 Fletcher CDM. Haemangiopericytoma – a dying breed? Reappraisal of an "entity" and its variants. A hypothesis. Curr Diagn Pathol 1994, **1**: 19–23.

859a Folpe AL, Weiss SW. Hemangiopericytomas and solitary fibrous tumors of soft tissue: a study of 69 cases. (Abstract) Mod Pathol 2003, **16**: 12A.

860 Granter SR, Badizadegan K, Fletcher CD. Myofibromatosis in adults, glomangiopericytoma, and myopericytoma: a spectrum of tumors showing perivascular myoid differentiation. Am J Surg Pathol 1998, **22**: 513–525.

861 Kuhn C III, Rosai J. Tumors arising from pericytes. Ultrastructure and organ culture of a case. Arch Pathol 1969, **88**: 653–663.

862 McMenamin ME, Fletcher CD. Malignant myopericytoma: expanding the spectrum of tumours with myopericytic differentiation. Histopathology 2002, **41**: 450–460.

863 Nemes Z. Differentiation markers in hemangiopericytoma. Cancer 1992, **69**: 133–140.

864 Nielsen GP, Dickersin GR, Provenzal JM, Rosenberg AE. Lipomatous hemangiopericytoma. A histologic, ultrastructural and immunohistochemical study of a unique variant of hemangiopericytoma. Am J Surg Pathol 1995, **19**: 748–756.

865 Stout AP. Hemangiopericytoma (a study of 25 new cases). Cancer 1949, **2**: 1027–1054.

866 Stout AP. Tumors featuring pericytes. Glomus tumor and hemangiopericytoma. Lab Invest 1965, **5**: 217–223.

867 Tsuneyoshi M, Daimaru Y, Enjoji M. Malignant hemangiopericytoma and other sarcomas with hemangiopericytoma-like pattern. Pathol Res Pract 1984, **178**: 446–453.

Hemangioendothelioma

868 Allen PW, Ramakrishna B, MacCormac LB. The histiocytoid hemangiomas and other controversies. Pathol Annu 1992, **27**(Pt 2): 51–87.

869 Angervall L, Kindblom L-G, Karlsson K, Stener B. Atypical hemangioendothelioma of venous origin. A clinicopathologic, angiographic, immunohistochemical, and ultrastructural study of two endothelial tumors within the concept of histiocytoid hemangioma. Am J Surg Pathol 1985, **9**: 504–516.

870 Arnold G, Klein PJ, Fischer R. Epithelioid hemangioendothelioma. Report of a case with immuno-lectin histochemical and ultrastructural demonstration of its vascular nature. Virchows Arch [A] 1986, **408**: 435–443.

871 Billings SD, Folpe AL, Weiss SW. Epithelioid sarcoma-like hemangioendothelioma. Am J Surg Pathol 2002, **27**: 48–57.

872 Cooper PH. Is histiocytoid hemangioma a specific pathologic entity? Am J Surg Pathol 1988, **12**: 815–817.

873 Dabska M. Malignant endovascular papillary angioendothelioma of the skin in childhood. Clinicopathologic study of six cases. Cancer 1969, **24**: 503–510.

874 Ellis GL, Kratochvil FJ III. Epithelioid hemangioendothelioma of the head and neck. A clinicopathologic report of twelve cases. Oral Surg Oral Med Oral Pathol 1986, **61**: 61–68.

874a Fanburg-Smith JC, Michal M, Partanen TA, Alitalo K, Miettinen M. Papillary intralymphatic angioendothelioma (PILA): a report of twelve cases of a distinctive vascular tumor with phenotypic features of lymphatic vessels. Am J Surg Pathol 1999, **23**: 1004–1010.

875 Fetsch JF, Weiss SW. Observations concerning the pathogenesis of epithelioid hemangioma (angiolymphoid hyperplasia). Mod Pathol 1991, **4**: 449–455.

876 Gray MH, Rosenberg AE, Dickersin GR, Bhan AK. Cytokeratin expression in epithelioid vascular neoplasms. Hum Pathol 1990, **21**: 212–217.

877 Malecha M, Rubin R. Aneurysms of the carotid arteries associated with von Recklinghausen's neurofibromatosis. Pathol Res Pract 1992, **188**: 145–147.

878 Mentzel T, Beham A, Calonje E, Katenkamp D, Fletcher CD. Epithelioid hemangioendothelioma of skin and soft tissues: clinicopathologic and immunohistochemical study of 30 cases. Am J Surg Pathol 1997, **21**: 363–374.

879 Morgan J, Robinson MJ, Rosen LB, Unger H, Niven J. Malignant endovascular papillary angioendothelioma (Dabska tumor). A case report and review of the literature. Am J Dermatopathol 1989, **11**: 64–68.

880 Nayler SJ, Rubin BP, Calonje E, Chan JK. Composite hemangioendothelioma: a complex, low grade vascular lesion mimicking angiosarcoma. Am J Surg Pathol 2000, **24**: 352–361.

881 Patterson K, Chandra RS. Malignant endovascular papillary angioendothelioma. Cutaneous borderline tumor. Arch Pathol Lab Med 1985, **109**: 671–673.

882 Rosai J, Gold J, Landy R. The histiocytoid hemangiomas. A unifying concept embracing several previously described entities of skin, soft tissue, large vessels, bone and heart. Hum Pathol 1979, **10**: 707–730.

883 Tsang WY, Chan JK. The family of epithelioid vascular tumors. Histopathology 1993, **8**: 187–212.

884 Urabe A, Tsuneyoshi M, Enjoji M. Epithelioid hemangioma versus Kimura's disease. A comparative clinicopathologic study. Am J Surg Pathol 1987, **11**: 758–766.

885 Weiss SW, Enzinger FM. Epithelioid hemangioendothelioma. A vascular tumor often mistaken for a carcinoma. Cancer 1982, **50**: 970–981.

886 Weiss SW, Ishak KG, Dail DH, Sweet DE, Enzinger FM. Epithelioid hemangioendothelioma and related lesions. Semin Diagn Pathol 1986, **3**: 259–287.

887 Williams SB, Butler BC, Gilkey FW, Kapadia SB, Burton DM. Epithelioid hemangioendothelioma with osteoclastlike giant cells. Arch Pathol Lab Med 1993, **117**: 315–318.

888 Yousem SA, Hochholzer L. Unusual thoracic manifestations of epithelioid hemangioendothelioma. Arch Pathol Lab Med 1987, **111**: 459–463.

Angiosarcoma

889 Abratt RP, Williams M, Dodd NF, Uys CJ. Angiosarcoma of the superior vena cava. Cancer 1983, **52**: 740–743.

890   Baker PB, Goodwin RA. Pulmonary artery sarcomas. A review and report of a case. Arch Pathol Lab Med 1985, **109:** 35–39.

891   Burke AP, Virmani R. Sarcomas of the great vessels. A clinicopathologic study. Cancer 1993, **71:** 1761–1773.

892   Byers RJ, McMahon RF, Freemont AJ, Parrott NR, Newstead CG. Epithelioid angiosarcoma arising in an arteriovenous fistula. Histopathology 1992, **21:** 87–89.

893   Chaudhuri B, Ronan SG, Manaligod JR. Angiosarcoma arising in a plexiform neurofibroma. A case report. Cancer 1980, **46:** 605–610.

894   Davies JD, Rees GJG, Mera SL. Angiosarcoma in irradiated post-mastectomy chest wall. Histopathology 1983, **7:** 947–956.

895   Fitzmaurice RJ, McClure J. Aortic intimal sarcoma. An unusual case with pulmonary vasculature involvement. Histopathology 1990, **17:** 457–462.

896   Fletcher CD, Beham A, Bekir S, Clarke AM, Marley NJ. Epithelioid angiosarcoma of deep soft tissue. A distinctive tumor readily mistaken for an epithelial neoplasm. Am J Surg Pathol 1991, **15:** 915–924.

897   Girard C, Johnson WC, Graham JH. Cutaneous angiosarcoma. Cancer 1970, **26:** 868–883.

898   Hayman J, Huygens H. Angiosarcoma developing around a foreign body. J Clin Pathol 1986, **36:** 515–518.

899   Hottenrott G, Mentzel T, Peters A, Schrader A, Katenkamp D. Intravascular ("intimal") epithelioid angiosarcoma: clinicopathological and immunohistochemical analysis of three cases. Virchows Arch 2000, **435:** 473–478.

900   Jennings TA, Peterson L, Friedlaender GE, Cooke RA, Axiotis A, Hayman JA, Rosai J. Angiosarcoma associated with foreign bodies. Report of three cases. Cancer 1988, **62:** 2436–2444.

901   Mackay B, Ordóñez NG, Huang WL. Ultrastructural and immunocytochemical observations on angiosarcomas. Ultrastruct Pathol 1989, **13:** 97–110.

902   Maddox JC, Evans HL. Angiosarcoma of skin and soft tissue. A study of 44 cases. Cancer 1981, **48:** 1907–1921.

903   McGlennen RC, Manivel JC, Stanley SJ, Slater DL, Wick MR, Dehner LP. Pulmonary artery trunk sarcoma. A clinicopathologic, ultrastructural, and immunohistochemical study of four cases. Mod Pathol 1989, **2:** 486–494.

904   McWilliam LJ, Harris M. Granular cell angiosarcoma of the skin. Histology, electron microscopy and immunohistochemistry of a newly recognized tumor. Histopathology 1985, **9:** 1205–1216.

905   Meis-Kindblom JM, Kindblom LG. Angiosarcoma of soft tissue: a study of 80 cases. Am J Surg Pathol 1998, **22:** 683–697.

906   Millstein DI, Tang C-K, Campbell EW Jr. Angiosarcoma developing in a patient with neurofibromatosis (von Recklinghausen's disease). Cancer 1981, **47:** 950–954.

907   Nanus DM, Kelsen D, Clark DGC. Radiation-induced angiosarcoma. Cancer 1987, **60:** 777–779.

908   Rosai J, Sumner HW, Kostianovsky M, Perez-Mesa C. Angiosarcoma of skin. A clinicopathologic and fine structural study. Hum Pathol 1976, **7:** 83–109.

909   Rossi S, Fletcher CD. Angiosarcoma arising in hemangioma/vascular malformation: report of four cases and review of the literature. Am J Surg Pathol 2002, **26:** 1319–1329.

910   Stout AP. Hemangio-endothelioma. A tumor of blood vessels featuring vascular endothelial cells. Ann Surg 1943, **118:** 445–464.

911   Ulbright TM, Clark SA, Einhorn LH. Angiosarcoma associated with germ cell tumors. Hum Pathol 1985, **16:** 268–272.

912   Vuletin JC, Wajsbort RR, Ghali V. Primary retroperitoneal angiosarcoma with eosinophilic globules. A combined light-microscopic, immunohistochemical, and ultrastructural study. Arch Pathol Lab Med 1990, **114:** 618–622.

913   Wehrli BM, Janzen DL, Shokeir O, Masri BA, Bryne SK, O'Connel JX. Epithelioid angiosarcoma arising in a surgically constructed arteriovenous fistula: a rare complication of chronic immunosuppression in the setting of renal transplantation. Am J Surg Pathol 1998, **22:** 1154–1159.

914   Wilson-Jones E. Malignant vascular tumours. Clin Exp Dermatol 1976, **1:** 287–312.

915   Wright EP, Virmani R, Glick AD, Page DL. Aortic intimal sarcoma with embolic metastases. Am J Surg Pathol 1985, **9:** 890–897.

916   Zagzag D, Yang G, Seidman I, Lusskin R. Malignant epithelioid hemangioendothelioma arising in an intramuscular lipoma. Cancer 1993, **71:** 764–768.

Lymphangioma and lymphangiomyoma

917   Banner A, Carrington C, Emory W, Kittle F, Leonard G, Ringus J, Taylor P, Addington W. Efficacy of oophorectomy in lymphangioleiomyomatosis and benign metastasizing leiomyoma. N Engl J Med 1981, **305:** 204–210.

918   Byrne J, Blanc WA, Warburton D, Wigger J. The significance of cystic hygroma in fetuses. Hum Pathol 1984, **15:** 61–67.

919   Carlson KC, Parnassus WN, Klatt EC. Thoracic lymphangiomatosis. Arch Pathol Lab Med 1987, **111:** 475–477.

920   Chan JK, Tsang WY, Pau MY, Tang MC, Pang SW, Fletcher CD. Lymphangiomyomatosis and angiomyolipoma. Closely related entities characterized by hamartomatous proliferation of HMB-45-positive smooth muscle. Histopathology 1993, **22:** 445–455.

921   Chervenak FA, Isaacson G, Blakemore KJ, Breg WR, Hobbins JC, Berkowitz RL, Tortora M, Mayden K, Mahoney MJ. Fetal cystic hygroma. N Engl J Med 1983, **309:** 822–825.

922   Cornog JL Jr, Enterline HT. Lymphangiomyoma, a benign lesion of chyliferous lymphatics synonymous with lymphangiopericytoma. Cancer 1966, **19:** 1909–1930.

923   Enterline HT, Roberts D. Lymphangiopericytoma. Case report of a previously undescribed tumor type. Cancer 1955, **8:** 582–587.

924   Folpe AL, McKenney JK, Li Z, Smith SJ, Weiss SW. Clear cell myomelanocytic tumor of the thigh: report of a unique case. Am J Surg Pathol 2002, **26:** 809–812.

925   Gomez CS, Calonje E, Ferrar DW, Browse NL, Fletcher CDM. Lymphangiomatosis of the limbs: clinicopathologic analysis of a series with a good prognosis. Am J Surg Pathol 1995, **19:** 125–133.

926   Graham ML II, Spelsberg TC, Dines DE, Payne WS, Bjornsson J, Lie JT. Pulmonary lymphangiomyomatosis. With particular reference to steroid-receptor assay studies and pathologic correlation. Mayo Clin Proc 1984, **59:** 3–11.

927   Gross RE, Hurwitt ES. Cervicomediastinal and mediastinal cystic hygromas. Surg Gynecol Obstet 1948, **87:** 599–610.

928   Guillou L, Fletcher CD. Benign lymphangioendothelioma (acquired progressive lymphangioma): a lesion not to be confused with well-differentiated angiosarcoma and patch stage Kaposi's sarcoma: clinicopathologic analysis of a series. Am J Surg Pathol 2000, **24:** 1047–1057.

929   Jao J, Gilbert S, Messer R. Lymphangiomyoma and tuberous sclerosis. Cancer 1972, **29:** 1188–1192.

930   Kuo T-T, Gomez LG. Papillary endothelial proliferation in cystic lymphangiomas. Arch Pathol Lab Med 1979, **103:** 306–308.

931   McCarty KS Jr, Mossler JA, McLelland R, Sieker HO. Pulmonary lymphangiomyomatosis responsive to progesterone. N Engl J Med 1980, **303:** 1461–1465.

932   Ohori NP, Yousem SA, Sonmez-Alpan E, Colby TV. Estrogen and progesterone receptors in lymphangioleiomyomatosis, epithelioid hemangioendothelioma, and sclerosing hemangioma of the lung. Am J Clin Pathol 1991, **96:** 529–535.

933   Ramani P, Shah A. Lymphangiomatosis. Histologic and immunohistochemical analysis of four cases. Am J Surg Pathol 1993, **17:** 329–335.

934 Taylor JR, Ryu J, Colby TV, Raffin TA. Lymphangioleiomyomatosis. Clinical course in 32 patients. N Engl J Med 1990, **323**: 1254–1260.

935 Wolff M. Lymphangiomyoma. Clinicopathologic study and ultrastructural confirmation of its histogenesis. Cancer 1973, **31**: 988–1007.

Lymphangiosarcoma and related lesions

936 Capo V, Ozzello L, Fenoglio CM, Lombardi L, Rilke F. Angiosarcomas arising in edematous extremities. Immunostaining for factor VIII-related antigen and ultrastructural features. Hum Pathol 1985, **16**: 144–150.

937 Drachman D, Rosen L, Sharaf D, Weissmann A. Postmastectomy low-grade angiosarcoma. An unusual case clinically resembling a lymphangioma circumscriptum. Am J Dermatopathol 1988, **10**: 247–251.

938 Eby CS, Brennan MJ, Fine G. Lymphangiosarcoma. A lethal complication of chronic lymphedema. Arch Surg 1967, **94**: 223–230.

939 Fineberg S, Rosen PP. Cutaneous angiosarcoma and atypical vascular lesions of the skin and breast after radiation therapy for breast carcinoma. Am J Clin Pathol 1995, **102**: 757–763.

940 Hashimoto K, Matsumoto M, Eto H, Lipinski J, LaFond AA. Differentiation of metastatic breast carcinoma from Stewart–Treves angiosarcoma. Use of anti-keratin and anti-desmosome monoclonal antibodies and factor VIII-related antibodies. Arch Dermatol 1985, **121**: 742–746.

941 Herman JB. Lymphangiosarcoma of the chronically edematous extremity. Surg Gynecol Obstet 1965, **121**: 1107–1115.

942 Lagacé R, Leroy J-P. Comparative electron microscopic study of cutaneous and soft tissue angiosarcomas, post-mastectomy angiosarcoma (Stewart–Treves syndrome) and Kaposi's sarcoma. Ultrastruct Pathol 1987, **11**: 161–173.

943 McWilliam LJ, Harris M. Histogenesis of post-mastectomy angiosarcoma. An ultrastructural study. Histopathology 1985, **9**: 331–343.

944 Miettinen M, Lehto V-P, Virtanen I. Postmastectomy angiosarcoma (Stewart–Treves syndrome). Light-microscopic, immunohistological, and ultrastructural characteristic of two cases. Am J Surg Pathol 1983, **7**: 329–339.

945 Muller R, Hajdu SI, Brennan MF. Lymphangiosarcoma associated with chronic filarial lymphedema. Cancer 1987, **59**: 179–183.

946 Rosso R, Gianelli U, Carnevali L. Acquired progressive lymphangioma of the skin following radiotherapy for breast carcinoma. J Cutan Pathol 1995, **22**: 164–167.

947 Sener SF, Milos S, Feldman JL, Martz CH, Winchester DJ, Dieterich M, Locker GY, Khandekar JD, Brockstein B, Haid M, Michel A. The spectrum of vascular lesions in the mammary skin, including angiosarcoma, after breast conservation treatment for breast cancer. J Am Coll Surg 2001, **193**: 22–28.

948 Sordillo PP, Chapman R, Hajdu SI, Magill GB, Golbey RB. Lymphangiosarcoma. Cancer 1981, **48**: 1674–1679.

949 Stewart FW, Treves N. Lymphangiosarcoma in post-mastectomy lymphedema. A report of six cases in elephantiasis chirurgica. Cancer 1948, **1**: 64–81.

950 Woodward AH, Ivins JC, Soule EH. Lymphangiosarcoma arising in chronic lymphedematous extremities. Cancer 1972, **30**: 562–572.

Tumors of smooth muscle
Leiomyoma

951 Billings SD, Folpe AL, Weiss SW. Do leiomyomas of deep soft tissue exist? An analysis of highly differentiated smooth muscle tumors of deep soft tissue supporting two distinct subtypes. Am J Surg Pathol 2001, **25**: 1134–1142.

952 Carla TG, Filotico R, Filotico M. Bizarre angiomyomas of superficial soft tissues. Pathologica 1991, **83**: 237–242.

953 Fox SB, Heryet A, Khong TY. Angioleiomyomas. An immunohistological study. Histopathology 1990, **16**: 495–496.

954 Geddy PM, Gray S, Reid WA. Mast cell density and PGP 9.5-immunostained nerves in angioleiomyoma. Their relationship to painful symptoms. Histopathology 1993, **22**: 387–390.

955 Hachisuga T, Hashimoto H, Enjoji M. Angioleiomyoma. A clinicopathologic reappraisal of 562 cases. Cancer 1984, **54**: 126–130.

956 Hasegawa T, Seki K, Yang P, Hirose T, Hizawa K. Mechanism of pain and cytoskeletal properties in angioleiomyomas. An immunohistochemical study. Pathol Int 1994, **44**: 66–72.

957 Khalluf E, DeYoung BR, Swanson PE. Soft tissue leiomyoma with cartilaginous metaplasia. Report of an unusual phenomenon. Int J Surg Pathol 1994, **1**: 235–238.

958 Kilpatrick SE, Mentzel T, Fletcher CD. Leiomyoma of deep soft tissue. Clinicopathologic analysis of a series. Am J Surg Pathol 1994, **18**: 576–582.

959 Lendrum AC. Painful tumors of the skin. Ann R Coll Surg Engl 1947, **1**: 62–67.

960 MacDonald DM, Sanderson KV. Angioleiomyoma of the skin. Br J Dermatol 1974, **91**: 161–168.

961 Stout AP. Solitary cutaneous and subcutaneous leiomyoma. Am J Cancer 1987, **29**: 435–469.

962 Yokoyama R, Hashimoto H, Daimaru Y, Enjoji M. Superficial leiomyomas. A clinicopathologic study of 34 cases. Acta Pathol Jpn 1987, **37**: 1415–1422.

Leiomyosarcoma

963 Baker PB, Goodwin RA. Pulmonary artery sarcomas. A review and report of a case. Arch Pathol Lab Med 1985, **109**: 35–39.

964 Bayer-Garner I, Morgan M, Smoller BR. Caveolin expression is common among benign and malignant smooth muscle and adipocyte neoplasms. Mod Pathol 2002, **15**: 1–5.

965 Berlin O, Stener B, Kindblom L-G, Angervall L. Leiomyosarcomas of venous origin in the extremities. A correlated clinical, roentgenologic, and morphologic study with diagnostic and surgical implications. Cancer 1984, **54**: 2147–2159.

966 Brooks JJ. Immunohistochemistry of soft tissue tumors. Hum Pathol 1982, **13**: 969–974.

967 Brown DC, Theaker JM, Banks PM, Gatter KC, Mason DY. Cytokeratin expression in smooth muscle and smooth muscle tumours. Histopathology 1987, **11**: 477–486.

968 Bulmer JH. Smooth muscle tumors of limbs. J Bone Joint Surg (Br) 1967, **49**: 52–58.

969 Dahl I, Angervall L. Cutaneous and subcutaneous leiomyosarcoma. A clinicopathologic study of 47 patients. Pathol Europ 1974, **9**: 307–315.

970 Dahl I, Hagmar B, Angervall L. Leiomyosarcoma of the soft tissue. A correlative cytological and histological study of 11 cases. Acta Pathol Microbiol Immunol Scand (A) 1981, **89**: 285–291.

971 de Saint Aubain Somerhausen N, Fletcher CD. Leiomyosarcoma of soft tissue in children: clinicopathologic analysis of 20 cases. Am J Surg Pathol 1999, **23**: 755–763.

971a Deyrup AT, Haydon RC, Huo D, Ishikawa A, Peabody TD, He T-C, Montag AG. Myoid differentiation and prognosis in adult pleomorphic sarcomas of the extremity. An analysis of 92 cases. Cancer 2003, **98**: 805–813.

972 Donner L, DeLanerolle P, Costa J. Immunoreactivity of paraffin-embedded normal tissues and mesenchymal tumors for smooth muscle myosin. Am J Clin Pathol 1983, **80**: 677–681.

973 Dorfman HD, Fishel ER. Leiomyosarcomas of the greater saphenous vein. Am J Clin Pathol 1963, **39**: 73–78.

974 Fields JP, Helwig EB. Leiomyosarcoma of the skin and subcutaneous tissue. Cancer 1981, **47**: 156–169.

975 Fletcher CD. Pleomorphic malignant fibrous histiocytoma: fact

or fiction?: a critical reappraisal based on 159 tumors diagnosed as pleomorphic sarcoma. Am J Surg Pathol 1992, **16:** 213–228.

976 Goldsmith JD, Pawel B, Goldblum JR, Pasha TL, Roberts S, Nelson P, Khurana JS, Barr FG, Zhang PJ. Detection and diagnostic utilization of placental alkaline phosphatase in muscular tissue and tumors with myogenic differentiation. Am J Surg Pathol 2002, **26:** 1627–1633.

977 Hashimoto H, Daimaru Y, Tsuneyoshi M, Enjoji M. Leiomyosarcoma of the external soft tissues. A clinicopathologic, immunohistochemical, and electron microscopic study. Cancer 1986, **57:** 2077–2088.

978 Hisaoka M, Wei-Qi S, Jian W, Morio T, Hashimoto H. Specific but variable expression of H-caldesmon in leiomyosarcomas: an immunohistochemical reassessment of a novel myogenic marker. Appl Immunohistochem Mol Morphol 2001, **9:** 302–308.

979 Imakita M, Yutani C, Ishibashi-Ueda H, Hiraoka H, Naito H. Primary leiomyosarcoma of the inferior vena cava with Budd-Chiari syndrome. Acta Pathol Jpn 1989, **39:** 73–77.

980 Iwata J, Fletcher CD. Immunohistochemical detection of cytokeratin and epithelial membrane antigen in leiomyosarcoma: a systemic study of 100 cases. Pathol Int 2000, **50:** 7–14.

981 Jensen ML, Jensen OM, Michalski W, Nielsen OS, Keller J. Intradermal and subcutaneous leiomyosarcoma: a clinicopathological and immunohistochemical study of 41 cases. J Cutan Pathol 1997, **23:** 458–463.

981a Kelley TW, Borden E, Patel R, Prok A, Goldblum JR. Estrogen and progesterone receptor expression in uterine and extra-uterine leimyosarcomas (LMS): an immunohistochemcial study. (Abstract) Mod Pathol 2003, **16:** 15A.

982 Kevoskian J, Cento DP. Leiomyosarcoma of large arteries and veins. Surgery 1973, **73:** 390–400.

983 Lee ES, Locker J, Nalesnik M, Reyes J, Jaffe R, Alashari M, Nour B, Tzakis A, Dickman PS. The association of Epstein-Barr virus with smooth-muscle tumors occurring after organ transplantation. N Engl J Med 1995, **332:** 19–25.

984 Leu HJ, Makek M. Intramural venous leiomyosarcomas. Cancer 1986, **57:** 1395–1400.

985 Mackay B, Ro J, Floyd C, Ordóñez NG. Ultrastructural observations on smooth muscle tumors. Ultrastruct Pathol 1987, **11:** 593–607.

985a Mandhal N, Fletcher CDM, DalCin P, deWever I, Mertens F, Mitelman F, Rosai J, Rydholm A, Sciot R, Tallini G, van den Berghe H, Vanni R, Willen H. Comparative cytogenetic study of spindle cell and pleomorphic leiomyosarcomas of soft tissue. A report from the CHAMP study group. Cancer Genet Cytogenet 2000, **116:** 66–73.

986 McClain KL, Leach CT, Jenson HB, Joshi VV, Pollock BH, Parmley RT, Di Carlo FJ, Chadwick EG, Murphy SB. Association of Epstein-Barr virus with leiomyosarcomas in children with AIDS. N Engl J Med 1995, **332:** 12–18.

987 Mentzel T, Calonje E, Fletcher CD. Leiomyosarcoma with prominent osteoclastlike giant cells. Analysis of eight cases closely mimicking the so-called giant cell variant of malignant fibrous histiocytoma. Am J Surg Pathol 1994, **18:** 258–265.

988 Mentzel T, Wadden C, Fletcher CD. Granular cell change in smooth muscle tumours of skin and soft tissue. Histopathology 1994, **24:** 223–231.

989 Miettinen M, Lehto V-P, Badley RA, Virtanen I. Expression of intermediate filaments in soft-tissue sarcomas. Int J Cancer 1982, **30:** 541–546.

989a Miyajima K, Oda Y, Tamiya S, Shimizu K, Hachitanda Y, Tsuneyosi M. Cytogenetic and clinicopathological analysis of soft-tissue leiomyosarcomas. Pathol Int 2003, **53:** 163–168.

990 Montgomery E, Goldblum JR, Fisher C. Leiomyosarcoma of the head and neck: a clinicopathological study. Histopathology 2002, **40:** 518–525.

991 Nistal M, Paniagua R, Picazo ML, Cermeño deGiles F, Ramos Guerreira JL. Granular changes in vascular leiomyosarcoma. Virchows Arch [A] 1980, **386:** 239–248.

992 Norton AJ, Thomas JA, Isaacson PG. Cytokeratin-specific monoclonal antibodies are reactive with tumours of smooth muscle derivation. An immunocyto-chemical and biochemical study using antibodies to intermediate filament cytoskeletal proteins. Histopathology 1987, **11:** 487–499.

993 Ogawa K, Oguchi M, Yamabe H, Nakashima Y, Hamashima Y. Distribution of collagen type IV in soft tissue tumors. An immunohistochemical study. Cancer 1986, **58:** 269–277.

994 Oshiro Y, Shiratsuchi H, Oda Y, Toyoshima S, Tsuneyoshi M. Rhabdoid features in leiomyosarcoma of soft tissue: with special reference to aggressive behaviour. Mod Pathol 2001, **13:** 1211–1218.

995 Phelan JT, Sherer W, Perez-Mesa C. Malignant smooth-muscle tumors (leiomyosarcomas) of soft-tissue origin. N Engl J Med 1962, **266:** 1027–1030.

995a Ren B, Yu YP, Jing L, Liu L, Michalopoulos GK, Luo J-H, Rao UNM. Gene expression analysis of human soft tissue leiomyosarcomas. Hum Pathol 2003, **34:** 549–558.

996 Rubin BP, Fletcher CD. Myxoid leiomyosarcoma of soft tissue, an underrecognised variant. Am J Surg Pathol 2000, **24:** 927–936.

997 Saku T, Tsuda N, Anami M, Okabe H. Smooth and skeletal muscle myosins in spindle cell tumors of soft tissue. An immunohistochemical study. Acta Pathol Jpn 1985, **35:** 125–136.

998 Salm R, Evans DJ. Myxoid leiomyosarcoma. Histopathology 1985, **9:** 159–169.

999 Schürch W, Skalli O, Seemayer TA, Gabbiani G. Intermediate filament proteins and actin isoforms as markers for soft tissue tumor differentiation and origin. I. Smooth muscle tumors. Am J Pathol 1987, **128:** 91–103.

1000 Sreekantaiah C, Davis JR, Sandberg AA. Chromosomal abnormalities in leiomyosarcomas. Am J Pathol 1993, **142:** 293–305.

1001 Stout AP, Hill WT. Leiomyosarcoma of the superficial soft tissue. Cancer 1958, **11:** 844–854.

1002 Swanson PE, Wick MR, Dehner LP. Leiomyosarcoma of somatic soft tissues in childhood. An immunohistochemical analysis of six cases with ultrastructural correlation. Hum Pathol 1991, **22:** 569–577.

1003 Tauchi K, Tsutsumi Y, Yoshimura S, Watanabe K. Immunohistochemical and immunoblotting detection of cytokeratin in smooth muscle tumors. Acta Pathol Jpn 1990, **40:** 574–580.

1004 Thomas MA, Fine G. Leiomyosarcoma of veins. Report of 2 cases and review of the literature. Cancer 1960, **13:** 96–101.

1005 Tsukada T, McNutt MA, Ross R, Gown AM. HHF35, a muscle actin-specific monoclonal antibody. II. Reactivity in normal, reactive, and neoplastic human tissues. Am J Pathol 1987, **127:** 389–402.

1006 Varela-Duran J, Oliva H, Rosai J. Vascular leiomyosarcoma. The malignant counterpart of vascular leiomyoma. Cancer 1979, **44:** 1684–1691.

1007 Weiss SW, Langloss JM, Shmookler BM, Malawer MM, D'Avis J, Enzinger FM, Stanton R. Estrogen receptor protein in bone and soft tissue tumors. Lab Invest 1986, **54:** 689–694.

1008 Wile AG, Evans HL, Romsdahl MM. Leiomyosarcoma of soft tissue. A clinicopathologic study. Cancer 1981, **48:** 1022–1032.

1009 Wilkinson N, Fitzmaurice RJ, Turner PG, Freemont AJ. Leiomyosarcoma with osteoclast-like giant cells. Histopathology 1992, **20:** 446–449.

1010 Yannopoulos K, Stout AP. Smooth muscle tumors in children. Cancer 1962, **15:** 958–971.

Clear cell (epithelioid) smooth muscle tumors

1011 Chen KTK, Ma CK. Intravenous leiomyoblastoma. Am J Surg Pathol 1983, **7**: 591–596.

1012 Evans DJ, Lampert IA, Jacobs M. Intermediate filaments in smooth muscle tumors. J Clin Pathol 1983, **36**: 57–61.

1013 Suster S. Epithelioid leiomyosarcoma of the skin and subcutaneous tissue. Clinicopathologic, immunohistochemical, and ultrastructural study of five cases. Am J Surg Pathol 1994, **18**: 232–240.

Tumors of striated muscle

Rhabdomyoma

1014 Agamanolis DP, Dasu S, Krill CE. Tumors of skeletal muscle. Hum Pathol 1986, **17**: 778–795.

1015 Crotty PL, Nakhleh RE, Dehner LP. Juvenile rhabdomyoma. An intermediate form of skeletal muscle tumor in children. Arch Pathol Lab Med 1993, **117**: 43–47.

1016 Czernobilsky B, Cornog JL, Enterline HT. Rhabdomyoma. Report of case with ultrastructural and histochemical studies. Am J Clin Pathol 1968, **49**: 782–789.

1017 Dehner LP, Enzinger FM. Fetal rhabdomyoma. An analysis of nine cases. Cancer 1972, **30**: 160–166.

1018 di Sant'Agnese PA, Knowles DM II. Extracardiac rhabdomyoma. A clinicopathologic study and review of the literature. Cancer 1980, **46**: 780–789.

1019 Golz R. Multifocal adult rhabdomyoma. Case report and literature review. Pathol Res Pract 1988, **183**: 512–518.

1020 Kapadia SB, Enzinger FM, Heffner DK, Hyams VJ, Frizzera G. Crystal-storing histiocytosis associated with lymphoplasmacytic neoplasms: report of three cases mimicking adult rhabdomyoma. Am J Surg Pathol 1993, **17**: 461–467.

1021 Kapadia SB, Meis JM, Frisman DM, Ellis GL, Heffner DK. Fetal rhabdomyoma of the head and neck. A clinicopathologic and immunophenotypic study of 24 cases. Hum Pathol 1993, **24**: 754–765.

1022 Kapadia SB, Meis JM, Frisman DM, Ellis GL, Heffner DK, Hyams VJ. Adult rhabdomyoma of the head and neck. A clinicopathologic and immunophenotypic study. Hum Pathol 1993, **24**: 608–617.

1023 Kodet R, Fajstavr J, Kabelka Z, Koutecky J, Eckschlager T, Newton WA Jr. Is fetal cellular rhabdomyoma an entity or a differentiated rhabdomyosarcoma? A study of patients with rhabdomyoma of the tongue and sarcoma of the tongue enrolled in the intergroup rhabdomyosarcoma studies I, II, and III. Cancer 1991, **67**: 2907–2913.

1024 Konrad EA, Meister P, Hübner G. Extracardiac rhabdomyoma. Report of different types with light microscopic and ultrastructural studies. Cancer 1982, **49**: 898–907.

1025 Lehtonen E, Asikainen U, Badley RA. Rhabdomyoma. Ultrastructural features and distribution of desmin, muscle type of intermediate filament protein. Acta Pathol Microbiol Immunol Scand (A) 1982, **90**: 125–129.

1026 Morgan JJ, Enterline HT. Benign rhabdomyoma of the pharynx. A case report, review of the literature, and comparison with cardiac rhabdomyoma. Am J Clin Pathol 1964, **42**: 174–181.

1027 Scrivner D, Meyer JS. Multifocal recurrent adult rhabdomyoma. Cancer 1980, **46**: 790–795.

1028 Whitten RO, Benjamin DR. Rhabdomyoma of the retroperitoneum. A report of a tumor with both adult and fetal characteristics. A study by light and electron microscopy, histochemistry, and immunochemistry. Cancer 1987, **59**: 818–824.

1029 Willis J, Abdul-Karim FW, di Sant'Agnese PA. Extracardiac rhabdomyomas. Semin Diagn Pathol 1994, **11**: 15–25.

Rhabdomyosarcoma

1030 Agamanolis DP, Dasu S, Krill CE. Tumors of skeletal muscle. Hum Pathol 1986, **17**: 778–795.

1031 Altmannsberger M, Dirk T, Osborn M, Weber K. Immunohistochemistry of cytoskeletal filaments in the diagnosis of soft tissue tumors. Semin Diagn Pathol 1986, **3**: 306–316.

1032 Autio-Harmainen H, Apaja-Sarkkinen M, Martikainen J, Taipale A, Rapola J. Production of basement membrane laminin and type IV collagen by tumors of striated muscle. An immunohistochemical study of rhabdomyosarcomas of different histologic types and a benign vaginal rhabdomyoma. Hum Pathol 1986, **17**: 1218–1224.

1033 Bale PM, Parsons RE, Stevens MM. Diagnosis and behavior of juvenile rhabdomyosarcoma. Hum Pathol 1983, **14**: 596–611.

1034 Brooks JJ. Immunohistochemistry of soft tissue tumors. Myoglobin as a tumor marker for rhabdomyosarcoma. Cancer 1982, **50**: 1757–1763.

1035 Bundtzen JL, Norback DH. The ultrastructure of poorly differentiated rhabdomyosarcomas. A case report and literature review. Hum Pathol 1982, **13**: 301–313.

1036 Carstens PHB. Soft tissue tumor with prominent leptomeric fibrils and complexes (rhabdomyosarcoma). Ultrastruct Pathol 1986, **10**: 137–144.

1037 Carter RL, Jameson CF, Philp ER, Pinkerton CR. Comparative phenotypes in rhabdomyosarcomas and developing skeletal muscle. Histopathology 1990, **17**: 301–309.

1038 Carter RL, McCarthy KP, Machin LG, Jameson CF, Philp ER, Pinkerton CR. Expression of desmin and myoglobin in rhabdomyosarcomas and in developing skeletal muscle. Histopathology 1989, **15**: 585–595.

1039 Cavazzana AO, Schmidt D, Ninfo V, Harms D, Tollot M, Carli M, Treuner J, Betto R, Salviati G. Spindle cell rhabdomyosarcoma. A prognostically favorable variant of rhabdomyosarcoma. Am J Surg Pathol 1992, **16**: 229–235.

1040 Cessna MH, Zhou H, Perkins SL, Tripp SR, Layfield L, Daines C, Coffin CM. Are myogenin and MyoD1 expression specific for rhabdomyosarcoma? A study of 150 cases, with emphasis on spindle cell mimics. Am J Surg Pathol 2001, **25**: 1150–1157.

1041 Chan JK, Ng HK, Wan KY, Tsao SY, Leung TW, Tse KC. Clear cell rhabdomyosarcoma of the nasal cavity and paranasal sinuses. Histopathology 1989, **14**: 391–399.

1042 Cho KR, Olson JL, Epstein JI. Primitive rhabdomyosarcoma presenting with diffuse bone marrow involvement. An immunohistochemical and ultrastructural study. Modern Pathol 1988, **1**: 23–28.

1043 Choi J, Costa ML, Mermelstein CS, Chagas C, Holtzer S, Holtzer H. MyoD converts primary dermal fibroblasts, chondroblasts, smooth muscle, and retinal pigmented epithelial cells into striated mononucleated myoblasts and multinucleated myotubes. Proc Natl Acad Sci U S A 1990, **87**: 7988–7992.

1044 Churg A, Ringus J. Ultrastructural observations on the histogenesis of alveolar rhabdomyosarcoma. Cancer 1978, **41**: 1355–1361.

1045 Clement S, Orlandi A, Bocchi L, Pizzolato G, Foschini MP, Eusebi V, Gabbiani G. Actin isoform pattern expression: a tool for the diagnosis and biological characterization of human rhabdomyosarcoma. Virchows Arch 2003, **442**: 31–38.

1046 Crist WM, Raney RB Jr, Newton W, Lawrence W Jr, Tefft M, Foulkes MA. Intrathoracic soft tissue sarcomas in children. Cancer 1982, **50**: 598–604.

1047 D'Amore ES, Tollot M, Stracca-Pansa V, Menegon A, Meli S, Carli M, Ninfo V. Therapy associated differentiation in rhabdomyosarcomas. Mod Pathol 1994, **7**: 69–75.

1048 De Jong ASH, Albus-Lutter ChE, van Raamsdonk W, Voûte PA. Myosin and myoglobin as tumor markers in the diagnosis of rhabdomyosarcoma. Am J Surg Pathol 1984, **8**: 521–528.

1049 De Jong ASH, van Kessel-van Vark M, Albus-Lutter ChE. Pleomorphic rhabdomyosarcoma in adults. Immunohistochemistry as a tool for its diagnosis. Hum Pathol 1987, **18**: 298–303.

1050 De Jong ASH, van Kessel-van Vark M, Albus-Lutter ChE, van Raamsdonk W, Voûte PA. Skeletal muscle actin as tumor marker in the diagnosis of rhabdomyosarcoma in childhood. Am J Surg Pathol 1985, 9: 467–474.

1051 De Jong ASH, van Kessel-van Vark M, Albus-Lutter ChE, Voûte PA. Creatine kinase subunits M and B as markers in the diagnosis of poorly differentiated rhabdomyosarcomas in children. Hum Pathol 1985, 16: 924–928.

1052 de la Monte SM, Hutchins GM, Moore GW. Metastatic behavior of rhabdomyosarcoma. Pathol Res Pract 1986, 181: 148–152.

1053 Dias P, Chen B, Dilday B, Palmer H, Hosoi H, Singh S, Wu C, Li X, Thompson J, Parham D, Qualman S, Houghton P. Strong immunostaining for myogenin in rhabdomyosarcoma is significantly associated with tumors of the alveolar subclass. Am J Pathol 2000, 156: 399–408.

1054 Dias P, Dilling M, Houghton P. The molecular basis of skeletal muscle differentiation. Semin Diagn Pathol 1994, 11: 3–14.

1055 Dias P, Parham DM, Shapiro DN, Webber BL, Houghton PJ. Myogenic regulatory protein (MyoD1) expression in childhood solid tumors. Diagnostic utility in rhabdomyosarcoma. Am J Pathol 1990, 137: 1283–1291.

1056 Downing JR, Khandekar A, Shurtleff SA, Head DR, Parham DM, Webber BL, Pappo AS, Hulshof MG, Conn WP, Shapiro DN. Multiplex RT-PCR assay for the differential diagnosis of alveolar rhabdomyosarcoma and Ewing's sarcoma. Am J Pathol 1995, 146: 626–634.

1057 Driman D, Thorner PS, Greenberg ML, Chilton-MacNeill S, Squire J. MYCN gene amplification in rhabdomyosarcoma. Cancer 1994, 73: 2231–2237.

1058 Elomaa I, Lehto V-P, Selander R-K. Hypercalcemia and elevated serum parathyroid hormone level in association with rhabdomyosarcoma. Arch Pathol Lab Med 1984, 108: 701–703.

1059 Enterline HT, Horn RC. Alveolar rhabdomyosarcoma. A distinctive tumor type. Am J Clin Pathol 1958, 20: 356–366.

1060 Enzinger FM. Alveolar rhabdomyosarcoma. An analysis of 110 cases. Cancer 1969, 24: 18–31.

1061 Erlandson RA. The ultrastructural distinction between rhabdomyosarcoma and other undifferentiated "sarcomas." Ultrastruct Pathol 1937, 11: 83–101.

1062 Eusebi V, Bondi A, Rosai J. Immunohistochemical localization of myoglobin in nonmuscular cells. Am J Surg Pathol 1984, 8: 51–55.

1063 Eusebi V, Ceccarelli C, Gorza L, Schiaffino S, Bussolati G. Immunocytochemistry of rhabdomyosarcoma. The use of four different markers. Am J Surg Pathol 1986, 10: 293–299.

1064 Eusebi V, Damiani S, Pasquinelli G, Lorenzini P, Reuter VE, Rosai J. Small cell neuroendocrine carcinoma with skeletal muscle differentiation: report of three cases. Am J Surg Pathol 2000, 24: 223–230.

1065 Eusebi V, Rilke F, Ceccarelli C, Fedeli F, Schiaffino S, Bussolati G. Fetal heavy chain skeletal myosin. An oncofetal antigen expressed by rhabdomyosarcoma. Am J Surg Pathol 1986, 10: 680–686.

1065a Ferrari A, Dileo P, Casanova M, Bertulli R, Meazza C, Gandola L, Navarria P, Collini P, Gronchi A, Olmi P, Fossati-Bellani F, Casali PG. Rhabdomyosarcoma in adults. A retrospective analysis of 171 patients treated at a single institution. Cancer 2003, 98: 571–580.

1066 Flamant F, Hill C. The improvement in survival associated with combined chemotherapy in childhood rhabdomyosarcoma. Cancer 1984, 53: 2417–2421.

1067 Folpe AL, McKenney JK, Bridge JA, Weiss SW. Sclerosing rhabdomyosarcoma in adults: report of four cases of a hyalinizing matrix-rich variant of rhabdomyosarcoma that may be confused with osteosarcoma, chondrosarcoma, or angiosarcoma. Am J Surg Pathol 2002, 26: 1175–1183.

1068 Furlong MA, Fanburg-Smith JC. Pleomorphic

1069 Furlong MA, Fentzel T, Fanburg-Smith JC. Pleomorphic rhabdomyosarcoma in adults: a clinicopathologic study of 38 cases with emphasis on morphologic variants and recent skeletal muscle-specific markers. Mod Pathol 2001, 14: 595–603.

1070 Gaffney EF, Dervan PA, Fletcher CD. Pleomorphic rhabdomyosarcoma in adulthood. Analysis of 11 cases with definition of diagnostic criteria. Am J Surg Pathol 1993, 17: 601–609.

1071 Gonzalez-Crussi F, Black-Schaffer S. Rhabdomyosarcoma of infancy and childhood. Problems of morphologic classification. Am J Surg Pathol 1979, 3: 157–171.

1072 Hawkins HK, Camacho-Velasquez JV. Rhabdomyosarcoma in children. A correlation of form and prognosis in one institution's experience. Am J Surg Pathol 1987, 11: 531–542.

1073 Hayashi Y, Kikuchi F, Oka T, Itoyama S, Mohri N, Usuki K, Takaku F, Murakami T, Saitoh Y, Urano Y. Rhabdomyosarcoma with bone marrow metastasis simulating acute leukemia. Report of two cases. Acta Pathol Jpn 1988, 38: 789–798.

1074 Hays DM, Newton W Jr, Soule EH, Foulkes MA, Raney RB, Tefft M, Ragab A, Maurer HM. Mortality among children with rhabdomyosarcomas of the alveolar histologic subtype. J Pediatr Surg 1983, 18: 412–417.

1075 Hays DM, Soule EH, Lawrence W Jr, Gehan EA, Maurer HM, Donaldson M, Raney RB, Tefft M. Extremity lesions in the Intergroup Rhabdomyosarcoma Study (IRS-I). A preliminary report. Cancer 1982, 49: 1–8.

1075a Heffner DK. The truth about alveolar rhabdomyosarcoma. Ann Diagn Pathol 2003, 7: 259–263.

1076 Hollowood K, Fletcher CD. Rhabdomyosarcoma in adults. Semin Diagn Pathol 1994, 11: 47–57.

1077 Horn RC Jr, Enterline HT. Rhabdomyosarcoma. A clinicopathological study and classification of 39 cases. Cancer 1958, 11: 181–199.

1078 Horvat BL, Caines M, Fisher ER. The ultrastructure of rhabdomyosarcoma. Am J Clin Pathol 1970, 53: 555–564.

1079 Ishiguro N, Baba T, Ishida T, Takeuchi K, Osaki M, Araki N, Okada E, Takahashi S, Saito M, Watanabe M, Nakaba C, Tsukamoto Y, Sato K, Ito K, Fukayama M, Mori S, Ito H, Moriyama M. Carp, a cardiac ankyrin-repeated protein, and its new homologue, arpp, are differentially expressed in heart, skeletal muscle, and rhabdomyosarcomas. Am J Pathol 2002, 160: 1767–1778.

1080 Jaffe BF, Fox JE, Batsakis JG. Rhabdomyosarcoma of the middle ear and mastoid. Cancer 1971, 27: 29–37.

1081 Kahn HJ, Yeger H, Kassim O, Jorgensen AO, MacLennan DH, Baumal R, Smith CR, Phillips MJ. Immunohistochemical and electron microscopic assessment of childhood rhabdomyosarcoma. Increased frequency of diagnosis over routine histologic methods. Cancer 1983, 51: 1897–1903.

1082 Karcioglu Z, Someren A, Mathes SJ. Ectomesenchymoma. A malignant tumor of migratory neural crest (ectomesenchyme) remnants showing ganglionic, schwannian, melanocytic and rhabdomyoblastic differentiation. Cancer 1977, 39: 2486–2496.

1083 Kawamoto EH, Weidner N, Agostini RM Jr, Jaffe R. Malignant ectomesenchymoma of soft tissue. Report of two cases and review of the literature. Cancer 1987, 59: 1791–1802.

1084 Keyhani A, Booher RJ. Pleomorphic rhabdomyosarcoma. Cancer 1968, 22: 956–967.

1085 Kindblom L-G, Seidal T, Karlsson K. Immunohistochemical localization of myoglobin in human muscle tissue and embryonal and alveolar rhabdomyosarcoma. Acta Pathol Microbiol Immunol Scand [A] 1982, 90: 167–174.

1086 Kodet R, Kasthuri N, Marsden HB, Coad NAG, Raafat F. Gangliorhabdomyosarcoma. A histopathological and immunohistochemical study of three cases. Histopathology 1986, **10**: 181–193.

1087 Kodet R, Newton WA Jr, Hamoudi AB, Asmar L. Rhabdomyosarcomas with intermediate-filament inclusions and features of rhabdoid tumors. Light microscopic and immunohistochemical study. Am J Surg Pathol 1991, **15**: 257–267.

1088 Kodet R, Newton WA Jr, Hamoudi AB, Asmar L, Jacobs DL, Maurer HM. Childhood rhabdomyosarcoma with anaplastic (pleomorphic) features. A report of the Intergroup Rhabdomyosarcoma Study. Am J Surg Pathol 1993, **17**: 443–453.

1089 Koh S-J, Johnson WW. Antimyosin and antirhabdomyoblast sera. Their use for the diagnosis of childhood rhabdomyosarcoma. Arch Pathol Lab Med 1980, **104**: 118–122.

1090 Kumar S, Pelman E, Haris CA, Raffeld M, Tsokos M. Myogenin is a specific marker for rhabdomyosarcomas: an immunohistochemical study of paraffin-embedded tissues. Mod Pathol 2001, **13**: 988–993.

1091 La Quaglia MP, Heller G, Ghavimi F, Casper ES, Vlamis V, Hajdu S, Brennan MF. The effect of age at diagnosis on outcome in rhabdomyosarcoma. Cancer 1994, **73**: 109–117.

1092 Lawrence W, Hays DM, Heyn R, Tefft M, Crist W, Beltangady M, Newton W Jr, Wharam M. Lymphatic metastases with childhood rhabdomyosarcoma. A report from the Intergroup Rhabdomyosarcoma Study. Cancer 1987, **60**: 910–915.

1093 Leuschner I, Newton WA Jr, Schmidt D, Sachs N, Asmar L, Hamoudi A, Harms D, Maurer HM. Spindle cell variants of embryonal rhabdomyosarcoma in the paratesticular region. A report of the Intergroup Rhabdomyosarcoma Study. Am J Surg Pathol 1993, **17**: 221–230.

1094 Linscheid RL, Soule EH, Henderson ED. Pleomorphic rhabdomyosarcomata of the extremities and limb girdles. J Bone Joint Surg (Am) 1965, **47**: 715–726.

1095 Lloyd RV, Hajdu SI, Knapper WH. Embryonal rhabdomyosarcoma in adults. Cancer 1983, **51**: 557–565.

1096 Lombardi L, Pilotti S. Ultrastructural characterization of poorly differentiated rhabdomyosarcomas. Ultrastruct Pathol 1993, **17**: 669–680.

1097 Lundgren L, Angervall L, Stenman G, Kindblom LG. Infantile rhabdomyofibrosarcoma. A high-grade sarcoma distinguishable from infantile fibrosarcoma and rhabdomyosarcoma. Hum Pathol 1993, **24**: 785–795.

1098 Masson JK, Soule EH. Embryonal rhabdomyosarcoma of head and neck. Report of 88 cases. Am J Surg 1965, **110**: 585–591.

1099 Maurer HM, Beltangady M, Gehan EA, Crist W, Hammond D, Hays DM, Heyn R, Lawrence W, Newton W, Ortega J, Ragab AH, Raney RB, Ruymann FB, Soule E, Tefft M, Webber B, Wharam M, Vietti TJ. The Intergroup Rhabdomyosarcoma Study. I. A final report. Cancer 1988, **61**: 209–220.

1100 Maurer HM, Gehan EA, Beltangady M, Crist W, Dickman PS, Donaldson SS, Fryer C, Hammond D, Hays DM, Herrmann J, et al.: The Intergroup Rhabdomyosarcoma Study-II. Cancer 1993, **71**: 1904–1922.

1101 Mierau GW, Favara BE. Rhabdomyosarcoma in children. Ultrastructural study of 31 cases. Cancer 1980, **46**: 2035–2040.

1102 Miettinen M. Antibody specific to muscle actins in the diagnosis and classification of soft tissue tumors. Am J Pathol 1988, **130**: 205–215.

1103 Miettinen M, Rapola J. Immunohistochemical spectrum of rhabdomyosarcoma and rhabdomyosarcoma-like tumors. Expression of cytokeratin and the 68-kD neurofilament protein. Am J Surg Pathol 1989, **13**: 120–132.

1104 Molenaar WM, Dam-Meiring A, Kamps WA, Cornelisse CJ. DNA-aneuploidy in rhabdomyosarcomas as compared with other sarcomas of childhood and adolescence. Hum Pathol 1988, **19**: 573–579.

1105 Molenaar WM, Oosterhuis AM, Ramaekers FCS. The rarity of

rhabdomyosarcomas in the adult. A morphologic and immunohistochemical study. Pathol Res Pract 1985, **180**: 400–404.

1106 Molenaar WM, Oosterhuis JW, Kamps WA. Cytologic "differentiation" in childhood rhabdomyosarcomas following polychemotherapy. Hum Pathol 1984, **15**: 973–979.

1107 Molenaar WM, Oosterhuis JW, Oosterhuis AM, Ramaekers FCS. Mesenchymal and muscle-specific intermediate filaments (vimentin and desmin) in relation to differentiation in childhood rhabdomyosarcoma. Hum Pathol 1985, **16**: 838–843.

1108 Morales AR, Fine G, Horn RC Jr. Rhabdomyosarcoma. An ultrastructural appraisal. Pathol Annu 1972, **7**: 81–106.

1109 Mukai K, Rosai J, Hallaway BE. Localization of myoglobin in normal and neoplastic human skeletal muscle cells using an immunoperoxidase method. Am J Surg Pathol 1979, **3**: 373–376.

1110 Mukai K, Schollmeyer JV, Rosai J. Immunohistochemical localization of actin. Its applications in surgical pathology. Am J Surg Pathol 1981, **5**: 91–97.

1111 Mukai M, Iri H, Torikata C, Kageyama K, Morikawa Y, Shimizu K. Immunoperoxidase demonstration of a new muscle protein (Z-protein) in myogenic tumors as a diagnostic aid. Am J Pathol 1984, **114**: 164–170.

1112 Nakhleh RE, Swanson PE, Dehner LP. Juvenile (embryonal and alveolar) rhabdomyosarcoma of the head and neck in adults. A clinical, pathologic, and immunohistochemical study of 12 cases. Cancer 1991, **67**: 1019–1024.

1113 Om A, Ghose T. Use of anti-skeletal muscle antibody from myasthenic patients in the diagnosis of childhood rhabdomyosarcomas. Am J Surg Pathol 1987, **11**: 272–276.

1114 Osborn M, Hill C, Altmannsberger M, Weber K. Monoclonal antibodies to titin in conjunction with antibodies to desmin separate rhabdomyosarcomas from other tumor types. Lab Invest 1986, **55**: 101–108.

1115 Pappo AS, Crist WM, Kuttesch J, Rowe S, Ashmun RA, Maurer HM, Newton WA, Asmar L, Luo X, Shapiro DN. Tumor-cell DNA content predicts outcome in children and adolescents with clinical group III embryonal rhabdomyosarcoma. The Intergroup Rhabdomyosarcoma Study Committee of the Children's Cancer Group and the Pediatric Oncology Group. J Clin Oncol 1993, **11**: 1901–1905.

1116 Parham DM. Pathologic classification of rhabdomyosarcomas and correlations with molecular studies. Mod Pathol 2001, **14**: 506–514.

1117 Parham DM, Shapiro DN, Downing JR, Webber BL, Douglass EC. Solid alveolar rhabdomyosarcomas with the t(2; 13). Report of two cases with diagnostic implications. Am J Surg Pathol 1994, **18**: 474–478.

1118 Parham DM, Webber B, Holt H, Williams WK, Maurer H. Immunohistochemical study of childhood rhabdomyosarcomas and related neoplasms. Results of an Intergroup Rhabdomyosarcoma study project. Cancer 1991, **67**: 3072–3080.

1119 Peters E, Cohen M, Altini M, Murray J. Rhabdomyosarcoma of the oral and paraoral region. Cancer 1989, **63**: 963–966.

1120 Ragab AH, Heyn R, Tefft M, Hays DN, Newton WA Jr, Beltangady M. Infants younger than 1 year of age with rhabdomyosarcoma. Cancer 1986, **58**: 2606–2610.

1121 Raney RB Jr, Tefft M, Maurer HM, Ragab AH, Hays DM, Soule EH, Foulkes MA, Gehan EA. Disease patterns and survival rate in children with metastatic soft-tissue sarcoma. A report from the Intergroup Rhabdomyosarcoma Study (IRS)-I. Cancer 1988, **62**: 1257–1266.

1122 Reboul-Marty J, Quintana E, Mosseri V, Flamant F, Asselain B, Rodary C, Zucker JM. Prognostic factors of alveolar rhabdomyosarcoma in childhood. An International Society of Pediatric Oncology study. Cancer 1991, **68**: 493–498.

1123 Riopelle JL, Thériault JP. Sur une forme méconnue de sarcome des parties molles; le rhabdomyosarcome alvéolaire. Ann Anat Pathol (Paris) 1956, **1**: 88–111.

1124 Royds JA, Variend S, Timperley WR, Taylor CB. Comparison of β-enolase and myoglobin as histological markers of rhabdomyosarcoma. J Clin Pathol 1985, **38**: 1258–1260.

1125 Ruymann FB, Newton WA Jr, Ragab AH, Donaldson MH, Foulkes M. Bone marrow metastases at diagnosis in children and adolescents with rhabdomyosarcoma. A report from the Intergroup Rhabdomyosarcoma Study. Cancer 1984, **53**: 368–373.

1126 Sarnat HB, de Mello DE, Siddiqui SY. Diagnostic value of histochemistry in embryonal rhabdomyosarcoma. Am J Surg Pathol 1979, **3**: 177–183.

1127 Schmidt D, Fletcher CD, Harms D. Rhabdomyosarcoma with primary presentation in the skin. Pathol Res Pract 1993, **189**: 422–427.

1128 Schmidt D, Mackay B, Osborne BM, Jaffe N. Recurring congenital lesion of the cheek. Ultrastruct Pathol 1982, **3**: 85–90.

1129 Schmidt D, Reimann O, Treuner J, Harms D. Cellular differentiation and prognosis in embryonal rhabdomyosarcoma. A report from the Cooperative Soft Tissue Sarcoma Study 1981 (CWS 81). Virchows Arch [A] 1986, **409**: 183–194.

1129a Schurch W, Begin LR, Seemayer TA, Lagace R, Boivin JC, Lamoureux C, Bluteau P, Piche J, Gabbiani G. Pleomorphic soft tissue myogenic sarcomas of adulthood: a reappraisal in the mid-1990s. Am J Surg Pathol 1996, **20**: 131–147.

1130 Scupham R, Gilbert EF, Wilde J, Wiedrich TA. Immunohistochemical studies of rhabdomyosarcoma. Arch Pathol Lab Med 1980, **110**: 818–821.

1131 Seidal T, Kindblom L-G. The ultrastructure of alveolar and embryonal rhabdomyosarcoma. A correlative light and electron microscopic study of 17 cases. Acta Pathol Microbiol Immunol Scand (A) 1984, **92**: 231–248.

1132 Seidal T, Mark J, Hagmar B, Angervall L. Alveolar rhabdomyosarcoma. A cytogenetic and correlated cytological and histological study. Acta Pathol Microbiol Immunol Scand (A) 1982, **90**: 345–354.

1133 Shimada H, Newton WA Jr, Soule EH, Beltangady MS, Maurer HM. Pathology of fatal rhabdomyosarcoma. Report from Intergroup Rhabdomyosarcoma Study (IRS-I and IRS-II). Cancer 1987, **59**: 459–465.

1134 Skalli O, Gabbiani G, Babaï F, Seemayer TA, Pizzolato G, Schürch W. Intermediate filament proteins and actin isoforms as markers for soft tissue tumor differentiation and origin II. Rhabdomyosarcomas. Am J Pathol 1988, **130**: 515–531.

1135 Sorensen PH, Lynch JC, Qualman SJ, Tirabosco R, Lim JF, Maurer HM, Bridge JA, Crist WM, Triche TJ, Barr FG. PAX3-FKHR and PAX7-FKHR gene fusions are prognostic indicators in alveolar rhabdomyosarcoma: a report from the children's oncology group. J Clin Oncol 2002, **20**: 2672–2679.

1136 Soule EH, Geitz M, Henderson ED. Embryonal rhabdomyosarcoma of the limbs and limb-girdles. A clinicopathologic study of 61 cases. Cancer 1969, **23**: 1336–1346.

1137 Stout AP. Rhabdomyosarcoma of the skeletal muscles. Ann Surg 1946, **123**: 447–472.

1138 Tsokos M. The role of immunocytochemistry in the diagnosis of rhabdomyosarcoma. Arch Pathol Lab Med 1986, **110**: 776–778.

1139 Tsokos M. The diagnosis and classification of childhood rhabdomyosarcoma. Semin Diagn Pathol 1994, **11**: 26–38.

1140 Tsokos M, Howard R, Costa J. Immunohistochemical study of alveolar and embryonal rhabdomyosarcoma. Lab Invest 1983, **48**: 148–155.

1141 Tsokos M, Webber BL, Parham DM, Wesley RA, Miser A, Miser JS, Etcubanas E, Kinsella T, Grayson J, Glatstein E, et al. Rhabdomyosarcoma. A new classification scheme related to prognosis. Arch Pathol Lab Med 1992, **116**: 847–855.

1142 Variend S, Loughlin MA. An evaluation of enzyme histochemistry in the diagnosis of childhood rhabdomyosarcoma. Histopathology 1985, **9**: 389–400.

1143 Wesche WA, Fletcher CD, Dias P, Houghton PJ, Parham DM. Immunohistochemistry of MyoD1 in adult pleomorphic soft tissue sarcomas. Am J Surg Pathol 1995, **19**: 261–269.

1144 Wijnaendts LC, van der Linden JC, van Unnik AJ, Delemarre JF, Barbet JP, Butler-Browne GS, Meijer CJ. Expression of developmentally regulated muscle proteins in rhabdomyosarcomas. Am J Pathol 1994, **145**: 895–901.

1145 Wijnaendts LC, van der Linden JC, van Unnik AJ, Delemarre JF, Voute PA, Meijer CJ. Histopathological classification of childhood rhabdomyosarcomas. Relationship with clinical parameters and prognosis. Hum Pathol 1994, **25**: 900–907.

1146 Young RH, Scully RE. Alveolar rhabdomyosarcoma metastatic to the ovary. A report of two cases and a discussion of the differential diagnosis of small cell malignant tumors of the ovary. Cancer 1989, **64**: 899–904.

1147 Yun K. A new marker for rhabdomyosarcoma. Insulin-like growth factor II. Lab Invest 1992, **67**: 653–664.

1148 Zuppan CW, Mierau GW, Weeks DA. Lipid-rich rhabdomyosarcoma – a potential source of diagnostic confusion. Ultrastruct Pathol 1991, **15**: 353–359.

Tumors of pluripotential mesenchyme

1149 Brady MS, Perino GK, Tallini G, Russo P, Woodruff JM. Malignant mesenchymoma. Cancer 1996, **77** : 467–473.

1150 Bures C, Barnes L. Benign mesenchymomas of the head and neck. Arch Pathol Lab Med 1978, **102**: 237–241.

1151 Dorfman HD, Levin S, Robbins H. Cartilage-containing benign mesenchymomas of soft tissue. Report of two cases. J Bone Joint Surg (Am) 1980, **62**: 472–475.

1152 Hollingsworth H, Pogrebniak H, Baker A, Merino M. Unusual mesenchymoma with prominent chondro-osseous elements. Int J Surg Pathol 1993, **1**: 129–134.

1153 Milchgrub S, McMurry NK, Vuitch F, Dorfman HD. Chondrolipoangioma. A cartilage-containing benign mesenchymoma of soft tissue. Cancer 1990, **66**: 2636–2641.

1154 Nash A, Stout AP. Malignant mesenchymomas in children. Cancer 1961, **14**: 524–533.

1155 Newman PL, Fletcher CD. Malignant mesenchymoma. Clinicopathologic analysis of a series with evidence of low-grade behaviour. Am J Surg Pathol 1991, **15**: 607–614.

1156 Stout AP. Mesenchymoma, the mixed tumor of mesenchymal derivatives. Ann Surg 1948, **127**: 278–290.

Tumors of metaplastic mesenchyme

1157 Allan CJ, Soule EH. Osteogenic sarcoma of the somatic soft tissues. Clinicopathologic study of 26 cases and review of literature. Cancer 1971, **27**: 1121–1133.

1158 Antonescu CR, Argani P, Erlandson RA, Healey JH, Ladanyi M, Huvos AG. Skeletal and extraskeletal myxoid chondrosarcoma: a comparative clinicopathologic, ultrastructural, and molecular study. Cancer 1998, **83**: 1504–1521.

1159 Bane BL, Evans HL, Ro JY, Carrasco CH, Grignon DJ, Benjamin RS, Ayala AG. Extraskeletal osteosarcoma. A clinicopathologic review of 26 cases. Cancer 1990, **65**: 2762–2770.

1160 Bertoni F, Picci P, Bacchini P, Capanna R, Innao V, Bacci G, Campanacci M. Mesenchymal chondrosarcoma of bone and soft tissues. Cancer 1983, **52**: 533–541.

1161 Bhagavan BS, Dorfman HD. The significance of bone and cartilage formation in malignant fibrous histiocytoma of soft tissue. Cancer 1982, **49**: 480–488.

1162 Carstens PHB. Chordoid tumor. A light, electron microscopic, and immunohistochemical study. Ultrastruct Pathol 1995, **19**: 291–296.

1163 Cates JM, Rosenberg AE, O'Connel JX, Neilsen GP.

Chondroblastoma-like chondroma of soft tissue: an underrecognized variant and its differential diagnosis. Am J Surg Pathol 2001, **25**: 661–666.

1164 Chhieng DC, Erlandson RA, Antonescu C, Ladanyi M, Rosai J. Neuroendocrine differentiation in adult soft tissue sarcomas with features of extraskeletal myxoid chondrosarcoma: report of seven cases. (Abstract) Mod Pathol 1998, **10**: 8A.

1165 Chung EB, Enzinger FM. Chondroma of soft parts. Cancer 1978, **41**: 1414–1424.

1166 Chung EB, Enzinger FM. Extraskeletal osteosarcoma. Cancer 1987, **60**: 1132–1142.

1167 Dabska M. Parachordoma. A new clinicopathologic entity. Cancer 1977, **40**: 1586–1592.

1168 Dahlin DC, Salvador AH. Cartilaginous tumors of the soft tissues of the hands and feet. Mayo Clin Proc 1974, **49**: 721–726.

1169 D'Ambrosio RG, Shiu MH, Brennan MF. Intrapulmonary presentation of extraskeletal myxoid chondrosarcoma of the extremity. Report of two cases. Cancer 1986, **58**: 1144–1148.

1170 De Blois G, Wang S, Kay S. Microtubular aggregates within rough endoplasmic reticulum. An unusual ultrastructural feature of extraskeletal myxoid chondrosarcoma. Hum Pathol 1986, **17**: 469–475.

1171 Dei Tos AP, Wadden C, Fletcher CD. S-100 protein staining in liposarcoma: its diagnostic utility in the high-grade myxoid (round cell) variant. Appl Immunohistochem 1996, **4**: 95–101.

1171a Domanski HA, Carlén, Mertens F, Åkerman M. Extraskeletal myxoid chondrosarcoma with neuroendocrine differentiation : a case report with fine-needle aspiration biopsy, histopathology, electron microscopy, and cytogenetics. Ultrastruct Pathol 2003, **27**: 363–368.

1172 Enzinger FM, Shiraki M. Extra-skeletal myxoid chondrosarcoma. An analysis of 34 cases. Hum Pathol 1972, **3**: 421–435.

1173 Fanburg-Smith JC, Bratthauer GL, Miettinen M. Osteocalcin and osteonectin immunoreactivity in extraskeletal osteosarcoma: a study of 28 cases. Hum Pathol 1999, **30**: 32–38.

1174 Fine G, Stout AP. Osteogenic sarcoma of the extraskeletal soft tissues. Cancer 1956, **9**: 1027–1043.

1175 Fletcher CDM, Powell G, McKee PH. Extraskeletal myxoid chondrosarcoma. A histochemical and immunohistochemical study. Histopathology 1986, **10**: 489–499.

1176 Goh Y-W, Spagnolo DV, Platten M, Caterina P, Fisher C, Oliveira AM, Nascimento AG. Extraskeletal myxoid chondrosarcoma: a light microscopic, immunohistochemical, ultrastructural and immuno-ultrastructural study indicating neuroendocrine differentiation. Histopathology 2001, **39**: 514–524.

1177 Guccion JG, Font RL, Enzinger FM, Zimmerman LE. Extraskeletal mesenchymal chondrosarcoma. Arch Pathol 1973, **95**: 336–340.

1178 Hachitanda Y, Tsuneyoshi M, Daimaru Y, Enjoji M, Nakagawara A, Ikeda K, Sueishi K. Extraskeletal myxoid chondrosarcoma in young children. Cancer 1988, **61**: 2521–2526.

1179 Hoang MP, Suarez PA, Donner LR, Ro J, Ordonez NG, Ayala AG, Czerniak B. Mesenchymal chondrosarcoma: a small cell neoplasm cell polyphenotypic differentiation. Int J Surg Pathol 2001, **8**: 291–301.

1180 Hu B, McPhaul L, Cornford M, Gaal K, Mirra J, French SW. Expression of tau proteins and tubulin in extraskeletal myxoid chondrosarcoma, chordoma, and other chondroid tumors. Am J Clin Pathol 1999, **112**: 189–193.

1181 Humphreys S, Pambakian H, McKee PH, Fletcher CDM. Soft tissue chondroma. A study of 15 tumours. Histopathology 1986, **10**: 147–159.

1182 Huvos AG. Osteogenic sarcoma of bones and soft tissues in older persons. A clinicopathologic analysis of 117 patients older than 60 years. Cancer 1986, **57**: 1442–1449.

1183 Huvos AG, Woodard HQ, Cahan WG, Higinbotham NL, Stewart FW, Butler A, Bretsky SS. Postradiation osteogenic sarcoma of bone and soft tissues. A clinicopathologic study of 66 patients. Cancer 1985, **55**: 1244–1255.

1183a Isotalo Pa, Lae ME, Luzzato F, Rua AM, Lloyd RV, Sebo TJ, Riehle DL, Unni KK, Nascimento AG. Extraskeletal mesenchymal chondrosarcoma: a clinicopathologic and molecular study of 16 cases. (Abstract) Mod Pathol 2003, **16**: 15A.

1184 Jensen ML, Schumacher B, Jensen OM, Neilsen OS, Keller J. Extraskeletal osteosarcomas: a clinicopathologic study of 25 cases. Am J Surg Pathol 1998, **22**: 588–594.

1185 Kawaguchi S, Wada T, Nagoya S, Ikeda T, Isu K, Yamashiro K, Kawai A, Ishii T, Araki N, Myoui A, Matsumoto S, Umeda T, Yoshikawa H, Hasegawa T. Extraskeletal myxoid chondrosarcoma. A multi-institutional study of 42 cases in Japan. Cancer 2003, **97**: 1285–1292.

1186 Lichtenstein L, Goldman RL. Cartilage tumors in soft tissues, particularly in the hand and foot. Cancer 1964, **17**: 1203–1208.

1187 Lucas DR, Fletcher CD, Adsay NV, Zalupski MM. High-grade extraskeletal myxoid chondrosarcoma: a high-grade epithelioid malignancy. Histopathology 1999, **35**: 201–208.

1188 Mackenzie DH. The unsuspected soft tissue chondrosarcoma. Histopathology 1983, **7**: 759–766.

1189 Malhotra CM, Doolittle CH, Rodil JV, Vezeridis MP. Mesenchymal chondrosarcoma of the kidney. Cancer 1984, **54**: 2495–2499.

1190 Martin RF, Melnick PJ, Warner NE, Terry R, Bullock WK, Schwinn CP. Chordoid sarcoma. Am J Clin Pathol 1973, **59**: 623–635.

1191 Martinez-Tello FJ, Navas-Palacios JJ. Ultrastructural study of conventional chondrosarcomas and myxoid- and mesenchymal-chondrosarcoma. Virchows Arch [A] 1982, **396**: 197–211.

1192 Meis-Kindblom JM, Bergh P, Gunterberg B, Kindblom LG. Extraskeletal myxoid chondrosarcoma: a reappraisal of its morphologic spectrum and prognostic factors based on 117 cases. Am J Surg Pathol 1999, **23**: 636–650.

1193 Mirra JM, Fain JS, Ward WG, Eckardt JJ, Eilber F, Rosen G. Extraskeletal telangiectatic osteosarcoma. Cancer 1993, **71**: 3014–3019.

1194 Nakashima Y, Unni KK, Shives TC, Swee RG, Dahlin DC. Mesenchymal chondrosarcoma of bone and soft tissue. A review of 111 cases. Cancer 1986, **57**: 2444–2453.

1195 Oliveira AM, Sebo TJ, McGrory JE, Gaffey TA, Rock MG, Nascimento AG. Extraskeletal myxoid chondrosarcoma: a clinicopathologic, immunohistochemical, and ploidy analysis of 23 cases. Mod Pathol 2000, **13**: 900–908.

1196 Oshiro Y, Shiratsuchi H, Tamiy S, Oda Y, Toyoshima S, Tsuneyoshi M. Extraskeletal myxoid chondrosarcoma with rhabdoid features, with special reference to its aggressive behaviour. Int J Surg Pathol 2001, **8**: 145–152.

1197 Panagopoulos I, Mertens F, Isaksson M, Domanski HA, Brosjo O, Heim S, Bjerkehagen B, Sciot R, Dal Cin P, Fletcher JA, Fletcher CD, Mandahl N. Molecular genetic characterization of the EWS/CHN and RBP56/CHN fusion genes in extraskeletal myxoid chondrosarcoma. Genes Chromosomes Cancer 2002, **35**: 340–352.

1198 Payne C, Dardick I, Mackay B. Extraskeletal myxoid chondrosarcoma with intracisternal microtubules. Ultrastruct Pathol 1994, **18**: 257–261.

1198a Reid R, de Silva VC, Paterson L. Poorly differentiated extraskeletal myxoid chondrosarcoma with t(9;22)(q22;q11) translocation presenting initially as a solid variant devoid of myxoid areas. Int J Surg Pathol 2003, **11**: 137–141.

1199 Reiman HM, Dahlin DC. Cartilage- and bone-forming tumors of the soft tissues. Semin Diagn Pathol 1986, **3**: 288–305.

1200 Rubin BP, Fletcher JA. Skeletal and extraskeletal myxoid chondrosarcoma: related or distinct tumors? Adv Anat Pathol 1999, 6: 204–212.

1201 Saleh G, Evans HL, Ro JY, Ayala AG. Extraskeletal myxoid chondrosarcoma. A clinicopathologic study of ten patients with long-term follow-up. Cancer 1992, 70: 2827–2830.

1202 Sciot R, Dal Cin P, Fletcher C, Samson I, Smith M, De Vos R, Van Damme B, Van den Berghe H. t(9;22)(q22-31;q11-12) is a consistent marker of extraskeletal myxoid chondrosarcoma. Evaluation of three cases. Mod Pathol 1995, 8: 765–768.

1202a Sjögren H, Meis-Kindblom JM, Örndal C, Bergh P, Ptaszynski K, Åman P, Kindblom L-G, Stenman G. Studies on the molecular pathogenesis of extraskeletal myxoid chondrosarcoma - cytogenetic, molecular genetic, and cDNA microarray analyses. Am J Pathol 2003, 162: 781–792.

1203 Sordillo PP, Hajdu SI, Magill GB, Golbey RB. Extraosseous osteogenic sarcoma. A review of 48 patients. Cancer 1983, 51: 727–734.

1204 Stout AP, Verner EW. Chondrosarcoma of the extraskeletal soft tissue. Cancer 1953, 6: 581–590.

1205 Tsuneyoshi M, Enjoji M, Iwasaki H, Shinohara N. Extraskeletal myxoid chondrosarcoma. A clinicopathologic and electron microscopic study. Acta Pathol Jpn 1981, 31: 439–447.

1206 Weiss SW. Ultrastructure of the so-called "chordoid sarcoma." Evidence supporting cartilaginous differentiation. Cancer 1976, 37: 300–306.

1207 Wolford JF, Bedetti CI. Skeletal myxoid chondrosarcoma with microtubular aggregates within rough endoplasmic reticulin. Arch Pathol Lab Med 1988, 112: 77–81.

1208 Wu KK, Collon DJ, Guise ER. Extra-osseous chondrosarcoma. Report of five cases and review of the literature. J Bone Joint Surg (Am) 1980, 62: 189–194.

1209 Wu WQ, Lapi A. Primary non-skeletal intracranial cartilaginous neoplasm. Report of a chondroma and a mesenchymal chondrosarcoma. J Neurol Neurosurg Psychiatry 1970, 33: 469–475.

1210 Yi ES, Shmookler BM, Malawer MM, Sweet DE. Well-differentiated extraskeletal osteosarcoma. A soft-tissue homologue of parosteal osteosarcoma. Arch Pathol Lab Med 1991, 115: 906–909.

1211 Zucker DK, Horopian DS. Dural mesenchymal chondrosarcoma. Case report. J Neurosurg 1978, 48: 829–833.

Tumors resembling synovial tissue

1212 Abenoza P, Manivel JC, Swanson PE, Wick MR. Synovial sarcoma. Ultrastructural study and immunohistochemical analysis by a combined peroxidase-antiperoxidase/avidin-biotin-peroxidase complex procedure. Hum Pathol 1986, 17: 1107–1115.

1213 Antonescu CR, Busam KJ, Iversen K, Kolb D, Coplan K, Spagnoli GC, Ladanyi M, Old LJ, Jungbluth AA. MAGE antigen expression in monophasic and biphasic synovial sarcoma. Hum Pathol 2002, 33: 225–229.

1214 Antonescu CR, Kawai A, Leung DH, Lonardo F, Woodruff JM, Healey JH, Landanyi M. Strong association of SYT-SSX fusion type and morphologic epithelial differentiation in synovial sarcoma. Diagn Mol Pathol 2000, 9: 1–8.

1215 Argani P, Zakowski MF, Klimstra DS, Rosai J, Ladanyi M. Detection of the SYT-SSX chimeric RNA of synovial sarcoma in paraffin-embedded tissue and its application in problematic cases. Mod Pathol 1998, 11: 65–71.

1216 Batsakis JG, Nishiyama RH, Sullinger GD. Synovial sarcomas of the neck. Arch Otolaryngol 1967, 85: 327–331.

1217 Cagle LA, Mirra JM, Storm FK, Roe DJ, Eilber FR. Histologic features relating to prognosis in synovial sarcoma. Cancer 1987, 59: 1810–1814.

1217a Chan JA, McMenamin ME, Fletcher CDM. Synovial sarcoma in older patients : clinicopathological analysis of 32 cases with emphasis on unusual histological features. Histopathology 2003, 43: 72–83.

1218 Corson JM, Weiss LM, Banks-Schlegel SP, Pinkus GS. Keratin proteins and carcinoembryonic antigen in synovial sarcomas. An immunohistochemical study of 24 cases. Hum Pathol 1984, 15: 615–621.

1219 Crocker EW, Stout AP. Synovial sarcoma in children. Cancer 1959, 12: 1123–1133.

1220 Dal Cin P, Rao U, Jani-Sait S, Karakousis C, Sandberg AA. Chromosomes in the diagnosis of soft tissue tumors. I. Synovial sarcoma. Mod Pathol 1992, 5: 357–362.

1221 Dardick I, Ramjohn S, Thomas MJ, Jeans D, Hammar SP. Synovial sarcoma. Pathol Res Pract 1991, 187: 871–885.

1222 Dei Tos AP, Wadden C, Calonje E, Sciot R, Pauwels P, Knight JC, Dal Cin P, Fletcher CDM. Immunohistochemical demonstration of glycoprotein p30/32^{MIC2} (CD99) in synovial sarcoma. A potential cause of diagnostic confusion. Appl Immunohistochem 1995, 3: 168–173.

1222a de Silva MVC, McMahon AD, Paterson L, Reid R. Identification of poorly differentiated synovial sarcoma: a comparison of clinicopathological and cytogenetic features with those of typical synovial sarcoma. Histopathology 2003, 443: 220–230.

1223 Dickersin GR. Synovial sarcoma. A review and update, with emphasis on the ultrastructural characterization of the nonglandular component. Ultrastruct Pathol 1991, 15: 379–402.

1224 Dische FE, Darby AJ, Howard ER. Malignant synovioma. Electron microscopical findings in three patients and review of the literature. J Pathol 1978, 124: 149–155.

1225 el-Naggar AK, Ayala AG, Abdul-Karim FW, McLemore D, Ballance WW, Garnsey L, Ro JY, Batsakis JG. Synovial sarcoma. A DNA flow cytometric study. Cancer 1990, 65: 2295–2300.

1226 Fetsch JF, Meis JM. Synovial sarcoma of the abdominal wall. Cancer 1993, 72: 469–477.

1227 Fisher C. Synovial sarcoma. Ultrastructural and immunohistochemical features of epithelial differentiation in monophasic and biphasic tumors. Hum Pathol 1986, 17: 996–1008.

1228 Fisher C. Synovial sarcoma. Ann Diagn Pathol 1999, 2: 401–421.

1228a Fisher C, Montgomery E, Healy V. Calponin and h-caldesmon expression in synovial sarcoma; the use of calponin in diagnosis. Histopathology 2003, 42: 588–593.

1229 Fisher C, Schofield JB. S-100 protein positive synovial sarcoma. Histopathology 1991, 19: 375–377.

1230 Folpe AL, Schmidt RA, Chapman D, Gown AM. Poorly differentiated synovial sarcoma: immunohistochemical distinction from primitive peripheral nerve sheath tumors. Am J Surg Pathol 1998, 22: 673–682.

1231 Fritsch M, Epstein JI, Perlman EJ, Watts JC, Argani P. Molecularly confirmed primary prostatic synovial sarcoma. Hum Pathol 2000, 31: 246–250.

1232 Gabbiani G, Kaye GI, Lattes R, Majno G. Synovial sarcoma. Electron microscopic study of a typical case. Cancer 1971, 28: 1031–1039.

1233 Ghadially FN. Is synovial sarcoma a carcinosarcoma of connective tissue? Ultrastruct Pathol 1987, 11: 147–151.

1233a Guillou L, Benhattar J, Terrier P, Gallagher G, Jundt G, Stauffer E, de St Aubain N, Michels JJ, Ranchere VD, Bertrand G, Trassard M, Collin F, Coindre JM. SYT-SSX fusion type is not a prognostic factor in synovial sarcoma patients. A multi-institutional study of 182 cases. (Abstract) Mod Pathol 2003, 16: 13A.

1234 Guillou L, Coindre JM, Gallagher G, Terrier P, Gebhard S, de Saint Aubain Somerhausen NA, Michels J, Jundt G, Vince DR, Collin F, Trassard M, Le Doussai V, Benhattar J. Detection of the synovial sarcoma translocation t(X;18)(SYT;SSX) in paraffin-embedded tissues using transcriptase-polymerase chain reaction: a reliable and powerful diagnostic tool for pathologists: a molecular analysis of 221 mesenchymal tumors fixed in different fixatives. Hum Pathol 2001, **32**: 105–112.

1235 Guillou L, Wadden C, Kraus MD, Dei Tos AP, Fletcher CD. S-100 protein reactivity in synovial sarcomas – a potentially frequent diagnostic pitfall: immunohistochemical analysis of 100 cases. Appl Immunohistochem 1996, **4**: 167–175.

1236 Haagensen CD, Stout AP. Synovial sarcoma. Ann Surg 1944, **120**: 826–842.

1237 Ishida T, Kojima T, Iijima T, Oka T, Kuroda M, Horiuchi H, Imamura T, Machinami R. Synovial sarcoma with a predominant epithelial component. Int J Surg Pathol 1994, **1**: 261–268.

1238 Kawai A, Woodruff J, Healey JH, Brennan MF, Antonescu CR, Ladanyi M. SYT-SSX gene fusion as a determinant of morphology and prognosis in synovial sarcoma. N Engl J Med 1998, **338**: 153–160.

1239 Krall RA, Kostianovsky M, Patchefsky AS. Synovial sarcoma. A clinical, pathological, ultrastructural study of 26 cases supporting the recognition of a monophasic variant. Am J Surg Pathol 1981, **5**: 137–151.

1240 Krane JF, Bertoni F, Fletcher CD. Myxoid synovial sarcoma: an underappreciated morphologic subset. Mod Pathol 1999, **12**: 456–462.

1241 Ladenstein R, Treuner J, Koscielniak E, d'Oleire F, Keim M, Gadner H, Jurgens H, Niethammer D, Ritter J, Schmidt D. Synovial sarcoma of childhood and adolescence. Report of the German CWS-81 study. Cancer 1993, **71**: 3647–3655.

1242 Leader M, Patel J, Collins M, Kristin H. Synovial sarcomas. True carcinosarcomas? Cancer 1987, **59**: 2096–2098.

1243 Lewis JJ, Antonescu CR, Leung DH, Blumberg D, Healey JH, Woodruff JM, Brennan MF. Synovial sarcoma: a multivariate analysis of prognostic factors in 112 patients with primary localized tumors of the extremity. J Clin Oncol 2000, **18**: 2087–2094.

1244 Lombardi L, Rilke F. Ultrastructural similarities and differences of synovial sarcoma, epithelioid sarcoma, and clear cell sarcoma of the tendons and aponeuroses. Ultrastruct Pathol 1984, **6**: 209–219.

1245 Lopes JM, Bjerkehagen B, Holm R, Bruland O, Sobrinho-Simoes M, Nesland JM. Immunohistochemical profile of synovial sarcoma with emphasis on the epithelial-type differentiation. A study of 49 primary tumours, recurrences and metastases. Pathol Res Pract 1994, **190**: 168–177.

1246 Lopes JM, Bjerkehagen B, Sobrinho-Simoes M, Nesland JM. The ultrastructural spectrum of synovial sarcomas. A study of the epithelial type differentiation of primary tumors, recurrences, and metastases. Ultrastruct Pathol 1993, **17**: 137–151.

1247 Lopes JM, Nesland JM, Reis-Filho JS, Holm R. Differential Ki67 and bcl-2 immunoexpression in solid-glandular and spindle cell components of biphasic synovial sarcoma: a double immunostaining assessment with cytokeratin and vimentin. Histopathology 2002, **40**: 464–471.

1248 Mackenzie DH. Synovial sarcoma. A review of 58 cases. Cancer 1966, **19**: 169–180.

1249 Mackenzie DH. Monophasic synovial sarcoma – a histological entity? Histopathology 1977, **1**: 151–157.

1250 Majeste RM, Beckman EN. Synovial sarcoma with an overwhelming epithelial component. Cancer 1988, **61**: 2527–2531.

1251 Miettinen M. Keratin subsets in spindle cell sarcomas. Keratins are widespread but synovial sarcoma contains a distinctive keratin polypeptide pattern and desmoplakins. Am J Pathol 1991, **138**: 505–513.

1252 Miettinen M, Lehto V-P, Virtanen I. Monophasic synovial sarcoma of spindle cell type. Virchows Arch [A] 1983, **44**: 187–199.

1253 Miettinen M, Limom J, Niezabitowski A, Lasota J. Calretinin and other mesothelioma markers in synovial sarcoma: analysis of antigenic similarities and differences with malignant mesothelioma. Am J Surg Pathol 2001, **25**: 610–617.

1254 Miettinen M, Santavirta S, Släts P. Intravascular synovial sarcoma. Hum Pathol 1987, **18**: 1075–1077.

1255 Miettinen M, Virtanen I. Synovial sarcoma – a misnomer. Am J Pathol 1984, **117**: 18–25.

1256 Milchgrub S, Ghandur-Mnaymneh L, Dorfman HD, Albores-Saavedra J. Synovial sarcoma with extensive osteoid and bone formation. Am J Surg Pathol 1993, **17**: 357–363.

1257 Mirra JM, Wang S, Bhuta S. Synovial sarcoma with squamous differentiation of its mesenchymal glandular elements. A case report with light-microscopic, ultramicroscopic, and immunologic correlation. Am J Surg Pathol 1984, **8**: 791–796.

1258 Moberger G, Nilsonne U, Friberg S Jr. Synovial sarcoma. Histologic features and prognosis. Acta Orthop Scand (Suppl) 1968, **3**: 1–38.

1259 Nagao K, Ito H, Yoshida H. Chromosomal translocation t(X;18) in human synovial sarcomas analysed by fluorescence in situ hybridisation using paraffin-embedded tissue. Am J Pathol 1996, **148**: 601–609.

1260 Nakamura T, Nakata K, Hata S, Ono K, Katsuyama T. Histochemical characterization of mucosubstances in synovial sarcoma. Am J Surg Pathol 1984, **8**: 429–434.

1261 O'Connell JX, Browne WL, Groppr PT, Berean KW. Intraneural biphasic synovial sarcoma: an alternative "glandular" tumor of peripheral nerve. Mod Pathol 1997, **9**: 738–741.

1261a Nuciforo PG, Pellegrini C, Fasani R, Maggioni M, Coggi G, Parafioriti A, Bosari S. Molecular and immunohistochemical analysis of HER2/neu oncogene in synovial sarcoma. Hum Pathol 2003, **34**: 639–645.

1262 Oda Y, Hashimoto H, Tsuneyoshi M, Takeshita S. Survival in synovial sarcoma. A multivariate study of prognostic factors with special emphasis on the comparison between early death and long-term survival. Am J Surg Pathol 1993, **17**: 35–44.

1263 Ordóñez NG, Mahfouz SM, Mackay B. Synovial sarcoma. An immunohistochemical and ultrastructural study. Hum Pathol 1990, **21**: 733–749.

1264 Pappo AS, Fontanesi J, Luo X, Rao BN, Parham DM, Hurwitz C, Avery L, Pratt CB. Synovial sarcoma in children and adolescents. The St Jude Children's Research Hospital experience. J Clin Oncol 1994, **12**: 2360–2366.

1265 Pelmus M, Guillou L, Hostein I, Sierankowski G, Lussan C, Coindre JM. Monophasic fibrous and poorly differentiated synovial sarcoma: immunohistochemical reassessment of 60 t(X;18)(SYT-SSX)-positive cases. Am J Surg Pathol 2002, **26**: 1434–1440.

1266 Pinkus GS, Kurtin PJ. Epithelial membrane antigen – a diagnostic discriminant in surgical pathology. Immunohistochemical profile in epithelial, mesenchymal, and hematopoietic neoplasms using paraffin sections and monoclonal antibodies. Hum Pathol 1985, **16**: 929–940.

1267 Rooser B, Willen H, Hugoson A, Rydholm A. Prognostic factors in synovial sarcoma. Cancer 1989, **63**: 2182–2185.

1268 Roth JA, Enzinger FM, Tannenbaum M. Synovial sarcoma of the neck. A follow-up study of 24 cases. Cancer 1975, **35**: 1243–1253.

1269 Salisbury JR, Isaacson PG. Synovial sarcoma. An immunohistochemical study. J Pathol 1985, **147**: 49–57.

1269a Sandberg AA, Bridge JA. Updates on the cytogenetics and molecular genetics of bone soft tissue tumors. Synovial sarcoma. Cancer Genet Cytogenet 2002, **133**: 1–23.

1270 Schiffman R. Epithelioid sarcoma and synovial sarcoma in the same knee. Cancer 1980, **45**: 158–166.

1271 Shaw GR, Lais CJ. Fatal intravascular synovial sarcoma in a 31-year-old woman. Hum Pathol 1993, **24**: 809–810.

1272 Shipley J, Crew J, Birdsall S, Gill S, Clark J, Fisher C, Kelsey A, Nojima T, Sonobe H, Cooper C, Gusterson B. Interphase fluorescence in situ hybridisation and reverse transcription polymerase chain reaction as a diagnostic aid for synovial sarcoma. Am J Pathol 1996, **148**: 559–567.

1273 Shmookler BM. Retroperitoneal synovial sarcoma. Am J Clin Pathol 1982, **77**: 686–691.

1274 Shmookler BM, Enzinger FM, Brannon RB. Orofacial synovial sarcoma: a clinicopathologic study of 11 new cases and review of the literature. Cancer 1982, **50**: 269–272.

1275 Singer S, Baldini EH, Demetri GD, Fletcher JA, Corson JM. Synovial sarcoma: prognostic significance of tumor size, margin of resection, and mitotic activity for survival. J Clin Oncol 1996, **14**: 1201–1208.

1276 Soule EH. Synovial sarcoma. Am J Surg Pathol 1986, **10**(Suppl 1): 78–82.

1277 Suit HD, Russell WO, Martin RG. Management of patients with sarcoma of soft tissue in an extremity. Cancer 1973, **31**: 1247–1255.

1278 Trassard M, Le Doussal V, Hacene K, Terrier P, Ranchere D, Guillou L, Fiche M, Collin F, Vilain MO, Bertrand G, Jacquemier J, Sastre-Garau X, Bui NB, Bonichon F, Coindre JM. Prognostic factors in localized primary synovial sarcoma: a multicentre study of 128 adult patients. J Clin Oncol 2001, **19**: 525–534.

1279 Tsuneyoshi M, Yokoyama K, Enjoji M. Synovial sarcoma. A clinicopathologic and ultrastructural study of 42 cases. Acta Pathol Jpn 1983, **33**: 23–36.

1280 van Andel JG. Synovial sarcoma. A review and analysis of treated cases. Radiol Clin Biol 1972, **41**: 145–159.

1281 van de Rijn M, Barr FG, Xiong QB, Hedges M, Shipley J, Fisher C. Poorly differentiated synovial sarcoma: an analysis of clinical, pathologic, and molecular genetic features. Am J Surg Pathol 1999, **23**: 106–112.

1282 Varela-Duran J, Enzinger FM. Calcifying synovial sarcoma. A clinicopathologic study of 32 cases. Cancer 1982, **50**: 345–352.

1283 Witkin GB, Rosai J. A biphasic tumor of the mediastinum with features of synovial sarcoma. A report of 4 cases (abstract). Lab Invest 1988, **58**: 104A.

1284 Wright PH, Sim EH, Soule EH, Taylor WF. Synovial sarcoma. J Bone Joint Surg (Am) 1982, **64**: 112–122.

1285 Zeren H, Moran CA, Suster S, Fishback NF, Koss MN. Primary pulmonary sarcomas with features of monophasic synovial sarcoma: a clinicopathological, immunohistochemical, and ultrastructural study of 25 cases. Hum Pathol 1995, **26**: 474–480.

Tumors of extragonadal germ cells

1286 Berry CL, Keelnig J, Hilton C. Teratoma in infancy and childhood. A review of 91 cases. J Pathol 1969, **98**: 241–252.

1287 Billmire DF, Grosfeld JL. Teratomas in childhood. Analysis of 142 cases. J Pediatr Surg 1986, **21**: 548–551.

1288 Colton JJ, Batsakis JG, Work WP. Teratomas of the neck in adults. Arch Otolaryngol 1978, **104**: 271–272.

1289 Conklin J, Abell MR. Germ cell neoplasms of sacrococcygeal region. Cancer 1967, **20**: 2105–2117.

1290 Dehner LP. Intrarenal teratoma occurring in infancy. Report of a case with discussion of extragonadal germ cell tumors in infancy. J Pediatr Surg 1973, **8**: 369–378.

1291 Dehner LP, Mills A, Talerman A, Billman GF, Krous HF, Platz CE. Germ cell neoplasms of head and neck soft tissues. A pathologic spectrum of teratomatous and endodermal sinus tumors. Hum Pathol 1990, **21**: 309–318.

1292 Gonzalez-Crussi F, Winkler RF, Mirkin DL. Sacrococcygeal teratomas in infants and children. Relationship of histology and prognosis in 40 cases. Arch Pathol Lab Med 1978, **102**: 420–425.

1293 Mochizuki Y, Noguchi S, Yokoyama S, Murakami N, Moriuchi A, Aisaka K, Yamashita H, Nakayama I. Cervical teratoma in a fetus and an adult. Two case reports and review of literature. Acta Pathol Jpn 1986, **36**: 935–943.

1294 Tapper D, Lack EE. Teratomas in infancy and childhood. A 54-year experience at the Children's Hospital Medical Center. Ann Surg 1983, **198**: 398–410.

1295 Willis RA. Pathology of tumors, ed. 4. London, 1968, Butterworth.

Tumors of neural tissue (other than peripheral nerves)
Pigmented neuroectodermal tumor of infancy

1296 Argenyi ZB, Schelper RL, Balogh K. Pigmented neuroectodermal tumor of infancy. A light microscopic and immunohistochemical study. J Cutan Pathol 1991, **18**: 40–45.

1297 Borello ED, Gorlin RH. Melanotic neuroectodermal tumor of infancy – a neoplasm of neural crest origin. Report of a case associated with high urinary excretion of vanilmandelic acid. Cancer 1966, **19**: 196–206.

1298 Clark BE, Parsons H. An embryological tumor of retinal anlage involving the skull. Cancer 1951, **4**: 78–85.

1299 Dehner LP, Sibley RK, Sauk JJ Jr, Vickers RA, Nesbit ME, Leonard AS, Waite DE, Neeley JE, Ophoven J. Malignant melanotic neuroectodermal tumor of infancy. A clinical, pathologic, ultrastructural and tissue culture study. Cancer 1979, **43**: 1389–1410.

1300 Johnson RE, Scheithauer BW, Dahlin DC. Melanotic neuroectodermal tumor of infancy. A review of seven cases. Cancer 1983, **52**: 661–666.

1301 Koudstaal J, Oldhoff J, Panders AK, Hardonk MJ. Melanotic neuroectodermal tumor of infancy. Cancer 1968, **22**: 151–161.

1302 Neustein HB. Fine structure of a melanotic progonoma or retinal anlage tumor of the anterior fontanel. Exp Mol Pathol 1967, **6**: 131–142.

1303 Pettinato G, Manivel JC, d'Amore ES, Jaszez W, Gorlin RJ. Melanotic neuroectodermal tumor of infancy. A reexamination of a histogenetic problem based on immunohistochemical, flow cytometric, and ultrastructural study of 10 cases. Am J Surg Pathol 1991, **15**: 233–245.

1304 Raju U, Zarbo R, Regezi J, Krutchkoff D, Perrin E. Melanotic, neuroectodermal tumors of infancy. Intermediate filament-, neuroendocrine-, and melanoma-associated antigen profiles. Appl Immunohistochem 1993, **1**: 69–76.

1305 Scheck O, Ruck P, Harms D, Kaiserling E. Melanotic neuroectodermal tumor of infancy occurring in the left thigh of a 6-month-old female infant. Ultrastruct Pathol 1989, **13**: 23–33.

1306 Stirling RW, Powell G, Fletcher CD. Pigmented neuroectodermal tumour of infancy. An immunohistochemical study. Histopathology 1988, **12**: 425–435.

1307 Young S, Gonzalez-Crussi F. Melanocytic neuroectodermal tumor of the foot. Report of a case with multicentric origin. Am J Clin Pathol 1985, **84**: 371–378.

Other neural tumors

1308 Anderson MS. Myxopapillary ependymomas presenting in the soft tissue over the sacrococcygeal region. Cancer 1966, **19**: 585–590.

1309 Bain GO, Shnitka TK. Cutaneous meningioma (psammoma). Arch Dermatol 1956, **74**: 590–594.

1310 Helwig EB, Stern JB. Subcutaneous sacrococcygeal myxopapillary ependymoma. A clinicopathologic study of 32 cases. Am J Clin Pathol 1984, **81**: 156–161.

1311 King P, Cooper PN, Malcolm AJ. Soft tissue ependymoma. A report of three cases. Histopathology 1993, **22**: 394–396.

1312 McDermott MB, Glasner SD, Nielsen PL, Dehner LP. Soft tissue gliomatosis: morphologic unity and histogenetic diversity. Am J Surg Pathol 1996, **20**: 148–155.

1313 Pulitzer DR, Martin PC, Collins PC, Ralph DR. Subcutaneous sacrococcygeal ("myxopapillary") ependymal rests. Am J Surg Pathol 1988, **12**: 672–677.

1314 Shepherd NA, Coates PJ, Brown AA. Soft tissue gliomatosis – heterotopic glial tissue in the subcutis. A case report. Histopathology 1987, **11**: 655–660.

Tumors of hematopoietic tissue

1315 Abbondanzo SL, Devaney K. Hodgkin's disease involving bone and adjacent soft tissue in adults: a clinicopathologic and immunophenotypic study of seven cases. Int J Surg Pathol 1996, **3**: 147–154.

1316 Akosa AB, Ali MH. Extramedullary plasmacytoma of skeletal muscle. A case report with immunocytochemistry and ultrastructural study. Cancer 1989, **64**: 1504–1507.

1317 Axiotis CA, Fuks J, Jennings TA, Kadish AS. Peripheral T-cell lymphoma presenting as a soft-tissue mass of the extremity. Arch Pathol Lab Med 1988, **112**: 850–851.

1318 Condon WB, Safarik LR, Elzi EP. Extramedullary hematopoiesis simulating intrathoracic tumor. Arch Surg 1965, **90**: 643–648.

1319 D'Amore ES, Wick MR, Geisinger KR, Frizzera G. Primary malignant lymphoma arising in postmastectomy lymphedema. Another facet of the Stewart–Treves syndrome. Am J Surg Pathol 1990, **14**: 456–463.

1320 Lanham GR, Weiss SW, Enzinger FM. Malignant lymphoma. A study of 75 cases presenting in soft tissue. Am J Surg Pathol 1989, **13**: 1–10.

1321 Salamao DR, Nascimento AG, Lloyd RV, Chen MG, Habermann TM, Strickler JG. Lymphoma in soft tissue: a clinicopathologic study of 19 cases. Hum Pathol 1996, **27**: 253–257.

1322 Travis WD, Banks FM, Reiman HM. Primary extranodal soft tissue lymphoma of the extremities. Am J Surg Pathol 1987, **11**: 359–366.

Tumors of uncertain cell type
Fibrous hamartoma of infancy

1323 Enzinger FM. Fibrous hamartoma of infancy. Cancer 1965, **18**: 241–248.

1324 Fletcher CDM, Powell G, Van Noorden S, McKee PH. Fibrous hamartoma of infancy. A histochemical and immunohistochemical study. Histopathology 1988, **12**: 65–74.

1325 Groisman G, Lichtig C. Fibrous hamartoma of infancy. Am immunohistochemical and ultrastructural study. Hum Pathol 1991, **22**: 914–918.

1326 Maung R, Lindsay R, Trevenen C, Hwang WS. Fibrous hamartoma of infancy. Hum Pathol 1987, **18**: 652–653.

1327 Michal M, Mukensnabl P, Chlumska A, Kodet R. Fibrous hamartoma of infancy. A study of eight cases with immunohistochemical and electron microscopical findings. Pathol Res Pract 1992, **188**: 1049–1053.

Myxoma

1328 Allen PW, Dymock RB, MacCormac LB. Superficial angiomyxomas with and without epithelial components. Report of 30 tumors in 28 patients. Am J Surg Pathol 1988, **12**: 519–530.

1329 Calonje E, Guerin D, McCormick D, Fletcher CD. Superficial angiomyxoma: clinicopathologic analysis of a series of distinctive but poorly recognized cutaneous tumors with tendency for recurrence. Am J Surg Pathol 1999, **23**: 910–917.

1330 Carney JA, Gordon H, Carpenter PC, Shenoy BV, Go VLW. The complex of myxomas, spotty pigmentation, and endocrine overactivity. Medicine 1985, **64**: 270–283.

1331 Enzinger FM. Intramuscular myxoma. A review and follow-up study of 34 cases. Am J Clin Pathol 1965, **43**: 104–113.

1332 Feldman PS. A comparative study including ultrastructure of intramuscular myxoma and myxoid liposarcoma. Cancer 1979, **43**: 512–525.

1333 Hashimoto H, Tsuneyoshi M, Daimaru Y, Enjoji M, Shinohara N. Intramuscular myxoma. A clinicopathologic,

immunohistochemical, and electron microscopic study. Cancer 1986, **58**: 740–747.

1334 Ireland DCR, Soule EH, Ivins JC. Myxoma of somatic soft tissues. A report of 58 patients, 3 with multiple tumors and fibrous dysplasia of bone. Mayo Clin Proc 1973, **48**: 401–410.

1335 Johnson WC, Helwig EB. Cutaneous focal mucinosis. A clinicopathological and histochemical study. Arch Dermatol 1966, **93**: 13–20.

1336 Mackenzie DH. The myxoid tumors of somatic soft tissues. Am J Surg Pathol 1981, **5**: 443–458.

1337 Meis JM, Enzinger FM. Juxta-articular myxoma. A clinical and pathologic study of 65 cases. Hum Pathol 1992, **23**: 639–646.

1338 Miettinen M, Hockerstedt K, Reitamo J, Totterman S. Intramuscular myxoma. A clinicopathological study of twenty-three cases. Am J Clin Pathol 1985, **84**: 265–272.

1339 Nielsen GP, O'Connell JX, Rosenberg AE. Intramuscular myxoma: a clinicopathologic study of 51 cases with emphasis on hypercellular and hypervascular variants. Am J Surg Pathol 1998, **22**: 1222–1227.

1340 Stout AP. Myxoma, the tumor of primitive mesenchyme. Ann Surg 1948, **127**: 706–719.

1341 van Roggen JFG, McMenamin ME, Fletcher CD. Cellular myxoma of soft tissue: a clinicopathological study of 38 cases confirming indolent clinical behaviour. Histopathology 2001, **39**: 287–297.

1342 Wirth WA, Leavitt D, Enzinger FM. Multiple intramuscular myxomas. Another extraskeletal manifestation of fibrous dysplasia. Cancer 1971, **27**: 1167–1173.

Granular cell tumor

1343 Al-Sarraf M, Loud AV, Vaitkevicius VK. Malignant granular cell tumor. Histochemical and electron microscopic study. Arch Pathol 1971, **91**: 550–558.

1344 Bedetti CD, Martinez AJ, Beckford NS, May M. Granular cell tumor arising in myelinated peripheral nerves. Light and electron microscopy and immunoperoxidase study. Virchows Arch [A] 1983, **402**: 175–183.

1345 Bhawan J, Malhotra R, Naik DR. Gaucher-like cells in a granular cell tumor. Hum Pathol 1983, **14**: 730–733.

1346 Budzilovich GN. Granular cell "myoblastoma" of vagus nerve. Acta Neuropathol 1968, **10**: 162–169.

1347 Chandrasoma P, Fitzgibbons P. Granular cell tumor of the intrapancreatic common bile duct. Cancer 1984, **53**: 2178–2182.

1348 Christ ML, Ozzello L. Myogenous origin of a granular cell tumor of the urinary bladder. Am J Clin Pathol 1971, **56**: 736–749.

1349 Clark HB, Minesky JJ, Agrawal D, Agrawal HC. Myelin basic protein and P2 protein are not immunohistochemical markers for Schwann cell neoplasms. A comparative study using antisera to S-100, P2, and myelin basic proteins. Am J Pathol 1985, **121**: 96–101.

1350 Copas P, Dyer M, Hall DJ, Diddle AW. Granular cell myoblastoma of the uterine cervix. Diagn Gynecol Obstet 1981, **3**: 251–254.

1351 de la Monte SM, Radowsky M, Hood AF. Congenital granular-cell neoplasms. An unusual case report with ultrastructural findings and a review of the literature. Am J Dermatopathol 1986, **8**: 57–63.

1352 Demay RM, Kay S. Granular cell tumor of the breast. Pathol Annu 1984, **19**(Pt 2): 121–148.

1353 Fanburg-Smith JC, Meis-Kindblom JM, Fante R, Kindblom LG. Malignant granular cell tumor of soft tissue: diagnostic criteria and clinicopathologic correlation. Am J Surg Pathol 1998, **22**: 779–794.

1354 Fine SW, Li M. Expression of calretinin and the alpha-subunit of inhibin in granular cell tumors. Am J Clin Pathol 2003, **119**: 259–264.

1355 Finkel G, Lane B. Granular cell variant of neurofibromatosis. Ultrastructure of benign and malignant tumors. Hum Pathol 1982, **13**: 959–963.

1356 Fisher ER, Wechsler H. Granular cell myoblastoma – a misnomer. Electron microscopic and histochemical evidence concerning its Schwann cell derivation and nature (granular cell schwannoma). Cancer 1962, **15**: 936–957.

1357 Garancis JC, Komorowski RA, Kuzma JF. Granular cell myoblastoma. Cancer 1970, **25**: 542–550.

1358 Johnston J, Helwig EB. Granular cell tumours of the gastrointestinal tract and perianal region. A study of 74 cases. Dig Dis Sci 1981, **26**: 807–816.

1359 Kindblom L-G, Olsson K-M. Malignant granular cell tumor. A clinicopathologic and ultrastructural study of a case. Pathol Res Pract 1981, **172**: 384–393.

1360 Lack EE, Worsham GF, Callihan MD, Crawford BE, Klappenbach S, Rowden G, Chun B. Granular cell tumor. A clinicopathologic study of 110 patients. J Surg Oncol 1980, **13**: 301–316.

1361 Lack EE, Worsham GF, Callihan MD, Crawford BE, Vawter GF. Gingival granular cell tumors of the newborn (congenital "epulis"). A clinical and pathologic study of 21 patients. Am J Surg Pathol 1981, **5**: 37–46.

1362 Le Boit PE, Barr RJ, Burall S, Metcalf JS, Yen TS, Wick MR. Primitive polypoid granular-cell tumor and other cutaneous granular-cell neoplasms of apparent nonneural origin. Am J Surg Pathol 1991, **15**: 48–58.

1363 Lifshitz MS, Flotte TJ, Greco MA. Congenital granular cell epulis. Immunohistochemical and ultrastructural observations. Cancer 1984, **53**: 1845–1848.

1364 Matthews JB, Mason GI. Granular cell myoblastoma. An immunoperoxidase study using a variety of antisera to human carcinoembryonic antigen. Histopathology 1983, **7**: 77–82.

1365 Mazur MT, Shultz JJ, Myers JL. Granular cell tumor. Immunohistochemical analysis of 21 benign tumors and one malignant tumor. Arch Pathol Lab Med 1990, **114**: 692–696.

1366 McMahon JN, Rigby HS, Davies JD. Elastosis in granular cell tumours. Prevalence and distribution. Histopathology 1990, **16**: 37–41.

1367 McSwain GR, Colpitts R, Kreutner A, O'Brien PH, Spicer S. Granular cell myoblastoma. Surg Gynecol Obstet 1980, **150**: 703–710.

1368 McWilliam LJ, Harris M. Granular cell angiosarcoma of the skin. Histology, electron microscopy and immunohistochemistry of a newly recognized tumor. Histopathology 1985, **9**: 1205–1216.

1369 Miettinen M, Lehtonen E, Lehtola H, Ekblom P, Lehto V, Virtanen I. Histogenesis of granular cell tumor. An immunohistochemical and ultrastructural study. J Pathol 1984, **142**: 221–229.

1370 Mittal KR, True LD. Origin of granules in granular cell tumor. Intracellular myelin formation with autodigestion. Arch Pathol Lab Med 1988, **112**: 302–303.

1371 Moscovic EA, Azar HA. Multiple granular cell tumors ("myoblastomas"). Case report with electron microscopic observations and review of the literature. Cancer 1967, **20**: 2032–2047.

1372 Mukai M. Immunohistochemical localization of S-100 protein and peripheral nerve myelin proteins (P2 protein, PO protein) in granular cell tumors. Am J Pathol 1983, **112**: 139–146.

1373 Nakazato Y, Ishizeki J, Takahashi K, Yamaguchi H. Immunohistochemical localization of S-100 protein in granular cell myoblastoma. Cancer 1982, **49**: 1624–1628.

1374 Nathrath WBJ, Remberger K. Immunohistochemical study of granular cell tumours. Demonstration of neurone specific enolase, S 100 protein, laminin and alpha-1-antichymotrypsin. Virchows Arch [A] 1986, **408**: 421–434.

1375 Navarrette AR, Smith M. Ultrastructure of granular cell ameloblastoma. Cancer 1971, **27**: 948–955.

1376 Nielsen K, Paulsen SM, Johansen P. Carcinoembryonic antigen like antigen in granular cell myoblastomas. An immunohistochemical study. Virchows Arch [A] 1983, **401**: 159–162.

1377 Nistal M, Paniagua R, Picazo ML, Cermeño deGiles F, Ramos Guerreira L. Granular changes in vascular leiomyosarcoma. Virchows Arch [A] 1980, **386**: 239–248.

1378 Ordonez NG, Mackay B. Granular cell tumor: a review of the pathology and histogenesis. Ultrastruct Pathol 1999, **23**: 207–222.

1379 Park SH, Kim TJ, Chi JG. Congenital granular cell tumor with systemic involvement. Immunohistochemical and ultrastructural study. Arch Pathol Lab Med 1991, **115**: 934–938.

1380 Penneys NS, Adachi K, Ziegels-Weissman J, Nadji M. Granular cell tumors of the skin contain myelin basic protein. Arch Pathol Lab Med 1983, **107**: 302–303.

1381 Regezi JA, Zarbo RJ, Courtney RM, Crissman JD. Immunoreactivity of granular cell lesions of skin, mucosa, and jaw. Cancer 1989, **64**: 1455–1460.

1382 Robertson AJ, McIntosh W, Lamont P, Guthrie W. Malignant granular cell tumour (myoblastoma) of the vulva. Report of a case and review of the literature. Histopathology 1981, **5**: 69–79.

1383 Sakurama N, Matsukado Y, Marubayashi T, Kodama T. Granular cell tumour of the brain and its cellular identity. Acta Neurochir (Wien) 1981, **56**: 81–94.

1384 Seo IS, Azzarelli B, Warner TF, Goheen MP, Senteney GE. Multiple visceral and cutaneous granular cell tumors. Ultrastructural and immunocytochemical evidence of Schwann cell origin. Cancer 1984, **53**: 2104–2110.

1385 Shimamura K, Osamura RY, Ueyama Y, Hata J I, Tamaoki N, Machida N, Fukuda H, Uemura K. Malignant granular cell tumor of the right sciatic nerve. Report of an autopsy case with electron microscopic, immunohistochemical, and enzyme histochemical studies. Cancer 1984, **53**: 524–529.

1386 Sobel JH, Marquet E, Schwarz R. Granular degeneration of appendiceal smooth muscle. Arch Pathol 1971, **92**: 427–432.

1387 Stefansson K, Wollmann RL. S-100 protein in granular cell tumors (granular cell myoblastomas). Cancer 1982, **49**: 1834–1838.

1388 Strong EW, McDivitt RW, Brasfield RD. Granular cell myoblastoma. Cancer 1970, **25**: 415–422.

1389 Troncoso P, Ordonez NG, Raymond AK, Mackay B. Malignant granular cell tumor. Immunocytochemical and ultrastructural observations. Ultrastruct Pathol 1988, **12**: 137–144.

1390 Usui M, Ishii S, Yamawaki S, Sasaki T, Minami A, Hizawa K. Malignant granular cell tumor of the radial nerve. Cancer 1977, **39**: 1547–1555.

1391 Uzoaru I, Firfer B, Ray V, Hubbard-Shepard M, Rhee H. Malignant granular cell tumor. Arch Pathol Lab Med 1992, **116**: 206–208.

1392 Vance SF III, Hudson RP. Granular cell myoblastoma. Clinicopathologic study of 42 patients. Am J Clin Pathol 1969, **52**: 208–211.

Alveolar soft part sarcoma

1393 Argani P, Antonescu CR, Illei PB, Lui MY, Timmons CF, Newbury I, Reuter VE, Garvin AJ, Perez-Atayde AR, Fletcher JA, Beckwith JB, Bridge JA, Ladanyi M. Primary renal neoplasms with the ASPL-TFE3 gene fusion of alveolar soft part sarcoma: a distinctive tumor entity previously included among renal cell carcinomas of children and adolescents. Am J Pathol 2001, **159**: 179–192.

1393a Argani P, Lal P, Hutchinson B, Lui MY, Reuter VE, Ladanyi M. Aberrant nuclear immunoreactivity for TFE3 in neoplasms with TFE3 gene fusions. Am J Surg Pathol 2003, **27**: 750–761.

1394 Auerbach HE, Brooks JJ. Alveolar soft part sarcoma. A clinicopathologic and immunohistochemical study. Cancer 1987, **60**: 66–73.

1395 Carstens HB. Membrane-bound cytoplasmic crystals, similar to those in alveolar soft part sarcoma, in a human muscle spindle. Ultrastruct Pathol 1990, **14**: 423–428.

1396 DeSchryver-Kecskemeti K, Kraus FT, Engleman W, Lacy PE. Alveolar soft-part sarcoma – a malignant angioreninoma. Histochemical, immunocytochemical, and electron-microscopic study of four cases. Am J Surg Pathol 1982, **6**: 5–18.

1397 Evans HL. Alveolar soft-part sarcoma. A study of 13 typical examples and one with a histologically atypical component. Cancer 1985, **55**: 912–917.

1397a Fanburg-Smith JC, Miettinen M, Folpe AL, Weiss SW, Childers ELB. Alveolar soft part sarcoma of the tongue: 14 cases. (Abstract) Mod Pathol 2003, **16**: 11A.

1398 Fisher ER, Reidford H. Electron microscopic evidence suggesting the myogenous derivation of the so-called alveolar soft part sarcoma. Cancer 1971, **27**: 150–159.

1399 Font RL, Jurco S III, Zimmerman LE. Alveolar soft-part sarcoma of the orbit. A clinicopathologic analysis of 17 cases and a review of the literature. Hum Pathol 1982, **13**: 569–579.

1400 Foschini MP, Ceccarelli C, Eusebi V, Skalli O, Gabbiani G. Alveolar soft part sarcoma. Immunological evidence of rhabdomyoblastic differentiation. Histopathology 1988, **13**: 101–108.

1401 Foschini MP, Eusebi V. Alveolar soft-part sarcoma. A new type of rhabdomyosarcoma? Semin Diagn Pathol 1994, **11**: 58–68.

1402 Gray GF Jr, Glick AD, Kurtin PJ, Jones HW III. Alveolar soft part sarcoma of the uterus. Hum Pathol 1986, **17**: 297–300.

1403 Hirose T, Kudo E, Hasegawa T, Abe J, Hizawa K. Cytoskeletal properties of alveolar soft part sarcoma. Hum Pathol 1990, **21**: 204–211.

1404 Ladanyi M, Antonescu CR, Drobnjak M, Baren A, Lui MY, Golde DW, Cordon-Cardo C. The precrystalline cytoplasmic granules of alveolar soft part sarcoma contain monocarboxylate transporter 1 and CD147. Am J Pathol 2002, **160**: 1215–1221.

1405 Ladanyi M, Lui MY, Antonescu CR, Krause-Boehm A, Meindl A, Argani P, Healey JH, Ueda T, Yoshikawa H, Meloni-Ehrig A, Sorens PH, Mertens F, Mandahl N, van den Berghe H, Sciot R, Cin PD, Bride J. The der(17)t(X;17)(p11;q25) of human alveolar soft part sarcoma fuses the TFE3 transcription factor gene to ASPL, a novel gene at 17q25. Oncogene 2001, **20**: 48–57.

1406 Lieberman PH, Brennan MF, Kimmel M, Erlandson RA, Garin-Chesa P, Flehinger BY. Alveolar soft-part sarcoma. A clinico-pathologic study of half a century. Cancer 1989, **63**: 1–13.

1407 Lieberman PH, Foote FW, Stewart FW, Berg JW. Alveolar soft-part sarcoma. JAMA 1966, **198**: 1047–1051.

1408 Lillehei KO, Kleinschmidt-De Masters B, Mitchell DH, Spector E, Kruse CA. Alveolar soft part sarcoma. An unusually long interval between presentation and brain metastasis. Hum Pathol 1993, **24**: 1030–1034.

1409 Machinami R, Kikuchi F. Adenosine triphosphatase activity of crystalline inclusions in alveolar soft part sarcoma. An ultrahistochemical study of a case. Pathol Res Pract 1986, **181**: 357–361.

1410 Matsuno Y, Mukai K, Itabashi M, Yamauchi Y, Hirota T, Nakajima T, Shimosato Y. Alveolar soft part sarcoma. A clinicopathologic and immunohistochemical study of 12 cases. Acta Pathol Jpn 1990, **40**: 199–205.

1411 Miettinen M, Ekfors T. Alveolar soft part sarcoma. Immunohistochemical evidence for muscle cell differentiation. Am J Clin Pathol 1990, **93**: 32–38.

1412 Mukai M, Iri H, Nakajima T, Hirose S, Torikata C, Kageyama K, Ueno N, Murakami K. Alveolar soft-part sarcoma. A review on its histogenesis and furthere studies based on electron microscopy, immunohistochemistry, and biochemistry. Am J Surg Pathol 1983, **7**: 679–689.

1413 Mukai M, Torikata C, Iri H, Mikata A, Hanaoka H, Kato K, Kageyama K. Histogenesis of alveolar soft part sarcoma. An immunohistochemical and biochemical study. Am J Surg Pathol 1986, **10**: 212–218.

1414 Ogawa K, Nakashima Y, Yamabe H, Hamashima Y. Alveolar soft part sarcoma, granular cell tumor, and paraganglioma. An immunohistochemical comparative study. Acta Pathol Jpn 1986, **36**: 895–904.

1415 Ohno T, Park P, Higaki S, Miki H, Kamura S, Unno K. Smooth tubular aggregates associated with plasmalemmal invagination in alveolar soft part sarcoma. Ultrastruct Pathol 1994, **18**: 383–388.

1416 Ordóñez NG, Hickey RC, Brooks TE. Alveolar soft part sarcoma. A cytologic and immunohistochemical study. Cancer 1988, **61**: 525–531.

1417 Ordóñez NG, Ro JY, Mackay B. Alveolar soft part sarcoma. An ultrastructural and immunocytochemical investigation of its histogenesis. Cancer 1989, **63**: 1721–1736.

1418 Ordonez NG. Alveolar soft part sarcoma: a review and update. Adv Anat Pathol 1999, **6**: 125–139.

1419 O'Toole RV, Tuttle SE, Lucas JG, Sharma HM. Alveolar soft part sarcoma of the vagina. An immunohistochemical and electron microscopic study. Int J Gynecol Pathol 1985, **4**: 258–265.

1420 Persson S, Willems JS, Kindblom LG, Angervall L. Alveolar soft part sarcoma. An immunohistochemical, cytologic and electron-microscopic study and a quantitative DNA analysis. Virchows Arch [A] 1988, **412**: 499–513.

1421 Rosai J, Dias P, Parham DM, Shapiro DN, Houghton P. MyoD1 protein expression in alveolar soft part sarcoma as confirmatory evidence of its skeletal muscle nature. Am J Surg Pathol 1991, **15**: 974–981.

1421a Sandberg A, Bridge J. Updates on the cytogenetics and molecular genetics of bone soft tissue tumors: alveolar soft part sarcoma. Cancer Genet Cytogenet 2002, **136**: 1–9.

1422 Shipkey IH, Lieberman PH, Foote FW Jr, Stewart FW. Ultrastructure of alveolar soft part sarcoma. Cancer 1964, **17**: 821–830.

1423 Tsutsumi Y, Deng YL. Alveolar soft part sarcoma of the pulmonary vein. Acta Pathol Jpn 1991, **41**: 771–777.

1424 Wang NP, Bacchi CE, Jiang JJ, McNutt MA, Gown AM. Does alveolar soft-part sarcoma exhibit skeletal muscle differentiation? An immunocytochemical and biochemical study of myogenic regulatory protein expression. Mod Pathol 1997, **9**: 496–506.

1425 Yagihashi S, Yagihashi N, Hase Y, Nagai K, Alguacil-Garcia A. Primary alveolar soft-part sarcoma of stomach. Am J Surg Pathol 1991, **15**: 399–406.

Clear cell sarcoma of tendons and aponeuroses (malignant melanoma of soft parts)

1426 Angervall L, Stener B. Clear-cell sarcoma of tendons. A study of 4 cases. Acta Pathol Microbiol Scand 1969, **77**: 589–597.

1427 Antonescu CR, Tschernyavsky SJ, Woodruff JM, Jungbluth AA, Brennan MF, Ladanyi M. Molecular diagnosis of clear cell sarcoma: detection of EWS-ATF1 and MITF-M transcripts and histopathological and ultrastructural analysis of 12 cases. J Mol Diagn 2002, **4**: 44–52.

1428 Azumi N, Turner RR. Clear cell sarcoma of tendons and aponeuroses. Electron microscopic findings suggesting Schwann cell differentiation. Hum Pathol 1983, **14**: 1084–1089.

1429 Bearman RM, Noe J, Kempson RL. Clear cell sarcoma with melanin pigment. Cancer 1975, **36**: 977–984.

1430 Benson JD, Kraemer BB, Mackay B. Malignant melanoma of soft parts. An ultrastructural study of four cases. Ultrastruct Pathol 1985, **8**: 57–70.

1431 Bridge JA, Borek DA, Neff JR, Huntrakoon M. Chromosomal abnormalities in clear cell sarcoma. Implications for histogenesis. Am J Clin Pathol 1990, **93**: 26–31.

1432 Chung EB, Enzinger FM. Malignant melanoma of soft parts. A reassessment of clear cell sarcoma. Am J Surg Pathol 1983, **7:** 405–413.

1433 Deenik W, Mooi WJ, Rutgers EJ, Peterse JL, Hart AA, Kroon BB. Clear cell sarcoma (malignant melanoma) of soft parts: a clinicopathologic study of 30 cases. Cancer 1999, **86:** 969–975.

1434 Eckardt JJ, Pritchard DJ. Soule EH. Clear cell sarcoma. A clinicopathologic study of 27 cases. Cancer 1983, **52:** 1482–1488.

1435 el-Naggar AK, Ordonez NG, Sara A, McLemore D, Batsakis JG. Clear cell sarcomas and metastatic soft tissue melanomas. A flow cytometric comparison and prognostic implications. Cancer 1991, **67:** 2173–2179.

1436 Enzinger FM. Clear-cell sarcoma of tendons and aponeuroses. An analysis of 21 cases. Cancer 1965, **18:** 1163–1174.

1437 Hasegawa T, Hirose T, Kudo E, Hizawa K. Clear cell sarcoma. An immunohistochemical and ultrastructural study. Acta Pathol Jpn 1989, **39:** 321–327.

1438 Kindblom L-G, Lodding P, Angervall L. Clear-cell sarcoma of tendons and aponeuroses. An immunohistochemical and electron microscopic analysis indicating neural crest origin. Virchows Arch [A] 1983, **401:** 109–128.

1439 Lucas DR, Nascimento AG, Sim FH. Clear cell sarcoma of soft tissues. Mayo Clinic experience with 35 cases. Am J Surg Pathol 1992, **16:** 1197–1204.

1440 Montgomery E, Meis J, Ramos A, Frisman D, Mertz K. Clear cell sarcoma of tendons and aponeuroses. A clinicopathologic study of 58 cases with analysis of prognostic factors. Int J Surg Pathol 1993, **1.** 89–100.

1441 Mooi WJ, Deenik W, Peterse JL. Hogendoorn PCW. Keratin immunoreactivity in melanoma of soft parts (clear cell sarcoma). Histopathology 1995, **27:** 61–65.

1442 Mukai M, Torikata C, Iri H, Mikata A, Kawai T, Hanaoka H, Yakumaru K, Kageyama K. Histogenesis of clear cell sarcoma of tendons and aponeuroses. Am J Pathol 1984, **114:** 264–272.

1443 Ohno T, Park P, Utsunomiya Y, Hirahata H, Inoue K. Ultrastructural study of a clear cell sarcoma suggesting Schwannian differentiation. Ultrastruct Pathol 1986, **10:** 39–48.

1444 Pavlidis NA, Fisher C, Wiltshaw E. Clear-cell sarcoma of tendons and aponeuroses. A clinicopathologic study. Presentation of six additional cases with review of the literature. Cancer 1984, **54:** 1412–1417.

1444a Sandberg AA, Bridge JA. Updates on the cytogenetics and molecular genetics of bone soft tissue tumors: clear cell sarcoma (malignant melanoma soft parts). Cancer Genet Cytogenet 2001, **130:** 1–7.

1445 Sara AS, Evans HL, Benjamin RS. Malignant melanoma of soft parts (clear cell sarcoma). A study of 17 cases, with emphasis on prognostic factors. Cancer 1990, **65:** 367–374.

1446 Saw D, Tse CH, Chan J, Watt CY, Ng CS, Poon YF. Clear cell sarcoma of the penis. Hum Pathol 1986, **17:** 423–425.

1447 Swanson PE, Wick MR. Clear cell sarcoma. An immunohistochemical analysis of six cases and comparison with other epithelioid neoplasms of soft tissue. Arch Pathol Lab Med 1989, **113:** 55–60.

1448 Tsuneyoshi M, Enjoji M, Kubo T. Clear cell sarcoma of tendons and aponeuroses. A comparative study of 13 cases with a provisional subgrouping into the melanotic and synovial types. Cancer 1978, **42:** 243–252.

1449 Zambrano E, Reyes-Mugica M, Franchi A, Rosai J. An osteoclast-rich tumor of the gastrointestinal tract with features resembling clear cell sarcoma of parts: reports of six cases of a GIST simulator. Int J Surg Pathol 2003, **11:** 75–81.

Epithelioid sarcoma

1450 Arber DA, Kandalaft PL, Mehta P, Battifora H. Vimentin-negative epithelioid sarcoma. The value of an immunohistochemical panel that includes CD34. Am J Surg Pathol 1993, **17:** 302–307.

1451 Bloustein PA, Silverberg SG, Waddell WR. Epithelioid sarcoma. Case report with ultrastructural review, histogenetic discussion, and chemotherapeutic data. Cancer 1976, **38:** 2390–2400.

1452 Bryan RS, Soule EH, Dobyns JH, Pritchard DJ, Linscheid RL. Primary epithelioid sarcoma of the hand and forearm. J Bone Joint Surg (Am) 1974, **56:** 458–465.

1453 Chase DR, Enzinger FM. Epithelioid sarcoma. Diagnosis, prognostic indicators, and treatment. Am J Surg Pathol 1985, **9:** 241–263.

1454 Chase DR, Enzinger FM, Weiss SW, Langloss JM. Keratin in epithelioid sarcoma. An immunohistochemical study. Am J Surg Pathol 1984, **8:** 435–441.

1455 Chase DR, Enzinger FM, Weiss SW, Langloss JM. Coexpression of keratin and vimentin in epithelioid sarcoma. Am J Surg Pathol 1985, **9:** 460–463.

1456 Chetty R, Slavin JL. Epithelioid sarcoma with extensive chondroid differentiation. Histopathology 1994, **24:** 400–401.

1457 Daimaru Y, Hashimoto H, Tsuneyoshi M, Enjoji M. Epithelial profile of epithelioid sarcoma. An immunohistochemical analysis of eight cases. Cancer 1987, **59:** 134–141.

1457a den Bakker MA, Flood SJ, Kliffen M.. CD31 staining in epithelioid sarcoma. Virchows Arch 2003, **443:** 93–97.

1458 Enzinger FM. Epithelioid sarcoma. A sarcoma simulating a granuloma or a carcinoma. Cancer 1970, **25:** 1029–1041.

1459 Evans HL, Baer SC. Epithelioid sarcoma. A clinicopathologic and prognostic study of 26 cases. Semin Diagn Pathol 1993, **10:** 286–291.

1460 Fisher C. Epithelioid sarcoma. The spectrum of ultrastructural differentiation in seven immunohistochemically defined cases. Hum Pathol 1988, **19:** 265–275.

1461 Gabbiani G, Fu Y-S, Kaye GI, Lattes R, Majno G. Epithelioid sarcoma. A light and electron microscopic study suggesting a synovial origin. Cancer 1972, **30:** 486–499.

1462 Guillou L, Wadden C, Coindre JM, Krausz T, Fletcher CD. "Proximal-type" epithelioid sarcoma, a distinctive aggressive neoplasm showing rhabdoid features: clinicopathologic, immunohistochemical, and ultrastructural study of a series. Am J Surg Pathol 1997, **21:** 130–146.

1463 Halling AC, Wollan PC, Pritchard DJ, Vlasak R, Nascimento AG. Epithelioid sarcoma: a clinicopathologic review of 55 cases. Mayo Clin Proc 1996, **71:** 636–642.

1464 Hasegawa T, Matsuno Y, Shimoda T, Umeda T, Yokoyama R, Hirohashi S. Proximal-type epithelioid sarcoma: a clinicopathologic study of 20 cases. Mod Pathol 2001, **14:** 655–663.

1464a Laskin WB, Miettinen M. Epithelioid sarcoma. New insights based on an extended immunohistochemical analysis. Arch Pathol Lab Med 2003, **127:** 1161–1168.

1465 Manivel JC, Wick MR, Dehner LP, Sibley RK. Epithelioid sarcoma. An immunohistochemical study. Am J Clin Pathol 1987, **87:** 319–326.

1466 Miettinen M, Fanburg-Smith JC, Virolainen M, Shmookler BM, Fetsch JF. Epithelioid sarcoma: an immunohistochemical analysis of 112 classical and variant cases and discussion of the differential diagnosis. Hum Pathol 1999, **30:** 934–942.

1467 Miettinen M, Lehto V-P, Vartio T, Virtanen I. Epithelioid sarcoma. Ultrastructural and immunohistologic features suggesting a synovial origin. Arch Pathol Lab Med 1982, **106:** 620–623.

1468 Mills SE, Rosai J. Adamantinoma of the pretibial soft tissue. Clinicopathologic features, differential diagnosis, and possible relationship to intraosseous disease. Am J Clin Pathol 1985, **83:** 108–114.

1469 Mirra JM, Kessler S, Bhuta S, Eckardt J. The fibroma-like variant of epithelioid sarcoma. A fibrohistiocytic/myoid cell lesion often confused with benign and malignant spindle cell tumours. Cancer 1992, **69**: 1382–1395.

1470 Molenaar WM, De Jong B, Dam-Meiring A, Postma A, De Vries J, Hoekstra HJ. Epithelioid sarcoma or malignant rhabdoid tumor of soft tissue? Epithelioid immunophenotype and rhabdoid karyotype. Hum Pathol 1989, **20**: 347–351.

1471 Mukai M, Torikata C, Iri H, Hanaoka H, Kawai T, Yakumaru K, Shimoda T, Mikata A, Kageyama K. Cellular differentiation of epithelioid sarcoma – electron-microscopic, enzyme-histochemical, and immunohistochemical study. Am J Pathol 1985, **119**: 44–56.

1472 Peimer CA, Smith RJ, Sirota RL, Cohen BE. Epithelioid sarcoma of the hand and wrist. Patterns of extension. J Hand Surg 1977, **2**: 275–282.

1473 Perrone T, Swanson PE, Twiggs L, Ulbright TM, Dehner LP. Malignant rhabdoid tumor of the vulva. Is distinction from epithelioid sarcoma possible? A pathologic and immunohistochemical study. Am J Surg Pathol 1989, **13**: 848–858.

1474 Prat J, Woodruff JM, Marcove RC. Epithelioid sarcoma. An analysis of 22 cases indicating the prognostic significance of vascular invasion and regional lymph node metastasis. Cancer 1978, **41**: 1472–1487.

1475 Rose DSC, Fisher C, Smith MEF. Epithelioid sarcoma arising in a patient with neurofibromatosis type 2. Histopathology 1994, **25**: 379–380.

1476 Santiago H, Feinerman LK, Lattes R. Epithelioid sarcoma. A clinical and pathologic study of nine cases. Hum Pathol 1972, **3**: 133–147.

1477 Shimm DS, Suit HD. Radiation therapy of epithelioid sarcoma. Cancer 1983, **52**: 1022–1025.

1478 Shiratsuchi H, Oshiro Y, Saito T, Itakura E, Kinoshita Y, Tamiya S, Oda Y, Komiyama S, Tsuneyoshi M. Cytokeratin subunits of inclusion bodies in rhabdoid cells: immunohistochemical and clinicopathological study of malignant rhabdoid tumor and epithelioid sarcoma. Int J Surg Pathol 2001, **9**: 37–48.

1479 Sugarbaker PH, Auda S, Webber BL, Triche TJ, Shapiro E, Cook WJ. Early distant metastases from epithelioid sarcoma of the hand. Cancer 1981, **48**: 852–855.

1480 Weissmann D, Amenta PS, Kantor GR. Vulvar epithelioid sarcoma metastatic to the scalp. A case report and review of the literature. Am J Dermatopathol 1990, **12**: 462–468.

Giant cell tumor of soft parts

1481 Alguacil-Garcia A, Unni KK, Goellner JR. Malignant giant cell tumor of soft parts. An ultrastructural study of four cases. Cancer 1977, **40**: 244–253.

1482 Angervall L, Hagmar B, Kindblom L-G, Merck C. Malignant giant cell tumor of soft tissues. A clinicopathologic, cytologic, ultrastructural, angiographic, and microangiographic study. Cancer 1981, **47**: 736–747.

1483 Folpe AL, Morris RJ, Weiss SW. Soft tissue giant cell tumor of low malignant potential: a proposal for the reclassification of malignant giant cell tumor of soft parts. Mod Pathol 1999, **12**: 894–902.

1484 Gould E, Albores-Saavedra J, Rothe M, Mnaymneh W, Menedez-Aponte S. Malignant giant cell tumor of soft parts presenting as a skin tumor. Am J Dermatopathol 1989, **11**: 197–201.

1485 Guccion JG, Enzinger FM. Malignant giant cell tumor of soft parts. An analysis of 32 cases. Cancer 1972, **29**: 1518–1529.

1486 Kearney MM, Soule EH, Ivins JC. Malignant fibrous histiocytoma. A retrospective study of 167 cases. Cancer 1980, **45**: 167–178.

1487 O'Connell JX, Wehrli BM, Neilsen GP, Rosenberg AE. Giant cell tumors of soft tissue: a clinicopathologic study of 18 benign and malignant tumors. Am J Surg Pathol 2000, **24**: 386–395.

1488 Oliveira AM, Dei Tos AP, Fletcher CD, Nascimento AG. Primary giant cell tumor of soft tissues: a study of 22 cases. Am J Surg Pathol 2000, **24**: 248–256.

1489 Salm R, Sissons HA. Giant-cell tumours of soft tissues. J Pathol 1972, **107**: 27–39.

1490 Teot LA, O'Keefe RJ, Rosier RN, O'Connell JX, Fox EJ, Hicks DG. Extraosseous primary and recurrent giant cell tumors: transforming growth factor beta-1 and beta-2 expression may explain metaplastic bone formation. Hum Pathol 1996, **27**: 625–632.

Ossifying fibromyxoid tumor

1491 Donner LR. Ossifying fibromyxoid tumor of soft parts. Evidence supporting Schwann cell origin. Hum Pathol 1992, **23**: 200–202.

1492 Enzinger FM, Weiss SW, Liang CY. Ossifying fibromyxoid tumor of soft parts. A clinicopathological analysis of 59 cases. Am J Surg Pathol 1989, **13**: 817–827.

1492a Folpe AL, Weiss SW. Ossifying fibromyxoid tumor of soft parts. A clinicopathological study of 70 cases with emphasis on atypical malignant variants. Am J Surg Pathol 2003, 27: 421–431.

1493 Kilpatrick SE, Ward WG, Mozes M, Miettinen M, Fukunaga M, Fletcher CDM. Atypical and malignant variants of ossifying fibromyxoid tumor. Clinicopathologic analysis of six cases. Am J Surg Pathol 1995, **19**: 1039–1046.

1494 Miettinen M. Ossifying fibromyxoid tumor of soft parts. Additional observations of a distinctive soft tissue tumor. Am J Clin Pathol 1991, **95**: 142–149.

1495 Schofield JB, Krausz T, Stamp GW, Fletcher CD, Fisher C, Azzopardi JG. Ossifying fibromyxoid tumour of soft parts. Immunohistochemical and ultrastructural analysis. Histopathology 1993, **22**: 101–112.

1496 Yang P, Hirose T, Hasegawa T, Gao Z, Hizawa K. Ossifying fibromyxoid tumor of soft parts. A morphological and immunohistochemical study. Pathol Int 1994, **44**: 448–453.

Extraskeletal Ewing's sarcoma/PNET

1497 Ambros IM, Ambros PF, Strehl S, Kovar H, Gadner H, Salzer-Kuntschik M. MIC2 is a specific marker for Ewing's sarcoma and peripheral primitive neuroectodermal tumors. Evidence for a common histogenesis of Ewing's sarcoma and peripheral primitive neuroectodermal tumors from MIC2 expression and specific chromosome aberration. Cancer 1991, **67**: 1886–1893.

1498 Angervall L, Enzinger FM. Extraskeletal neoplasm resembling Ewing's sarcoma. Cancer 1975, **36**: 240–251.

1499 Askin FB, Rosai J, Sibley RK, Dehner LP, McAlister WH. Malignant small cell tumor of the thoracopulmonary region in childhood. A distinctive clinicopathologic entity of uncertain histogenesis. Cancer 1979, **43**: 2438–2451.

1500 Cavazzana AO, Ninfo V, Roberts J, Triche TJ. Peripheral neuroepithelioma. A light microscopic, immunocytochemical, and ultrastructural study. Mod Pathol 1992, **5**: 71–78.

1501 Collini P, Sampietro G, Bertulli R, Casali PG, Luksch R, Mezzelani A, Sozzi G, Pilotti S. Cytokeratin immunoreactivity in 41 cases of ES/PNET confirmed by molecular diagnostic studies. Am J Surg Pathol 2001, **25**: 273–274.

1502 Contesso G, Llombart-Bosch A, Terrier P, Peydro-Olaya A, Henry-Amar M, Oberlin O, Habrand JL, Dubousset J, Tursz T, Spielmann M, et al. Does malignant small round cell tumor of the thoracopulmonary region (Askin tumor) constitute a clinicopathologic entity? An analysis of 30 cases with immunohistochemical and electron-microscopic support treated at the Institute Gustave Roussy. Cancer 1992, **69**: 1012–1020.

1503 De Alava E, Pardo J. Ewing tumor: tumor biology and clinical applications. Int J Surg Pathol 2001, **9**: 7–17.

1504 Delattre O, Zucman J, Melot T, Garau XS, Zucker JM, Lenoir

GM, Ambros PF, Sheer D, Turc-Carel C, Triche TJ, et al. The Ewing family of tumors – a sub group of small-round-cell tumors defined by specific chimeric transcripts. N Engl J Med 1994, **331**: 294–299.

1505 Dickman PS, Triche TJ. Extraosseous Ewing's sarcoma versus primitive rhabdomyosarcoma. Diagnostic criteria and clinical correlation. Hum Pathol 1986, **17**: 881–893.

1506 Downing JR, Head DR, Parham DM, Douglass EC, Hulshof MG, Link MP, Motroni TA, Grier HE, Curcio-Brint AM, Shapiro DN. Detection of the (11; 22) (q24; q12) translocation of Ewing's sarcoma and peripheral neuroectodermal tumor by reverse transcription polymerase chain reaction. Am J Pathol 1993, **143**: 1294–1300.

1507 Fellinger EJ, Garin-Chesa P, Triche TJ, Huvos AG, Retting WJ. Immunohistochemical analysis of Ewing's sarcoma cell surface antigen p30/32MIC2. Am J Pathol 1991, **139**: 317–325.

1508 Folpe AL, Hill CE, Parham DM, O'Shea PA, Weiss SW. Immunohistochemical detection of Fli-1 protein expression: a study of 132 round cell tumors with emphasis on CD99-positive mimics of Ewing's sarcoma/primitive neuroectodermal tumors. Am J Surg Pathol 2000, **24**: 1657–1662.

1509 Gerald WL. A practical approach to the differential diagnosis of small round cell tumors of infancy using recent scientific and technical advances. Int J Surg Pathol 2000, **8**: 87–97.

1510 Gillespie JJ, Roth LM, Wills ER, Einborn LH, Willman J. Extraskeletal Ewing's sarcoma. Histologic and ultrastructural observations in three cases. Am J Surg Pathol 1979, **3**: 99–108.

1511 Gonzalez Crussi F, Wolfson SL, Misugi K, Nakajima T. Peripheral neuroectodermal tumors of the chest wall in childhood. Cancer 1984, **54**: 2519–2527.

1512 Gould VE, Moll R, Berndt R, Roessner A, Franke WW, Lee I. Immunohistochemical analysis of Ewing's tumors (abstract). Lab Invest 1987, **56**: 28A.

1513 Harris MD, Moore IE, Steart PV, Weller RO. Protein gene product (PGP) 9.5 as a reliable marker in primitive neuroectodermal tumors—an immunohistochemical study of 21 childhood cases. Histopathology 1990, **16**: 271–277.

1514 Hashimoto H, Tsuneyoshi M, Daimaru Y, Enjoji M. Extraskeletal Ewing's sarcoma. A clinicopathologic and electron microscopic analysis of 8 cases. Acta Pathol Jpn 1985, **35**: 1087–1098.

1515 Jürgens H, Bier V, Harms D, Beck J, Brandeis W, Etspüler G, Gadner H, Schmidt D, Treuner J, Winkler K, Göbel U. Malignant peripheral neuroectodermal tumors. A retrospective analysis of 42 patients. Cancer 1988, **61**: 349–357.

1516 Kawaguchi K, Koike M. Neuron-specific enolase and leu-7 immunoreactive small round-cell neoplasm. The relationship to Ewing's sarcoma in bone and soft tissue. Am J Clin Pathol 1986, **86**: 79–83.

1517 Kumar S, Pack S, Kumar D, Walker R, Quezado M, Zhuang Z, Meltzer P, Tsokos M. Detection of EWS-FLI-1 fusion in Ewing's sarcoma/peripheral primitive neuroectodermal tumor by fluorescence in situ hybridisation using formalin-fixed paraffin-embedded tissue. Hum Pathol 1999, **30**: 324–330.

1518 Ladanyi M, Heinemann FS, Huvos AG, Rao PH, Chen QG, Jhanwar SC. Neural differentiation in small round cell tumors of bone and soft tissue with the translocation t(11; 22)(q24; q12). An immunohistochemical study of 11 cases. Hum Pathol 1990, **21**: 1245–1251.

1519 Ladanyi M, Lewis R, Garin-Chesa P, Rettig WJ, Huvos AG, Healey JH, Jhanwar SC. EWS rearrangement in Ewing's sarcoma and peripheral neuroectodermal tumor. Molecular detection and correlation with cytogenetic analysis and MIC2 expression. Diagn Mol Pathol 1993, **2**: 141–146.

1520 Linnoila RI, Tsokos M, Triche TJ, Marangos PJ, Chandra RS. Evidence for neural origin and PAS-positive variants of the malignant small cell tumor of thoracopulmonary region ("Askin tumor"). Am J Surg Pathol 1986, **10**: 124–133.

1521 Navarro S, Cavazzana AO, Llombart-Bosch A, Triche TJ. Comparison of Ewing's sarcoma of bone and peripheral neuroepithelioma. An immunocyto-chemical and ultrastructural analysis of two primitive neuroectodermal neoplasms. Arch Pathol Lab Med 1994, **118**: 608–615.

1522 Pagani A, Fischer-Colbrie R, Sanfilippo B, Winkler H, Cerrato M, Bussolati G. Secretogranin II expression in Ewing's sarcomas and primitive neuroectodermal tumors. Diagn Mol Pathol 1992, **1**: 165–172.

1523 Parham DM, Hijazi Y, Sternberg SM, Meyer WH, Horowitz M, Tzen CY, Wexler LH, Tsokos M. Neuroectodermal differentiation in Ewing's sarcoma family of tumors does not predict tumor behaviour. Hum Pathol 1999, **30**: 911–918.

1524 Rud NP, Reiman HM, Pritchard DJ, Frassica FJ, Smithson WA. Extraosseous Ewing's sarcoma. A study of 42 cases. Cancer 1989, **64**: 1548–1553.

1525 Schmidt D, Harms D, Burdach S. Malignant peripheral neuroectodermal tumours of childhood and adolescence. Virchows Arch [A] 1985, **406**: 351–365.

1526 Selleri L, Hermanson GG, Eubanks JH, Lewis KA, Evans GA. Molecular localization of the t(11; 22)(q24; q12) translocation of Ewing sarcoma by chromosomal in situ suppression hybridization. Proc Natl Acad Sci U S A 1991, **88**: 887–891.

1527 Shimada H, Newton WA Jr, Soule EH, Qualman SJ, Aoyama C, Maurer HM. Pathologic features of extraosseous Ewing's sarcoma. A report from the Intergroup Rhabdomyosarcoma Study. Hum Pathol 1988, **19**: 442–453.

1528 Shishikura A, Ushigome S, Shimoda T. Primitive neuroectodermal tumors of bone and soft tissue. Histological subclassification and clinicopathologic correlations. Acta Pathol Jpn 1993, **43**: 176–186.

1529 Sorensen P, Liu X, Delattre O, Rowland J, Biggs C, Thomas G, Triche T. Reverse transcriptase PCR amplification of EWS/FLI-1 fusion transcripts as a diagnostic test for peripheral primitive neuroectodermal tumors of childhood. Diagn Mol Pathol 1993, **2**: 147–157.

1530 Soule EH, Newton W Jr, Moon TE, Tefft M. Extraskeletal Ewing's sarcoma – a preliminary review of 26 cases encountered in the intergroup rhabdomyosarcoma study. Cancer 1978, **42**: 259–264.

1531 Stevenson AJ, Chatten J, Bertoni F, Miettinen M. CD99 (p30/32MIC2) neuroectodermal/Ewing's sarcoma antigen as an immunohistochemical marker. Review of more than 600 tumors and the literature experience. Appl Immunohistochem 1994, **2**: 231–240.

1532 Suh CH, Ordonez NG, Hicks J, Mackay B. Ultrastructure of Ewing's sarcoma family of tumors. Ultrastruct Pathol 2002, **26**: 67–76.

1533 Thorner P, Squire J, Chilton-MacNeill S, Marrano P, Bayani J, Malkin D, Greenberg M, Lorenzana A, Zielenska M. Is the EWS/FLI-1 fusion transcript specific for Ewing sarcoma and peripheral primitive neuroectodermal tumor? A report of four cases showing the transcript in a wider range of tumor types. Am J Pathol 1996, **148**: 1125–1138.

1534 Triche TJ, Askin FB, Kissane JM. Neuroblastoma. Ewing's sarcoma, and the differential diagnosis of small-, round-, blue-cell tumors. In Finegold M (ed.): Pathology of neoplasia in children and adolescents, vol 18. Philadelphia, 1986, WB Saunders, p. 145.

1535 Turc-Carel C, Philip I, Berger MP, Philip T, Lenoir GM. Chromosome study of Ewing's sarcoma (ES) cell lines. Consistency of a reciprocal translocation t(11;22)(q24; = –q12). Cancer Genet Cytogenet 1984, **12**: 1–12.

1536 Vakar-Lopez F, Ayala AG, Raymond AK, Czerniak B. Epithelial phenotype in Ewing's sarcoma/primitive neuroectodermal tumor. Int J Surg Pathol 2000, **8**: 59–65.

1537 Variend S. Small cell tumors in childhood. A review. J Pathol 1985, **145**: 1–25.

1538 Weidner N, Tjoe J. Immunohistochemical profile of monoclonal antibody O13. Antibody that recognizes glycoprotein p30/32MIC2 and is useful in diagnosing Ewing's sarcoma and peripheral neuroepithelioma. Am J Surg Pathol 1994, **18:** 486–494.

1539 Wigger HJ, Salazar GH, Blane WA. Extraskeletal Ewing sarcoma. An ultrastructural study. Arch Pathol Lab Med 1977, **101:** 446–449.

1540 Yunis EJ. Ewing's sarcoma and related small round cell neoplasms in children. Am J Surg Pathol 1986, **10**(Suppl 1): 54–62.

Desmophilic small cell tumor

1541 Adsay V, Cheng J, Athanasian E, Gerald W, Rosai J. Primary desmoplastic small cell tumor of soft tissues and bone of the hand. Am J Surg Pathol 1999, **23:** 1408–1413.

Rhabdoid tumor

1542 Fanburg-Smith JC, Hengge M, Hengge UR, Smith JS, Miettinen M. Extrarenal rhabdoid tumors of soft tissue: a clinicopathologic and immunohistochemical study of 18 cases. Ann Diagn Pathol 1999, **2:** 351–362.

1543 Frierson HF, Mills SE, Innes DJ Jr. Malignant rhabdoid tumor of the pelvis. Cancer 1985, **55:** 1963–1967.

1544 Gururangan S, Bowman LC, Parham DM, Wilimas JA, Rao B, Pratt CB, Douglass EC. Primary extracranial rhabdoid tumors. Clinicopathologic features and response to ifosfamide. Cancer 1993, **71:** 2653–2659.

1545 Kent AL, Mahoney DH Jr, Gresik MV, Steuber CP, Fernbach DJ. Malignant rhabdoid tumor of the extremity. Cancer 1987, **60:** 1056–1059.

1546 Kodet R, Newton WA Jr, Sachs N, Hamoudi AB, Raney RB, Asmar L, Gehan EA. Rhabdoid tumors of soft tissues. A clinicopathologic study of 26 cases enrolled on the Intergroup Rhabdomyosarcoma Study. Hum Pathol 1991, **22:** 674–684.

1547 Parham DM, Weeks DA, Beckwith JB. The clinicopathologic spectrum of putative extrarenal rhabdoid tumors. An analysis of 42 cases studied with immunohistochemistry or electron microscopy. Am J Surg Pathol 1994, **18:** 1010–1029.

1548 Schmidt D, Leuschner I, Harms D, Sprenger E, Schafer HJ. Malignant rhabdoid tumor. A morphological and flow cytometric study. Pathol Res Pract 1989, **184:** 202–210.

1549 Sotelo-Avila C, Gonzalez-Crussi F, De Mello D, Vogler C, Gooch WM, Gale G, Pena R. Renal and extrarenal rhabdoid tumors in children. A clinicopathologic study of 14 patients. Semin Diagn Pathol 1986, **3:** 151–163.

1550 Tsokos M, Kouraklis G, Chandra RS, Bhagavan BS, Triche TJ. Malignant rhabdoid tumor of the kidney and soft tissues. Evidence for a diverse morphological and immunocytochemical phenotype. Arch Pathol Lab Med 1989, **113:** 115–120.

1551 Tsuneyoshi M, Daimaru Y, Hashimoto H, Enjoji M. Malignant soft tissue neoplasms with the histologic features of renal rhabdoid tumors. An ultrastructural and immunohistochemical study. Hum Pathol 1985, **16:** 1235–1242.

1552 Weeks DA, Beckwith JB, Mierau GW. Rhabdoid tumor. An entity or a phenotype? Arch Pathol Lab Med 1989, **113:** 113–114.

1553 Wick MR, Ritter JH, Dehner LP. Malignant rhabdoid tumors. A clinicopathologic review and conceptual discussion. Semin Diagn Pathol 1995, **12:** 233–248.

Phosphaturic mesenchymal tumor

1554 Cai Q, Hodgson SF, Kao PC, Lennon VA, Klee GG, Zinsmiester AR, Kumar R. Brief report. Inhibition of renal phosphate transport by a tumor product in a patient with oncogenic osteomalacia. N Engl J Med 1994, **330:** 1645–1649.

1554a Folpe AL, Fanburg-Smith JC, Wiess SW. Most phosphaturic mesenchymal tumors are a single entity: an analysis of 31 cases. Mod Pathol 2003, **16:** 12A.

1555 Weidner N. Review and update. Oncogenic osteomalacia-rickets. Ultrastruct Pathol 1991, **15:** 317–333.

1556 Weidner N, Bar RS, Weiss D, Strottmann MP. Neoplastic pathology of oncogenic osteomalacia/rickets. Cancer 1985, **55:** 1691–1705.

1557 Weidner N, Santa Cruz D. Phosphaturic mesenchymal tumors. A polymorphous group causing osteomalacia or rickets. Cancer 1987, **59:** 1442–1454.

Pleomorphic hyalinizing angioectatic tumor of soft parts

1557a Bridge JA, Gentry JD, Swarts SJ, Billings SD, Bridge RS Jr, Althof PA, Pickering D, Neff JR, Wiess SW. Supernumerary ring chromosomes in pleomorphic hyalinizing angiectatic tumor: a feature of potential diagnostic utility. (Abstract) Mod Pathol 2003, **16:** 9A.

1558 Smith ME, Fisher C, Weiss SW. Pleomorphic hyalinizing angiectatic tumor of soft parts: a low-grade neoplasm resembling neurilemoma. Am J Surg Pathol 1996, **20:** 21–29.

Myoepithelioma of soft tissue

1559 Dabska M. Parachordoma. A new clinicopathologic entity. Cancer 1977, **40:** 1586–1592.

1560 Fisher C, Miettinen M. Parachordoma: a clinicopathologic and immunohistochemical study of four cases of an unusual soft tissue neoplasm. Ann Diagn Pathol 1999, **1:** 3–10.

1560a Hornick JL, Fletcher CDM. Myoepithelial tumors of soft tissue. A clinicopathologic and immunohistochemical study of 101 cases with evaluation of prognostic parameters. Am J Surg Pathol 2003, **27:** 1183–1196.

1561 Ishida T, Oda H, Oka T, Imamura T, Machinami R. Parachordoma. An ultrastructural and immunohistochemical study. Virchows Arch [A] 1993, **422:** 239–246.

1562 Kilpatrick SE, Hitchcock MG, Kraus MD, Calonje E, Fletcher CD. Mixed tumors and myoepitheliomas of soft tissue: a clinicopathologic study of 19 cases with a unifying concept. Am J Surg Pathol 1997, **21:** 13–22.

1563 Michal M, Miettinen M. Myoepitheliomas of the skin and soft tissues. Report of 12 cases. Virchows Arch 1999, **434:** 393–400.

1564 Sanguesa OP, White CR Jr. Parachordoma. Am J Dermatopathol 1994, **16:** 185–188.

1565 Shin HJ, Mackay B, Ichinose H, Ayala AG, Romsdahl MM. Parachordoma. Ultrastruct Pathol 1994, **18:** 249–256.

Other tumors

1566 Polk P, Parker KM, Biggs PJ. Soft tissue oncocytoma. Hum Pathol 1996, **27:** 206–208.

Metastatic tumors

1567 Alexiou G, Papadopoulou-Alexiou M, Karakousis CP. Renal cell carcinoma presenting as skeletal muscle mass. J Surg Oncol 1984, **27:** 23–25.

1567a Perez-Montiel DM, Plaza JA, Wakely P, Suster S. Metastases to soft tissue sites: review of 86 cases over a 30 year period. (Abstract) Mod Pathol 2003, **16:** 19A.

Other tumorlike conditions

1568 Cabanne F, Chapuis JL, Duperrat B, Putelat R. L'infiltration cutanée par la polyvinylpyrrolidone. Ann Anat Pathol 1966, **11:** 385–396.

1569 Coleman WR, Homer RS, Kaplan RP. Branchial cleft heterotopia of the lower neck. J Cutan Pathol 1989, **16:** 353–358.

1570 Fetsch JF, Montgomery EA, Meis JM. Calcifying fibrous pseudotumor. Am J Surg Pathol 1993, **17:** 502–508.

1571 Fraga S, Helwig EB, Rosen SM. Bronchogenic cysts in the skin and subcutaneous tissue. Am J Clin Pathol 1971, **56:** 230–238.

1572 Harkness JW, Peters HJ. Tumoral calcinosis, a report of six cases. J Bone Joint Surg (Am) 1967, **49:** 721–731.

1573 Hizawa K, Inaba H, Nakanishi S, Otsuka H, Izumi K. Subcutaneous pseudosarcomatous polyvinylpyrrolidone granuloma. Am J Surg Pathol 1984, **8:** 393–398.

1574 Krishnan J, Chu WS, Elrod JP, Frizzera G. Tumoral presentation of amyloidosis (amyloidomas) in soft tissues. A report of 14 cases. Am J Clin Pathol 1993, **100:** 135–144.

1575 Kuo T-T, Hsueh S. Mucicarminophilic histiocytosis. A polyvinylpyrrolidone (PVP) storage disease simulating signet-ring cell carcinoma. Am J Surg Pathol 1984, **8:** 419–428.

1576 Lyles KW, Burkes EJ, Ellis GJ, Lucas EJ, Dolan EA, Drezner MK. Genetic transmission of tumoral calcinosis. Autosomal dominant with variable clinical expressivity. J Clin Endocrinol Metab 1985, **60:** 1093–1096.

1577 Montgomery E, Meis J, Ramos A, Frisman D, Mertz K. Clear cell sarcoma of tendons and aponeuroses. A clinicopathologic study of 58 cases with analysis of prognostic factors. Int J Surg Pathol 1993, **1:** 89–100.

1578 Nascimento AF, Ruiz R, Hornick JL, Fletcher CD. Calcifying fibrous "pseudotumor". Clinicopathologic study of 15 cases and analysis of its relationship to inflammatory myofibroblastic tumor. Int J Surg 2002, **10:** 189–196.

1579 Nielsen GP, Fletcher CD, Smith MA, Rybak L, Rosenberg AE. Soft tissue aneurysmal bone cyst: a clinicopathologic study of five cases. Am J Surg Pathol 2001, **26:** 64–69.

1580 Pakasa NM, Kalengayi RM. Tumoral calcinosis: a clinicopathological study of 111 cases with emphasis on the earliest changes. Histopathology 1997, **31:** 18–24.

1581 Rodriguez-Peralto JL, Lopez-Barea F, Sanchez-Herrera S, Atienza M. Primary aneurysmal cyst of soft tissues (extraosseous aneurysmal cyst). Am J Surg Pathol 1994, **18:** 632–636.

1582 Shareef DS, Salm R. Ectopic vestigial lesions of the neck and shoulders. J Clin Pathol 1981, **34:** 1155–1162.

1583 Sleater J, Mullins D. Subcutaneous Castleman's disease of the wrist. Am J Dermatopathol 1995, **17:** 174–178.

26 Peritoneum, retroperitoneum, and related structures

Peritoneum

Normal anatomy

The peritoneal cavity is lined by mesodermally derived tissues consisting of a layer of surface mesothelium resting on vascularized subserosal tissue and separated from it by a continuous basal lamina.[1a] It is characterized ultrastructurally by the presence of apical tight junctions, desmosomes, surface microvilli, and tonofilaments. Immunohistochemically, it exhibits strong reactivity to cytokeratin (including keratin 5/6), EMA, calretinin, thrombomodulin, and basal lamina components. It is negative for CEA, Leu-M1, Ber-EP4 and B72:3. The surprising fact that normal mesothelium expresses parathyroid hormone-like peptide activity has been recently reported.[3] Just as interesting is the fact that developing mesothelium in the embryo exhibits transient immunoreactivity for desmin before switching to its adult keratin-based intermediate filament profile, and that this capacity for desmin expression reappears under reactive conditions.[2]

The resting subserosal cells have the overall structure of fibroblasts, are negative for keratin, and express vimentin.[1] These cells are sometimes referred to as *multipotential subserosal cells* because they are thought to have the capacity to serve as replicative cells that can differentiate into surface mesothelium. In females, these subserosal cells can be conspicuous, especially in the pelvic parietal peritoneum and on the bladder dome. They are sensitive to sex hormones and are probably the progenitors of lesions such as endometriosis, endosalpingiosis, ectopic decidual reaction, leiomyomatosis peritonealis disseminata, and tumors of ovarian or uterine type[4] (see p. 2386). This large group of peritoneal disorders related to the female genital tract is also discussed in Chapter 19, Ovary and Uterus corpus.

Structures or regions topographically related to the peritoneum and retroperitoneum are the omentum, mesentery, hernia sacs, umbilicus, and sacrococcygeal region. Since an overlapping of pathologic processes exists among all of them, they are discussed in this chapter, with appropriate references to other sections of the text when indicated.

Inflammation

Chemical peritonitis can be caused by bile, pancreatic juice, gastric juice, meconium, and radiographic contrast media. Barium peritonitis has been seen following perforation of large bowel occurring during the course of radiographic examinations performed because of obstruction[15]; it is the result of the bacteria that accompany the contrast material.

Extravasation of *bile* as a result of trauma or disease of the gallbladder, bile ducts, or duodenum causes an acute or subacute peritonitis that is initially limited to the upper quadrant of the abdomen.[8] *Gastric juice* produces a severe peritoneal reaction because of its hydrochloric acid content, although it may be bacteriologically sterile. The release of *pancreatic juice* causes fat necrosis. The formation of calcium salts in large areas of fat necrosis may cause hypocalcemia.

Bacterial peritonitis may be either primary or secondary. The *primary* form usually is caused by streptococci and is seen more commonly in children (particularly in those affected by the nephrotic syndrome). Adult patients with ascites secondary to liver disease are also susceptible. This form of peritonitis tends to produce marked constitutional symptoms with minimal localizing findings. Aspiration of intra-abdominal fluid discloses an inflammatory exudate containing only a single type of organism. Large amounts of extracellular fluid are lost into the exudate, equivalent to those of a burn covering one half to three fourths of the cutaneous surface.[7]

Perforation of a viscus such as the colon produces *secondary* peritonitis. If the fluid is aspirated, a mixture of bacterial flora rather than a single organism is found. *Tuberculous peritonitis* may occur with few constitutional symptoms, despite extensive involvement of the peritoneum.[5,11,12,18] In a review of 47 cases, Singh et al.[17] found radiographic evidence of pulmonary parenchymal lesions in only 6% of the cases. The search for acid-fast organisms on a direct smear of ascitic fluid is often unrewarding. The best diagnostic methods are culture of the fluid and percutaneous biopsy of the peritoneum.[13,14] Singh et al.[17] found the latter to be useful in 64% of their cases. Chemotherapy is the treatment of choice; surgery is reserved for those cases associated with enteritis leading to bowel obstruction, perforation, fistula, or a mass that does not resolve with drug therapy.[16] Other specific forms of peritonitis are *coccidioidomycosis* and *actinomycosis*.[6] Exceptionally, *Oxyuris vermicularis* may escape from the appendix or other portions of the gastrointestinal tract into the peri-

toneal cavity and elicit the formation of granulomas.[20]

Meconium peritonitis is the result of perforation of the small bowel during intrauterine life. It may present in infants as intestinal obstruction requiring surgical intervention. With healing, only scattered calcific foci remain. These can be located in the main peritoneal cavity, inguinal region, or scrotum; the latter can simulate clinically a testicular tumor.[9,19]

Vernix caseosa peritonitis represents a rare complication of cesarean section, and it has distinctive microscopic features.[10]

Adhesions

Adhesions, with the possibility of subsequent intestinal obstruction, follow all intra-abdominal operations. They can be minimized by careful handling of tissues, reperitonealization where feasible, and removal of intraperitoneal blood clots. Ryan et al.[27] showed in an experimental model that drying of the serosa plus bleeding consistently resulted in the formation of adhesions. There is good experimental evidence to suggest that the formation of peritoneal adhesions is related to a local depression of peritoneal plasminogen activator, which is the principal peritoneal fibrin-clearing system known.[21]

Innumerable agents, including sodium citrate, heparin, olive oil, liquid paraffin, ACTH, cortisone, pepsin, fibrinolysin, and amniotic fluid, have been used over the years to prevent adhesions, but none has accomplished this goal in an entirely successful fashion. Adhesions become collagenous and strong as the cellularity of their fibrous tissue decreases with maturation. Postoperative adhesions are the most frequent cause of intestinal obstruction today.

Extensive peritoneal fibrosis (*sclerosing* or *fibrosing peritonitis*) also has been described as a reaction to asbestos, to silica in drug abusers,[23] in patients with the carcinoid syndrome, in patients with lupus,[26] in women with luteinized thecomas and related proliferative stromal lesions of the ovary,[24] and as a complication of the administration of beta-adrenergic-blocking drugs,[22] or of compounds containing fluoropyrimidines.[25] In many instances, the etiologic agent cannot be identified; some of these "idiopathic" cases are probably pathogenetically related to mesenteric panniculitis and—as such—are part of the spectrum of the inflammatory fibrosclerosis group of diseases (see p. 2389).

Reaction to foreign materials

The peritoneum reacts briskly to foreign substances. The most spectacular (and easiest to recognize) are those accompanying retained sponges and instruments after surgery, an event still haunting the laparotomy procedure and more likely to occur in emergency situations and/or in obese patients.[35a] Classically, one of the better known peritoneal reactions to foreign material is *talc powder granuloma*, which is secondary to the talc (hydrated magnesium silicate) used in the past on surgical gloves. Spillage of this material into the peritoneal cavity at surgery results in nodules that can be mistaken grossly for tuberculosis or metastatic carcinoma. Microscopically, they are formed by foreign body granulomas containing birefringent crystals. The latter are made apparent with polarizing lenses or simply by lowering the condenser of the microscope.

Talc used for surgical gloves has long been recognized as a hazard and has been replaced by other substances, such as modified starch. Although these materials elicit a lesser degree of reaction, intraperitoneal granulomas may still develop,[43] on average between 10 days and 4 weeks after a laparotomy. These usually have the appearance of foreign body granulomas but sometimes exhibit tuberculoid features with caseum-like necrosis.[42] At reoperation, the findings are ascites, miliary peritoneal nodules, serosal inflammation, and adhesions. The gross appearance can closely simulate metastatic carcinoma, tuberculosis, or Crohn's disease. The nature of the granulomas can be identified by the presence of granules that are PAS positive and birefringent (with a Maltese cross pattern) within the cytoplasm of histiocytes and foreign body giant cells.[33,35] Levison et al.[39] have pointed out that the Maltese cross pattern is characteristic of corn starch, whereas other types of starch particles may have different shapes, sizes, and surface markings. The diagnosis may be suspected through the finding of starch granules in the aspirated peritoneal fluid. Fortunately, the disease is usually self-limited.

Other sources of surgical contamination are the cellulose fibers derived from disposable surgical gowns and drapes and the oxidized regenerated cellulose used as a hemostatic agent.[37,44] Sometimes the starch found in peritoneal granulomas does not originate in surgical gloves but from food starch that has gained its access to the peritoneal cavity through perforation of the bowel[34] or from the material contained in contraceptive devices.[39]

Mineral oil or paraffin placed in the peritoneal cavity years ago to prevent adhesions was responsible for the formation of nodules that could be grossly mistaken for metastatic carcinoma.[40] Microscopically, these nodules exhibit foreign body giant cells, chronic inflammation, and foamy macrophages. Similar changes follow rupture of a cystic teratoma of the ovary, in which large amounts of oily material cause a profound nodular peritoneal reaction.[28] Ruptured ovarian teratomas can also be associated with peritoneal *melanosis*.[36]

Keratin from endometrioid adenocarcinomas with squamous differentiation (adenoacanthomas) of the endometrium, ovary, or both can detach from the main tumor, reach the peritoneal cavity (through the fallopian tube in the case of uterine tumors), and elicit a brisk foreign body-type granulomatous reaction. The presence of these keratin granulomas has no prognostic significance and should not be equated with the presence of viable tumor implants.[30,38]

Peritoneal endometriosis may result in the formation of *necrotic pseudoxanthomatous nodules*; this may follow diathermy ablation of the lesion, but it may also be seen spontaneously.[31,32]

Exceptionally, silicosis can involve the peritoneal serosa and simulate a tumor on gross examination.[41]

Although not a foreign body, one could mention here the curious phenomenon of implantation of normal splenic tissue in the peritoneal cavity following traumatic rupture of the spleen, a process known as *splenosis*[29] (see Chapter 22).

Cysts and loose bodies

Pseudocysts of the peritoneal cavity (lacking a mesothelial or epithelial lining) may follow inflammatory processes such as perforated colitis or perforated appendicitis.

Solitary cysts varying in size from 1 to 6 cm can be found incidentally within the peritoneal cavity, either attached to the wall or lying loose in the lower pelvis. They have a translucent wall, watery fluid in the lumen, and a lining composed of one or more layers of mesothelial cells[51] (Fig. 26.1). They probably represent acquired inclusion cysts related to chronic inflammation. A case of multilocular *melanotic* peritoneal cyst has been described.[47]

A probably related condition has been designated **cystic** or **multicystic benign mesothelioma**.[49,53,59] This process nearly always occurs in the pelvis of adult

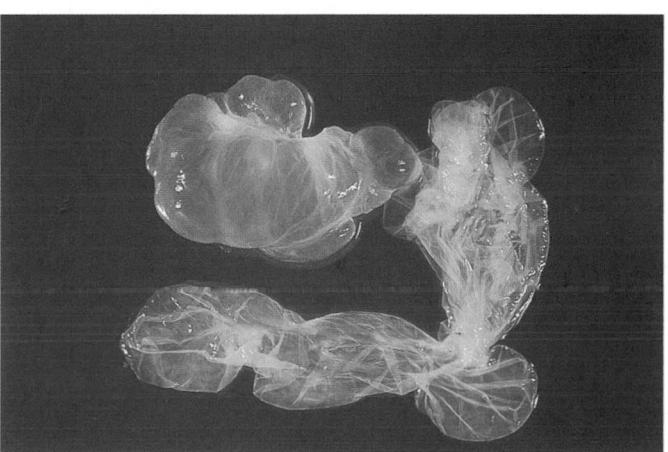

Fig. 26.1 Gross appearance of peritoneal cysts. They have a thin, translucent wall and contain a clear fluid. (Courtesy of Dr. Juan Jose Segura, San José, Costa Rica)

females, the average age at diagnosis being around 35 years. It has also been described involving most of the peritoneum, and a few cases have been seen in males. Often there is a history of previous pelvic surgery, endometriosis, or pelvic inflammatory disease. This entity may result in pelvic pain, present clinically as a mass, or be found incidentally at laparotomy (often at the time of a tubal ligation) or within a hernia sac. Grossly, multiple cysts are present, measuring up to 15 cm or more in diameter, attached to or engulfing pelvic organs (Fig. 26.2). Microscopically, the cysts are lined by flattened or cuboidal mesothelial cells. When flat, the cells closely simulate the appearance of endothelial cells. Intracellular hyaline globules may be present.[50] The mesothelial cells react immunohistochemically for keratin and calretinin; are negative for FVIII-related antigen and other endothelial markers; sometimes show focal reactivity for hormone receptors;[57a] and exhibit desmosomes, tonofibrils, and slender microvilli on ultrastructural examination.[53,58] The wall, which is devoid of smooth muscle, usually shows foci of chronic inflammation, hemorrhage, and fibrin deposition. Sometimes the

reactive mesothelial proliferation in the wall of these cysts is prominent enough to simulate a malignancy.[52]

The natural history of this disorder is characterized by a great tendency to local recurrence. This fact, plus the tumorlike appearance that these lesions exhibit grossly, is responsible for the assumption that they represent benign mesotheliomas. We agree with Ross et al.[56] that they probably are instead **multiple peritoneal inclusion cysts** forming as a result of peritoneal reactive proliferation. Their tendency for recurrence can be explained by persistence of the original inciting factor. Interestingly,

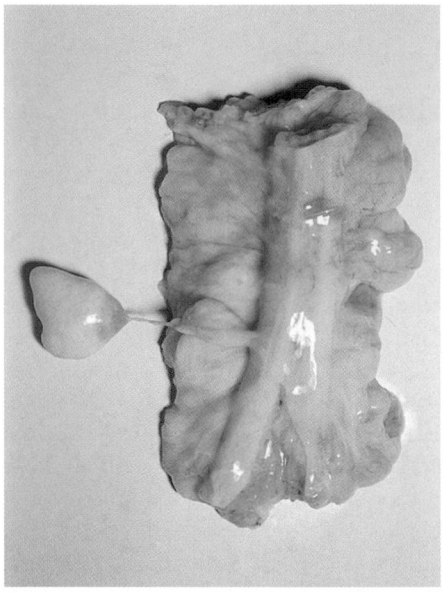

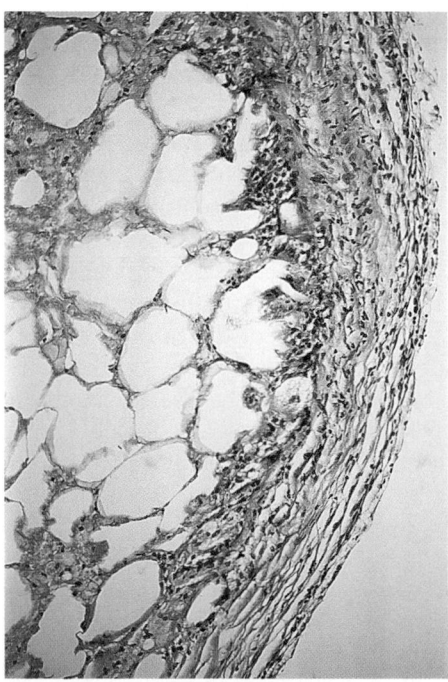

Fig. 26.3 Twisted appendix epiploica. **A,** Gross appearance. **B,** Microscopic appearance, showing inflammatory reaction to fat necrosis.

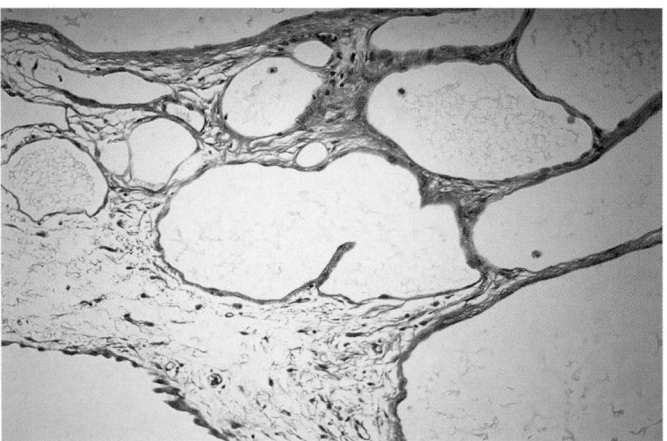

Fig. 26.2 So-called "multicystic benign mesothelioma". **A,** Gross appearance. **B,** Microscopic appearance. The flat shape of the mesothelium lining the cyst simulates the appearance of a lymphangioma.

this entity can be seen in association with adenomatoid tumor, another benign mesothelial lesion for which the neoplastic versus hyperplastic pathogenesis has been argued.[46] The main differential diagnosis is with cystic lymphangioma[45] (see pp. 2388, 2390, and 2398).

Cysts of müllerian origin can occur between the bladder and rectum in the true pelvis of males.[48] They result from persistence of müllerian duct derivatives and are usually lined by fallopian tube-type epithelium.[57] They have also been described in the mesentery and other portions of the abdominal cavity (see p. 2390). Occasionally, they may be the site of malignant transformation.[54]

Appendix epiploica may twist, undergo massive fat necrosis, and present as a sclerocalcified nodule either attached to its original site or free-floating in the abdominal cavity[60] (Fig. 26.3). Sometimes the fat necrosis has a *membranous* quality by virtue of the lining of the cysts by an eosinophilic membrane with pseudopapillary infoldings having the histochemical staining pattern of ceroid.[55]

Hyperplasia and metaplasia

The mesothelial lining surface has a great capacity to undergo florid hyperplastic changes when irritated. This hyperplasia can occur in a diffuse fashion throughout the peritoneal cavity in cases of liver cirrhosis, collagen vascular diseases (such as lupus erythematosus), and viral infections. Actually, mesothelial hyperplasia may supervene in any long-standing effusion regardless of its cause. It can also occur in a localized fashion as a response to injury. Hernia sacs can exhibit florid foci of **nodular mesothelial hyperplasia** following incarceration or some other mechanical insult; this is particularly common in children and may simulate malignancy[68] (Fig. 26.4). A similar change may occur in the serosa of an acutely inflamed appendix or a fallopian tube following rupture of an ectopic pregnancy, simulating implants from a serous papillary tumor of the ovary.[64b] The danger of misinterpreting these reactive mesothelial changes as neoplastic is even greater when they develop in association with ovarian neoplasms, sometimes in intimate closeness to them.[63]

Microscopically, these mesothelial hyperplastic changes may appear as papillary projections, solid nests, or tubular structures (Figs 26.5 and 26.6). They may project on the surface or interact in a complex fashion with the underlying stroma, simulating invasion.[66] Psammoma bodies may be present in the stroma of the papillary formations.[68] The cells may be vacuolated or have an entirely clear cytoplasm[66]; these vacuoles do not stain for mucin or fat.

A reactive change that has acquired a notoriety out of proportion with its clinical significance is that of **nodular histiocytic/mesothelial hyperplasia**. Among its many

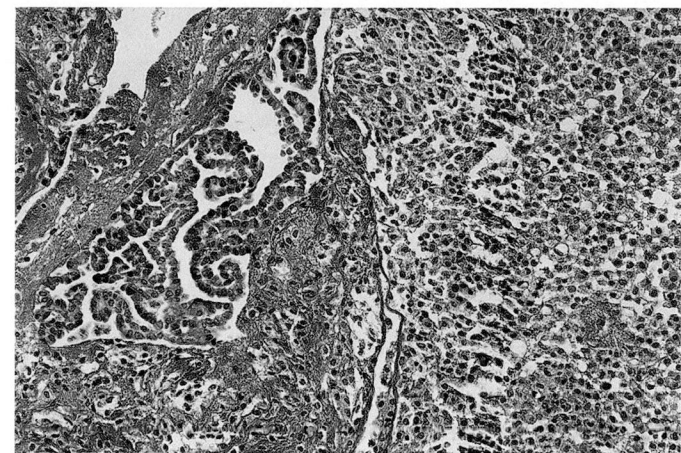

A

B

Fig. 26.4 A and **B**, Florid mesothelial hyperplasia in hernia sac. The complex papillary architecture may simulate a mesothelioma.

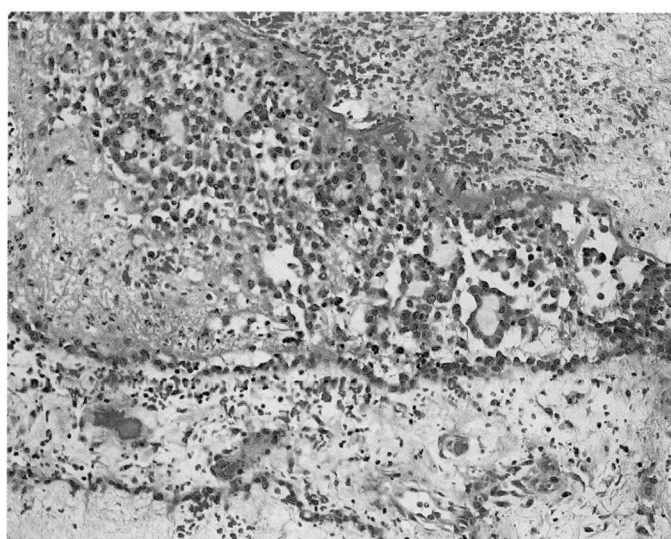

Fig. 26.5 Reactive mesothelial hyperplasia in a patient with granulosa cell tumor of the ovary. This should not be overinterpreted as a tumor implant.

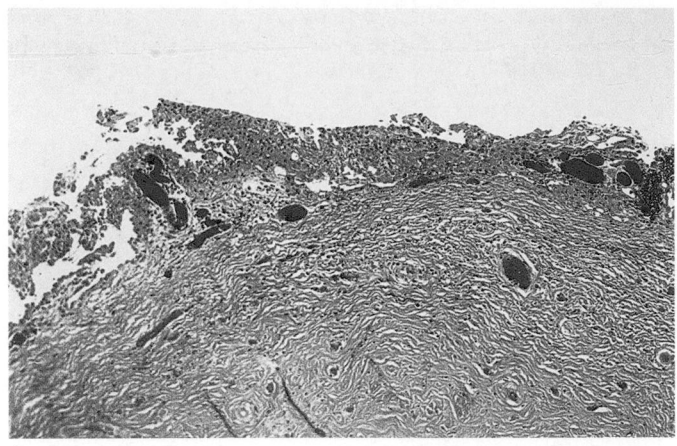

A

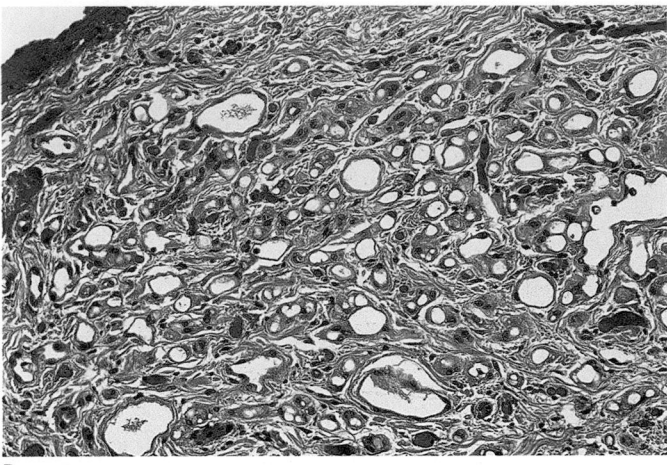

B

Fig. 26.6 A and **B**, Florid mesothelial hyperplasia with a pattern resembling adenomatoid tumor.

synonyms, the most picturesque is that of MICE (mesothelial/monocytic incidental cardiac excrescences), due to the fact that one of the sites in which it may be found is the heart[70] (see Chapter 27 for a more detailed account). Suffice it to say here that it can also present within the peritoneal cavity, nearly always as an incidental microscopic finding. It is microscopically composed of an admixture of CD68-positive histiocytes (which predominate) and keratin- and calretinin-positive mesothelial cells, the latter often appearing as clusters and micropapillae.[67] Its only importance derives from the fact that the pathologist unaware of its existence may overdiagnose it as mesothelioma, carcinoma, or worse.[62]

The differential diagnosis between reactive mesothelial hyperplasia and mesothelioma can be very difficult. Features favoring malignancy are the presence of *grossly visible* nodular or papillary foci, marked nuclear atypia, increase in nucleo-cytoplasmic ratio, and presence of necrosis in the desmoplastic areas.[66] The latter finding is one of the most useful signs, since it is extremely unusual in reactive processes.

Immunohistochemically, reactive mesothelial cells stain strongly for keratin of various molecular weights

and may regain the capacity for desmin expression normally exhibited by the developing mesothelium.[65] Reactive subserosal connective tissue cells retain their expression of vimentin but also acquire immunoreactivity for low-molecular-weight keratin and develop the ultrastructural features of myofibroblasts.[61] Unfortunately, these features are of little practical use in the differential diagnosis with mesothelioma. Instead, immunohistochemistry can be of value in the differential diagnosis between reactive mesothelial hyperplasia and epithelial tumor implants in patients with borderline or malignant ovarian serous neoplasms although the differences are not as sharp as those between pleural mesothelioma and lung adenocarcinoma (see under Differential diagnosis and in Chapters 7 and 19). It is important not to misinterpret as neoplastic the sometimes thick layer of keratin-positive reactive submesothelial fibroblasts that is often seen around or in between peritoneal tumor nodules of one type or another.

Mesothelial cells can also undergo metaplastic changes, the most important being *squamous metaplasia*[64,69] and *müllerian metaplasia*. The latter change is seen almost exclusively in females, predominates in the pelvic region, and is mainly represented by endometriosis, endosalpingiosis, and ectopic decidual reaction.[71] (This is further discussed on p. 2386 and in Chapter 19, Ovary.) Focal *cartilaginous metaplasia* also occurs, but this probably originates from the submesothelial mesenchymal elements rather than the mesothelium itself.[64a]

Tumors

Mesothelioma

The mesotheliomas seen in the peritoneum are qualitatively similar to those occurring in the pleural cavity (see Chapter 7), but the relative proportions among the various types and the criteria used for the differential diagnosis with metastatic carcinoma (ovary and lung, respectively) are somewhat different. Traditionally, peritoneal mesotheliomas have been divided into epithelial and fibrous, but the latter tumor is no longer considered a type of mesothelioma and is discussed separately (see p. 2384). The majority of true mesotheliomas are either solitary and benign or diffuse and malignant, but exceptions occur in both directions.

Benign mesothelioma

The benign form of mesothelioma usually presents as a solitary small papillary structure resembling grossly and microscopically the appearance of choroid plexus.[92] Most examples are incidental findings at the time of laparotomy. A few are pedunculated and may undergo torsion. We suspect that many of these lesions are reactive (i.e., examples of focal papillary mesothelial hyperplasia) rather than true neoplasms. There is no evidence that they undergo malignant transformation, and they are not related to asbestos exposure.

The above lesion is the only mesothelial proliferative process (other than the clearly reactive postinflammatory lesions) that we feel confident in regarding as benign. Solitary mesothelial proliferations having a predominantly *solid* pattern of growth and well-differentiated papillary mesothelial proliferations having a multicentric or diffuse quality are best regarded as malignant tumors (see next section).

The lesion known as **multicystic benign mesothelioma** has been discussed on p. 2375.

Malignant mesothelioma

General and clinical features. Most cases of peritoneal malignant mesothelioma occur in individuals past 40 years of age, but they have been described in young adults,[94] children,[74,98,124] and even neonates.[118] A definite male predominance has been noted. Their frequency is on the increase.[73] About half of the cases are associated with asbestos exposure[114a,119]; interestingly, peritoneal mesotheliomas are common in patients with heavy asbestos exposure, whereas pleural mesotheliomas predominate in the larger population of transiently exposed individuals. The average latency period is 15 years and over.[122] Major asbestos usage in the United States began around 1950 and continued through the 1960s, and therefore it is not unreasonable to expect a further increase in the incidence of this neoplasm. As a matter of fact, it has been estimated that the increase is likely to continue in the US and Western Europe well into the 21st century, at least until 2020.[81] Some peritoneal mesotheliomas have occurred after exposure to the contrast medium Thorotrast[109] and others following repeated mesothelial irritation.[82,114] In some instances, they have been found to coexist with pleural mesotheliomas.

The usual clinical presentation is in the form of recurrent ascites, which may be associated with abdominal cramps and increased abdominal girth.[93] Intermittent partial bowel obstruction is common. Occasionally, the disease may first manifest in a hernia sac, umbilicus, ovary, or large bowel wall.[79,85,87,116] In other instances, inguinal or cervical lymphadenopathy resulting from metastatic disease is the first sign of the tumor.[121] In yet other instances, the clinical presentation is in the form of a localized acute inflammatory process.[98a]

Gross features. Grossly, peritoneal mesothelioma usually appears as multiple plaques or nodules scattered over the visceral and parietal peritoneum.[96,128] It may be accompanied by dense intraperitoneal adhesions and shortening of the mesentery. Ascites is almost universally present. Coexisting fibrous pleural plaques are common, more so than with pleural mesotheliomas; sometimes fibrous plaques are also present within the abdominal cavity.[72] On rare occasions, the tumor presents as an isolated mass; such a lesion is distinguished

from benign mesothelioma by virtue of its more solid appearance and the presence of atypia, which may be very subtle.[89] As already indicated, one should be very careful before making the diagnosis of benign mesothelioma in the presence of a localized mesothelial proliferation with a predominantly solid appearance; we have seen several such cases in which recurrence developed in the form of disseminated peritoneal disease.

Microscopic features. The microscopic pattern of malignant mesothelioma is highly variable. The most common arrangement is that of papillae or tubules lined by atypical mesothelial cells, the former having vascularized fibrous cores that may contain psammoma bodies (Figs 26.7 and 26.8).[75] In other instances, the mesothelial-like cells alternate with sarcomatoid spindle cells in a biphasic fashion. The individual cells are, in general,

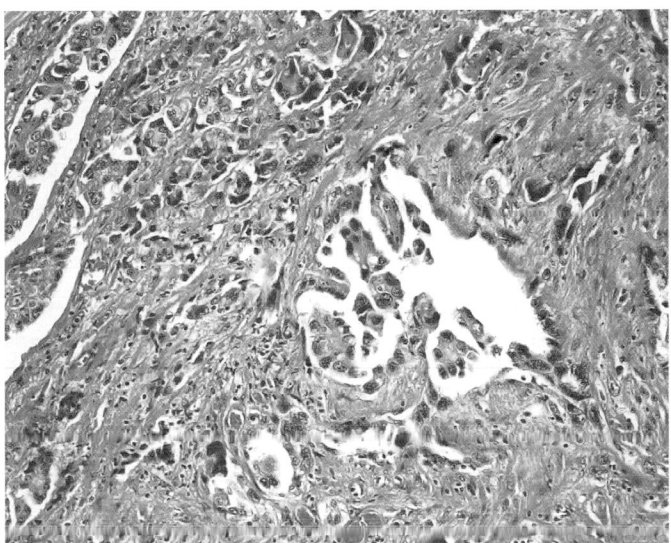

Fig. 26.7 Malignant mesothelioma with papillary formations and desmoplastic stromal reaction.

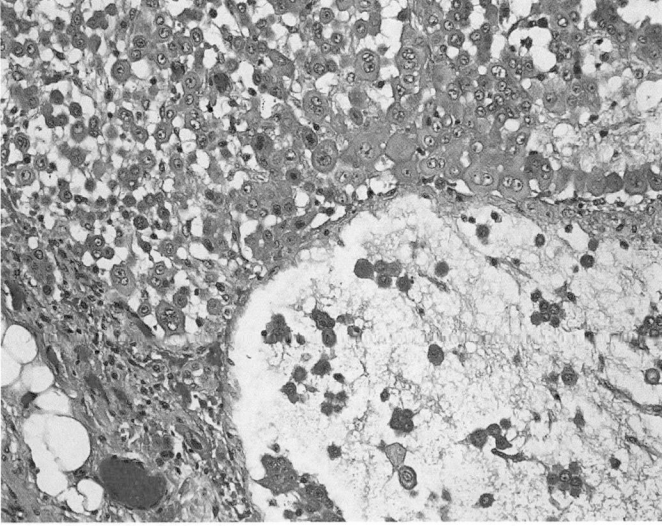

Fig. 26.8 Malignant mesothelioma combining hyper- and hypocellular areas.

fairly uniform, with acidophilic or vacuolated cytoplasm and large vesicular or hyperchromatic nuclei. In some cases, the tumor cells show prominent vacuoles or are entirely clear, as a result of hydropic changes. In other instances, the cells may appear foamy as a result of lipid accumulation; some of these are multinucleated and resemble Touton's giant cells.[101] Mitoses may be difficult to find. Exceptionally, the tumor may exhibit foci of cartilaginous or other types of stromal metaplasia.

Well-differentiated papillary mesothelioma shows a great predilection for women and is usually multifocal. Early descriptions emphasized the indolent clinical course and recommended a conservative approach,[90] but further studies have shown that it can behave in an aggressive fashion and that it should be regarded as a malignant tumor (see also under Therapy and prognosis).[83,99]

Mesothelioma with deciduoid features is a morphologic variant of malignant mesothelioma in which the tumors cell resemble decidualized stroma (Fig. 26.9). Although originally described in young women and unassociated with asbestos,[111] it has now been shown that it can be seen in both sexes and all age groups, that it can be related to asbestos, and that it can present focally in what is otherwise a conventional tubulopapillary mesothelioma.[113,117]

Lymphohistiocytoid mesothelioma similar to its pleural counterpart has been observed in the peritoneal cavity (Fig. 26.10).

Histochemical and immunohistochemical features. Malignant mesotheliomas usually contain extracellular mucosubstances, sometimes in large amounts. These represent acid mucopolysaccharides, since they stain with colloidal iron and Alcian blue, are removed at least partially by hyaluronidase digestion, and are PAS negative. Adenocarcinomas also may contain colloidal

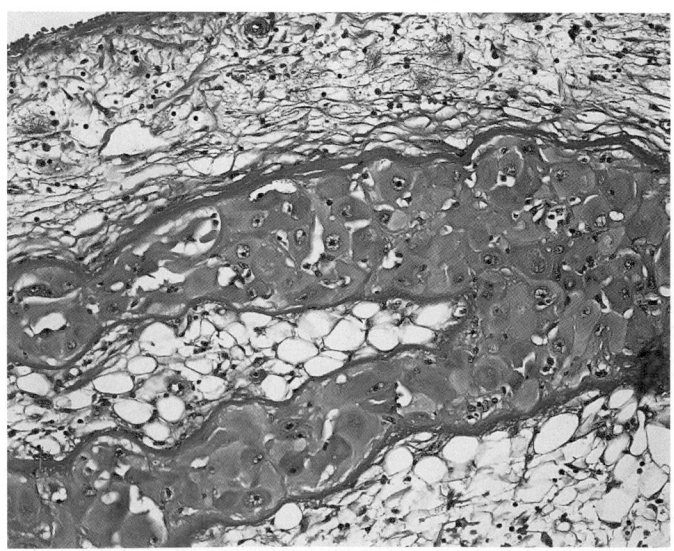

Fig. 26.9 So-called "deciduoid mesothelioma" combining hyper- and hypocellular areas.

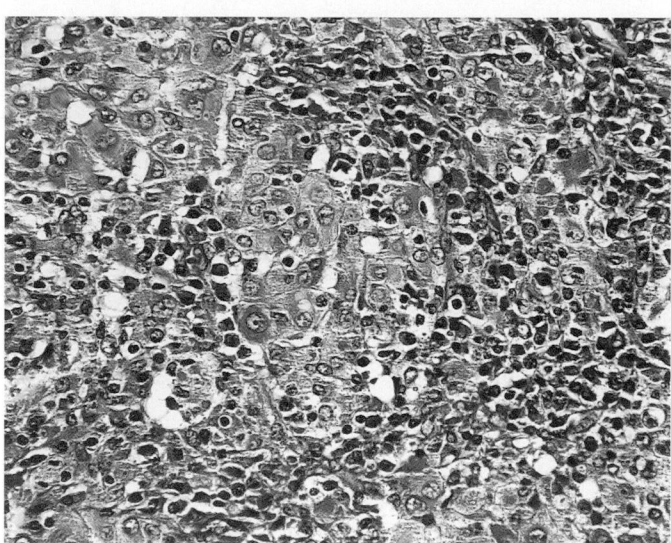

Fig. 26.10 So-called "lymphohistiocytoid mesothelioma". The tumor cells are admixed with numerous reactive lymphocytes and histiocytes.

iron-positive material, but hyaluronidase digestion would have little effect on the reaction. The detection of high levels of hyaluronic acid by histochemistry or biochemical extraction favors a diagnosis of mesothelioma, but it is not a specific finding.[86]

Immunohistochemically, the cells of malignant mesothelioma are generally positive for keratin (including keratin 5/6), EMA, calretinin, mesothelin, the WT1 gene product, thrombomodulin, HBME-1, vimentin, neural cell adhesion molecules, and basement membrane-related proteins (type IV collagen, laminin, and laminin receptors) (Fig. 26.11). They are generally negative for CEA, B72.3, the MOC31- and Ber-Ep4-defined glycoproteins, and Leu-M1 (and related "myelomonocytic" antigens).[95,104,106,120,127]

Some correlation exists between the expression of these markers and the histologic appearance of the tumor.[77] In sarcomatoid mesotheliomas some or all of the markers may be lost.[76]

Some mesotheliomas have been shown to express actin and desmin[103]; when the latter is the case, the tumors have been referred to as *leiomyoid mesotheliomas*.[110]

The application of these markers to the differential diagnosis of malignant mesothelioma with metastatic carcinoma and reactive mesothelial hyperplasia is discussed below.

Electron microscopic features. By electron microscopy, the cells of a well-differentiated mesothelioma exhibit polarity, abundant microvilli covered with fuzzy material, extracellular and intracellular neolumina formation, glycogen granules, junctional structures, tonofilaments, and basal lamina[123] (Fig. 26.12). Transitions are found between typical mesothelial cells and cells with a mesenchymal, fibroblast-like appearance.[80] At the

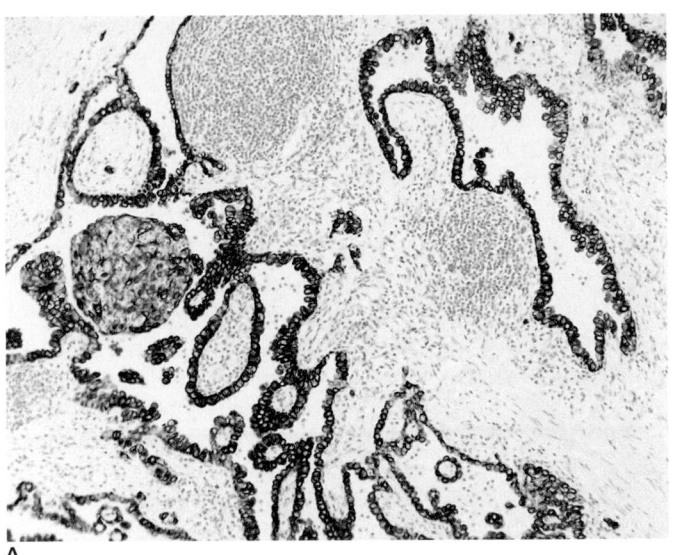
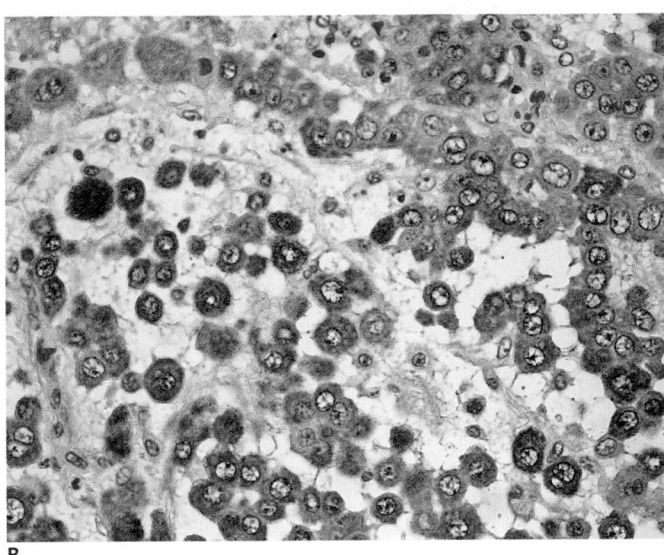

Fig. 26.11 Malignant mesothelioma cells show immunoreactivity for keratin 5/6 (**A**) and calretinin (**B**).

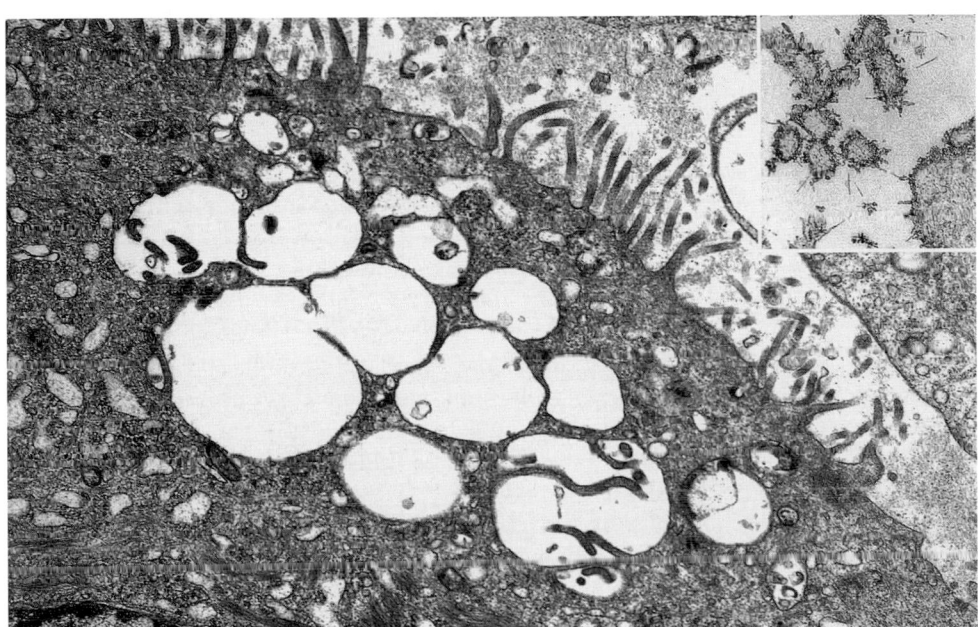

Fig. 26.12 Electron microscopic appearance of cell from malignant mesothelioma demonstrating numerous microvilli in luminal surface and intracellular vacuoles also equipped with microvilli. Inset shows microvilli coated with acid mucopolysaccharides. (×8000; inset, Hale's colloidal iron, ×45,000; from Suzuki Y, Churg J, Kannerstein M. Ultrastructure of human malignant diffuse mesothelioma. Am J Pathol 1976, **85**: 241–262)

ultrastructural level, the cytoplasmic appearance of the mesothelioma variant known as deciduoid is seen to be due to the accumulation of cytoplasmic intermediate filaments.[117a]

Molecular genetic features. Overexpression of p53 is common, whereas mutations of the *p53* gene are only rarely observed.[84] Some malignant melanomas express bcl-2 protein[115] and telomerase reverse transcriptase (TERT).[102,114b]

Differential diagnosis. The differential diagnosis of malignant mesothelioma is mainly with reactive mesothelial hyperplasia and with primary or metastatic adenocarcinoma (Fig. 26.13). As far as the former situation is concerned, the distinction is largely based on morphologic features, since special techniques are of little use

in this regard. Statistically speaking, strong immunoreactivity for EMA and overexpression of p53 is more common in malignant mesothelioma, but this is of no great value in the individual situation.[125] In terms of morphologic parameters, the US–Canadian Mesothelioma Reference Panel recently published an useful review article listing the most important distinguishing criteria.[125] They concluded that invasion of fat or of organ walls was the most reliable indicator of malignancy, as opposed to linear arrays of atypical mesothelial cells on the free surface, which should suggest a reactive process. They warned about the possible misinterpretation of reactive mesothelial cells in granulation tissue or between fat lobules, and emphasized the fact that cytologic atypia is not very helpful in this differential. Densely packed mesothe-

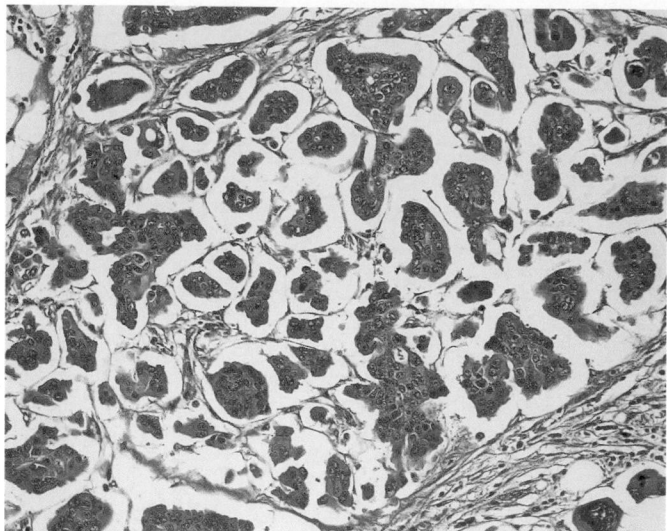

Fig. 26.13 Primary papillary serous carcinoma of peritoneum. The tumor is morphologically and immunohistochemically indistinguishable from its ovarian counterpart.

lial cells are of no great significance if within the peritoneal space but are a feature of malignancy if present embedded within the stroma.

Regarding the differential diagnosis between mesothelioma and carcinoma, special techniques play an important role, although the differences are not as clearcut as in the pleura.[100] The reason for this is simple: whereas in the pleura the main differential diagnosis is with lung adenocarcinoma (i.e., a tumor of an endodermally derived organ with no histogenetic connection with the mesothelium), in the peritoneum the main distinction is with (papillary) serous carcinoma of müllerian type (whether metastatic from ovary/uterus or primary in the peritoneum), i.e. a neoplasm of modified mesothelial cells. Be that as it may, important clinical and therapeutic differences exist between these tumors, and a distinction among the two should always be attempted. At the morphologic level, features that favor the diagnosis of mesothelioma over serous carcinoma are a prominent tubulopapillary pattern, polygonal cells with eosinophilic cytoplasm, absence of marked nuclear pleomorphism, and absence of a high nuclear rate.[99]

Histochemically, it is generally assumed that the presence of intracytoplasmic mucin (either PAS positive after diastase digestion or Mayer's mucicarmine positive) establishes the diagnosis of carcinoma. This feature is not as helpful in the peritoneum as it is in the pleura[97] and is of no absolute value, inasmuch as indubitable cases of mucin-positive mesotheliomas exist.[88]

At the immunohistochemical level, calretinin and the WT1 gene product seem to be the best mesothelioma markers, followed by thrombomodulin and keratin 5/6, whereas Ber-EP4 appears to be the best marker for carcinoma.[78,112] Ordóñez[112] concluded that the best evidence for mesothelioma was *negativity* for MOC-31, B72.3,

Ber-EP4, CA19-9 and Leu-M1, and commented that CEA, PLAP, EMA, vimentin, HBME-1 and S-100 protein have little or no utility in this situation.

As a final comment, it should be said that in cases in which the differential remains dubious, electron microscopic examination can play a decisive role.[91]

Spread and metastases. The characteristic pattern of spread of peritoneal mesothelioma is local, eventually leading to complete obliteration of the peritoneal cavity. In advanced stages, the tumor may locally invade the intestinal wall, hilum of the spleen and liver, gastric wall, pancreas, bladder, anterior abdominal wall, and retroperitoneum. Metastases to retroperitoneal or pelvic lymph nodes may develop, but metastases to lung or other distant sites are relatively rare. Peculiar instances of metastatic mesothelioma presenting as colonic polyps have been observed.[108]

Therapy and prognosis. The prognosis for malignant mesothelioma is extremely poor. Most patients die of the disease within 2 years of the diagnosis.[107,126] There is, however, a subset of diffuse mesotheliomas occurring in women and having well-differentiated features that behaves in an indolent fashion.[93] Unfortunately, it is very difficult to predict on the basis of the histology whether the tumor will behave aggressively or not.[99] Some encouraging results have been obtained with a combination of surgical debulking, combination chemotherapy, and whole-abdomen irradiation.[105]

Intra-abdominal desmoplastic small cell tumor

Intra-abdominal desmoplastic small cell tumor (DSCT) is a highly malignant neoplasm that characteristically presents as a single mass or multiple nodules within the abdominal cavity in adolescents and young adults, usually of the male sex.[141,153] However, it can also occur in the elderly.[161] One case has been reported in a patient with Peutz–Jeghers syndrome.[157] There is a definite predilection for the pelvic region, but sometimes there is extension to the entire peritoneal cavity, scrotum, and/or retroperitoneum. Sometimes the entire tumor is limited to the paratesticular region.[137,146] Accompanying ascites is the rule; malignant cells can be easily identified in the fluid.[136] Grossly, the tumor nodules are firm to hard, variously sized, and range in shape from plaque-like to spherical (Fig. 26.14). Invasion of intra-abdominal organs (such as the gastrointestinal tract) is usually restricted to the serosa. However, cases with prominent involvement of sites such as liver, pancreas, and ovary have been observed.[162] Lymph node metastases are rare but they have been well documented; occasionally, they represent the first manifestation of the disease.[133]

Microscopically, there are sharply outlined islands of tumor cells separated by a generally abundant stroma that tends to be very cellular ("desmoplastic") (Fig. 26.15). The tumor cells are usually small, round, and monotonous, with hyperchromatic nuclei, high mitotic

Fig. 26.14 Gross appearance of desmoplastic small cell tumor. There are multiple nodules, one of them of considerable size. Note the large areas of fibrosis.

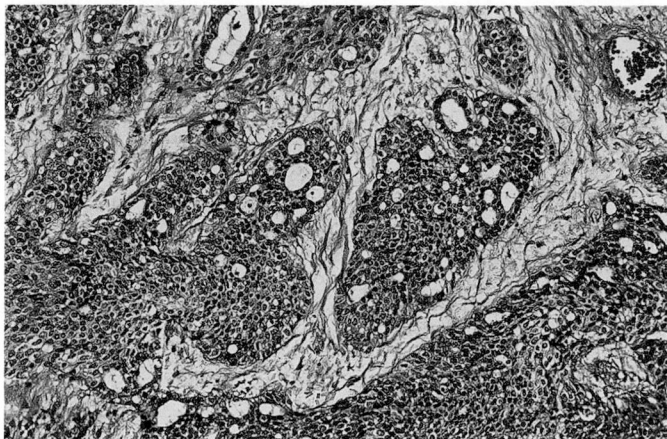

Fig. 26.16 Desmoplastic small cell tumor showing glandular formations at the periphery of the tumor nests.

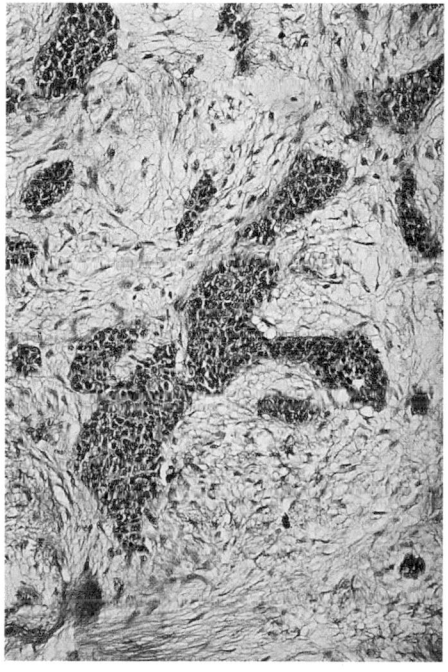

Fig. 26.15 Microscopic appearance of intra-abdominal desmoplastic small cell tumor. Low-power view showing well-defined tumor nests surrounded by cellular stroma.

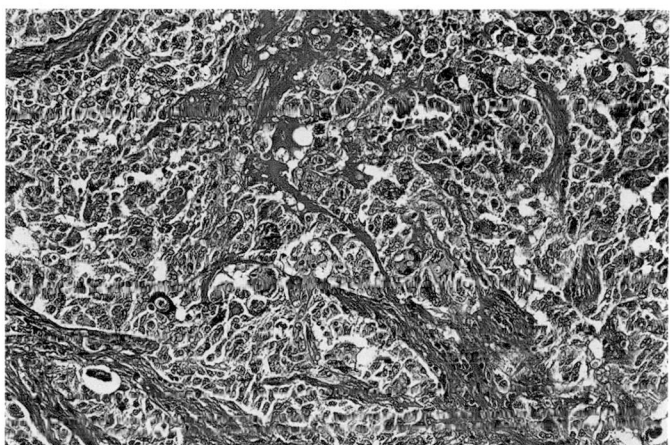

Fig. 26.17 Desmoplastic small cell tumor showing an unusual degree of pleomorphism. It was also unusual in the sense of occurring in a 76-year-old female and involving the outer uterine wall. The diagnosis was confirmed by demonstrating the EWS–WT1 gene fusion by PCR.

activity, and very scanty cytoplasm. Some of these cells may have a rhabdoid appearance. The stroma is largely made up of fibroblasts and myofibroblasts, but it also contains proliferating vessels sometimes exhibiting a lobular configuration. These structures are similar to those seen in other malignant tumors composed of primitive neuroepithelial/neuroendocrine cells and perhaps resulting from the secretion of angiogenic factor by the tumor cells.[140] Morphologic variations include tumors with very scanty stroma, presence of tubular or glandular formations, signet ring cells, and clusters of pleomorphic large tumor cells[139,148,150,152] (Figs 26.16 and 26.17).

The immunohistochemical profile of this neoplasm is distinctive in the sense that it displays simultaneous expression of epithelial (keratin, EMA) muscular (desmin), and neural (neuron-specific enolase) markers (Fig. 26.18). The keratin reactivity has a diffuse cytoplasmic quality, whereas that for desmin tends to have a localized, dotlike ("globoid") quality. The tumor is also positive for WT1, a feature resulting from the unique gene fusion that characterizes it.[135,144] It is crucial to use the appropriate antibody for this purpose (such as WT (C-19)); i.e. that directed against the C-terminal region of the WT1 protein, since the N-terminal region of the same molecule (detected with the WT (180) antibody) is not expressed.[134] Vimentin is also strongly expressed, but stains for actin and myogenin are characteristically negative. CD99 (an antigen associated with Ewing's sarcoma) is usually negative, although focal cytoplasmic staining may be observed. Stains for mesothelial markers such as calretinin and thrombomodulin are generally but not

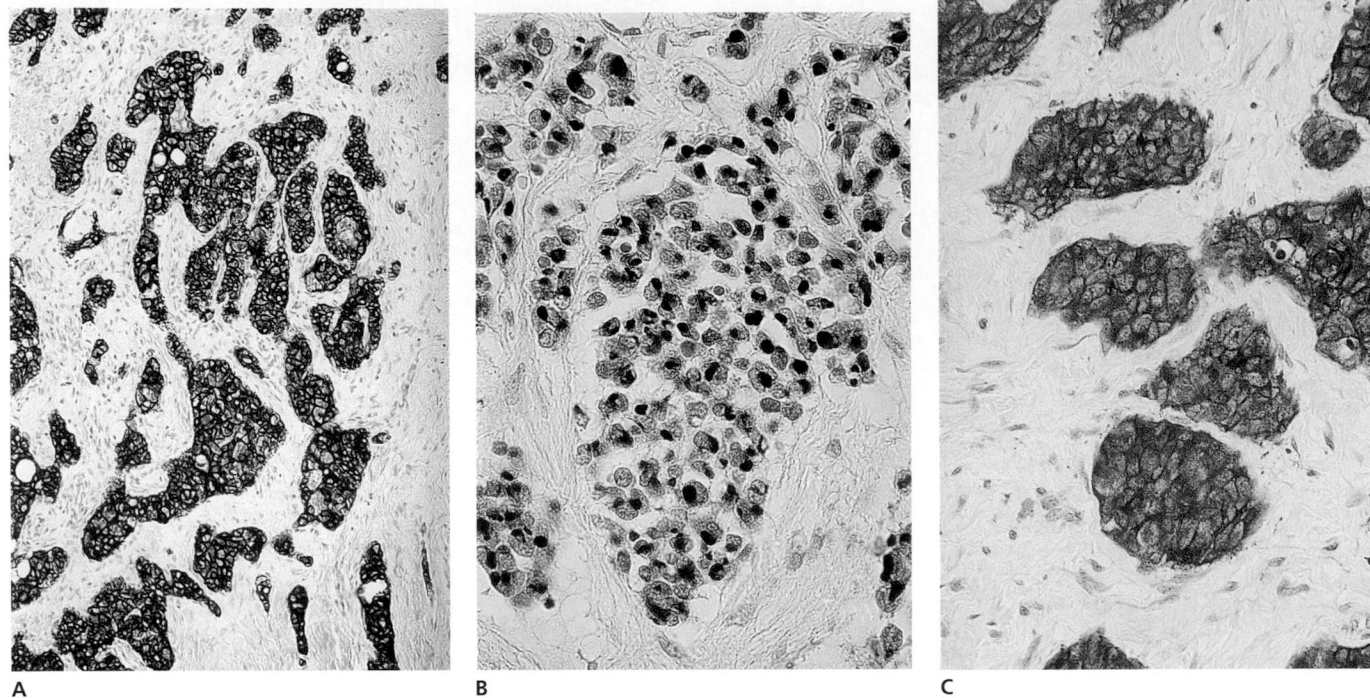

Fig. 26.18 Desmoplastic small cell tumor showing typical polyphenotypic reactivity for keratin (**A**), desmin (**B**), and neuron-specific enolase (**C**).

always negative.[151,162a] Occasional reactivity for chromogranin has also been described. At the ultrastructural level, the cells have a rather primitive appearance with a few specialized junctions, scattered membrane-bound dense-core cytoplasmic granules, and a variable amount of intermediate filaments that tend to cluster in a paranuclear location.

DSCT is associated with a unique karyotypic aberration involving the reciprocal translocation t (11;22) (p13; q12).[115,147a,156a] The genes involved are *EWS* (Ewing's sarcoma gene) in 22q12 and *WT1* (Wilms' tumor gene 1) in 11p13.[143] This finding is of practical importance in the differential diagnosis with other small round cell tumors of childhood,[132,138] particularly in the cases showing atypical morphologic or immunohistochemical features (such as negativity for keratin),[159] also because it can be carried out in the ascitic fluid.[155] Several molecular variants of the *EWS–WT1* gene fusion exist.[131] The involvement of these two genes may explain why the phenotypical features of this neoplasm overlap somewhat with those of Ewing's sarcoma/PNET and Wilms' tumor. The peculiar topographic distribution of DSCT also suggests a relationship with the mesothelial lining and the possibility that it may represent a "mesothelioblastoma."[141] The transient expression of desmin by the normal developing mesothelium (see p. 2373), the selective expression of *WT1* gene products in malignant mesothelioma,[130] and the description of three cases of desmoplastic small cell tumor in the pleural cavity[154] support this contention. On the other hand, the identification of a typical case of this entity in the cerebellum,[158] one in the parotid region,[161]

and another in the soft tissues and bone of the hand[129] casts some doubts on this hypothesis. It seems more likely that DSCT is related to the other small cell tumors of infancy and particularly Ewing's sarcoma/PNET, also in view of the existence of transitional or hybrid forms of these two tumors at a morphologic, immunohistochemical (DSCT with CD99 reactivity), and molecular level (DSCT with *EWS–FLI-1* or *EWS–ERG* rather than *EWS–WT1* gene fusion).[145,149]

The behavior of DSCT is extremely aggressive, perhaps more so than that of any other malignant small round cell tumor of infancy.[142,153,160] Most patients are dead of disease within 2 years of initial diagnosis. However, prolonged progression-free survival has been obtained in some cases with aggressive multimodality therapy.[147]

Other primary tumors

Primary peritoneal tumors other than mesotheliomas or DSCT not connected with either the omentum or the mesentery are extremely rare.

Solitary fibrous tumor (formerly known as solitary fibrous mesothelioma) is much less common in the peritoneal than in the pleural cavity, but its morphologic features are identical (see Chapter 7) (Fig. 26.19). It presents in adulthood and—like its pleural counterpart—may be accompanied by hypoglycemia. Most cases have followed a benign clinical course,[168,174] but a malignant counterpart has been well documented.[166] The phenotype of the tumor cell is the same as that of the normal submesothelial mesenchyme.

Angiosarcomas have been described, some following administration of radiation therapy[172] (Fig. 26.20). **Epithelioid hemangioendothelioma** can coat the peritoneal cavity in a diffuse fashion, simulating the pattern of growth of malignant mesothelioma, in a fashion similar to that seen in the pleural cavity[163,171] (Fig. 26.21). These tumors lack the herpesvirus-like DNA sequences that have been associated with Kaposi's sarcoma.[170]

Synovial sarcoma can occur within the peritoneal cavity; it needs to be distinguished mainly from biphasic mesothelioma. A molecular evaluation may be necessary for this purpose.[169]

Dendritic follicular cell tumor is being reported with an increasing frequency in the abdominal cavity; it has been claimed that it behaves more aggressively at this site than in others.[165,173]

Epithelioid angiomyolipoma (PEComa) is another neoplasm that is being recognized at a heightened rate, and this includes the peritoneal cavity. Most cases have occurred in the pelvis, often with no anatomic relation with any major organ, and some have been malignant.[164] They can simulate microscopically renal cell carcinoma, adrenal cortical carcinoma, oncocytoma, and a variety of pleomorphic sarcomas. HMB-45 positivity remains the key feature for the confirmation of the diagnosis.

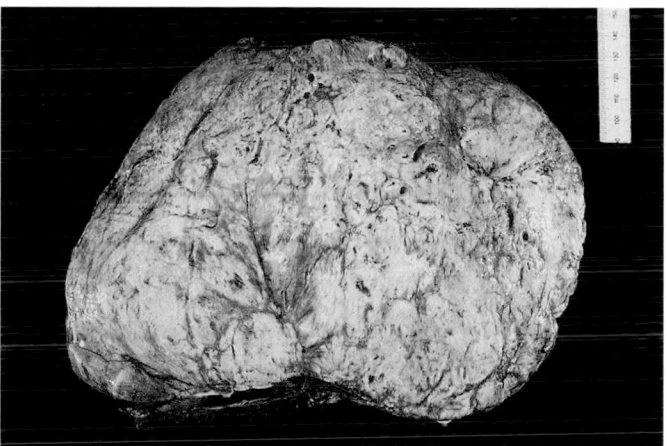

Fig. 26.19 Gross appearance of solitary fibrous tumor attached to the peritoneal side of the diaphragm.

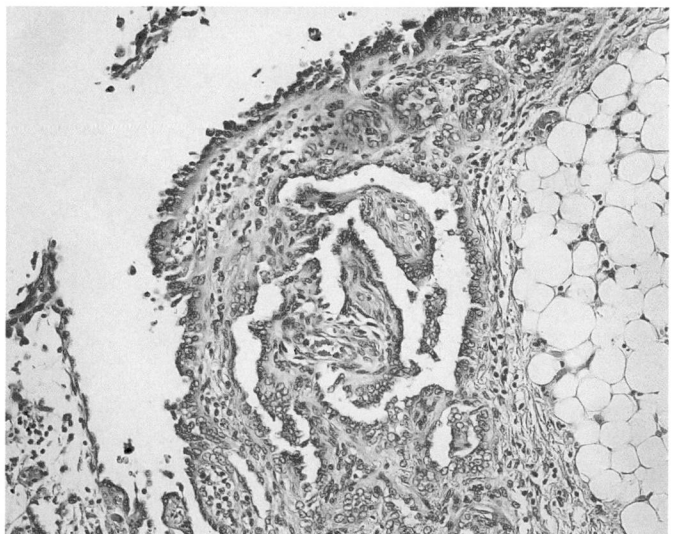

Fig. 26.20 Peritoneal angiosarcoma. The pattern of growth greatly simulates that of malignant mesothelioma.

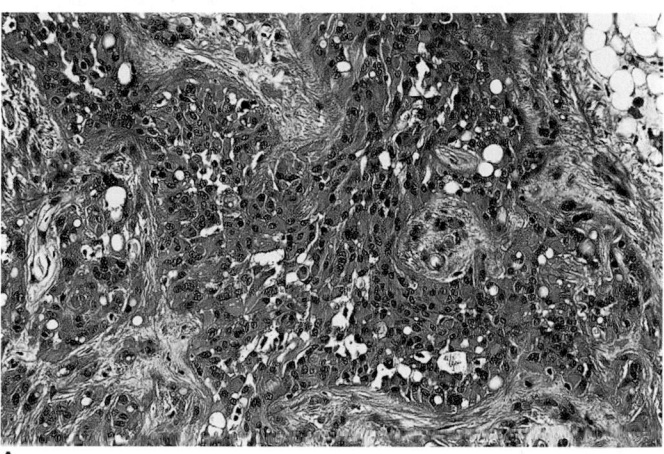

A

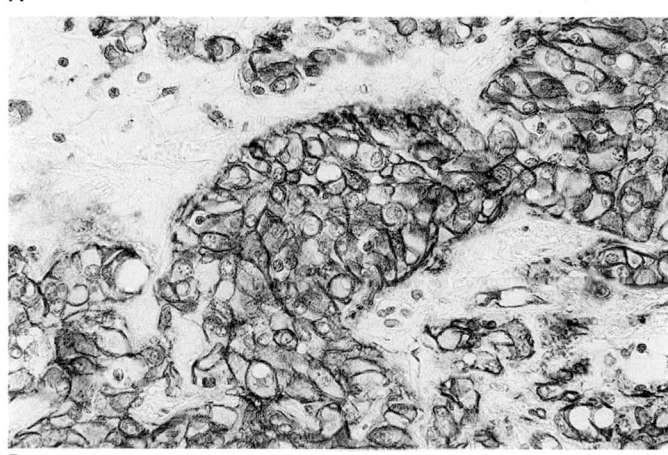

B

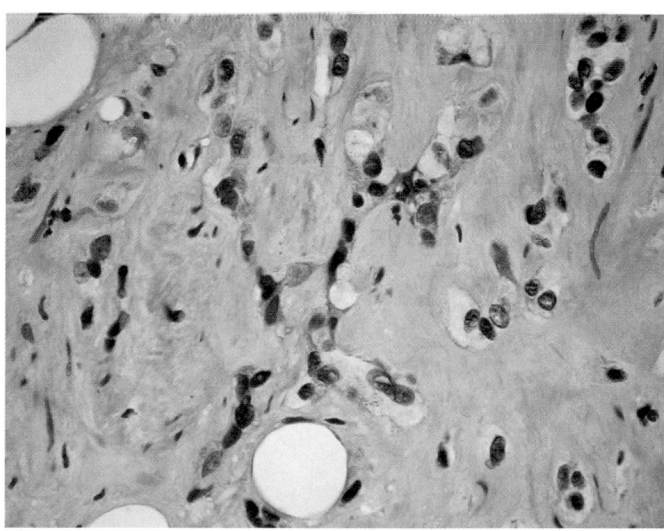

C

Fig. 26.21 Epithelioid hemangioendothelioma of peritoneum. **A**, Hematoxylin–eosin; **B**, CD31; **C**, FLI-1 (from another case of the same entity).

Undifferentiated sarcomas of undetermined histogenesis involving the peritoneal cavity of children have been described by Gonzalez-Crussi et al.[167]

Lesions of the secondary müllerian system

The term *secondary müllerian system* has been applied to the pelvic and lower abdominal mesothelium and the subjacent mesenchyme of females, on the basis of its close embryologic relationship with the primary müllerian system (i.e., the müllerian ducts).[189] The potentiality of this tissue is manifested by the existence in the peritoneal cavity (most often in the pelvic region but also in the omentum, mesentery, and retroperitoneum) of a large variety of metaplastic and neoplastic lesions that are analogous in all regards to those more commonly found in the ovary, uterus, or other organs of the female genital tract.[194] These lesions sometimes occur in association, not surprising in view of their related histogenesis and pathogenesis.[196]

1 **Endosalpingiosis.** This is discussed in Chapter 19.
2 **Endometriosis.** This is discussed in Chapter 19 (see also p. 2392).
3 **Ectopic decidual reaction.** It is most commonly seen in the pelvis and omentum, where it appears as tiny, gray submesothelial nodules.[177,179] Microscopically, the decidual cells may exhibit bizarre hyperchromatic nuclei and be confused with metastatic squamous cell carcinoma. Vascular changes may occur as an expression of regression.[177]
4 **Leiomyomatosis peritonealis disseminata.** This is a rare benign condition in which typical uterine leiomyomas are associated with multiple small nodules of mature smooth muscle distributed throughout the omentum and both visceral and parietal layers of the peritoneum (Fig. 26.22). A mistaken diagnosis of metastatic leiomyosarcoma may result. Rarely, the disease coexists with endometriosis. Exceptionally, a sex-cord-like pattern is observed within some of the leiomyomatous nodules.[190] Its clonal pattern is similar to that of uterine leiomyomas.[191] A strong association with pregnancy exists.[193] Steroid hormone receptors have been detected in the proliferating cells.[176,183] In most instances, spontaneous regression of the nodules occurs.
5 **(Papillary) serous tumors of the peritoneum.** They include peritoneal serous micropapillomatosis of low malignant potential, serous psammocarcinoma, and (extraovarian) serous carcinoma[175,181,184,185,187,188,195] (see Fig. 26.13). They are discussed in Chapter 19.
6 **Endometrial stromal sarcoma, müllerian adenosarcoma** (with and without sarcomatous overgrowth), and **malignant mixed müllerian tumor** (with or without neuroendocrine differentiation).[178,180,182,186,192] These are discussed in Chapter 19.

Metastatic tumors

All types of metastatic tumors may involve the peritoneal cavity. The most common sites of the primary tumors are the female genital tract (particularly ovary), followed by large bowel and pancreas.[198,208] The ovarian and uterine tumors resulting in peritoneal carcinomatosis are usually of the serous type; the primary uterine lesion can be very superficial or even in situ.[212] The gross pattern varies from single, well-defined nodules to a diffuse peritoneal thickening. Variations in consistency depend on cellularity, amount of fibrous tissue, and mucin content. Metastatic carcinoma may simulate closely the gross and microscopic appearance of malignant mesothelioma. This is particularly the case with papillary serous carcinoma of the ovary, but it can also occur with carcinoma of the lung, in conjunction with pleural spread.[209]

Pseudomyxoma peritonei is a distinctive form of tumor implant in which the peritoneal cavity contains large amounts of mucinous material[203,211] (Fig. 26.23). The bowel is relatively spared, but polypoid mucinous

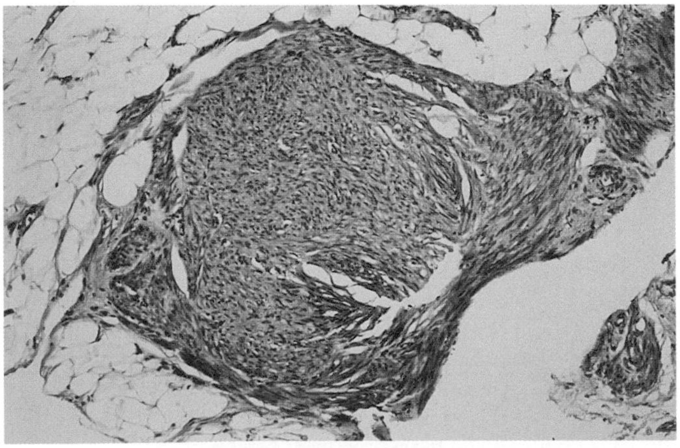

Fig. 26.22 Low-power view of leiomyomatosis peritonealis disseminata.

Fig. 26.23 Gross appearance of pseudomyxoma peritonei. The entire peritoneal cavity is occupied by a multinodular mucinous mass.

masses can develop on the peritoneal surface of the small bowel.[215] Mucinous cystic lesions can also be seen in the substance of the spleen.[200] Traditionally, it has been stated that the primary lesion may be a borderline or malignant mucinous neoplasm of the appendix, ovary, or pancreas (see Chapters 11, 15, and 19).[204] Several recent studies of the subject have led to the conclusion that the appendix is the primary site of origin of pseudomyxoma in the vast majority of the cases in both men and women.[205,206,219] The further suggestion has been made that the associated mucinous ovarian tumors—when present—are most likely additional implants from the appendiceal lesions rather than independent synchronous neoplasms.[205,206,219] The subject is further discussed in Chapter 19.

Microscopically, large pools of mucus are seen accompanied by hyperemic vessels and chronic inflammatory cells. *Viable epithelial glandular cells must be identified within the mucus to diagnose pseudomyxoma peritonei* (Fig. 26.24). These cells usually have a deceivingly bland appearance both on histologic and cytologic preparations and show no invasive properties.[202a,210] Because of these features, the suggestion has been made to designate this process as *adenomucinosis*, in order to distinguish it from the *peritoneal mucinous carcinomatosis* accompanied by cytologic atypia and resulting from an invasive mucinous adenocarcinoma usually located in the gastrointestinal tract.[207] We certainly agree that these two groups are associated with a different outcome (not surprisingly),[218] but are afraid that the neologism *adeno mucinous* may not contribute much to the understanding of what is clearly a neoplastic condition with low grade malignant features.

Immunohistochemically, the cells of pseudomyxoma characteristically show expression of MUC2, a mucin possessing the physicochemical property of being gel-forming.[204a]

Pseudomyxoma peritonei is characterized by a slow but relentless clinical course, with recurrent ascites that

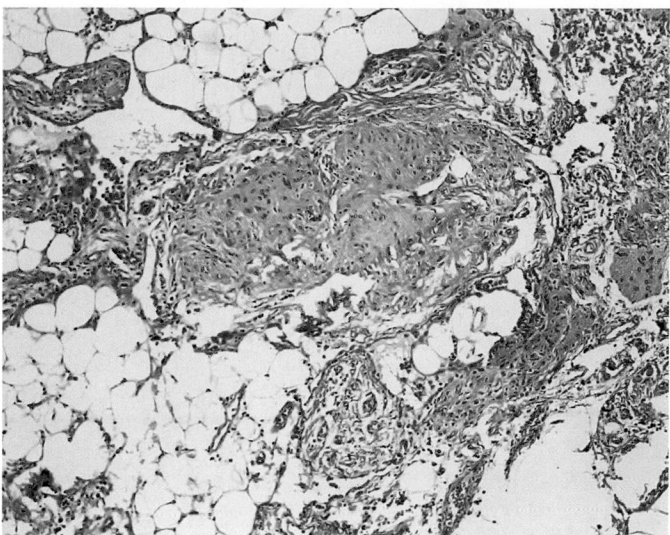

Fig. 26.25 So-called "peritoneal gliomatosis" resulting from rupture of an ovarian teratoma.

eventually reaches massive proportions ("jelly-belly syndrome"). Aggressive surgical resection is the treatment currently recommended, with most patients requiring multiple laparotomies, and in some including a total gastrectomy.[213,214] It should be noted that mucinous cystadenomas of the ovary and appendix can rupture and pour their content into the peritoneal cavity; the resulting condition, which is self-limited and microscopically lacks tumor cells, should not be designated as pseudomyxoma peritonei.[197,202] Pseudomyxoma-like changes (pseudo-pseudomyxoma, so to speak) have also been described in the stroma of prostatic adenocarcinoma following neoadjuvant androgen ablation therapy.[217]

Another very distinctive form of tumor implantation is the *gliomatosis peritonei* resulting from the selective growth of glial tissue from ovarian teratoma,[201] which in exceptional circumstances may undergo malignant transformation[199]; this is discussed in Chapter 19 (Fig. 26.25).

Metastatic carcinoma in the peritoneal cavity (often of ovarian origin) tends to be accompanied by recurrent ascites. This is sometimes treated by peritoneovenous shunting, by which the effusion is returned to the general circulation; amazingly, this technique has not resulted in an increase in the number of extra-abdominal metastases.[216]

Cytology

The diagnosis of metastatic carcinoma in the peritoneal cavity is possible in about 75% of the cases on the basis of cytologic examination of ascitic fluid.[220] This also applies to pseudomyxoma peritonei.[224a] With malignant lymphoma and leukemia, the overall yield is approximately 60%, these figures being slightly higher for large cell lymphoma.[226]

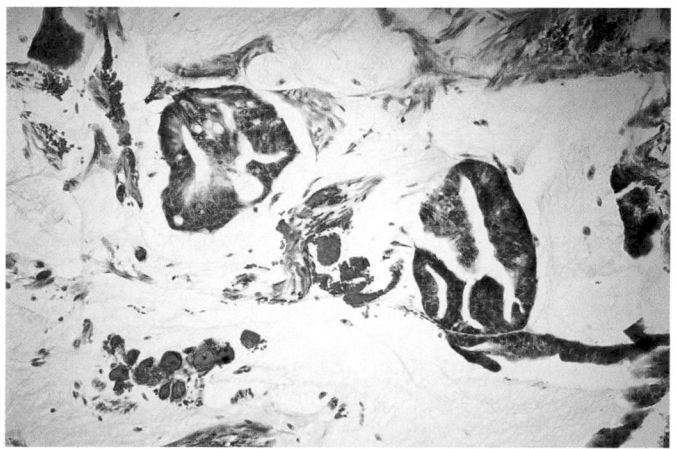

Fig. 26.24 Microscopic appearance of pseudomyxoma peritonei. Clusters of well-differentiated mucin-producing glandular cells are seen floating in a sea of mucin.

The two most difficult problems in cytology of ascitic fluid are the distinction between reactive and neoplastic mesothelium and that between malignant mesothelioma and metastatic carcinoma (Figs 26.26 to 26.28). False-positive diagnoses have been caused by liver cirrhosis and other disorders associated with

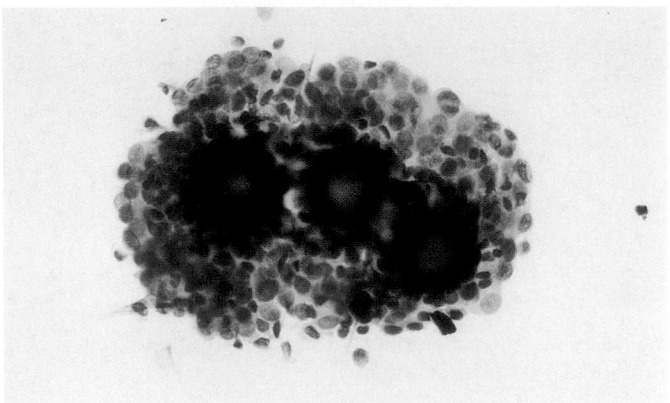

Fig. 26.26 Positive peritoneal cytology in a patient with serous carcinoma of the ovary. Note the psammomatous bodies.

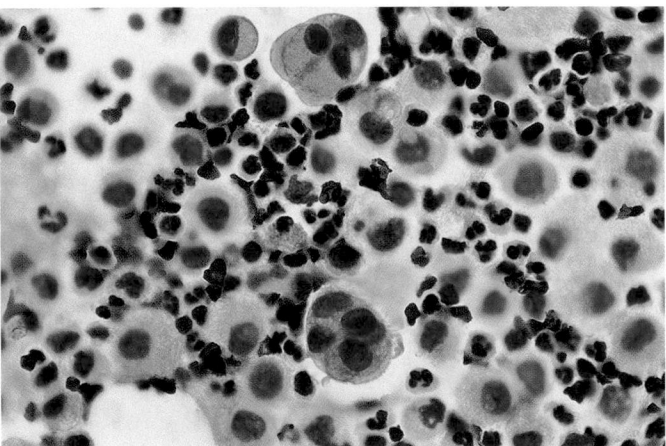

Fig. 26.27 Positive peritoneal cytology in a patient with pancreatic adenocarcinoma.

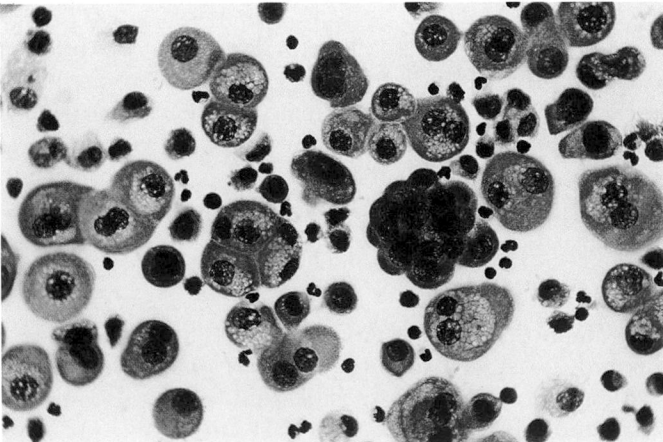

Fig. 26.28 Cytologic appearance of malignant mesothelioma. The clustering of tumor cells into morula-like structures is particularly characteristic.

mesothelial hyperplasia; confusion occurs because the reactive cells may form pseudoacini closely resembling the true acini of adenocarcinoma, have multiple nuclei or a signet ring appearance, or undergo mitotic division. Evaluation of the nucleo-cytoplasmic ratio and of nuclear features is essential in this differential diagnosis.

Malignant mesothelioma often grows in papillary clusters.[228] It differs from metastatic adenocarcinoma by the absence of true acini, a more frequent binucleation and multinucleation, and the presence of a range of differentiation among the mesothelial cells[225] (see Fig. 26.28). Electron microscopic and immunohistochemical techniques have been successfully applied to cytologic preparations in an effort to increase the diagnostic accuracy.[221–224,227,229]

Omentum

Hemorrhagic infarct of the omentum may result from torsion or strangulation in a hernia sac. *Primary idiopathic segmental infarction* of the greater omentum is an acute abdominal lesion of obscure etiology usually mistaken clinically for acute appendicitis or cholecystitis. Characteristically, the infarcted segment of omentum is on the right side adherent to the cecum, ascending colon, and anterior parietal peritoneum.[232]

Cystic lymphangioma represents the single most frequent tumor of the omentum in children[235]; its gross and microscopic appearance is analogous to that of the more common "cystic hygroma" of the neck.[233]

Primary solid tumors of the omentum are exceptionally rare. Smooth muscle tumors predominate among both the benign and malignant categories.[231,238] A high percentage of these tumors are of the epithelioid (clear cell or leiomyoblastoma) type and CD117-positive, and have therefore been incorporated into the GIST category (see Chapter 11).[238]

Myxoid or multicentric hamartoma is a peculiar lesion characterized by the formation of multiple nodules in the omentum and mesentery of children[234,235]; microscopically, plump mesenchymal cells are seen in a background of prominent myxoid and inflammatory changes. Whatever the nature of this lesion may ultimately prove to be, its behavior so far has been benign.

Metastatic carcinoma constitutes the most common malignant omental neoplasm in adults. Ovary, gastrointestinal tract, and pancreas are the most common sources of the primary tumor.

Diffuse malignant mesothelioma of the peritoneum consistently spreads into the omentum.

Other reported omental lesions include *teratoma* (usually mature),[236] *elastofibroma*,[239] *follicular deudritic cell tumor*,[239a] *cryptococcosis*, resulting in a tumorlike mass ("cryptococcoma"),[230] and *müllerian-type lesions* similar to those occurring in other portions of the peritoneal cavity and retroperitoneum.[237]

Mesentery

Mesenteric panniculitis (also called *isolated lipodystrophy of the mesentery, retractile mesenteritis,* and *sclerosing mesenteritis*) is a rare disorder grossly appearing as a diffuse, localized, or multinodular thickening of the mesentery of the small and/or large bowel.[250,257] The disease needs to be distinguished from the localized and nodular forms of panniculitis that can occur around colorectal carcinomas or diverticular disease,[241] and from the diffuse mesenteric fibrosis seen in association with chronic small bowel allograft rejection.[258a] The process may lead to retraction and distortion of the intestinal loops and the formation of adhesions between them. Microscopically, there is an infiltration by inflammatory cells, myofibroblasts, and foamy macrophages, the latter probably representing a reaction to fat necrosis[270] (Fig. 26.29). The vessels traversing the lesion are often inflamed and sometimes thrombosed. The differential diagnosis includes Weber–Christian disease and Whipple's disease. In 8 of the 53 patients reported by Kipfer et al.,[258] a malignant lymphoma ultimately developed; other series did not show such an association. Retrospectively, some of these cases might have been malignant lymphoma with a prominent degree of sclerosis, simulating an inflammatory condition. It is likely that at least some examples of mesenteric panniculitis represent a mesenteric extension of idiopathic retroperitoneal fibrosis and, as such, members of the family of disorders collectively known as *inflammatory fibrosclerosis.*[250,273]

Heterotopic mesenteric ossification has a morphologic appearance similar to that of myositis ossificans of soft tissues[278] (Fig. 26.30). The condition can result in intestinal obstruction. Most reported cases have occurred a short time following the performance of one or more intra-abdominal operations, such as the repair of an abdominal aortic aneurysm.

Inflammatory myofibroblastic tumor presents as an intra-abdominal mass in children and adolescents. It is often associated with fever, weight loss, and anemia, manifestations that often regress following excision of the mass.[249] Microscopically, there is a polymorphic infiltrate composed of plump myofibroblasts arranged in a vaguely fascicular fashion, plasma cells, lymphocytes, and other inflammatory elements (Fig. 26.31). It was originally reported as a pseudoneoplastic inflammatory process and designated as *inflammatory pseudotumor* because of the rich inflammatory component and the

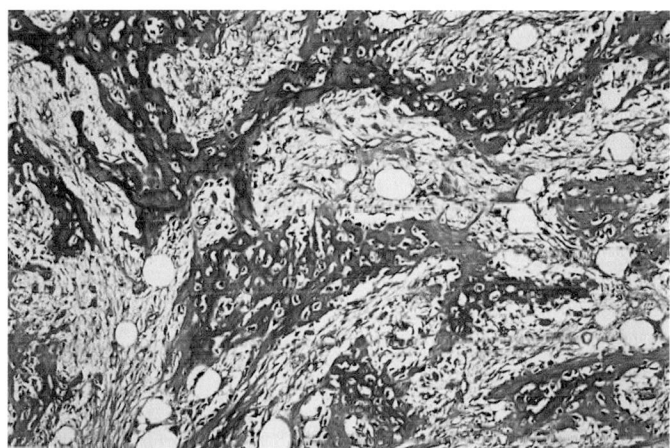

Fig. 26.30 Heterotopic mesenteric ossification. This section, which corresponds to the peripheral portion of the lesion, shows well-developed bone trabeculae.

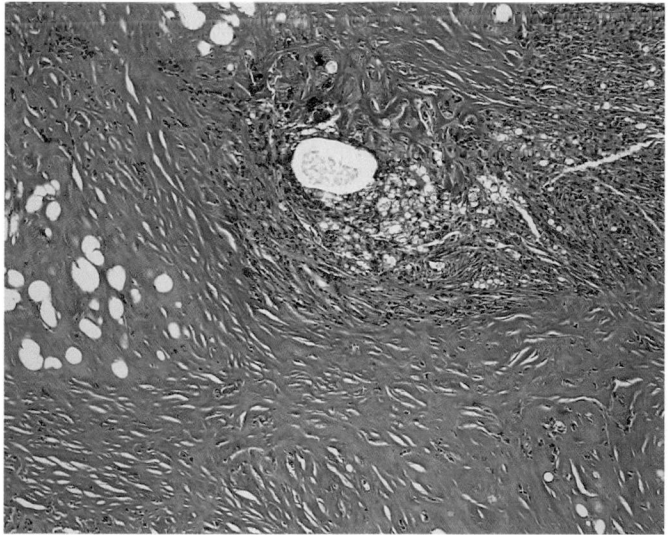

Fig. 26.29 Sclerosing mesenteritis. There is fibrosis with hyalinization, chronic inflammation, and fat necrosis surrounded by clusters of foamy macrophages.

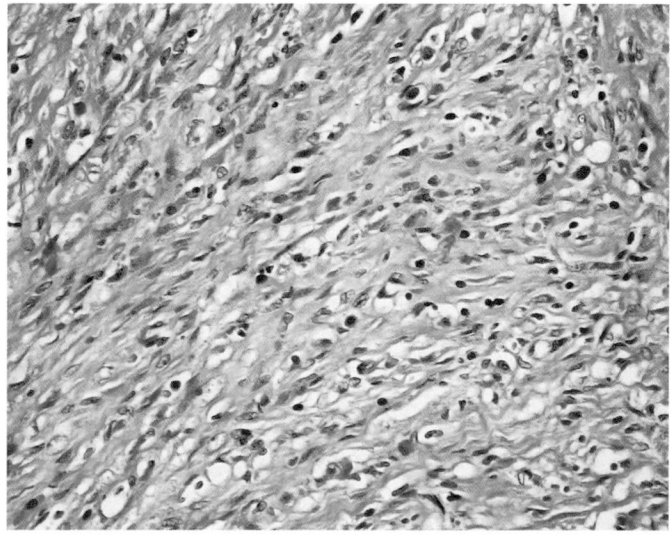

Fig. 26.31 Inflammatory pseudotumor showing an admixture of inflammatory cells in a fibrosed background.

generally favorable outcome following surgical excision. However, further experience has shown that these cases blend imperceptibly with others showing a more neoplastic appearance of the fibroblastic/myofibroblastic component and/or running an aggressive clinical course, including the development of metastases. The term *inflammatory fibrosarcoma*[265] has been proposed for the more neoplastic-appearing members of this group. There is also cytogenetic and molecular evidence that even some of the more inflammatory-appearing lesions may be neoplastic.[276] Because of these facts, we prefer the term *inflammatory myofibroblastic tumor*[249,272] for this process. It has been suggested that at least some of the reported cases of intra-abdominal *calcifying fibrous pseudotumor* (further discussed in Chapter 25) may represent the end stage of inflammatory pseudotumor.[248,259] However, the facts that the latter entity is usually immunoreactive for CD34 while negative for ALK and S-100 protein and that transitional forms between the two entities are rare are not supportive of such an association.[254a] Since local recurrence can supervene in calcifying fibrous pseudotumor, it has been further suggested that it be renamed *calcifying fibrous tumor*.[268] The group of conditions recently termed reactive *nodular fibrous pseudotumor* are part of this spectrum.[279a]

Mesenteric cysts are usually incidental findings, but they may be large enough to produce symptoms.[260,277] Some are seen as a component of the basal cell nevus syndrome.[251] They are round and smooth, with a thin wall and a content that may be a serous fluid resembling plasma or a white milky fluid, particularly if located near the jejunum. In the latter instance, they are referred to as *chylous cysts* (Fig. 26.32). Most of these cysts arise from lymph vessels and are lined by endothelium. When they are large and multilocular and/or have smooth muscle in their walls, we prefer to regard them as **cystic lymphangiomas**[247,264,274] and distinguish them from the HMB-45-positive **lymphangiomyomas**.[261]

Other types of mesenteric cysts occur. One is **bowel duplication**, in which the cyst is lined by intestinal mucosa, there is a layer of smooth muscle, and there is an anatomic connection with the bowel by way of an interlacing muscular wall and blood supply; over half of these are diagnosed before 6 months of age.[274] Other mesenteric cysts are lined by mesothelium and are examples of so-called **benign cystic (or multicystic) mesothelioma** (see p. 2375). Others are lined by *müllerian (fallopian tube-like) epithelium*, similar to those more commonly seen in the true pelvis[253,262] (see Chapter 19). Still others, seen in females who have had previous pelvic surgery, are lined by luteinized cells and have ovarian stroma in their wall; these are referred to as **ovarian remnant syndrome**[275] or **mesenteric cyst–ovarian implant syndrome**.[271] Another peculiar abnormality of müllerian nature and disputed pathogenesis (endometriotic versus malformative) that can occur in the mesentery is the so-called *uterus-like mass*.[255]

Cystic mucinous tumors of benign and borderline type have been described in the mesentery and retroperitoneum of females.[242] They are analogous in all regards to the homonymous tumors in the ovary, of which they can be regarded as the peritoneal counterparts.[242]

Primary solid tumors of the mesentery can be of various types, most of them of mesenchymal nature.[279] *Smooth muscle tumors*, when large, usually behave in a malignant fashion even if their mitotic count is low[254]; a high proportion of the tumors reported in the past as leiomyomas or leiomyosarcomas in this location (particularly those with an epithelioid or clear cell morphology) would be reclassified as GISTs today, a statement that also applies to tumors of the omentum and retroperitoneum. If one were to split GISTs from smooth muscle tumors, as currently proposed (see Chapter 11), the large majority of the mesenteric and omental tumors would fall into the former category, in contrast to the retroperitoneal situation (see p. 2388 and Chapter 11).

Fibromatosis (desmoid tumor) of the mesentery should always raise the suspicion of Gardner's syndrome, particularly if it develops following a surgical procedure[245,246,263] (Figs 26.33 and 26.34). During the past years we have seen several cases of fibromatosis misdiagnosed as GIST, the reasons being that they involved the bowel wall and were immunoreactive for CD34 and CD117 (c-kit).[266,280] The reactivity for CD117 is, however, only coarse cytoplasmic and not present with some of the newer antibodies against this marker. Furthermore, it has been recently shown that mesenteric fibromatosis shows

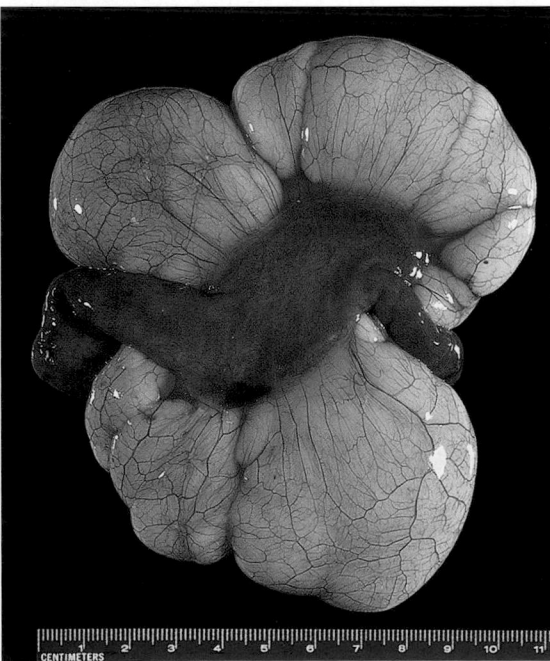

Fig. 26.32 Typical golden yellow color of chylous cyst. (Courtesy of Dr. RA Cooke, Brisbane, Australia; from Cooke RA, Stewart B: Colour Atlas of Anatomical Pathology. Edinburgh, Churchill Livingstone, 2004.)

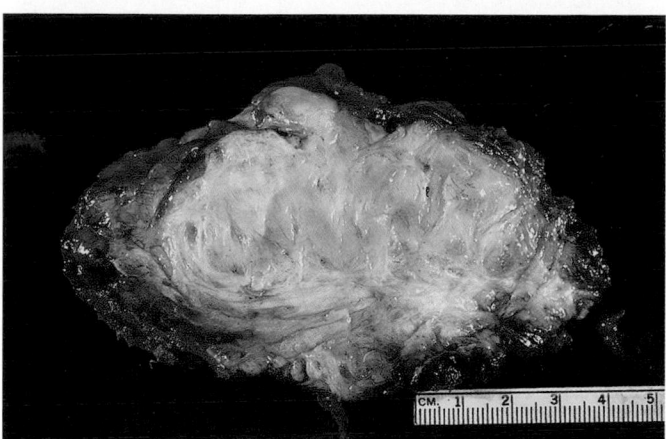

Fig. 26.33 Fibromatosis of mesentery involving the bowel wall. Cases like this are likely to be misinterpreted as GIST.

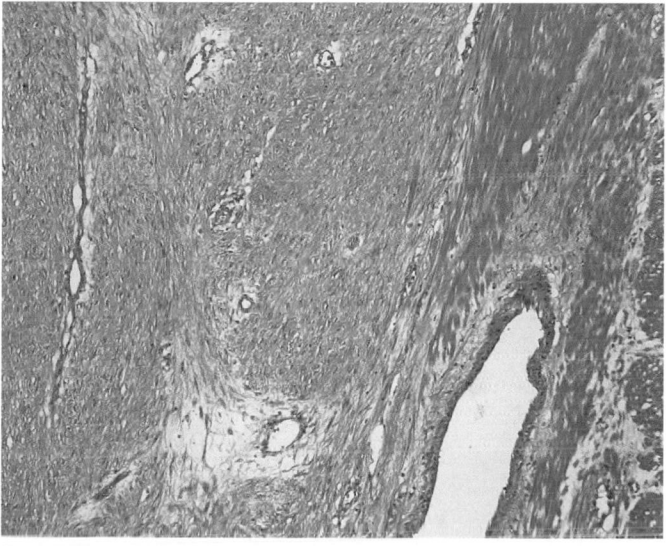

A

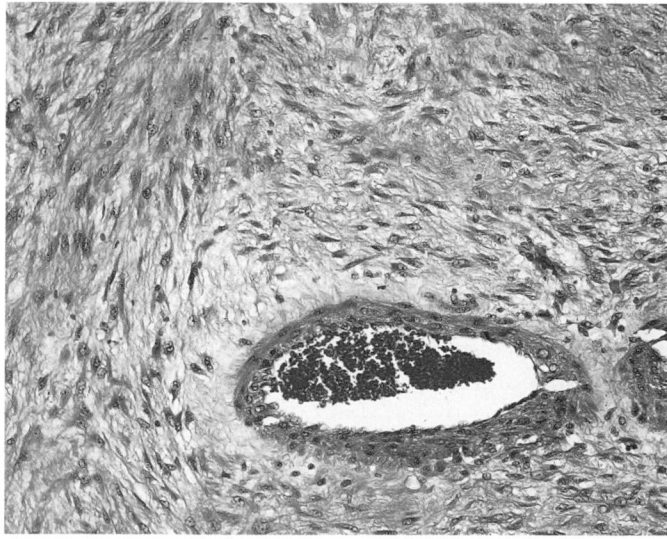

B

Fig. 26.34 Fibromatosis of mesentery. **A,** Entrapment of muscle fibers from bowel wall. **B,** Typical growth of myofibroblasts in a heavily collagenized background. Note the sharply etched thick-walled vessel.

consistent nuclear immunoreactivity for β-catenin, whereas GIST does not.[266a] The differential diagnosis is possible with plain H&E stains anyway in the large majority of cases.[240]

Adipose tissue tumors are usually of the atypical lipomatous tumor (well-differentiated liposarcoma) type, sometimes accompanied by secondary myxoid or inflammatory changes.

So-called "MFH" also occurs in this location, often having a polymorphous appearance and high content in foamy macrophages; it is likely that some of the cases previously reported as xanthogranulomas belong in this category.

Vascular tumors are represented by the already mentioned cystic lymphangioma, angiosarcoma, epithelioid hemangioendothelioma, and infantile hemangioendothelioma. The latter can be associated with thrombocytopenia.[252]

Peripheral nerve tumors are usually benign and represented both by schwannoma and neurofibroma.[279]

Other primary mesenteric tumors of which isolated cases have been reported include an allegedly primary *carcinoid tumor,*[243] *follicular dendritic cell tumor,*[267] paraganglioma (Fig. 26.35), and several examples of *germ cell tumor,* including yolk sac tumor[256] and mature cystic teratoma (dermoid cyst) associated with autoimmune hemolytic anemia.[244]

Tumorlike conditions of the mesentery include, in addition to those already mentioned, *Castleman's disease,* which can present as a mesenteric mass associated with hematologic disturbances,[269] and which in this location is often characterized by a rich stroma, hyalinization, and calcification (Fig. 26.36).

Metastatic carcinoma is the most common type of solid tumor of the mesentery; in most cases the primary tumor is in an intra-abdominal site.

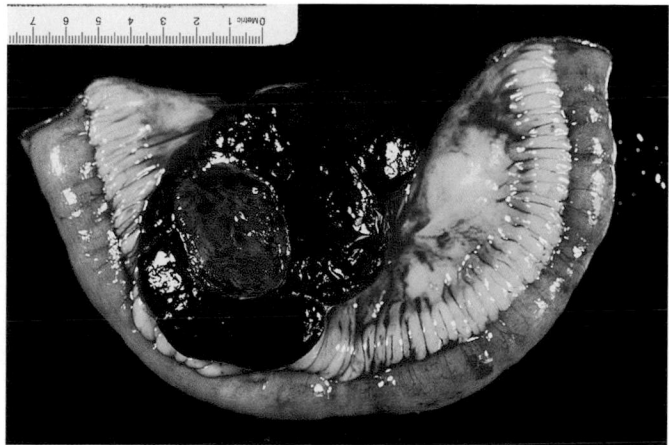

Fig. 26.35 Gross appearance of paraganglioma of the mesentery. This is a most unusual location for this tumor type. The associated hemorrhage due to the high degree of tumor vascularization is a common event.

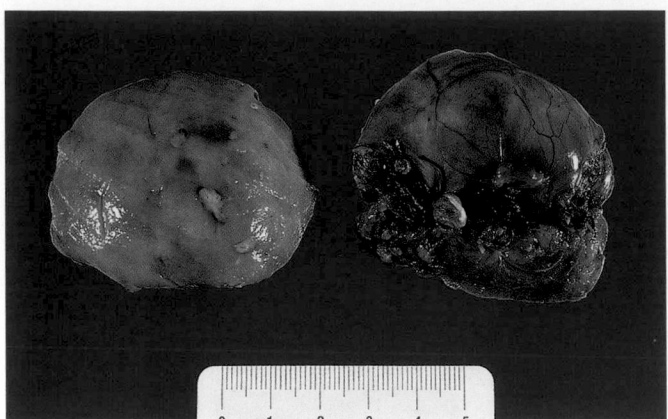

Fig. 26.36 Castleman's disease located in the root of the mesentery. This is a relatively common location for this entity.

Hernia sacs

This rather mundane specimen is one of the most common to be received in the surgical pathology laboratory. In most instances, there is not much of interest microscopically: an attenuated lining of mesothelial cells resting on a thin layer of connective tissue (corresponding to the processus vaginalis in indirect inguinal hernias), adipose tissue, dense fibrous tissue belonging to fascia and/or aponeurosis, and sometimes fascicles of skeletal muscle (from the transversus abdominis in the inguinal hernias). The preperitoneal fat that covers the sac may be abundant and be designated as "lipoma" by the surgeon, but it does not represent a neoplasm. Once in a while, however, the hernial sac will show one or more startling pathologic changes. *Mesothelial hyperplasia* resulting from trauma or another injury can be so extreme as to simulate a malignancy (see p. 2377); the accompanying inflammation, hyperemia, and fibrin deposition will point toward its reactive nature (see Fig. 26.4). Sometimes a *mesothelioma* or a *metastatic carcinoma* will first become evident from the study of a herniorrhaphy specimen. The most common sources for the primary are the gastrointestinal tract, ovary, prostate, and appendix.[282,286] The pseudomyxoma peritonei that sometimes accompanies appendiceal mucinous tumors may result in filling of the hernia sac by viscid mucin (see p. 2386).[291] The finding of mucinous material within the sac at the time of the hernia repair may be the first sign of the disease.[284] A particularly exotic tumor reported within an umbilical hernia sac is an *extragonadal sex-cord tumor with annular tubules*.[281] Parenthetically, the other reported case of extragonadal tumor of this type was located in the fallopian tube and associated with endometriosis.[285]

Other changes one may encounter in a hernia sac are *endometriosis* in females and *glandular inclusions* from wolffian or müllerian remnants in prepubertal males.

The latter are lined by ciliated epithelium and surrounded by a mantle of fibrous tissue; they should not be misinterpreted as portions of the vas deferens or epididymis.[287,290] Immunostaining for CD10 can provide some assistance, in the sense that the reaction is positive in the normal vas deferens and epididymis (at least focally) whereas it is always negative in the vas deferens-like inclusions and usually negative in the epididymis-like inclusions.[282a] In a microscopic study of 7314 herniorrhaphies in male children, Steigman et al.[289] found these embryonal rests in 30 (0.41%), whereas they detected vas deferens in 17 (0.23%) and epididymis in 22 (0.30%). This is one of several reasons why the routine microscopic evaluation of hernia sacs remains a worthwhile procedure, as eloquently pointed out by Dehner.[283]

Crystalline foreign particulate material largely composed of talc was consistently detected in hernia sacs by polarized microscopy and X-diffraction studies by Pratt et al.[288] They suggest that the source of this talc was ingestion with food or medication, but it seems to us that they did not satisfactorily rule out the alternative possibility that the source was the surgical procedure or the processing of the specimen.

Umbilicus

The umbilicus is subject to a variety of diseases resulting from its unique anatomy and the important structures with which it is connected during development. Foraker chose this structure for some of his satirical essays on the practice of surgical pathology, by creating the mythical figure of the omphalopathologist.[294] Excluding conditions such as hernias, omphaloceles, neonatal infections, and extensive fetal malformations, the group of disorders of importance to the surgical pathologist that can affect the umbilicus are those that follow.

Urachal remnant anomalies may present as a patent sinus between the umbilicus and the bladder, as blind sinuses at any level between these two structures, and as a closed but persistently attached urachus. Steck and Helwig[299] have suggested that most cases of granulomatous omphalitis, umbilical granuloma, and pilonidal sinus of the umbilicus are related to urachal anomalies because of the fact that an attached urachus is found in nearly half of these cases (see Chapter 17, Urinary bladder).

Omphalomesenteric duct remnant anomalies include patency of the duct, "umbilical polyp," sinus tract, attachment of Meckel's diverticulum to the umbilicus by an incompletely obliterated duct, and formation of a cyst in the umbilicus or along the course of the incompletely obliterated duct[296] (see Chapter 11, Small bowel) (Fig. 26.37).

Endometriosis of the umbilicus is the most common form of cutaneous endometriosis, except for that occurring in surgical scars[297] (see Chapter 19, Uterus corpus).

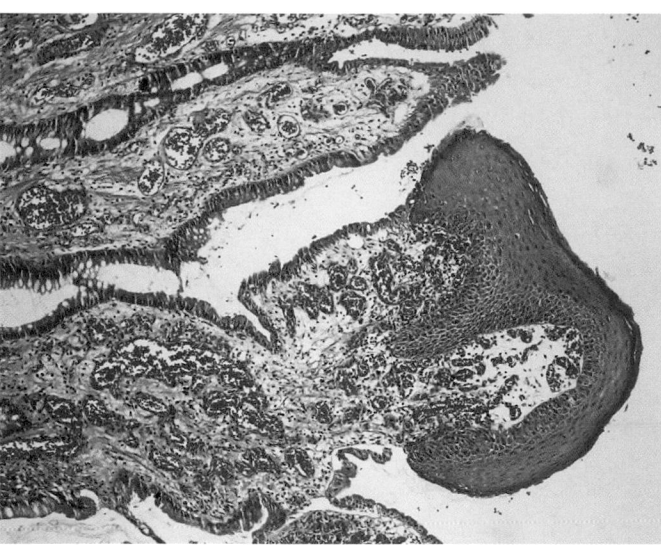

Fig. 26.37 Umbilical polyp partially lined by glandular epithelium derived from the omphalomesenteric duct.

Keratinous cysts of epidermal type are relatively common.[298]

Benign tumors of the umbilical region can be of various types; most of them belong to the category of benign melanocytic nevus and fibrous or fibroepithelial polyp.[298,301] The latter, which for some peculiar reason shows a marked male predominance, may be composed of dense fibrous tissue or have a nodular fasciitis-like appearance.[300]

Malignant tumors involving the umbilicus can be primary or metastatic. The most common primary malignant tumor is malignant melanoma, followed by basal cell carcinoma and adenocarcinoma.[295,298] Metastatic tumors are much more common. Most of them originate in the stomach, pancreas, large bowel, or ovary.[298] The colloquial term "Sister (Mary) Joseph's nodule" refers to umbilical metastases from malignancies of the female genital tract, usually ovarian carcinoma.[292] Several cases have been described of rapid development of umbilical metastases after laparoscopic cholecystectomy for unsuspected gallbladder carcinoma.[293]

Retroperitoneum

Normal anatomy

The retroperitoneal space is the portion of the lumboiliac region limited anteriorly by the peritoneal covering, posteriorly by the posterior abdominal wall, superiorly by the twelfth rib and vertebra, inferiorly by the base of the sacrum and iliac crest, and laterally by the side borders of the quadratus lumborum muscles. It contains, embedded in a meshwork of loose connective tissue, the adrenal glands, kidneys and ureters, aorta and its branches, inferior vena cava and its tributaries, and numerous lymph nodes.

This potentially large space allows both primary and metastatic tumors to grow silently before clinical signs and symptoms appear.

Non-neoplastic conditions

Inflammatory processes from the kidney (pyelonephritis), large bowel (diverticulitis), appendix, and pancreas may result in a retroperitoneal abscess, usually resulting from coliform bacteria. In children, nontuberculous psoas abscesses are, in most cases, due to gram-positive cocci originating from a focus of tonsillitis, otitis media, or cutaneous furuncle. Perforation of the biliary system may occur within the retroperitoneum, with formation of a bile-containing cystic mass. Infection from a tuberculous vertebra may form a retroperitoneal cold abscess, which is often confined to the psoas muscle. **Malakoplakia** can involve the retroperitoneum and be confused with malignant fibrous histiocytoma[328] (Fig. 26.38). Massive retroperitoneal **hemorrhage** in the adult is most often the result of a ruptured aortic aneurysm, trauma, hemorrhagic diathesis, or anticoagulant drug therapy.[317] Less commonly, it is of renal or adrenal origin. In five instances reported by Lawson et al.,[316] the adrenal gland was the site of a pheochromocytoma, but in the other five there was no demonstrable abnormality. We have also seen massive retroperitoneal hemorrhage as a complication of adrenal metastases of malignant melanoma. Sometimes **perirenal hemorrhagic cysts** contain equally spaced radial striations that are probably the expression of the Liesegang phenomenon and that have been confused with parasites,[327] whereas the lesions of so-called **myospherulosis** contain clusters of darkened red blood cells within baglike formations that simulate fungal organisms (see Chapter 7).[318]

Extravasation of urine from the upper urinary tract may result in an edematous or gelatinous tumefaction in the retroperitoneum around the renal pelvis. Microscopically, the early stages are characterized by fat necrosis and inflammation and so-called "urinary precipitates." An important diagnostic clue is the presence of Tamm–Horsfall protein, as detected immunohistochemically.[302]

Epithelium-lined peritoneal cysts unconnected to the adrenal gland or kidney can be of various types depending on the nature of the lining: mesothelial, mesonephric,[315] müllerian (either serous or mucinous),[307,314a] or bronchial. The latter, referred to as *bronchogenic cysts*, are usually found around the adrenal gland and may simulate a primary adrenal neoplasm.[308,320] They represent malformations of the embryonic foregut.

atypia commonly seen in the smooth muscle elements (see Chapter 17). The primarily intrarenal location, the admixture with mature fat and thick-walled blood vessels, and the immunoreactivity for HMB-45 should allow the recognition of this entity. It should also be noted that primary extrarenal examples of this tumor exist, some of them epithelioid and malignant.[362a]

Leiomyoma is very rare as a primary retroperitoneal neoplasm. When encountering a tumor in this region with a leiomyomatous appearance, one should consider the alternative possibilities of uterine leiomyoma extending posteriorly, well-differentiated leiomyosarcoma, benign or malignant GIST, lymphangiomyoma, and the previously discussed angiomyolipoma[340] (see p. 2397). It would appear that the majority of truly benign smooth muscle tumors presenting as retroperitoneal masses are anatomically and/or functionally related to the female genital tract (i.e., arising from hormonally sensitive smooth muscle), as suggested by the fact that there is a great predominance of females, a marked morphologic resemblance to uterine leiomyoma by virtue of hyaline change and trabecular pattern of growth, and frequent positivity for estrogen and progesterone receptors[341,360a,367] (Fig. 26.46).

Rhabdomyosarcoma of retroperitoneum is usually of the embryonal type (including its botryoid variety) and rarely of the alveolar type, and is limited for all practical purposes to infants and children.[344,371] Multimodality treatment has resulted in a greater than 50% tumor response, but the long-term prognosis remains poor.[344,371] The differential diagnosis of retroperitoneal rhabdomyosarcoma in children includes malignant lymphoma, Ewing's sarcoma/PNET in all its manifestations (including so-called "paravertebral round cell tumor"),[379,386] and (intra-abdominal) desmoplastic small cell tumor (i.e., the whole gamut of small cell tumors of childhood). The distinction between these various entities is often very difficult to make, to say the least, and it may be impossible in the individual case, even after performing ultrastructural and immunohistochemical studies.[345,349,380] This fact was clearly shown in a study from the Intergroup Rhabdomyosarcoma Study Committee,[344] in which almost 30% of 101 retroperitoneal soft tissue sarcomas were classified as undifferentiated or unspecified. The situation has greatly improved following the systematic evaluation of these tumors with cytogenetic and molecular techniques (see Chapter 25).

Rhabdomyoma is practically nonexistent in the retroperitoneum; however, a convincing case combining features of the fetal and adult types of this tumor has been reported in a neonate.[385]

Fibromatosis may occur, sometimes in association with mediastinal involvement. In contrast to idiopathic retroperitoneal fibrosis (a disorder with which it is often confused), it lacks a prominent inflammatory component, except for perivascular lymphocytic cuffing at the growing edge.

Fibrosarcoma is one of the rarest retroperitoneal tumors in our experience. We believe that most cases so designated in the literature would today be labeled liposarcomas, leiomyosarcomas, or malignant fibrous histiocytomas.

Solitary fibrous tumor can present as a primary retroperitoneal mass, sometimes accompanied by hypoglycemia (Fig. 26.47). Some of the reported cases were associated with independent pleural tumors of similar appearance.[358]

Vascular tumors of several types have been described, including hemangioma, hemangiopericytoma, lymphangioma, lymphangiomyoma, and angiosarcoma.[364] Some

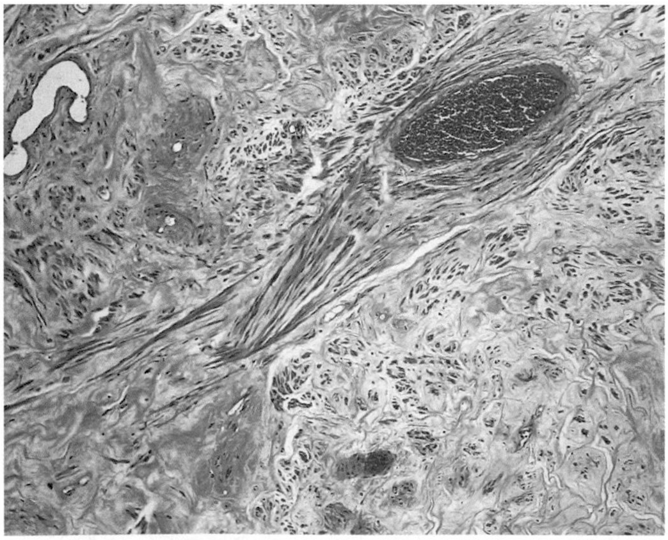

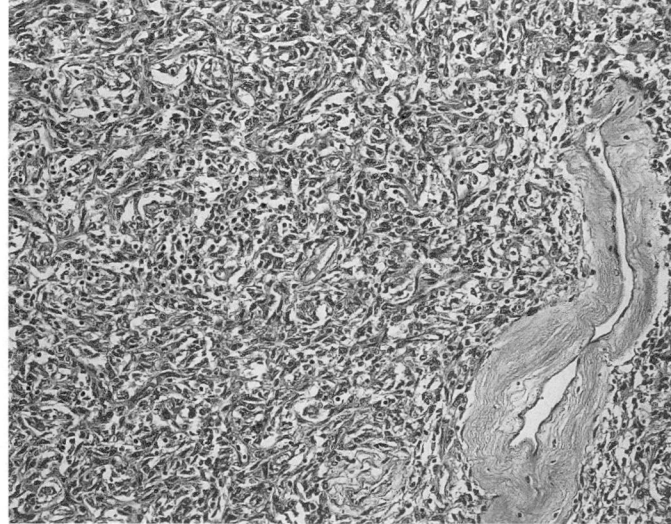

Fig. 26.46 Retroperitoneal smooth muscle tumor in pelvic region morphologically similar to uterine leiomyoma. Note the prominent hyalinization.

Fig. 26.47 Solitary fibrous tumor/hemangiopericytoma of the pelvic region. This is one of the most common locations for this tumor type.

of the angiosarcomas are of the epithelioid variety; prominent eosinophilic globules may be present in the cytoplasm of the tumor cells.[384] A peculiar variant of infantile hemangioendothelioma mimicking Kaposi's sarcoma and often accompanied by thrombocytopenia and hemorrhage (Kasabach–Merritt syndrome) has a special tendency for a retroperitoneal location.[350,381]

Peripheral nerve tumors of both benign and malignant type occur; as a matter of fact, the retroperitoneum is a relatively common site for their development. Among the benign tumors, there are *schwannomas, neurofibromas,* and (rarely but diagnosed with increasing frequency) *perineuriomas* (Fig. 26.48). *MPNSTs* usually present as paraspinal masses and tend to behave in an aggressive fashion[362] (Fig. 26.49). They may directly invade bone and metastasize distantly. Some of these tumors have arisen from retroperitoneal ganglioneuromas,[351] and others have had the phenotypic features of malignant perineurioma. A tumor histogenetically related to perineurioma is *meningioma*, which has been

reported to present exceptionally as a primary retroperitoneal lesion.[357]

Synovial sarcoma,[375] **alveolar soft part sarcoma,**[374] **extraskeletal osteosarcoma** and **endometrial stromal sarcoma**[365a] can present as primary retroperitoneal neoplasms.[342] There has also been a report of a **dendritic follicular tumor** arising extranodally from periduodenal retroperitoneal soft tissue.[356]

Germ cell tumors

Retroperitoneal germ cell tumors in children are represented by mature and immature teratoma, embryonal carcinoma, and yolk sac tumor.[388,391,392] Sometimes these occur in combination.[396] Their features merge with those of sacrococcygeal teratomas, which are discussed in more detail on p. 2401.

Retroperitoneal germ cell tumors in adults can theoretically arise in this location or represent metastases from primaries in the gonads[387,389,394] (Fig. 26.50). Both types are much more common in males. The entire microscopic gamut is represented, including seminoma (germinoma), embryonal carcinoma, teratocarcinoma, mature and immature teratoma, mature teratoma with malignant transformation, yolk sac tumor, and choriocarcinoma[395] (Fig. 26.51). The chances of a retroperitoneal germ cell tumor in a male being metastatic from a small testicular primary tumor are much higher than for a mediastinal tumor of the same type. The gross appearance of the tumor may give a clue in this regard: in general, primary retroperitoneal neoplasms are formed by a single mass, whereas those metastatic from the testis

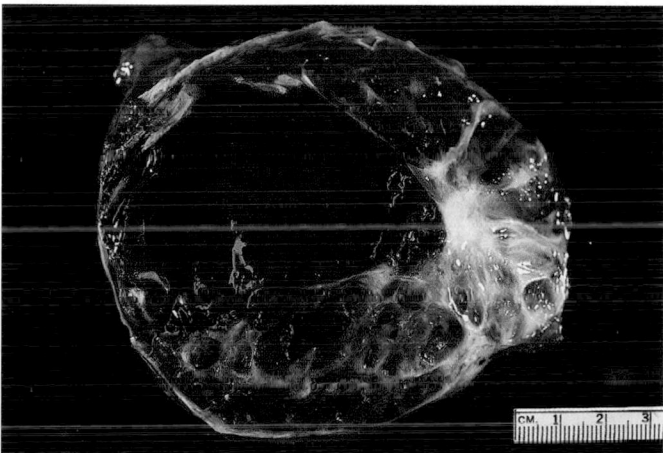

Fig. 26.48 Retroperitoneal schwannoma. The tumor is encapsulated and shows marked secondary hemorrhagic and cystic changes.

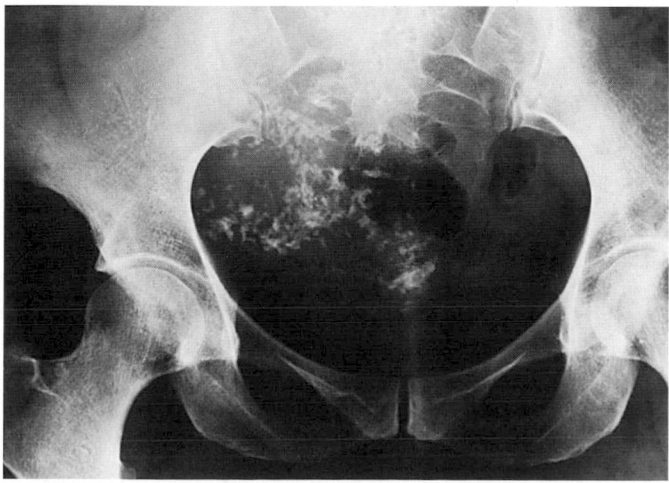

Fig 26.49 Partially calcified retroperitoneal malignant peripheral nerve sheath tumor.

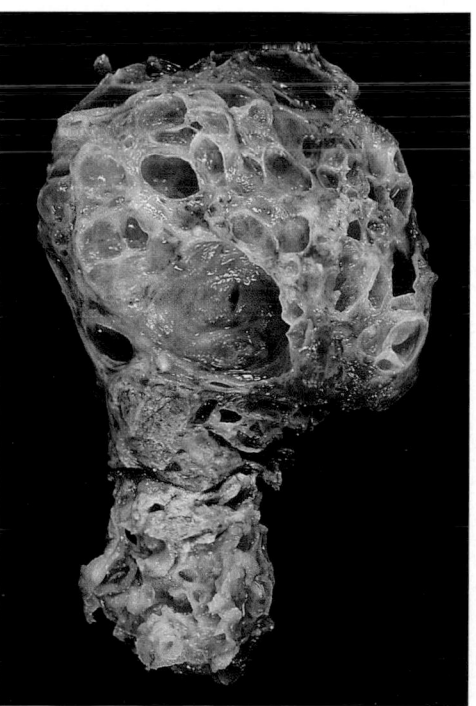

Fig. 26.50 Mature retroperitoneal teratoma. Gross appearance, showing multiple cystic spaces.

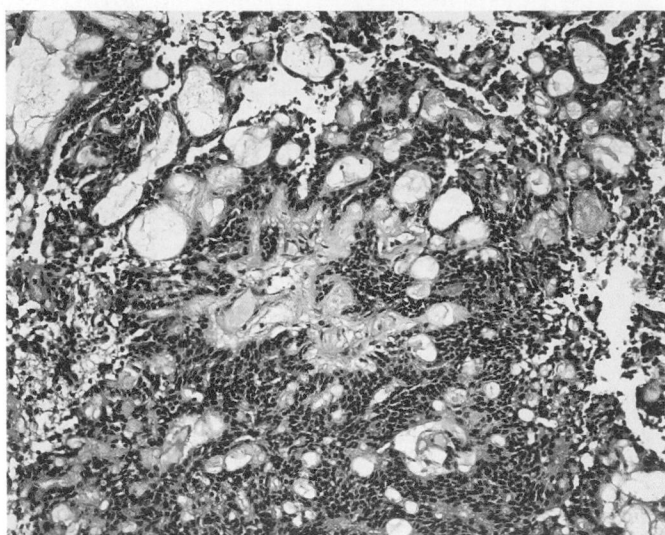

Fig. 26.51 Typical microscopic appearance of yolk sac tumor of sacrococcygeal region.

tend to involve several nodes, often on both sides of the peritoneum.[397] Also, seminomas are more likely to be primary than nonseminomatous germ cell tumors. The testicular primary tumor, when present, may be clinically apparent, may be occult, or may have been excised many years previously.[393] In some cases, only intratubular germ cell neoplasia is found in the testicle, suggesting the possibility of independent neoplastic events.[390] Careful palpation, roentgenograms, sonography, and scrotal thermography have been employed to detect occult testicular tumors; of these, sonography has proved to be the most useful.

Other primary tumors and tumorlike conditions

Tumors of sympathetic nervous tissue of the type more commonly seen in the adrenal gland can also be present in the retroperitoneum outside this gland, as indicated in

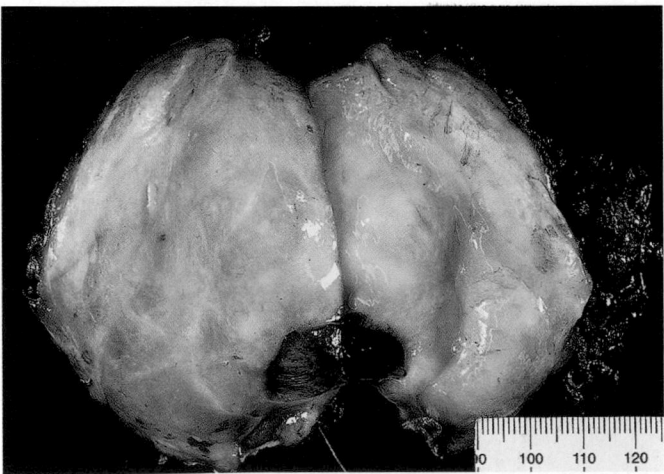

Fig. 26.52 Ganglioneuroma of retroperitoneum. The gross appearance is similar to that of neurofibroma.

Chapter 16. This includes neuroblastoma, ganglioneuroblastoma, ganglioneuroma, and their variants (Fig. 26.52). It is important to recognize that neuroblastoma can present in adult patients and to distinguish it from Ewing's sarcoma/PNET.[404]

Paragangliomas arise outside the adrenal gland in approximately 10% of the cases. They may occur anywhere along the midline of the retroperitoneum, the best known location being the body of Zuckerkandl (at the origin of the inferior mesenteric artery).[407,408] Tumors arising in **heterotopic adrenal cortex** have also been reported.

Myelolipomas similar to those of the adrenal glands can be encountered in the presacral area. They are well circumscribed, can attain a huge size, and are composed of a mixture of fat cells and normal marrow hematopoietic elements.[398] These are usually asymptomatic, whereas mass-forming foci of extramedullary hematopoiesis (which lack fat and are ill defined) are associated with myeloproliferative diseases, hemolytic anemia, or severe skeletal diseases.[401,402]

Carcinoid tumor has been described as a retroperitoneal neoplasm; whether it represents a metastasis from an undetected primary tumor, the expression of a monodermal teratoma, or a neoplasm from endocrine cells normally present in this location remains to be determined.[417]

Tumors of müllerian type are occasionally seen as primary retroperitoneal masses in the pelvis or rectovaginal septum (see Chapter 19, Ovary). They can be of serous, mucinous, or endometrioid subtype, and can be benign, borderline, or malignant[413] (Fig. 26.53). They also include mixed müllerian malignant tumor (müllerian carcinosarcoma).[412] They arise either from heterotopic ovarian tissue or, more likely, from invaginations of the peritoneal mesothelial layer with concurrent or subsequent müllerian metaplasia.[400,405,409,410,415] Some mucinous retroperitoneal tumors have shown evidence of gastric mucosal differentiation, suggesting a totally different histogenesis.[411]

Wilms' tumor has been reported in the retroperitoneum outside the kidney in the absence of teratomatous elements.[406,414,416] Some of these lesions may represent teratomas predominantly or exclusively composed of nephrogenic elements. Most of these cases have occurred in children, but they have also been recorded in adults.[403]

Myoepithelioma has been described, simulating microscopically the appearance of a schwannoma.[399]

Metastatic tumors

Secondary neoplasms may appear in the retroperitoneal space as a result of local extension or because of lymph node involvement. The former is mainly represented by pancreatic carcinoma and primary bone neoplasms, notably sacrococcygeal chordoma.

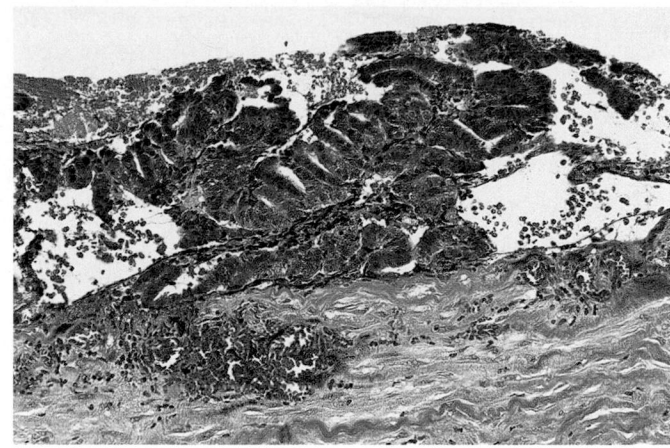

Fig. 26.53 A and **B**, Low-power and high-power appearance of müllerian-type cystadenocarcinoma located in the retroperitoneal region.

The carcinomas most commonly giving rise to retroperitoneal lymph node metastases are those originating in the testis, prostate, pancreas, uterine cervix, endometrium, and kidney.

Sacrococcygeal region

Developmental anomalies

A large and complex number of malformations can occur in the sacrococcygeal region, the most common being meningocele and spina bifida.[418,421] Some of these are discussed in Chapter 28.

Tailgut cyst (retrorectal cystic hamartoma) presents in the presacrococcygeal area, usually in adult patients but sometimes in children, as a multiloculated cyst lined by squamous, transitional, or glandular epithelium[419,422,423,425,427] (Figs 26.54 and 26.55). Disorganized fascicles of smooth muscle may be seen in the wall. Prominent glomus bodies may also be present.[426] This benign malformative lesion should be distinguished from teratoma, epidermal cyst, rectal or anal duplication, and anal gland cyst.[424,429] Malignant transformation can supervene in this malformation, in the form of adenocarcinoma or carcinoid tumor (see below).[428]

Ectopic prostatic tissue can occur in the presacral region and lead to extrinsic compression of the bowel.[420]

Germ cell tumors

Sacrococcygeal germ cell tumors in neonates and infants are nearly always primary.[431] From 75% to 90% of the cases occur in females. They can arise in the retroperitoneum proper, arise in the sacrococcygeal region, or involve both compartments.[436,438,446] Chromosomal analysis of these extragonadal teratomas suggests that they

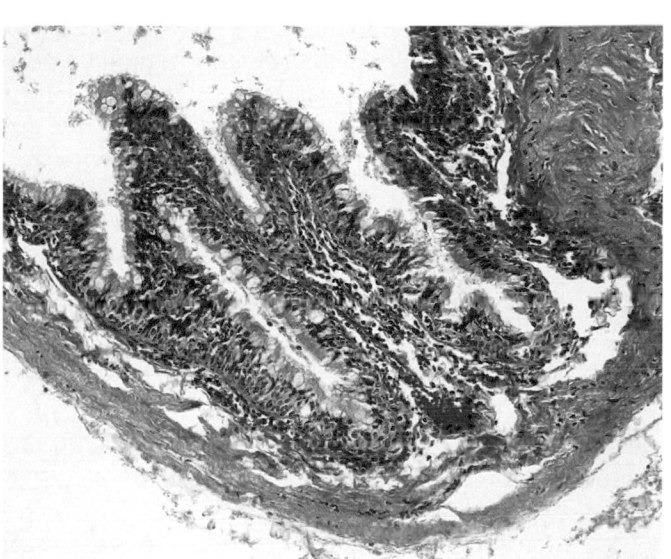

Fig. 26.54 Tailgut cyst lined by pseudostratified epithelium surrounded by a muscle wall.

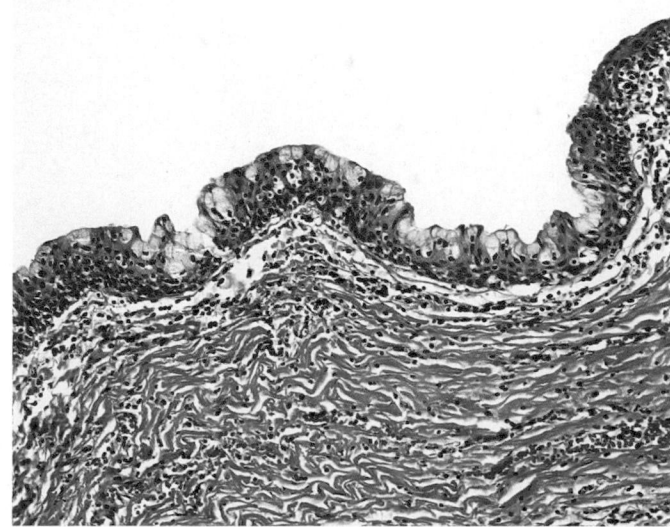

Fig. 26.55 Tailgut cyst lined by mucin-secreting well-differentiated epithelium with goblet cells.

have arisen from postmitotic, premeiotic cells.[439] The most common type is the **mature teratoma** presenting at birth in the sacrococcygeal region or protruding through the abdominal cavity (Fig. 26.56).[433,435] It may be very large, is usually cystic and multilocular, and may appear malignant to the surgeon because of its stubborn adherence to neighboring structures, but this fixation is usually of an inflammatory nature, caused by reaction to extravasated material. Total excision is curative; the tip of the coccyx should be removed as part of the operation to prevent recurrence.[451] Microscopically, this tumor is composed of mature tissues throughout. Hepatic tissue is present in one quarter of the cases.[444] The presence of immature elements in regard to amount and microscopic type should be evaluated with care.[450] If this immaturity is restricted to neuroectodermal components (which is often the case), the tendency is toward spontaneous differentiation. As a result, the behavior of this type of immature teratoma is usually benign, although occasional cases will recur or metastasize.[437,450]

Most of the clearly malignant teratomas in this age group have the appearance of **yolk sac (endodermal sinus) tumor**, either pure or associated with other germ cell components, and are accompanied by the production of oncofetal antigens[436,440,447] and expression of transcription factor GATA-4.[449] They often contain immature hepatic tissue.[444] These tumors run an extremely aggressive clinical course.[434,437,442] A renal component resembling Wilms' tumor is sometimes found in these teratomas. It may not be easy to decide in an individual case whether the lesion represents a teratoma with predominance of nephrogenic elements or a "teratoid" Wilms' tumor.

An interesting clinical observation is that the large majority of sacrococcygeal teratomas present at birth are benign, whereas tumors in the same general location

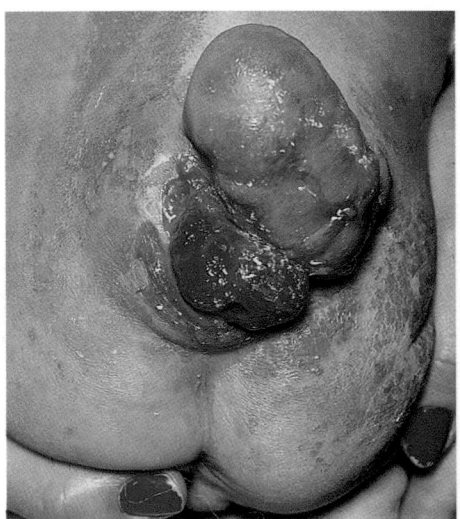

Fig. 26.56 Sacrococcygeal teratoma protruding as a polypoid, partially ulcerated mass.

discovered after the age of 2 months are often malignant.[435] This has been taken by some to indicate that a malignant transformation has supervened in that short period. We doubt that this is the case. It seems to us that this clinical observation can better be explained by postulating the existence of two groups of teratomas. One arises in the very distal portion of the sacrococcygeal region, is therefore clinically obvious at the time of birth, and is nearly always mature. The other arises more proximally, in the retrorectal or adjacent retroperitoneal region, is malignant from the start, and grows into the sacrococcygeal area to become clinically evident only some time after birth. It also grows within the abdominal cavity, this being responsible for the clinical observation that teratomas associated with marked bowel or bladder dysfunction are often malignant. Exceptions in both directions certainly occur, but the large majority of teratomas in this region fit into this scheme.

A sacrococcygeal presentation of teratoma in adults is exceptional.[445] Most are benign and probably have been there since birth. A few show malignant foci, either in the form of germ cell (trophoblastic, yolk sac) components or of adult-type carcinomatous tissues.[430,451] Mature teratomas excised in early life may recur in adulthood in the form of a microscopically similar neoplasm,[443] as a malignant germ cell tumor (such as yolk sac tumor),[448] or as a somatic-type malignant tumor, such as adenocarcinoma.[441]

The differential diagnosis of benign sacrococcygeal teratoma includes the already mentioned developmental abnormalities of this region, a discussion of which is beyond the scope of this book. A comprehensive review of these anomalies can be found in an article by Bale.[432]

Pilonidal disease

Pilonidal sinuses appear as small openings in the intergluteal fold about 3.5 to 5 cm posterior to the anal orifice. Hairs are sometimes seen protruding from them. The opening is continued by a sinus tract, which is directed upward in 93% of the cases.[456] The disease is most often seen in young white males with dark, straight hair. Although congenital anomalies related to the closure of the neural canal can certainly occur in this area, it is now believed that the large majority of pilonidal sinuses have an acquired pathogenesis.[453] Hairs penetrate areas of inflammation from without, lodge in the dermis, and elicit a foreign body type of reaction. The sinus is lined by granulation tissue. In approximately 25% of the cases, hairs are not found within the lesion.

Pilonidal sinuses also have been described in other areas where skin folds are prominent, such as the umbilicus, clitoris, and axilla.[452] A further observation favoring the theory of the acquired origin is the fact that barbers and hairdressers occasionally develop a disease equivalent to pilonidal sinus between their fingers, the sinuses containing somebody else's hairs!

Cases of **squamous cell carcinoma**[454,457] and **verrucous carcinoma** (giant condyloma acuminatum)[455] developing within pilonidal sinuses have been described.

Other tumors

Neoplasms other than germ cell tumors can involve the sacrococcygeal region primarily or as an extension from adjacent sites. Most cases of **cellular blue nevus** involve this area (see Chapter 4). Cases of coccydynia have been reported secondarily to **tumors of the coccygeal glomus**, although the neoplastic nature of this process and their role in producing symptoms have been questioned (see Chapter 25). Specifically, the point has been made that the normal glomus coccygeum can measure up to 4 mm in diameter and that its appearance is no different in cases of coccydynia than in those cases where it was incidentally removed in the course of operations for rectal or uterine carcinoma.[459] **Myxopapillary ependymoma** can involve the soft tissues of the buttock, unconnected with the spine[460,462] (see Chapter 28).

Carcinoid tumor can occur as a primary lesion in the presacral area. Most of these tumors probably arise from hindgut rests, as suggested by their documented association with tailgut cysts (see p. 2401).[458,461]

Chordoma arising in the sacrum can produce a large retrorectal or sacrococcygeal mass (see Chapter 24). Finally, **carcinomas** of the anus or rectum (particularly those of the mucinous adenocarcinoma type) can spread to this region by direct extension (see Chapter 11).

References

PERITONEUM
Normal anatomy

1   Bolen JLW, Hammar SP, McNutt MA. Reactive and neoplastic serosal tissue. A light-microscopic, ultrastructural, and immunocytochemical study. Am J Surg Pathol 1986, **10:** 34–47.

1a Carter D, True L, Otis CN. In: Sternberg S (Editor): Histology for pathologists, ed. 2. Philadelphia, 1997, Lippincott-Raven Publishers, pp. 223–242.

2   Kupryjanczyk J, Karpinska G. Desmin expression in reactive mesothelium: A potential aid in evaluation of gynecologic specimens. Int J Gynecol Pathol 1998, **17:** 123–128.

3   McAuley P, Asa SL, Chiu B, Henderson J, Goltzman D, Drucker DJ. Parathyroid hormone-like peptide in normal and neoplastic mesothelial cells. Cancer 1990, **66:** 1975–1979.

4   Ober WB, Black MB. Neoplasms of the subcoelomic mesenchyme. Arch Pathol 1955, **59:** 698–705.

Inflammation

5   Bastani B, Shariatzadeh MR, Dehdashti F. Tuberculous peritonitis. Report of 30 cases and review of the literature. QJM 1985, **56:** 549–557.

6   Chen KTK. Coccidioidal peritonitis. Am J Clin Pathol 1983, **80:** 514–516.

7   Davis JH. Current concepts of peritonitis. Am Surg 1967, **33:** 673–681.

8   Ellis H, Adair HM. Bile peritonitis. A report of fifteen patients. Postgrad Med J 1974, **50:** 713–717.

9   Forouhar F. Meconium peritonitis. Pathology, evolution, and diagnosis. Am J Clin Pathol 1982, **78:** 208–213.

10 George E, Leyser S, Zimmer HL, Simonowitz DA, Agress RL, Nordin DD. Vernix caseosa peritonitis. An infrequent complication of Cesarean section with distinctive histopathologic features. Am J Clin Pathol 1995, **103:** 681–684.

11 Gilinsky NH, Marks IN, Kottler RE, Price SK. Abdominal tuberculosis. A 10-year review. S Afr Med J 1983, **64:** 849–857.

12 Gonnella JS, Hudson EK. Clinical patterns of tuberculous peritonitis. Arch Intern Med 1966, **117:** 164–169.

13 Levine H. Needle biopsy of peritoneum in exudative ascites. Arch Intern Med 1967, **120:** 542–545.

14 Levine H. Needle biopsy diagnosis of tuberculous peritonitis. Am Rev Respir Dis 1968, **97:** 889–894.

15 Seaman WB, Wells J. Complications of the barium enema. Gastroenterology 1965, **48:** 728–737.

16 Sherman S, Rohwedder JJ, Ravikrishnan KP, Weg JLG. Tuberculous enteritis and peritonitis. Report of 36 general hospital cases. Arch Intern Med 1980, **140:** 506–507.

17 Singh MM, Bhargava AN, Jain KP. Tuberculous peritonitis. An evaluation of pathogenetic mechanisms, diagnostic procedures and therapeutic measures. N Engl J Med 1969, **281:** 1091–1094.

18 Sochocky S. Tuberculous peritonitis. A review of 100 cases. Am Rev Respir Dis 1967, **95:** 398–401.

19 Varkonyi I, Fliegel C, Rosslein R, Jenny P, Ohnacker H. Meconium periorchitis: case report and literature review. Eur J Pediatr Surg 2000, **10:** 404–407.

20 Vinuela A, Fernandez-Rojo F, Martinez-Merino A. Oxyuris granulomas of pelvic peritoneum and appendicular wall. Histopathology 1979, **3:** 69–77.

Adhesions

21 Bockman RF, Woods M, Sargent L, Gervin AS. A unifying pathogenetic mechanism in the etiology of intraperitoneal adhesions. J Surg Res 1976, **20:** 1–5.

22 Brown P, Baddeley H, Read AE, Davies JD, McGarry JMc. Sclerosing peritonitis. An unusual reaction to a β-adrenergic-blocking drug (Practolol). Lancet 1974, **2:** 1477–1481.

23 Castelli MJ, Armin A-R, Husain A, Orfei E. Fibrosing peritonitis in a drug abuser. Arch Pathol Lab Med 1985, **109:** 767–769.

24 Clement PB, Young RH, Hanna W, Scully RE. Sclerosing peritonitis associated with luteinized thecomas of the ovary. A clinicopathological analysis of six cases. Am J Surg Pathol 1994, **18:** 1–13.

25 Fata F, Ron IG, Maluf F, Klimstra D, Kemeny N. Intra-abdominal fibrosis after systemic and intraperitoneal therapy containing fluoropyrimidines. Cancer 2000, **88:** 2447–2451.

26 Finney AL, Spagnolo DV, Crawford GP, Shilkin KB. Pseudosarcomatous sclerosing peritonitis: A case report of an unusual form of chronic lupus peritonitis. Int J Surg Pathol 1996, **4:** 121–128.

27 Ryan GB, Grobety J, Majno G. Postoperative peritoneal adhesions. A study of the mechanisms. Am J Pathol 1971, **65:** 117–140.

Reaction to foreign materials

28 Auer EA, Dockerty MB, Mayo CW. Reaction to foreign material. Ruptured dermoid cyst of the ovary simulating abdominal carcinomatosis. Mayo Clin Proc 1951, **26:** 489–497.

29 Carr N, Turk E. The histological features of splenosis. Histopathology 1992, **21:** 549–554.

30 Chen KTK, Kostich ND, Rosai J. Peritoneal foreign body granulomas to keratin in uterine adenoacanthoma. Arch Pathol Lab Med 1978, **102**: 174–177.

31 Clarke TJ, Simpson RH. Necrotizing granulomas of peritoneum following diathermy ablation of endometriosis. Histopathology 1990, **16**: 400–402.

32 Clement PB, Young RH, Scully RE. Necrotic pseudoxanthomatous nodules of ovary and peritoneum in endometriosis. Am J Surg Pathol 1988, **12**: 330–397.

33 Coder DM, Olander GA. Granulomatous peritonitis caused by starch glove powder. Arch Surg 1972, **105**: 83–86.

34 Davies JD, Ansell ID. Food-starch granulomatous peritonitis. J Clin Pathol 1983, **36**: 435–438.

35 Davies JD, Neely J. The histopathology of peritoneal starch granulomas. J Pathol 1972, **107**: 265–278.

35a Gawande AA, Studdert DM, Orav EJ, Brennan TA, Zinner MJ. Risk factors for retained instruments and sponges after surgery. N Eng J Med 2003, **348**: 229–235

36 Jaworski RC, Boable R, Greg J, Cocks P. Peritoneal "melanosis" associated with a ruptured ovarian dermoid cyst: report of a case with electron-probe energy dispersive X-ray analysis. Int J Gynecol Pathol 2001, **20**: 386–389.

37 Kershisnik MM, Ro JY, Cannon GH, Ordóñez NG, Ayala AG, Silva EG. Histiocytic reaction in pelvic peritoneum associated with oxidized regenerated cellulose. Am J Clin Pathol 1995, **103**: 27–31.

38 Kim KR, Scully RE. Peritoneal keratin granulomas with carcinomas of endometrium and ovary and atypical polypoid adenomyoma of endometrium. A clinicopathological analysis of 22 cases. Am J Surg Pathol 1990, **14**: 925–932.

39 Levison DA, Crocker PR, Jones S, Owen RA, Barnard NJ. The varied appearances of starch particles in smears and paraffin sections. Histopathology 1988, **13**: 667–674.

40 Marshall SF, Rorse RA. Peritoneal adhesions. Report of a case of paraffinoma. Surg Clin North Am 1952, **32**: 903–908.

41 Miranda RN, McMillan PN, Pricolo VE, Finkelstein SD. Peritoneal silicosis. Arch Pathol Lab Med 1996, **120**: 300–302.

42 Nissim F, Ashkenazy M, Borenstein R, Czernobilsky B. Tuberculoid cornstarch granulomas with caseous necrosis. A diagnostic challenge. Arch Pathol Lab Med 1981, **105**: 86–88.

43 Saxen L, Saxen E. Starch granulomas as a problem in surgical pathology. Acta Pathol Microbiol Scand 1965, **64**: 55–70.

44 Tinker MA, Burdman D, Deysine M, Teicher I, Platt N, Aufses AH Jr. Granulomatous peritonitis due to cellulose fibers from disposable surgical fabrics. Laboratory investigations and clinical implications. Ann Surg 1974, **180**: 831–835.

Cysts and loose bodies

45 Carpenter HA, Lancaster JR, Lee RA. Multilocular cysts of the peritoneum. Mayo Clin Proc 1982, **57**: 634–638.

46 Chan JK, Fong MH. Composite multicystic mesothelioma and adenomatoid tumour of the uterus: Different morphological manifestations of the same process? Histopathology 1996, **29**: 375–377.

47 Drachenberg CB, Papadimitriou JC. Melanotic peritoneal cyst. Light-microscopic and ultrastructural studies. Arch Pathol Lab Med 1990, **114**: 463–467.

48 Eickhoff JH. Müllerian duct cyst. Report of a case and review of the literature. Scand J Urol Nephrol 1978, **12**: 89–92.

49 Katsube Y, Mukai K, Silverberg SG. Cystic mesothelioma of the peritoneum. Cancer 1982, **50**: 1615–1622.

50 Lamovec J, Sinkovec J. Multilocular peritoneal inclusion cyst (multicystic mesothelioma) with hyaline globules. Histopathology 1996, **28**: 466–469.

51 Lascano EF, Villamayor RD, Llauro JL. Loose cysts of the peritoneal cavity. Ann Surg 1960, **152**: 836–844.

52 McFadden DE, Clement PB. Peritoneal inclusion cysts with mural

mesothelial proliferation. A clinicopathological analysis of six cases. Am J Surg Pathol 1986, **10**: 844–854.

53 Moore JH Jr, Crum CP, Chandler JG, Feldman PS. Benign cystic mesothelioma. Cancer 1980, **45**: 2395–2399.

54 Novak RW, Raines RB, Sollee AN. Clear cell carcinoma in a müllerian duct cyst. Am J Clin Pathol 1981, **76**: 339–341.

55 Ramdial PK, Singh B. Membranous fat necrosis in appendices epiploicae. A clinicopathological study. Virchows Arch 1998, **432**: 223–227.

56 Ross MJ, Welch WR, Scully RE. Multilocular peritoneal inclusion cysts (so-called cystic mesotheliomas). Cancer 1989, **64**: 1336–1346.

57 Sarto GE, Simpson JL. Abnormalities of the müllerian and wolffian duct systems. Birth Defects 1978, **14**: 37–55.

57a Sawh RN, Malpica A, Deavers MT, Liu J, Silva EG. Benign cystic mesothelioma of the peritoneum: A clinicopathologic study of 17 cases and immunohistochemical analysis of estrogen and progesterone receptor status. Hum Pathol 2003, **34**: 369–374.

58 Schneider V, Partridge JR, Gutierrez F, Hurt WG, Maizels MS, Demay RM. Benign cystic mesothelioma involving the female genital tract. Report of four cases. Am J Obstet Gynecol 1983, **145**: 355–359.

59 Villaschi S, Autelitano F, Santeusanio G, Balistreri P. Cystic mesothelioma of the peritoneum. A report of three cases. Am J Clin Pathol 1990, **94**: 758–761.

60 Vuong PN, Guyot H, Moulin G, Houissa-Vuong S, Berrod JL. Pseudotumoral organization of a twisted epiploic fringe or 'hard-boiled egg' in the peritoneal cavity. Arch Pathol Lab Med 1990, **114**: 531–533.

Hyperplasia and metaplasia

61 Bolen JW, Hammar SP, McNutt MA. Reactive and neoplastic serosal tissue. A light-microscopic, ultrastructural, and immunocytochemical study. Am J Surg Pathol 1986, **10**: 34–47.

62 Chan JK, Loo KT, Yau BK, Lam SY. Nodular histiocytic/mesothelial hyperplasia: a lesion potentially mistaken for a neoplasm in transbronchial biopsy. Am J Surg Pathol 1997, **21**: 658–663.

63 Clement PB, Young RH. Florid mesothelial hyperplasia associated with ovarian tumors. A potential source of error in tumor diagnosis and staging. Int J Gynecol Pathol 1993, **12**: 51–58.

64 Crone L. Squamous metaplasia of the peritoneum. J Pathol Bacteriol 1950, **62**: 61–68.

64a Fadare O, Bifulco C, Carter D, Parkash V. Cartilaginous differentiation in peritoneal tissues: a report of two cases and a review of the literature. Mod Pathol 2002, **15**: 777–780.

64b Gupta A, Bhan AK, Bell DA. Can the implants of serous borderline tumors of the ovary be distinguished from mesothelial proliferations by use of immunohistochemistry? (Abstract) Mod Pathol 2003, **16**: 190A

65 Kupryjanczyk J, Karpinska G. Desmin expression in reactive mesothelium: A potential aid in evaluation of gynecologic specimens. Int J Gynecol Pathol 1998, **17**: 123–128.

66 McCaughey WTE, Al-Jabi M. Differentiation of serosal hyperplasia and neoplasia in biopsies. Pathol Annu 1986, **21**(Pt 1): 271–293.

67 Ordóñez NG, Ro JY, Ayala AG. Lesions described as nodular mesothelial hyperplasia are primarily composed of histiocytes. Am J Surg Pathol 1998, **22**: 285–292.

68 Rosai J, Dehner LP. Nodular mesothelial hyperplasia in hernia sacs. A benign reactive condition simulating a neoplastic process. Cancer 1975, **35**: 165–175.

69 Schatz JE, Colgan TJ. Squamous metaplasia of the peritoneum. Arch Pathol Lab Med 1991, **115**: 397–398.

70 Veinot JP, Tazelaar HD, Edwards WD, Colby TV. Mesothelial/monocytic incidental cardiac excrescences: cardiac MICE. Mod Pathol 1994, **7**: 9–16.

71 Zaytsev P, Taxy JB. Pregnancy-associated ectopic decidua. Am J Surg Pathol 1987, **11**: 526–530.

Tumors

Mesothelioma

72 Andrion A, Pira E, Mollo F. Peritoneal plaques and asbestos exposure. Arch Pathol Lab Med 1983, **107**: 609–610.

73 Antman KH. Malignant mesothelioma. N Engl J Med 1980, **303**: 200–202.

74 Armstrong GR, Raafat F, Ingram L, Mann JR. Malignant peritoneal mesothelioma in childhood. Arch Pathol Lab Med 1988, **112**: 1159–1162.

75 Attanoos RL, Gibbs AR. Pathology of malignant mesothelioma. Histopathology 1997, **30**: 403–418.

76 Attanoos RL, Dojcinov SD, Webb R, Gibbs AR. Antimesothelial markers in sarcomatoid mesothelioma and other spindle cell neoplasms. Histopathology 2000, **37**: 224–231.

77 Attanoos RL, Webb R, Dojcinov SD, Gibbs AR. Malignant epithelioid mesothelioma: ant-mesothelial marker expression correlates with histological pattern. Histopathology 2001, **39**: 584–588.

78 Attanoos RL, Webb R, Dojcinov SD, Gibbs AR. Value of mesothelial and epithelial antibodies in distinguishing diffuse peritoneal mesothelioma in females from serous papillary carcinoma of the ovary and peritoneum. Histopathology 2002, **40**: 237–244.

79 Bethwaite PB, Evans R, Naik DK, Delahunt B, Teague CA. Diffuse malignant mesothelioma arising in a paracolostomy hernial sac. Histopathology 1996, **29**: 282–284.

80 Bolen JW, Thorning D. Mesotheliomas. A light- and electron-microscopical study concerning histogenetic relationships between the epithelial and the mesenchymal variants. Am J Surg Pathol 1980, **4**: 451–464.

81 Britton M. The epidemiology of mesothelioma. Semin Oncol 2002, **29**: 18–25.

82 Brown JW, Kristensen KAB, Monroe LS. Peritoneal mesothelioma following pneumoperitoneum maintained for 12 years. Report of a case. Am J Dig Dis 1968, **13**: 830–835.

83 Butnor KJ, Sporn TA, Hammar SP, Roggli VL. Well-differentiated papillary mesothelioma. Am J Surg Pathol 2001, **25**: 1304–1309.

84 Carbone M, Kratzke RA, Testa JR. The pathogenesis of mesothelioma. Semin Oncol 2002, **29**: 2–17.

85 Chen KT. Malignant mesothelioma presenting as Sister Joseph's nodule. Am J Dermatopathol 1991, **13**: 300–303.

86 Chiu B, Churg A, Tengblad A, Pearce R, McCaughey WTE. Analysis of hyaluronic acid in the diagnosis of malignant mesothelioma. Cancer 1984, **54**: 2195–2199.

87 Clement PB, Young RH, Scully RE. Malignant mesotheliomas presenting as ovarian masses: A report of nine cases, including two primary ovarian mesotheliomas. Am J Surg Pathol 1996, **20**: 1067–1080.

88 Cook DS, Attanoos RL, Jalloh SS, Gibbs AR. "Mucin-positive" epithelial mesothelioma of the peritoneum: an unusual diagnostic pitfall. Histopathology 2000, **37**: 33–36.

89 Crotty TB, Myers JL, Katzenstein A-LA, Tazelaar HD, Swensen SJ, Churg A. Localized malignant mesothelioma. A clinicopathologic and flow cytometric study. Am J Surg Pathol 1994, **18**: 357–363.

90 Daya D, McCaughey WT. Well-differentiated papillary mesothelioma of the peritoneum. A clinicopathologic study of 22 cases. Cancer 1990, **65**: 292–296.

91 Eyden BP, Banik S, Harris M. Malignant epithelial mesothelioma of the peritoneum: observations on a problem case. Ultrastruct Pathol 1996, **20**: 337–344.

92 Goepel JR. Benign papillary mesothelioma of peritoneum. A histological, histochemical and ultrastructural study of six cases. Histopathology 1981, **5**: 21–30.

93 Goldblum J, Hart WR. Localized and diffuse mesotheliomas of the genital tract and peritoneum in women. A clinicopathologic study of nineteen true mesothelial neoplasms, other than adenomatoid tumors, multicystic mesotheliomas, and localized fibrous tumors. Am J Surg Pathol 1995, **19**: 1124–1137.

94 Kane MJ, Chahinian AP, Holland JF. Malignant mesothelioma in young adults. Cancer 1990, **65**: 1449–1455.

95 Kallianpur AR, Carstens PH, Liotta LA, Frey KP, Siegal GP. Immunoreactivity in malignant mesotheliomas with antibodies to basement membrane components and their receptors. Mod Pathol 1990, **3**: 11–18.

96 Kannerstein M, Churg J. Peritoneal mesothelioma. Hum Pathol 1977, **8**: 83–94.

97 Kannerstein M, Churg J, Magner D. Histochemistry in the diagnosis of malignant mesothelioma. Ann Clin Lab Sci 1973, **3**: 207–211.

98 Kauffman SL, Stout AP. Mesothelioma in children. Cancer 1964, **17**: 539–544.

98a Kerrigan SJA, Cagle P, Churg A. Malignant mesothelioma of the peritoneum presenting as an inflammatory lesion. Am J Surg Pathol 2003, **27**: 248–253.

99 Kerrigan SA, Turnnir RT, Clement PB, Young RH, Churg A. Diffuse malignant epithelial mesotheliomas of the peritoneum in women: a clinicopathologic study of 25 patients. Cancer 2002, **94**: 378–385.

100 King JE, Hasleton PS. (Commentary.)Immunohistochemistry and the diagnosis of malignant mesothelioma. Histopathology 2001, **38**: 471–476.

101 Kitazawa M, Kaneko H, Toshima M, Ishikawa H, Kobayashi H, Sekiya M. Malignant peritoneal mesothelioma with massive foamy cells. Codfish roe-like mesothelioma. Acta Pathol Jpn 1984, **34**: 687–692.

102 Kumaki F, Kawai T, Churg A, Galateau-Sallè P, Hasleton P, Henderson D, Roggli V, Travis WD, Cagle PT, Ferrans VJ. Expression of telomerase reverse transcriptase (TERT) in malignant mesotheliomas. Am J Surg Pathol 2002, **26**: 365–370.

103 Kung ITM, Thallas V, Spencer EJ, Wilson SM. Expression of muscle actin in diffuse mesotheliomas. Hum Pathol 1995, **26**: 565–570.

104 Lantuejoul S, Laverriere MH, Sturm N, Moro D, Frey G, Brambilla C, Brambilla E. NCAM (neural cell adhesion molecules) expression in malignant mesothelioma. Hum Pathol 2000, **31**: 415–421.

105 Lederman GS, Recht A, Herman T, Osteen R, Corson J, Antman KH. Long-term survival in peritoneal mesothelioma. The role of radiotherapy and combined modality treatment. Cancer 1987, **59**: 1882–1886.

106 Leong A S-Y, Vernon-Roberts E. The immunohistochemistry of malignant mesothelioma. Pathol Annu 1994, **29**(Pt 2): 157–159.

107 Lerner HJ, Schoenfeld DA, Martin A, Falkson G, Borden E. Malignant mesothelioma. The Eastern Cooperative Oncology Group (ECOG) experience. Cancer 1983, **52**: 1981–1985.

108 Masangkay AV, Susin M, Baker R, Ward R, Kahn E. Metastatic malignant mesothelioma presenting as colonic polyps. Hum Pathol 1997, **28**: 993–995.

109 Maurer R, Egloff B. Malignant peritoneal mesothelioma after cholangiography with Thorotrast. Cancer 1975, **36**: 1381–1385.

110 Mayall FG, Goddard H, Gibbs AR. Intermediate filament expression in mesotheliomas. Leiomyoid mesotheliomas are not uncommon. Histopathology 1992, **21**: 453–457.

111 Nascimento AG, Keeney GL, Fletcher CD. Deciduoid peritoneal mesothelioma. An unusual phenotype affecting young females. Am J Surg Pathol 1994, **18**: 439–445.

112 Ordóñez NG. Role of immunohistochemistry in distinguishing epithelial peritoneal mesotheliomas from peritoneal and ovarian serous carcinomas. Am J Surg Pathol 1998, **22**: 1203–1214.

113 Ordóñez NG. Epithelial mesothelioma with deciduoid features: report of four cases. Am J Surg Pathol 2000, **24**: 816–823.

114 Riddell RH, Goodman MJ, Moossa AR. Peritoneal malignant mesothelioma in a patient with recurrent peritonitis. Cancer 1981, **48:** 134–139.

114a Roggli VL, Sharma A, Butnor KJ, Sporn T, Vollmer RT. Malignant mesothelioma and occupational exposure to asbestos: A clinicopathological correlation of 1445 cases. Ultrastruct Pathol 2002, **26:** 55–65.

114b Sandberg AA, Bridge JA. Updates on the cytogenetics and molecular genetics of bone soft tissue tumors. Mesothelioma. Cancer Genet Cytogenet 2001, **127:** 93–110.

115 Segers K, Ramael M, Singh SK, Weyler J, Van Meerbeeck J, Vermeire P, Van Marck E. Immunoreactivity for bcl-2 protein in malignant mesothelioma and non-neoplastic mesothelium. Virchows Arch 1994, **424:** 631–634.

116 Shah IA, Somsin A, Wong SX, Gani OS, Chausow DD. Malignant mesothelioma presenting as colonic tumor. Hum Pathol 1998, **29:** 657.

117 Shanks JH, Harris M, Banerjee SS, Eyden BP, Joglekar VM, Nicol A, Hasleton PS, Nicholson AG. Mesotheliomas with deciduoid morphology: a morphologic spectrum and a variant not confined to young females. Am J Surg Pathol 2000, **24:** 285–294.

117a Shia J, Erlandson RA, Klimstra DS. Deciduoid mesothelioma: A report of 5 cases and literature review. Ultrastruct Pathol 2002, **26:** 355–363.

118 Silberstein MJ, Lewis JE, Blair JD, Graviss ER, Brodeur AE. Congenital peritoneal mesothelioma. J Pediatr Surg 1983, **18:** 243–246.

119 Smither WJ. Asbestos and mesothelioma of the pleura. Proc R Soc Med 1966, **59:** 57–61.

120 Strickler JG, Herndier BG, Rouse RV. Immunohistochemical staining in malignant mesotheliomas. Am J Clin Pathol 1987, **88:** 610–614.

121 Sussman J, Rosai J. Lymph node metastasis as the initial manifestation of malignant mesothelioma. Report of six cases. Am J Surg Pathol 1990, **14:** 819–828.

122 Suzuki Y. Diagnostic criteria for human diffuse malignant mesothelioma. Acta Pathol Jpn 1992, **42:** 767–786.

123 Suzuki Y, Churg J, Kannerstein M. Ultrastructure of human malignant diffuse mesothelioma. Am J Pathol 1976, **85:** 241–251.

124 Talerman A, Montero JR, Chilcote RR, Okagaki T. Diffuse malignant peritoneal mesothelioma in a 13-year-old girl. Report of a case and review of the literature. Am J Surg Pathol 1985, **9:** 73–80.

125 Churg A, Colby TV, Cagle P, Corson J, et al. The separation of benign and malignant mesothelial proliferations. Am J Surg Pathol 2000, **24:** 1183–1200.

126 Vogelzang NJ, Schultz SM, Iannucci AM, Kennedy BJ. Malignant mesothelioma. The University of Minnesota experience. Cancer 1984, **53:** 377–383.

127 Wick MR, Mills SE, Swanson PE. Expression of "myelomonocytic" antigens in mesotheliomas and adenocarcinomas involving the serosal surfaces. Am J Clin Pathol 1990, **94:** 18–26.

128 Winslow DJ, Taylor HB. Malignant peritoneal mesotheliomas. Cancer 1960, **13:** 127–136.

Intra-abdominal desmoplastic small cell tumor

129 Adsay V, Cheng J, Athanasian E, Gerald W, Rosai J. Primary desmoplastic small cell tumor of soft tissues and bone of the hand. Am J Surg Pathol 1999, **23:** 1408–1413.

130 Amin KM, Litzky LA, Smythe WR, Mooney AM, Morris JM, Mews DJY, Pass HI, Kari C, Rodeck U, Rauscher FJ III, Kaiser LR, Albelda SM. Wilms' tumor 1 susceptibility (WTI) gene products are selectively expressed in malignant mesothelioma. Am J Pathol 1995, **146:** 344–356.

131 Antonescu CR, Gerald WL, Magid MS, Ladany M. Molecular variants of the EWS–WT1 gene fusion in desmoplastic small round cell tumor. Diagn Mol Pathol 1998, **7:** 24–28.

132 Argatoff LH, O'Connell JX, Mathers JA, Gilks CB, Sorensen PH. Detection for the EWS/WT1 gene fusion by reverse transcriptase-polymerase chain reaction in the diagnosis of intra-abdominal desmoplastic small round cell tumor. Am J Surg Pathol 1996, **20:** 406–412.

133 Backer A, Mount SL, Zarka MA, Trask CE, Allen EF, Gerald WL, Sanders DA, Weaver DL. Desmoplastic small round cell tumour of unknown primary origin with lymph node and lung metastases: histological, cytological, ultrastructural, cytogenetic and molecular findings. Virchows Arch 1998, **432:** 135–141.

134 Barnoud R, Sabourin JC, Pasquier D, Ranchere D, Bailly C, Terrier-Lacombe MJ, Pasquier B. Immunohistochemical expression of WT1 by desmoplastic small round cell tumor: A comparative study with other small round cell tumors. Am J Surg Pathol 2000, **24:** 830–836.

135 Charles AK, Moore IE, Berry PJ. Immunohistochemical detection of the Wilms' tumour gene WT1 in desmoplastic small round cell tumour. Histopathology 1997, **30:** 312–314.

136 Crapanzano JP, Cardillo M, Lin O, Zakowski MF. Cytology of desmoplastic small round cell tumor. Cancer 2002, **96:** 21–32.

137 Cummings OW, Ulbright TM, Young RH, Dei Tos AP, Fletcher CDM, Hull MT. Desmoplastic small round cell tumors of the paratesticular region: a report of six cases. Am J Surg Pathol 1997, **21:** 219–225.

138 de Alava E, Ladanyi M, Rosai J, Gerald WL. Detection of chimeric transcripts in desmoplastic small round cell tumor and related developmental tumors by RT-PCR. A specific diagnostic assay. Am J Pathol 1995, **147:** 1584–1591.

139 Dorsey BV, Benjamin LE, Fauscher F, Klencke B, Venook AP, Warren RS, Weidner N. Intra-abdominal desmoplastic small round-cell tumor: Expansion of the pathologic profile. Mod Pathol 1996, **9:** 703–709.

140 Gaudin PB, Rosai J. Florid vascular proliferation associated with neural and neuroendocrine neoplasms. A diagnostic clue and potential pitfall. Am J Surg Pathol 1995, **19:** 642–652.

141 Gerald WL, Miller HK, Battifora H, Miettinen M, Silva EG, Rosai J. Intra-abdominal desmoplastic small round-cell tumor. Report of 19 cases of a distinctive type of high-grade polyphenotypic malignancy affecting young individuals. Am J Surg Pathol 1991, **15:** 499–513.

142 Gerald WL, Rosai J. Desmoplastic small cell tumor with multi-phenotypic differentiation. Zentralbl Pathol 1993, **139:** 141–151.

143 Gerald WL, Rosai J, Ladanyi M. Characterization of the genomic breakpoint and chimeric transcripts in the EWS–WT1 gene fusion of desmoplastic small round cell tumor. Proc Natl Acad Sci U S A 1995, **92:** 1028–1032.

144 Hill DA, Pfeifer JD, Marley EF, Dehner LP, Humphrey PA, Zhu X, Swanson PE. WT1 staining reliably differentiates desmoplastic small round cell tumor from Ewing sarcoma/primitive neuroectodermal tumor. An immunohistochemical and molecular diagnostic study. Am J Clin Pathol 2000, **114:** 345–353.

145 Katz RL, Quezado M, Senderowicz AM, Villalba L, Laskin WB, Tsokos M. An intra-abdominal small round cell neoplasm with features of primitive neuroectodermal and desmoplastic round cell tumor and a EWS/FLI-1 fusion transcript. Hum Pathol 1997, **28:** 502–509.

146 Kawano N, Inayama Y, Nagashima Y, Miyagi Y, Uemura H, Saitoh K, Kubota Y, Hosaka M, Tanaka Y, Nakatani Y. Desmoplastic small round-cell tumor of the paratesticular region: Report of an adult case with demonstration of EWS and WT1 gene fusion using paraffin-embedded tissue. Mod Pathol 1999, **12:** 729–734.

147 Kushner BH, LaQuaglia MP, Wollner N, Meyers PA, Lindsley KL, Ghavimi F, Merchant TE, Boulad F, Cheung NV, Bonilla MA, Crouch G, Felleher JF Jr, Steinherz PG, Gerald WL. Desmoplastic small round-cell tumor: Prolonged progression-free survival with

aggressive multimodality therapy. J Clin Oncol 1996, **14:** 1526–1531.

147a Lae ME, Roche PC, Jin L, Lloyd RV, Nascimento AG. Desmoplastic small round cell tumor: A clinicopathologic, immunohistochemical, and molecular study of 32 tumors. Am J Surg Pathol 2002, **26:** 823–835.

148 Pasquinelli G, Montanaro L, Martinelli GN. Desmoplastic small round-cell tumor: a case report on the large cell variant with immunohistochemical, ultrastructural and molecular genetic analysis. Ultrastruct Pathol 2000, **24:** 333–337.

149 Ordi J, de Alava E, Torne A, Mellado B, Pardo-Mindan J, Iglesias X, Cardesa A. Intra-abdominal desmoplastic small round cell tumor with EWS/ERG fusion transcript. Am J Surg Pathol 1998, **22:** 1026–1032.

150 Ordóñez NG. Desmoplastic small round cell tumor: I: A histopathologic study of 39 cases with emphasis on unusual histological patterns. Am J Surg Pathol 1998, **22:** 1303–1313.

151 Ordóñez NG. Desmoplastic small round cell tumor: II: An ultrastructural and immunohistochemical study with emphasis on new immunohistochemical markers. Am J Surg Pathol 1998, **22:** 1314–1327.

152 Ordóñez NG, Sahin AA. CA 125 production in desmoplastic small round cell tumor: Report of a case with elevated serum levels and prominent signet ring morphology. Hum Pathol 1998, **29:** 294–299.

153 Ordóñez NG, el-Naggar AK, Ro JY, Silva EG, Mackay B. Intra-abdominal desmoplastic small cell tumor. A light microscopic, immunocytochemical, ultrastructural, and flow cytometric study. Hum Pathol 1993, **24:** 850–865.

154 Parkash V, Gerald WL, Parma A, Miettinen M, Rosai J. Desmoplastic small round cell tumor of the pleura. Am J Surg Pathol 1995, **19:** 659–665.

155 Perez RP, Zhang PJ. Detection of EWS–WT1 fusion mRNA in ascites of a patient with desmoplastic small round cell tumor by RT-PCR. Hum Pathol 1999, **30:** 239–242.

156 Rodriguez E, Sreekantaiah C, Gerald W, Reuter VE, Motzer RJ, Chaganti RS. A recurring translocation, t(11;22)(p13;q11.2), characterizes intra-abdominal desmoplastic small round-cell tumors. Cancer Genet Cytogenet 1993, **69:** 17–21.

156a Sandberg AA, Bridge JA. Updates on the cytogenetics and molecular genetics of bone soft tissue tumors. Desmoplastic small round-cell tumors. Cancer Genet Cytogenet 2002, **138:** 1–10.

157 Shintaku M, Baba Y, Fujiwara T. Intra-abdominal desmoplastic small cell tumour in a patient with Peutz-Jeghers syndrome. Virchows Arch 1994, **425:** 211–215.

158 Tison V, Cerasoli S, Morigi F, Ladanyi M, Gerald WL, Rosai J. Intracranial desmoplastic small cell tumor. Report of a case. Am J Surg Pathol 1996, **20:** 112–117.

159 Trupiano JK, Machen SK, Barr FG, Goldblum JR. Cytokeratin-negative desmoplastic small round cell tumor: A report of two cases emphasizing the utility of reverse transcriptase-polymerase chain reaction. Mod Pathol 1999, **12:** 849–853.

160 Wills EJ. Peritoneal desmoplastic small round cell tumors with divergent differentiation. A review. Ultrastruct Pathol 1993, **17:** 295–306.

161 Wolf AN, Ladanyi M, Paull G, Blaugrund JE, Westra WH. The expanding clinical spectrum of desmoplastic small round-cell tumor: A report of two cases with molecular confirmation. Hum Pathol 1999, **30:** 430–435.

162 Young RH, Eichhorn JH, Dickersin GR, Scully RE. Ovarian involvement by the intra-abdominal desmoplastic small round cell tumor with divergent differentiation. A report of three cases. Hum Pathol 1992, **23:** 454–464.

162a Zhang PJ, Goldblum JR, Pawel BR, Fisher C, Pasha TL, Barr FG. Immunophenotype of desmoplastic small round cell tumors as detected in cases with EWS-WT1 gene fusion product. Mod Pathol 2003, **16:** 229–235.

Other primary tumors

163 Attanoos RL, Dallimore NS, Gibbs AR. Primary epithelioid haemangioendothelioma of the peritoneum: an unusual mimic of diffuse malignant mesothelioma. Histopathology 1997, **30:** 375–377.

164 Bonetti F, Martignoni G, Manfrin E, Colato C, Gambacorta M, Faleri M, Bacchi C, Sin VC, Wong NL, Coady M, Chan JKC. Abdominopelvic sarcoma of perivascular epithelioid cells. Report of four cases in young women, one with tuberous sclerosis. Mod Pathol 2001, **14:** 563–568.

165 Cheuk W, Chan JK, Shek TW, Chang JH, Tsou MH, Yuen NW, Ng WF, Chan AC, Prat J. Inflammatory pseudotumor-like follicular dendritic cell tumor: a distinctive low-grade malignant intra-abdominal neoplasm with consistent Epstein–Barr virus association. Am J Surg Pathol 2001, **25:** 721–731.

166 Fukunaga M, Naganuma H, Ushigome S, Endo Y, Ishikawa E. Malignant solitary fibrous tumour of the peritoneum. Histopathology 1996, **28:** 463–466.

167 Gonzalez-Crussi F, Sotelo-Avila C, de Mello DE. Primary peritoneal, omental, and mesenteric tumors in childhood. Semin Diagn Pathol 1986, **3:** 122–137.

168 Goodlad JR, Fletcher CD. Solitary fibrous tumour arising at unusual sites. Analysis of a series. Histopathology 1991, **19:** 515–522.

169 Kashima T, Matshushita H, Kuroda M, Takeuchi H, Udagawa H, Ishida T, Hara M, Machinami R. Biphasic synovial sarcoma of the peritoneal cavity with t(X:18) demonstrated by reverse transcriptase polymerase chain reaction. Pathol Int 1997, **47:** 637–641.

170 Lin BT, Chen YY, Battifora H, Weiss LM. Absence of Kaposi's sarcoma-associated herpesvirus-like DNA sequences in malignant vascular tumors of the serous membranes. Mod Pathol 1996, **9:** 1143–1146.

171 Lin BT, Colby T, Gown AM, Hammar SP, Mertens RB, Churg A, Battifora H. Malignant vascular tumors of the serous membranes mimicking mesothelioma: A report of 14 cases. Am J Surg Pathol 1996, **20:** 1431–1439.

172 McCaughey WTE, Dardick I, Barr JR. Angiosarcoma of serous membranes. Arch Pathol Lab Med 1983, **107:** 304–307.

173 Shek TW, Liu CL, Peh WC, Fan ST, Ng IO. Intra-abdominal follicular dendritic cell tumour, a rare tumour in need of recognition. Histopathology 1998, **33:** 465–470.

174 Young RH, Clement PB, McCaughey WT. Solitary fibrous tumors ('fibrous mesotheliomas') of the peritoneum. A report of three cases and a review of the literature. Arch Pathol Lab Med 1990, **114:** 493–495.

Lesions of the secondary müllerian system

175 Bell DA, Scully RE. Benign and borderline serous lesions of the peritoneum in women. Pathol Annu 1989, **24**(Pt 2): 1–21.

176 Butnor KJ, Burchette JL, Robboy SJ. Progesterone receptor activity in leiomyomatosis peritonealis disseminata. Int J Gynecol Pathol 1999, **18:** 259–264.

177 Buttner A, Bassler R, Theele C. Pregnancy-associated ectopic decidua (deciduosis) of the greater omentum. An analysis of 60 biopsies with cases of fibrosing deciduosis and leiomyomatosis peritonealis disseminata. Pathol Res Pract 1993, **189:** 352–359.

178 Chang KL, Crabtree GS, Lim-Tan SK, Kempson RL, Hendrickson MR. Primary extrauterine endometrial stromal neoplasms. A clinicopathologic study of 20 cases and a review of the literature. Int J Gynecol Pathol 1993, **12:** 282–296.

179 Clement PB, Young RH, Scully RE. Nontrophoblastic pathology of the female genital tract and peritoneum associated with pregnancy. Semin Diagn Pathol 1989, **6:** 372–406.

180 Cokelaere K, Michielsen P, De Vos R, Sciot R. Primary mesenteric malignant mixed mesodermal (mullerian) tumor with neuroendocrine differentiation. Mod Pathol 2001, **14:** 515–520.

181 Dalrymple JC, Bannatyne P, Russell P, Solomon HJ, Tattersall MH, Atkinson K, Carter J, Duval P, Elliott P, Friedlander M, et al. Extraovarian peritoneal serous papillary carcinoma. A clinicopathologic study of 31 cases. Cancer 1989, **64**: 110–115.

182 Dincer AD, Timmins P, Pietrocola D, Fisher H, Ambros RA. Primary peritoneal mullerian adenosarcoma with sarcomatous overgrowth associated with endometriosis: a case report. Int J Gynecol Pathol 2002, **21**: 65–68.

183 Due W, Pickartz H. Immunohistologic detection of estrogen and progesterone receptors in disseminated peritoneal leiomyomatosis. Int J Gynecol Pathol 1989, **8**: 46–53.

184 Fox H. Primary neoplasia of the female peritoneum. Histopathology 1993, **23**: 103–110.

185 Fromm GL, Gershenson DM, Silva EG. Papillary serous carcinoma of the peritoneum. Obstet Gynecol 1990, **75**: 89–95.

186 Garamvoelgyi E, Guillou L, Gebhard S, Salmeron M, Seematter RJ, Hadji MH. Primary malignant mixed Müllerian tumor (metaplastic carcinoma) of the female peritoneum. A clinical, pathologic, and immunohistochemical study of three cases and a review of the literature. Cancer 1994, **74**: 854–863.

187 Gu J, Roth LM, Younger C, Michael H, Abdul-Karim FW, Zhang S, Ulbright TM, Eble JN, Cheng L. Molecular evidence for the independent origin of extra-ovarian papillary serious tumors of low malignant potential. J Nat Cancer Inst 2001, **93**: 1147–1152.

188 Halperin R, Zehavi S, Hadas E, Habler L, Bukovsky I, Schneider D. Immunohistochemical comparison of primary peritoneal and primary ovarian serous papillary carcinoma. Int J Gynecol Pathol 2001, **20**: 341–345.

189 Lauchlan SC. The secondary müllerian system revisited. Int J Gynecol Pathol 1994, **13**: 73–79.

190 Ma KF, Chow LT. Sex cord-like pattern leiomyomatosis peritonealis disseminata. A hitherto undescribed feature. Histopathology 1992, **21**: 389–391.

191 Quade BJ, McLachlin CM, Soto-Wright V, Zuckerman J, Mutter GL, Morton CC. Disseminated peritoneal leiomyomatosis. Clonality analysis by X chromosome inactivation and cytogenetics of a clinically benign smooth muscle proliferation. Am J Pathol 1997, **150**: 2153–2166.

192 Shen D-H, Khoo US, Xue WC, Ngan HY, Wang JL, Liu VW, Chan YK, Cheung AN. Primary peritoneal malignant mixed mullerian tumors: a clinicopathologic, immunohistochemical, and genetic study. Cancer 2001, **91**: 1052–1060.

193 Tauber H-D, Wissner SE, Haskins AL. Leiomyomatosis peritonealis disseminata. An unusual complication of genital leiomyomata. Obstet Gynecol 1965, **25**: 561–574.

194 Thor AD, Young RH, Clement PB. Pathology of the fallopian tube, broad ligament, peritoneum, and pelvic soft tissues. Hum Pathol 1991, **22**: 856–867.

195 Weir MM, Bell DA, Young RH. Grade 1 peritoneal serous carcinomas: A report of 14 cases and comparison with 7 peritoneal serous psammocarcinomas and 19 peritoneal serous borderline tumors. Am J Surg Pathol 1998, **22**: 849–862.

196 Zotalis G, Nayar R, Hicks DG. Leiomyomatosis peritonealis disseminata, endometriosis, and multicystic mesothelioma: an unusual association. Int J Gynecol Pathol 1998, **17**: 178–182.

Metastatic tumors

197 Cariker M, Dockerty M. Mucinous cystadenomas and mucinous cystadenocarcinomas of the ovary. A clinical and pathological study of 355 cases. Cancer 1954, **7**: 302–310.

198 Chu DZ, Lang NP, Thompson C, Osteen PK, Westbrook KC. Peritoneal carcinomatosis in nongynecologic malignancy. A prospective study of prognostic factors. Cancer 1989, **63**: 364–367.

199 Dadmanesh F, Miller DM, Swenerton KD, Clement PB. Gliomatosis peritonei with malignant transformation. Mod Pathol 1997, **10**: 597–601.

200 Du Plessis DG, Louw JA, Wranz PA. Mucinous epithelial cysts of the spleen associated with pseudomyxoma peritonei. Histopathology 1999, **35**: 551–557.

201 Harms D, Janig U, Gobel U. Gliomatosis peritonei in childhood and adolescence. Pathol Res Pract 1989, **184**: 422–430.

202 Higa E, Rosai J, Pizzimbono CA, Wise L. Mucosal hyperplasia, mucinous cystadenoma and mucinous cystadenocarcinoma of appendix. A re-evaluation of appendiceal "mucocele." Cancer 1973, **32**: 1325–1341.

202a Jackson SL, Fleming RA, Loggie BW, Geisinger KR. Gelatinous ascites: A cytohistologic study of pseudomyxoma peritonei in 67 patients. Mod Pathol 2001, **14**: 664–671.

203 Kahn MA, Demopoulos RI. Mucinous ovarian tumors with pseudomyxoma peritonei. A clinicopathological study. Int J Gynecol Pathol 1992, **11**: 15–23.

204 Lee KR, Scully RE. Mucinous tumors of the ovary: a clinicopathologic study of 196 borderline tumors (of intestinal type) and carcinomas, including an evaluation of 11 cases with "pseudomyxoma peritonei." Am J Surg Pathol 2000, **24** 1447–1464.

204a O'Connell JT, Hacker CM, Barsky SH. MUC2 is a molecular marker for pseudomyxoma peritonei. Mod Pathol 2002, **15**: 958–972.

205 Prayson RA, Hart WR, Petras RE. Pseudomyxoma peritonei. A clinicopathologic study of 19 cases with emphasis on site of origin and nature of associated ovarian tumors. Am J Surg Pathol 1994, **18**: 591–603.

206 Ronnett BM, Kurman RJ, Zahn CM, Schmookler BM, Jablonski KA, Kass ME, Sugarbaker PH. Pseudomyxoma peritoneum in women. A clinicopathologic analysis of 30 cases with emphasis on site of origin, prognosis, and relationship to ovarian mucinous tumors of low malignant potential. Hum Pathol 1995, **26**: 509–524.

207 Ronnett BM, Yan H, Kurman RJ, Shmookler BM, Wu L, Sugarbaker PH. Patients with pseudomyxoma peritonei associated with disseminated peritoneal adenomucinosis have a significantly more favorable prognosis than patients with peritoneal mucinous carcinomatosis. Cancer 2001, **92**: 85–91.

208 Sadeghi B, Arvieux C, Glehen O, Beaujard AC, Rivoire M, Baulieux J, Fontaumard E, Brachet A, Caillot JL, Faure JL, Porcheron J, Peix JL, Francois Y, Vignal J, Gilly FN. Peritoneal carcinomatosis from non-gynecologic malignancies: Results of the EVOCAPE 1 multicentric prospective study. Cancer 2000, **88**: 358–363.

209 Shah IA, Salvatore JR, Kummet T, Gani OS, Wheeler LA. Pseudomesotheliomatous carcinoma involving pleura and peritoneum: a clinicopathologic and immunohistochemical study of three cases. Ann Diagn Pathol 1999, **3**: 148–159.

210 Shin HJ, Sneige N. Epithelial cells and other cytologic features of pseudomyxoma peritonei in patients with ovarian and/or appendiceal mucinous neoplasms. A study of 12 patients including 5 men. Cancer 2000, **90**: 17–23.

211 Smith JW, Kemeny N, Caldwell C, Banner P, Sigurdson E, Huvos A. Pseudomyxoma peritonei of appendiceal origin. The Memorial Sloan-Kettering Cancer Center experience. Cancer 1992, **70**: 396–401.

212 Soslow RA, Pirog E, Isacson C. Endometrial intraepithelial carcinoma with associated peritoneal carcinomatosis. Am J Surg Pathol 2000, **24**: 726–732.

213 Sugarbaker PH. Cytoreduction including total gastrectomy for pseudomyxoma peritonei. Br J Surg 2002, **89**: 208–212.

214 Sugarbaker PH, Chang D. Results of treatment of 385 patients with peritoneal surface spread of appendiceal malignancy. Ann Surg Oncol 1999, **6**: 727–731.

215 Sugarbaker PH, Yan H, Shmookler B. Pedunculated peritoneal surface polyps in pseudomyxoma peritonei syndrome. Histopathology 2001, **39**: 425–528.

216 Tarin D, Price JE, Kettlewell MGW, Souter RG, Vass ACR,

Crossley B. Mechanisms of human tumor metastasis studied in patients with peritoneovenous shunts. Cancer Res 1984, **44**: 3584–3592.

217 Tran TA, Jennings TA, Ross JS, Nazeer T. Pseudomyxoma ovariilike posttherapeutic alteration in prostatic adenocarcinoma: A distinctive pattern in patients receiving neoadjuvant androgen ablation therapy. Am J Surg Pathol 1998, **22**: 347–354.

218 Yan H, Pestieau SR, Shmookler BM, Sugarbaker PH. Histopathologic analysis in 46 patients with pseudomyxoma peritonei syndrome: failure versus success with a second-look operation. Mod Pathol 2001, **14**: 164–171.

219 Young RH, Gilks CB, Scully RE. Mucinous tumors of the appendix associated with mucinous tumors of the ovary and pseudomyxoma peritonei. A clinicopathological analysis of 22 cases supporting an origin in the appendix. Am J Surg Pathol 1991, **15**: 415–429.

Cytology

220 Cardozo PL. A critical evaluation of 3,000 cytologic analyses of pleural fluid, ascitic fluid and pericardial fluid. Acta Cytol (Baltimore) 1966, **10**: 455–460.

221 Benevolo M, Mariani L, Vocaturo G, Vasselli S, Natali PG, Mottolese M. Independent prognostic value of peritoneal immunocytodiagnosis in endometrial carcinoma. Am J Surg Pathol 2000, **24**: 241–247.

222 Chen LM, Lazcano O, Katzmann JA, Kimlinger TK, Li C-Y. The role of conventional cytology, immunocytochemistry, and flow cytometric DNA ploidy in the evaluation of body cavity fluids. A prospective study of 52 patients. Am J Clin Pathol 1998, **109**: 712–721.

223 Esteban JM, Yokota S, Husain S, Battifora H. Immunocytochemical profile of benign and carcinomatous effusions. A practical approach to difficult diagnosis. Am J Clin Pathol 1990, **94**: 698–705.

224 Hecht JL, Lee BH, Pinkus JL, Pinkus GS. The value of Wilms tumor susceptibility gene 1 in cytological preparations as a marker for malignant mesothelioma. Cancer Cytopathol 2002, **96**: 105–109.

224a Jackson SL, Fleming RA, Loggie BW, Geisinger KR. Gelatinous ascites: A cytohistologic study of pseudomyxoma peritonei in 67 patients. Mod Pathol 2001, **14**: 664–671.

225 Klempman S. The exfoliative cytology of diffuse pleural mesothelioma. Cancer 1962, **15**: 691–704.

226 Melamed MR. The cytological presentation of malignant lymphomas and related diseases in effusions. Cancer 1963, **16**: 413–431.

227 Nance KV, Silverman JF. Immunocytochemical panel for the identification of malignant cells in serous effusions. Am J Clin Pathol 1991, **95**: 867–874.

228 Roberts HG, Campbell GM. Exfoliative cytology of diffuse mesothelioma. J Clin Pathol 1972, **23**: 577–582.

229 Ruitenbeek T, Gouw AS, Poppema S. Immunocytology of body cavity fluids. MOC-31, a monoclonal antibody discriminating between mesothelial and epithelial cells. Arch Pathol Lab Med 1994, **118**: 265–269.

OMENTUM

230 Chong PY, Panabokke RG, Chew KH. Omental cryptococcoma. An unusual presentation of cryptococcosis. Arch Pathol Lab Med 1986, **110**: 239–241.

231 Dixon AY, Reed JS, Dow N, Lee SH. Primary omental leiomyosarcoma masquerading as hemorrhagic ascites. Hum Pathol 1984, **15**: 233–237.

232 Epstein LI, Lempke RE. Primary idiopathic segmental infarction of the greater omentum. Case report and collective review of the literature. Ann Surg 1968, **167**: 437–443.

233 Galifer RB, Pous JG, Juskiewenski S, Pasquie M, Gaubert J. Intra-abdominal cystic lymphangiomas in childhood. Prog Pediatr Surg 1978, **11**: 173–239.

234 Gonzalez-Crussi F, de Mello DE, Sotelo-Avila C. Omental-mesenteric myxoid hamartomas. Infantile lesions simulating malignant tumors. Am J Surg Pathol 1983, **7**: 567–578.

235 Gonzalez-Crussi F, Sotelo-Avila C, de Mello DE. Primary peritoneal, omental, and mesenteric tumors in childhood. Semin Diagn Pathol 1986, **3**: 122–137.

236 Ordóñez NG, Manning JT Jr, Ayala AG. Teratoma of the omentum. Cancer 1983, **51**: 955–958.

237 Quddus MR, Sung CJ, Lauchlan SC. Benign and malignant serous and endometrioid epithelium in the omentum. Gynecol Oncol 2000, **75**: 227–232.

238 Stout AP, Hendry J, Purdie FJ. Primary solid tumors of the great omentum. Cancer 1963, **16**: 231–243.

239 Tsutsumi A, Kawabata K, Taguchi K, Doi K. Elastofibroma of the greater omentum. Acta Pathol Jpn 1985, **35**: 233–241.

239a Yamakawa M, Andoh A, Masuda A, Miyauchi S, Kasajima T, Ohmori A, Oguma T, T'akasaki K. Follicular dendritic cell sarcoma of the omentum. Virchows Arch 2002, **440**: 660–663.

MESENTERY

240 Al-Nafussi A, Wong NACS. Intra-abdominal spindle cell lesions: a review and practical aids to diagnosis. Histopathology 2001, **38**: 387–402.

241 Bak M. Nodular intra-abdominal panniculitis: an accompaniment of colorectal carcinoma and diverticular disease. Histopathology 1996, **29**: 21–27.

242 Banerjee R, Gough J. Cystic mucinous tumours of the mesentery and retroperitoneum. Report of three cases. Histopathology 1988, **12**: 527–532.

243 Barnardo DE, Stavrou M, Bourne R, Bogomoletz W. Primary carcinoid tumor of the mesentery. Hum Pathol 1984, **15**: 796–798.

244 Buonanno G, Gonella F, Pettinato G, Castaldo C. Autoimmune hemolytic anemia and dermoid cyst of the mesentery. A case report. Cancer 1984, **54**: 2533–2536.

245 Burke AP, Sobin LH, Shekitka KM. Mesenteric fibromatosis. A follow-up study. Arch Pathol Lab Med 1990, **114**: 832–835.

246 Burke AP, Sobin LH, Shekitka KM, Federspiel BH, Helwig EB. Intra-abdominal fibromatosis. A pathologic analysis of 130 tumors with comparison of clinical subgroups. Am J Surg Pathol 1990, **14**: 335–341.

247 Carpenter HA, Lancaster JR, Lee RA. Multilocular cysts of the peritoneum. Mayo Clin Proc 1982, **57**: 634–638.

248 Chen KTK. Intraabdominal calcifying fibrous pseudotumor. Int J Surg Pathol 1996, **4**: 9–12.

249 Coffin CM, Watterson J, Priest JR, Dehner LP. Extrapulmonary inflammatory myofibroblastic tumor (inflammatory pseudotumor). A clinicopathologic and immunohistochemical study of 84 cases. Am J Surg Pathol 1995, **19**: 859–872.

250 Emory TS, Mohihan JM, Carr NJ, Sobin LH. Sclerosing mesenteritis, mesenteric panniculitis and mesenteric lipodystrophy: A single entity? Am J Surg Pathol 1997, **21**: 392–398.

251 Gorlin RJ, Sedano HO. The multiple nevoid basal cell carcinoma syndrome revisited. Birth Defects 1971, **7**: 140–148.

252 Hansen RC, Castelino RA, Lazerson J, Probert J. Mesenteric hemangioendothelioma with thrombocytopenia. Cancer 1973, **32**: 136–141.

253 Harpaz N, Gellman E. Urogenital mesenteric cyst with fallopian tubal features. Arch Pathol Lab Med 1987, **111**: 78–80.

254 Hashimoto H, Tsuneyoshi M, Enjoji M. Malignant smooth muscle tumors of the retroperitoneum and mesentery. A clinicopathologic analysis of 44 cases. J Surg Oncol 1985, **28**: 177–186.

254a Hill KA, Gonzalez-Crussi F, Chou PM. Calcifying fibrous pseudotumor versus inflammatory myofibroblastic tumor: A histological and immunohistochemical comparison. Mod Pathol 2001, **14**: 784–790.

255 Horie Y, Kato M. Uterus-like mass of the small bowel mesentery. Pathol Int 2000, **50**: 76–80.

256 Jones MA, Clement PB, Young RH. Primary yolk sac tumors of the mesentery. A report of two cases. Am J Clin Pathol 1994, **101**: 42–47.

257 Kelly JK, Hwang WS. Idiopathic retractile (sclerosing) mesenteritis and its differential diagnosis. Am J Surg Pathol 1989, **13**: 513–521.

258 Kipfer RE, Moertel CG, Dahlin DC. Mesenteric lipodystrophy. Ann Intern Med 1974, **80**: 582–588.

258a Klaus, A., Margreiter, R., Pernthaler, H., Klima, G., Offner, FA. Diffuse mesenterial sclerosis: a characteristic feature of chronic small-bowel allograft rejection. Virchows Arch 2003, **442**: 48–55.

259 Kocova L, Michal M, Sulc M, Zamecnik M. Calcifying fibrous pseudotumor of visceral peritoneum. Histopathology 1997, **31**: 182–184.

260 Kurtz RJ, Heimann TM, Holt J, Beck AR. Mesenteric and retroperitoneal cysts. Ann Surg 1986, **203**: 109–112.

261 Lamovec J, Bracko M. Infiltrating cavernous lymphangiomyoma of the mesentery: A case report. Int J Surg Pathol 1996, **3**: 275–282.

262 Lee J, Song SY, Park CS, Kim B. Mullerian cysts of the mesentery and retroperitoneum: A case report and literature review. Pathol Int 1998, **48**: 902–906.

263 Magid D, Fishman EK, Jones B, Hoover HC, Feinstein R, Siegelman SS. Desmoid tumors in Gardner syndrome. Use of computed tomography. AJR 1984, **142**: 1141–1145.

264 Mahle C, Schwartz M, Popek E, Bocklage T. Intra-abdominal lymphangiomas in children and adults: assessment of proliferative activity. Arch Pathol Lab Med 1997, **121**: 1055–1062.

265 Meis JM, Enzinger FM. Inflammatory fibrosarcoma of the mesentery and retroperitoneum. A tumor closely simulating inflammatory pseudotumor. Am J Surg Pathol 1991, **15**: 1146–1156.

266 Monihan JM, Carr NJ, Sobin LH. CD34 immunoexpression in stromal tumours of the gastrointestinal tract and in mesenteric fibromatoses. Histopathology 1994, **25**: 469–474.

266a Montgomery, E., Torbenson, MS., Kaushal, M,. Fisher, C., Ahraham, SC. ß-Catenin immunohistochemistry separates mesenteric fibromatosis from gastrointestinal stromal tumor and sclerosing mesenteritis. Am J Surg Pathol 2002, **26**: 1296–1301.

267 Moriki T, Takahashi T, Wada M, Ueda S, Ichien M, Yamane T, Hara H. Follicular dendritic cell tumor of the mesentery. Pathol Res Pract 1997, **193**: 629–639.

268 Nascimento AF, Ruiz R, Hornick JL, Fletcher CDM. Calcifying fibrous 'pseudotumor': clinicopathologic study of 15 cases and analysis of its relationship to inflammatory myofibroblastic tumor. Int J Surg Pathol 2002, **10**: 189–196.

269 Neerhout RC, Larson W, Mansur P. Mesenteric lymphoid hamartoma associated with chronic hypoferremia, anemia, growth failure and hypoglobulinemia. N Engl J Med 1969, **280**: 922–925.

270 Ogden WM, Bradburn DM, Rives JD. Mesenteric panniculitis. Review of 27 cases. Ann Surg 1965, **161**: 864–875.

271 Payan HM, Gilbert EF. Mesenteric cyst-ovarian implant syndrome. Arch Pathol Lab Med 1987, **111**: 282–284.

272 Pettinato G, Manivel JC, De Rosa N, Dehner LP. Inflammatory myofibroblastic tumor (plasma cell granuloma). Am J Clin Pathol 1990, **94**: 538–546.

273 Remmele W, Muller-Lobeck H, Paulus W. Primary mesenteritis, mesenteric fibrosis and mesenteric fibromatosis. Pathol Res Pract 1988, **184**: 77–85.

274 Ros PR, Olmstead WW, Moser RP Jr, Dachman AH, Hjermstad BH, Sobin LH. Mesenteric and omental cysts. Histologic classification with imaging correlation. Radiology 1987, **164**: 327–332.

275 Shemwell RE, Weed JC. Ovarian remnant syndrome. Obstet Gynecol 1970, **36**: 299–303.

276 Treissman SP, Gillis DA, Lee CL, Giacomantonio M, Resch L. Omental-mesenteric inflammatory pseudotumor. Cytogenetic demonstration of genetic changes and monoclonality in one tumor. Cancer 1994, **73**: 1433–1437.

277 Vanek VW, Phillips AK. Retroperitoneal, mesenteric, and omental cysts. Arch Surg 1984, **119**: 838–842.

278 Wilson JD, Montague CJ, Salcuni P, Bordi C, Rosai J. Heterotopic mesenteric ossification ('intraabdominal myositis ossificans'): Report of five cases. Am J Surg Pathol 1999, **23**: 1464–1470.

279 Yannopoulos K, Stout AP. Primary solid tumors of the mesentery. Cancer 1963, **16**: 914–927.

279a Yantiss RK, Nielsen GP, Lauwers GY, Rosenberg AE. Reactive nodular fibrous pseudotumor of the gastrointestinal tract and mesentery: A clinicopathologic study of five cases. Am J Surg Pathol 2003, **27**: 532–540.

280 Yantiss RK, Spiro IJ, Compton CC, Rosenberg AE. Gastrointestinal stromal tumor versus intra-abdominal fibromatosis of the bowel wall: a clinically important differential diagnosis. Am J Surg Pathol 2000, **24**: 947–957.

HERNIA SACS

281 Baron BW, Schraut WH, Azizi F, Talerman A. Extragonadal sex cord tumor with annular tubules in an umbilical hernia sac. A unique presentation with implications for histogenesis. Gynecol Oncol 1988, **30**: 71–75.

282 Bostwick D, Eble J. Prostatic adenocarcinoma metastatic to inguinal hernia sac. J Urol Pathol 1993, **1**: 193–200.

282a Cerilli LA, Sotelo-Avila C, Mills SE. Glandular inclusions in inguinal hernia sacs: Morphologic and immunohistochemical distinction from epididymis and vas deferens. Am J Surg Pathol 2003, **27**: 469–476.

283 Dehner LP. Inguinal hernia in the male child: Where the latest skirmish line has formed. Am J Surg Pathol 1999, **23**: 869–871.

284 Esquivel J, Sugarbaker PH. Pseudomyxoma peritonei in a hernia sac: analysis of 20 patients in whom mucoid fluid was found during a hernia repair. Eur J Surg Oncol 2001, **27**: 54–58.

285 Griffith LM, Carcangiu ML. Sex cord tumor with annular tubules associated with endometriosis of the fallopian tube. Am J Clin Pathol 1991, **96**: 259–262.

286 Nicholson CP, Donohue JH, Thompson GB, Lewis JE. A study of metastatic cancer found during inguinal hernia repair. Cancer 1992, **69**: 3008–3011.

287 Popek EJ. Embryonal remnants in inguinal hernia sacs. Hum Pathol 1990, **21**: 339–349.

288 Pratt PC, George MH, Mastin JP, Roggli VL. Crystalline foreign particulate material in hernia sacs. Hum Pathol 1985, **16**: 1141–1146.

289 Steigman CK, Sotelo-Avila C, Weber TR. The incidence of spermatic cord structures in inguinal hernia sacs from male children. Am J Surg Pathol 1999, **23**: 880–885.

290 Walker AN, Mills SE. Glandular inclusions in inguinal hernial sacs and spermatic cords. Müllerian-like remnants confused with functional reproductive structures. Am J Clin Pathol 1984, **82**: 85–89.

291 Young RH, Rosenberg AE, Clement PB. Mucin deposits within inguinal hernia sacs: A presenting finding of low-grade mucinous cystic tumors of the appendix. A report of two cases and a review of the literature. Mod Pathol 1997, **10**: 1228–1232.

UMBILICUS

292 Brustman L, Seltzer V. Sister Joseph's nodule. Seven cases of umbilical metastases from gynecologic malignancies. Gynecol Oncol 1984, **19**: 155–162.

293 Clair DG, Lautz DB, Brooks DC. Rapid development of umbilical

metastases after laparoscopic cholecystectomy for unsuspected galbladder carcinoma. Surgery 1993, **113**: 355–358.

294 Foraker AG. Job Plodd, Pathologist: his trials and tribulations. Oradell N.J., 1975, Medical Economics Company.

295 Ross JE, Hill RB Jr. Primary umbilical adenocarcinoma. A case report and review of literature. Arch Pathol 1975, **99**: 327–329.

296 Steck WD, Helwig EB. Cutaneous remnants of the omphalomesenteric duct. Arch Dermatol 1964, **90**: 463–470.

297 Steck WD, Helwig EB. Cutaneous endometriosis. JAMA 1965, **191**: 101–104.

298 Steck WD, Helwig EB. Tumors of the umbilicus. Cancer 1965, **18**: 907–915.

299 Steck WD, Helwig EB. Umbilical granulomas, pilonidal disease, and the urachus. Surg Gynecol Obstet 1965, **120**: 1043–1057.

300 Vargas SO. Fibrous umbilical polyp: a distinct fasciitis like proliferation of early childhood with a marked male predominance. Am J Surg Pathol 2001, **25**: 1438–1442.

301 Vicente J, Vazquez-Doval J, Quintanilla E. Fibroepithelial papilloma of the umbilicus. Int J Dermatol 1994, **33**: 791–792.

RETROPERITONEUM
Non-neoplastic conditions

302 Carr RA, Newman J, Antonakopulos GN, Parkinson MC. Lesions produced by the extravasation of urine from the upper urinary tract. Histopathology 1997, **30**: 335–340.

303 Catino D, Torack RM, Hagstrom JWC. Idiopathic retroperitoneal fibrosis. Histochemical evidence for lateral spread of the process from the midline. J Urol 1967, **98**: 191–194.

304 Comings DE, Skubi KB, van Eyes J, Motulsky AG. Familial multifocal fibrosclerosis. Findings suggesting that retroperitoneal fibrosis, mediastinal fibrosis, sclerosing cholangitis, Riedel's thyroiditis, and pseudo-tumor of the orbit may be different manifestations of a single disease. Ann Intern Med 1967, **66**: 884–892.

305 Cooksey G, Powell PH, Singh M, Yeates WK. Idiopathic retroperitoneal fibrosis. A long-term review after surgical treatment. Br J Urol 1982, **54**: 628–631.

306 Dehner LP, Coffin CM. Idiopathic fibrosclerotic disorders and other inflammatory pseudotumors. Semin Diagn Pathol 1998, **15**: 161–173.

307 de Peralta MN, Delahoussaye PM, Tornos CS, Silva EG. Benign retroperitoneal cysts of mullerian type. A clinicopathologic study of three cases and review of the literature. Int J Gynecol Pathol 1994, **13**: 273–278.

308 Doggett RS, Carty SE, Clarke MR. Retroperitoneal bronchogenic cyst masquerading clinically and radiologically as a phaeochromocytoma. Virchows Arch 1997, **431**: 73–76.

309 Graham JR, Suby HI, LeCompte PR, Sadowsky NL. Fibrotic disorders associated with methysergide therapy for headache. N Engl J Med 1966, **274**: 359–368.

310 Harbrecht PJ. Variants of retroperitoneal fibrosis. Ann Surg 1967, **165**: 388–401.

311 Hughes D, Buckley PJ. Idiopathic retroperitoneal fibrosis is a macrophage-rich process. Implications for its pathogenesis and treatment. Am J Surg Pathol 1993, **17**: 482–490.

312 Jones JH, Ross EJ, Matz LR, Edwards D, Davies DR. Retroperitoneal fibrosis. Am J Med 1970, **48**: 203–208.

313 Jonsson G, Lindstedt E, Rubin S-O. Two cases of metastasizing scirrhous gastric carcinoma simulating idiopathic retroperitoneal fibrosis. Scand J Urol Nephrol 1967, **1**: 299–302.

314 Kendall AR, Lakey WH. Sclerosing Hodgkin's disease vs. idiopathic retroperitoneal fibrosis. J Urol 1961, **35**: 284–291.

314a Konishi E, Nakashima Y, Iwasaki T. Immunohistochemical analysis of retroperitoneal Müllerian cyst. Hum Pathol 2003, **2**: 194–198

315 Kurtz RJ, Heiman TM, Holt J, Beck AR. Mesenteric and retroperitoneal cysts. Arch Surg 1986, **203**: 109–112.

316 Lawson DW, Corry RJ, Patton AS, Austen WG. Massive retroperitoneal adrenal hemorrhage. Surg Gynecol Obstet 1969, **129**: 989–994.

317 Leake R, Wayman TB. Retroperitoneal encysted hematomas. J Urol 1952, **68**: 69–73.

318 Le Gall F, Huerre M, Cipolla B, Shalev M, Ramee MP. A case of myospherulosis occurring in the peritoneal adipose tissue. Pathol Res Pract 1996, **192**: 172–178.

319 Lepor H, Walsh PC. Idiopathic retroperitoneal fibrosis. J Urol 1979, **122**: 1–6.

320 Meehan SM, Scully RE. Para-adrenal bronchogenic cyst: clinical dilemma, pathologic curiosity. J Urol Pathol 1996, **4**: 51–56.

321 Meyer S, Hausman R. Occlusive phlebitis in multifocal fibrosclerosis. Am J Clin Pathol 1976, **65**: 274–283.

322 Mitchinson MJ. The pathology of idiopathic retroperitoneal fibrosis. J Clin Pathol 1970, **23**: 681–689.

323 Mitchinson MJ. Retroperitoneal fibrosis revisited. Arch Pathol Lab Med 1986, **110**: 784–786.

324 Munro JM, van der Walt JD, Cox EL. A comparison of cytoplasmic immunoglobulins in retroperitoneal fibrosis and abdominal aortic aneurysms. Histopathology 1986, **10**: 1163–1169.

325 Osborn DE, Rao PN, Barnard RJ, Ackrill P, Ralston AJ, Best JJK. Surgical management of idiopathic retroperitoneal fibrosis. Br J Urol 1981, **53**: 292–296.

326 Osborne BM, Butler JJ, Bloustein P, Sumner G. Idiopathic retroperitoneal fibrosis (sclerosing retroperitonitis). Hum Pathol 1987, **18**: 735–739.

327 Sneige N, Dekmezian RH, Silva EG, Cartwright J Jr, Ayala AG. Pseudoparasitic Liesegang structures in perirenal hemorrhagic cysts. Am J Clin Pathol 1988, **89**: 148–153.

328 Terner JY, Lattes R. Malakoplakia of colon and retroperitoneum. Report of a case with a histochemical study of the Michaelis-Gutmann inclusion bodies. Am J Clin Pathol 1965, **44**: 20–31.

329 Thomas MH, Chisholm GD. Retroperitoneal fibrosis associated with malignant disease. Br J Cancer 1973, **28**: 453–458.

Tumors

330 Cafferty LL, Katz RL, Ordóñez NG, Carrasco CH, Cabanillas FR. Fine needle aspiration diagnosis of intraabdominal and retroperitoneal lymphomas by a morphologic and immunocytochemical approach. Cancer 1990, **65**: 72–77.

331 Gill W, Carter DC, Durie B. Retroperitoneal tumors. A review of 134 cases. J R Coll Surg Edinb 1970, **15**: 213–221.

332 Goldberg BB (ed.). Abdominal gray scale ultrasonography. New York, 1977, John Wiley & Sons.

333 Lofgren L. Primary retroperitoneal tumors. A histopathological, clinical and follow-up study supplemented by follow-up study of a series from the Finnish Cancer Register. Ann Acad Sci Fenn (Med) 1967, **129**: 5–86.

334 Parkinson MC, Chabrel CM. Clinicopathological features of retroperitoneal tumours. Br J Urol 1984, **56**: 17–23.

335 Stanley P. Computed tomographic evaluation of the retroperitoneum in infants and children. J Comput Tomogr 1983, **7**: 63–75.

336 Waldron JA, Magnifico M, Duray PH, Cadman EC. Retroperitoneal mass presentations of B-immunoblastic sarcoma. Cancer 1985, **56**: 1733–1741.

337 Waldron JA, Newcomer LN, Katz ME, Cadman E. Sclerosing variants of follicular center cell lymphomas presenting in the retroperitoneum. Cancer 1983, **52**: 712–720.

Soft tissue tumors

338 Antonescu CR, Elahi A, Humphrey M, Lui MY, Healey JH, Brennan MF, Woodruff JM, Jhanwar SC, Ladanyi M. Specificity of TLS-CHOP rearrangement for classic myxoid/round cell liposarcoma: absence in predominantly myxoid well-differentiated liposarcomas. J Mol Diagn 2000, **2**: 132–138.

339 Azumi N, Curtis J, Kempson RL, Hendrickson MR. Atypical and malignant neoplasms showing lipomatous differentiation. A study of 111 cases. Am J Surg Pathol 1987, **11**: 161–183.

340 Bhattacharyya AK, Balogh K. Retroperitoneal lymphangioleiomyomatosis. A 36-year benign course in a postmenopausal woman. Cancer 1985, **56**: 1144–1146.

341 Billings SD, Folpe AL, Weiss SW. Do leiomyomas of deep soft tissue exist? An analysis of highly differentiated smooth muscle tumors of deep soft tissue supporting two distinct subtypes. Am J Surg Pathol 2001, **25**: 1134–1142.

342 Chung EB, Enzinger FM. Extraskeletal osteosarcoma. Cancer 1987, **60**: 1132–1142.

343 Cody HS III, Turnbull AD, Fortner JG, Hajdu SI. The continuing challenge of retroperitoneal sarcomas. Cancer 1981, **47**: 2147–2152.

343a Coindre J-M, Mariani O, Chibon F, Mairal A, de Saint Aubain Somerhausen N, Favre-Guillevin E, Bui NB, Stoeckle E, Hostein I, Aurias A. Most malignant fibrous histiocytomas developed in the retroperitoneum are dedifferentiated liposarcomas: A review of 25 cases initially diagnosed as malignant fibrous histiocytoma. Mod Pathol 2003, **16**: 256–262.

344 Crist WM, Raney RB, Tefft M, Heyn R, Hays DM, Newton W, Beltangady M, Maurer HM. Soft tissue sarcomas arising in the retroperitoneal space in children. A report from the Intergroup Rhabdomyosarcoma Study (IRS) Committee. Cancer 1985, **56**: 2125–2132.

345 Dickman PS, Triche TJ. Extraosseous Ewing's sarcoma versus primitive rhabdomyosarcoma. Diagnostic criteria and clinical correlation. Hum Pathol 1986, **17**: 881–893.

346 Eble JN, Rosenberg AE, Young RH. Retroperitoneal xanthogranuloma in a patient with Erdheim-Chester disease. Am J Surg Pathol 1994, **18**: 843–848.

347 Elgar F, Goldblum JR. Well-differentiated liposarcoma of the retroperitoneum: a clinicopathologic analysis of 20 cases, with particular attention to the extent of low-grade dedifferentiation. Mod Pathol 1997, **10**: 113–120.

348 Enzinger FM, Winslow DJ. Liposarcoma. A study of 103 cases. Virchows Arch Pathol Anat 1962, **335**: 367–388.

349 Erlandson RA. The ultrastructural distinction between rhabdomyosarcoma and other undifferentiated "sarcomas." Ultrastruct Pathol 1987, **11**: 83–101.

350 Fukunaga M, Ushigome S, Ishikawa E. Kaposiform haemangioendothelioma associated with Kasabach-Merritt syndrome. Histopathology 1996, **28**: 281–284.

351 Ghali VS, Gold JE, Vincent RA, Cosgrove JM. Malignant peripheral nerve sheath tumor arising spontaneously from retroperitoneal ganglioneuroma. A case report, review of the literature, and immunohistochemical study. Hum Pathol 1992, **23**: 72–75.

352 Hasegawa T, Seki K, Hasegawa F, Matsuno Y, Shimada T, Hirose T, Sano T, Hirohashi S. Dedifferentiated liposarcoma of retroperitoneum and mesentery: varied growth patterns and histological grades—a clinicopathologic study of 32 cases. Hum Pathol 2000, **31**: 717–727.

353 Hashimoto H, Tsuneyoshi M, Enjoji M. Malignant smooth muscle tumors of the retroperitoneum and mesentery. A clinicopathologic analysis of 44 cases. J Surg Oncol 1985, **28**: 177–186.

354 Heslin MJ, Lewis JJ, Nadler E, Newman E, Woodruff JM, Casper ES, Leung D, Brennan MF. Prognostic factors associated with long-term survival for retroperitoneal sarcoma: implications for management. J Clin Oncol 1997, **15**: 2832–2839.

355 Hisaoka M, Morimitsu Y, Hashimoto H, Ishida T, Mukai H, Satoh H, Motoi T, Machinami R. Retroperitoneal liposarcoma with combined well-differentiated and myxoid malignant fibrous histiocytoma-like myxoid areas. Am J Surg Pathol 1999, **23**: 1480–1492.

356 Hollowood K, Stamp G, Zouvani J, Fletcher CDM. Extranodal follicular dendritic cell sarcoma of the gastrointestinal tract. Morphologic, immunohistochemical and ultrastructural analysis of two cases. Am J Clin Pathol 1995, **103**: 90–97.

356a Huang H-Y., Brennan MF, Antonescu CR. Metastatic retroperitoneal dedifferentiated liposarcomas are rapidly fatal: 6 cases with emphases on unusual spread to soft tissue and the low-grade myxofibrosarcoma-like pattern as an early sign of dedifferentiation. (Abstract) Mod Pathol 2003, **16**: 14a

357 Huszar M, Fanburg JC, Dickersin GR, Kirshner JJ, Rosenberg AE. Retroperitoneal malignant meningioma: A light microscopic, immunohistochemical, and ultrastructural study. Am J Surg Pathol 1996, **20**: 492–499.

358 Ibrahim NB, Briggs JC, Corrin B. Double primary localized fibrous tumours of the pleura and retroperitoneum. Histopathology 1993, **22**: 282–284.

359 Kahn LB. Retroperitoneal xanthogranuloma and xanthosarcoma (malignant fibrous xanthoma). Cancer 1973, **31**: 411–422.

360 Karakousis CP, Velez AF, Emrich LJ. Management of retroperitoneal sarcomas and patient survival. Am J Surg 1985, **150**: 376–380.

360a Kelley TW, Borden E, Patel R, Prok A, Goldblum JR. Estrogen (ER) and progesterone receptor expression in uterine and extra-uterine leiomyosarcomas: An Immunohistochemical study. (Abstract) Mod Pathol 2003, **16**: 15a.

361 Kinne DW, Chu FCH, Huvos AG, Yagoda A, Fortner JG. Treatment of primary and recurrent retroperitoneal liposarcoma. Twenty-five-year experience at Memorial Hospital. Cancer 1973, **31**: 53–64.

362 Kourea HP, Bilsky MH, Leung DHY, Lewis JJ, Woodruff JM. Subdiaphragmatic and intrathoracic paraspinal malignant peripheral nerve sheath tumors: a clinicopathologic study of 25 patients and 26 tumors. Cancer 1998, **82**: 2191–2203.

362a Lau SK, Marchevsky AM, McKenna Jr RJ, Luthringer DJ. Malignant monotypic epithelioid angiomyolipoma of the retroperitoneum. Int J Surg Pathol 2003, **11**: 223–228.

363 Lauwers GY, Erlandson RA, Casper ES, Brennan MF, Woodruff JM. Gastrointestinal autonomic nerve tumors. A clinicopathological, immunohistochemical, and ultrastructural study of 12 cases. Am J Surg Pathol 1993, **17**: 887–897.

364 Leonidas JC, Brill PW, Bhan I, Smith TH. Cystic retroperitoneal lymphangioma in infants and children. Radiology 1978, **127**: 203–208.

365 Michal M. Retroperitoneal myolipoma. A tumour mimicking retroperitoneal angiomyolipoma and liposarcoma with myosarcomatous differentiation. Histopathology 1994, **25**: 86–88.

365a Morrison C, Ramirez NC, Chan JKC, Wakely Jr P. Endometrial stromal sarcoma of the retroperitoneum. Ann Diagn Pathol 2002, **6**: 312–318.

366 Oberling C. Retroperitoneal xanthogranuloma. Am J Cancer 1935, **23**: 477–489.

367 Paal E, Miettinen M. Retroperitoneal leiomyomas: a clinicopathologic and immunohistochemical study of 56 cases with a comparison to retroperitoneal leiomyosarcomas. Am J Surg Pathol 2001, **25**: 1355–1363.

367a Patel R, Goldblum JR, Antonescu CR. Mutational analysis of c-kit in extragastrointestinal stromal tumors (EGIST): A molecular study of six cases. (Abstract) Mod Pathol 2003, **16**: 18a–19a.

368 Piana S, Roncaroli F. Epithelioid leiomyosarcoma of retroperitoneum with granular cell change. Histopathology 1994, **25**: 90–93.

369 Rajani B, Smith TA, Reith JD, Goldblum JR. Retroperitoneal leiomyosarcomas unassociated with the gastrointestinal tract: a clinicopathologic analysis of 17 cases. Mod Pathol 1999, **12**: 21–28.

370 Ranchod M, Kempson RC. Smooth muscle tumors of the gastrointestinal tract and retroperitoneum. A pathologic analysis of 100 cases. Cancer 1977, **39**: 255–262.

371 Ransom JL, Pratt CB, Hustu O, Kumar APM, Howarth CB, Bowles D. Retroperitoneal rhabdomyosarcoma in children. Results of multimodality therapy. Cancer 1980, **45**: 845–850.

372 Reith JD, Goldblum JR, Lyles RH, Weiss SW. Extragastrointestinal (soft tissue) stromal tumors: an analysis of 48 cases with emphasis on histologic predictors of outcome. Mod Pathol 2000, **13**: 577–585.

373 Roncaroli F, Eusebi V. Rhabdomyoblastic differentiation in a leiomyosarcoma of the retroperitoneum. Hum Pathol 1996, **27**: 310–312.

374 Schmidt D, Mackay B, Sinkovics JG. Retroperitoneal tumor with vertebral metastasis in a 25-year-old female. Ultrastruct Pathol 1981, **2**: 383–388.

375 Shmookler BM. Retroperitoneal synovial sarcoma. A report of four cases. Am J Clin Pathol 1982, **77**: 686–691.

376 Shmookler BM, Lauer DH. Retroperitoneal leiomyosarcoma. A clinicopathologic analysis of 36 cases. Am J Surg Pathol 1983, **7**: 269–280.

377 Stoeckle E, Coindre JM, Bonvalot S, Kantor G, Terrier P, Bonichon F, Nguyen Bui B. Prognostic factors in retroperitoneal sarcoma: a multivariate analysis of a series of 165 patients of the French Cancer Center Federation Sarcoma Group. Cancer 2001, **92**: 359–368.

378 Tallini G, Erlandson RA, Brennan MF, Woodruff JM. Divergent myosarcomatous differentiation in retroperitoneal liposarcoma. Am J Surg Pathol 1993, **17**: 546–556.

379 Tefft M, Vawter GF, Mitus A. Paravertebral "round cell" tumors in children. Radiology 1969, **92**: 1501–1509.

380 Triche RJ, Askin FB, Kissane JM. Neuroblastoma, Ewing's sarcoma, and the differential diagnosis of small-, round-, blue-cell tumors. In Finegold M (ed.): Pathology of neoplasia in children and adolescents, vol. 18 of Major problems in pathology. Philadelphia, 1986, W.B. Saunders.

381 Tsang WY, Chan JK. Kaposi-like infantile hemangioendothelioma. A distinctive vascular neoplasm of the retroperitoneum. Am J Surg Pathol 1991, **15**: 982–989.

382 van Doorn RC, Gallee MP, Hart AA, Gortzak E, Rutgers EJ, van Coevorden F, Keus RB, Zoetmulder FA. Resectable retroperitoneal soft tissue sarcomas. The effect of extent of resection and postoperative radiation therapy on local tumor control. Cancer 1994, **73**: 637–642.

383 Vilanova JR, Burgos-Bretones J, Simon R, Rivera-Pomar JM. Leukaemoid reaction and eosinophilia in "inflammatory fibrous histiocytoma." Virchows Arch [A] 1980, **388**: 237–243.

384 Vuletin JC, Wajsbort RR, Ghali V. Primary retroperitoneal angiosarcoma with eosinophilic globules. A combined light-microscopic, immunohistochemical, and ultrastructural study. Arch Pathol Lab Med 1990, **114**: 618–622.

385 Whitten RO, Benjamin DR. Rhabdomyoma of the retroperitoneum. A report of a tumor with both adult and fetal characteristics. A study by light and electron microscopy, histochemistry, and immunochemistry. Cancer 1987, **59**: 818–824.

386 Yunis EJ. Ewing's sarcoma and related small round cell neoplasms in children. Am J Surg Pathol 1986, **10**: S54–S62.

Germ cell tumors

387 Abell MR, Fayos JV, Lampe I. Retroperitoneal germinomas (seminomas) without evidence of testicular involvement. Cancer 1965, **18**: 273–290.

388 Berry CL, Keeling J, Hilton C. Teratoma in infancy and childhood. A review of 91 cases. J Pathol 1969, **98**: 241–252.

389 Buskirk SJ, Evans RG, Farrow GM, Earle JD. Primary retroperitoneal seminoma. Cancer 1982, **49**: 1934–1936.

390 Chen KT, Cheng AC. Retroperitoneal seminoma and intratubular germ cell neoplasia. Hum Pathol 1989, **20**: 493–495.

391 Hawkins EP, Finegold MJ, Hawkins HK, Krischer JP, Starling KA, Weinberg A. Nongerminomatous malignant germ cell tumors in children. A review of 89 cases from the pediatric oncology group, 1971–1984. Cancer 1986, **58**: 2579–2584.

392 Lack EE, Travis WD, Welch KJ. Retroperitoneal germ cell tumors in childhood. A clinical and pathologic study of 11 cases. Cancer 1985, **56**: 602–608.

393 Maatman T, Bukowski RM, Montie JE. Retroperitoneal malignancies several years after initial treatment of germ cell cancer of the testis. Cancer 1984, **54**: 1962–1965.

394 Montague DK. Retroperitoneal germ cell tumors with no apparent testicular involvement. J Urol 1975, **113**: 505–508.

395 Moss JF, Slayton RE, Economou SG. Primary retroperitoneal pure choriocarcinoma. Two long-term complete responders from a rare fatal disease. Cancer 1988, **62**: 1053–1054.

396 Ohno Y, Kanematsu T. An endodermal sinus tumor arising from a mature cystic teratoma in the retroperitoneum in a child: is a mature teratoma a premalignant condition? Hum Pathol 1998, **29**: 1167–1169.

397 Weissbach L, Boedefeld EA. Localization of solitary and multiple metastases in stage II nonseminomatous testis tumor as basis for a modified staging lymph node dissection in stage I. J Urol 1987, **138**: 77–82.

Other primary tumors and tumorlike conditions

398 Brietta LK, Watkins D. Giant extra-adrenal myelolipoma. Arch Pathol Lab Med 1994, **118**: 188–190.

399 Burke T, Sahin A, Johnson DE, Ordóñez NG, Mackay B. Myoepithelioma of the retroperitoneum. Ultrastruct Pathol 1995, **19**: 269–274.

400 Carabias E, Garcia Muñoz H, Dihmes FP, López Pino MA, Ballestin C. Primary mucinous cystadenocarcinoma of the retroperitoneum. Report of a case and literature review. Virchows Arch 1995, **426**: 641–645.

401 Chen KTK, Felix EL, Flam MS. Extraadrenal myelolipoma. Am J Clin Pathol 1982, **78**: 386–389.

402 Fowler MR, Williams GB, Alba JM, Byrd CR. Extra-adrenal myelolipomas compared with extra medullary hematopoietic tumors. A case of presacral myelolipoma. Am J Surg Pathol 1982, **6**: 363–374.

403 Fukutomi Y, Shibuya C, Yamamoto S, Okuno F, Nishiwaki S, Kashiki Y, Muto Y. Extrarenal Wilms' tumor in the adult patient. A case report and review of the world literature. Am J Clin Pathol 1988, **90**: 618–622.

404 Hasegawa T, Hirose T, Ayala AG, Ito S, Tomaru U, Matsuno Y, Shimoda T, Hirohashi S. Adult neuroblastoma of the retroperitoneum and abdomen: clinicopathologic distinction from primitive neuroectodermal tumor. Am J Surg Pathol 2001, **25**: 918–924.

405 Hyman MP. Extraovarian endometrioid carcinoma. Review of the literature and report of two cases with unusual features. Am J Clin Pathol 1977, **68**: 522–528.

406 Koretz MJ, Wang S, Klein FA, Lawrence W Jr. Extrarenal adult Wilms' tumor. Cancer 1987, **60**: 2484–2488.

407 Kryger-Baggesen N, Kjaergaard J, Sehested M. Nonchromaffin paraganglioma of the retroperitoneum. J Urol 1985, **134**: 536–538.

408 Olson JR, Abell MR. Nonfunctional nonchromaffin paragangliomas of the retroperitoneum. Cancer 1969, **23**: 1358–1367.

409 Park U, Han KC, Chang HK, Huh MH. A primary mucinous cystoadenocarcinoma of the retroperitoneum. Gynecol Oncol 1991, **42**: 64–67.

410 Pennell TC, Gusdon JP. Retroperitoneal mucinous cystadenoma. Am J Obstet Gynecol 1990, **160**: 1229–1231.

411 Rothacker D, Knolle J, Stiller D, Borchard F. Primary retroperitoneal mucinous cystadenomas with gastric epithelial differentiation. Pathol Res Pract 1993, **189**: 1195–1204.

412 Shintaku M, Matsumoto T. Primary mullerian carcinosarcoma of

the retroperitoneum: report of a case. J Gynecol Pathol 2001, **20:** 191–195.

413 Subramony C, Habibpour S, Hashimoto LA. Retroperitoneal mucinous cystadenoma. Arch Pathol Lab Med 2001, **125:** 691–694.

414 Tang C-K, Toker C, Wybel RE, Desai RG. An unusual pelvic tumor with benign glandular, sarcomatous, and Wilms' tumor-like components. Hum Pathol 1981, **12:** 940–944.

415 Ulbright TM, Morley DJ, Roth LM, Berkow RL. Papillary serous carcinoma of the retroperitoneum. Am J Clin Pathol 1983, **79:** 633–637.

416 Wakely PE Jr, Sprague RI, Kornstein MJ. Extrarenal Wilms' tumor. An analysis of four cases. Hum Pathol 1989, **20:** 691–695.

417 Yajima A, Toki T, Morinaga S, Sasano H, Sasano N. A retroperitoneal endocrine carcinoma. Cancer 1984, **54:** 2040–2042.

SACROCOCCYGEAL REGION
Developmental anomalies

418 Bale PM. Sacrococcygeal developmental abnormalities and tumors in children. Perspect Pediatr Pathol 1984, **1:** 9–56.

419 Berry CL, Keelnig J, Hilton C. Teratoma in infancy and childhood. A review of 91 cases. J Pathol 1969, **98:** 241–252.

420 Fulton RS, Rouse RV, Ranheim EA. Ectopic prostate: case report of a presacral mass presenting with obstructive symptoms. Arch Pathol Lab Med 2001, **125:** 286–288.

421 Harrist TY, Gang DL, Kleinman GM, Mihm MC Jr, Hendren WH. Unusual sacrococcygeal embryologic malformations with cutaneous manifestations. Arch Dermatol 1982, **118:** 643–648.

422 Hjernstad BM, Helwig EB. Tailgut cysts. Report of 53 cases. Am J Clin Pathol 1988, **89:** 139–147.

423 Hood DL, Petras RE, Grundfest-Broniatowski S, Jagelman DG. Retrorectal cystic hamartoma. Report of five cases with carcinoid tumor arising in two (abstract). Am J Clin Pathol 1988, **89:** 433.

424 MacLeod JH, Purves JKB. Duplications of the rectum. Dis Colon Rectum 1970, **13:** 133–137.

425 Marco V, Autonell J, Farre J, et al. Retrorectal cyst-hamartoma. Report of two cases with adenocarcinoma developing in one. Am J Surg Pathol 1982, **6:** 707–714.

426 McDermott NC, Newman J. Tailgut cyst (retrorectal cystic hamartoma) with prominent glomus bodies. Histopathology 1991, **18:** 265–266.

427 Mills SE, Walker AN, Stallings RG, Allen MS. Retrorectal cystic hamartoma. Report of three cases, including one with a perirenal component. Arch Pathol Lab Med 1984, **108:** 737–740.

428 Prasad AR, Amin MB, Randolph TL, Lee CS, Ma CK. Retrorectal cystic hamartoma: report of 5 cases with malignancy. Arch Pathol Lab Med 2000, **124:** 725–729.

429 Tagart REB. Congenital anal duplication. A cause of para-anal sinus. Br J Surg 1977, **64:** 525–528.

Germ cell tumors

430 Ahmed HA, Pollock DJ. Malignant sacrococcygeal teratoma in the adult. Histopathology 1985, **9:** 359–363.

431 Arnheim EE. Retroperitoneal teratomas in infancy and childhood. Pediatrics 1951, **8:** 309–327.

432 Bale PM. Sacrococcygeal developmental abnormalities and tumors in children. Perspect Pediatr Pathol 1984, **1:** 9–56.

433 Berry CL, Keelnig J, Hilton C. Teratoma in infancy and childhood. A review of 91 cases. J Pathol 1969, **98:** 241–252.

434 Chretien PB, Milam JD, Foote FW, Miller TR. Embryonal adenocarcinomas (a type of malignant teratoma) of the sacrococcygeal region. Clinical and pathologic aspects of 21 cases. Cancer 1970, **26:** 522–535.

435 Donnellan WA, Swenson O. Benign and malignant sacrococcygeal teratomas. Surgery 1968, **64:** 834–846.

436 Ein SH, Mancer K, Adeyemi SD. Malignant sacrococcygeal teratoma—endodermal sinus, yolk sac tumor—in infants and children. A 32-year review. J Pediatr Surg 1985, **20:** 473–477.

437 Gonzalez-Crussi F, Winkler RF, Mirkin DL. Sacrococcygeal teratomas in infants and children. Relationship of histology and prognosis in 40 cases. Arch Pathol Lab Med 1978, **102:** 420–425.

438 Hawkins EP, Finegold MJ, Hawkins HK, Krischer JP, Starling KA, Weinberg A. Nongerminomatous malignant germ cell tumors in children. A review of 89 cases from the pediatric oncology group, 1971–1984. Cancer 1986, **58:** 2579–2584.

439 Kaplan CG, Askin FB, Benirschke K. Cytogenetics of extragonadal tumors. Teratology 1979, **19:** 261–266.

440 Kuhajda FP, Taxy JB. Oncofetal antigens in sacrococcygeal teratomas. Arch Pathol Lab Med 1983, **107:** 239–242.

441 Lack EE, Glaun RS, Hefter LG, Seneca RP, Steigman C, Athari F. Late occurrence of malignancy following resection of a histologically mature sacrococcygeal teratoma. Report of a case and literature review. Arch Pathol Lab Med 1993, **117:** 724–728.

442 Lack EE, Travis WE, Welch KJ. Retroperitoneal germ cell tumors in childhood. A clinical and pathologic study of 11 cases. Cancer 1985, **56:** 602–608.

443 Lahdenne P, Heikinheimo M, Nikkanen V, Klemi P, Siimes MA, Rapola J. Neonatal benign sacrococcygeal teratoma may recur in adulthood and give rise to malignancy. Cancer 1993, **72:** 3727–3731.

444 Nakashima N, Fukatsu T, Nagasaka T, Sobue M, Takeuchi J. The frequency and histology of hepatic tissue in germ cell tumors. Am J Surg Pathol 1987, **11:** 682–692.

445 Ng EW, Porcu P, Loehrer PJ Sr. Sacrococcygeal teratoma in adults: case reports and a review of the literature. Cancer 1999, **86:** 1198–1202.

446 Noseworthy J, Lack EE, Kozakewich HPW, Vawter GF, Welch KJ. Sacrococcygeal germ cell tumors in childhood. An updated experience with 118 patients. J Pediatr Surg 1981, **16:** 358–364.

447 Olsen MM, Raffensperger JG, Gonzalez-Crussi F, Luck SR, Kaplan WE, Morgan ER. Endodermal sinus tumor. A clinical and pathological correlation. J Pediatr Surg 1982, **17:** 832–840.

448 Oosterhuis J, van Berlo R, de Jong B, Dam A, Buist J, Tamminga R, Zwierstra R. Sacral teratoma with late recurrence of yolk sac tumor. J Urol Pathol 1993, **1:** 257–268.

449 Siltanen S, Anttonen M, Heikkila P, Narita N, Laitinen M, Ritvos O, Wilson DB, Heikinheimo M. Transcription factor GATA-4 is expressed in pediatric yolk sac tumors. Am J Pathol 1999, **155:** 1823–1829.

450 Valdiserri RO, Yunis EJ. Sacrococcygeal teratomas. A review of 68 cases. Cancer 1981, **48:** 217–221.

451 Whalen TV Jr, Mahour GH, Landing BH, Woolley MM. Sacrococcygeal teratomas in infants and children. Am J Surg 1985, **150:** 373–375.

Pilonidal disease

452 Culp CE. Pilonidal disease and its treatment. Surg Clin North Am 1967, **47:** 1007–1014.

453 Davage ON. The origin of sacrococcygeal pilonidal sinuses based on an analysis of four hundred and sixty-three cases. Am J Pathol 1954, **30:** 1191–1205.

454 Lineaweaver WC, Brunson MB, Smith JF, Franzini DA, Rumley TO. Squamous carcinoma arising in a pilonidal sinus. J Surg Oncol 1984, **27:** 239–242.

455 Norris CS. Giant condyloma acuminatum (Buschke-Lowenstein tumor) involving a pilonidal sinus. A case report and review of the literature. J Surg Oncol 1983, **22:** 47–50.

456 Notaras MJ. A review of three popular methods of treatment of postanal (pilonidal) sinus disease. Br J Surg 1970, **57:** 886–890.

457 Pilipshen SJ, Gray G, Goldsmith E, Dineen P. Carcinoma arising in pilonidal sinuses. Ann Surg 1981, **193:** 506–512.

Other tumors

458 Addis BJ, Rao SG, Finnis D, Carvell JE. Pre-sacral carcinoid tumour. Histopathology 1991, **18:** 563–565.

459 Gatalica Z, Wang L, Lucio ET, Miettinen M. Glomus coccygeum in surgical pathology specimens: small troublemaker. Arch Pathol Lab Med 1999, **123:** 905–908.

460 Helwig EB, Stern JB. Subcutaneous sacrococcygeal myxopapillary ependymoma. A clinicopathologic study of 32 cases. Am J Clin Pathol 1984, **81:** 156–161.

461 Horenstein MG, Erlandson RA, Gonzalez-Cueto DM, Rosai J. Presacral carcinoid tumors: report of three cases and review of the literature. Am J Surg Pathol 1998, **22:** 251–255.

462 Lemberger A, Stein M, Doron J, Fried G, Goldsher D, Feinsod M. Sacrococcygeal extradural ependymoma. Cancer 1989, **64:** 1156–1159.

27 Cardiovascular system

Heart
Arteries
Veins
Lymph vessels

Heart

Introduction

Most operations for congenital cardiovascular malformations are directed toward improvement in the flow of oxygenated blood by such procedures as ligation or division of a patent ductus or the closure of interatrial and interventricular septal defects.[1] Methods have been devised to relieve pulmonary, aortic, and mitral valvular stenosis. Coronary artery bypass graft surgery has become a widely used and effective procedure for the symptomatic treatment of ischemic heart disease.[2] These various cardiac abnormalities and their methods of treatment will not be presented in detail.

Another cardiac operation that has become almost routine in some medical centers is cardiac transplantation; here the pathologist plays a very important role in monitoring the possibility of rejection.

Normal anatomy

The major histologic components of the heart are pericardium, myocardium, endocardium, and valves. The *pericardium* is divided into fibrous (parietal) and serous (visceral, epicardium) portions. It is lined by a single layer of mesothelial cells resting on a basement membrane. The *myocardium* consists of bundles of cardiac muscle fibers (myocytes) separated by fibrous bands.

These fibers form a syncytium with end-to-end junctions, called intercalated discs, and sometimes side-to-side junctions.[2a] The nuclei of myocytes are centrally located, in contrast to those of skeletal muscle fibers. The *endocardium* consists of a single layer of endothelial cells that are continuous with those of the major blood vessels. The *semilunar (pulmonary and aortic) valves* are composed of three layers: fibrosa (made of dense collagen), spongiosa (containing large amounts of proteoglycans, loosely arranged collagen fibers, and scattered fibroblasts), and ventricularis (identified by its profusion of elastic fibers). The *atrioventricular (mitral and tricuspid) valves* are composed of the annulus (a ring of circumferentially oriented collagen and elastic fibers), leaflets, chordae tendineae, and papillary muscles. The leaflets, like those of the semilunar valves, are composed of three layers: fibrosa, ventricularis (on the ventricular side, rich in elastic fibers), and the spongiosa (on the atrial side, rich in proteoglycans).

The morphologic features of blood vessels and lymph vessels are discussed in Chapter 25.

Myocardial biopsy

The performance of myocardial or endomyocardial biopsies has become a common procedure.[21,27,54] These biopsies can be obtained through a catheter inserted in a systemic vein through a transthoracic route or at the time of surgery for congenital or acquired heart disease.[39] Examination of multiple levels increases the sensitivity of the procedure, particularly in cases of myocarditis.[10,30] Ultrastructural examination can be of importance, especially for the evaluation of drug toxicity.[29]

The current complication rate with the intravascular procedure at specialized centers is less than 1%; the most common complication is hemopericardium (which rarely requires thoracotomy), and the most serious is cardiac perforation. The two most important indications of myocardial biopsy are monitoring of heart transplant recipients and grading of Adriamycin toxicity.[53] These and other diseases in which myocardial biopsy has provided useful information are discussed in the following paragraphs.[27,34,58]

Idiopathic hypertrophic cardiomyopathy. The main microscopic changes in this condition,[16,47] as seen in whole hearts, septal myomectomy specimens, or biopsies obtained at thoracotomy, are myofiber disarray and hypertrophy and interstitial fibrosis.[24,33a,50] Transvascular biopsy specimens are less informative, but they still show disarray of myofibrils and myofilaments within individual myocytes by ultrastructural examination. Unfortunately, these changes are not specific for this condition.[37,50] Another nonspecific change that is commonly found in idiopathic hypertrophic myocardiopathy is *basophilic degeneration* of myocardium. This appears as basophilic, finely granular material in the cytoplasm of isolated myocardial fibers and consists of polyglucosan deposits.[43,48]

Idiopathic dilated cardiomyopathy. Abnormalities in the myocardial biopsy are consistently present but, again, are of a nonspecific nature. They consist mainly of hypertrophy and degenerative changes of the myocardial fibers.[28,45,59]

A good correlation has been found between the severity of the condition clinically and the extent and degree of microscopic abnormalities, although the sometimes focal nature of the changes may be misleading. Leukocytic infiltrates are present in about one half of the myocardial biopsies in this condition, a fact to remember in the differential diagnosis with myocarditis.[49]

Restrictive (restrictive/obliterative) myocardiopathy. In the *eosinophilic* form of this disease in its active stage, a myocarditis with a heavy component of eosinophils is present (Fig. 27.1); in the inactive stage of this form and in the *noneosinophilic* form (the most common in the United States), the biopsy findings are nonspecific.[19]

Infiltrative myocardiopathies. This is the group of cardiac diseases in which endomyocardial biopsy can be particularly rewarding. This includes amyloidosis,[40] hemosiderosis,[9] hemochromatosis, and glycogenosis. However, the diagnosis of most of these conditions can be made more readily by biopsy of another, more readily accessible organ.[25]

Other myocardiopathies. *Ischemic myocardiopathy* is

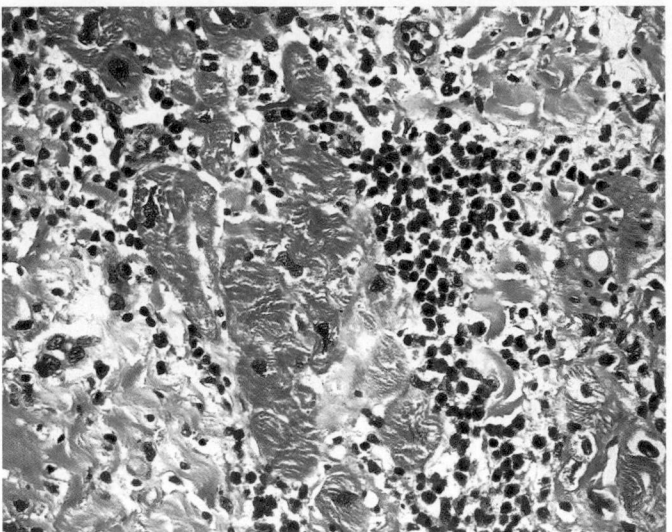

Fig. 27.1 Eosinophil-rich myocardial infiltrate in restrictive myocarditis.

secondary to severe coronary artery disease with myocardial infarct and is characterized by congestive heart failure and cardiac dilatation. Cases with similar features occurring in the absence of a myocardial infarct have been described.[6]

Right ventricular dysplasia is a strongly familial idiopathic cardiomyopathy that mainly involves the right ventricle. The anatomic substrate is variable infiltration of the right ventricular myocardium by adipose and fibrous tissue.[33]

Myocarditis. It is agreed that the diagnosis of myocarditis requires the presence of an inflammatory infiltrate *and* myocyte necrosis or degeneration ("Dallas criteria").[4,34] The infiltrate is usually of lymphocytic nature, easily identifiable, often admixed with histiocytes, and amenable to semiquantification in routine sections.[20] Most of the lymphocytes are of T-cell type.[12] Some authors have suggested the use of CD45 in immunohistochemical preparations to quantify the number of lymphocytes, but this seems hardly necessary.[46] In *hypersensitivity myocarditis*, the infiltrate is rich in eosinophils, is predominantly perivascular, and is accompanied by a lesser degree of necrotizing changes.[11,15,22]

The myocyte alterations can take the form of frank necrosis, vacuolization, or disruption and are better appreciated in longitudinal sections. The presence of edema should not be used as a criterion for myocarditis. Fibrosis, if present, should be quantified (mild, moderate, or severe) and qualified (interstitial, endocardial, or replacement).

Diagnostic terms to be used in subsequent biopsies, using the first specimen as a reference point, are *ongoing* or *persistent myocarditis* when both the myocyte damage and the inflammation persist, *resolving* or *healing myocarditis* when these changes are substantially reduced, and *resolved* or *healed myocarditis* when these changes are no longer present.[4] Fenoglio et al.[23] divided their cases of myocarditis into *acute, rapidly progressive,* and *chronic*; they found a good correlation between these types and the clinical course.

The etiology of myocarditis can be viral, bacterial, fungal, parasitic (particularly Chagas' disease and toxoplasmosis, the latter often seen in AIDS patients), caused by a collagen–vascular disease (especially rheumatic fever), drug-induced, radiation-induced, related to Whipple's disease, or an expression of transplant rejection.[3,5,14,38,42,52,56,57] Rare forms of granulomatous myocarditis include tuberculosis and sarcoidosis.[41,44] In many cases of myocarditis the condition remains idiopathic, although the recently introduced molecular diagnostic approach has allowed the identification of viruses (enteroviruses and adenoviruses) in a high proportion of cases of childhood myocarditis.[11a] *Giant cell myocarditis,* a different entity from sarcoidosis, is characterized by multicentric destruction of the cardiac myocytes by cytotoxic T cells and the multinucleated cells that define the entity (Fig. 27.2).[13,35] The latter have the immunohistochemical profile of histiocytes.[51] Another form of myocarditis that has been recently described is characterized by T lymphocytes that express the gamma-delta T-cell receptor and runs a fulminant clinical course.[17]

Drug-induced and radiation-induced cardiomyopathy. The myocardial changes resulting from *Adriamycin* toxicity have been well documented.[31,32] Vacuolization of cardiac myocytes, resulting from dilatation of the sarcotubular system, is the earliest change. This is followed by the appearance of the so-called "adria cell," characterized light microscopically by loss of cross striations and myofilamentous bundles and accompanied by a homogeneous basophilic staining ("myocytolysis"). Ultrastructurally, there is dissociation of sarcomeres and fragmentation and loss of myofilaments. Immunohistochemically, cells with myocytolysis retain reactivity for myoglobin and various enzymes, suggesting that the myocyte is viable and that the change may be reversible.[18] This alteration is in no way specific for Adriamycin toxicity but can be seen in a large variety of diseases.[18] Inflammation is nil or absent, this representing an important differential feature with other myocardial lesions (Figs 27.3 and 27.4).

The changes are rather diffuse but seem to predominate in the subendocardial region. They are dose dependent and are enhanced if radiation therapy has also been used. In the latter instance, the changes just described are superimposed on those resulting from the radiation, which are mainly located in the capillaries.[8] It could be added here that radiation-induced heart disease also includes constrictive pericarditis, myocardial fibrosis, and appreciable valvular and coronary artery lesions.[55]

Cyclophosphamide may produce hemorrhagic necrosis, extensive capillary thrombosis, interstitial hemorrhage and fibrin deposition, and necrosis of myocardial fibers.[7]

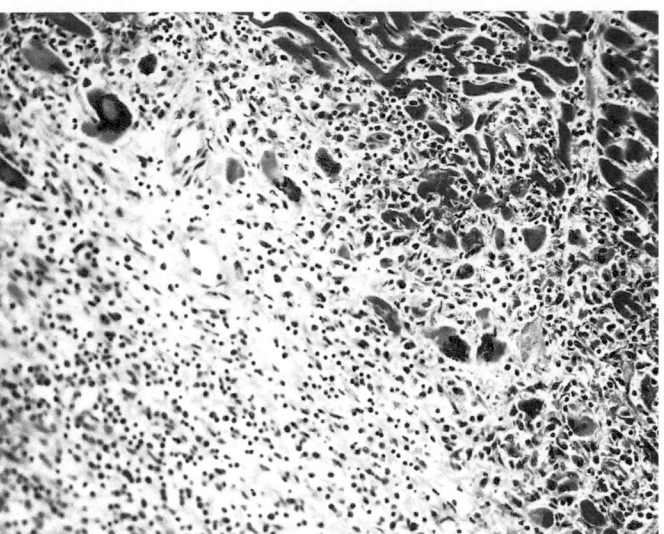

Fig. 27.2 Giant cell myocarditis. Scattered multinucleated giant cells accompanied by lymphocytes are seen in association with loss of myocardial fibers.

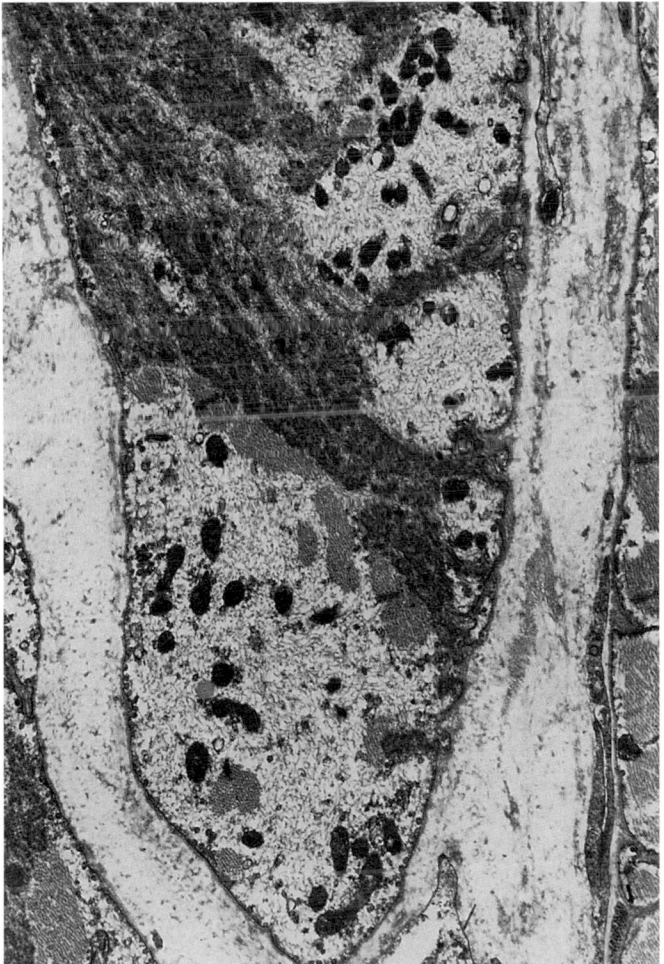

Fig. 27.3 Adriamycin cardiotoxicity. Myocyte in center ("adria cell") shows extensive pale areas of loss of myofibrils and fragmentation of myofilaments. Mitochondria (dark oval structures in same areas) are not qualitatively altered. Remnants of Z bands form a diagonal dense area in center. Note intact myocyte (right edge). (×5600; courtesy of Dr. L.F. Fajardo, Stanford, CA)

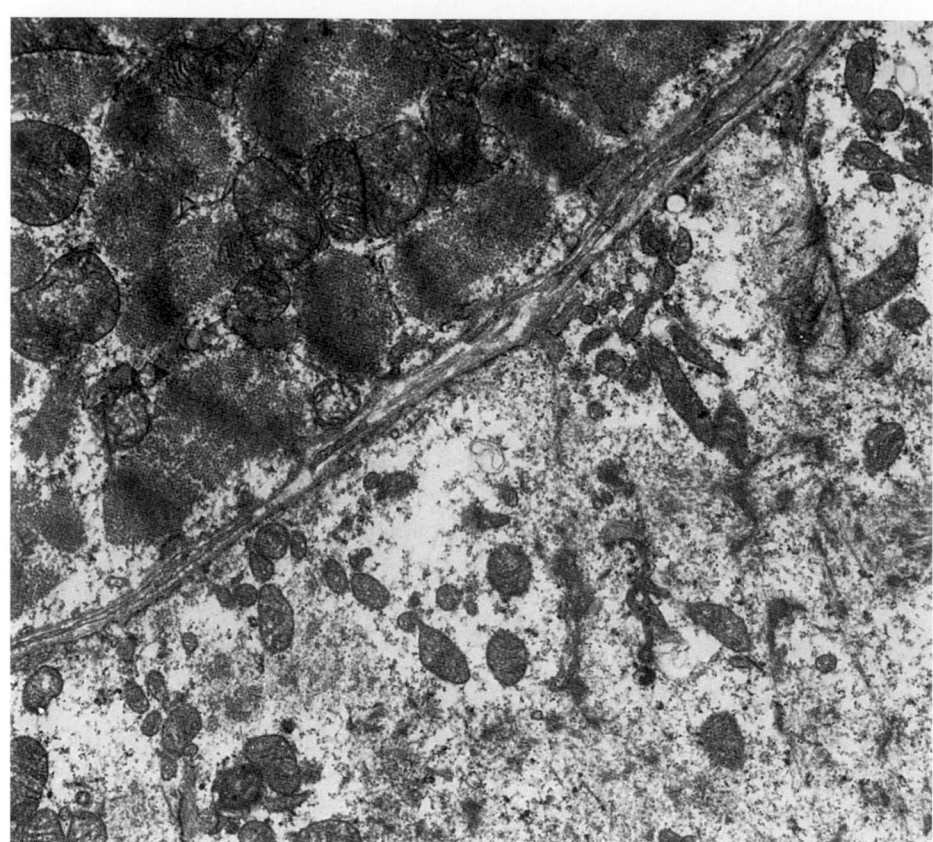

Fig. 27.4 Compare transverse section of normal cardiac myocyte (upper left) with myocyte severely affected by Adriamycin (lower right). There is complete disorganization of sarcomeres and extensive fragmentation of myofilaments. Mitochondria are small (compare with top). Remnants of Z bands are present near right edge. This complete loss of contractile elements in one myocyte, with preservation of adjacent cell, creates sharply defined amphophilic or basophilic areas that characterize "adria cells" in paraffin sections. (×8200; courtesy of Dr. L.F. Fajardo, Stanford, CA)

Tumors. Primary and metastatic tumors of the heart have been diagnosed with endomyocardial biopsy.[26]

Heart transplant

Myocardial biopsy is the most sensitive indicator of rejection.[64,67,69,75,76,79] The criteria used for the diagnosis depend on the immunosuppressive regimen used (i.e., cyclosporine-based or azathioprine-based).[65] The main microscopic sign of rejection is a perivascular and interstitial inflammatory infiltrate, predominantly lymphocytic, accompanied by focal necrosis of myocytes and edema. Clusters of neutrophils may be present around the necrotic myocytes.

One should be careful not to misinterpret a previous biopsy site as indicative of rejection; it appears as a sharply outlined area of necrotic myocytes, sometimes associated with a thrombus and granulation tissue. Rejection should also be distinguished from ischemic changes (Fig. 27.5A) and from *drug-induced hypersensitivity myocarditis*, a self-limited condition that does not cause heart failure and usually resolves without residual injury.[68]

The most widely used grading system of acute rejection episodes is that proposed by Billingham[62]:

Early rejection (reversible) (Fig. 27.5B)
   Endocardial and interstitial edema

Scanty perivascular and endocardial infiltrate of pyroninophilic lymphocytes with prominent nucleoli
Pyroninophilia of endocardial and endothelial cells

Moderate rejection (reversible) (Fig. 27.5C)
   Interstitial, perivascular, and endocardial infiltrate of pyroninophilic lymphocytes with prominent nucleoli
   Early focal myocytolysis

Severe rejection (irreversible or very difficult to reverse)
   Interstitial hemorrhage and infiltrate of pyroninophilic lymphocytes and polymorphonuclear leukocytes, vascular and myocyte necrosis

Resolving rejection (Fig. 27.5D)
   Active fibrosis, residual small lymphocytes (non-pyroninophilic), plasma cells, and hemosiderin deposits

Some modifications to this scheme have been proposed,[69,72,81] but it is not clear whether they represent an improvement over the original scheme.[71] Perhaps the most important of these additions is that of **vascular rejection**, a process that injures the endothelium in the absence of significant intramyocardial lymphocytic infiltration[74] (Fig. 27.5E).

The long-term successfully transplanted heart characteristically shows some degree of hypertrophy and

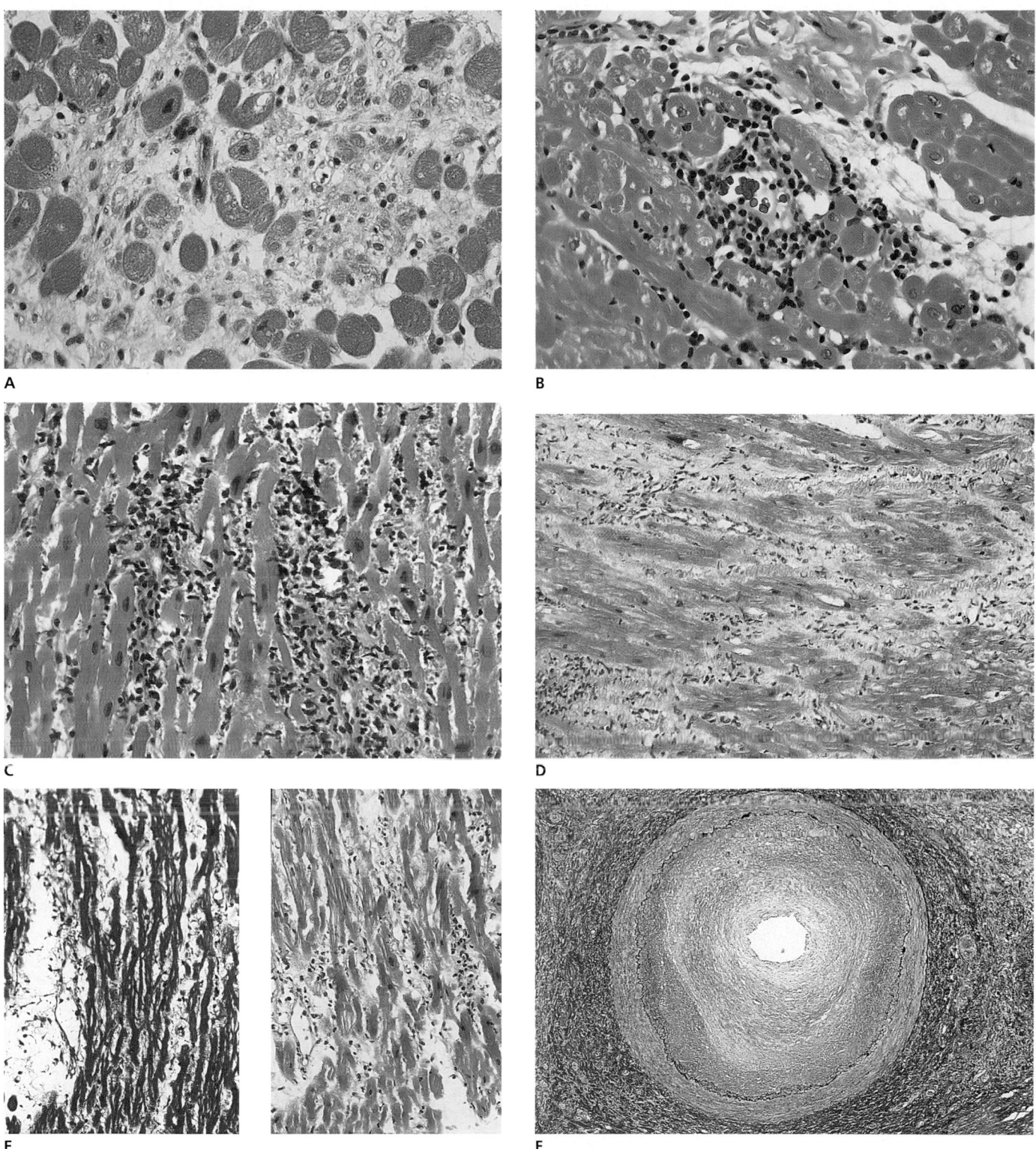

Fig 27.5 Various microscopic appearances of heart transplant. **A,** Endomyocardial biopsy with healing ischemic changes. There is focal dropout of myofibers with sparse infiltrate of mononuclear cells, including pigment-laden histiocytes. **B,** Mild acute cellular rejection. There is patchy perivascular lymphocytic infiltrate with no myocyte injury. **C,** Moderate acute rejection showing myocyte injury or damage. **D,** Resolving rejection. There is a diminished inflammatory infiltrate with interstitial fibrosis after treatment for moderate acute rejection. **E,** Acute vascular rejection. There is a sparse inflammatory infiltrate with dilated small vessels and edema, shown with H&E (left) and trichrome (right). **F,** Chronic rejection (transplant vasculopathy). There is concentric narrowing of epicardial coronary artery by fibromuscular intimal proliferation. Note the preservation of internal elastic lamina (EVG). (Courtesy of Dr. Richard N. Eisen, Greenwich, CT)

fibrosis of muscle fibers.[77,78] Accelerated arteriosclerosis is now the major long-term complication of heart transplantation. Gaudin et al.[66] have shown that ischemic injury to the heart during the peritransplant period—as detected in endomyocardial biopsies—contributes to the development of this complication (Fig. 27.5F).

In about 10% of heart transplant cases, endocardial lymphoid collections develop in which the presence of the Epstein–Barr virus genome can be demonstrated. When intense, this change has been referred to as *EBV-associated post-transplant lymphoproliferative disorder.*[60,70] In addition to the heart, the infiltrate may involve the lung, gastrointestinal tract, lymph nodes, and other sites.[63,73] The proliferating cells are B lymphocytes of host origin, and the process ranges from atypical lymphoid hyperplasia to malignant lymphoma.[63,80] Some of these cases (particularly when located in the lung and gastrointestinal tract) respond to a reduction in immunosuppression.[63]

Cytomegalovirus infection can be diagnosed through the demonstration of viral inclusion bodies, with immunohistochemical or in situ hybridization techniques, or by PCR. The latter method is the most sensitive; however, PCR demonstration of HCMV DNA in otherwise negative endomyocardial specimens is of questionable significance.[61]

Cardiac valves

Surgery to correct major defects of the valves by resection and prosthetic replacement is frequently performed (Fig. 27.6).[84,116] It should be emphasized that the most precise diagnosis will be made from the gross appearance of the valve and that usually the microscopic examination is of little value.[89,102,107,114] Photographic and radiographic examination of the specimen is also indicated. Careful examination of the gross specimen with knowledge of the clinical history often allows a distinction to be made between a rheumatic or congenital origin for a chronic valvulopathy.[103] Microscopically, both show fibrosis, calcification, occasional inflammatory cells, and sometimes foci of dystrophic amyloid deposition.[86]

The major etiologies of valvular disease, the gross morphologic assessment, and the etiologic assessment are shown in the box and Tables 27.1 and 27.2.[104]

Nearly all cases of *mitral valve* stenosis (with or without mitral insufficiency) are acquired and postinflammatory.[87] Among the cases of mitral insufficiency, Olson et al.[98] found that 38% were caused by a floppy valve (myxoid heart disease) and 31% by postinflammatory disease. They observed a floppy valve in 73% of the cases of chordal rupture and in 38% of the cases of infective endocarditis. They further noted that the relative frequency of floppy mitral valve as a cause of insufficiency has increased in recent years. Grossly, the floppy valve shows leaflet thickening and redundancy, leading to the formation of dome-like deformities reaching above the level of the annulus, which appears dilated. The chordae are often thin and attenuated, with fibrosis or fusion at the anchoring sites.[98,114,115] Chordal rupture is seen in over one half of the cases.[93] Microscopically, stromal accumulation of glycosaminoglycans is the distinguishing feature, leading to the appearance of "myxoid degeneration." A lesser degree of accumulation of this material is seen in the neural and conduction system of these patients, pointing to a more general myxoid alteration.[96] Whether this alteration is the result of a genetically determined disease or a degenerative process of nonspecific nature remains controversial. The existence of familial forms of this disorder points toward the former.[91]

Specimens of *aortic valves* removed because of stenosis may show calcification of congenitally bicuspid valves (48%), calcification of a normally tricuspid valve without commissural fusion (so-called "senile type") (28%), calcification of an acquired bicuspid valve (13%), a fibrous (rheumatic) type valve (10%), or calcification of congenitally unicuspid valves (1%).[99,100,112] Exceptionally, cartilaginous metaplasia is encountered.[92] In combined aortic stenosis and insufficiency, the most common changes are those of postinflammatory disease (69%) or calcification of congenitally bicuspid (19%) and unicommissural (6%) valves.[113] Pure aortic insufficiency is not related to calcification but to causes such as aortic root dilatation, bicuspid valve, and others.[88]

Specimens of *pulmonary valve* may be received in the surgical pathology laboratory because of pure pulmonary stenosis (the majority as a component of tetralogy of Fallot), pure pulmonary insufficiency, or combined stenosis and insufficiency. Congenital heart disease accounts for 95% of the cases, and tetralogy of Fallot is the most common form. Bicuspid pulmonary valve is the most common anomaly.[82]

Specimens of *tricuspid valve* can be the result of operations for pure insufficiency (by far the most common), combined stenosis and insufficiency, and pure stenosis

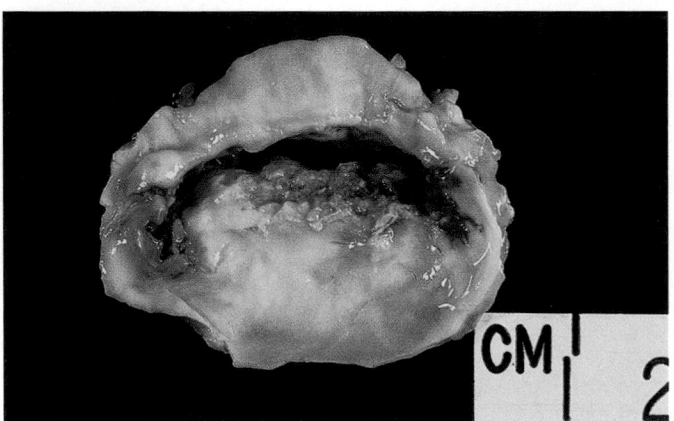

Fig. 27.6 Gross appearance of heavily fibrotic and calcified cardiac valve.

Table 27.1 Gross morphologic assessment of abnormal cardiac valvular function

Pathologic feature	Stenotic valve	Purely regurgitant valve
For all valves		
Valve weight	Increased	Normal or slightly increased or decreased
Fibrous thickening	Diffuse	Diffuse, focal, or none
Calcific deposits	None to heavy	Minimal (if any)
Tissue loss (perforation, indentation)	None	May be present
Vegetations	Minimal	May be present
Commissural fusion	May be present	Minimal (if any)
Annular circumference	Normal	Normal or increased
For aortic valves		
Number of cusps	One to three	Two or three
For mitral (or tricuspid) valves		
Abnormal papillary muscles	No	May be present
Chordae tendineae		
Fusion	Usually present	Absent
Elongation	Absent	May be present
Shortening	Usually present	May be present
Rupture	Absent	May be present

Table 27.2 Etiologic assessment of valvular heart disease

	Senile degeneration	Myxomatous degeneration	Rheumatic	Infective	Secondary
Gross features					
Leaflet/cuspal thickening	0	0/1	1	0	0
Calcification	1	0	0/1	0	0
Commissural chordal fusion	0	0	1	0	0
Leaflet cuspal redundancy	0	1	0	0	0
Leaflet cuspal defects	0	0	0	1	0
Chordal rupture	0	0/1	0	0/1	0
Histologic features					
Preservation of layered architecture	1	1	0	0/1	1
GAG accumulation in spongiosa	0	1	0	0	0/1
Thinned fibrosa	0	1	0	0	0
Neovascularization	0	0	0/1	0/1	0
Superficial fibrosis only	0/1	0/1	0	0/1	0/1

Abbreviations and symbols: 0, absent; 1, present; 0/1, present in some cases; GAG, glycosaminoglycan.
From Schoen FJ. Surgical pathology of removed natural and prosthetic heart valves. Hum Pathol, 1987, **18**: 558–567.

(very rare). The most common causes of insufficiency are postinflammatory diseases, congenital disorders, pulmonary venous hypertension, and infective endocarditis.[94]

An easy system for the identification by the pathologist of the many different types of *artificial heart valve prostheses* in existence in the mid 1970s has been developed.[111] Microscopic study of these prosthetic valves has shown that, following insertion, a neoendocardium develops at the junction with the heart wall, and from there it grows centripetally over the sewing cloth toward the valve lumen.

The pathologic changes that may be found in removed bioprosthetic heart valves include thrombosis, infection, cuspal tears and perforations, fibrous sheathing, calcification, intracuspal hematomas, and several others.[83,90,101,106,108,109] Mechanical valves may show thrombosis, infection, and various alterations associated with the valve design and the composition of the various elements.[105,110] Cuspal retraction without stenosis can also occur, leading to wide-open regurgitation.[97]

At the time of the correction of a mitral stenosis, the surgeon may perform a biopsy of the *atrial appendage*. These appendages are always abnormal, showing hypertrophy of the muscle and various other alterations. About one half of them show Aschoff nodules.[85] These

Major etiologies of acquired mitral and aortic valve disease
Mitral valve disease
Mitral stenosis
Postinflammatory scarring (rheumatic)
Calcification of mitral annulus
Mitral regurgitation
Abnormalities of leaflets and commissures
Postinflammatory scarring (rheumatic)
Infective endocarditis
Floppy mitral valve
Abnormalities of mitral apparatus
Rupture of papillary muscle
Papillary muscle dysfunction (fibrosis or ischemia)
Rupture of chordae tendineae
Left ventricular enlargement (e.g., congestive cardiomyopathy)
Calcification of mitral annulus
Aortic valve disease
Aortic stenosis
Calcification of congenitally deformed valve
Senile calcific aortic stenosis
Postinflammatory scarring (rheumatic)
Aortic regurgitation
Abnormalities of cusps and commissures
Postinflammatory scarring (rheumatic)
Infective endocarditis
Aortic disease
Syphilitic aortitis
Ankylosing spondylitis
Rheumatoid arthritis
Marfan's syndrome
Aortic dissection
Trauma

are formed by collections of plump cells arranged in a granuloma-like fashion. The cells are positive for vimentin and negative for actin and desmin, suggesting a mesenchymal but not myocardial derivation.[95] The presence of these nodules does not correlate with the postoperative course or with clinical evidence of activity of the rheumatic process.

Coronary artery bypass

A vast number of coronary artery bypass operations have been done during the past 30 years using a segment of saphenous vein to join the aorta to a segment of the coronary artery distal to the obstruction. The patency rate of these grafts is over 80% after 5 years. Graft failure necessitating reoperation may result from the intimal fibrous hyperplasia that develops after the first month in all grafts becoming occlusive or from atherosclerosis in older grafts.[120] This atherosclerosis is typically concentric, diffuse, without a fibrous cap, with numerous foamy and inflammatory cells (including multinucleated giant forms), and associated with erosion of the media.[118] Secondary thrombosis is common.[117,119]

Coarctation of aorta

Coarctation of aorta is divided into infantile (diffuse, preductal) and adult (localized, postductal) types (Figs 27.7 and 27.8).

In the first type, the coarctated segment lies proximal to the ductus arteriosus. In the second type, which is by far the most common, the short, narrowed segment of the aorta is at the level of the aortic insertion of the ductus or just distal to it. If resection is not done, about 60% of patients die before 40 years of age of aortic rupture,

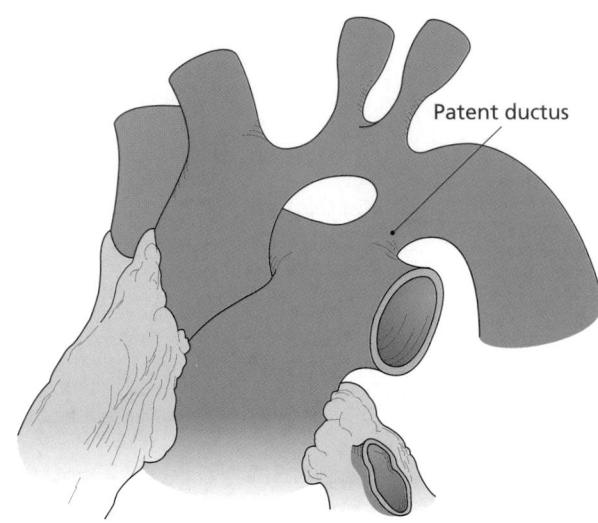

Fig. 27.7 Infantile (diffuse) type of coarctation of aorta. (From Burford TH. Symposium on clinical surgery. Coarctation of aorta and its treatment. Surg Clin North Am 1950, **30**: 1249–1258)

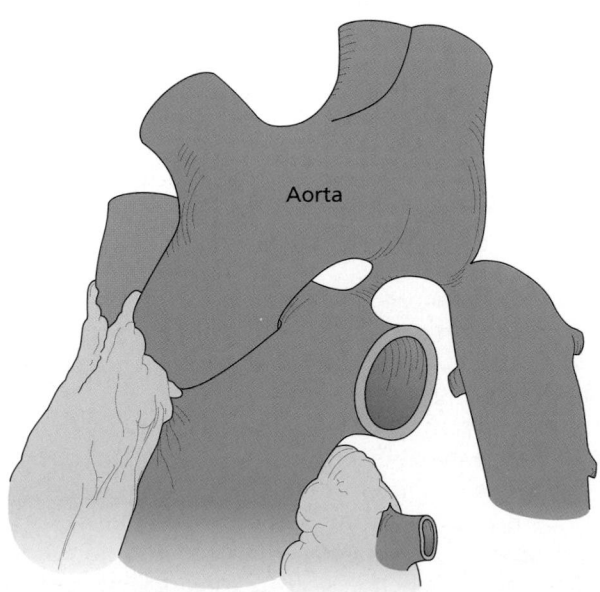

Fig. 27.8 Adult (localized) type of coarctation of aorta. (From Burford TH. Symposium on clinical surgery. Coarctation of aorta and its treatment. Surg Clin North Am 1950, **30**: 1249–1258)

endocarditis, hypertension, or congestive failure.[122] With present techniques, the operative risk is small, and the long-term results are excellent.[123,124] The operation, which consists in the removal of the coarctation with end-to-end anastomosis, is best done when the patient is between 5 and 7 years of age.[121,125]

Grossly, the vessel is narrowed at the point of insertion of the ligamentum arteriosum. On opening the aorta, a diaphragm-like structure lies across the lumen, through which there is an aperture usually 1 mm or less in diameter. Often there is localized subintimal thickening, and beneath this the media is distorted and thickened.

Operations for coarctation of the aorta are more difficult in older patients because of advanced arteriosclerotic changes in the aorta.

Cardiac tumors

Myxoma

Myxomas constitute approximately 50% of primary tumors of the heart. They occur in two settings: sporadic and familial.[130] The sporadic tumor occurs in middle-aged women (76%), usually in the left atrium (86%), nearly always as a single tumor, and without associated conditions. The familial variety is a disorder of young people, slightly more frequent in men, less commonly located in the left atrium (62%), multicentric in one third of the cases, and associated in 20% of the patients with extracardiac abnormalities. These include cutaneous and labial lentiginosis, eyelid and cutaneous myxomas, myxoid mammary fibroadenomas (often multiple and bilateral), adrenocortical nodular dysplasia associated with Cushing's syndrome, and large cell calcifying Sertoli cell tumor of the testis.[130] This genetically determined complex is known as *Carney's syndrome.*

Left-sided cardiac myxomas may present with signs of mitral stenosis or insufficiency, and right-sided tumors with dyspnea, syncope, distention of neck veins, and other symptoms. They may also lead to multiple emboli in the systemic or pulmonary circulation, depending on their location.[148] Myocardial, pulmonary, or cerebral infarcts may thus supervene. Some cases have resulted in polycythemia or hypergammaglobulinemia. A heart murmur that changes with time and position is a typical sign but is found in less than one half of the patients. The diagnosis can be established by echocardiography, gated radionuclide blood-pool scan, or cardiac catheterization.[146,156] Occasionally, the diagnosis is made by histologic examination of an embolus removed at operation.

Grossly, myxomas are soft, polypoid, pale, lobulated masses often attached by a stalk to the septum near the foramen ovale. Areas of hemorrhage may be present (Fig. 27.9). A papillary configuration may be apparent, especially if the specimen is examined under water. Calcification may occur, and this seems to be more com-mon in those located in the right atrium. Microscopically, round, polygonal, or stellate cells are seen surrounded by abundant loose stroma rich in acid mucopolysaccharides (Figs 27.10 and 27.11). Some of these cells form solid cords and vascular channels, sometimes continuous with the endocardial lining.[136] Mitoses, pleomorphism, or necrosis is absent or minimal. Other microscopic variations include surface thrombosis, Gamna–Gandy bodies, ossification ("petrified" myxoma), occurrence of cartilaginous tissue, extramedullary hematopoiesis, and presence of thymic and foregut remnants.[129,139,143,159] The latter may be somehow related to the most peculiar change that cardiac myxoma can exhibit, i.e., the presence of well-developed mucin-producing glands[137] (Fig. 27.12). This phenomenon, which has been referred to as *glandular myxoma,* should not be confused with metastatic adenocarcinoma.

The controversy that existed as to whether cardiac myxoma is a true neoplasm or an expression of exuberant thrombus formation[151] has been laid to rest.

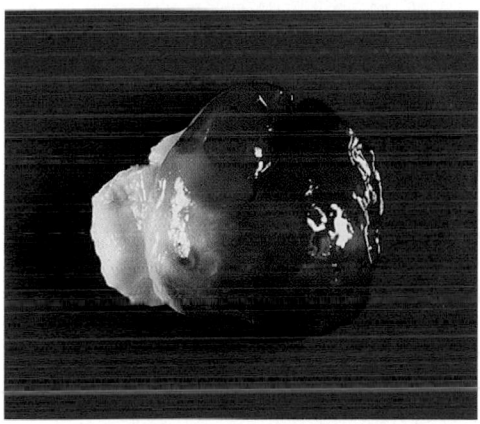

Fig. 27.9 Gross appearance of cardiac myxoma. The lesion has a polypoid shape and a hemorrhagic appearance.

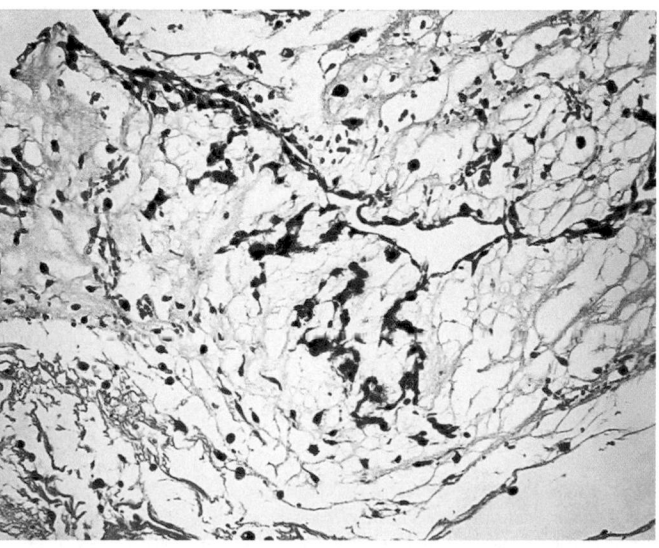

Fig. 27.10 Cardiac myxoma showing tumor cells concentrating beneath the surface, surrounded by a highly myxoid stroma.

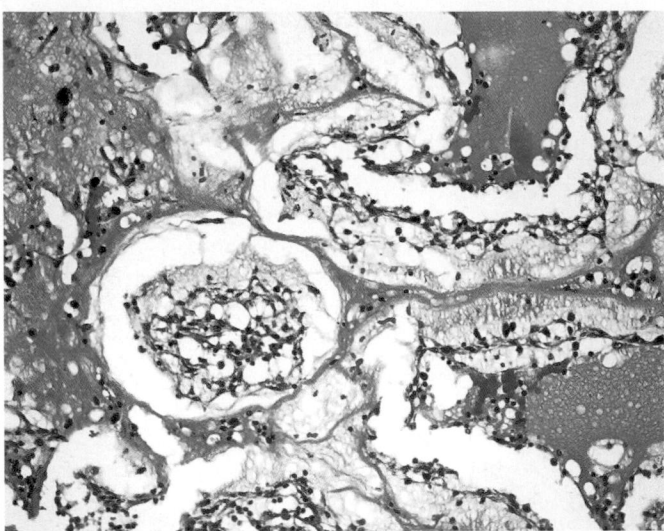

Fig. 27.11 Cardiac myxoma. The concentric arrangement of tumor cells around endocardium-lined spaces is characteristic of the entity.

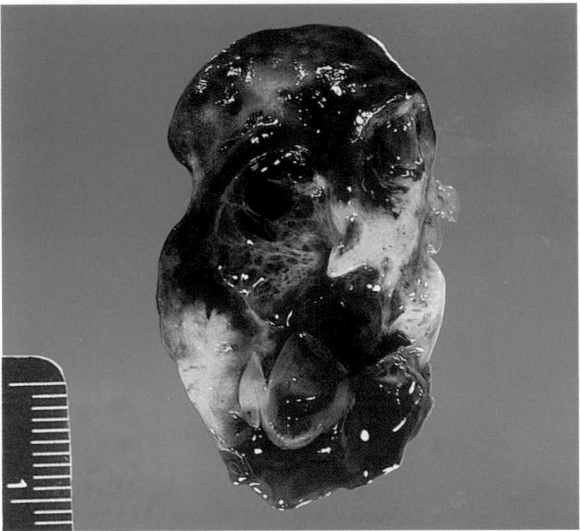

A

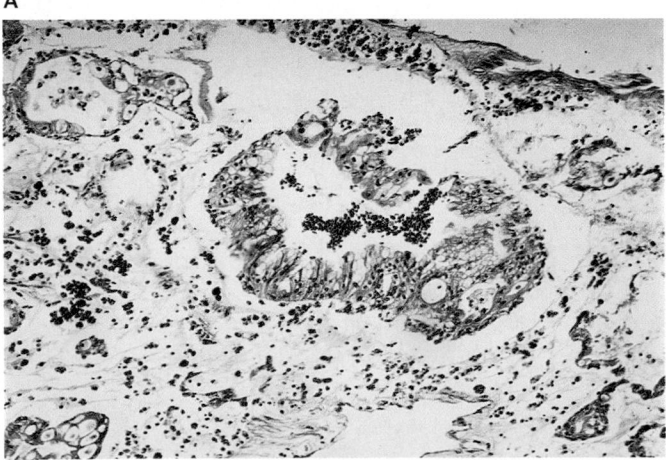

B

Fig. 27.12 Glandular myxoma. **A,** Gross appearance. Note the myxoid quality and extensive hemorrhage. **B,** Microscopic appearance. The epithelium is tall columnar and contains intracytoplasmic mucin. This rare type of myxoma should not be confused with metastatic adenocarcinoma.

Convincing evidence in favor of a neoplastic nature is provided by the existence of: (1) occasional aggressive examples with invasion of the chest wall or distant metastases[147,150,152,155]; (2) cases with malignant transformation at the morphologic level[140]; (3) cases with aneuploid DNA levels[154]; and (4) cases with chromosomal aberrations.[132] An interesting twist concerning the nature of cardiac myxoma is the recent suggestion of a possible pathogenetic role of herpes simplex virus type 1 infection.[142a]

The cell of origin has also been in dispute. Ultrastructural examinations have suggested that myxomas arise from multipotential mesenchymal cells.[134,135] Immunohistochemically, some endothelial markers—such as CD31 and CD34—are widely present, whereas others—such as factor VIII and Ulex—are more erratic in their expression pattern.[131,133,139,142,144] This has been taken to indicate a range in the status of maturation of mesenchymal cells toward endothelial (endocardial) cells.[133] In our experience, factor VIII staining is often present but usually restricted to cells lining invaginations rather than those embedded in the stroma. Positive staining has also been reported for vimentin, actin, desmin, smooth muscle myosin, α_1-antitrypsin, and α_1-antichymotrypsin.[128,138,142,157] More recently, it has been found that cardiac myxomas (in contrast to myxomas of jaw) stain consistently for calretinin; this somewhat unexpected result has led to the odd suggestion that the tumor may derive from endocardial sensory nerve tissue.[158] Also of interest is the finding that cardiac myxoma expresses several cardiomyocyte-specific transcription factors, thus suggesting the presence of cardiomyogenic differentiation.[141] The areas of glandular differentiation are positive for CEA, EMA, and keratin.[137,139,153] There may also be a minor neuroendocrine component.[146a] This combination of findings is in keeping with the interpretation that myxomas arise from mesenchymal cells with the capacity for multidirectional differentiation.[138,157] A purported origin of cardiac myxoma from subendothelial vasoformative reserve cells in the fossa ovalis known as Prichard's structures is not supported by the immunohistochemical profile.[126]

In addition to the neoplastic component, cardiac myxomas contain numerous reactive cells of histiocytic/dendritic type, including factor XIIIa-positive cells.[127]

Surgical excision of the ordinary myxoma is often curative.[145] Several instances of local recurrence have been reported in the past; with the routine performance of partial atrial septectomy, together with the excision of the tumor, they have become very rare.[149]

Other benign tumors and tumorlike conditions

Rhabdomyoma and **rhabdomyomatosis** are mostly seen during the first decade of life, and many are congenital.[169,199] However, they can also present in adult patients.[165a] Some of the patients have tuberous sclerosis, and others suffer from congenital heart disease.[168]

Grossly, rhabdomyomas present as one or more firm, white, well-circumscribed nodules. Microscopically, the most distinctive feature is the presence of "spider cells," so named because of their radial cytoplasmic extensions. Immunohistochemically, they show reactivity for myoglobin, actin, desmin, vimentin, and sometimes HMB-45.[168,207] The latter is of interest because of the link of rhabdomyoma with tuberous sclerosis and the morphologic similarities with angiomyolipoma, another HMB-45-positive lesion.[207] Rarely, cardiac rhabdomyomas in adults have a morphologic appearance similar to that of the extracardiac type of this tumor.[208]

Hamartoma of mature cardiac myocytes resembles microscopically hypertrophic cardiomyopathy but is a localized process characterized by myofiber disarray, focal scarring, and intramural coronary thickening. The usual but not exclusive location of this lesion is the left ventricle.[167,200]

Calcified amorphous tumor of the heart (cardiac CAT) is the name proposed for an endocardially based intracavitary cardiac mass characterized microscopically by nodular deposition of calcium in a background of degenerating blood cell elements and chronic inflammation.[195] The clinical course is benign. The pathogenesis is obscure, but an origin from mural thrombi has been suggested.[195]

Mesothelial/monocytic incidental cardiac excrescences ("cardiac MICE") are incidental microscopic findings at the time of cardiac surgery (usually for valvular disease) or in an endomyocardial biopsy. They may be found attached to the endocardium, free-floating in the pericardial cavity, or even inside an aortic dissecting aneurysm.[164,190,205] Ultrastructural and immunohisto-chemical studies have shown that the lesion is composed of an admixture of keratin-positive mesothelial cells and KP-1-positive histiocytes[190] (Fig. 27.13). Microscopically, the mesothelial cells form strips, tubular and micropapillary formations surrounded by the smaller histiocytes. Huge round vacuoles are often present. Except for the latter, the appearance is very similar to that of nodular mesothelial hyperplasia as seen in hernia sacs.[196]

The process is clearly benign, non-neoplastic, and clinically of no significance. The pathogenesis remains unclear. Ingrowth of pericardial cells along a perforation tract has been suggested.[190,205] Others have postulated an artifact produced by suctioning of the pericardial cavity during cardiac surgery,[171,206] a theory that we find difficult to accept. It has also been suggested that the process is mediated by adhesion molecules.[201] Their main practical importance resides in the fact that a pathologist unaware of their existence may mistake them for a metastatic carcinoma or some other neoplasm. We have seen a remarkable case in which a lesion of cardiac MICE contained within it a minute focus of metastatic adenocarcinoma.[163]

Cystic tumor of the atrioventricular nodal region was regarded as a mesothelioma for many years, but there is now conclusive evidence that it represents a developmental abnormality of epithelial nature and endodermal origin.[161,173,179] It may be associated with other congenital anomalies.[165] Because of its crucial location, it may result in complete heart block. All reported cases have been found at autopsy.

Microscopically, the lesion consists of ductular structures, cysts, and solid nests of epithelial-like cells, which on electron microscopy show desmosomes and microvilli

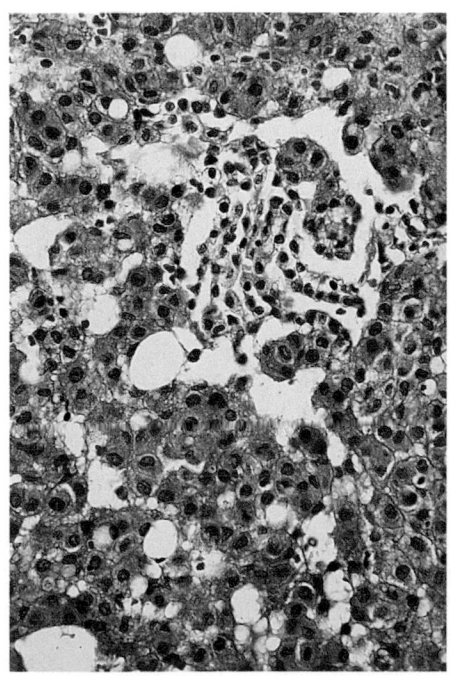
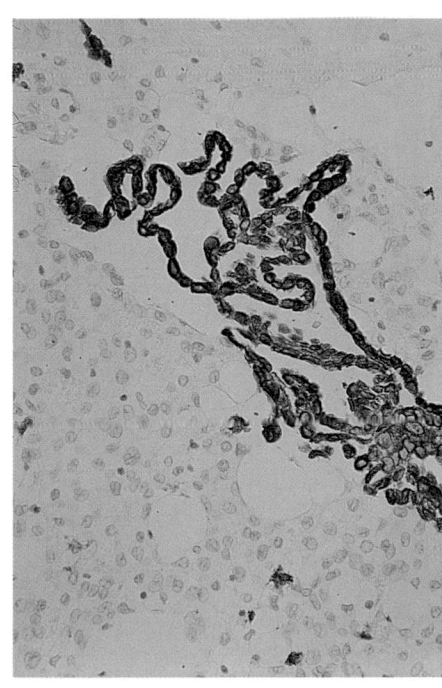

Fig. 27.13 So-called "cardiac MICE." **A,** This process is composed of an admixture of plump histiocytes and ribbons of small cuboidal mesothelial cells. **B,** The immunostain for keratin highlights the mesothelial cell component, which is surrounded by the negative histiocytes and other mononuclear cells.

A   B

(Fig. 27.14).[165,177] Immunohistochemically, the cells are reactive for keratin, CEA, and B72.3 but not for factor VIII, calretinin, WT-1, or thrombomodulin.[162,165,173,189] It should be pointed out that not all nodular lesions of the atrioventricular node are examples of this entity; some are of vascular or neural nature.[182,183]

Adenomatoid tumor analogous to its more common counterpart in the male and female genital system has been reported in the heart. Here too the lesion is of mesothelial nature (as opposed to the tumor described in the preceding paragraph).[193]

Papillary fibroelastoma (fibroelastic hamartoma, fibroma, papilloma, papillary fibroblastoma) is a small papillary growth that usually occurs on the surface of the valves but may also be seen in other endocardial locations[160] (Fig. 27.15A). It is nearly always an incidental finding at surgery or autopsy[181] and is formed microscopically by a lining of hyperplastic endocardial cells covering a core of hyalinized hypocellular stroma[175,198] (Fig. 27.15B). It probably represents the end stage of the organization of a mural thrombus rather than a true neoplasm, as supported by the fact that they are seen with increased frequency after cardiac surgery.[174,187a]

Paraganglioma can present as a primary intracardiac neoplasm. The left atrium is the most common location; hypertension and elevated urine catecholamine levels are often present, in which case the term extra-adrenal pheochromocytoma has been used. The microscopic, ultrastructural, and immunohistochemical features are similar to those of paraganglioma elsewhere, including an occasional pigmented example[184,191] (see Chapter 16).

Other primary tumors of the heart include *granular cell tumor* (not to be mistaken for rhabdomyoma),[176] *hemangioma*[203] (including the epithelioid or histiocytoid variety[172,187]), *lymphangioma, lipoma*[204] (to be distinguished from lipomatous hypertrophy of the atrial septum[166]), *angiolipoma*,[186] *schwannoma*,[192] *ganglioneuroma*,[178,194] and *benign teratoma*.[202]

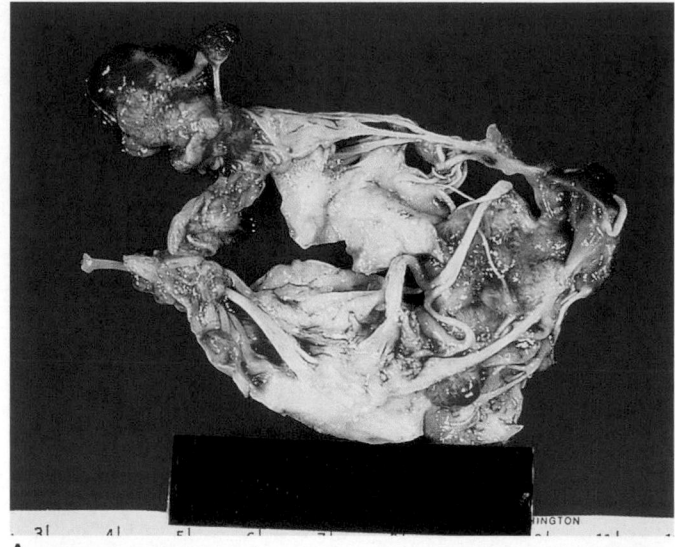

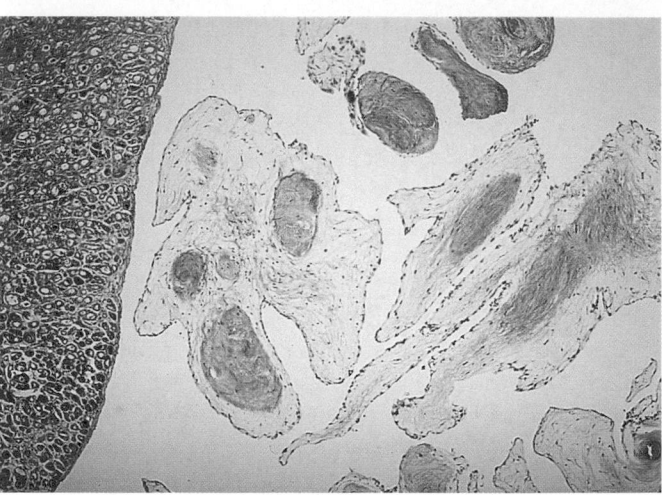

B

Fig. 27.15 So-called "papillary elastofibroma." **A**, Gross appearance. **B**, Low-power microscopic appearance. Notice the densely hyalinized central core and the flat endocardial lining.

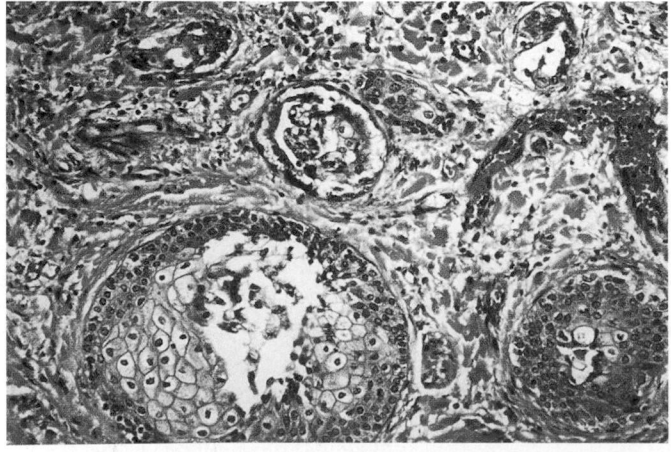

Fig. 27.14 So-called "cystic tumor" of the atrioventricular nodal region. In this case the lining of the cysts had a definite squamoid quality.

Other non-neoplastic conditions reported in the heart are *ectopic thyroid*,[185] *extramedullary hematopoiesis*,[180] and *plasma cell granuloma* (inflammatory pseudotumor).[170,197] As in other sites, the current tendency is to regard the latter entity as a true neoplasm and to rename it inflammatory myofibroblastic tumor.[188]

Primary malignant tumors

Sarcomas of the heart are exceptionally rare.[210,216,227] Some of them are highly pleomorphic and unclassifiable even with the help of ultrastructural and immunohistochemical techniques. Of those that can be placed into a specific category, *angiosarcoma* is probably the most common.[219,222] It is typically located in the atrium, where it presents as a large mass (Fig. 27.16). Its microscopic appearance may be similar to that of angiosarcoma elsewhere (see Chapter 25), but the majority are poorly

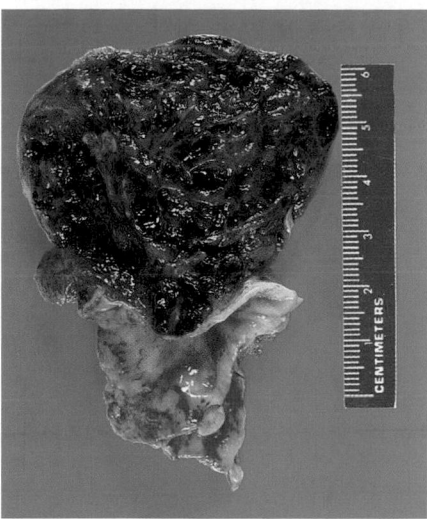

Fig. 27.16 Gross appearance of a large angiosarcoma of the heart.

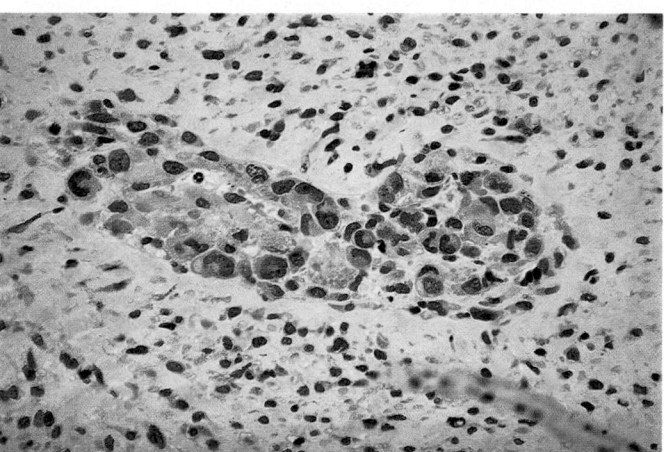

Fig. 27.18 High-grade sarcoma of heart, not further classifiable. It is not unusual for these tumors to show a ring of epithelioid large tumor cells in a perivascular location.

differentiated tumors. Ultrastructural and immunohisto-chemical features of endothelial differentiation can be demonstrated in some of the cases.[236] *Kaposi's sarcoma* can involve the heart in its generalized form, an event that seems to be more common in the AIDS setting. The second most common category of sarcoma is that of *myosarcoma*, either *leiomyosarcoma* or *rhabdomyosarcoma* (particularly the latter).[209] The leiomyosarcomas can have spindle cell, epithelioid, or myxoid features.[233,234] Some of them contain scattered osteoclast-like multinucleated giant cells, like those more commonly seen in the uterine corpus.[224] Other types described include *malignant fibrous histiocytoma*,[228,231] *osteosarcoma*,[211,237] *fibrosarcoma, liposarcoma, synovial sarcoma*[223,230] (Fig. 27.17), Ewing's sarcoma/PNET,[213] and *malignant peripheral nerve sheath tumor*.[232] It is possible that some of the sarcomas with prominent myxoid features represent the malignant

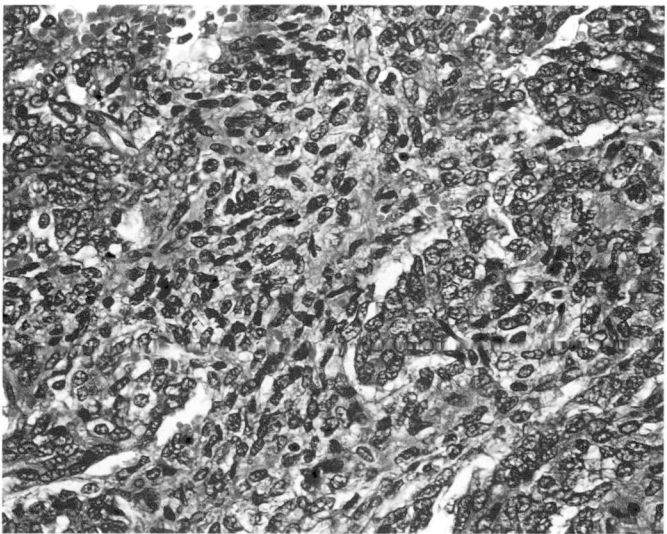

Fig. 27.17 Primary synovial sarcoma of heart showing typical biphasic appearance.

counterpart of cardiac myxoma.[225] A feature which, although not specific, is seen often in high-grade sarcomas of the heart and large vessel, is the presence of plump epithelioid cells in a perivascular location (Fig. 27.18). All of these tumor types occur almost always in adults, but a handful of pediatric cases are on record, including examples of *rhabdoid tumor*.[235]

Most patients with primary heart sarcomas present with intractable congestive heart failure, arrhythmias, or signs of superior vena cava obstruction. In rare cases, a metastatic lesion is the first manifestation of the disease.[218] It has been pointed out that malignant tumors are more frequently found in the right side of the heart and that benign neoplasms are more common on the left side.[209]

Malignant lymphoma presenting as a primary heart tumor is very rare.[212,215] Most of the reported cases have been of diffuse large cell type. AIDS and other immunocompromised patients are at an increased risk,[214,217,220] but these tumors also occur in immunocompetent individuals.[212a] Secondary cardiac involvement by advanced malignant lymphoma or leukemia is a relatively common event, although it is rarely detected ante mortem; in a few instances, it constitutes the immediate cause of death.[229] The lymphoproliferative lesion associated with EBV seen in cardiac transplant recipients is discussed on page 2422. Suffice it to say here that the majority of the lymphomas developing in the transplanted heart are of B-cell type with an important reactive T-cell component.[226] It should also be mentioned that the usual type of malignant lymphoma of the heart shows no association with EBV.[221]

Metastatic tumors

Involvement of the heart by metastatic carcinoma or by generalized malignant lymphoma is a more common event than primary malignancy of this organ, by a factor of 30 to 1[240,245]; however, it is rarely seen as a biopsy or

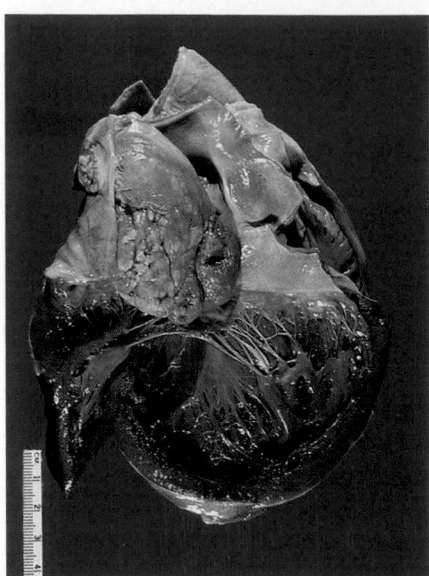

Fig. 27.19 Large metastatic carcinoma in left atrium that was continuous with tumor in left pulmonary vein. This mass simulated an atrial myxoma by echocardiography. The primary tumor was a mucoepidermoid carcinoma of left submaxillary gland.

surgical specimen unless the disease affects the pericardium preferentially.[239,244] Any portion of the heart can be involved, including the conducting system, the latter exceptionally resulting in complete cardiac block.[234a]

In the majority of the carcinomas metastatic to the heart, the primary tumor is in the thoracic cavity or contiguous areas, and the tumor reaches the heart by metastasizing to the mediastinal lymph nodes and from there extending in a retrograde fashion to the cardiac lymph vessels.[241] Malignant tumors with a marked tendency to spread to the heart by the hematogenous route are malignant melanoma; carcinomas of kidney, lung, and breast; choriocarcinomas; and childhood rhabdomyosarcoma.[238,243] Exceptionally, the metastatic heart lesion presents as an isolated nodule, amenable to surgical therapy (Fig. 27.19).[242]

Pericardium

Pericardial (coelomic) cysts are discussed together with all other mediastinal cysts in Chapter 9.

Other congenital abnormalities are extremely rare; they include the presence of ectopic tissue such as liver.[255]

Pericarditis is of importance to the surgical pathologist for several reasons. A diagnosis of tuberculous pericarditis or sarcoidosis can be made from a pericardial open biopsy. Acute nonspecific pericarditis[258] and purulent pericarditis[256] are rarely biopsied, but the former may be troublesome because of the sometimes extreme degree of mesothelial hyperplasia that accompanies it and that can simulate malignancy. Chronic pericarditis is often accompanied by fibrosis and calcification, which may

lead to constriction (so-called "constrictive pericarditis"). This may result from tuberculosis and other infections, collagen–vascular diseases, malignant tumors, trauma, surgery, radiation therapy, or chemotherapy.[263,265] Chronic pericarditis and pericardial constriction are the most common manifestations of radiation damage to the heart.[253,265,266] The interval between the radiation and the onset of the disease is usually between 50 and 125 months. Pathologic examination usually shows only dense fibrosis with deposits of calcium and a scanty inflammatory infiltrate. Residual granulomas may be found in the cases of tuberculous etiology, and atypical fibroblasts in those related to radiation.

Castleman's disease located within the pericardial sac has been described.[267]

Multilocular mesothelial inclusion cyst of the pericardium is morphologically and probably pathogenetically equivalent to the condition that bears the same name in the peritoneal cavity. Although originally designated as benign multicystic mesothelioma, it probably represents a reactive change secondary to chronic irritation.[250]

Mesotheliomas of the pericardium occur, but their frequency is much less than that for similar tumors in the pleura or peritoneum. They have been reported in the setting of tuberous sclerosis[259] and may present as a single well-circumscribed mass, as multiple tumors, or as a diffuse growth encasing the heart. Sometimes, they coexist with a pleural mesothelioma. Microscopically, the appearance varies from epithelial to spindle shaped, with a frequent admixture of these elements. Pure spindle-cell (sarcomatoid) mesotheliomas are particularly unusual.[252] As in the pleura, acid mucopolysaccharides are often produced by the tumor cells. The differential diagnosis is with mesothelial hyperplasia and metastatic carcinoma. Demonstration of continuity between the tumor and the mesothelial lining cells favors a mesothelial nature for the proliferation. Because of the extreme rarity of pericardial mesotheliomas and the fact that reactive mesothelial proliferation can be particularly florid in the pericardium, one should be very cautious in making a diagnosis of malignancy under these circumstances.

Most mesotheliomas of the pericardium occur in adults and are diffuse and malignant. They may locally infiltrate the superficial myocardium and even metastasize to the mediastinal lymph nodes and lungs.[251] Localized mesotheliomas are amenable to surgical excision.[261]

Other primary tumors of the pericardium are exceptionally rare. One such group is represented by *germ cell tumors*: both mature teratoma and yolk sac tumor (endodermal sac tumor) have been reported in this location.[249,260,262] *Angiosarcoma* of pericardium may coat the pericardium in a diffuse fashion, thus simulating the pattern of growth of mesothelioma[264]; some of these have been radiation induced.[254]

Myolipoma of the pericardium containing estrogen receptors has also been reported.[248]

Metastatic carcinoma to the pericardium usually originates in the lung in the form of direct extension or lymphatic permeation. It may result in constrictive "pericarditis" as a result of the associated intense desmoplastic reaction (see p. 2430). Other tumors that commonly give rise to pericardial metastases are breast carcinoma, malignant melanoma, and malignant lymphoma.[246,257] Cytology is the most important technique for the evaluation of malignant pericardial effusions. Pericardial biopsy may be necessary in some cases to confirm the diagnosis. The sensitivity of DNA ploidy is too low to be of practical utility.[247]

References

Introduction

1 Castaneda AR. Cardiac surgery of the neonate and infant. Philadelphia, 1994, W.B. Saunders.
2 Marks C. Fundamentals of cardiac surgery. London, 1993, Chapman & Hall.

Normal anatomy

2a Billingham MS. Normal Heart. In Sternberg S (ed): Histology for pathologists, ed. 2. Philadelphia, 1997, Lippincott-Raven Publishers, pp. 745–762.

Myocardial biopsy

3 Anderson DW, Virmani R. Emerging patterns of heart disease in human immunodeficiency virus infection. Hum Pathol 1990, **21**: 253–259.
4 Aretz HT. Myocarditis. The Dallas criteria. Hum Pathol 1987, **18**: 619–624.
5 Atkinson JB, Connor DH, Robinowitz M, McAllister HA, Virmani R. Cardiac fungal infections. Review of autopsy finding in 60 patients. Hum Pathol 1984, **15**: 935–942.
6 Atkinson JB, Virmani R. Congestive heart failure due to coronary artery disease without myocardial infarction. Clinicopathologic description of an unusual cardiomyopathy. Hum Pathol 1989, **20**: 1155–1162.
7 Billingham ME. Some recent advances in cardiac pathology. Hum Pathol 1979, **10**: 367–386.
8 Billingham ME, Bristow MR, Glatstein E, Mason JW, Masek MA, Daniels JR. Adriamycin cardiotoxicity. Endomyocardial biopsy evidence of enhancement by irradiation. Am J Surg Pathol 1977, **1**: 17–23.
9 Buja LM, Roberts WC. Iron in the heart, etiology and clinical significance. Am J Med 1971, **51**: 209–221.
10 Burke AP, Farb A, Robinowitz M, Virmani R. Serial sectioning and multiple level examination of endomyocardial biopsies for the diagnosis of myocarditis. Mod Pathol 1991, **4**: 690–693.
11 Burke AP, Saenger J, Mullick F, Virmani R. Hypersensitivity myocarditis. Arch Pathol Lab Med 1991, **115**: 764–769.
11a Calabrese F, Rigo E, Milanesi O, Boffa GM, Angelini A, Valente M, Thiene G. Molecular diagnosis of myocarditis and dilated cardiomyopathy in children: clinicopathologic features and prognostic implications. Diagn Mol Pathol 2002, **11**: 212–221.
12 Chow LH, Ye Y, Linder J, McManus BM. Phenotypic analysis of infiltrating cells in human myocarditis. An immunohistochemical study in paraffin-embedded tissue. Arch Pathol Lab Med 1989, **113**: 1357–1362.

13 Cooper LT Jr, Berry GJ, Shabetai R, for the Multicenter Giant Cell Myocarditis Study Group Investigators. Idiopathic giant-cell myocarditis—natural history and treatment. N Engl J Med 1997, **336**: 1860–1866.
14 d'Amati G, Di Gioia CR, Gallo P. Pathological findings of HIV-associated cardiovascular disease. Ann N Y Acad Sci 2001, **946**: 23–45.
15 Darcy T, Mullick F, Schell L, Virmani R. Distinguishing features of myocarditis. Hypersensitivity vs. idiopathic myocarditis (abstract). Lab Invest 1988, **58**: 21A.
16 Davies MJ, McKenna WJ. Hypertrophic cardiomyopathy. Pathology and pathogenesis. Histopathology 1995, **26**: 493–500.
17 Eck M, Greiner A, Kandolf R, Schumausser B, Marx A, Müller-Hermelink HK. Active fulminant myocarditis characterized by T-lymphocytes expressing the gamma-delta T-cell receptor: a new disease entity? Am J Surg Pathol 1997, **21**: 1109–1112.
18 Edwalds GM, Said JW, Block MI, Herscher LL, Siegel RJ, Fishbein MC. Myocytolysis (vacuolar degeneration) of myocardium. Immunohistochemical evidence of viability. Hum Pathol 1984, **15**: 753–756.
19 Edwards WD. Cardiomyopathies. Hum Pathol 1987, **18**: 625–635.
20 Edwards WD, Holmes DR Jr, Reeder GS. Diagnosis of active lymphocytic myocarditis by endomyocardial biopsy. Quantitative criteria for light microscopy. Mayo Clin Proc 1982, **57**: 419–425.
21 Fenoglio JJ, Marboe CC. Endomyocardial biopsy. An overview. Hum Pathol 1987, **18**: 609–612.
22 Fenoglio JJ Jr, McAllister HA Jr, Mullick FG. Drug related myocarditis. I. Hypersensitivity myocarditis. Hum Pathol 1981, **12**: 900–907.
23 Fenoglio JJ Jr, Ursell PC, Kellogg CF, Drusin RE, Weiss MB. Diagnosis and classification of myocarditis by endomyocardial biopsy. N Engl J Med 1983, **308**: 12–18.
24 Ferrans VJ, Morrow AG, Roberts WC. Myocardial ultrastructure in idiopathic hypertrophic subaortic stenosis. A study of operatively excised left ventricular outflow tract muscle in 14 patients. Circulation 1972, **45**: 769–792.
25 Ferrans VJ, Roberts WC. Myocardial biopsy. A useful diagnostic procedure or only a research tool? Am J Cardiol 1978, **41**: 965–967.
26 Flipse TR, Tazelaar HD, Holmes DR Jr. Diagnosis of malignant cardiac disease by endomyocardial biopsy. Mayo Clin Proc 1990, **65**: 1415–1422.
27 Frustaci A, Pieroni M, Chimenti C. The role of endomyocardial biopsy in the diagnosis of cardiomyopathies. Ital Heart J 2002, **3**: 348–353.
28 Gravanis MB, Ansari AA. Idiopathic cardiomyopathies. A review of pathologic studies and mechanism of pathogenesis. Arch Pathol Lab Med 1987, **111**: 915–929.
29 Hammond EH. Utility of ultrastructural studies of cardiac biopsy specimens. Ultrastruct Pathol 1994, **18**: 201–202.
30 Hauck AJ, Kearney DL, Edwards WD. Evaluation of postmortem endomyocardial biopsy specimens from 38 patients with lymphocytic myocarditis. Implications for role of sampling error. Mayo Clin Proc 1989, **64**: 1235–1245.
31 Henderson IC, Frei E III. Adriamycin and the heart (editorial). N Engl J Med 1979, **300**: 310–311.
32 Jaenke RS, Fajardo LF. Adriamycin-induced myocardial lesions. Report of a workshop. Am J Surg Pathol 1977, **1**: 55–60.
33 Kollo IJ, Edwards WD, Seward JB. Right ventricular dysplasia. The Mayo Clinic experience. Mayo Clin Proc 1995, **70**: 541–548.
33a Lamke GT, Allen RD, Edwards WD, Tazelaar HD, Danielson GK. Surgical pathology of subaortic septal myectomy associated with hypertrophic cardiomyopathy: a study of 229 cases (1996–2000) (Abstract). Mod Pathol 2003, **16**: 55A.
34 Lie JT. Diagnostic histology of myocardial disease in endomyocardial biopsies and at autopsy. Pathol Annu 1989, **24**(Pt 2): 255–293.

35 Litovsky SH, Burke AP, Virmani R. Giant cell myocarditis: an entity distinct from sarcoidosis characterized by multiphasic myocyte destruction by cytotoxic T cells and histiocytic giant cells. Mod Pathol 1996, **9**: 1126–1134.

36 Maisch B, Portig I, Ristic A, Hufnagel G, Pankuweit S. Definition of inflammatory cardiomyopathy (myocarditis): on the way to consensus. A status report. Herz 2000, **25**: 200–209.

37 Maron BJ, Bonow RO, Cannon RO III, Leon MB, Epstein SE. Hypertrophic cardiomyopathy. Interrelations of clinical manifestations, pathophysiology, and therapy. N Engl J Med 1987, **316**: 780–789; 844–852.

38 Mooney EE, Kenan DJ, Sweeney EC, Gaede JT. Myocarditis in Whipple's disease: An unsuspected cause of symptoms and sudden death. Mod Pathol 1997, **10**: 524–529.

39 Olsen EGJ. Endomyocardial biopsy. Invest Cell Pathol 1978, **1**: 139–157.

40 Olson LJ, Gertz MA, Edwards WD, Li C-Y, Pellikka PA, Holmes DR Jr, Tajik AJ, Kyle RA. Senile cardiac amyloidosis with myocardial dysfunction. Diagnosis by endomyocardial biopsy and immunohistochemistry. N Engl J Med 1987, **317**: 738–742.

41 Roberts WC, McAllister HA Jr, Ferrans VJ. Sarcoidosis of the heart. A clinicopathologic study of 35 necropsy patients (group I) and review of 78 previously reported necropsy patients (group II). Am J Med 1977, **63**: 86–108.

42 Roldan EO, Moskowitz L, Hensley GT. Pathology of the heart in acquired immunodeficiency syndrome. Arch Pathol Lab Med 1987, **111**: 943–946.

43 Rosai J, Lascano EF. Basophilic (mucoid) degeneration of myocardium. A disorder of glycogen metabolism. Am J Pathol 1970, **61**: 99–116.

44 Rose AG. Cardiac tuberculosis. A study of 19 patients. Arch Pathol Lab Med 1987, **111**: 422–426.

45 Rose AG, Beck W. Dilated (congestive) cardiomyopathy. A syndrome of severe cardiac dysfunction with remarkably few morphological features of myocardial damage. Histopathology 1985, **9**: 367–379.

46 Schnitt SJ, Ciano PS, Schoen FJ. Quantitation of lymphocytes in endomyocardial biopsies. Use and limitations of antibodies to leukocyte common antigen. Hum Pathol 1987, **18**: 796–800.

47 Spirito P, Chiarella F, Carratino L, Berisso MZ, Bellotti P, Vecchio C. Clinical course and prognosis of hypertrophic cardiomyopathy in an outpatient population. N Engl J Med 1989, **320**: 749–755.

48 Tamura S, Takahashi M, Kawamura S, Ishihara T. Basophilic degeneration of the myocardium. Histological, immunohistochemical and immunoelectronmicroscopic studies. Histopathology 1995, **26**: 501–508.

49 Tazelaar HD, Billingham ME. Leukocytic infiltrates in idiopathic dilated cardiomyopathy. A source of confusion with active myocarditis. Am J Surg Pathol 1986, **10**: 405–412.

50 Tazelaar HD, Billingham ME. The surgical pathology of hypertrophic cardiomyopathy. Arch Pathol Lab Med 1987, **111**: 257–260.

51 Theaker JM, Gatter KC, Brown DC, Heryet A, Davies MJ. An investigation into the nature of giant cells in cardiac and skeletal muscle. Hum Pathol 1988, **19**: 974–979.

52 Ursell PC, Albala A, Fenoglio JJ Jr. Diagnosis of acute rheumatic carditis by endomyocardial biopsy. Hum Pathol 1982, **13**: 677–679.

53 Ursell PC, Fenoglio JJ. Spectrum of cardiac disease diagnosed by endomyocardial biopsy. Pathol Annu 1984, **19**(Pt 2): 197–219.

54 Veinot JP. Diagnostic endomyocardial biopsy pathology: secondary myocardial diseases and other clinical indications—review. Can J Cardiol 2002, **18**: 287–296.

55 Veinot JP, Edwards WD. Pathology of radiation-induced heart disease. A surgical and autopsy study of 27 cases. Hum Pathol 1996, **27**: 766–773.

56 Weinstein C, Fenoglio JJ. Myocarditis. Hum Pathol 1987, **18**: 613–618.

57 Wijetunga M, Rockson S. Myocarditis in systemic lupus erythematosus. Am J Med 2002, **113**: 419–423.

58 Winters GL, Costanzo-Nordin MR. Pathological findings in 2300 consecutive endomyocardial biopsies. Mod Pathol 1991, **4**: 441–448.

59 Wu LA, Lapeyre AC III, Cooper LT. Current role of endomyocardial biopsy in the management of dilated cardiomyopathy and myocarditis. Mayo Clin Proc 2001, **76**: 1030–1038.

Heart transplant

60 Abu-Farsakh H, Cagle PT, Buffone GJ, Bruner JM, Weilbaecher D, Greenberg SD. Heart allograft involvement with Epstein-Barr virus-associated posttransplant lymphoproliferative disorder. Arch Pathol Lab Med 1992, **116**: 93–95.

61 Arbustini E, Grasso M, Diegoli M, Percivalle E, Grossi P, Bramerio M, Campana C, Goggi C, Gavazzi A, Vigano M. Histopathologic and molecular profile of human cytomegalovirus infections in patients with heart transplants. Am J Clin Pathol 1992, **98**: 205–213.

62 Billingham ME. Some recent advances in cardiac pathology. Hum Pathol 1979, **10**: 367–386.

63 Chen JM, Barr ML, Chadburn A, Frizzera G, Schenkel FA, Sciacca RR, Reison DS, Addonizio LJ, Rose EA, Knowles DM. Management of lymphoproliferative disorders after cardiac transplantation. Ann Thorac Surg 1993, **56**: 527–538.

64 Chomette G, Auriol M, Delcourt A, Karkouche B, Cabrol A, Cabrol C. Human cardiac transplants. Diagnosis of rejection by endomyocardial biopsy. Causes of death (about 30 autopsies). Virchows Arch [A] 1985, **407**: 295–307.

65 Forbes RD, Rowan RA, Billingham ME. Endocardial infiltrates in human heart transplants. A serial biopsy analysis comparing four immunosuppression protocols. Hum Pathol 1990, **21**: 850–855.

66 Gaudin PB, Rayburn BK, Hutchins GM, Kasper EK, Baughman KL, Goodman SN, Lecks LE, Baumgartner WA, Hruban RH. Peritransplant injury to the myocardium associated with the development of accelerated arteriosclerosis in heart transplant recipients. Am J Surg Pathol 1994, **18**: 338–346.

67 Hammond EH. Solid organ transplantation pathology. Major problems in pathology, vol. 30. Philadelphia, 1994, W.B. Saunders.

68 Hawkins ET, Levine TB, Goss SJ, Moosvi A, Levine AB. Hypersensitivity myocarditis in the explanted hearts of transplant recipients. Reappraisal of pathologic criteria and their clinical implications. Pathol Annu 1995, **30**(Pt 1): 287–304.

69 Kemnitz J, Cohnert T, Schnäfers H-J, Helmke M, Wahlers T, Herrmann G, Schmidt RM, Haverich A. A classification of cardiac allograft rejection. A modification of the classification by Billingham. Am J Surg Pathol 1987, **11**: 503–515.

70 Kottke-Marchant K, Ratliff NB. Endomyocardial lymphocytic infiltrates in cardiac transplant recipients. Incidence and characterization. Arch Pathol Lab Med 1989, **113**: 690–698.

71 Kottke-Marchant K, Ratliff NB. Endomyocardial biopsy. Pathologic findings in cardiac transplant recipients. Pathol Annu 1990, **25**(Pt 1): 211–244.

72 McAllister HA, Schnee MJ, Radiovancevic B, Frazier H. A system for grading cardiac allograft rejections. Tex Heart Inst J 1986, **13**: 1–2.

73 Morrison VA, Dunn DL, Manivel JC, Gajl-Peczalska KJ, Peterson BA. Clinical characteristics of post-transplant lymphoproliferative disorders. Am J Med 1994, **97**: 14–24.

74 Olsen SL, Wagoner LE, Hammond EH, Taylor DO, Yowell RL, Ensley RD, Bristow MR, O'Connell JB, Renlund DG. Vascular rejection in heart transplantation. Clinical correlation, treatment

options, and future considerations. J Heart Lung Transplant 1993, **12**: S135–142.

75 Pardo-Mindan FJ, Lozano MD, Contreras-Mejuto F, de Alava E. Pathology of heart transplant through endomyocardial biopsy. Semin Diagn Pathol 1992, **9**: 238–248.

76 Pomerance A, Stovin P. Heart transplant pathology. The British experience. J Clin Pathol 1985, **38**: 146–159.

77 Rowan RA, Billingham ME. Pathologic changes in the long-term transplanted heart. A morphometric study of myocardial hypertrophy, vascularity, and fibrosis. Hum Pathol 1990, **21**: 767–772.

78 Tazelaar HD, Gay RE, Rowan RA, Billingham ME, Gay S. Collagen profile in the transplanted heart. Hum Pathol 1990, **21**: 424–428.

79 Uys CJ, Rose AG. Cardiac transplantation. Aspects of the pathology. Pathol Annu 1982, **17**(Pt 2): 147–178.

80 Weissman DJ, Ferry JA, Harris NL, Louis DN, Delmonico F, Spiro I. Posttransplantation lymphoproliferative disorders in solid organ recipients are predominantly aggressive tumors of host origin. Am J Clin Pathol 1995, **103**: 748–755.

81 Zerbe TR, Arena V. Diagnostic reliability of endomyocardial biopsy for assessment of cardiac allograft rejection. Hum Pathol 1988, **19**: 1307–1314.

Cardiac valves

82 Altrichter PM, Olson LJ, Edwards WD, Puga FJ, Danielson GK. Surgical pathology of the pulmonary valve. A study of 116 cases spanning 15 years. Mayo Clin Proc 1989, **64**: 1352–1360.

83 Billingham ME. Some recent advances in cardiac pathology. Hum Pathol 1979, **10**: 367–386.

84 Carabello BA, Crawford FA Jr. Valvular heart disease. N Engl J Med 1997, **337**: 32–41.

85 Clark RM, Anderson W. Rheumatic activity in auricular appendages removed at mitral valvoplasty. Am J Pathol 1955, **31**: 809–819.

86 Cooper JH. Localized dystrophic amyloidosis of heart valves. Hum Pathol 1983, **14**: 649–653.

87 Dare AJ, Harrity PJ, Tazelaar HD, Edwards WD, Mullany CJ. Evaluation of surgically excised mitral valves. Revised recommendations based on changing operative procedures in the 1990s. Hum Pathol 1993, **24**: 1286–1293.

88 Dare AJ, Veinot JP, Edwards WD, Tazelaar HD, Schaff HV. New observations on the etiology of aortic valve disease. A surgical pathologic study of 236 cases from 1990. Hum Pathol 1993, **24**: 1330–1338.

89 Davies MJ. Pathology of cardiac valves. London, 1980, Butterworth.

90 Ferrans VJ, Tomita Y, Hilbert SL, Jones M, Roberts WC. Pathology of bioprosthetic cardiac valves. Hum Pathol 1987, **18**: 586–595.

91 Gravanis MB, Campbell WG Jr. The syndrome of prolapse of the mitral valve. Arch Pathol Lab Med 1982, **106**: 369–374.

92 Groom DA, Starke WR. Cartilaginous metaplasia in calcific aortic valve disease. Am J Clin Pathol 1990, **93**: 809–812.

93 Hanson TP, Edwards BS, Edwards JE. Pathology of surgically excised mitral valves. One hundred consecutive cases. Arch Pathol Lab Med 1985, **109**: 823–828.

94 Hauck AJ, Freeman DP, Ackermann DM, Danielson GK, Edwards WD. Surgical pathology of the tricuspid valve. A study of 363 cases spanning 25 years. Mayo Clin Proc 1988, **63**: 851–863.

95 Love GL, Restrepo C. Aschoff bodies of rheumatic carditis are granulomatous lesions of histiocytic origin. Mod Pathol 1988, **1**: 256–261.

96 Morales AR, Romanelli R, Boucek RJ, Tate LG, Alvarez RT, Davis JT. Myxoid heart disease. An assessment of extravalvular cardiac pathology in severe mitral valve prolapse. Hum Pathol 1992, **23**: 129–137.

97 Murphy SK, Rogler WC, Fleming WH, McManus BM. Retraction of bioprosthetic heart valve cusps. A cause of wide-open regurgitation in right-sided heart valves. Hum Pathol 1988, **19**: 140–147.

98 Olson LJ, Subramanian R, Ackermann DM, Orszulak TA, Edwards WD. Surgical pathology of the mitral valve. A study of 712 cases spanning 21 years. Mayo Clin Proc 1987, **62**: 22–34.

99 Passik CS, Ackermann DM, Pluth JR, Edwards WD. Temporal changes in the causes of aortic stenosis. A surgical pathologic study of 646 cases. Mayo Clin Proc 1987, **62**: 119–123.

100 Peterson MD, Roach RM, Edwards JE. Types of aortic stenosis in surgically removed valves. Arch Pathol Lab Med 1985, **109**: 829–832.

101 Robboy SJ, Kaiser J. Pathogenesis of fungal infection on heart valve prostheses. Hum Pathol 1975, **6**: 711–715.

102 Roberts WC, Morrow AG. Cardiac valves and the surgical pathologist. Arch Pathol 1966, **82**: 309–313.

103 Rose AG. Etiology of acquired valvular heart disease in adults. A survey of 18,132 autopsies and 100 consecutive valve-replacement operations. Arch Pathol Lab Med 1986, **110**: 385–388.

104 Schoen FJ. Surgical pathology of removed natural and prosthetic heart valves. Hum Pathol 1987, **18**: 558–567.

105 Schoen FJ, Hobson CE. Anatomic analysis of removed prosthetic heart valves. Causes of failure of 33 mechanical valves and 58 bioprostheses, 1980 to 1983. Hum Pathol 1985, **16**: 549–559.

106 Schoen FJ, Levy RJ, Piehler HR. Pathological considerations in replacement cardiac valves. Cardiovasc Pathol 1992, **1**: 29–52.

107 Schoen FJ, Sutton MSJ. Contemporary issues in the pathology of valvular heart disease. Hum Pathol 1987, **18**: 568–576.

108 Silver MD. Cardiac pathology. A look at the last five years. II. The pathology of cardiovascular prostheses. Hum Pathol 1974, **5**: 127–138.

109 Silver MD. Late complications of prosthetic heart valves. Arch Pathol Lab Med 1978, **102**: 281–284.

110 Silver MD, Butany J. Mechanical heart valves. Methods of examination, complications, and modes of failure. Hum Pathol 1987, **18**: 577–585.

111 Silver MD, Datta BN, Bowes VF. A key to identify heart valve prostheses. Arch Pathol 1975, **99**: 132–138.

112 Subramanian R, Olson LJ, Edwards WD. Surgical pathology of pure aortic stenosis. A study of 374 cases. Mayo Clin Proc 1984, **59**: 683–690.

113 Subramanian R, Olson LJ, Edwards WD. Surgical pathology of combined aortic stenosis and insufficiency. A study of 213 cases. Mayo Clin Proc 1985, **60**: 247–254.

114 van der Bel-Kahn J, Becker AE. The surgical pathology of rheumatic and floppy mitral valves. Distinctive morphologic features upon gross examination. Am J Surg Pathol 1986, **10**: 282–292.

115 Virmani R, Atkinson JB, Forman MB, Robinowitz M. Mitral valve prolapse. Hum Pathol 1987, **18**: 596–602.

116 Vongpatanasin W, Hillis LD, Lange RA. Prosthetic heart valves. N Engl J Med 1996, **335**: 407–416.

Coronary artery bypass

117 Kern WH, Wells WJ, Meyer BW. The pathology of surgically excised aortocoronary saphenous vein bypass grafts. Am J Surg Pathol 1981, **5**: 491–496.

118 Ratliff NB, Myles JL. Rapidly progressive atherosclerosis in aortocoronary saphenous vein grafts. Possible immune-mediated disease. Arch Pathol Lab Med 1989, **113**: 772–776.

119 Smith SH, Geer JC. Morphology of saphenous vein-coronary artery bypass grafts. Seven to 116 months after surgery. Arch Pathol Lab Med 1983, **107**: 13–18.

120 Yutani C, Imakita M, Ishibashi-Ueda H. Histopathological study of aorto-coronary bypass grafts with special reference to fibrin

deposits on grafted saphenous veins. Acta Pathol Jpn 1989, **39:** 425–432.

Coarctation of aorta

121 Bergdahl L, Bjork VO, Jonasson R. Surgical correction of coarctation of the aorta. Influence of age on late results. J Thorac Cardiovasc Surg 1983, **85:** 532–536.

122 Campbell M. Natural history of coarctation of the aorta. Br Heart J 1970, **32:** 633–640.

123 Gaynor JW. Management strategies for infants with coarctation and an associated ventricular septal defect. J Thorac Cardiovasc Surg 2001, **122:** 424–426.

124 Hornung TS, Benson LN, McLaughlin PR. Interventions for aortic coarctation. Cardiol Rev 2002, **10:** 139–148.

125 Lerberg DB, Hardesty RL, Siewers RD, Zuberbuhler JR, Bahnson HT. Coarctation of the aorta in infants and children. 25 years experience. Ann Thorac Surg 1982, **33:** 159–170.

Cardiac tumors

Myxoma

126 Acebo E, Val-Bernal JF, Gómez-Romàn JJ. Prichard's structures of the fossa ovalis are not histogenetically related to cardiac myxoma. Histopathology 2001, **39:** 529–535.

127 Berrutti L, Silverman JS. Cardiac myxoma is rich in factor XIIIa positive dendrophages: immunohistochemical study of four cases. Histopathology 1996, **28:** 529–535.

128 Boxer ME. Cardiac myxoma. An immunoperoxidase study of histogenesis. Histopathology 1984, **8:** 861–872.

129 Burke AP, Virmani R. Cardiac myxoma. A clinicopathologic study. Am J Clin Pathol 1993, **100:** 671–680.

130 Carney JA. Differences between nonfamilial and familial cardiac myxoma. Am J Surg Pathol 1985, **9:** 53–55.

131 Deshpande A, Venugopal P, Kumar AS, Chopra P. Phenotypic characterization of cellular components of cardiac myxoma: A light microscopy and immunohistochemistry study. Hum Pathol 1996, **27:** 1056–1059.

132 Dewald GW, Dahl RJ, Spurbeck JL, Carney JA, Gordon H. Chromosomally abnormal clones and nonrandom telomeric translocations in cardiac myxomas. Mayo Clin Proc 1987, **62:** 558–567.

133 Farrell DJ, Bulmer E, Angus B, Ashcroft T. Immunohistochemical expression of endothelial markers in left atrial myxomas: a study of six cases. Histopathology 1996, **28:** 147–152.

134 Feldman PS, Horvath E, Kovacs K. An ultrastructural study of seven cardiac myxomas. Cancer 1977, **40:** 2216–2232.

135 Ferrans VJ, Roberts WC. Structural features of cardiac myxomas. Histology, histochemistry and electron microscopy. Hum Pathol 1973, **4:** 111–146.

136 Fine G, Morales A, Horn RC Jr. Cardiac myxoma. A morphologic and histogenetic appraisal. Cancer 1968, **22:** 1156–1162.

137 Goldman BI, Frydman C, Harpaz N, Ryan SF, Loiterman D. Glandular cardiac myxomas. Histologic, immunohistochemical, and ultrastructural evidence of epithelial differentiation. Cancer 1987, **59:** 1767–1775.

138 Govoni E, Severi B, Cenacchi G, Laschi R, Pileri S, Rivano MT, Alampi G, Branzi A. Ultrastructural and immunohistochemical contribution to the histogenesis of human cardiac myxoma. Ultrastruct Pathol 1988, **12:** 221–233.

139 Johansson L. Histogenesis of cardiac myxomas. An immunohistochemical study of 19 cases, including one with glandular structures, and review of the literature. Arch Pathol Lab Med 1989, **113:** 735–741.

140 Kasugai T, Sakurai M, Yutani C, Hirota S, Waki N, Adachi S, Kitamura Y. Sequential malignant transformation of cardiac myxoma. Acta Pathol Jpn 1990, **40:** 687–692.

141 Kodama H, Hirotani T, Suzuki Y, Ogawa S, Yamazaki K. Cardiomyogenic differentiation in cardiac myxoma expressing lineage-specific transcription factors. Am J Pathol 2002, **161:** 381–389.

142 Landon G, Ordòñez NG, Guarda LA. Cardiac myxomas. An immunohistochemical study using endothelial, histiocytic, and smooth-muscle cell markers. Arch Pathol Lab Med 1986, **110:** 116–120.

142a Li Y, Pan Z, Ji Y, Sheppard M, Jeffries DJ, Archard LC, Zhang H. Herpes simplex virus type 1 infection associated with atrial myxoma. Am J Pathol 2003, **163:** 2407–2412.

143 Lie JT. Petrified cardiac myxoma masquerading as organized atrial mural thrombus. Arch Pathol Lab Med 1989, **113:** 742–745.

144 McComb RD. Heterogeneous expression of factor VIII/von Willebrand factor by cardiac myxoma cells. Am J Surg Pathol 1984, **8:** 539–544.

145 Perchinsky MJ, Lichenstein SV, Tyers GF. Primary cardiac tumors: forty years' experience with 71 patients. Cancer 1997, **79:** 1809–1815.

146 Pohost GM, Pastore JO, McKusick KA, Chiotellis PN, Kapellakis GZ, Meyers GS, Dinsmore RE, Block PC. Detection of left atrial myxoma by gated radionuclide cardiac imaging. Circulation 1977, **55:** 88–92.

146a Pucci A, Bartoloni G, Tessitore E, Carney JA, Papotti M. Cytokeratin profile and neuroendocrine cells in the glandular component of cardiac myxoma. Virchows Arch 2003, **443:** 618–624.

147 Read RC, White HJ, Murphy ML, Williams D, Sun CN, Flanagan WH. The malignant potentiality of left atrial myxoma. J Thorac Cardiovasc Surg 1974, **68:** 857–868.

148 Reed RJ, Utz MP, Terezakis N. Embolic and metastatic cardiac myxoma. Am J Dermatopathol 1989, **11:** 157–165.

149 Richardson JV, Brandt B III, Doty DB, Ehrenhaft JL. Surgical treatment of atrial myxomas. Early and late results of 111 operations and review of the literature. Ann Thorac Surg 1979, **28:** 354–358.

150 Rupp GM, Heyman RA, Martinez AJ, Sekhar LN, Jungreis CA. The pathology of metastatic cardiac myxoma. Am J Clin Pathol 1989, **91:** 221–227.

151 Salyer WR, Page DL, Hutchins GM. The development of cardiac myxomas and papillary endocardial lesions from mural thrombus. Am Heart J 1975, **89:** 14–17.

152 Samaratunga H, Searle J, Cominos D, Le Fevre I. Cerebral metastasis of an atrial myxoma mimicking an epithelioid hemangioendothelioma. Am J Surg Pathol 1994, **18:** 107–111.

153 Schmitt-Graff A, Borchard F. Cardiac myxoma with a cytokeratin-immunoreactive glandular component. Pathol Res Pract 1992, **188:** 221–225.

154 Seidman JD, Berman JJ, Hitchcock CL, Becker RL Jr, Mergner W, Moore GW, Virmani R, Yetter RA. DNA analysis of cardiac myxomas. Flow cytometry and image analysis. Hum Pathol 1991, **22:** 494–500.

155 Seo IS, Warner TFCS, Colyer RA, Winkler RF. Metastasizing atrial myxoma. Am J Surg Pathol 1980, **4:** 391–399.

156 Silverman NA. Primary cardiac tumors. Ann Surg 1980, **191:** 127–138.

157 Tanimura A, Kitazono M, Nagayama K, Tanaka S, Kosuga K. Cardiac myxoma. Morphologic, histochemical, and tissue culture studies. Hum Pathol 1988, **19:** 316–322.

158 Terracciano LM, Mhawech P, Suess K, D'Armiento M, Lehmann FS, Jundt G, Moch H, Sauter G, Mihatsch MJ. Calretinin as a marker for cardiac myxoma. Am J Clin Pathol 2000, **114:** 754–759.

159 Trotter SE, Shore DF, Olsen EG. Gamna-Gandy nodules in a cardiac myxoma. Histopathology 1990, **17:** 270–272.

Other benign tumors and tumorlike conditions

160 Almagro UA, Perry LS, Choi H, Pintar K. Papillary fibroelastoma of the heart. Report of six cases. Arch Pathol Lab Med 1982, **206:** 318–321.

161 Aqel NM, Shousha S. Glandular inclusions in fetal myocardium. Histopathology 1994, **24**: 85–87.

162 Arai T, Kurashima C, Wada S, Chida K, Ohkawa S. Histological evidence for cell proliferation activity in cystic tumor (endodermal heterotopia) of the atrioventricular node. Pathol Int 1998, **48**: 917–923.

163 Argani P, Sternberg SS, Burt M, Adsay NV, Klimstra DS. Metastatic adenocarcinoma involving a mesothelial/monocytic incidental cardiac excrescence (cardiac MICE). Am J Surg Pathol 1997, **21**: 970–974.

164 Bando Y, Kitagawa T, Uehara H, Sano N, Satake N, Onose Y, Kitaichi T, Miki O, Katoh I, Izumi K. So-called mesothelial/monocytic incidental cardiac excrescences obtained during valve replacement surgery: report of three cases and literature review. Virchows Arch 2000, **437**: 331–335.

165 Burke AP, Anderson PG, Virmani R, James TN, Herrera GA, Ceballos R. Tumor of the atrioventricular nodal region. A clinical and immunohistochemical study. Arch Pathol Lab Med 1990, **114**: 1057–1062.

165a Burke AP, Gatto-Weis C, Griego JE, Ellington KS, Virmani R. Adult cellular rhabdomyoma of the heart: a report of 3 cases. Hum Pathol 2002, **33**: 1092–1097.

166 Burke AP, Litovsky S, Virmani R. Lipomatous hypertrophy of the atrial septum presenting as a right atrial mass. Am J Surg Pathol 1996, **20**: 678–685.

167 Burke AP, Ribe JK, Bajaj AK, Edwards WD, Farb A, Virmani R. Hamartoma of mature cardiac myocytes. Hum Pathol 1998, **29**: 904–909.

168 Burke AP, Virmani R. Cardiac rhabdomyoma. A clinicopathologic study. Mod Pathol 1991, **4**: 70–74.

169 Chan HSL, Sonley MJ, Möes CAF, Daneman A, Smith CR, Martin DJ. Primary and secondary tumors of childhood involving the heart, pericardium, and great vessels. A report of 75 cases and review of the literature. Cancer 1985, **56**: 825–836.

170 Chou P, Gonzalez-Crussi F, Cole R, Reddy VB. Plasma cell granuloma of the heart. Cancer 1988, **62**: 1409–1413.

171 Courtice RW, Stinson WA, Walley VM. Tissue fragments recovered at cardiac surgery masquerading as tumoral proliferations. Evidence suggesting iatrogenic or artefactual origin and common occurrence. Am J Surg Pathol 1994, **18**: 167–174.

172 De Nictolis M, Brancorsini D, Goteri G, Prat J. Epithelioid haemangioma of the heart. Virchows Arch 1996, **428**: 119–123.

173 Duray PH, Mark EJ, Barwick KW, Madri JA, Strom RL. Congenital polycystic tumor of the atrioventricular node. Arch Pathol Lab Med 1985, **109**: 30–34.

174 Fekete PS, Nassar VH, Talley JD, Boedecker EA. Cardiac papilloma. Arch Pathol Lab Med 1983, **107**: 246–248.

175 Feldman PS, Meyer MW. Fibroelastic hamartoma (fibroma) of the heart. Cancer 1976, **38**: 314–323.

176 Fenoglio JJ, McAllister HA. Granular cell tumors of the heart. Arch Pathol Lab Med 1976, **100**: 276–278.

177 Fenoglio JJ Jr, Jacobs DW, McAllister HA Jr. Ultrastructure of the mesothelioma of the atrioventricular node. Cancer 1977, **40**: 721–727.

178 Fine G. Primary tumors of the pericardium and heart. In Edwards JE, et al. (eds): The heart. Baltimore, 1974, Williams & Wilkins, pp. 189–210.

179 Fine G, Raju U. Congenital polycystic tumor of the atrioventricular node (endodermal heterotopia, mesothelioma). A histogenetic appraisal with evidence for its endodermal origin. Hum Pathol 1987, **18**: 791–795.

180 Hill DA, Swanson PE. Myocardial extramedullary hematopoiesis: a clinicopathologic study. Mod Pathol 2000, **13**: 779–787.

181 Howard RA, Aldea GS, Shapira OM, Kasznica JM, Davidoff R. Papillary fibroelastoma: increasing recognition of a surgical disease. Ann Thorac Surg 1999, **68**: 1881–1885.

182 Hoyt JC, Hutchins GM. Angiomatous variants of so-called mesothelioma of the atrioventricular node. Arch Pathol Lab Med 1986, **110**: 851–852.

183 Jaffe R. Neuroma in the region of the atrioventricular node. Hum Pathol 1981, **12**: 375–376.

184 Johnson TL, Shapiro B, Beierwaltes WH, Orringer MB, Lloyd RV, Sisson JC, Thompson NW. Cardiac paragangliomas. A clinicopathologic and immunohistochemical study of four cases. Am J Surg Pathol 1985, **9**: 827–834.

185 Kantelip B, Lusson JR, De Riberolles C, Lamaison D, Bailly P. Intracardiac ectopic thyroid. Hum Pathol 1986, **17**: 1293–1296.

186 Kiaer HW. Myocardial angiolipoma. Acta Pathol Microbiol Immunol Scand (A) 1984, **92**: 291–292.

187 Kuo T-T, Hsueh S, Su I-J, Gonzalez-Crussi F, Chen J-S. Histiocytoid hemangioma of the heart with peripheral eosinophilia. Cancer 1985, **55**: 2854–2861.

187a Kurup AN, Tazelaar HD, Edwards WD, Burke AP, Virmani R, Klarich KW, Orszulak TA. Iatrogenic cardiac papillary fibroelastoma: a study of 12 cases (1990 to 2000). Hum Pathol 2003, **33**: 1165–1169.

188 Li L, Cerilli LA, Wick MR. Inflammatory pseudotumor (myofibroblastic tumor) of the heart. Ann Diagn Pathol 2002, **6**: 116–121.

189 Linder J, Shelburne JD, Sorge JP, Whalen RE, Hackel DB. Congenital endodermal heterotopia of the atrioventricular node. Evidence for the endodermal origin of so-called mesotheliomas of the atrioventricular node. Hum Pathol 1984, **15**: 1093–1098.

190 Luthringer DJ, Virmani R, Weiss SW, Rosai J. A distinctive cardiovascular lesion resembling histiocytoid (epithelioid) hemangioma. Evidence suggesting mesothelial participation. Am J Surg Pathol 1990, **14**: 993–1000.

191 Mikolaenko I, Galliani CA, Davis GG. Pigmented cardiac paraganglioma. Arch Pathol Lab Med 2001, **125**: 680–682.

192 Monroe B, Federman M, Balogh K. Cardiac neurilemoma. Report of a case with electron microscopic examination. Arch Pathol Lab Med 1984, **108**: 300–304.

193 Natarajan S, Luthringer DJ, Fishbein MC. Adenomatoid tumor of the heart: Report of a case. Am J Surg Pathol 1997, **21**: 1378–1380.

194 Prichard RW. Tumors of the heart. Review of the subject and report of one hundred and fifty cases. Arch Pathol 1951, **51**: 98–128.

195 Reynolds C, Tazelaar HD, Edwards WD. Calcified amorphous tumor of the heart (cardiac CAT). Hum Pathol 1997, **28**: 601–606.

196 Rosai J, Dehner LP. Nodular mesothelial hyperplasia in hernia sacs. A benign reactive condition simulating a neoplastic process. Cancer 1975, **35**: 165–175.

197 Rose AG, McCormick S, Cooper K, Titus JL. Inflammatory pseudotumor (plasma cell granuloma) of the heart: report of two cases and literature review. Arch Pathol Lab Med 1996, **120**: 549–554.

198 Rubin MA, Snell JA, Tazelaar HD, Lack EE, Austenfeld JL, Azumi N. Cardiac papillary fibroelastoma. An immunohistochemical investigation and unusual clinical manifestations. Mod Pathol 1995, **8**: 402–407.

199 Silverman JF, Kay S, McCue M, Lower RR, Brough AJ, Chang CH. Rhabdomyoma of the heart. Ultrastructural study of three cases. Lab Invest 1976, **35**: 596–606.

200 Sturtz CL, Abt AB, Leuenberger UA, Damiano R. Hamartoma of mature cardiac myocytes: a case report. Mod Pathol 1998, **11**: 496–499.

201 Suarez-Vilela D, Izquierdo-Garcia FM. Nodular histiocytic/mesothelial hyperplasia: a process mediated by adhesion molecules? Histopathology 2002, **40**: 299–300.

202 Swalwell CI. Benign intracardiac teratoma. A case of sudden death. Arch Pathol Lab Med 1993, **117**: 739–742.

203 Tabry IF, Nassar VH, Rizk G, Touma A, Dagher IK. Cavernous hemangioma of the heart. Case report and review of the literature. J Thorac Cardiovasc Surg 1975, **69**: 415–420.

204 Tazelaar HD, Locke TJ, McGregor CG. Pathology of surgically excised primary cardiac tumors. Mayo Clin Proc 1992, 67: 957–965.

205 Veinot JP, Tazelaar HD, Edwards WD, Colby TV. Mesothelial/monocytic incidental cardiac excrescences. Cardiac MICE. Mod Pathol 1994, 7: 9–16.

206 Walley VM, Peters HJ, Veinot JP, Courtice RW, Venance SL. The clinical and pathological manifestations of iatrogenically produced mesothelium-rich fragments of operative debris. Eur J Cardiothorac Surg 1997, 11: 328–332.

207 Weeks DA, Chase DR, Malott RL, Chase RL, Zuppan CW, Bekwith JB, Mierau GW. HMB-45 staining in angiomyolipoma, cardiac rhabdomyoma, other mesenchymal processes, and tuberous sclerosis-associated brain lesions. Int J Surg Pathol 1994, 1: 191–198.

208 Yu GH, Kussmaul WG, Di Sesa VJ, Lodato RF, Brooks JS. Adult intracardiac rhabdomyoma resembling the extracardiac variant. Hum Pathol 1993, 24: 448–451.

Primary malignant tumors

209 Bearman RM. Primary leiomyosarcoma of the heart. Report of a case and review of the literature. Arch Pathol 1974, 98: 62–65.

210 Burke AP, Cowan D, Virmani R. Primary sarcomas of the heart. Cancer 1992, 69: 387–395.

211 Burke AP, Virmani R. Osteosarcomas of the heart. Am J Surg Pathol 1991, 15: 289–295.

212 Cairns P, Butany J, Fulop J, Rakowski H, Hassaram S. Cardiac presentation of non-Hodgkin's lymphoma. Arch Pathol Lab Med 1987, 111: 80–83.

212a Chalabreysse L, Berger F, Loire R, Devouassoux G, Cordier JF, Thivolet-Bejui F. Primary cardiac lymphoma in immunocompetent patients: a report of three cases and review of the literature. Virchows Arch 2002, 441: 456–461.

213 Charney DA, Charney JM, Ghali VS, Teplitz C. Primitive neuroectodermal tumor of the myocardium: A case report, review of the literature, immunohistochemical and ultrastructural study. Hum Pathol 1996, 27: 1365–1369.

214 Constantino A, West TE, Gupta M, Loghmanee F. Primary cardiac lymphoma in a patient with acquired immune deficiency syndrome. Cancer 1987, 60: 2801–2805.

215 Curtsinger CR, Wilson MJ, Yoneda K. Primary cardiac lymphoma. Cancer 1989, 64: 521–525.

216 Fabian JT, Rose AG. Tumours of the heart. A study of 89 cases. S Afr Med J 1982, 61: 71–77.

217 Guarner J, Brynes RK, Chan WC, Birdsong G, Hertzler G. Primary non-Hodgkin's lymphoma of the heart in two patients with the acquired immunodeficiency syndrome. Arch Pathol Lab Med 1987, 111: 254–256.

218 Herhusky MJ, Gregg SB, Virmani R, Chun PKC, Bender H, Gray GF Jr. Cardiac sarcomas presenting as metastatic disease. Arch Pathol Lab Med 1985, 109: 943–945.

219 Herrmann MA, Shankerman RA, Edwards WD, Shub C, Schaff HV. Primary cardiac angiosarcoma. A clinicopathologic study of six cases. J Thorac Cardiovasc Surg 1992, 103: 655–664.

220 Holladay AO, Siegel RJ, Schwartz DA. Cardiac malignant lymphoma in acquired immune deficiency syndrome. Cancer 1992, 70: 2203–2207.

221 Ito M, Nakagawa A, Tsuzuki T, Yokoi T, Yamashita Y, Asai J. Primary cardiac lymphoma: No evidence for an etiologic association with Epstein-Barr virus. Arch Pathol Lab Med 1996, 120: 555–559.

222 Janigan DT, Husain A, Robinson NA. Cardiac angiosarcomas. A review and a case report. Cancer 1986, 57: 852–859.

223 Karn CM, Socinski MA, Fletcher JA, Corson JM, Craighead JE. Cardiac synovial sarcoma with translocation (X; 18) associated with asbestos exposure. Cancer 1994, 73: 74–78.

224 Katoh M, Shigematsu H. Leiomyosarcoma of the heart and its pulmonary metastasis, both with prominent osteoclast-like multinucleated giant cells expressing tartrate-resistant acid phosphatase activity. Pathol Int 1999, 49: 74–78.

225 Klima T, Milam JD, Bossart MI, Cooley DA. Rare primary sarcomas of the heart. Arch Pathol Lab Med 1986, 110: 1155–1159.

226 Kowal-Vern A, Swinnen L, Pyle J, Radvany R, Dizikes G, Michalov M, Molnar Z. Characterization of postcardiac transplant lymphomas: Histology, immunophenotyping, immunohistochemistry, and gene rearrangement. Arch Pathol Lab Med 1996, 120: 41–48.

227 Lam KY, Dickens P, Chan AC. Tumors of the heart. A 20-year experience with a review of 12,485 consecutive autopsies. Arch Pathol Lab Med 1993, 117: 1027–1031.

228 Laya MB, Mailliard JA, Bewtra C, Levin HS. Malignant fibrous histiocytoma of the heart. A case report and review of the literature. Cancer 1987, 59: 1026–1031.

229 McDonnell PJ, Mann RB, Bulkley BH. Involvement of the heart by malignant lymphoma. A clinicopathologic study. Cancer 1982, 49: 944–951.

230 Nicholson AG, Rigby M, Lincoln C, Meller S, Fisher C. Synovial sarcoma of the heart. Histopathology 1997, 30: 349–352.

231 Ovcak Z, Masera A, Lamovec J. Malignant fibrous histiocytoma of the heart. Arch Pathol Lab Med 1992, 116: 872–874.

232 Pauwels P, Dal Cin P, Sciot R, Lammens M, Penn O, Van Nes E, Kwee WS, van den Berghe H. Primary malignant peripheral nerve sheath tumor of the heart. Histopathology 1999, 34: 56–59.

233 Pins MR, Ferrell MA, Madsen JC, Piubello Q, Dickersin R, Fletcher CDM. Epithelioid and spindle-celled leiomyosarcoma of the heart: Report of 2 cases and review of the literature. Arch Pathol Lab Med 1999, 123: 782–788.

234 Pucci A, Gagliardotto P, Papandrea C, Di Rosa E, Morello M, di Summa M, Mollo F. An unusual myxoid leiomyosarcoma of the heart. Arch Pathol Lab Med 1996, 120: 583–586.

234a Shehata BM, Thomas JE, Doudenko-Rufforny I. Metastatic carcinoid to the conducting system – is it a rare or merely unrecognized manifestation of carcinoid cardiopathy? Arch Pathol Lab Med 2002, 126: 1538.

235 Small EJ, Gordon GJ, Dahms BB. Malignant rhabdoid tumor of the heart in an infant. Cancer 1985, 55: 2850–2853.

236 Yang H-Y, Wasielewski JF, Lee W, Lee E, Paik YK. Angiosarcoma of the heart. Ultrastructural study. Cancer 1981, 47: 72–80.

237 Zanella M, Falconieri G, Bussani R, Sinagra G, Libera D. Polypoid osteosarcoma of the left atrium: report of a new case with autopsy confirmation and review of the literature. Ann Diagn Pathol 1998, 2: 167–172.

Metastatic tumors

238 Gibbs P, Cebon JS, Calafiore P, Robinson WA. Cardiac metastases from malignant melanoma. Cancer 1999, 85: 78–84.

239 Hanfling SM. Metastatic cancer to the heart. Circulation 1960, 22: 474–483.

240 Klatt EC, Heitz DR. Cardiac metastases. Cancer 1990, 65: 1456–1459.

241 Kline IK. Cardiac lymphatic involvement by metastatic tumor. Cancer 1972, 29: 799–808.

242 Lagrange J-L, Despins P, Spielman M, Le Chevalier T, De Lajartre A-Y, Fontaine F, Sarrazin D, Contesso G, Génin J, Rouesse J, Grossetête R. Cardiac metastases. Case report on an isolated cardiac metastasis of a myxoid liposarcoma. Cancer 1986, 58: 2333–2337.

243 Pratt CB, Dugger DL, Johnson WW, Ainger LE. Metastatic involvement of the heart in childhood rhabdomyosarcoma. Cancer 1973, 31: 1492–1497.

244 Roberts WC, Glancy DL, DeVita VT Jr. Heart in malignant lymphoma (Hodgkin's disease, lymphosarcoma, reticulum cell sarcoma and mycosis fungoides). Study of 196 autopsy cases. Am J Cardiol 1968, 22: 85–107.

245 Smith C. Tumors of the heart. Arch Pathol Lab Med 1986, **110:** 371–374.

Pericardium

246 Adenle AD, Edwards JE. Clinical and pathologic features of metastatic neoplasms of the pericardium. Chest 1982, **81:** 166–169.

247 Bardales RH, Stanley MW, Schaefer RF, Liblit RA, Owens RB, Surhland MJ. Secondary pericardial malignancies. A critical appraisal of the role of cytology, pericardial biopsy, and DNA ploidy analysis. Am J Clin Pathol 1996, **106:** 29–34.

248 Ben-Izhak O, Elmalach I, Kerner H, Best LA. Pericardial myolipoma: a tumour presenting as a mediastinal mass and containing oestrogen receptors. Histopathology 1996, **29:** 184–185.

249 Cox JN, Friedli B, Mechmeche R, Ben Ismail M, Oberhaensli I, Faidutti B. Teratoma of the heart. A case report and review of the literature. Virchows Arch [A] 1983, **402:** 163–174.

250 Drut R, Quijano G. Multilocular mesothelial inclusion cysts (so-called benign multicystic mesothelioma) of pericardium. Histopathology 1999, **34:** 472–474.

251 Fine G. Primary tumors of the pericardium and heart. In Edwards JE et al. (eds): The heart. Baltimore, 1974, Williams & Wilkins, pp. 189–210.

252 Fukuda T, Ishikawa H, Ohnishi Y, Tachikawa S, Oguma F, Kasuya S, Sakashita I. Malignant spindle cell tumor of the pericardium. Evidence of sarcomatous mesothelioma with aberrant antigen expression. Acta Pathol Jpn 1989, **39:** 750–754.

253 Hancock EW. Heart disease after radiation (editorial). N Engl J Med 1983, **308:** 588.

254 Killion MJ, Brodovsky HS, Schwarting R. Pericardial angiosarcoma after mediastinal irradiation for seminoma: A case report and a review of the literature. Cancer 1996, **78:** 912–917.

255 Kinnunen P, Kumala P, Kaarteenaho-Wiik R, Vuopala K. Ectopic liver in the human pericardium. Histopathology 1997, **30:** 277–279.

256 Klacsmann PG, Bulkley BH, Hutchins GM. The changed spectrum of purulent pericarditis. An 86 year autopsy experience in 200 patients. Am J Med 1977, **63:** 666–673.

257 Mambo NC. Diseases of the pericardium. Morphologic study of surgical specimens from 35 patients. Hum Pathol 1981, **12:** 978–987.

258 Martin A. Acute non-specific pericarditis. A description of nineteen cases. BMJ 1966, **2:** 279–281.

259 Naramoto A, Itoh N, Nakano M, Shigematsu H. An autopsy case of tuberous sclerosis associated with primary pericardial mesothelioma. Acta Pathol Jpn 1989, **39:** 400–406.

260 Nelson E, Stenzel P. Intrapericardial yolk sac tumor in an infant girl. Cancer 1987, **60:** 1567–1569.

261 Sane AC, Roggli VL. Curative resection of a well-differentiated papillary mesothelioma of the pericardium. Arch Pathol Lab Med 1995, **119:** 266–267.

262 Sicari MC, Fyfe B, Parness I, Rossi A, Unger P. Intrapericardial yolk sac tumor associated with acute myocarditis. Arch Pathol Lab Med 1999, **123:** 241–243.

263 Stewart JR, Fajardo LF. Radiation-induced heart disease. An update. Prog Cardiovasc Dis 1984, **27:** 173–194.

264 Terada T, Nakanuma Y, Matsubara T, Suematsu T. An autopsy case of primary angiosarcoma of the pericardium mimicking malignant mesothelioma. Acta Pathol Jpn 1988, **38:** 1345–1351.

265 Tötterman KJ, Pesonen E, Sillanen P. Radiation-related chronic heart disease. Chest 1983, **83:** 875–878.

266 Veinot JP, Edwards WD. Pathology of radiation-induced heart disease: A surgical and autopsy study of 27 cases. Hum Pathol 1996, **27:** 766–773.

267 Virmani R, Bewtra C, McAllister HA, Schulte RD. Intrapericardial giant lymph node hyperplasia. Am J Surg Pathol 1982, **6:** 475–481.

Arteries

Normal anatomy

The reader is referred to standard textbooks and chapters on arteries, veins, capillaries, and lymph vessels for a description of the normal anatomy of these structures.[1]

Arteriosclerosis

Arteriosclerosis is a generalized progressive arterial disease associated with localized arterial occlusions and aneurysms. It is the principal cause of heart attack, stroke, and gangrene of the extremities and is responsible for about 50% of all deaths in the United States, Europe, and Japan. The lesions result from an excessive inflammatory and proliferative response to various forms of injury to the endothelium and smooth muscle of the arterial wall. Numerous growth factors, cytokines, and vasoregulatory molecules participate in the process.[9–11] The pathology of arteriosclerosis has gained greater surgical significance with the development of direct operative therapy for lesions of major arteries.

The pathology of arteriosclerosis primarily consists of the following[6]:

1 Formation of intimal *plaques*, composed of lipid deposits and proliferated spindle cells. The latter seem to be of heterogenous nature, fibroblasts and smooth muscle cells predominating.[8,12]
2 Reduplication and fragmentation of the internal elastic lamina.
3 Degeneration of the media indicated by fragmentation of elastic tissue network; by hyaline, mucinoid, and collagenous degeneration of the smooth muscle; and by medial calcification.
4 Adventitial fibrosis and chronic inflammatory cellular infiltration.

Arteriosclerosis may present as an occlusive process when the disease attacks the intima more rapidly than the media and adventitia, but may present as an aneurysm when the reverse is true. Occlusive disease and aneurysm may co-exist in the same arterial system.[7]

The pathogenesis of arteriosclerosis is probably multifactorial.[4,5,10] Factors thought important in its pathogenesis include changes in lipid metabolism, increased endothelial permeability to serum lipoprotein complexes, susceptibility of the intima to mechanical injury from flow turbulence at major bifurcations, and in the presence of hypertension, elastic tissue fragmentation and thrombosis or disruption of vasa vasorum.

The areas of the arterial tree involved by arteriosclerosis that are successfully treated surgically have rapidly increased so that only occlusions of the smaller peripheral arteries of the extremities remain outside the realm of operative attack.

Surgical therapy for occlusive disease of the coronary, carotid, and mesenteric arteries is now frequently undertaken. The principal manifestations of arteriosclerosis that at present are treated surgically with some success are fusiform and saccular aneurysms of the aorta or other major arteries; dissecting aneurysm; and occlusive disease of the abdominal aorta, the iliofemoral arterial system, and less often, the popliteal, subclavian, brachial, renal, and carotid arterial systems.[1a–3,13]

Aneurysms

Aortic aneurysms
Aneurysms secondary to arteriosclerosis occur most frequently in the abdominal aorta, but the mechanism of development and the pathologic changes are similar in other arteries.[15]

Arterial dilatation is likely initiated by a loss of elasticity or weakening of the recoil strength in the arterial wall, which results in elongation and tortuosity, as well as dilatation. Initially, this dilatation is most often fusiform. At the same intraluminal pressure, the larger the diameter of the artery the greater the tension in the arterial wall. The tendency for dilatation thus increases rapidly after it has begun.[23] The progressive dilatation often results in a break in the arterial wall and the development of sacculation of the aneurysm.[35] The sacculations nearly always are partially filled with laminated clot, which may be the source of emboli into the arteries peripheral to the aneurysm (Fig. 27.20).

Microscopically, there are medial fibrosis and calcification, atherosclerosis, periaortic fibrosis, and thickening of the vasa vasorum. Those aneurysms located in the ascending aorta have a high incidence of fragmentation of elastic fibers and cystic medial change.[32] A mild to moderate lymphoplasmacytic infiltrate may be seen in the adventitia; this is not necessarily indicative of a primary vasculitis (see p. 2447),[24,28,40] but it has been suggested that CMV may play a pathogenetic role in the induction and persistence of the inflammatory reaction.[44] The pattern of expression of the adhesion molecules suggests that they may play a role in the initiation and progression of the chronic inflammatory changes associated with advanced atherosclerosis.[38]

Superimposed bacterial infection may complicate an aortic aneurysm of arteriosclerotic origin.[25] Salmonella is the predominant organism, followed by Staphylococcus.[16,374] Cases of aortic aneurysm have also been reported secondary to lupus erythematosus.[42]

The patient with an abdominal aneurysm may be asymptomatic and without clinical findings except for prominent abdominal aortic pulsations. The majority, however, seek treatment because of dull midabdominal or back pain associated with a pulsating, tender epigastric or retroumbilical mass that has enlarged rapidly or has been noted only recently. Painful and rapidly enlarging aneurysms will soon rupture if operative therapy is not undertaken. Retroperitoneal hemorrhages from small aneurysms may produce severe back pain with few abdominal symptoms or signs. Fistulas may develop from these aneurysms; there may be leakage into the vena cava or the duodenum or other portions of small bowel.[39] Significantly, aortoenteric fistulas also may occur as a late complication of reconstructive aortic surgery.[31] Aneurysms of the hepatic artery may rupture into the common bile duct; those of the splenic artery into the stomach, colon, or pancreatic duct; and those of the internal iliac artery into the rectosigmoid.[14,18,27]

Patients with aneurysms of the thoracic aorta survive but a short time without surgical correction.[17] Kampmeir[29] showed the average life expectancy after onset of symptoms to be 6 to 8 months. The prognosis in abdominal aneurysm appears better than that in aneurysm of the thoracic aorta.[26,30,36]

Schatz et al.[41] reviewed 141 untreated cases of abdominal aortic aneurysms at the Mayo Clinic. The prognosis was poor when the aneurysms were accompanied by symptomatic heart disease, when they were symptomatic, and when they exceeded 7.5 cm in diameter. Only 20% of the patients with aneurysm associated with symptomatic heart disease survived 5 years. Of those in whom the cause of death was known, 44% died of ruptured aneurysm.

Klippel and Butcher[33] reported 30 patients with abdominal aortic aneurysms not treated operatively: only 2 died of rupture. Szilagyi et al.[43] compared 223 untreated abdominal aortic aneurysms with a group of 480 treated surgically. They were able to show that modern operative mortality was significantly less than the likelihood of rupture without operation.

It may be concluded that once an aneurysm of the aortic system is of significant size, its excision and aortic reconstitution are mandatory.[19–22,34]

Popliteal artery aneurysms

Arteriosclerotic aneurysms of arteries in the extremities are rare except for the popliteal and femoral arteries.[47] The pathologic changes and the progressive enlargement of these aneurysms are similar to those in larger arteries, although the rate of progressive dilatation usually is less. Their treatment is essential to avoid acute thrombosis, embolic phenomena, or rupture as causes of severe peripheral flow deficiency and gangrene.[48] Most patients with popliteal aneurysms are first seen because of these complications. Occasionally, such patients seek medical aid because of anterior tibial muscular necrosis. The popliteal arterial elongation associated with aneurysm formation may kink and occlude the anterior tibial artery as it passes through the interosseous membrane.[46]

Patients with popliteal aneurysms frequently have

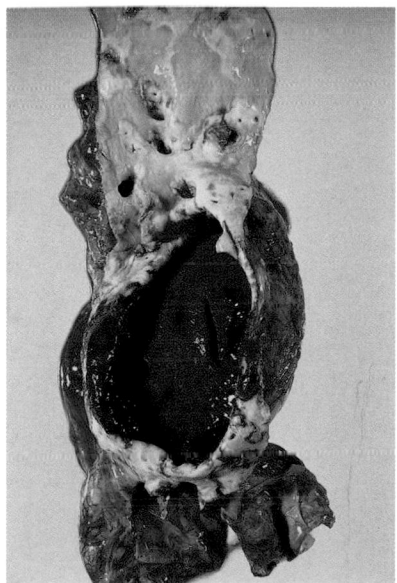

Fig. 27.20 Abdominal aortic aneurysm of arteriosclerotic origin containing a large thrombus. (Courtesy of Dr. RA Cooke, Brisbane, Australia; from Cooke RA, Stewart B: Colour Atlas of Anatomical Pathology. Edinburgh, Churchill Livingstone, 2004).

multiple aneurysms. In 69 patients having 100 popliteal aneurysms, hypertension and occlusive arterial disease were frequent.[45] Only 3 of these patients were women. Ninety-two of the aneurysms were considered purely arteriosclerotic. Syphilis, mycotic infections, and trauma entered into the diagnosis of the remaining ones. In the absence of extensive gangrene, popliteal aneurysms with or without the presence of complications are best treated by excision of the aneurysm and insertion of autologous vein grafts.

Dissecting aneurysms

Dissecting aneurysms of the aorta, if untreated, are associated with a rapidly fatal course in 75% to 90% of the patients. Their etiology is related to an underlying degeneration of the elements of the media. Factors associated with dissection are hypertension, Marfan's syndrome, pregnancy, bicuspid aortic valve, and traumatic, atherosclerotic, or inflammatory injuries of the aortic media.[49,56] This includes recently introduced procedures such as insertion of an intra-aortic balloon pump and aortic cannulation during cardiopulmonary bypass operation.

The process of dissection most commonly begins in a transverse intimal tear associated with an intimal plaque located either in the ascending aorta or in the upper descending thoracic aorta near the origin of the left subclavian artery.[52] Once this tear develops, the intramural layers of the aorta are rapidly separated by the force of the blood entering the wall. The dissection usually involves the entire circumference of the aorta as it progresses distally. Perforation often occurs through the adventitia, resulting in early death from hemorrhage into the pericardium or pleural cavity. Lower extremity symptoms and signs of acute occlusion of the abdominal aorta may be prominent because of distal aortic or iliac luminal occlusion by the leading point of the dissection. Diagnostic imaging is essential in the evaluation of suspected aortic dissection.[50]

Three major types of dissection are recognized depending on the location and extent.[52,53] Type I begins in the ascending aorta and extends beyond; type II is confined to the ascending aorta; type IIIA begins in the descending aorta and stops above the diaphragm; type IIIB also begins in the descending aorta but extends below the diaphragm. Dissecting aneurysms can also be classified according to their duration as acute, subacute, and chronic. The subacute type characteristically begins abruptly and then progresses gradually for several days before rupture and death (Fig. 27.21). The chronic form occurs in a few patients who develop a re-entry site from the dissected passage back into the lumen of the aorta. The occasional long-term survivor of dissecting aneurysm is encountered among these patients.

The objective of surgical treatment is to excise the intimal tear, obliterate entry into the false channel proximally and distally, and reconstitute the aorta, usually with the interposition of a synthetic sleeve graft; aortic valve repair or replacement may be also necessary in proximal dissections.[51,52] Medical therapy consists in

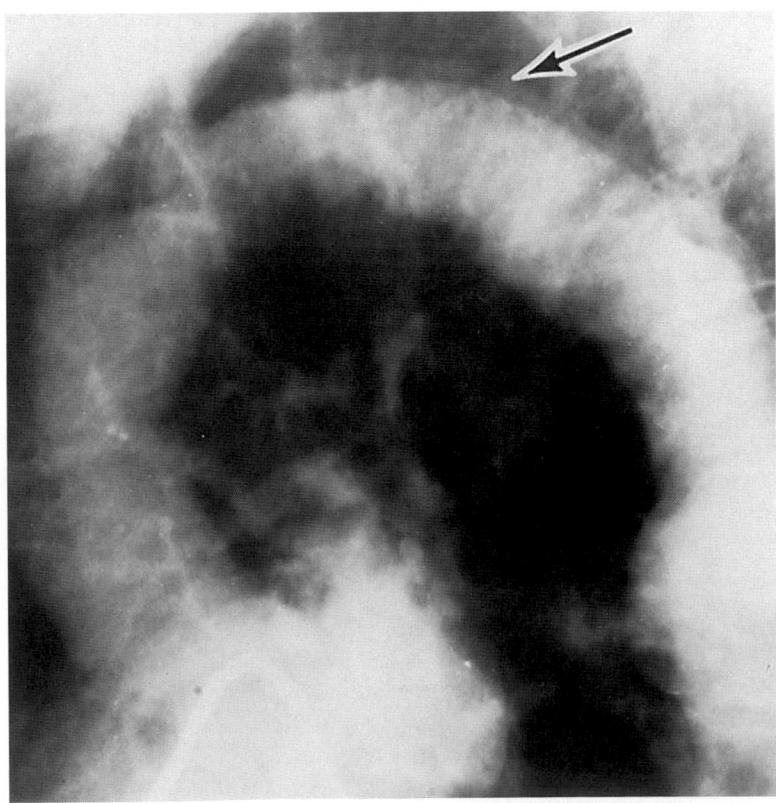

Fig. 27.21 Dissecting aneurysm in a 68-year-old man who died of rupture into pericardium on the way to the operating room. Double aortic shadow characteristic of dissecting aneurysm is indicated (arrow).

lowering the arterial blood pressure and diminishing the velocity of ventricular contraction.[54,55]

There is a need for proper selection in deciding surgical versus medical therapy. There is now general agreement that acute proximal dissections should be treated surgically whenever possible, whereas the treatment of distal dissections is more controversial.

Wheat et al.[55] reported the successful treatment of patients with acute dissecting aortic aneurysm by the use of antihypertensive agents. In a series of 33 patients so treated, McFarland et al.[54] reported that the survival rate was 52%, the mean follow-up period being more than 3 years. These authors emphasized the need for proper selection in deciding a surgical versus a medical therapy.

Exceptionally, dissecting aneurysms can occur in arteries other than the aorta, such as the renal, coronary, pulmonary, and carotid vessels.[57]

Diffuse arterial tortuosity and dilatation

Occasionally, a more or less generalized arterial dilatation and extreme tortuosity are seen in patients suffering from generalized arteriosclerosis (Fig. 27.22). Leriche[58] reported such instances as *dolicho et mega arteria*. The mechanism of the tortuosity and generalized dilatation is thought to relate to weakening of the arterial wall, but the cause for its generalized nature is not clearly understood.

One needs to know that such arterial dilatation and

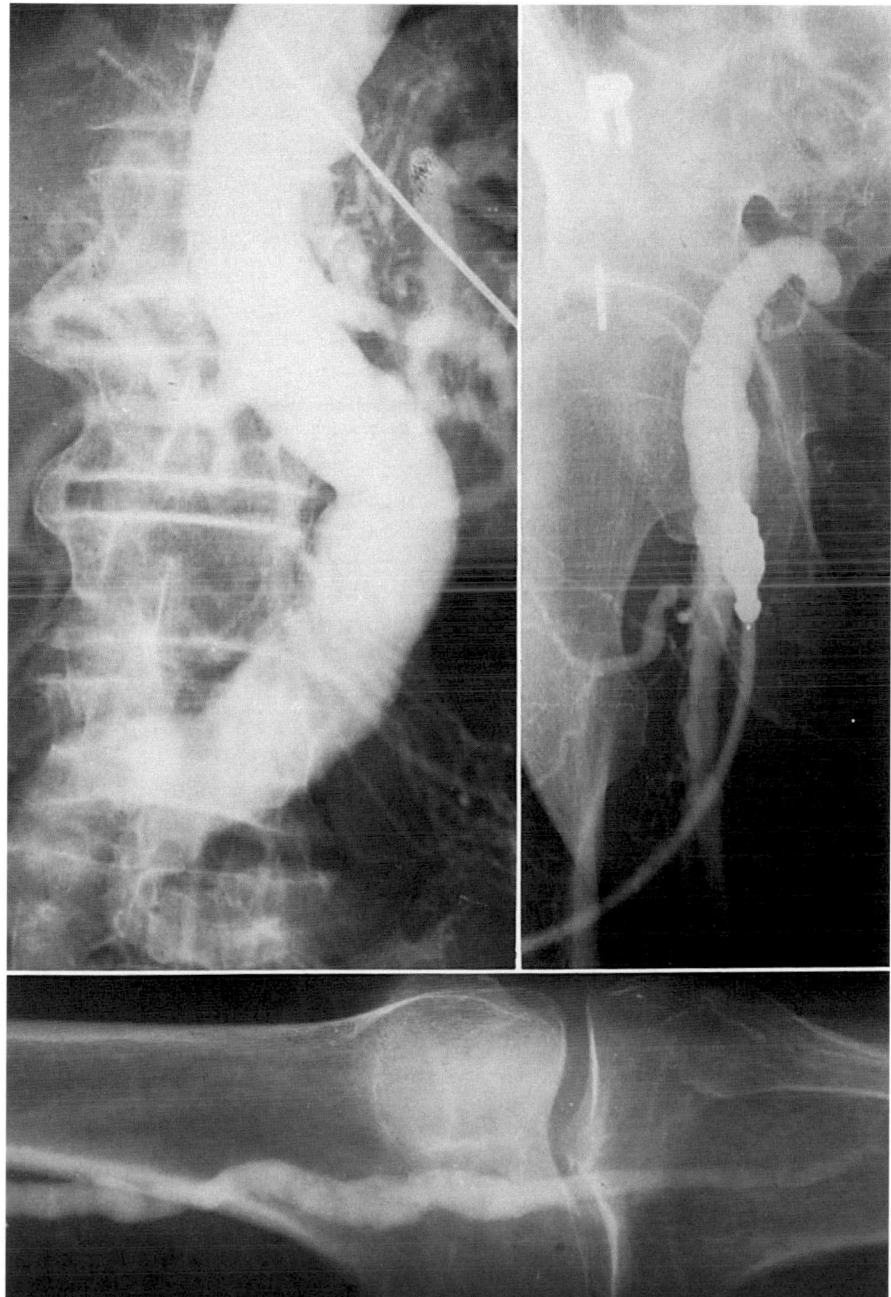

Fig. 27.22 Arteriograms of abdominal aorta and femoral and popliteal arteries illustrating generalized arterial dilatation and tortuosity in a patient who had a pulsating intra-abdominal mass initially diagnosed as aneurysm.

tortuosity may be mistaken for intra-abdominal aneurysm, since surgical attack on such generalized tortuosity is probably not warranted in the absence of complications.

Arterial substitution

Arteriosclerotic aneurysms of the abdominal aorta and the iliac arteries are best treated by excision and replacement of the involved arterial segment by synthetic prostheses.[60] Aneurysms of the popliteal arteries are probably best replaced by venous autografts. Arterial homografts are no longer used to replace diseased arterial segments because of the superiority of synthetic arterial prostheses.[59]

After implantation, homografts are partially replaced or encased by host collagenous tissue. In a few months, they lose much of their elasticity, although fragmented elastic tissue is still demonstrable histologically over a year after implantation. The evolution of the intimal surface of both homografts and synthetic cloth prostheses after implantation consists of the organization of the fibrin layer initially deposited and the development of a lining of flattened cells, which, by special staining techniques, appears nearly like normal vascular endothelium.[61] True endothelial ingrowth from the host artery occurs across the suture line for a variable distance.

Szilagyi et al.[62] reported late aneurysm formation in 2 of 55 aortic homografts and tortuous dilatation in 12 of 66 femoral homografts within 3 years after insertion. Calcification may appear in the wall of homografts after long implantation. Implantation of synthetic cloth prostheses is followed by their encasement with collagen and a decline in tensile strength of some of them.

Arterial occlusive disease

Thrombotic occlusions of the major arteries are often associated with arteriosclerotic changes such as calcification, atheromatosis, and ulceration of the intima.[73] The occlusive process is often insidious, although final thrombotic obliteration of the lumen is occasionally quite rapid and may be clinically indistinguishable from embolization. Indeed, the differentiation of the two pathologically and at surgery is quite difficult in older individuals in whom arteriosclerosis of the abdominal aorta is nearly universal. The process of occlusion probably begins in the iliac arteries near the aortic bifurcation from which thrombus formation propagates cephalad in the aorta, occasionally to the level of the renal arteries. Thrombi and emboli can become secondarily infected by fungi, particularly *Aspergillus* and *Mucor*.

The syndrome of distal aortic thrombosis (Leriche's syndrome) manifests itself with an insidious onset and gradual progression of symptoms of pain and easy fatigability in the legs, hips, and back; intermittent claudication; and sexual impotence.[77] In this condition, arterial insufficiency in the lower extremities usually is manifested clinically by the absence of pulses below the umbilicus. If the process is partial, weak pulsations may be felt or a characteristic systolic murmur heard over the abdominal aorta and the femoral arteries.

Despite the presence of intermittent claudication and the absence of pulses, many patients are found by arteriography to have near-normal distal arteries.[68] This patency of the peripheral arteries is probably responsible for the relative absence of muscular atrophy or of atrophy of skin appendages in the legs and feet of many of the patients despite their symptoms of peripheral blood flow insufficiency and lack of pulses.

Arteriosclerotic occlusive disease also frequently involves other major arterial bifurcations in the lower extremity such as those of the common iliac and common femoral arteries. In the latter instance, the intimal disease and thrombosis occur frequently in the external femoral artery just distal to the bifurcation. Other arterial segments in the lower extremity prone to early thrombotic occlusion are those associated with some degree of fascial fixation. Such areas exist (1) in the external iliac artery behind the inguinal ligament, (2) in the superficial femoral artery as it passes through the fascial ring beneath the adductor longus tendon, and (3) in the anterior tibial artery where it passes through the interosseous membrane.[69]

Although arteriosclerosis is a generalized arterial disease, the tendency for occlusive complications to develop early in its evolution at the sites just noted makes possible the successful treatment of patients with marked peripheral blood flow deficiency. Surgical correction of the obstructive disease, however, often only temporarily improves the peripheral blood flow because of the progressive nature of generalized arteriosclerosis.[81] Successful operative therapy of arterial occlusive disease relieves symptoms of ischemia but actually prevents amputation of but a few extremities. However, aggressive operative therapy in properly selected patients with limited gangrene of the extremities may permit healing after amputation of only the gangrenous part.[78]

The surgical treatment of major arterial occlusive disease is performed by using two general methods: arterial substitutes and thromboendarterectomy (intimectomy).

Thromboendarterectomy is superior to arterial replacement early after treatment of arterial occlusive disease of the aorta and iliac arteries.[66] Autogenous venous bypass for femoral arterial occlusive disease appears to be associated with patency rates superior to those following endarterectomy and synthetic bypass grafts.[67,76]

Successful results in 85% to 95% of patients with occlusions of the aortic and iliac arteries have been reported with both methods of treatment. Postoperative aneurysm formation and vascular thrombosis have also been reported following the use of both methods. The correction of femoral occlusive disease by endarterectomy or by the bypass arterial substitution technique has proved less beneficial than for larger arteries. Approximately 70% of the patients with femoral grafts develop late thrombosis.

The incidence of late failure of both endarterectomy and arterial grafting procedures will likely always be higher in the smaller femoral artery than in the aorta and iliac arteries.

Thromboendarterectomy of major arteries is a technique in which the diseased intima and thrombotic material filling the lumen are dissected from the inner portion of the media in a smooth and uniform manner so that the remaining adventitia and media of the artery can continue to conduct blood. The remaining arterial tube is lined rapidly by a fibrinoid layer that develops a pseudoendothelial surface similar to that lining an implanted arterial substitute. Likewise, early thrombosis does not occur in these segments if the transit time of the blood through them is rapid. Endarterectomized arterial segments, examined months after the operative procedure, show a fibrous type of intima with an endothelium-like covering and preservation of the remaining media and elastic tissue.[64]

Extensive medial calcification of the Mönckeberg type may occasionally be a contraindication to endarterectomy.

Studies of the elastic properties of normal human arteries and of arteriosclerotic arteries obtained at autopsy from patients of the same age have shown insignificant variations of elasticity coefficients between the two. The progressive encasement of synthetic prostheses with collagen and the similar encasement and invasion of fibrous tissue into the wall of homografts are associated with a reduction in the elastic properties of the implants. Their distensibility becomes much less after implantation.[65] Studies of both cloth prostheses and homografts at varying times after implantation indicate that the result is a collagen-like tube through which the blood flows. The response of the wall of the graft to distention is no longer that of the adjacent host vessels.

Arterial embolism of atheromatous origin is an important complication of arterial occlusive disease. It may occur spontaneously or following aortic surgery or angiographic procedures.[70,71,80] The complications vary according to the vessels affected and include livedo reticularis and gangrene of the lower extremities, ocular symptoms, cerebral infarct, gastrointestinal bleeding, renal hypertension, and renal failure.[63,72,74,75] The frequency of atheromatous embolism correlates with the severity of ulcerative atheromatous changes in the aorta. Simultaneous embolism to various organs may lead to a mistaken clinical diagnosis of polyarteritis nodosa.[79] Random biopsies of skeletal muscle may be diagnostic in these cases.[63]

Cystic adventitial degeneration

Cystic adventitial degeneration, a rare condition almost always affecting the popliteal artery, may cause luminal obstruction.[83,84] A collection of jelly-like material distends the wall and bulges into the lumen.[86] Most cases occur in young men without a history of trauma and without general arterial change. The microscopic appearance of the involved arterial segments is that of mucinous degeneration. The pathogenesis is probably related to that of soft tissue ganglion.[85] Other arteries may exceptionally be affected by this condition.[82]

Fibromuscular dysplasia

Fibromuscular dysplasia is a nonarteriosclerotic, noninflammatory vascular disease of unknown pathogenesis.[92] Humoral, mechanical, and genetic factors may play a role. It usually becomes manifest during the third or fourth decades of life, although it also can be seen in children.[94] It involves large and medium-sized muscular arteries, such as the renal, carotid, axillary, and mesenteric arteries, sometimes in a multicentric fashion.[90] Imaging techniques useful for the evaluation of this disease include CT scans, MRI, and angiography.[89] Morphologically, it is characterized by a disorderly arrangement and proliferation of the cellular and extracellular elements of the wall, particularly the media, with the resulting distortion of the vessel lumen.[87] The absence of necrosis, calcification, inflammation, and fibrinoid necrosis are important negative diagnostic features. Morphologic varieties with predominant intimal or adventitial involvement have been described.[88,91] Surgical techniques for this condition include graduated or balloon intraluminal dilatation (either isolated or associated with resection–anastomosis), saphenous graft, and reconstructive aneurysmorrhaphy.[93]

Mesenteric vascular occlusion

Mesenteric vascular occlusion may originate in veins or arteries. Rarely, occlusion of both occurs simultaneously. Arterial occlusion is the more frequent of the two[97,107] (62% of cases). After the initiation of arterial or venous thrombosis, hemorrhagic infarction of the intestine and its mesentery develops if the process is rapid in onset and extensive.

Venous mesenteric thrombosis often is associated with infection and cancer.[99,100] However, infection and cancer per se are not directly related to the mesenteric venous thrombosis.

The relative reduction in the frequency of mesenteric venous occlusion is probably due to antibiotic control of many intra-abdominal infections.

Occlusion of the mesenteric arterial system may be caused by emboli from thrombi in an arteriosclerotic aorta, from a fibrillating atrium, or from a mural thrombus secondary to myocardial infarction.[104] Mesenteric arterial occlusion also may follow arteriosclerotic change in the superior mesenteric artery with local thrombosis and such rare conditions as polyarteritis, septic arteritis, and thromboangiitis obliterans.[101] Mesenteric arteries can be involved in rheumatoid disease and cause infarction.[96] Arterial and venous thrombosis, followed by ulceration and necrosis of the bowel, has been described following surgical repair of aortic coarctation.[98] The pathogenesis of this condition, which has been erroneously designated as "mesenteric arteritis," is probably related to the occurrence of hypertension during the first 2 postoperative days.

The technique of color-flow Duplex imaging can detect the presence of significant arterial stenosis in over 80% of the cases.[105]

Infarction of the small intestine or colon, perforation, and peritonitis do not always follow mesenteric vascular occlusion, either arterial or venous. As a matter of fact, many patients with significant disease of the celiac and superior mesenteric arteries as detected by Doppler sonography are asymptomatic.[103] Johnson and Baggenstoss[99] reported the presence of infarction in only 52 of 99 patients found to have mesenteric vascular occlusions post mortem. Conversely, mesenteric infarct can be seen in the absence of arterial or venous occlusion.[102,106]

Infarction of the bowel depends on the location, extent of occlusion, rapidity of its onset, and state of the collateral circulation, as well as the general physical condition of the patient. Patients with cirrhosis of the liver and portal hypertension often have episodes of cramping abdominal pain associated with low-grade fever and moderate leukocytosis that gradually recede. Several such episodes may take place before a sufficient amount of the portal venous system is occluded to cause the clinical picture of intra-abdominal catastrophe.

The clinical diagnosis of mesenteric vascular thrombosis is difficult at times because the patient does not have the classic severe abdominal pain, distention, nausea, vomiting, leukocytosis, and shock. Such a picture depends on a massive sudden occlusion of the superior mesenteric artery or vein.

Acute occlusion of mesenteric arteries produces bowel necrosis without the early marked hypovolemic disturbances seen with extensive venous thrombosis. Bloody diarrhea is less common in arterial than in venous occlusions, but abdominal pain is generally more prominent in arterial occlusions. If the occlusion is sufficiently extensive to cause gangrene of the bowel, death from peritonitis follows if the bowel is not resected. A hypovolemic death in less than 24 hours, however, is often the outcome in the presence of massive venous occlusion.

Of the two types of occlusion, arterial embolic occlusion is more likely to be amenable to successful treatment than is venous thrombosis. The treatment of both conditions consists primarily of early abdominal exploration and resection of nonviable bowel. The determination of viability of laparotomy may be quite difficult. The extent of small bowel resection compatible with survival has been shown to be as much as three fourths of the organ.

To date, embolectomy has but rarely remedied occlusion of the superior mesenteric artery. However, because of the serious prognosis associated with extensive small intestinal and colonic resection, this procedure should probably be attempted more often.

Chronic intestinal ischemia produces the syndrome of abdominal angina. Segmental intestinal infarction may be incident to disease of small mesenteric arteries without involvement of the proximal superior mesenteric artery. So-called "nonocclusive intestinal infarction" is probably related to disease in these vessels in most instances.[95]

Renal artery disease and its relationship to hypertension are discussed in Chapter 17.

Traumatic and iatrogenic injuries

Rupture

Rupture of a major vessel in the absence of an aneurysm may follow open or blunt trauma; may exceptionally occur in a spontaneous fashion through an atheromatous plaque or an area destroyed by degeneration (as in Ehlers–Danlos syndrome) or inflammation[110–112]; or may be seen as a major complication of balloon dilatation, surgery, or radiation therapy.[108] Fajardo and Lee[109] reviewed 11 vascular ruptures in patients who had had previous treatment for carcinoma. The vessels involved were the aorta and the carotid and femoral arteries. Most patients were men who had been subjected to surgery and radiation therapy for epidermoid carcinomas of the oropharynx, esophagus, or genitalia. In most cases, the rupture was due to surgical rather than radiotherapeutic complications, such as necrosis of skin flaps, infections, and fistulas.

Thrombosis

Nonpenetrating trauma may result in occlusive thrombosis of a major artery such as the carotid artery following blunt trauma to the paratonsillar area.[114,116] In children, trauma and arteritis constitute the two most common causes of acquired occlusions of major arteries.[113,118] Organizing and recanalizing thrombi can exhibit a papillary pattern of anastomosing channels reminiscent of angiosarcoma[115] or else acquire a myxomatous appearance with primitive mesenchymal cells, similar to that of cardiac myxoma.[117]

Pulsating hematoma

Pulsating hematoma or false aneurysm usually results from a small perforation in the artery, usually produced by a sharp instrument or a small missile.[121] Traumatic aneurysms may also follow injury to an artery by blunt trauma.[119] The defect is only a few millimeters in diameter but is sufficiently large to allow the escape of blood into the immediately surrounding tissues.

Cohen[120] emphasized the role of the adventitial layer in the development of the aneurysmal sac because of its tendency to seal off the defect in the arterial wall. Of equal importance is the nature of the surrounding tissue and the strength of its fascial structures. When strong fascial surroundings are absent, the rate of aneurysmal enlargement is quite rapid. It is slower when the area of injury is within a circumscribed fascial channel such as Hunter's canal. The blood collects about the defect in the artery until the pressure within the hematoma approaches the mean blood pressure. Enlargement of the hematoma then slows because blood returns to the arterial lumen during diastole. It is this situation that produces the characteristic to-and-fro murmur heard over the pulsating hematoma. This murmur has a rather harsh systolic component and a softer diastolic component. The murmur is not constant as is the murmur of arteriovenous fistula. The walls of the pulsating hematoma contain varying amounts of laminated clot, which in turn is surrounded by a rather dense fibrous tissue reaction.

The operative treatment of pulsating hematoma is often not difficult. Usually the arterial wall defect can be closed by simple suture after evacuation of the hematoma and excision of the fibrotic aneurysmal sac. Occasionally, however, arterial substitution is required.

These lesions should be treated immediately on diagnosis to prevent continued enlargement, pain on compression of adjacent nerves and other structures, and ischemia of the tissues peripheral to them. Since ligation of the afflicted artery (if it is a major one) is no longer the treatment of choice, waiting for collateral vessels to develop is not indicated.

Acquired arteriovenous fistula

Acquired arteriovenous fistulas are seen most frequently during times of war and are produced in a manner quite similar to that of traumatic aneurysm. However, in this instance, the perforating injury involves both the artery and the adjacent vein. Such an injury usually results in a pulsating hematoma that communicates with both the arterial and venous lumina.[122]

Following trauma, the fistula may be established almost immediately. However, the communication between the arterial and venous systems is frequently delayed until the wound is partially organized and the thrombus in the hematoma surrounding the artery and vein is partially absorbed. Most patients present with a pulsating mass in the region of injury that can be differentiated from simple pulsating hematoma in several ways. The murmur over the pulsating region is usually continuous because of a continuous flow of arterial blood into the vein. In other words, during diastole the pressure in the pulsating hematoma about the arteriovenous communication is never sufficient to produce reversal of blood flow. In some slowly developing, long-standing arteriovenous communications in the absence of a pulsating hematoma, a massive sacculation of the adjacent vein may slowly develop.

Patients with an arteriovenous fistula usually show venous dilatation about and peripheral to the fistula, as well as increased skin temperature in the area of the fistula. Despite increased temperature near the lesion, the extremity peripheral to it is usually cooler than normal, since the actual peripheral blood flow is less.

When arteriovenous fistulas develop between smaller arteries and veins, the sac may be excised and the vessels ligated without difficulty. Those involving the larger arteries, such as the femoral, axillary, or popliteal artery, require the maintenance of arterial continuity. Some type of arterial substitution may be necessary occasionally in larger arteriovenous aneurysms, although transvenous closure of the defect in the arterial wall usually can be accomplished satisfactorily.

The dilatation of the major artery entering an arteriovenous fistula of long standing may be marked, and the degenerative changes in the arterial wall may be extensive. These changes consist of atherosclerosis, calcification, disruption of the elastic tissue network, and fibrosis. If the degeneration is sufficiently advanced, it is irreversible. In such arteries, aneurysms may develop despite the cure of the arteriovenous fistula. The dilatation of the artery entering the arteriovenous fistula is thought to result from the increased flow of blood through it.

Arteriovenous fistulas are associated with increase in cardiac output, pulse rate, and blood volume, which may lead to congestive heart failure (Fig. 27.23). Such systemic results rarely, if ever, develop from a single congenital arteriovenous fistula with the exception of those that appear in the pulmonary tree. Congenital arteriovenous fistulas usually present as tumefactions containing many relatively small arteries and veins surrounded by moderately large amounts of fibrous tissue. Their treatment is primarily excisional.

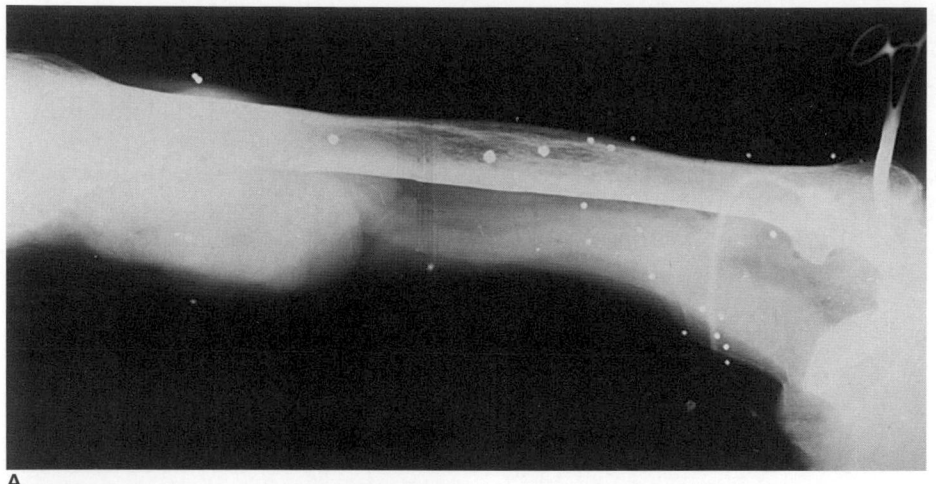

A

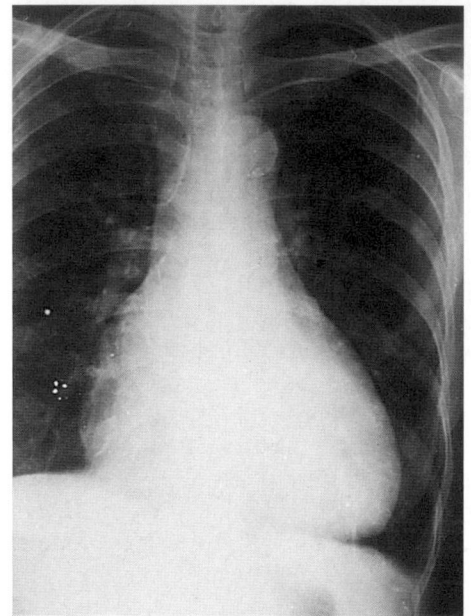

B

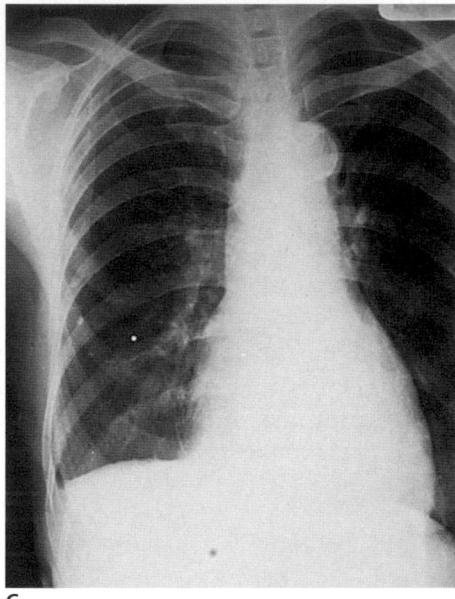

C

Fig. 27.23 Arteriovenous fistula in a 68-year-old woman. **A**, Arteriogram showing markedly enlarged femoral artery entering region of arteriovenous fistula. Pellets from original shotgun wound 30 years previously are visible. **B**, Radiograph before correction of arteriovenous fistula. **C**, Radiograph 5 days after operation.

Thromboangiitis obliterans

Thromboangiitis obliterans (Buerger's disease) is a rare thrombotic and inflammatory disease of the arteries and veins of unknown etiology that has no single diagnostic, clinical, or pathologic sign.[123,128,133] Its inflammatory component may involve entire neurovascular bundles. Although it is a generalized vascular disease, the involvement of the arteries of the lower extremities is usually most advanced, and the resultant flow deficiency is the usual reason for the patient to seek therapy. A form preferentially involving mesenteric vessels has also been described.[134] The onset of the condition occurs most often in men between 20 and 35 years of age and may be heralded by superficial migratory acute thrombophlebitis that is precipitated by undue exertion or exposure to cold. Study of biopsies of such involved veins shows the histologic changes associated with acute intravascular thrombosis. Pathologic involvement in the arterial tree is segmental and is usually present primarily in the smaller arteries. There is a paucity of collateral flow.[125] This process has a widespread geographic distribution[130] but has been reported with increased frequency in Korea and Japan.[129]

Microscopic examination of early arterial lesions shows panarteritis often associated with thrombosis. Endothelial proliferation and periarterial fibrosis soon become prominent. The inflammatory process attacks the entire thickness of the vessel wall and perivascular tissues.[128] Where nerves are in close proximity to the vascular tree, it involves the perineural stroma. Extension of the inflammatory process about peripheral sensory nerves may be responsible in part for the severe pain so common in afflicted extremities. Calcification in the arterial wall is absent. Arterial calcification on x-ray examination indicates arteriosclerosis rather than Buerger's disease.

The arterial and venous thrombosis associated with the angiitic process becomes partially recanalized. Cellularity of the organizing fibrous tissue replacing the thrombus is often prominent. Recanalization of thrombi is incomplete and is characterized by numerous small vascular channels passing through the remaining fibrous tissue.

The pathologic process ascribed to Buerger's disease may be difficult to distinguish microscopically from inflammatory and fibrotic changes that may accompany arteriosclerotic thromboses.[124,127]

The vascular process tends generally to be progressive, but in some instances the acute manifestation seems to subside, partially in patients who cease using tobacco.

Treatment is largely symptomatic and includes the control of pain, the avoidance of tobacco, and cleanliness of the extremity. Late in the disease, amputations may be necessary. Sympathectomy may benefit patients with cold, temperature-sensitive feet or hands and those with peripheral gangrenous ulcers.

The death of patients with Buerger's disease may follow complications attending gangrene of the extremities. However, many patients with this affliction die of myocardial infarction, renal insufficiency, occlusions of mesenteric vessels, and strokes.

With the use of arteriography and careful pathologic examination, a high proportion of cases of alleged Buerger's disease have actually been shown to be arteriosclerosis. This pathologic process can be mimicked with considerable exactitude by the development of embolism and thrombosis.[136] This has led some investigators to postulate that Buerger's disease is not a distinct entity but rather a peculiar manifestation of arteriosclerosis.[137] Although we agree that many cases originally diagnosed as Buerger's disease are indeed examples of arteriosclerosis, we believe that the entity thromboangiitis obliterans exists.[126,131,132,135,138]

Arteritis

Inflammatory diseases of the arteries have been classified on the basis of the etiologic agent involved, the caliber and location of the vessel affected, and the type of microscopic change observed.[138a,140a] The former is obviously the most desirable but, at present, impractical, since a specific etiologic agent can be detected for only a minority of the cases, such as in pneumococcal, syphilitic, mycotic, or tuberculous arteritis.[139,141] Imperfect as it is, a division based on the vessel caliber is quite useful. Within each group, the arteritides can be further subdivided into more or less specific types on the basis of the associated condition and/or pathologic appearance.[140]

Large vessel arteritis

A group of related nonsyphilitic diseases primarily affect the aorta and its main branches and are characterized by chronic inflammation and patchy destruction of the elements of the media.[145,160,164] They may result in aortic insufficiency, diffuse aortic tortuosity and elongation, the aortic arch syndrome, aneurysm formation, and dissection of the vessel (Fig. 27.24). They are more common in adults but have also been described in children.[148]

In some aortic aneurysms, there is a thick outer wall composed of fibroblasts and collagen that entrap fat, nerves, and lymph nodes and that are accompanied by a heavy lymphoplasmacytic infiltrate.[143] These have been referred to as *inflammatory aneurysms*,[146] but it is not clear whether they represent a distinct entity or simply a variant of atherosclerotic aneurysm, perhaps induced by antigens in the atheromatous plaque, and/or mediated by adhesion molecules (see p. 2439). The latter possibility seems the most likely,[155,161] although the possibility that CMV and HIV may play a pathogenetic role in some of the cases has been suggested.[144,166]

In the variety of arteritis known as **Takayasu's disease**, there is chronic inflammation and fibrosis of the arterial wall, which has a predilection for the aortic arch branches and results in the absence of pulses in the upper extremities, ocular changes, and neurologic symptoms (Figs 27.25 and 27.26).[149,151,157] In later stages, superimposed changes of arteriosclerosis may obscure the diagnosis.[150] In general, the possibility of an underlying arteritis should always be considered when arteriosclerotic changes in the aorta are seen in young or middle-aged individuals and when these changes are either segmental or occur at an unusual site. Most patients with Takayasu's disease are young, Asian, and female. The disease is rare in the United States, but it has been well documented.[152] In a series of 16 autopsy cases

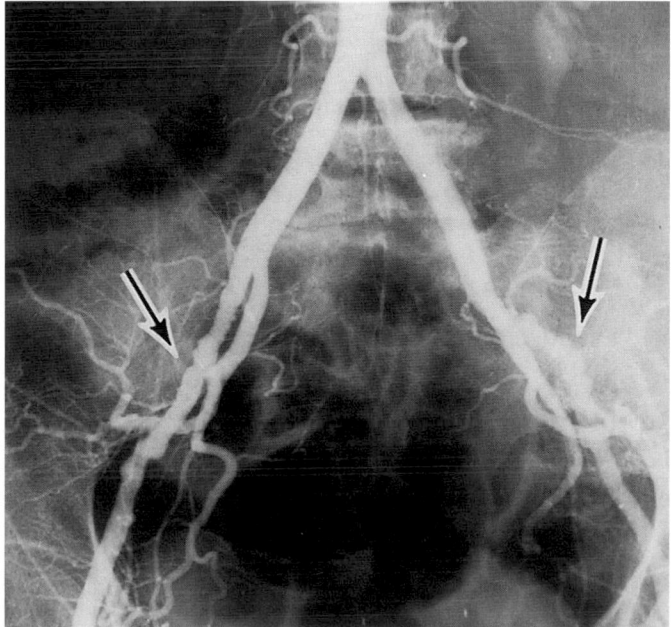

Fig. 27.24 Vasculitis in a 52-year-old woman showing scalloped irregularities limited to external iliac arteries.

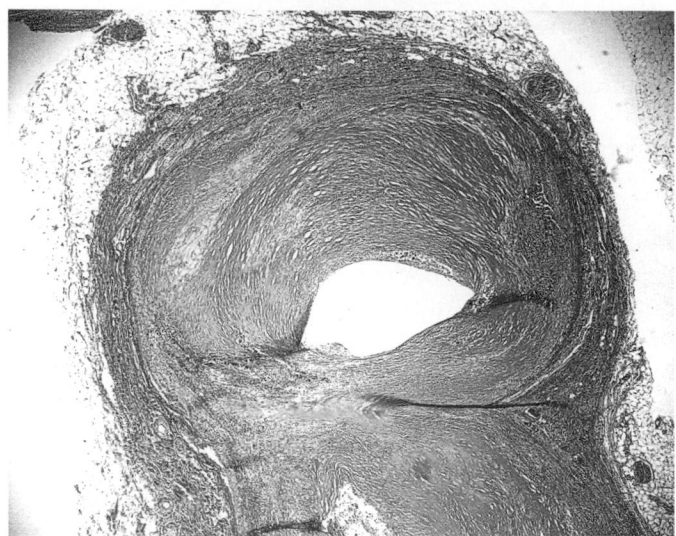

Fig. 27.25 Panoramic view of coronary artery in a case of Takayasu's arteritis. The massive hyaline thickening of the wall has led to marked narrowing of the lumen.

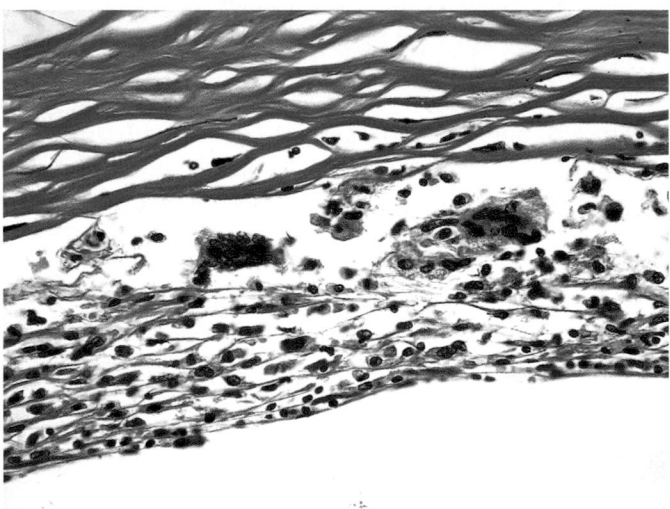

Fig. 27.26 Same case as Fig. 27.25. The high-power view shows subendothelial inflammation containing several multinucleated giant cells.

reported from South Africa,[162] there was segmental coronary arteritis in 3 patients, with development of coronary aneurysms in 2. There was coexistent tuberculosis in 37.5% of the patients, but this might well have been coincidental.

In Kawasaki's disease of infants, arterial changes are prominent and may result in sudden death from acute myocardial ischemia. Microscopically, the coronary and other arteries show reactive proliferative changes in the media, panarteritis, and frequent aneurysmal dilatation.[154] Marked fibrosis is present in the healed stage.[147] The etiology is unknown, but the pathologic changes are thought to be immune mediated.[142,153] Specifically, it has been suggested that the disease may be caused by a toxin that acts as a "superantigen."[156,159]

Aortic arteritis can be seen associated with rheumatoid arthritis, ankylosing spondylitis, and scleroderma.[163,165] There is a definite relationship between the type and location of the vessel and the frequency and etiology of the inflammatory diseases by which it may be affected. Tuberculosis characteristically involves small vessels; rarely, it may be seen in larger vessels and results in stenosis or aneurysms.[158]

Most of the reported cases of aneurysms of the superior mesenteric artery have been either syphilitic or mycotic; the majority of the latter were associated with bacterial endocarditis.

Medium-sized vessel arteritis

The classic example of medium-sized vessel arteritis is **polyarteritis nodosa**, classically described at autopsy as visible nodular lesions at the points of arterial branchings. This condition should be suspected clinically if there is a history suggesting hypersensitivity, with fever, eosinophilia, and involvement of many organ systems. Infrequently, there are skin manifestations. A muscle or peripheral nerve biopsy may be diagnostic.[178] A biopsy is most rewarding in the presence of a nodule. Rarely, organs such as the gallbladder, appendix, or colon may show unsuspected lesions typical of polyarteritis (see respective chapters).

In **Wegener's granulomatosis**, the arteritis is accompanied by necrosis and granulomatous reaction. The organs most commonly involved are the upper respiratory tract, lung, and kidney (see respective chapters).

Temporal arteritis (cranial arteritis, giant cell arteritis, Horton's disease) was originally thought to be restricted to the temporal, cerebral, and retinal arteries. However, many cases with generalized arterial involvement have been described, indicating that it is a systemic disease.[177,182] This condition, which is most common in the older age group, is characterized by pain in the distribution of the temporal artery and localized tenderness. In other patients, central nervous system manifestations predominate.[175] Sometimes, nodulations can be palpated along the course of the artery. Microscopically, partial destruction of the wall by an inflammatory infiltrate containing multinucleated giant cells is present.[176] Some of the multinucleated giant cells are of Langhans' type, and others are of foreign body type. Many of them are intimately associated with the internal elastic lamina, and some may even contain fragments of phagocytosed elastica in their cytoplasm. The presence of perivascular inflammation in the absence of inflammatory changes in the vessel wall is not diagnostic of temporal arteritis.[169] The pathogenesis of this disease remains unknown, but immune factors are thought to play an important role.[173]

Ultrastructurally, there is an accumulation of histiocytes, epithelioid cells, and giant cells at the intimal–medial junction, followed by fragmentation, degeneration, and dissolution of the internal elastic lamina.[181]

Immunohistochemical deposition of immunoglobulins and fibrinogen occurs in the vessel wall, but this is probably the result of diffusion from the lumen rather than a primary deposit of immune complexes.[168] It is important to emphasize that the changes are often segmental and that a negative biopsy does not rule out the diagnosis. In one series, only 60% of patients with clinical evidence of temporal arteritis had positive biopsies but the other 40% (showing arteriosclerosis or atherosclerosis) also responded to steroid therapy.[167]

Serial sections should always be performed[174] and contralateral biopsies should be considered in selected cases.[171] Angiography can be useful in guiding the surgeon to biopsy the diseased area.[170]

It should also be remembered that not all cases of arteritis involving the temporal artery represent examples of the entity temporal arteritis.[179,180]

The syndrome of *polymyalgia rheumatica*, characterized by muscle pain and tenderness involving mainly the muscles of the neck, shoulder, and pelvic girdle and accompanied by an elevated erythrocyte sedimentation rate, is often a manifestation of generalized giant cell arteritis.[172,183]

Degos' disease, a progressive subendothelial fibrous thickening of the wall of medium-sized arteries and arterioles, leads to vascular occlusions in many organs, particularly the skin and the digestive system, where ischemic infarcts result.[184]

Small vessel arteritis (arteriolitis)

Small vessel arteritis is the most common variety of arterial inflammation.[185] Most examples are secondary to hypersensitivity to drugs or bacterial antigens or appear as a component of one of the collagen–vascular diseases. The two most important morphologic features to be determined are the nature of the inflammatory infiltrate (whether lymphocytic or neutrophilic) and the presence or absence of necrosis of the vessel wall. In a large majority of the cases, skin manifestations are prominent (see Chapter 4). *Sneddon's syndrome* is an inflammatory syndrome of small arteries of unknown pathogenesis that is characteristically followed by smooth muscle proliferation.[186,187] The diagnosis can be suggested by skin biopsy.

Tumors

The general subject of vascular tumors is dealt with in Chapter 25. Only those neoplasms involving major vessels are discussed here.

Primary tumors of the *aorta* or *pulmonary artery* are almost invariably malignant and represent various types of sarcoma. Cases have been reported with names such as fibrosarcoma, leiomyosarcoma, rhabdomyosarcoma, fibromyxosarcoma, malignant fibrous histiocytoma, and malignant histiocytoma.[190,192,193,197,198,208,211] In some instances, abundant metaplastic cartilage and bone formation have been present.[189,201]

Some sarcomas are thought to originate from the intima and to represent a type of *angiosarcoma* (malignant hemangioendothelioma). The shape of the tumor cells ranges from spindle to epithelioid.[196] In contrast to those arising in smaller vessels, these tumors tend to have a predominantly solid pattern of growth, making the diagnosis very difficult.[209,210] Because of these interpretative problems and the fact that the clinical presentation correlates better with the location of the tumor than its microscopic type, it has been suggested that these sarcomas be simply classified as *intimal* (obstructive or nonobstructive) or *mural*.[191,200,214] Some of these tumors have arisen at the site of a vascular prosthesis,[189,194,213] and others at the site of a surgically constructed arteriovenous fistula. The latter, which represent a remarkable experiment of nature (if things done by surgeons qualify as such), have developed in the setting of chronic immunosuppression in renal transplant patients and have been of the epithelioid variety.[212] Embolic metastases are common.[203,207]

Most tumors arising in large veins are malignant and are largely represented by *leiomyosarcoma*[195,199,202] (see Chapter 25) (Fig. 27.27).

Additional primary tumors and tumorlike conditions that may exhibit a predominant or exclusive intravascular location are epithelioid hemangioendothelioma,[206] pyogenic granuloma, intravascular papillary endothelial hyperplasia, nodular fasciitis, so-called "systemic or malignant angioendotheliomatosis" (which in reality is an angiotropic malignant lymphoma), and synovial sarcoma. These entities are discussed in Chapters 4 and 25. We have also seen a case of entirely intravascular

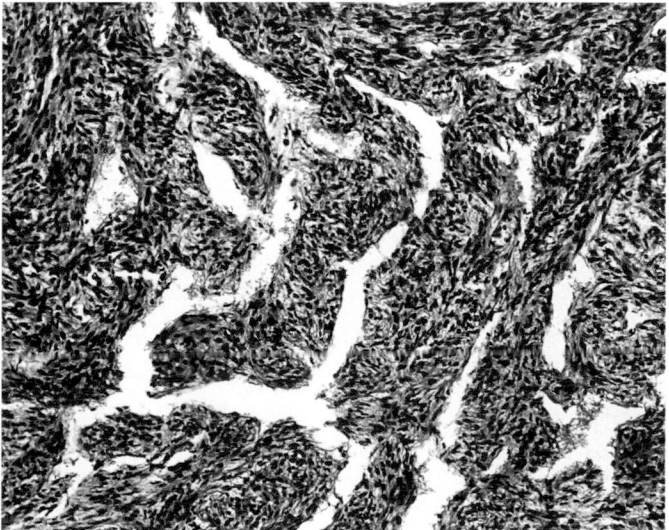

Fig. 27.27 Leiomyosarcoma of inferior vena cava. The vascular pattern of growth of the tumor is reminiscent of that seen in true hemangiopericytoma.

Kaposi's sarcoma. Arterial masses having a morphologic appearance similar to that of aneurysmal bone cyst have been recorded.[204]

Metastatic tumors can lodge in large vessels and produce occlusion. Cases of major arterial occlusion from carcinoma of lung and other sites have been well documented.[205]

References

Normal anatomy

1 Gallagher PJ. Blood vessels. In Sternberg S (ed.): Histology for pathologists, ed. 2. Philadelphia, 1997, Lippincott-Raven Publishers, pp. 763–788.

Arteriosclerosis

1a DeBakey ME, Crawford ES, Cooley DA, Morris GC Jr. Surgical considerations of occlusive disease of the abdominal aorta and iliac and femoral arteries. Analysis of 803 cases. Ann Surg 1958, **148**: 306–324.

2 DeBakey ME, Crawford ES, Cooley DA, Morris GC Jr, Garrett HE, Fields WS. Cerebral arterial insufficiency. One to 11-year results following arterial reconstructive operation. Ann Surg 1965, **161**: 921–945.

3 DeBakey ME, Crawford ES, Morris GC Jr, Cooley DA. Surgical considerations of occlusive disease of the innominate, carotid, subclavian, and vertebral arteries. Ann Surg 1961, **154**: 698–725.

4 Gimbrone MA Jr. Vascular endothelium, hemodynamic forces, and atherogenesis. Am J Pathol 1999, **155**: 1–5.

5 Gimbrone MA Jr, Topper JN, Nagel T, Anderson KR, Garcia-Cardena G. Endothelial dysfunction, hemodynamic forces, and atherogenesis. Ann N Y Acad Sci 2000, **902**: 230–239.

6 Hort W. Arteriosclerosis. Its morphology in the past and today. Basic Res Cardiol 1994, **89**: 1–15.

7 Kannel WB, Shurtleff D. The natural history of arteriosclerosis obliterans. Cardiovasc Clin 1971, **3**: 37–52.

8 Raines EW, Ross R. Smooth muscle cells and the pathogenesis of the lesions of atherosclerosis. Br Heart J 1993, **69**: S30–S37.

9 Ross R. Atherosclerosis. Current understanding of mechanisms and future strategies in therapy. Transplant Proc 1993, **25**: 2041–2043.

10 Ross R. The pathogenesis of atherosclerosis. A perspective for the 1990s. Nature 1993, **362**: 801–809.

11 Ross R. Rous-Whipple Award Lecture. Atherosclerosis. A defense mechanism gone awry. Am J Pathol 1993, **143**: 987–1002.

12 Stary HC, Chandler AB, Glagov S, Guyton JR, Insull W Jr, Rosenfeld ME, Schaffer SA, Schwartz CJ, Wagner WD, Wissler RW. A definition of initial, fatty streak, and intermediate lesions of atherosclerosis. A report from the Committee on Vascular Lesions of the Council on Arteriosclerosis, American Heart Association. Arterioscler Thromb 1994, **14**: 840–856.

13 Thompson JE, Kartchner MM, Austin DJ, Wheeler CG, Patman RD. Carotid endarterectomy for cerebrovascular insufficiency (stroke). Follow-up of 359 cases. Ann Surg 1966, **163**: 751–763.

Aneurysms

Aortic aneurysms

14 Ariyan S, Cahow CE, Greene FL, Stansel HC. Successful treatment of hepatic artery aneurysm with erosion into the common duct. Ann Surg 1975, **182**: 169–172.

15 Belkin M, Donaldson MC, Whittemore AD. Abdominal aortic aneurysms. Curr Opin Cardiol 1994, **9**: 581–590.

16 Bennett DE, Cherry JK. Bacterial infection of aortic aneurysms. A clinicopathological study. Am J Surg 1967, **113**: 321–326.

17 Borst HG, Laas J. Surgical treatment of thoracic aortic aneurysms. Adv Card Surg 1993, **4**: 47–87.

18 Bowers J, Koehler PR, Hammar SP, Nelson JA, Tolman KG. Rupture of a splenic artery aneurysm into the pancreatic duct. Gastroenterology 1976, **70**: 1152–1155.

19 Darling RC, Messina CR, Brewster DC, Ottinger LW. Autopsy study of unoperated abdominal aortic aneurysms. The case for early resection. Circulation 1977, **56**(Suppl): 161–164.

20 DeBakey ME, Cooley DA, Creech O Jr. Resection of aneurysms of thoracic aorta. Surg Clin North Am 1956, **36**: 969–982.

21 DeBakey ME, Crawford ES, Cooley DA, Morris GC Jr, Royster TS, Abbott WP. Aneurysm of abdominal aorta. Analysis of results of graft replacement therapy one to eleven years after operation. Ann Surg 1964, **160**: 622–639.

22 DeBakey ME, Creech O Jr, Morris GC Jr. Aneurysm of thoracoabdominal aorta involving the celiac, superior mesenteric, and renal arteries. Report of 4 cases treated by resection and homograft replacement. Ann Surg 1956, **144**: 549–573.

23 de Takats G, Pirani CL. Aneurysms. General considerations. Angiology 1954, **5**: 173–208.

24 De Vries DP, Van Schil PE, Vanmaele RG, Schoofs EL. Inflammatory aneurysms of the abdominal aorta. A five years experience. Acta Chir Belg 1994, **94**: 7–11.

25 Farkas JC, Fichelle JM, Laurian C, Jean-Baptiste A, Gigou F, Marzelle J, Goldstein FW, Cormier JM. Long-term follow-up of positive cultures in 500 abdominal aortic aneurysms. Arch Surg 1993, **128**: 284–288.

26 Hatswell EM. Abdominal aortic aneurysm surgery. I. An overview and discussion of immediate perioperative complications. Heart Lung 1994, **23**: 228–241.

27 Hirst AE Jr, Affeidt JE. Abdominal aortic aneurysm with rupture into the duodenum. A report of eight cases. Gastroenterology 1951, **17**: 504–514.

28 Imakita M, Yutani C, Ishibashi-Ueda H, Nakajima N. Atherosclerotic abdominal aneurysms. Comparative data of different types based on the degree of inflammatory reaction. Cardiovasc Pathol 1992, **1**: 65–73.

29 Kampmeir RH. Saccular aneurysm of the thoracic aorta. A clinical study of 633 cases. Ann Intern Med 1938, **12**: 624–651.

30 Kiell CS, Ernst CB. Advances in management of abdominal aortic aneurysm. Adv Surg 1993, **26**: 73–98.

31 Kiernan PD, Pairolero PC, Hubert JP Jr, Mucha P Jr, Wallace RB. Aortic graft-enteric fistula. Mayo Clin Proc 1980, **55**: 731–738.

32 Klima T, Spjut HJ, Coelho A, Gray AG, Wukasch DC, Reul GJ Jr, Cooley DA. The morphology of ascending aortic aneurysms. Hum Pathol 1983, **14**: 810–817.

33 Klippel AP, Butcher HR Jr. The unoperated abdominal aortic aneurysm. Am J Surg 1966, **111**: 629–631.

34 Kouchoukos NT, Dougenis D. Surgery of the thoracic aorta. N Engl J Med 1997, **336**: 1876–1888.

35 MacSweeney ST, Powell JT, Greenhalgh RM. Pathogenesis of abdominal aortic aneurysm. Br J Surg 1994, **81**: 935–941.

36 Money SR, Hollier LH. The management of thoracoabdominal aneurysms. Adv Surg 1994, **27**: 285–294.

37 Oskoui R, Davis WA, Gomes MN. Salmonella aortitis. A report of a successfully treated case with a comprehensive review of the literature. Arch Intern Med 1993, **153**: 517–525.

38 Ramshaw AL, Parums DV. The distribution of adhesion molecules in chronic periaortitis. Histopathology 1994, **24**: 23–32.

39 Reckless JPD, McColl I, Taylor GW. Aorto-enteric fistulae. An uncommon complication of abdominal aneurysms. Br J Surg 1972, **59**: 458–460.

40 Rose AG, Dent DM. Inflammatory variant of abdominal atherosclerotic aneurysm. Arch Pathol Lab Med 1981, **105**: 409–413.

41 Schatz IJ, Fairbairn JF II, Juergens JL. Abdominal aortic aneurysms. A reappraisal. Circulation 1962, **26**: 200–205.

42 Stehbens WE, Delahunt B, Shirer WC, Naik DK. Aortic aneurysm in systemic lupus erythematosus. Histopathology 1993, **22:** 275–277.

43 Szilagyi DE, Smith RF, DeRusso FJ, Elliott JP, Sherrin FW. Contribution of abdominal aortic aneurysmectomy to prolongation of life. Ann Surg 1966, **164:** 678–699.

44 Yonemitsu Y, Nakagawa K, Tanaka S, Mori R, Sugimachi K, Sueishi K. In situ detection of frequent and active infection of human cytomegalovirus in inflammatory abdominal aortic aneurysms: Possible pathogenic role in sustained chronic inflammatory reaction. Lab Invest 1996, **74:** 723–736.

Popliteal artery aneurysms

45 Gifford RW Jr, Hines EA Jr, Janes JM. An analysis and follow-up study of 100 popliteal aneurysms. Surgery 1953, **33:** 284–293.

46 Julian OC, Dye WS, Javid H. The use of vessel grafts in the treatment of popliteal aneurysms. Surgery 1955, **38:** 970–980.

47 Pappas G, Janes JM, Bernatz PE, Schirger A. Femoral aneurysms. Review of surgical management. JAMA 1964, **190:** 489–493.

48 Roggo A, Brunner U, Ottinger LW, Largiader F. The continuing challenge of aneurysms of the popliteal artery. Surg Gynecol Obstet 1993, **177:** 565–572.

Dissecting aneurysms

49 Cavanzo FJ, Taylor HB. Effect of pregnancy on the human aorta and its relationship to dissecting aneurysms. Am J Obstet Gynecol 1969, **105:** 567–568.

50 Cigarroa JE, Isselbacher EM, De Sanctis RW, Eagle KA. Diagnostic imaging in the evaluation of suspected aortic dissection. Old standards and new directions. N Engl J Med 1993, **328:** 35–43.

51 DeBakey ME, McCollum CH, Crawford ES, Morris GC Jr, Howell J, Noon GP, Lawrie G. Dissection and dissecting aneurysms of the aorta. Twenty-year follow-up of five hundred twenty-seven patients treated surgically. Surgery 1982, **92:** 1118–1134.

52 DeSanctis RW, Doroghazi RM, Austen WG, Buckley MJ. Aortic dissection. N Engl J Med 1987, **317:** 1060–1067.

53 Guilmet D, Bachet J, Goudot B, Dreyfus G, Martinelli GL. Aortic dissection. Anatomic types and surgical approaches. J Cardiovasc Surg (Torino) 1993, **34:** 23–32.

54 McFarland J, Willerson JT, Dinsmore RE, Austen WG, Buckley MJ, Sanders CA, DeSanctis RW. The medical treatment of dissecting aortic aneurysms. N Engl J Med 1972, **286:** 115–155.

55 Wheat MW Jr, Harris PD, Malm JR, Kaiser G, Bowman FO Jr, Palmer RF. Acute dissecting aneurysms of the aorta. Treatment and results in 64 patients. J Thorac Cardiovasc Surg 1969, **58:** 344–351.

56 Wilson SK, Hutchins GM. Aortic dissecting aneurysms. Causative factors in 204 subjects. Arch Pathol Lab Med 1982, **106:** 175–180.

57 Wychulis AR, Kincaid OW, Wallace RB. Primary dissecting aneurysms of peripheral arteries. Mayo Clin Proc 1969, **44:** 804–810.

Diffuse arterial tortuosity and dilatation

58 Leriche R. Physiologie, pathologique et traitement chirurgical des maladies artérielles de la vasomotricité. Paris, 1945, Masson.

Arterial substitution

59 Meade JW, Linton RR, Darling RC, Menendez CV. Arterial homografts. A long-term clinical follow-up. Arch Surg 1966, **93:** 392–399.

60 Stanley JC (ed.). Biologic and synthetic vascular prostheses. New York, 1982, Grune & Stratton.

61 Stump MM, Jordan GL Jr, DeBakey ME, Halpert B. The endothelial lining of homografts and Dacron prostheses in the canine aorta. Am J Pathol 1962, **40:** 487–491.

62 Szilagyi DE, McDonald RT, Smith RF, Whitcomb JG. Biologic fate of human arterial homografts. Arch Surg 1957, **75:** 506–529.

Arterial occlusive disease

63 Anderson WR, Richards AM, Weiss L. Hemorrhage and necrosis of stomach and small bowel due to atheroembolism. Am J Clin Pathol 1967, **48:** 30–38.

64 Barker WJ, Cannon JA, Zeldis LJ, Perry A. Anatomical results of endarterectomy. Surg Forum 1955, **6:** 266–269.

65 Bennett DE, Cherry JK. Bacterial infection of aortic aneurysms. A clinicopathological study. Am J Surg 1967, **113:** 321–326.

66 Darling RC, Linton RR. Aortoiliofemoral endarterectomy for atherosclerotic occlusive disease. Surgery 1964, **55:** 184–194.

67 DeWeese JA, Barner HB, Mahoney EB, Rob CG. Autogenous venous by-pass grafts and thromboendarterectomies for atherosclerotic lesions of the femoropopliteal arteries. Ann Surg 1966, **163:** 205–214.

68 DeWolfe VG, Beven EG. Arteriosclerosis obliterans in the lower extremities. Correlation of clinical and angiographic findings. Cardiovasc Clin 1971, **3:** 65–92.

69 Dible JH. The pathology of limb ischaemia. St. Louis, 1966, Warren H. Green.

70 Drost H, Buis B, Haan D, Hillers JA. Cholesterol embolism as a complication of left heart catheterization. Report of seven cases. Br Heart J 1984, **52:** 339–342.

71 Harrington JT, Sommers SC, Kassirer JP. Atheromatous emboli with progressive renal failure. Renal arteriography as the probable inciting factor. Ann Intern Med 1968, **68:** 152–160.

72 Hollenhorst RW. Vascular status of patients who have cholesterol emboli in the retina. Am J Ophthalmol 1966, **61:** 1159–1165.

73 Jorgensen L. Mechanisms of thrombosis. Pathobiol Annu 1972, **2:** 139–204.

74 Kalter DC, Rudolph A, McGavran M. Livedo reticularis due to multiple cholesterol emboli. J Am Acad Dermatol 1985, **13:** 235–242.

75 Kassirer JP. Atheroembolic renal disease. N Engl J Med 1969, **280:** 812–818.

76 Kouchoukos NT, Levy JF, Balfour JF, Butcher HR Jr. Operative therapy for femoral-popliteal arterial occlusive disease. A comparison of therapeutic methods. Circulation 1967, 35(Suppl 1): 174–182.

77 Krotovsky GS, Turpitko SA, Gerasimov VB, Zabelskaya TF, Mamedov DM, Klokov KI, Uchkin IG, Papandopoulos E. Surgical treatment and prevention of vasculopathic impotence in conjunction with revascularisation of the lower extremities in Leriche's syndrome. J Cardiovasc Surg 1991, **32:** 340–343.

78 Morris GC Jr, Wheeler CG, Crawford ES, Cooley DA, DeBakey ME. Restorative vascular surgery in the presence of impending and overt gangrene of the extremities. Surgery 1962, **51:** 50–57.

79 Richards AM, Eliot RS, Kanjuh VI, Bloemendaal RD, Edwards JE. Cholesterol embolism. A multiple system disease masquerading as polyarteritis nodosa. Am J Cardiol 1965, **15:** 696–707.

80 Stout C, Hartsuck JM, Howe J, Richardson JL. Atheromatous embolism after aortofemoral bypass and aortic ligation. Arch Pathol 1972, **93:** 271–275.

81 Warren R, Gomez RL, Marston JAP, Cox JST. Femoropopliteal arteriosclerosis obliterans. Arteriographic patterns and rates of progression. Surgery 1964, **55:** 135–143.

Cystic adventitial degeneration

82 Blackstrom CG, Linell F, Ostberg G. Cystic myxomatous adventitial degeneration of the radial artery with development of ganglion in the connective tissue. Acta Chir Scand 1965, **129:** 447–451.

83 Flanigan DP, Burnham SJ, Goodreau JJ, Bergan JJ. Summary of cases of adventitial cystic disease of the popliteal artery. Ann Surg 1979, **189:** 165–175.

84 Haid SP, Conn I Jr, Bergan JJ. Cystic adventitial disease of the popliteal artery. Arch Surg 1970, **101**: 765–770.

85 Lewis GJT, Douglas DM, Reid W, Watt JK. Cystic adventitial disease of the popliteal artery. BMJ 1967, **3**: 411–415.

86 Terry JD, Schenken JR, Lohff MR, Neis DD. Cystic adventitial disease. Hum Pathol 1981, **23**: 639–643.

Fibromuscular dysplasia

87 Claiborne TS. Fibromuscular hyperplasia. Report of a case with involvement of multiple arteries. Am J Med 1970, **49**: 103–105.

88 Crocker DW. Fibromuscular dysplasias of renal artery. Arch Pathol 1968, **85**: 602–613.

89 Furie DM, Tien RD. Fibromuscular dysplasia of arteries of the head and neck. Imaging findings. AJR Am J Roentgenol 1994, **162**: 1205–1209.

90 Harrison EG, Hung JC, Bernatz PE. Morphology of fibromuscular dysplasia of the renal artery in renovascular hypertension. Am J Med 1967, **43**: 97–112.

91 Hunt JC, Harrison EG Jr, Kincaid OW, Bernatz PE, Davis GP. Idiopathic fibrous and fibromuscular stenoses of the renal arteries associated with hypertension. Mayo Clin Proc 1962, **37**: 181–216.

92 Lüscher TF, Lie JT, Stanson AW, Houser OW, Hollier LH, Sheps SG. Arterial fibromuscular dysplasia. Mayo Clin Proc 1987, **62**: 931–952.

93 Moreau P, Albat B, Thevenet A. Fibromuscular dysplasia of the internal carotid artery. Long-term surgical results. J Cardiovasc Surg 1993, **34**: 466–472.

94 Price RA, Vawter GF. Arterial fibromuscular dysplasia in infancy and childhood. Arch Pathol 1972, **93**: 419–426.

Mesenteric vascular occlusion

95 Arosemena E, Edwards JE. Lesions of the small mesenteric arteries underlying intestinal infarction. Geriatrics 1967, **22**: 122–138.

96 Bienenstock H, Minick R, Rogoff B. Mesenteric arteritis and intestinal infarction in rheumatoid disease. Arch Intern Med 1967, **119**: 359–364.

97 Flaherty MJ, Lie JT, Haggitt RC. Mesenteric inflammatory veno-occlusive disease. A seldom recognized cause of intestinal ischemia. Am J Surg Pathol 1994, **18**: 779–784.

98 Ho ECK, Moss AJ. The syndrome of "mesenteric arteritis" following surgical repair of aortic coarctation. Report of 9 cases and review of literature. Pediatrics 1972, **49**: 40–45.

99 Johnson CC, Baggenstoss AH. Mesenteric vascular occlusion. I. Study of 99 cases of occlusion of veins. Mayo Clin Proc 1949, **24**: 628–636.

100 Johnson CC, Baggenstoss AH. Mesenteric vascular occlusion. II. Study of 60 cases of occlusion of arteries and of 12 cases of occlusion of both arteries and veins. Mayo Clin Proc 1949, **24**: 649–665.

101 Kempczinski RF, Clark SM, Blebea J, Koelliker DD, Fenoglio-Preiser C. Intestinal ischemia secondary to thromboangiitis obliterans. Ann Vasc Surg 1993, **7**: 354–358.

102 Ottinger LW, Austen WG. A study of 136 patients with mesenteric infarction. Surg Gynecol Obstet 1967, **124**: 251–261.

103 Roobottom CA, Dubbins PA. Significant disease of the celiac and superior mesenteric arteries in asymptomatic patients. Predictive value of Doppler sonography. AJR Am J Roentgenol 1993, **161**: 985–988.

104 Schneider TA, Longo WE, Ure T, Vernava AM. Mesenteric ischemia. Acute arterial syndromes. Dis Colon Rectum 1994, **37**: 1163–1174.

105 Volteas N, Labropoulos N, Leon M, Kalodiki E, Chan P, Nicolaides AN. Detection of superior mesenteric and coeliac artery stenosis with colour flow Duplex imaging. Eur J Vasc Surg 1993, **7**: 616–620.

106 Williams LF, Anastasia LF, Hasiotis CA, Bosniak MA, Byrne JJ. Nonocclusive mesenteric infarction. Am J Surg 1967, **114**: 376–381.

107 Wilson GSM, Block J. Mesenteric vascular occlusion. Arch Surg 1956, **73**: 330–345.

Traumatic and iatrogenic injuries
Rupture

108 Eeckhout E, Beuret P, Lobrinus A, Genton CY, Goy JJ. Coronary artery rupture during transluminal coronary recanalization and angioplasty in a case of acute myocardial infarction and shock. Clin Cardiol 1993, **16**: 355–356.

109 Fajardo LF, Lee A. Rupture of major vessels after radiation. Cancer 1975, **36**: 904–913.

110 Hasan RI, Krysiak P, Deiranyia AK, Hooper T. Spontaneous rupture of the internal mammary artery in Ehlers-Danlos syndrome (letter). J Thorac Cardiovasc Surg 1993, **106**: 184–185.

111 Rodriguez HF, Rivera E. Spontaneous rupture of the thoracic aorta through an atheromatous plaque. Ann Intern Med 1961, **54**: 307–313.

112 Worrell JT, Buja LM, Reynolds RC. Pneumococcal aortitis with rupture of the aorta. Report of a case and review of the literature. Am J Clin Pathol 1988, **89**: 565–568.

Thrombosis

113 Bickerstaff ER. Aetiology of acute hemiplegia in childhood. J Neurosurg 1964, **2**: 82–87.

114 Houck WS, Jackson JR, Odom GL, Young WG. Occlusion of internal carotid artery in neck secondary to closed trauma to head and neck. Report of two cases. Ann Surg 1964, **159**: 219–221.

115 Kuo T, Sayers CP, Rosai J. Masson's "vegetant intravascular hemangioendothelioma." A lesion often mistaken for angiosarcoma. Study of seventeen cases located in the skin and soft tissues. Cancer 1976, **38**: 1227–1236.

116 Pitner SE. Carotid thrombosis due to intraoral trauma. An unusual complication of a common childhood accident. N Engl J Med 1966, **274**: 764–767.

117 Salyer WR, Salyer DC. Myxoma-like features of organizing thrombi in arteries and veins. Arch Pathol 1975, **99**: 307–311.

118 Shillito J Jr. Carotid arteritis. Cause of hemiplegia in childhood. J Neurosurg 1964, **21**: 540–551.

Pulsating hematoma

119 Bennett DE, Cherry JK. The natural history of traumatic aneurysms of the aorta. Surgery 1967, **61**: 516–523.

120 Cohen SM. Peripheral aneurysm and arteriovenous fistula. Ann R Coll Surg Engl 1952, **11**: 1–30.

121 Gallen J, Wiss DA, Cantelmo N, Menzoin JO. Traumatic pseudoaneurysm of the axillary artery. Report of three cases and literature review. J Trauma 1984, **24**: 350–354.

Acquired arteriovenous fistula

122 Gomes MMR, Bernatz PE. Arteriovenous fistulas. A review of ten-year experience at the Mayo Clinic. Mayo Clin Proc 1970, **45**: 81–102.

Thromboangiitis obliterans

123 Colburn MD, Moore WS. Buerger's disease. Heart Dis Stroke 1993, **2**: 424–432.

124 Gore I, Burrows S. A reconsideration of the pathogenesis of Buerger's disease. Am J Clin Pathol 1958, **29**: 319–330.

125 Hershey FB, Pareira MD, Ahlvin RC. Quadrilateral peripheral vascular disease in the young adult. Circulation 1962, **26**: 1261–1269.

126 Ishikawa K, Kawase S, Mishima Y. Occlusive arterial disease in extremities, with special reference to Buerger's disease. Angiology 1962, **13**: 398–411.

127 Kelly PJ, Dahlin DJ, Janes JM. Clinicopathological study of ninety-four limbs amputated for occlusive vascular disease. J Bone Joint Surg 1958, **40**: 72–78.

128 Kurata A, Franke FE, Machinami R, Schulz A. Thromboangitis obliterans: classic and new morphological features. Virchows Arch 2000, **436**: 59–67.

129 McKusick VA, Harris WS. The Buerger syndrome in the Orient. Bull Johns Hopkins Hosp 1961, **109**: 241–291.

130 McKusick VA, Harris WS, Ottesen OE, Goodman RM. The Buerger syndrome in the United States. Bull Johns Hopkins Hosp 1962, **110**: 145–176.

131 McKusick VA, Harris WS, Ottesen OE, Shelley WM, Bloodwell DB. Buerger's disease. A distinct clinical and pathologic entity. JAMA 1962, **181**: 93–100.

132 Mills JL, Porter JM. Buerger's disease. A review and update. Semin Vasc Surg 1993, **6**: 14–23.

133 Olin JW. Thromboangiitis obliterans (Buerger's disease). N Engl J Med 2000, **343**: 864–869.

134 Schellong SM, Bernhards J, Ensslen F, Schafers HJ, Alexander K. Intestinal type of thromboangiitis obliterans (Buerger's disease). J Intern Med 1994, **235**: 69–73.

135 Shionoya S. Buerger's disease. Diagnosis and management. Cardiovasc Surg 1993, **1**: 207–214.

136 Theis FV. Thromboangiitis obliterans. A 30-year study. J Am Geriatr Soc 1958, **6**: 106–117.

137 Wessler S, Ming S-C, Guerwich V, Greiman DG. A critical evaluation of thromboangiitis obliterans. The case against Buerger's disease. N Engl J Med 1960, **262**: 1149–1160.

138 Williams G. Recent views on Buerger's disease. J Clin Pathol 1969, **22**: 573–577.

138a Hoffman GS, Weyand CM. Inflammatory diseases of blood vessels. New York, 2002, Marcel Dekker.

Arteritis

139 Manion WC. Infectious angiitis. In Orbison JL, Smith DE (eds): The peripheral blood vessels. Baltimore, 1963, Williams & Wilkins, pp. 221–231.

140 Parums DV. The arteritides. Histopathology 1994, **25**: 1–20.

140a Weyand CM, Goronzy JJ. Medium- and large-vessel vasculitis. N Engl J Med 2003, **349**: 160–169.

141 Worrell JT, Buja LM, Reynolds RC. Pneumococcal aortitis with rupture of the aorta. Report of a case and review of the literature. Am J Clin Pathol 1988, **89**: 565–568.

Large vessel arteritis

142 Arav-Boger R, Assia A, Jurgenson U, Spirer Z. The immunology of Kawasaki disease. Adv Pediatr 1994, **41**: 359–367.

143 Beckman EN. Plasma cell infiltrates in atherosclerotic abdominal aortic aneurysms. Am J Clin Pathol 1986, **85**: 21–24.

144 Chetty R, Batitang S, Nair R. Large artery vasculopathy in HIV-positive patients: another vasculitic enigma. Hum Pathol 2000, **31**: 374–379.

145 Domingo RT, Maramba MD, Torres LF, Wesolowski SA. Acquired aortoarteritis. A worldwide vascular entity. Arch Surg 1967, **95**: 780–790.

146 Feiner HD, Raghavendra BN, Phelps R, Rooney L. Inflammatory abdominal aortic aneurysm. Report of six cases. Hum Pathol 1984, **15**: 454–459.

147 Fujiwara H, Fujiwara T, Kao T-C, Ohshio G, Hamashima Y. Pathology of Kawasaki disease in the healed stage. Relationships between typical and atypical cases of Kawasaki disease. Acta Pathol Jpn 1986, **36**: 857–867.

148 Gonzalez-Cerna JL, Villavicencio L, Molina B, Bessudo L. Nonspecific obliterative aortitis in children. Ann Thorac Surg 1967, **4**: 193–204.

149 Hall S, Barr W, Lie JT, Stanson AW, Kazmier FJ, Hunder GG. Takayasu arteritis. A study of 32 North American patients. Medicine 1985, **64**: 89–99.

150 Ishikawa K, Maetani S. Long-term outcome for 120 Japanese patients with Takayasu's disease. Clinical and statistical analyses of related prognostic factors. Circulation 1994, **90**: 1855–1860.

151 Judge RD, Currier RD, Gracie WA, Figley MM. Takayasu arteritis and the aortic arch syndrome. Am J Med 1962, **32**: 379–392.

152 Kerr GS, Hallahan CW, Giordano J, Leavitt RY, Fauci AS, Rottem M, Hoffman GS. Takayasu arteritis. Ann Intern Med 1994, **120**: 919–929.

153 Leung DY. Kawasaki disease. Curr Opin Rheumatol 1993, **5**: 41–50.

154 Masuda H, Shozawa T, Naoe S, Tanaka N. The intercostal artery in Kawasaki disease. A pathologic study of 17 autopsy cases. Arch Pathol Lab Med 1986, **110**: 1136–1142.

155 Mitchinson MJ. Chronic periaortitis and periarteritis. Histopathology 1984, **8**: 589–600.

156 Nadel S, Levin M. Kawasaki disease. Curr Opin Pediatr 1993, **5**: 29–34.

157 Nasu T. Pathology of pulseless disease. A systematic study and critical review of 21 autopsy cases reported in Japan. Angiology 1963, **14**: 225–242.

158 O'Leary M, Nollet DJ, Blomberg DJ. Rupture of a tuberculous pseudoaneurysm of the innominate artery into the trachea and esophagus. Report of a case and review of the literature. Hum Pathol 1977, **8**: 458–467.

159 Pariser KM. Takayasu's arteritis. Curr Opin Cardiol 1994, **9**: 575–580.

160 Restrepo C, Tejeda C, Correa P. Nonsyphilitic aortitis. Arch Pathol 1969, **87**: 1–12.

161 Rose AG, Dent DM. Inflammatory variant of abdominal atherosclerotic aneurysm. Arch Pathol Lab Med 1981, **105**: 409–413.

162 Rose AG, Sinclair-Smith CC. Takayasu's arteritis. A study of 16 autopsy cases. Arch Pathol Lab Med 1980, **104**: 231–237.

163 Roth LM, Kissane JM. Panaortitis and aortic valvulitis in progressive systemic sclerosis (scleroderma). Report of case with perforation of an aortic cusp. Am J Clin Pathol 1964, **41**: 287–296.

164 Schrire V, Asherson RA. Arteritis of the aorta and its major branches. Q J Med 1964, **33**: 439–463.

165 Valaitis J, Pilz CG, Montgomery MM. Aortitis with aortic valve insufficiency in rheumatoid arthritis. Arch Pathol 1957, **63**: 207–212.

166 Yonemitsu Y, Nakagawa K, Tanaka S, Mori R, Sugimachi K, Sueishi K. In situ detection of frequent and active infection of human cytomegalovirus in inflammatory abdominal aortic aneurysms: Possible pathogenic role in sustained chronic inflammatory reaction. Lab Invest 1996, **74**: 723–736.

Medium-sized vessel arteritis

167 Allsop CJ, Gallagher PJ. Temporal artery biopsy in giant-cell arteritis. A reappraisal. Am J Surg Pathol 1981, **5**: 317–323.

168 Banks PM, Cohen MD, Ginsburg WW, Hunder GG. Immunohistologic and cytochemical studies of temporal arteritis. Arthritis Rheum 1983, **26**: 1201–1207.

169 Corcoran GM, Prayson RA, Herzog KM. The significance of perivascular inflammation in the absence of arteritis in temporal artery biopsy specimens. Am J Clin Pathol 2001, **115**: 342–347.

170 Elliott PD, Baker HL Jr, Brown AL Jr. The superficial temporal artery angiogram. Radiology 1972, **102**: 635–638.

171 Goodman BW Jr. Temporal arteritis. Am J Med 1979, **67**: 839–852.

172 Hamilton CR Jr, Shelley WM, Tumulty PA. Giant cell arteritis including temporal arteritis and polymyalgia rheumatica. Medicine (Baltimore) 1971, **50**: 1–27.

173 Hunder GG, Lie JT, Goronzy JJ, Weyand CM. Pathogenesis of giant cell arteritis. Arthritis Rheum 1993, **36**: 757–761.

174 Klein RG, Campbell RJ, Hunder GG, Carney JA. Skip lesions in temporal arteritis. Mayo Clin Proc 1976, **51**: 504–510.

175 Kolodny EH, Rebeiz JJ, Caviness VS, Richardson EP. Granulomatous angiitis of the central nervous system. Arch Neurol 1968, 19: 510–524.

176 Lie JT. Temporal artery biopsy diagnosis of giant cell arteritis: lessons from 1109 biopsies. Anat Pathol 1998, 1: 69–97.

177 Lie JT, Failoni DD, Davis DC Jr. Temporal arteritis with giant cell aortitis, coronary arteritis, and myocardial infarction. Arch Pathol Lab Med 1986, 110: 857–860.

178 Maxeiner SR, McDonald JR, Kirklin JW. Muscle biopsy in the diagnosis of periarteritis nodosa. Surg Clin North Am 1952, 32: 1225–1233.

179 Morgan GJ Jr, Harris ED Jr. Non-giant cell temporal arteritis. Arthritis Rheum 1978, 21: 362–366.

180 O'Brien JP. A concept of diffuse actinic arteritis. Br J Dermatol 1978, 98: 1–13.

181 Parker F, Healey LA, Wilske KR, Odland GF. Light and electron microscopic studies on human temporal arteries with special reference to alterations related to senescence, atherosclerosis and giant cell arteritis. Am J Pathol 1975, 79: 57–80.

182 Parums DV. The arteritides. Histopathology 1994, 25: 1–20.

183 Royster TS, DiRe JJ. Polymyalgia rheumatica and giant cell arteritis with bilateral axillary artery occlusion. Am Surg 1971, 37: 421–426.

184 Strole WE Jr, Clark WH, Isselbacher KJ. Progressive arterial occlusive disease (Kohlmeier-Degos). A frequently fatal cutaneosystemic disorder. N Engl J Med 1967, 276: 195–201.

Small vessel arteritis (arteriolitis)

185 Jennette JC, Falk RJ. Small-vessel vasculitis. N Engl J Med 1997, 337: 1512–1523.

186 Sepp N, Zelger B, Schuler G, Romani N, Fritsch P. Sneddon's syndrome. An inflammatory disorder of small arteries followed by smooth muscle proliferation. Immunohistochemical and ultrastructural evidence. Am J Surg Pathol 1995, 19: 448–453.

187 Zelger B, Sepp N, Stockhammer G, Dosch E, Hilty E, Ofner D, Aichner F, Fritsch PO. Sneddon's syndrome. A long-term follow-up of 21 patients. Arch Dermatol 1993, 129: 437–447.

Tumors

188 Baker PB, Goodwin RA. Pulmonary artery sarcomas. A review and report of a case. Arch Pathol Lab Med 1985, 109: 35–39.

189 Ben-Izhak O, Vlodavsky E, Ofer A, Engel A, Nitecky S, Hoffman A. Epithelioid angiosarcoma associated with a Dacron vascular graft. Am J Surg Pathol 1999, 23: 1418–1422.

190 Bleisch VR, Kraus FT. Polypoid sarcoma of the pulmonary trunk. Analysis of the literature and report of a case with leptomeric organelles and ultrastructural features of rhabdomyosarcoma. Cancer 1980, 46: 314–324.

191 Burke AP, Virmani R. Sarcomas of the great vessels. A clinicopathologic study. Cancer 1993, 71: 1761–1773.

192 Chen KTK. Primary malignant fibrous histiocytoma of the aorta. Cancer 1981, 48: 840–844.

193 Emmert-Buck MR, Stay EJ, Tsokos M, Travis WD. Pleomorphic rhabdomyosarcoma arising in association with the right pulmonary artery. Arch Pathol Lab Med 1994, 118: 1220–1222.

194 Fehrenbacher JW, Bowers W, Strate R, Pittman J. Angiosarcoma of the aorta associated with a Dacron graft. Ann Thorac Surg 1981, 32: 297–301.

195 Hines OJ, Nelson S, Quinones-Baldrich WJ, Eilber FR.

Leiomyosarcoma of the inferior vena cava: prognosis and comparison with leiomyosarcoma of other anatomic sites. Cancer 1999, 85: 1077–1083.

196 Hottenrott G, Mentzel T, Peters A, Schroder A, Katenkamp D. Intravascular ("intimal") epithelioid angiosarcoma: clinicopathological and immunohistochemical analysis of three cases. Virchows Arch 1999, 435: 473–478.

197 Iwasaki I, Iwase H, Horie H, Ide G, Saito T, Furukawa Y. Leiomyosarcoma of pulmonary truncus. Acta Pathol Jpn 1984, 34: 863–867.

198 Johansson L, Carlen B. Sarcoma of the pulmonary artery. Report of four cases with electron microscopic and immunohistochemical examinations, and review of the literature. Virchows Arch 1994, 424: 217–224.

199 Kaiser LR, Urmacher C. Primary sarcoma of the superior pulmonary vein. Cancer 1990, 66: 789–795.

200 Miracco C, Laurini L, Santopietro R, De Santi MM, Sassi C, Neri E, Pepi F, Luzi P. Intimal-type primary sarcoma of the aorta. Report of a case with evidence of rhabdomyosarcomatous differentiation. Histopathology 1999, 435: 62–66.

201 Murthy MSN, Meckstroth CV, Merkle BH, Huston JT, Cattaneo SM. Primary intimal sarcoma of pulmonary valve and trunk with osteogenic sarcomatous elements. Report of a case considered to be pulmonary embolus. Arch Pathol Lab Med 1976, 100: 649–651.

202 Oliai BR, Tazelaar HD, Lloyd RV, Doria MI, Trastek VF. Leiomyosarcoma of the pulmonary veins. Am J Surg Pathol 1999, 23: 1082–1088.

203 Patel KR, Niazi TBM, Griffiths AP, Hardy GJ, MacLaren CAN, Reid IN. Massive osteolytic bone metastases from a primary aortic sarcoma: a case report. Hum Pathol 1997, 28: 1306–1310.

204 Petrik PK, Findlay JM, Sherlock RA. Aneurysmal cyst, bone type, primary in an artery. Am J Surg Pathol 1993, 17: 1062–1066.

205 Prioleau PG, Katzenstein AA. Major peripheral arterial occlusion due to malignant tumor embolism. Cancer 1978, 42: 2009–2014.

206 Rosai J, Gold J, Landy R. The histiocytoid hemangiomas. A unifying concept embracing several previously described entities of skin, soft tissue, large vessels, bone and heart. Hum Pathol 1979, 10: 707–730.

207 Ruijter ET, Ten Kate FJ. Metastasising sarcoma of the aorta. Histopathology 1996, 29: 278–281.

208 Salm R. Primary fibrosarcoma of aorta. Cancer 1972, 29: 73–83.

209 Schmid E, Port J, Carroll RM, Freidman NB. Primary metastasizing aortic endothelioma. Cancer 1984, 54: 1407–1411.

210 Steffelaar JW, van der Heul RO, Blackstone E, Vos A. Primary sarcoma of the aorta. Arch Pathol 1975, 99: 139–142.

211 Stevenson JE, Burkhead H, Trueheart RE, McLaren J. Primary malignant tumor of the aorta. Am J Med 1971, 51: 553–559.

212 Wehrli BM, Janzen DL, Shokeir O, Masri BA, Byrne SK, O'Connell JX. Epithelioid angiosarcoma arising in a surgically constructed arteriovenous fistula: a rare complication of chronic immunosuppression in the setting of renal transplantation. Am J Surg Pathol 1998, 22: 1154–1159.

213 Weinberg DS, Maini BS. Primary sarcoma of the aorta associated with a vascular prosthesis. A case report. Cancer 1980, 46: 398–402.

214 Wright EP, Virmani R, Glick AD, Page DL. Aortic intimal sarcoma with embolic metastases. Am J Surg Pathol 1985, 9: 890–897.

Veins

Thrombophlebitis and thromboembolism

Thrombophlebitis is a thrombotic disease of veins accompanied by varying degrees of inflammation.[3a] The venous wall is edematous, the intima irregularly ulcerated, and the media infiltrated with chronic inflammatory cells. As the acute inflammatory phase of the disease subsides, varying amounts of fibrous tissue are deposited in the adventitia and in the media. During the acute phase, the thrombus becomes attached more or less firmly to the denuded intima.

The process of thrombophlebitis is associated with edema of the extremity, which may be minimal or marked. When there is but little edema and few or no clinical signs of acute inflammation in the extremity, the venous thrombosis has been termed *phlebothrombosis* or bland noninflammatory venous thrombosis.[10] The noninflammatory type of thrombophlebitis is probably more frequently associated with pulmonary emboli than is thrombophlebitis with more marked signs of inflammation. However, the rigid separation of phlebothrombosis from thrombophlebitis is neither pathologically possible nor clinically practical. In most instances, these two conditions are merely different degrees of the same process.

Thrombophlebitis may involve only the superficial veins such as the saphenous vein. The vein is acutely inflamed and tender, and the overlying skin is usually red. When such thrombosis of the superficial veins occurs, there is usually little edema. However, thrombophlebitic edema may develop with marked rapidity and may be of great volume if the process extends into the deep venous system. Rapid shifts of extracellular fluid into the leg may be sufficiently massive to cause shock. In such instances, the extremity may become so swollen that cutaneous blebs develop, followed by cutaneous necrosis (phlegmasia cerulea dolens).[14] Thrombophlebitis of this severity, however, is rare. The usual postoperative or post-traumatic acute thrombophlebitis initially causes painful, tender, swollen, cool, and mottled or grayish white extremity. Clinical examination is notoriously inaccurate in the diagnosis of deep vein thrombosis. Useful diagnostic tests are ascending contrast venography, radiolabeled fibrinogen leg scanning, and impedance plethysmography.[9]

Purulent or septic thrombophlebitis is occasionally seen in association with abscess or other infection usually occurring in the peritoneal cavity or pelvis. Stein and Pruitt[15] found this complication in 4.6% of 521 burned patients who had been treated by venous catheterization. Purulent thrombophlebitis at any location is associated with marked chills and high temperature because of the bacteremia arising from the infected intravascular thrombus.

There is a statistically significant association between deep vein thrombosis and the subsequent development of cancer (Trousseau's syndrome).[11] Many of the tumors have been mucin-producing adenocarcinomas, and most of them have arisen from the pancreas.

Pulmonary embolism is often thought to be primarily a complication of some surgical procedure or trauma such as fracture, particularly of the lower extremity, but the incidence of this complication is as high on medical as on surgical services.[7] Some of the factors thought to favor intravenous thrombosis and subsequent pulmonary embolism are neoplasms, cardiac disease, venous stasis from any cause, infection in the immediate area of veins, trauma, spasm of vessels, intimal injury, increased coagulability, and immobilization of the limbs.[3,16] The use of oral contraceptives with early regimens was found to be causally related to the presence of thromboembolic phenomena.[5,13,17] Irey et al.[6] described distinctive vascular lesions in association with thrombosis in arteries and veins of 20 young women receiving oral contraceptives. The incidence of this complication has greatly diminished with modifications in the type and dosage of contraceptive drugs.

Pulmonary embolism is seen in all forms of thrombophlebitis. Sudden massive pulmonary emboli frequently occur in patients without antecedent symptoms or signs of peripheral thrombophlebitis.

The greatest percentage of thrombi resulting in pulmonary embolization are thought to originate in the veins of the lower extremity. In a classic study, Rössle[12] found that 27% of patients over 20 years of age harbored thrombi in the veins of the calf at autopsy. The study of Hunter et al.[4] confirmed these observations and indicated that the thrombosis occurred in over 50% of middle-aged or older persons confined to bed.

McLachlin and Paterson[8] stressed the finding of intravascular thromboses arising in relationship to the valve pockets. In 100 complete dissections of the veins of the pelvis and lower extremities, they showed gross venous thrombi in 34%, and in over one half of these there were pulmonary emboli. In their series, the thrombi found in 34 patients totaled 76: 6 in the pelvic veins, 49 in the thigh veins, and 21 in the leg veins. They found that 75% of the venous thrombi arose in the veins of the thigh and pelvis and 25% in the smaller veins of the calf and feet, with 92% arising in the lower extremities. Similar findings were reported by Beckering and Titus.[1]

Crane[2] concluded that approximately 85% of fatal pulmonary emboli arise in the legs (90% in postsurgical patients and 80% in cardiac or medical patients).

Stasis ulcers

The chief immediate complication of thrombophlebitis is pulmonary embolus, and the principal long-term complication is stasis ulceration.

The treatment of acute thrombophlebitis attempts to limit the extension of the process and to prevent pulmonary embolization. Elevation, rest with the maintenance of good hydration, elastic support, and possibly anticoagulant therapy are the initial measures. The effectiveness of anticoagulant therapy as usually administered for thromboembolic disease has been questioned.[18] Ligation of the venous system above the area of intravascular clotting is occasionally indicated when lesser measures fail to prevent pulmonary embolus.

As the acute phase of the disease subsides, measures must be taken to avoid later stasis disease in the lower extremity. The use of elastic supports to help control any dependent edema in the extremity is imperative and may be required for many months or years. With the passage of time, collateral venous channels may develop and communicate with the superficial venous systems, resulting in secondary superficial varicosities. Recanalization of the major deep veins is usually associated with the process. Any significant varicosities in the postphlebitic extremity should be removed.

For reasons not clearly understood, the prevention and control of stasis ulceration are quite difficult in the presence of subcutaneous varicosities. The preventive measures directed toward control of dependent edema are not often carried out by patients suffering from thrombophlebitis, so after several years cutaneous pigmentation, brawny edema, dermal and subcutaneous fibrosis, extensive secondary varicosities, and ulceration of the skin in the lower one third of the leg develop. Although stasis ulcers are seen in patients who have a history of past thrombophlebitis, such a history is commonly absent. Even in patients having thrombophlebitis, the exact pathogenesis of the process leading to ulceration is unknown.

The diagnosis of stasis disease is not usually difficult. Only occasionally are ulceration, pigmentation, and surrounding fibrosis confused with other forms of ulceration. Before extensive treatment of a patient with advanced chronic leg ulcer, careful evaluation of the arterial blood supply should be made. Any significant arterial flow deficiency will likely result in failure of surgical therapy for ulceration. Correction of major arterial occlusion should be made when possible, before treatment of the stasis ulcer in those patients in whom both are present. Obviously, the other rare causes of ulceration such as specific infections and neoplasms must be excluded. All ulcers should be cultured and any unusual-appearing ones biopsied before excisional therapy is undertaken.

If ulceration has not yet appeared or is not extensive or chronic in nature, total removal of the varicose veins with ligation of perforating veins may control the process. If stasis ulceration is extensive, chronic, and long standing, it is best treated by excision and stripping of all superficial varicosities of the extremity after high ligation and division of the saphena magna and its tributaries at the saphenous–femoral junction. The ulcer and its base should be excised down to normal tissue, with removal of all the inelastic thickened skin and fascia about it. The cutaneous–fascial defect should then be covered with a partial thickness cutaneous autograft.

Advanced stasis ulceration often requires extensive excision. In most instances, the depth of the excision should include the fascia overlying the muscle, for the fascial fibrosis and thickening are quite extensive in the presence of long-standing stasis ulcers. This also facilitates ligation of the perforating veins that are invariably present beneath the area of stasis fibrosis.

Varicose veins

Varicose veins occur more frequently in women than in men. Their incidence is much higher in obese women, particularly those who have had several pregnancies. Varicosities developing in women after pregnancy may be secondary to deep venous thrombosis.

Larson and Smith[20] reported that 213 of 491 patients (43%) had a definite family history of varicose veins, indicating some hereditary disposition. The superficial veins of the leg become dilated and tortuous and lose valvular function. Microscopically, there is fibrosis beneath the endothelium and in the wall, with secondary elastosis and loss of muscle. Calcification may occur.

Primary or simple varicosities often develop in the second and third decades of life and may be present for many years without causing symptoms or complications. The likelihood of thrombosis with propagation into the deep venous system and the likelihood of the development of the postphlebitic syndrome are sufficiently great to warrant the removal of varicose veins. The use of sclerosing agents is contraindicated because of the danger of deep venous thrombosis, as well as the temporary nature of the superficial venous occlusion obtained. The surgical removal of varicosities is best performed by venous stripping techniques and excisions.[19,21]

Tumors

Tumors of large veins are discussed together with tumors of arteries on page 2449. Tumors of smaller vessels are discussed in Chapter 25 (Soft tissues).

References

Thrombophlebitis and thromboembolism

1 Beckering RE Jr, Titus JL. Femoral-popliteal venous thrombosis and pulmonary embolism. Am J Clin Pathol 1969, **52:** 530–537.
2 Crane C. Deep venous thrombosis and pulmonary embolism. N Engl J Med 1957, **257:** 147–157.
3 DeBakey ME. Critical evaluation of problem of thromboembolism. Int Abstr Surg 1954, **98:** 1–27.
3a Gloviczki P, Yao JST. Handbook of venous disorders: Guidelines of the American venous forum. London, 2001, Arnold.
4 Hunter WC, Krygier JJ, Kennedy JC, Sneedend VD. Etiology and prevention of thrombosis of the deep leg veins. Surgery 1945, **17:** 178–190.
5 Inman WHW, Vessey MP. Investigation of deaths from pulmonary coronary and cerebral thrombosis and embolism in women in childbearing age. BMJ 1968, **2:** 193–199.
6 Irey NS, Manion WC, Taylor HB. Vascular lesions in women taking oral contraceptives. Arch Pathol 1970, **89:** 1–8.
7 McCartney JS. Postoperative pulmonary embolism. N Engl J Med 1957, **257:** 147–157.
8 McLachlin J, Paterson JC. Some basic observations on venous thrombosis and pulmonary embolism. Surg Gynecol Obstet 1951, **93:** 1–8.
9 Mohr DN, Ryu JH, Litin SC, Rosenow EC III. Recent advances in the management of venous thromboembolism. Mayo Clin Proc 1988, **63:** 281–290.
10 Ochsner A, DeBakey ME, DeCamp PT. Venous thrombosis, analysis of 580 cases. Surgery 1951, **29:** 1–20.
11 Prandoni P, Lensing AW, Buller HR, Cogo A, Prins MH, Cattelan AM, Cuppini S, Noventa F, ten Cate JW. Deep-vein thrombosis and the incidence of subsequent symptomatic cancer. N Engl J Med 1992, **327:** 1128–1133.
12 Rössle R. Ueber die Bedeutung and die Entstehung der Wadenvenenthrombosen. Virchows Arch Pathol Anat 1937, **300:** 180–189.
13 Sartwell PE, Masi AT, Arthes FG, Greene GR, Smith HE. Thromboembolism and oral contraceptives. An epidemiological case-control study. Am J Epidemiol 1969, **90:** 365–380.
14 Stallworth JM, Bradham GB, Kletke RR, Price RG Jr. Phlegmasia cerulea dolens. A 10-year review. Ann Surg 1965, **161:** 802–811.
15 Stein JM, Pruitt BA Jr. Suppurative thrombophlebitis. A lethal iatrogenic disease. N Engl J Med 1970, **282:** 1452–1455.
16 Turpie AG, Chin BS, Lip GY. Venous thromboembolism: pathophysiology, clinical features, and prevention. BMJ 2002, **19:** 887–890.
17 Vessey MP, Doll R. Investigation of relation between use of oral contraceptives and thromboembolic disease. A further report. BMJ 1969, **2:** 651–657.

Stasis ulcers

18 Butcher HR Jr. Anticoagulant drug therapy for thrombophlebitis in the lower extremities. An evaluation. Arch Surg 1960, **80:** 864–875.

Varicose veins

19 Agrifoglio G, Edwards EA. Results of surgical treatment of varicose veins. JAMA 1961, **178:** 906–911.
20 Larson RA, Smith FS. Varicose veins. Evaluation of observations in 491 cases. Mayo Clin Proc 1943, **18:** 400–408.
21 Myers TT. Results of the stripping operation in the treatment of varicose veins. Mayo Clin Proc 1954, **29:** 583–590.

Lymph vessels

With the exception of tumors of lymph vessels, such as lymphangioma and lymphangiosarcoma (see Chapter 25), the only primary lymphatic disease encountered clinically with some frequency is lymphedema. Chylothorax and chyloascites also occur, but in nearly all instances these processes are secondary to trauma, neoplastic disease, or some infectious process.

Lymphedema

Lymphedema may be classified as postinfectious, posttraumatic, obstructive, and idiopathic. In some parts of the world, lymphedema resulting from *Schistosoma (Filaria)* is very common.[1] Obstructive lymphedema is most often seen following obstruction of regional lymph nodes by malignant tumor or following node removal, as in radical mastectomy or in radical groin dissection. The development of lymphedema of the arm after radical mastectomy is more common in patients in whom postoperative infection has produced fibrosis in the axilla or in patients having persistent cancer in the axilla. However, lymphedema can also be seen in patients who give a history of as little trauma as a severely sprained ankle or following such infections as a furuncle.

Many patients give no history of trauma or infection associated with the onset of their lymphedema. In such instances, the lymphedema is usually termed idiopathic.[3]

This type is further subdivided into *lymphedema congenita, praecox* (beginning before the age of 35 years), and *tarda*.[2,4] Congenital idiopathic lymphedema, also known as Milroy's disease, is inherited as an autosomal dominant trait.

Postmastectomy lymphedema and, to a lesser degree, Milroy's disease can be complicated by the development of lymphangiosarcoma (see Chapter 25). Curiously, this complication is extremely rare in the cases of lymphedema resulting from schistosomiasis, although cases have been described.

Pathology

The obstructive pathogenesis of neoplastic involvement of regional lymph nodes is obvious. Injection techniques combined with magnification radiography have served to delineate accurately normal fine lymphatic channels, as well as tumor involvement[8,9,11] (Fig. 27.28).

The swelling of lymphedema is usually slowly progressive. There is dilatation of the dermal lymphatics, as well as the deeper fascial lymphatics.[5] When the degree of swelling is advanced, there is a depression of hair follicles and gross dermal edema. In such cases, the cutaneous lymphatics may be sufficiently dilated to be associated with lymphorrhea following minor cutaneous abrasions or needle punctures. Tissue sections of such skin usually show markedly dilated dermal lymphatics.

All forms of lymphedema are probably in some way

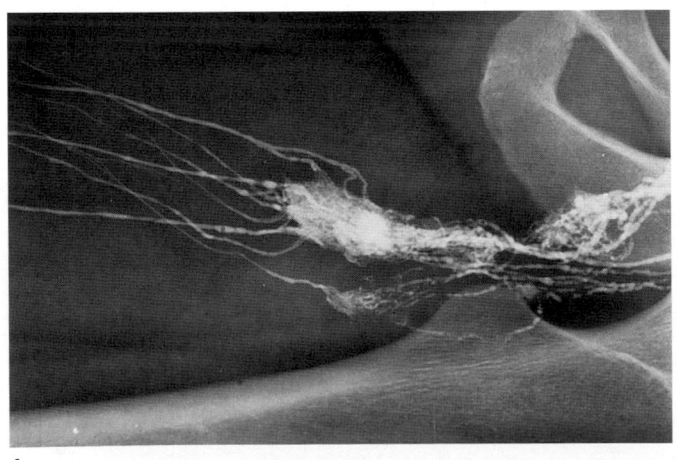
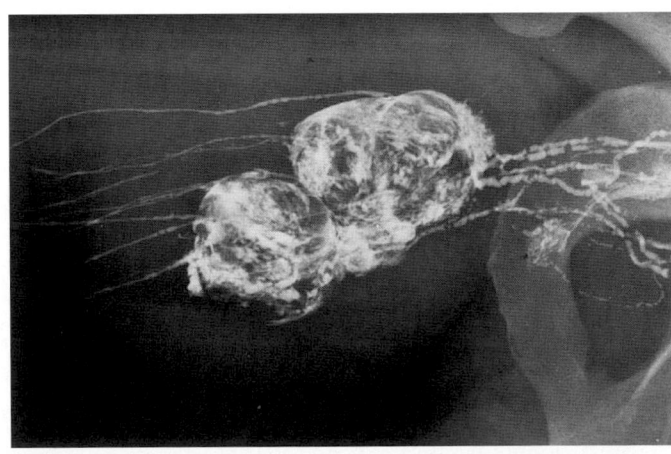

A

B

Fig. 27.28 A, Magnification radiograph of normal left superficial subinguinal lymph node with afferent and efferent lymphatic channels in a 40-year-old woman. **B**, Magnification radiograph of enlarged right superficial subinguinal lymph node with malignant infiltration secondary to primary melanoma of skin of heel. Same patient as shown in **A**. (From Isard HJ, Ostrum BJ, Cullinan JE. Magnification roentgenography. A "spot-film" technic. Med Radiogr Photogr 1962, **38**: 92–109)

associated with inadequate lymphatic drainage. Drinker and Yaffey[6] postulated that the increased protein content of the lymph present in chronic lymphatic stasis stimulates the deposition of fibrous tissue in the skin, subcutaneous tissue, and fascia. Such fibrosis aggravates the degree of inadequate lymphatic drainage and makes the disease slowly progressive.

Whatever the mechanism, the slowly progressive nature of lymphedema in many patients is associated with dermal thickening and collagenous deposition in the subcutaneous tissues and fascia. Bouts of superficial cellulitis and lymphangitis often become superimposed on the lymphedema in an extremity. In some patients, recurrent bouts of such infections are completely incapacitating. The presence of recurrent infection in such an extremity appears to hasten the deposition of collagen and may result in such a large amount of fibrotic replacement of subcutaneous fat and normal dermal structures as to make demonstration of dermal lymphatics impossible.

Kinmonth et al.[7] reported the presence of dilated, valveless, deep lymphatic channels in idiopathic lymphedema. These were visualized at operation after the injection of patent blue dye and by roentgenologic lymphangiography. Although many varicose-like lymphatic trunks were found in their patients, in none was a definite proximal site of lymphatic channel obstruction discovered.

In a few patients with idiopathic lymphedema having no clinical evidence or history of lymphangitis or cellulitis in the extremity, enlarged regional lymph nodes have been removed. Microscopically, they contain a mild chronic inflammatory response, sinusoidal fibrosis, and markedly dilated lymphatic channels. Direct communication between lymph nodes and veins has been demonstrated.[10]

Treatment

Treatment of lymphedema consists primarily of elevation of the extremity, compression, and massage, which must be maintained during many years of supervision. Recurrent bouts of streptococcal lymphangitis may be prevented by daily oral administration of antibiotics. Such conservative measures will control the lymphedema sufficiently to avoid operation in many patients.[12,13] Operative therapy is indicated only in about 15% of the cases when the extent of subcutaneous fibrosis, infection, and massive swelling is sufficient to markedly handicap the patient.[17,19]

The operation most commonly performed is the excision of the thickened fibrotic skin, the edematous subcutaneous tissue, and the thickened fascia overlying the muscles, followed by the immediate application of split-thickness cutaneous autografts.[16,18] The technique most frequently used is Kinmonth's modification of Homans' procedure.[15] A second group of operations,

referred to as physiologic, aim to provide or enhance lymph drainage[14]; these procedures are controversial and have not met with widespread acceptance.

In patients with sufficiently severe lymphedema to require excision of the skin, subcutaneous tissue, and fascia of the extremity, gross examination of the excised portions shows dense fibrotic bands and sheets extending through the markedly swollen subcutaneous tissue. Pockets of fluid may be found in the intervening tissue spaces at operation. The skin over the fibrotic dermis may be atrophic in some areas and hyperplastic and keratotic in others. The collagenous thickening of the dermis is usually extreme. Lymphatic channels as such are not often seen histologically in such skin and subcutaneous tissue. This is particularly true if the process has been associated with multiple episodes of dermal infection. Dilated dermal lymphatics may be demonstrated histologically and by dye injection techniques in the skin of a lymphedematous extremity unassociated with long-standing episodes of infection.

The dermal and subcutaneous fibrosis similar to that seen in advanced forms of lymphedema also occurs about long-standing chronic stasis ulcers. The obliteration of dermal lymphatics, however, cannot be related primarily to the etiology of stasis ulcers since similar obliteration occurs in the fibrotic skin of long-standing lymphedema, a condition rarely associated with chronic ulceration of the lower extremity.

Tumors

Benign and malignant tumors of lymph vessels are discussed in Chapter 25 (Soft tissues).

References

Lymphedema

1 Dandapat MC, Mohapatro SK, Mohanty SS. Filarial lymphoedema and elephantiasis of lower limb. A review of 44 cases. Br J Surg 1986, **73:** 451–453.

2 Lewis JM, Wald ER. Lymphedema praecox. J Pediatr 1984, **104:** 641–648.

3 Schirger A, Harrison EG Jr, Janes JM. Idiopathic lymphedema. JAMA 1962, **182:** 124–132.

4 Smeltzer DM, Stickler GB, Schirger A. Primary lymphedema in children and adolescents. A follow-up study and review. Pediatrics 1985, **76:** 206–218.

Pathology

5 Butcher HR Jr, Hoover AL. Abnormalities of human superficial cutaneous lymphatics associated with stasis ulcers, lymphedema, scars and cutaneous autografts. Ann Surg 1955, **142:** 633–653.

6 Drinker CK, Yaffey JM. Lymphatics, lymph and lymphoid tissue. Their physiological and clinical significance. Cambridge, Mass, 1941, Harvard University Press.

7 Kinmonth JB, Taylor GW, Tracy GD, Marsh JD. Primary lymphoedema. Clinical and lymphangiographic studies of a

series of 107 patients in which the lower limbs were affected. Br J Surg 1957, **95:** 1–10.

8 McPeak CJ, Constantinides SG. Lymphangiography in malignant melanoma. A comparison of clinicopathologic and lymphangiographic findings in 21 cases. Cancer 1964, **17:** 1586–1594.

9 Pomerantz M, Ketcham AS. Lymphangiography and its surgical applications. Surgery 1963, **53:** 589–597.

10 Pressman JJ, Simon MB. Experimental evidence of direct communications between lymph nodes and veins. Surgery 1961, **113:** 537–541.

11 Wallace S. Dynamics of normal and abnormal lymphatic systems as studied with contrast media. Cancer Chemother Rep 1968, **52:** 31–58.

Treatment

12 Browse NL. The diagnosis and management of primary lymphedema. J Vasc Surg 1986, **3:** 181–184.

13 Foldi E, Foldi M, Weissleder H. Conservative treatment of lymphoedema of the limbs. Angiology 1985, **36:** 171–180.

14 Huang GK, Hu RQ, Liu ZZ, Shen YL, Lan TD, Pan GP. Microlymphaticovenous anastomosis in the treatment of lower limb obstructive lymphedema. Analysis of 91 cases. Plast Reconstr Surg 1985, **76:** 671–685.

15 Kinmonth JB. The lymphatics. Surgery, lymphography and disease of the chyle and lymph systems, ed 2. London, 1982, Edward Arnold.

16 Savage RC. The surgical management of lymphedema. Surg Gynecol Obstet 1985, **160:** 283–290.

17 Schirger A, Harrison EG Jr, Janes JM. Idiopathic lymphedema. JAMA 1962, **182:** 124–132.

18 Servelle M. Surgical treatment of lymphedema. A report of 652 cases. Surgery 1987, **101:** 485–495.

19 Thompson N. Surgical treatment of chronic lymphedema of extremities. Surg Clin North Am 1967, **47:** 445–503.

28 Neuromuscular system

Marc K. Rosenblum, Juan M. Bilbao, and Lee-Cyn Ang

Central nervous system
Peripheral nerves
Skeletal muscle

Central nervous system
Marc K. Rosenblum

Normal anatomy

Dauntingly complex and characterized by extraordinary variation in regional architecture, the gross and microscopic anatomy of the human central nervous system (CNS) cannot be surveyed here in any methodic fashion. We preface this account of neurosurgical pathology with a brief review of those anatomic landmarks and topographic relationships that bear particularly on issues of differential diagnosis.[1] The cellular composition of the brain, the spinal cord, and their coverings are addressed only insofar as these topics are relevant to the current nosology of primary neoplasms arising in these locations, while considerations of traditional neurohistochemistry and immunohistology are deferred to those sections of this chapter dealing with specific tumor types and non-neoplastic conditions (e.g., demyelinating disease) that require application of such techniques for definitive classification.

Confined within the cranium and vertebral canal, the CNS is sheathed by connective tissue membranes that include a densely collagenous outer covering termed the pachymeninx or, more familiarly, dura mater and delicate inner investments known as the leptomeninges or pia-arachnoid. Under normal circumstances, these are closely apposed and loosely joined by a layer of dural border cells that are easily disrupted (artefactually or by expanding lesions such as hematomas) to yield a "subdural space" that is, in fact, only a potential tissue compartment. A sagittal dural fold referred to as the falx cerebri lies between the cerebral hemispheres, a second such fold—the tentorium cerebelli—separating the superior cerebellar surfaces from the overlying temporal lobes of the cerebrum. Enclosed within the cranial dura, in addition to meningeal artery branches, are venous sinuses that serve both to drain the cerebral veins and to carry away cerebrospinal fluid (CSF) transported from the subarachnoid space by arachnoid villi that project into these conduits. Termed pacchionian granulations as they achieve grossly visible proportions with normal aging, these villi are draped by specialized arachnoidal cells of interest to surgical pathologists as the likely progenitors of the meningioma, a relatively common, dura-based neoplasm. Whereas the dura adheres tightly to the endosteal surfaces of the skull, at spinal levels it is attached only anteriorly to the vertebral bodies and is surrounded on its lateral and posterior aspects by a true compartment—the epidural space—which contains segments of the spinal nerve roots, blood vessels, and a very modest amount of adipose tissue.

We introduce at this juncture several localizing terms current in clinical parlance that encode information of potential utility to the pathologist and that may be encountered in neuroimaging reports and on specimen requisitions. Because the substance of the brain and spinal cord constitutes the central "neuraxis," lesions localized to the neuroparenchyma proper are often described as intra-axial, whereas those that simply abut the CNS from a meningeal or juxtameningeal site are said to be extra-axial. The qualifiers intramedullary or extramedullary may be further invoked for masses lying within or adjacent to the spinal cord, respectively. The brain itself may be broadly but usefully parcelled into supratentorial versus infratentorial components, the former situated above and the latter below the tentorium cerebelli. The cerebellum and most of the brainstem, including the pons and medulla in their entirety, are infratentorial structures that may be collectively designated the posterior fossa contents. The supratentorial CNS consists of the cerebrum (subdivided into frontal, parietal, temporal, and occipital lobes) and deep nuclei of the basal ganglia, thalamus, and hypothalamus.

Within the CNS, connective tissue is scant and essentially restricted to the adventitia of blood vessels. There are no resident lymphoid elements. The parenchyma of the brain and spinal cord is composed principally of the bodies and cytoplasmic processes of neuroepithelial cell types, including neurons and various classes of glia. Subsumed under the latter designation are supporting astrocytes, myelinating oligodendrocytes, and ependymal cells that line ventricular surfaces. These all have their neoplastic counterparts, classified generically as gliomas and subclassified as astrocytomas, oligodendrogliomas, and ependymomas, respectively. Close kin of the ependyma are the specialized epithelial elements of the choroid plexus, which are responsible for the production of CSF and are represented among brain tumors by papillomas and carcinomas. The progenitory and differentiated neurosecretory parenchymal cells of the pineal gland, situated posterior to the roof (or "tectum") of the midbrain, may also be the targets of transformative events—thus the pineoblastoma and pineocytoma.

We close this necessarily truncated summary on a practical note. There can be no gainsaying the importance of lesion location in the formulation of differential clinical and histologic diagnoses, particularly when tumors are at issue. Meningioma, for example, should be a remote consideration for the pathologist confronted by neurosurgical material from an intra-axial mass but looms large if the lesion in question is dura-based or fills the cerebellopontine angle (where schwannoma might also be reasonably suspected). By contrast, astrocytomas of diffuse fibrillary type, oligodendrogliomas, and metastatic carcinoma account for most cerebral hemispheric tumors (particularly in adulthood). Pilocytic astrocytomas, which mainly affect young persons, exhibit a decided predilection for the cerebellum and third ventricular/hypothalamic region, whereas ependymomas frequent the fourth ventricles of children and the spinal cords of adults (where they constitute the most common intramedullary tumors). Primary CNS lymphomas are most often situated within deep, periventricular white matter structures or the basal ganglia, whereas germ cell tumors only exceptionally arise outside of a midline, pineal region–suprasellar axis and central neurocytomas are confined within the lateral ventricles. In a similar vein, the tapering conus medullaris and filum terminale of the distal spinal cord are the nearly exclusive hosts of myxopapillary ependymomas and CNS paragangliomas. Many other examples of regional CNS vulnerability to particular tumor types and non-neoplastic lesions are to be found in this chapter. The foregoing should serve to underscore the potential benefits of a dialogue among pathologists, neuroradiologists, and neurosurgeons.

Congenital abnormalities

Craniospinal dysraphism

Defective midline closure of the embryonic neural tube or its mesodermally derived coverings accounts for the varied malformations collectively referred to as **dysraphic states**. Expressions of craniospinal dysraphism range from trivial skeletal abnormalities that pass undetected through life to lethal anomalies of the nervous system proper that result in intrauterine fetal demise. Considered here are those representatives of this complex group most likely to be approached by the neurosurgeon.

The large majority of dysraphic malformations occur along the spinal axis, where they are chiefly localized, although by no means restricted, to the lumbosacral region.[1a,6] The minimal lesion—simple agenesis of the posterior vertebral arches—ranks among the most prevalent of congenital anomalies and is termed spina **bifida occulta**. Its presence may be suggested in otherwise asymptomatic cases by the finding of an overlying skin dimple or sinus tract, hyperpigmented patch, hairy tuft, angioma, or lipoma. **Spina bifida cystica** or **aperta** refers to the less common situation in which meningeal or neural tissues protrude through the osseous defect. The resulting lesion, generically designated a "**cystocele**,"

typically bulges from the posterior midline in saccular fashion and is subclassified according to the nature of its herniated elements, the major variants being **meningocele** and **meningomyelocele**. The latter, by definition, contains elements derived from the spinal cord, as well as its ensheathing meninges, and accounts for 80% to 90% of dysraphic cystoceles complicating spina bifida. Cystoceles may also present as ventrally positioned, pelvic, or laterally situated, paravertebral masses. The former are associated with sacral defects, the latter with hemivertebrae. It should be noted, however, that most "lateral meningoceles" are not true dysraphic lesions; instead, they represent arachnoidal diverticula that exit the spinal canal via widened neural foramina. These are most common at thoracic levels and are often encountered in the setting of type 1 neurofibromatosis.[5] Rarely, meningomyeloceles present as finger- or tail-like appendages in the lumbosacral region.[3,10]

The resected **meningocele** is a discoid mass covered on its external aspect by skin that may be attenuated but that is not usually ulcerated or otherwise disrupted. A narrow pedicle representing the cystocele's attachment to the spinal canal may hang from its smooth, membranous inner surface. The sac proper is composed of collagenous tissue containing meningothelial cells disposed along irregular clefts, around alveolar spaces, in nests and long cords. Distinct dural and arachnoid membranes are not formed. Some examples are associated with tumorous accumulations of mature adipose tissue ("**lipomeningocele**"), and the sac wall may also exhibit a disorganized proliferation of nerve twigs, smooth muscle bundles, and blood vessels. Displaced but otherwise normal spinal nerve roots may lie within the meningocele cavity but can often be successfully repositioned and thus do not usually appear in surgical specimens. The finding of neuroglial tissue in any form mandates a diagnosis of **meningomyelocele**.[1] This ranges in volume and organization from microscopic nests of glia embedded in the cystocele wall to recognizable, albeit deformed, spinal cord. Variants include the **lipomeningomyelocele** and the **syringomyelocele** (or **myelocystocele**), the latter characterized by gross distention of its included spinal cord's central canal. Rarely, meningomyeloceles are encountered in complex with intraspinal cysts lined by enteric epithelium—the so-called **split notochord syndrome**[4]—or with bona fide teratomas.[8] In any of these guises, the meningomyelocele is often covered by little more than a translucent membrane that represents atretic cutis and may contain plaques of ependymoglial tissue. This is prone to ulceration and predisposes to bacterial invasion of the CSF with ascending meningoventricular infection.

The outcome for infants afflicted by spina bifida cystica depends on the size and complexity of the malformation, particularly on the extent to which spinal cord elements participate in its genesis, and is frequently influenced by the presence of associated anomalies involving the spinal cord rostral to the cystocele, the cranium, and brain. Simple meningoceles are often unassociated with neurologic debility or attended by relatively mild paraparesis, are generally closed without incident, and only exceptionally prove fatal. Unfortunately, the far more common meningomyelocele is usually complicated by significant and irreversible impairment of lower extremity and bladder function. Furthermore, nearly all affected children also suffer an associated Arnold–Chiari malformation with hydrocephalus, the main structural features of this second anomaly being caudal displacement of the medulla and cerebellar vermis, kinking of the cervicomedullary junction, widening and shallowing of the posterior fossa, and, in many instances, deformation of the midbrain with aqueductal stenosis. Untreated, few patients survive childhood, and even with aggressive surgical intervention the mortality rate ranges from 30% to 60%. The leading immediate causes of death are meningitis, pyelonephritis, pneumonia, and progressive hydrocephalus. Rarely, squamous carcinomas arise from the chronically irritated epidermis overlying unattended cystoceles.[2]

To the externally evident malformations just described should be added various intraspinal and juxtaspinal anomalies, often referred to as occult or "closed" dysraphisms, that similarly occur in complex with spina bifida and its cutaneous stigmata but are imperceptible on physical examination because of their deep location. These, too, exhibit a decided predilection for the lumbosacral region, where they are typically discovered on neuroradiologic evaluation for myelopathy. It is fixation of the filum terminale or spinal roots to these abnormal structures, with resulting traction on the cord (as evidenced by displacement of the conus medullaris below the level of the L2 vertebral body), that is often responsible for their principal neurologic manifestations— disturbed gait, bladder spasticity or hypotonia, anococcygeal and perineal pain. Maldevelopmental lesions that may present as this "tethered cord" syndrome[1,6] include: intraspinal lipomas; dermoid, epidermoid, or hindgut cysts; intrasacral meningeal diverticula ("occult meningoceles"); and cystic intradural masses composed of neuroglial tissue ("occult meningomyeloceles"). The dividing collagenous or chondro-osseous septum characteristically present in cases of congenitally split spinal cord (diastematomyelia) is yet another potentially tethering anomaly, whereas the offending lesion in some instances is simply a short filum (typically thickened owing to fatty infiltration) or a fibrous band extending into the exposed spinal canal from the sacral subcutis. The latter is often associated with a telltale skin dimple or dermal sinus and may rarely exhibit a hamartomatous proliferation of included pacinian corpuscles.[1] Sizable thoracolumbar hamartomas that may contain nerves,

fat, muscle, cartilage, bone, glandular structures, and primitive urinary tract-type tissues have also been described as involving the spinal canal and exerting traction on the spinal cord.[9] Fortunately, many of these associated malformations are amenable to surgical correction, division of the immobilized filum frequently resulting in substantial neurologic improvement and relief of pain.

A distant second in incidence to the dysraphic cystoceles of the lumbosacral region are those involving the cranium.[6] These, too, hug the midline and, like their spinal counterparts, may contain meningeal derivatives alone or associated neural tissues. The latter, termed encephaloceles, vastly predominate. Approximately 80% of encephaloceles exit the cranial cavity in the region of the occiput via defects in the posterior wall of the foramen magnum or occipital bone. These are generally covered by intact scalp, subjacent to which are recognizable dural and leptomeningeal membranes, and may contain choroid plexus, cerebellar, and brainstem elements, in addition to substantial volumes of cerebral hemispheric tissue (Fig. 28.1). The extruded brain, which encloses a central CSF-filled chamber that may communicate freely with the ventricular system, can appear remarkably well formed but commonly exhibits microscopic abnormalities of cortical architecture, if not grossly anomalous gyration, and its covering leptomeninges frequently contain islands of heterotopic neuroglial tissue. Vascular compression at the level of the encephalocele's narrow intraosseous neck may result in secondary alterations such as hemorrhage and infarction. Excision and closure can often be effected without complication, but a regrettably large percentage of occipital encephaloceles are attended by malformations of the intracranial contents, microcephaly, and mental retardation.

Extraoccipital encephaloceles may protrude through defects in other portions of the cranial vault or bulge into the anterior or posterior fontanels but are more commonly of the sincipital or basilar types. Sincipital encephaloceles present as visible facial swellings in the region of the forehead, nasal bridge, or orbit, whereas basal variants are situated in the nasal cavity, sphenoid sinus, nasopharynx, or pterygopalatine fossa and therefore are not externally evident. The latter group includes transethmoidal encephaloceles that herniate through defects in the cribriform plate and constitute the most common polypoid intranasal masses encountered in the newborn. Prior to biopsy or resection, a congenital subcutaneous or submucosal mass in any of these locations must be carefully evaluated for evidence of extension into the cranial cavity. Inasmuch as the encephalocele communicates with the subarachnoid space via its associated osseous defect, intracranial repair with dural closure is required if CSF leakage and meningitis are to be avoided. Simple neuroglial heterotopias occurring in

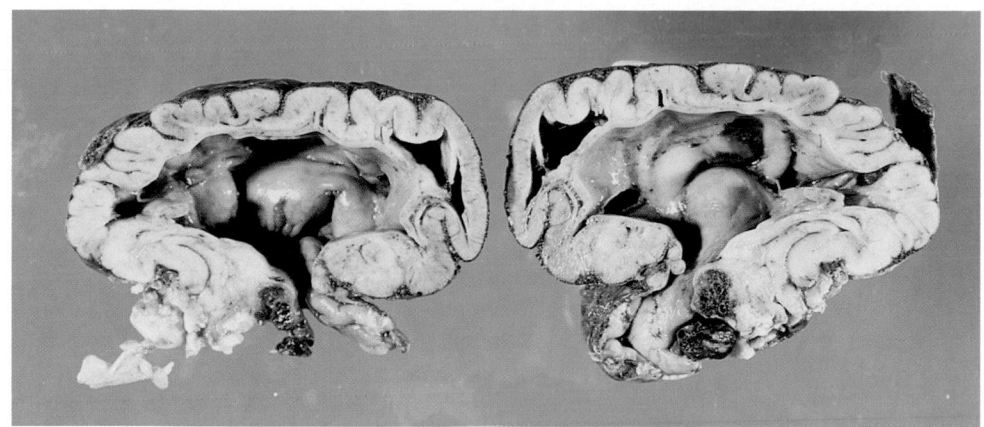

Fig. 28.1 Encephalocele. A well-developed, gyriform cortical mantle characterizes this neurosurgical specimen from the occipital region of a newborn. (Courtesy of Dr Humberto Cravioto, New York)

these same regions, by contrast, are defined as maintaining no open connection to the intracranial compartment and thus may be safely approached transnasally or transorally, depending on their precise situation. These are addressed separately later in this chapter. Suffice it to say that the results of neuroimaging study are often decisive in the classification of a given lesion because both the heterotopia and true encephalocele often consist solely of aggregated astroglia embedded in fibrous tissue. Either may contain admixed neurons. Heterotopias of the nasal region rarely if ever harbor ependymal elements, a feature of some encephaloceles, but these may be encountered in examples situated in other sincipital or basilar locations. Included meninges are an inconstant feature of specimens derived from extraoccipital encephaloceles, but, when identified, exclude heterotopia from further consideration.

Although this discussion is restricted to congenital anomalies, it should be noted that meningoceles and encephaloceles may be the acquired consequences of trauma or preceding neurosurgical procedures. "Endaural" examples may complicate chronic otitis media or mastoiditis and have been described as a late effect of cranial irradiation in childhood.[7]

Neuroglial and meningeal heterotopias

The **neuroglial heterotopia**, introduced in the preceding discussion of cranial dysraphism, is a displaced mass of mature central neuroepithelial tissue unconnected to the brain proper. Leptomeningeal examples constitute occasional incidental findings on post mortem examination and are frequently noted in association with major structural anomalies of the underlying nervous system (e.g., craniospinal cystoceles).[6,16] These are of little clinical import save for their hypothesized role as progenitors of the odd primary leptomeningeal glioma. Similarly, **intrapulmonary neuroglial rests** are an autopsy curiosity virtually restricted to fetuses and neonates harboring severe neural tube defects such as anencephaly.[17] The heterotopias most likely to engage the surgical pathologist frequent the same locations favored by sincipital and basal

encephaloceles—the bridge of the nose and nasal cavity, paranasal sinuses, palatal region, and nasopharynx—and are best regarded as "sequestered" variants of their obviously dysraphic counterparts.[19] By far the most common of these maldevelopmental lesions is the so-called **nasal glioma**, addressed in Chapter 7. Neuroglial heterotopias may also present in the cranial bones, scalp, orbit, and submandibular region.[19] Their structure varies. Most consist solely of solid glial nests embedded in fibrous tissues, only about 10% containing neurons and these rarely in abundance. Astrocytes usually predominate and are often the only neuroepithelial elements present in nasal examples. Pharyngeal lesions are typically more complex, often containing ependyma-lined clefts and choroid plexus-like formations. Pigmented neuroepithelial structures suggesting retinal differentiation may also be encountered in the latter. An intraorbital heterotopia composed of cerebellar tissue is on record.[13]

The neuroglial nature of the lesions under discussion is usually obvious in routinely prepared histologic sections but may be confirmed in a questionable case by immunolabeling of matrix and included astrocytic elements with antibodies to glial fibrillary acidic protein (GFAP).[19] The distinction of these rests from encephaloceles, a matter of considerable clinical significance, has already been addressed in the discussion of craniospinal dysraphism. It should be noted that neuroglial heterotopias occasionally exhibit worrisome cytologic abnormalities and troubling hypercellularity but are generally cured by simple excision. Even the small percentage that have reportedly recurred have been controlled with conservative local reoperation. Rare heterotopias interpreted as having undergone focal neoplastic transformation are to be found in the literature. The diminutive neoplasms purported to arise in this setting have included an oligodendroglioma,[12] a mixed glioma composed of oligodendroglial and astrocytic elements,[15] and a melanotic neuroectodermal tumor of infancy.[18] A probable instance of frontal lobe astrocytoma penetrating the cribriform plate to masquerade as a nasal glial heterotopia has also been depicted.[14]

In contrast to some sincipital and basal encephaloceles, neuroglial heterotopias do not contain elements derived from the meninges. Displaced meningothelium, however, may be encountered in curious lesions of the scalp variously interpreted as hamartomas or as meningeal dysraphias that have lost their connection to the intracranial compartment in the course of development ("**sequestered meningoceles**").[11,20] These extracranial meningeal heterotopias are often noted at birth but may not come to surgical attention until adulthood. They are situated most often in the dermis or subcutis of the midline occipital region, at the vertex, in the posterior fontanel, or overlying the lambdoid suture. Regional alopecia is a common associated finding. The lesion consists of collagenous tissue containing irregular slit-like spaces lined by flattened meningothelial cells. These may also form solid cords or, rarely, small nests. Central neuroepithelial derivatives are not present, but islands of necrotic cellular material that could conceivably represent degenerated neuroglial components have been described in some cases. Extracranial meningeal heterotopias may be misconstrued as melanocytic lesions, lymphangiomas, or even angiosarcomas[20] but can be distinguished in problematic cases by their expression of epithelial membrane antigen on immunocytochemical assay. These maldevelopmental lesions could theoretically serve as precursors to the rare bona fide meningiomas arising in the scalp, which are addressed along with other ectopic meningiomas in the discussion of meningothelial tumors.

The reader is referred to the section dealing with ependymal neoplasms for comment on myxopapillary ependymal rests of the sacrococcygeal region and their relationship to extramedullary ependymomas.

Choristomas and non-neuroepithelial hamartomas

Maldevelopmental rests composed of tissues foreign to the nervous system—"choristomas"—are only rarely encountered within the confines of the dura mater. **Ecchordosis physaliphora** is the term used to describe an intracranial heterotopia exhibiting the histologic and ultrastructural features characteristic of the notochord and its neoplastic offspring, the chordoma.[27,36] Ecchordoses are typically situated just ventral to the belly of the pons, are frequently connected to notochordal remnants in the adjacent clivus via attenuated transdural stalks, and usually take the form of bosselated, gelatinous nodules loosely adherent to the basilar artery. They generally measure no more than 1 to 2 cm in greatest dimension and, for the most part, are autopsy curiosities. Whether some larger, symptomatic examples are best regarded as "giant" ecchordoses or as bona fide intradural chordomas is questionable (see the section on chordoma). Neuroradiologically detected ecchordoses have been described as generally T_2-hyperintense and

nonenhancing on MRI, chordomas usually exhibiting contrast enhancement.[36] **Leptomeningeal rhabdomyomatosis** refers to microscopic aggregates of mature striated myofibers characteristically located in the prepontine region or cerebellopontine angles.[23] These may, in addition, harbor well-differentiated adipocytes, displaced neuroglial tissue, and aberrant peripheral nerve fibers and are usually detected in complex with major developmental anomalies of the CNS. Rarely, nodules composed of striated or smooth muscle are encountered in cranial nerve divisions.[21,29,37,38] These may contain admixed neuromatous elements and adipose tissue, can achieve considerable size and have been variously reported as **choristomas**, **neuromuscular** or **ectomesenchymal hamartomas**, **benign triton tumors** and **rhabdomyomas**. Also on record are several **müllerian choristomas of the lumbosacral region** associated with spina bifida, one intradural example containing endometrium, endocervical glands, and smooth muscle bundles.[32] We mention here isolated depictions of **intracerebral**[35] and **intraspinal**[30] **endometriosis**, although these are properly regarded as acquired, rather than developmental, lesions. Finally, there is the bizarre account of a minute adenoid cystic carcinoma arising in a cerebellopontine angle mass otherwise composed of mature salivary gland tissue.[22]

Meningioangiomatosis is the designation traditionally applied to what has long been regarded as an essentially hamartomatous or malformative process that usually occurs in sporadic fashion but that is clearly associated with type 2 neurofibromatosis (NF-2) as well.[39] Sporadic cases are nearly always solitary and found on evaluation for seizures, whereas NF-2-related examples are not infrequently multifocal and typically asymptomatic. The basic lesion (Fig. 28.2) is an en plaque proliferation of small blood vessels that dissects the cerebral cortex, halts abruptly at the gray–white junction and

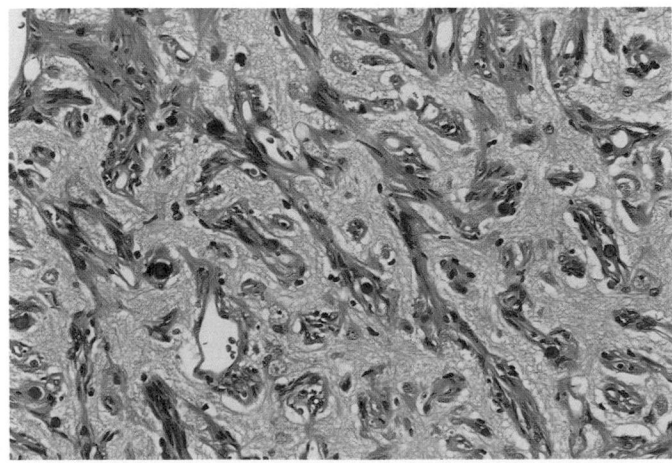

Fig. 28.2 Meningioangiomatosis. This typical example exhibits dissection of the cerebral cortex by small blood vessels with accompanying perivascular spindle cells and psammoma bodies.

is often accompanied by a spindle cell proliferation that may be tightly vasocentric or, in exuberantly cellular variants, arrayed in fascicular or storiform patterns. Loose whorling and schwannoma-like nuclear palisading may also be encountered. Extensive calcification is common, particularly conspicuous psammoma body formation, as are vascular hyalinization and regions of fibrous tissue overgrowth. A curious feature of the lesion is the tendency of entrapped neurons to develop Alzheimer-type neurofibrillary tangles.[26] Subcortical presentations have been described but are rare.[28] The term meningioangiomatosis notwithstanding, participating spindle cell populations have exhibited a meningothelial immunophenotype (specifically, labeling for epithelial membrane antigen) or ultrastructure (e.g., interdigitating cell processes with attaching desmosomes) in only a small minority of cases, are consistently reactive for vimentin alone, and have been interpreted as being predominantly fibroblastic by some observers.[25,39] Nonetheless, bona fide examples of meningioma arising in association with underlying meningioangiomatosis are on record.[24,33] Especially intriguing are reports that meningioangiomatosis may share with meningiomas allelic losses in the NF-2 gene region,[33,34] at least some of these "hamartomas" possibly representing clonal processes. The reader is referred to our discussion of meningothelial tumors for additional observations regarding this phenomenon, which must be considered in the differential diagnosis of meningeal tumors that appear to "infiltrate" subjacent cortex. We have encountered isolated examples of spindle cell hemangiopericytoma of the leptomeninges and high-grade cerebral fibrosarcoma in association with meningioangiomatosis, and note report of a neoplasm interpreted as an oligodendroglioma found adjacent to a focus of meningioangiomatosis as well.[31] Simple excision is the treatment of choice, but does not guarantee seizure control since patients with meningioangiomatosis may have complex electroencephalographic abnormalities indicative of multifocal, extralesional epileptogenic pathology.[39]

Cysts of the central neuraxis

Considered in this section are various non-neoplastic lesions, maldevelopmental or secondarily acquired, only some of which qualify as "true" (i.e., epithelium-lined) cysts. Chief among the latter are the **colloid cysts of the anterosuperior third ventricle**.[68,69] These generally present in the third through fifth decades of life with manifestations of ventricular outflow obstruction, a consequence of their intimate relation to the foramen of Monro (Fig. 28.3). Thin-walled and often draped by adherent choroid plexus, colloid cysts are filled with a viscous, mucoid material that rapidly congeals on fixation. Their lining epithelium is prone to a low cuboidal attenuation resulting from pressure exerted by the cyst contents, but when well preserved is found to be of

columnar type and is frequently populated by ciliated and goblet cell elements (Fig. 28.4). Only a basement membrane, inapparent at the light microscopic level, separates these from a delicate, fibrous capsule. The cyst contents are PAS positive and commonly include hyphae-like aggregates of degenerate nucleoproteins so characteristic of this entity as to be diagnostic in the absence of identifiable epithelium[78] (Fig. 28.5). An inflammatory reaction to the contents of ruptured colloid cysts is responsible for most, if not all, cases of so-called xanthogranuloma situated in the third ventricle.[71]

Ultrastructural[58] and immunocytochemical[65,87] investigations of the colloid cyst support an origin from misplaced endodermal tissues. Its constituent epithelial cell types correspond closely to those typical of respiratory mucosae, sporting an apical glycocalyx coating particularly characteristic of endodermally derived epithelia, and express cytokeratins, epithelial membrane antigen, and carcinoembryonic antigen, but not GFAP or the choroid plexus-associated transthyretin (prealbumin). Their occasional designation as "neuroepithelial" notwithstanding, similar histogenetic considerations apply to rare cysts of comparable structure situated within the posterior fossa,[12,46] supratentorial compartment,[40] and optic nerve.[61]

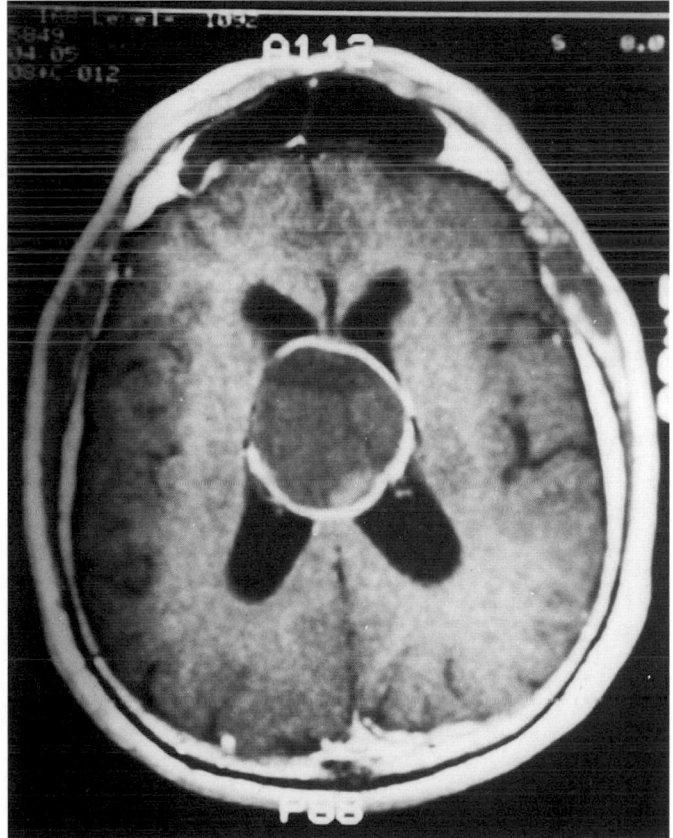

Fig. 28.3 Colloid cyst. The obstructive ventricular dilatation (hydrocephalus) associated with this large example is characteristic of these lesions. Note the well-delineated cyst wall, bright in this contrast-enhanced magnetic resonance image.

Adenocarcinomatous transformation of such cysts has rarely been recorded,[84] as has widespread craniospinal dissemination of a histologically conventional endodermal-type cyst via the CSF.[77] Although properly treated in the context of pituitary disorders (see Chapter 29), the **Rathke cleft cyst**,[88] a lesion having its origin in remnants of the stomodeum, is briefly noted here for the striking resemblance of its lining epithelium to that of the colloid cyst. Curiously, however, the latter rarely contains the metaplastic squamous elements common to Rathke cleft cysts and other cystic intracranial lesions putatively of endodermal lineage.

Intraspinal cysts resulting, in all likelihood, from the incomplete separation of developing endodermal and notochordal tissues in early embryonic life have been variously designated as "**neurenteric**," "**foregut**," "**enterogenous**," and "**teratomatous**."[69] These intradural lesions are typically situated anterior to the spinal cord, are often associated with local vertebral abnormalities, and may be encountered in complex with other evidences of faulty development such as intestinal malformations and dermal sinuses. An intramedullary presentation is well-recognized but far less frequently encountered.[66] Most examples exhibit a simple mural

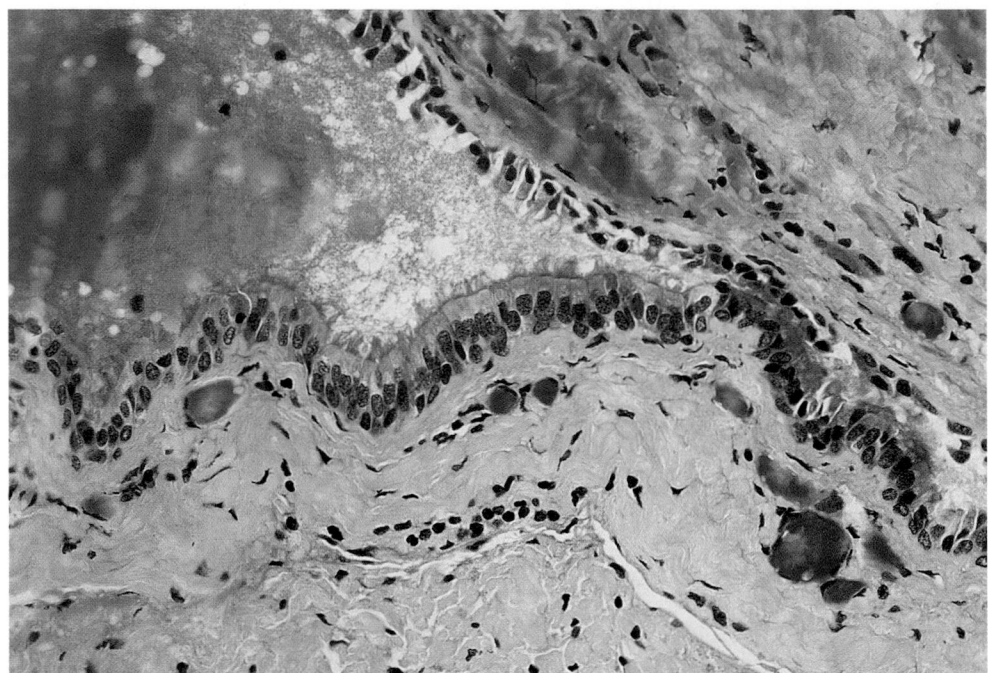

Fig. 28.4 Colloid cyst. A pseudostratified and ciliated columnar epithelium lines well-preserved colloid cysts. Note the supporting collagenous tissue of the cyst wall, yellow in this hematoxylin-phloxine-saffranin preparation.

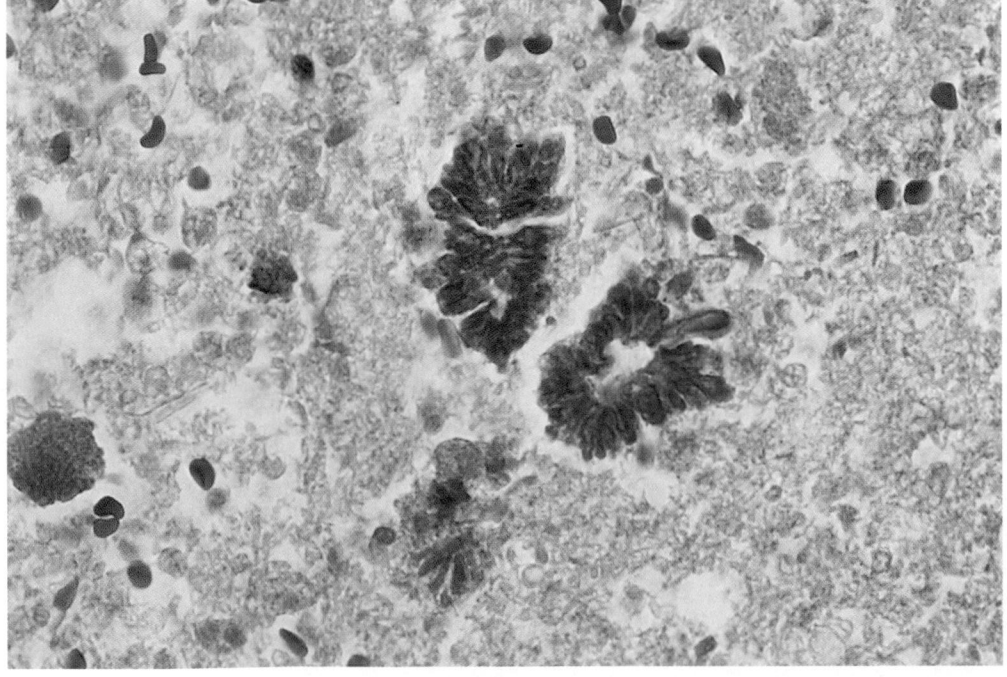

Fig. 28.5 Colloid cyst. The radiate, hyphae-like structures shown here are often found admixed with the liquid contents of colloid cysts and, for practical purposes, are diagnostic of this entity.

structure and columnar epithelial lining similar to that of the colloid cyst, but occasional variants are endowed with a specialized respiratory or gastroenteric-type "mucosa" and the organized supporting elements (e.g., seromucinous glands, muscularis, cartilaginous rings, ganglion cells) of the developed alimentary tract or tracheobronchial tree.[59]

Two major variants of ectodermally derived neuraxis cyst are recognized, both lined by keratinizing squamous epithelium. The **epidermoid cyst**, by definition, is devoid of cutaneous-type adnexal structures and filled by friable, often lamellated keratinous debris that radiates a pearly sheen as viewed through the thin, fibrous lesional capsule. **Dermoid cysts**, by contrast, are endowed with skin appendages, including pilosebaceous units, eccrine and, occasionally, apocrine glands, as well as mural adipose tissue foreign to the epidermoid type. They may contain a greasy, yellowish-gray material admixed with hairs or just friable, keratin-rich debris similar to that of their epidermoid counterparts. Cysts of both types are, for the most part, maldevelopmental in origin, presumably arising from surface ectodermal elements trapped in association with the developing central nervous system on closure of the neural groove or formation of the secondary cerebral vesicles. The occurrence of some examples, particularly dermoids, in complex with craniovertebral anomalies (e.g., spina bifida), malformations of the spinal cord, and dermal sinuses attests to their dysembryogenetic basis. Well documented, however, are acquired variants, most of them epidermoid, resulting from the traumatic[86] or iatrogenic[53] implantation of cutaneous tissues in the cranial or spinal subdural space.

Epidermoid and dermoid cysts are characterized by distinctive clinical as well as histologic features. The former affect subjects of all ages, most coming to attention in young adulthood or middle age, whereas the latter usually present in childhood or adolescence. Cysts of epidermoid type are widely distributed along the neuraxis, but the great majority are positioned intracranially, the cerebellopontine angle being their single most common location.[69] Rarely, posterior fossa examples conspicuously erode into, or lie embedded within, the cerebellum or brainstem. Supratentorial representatives exhibit a predilection for the parasellar region, but may also be situated within the ventricular system, in the cerebral hemispheres, suprasellar, or pineal regions.[69] Intraspinal epidermoid cysts are typically intradural and extramedullary in location but may on rare occasion lie entirely within the substance of the cord.[69]

Compared with its epidermoid counterpart, the dermoid cyst clings tightly to the midline. It, too, favors the posterior fossa but in this location characteristically occupies the cerebellar vermis or fourth ventricle.[69] When situated above the tentorium, the dermoid cyst tends to a frontal, paramedian position on the skull base.

An infantile, subgaleal variant typically resides in the anterior fontanel. Although generally outnumbered by epidermoid cysts, dermoids actually predominate at spinal levels. These exhibit a decided predilection for the lumbosacral region, where they constitute a manifestation of spinal dysraphism.

Although the clinical manifestations of dermoid and epidermoid cysts are principally referable to their local mass effects, either may present with signs and symptoms of "chemical" or infectious meningitis. The former results from cyst rupture and the spillage of irritating keratinous and lipid-rich debris into the ventricular system and subarachnoid space.[67] Repeated episodes of bacterial meningitis are a recognized complication of cysts associated with dermal sinuses offering access to the nervous system. Patients harboring posterior fossa dermoids and occipital sinuses may also suffer cerebellar abscesses. Neoplastic transformation is a well-documented but, fortunately, rare occurrence. In most cases, the underlying lesion is a cyst of epidermoid type and the secondary cancer a squamous carcinoma.[51,63] The bizarre phenomenon of an osteogenic sarcoma arising in association with a cerebellar epidermoid cyst has been recorded,[43] and isolated dermoid cysts have given rise to tumors described as anaplastic sebaceous carcinoma[50] or atypical hidradenoma.[62] A temporal lobe example containing islands of keratinized, anucleate-appearing ("shadow") cells similar to those seen in pilomatricomas has been depicted.[56] Even histologically conventional cysts can recur following incomplete resection of their walls. Spontaneous seeding of the CSF by apparently benign epidermoid cysts with development of intraventricular or subarachnoid "daughter" lesions is a recorded curiosity.[70]

Inasmuch as epidermoid cysts may arise, albeit rarely, in the suprasellar region, their differential diagnosis includes Rathke cleft cysts with extensive squamous metaplasia and craniopharyngiomas. The former will usually harbor scattered mucicarminophilic cells of cuboidal or low columnar configuration atop their squamous elements and do not evidence the advanced keratinization typical of the epidermoid cyst. The formation of cytoplasmic keratohyaline granules, typical of the epidermoid cyst's maturing squames, is generally foreign to the craniopharyngioma. Furthermore, epidermoid and Rathke cleft cysts lack the latter's islands of "ghost cell" keratinocytes and its "machinery oil"-like contents and do not exhibit the basaloid elements and stellate reticulum of the adamantinomatous craniopharyngioma or the filiform architecture of its papillary variant (see Chapter 29 for details). As regards further distinction of Rathke cleft cysts from craniopharyngiomas, study of a limited number of cases found immunolabeling for cytokeratins 8 and 20 to be characteristic of the former and generally foreign to the latter.[93] The exceptional dermoid cyst presenting in the pineal or suprasellar region should be separable from the mature cystic teratoma by its lack of glandular components (indicative of endodermal differentiation), muscle, or cartilage.

Glioependymal cysts are most commonly situated in the paraventricular white matter of the frontal and parietal lobes but may also lie within the cerebellum, brainstem, or spinal cord.[45,48,49,81] A derivation from ventricular lining elements displaced in the course of neuroembryogenesis seems most plausible for these intraparenchymal examples, rare variants positioned in the cerebellopontine angle and other extra-axial sites conceivably originating from subarachnoid neuroglial heterotopias.[57] As their name implies, glioependymal cysts are lined by cells resembling mature ependymocytes. Like the cells lining the more common cysts of endodermal type, these may be ciliated but differ in that they do not exhibit goblet cell differentiation, are not coated by an apical glycocalyx, and do not rest on a basal lamina, being directly apposed to fibrillary neuroglial tissue. Representatives presenting in the subarachnoid space may, however, contain "supporting" astrocytic elements that fashion a continuous basement membrane separating them from a delicate fibrous capsule, much as the normal glia limitans are delimited from the connective tissues of the pia-arachnoid by a basal lamina.[45,57]

The limited immunocytochemical studies reported to date suggest that the cells lining glioependymal cysts can express GFAP, S-100 protein, and, possibly, cytokeratin.[45,57,81] Failure to elaborate carcinoembryonic antigen or transthyretin (prealbumin) may serve to distinguish these lesions from cysts of endodermal or choroid plexus type, respectively. By definition, the latter are lined by cells having the immunohistochemical and fine structural attributes of the native plexus epithelium,[60,75] considered in the discussion of this structure's epithelial neoplasms. We mention only for the sake of completeness cystic alterations that are a transient feature of some fetal choroid plexi.[44] These are of no consequence to the surgical pathologist.

Rarely, intraparenchymal brain cysts exhibit no specialized lining elements and are not associated with historical or tissue evidence of underlying trauma, hemorrhage, infarction, neoplasia, demyelinating disease, or infection that might account for their genesis. Most numerous are examples termed "**simple**" or "**gliotic**" **cysts**, presenting in the cerebellar hemispheric white matter of middle-aged or elderly adults.[85,91] That at least some of these clinically benign lesions are not congenital anomalies but represent instead "burnt-out" pilocytic astrocytomas has been suggested in view of the latter tumor's proneness to macrocystic alterations and the presence around many simple cerebellar cysts of a dense mesh of glial processes rich in Rosenthal fibers and containing scattered atypical astrocytes.[85] Inasmuch as the neoplastic components of cerebellar cysts associated with pilocytic astrocytomas and hemangioblastomas may be confined to diminutive mural nodules, careful inspection of cystic lesions in this location following drainage at surgery is mandatory, and biopsy of various portions of their linings is prudent. Exceptional cysts arising outside the cerebellum are lined only by normal or mildly reactive neuroglial tissue, are juxtaventricular in location, and contain a fluid similar in its composition to CSF.[74,92] These likely derive from ventricular diverticula or represent collections of CSF that have dissected into the neuropil via congenital or acquired breaches in the ependyma. A congenital optic nerve cyst of simple glial type has been recorded.[64]

Particularly prone to cystic change is the normal human pineal gland, but only rarely does this alteration result in a lesion of symptomatic proportions.[47] **Pineal cysts** that come to neurosurgical attention generally do so in the third through fifth decades of life, their presenting manifestations being indistinguishable from those of neoplasms in this region and including evidences of obstructive hydrocephalus, as well as disturbances of ocular motility. Like the cerebellar lesions previously described, these are lined by a dense weave of piloid astroglial processes containing Rosenthal fibers and granular bodies but do not exhibit the microcystic architecture characteristic of the pilocytic astrocytoma or approach the latter in cellularity. A second differential diagnostic consideration is the pineocytoma, as the cysts under discussion regularly contain elements of residual pineal parenchyma within their walls. These usually retain the organoid appearances typical of the normal gland, but in some cases their uniform, telltale lobularity is obscured as a result of longstanding compression. Appreciation of a given lesion's neuroradiologic features and appearance at operation is quite helpful in this regard, as pineocytomas are nearly always solid masses rather than thin-walled cysts. Simple excision is curative.

Loculated accumulations of CSF enclosed by fibroconnective tissues derived from the leptomeninges are referred to as **arachnoid cysts**.[69] Etiologically diverse, some arachnoid cysts develop as sequelae of meningitis or trauma and are circumscribed by adhesions traversing the subarachnoid space. Most, however, are considered to begin as maldevelopmental clefts in the arachnoid membrane that subsequently undergoes cystic dilatation.[80] Lesions of this type are lined by an attenuated meningothelium resting on a layer of supporting fibrous tissue so thin as to be transparent at operation. These most commonly occupy the sylvian fissures, followed by the cisterna magna and cerebellopontine angles, but may occur in the suprasellar region and along the spinal neuraxis.[69] Intradiploic[90] and intramedullary[52] presentations have also been recorded. By virtue of their very gradual inflation, such lesions may produce striking deformities in neighboring neural tissues that are often unaccompanied by mass effects such as midline shifts or internal herniae and thus have a malformation-like appearance. **Dural cysts** (cystically dilated intradural clefts) are rare and described mainly as intraspinal causes of myelopathy.[54] Comparable intracranial lesions have been reported to produce sagittal sinus occlusions.[76]

Most arachnoid "cysts" presenting at spinal levels are actually meningeal diverticula that can be shown to communicate with the subarachnoid space.[72] These may lie within or outside the dural sleeve, are often multifocal, and can be lined by meningothelial cells or composed solely of membranous fibrous tissue. Only a minority achieve symptomatic proportions, producing myelopathy or radicular syndromes, at times associated with erosion of adjacent vertebral bodies or the sacrum. Extradural variants arising in association with the posterior spinal roots, typically at lumbosacral levels, are often eponymously designated as **Tarlov's perineurial cysts**.[89] Only exceptionally do these prompt neurosurgical intervention by causing perineal pain, sciatica, or bladder or bowel dysfunction. Rarely, cystically dilated or otherwise enlarged arachnoid granulations masquerade as dermoid (or other true) cysts[41] or produce sizable lytic skull defects that arouse suspicion of neoplastic disease.[82]

Yet another cystic lesion that may impinge on the spinal neuraxis is the **juxtafacet** or **"ganglion" cyst**, a collection of acellular and often myxoid material bound within a fibrous capsule devoid of specialized lining elements.[83] The term **synovial cyst** has been employed for essentially similar lesions interpreted as containing inflamed synovium. Cysts of comparable structure may rarely arise within the ligamentum flavum.[55] A degenerative abnormality, the juxtafacet cyst typically presents at lumbar levels in association with osteoarthritic changes of the vertebral column, but may rarely occur in the cervical region.[55] Mycloradiculopathy and bony erosion are its principal complications.

Finally, we mention the intracranial extension of sinonasal mucoceles and development of intracranial mucoceles in association with frontoethmoidal osteomas,[73] as well as report of a multiloculated, cystic frontal lobe mass having the appearance of allergic nasal polyposis, the latter associated with a bony abnormality of the anterior fossa floor and complicated by CSF rhinorrhea and meningitis.[79]

Cerebrovascular disorders

Cerebral infarction

Characterized by an abrupt loss of neurologic function ("stroke") referable to a circumscribed arterial territory within the affected brain, the common variety of **cerebral infarct** is an ischemic lesion of later adult life[94] confidently diagnosed at the bedside. Occasional examples, however, are silent at onset, evolve in subacute fashion as expansile intracranial "tumors" indistinguishable from neoplasms on conventional neuroradiologic assessment, and are consequently sampled by the neurosurgeon. Obviously, the histology of a given infarct will depend on the stage at which the dynamic cytologic and organizational alterations that follow irreversible ischemic injury are iatrogenically interrupted.[95] Biopsied tissues generally exhibit a spongy rarefaction reflecting the edema that is largely to blame for these lesions' associated mass effects, commonly evidence of intense vascular congestion, and may be frankly hemorrhagic. Neurons, if at all recognizable, persist only in faded, "ghost"-like profile or appear shrunken, angulated, and abnormally eosinophilic with a loss intranuclear detail. Neutrophilic exudates may be apparent early on, but most lesions approached surgically have evolved to the point where mononuclear phagocytes, including lipid-laden foam cells, constitute their principal reactive elements. These lend to organizing infarcts a potentially alarming hypercellularity that is all the more misleading when accompanied, as is often the case, by capillary proliferation and endothelial hypertrophy resembling glioma-associated vascular hyperplasia. Inasmuch as the cytologic features by which macrophages are recognized tend to be obscured in frozen sections but are immediately apparent in squash and smear preparations, routine use of the latter is urged for purposes of intraoperative consultation. Once a lesion has been identified as being rich in phagocytes, the major differential consideration is demyelinating disease, given detailed consideration elsewhere in this chapter. Suffice it to say that demyelinating pseudotumors only exceptionally progress to tissue necrosis, are usually characterized by perivascular lymphoid cuffing and a relative preservation of axons foreign to brain infarcts, and generally afflict patients younger than those at risk of ischemic cerebral events.

Intracranial aneurysms

The **saccular** or **"berry" aneurysm** ranks chief among surgically correctable cerebrovascular abnormalities and is unrivaled as a cause of massive subarachnoid hemorrhage in adults. These common lesions (their prevalence in the general population falls in the neighborhood of 5%) are somewhat more frequent in women and are encountered at all ages beyond puberty, although symptomatic examples cluster in the fifth through seventh decades of life.[103,106,112] Some 10–15% of cases have been estimated to occur on a familial basis.[107] The factors critical in initiating the formation of saccular intracranial aneurysms remain undefined, and the majority are unassociated with local or systemic conditions known to promote vascular injury, but hemodynamic stress probably plays the major role in their development and, on balance, the weight of evidence supports the hypothesis that these are primarily acquired, degenerative lesions rather than developmental anomalies.[94,112] Arterial hypertension is widely regarded as playing an aggravating role in their evolution and may underlie an association with the adult form of aortic coarctation, with type III polycystic kidney disease, and pheochromocytoma.[94,100,112] Connective tissue disorders that result in increased vascular fragility have mainly been associated with aneurysms of fusiform type but may also predispose to the development of saccular aneurysms, these having been described in the settings of type III collagen deficiency (Ehlers–Danlos syndrome type IV), pseudoxanthoma elasticum, and Marfan's syndrome.[94,112] Aneurysms of the saccular variety occasionally occur in complex with fibromuscular dysplasia of the renal arteries, intracranial arteriovenous malformations or fistulas, and persistent primitive carotid-basilar anastomoses or other anomalies of the circle of Willis.[94,112] The latter observations notwithstanding, the localization of most saccular aneurysms (discussed below) is at odds with the theory that they commonly originate in vestigial remnants of the embryonic cerebral vasculature.

Frequently multifocal, saccular intracranial aneurysms usually lie within 3 cm of the internal carotid artery termini at the circle of Willis, and 80% involve divisions of the cerebral vasculature ventral to the posterior communicating arteries.[106] It is clear from autopsy studies that the middle cerebral arteries are most commonly affected, but most clinical series are dominated by anterior communicating and internal carotid artery examples because these are more prone to rupture.[103,104,106,112] That saccular aneurysms almost invariably bulge from points of acute angle vascular bifurcation has been interpreted by some observers as the natural consequence of increased hemodynamic impact or turbulence at these points and by others as reflecting an inherent local weakness of the vessel wall secondary to focal gaps in the arterial media known to occur near circulatory forks.[94] Although such "defects" could theoretically influence the localization of some lesions, there actually appears to be little topographic concordance between their major distribution in the human cerebrovascular tree and that of saccular aneurysms.

On histologic examination, the walls of saccular intracranial aneurysms are composed principally of fibrous tissue, the muscular coats and elastic laminae of parent vessels typically terminating abruptly at the points of aneurysmal outpouching.[94,106] Atheromatous changes are common and may be florid but are characteristically confined to the aneurysmal sac and thus probably represent superimposed alterations of little direct etiologic significance. Much the same can be said of chronic inflammatory mural infiltration. Other secondary phenomena include partial or, in select instances, complete thrombotic occlusion, the latter presumably accounting for the occasional "disappearance" of untreated aneurysms assessed by periodic angiographic study.

Most saccular aneurysms remain asymptomatic, and

even frank rupture may be followed by spontaneous thrombotic closure of the aneurysmal sac and clinical resolution, but this is not to trivialize the associated risk of catastrophic intracranial hemorrhage. Long-term follow-up studies of patients with angiographically proven saccular aneurysms suggest a 1% to 2% annual incidence of rupture; approximately half of these bleeding episodes prove fatal.[104] Although subarachnoid hemorrhage alone may be lethal, it is the dissection of blood into the brain itself or ventricular system that kills in many cases. Massive intraparenchymal hematomas are most often a consequence of middle cerebral artery aneurysms, whereas anterior communicating examples are generally responsible for most episodes of fatal intraventricular hemorrhage (blood usually entering the anterior horn of the lateral ventricle after dissecting through the inferomedial frontal lobe). Another grave complication is cerebral infarction related to postrupture vasospasm, again encountered most commonly in patients harboring aneurysms of the anterior communicating arteries.

Although most observers have concluded that considerable risk of rupture is attached to saccular aneurysms exceeding 1 cm in diameter and relatively little to examples measuring 5 mm or less,[112] none of these lesions can be regarded as entirely innocent. In fact, nearly 70% of saccular aneurysms that ruptured in the course of one long-term follow-up study measured 6 mm or less in diameter on angiographic assessment.[104] Aneurysms that achieve "giant" proportions (usually defined as having diameters of at least 3 cm) typically present with cranial neuropathies, evidence of ventricular outflow obstruction or other mass effects, rather than hemorrhage. Rarely, the surgical management of saccular aneurysms is complicated by a local granulomatous response to shredded gauze employed as reinforcement following aneurysmal clipping.[98] These "**gauzomas**" can achieve considerable size, presenting as contrast-enhancing masses with significant accompanying edema, and may produce headache, fever, obstructive hydrocephalus, cranial nerve palsies, and endocrinopathy.

Although the designation of **mycotic aneurysm** would seem to specifically connote a fungal process, this term has been applied in practice to focal infectious arteritides of diverse cause having in common only an element of vascular dilatation. Most mycotic intracranial aneurysms are, in fact, bacterial in nature and evolve as complications of endocarditis or, less frequently, suppurating pulmonary infection.[94,96] Streptococci and staphylococcal species are the usual offenders. The resulting lesions, often multifocal, tend to be situated on distal branches of the cerebral vasculature, are more often fusiform or irregular than berry-like in configuration, and are frequently of diminutive proportions. Fungal aneurysms are specifically addressed in the discussion of CNS mycoses. In brief, these are most often caused by *Aspergillus* and *Candida* species, generally involve the large cerebral arteries at the base of the brain, and tend to have greater diameters on presentation than their bacterial counterparts.

Atherosclerotic intracranial aneurysms generally afflict older adults, usually arise in the setting of advanced and generalized cerebrovascular atheromatosis, typically involve supraclinoid portions of the internal carotid arteries or the basilar artery, and may assume saccular, fusiform, cylindrical, or conical configurations.[94] Fusiform lesions of the vertebrobasilar trunk are the single most common variant.[99,109] Atherosclerotic aneurysms are generally of large size and frequently achieve giant proportions. Their presenting manifestations are more often related to compression of neighboring CNS structures or ischemic complications of progressive thrombosis than to hemorrhage, although some observers assert that the associated risk of rupture is underestimated.[109] Far more common than discrete aneurysm formation is atherosclerotic **"dolichoectasia"**—diffuse dilatation and tortuous elongation of the basilar or internal carotid arteries—and the two processes may coexist.

Dissecting aneurysms of the intracranial vasculature are rarities.[94] Most documented cases are without satisfactory etiologic explanation, although some have been attributed to trauma, syphilis, cystic medionecrosis, arteriosclerosis, fibromuscular dysplasia, or other local abnormalities of vascular structure. Alpha-1-antitrypsin deficiency has been linked to intracranial arteriopathy potentially complicated by dissection or aneurysm formation.[108] Luminal stenosis secondary to the intramural accumulation of blood may result in bulbar or cerebral infarction; rupture typically produces catastrophic subarachnoid hemorrhage. Symptoms referable to mass effect constitute the least frequent manifestation of intracranial arterial dissection.

Exceptionally, tumors metastatic to the CNS present as "spontaneous" intracerebral or subarachnoid hemorrhages that ultimately prove the consequences of **neoplastic aneurysm** formation. Most neoplastic intracranial aneurysms result from the embolization of cardiac myxomas to the cerebral vasculature,[101] but examples caused by ovarian choriocarcinoma and non-small cell carcinoma of the lung are also on record.[102]

Considerable controversy surrounds the incidence of so-called **Charcot–Bouchard** (or **"miliary"**) **microaneurysms** and their clinical significance.[94,105] The latter are described as saccular or fusiform lesions most commonly involving lenticulostriate, perforating pontine and corticomedullary junction arteries measuring 25 to 250 microns in diameter. Said to be particularly prevalent in hypertensive subjects, their rupture is regarded by some as a major cause of basal ganglionic, bulbar and cerebellar hemorrhage in this patient cohort. That aneurysms of Charcot–Bouchard type have received little attention in the surgical pathology literature could reflect the specialized tissue handling requisite to their

identification. Studies from Japan in which surgically evacuated hematomas were subjected to meticulous examination under the dissecting microscope (and serial thin sectioning of suspect lesions) would suggest that microaneurysms are underappreciated as a factor predisposing to atraumatic lobar cerebral hemorrhage in both hypertensive and normotensive individuals.[110,111] Painstaking analysis in Caucasians, on the other hand, demonstrated most "microaneurysms" to actually represent complex vascular tortuosities and failed to establish a link between truly aneurysmal lesions and intracerebral hemorrhage.[97] Whether these discrepancies are simply methodological or have their basis in genetic or environmental factors is unclear. In practice, it is virtually impossible to conclusively identify microaneurysms in routinely processed paraffin sections.

Vascular malformations

Generically designated as vascular malformations are various non-neoplastic lesions resulting from focal anomalies in the development of the cerebrospinal circulation. These are usefully divided into four relatively discrete morphologic categories, namely, capillary telangiectases, angiomas of venous or cavernous type, and arteriovenous malformations.[94] Transitional or hybrid types, however, may be encountered.[117,129,138] Also considered in this section are arteriovenous fistulas, since these are, strictly speaking, malformations, although they are generally regarded as acquired, rather than developmental, abnormalities.

Capillary telangiectases exhibit a curious predilection for the basis pontis (particularly the region of the median raphe), but are occasionally found to involve the cerebral hemispheres and spinal cord.[94] They usually constitute incidental findings at autopsy and are only rarely complicated by symptomatic hemorrhage. On record is a massive pontomedullary case associated with a protracted history of bulbar dysfunction.[120] The lesion consists of loosely aggregated and variably ectatic capillary-type vessels (i.e., devoid of elastic or muscular mural elements) separated by normal or only mildly gliotic neuropil. A densely mineralized variant—the **"calcified telangiectatic hamartoma"** or **"hemangioma calcificans"**—is a recognized, albeit rare, cause of epilepsy, particularly of temporal lobe type.[147] Capillary telangiectases of the CNS complicate some examples of hereditary hemorrhagic telangiectasia, also known as Osler–Weber–Rendu disease.[94,140]

The **venous angioma** is a loose collection of dilated veins found typically in the digitate or deep white matter of the cerebral or cerebellar hemispheres.[94] The radial convergence of their ectatic vessels on a central draining varix lends to many of these lesions a diagnostic "caput medusae"-like profile on angiographic study. Although venous angiomas are the most common vascular malformations of the human central nervous system, it is the exceptional example that is responsible for intracranial hemorrhage or is otherwise symptomatic.[131]

The **cavernous angioma** differs from all other vascular malformations in that its constituent vessels are fashioned into a compact, globose mass devoid of intervening neural elements.[94] On gross inspection, a spongy core of blood-filled channels is encircled by a thin rind of indurated (because gliotic) and rusted-appearing (because hemosiderin-laden) neural parenchyma. Histologic study will reveal closely apposed, engorged vessels composed solely of fibrous tissue (Fig. 28.6). Secondary alterations such as thrombosis and dystrophic calcification are common, some lesions undergoing extensive metaplastic ossification as well. The existence of hybrid variants exhibiting in part the structure of capillary telangiectases, has fueled speculation that cavernous angiomas may evolve from malformations of the former type,[138] but the fact remains that "mixed" lesions are exceptional. Cavernous angiomas may be situated anywhere along the neuraxis. Most examples lie above the tentorium,[144] often in cerebral white matter subjacent to the motor strip, but the cerebellum and brainstem,[137,144] spinal cord,[118] cauda equina,[135] cranial nerves,[128] and epidural compartment[150] may also be involved. Multifocal cases are by no means rare. The designation of cavernous angioma has also been extended to certain extra-axial vascular malformations affecting dural venous sinuses, but these depart structurally from their counterparts positioned in the CNS proper in that they contain, in addition to compact cavernous elements, capillaries and muscular vessels of both arterial and venous type.[130] These distinctive lesions, which usually present as a consequence of cranial nerve compression and are generally mistaken for meningiomas on preoperative neuroimaging study, are not given further consideration here.

Cavernous angiomas may become manifest in childhood, but most symptomatic lesions are encountered in the third and fourth decades of life.[144] Familial cases transmitted in autosomal dominant fashion and linked to mutations involving chromosomes 7q (the KRIT 1 gene), 7p and 3q have been well-delineated,[94] an apparent excess involving Hispanic-American kindreds,[149] and include variants occurring in complex with cavernous angiomas of the retina[119] and hyperkeratotic venous malformations of the skin.[123] That seizures are their dominant clinical manifestation reflects the proximity of most such lesions to epileptogenic cerebrocortical tissues. Less frequent complaints include focal neurologic deficits and headache. Although catastrophic hemorrhage is decidedly rare, cavernous angiomas are a recognized cause of intracranial hematomas, including both acutely symptomatic[146] and "encapsulated" lobar types,[139] the latter resulting in all likelihood from repeated subclinical episodes of bleeding and subsequent organization. A confident preoperative diagnosis of cavernous angioma may be established by neuroradiologic means. The typical lesion, although "angiographically occult" (i.e., not apparent on arteriographic study), appears in T2-weighted magnetic resonance images as an irregularly hyperdense nodule unassociated with significant edema or mass effect but surrounded by a hypodense penumbra resulting from the accumulation of hemosiderin in adjoining neural tissues. Focal vascular lesions having a cavernous angioma-like neuroradiologic profile may develop in the brain or spinal cord as a consequence of

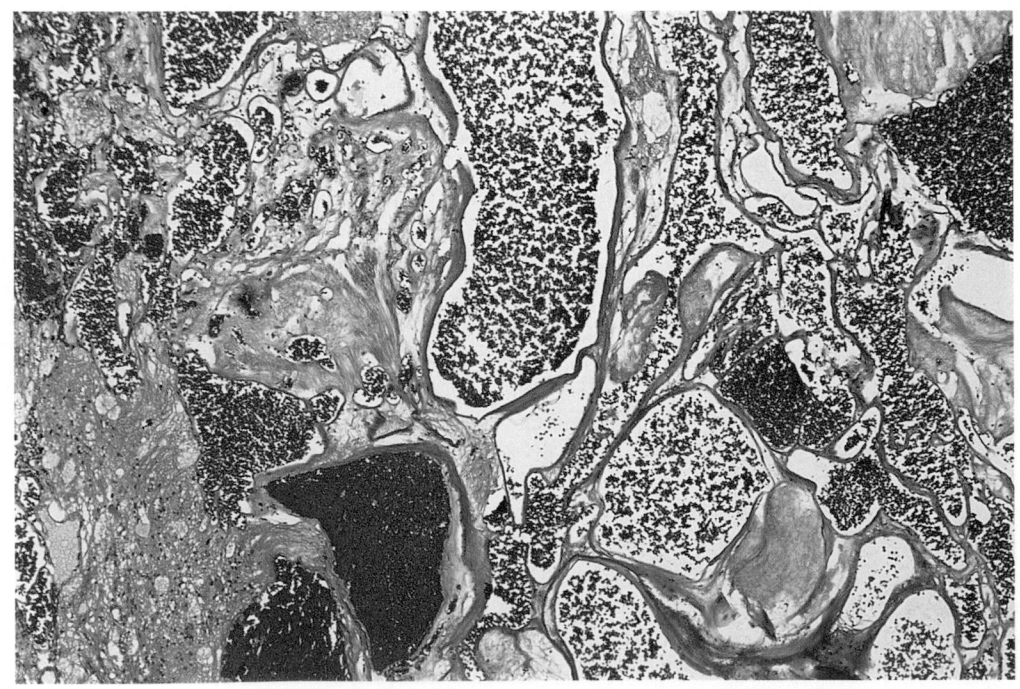

Fig. 28.6 Cavernous angioma. As illustrated, the cavernous angioma consists of ectatic and fibrous-walled vascular channels devoid of intervening neuroglial tissue. Neighboring brain parenchyma is present at lower left.

therapeutic CNS irradiation.[122,124] These seem more prone to hemorrhage than sporadic variants, develop most commonly in children and adolescents, and may exhibit transitional histologic features with regions of capillary and venous telangiectasis.

The most threatening of the congenital cerebrovascular anomalies under discussion is the **arteriovenous malformation** (AVM), a tangle of deformed arterial afferents and draining veins devoid of an interposed capillary bed.[94,127] AVMs may be situated in any region of the brain or spinal cord and can be restricted to the dura or choroid plexus,[116] but most lie within the distribution of the middle cerebral arteries and involve the hemispheric convexities in contiguity with their covering leptomeninges. A majority present in early and mid-adulthood as a consequence of intracranial hemorrhage, other common manifestations including seizures, focal sensorimotor deficits, and headaches not clearly referable to episodes of bleeding.[115,134] Familial cases have been described[113] and AVMs of the central neuraxis may be encountered in complex with Osler–Weber–Rendu disease (hereditary hemorrhagic telangiectasia).[140] The turbulent shunting of blood through AVMs of the brain is sometimes audible as a cranial or orbital bruit, can often be demonstrated to diagnostic advantage on angiographic study, and may precipitate high output cardiac failure in afflicted infants and children, particularly those harboring extensive lesions drained by aneurysmally dilated galenic veins. Unfortunately, AVMs are complicated by fatal rupture with distressing frequency. Long-term observations suggest that symptomatic examples carry a 2% to 4% risk of clinically significant hemorrhage per year and, left untreated, will eventuate in the deaths of at least one fourth of affected patients as a direct result of rupture.[115,134] Feeding arteries are prone to develop saccular aneurysms, and it is occasionally one of these, rather than the malformation itself, that is responsible for the lethal hemorrhagic ictus.

AVMs vary in size from cryptic lesions not demonstrable by angiographic means and discovered only on sampling of surgically evacuated hematomas[125] to enormous lobar examples that may focally span the full thickness of a cerebral hemisphere. As their tortuous, cirsoid vascular components form a complex network of blood-filled channels, the nature of these lesions is often apparent on casual gross inspection. Intervening neural tissues are typically attenuated, and there is evidence of rust-brown discoloration attesting to prior hemorrhage. Involved leptomeninges are thickened, opacified, and frequently siderotic as well. On histologic study (Fig. 28.7), the lesion is composed of variably ectatic and hyalinized veins, abnormally muscularized arteries, and structurally ambiguous vessels formed solely of fibrous tissue or displaying both arterial and venous characteristics.[94,127] Critical to the distinction of the true AVM from normal leptomeningeal vessels that may assume a malformative

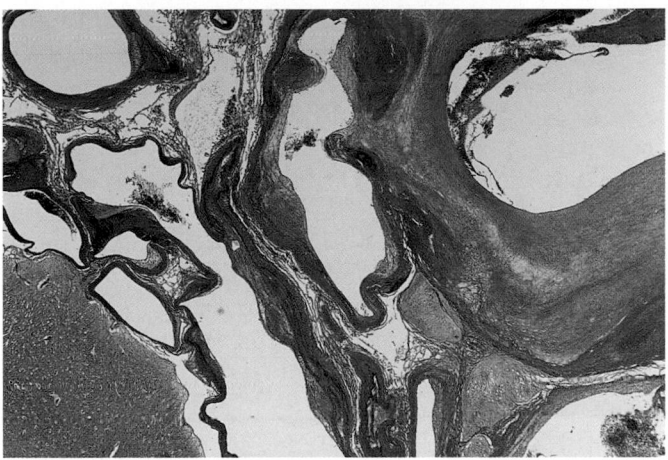

Fig. 28.7 Arteriovenous malformation. Ectatic, variably muscularized blood vessels with interrupted elastic lamina and fibrotic intimal thickening participate in this malformative lesion (Van Gieson stain).

appearance in neurosurgical material as a result of artefactual compaction are the former's conspicuous mural anomalies. Chief among these are striking fluctuations in medial thickness, architectural disarray or focal disappearance of the media altogether, or its separation into inner and outer coats by a seemingly aberrant elastic lamina.[127] Cushions of fibromuscular tissue may also appear to project in polypoid fashion into the lumens of these abnormal vessels, and focal duplications and disruptions of the internal elastic lamina are common. Superimposed alterations include mural fibroplasia and atheromatosis, aneurysmal dilatation, calcification, and thrombosis, which, if extensive, may preclude the visualization of even sizable malformations by angiographic methods.[125] Lesions subjected to preoperative embolization in an attempt to minimize blood loss during resection frequently exhibit an intraluminal foreign body response to the occluding material and may undergo focal necrosis,[143] radiosurgical treatment causing fibrointimal hyperplasia with progressive vaso-occlusion.[142] Entrapped neuropil usually manifests dense astrogliosis, neuronal depopulation, and ferruginous encrustation of included neuroglial elements. The reader's attention is also called to the presence, in the interstices of select AVMs, of oligodendroglioma-like regions that may be intrinsic to the underlying maldevelopmental process or the result of abnormal oligodendroglial aggregation caused by the ischemic contraction of entrapped white matter.[126,132] The association of AVMs and bona fide gliomas is discussed under the heading of "Gliomesenchymal tumors," as are malformation-like alterations occurring in the vascular stroma of neuroepithelial tumors.

To the sporadic and familial malformations mentioned in preceding paragraphs can be added a host of vascular anomalies constituting manifestations of certain neurocutaneous syndromes ("phakomatoses"), some clearly heritable and others the apparent result of spontaneous mutation. The most widely recognized of these disorders is **encephalo-trigeminal angiomatosis**, known by the eponym of **Sturge–Weber syndrome** and defined as a florid venocapillary proliferation involving the leptomeninges and cortical mantle of one cerebral hemisphere in complex with a cutaneous hemangioma ("port-wine stain") lying at least in part in the ophthalmic distribution of the ipsilateral trigeminal nerve.[94,148] Progressive mineralization of the involved cortex, centered initially on its abnormal perforating vessels, results in a gyriform, "tram-track" profile of radiologically demonstrable intracranial calcifications characteristic of the disease. Atrophy of the affected cerebral hemisphere is the rule, and patients typically suffer contralateral hemiparesis, often attended by motor seizures and mental retardation. The association of unilateral retinal angiomatosis and a cutaneous hemangioma in an ipsilateral trigeminal distribution with an AVM of the midbrain is referred to as **mesencephalo-oculo-facial angiomatosis** (also termed **neuroretinal angiomatosis**, **Bonnet–Dechaume–Blanc syndrome**, or **Wyburn–Mason syndrome**).[94] Capillary telangiectases and AVMs are also recognized, albeit rare, CNS manifestations of **hereditary hemorrhagic telangiectasia** (**Osler–Weber–Rendu** disease).[140]

Arteriovenous fistulas of the craniospinal vasculature are accorded only passing consideration here because their current management—surgical clipping or selective embolic occlusion of the offending communication—does not usually yield specimens for anatomic study. It is the absence of a plexiform, angiomatous nidus interposed between its feeding arteries and venous efferents that serves to distinguish the simple fistula from the AVM on angiographic and morphologic evaluation, although the latter's participating vessels may develop fistulous connections.[145] Trauma clearly figures in the genesis of many examples (particularly carotid-cavernous sinus and vertebrovertebral types), as does neurosurgical injury, and some complicate systemic disorders such as fibromuscular dysplasia and type IV Ehlers–Danlos syndrome.[94] Many arteriovenous fistulas, however, present in spontaneous fashion. Those involving the cerebral arteries proper typically come to attention in childhood or early adult life, their clinical manifestations including headache, seizures, focal sensorimotor deficits, cardiac decompensation, and intracranial hemorrhage. Catastrophic rupture, however, appears to be exceptional. Fistulas developing below the tentorium are often localized to the dural sheaths of spinal nerve roots in the low thoracic region.[114,141] Lesions of this sort afflict men far more commonly than women, usually become symptomatic in or beyond middle age, and result in an ischemic myelopathy characterized by progressive paraparesis, paresthesias of the lower extremities, and sphincter disturbances. Known eponymously as **Foix–Alajouanine syndrome** or **angiodysgenetic myelomalacia**, this disorder is typified by serpentine elongation and distention of veins coursing over the dorsal surface of the thoracic spinal cord and is likely the result of protracted local venous hypertension caused by an overlap in the vascular drainage of the adjacent dural fistula and the cord itself. Fistulas involving the perimedullary vascular plexus[145] or distantly situated in the cranial or sacral dura[136] may eventuate in a similar picture. Dural arteriovenous fistulas drained by ectatic or aneurysmally dilated cortical veins are particularly prone to hemorrhage.[121] Dural based arteriovenous fistulas have also been implicated in the pathogenesis of vascular malformations occupying the sigmoid and transverse sinuses.[133]

Primary angiitis

Among the less common forms of cerebrovascular disease is the idiopathic disorder variously described as "**isolated**," "**granulomatous**," or "**primary**" **angiitis of the CNS**.[152,153] Inasmuch as many histopathologically confirmed cases have not evidenced overtly granulomatous features and as autopsy studies have disclosed exceptional instances of extraneural vascular involvement, the last of these designations would seem the most accurate and is adopted here.

Primary angiitis of the CNS can occur at any age but usually afflicts young or middle-aged adults, its principal clinical manifestations including headache, mental status changes, and focal neurologic deficits (particularly hemiparesis) that may evolve in progressive fashion or present abruptly as "stroke." Signs and symptoms of myelopathy occasionally dominate the clinical picture, but only rarely is morphologic evidence of vascular injury accentuated at, or confined to, spinal levels.[151,154] If not promptly diagnosed and managed, the disorder generally proves progressive and fatal.

Short of biopsy for tissue confirmation, angiography is the most useful investigative procedure and findings typical of vasculitis—particularly multifocal, segmental stenosis, dilatation, or "beading" of small- to medium-caliber leptomeningeal arteries—are considered by some to constitute sufficient grounds for the institution of corticosteroid or cytotoxic therapy in the appropriate setting (i.e., when underlying infection and other systemic processes associated with secondary CNS angiitis have been excluded from further diagnostic consideration). However, arteriograms may be unrevealing even in the face of florid vascular disease.[152] Less commonly encountered neuroradiologic abnormalities include aneurysm formation and focal "mass" lesions secondary to infarction, often hemorrhagic.

Most observers regard biopsy as the sole means of confirming a presumptive clinical diagnosis of primary CNS angiitis, although false-negative samplings are a common consequence of the disorder's segmental distribution. Small and midsized leptomeningeal and intracortical arteries usually bear the brunt of the injury, but neighboring veins are often involved in concert, and the process may affect the large vessels at the base of the brain as well. Rarely, however, are inflammatory alterations confined to the latter. That the histologic presentation of primary CNS angiitis is subject to considerable variation merits emphasis.[152] Most frequently encountered are necrotizing, polyarteritis-like, or non-necrotizing lymphoplasmacytic variants. Mural infiltration by histiocytes, including epithelioid forms, and multinucleated giant cells of foreign body and Langhans' type characterize granulomatous examples, but, again, this is an inconstant feature (Fig. 28.8). When present, giant cells are not strictly associated with the elastic lamina and may lie in any part of the vessel wall. Secondary changes include thrombosis and, in longstanding cases, mural scarring and exuberant fibrointimal hyperplasia. The phenomenon of "mixed" granulomatous vasculitis and amyloid deposition is discussed below (see "Cerebral amyloid angiopathy" below).

Notwithstanding the fact that its histologic features are shared by cerebral vasculitides complicating a variety of systemic disorders,[152] primary angiitis of the CNS merits distinct nosologic status on clinical grounds. This is not to deny the possibility that this curious process might be triggered by diverse offenses to the cerebrospinal circulation. Although long suspected, an infectious etiology remains unproved. Noteworthy in this regard, however, is the epidemiologic association of primary CNS angiitis with cutaneous herpes zoster infection and with underlying conditions, chiefly Hodgkin's disease and other forms of hematolymphoid neoplasia, predisposing to this and other viral opportunists.[152,155] These observations are especially intriguing in view of the undisputed role of the varicella zoster virus as agent of a large vessel cerebral arteritis, poten-

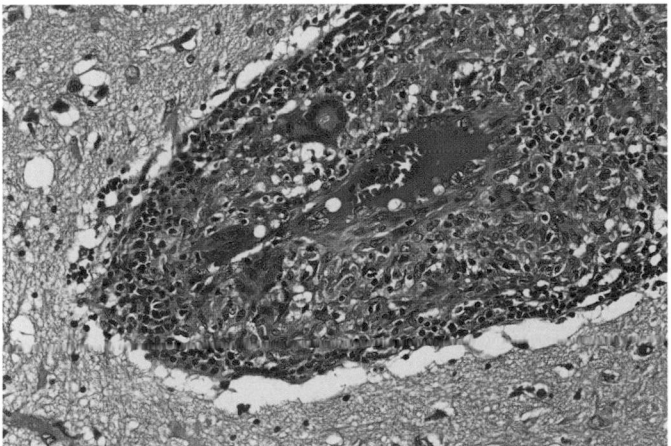

Fig. 28.8 Primary angiitis of the CNS. A frankly granulomatous inflammatory infiltrate replete with multinucleated giant cells expands the wall of this penetrating cerebrocortical blood vessel, found in biopsy material from a 34-year-old man with progressive encephalopathy.

tially indistinguishable from primary CNS angiitis, addressed in our discussion of viral disorders.

Cerebral amyloid angiopathy

The deposition of amyloid in the walls of cerebral blood vessels is a fact of aging and a conspicuous accompanying feature of varied neurologic disorders, including Alzheimer's disease, Down syndrome, dementia pugilistica, and certain types of spongiform encephalopathy. It is the association of this process—**cerebral amyloid angiopathy**—with intracranial hemorrhage that compels the attention of the neurosurgeon and surgical pathologist. Cerebral amyloid angiopathy is the most common nontraumatic cause of lobar cerebral hematoma in elderly subjects (the cohort at greatest risk) and has been estimated to account for some 5% to 10% of all primary, atraumatic brain hemorrhages.[94,160] The disorder is not a manifestation of systemic amyloidosis and typically presents in sporadic fashion, although kindreds afflicted by heritable (autosomal dominant) syndromes of florid cerebrovascular amyloidosis and early death due to recurrent intracerebral hemorrhage have been delineated.[160] β-amyloid peptide (βA4), found also in the infiltrated CNS vessels and neuritic plaques of asymptomatic senescence and Alzheimer's disease, constitutes the principal amyloid deposited in sporadic cases, in which it is apparently joined by amyloid derived from the cysteine protease inhibitor cystatin C.[160] Aberrant forms of βA4, cystatin C, transthyretin, gelsolin and other proteins resulting from point mutations in their encoding genes are the offending amyloidogenic agents in various heredofamilial types of CNS amyloidosis with vascular involvement.[160] While a substantial proportion of affected patients evidence dementia, cerebral amyloid angiopathy, even when severe, is not necessarily associated with cognitive impairment or with Alzheimer-type cerebrocortical alterations.

The peripheral, lobar location of amyloid-associated cerebral hematomas contrasts sharply with the basal ganglionic or bulbar situation typical of hypertensive hemorrhages and reflects the particular susceptibility of superficial cortical and leptomeningeal vessels to amyloidotic infiltration. Chiefly affected are small-caliber arteries and arterioles, but veins may be involved as well. These exhibit mural expansion and, in advanced cases, effacement by acellular, eosinophilic material deposited in the adventitia and media. By definition, this possesses the histochemical properties (Fig. 28.9) and fine structural attributes common to all amyloids. Definitive identification is most readily accomplished by demonstration of a dichroic, bluish-green birefringence in Congo red-stained sections viewed under polarized light. Other defining characteristics include thioflavin S or T fluorescence under ultraviolet light. Ultrastructural study should reveal randomly arrayed, nonbranching extracellular fibrils averaging 9 nm in diameter, but is not requisite to the diagnosis if the appropriate reactions are obtained on Congo red or thioflavin assay. Amyloid-laden cerebral vessels generally maintain their patency but are subject to a variety of "vasculopathic" alterations. These include "double-barreling" (a targetoid, vessel-within-vessel configuration produced by what would appear to be a circumferential cleft in the media), glomeruloid arteriolar changes, obliterative fibrointimal proliferation, perivascular or intramural lymphocytic infiltration, the development of microaneurysms, and, finally, fibrinoid necrosis.[159,161] Restricted to vessels bearing a heavy amyloid burden, this last abnormality appears to play a particularly significant role in the pathogenesis of vascular rupture.[161]

As is often the case in extracranial locations, amyloid deposited in the cerebral vasculature occasionally elicits a foreign body-type response replete with multinucleated giant cells that surround affected vessels and attempt to phagocytoze the offending material. Much rarer are examples of cerebral amyloid angiopathy associated with a true vasculitis of necrotizing and granulomatous type.[156,157] Such cases might represent idiosyncratic host reactions to the offending protein, but primary cerebral vasculitides could aggravate, if not trigger, local amyloidogenic processes. Instances of cerebral amyloid angiopathy and vasculitis occurring in patients with rheumatoid arthritis are noteworthy in this

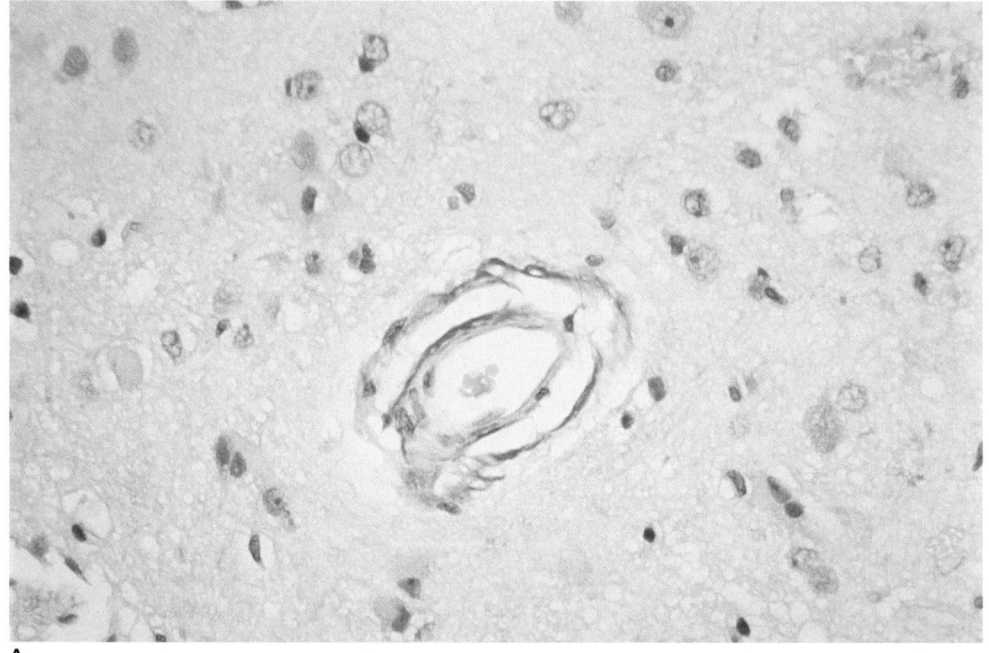

A

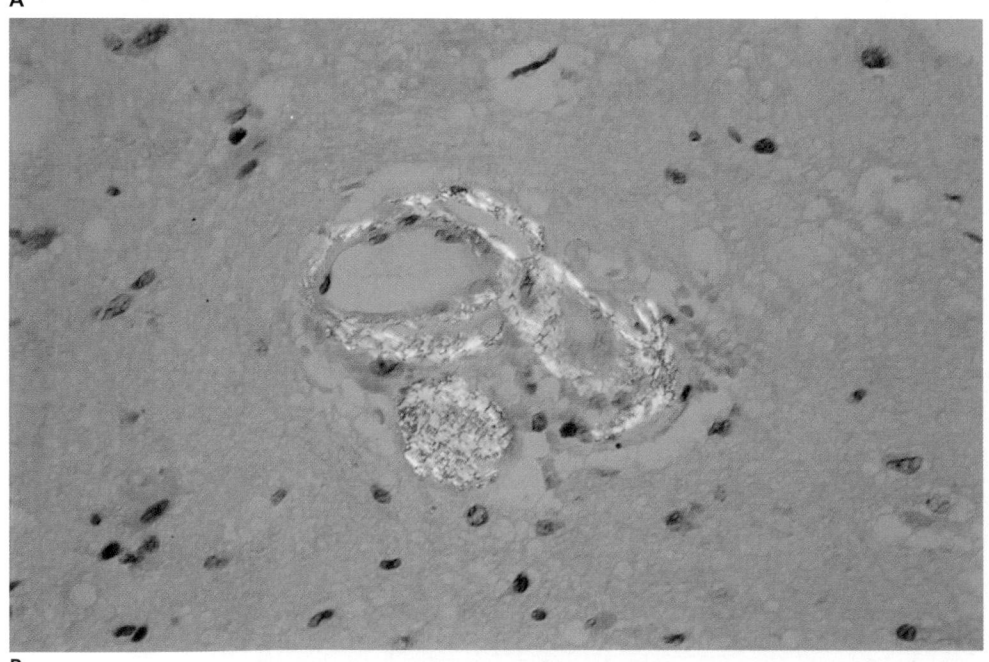

B

Fig. 28.9 Cerebral amyloid ("congophilic") angiopathy. As in extraneural locations, amyloid in the walls of cerebral vessels takes the Congo red stain (A) and exhibits an "apple green" birefringence when sections thus prepared are viewed under polarized light (B). The apparent "double-barrel" lumen evident in A is a common feature of amyloid-laden cerebral vessels.

regard.[158] Interestingly, the few examples of "angiitic" cerebrovascular amyloidosis that we have encountered presented not with hemorrhage but as pseudoneoplastic, infiltrative masses associated with seizures and focal neurologic deficits of a subacutely progressive nature. Much the same can be said of cases reported under the rubric of combined granulomatous angiitis and cerebral amyloid angiopathy.[156,157]

Cerebral autosomal dominant arteriopathy with subcortical infarcts and leukoencephalopathy (CADASIL)

Cerebral autosomal dominant arteriopathy with subcortical infarcts and leukoencephalopathy (CADASIL) is, as its name implies, a heritable condition.[162] Hundreds of affected kindreds have been delineated worldwide. The disorder has been linked to missense mutations or, rarely, small deletions involving the Notch 3 gene at chromosome 19p13, the product of which is a transmembrane receptor protein and transcriptional regulator selectively expressed in vascular smooth muscle cells. Isolated nonfamilial cases seemingly due to de novo Notch 3 mutations have been described. Clinical manifestations of CADASIL include migraine with aura (often the earliest neurologic complaint), subcortical ischemic strokes, psychiatric symptoms and cognitive deterioration eventuating in dementia. Most patients die within 15 to 25 years following their initial episodes of stroke. Nodular foci of periventricular T2 hyperintensity are characteristic and early changes seen in MR images, and are often apparent in presymptomatic individuals. With disease progression, lacunar white matter infarcts develop and confluent zones of increased T2-weighted MRI signal reflect a diffuse leukoencephalopathy.

CADASIL is a nonarteriosclerotic and nonamyloidotic vasculopathy that principally involves small and medium-sized arteries in the cerebral hemispheric white matter, but leptomeningeal and even systemic vessels are potentially affected by this generalized disorder.[162] Most recorded cases have been identified by brain biopsy, but sampling of skin, skeletal muscle and peripheral nerve may be informative as well. The hallmark of CADASIL is accumulation of a granular, basophilic and PAS-positive material in the tunica media of affected vessels with associated loss of medial smooth muscle cells, concentric mural sclerosis and luminal narrowing. At the ultrastructural level, this distinctive material consists of osmiophilic, electron-dense granules 10–15 mm in size that lie free between degenerating myocytes or cluster within pericellular indentations. These are illustrated in the following chapter on disorders of peripheral nerve. Irregular thickening of adjacent basal lamina is commonly apparent. While the exact composition of these granular deposits is not known, they may be labeled by monoclonal antibodies to the Notch 3 protein ectodomain, are specific for CADASIL, and may be identified in the presymptomatic phase of the disease. Accordingly, ultrastructural or immunohistochemical study of small dermal or subcutaneous arteries in skin biopsy specimens have been advocated as screening procedures for family members at risk as well as diagnostic methods in suspect cases. Formal genetic assessment (e.g., single strand conformational polymorphism analysis) may also be undertaken to confirm the diagnosis.

Epidural hematoma

The great majority of **epidural hematomas** follow cranial trauma complicated by temporal bone fracture and result from laceration of middle meningeal artery branches that penetrate the skull in the region of the pterion.[164] The accumulation of blood between the calvarium and endosteal surface of the dura mater is typically rapid, associated with acute deterioration of consciousness, and soon eventuates in death as a result of transtentorial herniation with brainstem compression if not promptly evacuated. Uncommon variants become symptomatic only long after their initiating injuries. Delimited by encapsulating neomembranes formed of vascularized fibrous tissue, chronic epidural hematomas of this sort are usually of venous origin.

Subdural hematoma

Subdural hematomas result from the dissection of blood into the potential space separating the arachnoid and dura mater, closely apposed under normal circumstances.[165] Most overlie the cerebral convexities in the frontoparietal region and are thought to follow rupture of delicate bridging veins that traverse the arachnoid-dura interface en route to the superior sagittal sinus.[164] These vessels are particularly susceptible to shearing forces generated by sudden angular acceleration of the head, as commonly occurs in the setting of trauma, and many subdural hematomas are clearly associated with cranial injury. Most "spontaneous" examples occur in the elderly, possibly because cerebral atrophy and resultant traction on these bridging vessels reduce their capacity to withstand otherwise trivial stresses. A similar phenomenon may promote the development of subdural hematomas following ventricular decompression for hydrocephalus. Patients who have received anticoagulants, who are thrombocytopenic, or who have been treated with long-term hemodialysis are also at increased risk of subdural hemorrhage.[166] A small subset of subdural hematomas result from arterial injury. These are usually associated with major craniocerebral trauma.

The pathology of the subdural hematoma is a function of its age. If evacuated within days of onset, it consists simply of clotted blood. Often, however, the original bleeding episode passes unnoticed, and the hematoma becomes symptomatic only after it has elicited an organizational response resulting in its enclosure within a discoid sac fashioned of grayish brown, collagenous neomembranes that adhere to the dura but develop no attachments to the underlying arachnoid. The latter feature reflects the fact that the mesenchymal elements responsible for encapsulation of the hematoma derive entirely from the dura, the leptomeninges remaining curiously unmoved by the presence of blood in the subdural space and playing no part in its organization. Inasmuch as the histologic maturation of these limiting membranes proceeds in temporally predictable fashion, the chronicity of a given lesion may be estimated by thorough assessment of the membranes.[164] Suffice it to say that the outer (juxtadural) membrane, which may attain a thickness of several millimeters, consists in the early stages of proliferating spindle cells and budding capillaries that penetrate the superficial aspect of the hematoma and come to lie in a loose connective tissue matrix containing admixed siderophages, scattered lymphocytes, and, in some cases, extramedullary hematopoietic elements (normoblasts). Infiltration by eosinophils may be striking. The inner membrane, by contrast, has a simpler structure and is thinner and relatively avascular. The precise cytogenesis of the spindly, fibroblastic elements populating these neomembranes and responsible for their ensuing collagenization remains a matter of speculation, but an origin from "dural border" cells that normally form a complex lamina apposed to the arachnoid has been suggested on the strength of fine structural observations.[163,165,167] In any event, both membranes undergo progressive hyalinization and, with complete resorption of the hematoma, fuse to form a thin fibrous rind closely resembling the adjacent dura mater on microscopic study. In exceptional instances, the hematoma sac is transformed into a calcific, even ossified, shell.

The capacity of the chronic subdural hematoma to present in clinically delayed fashion as an expanding intracranial mass would seem a paradox. Once completed, the enclosing hematoma sac could conceivably function as a semipermeable membrane and permit the ingress of fluid drawn by osmotic forces from the CSF compartment or the capillary network in its outer lamina. A prosaic (but, perhaps, more likely) explanation would incriminate these delicate vessels in episodes of rebleeding. Not infrequently, subdural hematomas that first come to attention in their chronic, encapsulated phases disclose evidence of recent, superimposed hemorrhage in the form of fresh blood layered subjacent to their vascularized outer membranes.

Inflammatory diseases

Demyelinating diseases

The idiopathic demyelinating diseases of the CNS, of which multiple sclerosis is by far the most common, are usually regarded as "medical" disorders diagnosed on clinical grounds or at autopsy. In fact, demyelinating lesions of the cerebral hemispheric white matter and spinal cord may present as space-occupying "tumors" associated with considerable mass effect, edema, and disruption of the blood–brain barrier evidenced, on CT or MR study, by diffuse or ring-like enhancement following administration of contrast media[170,174] (Fig. 28.10). Especially suspect on neuroradiologic grounds is the lesion that seems to fan out from a ventricular angle or that exhibits an "open" or "broken ring" profile characterized by the abrupt cessation of contrast enhancement where it abuts a ventricular surface or overlying cortex. Few patients harboring such lesions carry a diagnosis of multiple sclerosis when they present with symptoms and signs referable to an expanding intracranial mass. Solitary examples, not surprisingly, prompt consideration of aggressive glial neoplasia or abscess formation, whereas multifocal variants suggest metastatic disease or even cerebral parasitosis when lesions exhibit cystic characteristics on scan. Such **demyelinating "pseudo-**

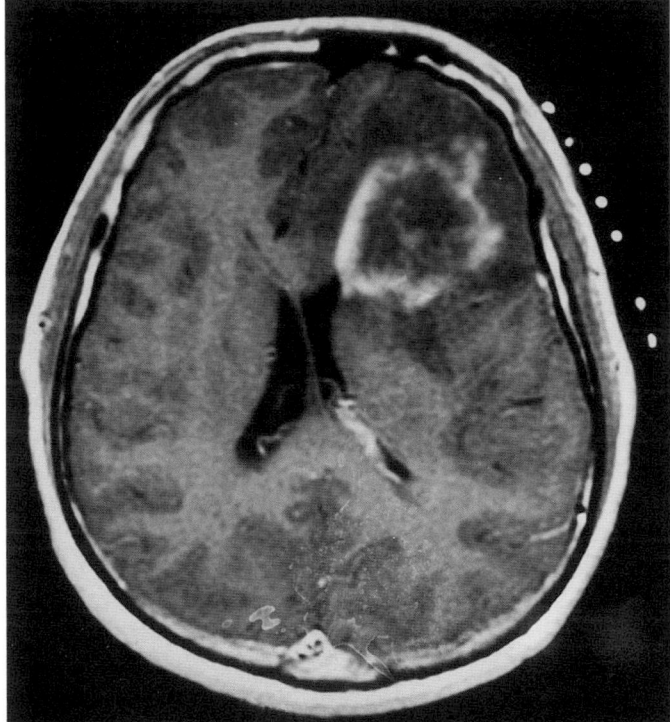

Fig. 28.10 Demyelinating pseudotumor. Taken following administration of a contrast agent that serves to delineate foci of blood–brain barrier breakdown as regions of bright signal, this magnetic resonance image demonstrates a lesion characterized by "ring" enhancement, conspicuous hypodensity of the surrounding white matter (indicative of edema), and mass effect evidenced by obliteration of the ipsilateral ventricular angle and shift of the neighboring cingulate gyrus across the midline. The neuroradiologic diagnosis was "probably glioblastoma, abscess also a possibility." The patient, a 32-year-old man with subacutely progressive hemiparesis and somnolence, recovered completely following limited biopsy and a short course of corticosteroids. He remains asymptomatic 9 years after diagnosis.

tumors" understandably occasion neurosurgical intervention for purposes of definitive diagnosis and thus enter the domain of the surgical pathologist.

The tumefactive demyelinating lesion shares with the active "plaque" typical of subacute multiple sclerosis[172] a sharp delineation from adjacent, uninvolved white matter evident in biopsy samples that include its perimeter. Affected tissues exhibit diffuse infiltration by foamy, lipid-laden macrophages, reactive astrocytosis of variable intensity, and perivascular aggregates of small (mostly T) lymphocytes and occasional plasma cells[170,174] (Fig. 28.11). The definitive characterization of the process as a demyelinating one ultimately requires the demonstration of relative axonal preservation in foci devoid of stainable myelin. This is readily accomplished by comparing serial sections assessed for myelin and axons by traditional neurohistochemical methods (Fig. 28.12) or assayed for components of the myelin sheath and axon using commercially available antibodies to myelin basic protein and neurofilaments, respectively. In the typical case, large numbers of axons will course uninterrupted through regions in which myelin, if at all demonstrable, persists only as phagocytized debris in the cytoplasm of macrophages. It should be pointed out, however, that a variable element of axonal depopulation is the rule, some particularly destructive examples progressing to cavitation.

In our experience, demyelinating pseudotumors are the non-neoplastic lesions most often misinterpreted on biopsy as gliomas, specifically as diffuse fibrillary astrocytomas or as oligodendrogliomas. The consequences to patients subjected to cerebral irradiation may be devastating.[173] The potential causes for error are many.[174] A

diagnosis of glioma may be prompted by the florid and cytologically atypical astrogliosis that characterizes some examples—an impression likely to be reinforced by the finding of scattered mitotic figures, as well as astrocytes that appear to be in atypical mitosis by virtue of a peculiar parcellation of their nuclear material (Fig. 28.13). Perivascular lymphoid infiltrates are an inconstant feature of demyelinating lesions sampled at craniotomy and even when conspicuous are no guarantee that a glial proliferation is not neoplastic. Even in their absence, however, the orderly spacing of gemistocytic astrocytes typical of hyperplastic states—a "logic" maintained in these lesions—should suggest a reactive process.

Especially confounding is failure to appreciate the high content of macrophages that lend to tissues undergoing demyelination their alarmingly hypercellular appearance. The voluminous foamy or granular cytoplasm typical of these cells when engaged in the digestion of phagocytozed myelin and useful in their distinction from glia may be obscured in suboptimally procured or processed samples. As this is particularly true of frozen sections, the use of cytologic preparations wherein these features are likely to be preserved is strongly advocated for purposes of intraoperative consultation (Fig. 28.14). Lectin or immunocytochemical assay for monocyte/macrophage markers such as HAM-56 (Fig. 28.15) and CD68 may also aid in circumventing problems of cell identification,[169] particularly as applied to neurosurgical specimens exhibiting artefactual distortion or dominated by newly arrived mononuclear cells interrupted in their labors and thus not evidencing the cytoplasmic characteristics of fully developed, lipid-

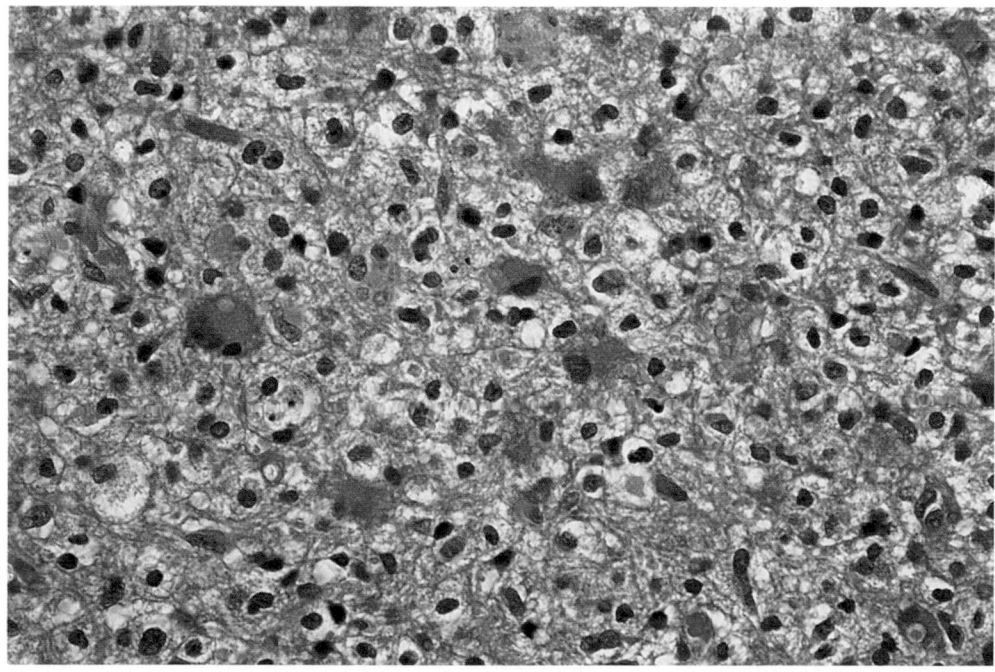

Fig. 28.11 Demyelinating pseudotumor. The hypercellularity of this lesion reflects infiltration by macrophages in large number, recognizable on careful study by their granular or foamy cytoplasm. Also apparent are several hyperplastic astrocytes.

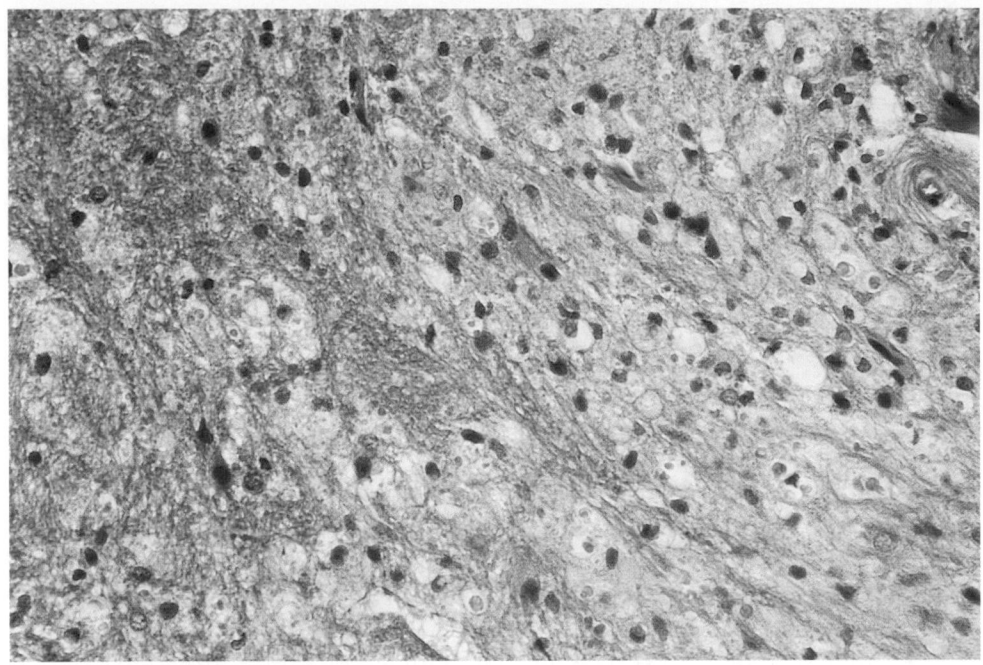

A

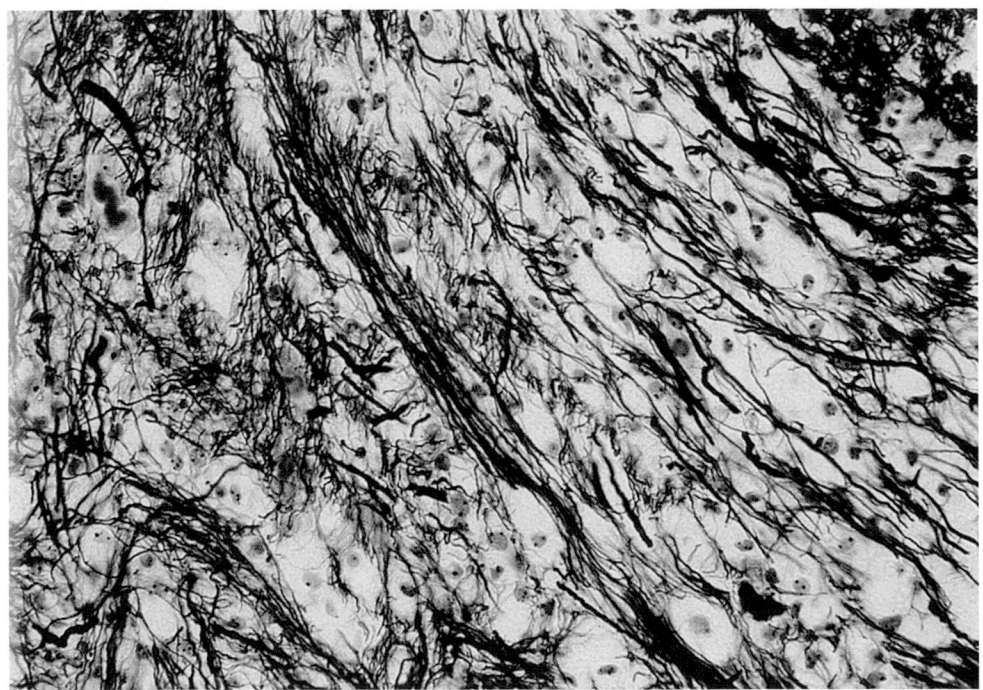

B

Fig. 28.12 Demyelinating pseudotumor. The interface of a demyelinated plaque (right) and normal white matter (left) is shown here in serial sections stained for myelin (**A**) and axons (**B**) by the Luxol fast blue and Bielschowsky methods, respectively. Myelin, blue in **A**, persists in the plaque only as globules present in the cytoplasm of macrophages. Axons, stained black in **B**, course uninterrupted into the region of demyelination.

engorged phagocytes. Diffuse infiltration by macrophages is so rarely a feature of the untreated glioma as to virtually exclude this diagnosis. The ready identification of such cells in smears, crush preparations, or tissue sections should instead suggest a non-neoplastic, necrotizing process (such as organizing infarction) or a selectively demyelinating disorder. Primary CNS lymphomas inadvertently treated by the preoperative administration of corticosteroids may vanish on neuroradiologic scan and can further simulate demyelinating disease by leaving behind only reactive lymphohistiocytic infiltrates but do not cause truly selective, regionally circumscribed myelin loss (see discussion of lymphoproliferative and myeloproliferative disorders for additional discussion and references). Patients suffering from multiple sclerosis on occasion do develop glial neoplasms,[171] but there is no compelling evidence that the incidence of the latter is increased in this population.

As mentioned, only exceptionally do tumefactive

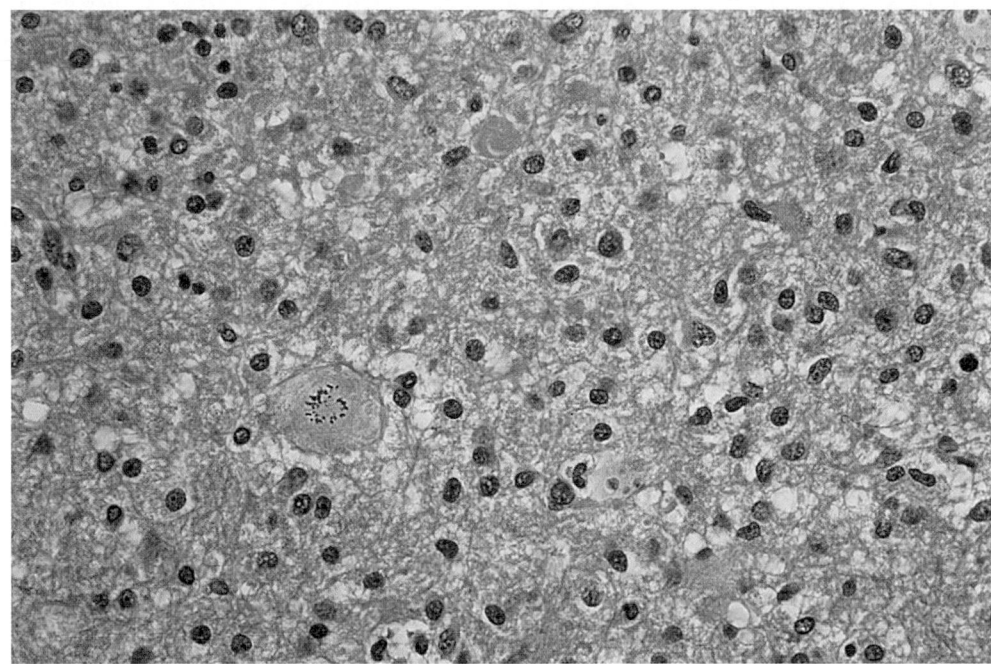

Fig. 28.13 Demyelinating pseudotumor. An apparently atypical mitotic figure and diffuse infiltrate of mononuclear cells lacking the cytoplasmic features of fully developed macrophages may lead to the incorrect diagnosis of glioma.

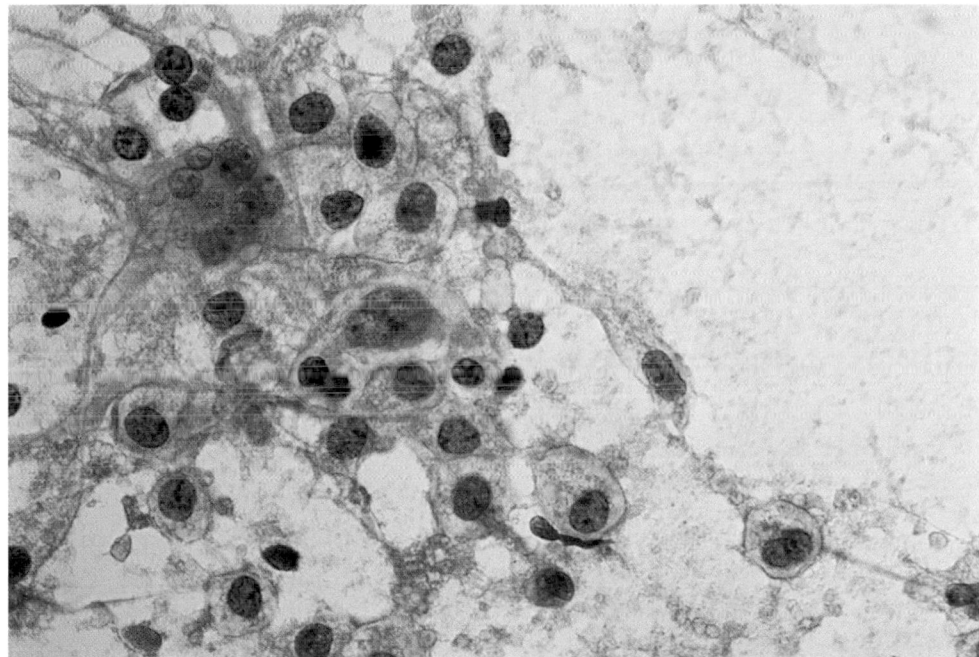

Fig. 28.14 Demyelinating pseudotumor. The presence of foamy macrophages in cytologic preparations argues strongly against a diagnosis of glioma at the time of intraoperative consultation. As shown here, somewhat atypical-appearing, multinucleate astrocytes are not uncommonly encountered in such specimens.

demyelinating lesions complicate the course of established multiple sclerosis. Interestingly, only 3 of 31 patients presenting with solitary or multifocal demyelinating pseudotumors in the series of Kepes[170] developed additional cerebral lesions during follow-up periods ranging from 9 months to 12 years. This intriguing observation suggests that the biology of pseudotumoral demyelinating disease differs significantly from that of classic multiple sclerosis and is perhaps more akin to that of the monophasic "allergic" encephalomyelitides triggered by viral infection or vaccination. A relapsing course, however, characterized a significant subset of cases in a smaller series.[167a] Last, mention is made of a **multifocal inflammatory leukoencephalopathy** described as complicating the chemotherapy of colorectal adenocarcinoma with 5-fluorouracil and levamisole.[168] The lesions in question are demyelinative and morphologically indistinguishable from active multiple sclerosis plaques. Whether one or both of these agents are directly responsible for this condition or somehow precipitate attacks of multiple sclerosis in patients predisposed to the disorder is unclear.

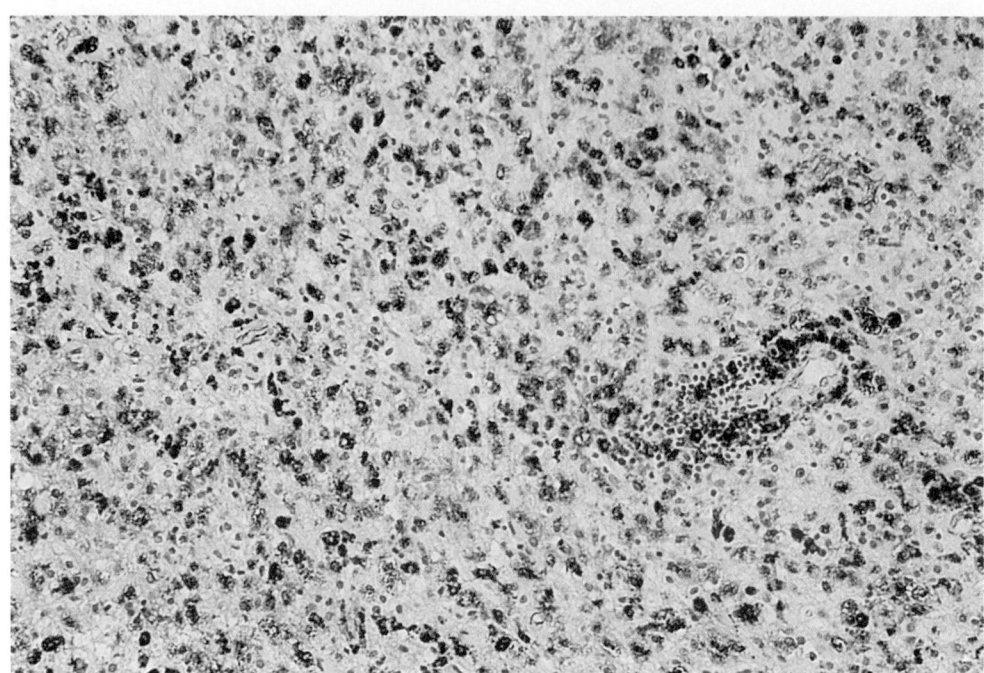

Fig. 28.15 Demyelinating pseudotumor. The density of infiltrating macrophages characteristic of demyelinating lesions is demonstrated in this immunoperoxidase assay for HAM-56.

Idiopathic inflammatory and reactive disorders, xanthomatous lesions, and "histiocytoses"

The various oddities collected in this section have little in common beyond their etiologic obscurity and inflammatory or otherwise "reactive" histologic appearances. Many are better known as systemic disorders and are given detailed consideration elsewhere in these volumes. Specific description is here accorded to only those entities unique to the nervous system.

Idiopathic hypertrophic cranial pachymeningitis is, as its name implies, an inflammatory and fibrosing disorder of unknown cause that affects the dura mater.[206,207] Clinical manifestations include headache, progressive cranial neuropathies, and cerebellar ataxia of adult onset occurring in association with radiographically demonstrable thickening and abnormal contrast enhancement of the peribulbar meninges, tentorium, and falx. The process can involve the dura over the cerebral convexities or extend into the cavernous sinus and orbit, causing painful ophthalmoplegia. **Idiopathic hypertrophic spinal pachymeningitis**, a disease of the cervicothoracic region typified by compressive myelopathy, may represent a variant of the same basic disorder.[178] A subset of afflicted patients evidence extradural abnormalities collected under the rubric of "**multifocal fibrosclerosis**," including inflammatory orbital pseudotumor, idiopathic mediastinal and retroperitoneal fibrosis, sclerosing cholangitis, Riedel's stroma, Peyronie's disease, Dupuytren's contracture, fibrosing orchitis, systemic vasculitis, and fibroinflammatory lesions of the subcutaneous tissues and lungs.[206,207] What may represent a localized pseudotumoral variant has been recorded.[187]

Dural biopsies in cases of idiopathic hypertrophic pachymeningitis disclose dispersed lymphoplasmacytic infiltrates, exuberant fibroplasia and, in some instances, necrosis and granuloma formation. Exclusion of tuberculosis, syphilis, mycotic infections, sarcoidosis, Wegener's granulomatosis, rheumatoid disease, and other defined causes of chronic fibrosing meningitis is required. Secondary intracranial extension of inflammatory orbital pseudotumor may also produce a similar meningeal picture.[186] The clinical course is variable, but often inexorably progressive. Corticosteroid administration and resection of compressing fibroinflammatory meningeal masses are of benefit to some patients. The reader should note that patients undergoing craniotomy, ventricular shunting, or even lumbar puncture alone may occasionally develop neuroradiologic evidence of diffuse meningeal thickening and enhancement that is typically asymptomatic and without clinical significance. We have seen biopsy material in one such case that exhibited subdural fibroplasia, neovascularization, hemosiderin deposition, and meningothelial hyperplasia.

Turning from the meninges to the brain proper, we briefly mention a form of chronic encephalitis, known eponymously as **Rasmussen's syndrome**, that is characterized by intractable unilateral focal seizures or epilepsia partialis continua of childhood onset, progressive cerebral hemiatrophy with hemiparesis, and cognitive decline.[216] Long suspected (but never convincingly shown) to represent a persistent viral infection, the disorder may have an autoimmune component—some afflicted patients harboring antibodies to native CNS antigens, including the glutamate GluR3 receptor. The neuropathologic substrate is nonspecific, consisting of perivascular and interstitial lymphoid infiltrates involving the cerebral cortex with microglial nodule formation, astrogliosis, and variable neuronal loss. High dose corticosteroids, intravenous gamma globulins, plasmapheresis, and surgery (including extended hemispherectomy) have all been investigated in the treatment of Rasmussen's syndrome and have proven beneficial to some patients. More localized and clinically benign forms of idiopathic chronic encephalitis have been described, particularly in adolescents and young adults, that may mimic cerebral neoplasms.[197] Whether these represent Rasmussen variants is unclear.

Limbic encephalitis is an amnestic syndrome of adulthood typically encountered as a paraneoplastic phenomenon[196] complicating small cell carcinoma of the lung, but the disorder has also been reported in association with other tumor types (e.g., nonsmall cell lung cancers, Hodgkin's disease, mammary adenocarcinomas, and testicular germ cell tumors) and, rarely, in the absence of demonstrable neoplasia.[180] Clinical manifestations progress in subacute fashion and consist principally of short-term memory loss, complex partial or generalized seizures, confusion, and disordered affect. Many examples evolve as one facet of a complex paraneoplastic disease that potentially involves the dorsal root ganglia, brainstem, cerebellum, spinal cord, autonomic ganglia, and myenteric plexi. MRI studies often disclose abnormal T2 hyperintensity of the medial temporal regions (with foci of pathologic contrast enhancement in some cases) and may prompt considerations of herpes simplex encephalitis or an infiltrative process. The brunt of the injury falls on the amygdaloid nuclei, hippocampi, and entorhinal cortices, biopsy material disclosing florid reactive astrocytosis, perivascular lymphoid cuffing, microglial or "neuronophagic" nodule formation, and in some cases, conspicuous neuronal depopulation. In contrast to herpes simplex encephalitis, the process is never overtly necrotizing, hemorrhagic, or attended by nuclear alterations indicative of a viral cytopathic effect.

Useful in the evaluation of suspected limbic encephalitis (the clinical manifestations of which often herald discovery of otherwise silent, low-stage tumors) is assay of serum and CSF for a specific autoantibody, designated anti-Hu, that is directed against neuronal nucleoproteins in the 35 to 40 kDa size range and strongly correlated with the presence of underlying small cell lung cancer.[196,219] Demonstration of this autoantibody constitutes compelling evidence for the paraneoplastic etiology of a patient's neurologic complaints and mandates a search for occult neoplastic disease that must begin with targeted investigation of the chest. Anti-Hu IgG appears to be elaborated in response to aberrant tumoral expression of this neuron-associated protein, prompting articulation of the hypothesis that an immunologic response directed initially against a triggering neoplasm comes ultimately to involve the nervous system in a cross-reaction having devastating neurologic consequences.[219] Another neuronal autoantibody known as anti-Ta has come to be recognized as a powerful marker of paraneoplastic limbic encephalitis in the setting of testicular germ cell neoplasia.[196] Tumor localization and treatment may effect neurologic improvement in patients with limbic encephalitis, which occasionally remits spontaneously, and is more effective than immune modulation in this regard.

The histologically distinctive masses reported as **"fibro-osseous lesions"** or **"calcifying pseudoneoplasms" of the neural axis** (Fig. 28.16) are composed principally of nonbirefringent, basophilic matrix materials that may assume an amorphous, somewhat chondromyxoid appearance or be deposited in coarsely fibrillar, ropey or plate-like fashion.[179,217] Rimming mononuclear and foreign body-type giant cells lend a granulomatous appearance to some examples. Matrix mineralization is at least focally apparent in most cases and many exhibit mature lamellar bone formation as well. Cerebrocortical alterations of meningioangiomatosis type (discussed in the section "Choristomas and non-neuroepithelial hamartomas") have been encountered adjacent to intracranial examples. These peculiar lesions are usually extra-axial and favor the spinal epidural compartment, but may arise from the cranial floor, within the leptomeninges or even brain. While properly regarded as non-neoplastic, they may be complicated by considerable neurologic morbidity resulting from spinal cord compression or skull base destruction with cranial nerve and cerebrovascular compromise. Ossified intracranial nodules lacking the defining matrix described above may be formed in nonspecific response to trauma, infection, or hemorrhage, and have been termed cerebral calculi or "brain stones." Rarely, symptomatic juxtaneural masses prove to be tophaceous lesions

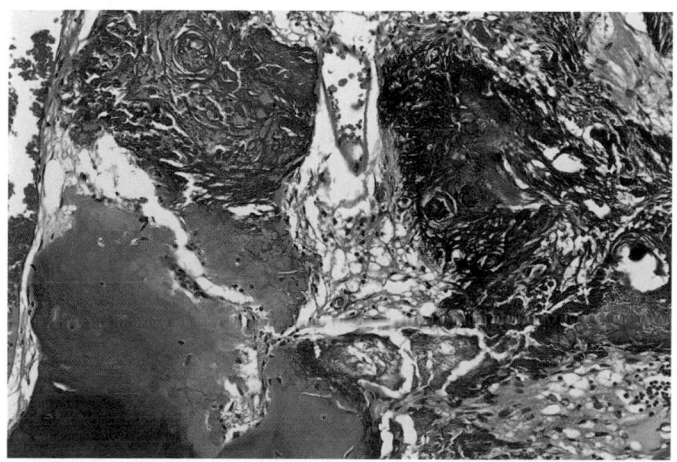

Fig. 28.16 Fibro-osseous lesion/calcifying pseudoneoplasm of the neuraxis. Fibroplasia, bone formation and the deposition of a highly characteristic basophilic matrix material in plate-like or ropey masses define this unusual process.

resulting from the crystalline deposition of sodium urate (gout), calcium pyrophosphate dihydrate (pseudo-gout) or calcium hydroxyapatite (tumoral calcinosis[194]).

Of those principally extraneural disorders that occasionally engage the talents of the neurosurgeon, most deserving of mention are Langerhans' cell histiocytosis ("eosinophilic granuloma"), sarcoidosis, and sinus histiocytosis with massive lymphadenopathy (Rosai–Dorfman disease). CNS involvement in **Langerhans' cell histiocytosis** typically follows infiltration of the calvarial floor and exhibits a striking tropism for the region of the hypothalamus and infundibulum, the eponym **Hand–Schüller–Christian disease** being applied to the classic clinical triad of diabetes insipidus, proptosis, and skull base defects on roentgenographic study. A similar topography is characteristic of those exceptional examples restricted (on presentation, at least) to the nervous system,[195] but lesions situated within the cerebral hemispheres are on record,[210] as are instances of brain invasion from contiguous primary foci in the cranial vault.[218]

Neurosarcoidosis most commonly assumes the form of a granulomatous basilar meningitis (Fig. 28.17) complicated by cranial neuropathies or, with extension of the process to the hypothalamic region, diabetes insipidus and other diencephalic syndromes. An accompanying granulomatous vasculitis may be apparent. While the overwhelming majority of patients have established systemic disease, primary CNS presentations have been described and can include pseudotumoral involvement of the meninges[175,199] as well as neuroparenchyma proper.[193] An example of necrotizing sarcoid granulomatosis presenting as a mass involving the temporal lobe

and cavernous sinus has been depicted.[221] In fact, only a subset of patients evaluated for granulomatous disease of the CNS that is not demonstrably infectious will prove to have clinical manifestations (e.g., interstitial lung involvement, mediastinal lymphadenopathy) or laboratory evidence (elevated serum/CSF angiotensin converting enzyme levels) supporting a diagnosis of sarcoidosis. Unclassifiable, "pathogen-free" granulomatous disorders were found in one study to share a tendency to diffuse neuraxial involvement, combined leptomeningeal and neuroparenchymal (particularly spinal cord) infiltration, attendant angiitis and a poor prognosis.[223]

Dura-based masses clinically indistinguishable from meningiomas constitute the usual pattern of CNS disease in cases of **Rosai–Dorfman disease** or **extranodal sinus histiocytosis with massive lymphadenopathy (SHML)**, though intramedullary involvement is on record.[177] These lesions can represent the sole manifestations of the disorder and may be multifocal. A similar predilection for the dura characterizes central neuraxial lesions that have been dubbed **inflammatory pseudotumors** or **plasma cell granulomas**,[184] although isolated cerebral[191] and choroid plexus[182] examples have been depicted. It is likely that at least some cases accorded these designations actually represent extranodal SHML. A unique falcine mass possibly analogous to the hyalinizing plasmacytic granuloma of pulmonary origin contained "raft-like" islands of acellular, hyaline connective tissue associated with a foreign body-type giant cell response.[211]

Collectively designated as "xanthomatous" are diverse lesions sharing only a conspicuous component of foamy, lipid-laden macrophages. Mention has already

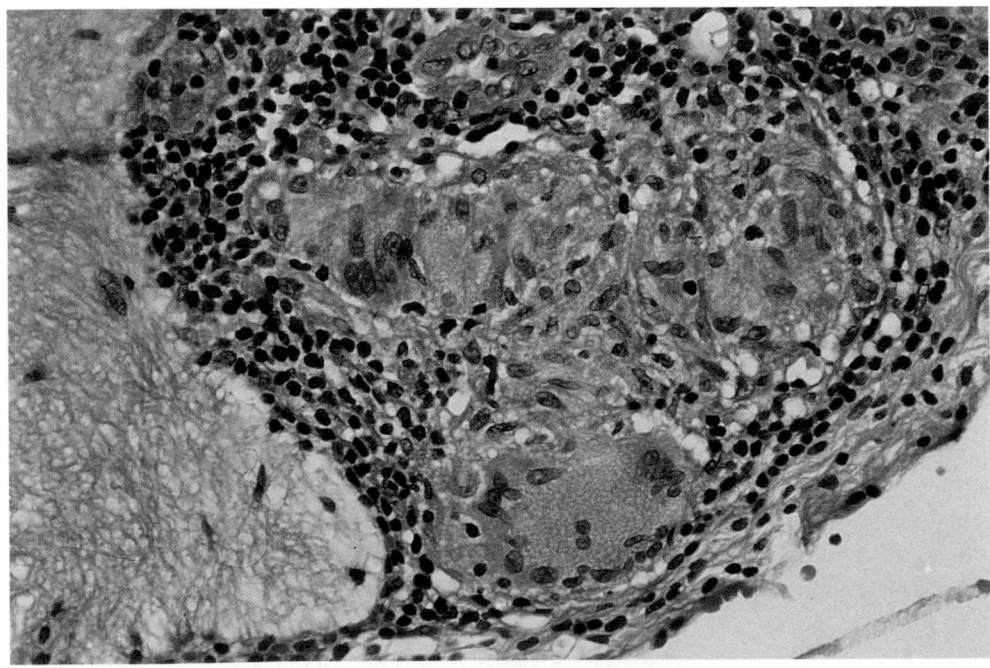

Fig. 28.17 Neurosarcoidosis. A non-necrotizing, granulomatous leptomeningitis replete with multinucleated giant cells of monocytic derivation characterizes this inflammatory disorder in its usual CNS presentation.

been made of **xanthogranulomas** forming in relation to colloid cysts of the third ventricle. Lesions similarly composed of foamy macrophages, foreign body-type giant cells, cholesterol clefts, and reactive lymphoid infiltrates commonly occur in the glomus of the choroid plexus but only rarely attain symptomatic proportions.[183] **Cholesterol granulomas of the petrous apex** that are believed to result from chronically impaired aeration of the petrous air cells may produce headache and palsies of cranial nerves V–VIII, prompting neurosurgical intervention.[188] Dura-based masses described as **xanthomas** or **xanthogranulomas**, some of immense proportions, have been encountered in otherwise healthy subjects,[205,224] in association with abnormalities of lipid metabolism such as familial hypercholesterolemia and phytosterolemia,[209,213,225] and in the setting of systemic Weber–Christian disease (relapsing nodular nonsuppurative panniculitis[215]). Some reported examples have complicated a disorder having the clinical features of Hand–Schüller–Christian disease.[200] A remarkable case interpreted as surgical dissemination of a parasellar xanthogranuloma to the convexity dura and falx has been depicted.[192] Xanthomatous CNS infiltrates may also complicate **Chester–Erdheim disease**, an enigmatic histiocytosis the hallmark of which is symmetric and bilateral sclerosis of the long tubular bones with colonization of the marrow spaces by lipid-laden macrophages.[176] On record, in addition, are xanthomas of probable traumatic etiology,[203] arguably neoplastic "**fibroxanthomas**"[201] and **juvenile xanthogranulomas**[181,214] involving the region of the Gasserian ganglion (Meckel's cave), meninges, brain, spinal cord, and ventricular system. CNS infiltration is a recognized complication of "**xanthoma dissemination**," a systemic syndrome characterized by the widespread eruption of juvenile xanthogranuloma-like lesions.[204]

Other odd processes that have been documented in neurosurgical material include **cerebral malakoplakia**,[190,198] the pseudoparasitic red blood cell alteration known as **myospherulosis**,[208] and a bizarre lesion reported as "**inflammatory myofibrohistiocytic proliferation simulating sarcoma in children**," one multifocal example of which presented with synchronous pulmonary and cerebral masses.[222] An isolated account depicts tumorous cerebellar infiltration by cytologically atypical histiocytes exhibiting immunoreactivity for S-100 protein and conspicuous lymphophagocytosis (emperipolesis), this possibly representing an unusual variant of extranodal SHML.[189] Lastly, we mention several described complications of systemic autoimmune (collagen vascular) disorders, including **rheumatoid meningeal nodules**,[202,220] extension of sinonasal **Wegener's granulomatosis** to the intracranial dura[212] and a low-grade, corticosteroid-responsive meningoencephalitis associated with cognitive impairment in the setting of **Sjögren's syndrome**.[185]

Infectious diseases

Bacterial infections

Bacteria are responsible for the overwhelming majority of suppurative infections involving the CNS and its coverings. Of particular concern to surgical pathologists are the common forms of localized suppuration: abscesses of the brain and spinal epidural space.

Approximately 20% of **brain abscesses** are unassociated with conditions predisposing to bacterial invasion of the nervous system, the remainder arising in patients with established pyogenic infections at extraneural sites, facilitating anatomic anomalies or histories of penetrating cranial trauma or prior neurosurgery.[230,247] Their demographic features, localization, number, and microbiologic characteristics vary with the risk factors operative in individual cases.

The extraneural bacterial infections predisposing to brain abscess are usefully divided into those involving contiguous meningeal or parameningeal sites versus those more distantly placed. Curious is the fact that cerebral abscesses rarely complicate bacterial meningitis, a notable exception to this rule being their significant association with neonatal leptomeningitides caused by *Proteus mirabilis* and *Citrobacter diversus*.[241,247] More frequently implicated among local sources of bacillary invasion are infected paranasal sinuses, middle ear cavities, and mastoids.[247] Although their pathogenesis remains imprecisely defined, abscesses associated with these various infections are commonly held to result from the retrograde thrombophlebitic carriage of organisms into the cranial cavity via emissary veins. Typically solitary, these tend to stereotyped topographic presentations. Thus, cerebral abscesses related to frontoethmoid sinusitis characteristically settle in the anterobasal frontal lobes, whereas "otitic" examples (including those associated with chronic mastoiditis) are usually encountered in the temporal lobes or cerebellar hemispheres. Lesions complicating sphenoid sinusitis frequent both the frontal and temporal regions. The organisms most often isolated from brain abscesses in these clinical circumstances include aerobic or microaerophilic streptococci (especially members of the *Streptococcus intermedius* "*milleri*" group), aerobic gram-negative bacilli (*Proteus, Escherichia coli, Klebsiella–Enterobacter*, and *Haemophilus* species), and *Bacteroides* species. Mixed infections are common. Other local suppurative processes associated with the subsequent development of brain abscess include dental sepsis and pyogenic infections of the face and scalp. Usually frontal in location, "odontogenic" abscesses typically follow tooth extraction or other dental manipulation and harbor mixed aerobic and anaerobic populations dominated by *Fusobacterium, Bacteroides*, and *Streptococcus* species. *Staphylococcus aureus* is the main offender when facial or scalp infections are incriminated; cerebral abscesses in this setting usually occur in cases complicated by cavernous sinus thrombosis. Mandibulofacial actinomycosis may also eventuate in brain abscess.[243] Spinal anomalies predispose to intramedullary abscesses, as do tumors of the spinal neuraxis, but such infections are decidedly rare.[244]

Hematogenous seeding of the CNS from distant foci of infection usually results in a multiplicity of abscesses that commonly lie within the territories subtended by the middle cerebral arteries. Most germinate at the junction of the cortical mantle and underlying white matter, but the cerebellum, basal ganglia, thalami, and brainstem may also be involved. "Metastatic" lesions of this sort most often have their origin in the thorax, chronic suppurating pulmonary disorders such as lung abscess and bronchiectasis leading the list of conditions predisposing to their development.[247] Much less common among underlying "donors" are bacterial endocarditis (characteristically acute), empyema, osteomyelitis, and infections of deep pelvic organs or abdominal viscera. Additional risk factors of note include various conditions in which the filtering function of the lung's capillary bed is abrogated (e.g., pulmonary arteriovenous fistulas) and cyanotic congenital heart diseases when complicated by right-to-left shunts (as encountered in tetralogy of Fallot, patent foramen ovale, ventricular septal defect, and transposition of the great vessels). The secondary polycythemia that regularly attends these anomalies may further promote the genesis of abscesses from infective emboli by causing microcirculatory sludging and regional brain hypoxia. Similar mechanisms may account for the significant risk of cerebral abscess in hereditary hemorrhagic telangiectasia (Osler–Weber–Rendu disease); most patients with this complication harbor pulmonary AVMs and exhibit hypoxemia with resultant cyanosis, clubbing, and polycythemia.[236] Among iatrogenic causes of metastatic brain abscess, instrumentation of the esophagus in attempts to relieve caustic strictures or treat varices by the endoscopic injection of sclerosing agents merits citation.[242]

The microbiology of the foregoing lesions is complex, but a few generalizations are possible. *Fusobacterium*, *Bacteroides*, and streptococci are the organisms most commonly recovered from brain abscesses associated with pulmonary sepsis, actinomycotic[243] and nocardial[237] lesions (the latter often encountered in debilitated and immunosuppressed subjects) also representing secondary deposits from foci of established lung infection in a majority of cases. Streptococci and *Haemophilus* species are the typical offenders in cases related to congenital heart disease, whereas *S. aureus* dominates isolates from examples complicating acute bacterial endocarditis.

With regard to the direct inoculation of bacteria into CNS tissues, abscess formation is probably the least frequent cerebral consequence of either penetrating cranial trauma or neurosurgery.[247] *S. aureus* is the organism most

often recovered from lesions arising in these circumstances, followed by *Streptococcus*, *Enterobacter*, and *Clostridium* species. *Propionibacterium acnes*, a gram-positive, anaerobic rod that causes a syndrome of shunt malfunction and immune-complex nephritis in patients with intraventricular catheters, has also emerged as an agent of traumatically and surgically acquired brain abscesses and epidural infection.[227,233] Trauma and intracranial hematoma accumulation, in addition, predispose to cerebral *Salmonella* abscess.[247]

Brain abscesses remain a diagnostic challenge to the clinician because their presenting manifestations and neuroradiologic appearances are nonspecific. Noteworthy is the fact that only 40% to 50% of patients are febrile on evaluation. The more common signs and symptoms are those of any expanding intracranial mass: headache, altered mental status, focal sensorimotor deficits, seizure, nausea, and vomiting.[230,247] Although central hypodensity, "ring" enhancement, and surrounding edema are characteristic on CT or MRI studies (Fig. 28.18), these appearances may be shared by malignant neoplasms and, on occasion, demyelinating disease.

Experimental, clinical, and histopathologic observa-

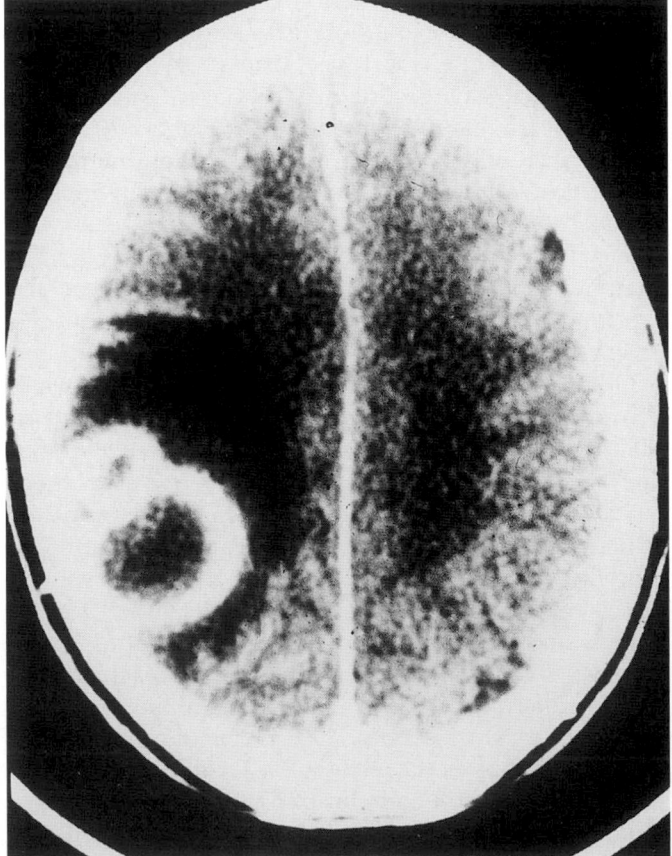

Fig. 28.18 Cerebral abscess. Ring enhancement of their developing pseudocapsules, budding of "daughter" lesions, and marked hypodensity of adjacent white matter reflecting severe edema are all characteristic of cerebral abscesses on CT or MR study. This example complicated mandibulofacial actinomycosis.

tions suggest that abscesses of the human brain begin as ill-defined zones of bacterial multiplication and polymorphonuclear leukocytic infiltration (cerebritis) most commonly situated in white matter immediately subjacent to the cortical ribbon or at the gray–white junction.[247] With time, proliferating fibroblasts come to surround a central mass of fibrinopurulent debris and fashion a collagenous capsule resembling the pyogenic membranes formed in response to suppurative infections outside the nervous system (Fig. 28.19). This, in turn, is bordered by edematous, chronically inflamed, and gliotic brain tissue that may evidence foci of acute cerebritis attesting to the host's failure to entirely wall off the primary locus of infection.

The rate at which encapsulation proceeds and its completeness vary considerably. Hematogenous bacterial seeding of the brain from distant sites of suppuration generally results in abscesses with capsules less developed than those that surround examples arising secondary to contiguous pyogenic processes. Especially notorious for their poor encapsulation are nocardial lesions. That capsular organization is typically most advanced along the superficial, juxtacortical perimeter of brain abscesses is reflected in the tendency of "daughter" lesions to bud from their deep aspects and in their tendency to rupture into the ventricular system rather than subarachnoid space. Because the mesenchymal elements responsible for capsule formation presumably derive from the adventitia of regional blood vessels and require oxygen for collagen fibrillogenesis, the relatively retarded organizational responses of paraventricular, as compared with cortical and paracortical, tissues may be a consequence of their less extensive vasculature. The intraventricular discharge of purulent material is among

the most feared of all abscess-related complications, often proving fatal.

In contrast to the largely intracranial localization of bacterial abscesses involving the CNS proper, 90% of epidural examples are situated at spinal levels.[231,234] Here a "true" (as opposed to potential) space, containing adipose tissue, nutrient arteries, and an elaborate venous plexus, expands posterior and lateral to the dura mater, whereas above the foramen magnum this fibrous sheath adheres tightly to the inner aspect of the skull. Anterior tethering of the dura to adjacent vertebral bodies presumably accounts for the fact that most **epidural abscesses** evolving along the length of the spinal cord are posteriorly or posterolaterally positioned. Approximately half of these settle in the thoracic, and one third in the lumbar, region. Less accommodating is the epidural space at cervical levels, where the spinal canal is nearly filled by the cord itself, and sacral lesions are rare.

Roughly 30–40% of spinal epidural abscesses arise "spontaneously," the remainder (like their neuroparenchymal counterparts) secondarily complicating infections established at contiguous or distant sites, trauma, intravenous drug abuse, spinal surgery or other invasive procedures, including epidural catheterization and lumbar puncture. Of particular importance among predisposing infections are contiguous foci of vertebral osteomyelitis, psoas and perinephric abscesses, decubitus ulcers, and other cutaneous and soft tissue suppurations. Diabetes mellitus, alcoholism, and renal failure are also recognized as significant risk factors. Presenting clinical manifestations typically include fever, malaise, and backache. If antimicrobial therapy and neurosurgical decompression are delayed, these early

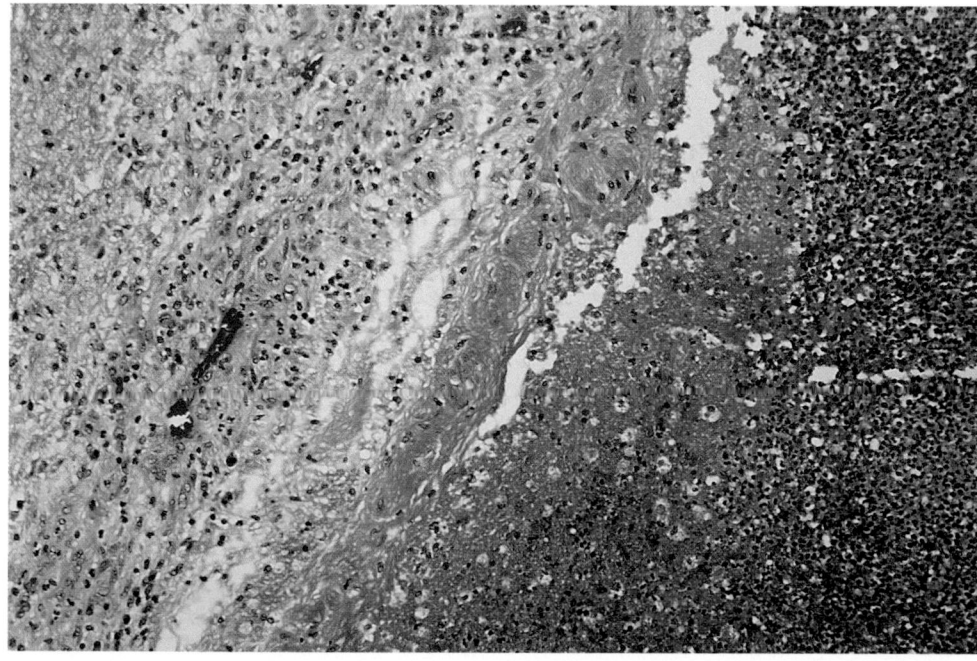

Fig. 28.19 Cerebral abscess. The lesion's purulent contents are separated from neighboring white matter by a granulation tissue-like zone of angioblastic and fibroblastic activity.

symptoms may progress in stepwise fashion to radiculopathy, sensorimotor and sphincter disturbances indicative of spinal cord dysfunction, and, finally, paralysis. *S. aureus* remains the most common culprit, distantly trailed by gram-negative aerobes such as *E. coli* and *Pseudomonas aeruginosa*, streptococci, and various anaerobes.

Although *Mycobacterium tuberculosis* is among the more common agents of spinal epidural abscess,[231,234,248] especially among intravenous drug abusers, the lesions it produces are typically granulomatous and caseating rather than suppurative. These usually arise in the low thoracic or lumbar region by extension from contiguous foci of tuberculous vertebral osteomyelitis or disk infection, but "primary" examples not associated with osseous, pulmonary, or other extraskeletal disease may be encountered. Diagnosis is complicated by the fact that patients often present with back pain of insidious onset and chronic evolution unattended by fever, leukocytosis, or evidence of tuberculosis on chest film. As with nontuberculous epidural abscesses, the consequence of delayed intervention is progressive neurologic dysfunction culminating in myelopathy or "Pott's paraplegia." Other localized forms of mycobacterial CNS infection include **tuberculoma**,[226,240,248] **focal tuberculous meningoencephalitis**,[245] and the rare **tuberculous abscess**.[246] **Subdural tuberculous empyema** has also been described.[228] Tuberculoma, defined as an encapsulated, granulomatous, and centrally caseating inflammatory mass, is by far the most common variant of neuroparenchymal tuberculosis, is usually unaccompanied by evidence of coextant meningeal infection, and may settle anywhere along the neuraxis but favors the intracranial contents. An excess of pediatric examples present in the cerebellum, constituting the posterior fossa "tumors" encountered most frequently in some countries (e.g., India) where tuberculosis is rampant. Exceptionally, tuberculomas are dura-based,[226] rather than intra-axial, or confined to the spinal cord.[240] At substantially increased risk of developing both tuberculous meningitis and neuroparenchymal tuberculomas are HIV-1-seropositive subjects,[248] instances of CNS infection by nontuberculous mycobacteria having also been documented in this setting.[229] Mycobacteria of the avium complex characteristically evoke a nongranulomatous response that may include conspicuous spindling of infected histiocytic elements—a phenomenon that can be confused with a mesenchymal or meningothelial neoplasm.[232]

Other distinctive bacterial infections of the nervous system proper include a bulbar encephalitis ("rhombencephalitis") caused by *Listeria monocytogenes*[239] and cerebral Whipple's disease, resulting from invasion of the neuropil by *Tropheryma whippelii*.[238] The latter process is characterized in the brain, as elsewhere, by infiltrates of foamy macrophages exhibiting an intense, granular PAS positivity of their cytoplasm (which has a peculiar blue–gray tint in hematoxylin-eosin sections) and containing numerous rod-shaped bacillary forms on ultrastructural study. A florid reactive astrogliosis is the rule. *Bartonella henselae* (agent of cat scratch disease and bacillary angiomatosis) has been described as causing space-occupying, inflammatory CNS lesions mainly in association with underlying immunodeficiency.[235]

Mycoses

The incidence of CNS mycosis has risen dramatically over the past several decades, reflecting the expanded population of immunocompromised patients susceptible to microbial opportunists. Still, neuroinvasive fungal infection only exceptionally occasions diagnostic operative intervention and thus remains a curiosity to the surgical pathologist. Most space-occupying intracranial and intraspinal lesions of mycotic etiology develop in association with diffuse meningeal or disseminated systemic infection and, consequently, are diagnosed by study of the CSF or, in the latter scenario, are treated empirically without recourse to tissue examination. Many are discovered only at autopsy. *Cryptococcus neoformans*, pathogenic molds, *Candida* species, and the dimorphic and dematiaceous fungi collectively account for the vast majority of lesions encountered in neurosurgical practice.[261]

C. neoformans, the agent of a diffuse leptomeningitis that is the single most common CNS mycosis, occasionally proliferates in localized neuroparenchymal or choroid plexus–based, intraventricular masses known as cryptococcomas.[259,261] Noteworthy is the fact that fewer than 5% of these unusual lesions arise in association with systemic disorders predisposing to opportunistic infection. Cryptococcal meningitis, by contrast, often afflicts immunosuppressed patients (e.g., HIV-1-seropositive adults, diabetics, organ transplant recipients, and patients being treated for hematologic or lymphoid neoplasia). The appearance of the cryptococcoma varies with the host's reaction, which may range from inertia to necrotizing granuloma formation and pronounced desmoplasia. When cryptococci hold the advantage, the lesion consists mainly of mucoid or gelatinous material that reflects the conspicuous elaboration of capsular mucopolysaccharides characteristic of these organisms. This is often traversed in honeycomb-like fashion by fibrous connective tissue septa. At the other extreme are sclerotic, granulomatous masses containing only rare yeast forms. Exceptional examples mimic bacterial abscesses, containing purulent debris bound by a well-developed pyogenic membrane. *Cryptococcus* is typically ovoid or spheric in profile, measures 2 to 15 µm in diameter, replicates by budding from a narrow base, and is reliably distinguished from other yeast by demonstration of its mucicarminophilic capsule (Fig. 28.20).

Fungi existing in pure hyphal form at both room

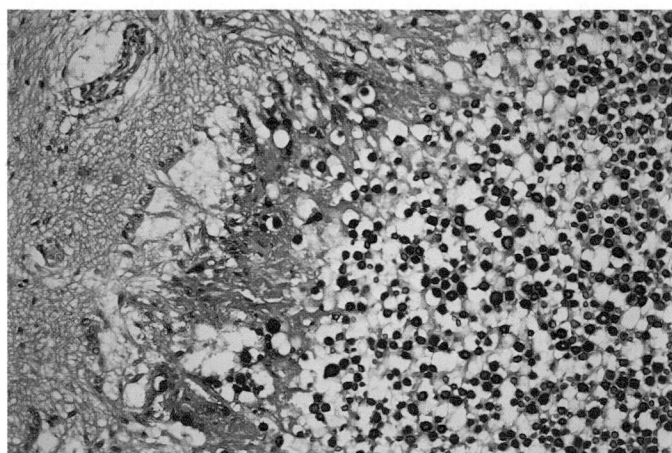

Fig. 28.20 Cryptococcoma. This neurosurgical specimen, from a previously healthy 54-year-old man with a "tumor" primarily involving the choroid plexus and wall of the right lateral ventricle, demonstrates numerous yeast forms identifiable as *Cryptococcus neoformans* by their mucicarmine-stained capsules.

temperature and 37°C are termed molds. The major CNS pathogens in this group include *Aspergillus* species, the Mucoraceae, and *Pseudallescheria boydii* (also referred to as *Scedosporium apiospermum*). *Fusarium*, *Paecilomyces*, and *Penicillium* species, *Streptomyces griseus*, and *Acremonium alabamensis* have also proved neuroinvasive on occasion.[261] Opportunists all, these ubiquitous organisms only rarely attack otherwise healthy individuals and share a particular predilection for patients receiving maintenance doses of broad-spectrum antibiotics through protracted periods of neutropenia, as commonly occurs in the management of leukemias and lymphomas. CNS infections that occur in such settings result from fungemia, are primarily intraparenchymal (as opposed to meningeal), are usually multifocal, and typically accompanied by evidence of systemic mycosis. The development of cerebral aspergillosis in patients treated for hematologic neoplasms, for example, is almost invariably preceded by symptomatic fungal infection of the lungs. Also at risk of blood-borne CNS seeding by pathogenic molds are patients taking corticosteroids, intravenous drug abusers, and, in the case of *P. boydii*,[255] victims of near drowning. Alcoholic liver disease and Cushing's syndrome have also been associated with CNS aspergillosis.[261] A second important form of meningeal and neuroparenchymal mycosis caused by these agents follows their direct intracranial spread from foci of orbital or paranasal sinus infection. This pattern of disease is typified by rhinocerebral mucormycosis, a disorder classically associated with diabetic ketoacidosis but also complicating other acidemic states (e.g., sepsis, profound dehydration, uremia), renal transplantation, and desferoxamine therapy.[261] Prior to the application of immunosuppressive chemotherapeutic regimens to the treatment of cancer, *Aspergillus* generally invaded the

CNS from primary foci of ocular, sinonasal, or middle ear infection. In addition, skull fracture, penetrating trauma, and craniotomy may set the stage for neural infection by molds.

The neurologic manifestations, distribution, and morphology of CNS lesions caused by these agents vary with the clinical circumstances surrounding infection and the immune status of the host. Particularly characteristic of cerebral disease evolving in the setting of disseminated systemic mycosis is a syndrome of multifocal stroke that reflects the shared tendency of pathogenic molds to occlude, invade, and trigger thrombosis of the leptomeningeal and perforating cerebral vasculature. The resulting lesions are basically infarcts, often hemorrhagic, that are secondarily colonized by fungi migrating through damaged blood vessel walls and that frequently exhibit little inflammatory reaction or limited superimposed suppuration. These are typically scattered in both cerebral hemispheres and often involve the deep nuclei, cerebellum, and brainstem. Contiguous fungal infiltration of the leptomeninges is common, but infection limited to these tissues is rare. Solitary lesions are exceptional, but examples produced by *Aspergillus* species,[251,265] *P. boydii*,[255] and other molds[261] are on record. These present with symptoms referable to an expanding intracranial mass, tend to occur in patients whose immune reflexes are relatively preserved, and may assume an abscess-like or even granulomatous character. Of particular note is a distinctive form of localized CNS mucormycosis characterized by a remarkably stereotypic predilection for the basal ganglia of intravenous drug abusers.[262] The more common rhinocerebral infections caused by advancing Mucoraceae are manifest as poorly delimited, necrotizing lesions again evidencing the ischemic and hemorrhagic qualities typical of these angioinvasive organisms. True mycotic aneurysm has also been described as a consequence of cerebral aspergillosis.[258]

The definitive taxonomic classification of molds requires their isolation in culture and cannot be accomplished on the basis of their morphology in tissue sections. Of the major CNS pathogens, both *Aspergillus* species and *P. boydii* appear in biopsy material as septate hyphae. *Aspergillus* species are usually somewhat stouter and branch (at acute angles) more frequently, but these are not reliably distinguishing features. By contrast, the Mucoraceae are broad, ribbon-like hyphal organisms that are nonseptate and branch at right angles.

Blastomyces dermatitidis, *Histoplasma capsulatum*, *Coccidioides immitis*, and *Paracoccidioides brasiliensis* are traditionally grouped as "dimorphic" fungi because of their growth as filamentous mycelia at room temperature and yeast at 37°C. All are capable of infecting the CNS, usually in the form of a chronic granulomatous meningitis in patients with coexistant, active systemic mycoses. Limited extension to the cerebral cortex from contiguous foci of leptomeningeal infection is common but typically of no clinical consequence. Only rarely do neuro-parenchymal lesions attain symptomatic proportions.[261] Again, these unusual fungal masses are generally, although not invariably, associated with evident infection of extraneural tissues. Examples have been described both in the obviously immunodeficient and in patients with no clear risk factors for opportunistic disease.[249,257,260,263,264] Worth noting are observations that roughly half of the intracranial blastomycomas and a majority of the histoplasmomas reported to date presented as solitary lesions. Brain invasion by *C. immitis* and *P. brasiliensis* is, by contrast, infrequently unifocal. The interested reader is referred to the cited literature for details regarding the pathogenesis and morphology of these curious lesions and the appearances of their causative agents. Suffice it to say that these organisms as a rule evoke a necrotizing, granulomatous tissue response replete with multinucleated giant cells and, in cases of blastomycoma and histoplasmoma, foci of caseation that may prompt considerations of tuberculous infection. A suppurative infiltrate of polymorphonuclear leukocytes is also commonly observed in otherwise granulomatous masses caused by *B. dermatitidis*. Cerebral endarteritis and mycotic intracranial aneurysm caused by *C. immitis* infection have been described,[252] as has massive dural and cerebral venous thrombosis associated with coccidioidal meningitis in an AIDS patient.[256]

The dermatiaceous fungi are a group of pigmented hyphal yeasts best known as the agents of chronic skin and subcutaneous infections such as Madura foot and tinea capitis. Extracutaneous disease is exceptional, but the brain is a common target in disseminated mycoses caused by these organisms. One member of the group, *Xylohypha bantiana* (*Cladosporium trichoides*), appears to be specifically neurotropic and is responsible for most CNS infections,[250] which are often classed with other deep mycoses caused by pigmented fungi under the rubric of phaeohyphomycosis. This organism is fully capable of invading the nervous systems of apparently immuno-competent hosts and, in many cases, does so in the absence of demonstrable foci of extraneural infection. Isolated patients have suffered immunosuppressive underlying conditions; exhibited pre-existent phaeohy-phomycotic infections of the paranasal sinuses, ear, or lungs; or have apparently acquired the infection through traumatic intracerebral implantation or intravenous drug abuse.[254] Neuroparenchymal lesions consist of necrotiz-ing granulomas, multifocal in about 50% of cases. A similar fraction are attended by fungal meningitis. In tissue sections, the agent appears as branching, septate hyphal, and yeast-like structures with a brown or olive-green hue. Isolation in culture is required for definitive classification. Other pigmented fungi that have been reported to cause CNS disease include *Drechslera–Bipolaris–Exserohilum* and *Curvularia* species, *Fonsecaea pedrosoi*, *Wangiella dermati-*

tidis, *Dactylaria constricta*, *Ramichloridium oboroideum*, and *Scopulariopsis brumptii*.[261]

If *Candida* species appear to receive short shrift in these pages, it is not because the threat they pose to the nervous system is trivial in epidemiologic terms. Actually, cerebral candidiasis has emerged in recent years as one of the most common CNS mycoses encountered in immunosuppressed patients.[261] The fact remains, however, that the great majority of cerebral *Candida* infections are discovered only at autopsy, resulting from fungemia in debilitated, moribund patients. The typical lesions are diminutive foci of suppuration scattered widely in the neuropil and associated in some cases with fungal meningitis. The formation of granulomas or macroabscesses, disease limited to the meninges, and vasculitis, with resultant infarction or the development of mycotic aneurysms,[258,261] have also been described, as has the extraordinary presentation of CNS candidiasis as a localized fungal mass.[253]

Parasitoses

The CNS parasitoses include a great variety of protozoal and helminthic infections. This discussion is limited to two representatives of particular importance to the surgical pathologist—neurocysticercosis and toxoplasmosis.

Neurocysticercosis, caused by larvae of the pork tapeworm, *Taenia solium*, is the most common parasitic cerebral infection encountered in worldwide neurosurgical practice.[268] Endemic to nearly all continents, the disease is particularly prevalent in Mexico (where it is the leading cause of space-occupying intracranial lesions), Central and South America, India, Africa, and China. An increasing incidence in the United States is largely attributable to cases occurring in immigrants from these regions. Infection is acquired by ingestion of food or water contaminated by feces containing the cestode's ova. These are partially digested in the host's stomach, evolving to oncospheres and subsequently penetrating the small intestinal mucosa to disseminate throughout the body, preferentially encysting in ocular tissues, striated muscle, and brain. The ensuing clinical disorder is named for the designation given the organism at this larval stage, *Cysticercus cellulosae*.

Cysticerci actually persist in parasitized tissues for long periods without eliciting symptoms of any kind. The active clinical phase of neurocysticercosis is triggered by the host's inflammatory response to the larva's death (approximately 18 months following primary infection). The high incidence of focal or generalized seizures associated with the disorder reflects the fact that oncospheres reaching the CNS settle mainly in the epileptogenic cerebral cortex, but they may also colonize the ventricular system and basal cisterns in a distinctive pattern of infestation ("racemose" cysticercosis) result-ing in obstructive hydrocephalus and consequent manifestations of elevated intracranial pressure. The presence of multifocal, rim-enhancing cerebral cysts on neuroimaging study suffices in many cases to prompt a diagnostic as well as therapeutic course of anti-helminthic chemotherapy, but a substantial proportion of patients present with solitary lesions, and the host's reaction to the decaying parasite may convert the cyst to a deceptively solid inflammatory pseudotumor. Neurosurgical intervention may be obviated by CSF or serologic assay for specific anticysticercal antibodies or antigens, but false-negative results may be encountered, especially in subjects with unifocal disease.[268]

When not completely obscured by secondary inflammatory changes, the gross appearance of cysticerci excised in toto is virtually pathognomonic (Fig. 28.21). Individual cysts are of small diameter, are circumscribed by a rubbery fibrous pseudocapsule, and contain a single larval scolex represented by a spheric or ovoid grayish-white nodule measuring no more than 3 to 4 mm in greatest dimension. By contrast, cestode larval cysts produced by the morphologically similar *Multiceps multiceps* contain numerous scolices and those caused by *Echinococcus granulosus* are considerably larger and endowed with a characteristically laminated wall. On histologic examination, the fibrous pseudocapsule is typically infiltrated by lymphocytes and plasma cells in large numbers, may contain eosinophils in abundance, and in some cases is the site of an active granulomatous reaction. The mummified remains of the degenerate scolex are covered by a wavy, somewhat refractile cuticle and consist largely of loose, reticular tissue containing numerous calcospherites. Relatively intact scolices possess a discernible subcuticular "pseudoepithelial" layer, small myofiber bundles, and four suckers armed with birefringent hooklets (Fig. 28.22). Racemose cysticerci evacuated from the ventricles or subarachnoid space present as grape-like clusters of interconnected larval "bladders" lacking organized scolices.

Toxoplasmosis is the generic designation applied to localized or systemic infections caused by the obligate intracellular protozoan *Toxoplasma gondii*. CNS involvement may assume a number of distinctive clinico-morphologic guises,[266] this discussion focusing on a "tumefactive" variant largely confined to immunocompromised hosts and typically unassociated with clinical manifestations of extraneural parasitosis. Once regarded as rare and encountered principally among patients treated for hematolymphoid neoplasms (Hodgkin's disease, particularly), this form of toxoplasmosis is now known to physicians the world over as a common AIDS-defining disorder and is in fact the leading cause of space-occupying intracranial lesions in the HIV-1 seropositive.[266,267] Bone marrow transplant recipients have also emerged in recent years as a population prone to CNS infections of this type. Common to the afflicted is a breakdown of cell-mediated immune surveillance thought, in most cases, to permit recrudescence of the agent in dormantly parasitized neural tissues. *T. gondii* is noted for its silent persistence in the brain following primary infection, which is usually asymptomatic and acquired by the consumption of inadequately cooked red meats containing encysted organisms or by the inadvertent ingestion of foodstuffs, soil, or other materials contaminated by protozoal oocytes shed in the feces of domestic cats.

The clinical and neuroradiologic features of CNS toxoplasmosis are quite variable, are nonspecific, and do not suffice for definitive diagnosis. Because *Toxoplasma* "abscesses" favor neuron-rich gray matter structures such as the cerebral cortex, basal ganglia, and brainstem, it should come as no surprise that seizures, progressive hemipareses, and cranial nerve deficits figure prominently among their initial manifestations. Many patients, however, present without localizing complaints, evidencing, instead, fever, headache, lethargy, and diffuse

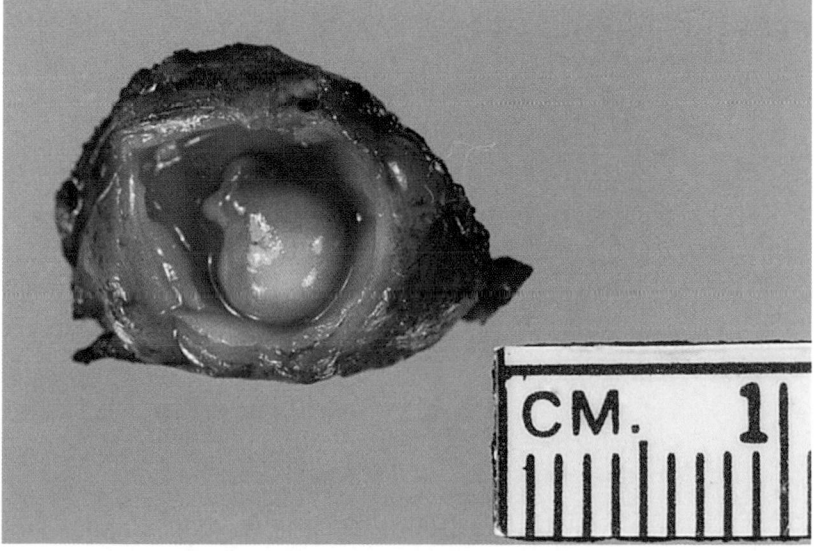

Fig. 28.21 Neurocysticercosis. Typical of cerebral *Taenia solium* infestation is the solitary, encysted scolex demonstrated in this neurosurgical specimen from the left frontal cortex of a 32-year-old Haitian man with a history of seizures.

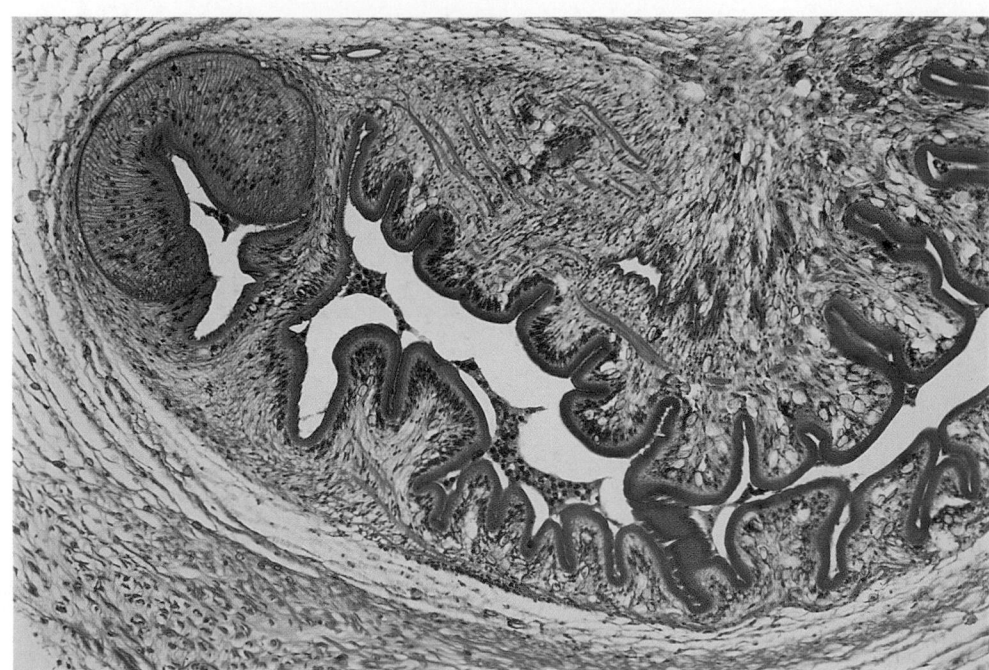

Fig. 28.22 Neurocysticercosis. The parasite's main structural features include a prominent investing tegument or "cuticle," aggregated subcuticular cells, smooth muscle fibers, and four suckers, one of which is depicted at upper left.

encephalopathy, subacute in its evolution. Cranial MR imaging typically discloses multifocal, nodular lesions characterized by ring-like peripheral enhancement, surrounding edema, and mass effect, but exceptional examples are nonenhancing or diffusely so, and solitary abscesses at presentation are not rare. Isolated involvement of the spinal cord has been described.[269] Studies in the HIV-1 seropositive have demonstrated that, in this population at least, cerebral toxoplasmosis only occasionally develops in patients lacking serologic evidence of contact with the organism.[266] A negative serum anti-toxoplasma IgG titer militates against, but does not exclude, the diagnosis in this setting. It has become common practice to institute antimicrobial therapy on empiric grounds in suspect cases and to reserve neurosurgical intervention for the patient who does not respond satisfactorily to such management. Most HIV-1-seropositive individuals whose intracranial masses fail to resolve on anti-toxoplasma chemotherapy prove to harbor primary CNS lymphomas.

The *Toxoplasma* "abscess", as it is commonly called, consists of a central mass of necrotic cellular debris surrounded by edematous and inflamed brain tissue typically exhibiting conspicuous vascular abnormalities. The latter include perivascular and intramural lymphoid infiltration, endothelial swelling, thrombosis, fibrinoid necrosis, and, in longstanding lesions, fibrous obliteration. It is within this perimeter zone that *Toxoplasma* are most numerous, the necrotic core often being devoid of identifiable organisms. Two protozoal forms are evident in active lesions. Responsible for tissue injury is the rapidly proliferating tachyzoite. This is faintly basophilic, measures approximately 4 to 8 μm in greatest

dimension, and typically exhibits a slightly crescentic or lunate profile (the Greek *toxon* means bow or arc). Because it is often difficult to visualize tachyzoites in routine histologic preparations and to confidently distinguish them from cellular detritus, the screening of suspect biopsy material with *Toxoplasma*-specific antibodies is strongly advised. More readily apparent, although present in lesser numbers, are intracellular pseudocysts and "true" (i.e., membrane-delimited) cysts that may attain diameters of up to 200 μm (Fig. 28.23). These are filled with minute, PAS-positive bradyzoites (named for their slow replicative cycles), are immunologically inert, and represent the form in which *Toxoplasma* chronically persist in brain and other tissues. Within the CNS, bradyzoites appear to collect preferentially within neurons and perivascular macrophages. Again, it is immune failure that is believed to somehow trigger their metamorphosis to tachyzoites and subsequent destructive invasion of neural tissues. Careful inspection of active lesions often reveals ruptured cysts that appear to be disgorging their content of protozoa into the neuropil. Like tachyzoites, bradyzoites are labeled by commercially available *Toxoplasma*-specific antibodies.

Spirochetal infections

The two major CNS spirochetoses are neurosyphilis,[270,271] caused by *Treponema pallidum*, and neuroborreliosis complicating infection by the agent of Lyme disease, *Borrelia burgdorferi*.[272,273] No attempt is made here to discuss the pathogenesis and varied clinical expressions of these complex syndromes, matters largely irrelevant to the surgical pathologist. Suffice it to say that intracerebral

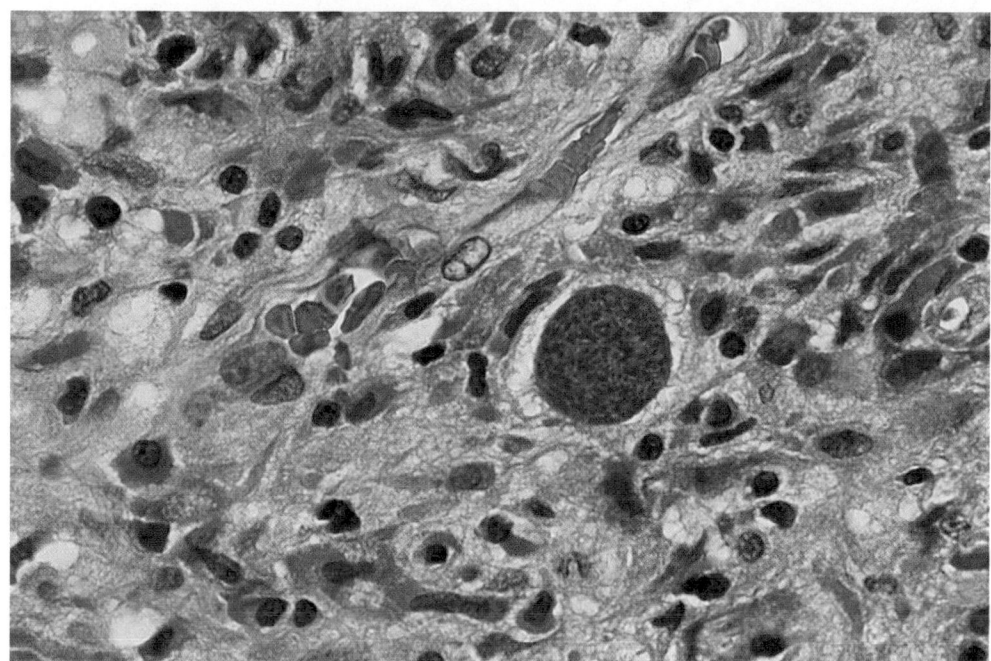

Fig. 28.23 Toxoplasmosis. Minute, basophilic structures representing bradyzoites fill a protozoal pseudocyst lying among infiltrating lymphocytes, plasma cells, and macrophages.

inflammatory pseudotumors (known as "gummas" in the case of treponemal disease and accompanied by necrosis and fibroplasia in this setting) are restricted to the late stages of systemic infection by these organisms, constitute their least common manifestations, and are usually approached surgically only when the diagnosis is unsuspected on clinical grounds and so not established by the appropriate serologic methods. The reader is referred to the cited literature for further details.

Viral infections

Herpes simplex encephalitis

Herpes viruses are responsible for a wide variety of neurologic infections, our concern here being with a distinctive form of focal, necrotizing, and hemorrhagic encephalitis caused principally by herpes simplex virus type 1 (HSV-1). **Herpes simplex encephalitis** (HSE) afflicts only 2 to 4 persons per 1,000,000 inhabitants a year but leads the list of potentially fatal, nonepidemic cerebral infections of viral etiology.[279] Individuals of any age may be affected. The disease is often fulminant in its evolution and is characterized by fever, disordered affect, dysphasia, seizure activity, and deterioration of consciousness. CSF pleocytosis is the rule and may be accompanied by xanthochromia, whereas abnormalities are usually localized to one or both frontotemporal regions on CT scan or MRI (Fig. 28.24). Brain biopsy is now generally obviated in the appropriate clinical circumstances by assay of CSF for HSV-specific antigens or genomic sequences. Polymerase chain reaction (PCR)-based amplification of HSV DNA has gained wide acceptance in this regard and, as the diagnostic method of choice, combines high degrees of both sensitivity and specificity.[279]

A remarkably stereotypic predilection for the anteromedial temporal lobes, orbitofrontal cortex, insulae, and cingulate gyri typifies HSE.[274,275] Experimental observations support the hypothesis that this "limbic" distribution reflects transolfactory spread of the agent to the CNS and suggest that at least some cases of HSE follow activation of virus residing latently in cerebral tissues. The histologic appearances of the disorder vary considerably with the duration of the clinical illness.[274,275] The earliest appreciable changes, evident prior to the arrival of inflammatory infiltrates, include neuronal shrinkage and eosinophilia accompanied by vascular congestion, spongy cortical rarefaction, and pallor. We have seen this picture, which closely mimics that of hypoxic-ischemic brain injury, misdiagnosed as acute cerebral infarction, although close scrutiny of these degenerating neurons often reveals a ground-glass alteration of their nucleoplasm that should suggest a viral cytopathic effect. It is during this early phase of symptomatic disease that careful search for the eosinophilic intranuclear inclusion bodies typical of herpetic infection is most likely to be rewarded (Fig. 28.25). These may be identified in the nuclei of cortical astrocytes and satellite oligodendroglia, as well as neurons, but are an inconstant feature of the disorder.

The pronounced inflammatory reaction characteristic of fully developed HSE is usually in evidence by the second week of clinical disease. Lymphocytes and plasma cells colonize the meninges, cuff penetrating blood vessels, and migrate into the devastated cortex. Mononuclear cells may converge on infected neurons to

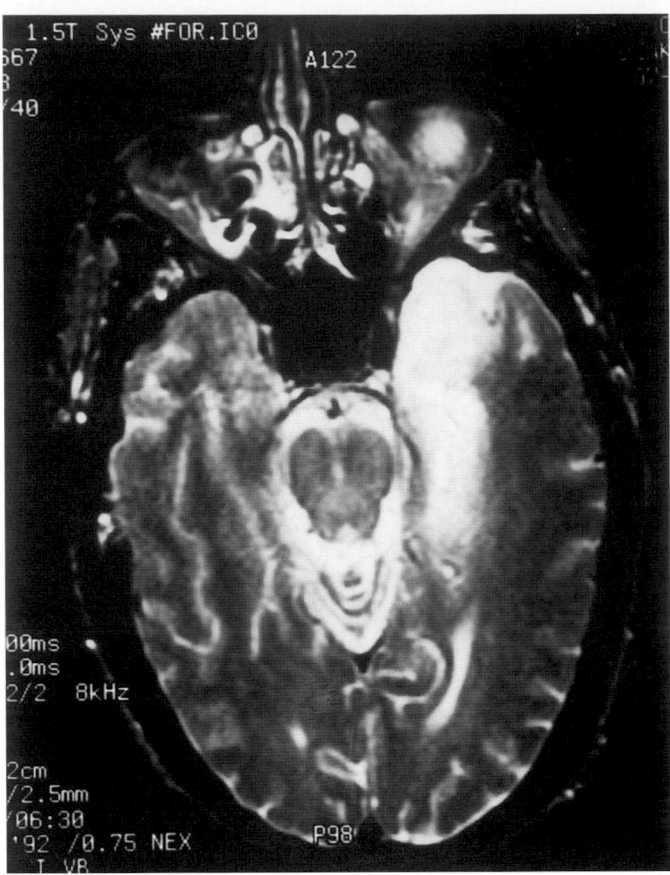

Fig. 28.24 HSE. This MRI, from a middle-aged man with headache, fever, and disordered affect, demonstrates the anteromedial temporal lobe localization of signal abnormalities ("bright" in this study) typical of HSE on neuroradiologic assessment.

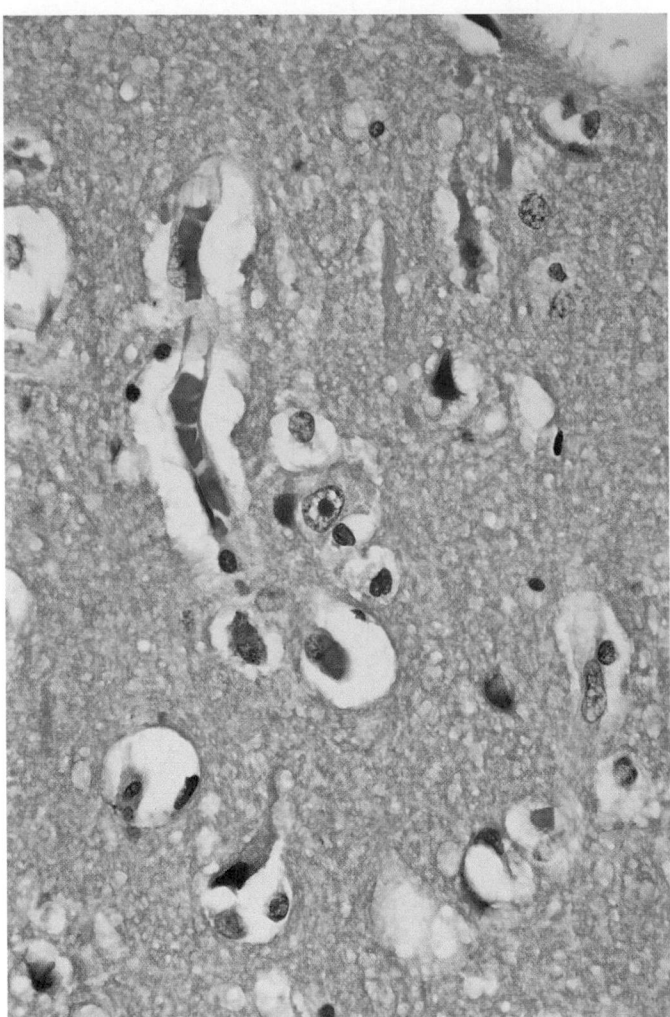

Fig. 28.25 HSE. As shown here, herpes simplex encephalitis may masquerade as a noninfectious, ischemic process (particularly if biopsied early in its clinical evolution). Note the noninflammatory appearance, neuronal shrinkage, pyknosis, and dissolution. The nucleus of an astrocyte in the center of this field contains a well-defined inclusion body.

form neuronophagic or so-called microglial nodules. These changes are often accompanied by hemorrhage and, in some cases, thrombosis and even fibrinoid necrosis of the cerebral vasculature. Foamy macrophages eventually come to dominate the invading cellular elements and ultimately clear the necrotic debris, only cavitated and gliotic remnants persisting at sites of prior infection.

Electron microscopy and immunocytochemistry may be profitably applied to the diagnosis of HSE and may in select cases provide evidence of HSV infection in biopsy material exhibiting little alteration at the light microscopic level.[278] Ultrastructural study is the more laborious and less sensitive of these methods but affords direct visualization of the agent in infected cells. Assembled in the nucleus, the mature HSV particle is an icosahedral nucleocapsid averaging 100 to 120 nm in diameter and containing a central density representing the agent's genomic DNA (Fig. 28.26). Virions typically acquire a lipid envelope derived from the host nuclear membrane on transport into the cytoplasm. Inasmuch as similar appearances are shared by other encephalitogenic herpes viruses, electron microscopy is of limited utility in specifically identifying the offender as HSV.

Commercially available antibodies to this agent are now routinely employed for this purpose, and immunohistochemical assessment is strongly recommended in all cases of clinically suspected HSE, regardless of whether inspection of biopsy material reveals evidence of an inflammatory process (Fig. 28.27). In fact, Esiri's elegant correlative studies indicate that attempts at HSV antigen detection are most likely to succeed during the first week of encephalitic symptoms.[274] Coincident with a mounting inflammatory reaction, antigen expression declines steadily through the second and third weeks of the clinical illness and is not usually demonstrable thereafter. We have noted, however, the unusual persistence of viral antigens beyond this period in cases of HSE involving immunocompromised hosts, including cancer patients and individuals with underlying infection by human immunodeficiency virus-type 1.[277] These appeared to be

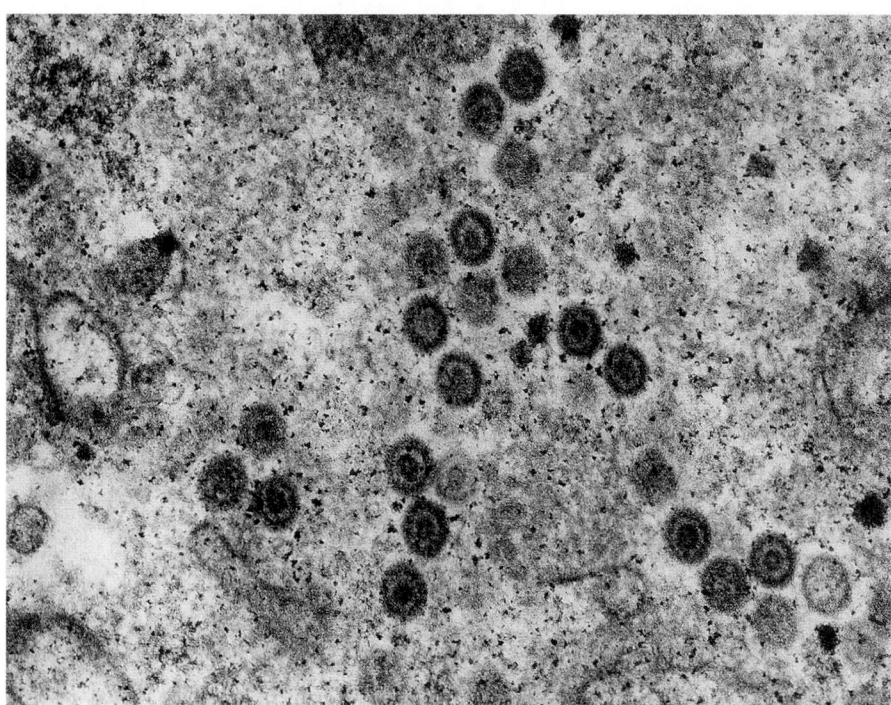

Fig. 28.26 HSE. This transmission electron photomicrograph reveals enveloped nucleocapsids with an average diameter of 100 nm in the cytoplasm of an infected cell. (×62,000)

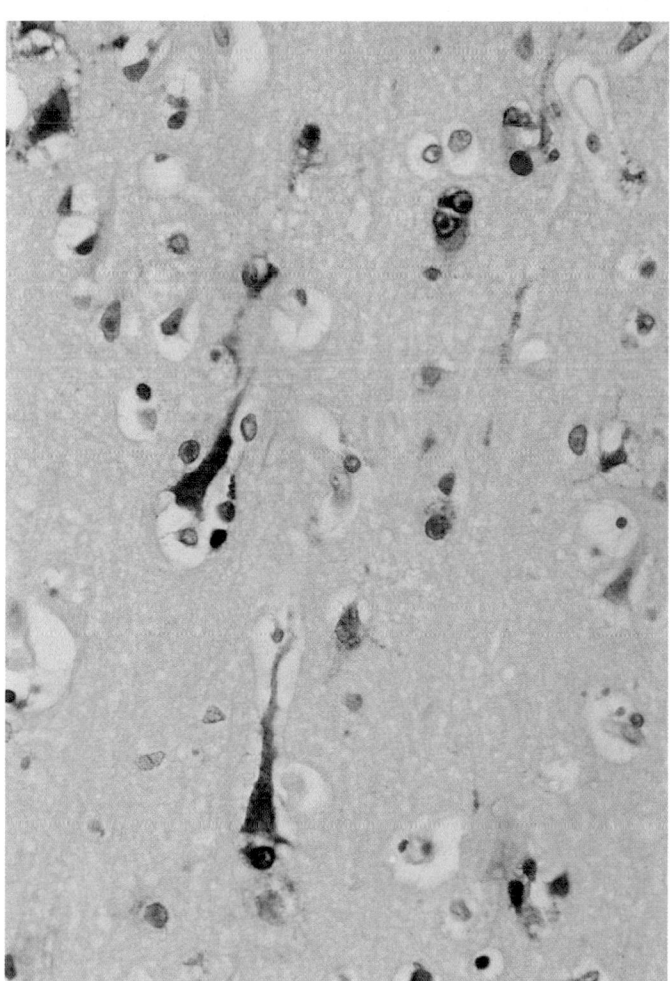

Fig. 28.27 HSE. In this immunoperoxidase preparation, the cytoplasm of neurons and inclusion bodies within the nuclei of satellite glia are labeled by antibodies to herpes simplex type 1.

arrested at the noninflammatory, pseudoischemic phase characteristic of early HSE in otherwise normal individuals. HSE has also been documented in patients with primary brain tumors,[276,277] raising the question of whether a neoplasm, its surgical or adjuvant management might trigger activation of latent CNS infection by HSV.

Progressive multifocal leukoencephalopathy

Progressive multifocal leukoencephalopathy (PML) is an opportunistic demyelinating disease of the CNS caused by DNA viruses of the polyoma group.[283] Nearly all clinical isolates responsible for the disorder have been strains of the ubiquitous JC virus (so designated for the initials of the first afflicted patient from whose brain the agent was recovered), with only exceptional cases linked to the related SV-40. Originally delineated as a paraneoplastic complication of Hodgkin's disease and chronic lymphocytic leukemia,[282] PML is almost always associated with defective cell-mediated immunity, is currently encountered most frequently in the setting of underlying human immunodeficiency virus type 1 (HIV-1) infection, and may be the presenting manifestation of AIDS. The disease is characterized by subacutely evolving neurologic symptoms indicative of a multifocal process. Chief among these are motor deficits, cognitive decline, and visual loss. Although tumefactive variants have been described,[285,289] neuroimaging studies usually provide a clue to the nature of the process by demonstrating scattered foci of white matter hypodensity not associated with mass effect or contrast enhancement (Fig. 28.28). Amplification of JC virus-specific DNA sequences from the CSF has emerged as a useful diagnostic procedure and has lessened reliance on brain biopsy.[283]

Any level of the central neuraxis may be affected in PML, but the cerebral hemispheric white matter gener-

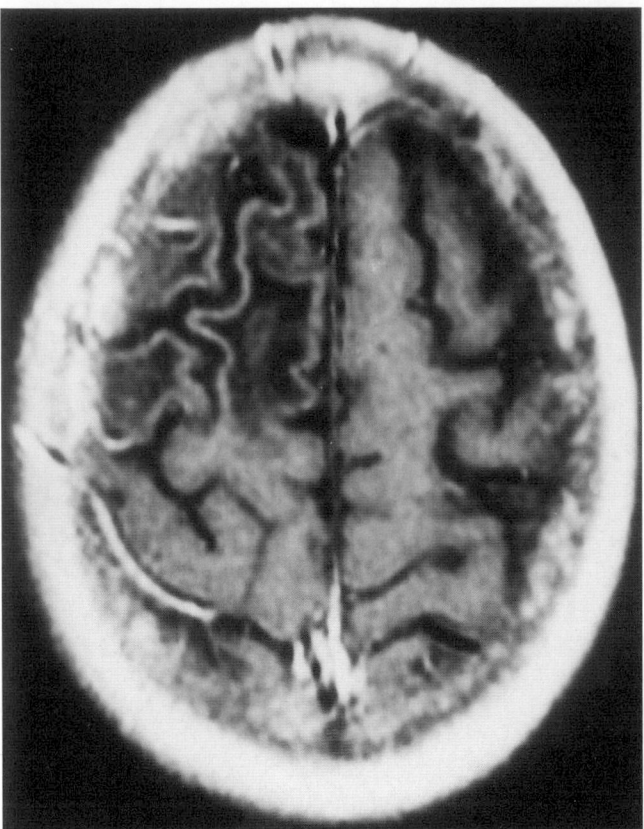

Fig. 28.28 Progressive multifocal leukoencephalopathy. A postcontrast injection MRI demonstrates the regional white matter hypodensity, absence of mass effect or abnormal enhancement, and cortical preservation that typify this demyelinating infection.

ally bears the brunt of the injury. Cerebellar and bulbar localizations are less common, and the spinal cord is usually spared. It is the remarkable tropism of the JC virus for, and its replication within, oligodendroglia that are responsible for the alterations pathognomonic of PML. Productive infection of these cells results in progressive enlargement of their nuclei, dissolution of their compacted chromatin, and its replacement by homogeneously dense and basophilic or "ground-glass," amphophilic material (Fig. 28.29). Considerably less common than this transformation of the entire nucleoplasm are demarcated eosinophilic inclusions of the sort that typify herpes virus infections. At the fine structural level, the oligodendrocytopathy characteristic of PML corresponds to a distention of the nucleus by nonenveloped, spheric or icosahedral particles measuring 33 to 45 nm in diameter. These are frequently aggregated in paracrystalline arrays and may be admixed with filamentous viral strands 15 to 25 nm in diameter (Fig. 28.30). Although immunocytochemical assay,[286] in situ hybridization,[286] and gene amplification techniques[288] may be used to confirm JC virus infection, the highly characteristic nature of the oligodendroglial karyomegaly and nucleoplasmic alterations typical of PML cannot be overemphasized.

With the ongoing infection and lysis of target cells, PML evolves as centrifugally expanding zones of oligodendroglial depletion and subsequent infiltration by foamy macrophages engaged in the scavenging and digestion of degenerating myelin sheaths. Early on, small plaques tend to a miliary clustering at the gray–white junction that probably reflects hematogenous seeding of the CNS following reactivation of the agent in sites of systemic latency. Geographic zones of demyelination,

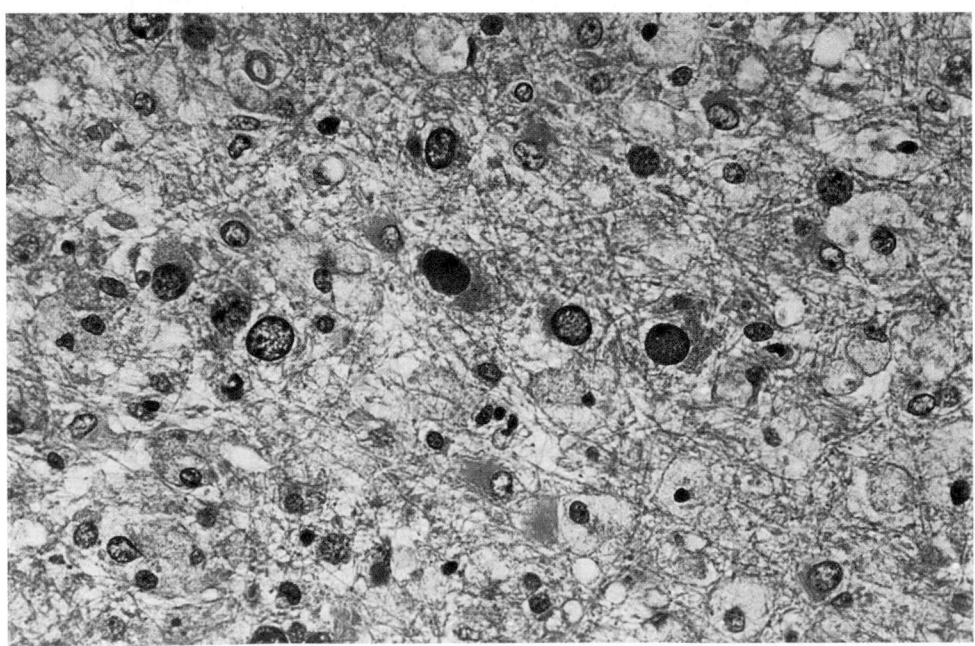

Fig. 28.29 Progressive multifocal leukoencephapathy. JC virus-infected oligodendrocytes in the center of this field exhibit the nuclear swelling, chromatin dissolution, and replacement by amphophilic, "ground-glass" inclusion material that are peculiar to this disorder. Note presence of scattered hyperplastic astrocytes and admixed foamy macrophages.

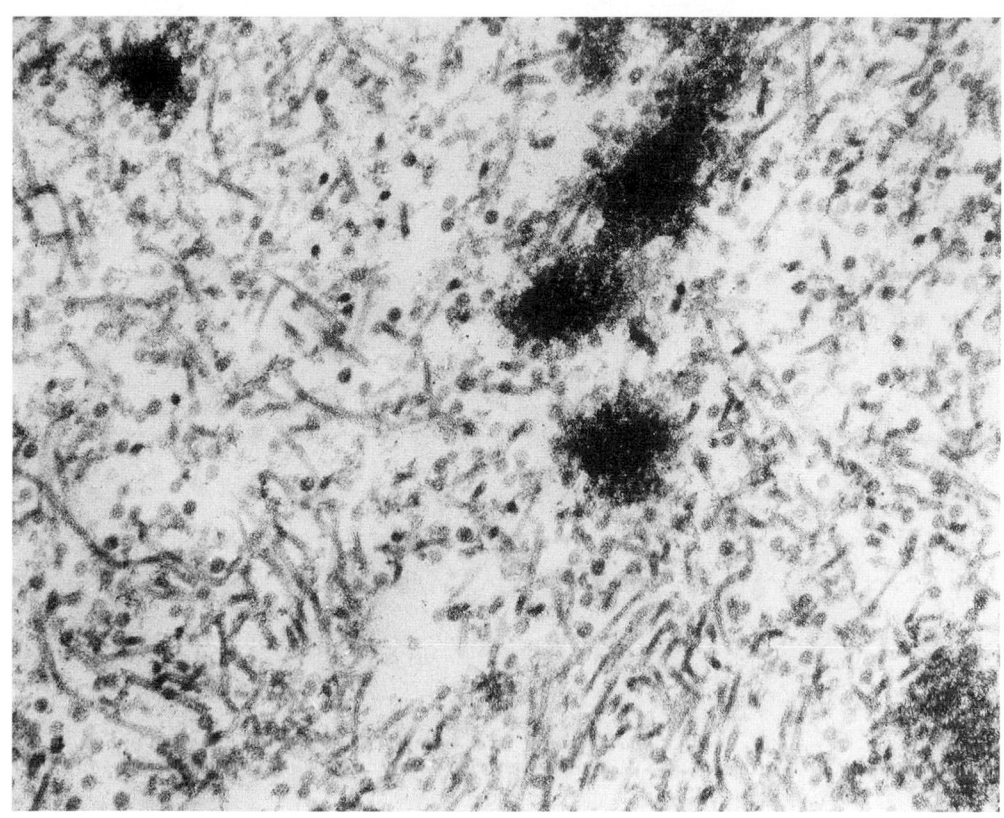

Fig. 28.30 Progressive multifocal leukoencephalopathy. This transmission electron micrograph of an oligodendrocyte's nucleus depicts nonenveloped virions of 37-nm diameter lying singly and in the filamentous arrays that are a common feature of JC infection. (×45,150)

resulting from the coalescence of these small lesions, become grossly evident as regions of white matter retraction, granularity, and yellowish-gray discoloration. In most cases, a relatively undisturbed cortical ribbon will span these devastated areas. This, and the characteristic persistence of axons in the face of total demyelination, reflect the resistance of neurons (cerebellar granule cells excepted) to JC virus infection. Some thinning of the axonal population, however, is the rule, and PML can progress to extensive white matter cavitation. Particularly widespread and destructive examples have been described in the setting of coinfection by HIV-1.[290]

A histologic feature of PML meriting further comment is atypical astrocytic hyperplasia (Fig. 28.31). In addition to florid astrogliosis—a constant finding—the demyelinating lesions of PML frequently contain greatly

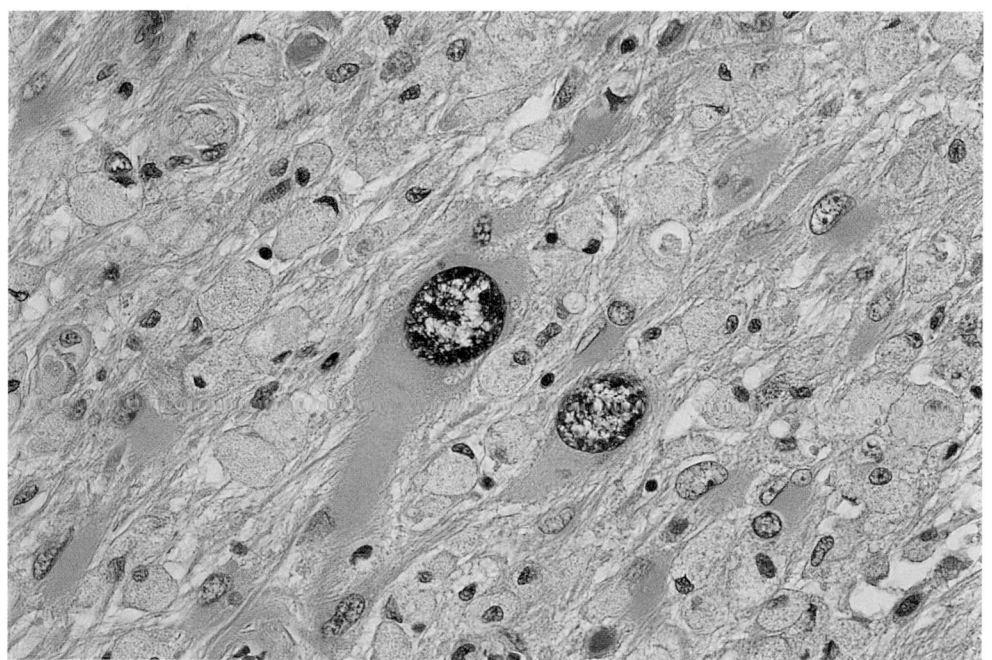

Fig. 28.31 Progressive multifocal leukoencephalopathy. Grotesque cytologic alterations may result from infection of astrocytes by the JC virus. An accompanying infiltrate of foamy macrophages should militate strongly against the diagnosis of neoplasia, despite the worrisome appearances of these bizarre cells.

enlarged astrocytes exhibiting bizarre nuclear abnormalities indistinguishable from those usually associated with neoplasia. These cytologic changes (often accompanied by morphologically atypical mitotic activity, Ki-67 expression[281] and abnormal nuclear immunoreactivity for p53[280]) are believed to reflect a form of nonpermissive infection in which the agent's genome is spliced into that of the host cell, a process integral to the recognized capacity of polyomaviruses, including JC virus isolates from patients with PML, to induce central neuroepithelial tumors in the experimental situation. The precise role, if any, of these viruses in the pathogenesis of human brain tumors remains to be clarified, but it is noteworthy that the association of PML with multifocal astrocytomas has been documented, albeit rarely.[287]

PML is usually characterized by minimal inflammatory response to the agent; however, some variants evidence intense perivascular and interstitial lymphoid infiltration. The latter often contain very few oligodendrocytes manifesting the nuclear cytopathic effects typical of JC virus infection and may prompt considerations of primary cerebral lymphoma, another recognized complication of the immunosuppressed state occurring with particular frequency in HIV-1-seropositive patients. It is this unusual form of PML that is most likely to present as a space-occupying, contrast-enhancing mass on CT or MRI study, further complicating the clinical delineation of these entities. A conspicuous inflammatory response typifies biopsy material from a small subset of AIDS patients surviving for considerably longer than the 3- to 6-month interval in which most cases of PML progress ineluctably to death.[284] The rare examples of spontaneously remitting PML that we have seen have been of this unusually inflammatory type and presumably reflect elimination or immunologic containment of the JC virus following a transitory abrogation of its enforced dormancy.

Varicella-zoster virus encephalitis and cerebral vasculitis

Varicella-zoster virus (VZV), agent of chickenpox and shingles, causes a rare form of encephalitis sharing certain clinical and histologic features with PML.[294–296] The condition has to date been described exclusively in immunocompromised hosts (including patients treated for Hodgkin's disease, other cancers, and AIDS) and may present months following resolution of cutaneous zoster or in the absence of a preceding exanthem. Described by some authors as a "leukoencephalitis," this chronic infection can settle anywhere along the central neuraxis, but exhibits a striking predilection for the cerebral hemispheric white matter. It is characterized by multifocal, centrifugally expanding, and coalescent foci of demyelination and variable axonal loss with little inflammatory reaction. Many cases also evidence small infarcts resulting from VZV-mediated vascular injury as further

discussed below. The nuclei of oligodendrocytes situated on the periphery of dymelinating lesions exhibit a ground-glass transformation or homogeneous filling by basophilic material superficially similar to the cytopathy induced in such cells by the JC virus but differ in not being conspicuously enlarged. Furthermore, neighboring astrocytes (and, in some cases, neurons and ependymal cells) infected by VZV contain well-demarcated Cowdry A-type intranuclear inclusions of the sort that typify herpes virus replication and are not driven to the atypical hyperplasia characteristic of PML. Fine structural study will disclose herpes-type nucleocapsids averaging approximately 100 nm in diameter within the nuclei of infected cells. These differ slightly from herpes simplex-type virions in that their core densities tend to be eccentrically positioned, but definitive identification of the agent requires immunocytochemical assay, molecular hybridization studies, or culture.

In addition to being an encephalitogen, VZV is recognized as a rare cause of cerebral vasculitis. This may involve large arteries at the base of the brain as well as smaller branches. Like the encephalitis associated with this agent, vasculitic complications of zoster typically follow resolution of the cutaneous exanthem. Two major variants have been described. One, a noninflammatory "angiopathy" afflicting immunocompromised hosts and associated in some cases with VZV encephalitis as just described, is characterized by striking fibrointimal proliferation, thrombosis, and, in some cases, disruption of the elastica and thinning of the media without evident necrosis of mural elements.[292] The other is an overtly inflammatory and necrotizing angiitis designated by some observers as "granulomatous" because of the presence of multinucleated histiocytes within damaged vessel walls.[291,293] This often presents as hemiplegic stroke weeks after an episode of contralateral zoster ophthalmicus in a patient with no major evidences of defective immunity.[291] In fact, we have seen several examples—all in patients seropositive for HIV-1—displaying both angiopathic and angiitic features, depending on the portion of vessel sampled, and suspect that the former simply represent the chronic sequelae of what is primarily an inflammatory process. In addition to thrombosis with consequent cerebral infarction, VZV angiitis may result in fusiform aneurysmal dilatation, mural rupture, and subarachnoid hemorrhage.[293] Definitive diagnosis requires localization of the agent by immunocytochemical assay or ultrastructural study to elements of the vessel wall, typically smooth muscle cells in the media or intimal (myo)fibroblasts. See our discussion of primary angiitis of the nervous system for further consideration of VZV as a cerebrovascular pathogen.

HIV-1 encephalomyelitis

HIV-1 encephalomyelitis is not a disorder likely to engage the surgical pathologist but demands, nevertheless, some consideration in view of the ongoing AIDS epidemic and the unique nature of the neuropathologic alterations associated with this retroviral infection.[297,298] HIV-1 is alone among viral encephalitogens in exhibiting no particular tropism for neuroectodermal cell types, its replication in the nervous system taking place largely within marrow-derived macrophages and microglia. CNS infection is characterized by loosely arrayed, vasocentric, or paravascular inflammatory infiltrates concentrated in the cerebral hemispheric white matter,

basal ganglia, and rostral brainstem (Fig. 28.32). These are dominated by mononucleated and multinucleated macrophages, the latter reflecting a process of virally mediated cell fusion that is the characteristic cytopathic effect of this and other members of the lentivirus subfamily of retroviruses. These cells, and their mononuclear precursors, harbor and release fully formed virions, which may be found budding from their plasmalemma, aggregated in membrane-delimited intracytoplasmic vacuoles, or lying free in the cytoplasm (Fig. 28.33). The

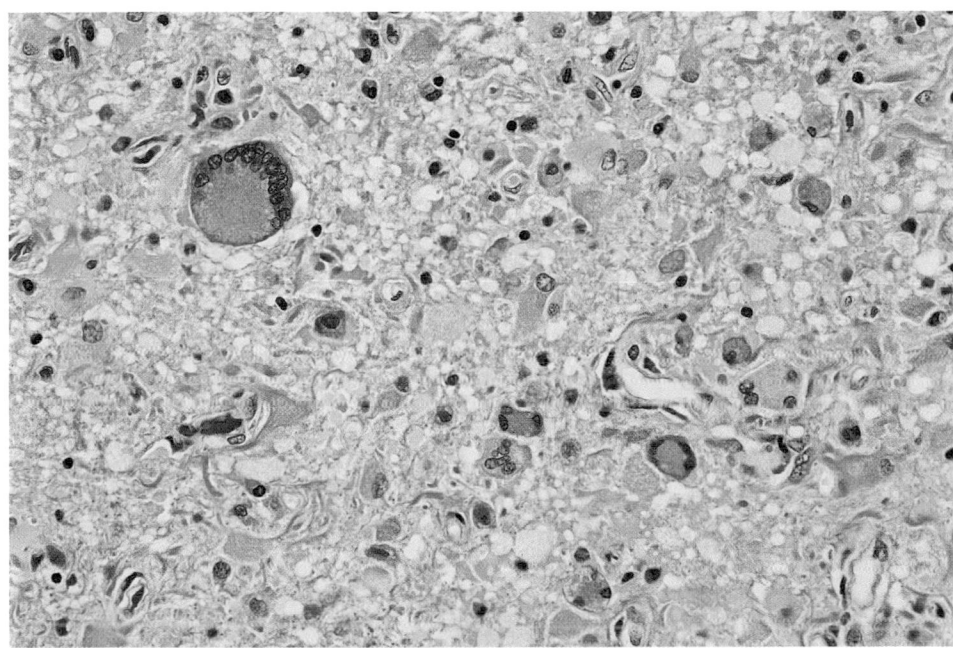

Fig. 28.32 HIV encephalitis. Nongranulomatous infiltrates centered loosely about blood vessels in the cerebral white matter (shown here) or basal ganglia and dominated by macrophages, including multinucleated forms resulting from retrovirally mediated cell fusion, characterize infection of the CNS by this agent. The associated astrogliosis and spongy rarefaction are common accompanying features.

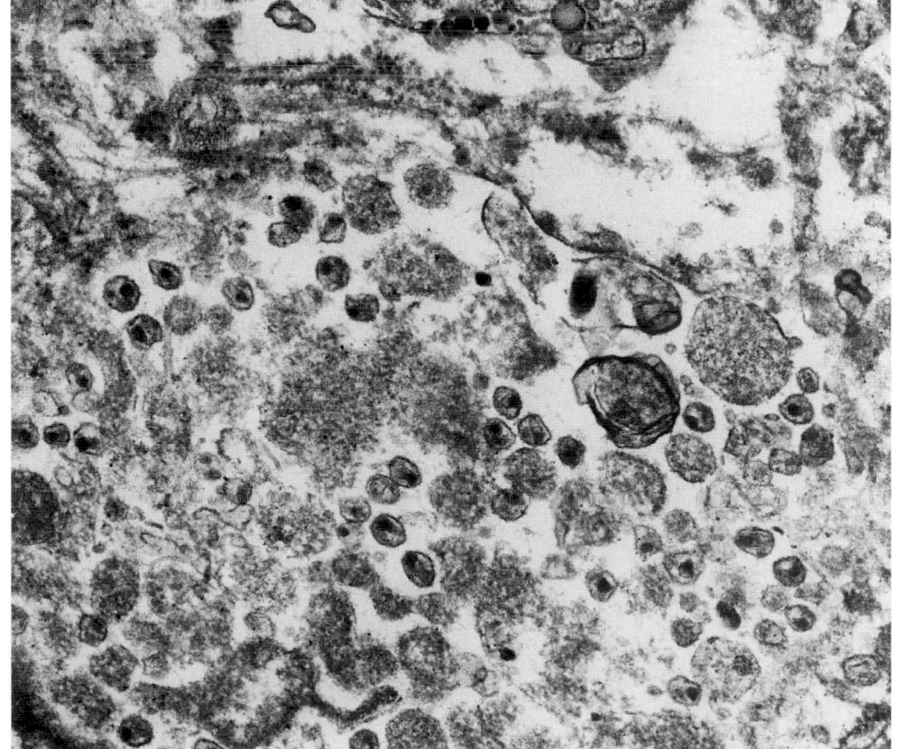

Fig. 28.33 HIV encephalitis. This transmission electron micrograph shows intracytoplasmic HIV particles measuring 110 to 120 nm in diameter. Note the well-defined envelopes and eccentrically positioned core densities. (×40,000) (Courtesy Dr Leroy Sharer, Newark, NJ)

mature particle is spherical, averages 100 to 120 mm in diameter, and possesses a cylindrical or bar-shaped nucleoid usually positioned eccentrically and enclosed by a limiting membrane. Attendant changes include diffuse astrogliosis and microglial activation, generalized pallor of the cerebral white matter, and brain atrophy. The precise relationship of local HIV-1 replication to these indices of widespread CNS injury is a subject of active investigation.[299]

Prion-associated diseases

Though long classed among viral disorders of the CNS, the unusual diseases collectively known as transmissible spongiform encephalopathies have resisted explication as conventional contagions and, in fact, occur in heritable and apparently sporadic, as well as clearly infectious, forms. The pathogenesis of these rare entities remains a subject of controversy and ongoing investigation, but they clearly share anomalies of a native cell membrane constituent—the prion protein (PrP)—expressed at particularly high levels by central neurons. Conformationally altered, abnormally protease-resistant and amyloidogenic PrP isoforms ("prions") characteristically accumulate in affected tissues, and there is much experimental evidence suggesting that these potentially host-derived proteins are capable of propagation and suffice for disease transmission in the absence of associated nucleic acids.[304] Prion-associated illnesses include **kuru** (linked to the practice of ritual cannibalism among the Fore tribespeople of Papua, New Guinea), **Creutzfeldt–Jakob disease (CJD)**, **"new variant" CJD** (most recently described of the group and cause of great public health concern as a putative manifestation of exposure to the agent of bovine spongiform encephalopathy or "mad cow" disease[308]), **Gerstmann–Straussler syndrome**, and **fatal familial insomnia**.[304] The following discussion is essentially limited to practical considerations in the diagnosis of CJD, the variant most commonly encountered in clinical practice.

The iatrogenic transmission of CJD via contaminated neurosurgical instruments, human growth hormone supplements, and a variety of allografts is well documented, but the large majority of cases involve middle-aged or older adults having no evident exposure to contaminated materials or other individuals suffering the disorder. A heredofamilial variant associated with PrP gene mutations accounts for 10% to 15% of cases.[304] The course of most patients is dominated by cognitive decline that progresses relentlessly in subacute fashion to profound dementia. Particularly characteristic accompanying features are generalized myoclonus and an electroencephalographic "burst suppression" pattern of periodic spike and wave complexes. The afflicted are typically left vegetive within 6 to 8 months of symptom onset and rarely survive longer than a year after diagnosis.

The appearance of brain biopsy material, usually secured from the nondominant frontal lobe, depends on disease duration.[304,306] The earliest change perceptible at the light microscopic level consists of spongy vacuolization of the cortex most pronounced in deeper laminae (Fig. 28.34). Rare vacuoles may be localizable to neuronal perikarya, but most appear randomly scattered in the neuropil. The latter are situated principally within neuronal processes on fine structural study, are often traversed by membrane-derived septa, and may contain granular or curled membranous profiles. With disease progression spongiform change becomes increasingly florid and is attended by conspicuous astrogliosis, neuronal shrinkage and depopulation. The end-stage cortex is left virtually devoid of recognizable neurons and largely replaced by the tangled processes of hyperplastic astrocytes. At no stage of the disorder is there evidence of an inflammatory response and white matter abnormalities are limited to secondary axonal loss save for rare variants exhibiting spongy leukoencephalopathy.[303] An arresting and diagnostic feature of prion-associated diseases, but one evident in only 5% of CJD cases, is the deposition of amyloid in "spiked ball" plaques that display radiate, spicular contours and are strongly PAS-positive (Fig. 28.35). Often referred to as "kuru" plaques, these are most often found in the cerebellar cortex (but may also be detected in cerebral gray matter) and are specifically recognized by antibodies to PrP.[304,307] Cerebrocortical examples may be numerous in familial CJD and have been described as a particularly conspicuous feature of "new variant" CJD cases.[308] Large, clustered deposits of PrP-immunoreactive amyloid in the cerebral and cerebellar cortices typify the dominantly inheritable Gerstmann–Straussler syndrome, also associated with PrP-encoding gene mutations and characterized clinically by a prominent component of progressive cerebellar ataxia.[304]

In the appropriate clinical setting (and in the absence of other potentially explanatory pathologic alterations), the presence of spongiform change alone suffices for a diagnosis of "probable" CJD. Definitive diagnosis requires satisfaction of any one of the following criteria: (1) finding of spiked ball-type PrP amyloid plaques; (2) demonstration of protease-resistant PrP in biopsy material by specific immunohistochemical or immunoblot methods; (3) detection of a PrP gene mutation that is recognized as pathogenic; (4) transmission of spongiform encephalopathy to an animal host. Readers are referred elsewhere for a fully annotated discussion of these specialized techniques.[304] A diagnosis of "probable" CJD should not be rendered on minimal histologic criteria inasmuch as scattered intracortical vacuoles and neuronal shrinkage are common artefacts of surgical manipulation. Furthermore, spongy cortical changes that may mimic CJD (but that are often restricted to the temporal cortex, insula, or amygdala, and unattended by

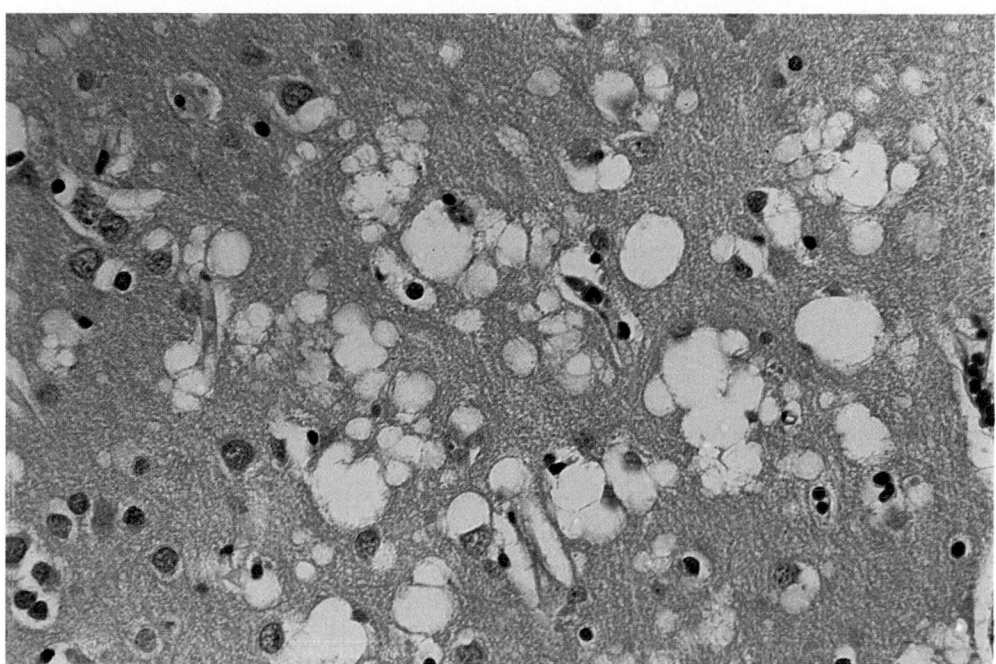

Fig. 28.34 Creutzfeldt–Jakob disease. Noninflammatory vacuolization of the cerebral cortex is the dominant alteration evident in this biopsy specimen from an elderly man with progressive dementia and myoclonus. This change typically precedes conspicuous neuronal dropout and astrogliosis, the other dominant findings in this prion-related disorder.

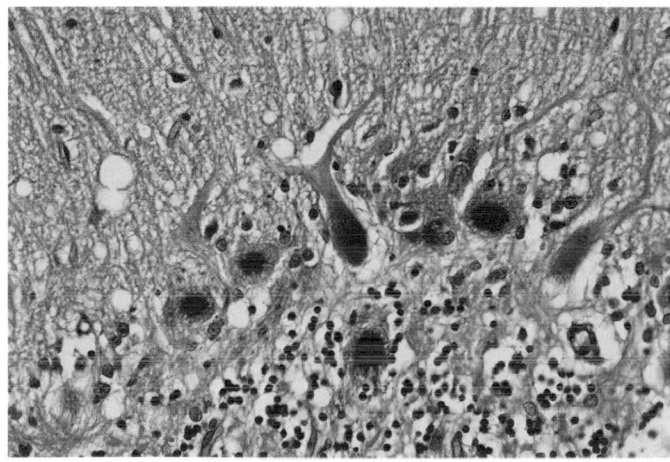

Fig. 28.35 Creutzfeldt–Jakob disease. Demonstrated in this cerebellar biopsy material are PAS-positive plaques of "spiked ball" type ("kuru" plaques). Note the spiculate radiations at the periphery of these deposits. Mild spongiform change is present in the overlying molecular layer white matter.

protease-resistant PrP deposition) can be encountered in otherwise typical examples of Alzheimer's disease, in cerebrocortical Lewy body disease, and in a dementing disorder combining morphologic features of both these entities.[305] Nontransmissible syndromes of aphasic presenile dementia with lower motor neuron disease may also be associated with superficial cortical vacuolization.[304] Conversely, an ostensibly negative biopsy should not reassure hospital staff handling tissues and fluids from suspect patients. The histopathologic alterations typical of CJD are not uniformly distributed in the involved brain and methods such as Western blot analysis have revealed protease-resistant PrP in neurosurgical specimens evidencing little or no spongiform change.[302]

Biopsy material from patients suspected to have CJD requires cautious handling, even formalinized and paraffin-embedded archival specimens retaining transmissibility. A simple protocol that eliminates virtually all infectivity is 48-hour fixation of biopsies in formalin, followed by immersion in 50–100 ml of pure formic acid for 1 hour and subsequent transfer to fresh formalin for an additional 48-hour period.[300] Continuous gentle agitation is employed throughout processing. This method yields histologic sections of excellent quality, preserves antigenic integrity, and may actually enhance PrP immunoreactivity. A minimum 4-week suspension in phenolized (15 g/dl) formalin has also been recommended, particularly for whole brain specimens.[301] Solid wastes and nondisposable instruments should be autoclaved for 4.5 hours at 132°C, as should liquid wastes following mixing in equal parts with 2N NaOH. Spills should be soaked with 1N NaOH three times, 30 minutes each.

Primary tumors

Glial tumors

Astrocytic neoplasms

Diffusely infiltrating astrocytomas

Currently classified as tumors of the astrocytic series are neoplasms varying considerably in their epidemiologic features, morphologic attributes, growth patterns, genetic profiles, and clinical behavior. Diffusely infiltrating astrocytomas—so designated in current World Health Organization (WHO) parlance for their permeative spread within the central neuroparenchyma[331]—

constitute the largest group and include the astrocytic tumors most prevalent in the adult brain. These differ from other members of the astrocytoma "family" (a fiction) not only in their insidious infiltration of CNS tissues but in an inherent tendency to biologic progression that reflects the predictably stepwise accumulation of certain nonrandom genetic abnormalities.[331] As detailed in the discussion to follow, the diffusely infiltrative astrocytomas have traditionally been divided on cytologic grounds into three basic variants—**fibrillary**, **gemistocytic**, and **protoplasmic**. The first of these is much the most frequently encountered species.

Named for the filamentous cytoplasmic processes that lend to their constituent cells a resemblance, however distorted, to the "fibrous" astrocytes populating the normal brain and spinal cord, fibrillary astrocytomas collectively constitute the most common primary neoplasms of the human CNS.[331] While most are unassociated with clearly predisposing factors, radiation-related cases are clearly recognized and occasional examples complicate type 1 neurofibromatosis, or the Li–Fraumeni (germline p53 gene mutation) syndrome.[331] Astrocytic neoplasms of fibrillary type also occur in complex with hereditary nonpolyposis colorectal carcinoma as defining components of type 1 Turcot syndrome,[331] linked to germline DNA mismatch repair gene mutations, and have been reported in association with the multiple enchondromatosis syndromes known as Ollier or Maffucci disease.[319,331] HIV-1-infected patients may additionally be at increased risk of developing central neuroepithelial tumors, including fibrillary astrocytomas.[310]

Diffuse fibrillary astrocytomas afflict subjects of all ages and may arise at any level of the central neuraxis, but there can be no doubt of their predilection for the cerebral hemispheres of adults. Here they are characteristically centered in white matter, a minority originating in deep gray structures such as the basal ganglia and thalami. Headaches, seizures, focal sensorimotor deficits, and alterations of affect are the principal clinical manifestations of these supratentorial lesions. The common variety of brainstem glioma, encountered in childhood or adolescence as progressive cranial nerve and long tract dysfunction associated with "pseudohypertrophic" enlargement of the pons on neuroradiologic investigation, is also an astrocytoma of diffuse fibrillary type.[318] Intraspinal examples figure prominently among primary tumors of the cervical and upper thoracic cord, but are vastly outnumbered by ependymomas at more caudal levels. Exceptional variants are situated entirely within the leptomeninges and subarachnoid space, where they may derive from heterotopic neuroglial rests.[327,346]

Neuro-oncologic practice demands that the diffuse fibrillary astrocytomas be subclassified according to their perceived biologic potential. Despite general agreement among observers as to the histologic features of greatest predictive value in this regard, a uniform system of grading and reporting has not been adopted to date, and various approaches to the subcategorization of these neoplasms are currently in use. We endorse the WHO format.[331] In this three-tiered system, fibrillary astroglial neoplasms are designated as **astrocytoma** or **diffuse astrocytoma (WHO grade II)**, **anaplastic astrocytoma (WHO grade III)**, or **glioblastoma multiforme (WHO grade IV)** according to histologic indices presently outlined. The reader will note that the diagnosis of glioblastoma is reserved for astrocytic tumors of the highest grade and is not applied to poorly differentiated gliomas that clearly exhibit oligodendroglial or ependymal differentiation. We would again emphasize the disheartening tendency of the diffuse fibrillary astrocytoma, however differentiated and indolent at inception, to grow increasingly alarming to the morphologist and clinically aggressive with the passage of time. A consequence of this inherent instability that bears on practical issues of diagnosis and management is the resulting regional heterogeneity for which this neoplasm is notorious, zonal variations in histologic appearance and proliferative activity potentially confounding the interpretation of observations based on limited tissue samples. The biology of astrocytoma progression is a complex topic beyond the scope of this survey, but we would be remiss to omit at this juncture mention of allelic loss and mutations involving the tumor-suppressing p53 gene (TP53) as early, genomically destabilizing events in the evolution of most low-grade fibrillary astrocytic neoplasms.[331]

Well-differentiated (WHO grade II) fibrillary astrocytic neoplasms, hereafter referred to simply as astrocytomas, typically present in the third or fourth decade of life and are decidedly uncommon after age 40 (beyond which, the overwhelming majority of fibrillary astrocytic tumors exhibit anaplastic histologic features or are frank glioblastomas). Particularly suggestive of a slowly evolving supratentorial astrocytoma (or other low-grade neoplasm) is a protracted preoperative course characterized by intermittent seizures or headache unassociated with focal neurologic deficits. Complaints referable to such lesions may be present for years prior to their discovery, although the advent of sophisticated neuroradiologic techniques has considerably shortened the average predetection interval. As low-grade astrocytomas do not usually provoke significant neovascularization of the infiltrated neural parenchyma, they appear in CT scans and T1-weighted MR images as regions of diminished density that are not opacified ("enhanced") by contrast media employed to define foci of blood–brain barrier disruption (Fig. 28.36). The presence of such enhancement suggests that a lesion shown by biopsy to be an astrocytoma has undergone focal anaplastic progression and should prompt careful review of postoperative neuroradiologic studies to ascertain the region of tumor sampled.

At operation, astrocytomas are spatially indistinct, producing a diffuse expansion and induration of permeated CNS structures along with a highly characteristic blurring or effacement of gray–white landmarks (Fig. 28.37). They may acquire a somewhat mucoid consistency as a result of myxoid change but are not prone to

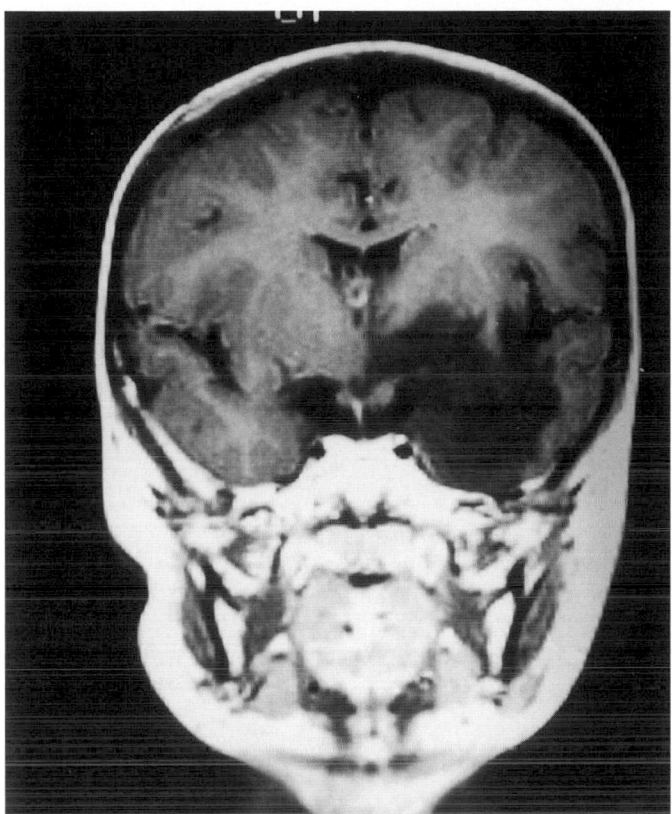

Fig. 28.36 Diffuse fibrillary astrocytoma. Neuroradiologic features common to the low grade fibrillary astrocytoma in postcontrast MRIs, such as this temporal example, include generalized expansion and hypodensity of infiltrated regions with only modest mass effect and no foci of bright signal enhancement that would indicate blood–brain barrier disruption (see Fig. 28.43 for comparison).

spontaneous hemorrhage or necrosis. Histologic study typically discloses a dyscohesive cellular infiltrate percolating through recognizable neuropil in a patternless array that stands in sharp contrast to the even distribution of hyperplastic astrocytes characteristic of reactive glial proliferations (Fig. 28.38). Samples of invaded cortex may disclose striking aggregation of tumor cells beneath the pia and about neurons, the latter phenomenon known as satellitosis, but it should be pointed out that these formations are shared by (and especially characteristic of) oligodendroglial tumors. A common architectural feature of immeasurable utility in establishing the neoplastic nature of the process in question is microcystic change (Fig. 28.39), an alteration to which a variety of glial neoplasms (generally low-grade) are prone but rarely, if ever, encountered in a reactive setting. A similar significance attaches to the finding of scattered calcospherites in biopsy material. A conspicuous admixture of foamy macrophages, on the other hand, militates strongly against the diagnosis of astrocytoma in the absence of prior therapy and should instead prompt considerations of demyelinating disease and infarction. Conspicuous lymphocytic cuffing of regional blood vessels, the hallmark of inflammatory CNS disorders, occasionally attends astrocytic neoplasms of the "garden variety" but among neuroepithelial tumors is far more often a feature of the gemistocytic astrocytoma, pleomorphic xanthoastrocytoma, and ganglioglioma. Finally, survey of a candidate for the diagnosis of WHO grade II astrocytoma should not reveal foci of dense cellularity, proliferation of vascular elements, mitotic activity (only the rare mitosis found on patient search can be tolerated), or zones of necrosis.

At the cytologic level, astrocytomas are composed, at least in part, of cells invested with delicate processes that taper from a modest perinuclear expanse of eosinophilic cytoplasm or are represented only as a background fibrillar meshwork in which "naked" nuclei appear to lie embedded (Fig. 28.38). Particularly arresting in smear or

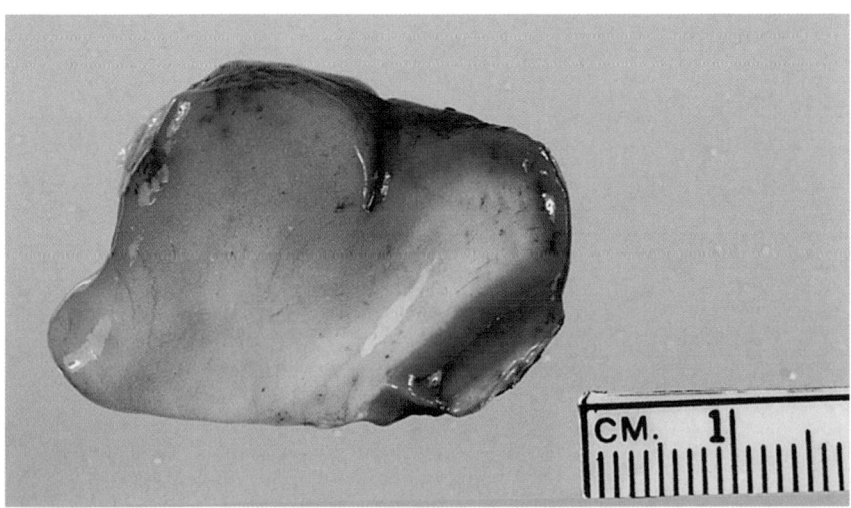

Fig. 28.37 Diffuse fibrillary astrocytoma. The insidious permeation typical of the fibrillary astrocytoma is illustrated in this anterior temporal lobectomy specimen. The gyrus at right maintains a clearly demarcated cortical ribbon over its digitate white matter. Moving to the left, there is diffuse gyral expansion and effacement of these landmarks, reflecting tumoral infiltration. No discrete mass is formed, and, as is characteristic of low-grade examples, there is no evident hemorrhage or necrosis (see Fig. 28.44 for comparison).

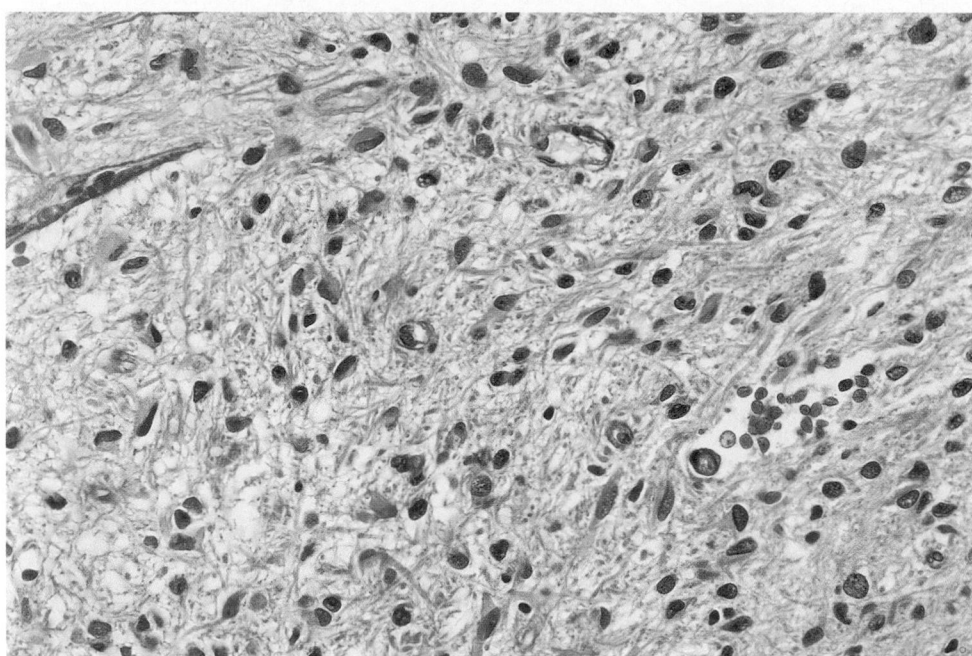

Fig. 28.38 Diffuse fibrillary astrocytoma. Conspicuous cytoplasmic processes, mild nuclear pleomorphism, and only modest hyperchromasia are evidenced by the cells of this well-differentiated astrocytoma. The absence of mitotic activity supports its classification as a low-grade lesion. Note the dyscohesive growth pattern.

crush preparations (Fig. 28.40), which are indispensable adjuncts (and expedient alternatives) to frozen section for purposes of intraoperative consultation, these may be unipolar or multipolar but, in contrast to the cytoplasmic extensions characteristic of hyperplastic astroglia, do not usually sprout from the cell body in the radial, stellate array for which the astrocyte is named.[313] On ultrastructural study,[349] these processes contain bundles of 7- to 11-nm ("intermediate") filaments composed of GFAP (Fig. 28.41), the principal cytoskeletal constituent elaborated by human astrocytes, and vimentin.[315,331] Nuclei are typically oval in configuration with smooth contours, do not contain conspicuous nucleoli, often have a vesicular

quality, but may be somewhat hyperchromatic. Mild variation in size and shape is to be expected, but conspicuous nuclear pleomorphism calls the diagnosis of low-grade astrocytoma into serious question.

The **anaplastic astrocytoma (WHO grade III)** often evolves from a well-differentiated precursor lesion of the type just described, a sequence in which losses of heterozygosity involving chromosomes 19q and 22q, retinoblastoma gene alterations and deletions of genes that encode p16 and other cell cycle regulators are implicated.[331] Accordingly, morphologic evidence of tumor progression may constitute a focal finding in what would otherwise qualify as a histologically favorable lesion.

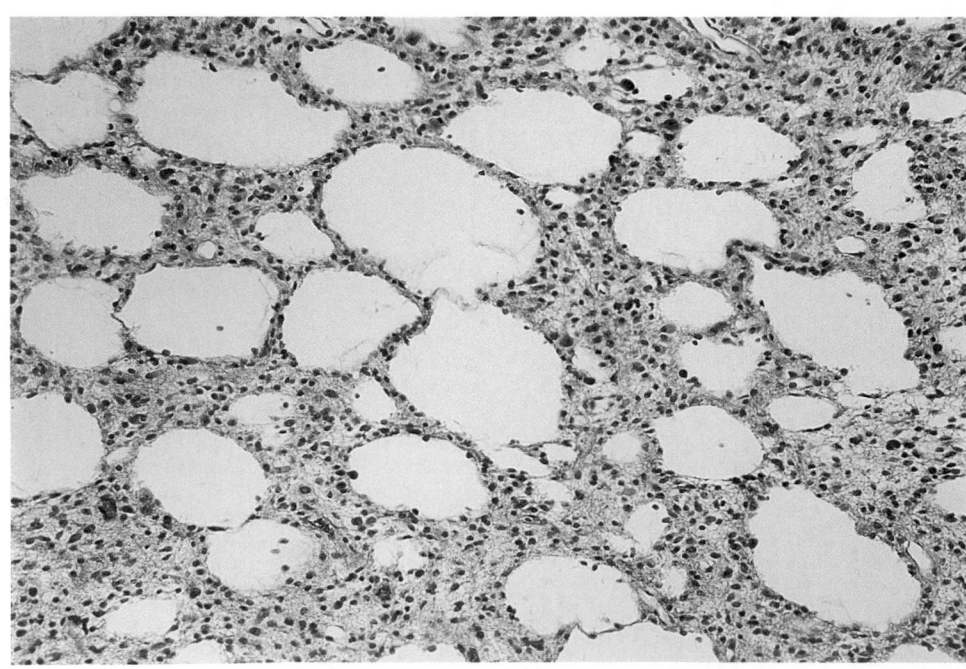

Fig. 28.39 Diffuse fibrillary astrocytoma. Foreign to reactive astroglial proliferations, microcystic change is a particularly conspicuous feature of some low-grade astrocytomas.

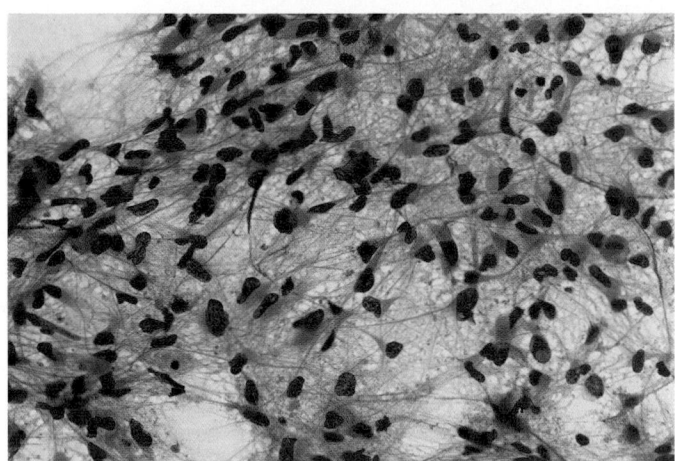

Fig. 28.40 Diffuse fibrillary astrocytoma. A lack of cellular cohesion and conspicuous cytoplasmic processes—features that serve to distinguish astrocytomas from metastatic carcinomas, lymphomas, and other neoplasms—are apparent in this intraoperative squash preparation.

Microscopic examination of the prototypical case reveals an infiltrate that is at a glance more alarmingly cellular and cytologically atypical than that of the low-grade astrocytoma (Fig. 28.42), although biopsies derived from the tumor – CNS interface may contain only scattered neoplastic elements. Nuclear alterations commonly include angulation, dense hyperchromasia, and considerable variation in contour and dimension. Mitotic figures can be demonstrated and most firmly establish the diagnosis. In this regard, we would stress that the solitary mitotic figure found on close scrutiny of a generous biopsy or resection specimen does not an anaplastic astrocytoma make. We will render this diagnosis, however, when confronted by any mitoses in a limited (e.g.,

stereotactic) neurosurgical sample demonstrating a fibrillary astrocytic neoplasm with pronounced nuclear abnormalities. An increase in regional blood vessels is permissible, as is hypertrophy of their lining endothelium, but complex and disorderly proliferation of vasoformative elements or zones of coagulative tumor necrosis in the setting of a cytologically malignant fibrillary astrocytic neoplasm mandate classification of the lesion as a glioblastoma.

Although its unfortunate title would imply a derivation from embryonal or stem cell elements, the **glioblastoma multiforme (WHO grade IV)** is now widely regarded as arising principally via the neoplastic transformation of mature astrocytes or committed astroglial progenitors. "Primary" and "secondary" variants are recognized, the former occurring de novo (i.e., unassociated with demonstrable precursor lesions), the latter resulting from the successful expansion of particularly aggressive clones generated within pre-existent, differentiated astrocytic neoplasms and often associated with chronic neurologic complaints indicative of a more protracted incubation.[331] Not surprisingly, the latter share with low-grade and anaplastic fibrillary astrocytomas a high incidence of mutations or deletions affecting TP53.[331,350] Such abnormalities are comparatively underrepresented among primary glioblastomas, these commonly evidencing (among other aberrations) loss of heterozygosity involving chromosome 10, amplification of the epidermal growth factor receptor (EGFR) gene on chromosome 7 and mutation of the tumor suppressor PTEN/MMAC 1 gene on chromosome 10q23.3.[331,350] Whether predictable differences in prognosis attach to these divergent oncogenetic pathways independent of patient age at diagnosis is controversial.[331,350] Secondary

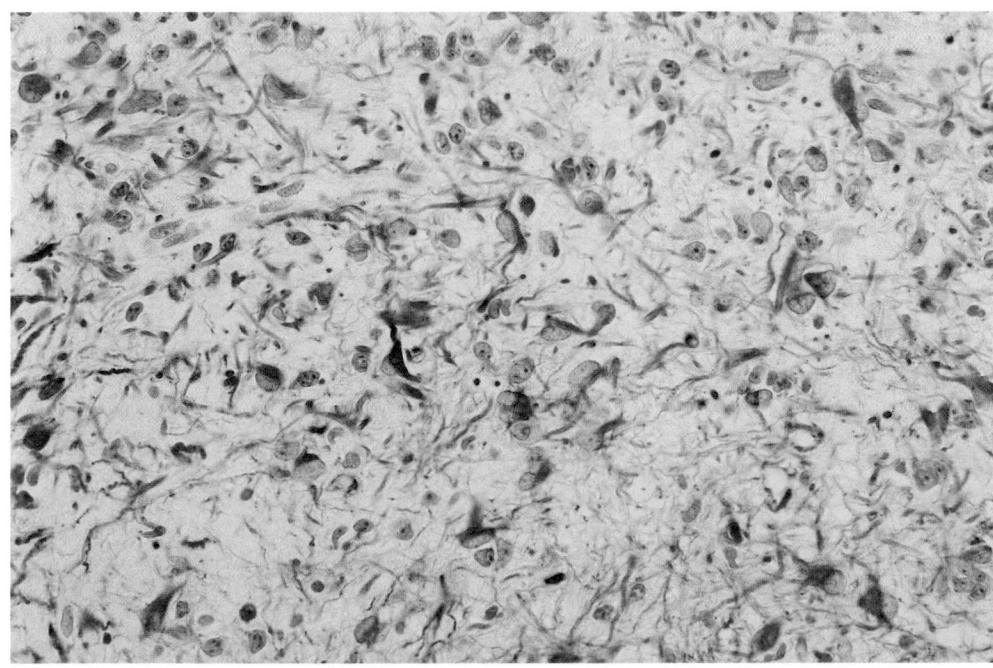

Fig. 28.41 Diffuse fibrillary astrocytoma. An immunoperoxidase preparation demonstrates labeling of tumor cell bodies and processes by a monoclonal antibody to glial fibrillary acidic protein.

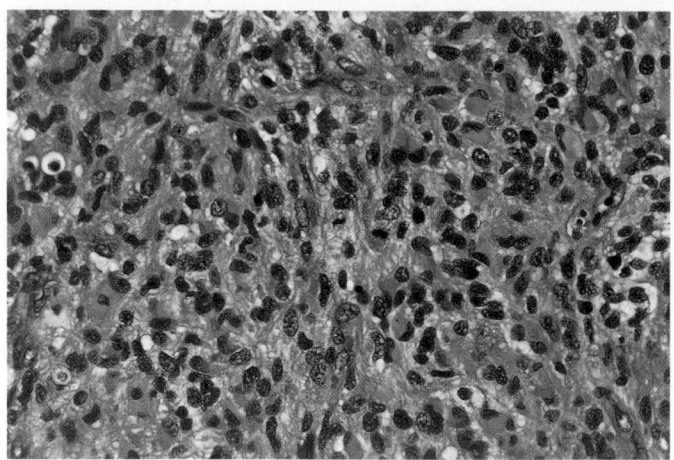

Fig. 28.42 Anaplastic astrocytoma. Compared with its low-grade counterpart (see Fig. 28.38), this lesion exhibits increased cellularity, the cytologic features of a fully malignant neoplasm, and, at center, mitotic figures.

glioblastomas tend to affect a significantly younger cohort than primary variants (mean ages at presentation being approximately 40 vs. 55 years, respectively) and by all accounts advancing age per se is inversely correlated with survival in the setting of fibrillary astrocytic neoplasia.[331] Yet another member of the glioblastoma group, the giant cell glioblastoma, shares with the secondary glioblastoma a younger patient age at onset, frequent TP53 mutation, and lack of EGFR amplification but, like the primary variant, arises in the absence of a differentiated precursor lesion, is associated with a brief predetection clinical interval and often manifests PTEN/MMAC 1 gene mutation.[331]

Like astrocytomas of lower grade, glioblastomas may be discovered on evaluation for seizures or headache but are often attended by subacutely evolving neurologic deficits indicative of their more rapid growth and destructive invasion. A subset present in sudden, stroke-like fashion as a consequence of intratumoral hemorrhage, and occasional examples mimic metastatic disease by virtue of their multifocality.[309] Especially characteristic on CT or MR evaluation is a pattern of ring-like contrast enhancement that reflects their abnormal vascularization and tendency to spontaneous central necrosis (Fig. 28.43). On gross inspection, these aggressive lesions may seem relatively circumscribed and often appear to be more clearly demarcated from neighboring tissues than their better-differentiated counterparts—deceptively so, inasmuch as neoplastic cells regularly invade neuropil well beyond the apparent tumor perimeter. Hemorrhagic discoloration and foci of yellow softening indicative of coagulative necrosis impart a variegated appearance to most examples that should immediately suggest their virulent nature (Fig. 28.44).

On histologic study, the glioblastoma is a highly cellular and mitotically active neoplasm. Its cytologic makeup

is subject to extreme variation. Differentiated elements may be intermingled with bizarre multinucleated tumor giant cells or small anaplastic forms altogether devoid of identifying astrocytic features (Fig. 28.45). The latter often come to dominate the histologic picture at recurrence, selectively repopulating tumors subjected to therapy, but may also constitute the nearly exclusive elements of select small cell glioblastomas at presentation. EGFR amplification appears to be significantly associated with this small cell phenotype.[312]

An arresting phenomenon common to many glioblastomas is a complex form of microvascular hyperplasia, apparently driven in paracrine fashion by tumor-derived mitogens (e.g., vascular endothelial growth factor and platelet-derived growth factor), in which proliferating blood vessels come to be lined by cells heaped up in disorderly fashion and are ultimately transformed into glomeruloid or solid tufts (Fig. 28.46). Although often referred to simply as "endothelial" hyperplasia, this process involves a number of vessel-associated cell types, prominent among which are pericytic/myoid elements expressing smooth muscle-related antigens.[322,354] Its identification in neurosurgical material from patients not previously subjected to radiation therapy suffices for a diagnosis of glioblastoma multiforme by WHO criteria, as does the finding of focal coagulative tumor necrosis regardless of whether neoplastic cells align themselves

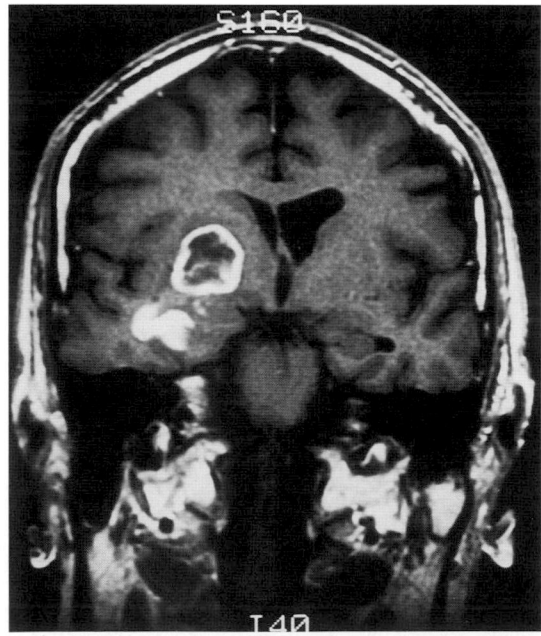

Fig. 28.43 Glioblastoma multiforme. In postcontrast injection CT or (shown here) MR studies, many glioblastomas are characterized by a bright ("enhancing") ring (representing intact, abnormally vascularized tumor tissue in which the blood–brain barrier is disrupted) that surrounds a region of hypodensity (central necrosis). The gyriform temporal lobe enhancement below this basal ganglionic example attests to neoplastic infiltration beyond the deceptively well-delimited ring margin.

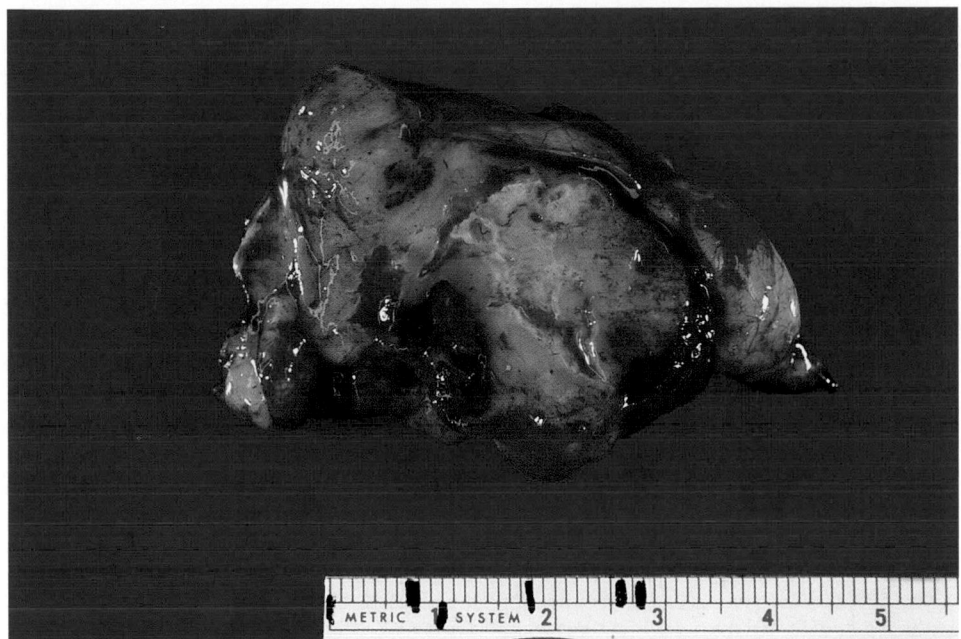

Fig. 28.44 Glioblastoma multiforme. Foci of hemorrhage and geographic yellow discoloration indicative of necrosis impart a variegated appearance to this example.

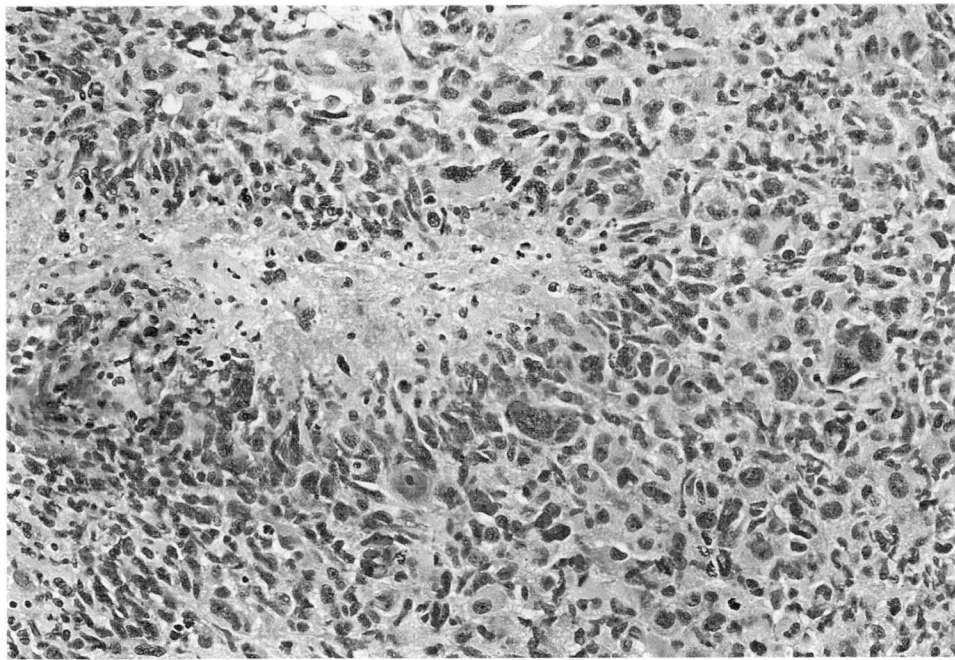

Fig. 28.45 Glioblastoma multiforme. Dense cellularity, striking pleomorphism, and zones of coagulative necrosis lined by "palisading" tumor cells characterize the prototypical glioblastoma.

about such zones in the prototypical palisades that are a "textbook" feature of this lesion[331] (Fig. 28.45).

Irradiation induces in the glioblastoma a variety of morphologic alterations, the most predictable being widespread necrosis unrelated to regional tumor cell density (usually much reduced) and vasculopathic changes that include ectasia, fibrinoid necrosis, and obliterative mural fibroplasia (Fig. 28.47). Florid astrogliosis and infiltration by macrophages, the latter identifiable by their immunoreactivity for HAM-56, CD68 and other histiocytic "markers," may complicate the recognition of neoplastic elements. Some re-resection specimens, in fact, consist solely of necrotic debris or contain only

scattered suspect cells exhibiting cytopathic alterations, presumably treatment-related, such as grotesque karyomegaly and dense hyperchromasia with chromatin smudging and nuclear vacuolization. Although we favor the view that these cells are neoplastic, albeit damaged, it is conceivable that they represent in some cases hyperplastic astrocytes displaying radiation atypia. Whatever their origin, these elements do not imply disease progression, and we report such specimens as exhibiting treatment effect with only minimal evidence of persistent, injured tumor. The diagnosis of recurrence rests on firmest grounds when aggregates of cytologically unaltered and mitotically active tumor cells can be

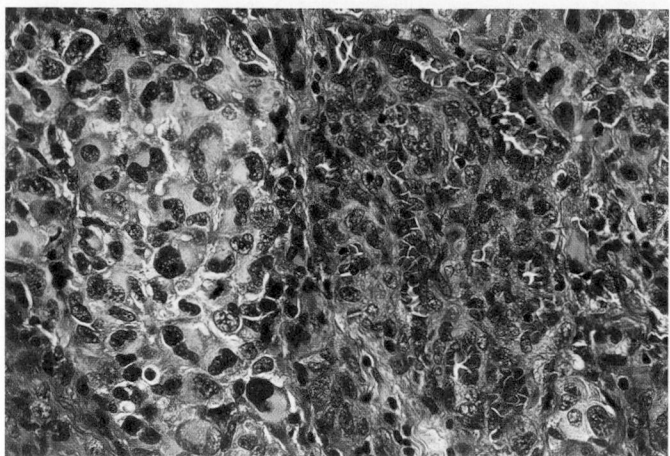

Fig. 28.46 Glioblastoma multiforme. Note the complex, "glomeruloid" quality of the microvascular proliferation at right. Astrocytic elements are seen at left.

demonstrated, cellular palisading about foci of necrosis also constituting unimpeachable testimony to treatment failure. In some instances, the necrotizing and vasculopathic changes described here will be found to involve brain tissue (typically white matter, which is particularly susceptible to ionizing irradiation) manifesting no tumoral infiltration. This toxic process (cerebral radionecrosis) characteristically interrupts a period of apparent remission and neurologic recovery measured in months (or, in some cases, years) and may mimic post-therapy relapse to clinical and neuroradiologic perfection.

Although most of the astrocytic neoplasms under discussion are confidently distinguished from primary cerebral sarcomas and tumors metastatic to the CNS by virtue of their characteristic cytologic features and typically dyscohesive patterns of infiltration, select variants may occasion considerable confusion in this regard. A case in point is the **giant cell glioblastoma**, a tumor noted for its unusual circumscription, sarcomatoid cytologic features, and reticulin-rich matrix.[335,342] Once regarded as a "monstrocellular" sarcoma, the glial nature of this neoplasm can be demonstrated by its immunohistochemical labeling for GFAP. The same can be said for spindle cell and "xanthosarcomatous," lipid-rich variants of glioblastoma.[330] We have seen a number of high-grade astrocytic neoplasms misclassified as fibrosarcomas or malignant fibrous histiocytomas when immunohistochemical studies demonstrated cytoplasmic labeling for such nonspecific antigens as vimentin, alpha-1-antitrypsin, or anti-chymotrypsin, but failed to include examination for GFAP expression. Still other aggressive and poorly differentiated astrocytic tumors contain gland-like ("adenoid") formations,[329,340] undergo squamous metaplasia,[339] or assume clear cell cytologic features (owing to cytoplasmic lipidization) and a cohesive disposition in nests and sheets that bring "balloon cell" melanoma and carcinomas of renal or adrenocortical origin to mind.[348] Immunolabeling for cytokeratin[315,316,341] and epithelial membrane antigen (EMA)[325] may further conspire to obscure the glial lineage of these and other astrocytic neoplasms. We emphasize in this regard the regular labeling of reactive and neoplastic astrocytes with the AE1/3 cytokeratin "cocktail," these usually proving nonreactive for CAM5.2, CK7, CK20, and the noncytokeratin epithelial marker BerEP4.[341] Again, assay for GFAP expression may be decisive in the unmasking of epithelioid glioblastoma variants, although the literature admittedly contains isolated depictions of carcinomas and meningiomas

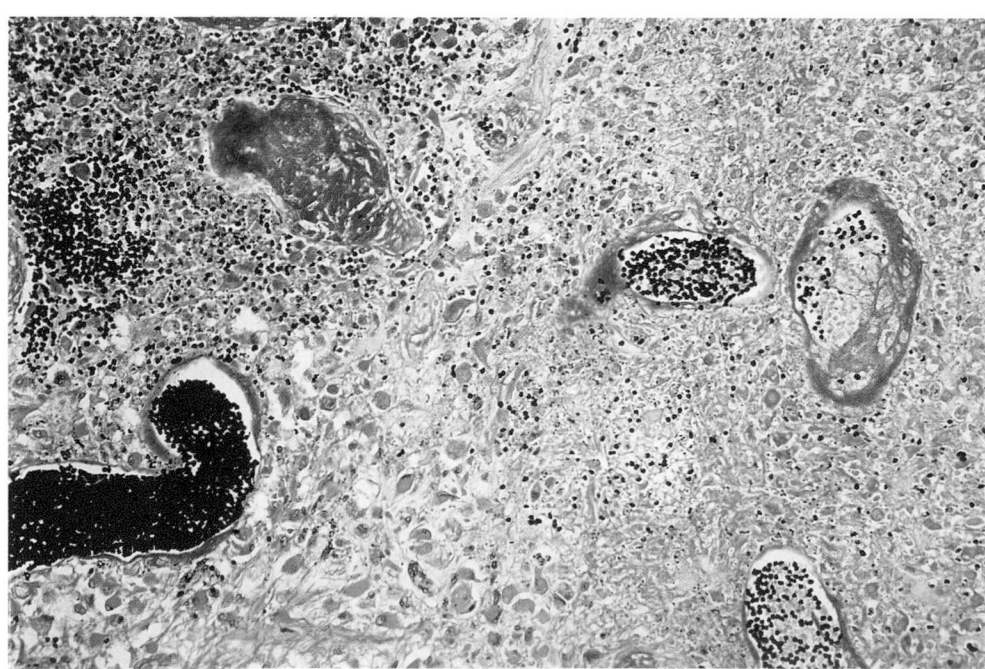

Fig. 28.47 Radiation effect. A marked reduction in cellularity, extensive necrosis, and necrotizing fibrinoid vasculopathy with vascular thrombosis and ectasia typify astrocytic neoplasms injured by irradiation.

that were focally decorated by antisera to this marker protein (see sections on meningothelial and secondary tumors). Glioblastomas may also harbor primitive-appearing papillary structures that invite confusion with the medulloepithelioma.[338] High-grade astrocytomas can contain ganglion cell-like forms or small cell elements of primitive appearance that potentially raise question of neuronal or neuroblastic differentiation, and may exhibit class III β-tubulin immunolabeling,[328] but are generally nonreactive for more neuron-restricted antigens such as synaptophysin[328] and the NeuN[355] and Hu[321] nuclear proteins. Lastly, we call the reader's attention to the existence of astrocytic tumors that undergo a striking granular cell metamorphosis resulting from the intracytoplasmic accumulation of engorged secondary lysosomes.[311] Although their granular cell components may in some cases exhibit remarkably benign cytologic features, these peculiar neoplasms are characterized by an aggressive clinical evolution. Immunolabeling of their cytoplasm for CD68 can result in the misidentification of such tumors as reactive histiocytic infiltrates.

The four-tiered Daumas–Duport scheme for the grading of diffuse fibrillary astrocytomas, also known as the St Anne–Mayo system, merits comment as an alternative to the WHO classification in that it requires of the pathologist only binary decisions regarding clearly defined and easily identified histologic variables.[317] Specimens are assessed for the presence of nuclear atypia (i.e., hyperchromasia or obvious variation in size or shape), mitotic figures, endothelial proliferation (defined as vascular lumina lined by at least two layers of piled-up or haphazardly arrayed endothelial cells), and foci of coagulative necrosis. Variables are simply scored as present or absent and astrocytomas assigned to grade 1 if none, grade 2 if any one, grade 3 if any two, and grade 4 if three or all of these features are identified. Although the equal weighting of such findings as nuclear atypism and necrosis would seem inappropriate in theory, this method succeeds in stratifying lesions in a hierarchy of escalating biologic potential precisely because the evaluated indices of anaplasia accrue to evolving astrocytic tumors in a predictable sequence. Thus it is nuclear atypism alone that comes in practice to distinguish the grade 2 from the grade 1 astrocytoma, the additional presence of any mitoses that defines the grade 3 lesion, and the superimposed appearance of endothelial proliferation or necrosis that characterizes tumors of grade 4. The last three Daumas–Duport grades generally correspond, then, to the tripartite astrocytoma–anaplastic astrocytoma–glioblastoma construct of the WHO classification, the former system also identifying a small subset of patients with particularly indolent (grade 1) lesions and favorable outcomes. The latter, unfortunately, are exceedingly rare. The interobserver reproducibility of this method and its ability to generate four distinct survival curves have been demonstrated in large studies of archival material,[317] but a potential drawback of the St Anne–Mayo scheme is its rigid categorization of the fibrillary astrocytoma containing only a rare mitotic figure as a grade 3 lesion. One retrospective series to have addressed this issue found that neoplasms designated as grade 3 on the finding of a solitary mitosis did not differ significantly in prognosis from grade 2 tumors.[320]

The prognosis of a given fibrillary astrocytic neoplasm is a complex function of both clinical and morphologic variables. Patient age, functional status on presentation, tumor location, and histology all affect the outcome of supratentorial examples.[331] Faring best are young subjects harboring low-grade lesions that are unassociated with focal neurologic deficits and that are situated in the cerebral hemispheres (as opposed to corpus callosum, basal ganglia, or thalami). Follow-up studies of patients identified and managed since the advent of CT imaging (i.e., in the era of "early" detection) suggest median survivals in the 7- to 10-year range under such relatively favorable circumstances, death typically following tumor "dedifferentiation."[331,334,336] Whether attempted resection or radiotherapy prolongs the lives of patients with low-grade cerebral hemispheric astrocytomas is a contentious matter; some neuro oncologists elect to simply follow affected individuals until there is clear clinical or neuroradiologic evidence of tumor progression. Comparably situated anaplastic astrocytomas and glioblastomas, by contrast, are unarguably aggressive neoplasms associated with median postoperative survival periods of 24 to 48 and 12 months, respectively, despite irradiation and adjuvant chemotherapy.[331] Again, young patients tend to live longer than middle-aged or elderly adults. Ultimately, however, the insidious manner in which these lesions permeate brain tissues beyond their neuroradiologically defined and grossly apparent confines frustrates operative attempts at local disease control and sets the stage for progressive infiltration of neighboring cerebral parenchyma by chemoresistant clones. This, the primary pattern of treatment failure, is occasionally complicated by the development of CSF-borne neuraxial metastases and, rarely, by spread to somatic sites, such as bone, lung, liver, or lymph node.[331,332] Most unusual, but well documented, are cases in which systemic metastases have been apparent on initial patient presentation,[332] and the bizarre phenomenon of inadvertent tumor transplantation via hepatic and renal allografts has also been the subject of isolated reports.[351]

Similarly dismal is the prognosis attached to diffusely invasive astrocytic neoplasms of the brainstem, most of which are high-grade at diagnosis.[318] It is the exceptional patient who remains alive more than 2 years from symptom onset. These lesions may mimic pilocytic astrocytomas in the generally limited biopsies secured from the bulbar region by virtue of a certain spindling imposed on their constituent cells as these infiltrate the compact fiber tracts of the pontine base. Dense hyperchromasia and conspicuous nuclear pleomorphism usually serve to distinguish these cells from well-differentiated piloid astrocytes, but in questionable cases their elongate nuclei can be shown by the appropriate histochemical methods to lie among myelinated axons rather than in a meshwork of bipolar, GFAP-immunoreactive cytoplasmic processes. It should also be pointed out that pilocytic astrocytomas (discussed later) tend at bulbar levels to a sharp circumscription and exophytic growth from the dorsal pontomedullary junction generally foreign to fibrillary astrocytic neoplasms of the brainstem. Not surprisingly, patients with high-grade astrocytomas of the cerebellum and spinal cord do very poorly, whereas a subset of indolent, well-differentiated lesions occurring in the latter location appear amenable to radical resection and are compatible with long-term survival.[314]

While the histologic grading of fibrillary astrocytic neoplasms remains, at the time of this writing, the "gold standard" for purposes of prognostication and treatment planning, quantifiable methods for the determination of proliferative potential are now in wide employ as adjuncts to conventional morphologic assessment. Immunohistochemical assay for the Ki-67 antigen, a non-histone nucleoprotein selectively expressed by actively cycling cells and demonstrable in paraffin-embedded material using the MIB-1 monoclonal antibody, has proven especially addicting to surgical neuropathologists in this regard (Fig. 28.48). Truth be told, the performance of this reagent is subject to all the technical vagaries that attend immunohistochemical methods, the calculation of MIB-1 labeling indices (i.e., fraction of decorated tumor cell nuclei) potentially influenced by antigen retrieval strategies, section thickness, choice of

region for quantitative analysis, number of cells assessed, use of automated versus manual counting techniques and level of nuclear staining intensity required for positive identification. Interpretation of the literature is complicated by the nonuniform manner in which studies have been conducted, but general survey[331] discloses a broad correlation of histologic grade and labeling index and reveals (unfortunately) overlapping index ranges for low-grade astrocytomas (<5%), anaplastic astrocytomas (5–10%), and glioblastomas (>10%). Ki-67/MIB-1 labeling fractions in excess of 5% to 7.5% emerge from select studies[331,337] as powerful predictors of relatively shortened survival in this patient cohort, but not all investigations support their utility as independent prognostic indicators[323,331] and their significance taken on an individual case basis has been called into question. In practice, we employ MIB-1 only in the evaluation of histologically low-grade or "borderline" fibrillary astrocytomas and simply append in our reporting of values above 5% a comment to the effect that such levels suggest a heightened proliferative potential.

Ongoing investigations into the targeted genomic and gene expression profiling of fibrillary astrocytic neoplasms merit additional comment, particularly those analyses employing techniques readily applicable in laboratories of diagnostic histopathology. Only a small selection of the most recently published efforts in this evolving area can be cited here.[323,324,343,347,350] Special interest has focussed, understandably, on the tumor-suppressing p53 gene. As mentioned, events that abrogate p53 function commonly occur early in the evolution of fibrillary astrocytomas.[331] Abnormal accumulation ("overexpression") of p53 in this setting is often evidenced by aberrant nuclear immunolabeling of

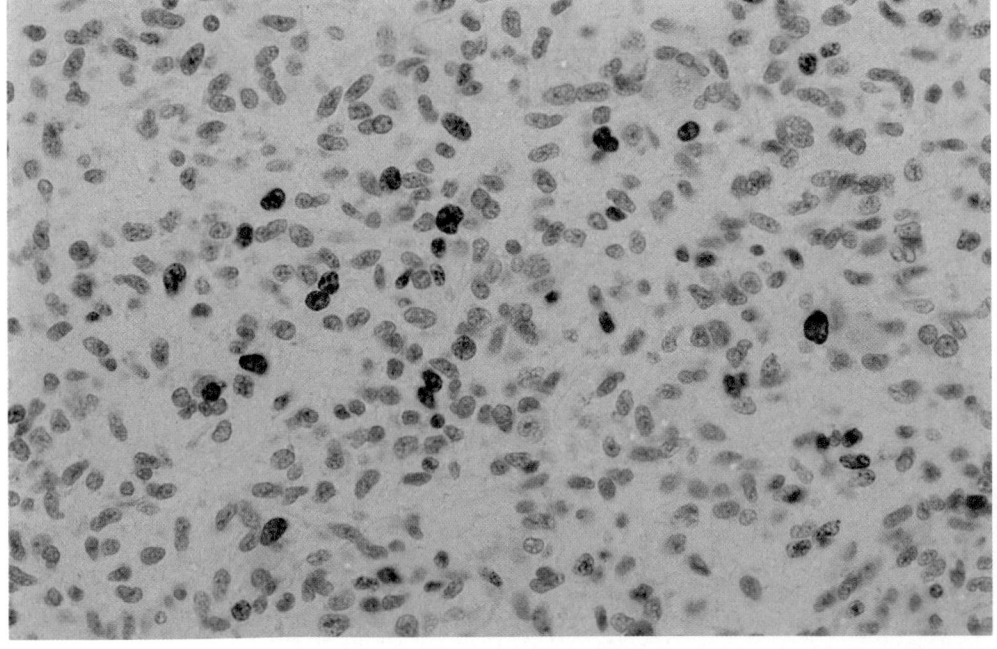

Fig. 28.48 Markers of cellular proliferation. Actively cycling tumor cells within a glioblastoma are identified in this immunoperoxidase preparation by their nuclear labeling with the MIB-1 monoclonal antibody.

neoplastic cells for this protein. The latter phenomenon does not necessarily reflect TP53 mutation but, on a practical note, may nonetheless be helpful in segregating diffuse astrocytic tumors from the general run of reactive processes (a notable exception being the regular p53 immunoreactivity of atypical astroglial cells associated with the demyelinating polyomaviral infection known as progressive multifocal leukoencephalopathy[356]) and, when widespread, distances fibrillary astrocytomas from the large majority of oligodendrogliomas (discussed in a later section). Requiring confirmation is a recent report suggesting that p53 overexpression as immunohistochemically defined characterizes a subset of high-grade pediatric astrocytomas with particularly poor progression-free survival.[343] Certainly, consensus is not to be found on the issue of whether p53 immunostatus or mutation bears independently on outcome with regards to adult-onset astrocytomas.[323,324,331,347] Loss of immunoreactivity for p16 or the retinoblastoma gene product was associated with relatively shortened survival in a series of histologically low-grade supratentorial astrocytomas deriving from patients 19 years of age or older,[324] but only a small minority of the tumors assessed evidenced either of these abnormalities and so further validation of these data is needed. A limited subset of high-grade, ostensibly astrocytic neoplasms (including glioblastomas) manifesting deletions of chromosome 1p in isolation or combined with losses on chromosome 19q may be somewhat more treatment-responsive (and amenable to longer clinical control) than their genetically conventional counterparts.[326,350] As presently discussed, such deletions are far more characteristic of oligodendrogliomas and define a group of particularly chemosensitive anaplastic oligodendroglial neoplasms.

Diffuse astrocytic neoplasms of fibrillary type may contain large tumor cells characterized by globose masses of glassy eosinophilic cytoplasm and peripherally displaced nuclei that seem on the verge of extrusion from their parent cell bodies (Fig. 28.49). Termed gemistocytes (from the Greek gemistos for laden or full), these result from an accumulation of glial-type intermediate filaments that form compacted paranuclear whorls and extend into stout cytoplasmic processes. Only exceptionally do such cells dominate the histologic picture. The designation of gemistocytic astrocytoma has been subjectively applied to tumors harboring these elements in varying density, current WHO guidelines[331] endorsing the suggestion[333] that gemistocytes constitute at least 20% of the neoplastic population if this diagnosis is to be entertained.

Gemistocyte-rich astrocytomas are virtually restricted to the cerebral hemispheres of adults. They often exhibit conspicuous perivascular infiltration by lymphocytes and typically contain small, poorly differentiated neoplastic cells that emerge from MIB-1 (Ki-67) immunolabeling studies as more actively proliferative than their large-bodied companions.[353] Aberrant nuclear immunolabeling for p53 is commonly seen, a phenomenon that presumably reflects the particular prevalence of TP53 gene mutations in astrocytomas of gemistocytic type.[352] Gliovascular structuring may be apparent, radially arranged gemistocytes projecting short cytoplasmic processes towards centering blood vessels to form pseudorosettes that may bring ependymoma or astroblastoma to mind. The latter tumor types do not permeate

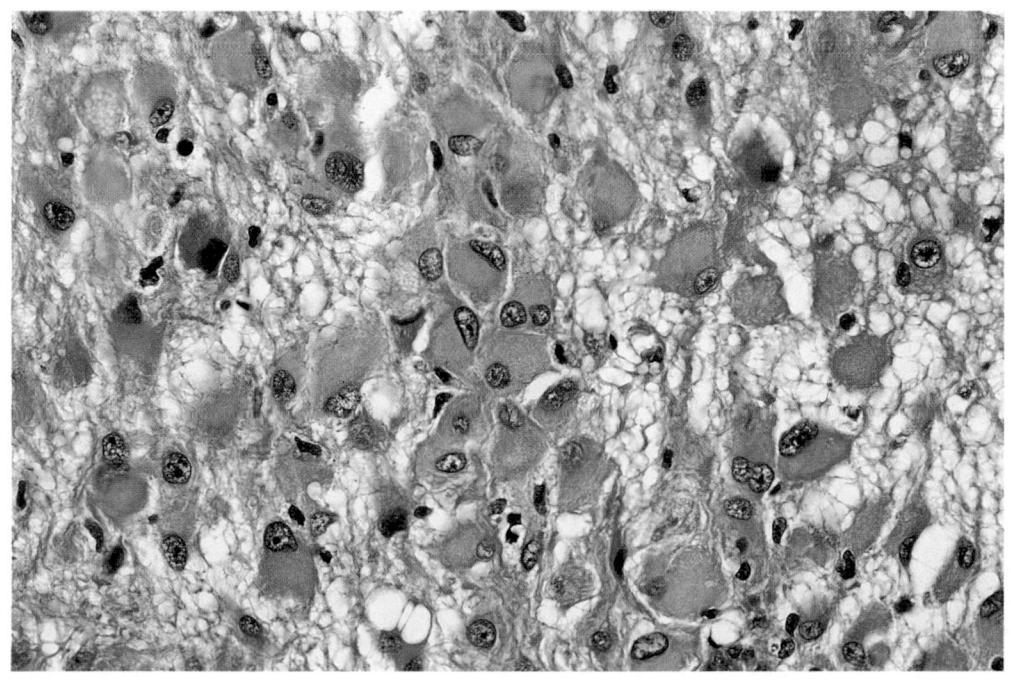

Fig. 28.49 Gemistocytic astrocytoma. Heavily dominated on initial resection by the large gemistocytes shown here, this example recurred 11 months after radiotherapy and chemotherapy. Re-resection demonstrated progression to glioblastoma. Note that these cells retain the oval and somewhat vesicular nuclei of astrocytes. For a comparison with the "minigemistocytic" variant of oligodendroglioma, see Fig. 28.62B.

neuroparenchyma in the diffuse fashion of the gemisto-cytic astrocytoma, true gemistocyte formation being foreign to the astroblastoma and only rarely encountered as a focal finding in ependymal neoplasms of otherwise conventional appearance. Care must also be taken lest the designation of gemistocytic astrocytoma be applied to oligodendroglial tumors composed of diminutive "mini"-gemistocytes or to the exceptional oligodendroglioma undergoing macrogemistocytic change with tumor progression. These usually do not manifest perivascular lymphocytic cuffing, may exhibit a distinctively lobular or pavement-like architecture, and almost invariably harbor telltale oligodendroglial elements of classic clear cell type. Furthermore, oligodendrogliomas usually display little or no nuclear p53 immunoreactivity (TP53 mutations are uncommon in this tumor group) and often evidence signature genetic abnormalities—specifically, combined chromosomal 1p and 19q deletions. The reader is referred to the section on oligodendrogliomas for further details and references.

Gemistocyte-rich astrocytomas that do not exhibit mitotic activity, complex microvascular proliferation or necrosis are currently accorded WHO grade II status.[331] We, however, cannot recommend the grading of these lesions. While acknowledging that such tumors do not necessarily behave in a highly aggressive fashion, our experience conforms to that of other observers who have found gemistocytic astrocytomas especially prone to histologic and clinical progression as compared to other ostensibly "grade II" astrocytic neoplasms.[333,353] We simply append to the diagnosis a statement acknowledging this increased biologic potential. Mitotically active variants can be reported as anaplastic gemistocytic astrocytomas (WHO grade III), examples displaying microvascular hyperplasia or necrosis qualifying as gemistocytic glioblastomas (WHO grade IV).

In contrast to the fibrous astrocyte, assumed progenitor of the fibrillary astrocytoma, the "protoplasmic" astrocyte principally resides in gray, rather than white, matter and fashions elongated, GFAP-rich cytoplasmic processes only in pathologic circumstances. Process-poor tumor cells resembling protoplasmic astrocytes are often apparent in foci of cortical invasion by conventional fibrillary astrocytomas and, as presently discussed, populate the microcystic regions common to astrocytomas of pilocytic type. Uncommon neoplasms that have traditionally been dubbed **protoplasmic astrocytomas** are composed exclusively of such cells.[331,344] Generally arising in the cerebral cortices of children and young adults, these present as superficially situated masses of gelatinous gray tissue. Histologic study reveals cytologically uniform cells evenly suspended in a cobweb-like matrix of short cytoplasmic fibrils and myxoid material that accumulates in microcysts of varying diameter. Nuclei, typically monomorphous, are round or slightly oval, mitotic activity is exceptional, and MIB-1 labeling

indices are low (with a mean <1% in one analysis[345]). Complex microvascular hyperplasia and necrosis, furthermore, are foreign to these slow-growing, WHO grade II lesions. In practice, we find the distinction of so-called protoplasmic astrocytomas from largely microcystic variants of oligodendroglioma and pilocytic astrocytoma to be problematic.

Pilocytic astrocytomas

Pilocytic astrocytomas typically present in childhood, adolescence, or early adult life—hence their common designation by the prefacing "juvenile"—and exhibit a decided predilection for the cerebellum, third ventricular/hypothalamic region, and anterior optic pathway.[359] They constitute the great majority of tumors collected under the traditional appellations of "cerebellar astrocytoma" and "optic nerve glioma," including those examples of the latter, often bilateral, complicating type 1 neurofibromatosis (NF-1 or von Recklinghausen disease). NF-1 patients are also at risk of developing cerebellar, and other extraoptic, astrocytomas of pilocytic type. Pilocytic astrocytomas may arise within the cerebral hemispheres,[361,373] basal ganglia/thalami,[368] or spinal cord[369] and are overrepresented within a clinically distinctive subset of bulbar tumors that deviate from the diffuse, fibrillary astrocytic neoplasms typical of the brainstem by virtue of their circumscription, by their tendency to bulge into the fourth ventricle in "dorsally exophytic" fashion, and far more favorable prognosis.[318]

Save for those tumors positioned in the anterior visual pathway, which produce a fusiform, "pseudohypertrophic" expansion of the optic nerve, and a subset of cerebellar examples having diffusely invasive components,[362] pilocytic astrocytomas tend to be relatively demarcated, to be nodular in contour, and frequently project into sizable cysts that may account for most of their mass effect and associated neurologic symptoms. Homogeneous contrast enhancement typifies the solid elements of the pilocytic astrocytoma, a feature serving, along with the tendency to macrocystic change and the high signal intensity often displayed on both T1- and T2-weighted MRI study, to distinguish this lesion from the diffuse fibrillary astrocytoma on neuroradiologic examination (Fig. 28.50).

The prototypical pilocytic astrocytoma is an architecturally and cytologically biphasic neoplasm composed of tumor cells in both fascicular and microcystic array (Fig. 28.51). The former component is fashioned of elements bearing the delicate, bipolar cytoplasmic processes for which the tumor is named, the adjectival pilocytic deriving from the Greek root for hair. These are typically woven in a dense fibrillar matrix in which oval or spindly tumor cell nuclei appear to lie embedded, a given cell's slender and remarkably elongated processes being optimally visualized in cytologic preparations that are useful adjuncts to the study of frozen sections during intraoper-

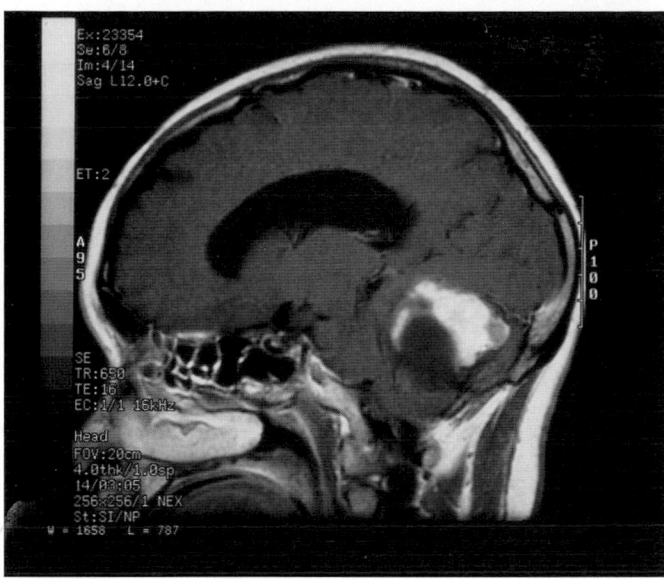

Fig. 28.50 Pilocytic astrocytoma. This typical cerebellar example is characterized by a solid, brightly contrast-enhancing mural component and associated cyst.

ative consultation. In microcystic regions, neoplastic cells are arranged about, or float suspended in, pools of basophilic, myxoid material. Here a "protoplasmic" cytology is assumed, tumor cells exhibiting rounded nuclear contours and manifesting little tendency to elaborate cytoplasmic extensions. It should be noted that the relative admixture of piloid and microcystic elements varies greatly from case to case. The latter are particularly likely to dominate cerebellar examples in children. Other common histologic features include oligodendroglioma-like clear cell foci and an angiomatoid vasculature characterized by complex arborization, hyaline mural

fibroplasia, and ectasia. Microcalcifications may be encountered at the histologic level, though neuroradiologically evident tumoral calcification is rare. Mitotic activity is generally nil or difficult to demonstrate (some 30% of cases evidence 1–2 mitoses per 50 high power fields[320]) and MIB-1 labeling indices usually do not exceed 1–3%.[320] A melanotic astroglial neoplasm with features of pilocytic astrocytoma has been recorded.[376]

Classically associated with the juvenile pilocytic astrocytoma are the cytoplasmic structures known as Rosenthal fibers and eosinophilic granular bodies. Vermiform acidophilic densities typically restricted to the tumor's richly fibrillated regions (Fig. 28.52), Rosenthal fibers represent masses of granular, electron-dense material surrounded by glial filaments (Fig. 28.53). They may be labeled by antisera to alpha B-crystallin and a related 27-kDa heat shock protein but are not immunoreactive in GFAP preparations.[365,367] Eosinophilic granular bodies are clustered acidophilic globules (Fig. 28.54) that probably derive from lysosomes and are immunoreactive for alpha-1-antitrypsin, alpha-1-antichymotrypsin, ubiquitin, and alpha B-crystallin.[366,370] At the ultrastructural level, granular bodies represent membrane-bound collections of amorphous osmiophilic material and myelin-like figures lying within the cytoplasm of tumor cells[366,370] (Fig. 28.55). It is important to note that neither of these cytoplasmic alterations is constant to, or pathognomic of, the pilocytic astrocytoma. Rosenthal fibers, for example, typically abound in the gliotic tissues adjacent to hemangioblastomas and craniopharyngiomas, whereas eosinophilic granular bodies are a conspicuous feature of many gangliogliomas and pleomorphic xanthoastrocytomas, as discussed in the sections dealing with these entities.

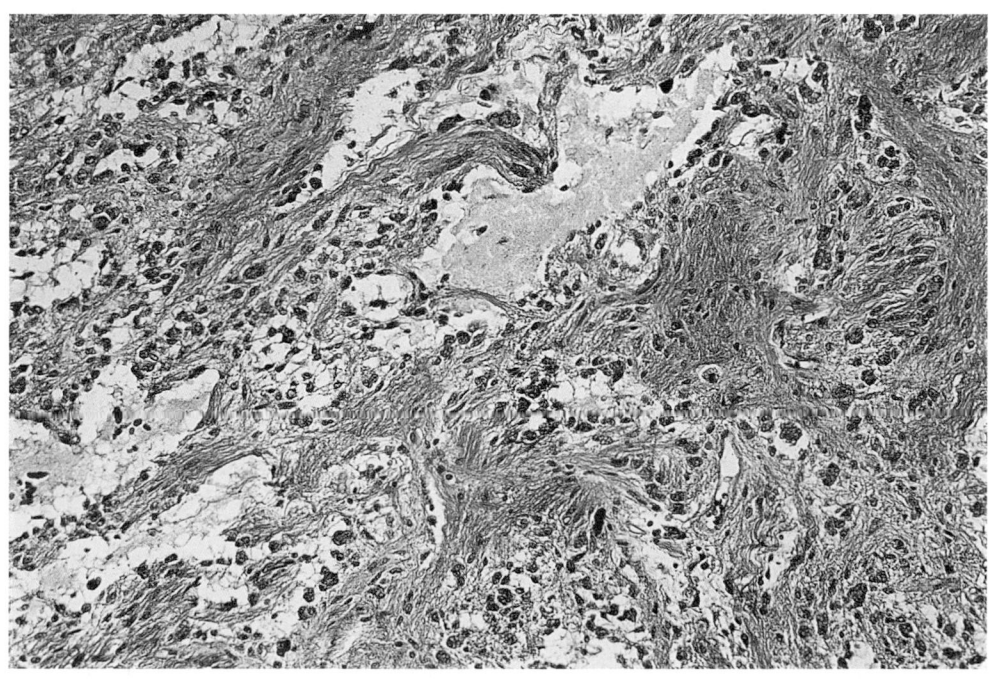

Fig. 28.51 Pilocytic astrocytoma. The biphasic cellular populations and architecture of the classic pilocytic astrocytoma are in evidence. The lesion's process-bearing spindle cell ("piloid") constituents fashion a densely fibrillar matrix, whereas its process-poor ("protoplasmic") elements aggregate in regions of myxoid change that often progress to microcyst formation.

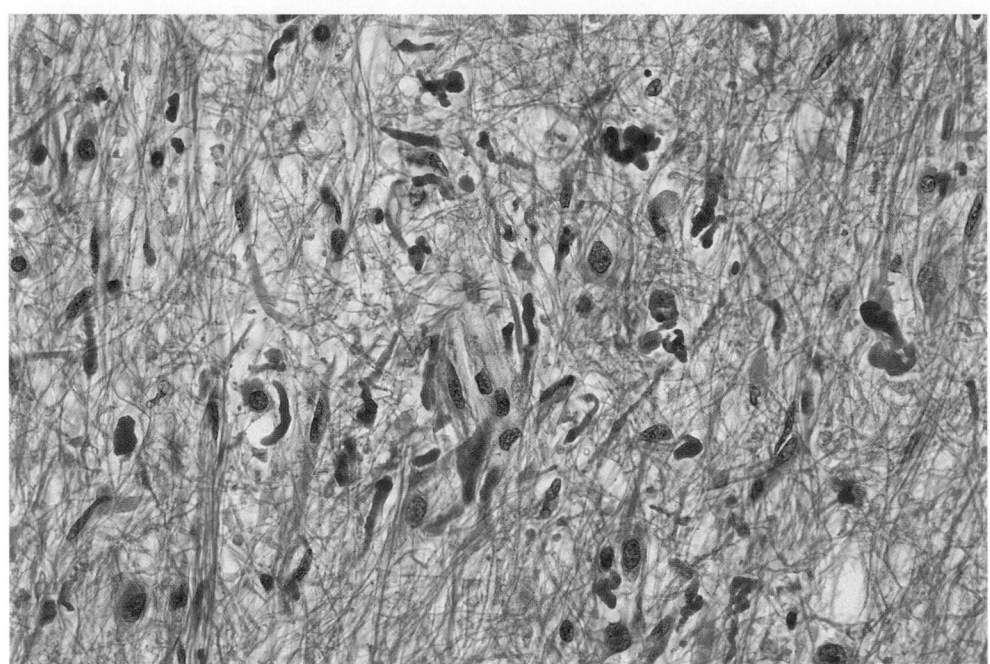

Fig. 28.52 Pilocytic astrocytoma. Varicose Rosenthal fibers lie among the otherwise delicate and hair-like cytoplasmic processes for which the pilocytic astrocytoma is named.

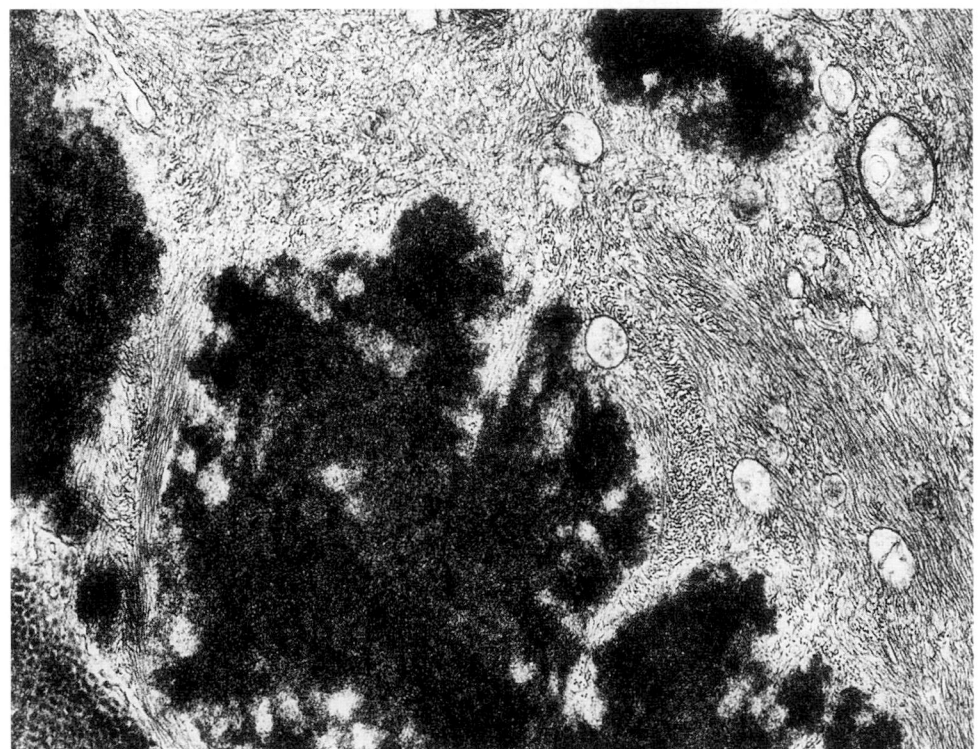

Fig. 28.53 Pilocytic astrocytoma. On transmission electron microscopic study, Rosenthal fibers are intracytoplasmic aggregates of granular, electron-dense material intimately associated with intermediate filaments, the latter composed principally of glial fibrillary acidic protein. (×25,350)

The exacting histologic indices by which the biologic potential of the diffuse fibrillary astrocytoma is gauged simply cannot be applied to the juvenile pilocytic variant, a WHO grade I neoplasm that is among the most indolent of all central neuroepithelial tumors.[359] Isolated mitotic figures, glomeruloid vascular proliferation, multinucleated giant cell formation, and nuclear atypism (at times alarming, particularly in microcystic regions) are divorced, in this setting, from sinister prognostic import, as is the rather common finding of extension into the subarachnoid space. This is not to deny the existence of potentially aggressive lesions meriting the designation of "anaplastic" pilocytic astrocytoma[375] by virtue of their conspicuous mitotic activity, dense cellularity, and foci of coagulative necrosis, but such cases are rare and actually seem more amenable to surgical control than diffuse astrocytomas exhibiting comparable features (i.e., glioblastomas).

Pilocytic astrocytomas confined to the optic nerve[357] and cerebellum[362] lend themselves to curative neuro-

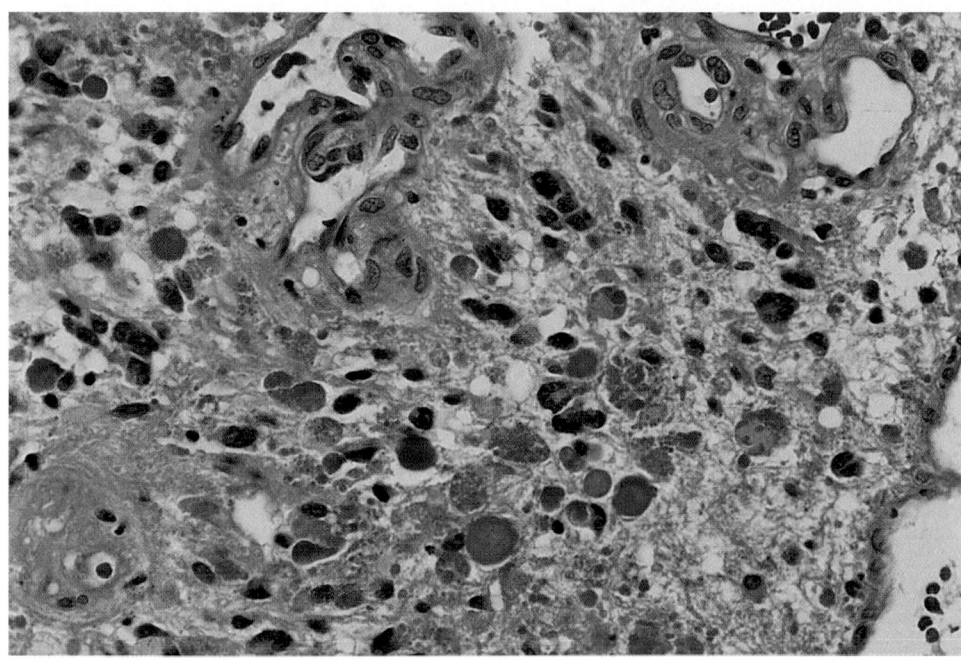

Fig. 28.54 Pilocytic astrocytoma. Eosinophilic, hyaline globular bodies are typically associated with, although not restricted to, three indolent neuroepithelial tumors: the pilocytic astrocytoma, pleomorphic xanthoastrocytoma, and ganglioglioma.

surgical resection, as do those arising in accessible cerebral hemispheric sites,[361,373] though instances of recurrence (even decades) after radical removal are on record.[371] An increased biologic potential has characterized some cerebellar examples associated with NF-1.[363] A less favorable prognosis attaches, understandably, to lesions involving the optic chiasm, hypothalamus, and other regions that preclude concerted neurosurgical attack,[359] but even in these loci the clinical evolution of subtotally resected pilocytic astrocytomas is typically protracted and may extend over a decade or more. Evidence from bromodeoxyuridine studies suggests that the proliferative activity of pilocytic astrocytomas may actually diminish over time,[364] rare instances of spontaneous regression being on record.[358] Dissemination via the CSF, principally complicating optico-hypothalamic lesions, is exceptional despite the fact that pilocytic astrocytomas frequently infiltrate the adjacent subarachnoid space and leptomeninges extensively.[372,375] Metastatic deposits may remain remarkably stable and are not necessarily associated with early death. "Malignant degeneration" remains the stuff of which case reports are made.[360,375] Radiation therapy may play a role in the latter development, as nearly all tumors evidencing such biologic progression were subjected to this treatment years prior to recurring in anaplastic and aggressive form. In fact, some may have represented independent, radiation-induced glioblastomas. Extracranial spread of optico-hypothalamic pilocytic astrocytoma to the abdominal cavity via a ventriculoperitoneal shunt has been described,[374] but is a curiosity. We refer the reader to our discussion of pilomyxoid astrocytomas (see below) for further comments on a potentially aggressive glioma of

childhood that has only recently been separated from the pilocytic astrocytoma group.

We close this discussion of the pilocytic astrocytoma by emphasizing the importance of segregating this surgically curable neoplasm from the diffuse fibrillary astrocytoma, which may arise in the cerebellum. The latter is typically resistant to all forms of therapy and, with rare exception, progresses inexorably to death. Pilocytic astrocytomas of the cerebellum occasionally consist in part of diffusely permeative elements that are indistinguishable from neoplastic cells of fibrillary astrocytic type, but these are noteworthy for their remarkable cytologic uniformity and lack of atypism.[362] The finding of such components, particularly in a pediatric case, should prompt a careful search for piloid or microcystic foci and a review of preoperative neuroimaging studies. The sharp demarcation, largely cystic configuration, and homogeneously contrast-enhancing solid components often evidenced by the pilocytic astrocytoma are generally foreign to astrocytic neoplasms of the diffuse fibrillary variety. Similar neuroradiologic considerations apply above the tentorium (i.e., to cerebral hemispheric lesions), as discussed previously.

Pilomyxoid astrocytoma

Retrospective analyses suggest that certain tumors historically included in the pilocytic astrocytoma group merit recognition as representatives of a distinct biologic, as well as morphologic, entity. **Pilomyxoid astrocytoma** is the designation most recently proposed for this incompletely characterized neoplasm,[378] which usually arises in the hypothalamus or optic chiasm of an infant or young child. The pilomyxoid lesion shares with the clas-

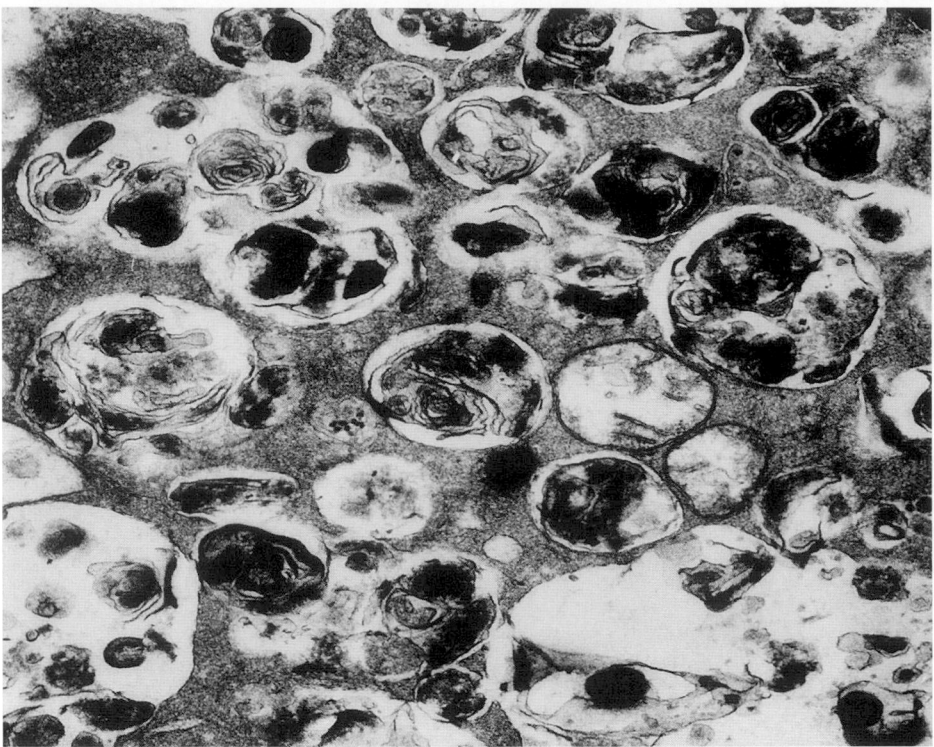

A

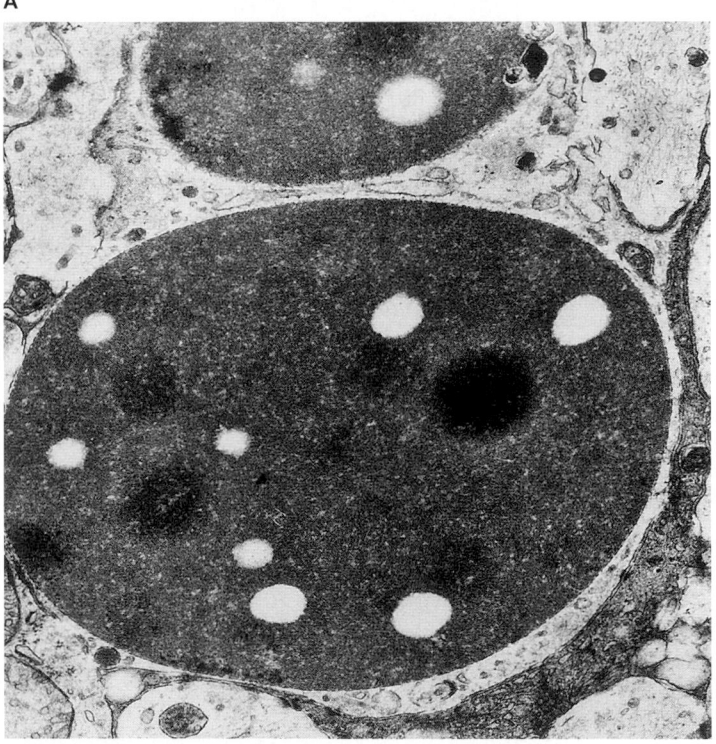

B

Fig. 28.55 Pilocytic astrocytoma. At the ultrastructural level, eosinophilic globular bodies appear to represent engorged lysosomes containing membranous debris ("myelin figures") (**A**) or amorphous, variably electron-dense material (**B**). (**A**, ×26,500; **B**, ×14,200)

sic pilocytic astrocytoma a population of spindly, bipolar glial cells but does not evidence a biphasic alternation of solid and microcystic growth patterns, instead exhibiting diffuse and prominent myxomatous change, does not contain Rosenthal fibers, and usually lacks eosinophilic granular bodies. Many such tumors deviate further from conventional pilocytic histology in containing pseudorosette-like formations of neoplastic cells that appear to radiate from stromal blood vessels (Fig. 28.56). Mitoses are often in evidence, though not numerous, and necrosis (without pseudopalisading) may be encountered.

Precise definition of the so-called pilomyxoid astrocytoma as a biologic entity awaits additional study, as does

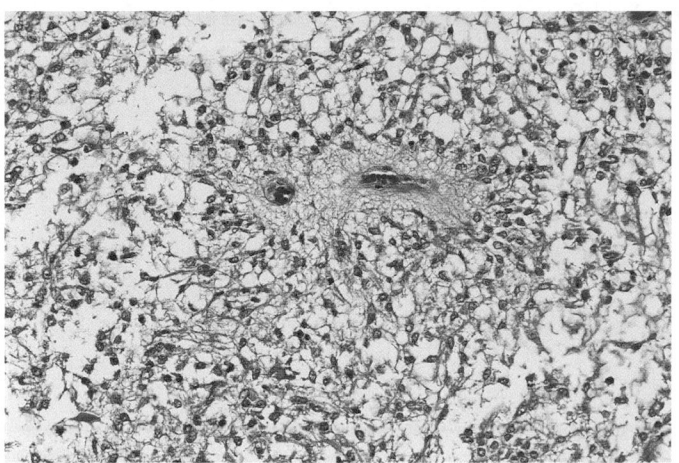

Fig. 28.56 Pilomyxoid astrocytoma. Spindled cytologic features, diffuse myxoid change, and focal perivascular pseudorosetting (center top) characterize this emerging entity.

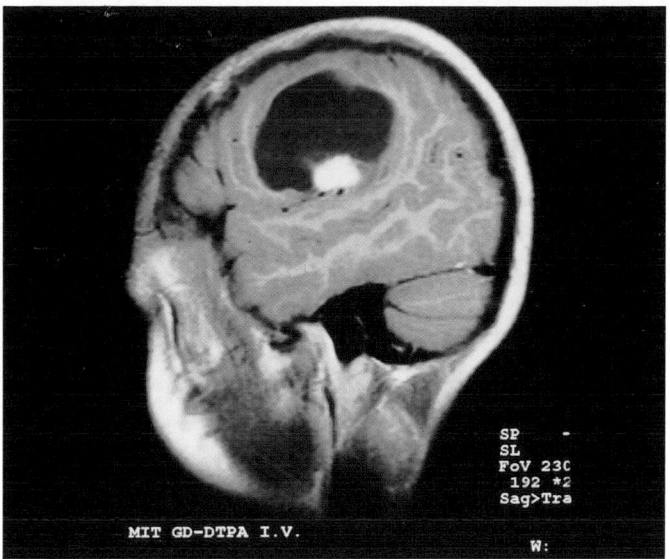

Fig. 28.57 Pleomorphic xanthoastrocytoma. This frontal lobe example is represented by a sharply delimited, intensely and homogenously contrast-enhancing nodule that projects into a large cyst. Pilocytic astrocytomas and gangliogliomas may exhibit identical neuroradiologic profiles and are the major differential diagnostic considerations in this setting.

clarification of its relationship, if any, to the classic pilocytic lesion. We have encountered tumors manifesting hybrid pilomyxoid/pilocytic features as well as neoplasms conforming in all respects to the pilomyxoid astrocytoma that evidenced more conventionally pilocytic histology on recurrence. To complicate matters, a subset of pilomyxoid suprasellar neoplasms proved in one study to share certain fine structural attributes suggesting ependymal differentiation and raising question of their origin from specialized paraventricular cells known as tanycytes.[377] These included lengthy, bipolar cytoplasmic extensions with surface microvilli, rare cilia, blebs, coated vesicles and pits, "synaptoid" complexes, intercellular junctions and foot processes terminating on delimiting, perivascular basement membranes. It must be admitted that the diagnosis of pilomyxoid astrocytoma may have been extended to tumors of nonuniform cytogenesis allied by spindle cell morphology and a propensity to myxoid change. Whatever their origins, pediatric neoplasms of the pilomyxoid astrocytoma group seem to carry a higher risk of local progression, symptomatic CSF seeding and tumor-related death than pilocytic astrocytomas of the usual variety.[378]

Pleomorphic xanthoastrocytoma

The **pleomorphic xanthoastrocytoma** is a histologically alarming, yet biologically favorable, neoplasm that typically presents in later childhood or early adult life and exhibits a predilection for the cerebral hemispheres, particularly the temporal lobes.[379,383] Cerebellar,[392] intramedullary[381] and retinal[393] examples have been described, as have morphologically similar tumors of the pineal region reported under the rubric of "pleomorphic granular cell astrocytoma."[390] Especially suggestive is neuroradiologic demonstration of a well-demarcated and partially cystic lesion containing superficially positioned, contrast-enhancing mural components of nodular or plaque-like contour (Fig. 28.57). Usually

unaccompanied by significant mass effect or edema, the latter may adhere to dura and can appear at operation to lie largely above the cortical mantle.

Evaluation of surgical specimens often shows much of the pleomorphic xanthoastrocytoma to occupy the leptomeninges and subarachnoid space, but invariably discloses foci of brain parenchymal invasion in which neoplastic cells permeate Virchow–Robin spaces and the neuropil proper. The tumor is named for its potentially bizarre cytologic characteristics and the tendency of its constituent cells to intracytoplasmic lipid accumulation, although the latter is not a uniformly conspicuous feature. Most examples are composed of spindle-shaped elements in fascicular array admixed with tumor giant cells displaying worrisome, even grotesque, nuclear abnormalities (Fig. 28.58). The abundant cytoplasm of these cells may appear foamy or coarsely vacuolated—attesting to advanced lipidization—but more commonly assumes a ground-glass, finely granular or hyalin quality. Reactive lymphoid infiltrates, at times extensive, and aggregated eosinophilic granular bodies representing lysosomes distended by autophagic debris or imbibed proteinaceous material round out the histologic picture. The latter, an important clue to the diagnosis, are shared by certain other slowly growing neuroepithelial neoplasms, notably the pilocytic astrocytoma and ganglioglioma, and so likely reflect a process of cellular senescence. In fact, "composite" tumors harboring gangliogliomatous and xanthoastrocytomatous components are on record[387] and we have rarely encountered cerebral hemispheric astrocytomas of pilocytic type with foci of

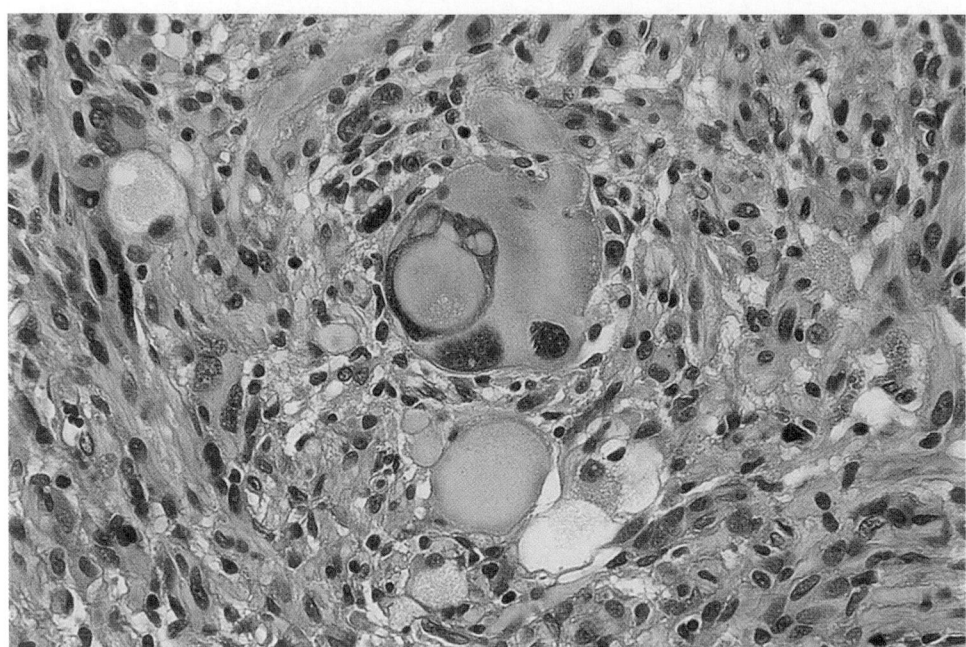

Fig. 28.58 Pleomorphic xanthoastrocytoma. Spindle and giant cells, including bizarre multinucleated forms, combine to give this relatively indolent neoplasm a most disturbing appearance. Note hyaline, granular, and vacuolar cytoplasmic alterations, the last attesting to lipid accumulation.

leptomeningeal spread conforming to the histology of the pleomorphic xanthoastrocytoma in unalloyed form. Additional features described in select cases include a cohesive, nesting or alveolar growth pattern[382] and a hyalinizing, angiomatoid stromal vascular response.[391]

The sarcomatoid histologic presentation of the pleomorphic xanthoastrocytoma may be rendered all the more misleading by an intricate pericellular pattern of reticulin deposition in flagrant violation of the neurohistochemical principle that such staining in glial, as opposed to mesodermally derived, neoplasms typically remains confined to supporting vasculature. This feature actually reflects the elaboration by tumor cells of encircling basal lamina material, demonstrable at the ultrastructural level or by recourse to antibodies directed against type IV collagen or laminin,[382] and has been taken, along with the characteristically superficial location of the xanthoastrocytoma, as evidence of its derivation from a specialized class of subpial astrocytes having radially oriented cytoplasmic processes that are normally invested by basement membranes.[383] GFAP expression, mandatory for definitive diagnosis, effectively segregates this tumor from mesenchymal neoplasms,[380,383,384] though typical examples may contain relatively few immunolabeled elements. Diffuse cytoplasmic immunoreactivity for S-100 protein is the rule and tumor cells may be labeled by antisera to alpha-1-antitrypsin, antichymotrypsin, and other "histiocytic" markers.[384] The latter reagents decorate a variety of neoplastic (including glial) cell types and are of notoriously little discriminatory value when applied to neurosurgical material. Noteworthy, given the association of xanthoastrocytomatous components with neuronal malformations (cortical dysplasia), hamartomas, and

neoplasms,[385,387] is the observation that the tumors under discussion often harbor cells that bind antibodies to synaptophysin (among other neuronal antigens) and that can exhibit ultrastructural features of neuronal differentiation (including clear (synaptic-type) and dense core vesicles).[380] This would suggest that pleomorphic xanthoastrocytomas are capable of divergent glioneuronal differentiation and would serve, along with shared clinicobiologic features, to further ally these curious neoplasms with gangliogliomas (discussed in the section devoted to ganglion cell tumors).

Despite their disturbing morphology, pleomorphic xanthoastrocytomas tend to behave in relatively benign clinical fashion, gross total resection usually sufficing to achieve long-term tumor control. A closely characterized series of 71 cases revealed recurrence-free survivals of 72% and 61% at 5 and 10 years, respectively, with overall survival figures of approximately 80% and 70% at these same postoperative intervals.[379] Extent of tumor removal bears critically on the risk of regrowth. The presence of scattered mitotic figures does not seem to constitute an ominous prognostic sign in this setting, but proliferative activity in excess of 5 mitoses per 10 high power fields proved a predictor of shortened survival in the sizable study to which we have just referred. The emergence of poorly differentiated small cell components and the presence of necrosis have also been associated with fatal outcomes, some pleomorphic xanthoastrocytomas degenerating into glioblastoma-like histology.[379,388] Tumors exhibiting these indices of potentially aggressive evolution can be termed "pleomorphic xanthoastrocytomas with anaplastic features." A recurring example with histologic evidence of anaplasia and an extensive clear cell component as well as focally papillary growth has been recorded.[389] Local failure is the rule, CSF-borne spread being a rarity.[386]

Subependymal giant cell astrocytoma (tuberous sclerosis)

The **subependymal giant cell astrocytoma** typically presents in the first or second decade of life as an intraventricular mass associated with obstructive hydrocephalus, a consequence of its practically unvarying situation near the foramen of Monro (Fig. 28.59). While not restricted to this setting, it is the intracranial tumor classically associated with **tuberous sclerosis**, a disorder transmissible in autosomal dominant fashion via loci on chromosomes 9q34 and 16p13.3 but often encountered in a nonfamilial form resulting from spontaneous mutation.[400] Traditionally defined by the triad of mental retardation, epilepsy, and midfacial angiofibromatosis ("adenoma sebaceum"), this phakomatosis is named for distinctive foci of gyral expansion ("tubers") which are populated by dysmorphic neurons and giant astrocytes in architectural disarray and possessed of an abnormal firmness ("sclerosis") resulting from glial overgrowth. Also characteristic are periventricular "candle gutterings," essentially miniature versions of the tumors under discussion, composed of outsized astrocytes aggregated in a fibrillary matrix prone to calcification. Dominant extracranial manifestations of the tuberous sclerosis complex include renal angiomyolipomas, cardiac rhabdomyomas, pulmonary lymphangioleiomyomatosis, fibrous dysplasia of bone, microhamartomatous rectal polyps, and various cutaneous lesions (hypopigmented macules, shagreen patches, subungual fibromas and, as mentioned, facial angiofibromas). Some afflicted patients also harbor retinal hamartomas similar to the subependymal nodules just described or larger masses that would qualify as retinal giant cell astrocytomas.

A sharply delineated, spherical or multinodular mass of fleshy, gray–pink tissue, the subependymal giant cell astrocytoma is anchored to the ventricular wall over a broad front. Calcifications are common, some examples exhibiting foci of cystic change. Constituent cells are large, closely apposed and characterized by polygonal (ganglion cell-like), rounded (gemistocyte-like), or spindly profiles (Fig. 28.60). Their eosinophilic cytoplasm often has a glassy or hyaline appearance and their eccentrically positioned, vesicular nuclei and prominent nucleoli distinctly resemble those of large neurons or ganglion cells. An intersecting fibrovascular stroma lends a lobular architecture to many examples and tumor cell processes often condense about blood vessels in ependymomatous fashion. A curious feature of many cases is infiltration by mast cells. Immunohistochemical assessment may reveal

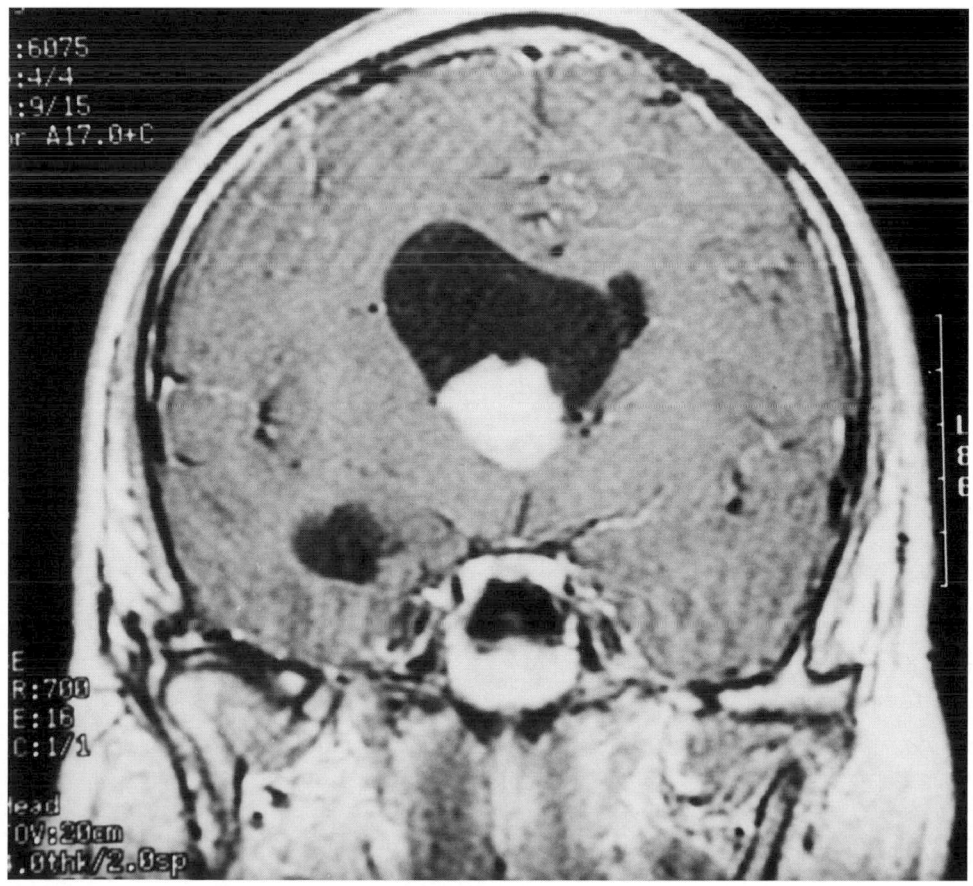

Fig. 28.59 Subependymal giant cell astrocytoma. This postcontrast injection MRI demonstrates the subependymal giant cell astrocytoma's typically intraventricular location near the foramen of Monro (with resulting obstructive hydrocephalus), as well as its characteristic circumscription. This example was not associated with other features of tuberous sclerosis.

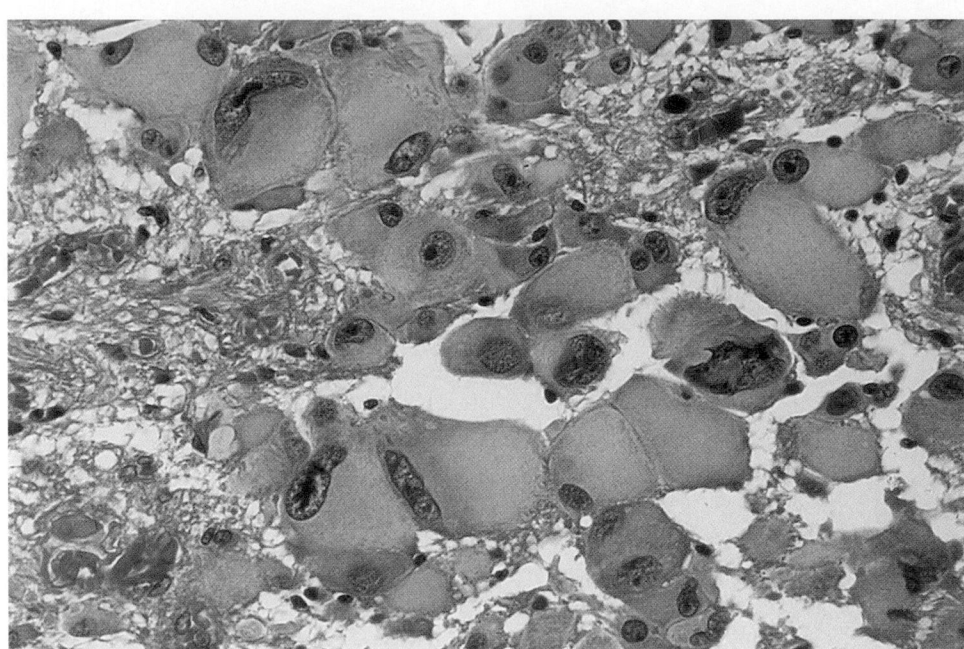

Fig. 28.60 Subependymal giant cell astrocytoma. Tumor cells that achieve truly giant proportions, often polygonal in contour and closely apposed in lobular array, are responsible for this neoplasm's name (but not evident in all cases).

only few GFAP-positive elements and—designation of this neoplasm as an astrocytoma notwithstanding—may show some tumor cells to colabel for (or exclusively express) such neuronal antigens as class III β-tubulin and neurofilament proteins.[396,397] Ultrastructural studies have demonstrated the presence of dense-core granules and synaptic formations in select cases, confirming the ability of subependymal giant cell astrocytomas to differentiate along neuronal, as well as glial, lines.[396] Accordingly, some neuropathologists prefer to designate these neoplasms simply as subependymal giant cell tumors. Ambiguous glioneuronal features also characterize the giant "astrocytes" seen in cortical tubers, suggesting a disturbance of normal lineage commitment.[396] Subependymal giant cell astrocytomas do not exhibit immunolabeling for HMB-45 and typically evidence low MIB-1 indices.[395]

Subependymal giant cell astrocytomas enlarge slowly, are reluctant to invade adjacent cerebral structures and do not exploit the CSF as a means of escaping their ventricular confines.[399,400] Recurrence following gross total resection is rare and these indolent neoplasms are not prone to malignant transformation. Although reported examples are few, cases evidencing mitotic activity and foci of necrosis do not appear to behave in particularly sinister fashion.[394,399] Neoplasms interpreted as overtly malignant subependymal giant cell astrocytomas or glioblastomas have been described in the setting of tuberous sclerosis but are clearly exceptional.[398]

Desmoplastic infantile astrocytoma

The desmoplastic cerebral astrocytoma of infancy or desmoplastic infantile astrocytoma is a rare lesion now recognized as belonging to a tumor family capable of divergent and advanced glioneuronal differentiation.

Accordingly, we address this entity along with its variant—the desmoplastic infantile ganglioglioma—in our discussion of neuronal and glioneuronal tumors.

Oligodendrogliomas

The tumors of the oligodendroglioma group are named for the resemblance of their constituent cells to native oligodendrocytes, although the assumption that these neoplasms derive from the latter or from progenitors committed to differentiate along oligodendroglial lines remains unproven. Characteristic clinical features include a predilection for young and middle-aged adults, a cerebral hemispheric localization (the frontal and temporal lobes being principally affected), an often protracted preoperative history of intermittent seizures or headache, and partial calcification on neuroradiologic study[421] (Fig. 28.61). Only exceptionally do oligodendroglial neoplasms arise below the tentorium, but no division of the CNS is immune and the literature even includes accounts of tumors interpreted as oligodendrogliomas of leptomeningeal[403,422] and retinal origin.[415] We note in passing the description of oligodendroglioma-like proliferations in association with AVMs[126,132] and report of an oligodendroglioma arising adjacent to a focus of meningioangiomatosis.[31]

Oligodendrogliomas are usually found to lie mainly within white matter at operation, but extension into overlying cortex is the rule. Composed of soft, gray–pink tissue that often acquires a gelatinous consistency owing to the accumulation of myxoid matrix materials, these may evidence cystic change and can contain foci of dense calcium deposition that are palpably gritty or even rock-hard. A vulnerability to artefactual cytoplasmic dissolution accounts for the histologic presentation of

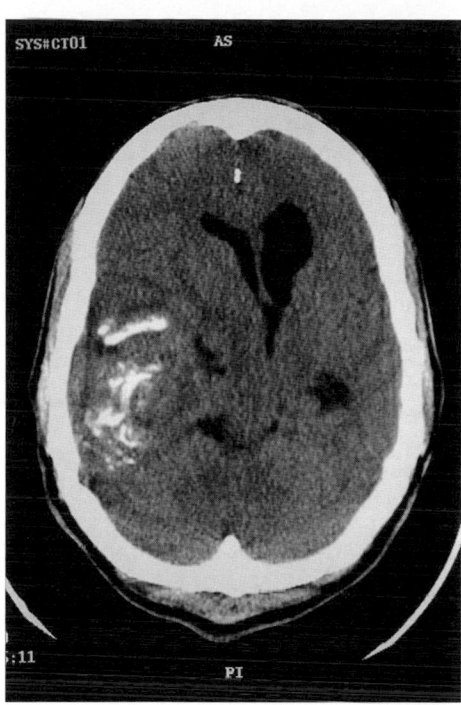

Fig. 28.61 Oligodendroglioma. The bright signal abnormalities seen in this nonenhanced CT study of a large right cerebral oligodendroglioma represent foci of intratumoral calcification. While evidenced by only a minority of oligodendroglial neoplasms, linear or plate-like calcifications of this sort are most suggestive of the diagnosis.

classic oligodendrogliomas as permeative or, in some cases, sheet-like proliferations of uniform, small round nuclei surrounded by optically clear halos (Fig. 28.62A). A fusiform spindling of tumor cells is occasionally apparent and some high-grade, "polymorphous" variants harbor markedly pleomorphic, giant cell subpopulations.[421] A majority of oligodendrogliomas contains scattered calcospherites, which may be clustered in laminar fashion within cerebral cortex along the advancing tumoral perimeter, and many are subtended by a plexiform ("chicken wire") network of thin-walled blood vessels. Of additional diagnostic utility is a tendency to perineuronal tumor cell aggregation ("satellitosis"). Perivascular and subpial growth are also commonly encountered, as are myxoid changes, microcyst formation, and nodular foci of increased cell density. In exceptional instances, tumor cells are segregated into prominent lobules by fibrovascular stromal elements or stagger across the microscopic field in rhythmic palisades.

That the "fried egg" cellular profile of the prototypical oligodendroglioma is an artefact not seen in conventional frozen sections, intraoperative smears or crush preparations merits emphasis. The first of these techniques almost invariably produces misleading nuclear angulations, whereas the latter preserve the rounded profiles of tumor cell nuclei which appear either naked

or irregularly encircled by pale eosinophilic cytoplasm in modest quantity. Distinct cytoplasmic expanses and cell membranes are also appreciable in paraffin sections prepared from very promptly fixed surgical material. Perinuclear halos, on the other hand, constitute (along with nuclear shrinkage and oligodendrocyte-like rounding) deceptive artefacts potentially imposed on astrocytomas and other nonoligodendroglial neoplasms by the common practice of ultrasonic tumor aspiration. Inspection of manually resected specimens should serve as the basis for histologic subclassification.

Oligodendrogliomas often contain intensely GFAP-positive "mini-gemistocytes"[408,413] that may harbor inclusion-like, whorled intracytoplasmic bodies of filamentous substructure (Fig. 28.62B). These are of no proven prognostic significance per se but tend to be particularly numerous in high-grade oligodendroglial tumors (as defined presently) and may evidence transition to large and pleomorphic gemistocytes of astroglial type that have been associated with aggressive behavior.[413] So-called "gliofibrillary oligodendrocytes," elements of conventional clear cell type characterized by perinuclear rims of GFAP-immunoreactive cytoplasm that may taper into short, unipolar cell processes, may also be apparent.[408] Neoplastic transformation of a glial progenitor credited with the normal spawning of oligodendroglia and a subset of astrocytes has been posited to account for these observations and could explain the frequency with which oligodendrogliomas are colonized by tumor cells evidencing transition to fibrillary astroglial morphology.[405,421] As discussed in the section dealing with "mixed" gliomas, the point at which the diagnosis of oligoastrocytoma is invoked in recognition of this common phenomenon is a subjective affair. Other cytologic alterations that may be encountered in oligodendroglial neoplasms include cytoplasmic distension by a PAS-positive mucosubstance, the formation of eosinophilic granular cells stuffed with autophagic vacuoles[426] or truncated Rosenthal fibers,[411] and "signet ring" change resulting from the intracytoplasmic accumulation of degenerating mitochondria[412] or of dilated profiles of rough endoplasmic reticulum.[416]

Unfortunately, there does not exist at present an immunocytochemical reagent that consistently and specifically identifies neoplastic cells as oligodendroglial. Immunolabeling for S-100 protein, membranous Leu7 (CD57) reactivity and expression of carbonic anhydrase C are characteristic but shared by other tumor types.[419,421] Cytoplasmic galactocerebroside labeling is of some diagnostic utility,[405] but inconstant, and only exceptionally are tumor cells (even those of highly differentiated appearance) decorated by antibodies to myelin-associated glycoprotein or other oligodendrocyte-restricted markers.[419,421] Definitive ultrastructural indices of oligodendroglial maturation are similarly lacking in most cases, though careful search may rarely reveal cytoplasmic

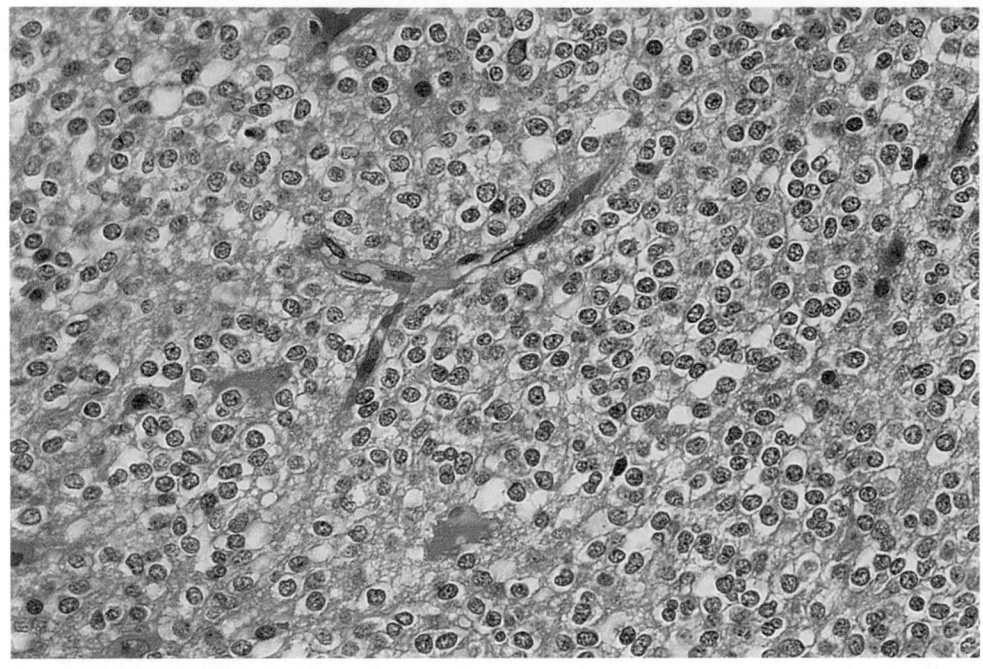

A

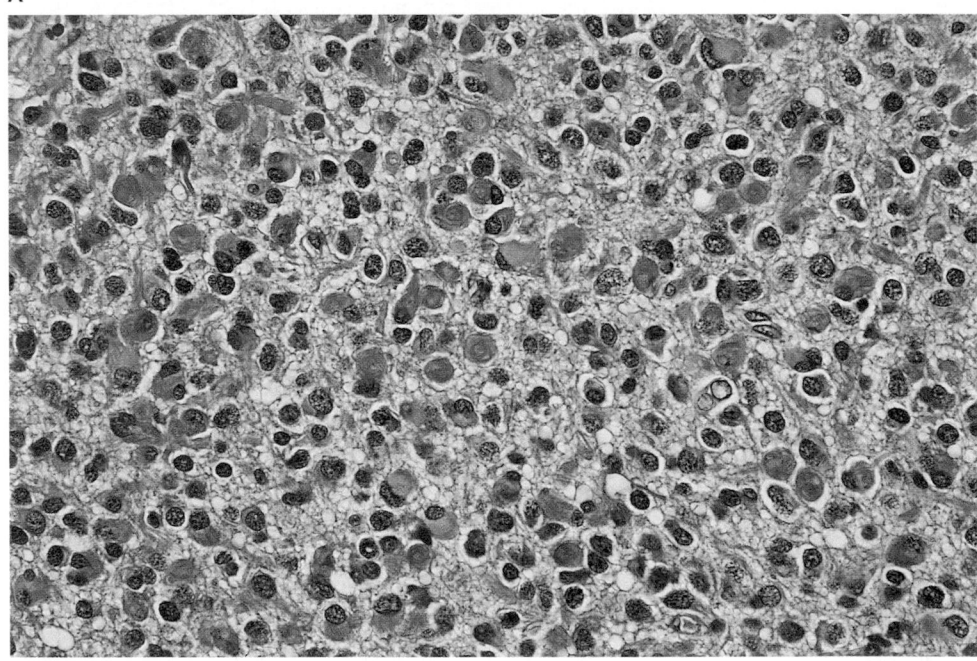

B

Fig. 28.62 Oligodendroglioma. Uniform, round nuclei and clear perinuclear halos (artefacts of delayed fixation) typify well-differentiated oligodendrogliomas **(A)**. "Minigemistocytic" variants **(B)** maintain oligodendroglial nuclear features while amassing globose paranuclear expanses of eosinophilic, hyaline or whorling fibrillar cytoplasm. Compare the size of these cells and their cytologic features with those of the gemistocytic astrocytoma depicted at identical magnification in Fig. 28.49.

processes compacted in a concentric lamellar fashion reminiscent of myelin sheath formation.[417] Microtubules, free ribosomes and mitochondria constitute the usual cytoplasmic contents and are unaccompanied by any unique organellar structures.

It is, in fact, what the oligodendroglioma fails to accomplish at the ultrastructural level or by way of antigen expression that often proves most useful in its distinction from certain mimickers that may assume astonishingly similar histologic guises. Specifically, it does not fashion the elaborate zonulae adherentes-type intercellular junctions, microlumens, microvillous or ciliary arrays of the clear cell ependymoma, nor the clear synaptic or dense-core vesicles that betray the neuronal nature of central and extraventricular neurocytomas. The latter are further (and, in most cases, more efficiently) distinguished by a neuronal immunophenotype that includes conspicuous matrix labeling for synaptophysin and, in many instances, immunoreactivity for the neuronal nuclear antigens Hu[321] and NeuN.[355] This is not to dismiss various lines of evidence, given more detailed treatment elsewhere,[410,420,427,428] that oligodendrogliomas occasionally exercise a potential for neuronal differentiation. We acknowledge reports that document the (generally limited) labeling of some examples for a variety of neuron-associated antigens,[406,410,427,428] including synaptophysin, and note a particularly thought-provoking account of otherwise "acceptable" oligodendrogliomas harboring unarguably neurocytic elements in rosetted array.[420] Such phenomena necessarily raise questions regarding the cytogenesis of the neoplasms currently regarded as oligodendroglial, but are certainly exceptional and of no special clinical significance. We would emphasize that close scrutiny is required lest neoplastic infiltration of synaptophysin-rich cortex (a frequent event) be seized upon as evidence of tumoral differentiation along neuronal lines. Again, NeuN assessment is useful in this regard, as immunoreactivity for this protein is generally foreign to oligodendrogliomas and serves to highlight remaining native neurons in colonized gray matter. Focal NeuN labeling has also been described as segregating some examples of the decidedly oligodendroglioma-like dysembryoplastic neuroepithelial tumor,[428] a lesion that further departs from the neoplasms under discussion in its predilection for subjects younger than 20 years of age, largely cortical topography, content of intracortical nodules with a "patterned" alveolar architecture, and apparently intact chromosome 1p status.

Unlike clear cell meningiomas (usually extra-axial and dura-based), oligodendrogliomas are typically EMA-negative, are not heavily glycogenated, and lack well-developed intercellular junctions at the electron microscopic level. Similar considerations apply to the identification of clear cell carcinomas, which may also exhibit cytokeratin reactivity. A major problem that cannot be entirely resolved by either immunohistochemical or ultrastructural assessment is appropriate subclassification of the glioma manifesting ambiguous histologic features—i.e., not falling clearly into the oligodendroglial versus diffuse astrocytic camp. Oligodendrogliomas may contain minor populations that exhibit nuclear immunoreactivity for p53, but when widespread this phenomenon is far more characteristic of the astrocytoma group and tends to an inverse correlation with those genetic abnormalities, presently discussed, that have come to define a subset of chemoresponsive oligodendroglial neoplasms.[401]

A variety of grading strategies have emerged from correlative studies of oligodendroglioma histology and outcome,[406,407] a two-tiered segregation into low- versus high-grade variants forming the basis of the WHO classification and finding wide application among neuropathologists.[407,421] Reported simply as "oligodendroglioma" or "oligodendroglioma, WHO grade II" is the well-differentiated tumor that exhibits little in the way of mitotic activity and is devoid of proliferative microvascular alterations or necrosis. Nodular foci of increased cellularity alone are compatible with this diagnosis. Endothelial hypertrophy, complex microvascular prolif-

eration, and conspicuous mitotic activity—joined, in some cases, by necrosis and often accompanied by dense cellularity and obvious nuclear atypism—are features of the clinically aggressive, "**anaplastic oligodendroglioma**" (or "anaplastic oligodendroglioma, WHO grade III") (Fig. 28.63). The latter may evolve from a progenitory low-grade oligodendroglioma, i.e., anaplastic components may be found in an otherwise well-differentiated lesion. Some neuropathologists extend a WHO grade IV designation to anaplastic oligodendrogliomas exhibiting particularly florid microvascular hyperplasia and glioblastoma-like necrosis with palisading, but this decision does not bear on issues of clinical management and so there is no compelling reason at present to attempt a subclassification of high-grade oligodendroglial neoplasms. Other variables associated with an unfavorable clinical course include advancing patient age, contrast enhancement on neuroradiologic assessment (a ring enhancing profile seems especially ominous) and, in some studies, MIB-1 labeling indices in excess of 5%.[404,421]

Median survivals of 3 to 5 years have historically characterized oligodendroglial neoplasms considered as a group, but recent investigations demonstrate that a far more favorable prognosis attaches to examples harboring select molecular genetic anomalies.[402,409,425] Specifically, combined and isolated allelic losses involving chromosomes 1p and 19q—a "signature" strongly (though not invariably or exclusively) associated with oligodendrogliomatous tumor morphology[423–425]—are predictive of relatively prolonged patient survival and seem to identify a subset of anaplastic oligodendroglial neoplasms that can be driven into chemotherapy-induced remissions of gratifying durability. A variety of methods may be applied to the demonstration of these deletions,[401,423,424] including microsatellite analysis, comparative genomic hybridization, and fluorescence in situ hybridization (Fig. 28.64). An intact chromosome 1p

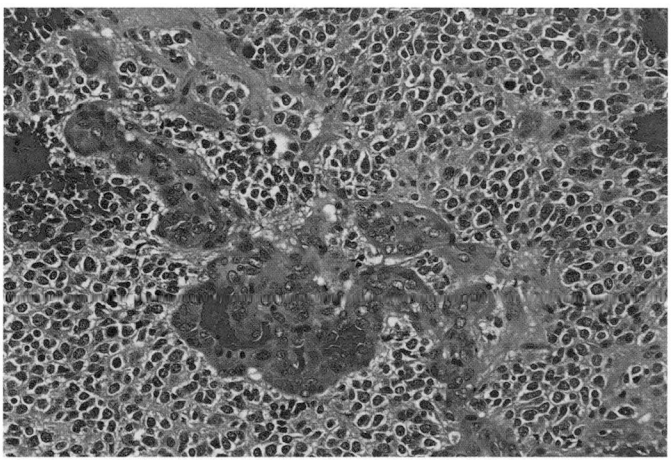

Fig. 28.63 Anaplastic oligodendroglioma. Microvascular proliferation, readily apparent mitotic activity and cytologic atypism are features of this example.

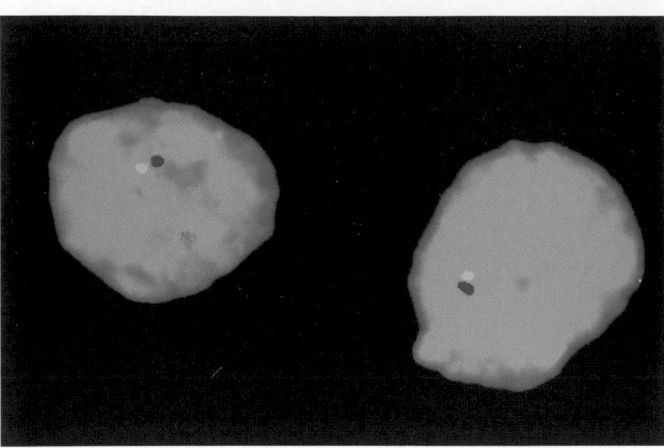

Fig. 28.64 Chromosomal deletion in oligodendrogliomas (same case as illustrated in Fig. 28.63). Fluorescence in situ hybridization utilizing centromeric (green) and telomeric (red) probes to chromosome 1p reveals only one signal pair in each of these tumor cells, indicating that both have lost the second 1p copy. This case also exhibited 19q deletion, commonly an accompanying event. The patient achieved complete remission on a regimen of procarbazine, CCNU, and vincristine.

profile accompanied by TP53 mutation (occurring in only a small fraction of oligodendrogliomas) has been correlated with a much reduced likelihood of chemoresponsiveness as well as brief intervals to recurrence and decreased overall survival, while a particularly refractory and aggressive clinical course characterizes a subset of high-grade oligodendroglial tumors in which 1p preservation is found in combination with PTEN mutation, 10q loss, EGFR amplification, and CDKN2A deletion.[409] The latter often exhibit glioblastoma-like ring enhancement on neuroradiologic study. Curiously, chromosomal 1p/19q co-deletions are evidenced by most oligodendrogliomas arising in the frontal, parietal and occipital lobes, but only a minority of histologically identical neoplasms (and "oligoastrocytomas") localized to the temporal lobes, insula, or diencephalon.[418,429]

Oligodendrogliomas usually kill by virtue of progressive neuroparenchymal infiltration following local recurrence. Leptomeningeal dissemination via the CSF is exceptional and distant metastasis vanishingly rare.[414,421] The progressive overgrowth of recurring tumors by high-grade elements of astroglial phenotype can eventuate in a histologic picture indistinguishable from that of glioblastoma. Gliosarcomatous transformation has been recorded (see section "Gliomesenchymal tumors").

Ependymal tumors

Ependymomas constitute no more than 5% to 9% of primary CNS neoplasms, but their prevalence relative to other tumor types varies considerably with patient age and presenting location.[471] A majority of intracranial examples arise in childhood, whereas intramedullary variants usually afflict adults. The incidence of the for-

mer peaks in the first decade of life, ependymomas comprising approximately 10% of intracranial neoplasms in the pediatric population and up to 30% of those encountered in children under 3 years of age. At least two thirds of these childhood tumors are situated within the fourth ventricle and consequently present with evidence of increased intracranial pressure secondary to obstructive hydrocephalus. Supratentorial lesions are more evenly distributed among children and adults and are more likely to be associated with seizures and focal motor deficits.

Ependymomas of the spinal cord usually arise within cervicothoracic segments and exhibit a predilection for the fourth and fifth decades of life, constituting the most common intramedullary neoplasms of adulthood and some 60% to 70% of tumors so situated.[439,471] Principal clinical manifestations include pain localized to the neck or back, numbness and paresthesias of the distal extremities, atrophy of hand musculature, and gait disturbances. An intramedullary location and multifocality characterize ependymomas complicating type 2 neurofibromatosis (NF-2), sporadic spinal cord examples apparently sharing with these predetermined variants alterations of the NF-2 tumor suppressor gene on chromosome 22q12.[471] Ependymomas may rarely arise within cranial nerves[449] and have been reported to originate in the ovary,[442] uterosacral ligament,[438] mediastinum,[458] and lung,[436] though female genital tract and mediastinal cases may well represent "lopsided" (i.e., monodermal) teratomas. We allude in passing to controversy over the role of simian virus 40 (SV40) in the genesis of ependymal tumors.[471] Reports that childhood ependymomas (and choroid plexus tumors) harbor SV40 or SV40-specific DNA sequences intrigue given the recognized ability of this agent to induce such neoplasms in animal hosts, but have not been replicated in all laboratories and could reflect "bystander" passage rather than an etiologically relevant phenomenon.

Wherever situated, ependymomas tend to be well-circumscribed and contrast-enhancing on neuroradiologic study. Supratentorial examples are often, but not invariably, found to communicate with the ventricular system, lobar types frequently exhibiting cystic change and focal calcification.[430,471] The latter is also a relatively common feature of posterior fossa lesions, which tend to be anchored to the floor of the fourth ventricle. Medulloblastomas, by contrast, only exceptionally undergo any appreciable mineralization and usually hang from the fourth ventricular roof when localized to the midline. Ependymomas may exploit CSF exit foramina to escape the restrictive confines of the fourth ventricle and, in so doing, can encircle the medulla and cervical spinal cord. Intramedullary variants produce a fusiform widening of involved segments and commonly precipitate syrinx formation, cystic dissection of the spinal cord usually progressing rostrally. MRI demonstration of a T2-

hypointense "hemosiderin cap" atop the rostral pole of a well-delimited and enhancing intramedullary mass is particularly suggestive.

The conventional **ependymoma** is typified by a dense meshwork of fibrillary cytoplasmic processes that condense, collar-like, about stromal blood vessels in formations known as perivascular pseudorosettes (Fig. 28.65). These are accompanied in a minority of cases by canals, tubules or actual rosettes lined by cells closely resembling normal ependymocytes (Fig. 28.66). The term "cellular ependymoma" may be used for densely populated examples with relatively narrow pseudorosettes but little

mitotic activity, though this conveys no clinically useful information. Tumor cell nuclei are rounded or spindled, characteristically exhibit an evenly granular chromatin distribution, generally lack nucleoli, and may contain invaginated cytoplasmic pseudoinclusions or exhibit longitudinal nuclear grooving.[435] Optimally visualized in cytologic preparations, the last feature—along with the tendency of neoplastic ependymal cells to remain attached to delicate blood vessels in papillary fashion when subjected to smearing or crushing—facilitates intraoperative diagnosis. While nuclear uniformity is the rule, ependymomas may contain scattered pleomorphic

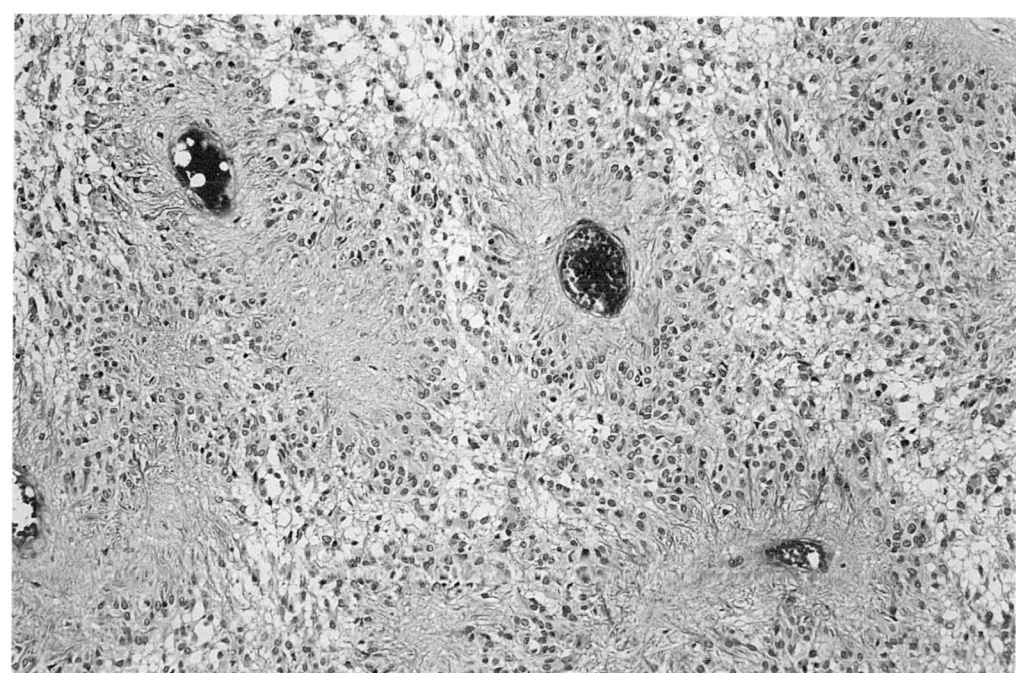

Fig. 28.65 Ependymoma. The cytoplasmic processes of ependymal tumor cells condense about blood vessels to form pseudorosettes.

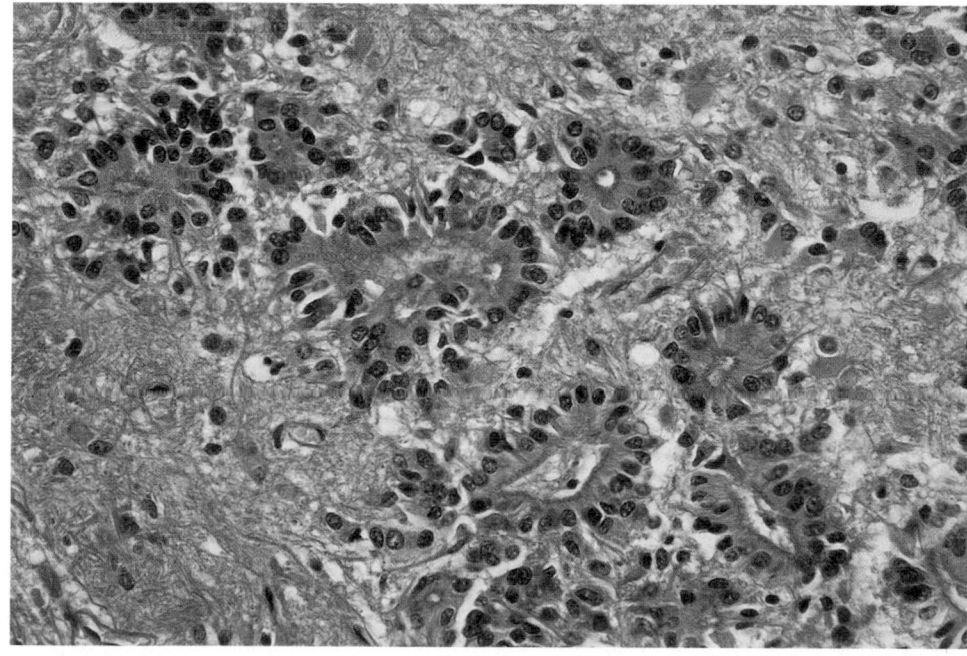

Fig. 28.66 Ependymoma. The true ependymal rosette contains a well-defined central lumen. Clustered ciliary basal bodies ("blepharoplasts") are responsible for the enhanced, granular staining of tumor cell apices.

elements and "giant cell" variants have been described within the cranial compartment[433] and in the filar region (see discussion of myxopapillary ependymoma below[472]). Dystrophic calcification is a common finding, and some examples undergo osseous or chondroid metaplasia.[454] Melanotic ependymomas have been depicted,[462] as have "xanthomatous" variants containing intracytoplasmic lipid droplets[467] and examples harboring adipocyte-like, "lipomatous" elements.[463] We have rarely encountered extensive gemistocytic change in ependymomas, one report describing a case exhibiting globular, inclusion-like cytoplasmic bodies immunoreactive for GFAP.[469]

At the ultrastructural level, ependymomas exhibit a number of specialized cytoplasmic features characteristic of non-neoplastic ependyma.[465] Elaborate, zipper-like junctional complexes (zonulae adherentes) bind their constituent cells and are likely responsible in some measure for the cohesive growth pattern and "pushing" margins typical of such tumors. Slender microvilli and (in smaller numbers) cilia sprout into the lumina of rosettes or intercellular clefts, again framed by membrane junctions of zonula adherens type (Fig. 28.67). Intracytoplasmic granules ("blepharoplasts") that are often apprehended by light microscopy along the apices of rosette-forming tumor cells in fact represent anchoring ciliary basal bodies. Also commonly observed on fine structural study is intracytoplasmic lumen formation, a phenomenon responsible in particularly pronounced cases for signet ring cell variants of ependymoma.[473] Intermediate filaments composed principally of vimentin

and GFAP[455,470] are additional cytoskeletal elements conspicuous in the cell processes of ependymal neoplasms, which, in select cases, may be coated by basal lamina material where they abut blood vessel walls.

While maintaining a diagnostic ultrastructural fidelity to the ependymal line, a subset of ependymomas exhibit distinctly confounding histologic features.[471] **Tanycytic ependymomas** (from the Greek *tanyos*—to stretch) may be confused with schwannomas, meningiomas, and fibrillary or pilocytic astrocytomas by virtue of their spindly cytologic features, fascicular growth patterns and poorly developed, inconspicuous pseudorosettes. Such tumors are typically encountered at spinal levels. Ependymomas commonly contain, in addition to admixed elements of astrocytic appearance, cells characterized by rounded nuclear profiles and perinuclear cytoplasmic clearing. Variants dominated by the latter, **clear cell ependymomas**,[456] are practically restricted to the supratentorial compartment and often misconstrued as oligodendroglial, a mischance made all the more inviting by the frequent presence of intratumoral calcospherules and a plexiform vascular network. Again, these retain identifying ependymal attributes at the electron microscopic level and so are readily segregated from oligodendrogliomas and other potentially clear cell neoplasms, including intra- and extraventricular tumors of neurocytic type. Discussed elsewhere in this chapter, the latter evidence neuronal specializations at the ultrastructural level and synaptophysin immunolabeling—both foreign to tumors of the ependymal series.

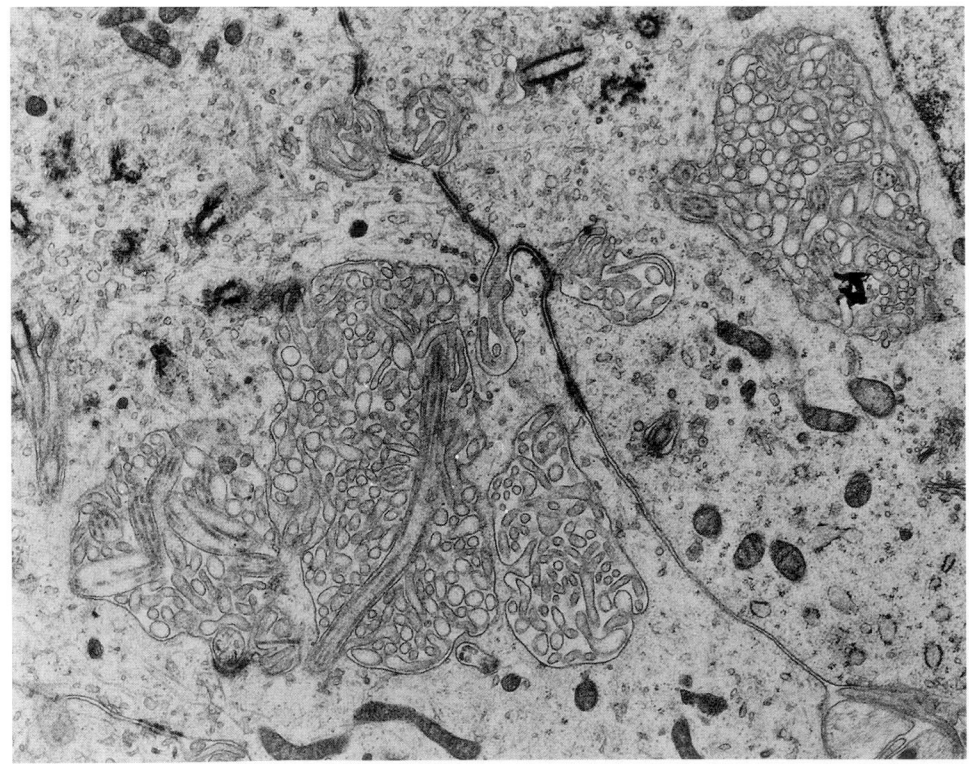

Fig. 28.67 Ependymoma. Features indicative of ependymal differentiation at the ultrastructural level include the joining of tumor cells by elongated junctional complexes and the formation of lumens filled with microvilli and, in lesser number, cilia. (×8800)

True **papillary ependymomas**—i.e., tumors in which neoplastic ependymal cells assume a columnar configuration and are supported by fibrovascular cores rather than a fibrillary glial "stroma"—are very rare and need be distinguished from metastatic papillary carcinomas, choroid plexus papillomas, and papillary meningiomas. Immunohistochemistry may be applied to this problem and obviates more laborious electron microscopic study.[432,452,455,470] Like other ependymomas, papillary variants label for S-100 protein, vimentin, and GFAP. Apical EMA reactivity (a feature potentially shared by ependymal rosettes) may be apparent, as may cytoplasmic decoration with the AE1/3 anti-keratin "cocktail," but ependymomas usually do not immunolabel for CAM 5.2, CK7, CK20, or CK903.[470] If present at all, tumor cells positive for such cytokeratins are typically few in number.[470] Epithelial neoplasms of the choroid plexus may harbor decidedly ependymocytic populations with elongated and tapering cytoplasmic processes that are GFAP-immunoreactive, but this phenomenon (which underscores a shared neurocytogenesis) characteristically constitutes a focal finding when manifest. Choroid plexus papillomas, furthermore, generally depart from intracranial ependymomas in their more diffuse labeling for CAM 5.2 and CK7, transthyretin expression, and elaboration of continuous basement membranes demonstrable by immunohistochemical assessment for laminin.[441] Tumors of this group are given full consideration later, as is the papillary glial neoplasm known as astroblastoma. Select papillary meningiomas have been described as GFAP immunoreactive (see "Meningothelial tumors"), but these are extra-axial, dural-based neoplasms and do not evidence ependymal characteristics by electron microscopy.

A relatively protracted clinical evolution characterizes most ependymomas, these generally expanding slowly and, save for exceedingly rare variants of more diffusely invasive character, remaining circumscribed in their growth patterns. Cited here is only a limited sampling of the more recent series bearing on prognostic variables in this setting. Location weighs heavily on outcome. Whereas intramedullary examples are generally curable by excision alone in experienced hands,[439] few posterior fossa ependymomas lend themselves to truly complete resection owing to their colonization of critical bulbar tissues along the floor of the fourth ventricle. Consequently, the long-term prognosis for patients afflicted with such tumors is poor.[440,446,461] An especially dismal outcome appears to be associated with a posterior fossa presentation prior to 3 years of age, whereas older patients with resectable supratentorial ependymomas often experience long postsurgical remissions (but remain at risk for late recurrence). Whether specific histologic features have an impact on survival separable from considerations of tumor site, extent of resection and patient age at diagnosis is quite controversial.[440,446,461] Unfortunately,

meaningful analysis of the pertinent literature is complicated by the application of nonuniform and irreproducible grading parameters to this problem. Poorly differentiated tumors exhibiting dense cellularity and conspicuous mitotic activity (which may be accompanied by complex microvascular proliferation and necrosis with pseudopalisading) certainly merit the designation of **anaplastic ependymoma** on morphologic grounds and have proven more aggressive than their low-grade counterparts in some studies, but these histologic findings are not consistently predictive of an accelerated course. Interestingly, features of anaplasia are especially common in the intracranial ependymomas of young children and only rarely encountered in adult-onset ependymomas of the spinal cord. Regional necrosis without pseudopalisades is a common finding in posterior fossa ependymomas and alone does not brand a lesion as anaplastic. An elevated MIB-1 labeling index has been correlated with aggressive histology and poor outcome, but requires verification as an independent prognostic variable and is currently irrelevant to treatment planning.[440,159,171]

Despite their preferential distribution in and around the ventricular system, intracranial ependymomas only occasionally give rise to symptomatic CSF-borne metastasis; the utility of histologic assessment in predicting this complication is, again, open to question. Distant extraneural metastasis is rare, fatal ependymomas usually killing by virtue of uncontrollable progression at the primary site. Reproducibly effective forms of adjuvant treatment for this disease are yet to be devised.

The **myxopapillary ependymoma** is a morphologically distinctive variant virtually restricted to the region of the conus medullaris and filum terminale.[466,471] An origin in cervicothoracic segments of the spinal cord is exceptional, an intracranial presentation exceedingly rare.[453] Typically of myxopapillary type are unusual extradural ependymomas that arise in the subcutaneous tissues overlying the sacrococcyx[443,448] or, less often, in the sacrum proper.[457] These curious lesions probably originate from ependymal rests representing remnants of the extradural filum terminale or coccygeal medullary vestige, a derivative of the caudal neural tube persisting beneath the skin of the postanal pit as an ependyma-lined cleft. Such rests can exhibit myxopapillary features and should not be construed as neoplastic by sole virtue of this growth pattern.[460]

Myxopapillary ependymomas share with other intramedullary tumors of the ependymal series a predilection for adults in the third to fifth decades of life, though nearly one fifth of those in a large Mayo Clinic series[466] involved patients younger than 20 years of age (some of them children). Nearly all produce low back pain, other manifestations including sciatica, sensorimotor deficits, impotence, urinary, and fecal incontinence. Neuroimaging studies usually demonstrate a sharply delimited, contrast-enhancing mass. Surgical exploration typically discloses a highly vascularized, ovoid or sausage-shaped mass that may be invested by a fibrous pseudocapsule derived from the stroma of the filum. Advanced examples can envelop the cauda equina, erode into neighboring bony structures, and infiltrate paraspinal soft tissues. A gelatinous appearance is characteristic on sectioning, many examples evidencing hemorrhagic discoloration.

The myxopapillary ependymoma is named for the manner in which cuboidal tumor cells drape themselves about a basophilic, mucinous material that in turn collars stromal blood vessels and collects in microcystic spaces (Fig. 28.68). Many examples contain, in addition, spindly elements that may engage in the formation of gliovascular pseudorosettes. A report of "giant cell" ependymomas arising in the filum terminale includes depiction of an example containing conventional myxopapillary components.[472] Present in select cases are eosinophilic spherules ("balloons") possibly representing amalgamated collagen fibrils, myxoid matrix components, and basal lamina materials.[466] Common degenerative alterations include vascular sclerosis, hemorrhage, and hemosiderin deposition. Longstanding cases are at times characterized by extensive fibrous tissue overgrowth and virtual obliteration of their neoplastic cellular elements.

The histologic presentation of the myxopapillary ependymoma is in most cases sufficiently distinctive as to render it instantly recognizable to the pathologist familiar with this entity. Particularly myxomatous variants may assume a chordoma-like appearance whereas examples dominated by spindle cell elements may be mistaken for schwannomas of spinal nerve root origin. A characteristic immunophenotype, as well as a patently ependymal fine structure, distinguishes myxopapillary ependymomas from these neoplasms, from mucinous carcinomas, myxochordoid meningiomas, and paragangliomas of the cauda equine region.[434,466,470] The former share with other ependymomas the coexpression of vimentin, S-100 protein, and GFAP, but do not elaborate EMA, chromogranin, or carcinoembryonic antigen (CEA) and exhibit little, if any, labeling for CAM 5.2, CK7, or CK20. The ultrastructural specializations previously detailed in reference to other ependymomas are similarly evidenced by myxopapillary variants, though the latter are often less conspicuously endowed with cilia and microvilli, consistently elaborate basal lamina material that may invest cells as a continuous basement membrane, and may contain a unique and specific ultrastructural marker consisting of microtubules aggregated within cisternae of rough endoplasmic reticulum.[445]

Myxopapillary ependymomas are indolent and generally amenable to surgical cure. Five of seventy-seven (6.5%) afflicted patients described in the Mayo Clinic series[466] died of their disease but did so following repeated local recurrences over periods ranging from 12 to 15 years. The presence of cytologic atypism and modest mitotic activity did not alter the prognosis in this study, whereas lesions amenable only to subtotal resection recurred and progressed more frequently than tumors lending themselves to complete removal. The need for prolonged postoperative surveillance is underscored by the fact that 15% of patients experienced late recurrences that became manifest an average of 5.8 years following gross total excision. Myxopapillary ependymomas occasionally spread to higher levels of the central neuraxis via the CSF and rarely metastasize to the lungs,

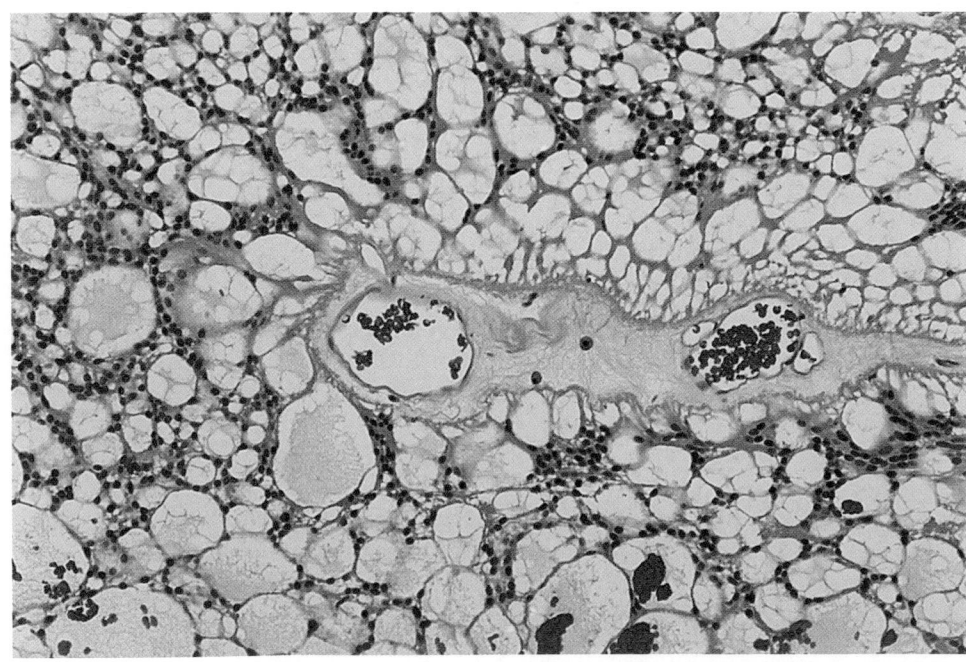

Fig. 28.68 Myxopapillary ependymoma. Note the manner in which mucinous material separates draping tumor cells from a hyalinized vascular core and accumulates in rounded microcysts.

liver, lymph nodes, or bone.[437,471] The latter phenomenon typically complicates stubbornly recurring tumors that have gained access to extravertebral soft tissues, and is encountered at substantially increased frequency in patients with extradural variants arising in the sacrococcygeal region.[448,457] Neuroradiologic survey of the spinal axis is mandatory before a diagnosis of primary intracranial myxopapillary ependymoma can be accepted. We have seen neurosurgical intervention prompted by complaints referable to expanding cerebellopontine angle or suprasellar myxopapillary ependymomas that proved to represent secondary deposits from filar region primaries. As was the case in one reported example,[431] the patients in question only later admitted to years of lower back pain.

We defer consideration of the ependymoblastoma to our discussion of primitive neuroepithelial neoplasms and conclude this section with a brief account of the **subependymoma**, a lesion named for the resemblance of its constituent cells to, and proposed origin from, subependymal neuroglia distributed along the ventricular system.[471] Most such tumors are confined to the fourth ventricle and are diminutive lesions discovered incidentally at autopsy of older men, but occasional examples attain obstructing proportions.[450] More likely to achieve symptomatic size are those exceptional subependymomas situated in the lateral ventricles (particularly tumors originating about the foramen of Monro or from the septum pellucidum), third ventricle, cerebral aqueduct, or spinal cord.[447,450] The remarkable indolence of subependymomas and their histologic resemblance to the ependymal granulations that result from chronic irritation of the ventricular surfaces have been taken as

evidence that some may have a reactive or hamartomatous etiology. Noteworthy in this regard is report of a third ventricular example developing adjacent to a craniopharyngioma, a neoplasm that consistently provokes a proliferative glial reaction.[444] As pointed out by the authors, local irradiation may also have played a role in the genesis of this unique lesion. Rare familial cases are on record.[464]

Subependymomas are usually characterized by well-delimited, lobulated contours. Small examples are typically solid and composed of rubbery or tough white tissue, whereas larger lesions often exhibit cystic change and foci of hemorrhagic discoloration. Calcification is common and may be extensive. Histologic examination discloses a multinodular growth pattern with small aggregates of tumor cells haphazardly disposed in a voluminous, hypovascular fibrillary meshwork that may be densely compacted or evidence spongy, microcystic rarefaction (Fig. 28.69). Tumor cell nuclei are generally uniform, having delicate oval contours and a punctate chromatin distribution. The occasional formation of ependymal rosettes, the occurrence of transitional or hybrid tumors containing elements of conventional ependymoma, and demonstrable ependymocytic specializations (e.g., zonulae adherentes, ciliary and microvillus arrays) on electron microscopy all serve to ally the neoplasms under discussion with other members of the ependymoma family. These evidences of ependymal differentiation notwithstanding, many subependymomas contain elements of astrocytic appearance that may assume fibrillary or gemistocytic profiles and that are devoid of prognostic import. We would emphasize that some of these benign (WHO grade I) neoplasms

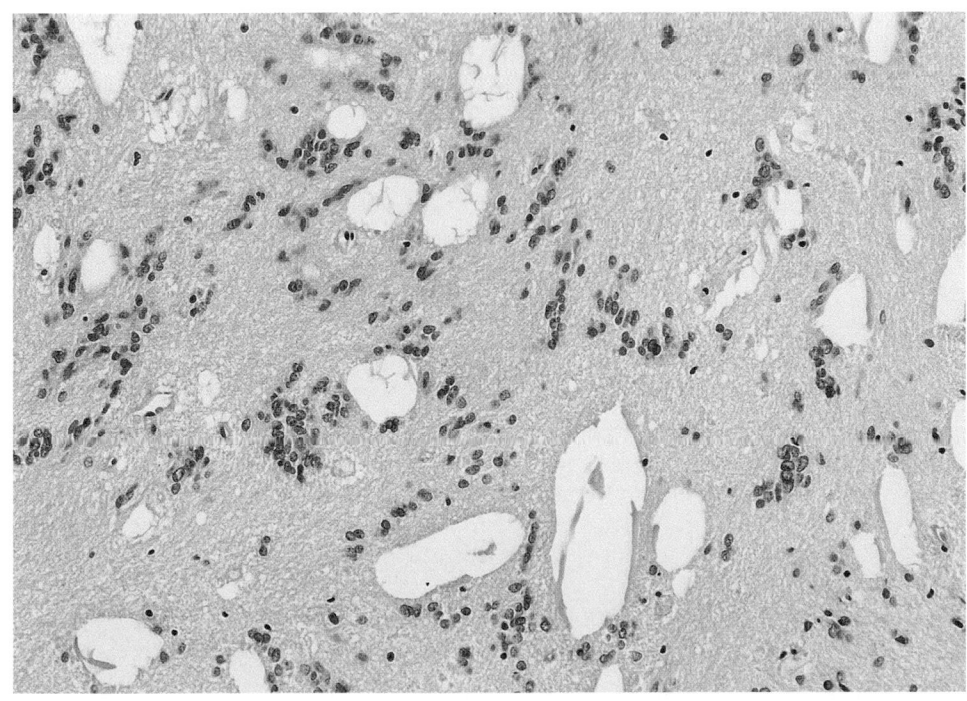

Fig. 28.69 Subependymoma. Characteristic of this entity is the huddling of small tumor cells in an expansive fibrillar meshwork. Microcystic changes commonly round out the histologic picture.

contain a subset of cells with conspicuously enlarged and atypical nuclei, manifest modest mitotic activity, and exhibit foci of coagulative necrosis without pseudopalisading. These findings are not predictive of an aggressive course.[450] A melanotic example has been depicted,[462] as have cases containing sarcomatous elements.[451,468]

Excision is the treatment of choice for subependymomas, usually sufficing for cure.[447,450] Tumors of mixed subependymoma/ependymoma morphology appear to carry a somewhat higher risk of recurrence. It is our practice, in common with many neuropathologists, to report these as ependymomas (WHO grade II) while acknowledging their subependymomatous components.

Mixed gliomas

Although there can be no disclaiming the presence within many gliomas of elements suggesting differentiation along more than a single cell line, the point at which this phenomenon merits recognition in the reporting of neurosurgical specimens remains very much a matter of subjective interpretation and personal prejudice. Some observers have insisted that constituent populations be regionally segregated, as well as cytologically distinct, or that dissimilar cell types, when closely intermingled, be represented in roughly equivalent proportion if the status of mixed glioma is to be granted. Most common in either guise are "**oligoastrocytomas**"—i.e., neoplasms exhibiting combined oligodendroglial and astrocytic appearances.[474–479] These are largely supratentorial tumors of adulthood that favor the frontal and temporal lobes. They may be divided into low-grade and anaplastic variants, the latter characterized by high cellularity, conspicuous cytologic atypism, readily apparent mitotic activity and, in some cases, microvascular proliferation and necrosis. These diagnoses should be reserved for tumors harboring neoplastic astrocytes that exhibit the cytologic features expected of the conventional fibrillary or gemistocytic astrocytoma. Oligodendrogliomas composed in part of GFAP-positive, "minigemistocytic" elements retaining the oligodendrocyte's rounded nuclear profile and compacted chromatin do not qualify. In a similar vein, oligodendroglioma-like regions are not infrequently encountered in pilocytic astrocytomas and in dysembryoplastic neuroepithelial tumors (discussed in a later section) but, in these settings, are considered part of the diagnosis.

Given the subjective nature of judgments regarding just what qualifies as astrocytic versus oligodendroglial (and how much of either compels acknowledgment), it should come as no surprise that oligoastrocytoma is among the least reproducible diagnoses in surgical neuropathology and that oligoastrocytic neoplasms as morphologically defined do not constitute a homogeneous biologic entity. Two distinct genetic variants have been delineated.[478] One, often composed in the main of classic oligodendrogliomatous elements, shares with the majority of pure oligodendrogliomas combined deletions of chromosomes 1p and 19q that are generally unaccompanied by TP53 abnomalities. These deletions are far more characteristic of oligoastrocytomas arising in the frontal, parietal and occipital regions than of those situated in the temporal lobes or basal ganglia.[418] The second, frequently astrocyte-predominant, exhibits TP53 mutations or loss of heterozygosity involving chromosome 17p with intact 1p/19q status—i.e., the genotype characterizing most fibrillary and gemistocytic astrocytomas. Treatment responsiveness and survival intervals exceeding those associated with purely astrocytic neoplasms of diffuse type would further ally a subset of oligoastrocytic tumors with oligodendrogliomas in unalloyed form.[475,477,479] Accordingly, we agree that even minor components of conventionally oligodendrogliomatous appearance should be "captured" in the reporting of neurosurgical material[474] and so apply the label oligoastrocytoma rather liberally. As mentioned previously, isolated 1p/19q chromosomal deletions are a marker of chemosensitivity and prolonged survival when deleted in pure oligodendrogliomas.[402,409,425] Should such deletions prove to consistently identify "mixed" lesions of comparable clinical biology, ration might be imposed on the management of affected patients. Similar considerations apply to a distressingly common group of "transitional" neoplasms populated by elements that resist rigid classification as either oligodendrocytic or astroglial. We simply term these infiltrative gliomas and comment on their ambiguous features.

As previously discussed, clear cell components histologically identical to oligodendroglioma may be found within otherwise conventional ependymomas, particularly supratentorial examples. The demonstration that these elements retain ependymocytic features at the ultrastructural level calls into question descriptions of mixed oligodendroglial and ependymal tumors.[476] In fact, we have not encountered a glioma that could be proved to differentiate along divergent, oligoependymal lines. With regard to other forms of mixed glial neoplasia, we have on occasion resorted halfheartedly to the diagnosis of ependymoastrocytoma for infiltrative tumors of partially astrocytic aspect exhibiting foci of conspicuous pseudorosette formation. The neoplastic cells forming such gliovascular structures, however, often retain astrocytic nuclear features and elaborate cytoplasmic processes considerably coarser than those of the classic ependymoma. The diagnosis of ependymoastrocytoma should not be extended to the common fourth ventricular ependymoma harboring minor components of astrocytic appearance.

Astroblastoma

The **astroblastoma** is a rare and somewhat controversial glial neoplasm that usually presents as a well-demarcated, contrast-enhancing mass in the cerebral hemisphere of a child, adolescent, or young adult.[480,481,486] The lesion is characterized by a papilliform architecture, its radially arranged cellular elements directing unipolar cytoplasmic processes toward centrally placed stromal blood vessels (Fig. 28.70). The latter are prone to progressive collagenous thickening and hyalinization, a striking feature of most cases that may advance to partial fibrous obliteration of the neoplastic tissue. Astroblastomatous cell processes are shorter, stouter and less tapering than those forming ependymal-type pseudorosettes, differing further in their termination on target vessels as expanded footplates. Whereas ependymomatous pseudorosettes generally lie embedded in a dense fibrillar matrix, the gliovascular structures of the astroblastoma are only tenuously supported by an intervening population of astrocyte-like tumor cells or appear to float unanchored in tissue sections. Cytoplasmic immunolabeling for vimentin, S-100 protein, and GFAP are the rule, though the last may be faint or only focally demonstrable.[480–484] Reactivity for low molecular weight cytokeratins[482] and EMA[482] has also been depicted, but expression of synaptophysin has not been demonstrated.

Described ultrastructural attributes of the astroblastoma include a rich cytoplasmic complement of intermediate filaments, intercellular junctional complexes that may be well developed but that usually fall short of the elaborate zonulae adherentes characterizing ependymomas, and an investing basal lamina separating polar cell processes from adjoining stromal vessels.[480,483,485] In select cases constituent cells have been found to display certain ultrastructural features characteristic of "tanycytes," ventricular lining elements that normally extend basal cytoplasmic processes towards regional capillaries.[485] These include "purse string"-like constrictions of cell apices and crowning microvilli as well as lamellar cytoplasmic interdigitations ("pleats") along lateral cell borders. Evidence of neuronal differentiation has not been detected.

Inasmuch as conventional astrocytomas of diffuse type (particularly gemistocytic variants) may occasionally harbor gliovascular formations comparable to those of the astroblastoma, the latter designation is best reserved for tumors with a pure, or at least dominant, architecture of the type just described and a circumscribed, compact growth pattern. These may be divided into prognostically favorable and unfavorable types, although the correlation of histology and outcome is, admittedly, imperfect.[480,481,486] Tumors of orderly histologic aspect throughout and inconspicuous mitotic activity appear to be amenable to long-term control by surgical resection, the role of adjuvant therapy being unclear. Examples manifesting a breakdown in astroblastomatous architecture with regions of solid growth, conspicuous mitotic activity, and cellular atypia (accompanied, in some cases, by microvascular proliferation and large zones of coagulative necrosis) are overrepresented among recurring and fatal cases. These "anaplastic astroblastomas" may develop diffusely infiltrating components, some seeding the CSF. That aggressive-looking variants may yet retain the circumscription typical of well-differentiated astroblastomas, rendering operative extirpation feasible, probably accounts for instances of unexpectedly long disease-free survival and cure in this setting, though most recorded cases have also been subjected to irradiation.

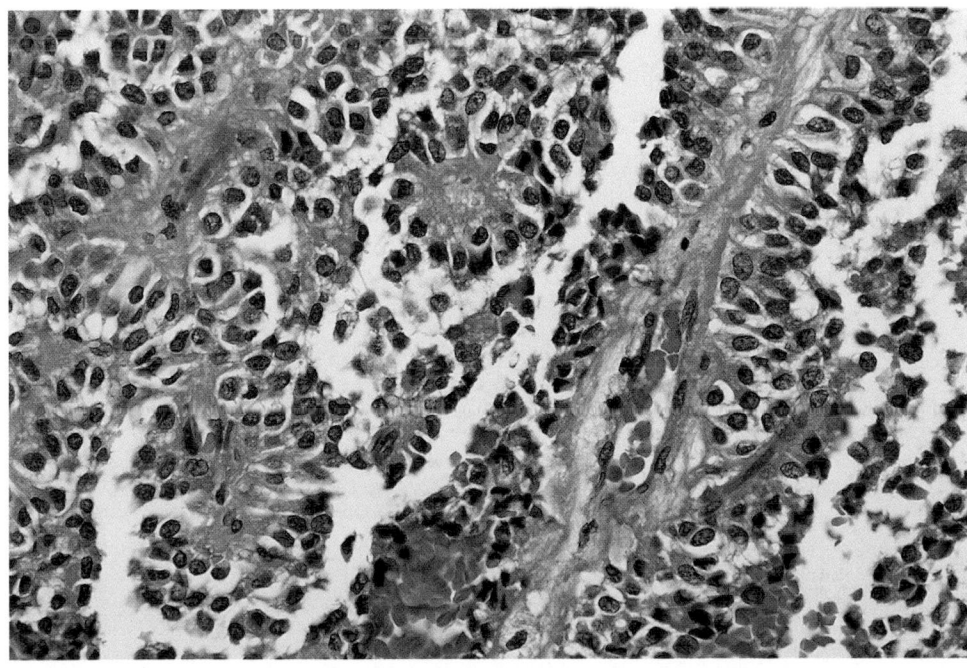

Fig. 28.70 Astroblastoma. The stout cytoplasmic processes of this papillary neoplasm's constituent cells taper rapidly toward supporting vascular cores.

Whether astroblastomas constitute an entity sui generis is controversial, some neuropathologists viewing these as simply variants of astrocytoma or ependymoma. A recent study suggests that combined gains of chromosomes 19 and 20q, generally foreign to conventional astrocytic and ependymal neoplasms, are particularly frequent in this rare tumor group.[481] Though this does not speak to the cytogenesis of astroblastomas, it does argue for their being accorded distinct nosologic status.

Chordoid glioma of the third ventricle

The rare neoplasms reported as **chordoid gliomas of the third ventricle** have occurred almost exclusively in adults, an excess affecting women.[487–492] As implied by their site-specific designation, these have been limited to the third ventricular/suprasellar compartment. Here they present on neuroradiologic study as large, solid, sharply circumscribed and homogeneously contrast-enhancing masses producing obstructive hydrocephalus and an array of clinical manifestations that potentially include headache, ataxia, visual and endocrine disturbances, marked fluctuations of weight and psychotic/organic brain syndromes.

The chordoid glioma is noninfiltrative in its growth pattern and composed of epithelioid, oval to polygonal cells disposed as irregular cords or nests within a basophilic, myxoid matrix prone to coarse vacuolation (Fig. 28.71A). The latter may be PAS/DPAS-positive and faintly mucicarminophilic. Tumor cells possess eosinophilic cytoplasm and round or oval nuclei with finely granular or clumped chromatin and small nucleoli. Cell cords and nests may be outlined by reticulin fibers. An additional, near constant feature of this peculiar neoplasm is interstitial and perivascular infiltration by lymphocytes and Russell body-bearing plasma cells.

A unique pediatric example manifesting chondroid metaplasia has been recorded.[488] Pertinent to the differential diagnosis (which includes metastatic carcinoma, intradural chordoma, and chordoid meningioma) is the absence of true gland formation, physaliphorous cells, cellular whorls, intranuclear pseudoinclusions, and psammoma bodies. Mitoses are not found or are rare (MIB-1 labeling indices generally fall in the 0–1.5% range), conspicuous pleomorphism, microvascular proliferation, and necrosis also being foreign to these lesions. Adjacent brain tissue typically manifests reactive gliosis with Rosenthal fiber formation.

A characteristic immunoprofile segregates chordoid gliomas from potential mimickers.[487–489] The former consistently evidence diffuse cytoplasmic labeling for GFAP (Fig. 28.71B) as well as vimentin, express CD34 (with cell membrane accentuation), and may be focally S-100 protein-positive, but are EMA-negative or only focally EMA-immunoreactive. Limited labeling for a variety of cytokeratins has been reported,[487,492] though the AE1/3 "cocktail" may yield a pattern overlapping with that of GFAP preparations. Cytoplasmic immunolabeling for epidermal growth factor receptor and merlin/schwannomin have also been recorded, but examples assessed to date have not evidenced reactivity for synaptophysin, neurofilament proteins, estrogen or progesterone receptors, desmin, chromogranin or p53.[492] The limited ultrastructural experience communicated thus far suggests that chordoid gliomas differentiate along ependymal lines. While such pathognomonic ependymal specializations as microlumens delimited by intercellular junctional complexes of zonula adherens type have not been depicted, the formation of desmosome-like cytoplasmic attachments, microvilli, partially investing basal lamina and, in one case,[490] aberrant

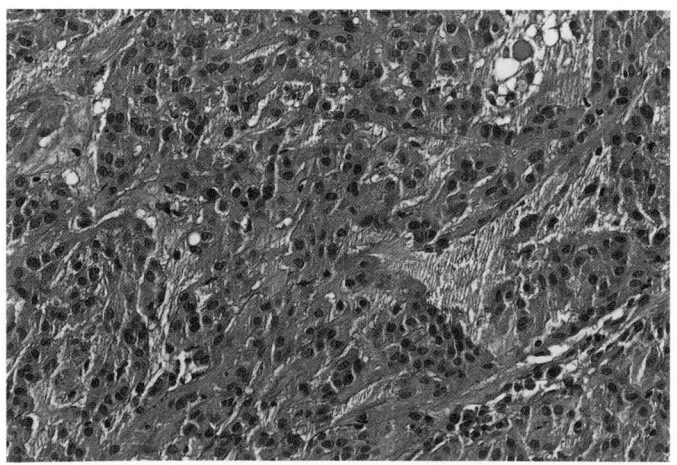

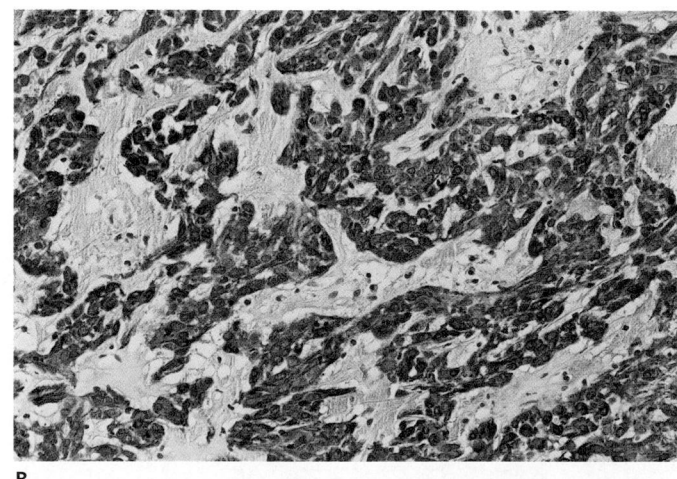

A **B**

Fig. 28.71 Chordoid glioma of the third ventricle. Nests and anastomosing cords of epithelioid tumor cells arrayed against a variably myxoid stromal background typify this lesion (**A**), which is distinguished from other chordoid neoplasms by its diffuse cytoplasmic immunolabeling for GFAP (**B**). Note also in **A** the presence of plasma cells at lower right. These are often present in more conspicuous numbers.

juxtanuclear cilia would seem to ally these unusual tumors with neoplasms of the ependymocytic series and to distance them from the astrocytic and oligodendroglial families.[487,489,491] In this connection, we would mention personal experience with an example containing papillary perivascular pseudorosettes and alveolus-like structures.[491] Chordoid gliomas have been described in one report as sharing certain ultrastructural properties with specially modified ependymal cells that constitute the subcommissural organ—an ostensibly secretory body, situated in the dorsocaudal aspect of the third ventricle, that develops fully during human embryonic life and undergoes postnatal involution.[489] Common features included zonation of cell bodies into: a perinuclear region containing prominent profiles of rough endoplasmic reticulum and Golgi apparatus; an intermediate region occupied principally by mitochondria, smooth endoplasmic reticulum and secretory-type granules; and an apical zone displaying a rich complement of intermediate filaments and crowning microvilli.

Chordoid gliomas of the third ventricle grow slowly, do not invade surrounding tissues, and have not been reported to metastasize via the CSF, but their attachment to hypothalamic/suprasellar structures complicates removal. Curiously, pulmonary thromboembolism has accounted for a disproportionate share of deaths occurring in the immediate postoperative period.[487,492] Incompletely resected examples may remain relatively stable but can regrow and eventually prove fatal.[487] The role of adjuvant therapy is undefined.

Gliomatosis cerebri

Gliomatosis cerebri, as traditionally and stringently defined, is a rare condition in which large portions of the brain are permeated by neoplastic cells in such manner as to suggest a transformative "field effect" rather than the centrifugal spread of an initially localized glial tumor.[493,498] Affected regions are typically expanded in nondestructive ("pseudohypertrophic") fashion without formation of appreciable tumor nodules. The process may be remarkably extensive at presentation, potentially involving the entire central neuraxis.[495] Formerly reserved for cases examined at autopsy, this diagnosis is now rendered on clinical grounds when biopsy material demonstrating a diffusely infiltrative glioma derives from a patient evidencing particularly widespread neuroradiologic abnormalities. Confluent multilobar and bihemispheric zones of T2 signal hyperintensity are characteristic on MRI.[496–498]

Gliomatosis cerebri is neither a uniform morphologic entity nor a condition that can be reliably identified on cytologic or histologic grounds alone. While most examples exhibit fibrillary astroglial features, participating gemistocytic populations have been described,[499] as has "oligodendrogliomatosis."[494] Unusually elongated nuclear profiles in parallel array (the result of tumor cell infiltration between compacted nerve fibers) and a tendency to pronounced subpial, perivascular and circumneuronal cellular aggregation are often emphasized as especially characteristic, but are by no means specific, or even constant, attributes.[493] There is, moreover, considerable variation in GFAP expression (not demonstrable in some cases), in mitotic activity and proliferative potential as assessed by MIB-1 (Ki-67) immunolabeling.[497,498]

It should come as no surprise, given the foregoing observations, that the clinical course of gliomatosis cerebri is not strictly predictable (apart from the generally poor prognosis and eventual lethality of bona fide cases). A comprehensive review of reported patients found that 52% died within 12 months, and 73% within 3 years, of symptom onset.[496] A more protracted evolution, however, characterizes some cerebral gliomatoses of low histologic grade. Limited Ki-67 immunolabeling has also been correlated with less aggressive behavior.[497] Focal or multicentric progression to the picture of anaplastic astrocytoma or glioblastoma may complicate otherwise well-differentiated examples. The reader interested in issues of histogenesis (unknown) and pertinent genetic data (fragmentary) is referred elsewhere.[498] Suffice it to say that the latter generally support the clonal nature of gliomatosis and provide some evidence for a potential cellular origin or pathogenesis distinct from that of the conventional astrocytomas of diffuse type.

Pituicytoma

We briefly mention a very rare neoplasm of the sellar and suprasellar compartments that is believed to derive from specialized glial elements, known as "pituicytes," native to the neurohypophysis and infundibulum. The **pituicytoma** seems to be a tumor of adulthood with presenting manifestations (principally headache and visual disturbances) indistinguishable from those attending nonfunctional pituitary adenomas.[500] Composed of spindled cells in compact fascicular or storiform array, this may be misconstrued as a "fibrous histiocytoma," meningioma, schwannoma or pilocytic astrocytoma. Immunolabeling for S-100 protein, variable GFAP reactivity, a general absence of intercellular reticulin or type IV collagen and failure to fashion Rosenthal fibers, eosinophilic granular bodies or microcysts collectively serve to distinguish this oddity from such mimickers. Immunonegativity for chromogranin, synaptophysin and adenohypophyseal hormones further distances this lesion from spindled variants of pituitary adenoma,[500,501] though one studied case exhibited evidence of neuroendocrine differentiation (including secretory granule formation) at the ultrastructural level.[501] The latter raises the possibility that at least some pituicytomas in fact derive from pluripotent folliculostellate cells of the anterior pituitary[501]—interstitial elements recently forwarded as the progenitors of select "spindle cell oncocytomas" arising in the latter location.[502] Unlike the normal neurohypophysis, which also contains prominent spindle cell elements, the pituicytoma is devoid of bundled axons and does not harbor the granular axonal swellings termed Herring bodies. Mitoses are usually not demonstrable or are rare, the overall appearance being that of a histologically benign (though potentially rather cellular) lesion. Gross total resection is the treatment of choice, incompletely excised examples having the potential for local regrowth. Of note, one affected patient had previously been treated for endocrine tumors that included parathyroid adenoma and follicular carcinoma of the thyroid.[503]

Gliomesenchymal tumors

A variety of unusual tumors are characterized by "mixed" neuroepithelial (specifically glial) and mesenchymal features. The most common of these peculiar neoplasms is the **gliosarcoma**,[506,514,518] traditionally regarded as a variant of glioblastoma multiforme in which proliferating mesodermal elements associated with the latter's hyperplastic microvasculature secondarily undergo neoplastic transformation. Sarcomatous change has been estimated to occur in some 2% of glioblastomas.[514] The designation of sarcoglioma has been extended to exceedingly rare, malignant gliomesenchymal tumors for which the reverse of the foregoing scenario is postulated (i.e., intracranial sarcomas and meningiomas complicated by the progression to neoplasia of commingled, reactive astrocytic elements).[513,515]

The clinical profile of the gliosarcoma is essentially that of the primary glioblastoma.[514,518] Most tumors arise in the absence of recognized predisposing factors, but gliosarcomas have been associated with prior irradiation,[518] including the intracranial instillation of Thorotrast.[524] At operation, many are initially mistaken for cerebral metastases or (when attached to the dura) meningiomas, errors resulting from their characteristic circumscription and firm textures. These attributes in turn reflect the high content of connective tissue fibers typical of the gliosarcoma but foreign to most other neuroepithelial neoplasms. A marmoreal admixture of gliomatous and sarcomatous tissues lends to these tumors a strikingly biphasic architecture on histologic study (Fig. 28.72A). The former are nearly always astrocytic and overtly high-grade, most exhibiting the features of full-blown glioblastoma, although examples derived from oligodendrogliomas[516] and subependymomas[451,468] are on record. Gland-like or "adenoid" formations and squamous metaplasia may be observed in the glial portions of select cases.[329,339] Mesenchymal components usually evidence appearances that would prompt the diagnosis of fibrosarcoma or malignant fibrous histiocytoma in a soft tissue setting. A subset contain chondroosseous,[510] muscle,[504] or mixed mesenchymal[517] elements and differentiation along endothelial lines has also been described.[522] A unique example of multifocal intramedullary "astrolipoma" composed of low-grade astroglial and well-differentiated adipocyte-like elements has also been recorded.[521] We have previously alluded to admixed lipoma-like components in ependymomas.[463]

Distinction of the gliosarcoma's neuroepithelial and mesenchymal constituents can be accomplished using a combination of traditional histochemical and immunocytochemical techniques.[508,514,518] The latter are richly invested with connective tissue fibers demonstrable by reticulin impregnation methods and preparations for collagen, such as the Mallory trichrome stain, but do not express GFAP, the reverse being true of the glial population (Fig. 28.72B). The identification of an architecturally and cytologically distinct, GFAP-negative component is requisite to the segregation of the true gliosarcoma from collagenized, spindle cell ("desmoplastic") glioblastomas and gliomas associated with a florid fibroblastic reaction by virtue of meningeal invasion. Similar considerations apply to "metaplastic" variants of astrocytoma and ependymoma that give rise to GFAP-immunoreactive, cartilaginous elements.[512]

As previously discussed in connection with the astrocytomas of diffuse type, the complex microvascular proliferation characteristic of glioblastomas is driven by the tumoral elaboration of mitogens that act on endothelium, pericytes, smooth muscle cells, and fibroblasts. Each of these cell types has been championed as the target of neoplastic transformation within evolving gliosarcomas, as have histiocytes, myofibroblasts and uncommitted adventitial elements. That this autocrine phenomenon eventuates in sarcomatous outgrowth—a notion originally based on perceived histologic transitions from the hyperplastic to unarguably malignant—has received qualified support from immunohistochemical observations. Reports that the sarcomatous constituents of the gliosarcoma label for endothelial markers (Factor VIII-related antigen and the UEA-1 lectin) or contain Weibel–Palade bodies on ultrastructural study[522] have not proven generally reproducible,[508] but we agree that these populations often exhibit focal immunoreactivity for smooth muscle actin[509,518]—a feature shared by cells of pericytic/myoid type which dominate the glomeruloid microvascular formations typical of the glioblastoma.[322,354]

A rival histogenetic view of the gliosarcoma would have neoplastic glial cells simply undergoing phenotypic shift with tumor progression, losing GFAP expression and assuming mesenchymal attributes.[511,520] Powerful backing for this scenario derives from molecular genetic studies demonstrating that gliomatous and sarcomatous components may harbor identical TP53 and PTEN mutations, p16 (CDKN2A) deletions and coamplifications of CDK4 and MDM2.[520] Whether a subset of tumors accorded this designation might still represent true composites is arguable.

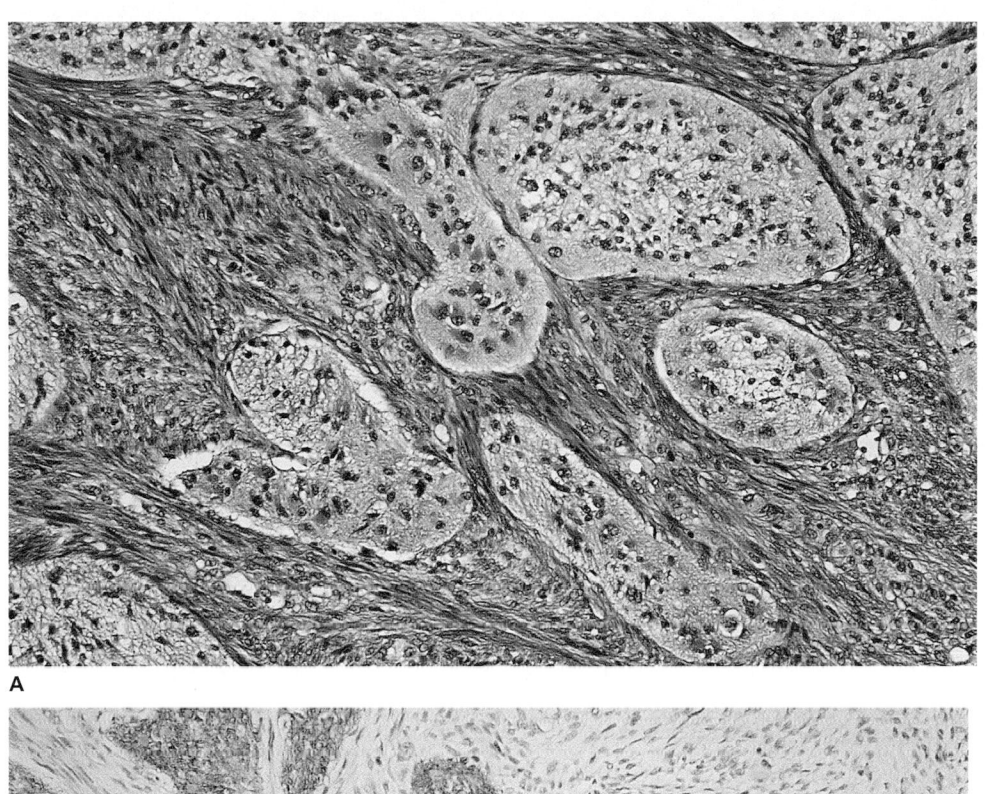

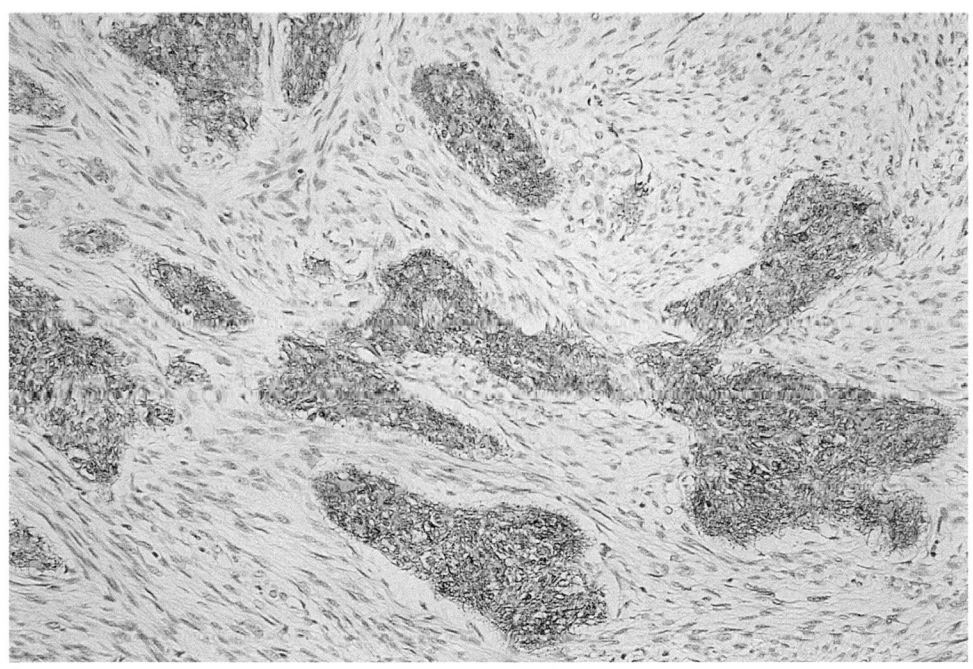

Fig. 28.72 Gliosarcoma. Islands of astrocytic tumor tissue lie embedded in what otherwise appears to be a spindle cell sarcoma (**A**). On immunoperoxidase assay (**B**), only astrocytic elements are labeled for glial fibrillary acidic protein.

The designation "**gliofibroma**" has been extended to a somewhat heterogeneous group of neoplasms encountered for the most part in childhood and having in common a population of astrocytes invested by basal lamina material and embedded in a variably collagenized matrix.[506] Some appear to represent desmoplastic astrocytomas in which neoplastic glia, unaided by mesenchymal derivatives, are directly responsible for the elaboration of connective tissues,[519] whereas other examples contain a second cellular population variously interpreted as fibroblastic[506] or schwannian.[523] The rarity and disparate morphologic features of the tumors reported under this rubric obviously preclude useful generalizations regarding their histogenesis and clinical biology. A number of recorded cases have evidenced conspicuous cytologic atypism and mitotic activity, pursuing an aggressive course (with CSF-borne metastasis) and ending fatally, the benign connotations of the term gliofibroma notwithstanding.[506] A more favorable outcome seems to be attached to those lacking features of histologic anaplasia.

This discussion of gliomesenchymal tumors is concluded with passing reference to the various uses of the term "**angioglioma**." Originally applied to what would now be classified as the cellular variant of cerebellar hemangioblastoma, this designation has been most frequently invoked in reference to gliomas exhibiting degenerative vascular alterations resembling AVMs or cavernous angiomas.[126] Slow-growing lesions such as pilocytic astrocytomas, oligodendrogliomas and gangliogliomas seem especially prone to such changes. These may appear hypervascular on angiographic study, exhibiting a tumoral "blush," but as a rule do not evidence the shunting characteristic of true AVMs. Only exceptionally are the latter found in contiguity with glial neoplasms. Most such lesions are regarded as "collision" tumors in which gliomatous and malformative tissues are fortuitously associated, but isolated reports of glial neoplasms secondarily arising at the sites of pre-existent AVMs and angiomas suggest that the gliotic reaction typical of tissues surrounding such longstanding vascular anomalies may rarely progress to neoplasia.[507] A strikingly increased concentration of oligodendrocytes in and around some AVMs appears to result from "collapse" of chronically edematous and ischemic white matter or to represent part of the malformation process and should not necessarily prompt a diagnosis of oligodendroglioma.[126,132] Finally, we call attention to a group of exceedingly uncommon tumors interpreted as containing both gliomatous and hemangioblastomatous elements.[505] These, too, have been described as a form of "angioglioma," a nonspecific and potentially misleading term that is probably best abandoned.

Choroid plexus tumors

A secretory organ responsible for the production of CSF, the choroid plexus consists of a richly vascularized fibrous stroma draped by an epithelium that derives from neuroectodermal cells abutting the embryonic ventricular system. Only rarely do its specialized epithelial elements give rise to neoplasms, these generally affecting children and presenting in sporadic fashion. Tumors of the choroid plexus, however, are known to occasionally complicate the familial Li–Fraumeni (germline p53 mutation) syndrome[525,548] and have been recorded in connection with a complex of infantile flexor spasms, agenesis of the corpus callosum and chorioretinal anomalies known as Aicardi syndrome.[543] That human choroid plexus tumors, like ependymomas, may harbor simian virus 40-type DNA sequences is intriguing, given the fact that expression of this agent's T antigen is specifically associated with choroid plexus neoplasia in transgenic murine models, but an etiologic link in the former scenario (as opposed to passenger effect) is yet to be established.[525] Of special note is the reported association of human choroid plexus carcinomas with germline and somatic alterations affecting a gene—hSNF5/INI1—located at chromosome 22q11.2 and implicated in the genesis of renal and extrarenal rhabdoid tumors, including the atypical teratoid/rhabdoid tumor indigenous to

the CNS.[545,550] Interestingly, a subset of the lesions in question have manifested rhabdoid cytologic profiles as well as complex immunophenotypes somewhat similar to those characteristic of the latter entity.[550]

Tumors derived from the epithelium of the choroid plexus exhibit considerable morphologic and biologic diversity. The great majority, however, are benign neoplasms that replicate the villous architecture of the parent organ and are consequently termed **choroid plexus papillomas**.[525,541,542] Most of the latter come to attention during early childhood, displaying a predilection for the lateral ventricles. Adult cases, by contrast, are situated more often in the fourth ventricle or its lateral recesses, some presenting as tumors of the cerebellopontine angle. A multifocal presentation is on record,[551] as are ectopic intraparenchymal and primary suprasellar examples.[537] Associated clinical manifestations are largely those of hydrocephalus resulting from ventricular outflow obstruction or the excessive production of CSF by these highly differentiated neoplasms. Rarely, plexus-related hydrocephalus is caused by villous hyperplasia of this organ.[527]

On gross inspection, the choroid plexus papilloma is a friable mass having a villiform or bosselated surface often likened to that of a cauliflower (Fig. 28.73). Calcification, common to these tumors, imparts to some a gritty consistency or, when extensive, stony hardness that may hinder sectioning in the undecalcified state. Histologic examination typically discloses a complex array of branching fibrovascular fronds covered by a monolayer of uniform cuboidal or columnar epithelial cells exhibiting minimal nuclear atypism and little, if any, mitotic activity (Fig. 28.74). On ultrastructural study these cells rest on an uninterrupted basement membrane, are joined at their apices by elaborate junctional complexes, are crowned by microvilli, and may be ciliated.[538] The tumoral stroma, like that of the normal choroid

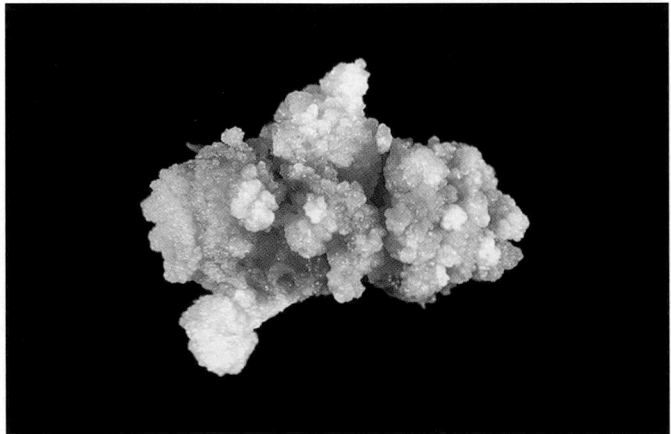

Fig. 28.73 Choroid plexus papilloma. Note the characteristically bosselated surface of this surgically resected example. Deprived of its blood supply, the tumor tissue loses its normally hyperemic appearance and may assume a tan or golden hue.

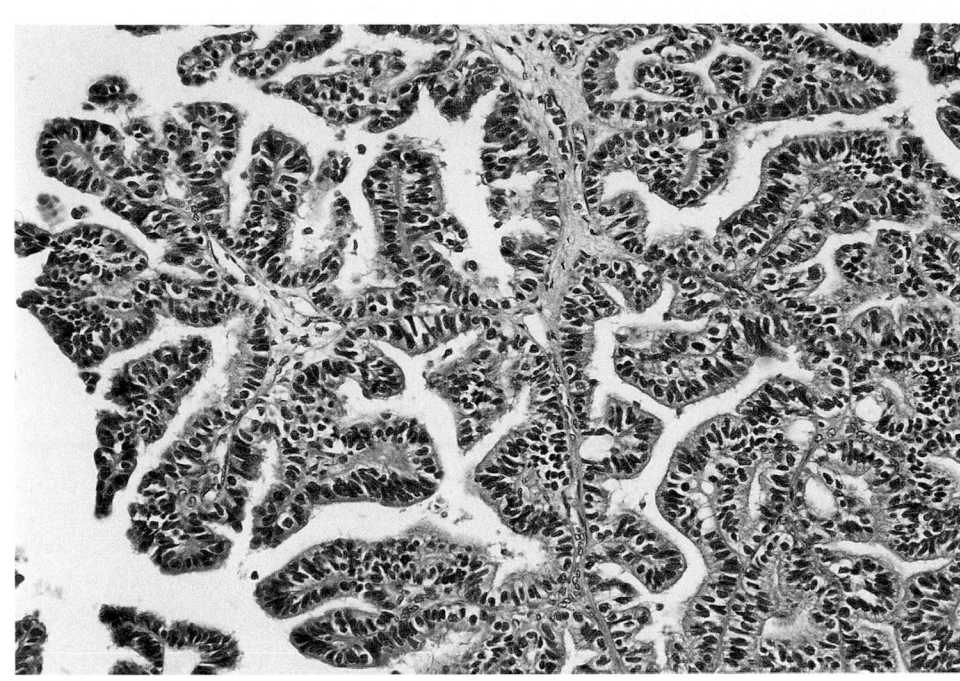

Fig. 28.74 Choroid plexus papilloma. This example's delicate fibrovascular fronds are covered by an orderly, low columnar epithelium.

plexus, may be conspicuously infiltrated by foamy macrophages and is, in select cases, the site of metaplastic bone or cartilage formation.[544] The epithelial elements of some tumors undergo oncocytic change (one reported example progressing to malignant "oncocytoma"[529]) and a rare melanotic variant of the choroid plexus papilloma has also been described.[549] These neoplasms may, in addition, evidence limited ependymal differentiation, signaled by foci in which tumor cells extend tapering, GFAP-immunoreactive cytoplasmic processes toward their fibrovascular cores. This finding presumably reflects the ontogeny of the plexus epithelium as a form of specialized ependyma, but choroid plexus papillomas do not elaborate the fibrillary glial "stroma" characteristic of ependymomas—an important differential diagnostic feature. Exceptional cases exhibit a glandular, rather than papillary, growth pattern—an arrangement for which the designations of acinar or tubular choroid plexus adenoma have been invoked.[531,547] Some of these curious variants have been mucin-producing.

The well-differentiated choroid plexus papilloma is a noninvasive growth that is usually amenable to curative resection.[525] The capacity of otherwise conventional examples to seed the CSF and metastasize along the central neuraxis is a recognized but, fortunately, uncommon phenomenon. More problematic is a subset of tumors, often dubbed **atypical choroid plexus papillomas**, that fall short of overt histologic malignancy while evidencing an unexpectedly complex architecture, cytologic atypism, and increased mitotic activity or penetration of juxtatumoral brain tissue.[525,541] Some have noted an increased likelihood of recurrence and progression to histologic anaplasia on the part of tumors exhibiting

worrisome morphologic traits of this sort,[541] but this is a murky and controversial area. It has been our experience, in fact, that "invasive" tumoral deposits are not infrequently found along the perimeter of perfectly benign-appearing papillomas, where they are typically associated with a Rosenthal fiber-rich pilocytic astrogliosis attesting to a chronic and indolent process. We can attach no significance to this phenomenon.

Choroid plexus carcinoma is the appropriate designation for frankly malignant epithelial neoplasms of plexus origin. The overwhelming majority of these rare tumors present in infancy or childhood and are situated in a lateral ventricle.[540,542] In contrast to their benign counterparts, choroid plexus carcinomas are invasive, destructive, and typified by geographic foci of necrosis and hemorrhage. Many, while focally maintaining a half-hearted fidelity to the villiform architecture of the native plexus, contain foci in which their papillary structure breaks down and is replaced by nests and patternless sheets of anaplastic cells exhibiting alarming pleomorphism and mitotic activity. As previously mentioned, some have been reportedly populated by rhabdoid components associated with chromosome 22q deletion.[550] Isolated cases have been described as containing melanotic cytoplasmic pigments[530] or eosinophilic, PAS-positive and diastase-resistant globules.[539] These aggressive neoplasms often prove fatal, some escaping the confines of the ventricular system and seeding the subarachnoid space, but cure of localized examples may be effected by gross total removal.[540,542]

Application of an appropriate antibody panel can be recommended for purposes of distinguishing choroid plexus tumors from potential mimickers. The former often evidence cytoplasmic colabeling for vimentin, cytokeratins (CAM 5.2 and AE1/3 reactivity are the rule, though highly variable in extent, one study[534] describing a CK7+/CK20- immunophenotype as characterizing most plexus papillomas), and S-100 protein (potentially expressed in nuclei as well).[432,452,455,528,541] Neoplasms of the choroid plexus may, in addition, facilitate recognition of their neuroepithelial lineage by expressing GFAP (usually in focal fashion),[452,455,528,541] and the labeling of these tumors for synaptophysin has also been depicted.[536] The basis for the latter finding is unclear, as this phenomenon is divorced from fine structural indices of neuronal differentiation. As previously discussed, intracranial ependymomas (including papillary variants) often exhibit widespread GFAP reactivity, contain few, if any, CAM 5.2- or CK7-positive elements and are synaptophysin-negative. As compared to primary choroid plexus tumors, metastatic carcinomas are far more likely to exhibit immunoreactivity for EMA and the surface epithelial antigens identified by monoclonal antibodies HEA 125 and Ber EP4,[533] are less often S-100 protein-positive and (with rare exception) are GFAP-negative. Cytoplasmic labeling for transthyretin, a 55-kDa protein involved in thyroxine and retinol transport, seems to be the most restricted (i.e., specific) feature of choroid plexus tumor immunophenotype, but is inconstant and shared by a minority of epithelial tumors metastatic to brain.[526]

We stress that the diagnosis of choroid plexus carcinoma in an adult must be regarded with considerable skepticism (regardless of tumor location, morphology, or immunohistochemical characteristics) as this entity is vanishingly rare beyond childhood and older patients presenting with intracranial carcinomas, including well-differentiated lesions of papillary configuration, almost invariably prove to harbor lung or other systemic primaries. With regard to the prognostic implications of immunophenotype in the setting of choroid plexus neoplasia, we would emphasize that the benign and malignant cannot be reliably distinguished on the basis of antigenic profile, though dampened expression of transthyretin and S-100 protein seem to be more characteristic of plexus carcinomas and of papillomas that recur following resection.[528,541] Carcinomas may also be somewhat more prone to express CEA,[528] though this is generally foreign to tumors of the choroid plexus family,[541] and appear more likely to exhibit widespread nuclear p53 labeling[535] and MIB-1 (Ki-67) indices in excess of 5% to 10%.[546]

The reader's attention is called to a recent report describing as "**pigmented papillary epithelial neoplasm of the pituitary fossa**" a melanotic sellar tumor that underwent anaplastic spindle cell transformation following repeated resections and radiotherapy.[532] As suggested by the authors, this curiosity may represent an ectopic form of choroid plexus neoplasm.

Neuronal and glioneuronal tumors, hamartomas, and related lesions

Gangliocytoma and ganglioglioma

A biologically heterogeneous assortment of CNS tumors, including primitive neuroepithelial neoplasms of potentially aggressive character, are capable of neuronal differentiation and may spawn ganglion cell-like forms. The uncommon entities known as **gangliocytoma** and **ganglioglioma** (collectively termed "ganglion cell tumors") are typically indolent lesions that share a complement of large and essentially mature neurons unassociated, by definition, with recognizably embryonal elements. Much the more prevalent species, the ganglioglioma harbors an admixed glial population whereas the gangliocytoma is composed exclusively of differentiated neurons.[559] Ganglion cell tumors usually come to neurosurgical intervention within the first three decades of life,[555,565,571,576] but may be encountered in older adults.[561] By most accounts, they favor the supratentorial compartment, but examples have been described at all levels of the central neuraxis and we concur in the observation that gangliogliomas constitute a significant percentage of pediatric tumors presenting in the brainstem and spinal cord.[314,567] Even cranial nerve cases have been depicted.[553,567a] A predilection for the temporal lobes accounts for the discovery of many ganglion cell tumors in the course of evaluation for partial complex epilepsy, often of protracted duration. Albeit nonspecific, neuroradiologic presentation as a well-demarcated, partially cystic mass evidencing contrast enhancement of its solid components and foci of calcification is especially suggestive. The cerebral hemispheric lesion presenting as a discrete mural nodule within a cyst usually proves to be a ganglion cell tumor, pilocytic astrocytoma, or pleomorphic xanthoastrocytoma (for illustration of this profile see Fig. 28.57).

Common to the gangliocytoma and ganglioglioma is the irregular distribution of variably sized neurons, some of ganglion cell-like profile, in a delicate fibrillar matrix that is prone to spongy rarefaction and that often contains scattered calcospherules (Fig. 28.75). Microcystic changes are common in regions of predominantly glial composition. Whereas native neurons trapped in an advancing glial neoplasm generally manifest little cytologic alteration and tend to an even distribution and orderly polarity, the neuronal populace of the ganglion cell tumor often displays, in addition to obvious architectural disarray and anomalous clustering, conspicuous morphologic abnormalities that include striking pleomorphism, multinucleation, cytoplasmic vacuolization and, in some cases, gigantism. Rare examples have been reported to contain Alzheimer disease-type neurofibrillary tangles and other cytoplasmic inclusions seen in neurodegenerative and neuronal storage disorders.[573] Melanotic variants have been described,[572] as have

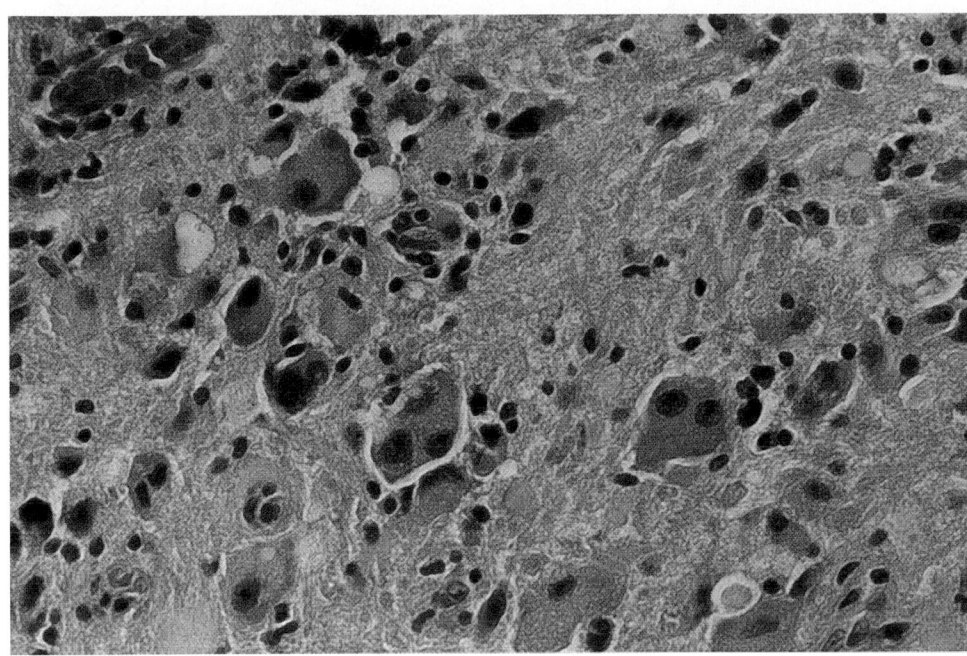

Fig. 28.75 Ganglioglioma. The neoplastic nature of the ganglion cell tumor's large neurons is readily apparent when abnormal clustering and cytologic abnormalities such as multinucleation are in evidence. Note admixed small lymphocytes, a common feature. Elsewhere this example harbored astrocytic elements.

ganglion cell tumors associated with (possibly progenitory) glioneuronal hamartomas,[554,555] with other maldevelopmental cerebrocortical anomalies[569] and with the curious lesions known as dysembryoplastic neuroepithelial tumors (see later discussion).

The glial component of the ganglioglioma is typically astrocytic, GFAP-positive, and well-differentiated, usually assuming the guise of a low-grade fibrillary or pilocytic astrocytoma.[563,575] Gemistocytic elements may be encountered, but if prominent call the diagnosis into question. Gangliogliomas may contain pleomorphic xanthoastrocytomatous components, reference having previously been made in our discussion of the latter tumor type to "composite" lesions.[387] While gangliogliomas may harbor constituents indistinguishable from conventional oligodendroglioma, the oligodendrocyte-like clear cells present in select ganglion cell tumors actually represent "neurocytes," i.e., diminutive neurons.[568] A remarkable example of tanycytic ependymal differentiation on the part of a ganglioglioma is also on record.[562] Only exceptionally do gangliogliomas exhibit high-grade histologic features, "malignant degeneration" typically involving their astroglial components and potentially resulting in a glioblastoma-like picture.[557] Anaplastic ganglioglioma is the designation appropriate to the tumor densely populated by mitotically active glial cells (microvascular proliferation and necrosis may also be encountered), cytologic atypism alone, even if pronounced, not constituting grounds for this diagnosis. Elements of anaplastic oligodendrogliomatous appearance have exceptionally been observed in malignant ganglioglial tumors.[552] The recurrence of a ganglioglioma (3 years after subtotal resection and irradiation) as a high-grade neoplasm composed of cells exhibiting a hybrid neuronal/astrocytic phenotype on immunocytochemical and ultrastructural study has also been documented,[564] as has a neuroblastoma-like picture at relapse.[558]

Certain recurring histologic features merit emphasis as clues to ganglion cell tumor diagnosis. Eosinophilic globular bodies of lysosomal derivation that appear to aggregate in the matrices of many such tumors are noteworthy in this regard, only the pilocytic astrocytoma and pleomorphic xanthoastrocytoma exhibiting this presumably degenerative alteration with comparable frequency (see Fig. 28.54 for an illustration of these structures). Lymphoid infiltration can also be of some diagnostic utility to the pathologist not distracted by this common, "pseudoencephalitic" phenomenon. In fact, a florid inflammatory reaction extending into the substance of the lesion (i.e., not simply confined to the perivascular compartment) is characteristic among central neuroepithelial tumors only of this entity and the pleomorphic xanthoastrocytoma, the more so if plasma cells are found to participate. Desmoplasia, uncommonly associated with neoplasms of neuroepithelial lineage, need be mentioned as imposing a disfiguring and deceptive spindling and fascicular or vaguely storiform architecture on the constituent cellular elements of some ganglion cell tumors. Stromal blood vessels, often prominent, frequently undergo sclerosis—ganglion cell tumors potentially masquerading as vascular malformations on angiographic and gross neurosurgical assessment.

Given their differentiated appearances, it should come as no surprise that the tumoral neurons under discussion elaborate cytoplasmic processes that contain parallel microtubular arrays and clear, synaptic-type vesicles on ultrastructural examination, and that occasionally terminate in well-developed synaptic complexes.[563] These neoplastic elements often harbor dense-core neurosecretory granules as well, a feature generally foreign to native cortical neurons.[563] While tumors of astrocytic lineage may assume ganglion cell-like cytologic profiles, they manifest none of these specialized neuronal features and in most instances are readily unmasked by their expression of GFAP.

The formation of aberrant axosomatic synapses is apparently responsible for the presence in many ganglion cell tumors of large neurons displaying a coarsely granular or linear deposition of reaction product about their perikarya on immunocytochemical assay for synaptophysin (Fig. 28.76), a glycoprotein component of the presynaptic vesicle membrane.[563,568] This phenomenon bears significantly on the problem of distinguishing tumoral and native neurons—a comparable reaction pattern is not observed on antisynaptophysin immunoassessment of normal cerebral cortex—but must be cautiously interpreted. Circumperikaryal synaptophysin labeling is a recognized attribute of some striatal, cerebellar, bulbar and intramedullary neurons.[570,577] Furthermore, cerebrocortical neurons entrapped within arteriovenous malformations can evidence this immunoprofile[570] and an identical labeling pattern has been depicted in a lesion of the cerebral cortex reported as postradiation neuronal gigantism,[556] suggesting that chronic, nonspecific neuronal injury may rarely provoke anomalous synaptic remodeling.

Additional, and somewhat more specific (albeit inconstant), immunohistochemical evidence for the tumoral nature of a suspect neuronal population is intense and diffuse perikaryal labeling for chromogranin A (Fig. 28.77)—a reflection of the dense core granule formation noted above.[563] Native CNS neurons outside the brainstem and cerebellum, by contrast, either fail to react (as do glia) or display only punctate and relatively weak partial labeling of their perikarya for this antigen. Many gangliogliomas (and glioneuronal hamartomas) further depart from the normal in exhibiting matrix and perikaryon-associated immunoreactivity for CD34, an antigen expressed in the CNS by neural stem cells and endothelium but apparently not by differentiated neuroepithelial cell types.[554,555] The reader who consults the references provided on this score will unfortunately find rather contradictory statements as to CD34 expression in glial neoplasms. The neuronal constituents of ganglion cell tumors may also exhibit immunoreactivity for neurofilament proteins, microtubule-associated protein 2, class III β-tubulin, the neuronal nuclear proteins designated as NeuN[355] and Hu,[321] various neuropeptides, enzymes integral to catecholamine metabolism and other neuron-associated antigens.[563,575] As previously mentioned in connection with the diffuse astrocytomas, high-grade neoplasms of patently astrocytic character may contain ganglion cell-like forms and can display potentially confusing class III β-tubulin labeling.[328]

Ganglion cell tumors are, in the main, remarkably indolent and only exceptionally spread via the CSF or kill.[555,561,565–567,571,576] Supratentorial examples, if accessible, are generally cured by resection alone. Bulbar and intramedullary variants are somewhat more prone to symptomatic regrowth following operation, possibly owing to surgical limitations imposed by their physical circumstances, but run a protracted clinical course.[314,567] Noteworthy is the observation that the presence of frankly malignant glial elements does not necessarily augur poorly in this setting,[566,567,568] a happy discrepancy

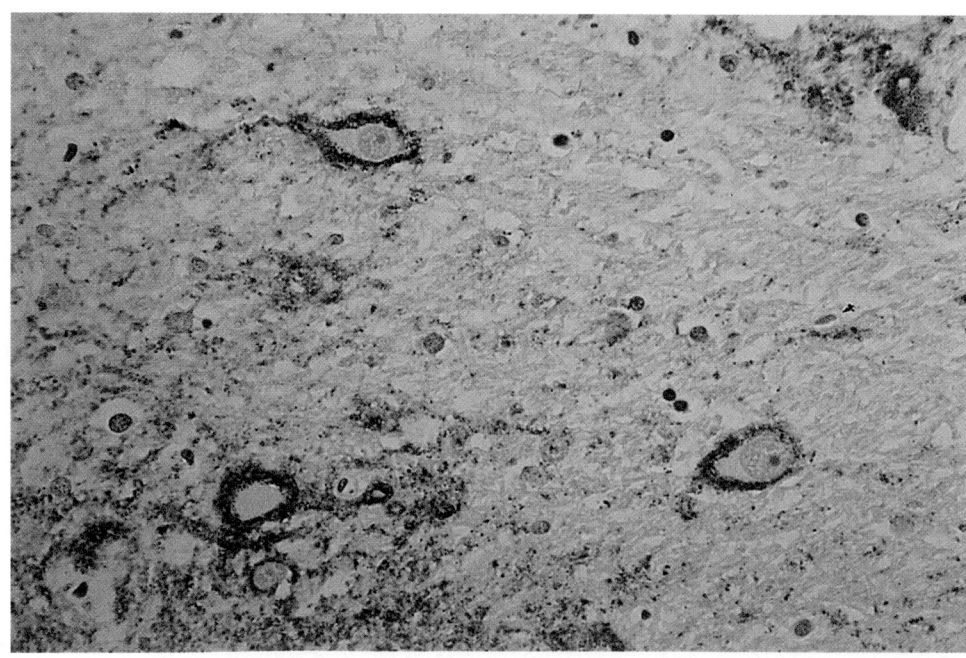

Fig. 28.76 Ganglioglioma. Surface perikaryal labeling for synaptophysin characterizes the neuronal elements of some ganglion cell tumors on immunohistochemical assay.

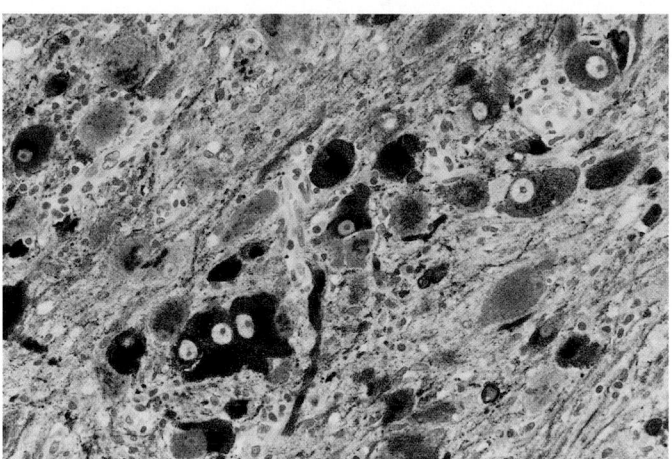

Fig. 28.77 Ganglioglioma. Diffuse and strong cytoplasmic immunoreactivity for chromogranin A, a feature foreign to native cerebrocortical neurons, characterizes the neoplastic neuronal perikarya of some ganglion cell tumors.

likely resulting from the fact that gangliogliomas tend to expand in a compact, relatively noninvasive fashion that lends itself to the purposes of the neurosurgeon. The optimal management of anaplastic gangliogliomas remains in doubt owing to their rarity, but a number of observers have concluded that neuroradiologic surveillance alone is reasonable following gross total excision.[566,567] Certainly, subtotally resected lesions exhibiting histologic anaplasia carry a significant risk of fatal progression due to locally aggressive growth and, in some cases, leptomeningeal seeding.[571] The role of adjuvant treatment in such cases is unclear. A remarkable example of diffuse leptomeningeal gangliogliomatosis may actually have represented advanced glioneuronal maturation of a metastasizing cerebellar medulloblastoma, as noted by the authors.[574] Whether immunohistochemical assessments of proliferative activity or p53 expression bear on outcome as independent factors following gross surgical extirpation of gangliogliomas is far from clear.[563,569,575] The reader interested in these issues is encouraged to consult the cited literature. As a rule, gangliogliomas manifest low MIB-1 labeling indices, reported mean values falling in the 1 to 3% range.[563,569,575] Histologically anaplastic variants and recurrent lesions have been noted by some observers to evidence higher indices,[563] but, again, the independent predictive power of proliferation assays is not settled. MIB-1 reactivity is typically restricted to cells of glial appearance though, as previously mentioned, malignant elements of neuronal immunophenotype have been reported to emerge from gangliogliomas.[558,564]

Much speculation has centered on whether ganglion cell tumors represent neoplasms, hamartomatous proliferations, or combinations thereof. A frequent association with maldevelopmental cortical abnormalities and their often remarkable clinical stability have prompted some to suggest that gangliogliomas essentially represent tumoral forms of cortical dysplasia or benign neoplasms arising in dysembryogenetic tissues.[554,569] The shared CD34 expression alluded to previously has been taken as evidence that gangliogliomas and glioneuronal hamartomas are linked by an origin from developmentally dysregulated neural stem cells. One scenario would have the forces of neoplastic transformation selectively targeting glial elements residing within such hamartomas.[555] A majority of gangliogliomas assessed in one molecular genetic analysis appeared to be monoclonal,[578] supporting their neoplastic nature and the origin of their glioneuronal populations in a common, bipotential precursor. The additional genetic events responsible for malignant progression in this setting await clarification.

We briefly call the reader's attention to the occurrence of "intrasellar gangliocytomas"—a heterogeneous collection of benign lesions most of which arise via neuronal transdifferentiation within growth hormone-producing (or, less commonly, other pituitary) adenomas.[560] A small minority of these curious masses may represent ganglion cell tumors ab initio or ectopic, hypothalamic-type neuronal hamartomas. Given separate consideration below are the distinctive entities known as desmoplastic infantile ganglioglioma and dysplastic gangliocytoma of the cerebellum (Lhermitte–Duclos disease).

Desmoplastic infantile ganglioglioma/desmoplastic infantile astrocytoma

Though originally characterized as distinct entities,[587,589] the **desmoplastic infantile astrocytoma** and **desmoplastic infantile ganglioglioma** are allied by common (and stereotypic) clinical, neuroradiologic, morphologic, and biologic features.[500] Accordingly, they are given joint treatment in this section. Characteristic of these rare neoplasms are a presentation in the first two years of life (mean patient age at tumor discovery being 6 months), a supratentorial localization (usually frontoparietal), and associated manifestations of increased intracranial pressure that include irritability, vomiting, macrocephaly, bulging fontanels, and forced downwards deviation of the eyes (the "sunset" sign). Virtually pathognomonic of this tumor family in the clinical setting just described is CT or MR demonstration of a superficially positioned, nodular or plaque-like mass that broadly adheres to the dura, exhibits homogeneous contrast enhancement, and is associated with a prominent subjacent cystic component of uni- or multilocular aspect (Fig. 28.78). Most examples are quite large at operation (these often measuring 10 or more centimeters in greatest span), are composed of tan-white tissue that is rubbery or firm to palpation owing to associated fibroplasia, and appear to lie largely outside the cerebrum proper.

Histologic study of desmoplastic infantile astrocytomas and gangliogliomas generally confirms their dural attachment and predilection for supracerebral growth,

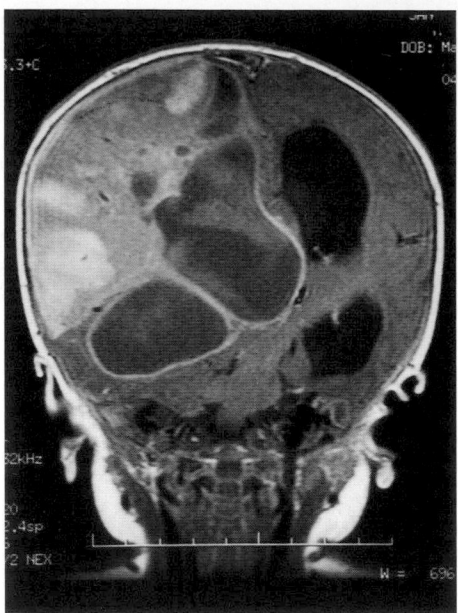

Fig. 28.78 Desmoplastic infantile ganglioglioma/astrocytoma. As demonstrated by this example in an 8-week-old boy, tumors of the desmoplastic infantile ganglioglioma/astrocytoma group are typically large cerebral growths exhibiting dural attachment of their superficially located and contrast-enhancing solid components with the formation of prominent underlying cysts.

while invariably revealing tumor colonization of the adjoining cortex and frequently demonstrating spread along Virchow–Robin spaces. Common to these tumors are collagenized components of pseudomesenchymal appearance as well as recognizably neuroepithelial elements (Fig. 28.79). The former, usually predominant, are populated by variably pleomorphic spindle cells in loose fascicular or storiform array, these patterns inviting

confusion with bona fide fibrohistiocytic neoplasms, intracranial fibromatosis, or fibroblastic meningioma. Immunohistochemical assessment typically discloses a large complement of GFAP-positive astroglial forms within these desmoplastic regions, where they are admixed with nonlabeling elements that have proven on electron microscopic study to include fibroblasts.[579,585,587,589] Ultrastructural analyses have further shown that these neoplastic astrocytes are invested by basal lamina material, which accounts for a pericellular, reticulin-impregnable network immunoreactive for basement membrane-associated antigens such as type IV collagen.[579,585] As discussed in connection with the pleomorphic xanthoastrocytoma, this finding may signal differentiation along specialized subpial astrocytic lines.

In addition to sharing collagen-rich zones evidencing astrocytic outgrowth, the neoplasms under discussion are allied by the regular presence of seemingly undifferentiated small cell populations that inhabit reticulin-free islands or broader tissue expanses (Fig. 28.79). These may achieve considerable density and can exhibit mitotic activity (usually at low or modest level). High mitotic rates, microvascular proliferation and necrosis are clearly exceptional, but occasionally encountered.[581,583,584] These small cell components, which appear to be primitive neuroepithelial constituents capable of divergent differentiation, can exhibit cytologic transition to fibrillary astroglial, gemistocytic or neuronal morphology and may label for GFAP, various neuron-associated antigens (e.g., synaptophysin, class III β-tubulin, neurofilament proteins, MAP–2, Hu), and desmin.[588,589] The specific diagnosis of desmoplastic infantile ganglioglioma is reserved for tumors containing recognizable neurons, but the expression of neuron-restricted epitopes by the

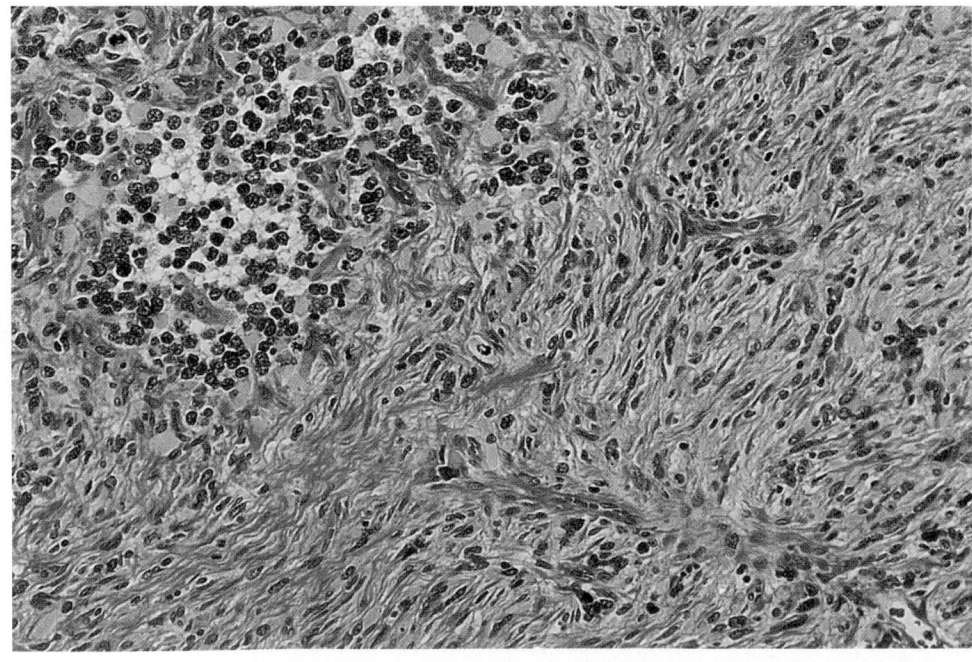

Fig. 28.79 Desmoplastic infantile ganglioglioma/astrocytoma. Distinctive features include collagenized regions dominated by spindly astrocytes in fascicular or storiform array and admixed small cells of primitive appearance in nodular aggregates.

ostensibly uncommitted small cells populating examples devoid of patently differentiated neuronal elements exposes the artifice in so subclassifying these unusual neoplasms of early life. When present, neuronal forms include mature, atypical and ganglion cell-sized variants. While most prevalent in noncollagenized regions, these can be detected in desmoplastic areas as well (particularly with the aid of immunoscreening for synaptophysin and neurofilament epitopes). A deep-seated example containing components of conventional ganglioglioma, gangliocytomatous foci, pilocytic astrocytoma-like regions and elements suggesting Schwann cell differentiation has been recorded.[582]

Desmoplastic infantile gangliogliomas and astrocytomas may represent neoplasms of essentially embryonal character programmed to advanced maturation along glioneuronal lines. Their proliferative small cell components notwithstanding, a most favorable prognosis attaches to cases amenable to gross total resection and so these peculiar tumors are accorded WHO grade I status.[588] Even frankly malignant histologic features (e.g., conspicuous mitotic activity and necrosis with palisading) do not necessarily augur in ominous fashion if surgical removal can be effected,[581,583] but we would caution that very few "anaplastic" cases have been recorded to date. Recurrence following complete excision is exceptional, though subtotally removed examples may occasionally regrow over relatively brief intervals and prove fatal.[582] CSF-borne metastasis at presentation has been described,[580,586] the diagnosis in one of these reports[586] being open to much question on both clinical and morphologic grounds. A second account of this phenomenon[580] detailed the virulent behavior of an example atypical by virtue of its subcortical, partly intraventricular localization and the unusually florid proliferative activity (including a MIB-1/Ki-67 labeling index of 45%) evidenced by anaplastic small cell elements that constituted one third of the tumor bulk. It would appear that adjuvant therapy can be reserved for refractory lesions that cannot be extirpated by surgical means alone.[581] It has been suggested that basal lamina formation by astrocytic elements may exert a restraining influence on the proliferation of these neoplasms, basement membrane-associated proteins apparently promoting cell differentiation and growth arrest when applied to human glioma lines.[585]

Central neurocytoma and extraventricular neurocytic neoplasms

Characterized by an intraventricular location, attendant manifestations of obstructive hydrocephalus, a peak incidence in adults aged 20 to 40 years, and deceptively oligodendroglioma-like histology, the **central neurocytoma** is a neoplasm composed of highly differentiated, albeit diminutive, neuronal elements.[593,594] It may be situated anywhere within the ventricular confines, possibly deriving from remnants of the subependymal matrix that retain postnatal proliferative capacity, but most often inhabits anterior portions of the lateral ventricles in the foramen of Monro region and frequently involves the septum pellucidum. Common neuroradiologic features include cystic change, contrast enhancement of solid components, and conspicuous calcification (Fig. 28.80).

The central neurocytoma is remarkable for the cytologic conformity of its constituent cells (Fig. 28.81), which possess monomorphic nuclei of small diameter, rounded contour, and evenly granular chromatin content. Perinuclear clearing, a plexiform capillary microvasculature and admixed calcospherules often conspire to render this lesion indistinguishable from the oligodendroglioma, though the central neurocytoma usually differs in its elaboration of a fine, neuropil-like fibrillar matrix that may separate streaming tumor cells, punctuate foci of sheet-like growth as anuclear islands, collar stromal blood vessels in pseudoependymomatous fashion, or (rarely) constitute the cores of Homer–Wright-like rosettes. This unusual neoplasm can attain dense cellularity, but the typical example is virtually devoid of mitotic activity and does not exhibit micro-

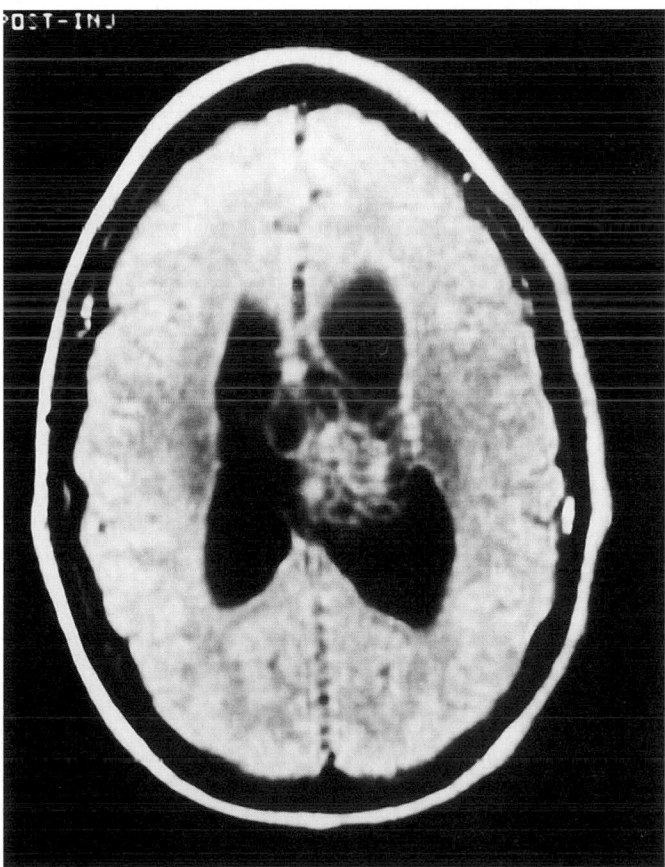

Fig. 28.80 Central neurocytoma. This postcontrast injection MRI shows the neurocytoma's predilection for the lateral ventricles, its tendency to be centered about the septum pellucidum, its often multicystic structure, regions of bright enhancement, and associated ventriculomegaly indicative of obstructive hydrocephalus.

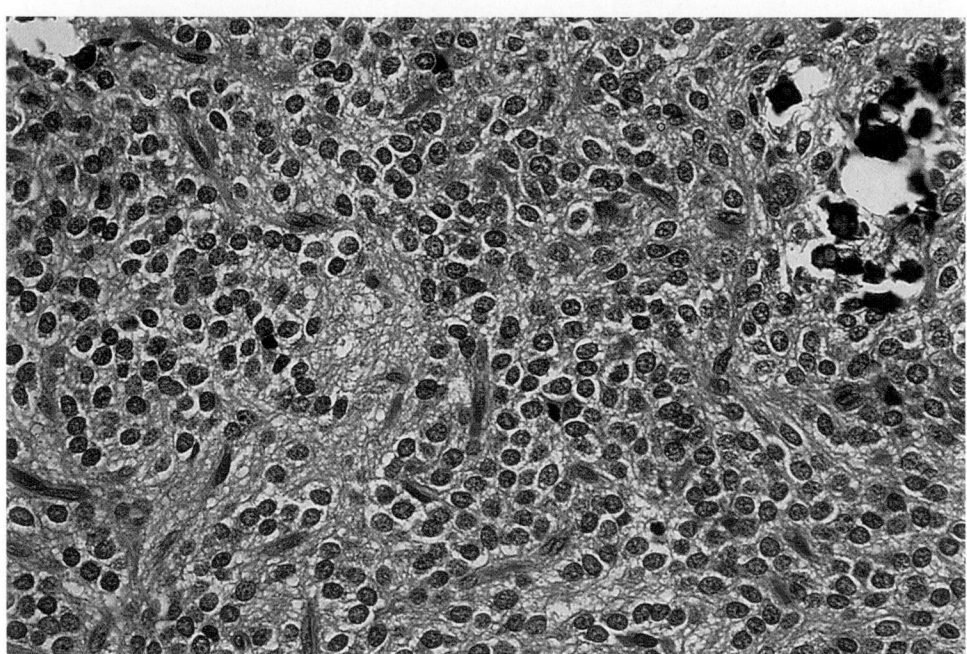

Fig. 28.81 Central neurocytoma. The typical neurocytoma is rather densely populated by small, monomorphous cells embedded in a variably abundant, delicate fibrillar matrix. Rounded nuclear contours, perinuclear clearing, a plexiform capillary arcade, and associated microcalcifications (the basophilic structures present at upper right) impart an oligodendroglioma-like appearance to this small cell neuronal neoplasm.

vascular proliferation or necrosis. Admixed ganglion cell,[594,608] adipocyte-like[595,599] and melanotic[605] components have been recorded, as has an example associated with a fourth ventricular tumor of medulloblastomatous appearance[599] and a case interpreted as evidencing gangl;gliogliomatous differentiation on recurrence.[610]

Cytoplasmic processes replete with parallel microtubular arrays, clear vesicles and membrane-bound neurosecretory granules (the last typically in small number) attest to the neuronal nature of the central neurocytoma on electron microscopy (Fig. 28.82), synapse formation signalling the particularly advanced maturation of some representatives.[593,608] Such findings effectively distinguish this entity from the oligodendroglioma and clear cell ependymoma, though we note one fine structural study depicting an unusual variant with oligodendrocyte-like lamellar cytoplasmic structuring[607] and a second documenting an intraventricular neoplasm with both neuronal and ependymal specializations.[603] We have also previously alluded to neurocytomatous components

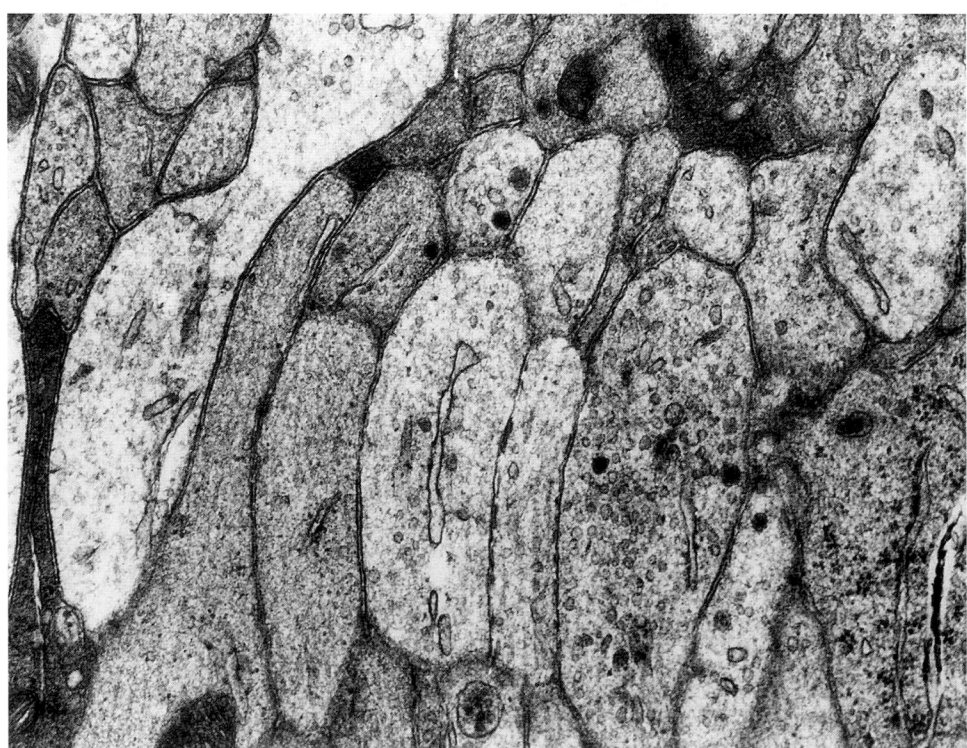

Fig. 28.82 Central neurocytoma. This transmission electron micrographic study readily discloses the neuronal nature of this neoplasm, demonstrating arrays of "neuritic" processes replete with microtubules, clear synaptic-type vesicles, and dense-core neurosecretory granules. (×327,000)

within otherwise acceptable oligodendrogliomas, but this is a clearly exceptional phenomenon.[420] That the central neurocytoma, unless subjected to prolonged formalin fixation, almost invariably manifests immunolabeling of its fibrillary matrix for synaptophysin merits particular emphasis as confirming this diagnosis in the appropriate setting while obviating more costly and time-consuming ultrastructural assessment.[593,608] Central neurocytomas often exhibit labeling for the Hu[321] and NeuN[355] neuronal nuclear proteins (Fig. 28.83) as well, though chromogranin A and neurofilament protein expression seem restricted to the rare variant exhibiting transition to ganglion cell-like morphology.[593,594,608] Chromogranin A immunoreactivity, by contrast, is a frequent attribute of pineocytomas and of pineal parenchymal tumors of intermediate differentiation that may be difficult to distinguish from central neurocytomas on histologic grounds alone and that share synaptophysin positivity. The reader is referred to our treatment of pineal parenchymal neoplasms for reference to specific fine structural features that further segregate such tumors from neoplasms of conventional neuronal type. Central neurocytomas seem capable of glial differentiation,[600,609,611,614] but cytoplasmic GFAP immunolabeling is foreign to most and, if present, limited to tumor cells in relatively small number.

The prognosis for patients with central neurocytomas is generally favorable, complete excision alone effecting long-term tumor control in most cases.[593,594,609] Gross invasion of periventricular structures, dissemination via the CSF and fatal progression are exceptional[591,592,608] and not necessarily predicted by lesion histology, though "atypical central neurocytomas" characterized by features including readily apparent mitotic activity, macronucleoli, microvascular proliferation, necrosis and

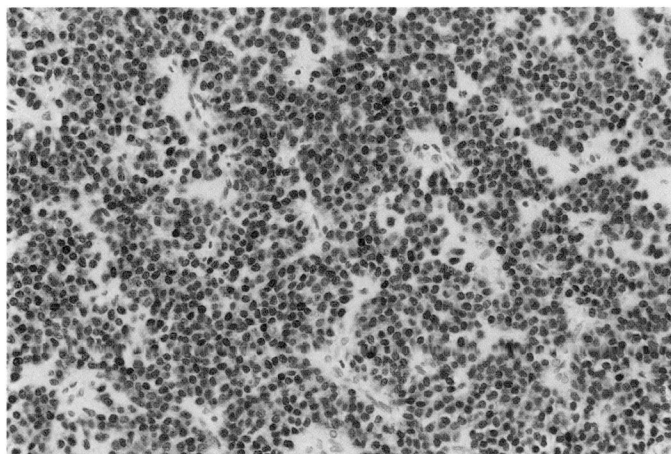

Fig. 28.83 Central neurocytoma. A phenomenon restricted in the normal CNS to advanced stages of neuronal maturation, immunolabeling for the NeuN nuclear antigen is shared by many central neurocytomas and attests to their well-differentiated nature.

elevated MIB-1 labeling indices (typically below 2% in conventional cases) have been overrepresented among clinically aggressive lesions.[602,611] An excess of cases with poor outcome seem to have been GFAP-positive,[591,592,611] though this requires further study. Adjuvant therapy, particularly irradiation, may prove beneficial to some patients with disease refractory to surgical management.

While the specific diagnosis of central neurocytoma should be reserved for the intraventricular neoplasm described above, tumors of comparable morphology may arise within the substance of the brain[590,596] or spinal cord.[613] These can harbor admixed ganglion cell and astroglial elements,[590,596] a remarkable cerebellar example exhibiting rhabdomyomatous differentiation.[606] The clinical biology of these **extraventricular neurocytomas** and "**ganglio/glioneurocytomas**" remains to be fully characterized, but most reported to date have exhibited limited proliferative activity and have behaved in relatively benign fashion. Gross total resection of these generally demarcated tumors is the treatment of choice and may serve to control at least some cases manifesting obvious proliferative activity, necrosis, and other atypical features.[590] The nosology of aggressive, small cell glioblastoma-like neoplasms reported as malignant neurocytic tumors[604] is unclear.

Cerebellar liponeurocytoma is the consensus WHO designation[601] for an unusual lesion previously regarded as embryonal in nature and variously termed a "lipomatous" or "lipidized" medulloblastoma, medullocytoma, neurolipocytoma, or lipomatous glioneurocytoma.[597,612] To date, this has been encountered only in adults (with a mean age at diagnosis of approximately 50 years). CT/MRI study typically discloses a relatively well-demarcated, contrast-enhancing cerebellar mass (vermian or hemispheric) with foci of bright signal on precontrast T1-weighted images reflecting the fatty component. The latter, variably represented, consists of cells that resemble mature or multivacuolated adipocytes grouped within a tumor otherwise of central neurocytoma-like histology, immunophenotype and fine structure. Oddly, however, GFAP-immunoreactive glial elements are often present and concentrated in "lipomatous" regions. An example evidencing myoid differentiation is on record.[598] There is typically little mitotic activity and only low level MIB-1 labeling. Most reported patients followed for 5 years or more have remained disease-free following resection, irrespective of adjuvant radiotherapy, and CSF seeding has not been described. Accordingly, the cerebellar liponeurocytoma has been accorded WHO grade I status.[601]

Dysembryoplastic neuroepithelial tumor
Dysembryoplastic neuroepithelial tumors (DNTs) are strongly associated with pharmacoresistant partial seizures in young subjects and only exceptionally come to attention in patients older than 20 years of age.[617,618,626,628]

While the great majority are supratentorial and cerebral in position, the temporal lobes being particularly prone, lesions of strikingly similar morphology involving the septum pellucidum,[615] caudate nucleus,[616] brainstem and cerebellum[621] have been recorded. Multifocal presentations have also been described.[629] Neuroradiologic features of great utility in suggesting the diagnosis and in serving to distinguish DNTs from conventional glial neoplasms (particularly oligodendrogliomas) with which they may be confused on histologic study are their tendency to lie largely, if not entirely, within an expanded cortical ribbon (Fig. 28.84) and their multinodular bright signal qualities in T2-weighted MRIs. Remodelling of the adjacent calvarium often attests to the indolent expansion of these unusual lesions, which are typically T1 hypointense and devoid of mass effect or associated edema. A minority exhibit discrete foci of nodular or ring enhancement.

"Simple" and "complex" histologic variants of DNT are recognized.[617,618,626,628] Common to both and required for morphologic diagnosis is the presence of what has been termed the "specific glioneuronal element,"—a characteristically multinodular proliferation of oligodendrocyte-like cells (OLCs) that appear to be arranged along bundled axons and ramifying capillaries (often coursing perpendicular to the cortical surface) and that are separated by a myxoid matrix in which well-differentiated neurons seem to float (Fig. 28.85). Mitoses are absent or exceedingly rare and MIB-1 labeling indices do not usually exceed 1–2%. Readily apprehended on low power examination, such "patterned" nodules colonize a

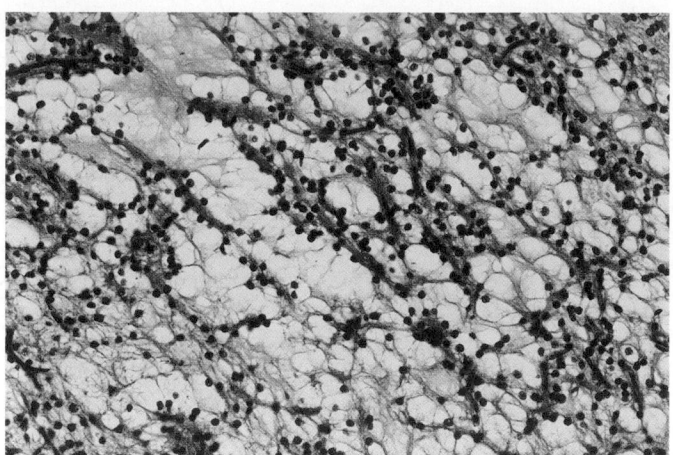

Fig. 28.85 Dysembryoplastic neuroepithelial tumor. Extensive myxoid change and the disposition of small, oligodendrocyte-like cells along axonal fiber bundles and capillaries lend an alveolar or "patterned" appearance to the specific glioneuronal element of this distinctive lesion. Not shown here, mature neurons often appear to float in the mucoid matrix.

cortex that frequently exhibits background architectural disorganization (dysplasia). OLCs can also be disposed about myxoid microcysts in alveolar fashion or about a fine fibrillar meshwork in cribriform, rosetted array. Stellate, GFAP-immunoreactive astrocytes may be found within the specific glioneuronal element of simple DNTs, complex variants harboring, in micronodular or more diffuse arrangement, additional glial components that may be indistinguishable from conventional oligodendroglioma, pilocytic or fibrillary astrocytoma. These can exhibit considerable cytologic atypism and have been described in some cases as manifesting low level mitotic activity, microvascular proliferation and, rarely, necrosis.[617] An anomalous vasculature of hamartomatous aspect may be encountered. Curiosities include examples of DNT admixed with ganglioglioma[624] and a lesion interpreted as a melanotic DNT variant.[620]

The characteristically superficial localization of the DNT, common association with cortical dysplasia and young patient age at presentation have been taken as evidence of an origin from the secondary germinal layer during embryogenesis.[617] Whether the OLCs that dominate its specific glioneuronal element actually represent oligodendroglia is unclear. Some observers have found these cells, which are usually S-100 protein-positive and GFAP-negative, to be immunoreactive for myelin oligodendrocyte glycoprotein,[622] others noting subsets labeling for such neuron-associated antigens as NeuN and the N-methyl-D-aspartate receptor subunit NR1[428] or evidencing dense core granule and axo-somatic synapse formation at the ultrastructural level.[625] These may, then, be capable of divergent differentiation. As previously mentioned, NeuN labeling is typically foreign to oligodendrogliomas.[428] The latter, however, may contain

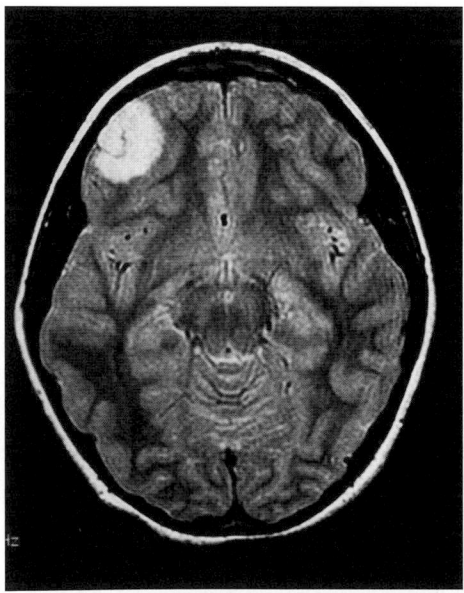

Fig. 28.84 Dysembryoplastic neuroepithelial tumor. A gyriform focus of increased signal attests to the largely cortical localization of this superficial lesion, seen in a FLAIR MR sequence. Also characteristic is the absence of mass effect or white matter changes indicative of edema.

trapped, NeuN-positive neurons of small size that complicate segregation of these entities by immunohistochemical means alone. It has been suggested that chromosome 1p deletion, commonly encountered in oligodendrogliomas, is generally foreign to DNTs.[627] The reader is referred to the section on "Oligodendroglial neoplasms" for further discussion of this differential.

Patients with DNTs of both simple and complex type are usually cured by simple excision alone, subtotally resected examples usually remaining stable on neuroradiologic surveillance.[617,618,626,628] While a comparably favorable outcome has been recorded following complete surgical extirpation of complex variants exhibiting mitotic activity, microvascular proliferation or necrosis,[617] few such lesions have been recorded and judgment regarding their biologic potential must be reserved. An example of complex DNT progressing to frank clinical, as well as histologic, malignancy has been described,[623] suggesting that this otherwise benign entity—viewed by some, in fact, as hamartomatous—can rarely act as the substrate from which a bona fide glioma of aggressive nature may arise.

It has been proposed that certain DNT variants evidence neither a specific glioneuronal element nor a multinodular growth pattern, assuming, instead, the guises of oligodendroglioma, oligoastrocytoma, pilocytic or fibrillary (including high-grade) astrocytoma in unalloyed form.[619] The criteria posited for the identification of such "nonspecific" DNTs, which are said to be clinically benign and nonrecurring after simple removal irrespective of their histologic attributes are: (1) association with partial seizures (with or without secondary generalization) beginning prior to 20 years of age; (2) absence of associated neurologic deficits or presence of a nonprogressive congenital deficit only; (3) supratentorial localization and cortical topography on CT/MRI; (4) absence of associated edema or mass effect other than that related to cystic components. This is, understandably, a controversial notion.

Other glioneuronal neoplasms

We mention here three emerging clinicopathologic entities of recent description—the papillary glioneuronal tumor, the glioneuronal tumor with neuropil-like islands (also known as rosetted glioneuronal tumor), and the rosette-forming glioneuronal tumor of the fourth ventricle. The reader is referred to the section on oligodendrogliomas for discussion of neurocytic differentiation in the latter.

The **papillary glioneuronal tumor** seems to have a predilection for young adults and tendency to a subcortical cerebral hemispheric localization.[630,633] Neuroradiologic features include circumscription, contrast-enhancing solid components with associated cysts and little in the way of accompanying mass effect or edema. A biphasic morphology is characteristic. The glial element, papillary in architecture, is represented by GFAP-immunolabeling cells of flattened to low cuboidal profile draped in monolayered or pseudostratified fashion over branching, hyalinized vascular cores. Admixed or regionally segregated are synaptophysin-rich, nonpapillary neuronal populations that include neurocytes, large neurons of mature appearance and intermediate forms. Myxoid change is common. Mitoses are absent or rare, there is no microvascular proliferation or necrosis, MIB-1 labeling indices do not usually exceed 1–2% of tumor cell nuclei, and there have been no recorded recurrences following excision alone.

A single case involving the cervicothoracic spinal cord excepted,[631] all examples of the **glioneuronal tumor with neuropil-like islands/rosetted glioneuronal tumor** recorded to date have arisen in the cerebral hemispheres of young or middle-aged adults.[632,635,636] There are no suggestive neuroradiologic features. The lesion is defined by its content of synaptophysin-immunoreactive islands of delicate, neuropil-like matrix embedded within a tumor otherwise composed of conventional, GFAP-positive astrocytic elements. The latter may be of fibrillary, gemistocytic or protoplasmic appearance and can exhibit mitotic activity. The neuropil-like islands are rimmed in rosetted fashion or irregularly populated by small, oligodendrocyte-like cells and larger, atypical and hyperchromatic forms that have been shown to label for the neuron-associated NeuN and Hu nuclear antigens. The prognosis is guarded, as this tumor is capable of diffuse cerebral infiltration and biologic progression. Local recurrence and death due to bihemispheric invasion (in a patient with an unresectable lesion exhibiting anaplastic glial histology) have been recorded,[636] as has CSF dissemination of the intramedullary example noted above.[631] It would appear that even tumors of low-grade histologic aspect may behave in unexpectedly aggressive fashion.

Rosette-forming glioneuronal tumors of the fourth ventricle, which may also involve the cerebellar vermis and cerebral aqueduct, are low-grade neoplasms composed of pilocytic astrocytoma-like glial elements and neurocytic populations that engage in the formation of diminutive, synaptophysin-immunoreactive rosettes.[634] These have been encountered in children and adults, typically presenting as relatively discrete and partially contrast-enhancing masses associated with symptomatic hydrocephalus.

Hypothalamic neuronal hamartoma

The **hypothalamic neuronal hamartoma** typically presents as a rubbery grayish-white nodule no more than 1 or 2 cm in diameter that bulges into the suprasellar cistern from a broad-based stalk anchoring it to the tuber cinereum or mammillary body.[639–641] The lesion is usually discovered on evaluation of a boy for precocious puberty, but young females and older individuals may be affected, and associations with other endocrinologic syndromes (principally acromegaly) and with spontaneous fits of laughter known as "gelastic" seizures are recognized. The hamartoma consists of large, mature neurons that may closely resemble those populating the principal hypothalamic nuclei. The former are embedded in a matrix of myelinated and nonmyelinated axons. Some examples have a gliotic appearance, but astrocytes and oligodendroglia are only minor cellular elements. That their misplaced neurons retain hypothalamic hormonal activity is currently the most attractive hypothesis regarding the functional manifestations of these unusual lesions. Immunohistochemical assay of select examples, among them cases associated with sexual precocity, has revealed reactivity of their neuronal elements for gonadotropin-releasing hormones, including luteinizing hormone-releasing factor.[639,641] Hamartomas (described as hypothalamic "gangliocytomas") harbored by acromegalic patients have been found to elaborate growth hormone-releasing factor[637] and, in so doing, are postulated to rarely drive the adenohypophysis to neoplasia, as suggested by their reported association with growth hormone-producing pituitary adenomas.[642] Congenital hypothalamic hamartomas are found as part of a complex malformative process—the **Pallister–Hall syndrome**—that includes imperforate anus, cryptorchidism, polydactyly, pituitary aplasia, hypoplasia of the adrenal and thyroid glands, and various cardiac and renal anomalies.[638,643] In affected infants, the hypothalamic lesion may contain small, immature-appearing neuroepithelial elements and has accordingly been termed "**hypothalamic hamartoblastoma**." Resection specimens from patients surviving infancy exhibit more mature neuronal features.[643]

Glioneuronal hamartomas, cortical dysplasias, and other epileptogenic lesions

Many published series and reviews attest to an ongoing interest in the neurosurgical management of refractory seizure disorders and the delineation of their anatomic substrates.[644–649] Inasmuch as operative approaches to this problem are practiced largely in specialized referral centers and so do not engage the general surgical pathologist, we specifically consider here only one of the more commonly encountered lesions not addressed elsewhere in this text, the glioneuronal hamartoma.

Although by no means restricted to this site, **glioneuronal hamartomas** figure prominently among seizure-associated lesions in series detailing the surgical treatment of chronic temporal lobe epilepsy.[646,648] Ranging from microscopic lesions ("**hamartias**") to expansile gray nodules that may be grossly evident on evaluation of lobectomy specimens and visualized by neuroradiographic means, these are sometimes found to be multifocal, are often associated with other evidences of faulty development (such as patchy cortical dysgene-

sis and neuronal ectopias in the temporal white matter), and may occur in complex with low-grade neuroepithelial neoplasms of varied type. Whether they serve as the progenitors of select gliomas, gangliogliomas, or dysembryoplastic neuroepithelial tumors (the more commonly associated lesions) is open to question. As noted previously, gangliogliomas do often share with these dysgenetic lesions expression of CD34, restricted in the normal CNS to embryonic neural stem cells and endothelium.[554,555] Populated, in most cases rather sparsely, by neurons of medium to large size and admixed astrocytes that may exhibit hyperplastic features, glioneuronal hamartomas do not evidence the cellularity, pleomorphism, or conspicuous inflammatory infiltration of the bona fide ganglioglioma, nor do they manifest alveolar patterning or the myxoid alterations characteristic of the dysembryoplastic neuroepithelial tumor. Some, like the latter, harbor aggregated oligodendrocyte-like clear cell elements, but these are a minor component and further deviate in evidencing no special relationship to regional axons or the stromal vasculature. Spongiform change may be apparent within the lesion and can involve associated cortex in patchy fashion, this possibly representing a seizure-induced tissue disturbance. Finally, select variants contain dysmorphic cells of neuronal, astrocytic, or indeterminate lineage resembling those of the cortical tuber (the tuberous sclerosis complex is discussed in relation to subependymal giant cell astrocytomas). These include cells exhibiting a characteristically "ballooned" appearance. Such cells are also the hallmark of a form of **focal cortical dysplasia** (known eponymously as **Taylor's cortical dysplasia**) that is strongly associated with refractory seizures in childhood and that appears to represent a disorder of neuronal migration and differentiation.[644,645]

Dysplastic gangliocytoma of the cerebellum (Lhermitte–Duclos disease)

The **dysplastic gangliocytoma of the cerebellum**, also known by the eponymous **Lhermitte–Duclos disease**, principally affects adults in the third and fourth decades of life, usually coming to attention on evaluation for progressive ataxia or symptoms of intracranial hypertension reflecting mass effect on the fourth ventricle.[657] Virtually diagnostic on MRI assessment is the demonstration of regionally thickened and abnormally T2 bright cerebellar folia without associated contrast enhancement. The histologic substrate of this curious disorder is variable replacement of the granule cell layer by a seemingly disorganized array of large neurons with attendant expansion and aberrant myelination of the overlying molecular layer. The latter is prone to coarse spongy change and dystrophic microcalcification, often blood vessel-associated, while the subjacent folial white matter is typically thinned, if not cavitated. Neuronal elements are generally well-differentiated in appearance and may include Purkinje cell-like forms, some examples containing neurons of atypical aspect. Axons emanating from these populations are oriented (relative to the pial surface) in parallel stacks within the deep molecular zone and in perpendicular array more superficially.

The neuronal constituents of the dysplastic gangliocytoma of the cerebellum appear to be of heterogeneous character. The molecular layer orientation of their axons, the appearances of these in Golgi preparations,[650] and observed patterns of neurofilament protein expression on immunoassay[659] suggest that most of the abnormal neurons in this disorder are outsized caricatures of the granule cells that they would seem to replace. One histogenetic hypothesis, in fact, has these neuronal elements representing native granule cells reduced in numbers owing to faulty development of the fetal external granular cell layer and so stimulated to compensatory hypertrophy. Noteworthy, in this regard, is report of a congenital example evidencing selective depletion of external granule cells in regions of dysplastic gangliocytomatous change.[654] That the dysplastic gangliocytoma is a complex hamartomatous lesion, rather than an internal granule cell response to dysembryogenetic events, has been suggested to account for the demonstration that a subset of its neuronal populace exhibits a Purkinje cell-like immunophenotype. This includes the binding of antibodies to Leu-4, PEP-19, L7, and calbindin, as well as surface perikaryal immunolabeling for such synaptic vesicle-associated antigens as SV2 and synaptophysin.[651,652,655]

While the dysplastic gangliocytoma of the cerebellum usually occurs in sporadic fashion, it is now recognized as a potential manifestation of **Cowden syndrome**.[653,657] An autosomal dominant phakomatosis linked to germline mutations of the PTEN/MMAC 1 gene on chromosome 10q23, this disease complex is chiefly characterized by multiple cutaneous tricholemmomas, oral papillomatosis, acral keratoses, macrocephaly/megalencephaly, gastrointestinal polyps of various types, thyroid abnormalities (principally goiter, but including follicular neoplasms), and a substantially increased risk of mammary adenocarcinoma (as well as benign fibroepithelial and papillomatous proliferations of the female breast).[657] Cowden syndrome patients should be investigated for cerebellar abnormalities, the fact that dysplastic gangliocytomas occasionally prefigure other stigmata of this heritable disorder having obvious screening implications as well (particularly mandating targeted investigation of the breast in affected women). Gross total excision is the treatment of choice and usually proves curative, but recurrences have been recorded.[656,658] The latter raise the possibility, though this would seem unlikely, that dysplastic gangliocytomas of the cerebellum are neither hyperplastic nor hamartomatous but instead represent neoplasms of a remarkably orchestrated nature.

Embryonal neuroepithelial tumors

Collectively described as "embryonal" are diverse neoplasms sharing, in addition to a postulated derivation from primitive neuroepithelial precursors, a peak incidence in the early years of life and an aggressive clinical biology. Most such tumors are dominated by small, anaplastic cells apparently uncommitted to any particular cytogenetic pathway on conventional histologic assessment, but the capacity of these lesions to differentiate along neuronal, glial, and, on occasion, mesenchymal lines has long been recognized and is manifest in their bewildering morphologic and immunophenotypic heterogeneity.

Few subjects in surgical neuropathology have occasioned controversy as heated as that surrounding the nomenclature appropriate to these complex neoplasms. Their original designations were predicated on the theory that the histologic appearances of CNS tumors reflect the neoplastic transformation of specific cell types at recognizable stages of neuroembryogenesis.[663] Thus, medulloepithelioma was the name given to a tumor harboring structures resembling, and so presumed to originate from, the primitive medullary epithelium of the neural tube, whereas ependymoblastoma was used for an embryonal neoplasm seemingly committed to differentiation along ependymal lines alone, and so forth. The theoretical underpinnings of this scheme have been justly questioned and an alternative, operational approach suggested in which the generic primitive neuroectodermal tumor (PNET) is accorded all such neoplasms and then qualified to indicate a given lesion's site and differentiating characteristics.[662] Implied is the common origin of embryonal tumors from indifferent stem cells that either remain undifferentiated or exercise any of a number of maturational options following neoplastic transformation. Specifically, targeting of undifferentiated neuroepithelial cells known to persist in the subependymal plate and pineal anlage is hypothesized to account for the occurrence of histologically similar neoplasms of primitive character at various sites along the neuraxis.

Simply stated, the cytogenesis of these embryonal tumors remains, at present, wholly speculative and genomic expression analyses do not support a common pathogenesis for the members of this group.[661] It is our practice, in accord with WHO guidelines,[660] to employ the time-honored designations first applied to these neoplasms, flawed as they may be. The pineoblastoma is treated under pineal parenchymal neoplasms.

Medulloblastoma

The cerebellar tumors traditionally termed **medulloblastomas** are the most common of primitive neuroepithelial neoplasms arising in the CNS. These occur throughout life but are characterized by a peak incidence in children between 5 and 10 years of age.[678,695] Approximately 25%

of afflicted patients are beyond their teenage years,[684] adult-onset cases clustering in the third and fourth decades, and 65% are male. At least 75% of childhood medulloblastomas arise in the cerebellar vermis, often expanding to fill the fourth ventricle and so producing manifestations of obstructive hydrocephalus (lethargy, headache, and morning emesis) in addition to truncal ataxia and disturbed gait. The relative proportion of laterally positioned, hemispheric examples increases with age. As visualized in CT and MR images, medulloblastomas are usually solid and contrast-enhancing. Unlike ependymomas, the main differential diagnostic considerations in the fourth ventricular region, they are not prone to calcification and midline examples often appear to hang from the roof of this chamber rather than bulging upwards from its floor.

While usually sporadic, medulloblastomas are known to complicate certain heritable disorders.[696] **Type 2 Turcot's syndrome**, an autosomal dominant condition, is defined by the occurrence of medulloblastoma in association with adenomatous polyposis of the colon and germline mutations of the adenomatous polyposis coli (APC) gene on chromosome 5q21. A greatly increased risk of medulloblastoma also characterizes the **nevoid basal cell carcinoma**—or "**Gorlin's**"—**syndrome**, an autosomal dominant complex caused by germline mutations of the Patched (PTCH) gene (chromosome 9q22.3) and including among its many manifestations odontogenic keratocysts, dyskeratotic pitting of the palms and soles, craniomegaly and other skeletal anomalies, lamellar calcium deposition in the falx cerebri and diaphragma sellae, calcifying ovarian fibromas and multifocal basal cell carcinomas notable for their early age at onset, involvement of both sun-exposed and hidden skin, melanotic pigmentation, associated calcifications, and clinical indolence. Medulloblastomas may arise in the setting of **germline p53 gene mutation** (including **Li–Fraumeni syndrome**), previously mentioned as predisposing to astrocytic neoplasms and other tumor types, and may occur at increased frequency (along with oligodendrogliomas and meningiomas) in **Rubinstein–Taybi syndrome**. The latter, due to mutations in the CREB-binding protein gene on chromosome 16p13.3, is typified by congenital cognitive impairment, growth retardation, microcephaly with abnormal facies, broad thumbs and toes.

We emphasize that the designation of medulloblastoma is currently extended to tumors of heterogeneous morphology and genomic profile that may not share a unifying pathogenesis or cellular lineage. Remnants of the fetal external granular layer, elements of the posterior medullary velum and stem cells in the subependymal matrix have all been championed as progenitors, but the histogenesis of medulloblastomas remains a matter of conjecture.[678] At the time of this writing, histologic subtyping is not considered in treatment protocols—a situation that may well change with the additional characterization of certain subtypes that seem to constitute biologically distinctive entities (see below). The tumor group under discussion is vastly dominated by the "classical" medulloblastoma, the "desmoplastic" or "nodular" medulloblastoma trailing in prevalence and all other forms being decidedly uncommon. Recent studies indicate that the classic and desmoplastic subtypes coexpress genes encoding cerebellar granule cell-specific transcription factors,[661] suggesting a common origin in such cells or, at least, shared activation of the granule cell differentiation program.

Classic medulloblastomas are solid masses of friable, gray–white tissue composed, at their most primitive, of small, ostensibly undifferentiated cells closely arrayed in packed sheets (Fig. 28.86). Nuclei are often densely hyperchromatic, round or angulated, invested with little or no definable cytoplasm and so prone to deformation ("molding") by their neighbors. A swirling or fascicular architecture may be encountered, as may nuclei disposed in tight perivascular pseudorosettes or regimented in compact, rhythmic palisades. Stromal elements are typically scant, consisting of small blood vessels that only exceptionally exhibit proliferative changes (and these rarely comparable to the glomeruloid alterations characteristic of high-grade gliomas). Mitotic figures may abound, MIB-1 (Ki-67) labeling indices often exceeding 50%, but most medulloblastomas exhibit surprisingly little in the way of geographic necrosis. When present, however, necrotic zones may be rimmed by pseudopalisading tumor cells in glioblastoma-like fashion. Patterns of local spread commonly evident in neurosurgical material include diffuse permeation of adjoining neuroparenchyma, arresting subpial accumulations of neoplastic cells that invite comparison to a persistent fetal external granular layer and extension into the subarachnoid compartment with reinvasion of the underlying cerebellar cortex along a broad front or via penetrating perivascular spaces. Contact with the pia-arachnoid may incite considerable fibroplasia, in florid cases forcing tumor cells into single file, trabecular or even storiform arrays.

Desmoplastic medulloblastomas may occupy the vermis and present in childhood, but are overrepresented among laterally situated, cerebellar hemispheric tumors of adult onset. We refer the interested reader elsewhere for detailed discussion of certain shared antigenic attributes that would make these distinctive neoplasms especially strong candidates for an external granule cell lineage in the assessment of some observers.[668] Noteworthy, given the fact that desmoplastic variants constitute the majority of medulloblastomas complicating the nevoid basal cell carcinoma syndrome, is evidence that PTCH gene mutations occur preferentially in this group.[678] At operation, these neoplasms may seem leptomeninges-based and are often lobulated, sharply demarcated and firm owing to the associated deposition of reticulin and collagen for which they are named. Desmoplastic medulloblastomas, however, depart from classical variants evidencing collagenization due simply to arachnoidal infiltration in their conspicuous content of "pale islands"—micronodular, reticulin-free zones that lend to many a low magnification appearance likened to follicular lymphoid hyperplasia (Fig. 28.87). Characterized by reduced cellularity, a rarefied fibrillar matrix, the emergence of an oligodendrocyte-like (but, in fact, neuronal) populace and downregulated bcl-2 expression with increased apoptosis and a sharp decline

in mitotic activity and MIB-1 (Ki-67) immunolabeling,[674] the pale island is not merely free of connective tissues but represents a locus of progressive neuronal maturation and potential glial differentiation (as further addressed below). In recognition of this defining phenomenon (and to avoid confusion with sclerotic medulloblastomas of otherwise classic appearance), some neuropathologists prefer the designation of "**nodular**" **medulloblastoma** for the desmoplastic subtype.

Although medulloblastomas in both classic and desmoplastic form are unarguably capable of differentiating along glial, as well as neuronal, lines, it is the latter

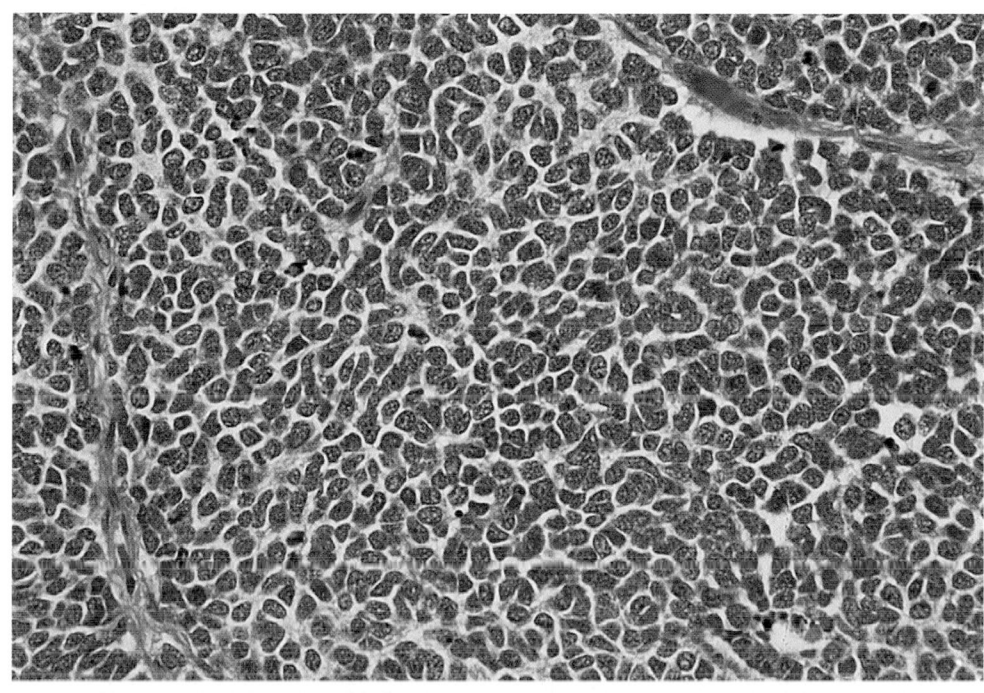

Fig. 28.86 Medulloblastoma. The classic medulloblastoma is a highly cellular neoplasm composed of diminutive, undifferentiated-looking elements possessed of little definable cytoplasm and prone to nuclear molding.

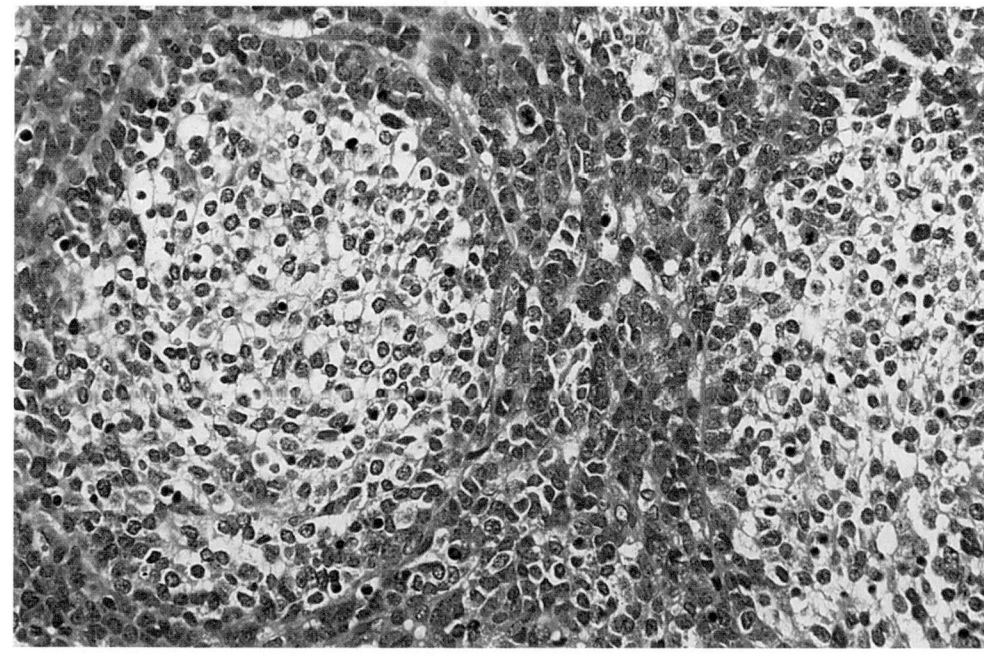

Fig. 28.87 Desmoplastic medulloblastoma. Micronodular zones of reduced cellularity ("pale islands") are a striking feature of this medulloblastoma variant.

option that is far more frequently exercised. While overt ganglion cell maturation is exceptional, the overwhelming majority of medulloblastomas (including those of thoroughly undifferentiated histologic aspect) exhibit at least focal immunolabeling for synaptophysin.[670,693] Reliable indices of neuronal differentiation that can be apprehended at the light microscopic level include, in addition to the pale islands just described, Homer Wright rosettes—radial arrangements of tumor cell nuclei about small tangles of fibrillar material devoid of a centering lumen (Fig. 28.88). Ultrastructural studies have confirmed that the cores of such structures and the neuropil-like matrix of the pale island consist of neuritic cytoplasmic processes laden with microtubules in parallel array and joined by specialized adhesion plaques, features restricted in combination to embryonal neurons.[690] Furthermore, both the Homer Wright rosette and pale island constitute loci of concentrated immunoreactivity for synaptophysin and other neuron-associated cytoplasmic antigens that include class III β-tubulin and microtubule-associated protein 2,[689] pale islands also evidencing upregulated immunoexpression of the TrkA and TrkC neurotrophin receptors.[674] Medulloblastomas may also contain populations immunoreactive for neurofilament proteins[678,686] as well as the Hu[321] and NeuN[355] neuronal nuclear antigens. Labeling for the latter reveals the oligodendrocyte-like elements of the pale island to be diminutive neuronal or "neurocytic" forms.

Advanced neurocytic maturation characterizes the rare tumors referred to as "**cerebellar neuroblastomas**," "**neuroblastic medulloblastomas**," or "**medulloblastomas with extensive nodularity**."[678,679] These resemble desmoplastic medulloblastomas but exhibit a more strikingly lobular microarchitecture, their outsized reticulin-free zones having unusually elongated profiles, being particularly rich in synaptophysin-immunoreactive fibrillary matrix material and boasting a population of small, amitotic and uniformly rounded cells arrayed in linear streams (Fig. 28.89). The differentiated neuronal nature of this population is apparent in that such cells elaborate cytoplasmic processes replete with clear and dense-cored secretory vesicles that may terminate in synaptic contacts. Some examples contain recognizable neurons of intermediate to large size and this embryonal neoplasm may rarely undergo sequential maturation to benign ganglioneurocytic or gangliogliomatous histology,[672,677] a phenomenon (possibly treatment-driven) recorded in isolated cases of conventional medulloblastoma as well.[669] Medulloblastomas of this sort seem to have a predilection for children younger than 3 years of age and to carry a more favorable prognosis than other subtypes (particularly in this patient cohort).[675,679] Though not all such tumors comply, neuroradiologic presentation as a cerebellar mass composed of contrast-enhancing nodules clustered in grape-like fashion is virtually diagnostic.[679] "Neuroblastic" foci may be found in otherwise conventional and desmoplastic/nodular medulloblastomas, having no clear clinical import in these settings.

Classical medulloblastomas are often found on immunohistochemical assessment to be colonized by GFAP-positive elements that tend to lie near stromal blood vessels and to display the stellate cytoplasmic configurations typical of reactive astroglia. These are generally taken to be entrapped, though the identification of similar cells in metastatic deposits raises the possibility that at least some represent neoplastic astrocytes of terminally differentiated nature.[678] GFAP-labeling cells of

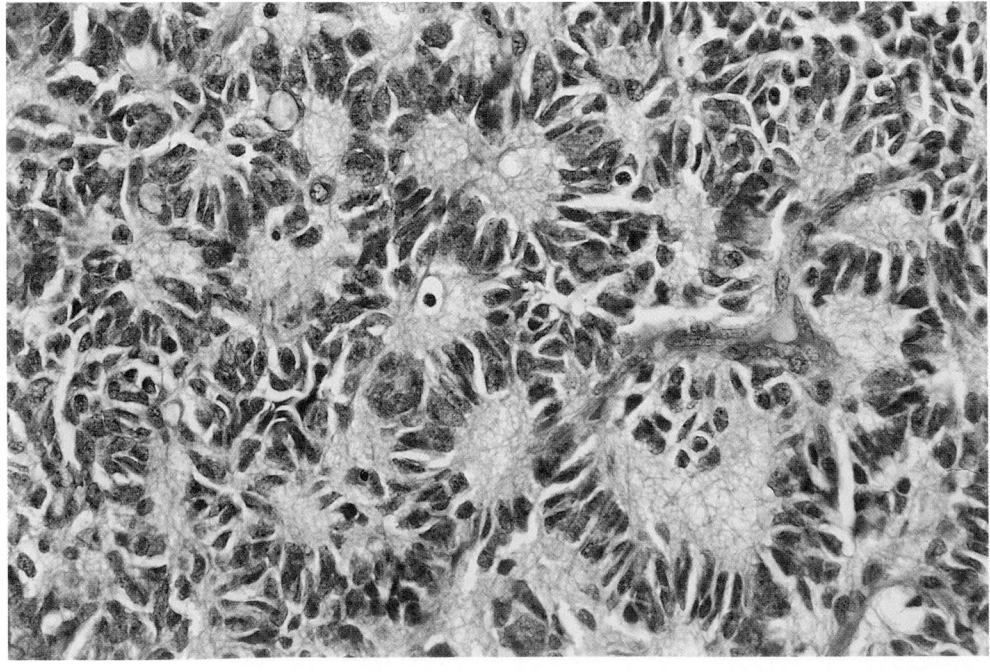

Fig. 28.88 Medulloblastoma. Homer Wright rosettes consist of tumor cell nuclei disposed in circular fashion about tangled cytoplasmic processes. These structures are indicative of differentiation along neuronal lines.

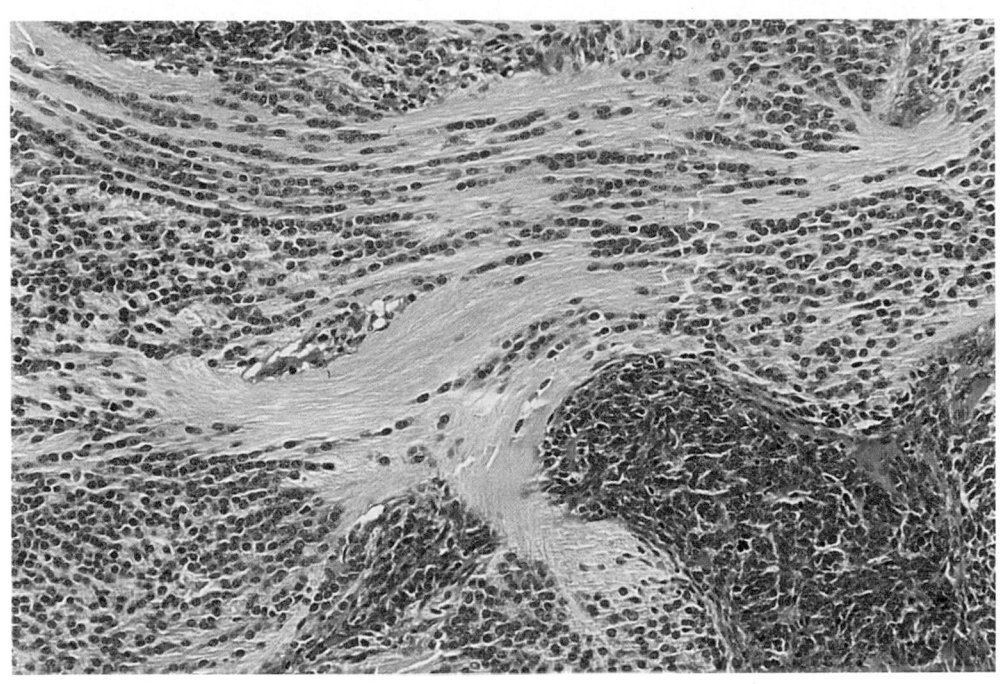

Fig. 28.89 "Neuroblastic" medulloblastoma. This variant of medulloblastoma is typified by the linear streaming of rounded, "neurocytic" tumor cell nuclei within amassed cytoplasmic processes.

indisputably neoplastic morphology are much less frequently encountered,[678,606,693] glial differentiation sufficiently advanced as to be obvious on routine microscopic inspection being most exceptional. A conspicuous network of fibrillary, GFAP-reactive cells is often localized to the pale islands of desmoplastic medulloblastomas, suggesting that these micronodules are organized centers of divergent astroglial, as well as neuronal, outgrowth.[689] We mention in passing the immunolabeling of some medulloblastomas for photoreceptor-associated proteins, including rod-opsin and retinal S-antigen,[671,685,693] as well as curious variants containing neurosensory rosettes of Flexner–Wintersteiner type.[685] Shared by retinoblastomas and pineoblastomas, such evidences of photosensory differentiation have been taken to support the unified cytogenesis of these embryonal neoplasms but, as discussed previously, this is an embattled hypothesis. The immunophenotypic potential of the medulloblastoma further includes reactivity for vimentin, desmin (typically limited to minor tumor cell subsets), nestin (a class VI intermediate filament protein expressed by many embryonic cell types, including neuroepithelial progenitors in the developing CNS), neural cell adhesion molecules, nerve growth factors and their receptors.[678] Even cytoplasmic actin labeling has been described,[666] a finding that we can confirm, and exceptional cases may evidence cytokeratin (AE1/3) reactivity.[694] The latter, when present, is usually a focal finding.

Regarding immunophenotype and its bearing on differential diagnosis, we would emphasize the labeling of nearly all medulloblastomas (including those of thoroughly undifferentiated histologic aspect) for synaptophysin as a property that may be exploited to exclude from further consideration such potentially confounding lesions as the poorly differentiated fourth ventricular ependymoma, other anaplastic gliomas, and primary cerebellar lymphoma (typified by a B-cell profile). A pertinent "negative" is the general failure of medulloblastomas to express thyroid transcription factor-1 (TTF-1), as metastatic small cell carcinoma of pulmonary origin potentially complicates the diagnostic picture when one is dealing with adult neurosurgical material (and shares synaptophysin labeling) but is usually TTF-1-reactive.[694] We have not encountered a solitary cerebellar metastasis as the presenting manifestation of an otherwise occult small cell carcinoma. The reader is advised to consult the section dealing with atypical teratoid/rhabdoid tumors for differential diagnostic discussion of an embryonal neoplasm that often arises in the cerebellum and frequently harbors medulloblastoma-like small cell components.

We have elected to cite here only a small sample of the many studies detailing the immunohistochemical profile of medulloblastomas and make no attempt to dissect the conflicting (and, at present, clinically immaterial) data that have emerged from efforts to correlate the expression of neuronal, glial and photosensory antigens with tumor behavior.[671,686,693] Simply put, neither immunophenotypic nor conventional light microscopic indices of differentiation along specific cellular lines have proven predictive of tumor biology in sufficiently consistent fashion as to figure in current treatment planning, although the medulloblastoma with extensive nodularity/neuroblastic medulloblastoma may emerge as a variant amenable to less aggressive management than other subtypes. Conspicuous mitotic activity, necrosis, diploidy, high proliferative indices and c-myc gene amplification have been correlated with decreased survival in some investigations,[678] but none of these variables has found general application in clinical practice and all medulloblastomas are currently approached as high-grade neoplasms with a propensity for CSF-borne metastasis as well as local recurrence. High-level expression by medulloblastomas of mRNA encoding the TrkC neurotrophin receptor appears to be strongly associated with favorable outcome,[682] but this observation requires validation in prospective, randomized trials. Especially thought provoking is the predictive power demonstrated for oligonucleotide microarray analyses of medulloblastoma gene expression.[661] Details may be found in the cited reference.

At present, the therapeutic approach to medulloblastomas is predicated solely on clinical variables.[684,695] The "standard risk" patient is generally defined as a subject 3 years of age or older who has undergone complete (or near-total) resection of a tumor confined to the posterior fossa. Protocols combining chemotherapy and whole neuraxis irradiation have achieved 5-year survivals exceeding 80% in this relatively favorable clinical setting, very few such patients experiencing late relapse. Children below the age of 3 years at diagnosis, individuals of any age with evident CSF dissemination (found in approximately 30% of cases on initial evaluation), or with bulky residual disease after surgery—"poor risk" patients—do not fare as well. Whether the excess mortality noted in the very young reflects intrinsic tumor biology or the reluctance of neuro-oncologists to expose the immature nervous system to the predictably toxic doses of radiation that have been considered requisite to achieving disease control is unclear. Certainly, the price exacted of childhood medulloblastoma survivors by conventional radiotherapy—growth failure, endocrinopathy, significant intellectual impairment, behavioral disturbances, and the induction of secondary neoplasms that include meningiomas, sarcomas and glioblastomas—has been disheartening and continues to drive investigations aimed at reducing CNS radiation exposure in the pediatric cohort.[695] Whereas treatment failure in the posterior fossa or along the craniospinal axis is the rule, medulloblastomas do occasionally travel to more distant sites. Skeletal deposits, often widespread, account for over 90% of systemic metastases, but the liver, lymph nodes and lungs may be involved as may the abdominal cavity (via ventriculoperitoneal shunts placed to relieve obstructive hydrocephalus). While late relapses may be encountered, medulloblastomas usually conform to the principle (Collins' law) that defines the period of risk for recurrence of embryonal childhood neoplasms as equal to the patients' age at diagnosis plus 9 months.

Particularly aggressive behavior and treatment resistance characterize tumors reported as "**large cell**" or "**anaplastic**" medulloblastomas (Fig. 28.90).[667,675,680,691,694a] The former descriptor has been applied to neoplasms

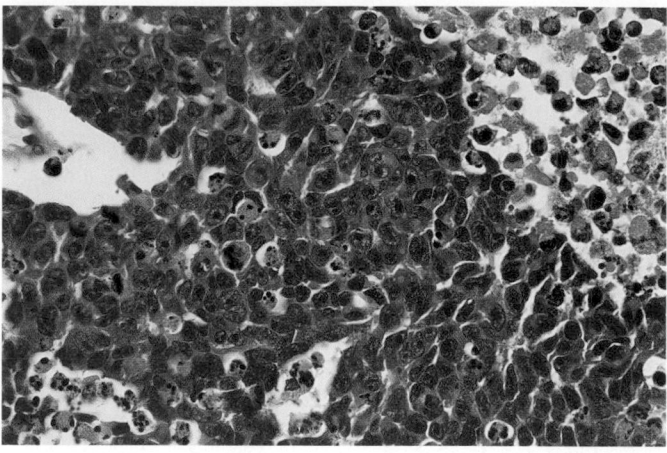

Fig. 28.90 Large cell/anaplastic medulloblastoma. Cellular enlargement, often prominent nucleoli, and pronounced mitotic and apoptotic activity are features of this virulent medulloblastoma subtype.

conspicuously or wholly populated by monomorphic cells with large, rounded and vesicular nuclei, prominent nucleoli and variably abundant eosinophilic cytoplasm. The adjective "anaplastic" recognizes tumors exhibiting marked variation in nuclear size and contour, multinucleated and bizarre giant cells inhabiting some examples. The cannibalistic wrapping of tumor cells about one another is a striking feature of many cases.[667,675] In fact, large cell and anaplastic medulloblastomas evidence considerable cytologic overlap and appear to constitute a unified entity. High mitotic rates are the rule and apoptotic cellular remains, typically abundant, may form confluent lakes and serpiginous seams. Cytoplasmic immunolabeling for synaptophysin is generally retained and reactivity for neurofilament proteins and chromogranin may also be demonstrable. Focal GFAP expression has been documented, but is exceptional. Large cell/anaplastic features may be apparent at presentation or appear only at relapse and can be encountered in medulloblastomas of otherwise classic or desmoplastic/nodular type as well as medullomyoblastomas (discussed below).[691] Of differential diagnostic utility are the observations that large cell/anaplastic medulloblastomas do not manifest the inclusion-like cytoplasmic bodies, EMA immunoreactivity or chromosome 22 abnormalities of the atypical teratoid/rhabdoid tumor.[667,691] That the former are members of the medulloblastoma series is supported by the demonstration that at least some of these unusual neoplasms exhibit allelic losses of chromosome 17p with isochromosome 17q formation (the most common genetic alterations associated with classical medulloblastomas).[667,680,691] Myc oncogene amplifications, previously mentioned as an adverse prognostic indicator, may be especially prevalent in this medulloblastoma subset.[667,676,680,691]

Certain rare neoplasms classed as medulloblastoma variants merit additional comment. The **melanotic** medulloblastoma is defined by its content of pigmented cells disposed in tubules, papillae, or nests.[673,687] These are stained by conventional histochemical methods for the demonstration of melanin, can be shown to contain melanosomes in varying stages of maturation, and may represent differentiation along the lines of the ocular pigment epithelium. Although this lesion bears some histologic resemblance to the indolent melanotic neuroectodermal tumors of infancy that arise in the maxillary and epididymal regions, it is a virulent neoplasm prone to early and widespread neuraxis dissemination along CSF pathways. The medullomyoblastoma is named for its heterologous rhabdomyoblastic elements.[665,683,692] This curious entity has been variously interpreted as a medulloblastoma evidencing the extreme plasticity of its multipotential neuroepithelial precursors, as a tumor derived from neural crest (ectomesenchymal) progenitors recognized for their ability to differentiate along striated muscle lines, as a composite neoplasm populated by myoblastic constituents that arise via the secondary neoplastic induction of leptomeningeal or stromal elements, and, finally, as a lopsided, bidermal teratoma. Several examples reported under this designation have harbored cystic components with the appearance of mature, tridermal teratoma.[692] Some medullomyoblastomas have been found to harbor an isochrome 17q,[691] suggesting that at least a subset is allied with the more conventional medulloblastoma subtypes. Variants containing both muscular and melanotic elements have been described,[688] as has medulloblastoma with chondroid differentiation.[664] A group of adult-onset tumors originally characterized as "lipomatous medulloblastomas" is now recognized to be more closely allied with neoplasms of neurocytic type.

These are termed cerebellar liponeurocytomas in current WHO nomenclature and are discussed elsewhere under that designation (see "Central neurocytomas and extraventricular neurocytic neoplasms"). Conventional medulloblastomas may rarely contain lipid-laden cells in conspicuous numbers, these usually representing macrophages.[681]

Medulloepithelioma

The medulloepithelioma is a highly aggressive neoplasm that typically arises in the cerebrum of an infant or child younger than 5 years of age.[703] Particularly characteristic is a deep, paraventricular localization—a topography adduced in support of a postulated origin from the lining germinal matrix of the developing forebrain—but medulloepitheliomas may also originate in the third ventricular/thalamostriate regions, cerebellum, brainstem, and cauda equina.[703] Ocular neoplasms of comparable morphology are well recognized and rare examples presenting as sciatic nerve[704] or pelvic[698,701] growths are on record. These extraneural variants are not further considered here.

Often attaining massive proportions, medulloepitheliomas are usually well circumscribed and composed of friable, gray–pink tissue evidencing hemorrhage, necrosis and, in some cases, cystic change. Their defining feature is the formation of tubules, ribbons or, less frequently, papillae resembling, and believed to represent a recapitulation of, the medullary epithelial structuring of the primitive neural tube (Fig. 28.91). These are fashioned of pseudostratified columnar cells that rest on a continuous, PAS-positive basement membrane and are sometimes capped by apical cytoplasmic blebs. PAS-positive material may also coat luminal surfaces as an

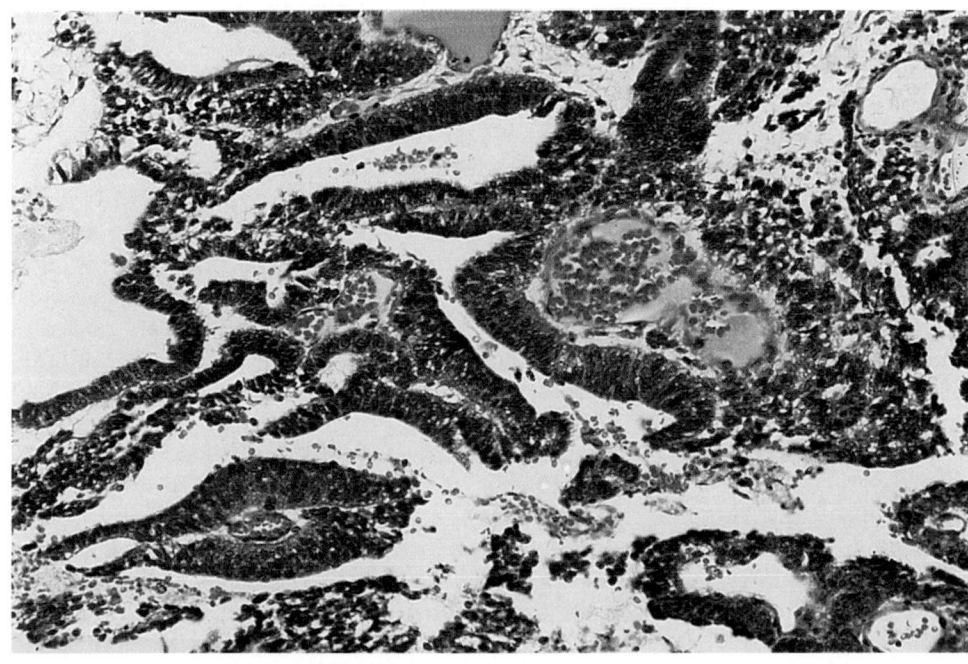

Fig. 28.91 Medulloepithelioma. A tubulopapillary disposition of its columnar elements characterizes this primitive neuroepithelial neoplasm.

ill-defined, granular pseudomembrane. Mitotic figures are readily identifiable and generally abluminal in location, a pattern reminiscent of the juxtaventricular proliferative activity characterizing early neurocytogenesis. Selective labeling of these inner, mitotically active elements for nestin and full thickness immunoreactivity of this neoplastic neuroepithelium for vimentin and microtubule-associated protein type 5 (MAP–5) are additional antigenic features shared with the embryonic neural tube.[702] Some observers have found focal labeling for GFAP, class III β-tubulin and neurofilament protein epitopes within these arrays, but this would appear to be exceptional.[699] Also described are instances of apical immunoreactivity for EMA and focal cytoplasmic labeling for NSE and cytokeratins.[699,702,707] It should be noted that medulloepithelial structures vary greatly in extent from case to case and may constitute only a regionally limited finding in an otherwise patternless, small cell neoplasm of thoroughly undifferentiated aspect.

In keeping with their proposed stem cell derivation, medulloepitheliomas often manifest divergent differentiation and maturation, at times advanced, along astrocytic, ependymal, neuronal and, rarely, oligodendroglial lines.[699,700,703,705] A tubulopapillary, melanotic fourth ventricular neoplasm interpreted as a pigmented medulloepithelioma is on record,[706] as is an example containing chondroid, osseous and skeletal muscle elements.[697] The exact nosologic position of the latter in relation to the immature teratoma, which may harbor medullary-type neuroepithelial formations, is problematic. Obviously, the presence of admixed nonteratomatous germ cell components and evidence of endodermal or somatic ectodermal differentiation should be sought and excluded before a diagnosis of medulloepithelioma is rendered, particularly if neoplastic mesenchymal tissues are identified.

The differential diagnosis of the medulloepithelioma must also include the ependymoblastoma and choroid plexus carcinoma. Medulloepitheliomas may contain elements of ependymoblastoma (described below), but their neuromedullary components rest on basement membranes foreign to ependymoblastic rosettes and do not fashion at the EM level such ependymal specializations as crowning cilia, microvilli, or complex intercellular junctions of zonula adherens type.[707] Ependymoblastomas, by definition, do not manifest divergent differentiation along astrocytic or neuronal lines. The same is true of choroid plexus carcinomas which, in addition, tend to a more obviously villiform architecture than is displayed by most medulloepitheliomas and, unlike the latter, may display widespread immunoreactivity for S-100 protein and cytokeratins. We have previously cited, in our discussion of fibrillary astrocytic neoplasms, reference to glioblastomas harboring medulloepithelioma-like structures.

The medulloepithelioma is highly malignant and typically kills within 1 to 2 years of diagnosis. Uncontrollable growth at the primary site is the usual cause of death, but widespread leptomeningeal metastasis is frequent as well and may occur early in the disease course.

Central neuroblastic tumors

The diagnosis of **neuroblastoma** should be reserved for extracerebellar neoplasms of embryonal appearance that can be shown to differentiate solely along neuronal lines. Neuroblastomas of the central neuraxis are typified by a presentation in the first decade of life (usually prior to age 5 years) and localization to the cerebral hemispheres,[709,712] though they may arise within the ventricular system[716] and intraspinal compartment.[713,717]

Consisting of friable gray tissue prone to necrosis, hemorrhage and cystic change, neuroblastomas often achieve enormous proportions by the time they are discovered but tend to appear relatively circumscribed. Induction of a collagenous stroma lends to some examples a firm consistency and unusually lobulated contours. Although there is no biologic import to this division, several histologic variants are recognized. The **"classic"** neuroblastoma is composed of small, mitotically active cells possessed of densely hyperchromatic nuclei and disposed in highly populous sheets. Variably represented is a delicate fibrillary matrix consisting of tangled cytoplasmic processes. It is this subtype that is most likely to contain Homer Wright rosettes and large neurons of ganglion cell type. Occasional examples manifest a compact palisading of tumor cell nuclei within their neuropil-like matrices.[715] Tumor cells may also palisade about foci of necrosis, imparting a small cell glioblastoma-like histology to some examples.[714] The **"desmoplastic"** neuroblastoma is defined by a fibrous stroma, most developed where tumor contacts the leptomeninges, that imposes lobular, trabecular or single-file arrangements on its constituent cells. Larger than classic neuroblasts, the latter are characterized by vesicular nuclei, distinct nucleoli and, in some cases, a modest paranuclear expanse of hematoxyphilic or plum-colored cytoplasm. The **"transitional"** neuroblastoma combines features of both the classic and desmoplastic variants. Only exceptionally do central neuroblastic tumors evidence the graded maturational alterations so often displayed by their retroperitoneal and posterior mediastinal counterparts, meriting designation as ganglioneuroblastomas.[708,711,717–719]

In the absence of Homer Wright rosettes or an unarguably neoplastic (as opposed to entrapped) neuronal population, the diagnosis of neuroblastoma needs ultrastructural or immunocytochemical defending. Neurite-like cytoplasmic processes containing microtubules in parallel array, dense-core and clear, synaptic-type vesicles signal neuronal differentiation. Attempts at synapse formation, usually abortive, are apparent in only a small minority of cases. Immunohistochemical assessment obviates the need for electron microscopic study if cytoplasmic synaptophysin or neurofilament protein labeling can be demonstrated. Synaptophysin reactivity is far the more sensitive index and typically concentrated in the fibrillar matrix. GFAP expression should be limited to cells reasonably interpreted as reactive astrocytes. These possess stellate cytoplasmic processes, are most numerous at the tumor–brain interface and, when present deeper within a lesion, usually lie near penetrating blood vessels. Some observers have credited central neuroblastic tumors with the capacity to generate GFAP-immunoreactive schwannian elements,[711] but the exact nature of the cells in question is far from clear.[718]

The interpretation of survival data reported for patients with cerebral neuroblastomas is complicated by the inclusion in some series of cases that would now be regarded as examples of central neurocytoma or desmoplastic infantile ganglioglioma, both associated with a favorable prognosis, as well as anaplastic small cell tumors not further characterized as to differentiating potential.[709,712,716] Still, neuroblastomas seem more amenable to surgical and radiotherapeutic management than other primitive extracerebellar neoplasms,[709] some observers recording a particularly gratifying outcome following resection of largely cystic examples.[710] The risks of local regrowth and CSF-borne metastasis, however, are high and spread to extraneural sites is occasionally seen.[709,712] Noteworthy are isolated instances of late local recurrence in which reoperation has demonstrated maturation of central neuroblastomas to differentiated ganglion cell tumors.[708,719]

Ependymoblastoma

A high-grade neoplasm of infancy and early childhood, the **ependymoblastoma** tends to a paraventricular localization deep within the cerebral hemispheres but may arise in the posterior fossa.[720,722] Primary leptomeningeal[724] and extradural, sacrococcygeal[723] presentations have been described, the latter associated with elevated serum α-fetoprotein levels. The tumor is densely populated by small, monomorphous cells disposed in sheets and broad, anastomosing cords punctuated by "ependymoblastic" rosettes. These defining structures lack the PAS-positive basement membranes of medulloepitheliomatous arrays and are distinguished from rosettes of mature ependymal type by a multilayered stratification of their encircling nuclei and by manifest proliferative activity, mitoses often lying in a juxtaluminal position. Perivascular pseudorosettes are not in evidence or only poorly developed. Necrosis is common but not associated with cellular palisading and there is generally no microvascular proliferation—additional features separating these embryonal neoplasms from anaplastic ependymomas. Ultrastructural studies

have confirmed that rosette-forming elements are ependymal in nature, sporting elaborate apical cell junctions, microvilli, and cilia.[720,721,723] These may exhibit focal GFAP immunolabeling, but this is an inconstant finding.[720,721] We have alluded to regional ependymoblastic differentiation within medulloepitheliomas. Ependymoblastomas, by definition, are devoid of medullary epithelial structures and incapable of divergent neuronal differentiation. Disseminated CSF-borne metastasis is common and most examples prove fatal within 1 to 2 years of diagnosis.

Polar spongioblastoma

It is in deference to a traditional view[727] that the so-called **polar spongioblastoma** represents a primitive neuroepithelial neoplasm of distinctive character that we briefly address it here, but there is, in fact, considerable controversy as to whether the peculiar tumors awarded this designation constitute a unified entity[728] and this diagnosis has actually been deleted from the current WHO nosology.[660] A tendency to arise in the walls of the third and fourth ventricles in childhood has been asserted,[727] but no generalizations as regards clinical course emerge from the literature. The tumor is composed of spindled cells with fusiform nuclei that appear suspended in compact palisades between delicate uni- or bipolar cytoplasmic processes in close parallel array. This arresting disposition has been likened to the radial arrangement of migrating glia ("spongioblasts") that characterizes the 16- to 18-week stage of human neuroembryogenesis.[727] Skeptics point to the fact that a comparably rhythmic architecture may be encountered in neoplasms that otherwise qualify as classic oligodendrogliomas, pilocytic astrocytomas, glioblastomas, ependymomas, neuroblastomas, and medulloblastomas.[728] To believers, however, a frequent admixture of conventional oligodendroglial and astrocytic elements has simply constituted evidence that the polar spongioblastoma derives from embryonic forbears committed to differentiate along glial lines. Uncritical acceptance of this entity is further complicated by its lack of defining immunohistochemical or ultrastructural features. The presumed spongioblastic constituents are said to be GFAP-negative, consonant with their putatively primitive nature.[726,727] Whether examples reported to contain intracytoplasmic dense-core vesicles and microtubules[725] are not better regarded as neuroblastoma variants is open to question.

It is our view that the diagnosis of polar spongioblastoma, if resorted to at all, should be reserved for neoplasms that exhibit a compact, palisaded growth pattern throughout. Careful search should be made for telltale foci exhibiting the features of any of the conventional tumor types mentioned above and classification based on the histology of such areas, however limited in volume. Immunoassessment for synaptophysin expression and, if that proves negative, ultrastructural examination are required to exclude palisaded cerebral neuroblastoma.

Assorted primitive neuroectodermal tumors

The term **primitive neuroectodermal tumor (PNET)** was originally coined not as a generic appellation for embryonal neoplasms of every stripe, which it was to become, but to designate a cerebral tumor of infancy and childhood characterized by medulloblastoma-like histology and a propensity to disseminate along CSF pathways.[734] As initially defined, at least 90% of the tumor qualifying for this diagnosis had to consist of uniformly small and densely hyperchromatic cells of entirely undifferentiated appearance disposed in patternless sheets. Additionally described in many cases were desmoplastic mesenchymal components, sharp tumor circumscription, high mitotic rates, necrosis, and cystic change. Often noted, as well, were limited foci of apparent glial, neuronal or bidirectional differentiation.

The problems inherent in defining a neoplasm largely on the basis of its undifferentiated appearances should be obvious. The diagnosis of PNET rests on firmest ground when applied to extracerebellar tumors of embryonal aspect exhibiting divergent neuronoglial differentiation. The demonstration of a polymorphous immunophenotype is useful in this regard, some PNETs clearly coexpressing synaptophysin and multiple intermediate filament proteins (most often the complex of vimentin–GFAP–neurofilament protein but, occasionally, cytokeratins and desmin as well[732]). Murky is the distinction of putative PNETs evidencing GFAP immunolabeling alone from highly anaplastic gliomas. In practice, we find ourselves applying the former label to largely monomorphic, small cell neoplasms of childhood containing GFAP-positive elements but manifesting neither the complex microvascular proliferation nor perinecrotic cellular palisading that typify high-grade glial neoplasms (particularly astrocytomas) of conventional type. Immunoreactive cells often huddle in small clusters or aggregate about stromal blood vessels, are poorly fibrillated and may assume a microgemistocytic or miniature rhabdoid appearance. We caution the reader against the low percentage diagnosis of PNET in an adult, the patient so labeled almost invariably proving to harbor a glioblastoma with small cell features at reoperation or autopsy. Convincing ultrastructural or immunohistochemical evidence of divergent glioneuronal differentiation must be forwarded to support the diagnosis in this setting.

Neoplasms interpreted as PNET variants have been reported to follow prophylactic cranial irradiation for childhood leukemia and lymphoma,[730] to arise in the leptomeninges[739] and cauda equina,[713] to evidence choroid plexus differentiation,[735] and to contain smooth muscle,[740] rhabdomyoblastic[729] or adipocytic[737,740] elements. Noteworthy as well, though of uncertain nosologic status, are composite tumors described as harboring admixtures of neuroblastoma/ganglioneuroblastoma and variably differentiated astrocytoma.[738] We have encountered cerebral neoplasms similar to a unique cerebellar lesion descriptively designated as a "**desmoplastic primitive neuroectodermal tumor with divergent differentiation.**"[743] The recorded case was characterized by nests and cords of small neuroepithelial cells (some labeling for synaptophysin, neurofilament protein epitopes, GFAP, and cytokeratins) embedded in a cellular "stroma" populated by desmin-immunoreactive elements. At recurrence, this exhibited strikingly epithelioid features and overt neuronal (ganglion cell) differentiation. Curiosities that potentially complicate the differential diagnosis of central PNETs include intracranial examples of the **melanotic neuroectodermal tumor of infancy,**[744] the **desmoplastic small round-cell tumor** of Gerald and Rosai,[741] and the **Ewing sarcoma/"peripheral" PNET.**[731] The last two of these entities are characterized by specific t(11;22) chromosomal translocations foreign to embryonal tumors of central neuroepithelial type[736] and critical to definitive tumor classification. The limited studies communicated to date report that immunolabeling for the MIC2 gene product CD99, a characteristic feature of the Ewing sarcoma/"peripheral" PNET family, is not shared by central PNETs or medulloblastomas,[733] but we have rarely encountered exceptions to this rule. Genetically confirmed intracranial examples of Ewing sarcoma/ "peripheral" PNET have been described mainly as dura-based lesions,[731] though an intramedullary case is also on record.[742]

Atypical teratoid/rhabdoid tumor

The **atypical teratoid/rhabdoid tumor (AT/RT)** is a highly aggressive neoplasm encountered principally in the posterior fossa of infancy and early childhood.[748,750] Over 90% of afflicted patients reported to date have been less than 5 years of age at diagnosis (mean = 20 months) and approximately 50% have harbored tumors of the cerebellum or cerebellopontine angle, often with contiguous brainstem involvement. Supratentorial (cerebral or suprasellar), pineal region and intraspinal examples account for some 40%, 5%, and 2% of recorded cases, respectively. MRI typically discloses a bulky mass, often partly cystic and hemorrhagic, with a profile indistinguishable from that of the medulloblastoma/PNET—T1 hypointensity, T2 iso/hypointensity and contrast enhancement being the rule. Approximately one third of patients have evidence of CSF dissemination at diagnosis, half succumb to disease within 6 months, and survival beyond 1 year is exceptional.

AT/RTs are so designated in acknowledgment of their potentially complex histology.[748,750] In fact, only a minority consist solely of rhabdoid cells and the latter (characterized in classic form by distinct cell borders, large and vesicular nuclei, macronucleoli and globose, paranuclear cytoplasmic inclusions of hyalin appearance) may be only sparsely represented among tumor cells with uniformly dense and eosinophilic, finely granular, vacuolated, wispy or water-clear cytoplasm (Fig. 28.92A). These nonrhabdoid, large cell elements may include variably spindled, polygonal and bizarre, multinucleated cells disposed in nests or sheets. Bands of hyalinized collagen traverse some examples, while others exhibit myxoid change and a chordoid growth pattern. The adjectival "teratoid" reflects the presence, in many tumors of this group, of varied neoplastic tissue components (Fig. 28.92B). Most prominently represented are small cell elements of embryonal appearance indistinguishable from those that typify the medulloblastoma/PNET. The latter, encountered in 60–70% of cases—and the vastly dominant component in some examples—usually assume an undifferentiated histologic profile but may fashion rosettes of Homer Wright, Flexner–Wintersteiner or ependymoblastic type, some AT/RTs containing ependymal canals or neural tube-like structures within their primitive neuroepithelial compartment. Approximately 30% harbor spindle cell mesenchymal components (these often having a fetal mesenchyme-like appearance) and roughly 25% contain epithelial elements that may be represented by cohesive cell nests, glands, adenoid structures or keratinizing squamous islands. Differentiation along striated muscle lines has not been reported.

Immunohistochemical assessment is critical to the distinction of AT/RTs from a variety of neoplasms that may assume rhabdoid cytologic features. A complex immunophenotype is the rule.[748,750] Rhabdoid and nonrhabdoid large cell elements invariably display labeling for vimentin (with intense decoration of cytoplasmic inclusions, when present), are nearly always immunoreactive for epithelial membrane antigen (EMA), and commonly label for glial fibrillary acidic protein (GFAP) and smooth muscle actin (SMA) as well. The percentage of cells reactive for each antigen is highly variable. EMA labeling may be diffuse or confined to cytoplasmic membranes, antibodies to SMA occasionally decorating a peripheral cytoplasmic ring with particular intensity (a pattern encountered in some smooth muscle tumors). In this connection, we would cite gene expression studies confirming the activation of a myogenic differentiation program in AT/RTs.[661] Also common is immunoreactivity of the large cell components for cytokeratins (AE1/3; CAM 5.2) and some may be decorated by antibodies to neurofilament protein (NFP) and synaptophysin (SYN). Desmin reactivity, present in only a minority of cases, is usually restricted to mesenchymal or PNET-like regions (which may also label for NFP, SYN, and GFAP). Epithelial elements, not surprisingly, label for cytokeratins and, less commonly, EMA. Finely granular α-fetoprotein staining of large cell elements has been reported,[748] but AT/RTs assessed for placental alkaline phophatase (PLAP) and beta-human chorionic gonadotropin (β-HCG) immunoreactivity have been uniformly negative.

That the polymorphous neoplasms yoked under the AT/RT designation constitute a unified entity is supported by cytogenetic and molecular genetic observations.[545,745] Over 90% of the AT/RTs assessed to date have been characterized by monosomy/deletions or mutations involving chromosome 22q on fluorescence in situ hybridization (FISH) or loss of heterozygosity (LOH) analysis. FISH may be applied to paraffin-embedded tissues for this purpose.[747,748] The apparently responsible gene—hSNF5/INI 1—maps to 22q11.2 and codes for a ubiquitously expressed protein that is a member of the SWI/SNF complex.[545,745] Proteins of the latter family apparently effect conformational alterations in the nucleosome that influence histone–DNA binding, thus facili

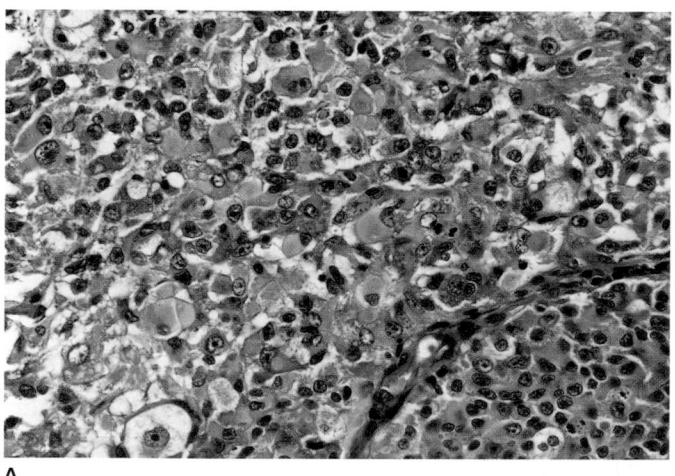
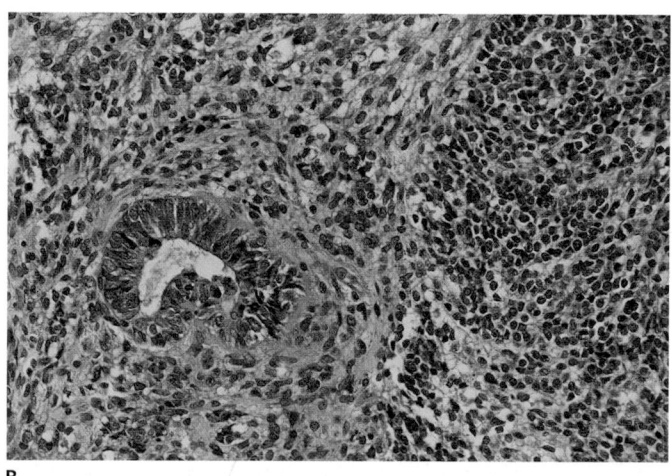

A

B

Fig. 28.92 Atypical teratoid/rhabdoid tumor. Neoplasms of this family typically contain at least some cells of large, rhabdoid phenotype (A). A second example (B) harbors, at right, small cell elements of primitive neuroepithelial appearance and a differentiated glandular structure, at left, embedded in a neoplastic component of mesenchymal aspect.

tating transcription factor access. It would appear that INI 1 functions as a tumor suppressor gene in the development of both AT/RTs and the extra-CNS RTs (including renal examples) of infancy and early childhood,[545,745] INI 1 alterations also characterizing a subset of choroid plexus carcinomas and select tumors histologically indistinguishable from medulloblastomas and supratentorial PNETs.[545] The familial occurrence of these tumor types in various combination constitutes a syndrome associated with germline INI 1 mutation.[749,751] As previously mentioned in our discussion of choroid plexus carcinomas, the latter may share with AT/RTs a rhabdoid cytologic profile and potentially complex immunophenotype as well as chromosome 22q/INI 1 abnormalities.[550]

Mesenchymal, neuroectomesenchymal, meningeal, stem and germ cells have all been forwarded as progenitors of the AT/RT. As regards a germinal origin, it should be pointed out that no CNS tumor evidencing the histology, immunophenotype or molecular genetic profile of the AT/RT has ever been reported to contain elements of germinoma, embryonal carcinoma, yolk sac tumor, choriocarcinoma, syncytiotrophoblastic giant cells or the organoid structures (e.g., miniature gut- or bronchus-like formations) found in many bona fide teratomas. Only a small minority of AT/RTs arise along the midline suprasellar-pineal axis in which 90% of intracranial germ cell tumors originate.

The differential diagnosis of the AT/RT includes, in addition to rhabdoid variants of choroid plexus carcinoma and germ cell tumors, neoplasms of disparate histogenesis that can assume rhabdoid guises and arise within, or secondarily involve, the CNS. Principal considerations, given the locations favored by the AT/RT, the age group at risk and frequent presence within this neoplasm of embryonal neuroepithelial elements that may dominate the histologic picture, are the medulloblastoma, including its "large cell" variant, pineoblastoma and other primitive neuroepithelial tumors (central PNETs) arising within the supratentorial and intraspinal compartments. Thought provoking is the possibility that some neoplasms of ostensibly pure, medulloblastomatous or PNET-like appearance actually represent "lopsided" variants of AT/RT. Occasional tumors so diagnosed will be found to display monosomy 22 or deletions/mutations involving INI 1[749,751]—genetic alterations otherwise foreign to primitive neuroepithelial neoplasms and, as discussed above, characteristic of the AT/RT. At least some tumors reported as medulloblastomas or pineoblastomas arising in association with renal RTs of infancy and early childhood[746] may actually have been AT/RTs of exclusively neuroepithelial appearance complicating constitutional INI 1 mutations. On a practical note, we would emphasize that the complex immunophenotype evidenced by most AT/RTs—particularly colabelling of their large cell elements for VIM, EMA, GFAP, and SMA—segregates these from the conventional embryonal neoplasms of central neuroepithelial derivation and from other tumor types (sarcomas, meningiomas, gliomas, melanomas, and carcinomas) that occasionally exhibit rhabdoid features. Assessment of chromosome 22/INI 1 status may be required in ambiguous cases,[747] and serves to unmask AT/RTs presenting as medulloblastomas/PNETs of infancy.

Pineal parenchymal tumors

The pineal gland is populated in the main by specially modified neuronal elements, known as pineal parenchymal cells or "pineocytes," that number among their functions the secretion of melatonin—a potent regulator of gonadotrophic and other endocrine hormonal activity. Tumors of pineal parenchymal lineage include the embryonal pineoblastoma, the mature pineocytoma, and lesions exhibiting mixed histology or intermediate degrees of differentiation.[758,762,765] As a rule, such neoplasms present as solid, contrast-enhancing masses associated with manifestations of obstructive hydrocephalus owing to aqueductal compression or disturbances of ocular motility (classically including the upwards gaze paresis termed Parinaud's syndrome) resulting from pressure on the mesencephalic tectum.

The **pineoblastoma** is characterized by a predilection for children and adolescents, aggressive local growth with destructive invasion of neighboring structures, and a proclivity for dissemination via the CSF. Primitive in appearance, it is densely populated by diminutive cells with hyperchromatic, round or variably angulated and molded nuclei. These may exhibit brisk mitotic activity and are disposed in patternless sheets or lobules that are often punctuated by zones of coagulative necrosis and dystrophic calcification. The monotony may be relieved by the formation of Homer Wright rosettes, identical to those of the neuroblastoma and medulloblastoma, that attest (along with frequent tumoral synaptophysin immunoreactivity) to a shared capacity for neuronal differentiation. Rare variants have been described as containing mature ganglion cell and glial elements,[767] occasional examples evincing an atavistic potential for photosensory differentiation that recapitulates the phylogenesis of the pineal gland as the primary photoreceptor of low vertebrates and "third" eye of some mammalian species. The pineoblastoma may thus fashion Flexner–Wintersteiner rosettes and fleurettes a la the retinoblastoma, can elaborate club-shaped cilia with the 9+0 axonemal array characteristic of photosensory cells,[763] and is capable of expressing various retinal antigens (including the rhodopsin-binding S antigen or "arrestin," normally involved in visual signal transduction[762]).

The vestigial photosensory attributes of the human pineal gland are also obliquely evidenced by the occurrence of pineoblastomas, some exhibiting photoreceptor-associated features, in complex with retinoblastomas.

Afflicted patients typically carry germline mutations of the retinoblastoma tumor-suppressor gene and their ocular neoplasms are usually bilateral—hence, designation of this curious phenomenon as the **"trilateral retinoblastoma"** syndrome.[752,760] Rare pineoblastomas actually harbor melanotic elements in tubular array that have been likened to pigmented ciliary or retinal-type epithelium,[764,766] similar cellular components transiently populating the fetal pineal gland and, parenthetically, typifying the melanotic neuroectodermal ("retinal anlage") tumor of infancy.[754] That the human gland is also home to an enigmatic population of myoid, striated muscle-type cells is noteworthy given the presence of rhabdomyoblastic differentiation in the "pineal anlage tumor"—a complex, pineoblastomatous neoplasm that may also contain melanotic and even chondroblastic elements.[761,766] The similarity of such tumors to neoplasms derived from the primitive medullary epithelium of the optic vesicle (teratoid ocular medulloepitheliomas or "diktyomas") has been noted.

The appellation of **pineocytoma** has been extended over the years to neoplasms of varying histology and disparate biologic potential. We concur in the view that this diagnosis is best reserved for the tumor in which neoplastic cells are arrayed about a conspicuous, anuclear meshwork of delicate, synaptophysin-immunoreactive cytoplasmic processes in formations dubbed "pineocytomatous" rosettes.[758,762,765] Looking like outsized versions of the Homer Wright rosette but often of less regular contour (Fig. 28.93), these are frequently found in confluent arrangements alongside regions of uninterrupted, sheet-like or lobular tumor growth. Such lesions are largely devoid of mitotic activity, do not exhibit necrosis and are typically dominated by monomorphous, cytologically benign-appearing elements with rounded nuclear profiles. They can, however, harbor

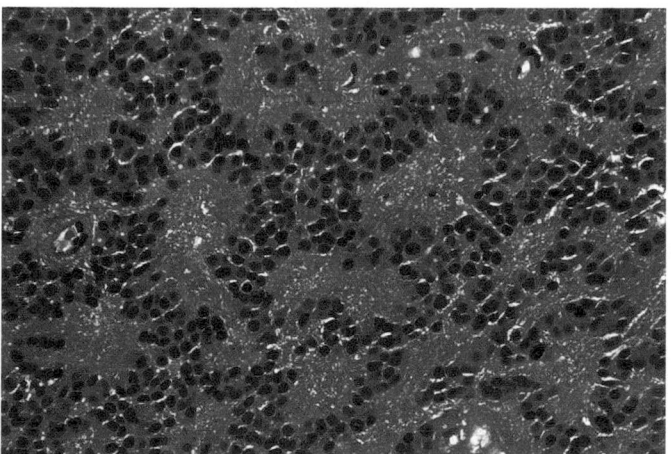

Fig. 28.93 Pineocytoma. Shown here are the conspicuous rosettes that constitute a defining feature of this neoplasm. Note the benign nuclear features, monomorphism, and absence of mitotic activity.

admixed tumor giant cells (including hyperchromatic and multinucleated forms) to which no prognostic import attaches.[758,759] Ganglion cells may be identified within **"pleomorphic pineocytomas"** of the latter type.[759]

Ultrastructural studies have demonstrated that the cytoplasmic processes elaborated by pineocytoma cells distinctly resemble those of native pineocytes in the tendency of microtubule-laden, neurite-like cellular extensions to end as bulbous expansions containing clear vesicles of synaptic type, dense core ("neurosecretory") vesicles and vesicle-crowned rodlets.[755,757,763] The last, also known as synaptic ribbons and recognized as a distinctive feature of mammalian pineocytes, consist of closely apposed, bar-like osmiophilic densities measuring approximately 700 nm in length by 50 nm in width that are surrounded by clear vesicles 60 nm in diameter. A further specialization shared with pineal parenchymal cells are paired cytoplasmic filaments, 8 nm in diameter, arrayed in helices of 26–30 nm periodicity.[757,763] Synaptic junctions and such photosensory attributes as annulate lamellae and cilia of 9+0 configuration may also be apparent. A variety of metallic impregnation methods may be used to visualize these unipolar cell processes and their rounded, varicose terminals at the light microscopic level, but such techniques are now mainly of historical interest.[753]

Given the fine structural profile just delineated, it should come as no surprise that the fibrillar matrix of the pineocytoma is GFAP-negative but often immunolabels for neurofilament protein epitopes, class III β-tubulin, PGP 9.5, and chromogranin A as well as synaptophysin.[758,762] Rhodopsin and retinal S-antigen immunoreactivity have also been documented[758,762] and further attest to the photosensory differentiating potential of pineal parenchymal tumors. Intriguing in this connection is report of a pineocytoma associated with uveoretinitis.[756] Lastly, the differentiated nature of the pineocytoma is reflected in the observation[755] that its constituent cells may evidence immunoreactivity for, or express messenger RNA encoding, enzymes involved in melatonin synthesis (including tryptophan hydroxylase, serotonin N-acetyltransferase and hydroxyindole-O-methyltransferase).

Restriction of the term pineocytoma to the distinctively rosetted neoplasm described above identifies a surgically curable tumor that typically presents in young or middle-aged adults and that remains confined to the pineal region, expanding slowly and in noninvasive fashion.[758,762,765] The same cannot be said for exceedingly rare tumors described as harboring "mixed" pineocytomatous and pineoblastomatous elements,[758,765] these having the potential for aggressive behavior with CSF dissemination,[765] or for curiosities published as **"papillary"** pineocytomas.[768,769] Rapid progression characterized one partly papillary tumor accorded the latter designation, this particular example manifesting foci of solid, sheet-like growth, necrosis and the formation of fleurettes and rosettes of Flexner–Wintersteiner (but not pineocytomatous) type.[768] We have rarely encountered papillary formations lined by columnar tumor cells in neoplasms otherwise having the appearances of conventional pineoblastoma. The reader's attention is called to recent description of a distinctive **papillary tumor of the pineal region**[756a] posited to derive from specialized ependymocytes of the subcommissural organ, previously mentioned as possible progenitors of the third ventricular chordoid glioma.

Falling within an incompletely characterized group now designated as **pineal parenchymal tumors of intermediate differentiation** are certain neoplasms that occupy a rather broad middle ground between the mature and embryonal extremes.[758,762,765] One variant is characterized by a neuroendocrine histologic profile in which small tumor cells are segregated into lobules subtended by a delicate vasculature, a second by a more sheet-like proliferation of neoplastic elements in a scant fibrillary matrix. Cytoplasmic clearing lends an oligo-dendrogliomatous aspect to some examples, the differential including third ventricular neurocytoma. A neuronal/neuroendocrine immunoprofile similar to that of the pineocytoma puts the former issue to rest,[758] neurocytic neoplasms sharing synaptophysin expression but usually proving chromogranin-negative (save for examples with ganglion cell components). Some neuro-pathologists[758] include in this family "transitional" cases in which focal pineocytomatous rosette formation is apparent against a background of solid, lobular or diffuse growth. As a group, these pineocytic neoplasms can achieve relatively dense cellularity, occasionally evidence necrosis and may exhibit mitotic activity, but fall short of the frank anaplasia and conspicuous proliferative activity that typifies pineoblastomas. Many behave in relatively low-grade fashion,[758,765] but some frustrate all attempts at local control and CSF-borne metastasis has been documented as an exceptional occurrence.[765] One analysis suggests that the best prognosis attaches to examples displaying fewer than 6 mitoses per 10 high power microscopic fields and immunoreactivity for 70 and 200 kDa neurofilament proteins.[758] Relatively favorable as well seems the outlook when regional rosetting of pineocytomatous type is apparent.[758] Some would argue that the latter are essentially pineocytoma variants.

Meningiomas

The designation of meningioma has been extended through the years to diverse neoplasms sharing only a tendency to arise within the histogenetically complex tissues of the leptomeninges or dura mater. Thus, such dissimilar entities as the meningeal hemangiopericy-toma and hemangioblastoma—currently accorded separate nosologic status among tumors of the CNS and its coverings—were once yoked under the regrettable rubric of "angioblastic" meningioma and widely assumed to derive from a common progenitor. Neuro-pathologists now label as meningiomas only those neoplasms exhibiting morphologic or immunopheno-typic evidence of an origin from meningothelial cells, specialized elements that populate the arachnoid membranes and cap the arachnoidal villi associated with intradural venous sinuses and their tributaries.

Meningiomas may make their appearance in childhood or adolescence,[780,809] but most are encountered in middle or later adult life.[788,795,797] Females are afflicted more commonly than males (especially at spinal levels), and some studies suggest a particularly increased prevalence in women with mammary carcinomas,[795] rare meningiomas actually harboring metastatic deposits derived from breast primaries.[828] Coupled with their frequent expression of progesterone (as well as androgen) receptors[797] and the rapid enlargement of some examples during pregnancy or the luteal phase of the menstrual cycle, these observations indicate that the growth of meningiomas is subject to hormonal influence. Noteworthy is the association of multifocal meningiomas with type 2 ("central") neurofibromatosis (NF-2),[797] the genetic locus for which resides on chromosome 22q12. Allelic loss involving this band is a frequent feature of meningiomas, including sporadic variants, as are NF-2 gene mutations (particularly common in fibroblastic and transitional variants). The presentation of a meningioma in childhood or adolescence should trigger investigation for underlying NF-2.[809] Familial examples occurring outside the setting of classic NF-2 have also been described.[797] Ionizing cranial irradiation emerges from a number of epidemiologic studies as conferring significant risk for subsequent meningioma development,[795] radiation-related lesions being more often multiple, histologically atypical, and clinically aggressive than those arising in sporadic fashion.[782,797] Less clear is the etiologic role of craniocerebral trauma,[795] but the presentation of select meningiomas in the immediate vicinity of a prior skull fracture or in close physical association with traumatically implanted foreign bodies has been convincingly documented.[772,819] Also on record are meningiomas found to lie just over a glioblastoma or other glioma.[800] Most "collision" tumors of this sort are undoubtedly fortuitous lesions, but it is conceivable that the occasional meningioma evokes a hyperplastic glial reaction that subsequently progresses to neoplasia. As noted in our discussion of gliomesenchymal neoplasms, the term *sarcoglioma* has been extended to some mixed tumors postulated to have arisen in this fashion.[513] As mentioned in our prior discussion of hamartomatous lesions, meningiomas very occasionally arise in association with foci of meningioangiomatosis.[24,33]

Most meningiomas arise within the cranial cavity, are dura-based, and are found in the vicinity of the superior sagittal sinus, over the cerebral convexities or in contact with the falx cerebri. Basally positioned examples favor the sphenoid ridge, olfactory grooves, tuberculum sellae, and parasellar region. Still others are anchored to the petrous ridge, presenting as cerebellopontine angle tumors when posteriorly situated. Intracranial meningiomas may also originate within the tela choroidea or stroma of the choroid plexus and rest entirely within the ventricular system. At spinal levels, meningiomas clearly favor the thoracic region, cervical examples being uncommon and lumbar lesions rare. Also recognized are epidural (intradiploic), calvarial, and intrapetrous meningiomas as well as variants located entirely outside the craniospinal confines. The latter are usually encountered in the head and neck region and include orbital (i.e., optic sheath), glabellar, sinonasal, oropharyngeal, subgaleal, juxtaparotid, and cutaneous examples.[792,823] Rarely, ectopic meningiomas are situated at even greater removes from the central neuraxis (e.g., in the mediastinum,[826] lung,[794,814] or brachial plexus[775]). As discussed elsewhere in these volumes, the so-called minute pulmonary chemodectoma is actually composed of cells having the ultrastructure and immunophenotype of meningothelium.

On neuroradiologic (Fig. 28.94) and gross assessment (Fig. 28.95), the typical meningioma is a solid, lobulated, or globose mass that is broadly anchored to the dura mater. Cystic variants, although uncommon, are well recognized,[806] and the term meningioma en plaque may be invoked for the occasional lesion that presents (usually over the sphenoid ridge) as a poorly delimited, blanket-like growth. Adjoining neural tissues are generally deflected at the "pushing" perimeters of these tumors, but grossly evident dural infiltration or invasion of nearby venous sinuses is not uncommon. Some exam-

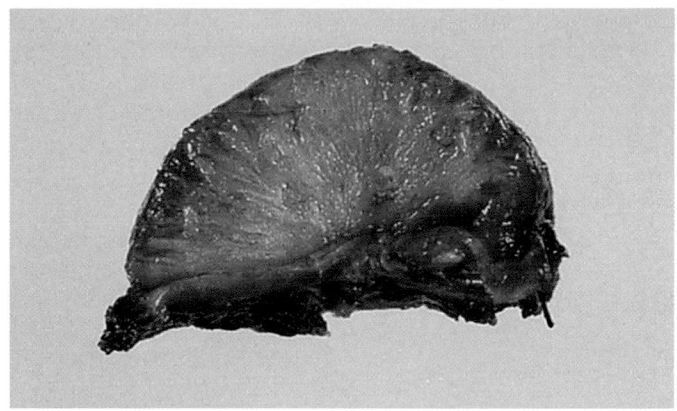

Fig. 28.95 Meningioma. The broad dural base depicted here is characteristic.

ples insidiously permeate the neighboring skull, provoking a highly characteristic form of osteoplastic expansion and bony remodeling known as hyperostosis or, neglected, come to attention as visible masses in the scalp. None of these findings brand a meningioma as atypical or anaplastic, although involvement of the cranial floor greatly prejudices matters against the neurosurgeon and so predisposes to tumor recurrence and progression following attempted resection. Highly suspect, however, is the lesion that cannot be easily separated from the adjacent brain or spinal cord, as this implies transgression of the pia-arachnoid and invasion of the neuroparenchyma proper—traditionally regarded as prima facie evidence of aggressive biologic potential in the setting of meningothelial neoplasia. Neuroradiologic features that should prompt concern include indistinct tumoral margins, a "mushrooming" growth pattern characterized by multinodular projections from the main mass, foci that fail to enhance on contrast administration (these representing regions of necrosis), and edema of the neighboring brain on CT or MR study.[786]

On sectioning, most meningiomas are grayish-tan and soft, but collagenized examples have a rubbery texture and a whorled or trabeculated cut surface (resembling that of the leiomyoma), whereas variants rich in stromal mucopolysaccharides acquire a somewhat gelatinous consistency. Calcification is often readily apparent and infiltration by foamy macrophages at times results in foci of yellow discoloration, a phenomenon that may also reflect the accumulation of lipids within tumor cells.

Meningiomas are notorious for the variety of their cytologic and histologic presentations, but most assume one of several prototypical guises.[788,797] "**Meningotheliomatous**" variants are characterized by a lobular microarchitecture and are populated by cells having delicate round or oval nuclei, inconspicuous nucleoli, lightly eosinophilic cytoplasm, and indistinct cytoplasmic borders (thus their alternative designation as syncytial meningiomas). Common to these (and other

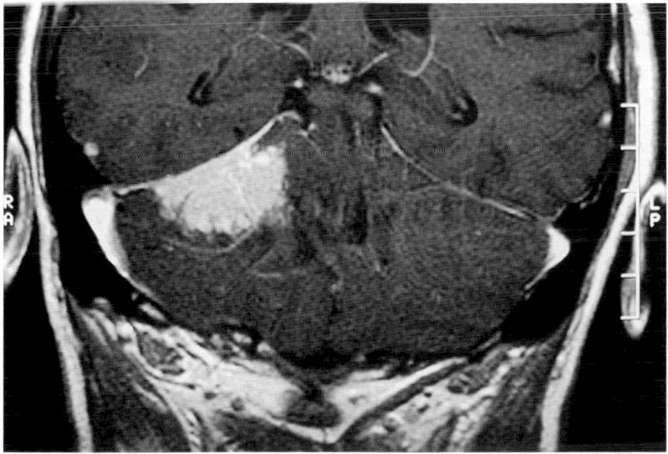

Fig. 28.94 Meningioma. Circumscription, homogeneous contrast enhancement and anchorage to the dura (in this case, the tentorium) typify the meningioma. This MRI also demonstrates thickened and abnormally enhancing dural "tails" extending from the lesional borders—a finding suggestive, though not diagnostic, of this tumor entity.

subtypes) are tumor cells concentrically wrapped in tight whorls, nuclear clearing and pale nuclear "pseudoinclusions" consisting of invaginated cytoplasm, and the lamellated calcospherules known as psammoma bodies (Fig. 28.96). While none of these features are pathognomonic of meningioma, their demonstration in the setting of an extra-axial, dura-based mass carries considerable diagnostic weight. In contrast to the epithelioid appearances of meningotheliomatous variants, **fibrous (or fibroblastic) meningiomas** adopt a mesenchymal profile, being variably collagenized and consisting of spindly tumor cells in fascicular or storiform array (Fig. 28.97). An example containing crystalline structures rich in tyrosine has been depicted.[777] **Transitional meningiomas**, as their name implies, are hybrids, maintaining a lobular arrangement but evidencing a tendency to cellular elongation and streaming. These are often particularly rich in compact cellular whorls and endowed with psammoma bodies in conspicuous numbers. When the latter are present in profusion, the term *psammomatous meningioma* may be applied. Tumors of this type characteristically occur in middle-aged women and exhibit a

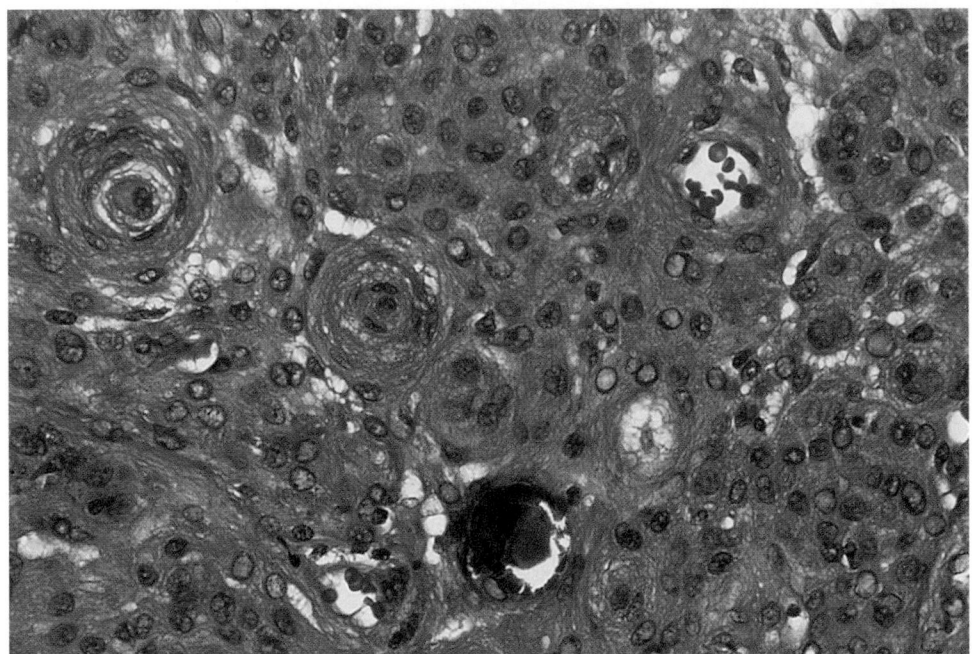

Fig. 28.96 Meningioma. Indistinct cytoplasmic boundaries, nuclear clearing ("pseudoinclusions"), cellular whorls, and a psammoma body are all apparent in this view of a meningotheliomatous (syncytial) meningioma.

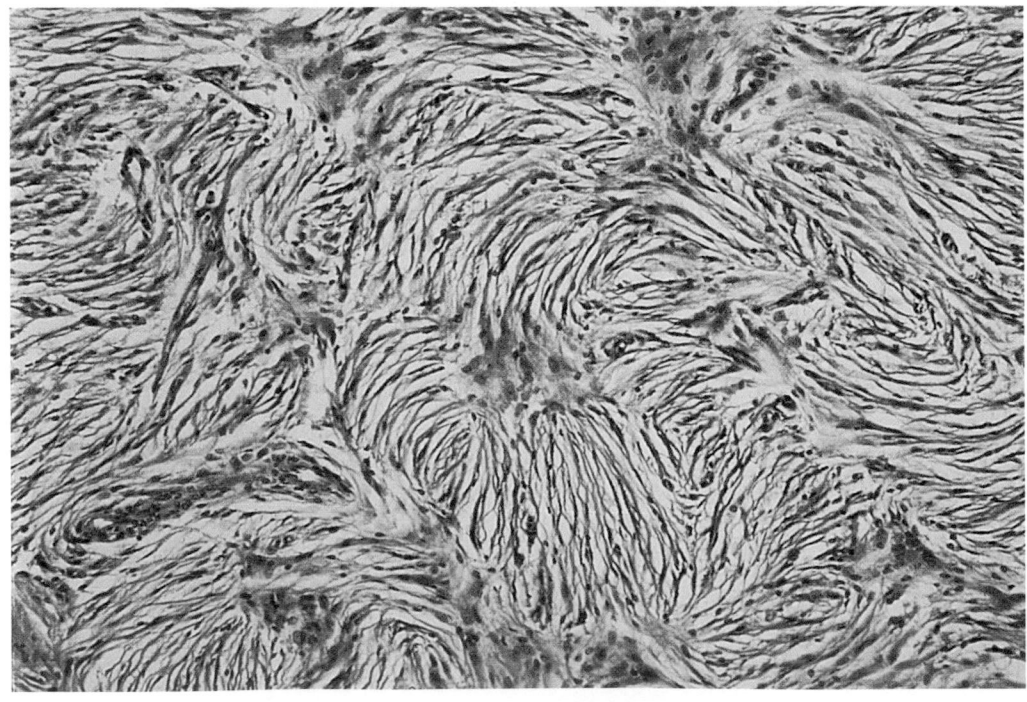

Fig. 28.97 Meningioma. Cellular spindling and a fascicular or storiform architecture are evidenced by meningiomas of "fibroblastic" type.

particular predilection for the intraspinal compartment. It should be noted that none of the foregoing growth patterns is of any special biologic significance, most neuropathologists dispensing with these qualifying adjectives in their reporting of surgical material.

To these classic subtypes of meningioma can be added histologic variants too numerous to be accorded (and too uncommon to merit) detailed discussion or depiction here. Only the more distinctive are acknowledged. Unless otherwise stated, these depart in no way from the benign course pursued by meningiomas of more conventional appearance.

The **microcystic meningioma**[801,804] is named for its content of variably sized intercellular vacuoles, these often appearing empty but in some instances containing a lightly PAS-positive fluid derived in all likelihood via the transudation of plasma across a characteristically rich, and frequently hyalinized, stromal vasculature. Some examples actually progress to the formation of macrocysts and harbor only minor solid components. Constituent cells may exhibit cytoplasmic clearing due to glycogen or lipid accumulation and often assume spindly or stellate profiles that, along with their tendency to disaggregation, can prompt consideration of a low-grade, microcystic astrocytoma in the differential diagnosis. Nuclear pleomorphism, karyomegaly, and a smudgy hyperchromasia may be in evidence but are unattended by mitotic activity and are divorced from any sinister prognostic import. We mention report of a mixed testicular germ cell tumor harboring components of microcystic meningioma.[771]

The **secretory meningioma**,[815] a variant of the meningotheliomatous subtype, is distinguished by its content of "pseudopsammoma bodies"—globular hyaline inclusions that are eosinophilic, intensely PAS positive, and diastase resistant (Fig. 28.98A). On ultrastructural study, these can be shown to lie within microvillus-lined intracellular lumina and may be immunolabeled for human secretory component, IgM, IgA, and CEA (Fig. 28.98B). Nearly always benign, the secretory meningioma may yet masquerade as a malignant neoplasm by virtue of its occasional association with elevated serum CEA levels,[796] an especially confounding phenomenon in the patient with a prior history of systemic cancer, and with subacutely progressive neurologic deficits referable to severe edema of juxtatumoral cerebral tissues. The latter, generally foreign to conventional meningiomas and usually encountered as a complication of malignant meningeal neoplasms (primary or metastatic), may be associated with a curious pericytic proliferation occurring in the tumoral vascular bed.[816]

The **lymphoplasmacyte-rich meningioma** is a tumor infiltrated by chronic inflammatory elements, at times so heavily that its meningothelial (and neoplastic) nature is obscured.[781,785] There can be no doubt that at least some

reported cases would be better classified as dura-based examples of inflammatory pseudotumor ("plasma cell granuloma") or sinus histiocytosis with massive lymphadenopathy (Rosai–Dorfman disease). Peritumoral lymphoplasmacytic infiltrates with germinal center formation are also conspicuous features of a peculiar meningeal tumor noteworthy for its **chordoid histology** and presentation in childhood or adolescence with manifestations of the **Castleman syndrome**—polyclonal dysgammaglobulinemia, iron-refractory anemia, hepatosplenomegaly, and retarded growth and sexual maturation.[789,791] Resection typically effects a remission of the systemic disorder, but this obscure neoplasm may recur and behave in locally aggressive fashion. The relationship of this lesion to adult-onset **chordoid meningiomas**,[776] which typically are unaccompanied by conspicuous inflammatory components and potentially masquerade as chordomas or metastatic mucinous carcinomas, is unclear. The latter, also reported as "**myxoid**" or "**mucinous**" meningiomas, proved in one analysis to be more prone to local regrowth following subtotal resection than meningothelial tumors of conventional type.[776]

Metaplastic meningiomas can contain bone, cartilage, or adipocytic elements.[788,797] Progressive xanthomatous change, i.e., nonspecific cytoplasmic lipidization, rather than true metaplasia seems to account for so-called **lipomatous meningiomas**.[818] We would call particular attention to rare variants that may be misconstrued as sarcoma owing to potentially lipoblastic cytologic features and the occurrence in some examples of troubling nuclear abnormalities that are almost certainly degenerative in nature.[793,818] Neoplasms exhibiting meningothelial and rhabdomyosarcomatous[779] or leiomyosarcomatous[821] differentiation are also on record. Still other meningiomas evidence foci of schwannoma-like nuclear palisading; pseudoglandular structures[790], a nesting arrangement reminiscent of paraganglioma; or a hyalinized stromal vasculature so exuberant and domineering as to suggest a malformative process (**angiomatous meningioma**).[788,797] A **sclerosing subtype** that appears to undergo progressive fibrous obliteration is noteworthy for its presentation in the pediatric group and favorable outcome despite a tendency to foci of disturbing hypercellularity, pleomorphism, and cerebrocortical infiltration.[778] Some observers have suggested that at least a subset of sclerosing childhood meningiomas are pseudoinvasive lesions arising within cortical foci of meningioangiomatosis.[24]

A subset of meningothelial neoplasms evidence clear cell, oncocytic or rhabdoid features. The significance of such alterations when encountered only focally is unsettled, but tumors exhibiting prominent changes of this sort merit distinct designation owing to their potential for mischief. **Clear cell meningiomas** are the most deceptive of the lot.[783,822,828a] These are characterized by a predilection for young subjects (including children) and

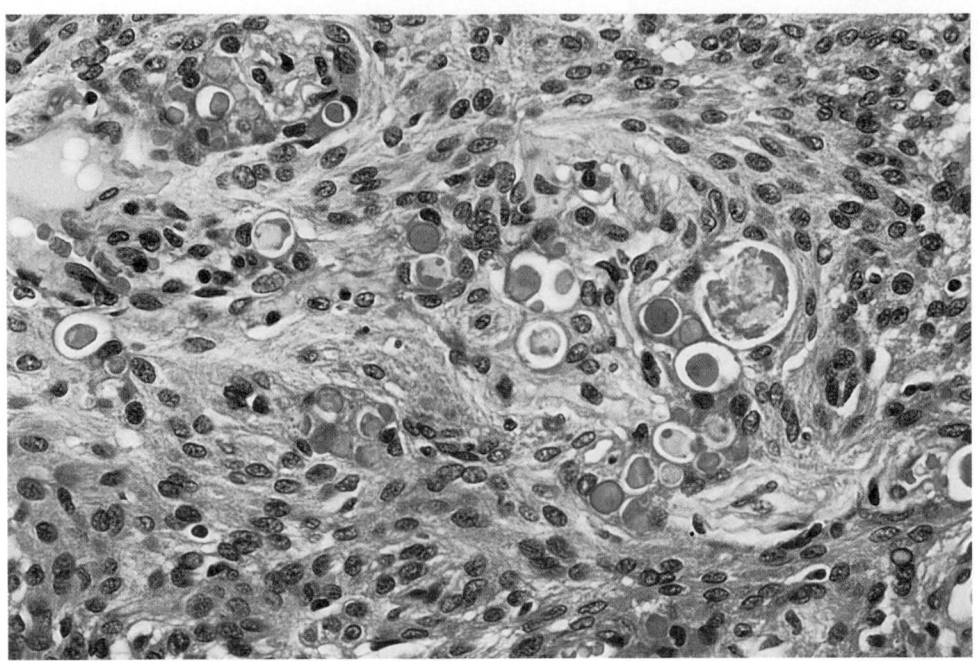

A

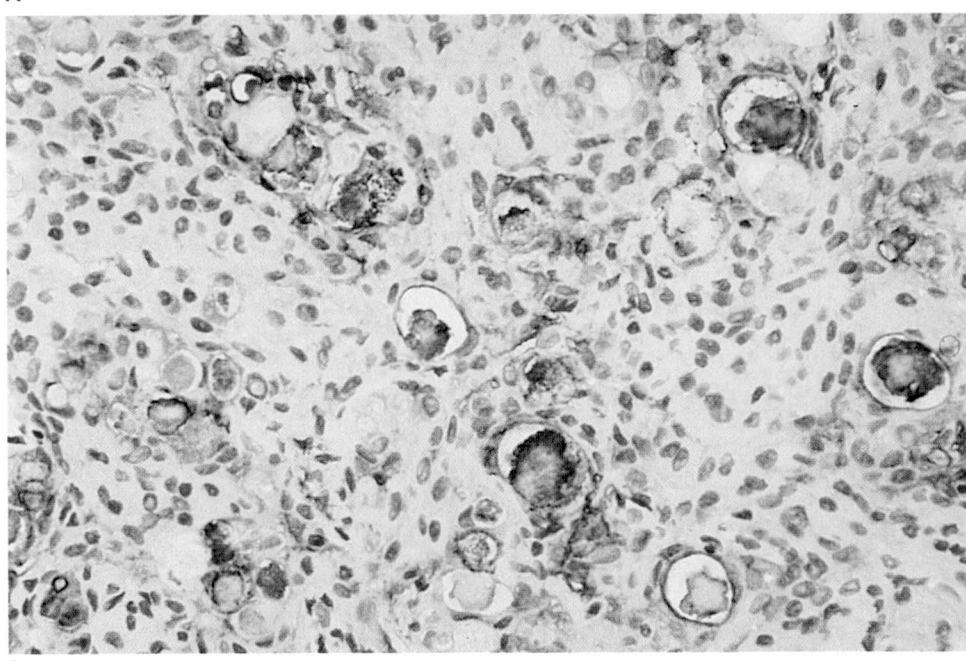

B

Fig. 28.98 Secretory meningioma. This variant of meningotheliomatous meningioma harbors eosinophilic globules (**A**) that label with antibodies to carcinoembryonic antigen (**B**).

are most often found in the spinal canal, cerebellopontine angle, or foramen magnum region. They are usually extra-axial and dura-based, but may be associated with cranial nerves, spinal roots, or the cauda equina. A fourth ventricular presentation has been described.[774a] We have encountered a bulbar example in a 2-year-old child.[822] Composed of glycogen-rich, water-clear cells that are often disposed in patternless sheets traversed by bands of hyalinized collagen (Fig. 28.99), these unusual tumors typically manifest little or nothing in the way of classic meningothelial attributes (e.g., whorls or nuclear pseudoinclusions) and may be only focally and faintly immunoreactive for epithelial membrane antigen

(EMA), a marker of specialized arachnoidal cells expressed by most meningiomas in diffuse fashion. High recurrence rates and increased mortality characterize this intrinsically aggressive meningioma variant, this despite the fact that most examples do not evidence conspicuously increased mitotic activity, necrosis or other histologic features that would arouse suspicion.

That rhabdoid cytology is, in general, a marker of increased biologic potential is borne out by the discouraging behavior of most meningiomas displaying this profile, which may be evident on initial presentation or appear only in recurrent material.[797,810] **Rhabdoid meningiomas** in fully developed form usually retain

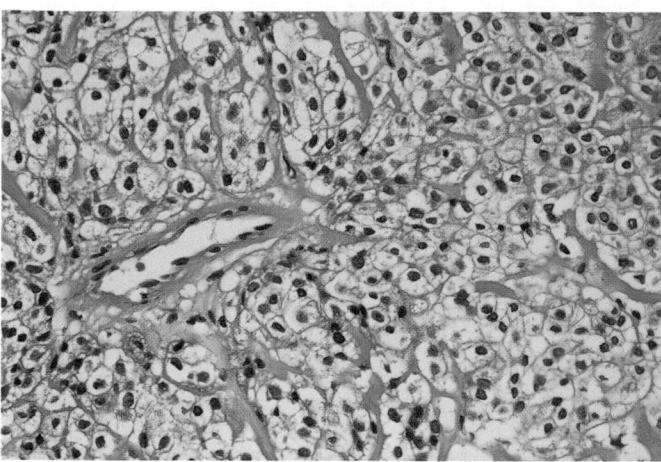

Fig. 28.99 Clear cell meningioma. The example shown here arose from the filum terminale of a 9-year-old girl. Note cytoplasmic clearing, traversing collagenous bands, and absence of meningothelial-type whorls.

meningotheliomatous regions but boast a prominent population of cells with vesicular nuclei, prominent nucleoli, and globose, paranuclear inclusion-like bodies representing compacted cytoplasmic vimentin filaments. These cells usually lie in lobules or sheets, but a papillary growth pattern may be encountered.[784] Conspicuously increased mitotic activity is the rule, and brain invasion common, most such tumors qualifying as atypical or frankly anaplastic by the WHO/Mayo Clinic criteria presently discussed. In one reported series, 87% of afflicted patients experienced at least one recurrence and 53% died of tumor progression.[810] The prognosis for examples evidencing rhabdoid change in the absence of elevated proliferative activity or other aggressive indica-

tors does not appear to be as poor, but these need close watching. Similar considerations seem to apply to **oncocytic meningiomas**, i.e., meningothelial neoplasms demonstrating fine cytoplasmic granularity due to an accumulation of mitochondria.[817] High mitotic rates, necrosis, brain invasion and recurrence have been over-represented in the few cases recorded to date and in examples that we have encountered in consultation.

A final variant meriting specific comment in view of its distinctive histology and clinical biology is the **papillary meningioma**, a tumor characterized by the ependymoma-like perivascular structuring of its constituent cells.[773,798,807] The latter can be seen to extend variably elongated cytoplasmic processes toward vessel walls, fashioning pseudorosette-like structures that disaggregate and come to float unanchored in tissue sections (Fig. 28.100). Regions exhibiting a more conventional meningothelial appearance are nearly always identifiable but usually depart from the typical in evidencing worrisome hypercellularity, mitotic activity, and, in some cases, foci of coagulative necrosis. Stubborn local recurrence, a capacity for extraneural metastasis, and often fatal outcome characterize papillary meningiomas. An excess of reported cases have presented in childhood or adolescence.

Distinction of the meningioma from potential counterfeits occasionally requires the use of the electron microscope or immunohistochemical assay. The most constant and distinctive ultrastructural feature of meningothelial neoplasms is the complex interdigitation of tumor cell processes without intervening basal lamina material (elaborated by both the meningeal hemangiopericytoma and schwannoma), although fibroblastic variants tend to a more parallel alignment. Intercellular junctional com-

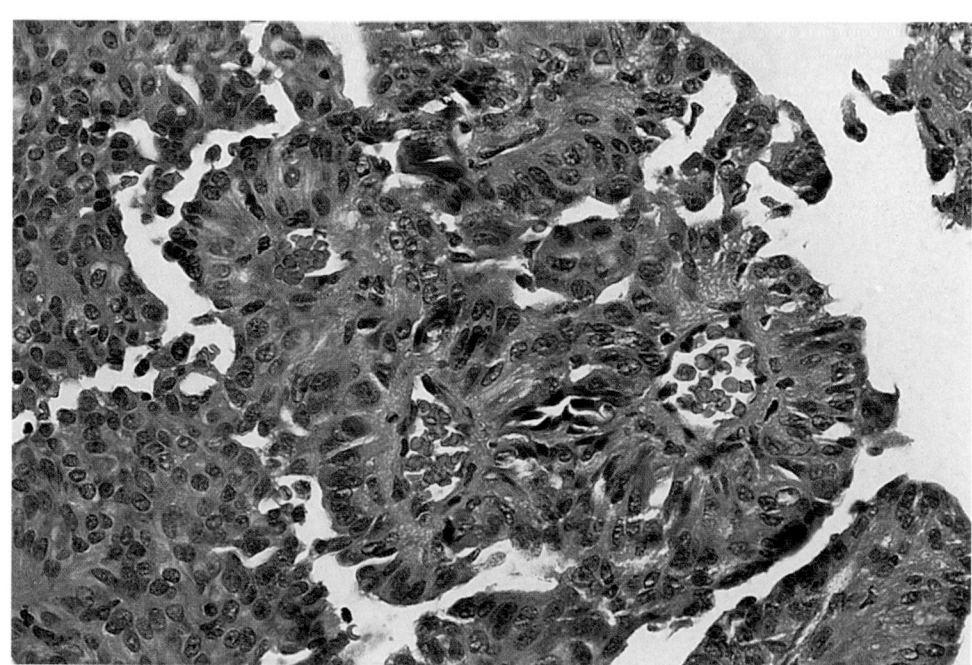

Fig. 28.100 Papillary meningioma. This instraspinal example, which elsewhere exhibited the histology of an atypical meningotheliomatous meningioma with increased mitotic activity and foci of necrosis, metastasized to lung, lymph node, and bone.

plexes are frequent and include well-developed desmosomes, a conspicuous cytoplasmic complement of intermediate filaments rounding out the ultrastructural picture (Fig. 28.101). The latter consist of vimentin, regularly demonstrable by immunohistochemical methods regardless of tumor subtype.[797] Of particular diagnostic utility is the observation that a large majority of meningiomas exhibit (at least focally) membranous, as well as diffuse, cytoplasmic immunolabeling for EMA[797] (Fig.

28.102), a feature foreign to the hemangiopericytoma, to nerve sheath tumors other than the rare perineurioma, the solitary fibrous tumor, and other fibroblastic neoplasms. Nuclear immunoreactivity for progesterone receptors is also common.[797] Reactivity for S-100 protein, if present, is usually limited to the cytoplasm of a subset of neoplastic cells but may occasionally be encountered in diffuse form. As regards cytokeratin expression, meningiomas often share with native arachnoidal lining

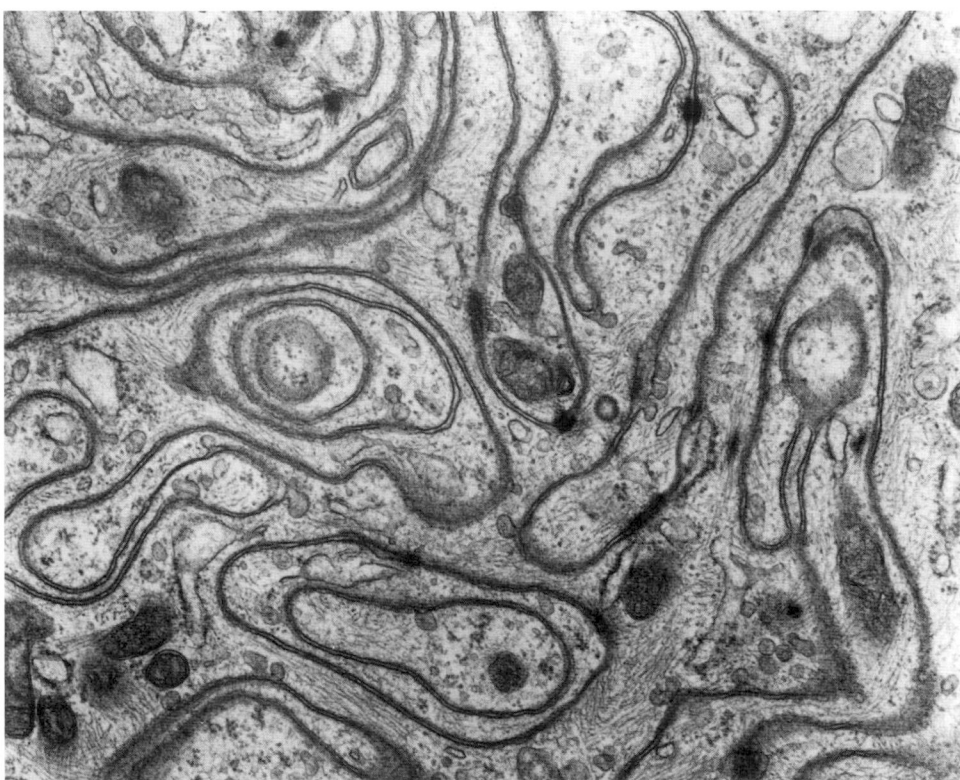

Fig. 28.101 Meningioma. Ultrastructural examination of meningiomas will often disclose complex, jigsaw puzzle-like arrays of interdigitated cytoplasmic processes laden with intermediate filaments and joined by desmosomes. As demonstrated here, neoplastic meningothelial cells are not typically coated by basement membranes (a feature of Schwann cells), nor does basal lamina material accumulate in their matrices (a characteristic of the hemangiopericytoma illustrated in Fig. 28.104). (×18,000)

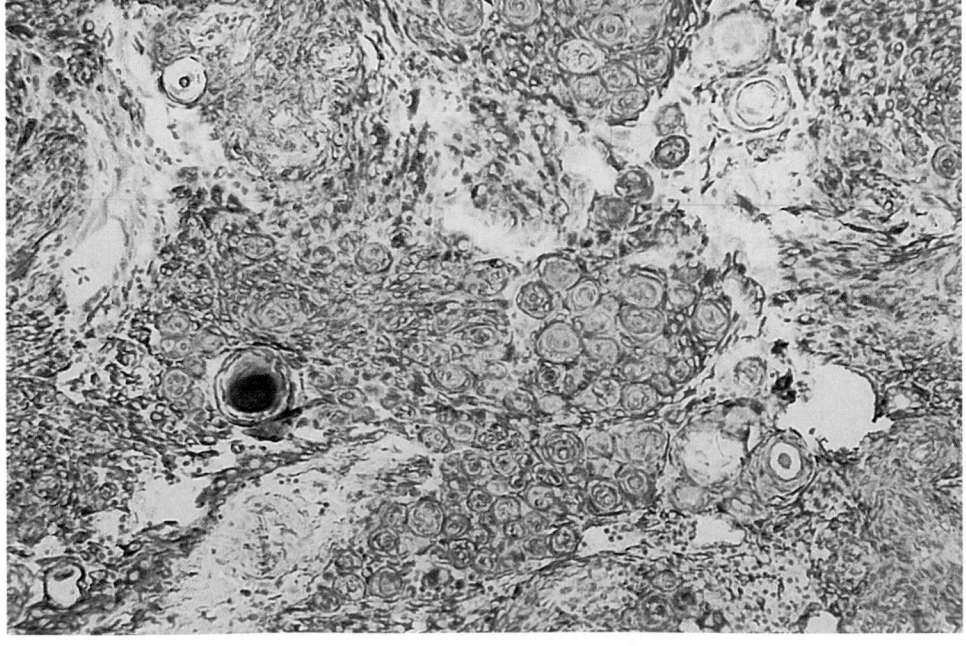

Fig. 28.102 Meningioma. Cytoplasmic labeling for epithelial membrane antigen on immunoperioxidase assay, depicted here, characterizes the overwhelming majority of meningiomas, regardless of their histologic subtype.

cells (and with epithelial cancers) immunolabeling for CK18, but are typically CK20-negative regardless of histologic pattern.[802] Focal reactivity for CK7, CK8 (CAM 5.2), CK19 and AE1/3 may be encountered (and is a consistent feature of the inclusion-bearing elements that define meningiomas of secretory type), but widespread labeling for these antigens suggests that a dura-based mass represents metastatic carcinoma.[802] GFAP-labeling meningiomas of papillary[774] and rhabdoid[784,810,820] type have been depicted but are curiosities. Whether this phenomenon actually reflects GFAP expression is open to question. In fact, one report depicting GFAP reactivity in a tumor interpreted as meningothelial[825] seems instead to represent the first account of the neoplasm now recognized as chordoid glioma of the third ventricle.[487] As previously noted, meningiomas rarely exercise an ability to differentiate along myogenic lines[779,821] and some otherwise conventional examples focally label for muscle-associated actins.[824]

Meningiomas of conventional histologic type grow slowly and are amenable to surgical cure when complete excision can be effected, as is usually the case for examples arising over the cerebral convexities or along the spinal axis. Even tumors so favorably situated, however, may recur following gross total resection, the magnitude of this risk emerging only on long-term observation. In one study, for example, respective 5-, 15-, and 25-year relapse rates for histologically benign and completely excised intracranial meningiomas were 3%, 15%, and 21%.[786] By all accounts, the likelihood of regrowth is considerably higher for the less accessible olfactory groove and sphenoid wing meningiomas, en plaque examples and lesions invasive of the cranial floor proving particularly troublesome.[787] But while there can be no gainsaying the influence of tumor location on outcome in this setting, it is clear that certain morphologic features serve to independently define a subset of high-risk meningiomas to which a substantially increased likelihood of postoperative recurrence attaches. Recognizing that a number of grading strategies have proven useful in the identification of potentially aggressive meningothelial neoplasms,[786,799] we can endorse with minor reservations a Mayo Clinic proposal[811,812] adopted with little modification in the 2000 WHO formulation.[797]

Application of the WHO/Mayo Clinic criteria outlined below broadly stratifies meningothelial tumors into three tiers of increasing biologic potential— **meningioma**, **atypical meningioma**, and **anaplastic meningioma** (WHO grades I, II, and III, respectively). The stated criteria are applied whether present as focal findings (often the case) or in more diffuse form. In this scheme, atypical meningiomas are defined as:

(1) containing 4 or more mitotic figures per 10 high power microscopic fields (0.16 mm²)

or

(2) exhibiting at least three of the following features:

(a) hypercellularity
(b) patternless, sheet-like growth
(c) macronucleoli
(d) small cell components with high nuclear : cytoplasmic ratio
(e) zones of necrosis.

Anaplastic meningiomas are defined as:

(1) containing 20 or more mitoses per 10 high power microscopic fields (0.16 mm²)

or

(2) exhibiting a loss of differentiated features resulting in carcinoma-, melanoma-, or sarcoma-like appearances.

We would emphasize that the preoperative embolization of meningiomas, undertaken to reduce their blood supplies and facilitate removal, often results in regions of necrosis with evident mitotic activity (and increased MIB-1 reactivity) in adjoining tumor tissue.[808] Potentially rendering problematic application of the foregoing criteria, this phenomenon is often, though not invariably, signaled by the presence of clearly foreign material within the tumoral vasculature. The finding of multiple zones of necrosis that appear to be at the same acute stage of development suggests such intervention but, in any case, pathologists should consult their clinical colleagues on this issue prior to releasing reports. The study cited above suggests that WHO/Mayo Clinic mitotic criteria remain valid in these circumstances, but confirmation in additional large series would be reassuring.

The reader may well wonder at our silence thus far on the issue of neuroparenchymal infiltration and tumor grading. Brain-invasive meningiomas, in fact, span the histologic spectrum, some being of otherwise typical appearance.[797,811] The demonstration of brain invasion per se adds relatively little to the predictive power of the WHO/Mayo Clinic scheme as a prognostic model once a given tumor has satisfied the listed criteria for designation as atypical or anaplastic. Meningothelial tumors of conventionally benign histologic aspect that infiltrate brain, on the other hand, appear to behave much in the manner of morphologically atypical meningiomas (see below) and so we endorse the Mayo Clinic suggestion[811] that they be so designated, though this is not specifically advocated by the WHO.[797]

In the experience that served as the basis for these recommendations, respective 5-year recurrence rates for conventional versus atypical meningiomas (the latter including brain-invasive but otherwise benign examples) were 12% and 41% following gross total resection.[811,812] Atypical tumors carried a 5-year mortality rate of approximately 20%. Anaplastic meningiomas, by contrast, recurred in the large majority of cases (ostensibly complete excision notwithstanding), were associated with a 68% 5-year mortality rate, and a median survival of only 18 months. Other findings that have been correlated with worrisome histology and increased biologic potential in the setting of meningothelial neoplasia include elevated MIB-1 labeling indices and, in some studies, failure to express progesterone receptors.[797] Regarding the former, meningiomas of conventional type and indolent behavior usually have MIB-1 labeling indices below 4–5% but there is overlap in the values recorded for benign, atypical and anaplastic lesions as well as for recurring versus nonrecurring tumors.[770,803,813] Consequently, the predictive power of this assessment in the individual case is somewhat compromised. Noteworthy is the observation that disturbing histologic features, including elevated mitotic MIB-1 indices and brain invasion, seem to be overrepresented among meningiomas occurring in the pediatric group.[809] As detailed elsewhere,[809] most studies have found these morphologic attributes to correlate with an increased risk of recurrence and fatal outcome in this patient cohort, but this has not been the experience of all.[780] Progression-associated genetic markers, such as chromosome 1p and 14q deletions, may also be more prevalent in meningiomas of childhood and adolescence compared to adult-onset examples.[809] The reader is referred elsewhere for more comprehensive discussion of genetic alterations associated with meningioma progression.[797] At the time of this writing, these have no generally accepted role in patient management.

While application of the WHO/Mayo Clinic guidelines discussed above can be recommended as a means of stratifying affected patients into groups at increasing risk of recurrence and meningioma-related death, pathologists and attending clinicians must realize that prognostic certainty is not to be found in the proposed criteria—particularly in the mitotic thresholds that separate the typical, atypical, and anaplastic. It has long been our practice to specifically comment when confronted by any meningioma containing more than the very occasional mitosis found on careful scrutiny, close neuroradiologic surveillance being prudent in this circumstance even if a gross total excision has been effected. It also bears emphasizing that within the broad spectrum of meningiomas that qualify as merely "atypical" by WHO/Mayo Clinic criteria are to be found examples (e.g., the tumor exhibiting 14 mitoses per 10 high-power microscopic fields, necrosis, and cerebrocortical invasion) that may not be as predictably virulent as anaplastic variants but that are capable of frankly malignant clinical behavior. The last words have not been written on these issues.

Although local regrowth is the major pattern of treatment failure, aggressive meningioma variants can spread via the CSF and, on occasion, travel to extraneural sites such as the lung, liver, bone, and lymph node.[788,797] We would point out, however, that an excess of distant metastases recorded in the literature have derived from "angioblastic" variants that would now be classified as meningeal hemangiopericytomas. Examples of "**benign metastasizing meningioma**" have been well documented but remain curiosities.[805] As noted, venous sinus invasion is a feature of many meningiomas and is not predictive of hematogenous dissemination or germane to the designation of a given lesion as atypical or anaplastic. In a similar vein, little significance attaches to foci of pronounced nuclear pleomorphism, provided that nucleolar enlargement, mitotic activity, or other atypical features are not in evidence. X-chromosome inactivation studies and NF-2 gene mutation analyses suggest that at least some sporadic cases of "multifocal" meningioma (particularly those characterized by the presence of three or more spatially distinct tumors) actually represent clonal proliferations with subarachnoid spread.[797]

Nonmeningothelial mesenchymal tumors

Excepting the obscure process known as primary meningeal sarcomatosis and the congenital lipomatous tumors of the lumbosacral spinal canal and cranial cavity, the varied lesions surveyed in this section represent the homologs of neoplasms encountered far more frequently in the somatic soft tissues and bones than along the central neuraxis.[829,830] Accordingly, little attempt is made to describe or depict their histopathologic, ultrastructural, and immunophenotypic profiles, all of which are given detailed attention elsewhere in these volumes. However, we would emphasize the hazards in diagnosis occasioned by the existence of both neuroepithelial and meningothelial tumors that pretend to inclusion among the select company under discussion. Whereas CNS neoplasms exhibiting spindly or bizarre, "monstrocellular" cytologic features were once presumed to be mesodermal in derivation if they could be shown to elaborate an intercellular reticulin network, it is now clear that candidates fulfilling this criterion must be subjected to immunohistochemical assay for evidence of cytoplasmic GFAP expression if entities such as the sarcomatoid or "giant cell" glioblastoma, desmoplastic cerebral astrocytoma, and pleomorphic xanthoastrocytoma are to be unmasked. In addition, the possibility has always to be borne in mind, particularly in adult cases, that the biopsy ostensibly demonstrating sarcoma derives, in fact, from a malignant gliomesenchymal tumor (i.e., a gliosarcoma). Especially suspect in this regard are limited specimens evidencing the features of fibrosarcoma or malignant fibrous histiocytoma, but the gliosarcoma, as already indicated, may also contain angiosarcomatous, osteosarcomatous, chondrosarcomatous, and myosarcomatous components. Inasmuch as primitive neuroepithelial neoplasms such as the medullomyoblastoma and certain variants of pineoblastoma contain striated muscle elements, putative embryonal rhabdomyosarcomas of the CNS must be screened for telltale evidence of neural differentiation at the ultrastructural level or for the expression of GFAP, synaptophysin, neurofilament proteins, and other neuroepithelial antigens. Finally, electron microscopic study and immunocytochemical assessment for EMA labeling may serve to distinguish the fibrosarcoma- or hemangiopericytoma-like meningioma from the genuine article. These guidelines are offered, of course, with the full realization that malignant neoplasms readily forego such luxury functions as the display of marker antigens convenient to the surgical pathologist.

Lipoma and liposarcoma

Intradural tumors composed of mature adipose tissue may be encountered anywhere along the neuraxis but are most common at spinal levels, where they can be divided into a congenital, maldevelopmental group situated principally in the lumbosacral region and a smaller, arguably neoplastic subset tending to a thoracic location. The former have already been discussed as manifestations of spinal dysraphism. Commonly occurring in complex with spina bifida and its cutaneous stigmata, "lipomas" of this type figure prominently among intraspinal anomalies complicated by fixation of the filum terminale, caudal displacement of the conus medullaris, and the traction induced myelopathy known as the "tethered cord" syndrome. These malformative lesions not infrequently contain heterotopic components such as smooth and striated muscle ("myolipoma"),[833] aberrant peripheral nerve fibers, meningothelial derivatives ("occult" lipomeningocele), ependyma, and other neuroglial elements ("occult" lipomeningomyelocele).[849] We have encountered an example that harbored mesonephroid tubules and glomeruloid structures lined by an orderly cuboidal epithelium. Although entrapment of the cauda equina and permeation of the conus usually preclude thorough resection of these intraspinal masses, dramatic neurologic improvement can often be effected by debulking, division of the tethered filum, and dural reconstruction.

In contrast to the congenital lipomatous tumors of the lumbosacral canal, lipomas occurring at higher levels of the spinal axis are typically unassociated with regional anomalies of the vertebrae or intraspinal contents and consist solely of mature fat. Only rarely are these entirely intramedullary.[841] Much more common are leptomyelolipomas,[840] which present as subpial masses plastered over a highly variable length of the spinal cord, incorporating nerve roots and blending into the neuroparenchyma proper. These features frustrate attempts at complete excision, but, again, long-term symptomatic relief is often achieved by simple debulking. Uncommon examples contain conspicuous vascular elements and are dubbed angiolipomas or angiomyolipomas, but such lesions are more often epidural in location.[845] An extradural location also characterized an intraspinal

example of osteolipoma arising in the cervical region.[842] Symptomatic accumulation of adipose tissue in this compartment is also a recognized, albeit rare, complication of natural obesity and of corticosteroid administration. Known as spinal epidural lipomatosis,[839] this may consist of brown fat ("hibernoma").[843] Intradural hibernoma has also been described.[835]

Intracranial lipomas are usefully segregated into a midline group and laterally situated variants, most of which involve the eighth cranial nerve. The former exhibit a decided predilection for the region of the corpus callosum but may also settle along the tuber cinereum, above the quadrigeminal plate, in the ambient cisterns, and in the third ventricle.[834] Most are incidentally discovered at autopsy, but epileptogenic callosal examples are well-recognized, tuberal variants may eventuate in hypothalamic dysfunction, and lesions impinging on the third ventricle or aqueduct of Sylvius may be complicated by progressive hydrocephalus. Sleep apnea has exceptionally been recorded in association with lipomas involving the mesencephalic tectum and rostral pons.[846] In any of these locations, the midline lipoma is clearly maldevelopmental, being frequently associated with structural anomalies of neighboring neural tissues (e.g., agenesis of the corpus callosum) and occasionally occurring in complex with cranial defects or congenital intracranial cysts of colloid or epidermoid type. The added presence, in some instances, of cartilage, bone, smooth or striated muscle, heterotopic peripheral nerves, ganglion cells, neuroglia, and choroid plexus further attests to their malformative basis, although some observers have speculated that these more complex lesions may represent teratomas or teratoid neoplasms.[848] As in the spinal compartment, exceptional variants merit designation as angiolipomas,[844] or osteolipoma.[832]

Intracranial lipomas situated off the midline tend to present in the cerebellopontine angle[831,836] or internal auditory canal[831] and are usually mistaken for acoustic schwannomas on clinical evaluation. The eighth cranial nerve is typically permeated in diffuse fashion, its fibers divided into small fascicles embedded in mature adipose tissue, and other cranial nerves may be engulfed in like manner by large lesions lying adjacent to the brainstem. On rare occasions, intracranial lipomas settle in the region of the sylvian fissure, encasing middle cerebral artery branches and infiltrating temporal cortex.[838] As attempts at en bloc resection may result in severe neurologic injury, it has been suggested that these and cerebellopontine angle examples be subjected to the minimum debulking required to relieve local mass effects. The intrinsically high signal characteristic of fat on T1-weighted MR study may facilitate the accurate preoperative identification of neuraxial masses as lipomas.

Liposarcomas are among the least common of all malignant mesenchymal tumors reported to involve the CNS or its coverings. Only isolated meningeal examples are on record.[829,837,847] The reader is reminded that atypical cells resembling lipoblasts may be encountered in hemangioblastomas as well as "lipidized" neoplasms of meningothelial and astrocytic lineage.

Osseous and cartilaginous tumors

Osseous plaques adherent to the falx cerebri and undersurface of the dura in the region of the superior sagittal sinus are common incidental findings at autopsy and are generally asymptomatic. Although termed **osteomas**, these almost certainly represent reactive, metaplastic lesions and may occur with increased frequency in the setting of chronic renal failure.[854] In a similar vein, the spinal arachnoid frequently undergoes patchy ossification but only rarely is this process so extensive as to produce myelopathy.[857] Examples of bona fide **osteogenic sarcoma** arising from the dura or brain have been depicted, but are most uncommon.[850,853,863] Bosselated masses of mature hyaline cartilage known as **chondromas** (or **osteochondromas** when they contain bony elements) may bulge into the cranial cavity from its floor or, much less commonly, may arise from the dura.[856,859] Examples complicating the generalized skeletal chondromatoses designated as **Maffucci's syndrome**[852] and **Ollier's disease**[864] have also been depicted.

Intracranial chondrosarcomas of conventional type usually originate in the skull base,[855] but meningeal and neuroparenchymal primaries are recognized, reports including isolated cases following cranial irradiation[851] and evolving from chondromas.[858] Curiously, the mesenchymal chondrosarcoma seems to have a special predilection for the dura among extraosseous sites.[861] Examples arising in the leptomeninges and brain[860] are also on record. Rarest of all cartilaginous intracranial neoplasms is the **extraskeletal myxoid chondrosarcoma**.[862]

Fibroblastic and "fibrohistiocytic" tumors

Solitary fibrous tumors (SFTs) in all respects identical to those originating in the pleura and extrapleural somatic tissues constitute in our experience the most common neuraxial neoplasms composed of fibroblasts or related cell types.[881a] Usually dura-based[867] (and so taken for meningiomas on preoperative assessment), these may also arise within the lateral ventricles or the substance of the spinal cord.[865,881a] A postradiation example has been documented.[881] Most such tumors are benign in appearance and clinical evolution, gross total resection usually proving curative; only exceptional cases evidencing aggressive morphologic features (e.g., conspicuous mitotic activity) or behavior (local invasion of brain or, distant metastasis following repeated local recurrence) are on record.[867a,875,881a] Neuraxial SFTs share with their systemic counterparts a characteristic immunophenotype[867,881a] including strong and diffuse cytoplasmic labeling for CD34, frequently intense bcl-2 reactivity, and failure to express S-100 protein or epithelial membrane

antigen (EMA)—that facilitates their distinction from schwannomas (S-100 protein-positive) and fibrous meningiomas (usually EMA-reactive). More problematic in differential diagnostic terms is the meningeal hemangiopericytoma, discussed further below. CD34 expression in the latter setting is generally weaker and less widespread, but there is potential immunophenotypic overlap.[867,881a]

Benign neuraxial neoplasms of fibroblastic or myofibroblastic type reported underdesignations other than SFT are exceedingly rare; whether at least some such cases represent examples of the latter is arguable. The literature thus contains accounts of CNS "**fibroma**"[878,880] (sometimes referred to as fibromyxoma owing to mucoid stromal alterations) and "**sclerosing fibrous tumor**"[869] as well as **angiofibroma**[870] and **myofibroblastoma**.[879] **Dural fibromatosis**[874] has also been described, in some cases as a complication of neurosurgery, as has the intracranial presentation of **childhood cranial fasciitis**.[877] Fibroblasts additionally participate in the formation of so-called intracranial "**fibroxanthomas**," but these, often dominated by foam cells, may be reactive in nature and are considered under the rubric of xanthomatous lesions.

Fibrosarcomas of the CNS are commonly attached to the dura or leptomeninges, but some examples are situated entirely within the substance of the cerebrum or cerebellum.[829,868,873] Radiation is clearly recognized as predisposing,[868,876] especially to sellar fibrosarcoma in patients so treated for pituitary adenomas, but spontaneous development of this tumor in the confines of the sella turcica has been described.[871] Symptomatic local recurrence is the rule even after gross total resection of circumscribed, superficially positioned lesions, and patients with high-grade lesions usually succumb to their disease within several years of diagnosis, some developing leptomeningeal and distant, extracranial metastases. Low-grade variants seem more amenable to surgical control.[829] Similar considerations apply to the intracranial **malignant fibrous histiocytoma** (a dubious entity from the histogenetic perspective and probably better regarded as a pleomorphic variant of fibrosarcoma).[829,872] The spectrum of malignant fibroblastic tumors encountered along the neuraxis includes an example of **low-grade fibromyxoid sarcoma** histologically similar to its soft tissue counterpart[830] and **sclerosing epithelioid fibrosarcoma**.[866] The latter may assume a deceptively benign, hypocellular and amitotic appearance, but seems prone to local recurrence and distant metastasis.

To our opening caveats regarding neuroglial tumors that may masquerade as neoplasms of fibroblastic or fibrohistiocytic lineage, we would add the warning that astrocytic lesions routinely exhibit immunolabeling with antisera to vimentin and may also be positive on assay for alpha-1-antitrypsin and antichymotrypsin. No differential diagnostic significance should be attached to these findings.

Endothelial tumors

The overwhelming majority of vasoformative tumors involving the CNS are maldevelopmental anomalies (previously considered in our discussion of vascular malformations). Endothelial neoplasms of the neuraxis include **hemangiomas** (typically of capillary type with lobular growth features),[890–892] **hemangioendotheliomas** of spindled, epithelioid and polymorphous types (the first arguably benign and the latter two best regarded as low malignant potential lesions),[889,893] and aggressive **angiosarcomas** of conventional type.[888,895] Also on record is a unique cerebral neoplasm exhibiting hybrid components of "angiogenic" leiomyosarcoma and epithelioid angiosarcoma[887] and CNS involvement by AIDS-associated **Kaposi's sarcoma** has been documented.[884] We have not encountered an example of cutaneous or visceral angiosarcoma presenting as a neuraxial mass, but metastatic atrial myxoma may masquerade as intracranial epithelioid hemangioendothelioma.[894]

The designation of hemangioendothelioma has been extended to certain benign vasogenic meningocerebral lesions that structurally resemble the cellular ("juvenile") capillary hemangiomas encountered as cutaneous "nevi" in infancy.[890] We have also had the opportunity to study an epileptogenic frontal lobe mass, associated with a history of antecedent cranial trauma, which exhibited the features of lobular capillary hemangioma (or so-called pyogenic granuloma) and are familiar with a case in which morphologically similar, but multifocal cerebral hemispheric lesions regressed after corticosteroid administration.[882] Multifocal involvement of the spinal cord and cauda equina by lesions having capillary hemangiomatous features has also been described.[885,891] Finally, the spectrum of primary endothelial prolifera-

tions potentially involving the nervous system includes the process known as **intravascular papillary endothelial hyperplasia** or **Masson's vegetant intravascular hemangioendothelioma**.[883,886] Intracranial variants, which may evolve from pre-existing vascular malformations or develop within dural venous sinuses, can achieve enormous proportions, may regrow if subtotally excised, and have occasionally proved fatal as a result of associated mass effects.

Meningeal hemangiopericytoma

Although their cytogenesis remains a contentious issue, select dura-based tumors long regarded as "angioblastic" variants of meningioma are immunophenotypically, as well as morphologically, indistinguishable from hemangiopericytomas arising in the somatic soft tissues[896–898] (Fig. 28.103). **Meningeal hemangiopericytomas** are largely tumors of adulthood that do not exhibit the distinct predilection for women characteristic of meningiomas and that strongly favor the intracranial compartment. Their distinction from meningiomas evidencing potentially misleading pericytomatous growth patterns is usually straightforward as the latter often contain psammomatous calcospherites and tumor cells concentrically arrayed in tight whorl formations—both foreign to the hemangiopericytoma, as are the intranuclear pseudoinclusions typical of meningothelial elements and their neoplastic derivatives. Also alien to the meningioma, but a feature of many hemangiopericytomas, is a network of "reticulin" investing individual tumor cells. This appears to represent basal lamina material at the ultrastructural level[897,898] (Fig. 28.104). The hemangiopericytoma further departs from the meningioma on electron microscopic study in that the

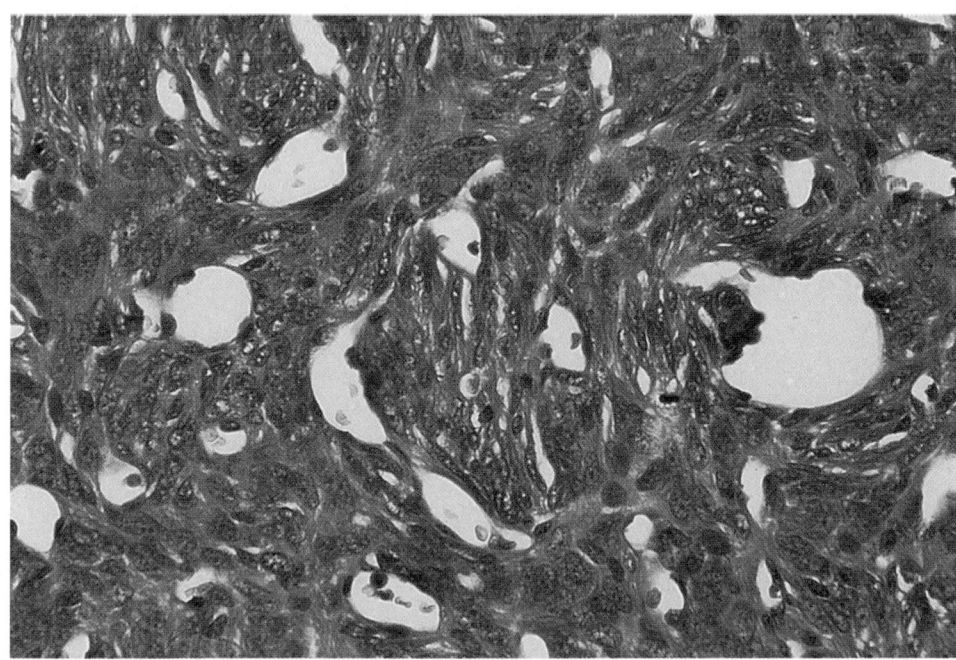

Fig. 28.103 Meningeal hemangiopericytoma. Long regarded as a form of "angioblastic" meningioma, this lesion is now widely accepted as the homolog of its extraneural soft tissue counterpart.

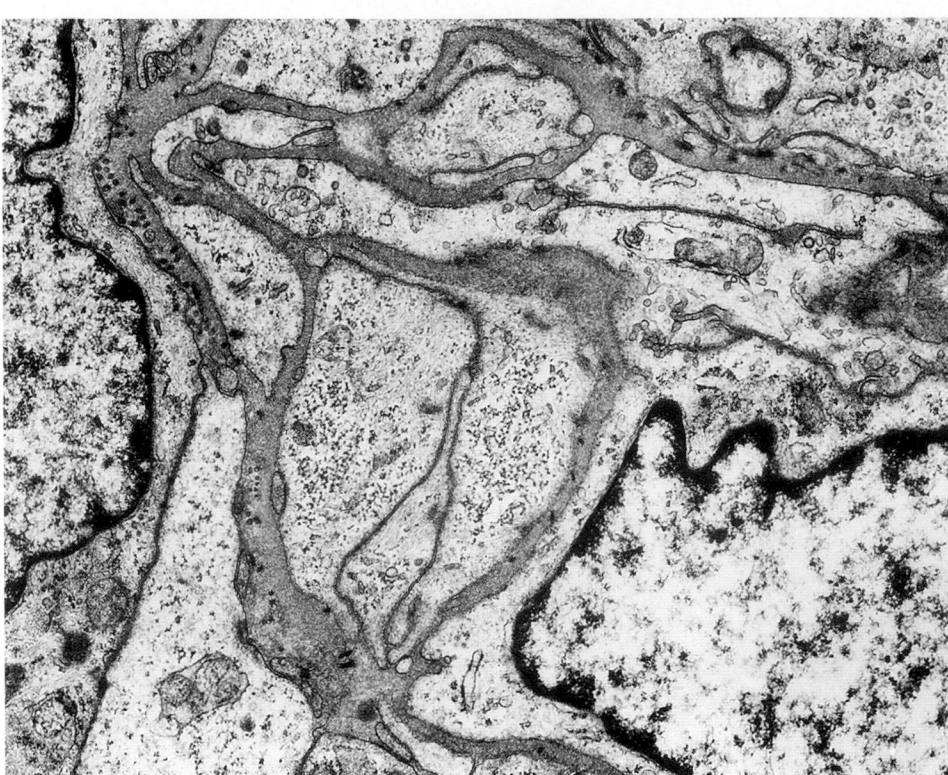

Fig. 28.104 Meningeal hemangiopericytoma. Unlike the cytoplasmic processes of meningothelial tumor cells (compare Fig. 28.101), those of the hemangiopericytoma's constituent neoplastic elements are separated by basal lamina material demonstrable on ultrastructural examination. (×11,360)

cytoplasmic processes elaborated by its constituent cells, although joined by rudimentary junctions, are neither bound by well-developed desmosomes nor intertwined in complex fashion. Serving also to segregate these lesions from neoplasms of meningothelial lineage is their failure to express EMA on immunohistochemical assessment.[827,898,899] Mesenchymal chondrosarcomas of dural origin routinely harbor anaplastic small cell elements in pericytomatous architectural array and thus enter the differential diagnosis, but the meningeal hemangiopericytoma lacks chondroid components. As mentioned above, meningeal hemangiopericytomas may evidence labeling for CD34 but this is usually weak and patchy as opposed to the diffuse and often strong cytoplasmic reactivity typical of solitary fibrous tumors.[881a,899] In problematic cases, the demonstration of pericellular basal lamina material in our view excludes solitary fibrous tumor from further consideration.

Regrowth at the primary site despite seemingly complete initial resection is typical of the meningeal hemangiopericytoma, although this may take years to become clinically apparent. Even with the addition of postoperative radiotherapy, many afflicted patients die as a direct result of intracranial tumor progression, often after a protracted course characterized by repeated local recurrence.[896–898] Extracranial metastasis, usually a late complication, occurs with surprising frequency. Most often seeded are the lungs, bones, and liver, but retroperitoneal organs, such as kidney and pancreas, may also be involved.[898] Some observers have found such features as conspicuous mitotic activity and foci of necrosis to be of ominous prognostic import,[898] whereas others have been unable to correlate outcome with histology.[896] In our view, all meningeal hemangiopericytomas are best regarded as potentially aggressive.

Myogenous tumors

Embryonal rhabdomyosarcomas account for most primary myogenous neoplasms of the CNS reported to date.[900–901] These tend to segregate into a posterior fossa subset, characterized by a presentation in childhood and a predilection for the cerebellum, and a supratentorial group of adult onset typified by a cerebral hemispheric localization. Rare cases of **pleomorphic** and **alveolar rhabdomyosarcoma** have been documented to arise in the cerebrum as well.[829] The midline, vermal position of many intracranial rhabdomyosarcomas arising in the pediatric population and the recognized capacity of the cerebellar medulloblastoma to differentiate along skeletal muscle lines ("medullomyoblastoma") have prompted speculation that both tumor types might originate from a common, primordial progenitor in the rhombic roof. Whatever their histogenesis, primary rhabdomyosarcomas of the CNS are high-grade neoplasms; few patients remain alive 2 years after diagnosis despite aggressive irradiation and chemotherapy. Neuraxis dissemination and extracranial metastasis may complicate local tumor progression. Mention should be made of a diffuse leptomeningeal variant unassociated with a demonstrable neuroparenchymal component,[910] but this diagnosis requires rigorous exclusion of an occult primary focus in the orbit, paranasal sinuses, nasopharynx, or middle ear since rhabdomyosarcomas originating in these parameningeal regions frequently seed the subarachnoid space. The cited example is of note for its occurrence in a child with the neurocristopathy known as hypomelanosis of Ito. Non-neoplastic, cranial nerve-associated proliferations of skeletal and, in some instances, smooth, muscle have been variously designated as **rhabdomyomas, neuromuscular hamartomas/choristomas**, and **benign ectomesenchymomas/Triton tumors**. These have been previously treated in our discussion of hamartomas and choristomas.

Sporadic instances of **leiomyoma**[906] or **leiomyosarcoma**[829,907] originating from the meninges or within the neuroparenchyma have been depicted, these exceedingly rare neoplasms including such oddities as **diffuse leptomeningeal leiomyomatosis**,[902] **pleomorphic angioleiomyoma**,[905] and the **composite leiomyosarcoma-epithelioid angiosarcoma**[887] to which we have previously referred. At special risk of developing neuraxial (as well as systemically situated) smooth muscle tumors are the immunocompromised, particularly patients with AIDS.[903,904,909] Such tumors are usually associated with the dura or situated in juxta-neuraxial sites such as the parasellar region or cavernous sinus, but may involve the brain.[908] They range in appearance from highly differentiated leiomyomas to frank leiomyosarcomas and, in our experience, include epithelioid variants of small, clear cell cytologic type that may be difficult to recognize as being of smooth muscle character. As is the case for their systemic counterparts arising in a background of immunosuppression, neuraxial variants consistently harbor Epstein–Barr virus (EBV) as evidenced by nuclear labeling for EBV-associated nuclear antigen 2 (EBNA–2) and EBV-encoded RNA–1 (EBER–1) on immunohistochemical and in situ hybridization assessment, respectively.

Other mesenchymal neoplasms

In addition to the varied forms of CNS mesenchymal neoplasia exhibiting specific diagnostic features, there is a disparate collection of anaplastic tumors to which only descriptive appellations such as high-grade "spindle cell," "pleomorphic," or "undifferentiated" sarcoma can be given.[829] Reported under the rubric of **primary leptomeningeal sarcomatosis** are poorly characterized variants typified by diffuse tumoral proliferation restricted to the subarachnoid space and unaccompanied by dominant foci of bulky disease.[911,915] These may present with signs and symptoms of polyradiculopathy, spinal cord compression, or intracranial mass effect and are often misdiagnosed initially as chronic meningitides of infectious etiology or as manifestations of neurosarcoidosis or other inflammatory disorders. The differential diagnosis includes leptomeningeal carcino-

matosis, gliomatosis, lymphomatosis, melanomatosis, and medulloblastomatosis. Neoplasms that seem to represent the intracranial equivalents of soft tissue and skeletal **myxomas** have been described,[913] but myxoid meningioma and metastatic atrial myxoma must be excluded before this diagnosis can be accepted. Last, we mention report of a dural **epithelioid sarcoma**[914] and the bizarre phenomenon of a **phosphaturic mesenchymal tumor** (a lesion recognized for its association with paraneoplastic osteomalacia secondary to tumor-induced renal phosphate wasting) masquerading as a subfrontal meningioma.[912]

Nerve sheath tumors of the craniospinal axis

Inasmuch as nerve sheath tumors arising within the cranial cavity and spinal canal are the morphologic and biologic homologs of their more common, peripherally situated counterparts, the reader is referred to Chapter 25 of this text for a detailed treatment of their diagnostic structural and immunophenotypic features.

Schwannomas are the most frequent variant to abut the central neuraxis, usually presenting in adulthood as tumors of the cerebellopontine angle or lumbosacral spinal extramedullary space.[949] Nearly all cerebellopontine angle tumors originate in the vestibular branch of cranial nerve VIII (acoustic schwannoma or neuroma) and produce hearing loss. Schwannomas arising at spinal levels exhibit a similar predilection for sensory divisions of the neuraxis, typically involving the posterior roots. These often assume a "dumbbell" configuration as they squeeze through adjacent intervertebral foramina and expand into the paravertebral soft tissues. Schwannomas rarely lie within the central neuroparenchyma proper,[919] can present as intraventricular masses,[948d] and may involve cranial nerves other than the acoustic. Bilateral eighth nerve examples are a defining feature of **neurofibromatosis type 2 (NF-2)**, an autosomal dominant disorder linked to inherited or newly acquired mutations involving a gene localized to chromosome 22q12.[936] Affected kindreds are prone to an assortment of neoplasms, all typified in this setting by multifocality, that includes craniospinal schwannomas, meningiomas, and intramedullary ependymomas. Inactivating mutations of the NF-2 gene on chromosome 22 also characterize most acoustic schwannomas occurring in sporadic fashion.[949] Multifocal, nonacoustic schwannomas divorced from other manifestations of NF-2 constitute a syndrome known as **schwannomatosis**.[944,949]

The schwannoma's characteristic Antoni A and B structure, nuclear palisading (Verocay bodies), infiltration by foamy macrophages, and vascular hyalinization usually suffice for its recognition, NF-2-associated variants often evidencing a multilobulated growth pattern on gross and microscopic assessment.[946] Rosenthal fibers and eosinophilic granular bodies may rarely be encountered in acoustic examples,[916] in all likelihood reflecting chronic stimulation of astrocytes native to the central portion of cranial nerve VIII.[933] Meningiomas on occasion exhibit schwannoma-like features and are the most frequent counterfeit. Immunocytochemical techniques and electron microscopic study may both be usefully applied to this problem and to the elimination of solitary fibrous tumor from the differential. Schwannomas are characterized by diffuse cytoplasmic S-100 protein expression and pericellular immunolabeling for laminin and type IV collagen, the latter reflecting investment of their elongated cellular processes by a continuous basal lamina foreign to the typical meningioma. Cytoplasmic expression of EMA—a regular feature of meningothelial tumors—is usually absent from the schwannoma or restricted to normal perineurial cells incorporated into the latter's capsule and thus limited to its periphery.[941] Admittedly, however, some observers have described EMA-reactive neoplastic elements in the substance of occasional schwannomas.[827] These are said to exhibit diffuse cytoplasmic reactivity without the cell membrane accentuation characteristic of meningothelial tumors. It is worth remembering that meningiomas only rarely present in the lumbosacral regions favored by schwannomas of the spinal roots. Solitary fibrous tumors are typically nonreactive for S-100 protein and EMA, instead labeling for CD34, and their constituent fibroblastic cells do not elaborate basal lamina material.[867]

A variant of schwannoma recognized for its elaboration of melanosomal melanin exhibits a decided predilection for the spinal nerve roots.[934,948] An intramedullary presentation has also been recorded.[937] Most of the **melanotic schwannomas** reported to date were stated to evolve in benign fashion, though recorded follow-up intervals for many of these cases were limited. The risk of local recurrence following incomplete resection is actually substantial,[934] and an aggressive course characterized by visceral and cerebral metastases has been documented.[923,948] A subset of melanotic schwannomas containing psammomatous concretions constitutes part of the heritable **Carney complex**,[917] which includes cardiac, cutaneous, and mammary myxomas; spotty pigmentation; large cell calcifying Sertoli cell tumors of the testis; and evidence of endocrine hyperfunction (principally Cushing's syndrome and acromegaly, the former associated with primary pigmented nodular adrenocortical disease).

A small minority of intracranial and intraspinal schwannomas are of the "cellular" type.[920,924,942] In contrast to its histologically conventional counterpart, the cellular schwannoma is a densely populated spindle cell tumor, typically devoid of Antoni B areas and Verocay bodies, that may contain foci of mitotic activity and is likely to be misconstrued as a sarcoma. The lesion shares with the classical schwannoma foci of vascular hyalinization, infiltration by lymphocytes and foamy macrophages, diffuse S-100 protein immunoreactivity, and highly differentiated Schwann cell features at the

ultrastructural level. Such tumors may recur locally following excision, but a metastasizing example has never been described. Finally, **granular cell tumors of schwannian lineage** have been noted to involve the trigeminal nerve and to present as intracranial masses.[918]

Most craniospinal **neurofibromas** represent manifestations of neurofibromatosis type 1 (NF-1 ("peripheral" or classic von Recklinghausen's disease)), transmitted in autosomal dominant fashion by a locus on chromosome 17q12.[943] This complex disorder includes, in addition to multifocal cutaneous and more deeply situated plexiform neurofibromas, dermatologic abnormalities (café au lait spots and axillary freckling), pigmented hamartomas of the iris (Lisch nodules), various skeletal defects, and glial neoplasms, chief among which are pilocytic astrocytomas of the anterior optic pathways. Spinal neurofibromas arising in this setting typically do so at multiple levels. Only rarely are cranial nerves involved. Curious lesions interpreted as plexiform neurofibromas of the cauda equina have been reported in patients without evidence of NF-1.[939]

Well-documented, but exceedingly uncommon, are **malignant nerve sheath tumors** originating in cranial or spinal nerve roots. The former are said to arise most commonly within the trigeminal nerve[927,950] or gasserian ganglion.[935] "Acoustic" examples are on record,[938] including neoplasms interpreted as so-called **Triton tumors** (i.e., variants exhibiting rhabdomyoblastic differentiation)[922,929] and rare cases in which conventional vestibular schwannomas apparently underwent malignant transformation.[922,930] Radiosurgery has preceded the latter event in isolated cases.[922] Also noteworthy are reports of malignant nerve sheath tumors arising in the cerebral parenchyma[945,947] or a lateral ventricle.[931] Malignant nerve sheath tumors often originate in neurofibromas, particularly those of plexiform type, and so are strongly associated with NF-1.[926] Rare craniospinal examples unassociated with neurofibromas or schwannomas have also followed local irradiation.[925]

Other reported lesions relevant to the present discussion include an intraventricular **perineurioma** of soft tissue type,[928] **nerve sheath "myxoma"** or **"neurothekeoma"** that involved the gasserian ganglion[940] or cauda equina,[932] and examples of **localized hypertrophic mononeuropathy** affecting cranial nerves[921] or spinal roots.[951] The latter exhibit segmental expansion of the involved nerves secondary to "onion bulb," periaxonal Schwann cell proliferations.

Lymphoproliferative and myeloproliferative disorders

As secondary spread of systemic lymphoproliferative and myeloproliferative disorders to the CNS does not often occasion neurosurgical intervention for diagnostic purposes, only a few general observations on this problem are offered. At greatest risk of such dissemination are patients suffering from acute leukemias,[961] particularly of lymphoblastic type; diffuse leptomeningeal infiltration is the dominant pattern of CNS involvement encountered in this setting. In some cases, extensive permeation of cranial and spinal nerve roots accompanies the unrestrained proliferation of leukemic cells in the subarachnoid compartment. Circumscribed, dura-based, or (rarely) intracerebral masses composed of leukemic cells principally complicate the acute myelogenous leukemias but have virtually disappeared from clinical practice since the advent of modern cytoreductive therapy. Variously designated as **chloromas**, **granulocytic sarcomas**, or **myeloblastomas**, these tumors usually develop in subjects who are demonstrably leukemic but exceptionally constitute the initial manifestation of relapse following apparently successful treatment or arise in otherwise normal individuals as harbingers of subsequent bone marrow and peripheral blood involvement.[971,1000,1003] Parameningeal masses of **extramedullary hematopoietic** tissue have been reported to produce neurologic dysfunction, mainly as a result of spinal cord compression, in patients with thalassemia or myelofibrosis.[966,994]

Involvement of the CNS in the course of node-based non-Hodgkin lymphoma is uncommon and usually limited to permeation of the leptomeninges ("lymphomatous meningitis") or, less often, infiltration of the spinal epidural space.[980] Cerebral infiltrates are decidedly unusual in this setting and typically complicate advanced (stage IV) disease, an excess of cases occurring in patients with diffuse large cell or lymphoblastic subtypes and involvement of other extranodal sites.[980] By contrast, patients presenting with non-Hodgkin lymphoma of the eye—an extension of the CNS—frequently develop lymphomatous lesions of the brain proper.[998] A subset of malignant lymphomas, principally non-Hodgkin's variants, are confined at diagnosis to the epidural compartment and paraspinal tissues, usually arising in the midthoracic region and prompting evaluation for compressive myelopathy.[975] Only exceptionally are the meninges colonized or the neural parenchyma penetrated in the course of systemic **Hodgkin's disease**,[999] **plasma cell myeloma**,[991,1001] **Waldenström's macroglobulinemia**,[972] or **mycosis fungoides**.[960]

The designation of **primary central nervous system lymphoma (PCNSL)** is reserved for malignant lymphoid neoplasms restricted at presentation to the brain, spinal cord, or meninges.[996] Although the association of PCNSL with states of diminished immune responsiveness has long been appreciated and its particular predilection for victims of AIDS firmly established,[962] the majority of afflicted patients suffer no predisposing illness.[963,992,996] Sporadic cases most often present in the sixth or seventh decades of life and manifest a 1.5:1 to 2:1 male/female ratio, whereas AIDS-related examples are characterized by a younger age at onset and an overwhelming pre-

dominance in men, reflecting the demography of HIV-1 infection. Most patients suffer the usual symptoms of an expanding intracranial mass, although PCNSLs tend to arise in the deep cerebral hemispheric white matter, corpus callosum, and basal ganglia and thus are not as prone to produce seizures as gliomas or metastatic deposits that involve epileptogenic cortical tissues. Frontocallosal and periventricular examples may prompt evaluation for personality change, depression, progressive psychomotor retardation, or frank psychosis. Some tumors are discovered in the course of workup for persistent uveocyclitides unresponsive to conventional ophthalmologic treatment, a manifestation of ocular involvement that often occurs in complex with cerebral infiltration.[998]

Neuroradiologic features (Fig. 28.105) that suggest the diagnosis of PCNSL on CT or MR study include tumoral hyperdensity in precontrast images, diffuse (as opposed to rim) enhancement on administration of contrast media, evidence of widespread subependymal infiltration, and multifocality. The last is apparent in some 25% to 40% of sporadic, and the majority of HIV-1-associated, cases.[996] Especially suspect in older adults are masses that regress substantially with corticosteroid administration alone prior to biopsy, occasional lymphomas

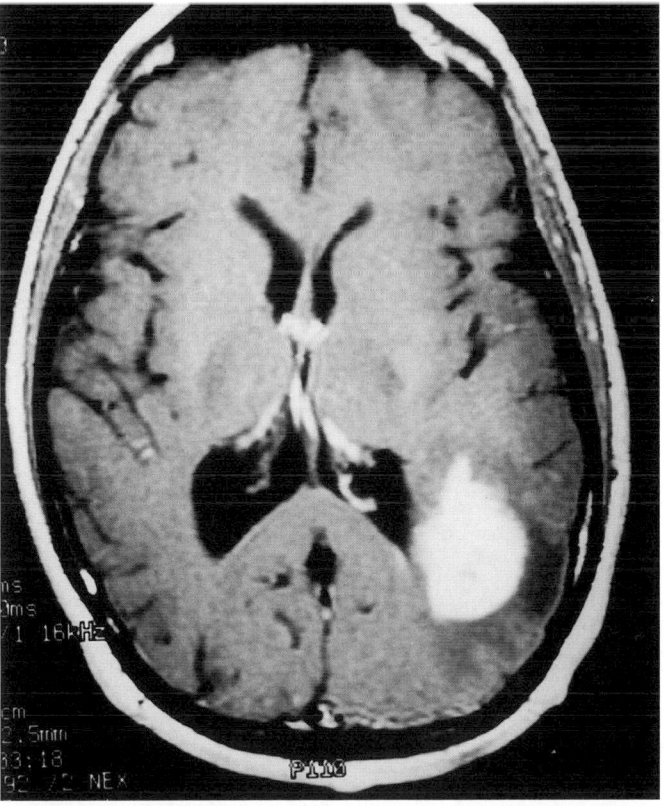

Fig. 28.105 Primary CNS lymphoma. As demonstrated in this postcontrast injection MRI, primary cerebral lymphomas exhibit a predilection for the deep, paraventricular white matter and tend to striking and fairly homogeneous enhancement in "sporadic" (as opposed to AIDS-related) cases.

disappearing (transiently) with such treatment and masquerading as multiple sclerosis.[953] Inasmuch as extensive central necrosis lends to many HIV-1-associated PCNSLs a "ring"-enhancing radiologic appearance indistinguishable from *Toxoplasma* abscesses, it has become common practice in this setting to offer patients what amounts to a diagnostic as well as therapeutic trial of antimicrobial therapy. Lesions that do not respond promptly must be regarded as lymphomas until proved otherwise. A definitive diagnosis of PCNSL usually requires biopsy, but may be accomplished by demonstration of malignant lymphoid cells in CSF.

PCNSLs may arise anywhere along the neuraxis. Roughly 75% are situated in the supratentorial compartment, these favoring the deep structures enumerated above. Most of the remainder involve the cerebellum or brainstem, only rare examples being isolated to the spinal cord.[996,1002] A small fraction present as diffuse leptomeningeal infiltrates in the absence of demonstrable intraparenchymal disease,[976,986] the literature including description of **human herpesvirus 8-associated "primary effusion lymphoma"** of the subarachnoid space as a complication of AIDS.[973] Lesions of the CNS proper are poorly defined in most instances and composed of dry, granular tan-white or grayish-pink tissue that may evidence small foci of necrotic softening or hemorrhagic discoloration. Extensive necrosis and conspicuous hemorrhage are most commonly encountered in AIDS-related cases, which may closely mimic *Toxoplasma* abscesses on gross examination (particularly after irradiation). Some examples diffusely permeate the neuropil, producing little architectural distortion save for a slight pallor of gray matter landmarks and expansion of involved structures ("**lymphomatosis cerebri**").[958] A striking histologic feature of many cases is the tendency

for tumor cells to aggregate in Virchow–Robin spaces and to infiltrate the walls of cerebral vessels (Fig. 28.106). Most PCNSLs are high-grade non-Hodgkin's lesions of diffuse large cell type,[962,963,992,996] although all major cytologic variants have been reported in this location, including such oddities as **signet-ring cell**[995] and **anaplastic large cell (Ki-1)**[952,997] **lymphoma**. Follicular (nodular) lymphoid neoplasms, however, are foreign to the neuroparenchyma. Some observers have noted an overrepresentation of immunoblastic and small noncleaved Burkitt-like cell types among PCNSLs, particularly those involving AIDS patients and other immunosuppressed hosts, compared with node-based or other extranodal primary tumors.[962,996] Regardless of the cytologic variety, touch preparations are useful in establishing the lymphoid nature of a given tumor at the time of intraoperative consultation (Fig. 28.107).

The overwhelming majority (>95%) of PCNSLs exhibit a B-cell immunophenotype,[962,963,992,996] including labeling for CD20 and CD79a in the absence of CD3 or CD45RO expression (Fig. 28.108). Other evidences of their B-lymphocytic lineage include clonal IgH gene rearrangements and certain characteristics shared with germinal center B cells, including frequent alterations of 5' noncoding regions of the BCL6 gene and bcl-6 protein expression.[988,996] Such lesions often harbor a conspicuous complement of admixed T cells that can confound interpretation of the histologic and immunohistochemical picture, but these reactive elements usually appear as small, well-differentiated lymphocytes that are readily distinguished from the large, atypical B cells on which the diagnosis rests. Particularly deceptive are biopsies deriving from the perimeter of PCNSLs, where reactive T lymphocytes often constitute a dominant and obscuring population, or from masses evidencing regression on

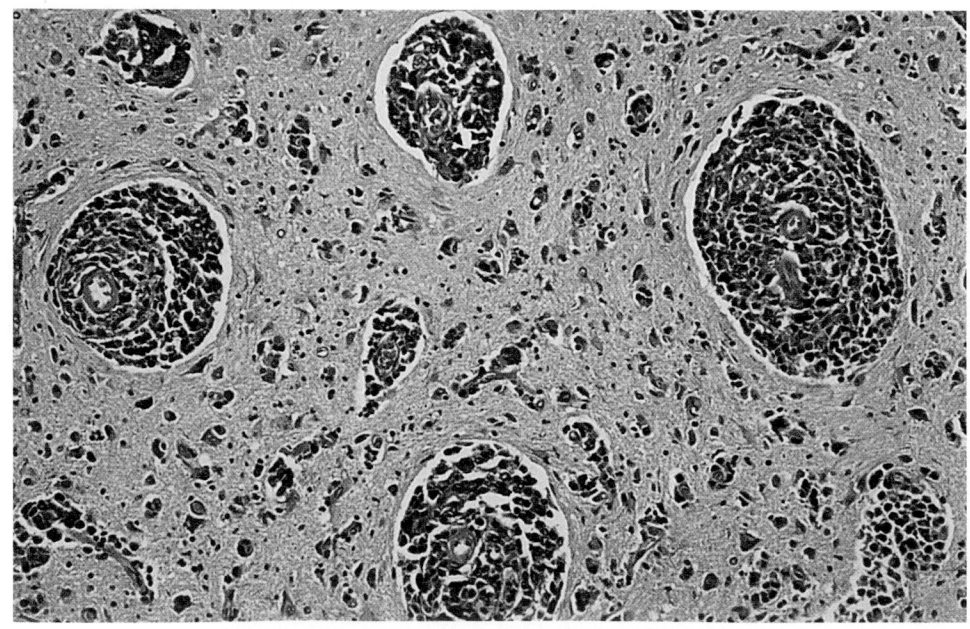

Fig. 28.106 Primary CNS lymphoma. Although not apparent in all cases, a vasocentric growth pattern with tumoral infiltration of blood vessel walls and Virchow–Robin spaces is common to primary CNS lymphomas. Systemic lymphomas secondarily involving the neuroparenchyma may also preferentially grow in this fashion.

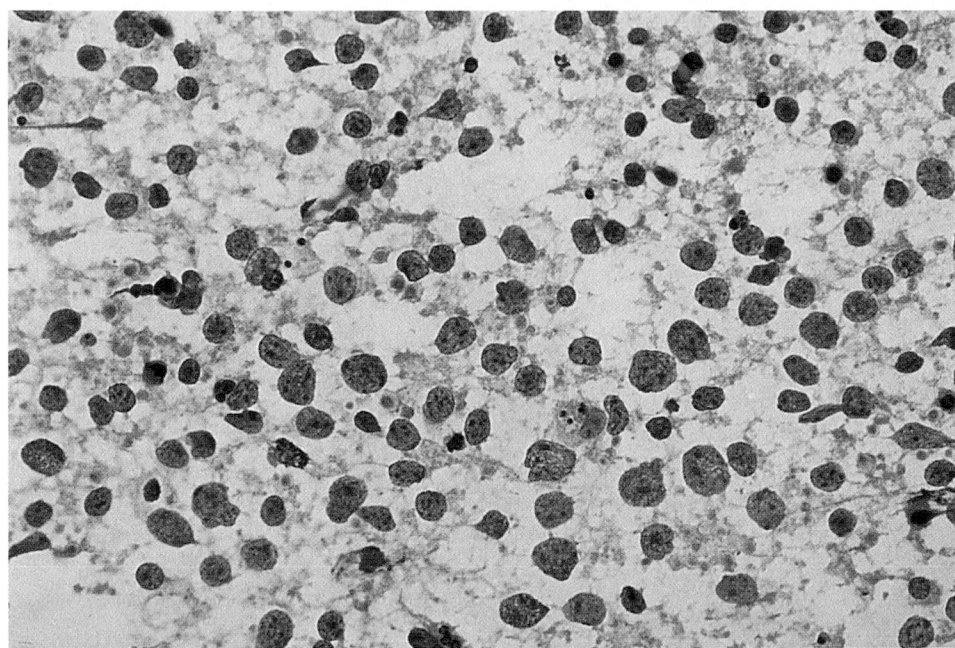

Fig. 28.107 Primary CNS lymphoma. An intraoperative smear preparation demonstrates the large cell cytology and nuclear features characteristic of CNS lymphoma. The lack of cellular cohesion or cytoplasmic processes, respectively, are useful in discriminating this tumor from metastatic carcinoma and glioblastoma multiforme, two neoplasms that commonly enter the clinical differential diagnosis.

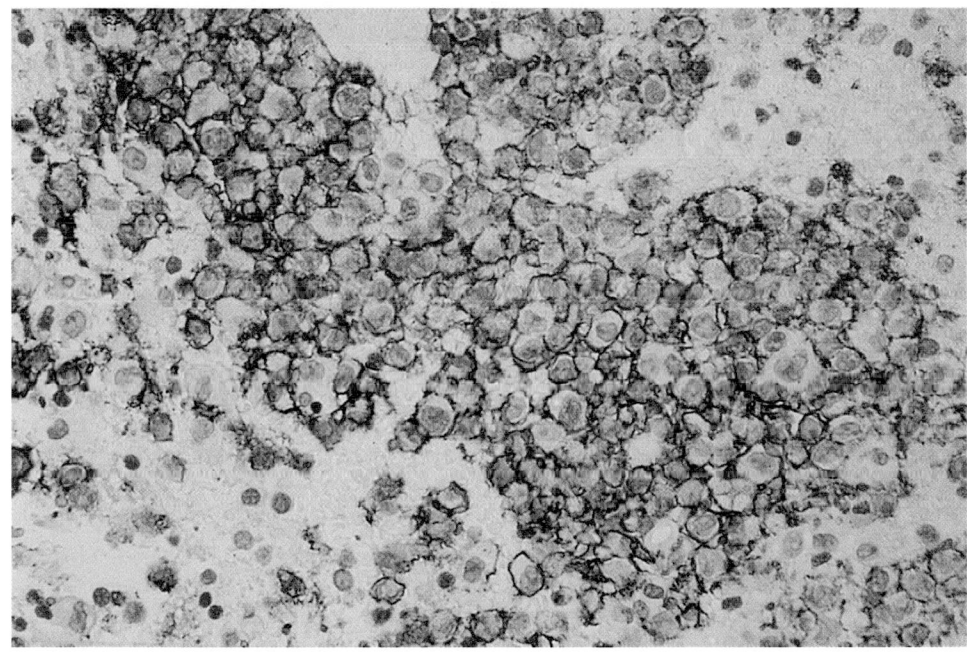

Fig. 28.108 Primary CNS lymphoma. The great majority of lymphomas arising in the CNS are of B-cell type and, as shown here, label for CD20 on immunoperoxidase (L–26) assay.

preoperative corticosteroid administration. These "sentinel lesions" may be selectively relieved of their neoplastic B-cell components, heavily infiltrated by foamy macrophages, and partially demyelinated, a phenomenon that may prompt, along with their radiologic and clinical resolution, acceptance of multiple sclerosis or demyelinating pseudotumor as the primary disease process.[953] It is worth remembering that multiple sclerosis is, for the most part, a disorder of the young. Furthermore, it has been our experience that inadvertently "treated" lymphomas do not leave behind the sharply demarcated zones of selective and total myelin loss with axonal preservation typical of multiple

sclerosis or demyelinating pseudotumors. Clonal B-cell populations have rarely been described as participants in multiple sclerosis,[1005] but atypical B lymphocytes should not be seen in this disorder. **Primary T-cell lymphomas of the CNS** (including anaplastic large cell variants[997]) may be encountered but are clearly exceptional.[957,963,974,976,989a] The latter seem to be overrepresented among leptomeningeal and infratentorial (particularly cerebellar) primaries. An increased incidence of T-cell CNS lymphomas in Koreans is suggested by one recent report, these, as compared to B-cell tumors in this cohort, tending to a more superficial intracerebral presentation, often exhibiting rim enhancement on MRI, harboring mixed neoplastic elements of small and intermediate size, and forming loose vasocentric aggregates rather than sheet-like proliferations.[964a]

Attempts to correlate morphologic subtype with outcome in the setting of neuroparenchymal or leptomeningeal PCNSL have yielded conflicting results,[963,992,996] histologic subclassification currently having no relevance to disease management. Much the same can be said for measures of proliferative activity and genetic profiling, though this is an area of active investigation.[996] All PCNSLs are now approached as high-risk neoplasms and the outlook for affected patients is generally poor. Tumors occurring in otherwise healthy adults typically regress following irradiation and chemotherapy, but frequently recur (often at CNS sites remote from the initial focus) and are associated with reported median survival intervals of 18 to 45 months and overall survivorship of 25 to 45% at 5 years.[996] The prognosis for affected AIDS patients is particularly grim. The usual pattern of treatment failure is progressive, frequently multifocal infiltration of the CNS proper attended, in some cases, by leptomeningeal dissemination. Ocular involvement is experienced by many patients as the disease evolves,[998] but systemic lymphomatous infiltrates develop in no more than 10% of cases.

As the central neuraxis normally lacks a resident lymphoid population, the histogenesis of PCNSLs is obscure. Specifically, whether primary neuroparenchymal and leptomeningeal lymphomas actually arise in these locales or are peripherally generated and selectively home to (or opportunistically colonize and, shielded from immune surveillance, persist within) the CNS is unclear. As mentioned, PCNSLs exhibit antigenic characteristics and genetic alterations typical of germinal center-derived B lymphocytes.[988,996] Infections or other inflammatory processes could summon lymphocytes to the CNS and thus set the stage for their subsequent neoplastic transformation (a particularly plausible scenario in the immunodeficient), but only exceptionally has PCNSL been described in patients with proven neurological infections or other unarguably reactive processes characterized by lymphoid infiltration.[956] Given the recognized ability of the Epstein–Barr virus (EBV) to immortalize B cells in vitro and to drive a polyclonal, systemic lymphoproliferation that may evolve to frank lymphoma in immunocompromised hosts, it is noteworthy that AIDS-related PCNSLs[962,996] and post-transplant lymphoproliferative disease involving the CNS[990] regularly harbor this agent whereas sporadic PCNSLs rarely do.[963] EBV has also been incriminated in a low-grade lymphoproliferative disorder resembling polymorphic B-cell hyperplasia in an HIV-1-infected child,[983] and in a polyclonal cerebellar lymphoproliferation that progressed to lymphoma in an apparently immunocompetent adult.[967] On a practical note, the demonstration of EBV DNA in the CSF of AIDS patients by polymerase chain reaction assay has emerged as a reasonably specific and sensitive indicator of PCNSL in this cohort.[965]

Primary lymphoproliferative disorders of the CNS other than non-Hodgkin lymphoma of the neuroparenchyma and leptomeninges merit little discussion. **Primary dural lymphomas** are uncommon lesions that typically mimic meningiomas and that are usually B-cell tumors of **low-grade, mucosa-associated lymphoid tissue (MALT) type**.[985] Other variants have been described in this setting,[993] including **T-cell-rich B-cell lymphoma**[954] and **marginal zone-type lymphoma with amyloid deposition**.[989] Only rarely is **Hodgkin's disease** confined, on presentation, to the CNS.[963,984] PCNSLs derived from immunodeficient hosts, however, not infrequently harbor pleomorphic cellular elements that may be misconstrued as Reed-Sternberg cells. The peculiar disorder described as **neoplastic angioendotheliomatosis**, formerly regarded as an intravascular variant of angiosarcoma, is now known to be an unusual form of malignant lymphoma, usually of large B-cell type, exhibiting a remarkable tropism for blood vessels in the skin, adrenal glands, and CNS.[968,996] More accurate designations for this process are **angiotropic lymphoma** or **intravascular malignant lymphomatosis**. Patients often present with neurologic dysfunction—progressive encephalopathy, dementia, or stroke—that reflects multifocal cerebral infarction resulting from occlusion of vascular lumina by malignant lymphoid cells (Fig. 28.109). Rare cases have been described as limited to the brain or spinal cord,[970] one of which occurred in a child with AIDS.[969]

Other oddities include **Castleman's disease** confined to the meninges,[977,979] primary dural[959] or intracerebral[1004] **plasmacytoma** (including cases described as developing against a background of **atypical plasma cell hyperplasia**),[981] and CNS **amyloidomas**,[987] neither of the latter appearing to herald systemic myeloma. Tumors interpreted as **true histiocytic neoplasms** of the brain have also been depicted.[964,982,1002a] Finally, there is so-called **lymphomatoid granulomatosis**, an angiocentric and necrotizing lymphoproliferative disorder historically described as a prelymphomatous condition involving the CNS in association with pulmonary disease but occasionally reported to localize in brain alone.[955,978] Several of these isolated cerebral variants involved patients with AIDS[955] and a number eventuated in recognizable lymphoma. Arguably, at least some of these cases represented angiocentric forms of malignant lymphoma ab initio. The participation of EBV in this process has been documented.[978]

Germ cell tumors

Whether **germ cell tumors** of the CNS derive, as long presumed, from primordial germ cells that aberrantly migrate to the developing central neuraxis from the fetal

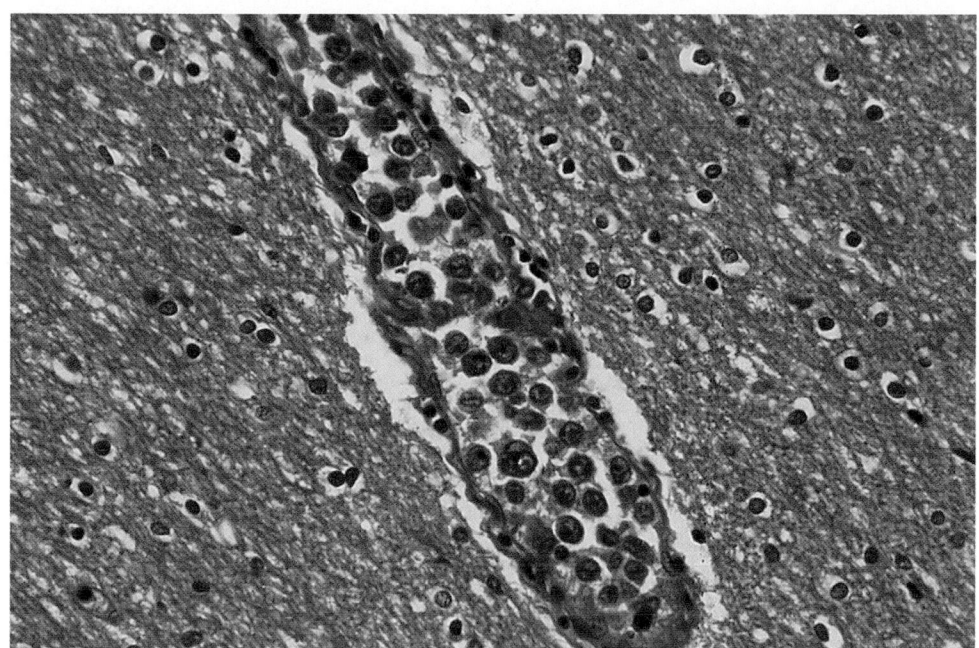

Fig. 28.109 Angiotropic lymphoma/intravascular malignant lymphomatosis. Large, highly atypical cells fill a small blood vessel in the white matter of a 63-year-old woman subjected to brain biopsy for progressive cognitive impairment. Positive immunoassays for leukocyte common antigen and CD20 confirmed their lymphoid nature and B-cell phenotype, respectively.

yolk sac remains a speculative and controversial matter,[1028] but the fact remains that these uncommon neoplasms are the morphologic homologs of germinal tumors arising in the gonads (as well as other extragonadal sites) and at least a subset manifest genetic abnormalities, such as X chromosome gains and isochromosome 12p, characteristic of testicular (and mediastinal) primaries.[1024,1028] Approximately 90% of CNS germ cell tumors are discovered in the first two decades of life, case rates peaking in 10 to 12 year olds. In Western series, these account for no more than 0.5% of all primary intracranial neoplasms and 3% of those encountered in children, but their incidence is increased some fivefold in Japan and Taiwan.[1019,1028] Sharing with other extragonadal germ cell tumors a predilection for the midline, at least 80% to 90% of CNS examples arise along an axis extending from the suprasellar cistern and infundibulum to the pineal gland (these constituting the most common neoplasms encountered in the latter location). A synchronous suprasellar and pineal region presentation is well recognized, though exceptional, as are rare cases confined to the cerebral hemispheres, basal ganglia or thalami (these may be bilateral), ventricles, spinal cord and sella turcica. Males are afflicted more than twice as frequently as females when all sites are considered, but gender distribution varies with tumor localization: the large majority of pineal examples affect boys, suprasellar lesions occurring more often in girls.

CNS germ cell tumors generally arise in sporadic fashion, but are recognized to complicate Klinefelter's syndrome[1012] and their incidence may prove to be somewhat increased in the setting of Down syndrome as well.[1011,1028] Suprasellar examples produce visual field defects, diabetes insipidus and hypothalamopituitary failure, whereas pineal region tumors compress the tectal plate and aqueduct, presenting with symptoms and signs of obstructive hydrocephalus that are often accompanied by a vertical gaze paresis known eponymously as Parinaud's syndrome. The secretion of β-human chorionic gonadotropin (β-HCG) by neoplastic syncytiotrophoblast[1006,1014] may stimulate testosterone production in boys and result in "precocious puberty" (isosexual pseudoprecocity), as may release of the immature testes from tonic inhibitory controls secondary to pineal and hypothalamic injury. The additional elaboration of cytochrome p450 aromatase, which catalyzes estrogen formation from C19 steroids, may explain the exceptional occurrence of precocious puberty in girls with HCG-producing intracranial germ cell tumors.[1025]

The macroscopic features, histologic and immunohistochemical criteria governing the identification and subclassification of CNS germ cell tumors differ in no way from those previously articulated in discussion of their more common gonadal counterparts and are not systematically reprised here.[1008,1028,1029] Exceeding in incidence all other tumor types is the **germinoma**. This neoplasm is histologically identical to the seminoma and, like its testicular homolog, demonstrates cytoplasmic immunolabeling (often membranous) for placental alkaline phophatase (PLAP) but not α-fetoprotein (α-FP) or β-HCG. Germinomas may be somewhat more likely than seminomas to express cytokeratins and to evidence differentiation along epithelial lines at the fine structural level,[1020,1028] though no clinical significance has been attached to such findings. We can confirm that germinomas may exhibit limited cytoplasmic CAM 5.2 labeling (often paranuclear and only focally apparent when present), but are typically AE1/3 negative. While the histologic diagnosis is usually straightforward, the germinoma that has elicited a florid lymphoplasmacytic and granulomatous reaction may masquerade as tuberculosis, sarcoidosis or other inflammatory process.[1018] Immunohistochemical screening for PLAP may aid in the visualization of tumor cells obscured by such an infiltrate and is mandatory when dealing with inflamed biopsy material deriving from the suprasellar–pineal axis (a unique report of apparently **idiopathic "pinealitis"** notwithstanding[1022]), but the potential for sampling error and the failure of some 5 to 10% of germinomas to express this antigen complicate matters considerably. We have found germinomas to exhibit cell membrane immunolabeling for CD 117 (c-kit) that is more constant and intense than that apparent in PLAP preparations and can recommend this in difficult circumstances. A minority of otherwise pure germinomas harbor syncytiotrophoblastic giant cell elements that are β-HCG-immunoreactive and associated with elevated levels of this oncoprotein in serum and CSF. The prognostic implications of this phenomenon are addressed below.

Apart from germinoma, only CNS germ cell tumors of the teratoma family are likely to be encountered in pure form.[1019,1028] **Teratomas** constitute the majority of congenital CNS germ cell tumors,[1009] one account describing the remarkable discovery of a primary intracranial example in the fetus of a woman with an independent ovarian teratoma.[1026] This tumor group includes the **mature teratoma** (composed entirely of adult-type tissues), the **immature teratoma** (defined by a content of incompletely differentiated components exhibiting fetal appearances), and the **teratoma with malignant transformation** (i.e., one spawning a secondary cancer of conventional somatic type). As regards the last entity, sarcomas of undifferentiated or rhabdomyosarcomatous aspect,[1008,1019,1027,1029] leiomyosarcoma,[1032] adenocarcinomas of enteric type,[1010] squamous carcinoma[1019] and erythroleukemia[1013] have all been reported to arise from intracranial, teratoma-containing germ cell tumors and we have seen in consultation a mature pineal teratoma partially overgrown by malignant hemangioendothelioma. A carcinoid has been encountered within a teratomatous tumor of the spinal axis,[1016] though some argue that intraspinal "teratomas" are complex malformations rather than true germinal neoplasms.[1007,1017] Rarely, intracranial teratomas achieve extraordinary degrees of organization and contain fetus-like bodies.[1021] The spontaneous maturation of teratomas has also been recorded,[1031] but re-resection specimens composed entirely of fully differentiated somatic tissue elements usually derive from initially immature teratomatous neoplasms or mixed germ cell tumors subjected to adjuvant therapy. The apparent maturation in such circumstances may simply reflect the selective ablation of incompletely differentiated cellular components. The progressive, seemingly paradoxical enlargement of these ostensibly mature neoplasms has been referred to as the "growing teratoma syndrome."[1023]

Embryonal carcinoma, **yolk sac tumor** and **choriocarcinoma** may all arise within the CNS, but only rarely are these encountered in unalloyed form. Far more frequent is their presence within mixed germ cell tumors, which often contain elements of germinoma and teratoma as well. We again emphasize the importance of immunohistochemical assessment in the evaluation of such lesions. Specifically, screening for α-FP is critical if minor components of yolk sac tumor are not to be overlooked (bearing in mind, however, that teratomatous glands of enteric type may also label for this antigen). The pathologist reporting a mixed germ cell neoplasm should specify the participating tumor types and their relative representation.

Histologic subtype emerges from a number of multivariate analyses as bearing most heavily on CNS germ cell tumor prognosis.[1019,1030] The best outcomes attach to pure germinomas in localized form (which are generally radiocurable as well as chemosensitive) and to mature teratomas that can be completely resected. The spontaneous regression of germinoma has been recorded,[1015] a phenomenon that may well be mediated by the tumor-infiltrating lymphocytes characteristic of this neoplasm. The presence of syncytiotrophoblastic giant cells within germinomas has been associated in some studies with an increased risk of local failure and modest decrement in survival following irradiation.[1019] Yolk sac tumors, embryonal carcinomas, choriocarcinomas and mixtures thereof frequently resist both surgery and adjuvant treatment, carrying a high mortality. These destructively infiltrate local structures and may disseminate via the CSF, as can the germinoma. Extraneural spread is a rare complication that includes spontaneous systemic metastasis (mainly to lung and bone) as well as seeding of the peritoneal cavity via ventriculoperitoneal shunts placed for relief of obstructive hydrocephalus. Some observers have found immature teratomas and mixed tumors composed mainly of germinoma and teratomatous elements to be associated with an "intermediate" risk of recurrence and progression.[1019]

Melanocytic tumors

We have previously mentioned melanogenesis as a function occasionally exercised by nerve sheath tumors as well as central neuroepithelial neoplasms of varying types. The CNS and its coverings also host tumors posited to derive from dendritic melanocytes of neural crest origin that normally populate the pia-arachnoid. The latter are especially numerous over the ventral medulla and high cervical spinal cord, regions that often evidence a peppery discoloration on gross inspection, but the growths for which they are held accountable are by no means restricted to these areas and, while largely leptomeninges-based, may be anchored to the dura mater or situated in the substance of the brain, spinal cord, or pineal gland. Most such lesions fall into one of several fairly homogeneous diagnostic categories. As described below, these include well-differentiated and relatively indolent tumors that are termed melanocytomas as well as frankly malignant melanomas occurring in either localized or diffuse leptomeningeal form. Melanocytic neoplasms of the CNS may constitute manifestations of a generalized neurocristopathy. The syndrome of **neurocutaneous melanosis** is defined by the association of giant or multifocal nevi of congenital type with discrete meningeal melanomas or, more commonly, an unrestrained (and ultimately fatal) proliferation of melanocytic elements, often deceptively benign in appearance, throughout the subarachnoid compartment and within Virchow–Robin spaces.[1035,1045] In addition, meningeal melanocytomas[1044] and melanomas[1048] have been reported in complex with nevus of Ota, characterized by congenital cutaneous, ocular and retrobulbar soft tissue hyperpigmentation in a maxillo-ophthalmic trigeminal nerve distribution. Intracranial melanoma has also been described in the setting of NF-1.[1040]

Melanocytomas usually present in middle age or later adult life as circumscribed, extra-axial masses attached to the leptomeninges. Most arise along the spinal neuraxis (some in association with nerve roots), intracranial examples exhibiting a decided predilection for the posterior fossa and Meckel's cave.[1036,1042,1043] Only exceptionally do such tumors involve higher levels of the intracranial compartment.[1036,1037,1043] Consisting grossly of tan-brown to coal-black tissue, melanocytomas are frequently composed of uniform spindle cells arrayed in fascicles and compactly whorled nests (the latter accounting for the once prevalent perception of these tumors as pigmented meningiomas) (Fig. 28.110). Whorling formations may be centered on delicate stromal blood vessels, cellular dehiscence often producing a pseudopapillary appearance at low magnification. Epithelioid forms may be admixed, but only exceptionally do these dominate the histologic picture. Tumor cell nuclei may exhibit longitudinal grooving when spindled and typically contain centrally positioned eosinophilic nucleoli that are easily apprehended but of relatively small diameter. Candidates for the diagnosis of melanocytoma should not harbor macronucleoli, evidence conspicuous nuclear atypia or pleomorphism, contain more than the (very) occasional mitotic figure, or exhibit necrosis. Cytoplasmic melanization is usually advanced, particularly at the periphery of whorled nests (which are often bordered by clustered melanophages), and can obscure all cytologic detail. Virtually amelanotic examples may be encountered but are exceptional. Ultrastructural studies will confirm the presence of mature melanosomes and may show basement membrane material (also demonstrable in type IV collagen immunopreparations) to incompletely invest some cellular processes or to surround groups of neoplastic melanocytes,[1034] though the extensive basal lamina formation about individual cells and complex cytoplasmic interdigitation characteristic of the melanotic schwannoma are foreign to the melanocytoma. Immunoreactivity for vimentin, S-100 protein, and HMB-45 are regularly present, melanocytomas—in contradistinction to meningiomas—being epithelial membrane antigen-negative.[1036,1043] A curious oncocytic (i.e., mitochondrion-rich) neoplasm of apparently melanocytomatous nature has been reported.[1038]

Melanocytomas are slowly expanding and generally

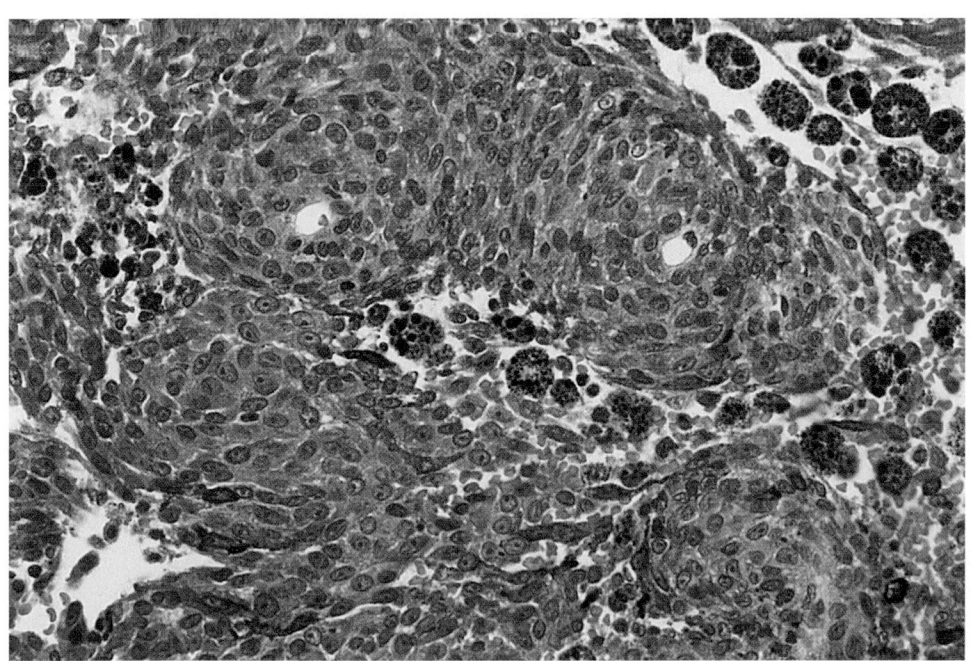

Fig. 28.110 Meningeal melanocytoma. The tendency to cellular whorling manifested by this example, resected from the cervical region of a 34-year-old man with a protracted history of neck pain and gait disturbance, accounts for the potential misclassification of melanocytomas as melanotic meningiomas. Note finely divided brown pigment in the cytoplasm of some tumor cells (as opposed to coarse pigment granules in melanophages), delicate and monomorphous nuclear features, lack of mitotic activity, and absence of necrosis.

amenable to surgical control if gross total removal can be accomplished. They have been reported to recur following resection and to invade adjoining neuroparenchyma, but the literature on this score is difficult to interpret owing to the rarity of melanocytic tumors of CNS origin and the application of nonuniform diagnostic criteria to these unusual lesions.[1036] The largest and most closely analyzed series to date included, under the rubric of melanocytoma, only well-differentiated leptomeningeal neoplasms with minimal cytologic atypism, small nucleoli, low mitotic counts (maximally 1 per 10 high power fields and below this level in most cases), MIB-1 labeling indices not exceeding 2%, no necrosis or invasion of CNS proper.[1036] None regrew following gross total excision or subtotal resection, irrespective of adjuvant radiotherapy (median follow-up period of 36 months). We have encountered, however, a fatal tumor meeting all of the foregoing criteria that widely seeded the CSF, as well as neoplasms otherwise acceptable as melanocytomas that partially colonized the spinal cord (extending along perivascular spaces and associated with florid Rosenthal fiber formation in testament to their chronicity) or that proved, in the main, to be intramedullary at operation.[1039] It is our impression that the latter, which may cause debilitating myelopathy, are far more likely than their wholly leptomeningeal counterparts to recur after resection but nonetheless pursue a protracted course. A recent report further describes late local recurrence and hepatic metastasis complicating the course of a foramen magnum region tumor exhibiting melanocytomatous histology.[1041] Given the morphologic attributes and relatively favorable clinical biology of most melanocytomas, it should come as no surprise that these have been likened to ocular melanomas of spindle A and B types, as well as to cellular blue nevi.

Malignant melanomas of the CNS may present as diffuse leptomeningeal growths ("**melanomatosis**") or discrete masses. Proliferations of the former sort are particularly characteristic of childhood examples occurring as part of the **neurocutaneous melanosis** complex[1035,1045] but may be encountered at any age and in the absence of unusual dermal nevi. Clinical manifestations of intracranial hypertension, cranial nerve deficits, a meningitic or subarachnoid hemorrhage-like picture and diffuse leptomeningeal enhancement on CT or MRI are typical of **primary leptomeningeal melanomatosis**, which can be diagnosed by demonstration in CSF samples of tumor cells that are melanin-laden or immunoreactive for S-100 protein and HMB-45.[1049] Death within months of diagnosis is the rule. Solitary variants of CNS melanoma (other than those complicating neurocutaneous melanosis) mainly afflict adults, and become symptomatic by virtue of their compression or invasion of neural structures. These generally share with melanocytomas an origin in the pia-arachnoid and a predilection for the posterior fossa and intraspinal compartment that stand in contrast to the intracerebral distribution characteristic of melanomas metastatic to the central neuraxis.[1036,1046] Still, meticulous search for a cutaneous, mucosal or ocular primary must prove unrevealing before a malignant melanoma can be accepted as indigenous to the CNS. Spindle cell, epithelioid and mixed cytologic features may be encountered, evidences of malignancy including nuclear and nucleolar enlargement, coarse hyperchromatism, readily apparent mitotic activity, necrosis, and neuroparenchymal invasion.

High rates of regional recurrence, a potential for subarachnoid dissemination and substantial mortality attach to localized CNS melanomas that cannot be surgically extirpated (unfortunately, a majority of cases). Some observers, however, have found a low incidence of CSF-borne metastasis as well as unexpectedly favorable outcomes following gross total resection in this setting, drawing parallels to the histology and behavior of spindle B, epithelioid and mixed ocular melanomas.[1036] Again, the literature on this subject is difficult to parse owing to the almost certain inclusion in reported series of cases better classified as melanocytomas.

We close this discussion with the admission that melanocytic tumors of the central neuraxis occasionally defy ready placement in either the melanocytoma or melanoma camp, maintaining relatively reassuring cytologic profiles while exhibiting modest mitotic activity and, in some cases, invasive growth. These "**atypical**," "**borderline**" or "**intermediate grade**" **melanocytic neoplasms** are capable of recurrence, but the magnitude of this risk is unclear.[1036] In addition, some examples contain both well-differentiated and clearly malignant components that raise the question of biologic progression within a progenitory neoplasm of melanocytomatous character.[1047] On record is an intracerebral **balloon cell melanoma** that may have arisen from a meningocortical melanocytic "nevus."[1033]

Paraganglioma

Primary **paragangliomas** of the craniospinal axis usually arise in the region of the cauda equina, presenting as delicately encapsulated intradural masses attached to the filum terminale or, less commonly, spinal roots.[1053,1058] Afflicted patients are typically in their fifth or sixth decades and commonly complain of chronic low back pain that may be accompanied by sciatica, sensorimotor deficits, and sphincter disturbances. Paragangliomas have also been reported to originate at cervicothoracic levels,[1053] in the pineal region,[1057] cerebellopontine angle,[1052] and sella turcica,[1055] an intrasellar presentation in the setting of von Hippel–Lindau disease being on record.[1056] While intraoperative, cardiovascular abnormalities presumed to reflect the release of biogenic amines upon tumor manipulation have been described,[1060] CNS paragangliomas are nearly always functionally silent. Simple resection usually suffices to cure these uncommon neoplasms, which are generally indolent and noninvasive, but exceptional instances of recurrence in the face of ostensibly complete removal, erosion into neighboring bone, CSF-borne spread, osseous metastasis and tumor-related death following inadequate excision are well documented.[1053,1054,1059]

Apart from a more frequently realized potential to differentiate along ganglion cell lines (a phenomenon of no clinical import but one recognized in the designation of some examples as "gangliocytic"), paragangliomas of the CNS are histologically, ultrastructurally and immunophenotypically comparable to their systemic counterparts.[1053,1058] Accordingly, we do not describe these neoplasms here other than to emphasize that some depart from the classic arrangement of epithelioid tumor cells in cohesive nests ("zellballen") and display, instead, spindled cytology and vaguely storiform growth or a vasocentric, pseudopapillary architecture superficially similar to that of the myxopapillary ependymoma but unaccompanied by mucoid change. Paragangliomas are readily distinguished from the latter (and from other tumors that may share a similar intraspinal topography, such as schwannomas and meningiomas) by virtue of their argyrophilia, content of dense-core granules on ultrastructural study, and immunolabeling for synaptophysin and chromogranin. A neoplasm of the cauda equina evidencing both ependymal and paraganglionic differentiation has been depicted,[1050] but is a curiosity. Paragangliomas have been reported to variably express neurofilament proteins, GFAP, keratins, serotonin, somatostatin, and other neuropeptides.[1053,1059] Melanotic and oncocytic examples are on record,[1053] one of the latter exhibiting locally aggressive growth.[1051]

Chordoma

Chordomas are familiar to all pathologists as destructive tumors of the clivus and sacrococcygeum generally thought to originate from remnants of the primitive notochord persisting at these sites. Attention is called to entirely extraosseous, intradural variants that typically lie ventral to the brainstem and that present in adulthood by reason of progressive hydrocephalus, bulbar dysfunction, or intratumoral hemorrhage.[1063,1064,1066] Chordomas have also been described as originating in the intraspinal compartment (including a remarkable example associated with the filum terminale[1061]), as occupying the anterior third ventricle,[1062] and as arising from the tentorium.[1065] The relationship of the intradural chordoma to the ecchordosis physaliphora,[27,36] a notochordal heterotopia of comparable morphology that also favors the prepontine regions, remains a subject of debate.[1066] Although some lesions designated as intradural chordomas are clearly neoplasms and are likely derived from displaced notochordal remnants, others may simply represent outsized, symptomatic ecchordoses. Ecchordoses have been described as failing to exhibit the contrast

enhancement typical of chordomas on neuroradiologic assessment,[36] but the number of studied examples has been quite limited. The differential diagnosis necessarily includes the rare intracranial myxoid chondrosarcoma. Intradural chordomas share with their osseous counterparts expression of cytokeratins and EMA, both alien to the chondrosarcoma, and so are readily distinguished by immunohistochemical study. The number of reported cases is small, but gross total excision of these circumscribed masses seems to hold the promise of cure.

Hemangioblastoma (von Hippel–Lindau disease)

Hemangioblastomas are familiar to most physicians as the hallmark of **von Hippel–Lindau (VHL) disease**, variants associated with this heritable condition constituting some 20–25% of examples encountered in clinical practice.[1068] An autosomal dominant disorder caused by germline mutations of a tumor suppressor gene localized to chromosome 3p25-26, the VHL complex classically includes, in addition to hemangioblastomas of the CNS and retina, visceral cysts (particularly of the kidney, liver and pancreas), renocortical carcinomas of conventional clear cell type, adrenal pheochromocytomas, and papillary cystadenomas of the epididymis. Affected individuals may also develop endolymphatic sac tumors of the inner ear; hepatocellular adenomas and carcinomas; paragangliomas; endocrine tumors of the pancreas, thyroid gland and gastrointestinal tract; central neuroepithelial neoplasms; visceral angiomas, and papillary cystadenomas of probable mesonephric origin involving the female genital adnexae. Even sporadic hemangioblastomas commonly harbor mutations of the VHL gene, which appears to be normally involved in aspects of angiogenesis and cell cycle regulation.[1068]

The large majority of hemangioblastomas arise within the cerebellum and produce the neurologic manifestations expected of an expanding posterior fossa mass, extracerebellar examples favoring the medulla and spinal cord (including its covering leptomeninges, nerve roots, and cauda equina).[1068] No division of the central neuraxis is entirely immune and these curious neoplasms have rarely been documented to originate in the optic nerve,[1085] cerebrum,[1083] ventricular system,[1077,1082] sella turcica,[1079] spinal extradural compartment or at considerably further remove from the CNS (e.g., in association with the radial[1070] or sciatic nerves,[1075] within the pancreas, kidney, bladder, or retroperitoneum[1073]). Underlying VHL disease carries a special risk of multifocal (including retinal) hemangioblastomas and an increased incidence of extracerebellar primaries. The mean age at diagnosis of VHL disease-associated hemangioblastomas is approximately 30 years, sporadic examples peaking in incidence about a decade later.

The hemangioblastoma often constitutes a sharply circumscribed mural nodule, at times diminutive, in what is otherwise a smooth-walled cyst or, at spinal levels, syrinx

(Fig. 28.111). A clear demarcation from adjacent native tissues is typical of the hemangioblastoma, its characteristic reddish-brown and yellow coloration reflecting, respectively, a rich vasculature and high lipid content. The former component, an anastomosing network of delicate, capillary-like channels supplied by feeding vessels of larger caliber, is responsible for the naming of this entity and its traditional classification as a primary vascular neoplasm. In fact, the sole neoplastic element of the hemangioblastoma—known as the "stromal cell"—inhabits the interstices between ramifying vascular arcades and is recognized by a pale cytoplasm often rich in neutral fats and, as a consequence, vacuolated or foamy in appearance (Fig. 28.112). Aggregation of stromal cells in cohesive nests and lobules lends to "cellular" hemangioblastomas an epithelioid histologic presentation that invites confusion with metastatic renocortical carcinoma of clear cell type (these tumors, parenthetically, may collide in the setting of VHL disease[1069]), whereas their paucity in "reticular" variants results in a picture that may be misconstrued as simply angiomatous. Potentially misleading as well is the tendency of stromal cell to exhibit conspicuous nuclear abnormalities, presumably degenerative, reminiscent of those encountered in neoplasms of neuroendocrine type. These changes, which may include alarming karyomegaly, pleomorphism and chromatin smudging, are typically unaccompanied by mitotic activity and are of no prognostic import. Regular features of additional note include infiltration by mast cells and, at the tumor–brain interface, a florid piloid astrogliosis replete with Rosenthal fibers but lacking the microcystic elements typical of the juvenile pilocytic astrocytoma. Foci of extramedullary normopoiesis may be found in hemangioblastomas, a

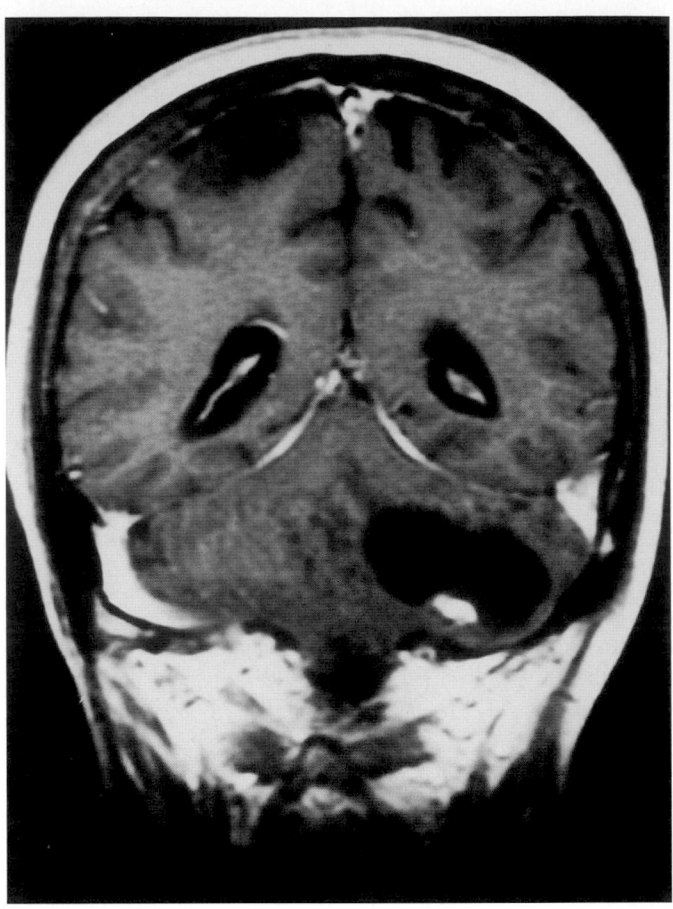

Fig. 28.111 Hemangioblastoma. Most hemangioblastomas arise in the cerebellar hemispheres, where, as emphasized in this postcontrast injection MRI, they present as diminutive, brightly enhancing, and sharply delimited mural nodules projecting into sizable cysts.

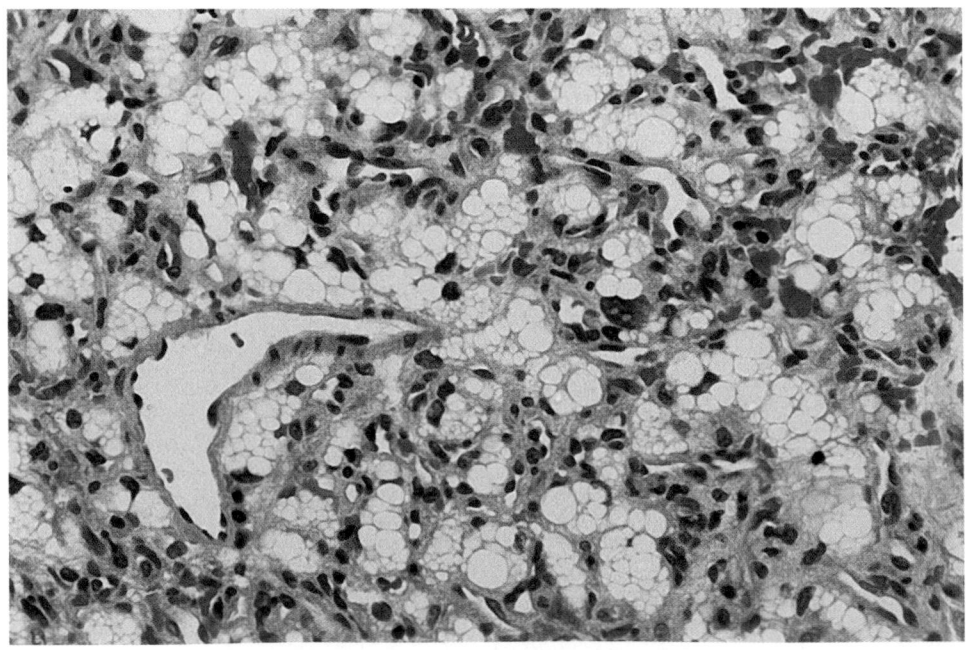

Fig. 28.112 Hemangioblastoma. The neoplasm's defining "stromal" cells are most readily visualized when lipid accumulation imparts a foamy or vacuolated quality to their pale cytoplasm.

minority of which present with erythrocytosis in consequence of erythropoietin production by stromal cells. Examples of hemangioblastoma arising in association with AVM have been reported[1081] and, as mentioned in our discussion of gliomesenchymal neoplasms, the designation "angioglioma" has been extended to rare tumors interpreted as containing a mixture of hemangioblastomatous and neoplastic glial tissues.

Repeated investigations into the ultrastructure and antigenic profile of the stromal cell have not settled the matter of its cytogenesis,[1067,1068,1074,1076] evidence to support a long-assumed derivation from angiogenic elements being fragmentary and controversial. Characteristic electron microscopic findings include intracytoplasmic lipid droplets, microfilaments, and profiles of smooth and rough endoplasmic reticulum.[1068,1078] Vasoformative features depicted in isolated studies[1080] have included electron-dense cytoplasmic structures resembling the Weibel–Palade bodies normally restricted to endothelial cells (some of these Factor VIII-labeling by the immunogold technique), intracytoplasmic caveolae suggesting abortive capillary-type lumen formation, and such pericytic/myoid specializations as subplasmalemmal densities, pinocytotic vesicles and cell processes partially invested by basement membrane material. Stromal cells, on the other hand, do not label for such endothelial "markers" as CD31 and CD34 and only exceptionally have been described as binding (and then in small numbers) antibodies to Factor VIII-related antigen or the lectins Ulex europaeus agglutinin-I or Ricinus communis agglutinin.[1068]

We emphasize certain aspects of hemangioblastoma immunophenotype that are of practical significance. GFAP reactivity is typically restricted to entrapped astrocytes or to stromal cells preferentially distributed along the tumor–neuroparenchymal border, a phenomenon reasonably interpreted as reflecting nonspecific adsorption of antigen produced in adjoining gliotic tissues. The occurrence of hemangioblastomas outside the CNS (all GFAP-negative) further militates against a glial histogenesis or differentiating capacity. That stromal cells often label for S-100 protein and neuron-specific enolase facilitates the distinction of hemangioblastomas from hemangiopericytomas and angiomas.[1067] The latter phenomena, along with reported immunoreactivity for a variety of neuropeptides[1067] and sightings of dense core intracytoplasmic granules on ultrastructural study,[1078] suggest that stromal cells may differentiate along neuroendocrine lines. Particularly important is the observation that stromal cells can exhibit cytokeratin immunoreactivity but typically fail to express epithelial membrane antigen, the latter distinguishing the hemangioblastoma from metastatic renocortical carcinoma and lipidized, angiomatous meningiomas.[1076] A recent study found cytoplasmic labeling for inhibin alpha to further distinguish the hemangioblastoma from clear cell carcinoma of renal origin.[1075a] We refer the reader elsewhere for further discussion of stromal cell biology, which includes upregulated production of vascular endothelial growth factor and other promoters of angiogenesis.[1068]

Hemangioblastomas are benign neoplasms that usually lend themselves to curative resection. Excised examples may exceptionally recur, however, and patients afflicted with von Hippel–Lindau disease are prone to develop additional primaries.[1068,1071,1072] One study found a solid gross configuration and paucity of stromal cells to be correlated with symptomatic tumor regrowth,[1071] but this has not been confirmed. CSF dissemination by histologically conventional hemangioblastomas has only rarely been recorded, this potentially occurring years after ostensibly successful resection of cerebellar examples.[1086] An example of "multifocal" hepatic and pulmonary hemangioblastomatosis complicating VHL disease after several craniotomies for cerebellar hemangioblastoma is also on record.[1084] This could be interpreted, though, as an instance of "benign hematogenesis metastasis" facilitated by surgery.

Other primary tumors

The list of neoplastic oddities that have been encountered along the central neuraxis includes a spinal nerve root "**oncocytoma**" of indeterminate lineage,[1088] an intraspinal mass interpreted as a misplaced **adrenocortical adenoma**,[1087] a lesion of the sellar region described as a **heterotopic follicular carcinoma of thyroid gland type**,[1091] and a number of **ectopic, suprasellar pituitary adenomas** situated in the third ventricle/hypothalamic region.[1089,1090] A survey of intracranial sarcomas previously cited in the discussion of nonmeningothelial, mesenchymal neoplasms includes an example of cerebral **ectomesenchymoma**—a tumor composed of ganglion cell and rhabdomyosarcomatous elements.[830]

Secondary tumors

Secondary involvement of the CNS by direct extension or hematogenous metastasis is a common complication of systemic cancer and a phenomenon that frequently prompts diagnostic, as well as palliative, neurosurgical intervention. Because we have already touched on this subject in reference to lymphoproliferative and myeloproliferative disorders, this discussion is concerned only with invasion of the central neuraxis by solid tumors.

That neoplasms arising in and around the skeletal confines of the brain and spinal cord often come to impinge on these structures should come as no surprise. Examples include the pituitary adenoma with suprasellar or retrosellar expansion, the glomus jugulare tumor (paraganglioma) that exploits neighboring foramina of the calvarial floor to present as a mass in the pontocerebellar angle, and sacrococcygeal chordomas that engulf the roots of the cauda equina. Ceruminous gland carcinomas and other neoplasms arising in the ear may occasionally billow into the middle cranial fossa to present as intracranial masses.[1096,1110] A substantial risk of local skull base destruction and invasion of contiguous meninges, potentially complicated by dissemination in the subarachnoid space, is seen in embryonal rhabdomyosarcomas originating in head and neck sites, particularly the nasopharynx, paranasal sinuses, and middle ear.[1093] Similarly situated carcinomas of mucosal or minor salivary gland derivation may behave in like fashion, but some of the latter instead track insidiously along regional nerve fiber bundles to achieve radiologically detectable proportions only within the cranial compartment.[1099,1113] Neglected, basal cell or squamous carcinomas of the face and scalp may also reach the CNS by permeating the calvarium or by propagation within perineural spaces.[1115] The neurotropic spread of a malignant mesothelioma to the spinal cord via the brachial plexus is also on record.[1119] Cancers arising in more distant sites may secondarily infiltrate the nervous system after first metastasizing to juxtaneural structures, the vertebral column apparently serving as an especially important way station in this regard. Epidural spinal cord compression by malignant tumors, for example, is most frequently caused by carcinomas of pulmonary, prostatic, or mammary origin that have spread to the vertebrae, neoplastic cells commonly entering the spinal canal via the bony foramina traversed by vertebral veins.[1094] A similar sequence of events is postulated to account for the high incidence of vertebral and paravertebral metastases in cancer patients developing diffuse leptomeningeal carcinomatosis, principally a complication of adenocarcinomas derived from the lung and breast.[1103] This diagnosis is usually established by the demonstration of malignant cells on cytologic inspection of the CSF.

More common than instances of secondary CNS infiltration by contiguous malignant tumors are blood-borne neuraxial metastases. The principal offenders in this regard are carcinomas of the lung and breast, followed by malignant melanomas, renocortical carcinomas, and adenocarcinomas of colorectal origin.[1114] Carcinomas of the lung are the systemic cancers most likely to present initially as intracerebral tumors, accounting for roughly half of all such cases[1104] and up to 85% of lesions exhibiting adenocarcinomatous histology.[1107] Increasingly effective management of systemic disease may account for perceived rises in the incidence of intracranial deposits from ovarian carcinomas[1105] and osseous or soft tissue sarcomas,[1100,1106] but the latter remain rare as neurosurgical specimens. Sarcomas typically spread to the lungs en route to the brain but may give rise to isolated cerebral or dura-based metastases that, in exceptional instances, herald discovery of the primary tumor.[1112] Noteworthy is the prominence in some series of alveolar

soft part sarcoma, one of the rarest tumor types, among mesenchymal neoplasms giving rise to intracranial metastases.[1106,1112] Mention should also be made of HIV-1-associated Kaposi's sarcoma traveling to the cranial compartment,[1092] but this remains a curiosity even in the presence of widespread cutaneous and visceral involvement.

Although blood-borne tumor emboli may lodge at any level of the central neuraxis, a few useful generalizations can be made regarding the topography of metastatic lesions. Intramedullary metastases (i.e., those involving the spinal cord parenchyma) are rare,[1097,1114] the great majority of metastatic deposits coming to lie in the supratentorial or infratentorial compartments. In general, the distribution of metastases within the latter conforms to their relative volumes and blood supply.[1098,1114] Thus, most lesions settle within frontoparietal cerebral tissues subtended by the middle cerebral artery (the dominant tributary of the circle of Willis); tumor emboli often lodge within the "watershed" zone representing the terminus of this vascular territory. For reasons that are not clear, colorectal, uterine, and renocortical carcinomas are overrepresented among cancers seeding the cerebellum.[1098] Prostatic adenocarcinomas also exhibit a curious predilection for this structure when they metastasize to the brain, but their deposits are more typically dura-based and only exceptionally involve the neural parenchyma proper.[1095,1102] Dural metastases in women most often derive from mammary carcinomas.[1102,1114,1120] As a rule, those tumors that frequently travel to the CNS (e.g., malignant melanoma and carcinomas of the lung) tend to produce multiple metastases, whereas cancers that only occasionally involve the brain (e.g., gastrointestinal adenocarcinomas) are often represented by solitary deposits. Noteworthy is a clinical study in which nearly one half of cancer patients with brain metastases were found to have unifocal lesions on neuroradiologic assessment.[1098] A particularly compelling case for neurosurgical intervention can be made in this setting because metastatic lesions are usually compact in their growth patterns and thus lend themselves to excision. Patients who undergo surgical extirpation of single metastases (usually followed by radiotherapy) may be restored to many months (or even years) of useful function, live longer, and enjoy a better quality of life than those whose tumors are simply irradiated.[1109,1114] Refined stereotactic and radiosurgical techniques may improve the outlook for patients with deep-seated or multifocal lesions.

In contrast to the common glial neoplasms of adulthood, metastatic nodules tend to be sharply circumscribed and possessed of "pushing" margins (Fig. 28.113). Much of their mass effect may be derived from edematous expansion of neighboring white matter, often disproportionate to the small size of the offending deposits and usually more pronounced than the edema

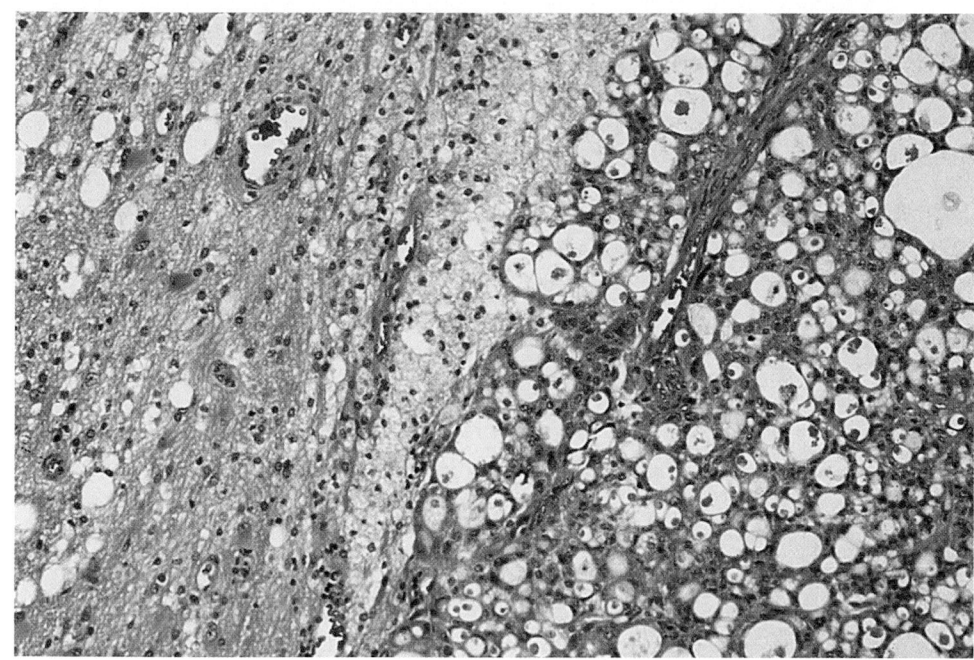

Fig. 28.113 Metastatic carcinoma. A cohesive growth pattern and clearly delimited tumor–CNS interface are hallmarks of neoplasms metastatic to the brain. The adenocarcinoma (right), derived from a primary in the left lung, "pushes" against adjacent cerebral white matter.

accompanying primary brain tumors. Most metastases are relatively superficial in location, straddling the gray–white junction to involve both cerebral cortex (thus the high incidence of associated seizures) and digitate white matter. Intralesional hemorrhage occasionally brings brain metastases to light, an especially common phenomenon in the settings of germ cell neoplasia and melanoma.[1116]

On histologic examination, most secondary cancers conform to the histology of their donor tumors and are readily distinguished from primary neoplasms of the brain or meninges on casual inspection. Features that aid in the segregation of poorly differentiated carcinomas from anaplastic gliomas include a cohesive architecture, abrupt interface with adjacent neural tissue, "peritheliomatous" pattern of tumor cell preservation about stromal blood vessels in cases evidencing coagulative necrosis, and absence of complex microvascular hyperplasia. The last, however, is an arresting feature of some metastatic small cell carcinomas derived from the lung. A confident diagnosis of metastatic carcinoma can often be made at the time of surgery by examination of smear or crush preparations in which the cellular cohesion of most epithelial neoplasms is preserved (Fig. 28.114). The

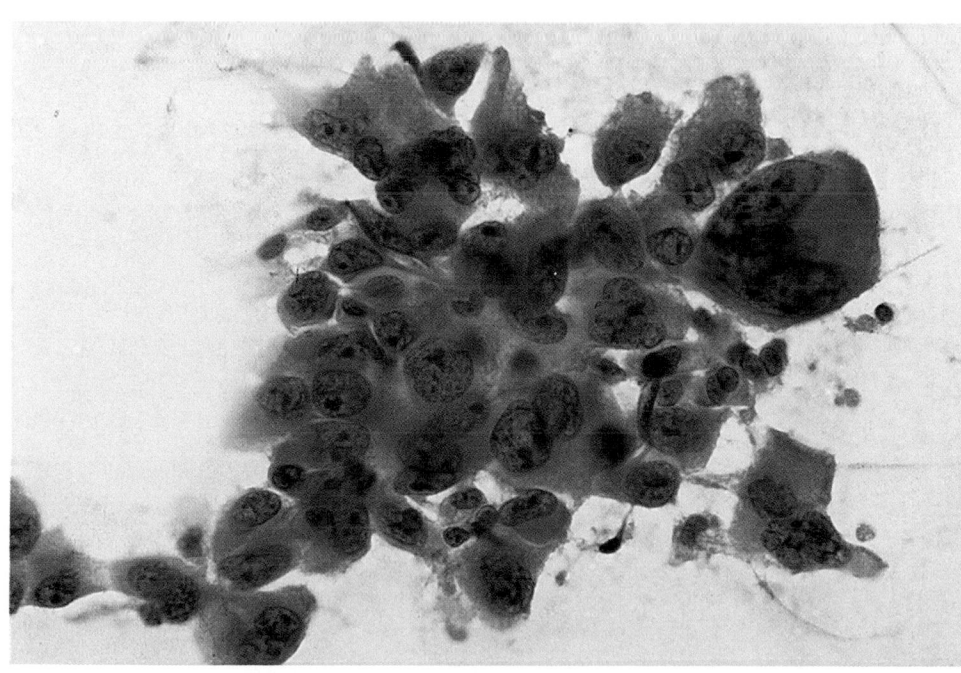

Fig. 28.114 Metastatic carcinoma. The cellular cohesion characteristic of most epithelial neoplasms and foreign to gliomas and lymphomas is generally maintained in cytology preparations, facilitating rapid intraoperative diagnosis. Note also the absence of cytoplasmic processes and presence of conspicuous nucleoli, the latter also alien to most neuroepithelial tumors, in this smear preparation of a poorly differentiated pulmonary adenocarcinoma that presented as a solitary, right frontal lobe brain mass.

reader is reminded that glial neoplasms of varied type, including fibrillary astrocytomas, may be labeled by antibodies to cytokeratins (particularly the AE1/3 "cocktail")[315,316,341] and, on occasion, EMA.[325] It would appear that CAM 5.2, CK7, CK20, and Ber EP4 perform in more discriminating fashion as epithelial markers in this regard.[341,1111] GFAP labeling of metastatic carcinomas, while documented, is a most exceptional event.[341,774,1111] As metastases usually remain faithful to the donor immunophenotype, immunohistochemical assessment may focus the search for a systemic primary in the patient who does not have a history of cancer. Nuclear labeling for thyroid transcription factor-1, for example, seems nearly restricted to metastatic deposits derived from differentiated carcinomas of the thyroid gland and nonsquamous carcinomas of the lung.[1118] Depending on the histologic findings in a given case, the differential diagnosis of a suspected metastasis may include, in addition to an epithelioid or sarcomatoid glioblastoma, the capillary hemangioblastoma, papillary ependymoma, choroid plexus tumor, and meningioma. Each of these is considered separately elsewhere in this chapter. We refer the reader to the foregoing discussion of fibrillary astrocytic neoplasms for a brief account of lipid-rich, adenoid or partially squamous glioblastomas and gliosarcomas that may masquerade as cerebral metastases.

In closing, mention is made of certain unusual forms or presentations of secondary CNS involvement by malignant neoplasms. These include diffuse seeding of the periventricular tissues by metastatic small cell carcinomas of the lung[1121] (a pattern of spread mimicking the topography of some primary CNS lymphomas), miliary or "encephalitic" cerebral carcinomatosis or melanomatosis with widespread vascular cuffing by tumor cells on microscopic study but no conspicuous mass lesions,[1101,1117] and occlusion of major cerebral vessels by neoplastic emboli resulting in ischemic stroke.[1108] Intracardiac tumors such as myxomas are the lesions most often implicated in cerebral infarction secondary to neoplastic embolization, but this phenomenon has also been recorded in association with carcinomas arising in the head and neck, lungs, colon, and other visceral sites. As mentioned in the discussion of primary mesenchymal tumors of the CNS, deposits derived from occult atrial myxomas may be misconstrued as cerebral epithelioid hemangioendotheliomas.[894] Atrial myxomas are also responsible for most neoplastic cerebrovascular aneurysms,[101,102] a metastatic complication of cancer noted in our prior treatment of vascular disorders. Yet another vascular complication of intracranial metastasis is subdural hemorrhage secondary to dura-based lesions.[1102]

Acknowledgments

Donna Bauer prepared the manuscript, hunted down references, and propped me up throughout. Kin Kong's expertise as a medical photographer should be plain. Dr Rosemary Purrazzella, my wife, was patience itself and will hopefully find this useful in her own practice of surgical pathology (small reward).

REFERENCES

Normal anatomy

1 Fuller GN, Burger PC. Central Nervous System. Histology for Pathologists 1997, 2: 243–284.

Congenital abnormalities
Craniospinal dysraphism

1a Bale PM. Sacrococcygeal developmental abnormalities and tumors in children. Perspect Pediatr Pathol 1984, 8: 9–56.
2 Chadduck WM, Uthman EO. Squamous cell carcinoma and meningomyelocele. Neurosurgery 1984, 14: 601–603.
3 Chakrabortty S, Oi S, Yoshida Y, Yamada H, Yamaguchi M, Tamaki N, Matsumoto S. Myelomeningocele and thick filum terminale with tethered cord appearing as a human tail. Case report. J Neurosurg 1993, 78: 966–969.
4 Ebisu T, Odake G, Fujimoto M, Ueda S, Tsujii H, Morimoto M, Sawada T. Neurenteric cysts with meningomyelocele or meningocele. Split notochord syndrome. Childs Nerv Syst 1990, 6: 465–467.
5 Erkulvrawatr S, El Gammal T, Hawkins J, Green JB, Srinivasan G. Intrathoracic meningoceles and neurofibromatosis. Arch Neurol 1979, 36: 557–559.
6 Harding B, Copp AJ. Malformations. In Graham DI, Lantos PL (eds): Greenfield's Neuropathology, vol. 1, ed 7. London, 2002, Arnold, pp. 357–483.
7 Lalwani AK, Jackler RK, Harsh GR 4th, Butt FY. Bilateral temporal bone encephaloceles after cranial irradiation. Case report. J Neurosurg 1993, 79: 596–599.
8 Mitgang RN. Teratoma occurring within a myelomeningocele. Case report. J Neurosurg 1972, 37: 448–451.
9 Morris GF, Murphy K, Rorke LB, James HE. Spinal hamartomas. A distinct clinical entity. J Neurosurg 1998, 88: 954–961.
10 Yamada S, Mandybur GT, Thompson JR. Dorsal midline proboscis associated with diastematomyelia and tethered cord syndrome. Case report. J Neurosurg 1996, 85: 709–712.

Neuroglial and meningeal heterotopias

11 Bale PM, Hughes L, de Silva M. Sequestrated meningoceles of scalp. Extracranial meningeal heterotopia. Hum Pathol 1990, 21: 1156–1163.
12 Bossen EH, Hudson WR. Oligodendroglioma arising in heterotopic brain tissue of the soft palate and nasopharynx. Am J Surg Pathol 1987, 11: 571–574.
13 Call NB, Baylis HI. Cerebellar heterotopia in the orbit. Arch Ophthalmol 1980, 98: 717–719.
14 Chan JK, Lau WH. Nasal astrocytoma or nasal glial heterotopia? Arch Pathol Lab Med 1989, 113: 943–945.
15 Gold AH, Sharer LR, Walden RH. Central nervous system heterotopia in association with cleft palate. Plast Reconstr Surg 1980, 66: 434–441.
16 Hirano S, Houdou S, Hasegawa M, Kamei A, Takashima S. Clinicopathologic studies on leptomeningeal glioneuronal heterotopia in congenital anomalies. Pediatr Neurol 1992, 8: 441–444.
17 Kershisnik MM, Kaplan C, Craven CM, Carey JC, Townsend JJ, Knisely AS. Intrapulmonary neuroglial heterotopia. Arch Pathol Lab Med 1992, 116: 1043–1046.
18 Lee SC, Henry MM, Gonzalez-Crussi F. Simultaneous

occurrence of melanotic neuroectodermal tumor and brain heterotopia in the oropharynx. Cancer 1976, **38**: 249–253.

19 Patterson K, Kapur S, Chandra RS. "Nasal gliomas" and related brain heterotopias. A pathologist's perspective. Pediatr Pathol 1986, **5**: 353–362.

20 Suster S, Rosai J. Hamartoma of the scalp with ectopic meningothelial elements. A distinctive benign soft tissue lesion that may simulate angiosarcoma. Am J Surg Pathol 1990, **14**: 1–11.

Choristomas and non-neuroepithelial hamartomas

21 Apostolides PJ, Spetzler RF, Johnson PC. Ectomesenchymal hamartoma (benign "ectomesenchymoma") of the VIIIth nerve: case report. Neurosurgery 1995, **37**: 1204–1207.

22 Curry B, Taylor CW, Fisher AW. Salivary gland heterotopia. A unique cerebellopontine angle tumor. Arch Pathol Lab Med 1982, **106**: 35–38.

23 Fix SE, Nelson J, Schochet SS, Jr: Focal leptomeningeal rhabdomyomatosis of the posterior fossa. Arch Pathol Lab Med 1989, **113**: 872–873.

24 Giangaspero F, Guiducci A, Lenz FA, Mastronardi L, Burger PC. Meningioma with meningioangiomatosis. A condition mimicking invasive meningiomas in children and young adults. Report of two cases and review of the literature. Am J Surg Pathol 1999, **23**: 872–875.

25 Goates JJ, Dickson DW, Horoupian DS. Meningioangiomatosis. An immunocytochemical study. Acta Neuropathol (Berl) 1991, **82**: 527–532.

26 Halper J, Scheithauer BW, Okazaki H, Laws ER, Jr: Meningioangiomatosis. A report of six cases with special reference to the occurrence of neurofibrillary tangles. J Neuropathol Exp Neurol 1986, **45**: 426–446.

27 Ho KL. Ecchordosis physaliphora and chordoma. A comparative ultrastructural study. Clin Neuropathol 1985, **4**: 77–86.

28 Kollias SS, Crone KR, Ball WS, Jr., Prenger EC, Ballard ET. Meningioangiomatosis of the brain stem. Case report. J Neurosurg 1994, **80**: 732–735.

29 Lena G, Dufour T, Gambarelli D, Chabrol B, Mancini J. Choristoma of the intracranial maxillary nerve in a child. Case report. J Neurosurg 1994, **81**: 788–791.

30 Lombardo L, Mateos JH, Barroeta FF. Subarachnoid hemorrhage due to endometriosis of the spinal canal. Neurology 1968, **18**: 423–426.

31 Lopez JI, Ereno C, Oleaga L, Areitio E. Meningioangiomatosis and oligodendroglioma in a 15-year-old boy. Arch Pathol Lab Med 1996, **120**: 587–590.

32 Molleston MC, Roth KA, Wippold FJ, 2nd, Grubb RL, Jr: Tethered cord syndrome from a choristoma of mullerian origin. Case report. J Neurosurg 1991, **74**: 497–500.

33 Sinkre P, Perry A, Cai D, Raghavan R, Watson M, Wilson K, Barton Rogers B. Deletion of the NF2 region in both meningioma and juxtaposed meningioangiomatosis. Case report supporting a neoplastic relationship. Pediatr Dev Pathol 2001, **4**: 568–572.

34 Takeshima Y, Amatya VJ, Nakayori F, Nakano T, Sugiyama K, Inai K. Meningioangiomatosis occurring in a young male without neurofibromatosis. With special reference to its histogenesis and loss of heterozygosity in the NF2 gene region. Am J Surg Pathol 2002, **26**: 125–129.

35 Thibodeau LL, Prioleau GR, Manuelidis EE, Merino MJ, Heafner MD. Cerebral endometriosis. Case report. J Neurosurg 1987, **66**: 609–610.

36 Toda H, Kondo A, Iwasaki K. Neuroradiological characteristics of ecchordosis physaliphora. Case report and review of the literature. J Neurosurg 1998, **89**: 830–834.

37 Vajramani G, Devi I, Santosh V, Hegde T, Das BS, Das S, Shankar SK. Benign triton tumor of the trigeminal nerve. Childs Nerv Syst 1999, **15**: 140–144.

38 Vandewalle G, Brucher JM, Michotte A. Intracranial facial nerve rhabdomyoma. Case report. J Neurosurg 1995, **83**: 919–922.

39 Wiebe S, Munoz DG, Smith S, Lee DH. Meningioangiomatosis. A comprehensive analysis of clinical and laboratory features. Brain 1999, **122 (Pt 4)**: 709–726.

Cysts of the central neuraxis

40 Bavetta S, El-Shunnar K, Hamlyn PJ. Neurenteric cyst of the anterior cranial fossa. Br J Neurosurg 1996, **10**: 225–227.

41 Beatty RM, Hornig GW, Hanson EJ, Jr.: Protruding arachnoid granulations mimicking dermoid cysts. J Pediatr Surg 1989, **24**: 411–413.

42 Bejjani GK, Wright DC, Schessel D, Sekhar LN. Endodermal cysts of the posterior fossa. Report of three cases and review of the literature. J Neurosurg 1998, **89**: 326–335.

43 Cannon TC, Bane BL, Kistler D, Schoenhals GW, Hahn M, Leech RW, Brumback RA. Primary intracerebellar osteosarcoma arising within an epidermoid cyst. Arch Pathol Lab Med 1998, **122**: 737–739.

44 Chitkara U, Cogswell C, Norton K, Wilkins IA, Mehalek K, Berkowitz RL. Choroid plexus cysts in the fetus. A benign anatomic variant or pathologic entity? Report of 41 cases and review of the literature. Obstet Gynecol 1988, **72**: 185–189.

45 Ciricillo SF, Davis RL, Wilson CB. Neuroepithelial cysts of the posterior fossa. Case report. J Neurosurg 1990, **72**: 302–305.

46 Del Bigio MR, Jay V, Drake JM. Prepontine cyst lined by respiratory epithelium with squamous metaplasia. Immunohistochemical and ultrastructural study. Acta Neuropathol (Berl) 1992, **83**: 564–568.

47 Fain JS, Tomlinson FH, Scheithauer BW, Parisi JE, Fletcher GP, Kelly PJ, Miller GM. Symptomatic glial cysts of the pineal gland. J Neurosurg 1994, **80**: 454–460.

48 Friede RL, Yasargil MG. Supratentorial intracerebral epithelial (ependymal) cysts: review, case reports, and fine structure. J Neurol Neurosurg Psychiatry 1977, **40**: 127–137.

49 Gherardi R, Lacombe MJ, Poirier J, Roucayrol AM, Wechsler J. Asymptomatic encephalic intraparenchymatous neuroepithelial cysts. Acta Neuropathol (Berl) 1984, **63**: 264–268.

50 Gluszcz A. A cancer arising in a dermoid of the brain. A case report. J Neuropathol Exp Neurol 1962, **21**: 383–387.

51 Goldman SA, Gandy SE. Squamous cell carcinoma as a late complication of intracerebroventricular epidermoid cyst. Case report. J Neurosurg 1987, **66**: 618–620.

52 Goyal A, Singh AK, Singh D, Gupta V, Tatke M, Sinha S, Kumar S. Intramedullary arachnoid cyst. Case report. J Neurosurg (Spine 1) 2002, **96**: 104–106.

53 Halcrow SJ, Crawford PJ, Craft AW. Epidermoid spinal cord tumour after lumbar puncture. Arch Dis Child 1985, **60**: 978–979.

54 Hamburger CH, Buttner A, Weis S. Dural cysts in the cervical region. Report of three cases and review of the literature. J Neurosurg 1998, **89**: 310–313.

55 Hatem O, Bedou G, Negre C, Bertrand JL, Camo J. Intraspinal cervical degenerative cyst. Report of three cases. J Neurosurg 2001, **95**: 139–142.

56 Hitchcock MG, Ellington KS, Friedman AH, Provenzaie JM, McLendon RE. Shadow cells in an intracranial dermoid cyst. Arch Pathol Lab Med 1995, **119**: 371–373.

57 Ho KL, Chason JL. A glioependymal cyst of the cerebellopontine angle. Immunohistochemical and ultrastructural studies. Acta Neuropathol (Berl) 1987, **74**: 382–388.

58 Ho KL, Garcia JH. Colloid cysts of the third ventricle. Ultrastructural features are compatible with endodermal derivation. Acta Neuropathol (Berl) 1992, **83**: 605–612.

59 Ho KL, Tiel R. Intraspinal bronchogenic cyst: ultrastructural study of the lining epithelium. Acta Neuropathol (Berl) 1989, **78**: 513–520.

60 Inoue T, Matsushima T, Fukui M, Matsubara T, Kitamoto T. Choroidal epithelial cyst of the cerebral hemisphere. An immunohistochemical study. Surg Neurol 1987, **28**: 119–122.

61 Isla A, Palacios J, Roda JM, Gutierrez M, Gonzalez C, Blazquez MG. Neuroepithelial cyst in the optic nerve. Case report. J Neurosurg 1987, **67**: 137–139.

62 Keogh AJ, Timperley WR. Atypical hidradenoma arising in a dermoid cyst of the spinal canal. J Pathol 1975, **117**: 207–209.

63 Khan RB, Giri DD, Rosenblum MK, Petito FA, DeAngelis LM. Leptomeningeal metastasis from an intracranial epidermoid cyst. Neurology 2001, **56**: 1419–1420.

64 Kim KM, Kang SJ, Kim DS, Chi JG, Kim SM. Congenital intraorbital optic nerve cyst. Case report. J Neurosurg 1999, **91**: 325–327.

65 Lach B, Scheithauer BW, Gregor A, Wick MR. Colloid cyst of the third ventricle. A comparative immunohistochemical study of neuraxis cysts and choroid plexus epithelium. J Neurosurg 1993, **78**: 101–111.

66 Lippman CR, Arginteanu M, Purohit D, Naidich TP, Camins MB. Intramedullary neurenteric cysts of the spine. Case report and review of the literature. J Neurosurg 2001, **94**: 305–309.

67 Lunardi P, Missori P, Rizzo A, Gagliardi FM. Chemical meningitis in ruptured intracranial dermoid. Case report and review of the literature. Surg Neurol 1989, **32**: 449–452.

68 Mathiesen T, Grane P, Lindgren L, Lindquist C. Third ventricle colloid cysts: a consecutive 12-year series. J Neurosurg 1997, **86**: 5–12.

69 McLendon RE, Tien RD. Tumors and tumor-like lesions of maldevelopmental origin. In Bigner DD, McLendon RE, Bruner JM (eds): Russell and Rubinstein's pathology of tumors of the nervous system, vol. 2. London, 1998, Arnold, pp. 327–370.

70 Miyagi Y, Suzuki SO, Iwaki T, Ishido K, Araki T, Kamikaseda K. Magnetic resonance appearance of multiple intracranial epidermoid cysts. Intrathecal seeding of the cysts? Case report. J Neurosurg 2000, **92**: 711–714.

71 Montaldi S, Deruaz JP, Cai ZT, de Tribolet N. Symptomatic xanthogranuloma of the third ventricle. Report of two cases and review of the literature. Surg Neurol 1989, **32**: 200–205.

72 Nabors MW, Pait TG, Byrd EB, Karim NO, Davis DO, Kobrine AI, Rizzoli HV. Updated assessment and current classification of spinal meningeal cysts. J Neurosurg 1988, **68**: 366–377.

73 Nakajima Y, Yoshimine T, Ogawa M, Takanashi M, Nakamuta K, Maruno M, Hasegawa H, Yokota J. A giant intracranial mucocele associated with an orbitoethmoidal osteoma. Case report. J Neurosurg 2000, **92**: 697–701.

74 Nakasu Y, Handa J, Watanabe K. Progressive neurological deficits with benign intracerebral cysts. Report of two cases. J Neurosurg 1986, **65**: 706–709.

75 Odake G, Tenjin H, Murakami N. Cyst of the choroid plexus in the lateral ventricle. Case report and review of the literature. Neurosurgery 1990, **27**: 470–476.

76 Ojemann JG, Moran CJ, Gokden M, Dacey RG, Jr: Sagittal sinus occlusion by intraluminal dural cysts. Report of two cases. J Neurosurg 1999, **91**: 867–870.

77 Perry A, Scheithauer BW, Zaias BW, Minassian HV. Aggressive enterogenous cyst with extensive craniospinal spread: case report. Neurosurgery 1999, **44**: 401–404; discussion 404–405.

78 Powers JM, Dodds HM. Primary actinomycoma of the third ventricle—the colloid cyst. A histochemical and ultrastructural study. Acta Neuropathol (Berl) 1977, **37**: 21–26.

79 Reddy PK, Rao GP, Prakasham A, Purnanand A, Sulochana C, Kumar RS, Reddy YR, Chandramala, Indumathi D. Intracerebral polyposis. Case report. J Neurosurg 1993, **78**: 294–296.

80 Rengachary SS, Watanabe I. Ultrastructure and pathogenesis of intracranial arachnoid cysts. J Neuropathol Exp Neurol 1981, **40**: 61–83.

81 Robertson DP, Kirkpatrick JB, Harper RL, Mawad ME. Spinal intramedullary ependymal cyst. Report of three cases. J Neurosurg 1991, **75**: 312–316.

82 Rosenberg AE, O'Connell JX, Ojemann RG, Plata MJ, Palmer WE. Giant cystic arachnoid granulations. A rare cause of lytic skull lesions. Hum Pathol 1993, **24**: 438–441.

83 Sabo RA, Tracy PT, Weinger JM. A series of 60 juxtafacet cysts: clinical presentation, the role of spinal instability, and treatment. J Neurosurg 1996, **85**: 560–565.

84 Sahara Y, Nagasaka T, Takayasu M, Takagi T, Hata N, Yoshida J. Recurrence of a neurenteric cyst with malignant transformation in the foramen magnum after total resection. Case report. J Neurosurg 2001, **95**: 341–345.

85 Silverberg GD. Simple cysts of the cerebellum. J Neurosurg 1971, **35**: 320–327.

86 Smith CM, Timperley WR. Multiple intraspinal and intracranial epidermoids and lipomata following gunshot injury. Neuropathol Appl Neurobiol 1984, **10**: 235–239.

87 Tsuchida T, Hruban RH, Carson BS, Phillips PC. Colloid cysts of the third ventricle. Immunohistochemical evidence for nonneuroepithelial differentiation. Hum Pathol 1992, **23**: 811–816.

88 Voelker JL, Campbell RL, Muller J. Clinical, radiographic, and pathological features of symptomatic Rathke's cleft cysts. J Neurosurg 1991, **74**: 535–544.

89 Voyadzis JM, Bhargava P, Henderson FC. Tarlov cysts. A study of 10 cases with review of the literature. J Neurosurg (Spine 1) 2001, **95**: 25–32.

90 Weinand ME, Rengachary SS, McGregor DH, Watanabe I. Intradiploic arachnoid cysts. Report of two cases. J Neurosurg 1989, **70**: 954–958.

91 Weisberg LA. Non-neoplastic gliotic cerebellar cysts: clinical and computed tomographic correlations. Neuroradiology 1982, **24**: 53–57.

92 Wilkins RH, Burger PC. Benign intraparenchymal brain cysts without an epithelial lining. J Neurosurg 1988, **68**: 378–382.

93 Xin W, Rubin MA, McKeever PE. Differential expression of cytokeratins 8 and 20 distinguishes craniopharyngioma from Rathke cleft cyst. Arch Pathol Lab Med 2002, **126**: 1174–1178.

Cerebrovascular disorders

Cerebral infarction

94 Kalimo H, Kaste M, Haltia M. Vascular diseases. In Graham DI, Lantos PL (eds): Greenfield's Neuropathology, vol. 1, ed 7. London, 2002, Arnold, pp. 281–355.

95 Chuaqui R, Tapia J. Histologic assessment of the age of recent brain infarcts in man. J Neuropathol Exp Neurol 1993, **52**: 481–489.

Intracranial aneurysms

96 Bohmfalk GL, Story JL, Wissinger JP, Brown WE, Jr: Bacterial intracranial aneurysm. J Neurosurg 1978, **48**: 369–382.

97 Challa VR, Moody DM, Bell MA. The Charcot-Bouchard aneurysm controversy: impact of a new histologic technique. J Neuropathol Exp Neurol 1992, **51**: 264–271.

98 Chambi I, Tasker RR, Gentili F, Lougheed WM, Smyth HS, Marshall J, Young I, Deck J, Shrubb J. Gauze-induced granuloma ("gauzoma"). An uncommon complication of gauze reinforcement of berry aneurysms. J Neurosurg 1990, **72**: 163–170.

99 Drake CG, Peerless SJ. Giant fusiform intracranial aneurysms. Review of 120 patients treated surgically from 1965 to 1992. J Neurosurg 1997, **87**: 141–162.

100 Erbengi A, Inci S. Pheochromocytoma and multiple intracranial aneurysms. Is it a coincidence? Case report. J Neurosurg 1997, **87**: 764–767.

101 Furuya K, Sasaki T, Yoshimoto Y, Okada Y, Fujimaki T, Kirino T. Histologically verified cerebral aneurysm formation

secondary to embolism from cardiac myxoma. Case report. J Neurosurg 1995, **83**: 170–173.

102 Ho KL. Neoplastic aneurysm and intracranial hemorrhage. Cancer 1982, **50**: 2935–2940.

103 Inagawa T, Hirano A. Ruptured intracranial aneurysms. An autopsy study of 133 patients. Surg Neurol 1990, **33**: 117–123.

104 Juvela S, Porras M, Poussa K. Natural history of unruptured intracranial aneurysms. Probability of and risk factors for aneurysm rupture. J Neurosurg 2000, **93**: 379–387.

105 Lammie GA. Hypertensive cerebral small vessel disease and stroke. Brain Pathol 2002, **12**: 358–370.

106 McCormick WF, Nofzinger JD. Saccular intracranial aneurysms. An autopsy study. J Neurosurg 1965, **22**: 155–159.

107 Ronkainen A, Hernesniemi J, Tromp G. Special features of familial intracranial aneurysms. Report of 215 familial aneurysms. Neurosurgery 1995, **37**: 43–46; discussion 46–47.

108 Schievink WI, Puumala MR, Meyer FB, Raffel C, Katzmann JA, Parisi JE. Giant intracranial aneurysm and fibromuscular dysplasia in an adolescent with alpha 1-antitrypsin deficiency. J Neurosurg 1996, **85**: 503–506.

109 Shokunbi MT, Vinters HV, Kaufmann JC. Fusiform intracranial aneurysms. Clinicopathologic features. Surg Neurol 1988, **29**: 263–270.

110 Wakai S, Kumakura N, Nagai M. Lobar intracerebral hemorrhage. A clinical, radiographic, and pathological study of 29 consecutive operated cases with negative angiography. J Neurosurg 1992, **76**: 231 238.

111 Wakai S, Nagai M. Histological verification of microaneurysms as a cause of cerebral haemorrhage in surgical specimens. J Neurol Neurosurg Psychiatry 1989, **52**: 595–599.

112 Weir B. Unruptured intracranial aneurysms. A review. J Neurosurg 2002, **96**: 3–42.

Vascular malformations

113 Amin-Hanjani S, Robertson R, Arginteanu MS, Scott RM. Familial intracranial arteriovenous malformations. Case report and review of the literature. Pediatr Neurosurg 1998, **29**: 208–213.

114 Benhaiem N, Poirier J, Hurth M. Arteriovenous fistulae of the meninges draining into the spinal veins. A histological study of 28 cases. Acta Neuropathol (Berl) 1983, **62**: 103–111.

115 Brown RD, Jr., Wiebers DO, Forbes G, O'Fallon WM, Piepgras DG, Marsh WR, Maciunas RJ. The natural history of unruptured intracranial arteriovenous malformations. J Neurosurg 1988, **68**: 352–357.

116 Carleton CC, Cauthen JC. Vascular ("arteriovenous") malformations of the choroid plexus. Arch Pathol 1975, **99**: 286–288.

117 Chang SD, Steinberg GK, Rosario M, Crowley RS, Hevner RF. Mixed arteriovenous malformation and capillary telangiectasia. A rare subset of mixed vascular malformations. Case report. J Neurosurg 1997, **86**: 699–703.

118 Deutsch H, Jallo GI, Faktorovich A, Epstein F. Spinal intramedullary cavernoma. Clinical presentation and surgical outcome. J Neurosurg 2000, **93**: 65–70.

119 Dobyns WB, Michels VV, Groover RV, Mokri B, Trautmann JC, Forbes GS, Laws ER, Jr: Familial cavernous malformations of the central nervous system and retina. Ann Neurol 1987, **21**: 578–583.

120 Farrell DF, Forno LS. Symptomatic capillary telangiectasis of the brainstem without hemorrhage. Report of an unusual case. Neurology 1970, **20**: 341–346.

121 Hamada J, Yano S, Kai Y, Koga K, Morioka M, Ishimaru Y, Ushio Y. Histopathological study of venous aneurysms in patients with dural arteriovenous fistulas. J Neurosurg 2000, **92**: 1023–1027.

122 Heckl S, Aschoff A, Kunze S. Radiation-induced cavernous hemangiomas of the brain. A late effect predominantly in children. Cancer 2002, **94**: 3285–3291.

123 Labauge P, Enjolras O, Bonerandi JJ, Laberge S, Dandurand M, Joujoux JM, Tournier-Lasserve E. An association between autosomal dominant cerebral cavernomas and a distinctive hyperkeratotic cutaneous vascular malformation in 4 families. Ann Neurol 1999, **45**: 250–254.

124 Larson JJ, Ball WS, Bove KE, Crone KR, Tew JM, Jr: Formation of intracerebral cavernous malformations after radiation treatment for central nervous system neoplasia in children. J Neurosurg 1998, **88**: 51–56.

125 Lobato RD, Perez C, Rivas JJ, Cordobes F. Clinical, radiological, and pathological spectrum of angiographically occult intracranial vascular malformations. Analysis of 21 cases and review of the literature. J Neurosurg 1988, **68**: 518–531.

126 Lombardi D, Scheithauer BW, Piepgras D, Meyer FB, Forbes GS. "Angioglioma" and the arteriovenous malformation-glioma association. J Neurosurg 1991, **75**: 589–596.

127 Mandybur TI, Nazek M. Cerebral arteriovenous malformations. A detailed morphological and immunohistochemical study using actin. Arch Pathol Lab Med 1990, **114**: 970–973.

128 Matias-Guiu X, Alejo M, Sole T, Ferrer I, Noboa R, Bartumeus F. Cavernous angiomas of the cranial nerves. Report of two cases. J Neurosurg 1990, **73**: 620–622.

129 Meyer B, Stangl AP, Schramm J. Association of venous and true arteriovenous malformation. A rare entity among mixed vascular malformations of the brain. Case report. J Neurosurg 1995, **83**: 141–144.

130 Meyer FB, Lombardi D, Scheithauer B, Nichols DA. Extra-axial cavernous hemangiomas involving the dural sinuses. J Neurosurg 1990, **73**: 187–192.

131 Naff NJ, Wemmer J, Hoenig-Rigamonti K, Rigamonti DR. A longitudinal study of patients with venous malformations. Documentation of a negligible hemorrhage risk and benign natural history. Neurology 1998, **50**: 1709–1714.

132 Nazek M, Mandybur TI, Kashiwagi S. Oligodendroglial proliferative abnormality associated with arteriovenous malformation. Report of three cases with review of the literature. Neurosurgery 1988, **23**: 781–785.

133 Nishijima M, Takaku A, Endo S, Kuwayama N, Koizumi F, Sato H, Owada K. Etiological evaluation of dural arteriovenous malformations of the lateral and sigmoid sinuses based on histopathological examinations. J Neurosurg 1992, **76**: 600–606.

134 Ondra SL, Troupp H, George ED, Schwab K. The natural history of symptomatic arteriovenous malformations of the brain. A 24-year follow-up assessment. J Neurosurg 1990, **73**: 387–391.

135 Pagni CA, Canavero S, Forni M. Report of a cavernoma of the cauda equina and review of the literature. Surg Neurol 1990, **33**: 124–131.

136 Partington MD, Rufenacht DA, Marsh WR, Piepgras DG. Cranial and sacral dural arteriovenous fistulas as a cause of myelopathy. J Neurosurg 1992, **76**: 615–622.

137 Porter RW, Detwiler PW, Spetzler RF, Lawton MT, Baskin JJ, Derksen PT, Zabramski JM. Cavernous malformations of the brainstem. Experience with 100 patients. J Neurosurg 1999, **90**: 50–58.

138 Rigamonti D, Johnson PC, Spetzler RF, Hadley MN, Drayer BP. Cavernous malformations and capillary telangiectasia. A spectrum within a single pathological entity. Neurosurgery 1991, **28**: 60–64.

139 Roda JM, Carceller F, Perez-Higueras A, Morales C. Encapsulated intracerebral hematomas: a defined entity. J Neurosurg 1993, **78**: 829–833.

140 Román G, Fisher M, Perl DP, Poser CM. Neurological manifestations of hereditary hemorrhagic telangiectasia (Rendu-Osler-Weber disease). Report of 2 cases and review of the literature. Ann Neurol 1978, **4**: 130–144.

141 Rosenblum B, Oldfield EH, Doppman JL, Di Chiro G. Spinal

arteriovenous malformations. A comparison of dural arteriovenous fistulas and intradural AVMs in 81 patients. J Neurosurg 1987, **67**: 795–802.

142 Schneider BF, Eberhard DA, Steiner LE. Histopathology of arteriovenous malformations after gamma knife radiosurgery. J Neurosurg 1997, **87**: 352–357.

143 Schweitzer JS, Chang BS, Madsen P, Vinuela F, Martin NA, Marroquin CE, Vinters HV. The pathology of arteriovenous malformations of the brain treated by embolotherapy. II. Results of embolization with multiple agents. Neuroradiology 1993, **35**: 468–474.

144 Simard JM, Garcia-Bengochea F, Ballinger WE, Jr., Mickle JP, Quisling RG. Cavernous angioma. A review of 126 collected and 12 new clinical cases. Neurosurgery 1986, **18**: 162–172.

145 Tomlinson FH, Rufenacht DA, Sundt TM, Jr., Nichols DA, Fode NC. Arteriovenous fistulas of the brain and the spinal cord. J Neurosurg 1993, **79**: 16–27.

146 Tung H, Giannotta SL, Chandrasoma PT, Zee CS. Recurrent intraparenchymal hemorrhages from angiographically occult vascular malformations. J Neurosurg 1990, **73**: 174–180.

147 Vaquero J, Manrique M, Oya S, Cabezudo JM, Bravo G. Calcified telangiectatic hamartomas of the brain. Surg Neurol 1980, **13**: 453–457.

148 Wohlwill FJ, Yakovlev PI. Histopathology of meningofacial angiomatosis (Sturge–Weber's disease). Report of four cases. J Neuropathol Exp Neurol 1957, **16**: 341–364.

149 Zabramski JM, Wascher TM, Spetzler RF, Johnson B, Golfinos J, Drayer BP, Brown B, Rigamonti D, Brown G. The natural history of familial cavernous malformations. Results of an ongoing study. J Neurosurg 1994, **80**: 422–432.

150 Zevgaridis D, Buttner A, Weis S, Hamburger C, Reulen HJ. Spinal epidural cavernous hemangiomas. Report of three cases and review of the literature. J Neurosurg 1998, **88**: 903–908.

Primary angiitis

151 Caccamo DV, Garcia JH, Ho KL. Isolated granulomatous angiitis of the spinal cord. Ann Neurol 1992, **32**: 580–582.

152 Lie JT. Primary (granulomatous) angiitis of the central nervous system. A clinicopathologic analysis of 15 new cases and a review of the literature. Hum Pathol 1992, **23**: 164–171.

153 Rhodes RH, Madelaire NC, Petrelli M, Cole M, Karaman BA. Primary angiitis and angiopathy of the central nervous system and their relationship to systemic giant cell arteritis. Arch Pathol Lab Med 1995, **119**: 334–349.

154 Yoong MF, Blumbergs PC, North JB. Primary (granulomatous) angiitis of the central nervous system with multiple aneurysms of spinal arteries. Case report. J Neurosurg 1993, **79**: 603–607.

155 Yuen RW, Johnson PC. Primary angiitis of the central nervous system associated with Hodgkin's disease. Arch Pathol Lab Med 1996, **120**: 573–576.

Cerebral amyloid angiopathy

156 Gray F, Vinters HV, Le Noan H, Salama J, Delaporte P, Poirier J. Cerebral amyloid angiopathy and granulomatous angiitis: immunohistochemical study using antibodies to the Alzheimer A4 peptide. Hum Pathol 1990, **21**: 1290–1293.

157 Le Coz P, Mikol J, Ferrand J, Woimant F, Masters C, Beyreuther K, Haguenau M, Cophignon J, Pepin B. Granulomatous angiitis and cerebral amyloid angiopathy presenting as a mass lesion. Neuropathol Appl Neurobiol 1991, **17**: 149–155.

158 Mandybur TI. Cerebral amyloid angiopathy. Possible relationship to rheumatoid vasculitis. Neurology 1979, **29**: 1336–1340.

159 Mandybur TI. Cerebral amyloid angiopathy. The vascular pathology and complications. J Neuropathol Exp Neurol 1986, **45**: 79–90.

160 Revesz T, Holton JL, Lashley T, Plant G, Rostagno A, Ghiso J, Frangione B. Sporadic and familial cerebral amyloid angiopathies. Brain Pathol 2002, **12**: 343–357.

161 Vonsattel JP, Myers RH, Hedley-Whyte ET, Ropper AH, Bird ED, Richardson EP, Jr: Cerebral amyloid angiopathy without and with cerebral hemorrhages. A comparative histological study. Ann Neurol 1991, **30**: 637–649.

CADASIL

162 Kalimo H, Ruchoux MM, Viitanen M, Kalaria RN. CADASIL. A common form of hereditary arteriopathy causing brain infarcts and dementia. Brain Pathol 2002, **12**: 371–384.

Epidural and subdural hematoma

163 Friede RL, Schachenmayr W. The origin of subdural neomembranes. II. Fine structure of neomembranes. Am J Pathol 1978, **92**: 69–84.

164 Hardman JM. Cerebrospinal trauma. In Davis RL, Robertson DM (eds): Textbook of neuropathology, ed. 3. Baltimore, 1997, William & Wilkins, pp. 1195–1201.

165 Schachenmayr W, Friede RL. The origin of subdural neomembranes. I. Fine structure of the dura-arachnoid interface in man. Am J Pathol 1978, **92**: 53–68.

166 Wintzen AR. The clinical course of subdural haematoma. A retrospective study of aetiological, chronological and pathological features in 212 patients and a proposed classification. Brain 1980, **103**: 855–867.

167 Yamashima T, Yamamoto S. The origin of inner membranes in chronic subdural hematomas. Acta Neuropathol (Berl) 1985, **67**: 219–225.

Inflammatory diseases
Demyelinating diseases

167a Annesley-Williams D, Farrell A, Staunton H, Brett FM. Acute demyelination, neuropathological diagnosis, and clinical evolution. J Neuropathol Exp Neurol 2000, **59**: 477–489.

168 Hook CC, Kimmel DW, Kvols LK, Scheithauer BW, Forsyth PA, Rubin J, Moertel CG, Rodriguez M. Multifocal inflammatory leukoencephalopathy with 5-fluorouracil and levamisole. Ann Neurol 1992, **31**: 262–267.

169 Hulette CM, Downey BT, Burger PC. Macrophage markers in diagnostic neuropathology. Am J Surg Pathol 1992, **16**: 493–499.

170 Kepes JJ. Large focal tumor-like demyelinating lesions of the brain. Intermediate entity between multiple sclerosis and acute disseminated encephalomyelitis? A study of 31 patients. Ann Neurol 1993, **33**: 18–27.

171 Nahser HC, Vieregge P, Nau HE, Reinhardt V. Coincidence of multiple sclerosis and glioma. Clinical and radiological remarks on two cases. Surg Neurol 1986, **26**: 45–51.

172 Nesbit GM, Forbes GS, Scheithauer BW, Okazaki H, Rodriguez M. Multiple sclerosis: histopathologic and MR and/or CT correlation in 37 cases at biopsy and three cases at autopsy. Radiology 1991, **180**: 467–474.

173 Peterson K, Rosenblum MK, Powers JM, Alvord E, Walker RW, Posner JB. Effect of brain irradiation on demyelinating lesions. Neurology 1993, **43**: 2105–2112.

174 Zagzag D, Miller DC, Kleinman GM, Abati A, Donnenfeld H, Budzilovich GN. Demyelinating disease versus tumor in surgical neuropathology. Clues to a correct pathological diagnosis. Am J Surg Pathol 1993, **17**: 537–545.

Idiopathic inflammatory and reactive disorders, xanthomatous lesions, and "histiocytoses"

175 Abrey LE, Rosenblum MK, DeAngelis LM. Sarcoidosis of the cauda equina mimicking leptomeningeal malignancy. J Neurooncol 1998, **39**: 261–265.

176 Adle-Biassette H, Chetritt J, Bergemer-Fouquet AM, Wechsler J,

Mussini JM, Gray F. Pathology of the central nervous system in Chester-Erdheim disease. Report of three cases. J Neuropathol Exp Neurol 1997, 56: 1207–1216.

177 Andriko JA, Morrison A, Colegial CH, Davis BJ, Jones RV. Rosai-Dorfman disease isolated to the central nervous system: a report of 11 cases. Mod Pathol 2001, 14: 172–178.

178 Ashkenazi E, Constantini S, Pappo O, Gomori M, Averbuch-Heller L, Umansky F. Hypertrophic spinal pachymeningitis. Report of two cases and review of the literature. Neurosurgery 1991, 28: 730–732.

179 Bertoni F, Unni KK, Dahlin DC, Beabout JW, Onofrio BM. Calcifying pseudoneoplasms of the neural axis. J Neurosurg 1990, 72: 42–48.

180 Bien CG, Schulze-Bonhage A, Deckert M, Urbach H, Helmstaedter C, Grunwald T, Schaller C, Elger CE. Limbic encephalitis not associated with neoplasm as a cause of temporal lobe epilepsy. Neurology 2000, 55: 1823–1828.

181 Bostrom J, Janssen G, Messing-Junger M, Felsberg JU, Neuen-Jacob E, Engelbrecht V, Lenard HG, Bock WJ, Reifenberger G. Multiple intracranial juvenile xanthogranulomas. Case report. J Neurosurg 2000, 93: 335–341.

182 Bramwit M, Kalina P, Rustia-Villa M. Inflammatory pseudotumor of the choroid plexus. AJNR Am J Neuroradiol 1997, 18: 1307–1309.

183 Brück W, Sander U, Blanckenberg P, Friede RL. Symptomatic xanthogranuloma of choroid plexus with unilateral hydrocephalus. Case report. J Neurosurg 1991, 75: 324–327.

184 Cannella DM, Prezyna AP, Kapp JP. Primary intracranial plasma-cell granuloma. Case report. J Neurosurg 1988, 69: 785–788.

185 Caselli RJ, Scheithauer BW, Bowles CA, Trenerry MR, Meyer FB, Smigielski JS, Rodriguez M. The treatable dementia of Sjögren's syndrome. Ann Neurol 1991, 30: 98–101.

186 de Jesus O, Inserni JA, Gonzalez A, Colon LE. Idiopathic orbital inflammation with intracranial extension. Case report. J Neurosurg 1996, 85: 510–513.

187 Deprez M, Born J, Hauwaert C, Otto B, Reznik M. Idiopathic hypertrophic cranial pachymeningitis mimicking multiple meningiomas. Case report and review of the literature. Acta Neuropathol (Berl) 1997, 94: 385–389.

188 Eisenberg MB, Haddad G, Al-Mefty O. Petrous apex cholesterol granulomas: evolution and management. J Neurosurg 1997, 86: 822–829.

189 Figarella-Branger D, Gambarelli D, Perez-Castillo M, Regis J, Peragut JC, Pellissier JF. Atypical inflammatory histiocytic tumor of the cerebellum. A histological, immunohistochemical, and ultrastructural study. Am J Surg Pathol 1990, 14: 778–783.

190 Gal R, Gukovsky-Oren S, Sandbank U, Baharav E, Kessler E. Michaelis-Gutmann bodies in a healing brain infarct. Stroke 1987, 18: 947–950.

191 Gochman GA, Duffy K, Crandall PH, Vinters HV. Plasma cell granuloma of the brain. Surg Neurol 1990, 33: 347–352.

192 Goto T, Kitazawa K, Tada T, Tanaka Y, Hongo K, Kobayashi S. Surgical dissemination of intracranial xanthogranulomas. Case illustration. J Neurosurg 2001, 95: 537.

193 Graf M, Wakhloo A, Schmidtke K, Bloss H, Volk B. Sarcoidosis of the spinal cord and medulla oblongata. A pathological and neuroradiological case report. Clin Neuropathol 1994, 13: 19–25.

194 Grant GA, Wener MH, Yaziji H, Futran N, Bronner MP, Mandel N, Mayberg MR. Destructive tophaceous calcium hydroxyapatite tumor of the infratemporal fossa. Case report and review of the literature. J Neurosurg 1999, 90: 148–152.

195 Grois NG, Favara BE, Mostbeck GH, Prayer D. Central nervous system disease in Langerhans cell histiocytosis. Hematol Oncol Clin North Am 1998, 12: 287–305.

196 Gultekin SH, Rosenfeld MR, Voltz R, Eichen J, Posner JB, Dalmau J. Paraneoplastic limbic encephalitis. Neurological symptoms, immunological findings and tumour association in 50 patients. Brain 2000, 123 (Pt 7): 1481–1494.

197 Hart YM, Andermann F, Fish DR, Dubeau F, Robitaille Y, Rasmussen T, Berkovic S, Marino R, Yakoubian EM, Spillane K, Scaravilli F. Chronic encephalitis and epilepsy in adults and adolescents. A variant of Rasmussen's syndrome? Neurology 1997, 48: 418–424.

198 Ho KL. Morphogenesis of Michaelis-Gutmann bodies in cerebral malacoplakia. An ultrastructural study. Arch Pathol Lab Med 1989, 113: 874–879.

199 Jackson RJ, Goodman JC, Huston DP, Harper RL. Parafalcine and bilateral convexity neurosarcoidosis mimicking meningioma: case report and review of the literature. Neurosurgery 1998, 42: 635–638.

200 Jamjoom ZA, Raina V, al-Jamali A, Jamjoom AB, Yacub B, Sharif HS. Intracranial xanthogranuloma of the dura in Hand-Schuller-Christian disease. Case report. J Neurosurg 1993, 78: 297–300.

201 Kamiryo T, Abiko S, Orita T, Aoki H, Watanabe Y, Hiraoka K. Bilateral intracranial fibrous xanthoma. Surg Neurol 1988, 29: 27–31.

202 Kim RC, Collins GH. The neuropathology of rheumatoid disease. Hum Pathol 1981, 12: 5–15.

203 Kimura H, Oka K, Nakayama Y, Tomonaga M. Xanthoma in Meckel's cave. A case report. Surg Neurol 1991, 35: 317–320.

204 Knobler RM, Neumann RA, Gebhart W, Radaskiewicz T, Ferenci P, Widhalm K. Xanthoma disseminatum with progressive involvement of the central nervous and hepatobiliary systems. J Am Acad Dermatol 1990, 23: 341–346.

205 Koyama S, Tsubokawa T, Katayama Y, Hirota H. A huge intracranial xanthogranuloma in the middle cranial fossa. Case report. Neurosurgery 1991, 28: 436–439.

206 Mamelak AN, Kelly WM, Davis RL, Rosenblum ML. Idiopathic hypertrophic cranial pachymeningitis. Report of three cases. J Neurosurg 1993, 79: 270–276.

207 Masson C, Henin D, Hauw JJ, Rey A, Raverdy P, Masson M. Cranial pachymeningitis of unknown origin: a study of seven cases. Neurology 1993, 43: 1329–1334.

208 Mills SE, Lininger JR. Intracranial myospherulosis. Hum Pathol 1982, 13: 596–597.

209 Miyachi S, Kobayashi T, Takahashi T, Saito K, Hashizume Y, Sugita K. An intracranial mass lesion in systemic xanthogranulomatosis: case report. Neurosurgery 1990, 27: 822–826.

210 Montine TJ, Hollensead SC, Ellis WG, Martin JS, Moffat EJ, Burger PC. Solitary eosinophilic granuloma of the temporal lobe. A case report and long-term follow-up of previously reported cases. Clin Neuropathol 1994, 13: 225–228.

211 Nazek M, Mandybur TI, Sawaya R. Hyalinizing plasmacytic granulomatosis of the falx. Am J Surg Pathol 1988, 12: 308–313.

212 Nishino H, Rubino FA, DeRemee RA, Swanson JW, Parisi JE. Neurological involvement in Wegener's granulomatosis: an analysis of 324 consecutive patients at the Mayo Clinic. Ann Neurol 1993, 33: 4–9.

213 Okabe H, Ishizawa M, Matsumoto K, Ogata M, Nishioka J, Hukuda S, Hidaka H, Yasuda H, Ochi Y. Immunohistochemical analysis of spinal intradural xanthomatosis developed in a patient with phytosterolemia. Acta Neuropathol (Berl) 1992, 83: 554–558.

214 Paulus W, Kirchner T, Michaela M, Kuhl J, Warmuth-Metz M, Sorensen N, Muller-Hermelink HK, Roggendorf W. Histiocytic tumor of Meckel's cave. An intracranial equivalent of juvenile xanthogranuloma of the skin. Am J Surg Pathol 1992, 16: 76–83.

215 Pick P, Jean E, Horoupian D, Factor S. Xanthogranuloma of the dura in systemic Weber–Christian disease. Neurology 1983, 33: 1067–1070.

216 Prayson RA, Frater JL. Rasmussen encephalitis. A

clinicopathologic and immunohistochemical study of seven patients. Am J Clin Pathol 2002, **117**: 776–782.

217 Qian J, Rubio A, Powers JM, Rosenblum MK, Pilcher WH, Shrier DA, Stein BM, Ito M, Iannucci A. Fibro-osseous lesions of the central nervous system. Report of four cases and literature review. Am J Surg Pathol 1999, **23**: 1270–1275.

218 Reznik M, Stevenaert A, Bex V, Kratzenberg E. Focal brain invasion as the first manifestation of Langerhans cell histiocytosis in an adult. Case report. Clin Neuropathol 1993, **12**: 179–183.

219 Rosenblum MK. Paraneoplasia and autoimmunologic injury of the nervous system: the anti-Hu syndrome. Brain Pathol 1993, **3**: 199–212.

220 Spurlock RG, Richman AV. Rheumatoid meningitis. A case report and review of the literature. Arch Pathol Lab Med 1983, **107**: 129–131.

221 Strickland-Marmol LB, Fessler RG, Rojiani AM. Necrotizing sarcoid granulomatosis mimicking an intracranial neoplasm: clinicopathologic features and review of the literature. Mod Pathol 2000, **13**: 909–913.

222 Tang TT, Segura AD, Oechler HW, Harb JM, Adair SE, Gregg DC, Camitta BM, Franciosi RA. Inflammatory myofibrohistiocytic proliferation simulating sarcoma in children. Cancer 1990, **65**: 1626–1634.

223 Thomas G, Murphy S, Staunton H, O'Neill S, Farrell MA, Brett FM. Pathogen-free granulomatous diseases of the central nervous system. Hum Pathol 1998, **29**: 110–115.

224 Vaquero J, Leunda G, Cabezudo JM, De Juan M, Herrero J, Bravo G. Posterior fossa xanthogranuloma. Case report. J Neurosurg 1979, **51**: 718–722.

225 Yamada H, Kurata H, Nomura K, Utsunomiya K, Shimizu M, Isogai Y. Adult xanthogranulomatous intracranial lesion involving familial hypercholesterolemia. Jpn J Med 1989, **28**: 757–761.

Infectious diseases

Bacterial infections

226 Bauer J, Johnson RF, Levy JM, Pojman DV, Ruge JR. Tuberculoma presenting as an en plaque meningioma. Case report. J Neurosurg 1996, **85**: 685–688.

227 Berenson CS, Bia FJ. Propionibacterium acnes causes postoperative brain abscesses unassociated with foreign bodies: case reports. Neurosurgery 1989, **25**: 130–134.

228 Cayli SR, Onal C, Kocak A, Onmus SH, Tekiner A. An unusual presentation of neurotuberculosis. Subdural empyema. Case report. J Neurosurg 2001, **94**: 988–991.

229 Cegielski JP, Wallace Jr RJ. Infections due to nontuberculous mycobacteria. In Scheld WM, Whitley RJ, Durack DT (eds): Infections of the central nervous system, ed. 2. Philadelphia, 1997, Lippincott-Raven, pp. 445–461.

230 Chun CH, Johnson JD, Hofstetter M, Raff MJ. Brain abscess. A study of 45 consecutive cases. Medicine (Baltimore) 1986, **65**: 415–431.

231 Del Curling O, Jr., Gower DJ, McWhorter JM. Changing concepts in spinal epidural abscess: a report of 29 cases. Neurosurgery 1990, **27**: 185–192.

232 Di Patre PL, Radziszewski W, Martin NA, Brooks A, Vinters HV. A meningioma-mimicking tumor caused by Mycobacterium avium complex in an immunocompromised patient. Am J Surg Pathol 2000, **24**: 136–139.

233 Ekseth K, Boström S. Late complications of Silastic duraplasty. Low-virulence infections. Case report. J Neurosurg 1999, **90**: 559–562.

234 Gellin BG, Weingarten K, Gamache Jr FW, Hartman BJ. Epidural abscess. In Scheld WM, Whitley RJ, Durack DT (eds): Infections of the central nervous system, ed. 2. Philadelphia, 1997, Lippincott-Raven, pp. 507–522.

235 George TI, Manley G, Koehler JE, Hung VS, McDermott M, Bollen A. Detection of Bartonella henselae by polymerase chain reaction in brain tissue of an immunocompromised patient with multiple enhancing lesions. Case report and review of the literature. J Neurosurg 1998, **89**: 640–644.

236 Hall WA. Hereditary hemorrhagic telangiectasia (Rendu-Osler-Weber disease) presenting with polymicrobial brain abscess. Case report. J Neurosurg 1994, **81**: 294–296.

237 Mamelak AN, Obana WG, Flaherty JF, Rosenblum ML. Nocardial brain abscess. Treatment strategies and factors influencing outcome. Neurosurgery 1994, **35**: 621–631.

238 Mendel E, Khoo LT, Go JL, Hinton D, Zee CS, Apuzzo ML. Intracerebral Whipple's disease diagnosed by stereotactic biopsy: a case report and review of the literature. Neurosurgery 1999, **44**: 203–209.

239 Pollock SS, Pollock TM, Harrison MJ. Infection of the central nervous system by Listeria monocytogenes. A review of 54 adult and juvenile cases. Q J Med 1984, **53**: 331–340.

240 Ratliff JK, Connolly ES. Intramedullary tuberculoma of the spinal cord. Case report and review of the literature. J Neurosurg (Spine 1) 1999, **90**: 125–128.

241 Renier D, Flandin C, Hirsch E, Hirsch JF. Brain abscesses in neonates. A study of 30 cases. J Neurosurg 1988, **69**: 877–882.

242 Schlitt M, Mitchem L, Zorn G, Dismukes W, Morawetz RB. Brain abscess after esophageal dilation for caustic stricture. Report of three cases. Neurosurgery 1985, **17**: 947–951.

243 Smego RA, Jr: Actinomycosis of the central nervous system. Rev Infect Dis 1987, **9**: 855–865.

244 Thomé C, Krauss JK, Zevgaridis D, Schmiedek P. Pyogenic abscess of the filum terminale. Case report. J Neurosurg 2001, **95**: 100–104.

245 Trautmann M, Lindner O, Haase C, Bruckner O. Focal tuberculous meningoencephalitis. Eur Neurol 1983, **22**: 417–420.

246 Whitener DR. Tuberculous brain abscess. Report of a case and review of the literature. Arch Neurol 1978, **35**: 148–155.

247 Wispelwey B, Dacey Jr RG, Scheld WM. Brain abscess. In Scheld WM, Whitley RJ, Durack DT (eds): Infections of the central nervous system, ed. 2. Philadelphia, 1997, Lippincott-Raven, pp. 463–493.

248 Zuger A, Lowy FD. Tuberculosis. In Scheld WM, Whitley RJ, Durack DT (eds): Infections of the central nervous system, ed. 2. Philadelphia, 1997, Lippincott-Raven, pp. 417–443.

Mycoses

249 Araujo JC, Werneck L, Cravo MA. South American blastomycosis presenting as a posterior fossa tumor. Case report. J Neurosurg 1978, **49**: 425–428.

250 Dixon DM, Walsh TJ, Merz WG, McGinnis MR. Infections due to *Xylohypha bantiana* (*Cladosporium trichoides*). Rev Infect Dis 1989, **11**: 515–525.

251 Goodman ML, Coffey RJ. Stereotactic drainage of Aspergillus brain abscess with long-term survival. Case report and review. Neurosurgery 1989, **24**: 96–99.

252 Hadley MN, Martin NA, Spetzler RF, Johnson PC. Multiple intracranial aneurysms due to Coccidioides immitis infection. Case report. J Neurosurg 1987, **66**: 453–456.

253 Ilgren EB, Westmorland D, Adams CB, Mitchell RG. Cerebellar mass caused by Candida species. Case report. J Neurosurg 1984, **60**: 428–430.

254 Kasantikul V, Shuangshoti S, Sampatanukul P. Primary chromoblastomycosis of the medulla oblongata. Complication of heroin addiction. Surg Neurol 1988, **29**: 319–321.

255 Kershaw P, Freeman R, Templeton D, DeGirolami PC, DeGirolami U, Tarsy D, Hoffmann S, Eliopoulos G, Karchmer AW. Pseudallescheria boydii infection of the central nervous system. Arch Neurol 1990, **47**: 468–472.

256 Kleinschmidt-DeMasters BK, Mazowiecki M, Bonds LA, Cohn

DL, Wilson ML. Coccidioidomycosis meningitis with massive dural and cerebral venous thrombosis and tissue arthroconidia. Arch Pathol Lab Med 2000, **124**: 310–314.

257 Mendel E, Milefchik EN, Amadi J, Gruen P. Coccidioidomycosis brain abscess. Case report. J Neurosurg 1994, **81**: 614–616.

258 Mielke B, Weir B, Oldring D, von Westarp C. Fungal aneurysm. Case report and review of the literature. Neurosurgery 1981, **9**: 578–582.

259 Penar PL, Kim J, Chyatte D, Sabshin JK. Intraventricular cryptococcal granuloma. Report of two cases. J Neurosurg 1988, **68**: 145–148.

260 Roos KL, Bryan JP, Maggio WW, Jane JA, Scheld WM. Intracranial blastomycoma. Medicine (Baltimore) 1987, **66**: 224–235.

261 Sepkowitz K, Armstrong D. Space-occupying fungal lesions. In Scheld WM, Whitley RJ, Durack DT (eds): Infections of the central nervous system, ed. 2. Philadelphia, 1997, Lippincott-Raven, pp. 741–762.

262 Stave GM, Heimberger T, Kerkering TM. Zygomycosis of the basal ganglia in intravenous drug users. Am J Med 1989, **86**: 115–117.

263 Venger BH, Landon G, Rose JE. Solitary histoplasmoma of the thalamus. Case report and literature review. Neurosurgery 1987, **20**: 784–787.

264 Voelker JL, Muller J, Worth RM. Intramedullary spinal Histoplasma granuloma. Case report. J Neurosurg 1989, **70**: 959–961.

265 Yanai Y, Wakao T, Fukamachi A, Kunimine H. Intracranial granuloma caused by *Aspergillus fumigatus*. Surg Neurol 1985, **23**: 597–604.

Parasitoses

266 Dukes CS, Luft BJ, Durack DT. Toxoplasmosis. In Scheld WM, Whitley RJ, Durack DT (eds): Infections of the central nervous system, ed. 2. Philadelphia, 1997, Lippincott-Raven, pp. 785–806.

267 Navia BA, Petito CK, Gold JW, Cho ES, Jordan BD, Price RW. Cerebral toxoplasmosis complicating the acquired immune deficiency syndrome: clinical and neuropathological findings in 27 patients. Ann Neurol 1986, **19**: 224–238.

268 Pittella JE. Neurocysticercosis. Brain Pathol 1997, **7**: 681–693.

269 Resnick DK, Comey CH, Welch WC, Martinez AJ, Hoover WW, Jacobs GB. Isolated toxoplasmosis of the thoracic spinal cord in a patient with acquired immunodeficiency syndrome. Case report. J Neurosurg 1995, **82**: 493–496.

Spirochetal infections

270 Hook III EW. Syphillis. In Scheld WM, Whitley RJ, Durack DT (eds): Infections of the central nervous system, ed. 2. Philadelphia, 1997, Lippincott-Raven, pp. 669–684.

271 Horowitz HW, Valsamis MP, Wicher V, Abbruscato F, Larsen SA, Wormser GP, Wicher K. Brief report. Cerebral syphilitic gumma confirmed by the polymerase chain reaction in a man with human immunodeficiency virus infection. N Engl J Med 1994, **331**: 1488–1491.

272 Murray R, Morawetz R, Kepes J, el Gammal T, LeDoux M. Lyme neuroborreliosis manifesting as an intracranial mass lesion. Neurosurgery 1992, **30**: 769–773.

273 Reik Jr L. Lyme Disease. In Scheld WM, Whitley RJ, Durack DT (eds): Infections of the central nervous system, ed. 2. Philadelphia, 1997, Lippincott-Raven, pp. 685–718.

Viral infections

Herpes simplex encephalitis

274 Esiri MM. Herpes simplex encephalitis. An immunohistological study of the distribution of viral antigen within the brain. J Neurol Sci 1982, **54**: 209–226.

275 Kennedy PG, Adams JH, Graham DI, Clements GB. A clinico-pathological study of herpes simplex encephalitis. Neuropathol Appl Neurobiol 1988, **14**: 395–415.

276 Molloy S, Allcutt D, Brennan P, Farrell MA, Perryman R, Brett FM. Herpes simplex encephalitis occurring after chemotherapy, surgery, and stereotactic radiotherapy for medulloblastoma. Arch Pathol Lab Med 2000, **124**: 1809–1812.

277 Schiff D, Rosenblum MK. Herpes simplex encephalitis (HSE) and the immunocompromised. A clinical and autopsy study of HSE in the settings of cancer and human immunodeficiency virus-type 1 infection. Hum Pathol 1998, **29**: 215–222.

278 White CL, 3rd, Taxy JB. Early morphologic diagnosis of herpes simplex virus encephalitis. Advantages of electron microscopy and immunoperoxidase staining. Hum Pathol 1983, **14**: 135–139.

279 Whitley RJ. Herpes simplex virus. In Scheld WM, Whitley RJ, Durack DT (eds): Infections of the central nervous system, ed. 2. Philadelphia, 1997, Lippincott-Raven, pp. 73–89.

Progressive multifocal leukoencephalopathy

280 Ariza A, Mate JL, Fernandez-Vasalo A, Gomez-Plaza C, Perez-Piteira J, Pujol M, Navas-Palacios JJ. p53 and proliferating cell nuclear antigen expression in JC virus-infected cells of progressive multifocal leukoencephalopathy. Hum Pathol 1994, **25**: 1341–1345.

281 Ariza A, Mate JL, Isamat M, Calatrava A, Fernandez-Vasalo A, Navas-Palacios JJ. Overexpression of Ki-67 and cyclins A and B1 in JC virus-infected cells of progressive multifocal leukoencephalopathy. J Neuropathol Exp Neurol 1998, **57**: 226–230.

282 Astrom K-E, Mancall EL, Richardson EP Jr: Progressive multifocal leukoencephalopathy. A hitherto unrecognized complication of chronic lymphatic leukaemia and Hodgkin's disease. Brain 1958, **81**: 93–111.

283 Finkelstein SD. Polyomaviruses and progressive multifocal leukoencephalopathy. In Connor DH, Chandler FW, Schwartz DA, Manz HJ, Lack EE (eds): Pathology of infectious diseases, vol. 1. Stamford, 1997, Appleton and Lange, pp. 265–272.

284 Hair LS, Nuovo G, Powers JM, Sisti MB, Britton CB, Miller JR. Progressive multifocal leukoencephalopathy in patients with human immunodeficiency virus. Hum Pathol 1992, **23**: 663–667.

285 Preskorn SH, Watanabe I. Progressive multifocal leukoencephalopathy. Cerebral mass lesions. Surg Neurol 1979, **12**: 231–234.

286 Schmidbauer M, Budka H, Shah KV. Progressive multifocal leukoencephalopathy (PML) in AIDS and in the pre-AIDS era. A neuropathological comparison using immunocytochemistry and in situ DNA hybridization for virus detection. Acta Neuropathol (Berl) 1990, **80**: 375–380.

287 Sima AA, Finkelstein SD, McLachlan DR. Multiple malignant astrocytomas in a patient with spontaneous progressive multifocal leukoencephalopathy. Ann Neurol 1983, **14**: 183–188.

288 Ueki K, Richardson EP, Jr., Henson JW, Louis DN. In situ polymerase chain reaction demonstration of JC virus in progressive multifocal leukoencephalopathy, including an index case. Ann Neurol 1994, **36**: 670–673.

289 Vanneste JA, Bellot SM, Stam FC. Progressive multifocal leukoencephalopathy presenting as a single mass lesion. Eur Neurol 1984, **23**: 113–118.

290 Vazeux R, Cumont M, Girard PM, Nassif X, Trotot P, Marche C, Matthiessen L, Vedrenne C, Mikol J, Henin D, et al. Severe encephalitis resulting from coinfections with HIV and JC virus. Neurology 1990, **40**: 944–948.

Varicella-zoster virus encephalitis and cerebral vasculitis

291 Doyle PW, Gibson G, Dolman CL. Herpes zoster ophthalmicus with contralateral hemiplegia: identification of cause. Ann Neurol 1983, **14**: 84–85.

292   Eidelberg D, Sotrel A, Horoupian DS, Neumann PE, Pumarola-Sune T, Price RW. Thrombotic cerebral vasculopathy associated with herpes zoster. Ann Neurol 1986, **19**: 7–14.

293   Fukumoto S, Kinjo M, Hokamura K, Tanaka K. Subarachnoid hemorrhage and granulomatous angiitis of the basilar artery. Demonstration of the varicella-zoster-virus in the basilar artery lesions. Stroke 1986, **17**: 1024–1028.

294   Horten B, Price RW, Jimenez D. Multifocal varicella-zoster virus leukoencephalitis temporally remote from herpes zoster. Ann Neurol 1981, **9**: 251–266.

295   Kleinschmidt-DeMasters BK, Amlie-Lefond C, Gilden DH. The patterns of varicella zoster virus encephalitis. Hum Pathol 1996, **27**: 927–938.

296   Weaver S, Rosenblum MK, DeAngelis LM. Herpes varicella zoster encephalitis in immunocompromised patients. Neurology 1999, **52**: 193–195.

HIV-1 encephalomyelitis

297   Rosenblum MK. Human immunodeficiency virus lesions of the central nervous system. In Connor DH, Chandler FW, Schwartz DA, Manz HJ, Lack EE (eds): Pathology of infectious diseases, vol. 1. Stamford, 1997, Appleton and Lange, pp. 183–197.

298   Sharer LR. Pathology of HIV–1 infection of the central nervous system. A review. J Neuropathol Exp Neurol 1992, **51**: 3–11.

299   Sotrel A, Dal Canto MC. HIV–1 and its causal relationship to immunosuppression and nervous system disease in AIDS. A review. Hum Pathol 2000, **31**: 1274–1298.

Prion-associated diseases

300   Brown P, Wolff A, Gajdusek DC. A simple and effective method for inactivating virus infectivity in formalin-fixed tissue samples from patients with Creutzfeldt–Jakob disease. Neurology 1990, **40**: 887–890.

301   Brumback RA. Routine use of phenolized formalin in fixation of autopsy brain tissue to reduce risk of inadvertent transmission of Creutzfeldt–Jakob disease. N Engl J Med 1988, **319**: 654.

302   Castellani RJ, Parchi P, Madoff L, Gambetti P, McKeever P. Biopsy diagnosis of Creutzfeldt–Jakob disease by western blot. A case report. Hum Pathol 1997, **28**: 623–626.

303   Cruz-Sanchez F, Lafuente J, Gertz HJ, Stoltenburg-Didinger G. Spongiform encephalopathy with extensive involvement of white matter. J Neurol Sci 1987, **82**: 81–87.

304   De Armond SJ, Kretzschmar HA, Prusiner SB. Prion diseases. In Graham DI, Lantos PL (eds): Greenfield's neuropathology, ed. 7. London, 2002, Arnold, pp. 273–323.

305   Hansen LA, Masliah E, Terry RD, Mirra SS. A neuropathological subset of Alzheimer's disease with concomitant Lewy body disease and spongiform change. Acta Neuropathol (Berl) 1989, **78**: 194–201.

306   Masters CL, Richardson EP, Jr: Subacute spongiform encephalopathy (Creutzfeldt–Jakob disease). The nature and progression of spongiform change. Brain 1978, **101**: 333–344.

307   Piccardo P, Safar J, Ceroni M, Gajdusek DC, Gibbs CJ, Jr. Immunohistochemical localization of prion protein in spongiform encephalopathies and normal brain tissue. Neurology 1990, **40**: 518–522.

308   Will RG, Ironside JW, Zeidler M, Cousens SN, Estibeiro K, Alperovitch A, Poser S, Pocchiari M, Hofman A, Smith PG. A new variant of Creutzfeldt–Jakob disease in the UK. Lancet 1996, **347**: 921–925.

Primary tumors

Diffusely infiltrating astrocytomas

309   Barnard RO, Geddes JF. The incidence of multifocal cerebral gliomas. A histologic study of large hemisphere sections. Cancer 1987, **60**: 1519–1531.

310   Blumenthal DT, Raizer JJ, Rosenblum MK, Bilsky MH, Hariharan S, Abrey LE. Primary intracranial neoplasms in patients with HIV. Neurology 1999, **52**: 1648–1651.

311   Brat DJ, Scheithauer BW, Medina-Flores R, Rosenblum MK, Burger PC. Infiltrative astrocytomas with granular cell features (granular cell astrocytomas). A study of histopathologic features, grading, and outcome. Am J Surg Pathol 2002, **26**: 750–757.

312   Burger PC, Pearl DK, Aldape K, Yates AJ, Scheithauer BW, Passe SM, Jenkins RB, James CD. Small cell architecture—a histological equivalent of EGFR amplification in glioblastoma multiforme? J Neuropathol Exp Neurol 2001, **60**: 1099–1104.

313   Burger PC, Vogel FS. Frozen section interpretation in surgical neuropathology. II. Intraspinal lesions. Am J Surg Pathol 1978, **2**: 81–95.

314   Constantini S, Miller DC, Allen JC, Rorke LB, Freed D, Epstein FJ. Radical excision of intramedullary spinal cord tumors. Surgical morbidity and long-term follow-up evaluation in 164 children and young adults. J Neurosurg 2000, **93**: 183–193.

315   Cosgrove M, Fitzgibbons PL, Sherrod A, Chandrasoma PT, Martin SE. Intermediate filament expression in astrocytic neoplasms. Am J Surg Pathol 1989, **13**: 141–145.

316   Cosgrove MM, Rich KA, Kunin SA, Sherrod AE, Martin SE. Keratin intermediate filament expression in astrocytic neoplasms. analysis by immunocytochemistry, western blot, and northern hybridization. Mod Pathol 1993, **6**: 342–347.

317   Daumas-Duport C, Scheithauer B, O'Fallon J, Kelly P. Grading of astrocytomas. A simple and reproducible method. Cancer 1988, **62**: 2152–2165.

318   Fisher PG, Breiter SN, Carson BS, Wharam MD, Williams JA, Weingart JD, Foer DR, Goldthwaite PT, Tihan T, Burger PC. A clinicopathologic reappraisal of brain stem tumor classification. Identification of pilocystic astrocytoma and fibrillary astrocytoma as distinct entities. Cancer 2000, **89**: 1569–1576.

319   Frappaz D, Ricci AC, Kohler R, Bret P, Mottolese C. Diffuse brain stem tumor in an adolescent with multiple enchondromatosis (Ollier's disease). Childs Nerv Syst 1999, **15**: 222–225.

320   Giannini C, Scheithauer BW, Burger PC, Christensen MR, Wollan PC, Sebo TJ, Forsyth PA, Hayostek CJ. Cellular proliferation in pilocytic and diffuse astrocytomas. J Neuropathol Exp Neurol 1999, **58**: 46–53.

321   Gultekin SH, Dalmau J, Graus Y, Posner JB, Rosenblum MK. Anti-Hu immunolabeling as an index of neuronal differentiation in human brain tumors. A study of 112 central neuroepithelial neoplasms. Am J Surg Pathol 1998, **22**: 195–200.

322   Haddad SF, Moore SA, Schelper RL, Goeken JA. Vascular smooth muscle hyperplasia underlies the formation of glomeruloid vascular structures of glioblastoma multiforme. J Neuropathol Exp Neurol 1992, **51**: 488–492.

323   Hilton DA, Love S, Barber R, Ellison D, Sandeman DR. Accumulation of p53 and Ki-67 expression do not predict survival in patients with fibrillary astrocytomas or the response of these tumors to radiotherapy. Neurosurgery 1998, **42**: 724–729.

324   Hilton DA, Penney M, Evans B, Sanders H, Love S. Evaluation of molecular markers in low-grade diffuse astrocytomas. Loss of p16 and retinoblastoma protein expression is associated with short survival. Am J Surg Pathol 2002, **26**: 472–478.

325   Hitchcock E, Morris CS. Cross reactivity of anti-epithelial membrane antigen monoclonal for reactive and neoplastic glial cells. J Neurooncol 1987, **4**: 345–352.

326   Ino Y, Zlatescu MC, Sasaki H, Macdonald DR, Stemmer-Rachamimov AO, Jhung S, Ramsay DA, von Deimling A, Louis DN, Cairncross JG. Long survival and therapeutic responses in patients with histologically disparate high-grade gliomas demonstrating chromosome 1p loss. J Neurosurg 2000, **92**: 983–990.

327 Kakita A, Wakabayashi K, Takahashi H, Ohama E, Ikuta F, Tokiguchi S. Primary leptomeningeal glioma. Ultrastructural and laminin immunohistochemical studies. Acta Neuropathol (Berl) 1992, 83: 538–542.

328 Katsetos CD, Del Valle L, Geddes JF, Assimakopoulou M, Legido A, Boyd JC, Balin B, Parikh NA, Maraziotis T, de Chadarevian JP, Varakis JN, Matsas R, Spano A, Frankfurter A, Herman MM, Khalili K. Aberrant localization of the neuronal class III beta-tubulin in astrocytomas. Arch Pathol Lab Med 2001, 125: 613–624.

329 Kepes JJ, Fulling KH, Garcia JH. The clinical significance of "adenoid" formations of neoplastic astrocytes, imitating metastatic carcinoma, in gliosarcomas. A review of five cases. Clin Neuropathol 1982, 1: 139–150.

330 Kepes JJ, Rubinstein LJ. Malignant gliomas with heavily lipidized (foamy) tumor cells. A report of three cases with immunoperoxidase study. Cancer 1981, 47: 2451–2459.

331 Kleihues P, Cavenee WK (eds): World Health Organization classification of tumours. Pathology and genetics—tumours of the nervous system. Lyon, 2000, IARC Press, pp. 9–41.

332 Kleinschmidt-Demasters BK. Diffuse bone marrow metastases from glioblastoma multiforme. The role of dural invasion. Hum Pathol 1996, 27: 197–201.

333 Krouwer HG, Davis RL, Silver P, Prados M. Gemistocytic astrocytomas. A reappraisal. J Neurosurg 1991, 74: 399–406.

334 Lunsford LD, Somaza S, Kondziolka D, Flickinger JC. Survival after stereotactic biopsy and irradiation of cerebral nonanaplastic, nonpilocytic astrocytoma. J Neurosurg 1995, 82: 523–529.

335 Margetts JC, Kalyan-Raman UP. Giant-celled glioblastoma of brain. A clinico-pathological and radiological study of ten cases (including immunohistochemistry and ultrastructure). Cancer 1989, 63: 524–531.

336 McCormack BM, Miller DC, Budzilovich GN, Voorhees GJ, Ransohoff J. Treatment and survival of low-grade astrocytoma in adults-1977–1988. Neurosurgery 1992, 31: 636–642; discussion 642.

337 Montine TJ, Vandersteenhoven JJ, Aguzzi A, Boyko OB, Dodge RK, Kerns BJ, Burger PC. Prognostic significance of ki-67 proliferation index in supratentorial fibrillary astrocytic neoplasms. Neurosurgery 1994, 34: 674–678; discussion 678–679.

338 Mork SJ, Rubinstein LJ, Kepes JJ. Patterns of epithelial metaplasia in malignant gliomas. I. Papillary formations mimicking medulloepithelioma. J Neuropathol Exp Neurol 1988, 47: 93–100.

339 Mork SJ, Rubinstein LJ, Kepes JJ, Perentes E, Uphoff DF. Patterns of epithelial metaplasia in malignant gliomas. II. Squamous differentiation of epithelial-like formations in gliosarcomas and glioblastomas. J Neuropathol Exp Neurol 1988, 47: 101–118.

340 Mueller W, Lass U, Herms J, Kuchelmeister K, Bergmann M, von Deimling A. Clonal analysis in glioblastoma with epithelial differentiation. Brain Pathol 2001, 11: 39–43.

341 Oh D, Prayson RA. Evaluation of epithelial and keratin markers in glioblastoma multiforme. An immunohistochemical study. Arch Pathol Lab Med 1999, 123: 917–920.

342 Palma L, Celli P, Maleci A, Di Lorenzo N, Cantore G. Malignant monstrocellular brain tumours. A study of 42 surgically treated cases. Acta Neurochir (Wien) 1989, 97: 17–25.

343 Pollack IF, Finkelstein SD, Woods J, Burnham J, Holmes EJ, Hamilton RL, Yates AJ, Boyett JM, Finlay JL, Sposto R. Expression of p53 and prognosis in children with malignant gliomas. N Engl J Med 2002, 346: 420–427.

344 Prayson RA, Estes ML. Protoplasmic astrocytoma. A clinicopathologic study of 16 tumors. Am J Clin Pathol 1995, 103: 705–709.

345 Prayson RA, Estes ML. MIB1 and p53 immunoreactivity in protoplasmic astrocytomas. Pathol Int 1996, 46: 862–866.

346 Ramsay DA, Goshko V, Nag S. Primary spinal leptomeningeal astrocytoma. Acta Neuropathol (Berl) 1990, 80: 338–341.

347 Rasheed A, Herndon JE, Stenzel TT, Raetz JG, Kendelhardt J, Friedman HS, Friedman AH, Bigner DD, Bigner SH, McLendon RE. Molecular markers of prognosis in astrocytic tumors. Cancer 2002, 94: 2688–2697.

348 Rosenblum MK, Erlandson RA, Budzilovich GN. The lipid-rich epithelioid glioblastoma. Am J Surg Pathol 1991, 15: 925–934.

349 Scheithauer BW, Bruner JM. The ultrastructural spectrum of astrocytic neoplasms. Ultrastruct Pathol 1987, 11: 535–581.

350 Schmidt MC, Antweiler S, Urban N, Mueller W, Kuklik A, Meyer-Puttlitz B, Wiestler OD, Louis DN, Fimmers R, von Deimling A. Impact of genotype and morphology on the prognosis of glioblastoma. J Neuropathol Exp Neurol 2002, 61: 321–328.

351 Val-Bernal F, Ruiz JC, Cotorruelo JG, Arias M. Glioblastoma multiforme of donor origin after renal transplantation. Report of a case. Hum Pathol 1993, 24: 1256–1259.

352 Watanabe K, Peraud A, Gratas C, Wakai S, Kleihues P, Ohgaki H. p53 and PTEN gene mutations in gemistocytic astrocytomas. Acta Neuropathol (Berl) 1998, 95: 559–564.

353 Watanabe K, Tachibana O, Yonekawa Y, Kleihues P, Ohgaki H. Role of gemistocytes in astrocytoma progression. Lab Invest 1997, 76: 277–284.

354 Wesseling P, Schlingemann RO, Rietveld FJ, Link M, Burger PC, Ruiter DJ. Early and extensive contribution of pericytes/vascular smooth muscle cells to microvascular proliferation in glioblastoma multiforme. An immuno-light and immuno-electron microscopic study. J Neuropathol Exp Neurol 1995, 54: 304–310.

355 Wolf HK, Buslei R, Schmidt-Kastner R, Schmidt-Kastner PK, Pietsch T, Wiestler OD, Bluhmke I. NeuN. A useful neuronal marker for diagnostic histopathology. J Histochem Cytochem 1996, 44: 1167–1171.

356 Yaziji H, Massarani-Wafai R, Gujrati M, Kuhns JG, Martin AW, Parker JC, Jr. Role of p53 immunohistochemistry in differentiating reactive gliosis from malignant astrocytic lesions. Am J Surg Pathol 1996, 20: 1086–1090.

Pilocytic astrocytomas

357 Alvord EC, Jr., Lofton S. Gliomas of the optic nerve or chiasm. Outcome by patients' age, tumor site, and treatment. J Neurosurg 1988, 68: 85–98.

358 Balkhoyor KB, Bernstein M. Involution of diencephalic pilocytic astrocytoma after partial resection. Report of two cases in adults. J Neurosurg 2000, 93: 484–486.

359 Burger PC, Scheithauer BW, Paulus W, Szymas J, Giannini C, Kleihues P. Pilocytic astrocytoma. In Kleihues P, Cavenee WK (eds): World Health Organization classification of tumours. Pathology and genetics—tumours of the nervous system. Lyon, 2000, IARC Press, pp. 45–51.

360 Dirks PB, Jay V, Becker LE, Drake JM, Humphreys RP, Hoffman HJ, Rutka JT. Development of anaplastic changes in low-grade astrocytomas of childhood. Neurosurgery 1994, 34: 68–78.

361 Forsyth PA, Shaw EG, Scheithauer BW, O'Fallon JR, Layton DD, Jr., Katzmann JA. Supratentorial pilocytic astrocytomas. A clinicopathologic, prognostic, and flow cytometric study of 51 patients. Cancer 1993, 72: 1335–1342.

362 Hayostek CJ, Shaw EG, Scheithauer B, O'Fallon JR, Weiland TL, Schomberg PJ, Kelly PJ, Hu TC. Astrocytomas of the cerebellum. A comparative clinicopathologic study of pilocytic and diffuse astrocytomas. Cancer 1993, 72: 856–869.

363 Ilgren EB, Kinnier-Wilson LM, Stiller CA. Gliomas in neurofibromatosis. A series of 89 cases with evidence for enhanced malignancy in associated cerebellar astrocytomas. Pathol Annu 1985, 20 Pt 1: 331–358.

364 Ito S, Hoshino T, Shibuya M, Prados MD, Edwards MS, Davis RL. Proliferative characteristics of juvenile pilocytic astrocytomas determined by bromodeoxyuridine labeling. Neurosurgery 1992, **31**: 413–419.

365 Iwaki T, Iwaki A, Tateishi J, Sakaki Y, Goldman JE. Alpha b-crystallin and 27-kd heat shock protein are regulated by stress conditions in the central nervous system and accumulate in Rosenthal fibers. Am J Pathol 1993, **143**: 487–495.

366 Katsetos CD, Krishna L, Friedberg E, Reidy J, Karkavelas G, Savory J. Lobar pilocytic astrocytomas of the cerebral hemispheres. II. Pathobiology—morphogenesis of the eosinophilic granular bodies. Clin Neuropathol 1994, **13**: 306–314.

367 Lach B, Sikorska M, Rippstein P, Gregor A, Staines W, Davie TR. Immunoelectron microscopy of Rosenthal fibers. Acta Neuropathol (Berl) 1991, **81**: 503–509.

368 McGirr SJ, Kelly PJ, Scheithauer BW. Stereotactic resection of juvenile pilocytic astrocytomas of the thalamus and basal ganglia. Neurosurgery 1987, **20**: 447–452.

369 Minehan KJ, Shaw EG, Scheithauer BW, Davis DL, Onofrio BM. Spinal cord astrocytoma. Pathological and treatment considerations. J Neurosurg 1995, **83**: 590–595.

370 Murayama S, Bouldin TW, Suzuki K. Immunocytochemical and ultrastructural studies of eosinophilic granular bodies in astrocytic tumors. Acta Neuropathol (Berl) 1992, **83**: 408–414.

371 Pagni CA, Giordana MT, Canavero S. Benign recurrence of a pilocytic cerebellar astrocytoma 36 years after radical removal. Case report. Neurosurgery 1991, **28**: 606–609.

372 Perilongo G, Carollo C, Salviati L, Murgia A, Pillon M, Basso G, Gardiman M, Laverda A. Diencephalic syndrome and disseminated juvenile pilocytic astrocytomas of the hypothalamic-optic chiasm region. Cancer 1997, **80**: 142–146.

373 Pollack IF, Claassen D, al-Shboul Q, Janosky JE, Deutsch M. Low-grade gliomas of the cerebral hemispheres in children. An analysis of 71 cases. J Neurosurg 1995, **82**: 536–547.

374 Pollack IF, Hurtt M, Pang D, Albright AL. Dissemination of low-grade intracranial astrocytomas in children. Cancer 1994, **73**: 2869–2878.

375 Tomlinson FH, Scheithauer BW, Hayostek CJ, Parisi JE, Meyer FB, Shaw EG, Weiland TL, Katzmann JA, Jack CR, Jr: The significance of atypia and histologic malignancy in pilocytic astrocytoma of the cerebellum. A clinicopathologic and flow cytometric study. J Child Neurol 1994, **9**: 301–310.

376 Vajtai I, Yonekawa Y, Schäuble B, Paulus W. Melanotic astrocytoma. Acta Neuropathol (Berl) 1996, **91**: 549–553.

Pilomyxoid astrocytoma

377 Fuller CE, Frankel B, Smith M, Rodziewitz G, Landas SK, Caruso R, Schelper R. Suprasellar monomorphous pilomyxoid neoplasm. An ultastructural analysis. Clin Neuropathol 2001, **20**: 256–262.

378 Tihan T, Fisher PG, Kepner JL, Godfraind C, McComb RD, Goldthwaite PT, Burger PC. Pediatric astrocytomas with monomorphous pilomyxoid features and a less favorable outcome. J Neuropathol Exp Neurol 1999, **58**: 1061–1068.

Pleomorphic xanthoastrocytoma

379 Giannini C, Scheithauer BW, Burger PC, Brat DJ, Wollan PC, Lach B, O'Neill BP. Pleomorphic xanthoastrocytoma. What do we really know about it? Cancer 1999, **85**: 2033–2045.

380 Giannini C, Scheithauer BW, Lopes MB, Hirose T, Kros JM, VandenBerg SR. Immunophenotype of pleomorphic xanthoastrocytoma. Am J Surg Pathol 2002, **26**: 479–485.

381 Herpers MJ, Freling G, Beuls EA. Pleomorphic xanthoastrocytoma in the spinal cord. Case report. J Neurosurg 1994, **80**: 564–569.

382 Iwaki T, Fukui M, Kondo A, Matsushima T, Takeshita I. Epithelial properties of pleomorphic xanthoastrocytomas determined in ultrastructural and immunohistochemical studies. Acta Neuropathol (Berl) 1987, **74**: 142–150.

383 Kepes JJ, Rubinstein LJ, Eng LF. Pleomorphic xanthoastrocytoma. A distinctive meningocerebral glioma of young subjects with relatively favorable prognosis. A study of 12 cases. Cancer 1979, **44**: 1839–1852.

384 Kros JM, Vecht CJ, Stefanko SZ. The pleomorphic xanthoastrocytoma and its differential diagnosis. A study of five cases. Hum Pathol 1991, **22**: 1128–1135.

385 Lach B, Duggal N, DaSilva VF, Benoit BG. Association of pleomorphic xanthoastrocytoma with cortical dysplasia and neuronal tumors. A report of three cases. Cancer 1996, **78**: 2551–2563.

386 McLean CA, Jellinek DA, Gonzales MF. Diffuse leptomeningeal spread of pleomorphic xanthoastrocytoma. J Clin Neurosci 1998, **5**: 230–233.

387 Perry A, Giannini C, Scheithauer BW, Rojiani AM, Yachnis AT, Seo IS, Johnson PC, Kho J, Shapiro S. Composite pleomorphic xanthoastrocytoma and ganglioglioma. Report of four cases and review of the literature. Am J Surg Pathol 1997, **21**: 763–771.

388 Prayson RA, Morris HH, 3rd. Anaplastic pleomorphic xanthoastrocytoma. Arch Pathol Lab Med 1998, **122**: 1082–1086.

389 Primavera J, Nikas DC, Zamani AA, Shafman T, Alexander E, 3rd, De Girolami U, Louis DN. Clear cell pleomorphic xanthoastrocytoma. Case report. Acta Neuropathol (Berl) 2001, **102**: 404–408.

390 Snipes GJ, Horoupian DS, Shuer LM, Silverberg GD. Pleomorphic granular cell astrocytoma of the pineal gland. Cancer 1992, **70**: 2159–2165.

391 Sugita Y, Kepes JJ, Shigemori M, Kuramoto S, Reifenberger G, Kiwit JC, Wechsler W. Pleomorphic xanthoastrocytoma with desmoplastic reaction. Angiomatous variant. Report of two cases. Clin Neuropathol 1990, **9**: 271–278.

392 Wasdahl DA, Scheithauer BW, Andrews BT, Jeffrey RA, Jr: Cerebellar pleomorphic xanthoastrocytoma. Case report. Neurosurgery 1994, **35**: 947–950.

393 Zarate JO, Sampaolesi R. Pleomorphic xanthoastrocytoma of the retina. Am J Surg Pathol 1999, **23**: 79–81.

Subependymal giant cell astrocytoma (tuberous sclerosis)

394 Chow CW, Klug GL, Lewis EA. Subependymal giant-cell astrocytoma in children. An unusual discrepancy between histological and clinical features. J Neurosurg 1988, **68**: 880–883.

395 Gyure KA, Prayson RA. Subependymal giant cell astrocytoma: A clinicopathologic study with HMB-45 and MIB-1 immunohistochemical analysis. Mod Pathol 1997, **10**: 313–317.

396 Hirose T, Scheithauer BW, Lopes MB, Gerber HA, Altermatt HJ, Hukee MJ, VandenBerg SR, Charlesworth JC. Tuber and subependymal giant cell astrocytoma associated with tuberous sclerosis. An immunohistochemical, ultrastructural, and immunoelectron microscopic study. Acta Neuropathol (Berl) 1995, **90**: 387–399.

397 Lopes MB, Altermatt HJ, Scheithauer BW, Shepherd CW, VandenBerg SR. Immunohistochemical characterization of subependymal giant cell astrocytomas. Acta Neuropathol (Berl) 1996, **91**: 368–375.

398 Padmalatha C, Harruff RC, Ganick D, Hafez GB. Glioblastoma multiforme with tuberous sclerosis. Report of a case. Arch Pathol Lab Med 1980, **104**: 649–650.

399 Shepherd CW, Scheithauer BW, Gomez MR, Altermatt HJ, Katzmann JA. Subependymal giant cell astrocytoma. A clinical, pathological, and flow cytometric study. Neurosurgery 1991, **28**: 864–868.

400 Wiestler OD, Lopes BS, Green AJ, Vinters HV. Tuberous sclerosis complex and subependymal giant cell astrocytoma. In Kleihues P, Cavenee WK (eds): World Health Organization

classification of tumours. Pathology and genetics—tumours of the nervous system. Lyon, 2000, IARC Press, pp. 227–230.

Oligodendrogliomas

401 Burger PC, Minn AY, Smith JS, Borell TJ, Jedlicka AE, Huntley BK, Goldthwaite PT, Jenkins RB, Feuerstein BG. Losses of chromosomal arms 1p and 19q in the diagnosis of oligodendroglioma. A study of paraffin-embedded sections. Mod Pathol 2001, **14**: 842–853.

402 Cairncross JG, Ueki K, Zlatescu MC, Lisle DK, Finkelstein DM, Hammond RR, Silver JS, Stark PC, Macdonald DR, Ino Y, Ramsay DA, Louis DN. Specific genetic predictors of chemotherapeutic response and survival in patients with anaplastic oligodendrogliomas. J Natl Cancer Inst 1998, **90**: 1473–1479.

403 Chen R, Macdonald DR, Ramsay DA. Primary diffuse leptomeningeal oligodendroglioma. Case report. J Neurosurg 1995, **83**: 724–728.

404 Coons SW, Johnson PC, Pearl DK. The prognostic significance of Ki-67 labeling indices for oligodendrogliomas. Neurosurgery 1997, **41**: 878–884.

405 de la Monte SM. Uniform lineage of oligodendrogliomas. Am J Pathol 1989, **135**: 529–540.

406 Dehghani F, Schachenmayr W, Laun A, Korf HW. Prognostic implication of histopathological, immunohistochemical and clinical features of oligodendrogliomas. A study of 89 cases. Acta Neuropathol (Berl) 1998, **95**: 493–504.

407 Giannini C, Scheithauer BW, Weaver AL, Burger PC, Kros JM, Mork S, Graeber MB, Bauserman S, Buckner JC, Burton J, Riepe R, Tazelaar HD, Nascimento AG, Crotty T, Keeney GL, Pernicone P, Altermatt H. Oligodendrogliomas. Reproducibility and prognostic value of histologic diagnosis and grading. J Neuropathol Exp Neurol 2001, **60**: 248–262.

408 Herpers MJ, Budka H. Glial fibrillary acidic protein (GFAP) in oligodendroglial tumors. Gliofibrillary oligodendroglioma and transitional oligoastrocytoma as subtypes of oligodendroglioma. Acta Neuropathol (Berl) 1984, **64**: 265–272.

409 Ino Y, Betensky RA, Zlatescu MC, Sasaki H, Macdonald DR, Stemmer-Rachamimov AO, Ramsay DA, Cairncross JG, Louis DN. Molecular subtypes of anaplastic oligodendroglioma. Implications for patient management at diagnosis. Clin Cancer Res 2001, **7**: 839–845.

410 Katsetos CD, Del Valle L, Geddes JF, Aldape K, Boyd JC, Legido A, Khalili K, Perentes E, Mork SJ. Localization of the neuronal class III beta-tubulin in oligodendrogliomas. Comparison with Ki-67 proliferative index and 1p/19q status. J Neuropathol Exp Neurol 2002, **61**: 307–320.

411 Kros JM, de Jong AA, van der Kwast TH. Ultrastructural characterization of transitional cells in oligodendrogliomas. J Neuropathol Exp Neurol 1992, **51**: 186–193.

412 Kros JM, van den Brink WA, Loon-van Luyt JJ, Stefanko SZ. Signet-ring cell oligodendroglioma. Report of two cases and discussion of the differential diagnosis. Acta Neuropathol (Berl) 1997, **93**: 638–643.

413 Kros JM, Van Eden CG, Stefanko SZ, Waayer-Van Batenburg M, van der Kwast TH. Prognostic implications of glial fibrillary acidic protein containing cell types in oligodendrogliomas. Cancer 1990, **66**: 1204–1212.

414 Macdonald DR, O'Brien RA, Gilbert JJ, Cairncross JG. Metastatic anaplastic oligodendroglioma. Neurology 1989, **39**: 1593–1596.

415 Marek J, Jakubaszko-Turkiewicz J, Oficjalska-Mlynczak J, Markowska-Woyciechowska A. Retinal oligodendroglioma. Am J Ophthalmol 1999, **128**: 389–391.

416 Mikami Y, Shirabe T, Hata S, Watanabe A. Oligodendroglioma with signet-ring cell morphology. A case report with an immunohistochemical and ultrastructural study. Pathol Int 1998, **48**: 144–150.

417 Min KW, Scheithauer BW. Oligodendroglioma. The ultrastructural spectrum. Ultrastruct Pathol 1994, **18**: 47–60.

418 Mueller W, Hartmann C, Hoffmann A, Lanksch W, Kiwit J, Tonn J, Veelken J, Schramm J, Weller M, Wiestler OD, Louis DN, von Deimling A. Genetic signature of oligoastrocytomas correlates with tumor location and denotes distinct molecular subsets. Am J Pathol 2002, **161**: 313–319.

419 Nakagawa Y, Perentes E, Rubinstein LJ. Immunohistochemical characterization of oligodendrogliomas. An analysis of multiple markers. Acta Neuropathol (Berl) 1986, **72**: 15–22.

420 Perry A, Scheithauer BW, Macaulay R, Raffel C, Roth KA, Kros JM. Oligodendrogliomas with neurocytic differentiation. A report of four cases with diagnostic and histogenetic implications. J Neuropathol Exp Neurol 2002, **61**: 947–955.

421 Reifenberger G, Kros JM, Burger PC, Louis DN, Collins VP. Oligodendroglial tumours. In Kleihues P, Cavenee WK (eds): World Health Organization classification of tumours. Pathology and genetics—tumours of the nervous system. Lyon, 2000, IARC Press, pp. 56–64.

422 Rogers LR, Estes ML, Rosenbloom SA, Harrold L. Primary leptomeningeal oligodendroglioma. Case report. Neurosurgery 1995, **36**: 166–168.

423 Sasaki H, Zlatescu MC, Betensky RA, Johnk LB, Cutone AN, Cairncross JG, Louis DN. Histopathological-molecular genetic correlations in referral pathologist-diagnosed low-grade "oligodendroglioma". J Neuropathol Exp Neurol 2002, **61**: 58–63.

424 Smith JS, Alderete B, Minn Y, Borell TJ, Perry A, Mohapatra G, Hosek SM, Kimmel D, O'Fallon J, Yates A, Feuerstein BG, Burger PC, Scheithauer BW, Jenkins RB. Localization of common deletion regions on 1p and 19q in human gliomas and their association with histological subtype. Oncogene 1999, **18**: 4144–4152.

425 Smith JS, Perry A, Borell TJ, Lee HK, O'Fallon J, Hosek SM, Kimmel D, Yates A, Burger PC, Scheithauer BW, Jenkins RB. Alterations of chromosome arms 1p and 19q as predictors of survival in oligodendrogliomas, astrocytomas, and mixed oligoastrocytomas. J Clin Oncol 2000, **18**: 636–645.

426 Takei Y, Mirra SS, Miles ML. Eosinophilic granular cells in oligodendrogliomas. An ultrastructural study. Cancer 1976, **38**: 1968–1976.

427 Wharton SB, Chan KK, Hamilton FA, Anderson JR. Expression of neuronal markers in oligodendrogliomas. An immunohistochemical study. Neuropathol Appl Neurobiol 1998, **24**: 302–308.

428 Wolf HK, Buslei R, Blumcke I, Wiestler OD, Pietsch T. Neural antigens in oligodendrogliomas and dysembryoplastic neuroepithelial tumors. Acta Neuropathol (Berl) 1997, **94**: 436–443.

429 Zlatescu MC, TehraniYazdi A, Sasaki H, Megyesi JF, Betensky RA, Louis DN, Cairncross JG. Tumor location and growth pattern correlate with genetic signature in oligodendroglial neoplasms. Cancer Res 2001, **61**: 6713–6715.

Ependymal tumors

430 Afra D, Muller W, Slowik F, Wilcke O, Budka H, Turoczy L. Supratentorial lobar ependymomas. Reports on the grading and survival periods in 80 cases, including 46 recurrences. Acta Neurochir (Wien) 1983, **69**: 243–251.

431 al Moutaery K, Aabed MY, Ojeda VJ. Cerebral and spinal cord myxopapillary ependymomas. A case report. Pathology 1996, **28**: 373–376.

432 Ang LC, Taylor AR, Bergin D, Kaufmann JC. An immunohistochemical study of papillary tumors in the central nervous system. Cancer 1990, **65**: 2712–2719.

433 Brown DF, Chason DP, Schwartz LF, Coimbra CP, Rushing EJ. Supratentorial giant cell ependymoma. A case report. Mod Pathol 1998, **11**: 398–403.

434 Coffin CM, Swanson PE, Wick MR, Dehner LP. An immunohistochemical comparison of chordoma with renal cell carcinoma, colorectal adenocarcinoma, and myxopapillary ependymoma. A potential diagnostic dilemma in the diminutive biopsy. Mod Pathol 1993, **6**: 531–538.

435 Craver RD, McGarry P. Delicate longitudinal nuclear grooves in childhood ependymomas. Arch Pathol Lab Med 1994, **118**: 919–921.

436 Crotty TB, Hooker RP, Swensen SJ, Scheithauer BW, Myers JL. Primary malignant ependymoma of the lung. Mayo Clin Proc 1992, **67**: 373–378.

437 Davis C, Barnard RO. Malignant behavior of myxopapillary ependymoma. Report of three cases. J Neurosurg 1985, **62**: 925–929.

438 Duggan MA, Hugh J, Nation JG, Robertson DI, Stuart GC. Ependymoma of the uterosacral ligament. Cancer 1989, **64**: 2565–2571.

439 Epstein FJ, Farmer JP, Freed D. Adult intramedullary spinal cord ependymomas. The result of surgery in 38 patients. J Neurosurg 1993, **79**: 204–209.

440 Figarella-Branger D, Civatte M, Bouvier-Labit C, Gouvernet J, Gambarelli D, Gentet JC, Lena G, Choux M, Pellissier JF. Prognostic factors in intracranial ependymomas in children. J Neurosurg 2000, **93**: 605–613.

441 Furness PN, Lowe J, Tarrant GS. Subepithelial basement membrane deposition and intermediate filament expression in choroid plexus neoplasms and ependymomas. Histopathology 1990, **16**: 251–255.

442 Guerrieri C, Jarlsfelt I. Ependymoma of the ovary. A case report with immunohistochemical, ultrastructural, and DNA cytometric findings, as well as histogenetic considerations. Am J Surg Pathol 1993, **17**: 623–632.

443 Helwig EB, Stern JB. Subcutaneous sacrococcygeal myxopapillary ependymoma. A clinicopathologic study of 32 cases. Am J Clin Pathol 1984, **81**: 156–161.

444 Ho KC, Meyer G, Caya J, Tieu TM, Prentiss A. Craniopharyngioma and "reactive" subependymoma of the third ventricle. A case report. Clin Neuropathol 1987, **6**: 12–15.

445 Ho KL. Microtubular aggregates within rough endoplasmic reticulum in myxopapillary ependymoma of the filum terminale. Arch Pathol Lab Med 1990, **114**: 956–960.

446 Horn B, Heideman R, Geyer R, Pollack I, Packer R, Goldwein J, Tomita T, Schomberg P, Ater J, Luchtman-Jones L, Rivlin K, Lamborn K, Prados M, Bollen A, Berger M, Dahl G, McNeil E, Patterson K, Shaw D, Kubalik M, Russo C. A multi-institutional retrospective study of intracranial ependymoma in children. Identification of risk factors. J Pediatr Hematol Oncol 1999, **21**: 203–211.

447 Jallo GI, Zagzag D, Epstein F. Intramedullary subependymoma of the spinal cord. Neurosurgery 1996, **38**: 251–257.

448 Kline MJ, Kays DW, Rojiani AM. Extradural myxopapillary ependymoma. Report of two cases and review of the literature. Pediatr Pathol Lab Med 1996, **16**: 813–822.

449 Little NS, Morgan MK, Eckstein RP. Primary ependymoma of a cranial nerve. Case report. J Neurosurg 1994, **81**: 792–794.

450 Lombardi D, Scheithauer BW, Meyer FB, Forbes GS, Shaw EG, Gibney DJ, Katzmann JA. Symptomatic subependymoma. A clinicopathological and flow cytometric study. J Neurosurg 1991, **75**: 583–588.

451 Louis DN, Hedley-Whyte ET, Martuza RL. Sarcomatous proliferation of the vasculature in a subependymoma. A follow-up study of sarcomatous dedifferentiation. Acta Neuropathol (Berl) 1990, **80**: 573–574.

452 Mannoji H, Becker LE. Ependymal and choroid plexus tumors. Cytokeratin and GFAP expression. Cancer 1988, **61**: 1377–1385.

453 Maruyama R, Koga K, Nakahara T, Kishida K, Nabeshima K. Cerebral myxopapillary ependymoma. Hum Pathol 1992, **23**: 960–962.

454 Mathews T, Moossy J. Gliomas containing bone and cartilage. J Neuropathol Exp Neurol 1974, **33**: 456–471.

455 Miettinen M, Clark R, Virtanen I. Intermediate filament proteins in choroid plexus and ependyma and their tumors. Am J Pathol 1986, **123**: 231–240.

456 Min KW, Scheithauer BW. Clear cell ependymoma. A mimic of oligodendroglioma. Clinicopathologic and ultrastructural considerations. Am J Surg Pathol 1997, **21**: 820–826.

457 Miralbell R, Louis DN, O'Keeffe D, Rosenberg AE, Suit HD. Metastatic ependymoma of the sacrum. Cancer 1990, **65**: 2353–2355.

458 Nobles E, Lee R, Kircher T. Mediastinal ependymoma. Hum Pathol 1991, **22**: 94–96.

459 Prayson RA. Clinicopathologic study of 61 patients with ependymoma including MIB-1 immunohistochemistry. Ann Diagn Pathol 1999, **3**: 11–18.

460 Pulitzer DR, Martin PC, Collins PC, Ralph DR. Subcutaneous sacrococcygeal ("myxopapillary") ependymal rests. Am J Surg Pathol 1988, **12**: 672–677.

461 Robertson PL, Zeltzer PM, Boyett JM, Rorke LB, Allen JC, Geyer JR, Stanley P, Li H, Albright AL, McGuire-Cullen P, Finlay JL, Stevens KR, Jr, Milstein JM, Packer RJ, Wisoff J. Survival and prognostic factors following radiation therapy and chemotherapy for ependymomas in children. A report of the Children's Cancer Group. J Neurosurg 1998, **88**: 695–703.

462 Rosenblum MK, Erlandson RA, Aleksic SN, Budzilovich GN. Melanotic ependymoma and subependymoma. Am J Surg Pathol 1990, **14**: 729–736.

463 Ruchoux MM, Kepes JJ, Dhellemmes P, Hamon M, Maurage CA, Lecomte M, Gall CM, Chilton J. Lipomatous differentiation in ependymomas. A report of three cases and comparison with similar changes reported in other central nervous system neoplasms of neuroectodermal origin. Am J Surg Pathol 1998, **22**: 338–346.

464 Ryken TC, Robinson RA, VanGilder JC. Familial occurrence of subependymoma. Report of two cases. J Neurosurg 1994, **80**: 1108–1111.

465 Sara A, Bruner JM, Mackay B. Ultrastructure of ependymoma. Ultrastruct Pathol 1994, **18**: 33–42.

466 Sonneland PR, Scheithauer BW, Onofrio BM. Myxopapillary ependymoma. A clinicopathologic and immunocytochemical study of 77 cases. Cancer 1985, **56**: 883–893.

467 Takahashi H, Goto J, Emura I, Honma T, Hasegawa K, Uchiyama S. Lipidized (foamy) tumor cells in a spinal cord ependymoma with collagenous metaplasia. Acta Neuropathol (Berl) 1998, **95**: 421–425.

468 Tomlinson FH, Scheithauer BW, Kelly PJ, Forbes GS. Subependymoma with rhabdomyosarcomatous differentiation: Report of a case and literature review. Neurosurgery 1991, **28**: 761–768.

469 Twiss JL, Anderson LJ, Horoupian DS. Globular glial fibrillary acidic protein-reactive cytoplasmic inclusions in ependymoma. An immunoelectron-microscopic study. Acta Neuropathol (Berl) 1993, **85**: 658–662.

470 Vege KD, Giannini C, Scheithauer BW. The immunophenotype of ependymomas. Appl Immunohistochem Mol Morphol 2000, **8**: 25–31.

471 Wiestler OD, Schiffer D, Coons SW, Prayson RA, Rosenblum MK. Ependymal tumors. In Kleihues P, Cavenee WK (eds): World Health Organization classification of tumours. Pathology and genetics—tumours of the nervous system. Lyon, 2000, IARC Press, pp. 71–81.

472 Zec N, De Girolami U, Schofield DE, Scott RM, Anthony DC. Giant cell ependymoma of the filum terminale. A report of two cases. Am J Surg Pathol 1996, **20**: 1091–1101.

473 Zuppan CW, Mierau GW, Weeks DA. Ependymoma with signet-ring cells. Ultrastruct Pathol 1994, **18**: 43–46.

Mixed gliomas

474 Coons SW, Johnson PC, Scheithauer BW, Yates AJ, Pearl DK. Improving diagnostic accuracy and interobserver concordance in the classification and grading of primary gliomas. Cancer 1997, **79**: 1381–1393.

475 Donahue B, Scott CB, Nelson JS, Rotman M, Murray KJ, Nelson DF, Banker FL, Earle JD, Fischbach JA, Asbell SO, Gaspar LE, Markoe AM, Curran W. Influence of an oligodendroglial component on the survival of patients with anaplastic astrocytomas: a report of Radiation Therapy Oncology Group 83–02. Int J Radiat Oncol Biol Phys 1997, **38**: 911–914.

476 Hart MN, Petito CK, Earle KM. Mixed gliomas. Cancer 1974, **33**: 134–140.

477 Kim L, Hochberg FH, Thornton AF, Harsh GR 4th, Patel H, Finkelstein D, Louis DN. Procarbazine, lomustine, and vincristine (PCV) chemotherapy for grade III and grade IV oligoastrocytomas. J Neurosurg 1996, **85**: 602–607.

478 Maintz D, Fiedler K, Koopmann J, Rollbrocker B, Nechev S, Lenartz D, Stangl AP, Louis DN, Schramm J, Wiestler OD, von Deimling A. Molecular genetic evidence for subtypes of oligoastrocytomas. J Neuropathol Exp Neurol 1997, **56**: 1098–1104.

479 Shaw EG, Scheithauer BW, O'Fallon JR, Davis DH. Mixed oligoastrocytomas: a survival and prognostic factor analysis. Neurosurgery 1994, **34**: 577–582.

Astroblastoma

480 Bonnin JM, Rubinstein LJ. Astroblastomas: A pathological study of 23 tumors, with a postoperative follow-up in 13 patients. Neurosurgery 1989, **25**: 6–13.

481 Brat DJ, Hirose Y, Cohen KJ, Feuerstein BG, Burger PC. Astroblastoma: Clinicopathologic features and chromosomal abnormalities defined by comparative genomic hybridization. Brain Pathol 2000, **10**: 342–352.

482 Cabello A, Madero S, Castresana A, Diaz-Lobato R. Astroblastoma: Electron microscopy and immunohistochemical findings: Case report. Surg Neurol 1991, **35**: 116–121.

483 Jay V, Edwards V, Squire J, Rutka J. Astroblastoma: Report of a case with ultrastructural, cell kinetic, and cytogenetic analysis. Pediatr Pathol 1993, **13**: 323–332.

484 Pizer BL, Moss T, Oakhill A, Webb D, Coakham HB. Congenital astroblastoma: An immunohistochemical study. Case report. J Neurosurg 1995, **83**: 550–555.

485 Rubinstein LJ, Herman MM. The astroblastoma and its possible cytogenic relationship to the tanycyte. An electron microscopic, immunohistochemical, tissue- and organ-culture study. Acta Neuropathol (Berl) 1989, **78**: 472–483.

486 Thiessen B, Finlay J, Kulkarni R, Rosenblum MK. Astroblastoma: Does histology predict biologic behavior? J Neurooncol 1998, **40**: 59–65.

Chordoid glioma of the third ventricle

487 Brat DJ, Scheithauer BW, Staugaitis SM, Cortez SC, Brecher K, Burger PC. Third ventricular chordoid glioma. A distinct clinicopathologic entity. J Neuropathol Exp Neurol 1998, **57**: 283–290.

488 Castellano-Sanchez AA, Schemankewitz E, Mazewski C, Brat DJ. Pediatric chordoid glioma with chondroid metaplasia. Pediatr Dev Pathol 2001, **4**: 564–567.

489 Cenacchi G, Roncaroli F, Cerasoli S, Ficarra G, Merli GA, Giangaspero F. Chordoid glioma of the third ventricle. An ultrastructural study of three cases with a histogenetic hypothesis. Am J Surg Pathol 2001, **25**: 401–405.

490 Pasquier B, Peoc'h M, Morrison AL, Gay E, Pasquier D, Grand S, Sindou M, Kopp N. Chordoid glioma of the third ventricle. A report of two new cases, with further evidence supporting an ependymal differentiation, and review of the literature. Am J Surg Pathol 2002, **26**: 1330–1342.

491 Raizer JJ, Shetty T, Gutin P, Obbens E, Holodny A, Antonescu CR, Rosenblum MK. Chordoid glioma. Report of a case with unusual histologic features, ultrastructural study and review of the literature. J Neurooncol 2003, **63**: 39–47.

492 Reifenberger G, Weber T, Weber RG, Wolter M, Brandis A, Kuchelmeister K, Pilz P, Reusche E, Lichter P, Wiestler OD. Chordoid glioma of the third ventricle. Immunohistochemical and molecular genetic characterization of a novel tumor entity. Brain Pathol 1999, **9**: 617–626.

Gliomatosis cerebri

493 Artigas J, Cervos-Navarro J, Iglesias JR, Ebhardt G. Gliomatosis cerebri. Clinical and histological findings. Clin Neuropathol 1985, **4**: 135–148.

494 Balko MG, Blisard KS, Samaha FJ. Oligodendroglial gliomatosis cerebri. Hum Pathol 1992, **23**: 706–707.

495 Cummings TJ, Hulette CM, Longee DC, Bottom KS, McLendon RE, Chu CT. Gliomatosis cerebri. Cytologic and autopsy findings in a case involving the entire neuraxis. Clin Neuropathol 1999, **18**: 190–197.

496 Jennings MT, Frenchman M, Shehab T, Johnson MD, Creasy J, LaPorte K, Dettbarn WD. Gliomatosis cerebri presenting as intractable epilepsy during early childhood. J Child Neurol 1995, **10**: 37–45.

497 Kim DG, Yang HJ, Park IA, Chi JG, Jung HW, Han DH, Choi KS, Cho BK. Gliomatosis cerebri. Clinical features, treatment, and prognosis. Acta Neurochir (Wien) 1998, **140**: 755–762.

498 Lantos PL, Bruner JM. Gliomatosis cerebri. In Kleihues PL, Cavanee WK (eds): World Health Organization classification of tumors. Pathology and genetics—tumours of the nervous system. Lyon, 2000, IARC Press, pp. 92–93.

499 Nishioka H, Ito H, Miki T. Difficulties in the antemortem diagnosis of gliomatosis cerebri. Report of a case with diffuse increase of gemistocyte-like cells, mimicking reactive gliosis. Br J Neurosurg 1996, **10**: 103–107.

Pituicytoma

500 Brat DJ, Scheithauer BW, Staugaitis SM, Holtzman RN, Morgello S, Burger PC. Pituicytoma. A distinctive low-grade glioma of the neurohypophysis. Am J Surg Pathol 2000, **24**: 362–368.

501 Cenacchi G, Giovenali P, Castrioto C, Giangaspero F. Pituicytoma. Ultrastructural evidence of a possible origin from folliculo-stellate cells of the adenohypophysis. Ultrastruct Pathol 2001, **25**: 309–312.

502 Roncaroli F, Scheithauer BW, Cenacchi G, Horvath E, Kovacs K, Lloyd RV, Abell-Aleff P, Santi M, Yates AJ. "Spindle cell oncocytoma" of the adenohypophysis. A tumor of folliculostellate cells? Am J Surg Pathol 2002, **26**: 1048–1055.

503 Schultz AB, Brat DJ, Oyesiku NM, Hunter SB. Intrasellar pituicytoma in a patient with other endocrine neoplasms. Arch Pathol Lab Med 2001, **125**: 527–530.

Gliomesenchymal tumors

504 Barnard RO, Bradford R, Scott T, Thomas DG. Gliomyosarcoma. Report of a case of rhabdomyosarcoma arising in a malignant glioma. Acta Neuropathol (Berl) 1986, **69**: 23–27.

505 Bonnin JM, Pena CE, Rubinstein LJ. Mixed capillary hemangioblastoma and glioma. A redefinition of the "angioglioma". J Neuropathol Exp Neurol 1983, **42**: 504–516.

506 Cerda-Nicolas M, Kepes JJ. Gliofibromas (including malignant forms), and gliosarcomas. A comparative study and review of the literature. Acta Neuropathol (Berl) 1993, **85**: 349–361.

507 Goodkin R, Zaias B, Michelsen WJ. Arteriovenous malformation and glioma. Coexistent or sequential? Case report. J Neurosurg 1990, 72: 798–805.

508 Grant JW, Steart PV, Aguzzi A, Jones DB, Gallagher PJ. Gliosarcoma. An immunohistochemical study. Acta Neuropathol (Berl) 1989, 79: 305–309.

509 Haddad SF, Moore SA, Schelper RL, Goeken JA. Smooth muscle can comprise the sarcomatous component of gliosarcomas. J Neuropathol Exp Neurol 1992, 51: 493–498.

510 Hayashi K, Ohara N, Jeon HJ, Akagi S, Takahashi K, Akagi T, Namba S. Gliosarcoma with features of chondroblastic osteosarcoma. Cancer 1993, 72: 850–855.

511 Jones H, Steart PV, Weller RO. Spindle-cell glioblastoma or gliosarcoma? Neuropathol Appl Neurobiol 1991, 17: 177–187.

512 Kepes JJ, Rubinstein LJ, Chiang H. The role of astrocytes in the formation of cartilage in gliomas. An immunohistochemical study of four cases. Am J Pathol 1984, 117: 471–483.

513 Lalitha VS, Rubinstein LJ. Reactive glioma in intracranial sarcoma. A form of mixed sarcoma and glioma ("sarcoglioma"). Report of eight cases. Cancer 1979, 43: 246–257.

514 Meis JM, Martz KL, Nelson JS. Mixed glioblastoma multiforme and sarcoma. A clinicopathologic study of 26 radiation therapy oncology group cases. Cancer 1991, 67: 2342–2349.

515 Montpetit VJ, Pokrupa R, Richard MT, Clapin DF. Myofibroblastic differentiation of a primary intracerebral sarcoma with gliomatous reaction. Clin Neuropathol 1988, 7: 1–9.

516 Pasquier B, Couderc P, Pasquier D, Panh MH, N'Golet A. Sarcoma arising in oligodendroglioma of the brain. A case with intramedullary and subarachnoid spinal metastases. Cancer 1978, 42: 2753–2758.

517 Paulus W, Jellinger K. Mixed glioblastoma and malignant mesenchymoma, a variety of gliosarcoma. Histopathology 1993, 22: 277–279.

518 Perry JR, Ang LC, Bilbao JM, Muller PJ. Clinicopathologic features of primary and postirradiation cerebral gliosarcoma. Cancer 1995, 75: 2910–2918.

519 Prayson RA. Gliofibroma. A distinct entity or a subtype of desmoplastic astrocytoma? Hum Pathol 1996, 27: 610–613.

520 Reis RM, Konu-Lebleblicioglu D, Lopes JM, Kleihues P, Ohgaki H. Genetic profile of gliosarcomas. Am J Pathol 2000, 156: 425–432.

521 Roda JM, Gutierrez-Molina M. Multiple intraspinal low-grade astrocytomas mixed with lipoma (astrolipoma). Case report. J Neurosurg 1995, 82: 891–894.

522 Slowik F, Jellinger K, Gaszo L, Fischer J. Gliosarcomas. Histological, immunohistochemical, ultrastructural, and tissue culture studies. Acta Neuropathol (Berl) 1985, 67: 201–210.

523 Vazquez M, Miller DC, Epstein F, Allen JC, Budzilovich GN. Glioneurofibroma. Renaming the pediatric "gliofibroma". A neoplasm composed of schwann cells and astrocytes. Mod Pathol 1991, 4: 519–523.

524 Wargotz ES, Sidawy MK, Jannotta FS. Thorotrast-associated gliosarcoma. Including comments on thorotrast use and review of sequelae with particular reference to lesions of the central nervous system. Cancer 1988, 62: 58–66.

Choroid plexus tumors

525 Aguzzi A, Brandner S, Paulus W. Choroid plexus tumours. In Kleihues P, Cavenee WK (eds): World Health Organization classification of tumours. Pathology and genetics—tumours of the nervous system. Lyon, 2000, IARC Press, pp. 84–86.

526 Albrecht S, Rouah E, Becker LE, Bruner J. Transthyretin immunoreactivity in choroid plexus neoplasms and brain metastases. Mod Pathol 1991, 4: 610–614.

527 Britz GW, Kim DK, Loeser JD. Hydrocephalus secondary to diffuse villous hyperplasia of the choroid plexus. Case report and review of the literature. J Neurosurg 1996, 85: 689–691.

528 Coffin CM, Wick MR, Braun JT, Dehner LP. Choroid plexus neoplasms. Clinicopathologic and immunohistochemical studies. Am J Surg Pathol 1986, 10: 394–404.

529 Diengdoh JV, Shaw MD. Oncocytic variant of choroid plexus papilloma. Evolution from benign to malignant "oncocytoma". Cancer 1993, 71: 855–858.

530 Dobin SM, Donner LR. Pigmented choroid plexus carcinoma. A cytogenetic and ultrastructural study. Cancer Genet Cytogenet 1997, 96: 37–41.

531 Duckett S, Osterholm J, Schaefer D, Gonzales C, Schwartzman RJ. Ossified mucin-secreting choroid plexus adenoma. Case report. Neurosurgery 1991, 29: 130–132.

532 Fuller CE, Smith M, Miller DC, Schelper R. Pigmented papillary epithelial neoplasm of the pituitary fossa. A distinct lesion of uncertain histogenesis. Arch Pathol Lab Med 2001, 125: 1242–1245.

533 Gottschalk J, Jautzke G, Paulus W, Goebel S, Cervos-Navarro J. The use of immunomorphology to differentiate choroid plexus tumors from metastatic carcinomas. Cancer 1993, 72: 1343–1349.

534 Gyure KA, Morrison AL. Cytokeratin 7 and 20 expression in choroid plexus tumors. Utility in differentiating these neoplasms from metastatic carcinomas. Mod Pathol 2000, 13: 638–643.

535 Jay V, Ho M, Chan F, Malkin D. p53 expression in choroid plexus neoplasms. An immunohistochemical study. Arch Pathol Lab Med 1996, 120: 1061–1065.

536 Kepes JJ, Collins J. Choroid plexus epithelium (normal and neoplastic) expresses synaptophysin. A potentially useful aid in differentiating carcinoma of the choroid plexus from metastatic papillary carcinomas. J Neuropathol Exp Neurol 1999, 58: 398–401.

537 Kimura M, Takayasu M, Suzuki Y, Negoro M, Nagasaka T, Nakashima N, Sugita K. Primary choroid plexus papilloma located in the suprasellar region. Case report. Neurosurgery 1992, 31: 563–566.

538 Matsushima T. Choroid plexus papillomas and human choroid plexus. A light and electron microscopic study. J Neurosurg 1983, 59: 1054–1062.

539 McComb RD, Burger PC. Choroid plexus carcinoma. Report of a case with immunohistochemical and ultrastructural observations. Cancer 1983, 51: 470–475.

540 Packer RJ, Perilongo G, Johnson D, Sutton LN, Vezina G, Zimmerman RA, Ryan J, Reaman G, Schut L. Choroid plexus carcinoma of childhood. Cancer 1992, 69: 580–585.

541 Paulus W, Jänisch W. Clinicopathologic correlations in epithelial choroid plexus neoplasms. A study of 52 cases. Acta Neuropathol (Berl) 1990, 80: 635–641.

542 Pencalet P, Sainte-Rose C, Lellouch-Tubiana A, Kalifa C, Brunelle F, Sgouros S, Meyer P, Cinalli G, Zerah M, Pierre-Kahn A, Renier D. Papillomas and carcinomas of the choroid plexus in children. J Neurosurg 1998, 88: 521–528.

543 Robinow M, Johnson GF, Minella PA. Aicardi syndrome, papilloma of the choroid plexus, cleft lip, and cleft of the posterior palate. J Pediatr 1984, 104: 404–405.

544 Salazar J, Vaquero J, Aranda IF, Menendez J, Jimenez MD, Bravo G. Choroid plexus papilloma with chondroma. Case report. Neurosurgery 1986, 18: 781–783.

545 Sevenet N, Lellouch-Tubiana A, Schofield D, Hoang-Xuan K, Gessler M, Birnbaum D, Jeanpierre C, Jouvet A, Delattre O. Spectrum of hSNF5/INI1 somatic mutations in human cancer and genotype-phenotype correlations. Hum Mol Genet 1999, 8: 2359–2368.

546 Vajtai I, Varga Z, Aguzzi A. MIB-1 immunoreactivity reveals different labelling in low-grade and in malignant epithelial neoplasms of the choroid plexus. Histopathology 1996, 29: 147–151.

547 Varga Z, Vajtai I, Marino S, Schauble B, Yonekawa Y, Aguzzi A.

Tubular adenoma of the choroid plexus. Evidence for glandular differentiation of the neuroepithelium. Pathol Res Pract 1996, **192:** 840–844.

548 Vital A, Bringuier PP, Huang H, San Galli F, Rivel J, Ansoborlo S, Cazauran JM, Taillandier L, Kleihues P, Ohgaki H. Astrocytomas and choroid plexus tumors in two families with identical p53 germline mutations. J Neuropathol Exp Neurol 1998, **57:** 1061–1069.

549 Watanabe K, Ando Y, Iwanaga H, Ochiai C, Nagai M, Okada K, Watanabe N. Choroid plexus papilloma containing melanin pigment. Clin Neuropathol 1995, **14:** 159–161.

550 Wyatt-Ashmead J, Kleinschmidt-DeMasters B, Mierau GW, Malkin D, Orsini E, McGavran L, Foreman NK. Choroid plexus carcinomas and rhabdoid tumors. Phenotypic and genotypic overlap. Pediatr Dev Pathol 2001, **4:** 545–549.

551 Yoshino A, Katayama Y, Watanabe T, Kurihara J, Kimura S. Multiple choroid plexus papillomas of the lateral ventricle distinct from villous hypertrophy. Case report. J Neurosurg 1998, **88:** 581–585.

Neuronal and glioneuronal tumors, hamartomas, and related lesions

Gangliocytoma and ganglioglioma

552 Allegranza A, Pileri S, Frank G, Ferracini R. Cerebral ganglioglioma with anaplastic oligodendroglial component. Histopathology 1990, **17:** 439–441.

553 Athale S, Hallet KK, Jinkins JR. Ganglioglioma of the trigeminal nerve. MRI. Neuroradiology 1999, **41:** 576–578.

554 Blümcke I, Löbach M, Wolf HK, Wiestler OD. Evidence for developmental precursor lesions in epilepsy-associated glioneuronal tumors. Microsc Res Tech 1999, **46:** 53–58.

555 Blümcke I, Wiestler OD. Gangliogliomas: an intriguing tumor entity associated with focal epilepsies. J Neuropathol Exp Neurol 2002, **61:** 575–584.

556 Caccamo D, Herman MM, Urich H, Rubinstein LJ. Focal neuronal gigantism and cerebral cortical thickening after therapeutic irradiation of the central nervous system. Arch Pathol Lab Med 1989, **113:** 880–885.

557 Dash RC, Provenzale JM, McComb RD, Perry DA, Longee DC, McLendon RE. Malignant supratentorial ganglioglioma (ganglion cell-giant cell glioblastoma). A case report and review of the literature. Arch Pathol Lab Med 1999, **123:** 342–345.

558 David KM, de Sanctis S, Lewis PD, Noury AM, Edwards JM. Neuroblastomatous recurrence of ganglioglioma. Case report. J Neurosurg 2000, **93:** 698–700.

559 Felix I, Bilbao JM, Asa SL, Tyndel F, Kovacs K, Becker LE. Cerebral and cerebellar gangliocytomas. A morphological study of nine cases. Acta Neuropathol (Berl) 1994, **88:** 246–251.

560 Geddes JF, Jansen GH, Robinson SF, Gömöri E, Holton JL, Monson JP, Besser GM, Révész T. "Gangliocytomas" of the pituitary. A heterogeneous group of lesions with differing histogenesis. Am J Surg Pathol 2000, **24:** 607–613.

561 Hakim R, Loeffler JS, Anthony DC, Black PM. Gangliogliomas in adults. Cancer 1997, **79:** 127–131.

562 Hayashi S, Kameyama S, Fukuda M, Takahashi H. Ganglioglioma with a tanycytic ependymoma as the glial component. Acta Neuropathol (Berl) 2000, **99:** 310–316.

563 Hirose T, Scheithauer BW, Lopes MB, Gerber HA, Altermatt HJ, VandenBerg SR. Ganglioglioma. An ultrastructural and immunohistochemical study. Cancer 1997, **79:** 989–1003.

564 Jay V, Squire J, Becker LE, Humphreys R. Malignant transformation in a ganglioglioma with anaplastic neuronal and astrocytic components. Report of a case with flow cytometric and cytogenetic analysis. Cancer 1994, **73:** 2862–2868.

565 Johnson JH Jr, Hariharan S, Berman J, Sutton LN, Rorke LB, Molloy P, Phillips PC. Clinical outcome of pediatric gangliogliomas. Ninety-nine cases over 20 years. Pediatr Neurosurg 1997, **27:** 203–207.

566 Krouwer HG, Davis RL, McDermott MW, Hoshino T, Prados MD. Gangliogliomas. A clinicopathological study of 25 cases and review of the literature. J Neurooncol 1993, **17:** 139–154.

567 Lang FF, Epstein FJ, Ransohoff J, Allen JC, Wisoff J, Abbott IR, Miller DC. Central nervous system gangliogliomas. Part 2. Clinical outcome. J Neurosurg 1993, **79:** 867–873.

567a Lu WY, Goldman M, Young B, Davis DG. Optic nerve ganglioglioma. Case report. J Neurosurg 1993, **78:** 979–982.

568 Miller DC, Lang FF, Epstein FJ. Central nervous system gangliogliomas. Part 1. Pathology. J Neurosurg 1993, **79:** 859–866.

569 Prayson RA, Khajavi K, Comair YG. Cortical architectural abnormalities and MIB1 immunoreactivity in gangliogliomas. A study of 60 patients with intracranial tumors. J Neuropathol Exp Neurol 1995, **54:** 513–520.

570 Quinn B. Synaptophysin staining in normal brain. Importance for diagnosis of ganglioglioma. Am J Surg Pathol 1998, **22:** 550–556.

571 Selch MT, Goy BW, Lee SP, El-Sadin S, Kincaid P, Park SH, Withers HR. Gangliogliomas. Experience with 34 patients and review of the literature. Am J Clin Oncol 1998, **21:** 557–564.

572 Soffer D, Lach B, Constantini S. Melanotic cerebral ganglioglioma. Evidence for melanogenesis in neoplastic astrocytes. Acta Neuropathol (Berl) 1992, **83:** 315–323.

573 Soffer D, Umansky F, Goldman JE. Ganglioglioma with neurofibrillary tangles (NFTs). Neoplastic NFTs share antigenic determinants with NFTs of Alzheimer's disease. Acta Neuropathol (Berl) 1995, **89:** 451–453.

574 Wacker MR, Cogen PH, Etzell JE, Daneshvar L, Davis RL, Prados MD. Diffuse leptomeningeal involvement by a ganglioglioma in a child. Case report. J Neurosurg 1991, **77:** 302–306.

575 Wolf HK, Müller MB, Spänle M, Zentner J, Schramm J, Wiestler OD. Ganglioglioma. A detailed histopathological and immunohistochemical analysis of 61 cases. Acta Neuropathol (Berl) 1994, **88:** 166–173.

576 Zentner J, Wolf HK, Ostertun B, Hufnagel A, Campos MG, Solymosi L, Schramm J. Gangliogliomas. Clinical, radiological, and histopathological findings in 51 patients. J Neurol Neurosurg Psychiatry 1994, **57:** 1497–1502.

577 Zhang PJ, Rosenblum MK. Synaptophysin expression in the human spinal cord. Diagnostic implications of an immunohistochemical study. Am J Surg Pathol 1996, **20:** 273–276.

578 Zhu JJ, Leon SP, Folkerth RD, Guo SZ, Wu JK, Black PM. Evidence for clonal origin of neoplastic neuronal and glial cells in gangliogliomas. Am J Pathol 1997, **151:** 565–571.

Desmoplastic infantile ganglioglioma/desmoplastic infantile astrocytoma

579 Aydin F, Ghatak NR, Salvant J, Muizelaar P. Desmoplastic cerebral astrocytoma of infancy. A case report with immunohistochemical, ultrastructural and proliferation studies. Acta Neuropathol (Berl) 1993, **86:** 666–670.

580 de Munnynck K, van Gool S, van Calenbergh F, Demaerel P, Uyttebroeck A, Buyse G, Sciot R. Desmoplastic infantile ganglioglioma. A potentially malignant tumor? Am J Surg Pathol 2002, **26:** 1515–1522.

581 Duffner PK, Burger PC, Cohen ME, Sanford RA, Krischer JP, Elterman R, Aronin PA, Pullen J, Horowitz ME, Parent A, et al. Desmoplastic infantile gangliogliomas. An approach to therapy. Neurosurgery 1994, **34:** 583–589; discussion 589.

582 Komori T, Scheithauer BW, Parisi JE, Watterson J, Priest JR. Mixed conventional and desmoplastic infantile ganglioglioma. An autopsied case with 6-year follow-up. Mod Pathol 2001, **14:** 720–726.

583 Kuchelmeister K, Schonmeyr R, Albani M, Schachenmayr W. Anaplastic desmoplastic infantile ganglioglioma. Clin Neuropathol 1998, **17**: 269.

584 Kuchelmeister K, Steinhauser A, Korf B, Wagner D, Prey N, Schachenmayr W. Anaplastic desmoplastic infantile ganglioglioma. A case report. Clin Neuropathol 1996, **15**: 280.

585 Louis DN, von Deimling A, Dickersin GR, Dooling EC, Seizinger BR. Desmoplastic cerebral astrocytomas of infancy. A histopathologic, immunohistochemical, ultrastructural, and molecular genetic study. Hum Pathol 1992, **23**: 1402–1409.

586 Setty SN, Miller DC, Camras L, Charbel F, Schmidt ML. Desmoplastic infantile astrocytoma with metastases at presentation. Mod Pathol 1997, **10**: 945–951.

587 Taratuto AL, Monges J, Lylyk P, Leiguarda R. Superficial cerebral astrocytoma attached to dura. Report of six cases in infants. Cancer 1984, **54**: 2505–2512.

588 Taratuto AL, Vandenberg S, Rorke L. Desmoplastic infantile astrocytoma and ganglioglioma. In Kleihues P, Cavanee WK (eds): World Health Organization classification of tumours. Pathology and genetics—tumours of the nervous system. Lyon, 2000, IARC Press, pp. 99–102.

589 VandenBerg SR, May EE, Rubinstein LJ, Herman MM, Perentes E, Vinores SA, Collins VP, Park TS. Desmoplastic supratentorial neuroepithelial tumors of infancy with divergent differentiation potential ("desmoplastic infantile gangliogliomas"). Report on 11 cases of a distinctive embryonal tumor with favorable prognosis. J Neurosurg 1987, **66**: 58–71.

Central neurocytoma and extraventricular neurocytic neoplasms

590 Brat DJ, Scheithauer BW, Eberhart CG, Burger PC. Extraventricular neurocytomas. Pathologic features and clinical outcome. Am J Surg Pathol 2001, **25**: 1252–1260.

591 Elek G, Slowik F, Eross L, Toth S, Szabo Z, Balint K. Central neurocytoma with malignant course. Neuronal and glial differentiation and craniospinal dissemination. Pathol Oncol Res 1999, **5**: 155–159.

592 Eng DY, DeMonte F, Ginsberg L, Fuller GN, Jaeckle K. Craniospinal dissemination of central neurocytoma. Report of two cases. J Neurosurg 1997, **86**: 547–552.

593 Figarella-Branger D, Pellissier JF, Daumas-Duport C, Delisle MB, Pasquier B, Parent M, Gambarelli D, Rougon G, Hassoun J. Central neurocytomas. Critical evaluation of a small-cell neuronal tumor. Am J Surg Pathol 1992, **16**: 97–109.

594 Figarella-Branger D, Soylemezoglu F, Kleihues P, Hassoun J. Central neurocytoma. In Kleihues P, Cavenee WK (eds): World Health Organization classification of tumours. Pathology and genetics—tumours of the nervous system. Lyon, 2000, IARC Press, pp. 107–109.

595 George DH, Scheithauer BW. Central liponeurocytoma. Am J Surg Pathol 2001, **25**: 1551–1555.

596 Giangaspero F, Cenacchi G, Losi L, Cerasoli S, Bisceglia M, Burger PC. Extraventricular neoplasms with neurocytoma features. A clinicopathological study of 11 cases. Am J Surg Pathol 1997, **21**: 206–212.

597 Giangaspero F, Cenacchi G, Roncaroli F, Rigobello L, Manetto V, Gambacorta M, Allegranza A. Medullocytoma (lipidized medulloblastoma). A cerebellar neoplasm of adults with favorable prognosis. Am J Surg Pathol 1996, **20**: 656–664.

598 Gonzalez-Campora R, Weller RO. Lipidized mature neuroectodermal tumour of the cerebellum with myoid differentiation. Neuropathol Appl Neurobiol 1998, **24**: 397–402.

599 Horoupian DS, Shuster DL, Kaarsoo-Herrick M, Shuer LM. Central neurocytoma. One associated with a fourth ventricular PNET/medulloblastoma and the second mixed with adipose tissue. Hum Pathol 1997, **28**: 1111–1114.

600 Ishiuchi S, Tamura M. Central neurocytoma. An immunohistochemical, ultrastructural and cell culture study. Acta Neuropathol (Berl) 1997, **94**: 425–435.

601 Kleihues P, Chimelli L, Giangaspero F. Cerebellar liponeurocytoma. In Kleihues P, Cavenee WK (eds): World Health Organization classification of tumours. Pathology and genetics—tumours of the nervous system. Lyon, 2000, IARC Press, pp. 110–111.

602 Mackenzie IR. Central neurocytoma. Histologic atypia, proliferation potential, and clinical outcome. Cancer 1999, **85**: 1606–1610.

603 Mierau GW, Scheithauer BW, Hukee MJ, Orsini EN. Mixed ependymoma-neuroendocrine tumor of the lateral ventricle. Ultrastruct Pathol 1996, **20**: 47–53.

604 Mrak RE. Malignant neurocytic tumor. Hum Pathol 1994, **25**: 747–752.

605 Ng TH, Wong AY, Boadle R, Compton JS. Pigmented central neurocytoma. Case report and literature review. Am J Surg Pathol 1999, **23**: 1136–1140.

606 Pal L, Santosh V, Gayathri N, Das S, Das BS, Jayakumar PN, Shankar SK. Neurocytoma/rhabdomyoma (myoneurocytoma) of the cerebellum. Acta Neuropathol (Berl) 1998, **95**: 318–323.

607 Park SH, Ostrzega N, Akers MA, Vinters HV. Intraventricular neurocytoma with prominent myelin figures. Ultrastruct Pathol 1999, **23**: 311–317.

608 Robbins P, Segal A, Narula S, Stokes B, Lee M, Thomas W, Caterina P, Sinclair I, Spagnolo D. Central neurocytoma. A clinicopathological, immunohistochemical and ultrastructural study of 7 cases. Pathol Res Pract 1995, **191**: 100–111.

609 Schild SE, Scheithauer BW, Haddock MG, Schiff D, Burger PC, Wong WW, Lyons MK. Central neurocytomas. Cancer 1997, **79**: 790–795.

610 Schweitzer JB, Davies KG. Differentiating central neurocytoma. Case report. J Neurosurg 1997, **86**: 543–546.

611 Soylemezoglu F, Scheithauer BW, Esteve J, Kleihues P. Atypical central neurocytoma. J Neuropathol Exp Neurol 1997, **56**: 551–556.

612 Soylemezoglu F, Soffer D, Onol B, Schwechheimer K, Kleihues P. Lipomatous medulloblastoma in adults. A distinct clinicopathological entity. Am J Surg Pathol 1996, **20**: 413–418.

613 Tatter SB, Borges LF, Louis DN. Central neurocytomas of the cervical spinal cord. Report of two cases. J Neurosurg 1994, **81**: 288–293.

614 Tsuchida T, Matsumoto M, Shirayama Y, Imahori T, Kasai H, Kawamoto K. Neuronal and glial characteristics of central neurocytoma. Electron microscopical analysis of two cases. Acta Neuropathol (Berl) 1996, **91**: 573–577.

Dysembryoplastic neuroepithelial tumor

615 Baisden BL, Brat DJ, Melhem ER, Rosenblum MK, King AP, Burger PC. Dysembryoplastic neuroepithelial tumor-like neoplasm of the septum pellucidum. A lesion often misdiagnosed as glioma. Report of 10 cases. Am J Surg Pathol 2001, **25**: 494–499.

616 Cervera-Pierot P, Varlet P, Chodkiewicz JP, Daumas-Duport C. Dysembryoplastic neuroepithelial tumors located in the caudate nucleus area. Report of four cases. Neurosurgery 1997, **40**: 1065–1069; discussion 1069–1070.

617 Daumas-Duport C. Dysembryoplastic neuroepithelial tumours. Brain Pathol 1993, **3**: 283–295.

618 Daumas-Duport C, Scheithauer BW, Chodkiewicz JP, Laws ER, Jr., Vedrenne C. Dysembryoplastic neuroepithelial tumor. A surgically curable tumor of young patients with intractable partial seizures. Report of thirty-nine cases. Neurosurgery 1988, **23**: 545–556.

619 Daumas-Duport C, Varlet P, Bacha S, Beuvon F, Cervera-Pierot P, Chodkiewicz JP. Dysembryoplastic neuroepithelial tumors.

Nonspecific histological forms. A study of 40 cases. J Neurooncol 1999, **41:** 267–280.

620 Elizabeth J, Bhaskara RM, Radhakrishnan VV, Radhakrishnan K, Thomas SV. Melanotic differentiation in dysembryoplastic neuroepithelial tumor. Clin Neuropathol 2000, **19:** 38–40.

621 Fujimoto K, Ohnishi H, Tsujimoto M, Hoshida T, Nakazato Y. Dysembryoplastic neuroepithelial tumor of the cerebellum and brainstem. Case report. J Neurosurg 2000, **93:** 487–489.

622 Gyure KA, Sandberg GD, Prayson RA, Morrison AL, Armstrong RC, Wong K. Dysembryoplastic neuroepithelial tumor. An immunohistochemical study with myelin oligodendrocyte glycoprotein. Arch Pathol Lab Med 2000, **124:** 123–126.

623 Hammond RR, Duggal N, Woulfe JM, Girvin JP. Malignant transformation of a dysembryoplastic neuroepithelial tumor. Case report. J Neurosurg 2000, **92:** 722–725.

624 Hirose T, Scheithauer BW. Mixed dysembryoplastic neuroepithelial tumor and ganglioglioma. Acta Neuropathol (Berl) 1998, **95:** 649–654.

625 Hirose T, Scheithauer BW, Lopes MB, VandenBerg SR. Dysembryoplastic neuroepithelial tumor (DNT). An immunohistochemical and ultrastructural study. J Neuropathol Exp Neurol 1994, **53:** 184–195.

626 Honavar M, Janota I, Polkey CE. Histological heterogeneity of dysembryoplastic neuroepithelial tumour. Identification and differential diagnosis in a series of 74 cases. Histopathology 1999, **34:** 342–356.

627 Prayson RA, Castilla EA, Hartke M, Pettay J, Tubbs RR, Barnett GH. Chromosome 1p allelic loss by fluorescence in situ hybridization is not observed in dysembryoplastic neuroepithelial tumors. Am J Clin Pathol 2002, **118:** 512 517.

628 Raymond AA, Halpin SF, Alsanjari N, Cook MJ, Kitchen ND, Fish DR, Stevens JM, Harding BN, Scaravilli F, Kendall B. Dysembryoplastic neuroepithelial tumor. Features in 16 patients. Brain 1994, **117:** 461–475.

629 Whittle IR, Dow GR, Lammie GA, Wardlaw J. Dysembryoplastic neuroepithelial tumour with discrete bilateral multifocality. Further evidence for a germinal origin. Br J Neurosurg 1999, **13:** 508–511.

Other glioneuronal neoplasms

630 Bouvier-Labit C, Daniel L, Dufour H, Grisoli F, Figarella-Branger D. Papillary glioneuronal tumour. Clinicopathological and biochemical study of one case with 7-year follow up. Acta Neuropathol (Berl) 2000, **99:** 321–326.

631 Harris BT, Horoupian DS. Spinal cord glioneuronal tumor with "rosetted" neuropil islands and meningeal dissemination. A case report. Acta Neuropathol (Berl) 2000, **100:** 575–579.

632 Keyvani K, Rickert CH, von Wild K, Paulus W. Rosetted glioneuronal tumor. A case with proliferating neuronal nodules. Acta Neuropathol (Berl) 2001, **101:** 525–528.

633 Komori T, Scheithauer BW, Anthony DC, Rosenblum MK, McLendon RE, Scott RM, Okazaki H, Kobayashi M. Papillary glioneuronal tumor. A new variant of mixed neuronal-glial neoplasm. Am J Surg Pathol 1998, **22:** 1171–1183.

634 Komori T, Scheithauer BW, Hirose T. A rosette-forming glioneuronal tumor of the fourth ventricle. Infratentorial form of dysembryoplastic neuroepithelial tumor? Am J Surg Pathol 2002, **26:** 582–591.

635 Prayson RA, Abramovich CM. Glioneuronal tumor with neuropil-like islands. Hum Pathol 2000, **31:** 1435–1438.

636 Teo JG, Gultekin SH, Bilsky M, Gutin P, Rosenblum MK. A distinctive glioneuronal tumor of the adult cerebrum with neuropil-like (including "rosetted") islands. Report of 4 cases. Am J Surg Pathol 1999, **23:** 502–510.

Hypothalamic neuronal hamartoma

637 Asa SL, Scheithauer BW, Bilbao JM, Horvath E, Ryan N, Kovacs K, Randall RV, Laws ER, Jr., Singer W, Linfoot JA, et al. A case for hypothalamic acromegaly. A clinicopathological study of six patients with hypothalamic gangliocytomas producing growth hormone-releasing factor. J Clin Endocrinol Metab 1984, **58:** 796–803.

638 Clarren SK, Alvord EC, Jr., Hall JG. Congenital hypothalamic hamartoblastoma, hypopituitarism, imperforate anus, and postaxial polydactyly—a new syndrome? Part II. Neuropathological considerations. Am J Med Genet 1980, **7:** 75–83.

639 Culler FL, James HE, Simon ML, Jones KL. Identification of gonadotropin-releasing hormone in neurons of a hypothalamic hamartoma in a boy with precocious puberty. Neurosurgery 1985, **17:** 408–412.

640 Nishio S, Fujiwara S, Aiko Y, Takeshita I, Fukui M. Hypothalamic hamartoma. Report of two cases. J Neurosurg 1989, **70:** 640–645.

641 Price RA, Lee PA, Albright AL, Ronnekleiv OK, Gutai JP. Treatment of sexual precocity by removal of a luteinizing hormone-releasing hormone secreting hamartoma. JAMA 1984, **251:** 2247–2249.

642 Scheithauer BW, Kovacs K, Randall RV, Horvath E, Okazaki H, Laws ER, Jr. Hypothalamic neuronal hamartoma and adenohypophyseal neuronal choristoma. Their association with growth hormone adenoma of the pituitary gland. J Neuropathol Exp Neurol 1983, **42:** 648–663.

643 Squires LA, Constantini S, Miller DC, Wisoff JH. Hypothalamic hamartoma and the Pallister–Hall syndrome. Pediatr Neurosurg 1995, **22:** 303–308.

Glioneuronal hamartomas, cortical dysplasias, and other epileptogenic lesions

644 Garbelli R, Munari C, De Biasi S, Vitellaro-Zuccarello L, Galli C, Bramerio M, Mai R, Battaglia G, Spreafico R. Taylor's cortical dysplasia. A confocal and ultrastructural immunohistochemical study. Brain Pathol 1999, **9:** 445–461.

645 Mischel PS, Nguyen LP, Vinters HV. Cerebral cortical dysplasia associated with pediatric epilepsy. Review of neuropathologic features and proposal for a grading system. J Neuropathol Exp Neurol 1995, **54:** 137–153.

646 Plate KH, Wieser HG, Yasargil MG, Wiestler OD. Neuropathological findings in 224 patients with temporal lobe epilepsy. Acta Neuropathol (Berl) 1993, **86:** 433–438.

647 Prayson RA, Estes ML. Cortical dysplasia. A histopathologic study of 52 cases of partial lobectomy in patients with epilepsy. Hum Pathol 1995, **26:** 493–500.

648 Wolf HK, Campos MG, Zentner J, Hufnagel A, Schramm J, Elger CE, Wiestler OD. Surgical pathology of temporal lobe epilepsy. Experience with 216 cases. J Neuropathol Exp Neurol 1993, **52:** 499–506.

649 Wolf HK, Zentner J, Hufnagel A, Campos MG, Schramm J, Elger CE, Wiestler OD. Surgical pathology of chronic epileptic seizure disorders. Experience with 63 specimens from extratemporal corticectomies, lobectomies and functional hemispherectomies. Acta Neuropathol (Berl) 1993, **86:** 466–472.

Dysplastic gangliocytoma of the cerebellum (Lhermitte–Duclos disease)

650 Ferrer I, Isamat F, Acebes J. A Golgi and electron microscopic study of a dysplastic gangliocytoma of the cerebellum. Acta Neuropathol (Berl) 1979, **47:** 163–165.

651 Ferrer I, Isamat F, Lopez-Obarrio L, Conesa G, Rimbau J, Alcantara S, Espanol I, Zujar MJ. Parvalbumin and calbindin D–28K immunoreactivity in central ganglioglioma and dysplastic gangliocytoma of the cerebellum. Report of two cases. J Neurosurg 1993, **78:** 133–137.

652 Hair LS, Symmans F, Powers JM, Carmel P. Immunohistochemistry and proliferative activity in Lhermitte–Duclos disease. Acta Neuropathol (Berl) 1992, **84**: 570–573.

653 Koch R, Scholz M, Nelen MR, Schwechheimer K, Epplen JT, Harders AG. Lhermitte–Duclos disease as a component of Cowden's syndrome. Case report and review of the literature. J Neurosurg 1999, **90**: 776–779.

654 Roessmann U, Wongmongkolrit T. Dysplastic gangliocytoma of cerebellum in a newborn. Case report. J Neurosurg 1984, **60**: 845–847.

655 Shiurba RA, Gessaga EC, Eng LF, Sternberger LA, Sternberger NH, Urich H. Lhermitte–Duclos disease. An immunohistochemical study of the cerebellar cortex. Acta Neuropathol (Berl) 1988, **75**: 474–480.

656 Stapleton SR, Wilkins PR, Bell BA. Recurrent dysplastic cerebellar gangliocytoma (Lhermitte–Duclos disease) presenting with subarachnoid haemorrhage. Br J Neurosurg 1992, **6**: 153–156.

657 Wiestler OD, Padberg GW, Steck PA. Cowden disease and dysplastic gangliocytoma of the cerebellum/Lhermitte–Duclos disease. In Kleihues P, Cavanee WK (eds): World Health Organization classification of tumours. Pathology and genetics—tumours of the nervous system. Lyon, 2000, IARC Press, pp. 235–237.

658 Williams DW, 3rd, Elster AD, Ginsberg LE, Stanton C. Recurrent Lhermitte–Duclos disease. Report of two cases and association with Cowden's disease. AJNR Am J Neuroradiol 1992, **13**: 287–290.

659 Yachnis AT, Trojanowski JQ, Memmo M, Schlaepfer WW. Expression of neurofilament proteins in the hypertrophic granule cells of Lhermitte–Duclos disease. An explanation for the mass effect and the myelination of parallel fibers in the disease state. J Neuropathol Exp Neurol 1988, **47**: 206–216.

Embryonal neuroepithelial tumors

660 Kleihues P, Cavanee WK. World Health Organization classification of tumours. Pathology and genetics—tumours of the nervous system. Lyon: IARC Press, 2000.

661 Pomeroy SL, Tamayo P, Gaasenbeek M, Sturla LM, Angelo M, McLaughlin ME, Kim JY, Goumnerova LC, Black PM, Lau C, Allen JC, Zagzag D, Olson JM, Curran T, Wetmore C, Biegel JA, Poggio T, Mukherjee S, Rifkin R, Califano A, Stolovitzky G, Louis DN, Mesirov JP, Lander ES, Golub TR. Prediction of central nervous system embryonal tumour outcome based on gene expression. Nature 2002, **415**: 436–442.

662 Rorke LB. The cerebellar medulloblastoma and its relationship to primitive neuroectodermal tumors. J Neuropathol Exp Neurol 1983, **42**: 1–15.

663 Rubinstein LJ. Embryonal central neuroepithelial tumors and their differentiating potential. A cytogenetic view of a complex neuro-oncological problem. J Neurosurg 1985, **62**: 795–805.

Medulloblastoma

664 Anwer UE, Smith TW, DeGirolami U, Wilkinson HA. Medulloblastoma with cartilaginous differentiation. Arch Pathol Lab Med 1989, **113**: 84–88.

665 Bergmann M, Pietsch T, Herms J, Janus J, Spaar HJ, Terwey B. Medullomyoblastoma: A histological, immunohistochemical, ultrastructural and molecular genetic study. Acta Neuropathol (Berl) 1998, **95**: 205–212.

666 Biggs PJ, Powers JM. Neuroblastic medulloblastoma with abundant cytoplasmic actin filaments. Arch Pathol Lab Med 1984, **108**: 326–329.

667 Brown HG, Kepner JL, Perlman EJ, Friedman HS, Strother DR, Duffner PK, Kun LE, Goldthwaite PT, Burger PC. "Large cell/anaplastic" medulloblastomas. A Pediatric Oncology Group Study. J Neuropathol Exp Neurol 2000, **59**: 857–865.

668 Bühren J, Christoph AH, Buslei R, Albrecht S, Wiestler OD, Pietsch T. Expression of the neurotrophin receptor p75NTR in medulloblastomas is correlated with distinct histological and clinical features. Evidence for a medulloblastoma subtype derived from the external granule cell layer. J Neuropathol Exp Neurol 2000, **59**: 229–240.

669 Cai DX, Mafra M, Schmidt RE, Scheithauer BW, Park TS, Perry A. Medulloblastomas with extensive posttherapy neuronal maturation. Report of two cases. J Neurosurg 2000, **93**: 330–334.

670 Coffin CM, Braun JT, Wick MR, Dehner LP. A clinicopathologic and immunohistochemical analysis of 53 cases of medulloblastoma with emphasis on synaptophysin expression. Mod Pathol 1990, **3**: 164–170.

671 Czerwionka M, Korf HW, Hoffmann O, Busch H, Schachenmayr W. Differentiation in medulloblastomas. Correlation between the immunocytochemical demonstration of photoreceptor markers (S-antigen, rod-opsin) and the survival rate in 66 patients. Acta Neuropathol (Berl) 1989, **78**: 629–636.

672 de Chadarevian JP, Montes JL, O'Gorman AM, Freeman CR. Maturation of cerebellar neuroblastoma into ganglioneuroma with melanosis. A histologic, immunocytochemical, and ultrastructural study. Cancer 1987, **59**: 69–76.

673 Dolman CL. Melanotic medulloblastoma. A case report with immunohistochemical and ultrastructural examination. Acta Neuropathol (Berl) 1988, **76**: 528–531.

674 Eberhart CG, Kaufman WE, Tihan T, Burger PC. Apoptosis, neuronal maturation, and neurotrophin expression within medulloblastoma nodules. J Neuropathol Exp Neurol 2001, **60**: 462–469.

675 Eberhart CG, Kepner JL, Goldthwaite PT, Kun LE, Duffner PK, Friedman HS, Strother DR, Burger PC. Histopathologic grading of medulloblastomas: a Pediatric Oncology Group study. Cancer 2002, **94**: 552–560.

676 Eberhart CG, Kratz JE, Schuster A, Goldthwaite P, Cohen KJ, Perlman EJ, Burger PC. Comparative genomic hybridization detects an increased number of chromosomal alterations in large cell/anaplastic medulloblastomas. Brain Pathol 2002, **12**: 36–44.

677 Geyer JR, Schofield D, Berger M, Milstein J. Differentiation of a primitive neuroectodermal tumor into a benign ganglioglioma. J Neurooncol 1992, **14**: 237–241.

678 Giangaspero F, Bigner SH, Kleihues P, Pietsch T, Trojanowski JQ. Medulloblastoma. In Kleihues P, Cavenee WK (eds): World Health Organization classification of tumours. Pathology and genetics—tumors of the nervous system. Lyon: IARC Press, 2000, pp. 129–137.

679 Giangaspero F, Perilongo G, Fondelli MP, Brisigotti M, Carollo C, Burnelli R, Burger PC, Garre ML. Medulloblastoma with extensive nodularity. A variant with favorable prognosis. J Neurosurg 1999, **91**: 971–977.

680 Giangaspero F, Rigobello L, Badiali M, Loda M, Andreini L, Basso G, Zorzi F, Montaldi A. **Large-cell medulloblastomas**. A distinct variant with highly aggressive behavior. Am J Surg Pathol 1992, **16**: 687–693.

681 Giordana MT, Schiffer P, Boghi A, Buoncristiani P, Benech F. Medulloblastoma with lipidized cells versus lipomatous medulloblastoma. Clin Neuropathol 2000, **19**: 273–277.

682 Grotzer MA, Janss AJ, Fung K, Biegel JA, Sutton LN, Rorke LB, Zhao H, Cnaan A, Phillips PC, Lee VM, Trojanowski JQ. TrkC expression predicts good clinical outcome in primitive neuroectodermal brain tumors. J Clin Oncol 2000, **18**: 1027–1035.

683 Holl T, Kleihues P, Yasargil MG, Wiestler OD. Cerebellar medullomyoblastoma with advanced neuronal differentiation and hamartomatous component. Acta Neuropathol (Berl) 1991, **82**: 408–413.

684 Hubbard JL, Scheithauer BW, Kispert DB, Carpenter SM, Wick MR, Laws ER, Jr. Adult cerebellar medulloblastomas. The pathological, radiographic, and clinical disease spectrum. J Neurosurg 1989, **70**: 536–544.

685 Jaffey PB, To GT, Xu HJ, Hu SX, Benedict WF, Donoso LA, Campbell GA. Retinoblastoma-like phenotype expressed in medulloblastomas. J Neuropathol Exp Neurol 1995, **54**: 664–672.

686 Janss AJ, Yachnis AT, Silber JH, Trojanowski JQ, Lee VM, Sutton LN, Perilongo G, Rorke LB, Phillips PC. Glial differentiation predicts poor clinical outcome in primitive neuroectodermal brain tumors. Ann Neurol 1996, **39**: 481–489.

687 Jimenez CL, Carpenter BF, Robb IA. Melanotic cerebellar tumor. Ultrastruct Pathol 1987, **11**: 751–759.

688 Kalimo H, Paljarvi L, Ekfors T, Pelliniemi LJ. Pigmented primitive neuroectodermal tumor with multipotential differentiation in cerebellum (pigmented medullomyoblastoma). A case with light- and electron-microscopic, and immunohistochemical analysis. Pediatr Neurosci 1987, **13**: 188–195.

689 Katsetos CD, Herman MM, Frankfurter A, Gass P, Collins VP, Walker CC, Rosemberg S, Barnard RO, Rubinstein LJ. Cerebellar desmoplastic medulloblastomas. A further immunohistochemical characterization of the reticulin-free pale islands. Arch Pathol Lab Med 1989, **113**: 1019–1029.

690 Katsetos CD, Liu HM, Zacks SI. Immunohistochemical and ultrastructural observations on Homer Wright (neuroblastic) rosettes and the "pale islands" of human cerebellar medulloblastomas. Hum Pathol 1988, **19**: 1219–1227.

691 Leonard JR, Cai DX, Rivet DJ, Kaufman BA, Park TS, Levy BK, Perry A. Large cell/anaplastic medulloblastomas and medullomyoblastomas: clinicopathological and genetic features. J Neurosurg 2001, **95**: 82–88.

692 Mahapatra AK, Sinha AK, Sharma MC. Medullomyoblastoma. A rare cerebellar tumour in children. Childs Nerv Syst 1998, **14**: 312–316.

693 Maraziotis T, Perentes E, Karamitopoulou E, Nakagawa Y, Gessaga EC, Probst A, Frankfurter A. Neuron-associated class III beta-tubulin isotype, retinal S-antigen, synaptophysin, and glial fibrillary acidic protein in human medulloblastomas. A clinicopathological analysis of 36 cases. Acta Neuropathol (Berl) 1992, **84**: 355–363.

694 McKenney JK, Varma VA, Hunter SB. Distinguishing metastatic small cell carcinoma (SCC) from a primary cerebellar medulloblastoma (MB) in an adult. An immunohistochemical study of thyroid transcription factor (TTF), cytokeratin AE1/3 (AE1/3), and epithelial membrane antigen (EMA). J Neuropathol Exp Neurol 2000, **59**: 420 (Abstract).

694a McManamy CS, Lamont JM, Taylor RE, Cole M, Pearson AD, Clifford SC, Ellison DW. Morphophenotypic variation predicts clinical behavior in childhood nondesmoplastic medulloblastomas. J Neuropathol Exp Neurol 2003, **62**: 627–632.

695 Packer RJ. Childhood medulloblastoma: progress and future challenges. Brain Dev 1999, **21**: 75–81.

696 Taylor MD, Mainprize TG, Rutka JT. Molecular insight into medulloblastoma and central nervous system primitive neuroectodermal tumor biology from hereditary syndromes. A review. Neurosurgery 2000, **47**: 888–901.

Medulloepithelioma

697 Auer RN, Becker LE. Cerebral medulloepithelioma with bone, cartilage, and striated muscle. Light microscopic and immunohistochemical study. J Neuropathol Exp Neurol 1983, **42**: 256–267.

698 Bruggers CS, Welsh CT, Boyer RS, Byrne JL, Pysher TJ. Successful therapy in a child with a congenital peripheral medulloepithelioma and disruption of hindquarter development. J Pediatr Hematol Oncol 1999, **21**: 161–164.

699 Caccamo DV, Herman MM, Rubinstein LJ. An immunohistochemical study of the primitive and maturing elements of human cerebral medulloepitheliomas. Acta Neuropathol (Berl) 1989, **79**: 248–254.

700 Deck JH. Cerebral medulloepithelioma with maturation into ependymal cells and ganglion cells. J Neuropathol Exp Neurol 1969, **28**: 442–454.

701 Donner LR, Teshima I. Peripheral medulloepithelioma. An immunohistochemical, ultrastructural, and cytogenic study of a rare, chemotherapy-sensitive, pediatric tumor. Am J Surg Pathol 2003, **27**: 1008–1012.

702 Khoddami M, Becker LE. Immunohistochemistry of medulloepithelioma and neural tube. Pediatr Pathol Lab Med 1997, **17**: 913–925.

703 Molloy PT, Yachnis AT, Rorke LB, Dattilo JJ, Needle MN, Millar WS, Goldwein JW, Sutton LN, Phillips PC. Central nervous system medulloepithelioma. A series of eight cases including two arising in the pons. J Neurosurg 1996, **84**: 430–436.

704 Nakamura Y, Becker LE, Mancer K, Gillespie R. Peripheral medulloepithelioma. Acta Neuropathol (Berl) 1982, **57**: 137–142.

705 Scheithauer BW, Rubinstein LJ. Cerebral medulloepithelioma. Report of a case with multiple divergent neuroepithelial differentiation. Childs Brain 1979, **5**: 62–71.

706 Sharma MC, Mahapatra AK, Gaikwad S, Jain AK, Sarkar C. Pigmented medulloepithelioma. Report of a case and review of the literature. Childs Nerv Syst 1998, **14**: 74–78.

707 Troost D, Jansen GH, Dingemans KP. Cerebral medulloepithelioma. Electron microscopy and immunohistochemistry. Acta Neuropathol (Berl) 1990, **80**: 103–107.

Central neuroblastic tumors

708 Ahdevaara P, Kalimo H, Torma T, Haltia M. Differentiating intracerebral neuroblastoma. Report of a case and review of the literature. Cancer 1977, **40**: 784–788.

709 Bennett JP, Jr, Rubinstein LJ. The biological behavior of primary cerebral neuroblastoma. A reappraisal of the clinical course in a series of 70 cases. Ann Neurol 1984, **16**: 21–27.

710 Berger MS, Edwards MS, Wara WM, Levin VA, Wilson CB. Primary cerebral neuroblastoma. Long-term follow-up review and therapeutic guidelines. J Neurosurg 1983, **59**: 418–423.

711 Dehner LP, Abenoza P, Sibley RK. Primary cerebral neuroectodermal tumors. Neuroblastoma, differentiated neuroblastoma, and composite neuroectodermal tumor. Ultrastruct Pathol 1988, **12**: 479–494.

712 Horten BC, Rubinstein LJ. Primary cerebral neuroblastoma. A clinicopathological study of 35 cases. Brain 1976, **99**: 735–756.

713 Kepes JJ, Belton K, Roessmann U, Ketcherside WJ. Primitive neuroectodermal tumors of the cauda equina in adults with no detectable primary intracranial neoplasm—three case studies. Clin Neuropathol 1985, **4**: 1–11.

714 Ojeda VJ, Spagnolo DV, Kakulas BA. Cerebral gliomas with palisading necrosis. Glioblastoma multiforme or high-grade cerebral neuroblastoma? A light and electron microscopical study of three cases. Pathology 1987, **19**: 167–172.

715 Ojeda VJ, Spagnolo DV, Vaughan RJ. Palisades in primary cerebral neuroblastoma simulating so-called polar spongioblastoma. A light and electron microscopical study of an adult case. Am J Surg Pathol 1987, **11**: 316–322.

716 Rhodes RH, Cole M, Takaoka Y, Roessmann U, Cotes EE, Simon J. Intraventricular cerebral neuroblastoma. Analysis of subtypes and comparison with hemispheric neuroblastoma. Arch Pathol Lab Med 1994, **118**: 897–911.

717 Sibilla L, Martelli A, Farina L, Uggetti C, Zappoli F, Sessa F, Rodriguez Baena R, Gaeltani P. Ganglioneuroblastoma of the spinal cord. AJNR Am J Neuroradiol 1995, **16**: 875–877.

718 Takahashi M, Ishihara T, Yokota T, Uchino F, Yokoyama T,

Matsumoto N. A case of cerebral composite ganglioneuroblastoma. An immunohistochemical and ultrastructural study. Acta Neuropathol (Berl) 1990, **80**: 98–102.

719 Torres LF, Grant N, Harding BN, Scaravilli F. Intracerebral neuroblastoma. Report of a case with neuronal maturation and long survival. Acta Neuropathol (Berl) 1985, **68**: 110–114.

Ependymoblastoma

720 Cruz-Sanchez FF, Haustein J, Rossi ML, Cervos-Navarro J, Hughes JT. Ependymoblastoma. A histological, immunohistological and ultrastructural study of five cases. Histopathology 1988, **12**: 17–27.

721 Langford LA. The ultrastructure of the ependymoblastoma. Acta Neuropathol (Berl) 1986, **71**: 136–141.

722 Mork SJ, Rubinstein LJ. Ependymoblastoma. A reappraisal of a rare embryonal tumor. Cancer 1985, **55**: 1536–1542.

723 Murphy MN, Dhalla SS, Diocee M, Halliday W, Wiseman NE, de Sa DJ. Congenital ependymoblastoma presenting as a sacrococcygeal mass in a newborn. An immunohistochemical, light and electron microscopic study. Clin Neuropathol 1987, **6**: 169–173.

724 Wada C, Kurata A, Hirose R, Tazaki Y, Kan S, Ishihara Y, Kameya T. Primary leptomeningeal ependymoblastoma. Case report. J Neurosurg 1986, **64**: 968–973.

Polar spongioblastoma

725 de Chadarévian JP, Guyda HJ, Hollenberg RD. Hypothalamic polar spongioblastoma associated with the diencephalic syndrome. Ultrastructural demonstration of a neuroendocrine organization. Virchows Arch A Pathol Anat Histopathol 1984, **402**: 465–474.

726 Jansen GH, Troost D, Dingemans KP. Polar spongioblastoma. An immunohistochemical and electron microscopical study. Acta Neuropathol (Berl) 1990, **81**: 228–232.

727 Russell DS, Rubinstein LJ. Pathology of tumours of the nervous system, 5th ed. Baltimore, 1989, Williams & Wilkins, pp. 169–172.

728 Schiffer D, Cravioto H, Giordana MT, Migheli A, Pezzulo T, Vigliani MC. Is polar spongioblastoma a tumor entity? J Neurosurg 1993, **78**: 587–591.

Assorted primitive neuroectodermal tumors

729 Abenoza P, Wick MR. Primitive cerebral neuroectodermal tumor with rhabdomyoblastic differentiation. Ultrastruct Pathol 1986, **10**: 347–354.

730 Brüstle O, Ohgaki H, Schmitt HP, Walter GF, Ostertag H, Kleihues P. Primitive neuroectodermal tumors after prophylactic central nervous system irradiation in children. Association with an activated K-ras gene. Cancer 1992, **69**: 2385–2392.

731 Dedeurwaerdere F, Giannini C, Sciot R, Rubin BP, Perilongo G, Borghi L, Ballotta ML, Cornips E, Demunter A, Maes B, Dei Tos AP. Primary peripheral PNET/Ewing's sarcoma of the dura. A clinicopathologic entity distinct from central PNET. Mod Pathol 2002, **15**: 673–678.

732 Gould VE, Jansson DS, Molenaar WM, Rorke LB, Trojanowski JQ, Lee VM, Packer RJ, Franke WW. Primitive neuroectodermal tumors of the central nervous system. Patterns of expression of neuroendocrine markers, and all classes of intermediate filament proteins. Lab Invest 1990, **62**: 498–509.

733 Gyure KA, Prayson RA, Estes ML. Extracerebellar primitive neuroectodermal tumors. A clinicopathologic study with bcl–2 and CD99 immunohistochemistry. Ann Diagn Pathol 1999, **3**: 276–280.

734 Hart MN, Earle KM. Primitive neuroectodermal tumors of the brain in children. Cancer 1973, **32**: 890–897.

735 Janzer RC, Kleihues P. Primitive neuroectodermal tumor with choroid plexus differentiation. Clin Neuropathol 1985, **4**: 93–98.

736 Jay V, Pienkowska M, Becker L, Zielenska M. Primitive neuroectodermal tumors of the cerebrum and cerebellum. Absence of t(11;22) translocation by RT-PCR analysis. Mod Pathol 1995, **8**: 488–491.

737 Krishnamurthy S, Powers SK, Towfighi J. Primitive neuroectodermal tumor of cerebrum with adipose tissue. Arch Pathol Lab Med 2001, **125**: 264–266.

738 McLendon RE, Bentley RC, Parisi JE, Tien RD, Harrison JC, Tarbell NJ, Billitt AL, Gualtieri RJ, Friedman HS. Malignant supratentorial glial-neuronal neoplasms. Report of two cases and review of the literature. Arch Pathol Lab Med 1997, **121**: 485–492.

739 Mendal RC, Pollay M, Bobele GB, Leech RW, Brumback RA. Primary primitive neuroectodermal tumor of the leptomeninges. J Child Neurol 1996, **11**: 404–407.

740 Selassie L, Rigotti R, Kepes JJ, Towfighi J. Adipose tissue and smooth muscle in a primitive neuroectodermal tumor of cerebrum. Acta Neuropathol (Berl) 1994, **87**: 217–222.

741 Tison V, Cerasoli S, Morigi F, Ladanyi M, Gerald WL, Rosai J. Intracranial desmoplastic small-cell tumor. Report of a case. Am J Surg Pathol 1996, **20**: 112–117.

742 Weil RJ, Zhuang Z, Pack S, Kumar S, Helman L, Fuller BG, Mackall CL, Oldfield EH. Intramedullary Ewing sarcoma of the spinal cord. Consequences of molecular diagnostics. Case report. J Neurosurg (Spine 2) 2001, **95**: 270–275.

743 Yachnis AT, Rorke LB, Biegel JA, Perilongo G, Zimmerman RA, Sutton LN. Desmoplastic primitive neuroectodermal tumor with divergent differentiation. Broadening the spectrum of desmoplastic infantile neuroepithelial tumors. Am J Surg Pathol 1992, **16**: 998–1006.

744 Yu JS, Moore MR, Kupsky WJ, Scott RM. Intracranial melanotic neuroectodermal tumor of infancy. Two case reports. Surg Neurol 1992, **37**: 123–129.

Atypical teratoid/rhabdoid tumor

745 Biegel JA, Zhou JY, Rorke LB, Stenstrom C, Wainwright LM, Fogelgren B. Germ-line and acquired mutations of INI1 in atypical teratoid and rhabdoid tumors. Cancer Res 1999, **59**: 74–79.

746 Bonnin JM, Rubinstein LJ, Palmer NF, Beckwith JB. The association of embryonal tumors originating in the kidney and in the brain. A report of seven cases. Cancer 1984, **54**: 2137–2146.

747 Bruch LA, Hill DA, Cai DX, Levy BK, Dehner LP, Perry A. A role for fluorescence in situ hybridization detection of chromosome 22q dosage in distinguishing atypical teratoid/rhabdoid tumors from medulloblastoma/central primitive neuroectodermal tumors. Hum Pathol 2001, **32**: 156–162.

748 Burger PC, Yu IT, Tihan T, Friedman HS, Strother DR, Kepner JL, Duffner PK, Kun LE, Perlman EJ. Atypical teratoid/rhabdoid tumor of the central nervous system. A highly malignant tumor of infancy and childhood frequently mistaken for medulloblastoma. A Pediatric Oncology Group study. Am J Surg Pathol 1998, **22**: 1083–1092.

749 Fernandez C, Bouvier C, Sevenet N, Liprandi A, Coze C, Lena G, Figarella-Branger D. Congenital disseminated malignant rhabdoid tumor and cerebellar tumor mimicking medulloblastoma in monozygotic twins. Pathologic and molecular diagnosis. Am J Surg Pathol 2002, **26**: 266–270.

750 Rorke LB, Packer RJ, Biegel JA. Central nervous system atypical teratoid/rhabdoid tumors of infancy and childhood. Definition of an entity. J Neurosurg 1996, **85**: 56–65.

751 Sevenet N, Sheridan E, Amram D, Schneider P, Handgretinger R, Delattre O. Constitutional mutations of the hSNF5/INI1 gene predispose to a variety of cancers. Am J Hum Genet 1999, **65**: 1342–1348.

Pineal parenchymal tumors

752 Amoaku WM, Willshaw HE, Parkes SE, Shah KJ, Mann JR. Trilateral retinoblastoma. A report of five patients. Cancer 1996, **78**: 858–863.

753 De Girolami U, Zvaigzne O. Modification of the Achucarro-Hortega pineal stain for paraffin-embedded formalin-fixed tissue. Stain Technol 1973, **48**: 48–50.

754 Dooling EC, Chi JG, Gilles FH. Melanotic neuroectodermal tumor of infancy. Its histological similarities to fetal pineal gland. Cancer 1977, **39**: 1535–1541.

755 Fevre-Montange M, Jouvet A, Privat K, Korf HW, Champier J, Reboul A, Aguera M, Mottolese C. Immunohistochemical, ultrastructural, biochemical and in vitro studies of a pineocytoma. Acta Neuropathol (Berl) 1998, **95**: 532–539.

756 Illum N, Korf HW, Julian K, Rasmussen T, Herning M, Krabbe S. Concurrent uveoretinitis and pineocytoma in a child suggests a causal relationship. Br J Ophthalmol 1992, **76**: 574–576.

756a Jovet A, Fauchon F, Liberski P, Saint-Pierre G, Didier-Bazes M, Heitzmann A, Delisle M-B, Biassette HA, Vincent S, Mikol J, Streichenberger N, Ahboucha S, Brisson C, Belin M-F, Fevre-Montange M. Papillary tumor of the pineal region. Am J Surg Pathol 2003, **4**: 505–512.

757 Jouvet A, Fevre-Montange M, Besancon R, Derrington E, Saint-Pierre G, Belin MF, Pialat J, Lapras C. Structural and ultrastructural characteristics of human pineal gland, and pineal parenchymal tumors. Acta Neuropathol (Berl) 1994, **88**: 334–348.

758 Jouvet A, Saint-Pierre G, Fauchon F, Privat K, Bouffet E, Ruchoux MM, Chauveinc L, Fevre-Montange M. Pineal parenchymal tumors. A correlation of histological features with prognosis in 66 cases. Brain Pathol 2000, **10**: 49–60.

759 Kuchelmeister K, von Borcke, IM, Klein H, Bergmann M, Gullotta F. Pleomorphic pineocytoma with extensive neuronal differentiation. Report of two cases. Acta Neuropathol (Berl) 1994, **88**: 448–453.

760 Marcus DM, Brooks SE, Leff G, McCormick R, Thompson T, Anfinson S, Lasudry J, Albert DM. Trilateral retinoblastoma. Insights into histogenesis and management. Surv Ophthalmol 1998, **43**: 59–70.

761 McGrogan G, Rivel J, Vital C, Guerin J. A pineal tumour with features of "pineal anlage tumour". Acta Neurochir (Wien) 1992, **117**: 73–77.

762 Mena H, Rushing EJ, Ribas JL, Delahunt B, McCarthy WF. Tumors of pineal parenchymal cells. A correlation of histological features, including nucleolar organizer regions, with survival in 35 cases. Hum Pathol 1995, **26**: 20–30.

763 Min KW, Scheithauer BW, Bauserman SC. Pineal parenchymal tumors. An ultrastructural study with prognostic implications. Ultrastruct Pathol 1994, **18**: 69–85.

764 Raisanen J, Vogel H, Horoupian DS. Primitive pineal tumor with retinoblastomatous and retinal/ciliary epithelial differentiation. An immunohistochemical study. J Neurooncol 1990, **9**: 165–170.

765 Schild SE, Scheithauer BW, Schomberg PJ, Hook CC, Kelly PJ, Frick L, Robinow JS, Buskirk SJ. Pineal parenchymal tumors. Clinical, pathologic, and therapeutic aspects. Cancer 1993, **72**: 870–880.

766 Schmidbauer M, Budka H, Pilz P. Neuroepithelial and ectomesenchymal differentiation in a primitive pineal tumor ("pineal anlage tumor"). Clin Neuropathol 1989, **8**: 7–10.

767 Sobel RA, Trice JE, Nielsen SL, Ellis WG. Pineoblastoma with ganglionic and glial differentiation. Report of two cases. Acta Neuropathol (Berl) 1981, **55**: 243–246.

768 Trojanowski JQ, Tascos NA, Rorke LB. Malignant pineocytoma with prominent papillary features. Cancer 1982, **50**: 1789–1793.

769 Vaquero J, Coca S, Martinez R, Escandon J. Papillary pincocytoma. Case report. J Neurosurg 1990, **73**: 135–137.

Meningiomas

770 Abramovich CM, Prayson RA. Histopathologic features and MIB-1 labeling indices in recurrent and nonrecurrent meningiomas. Arch Pathol Lab Med 1999, **123**: 793–800.

771 Allen EA, Burger PC, Epstein JI. Microcystic meningioma arising in a mixed germ cell tumor of the testis. A case report. Am J Surg Pathol 1999, **23**: 1131–1135.

772 Barnett GH, Chou SM, Bay JW. Posttraumatic intracranial meningioma. A case report and review of the literature. Neurosurgery 1986, **18**: 75–78.

773 Bouvier C, Zattara-Canoni H, Daniel L, Gentet JC, Lena G, Figarella-Branger D. Cerebellar papillary meningioma in a 3-year-old boy. The usefulness of electron microscopy for diagnosis. Am J Surg Pathol 1999, **23**: 844–848.

774 Budka H. Nonglial specificities of immunocytochemistry for the glial fibrillary acidic protein (GFAP). Triple expression of GFAP, vimentin and cytokeratins in papillary meningioma and metastasizing renal carcinoma. Acta Neuropathol (Berl) 1986, **72**: 43–54.

774a Carlotti Jr CG, Neder L, Colli BO, dos Santos MB, Scaff Garcia A, Elias Jr J, Chimelli LC. Clear cell meningioma of the fourth ventricle. Am J Surg Pathol 2003, **27**: 131–135.

775 Coons SW, Johnson PC. Brachial plexus meningioma. Report of a case with immunohistochemical and ultrastructural examination. Acta Neuropathol (Berl) 1989, **77**: 445–448.

776 Couce ME, Aker FV, Scheithauer BW. Chordoid meningioma. A clinicopathologic study of 42 cases. Am J Surg Pathol 2000, **24**: 899–905.

777 Couce ME, Perry A, Webb P, Kepes JJ, Scheithauer BW. Fibrous meningioma with tyrosine-rich crystals. Ultrastruct Pathol 1999, **23**: 341–345.

778 Davidson GS, Hope JK. Meningeal tumors of childhood. Cancer 1989, **63**: 1205–1210.

779 Ferracini R, Poggi S, Frank G, Azzolini U, Sabattini E, Spagnotti F, Cenacchi G, Pileri S. Meningeal sarcoma with rhabdomyoblastic differentiation. Case report. Neurosurgery 1992, **30**: 782–785.

780 Germano IM, Edwards MS, Davis RL, Schiffer D. Intracranial meningiomas of the first two decades of life. J Neurosurg 1994, **80**: 447–453.

781 Gi H, Nagao S, Yoshizumi H, Nishioka T, Uno J, Shingu T, Fujita Y. Meningioma with hypergammaglobulinemia. Case report. J Neurosurg 1990, **73**: 628–629.

782 Harrison MJ, Wolfe DE, Lau TS, Mitnick RJ, Sachdev VP. Radiation-induced meningiomas. Experience at the Mount Sinai Hospital and review of the literature. J Neurosurg 1991, **75**: 564–574.

783 Heth JA, Kirby P, Menezes AH. Intraspinal familial clear cell meningioma in a mother and child. Case report. J Neurosurg 2000, **93**: 317–321.

784 Hojo H, Abe M. Rhabdoid papillary meningioma. Am J Surg Pathol 2001, **25**: 964–969.

785 Horten BC, Urich H, Stefoski D. Meningiomas with conspicuous plasma cell-lymphocytic components. A report of five cases. Cancer 1979, **43**: 258–264.

786 Jaaskelainen J, Haltia M, Servo A. Atypical and anaplastic meningiomas. Radiology, surgery, radiotherapy, and outcome. Surg Neurol 1986, **25**: 233–242.

787 Kallio M, Sankila R, Hakulinen T, Jaaskelainen J. Factors affecting operative and excess long-term mortality in 935 patients with intracranial meningioma. Neurosurgery 1992, **31**: 2–12.

788 Kepes JJ. Meningiomas. Biology, Pathology and Differential Diagnosis. New York: Masson, 1982.

789 Kepes JJ, Chen WY, Connors MH, Vogel FS. "Chordoid"

meningeal tumors in young individuals with peritumoral lymphoplasmacellular infiltrates causing systemic manifestations of the Castleman syndrome. A report of seven cases. Cancer 1988, 62: 391–406.

790 Kepes JJ, Goldware S, Leoni R. Meningioma with pseudoglandular pattern. A case report. J Neuropathol Exp Neurol 1983, 42: 61–68.

791 Kobata H, Kondo A, Iwasaki K, Kusaka H, Ito H, Sawada S. Chordoid meningioma in a child. Case report. J Neurosurg 1998, 88: 319–323.

792 Lang FF, Macdonald OK, Fuller GN, DeMonte F. Primary extradural meningiomas. A report on nine cases and review of the literature from the era of computerized tomography scanning. J Neurosurg 2000, 93: 940–950.

793 Lattes R, Bigotti G. Lipoblastic meningioma. "Vacuolated meningioma". Hum Pathol 1991, 22: 164–171.

794 Lockett L, Chiang V, Scully N. Primary pulmonary meningioma. Report of a case and review of the literature. Am J Surg Pathol 1997, 21: 453–460.

795 Longstreth WT, Jr., Dennis LK, McGuire VM, Drangsholt MT, Koepsell TD. Epidemiology of intracranial meningioma. Cancer 1993, 72: 639–648.

796 Louis DN, Hamilton AJ, Sobel RA, Ojemann RG. Pseudopsammomatous meningioma with elevated serum carcinoembryonic antigen. A true secretory meningioma. Case report. J Neurosurg 1991, 74: 129–132.

797 Louis DN, Scheithauer BW, Budka H, von Deimling A, Kepes JJ. Meningiomas. In Kleihues P, Cavanee W (eds): World Health Organization classification of tumours. Pathology and genetics—tumours of the nervous system. Lyon, 2000, IARC Press, pp. 175–184.

798 Ludwin SK, Rubinstein LJ, Russell DS. Papillary meningioma. A malignant variant of meningioma. Cancer 1975, 36: 1363–1373.

799 Mahmood A, Caccamo DV, Tomecek FJ, Malik GM. Atypical and malignant meningiomas. A clinicopathological review. Neurosurgery 1993, 33: 955–963.

800 Matyja E, Kuchna I, Kroh H, Mazurowski W, Zabek M. Meningiomas and gliomas in juxtaposition. Casual or causal coexistence? Report of two cases. Am J Surg Pathol 1995, 19: 37–41.

801 Michaud J, Gagne F. Microcystic meningioma. Clinicopathologic report of eight cases. Arch Pathol Lab Med 1983, 107: 75–80.

802 Miettinen M, Paetau A. Mapping of the keratin polypeptides in meningiomas of different types. An immunohistochemical analysis of 463 cases. Hum Pathol 2002, 33: 590–598.

803 Nakasu S, Li DH, Okabe H, Nakajima M, Matsuda M. Significance of MIB-1 staining indices in meningiomas. Comparison of two counting methods. Am J Surg Pathol 2001, 25: 472–478.

804 Ng HK, Tse CC, Lo ST. Microcystic meningiomas. An unusual morphological variant of meningiomas. Histopathology 1989, 14: 1–9.

805 Ng TH, Wong MP, Chan KW. Benign metastasizing meningioma. Clin Neurol Neurosurg 1990, 92: 152–154.

806 Odake G. Cystic meningioma. Report of three patients. Neurosurgery 1992, 30: 935–940.

807 Pasquier B, Gasnier F, Pasquier D, Keddari E, Morens A, Couderc P. Papillary meningioma. Clinicopathologic study of seven cases and review of the literature. Cancer 1986, 58: 299–305.

808 Perry A, Chicoine MR, Filiput E, Miller JP, Cross DT. Clinicopathologic assessment and grading of embolized meningiomas. A correlative study of 64 patients. Cancer 2001, 92: 701–711.

809 Perry A, Giannini C, Raghavan R, Scheithauer BW, Banerjee R, Margraf L, Bowers DC, Lytle RA, Newsham IF, Gutmann DH. Aggressive phenotypic and genotypic features in pediatric and NF2-associated meningiomas. A clinicopathologic study of 53 cases. J Neuropathol Exp Neurol 2001, 60: 994–1003.

810 Perry A, Scheithauer BW, Stafford SL, Abell-Aleff PC, Meyer FB. "Rhabdoid" meningioma. An aggressive variant. Am J Surg Pathol 1998, 22: 1482–1490.

811 Perry A, Scheithauer BW, Stafford SL, Lohse CM, Wollan PC. "Malignancy" in meningiomas. A clinicopathologic study of 116 patients, with grading implications. Cancer 1999, 85: 2046–2056.

812 Perry A, Stafford SL, Scheithauer BW, Suman VJ, Lohse CM. Meningioma grading. An analysis of histologic parameters. Am J Surg Pathol 1997, 21: 1455–1465.

813 Perry A, Stafford SL, Scheithauer BW, Suman VJ, Lohse CM. The prognostic significance of MIB-1, p53, and DNA flow cytometry in completely resected primary meningiomas. Cancer 1998, 82: 2262–2269.

814 Prayson RA, Farver CF. Primary pulmonary malignant meningioma. Am J Surg Pathol 1999, 23: 722–726.

815 Probst-Cousin S, Villagran-Lillo R, Lahl R, Bergmann M, Schmid KW, Gullotta F. Secretory meningioma. Clinical, histologic, and immunohistochemical findings in 31 cases. Cancer 1997, 79: 2003–2015.

816 Robinson JC, Challa VR, Jones DS, Kelly DL, Jr. Pericytosis and edema generation. A unique clinicopathological variant of meningioma. Neurosurgery 1996, 39: 700–706; discussion 706–707.

817 Roncaroli F, Riccioni L, Cerati M, Capella C, Calbucci F, Trevisan C, Eusebi V. Oncocytic meningioma. Am J Surg Pathol 1997, 21: 375–382.

818 Roncaroli F, Scheithauer BW, Laeng RH, Cenacchi G, Abell-Aleff P, Moschopulos M. Lipomatous meningioma. A clinicopathologic study of 18 cases with special reference to the issue of metaplasia. Am J Surg Pathol 2001, 25: 769–775.

819 Saleh J, Silberstein HJ, Salner AL, Uphoff DF. Meningioma. The role of a foreign body and irradiation in tumor formation. Neurosurgery 1991, 29: 113–118; discussion 118–119.

820 Su M, Ono K, Tanaka R, Takahashi H. An unusual meningioma variant with glial fibrillary acidic protein expression. Acta Neuropathol (Berl) 1997, 94: 499–503.

821 Sugita Y, Shigemori M, Harada H, Wada Y, Hayashi I, Morimastu M, Okamoto Y, Kajiwara K. Primary meningeal sarcomas with leiomyoblastic differentiation. A proposal for a new subtype of primary meningeal sarcomas. Am J Surg Pathol 2000, 24: 1273–1278.

822 Teo JG, Goh KY, Rosenblum MK, Muszynski CA, Epstein FJ. Intraparenchymal clear cell meningioma of the brainstem in a 2-year-old child. Case report and literature review. Pediatr Neurosurg 1998, 28: 27–30.

823 Thompson LD, Gyure KA. Extracranial sinonasal tract meningiomas. A clinicopathologic study of 30 cases with a review of the literature. Am J Surg Pathol 2000, 24: 640–650.

824 Tsuchida T, Matsumoto M, Shirayama Y, Kasai H, Kawamoto K. Immunohistochemical observation of foci of muscle actin-positive tumor cells in meningiomas. Arch Pathol Lab Med 1996, 120: 267–269.

825 Wanschitz J, Schmidbauer M, Maier H, Rossler K, Vorkapic P, Budka H. Suprasellar meningioma with expression of glial fibrillary acidic protein. A peculiar variant. Acta Neuropathol (Berl) 1995, 90: 539–544.

826 Wilson AJ, Ratliff JL, Lagios MD, Aguilar MJ. Mediastinal meningioma. Am J Surg Pathol 1979, 3: 557–562.

827 Winek RR, Scheithauer BW, Wick MR. Meningioma, meningeal hemangiopericytoma (angioblastic meningioma), peripheral hemangiopericytoma, and acoustic schwannoma. A comparative immunohistochemical study. Am J Surg Pathol 1989, 13: 251–261.

828 Zon LI, Johns WD, Stomper PC, Kaplan WD, Connolly JL,

Morris JH, Harris JR, Henderson IC, Skarin AT. Breast carcinoma metastatic to a meningioma. Case report and review of the literature. Arch Intern Med 1989, **149**: 959–962.

828a Zorludemir S, Scheithauer BW, Hirose T, Van Houten C, Miller G, Meyer FB. Clear cell meningioma. A clinicopathologic study of a potentially aggressive variant of meningioma. Am J Surg Pathol 1995, **19**: 493–505.

Nonmeningothelial mesenchymal tumors

829 Oliveira AM, Scheithauer BW, Salomao DR, Parisi JE, Burger PC, Nascimento AG. Primary sarcomas of the brain and spinal cord. A study of 18 cases. Am J Surg Pathol 2002, **26**: 1056–1063.

830 Paulus W, Slowik F, Jellinger K. Primary intracranial sarcomas. Histopathological features of 19 cases. Histopathology 1991, **18**: 395–402.

Lipoma and liposarcoma

831 Bigelow DC, Eisen MD, Smith PG, Yousem DM, Levine RS, Jackler RK, Kennedy DW, Kotapka MJ. Lipomas of the internal auditory canal and cerebellopontine angle. Laryngoscope 1998, **108**: 1459–1469.

832 Bognar L, Balint K, Bardoczy Z. Symptomatic osteolipoma of the tuber cinereum. Case report. J Neurosurg 2002, **96**: 361–363.

833 Brown PG, Shaver EG. Myolipoma in a tethered cord. Case report and review of the literature. J Neurosurg (Spine 2) 2000, **92**: 214–216.

834 Budka H. Intracranial lipomatous hamartomas (intracranial "lipomas"). A study of 13 cases including combinations with medulloblastoma, colloid and epidermoid cysts, angiomatosis and other malformations. Acta Neuropathol (Berl) 1974, **28**: 205–222.

835 Chitoku S, Kawai S, Watabe Y, Nishitani M, Fujimoto K, Otsuka H, Fushimi H, Kotoh K, Fuji T. Intradural spinal hibernoma. Case report. Surg Neurol 1998, **49**: 509–512.

836 Christensen WN, Long DM, Epstein JI. Cerebellopontine angle lipoma. Hum Pathol 1986, **17**: 739–743.

837 Cinalli G, Zerah M, Carteret M, Doz F, Vinikoff L, Lellouch-Tubiana A, Husson B, Pierre-Kahn A. Subdural sarcoma associated with chronic subdural hematoma. Report of two cases and review of the literature. J Neurosurg 1997, **86**: 553–557.

838 Feldman RP, Marcovici A, LaSala PA. Intracranial lipoma of the sylvian fissure. Case report and review of the literature. J Neurosurg 2001, **94**: 515–519.

839 Haddad SF, Hitchon PW, Godersky JC. Idiopathic and glucocorticoid-induced spinal epidural lipomatosis. J Neurosurg 1991, **74**: 38–42.

840 Harrison MJ, Mitnick RJ, Rosenblum BR, Rothman AS. Leptomyelolipoma. Analysis of 20 cases. J Neurosurg 1990, **73**: 360–367.

841 Lee M, Rezai AR, Abbott R, Coelho DH, Epstein FJ. Intramedullary spinal cord lipomas. J Neurosurg 1995, **82**: 394–400.

842 Lin YC, Huang CC, Chen HJ. Intraspinal osteolipoma. Case report. J Neurosurg 2001, **94**: 126–128.

843 Perling LH, Laurent JP, Cheek WR. Epidural hibernoma as a complication of corticosteroid treatment. Case report. J Neurosurg 1988, **69**: 613–616.

844 Pirotte B, Krischek B, Levivier M, Bolyn S, Brucher JM, Brotchi J. Diagnostic and microsurgical presentation of intracranial angiolipomas. Case report and review of the literature. J Neurosurg 1998, **88**: 129–132.

845 Preul MC, Leblanc R, Tampieri D, Robitaille Y, Pokrupa R. Spinal angiolipomas. Report of three cases. J Neurosurg 1993, **78**: 280–286.

846 Sheridan F, Scharf D, Henderson VW, Miller CA. Lipomas of

the mesencephalic tectum and rostral pons associated with sleep apnea syndrome. Clin Neuropathol 1990, **9**: 152–156.

847 Sima A, Kindblom LG, Pellettieri L. Liposarcoma of the meninges. A case report. Acta Pathol Microbiol Scand (A) 1976, **84**: 306–310.

848 Tresser N, Parveen T, Roessmann U. Intracranial lipomas with teratomatous elements. Arch Pathol Lab Med 1993, **117**: 918–920.

849 Walsh JW, Markesbery WR. Histological features of congenital lipomas of the lower spinal canal. J Neurosurg 1980, **52**: 564–569.

Osseous and cartilaginous tumors

850 Bauman GS, Wara WM, Ciricillo SF, Davis RL, Zoger S, Edwards MS. Primary intracerebral osteosarcoma. A case report. J Neurooncol 1997, **32**: 209–213.

851 Bernstein M, Perrin RG, Platts ME, Simpson WJ. Radiation-induced cerebellar chondrosarcoma. Case report. J Neurosurg 1984, **61**: 174–177.

852 Chakrabortty S, Tamaki N, Kondoh T, Kojima N, Kamikawa H, Matsumoto S. Maffucci's syndrome associated with intracranial enchondroma and aneurysm. Case report. Surg Neurol 1991, **36**: 216–220.

853 Cohen IJ, Kornreich L. Intracranial osteosarcoma. Report of four cases and review of the literature. J Neurooncol 1999, **43**: 93.

854 Fallon MD, Ellerbrake D, Teitelbaum SL. Meningeal osteomas and chronic renal failure. Hum Pathol 1982, **13**: 449–453.

855 Korten AG, ter Berg HJ, Spincemaille GH, van der Laan RT, Van de Wel AM. Intracranial chondrosarcoma. Review of the literature and report of 15 cases. J Neurol Neurosurg Psychiatry 1998, **65**: 88–92.

856 Lacerte D, Gagne F, Copty M. Intracranial chondroma. Report of two cases and review of the literature. Can J Neurol Sci 1996, **23**: 132–137.

857 Mello LR, Bernardes CI, Feltrin Y, Rodacki MA. Thoracic spine arachnoid ossification with and without cord cavitation. Report of three cases. J Neurosurg (Spine 1) 2001, **94**: 115–120.

858 Miyamori T, Mizukoshi H, Yamano K, Takayanagi N, Sugino M, Hayase H, Ito H. Intracranial chondrosarcoma. Case report. Neurol Med Chir (Tokyo) 1990, **30**: 263–267.

859 Nakayama M, Nagayama T, Hirano H, Oyoshi T, Kuratsu J. Giant chondroma arising from the dura mater of the convexity. Case report and review of the literature. J Neurosurg 2001, **94**: 331–334.

860 Parker JR, Zarabi MC, Parker JC, Jr. Intracerebral mesenchymal chondrosarcoma. Ann Clin Lab Sci 1989, **19**: 401–407.

861 Rushing EJ, Armonda RA, Ansari Q, Mena H. Mesenchymal chondrosarcoma. A clinicopathologic and flow cytometric study of 13 cases presenting in the central nervous system. Cancer 1996, **77**: 1884–1891.

862 Sato K, Kubota T, Yoshida K, Murata H. Intracranial extraskeletal myxoid chondrosarcoma with special reference to lamellar inclusions in the rough endoplasmic reticulum. Acta Neuropathol (Berl) 1993, **86**: 525–528.

863 Sipos EP, Tamargo RJ, Epstein JI, North RB. Primary intracerebral small-cell osteosarcoma in an adolescent girl. Report of a case. J Neurooncol 1997, **32**: 169–174.

864 Traflet RF, Babaria AR, Barolat G, Doan HT, Gonzalez C, Mishkin MM. Intracranial chondroma in a patient with Ollier's disease. Case report. J Neurosurg 1989, **70**: 274–276.

Fibroblastic and "fibrohistiocytic" tumors

865 Alston SR, Francel PC, Jane JA, Jr. Solitary fibrous tumor of the spinal cord. Am J Surg Pathol 1997, **21**: 477–483.

866 Bilsky MH, Schefler AC, Sandberg DI, Dunkel IJ, Rosenblum MK. Sclerosing epithelioid fibrosarcomas involving the neuraxis. Report of three cases. Neurosurgery 2000, **47**: 956–959.

867 Carneiro SS, Scheithauer BW, Nascimento AG, Hirose T, Davis DH. Solitary fibrous tumor of the meninges. A lesion distinct from fibrous meningioma. A clinicopathologic and immunohistochemical study. Am J Clin Pathol 1996, **106:** 217–224.

867a Castilla EA, Prayson RA, Stevens GHJ, Barnet GH. Brain-invasive solitary fibrous tumor of the meninges: report of a case. Int J Surg Pathol 2002, **10:** 217–221.

868 Gaspar LE, Mackenzie IR, Gilbert JJ, Kaufmann JC, Fisher BF, Macdonald DR, Cairncross JG. Primary cerebral fibrosarcomas. Clinicopathologic study and review of the literature. Cancer 1993, **72:** 3277–3281.

869 Hisaoka M, Furuta A, Rikimaru S. Sclerosing fibrous tumor of the cauda equina. A fibroblastic variant of peripheral nerve tumor? Acta Neuropathol (Berl) 1993, **86:** 193–197.

870 Iyer GV, Vaishya ND, Bhaktaviziam A, Taori GM, Abraham J. Angiofibroma of the middle cranial fossa. Case report. J Neurosurg 1971, **35:** 90–94.

871 Lopes MB, Lanzino G, Cloft HJ, Winston DC, Vance ML, Laws ER, Jr. Primary fibrosarcoma of the sella unrelated to previous radiation therapy. Mod Pathol 1998, **11:** 579–584.

872 Martinez-Salazar A, Supler M, Rojiani AM. Primary intracerebral malignant fibrous histiocytoma. Immunohistochemical findings and etiopathogenetic considerations. Mod Pathol 1997, **10:** 149–154.

873 McDonald P, Guha A, Provias J. Primary intracranial fibrosarcoma with intratumoral hemorrhage. Neuropathological diagnosis with review of the literature. J Neurooncol 1997, **35:** 133–139.

874 Mitchell A, Scheithauer BW, Ebersold MJ, Forbes GS. Intracranial fibromatosis. Neurosurgery 1991, **29:** 123–126.

875 Ng HK, Choi PC, Wong CW, To KF, Poon WS. Metastatic solitary fibrous tumor of the meninges. Case report. J Neurosurg 2000, **93:** 490–493.

876 Nishio S, Morioka T, Inamura T, Takeshita I, Fukui M, Sasaki M, Nakamura K, Wakisaka S. Radiation-induced brain tumours. Potential late complications of radiation therapy for brain tumours. Acta Neurochir (Wien) 1998, **140:** 763–770.

877 Pagenstecher A, Emmerich B, van Velthoven V, Korinthenberg R, Volk B. Exclusively intracranial cranial fasciitis in a child. Case report. J Neurosurg 1995, **83:** 744–747.

878 Palma L, Spagnoli LG, Yusuf MA. Intracerebral fibroma. Light and electron microscopic study. Acta Neurochir (Wien) 1985, **77:** 152–156.

879 Prayson RA, Estes ML, McMahon JT, Kalfas I, Sebek BA. Meningeal myofibroblastoma. Am J Surg Pathol 1993, **17:** 931–936.

880 Reyes-Mugica M, Chou P, Gonzalez-Crussi F, Tomita T. Fibroma of the meninges in a child. Immunohistological and ultrastructural study. Case report. J Neurosurg 1992, **76:** 143–147.

881 Slavik T, Bentley RC, Gray L, Fuchs HE, McLendon RE. Solitary fibrous tumor of the meninges occurring after irradiation of a mixed germ cell tumor of the pineal gland. Clin Neuropathol 1998, **17:** 55–60.

881a Tihan T, Viglione M, Rosenblum MK, Olivi A, Burger PC. Solitary fibrous tumors in the central nervous system. A clinicopathologic review of 18 cases and comparison to meningeal hemangiopericytomas. Arch Pathol Lab Med, **127:** 432–439.

Endothelial tumors

882 Abe M, Tabuchi K, Takagi M, Matsumoto S, Shimokama T, Kishikawa T. Spontaneous resolution of multiple hemangiomas of the brain. Case report. J Neurosurg 1990, **73:** 448–452.

883 Avellino AM, Grant GA, Harris AB, Wallace SK, Shaw CM. Recurrent intracranial Masson's vegetant intravascular hemangioendothelioma. Case report and review of the literature. J Neurosurg 1999, **91:** 308–312.

884 Buttner A, Marquart KH, Mehraein P, Weis S. Kaposi's sarcoma in the cerebellum of a patient with AIDS. Clin Neuropathol 1997, **16:** 185–189.

885 Hida K, Tada M, Iwasaki Y, Abe H. Intramedullary disseminated capillary hemangioma with localized spinal cord swelling. Case report. Neurosurgery 1993, **33:** 1099–1101.

886 Kristof RA, Van Roost D, Wolf HK, Schramm J. Intravascular papillary endothelial hyperplasia of the sellar region. Report of three cases and review of the literature. J Neurosurg 1997, **86:** 558–563.

887 Lach B, Benoit BG. Primary composite angiogenic leiomyosarcoma-epithelioid angiosarcoma of the brain. Ultrastruct Pathol 2000, **24:** 339–346.

888 Mena H, Ribas JL, Enzinger FM, Parisi JE. Primary angiosarcoma of the central nervous system. Study of eight cases and review of the literature. J Neurosurg 1991, **75:** 73–76.

889 Nora FE, Scheithauer BW. Primary epithelioid hemangioendothelioma of the brain. Am J Surg Pathol 1996, **20:** 707–714.

890 Pearl GS, Takei Y, Tindall GT, O'Brien MS, Payne NS, Hoffman JC. Benign hemangioendothelioma involving the central nervous system. "Strawberry nevus" of the neuraxis. Neurosurgery 1980, **7:** 249–256.

891 Roncaroli F, Scheithauer BW, Deen HG, Jr. Multiple hemangiomas (hemangiomatosis) of the cauda equina and spinal cord. Case report. J Neurosurg (Spine 2) 2000, **92:** 229–232.

891a Roncaroli F, Scheithauer BW, Krauss WE. Hemangioma of spinal nerve root. J Neurosurg (Spine 2) 1999, **91:** 175–180.

892 Roncaroli F, Scheithauer BW, Krauss WE. Capillary hemangioma of the spinal cord. Report of four cases. J Neurosurg (Spine 1) 2000, **93:** 148–151.

893 Roncaroli F, Scheithauer BW, Papazoglou S. Primary polymorphous hemangioendothelioma of the spinal cord. Case report. J Neurosurg (Spine 1) 2001, **95:** 93–95.

894 Samaratunga H, Searle J, Cominos D, Le Fevre I. Cerebral metastasis of an atrial myxoma mimicking an epithelioid hemangioendothelioma. Am J Surg Pathol 1994, **18:** 107–111.

895 Suzuki Y, Yoshida YK, Shirane R, Yoshimoto T, Watanabe M, Moriya T. Congenital primary cerebral angiosarcoma. Case report. J Neurosurg 2000, **92:** 466–468.

Meningeal hemangiopericytoma

896 Guthrie BL, Ebersold MJ, Scheithauer BW, Shaw EG. Meningeal hemangiopericytoma. Histopathological features, treatment, and long-term follow-up of 44 cases. Neurosurgery 1989, **25:** 514–522.

897 Jääskeläinen J, Louis DN, Paulus W, Haltia MJ. Haemangiopericytoma. In Kleihues P, Cavanee WK (eds): World Health Organization classification of tumours. Pathology and genetics—tumours of the nervous system. Lyon, 2000, IARC Press, pp. 190–192.

898 Mena H, Ribas JL, Pezeshkpour GH, Cowan DN, Parisi JE. Hemangiopericytoma of the central nervous system. A review of 94 cases. Hum Pathol 1991, **22:** 84–91.

899 Perry A, Scheithauer BW, Nascimento AG. The immunophenotypic spectrum of meningeal hemangiopericytoma. A comparison with fibrous meningioma and solitary fibrous tumor of meninges. Am J Surg Pathol 1997, **21:** 1354–1360.

Myogenous tumors

900 Caputo V, Repetti ML, Grimoldi N, Lazzarini G, Masini B, Radice F. Cerebral rhabdomyosarcoma with rhabdoid tumor-like features. J Neurooncol 1997, **32:** 81–86.

900a Dropcho EJ, Allen JC. Primary intracranial rhabdomyosarcoma.

Case report and review of the literature. J Neurooncol 1987, **5**: 139–150.

901 Herva R, Serlo W, Laitinen J, Becker LE. Intraventricular rhabdomyosarcoma after resection of hyperplastic choroid plexus. Acta Neuropathol (Berl) 1996, **92**: 213–216.

902 Janisch W, Janda J, Link I. (Primary diffuse leptomeningeal leiomyomatosis). Zentralbl Pathol 1994, **140**: 195–200.

903 Karpinski NC, Yaghmai R, Barba D, Hansen LA. Case of the month. March 1999—A 26 year old HIV positive male with dura based masses. Brain Pathol 1999, **9**: 609–610.

904 Kleinschmidt-DeMasters BK, Mierau GW, Sze CI, Breeze RE, Greffe B, Lillehei KO, Stephens JK. Unusual dural and skull-based mesenchymal neoplasms. A report of four cases. Hum Pathol 1998, **29**: 240–245.

905 Lach B, Duncan E, Rippstein P, Benoit BG. Primary intracranial pleomorphic angioleiomyoma—a new morphologic variant. An immunohistochemical and electron microscopic study. Cancer 1994, **74**: 1915–1920.

906 Lin SL, Wang JS, Huang CS, Tseng HH. Primary intracerebral leiomyoma. A case with eosinophilic inclusions of actin filaments. Histopathology 1996, **28**: 365–369.

907 Louis DN, Richardson EP, Jr, Dickersin GR, Petrucci DA, Rosenberg AE, Ojemann RG. Primary intracranial leiomyosarcoma. Case report. J Neurosurg 1989, **71**: 279–282.

908 Mierau GW, Greffe BS, Weeks DA. Primary leiomyosarcoma of brain in an adolescent with common variable immunodeficiency syndrome. Ultrastruct Pathol 1997, **21**: 301–305.

909 Ritter AM, Amaker BH, Graham RS, Broaddus WC, Ward JD. Central nervous system leiomyosarcoma in patients with acquired immunodeficiency syndrome. Report of two cases. J Neurosurg 2000, **92**: 688–692.

910 Xu F, De Las Casas LE, Dobbs Jr. LJ. Primary meningeal rhabdomyosarcoma in a child with hypomelanosis of Ito. Arch Pathol Lab Med 2000, **124**: 762–765.

Other mesenchymal neoplasms

911 Budka H, Pilz P, Guseo A. Primary leptomeningeal sarcomatosis. Clinicopathological report of six cases. J Neurol 1975, **211**: 77–93.

912 David K, Revesz T, Kratimenos G, Krausz T, Crockard HA. Oncogenic osteomalacia associated with a meningeal phosphaturic mesenchymal tumor. Case report. J Neurosurg 1996, **84**: 288–292.

913 Graham JF, Loo SY, Matoba A. Primary brain myxoma, an unusual tumor of meningeal origin. Case report. Neurosurgery 1999, **45**: 166–170.

914 Kurtkaya-Yapicier O, Scheithauer BW, Dedrick DJ, Wascher TM. Primary epithelioid sarcoma of the dura. Case report. Neurosurgery 2002, **50**: 198–202.

915 Thibodeau LL, Ariza A, Piepmeier JM. Primary leptomeningeal sarcomatosis. Case report. J Neurosurg 1988, **68**: 802–805.

Nerve sheath tumors of the craniospinal axis

916 Brown DF, Rushing EJ. Rosenthal fibers and eosinophilic granular bodies in a classic acoustic schwannoma. Arch Pathol Lab Med 1997, **121**: 1207–1209.

917 Carney JA. Psammomatous melanotic schwannoma. A distinctive, heritable tumor with special associations, including cardiac myxoma and the Cushing syndrome. Am J Surg Pathol 1990, **14**: 206–222.

918 Carvalho GA, Lindeke A, Tatagiba M, Ostertag H, Samii M. Cranial granular-cell tumor of the trigeminal nerve. Case report. J Neurosurg 1994, **81**: 795–798.

919 Casadei GP, Komori T, Scheithauer BW, Miller GM, Parisi JE, Kelly PJ. Intracranial parenchymal schwannoma. A clinicopathological and neuroimaging study of nine cases. J Neurosurg 1993, **79**: 217–222.

920 Casadei GP, Scheithauer BW, Hirose T, Manfrini M, Van Houten C, Wood MB. Cellular schwannoma. A clinicopathologic, DNA flow cytometric, and proliferation marker study of 70 patients. Cancer 1995, **75**: 1109–1119.

921 Chang Y, Horoupian DS, Jordan J, Steinberg G. Localized hypertrophic mononeuropathy of the trigeminal nerve. Arch Pathol Lab Med 1993, **117**: 170–176.

922 Comey CH, McLaughlin MR, Jho HD, Martinez AJ, Lunsford LD. Death from a malignant cerebellopontine angle triton tumor despite stereotactic radiosurgery. Case report. J Neurosurg 1998, **89**: 653–658.

923 Cras P, De Groote GC, Van Vyve M, Vercruyssen A, Martin JJ. Malignant pigmented spinal nerve root schwannoma metastasizing in the brain and viscera. Clin Neuropathol 1990, **9**: 290–294.

924 Deruaz JP, Janzer RC, Costa J. Cellular schwannomas of the intracranial and intraspinal compartment. Morphological and immunological characteristics compared with classical benign schwannomas. J Neuropathol Exp Neurol 1993, **52**: 114–118.

925 Ducatman BS, Scheithauer BW. Postirradiation neurofibrosarcoma. Cancer 1983, **51**: 1028–1033.

926 Ducatman BS, Scheithauer BW, Peipgras DG, Reiman HM, Illustrup DM. Malignant peripheral nerve sheath tumors. A clinicopathologic study of 120 cases. Cancer 1986, **57**: 2006–2021.

927 Franks AJ. Epithelioid neurilemmoma of the trigeminal nerve. An immunohistochemical and ultrastructural study. Histopathology 1985, **9**: 1339–1350.

928 Giannini C, Scheithauer BW, Steinberg J, Cosgrove TJ. Intraventricular perineurioma. Case report. Neurosurgery 1998, **43**: 1478–1481.

929 Han DH, Kim DG, Chi JG, Park SH, Jung HW, Kim YG. Malignant triton tumor of the acoustic nerve. Case report. J Neurosurg 1992, **76**: 874–877.

930 Hanabusa K, Morikawa A, Murata T, Taki W. Acoustic neuroma with malignant transformation. Case report. J Neurosurg 2001, **95**: 518–521.

931 Jung JM, Shin HJ, Chi JG, Park IS, Kim ES, Han JW. Malignant intraventricular schwannoma. Case report. J Neurosurg 1995, **82**: 121–124.

932 Kaar GF, Bashir SH, N'Dow JM, Best PV, Gomersall LN. Neurothekeoma of the cauda equina. J Neurol Neurosurg Psychiatry 1996, **61**: 530–531.

933 Kepes JJ. Rosenthal fibers in a classic acoustic schwannoma. Arch Pathol Lab Med 1998, **122**: 673–674, (Letter).

934 Killeen RM, Davy CL, Bauserman SC. Melanocytic schwannoma. Cancer 1988, **62**: 174–183.

935 Levy WJ, Ansbacher L, Byer J, Nutkiewicz A, Fratkin J. Primary malignant nerve sheath tumor of the gasserian ganglion. A report of two cases. Neurosurgery 1983, **13**: 572–576.

936 Louis DN, Stemmer-Rachamimov A, Wiestler OD. Neurofibromatosis type 2. In Kleihues P, Cavenee WK (eds): World Health Organization classification of tumours. Pathology and genetics—tumours of the nervous system. Lyon, 2000, IARC Press, pp. 219–222.

937 Marchese MJ, McDonald JV. Intramedullary melanotic schwannoma of the cervical spinal cord. Report of a case. Surg Neurol 1990, **33**: 353–355.

938 Mrak RE, Flanigan S, Collins CL. Malignant acoustic schwannoma. Arch Pathol Lab Med 1994, **118**: 557–561.

939 Nadkarni TD, Rekate HL, Coons SW. Plexiform neurofibroma of the cauda equina. Case report. J Neurosurg 1999, **91**: 112–115.

940 Paulus W, Warmuth-Metz M, Sorensen N. Intracranial neurothekeoma (nerve-sheath myxoma). Case report. J Neurosurg 1993, **79**: 280–282.

941 Perentes E, Nakagawa Y, Ross GW, Stanton C, Rubinstein LJ. Expression of epithelial membrane antigen in perineurial cells

Clinicopathological study of seven cases of spinal cord teratoma. A possible germ cell origin. Histopathology 1998, **32:** 51–56.

1008 Bjornsson J, Scheithauer BW, Okazaki H, Leech RW. Intracranial germ cell tumors. Pathobiological and immunohistochemical aspects of 70 cases. J Neuropathol Exp Neurol 1985, **44:** 32–46.

1009 Ferreira J, Eviatar L, Schneider S, Grossman R. Prenatal diagnosis of intracranial teratoma. Prolonged survival after resection of a malignant teratoma diagnosed prenatally by ultrasound. A case report and literature review. Pediatr Neurosurg 1993, **19:** 84–88.

1010 Freilich RJ, Thompson SJ, Walker RW, Rosenblum MK. Adenocarcinomatous transformation of intracranial germ cell tumors. Am J Surg Pathol 1995, **19:** 537–544.

1011 Hashimoto T, Sasagawa I, Ishigooka M, Kubota Y, Nakada T, Fujita T, Nakai O. Down's syndrome associated with intracranial germinoma and testicular embryonal carcinoma. Urol Int 1995, **55:** 120–122.

1012 Hasle H, Mellemgaard A, Nielsen J, Hansen J. Cancer incidence in men with Klinefelter syndrome. Br J Cancer 1995, **71:** 416–420.

1013 Heimdal K, Evensen SA, Fossa SD, Hirschberg H, Langholm R, Brogger A, Moller P. Karyotyping of a hematologic neoplasia developing shortly after treatment for cerebral extragonadal germ cell tumor. Cancer Genet Cytogenet 1991, **57:** 41–46.

1014 Hisa S, Morinaga S, Kobayashi Y, Ojima M, Chikaoka H, Sasano N. Intramedullary spinal cord germinoma producing HCG and precocious puberty in a boy. Cancer 1985, **55:** 2845–2849.

1015 Ide M, Jimbo M, Yamamoto M, Hagiwara S, Aiba M, Kubo O. Spontaneous regression of primary intracranial germinoma. A case report. Cancer 1997, **79:** 558–563.

1016 Ironside JW, Jefferson AA, Royds JA, Taylor CB, Timperley WR. Carcinoid tumour arising in a recurrent intradural spinal teratoma. Neuropathol Appl Neurobiol 1984, **10:** 479–489.

1017 Koen JL, McLendon RE, George TM. Intradural spinal teratoma. Evidence for a dysembryogenic origin. Report of four cases. J Neurosurg 1998, **89:** 844–851.

1018 Kraichoke S, Cosgrove M, Chandrasoma PT. Granulomatous inflammation in pineal germinoma. A cause of diagnostic failure at stereotaxic brain biopsy. Am J Surg Pathol 1988, **12:** 655–660.

1019 Matsutani M, Sano K, Takakura K, Fujimaki T, Nakamura O, Funata N, Seto T. Primary intracranial germ cell tumors. A clinical analysis of 153 histologically verified cases. J Neurosurg 1997, **86:** 446–455.

1020 Min KW, Scheithauer BW. Pineal germinomas and testicular seminoma. A comparative ultrastructural study with special references to early carcinomatous transformation. Ultrastruct Pathol 1990, **14:** 483–496.

1021 Naudin ten Cate L, Vermeij-Keers C, Smit DA, Cohen-Overbeek TE, Gerssen-Schoorl KB, Dijkhuizen T. Intracranial teratoma with multiple fetuses: pre- and post-natal appearance. Hum Pathol 1995, **26:** 804–807.

1022 Nikas DC, De Girolami U, Zamani AA, Pinkus GS, Bello L, Kirsch M, Black PM. Idiopathic pinealitis. Case report. J Neurosurg 1999, **91:** 330–334.

1023 O'Callaghan AM, Katapodis O, Ellison DW, Theaker JM, Mead GM. The growing teratoma syndrome in a nongerminomatous germ cell tumor of the pineal gland. A case report and review. Cancer 1997, **80:** 942–947.

1024 Okada Y, Nishikawa R, Matsutani M, Louis DN. Hypomethylated X chromosome gain and rare isochromosome 12p in diverse intracranial germ cell tumors. J Neuropathol Exp Neurol 2002, **61:** 531–538.

1025 O'Marcaigh AS, Ledger GA, Roche PC, Parisi JE, Zimmerman D. Aromatase expression in human germinomas with possible biological effects. J Clin Endocrinol Metab 1995, **80:** 3763–3766.

1026 Poremba C, Dockhorn-Dworniczak B, Merritt V, Li CY, Heidl G, Tauber PF, Bocker W, Yandell DW. Immature teratomas of different origin carried by a pregnant mother and her fetus. Diagn Mol Pathol 1993, **2:** 131–136.

1027 Preissig SH, Smith MT, Huntington HW. Rhabdomyosarcoma arising in a pineal teratoma. Cancer 1979, **44:** 281–284.

1028 Rosenblum MK, Matsutani M, Van Meir EG. CNS germ cell tumours. In Kleihues P, Cavenee WK (eds): World Health Organization classification of tumours. Pathology and genetics—tumours of the nervous system. Lyon, 2000, IARC Press, pp. 207–214.

1029 Rueda-Pedraza ME, Heifetz SA, Sesterhenn IA, Clark GB. Primary intracranial germ cell tumors in the first two decades of life. A clinical, light-microscopic, and immunohistochemical analysis of 54 cases. Perspect Pediatr Pathol 1987, **10:** 160–207.

1030 Schild SE, Scheithauer BW, Haddock MG, Wong WW, Lyons MK, Marks LB, Norman MG, Burger PC. Histologically confirmed pineal tumors and other germ cell tumors of the brain. Cancer 1996, **78:** 2564–2571.

1031 Shaffrey ME, Lanzino G, Lopes MB, Hessler RB, Kassell NF, VandenBerg SR. Maturation of intracranial immature teratomas. Report of two cases. J Neurosurg 1996, **85:** 672–676.

1032 Skullerud K, Stenwig AE, Brandtzaeg P, Nesland JM, Kerty E, Langmoen I, Saeter G. Intracranial primary leiomyosarcoma arising in a teratoma of the pineal area. Clin Neuropathol 1995, **14:** 245–248.

Melanocytic tumors

1033 Adamek D, Kaluza J, Stachura K. Primary balloon cell malignant melanoma of the right temporo-parietal region arising from meningeal naevus. Clin Neuropathol 1995, **14:** 29–32.

1034 Alameda F, Lloreta J, Galito E, Roquer J, Serrano S. Meningeal melanocytoma. A case report and literature review. Ultrastruct Pathol 1998, **22:** 349–356.

1035 Allcutt D, Michowiz S, Weitzman S, Becker L, Blaser S, Hoffman HJ, Humphreys RP, Drake JM, Rutka JT. Primary leptomeningeal melanoma. An unusually aggressive tumor in childhood. Neurosurgery 1993, **32:** 721–729.

1036 Brat DJ, Giannini C, Scheithauer BW, Burger PC. Primary melanocytic neoplasms of the central nervous system. Am J Surg Pathol 1999, **23:** 745–754.

1037 Chow M, Clarke DB, Maloney WJ, Sangalang V. Meningeal melanocytoma of the planum sphenoidale. Case report and review of the literature. J Neurosurg 2001, **94:** 841–845.

1038 Gelman BB, Trier TT, Chaljub G, Borokowski J, Nauta HJ. Oncocytoma in melanocytoma of the spinal cord. Case report. Neurosurgery 2000, **47:** 756–759.

1039 Glick R, Baker C, Husain S, Hays A, Hibshoosh H. Primary melanocytomas of the spinal cord. A report of seven cases. Clin Neuropathol 1997, **16:** 127–132.

1040 Haddad FS, Jamali AF, Rebeiz JJ, Fahl M, Haddad GF. Primary malignant melanoma of the gasserian ganglion associated with neurofibromatosis. Surg Neurol 1991, **35:** 310–316.

1041 Koenigsmann M, Jautzke G, Unger M, Theallier-Janko A, Wiegel T, Stoltenburg-Didinger G. June 2002. 57-year-old male with leptomeningeal and liver tumors. Brain Pathol 2002, **12:** 519–520.

1042 Matsumoto S, Kang Y, Sato S, Kawakami Y, Oda Y, Araki M, Kawamura J, Uchida H. Spinal meningeal melanocytoma presenting with superficial siderosis of the central nervous system. Case report and review of the literature. J Neurosurg 1998, **88:** 890–894.

1043 O'Brien TF, Moran M, Miller JH, Hensley SD. Meningeal melanocytoma. An uncommon diagnostic pitfall in surgical neuropathology. Arch Pathol Lab Med 1995, **119:** 542–546.

1044 Piercecchi-Marti MD, Mohamed H, Liprandi A, Gambarelli D,

Grisoli F, Pellissier JF. Intracranial meningeal melanocytoma associated with ipsilateral nevus of Ota. Case report. J Neurosurg 2002, **96**: 619–623.

1045 Reyes-Mugica M, Chou P, Byrd S, Ray V, Castelli M, Gattuso P, Gonzalez-Crussi F. Nevomelanocytic proliferations in the central nervous system of children. Cancer 1993, **72**: 2277–2285.

1046 Salpietro FM, Alafaci C, Gervasio O, La Rosa G, Baio A, Francolini DC, Batolo D, Tomasello F. Primary cervical melanoma with brain metastases. Case report and review of the literature. J Neurosurg 1998, **89**: 659–666.

1047 Suzuki T, Yasumoto Y, Kumami K, Matsumura K, Kumami M, Mochizuki M, Suzuki H, Kojima H. Primary pineal melanocytic tumor. Case report. J Neurosurg 2001, **94**: 523–527.

1048 Theunissen P, Spincemaille G, Pannebakker M, Lambers J. Meningeal melanoma associated with nevus of Ota. Case report and review. Clin Neuropathol 1993, **12**: 125–129.

1049 Tosaka M, Tamura M, Oriuchi N, Horikoshi M, Joshita T, Sugawara K, Kobayashi S, Kohga H, Yoshida T, Sasaki T. Cerebrospinal fluid immunocytochemical analysis and neuroimaging in the diagnosis of primary leptomeningeal melanoma. Case report. J Neurosurg 2001, **94**: 528–532.

Paraganglioma

1050 Caccamo DV, Ho KL, Garcia JH. Cauda equina tumor with ependymal and paraganglionic differentiation. Hum Pathol 1992, **23**: 835–838.

1051 Gaffney EF, Doorly T, Dinn JJ. Aggressive oncocytic neuroendocrine tumour ("oncocytic paraganglioma") of the cauda equina. Histopathology 1986, **10**: 311–319.

1052 Jamjoom ZA, Sadiq S, Naim UR, Malabary T. Cerebello-pontine angle paraganglioma simulating an acoustic neurinoma. Br J Neurosurg 1991, **5**: 307–312.

1053 Moran CA, Rush W, Mena H. Primary spinal paragangliomas. A clinicopathological and immunohistochemical study of 30 cases. Histopathology 1997, **31**: 167–173.

1054 Roche PH, Figarella-Branger D, Regis J, Peragut JC. Cauda equina paraganglioma with subsequent intracranial and intraspinal metastases. Acta Neurochir (Wien) 1996, **138**: 475–479.

1055 Sambaziotis D, Kontogeorgos G, Kovacs K, Horvath E, Levedis A. Intrasellar paraganglioma presenting as nonfunctioning pituitary adenoma. Arch Pathol Lab Med 1999, **123**: 429–432.

1056 Scheithauer BW, Parameswaran A, Burdick B. Intrasellar paraganglioma. Report of a case in a sibship of von Hippel–Lindau disease. Neurosurgery 1996, **38**: 395–399.

1057 Smith WT, Hughes B, Ermocilla R. Chemodectoma of the pineal region, with observations on the pineal body and chemoreceptor tissue. J Pathol Bacteriol 1966, **92**: 69–76.

1058 Sonneland PR, Scheithauer BW, LeChago J, Crawford BG, Onofrio BM. Paraganglioma of the cauda equina region. Clinicopathologic study of 31 cases with special reference to immunocytology and ultrastructure. Cancer 1986, **58**: 1720–1735.

1059 Strommer KN, Brandner S, Sarioglu AC, Sure U, Yonekawa Y. Symptomatic cerebellar metastasis and late local recurrence of a cauda equina paraganglioma. Case report. J Neurosurg 1995, **83**: 166–169.

1060 Toyota B, Barr HW, Ramsay D. Hemodynamic activity associated with a paraganglioma of the cauda equina. Case report. J Neurosurg 1993, **79**: 451–455.

Chordoma

1061 Bayar MA, Erdem Y, Tanyel O, Ozturk K, Buharali Z. Spinal chordoma of the terminal filum. Case report. J Neurosurg (Spine 2) 2002, **96**: 236–238.

1062 Commins D, Baran GA, Molleston M, Vollmer D. Hypothalamic chordoma. Case report. J Neurosurg 1994, **81**: 130–132.

1063 Katayama Y, Tsubokawa T, Hirasawa T, Takahata T, Nemoto

N. Intradural extraosseous chordoma in the foramen magnum region. Case report. J Neurosurg 1991, **75**: 976–979.

1064 Nishigaya K, Kaneko M, Ohashi Y, Nukui H. Intradural retroclival chordoma without bone involvement. No tumor regrowth 5 years after operation. Case report. J Neurosurg 1998, **88**: 764–768.

1065 Warnick RE, Raisanen J, Kaczmar T, Jr., Davis RL, Prados MD. Intradural chordoma of the tentorium cerebelli. Case report. J Neurosurg 1991, **74**: 508–511.

1066 Wolfe III JT, Scheithauer BW. "Intradural chordoma" or "giant ecchordosis physaliphora"? Report of two cases. Clin Neuropathol 1989, **6**: 98–103.

Hemangioblastoma (von Hippel–Lindau disease)

1067 Becker I, Paulus W, Roggendorf W. Histogenesis of stromal cells in cerebellar hemangioblastomas. An immunohistochemical study. Am J Pathol 1989, **134**: 271–275.

1068 Böhling T, Plate KH, Haltia MJ, Alitalo K, Neumann HPH. Von Hippel-Lindau disease and capillary hemangioblastoma. In Kleihues P, Cavenee WK (eds): World Health Organization classification of tumours. Pathology and genetics—tumours of the nervous system. Lyon, 2000, IARC Press, pp. 223–226.

1069 Bret P, Streichenberger N, Guyotat J. Metastasis of renal carcinoma to a cerebellar hemangioblastoma in a patient with von Hippel Lindau disease. A case report. Br J Neurosurg 1999, **13**: 413–416.

1070 Brodkey JA, Buchignani JA, O'Brien TF. Hemangioblastoma of the radial nerve. Case report. Neurosurgery 1995, **36**: 198–200.

1071 de la Monte SM, Horowitz SA. Hemangioblastomas. Clinical and histopathological factors correlated with recurrence. Neurosurgery 1989, **25**: 695–698.

1072 Eniss J, Wild G, Schroth G, Heiss E, Melms A. Multiple supratentorial hemangioblastomas following primary infratentorial manifestation. Clin Neuropathol 1991, **10**: 21–25.

1073 Fanburg-Smith JC, Gyure KA, Michal M, Katz D, Thompson LD. Retroperitoneal peripheral hemangioblastoma. A case report and review of the literature. Ann Diagn Pathol 2000, **4**: 81–87.

1074 Frank TS, Trojanowski JQ, Roberts SA, Brooks JJ. A detailed immunohistochemical analysis of cerebellar hemangioblastoma. An undifferentiated mesenchymal tumor. Mod Pathol 1989, **2**: 638–651.

1075 Giannini C, Scheithauer BW, Hellbusch LC, Rasmussen AG, Fox MW, McCormick SR, Davis DH. Peripheral nerve hemangioblastoma. Mod Pathol 1998, **11**: 999–1004.

1075a Hoang MP, Amirkhan RH. Inhibin alpha distinguishes hemangioblastoma from clear cell renal cell carcinoma. Am J Surg Pathol 2003, **27**: 1152–1156.

1076 Hufnagel TJ, Kim JH, True LD, Manuelidis EE. Immunohistochemistry of capillary hemangioblastoma. Immunoperoxidase-labeled antibody staining resolves the differential diagnosis with metastatic renal cell carcinoma, but does not explain the histogenesis of the capillary hemangioblastoma. Am J Surg Pathol 1989, **13**: 207–216.

1077 Isaka T, Horibe K, Nakatani S, Maruno M, Yoshimine T. Hemangioblastoma of the third ventricle. Neurosurg Rev 1999, **22**: 140–144.

1078 Ismail SM, Jasani B, Cole G. Histogenesis of haemangioblastomas. An immunocytochemical and ultrastructural study in a case of von Hippel–Lindau syndrome. J Clin Pathol 1985, **38**: 417–421.

1079 Kachhara R, Nair S, Radhakrishnan VV. Sellar-sphenoid sinus hemangioblastoma. Case report. Surg Neurol 1998, **50**: 461–463.

1080 Lach B, Gregor A, Rippstein P, Omulecka A. Angiogenic histogenesis of stromal cells in hemangioblastoma. Ultrastructural and immunohistochemical study. Ultrastruct Pathol 1999, **23**: 299–310.

1081 Medvedev YA, Matsko DE, Zubkov YN, Pak VA, Alexander LF. Coexistent hemangioblastoma and arteriovenous malformation of the cerebellum. Case report. J Neurosurg 1991, 75: 121–125.

1082 Naik RT, Purohit AK, Dinakar I, Ratnakar KS. Hemangioblastoma of the IV ventricle. Childs Nerv Syst 1995, 11: 499–500.

1083 Richmond BK, Schmidt III JH. Congenital cystic supratentorial hemangioblastoma. Case report. J Neurosurg 1995, 82: 113–115.

1084 Rojiani AM, Owen DA, Berry K, Woodhurst B, Anderson FH, Scudamore CH, Erb S. Hepatic hemangioblastoma. An unusual presentation in a patient with von Hippel–Lindau disease. Am J Surg Pathol 1991, 15: 81–86.

1085 Rubio A, Meyers SP, Powers JM, Nelson CN, de Papp EW. Hemangioblastoma of the optic nerve. Hum Pathol 1994, 25: 1249–1251.

1086 Weil RJ, Vortmeyer AO, Zhuang Z, Pack SD, Theodore N, Erickson RK, Oldfield EH. Clinical and molecular analysis of disseminated hemangioblastomatosis of the central nervous system in patients without von Hippel–Lindau disease. Report of four cases. J Neurosurg 2002, 96: 775–787.

Other primary tumors

1087 Kepes JJ, O'Boynick P, Jones S, Baum D, McMillan J, Adams ME. Adrenal cortical adenoma in the spinal canal of an 8-year-old girl. Am J Surg Pathol 1990, 14: 481–484.

1088 Kim SH, Paik S, Yoon DH, Kim TS. Oncocytoma of the spinal cord. Case report. J Neurosurg (Spine 2) 2001, 94: 310–312.

1089 Kleinschmidt-DeMasters BK, Winston KR, Rubinstein D, Samuels MH. Ectopic pituitary adenoma of the third ventricle. Case report. J Neurosurg 1990, 72: 139–142.

1090 Lindboe CF, Unsgard G, Myhr G, Scott H. ACTH and TSH producing ectopic suprasellar pituitary adenoma of the hypothalamic region. Case report. Clin Neuropathol 1993, 12: 138–141.

1091 Ruchti C, Balli-Antunes M, Gerber HA. Follicular tumor in the sellar region without primary cancer of the thyroid. Heterotopic carcinoma? Am J Clin Pathol 1987, 87: 776–780.

Secondary tumors

1092 Ariza A, Kim JH. Kaposi's sarcoma of the dura mater. Hum Pathol 1988, 19: 1461–1463.

1093 Berry MP, Jenkin RD. Parameningeal rhabdomyosarcoma in the young. Cancer 1981, 48: 281–288.

1094 Byrne TN. Spinal cord compression from epidural metastases. N Engl J Med 1992, 327: 614–619.

1095 Castaldo JE, Bernat JL, Meier FA, Schned AR. Intracranial metastases due to prostatic carcinoma. Cancer 1983, 52: 1739–1747.

1096 Cilluffo JM, Harner SG, Miller RH. Intracranial ceruminous gland adenocarcinoma. J Neurosurg 1981, 55: 952–956.

1097 Costigan DA, Winkelman MD. Intramedullary spinal cord metastasis. A clinicopathological study of 13 cases. J Neurosurg 1985, 62: 227–233.

1098 Delattre JY, Krol G, Thaler HT, Posner JB. Distribution of brain metastases. Arch Neurol 1988, 45: 741–744.

1099 Dolan EJ, Schwartz ML, Lewis AJ, Kassel EE, Cooper PW. Adenoid cystic carcinoma. An unusual neurosurgical entity. Can J Neurol Sci 1985, 12: 65–68.

1100 Espat NJ, Bilsky M, Lewis JJ, Leung D, Brennan MF. Soft tissue sarcoma brain metastases. Cancer 2002, 94: 2706–2711.

1101 Floeter MK, So YT, Ross DA, Greenberg D. Miliary metastasis to the brain. Clinical and radiologic features. Neurology 1987, 37: 1817–1818.

1102 Kleinschmidt-DeMasters BK. Dural metastases. A retrospective surgical and autopsy series. Arch Pathol Lab Med 2001, 125: 880–887.

1103 Kokkoris CP. Leptomeningeal carcinomatosis. How does cancer reach the pia-arachnoid? Cancer 1983, 51: 154–160.

1104 Le Chevalier T, Smith FP, Caille P, Constans JP, Rouesse JG. Sites of primary malignancies in patients presenting with cerebral metastases. A review of 120 cases. Cancer 1985, 56: 880–882.

1105 LeRoux PD, Berger MS, Elliott JP, Tamimi HK. Cerebral metastases from ovarian carcinoma. Cancer 1991, 67: 2194–2199.

1106 Lewis AJ. Sarcoma metastatic to the brain. Cancer 1988, 61: 593–601.

1107 Mrak RE. Origins of adenocarcinomas presenting as intracranial metastases. An ultrastructural study. Arch Pathol Lab Med 1993, 117: 1165–1169.

1108 O'Neill BP, Dinapoli RP, Okazaki H. Cerebral infarction as a result of tumor emboli. Cancer 1987, 60: 90–95.

1109 Patchell RA, Tibbs PA, Walsh JW, Dempsey RJ, Maruyama Y, Kryscio RJ, Markesbery WR, Macdonald JS, Young B. A randomized trial of surgery in the treatment of single metastases to the brain. N Engl J Med 1990, 322: 494–500.

1110 Paulus W, Romstock J, Weidenbecher M, Huk WJ, Fahlbusch R. Middle ear adenocarcinoma with intracranial extension. Case report. J Neurosurg 1999, 90: 555–558.

1111 Perry A, Parisi JE, Kurtin PJ. Metastatic adenocarcinoma to the brain. An immunohistochemical approach. Hum Pathol 1997, 28: 938–943.

1112 Perry JR, Bilbao JM. Metastatic alveolar soft part sarcoma presenting as a dural-based cerebral mass. Neurosurgery 1994, 34: 168–170.

1113 Piepmeier JM, Virapongse C, Kier EL, Kim J, Greenberg A. Intracranial adenocystic carcinoma presenting as a primary brain tumor. Neurosurgery 1983, 12: 348–352.

1114 Posner JB. Neurologic complications of cancer. Philadelphia, 1995, FA Davis.

1115 Redman BG, Tapazoglou E, Al-Sarraf M. Meningeal carcinomatosis in head and neck cancer. Report of six cases and review of the literature. Cancer 1986, 58: 2656–2661.

1116 Retsas S, Gershuny AR. Central nervous system involvement in malignant melanoma. Cancer 1988, 61: 1926–1934.

1117 Scully RE ed: Case records of the Massachusetts General Hospital. Weekly clinicopathological exercises. Case 28–1992. A 45-year-old man with confusion, seizures, and few focal findings. N Engl J Med 1992, 327: 107–116.

1118 Srodon M, Westra WH. Immunohistochemical staining for thyroid transcription factor-1. A helpful aid in discerning primary site of tumor origin in patients with brain metastases. Hum Pathol 2002, 33: 642–645.

1119 Steel TR, Allibone J, Revesz T, D'Arrigo C, Crockard HA. Intradural neurotropic spread of malignant mesothelioma. Case report and review of the literature. J Neurosurg 1998, 88: 122–125.

1120 Tsukada Y, Fouad A, Pickren JW, Lane WW. Central nervous system metastasis from breast carcinoma. Autopsy study. Cancer 1983, 52: 2349–2354.

1121 Vannier A, Gray F, Gherardi R, Marsault C, Degos JD, Poirier J. Diffuse subependymal periventricular metastases. Report of three cases. Cancer 1986, 58: 2720–2725.

Peripheral nerves
Juan M. Bilbao, M.D.

Introduction

The peripheral nervous system may be affected by a variety of multifocal and systemic disorders, and in selected patients, the biopsy of a peripheral nerve is a valuable method for the evaluation of peripheral neuropathy. The mere demonstration of peripheral nerve dysfunction by clinical examination is not an indication for nerve biopsy. The latter is more informative in patients in whom a proper clinical history, thorough physical examination, evaluation of kindred (even of patients without a phenotype suggestive of inherited neuropathy), examination of CSF, and electrophysiologic and immunologic studies have failed to determine the cause of nerve disorder. Conditions masquerading as a cryptogenic neuropathy, such as chronic inflammatory neuropathy, amyloidosis, and vasculitis, are occasionally revealed only at biopsy. In many of the metabolic and toxic neuropathies, history and biochemical analysis alone are sufficient to make a diagnosis. Included in these are the neuropathies of chronic alcoholism and malnutrition, porphyria, renal failure, toxic agents and pharmaceuticals, and diabetes mellitus. In our institution the three most common indications for nerve biopsy are a search for a specific interstitial nerve change (e.g., vasculitis, amyloidosis, granuloma), confirmation of inflammatory demyelination polyneuropathy, and diagnosis of hereditary neuropathy. Some of the inherited metabolic diseases (such as Fabry's disease, Krabbe's disease, and metachromatic leukodystrophy) that produce pathognomonic morphologic and histochemical changes in nerves[1] are now readily identified by biochemical analysis of tissue samples. Furthermore, neuropathies caused by amyloidosis or vasculitis can be diagnosed by biopsy of other tissues (see later discussion, p. 2578).

The diagnostic yield of the peripheral nerve biopsy varies considerably.[2–4,6,7] It is important to recognize that in many specimens the morphologic abnormality will be nonspecific, without providing clues as to a definite etiology. Nerve biopsy provides only a small window into the pathology of the peripheral nervous system and in many instances histologic change, however specific proximal to the biopsy site, may be associated with downstream (at biopsy site) nonspecific axonal degeneration. Over a 30-year-period (1972 to 2003) 897 consecutive subcutaneous nerve biopsies were performed in adult patients at St Michael's Hospital, University of Toronto. The sural nerve was selected in 880 patients, a branch of the radial nerve in nine, a branch of the ulnar nerve in three, and the lateral peroneal nerve in five. Eight additional specimens showed no nerve. A specific diagnosis was made in 29% of cases (Table 28.1). Specimens were either normal or showed minimal change in 14% of biopsies. Cases with normal histology included nerve biopsies in patients suspected of having vasculitis but with no clinical evidence of peripheral neuropathy; other patients with symptoms thought to represent neuropathy were found to have disorders of the spinal cord or muscle. Of the remaining 57% of cases the histologic abnormalities, although significant, were considered to be nonspecific (Table 28.2). Many of the patients in the latter group had a distal symmetric neuropathy of the type associated with most nutritional or metabolic-toxic conditions. In these cases,

Table 28.1 Specific diagnoses among 897 nerve biopsies

Guillain–Barré, CIDP	71
Vasculitis	85
CMT AND HSAN	34
Leprosy	10
Diabetic neuropathy—angiopathy	11
Amyloid	11
Tomaculous neuropathy	9
Paraprotein neuropathy	6
Granulomatous (nonleprosy)	7
Amiodarone neuropathy	3
Niemann–Pick disease	3
Filamentous axonopathy (disulfiram)	2
Sensory perineuritis	1
Fabry's disease	1
Fungal neuritis—vasculitis	1
Lymphoma	1
Chloroquine neuropathy	3
Perineurioma	1

Table 28.2 Diagnostic sensitivity of sural nerve biopsy (*N* = 897 cases)

	Cases (no.)	%
Specific diagnosis	260	29
Axonal degeneration	397	43
Mixed axonal degeneration–demyelination	70	8
Focal chronic inflammation and axonal degeneration	53	6
Normal or minimal change	127	14

interaction between physician and pathologist is essential in reaching a final diagnosis.[2,3,5]

Removal of a segment of peripheral nerve for diagnostic purposes should result in only a minimal morbidity.

Because of the muscular deficit that its resection induces, physicians request biopsy of a terminal motor nerve in very special circumstances.[4] The site of biopsy must avoid areas where previous local trauma to nerve may produce changes or artifacts that may be confused with a polyneuropathy. Pathologists favor a distal nerve because in most neuropathies the longest fibers are more often affected. The selected nerve should be accessible to conduction studies and have a constant anatomic course and fascicular composition. The **sural nerve**, a purely sensory subcutaneous nerve, combines all of these requirements and is therefore the most common biopsy site. Alternatively, the saphenous nerve, the superficial peroneal nerve, or a cutaneous branch of the radial nerve at the wrist are used. The sural nerve (derived mostly from the tibial nerve plus a small component from the

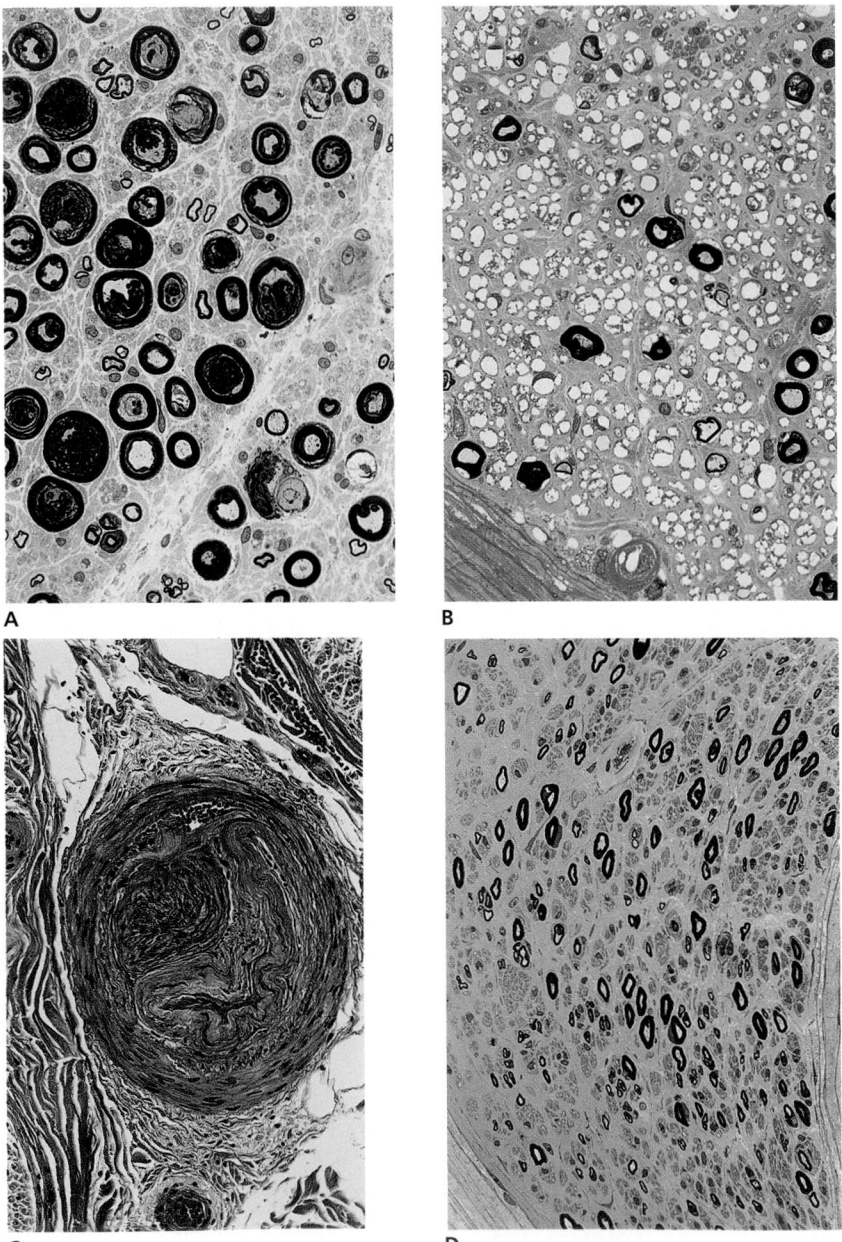

A   B

C   D

Fig. 28.115 Artifacts: **(A)** crush injury has some of the attributes of recent Wallerian degeneration; **(B)** electrocauterization mimicks infarct; **(C)** crushed vessel resembles healed vasculitis; **(D)** shrinkage caused by hyperosmolar fixative; compare with Figs 28.123B and 28.124A. (**A, B, D**, plastic resin, **C**, paraffin; HPS, hematoxylin-phloxin-saffron)

peroneal nerve) consists of 6 to 16 fascicles. It lies superficial to deep fascia, in the lateral retromalleolar region adjacent to the lesser saphenous vein, between the Achilles tendon and the tendon of the peroneus longus muscle.[6] Although a technique for fascicular biopsy of the sural nerve has been described, removal of a 5- to 7-cm-long segment of the entire nerve is preferable. Complications of the procedure include unpleasant paresthesia and pain persisting for 6 months or longer and in 10% or more of patients, and significant wound infections or traumatic neuroma in 1 to 2%. The four types of preparations needed for a proper evaluation of a nerve specimen are: paraffin embedding after B5 fixation, teased nerve fibers, cryostat sections after "quench" freezing in isopentane-liquid nitrogen, and plastic resin embedding for light and transmission electron microscopy. Because large fibers are greatly susceptible to artifacts, indelicate handling (Fig. 28.115) and the use of hyperosmolar fixatives are to be avoided (Fig. 28.122B). The segment of nerve selected for electron microscopy is received slightly stretched on a wooden stick and immediately immersed in chilled 2.5% glutaraldehyde in 0.05 M cacodylate buffer at pH 7.4 with an osmolarity of 340 mOs, where it is left undisturbed for at least 2 hours before trimming. In the paraffin-embedded tissue, we routinely use H&E, Luxol fast blue, leukocyte common antigen (LCA), lymphocyte markers, smooth muscle actin, ulex and CD34 immunostains, PAS, fibrin and Congo Red histostains. Of the plastic blocks four contain segments of nerve that comprise the entire cross-sectional area, and four represent fascicles in longitudinal orientation; the remaining blocks include one to three fascicles in transverse orientation. Examination of plastic resin-embedded (20 to 30 blocks), semithin sec-

tions counterstained with Toluidine Blue is essential in assessing a nerve specimen. Few structural changes will be found by electron microscopy if they were not first appreciated in semithin sections, particularly if viewing was done under oil immersion. Examination of "teased" nerve fiber preparation may unveil unique morphologic features in some cases, however the method is laborious and not economical. We recommend post-fixation in osmium tetroxide of a 12-mm segment of nerve, followed by maceration in glycerine for 48 hours before dissection. However gentle, the separation of single nerve fibers from their fascicular bundles with forceps may produce artifacts. This time-consuming technique requires an experienced dissector for at least 100 fibers of 10 internodes in length each (about 1 cm) should be examined to obtain meaningful data.

Normal anatomy

Three areas can be defined in peripheral nerves[24] (Fig. 28.116). The intrafascicular compartment contains myelinated and unmyelinated nerve fibers (Fig. 28.117; see also Figs 28.123 and 28.124), Schwann cells, microvessels and venules, fibroblasts, mast cells, macrophages,[16] collagen, oxytalan filaments (Fig. 28.118), and endoneurial ground substance. The presence of more than a few endoneurial cells (per fascicle on cross section) labeled with LCA is an abnormal finding. Endoneurial vessels differ from their counterpart in muscle in that they invariably have a pericytic complement (thus a microvessel rather than a capillary) and that their endothelium is nonfenestrated and displays tight junctions. Like the endothelium of brain, it is impermeable to

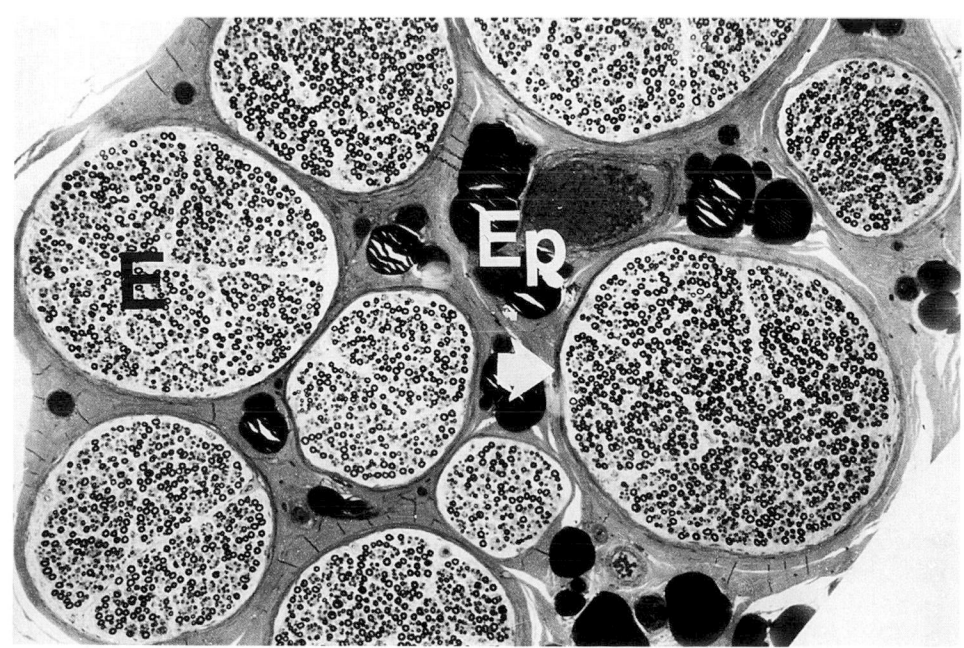

Fig. 28.116 Cross section of normal sural nerve: epineurium (Ep), perineurium (arrow), and endoneurium (E). (Plastic)

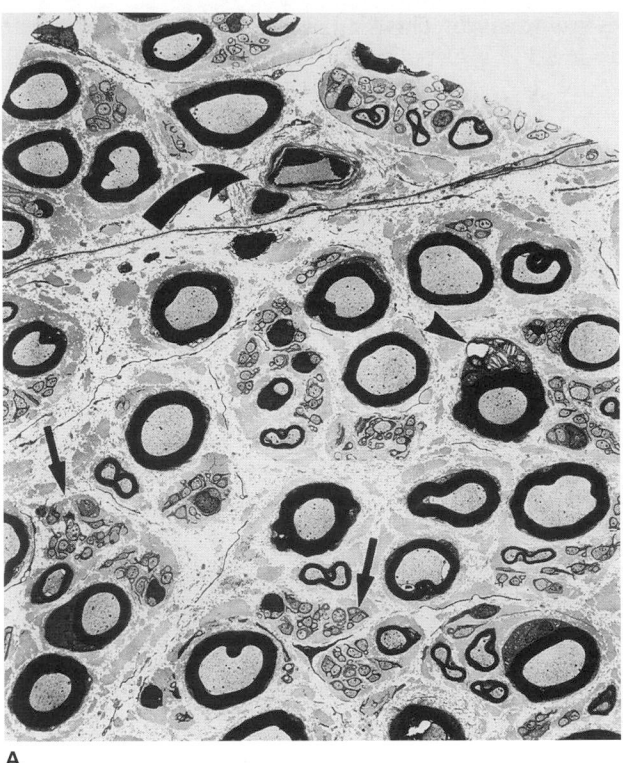 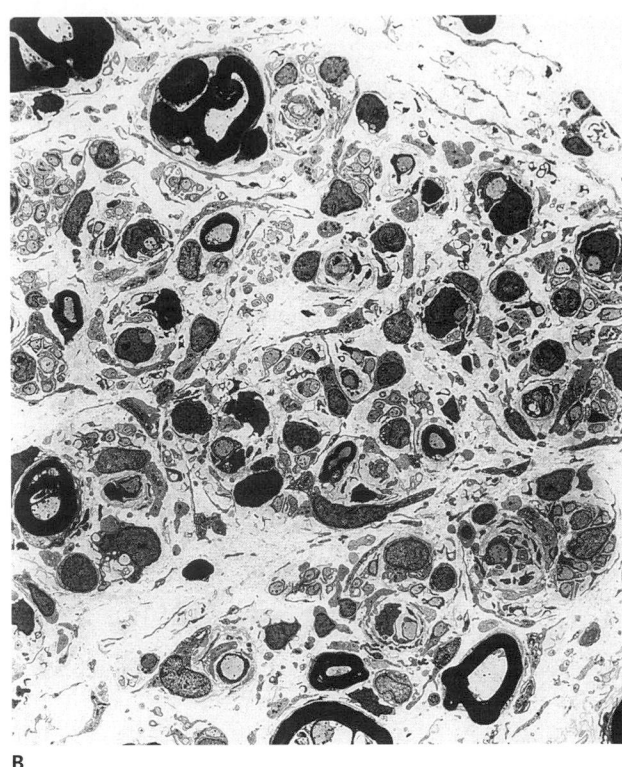

A **B**

Fig. 28.117 Sural nerve. **(A)** Normal. Note the unmyelinated fibers (arrow), Reich's pi-granule (arrowhead), a macrophage, and a mast cell adjacent to microvessel (open arrow). (×990) **(B)** Dropout of fibers and hypercellularity in CIDP. (×990)

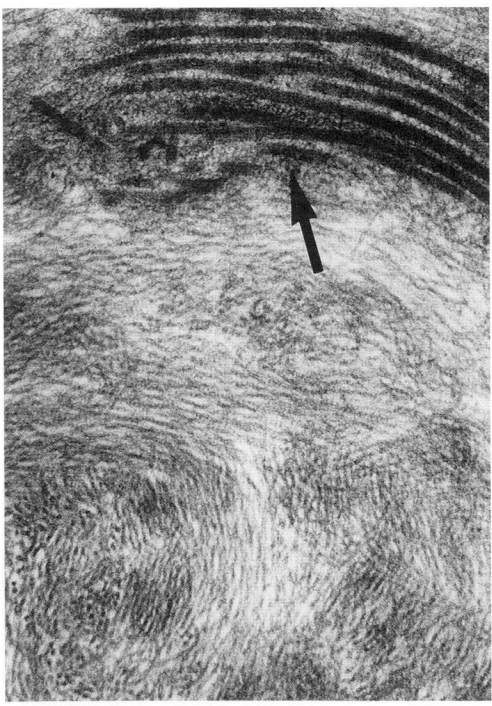

Fig. 28.118 Bundles of oxytalan filaments in endoneurium should not be confused with amyloid deposits. Compare size of oxytalan with collagen (arrow) (×21,000)

the transport of protein tracers.[21] An exception is the spinal ganglia, where there is always leakage to most substances. Poorly visualized in paraffin sections, Renaut bodies are enigmatic structures that intrude into the endoneurium. In semithin sections, they appear as whorled "cushions" adjacent to inner perineurium and consist of ground substance, randomly oriented fibrils, and fibroblasts with slender processes[9] (Fig. 28.119). In transverse sections, Renaut bodies may be seen to involve several fascicles; in some they extend for the entire circumference of subperineurium. In longitudinal sections Renaut bodies are seen to extend for variable distances. Ultrastructurally, Renaut bodies contain abundant extracellular filaments of 8 to 14 nm in diameter corresponding in size to the microfibrils described by Haust[17] and to the oxytalan filament of elastic fibers[27](Fig. 28.118). Renaut bodies are not seen during fetal life and seem to increase in number during age, particularly near or at entrapment sites, suggesting that repetitive trauma may play a role in their pathogenesis.

Each nerve fascicle is ensheathed by the perineurium, which consists of overlapping layers of flattened cells with interleaved collagen and elastin[23] (Fig. 28.120). Ultrastructurally, the perineurial cell features prominent pinocytotic vesicles, bundles of cytoplasmic filaments, and a continuous basal lamina on the free surface that allows extensive zonulae occludentes at points of contact between cells,[13] thus conferring on the perineurium the characteristics of a bidirectional diffusion barrier.[21] At the neuromuscular junction, the perineurial sleeve terminates before it reaches the end-plate.[13] At this point the perineurium is open ended, and the endoneurium and epineurium are continuous, without an intervening

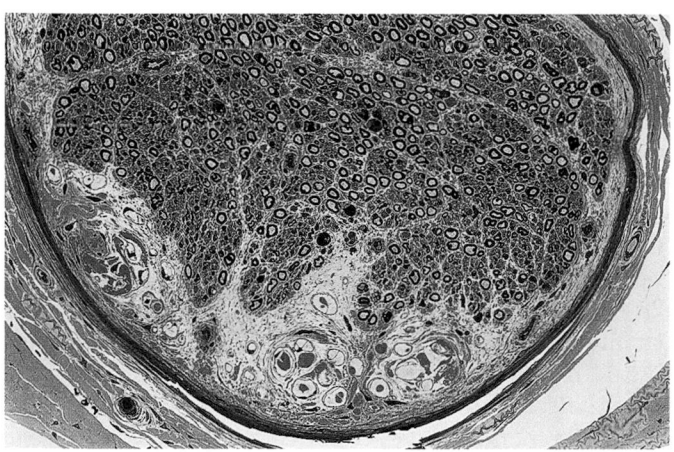

Fig. 28.119 Normal sural nerve. Renaut body. (Plastic resin)

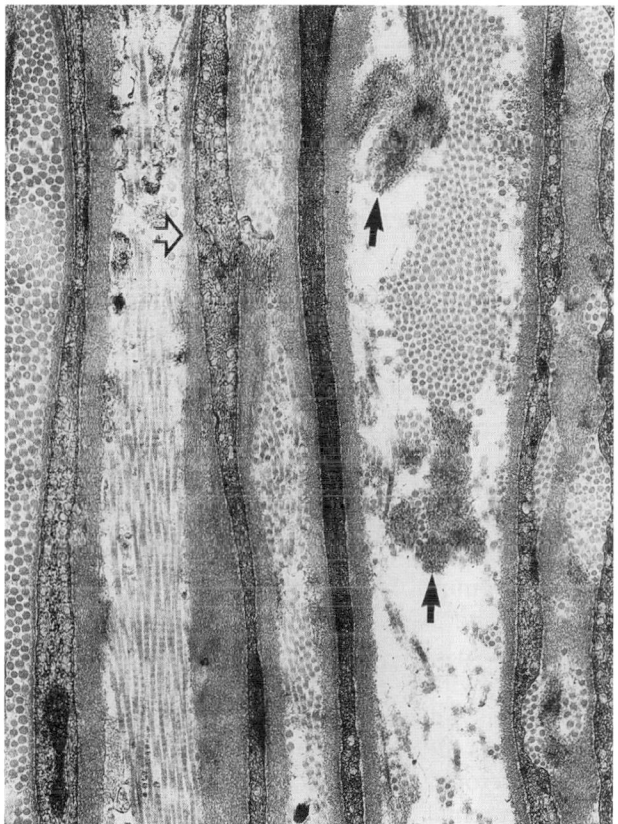

Fig. 28.120 Cross section of perineurium. Perineurial cells are linked by tight junctions (open arrow). Note intervening elaunin (arrows) and collagen fibers oriented longitudinally and circumferentially. Cell membrane shows pinocytotic vesicles. (×12,800)

structural barrier. Perineurial cell lineage studies using a recombinant retroviral vector in tissue cultures have elucidated the embryogenesis of this structure. Fibroblasts infected with a recombinant retrovirus (having an *E. coli* Lac Z gene that encodes beta-galactosidase) give rise to Lac Z-positive perineurial cells, whereas Schwann cells do not.[22] Immunopositivity for epithelial membrane antigen and lack of immunoreaction for S-100 protein are characteristics that distinguish the perineurial cell from

the Schwann cell.[8] The epineurium is the outermost covering of the peripheral nerves and consists of loose connective tissue, fat cells, and rare elastic fibers. Nerves are richly vascularized structures. Branches from the nearest limb artery bifurcate into ascending and descending rami that give off vasa nervorum that connect with longitudinal epineurial plexuses. The veins follow a similar course. A lymphatic system in the epineurium has been described.

Schwann cells originate from the neural crest and migrate into the peripheral nervous system to ensheath every myelinated and unmyelinated nerve fiber (Fig. 28.117) from the roots to the axonal termination. These cells display a continuous basal lamina,[12,14] and their nucleus lies lengthwise on the nerve fiber. The perinuclear cytoplasm accumulates lysosomal metachromatic lipid inclusions (pi-granule of Reich)[26] (Fig. 28.117) and Marchi-positive globules (Elzholz body) during aging, and abnormal deposits in many lipid storage diseases. Lipofuscin is seen in the Schwann cell cytoplasm of unmyelinated fibers. Schwann cells readily proliferate in response to axonal damage and myelin disintegration. They exhibit a passive response to invasion by *Mycobacterium leprae*, with long-term bacterial survival and proliferation.

Myelin is a proteophospholipid spiral formed by the invagination of the apposed and compacted Schwann cell membrane. The major protein components of peripheral myelin are protein 0, myelin-associated glycoprotein (antibodies against this protein cause demyelinating neuropathy in some IgM paraproteinemias), P1 protein (myelin basic protein), P2 glycoprotein (the major antigen in the production of experimental allergic neuritis), and peripheral myelin protein 22. Compact myelin corresponds to a sequence to two layers of fused Schwann cell membrane without intervening cytoplasm, which during formation is extruded to a paranodal and perinuclear position and to the intramyelinic incisures (or cytoplasmic pockets) of Schmidt–Lanterman.[18] The repetitive structures or periodicity of compact myelin comprises the major dense line (derived from the opposed cytoplasmic aspect of each pair of membranes) and the intraperiod line (formed by the opposed outer surface of each pair of membranes). The thickness of the myelin sheath and internodal length is proportional to axonal diameter. The basic myelinating unit of the peripheral nervous system is the internodal segment, which is delineated by the node of Ranvier, the latter defined as the point of separation of two contiguous Schwann cell territories.

Myelinated nerve fibers vary in outside diameter from 2 to 18 mm (Fig. 28.117). Intra-axonal structures analogous to corpora amylacea are incidentally found within myelinated fibers in peripheral nerves of older individuals (Fig. 28.159). These polyglucosan bodies are composed partly of glucose polymers and an unidentified protein; they stain strongly with PAS and variably

bulbs also occur in chronic inflammatory and demyelinating polyneuropathy (Figs 28.126 and 28.127D) and to a lesser extent in diabetic neuropathy.

Dejerine–Sottas disease (formerly classified as hereditary motor-sensory neuropathy type III) appears in childhood and is autosomal-recessive. The clinical features include sensory motor neuropathy, skeletal abnormalities, and markedly enlarged nerves. The CSF protein content is elevated, presumably because the spinal roots are involved. A progressive and debilitating clinical course is the rule. Electrophysiology discloses very slow conduction velocities (less than 10 m/s).

Nerve biopsy shows large numbers of onion bulbs, endoneurial fibrosis, loss of axons, and specifically hypomyelination: many fibers that for axon diameter should be myelinated are amyelinate or show disproportionately thin myelin sheaths[44] (Fig. 28.123C). This is a genetically complex syndrome caused in some patients by point mutations of the peripheral myelin protein 22 gene and in others by mutations in the gene of Po myelin protein; these are dominantly inherited. Some patients with a similar phenotype have no abnormality for the PMP 22 and Po genes but have a mutation of the early growth response gene. Nerve pathology in a group of

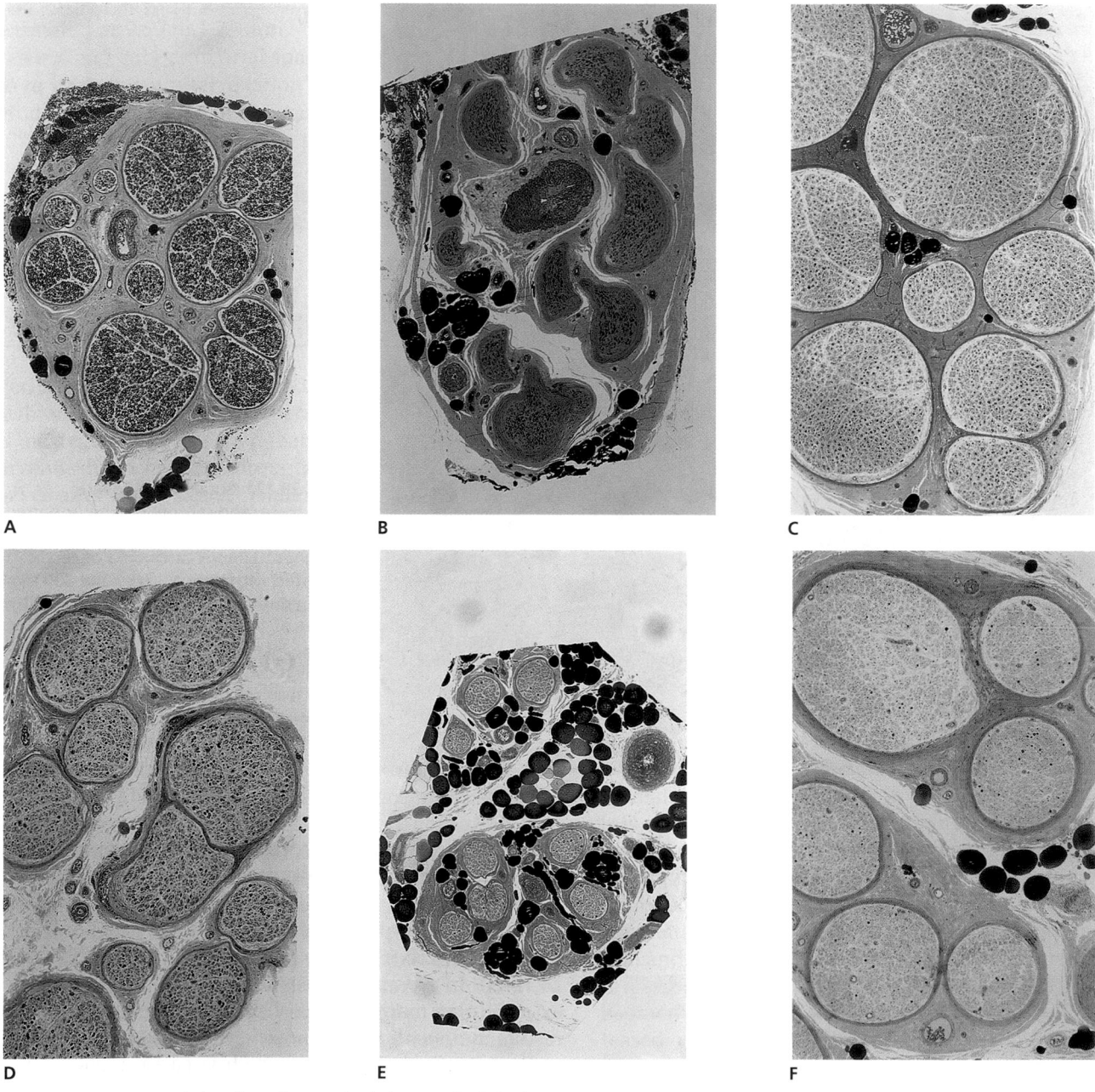

Fig. 28.122 Cross sections of sural nerve in: (**A**) normal adult; (**B**) shrinkage by hyperosmolar fixative, note lack of circularity of fascicles; (**C**) CMT-1; (**D**) amyloid neuropathy; (**E**) HSAN-II, note hypoplasia of fascicles; (**F**) HSAN-I. (Plastic resin. All pictures taken at same magnification, ×16.)

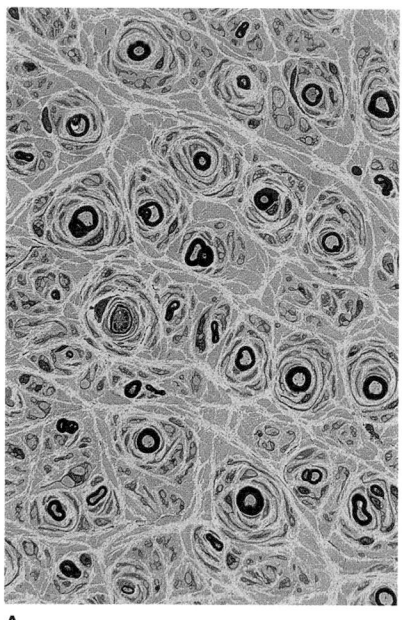 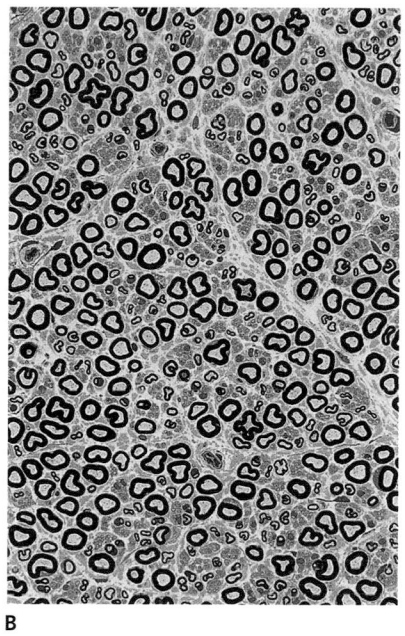 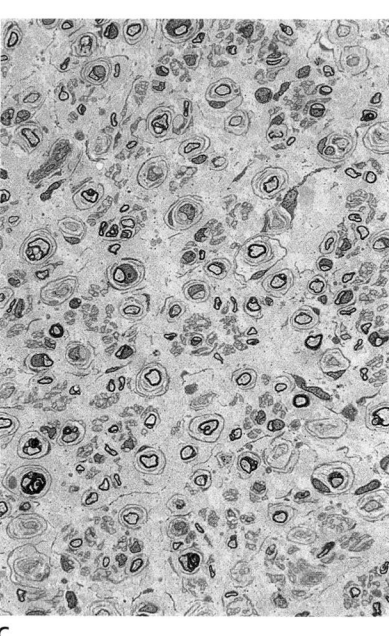

A   B   C

Fig. 28.123 Cross section of sural nerve in: (A) CMT-1: onion bulbs: (B) normal: (C) Dejerine–Sottas—hypomyelination. (Plastic resin. All pictures taken at same magnification: ×202. Oil immersion.)

patients with this condition who do not show mutations in any of the above genes shows onion bulbs formed mostly by basal lamina; in others focally folded myelin is prominent.

Charcot–Marie–Tooth disease (CMT) has historically been divided into the neuronal forms (characterized by normal or slightly slowed nerve conduction velocity) and the demyelinating or hypertrophic forms (in which nerve conduction velocity is markedly and diffusely reduced). The most common variant of Charcot–Marie–Tooth disease is type 1, characterized by conduction velocity slowing and autosomal dominant inheritance. CMT-2 refers to the autosomal dominant neuronal form of the disease. Autosomal recessive forms are classified as CMT-4 and most would fit the classic definition of Dejerine–Sottas syndrome, with a severe clinical phenotype and dramatic hypomyelination.

Clinical onset in CMT-1 is during the first to fourth decades of life, and the course is indolent. Patients develop weakness and wasting distally in lower extremities, associated with areflexia and sensory loss. The upper extremities are involved at a later stage. Pes cavus and scoliosis may be present as an early manifestation from childhood. Marked slowing of nerve conduction is always demonstrated. The histology is similar to that of Dejerine–Sottas disease, except that many fibers exhibit full myelination[47,48,52] (Figs 28.123A, 28.124B and 28.125A). Variable amounts of chronic inflammation can be found in some cases (see later). CMT-1 has several discrete genetic loci. The commonest, accounting for 70% to 80% of all CMT-1 patients, is due to a defect in expression.[53] Messenger RNA for PMP-22 is significantly elevated in nerve biopsies of patients with HMSN-Ia.[57] In CMT-1B, the defect is in another peripheral myelin protein, the P_0 protein, located on chromosome 1. These patients are clinically indistinguishable from patients with CMT-1A. The light microscopic features are also indistinguishable, but an ultrastructural finding which suggests the diagnosis of the P_0 mutation (CMT-1B) is the presence of uncompacted myelin.[43] Recently described is Charcot–Marie–Tooth type 1C due to a mutation of Early Growth Response 2 gene, and other families with CMT-1 do not appear to link to any of these genes, implying further genetic heterogeneity.

Charcot–Marie–Tooth disease type 2, for which there are multiple genetic loci, is usually clinically very similar to CMT-1, although on average the phenotype is milder. Histologically this disorder displays mostly chronic axonal loss with abundant regenerating clusters and no hypertrophy[39,45,49] (Fig. 28.124C).

Another genetically separate group of CMT phenotype patients is X-linked. More than 50 mutations of the Connexin 32 gene have been found to cause this syndrome. CMT-X males display a more severe clinical, electrophysiologic and histopathologic disease than females, befitting the notion that having two X chromosomes confers some protection. The pathology is somewhat nonspecific, but just as the condition is often considered "intermediate" between CMT-1 and CMT-2, so too is its pathology.[51,56] Classic onion bulbs are not very frequent, but "pseudo onion bulbs" are quite typical. In these formations a regenerating cluster is centered by a myelinated fiber and surrounded by several unmyelinated axons with their associated Schwann cells. Axon numbers are often relatively preserved in CMT-X, as large myelinated fibers degenerate or atrophy, but

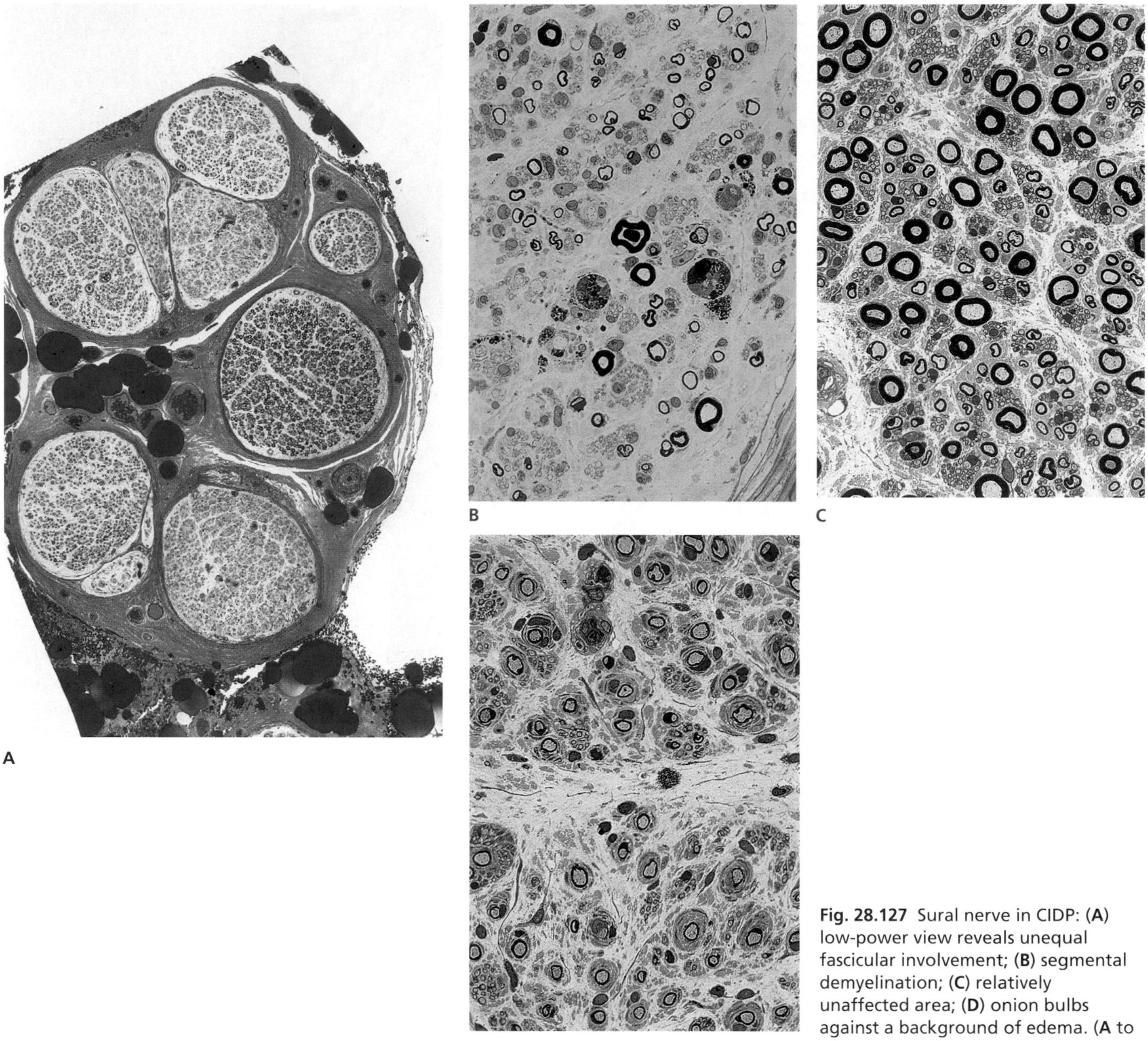

Fig. 28.127 Sural nerve in CIDP: (**A**) low-power view reveals unequal fascicular involvement; (**B**) segmental demyelination; (**C**) relatively unaffected area; (**D**) onion bulbs against a background of edema. (**A** to **D**, plastic resin)

consist of straight or curved prismatic or tubular inclusions[54] (Fig. 28.130). Depending on the plane of section they may appear as empty clefts or hollow, needle-like structures.

Metachromatic leukodystrophy is transmitted as an autosomal recessive trait and is characterized by the accumulation of galactosyl sulfatide in the white matter of brain and in peripheral nerves. Most cases are due to a deficiency of arylsulfatase A. Regardless of age of onset, most patients show evidence of demyelinating polyneuropathy, with onion bulb formation being more obvious in older individuals. The salient feature of the neuropathy is the accumulation of granules in Schwann cells and endoneurial macrophages (Fig. 28.131A). Such lipid deposits give a brown metachromasia when a frozen sec-

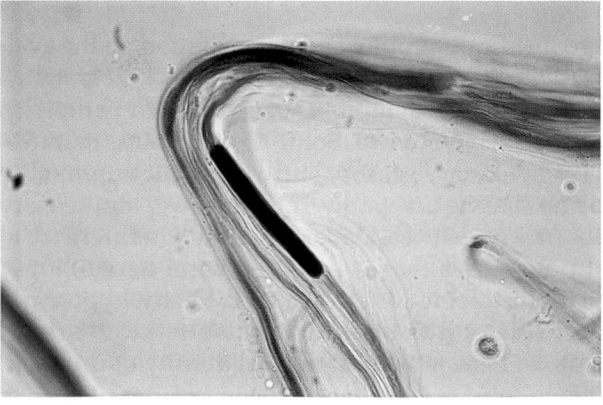

Fig. 28.128 Tomaculous neuropathy. (Teased nerve fiber preparation, osmium tetroxide)

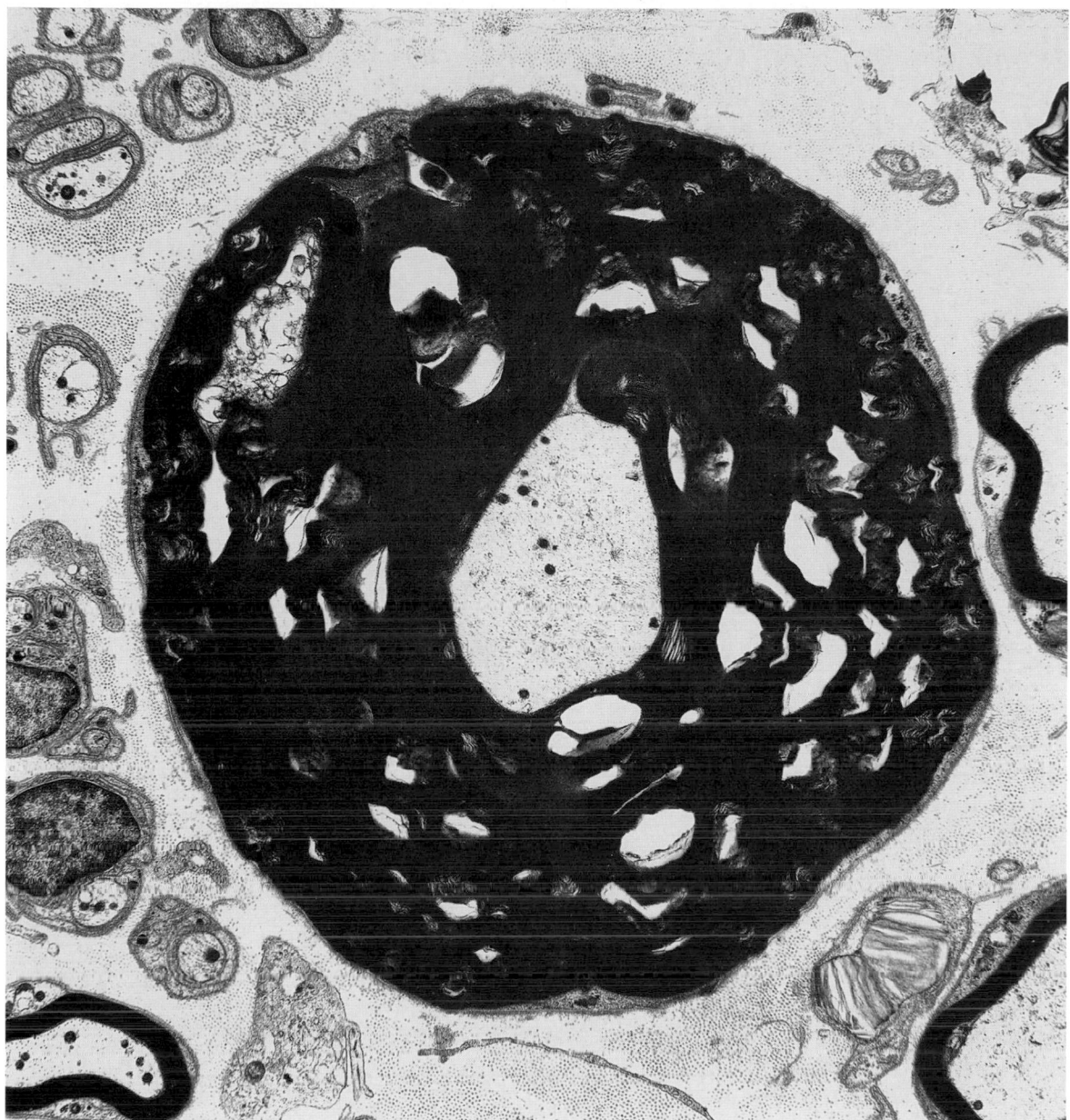

Fig. 28.129 Since the age of 12, a 42-year-old man has had recurrent episodes of peripheral nerve dysfunction considered typical of inherited liability to pressure palsies. Two sons are clinically normal but have slow nerve conduction velocities. Transverse section showing typical "jelly rolls" as shown in Fig. 28.124D. These consist of compacted and apposed redundant loops of myelin, characteristic of tomaculous neuropathy. (Electron micrograph. ×14,200)

tion is treated with a solution of acidified cresyl violet or when stained with toluidine blue or thionine; with pseudo-isocyanine the stored material develops a red-violet metachromasia.[38] Pretreatment of sections with lipid solvents abolishes the metachromatic reaction. By electron microscopy, many lysosomal lamellated inclusions can be seen, the most characteristic being the "**tuffstone**" **bodies**[55] (Fig. 28.131B).

Fabry's disease is a sex-linked inborn error of glycosphingolipid catabolism resulting from the deficiency of the lysosomal hydrolase alphagalactosidase in tissues. Affected males have extensive deposition of globotriao-

sylceramide (Gb Ose3 Cer) in the lysosomes of endothelium, pericytes, and smooth muscle cells of blood vessels. There is also deposition in the ganglion cells, heart, kidneys, cornea, and most other tissues. Clinical manifestations include painful neuropathy, corneal whorl dystrophy (Fig. 28.132A), renal failure, cutaneous angiokeratomata, and cardiac and cerebral vascular disease. In nerve biopsies there is massive accumulation of glycosphingolipids in perineurium, endothelial cells, and smooth muscle cells but not in Schwann cells[50] (Figs 28.132B and 28.133). Frozen sections examined under polarized light disclose birefringent "Maltese crosses"

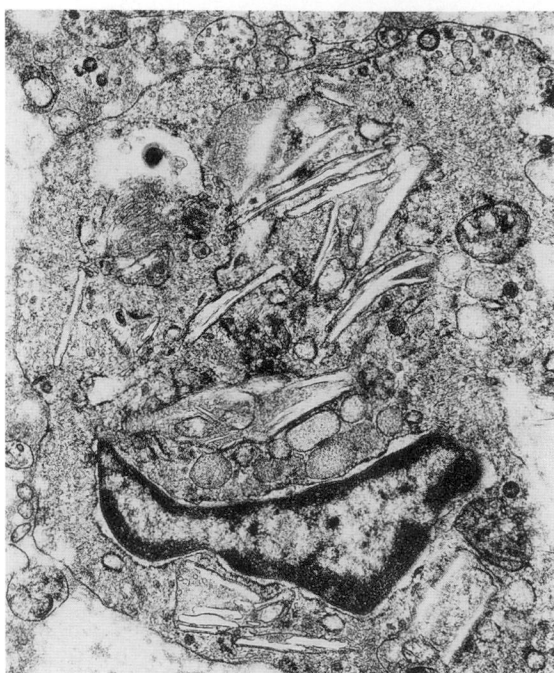

Fig. 28.130 Krabbe's disease. Characteristic inclusions in endoneurial macrophage. (×17,680)

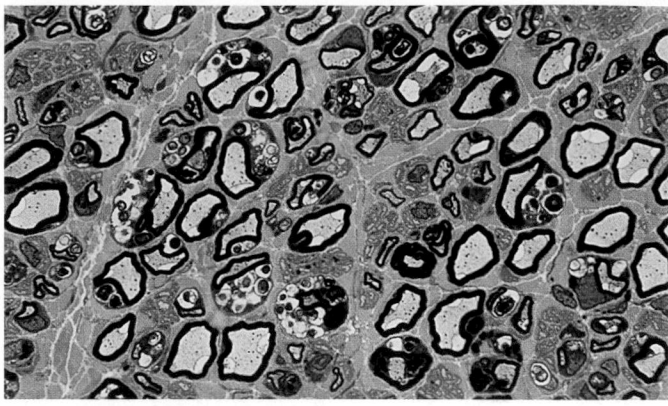

A

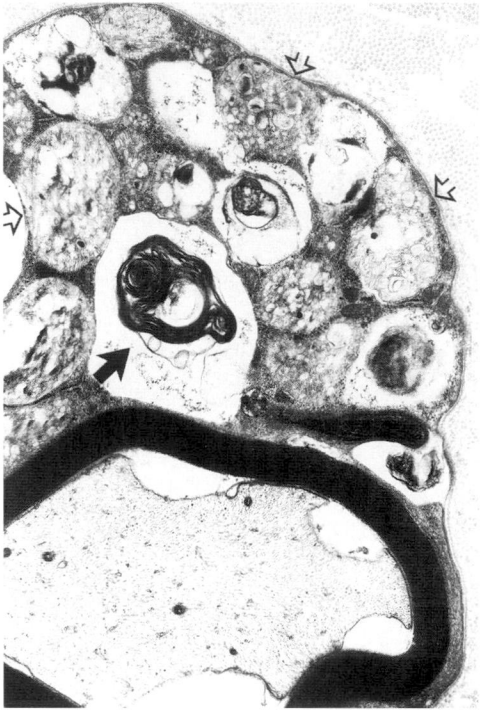

B

Fig. 28.131 (A) Large lysosomal bodies and lipid inclusions in cytoplasm of Schwann cell in metachromatic dystrophy. (Plastic resin) (B) Metachromatic leukodystrophy. Schwann cell cytoplasm is distended with "tuffstone" bodies (open arrows) and a myeloid body (arrow). (×8800)

(Fig. 28.132). The stored lipid stains, in frozen section, with lipid-soluble dyes, and in paraffin section with PAS and Luxol Fast Blue. Treatment of formalin-fixed tissue with 3% potassium chromate helps preserve the lipid. Ultrastructurally the lipid inclusions display a typical pattern of concentric lamellar inclusions with alternating light- and dark-staining bands having a periodicity of 6.3 nm (Fig. 28.133A). In some areas the deposit has a spiral configuration[42] (Fig. 28.133B). Assay for alpha-galactosidase A in serum or leukocytes typically measures 10% or less of the normal value in affected individuals, and 50% of the normal value in heterozygous females.

Tangier disease is a rare autosomal-recessive disorder of lipid metabolism characterized by a low serum cholesterol level, a normal or elevated triglyceride level, and almost absent high-density lipoprotein (HDL) and apolipoprotein A-I, A-II. One half of patients with Tangier disease present with symptoms of peripheral neuropathy—this includes multiple mononeuropathies, distal symmetrical polyneuropathy, and a syringomyelia-like syndrome. Paraffin sections of peripheral nerve reveal dissolution of a stored lipid resulting in vacuolation of Schwann cells, pericytes, and endothelium. With fresh frozen sections, the material stains bright red with oil-red-O.

Inflammatory neuropathy

Guillain–Barré syndrome (GBS) is an acute or subacute paralytic illness often but not always associated with an autoimmune disorder of T-cell lymphocyte activation as an aberrant response to a precipitating trivial viral infec-

tion or another immunologic stimulus such as immunization. The syndrome characteristically has a monophasic course; it begins with paresthesias in toes or fingertips, followed by weakness that usually ascends from the legs to the arms in a matter of days, associated with loss of reflexes. The typical patient becomes bedridden, and in severe cases difficulties in swallowing and respiratory failure ensue. Conduction block is demonstrated in the motor nerves, and the CSF shows few lymphocytes and usually a high protein concentration.

Although this syndrome is well defined clinically, nerve biopsy is sometimes indicated.[70,71] The histologic changes range from no significant abnormality to wide-

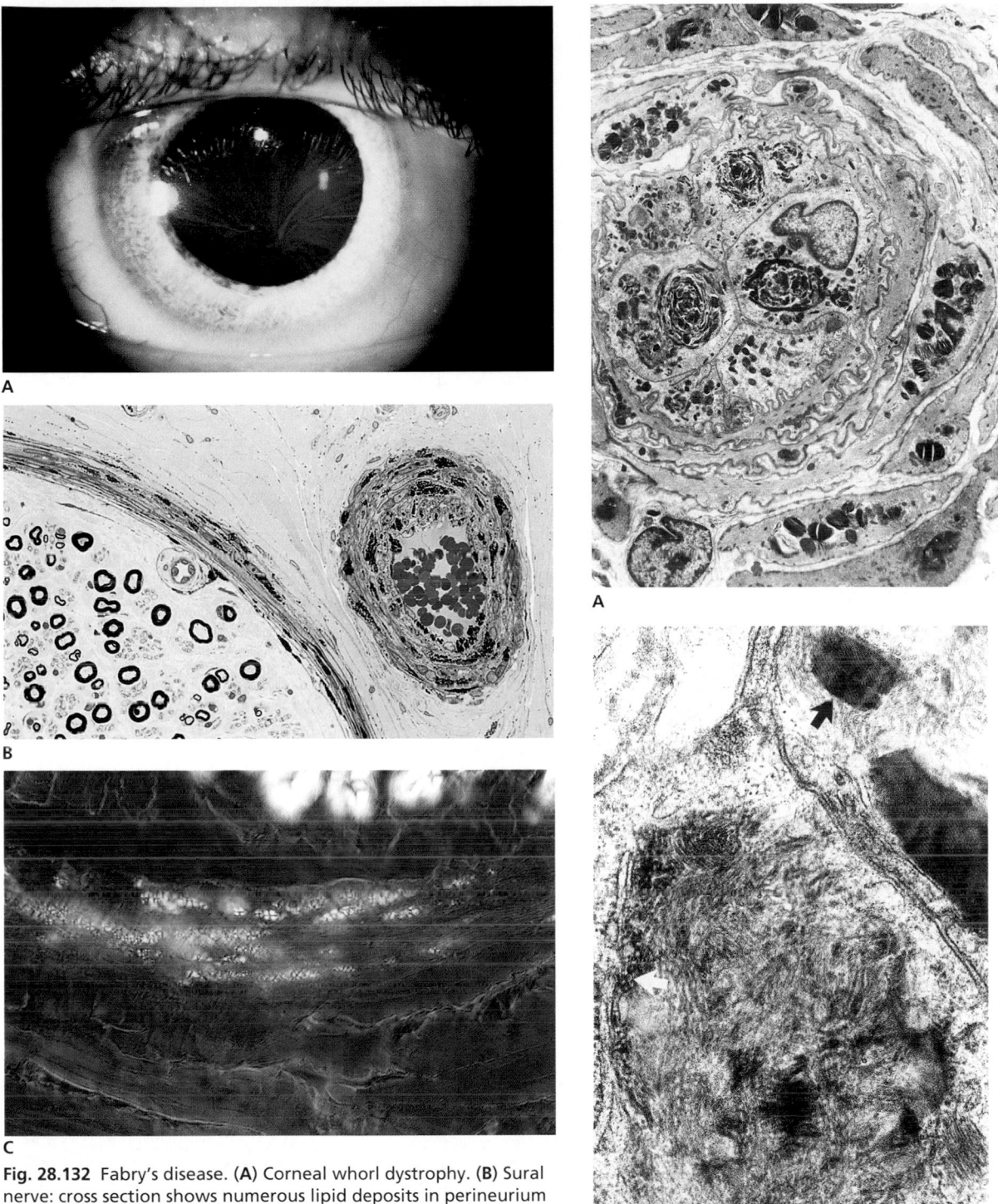

Fig. 28.132 Fabry's disease. **(A)** Corneal whorl dystrophy. **(B)** Sural nerve: cross section shows numerous lipid deposits in perineurium and epineurial vessel. (Plastic) **(C)** Unstained frozen section photographed under polarized light: Maltese crosses are demonstrated along perineurium.

Fig. 28.133 Fabry's disease. **(A)** Lipid inclusions in the endothelial cells and pericytes. (×4800) **(B)** Inclusions with alternating bands (solid arrow) and curvilinear profiles (arrow) in endothelial cells. (×59,100)

spread focal and perivascular lymphohistiocytic infiltration in the endoneurium (Fig. 28.134A and B). In many cases, the only telltale evidence of inflammation is macrophages that permeate into the fascicles. The changes are more pronounced in the proximal segments of the peripheral nervous system, such as the spinal roots and plexuses; however, the sural nerve may show a sub-

tle mononuclear cell infiltration.[58] In semithin sections, the endoneurium appears hypercellular because of the presence of numerous debris-laden macrophages that surround denuded axons (Fig. 28.135). Other nerve fibers exhibit disproportionately thin myelin sheaths[78] (Figs

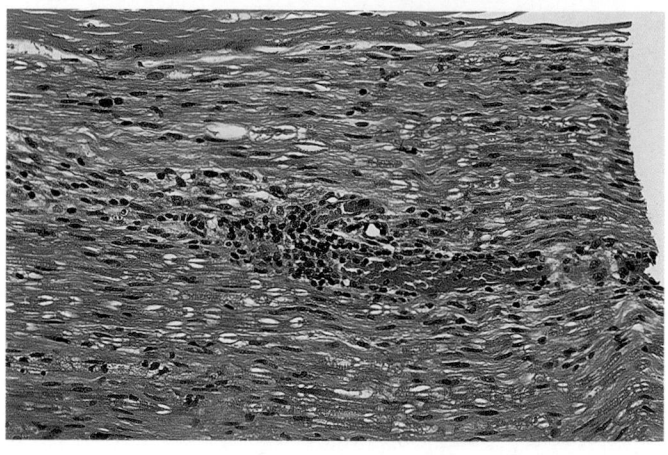

A

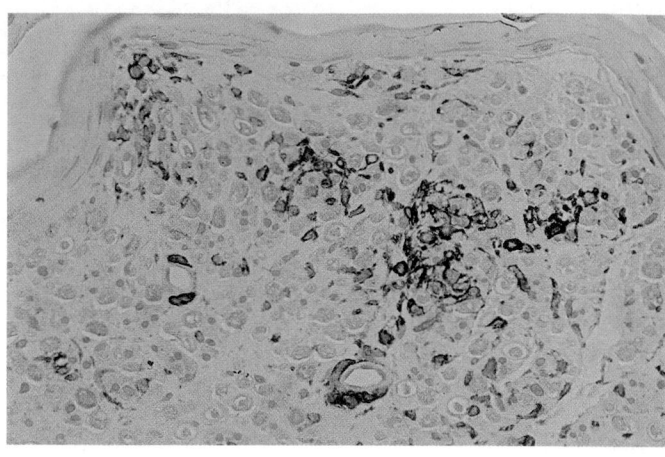

B

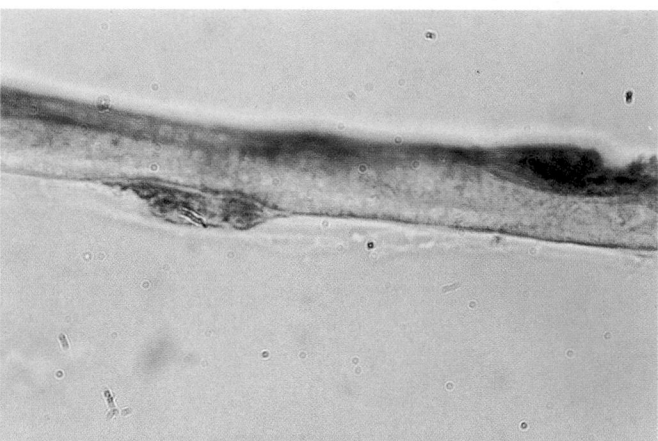

C

Fig. 28.134 Guillain–Barré: (**A**) perivascular lymphocytic infiltrate (H&E); (**B**) endoneurial diffuse lymphocytic infiltrate (immunostaining for LCA, methyl green counterstain); (**C**) macrophage attached to surface of myelinated fiber (fresh teased nerve fiber incubated for acid phosphatase).

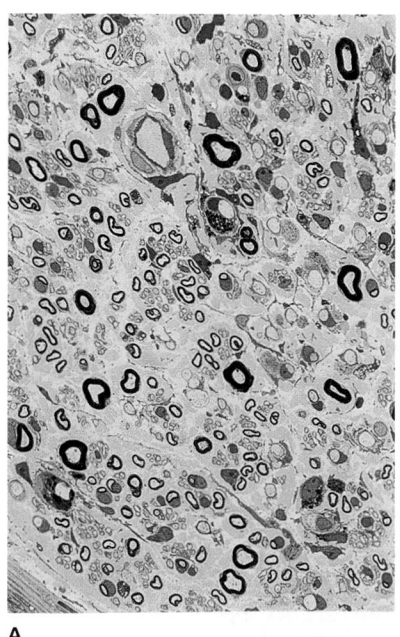

A

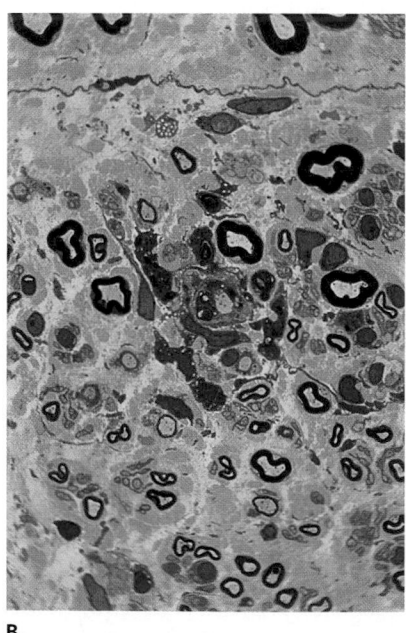

B

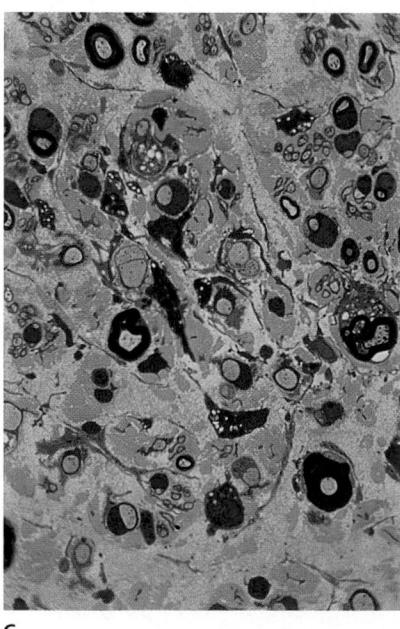

C

Fig. 28.135 Guillain–Barré: hypercellularity of endoneurium is caused by invading macrophages. Note denuded axons, myelin debris, and attenuated myelin sheaths (Compare with normal sural nerve Fig. 28.123B). (**A** to **C**, plastic resin (oil))

28.135 and 28.136A). In patients with no clinical or electrophysiologic evidence of sensory nerve involvement, examination of a terminal motor nerve may be more informative albeit rarely indicated.[67]

Ultrastructural studies reveal a cell-mediated demyelination; macrophage tongues disrupt and penetrate the Schwann cell basal lamina and displace Schwann cell cytoplasm (Figs 28.134C and 28.136B). Macrophage processes, now intratubal (i.e., within the perimeter of Schwann cell basal lamina), begin to dissect along the intraperiod line and strip and engulf the normal myelin with the axon usually being unaffected[78] (Fig. 28.136B). Recovery, which is common, is associated with remyelination. When inflammation is particularly severe, axonal damage occurs as a bystander effect.[63,70] Treatment in the early stages with plasmapheresis and, more recently, intravenous immune globulin has been shown to improve outcome.[74] Some patients infected with *Campylobacter jejuni* are prone to developing a variant of GBS known as acute motor-sensory axonal neuropathy. Because of molecular mimicry *C. jejuni* induces the production of anti-GM1 antibodies which may react with antigens in the nodal region of motor and sensory axons. Axonal degeneration follows activation of complement and macrophage invasion.[65]

A clinical related disorder of the GBS is chronic inflammatory demyelinating polyneuropathy (CIDP) with its more gradual onset and progressive or relapsing course. Nerve biopsy shows axonal degeneration, hyper-

cellularity (Figs 28.117B and 28.127), fenestration of endothelium in intrafascicular microvessels resulting in endoneurial edema, widespread macrophage-mediated segmental demyelination, and occasionally prominent hypertrophic changes[79] (Figs 28.126 and 28.127D). Nerve involvement in CIDP lacks uniformity. Although some fascicles are relatively spared, others show changes of varying severity[61,73] (Fig. 28.127). Chronic inflammation in the form of perivascular collars varies considerably from case to case (Fig. 28.126). The use of serial sections and immunohistochemical markers may help detect inconspicuous lymphocytic infiltrates, typically located in the endoneurium. Not uncommonly, however, perivascular lymphocytes may be confined to the epineurium with no inflammation demonstrable in the endoneurium. In the absence of clear-cut signs of segmental demyelination, the demonstration of occasional mononuclear cells in a nerve biopsy should not be taken as evidence for CIDP. A small number of perivascular lymphocytes in epineurium is considered a normal finding. Some patients with CIDP improve in response to steroid treatment, plasmapheresis, or immunoglobulin. A false-positive diagnosis of CIDP is possible in patients with inherited neuropathy because of the demonstration of focal lymphocytic infiltrates in up to 12% of sural nerve specimens of patients with CMT 1.[64] Whereas CSF protein is consistently elevated in CIPD, a normal value is the rule in CMT-1.

Acute and chronic inflammatory demyelinating

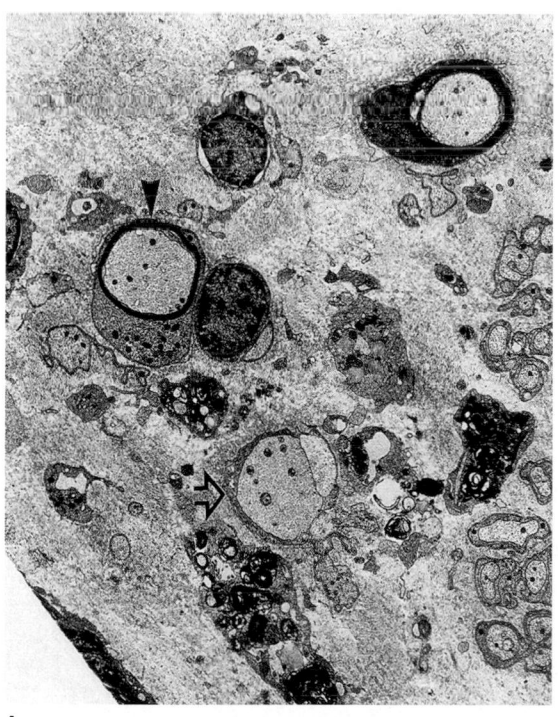
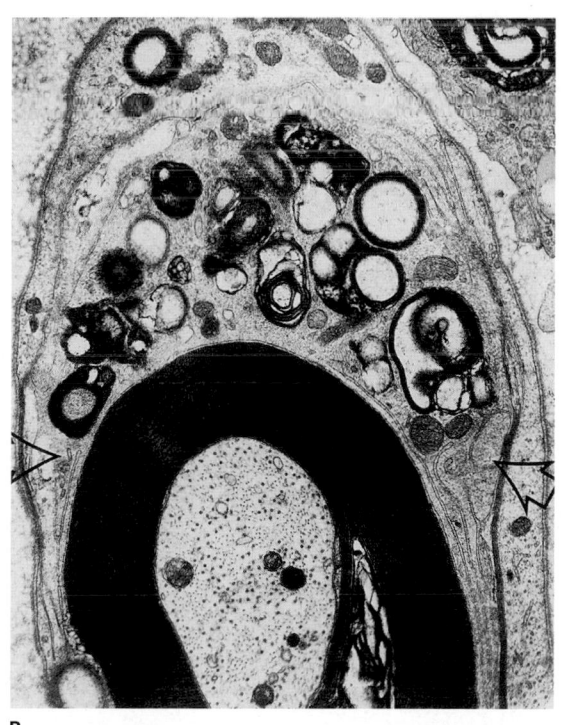

Fig. 28.136 Ultrastructural features of the Guillain–Barré syndrome. **(A)** Low-power view of endoneurium shows macrophage processes laden with myelin debris and axons that are demyelinated (open arrow) and remyelinating (arrowhead). (×4500) **(B)** Macrophagic processes penetrate Schwann cell tube and separate and strip myelin (open arrows) off nerve fiber. The axon is spared. (×5700)

polyneuropathies are not uncommon complications during the early stages of infection with the human immunodeficiency virus. Except for pleocytosis in CSF, these cases are clinically indistinguishable from GBS and CIDP. Histologically, the chronic inflammation in subcutaneous nerves is much more intense.[60] A more common neuropathy in AIDS appears late in the disease and is characterized by painful dysesthesias, symmetric distal sensory loss, and areflexia.[60,62] Peripheral nerves show axonal degeneration, demyelination, sparse chronic inflammation, and occasionally necrotizing vasculitis[82] (Fig. 28.137C), which is associated with distinctive tubuloreticular inclusions in the endothelium (Fig. 28.138). A multifocal, necrotizing, inflammatory neuropathy with

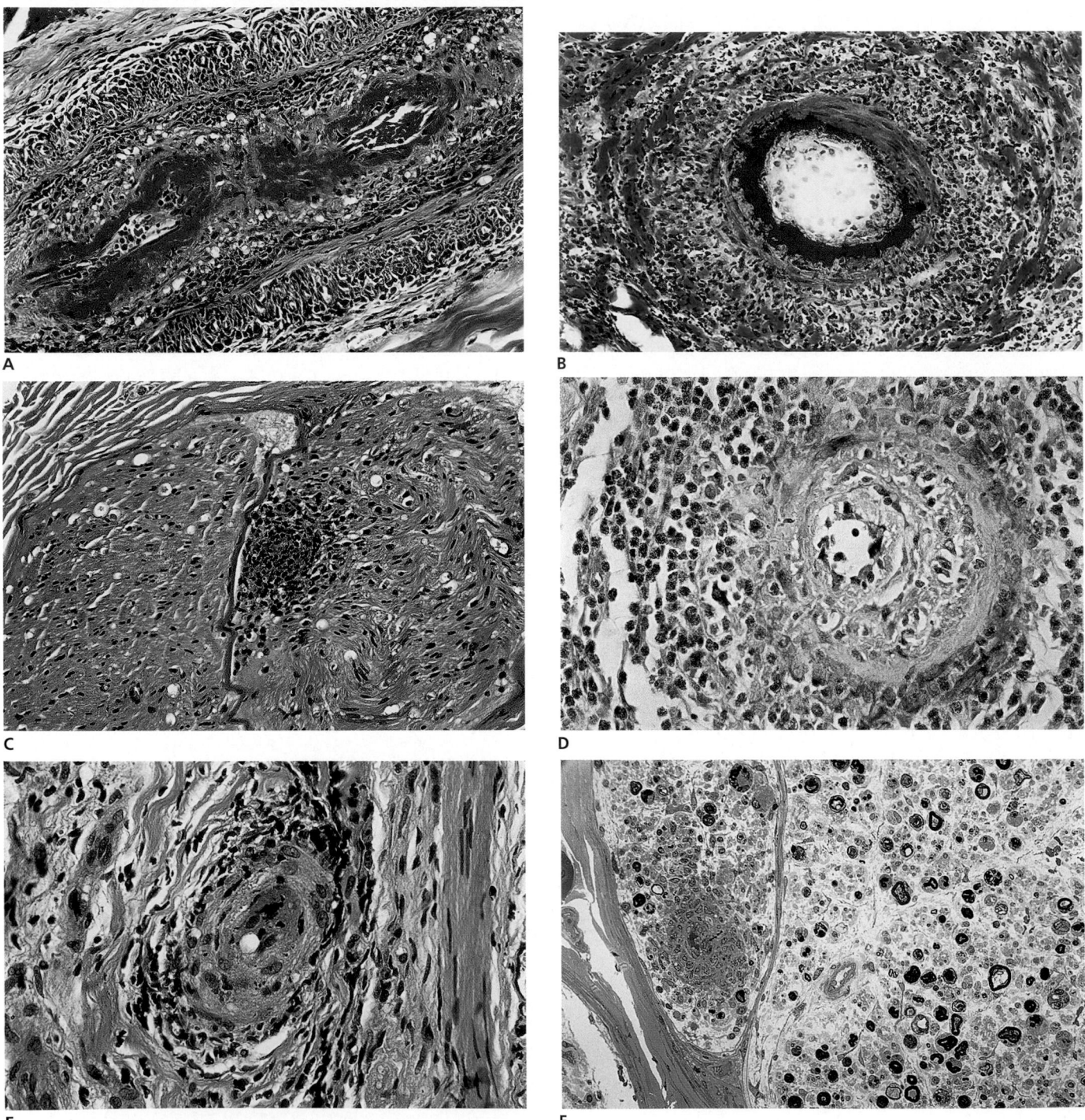

Fig. 28.137 Necrotizing angiitis: (**A**) polyarteritis nodosa showing a sleeve of fibrinoid necrosis; (**B**) Martius Scarlet Blue stain highlights fibrinoid necrosis; (**C**) acute vasculitis affecting endoneurial microvessel in a patient with AIDS; (**D**) Giemsa preparation shows numerous eosinophils in Churg–Strauss vasculitis; (**E**) acute necrotizing vasculitis in borderline lepromatous neuropathy; (**F**) endoneurial microvasculitis (Churg–Strauss syndrome). (**A**, HPS; **C** and **E**, H&E; **F**,plastic resin)

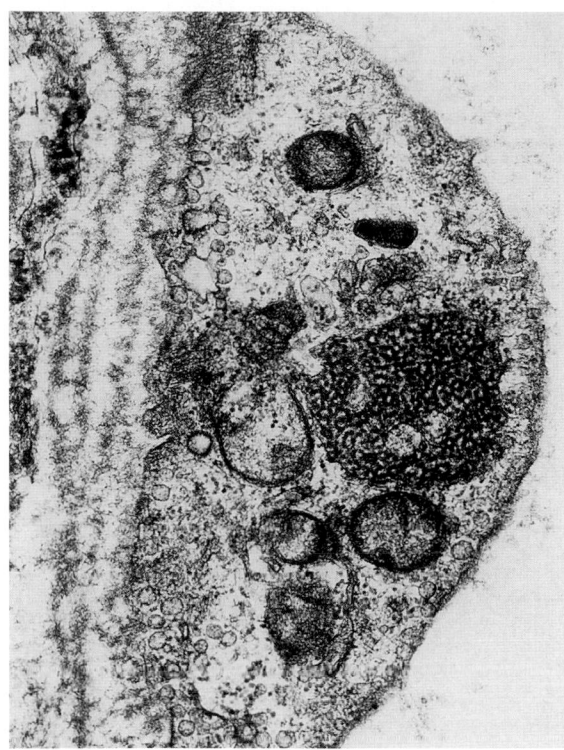

Fig. 28.138 Sural nerve. Tubuloreticular inclusions in endothelium. (×33,516)

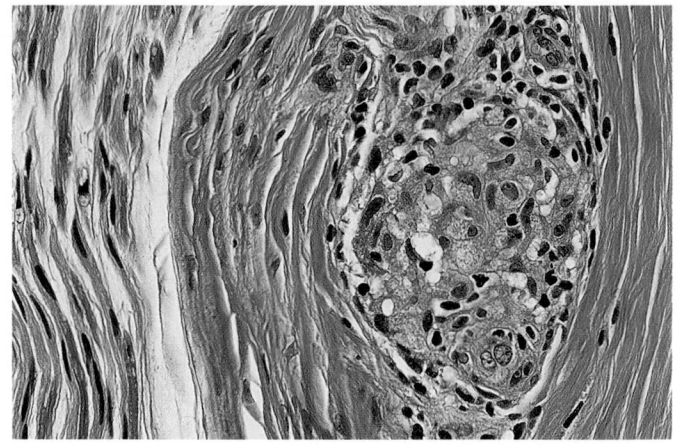

A

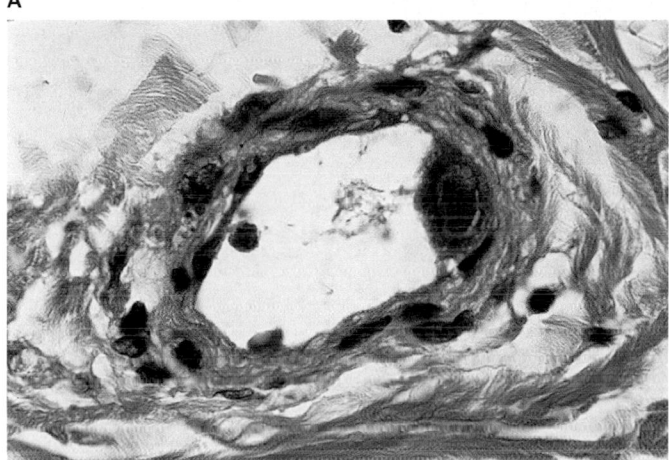

B

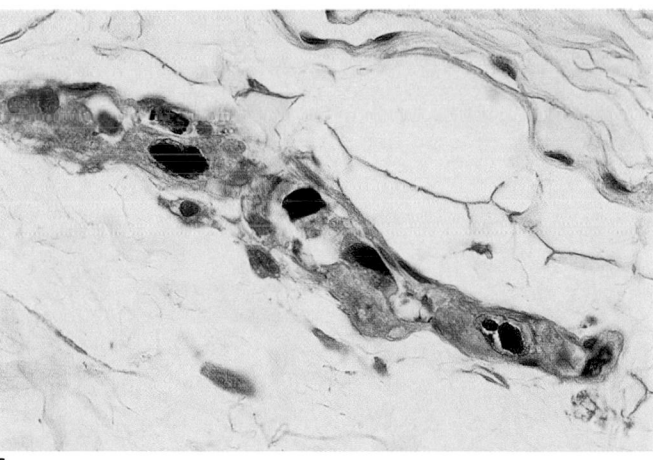

C

Fig. 28.139 Sural nerve: (**A**) sarcoidosis: "naked" epithelioid granuloma adjacent to nerve fascicle; (**B,C**) cytomegalovirus in immunosuppressed patient. (**A** and **B**, H&E; **C**, immunostain for CMV)

associated endoneurial cytomegalovirus cytopathy has also been reported in patients with AIDS.[83] The inflammatory infiltrate is composed of mononuclear and polymorphonuclear leukocytes. The diagnosis of CMV-mediated neuropathy is important because its treatment may be lifesaving[72] (Fig. 28.139B and C).

Nerve biopsies in patients with Lyme borreliosis and neuropathy have shown nonspecific perivascular (endoneurial, perineurial, and epineurial) lymphoplasmacytic cuffings and endarteritis obliterans.[75] Although spirochetes have never been observed in nerve tissue of patients infected with *Borrelia burgdorferi*, relief of signs and symptoms of neuropathy follows antibiotic therapy.

Sural nerve biopsies of patients affected by the toxic syndrome produced by ingestion of adulterated rapeseed oil have shown prominent perineurial mononuclear cell infiltrates, as well as perivenular and pericapillary lymphocytic cuffings mostly in epineurium, in the absence of vasculitis.[81]

About 5% of the patients with sarcoidosis develop symptoms of neurologic involvement. The most salient clinical feature of sarcoidosis of the peripheral nervous system is the occurrence of a fluctuating cranial polyneuritis, the facial nerve being most often involved. A symmetric peripheral neuropathy has also been described.[86] Sural nerve biopsy in at least five such cases has shown epithelioid cell granulomas in epineurium and endoneurium[59,76,77,88] (Fig. 28.139A); multinucleated giant cells are uncommon in nerve lesions. A granulomatous angiitis and periangiitis have been proposed as a mechanism for nerve damage.[77,80] Nerve biopsy alone is not advisable for the diagnosis of sarcoidosis. Diagnostic pathology is more likely to be found in combined muscle-nerve biopsy in patients with active disease.[84,85]

Focal perivascular collections of lymphocytes have been shown in peripheral nerves in patients with the eosinophilia-myalgia syndrome.[69]

Patients suffering from carcinomas of various sites may develop neuropathies not related to direct invasion by neoplastic cells. In paraneoplastic subacute sensory neuropathy, there are neuronal cell loss and perivascular lymphocytic infiltrates in spinal ganglia. In other patients, a nonmetastatic carcinomatous sensory motor polyneuropathy may develop. In these cases the sural nerve shows axonal degeneration and rarely sparse chronic inflammation.

Although benign lymphocytic aggregates are relatively common in nerve biopsies, pathologists should be aware that selective and extensive lymphocytic infiltration of peripheral nerves may be the initial manifestation of malignant lymphoma. The patients may present with a progressive or relapsing subacute and asymmetric painful neuropathy. Pathologically this neurolymphomatosis is widespread and involves nerves, roots, and plexuses. The diagnosis lies in the recognition of the atypical features and the immunophenotype of the mononuclear cell infiltrate.[66,87] Peripheral nerves can be involved in malignant angioendotheliomatosis (angiotropic large cell lymphoma)[68] and in lymphomatoid granulomatosis (Fig. 28.140).

Leprous neuritis

Mycobacterium leprae has an unexplained tropism for peripheral nerves that are affected in all forms and stages of leprosy[94,97] (Figs 28.141 and 28.142). In a patient with leprosy, biopsy of a subcutaneous nerve may reveal pathologic changes that are greater than (or at variance with) those suggested by skin biopsy or clinical examination.[90,100] The tissue response to *M. leprae* infection is largely determined by the natural resistance of the host, the bacillus itself being of low pathogenicity.[99] A two-stage model for genetic control of innate susceptibility to leprosy has been proposed. The expression of a single recessive autosomal gene may determine the susceptibility to disease per se,[101] whereas the progression of the disease and the histologic reaction ultimately developed are associated with genes of the major histocompatibility complex.[96]

The histologic lesions of leprosy are classified within the spectrum of the pure tuberculoid (paucibacillary) and the pure lepromatous (pluribacillary) poles. The true borderline form is most unstable, with downgrading (toward lepromatous form) in the absence of treatment, or upgrading (toward tuberculoid form) with treatment. In tuberculoid leprosy there is an exuberant inflammatory response; lesions occur early during the disease and may be confined to a single nerve trunk near the portal of entry of the bacillus. The subcutaneous nerve is thickened, with obliteration of the fascicular anatomy by confluent granulomas composed of epithelioid histiocytes, multinucleated giant cells, and lymphocytes (Fig. 28.141C). This may affect the whole cross section of nerve, to the point that the structure becomes unrecognizable. In this instance, immunohistochemical studies for EMA and S-100 protein may help detect residual perineurium and Schwann cells. Caseation necrosis centered in nerves may occur (Fig. 28.141C). The finding of normal or marginally affected nerve bundles within a granuloma almost excludes the possibility of leprosy. In tuberculoid leprosy, bacilli are very rarely demonstrable with conventional stains. A specific DNA probe and polymerase chain reaction for the detection of picogram quantities of *M. leprae* in tissues has been developed.[95,102]

Lepromatous leprosy is characterized by a selective anergy to *M. leprae* and its antigens.[93] A defect in cell-mediated immunity associated with decreased interferon-gamma production leads to unchecked bacillary proliferation in dermal macrophages, hematogenous spread, and eventually colonization of subcutaneous nerves. A symmetric polyneuropathy develops late in the disease with a peculiar pattern of sensory loss involving the legs (sparing the soles of the feet), dorsal aspect of the forearms, pinnae of the ears, nose, and supraorbital

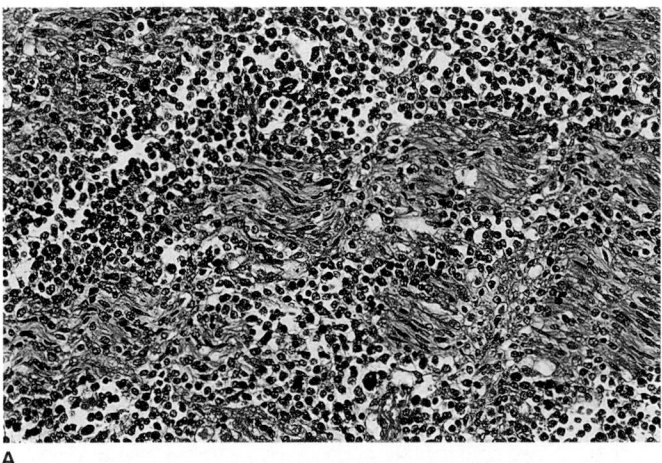

A

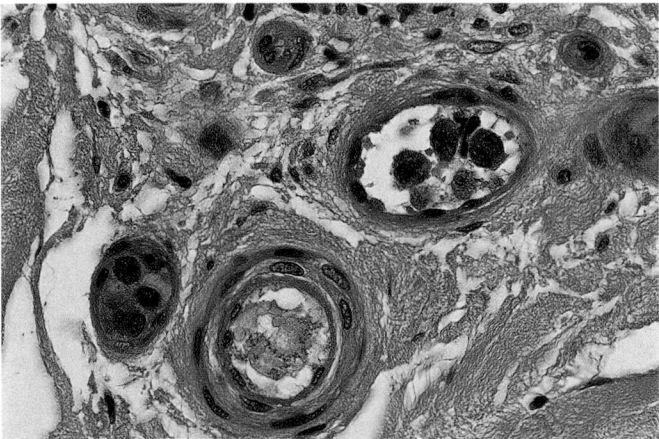

B

Fig. 28.140 (A) Neurolymphomatosis—polyneuropathy was the first manifestation of B-cell lymphoma in this patient; **(B)** malignant lymphoid cells are seen in vascular lumen in a sural nerve specimen of a patient with angiotrophic large cell lymphoma and polyneuropathy. **(A**, HPS; **B**, H&E) (Case B courtesy of Dr Robert E. Schmidt, St Louis, MO)

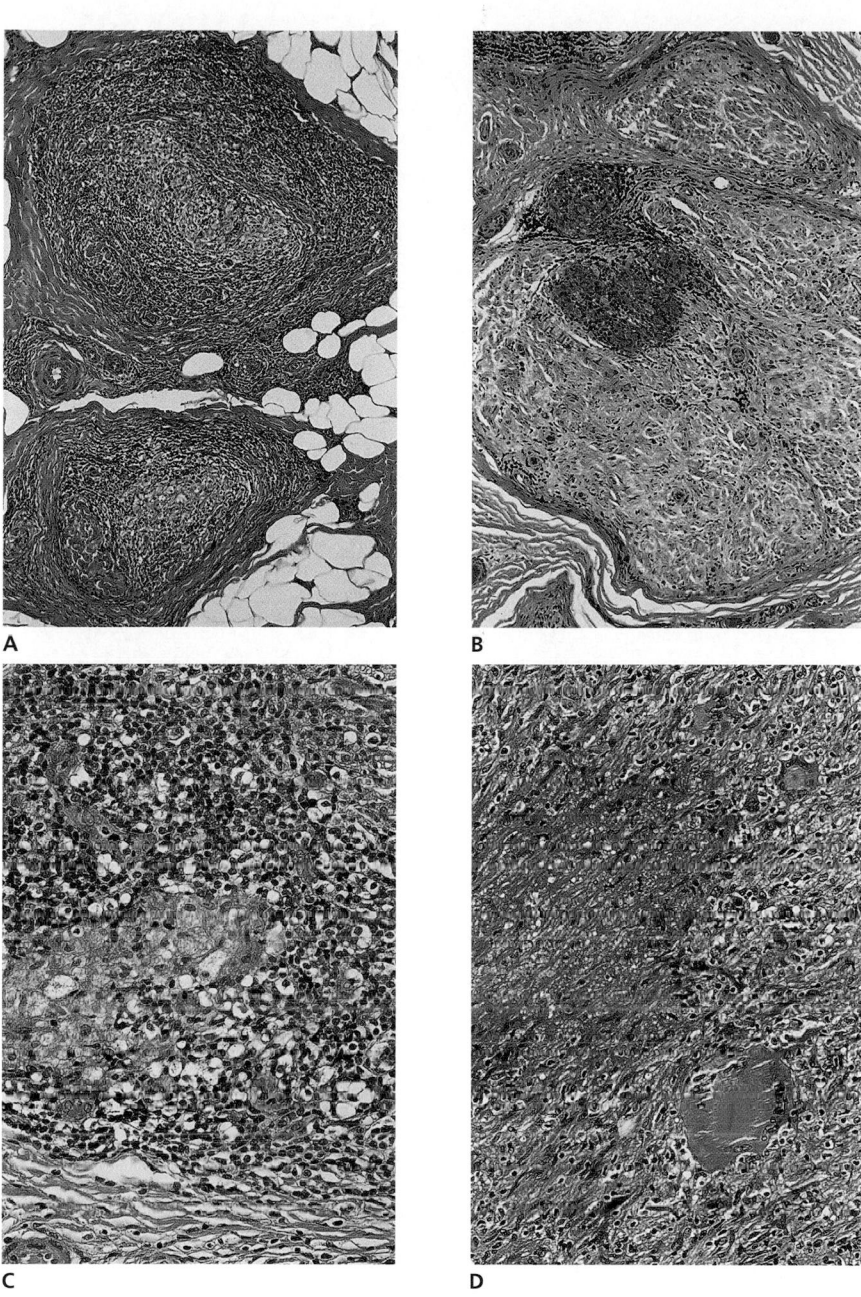

Fig. 28.141 Leprous neuropathy. (**A,B**) Borderline tuberculoid. In A epithelioid granulomas are centered in fascicles and surrounded by mononuclear cells, severe destruction of axons was seen. In B there is a "naked" endoneurial granuloma. (**C**) Tuberculoid; note focal necrosis and multinucleated giant cells. (**D**) Borderline lepromatous in a patient noncompliant to treatment; few organisms could be demonstrated in foamy macrophages, note rich lymphoid infiltrate. (**A** to **D**, H&E)

regions. This distribution depends on temperature gradients—*M. leprae* proliferates more freely in cooler areas. Superficial nerves are enlarged, often with an abrupt transition with normal deeper segments. In transverse sections, there appears an uneven involvement of fascicles, with some being heavily infiltrated by foamy histiocytes and a variable number of plasma cells.[92] Lymphocytes may increase after treatment. Large numbers of bacilli are demonstrable in macrophages, Schwann cells, perineurial cells (Fig. 28.142G), endothelium (Fig. 28.142E), and perhaps axons (Fig. 28.143A). The bacilli are mainly found in "globi" that contain dozens and even hundreds of organisms (Figs 28.142C,D and 28.143B) in the cytoplasm, the affected cells in paraffin-embedded preparations acquire a typical foamy con-

figuration that is designated "lepra cell". The widespread bacillary multiplication may change to fibrosis and atrophy of nerve bundles. Bacilli may persist in nerves even after years of apparently successful treatment.[90] Following treatment and even as part of the natural history of the disease, the subsiding inflammation unveils the devastation of the nerve, although the fascicular anatomy is still discernible the endoneurium is now devoid of native elements (axons and Schwann cells) and nerve bundles now consist of chords of hyalinized connective tissue. Regressive changes include large vacuolated cells that contain much lipid and sometimes remnants of bacilli (Fig. 28.142H). Both axonal loss and demyelination are prominent in lepromatous leprosy, but the mechanism of damage is not well understood.

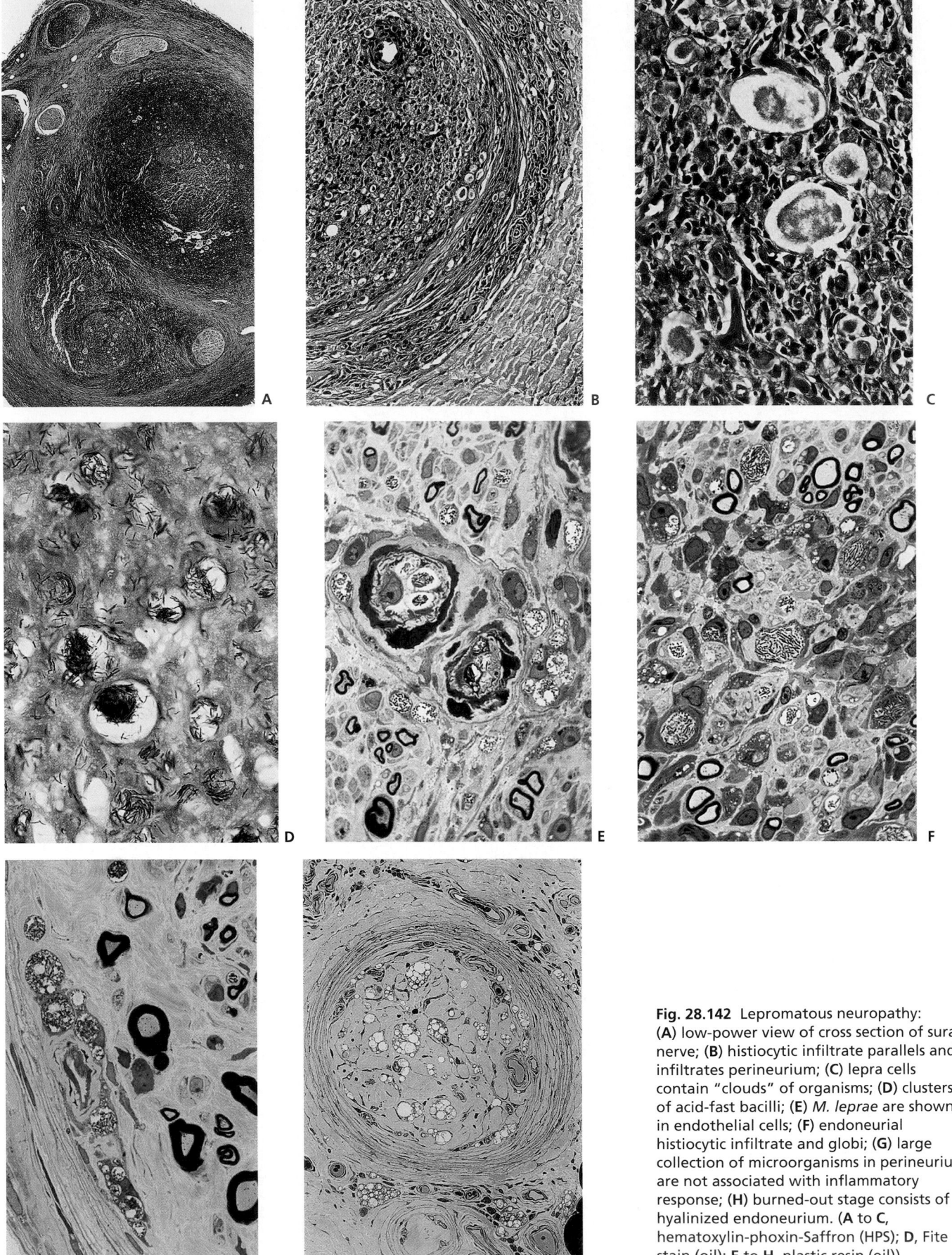

Fig. 28.142 Lepromatous neuropathy: (**A**) low-power view of cross section of sural nerve; (**B**) histiocytic infiltrate parallels and infiltrates perineurium; (**C**) lepra cells contain "clouds" of organisms; (**D**) clusters of acid-fast bacilli; (**E**) *M. leprae* are shown in endothelial cells; (**F**) endoneurial histiocytic infiltrate and globi; (**G**) large collection of microorganisms in perineurium are not associated with inflammatory response; (**H**) burned-out stage consists of hyalinized endoneurium. (**A** to **C**, hematoxylin-phoxin-Saffron (HPS); **D**, Fite stain (oil); **E** to **H**, plastic resin (oil))

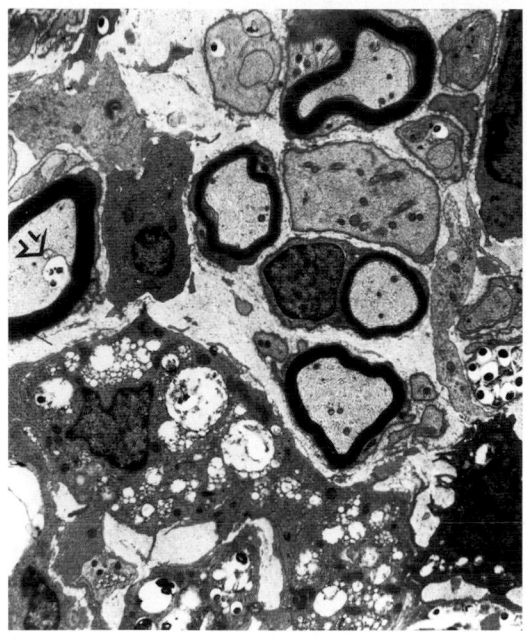
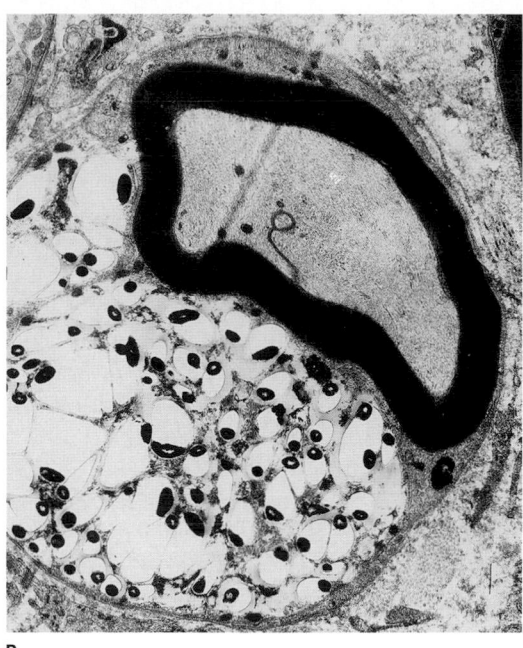

Fig. 28.143 Electron micrographs. **(A)** Low-power view of endoneurium shows *M. leprae* in macrophages, Schwann cells, and axon (arrow). (×3960) **(B)** This view illustrates tolerance of Schwann cells to *M. leprae*. Numerous organisms are seen within a single viable cell. (×6200)

The perineurium is often greatly involved with lamination by foamy macrophages and separation of the perineurial leaves (Fig. 28.142B).

Vasculitic lesions may occur within cutaneous nerves in erythema nodosum leprosum. Typically, arterioles in the vicinity of perineurium are involved; they show fibrinoid necrosis and acute inflammation indistinguishable from those of hypersensitivity vasculitis. In borderline leprosy, where the immunologic polarity is only partially expressed, the lesions are often early, widespread, and severe. The histologic features of this form of leprous neuropathy may have an incongruous appearance, with both lepromatous and tuberculoid patterns being present in the same specimen[98] (Fig. 28.141). Lymphocytes are most abundant in borderline leprosy (Fig. 28.141A and D). They may appear densely packed in the epineurium or in the endoneurium adjacent to granulomas or may infiltrate the perineurium. Bacilli are almost always found in borderline lesions.[89]

Patients with pure neuritic leprosy display no skin lesions and are skin smear negative for acid-fast bacilli. The diagnosis of this imperfectly known form of leprosy depends exclusively on nerve biopsy,[91] in which the entire spectrum of leprosy lesions can be observed. In a nerve biopsy study of 39 such patients, a significant proportion showed lepromatous histology and nearly two thirds had a moderate to heavy bacterial load within the nerves.[94]

Vasculitis

Although peripheral nerves are resistant to the development of infarcts secondary to large vessel occlusive disease, sensory motor polyneuropathy is not an uncommon syndrome either in established systemic vasculitis or as the first manifestation of the disease. In most cases, nerve biopsy alone cannot distinguish the necrotizing vasculitis of polyarteritis nodosa (PAN), rheumatoid arthritis, and most other systemic vasculitis because they are morphologically, immunohistochemically, and probably pathogenetically similar.[109,114] The necrotizing angiitis involves arterioles (up to 300 μm in diameter) and occasionally veins of the epineurial compartment. In isolated peripheral nerve vasculitis, the process seems to affect smaller epineurial arterioles.[105] Capillaries and venules are as a rule spared. Acute lesions display segmental fibrinoid necrosis of the vessel and transmural infiltration of polymorphonuclear leukocytes and mononuclear cells (Fig. 28.137). In some cases, the only evidence of necrosis is karyorrhexis within the vascular inflammatory infiltrate. The observation of necrotizing vasculitis with numerous eosinophils and perivascular collections of plasma cells and monocytes argues for the Churg–Strauss syndrome (CSS),[103,110] (Fig. 28.137D) although this is only detected in about half of biopsies showing necrotizing vasculitis in CSS. Step sections are essential in the search for vasculitis when the original sample shows perivascular mononuclear cell infiltration without destruction of arterial wall. We have obtained good results by cutting serial sections through the block and staining them in succession with H&E, elastica, Perl's Prussian Blue (Fig. 28.144B), Martius Scarlet Blue (Fig. 28.137B), and leukocyte common antigen. Perivascular aggregates of mononuclear cells without transmural inflammation and necrosis are not diagnostic of vasculitis because similar changes are demonstrable in inflammatory neuropathies. However, studies on simultaneous muscle and nerve biopsies have indicated that in the proper clinical setting the diagnosis of probable vasculitis can be made when massive Wallerian degeneration is associated with perivascular cuffing of mononuclear cells, whereas in inflammatory neuropathy endoneurial subtle inflammatory infiltrates and segmental demyelination are seen. Older vasculitic lesions are sometimes shown by recanalized vessels with fragmentation of internal elastica (Fig. 28.144A) and by obliteration and calcification of microvessels (Fig. 28.144C). Hemosiderin-laden macrophages may be found around these older lesions. In acute cases there is obvious Wallerian degeneration, predominantly in central fascicular areas, but clear-cut infarction is exceptional (Fig. 28.145A and B). Vasculitic neuropathy may be an early manifestation of polyarteritis nodosa, whereas in rheumatoid arthritis necrotizing vasculitis is a late development; most cases occuring after many years of chronic arthritis.

The classic clinical feature of vasculitis is that of mononeuritis multiplex, a term that indicates focal and painful involvement of several nerves.[107] Although most often the neurologic deficit is asymmetric, the lesions may summate to produce a symmetric picture. The value of nerve biopsy for the diagnosis of vasculitis depends on: (i) clinical evidence of neuropathy; (ii) electrodiagnostic studies to demonstrate the extent and distribution of nerve involvement and to help in the selection of nerve for biopsy; and (iii) the amount of tissue removed.[108,112] We favor a combination biopsy, through a single incision, of the sural nerve and the gastrocnemius muscle. For this procedure the nerve is found as it courses in the midline of dorsal calf between the two heads of the muscle. Delay in wound healing at the biopsy site may be seen in some patients as the result of corticosteroid therapy. Although good functional recovery follows vasculitic neuropathy, long-term survival varies considerably from patient to patient.[104]

About 15% of patients with systemic lupus erythematosus develop peripheral neuropathy, some of which is due to microvasculitis affecting the endoneurial capillaries. We have seen prominent tubuloreticular inclusions in endoneurial endothelium in a case of lupus vasculitis. A microvasculitis causing neuropathy as a remote effect of cancer has recently emerged.[111] A microvasculitis in cutaneous nerves has been described in patients with diabetic and nondiabetic lumbosacral radiculoplexus neuropathies.[106,113] Whether this represents a primary vasculitis or a reactive change to obliterated vessels remains to be determined. Elsewhere in this chapter reference is made to the peripheral nerve

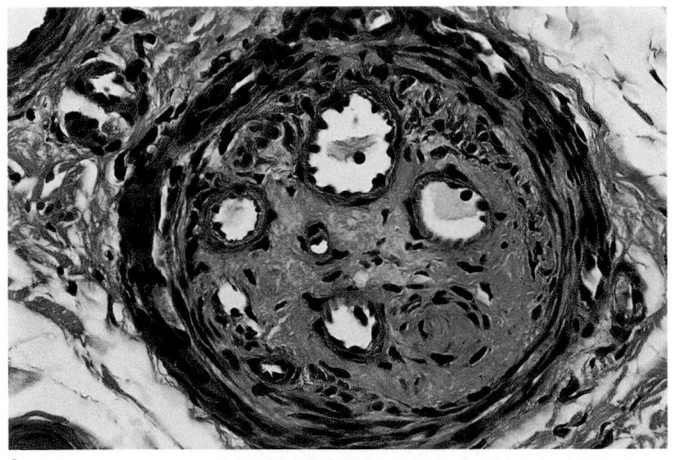

A

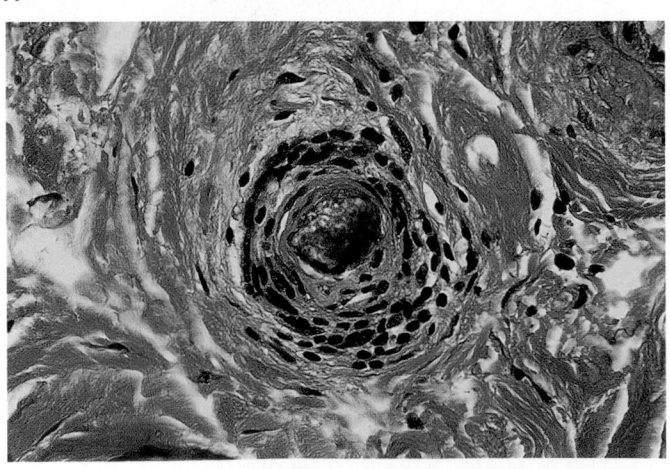

C

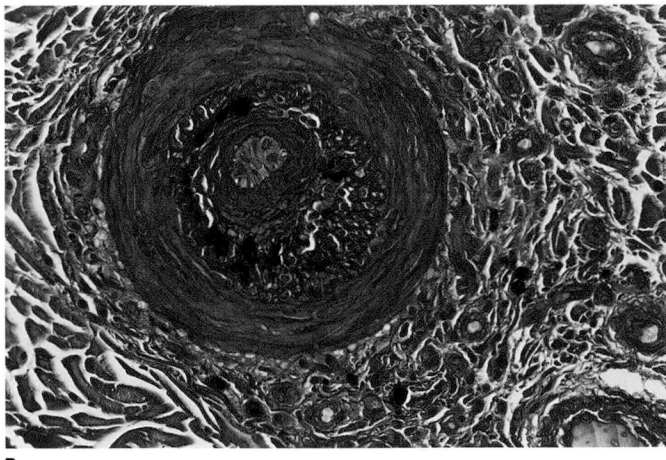

B

Fig. 28.144 Healed vasculitis. **(A)** Polyarteritis nodosa (PAN): lumen obliteration and recanalization. **(B)** PAN: scarred vessel harboring residual iron. **(C)** Systemic lupus erythematosus (SLE): scarring and calcification of epineurial microvessel. (**A**, HPS; **B**, Prussian Blue for iron; **C**, H&E)

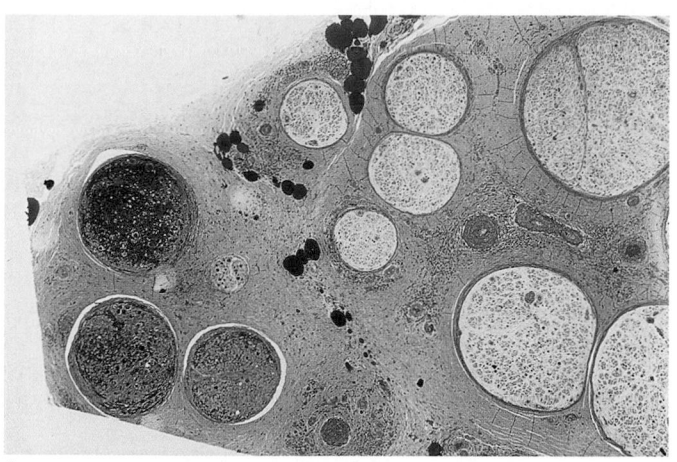

A

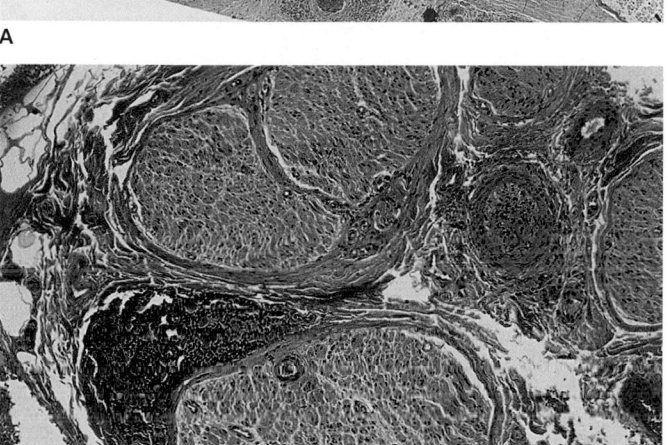

C

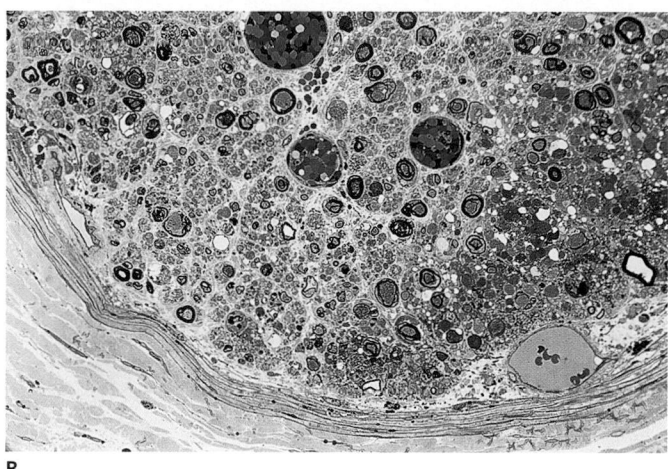

B

Fig. 28.145 PAN. (**A,B**) Recent infarct involves three fascicles. (**C**) Note scarred arteriole distant from a nonspecific pool of lymphocytes. (**A** and **B**, plastic resin; **C**, H&E)

vasculitis of mixed cryoglobulinemia, leprous neuritis, AIDS, Lyme borreliosis, and sarcoidosis.

Amyloidosis

Involvement of the peripheral nerve is found in **primary amyloidosis** (now defined as **plasma cell dyscrasia**), in amyloidosis secondary to **myeloma** and other **B-cell lymphomas**, and in the **hereditary forms of amyloidosis**. The precursor protein of most types of familial amyloidotic polyneuropathy (FAP) has been identified as variant types of transthyretin (TTR; originally called prealbumin), an acronym for a serum transport protein that binds thyroxin and vitamin A (retinoic acid).[116] Over 90% of TTR is generated in the liver and the remaining 10% is produced in the choroid plexus and the retina. Mutations of a single copy gene on chromosome 18 are associated with most of the autosomal dominant hereditary amyloidosis. Each mutation in the transthyretin protein is the result of a single nucleotide change. Thus far, 72 different point mutations in the TTR gene have been associated with the deposition of TTR as the amyloid major protein. The substitution of methionine for valine at position 30 of the prealbumin molecule is the most common form of FAP (type I), resulting in a peripheral neuropathy (Portuguese, Swedish, and Japanese types).[122,123] Carriers of variant TTR can be detected by

Southern blot analysis of isolate DNA from peripheral blood leukocytes,[124] or by amplification of the relevant sequence, using either PCR and restriction analysis, allelic-specific PCR or MMP-PCR. These have been superseded by recent commercial tests that sequence the whole gene. Endoneurial deposits of amyloid in secondary (reactive) amyloidosis have not been properly documented. Peripheral neuropathy occurs in 15% to 35% of patients with primary amyloidosis and is the presenting feature in 10%.

The clinical picture of the neuropathy of light chain amyloidosis and of FAP type I is similar except that in immune amyloidosis the clinical progression is somewhat faster. The patients experience a progressive distal symmetric sensory polyneuropathy affecting primarily the lower limbs. Spontaneous pain occurs, and there are associated autonomic features (dysautonomia) consisting of orthostatic hypotension, sexual dysfunction, and urinary hesitancy. Motor involvement is early but masked by sensory dysfunction. Damage to smaller fibers, both unmyelinated and myelinated, occurs initially, with a dissociation of sensory abnormality: there is loss of sensation to pain and temperature and preservation of position and vibratory senses (Figs 28.122D and 28.146D). As the disease progresses all sensory modalities become impaired. Noteworthy in the differential diagnosis with other conditions that cause selective depletion of small myelinated and unmyelinated fibers are: Fabry's disease, Tangier disease, diabetes, and idiopathic small fiber neuropathy.

Atypical patterns of immune amyloid neuropathy include motor-predominant forms without demyelinating features, motor neuron disease-like, asymmetric lumbosacral polyradiculopathy or plexopathy, mononeuritis multiplex, and **amyloidomas** of the facial, trigeminal and sciatic nerves. In the peripheral nerve the amyloid deposits of light chain protein and TTR are indistinguishable without immunohistochemistry.[123] They are extremely variable in amount and may be pre-

sent in the vessel wall and perivascular spaces of the epineurium and endoneurium (Fig. 28.146), along the perineurium (Fig. 28.147), and as masses of amyloid in the endoneurium, presumably an extension of perivascular deposits[121] (Fig. 28.146).

Although the sensitivity of sural nerve biopsy for the diagnosis of amyloidosis with peripheral neuropathy is undetermined, we have seen three patients in whom no amyloid was detected in sural nerves, and yet amyloidosis was diagnosed in concomitant muscle biopsy in two and by autopsy a year later in another. Some authors claim a higher yield of positive diagnosis with biopsy of either muscle or abdominal fat pad. The binding capacity

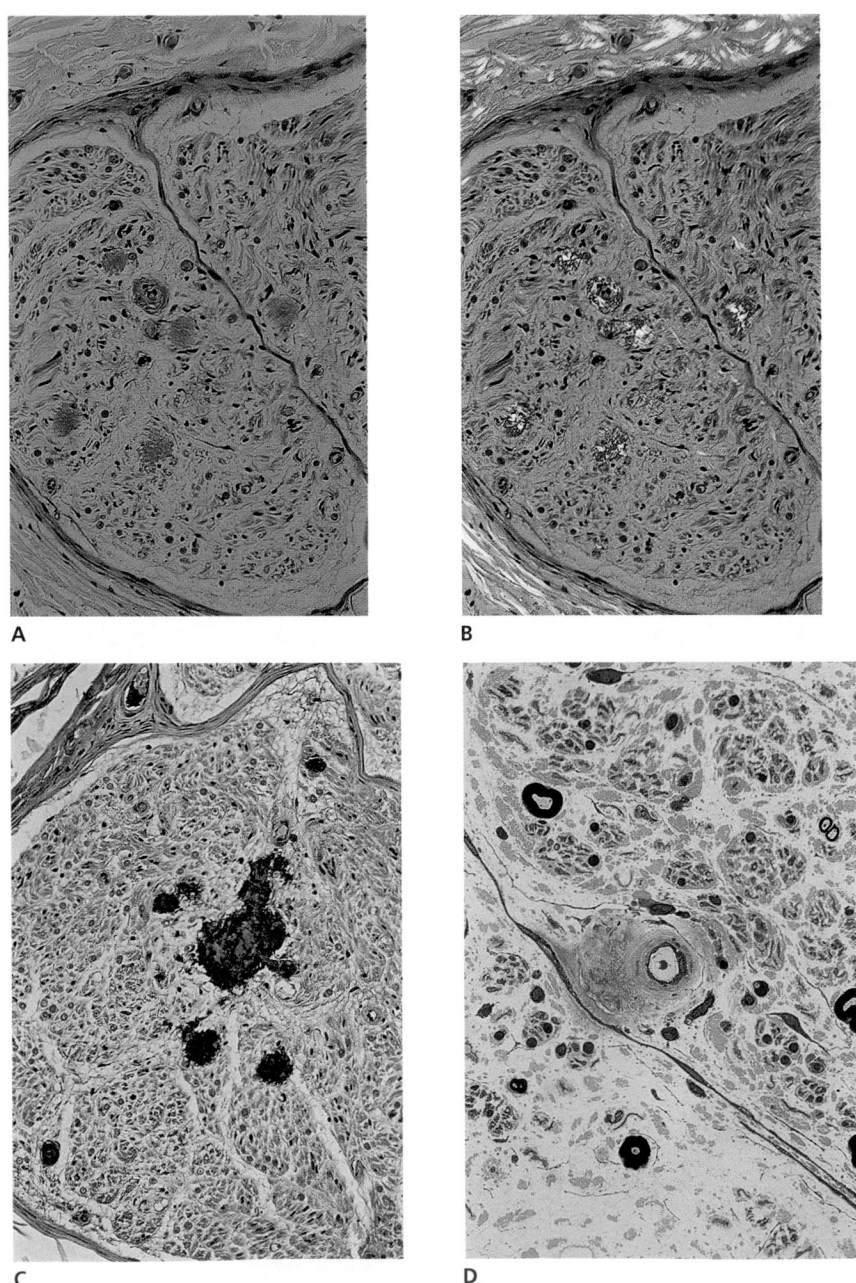

Fig. 28.146 Amyloid neuropathy: (**A,B**) scattered Congo Red positive material in endoneurium displays apple green birefringence under polarized light; (**C**) positive immunostaining for transthyretin; (**D**) depletion of myelinated fibers and perivascular amyloid deposit. (**A**, Congo Red; **B**, Congo Red and polarized light; **C**, immunoperoxidase; **D**, plastic resin)

of Congo Red for amyloid (which results in the typical apple green–yellow birefringence) (Fig. 28.146B) is best demonstrated on fresh frozen sections, whereas prolonged formalin fixation interferes with this reaction. The use of fluorochromic dyes is also a reliable method for the screening of amyloid in paraffin and frozen sections.[128] In both light chain amyloid and TTR amyloid, affinity for Congo Red stain is preserved after treatment with potassium permanganate.

Nerve deposits in FAP show positive immunostaining with antihuman TTR antiserum[124] (Fig. 28.146C). The majority of light chain amyloid-containing biopsies can be characterized as to light chain type by using anti-light chain antisera. The use of commercially available anti-

bodies is valuable in the categorization of sporadic amyloidotic neuropathy because light chain amyloid may be detected in patients without biochemical evidence of light chain disease, and TTR amyloid may be demonstrable in the nerve of patients without history of an inherited disorder. Dalakas and Cunningham[118] characterized the deposits in 15 cases of "sporadic" (nonfamilial or plasma cell dyscrasia) amyloidotic neuropathy. Eleven had antigenic determinants for light chain and three for prealbumin. They concluded that characterization of amyloid protein in tissues is useful in sporadic cases because those who were shown to have TTR could receive genetic counseling and those who had light chain amyloid might receive chemotherapy.

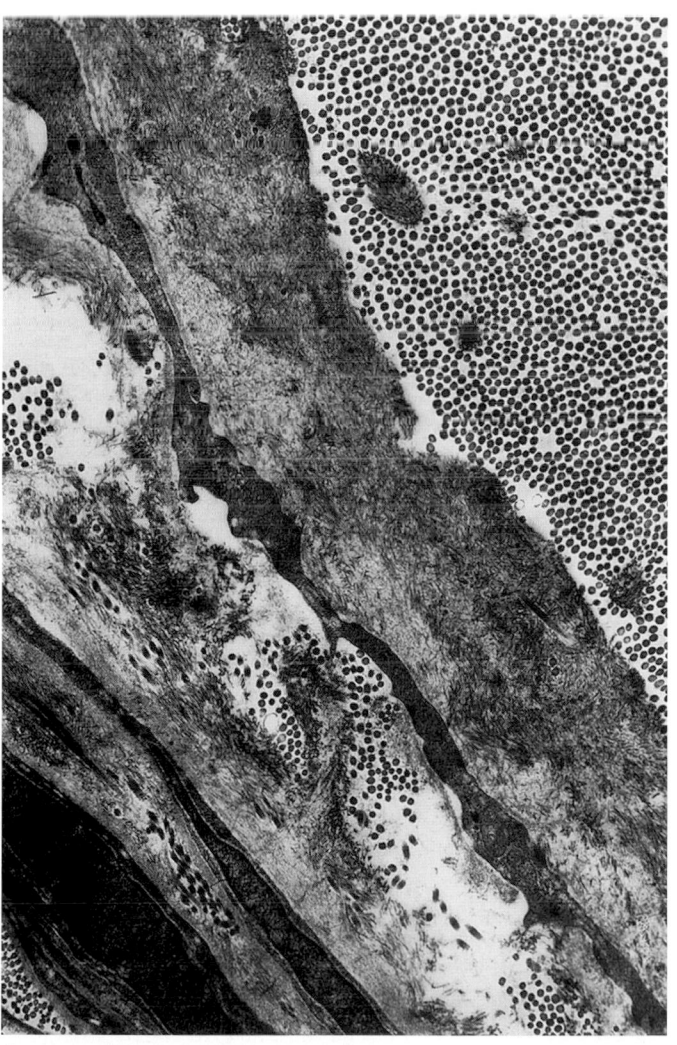

A

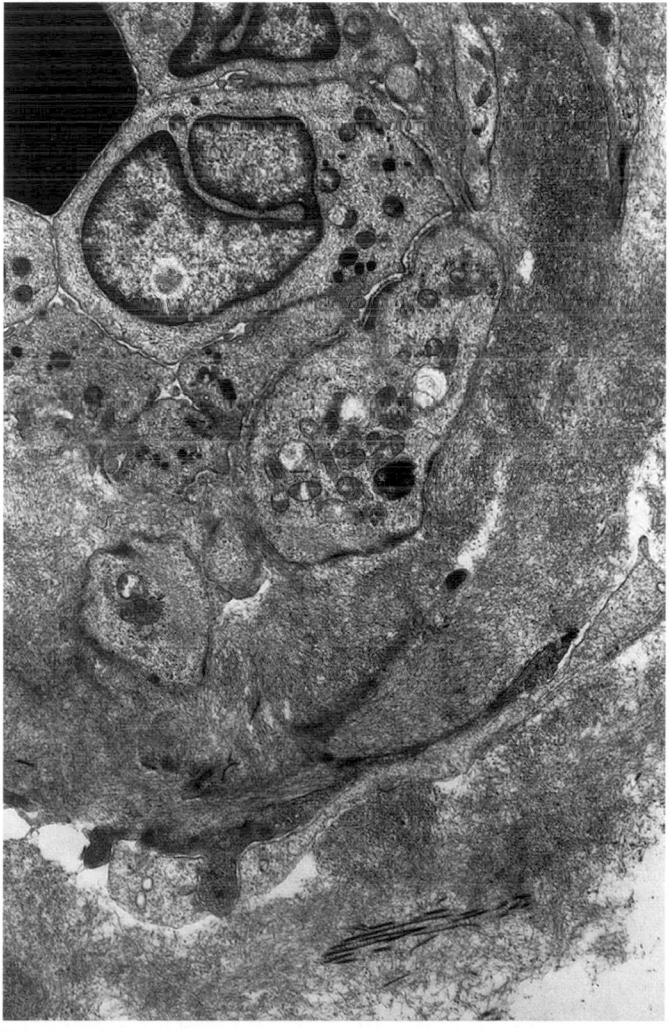

B

Fig. 28.147 FAP. **(A,B)** Electron micrographs show amyloid fibrils in perineurium and perivascular spaces. Basal lamina of perineural and endothelial cells is focally effaced at points of contact with amyloid. Note intervening collagen fibers.

In amyloidotic neuropathy, the degree of fiber loss as seen on histologic sections depends largely on the evolution of the disease. In severe cases, no myelinated or unmyelinated fibers may be detectable, whereas in the early stage there is preservation of fibers of larger diameter. This pattern of predominantly small fiber vulnerability is so characteristic of amyloid neuropathy that notwithstanding negative staining (and this must comprise step sections of the entire block) the diagnosis of amyloidosis is likely to be made with biopsy of other sites. Ultrastructurally the deposits consist of 10-nm unbranched "rigid" or straight fibrils in irregular arrangement or forming fan-shaped clusters. In the intercellular matrix of endoneurium, perivascular spaces, and perineurium, oxytalan filaments of 8 to 14 nm in diameter may simulate amyloid fibrils (Fig. 28.147). They are distinguished by their wavy or curved shape and by a slightly larger size. In the pathogenesis of amyloid neuropathy, ischemia ascribed to vascular involvement and mechanical damage of nerve fibers resulting from the accumulation of large endoneurial deposits have been proposed. However, autopsy studies have shown massive deposition of amyloid in spinal and autonomic ganglia, which may account for neuronal death and secondary axonal degeneration.

Another type of familial amyloidotic polyneuropathy (type II, Rukayina or Indiana form) presents with carpal tunnel syndrome related to deposits (TTR mutation: serine 84) in the flexor retinaculum, causing compression of the median nerve. The carpal tenosynovium is also the site of localized amyloid deposits in patients on long-term hemodialysis. Beta$_2$-microglobulin has been identified by immunoperoxidase as the main protein of this peculiar form of amyloid.[117,119,120] Transthyretin is not involved in FAP type III (Van Allen or Iowa form), which presents as a symmetric polyneuropathy, duodenal ulceration, and renal failure. The amyloid deposits here are derived from a variant of apolipoprotein AI formed from an arginine to glycine substitution at position 26 of the gene (chromosome 11).[125] Regardless of ethnic background the amyloid protein in FAP type IV is related to a mutation of gelsolin, an actin-modulating protein encoded in a single copy gene located on the long arm of chromosome 9. The amyloid protein deposited in the tissues is an abnormal degradation product of the mutant gelsolin. Although amyloid deposits may be detected throughout the peripheral nervous system, FAP IV (Finnish and Japanese types) is clinically characterized by progressive cranial neuropathy and corneal lattice dystrophy.[126]

Neuropathy of dysproteinemia

Sixty percent of patients with paraproteinemia have a monoclonal gammopathy of unknown significance (MGUS), which denotes a serum protein value of less than 3 g/liter, fewer than 5% of plasma cells in the bone marrow, no proteinuria, normal hematology, and absence of systemic signs and symptoms.[134] About 5% of patients with peripheral neuropathy are found to have MGUS. Conversely, about one third of patients with MGUS display peripheral neuropathy. While IgG is the most common class of paraprotein in patients with benign paraproteinemia, IgM is more common in those with neuropathy (60%) followed by IgG (30%) and IgA (10%).[131,133,135,137] The neuropathy may be the presenting feature before an underlying plasma cell dyscrasia becomes detectable, or it may develop during established multiple myeloma, solitary plasmacytoma, or Waldenström's macroglobulinemia. The peripheral nerve deficit may be sensory, motor, or mixed sensory motor. The mechanism of nerve damage in the setting of monoclonal gammopathy is not invariably caused by amyloidosis (see above); lymphocytic infiltration of nerve and damage on an immunologic-inflammatory basis are also important.[134,135] Studies have demonstrated binding to normal peripheral nerve structures of paraproteins from the patient's serum. Approximately one half of patients with peripheral neuropathy and IgM monoclonal gammopathy have IgM antibodies that bind to myelin. The most prevalent antibody activity among these IgM proteins is directed against myelin-associated glycoprotein (MAG).[136] and/or sulfate-3 glucuronyl paragloboside. The patients whose IgM binds to MAG form a major and well-characterized subgroup, associated with a distinct clinical picture: Elderly individuals are usually affected; the onset of the neuropathy is insidious and progressive, initially it has predominantly demyelinating features affecting large sensory fibers (loss of joint and position sense with ataxia and tremor) and late development of distal limb weakness. The disease in some patients progresses slowly but inexorably over decades, mimicking a genetically determined condition. Nerve conduction tracing discloses low velocities and CSF levels of protein are commonly elevated. The differentiation of paraproteinemic (anti-MAG) neuropathy from chronic inflammatory demyelinating polyneuropathy (CIDP) is sometimes difficult because: (i) about 20% of patients with CIDP also have a paraproteinemia; (ii) both neuropathies respond to immunosuppressants[137]; and (iii) in both conditions there is increase protein in CSF. Electrophysiologic studies are of some help in that CIDP shows focal block of conduction in motor nerves whereas in the anti-MAG paraprotein-associated neuropathy, sensory fibers are severely affected, and conduction slowing (without block) is more diffuse and distally predominant. Pathologically, both axonal degeneration and segmental demyelination with occasional hypertrophic changes have been documented in nerve biopsies (Fig. 28.148A). By immunofluorescence specific changes can be visualized: anti-MAG antibody can be localized to areas of myelin splitting[136] (Figs 28.148B and 28.150B). Ultrastructurally, this is termed widely spaced myelin (WSM) (Figs 28.149 and 28.150A)

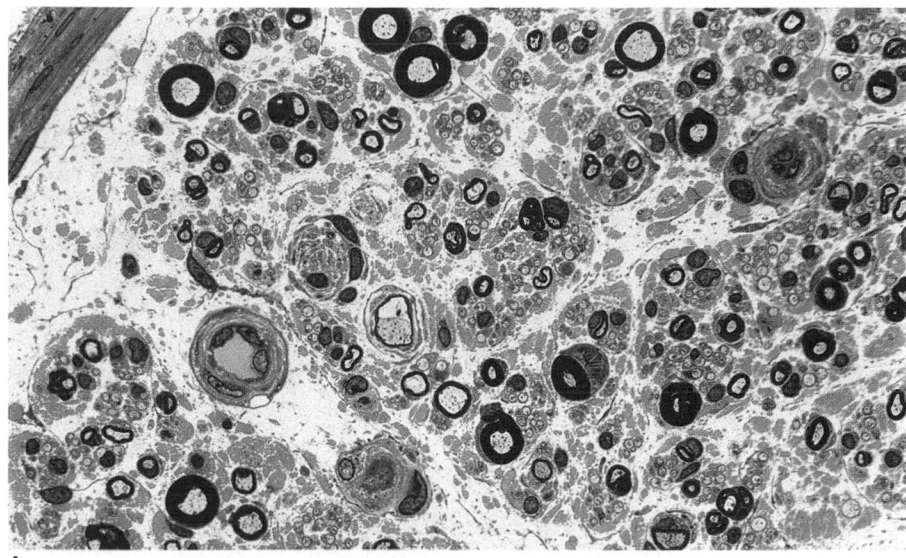

Fig. 28.148 Anti-MAG IgM paraproteinemic neuropathy: (**A**) note dropout of fibers, attenuation of myelin sheaths, and onion bulbs; (**B**) immunofluorescence outlines most myelinated fibers. (**A**, plastic resin; **B**, fresh frozen.)

and represents focal separation of the intraperiod line (this line that represents a virtual extracellular space is composed of two thin leaflets 2 to 4 nm apart), brought about by the intrusion of anti-MAG antibodies that "open up" the intraperiod line giving a characteristic wide spacing between the myelin lamellae (between 20 and 30 nm) that lead to myelin breakdown and remodeling; this is considered to be a unique feature of dysglobulinemic neuropathy[138] and has been proven elegantly by electron immunohistochemistry (Fig. 28.150B). By contrast, a superficially similar abnormality—uncompacted myelin—consists of widening of the major dense line and is an uncommon finding in diverse neuropathies.

Nonamyloid light chain deposition may occur in the setting of myeloma, Waldenström's macroglobulinemia, and monoclonal gammopathy of undetermined significance. The deposits appear as coalescent amorphous eosinophilic pools within the endoneurium associated with blood vessels and appear as hyaline bluish deposits in the Toluidine Blue semithin plastic sections[132] (Fig. 28.151). This material is PAS positive, resistant to diastase digestion, and Congo Red negative. Most of the

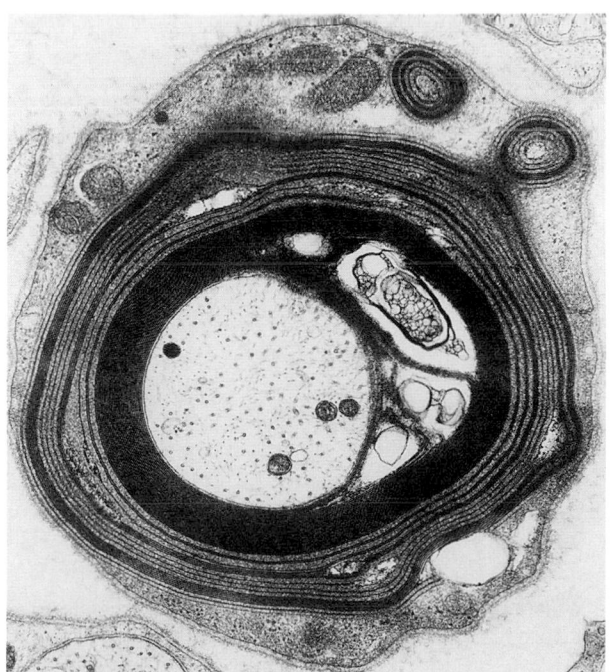

Fig. 28.149 Sural nerve. Widely spaced myelin is typical of the neuropathy associated with IgM paraproteinemia. (×19,600)

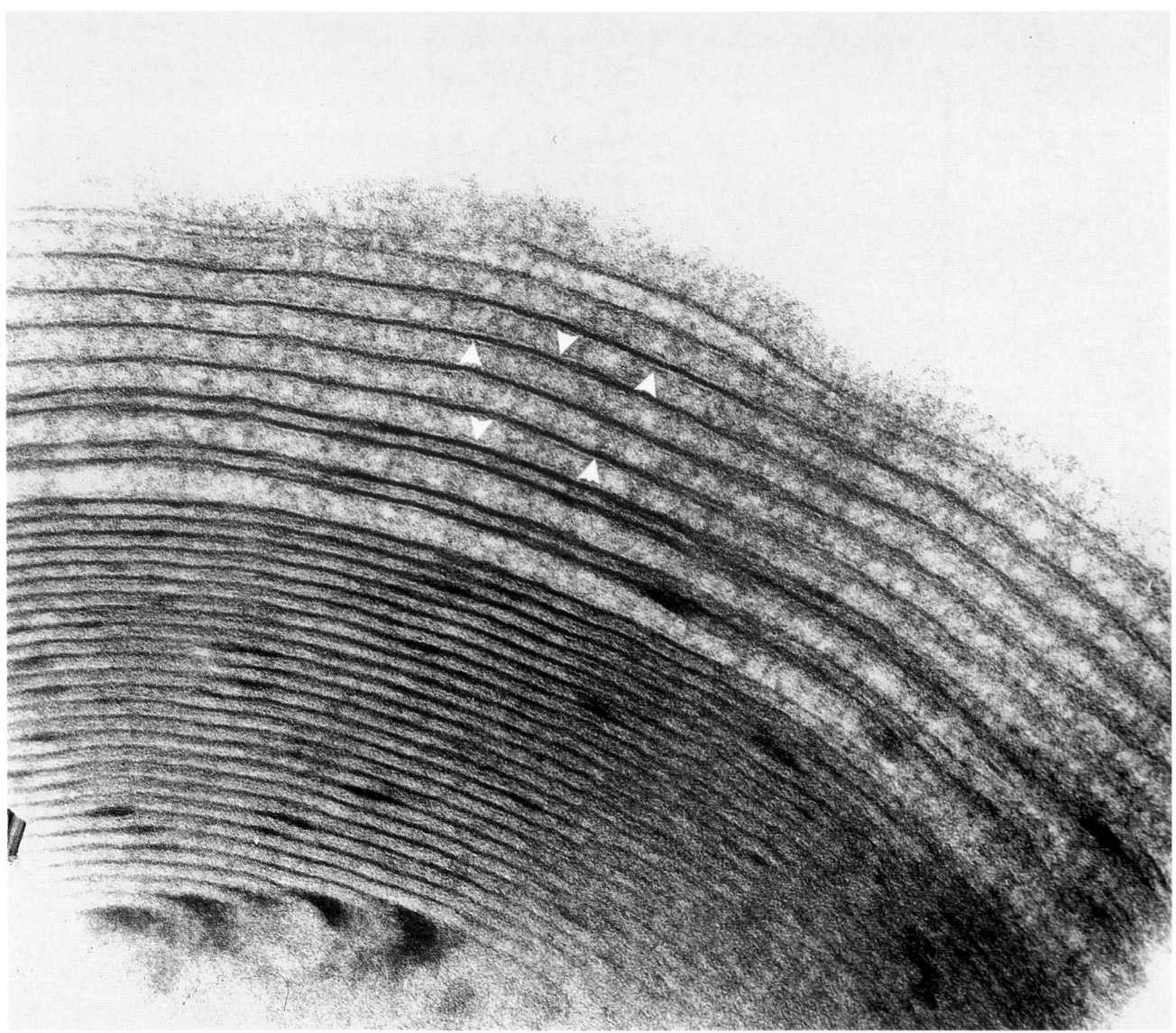

A

Fig. 28.150 Anti-MAG paraproteinemic neuropathy: **(A)** separation of intraperiod line causes widely spaced myelin (arrowheads) (×126,040) *continued*

cases exhibit positive immunoreactivity for kappa light chain (Fig. 28.117B). Ultrastructurally, nonamyloid deposits are amorphous granular or finely reticulated.

Curved tubular structures arranged in a fingerprint pattern may be seen in the endoneurium adjacent to Schwann cells and in the cytoplasm of endothelial cells and pericytes in cases of IgG myeloma with cryoglobulinemia.[139,140] A vasculitis involving peripheral nerves resulting in ischemic neuropathy has been described in mixed cryoglobulinemia.[141] Ischemia of nerve may also be caused by intravascular cryoglobulin deposition in the absence of inflammation.[130]

A chronic demyelinating polyneuropathy with predominant and severe motor dysfunction is the salient clinical feature in osteosclerotic myeloma and the POEMS syndrome (polyneuropathy, organomegaly, endocrinopathy, M-protein, and skin changes).[129] The M protein in these rare variants of multiple myeloma is usually of the IgG or IgA heavy chain class; most are lambda light chain type.

Toxic-metabolic neuropathy

Axonal degeneration of varying severity is the usual pathologic finding in the neuropathy caused by systemic metabolic disorders (vitamin deficiency, uremia, porphyria),[149] exogenous toxins and pharmaceuticals such as alcohol,[147,150] isoniazid, metronidazole, misonidazole,[144] cis-platinum, taxol,[142] thalidomide, heavy metals (arsenic, thallium, mercury), and chemical agents.[148] In the sural nerve, chronic axonal degeneration is manifested by loss of myelinated fibers. Fibers of larger diameter are always more severely affected. In the acute

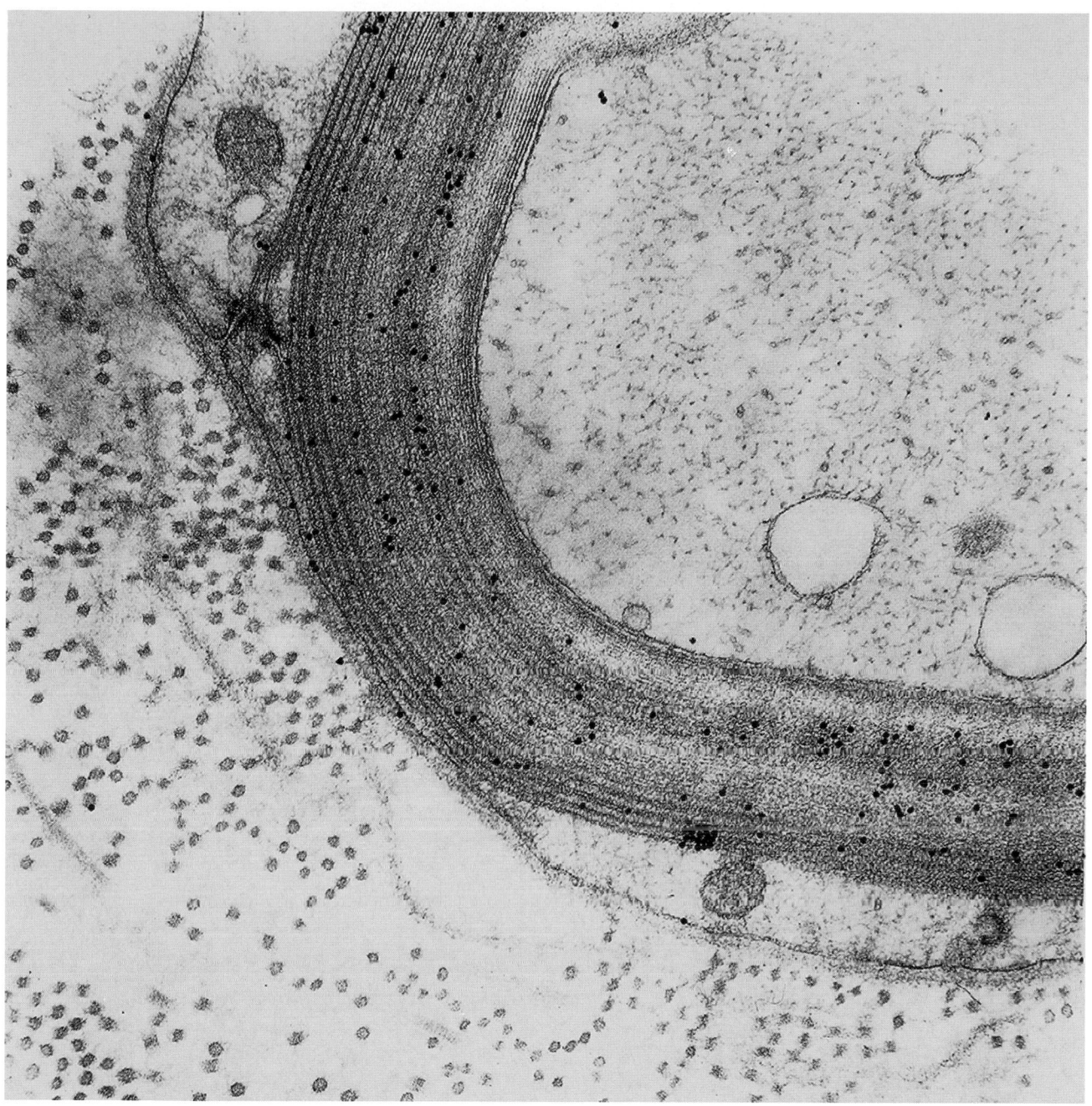

Fig. 28.150 *Continued:* Anti-MAG paraproteinemic neuropathy: **(B)** immunogold co-localizes with widely spaced myelin (×38,600).

stage, degeneration may affect a few fibers or the vast majority of them. The breakdown of myelin is best seen on longitudinal sections as rows of osmiophilic debris. Later, fat-laden macrophages appear. In longstanding neuropathy the salient features are fiber loss, denervated Schwann cells, and clusters of myelinated fibers of complementary shapes indicative of regeneration.

Only in rare instances does a toxin induce tissue changes that may be pathognomonic or highly suggestive of a particular compound. Hexacarbons and glue-sniffing neuropathy (and rarely disulfiram) will produce characteristic segmental distention of axons as a result of the accumulation of neurofilaments.[142] The diiodinated benzofuran derivative amiodarone, used in the treatment of cardiac rhythm abnormalities, occasionally gives rise to a sensory motor neuropathy[143]; this typically occurs in a patient who has been taking the drug for several months at a dosage of 200 to 600 mg per day. Sural nerve biopsy discloses, in addition to axonal degeneration and rare segmental demyelination, phospholipid-containing cytosomes in Schwann cells, perineurium, vascular endothelial cells, and nerve fibers.[145] Amiodarone and its metabolite desethyl-amiodarone pass readily into human nerves, either directly or following endothelial injury. The drug inhibits lysosomal phospholipases leading to the formation of typical whorled, lamellar and paracrystalline inclusions (Fig. 28.152). Chronic treatment with chloroquine even when prophylactic doses are given may cause neuromyopathy; studies of sural nerve biopsies have shown axonal degeneration and demyelination. Chloroquine, an amphiphilic cationic compound, binds to acidic phospholipids of membranes forming a complex that is not digested by lysosomes and is rearranged into concentric lamellar or crystalid myeloid bodies in Schwann cells (Fig. 28.153A), pericytes and smooth muscle cells of blood vessels. Ultrastructurally besides myeloid bodies, curvilinear structures (Fig. 28.153B) are conspicuous and similar to those described in ceroid lipofuscinosis (Fig. 28.153B). Experimental studies have shown the susceptibility of spinal ganglion neurons to chloroquine-induced inclusions; this may lead to degeneration of their axons,

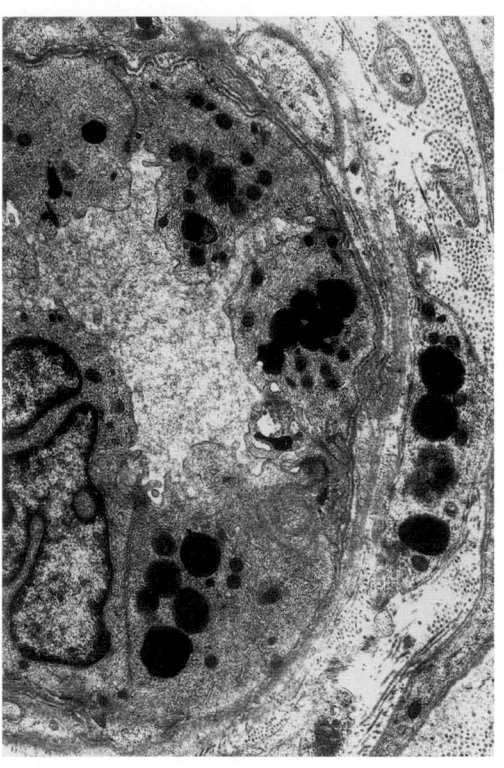

A

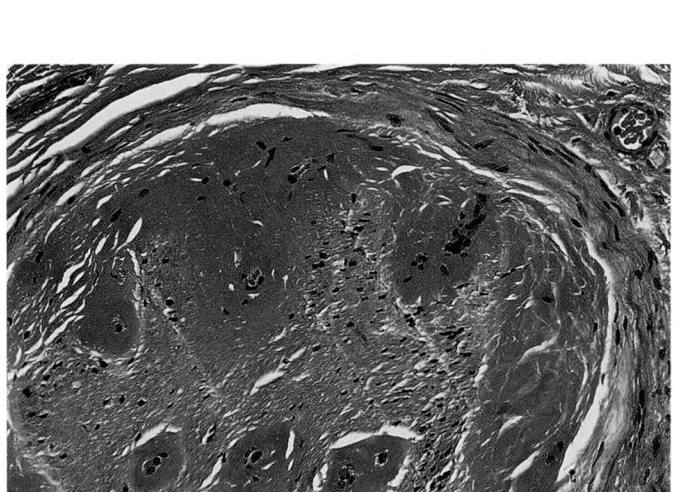

A

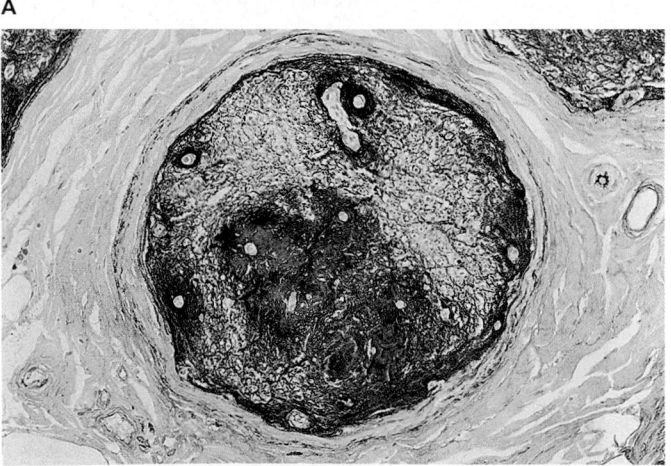

B

Fig. 28.151 Sural nerve in IgM paraproteinemia. **(A,B)** Kappa chain neuropathy, the endoneurium is depleted of nerve fibers and contains pools of Congo Red negative amorphous material which immunoreacts for kappa chain. **(A,** HPS; **B,** immunoperoxidase)

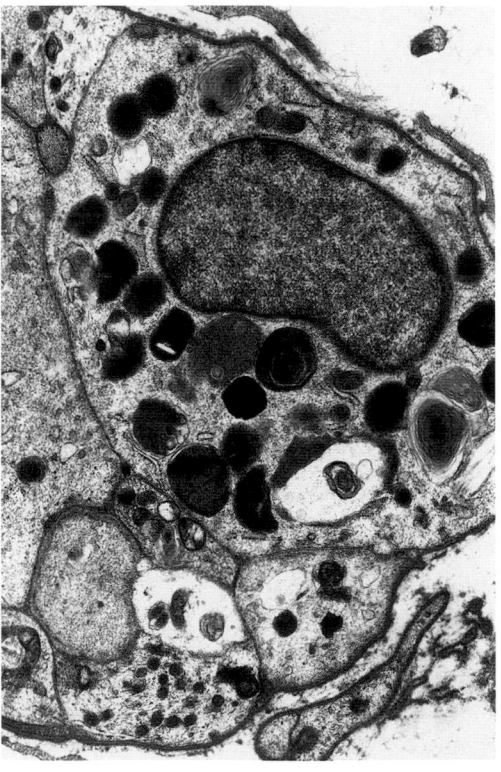

B

Fig. 28.152 Amiodarone neuropathy. Viewed under the electron microscope this sural nerve reveals lysosomal inclusions in the form of osmiophilic bodies and lamellar and paracrystalline structures in endothelium, pericytes **(A)**, and Schwann cells **(B)**. **(A,** ×12,100; **B,** ×12,100)

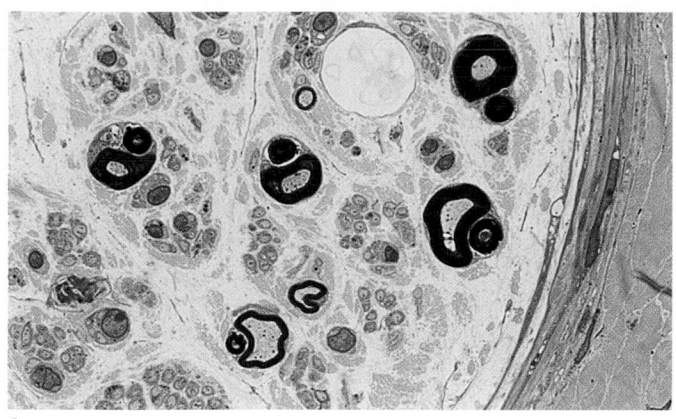

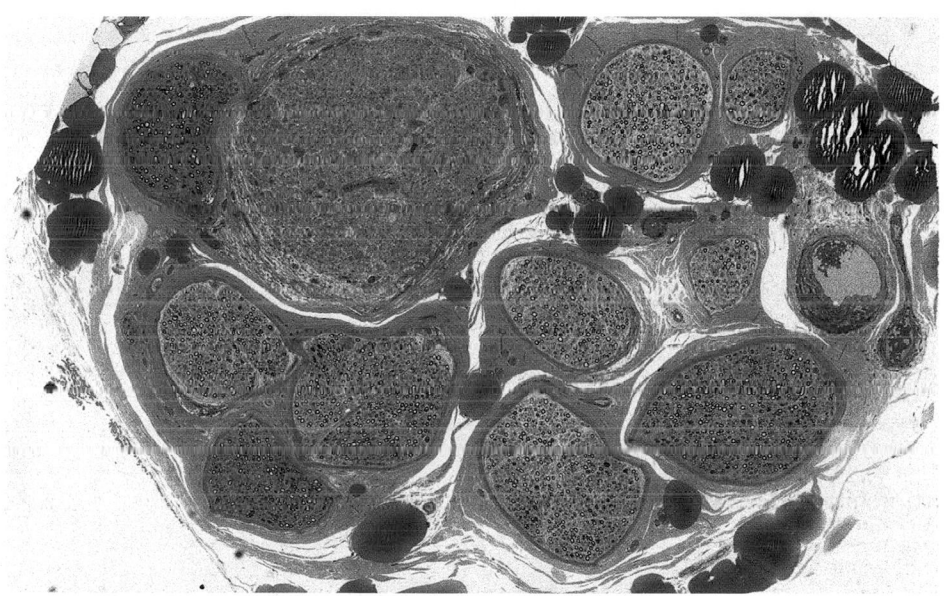

Fig. 28.153 Chloroquine neuropathy. (**A**) Large lysosomal inclusions in myelinated nerve fibers (plastic resin (oil). (**B**) Electron photomicroscopy shows curvilinear and osmiophilic bodies (×31,834).

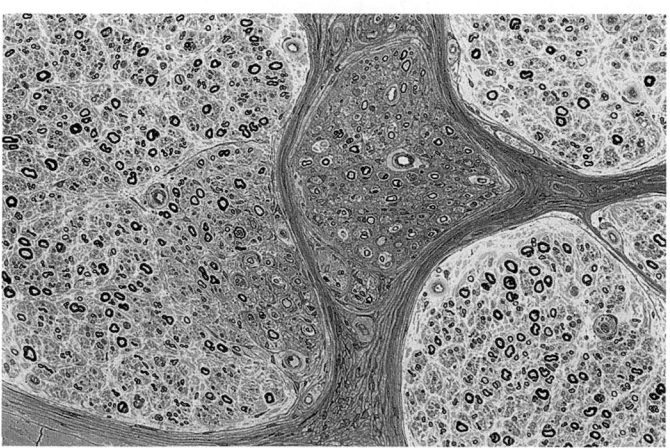

Fig. 28.154 (**A,B**) Focal fascicular damage and minineuroma in diabetic neuropathy. (**A** and **B**, plastic resin)

thus providing a pathogenesis for an axonal polyneuropathy. The absence of a blood–brain barrier to dorsal root ganglia explains the significant accumulation of inclusion in neurons. Diphtheria toxin and perhexilene maleate induce a primary demyelination,[146] an unusual feature in toxic neuropathy. An inflammatory demyelinating neuropathy has been reported in patients treated with Suramin.

Other neuropathies

The most common known cause of peripheral neuropathy in North America is **diabetes mellitus**. Two types of neuropathies have been described in longstanding diabetes: (i) a focal and multifocal neuropathy affecting proximal nerves and, (ii) more commonly, a symmetric distal polyneuropathy[155] in which the sural nerve biopsy displays a mixture of axonal degeneration, segmental demyelination (Fig. 28.155B) and hypertrophy, and regeneration clusters (Fig. 28.154) suggesting a dying-back process.[166,179,180] Electron microscopy has revealed thickening of the basal lamina of Schwann cells and perineurium[166] and—more importantly—thickening of the walls of endoneurial microvessels by layers of duplicated basal lamina (Fig. 28.155A). Autopsy studies in diabetics with neuropathy have shown focal areas of myelinated fiber loss, perineurial damage, miniature neuroma formation, and microangiopathy in the sciatic nerve suggesting a vascular lesion. It is postulated that in some cases the accumulation of many proximal insults causes a severe and diffuse fiber loss distally to produce a symmetric neuropathy. It seems likely, however, that both metabolic and ischemic factors are involved in the pathogenesis of diabetic neuropathy. We have occasionally observed perivascular lymphocytic cuffing in sural nerves from patients with diabetic polyneuropathy.[178]

Nerve biopsy may yield clues to a specific diagnosis or show significant abnormality in the following conditions: **adrenoleukodystrophy** (lamellar inclusions consisting of two parallel electron-dense 2- to 5-nm leaflets separated by a clear space varying from 2 to 7 nm in width in Schwann cells),[174,175] **cerebrotendinous xanthomatosis**,[172] **ceroid lipofuscinosis** (curvilinear bodies and fingerprint structures),[160,167] **CADASIL**[176] (Fig. 28.156), **Chediak–Higashi disease** (giant lysosomes in Schwann cells),[170,171] **chloroquine neuropathy**,[181] **Farber's disease**[185] (Fig. 28.157), **gangliosidosis**,[169] **Gaucher's disease**, **giant axonal neuropathy**[159,161] (Fig. 28.158), **leukemic infiltrate**,[184] **neurofibromatous neuropathy**,[182] **Niemann–Pick disease**,[151,165] **polyglucosan body disease** (hyaline concentrically laminated PAS-

A

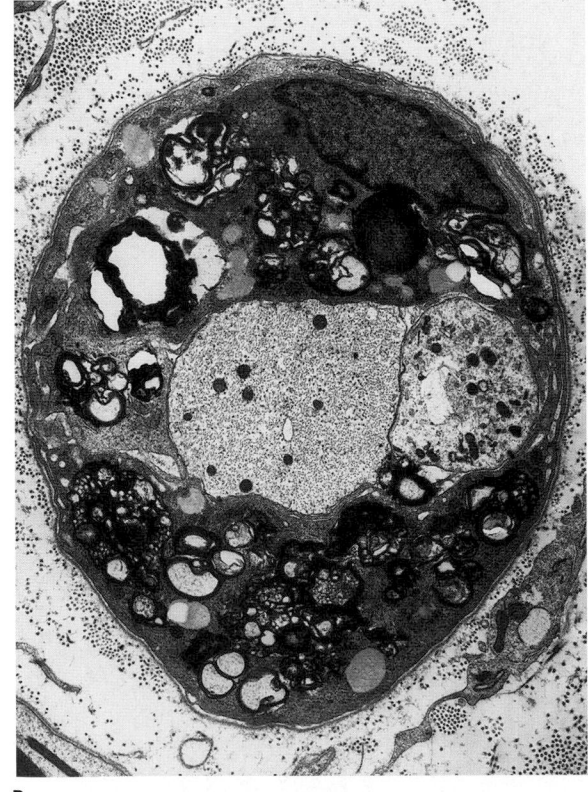

B

Fig. 28.155 Diabetic neuropathy. Electron micrographs of endoneurium show reduplication of basal lamina about microvessel (**A**) and segmental demyelination (**B**). Axon at center is unaffected while myelin is breaking down. (**A**, 7370; **B**, 9300)

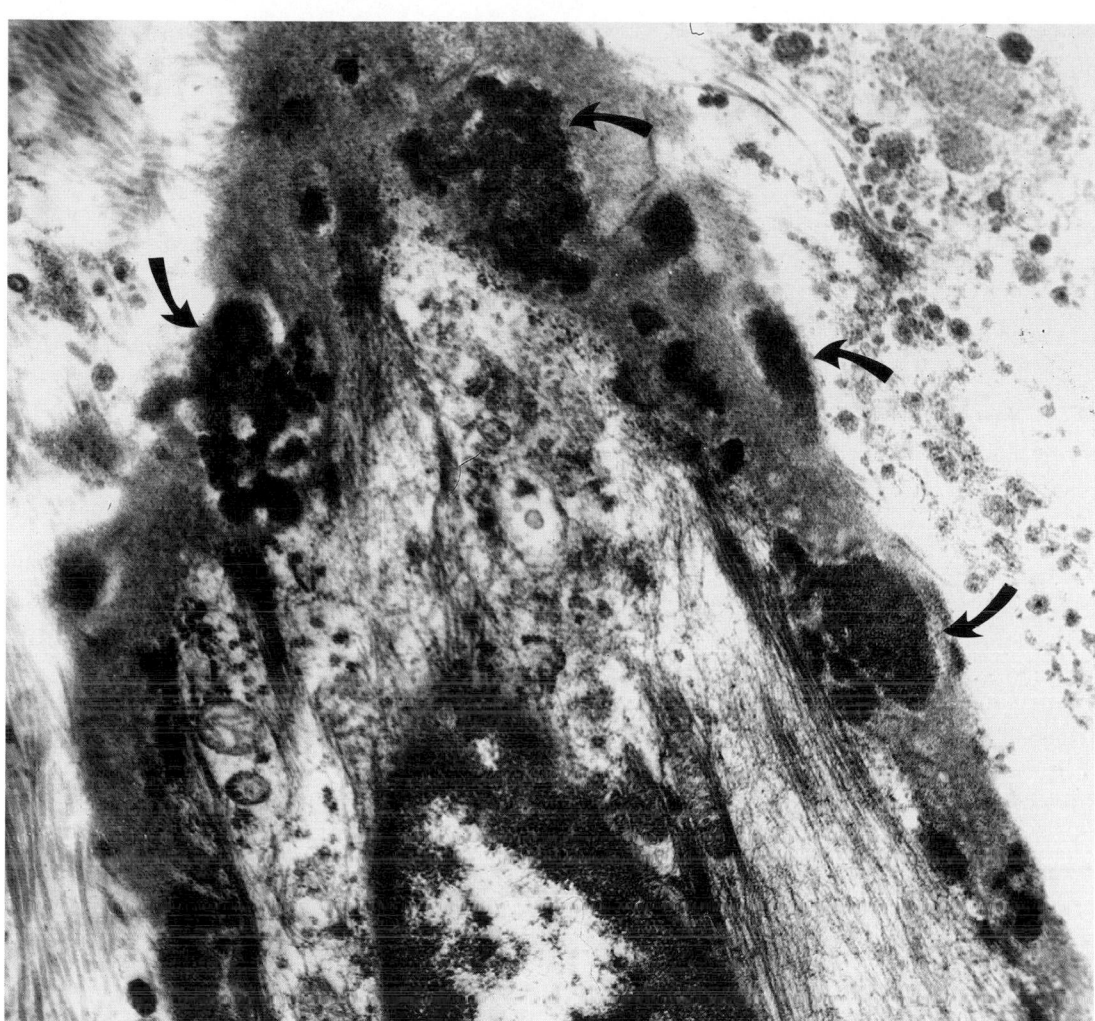

Fig. 28.156 Electron photomicrograph. CADASIL: characteristic extracellular granular osmiophilic material adjacent to smooth muscle cell (arrows). (×48,500)

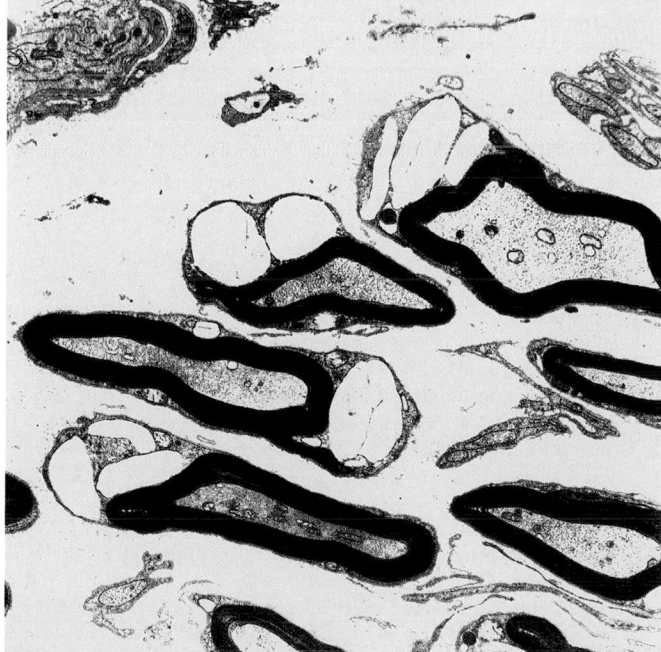

Fig. 28.157 Sural nerve. Electron photomicrograph. Farber's disease. Typical "banana" bodies in cytoplasm of Schwann cell. (×13,490)

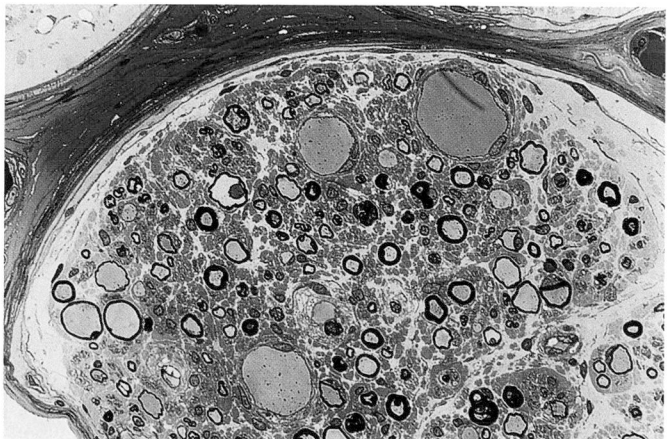

Fig. 28.158 Giant axonal neuropathy. Sural nerve: axons distended by filaments are surrounded by attenuated myelin or are devoid of myelin. (Plastic resin)

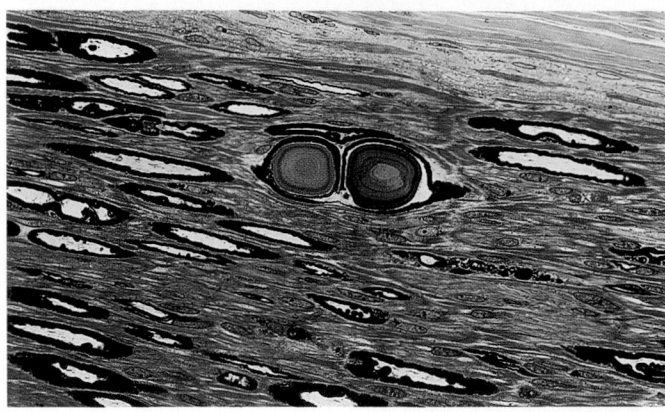

Fig. 28.159 Sural nerve: intra-axonal polyglucosan bodies. (Plastic resin (oil))

positive intra-axonal bodies)[156,158,165,186] (Fig. 28.159), **Pompe's disease,**[152,164] **primary hyperoxaluria,**[153] **Refsum's disease** (abundant though nonspecific paracrystaline inclusions in Schwann cells),[163] **Tangier disease** (lipid droplets and pleomorphic inclusions in the cytoplasm of Schwann cells),[162,168,173] **vincristine toxicity,**[154,177] **Wolman's disease,**[157] and **xanthomatous neuropathy in primary biliary cirrhosis.**[183]

References

Introduction

1 Bischoff A. The peripheral nerves. In Johannessen JV (ed.): Electron Microscopy in Human Medicine, vol. 6, Nervous System, Sensory Organs, and Respiratory Tract. New York, 1979, McGraw-Hill.

2 Dyck PJ, Oviatt KF, Lambert EH. Intensive evaluation of referred unclassified neuropathies yields improved diagnosis. Ann Neurol 1981, **10:** 222–226.

3 Fagius J. Chronic cryptogenic polyneuropathy. The search for a cause. Acta Neurol Scand 1983, **67:** 173–180.

4 Hall SM, Hughes RA, Atkinson PF, McColl I, Gale A. Motor nerve biopsy in severe Guillain–Barré syndrome. Ann Neurol 1992, **31:** 441–444.

5 McLeod JG, Tuck RR, Pollard JD, Cameron J, Walsh JC. Chronic polyneuropathy of undetermined cause. J Neurol Neurosurg Psychiatry 1984, **47:** 530–535.

6 Midroni G, Bilbao JM. Biopsy diagnosis of peripheral neuropathy. Boston, 1995, Butterworth-Heinemann, p. 14.

7 Said G. Indications and usefulness of nerve biopsy. Arch Neurol 2002, **59:** 1532–1535.

Normal anatomy

8 Ariza A, Bilbao JM, Rosai J. Immunohistochemical detection of epithelial membrane antigen in normal perineurial cells and perineurioma. Am J Surg Pathol 1988, **12:** 678–683.

9 Asbury AK, Johnson PC. Pathology of peripheral nerve. In Bennington JL (ed.): Major Problems in Pathology, vol. 9. Philadelphia, 1978, WB Saunders pp. 1–311.

10 Behse F. Morphometric studies on the human sural nerve. Acta Neurol Scand Suppl 1990, **132:** 1–38.

11 Behse F, Buchtal F, Carlsen F, Knappeis GG. Endoneurial space and its constituents in the sural nerve of patients with neuropathy. Brain 1974, **97:** 773–784.

12 Bunge MB, Bunge RP. Linkage between Schwann cell extracellular matrix production and ensheathment function. Ann NY Acad Sci 1986, **486:** 241–247.

13 Burkel WE. The histological fine structure of perineurium. Anat Rec 1967, **158:** 177–189.

14 Dziadek M, Edgar D, Paulsson M, Timpl R, Fleischmajer R. Basement membrane proteins produced by Schwann cells and in neurofibromatosis. Ann NY Acad Sci 1986, **486:** 248–259.

15 Gray F, Gherardi R, Marshall A, Janota I, Poirier J. Adult polyglucosan body disease (APBD). J Neuropathol Exp Neurol 1988, **47:** 459–474.

16 Griffin JW, George R, Ho T. Macrophage systems in peripheral nerves. A review. J Neuropathol Exp Neurol 1993, **52:** 553–560.

17 Haust Daria M. Fine fibrils of extracellular space (microfibrils), their structure and role in connective tissue organization. Am J Pathol 1965, **47:** 1113–1136.

18 Mugnaini E, Osen KK, Schnapp B, Friedrich VL Jr. Distribution of Schwann cell cytoplasm and plasmalemmal vesicles (caveolae) in peripheral myelin sheaths. An electron microscopic study with thin sections and freeze fracturing. J Neurocytol 1977, **6:** 647–648.

19 Ochoa J, Mair WG. The normal sural nerve in man. I. Ultrastructure and numbers of fibres and cells. Acta Neuropathol 1969, **13:** 197–216.

20 Ochoa J, Mair WG. The normal sural nerve in man. II. Changes in the axons and Schwann cells due to aging. Acta Neuropathol 1969, **13:** 217–239.

21 Olsson Y, Reese TS. Permeability of vasa nervorum and perineurium in mouse sciatic nerve studied by fluorescence and electron microscopy. J Neuropathol Exp Neurol 1971, **30:** 105–119.

22 Sanes JR. Analyzing cell lineage with a recombinant retrovirus. Trends Neurosci 1989, **12:** 21–28.

23 Shanta TR, Bourne GH. The perineurial epithelium—a new concept. In Bourne GH (ed.): The structure and function of nervous tissue. Structure I. New York, 1968, Academic Press.

24 Sunderland S. Nerve and nerve injuries, ed 2. New York, 1978, Churchill Livingstone.

25 Tohgi H, Tsukagoshi H, Toyokura Y. Quantitative changes with age in normal sural nerves. Acta Neuropathol 1977, **38:** 213–220.

26 Tomonaga M, Sluga E. The ultrastructure of protagen(pi) granules. Acta Neuropathol 1970, **15:** 56–69.

27 Weis J, Alexianu ME, Heide G, Schroder JM. Renaut bodies contain elastic fiber components. J Neuropathol Exp Neurol 1993, **52:** 444–451.

Basic pathologic mechanisms

28 Asbury AK, Johnson PC. Pathology of peripheral nerve. In Bennington JL (ed.): Major problems in pathology, vol. 9. Philadelphia, 1978, WB Saunders.

29 Beuche W, Friede RL. The role of nonresident cells in Wallerian degeneration. J Neurocytol 1984, **13:** 767–796.

30 Cavanagh JB. The "dying-back" process. A common denominator in many naturally occurring and toxic neuropathies. Arch Pathol Lab Med 1979, **103:** 659–664.

31 Heumann R, Lindholm D, Bandtlow C, et al. Differential regulation of mRNA encoding nerve growth factor and its receptor in rat sciatic nerve during development, degeneration, and regeneration. Role of macrophages. Proc Natl Acad Sci USA 1987, **84:** 8735–8739.

32 Johnson FM Jr., Taniuchi M, DiStefano PS. Expression and possible function of nerve growth factor receptors on Schwann cells. Trends Neurosci 1988, **11:** 299–304.

33 Lubinska L. Patterns of Wallerian degeneration of myelinated fibres in short and long peripheral stumps and in isolated segments of rat phrenic nerve. Interpretation of the role of axoplasmic flow of the trophic factor. Brain Res 1982, **233:** 227–240.

34 Malbouisson AM, Ghabriel MN, Allt G. The nondirectional

pattern of axonal changes in Wallerian degeneration. A computer-aided morphometric analysis. J Anat 1984, **139:** 159–174.

35 Spencer PS, Schaumburg HH. Central and peripheral nervous system degeneration produced by pure n-hexane. Trans Am Neurol Assoc 1977; **101:** 153–156.

36 Weller RO. Diphtheritic neuropathy in the chicken, an electron microscopic study. J Pathol Bacteriol 1965, **89:** 591–598.

Neuropathies
Inherited neuropathy

37 Behse F, Buchthal F, Carlsen F, Knappeis GG. Hereditary neuropathy with liability to pressure palsies. Electrophysiological and histopathological aspects. Brain 1972, **95:** 777–794.

38 Benz HU, Harzer K. Metachromatic reaction of pseudoisocyanine with sulfatides in metachromatic leukodystrophy. I. Technical and histochemical staining. Acta Neuropathol 1974, **27:** 177–180.

39 Berciano J, Combarros O, Figols J, Calleja J, Cabello A, Silos I, Coria F. Hereditary motor and sensory neuropathy type II. Clinicopathological study of a family. Brain 1986, **109:** 897–914.

40 Bischoff A, Ulrich J. Peripheral neuropathy in globoid cell leukodystrophy (Krabbe's disease). Ultrastructural and histochemical findings. Brain 1969, **92:** 861–870.

41 Chance PF, Alderson MK, Leppig KA, Lensch MW, Matsunami N, Smith B, Swanson PD, Odelberg SJ, Disteche CM, Bird TD. DNA deletion associated with hereditary neuropathy with liability to pressure palsies. Cell 1993, **72:** 143–151.

42 Desnick RJ, Bishop DF. Fabry's disease. Alpha galactosidase deficiency. Schindler disease. Alpha-N-acetyl galactosaminidase deficiency. In Scriver CR, Beaudet AL, Sly WS, Valle D (eds): The Metabolic Basis of Inherited Disease. New York, 1989, McGraw-Hill.

43 Gabreels-Feston AAWM, Hoogendijk JE, Meijerink HHS, Gabreels FJM, Bolhuis PA, van Beersum S, Kulkens T, Nelis E, Jennekens FGI, de Viser M, van Engelen BGM, Van Broeckhoven C, Mariman ECM. Two divergent types of nerve pathology in patients with different P0 mutations in Charcot–Marie–Tooth disease. Neurology 1996, **47:** 761–765.

44 Guzzetta F, Ferriere G, Lyon G. Congenital hypomyelination polyneuropathy. Pathological findings compared with polyneuropathies starting later in life. Brain 1982, **105:** 395–416.

45 Hahn AF. Hereditary motor and sensory neuropathy. HMSN type 11 (neuronal type and X-linked HMSN). Brain Pathol 1993, **3:** 147–155.

46 Madrid R, Bradley WG. The pathology of neuropathies with focal thickening of the myelin sheath (tomaculous neuropathy). J Neurol Sci 1975, **25:** 415–448.

47 Madrid R, Bradley WG, Davis CJ. The peroneal muscular atrophy syndrome. Clinical, genetic, electrophysiological and nerve biopsy studies. Part 2. Observations on pathological changes in sural nerve biopsies. J Neurol Sci 1977, **32:** 91–122.

48 Ouvrier RA, McLeod JG, Conchin TE. The hypertrophic forms of hereditary motor and sensory neuropathy. A study of hypertrophic Charcot–Marie–Tooth disease (HMSN type I) and Dejerine–Sottas disease (HMSN type III) in childhood. Brain 1987, **110:** 121–148.

49 Ouvrier RA, McLeod JG, Morgan GJ, Wise GA, Conchin TE. Hereditary motor and sensory neuropathy of neuronal type with onset in early childhood. J Neurol Sci 1981, **51:** 181–197.

50 Pellissier JF, Van Hoof F, Bourdet-Bonerandi D, Monier-Faugere MC, Toga M. Morphological and biochemical changes in muscle and peripheral nerve in Fabry's disease. Muscle Nerve 1981, **4:** 381–387.

51 Sander S, Nicholson GA, Ouvrier RA, McLeod JG, Pollard JD. Charcot–Marie–Tooth disease: histopathological features of the peripheral myelin protein (PMP22) duplication (CMT1A) and Connexin32 mutations (CMTX1). Muscle Nerve 1998; **21:** 217–225.

52 Smith TW, Bhawan J, Keller RB, DeGirolami U. Charcot–Marie–Tooth disease associated with hypertrophic neuropathy. A neuropathologic study of two cases. J Neuropathol Exp Neurol 1980, **39:** 420–440.

53 Suter U, Welcher AA, Snipes GJ. Progress in the molecular understanding of hereditary peripheral neuropathies reveals new insights into the biology of the peripheral nervous system. Trends Neurosci 1993, **16:** 50–56.

54 Suzuki K, Suzuki Y. Galactosylceramide lipidosis. Globoid-cell leukodystrophy (Krabbe's disease). In Scriver CR, Beaudet AL, Sly WS, Valle D (eds): The Metabolic Basis of Inherited Disease. New York, 1989, McGraw-Hill.

55 Thomas PK, King RH, Kocen RS, Brett EM. Comparative ultrastructural observations on peripheral nerve abnormalities in the late infantile, juvenile and late onset forms of metachromatic leukodystrophy. Acta Neuropathol 1977, **39:** 237–245.

56 Vital A, Ferrer X, Lagueny A, Vandenberghe A, Latour P, Goizet C, Canron MH, Louset P, Petry KG, Vital C. Histolopathological features of X-linked Charcot–Marie–Tooth disease in 8 patients from 6 families with different connexin32 mutations. J Periph Nerv System 2001, **6:** 79–84.

57 Yoshikawa H, Nishimura T, Nakatsuji Y, Fujimura H, Himoro M, Hayasaka K, Sakoda S, Yanagihara T. Elevated expression of messenger RNA for peripheral myelin protein 22 in biopsied peripheral nerves of patients with Charcot–Marie–Tooth disease type 1A. Ann Neurol 1994, **35:** 445–450.

Inflammatory neuropathy

58 Asbury AK, Arnason BG, Adams RD. The inflammatory lesion in idiopathic polyneuritis. Its role in pathogenesis. Medicine 1969, **48:** 173–215.

59 Brochet B, Louiset P, Lagueny A, Coquet M, Vital C, Loiseau P. Peripheral neuropathies disclosing sarcoidosis. Rev Neurol 1988, **144:** 590–595.

60 Cornblath D, McArthur JC, Kennedy PG, Witte AS, Griffin JW. Inflammatory demyelinating peripheral neuropathies associated with human T-cell lymphotropic virus type III infection. Ann Neurol 1987, **21:** 32–40.

61 Cusimano MD, Bilbao JM, Cohen SM. Hypertrophic brachial plexus neuritis. A pathological study of two cases. Ann Neurol 1988, **24:** 615–622.

62 Dalakas MC, Pezeshkpour GH. Neuromuscular diseases associated with human immunodeficiency virus infection. Ann Neurol 1988, **23(Suppl):** S38–S48.

63 Dyck PJ. Is there an axonal variety of GBS? Neurology 1993, **43:** 1277–1280.

64 Gabreels-Festen AA, Gabreels FJ, Hoogendijk DA, Bolhuis PA, Jongen PJ, Vingerhoets HM. Chronic inflammatory demyelinating polyneuropathy or hereditary motor and sensory neuropathy? Diagnostic value of morphological criteria. Acta Neuropathol 1993, **86:** 630–635.

65 Griffin JW, Li CY, Ho TW, Tian M, Gao CY, Xue P, Mishu B, Conblath DR, Macko C, McKhann GM, Asbury AK. Pathology of the motor-sensory axonal Guillain–Barré syndrome. Ann Neurol 1996, **39:** 17–28.

66 Guberman A, Rosenbaum H, Braciale T, Schlaepfer WW. Human neurolymphomatosis. J Neurol Sci 1978, **36:** 1–12.

67 Hall SM, Hughes RA, Atkinson PF, McColl I, Gale A. Motor nerve biopsy in severe Guillain–Barré syndrome. Ann Neurol 1992, **31:** 441–444.

68 Harris CP, Sigman JD, Jaeckle KA. Intravascular malignant lymphomatosis. Amelioration of neurological symptoms with plasmapheresis. Ann Neurol 1994, **35:** 357–359.

69 Heiman-Patterson TD, Bird SJ, Parry GI, Varga J, Shy ME, Culligan NW, Edelsohn L, Tatarian GT, Heyes MP, Garcia CA, Tahmoush AJ. Peripheral neuropathy associated with eosinophilia-myalgia syndrome. Ann Neurol 1990, **28:** 522–528.

70 Hughes R, Atkinson P, Coates P, Hall S, Leibowitz S. Sural nerve biopsies in Guillain–Barré syndrome. Axonal degeneration and macrophage-associated demyelination and absence of cytomegalovirus genome. Muscle Nerve 1992, **15:** 568–575.

71 Krendel DA, Parks HP, Anthony DC, St. Clair MB, Graham DG. Sural nerve biopsy in chronic inflammatory demyelinating polyradiculoneuropathy. Muscle Nerve 1989, **12:** 257–264.

72 Lange DJ. Neuromuscular diseases associated with HIV–1 infection. Muscle Nerve 1994, **17:** 16–30.

73 Lewis RA, Sumner AJ, Brown MJ, Asbury AK. Multifocal demyelinating neuropathy with persistent conduction block. Neurology 1982, **32:** 958–964.

74 van der Meche, FG, Schmitz PI, and the Dutch Guillain–Barré Study Group. A randomized trial comparing intravenous immune globulin and plasma exchange in Guillain–Barré syndrome. N Engl J Med 1992, **326:** 1123–1129.

75 Meier C, Grahmann F, Engelhardt A, Dumas M. Peripheral nerve disorders in Lyme-borreliosis. Nerve biopsy studies from eight cases. Acta Neuropathol 1989, **79:** 271–278.

76 Nemni R, Galassi G, Cohen M, Hays AP, Gould R, Singh N, Bressman S, Gamboa ET. Symmetric sarcoid polyneuropathy. Analysis of a sural nerve biopsy. Neurology 1981, **31:** 1217–1223.

77 Oh SJ. Sarcoid polyneuropathy. A histologically proved case. Ann Neurol 1980, **7:** 178–181.

78 Prineas JW. Pathology of the Guillain–Barre syndrome. Ann Neurol 1981, **9(Suppl):** 6–19.

79 Prineas JW, McLeod JG. Chronic relapsing polyneuritis. J Neurol Sci 1976, **27:** 427–458.

80 Reske-Nielsen E, Harmsen A. Periangiitis and panangiitis as a manifestation of sarcoidosis of the brain. Report of a case. J Nerve Ment Dis 1962, **135:** 399–412.

81 Ricoy JR, Cabello A, Rodriguez J, Tellez I. Neuropathological studies on the toxic syndrome related to adulterated rapeseed oil in Spain. Brain 1983, **106:** 817–835.

82 Said G, Lacroix C, Andrieu JM, Leibowitch J. Necrotizing arteritis in patients with inflammatory neuropathy and immunodeficiency virus (HIV-III) infection. Neurology 1987, **37(Suppl I):** 176.

83 Said G, Lacroix C, Chemouilli P, Goulon-Goeau C, Roullet E, Penaud D, de Broucker T, Meduri G, Vincent D, Torchet M, Vittcoq D, Leport C, Vilde JL. Cytomegalovirus neuropathy in acquired immunodeficiency syndrome. A clinical and pathological study. Ann Neurol 1991, **29:** 139–146.

84 Said G, Lacroix C, Plante-Bordeneuve V, Le Page L, Pico F, Presles O, Senant J, Remy P, Rondepierre P, Mallecourt J. Nerve granulomas and vasculitis in sarcoid peripheral neuropathy. A clinicopathological study of 11 patients. Brain 2002, Feb; **125(Pt2):** 264–275.

85 Silverstein A, Siltzbach LE, et al. Muscle involvement in sarcoidosis. Asymptomatic, myositis, and myopathy. Arch Neurol 1969, **21:** 235–241.

86 Stern BJ, Krumholz A, John C, Scott P, Nissim J. Sarcoidosis and its neurological manifestations. Arch Neurol 1985, **42:** 909–917.

87 Thomas FP, Vallejos U, Foitl DR, Miller JR, Barrett R, Fetell MR, Knowles DM, Latov N, Hays AP. B cell small lymphocytic lymphoma and chronic lymphocytic leukemia with peripheral neuropathy. Two cases with neuropathological findings and lymphocyte marker analysis. Acta Neuropathol 1990, **80:** 198–203.

88 Vital C, Aubertin J, Ragnault JM, Amigues H, Mouton L, Bellance R. Sarcoidosis of the peripheral nerve. A histological and ultrastructural study of two cases. Acta Neuropathol 1982, **58:** 111–114.

Leprous neuritis

89 Finlayson MH, Bilbao JM, Lough JO. The pathogenesis of the neuropathy in dimorphous leprosy. Electron microscopic and cytochemical studies. J Neuropathol Exp Neurol 1974, **33:** 446–455.

90 Haimanot RT, Mshana RN, McDougall AC, Andersen JO. Sural nerve biopsy in leprosy patients after varying periods of treatment. Histopathological and bacteriological findings on light microscopy. Int J Lepr 1984, **52:** 163–170.

91 Jacob M, Mathai R. Diagnostic efficacy of cutaneous nerve biopsy in primary neuritic leprosy. Int J Lepr Myobact Dis 1988, **56:** 56–60.

92 Job CK, Desikan KV. Pathologic changes and their distribution in peripheral nerves in lepromatous leprosy. Int J Lepr 1968, **36:** 257–270.

93 Kaplan G. Recent advances in cytokine therapy in leprosy. J Infect Dis 1993, **167(Suppl 1):** S18–S22.

94 Kaur G. Girdhar BK, Girdhar A, Malaviya ON, Mukherjee A, Sengupta V, Desikan KV. A clinical, immunological, and histological study of neuritic leprosy patients. Int J Lepr Other Mycobact Dis 1991, **59:** 385–391.

95 Nishimura M, Kwon KS, Shibuta K, Yoshikawa Y, Oh CK, Suzuki T, Chung TA, Hori Y. An improved method for DNA diagnosis of leprosy using formaldehyde-fixed, paraffin embedded skin biopsies. Mod Pathol 1994, **7:** 253–256.

96 Ohenhoff TH, DeVrieS RR. HLA class II immune response and suppression genes in leprosy. Int J Lepr Other Mycobact Dis 1987, **55:** 521–534.

97 Pearson JM, Ross WF. Nerve involvement in leprosy: pathology, differential diagnosis and principles of management. Lepr Rev 1975, **46:** 199–212.

98 Ridley DS. Skin Biopsy in Leprosy. Histological Interpretation and Clinical Application. Basel, 1977, Ciba-Geigy.

99 Ridley DS. Pathogenesis of Leprosy and Related Diseases. London, 1988, Wright.

100 Ridley DS, Ridley MJ. Classification of nerves is modified by the delayed recognition of *Mycobacterium leprae*. Int J Lepr 1986, **54:** 596–606.

101 Shields ED, Russell DA, Pericak-Vance MA. Genetic epidemiology of the susceptibility to leprosy. J Clin Invest 1987, **79:** 1139–1143.

102 Williams DL, Gillis TP, Booth RJ, Looker D, Watson JD. The use of a specific DNA probe and polymerase chain reaction for the detection of *Mycobacterium leprae*. J Infect Dis 1990, **162:** 193–200.

Vasculitis

103 Churg J, Strauss L. Allergic granulomatosis, allergic angitis, and periarteritis nodosa. Am J Pathol 1951, **27:** 277–301.

104 Cohen RD, Conn DL, Ilstrup DM. Clinical features, prognosis, and response to treatment in polyarteritis. Mayo Clin Proc 1980, **55:** 146–155.

105 Dyck PJ, Benstead TJ, Conn DL, Stevens JC, Windebank AJ, Low PA. Nonsystemic vasculitic neuropathy. Brain 1987, **110:** 843–854.

106 Dyck PJ, Windebank AJ. Diabetic and nondiabetic lumbosacral radiculoplexus neuropathies: new insights into pathophysiology and treatment. Muscle Nerve 2002, **25:** 477–491.

107 Hawke SH, Davies L, Pamphlett R, Guo YD, Pollard JD, McLeod JG. Vasculitic neuropathy. A clinical and pathological study. Brain 1991, **114:** 2175–2190.

108 Kissel JT, Mendell JR. Vasculitic neuropathy. In Dyck PJ (ed.): Peripheral Neuropathy. New Concepts and Treatments. Neurol Clin 1992, **10:** 761–781.

109 Kissel JT, Riethman JL, Omerza J, Rammohan KW, Mendell JR. Peripheral nerve vasculitis. Immune characterization of the vascular lesions. Ann Neurol 1989, **25:** 291–297.

110 Lanham JG, Churg J. Churg–Strauss syndrome. In Churg A, Churg J, eds. Systemic Vasculitides. New York, 1991, Igaku-Shoin Medical.

111 Oh SJ, Slaughter R, Harrell L. Paraneoplastic vasculitic neuropathy. A treatable neuropathy. Muscle Nerve 1991, **14:** 152–156.

112 Said G, Lacroix-Ciaudo C, Fujimura H, Blas C, Faux N. The peripheral neuropathy of necrotizing arteritis. A clinicopathological study. Ann Neurol 1988, **23**: 461–465.

113 Said G, Lacroix C, Lozeron P, Ropert A, Plante V, Adams D. Inflammatory vasculopathy in multifocal diabetic neuropathy. Brain 2003, Feb; **126(Pt2):** 376–385.

114 Wees SJ, Sunwoo IN, Oh SJ. Sural nerve biopsy in systemic necrotizing vasculitis. Am J Med 1981, **71:** 525–532.

Amyloidosis

115 Benson MD. Familial amyloidotic polyneuropathy. Trends Neurosci 1989, **12:** 88–92.

116 Buxbaum JN, Tagoe CE. The genetics of the amyloidoses. Annu Rev Med 2000, **51:** 543–569.

117 Clanet M, Mansat M, Durroux R, Testut MF, Guiraud B, Rascol A, Conte J. Carpal tunnel syndrome, amyloid tenosynovitis and periodic hemodialysis. Rev Neurol 1981, **137:** 613–624.

118 Dalakas M, Cunningham G. Characterization of amyloid deposits in biopsies of 15 patients with "sporadic" (nonfamilial or plasma cell dyscrasia) amyloid polyneuropathy. Acta Neuropathol 1986, **69:** 66–72.

119 Gagnon RF, Lough JO, Bourgouin PA. Carpal tunnel syndrome and amyloidosis associated with continuous ambulatory peritoneal dialysis. Can Med Assoc J 1988, **139:** 753–755.

120 Gorevic PD, Munoz PC, Casey TT, DiRaimondo CR, Stone WJ, Prelli FC, Rodrigues MM, Poulik MD, Frangione B. Polymerization of intact beta 2-microglobulin in tissue causes amyloidosis in patients on chronic hemodialysis. Proc Natl Acad Sci USA 1986, **83:** 7908–7912.

121 Hanyu N, Ikeda S, Nakadai A, Yanagisawa N, Powell HC. Peripheral nerve pathological findings in familial amyloid polyneuropathy. A correlative study of proximal sciatic nerve and sural nerve lesions. Ann Neurol 1989, **25:** 340–350.

122 Ikeda S, Hanyu N, Hongo M, Yoshioka J, Oguchi H, Yanagisawa N, Kobayashi T, Tsukagoshi H, Ito N, Yokota T. Hereditary generalized amyloidosis with polyneuropathy. A clinicopathological study of 65 Japanese patients. Brain 1987, **110:** 315–337.

123 Li K, Kyle RA, Dyck PJ. Immunohistochemical characterization of amyloid proteins in sural nerves and clinical associations in amyloid neuropathy. Am J Pathol 1992, **141:** 217–226.

124 Murakami T, Yi S, Yamamoto K, Maruyama S, Araki S. Familial amyloidotic polyneuropathy. Report of patients heterozygous for the transthyretin Gly42 gene. Ann Neurol 1992, **31:** 340–342.

125 Nichols WC, Gregg RE, Brewer HB, Benson MD. A mutation in apolipoprotein A1 in the Iowa type of familial amyloidotic polyneuropathy. Genomics 1990, **8:** 318–323.

126 Sunada Y, Shimizu T, Nakase H, Shigeo O, Asaoka T, Amano S, Sawa M, Kagawa Y, Karasawa I, Mannen T. Inherited amyloid polyneuropathy type IV (Gelsolin variant) in a Japanese family. Ann Neurol 1993, **33:** 57–62.

127 Takahashi K, Yi S, Kimura Y, Araki S. Familial amyloidotic polyneuropathy type I in Kumamoto, Japan. A clinicopathologic, histochemical, immunohistochemical, and ultrastructural study. Hum Pathol 1991, **22:** 519–527.

128 Waldrop FS, Puchtler H, Valentine LS. Fluorescent microscopy of amyloid using mixed illumination. Arch Pathol 1973, **95:** 37–41.

Neuropathy of dysproteinemia

129 Scully RE (ed.). Case records of the Massachusetts General Hospital #21–1993. N Engl J Med 1993, **328:** 1550–1558.

130 Chad D, Pariser K, Bradley WG, Adelman LS, Pinn VW. The pathogenesis of cryoglobulinemic neuropathy. Neurology 1982, **32:** 725–729.

131 Feiner HD. Pathology of dysproteinemia. Light chain amyloidosis, non amyloid immunoglobulin deposition disease, cryoglobulinemia syndromes, and macroglobulinemia of Waldenström. Hum Pathol 1988, **19:** 1255–1272.

132 Jay V, Bilbao JM. Peripheral neuropathy associated with monoclonal gammopathy. Anat Pathol II, APII 91–6 (APII–174), 15, 1991.

133 Kelly JJ, Kyle RA, Latov N. Polyneuropathies Associated with Plasma Cell Dyscrasia. Boston, 1987, Martinus Nijhoff.

134 Kyle R, Rajkumar SV. Monoclonal gammopathies of undetermined significance. Immunol Rev 2003, **194:** 112–139.

135 Meier C, Vandevelde M, Steck A, Zurbriggen A. Demyelinating polyneuropathy associated with monoclonal IgM-paraproteinaemia. J Neurol Sci 1983, **63:** 353–367.

136 Mendell JR, Sahenk Z, Whitaker JN, Trapp BD, Yates AJ, Griggs RC, Quarles RH. Polyneuropathy and IgM monoclonal gammopathy. Studies on the pathogenetic role of anti-myelin-associated glycoprotein antibody. Ann Neurol 1985, **17:** 243–254.

137 Ropper AH, Gorson KC. Neuropathies associated with paraproteinemia. N Engl J Med 1998, **338:** 1601–1607.

138 Smith IS, Kahn SM, Lacey BW. Chronic demyelinating neuropathy associated with benign IgM paraproteinemia. Brain 1983, **106:** 169–195.

139 Vallat JM, Desproges-Gotteron R, Leboutet MJ, Loubet A, Gualde N, Treves R. Cryoglobulinemic neuropathy. A pathological study. Ann Neurol 1980, **8:** 179–185.

140 Vital A, Vital C, Ragnaud JM, Baquey A, Aubertin J. IgM cryoglobulin deposits in the peripheral nerve. Virchows Arch [A] 1991, **418:** 83–85.

141 Vital C, Vallat JM, Deminiere C, Loubet A, Leboutet MJ. Peripheral nerve damage during multiple myeloma and Waldenström's macroglobulinemia. An ultrastructural and immunopathologic study. Cancer 1982, **50:** 1491–1497.

Toxic-metabolic neuropathy

142 Bilbao JM, Briggs SJ, Gray TA. Filamentous axonopathy in disulfiram neuropathy. Ultrastruct Pathol 1984, **7:** 295–300.

143 Jacobs JM, Costa-Jussa FR. The pathology of amiodarone neurotoxicity. II. Peripheral neuropathy in man. Brain 1985, **108:** 753–769.

144 Melgaard B, Hansen HS, Kamieniecka Z, Paulson OB, Pedersen AG, Tang X, Trojaborg W. Misonidazole neuropathy. A clinical, electrophysiological, and histological study. Ann Neurol 1982, **12:** 10–17.

145 Pellissier JF, Pouget J, Cros D, De Victor B, Serratrice G, Toga M. Peripheral neuropathy induced by amiodarone chlorhydrate. A clinicopathological study. J Neurosci 1984, **63:** 251–266.

146 Said G. Perhexiline neuropathy. A clinicopathological study. Ann Neurol 1978, **3:** 259–266.

147 Shields RW Jr. Alcoholic polyneuropathy. Muscle Nerve 1985, **8:** 183–187.

148 Spencer PS, Schaumburg HH (eds): Experimental and Clinical Neurotoxicology. Baltimore, 1980, Williams & Wilkins.

149 Thorner PS, Bilbao JM, Sima AA, Briggs S. Porphyric neuropathy. An ultrastructural and quantitative case study. Can J Neurol Sci 1981, **8:** 281–287.

150 Tredici G, Minazzi M. Alcoholic neuropathy. An electron-microscopic study. J Neurol Sci 1975, **25:** 333–346.

Other neuropathies

151 Anzil AP, Blinzinger K, Mehraein P, Dozic S. Niemann–Pick case report with ultrastructural findings. Neuropaediatrie 1973, **4:** 207–225.

152 Araoz C, Sun CN, Shenefelt R, White HJ. Glycogenosis type II (Pompe's disease). Ultrastructure of peripheral nerves. Neurology 1974, **24:** 739–742.

153 Bilbao JM, Berry H, Marotta J, Ross RC. Peripheral neuropathy in oxalosis. A case report with electron microscopic observations. Can J Neurol Sci 1976, **3:** 63–67.

154 Bradley WG, Lassman LP, Pearce GW, Walton JN. The neuromyopathy of vincristine in man. Clinical, electrophysiological and pathological studies. J Neurol Sci 1970, **10**: 107–131.

155 Brown MJ, Asbury AK. Diabetic neuropathy. Ann Neurol 1984, **15**: 2–12.

156 Busard HL, Gabreels-Festen AA, van't Hof MA, Renier WO, Gabreels FJ. Polyglucosan bodies in sural nerve biopsies. Acta Neuropathol 1990, **80**: 554–557.

157 Byrd JC, Powers JM. Wolman's disease. Ultrastructural evidence of lipid accumulation in central and peripheral nervous system. Acta Neuropathol 1979, **45**: 37–42.

158 Cafferty MS, Lovelace RE, Hays AP, Servidei S, Dimauro S, Rowland LP. Polyglucosan body disease. Muscle Nerve 1991, **14**: 102–107.

159 Carpenter S, Karpati G, Andermann F, Gold R. Giant axonal neuropathy. A clinically and morphologically distinct neurological disease. Arch Neurol 1974, **31**: 312–316.

160 Carpenter S, Karpati G, Andermann F, Jacob JC, Andermann E. The ultrastructural characteristics of the abnormal cytosomes in Batten-Kuf's disease. Brain 1977, **100**: 137–156.

161 Donaghy M, King RH, Thomas PK, Workman JM. Abnormalities of the axonal cytoskeleton in giant axonal neuropathy. J Neurocytol 1988, **17**: 197–208.

162 Dyck PJ, Ellefson RD, Yao JK, Herbert PN. Adult-onset Tangier disease. Morphometric and pathologic studies suggesting delayed degradation of neutral lipids after fiber degeneration. J Neuropathol Exp Neurol 1978, **37**: 119–137.

163 Fardeau M, Abelanet R, Laudat P, Bonduelle M. Refsum's disease. Histological, ultrastructural and biochemical study of a peripheral nerve biopsy. Rev Neurol 1970, **122**: 185–196.

164 Gambetti P, DiMauro S, Baker L. Nervous system in Pompe's disease. Ultrastructure and biochemistry. J Neuropathol Exp Neurol 1971, **30**: 412–430.

165 Gumbinas M, Larsen M, Mei Liu H. Peripheral neuropathy in classic Niemann–Pick disease. Ultrastructure of nerves and skeletal muscles. Neurology 1975, **25**: 107–113.

166 Johnson PC. Diabetic neuropathy. In Adachi M, Hirano A, Aronson SM (eds): The Pathology of the Myelinated Axon. New York, 1985, Igaku-Shoin.

167 Joosten E, Gabreels F, Stadhouders A, Bolmers D, Gabreels-Festen A. Involvement of sural nerve in neuronal ceroid-lipofuscinoses. Report of two cases. Neuropaediatrie 1973, **4**: 98–110.

168 Kocen RS, King RH, Thomas PK, Haas LF. Nerve biopsy findings in two cases of Tangier disease. Acta Neuropathol 1973, **26**: 317–327.

169 Kristensson K, Olsson Y, Sourander P. Peripheral nerve changes in Tay–Sachs and Batten–Spielmeyer–Vogt disease. Acta Pathol Microbiol Scand 1967, **70**: 630–632.

170 Lockman LA, Kennedy WR, White JG. The Chediak–Higashi syndrome. Electrophysiological and electron microscopic observations on the peripheral neuropathy. J Pediatr 1967, **70**: 942–951.

171 Misra VP, King RH, Harding AE, Muddle JR, Thomas PK. Peripheral neuropathy in the Chediak–Higashi syndrome. Acta Neuropathol 1991, **81**: 354–358.

172 Ohnishi A, Yamashita Y, Goto I, Kuriowa Y, Murakami S, Ikeda M. De- and remyelination and onion bulb in cerebrotendinous xanthomatosis. Acta Neuropathol 1979, **45**: 43–45.

173 Pollock M, Nukada H, Frith RW, Simcock JP, Allpress S. Peripheral neuropathy in Tangier disease. Brain 1983, **106**: 911–928.

174 Powers JM, Schaumburg HH. Adrenoleukodystrophy. Similar ultrastructural changes in adrenal cortical and Schwann cells. Arch Neurol 1974, **302**: 406–408.

175 Probst A, Ulrich J, Heitz PU, Herschkowitz N. Adrenomyeloneuropathy. A protracted pseudosystematic variant of adrenoleukodystrophy. Acta Neuropathol 1980, **49**: 105–115.

176 Ruchoux M-M, Maurage CA. CADASIL: Cerebral Autosomal Dominant Arteriopathy with Subcortical Infarcts and Leukoencephalopathy. J Neuropathol Exp Neurol 1997, **56**: 947–964.

177 Sahenk Z, Brady ST, Mendell JR. Studies on the pathogenesis of vincristine-induced neuropathy. Muscle Nerve 1987, **10**: 80–84.

178 Said G, Goulon-Goeau C, Lacroix C, Moulonguet A. Nerve biopsy findings in different patterns of proximal diabetic neuropathy. Ann Neurol 1994, **35**: 559–569.

179 Said G, Goulon-Goeau C, Slama G, Tchobroutsky G. Severe early-onset polyneuropathy in insulin-dependent diabetes mellitus. A clinical and pathological study. N Engl J Med 1992, **326**: 1257–1263.

180 Sugimura K, Dyck PJ. Multifocal fiber loss in proximal sciatic nerve in symmetric distal diabetic neuropathy. J Neurol Sci 1982, **53**: 501–509.

181 Tegner R, Tome FM, Godeau P, Lhermitte F, Fardeau M. Morphological study of peripheral nerve changes induced by chloroquine treatment. Acta Neuropathol 1988, **75**: 253–260.

182 Thomas PK, King RH, Chiang TR, Scaravilli F, Sharma AK, Downie AW. Neurofibromatous neuropathy. Muscle Nerve 1990, **13**: 93–101.

183 Thomas PK, Walker JG. Xanthomatous neuropathy in primary biliary cirrhosis. Brain 1965, **88**: 1079–1088.

184 Vital A, Vital C, Ellie E, Ferrer X, Lagueny A, Ferrer AM, Broustet A, Gbikpi-Benissan G. Malignant infiltration of peripheral nerves in the course of acute myelomonoblastic leukemia—neuropathological study of two cases. Neuropathol Appl Neurobiol 1993, **19**: 159–163.

185 Vital C, Battin J, Rivel J, Hehunstre JP. Ultrastructural aspects of peripheral nerve lesions in one case of Farber's disease. Rev Neurol 1976, **132**: 419–423.

186 Vos AJ, Joosten EM, Gabreels-Festen AA. Adult polyglucosan body disease. Clinical and nerve biopsy findings in two cases. Ann Neurol 1983, **13**: 440–444.

Skeletal muscle

Lee-Cyn Ang, Juan M. Bilbao

A skeletal muscle biopsy is important for the diagnosis of diseases of the motor unit, systemic diseases such as vasculitis, and disorders of metabolic mechanism such as glycogenosis. When interpreting a muscle biopsy, the pathologist must have knowledge of the patient's clinical and family history, physical examination findings, and results of salient laboratory tests such as EMG, nerve conduction, and serum creatinine phosphokinase. The biopsy site should be selected from a muscle that is moderately involved by the disease process. It should not be taken from a severely affected site having only fat and fibrous tissue, with few, if any, myofibers left.[2] Conversely, a biopsy specimen from a site where the muscle is minimally involved may show no diagnostic changes. The physician ordering the biopsy should clearly indicate a site for the procedure on the request form. A muscle that has been previously traumatized, for instance by EMG needles, should be avoided. Interpretation is easier if biopsies are taken consistently from the same muscles (e.g., from the biceps brachialis in the upper limbs and the quadriceps femoris in the lower limbs). Equally important is that the biopsy be taken from the belly of the muscle and not at the tendon insertion where there are features that simulate myopathic changes, such as increased number of internal nuclei, variability of myofiber size, and endomysial fibrosis. The muscle sample can be obtained through an open biopsy or a needle biopsy. While an open biopsy provides larger samples, a needle biopsy is less painful and leaves behind a smaller scar and is cosmetically more acceptable.

The biopsy must be performed with great care and the least traumatization. The size of tissue sample must be adequate for cryostat sectioning, resin and paraffin embedding. For an open biopsy, the ideal specimen measures $2.0 \times 0.5 \times 0.5$ cm in size. Sections selected for cryostat preparation should be oriented for transverse sectioning and are "quench" frozen in liquid nitrogen–isopentane. Improper freezing technique will give rise to ice crystal growth with vacuolation of the sarcoplasm, a common artefact in muscle biopsy.[1] Serial cryostat sections are prepared routinely for the following stains: H&E, Congo Red, modified Gomori trichrome,[3]

NADH-TR, succinic dehydrogenase (SDH), cytochrome oxidase, acid phosphatase, PAS, oil red O, and ATPase preincubated at pH 9.4, 4.6, and 4.3. Immunohistochemistry for the dystrophins, sarcoglycans and merosin should be performed on the cryostat sections when indicated. Transverse and longitudinal sections of muscle are obtained from the plastic resin blocks for electron microscopy. If there is insufficient tissue, priority should be given to the preparation of cryostat sectioning.

Normal anatomy

The transverse sections of muscle fascicle show polygonal myofibers fitting snugly against each other with little intervening endomysial connective tissue between (Fig. 28.160). A mature myocyte is a syncytial element with the nuclei located subsarcolemally. Up to 4% of muscle fibers in the normal adult fascicle may show internalization of the nuclei. Satellite cells display scanty cytoplasm and are seen closely applied to the periphery of the myofibers.[6] Ultrastructurally, these reserve cells lie between the plasma membrane and the basal lamina of the myofiber. The diameter of individual fibers can vary from 20 to 50 µm. In adult males, the larger fibers are found in proxi-

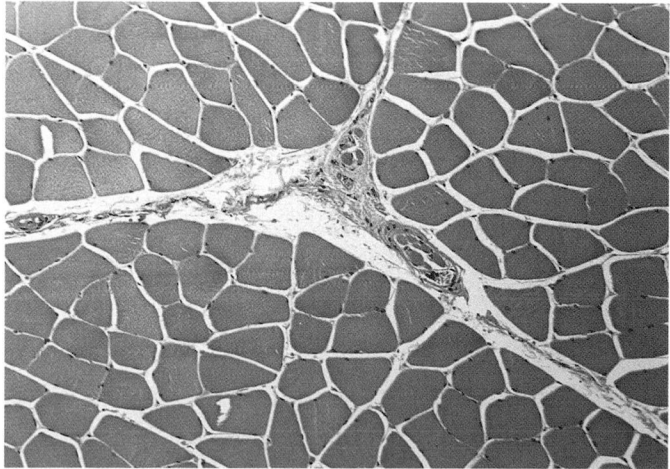

Fig. 28.160 Cryostat transverse section of a muscle fascicle with polygonal myofibers with mostly subsarcolemmal nuclei. (H&E)

mal muscles and in muscles subjected to prolonged exercise. The fascicle is wrapped by a layer of collagen tissue known as a perimysium where the arterioles, venules, and nerve bundles are located. Muscle spindles consisting of smaller-diameter striated myofibers covered with a fibrous capsule are occasionally seen in the perimysium. A number of fascicles are in turn bound by the epimysium in which the larger blood vessels and nerves are present. Capillaries are located in the endomysial connective tissue, averaging one to two per muscle fiber. In the longitudinal section, the fascicular arrangement of the myofiber is not apparent, but the cross striations of the fibers are well visualized (Fig. 28.161).

Ultrastructurally, the myofibril, a major component of each individual myofiber, is made up of repeating units

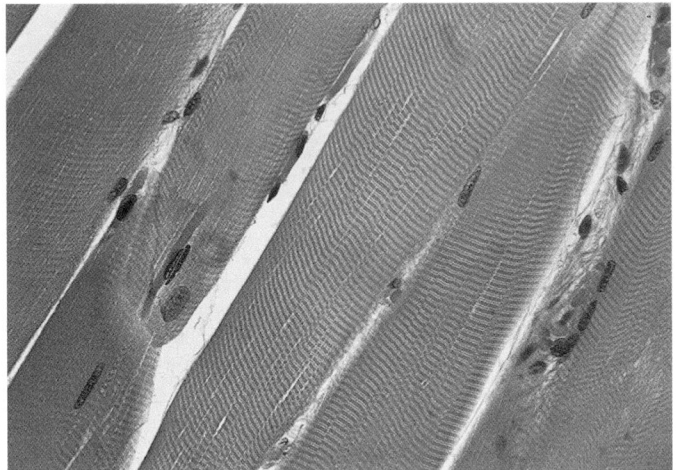

Fig. 28.161 Longitudinal section with cross striation of myofibers. (H&E)

of regularly aligned sarcomeres. The sarcomere, the functional unit of the muscle fiber, can be defined as the myofibrillary element between two consecutive Z lines.[4] It consists of alternating light (I) and dark (A) bands (Fig. 28.162). In the middle of the A band is the M line, which is flanked by the narrower and lighter H zone. In the middle of the I band is the dense Z line, where the thin actin filaments are anchored. The lighter I band has only the actin filaments traversing it, whereas the darker A band consists of the interdigitation of both the actin and myosin filaments. The H zone is where the actin filaments end, and the M line is where the thickening of myosin filaments occurs. When the muscle contracts, the actin filaments slide past the myosin filaments leading to the shortening of the sarcomeres.

In addition to the myofibrils, the muscle fiber contains mitochondria, sarcoplasmic reticulum, transverse tubular system (T-system) that is an extension of the extracellular space[5] (Fig. 28.162), glycogen granules, lipid inclusions, and lysosomes.

Histochemistry

To interpret a muscle biopsy, the pathologist must be acquainted with the changes that are seen in the histochemical stains. The ATPase reaction is very useful for distinguishing fiber types[8] (Fig. 28.163). The type I (slow twitch or red) fibers, which contain more mitochondria and myoglobin, utilize aerobic oxidation for their energy requirement. The type II (fast twitch or white) fibers, which contain more glycogen, produce energy through

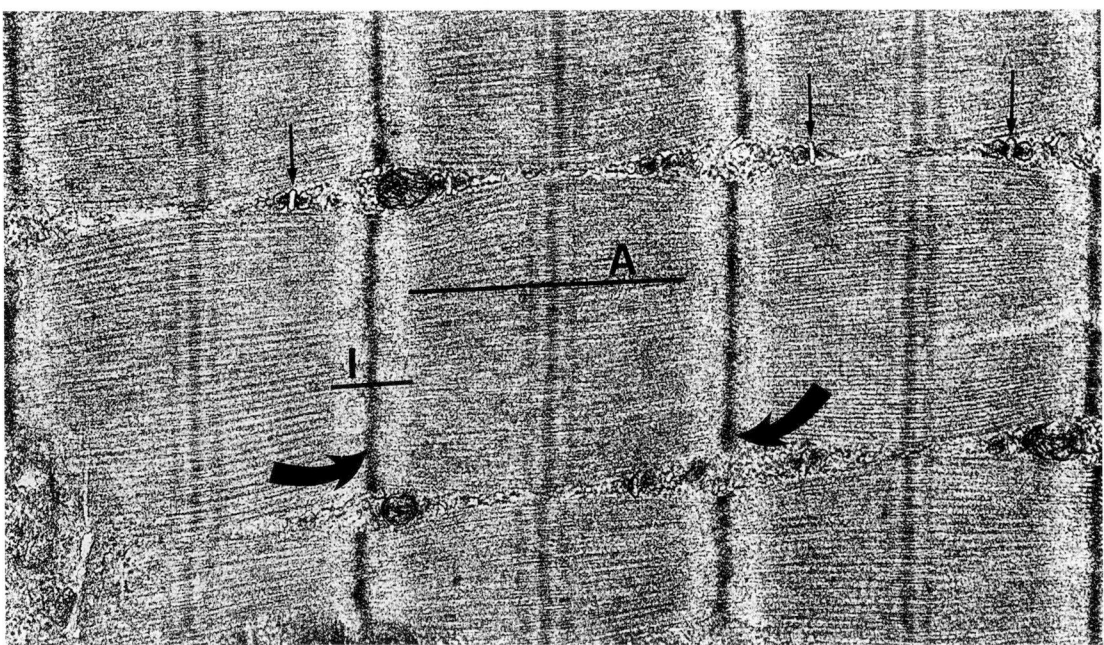

Fig. 28.162 Longitudinal section of normal rat skeletal muscle. The I band is centered by the Z line (open arrows). The A band is bisected by the M line. The T tubules forming triads are shown (arrows). (×33,858)

Fig. 28.163 Normal muscle. In routine ATPase reaction (pH 9.4), type I fibers are light and type II fibers are dark. (Cryosection)

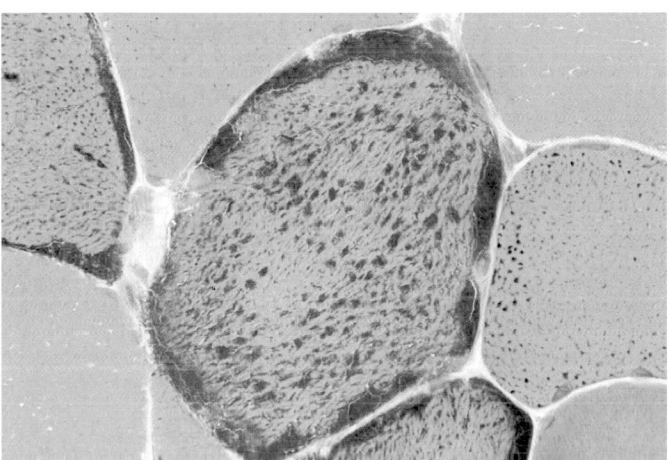

Fig. 28.164 On cryosections, ragged red fibers appear hematoxyphilic with H&E and red with modified Gomori trichrome (as shown) and display intense reaction with oxidative enzymes.

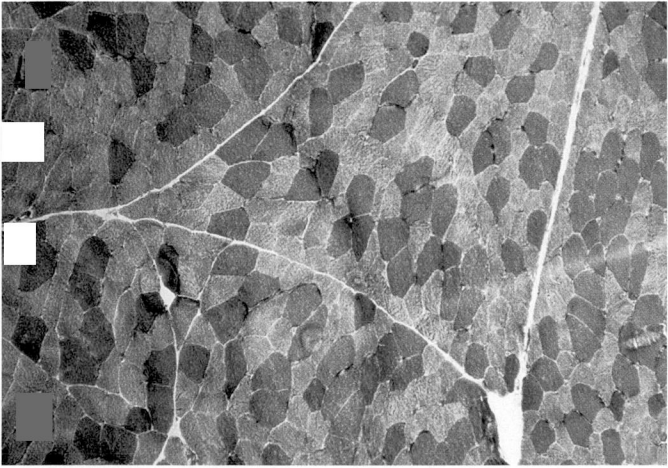

Fig. 28.165 In cryosection the type I fibers appear darker than type II fibers with nicotinamide adenine dinucleotide tetrazolium reductase (NADH-TR)

the anerobic glycolysis pathway. With the ATPase reaction at pH 9.4, the type I fibers are pale, and type II fibers are dark. At pH 4.3, this reaction is reversed, with type I fibers appearing dark and the type II fibers pale. The ATPase reaction at pH 4.6 highlights the type I and type IIb fibers as darkly stained and the IIa as lightly stained. In the normal muscle, the type I and II fibers are well intermixed in a "checkerboard" pattern (Fig. 28.163).

In most muscles such as the quadriceps, the proportion of the different fiber types is roughly divided into thirds—one third type I, one third type IIA, and one third type IIB.[7] However, the proportion of type I fibers is higher in muscles that can sustain long contractions such as postural muscles. The proportion of type II is higher in muscles that require fast, powerful, and short contractions. In reinnervation, there is loss of the "checkerboard" pattern with an excessive grouping of one type of fiber, the so-called fiber type grouping.

The modified Gomori trichrome stain is useful for showing ragged red fibers, which are most frequently associated with mitochondrial myopathy (Fig. 28.164). The inclusions in rod (nemaline) myopathy appear dark red to purple in this stain. PAS and oil red O stains are used to demonstrate an increase of glycogen and lipid stores, respectively. Acid phosphatase is useful in identifying enzymes in the lysosomes which are present in abundance in fiber breakdown.

NADH-TR also identifies the fiber type by virtue of the fact that it reflects the oxidative enzyme activities, although it is less specific than ATPase. The type I fibers appear darker than the type II fibers (Fig. 28.165). Because it also highlights the distribution of subcellular organelles such as mitochondria and sarcoplasmic reticulum (which are heavily stained), it is a useful stain in the diagnosis of mitochondrial myopathy and structural myopathy such as central core disease. In denervation, target and targetoid fibers are also best demonstrated by NADH-TR. Both the succinic dehydrogenase and the cytochrome oxidase (COX) stain the type I fibers darker than type II fibers as the NADH-TR stain. The ragged red fibers are highlighted by both NADH-TR and SDH, whereas COX is absent in these fibers.

Working classification

Although the recent advances in cell biology and molecular genetics have contributed immensely to new understanding and reclassification of many muscle diseases, for practical reasons we still propose a simple approach for the diagnosis of non-neoplastic skeletal muscle diseases by dividing them into three broad categories: neurogenic atrophy, neuromuscular junction disorders, and primary myopathic diseases.[9,10] Because muscle biopsies are rarely performed for neuromuscular junction diseases such as myasthenia gravis, the first step in diagnosis is usually to differentiate between neurogenic atrophy and primary myopathic changes. In general, primary myopathic changes are characterized by marked variation of individual fiber size and endomysial fibrosis, with or without necrotic and regenerative fibers.[9] Often the myopathic changes in a biopsy may be so minimal that it is difficult to distinguish a myopathy from denervation. In such circumstances, access to clinical information, EMG findings, and serum creatine kinase (CK) levels is essential before the final interpretation of the biopsy.

The primary myopathic group can be further subdivided into the inflammatory myopathies and noninflammatory myopathies. Polymyositis, dermatomyositis, and inclusion body myositis are the more common forms of inflammatory myopathies encountered in biopsies. There are many more diseases in the noninflammatory group, which can be roughly subdivided into five categories: muscular dystrophies, developmental disorders of the muscle, myofibrillary myopathies, metabolic myopathies, and toxic and drug-induced myopathies.

Neurogenic atrophy (denervation)

Neurogenic atrophy can be seen in diseases affecting the lower motor neuron such as poliomyelitis, amyotrophic lateral sclerosis, spinal muscular atrophy (Werdnig–Hoffmann and Kugelberg–Welander disease), and predominantly in peripheral neuropathy.[11]

Early denervation changes in a muscle are characterized by random atrophy of both fiber types, mainly type II fibers that are angulated on transverse sections. The ATPase reaction shows a mixture of both type I and type II fibers amongst the atrophied angulated fibers (Fig. 28.166). With NADH-TR, however, all these atrophied fibers, regardless of the types, are stained darkly. Denervated fibers have little PAS-stainable glycogen.

A more specific change of denervation is the formation of small and later large groups of atrophied fibers. In Werdnig–Hoffmann disease the markedly atrophic fibers have a rounded contour (Fig. 28.167). In about 20% to 30% of cases of denervation atrophy, the NADH-TR or SDH reaction may show target fibers, which have central pallor surrounded by a very darkly stained rim that in turn is surrounded by normal-staining sarcoplasm (Fig. 28.168). Fibers with central pallor in the absence of the darkly stained rim are referred to as targetoid fibers. Target fibers are more common in chronic polyneuropathies than in amyotrophic lateral sclerosis (Fig. 28.169). As a consequence of denervation and reinnervation from collateral sprouting of surviving axons, the typical "checkerboard" pattern is lost. As the motor unit territory enlarges, the newly recruited fibers are converted to single histochemical type, thus forming fiber type grouping (Fig. 28.170). After longstanding denervation, muscle may show hypertrophic fibers, fiber

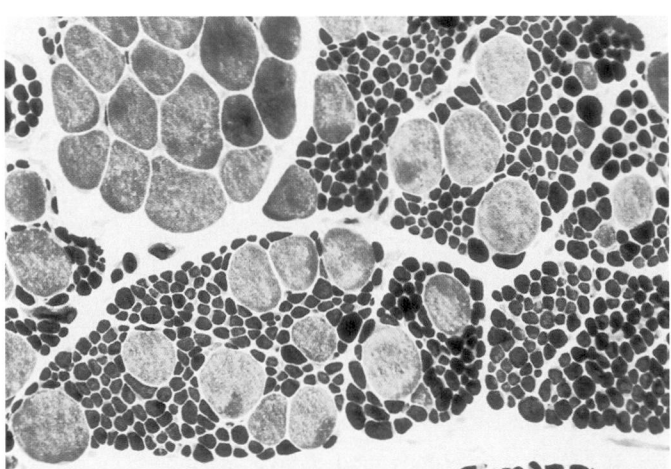

Fig. 28.167 Werdnig–Hoffman disease. Large group atrophy. Unlike other forms of neurogenic atrophy the small fibers are only occasionally angulated. (Cryosection, routine ATPase)

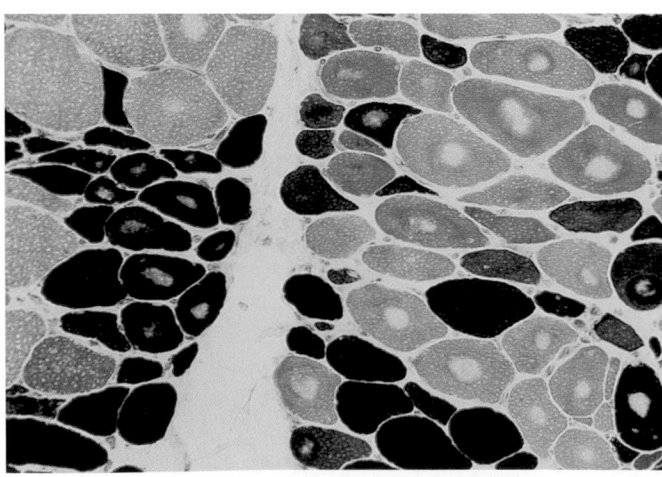

Fig. 28.166 Cryosection showing angular atrophied fibers of both types. Also note the target fibers. (Routine ATPase)

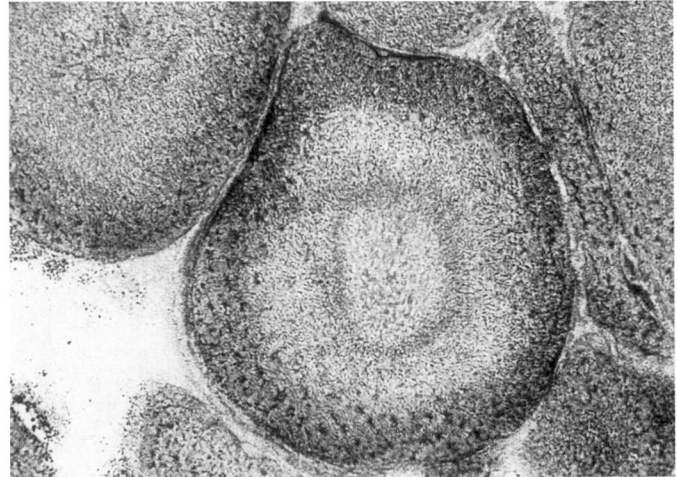

Fig. 28.168 "Target" fiber. Succinic acid dehydrogenase (SDH) reveals the typical pattern. (Cryosection)

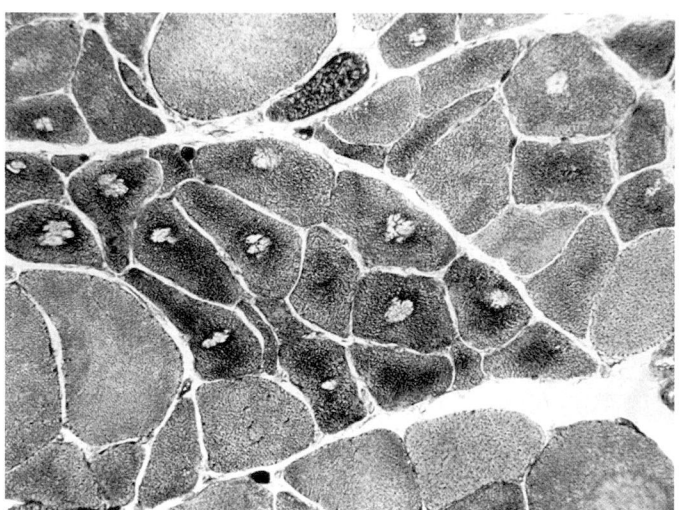

Fig. 28.169 Neurogenic atrophy with reinnervation. Fiber type grouping and "targets" in most type I fibers are shown (Cryosection, SDH)

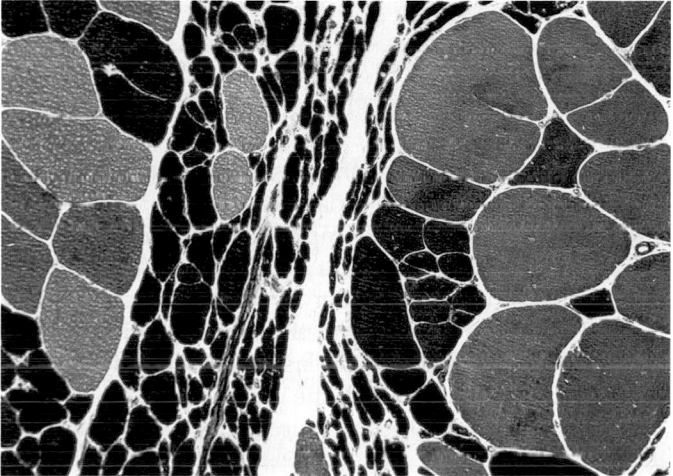

Fig. 28.170 Chronic neurogenic atrophy with reinnervation. The "checkerboard" staining pattern is lost and fiber type grouping is seen. (Cryosection, routine ATPase)

splitting, and even necrotic fibers giving rise to a pseudomyopathic picture.[12] In cases of advanced neurogenic atrophy, very little muscle may be visualized in a biopsy. Small, inconspicuous bundles of atrophic fibers may be found mingled with adipose tissue.

Inflammatory myopathies

Inflammatory myopathy is a heterogeneous group of acquired muscle diseases among which three should be emphasized.[16] Polymyositis has an insidious onset without a precipitating event and a subacute or chronic course. The patient complains of symmetric weakness involving the proximal muscles; dysphagia develops later. The histologic appearance is nonspecific; thus polymyositis is a diagnosis of exclusion. The mononuclear cell infiltrate that consists mostly of T cells, particularly activated CD8 cells, with few or no B cells, is intrafascicular (endomysial) surrounding or invading

individual non-necrotic muscle fibers.[16,17] Necrotic and regenerating fibers are scattered within the fascicle. In the early phase, the sarcoplasm of the necrotic fibers appears hypereosinophilic and granular with nuclear pyknosis and karyorrhexis. Later, the fibers become pale and vacuolated and undergo phagocytosis (myophagia) (Fig. 28.171). Like the other destructive myopathies, the regenerating fibers are characterized by large vesicular nuclei with prominent nucleoli and basophilia of sarcoplasm (Fig. 28.172). HIV-associated polymyositis has a similar histologic picture.

Dermatomyositis is a distinct clinical entity characterized by skin rash heralding the onset of muscle weakness. This myositis may occur alone or can be associated with mixed connective tissue diseases or malignant conditions. The inflammatory infiltrate consists of mainly lymphocytes with few plasma cells. The immunophenotyping of the lymphocytes discloses a high percentage of B cells, and the T cells are mostly CD4 lymphocytes.[16,17] The inflammation is predominantly

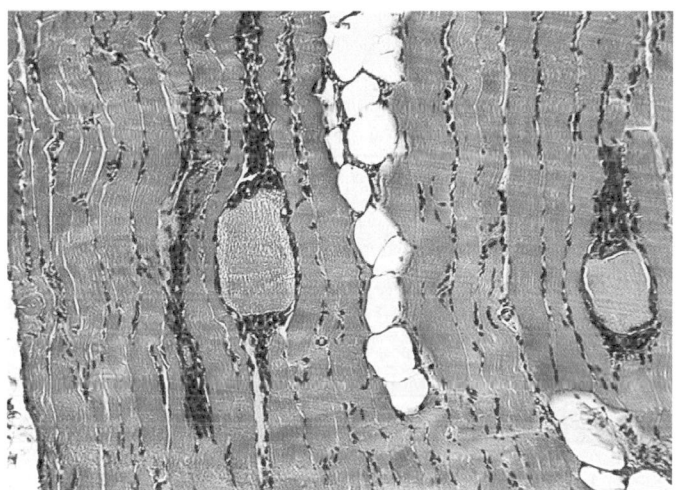

Fig. 28.171 Two necrotic myofibers with pale sarcoplasm. (H&E)

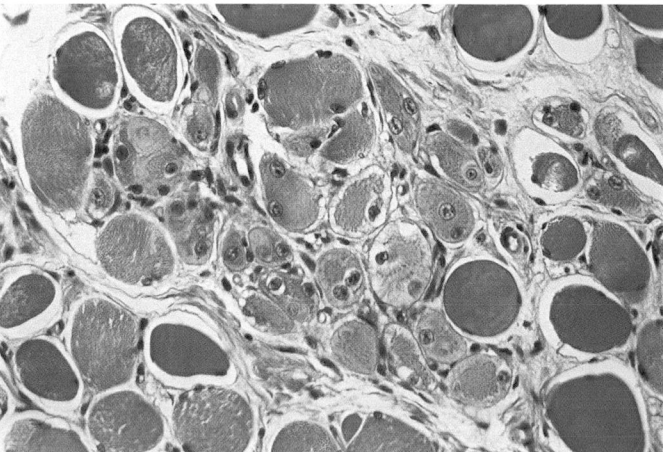

Fig. 28.172 Duchenne's muscular dystrophy. Regenerating myofibers characterized by vesicular nuclei with prominent nucleoli and sarcoplasmic basophilia. (H&E)

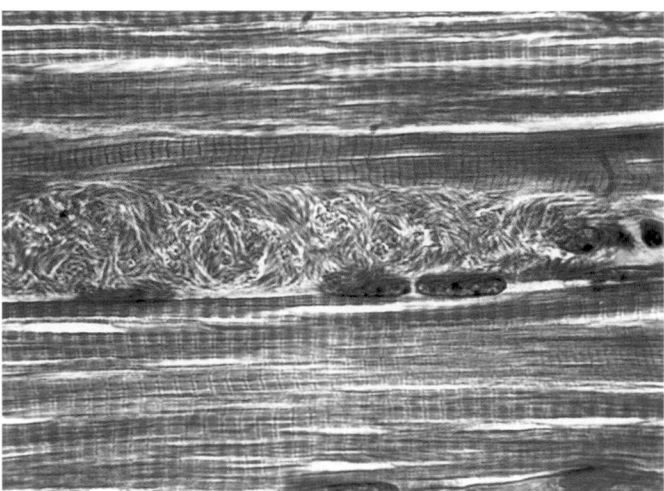

Fig. 28.189 Nemaline myopathy. Thread-like subsarcolemmal aggregates are shown on longitudinal sections. (Phoshphotungstic acid hematoxylin)

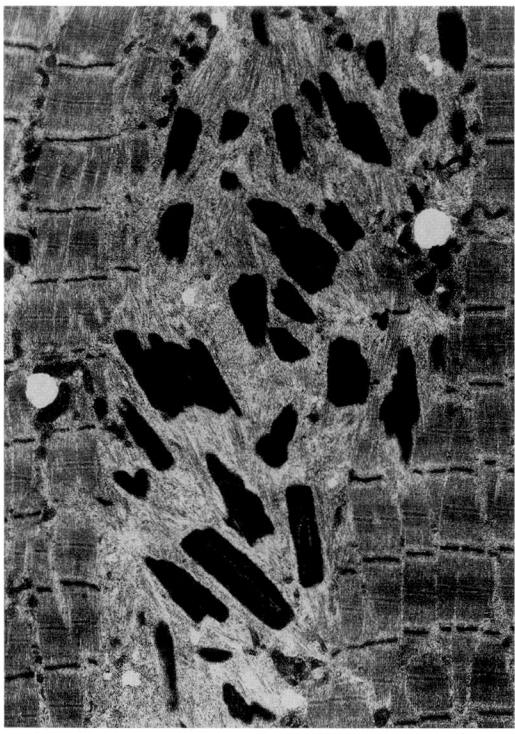

Fig. 28.190 Nemaline myopathy. Rods appear to originate from the Z disks. (×6160)

appear elongated or rectangular in the longitudinal sections and polygonal in transverse sections have a similar density to the Z lines[46,51,56] (Fig. 28.190). Genetic alterations involving α-tropomysin (1q21–23), β-tropomysin (9p13.2), nebulin (2q21–22), and sarcomeric actin (1q42.1) have been reported in some but not all forms of rod myopathy.[45]

Patients who receive a combination of high-dose corticosteroids and nondepolarizing neuromuscular blocking agents (vecuronium use in status asthmaticus patient) may develop an acute flaccid quadriparesis and muscle

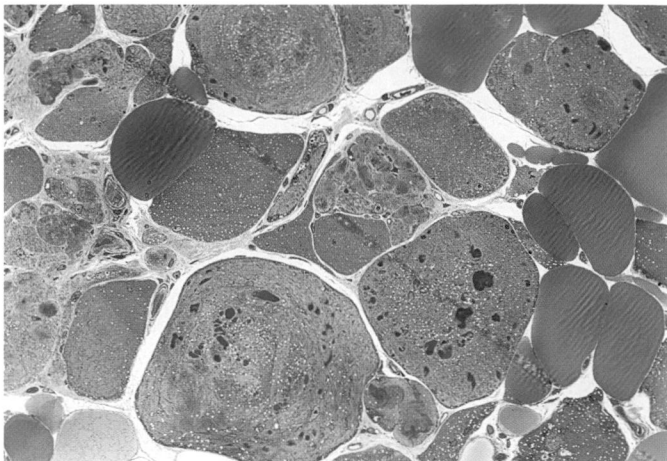

Fig. 28.191 Cytoplasmic bodies in desmin-related myopathy. (Plastic resin)

wasting with an elevated CK level. Slow recovery follows pharmacologic paralysis. Muscle biopsy has shown a non-necrotizing noninflammatory myopathy with patchy loss of myofibrillar ATPase staining and selective loss of myosin filaments.[53,55] The type II fibers are more affected than the type I fibers. Ultrastructural examination confirms the selective loss of the thick myofilaments (myosin) in the myofibers. Because of the pathologic features, this acute quadriplegic myopathy is also known as myosin heavy chain depletion syndrome. Interestingly, not all patients with this syndrome have been exposed to these drugs.[53]

There is also a group with variable abnormalities in the skeletal muscles, including cytoplasmic bodies, Z-disc streaming, spheroid bodies, granulofilamentous material, and hyaline structures. This group is earmarked by the accumulation of desmin, demonstrated by immunohistochemistry, and designated as the desminopathy or desmin-related myopathy (Fig. 28.191).[40,45,48] Some patients with desminopathies present with cardiomyopathy. Recently, most of the congenital myopathies with granular or filamentous inclusions/bodies are being categorized into a group as "surplus protein myopathies."[49]

Metabolic and mitochondrial myopathies

This category consists of many different conditions. Only the myopathies associated with periodic paralysis, glycogen storage, lipid storage, and mitochondrial diseases will be discussed here. Periodic paralysis may be familial (autosomal dominant) or associated with thyrotoxicosis. The periodicity of the paralysis is related to abnormalities in influx and efflux of potassium ions in the muscle fibers, leading to failure in propagation of the action potential. Familial forms are subdivided according to the serum potassium level during the attack into hypokalemic, hyperkalemic, and normokalemic periodic paralysis. The abnormal membrane excitability in skeletal muscle could be attributed to genetic alteration. This affects the functions in sodium ion channels (17q23) in sarcolemma and the T-tubule membrane in hyperkalemic and normokalemic periodic paralysis,[72] and the dihydropyridine receptor (1q32), a voltage-gated calcium channel in the T-tubule membrane in another subset of hypokalemic periodic paralysis.[70] In the hypokalemic form, the attack of paralysis occurs after a long period of rest such as after a good night's sleep with the patient unable to move on awakening. These attacks usually last from a few hours to one day. In the hyperkalemic form, attacks occur about half an hour after exercise, and each one lasts approximately a few hours. The normokalemic attacks of paralysis are similar to the hyperkalemic but are more severe and can last for days or weeks. The thyrotoxic periodic paralysis may be sporadic or has HLA antigenic association. Biopsy specimens taken during or shortly after periodic paralysis show vacuolar changes, either single or multiple, in the affected fibers (Fig. 28.192). Other changes such as variability in fiber size, endomysial fibrosis, fiber degeneration, increased internal nuclei, and regeneration can accompany the vacuolar myopathy. Ultrastructural examination reveals membrane-bound vacuoles that either can be empty or can contain granular material. These vacuoles are the dilated sacs of the sarcoplasmic reticulum. Occasionally there are ultrastructural tubular aggregates that are dense collections of tubules arranged in hexagonal array. These are thought to be derived from the sarcoplasmic reticulum. In both the autosomal form (Thomsen) and recessive form (Becker) of congenital myotonia, genetic alterations have also been identified in the calcium channels of skeletal muscle. Because of the ion channel defects, the periodic paralysis, congenital myotonia, and central core myopathy are now classified as channelopathies.

Glycogen storage diseases (glycogenoses) are a group of inherited (autosomal recessive) diseases characterized by deficiencies of enzymes that degrade glycogen. This leads to the accumulation of glycogen in different organs such as the liver, heart, and skeletal muscle. The skeletal muscle is affected in at least four types of glycogenoses—acid maltase deficiency, amylo-1,6-glucosidase (debranching enzyme) deficiency, myophosphorylase deficiency, and phosphofructokinase deficiency.[62,66] In all cases, the ultimate diagnosis can only be confirmed by biochemical assay of the enzyme involved.

Acid maltase (α1,4 lysosomal α-glucosidase) deficiency, also known as type II glycogenosis, can present at the early infantile, late infantile (Pompe's disease), juvenile, or adult period. The early infantile form is most severe with involvement of the cardiac muscle, usually leading to cardiac failure and death within the first 2 years of life. The other forms are less severe, and patients survive to adulthood with a progressive myopathy. Vacuolar change is present in all forms, but vacuoles have a tendency to coalesce in the early infantile form, leading to larger vacuoles in most fibers, whereas in the late-onset forms, vacuoles are less conspicuous and may affect selectively type I fibers (Figs 28.193A and 28.194A).

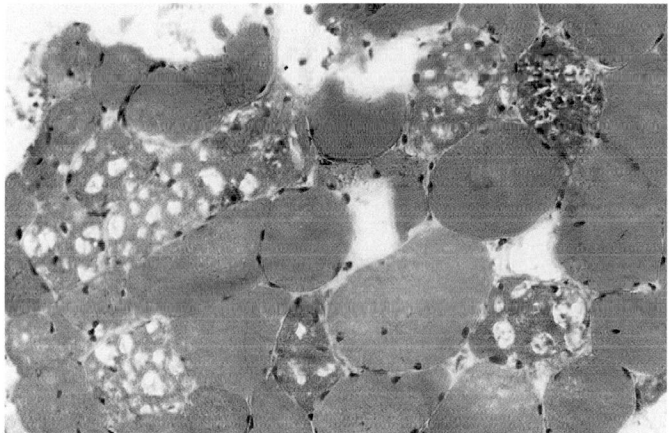

A

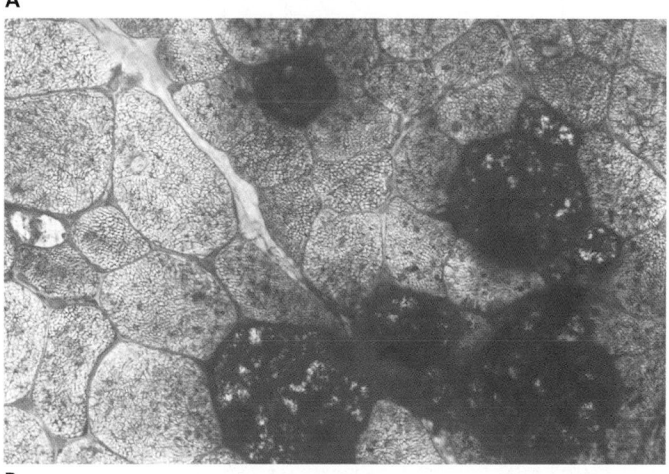

B

Fig. 28.193 Acid maltase deficiency. (**A**) Sarcoplasmic vacuoles in a patient with acid maltase deficiency. (Cryosection, H&E) (**B**) Vacuoles filled with glycogen. (Cryosection, PAS)

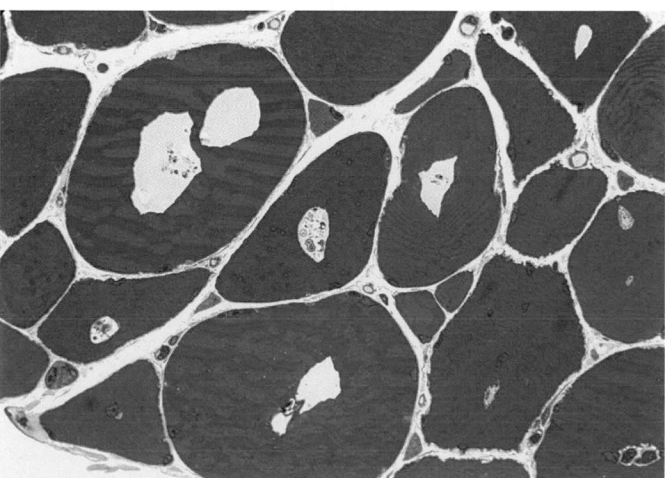

Fig. 28.192 Hypokalemic periodic paralysis. Many fibers display large, optically empty vacuoles. (Plastic resin)

In the adult form the biopsy may appear normal. PAS stain with diastase digestion is useful in demonstrating glycogen in the vacuoles (Figs 28.193B and 28.194B). Because acid maltase is a lysosomal enzyme, the acid phosphatase is also reactive, even in the absence of obvious glycogen storage. Electron microscopy distinguishes this type of glycogenosis from the other types in that some of the glycogen granules in maltase deficiency are bound within lysosomal membranes.

In debranching deficiency (type III glycogenosis) the skeletal muscle is mildly affected although the patient may have growth retardation, hepatomegaly, and hypoglycemia. Vacuolar myopathy is noted in the biopsy, and the vacuoles contain glycogen. Ultrastructural studies reveal storage of free glycogen, not bound by any membrane.

Myophosphorylase deficiency (type IV glycogenosis) causes a mild myopathy; the patients' main complaints are related to cramps and pains in their muscles, especially those of the calf, during exercise. Myophosphorylase deficiency prevents the muscle from utilizing glycogen during exercise; thus in severe cases,

prolonged exercise may lead to rhabdomyolysis. The muscle biopsy usually is normal except that there may be some increase in subsarcolemmal accumulation of glycogen. This is best demonstrated ultrastructurally. The demonstration of the myophosphorylase in the muscle by histochemistry is essential for diagnosis of this condition (Fig. 28.195). The genetic alteration for this disease has been identified in chromosome 11q13.[75]

Clinically, phosphofructokinase deficiency (type VII glycogenosis) has the same presentation as type IV glycogenosis and the muscle alterations are very similar except that histochemically there is an absence of phosphofructokinase instead of myophosphorylase.

An increase in the number and size of lipid droplets in lipid myopathies are best demonstrated with the use of oil red O preparation on cryostat sections. Although an increase in lipid storage in the skeletal muscle is seen secondarily in steroid myopathy and acute alcoholic myopathy, there are conditions in which the myopathies are the direct result of abnormalities in the lipid metabolic pathway, namely carnitine deficiency.[64] A number

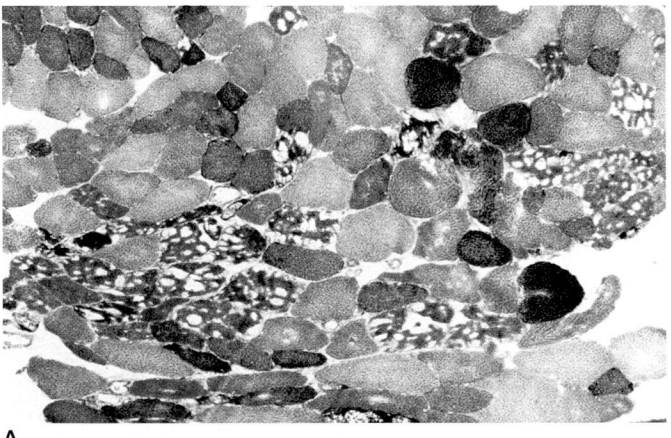

A

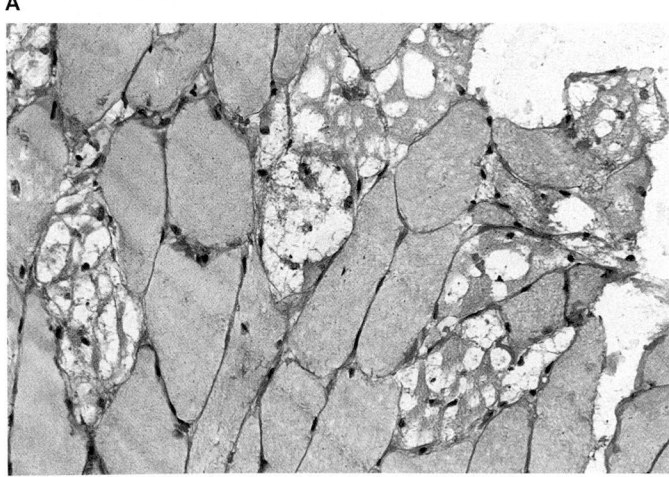

B

Fig. 28.194 Acid maltase deficiency. In adult onset the type I fibers are predominantly affected. Cryosection with SDH demonstrates type I fiber involvement (**A**) and PAS-diastase shows no staining of vacuoles (**B**).

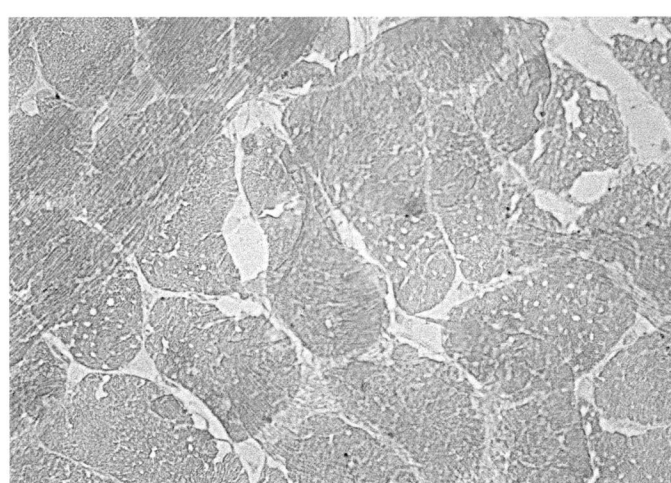

A

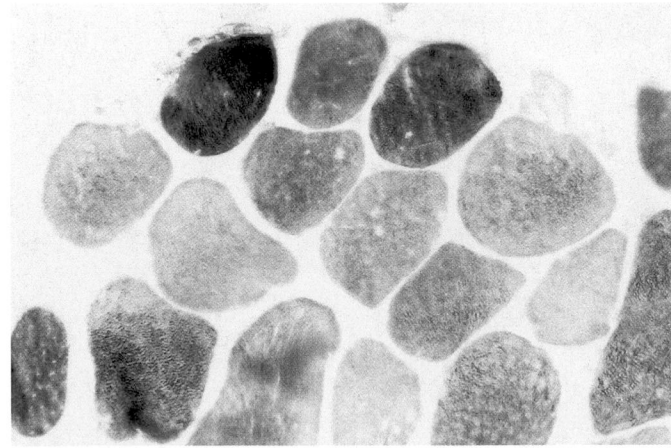

B

Fig. 28.195 McArdle's disease. Loss of myophosphorylase activity in patient with McArdle's disease ((**A**) compared to control (**B**) cryosection, myophosphorylase).

of mitochondrial myopathies can also secondarily lead to increased sarcoplasmic lipid deposition.

Carnitine deficiency primarily affects the skeletal muscle causing weakness or systemically giving rise to hypoglycemia, cardiomyopathy, bowel dysfunctions, hypochromic anemia, seizures, psychomotor retardation, and failure to thrive. Carnitine is essential for the transport of long chain fatty acids across the inner membrane of the mitochondria; when it is deficient, lipid accumulates in the sarcoplasm. This deficiency can occur as a primary defect in the carrier-mediated carnitine or secondary to disorders of beta-oxidation and defects in the respiratory chain. The muscle biopsy shows excessive lipid droplets, but the definitive diagnosis is based on assay of the muscle carnitine.

Carnitine palmitoyl transferase deficiency will affect the transfer of long chain fatty acids into the mitochondria and the beta-oxidation pathway. Mutations on chromosome 1p11–13 are found to be responsible for the deficiency in one of the isoforms of this enzyme.[74] Some patients have exercise intolerance and exercise-induced muscle pain. In severe cases, this may be followed by rhabdomyolysis and myoglobinuria. The muscle usually appears normal with light and electron microscopy and therefore the diagnosis is dependent on the biochemical assay.

Mitochondrial myopathy is a large and heterogeneous group of diseases characterized by abnormal sarcoplasmic accumulation of mitochondria, most of which are ultrastructurally abnormal. The modified Gomori trichrome stain identifies this abnormal accumulation in affected myofibers as intense red granular staining of the sarcoplasm. When the intermyofibrillary deposits are very numerous, the fiber will have a fragmented appearance; hence the name ragged red fiber[60,68] (Fig. 28.164). These fibers also display intense reaction with NADH-TR and SDH. A modified SDH with phenazine methylsulfate is more specific for abnormal mitochondria. The COX reaction is negative in fibers with mitochondrial t-RNA mutations that reduce COX biogenesis. Ultrastructurally, not only is there an increase in the number and size of mitochondria, but also there is an abnormal configuration, paracrystalline intermembranous inclusions, and abnormal cristae with excessive branching[73] (Fig. 28.196). Most of the mitochondrial diseases with known genetic defects involve either the mitochondrial genes[65] or nuclear genes encoding the respiratory chain polypeptides and Krebs' cycle enzymes.[67] Those with mitochondrial gene mutations are maternally inherited.[59] Even though identification of the genetic defects, deficient enzymes, or polypeptides will provide the final diagnosis, the muscle biopsy very often provides the first clue. The pathologist should also be cognizant of the fact that a negative biopsy may not exclude a mitochondrial myopathy.

With the increased understanding of the metabolic

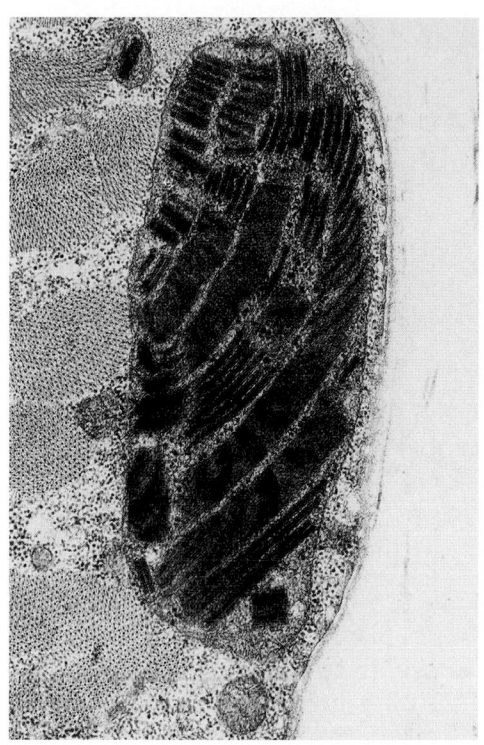

Fig. 28.196 Mitochondrial myopathy. This giant mitochondrion contains paracrystalline arrays (×19,426)

pathways in the mitochondria, this group of diseases can be classified according to the types of metabolic defect[67]; for instance, there are derangements in energy transduction[61] (e.g., Luft's disease), substrate utilization[63] (e.g., Leigh's disease), and the mitochondrial respiratory chain[69] (e.g., MELAS, MERRF,[60] Leigh's disease and Kearns–Sayre syndromes[71]). Some of these diseases, in addition to myopathy, involve other organs such as the heart and brain, resulting in cardiomyopathy, gastrointestinal disorders, stroke-like syndromes, encephalopathies, seizures, ophthalmoplegia, and deafness.[67,69,76] Interestingly, the phenotypes of a number of these diseases, such as MELAS and Leigh's disease, can be the result of more than one form of genotypic alteration.[76]

Toxic and drug-induced myopathies

Rhabdomyolysis is one of the most serious toxic effects of alcohol, amphetamine, heroin, barbiturate, methadone, amphotericin B, clofibrate, lovastatin, and other cholesterol-lowering agents (β-hydroxyl-β-methylglutaryl coenzyme A reductase inhibitors)[77,80,81] (Fig. 28.197). This is also a manifestation of malignant hyperthermia, which can be precipitated by general anesthetic agents, such as halothane and succinylcholine,[80] and neuroleptic malignant syndrome following the administration of drugs, such as haloperidol or chlorpromazine.[79] Snake, wasp, and spider venoms introduced into the body can also lead to rhabdomyolysis.[80,81] There is massive acute necrosis of myofibers and, depending on the duration, scattered areas of fiber regeneration may be seen. Any

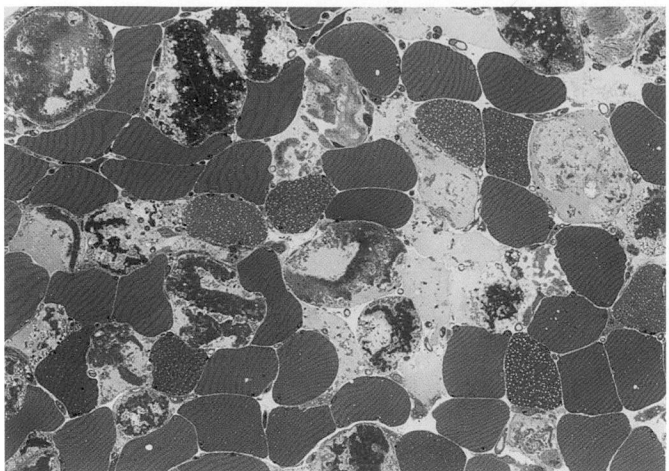

Fig. 28.197 Lovastatin toxicity. About 40% of the myofibers are undergoing necrosis. (Plastic resin)

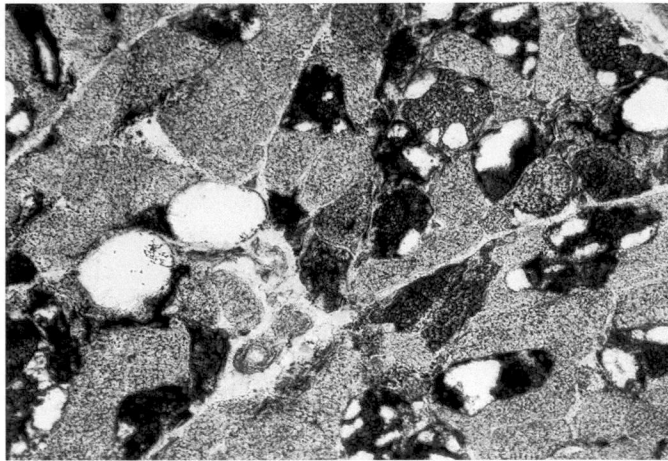

A

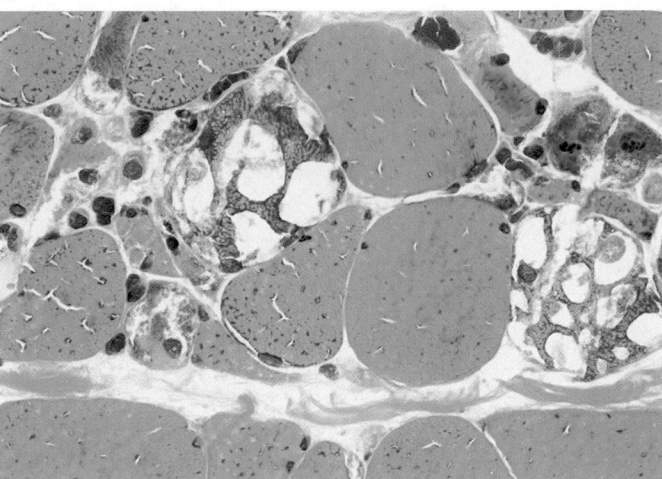

B

Fig. 28.198 Chloroquine myopathy. Severe vacuolization of myofibers with most of the affected fibers are type I in (**A**) with SDH and in (**B**) with modified Gomori trichrome. (Cryosection)

inflammatory changes present are considered as only a reaction to the necrosis. In addition to rhabdomyolysis, the other clinical manifestations of cholesterol-lowering agents include elevated serum CK alone, generalized myalgia unrelated to activity, and exercise-induced muscle pain.[77] Other drugs, such as azidothymidine (AZT), emetine, clofibrate, epsilon-aminocaproic acid, and alcohol, can cause subacute necrotizing myopathy.[80] In the case of AZT, there are changes in the mitochondria, such as ragged red fibers, accompanied by ultrastructural abnormalities.[84] Toxic reaction to chloroquine and hydroxylchloroquine results in a vacuolar myopathy associated with proximal weakness.[81] These vacuoles are present mainly in type I fibers and contain PAS-positive and acid phosphatase-positive lysosomal inclusions (Fig. 28.198). Ultrastructurally, these lysosomal inclusions can be membranous bodies, myelin figures, or curvilinear inclusions.[86] Vacuolar change and lysosomal inclusions have also been described in colchicine-induced myopathy[82] (Fig. 28.199). Agents such as procainamide, emetine, and D-penicillamine are linked to a form of inflammatory myopathy.[80] In eosinophilia-myalgia syndrome associated with L-tryptophan ingestion, the inflammatory infiltrate consists of lymphocytes, histiocytes, and eosinophils involving mainly the fascia and interstitium.[85]

Although type II fiber atrophy is very nonspecific, it is a relatively common finding in a muscle biopsy. The most common causes are related to prolonged steroid therapy and disuse related to prolonged bed rest or joint diseases (Fig. 28.200). The other conditions associated with type II atrophy are collagen vascular diseases, polymyalgia rheumatica, and myasthenia gravis.[78] ATPase is essential for the diagnosis and identifies the type II fibers that are angular and only about half the diameter of the normal-looking type I fibers. The diagnosis of acute quadriplegic myopathy which is previously

mentioned under myofibrillary myopathies should also be considered in patients with exposure to steroids and nondepolarizing neuromuscular blocking agents.[77,83]

Neuromuscular junction disorders

Myasthenia gravis is an autoimmune disease resulting from autoantibodies produced against the acetylcholine receptors at the motor endplate, causing a defect in neuromuscular transmission.[88,91] Patients usually suffer from a relapsing and remitting disease with muscle weakness and fatigue. Considerable difference exists in the severity and in the groups of muscles affected. The extraocular muscles are most commonly involved, producing ptosis and diplopia. Depending on the different muscles affected, patients may have dysphagia or even respiratory insufficiency. Typically, the patient is a young female, but when the patient is an elderly male, the presence of a thymoma should be excluded. Muscle biopsy is usually nondiagnostic, although findings such as type II fiber atrophy[78] and scattered collections of lymphocytes

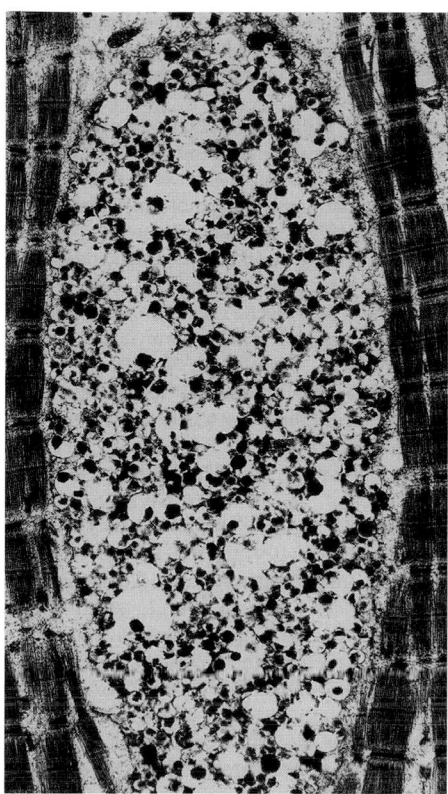

Fig. 28.199 Colchicine myopathy. Vacuoles are formed by aggregates of secondary lysosomes. (×8800)

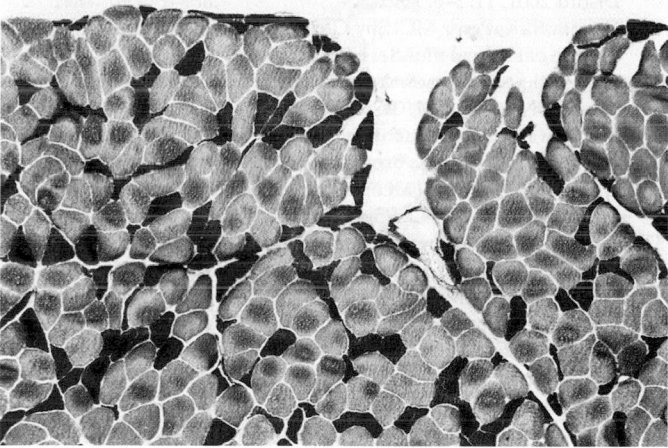

Fig. 28.200 Type II atrophy. This is a consistent finding in steroid-induced myopathy. (Cryosection, routine ATPase)

without evidence of fiber necrosis have been described.[89] Gammaglobulin and complements can be localized in the synaptic folds at the receptor sites. Changes in the neuromuscular junctions such as loss of secondary sarcolemmal folds and widening of the clefts are apparent only on electron microscopy.[90] Unfortunately, in most routine muscle biopsies the neuromuscular junctions are rarely sampled, rendering muscle biopsy unsuitable as a means for the diagnosis of myasthenia gravis.

Similarly, in Eaton–Lambert syndrome, a paraneoplastic syndrome associated with a defect in the release of acetylcholine from the nerve terminals at the neuromuscular junctions, the muscle biopsy is generally unhelpful. At most, nonspecific changes such as type II fiber atrophy are demonstrated.[87] The pathogenesis of this disease has been attributed to autoantibodies against the presynaptic voltage-gated calcium channels.[91]

Acknowledgments

The authors are grateful to Beverley Young, Karen Mackie, and Kris Milne for their assistance in the preparation of the manuscript and photographs.

References

1 Carpenter S, Karpati G. Methods of Tissue Removal and Preparation. Pathology of Skeletal Muscle, ed 2. Oxford, 2001, Oxford University, pp. 8–27.
2 Dubowitz V. Procedure of Muscle Biopsy. A Practical Approach, ed 2. London, 1985, Baillière Tindall, pp. 3–40.
3 Engel WK, Cunningham GG. Rapid examination of muscle tissue. An improved trichrome method for fresh-frozen biopsy sections. Neurology 1963, **13:** 919–923.

Normal anatomy

4 Craig R. The structure of the contractile filaments. In Engel AG, Franzini-Armstrong C (eds): Myology, ed. 2. New York, 1994, McGraw-Hill, pp. 134–175.
5 Franzini-Armstrong C. The sarcoplasmic reticulum and the transverse tubules. In Engel AG, Franzini-Armstrong C (eds): Myology, ed 2. New York, 1994, McGraw-Hill, pp. 176–222.
6 Schmalbruch H, Hellhammer U. The number of satellite cells in normal human muscle. Anat Rec 1976, **185:** 279–287.

Histochemistry

7 Johnson MA, Polgar J, Weightman D, Appelton D. Data on the distribution of fiber types in thirty-six human muscles. An autopsy study. J Neurol Sci 1973, **18:** 111–129.
8 Round JM, Matthews Y, Jones DA. A quick, simple and reliable histochemical method for ATPase in human muscle preparations. Histochem J 1980, **12:** 707–709.

Working classification

9 Karpati G. General pathological, immunopathological and genetic background of skeletal muscle disorders. In Karpti G (ed.) Structural and Molecular Basis of Skeletal Muscle Disease. Basel, 2002, ISN Neuropath Press, pp. 1–3.
10 Weller RO, Cumming WJK, Mahon M, Ellison DW. Diseases of muscle. In Graham DI, Lantos PL (eds): Greenfield's Neuropathology, vol. 2. London, 2002, Arnold, pp. 677–765.

Neurogenic atrophy (denervation)

11 Brooke MH, Engel WK. The histographic analysis of human muscle biopsies with regard to fiber types. 2. Diseases of the upper and lower motor neuron. Neurology 1969, **19:** 378–393.
12 Drachman DB, Murphy SR, Nigam MP, Hills JR. "Myopathic" changes in chronically denervated muscle. Arch Neurol 1967, **16:** 14–24.

Inflammatory myopathies

13 Albrecht S, Bilbao JM. Ubiquitin expression in inclusion-body myositis. Arch Pathol Lab Med 1993, **117:** 789–793.
14 Askanas V, Engel WK. Inclusion-body myositis, newest concepts of pathogenesis and relation to aging and Alzheimer's disease. Review. J Neuropathol Exp Neurol 2001, **60:** 1–14.

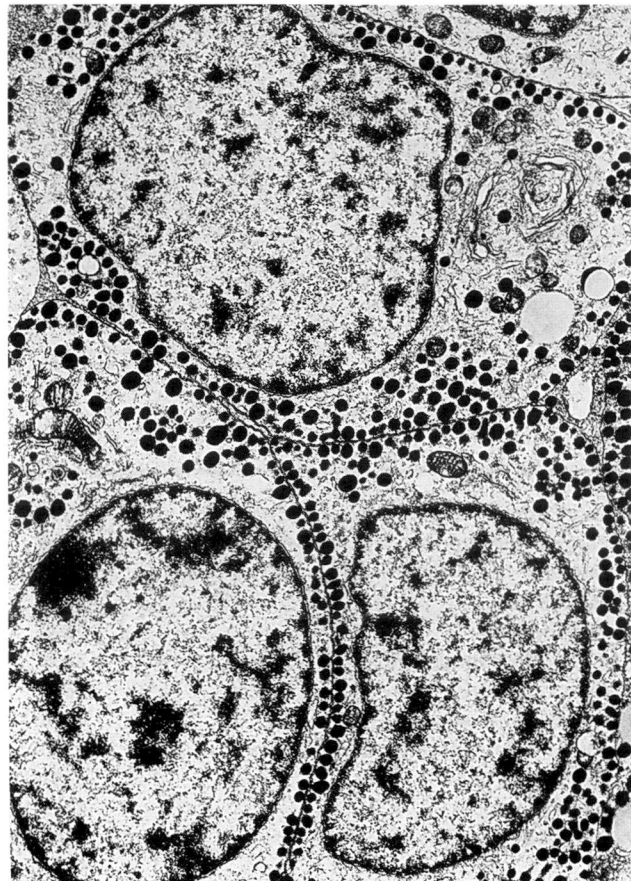

Fig. 29.1 Growth hormone cells have well-developed Golgi complexes and are densely granulated with evenly electron-dense spherical secretory granules measuring 350 to 500 nm in diameter. (Electron micrograph, ×6150) (Courtesy of Dr. E Horvath, Toronto.)

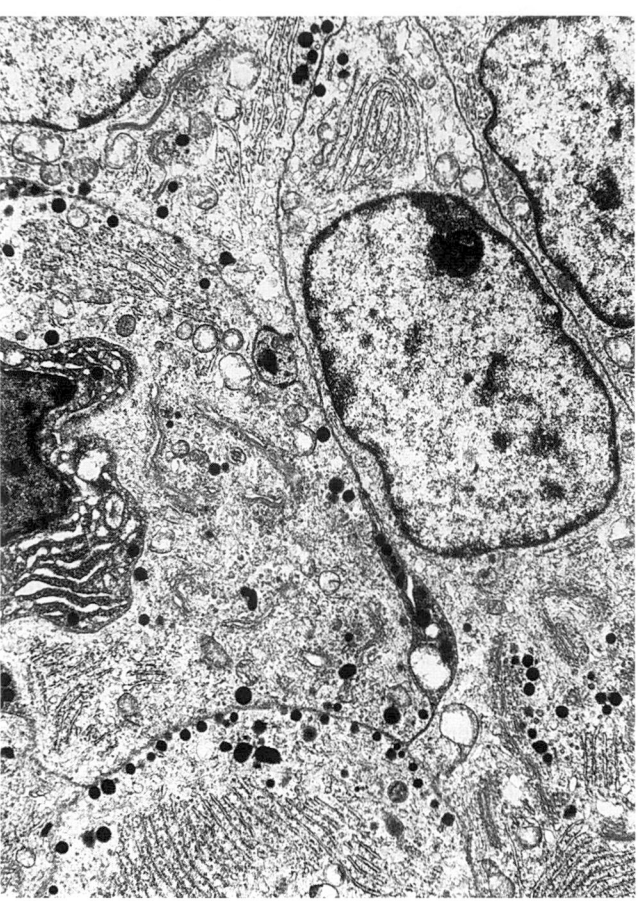

Fig. 29.2 Cytoplasm of prolactin cells displays stacks of well-developed RER and sparse secretory granules measure up to 300 nm. (Electron micrograph, ×5896) (Courtesy of Dr. E Horvath, Toronto.)

Cystic structures of variable dimensions lined by cuboidal ciliated epithelium are often found interposed between neurohypophysis and the pars distalis. These are thought to be remnants of Rathke's pouch. Surgical pathologists should be aware of salivary gland rests[9] and nests of granular cells[5] that can rarely be found in the neurohypophysis.

Pituitary adenoma

General and clinical features

Pituitary neoplasms have traditionally made up 10% of the intracranial tumors, but their relative incidence has risen to almost 25% in some institutions as a result of refinement in radioimmunoassay, imaging techniques, and transsphenoidal microsurgery.[17,25,26] They arise from the cells of the adenohypophysis and are designated as pituitary adenomas. Most examples are found within the confines of the sella turcica. However, since aberrant adenohypophysial cells are known to occur in the diencephalic infundibulum, pituitary stalk,[13] and sphenoid bone between the nasopharynx and pituitary fossa, the appearance of pituitary adenomas in one of these locations (including the root of the nasal cavity) is not unexpected, even if exceptional.[18,19]

The pathogenesis of pituitary adenoma is complex and most data are derived from animal models.[10] Unlike experimental animals, it appears that the human adenomas are rarely preceded by glandular hyperplasia. There are examples of human GH cell adenoma that are linked to G-protein mutation, which promotes tumor proliferation and survival.[19] The pituitary adenomas associated with multiple endocrine neoplasm are associated with the inactivation of the tumor suppressor MEN1 gene in chromosome 11q13.[10]

Although pituitary adenomas are usually benign lesions, their growth rate is highly variable and unpredictable. Whereas some microadenomas may exhibit little or no detectable change in size over time, others show rapid expansion and invasion of adjacent meninges, bone, sinuses, and brain. Pituitary adenomas may synthesize and release hormones, and in about 70% of cases, there is clinical and/or biochemical evidence of a characteric hypersecretory syndrome.[25] Some patients

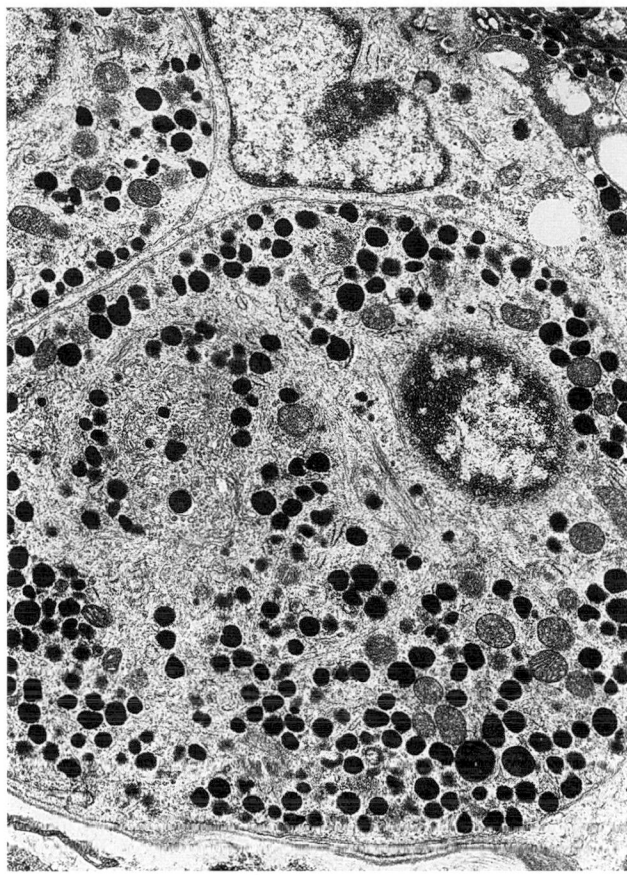

Fig. 29.3 Corticotroph cells show widely distributed RER membranes and prominent Golgi complex displays dilated saccule containing developing secretory granules. Secretory granules are irregular in shape and measure between 300 and 350 nm. Bundles of filaments are present in perinuclear cytoplasm. (Electron micrograph, ×7480) (Courtesy of Dr. E Horvath, Toronto.)

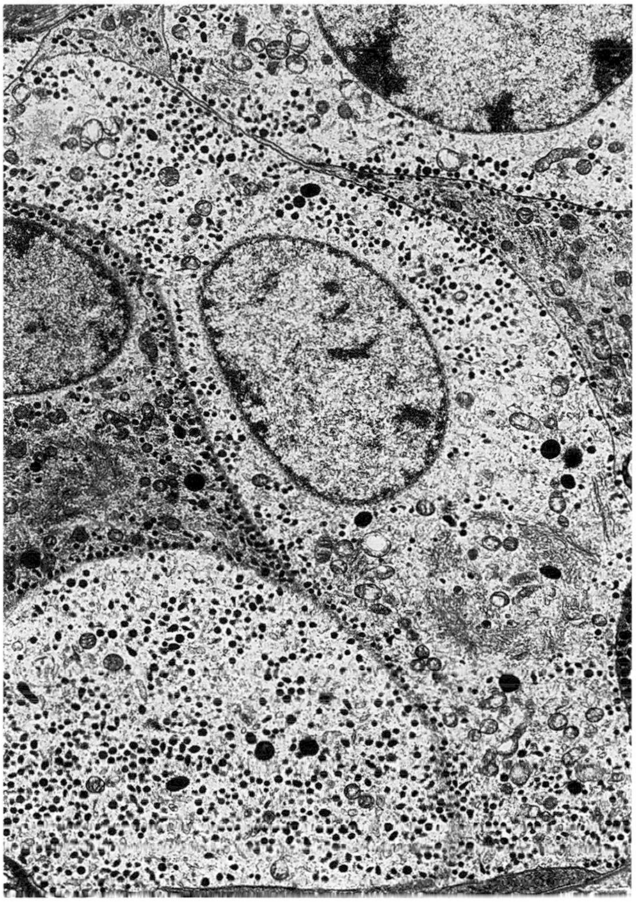

Fig. 29.4 Thyrotroph cells are of medium to large size with angular shape and long processes. Secretory granules measure 150 to 200 nm. (Electron micrograph, ×4500) (Courtesy of Dr. E Horvath, Toronto.)

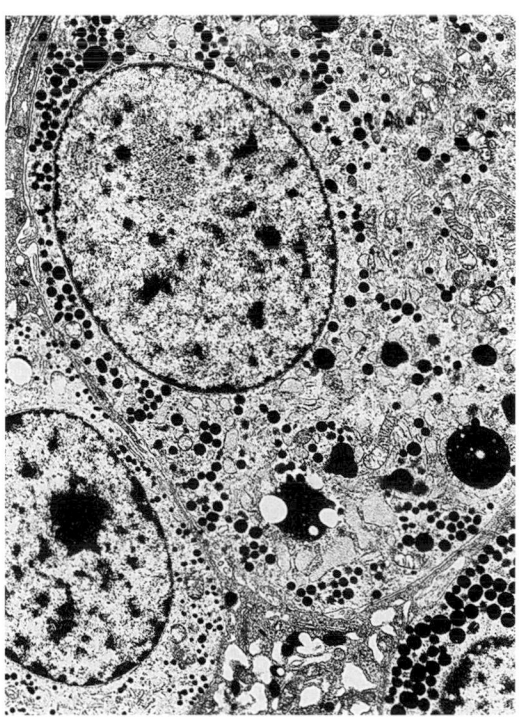

Fig. 29.5 Gonadotroph cells exhibit network of dilated RER and secretory granules whose number, size, electron density, and morphology vary considerably. (Electron micrograph, ×5700) (Courtesy of Dr. E Horvath, Toronto.)

harboring pituitary adenomas may present to the clinician with insidious symptoms of hypopituitarism (secondary to destruction of the normal gland or interference with the delivery of hypothalamic hormones) affecting one or more pituitary hormones.

Pituitary adenomas with suprasellar extension occur in about 10% to 20% of cases (Fig. 29.6). This may give rise to a constellation of neurologic signs and symptoms, not uncommonly as the first manifestation of the disease, related to compression of optic nerves, chiasm, cavernous sinus, and oculomotor nerves. The term pituitary apoplexy is reserved for those cases with the abrupt onset of headache, ocular deficits, and altered consciousness. This uncommon but well-known neurosurgical emergency results from hemorrhage and necrosis in an adenoma.[11]

Pituitary adenomas as a group are more frequent in adults and show no major gender difference. Adenomas in younger patients are uncommon.[16,22] Microadenomas

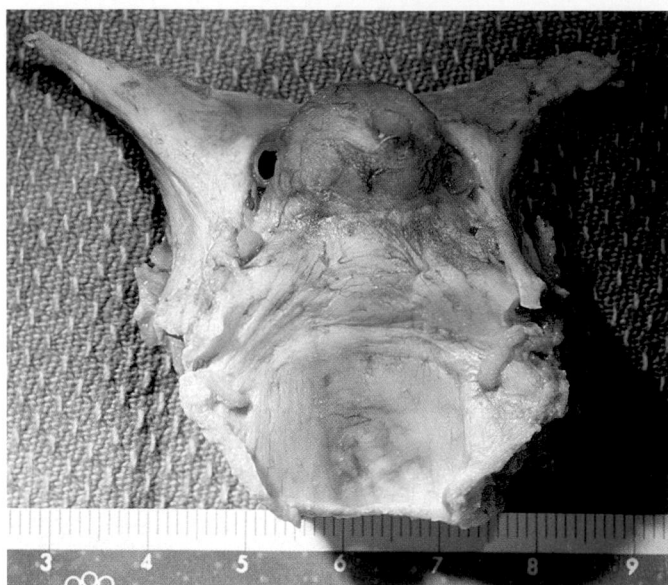

Fig. 29.6 Gross appearance of pituitary adenoma with suprasellar extension through the diaphragm of the sella.

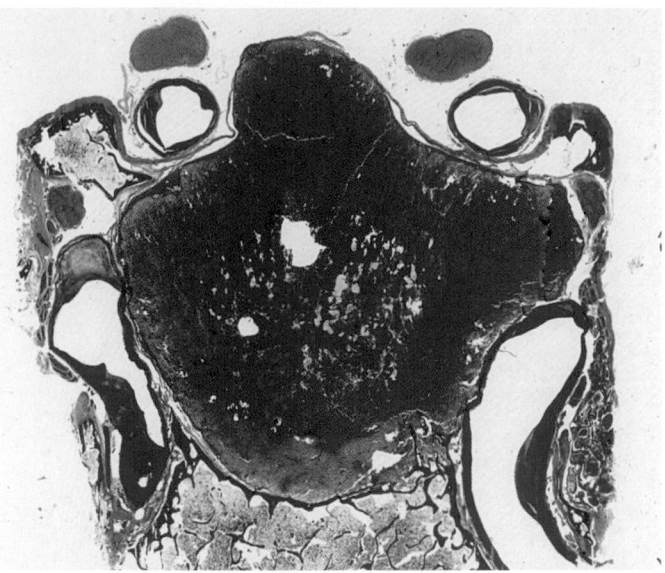

Fig. 29.7 Incidental finding at autopsy of null cell adenoma in a 78-year-old woman. Coronal section of sella showing diffuse tumor that fills sella and compresses residual pituitary tissue into thin peripheral rim (see also Fig. 29.12). Note moderate suprasellar extension. (Whole mount, H&E) (Courtesy of Dr. William Halliday, Winnipeg.)

are detected in about one fourth of autopsies.[12,23] In a small percentage of patients, the pituitary tumor is one of the components of the multiple endocrine neoplasia syndrome type I.[24] Endocrinologically silent (clinically and biochemically nonfunctional) adenomas tend to be large and constitute about one third of surgically removed pituitary tumors. By contrast, the vast majority of pituitary adenomas in childhood and adolescence are functional.[15]

Enlargement and erosion of the floor of the sella turcica are common findings and important radiologic signs. Currently, magnetic resonance imaging is regarded as the method of choice for the imaging diagnosis of pituitary lesions because of its sensitivity and high resolution.[27]

On the basis of these newer imaging techniques, an anatomic classification of pituitary tumors has been devised.[14,21] Accordingly, microadenomas are intrasellar tumors less than 10 mm in diameter. Macroadenomas with suprasellar extension (SSE) include the following subtypes: grade A (moderate SSE within 10 mm above the jugum sphenoidale, filling the chiasmatic cistern), grade B (large SSE, up to 20 mm, elevating the anterior recess of the third ventricle), grade C (very large SSE, up to 30 mm, filling the anterior third ventricle), and grade D (huge SSE, in excess of 30 mm, above the level of the foramen of Monro, or grade C with asymmetric lateral or multiple expansion).

Gross features

Grossly, pituitary adenomas are usually solid and soft. Their color varies from gray to red according to the degree of vascularity. Cystic, hemorrhagic, and necrotic changes may occur. A characteristic gross appearance is that of a tumor occupying both the intrasellar and

suprasellar areas (Fig. 29.7), with a central constriction produced by the diaphragm and the circle of Willis.

Terms that are sometimes used for pituitary adenomas are enclosed (when encased within the dural covering of the sella), invasive (when infiltrating the dura, the floor of the sella, nasal sinuses, or other structures), and giant (when the superior growing edge of the tumor is 20 mm above the jugum sphenoidale)[29] (Fig. 29.8). The most common pattern of gross local invasion is lateral extension and penetration of the cavernous sinus.[30] Even invasive adenomas tend to displace rather than infiltrate the brain. The invasive tendencies of the adenoma can be

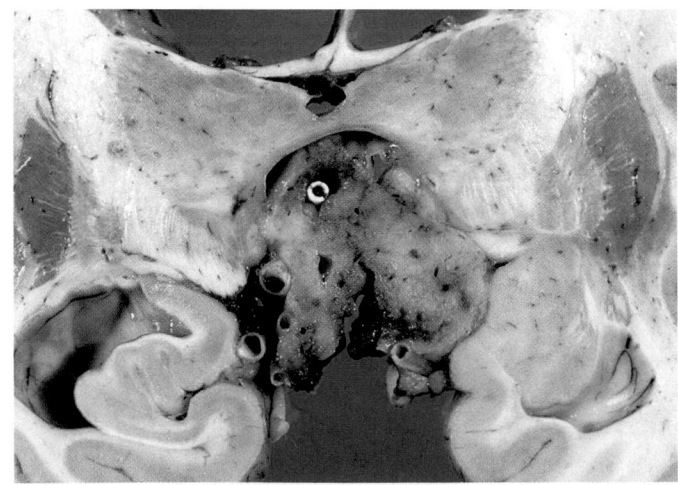

Fig. 29.8 Gross appearance of giant mixed PRL and GH cell adenoma intruding into brain in 74-year-old female with 2-year history of dementia and visual impairment.

identified by neuroimaging, by direct inspection at the time of surgery, or by histologic examination if the tissue sample is adequate (Fig. 29.9). Some of the larger adenomas may undergo suprasellar extension, with intrusion into brain mimicking a primary intraventricular tumor if the brain specimen is viewed in isolation (Fig. 29.8). When massive parasellar extension occurs the tumor may grow intradurally into all the compartments of the base of the brain.

Microscopic features

The microscopic pattern in H&E sections varies from case to case, the differences being based on the relative degrees of cellularity and vascularity. The pattern of growth may be diffuse (solid) (Fig. 29.10), sinusoidal (trabecular) (Fig. 29.11), or papillary (pseudopapillary). Glandular arrangement of cells is unusual and suggestive of gonadotroph adenoma. Some lesions are hypocellular with marked sclerohyalinization of the stroma. The use of reticulin stains facilitates the identifi-

cation of the tumor–gland interface, with no fibrous capsule in between. The pituitary tissue at the periphery of the adenoma is compressed with condensation of the reticulin network, which is disrupted in the tumor (Fig. 29.12).

The tumor cells are generally round or polygonal and less commonly elongated (Fig. 29.13A, C and D). They have a round or oval nucleus and a variable amount of cytoplasm, which may be basophilic, acidophilic, amphophilic, or chromophobic. In intraoperative touch and smear preparations, nuclear pleomorphism and multinucleated cells are readily detected (Fig. 29.13B). Mitoses are scanty or absent (Fig. 29.13A). Occasional bizarre hyperchromatic nuclei may occur, including giant and ring forms with prominent nucleoli (Fig. 29.13B). Poor correlation exists between histopathologic findings and the aggressiveness of pituitary adenomas. In a study including nonrecurrent and recurrent tumors, the proliferating cell nuclear antigen index was found to

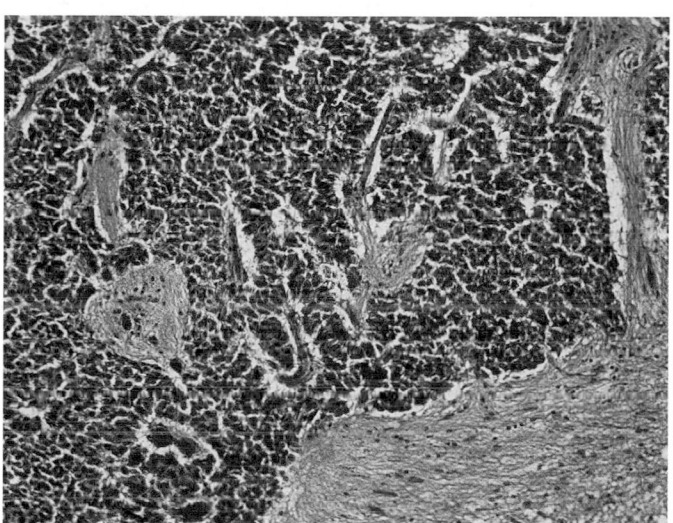

Fig. 29.9 Pituitary adenoma invasive to brain. (H&E, same case as in Fig. 29.8.)

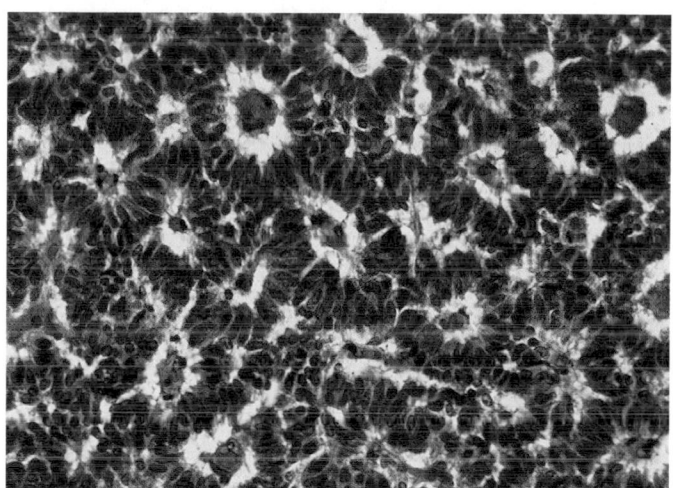

Fig. 29.11 Pituitary adenoma. Sinusoidal pattern. (H&E.)

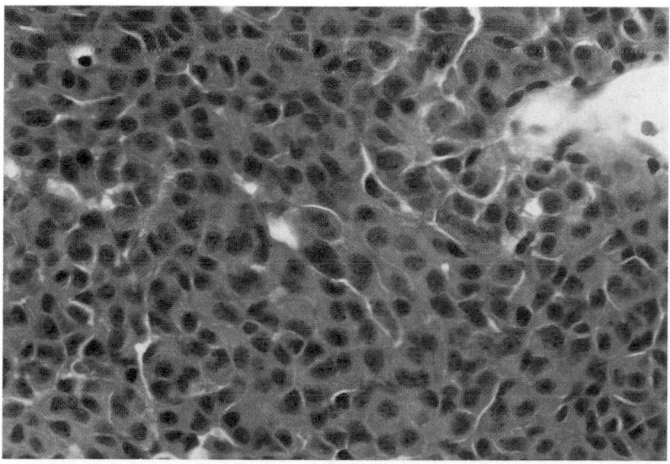

Fig. 29.10 Pituitary adenoma. Diffuse pattern. (H&E.)

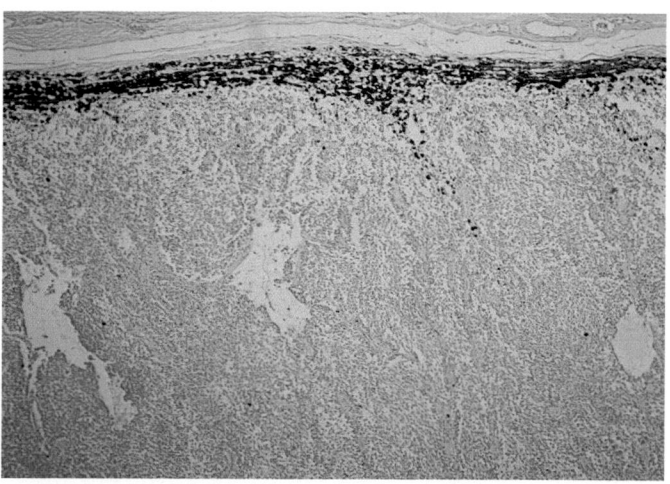

Fig. 29.12 Pituitary adenoma. Immunostaining of GH highlights compressed residual adenohypophysis at the periphery of adenoma. (Same case as in Fig. 29.7.)

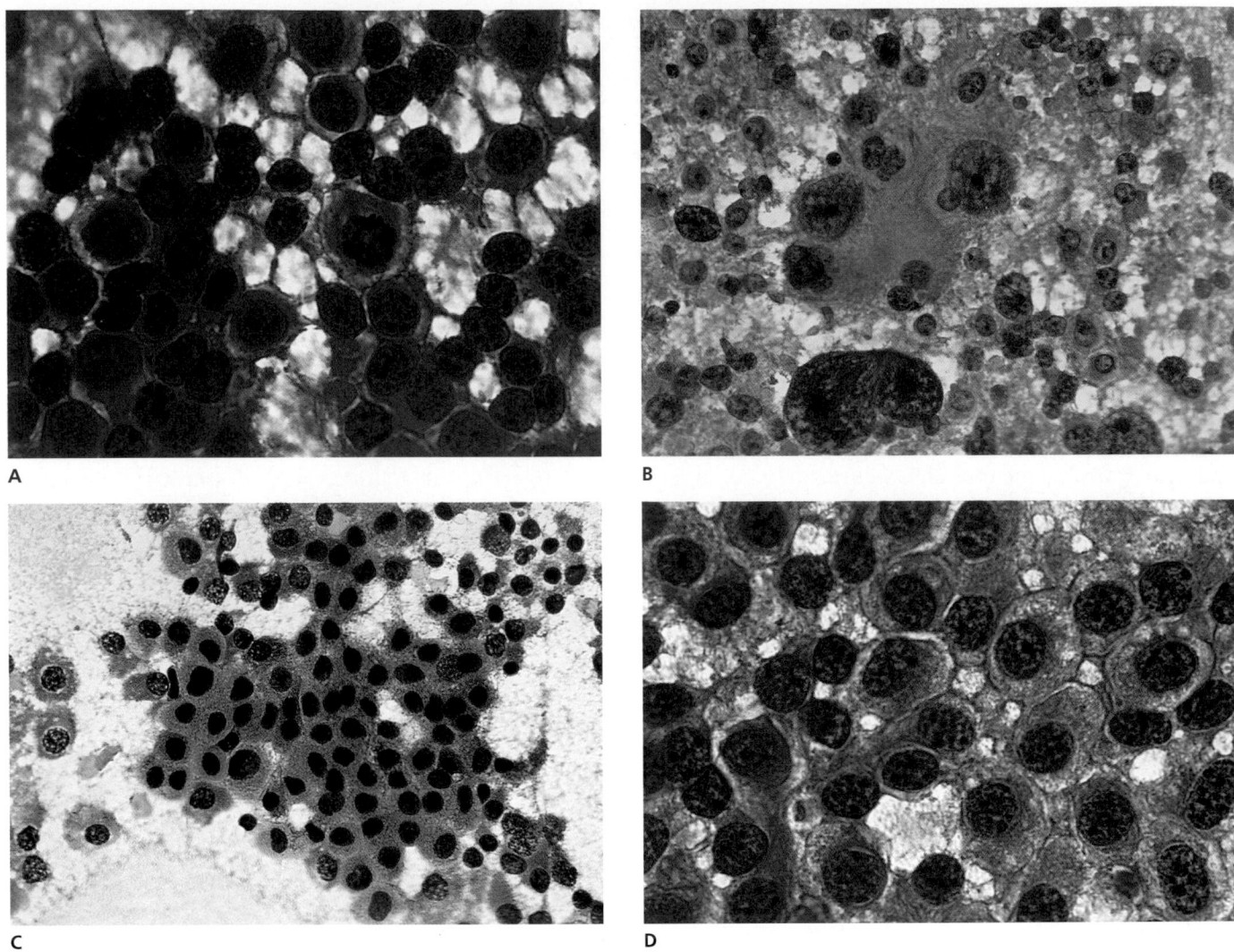

Fig. 29.13 Intraoperative touch and smear preparation of pituitary adenomas showing mitosis **A**, binucleation and atypical nuclei **B**, and oncocytoma **C**, **D**.

be highest among recurrent tumors and in macro-adenomas.[31] In some cases, the tumor cells have the morphologic appearance of oncocytes. Calcification occurs in about 7% of pituitary adenomas (Fig. 29.14B), primarily in PRL-secreting neoplasms.[33] The deposition of endocrine amyloid has also been documented in some of these tumors; such deposits are seen mainly in PRL cell adenomas[30,32] (Fig. 29.14A). In tumors that have undergone hemorrhage and necrosis, the specimen may have the appearance of altered blood, making identification of the adenoma difficult.

Pituitary adenomas composed of uniform cells of clear cytoplasm may be confused with oligodendrogliomas, whereas those consisting of oval cells with acidophilic cytoplasm and eccentric nucleus may be mistaken for plasma cell myeloma. The most common error, however, is the misinterpretation of a papillary type of pituitary adenoma as an ependymoma.

Classification

The traditional classification of pituitary adenomas into chromophobe, acidophil, and basophil variants corre-lates so poorly with the specific cell types and the corresponding patterns of hormone secretion that there is little use in maintaining it. It has become evident that most normal "chromophobe" cells simply represent spe-cific cells of one kind or another in which the granules are not numerous enough to be obvious at the light microscopic level. The same is true of the so-called chro-mophobe adenomas. Ultrastructural studies have demonstrated that truly agranular adenomas do not exist.[36–38] Acidophilic pituitary tumors also have been shown to be highly heterogeneous. Immuno-histochemical studies have demonstrated no detectable hormones in some tumors, whereas others display immunopositivity for GH, PRL, or both.

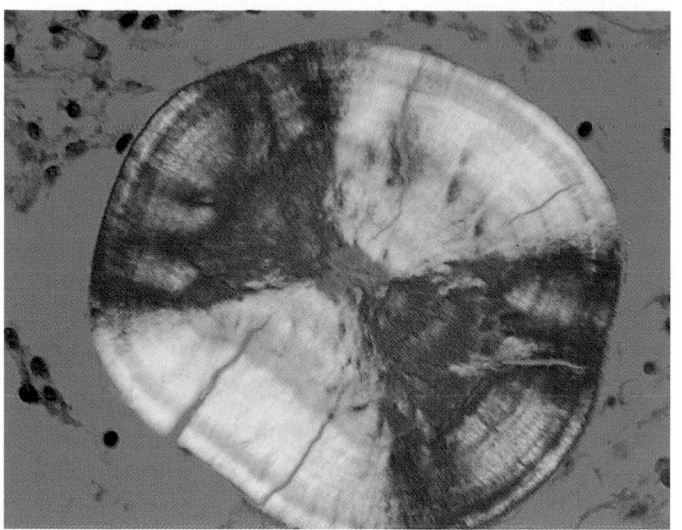
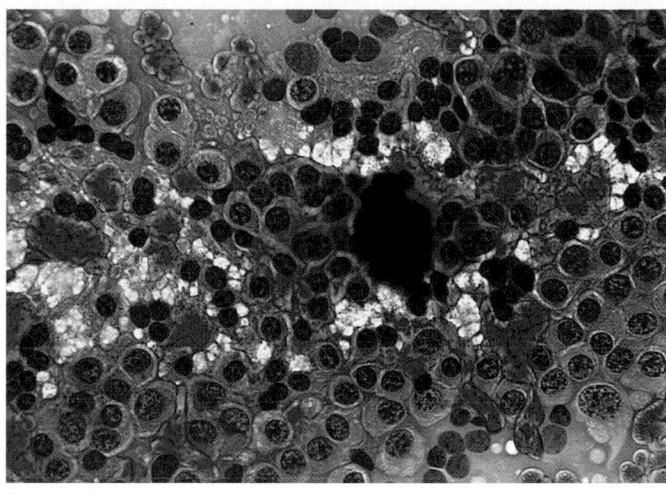

A
B

Fig. 29.14 Prolactinomas with amyloid deposition (Congo red) in the form of large spheroids **A** and scattered calcospherites **B**.

There is now general agreement that the hormones of the nontumorous adenohypophysis are secreted by a single cell type. The identification of these cells and the correlation with a given hormone have been achieved by careful immunohistochemical and electron microscopic studies under normal and abnormal conditions. The same approach should be followed in the case of neoplasms.[36,41] H&E stains should be routinely supplemented by PAS stain, immunohistochemical (Fig. 29.15), and electron microscopic examination. The contribution of these techniques to the characterization of nonfunctioning or "silent" pituitary adenomas is essential.[34,35,42] The substantial majority of clinically nonsecreting adenomas are found to correspond to null cell adenomas, oncocytomas, or gonadotroph adenomas.[39]

The current classification of pituitary adenomas is based on cell type, largely ascertained by immunohistochemical reactions against the specific hormones and by electron microscopy[37,38,41] (Table 29.1). Some pituitary adenomas are also immunoreactive for alpha-subunit, neuron-specific enolase, chromogranin, synaptophysin, and estrogen receptor.[43] Most pituitary adenomas, even those with a plurihormonal phenotype, are considered to be distinct and uniform neoplasms. The occurrence of double adenomas, that is, two morphologically and/or imunocytologically distinct patterns in the same surgical specimen, is infrequent.[40]

PRL cell adenoma

PRL cell adenoma is the most common neoplasm arising in the adenohypophysis, accounting for 50% of tumors found incidentally at autopsy[45] and for about 30% of

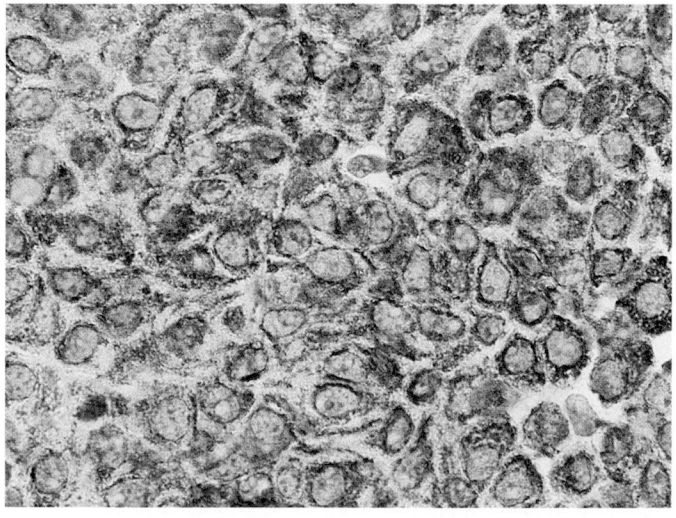
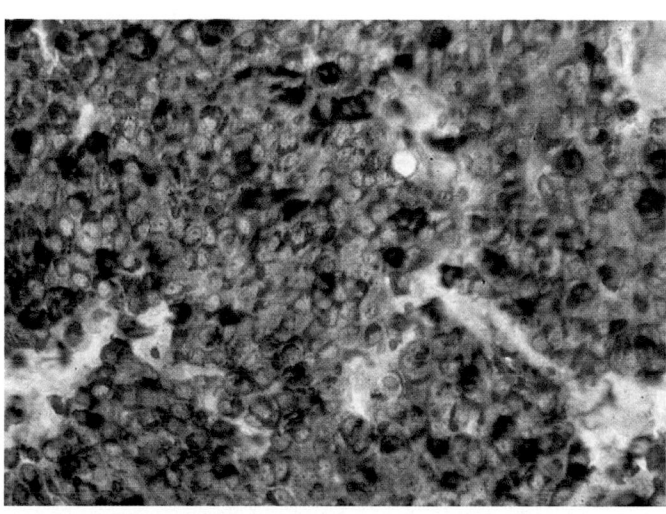

A
B

Fig. 29.15 Pituitary adenoma. Note different patterns of immunoreactivity of secretory granules, which are restricted to peripheral parts of cytoplasm in ACTH adenoma **A** and form typical perinuclear crescents in prolactinoma **B**. (**B**, courtesy of Dr. K Kovacs, Toronto)

Table 29.1 Classification of pituitary adenomas.* (Data from Dr K. Kovacs and Dr. E. Horvath, St Michael's Hospital, Toronto, 1994)

Cell type	Incidence
Sparsely granulated PRL cell adenoma	26%
Densely granulated PRL cell adenoma	1%
Sparsely granulated GH cell adenoma	7%
Densely granulated GH cell adenoma	7%
Mixed PRL and GH synthesizing adenomas	6%
Acidophil stem cell adenoma	2%
Functioning corticotroph cell adenoma	8%
Silent "corticotroph" cell adenomas	6%
Gonadotroph adenoma	6%
Thyrotroph adenoma	1%
Null cell adenoma (oncocytoma)	26%
Unclassified plurihormonal adenomas	4%

* Relative frequency of each tumor subtype in a series of over 3000 surgically removed pituitary adenomas.

those encountered by the neurosurgeon.[49] The latter group is composed mostly of women of childbearing age who present with the galactorrhea-amenorrhea syndrome (Chiari–Frommel syndrome or Forbes–Albright syndrome). The implementation of dopamine agonists as a proven nonsurgical therapeutic alternative for many prolactinomas may explain a decline in their numbers in current surgical series.

Serum level values of PRL above 200 ng/ml are considered diagnostic of PRL-secreting adenomas. Elevation of PRL serum levels up to 150 ng/ml may be the result of a "stalk effect".[50]

In women of childbearing age, prolactinomas are usually encountered in the microadenoma stage, whereas in males and elderly females prolactinomas may acquire large sizes, have a higher incidence of dural invasion, and have usually transgressed the confines of the sella turcica at presentation.

Histologically, these neoplasms are chromophobic or slightly acidophilic, are PAS negative, and exhibit a diffuse or, less commonly, papillary pattern. Some tumors possess a prominent hyalinized stroma, and microcalcification is shown in about one fifth of cases (Fig. 29.14B). Coarse mineral deposition and ossification with the development of "pituitary stones" rarely occur.[51,52] Endocrine amyloid is not an uncommon feature of PRL-producing adenomas. Amyloid may be present in "wisps" detectable only by electron microscopy both intracellularly and extracellularly[44] or seen in the formation of large extracellular spherules that are pathognomic for this type of neoplasm (Fig. 29.14A). Prolactin immunopositivity is demonstrated in perinuclear areas corresponding to the prominent Golgi complex, resulting in a crescent-shaped pattern[46] (Fig. 29.15B).

Ultrastructurally, the cells are irregular and form intricate processes that interdigitate.[48,53] The rough endoplasmic reticulum (RER) is abundant and consists of parallel arrays of delicate cisternae. A whorl arrange-

ment of RER (nebenkern) is typical of this tumor. In keeping with the chromophobic appearance on H&E stain, the secretory granules are sparse in the range of 150 to 300 nm in diameter. Some of these granules are extruded in the extracellular space between two cells, a phenomenon known as "misplaced exocytosis," and not in the perivascular spaces[47] (Fig. 29.16). A rare variant of PRL adenoma shows marked acidophilia of cytoplasmic granules and, on electron microscopy, densely granulated cells.[47] The sparsely granulated PRL adenoma may occur in the form of a microadenoma typically located laterally in the gland. The macroadenomas may simply expand the sella, whereas others have a predilection of growth downward through sphenoid bone and into the nasopharynx. Dopamine agonists used for the control of hyperprolactinemic states lead to reduction of serum levels of PRL and of the tumor mass. Histologically, such tumors appear to be more cellular because of the involution of the cytoplasm, particularly the RER and Golgi membranes. Tumor fibrosis has been described in long-term treatment with bromocriptine.

GH cell adenoma

Pure adenomas of GH cell type are the densely granulated and sparsely granulated variants. They account for about 14% of all surgically resected pituitary adenomas and may result in gigantism or acromegaly if functioning at a clinical level or, less commonly, unaccompanied by

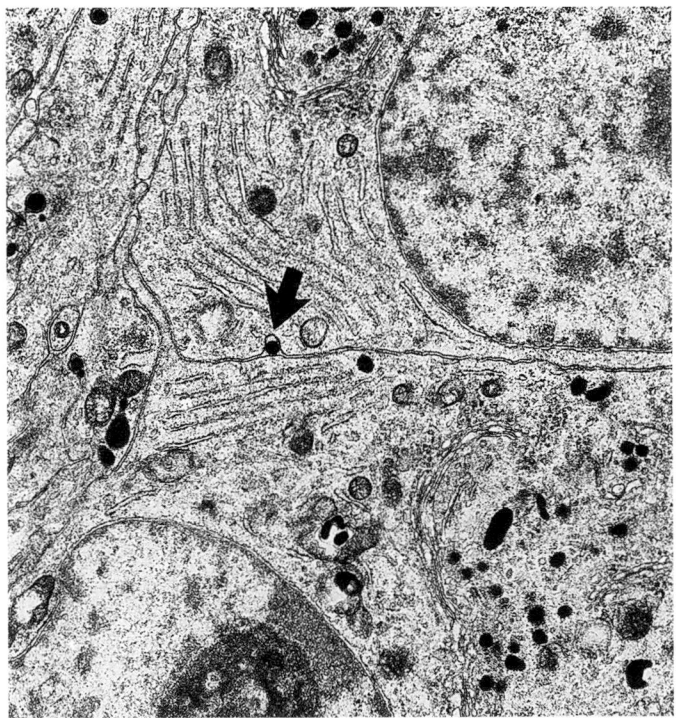

Fig. 29.16 Sparsely granulated PRL cell adenoma showing misplaced exocytosis and pleomorphic granules within the Golgi sacculi. (Electron micrograph, ×4400) (Courtesy of Dr. E Horvath, Toronto.)

clinical signs of hyperfunction.[54,58,59] Other GH-secreting tumors are bihormonal or plurihormonal and cosecrete PRL, TSH, alpha-subunit, and sometimes other hormones.[56,57,67] These will be discussed elsewhere. Notwithstanding, in situ hybridization studies of mRNA have shown that tumors causing acromegaly not expressing PRL are rare.[55]

The densely granulated somatotroph adenoma corresponds to the classic acidophilic adenoma of acromegaly. Cytoplasmic granules are plentiful and stain strongly with eosin. By immunostaining they display a diffuse pattern much like normal somatotrophs. No definite correlation exists between serum levels of GH and the intensity of staining for this hormone in the tumor cells. The significant ultrastructural feature is the abundance of large spherical secretory granules measuring 300 to 600 nm.[60,64,65]

The sparsely granulated GH cell adenoma is chromophobic when stained with H&E,[66] and immunopositivity for GH is meager. When viewed under the electron microscope, scanty secretory granules measure 100 to 300 nm. The area normally occupied by the Golgi region displays a skein of intermediate filaments that immunoreact for keratin[62] (Fig. 29.17A) and ubiquitin. These fibrous bodies (Fig. 29.17B) and multiple centrioles are the distinguishing features of the sparsely granulated variant of GH adenoma.

In both types of GH cell adenomas, tubuloreticular inclusions within capillary endothelium and the accumulation of endocrine amyloid may occur, although these changes are poorly understood.[61] Both types of GH cell adenomas are considered variants of the same tumor.[60] From the clinical standpoint, however, the separation of these two types is important because of a

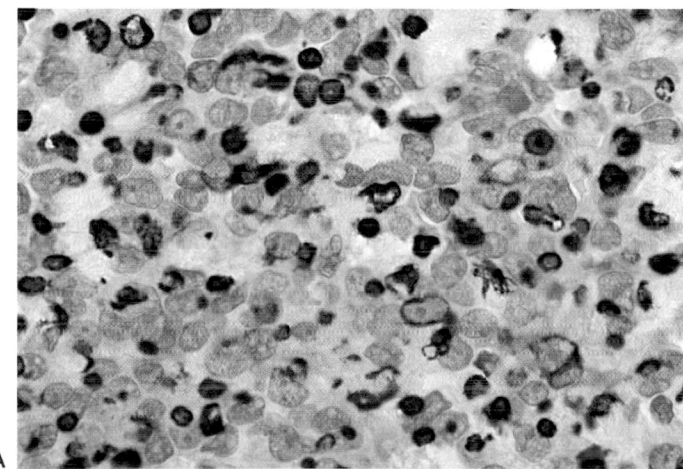

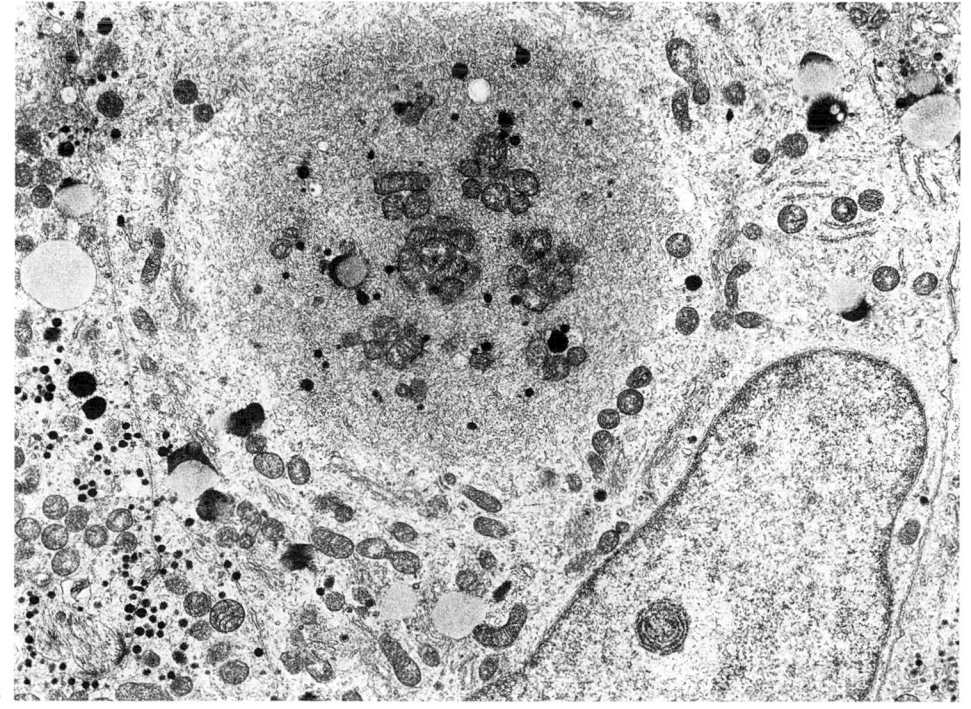

Fig. 29.17 Growth hormone cell adenoma. **A**, Fibrous bodies immunolabeled with keratin. **B**, Characteristic appearance of sparsely granulated GH cell adenoma. Note fibrous body. (Electron micrograph, ×7200) (Courtesy of Dr. E Horvath, Toronto.)

treatment. By contrast, cytoplasmic filaments are not found in tumor cells of Nelson's syndrome because levels of circulating glucocorticoids decline after adrenalectomy. Corticotroph adenomas are usually monohormonal, and immunohistochemically, there is positivity for ACTH (Fig. 29.15A) and for beta-lipotropic hormone, melanocyte-stimulating hormone, and beta-endorphin in the cytoplasm of adenoma cells.[79,81,82,89]

About 6% of basophil densely granulated adenomas that are immunoreactive for ACTH are endocrinologically silent; the reason for this lack of function or hormone release is not known.[81] Some of these silent ACTH adenomas have a proclivity to hemorrhage with sudden tumor expansion, leading to the known clinical presentation of pituitary apoplexy. Hyperplasia of corticotroph cells as a cause of Cushing's disease poses a most difficult problem for both neurosurgeons and pathologists.[83,87] Corticotroph hyperplasia is assumed to be the result of hypothalamic dysregulation but may also be secondary to ectopic production of corticotropin-releasing hormone.[78] Ectopic production of ACTH by a neuroendocrine tumor elsewhere in the body may result in Cushing's disease with a pituitary gland of normal size.

Glycoprotein hormone-producing adenomas

The glycoprotein hormone-producing cells of the pituitary gland are gonadotrophs and thyrotrophs. These cells normally synthesize the hormones in a heterodimeric configuration, consisting of an "alpha" subunit common to all members of the class and a "beta" subunit that lends biochemical, immunologic, and functional specificity to the molecule.[91] Abnormal hormone synthesis in gonadotroph and thyrotroph adenomas results in excess production of the alpha-subunit, which can be measured as a diagnostic marker for glycoprotein-producing adenomas[95] and to monitor follow-up after treatment.

The presence of adenomas of TSH cell type had been proved by the reports of pituitary adenomas associated with hyperthyroidism and confirmed by Hamilton et al.[93] by the finding of elevated serum TSH levels on radioimmunoassay. However, several of these adenomas arise in patients with longstanding hypothyroidism.[101,104] They are the least common pituitary tumor type, representing only 1% of all neoplasms, with about 100 cases reported so far.[90,92,98,100] Tumors are usually large but may also present as microadenomas. By light microscopy they display a sinusoidal growth pattern. Immunohistochemical reactivity for TSH is essential for diagnosis. The alpha-subunit of the pituitary glycoprotein hormones (TSH, FSH, and LH) can be labeled with immunoreagents in many of the glycoprotein-producing pituitary adenomas. Ultrastructurally, most thyrotroph tumors are well differentiated, the cells resembling nonadenomatous TSH elements[92] with minute secretory granules.

Adenomas of FSH/LH cell type, gonadotroph adenomas, represent about 6% of all pituitary adenomas.[99,102,103] These tumors are slow growing, show no evidence of gross invasion, tend to be large at presentation, and rarely are associated with high serum gonadotropin levels. Neoplastic gonadotroph cells have few secretory granules and are therefore rendered chromophobic by conventional stains. Ultrastructurally, the secretory granules have a mean diameter of 150 nm. Immunohistochemically, Trouillas et al.[103] found reactivity for both FSH and LH in 14 cases, for FSH in seven, and for alpha-subunit in five. The existence of pure alpha-subunit-secreting adenomas has also been documented by other groups.[94,97] Pure LH-producing adenomas are rare. Horvath et al.[96] found, ultrastructurally, a distinctive vesicular dilatation of the Golgi complex ("honeycomb Golgi") in gonadotropin adenomas occurring in women. Other tumors are less differentiated and resemble null cell adenomas.

Plurihormonal adenoma

Pituitary tumors that produce two or more hormones are designated plurihormonal adenomas. The hormones produced may be demonstrated within the same tumor cell, or the tumor may be composed of multiple cell clones, each engaged in the processing of a different hormone.[105,106,108] Most of the plurihormonal adenomas are found in patients with acromegaly. These tumors usually coexpress GH and PRL[107] and have already been discussed. Not regarded as plurihormonal are adenomas containing ACTH and related proopiomelanocortin peptides because such substances are normally produced in the same cell. In the assessment of the plurihormonality of an adenoma, stringent laboratory methods are essential to avoid spurious labeling caused by cross-reactivity. Nonetheless, there remains a small group of adenomas that cosecrete GH, TSH,[109] alpha-subunit, and any combination of LH, FSH, alpha-subunit, TSH, GH, and PRL. The hormones produced by these tumors are not always accompanied by corresponding elevation in serum hormone levels. Plurihormonal adenomas tend to be large at presentation and have a more aggressive clinical course.

Null cell adenoma and oncocytoma

These tumors are pituitary adenomas that manifest no clinical or biochemical evidence of hormone production, show no or faint hormonal immunoreactivity, and when examined under the electron microscope, lack features indicative of any of the five known pituitary cells, showing instead a rudimentary Golgi apparatus and rare secretory granules. Most of such tumors are designated null cell adenomas[113] and are found often as slow-growing sellar and parasellar neoplasms affecting elderly individuals (Fig. 29.7) who seek medical attention because of progressive loss of vision and hypopituitarism.

These chromophobe tumors are often focally immunoreactive for FSH, LH, TSH, and alpha-subunit[111] and have been found to contain dopamine receptors[115] and estrogen receptors; ultrastructurally they are nononcocytic (Fig. 29.20). The demonstration of gonadotropin release by null cell adenomas maintained in tissue culture has strengthened the hypothesis that null cell adenomas may have a gonadotrophic lineage.[110]

Adenomas having the same morphologic and immuno-histochemical attributes as null cell adenomas with added oncocytic change (Fig. 29.13C and D) affecting more than 50% of cells have been designated pituitary oncocytomas.[112] When viewed under the electron microscope, mitochondria are found to occupy up to 50% of the cytoplasmic area[114] (Fig. 29.21). These adenomas most likely represent a heterogeneous group, but many, if not most, are transformed null cell adenomas.

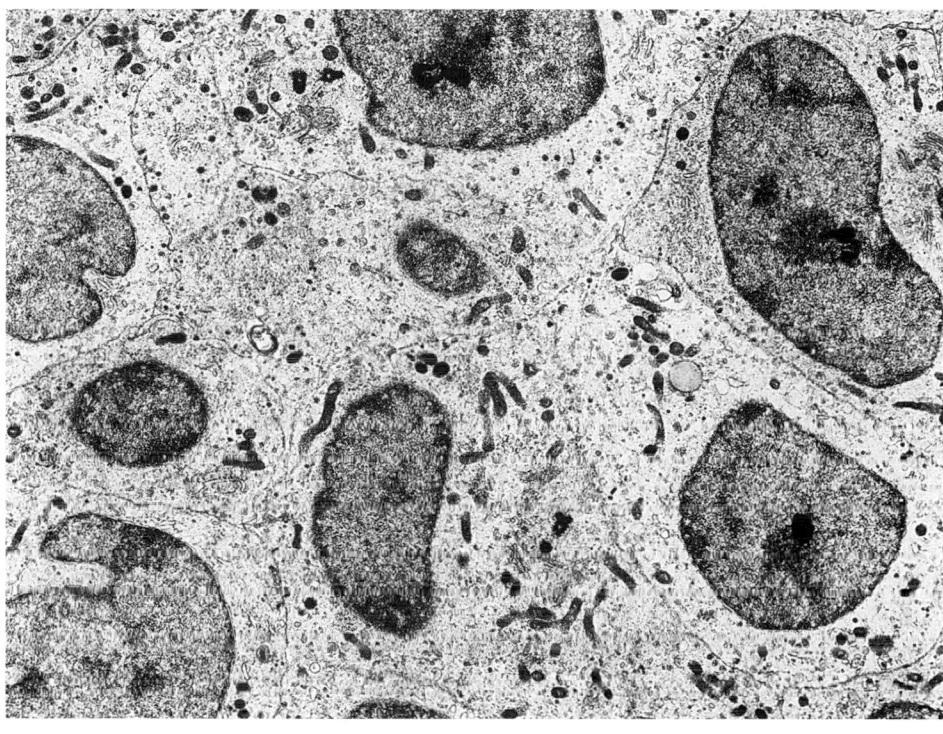

Fig. 29.20 Cytoplasm of null cell adenoma cells contains scanty organelles and small secretory granules. (Electron micrograph, ×5400) (Courtesy of Dr. E Horvath, Toronto.)

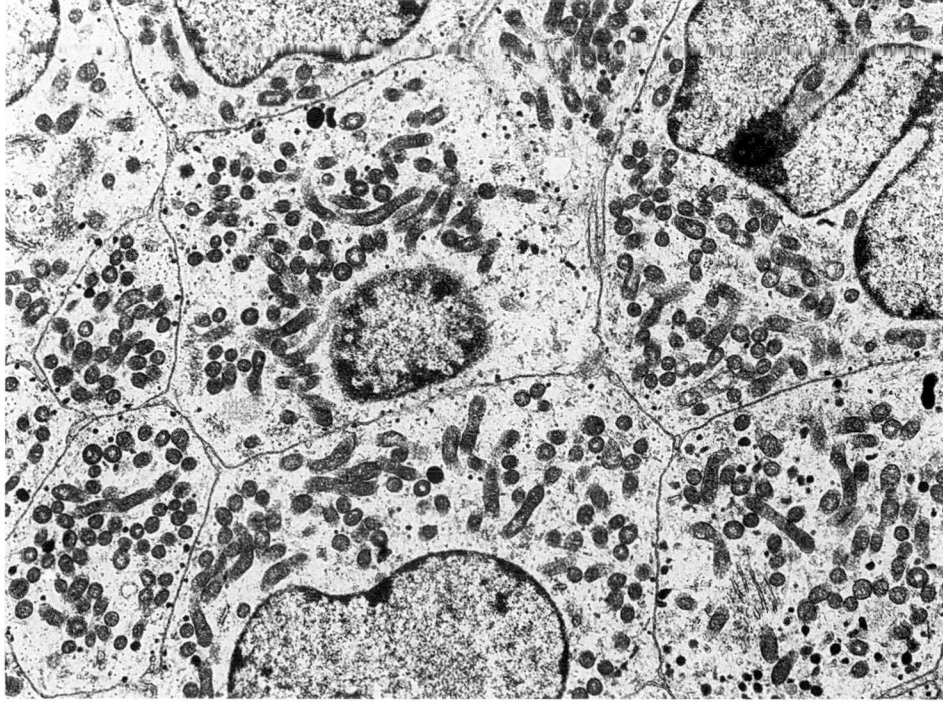

Fig. 29.21 Large numbers of mitochondria and paucity of secretory granules are typical of oncocytoma. (Electron micrograph, ×6000. Courtesy of Dr. E Horvath, Toronto.)

Natural history, spread, and metastases

Pituitary apoplexy is a rare complication of adenomas.[116] It represents a spontaneous massive hemorrhagic infarct within a large tumor and is most often seen in nonfunctioning adenomas and in tumors producing ACTH. Pituitary apoplexy often presents as a neurosurgical emergency because of the rapid expansion of the mass upward with compression of anterior hypothalamic area (Fig. 29.22). Bromocriptine treatment may induce the development of pituitary apoplexy in some patients.[120]

In many pituitary tumors, actual invasion of neighboring structures is encountered; these structures may include: the brain; anterior, middle, or posterior fossa; cavernous sinus and dura mater; optic nerve; chiasm; sphenoid bone; nasopharynx; and nasal cavity. These tumors should be designated as invasive adenomas and not as carcinomas. Exceptionally, pituitary neoplasms are found to implant along the subarachnoid space[117,119] and even to metastasize distantly, to the liver, bone, or other organs. In the case of hematogenous metastasis, tumor permeation into the cavernous sinus provides a venous access to the internal jugular vein via the petrosal system.[121] This phenomenon has been reported with nonfunctioning tumors, as well as with neoplasms associated with Nelson's syndrome, acromegaly, and hyperprolactinemia. The behavior of pituitary carcinomas suggests that some tumors result from malignant transformation in a preexisting benign tumor, whereas others represent de novo malignancy.[118] As in most other endocrine tumors, the correlation between microscopic appearance and biologic behavior is poor. Some of the invasive or metastasizing neoplasms have an obviously malignant cytologic appearance, but the majority do not appreciably differ from the ordinary pituitary adenoma.

Evaluation of cell-proliferation markers such as MIB-1 or immunoreactivity for p53, the mutated form of a tumor-suppressor gene product, may provide useful information in the assessment of biologic behavior of adenomas.[122] Death from pituitary carcinoma is usually caused by extensive intracranial disease.

Treatment

The therapeutic approach to pituitary adenomas varies in different clinics. Both surgical excision and radiation therapy can be used. The choice of therapy sometimes depends on the patient's age, on clinical circumstances, and on the evaluation of postradiation risk of development of malignant bony tumors and hypopituitarism. Radiation results in fibrosis and sometimes cavitation of the adenoma. Transsphenoidal surgery is established as a procedure of low morbidity and mortality.[125,126] A valuable form of therapy, used successfully in cases of adenomas of PRL type, consists of the administration of bromocriptine, a dopamine agonist.[124,128] This results in shrinkage and fibrosis of the mass, recovery of visual field defect, and normalization of the PRL blood level. Clinical symptoms disappear with fertility being restored; this is a reversible effect.

Although no significant shrinkage of the mass has been shown to occur, the long-acting somatostatin analog octreotide has been used with good results in the treatment of patients with acromegaly and pituitary adenomas.[123,124] It is not, however, currently viewed as an alternative to surgery in most patients, but rather as adjuvant therapy.[126] Preoperative treatment with octreotide may prove to be useful in facilitating tumor removal. Refractory acromegaly after surgery can be effectively treated with radiotherapy.[127]

Other lesions

Gangliocytoma

Gangliocytomas are rare hypothalamic and/or intrasellar tumors composed of large mature nerve cells with a glial stroma.[130,133,135] These lesions exhibit progressive growth, and a number of them are part of a mixed adenoma-gangliocytoma (Fig. 29.23) causing acromegaly[131,136,137] and less often Cushing's disease.[129,138,143] The nerve cells that have morphologic characteristics of hypothalamic elements have been shown to contain not only pituitary hormones and other peptides, but also releasing factors such as GHRH and GnRH.[144] Two theories have been suggested concerning the pathogenesis of adenoma-gangliocytoma: (i) Neurons having a hypothalamic phenotype stimulate GH cells, resulting in adenoma formation; and (ii) neuron-like cells may represent transformed adenoma cells.

Gangliocytoma should be differentiated from the neuronal hypothalamic hamartoma,[139,140] usually seen in

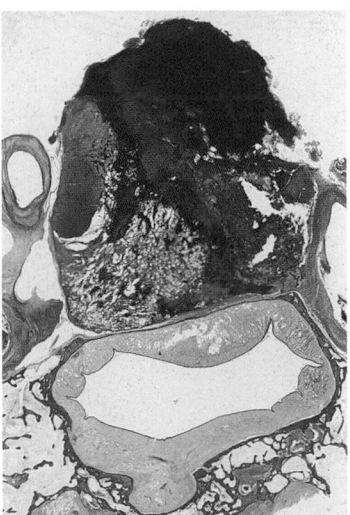

Fig. 29.22 Pituitary apoplexy in 76-year-old man with null cell adenoma. Coronal section of sella and cavernous sinuses showing large intratumoral hemorrhage and necrosis with suprasellar extension.

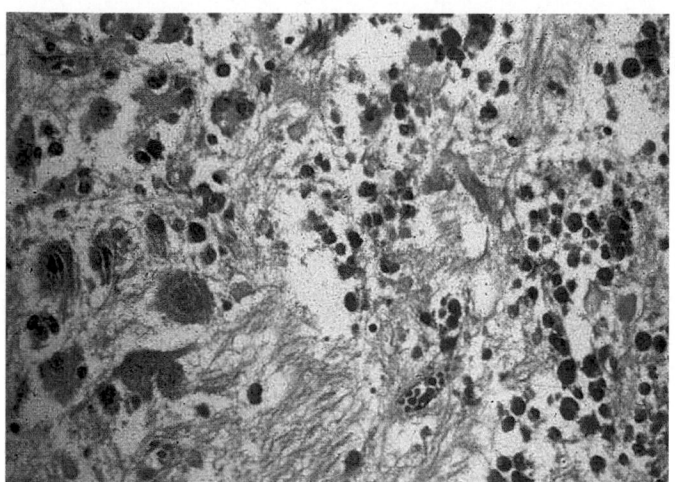

Fig. 29.23 Intrasellar mixed gangliocytoma-adenoma. Large neurons (left) with glial stroma in tumor and adjacent adenoma cells (right). (H&E.) (Courtesy of Dr. K Kovacs, Toronto.)

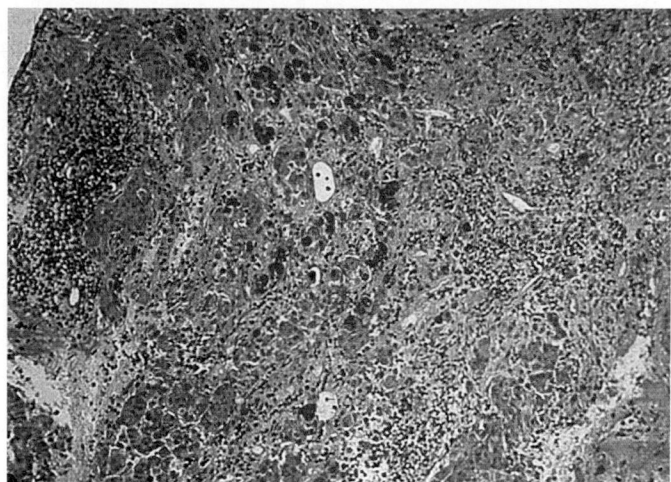

Fig. 29.24 Lymphocytic hypophysitis. Note disorganization of normal histology caused by infiltration of lymphocytes and plasma cells. (Courtesy of Dr. K Kovacs, Toronto.)

children with the syndrome of precocious puberty[134] and gelastic seizures.[132,142] Histologically, this lesion is composed of a mixture of mature neurons, astrocytes, and oligodendrocytes arranged with a varying degree of organization.

Hypothalamic tumors containing immature neurons are designated hamartoblastomas. The constellation of hypothalamic hamartoblastoma with craniofacial anomalies, limb anomalies, and imperforate anus along with hypopituitarism secondary to pituitary dysplasia constitutes the Pallister–Hall syndrome.[141]

Lymphocytic hypophysitis

Lymphocytic adenohypophysitis is a rare autoimmune endocrine disease[153] with only about 50 reported cases.[149,148,154] Women in late pregnancy or the immediate postpartum period are primarily affected. The occurrence of this syndrome is rare in males.[149] Patients may present with symptoms of an expanding pituitary mass[151] and/or varying degrees of pituitary dysfunction. Regardless of the form of presentation, most patients will have evidence of partial hypopituitarism or panhypopituitarism at some time during the course of the disease before surgical intervention. About one third of patients develop visual field defects.

Magnetic resonance imaging discloses enlargement of the pituitary fossa with suprasellar extension in most cases.[152] In the initial stages, the pituitary has a firm, tough appearance, very different from that of an adenoma. The salient histologic picture is a polymorphic lymphoplasmacytic infiltration associated with destruction of the anterior pituitary cells[145] (Fig. 29.24). In rare instances, lymphoid follicles with germinal centers are formed.[147] The later stages of the disease are characterized by fibrosis, parenchymal atrophy, and residual lymphocytic aggregates. Electron microscopy has shown inter-

digitation of mononuclear cells with adenohypophysial cells.[145] Antibodies to pituitary cell have been detected in some cases, and about one third of the patients had other endocrine or immune diseases or chronic lymphocytic infiltration of other endocrine organs at autopsy.

Corticosteroid therapy may be beneficial, with full endocrinologic recovery well documented in one patient.[147,150] Some cases may require surgical decompression and replacement therapy for residual hypopituitarism.[145,146] Indirect evidence suggests spontaneous resolution in some cases.

Rathke's cleft cyst

Cysts of the hypophysial cleft, arising from the remnants of Rathke's pouch, are usually incidental post mortem findings within the pituitary gland.[158,162] On occasion they reach a large size (Fig. 29.25A) and may exhibit suprasellar extension. Thus they become clinically apparent with compression of the hypothalamus and optic chiasm.[159] Some purely suprasellar cases have been described.[155] In a review of symptomatic cases, the presenting symptoms included visual disturbances, diabetes insipidus, hypopituitarism, and hydrocephalus.[163,164] Some cases are associated with septic meningitis.[161] The smaller cyst can be found in up to 20% of pituitaries obtained at autopsy. They usually measure less that 5 mm in diameter.

Histologically, the cysts are lined by predominantly columnar ciliated cells (Fig. 29.25B), rare goblet cells, and adenohypophysial cells. Foci of squamous differentiation are also demonstrable. Lining cells exhibit strong immunopositivity for low-molecular-weight keratin and focal immunoreaction for S-100 protein. Rare cells may immunoreact for GFAP and vimentin. Evidence of old hemorrhage may be seen in up to 40% of cases.[159] Confusion with craniopharyngioma is possible because

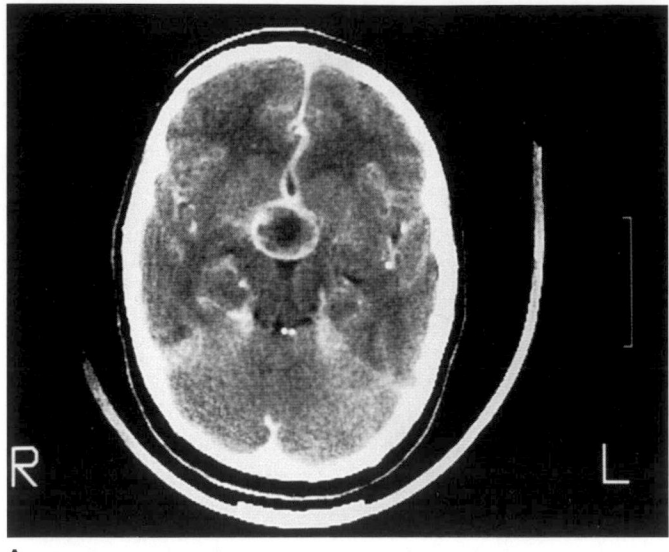

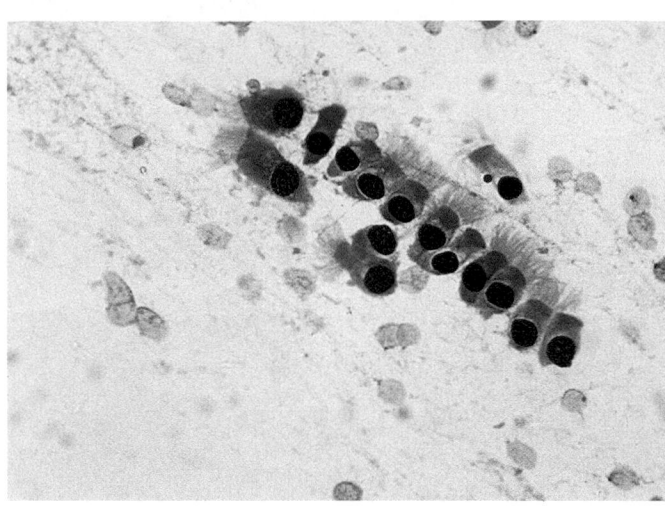

Fig. 29.25 Intrasellar Rathke's cleft cyst within the pituitary gland. **A**, The unilocular lesion on imaging. **B**, Ciliated cells are readily demonstrable on a needle aspirate. (H&E.)

of a calcified rim in some Rathke's pouch cysts. Magnetic resonance imaging has a high sensitivity in disclosing the lesion.[159] The cyst content has a high T1- and T2-weighted image on magnetic resonance imaging.[157,165] Association with pituitary adenoma has been reported (Fig. 29.26).[160] Surgical drainage and excision is the treatment of choice; recurrence is unusual.[156,159]

Craniopharyngioma

Most patients with craniopharyngioma are in the first or second decades of life,[175] although some are in their seventies and eighties.[178] The tumor has also been reported in fetuses and newborns.[167,176] Its location is usually suprasellar, although it may occupy the sella as well (Figs 29.27 and 29.29A). It may develop dorsal or ventral

to the optic chiasm and, in rare cases, within the chiasm itself.[170,171] Occasional cases located within the third ventricle have been reported.[177] The tumor may achieve giant proportions, growing in the parasellar region and into brain.[187] Craniopharyngiomas can be implanted in other areas of the brain by repeated needle aspiration.[168] Craniopharyngioma constitutes about 3% of all brain tumors.[181]

Cystic degeneration is an extremely common finding, the content of the cyst being a viscous fluid resembling "machinery oil" sparkling with cholesterol crystals (Fig. 29.28). Focal calcification is almost invariably present. In about 75% of the cases, it is prominent enough to be detectable by X-ray studies. The microscopic appearance resembles that of ameloblastoma of the jaws.

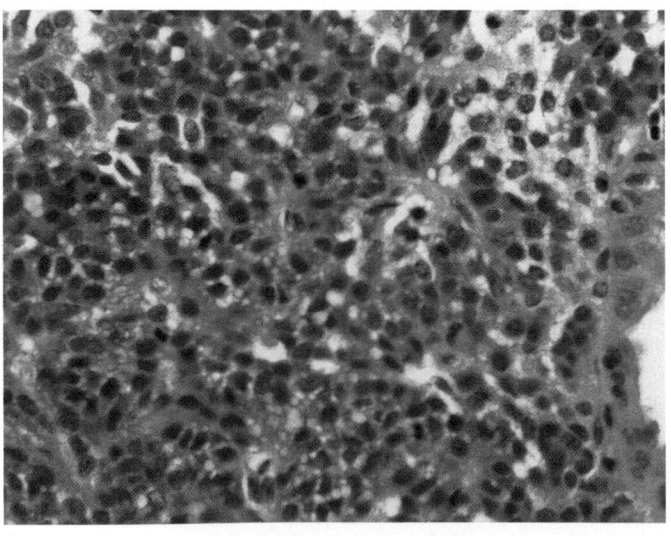

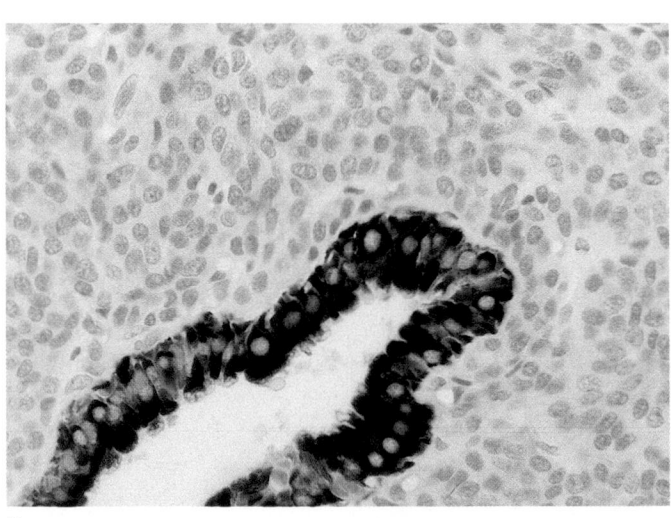

Fig. 29.26 Mixed Rathke's cleft cyst and null cell adenoma. **A**, H&E. **B**, Cytokeratin immunolabeling cyst lining but not the tumor.

Anastomosing epithelial islands with a palisaded layer of cells and a center of stellate cells are characteristic (Fig. 29.29B). Foci of squamous metaplasia with solid nests of keratinization (Fig. 29.29C), degenerative changes, calcification, and a mixed inflammatory reaction that may be granulomatous are often found.

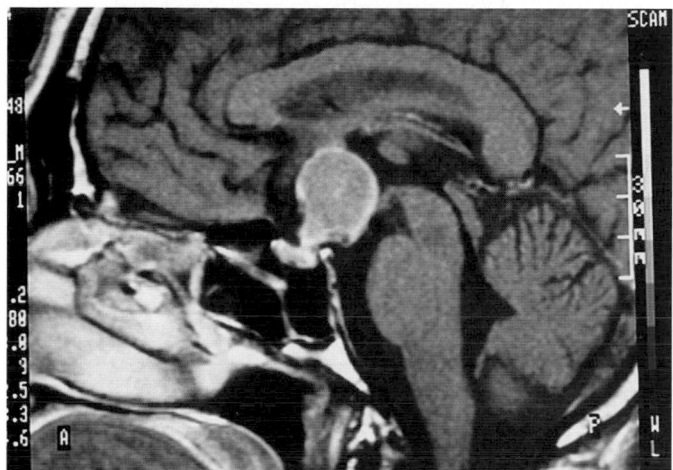

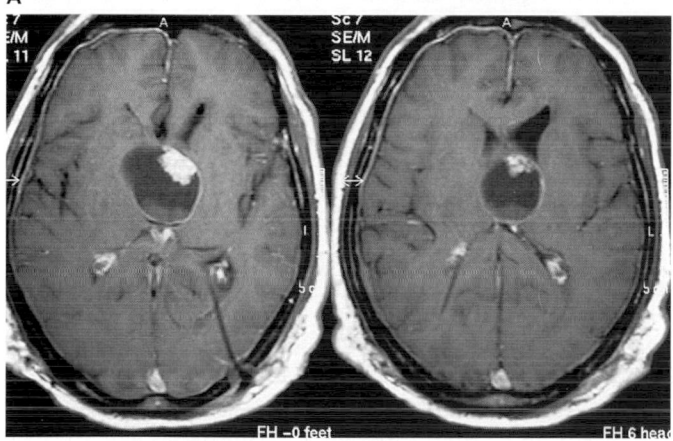

Fig. 29.27 Classic MRI features of craniopharygioma. **A**, Sagittal view of mainly solid component. **B**, Horizontal view of both solid and cystic component.

Fig. 29.28 Craniopharygioma. Cholesterol crystals in the aspirate of cyst content. (Polarized light micrograph.)

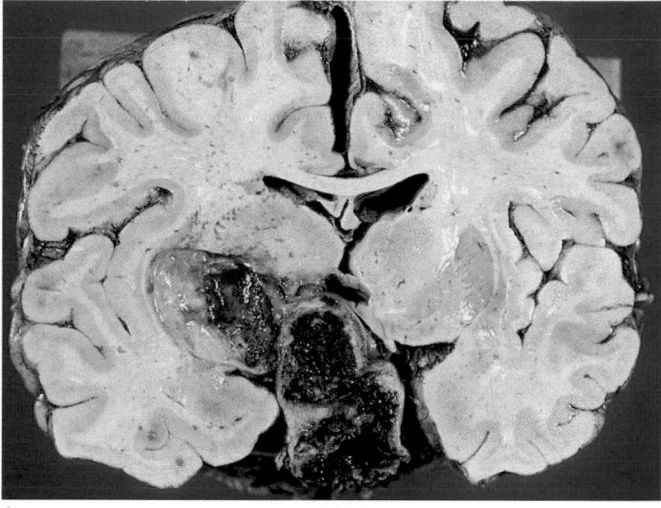

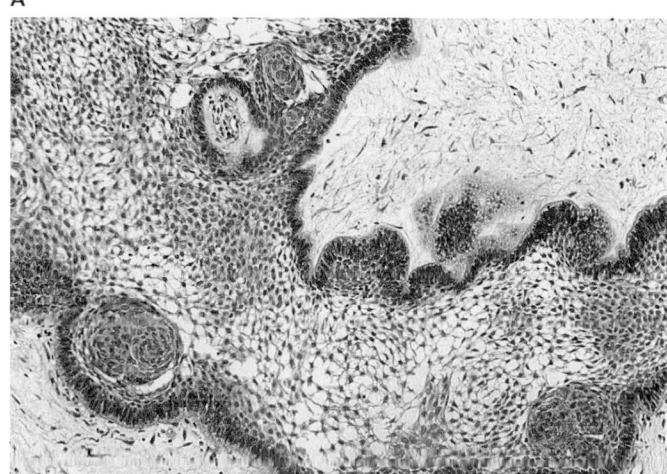

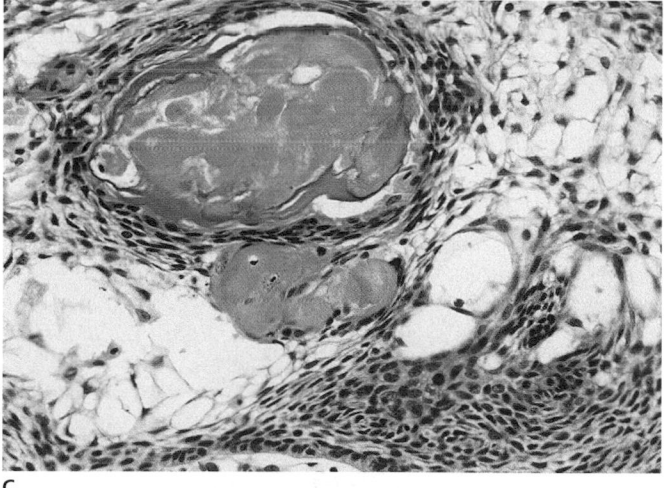

Fig. 29.29 Suprasellar craniopharyngioma in 47-year-old man who had surgery 15 years previously, but tumor could not be excised because of its size. Despite subsequent radiation therapy, progressive tumor growth led to compression of optic chiasm, pituitary gland, and cerebral peduncles. **A**, Note good circumscription of tumor and its variegated appearance. **B** and **C**, Microscopic appearance of craniopharyngioma of suprasellar region. Solid epithelial nests with calcification, keratinization, collections of "shadow cells," and peripheral palisading alternate with cystic areas. (H&E.)

Gliosis with Rosenthal fiber formation in the adjacent brain may be so intense as to be mistaken for a pilocytic astrocytoma. Small epithelial strands trapped in the peripheral reactive glial tissue may result in a mistaken diagnosis of carcinoma. Cystic craniopharyngiomas should also be distinguished from epidermoid and other cysts occurring in this region, although this may prove difficult in a small sample. The most important features that favor a diagnosis of craniopharyngioma are the basal palisading, the absence of keratohyaline granules, the stratified masses of keratin, and the stellate reticulum. Cavitation may develop from dissociation of the stellate cells, from degeneration of the stromal elements, and from accumulation of desquamated debris. The electron microscopic appearance of craniopharyngioma has been described by Ghatak et al.[173]

In about 10% of cases, seen only in adults, the tumor has a macroscopic papillary appearance, lacks calcification and nodules of keratin (Fig. 29.30A), and is composed microscopically of solid, well-differentiated pseudopapillary squamous epithelium with keratinization of individual cells[174] (Fig. 29.30B). Malignant transformation in craniopharyngiomas is a rarity.[180]

Although some microscopic differences exist between craniopharyngioma and ameloblastoma of the jaws, the striking morphologic similarity of craniopharyngioma to another odontogenic lesion, the "calcifying odontogenic cyst of Gorlin,"[171,172] and the finding in several cases of craniopharyngioma of undeniable tooth structures[183] is supportive evidence of a related embryologic origin, the intracranial tumor probably arising from a buccal equivalent of the embryonic enamel organ present in Rathke's pouch. Squamous cell nests found in the pars tuberalis in about 24% of autopsy cases, once thought to be precursors of craniopharyngiomas, are now considered to be unrelated. The simultaneous immunohistochemical demonstration of keratin and pituitary hormones in these squamous cells indicates a metaplastic derivation from adenohypophysial cells.[184]

Symptoms are dominated by those of hydrocephalus, especially in the younger patients, and of pressure on the chiasm and optic tracts. Craniopharyngiomas can also present with signs of dwarfism, hypogonadism, panhypopituitarism, diabetes insipidus, and hyperprolactinemia caused by a compression of the pituitary stalk. The diagnosis is often delayed until visual disturbances occur. Magnetic resonance imaging is thought to be superior to CT scan in outlining the lesion and in distinguishing scarring from recurrent tumor.[182]

Total or subtotal surgical excision, in some cases followed by radiation therapy, is the treatment of choice.[185,186] In one series, most postoperative morbidity and all postoperative mortality occurred after the second and third operations for recurrent tumor. Some authors also achieved good results with stereotactic endocavitary irradiation.[179] Depending on the therapy instituted, recurrence takes place in 20% to 30% of patients. Better results have been reported for the papillary variant of craniopharyngioma.[166] Severe mental retardation may follow radiotherapy in children.

Granular cell tumor and pituicytoma

Granular cell tumors (also known as choristoma of neurohypophysis or granular cell pituicytoma) arising from the stalk or posterior lobe of the pituitary (Fig. 29.31A) usually represent incidental autopsy findings in adults,[194] but in a few cases they have attained sufficient size to produce symptoms of visual impairment requiring surgical intervention.[201,202] Diabetes insipidus was the initial manifestation in one case.[196] Shanklin,[197] in a detailed study of pituitaries obtained post mortem, demonstrated small clusters of granular cells that he

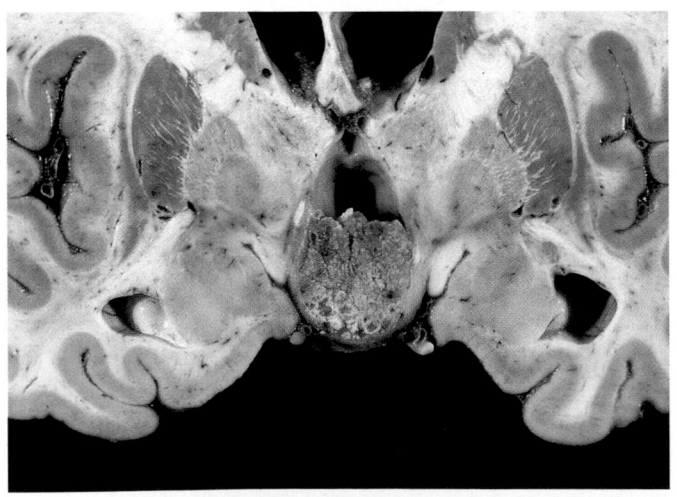

A

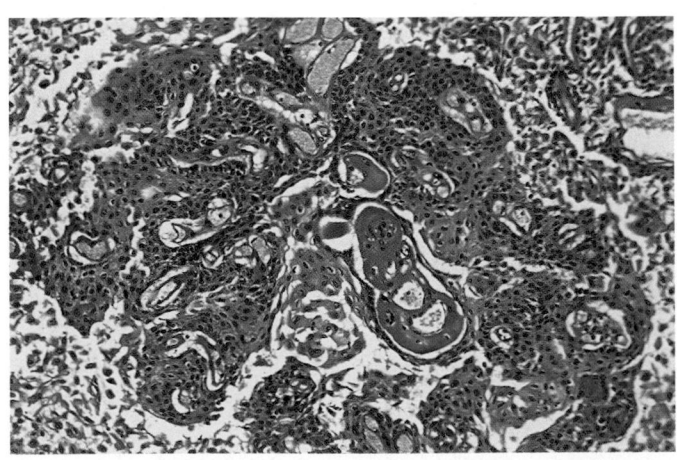

B

Fig. 29.30 Intraventricular craniopharyngioma of papillary type. **A,** Grossly, this tumor is a well-demarcated solid lesion showing no calcification. **B,** Separation and desquamation of the epithelium along artefactual fissures results in pseudopapillary formation in this craniopharyngioma. Note absence of keratin nodules. (H&E.)

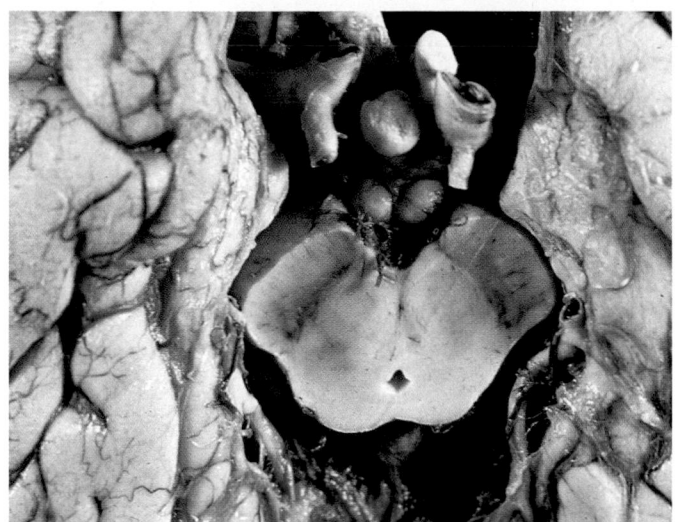
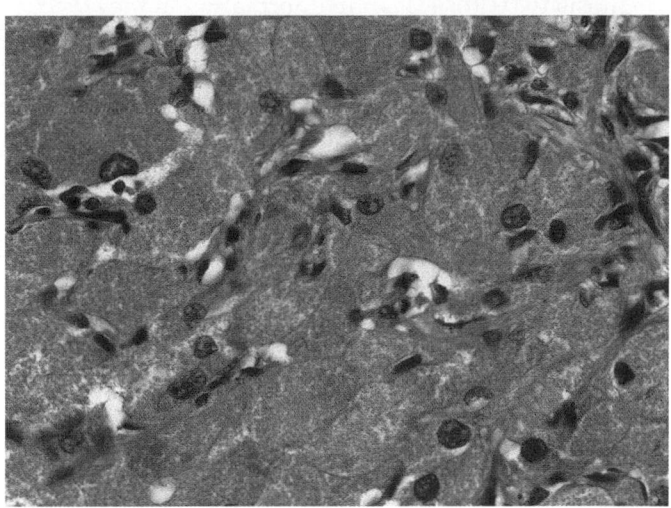

A   B

Fig. 29.31 Granular cell tumor. **A** Grossly, a nodular swelling at the pituitary stalk, anterior to mamillary bodies. **B** Tightly packed polyhedral cells with granular cytoplasm. (H&E.)

designated "tumorettes" in up to 17% of unselected specimens; they were found within the posterior pituitary or in the infundibulum. The absence of these nodules in the first and second decades of life suggests that they are acquired rather than congenital.

The histologic and ultrastructural appearance and histochemical reactions of granular cell tumors of neurohypophysis are similar to those of their more common peripheral counterpart: namely, tightly packed polyhedral cells arranged in sheets or ill-defined lobules. They display an abundant granular cytoplasm (Fig. 29.31B) that is PAS positive–diastase resistant. For some authors the immunophenotype seems to be consistent with Schwannian differentiation.[189] Others have not been able to confirm this finding.[200] Although this lesion is consistently negative when stained for GFAP,[193,200] Nishioka[195] has provided immunohistochemical evidence in support of the hypothesis that granular cell tumors of the neurohypophysis may originate from granular pituicytes, modified glial cells.

The association of granular cell tumors of the pituitary with pituitary adenomas[198] and multiple endocrine neoplasia[199] must be interpreted as fortuitous rather than evidence for a common precursor cell. Hypothalamic granular cell tumors should be differentiated from similar tumors in the cerebral hemispheres where an astrocytic differentiation can be demonstrated by immunohistochemistry.[190] Of the symptomatic cases reported in the literature, most present in the fifth decade and affect females predominantly.[192,201]

The other rare tumor of the neurohypophysis and pituitary stalk is the pituicytoma which presumably arises from the pituicyte, a specialized glial cell found in posterior pituitary. The tumor presents as a suprasellar or sellar mass with symptoms of headache, hypopituitarism, or visual field defect. Histologically, this is a solid tumor composed of spindle cells with round to elongated nuclei forming either interlacing or storiform pattern.[188,191] There is a rich capillary network within the tumor. Mitotic activity is low and invasion into adjacent tissue is rare. This tumor consistently expresses vimentin and S-100, whereas EMA, synaptophysin, and chromogranin are absent. Although, it is considered to be a type of low-grade glioma, the expression of GFAP is not consistent, ranging from diffuse to focal and virtually absent.[188] The ultrastructural features consist of intermediate filaments, mitochondria, and junctional complexes in tumor cells, and basal lamina surrounding tumor cells and blood vessel.[191] Tumor recurrence is rare after total resection and metastasis has not been reported so far. This tumor is distinguished from granular cell tumor by its lack of cytoplasmic PAS staining and from pilocytic astrocytoma by absence of microcytic changes, piloid processes, Rosenthal fibers, and granular bodies.[192]

Postradiation tumors

Malignant gliomas in the parasellar area have been reported following radiotherapy for pituitary adenoma, craniopharyngioma, suprasellar germinoma, and acute lymphoblastic leukemia.[205,207–215,219,220] Except for a single oligodendroglioma, most cases described are astrocytomas.[206] The latency period ranges from 5 to 25 years, and the radiation doses range from 42.5 to 66 Gy. Osteosarcoma and fibrosarcoma of the sphenoid bone and skull have been described following radiotherapy for pituitary adenoma and craniopharyngioma.[203,204,212,218] Postirradiation malignant gliomas are aggressive, with most patients dying within a few months after histologic diagnosis. Meningiomas have rarely been reported following irradiation for pituitary adenoma and craniopharyngioma.[216,217]

Metastatic tumors

Autopsy data indicate that metastasis to the pituitary is not rare; the prevalence is 3% to 5%.[224,226,227] Metastatic carcinoma is more common in the neurohypophysis[222] (Fig. 29.32), with many patients displaying diabetes insipidus.[225] Carcinoma of the breast, lung, or GI tract is the most frequent primary lesion.[221,223,230] Occasionally, no primary tumor can be identified, even at autopsy.

Most pituitary metastases are asymptomatic and constitute incidental findings at autopsy in patients with widespread cancer.[229] However, nine of 14 patients in one series presented with symptomatic pituitary metastasis with no prior history of malignancy.[221] Metastatic carcinoma to pituitary adenoma has also been reported.[228]

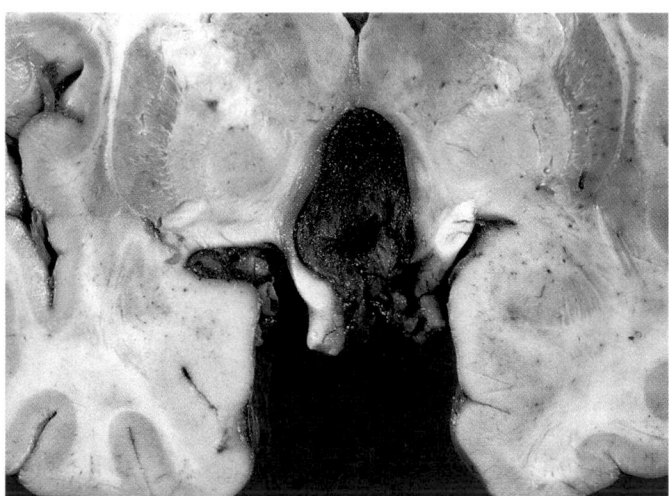

A

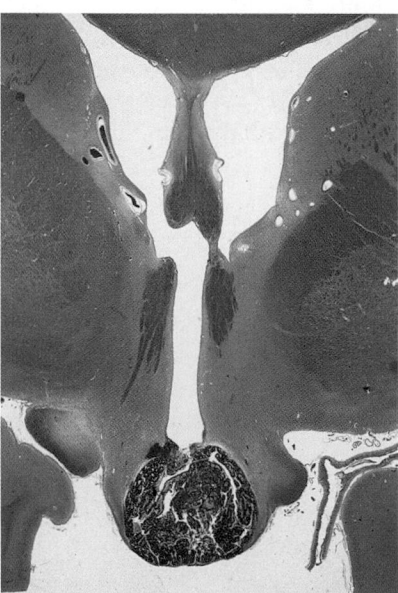

B

Fig. 29.32 Metastatic malignant carcinoid to posterior pituitary gland extending into hypothalamus. **A**, Gross appearance. **B**, Whole mount.

Miscellaneous lesions

Although involvement of the hypothalamic–pituitary axis in disseminated Langerhans' cell histiocytosis is not uncommon (Fig. 29.33),[245,265] isolated lesions are extremely rare and probably analogous to Gagel's hypothalamic granuloma and Ayala's disease.[253,264]

In about half the cases of adult acute lymphoblastic leukemia, periglandular (subcapsular) pituitary infiltration is demonstrable.[257] However, true intraparenchymal deposits are a rarity. Massive leukemic infiltrate of the sella mimicking pituitary adenoma has been reported in chronic lymphocytic leukemia.[263] When lymphoma, primary CNS or secondary, involves the anterior hypothalamus and pituitary stalk, evidence of hypopituitarism and chiasmal syndrome may develop (Fig. 29.34).[244,259]

Plasmacytoma may develop in the area of the sphenoid bone and thus mimic pituitary adenoma.[243] Most of the patients reported eventually developed multiple myeloma. Ultrastructural and immunohistochemical studies are essential in differentiating plasmacytoma from plasma cell granuloma (inflammatory pseudotumor),[248] which is assumed to be a reactive lesion composed of a mixed inflammatory infiltrate.

Other tumors of bone that may arise at the base of the skull involving the sellar and parasellar region are giant cell tumors,[287] chondromyxoid fibroma,[284] chordoma (Fig. 29.35),[234,258] (en)chondroma,[231,260] and chondrosarcoma (Fig. 29.36).[281] Even a bony spur may become significant when located in the sella.[269]

Schwannomas have been reported in both the intrasellar compartment and the parasellar region.[251,268,285] Most uncommon are hemangioblastoma,[240] hemangiopericytoma,[256] hemangioma (cavernous) (Fig. 29.37),[238,276] glomangioma,[232] paraganglioma,[235,282] neurocytoma,[255] primary melanoma,[239,262,279] ectopic salivary gland tissue in the pituitary gland,[278] primary sellar thyroid follicular tumor,[274] and sphenoid sinus mucocele presenting as pituitary adenoma.[249]

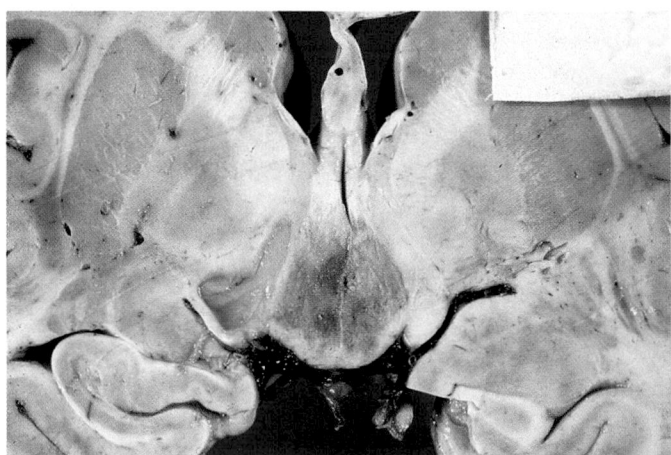

Fig. 29.33 Gross appearance of Langerhans' cell histiocytosis involving the hypothalamus.

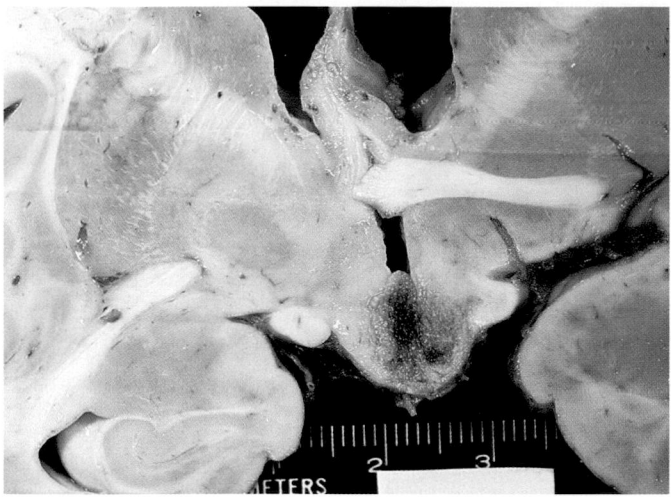

Fig. 29.34 Gross appearance of systemic lymphoma with secondary involvement of hypothalamus.

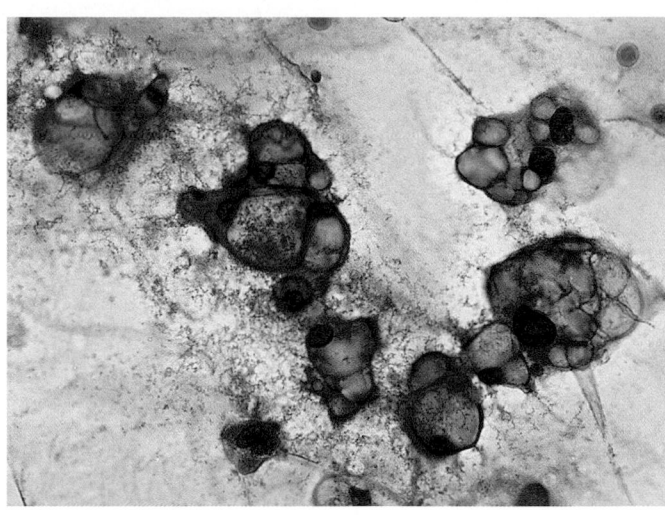

Fig. 29.35 Chordoma. An imprint smear preparation showing classic physaliferous cells in parasellar chordoma. (H&E.)

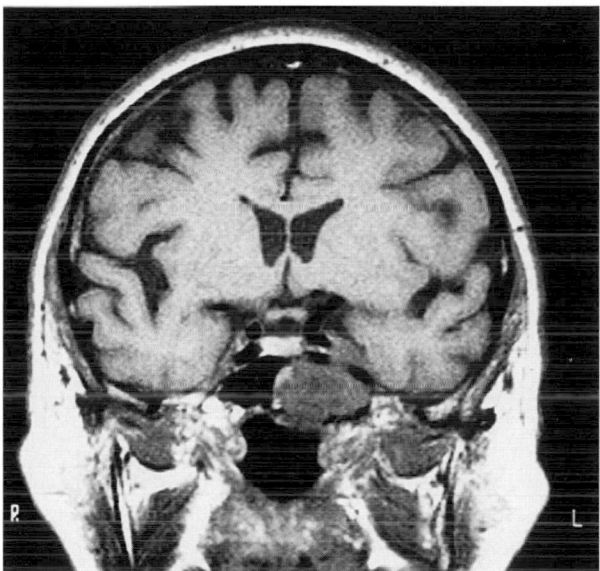

A

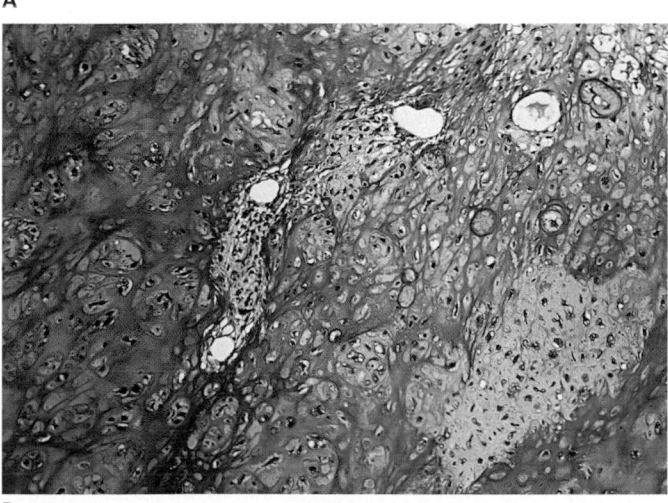

B

Fig. 29.36 Chondrosarcoma. **A**, MRI shows an off-midline suprasellar mass. **B**, Microscopic appearance of atypical chondrocytes. (H&E.)

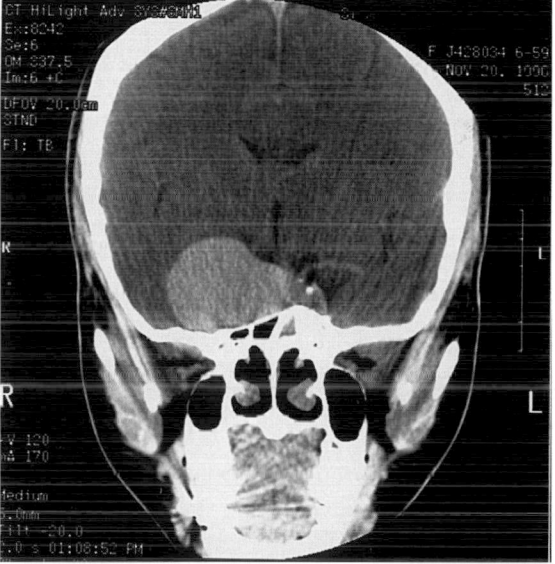

A

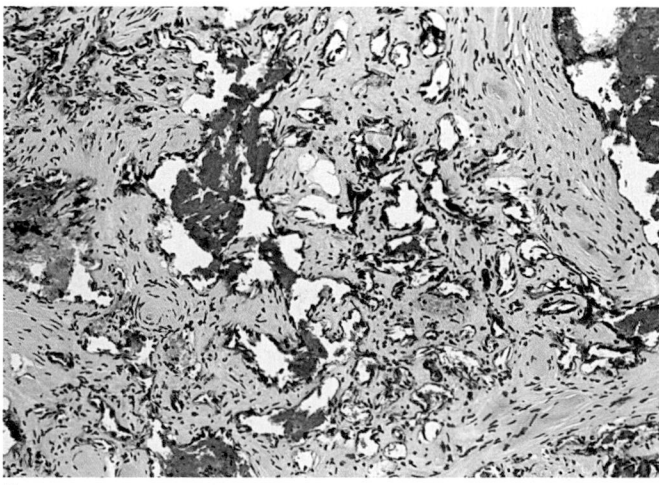

B

Fig. 29.37 Cavernous hemangioma. **A**, CT scan shows suprasellar mass. **B**, Thin-walled vascular channels are highlighted by CD31 immunohistochemistry in a sclerotic stroma.

Purely intrasellar meningiomas are a rarity[252]; more often the pituitary gland is involved by extension of a suprasellar meningioma (Fig. 29.38).[254,272] Also uncommon are gliomas infiltrating the pituitary gland or the sella turcica.[286] Radiologically and clinically they mimic adenomas.[273] The recently described chordoid glioma of the third ventricle can also present as a suprasellar mass.[271] This tumor is characterized by cords and lobules of epithelioid cells with eosinophilic cytoplasm embedded in a rich mucinous extracellular matrix (Fig. 29.39). Usually, a prominent lymphoplasmacytic infiltrate is noted. There is strong GFAP, CD34, and vimentin expression, and focal S-100 and EMA immunoreactivity.[236] The electron microscopy confirms its glial nature with cytoplasm filled with intermediate filaments and recent works suggest an ependymal origin for this tumor.[268] Even though, histologically it is a low-grade neoplasm, its location near the hypothalamus makes complete resection extremely difficult and tumor recurrence a distinct possibility.[236]

Germ cell tumors account for 0.3% to 0.7% of intracranial tumors,[275] and the most commonly involved sites are the epithalamus and the parasellar area (Fig. 29.40). Three reports describe the distinctly uncommon situation of a germ cell tumor limited to the pituitary fossa.[247,250,270] Morphologically, these neoplasms are indistinguishable from their gonadal and extragonadal counterparts, with germinomas predominating.

Sarcoidosis may involve the cranial and spinal leptomeninges throughout and the parasellar area affecting the anterior hypothalamus, resulting in hypopituitarism.[237,261,280,283] Furthermore, both the anterior and posterior lobes of the pituitary may be affected in this condition, leading to a complex pattern of endocrine disturbance.

In some patients well-formed non-necrotizing granulomas without a lymphocytic component remain confined to the region. Giant cell granulomatous hypophysitis is considered by some to be a distinct clinicopathologic entity.[233,277,288] In another form of hypophysitis known as xanthomatous hypophysitis, the anterior pituitary is heavily infiltrated by granular to foamy histiocytes which are immunoreactive for CD68, and immunonegative for S-100 and CD1a (Fig. 29.41).[242,246] Its presentation is quite variable and the majority of patients described in the literature are females. Like the granulomatous hypophysitis, the diagnosis of xanthomatous hypophysitis is made after the presence of acid-fast bacilli, spirochetes, other bacteria and fungi has been excluded. Isolated reports document intrasellar cysticercosis[241] and hydatid cyst.[266]

Acknowledgments

The authors are indebted to Dr Kalman Kovacs (Toronto) for his invaluable contribution to this chapter, and grateful to Beverley Young and Kris Milne for their assistance in the preparation of the manuscript and photographs.

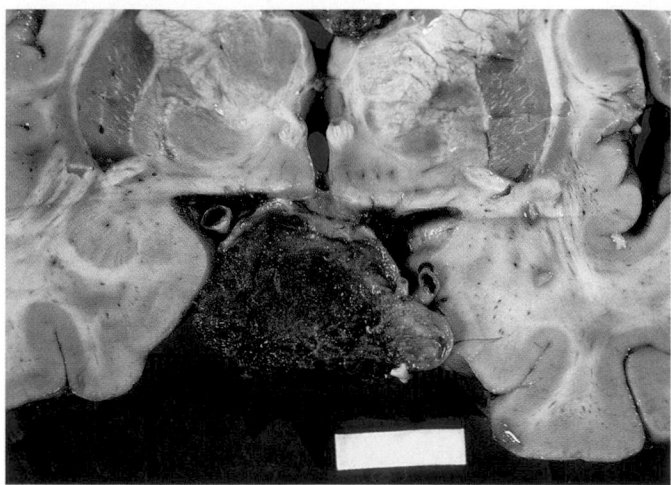

Fig. 29.38 Meningioma involving the parasellar and suprasellar region with compression of hypothalamus.

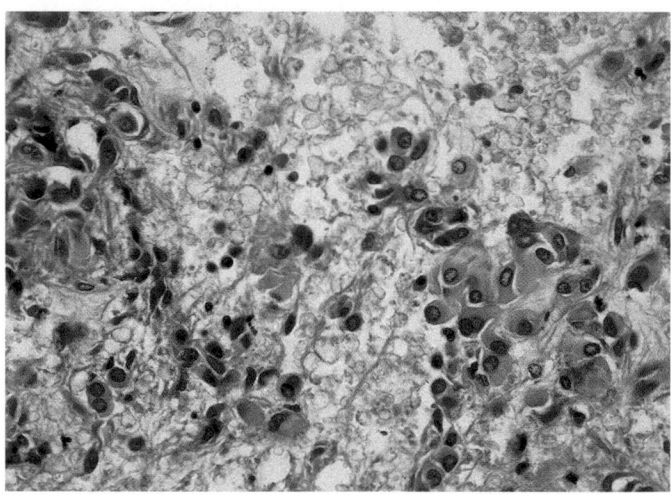

Fig. 29.39 Chordoid glioma. Neoplastic glial cells arranged in chordoid configuration within a rich mucinous extracellular matrix. (H&E.)

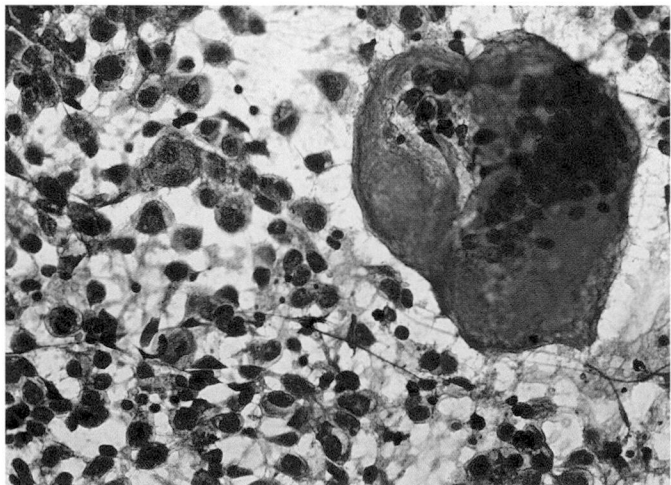

Fig. 29.40 Suprasellar germinoma. An imprint smear showing a multinucleated giant cell, not uncommon in such a tumor of this location. (H&E.)

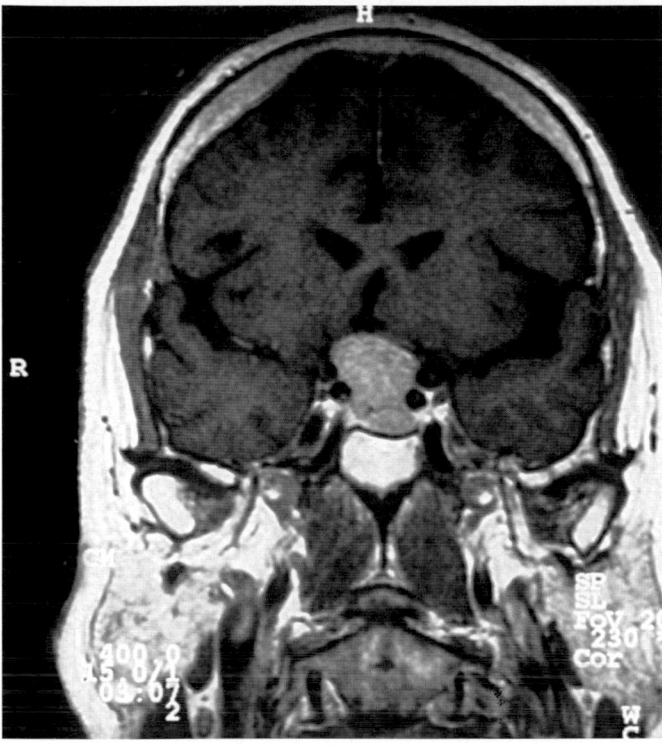

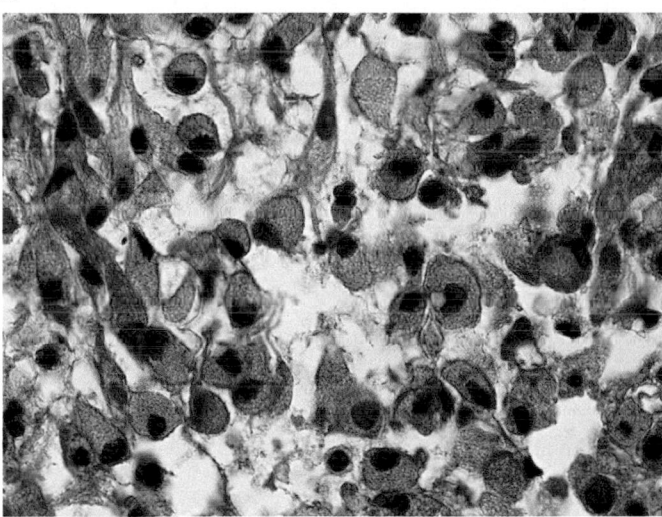

Fig. 29.41 Xanthomatous hypophysitis. **A,** An MRI shows suprasellar mass. **B,** The infiltrate consists of a monomorphous population of foamy histiocyte. (H&E.)

REFERENCES

Normal anatomy

1 Asa SL, Kovacs K, Bilbao JM. The pars tuberalis of the human pituitary. A histologic, immunohistochemical, ultrastructural, and immunoelectron microscopic analysis. Virchows Arch A Pathol Anat Histopathol 1983, **399:** 49–59.

2 Horvath E, Kovacs K. Fine structural cytology of the adenohypophysis in rat and man. J Electron Microsc Technol 1989, **8:** 401–432.

3 Horvath E. The adenohypophysis. In Kovacs K (ed): Functional Endocrine Pathology. Boston, 1991, Blackwell, pp. 245–281.

4 Lloyd RV, D'Amato CJ, Thiny MT, Jin L, Hicks SP, Chandler WF. Corticotroph (basophil) invasion of the pars nervosa in the human pituitary. Localization of proopiomelanocortin peptides, galanin, and peptidylglycine alpha-amidating monoxygenase-like immunoreactivities. Endocr Pathol 1993, **4:** 86–94.

5 Luse SA, Kernohan JW. Granular-cell tumors of the stalk and posterior lobe of the pituitary gland. Cancer 1955, **8:** 616–622.

6 Luse SA, Kernohan JW. Squamous nests of the pituitary gland. Cancer 1955, **8:** 616–622.

7 Nishioka H, Llena JF, Hirano A. Immunohistochemical study of folliculo-stellate cells in pituitary lesions. Endocr Pathol 1991, **2:** 155–160.

8 Pelletier G, Robert F, Hardy J. Identification of human anterior pituitary cells by immunoelectron microscopy. J Clin Endocrinol Metab 1979, **46:** 534–542.

8a Pernicone PJ, Scheithauer BW, Horvath E, Kovacs K. Pituitary and sellar region. In: Sternberg S (ed.). Histology for Pathologists Lippincott–Raven Publishers 1997, pp. 1053–1074.

9 Schochet SS, McCormick WF, Halmi NS. Salivary gland rests in the human pituitary. Arch Pathol 1974, **98:** 193–200.

Pituitary adenoma
General and clinical features

10 Asa SL, Ezzat S. Pathogenesis of pituitary tumors. Natl Rev Cancer 2002, **2:** 836–849.

11 Bills DC, Meyer FB, Laws ER Jr, Davis DH, Ebersold MJ, Scheithauer BW, Ilstrup DM, Abboud CF. A retrospective analysis of pituitary apoplexy. Neurosurgery 1993, **33:** 602–608.

12 Burrow G, Wortzman G, Rewcastle B, Holgate RC, Kovacs K. Microadenomas of the pituitary and abnormal sellar tomograms in an unselected autopsy series. N Engl J Med 1981, **304:** 156–158.

13 Colohan ART, Grady MS, Bonnin JM, Thorner MO, Kovacs K, Jane JA. Ectopic pituitary gland simulating a suprasellar tumor. Neurosurgery 1987, **20:** 43–48.

14 Hardy J, Vezina JL. Transsphenoidal neurosurgery of intracranial neoplasms. In Thompson RA, Green JR (eds): Advances in Neurology. New York, 1976, Raven Press, pp. 261–274.

15 Kane LA, Leinung MC, Scheithauer BW, Groover RV, Rini JN, Bergstralh EJ, Laws ER Jr, Kovacs K, Horvath E, Zimmerman D. Pituitary adenomas in childhood and adolescence. A clinicopathologic study of the Mayo Clinic experience. Endocr Pathol 1992, **3:** 517–518.

16 Kanter SL, Mickle P, Hunter SB, Rhoton AL. Pituitary adenomas in pediatric patients. Are they more invasive? Pediatr Neurosci 1987, **12:** 202–204.

17 Klibanski A, Zervas NT. Diagnosis and management of hormone-secreting pituitary adenomas. New Engl J Med 1991, **324:** 822–831.

18 Lloyd RV, Chandler WF, Kovacs K, Ryan N. Ectopic pituitary adenomas with normal anterior pituitary glands. Am J Surg Pathol 1986, **10:** 546–552.

19 Lyons J, Landis CA, Harsh G, Vallar L, Grunewald K, Feichtinger H, Duh QY, Clark OH, Kawasaki E, Bourne HR. Two G protein oncogenes in human endocrine tumors. Science 1990, **249:** 655–659.

20 McGrath P. Volume and histology of the human pharyngeal hypophysis. Anat NZ J Surg 1967, **37:** 16–27.

21 Mohr G, Hardy J, Comtois R, Beauregard H. Surgical management of giant pituitary adenomas. Can Neurol Sci 1990, **17:** 62–66.

22 Mukai K, Seljeskog L, Dehner LP. Pituitary adenomas in patients under 20 years old. A clinicopathological study of 12 cases. J Neurooncol 1986, **4:** 79–89.

23 Parent AD, Brown B, Smith EE. Incidental pituitary adenomas. A retrospective study. Surgery 1982, **92:** 880–883.

24 Scheithauer BW, Laws ER, Kovacs K, Horvath E, Randall RV,

Carney JA. Pituitary adenomas of the multiple endocrine neoplasia type I syndrome. Semin Diagn Pathol 1987, **4**: 205–211.

25 Thapar K, Kovacs K, Laws ER, Muller P. Pituitary adenomas. Current concepts in classification, histopathology and molecular biology. Endocrinologist 1993, **3**: 39–57.

26 Thapar K, Kovacs K, Muller PJ. Clinical–pathological correlations of pituitary tumours. Bailliere's Clin Endocrin Metab 1995, **9**: 243–270.

27 Zimmerman RA. Imaging of intrasellar, suprasellar and parasellar tumors. Semin Roentgenol 1990, **25**: 174–197.

Gross features

28 Knosp E, Steiner E, Kitz K, Matula C. Pituitary adenomas with invasion of the cavernous sinus space. A magnetic resonance imaging classification compared with surgical findings. Neurosurgery 1993, **33**: 610–618.

29 Kovacs K, Horvath E. Tumors of the pituitary gland. In Atlas of Tumor Pathology, Series 2, vol. 21. Washington, DC, 1986, Armed Forces Institute of Pathology.

Microscopic features

30 Bilbao JM, Horvath E, Hudson AR, Kovacs K. Pituitary adenomas producing amyloid-like substance. Arch Pathol 1975, **99**: 411–415.

31 Hsu DW, Hakim F, Biller BMK, de la Monte S, Zervas NT, Klibanski A, Hedley-White ET. Significance of proliferating cell nuclear antigen index in predicting pituitary adenoma recurrence. J Neurosurg 1993, **78**: 753–761.

32 Landolt AM, Kleihues P, Heitz PU. Amyloid deposits in pituitary adenomas. Arch Pathol Lab Med 1987, **111**: 453–458.

33 Landolt AM, Rothenbuhler V. Pituitary adenoma calcification. Arch Pathol Lab Med 1977, **101**: 22–27.

Classification

34 Black PM, Hsu DW, Klibanski A, Kliman B, Jameson JL, Ridgway EC, Hedley-Whyte ET, Zervas NT. Hormone production in clinically nonfunctioning pituitary adenomas. J Neurosurg 1987, **66**: 244–250.

35 Croue A, Beldent V, Rousselet MC, Guy G, Rohmer V, Bigorgne JC, Saint-Andre JP. Contribution of immunohistochemistry, electron microscopy, and cell culture to the characterization of nonfunctioning pituitary adenomas. A study of 40 cases. Hum Pathol 1992, **23**: 1332–1339.

36 Girod C, Mazzuca M, Trouillas J, et al. Light microscopy, fine structure and immunohistochemistry studies of 278 pituitary adenomas. In Derome PJ, Gedynak CP, Peillon F (eds): Pituitary Adenomas. Paris, 1980, Esdefrios Publishing.

37 Heitz PU, Landolt AM, Zenklusen HR, Kasper M, Reubi JC, Oberholzer M, et al. Immunocytochemistry of pituitary tumors. J Histochem Cytochem 1987, **35**: 1005–1011.

38 Horvath E, Kovacs K. The adenohypophysis. In Kovacs K, Asa SL (eds): Functional Endocrine Pathology. Boston, 1991, Blackwell, pp. 245–281.

39 Kontogeorgos G, Kovacs K, Horvath E, Scheithauer BW. Null cell adenomas, oncocytomas, and gonadotroph adenomas of the human pituitary. An immunocytochemical and ultrastructural analysis of 300 cases. Endocr Pathol 1993, **4**: 20–27.

40 Kontogeorgos G, Scheithauer BW, Horvath E, Kovacs K, Lloyd RV, Smyth HS, Rologis D. Double adenomas of the pituitary. A clinicopathological study of 11 tumors. Neurosurgery 1992, **31**: 840–849.

41 Mukai K. Pituitary adenomas. Immunocytochemical study of 150 tumors with clinicopathologic correlations. Cancer 1983, **52**: 648–653.

42 Saeger W, Gunzl H, Meyer M, et al. Immunohistological studies on clinically silent pituitary adenomas. Endocr Pathol 1990, **1**: 37–44.

43 Stefaneanu L, Kovacs K, Horvath E, Lloyd RV, Buchfelder M, Fahlbusch R, Smyth H. In situ hybridization study of estrogen receptor messenger ribonucleic acid in human adenohypophysial cells and pituitary adenomas. J Clin Endocrinol Metab 1994, **78**: 83–88.

PRL cell adenoma

44 Bilbao JM II, Horvath E, Hudson AR, Kovacs K. Pituitary adenoma producing amyloid-like substance. Arch Pathol 1975, **99**: 411–415.

45 Burrow GN, Wortzman G, Rewcastle NB, Holgate RC, Kovacs K. Microadenomas of the pituitary and abnormal sellar tomograms in an unselected autopsy series. N Engl J Med 1981, **304**: 156–158.

46 Esiri MM, Adams CBT, Burke C, Underdown R. Pituitary adenomas. Immunohistology and ultrastructural analysis of 118 tumors. Acta Neuropathol (Berl) 1983, **62**: 1–14.

47 Horvath E, Kovacs K. The adenohypophysis. In Functional Endocrine Pathology. Boston, 1991, Blackwell, pp. 245–281.

48 Kameya T, Tsumuraya M, Adachi I, Abe K, Ichikizaki K, Toya S, Demura R. Ultrastructure, immunohistochemistry and hormone release of pituitary adenomas in relation to prolactin production. Virchows Arch [A] 1980, **387**: 31–46.

49 Kovacs K, Horvath E. Tumors of the pituitary gland. In Hartmann WH (ed.): Atlas of Tumor Pathology, Series 2, fasc. XXI. Washington, DC, 1986, Armed Forces Institute of Pathology, pp. 1–264.

50 Lees PD, Pickard JD, Chir M. Hyperprolactinemia, intrasellar pituitary tissue pressure, and the pituitary stalk compression syndrome. J Neurosurg 1987, **67**: 192–196.

51 Mukada K, Ohta M, Uozumi T, Arita K, Kurisu K, Inai K. Ossified prolactinoma. Case report. Neurosurgery 1987, **20**: 473–475.

52 Rasmussen C, Larsson SG, Bergh T. The occurrence of macroscopical pituitary calcifications in prolactinomas. Neuroradiology 1990, **31**: 507–511.

53 Saeger W, Mohr K, Caselitz J, Ludecke DK. Light and electron microscopical morphometry of pituitary adenomas in hyperprolactinemia. Pathol Res Pract 1986, **181**: 544–550.

GH cell adenoma

54 Asa SL, Kovacs K. Pituitary pathology in acromegaly. Endocrinol Metab Clin North Am 1992, **21**: 553–574.

55 Furuhata S, Kameya T, Otani M, Toya S. Prolactin presents in all pituitary tumors of acromegalic patients. Hum Pathol 1993, **24**: 10–15.

56 Halmi NS. Occurrence of both growth hormone- and prolactin-immunoreactive material in the cells of human somatotropic pituitary adenomas containing mammotropic elements. Virchows Arch [A] 1982, **398**: 19–31.

57 Kanie N, Kageyama N, Kuwayama A, Nakane T, Watanabe M, Kawea A. Pituitary adenomas in acromegalic patients: an immunohistochemical and endocrinological study with special reference to prolactin-secreting adenoma. J Clin Endocrinol Metab 1983, **57**: 1093–1101.

58 Klibanski A, Zeras NT, Kovacs K, Ridgway EC. Clinically silent hypersecretion of growth hormone in patients with pituitary tumors. J Neurosurg 1987, **66**: 806–811.

59 Kovacs K. Pathology of growth hormone excess. Pathol Res Pract 1988, **183**: 565–568.

60 Kovacs K, Horvath E. Pathology of growth hormone-producing tumors of the human pituitary. Semin Diagn Pathol 1986, **3**: 18–33.

61 Mori H, Mori S, Saitoh Y, Moriwaki K, Iida S, Matsumoto K. Growth hormone-producing pituitary adenoma with crystal-like amyloid immunohistochemically positive for growth hormone. Cancer 1985, **55**: 96–102.

62 Neumann PE, Goldman JE, Horoupian DS, Hess MA. Fibrous

bodies in growth hormone-secreting adenomas contain cytokeratin filaments. Arch Pathol Lab Med 1985, **109:** 505–508.

63 Robert F. Electron microscopy of pituitary tumors. In Tindall GT, Collins WF (eds): Clinical Management of Pituitary Disorders. New York, 1979, Raven Press, pp. 113–131.

64 Saeger W. Pathology of the pituitary gland. In Belchetz PE (ed.): Management of Pituitary Disease. London, 1984, Chapman & Hall, pp. 253–289.

65 Saeger W, Rubenach-Gerz K, Caselitz J, Ludecke DK. Electron microscopical morphometry of GH producing pituitary adenomas in comparison with normal GH cells. Virchows Arch [A] 1987, **411:** 467–472.

66 Trouillas J, Girod C, Lheritier M, Claustrat B, Dubois MP. Morphological and biochemical relationships in 31 human pituitary adenomas with acromegaly. Virchows Arch [A] 1980, **389:** 127–142.

67 Yamada S, Aiba T, Sano T, Kovacs K, Shishiba Y, Sawano S, Takada K. Growth hormone-producing pituitary adenomas: correlations between clinical characteristics and morphology. Neurosurgery 1993, **33:** 20–27.

Mixed PRL- and GH-producing adenomas

68 Bassetti M, Spada A, Arosio M, Vallar L, Brina M, Giannattasio G. Morphologic studies on mixed growth hormone (GH) and prolactin (PRL) secreting human pituitary adenomas. Coexistence of GH and PRL in the same secretory granule. J Clin Endocrinol Metab 1986, **62:** 1093–1100.

69 Felix IA, Horvath E, Kovacs K, Smyth HS, Killinger DW, Vale J. Mammosomatotroph adenoma of the pituitary associated with gigantism and hyperprolactinemia. A morphological study including immunoelectron microscopy. Acta Neuropathol (Berl) 1986, **71:** 76–82.

70 Frawley LS, Boockfor FR. Mammosomatotropes. Presence and functions in normal and neoplastic pituitary tissue. Endocr Rev 1991, **12:** 337–355.

71 Furuhata S, Kameya T. Subdivisions of 26 mixed growth hormone and prolactin-producing pituitary adenomas. Endocr Pathol 1992, **3:** 812–813.

72 Halmi NS. Occurrence of both growth hormone- and prolactin-immunoreactive material in the cells of human somatotropic pituitary adenomas containing mammotropic elements. Virchows Arch [A] 1982, **398:** 19–31.

73 Horvath E, Kovacs K, Killinger DW, Smyth HS, Weiss MH, Ezrin C. Mammo somatotroph cell adenoma of the human pituitary: a morphologic entity. Virchows Arch [A] 1983, **398:** 277–289.

74 Li J, Stefaneanu L, Kovacs K, Horvath E, Smyth H. Growth hormone (GH) and prolactin (PRL) gene expression and immunoreactivity in GH- and PRL-producing human pituitary adenomas. Virchows Arch [A] 1993, **422:** 193–201.

Acidophilic stem cell adenoma

75 Horvath E, Kovacs K, Singer W, Smyth HS, Killinger DW, Ezrin C, Weiss MH. Acidophil stem cell adenoma of the human pituitary. Clinicopathological analysis of 15 cases. Cancer 1981, **47:** 761–771.

76 Li J, Stefaneanu L, Kovacs K, Horvath E, Smyth H. Growth hormone (GH) and prolactin (PRL) gene expression and immunoreactivity in GH- and PRL-producing human pituitary adenomas. Virchows Archiv [A] 1993, **422:** 193–201.

77 McNicol AM, Walker E, Farguharson MA, Teasdale GM. Pituitary macroadenomas associated with hyperprolactinaemia: immunocytochemical and in situ hybridization studies. Clin Endocrinol 1991, **35:** 239–244.

ACTH cell adenoma

78 Belsky JL, Cuello B, Swanson LW, Simmons DM, Jarrett RM, Braza F. Cushing's syndrome due to ectopic production of corticotropin-releasing factor. J Clin Endocrinol Metab 1985, **60:** 496–500.

79 Charpin C, Hassoun J, Oliver C, Jacquet P, Argemi B, Grisoli F, Toga M. Immunohistochemical and immunoelectron-microscopic study of pituitary adenomas associated with Cushing's disease. A report of 13 cases. Am J Pathol 1982, **109:** 1–7.

80 Findling JW, Aron DC, Tyrrell JB. Cushing's disease. In Imura H (ed.): The Pituitary Gland. New York, 1985, Raven Press, pp. 441–466.

81 Kovacs K. The pathology of Cushing's disease. J Steroid Biochem Mol Biol 1993, **45:** 179–182.

82 Lloyd RV, Chandler WF, McKeever PE, Schteingart DE. The spectrum of ACTH-producing pituitary lesions. Am J Surg Pathol 1986, **10:** 618–626.

83 McKeever PE, Koppelman MCS, Metcalf D, Quindlen E, Kornblith PL, Strott CA, Howard R, Smith BH. Refractory Cushing's disease caused by multinodular ACTH-cell hyperplasia. J Neuropathol Exp Neurol 1982, **41:** 490–499.

84 Nelson DH, Meakin JW, Thorn GW. ACTH-producing pituitary tumors following adrenalectomy for Cushing's syndrome. Ann Intern Med 1960, **52:** 560–569.

85 Neumann PE, Horoupian DS, Goldman JE, Hess MA. Cytoplasmic filaments of Crooke's hyaline change belong to the cytokeratin class. An immunocytochemical and ultrastructural study. Am J Pathol 1984, **116:** 214–222.

86 Robert F, Hardy J. Human corticotroph cell adenomas. Semin Diagn Pathol 1986, **3:** 34–41.

87 Schnall AM, Kovacs K, Brodkey JS, Pearson OH. Pituitary Cushing's disease without adenoma. Acta Endocrinol (Copenh) 1980, **94:** 297–303.

88 Thapar K, Smith MV, Elliot E, Kovacs K, Laws E. Corticotroph adenomas of the pituitary. Long term results of operative treatment. Endocr Pathol 1992, **3:** S51–S53.

89 Wowra B, Peiffer J. An immunoperoxidase study of a human pituitary adenoma associated with Cushing's syndrome. Pathol Res Pract 1984, **178:** 349–354.

Glycoprotein hormone-producing adenomas

90 Gesundheit N, Petrick PA, Nissim M, Dahlberg PA, Doppman JL, Emerson GH, Braverman LF, Oldfield EH, Weintraub BD. Thyrotropin-secreting pituitary adenomas. Clinical and biochemical heterogeneity. Case reports and follow-up of nine patients. Ann Intern Med 1989, **111:** 827–835.

91 Gharib SD, Weirman MF, Shupnik MA, Chin WW. Molecular biology of pituitary gonadotropins. Endocr Rev 1990, **11:** 177–199.

92 Girod C, Trouillas J, Claustrat B. The human thyrotropic adenoma: pathologic diagnosis in five cases and critical review of the literature. Semin Diagn Pathol 1986, **3:** 58–68.

93 Hamilton CRJ, Adams LC, Maloof F. Hyperthyroidism due to thyrotropin-producing pituitary chromophobe adenoma. N Engl J Med 1970, **283:** 1077–1080.

94 Klibanski A, Ridgway EC, Zervas NT. Pure alpha subunit-secreting pituitary tumors. J Neurosurg 1983, **59:** 585–589.

95 Klibanski A, Zervas N. Diagnosis and management of hormone-secreting pituitary adenomas. N Engl J Med 1991, **324:** 822–831.

96 Kovacs K, Asa SL (eds): The Adenohypophysis. Functional Endocrine Pathology. Boston, 1991, Blackwell, pp. 245–281.

97 Landolt AM, Heitz PU. Alpha-subunit-producing pituitary adenomas. Immunocytochemical and ultrastructural studies. Virchows Arch [A] 1986, **409:** 417–431.

98 McCutcheon IA, Weitraub BE, Oldfield EH. Surgical treatment of thyrotropin-secreting pituitary adenomas. J Neurosurg 1990, **73:** 674–683.

99 Miura M, Matsukado Y, Kodama T, Mihara Y. Clinical and histopathological characteristics of gonadotropin-producing pituitary adenomas. J Neurosurg 1985, **62:** 376–382.

100 Saeger W, Ludecke DK. Pituitary adenomas with hyperfunction

of TSH. Frequency, histological classification, immunocytochemistry and ultrastructure. Virchows Arch [A] 1982, **394**: 255–267.

101 Samaan NA, Osborne BM, Mackay B, Leavens ME, Duello T, Halmi NS. Endocrine and morphologic studies of pituitary adenomas secondary to primary hypothyroidism. J Clin Endocrinol Metab 1977, **45**: 903–911.

102 Snyder PJ. Gonadotroph cell adenomas of the pituitary. Endocr Rev 1985, **6**: 552–563.

103 Trouillas J, Girod C, Sassolas G, Claustrat B. The human gonadotropic adenoma: pathologic diagnosis and hormonal correlations in 26 tumors. Semin Diagn Pathol 1986, **3**: 42–57.

104 Wajchenberg BL, Tsanaclis AMC, Marino R Jr. TSH-containing pituitary adenoma associated with primary hypothyroidism manifested by amenorrhoea and galactorrhoea. Acta Endocrinol (Copenh) 1984, **106**: 61–66.

Plurihormonal adenoma

105 Giannattasio G, Bassetti M. Human pituitary adenomas. Recent advances in morphological studies. J Endocrinol Invest 1990, **13**: 435–454.

106 Kovacs K, Horvath E, Asa SL, et al. Pituitary cells producing more than one hormone. Human pituitary adenomas. Trends Endocrinol Metab 1989, **1**: 104–107.

107 Lloyd RV, Cano M, Chandler WF, Barkan AL, Horvath E, Kovacs K. Human growth hormone and prolactin secreting pituitary adenomas analyzed by in situ hybridization. Am J Pathol 1989, **134**: 605–613.

108 Thapar K, Stefaneanu L, Kovacs K, Horvath E, Asa SL. Plurihormonal pituitary tumors. Beyond the one cell-one hormone theory. Endocr Pathol 1993, **4**: 1–3.

109 Yamada S, Aiba T, Sano T, Kovacs K, Shishiba Y, Sawano S, Takada K. Growth hormone-producing pituitary adenomas: correlations between clinical characteristics and morphology. Neurosurgery 1993, **33**: 20–27.

Null cell adenoma and oncocytoma

110 Asa SL, Cheng Z, Ramyar L, Singer W, Kovacs K, Smyth HS, Muller P. Human pituitary null cell adenomas and oncocytomas in vitro: effects of adenohypophysiotropic hormone and gonadal steroids on hormone secretion and tumor cell morphology. J Clin Endocrinol Metab 1992, **74**: 1128–1134.

111 Kontogeorgos G, Kovacs K, Horvath E, Scheithauer B. Null cell adenomas, oncocytomas and gonadotroph cell adenomas of the human pituitary. An immunocytochemical and ultrastructural analysis of 300 cases. Endocr Pathol 1993, **4**: 20–27.

112 Kovacs K, Horvath E. Pituitary "chromophobe" adenoma composed of oncocytes. A light and electron microscopic study. Arch Pathol 1973, **95**: 235–239.

113 Kovacs K, Horvath E, Ryan N, Ezrin C. Null cell adenoma of the human pituitary. Virchows Arch [A] 1980, **387**: 165–174.

114 Landolt AM, Oswald UW. Histology and ultrastructure of an oncocytic adenoma of the human pituitary. Cancer 1973, **31**: 1099–1105.

115 Lloyd RV, Anagnostou D, Chandler WF. Dopamine receptors in immunohistochemically characterized null cell adenomas and normal human pituitaries. Mod Pathol 1988, **1**: 51–56.

Natural history, spread, and metastases

116 Ahmed M, Rifai A, Al-Jurf M, Akhtar M, Woodhouse N. Classical pituitary apoplexy. Presentation and follow-up of 13 patients. Horm Res 1989, **31**: 125–132.

117 Hashimoto N, Handa H, Nishi S. Intracranial and intraspinal dissemination from a growth hormone-secreting pituitary tumor. J Neurosurg 1986, **64**: 140–144.

118 Mountcastle RB, Roof BS, Mayfield RK, Mordes DB, Sagel J, Biggs PJ, Rawe SE. Pituitary adenocarcinoma in an acromegalic

patient: response to bromocriptine and pituitary testing. A review of the literature on 36 cases of pituitary carcinoma. Am J Med Sci 1989, **298**: 109–118.

119 Plangger CA, Twerdy K, Grunert V, Weiser G. Subarachnoid metastases from a prolactinoma. Neurochirurgia 1985, **28**: 235–237.

120 Shirataki K, Chihara K, Shibata Y, Tamaki N, Matsumoto S, Fujita T. Pituitary apoplexy manifested during a bromocriptine test in a patient with a growth hormone and prolactin producing pituitary adenoma. Neurosurgery 1988, **23**: 395–398.

121 Thapar K, Kovacs K, Laws ER. The Classification and Molecular Biology of Pituitary Adenomas. Advances and Technical Standards in Neurosurgery. Wein-Vienna, 1995, Springer-Verlag.

122 Thapar K, Kovacs K, Scheithauer BW, Stefaneanu L, Horvath E, Pernicone PJ, Murray D, Laws ER Jr. Proliferative activity and invasiveness among pituitary adenomas and carcinomas. An analysis using the MIB-1 antibody. Neurosurgery 1996, **38**: 99–106.

Treatment

123 Beckers A, Kovacs K, Horvath E, Abs R, Reznik M, Stevenaert A. Effect of treatment with octreotide on the morphology of growth hormone-secreting pituitary adenomas. Study of 24 cases. Endocr Pathol 1991, **2**: 123–131.

124 Bevan JS, Adams CBT, Burke CW, Morton KE, Molyneux AJ, Moore RA, Esiri MM. Factors in the outcome of transsphenoidal surgery for prolactinoma and nonfunctioning pituitary tumor, including pre-operative bromocriptine therapy. Clin Endocrinol 1987, **26**: 541–556.

125 Black PM, Zervas NT, Candia GL. Incidence and management of complications of transsphenoidal operation for pituitary adenomas. Neurosurgery 1987, **20**: 920–924.

126 Davis DH, Laws ER Jr, Ilstrup DM, Speed JK, Caruso M, Shaw EG, Abboud CF, Scheithauer BW, Rott LM, Schleck C. Results of surgical treatment for growth hormone-secreting pituitary adenomas. J Neurosurg 1993, **79**: 70–75.

127 Goffman TE, Dewan R, Arakaki R, Gorden P, Oldfield EH, Glatstein E. Persistent or recurrent acromegaly. Long-term endocrinologic efficacy and neurologic safety of postsurgical radiation therapy. Cancer 1992, **69**: 271–275.

128 Schettini G, Lombardi G, Merola B, Colao A, Miletto P, Caruso E, Lancranjan I. Rapid and longlasting suppression of prolactin secretion and shrinkage of prolactinomas after infection of long-acting repeatable form of bromocriptine (Parlodel Lar). Clin Endocrinol 1990, **33**: 161–169.

Other lesions
Gangliocytoma

129 Asa SL, Kovacs K, Tindall GT, Barrow DL, Horvath E, Vecsei P. Cushing's disease associated with an intrasellar gangliocytoma producing corticotrophin-releasing factor. Ann Intern Med 1984, **101**: 789–793.

130 Asa SL, Scheithauer BW, Bilbao JM, Horvath E, Ryan N, Kovacs K, Randall RV, Laws ER Jr, Singer W, Linfoot JA. A case for hypothalamic acromegaly: a clinicopathological study of six patients with hypothalamic gangliocytomas producing growth hormone-releasing factor. J Clin Endocrinol Metab 1984, **58**: 796–803.

131 Bevan JS, Asa SL, Rossi ML, Esiri MM, Adams CB, Burke CW. Intrasellar gangliocytoma containing gastrin and growth hormone-releasing hormone associated with a growth hormone-secreting pituitary adenoma. Clin Endocrinol 1989, **30**: 213–224.

132 Curatolo P, Cusmai R, Finocchi G, Boscherini B. Gelastic epilepsy and true precocious puberty due to hypothalamic hamartoma. Dev Med Child Neurol 1984, **26**: 509–514.

133 Fischer EG, Morris JH, Kettyle WM. Intrasellar gangliocytoma and syndromes of pituitary hypersecretion. Case report. J Neurosurg 1983, **59**: 1071–1075.

134 Pescovitz OH, Comite F, Hench K, Barnes K, McNemar A, Foster C, Kenigsberg D, Loriaux DL, Cutler GB Jr. The NIH experience with precocious puberty: diagnostic subgroups and response to short-term luteinizing hormone releasing hormone analogue therapy. J Pediatr 1986, **108:** 47–54.

135 Jakumeit HD, Zimmerman V, Guiot G. Intrasellar gangliocytomas. Report of four cases. J Neurosurg 1974, **40:** 626–630.

136 Kamel OW, Horoupian DS, Silverberg GD. Mixed gangliocytoma-adenoma. A distinct neuroendocrine tumor of the pituitary fossa. Hum Pathol 1989, **20:** 1198–1203.

137 Kurosaki M, Saeger W, Ludecke DK. Intrasellar gangliocytoma associated with acromegaly. Brain Tumor Pathol 2002, **19:** 63–67.

138 Li JY, Racadot O, Kujas M, Kouadri M, Peillon F, Racadot J. Immunocytochemistry of four mixed pituitary adenomas and intrasellar gangliocytomas associated with different clinical syndromes. Acromegaly, amenorrhea-galactorrhea, Cushing's disease and isolated tumoral syndrome. Acta Neuropathol 1989, **77:** 320–328.

139 Markin RS, Leibrock LG, Huseman CA, McComb RD. Hypothalamic harmartoma. A report of two cases. Pediatr Neurosci 1987, **13:** 19–26.

140 Nishio S, Fujiwara S, Aiko Y, Takeshita I, Fukui M. Hypothalamic hamartoma. Report of two cases. J Neurosurg 1989, **70:** 640–645.

141 Pallister PD, Hecht F, Herrman J. Three additional cases of the congenital hypothalamic "hamartoblastoma" (Pallister–Hall) syndrome (letter). Am J Med Genet 1989, **33:** 500–501.

142 Ponsot G, Diebler C, Plouin P, Nardou M, Dulac O, Chaussain JL, Arthuis M. Hypothalamic hamartoma and gelastic crises. Apropos of 7 cases. Arch Fr Pediatr 1983, **40:** 757–761.

143 Puchner MJA, Ludecke DK, Valdueza JM, Saeger W, Willig RP, Stalla GK, Odink RJ. Cushing's disease in a child caused by a corticotropin releasing hormone–secreting intrasellar gangliocytoma associated with an adrenocorticotropic hormone-secreting pituitary adenoma. Neurosurgery 1993, **33:** 920–925.

144 Yamada S, Stefaneanu L, Kovacs K, Aiba T, Shishiba Y, Hara M. Intrasellar gangliocytoma with multiple immunoreactives. Endocr Pathol 1990, 1:58–63.

Lymphocytic hypophysitis

145 Asa SL, Bilbao JM, Kovacs K, Josse RG, Kreines K. Lymphocytic hypophysis in pregnancy resulting in hypopituitarism. A distinct clinicopathologic entity. Ann Intern Med 1981, **95:** 166.

146 Bitton RN, Slavin M, Decker RE, Zito J, Schneider BS. The course of lymphocytic hypophysitis. Surg Neurol 1991, **36:** 40–43.

147 Cosman F, Post KD, Holub DA, Wardlaw SL. Lymphocytic hypophysitis. Report of three new cases and review of the literature. Medicine 1989, **68:** 240–256.

148 Feigenbaum SL, Martin MC, Wilson Ch B, Jaffe RB. Lymphocytic adenohypophysitis. A pituitary mass lesion occurring in pregnancy. Am J Obstet Gynecol 1991, **164:** 1549–1555.

149 Lee JI, Laws ER, Guthrie BL, Dina TS, Nochomovitz LE. Lymphocytic hypophysitis. Occurrence in two men. Neurosurgery 1994, **34:** 159–163.

150 Megrail KM, Beyerl BD, Black PM, Klibanski A, Zervas NT. Lymphocytic adenohypophysitis of pregnancy with complete recovery. Neurosurgery 1987, **20:** 791–793.

151 Meichner RH, Riggio S, Manz HJ, Earll JM. Lymphocytic adenohypophysitis causing pituitary mass. Neurology 1987, **37:** 158–161.

152 Nussbaum CE, Okawara SH, Jacobs LS. Lymphocytic hypophysitis with involvement of the cavernous sinus and hypothalamus. Neurosurgery 1991, **28:** 440–444.

153 Pestell RG, Best JD, Alford FP. Lymphocytic hypophysitis. The clinical spectrum of the disorder and evidence for an autoimmune pathogenesis. Clin Endocrinol 1990, **33:** 457–466.

154 Reusch JEB, Kleinschmidt-DeMasters BK, Lillehei KO, Rappe D, Gutierrez-Hartmann A. Preoperative diagnosis of lymphocytic hypophysitis (adenohypophysitis) unresponsive to short course dexamethasone. Case report. Neurosurgery 1992, **30:** 268–272.

Rathke's cleft cyst

155 Barrow DL, Spector RH, Takei Y, Tindall GT. Symptomatic Rathke's cleft cysts located entirely in the suprasellar region. Review of diagnosis, management and pathogenesis. Neurosurgery 1985, **16:** 766–772.

156 Baskin DS, Wilson CB. Transsphenoidal treatment of non-neoplastic intrasellar cysts. Report of 38 cases. J Neurosurg 1984, **60:** 8–13.

157 Kucharczyk W, Peck WW, Kelly WM, Norman D, Newton TH. Rathke cleft cysts: CT, MR imaging, and pathologic features. Radiology 1987, **165:** 491–495.

158 McGrath P. Cysts of sellar and pharyngeal hypophyses. Pathology 1971, **3:** 123–131.

159 Midha R, Jay V, Smyth HS. Transsphenoidal management of Rathke's cleft cysts. A clinicopathological review of 10 cases. Surg Neurol 1991, **35:** 446–454.

160 Nishio S, Mizuno J, Barrow DL, Takei Y, Tindall GT. Pituitary tumors composed of adenohypophysial adenoma and Rathke's cleft cyst elements. A clinicopathological study. Neurosurgery 1987, **21:** 371–377.

161 Obenchain TG, Becker DP. Abscess formation in a Rathke's cleft cyst. Case report. J Neurosurg 1972, **36:** 359–362.

162 Shuangshoti S, Netsky MG, Nashold BS. Epithelial cysts related to sella turcica. Proposed origin from neuroepithelium. Arch Pathol 1970, **90:** 444–450.

163 Steinberg GK, Koenig GH, Golden JB. Symptomatic Rathke's cleft cysts. Report of two cases. J Neurosurg 1982, **56:** 290–295.

164 Yoshida J, Kobayashi T, Kageyama N, Kanzaki M. Symptomatic Rathke's cleft cyst. Morphological study with light and electron microscopy and tissue culture. J Neurosurg 1977, **47:** 451–458.

165 Zimmerman RA. Imaging of intrasellar, suprasellar and parasellar tumors. Semin Roentgenol 1990, **25.** 174–197.

Craniopharyngioma

166 Adamson TE, Wiestler OD, Kleihues P, Yasargil MG. Correlation of clinical and pathological features in surgically treated craniopharyngiomas. J Neurosurg 1990, **73:** 12–17.

167 Azar-Kia B, Krishnan UR, Schechter MM. Neonatal craniopharyngioma. Case report. J Neurosurg 1975, **42:** 91–93.

168 Barloon TJ, Yuh WTC, Sato Y, Sickels WJ. Frontal lobe implantation of craniopharyngioma by repeated needle aspirations. Am J Neuroradiol 1988, **9:** 406–407.

169 Berstein ML, Buchino JJ. The histologic similarity between craniopharyngioma and odontogenic lesions. A reappraisal. Oral Surg 1983, **56:** 502–511.

170 Brodsky MC, Hoyt WF, Barnwell SL, Wilson CB. Intrachiasmatic craniopharyngioma. A rare cause of chiasmal thickening. Case report. J Neurosurg 1988, **68:** 300–302.

171 Duff TA, Levine R. Intrachiasmatic craniopharyngioma. Case report. J Neurosurg 1983, **59:** 176–178.

172 Freedman PD, Lumerman H, Gee JK. Calcifying odontogenic cyst. Oral Surg 1975, **40:** 93–106.

173 Ghatak NY, Hirano A, Zimmerman HM. Ultrastructure of a craniopharyngioma. Cancer 1971, **27:** 1465–1475.

174 Giangaspero F, Burger PC, Osborne DR, Stein RB. Suprasellar papillary squamous epithelium ("papillary craniopharyngioma"). Am J Surg Pathol 1984, **8:** 57–64.

175 Hoffman HJ. Craniopharyngiomas. Can J Neurol Sci 1985, **12:** 348–352.

176 Janish W, Flegel HG. Kranipharingiom bei einem Feten. Zentralbl Allg Pathol 1989, **135:** 65–69.

177 Kunishio K, Yamamoto Y, Sunami N, Asari S, Akagi T, Ohtsuki Y. Craniopharyngioma in the third ventricle. Necropsy findings and histogenesis. J Neurol Neurosurg Psychiatry 1987, **50:** 1053–1056.

178 Lederman GS, Recht A, Loeffler JS, Dubuisson D, Kleefield J, Schnitt SJ. Craniopharyngioma in an elderly patient. Cancer 1987, **60**: 1077–1080.

179 Munari C, Landre E, Musolino A, Turak B, Habert MO, Chodkiewicz JP. Long term results of stereotactic endocavitary beta irradiation of craniopharyngioma. J Neurosurg Sci 1989, **33**: 99–105.

180 Nelson GA, Bastian FO, Schlitt M, White RL. Malignant transformation in craniopharyngioma. Neurosurgery 1988, **22**: 427–429.

181 Petito CK, DeGirolami U, Earle KM. Craniopharyngiomas. A clinical and pathological review. Cancer 1976, **37**: 1944–1952.

182 Pigeau I, Sigal R, Halimi P, Comoy J, Doyon D. MRI features of craniopharyngiomas at 1.5 tesla. J Neuroradiol 1988, **15**: 276–287.

183 Seemayer TA, Blundell JS, Wiglesworth FW. Pituitary craniopharyngioma with tooth formation. Cancer 1972, **29**: 423–430.

184 Sumi T, Stefaneanu L, Kovacs K. Squamous-cell nests in the pars tuberalis of the human pituitary. Immunocytochemical and in situ hybridization studies. Endocr Pathol 1993, **4**: 155–161.

185 Weiss M, Sutton L, Marcial V, Fowble B, Packer R, Zimmerman R, Schut L, Bruce D, D'Angio G. The role of radiation therapy in the management of childhood craniopharyngioma. Int J Radiat Oncol Biol Phys 1989, **17**: 1313–1321.

186 Yasargil MG, Curcic M, Kis M, Siegenthaler G, Teddy PJ, Roth P. Total removal of craniopharyngiomas. Approaches and long-term results in 144 patients. J Neurosurg 1990, **73**: 3–11.

187 Young SC, Zimmerman RA, Nowell MA, Bilaniuk LT, Hackney DB, Grossman RI, Goldberg HI. Giant cystic craniopharyngiomas. Neuroradiology 1987, **29**: 468–473.

Granular cell tumor and pituicytoma

188 Brat DJ, Scheithauer BW, Staugaitis SM, Holtzman RN, Morgello S, Burger PC. Pituicytoma: a distinctive low-grade glioma of the neurohypophysis. Am J Surg Pathol 2000, **24**: 362–369.

189 Buley ID, Gatter KC, Kelly PMA, Heryet A, Millard PR. Granular cell tumors revisited. An immunohistochemical and ultrastructural study. Histopathology 1988, **12**: 263–274.

190 Dickson DW, Suzuki KI, Kanner R, Weitz S, Horoupian DS. Cerebral granular cell tumor. Immunohistochemical and electron microscopic study. J Neuropathol Exp Neurol 1986, **45**: 304–314.

191 Figarella-Branger D, Dufour H, Fernandez C, Bouvier-Labit C, Grisoli F, Pellissier JF. Pituicytomas: a misdiagnosed benign tumor of the neurohypophysis. Report of three cases. Acta Neuropathol 2002, **104**: 313–319.

192 Katsuta T, Inoue T, Nakagaki H, Takeshita M, Morimoto K, Iwaki T. Distinctions between pituicytoma and ordinary pilocytic astrocytoma. Case report. J Neurosurg 2003, **98**: 404–406.

193 Landolt A. Granular cell tumors of the neurohypophysis. Acta Neurochir (Wien) 1975, **22(suppl)**: 120–128.

194 Luse SA, Kernohan JW. Granular cell tumors of the stalk and posterior lobe of the pituitary gland. Cancer 1955, **8**: 616–622.

195 Nishioka H. Immunohistochemical study of granular cell tumors and granular pituicytes of the neurohypophysis. Endocr Pathol 1993, **4**: 140–145.

196 Schlachter LB, Tindall GT, Pearl GS. Granular cell tumor of the pituitary gland associated with diabetes insipidus. Neurosurgery 1980, **6**: 418–421.

197 Shanklin WM. The origin, histology and senescence of tumorettes in the human neurohypophysis. Acta Anat 1953, **18**: 1–20.

198 Tomita T, Kuziez M, Watanabe I. Double tumors of anterior and posterior pituitary gland. Acta Neuropathol (Berl) 1981, **54**: 161–164.

199 Tuch BE, Carter JN, Armellin GM, Newland RC. The association of a tumor of the posterior pituitary gland with multiple endocrine neoplasia type 1. Aust NZ J Med 1982, **12**: 179–181.

200 Ulrich J, Heitz PU, Fischer T, Obrist E, Gullotta F. Granular cell tumors. Evidence for heterogeneous tumor cell differentiation. An immunocytochemical study. Virchows Arch [Cell Pathol] 1987, **53**: 52–57.

201 Vaquero J, Leunda G, Cabezudo JM, Solazar AR, Miguel J. Granular pituicytomas of the pituitary stalk. Acta Neurochir (Wien) 1981, **59**: 209–215.

202 Waller RR, Riley FC, Sundt TM. A rare cause of the chiasmal syndrome. Arch Ophthalmol 1972, **88**: 269–272.

Postradiation tumors

203 Ahmad K, Fayos JV. Pituitary fibrosarcoma secondary to radiation therapy. Cancer 1978, **42**: 107–110.

204 Amine ARC, Sugar O. Suprasellar osteogenic sarcoma following radiation for pituitary adenoma. Case report. J Neurosurg 1976, **44**: 88–91.

205 Fontana M, Stanton C, Pompili A, Amadori S, Mandelli F, Meloni G, Riccio A, Rubinstein LJ. Late multifocal gliomas in adolescents previously treated for acute lymphoblastic leukemia. Cancer 1987, **60**: 1510–1518.

206 Huang CI, Chiou WH, Ho DM. Oligodendroglioma occurring after radiation therapy for pituitary adenoma. J Neurol Neurosurg Psychiatry 1987, **50**: 1619–1624.

207 Hufnagel TJ, Kim JH, Lesser R, Miller JM, Abrahams JJ, Piepmeier J, Manuelidis EE. Malignant glioma of the optic chiasm eight years after radiotherapy for prolactinoma. Arch Ophthalmol 1988, **106**: 1701–1705.

208 Kitanaka C, Shitara N, Nakagomi T, Nakamura H, Genka S, Nakagawaw K, Akanuma A, Aoyama H, Takakura K. Postradiation astrocytoma. Report of two cases. J Neurosurg 1989, **70**: 469–474.

209 Liwnicz BH, Berger TS, Liwnicz RG, Aron BS. Radiation-associated gliomas. A report of four cases and analysis of postradiation tumors of the central nervous system. Neurosurgery 1985, **17**: 436–445.

210 Maat-Schieman ML, Bots GT, Thomeer RT, Vielvoye GJ. Malignant astrocytoma following radiotherapy for craniopharyngioma. Br J Radiol 1985, **58**: 480–482.

211 Marus G, Levin CV, Rutherfoord GS. Malignant glioma following radiotherapy for unrelated primary tumors. Cancer 1986, **58**: 886–894.

212 Meredith JM, Mandeville FB, Kay S. Osteogenic sarcoma of the skull following roentgen-ray therapy for benign pituitary tumor. J Neurosurg 1960, **17**: 792–799.

213 Piatt JH, Blue JM, Schold SC, Burger PC. Glioblastoma multiforme after radiotherapy for acromegaly. Neurosurgery 1983, **13**: 85–89.

214 Ron E, Modan B, Boice JD, Alfandary E, Stovall M, Chetrit A, Katz L. Tumors of the brain and nervous system after radiotherapy in childhood. N Engl J Med 1988, **319**: 1033–1039.

215 Sogg RL, Donaldson SS, Yorke CH. Malignant astrocytoma following radiotherapy of a craniopharyngioma. J Neurosurg 1978, **48**: 622–627.

216 Spallone A. Meningioma as a sequel to radiotherapy for pituitary adenoma. Neurochirurgia (Stuttg) 1982, **25**: 68–72.

217 Sridhar K, Ramamurthi B. Intracranial meningioma subsequent to radiation for a pituitary tumor. Case report. Neurosurgery 1989, **25**: 643–645.

218 Tanaka S, Nishio S, Morioka T, Fukui M, Kitamura K, Hikita K. Radiation-induced osteosarcoma of the sphenoid bone. Neurosurgery 1989, **25**: 640–643.

219 Ushio Y, Arita N, Yoshimine T, Nagatani M, Mogami H. Glioblastoma after radiotherapy for craniopharyngioma. Case report. Neurosurgery 1987, **21**: 33–38.

220 Zampieri P, Zorat PL, Migrino S, Soattin GB. Radiation-associated cerebral gliomas. A report of two cases and review of the literature. J Neurosurg Sci 1989, **33**: 271–279.

Metastatic tumors

221 Branch CL, Laws ER. Metastatic tumors of the sella turcica masquerading as primary pituitary tumors. J Clin Endocrinol Metab 1987, **65**: 469–474.

222 Felix IA. Pathology of the neurohypophysis. Pathol Res Pract 1988, **183**: 535–537.

223 Gurling KJ, Scott GBD, Baron DN. Metastasis in pituitary tissue removed at hypophysectomy in women with mammary carcinoma. Br J Cancer 1957, **11**: 519–523.

224 Kattah JC, Silgals RM, Manz H, Toro JG, Dritschilo A, Smith FP. Presentation and management of parasellar and suprasellar metastatic mass lesions. J Neurol Neurosurg Psychiatry 1985, **48**: 44–49.

225 Kimmel DW, O'Neill BP. Systemic cancer presenting as diabetes insipidus. Clinical and radiographic features of 11 patients with a review of metastatic-induced diabetes insipidus. Cancer 1983, **52**: 2355–2358.

226 Max MB, Deck MDF, Rottenberg DA. Pituitary metastasis. Incidence in cancer patients and clinical differentiation from pituitary adenoma. Neurology 1981, **31**: 998–1002.

227 McCormick PC, Post KD, Kandji AD, Hays AP. Metastatic carcinoma to the pituitary gland. Br J Neurosurg 1989, **3**: 71–79.

228 Post KD, McCormick PC, Hays AP, Kandji AD. Metastatic carcinoma to pituitary adenoma. Report of two cases. Surg Neurol 1988, **30**: 286–292.

229 Roessmann U, Kaufman B, Friede RL. Metastatic lesions in the sella turcica and pituitary gland. Cancer 1970, **25**: 478–480.

230 Teears RJ, Silverman EM. Clinicopathologic review of 88 cases of carcinoma metastatic to the pituitary gland. Cancer 1975, **36**: 216–220.

Miscellaneous lesions

231 Angiari P, Torcia E, Botticelli RA, Villani M, Merli GA, Crisi G. Ossifying parasellar chondroma. Case report. J Neurosurg Sci 1987, **31**: 59–63.

232 Asa SL, Kovacs K, Horvath E, Ezrin C, Weiss MH. Sellar glomangioma. Ultrastruct Pathol 1984, **7**: 49–54.

233 Bachour E, Perrin G, Ciriano P, Trouillas J, Sassolas G, Tommasi M, Goutelle A. Idiopathic giant cell granulomas of the pituitary gland. Apropos of 2 cases. J Neurosurg 1991, **37**: 253–257.

234 Belza J. Double midline intracranial tumors of vestigial origin. Contiguous intrasellar chordoma and suprasellar craniopharyngioma. Case report. J Neurosurg 1966, **25**: 199–204.

235 Bilbao JM, Horvath E, Kovacs K, Singer W, Hudson AR. Intrasellar paraganglioma associated with hypopituitarism. Arch Pathol Lab Med 1978, **102**: 95–98.

236 Brat DJ, Scheithauer BW, Staugaitis SM, Cortez SC, Brecher K, Burger PC. Third ventricular chordoid glioma. J Neuropathol Exp Neurol 1999, **57**: 283–290.

237 Capellan JIL, Olmedo LC, Martin JM, et al. Intrasellar mass with hypopituitarism as a manifestation of sarcoidosis. Case report. J Neurosurg 1990, **73**: 283–286.

238 Castel JP, Delorge-Kerdiles C, Rivel J. Cavernous angioma of the optic chiasma. J Neurosurg 1989, **35**: 252–256.

239 Copeland DD, Sink JD, Seigler HF. Primary intracranial melanoma presenting as a suprasellar tumor. Neurosurgery 1980, **6**: 542–545.

240 Dan NG, Smith DE. Pituitary hemangioblastoma in a patient with von Hippel–Lindau disease. J Neurosurg 1975, **42**: 232–235.

241 Del Brutto OH, Guevara J, Sotelo J. Intrasellar cysticercosis. J Neurosurg 1988, **69**: 58–60.

242 Deodhare SS, Bilbao JM, Kovacs K, Horvath E, Nomikos P, Buchfelder M, Reschke K, Lehnert H. Xanthomatous hypophysitis: a novel entity of obscure etiology. Endocr Pathol 1999, **10**: 237–241.

243 Dhanani AN, Bilbao JM, Kovacs K. Multiple myeloma presenting as a sellar plasmacytomas mimicking a pituitary tumor. Report of a case and review of the literature. Endocr Pathol 1990, **1**: 245–248.

244 Duchen LW, Treip CS. Microgliomatosis presenting with dementia and hypopituitarism. J Pathol 1969, **98**: 143–146.

245 Favara BE, Jaffe R. Pathology of Langerhans cell histiocytosis. Hematol Oncol Clin North Am 1987, **1**: 75–97.

246 Folkerth RD, Price DL Jr, Schwartz M, Black PM, De Girolami U. Xanthomatous hypophysis. Am J Surg Pathol 1998, **22**: 736–741.

247 Furukawa F, Haebara H, Hamashima Y. Primary intracranial choriocarcinoma arising from the pituitary fossa. Report of an autopsy case with literature review. Acta Pathol Jpn 1986, **36**: 773–781.

248 Gartman JJ, Powers SK, Fortune M. Pseudotumor of the sellar and parasellar areas. Neurosurgery 1989, **24**: 896–901.

249 Gerlings PG. Sphenoid sinus mucocele presenting as hypophyseal tumor. Acta Neurochir 1982, **61**: 167–171.

250 Ghatak NR, Hirano A, Zimmerman HM. Intrasellar germinomas. A form of ectopic pinealoma. J Neurosurg 1969, **31**: 670–675.

251 Goebel HH, Shimokawa K, Schaake T, Kremp A. Schwannoma of the sellar region. Acta Neurochir (Wien) 1979, **48**: 191–198.

252 Grisoli F, Vincentelli F, Raybaud C, Harter M, Guibout M, Baldini M. Intrase-lar meningioma. Surg Neurol 1983, **20**: 36–41.

253 Kepes JJ, Kepes M. Predominantly cerebral forms of histiocytosis-X. A reappraisal of "Gagel's hypothalamic granuloma," "granuloma infiltrans of the hypothalamus," and "Ayala's disease" with a report of four cases. Acta Neuropathol (Berl) 1969, **14**: 77–98.

254 Kinjo T, al-Mefty O, Ciric I. Diaphragma sella meningiomas. Neurosurgery 1995, **36**: 1082–1092.

255 Maguire JA, Bilbao JM, Kovacs K, Resch L. Hypothalamic neurocytoma with vasopressin immunoreactivity. Immunohistochemical and ultrastructural observations. Endocr Pathol 1992, **3**: 93–96.

256 Mangiardi JR, Flamm ES, Cravioto H, Fisher B. Hemangiopericytoma of the pituitary fossa. Case report. Neurosurgery 1983, **13**: 58–61.

257 Masse SR, Wolk RW, Conklin RH. Peripituitary gland involvement in acute leukemia in adults. Arch Pathol 1973, **96**: 141–142.

258 Mathews W, Wilson CB. Ectopic intrasellar chordoma. Case report. J Neurosurg 1974, **40**: 260.

259 Miauri F. Primary cerebral lymphoma presenting as steroid-responsive chiasmal syndrome. Br J Neurosurg 1987, **1**: 499–502.

260 Miki K, Kawamoto K, Kawamura Y, Matsumura H, Asada Y, Hamada A. A rare case of Maffucci's syndrome combined with tuberculum sellae enchondroma, pituitary adenoma and thyroid adenoma. Acta Neurochir (Wien) 1987, **87**: 79–85.

261 Missler U, Mack M, Nowak G, Muller-Esch G, Reusche E, Borgis KJ, Lohrs U, Arnold H. Pituitary sarcoidosis. Klin Wochenschr 1990, **68**: 342–345.

262 Neilson JM, Moffat AD. Hypopituitarism caused by a melanoma of the pituitary gland. J Clin Pathol 1963, **16**: 144–149.

263 Nemato K, Ohnishi Y, Tsukada T. Chronic lymphocytic leukemia showing pituitary tumor with massive leukemic cell infiltration, and special reference to clinicopathological findings of CLL. Acta Pathol Jpn 1978, **28**: 797–805.

264 Nishio S, Mizuno J, Barrow DL, Takei Y, Tindall GT. Isolated histocytosis X of the pituitary gland. Case report. Neurosurgery 1987, **21**: 718–721.

265 Ober KP, Alexander E, Challa VR, Ferree C, Elster A. Histiocytosis X of the hypothalamus. Neurosurgery 1989, **24**: 93–95.

266 Ozgen T, Bertan V, Kansu T, Akalin S. Intrasellar hydatid cyst. Case report. J Neurosurg 1984, **60**: 647–648.

267 Pasquier B, Peoc'h M, Morrison AL, Gay E, Pasquier D, Grand S, Sinden M, Kopp N. Chordoid glioma of the third ventricle: a report of two new cases, with further evidence supporting an

ependymal differentiation, and review of the literature. Am J Surg Pathol 2002, **26**: 1330–1342.

268 Perone TP, Robinson B, Holmes SM. Intrasellar schwannoma. Case report. Neurosurgery 1984, **14**: 71–73.

269 Petrus M, Mignonat M, Netter JC, Bat P, Chateaneuf R, Bildstein G. Association epine intrasellaire et hyperprolactinemie. Ann Pediatr (Paris) 1988, **35**: 201–203.

270 Poon W, Ng HK, Wong K, South JR. Primary intrasellar germinoma presenting with cavernous sinus syndrome. Surg Neurol 1988, **30**: 402–405.

271 Ricoy JR, Lobato RD, Baez B, Cabello A, Martinez MA, Rodriguez G. Suprasellar chordoid glioma. Acta Neuropathol 2000, **99**: 699–703.

272 Rohringer M, Sutherland GR, Louw DF, Sima AAF. Incidence and clinicopathological features of meningioma. J Neurosurg 1989, **71**: 665–672.

273 Rossi ML, Bevan JS, Esiri MM, Hughes JT, Adams CBT. Pituicytoma (pilocytic astrocytoma). Case report. J Neurosurg 1987, **67**: 768–772.

274 Ruchti C, Balli-Antunes M, Gerber HA. Follicular tumor in the sellar region without primary cancer of the thyroid. Heterotopic carcinoma? Am J Clin Pathol 1987, **87**: 776–780.

275 Rueda-Pedraza ME, Heifetz SA, Sesterhenn IA, Clark GB. Primary intracranial germ cell tumors in the first two decades of life. Perspect Pediatr Pathol 1987, **10**: 160–207.

276 Sansone ME, Liwnicz BH, Mandybur TI. Giant pituitary cavernous hemangioma. Case report. J Neurosurg 1980, **53**: 124–126.

277 Scanarini M, D'Avella D, Rotilio A, Kitromilis N, Mingrino S. Giant cell granulomatous hypophysitis. A distinct clinicopathological entity. J Neurosurg 1989, **71**: 681–686.

278 Schochet SS, McCormick WF, Halmi NS. Salivary gland rests in the human pituitary. Light and electron microscopical study. Arch Pathol 1974, **98**: 193–200.

279 Scholtz CL, Siu K. Melanoma of the pituitary. Case report. J Neurosurg 1976, **45**: 101–103.

280 Scott IA, Stocks AE, Saines N. Hypothalamic/pituitary sarcoidosis. Aust NZ J Med 1987, **17**: 243–245.

281 Sindou M, Daher A, Vighetto A, Goutelle A. Chondrosarcoma parasellaire rapport d'un cas opere par voie pterionotemporale et reuve de la litterature. Neurochirurgie 1989, **35**: 186–190.

282 Steel TR, Dailey AT, Born D, Berger MS, Mayberg MR. Paragangliomas of the sellar region. Report of two cases. Neurosurgery 1993, **32**: 844–847.

283 Vesley DL. Hypothalamic sarcoidosis. A new cause of morbid obesity. South Med J 1989, **82**: 758–761.

284 Viswanathan R, Jegathraman AR, Ganapathy K, Bharati AS, Govindan R. Parasellar chondromyxoid fibroma with ipsilateral total internal carotid artery occlusion. Surg Neurol 1987, **28**: 141–144.

285 Wilberger JE. Primary intrasellar schwannoma. Case report. Surg Neurol 1989, **32**: 156–158.

286 Winer JB, Lidov H, Scaravilli F. An ependymoma involving the pituitary fossa. J Neurol Neurosurg Psychiatry 1989, **52**: 1443–1444.

287 Wolfe JT, Scheithauer BW, Dahlin DC. Giant cell tumor of the sphenoid bone. Review of ten cases. J Neurosurg 1983, **59**: 322–327.

288 Yamada S, Sawano S, Aiba T, Shishiba Y, Sano T, Takahashi S, Takebe K, Yanagiya S. Idiopathic giant-cell granuloma of the pituitary with unusual clinical and histologic features. Endocr Pathol 1993, **4**: 169–173.

30 Eye and ocular adnexa

This chapter will cover primarily those entities that come to the attention of the surgical pathologist; therefore entities seen most often at post mortem examination will be excluded. For a more detailed description of these and other entities, the reader is referred to one of the many specialized textbooks available.[1–10] As with all surgical specimens, a complete description of the lesion and a meaningful clinical history are invaluable. Clinical photographs are especially helpful in ophthalmic pathology.

Normal anatomy

The *eyelids* are divided into a cutaneous and a conjunctival portion. The former is composed of stratified squamous epithelium and the latter of a much thinner conjunctival epithelium. Skin appendages of eyelids include the sebaceous glands (glands of Zeis and meibomian glands), apocrine glands (glands of Moll), and eccrine sweat glands.[5a]

The *lacrimal gland* is largely of serous type, with a minor mucinous component in the ductal portion and a layer of myoepithelial cells in the larger peripheral ducts.

The *orbit* contains, in addition to the ocular globe and the lacrimal gland, the following structures: the optic nerve and its meningeal covering, Tenon's capsule, the extraocular muscles, blood vessels, and a delicate framework of fibroadipose connective tissue.

The *conjunctiva* is a thin mucous membrane that lines the inner surface of the eyelids and most of the anterior surface of the ocular globe. The conjunctival epithelium is composed of two to five layers of columnar cells that rest on a continuous basal lamina. This epithelium contains mucin-secreting goblet cells and melanocytes.

The *cornea* consists of six distinct layers: epithelium, epithelial basal lamina, Bowman's layer (an acellular structure made up of collagen fibers), stroma, Descemet's membrane (a true basal lamina produced by the underlying corneal endothelial cells), and a single layer of very flat cells traditionally known as "endothelium."[5a]

The *sclera* is mainly composed of a dense collagenous stroma admixed with occasional elastic fibers and scattered fibroblasts.

The *intraocular tissues* comprise the uveal tract (iris, ciliary body, and choroid), the retina, the crystalline lens, and the various intraocular compartments. A detailed description of these structures is beyond the scope of this book.

Eyelids

Most of the pathologic processes that involve the eyelids are those that involve the skin in general and are considered in detail in Chapter 4. Some consideration, however, is given in this chapter to those lesions that either are peculiar to the lids or present particular problems in this location.

Developmental anomalies

Dermoid cysts typically involve the upper eyelid along the brow margin and may represent forward extension of a mass that is primarily intraorbital (Fig. 30.1). These lesions rest on and are often firmly attached to the periosteum of the bony orbital rim. They are soft, nontender, oval or round, and usually about 1 cm in diameter.

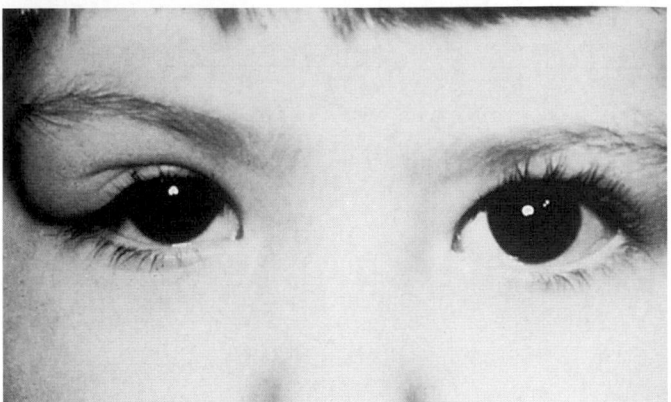

Fig. 30.1 Dermoid cyst of right upper eyelid.

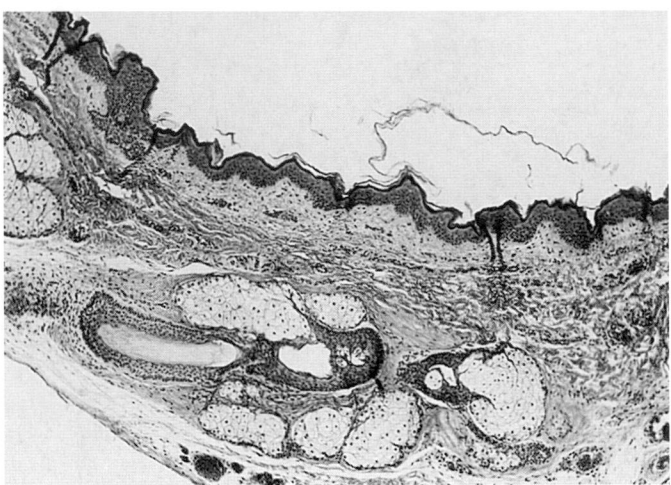

Fig. 30.2 Dermoid cyst of eyelid and brow. The cyst lumen is located in the upper right corner.

Microscopically, the cysts are lined by well-differentiated epidermal and dermal tissues containing all of the usual skin appendages (Fig. 30.2). The lumen is filled with keratinous debris, sebum, and hairs. In places where these contents have been extruded into the surrounding tissues, a severe foreign body inflammatory reaction may be observed.

Inflammation

Inflammation of the eyelids may be the result of viral, rickettsial, bacterial, mycotic, or parasitic infections; chemical or physical irritants; hypersensitivity states; or systemic dermatologic disorders. These inflammatory processes are rarely biopsied and are of relatively little practical significance to pathologists.

Pseudorheumatoid nodules (deep granuloma annulare) can involve the eyelid and eyebrow and rarely the episcleral and orbital tissues.[13]

Necrobiotic xanthogranuloma with paraproteinemia is characterized by multiple nodules or plaques that involve the periorbital areas (including eyelids) along with other parts of the body. A dysproteinemia caused by an IgG paraprotein is consistently present. Microscopically, the granulomas are characterized by collagen "necrobiosis" together with foamy macrophages and Touton giant cells.[11]

Silica granulomas are of noncaseating type and composed of epithelioid cells and multinucleated giant cells and birefringent crystals. They are surrounded by areas of fibrosis.[12]

Chalazion

Chalazion is an extremely common lesion. It represents a lipogranuloma that develops in and about a meibomian

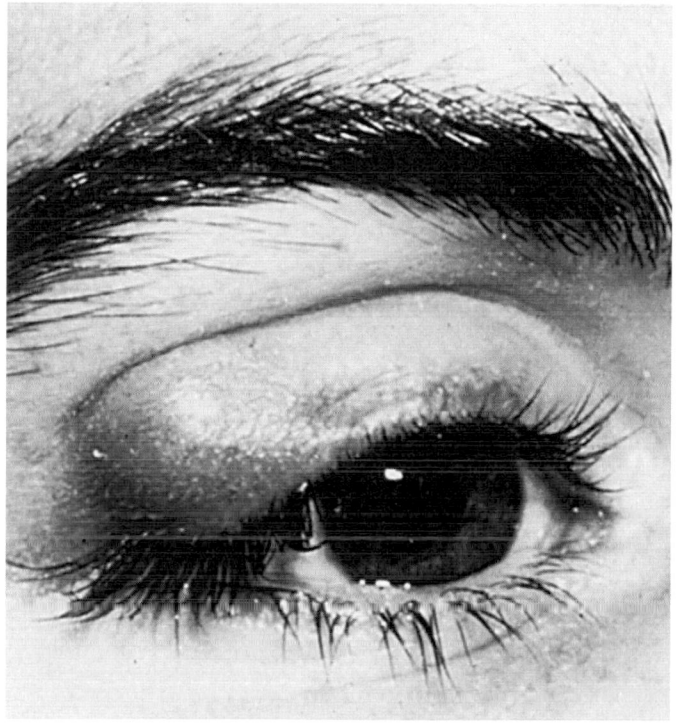

Fig. 30.3 Chalazion of right upper eyelid.

gland, presumably as a consequence of the combined effects of obstruction and nonspecific infection of the excretory passages of the gland. The sebaceous material discharged into the tarsus provokes an intense granulomatous inflammatory reaction (Fig. 30.3).

Although chalazion begins as a deep-seated process, not infrequently it erupts through the conjunctival surface of the eyelid. Ordinarily, this lesion is readily recognized and treated, but if, after curettage, one or more recurrences develop, the clinician should be alert to the possibility of a meibomian gland tumor that has previously escaped recognition. In such cases, excision and histopathologic study are indicated.

Microscopically, the typical chalazion reveals multiple foci of granulomatous inflammation (Fig. 30.4). In the center of many of the focal granulomas there is a small globule of fat, which in paraffin sections presents as an empty round to ovoid space (Fig. 30.5).

Cysts

Benign cysts of the skin of the eyelids and along the lid margins are relatively common, comprising approximately one third of lesions removed from the lids. The most common of these are the *keratinous cysts* discussed in Chapter 4. Another relatively frequent lesion is the *cyst of Moll's glands*, often referred to as sudoriferous cyst or simply ductal cyst. These present as thin-walled transparent vesicles at the lid margin. Microscopically, they are simple cysts lined by atrophic cuboidal or flattened epithelial cells with an empty lumen (Fig. 30.6).

Tumors and tumorlike lesions

Tumors and tumorlike lesions of surface epithelium

Basal cell carcinoma is by far the most frequent neoplasm arising in any of the palpebral tissues.[14,15] The over-

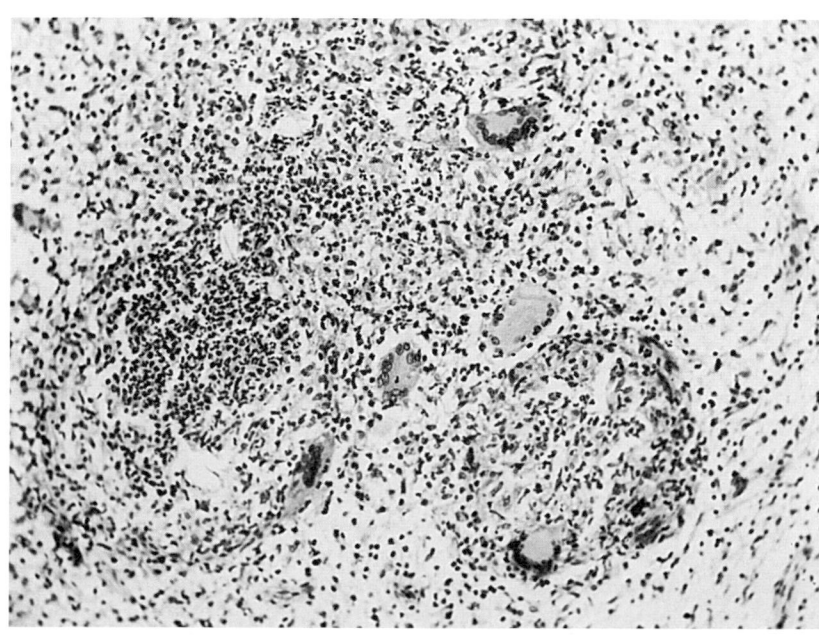

Fig. 30.4 Multiple foci of granulomatous inflammation with microabscesses and multinucleated giant cells in chalazion.

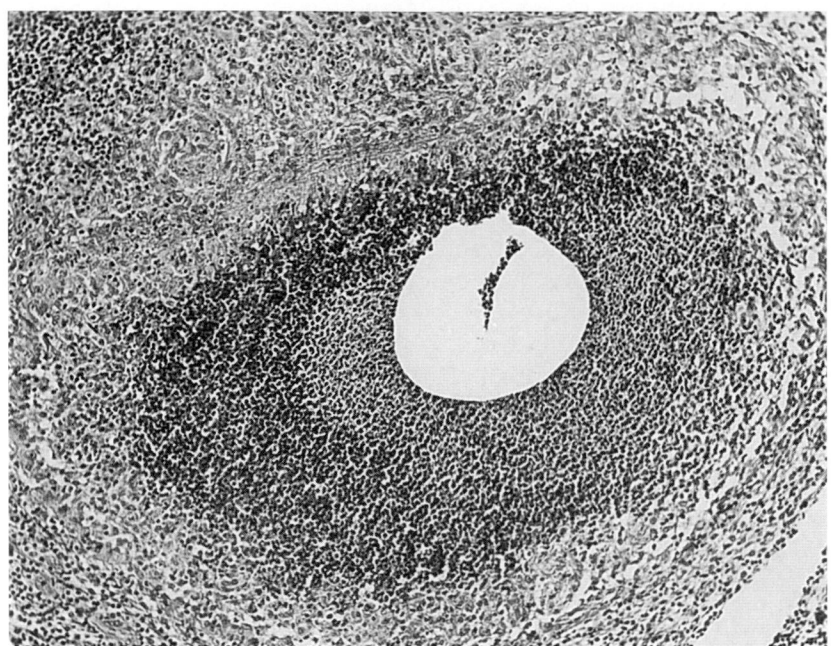

Fig. 30.5 The presence of pools of fat in the center of many of the granulomas is characteristic of chalazion.

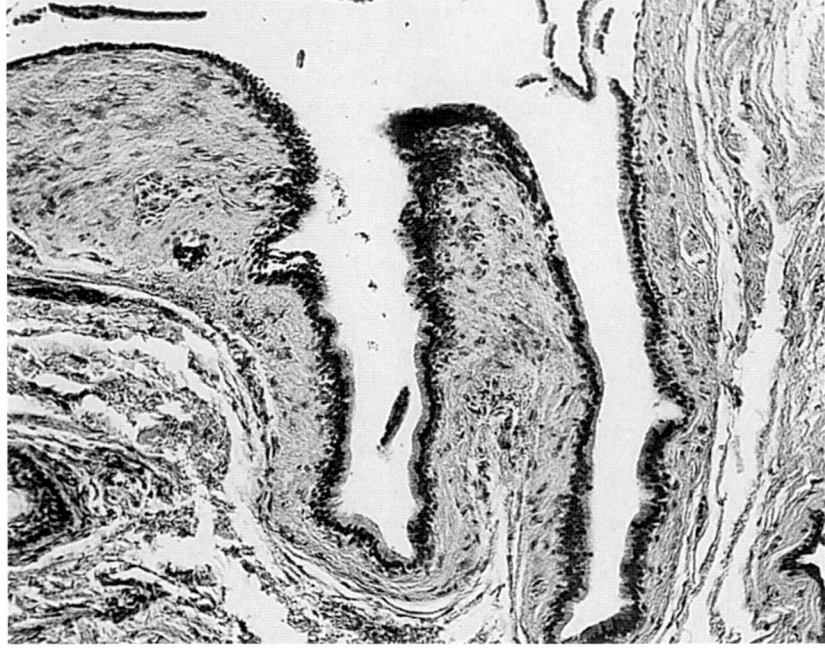

Fig. 30.6 Simple cyst of eyelid margin believed to be secondary to obstruction of the duct of Moll's gland (sudoriferous cyst).

whelming majority are easily excised without sequelae. On rare occasions, they may invade the orbit, nose, or both, and exenteration of the orbit may become necessary. Microscopic examination of the margins by frozen section at the time of surgery is a useful technique for ensuring that total removal of the tumor has been achieved.[19]

Basal cell carcinomas arise from the cutaneous surface of the eyelids and rarely, if ever, from the conjunctiva. This point is of some diagnostic significance, for a *papilloma* of the palpebral conjunctiva may resemble basal cell carcinoma. When such a lesion is excised and sectioned in such a way that its topographic orientation in relation to the conjunctival surface of the lid is not apparent and

if the pathologist is not informed of the clinical appearance of the tumor, an erroneous diagnosis of basal cell carcinoma can result (Fig. 30.7).

Squamous cell carcinoma is said to be responsible for approximately 10% to 20% of all malignant epithelial tumors of the eyelid.[22] Most cases are located in the lower lid.[20] A small percentage of these tumors are of the adenoid (pseudoglandular) type.[18]

Merkel cell carcinoma can occur in the eyelid, its morphologic appearance being the same as elsewhere in the skin.[21] Most reported cases have been located in the upper eyelid, where they have presented as large, nontender, red, or violaceous masses.[23]

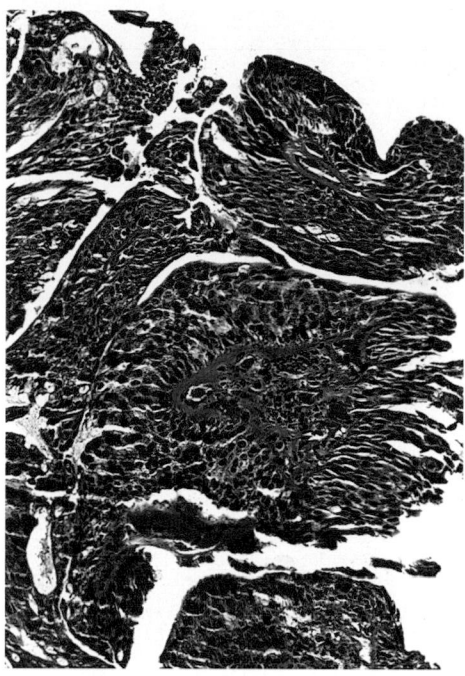

Fig. 30.7 Papilloma of conjunctiva. An exophytic growth of well-differentiated epithelial cells is supported by a prominent central fibrovascular core. The complex pattern of growth may simulate a carcinoma.

Non-neoplastic keratotic lesions may closely resemble squamous cell carcinomas. They include such entities as papilloma, pseudoepitheliomatous hyperplasia, keratoacanthoma, inverted follicular keratosis, seborrheic keratosis, actinic keratosis, and cutaneous horns.[16,17] The histopathologic features of these lesions are described in Chapter 4.

Adnexal tumors

Sebaceous gland adenomas and adenocarcinomas may arise from the cutaneous sebaceous glands, the glands of Zeis, or the meibomian glands (Fig. 30.8).[25] Some of the carcinomas have been seen as a second malignancy following radiation therapy for retinoblastoma.[27]

Solitary adenomas of the meibomian and Zeis glands are rarely seen in the laboratory, although they may be more common than is generally believed. The meibomian gland tumors, for example, may simulate a chalazion and be removed by curettage. Such curettings are rarely submitted for microscopic examination. Hence, one does not know how often such tumors are missed. In the case of malignant tumors, however, recurrence is likely. It is for this reason that recurrent chalazia are often excised and sent to the pathology laboratory. In reviewing the histories of patients with meibomian gland carcinomas, it is impressive that the usual story is one of repeated curettage for chalazia before a neoplasm is suspected and a biopsy obtained.[37]

Malignant meibomian gland tumors show considerable histologic and cytologic variation, merging with adenomas on the one hand and with very anaplastic

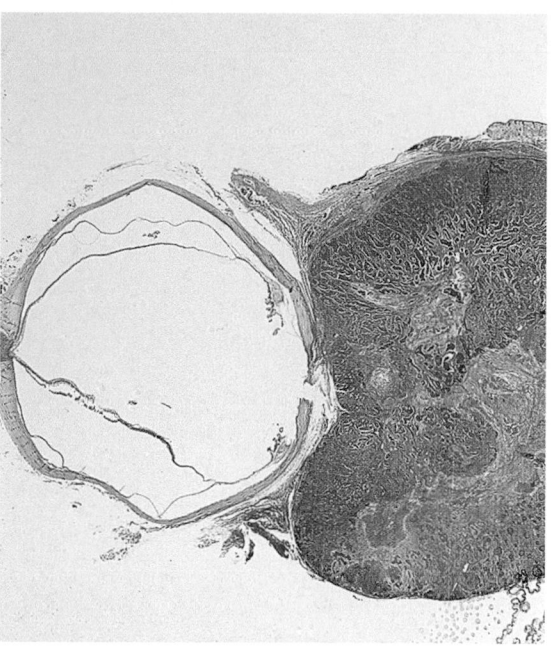

Fig. 30.8 Whole mount of sebaceous gland carcinoma compressing but not infiltrating the ocular globe. The tumor is sharply circumscribed and very cellular and has areas of necrosis.

epithelial tumors of uncertain histogenesis on the other. The former are easily recognized, first by their position within the tarsus and their obvious anatomic relation to the meibomian gland, and second by their cytologic characteristics. In such tumors the cells continue to exhibit sebaceous differentiation, which is very dramatically brought out by frozen sections stained for fat. More rapidly growing tumors may be characterized by extensive necrosis of the central areas of neoplastic lobules, giving rise to a comedocarcinoma pattern (Fig. 30.9). Pagetoid involvement of the overlying skin can occur, resulting in a clinical picture of chronic blepharoconjunctivitis.[24,33]

In the series of Rao et al.,[31] 23 out of 104 patients died from metastatic disease, confirming the fact that sebaceous carcinoma is a more aggressive neoplasm when located in the ocular adnexa. Features indicative of a poor prognosis were orbital or vascular invasion, involvement of both eyelids, poor differentiation, multicentric origin, large size, a highly infiltrative pattern, and pagetoid spread.[31]

Trichilemmoma, a benign adnexal tumor believed to originate from the outer hair sheath (trichilemma) and mostly composed of glycogen-rich clear cells, can involve the eyelid and eyebrow[26] (see Chapter 4).

Benign sweat gland tumors of the region include apocrine hidrocystoma[29] and papillary oncocytoma.[32] It is likely that the unique case of fibroadenoma of eyelid that has been recently reported was of sweat gland derivation.[30]

Malignant sweat gland tumors include apocrine adenocarcinoma[34] and mucinous adenocarcinoma. The latter

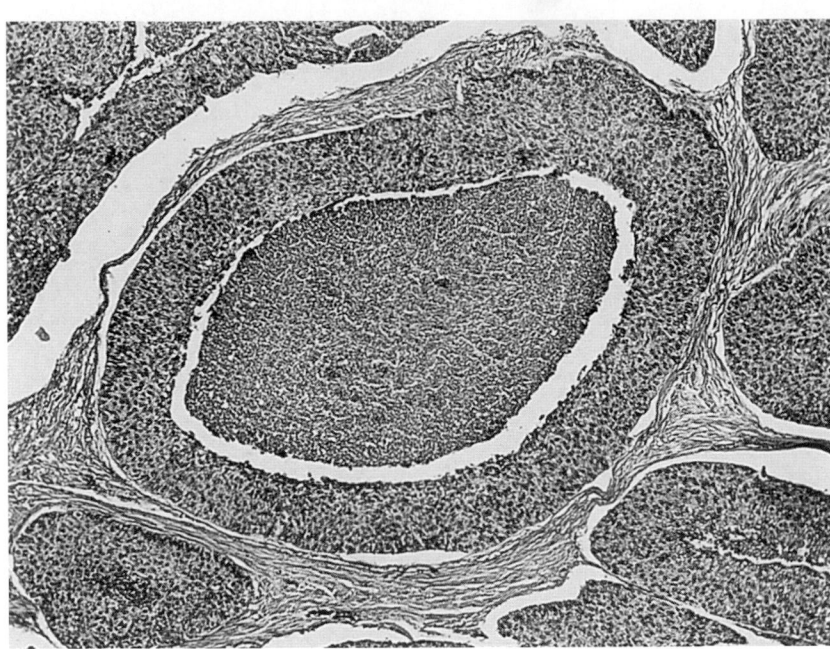

Fig. 30.9 Adenocarcinoma of meibomian gland. Plugs of necrotic tumor fill central portions of ductlike tubular masses of neoplastic tissue.

is homologous to the adenocystic carcinoma of the skin seen in other locations[35,37] (see Chapter 4). Local recurrence is common, but distant metastases occurred in only one of the 21 cases reported by Wright and Font.[38]

Signet ring carcinoma primary in the eyelid has been reported.[28] Before making this diagnosis, the statistically more likely possibility of a metastasis from breast carcinoma needs to be ruled out[36] (see p. 2720).

Melanocytic tumors

Melanocytic nevi may be observed in either the cutaneous or the conjunctival surface of the eyelids. The lid margin is a particularly common site (Fig. 30.10). Most are of the junctional or compound type. Like those in other areas, they may give rise to malignant melanoma. Fortunately, this is a very rare event.

A more diffuse and deeply situated melanotic lesion of the lids is the *nevus of Ota* (congenital oculodermal melanosis). This is a form of extrasacral mongolian spot involving the face in areas supplied by the first and second branches of the trigeminal nerve. This type of nevus occurs more frequently in Orientals and blacks than in whites. The latter have an increased incidence of ocular and orbital melanomas.[40]

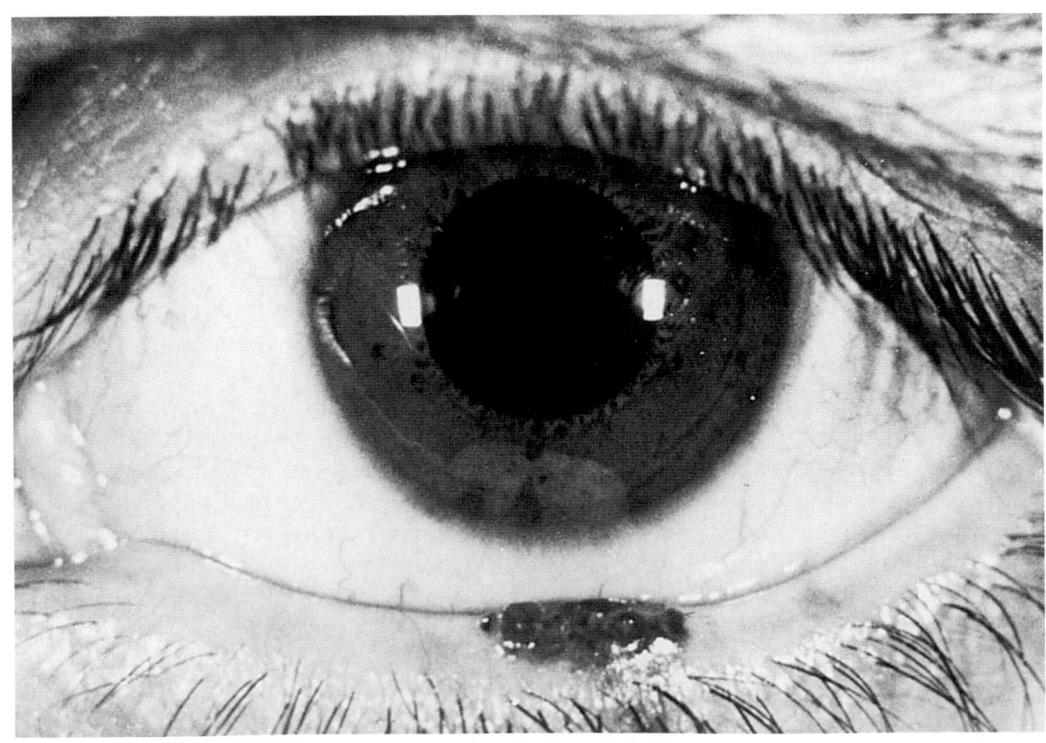

Fig. 30.10 Nevus of margin of lower eyelid.

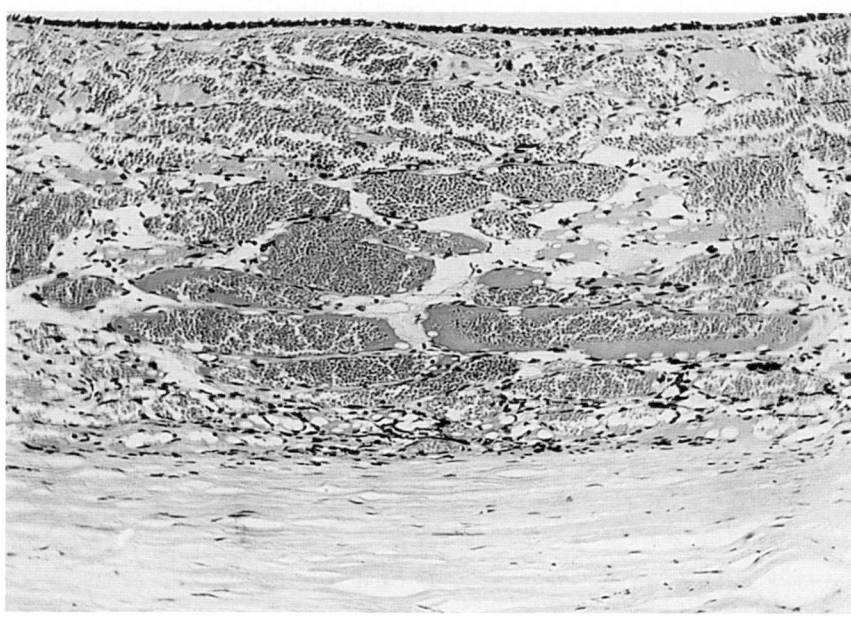

Fig. 30.11 Hemangioma of choroid in eye enucleated from a 42-year-old woman who had had a port-wine facial hemangioma since birth and ipsilateral glaucoma since early childhood.

Melanosis oculi (ocular melanocytosis) is an uncommon congenital anomaly characterized by variable hyperpigmentation of the conjunctiva, episclera, sclera, uveal tract and, occasionally, the optic nerve. It is generally regarded as a variant of nevus of Ota. Patients with this disorder have an increased incidence of ocular malignant melanoma.[41]

So-called **acquired melanosis** is a disorder that may involve either surface or both surfaces of the eyelid in association with the conjunctiva and is described in the section on the conjunctiva (p. 2734).

Malignant melanoma of the eyelid is rare.[42] It may originate from a nevus that has been present for many years, from an acquired melanosis of variable duration, or de novo.

In general, malignant melanomas of the lid carry a grave prognosis because they tend to metastasize early by the lymphatics and bloodstream. This is in contrast to malignant melanomas of the bulbar conjunctiva (p. 2734) and of the uvea (p. 2751), which have a more favorable prognosis. The procedure of sentinel lymph node biopsy, now routinely done for melanoma of the skin, has also been applied to melanoma of the eyelid and conjunctiva.[39]

Lymphoid tumors and tumorlike conditions

The morphologic appearances and diagnostic problems presented by these lesions when located in the eyelid are largely similar to those of analogous lesions of the conjunctiva and orbit and are fully discussed on p. 2728. The only difference of note is that the percentage of malignant tumors seems to be higher for lymphoid masses in the eyelid than for those in the other sites.

Eyelid involvement is not an uncommon finding in late cases of *mycosis fungoides*.[43]

Mesenchymal tumors and tumorlike conditions

Angiomas may present as small lesions confined to the eyelid or may extend deep into the orbit.[45] Hemangiomas are more common than lymphangiomas. Their histopathologic characteristics are described in Chapter 4.

The so-called *port-wine stain* (nevus flammeus) is of special interest not only because of its great cosmetic effect, but also because it may be associated with malformations in other tissues (Fig. 30.11). In the *Sturge–Weber syndrome*, the facial hemangioma may be associated with a choroidal hemangioma, glaucoma, and a meningeal hemangioma, all on the ipsilateral side (Fig. 30.12).

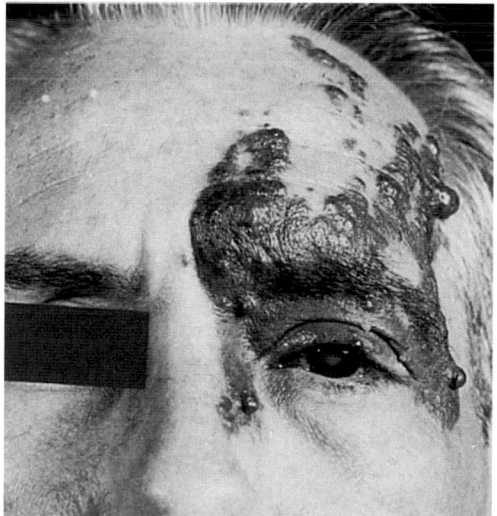

Fig. 30.12 Sturge–Weber syndrome. The patient, a 42-year-old man, had had facial hemangioma all his life and was blind in the ipsilateral eye because of retinal degeneration, glaucoma, and cataract. Choroidal hemangioma was found in the enucleated eye, but clinical study failed to disclose evidence of an intracranial lesion. (Courtesy of the Veterans Administration Hospital, Hines, IL)

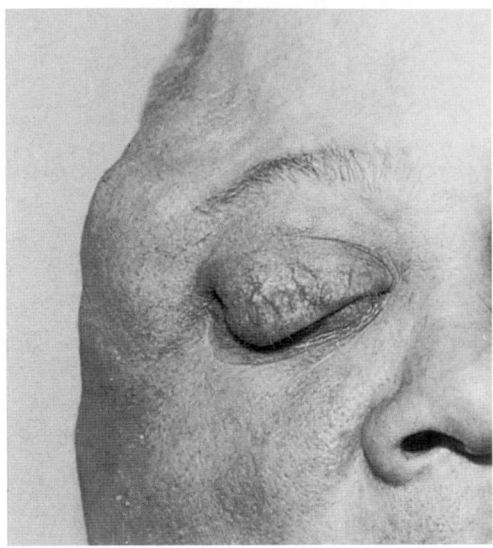

Fig. 30.13 Severe unilateral deformity of face in a patient with Recklinghausen's neurofibromatosis. (Courtesy of Dr. L.L. Calkins, Kansas City, KS)

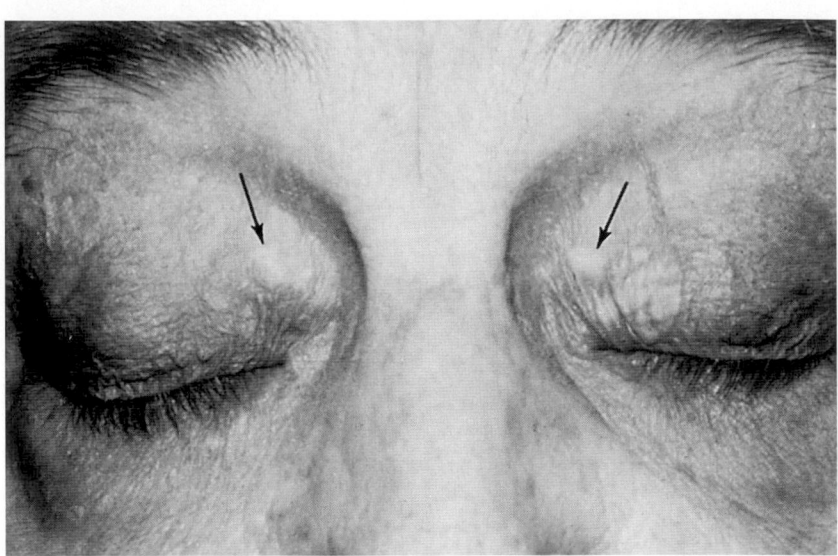

Fig. 30.14 Xanthelasma of upper eyelids in a patient who had no other systemic findings (arrows).

Masson's hemangioma (intravascular papillary endothelial hyperplasia) can develop in the eyelid, either de novo or engrafted on a preexisting vascular lesion.[47]

Neurofibromas can present as isolated lesions or as a component of Recklinghausen's disease. Although believed to be present from birth, these tumors frequently show accelerated growth during childhood or later. When associated with Recklinghausen's disease, there may be marked asymmetry of the face caused by diffuse hypertrophy and pendulousness of all of the facial tissues on one side (Fig. 30.13).

Xanthelasmas are slightly elevated yellow plaques located on the medial aspect of the upper and lower eyelids (Fig. 30.14). They are rarely indicative of any serious systemic disturbance and are usually removed for

cosmetic reasons. Most of the patients are in the fifth or sixth decade of life. Patients with familial hypercholesterolemia may develop these lesions at a younger age.

Microscopically, these lesions show large, pale-staining, fat-laden histiocytes throughout the subepithelial tissues (Fig. 30.15).

Amyloidosis can occur in the eyelid and conjunctiva as a localized mass. It presents as a chronic painless tumefaction usually not associated with any systemic disease.[44,46]

Metastatic tumors

Carcinomas from various sites can metastasize to one or both eyelids, sometimes as the first manifestation of the disease. A notorious diagnostic trap in this area is the mammary lobular carcinoma having striking histiocytoid features and simulating an inflammatory process.[47a]

Lacrimal passages

Diseases of the lacrimal passages that are of importance to the surgical pathologist are characterized by epiphora (the imperfect drainage of tears so that they flow over the lid margin onto the cheek) and by varying degrees of swelling, induration, and inflammation of the lower eyelid at its nasal end. Although inflammatory obstructions of these passages are common, neoplastic lesions are rare.

Canaliculitis and dacryocystitis

Canaliculitis and dacryocystitis may be the result of direct spread of inflammatory processes in neighboring structures such as the conjunctiva or nose, but more often their pathogenesis is obscure. Acute and chronic types are recognized, and the inflammatory reaction may be suppurative, granulomatous, or necrotizing, with the

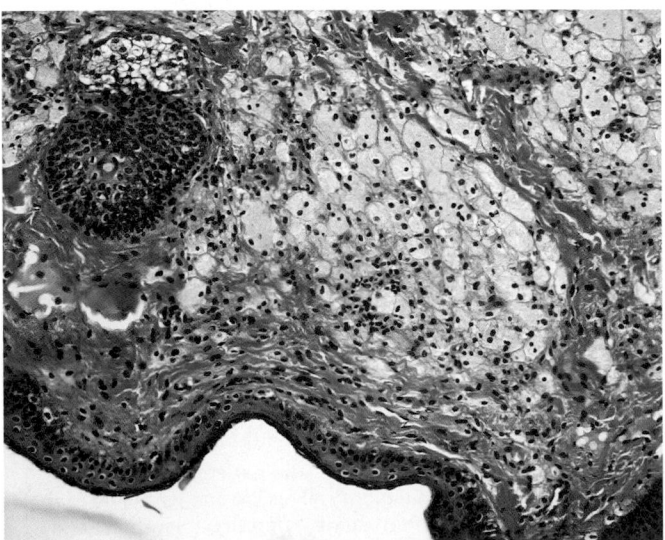

Fig, 30.15 Xanthelasma of eyelid. Clusters of foamy macrophages are seen in the dermis in association with a few lymphocytes.

formation of fistulous tracts to the skin surface below the eyelid near the base of the nose.

The lacrimal passages become filled with purulent exudate in the acute suppurative types, whereas in the chronic forms the passages are narrowed by inflammatory thickening of the walls of the lacrimal canal or sac. Frequently there are also hyperplasia of the lining epithelium and hypersecretion of mucus. At times, the degree of papillomatous or adenomatous hyperplasia of the sac may give rise to difficulties in differential diagnosis.

Sarcoidosis may involve the lacrimal sac as an extension of upper respiratory tract disease.[48]

Mucocele

Lacrimal mucocele is another complication of chronic inflammation of the lacrimal sac. A low-grade obstructive lesion with a relatively intact and possibly hypersecreting mucosa may lead to great distention of the sac by accumulated secretions.

The contents of the cyst may be clear or milky, fluid or gelatinous, fibrinous or flocculent, sterile or infected. Microscopically, the cyst wall reveals varying degrees of atrophy, degeneration, hyperplasia, hypersecretion of the mucosa, and chronic inflammation of the subepithelial tissues.

Dacryolithiasis

Dacryolithiasis and concretions in the lacrimal canaliculus ("tear stones") are of uncertain pathogenesis, but they are generally believed to be the result of low-grade inflammatory processes, including mycoses. If such concretions are crushed and examined microscopically, they will be seen to contain myriad mycelial elements embedded in a relatively acellular matrix. Others are laminated, mineralized stones with recognizable fungous or bacterial forms.

Tumors

Neoplasms of the lacrimal passages are rare. **Papillomas** similar to those arising in the conjunctival surface of the eyelid (p. 2715) may form in the punctum, within the canaliculus, or in the sac. Inflammatory pseudoepitheliomatous hyperplasia, however, is seen more often.

From the clinical point of view, it is usually not possible to distinguish malignant tumors of the lacrimal passages from benign neoplasms and pseudotumors. Dacryocystography has become an important part of the clinical evaluation of lacrimal sac tumors.

Oncocytomas (oxyphil cell adenomas) may develop in the lacrimal sac or in the caruncle. Most of the cases have been seen in elderly women, and local excision has been curative.[50]

All malignant tumors of the lacrimal passages except carcinoma are exceedingly rare, and even carcinoma is distinctly uncommon. These tumors are usually moderately well differentiated **squamous cell carcinomas**, similar in appearance to those arising from the mucosa of the nose or in the conjunctiva. They tend to form papillary projections into the lumen and spread along natural surfaces, but they also infiltrate directly into adjacent tissues.[55]

Other reported malignancies of the lacrimal sac include **mucoepidermoid carcinoma,**[54] **lymphoepithelioma-like carcinoma,**[52] **malignant lymphoma,**[53] and **malignant melanoma.**[49,51]

Lacrimal gland

Lacrimal gland lesions are divided into nonepithelial and epithelial. The nonepithelial lesions, which make up about 65% of the cases, include inflammatory pseudotumor, lymphoid hyperplasia, nonspecific dacryoadenitis, Sjögren's syndrome, sarcoidosis, malignant lymphoma, and leukemia. Of the epithelial tumors, benign mixed cell tumor (pleomorphic adenoma) is the most common.

Mikulicz's disease

When chronic dacryoadenitis is associated with enlargement of the parotid or other salivary glands, it has been referred to as *Mikulicz's syndrome*. This may be the result of Mikulicz's disease or a variety of other specific diseases, including sarcoidosis, tuberculosis, syphilis, mumps, Graves' disease, malignant lymphoma, and leukemia.

Mikulicz's disease (benign lymphoepithelial lesion) is the most common cause of Mikulicz's syndrome.[56-58] Microscopically, the two essential features are lymphocytic infiltration and formation of lymphoepithelial lesions. The appearance is thus similar to that seen in a more exuberant form in the salivary glands. Sometimes these changes affect only one lacrimal gland, with no salivary gland involvement or systemic manifestations. In fact, this is the type of dacryoadenitis the pathologist sees most frequently.

When Mikulicz's disease is accompanied by failure of lacrimal and conjunctival secretions and consequent keratoconjunctivitis sicca, the term *Sjögren's syndrome* is used. Most of the cases are seen in postmenopausal women.

The reader is referred to the chapter on the salivary glands (see p. 873) for a more detailed discussion of the nature of Mikulicz's disease and its relationship to malignant lymphoma.

Tumors

Most neoplasms of the lacrimal gland arise in the orbital lobe where the gland is firmly attached to the orbital rim about the lacrimal fossa. The bone tends to restrict growth in its direction. Hence the enlarging tumor characteristically displaces the eye downward and nasally (Fig. 30.16).

The histopathologic, ultrastructural, and immunohistochemical characteristics of lacrimal gland tumors are similar to those of the salivary glands[63,66] (see Chapter 12). **Benign mixed tumors** account for approximately 50% to 60%, **malignant mixed tumors** for 5% to 10%,

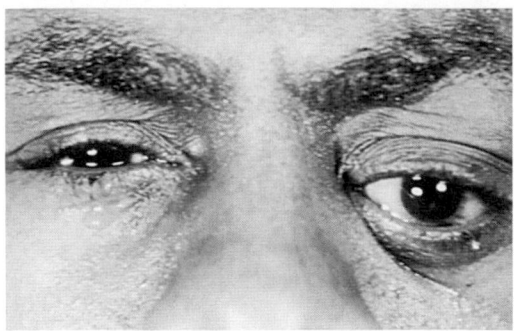

Fig. 30.16 Benign mixed tumor of left lacrimal gland in a 38-year-old man. Proptosis was accompanied by severe visual loss.

adenoid cystic carcinomas for 20% to 30%, and other carcinomas for 5% to 10%.[60,64,68] Many of the mixed tumors have a predominant component of hyaline cells of presumed myoepithelial nature (Fig. 30.17). Oncocytomas have also been reported.[65,67] Gamel and Font[62] found that adenoid cystic carcinomas with a basaloid pattern of growth had a decidedly worse prognosis than the nonbasaloid type. Because so many of these lacrimal gland tumors are not completely and adequately removed at the initial operation, there has been an excessively high recurrence rate.[70] It is even more difficult to treat the recurrences, for they are often multiple. The carcinomas have a very poor prognosis.[61,72]

In addition to the epithelial tumors of the lacrimal gland, **malignant lymphomas, lymphoid hyperplasias**, and **chronic inflammatory processes** are important causes of enlargement of the gland. In a patient who is in good general health and who presents no evidence of a systemic disease, the discovery of a lymphoid mass in the lacrimal fossa rarely heralds the development of malignant lymphoma or leukemia. In fact, in the majority of cases there is a polymorphism suggestive of a reactive inflammatory process, although in other cases the rather pure proliferation of lymphocytes makes it quite impossible to rule out a lymphocytic lymphoma or leukemia. The lacrimal glands may, of course, become involved along with other tissues in a leukemia or malignant lymphoma.

Mesenchymal tumors of the lacrimal gland are exceptional and include a few case reports of solitary fibrous tumor,[59] giant cell angiofibroma,[71] and granular cell tumor.[69]

Orbit

The clinical hallmark of disease of the orbit is exophthalmos. This may not necessarily be caused by a true neoplasm, and therefore the surgical pathologist may never see any specimen from the many patients who present with this finding. For example, the most common cause of exophthalmos is dysthyroid ophthalmopathy, and rarely is a biopsy taken in such a circumstance.

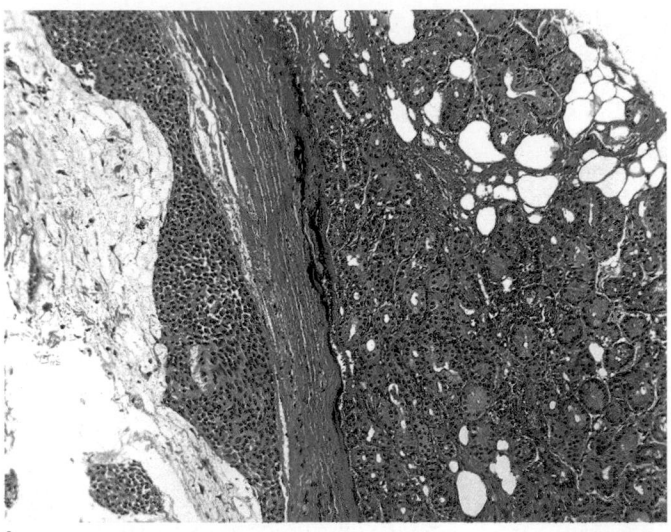

A

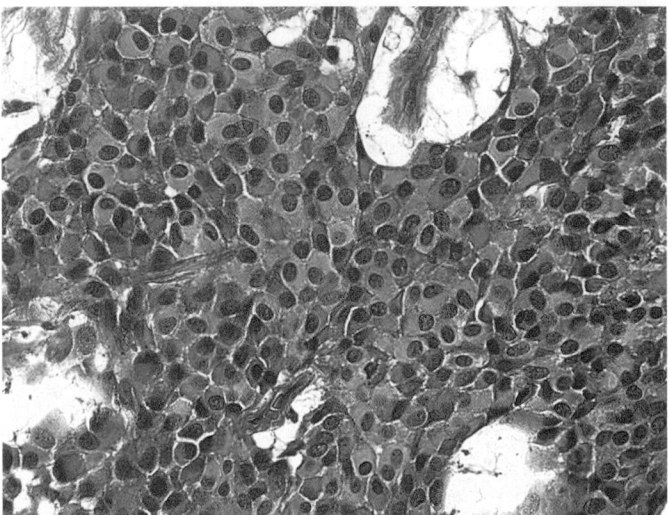

B

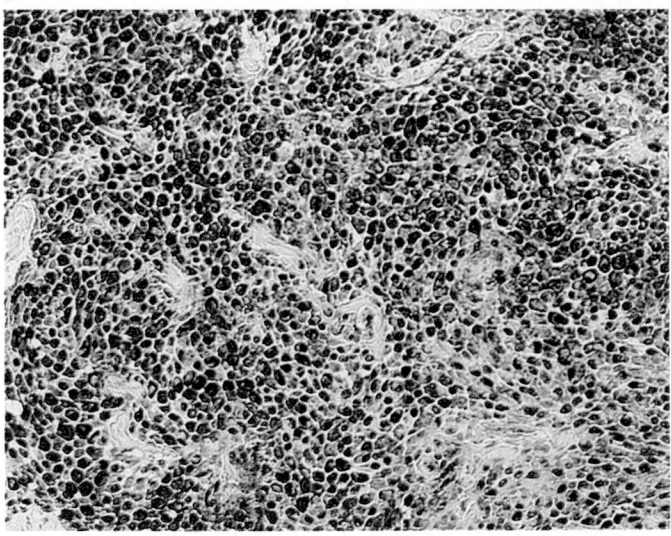

C

Fig. 30.17 Benign mixed tumor of lacrimal gland largely composed of so-called "hyaline cells": **A**, low-power view showing encapsulated quality; **B**, high-power view showing a diffuse eosinophilic appearance of the cytoplasm; **C**, strong immunoreactivity for S-100 protein.

As for the relative frequency of lesions that cause exophthalmos, many of the statistics that have been reported merely reflect the bias of the specialist involved. To the radiologist, for example, one of the most common orbital lesions producing displacement of the eye is a mucocele arising from a paranasal sinus. The ophthalmologist, however, would place mucocele far below such entities as dysthyroid ophthalmopathy, hemangioma, and inflammatory pseudotumor.[74] Procedures useful for the diagnostic evaluation of orbital masses include CT scan, MRI, and fine needle aspiration.[73,75]

Dysthyroid ophthalmopathy

The most common cause of orbital disease and of exophthalmos is dysthyroid ophthalmopathy in which there is a dysfunction of the pituitary–thyroid axis.[76] When seen because of ocular problems, the patient may be hyperthyroid, hypothyroid, or euthyroid. There is often a history of hyperthyroidism or some form of treatment.

Unilateral orbital involvement occurs with sufficient frequency in both forms of dysthyroid ophthalmopathy to warrant this condition always being considered in the differential diagnosis of orbital tumors (Fig. 30.18).

Histopathologic changes observed in severe cases, which are most likely to come to the attention of surgical pathologists, include widespread edema and chronic inflammation of all the orbital tissues. The most striking gross alterations are observed in the extraocular muscles, which may be massively enlarged. Muscle fibers degenerate and become hyalinized. A great increase in the interstitial connective tissue, including both cellular

elements and ground substance, is observed particularly in the muscles but also in the other orbital tissues.

Inflammatory processes

Secondary inflammation of the orbit can occur from lesions arising in the face, eyes, nose, sinuses, orbital bones, blood vessels, brain, and meninges.[83] Generally, it is only when such inflammations simulate neoplasms that orbital exploration is undertaken and tissue is obtained for histopathologic diagnosis.

Specific granulomas, including those of tuberculosis, mycosis, sarcoidosis, and Wegener's granulomatosis are rare (Fig. 30.19).

Mucocele is the result of chronic inflammatory disease of the frontal or ethmoid sinuses. The lesion erodes through the wall of the sinus to produce an inferolateral displacement of the globe. The onset is usually insidious, and the enlargement is symptomless and slow (Fig. 30.20).

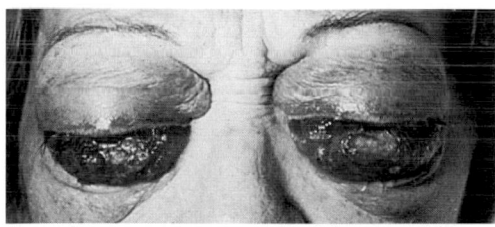

A

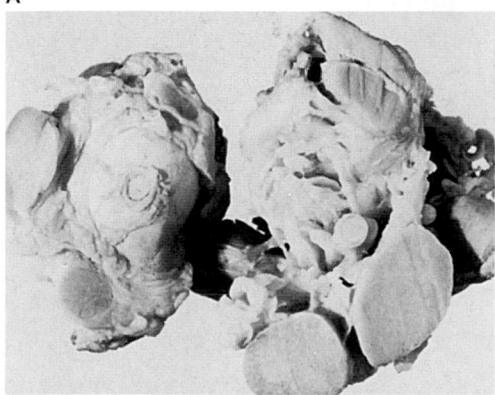

B

Fig. 30.18 A, Exophthalmos of approximately 10 months duration in a 65-year-old woman who finally died of congestive heart failure. **B,** At autopsy, extraocular muscles were found to be massively thickened.

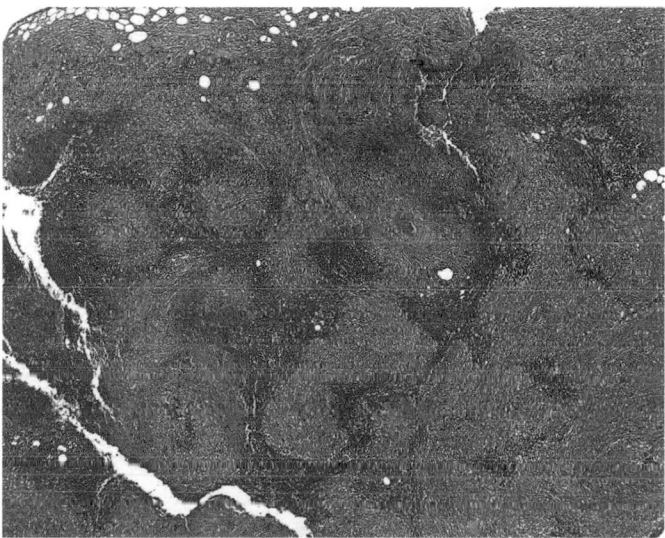

A

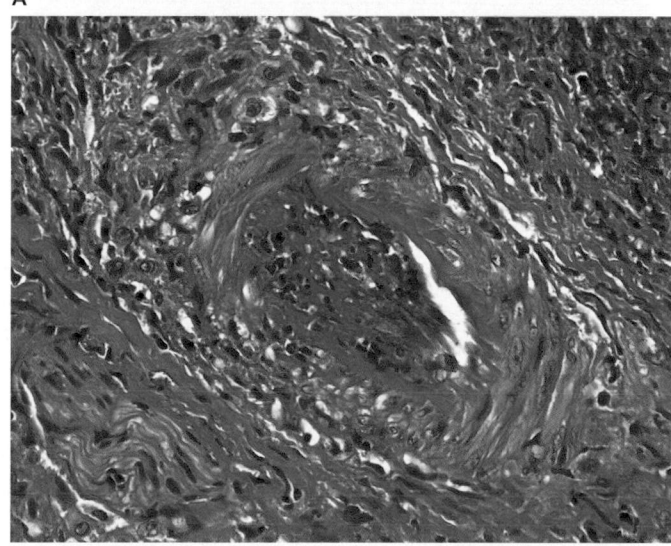

B

Fig. 30.19 Wegener's granulomatosis involving orbit: **A,** multiple confluent granulomas; **B,** vasculitis with thrombosis.

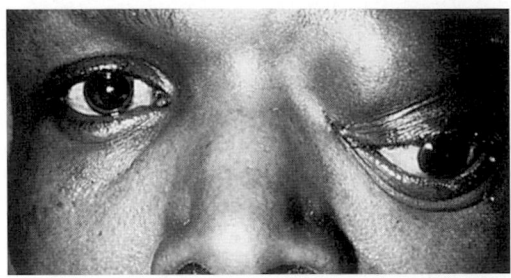

Fig. 30.20 Mucocele producing downward and lateral displacement of left eye. (From del Regato JA, Spjut HJ. Ackerman and del Regato's cancer, ed. 6. St. Louis, 1985, Mosby)

Histopathologically, this cystic mass is lined by mucus-secreting sinus mucosa with variable degrees of inflammation and scarring.

Inflammatory pseudotumors of the orbit are much more frequent than the specific infectious granulomas. These pseudotumors undoubtedly represent an etiologically and pathogenetically heterogeneous group.[77,84] In some instances, they have been found associated with involvement of paranasal sinuses.[78] In others, they have been the orbital manifestation of Rosai–Dorfman disease[79] (sinus histiocytosis with massive lymphadenopathy) (Fig. 30.21). Still others represent the orbital manifestation of inflammatory fibrosclerosis (idiopathic sclerosing inflammation), a process that may also involve the retroperitoneum, mediastinum, extrahepatic bile ducts, and thyroid.[85] The pathologic features they share include the following:

1 The formation of an indurated orbital mass often surrounding the optic nerve and incorporating one or more of the extraocular muscles.
2 A tissue reaction that includes exudation of fluid, excessive production of ground substance, mobilization of chronic inflammatory cells, vascular proliferation, and hyperplasia of connective tissue.
3 The absence of demonstrable etiologic agents or of otherwise diagnostic histopathologic alterations indicative of specific disease entities such as Hodgkin's lymphoma, temporal arteritis, or lupus erythematosus.[82]

This is not to say, however, that the microscopic features are uniform from case to case (Fig. 30.22). In some instances the proliferation of blood vessels and ground substance resembles that of exuberant granulation tissue.[81] At times, there is lymphoid hyperplasia with follicle formation (p. 2728). Other cases with prominent involvement of extraocular muscles suggest the possibility of dysthyroid ophthalmopathy. In cases that are caused by Rosai–Dorfman disease the infiltrate is composed of large histiocytes (some exhibiting lymphocytophagocytosis), lymphocytes, and plasma cells; fibrosis can be very prominent.[79] Other types of inflammatory pseudotumors are composed of cholesterol granulomas or accumulation of keratin ("epidermoid cholesteatomas").[86]

A well-developed granulomatous reaction about small pools of fat is observed in certain cases. Such lesions may suggest traumatic fat necrosis. Others containing large numbers of cholesterol clefts and many foamy macrophages and giant cells suggest an area of old suppuration or hemorrhage. Periphlebitis is prominent in certain cases, and some of these may present a significant tissue eosinophilia, suggesting the possibility of a hypersensitivity angiitis, a parasitic infection,

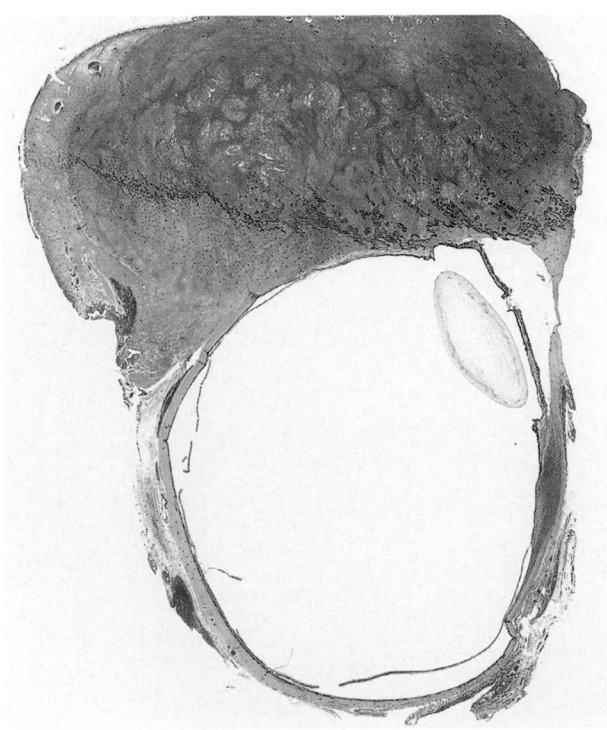

Fig. 30.21 Large intraorbital mass in a case of Rosai–Dorfman disease.

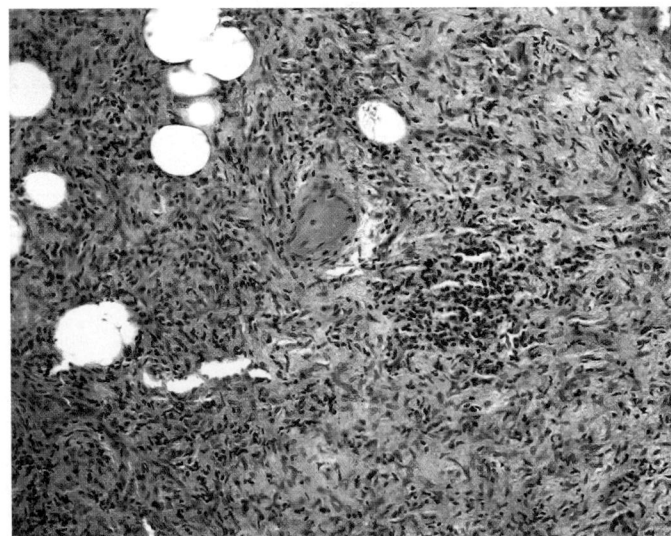

Fig 30.22 Inflammatory pseudotumor of orbit. Lymphocytes and spindle cells of fibroblastic/myofibroblastic appearance permeate the adipose tissue of the orbit.

Kimura's disease, or angiolymphoid hyperplasia with eosinophilia.

Patients with pseudotumors are usually in the third to fifth decade and in good health. The exophthalmos is of relatively sudden onset and in at least one half of the patients is associated with moderate to severe orbital pain and with lid and conjunctival edema. Diplopia is often present secondary to limitation of ocular motility in one or more fields of gaze, but visual acuity is usually unimpaired. Intracranial extension can occur.[80]

The lesion often can be palpated through the eyelids; if so, the surgeon may be able to reach it easily for a biopsy. Deeper lesions are not so readily accessible for biopsy, and if the clinical signs and symptoms are characteristic of inflammatory pseudotumor, steroids are often given without a biopsy, especially since systemic steroids often produce dramatic alleviation of signs and symptoms. The CT scan can be helpful in localizing the lesion.

Primary tumors

Mesenchymal tumors and tumorlike conditions

Rhabdomyosarcoma is the most common soft tissue sarcoma of the orbit in childhood.[103] The types seen in this age group are embryonal and alveolar, the latter being associated with a more aggressive clinical course. Some cases have occurred as a second primary tumor following irradiation for bilateral retinoblastoma.[99]

Hemangiopericytoma and **solitary fibrous tumor** are closely related and part of a morphologic continuum.[97] The former term has been used when the vascularity is prominent, while the latter has been generally employed when the tumor is solid, with keloid-like collagen and an alternation of hyper- and hypocellular areas[100,103,107] (Fig. 30.23). Strong immunoreactivity for CD34 and bcl-2 is present, particularly in the cases with a solitary fibrous tumor pattern.[90,110] In the series reported as hemangiopericytoma by Croxatto et al.,[88] the recurrence rate

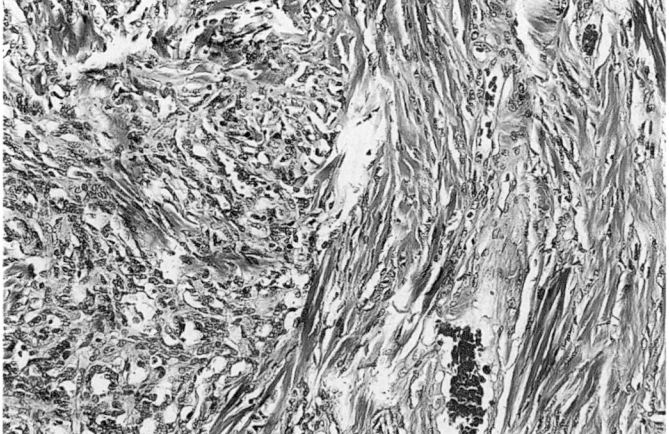

Fig. 30.23 Solitary fibrous tumor of orbit. The alternation of hypercellular and hypocellular areas is characteristic. The collagen has a keloid-type quality. This tumor was strongly immunoreactive for CD34.

was 30% and the metastatic rate was 15%, with most of the metastases developing late in the course of the disease. Some of the cases classified as solitary fibrous tumor have also followed an aggressive clinical course.[106]

Giant cell angiofibroma shares morphologic features of solitary fibrous tumor and giant cell fibroblastoma.[96] It is characterized by a richly vascularized proliferation of spindle cells containing pseudovascular spaces and multinucleated giant cells, often of the so-called "floret type."[89] CD34 is positive. This lesion, which is not limited to the orbit,[105] may represent a variant of solitary fibrous tumor rich in giant cells.[98]

Fibrous histiocytoma used to be regarded as the most common primary mesenchymal orbital tumor in adults, the upper and nasal portions of the orbit said to be the most common sites. Font et al.[91] divided their cases into benign, locally aggressive, and malignant: the 10-year survival rate was 100%, 92%, and 23% respectively. At present, it is likely that many of these cases would be placed in another category. However, some lesions having an admixture of fibroblast-like and histiocyte-like cells and a storiform pattern of growth remain, there being no better alternative diagnosis.

Alveolar soft-part sarcoma can present as a primary orbital tumor.[93] The age of occurrence, microscopic appearance, and evolution are similar to those seen in the other location of this tumor (see Chapter 25) (Fig. 30.24). The clinical course is indolent, distant metastases sometimes occurring 10 years or more after initial therapy.[93]

Osteosarcoma has been reported most often as a late complication of radiation therapy to the area.[95]

Other malignant mesenchymal tumors, all extremely rare, include **leiomyosarcoma**,[112] **liposarcoma**,[87] **fibrosarcoma**,[109] **mesenchymal chondrosarcoma**,[102] **angiosarcoma**,[101] and **Ewing's sarcoma/PNET**.[111]

Angiomas are relatively common orbital tumors, with hemangiomas occurring much more commonly than lymphangiomas.[113]

In the infant, these soft, blue, compressible tumors are diffuse throughout the orbit and often extend forward into the eyelids (Fig. 30.25). Surgical removal is difficult; fortunately, however, most hemangiomas spontaneously regress by 4 years of age. If the tumor is so large that the visual axis of the eye is covered and the eye is at risk for the development of deprivation amblyopia, such lesions can often be reduced in size following a short course of systemic steroids or small doses of radiotherapy.

In the adult, these tumors are usually encapsulated, are situated close to the back of the eye, and can be surgically "shelled" out. The CT scan reveals a discrete round mass that is enhanced by contrast dye (Fig. 30.26).

These tumors rarely present difficulties in histopathologic diagnosis, for they are not significantly dissimilar from angiomas elsewhere. In the infant, the lesion is usually of capillary type and in the adult of cavernous type.

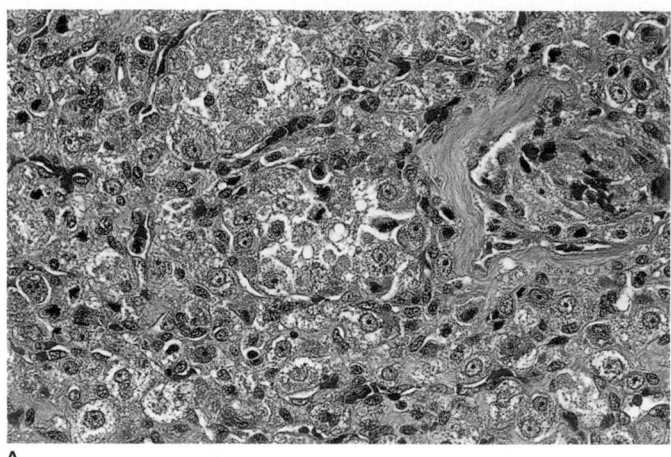
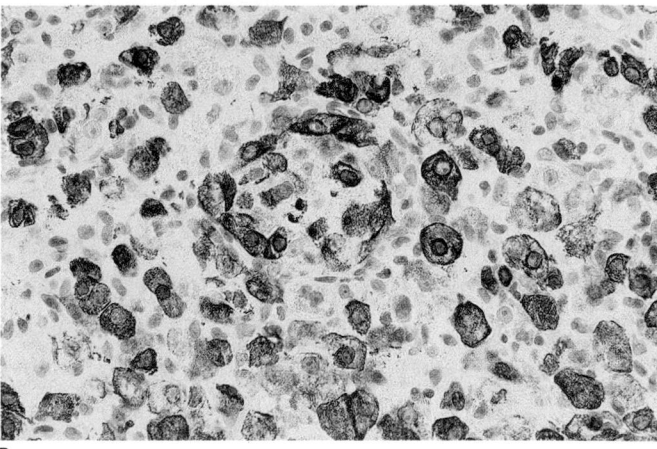

A   B

Fig. 30.24 A and **B**, Alveolar soft part sarcoma of orbit. **A**, Hematoxylin–eosin. **B**, Desmin immunostain. This degree of positivity for this marker is unusual but it constitutes strong evidence for muscle differentiation.

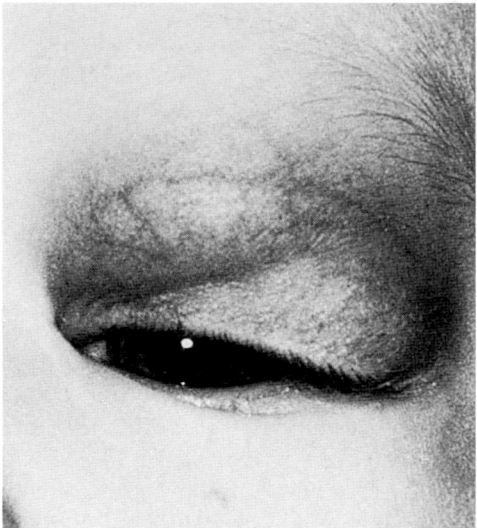

Fig. 30.25 Capillary hemangioma of left orbit and eyelid.

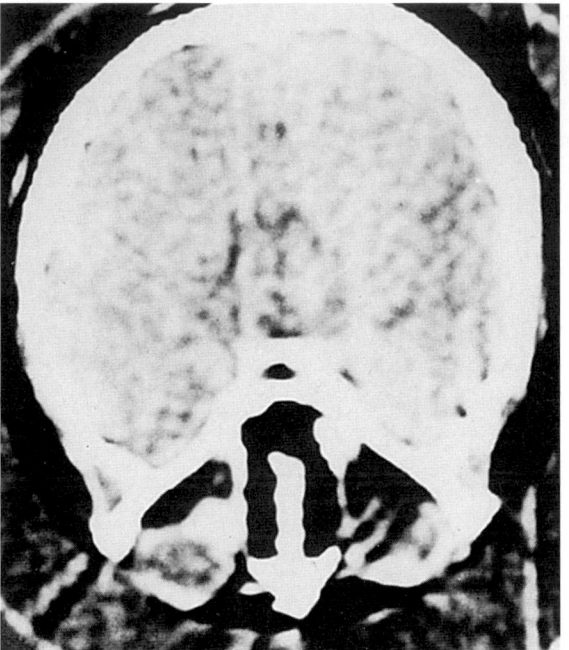

Fig. 30.26 CT scan showing hemangioma of right orbit.

Schwannoma and **neurofibroma** represent a small percentage of orbital tumors. Almost all orbital schwannomas are well-encapsulated tumors which can be completely removed surgically by orbitotomy.[108] Orbital neurofibromas are usually but not always an expression of Recklinghausen's disease.[104] There may be a gross deformity of the orbit and eyelid and, on palpation, the lid has been referred to as "a bag of worms."

Other benign mesenchymal tumors that have been observed at this site are **lipoma, chondroma**, and **osteoma**.

Tumorlike proliferations also occur within the orbit, including **nodular fasciitis**[92] and **intravascular papillary endothelial hyperplasia** (Masson's hemangioma).[94]

Langerhans' cell histiocytosis can involve the orbit and result in prominent exophthalmos.

Glioma of optic nerve

Gliomas of the optic nerve are relatively rare, slow-growing tumors that usually arise within the orbital segment of the nerve.

Considerable cytologic variation exists among the gliomas, not only from case to case but also in different portions of a given tumor. Varying degrees of cellularity are observed, but generally these neoplasms are characterized by a low order of anaplasia. This is especially true about the margins of the tumor, where it is often impossible to be certain where reactive gliosis ends and neoplasia begins. There are typically areas of intense mucinous degeneration within the tumor. In such areas the tumor cells frequently appear to be virtually lost in the abundant hyaluronidase-sensitive mucoid accumulations.

Small tumors limited to the optic nerve can be adequately managed by resection alone; for the more extensive lesions, biopsy followed by definitive irradiation is recommended.[115,117]

As these gliomas increase in size, they tend to form a bulbous enlargement of the nerve (Fig. 30.27). They also extend along the nerve peripherally toward the eye and centrally toward the brain. In so doing, they often produce great enlargement of the optic canal, an important diagnostic sign for the radiologist. In such cases the optic nerve fibers are likely to be completely destroyed, and the optic disc typically presents the ophthalmoscopic characteristics of primary optic atrophy.

Another growth pattern exhibited by a majority of optic nerve gliomas is infiltration through the pia. This leads to great thickening of the arachnoid (Fig. 30.28). This is partly the result of more exuberant growth of the tumor cells once they have reached the arachnoid, but equally important is the reactive proliferation of arachnoidal cells. At times, this has created difficulties in differential diagnosis between glioma and meningioma.

Microscopically, almost all optic gliomas are *low-grade pilocytic astrocytomas*, similar to those occurring in the cerebellum and in the region of the third ventricle.[114,116]

Rarely, malignant tumors characterized by dense cellularity, high mitotic index, marked pleomorphism, necrosis, and vascular proliferation are encountered.[116]

Gliomas of the optic nerve typically make their presence known during the first decade of life with minimal exophthalmos, optic nerve atrophy, or papilledema, and with a characteristic thickening of the nerve on CT scan. There is a distinct association of these tumors and Recklinghausen's disease. The majority of optic nerve gliomas are so slow growing that surgical intervention is seldom warranted.

Meningioma

Meningiomas of the orbit arising from the meninges of the optic nerve are thought to be more aggressive tumors than the meningiomas of the sphenoidal ridge[118] (Fig. 30.29). However, some authors believe that they need not be operated on unless severe proptosis or proof of posterior extension occurs.

Those tumors arising from the orbital meninges generally produce some visual loss, optic atrophy, and exophthalmos. Those arising from the inner portion of the

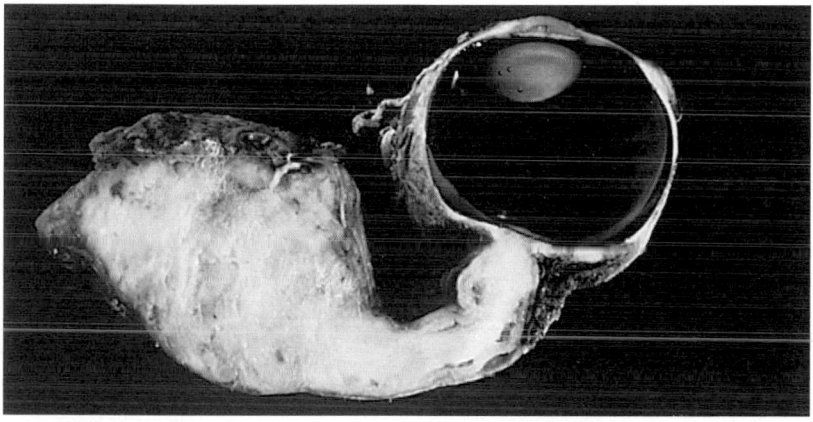

Fig. 30.27 Glioma that has produced massive enlargement of the orbital segment of the optic nerve. The tumor has completely effaced characteristic architectural features of the nerve and its meninges.

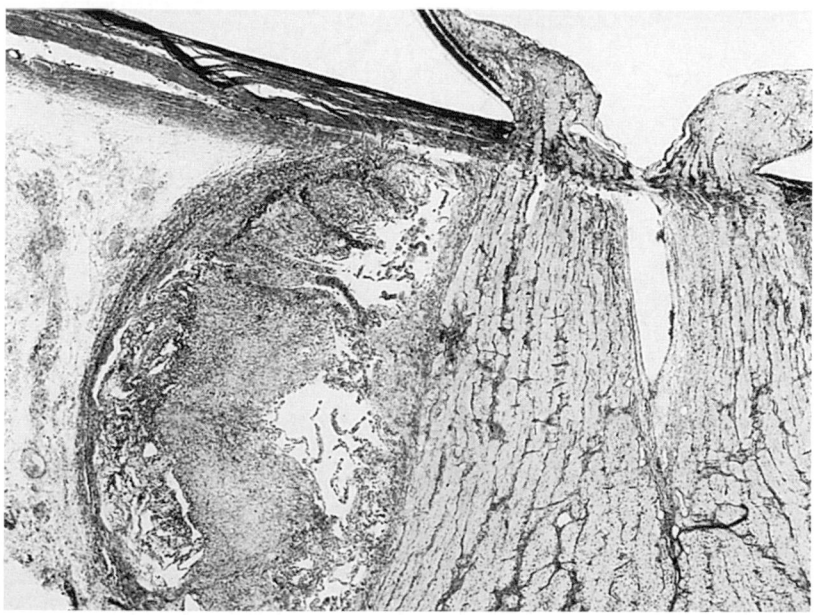

Fig. 30.28 Section through the optic nerve just anterior to the main mass of this glioma reveals minimal alteration of the parenchyma of the nerve but greatly thickened meninges. The combination of infiltrating tumor and arachnoidal proliferation is responsible for this meningeal thickening.

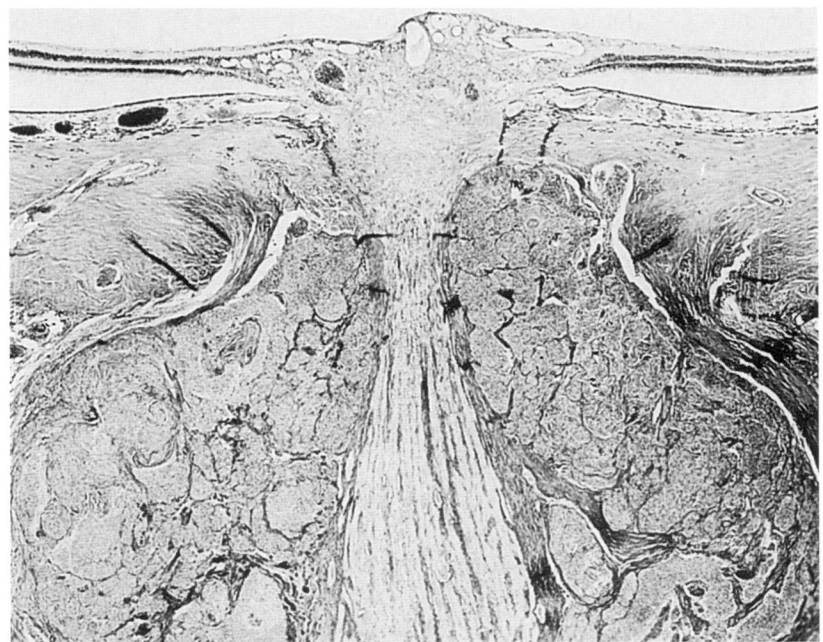

Fig. 30.29 Meningioma of optic nerve. The meninges are greatly thickened, and the optic nerve reveals severe compression atrophy.

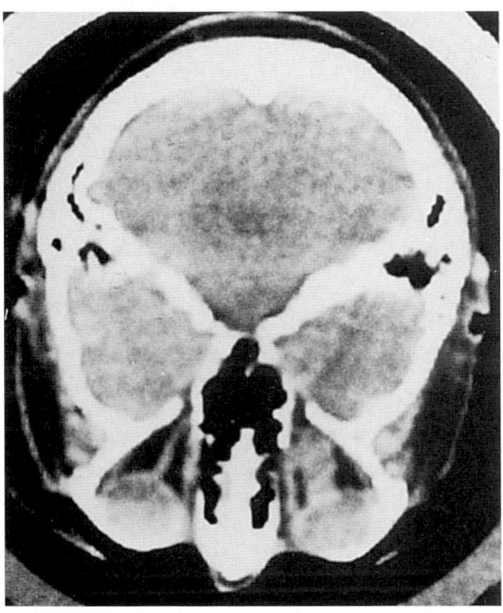

Fig. 30.30 CT scan showing perioptic meningioma of left orbit.

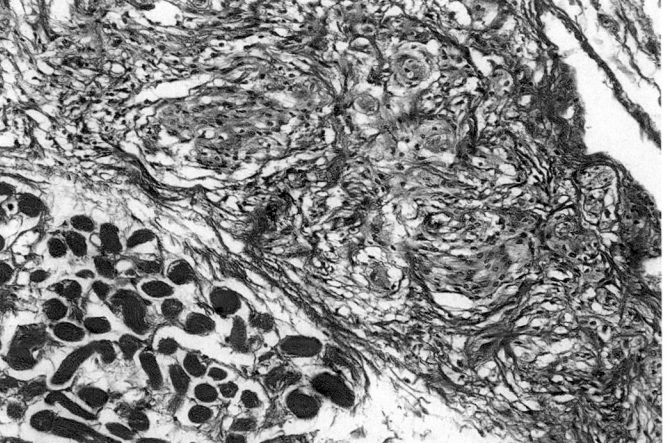

Fig. 30.31 Meningioma of orbit. The tumor has a typical meningothelial appearance.

sphenoidal ridge produce more severe compression of the optic nerve within the optic canal, resulting in papilledema or optic atrophy before proptosis. The CT scan has facilitated the diagnosis and localization of these tumors (Fig. 30.30). Microscopically, most orbital meningiomas are of the meningothelial type (Fig. 30.31). The differential diagnosis includes exuberant arachnoidal hyperplasia, fibrous histiocytoma, hemangiopericytoma/solitary fibrous tumor, and metastatic carcinoma.[119]

Lymphoid tumors and tumorlike conditions

Lymphoid lesions of the orbit and other ocular sites may present great difficulties in histopathologic diagnoses.

Some of these lesions develop in the course of a previously recognized malignant lymphoma or leukemia.[134] Others present initially in the orbit, but thorough clinical and laboratory examination reveals the presence of systemic involvement.[121,126] Still others, perhaps the majority, show involvement of the orbit, conjunctiva, or eyelid not accompanied by any clinical or hematologic evidence of systemic disease.[133]

Microscopically, the latter lesions fall into three groups:

1 Those lesions that are quite obviously of malignant nature, usually non-Hodgkin's lymphomas.[135]
2 Those lesions that are fairly obvious examples of reactive hyperplasia with considerable polymorphism, a variety of cell types, vascular proliferation, and prominent follicles with germinal centers.

3 Those lesions that are characterized by a rather uniform and monotonous but widespread proliferation of lymphocytes (small lymphocytic proliferations), frequently associated with involvement of orbital fat, blood vessels, and nerves (Figs 30.32 and Fig. 30.33). It is this group that presents the most difficult problems in differential diagnosis.[120,123,131] Some of these lesions are accompanied by plasmacytoid differentiation, Dutcher bodies, and an associated serum paraproteinemia.[122] At present, most of these lesions are thought to belong to the category of MALT lymphoma.[119a,137]

Most studies that have been carried out with the third group of lesions have shown that it is very difficult to predict which of them will develop into systemic lym-

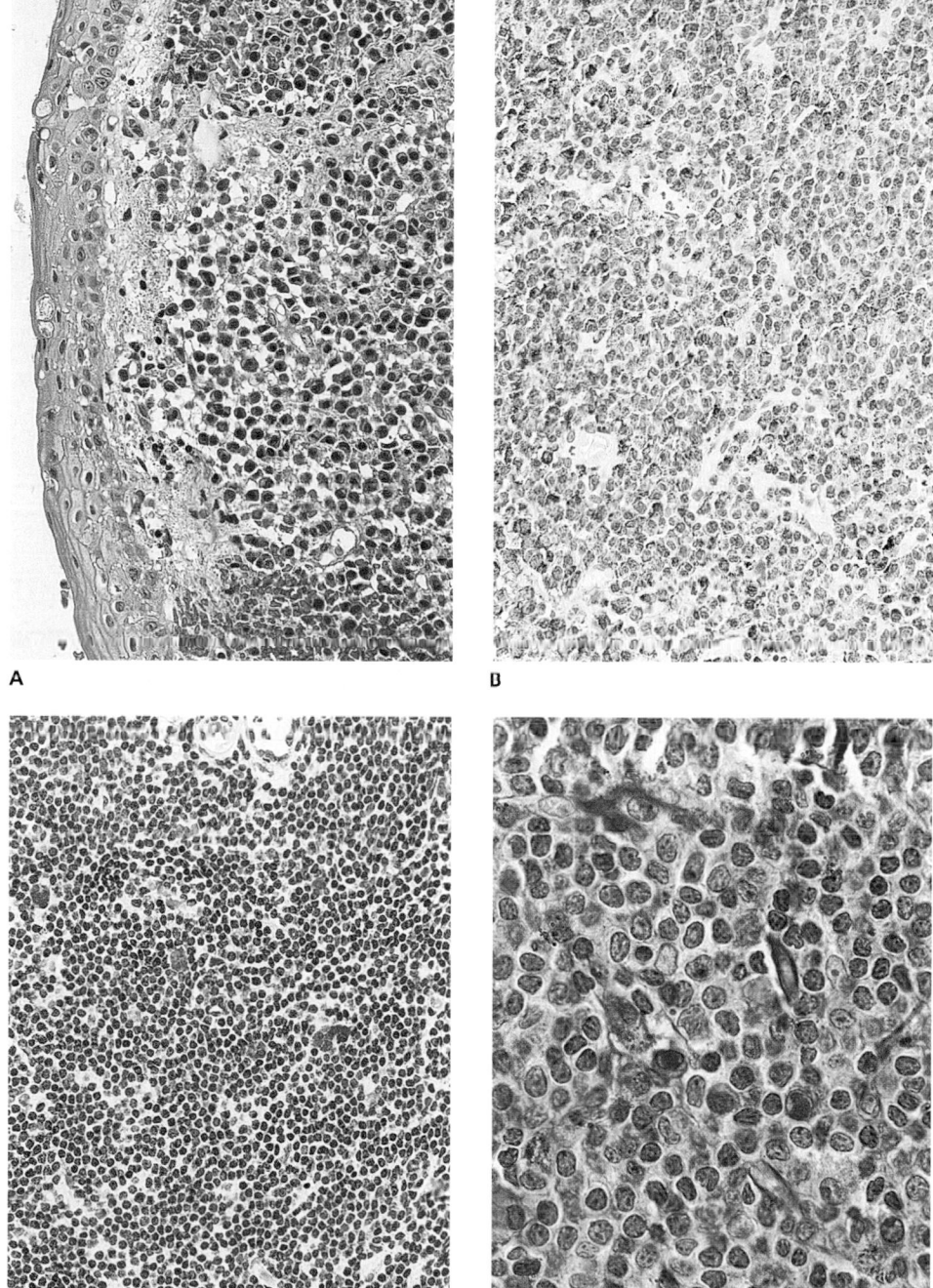

A B

Fig. 30.32 A and **B,** Malignant lymphoid proliferation of conjunctiva composed of small tumor cells with prominent plasmacytoid features: **B** shows strong immunoreactivity for kappa light chain.

A B

Fig. 30.33 A and **B,** Small lymphocytic proliferation of orbit. **A,** Low-power appearance showing a monotonous infiltrate of small lymphoid cells. **B,** PAS stain in another case, showing PAS-positive intranuclear inclusions composed of inspissated immunoglobulin (Dutcher bodies). The occurrence of these formations is strong evidence in favor of a neoplastic nature for the proliferation.

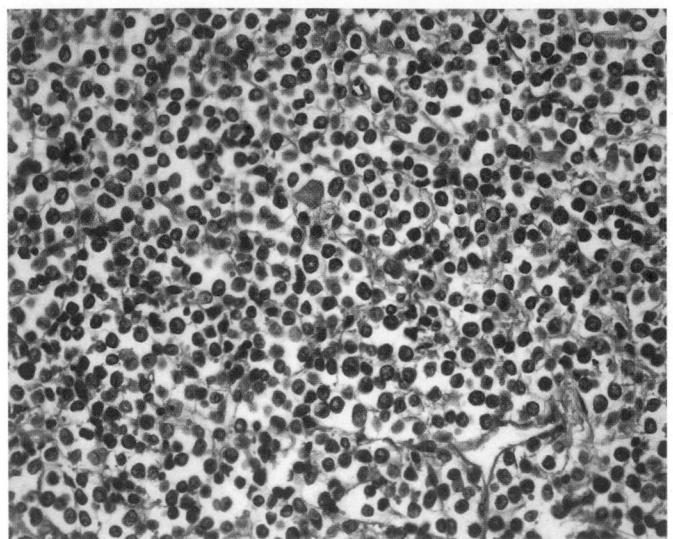

Fig. 30.34 So-called granulocytic sarcoma of orbit. This represents a localized focus of acute myelocytic leukemia.

phomas, whether one evaluates them by standard morphologic criteria, by cell marker analysis, or by gene rearrangement techniques.[124,128,132,136] Other studies have shown a better correlation between immunohistochemical features and outcome,[129,130] but perhaps the most important conclusion of all these studies is that the majority of patients with small lymphocytic proliferations localized to the ocular tissues enjoy an indolent clinical course and long survival with only minimal therapeutic intervention whether they are of polyclonal or monoclonal nature.[124,127] Lymphoid infiltrates of the conjunctiva are associated with a lower incidence of extraocular lymphoma (20%) than those of the orbit (35%) or eyelid (67%).[125] The most important prognostic factor is the extent of the disease at the time of presentation.[125]

Acute myelocytic leukemia can involve the orbit as an initially localized lesion (granulocytic sarcoma) (Fig. 30.34).

Metastatic tumors

Direct spread from adjacent structures can occur with primary intraocular tumors such as retinoblastoma or uveal malignant melanomas. Carcinomas of the paranasal sinuses may also fail to produce diagnostic symptoms until orbital extension has occurred.

Hematogenous metastases to the orbit may be seen with many different tumors, but only rarely are these the initial manifestations of a carcinoma. Even neuroblastoma, which has a notorious reputation for metastasizing to the orbit, rarely does so before other diagnostic signs appear.

Most important in this regard is the distinct possibility that a primary embryonal rhabdomyosarcoma might be misinterpreted as a metastatic tumor. Another important possibility to be considered when an undifferentiated "round cell sarcoma" is found in a child's orbital tissues is acute leukemia. Such orbital lesions may make their appearance before peripheral blood studies are diagnostic, but bone marrow aspirates will usually furnish a conclusive answer. In the case of adults an orbital metastasis may, on rare occasions, be the initial manifestation of carcinoma of the breast, bronchus, kidney, or prostate.[138,139]

Carcinoid tumors of the lung or small bowel can also metastasize to the orbit or ocular globe; occasionally an orbital carcinoid tumor is found in the absence of any other disease, suggesting the possibility that it may be primary at this site.[140,141]

Conjunctiva

Lesions of the conjunctiva are thin and tend to fold into distorted patterns when placed into fixative. To prepare the tissue so that the pathologist can orient it properly, the surgeon should spread the lesion onto a small piece of filter paper and allow it to dry for a few seconds before gently placing the filter paper with the adherent specimen into the jar of fixation. Specimens should never be put onto sponges of any kind since these will expand when placed into the fixative, thus distorting the specimen.

Developmental anomalies

Dermoid tumors of the bulbar conjunctiva are firm, localized, elevated opaque masses that typically occur at the limbus, often encroaching on the cornea (Fig. 30.35). These are solid choristomatous masses, not to be confused with dermoid cysts of the orbit.

Over the lesion, the surface epithelium and the subepithelial connective tissue present the histologic features characteristic of epidermis and dermis, respectively. A few hairs typically project from the tumor. The bulk of the mass is composed of thick bundles of collagen. In some lesions, skin appendages are few, and adipose tissue is abundant. These are known as *dermolipomas*, and they are usually situated in the upper outer fornix. Ocular dermoids may be part of *Goldenhar's syndrome* in which there are extra-auricular appendages and vertebral abnormalities.

Cysts

Benign epithelium-lined inclusion cysts of the conjunctiva usually arise after accidental or surgical trauma or, rarely, de novo.

Degeneration

Pinguecula is a very common degenerative process affecting primarily the subepithelial connective tissues of the bulbar conjunctiva in the interpalpebral region. This gives rise to an elevated yellowish lesion over which the

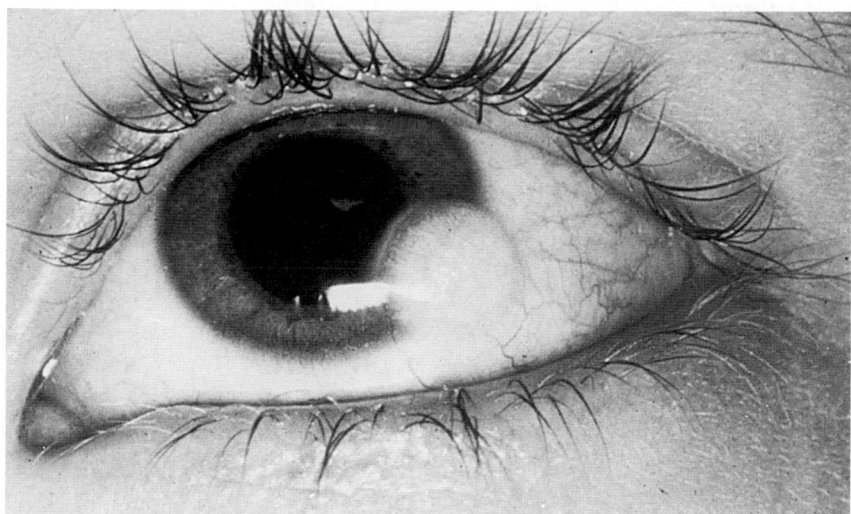

Fig. 30.35 Limbal dermoid in a child.

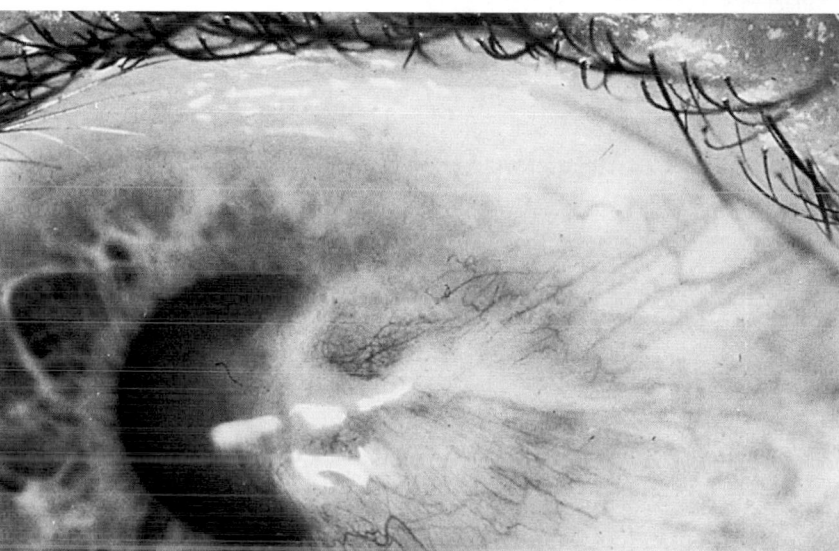

Fig. 30.36 Pterygium that has grown over the pupillary axis and has interfered with vision.

epithelium may become atrophic or thickened. Since these lesions are not progressive, they are seldom excised.

Histologically, the most characteristic feature is actinic elastosis affecting a bandlike zone beneath the epithelium. Secondary hyalinization and calcareous degeneration also may be observed. The epithelium over pingueculae typically becomes atrophic, but at times it becomes so acanthotic and dyskeratotic that the erroneous diagnosis of carcinoma may be made.

Pterygium extends into the cornea and is therefore a more important lesion than the pinguecula (Fig. 30.36). Microscopically, there is usually some actinic elastosis but also a variable amount of acute and chronic inflammation and congestion of blood vessels.

A morphologically somewhat similar lesion of the conjunctiva has been interpreted as the ocular equivalent of *elastofibroma*.[142]

Graft-versus-host disease

The major histopathologic changes seen in the eyes of patients undergoing bone marrow transplantation involve the conjunctiva, cornea, choroid, and lacrimal gland. The major change in the cornea is keratinization, as appreciated in biopsy specimens.[143]

Inflammation

Inflammatory lesions of the conjunctiva seldom give rise to the type of diagnostic or therapeutic problem that requires excision and histopathologic study. One lesion that deserves mention is the noncaseating granulomatous inflammation found in approximately one fourth of patients with **sarcoidosis**[144] (Fig. 30.37). **Ligneous conjunctivitis** is a peculiar form of chronic pseudomembranous conjunctivitis that presents as a woody induration of the eyelids together with the formation of a pseudomembrane on the tarsal conjunctiva. The cardinal feature histologically is the presence of large hyaline masses that may simulate amyloid.[145,146]

Inclusion conjunctivitis is seen in adults as an acute or chronic infection. It is produced by *Chlamydia*, and it shows the microscopic appearance of follicular conjunctivitis indistinguishable from viral infection. The

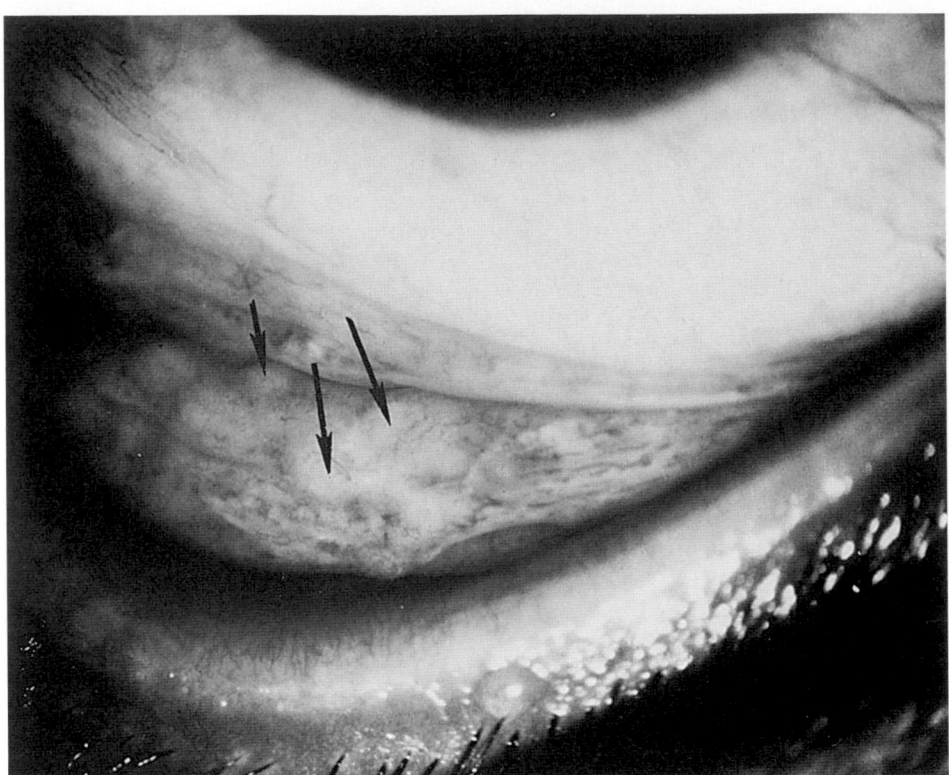

Fig. 30.37 Conjunctival granulomas in sarcoidosis (arrows).

diagnosis is based on the finding of so-called "Halberstaedter–Prowazek inclusions" on conjunctival scrapings.[149]

Actinic granuloma can develop in the conjunctiva, its microscopic appearance being equivalent to that of its more common cutaneous counterpart.[148]

Sjögren's syndrome manifests itself in the conjunctiva by metaplasia of the epithelium, associated with a decreased number of goblet cells and a polymorphic inflammatory infiltrate in the stroma.[147]

Tumors and tumorlike conditions

Tumors of surface epithelium

Papillomas are relatively common lesions of the conjunctiva with a tendency for recurrence after apparent complete excision. In children the papillomas are often multiple. The lesions have a typical papillomatous or "mulberry" surface appearance with small vessels coming up to the surface (Fig. 30.38).

Microscopically, the typical papilloma reveals pronounced acanthosis and varying degrees of keratinization, koilocytosis, and nonspecific inflammation (see Fig. 30.7). Human papillomavirus type 6/11 has been found in these lesions by in situ hybridization techniques.[154]

Carcinoma in situ of the bulbar conjunctiva varies considerably in its clinical appearance. It may present as an area of leukoplakia, as a papilloma, or as a complication of pterygium or pinguecula (Fig. 30.39).

The histopathologic characteristics of carcinoma in situ of the conjunctiva and cornea are similar to those observed elsewhere in the mucous membranes, or the

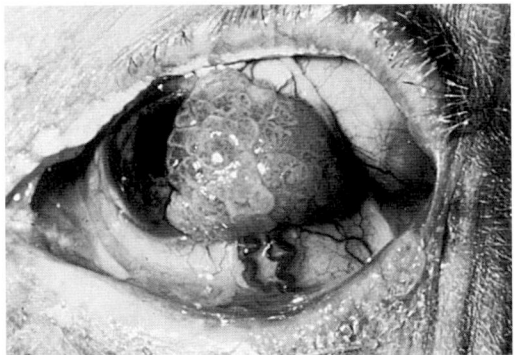

Fig. 30.38 Extensive papilloma of bulbar conjunctiva.

lesion may resemble Bowen's disease or Paget's disease of the skin[152] (Fig. 30.40).

There are many lesions removed from the conjunctiva that do not fall clearly into either of the categories of papilloma or carcinoma in situ. They are often not quite so benign as to be called papilloma, yet there are not enough changes to warrant a classification of carcinoma in situ. These are referred to as *dysplasia* of the conjunctiva; the suggestion has been made that these lesions be placed within a spectrum of *conjunctival (or corneal) intraepithelial neoplasia*.[156] The dysplastic lesions have been found to contain HPV type 16 in a substantial number of cases.[153]

Invasive squamous cell carcinoma of the conjunctiva is rare but is still more common than basal cell carcinoma at this site.[150] Clinically, carcinomas of the conjunctiva with significant infiltration are seldom observed in the

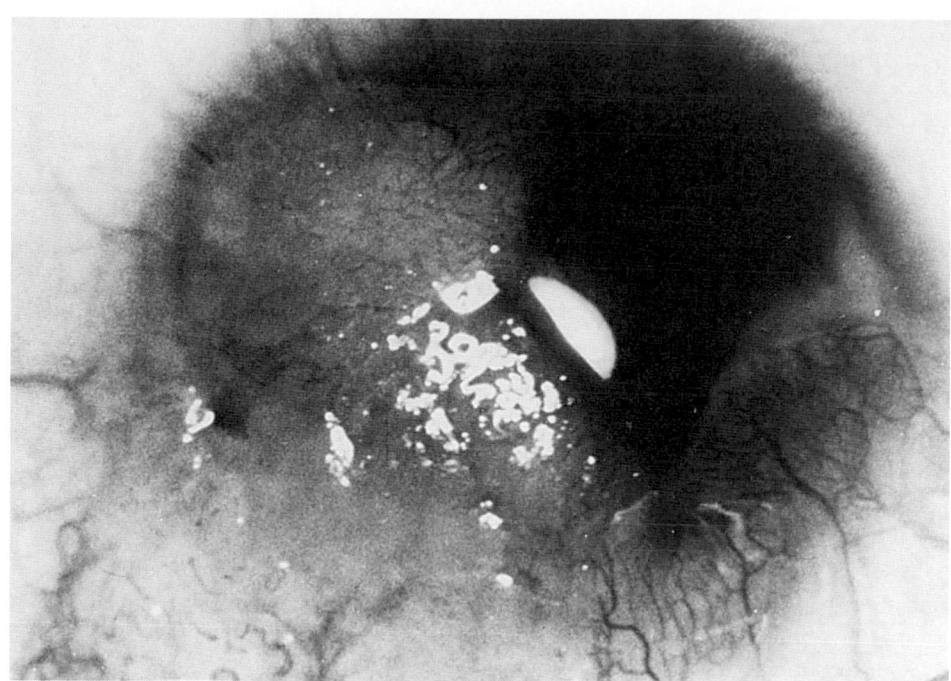

Fig. 30.39 Carcinoma in situ of conjunctiva and cornea.

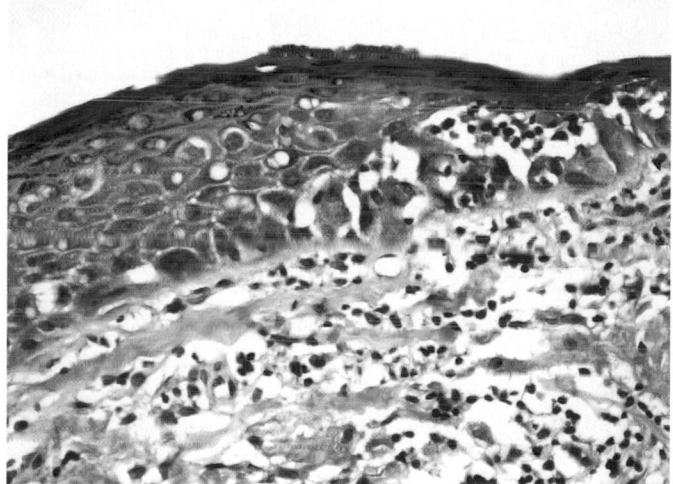

Fig. 30.40 Carcinoma of conjunctiva with pagetoid pattern of growth.

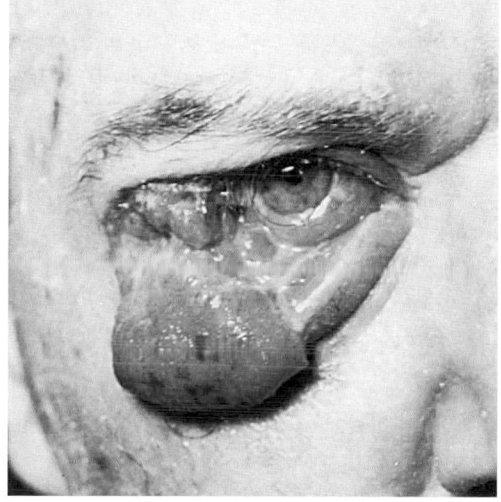

Fig. 30.41 Squamous cell carcinoma of conjunctiva. The tumor grew rapidly over a 4-month period.

United States, probably because it is common practice to excise early "precancerous" or "in situ cancerous" lesions long before this stage occurs (Figs 30.41 and 30.42). Such lesions, as well as the majority of early invasive carcinomas of the limbal area, can be adequately controlled by excisional therapy. If untreated, these tumors will invade the anterior chamber and other portions of the ocular globe. A high proportion of the deeply invasive conjunctival carcinomas have *adenosquamous* ("mucoepidermoid") features.[151,155] Radical surgery is necessary in these cases.[152]

Melanocytic tumors and tumorlike conditions

Nevi. Nevi of the bulbar conjunctiva, like those of the skin, may be observed from birth, or they may become noticeable at any time during childhood, adolescence, or later.[166,167] At times a nevus known to have been present since infancy appears to become much larger and more pigmented at puberty (Fig. 30.43).

Characteristically, conjunctival nevi are discrete, flat, or slightly elevated lesions located on the globe in the interpalpebral zone near the limbus, but they vary greatly in size, shape, and position. They also exhibit much variation in degree of pigmentation, approximately one third being essentially amelanotic.

Microscopically, conjunctival nevi are almost always of the junctional or compound variety. Counterparts of the common dermal nevus of the skin are rarely observed. A few of the conjunctival nevi are of Spitz type.[164] Frequently, there are numerous solid and cystic

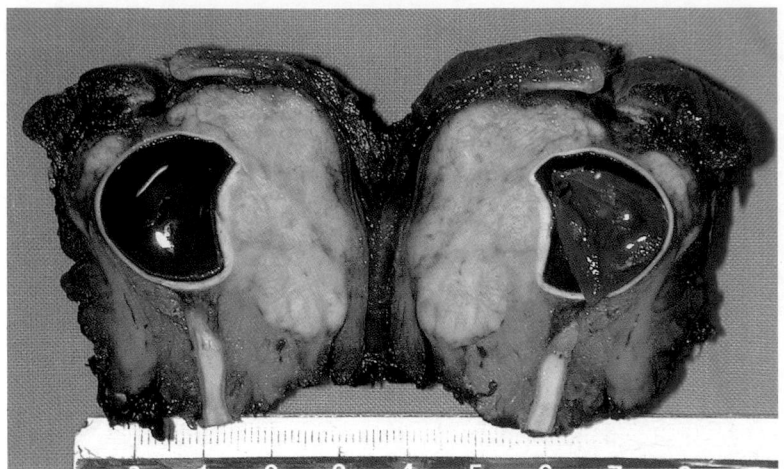

Fig. 30.42 Squamous cell carcinoma of conjunctiva growing extensively inside the orbit and compressing the ocular globe.

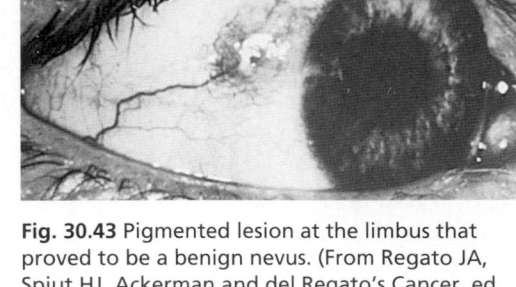

Fig. 30.43 Pigmented lesion at the limbus that proved to be a benign nevus. (From Regato JA, Spjut HJ. Ackerman and del Regato's Cancer, ed. 5. St. Louis, 1977, Mosby; courtesy of the Registry of Ophthalmic Pathology, Armed Forces Institute of Pathology, Washington, D.C.)

inclusions of conjunctival epithelium intimately incorporated into the subepithelial component of these nevi. At times, the epithelial inclusions may so dominate the clinical and histopathologic picture that the nevoid nature of the lesion is overlooked (Fig. 30.44). The presence of the epithelial inclusions is supportive evidence for benignity, since they are rare in melanomas.

Malignant melanoma. Malignant melanoma of the conjunctiva, a very rare lesion, may arise without an apparent precursor lesion, or it may be the sequela of a nevus or of so-called "acquired melanosis" (see later discussions)[165,166,168] (Figs 30.45 and 30.46). The microscopic appearance is similar to that of its cutaneous counterpart. The prognosis is closely related to the subsite and size of the primary tumor.[172] Small localized bulbar tumors have an excellent prognosis, diffuse bulbar melanomas have an intermediate prognosis, and melanomas of the fornix and caruncle have a poor prognosis.[166] Metastatic spread is very uncommon with melanomas less than 1.5 cm in maximum thickness. In the series of 131 cases reported by Folberg et al.[162] the overall mortality was 26%; no prognostic differences were found among the melanomas arising de novo, those with an accompanying nevus, and those associated with so-called "acquired melanosis."

The treatment varies from local excision to exenteration of the eye, depending on the extent of the disease.

So-called "acquired melanosis." Acquired melanosis is the term most commonly used among ophthalmologists and ophthalmic pathologists for a melanocytic proliferative lesion of the conjunctiva that has also been referred to as primary acquired melanosis, precancerous melanosis, atypical melanocytic hyperplasia, and malignant melanoma in situ.[157,160,169,171] Most cases are seen in the fifth decade of life or later, and the typical presentation is that of a diffuse nonelevated granular pigmentation of the conjunctiva. The most common site of involvement is the bulbar conjunctiva, but it can also

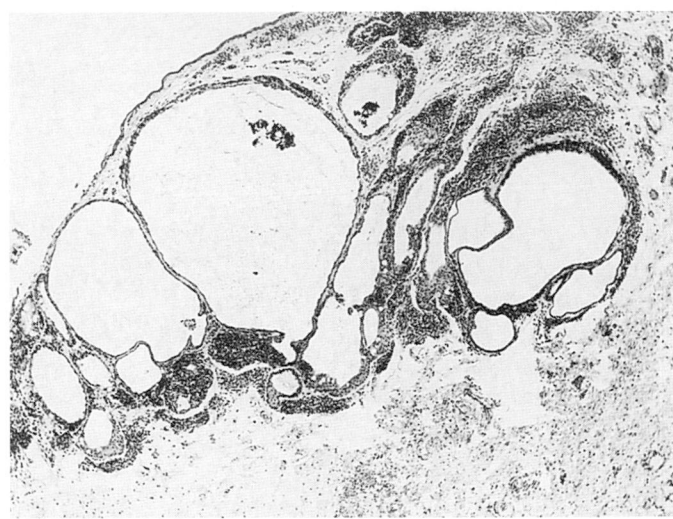

Fig. 30.44 Conjunctival nevus with many associated cystic epithelial inclusions. Small round cells about large cysts are not inflammatory cells but nevus cells. This epibulbar lesion may be analogous to hair dermal nevus of skin.

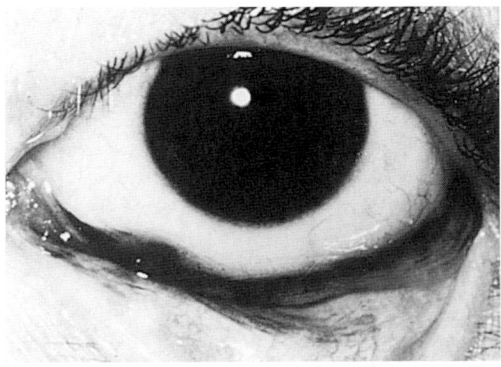

Fig. 30.45 Malignant melanoma of conjunctiva in lower cul-de-sac arising from a lesion of acquired melanosis. (From Zimmerman LE. Discussion of pigmented tumors of the conjunctiva. In Boniuk M (ed.): Ocular and adnexal tumors. St. Louis, 1964, Mosby; courtesy of the Registry of Ophthalmic Pathology, Armed Forces Institute of Pathology, Washington, D.C.)

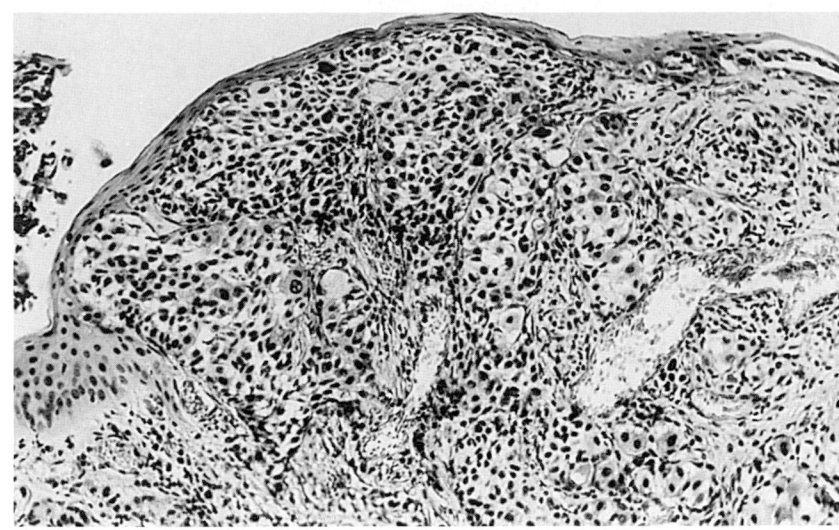

Fig. 30.46 Malignant melanoma arising in a nevus known to have been present since childhood. The patient, a 59-year-old woman, stated that the lesion suddenly became quite large several months before it was excised.

be present in the cornea, palpebral conjunctiva, or skin of the eyelid. The extent of the lesion and the degree of pigmentation may fluctuate during the course of the years.

Microscopically, an increase in the number of melanocytes is seen along the basal layer, individually or in clusters, associated with various degrees of atypicality[161] (Fig. 30.47).

The nature and significance of this lesion have been controversial. Considerations that have been made are similar to those expressed for other acquired melanocytic proliferations of the skin, notably Hutchinson's freckle. Specifically, it has been postulated that all cases of acquired melanosis (at least those exhibiting atypia) are malignant melanomas in situ.[157] Guillén and co-workers[163,170] have divided these conjunctival lesions into three groups: (1) conjunctival hypermelanosis (with or without melanocytic hyperplasia but lacking atypia), (2) atypical melanocytic hyperplasia, and (3) malignant melanoma. From a practical standpoint, the important fact to remember is that the propensity for the development of invasive melanoma is directly related to the presence and degree of atypia.[159,161] In the series of Folberg et al.,[161] none of the lesions without atypia progressed to invasive melanoma, whereas 40% of those with atypia did. Accordingly, the recommendation has been made to extirpate all of these lesions by excision or cryotherapy.[158,161]

Lymphoid tumors and tumorlike conditions

The morphologic appearances and diagnostic problems posed by these lesions when they present in the conjunctiva are similar to those of analogous lesions of the eyelid and orbit and are discussed on p. 2728. The clinical appearance of the conjunctival lesions is that of salmon-colored, smooth masses[173] (Fig. 30.48).

Other tumors

Myxoma has been reported as a primary tumor in the conjunctiva, cornea, eyelid, and orbit. Grossly, the conjunctival lesions have a smooth, fleshy, gelatinous appearance. Local excision is curative.[176]

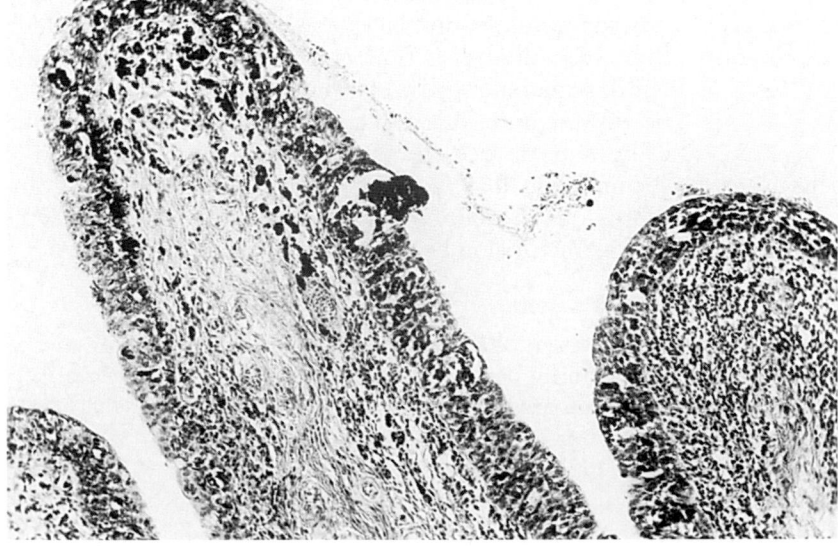

Fig. 30.47 Widespread acquired melanosis of conjunctiva.

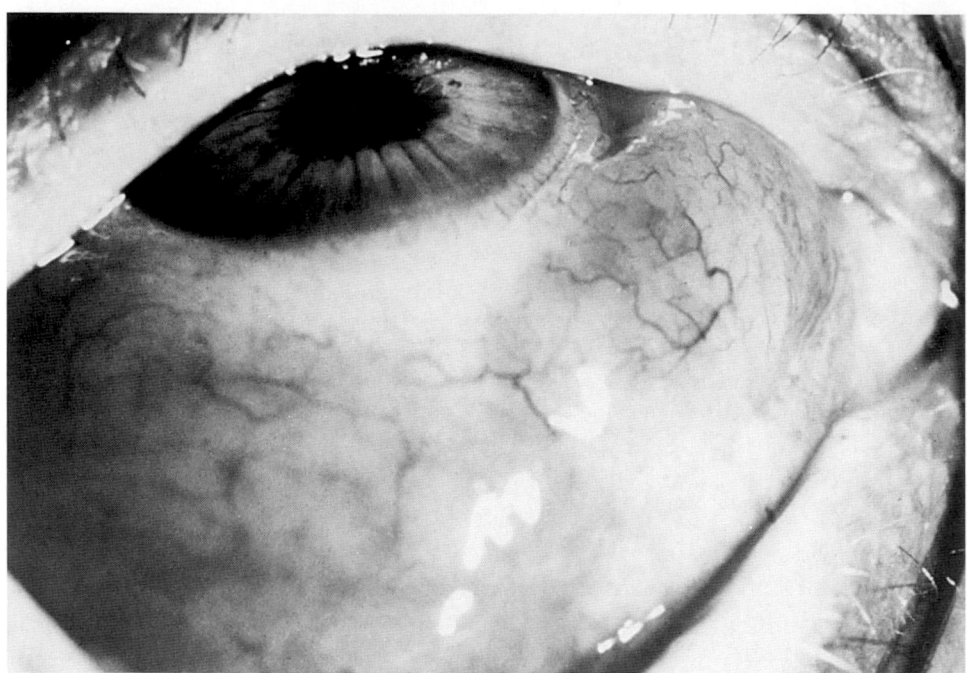

Fig. 30.48 Lymphoid infiltration of conjunctiva.

Intravenous pyogenic granuloma has been observed in the region of the canthus and in the lacrimal sac.[177]

Vascular tumors of various types can also involve the conjunctiva. They include hemangioma, Kaposi's sarcoma,[175] and angiosarcoma.[174]

Cornea

A major source of knowledge about corneal pathology comes from the study of corneal "buttons" submitted to the laboratory after corneal transplantation (keratoplasty). The most common diseases that account for keratoplasties are primary and secondary endothelial decompensation, fibrosis and vascularization (such as herpes simplex keratitis), keratoconus, and failed previous grafts.

Other entities for which keratoplasties are sometimes done include interstitial keratitis and the various hereditary dystrophies.

Endothelial decompensation

When the endothelium of the cornea decompensates, it leads to chronic edema of the stroma and epithelium. Bullae of the epithelium break down, causing severe pain, and eventually there is diffuse scarring with reduced vision. When the process is primary (i.e., with no apparent antecedent factors), it is referred to as *Fuchs' dystrophy* and occurs most frequently in females over 50 years of age. It is a bilateral process, although often asymmetric.

When the endothelial decompensation occurs some time after intraocular surgery, especially after cataract extraction, it is often clinically referred to as *aphakic bullous keratopathy*. The clinical appearance and the histopathologic appearance of these buttons are similar in both situations.

Microscopically, there are a paucity of endothelial cells, a thickening of Descemet's membrane, and the formation of excrescences of Descemet's membrane, clinically referred to as guttata (Fig. 30.49). If the process has been severe, changes in the epithelium occur, including edema of the basal cells, bullae formation, and pannus formation. A pannus is a fibrovascular ingrowth between the epithelium and Bowman's membrane.[178]

Fibrosis and vascularization

Many buttons from keratoplasty procedures show a diffuse, nonspecific fibrosis and vascularization throughout the corneal stroma. Such a histopathologic picture can be seen with traumatic scars, chemical burns, or healed ulcerative keratitis secondary to infections. One particular common infection is *herpes simplex keratitis*, in which the histopathology is characterized by irregularity of the epithelium, patchy loss of Bowman's membrane, infiltration of the anterior stroma by lymphocytes and plasma cells, and diffuse fibrosis and vascularization of the stroma (Fig. 30.50). In severe cases, there is often a granulomatous reaction surrounding Descemet's membrane.[179] Inclusion bodies are only occasionally seen.

Keratoconus

Keratoconus is a congenital ectasia of the central cornea that usually becomes manifest in the first decade of life. It tends to progress until fibrosis decreases the vision and necessitates corneal transplantation. Histopathologically, there is central thinning and fibrosis. Often the "button" will appear wrinkled on the slide, and this artifact is an instant clue to the diagnosis.

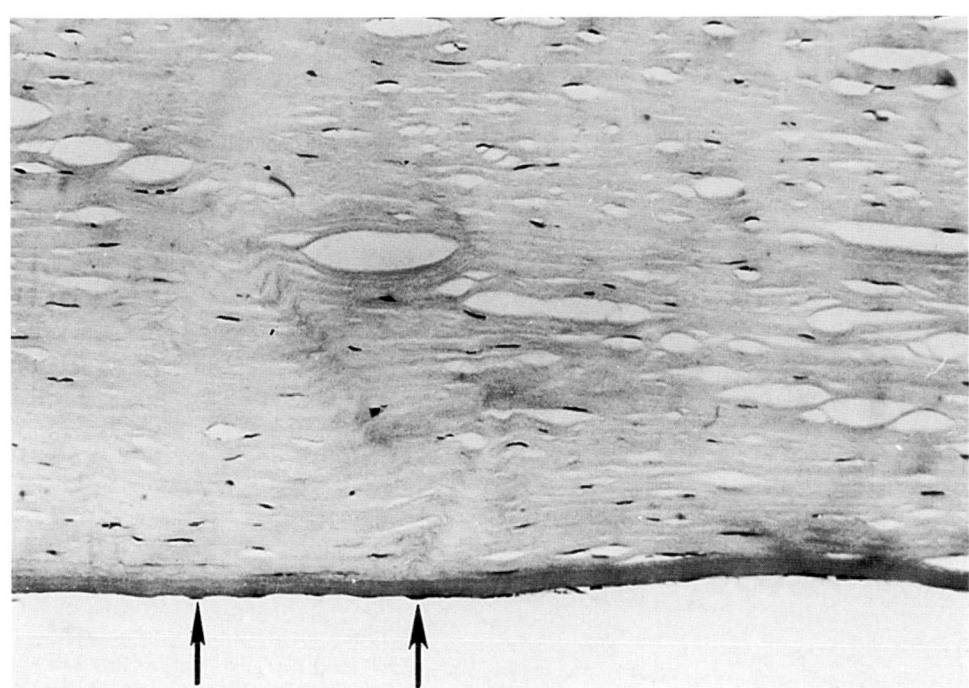

Fig. 30.49 Endothelial decompensation. There is a paucity of endothelial cells. Descemet's membrane is thickened, and there are excrescences along its posterior edge (arrows).

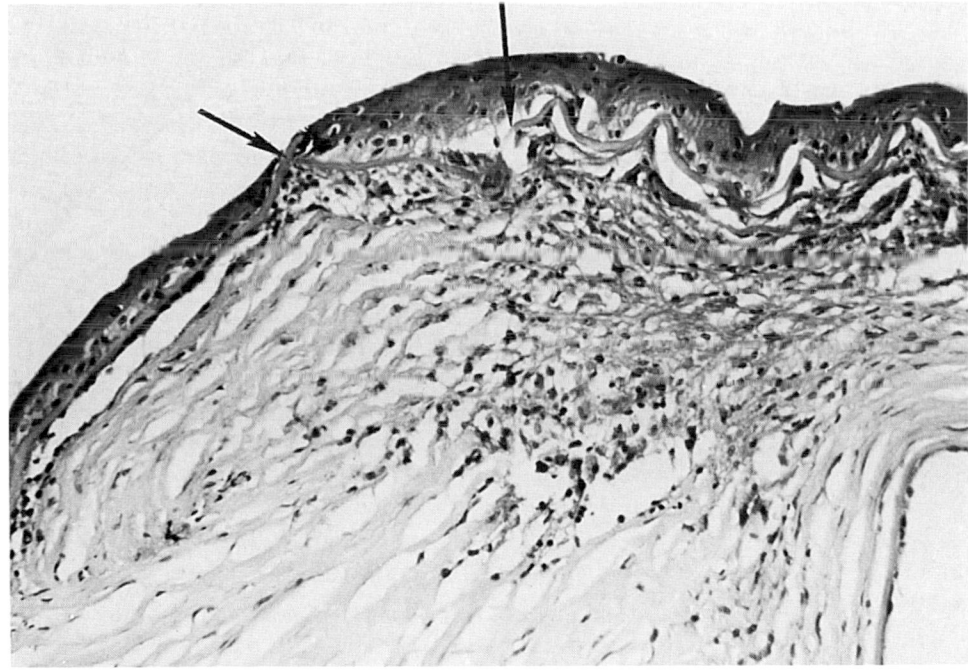

Fig. 30.50 Herpes simplex keratitis. The epithelium is irregular, and there is fragmentation of Bowman's membrane (arrows). Chronic inflammatory cells infiltrate the anterior stroma.

Failed previous grafts

For a variety of reasons, corneal grafts may become opaque, and a second graft is done. The button from the second procedure will often show nonspecific changes such as fibrosis, vascularization, and inflammatory cell infiltration throughout the stroma. At the peripheral edges of the button are the full-thickness scars of the previous procedure. A fibrous retrocorneal membrane is present in approximately one half of the cases (Fig. 30.51).

Intraocular tissues

Surgical pathology of the eye itself differs from most of the rest of surgical pathology for several important reasons.

In the first place, biopsies of intraocular tissues are rarely feasible. The important exceptions are the iris and the ciliary body. Lesions of the iris and ciliary body can be removed by iridectomy or iridocyclectomy. This is especially true for melanomas confined to these structures.

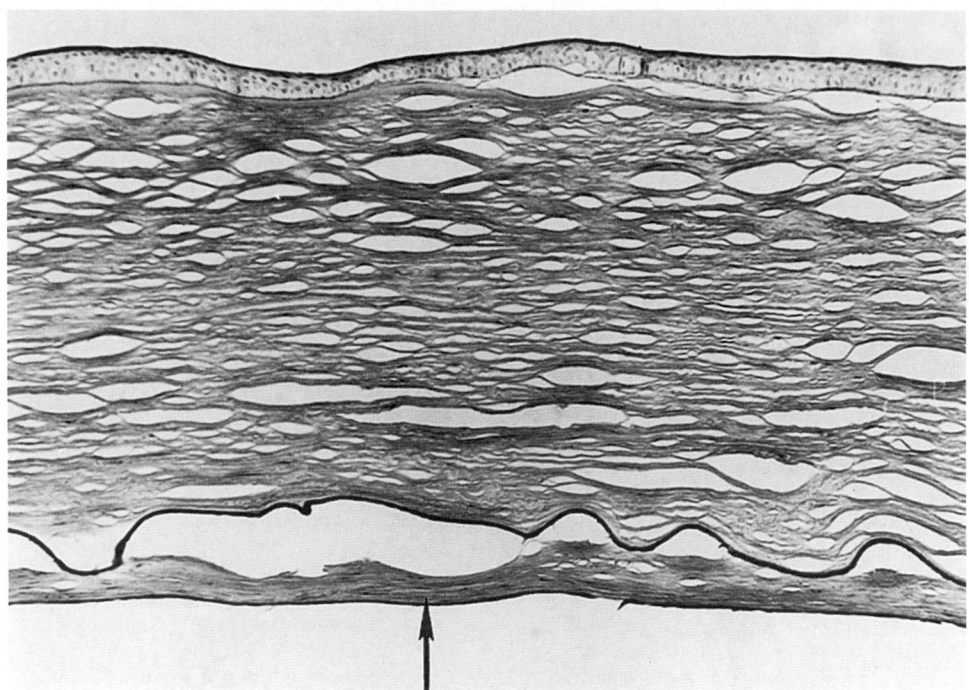

Fig. 30.51 Re-graft of corneal button. Note the fibrous retrocorneal membrane posterior to Descemet's membrane (arrow).

In the second place, most of the eyes reaching the surgical pathology laboratory are obtained as a result of enucleation. Usually the globe is intact but free of such accessory tissues as the extraocular muscles and orbital fat. Much less often, the eye is eviscerated, and only fragments of the intraocular tissues are submitted for microscopic study; it is rarely possible to arrive at a satisfactory diagnosis and clinicopathologic correlation in such cases. Eyes that are enucleated or eviscerated usually have been diseased for a long time and have become blind. Severe pain and unsightliness are the common immediate reasons for removing the eye. In these cases it is the responsibility of the pathologist not merely to arrive at a definitive diagnosis but also to reconstruct the sequence of events that took place from the onset of ocular disease to the final stages that led to enucleation.

This brings us to another distinctive characteristic of ophthalmic pathology. The initial pathologic process frequently becomes completely obscured by the subsequent series of events. For example, the patient may first complain of visual disturbance produced by a cataract. The lens opacification progresses, and cataract extraction is performed. Defective wound healing follows, and surface epithelium grows down into the anterior chamber. This leads to secondary glaucoma for which one or more additional surgical procedures are performed. These, in turn, may be complicated by hemorrhage, infection, or retinal detachment. Finally, the eye may become shrunken (phthisic) and disfiguring. A period of several years to a decade or more is usually required for such a series of events to take place.

Intraocular neoplasms represent an exception to the generalization just given. Since only in the case of iris and small ciliary body tumors is it ordinarily possible to excise the neoplasm, the procedure usually followed is to recommend enucleation for other uveal and retinal neoplasms. The aim here is to arrive at a correct clinical diagnosis early, long before such secondary pathologic processes as cataract formation, massive retinal detachment, glaucoma, uveitis, or phthisis complicate the picture. Therefore the pathologist often observes a much less confusing array of pathologic changes and has less difficulty making a diagnosis in eyes removed because of intraocular neoplasms rather than in other enucleated eyes. This, however, is not invariably the case, for if the tumor has been present and growing for a long time, it, too, may lead to a wide assortment of secondary processes that sometimes confuse the pathologist as well as the clinician.

Developmental anomalies

Most congenital and developmental malformations of the eye are not seen by the surgical pathologist but rather at post mortem examination.[180] Congenital abnormalities typify the point made earlier—that is, the initial pathologic process becomes completely obscured by the subsequent series of events occurring in that eye.

Congenital glaucoma

Congenital glaucoma is characterized by an elevation in the intraocular pressure caused by a malformation of the tissues in the region of the anterior chamber angle. The precise nature of this malformation is still not clear, but there seems to be either an incomplete separation of the iris root from the trabeculae or the retention of an embryonic membrane, or both.

The increased intraocular pressure leads to retinal and optic nerve degeneration, corneal edema and scarring, and global enlargement (buphthalmos). Unilateral congenital glaucoma may occur in Recklinghausen's disease or in the Sturge–Weber syndrome.

When there is a more obvious architectural distortion of the iris and angle of the anterior chamber, it is referred to as the anterior chamber cleavage syndrome[181] or iridogoniodysgenesis. Depending on the degree of angle malformation, various other designations are used (e.g., Rieger's syndrome and Axenfeld's syndrome). This group of malformations is also often associated with a developmental glaucoma.

Retrolental fibroplasia

Retrolental fibroplasia, also called the retinopathy of prematurity, is an acquired form of developmental disorder resulting from the unique sensitivity of retinal blood vessels of the premature retina to oxygen.[182]

Much of the retinal periphery of a baby born after only 6 or 7 months of gestation is completely avascular. If such a premature infant is given high concentrations of oxygen, normal vascularization of the retinal periphery may be inhibited. Vasoconstriction and actual obliteration of the terminal vessels may follow prolonged oxygen therapy. Later, on withdrawal of oxygen, pathologic neovascularization occurs. These newly formed vessels frequently invade the vitreous, leak serum or blood, and eventually lead to organization of the vitreous, retinal detachment, and blindness.

Phakoma

Phakomas are hamartomatous malformations often associated with extraocular lesions as a part of well-defined clinicopathologic syndromes.[183] These include tuberous sclerosis (Bourneville's syndrome), Recklinghausen's disease (neurofibromatosis), Sturge–Weber syndrome (encephalotrigeminal angiomatosis), von Hippel–Lindau disease (angiogliomatosis), ataxia–telangiectasia, and Wyburn–Mason syndrome.

In tuberous sclerosis the most characteristic intraocular lesions are glial plaques and nodules in the nerve fiber layer of the retina, which clinically may simulate a retinoblastoma (Fig. 30.52). Neurofibromas (including the plexiform variety) of the eyelid and orbit and gliomas of the optic nerve are the usual lesions observed in neurofibromatosis.

Hemangioma of the choroid is the most common intraocular lesion of the Sturge–Weber syndrome. Ipsilateral glaucoma is often associated with the Sturge–Weber syndrome or Recklinghausen's disease. Abnormally large tortuous arteries and veins leading to a retinal nodule composed of vascular, endothelial, and glial tissues are characteristic of von Hippel–Lindau disease. Vitreous disturbance and retinal detachment are common complications. In ataxia–telangiectasia there are telangiectatic conjunctival vessels, and in the

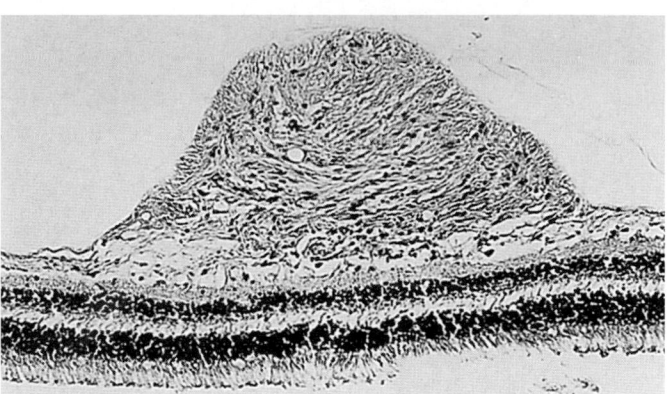

Fig. 30.52 Tuberous sclerosis showing a glial nodule or hamartoma projecting against the vitreous body from the nerve fiber layer of the retina.

Wyburn–Mason syndrome there are arteriovenous shunts of the retinal vessels.

Persistent hyperplastic primary vitreous

A congenital condition, persistent hyperplastic primary vitreous refers to the persistence and hyperplasia of the fibrovascular tunic of the lens and part of the hyaloid vascular system.[184] It is usually unilateral and occurs in a microphthalmic eye. This anomaly is manifested clinically by a white reflex behind the pupil (leukokoria). Varying degrees of fibrous tissue are seen behind the lens, and often there is a cataract. Distinction from retinoblastoma is not so great a problem as in the past, but occasionally these eyes are enucleated because retinoblastoma cannot be ruled out.

Histologically, there is a dense fibrovascular retrolental mass, and the elongated ciliary processes are enmeshed in this tissue. Remnants of the hyaloid artery system are present, and the retina may appear normal or show evidence of retinal dysplasia (Fig. 30.53).

Retinal dysplasia

Retinal dysplasia is a congenital anomaly that may occur as part of the 13–15 trisomy syndrome or merely in a unilateral malformed eye not associated with other systemic anomalies.[185,186] An example of the latter situation would be in the case of persistent hyperplastic primary vitreous, as previously mentioned.

Dysplastic retina is characterized histologically by a series of straight branching tubes composed of abortive elements of the rod and cone layers (see Fig. 30.54). It is believed that it is the result of disturbed differentiation of neural ectoderm.

Other developmental anomalies

Other congenital entities that are only rarely seen by the surgical pathologist include the rubella syndrome,[187,190] Lowe's syndrome, Fabry's syndrome,[188] and aniridia, in which the nonfamilial case may be associated with Wilms' tumor.[189]

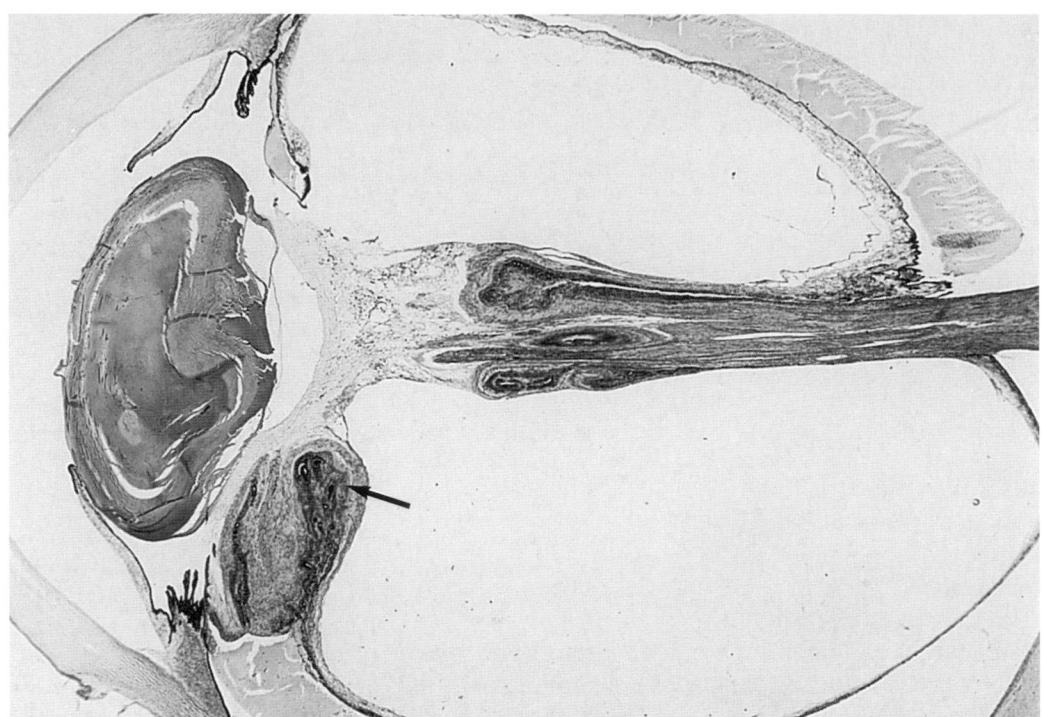

Fig. 30.53 Persistent hyperplastic primary vitreous. Behind the lens lies a fibrovascular mass, to which a remnant of the hyaloid system attaches. In some cases of persistent hyperplastic primary vitreous, there may be areas of retinal dysplasia (arrow).

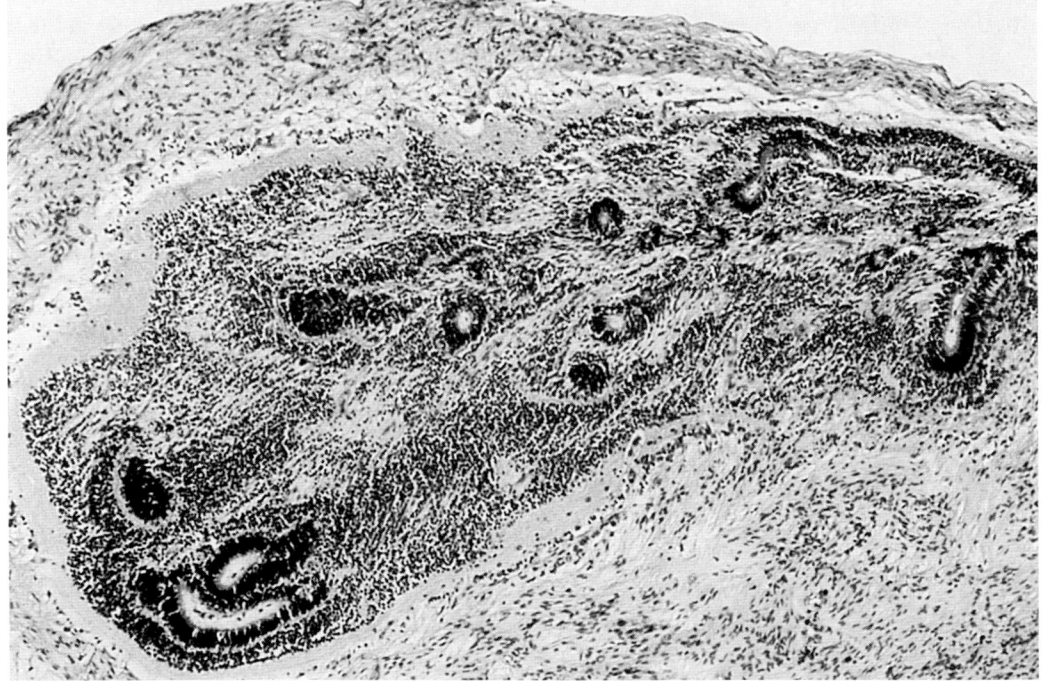

Fig. 30.54 Retinal dysplasia. Within the retina are branching tubes composed of abortive elements of the rod and cone layer.

Trauma

Trauma to the globe can be accidental or surgical. The complications that may ensue after severe trauma may eventually lead to blindness and pain, necessitating enucleation. In fact, ocular trauma is the most common reason for eyes reaching the ophthalmic pathology laboratory of a general hospital. Often there are instances in which the surgical pathologist will be expected to identify tissue that has been removed from an eye that is being sutured following a severe laceration. What the ophthalmic surgeon wants to know is whether any retina is extruded through the wound. If so, this information may influence further management of the case.

Although some eyes are so extensively damaged that immediate removal is necessary, most of the injured eyes are removed at varying intervals because of secondary changes such as organization of hemorrhage, glaucoma, retinal detachment, infections, inflammation, or complete atrophy (phthisis bulbi) (Fig. 30.55).

Histopathologic diagnosis is not usually a problem,

but a search should be made for retained intraocular foreign bodies such as metal, vegetation, and cilia. Retained intraocular iron and copper may produce siderosis and chalcosis, respectively.

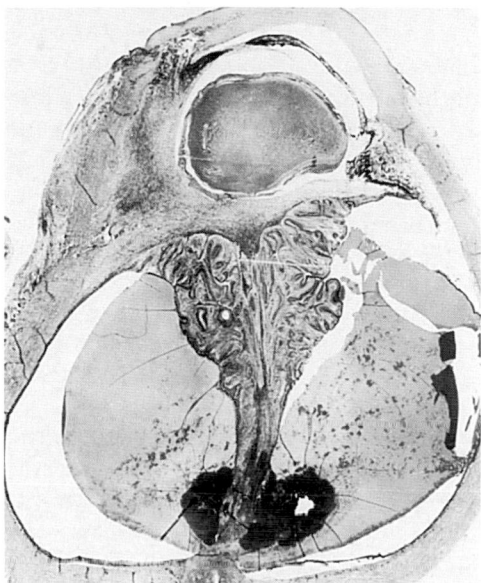

Fig. 30.55 A penetrating wound of the eye and multiple minute intraocular foreign bodies (palm splinters) led to the formation of a dense mass of inflammatory tissue in the anterior segment on one side. Organization of the vitreous has been complicated by retinal detachment. Blood clots are attached to the stalk of the detached retina near the optic disc.

Beside the aforementioned secondary changes (e.g., diffuse fibrosis, secondary glaucoma, inflammation), certain specific complications associated with trauma include sympathetic ophthalmia, phacoanaphylactic endophthalmitis, postcontusion angle deformity, fibrous downgrowth, and epithelial downgrowth. These are considered subsequently under other headings.

Inflammation

Inflammation of the eye, as elsewhere, may be acute or chronic, granulomatous or nongranulomatous.

Acute inflammation

Acute intraocular inflammation is often infectious in origin. The causative organism is usually a bacterium or fungus and is generally introduced through a perforating wound (Fig. 30.56). Occasionally, however, the infection is hematogenous. There have been reports of endogenous fungous endophthalmitis,[191,193] and metastatic endophthalmitis also has been reported after injection of addictive drugs.[194]

Initially there is a massive purulent reaction in the anterior and vitreous chambers, and the process is called *endophthalmitis*. As the infection spreads, other intraocular tissues, such as the retina, uvea, and eventually the cornea and sclera, may become involved. At this stage the term *panophthalmitis* is applicable. Before the advent of antibiotic therapy, eyes affected by severe panophthalmitis were frequently eviscerated or enucleated

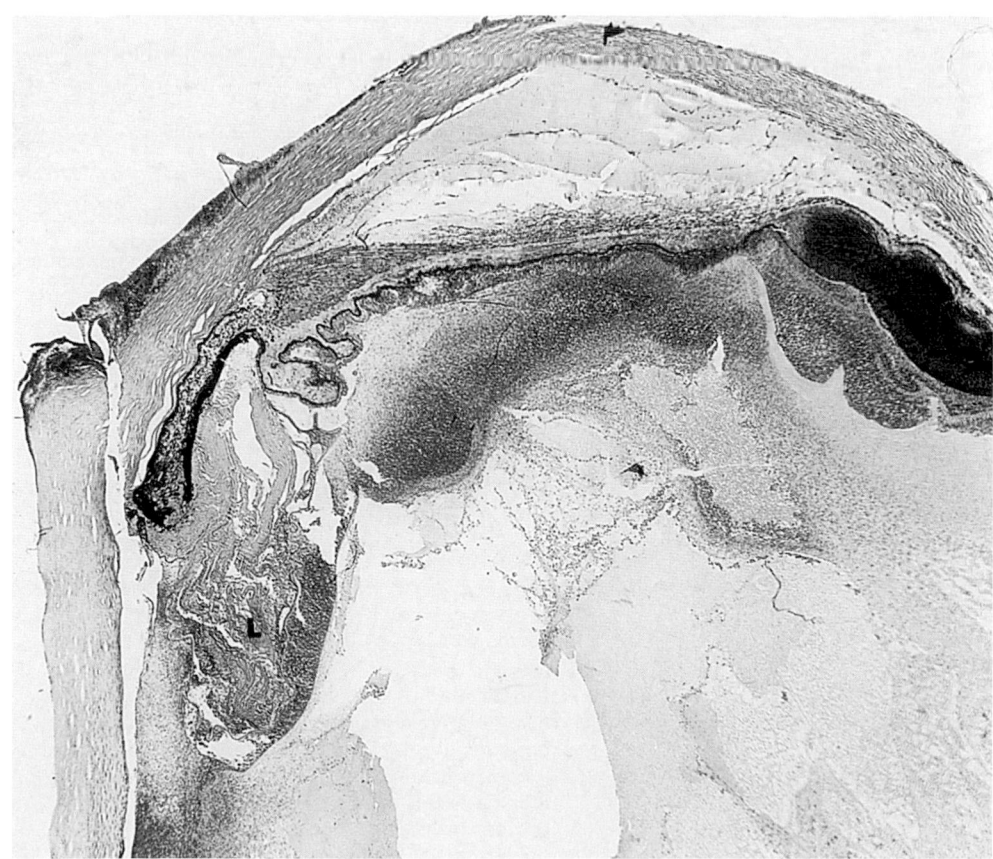

Fig. 30.56 Endophthalmitis showing infiltration of all intraocular structures by acute inflammatory cells. The lens, L, is necrotic. The organism presumably gained entrance through a corneal wound.

early. Today the infection can often be controlled, but subsequent organization of the exudate leads to *phthisis bulbi* (see p. 2746). A common cause of noninfectious endophthalmitis or panophthalmitis is massive necrosis of a uveal malignant melanoma or a metastatic carcinoma.[192]

Chronic nongranulomatous inflammation

In chronic nongranulomatous inflammation of the eye, the uveal tract is primarily involved. In *anterior uveitis (iridocyclitis)*, the tissues are typically infiltrated by plasma cells in a rather diffuse fashion (Fig. 30.57A), but occasionally the inflammation is in the form of nodular lymphocytic infiltrates. In *posterior uveitis (choroiditis)* the round cell infiltration may also be diffuse, but frequently it is focal or scattered as multiple discrete lesions. In *choroiditis* the overlying retina is usually involved by spread of the inflammatory reaction—hence the alternative term *chorioretinitis*. A complication of inflammatory diseases of the uveal tract is the formation of a *cyclitic membrane* that can contract and lead to detachment of the retina and ciliary body.[195]

In choroiditis, even if prolonged, enucleation is not often necessary, for the eyes do not become painful. However, with recurrent iridocyclitis the inflammatory reaction often produces adhesions between the iris and the cornea (anterior synechiae; Fig. 30.57B) or between the iris and the lens (posterior synechiae; Fig. 30.58), and secondary glaucoma results. If this condition is intractable, enucleation is almost inevitable. Often the process is of such a long-term nature that when the eye is enucleated, all that is recognized is the massive scarring that is found in phthisis bulbi, which is due to any cause.

The etiology and pathogenesis of nongranulomatous uveitis can rarely be ascertained clinically or pathologically. Occasionally an entity presents a characteristic picture such as is seen in *herpes zoster ophthalmicus* in which there is a chronic inflammatory cell infiltration around the posterior ciliary nerves and vessels.[196] *Behçet's disease* produces an obliterative vasculitis of the retinal vessels.

Granulomatous inflammation

Granulomatous inflammation may be the result of a specific infection such as toxoplasmosis, tuberculosis, syphilis, nematodiasis, and cytomegalic inclusion disease. Also associated with granulomatous reactions are entities such as sarcoidosis and the collagen diseases. It should be kept in mind, however, that as with the nongranulomatous cases, the etiology cannot often be

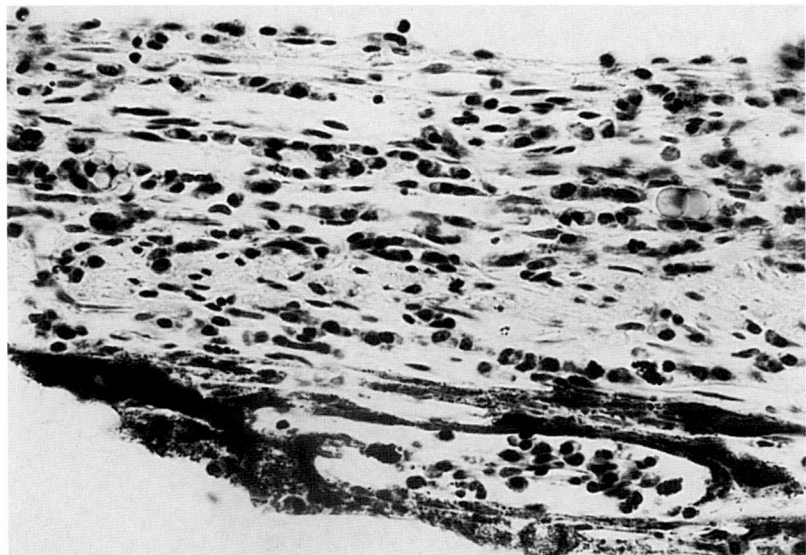

A

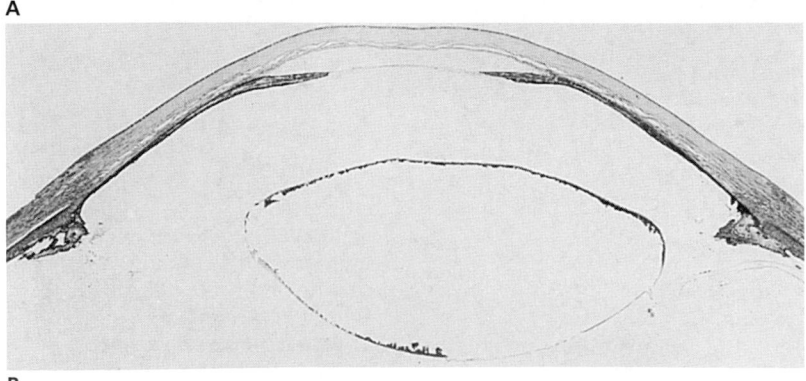

B

Fig. 30.57 A, Nongranulomatous iritis in which the atrophic iris is diffusely infiltrated by plasma cells, and several Russell bodies are present. Irregular degenerative and proliferative changes may be observed in the pigment epithelium. **B,** The same lesion illustrated in **A** showing that the chronically inflamed iris is almost completely adherent to the cornea and the anterior chamber is virtually obliterated.

Fig. 30.58 Nongranulomatous iritis with posterior synechiae. The iris is firmly attached to the lens, which reveals widespread degeneration of its cortex and fibrous metaplasia of its subcapsular epithelium.

ascertained. This is the case with the entity designated as *idiopathic solitary granuloma* of the uveal tract.[197] This disorder is unilateral, accompanied by uveal effusion and total retinal detachment, and typically located between the pars plana ciliaris and the equator.[197]

The inflammatory process in granulomatous uveitis may be diffuse, or there is a more localized area of destruction in which the causative agent or otherwise diagnostic lesion will be found.

The term granulomatous uveitis is misleading, for often the most diagnostic lesions are not found in the iris, ciliary body, or choroid but rather in the retina, vitreous, or sclera. The diagnostic lesions of toxoplasmosis are found in the retina, those of nematodiasis in the vitreous or retina, and those of the rheumatoid group in the sclera between the limbus and the equator.

Toxoplasmosis. Although ocular toxoplasmosis is an important entity, it is actually quite rare to receive such globes in the pathology laboratory. The histopathology is characterized by a focal area of coagulative necrosis of the retina surrounded by a granulomatous inflammation in the adjacent choroid and sclera. Within the area of necrotic retina, cysts of *Toxoplasma gondii* can be found[199] (Fig. 30.59). Cases of toxoplasmosis resulting in diffuse retinal necrosis have been observed in patients with AIDS.[198]

Nematodiasis. Nematodiasis is a broad term encompassing a variety of parasitic diseases. The one form of ocular nematodiasis that has been found with considerable frequency in the United States and Great Britain is a type of visceral larva migrans, produced in most cases by wandering larvae of *Toxocara canis*. This is principally an infection of children between the ages of 3 and 14 years.[200]

Almost without exception, those children who have had ocular infection have not had clinical evidence of systemic visceral larva migrans, and those who have had the systemic form have not had ocular lesions. Typically, a single migrating larva finds its way, hematogenously, into the eye and comes to rest in the vitreous or on the inner surface of the retina (Fig. 30.60).

A pronounced infiltration by acute and chronic inflammatory cells, often with intense eosinophilia, is observed in these tissues.

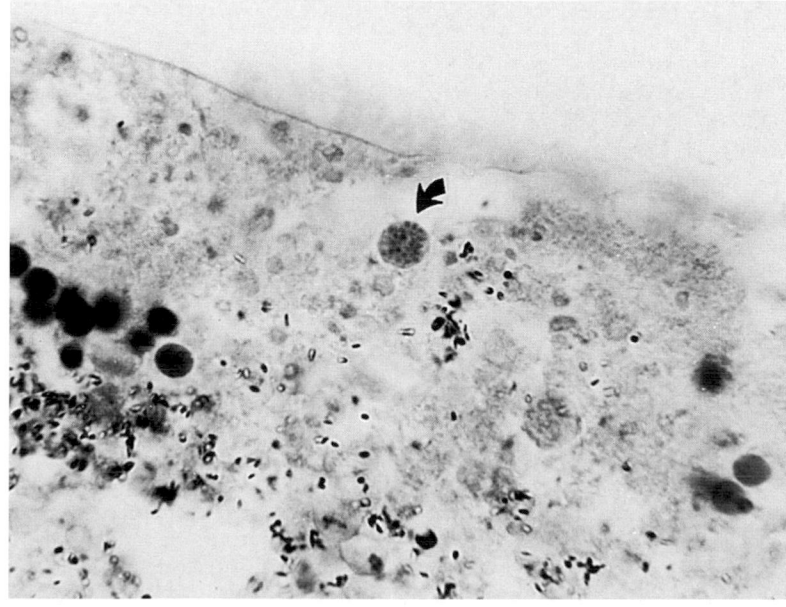

Fig. 30.59 Encysting proliferative forms (arrow) of *Toxoplasma gondii* found in necrotic retina. The small particles are pigment granules from necrotic retinal pigment epithelium, whereas the larger round structures represent pyknotic retinal nuclei.

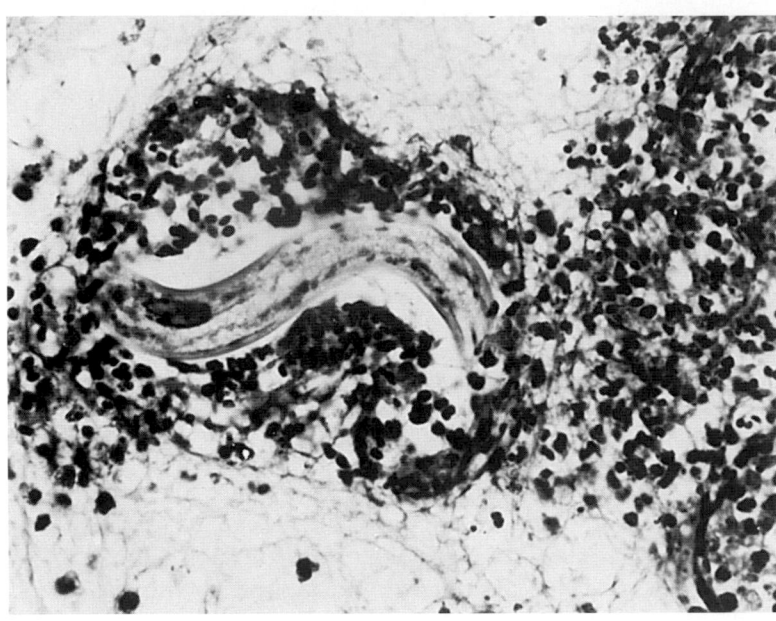

Fig. 30.60 Nematode larva, probably *Toxocara canis*, surrounded by inflammatory cells in the vitreous body.

The inflammatory reaction in the vitreous eventually leads to organization and contracture of this structure with consequent detachment of the retina (Fig. 30.61). This leads to leukokoria, and the eye is enucleated because retinoblastoma cannot be ruled out.

As the nematode larvae die, they often stimulate the formation of a typical granulomatous inflammatory reaction about them. It is usually necessary to make serial sections to find these minute granulomas. The typical inflammatory reaction with intense eosinophilia observed in the vitreous is presumptive evidence of nematodiasis.

Post-traumatic uveitis

Following penetrating injury of the eye, the development of a granulomatous uveitis always causes great concern because of the possibility of *sympathetic uveitis*, a dreaded disease in which injury to one eye gives rise to severe inflammation that sometimes progresses to blindness in the uninjured eye as well as in the injured eye. Fortunately, sympathetic uveitis is extremely rare today. Other causes of post-traumatic granulomatous inflammation are lens-induced endophthalmitis (phacoanaphylaxis), foreign bodies, and blood in the vitreous.

Sympathetic uveitis. Sympathetic uveitis is probably the best example of a pure granulomatous uveitis, for the significant lesion in this disease is confined to the uveal tissues. The process typically involves the entire uveal tract. There may, of course, be associated inflammatory lesions in other tissues attributable to the original trauma or to the presence of foreign bodies, but the reaction of sympathetic uveitis itself is purely uveal.

There is a dense, diffuse infiltration of the choroid by

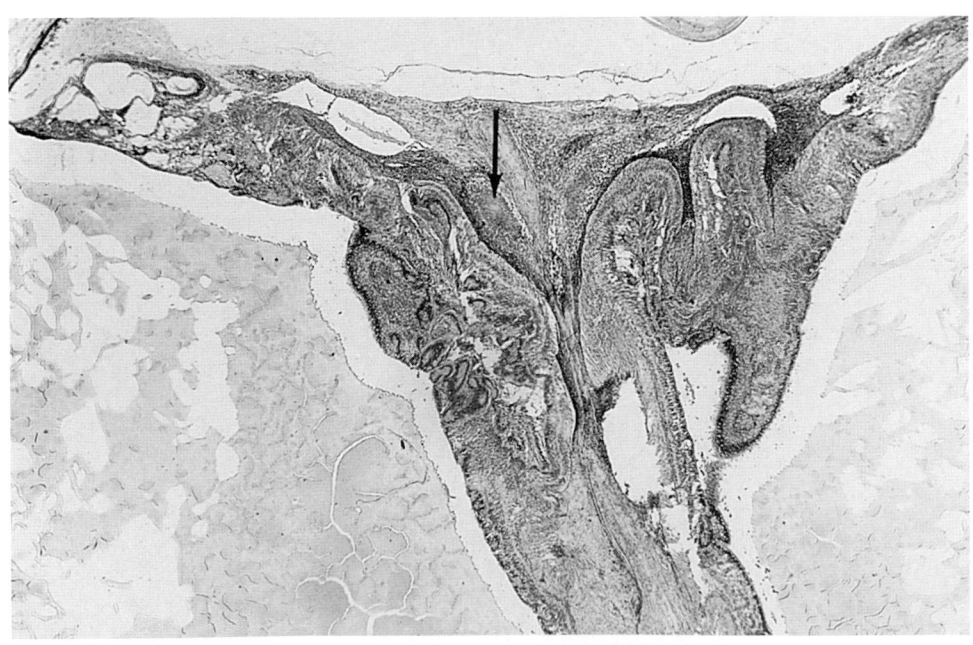

Fig. 30.61 Nematode endophthalmitis in which inflammatory reaction in the vitreous has led to retinal detachment. The parasite was found in an area of necrosis (arrow).

lymphocytes (Fig. 30.62), and often the ciliary body and iris are similarly involved. Superimposed on this lymphocytic infiltrate are small, irregular, patchy accumulations of large, pale-staining epithelioid cells, which on high magnification will often be found to contain finely dispersed melanin granules (Fig. 30.63). Polymorphonuclear leukocytes are characteristically lacking, and plasma cells are rare, but eosinophils are often included in moderate numbers.

The reaction involves the outer and middle coats of the choroid, extending into the scleral canals along ciliary vessels and nerves, sometimes to the episcleral surface. The choriocapillaris, on the other hand, is typically uninvolved. Clusters of epithelioid cells between Bruch's membrane and the retinal pigment epithelium, referred to as Dalen–Fuchs nodules, are often seen.

Phacoanaphylaxis. Phacoanaphylactic endophthalmitis usually follows penetrating injury to the lens, but a few cases have been observed following spontaneous rupture of a swollen cataractous lens. It is characterized by a granulomatous inflammatory reaction centered about an area of lens perforation. The process is believed to be the result of acquired hypersensitivity to lens protein.

A typical zonal pattern of inflammatory reaction is observed in most cases (Fig. 30.64A). In the area in which the lens capsule is broken, there is massive invasion of the lens by inflammatory cells. Centrally and immediately surrounding individual lens fibers are polymorphonuclear leukocytes. Peripheral to this is a wall of epithelioid and giant cells about which is a broader, more diffuse zone of granulation tissue and round cell infiltration (Fig. 30.64B). The iris reveals a variable degree of plasma

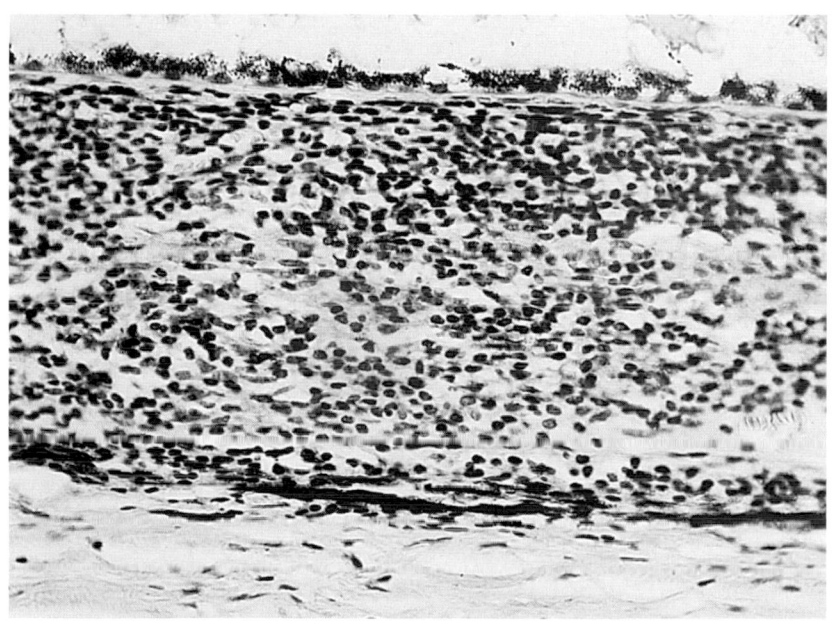

Fig. 30.62 Sympathetic uveitis. The uveal tissues are diffusely infiltrated by lymphocytes, and there are small, irregular collections of pale-staining epithelioid cells.

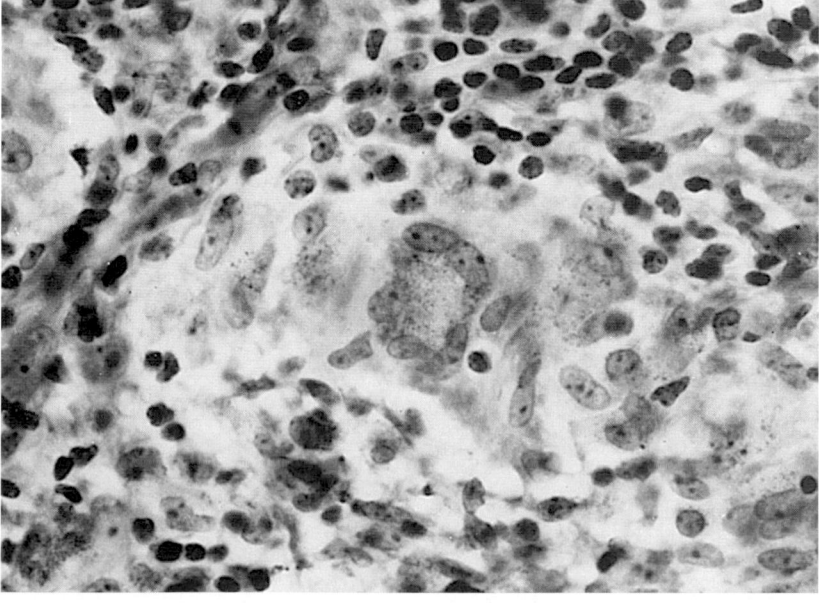

Fig. 30.63 Epithelioid cells and giant cells containing finely dispersed uveal pigment granules that are characteristically present in sympathetic uveitis. (From Friedenwald JS, Wilder HC, Maumenee AE, Sanders TE, Keyes JEL, Hogan MJ, Owens WC, Owens EU. Ophthalmic pathology. An atlas and textbook. Philadelphia, 1952, W.B. Saunders)

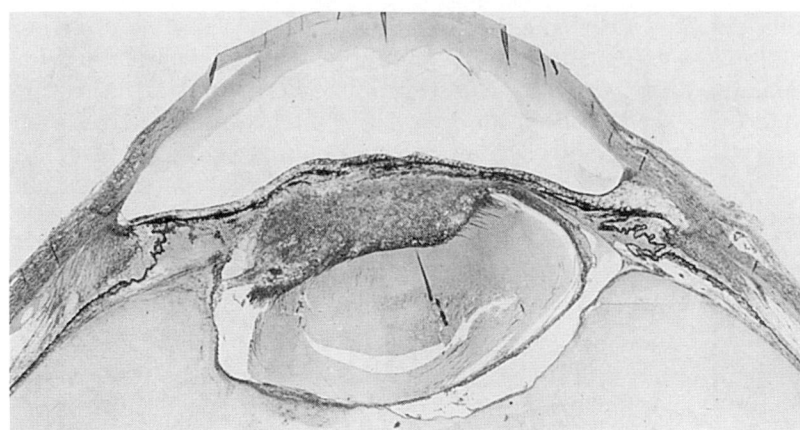

A

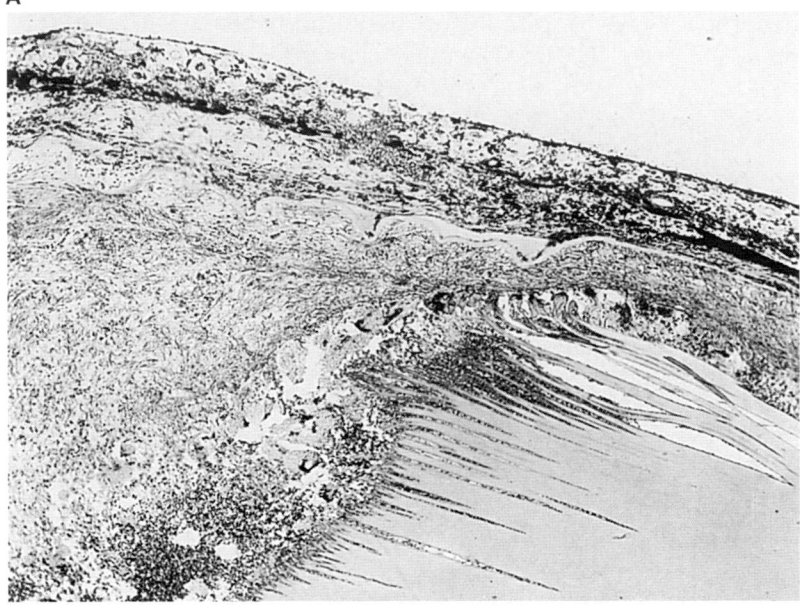

B

Fig. 30.64 A, Phacoanaphylactic endophthalmitis resulting from a penetrating wound that ruptured the capsule of the anterior lens. A dense infiltrate of acute and chronic inflammatory cells is present in the area of lens damage. **B**, Higher magnification of the lesion illustrated in **A**. Polymorphonuclear leukocytes are present in and about disintegrating lens fibers. Peripheral to them is a wall of macrophages, epithelioid cells, and giant cells, and there is a broad zone of granulation tissue around the entire lesion.

cell infiltration, and posterior synechiae are commonly formed.

Ordinarily the posterior uveal tract is not inflamed, but characteristically there is a perivasculitis of the retinal vessels. In a considerable number of cases, however, phacoanaphylactic endophthalmitis and sympathetic uveitis coexist.[201]

Degeneration

Degenerative changes are usually the result of other primary processes such as trauma or inflammation. The most advanced stage of ocular degeneration in which all tissues are involved is called phthisis bulbi.

Phthisis bulbi

Phthisis bulbi represents the final stage of ocular degeneration in which the production of aqueous humor is so markedly reduced that the intraocular pressure falls (hypotony) and the globe shrinks (Fig. 30.65). The causes of phthisis bulbi are myriad, but most phthisic eyes reaching the surgical pathology laboratory

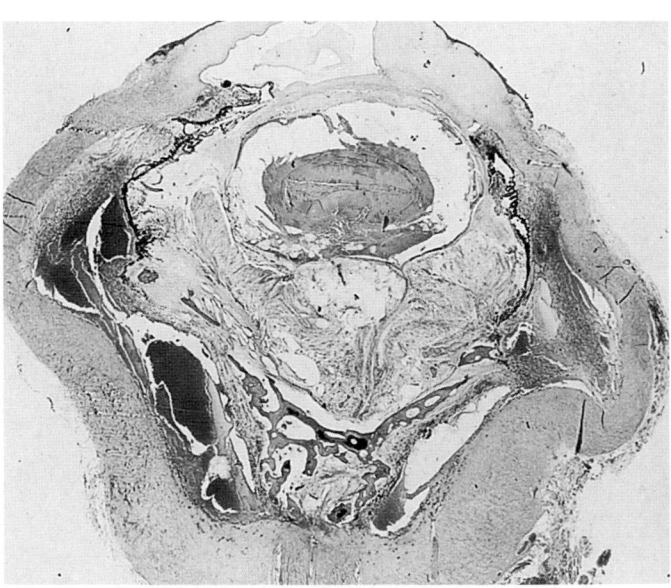

Fig. 30.65 Phthisis bulbi, in which the globe is markedly shrunken, the sclera is wrinkled, and all intraocular tissues reveal severe degenerative changes, including foci of ossification.

have been injured, either accidentally or as a result of surgical procedures.

Phthisic eyes are enucleated for several reasons. Many are enucleated because they are disfiguring and others because they become irritated as a result of periodic hemorrhages or bouts of uveitis. Some are enucleated for prophylactic reasons—the fear of sympathetic uveitis or malignant melanoma, either of which may develop long after the eye has become blind and phthisic.

All tissues are affected to varying degrees in phthisis bulbi, and the degree of shrinkage is also variable. The eye may be soft and spongy or stony hard because of calcification and ossification. Typically, the media are opaque. Corneal scars, exudates in the anterior and posterior chambers, and advanced cataract formation prevent visualization of the inner eye. The vitreous is usually destroyed, and the retina is completely detached. Extensive areas of osseous metaplasia are frequently observed along the inner surface of the choroid posteriorly. The uvea is often edematous, and pools of serous exudate may separate it from the wrinkled sclera.

In phthisis bulbi that has followed extensive endophthalmitis or panophthalmitis, the various intraocular tissues are often so necrotic and replaced by scar tissue that most of the internal architecture of the eye is effaced.

Glaucoma

Glaucoma is conveniently placed here, since it represents another condition of diverse etiology characterized by widespread degeneration of ocular tissues. The essential feature of the glaucomas is an unphysiologic state of increased intraocular pressure, caused in almost all cases by impaired outflow of aqueous humor. Aqueous humor is produced by the ciliary processes and discharged into the posterior chamber. It flows forward between the lens and the iris, through the pupil, and into the anterior chamber. Aqueous humor leaves the anterior chamber via the trabecular meshwork, which is present in the deep layers of the peripheral cornea, just in front of the anterior chamber angle (Fig. 30.66). After passing through the trabecula, aqueous humor enters Schlemm's canal and leaves the eye via the plexus of intrascleral and episcleral veins along the corneoscleral limbus. When the impaired aqueous drainage follows some known or suspected antecedent disease, the condition is known as secondary glaucoma. Here the surgical pathologist may play an important role in determining the antecedent disease.

Primary glaucoma. The primary glaucomas are not associated with antecedent disease but are of either the "chronic simple" type or the "angle-closure" type. In the former, there are certain degenerative changes in the trabecular meshwork and the connective tissues about Schlemm's canal. The exact nature of these changes remains obscure. These eyes seldom reach the pathology laboratory, since the process is usually insidious and often does not cause enough pain to necessitate enucleation.

Acute and chronic angle-closure glaucoma is caused by anatomic and physiologic peculiarities of the tissues and the spaces of the anterior chamber that predispose to blockage of the outflow channels by the iris root. Chronic attacks of angle-closure glaucoma may lead to extensive adhesions of the iris root to the trabecular meshwork (peripheral anterior synechia, Fig. 30.67), and if this glaucoma becomes intractable, it may necessitate enucleation because of pain.

Secondary glaucoma. Secondary glaucoma may be a complication of numerous primary processes, including trauma, inflammation, neoplasia, and malformation. The

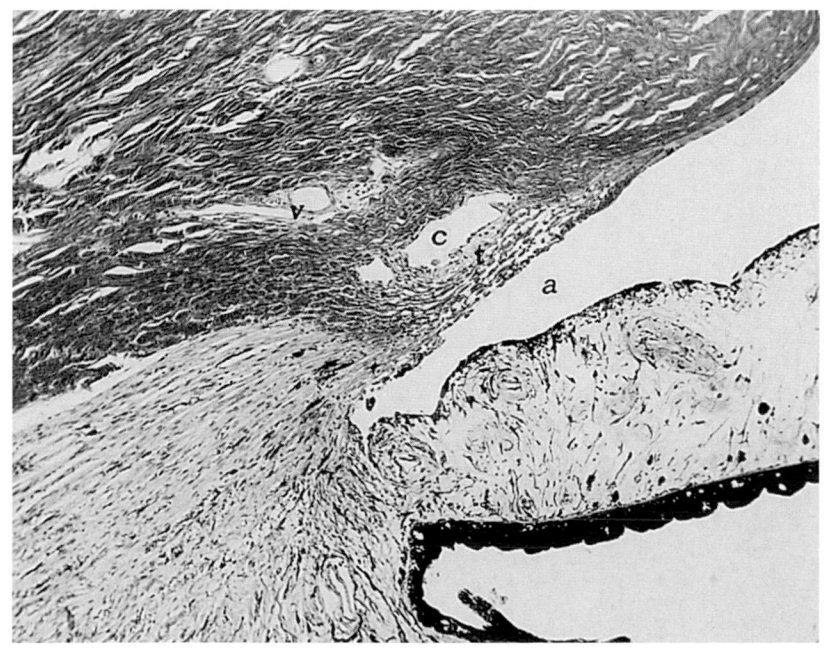

Fig. 30.66 Normal outflow channels for the passage of aqueous humor from the anterior chamber angle (a) include corneoscleral trabecula (r), Schlemm's canal (c), and the intrascleral plexus of veins (v). (Verhoeff–van Gieson)

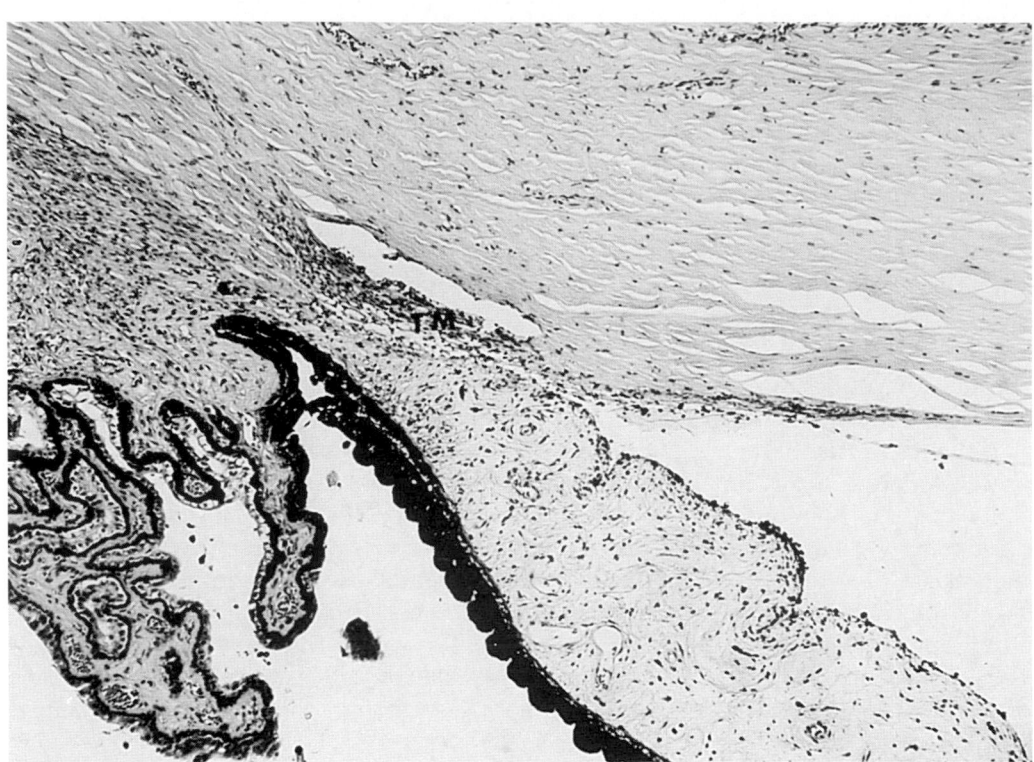

Fig. 30.67 Peripheral aspect of iris lying against trabecular meshwork (TM) producing peripheral anterior synechia and blocking the outflow of aqueous humor.

sites of obstruction to the outflow of aqueous humor are numerous, but the most vulnerable areas are the pupil and the angle of the anterior chamber. Formation of pupillary membranes as a result of organization of hemorrhages and exudates or the development of extensive adhesions between the iris and the lens (posterior synechiae) as a consequence of iritis) are the usual mechanisms leading to pupillary obstruction.

The outflow channels in the anterior chamber angle may become obstructed by particulate matter or by the formation of extensive adhesions between the root of the iris and the peripheral cornea (peripheral anterior synechiae) (see Fig. 30.68). Particulate matter clogging the passages between the anterior chamber and Schlemm's canal is usually cellular—red blood cells after massive hemorrhage into the anterior chamber,[202] leukocytes in certain types of uveitis[203] (Fig. 30.69), or tumor cells, particularly with diffuse melanomas of the iris. Following accidental trauma or surgery, conjunctival and/or corneal epithelium may grow between the wound edges and eventually line the anterior chamber and iris, thus blocking the outflow of aqueous (clinically referred to as "epithelial downgrowth"; Fig. 30.70). Fibrous downgrowth is the extension of dense fibrous tissue from the cornea into the anterior chamber through a gap in the posterior aspect of a corneal wound.

Fig. 30.68 Outflow channels blocked by macrophages in the anterior chamber in phacolytic glaucoma (glaucoma secondary to lysis and escape of lens protein into aqueous humor). (From Flocks M, Littwin CS, Zimmerman LE. Phacolytic glaucoma. Clinicopathologic study of 138 cases of glaucoma associated with hypermature cataract. Arch Ophthalmol 1955, **54**: 37–45)

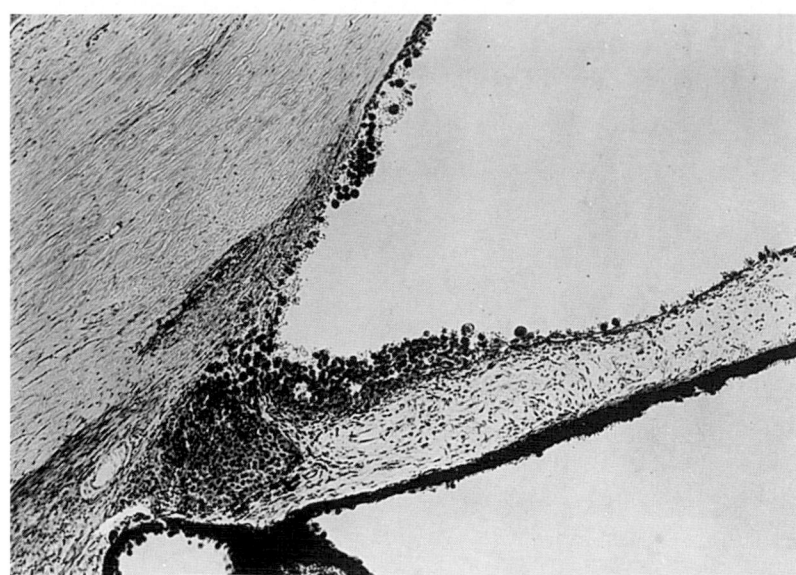

Fig. 30.69 Anterior chamber angle and outflow channels filled with deeply pigmented cells dispersed into the aqueous humor from a malignant melanoma of iris.

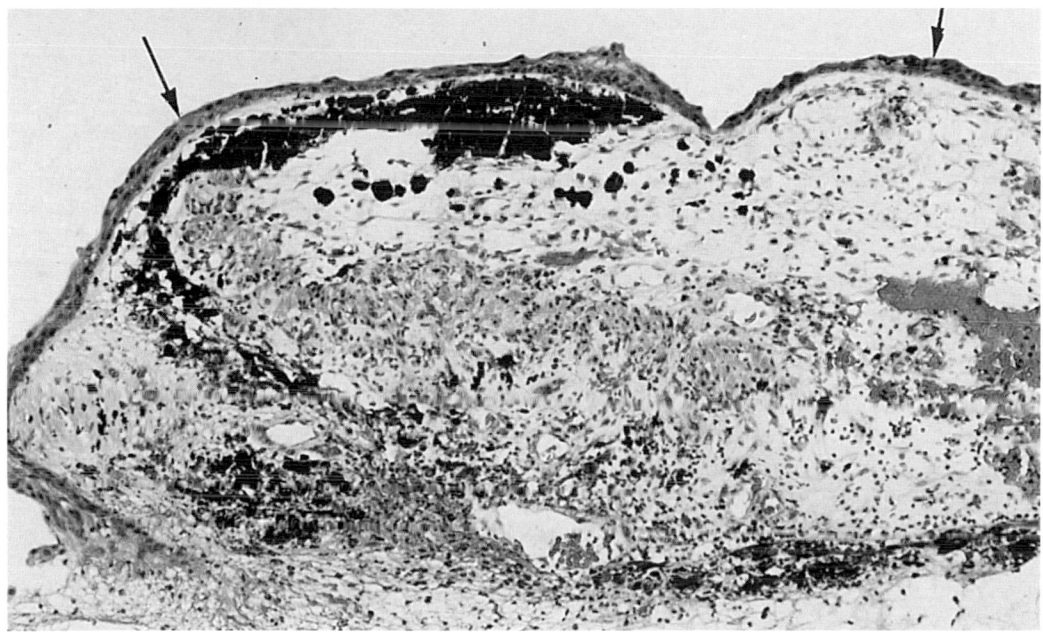

Fig. 30.70 In this case of postcataract extraction, a layer of epithelium has grown down the wound into the anterior chamber to lie on the surface of the iris (arrows).

One of the common causes of secondary glaucoma encountered by the ophthalmic pathologist is the development of a neovascular membrane on the surface of the iris. This membrane, known as *rubeosis iridis*, is eventually associated with some degree of peripheral anterior synechia, thus causing blockage of the outflow channels (Fig. 30.71).

Rubeosis iridis can occur following several different conditions. It occurs most commonly in diabetes or following occlusion of the central retinal artery or vein. Other conditions associated with rubeosis include carotid artery occlusion, longstanding retinal detachment, chronic uveitis, and intraocular neoplasms.

Damage to the outflow channels may occur as a result of blunt trauma to the eye and give rise to chronic glaucoma. This situation is often associated with a recession of the anterior chamber angle. Histologically, the iris root insertion appears retrodisplaced, and there is atrophy of the ciliary body (Fig. 30.72).

Regardless of the type and cause of glaucoma, certain degenerative changes are typically produced after periods of variable duration. When glaucoma begins in childhood, the tissues tend to stretch, and the globe may become greatly enlarged (buphthalmos). When its onset is in adult life, however, the tissues tend to resist stretching, and normal ocular dimensions are maintained.

The elevated intraocular pressure typically affects the inner retinal layers to a more pronounced degree than it does the outer layers. A common observation is the presence of rather well preserved rods and cones and an intact outer nuclear layer when virtually all ganglion cells have disappeared and the nerve fiber and inner nuclear layers have become reduced to one half or one third their normal thickness (Fig. 30.73).

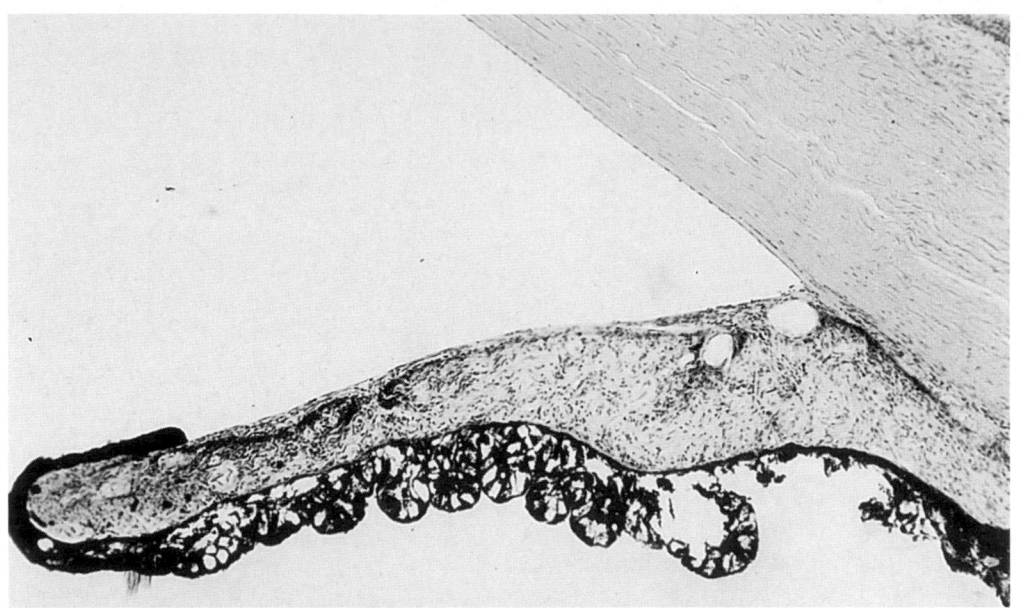

Fig. 30.71 Rubeosis iridis in diabetes. The angle of the anterior chamber is occluded by peripheral anterior synechia, and a fibrovascular membrane (rubeosis iridis) covers the anterior surface of the iris. Contraction of this membrane has pulled the pigment epithelium anteriorly to produce "ectropion uvea." There is marked diabetic vacuolization of pigment epithelial cells.

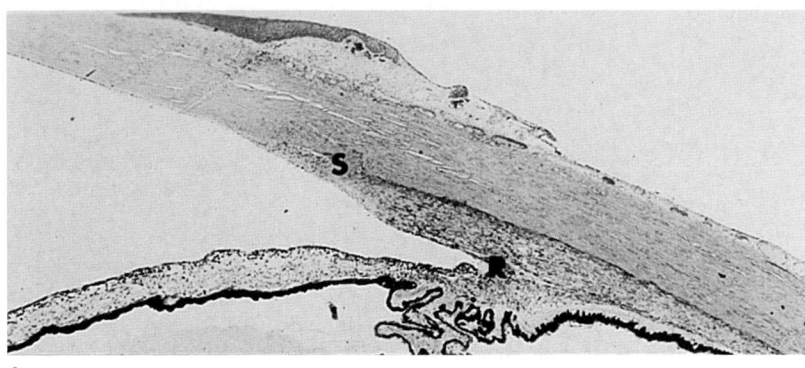

A

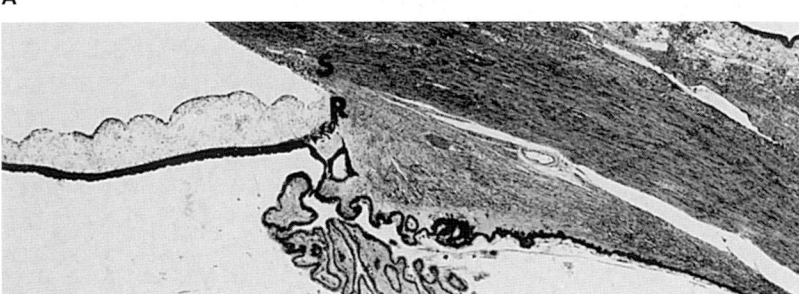

B

Fig. 30.72 A, Recession of angle of anterior chamber. **B,** Normal angle. In **A,** the iris root (R) is retrodisplaced with reference to the scleral spur (S), and the contour of the atrophic ciliary body is fusiform instead of a normal wedge shape.

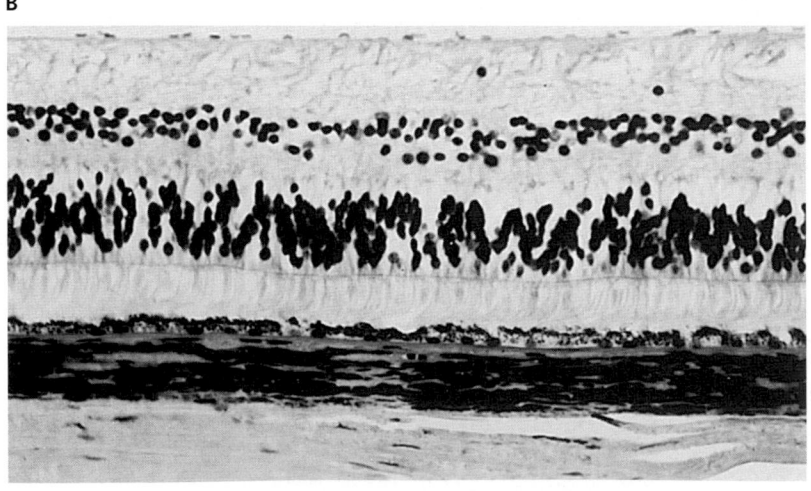

Fig. 30.73 Retina in chronic glaucoma revealing widespread loss of ganglion cells and nerve fibers and reduction of cells in the inner nuclear layer but relatively well-preserved visual cells. (From Friedenwald JS, Wilder HC, Maumenee AE, Sanders TE, Keyes JEL, Hogan MJ, Owens WC, Owens EU. Ophthalmic pathology. An atlas and textbook. Philadelphia, 1952, W.B. Saunders)

Degeneration of nerve fibers is especially noteworthy in the region of the optic disc. This leads to excavation or cupping of the nerve head, posterior bowing of the lamina cribrosa, and severe atrophy of the optic nerve (Fig. 30.74). Often, discrete areas of scleral ectasia are observed, particularly in the equatorial regions. These are lined by uveal tissue and therefore have a bluish color—hence the name *staphyloma* (grape-like swelling).

Diabetes

Ocular diabetes has become one of the most common causes of blindness in Western society. Diabetes can cause a variety of pathologic conditions within the eye. These conditions may lead to complete blindness and, if associated with pain, the eyes often reach the pathology laboratory.[205]

The retina often shows scattered hemorrhages and exudates, and there may be the development of neovascular tissue that grows from the inner surface of the retina into the vitreous (Fig. 30.75A). This condition, known as *proliferative retinopathy*, can cause a retinal detachment that usually does not respond well to surgical treatment (Fig. 30.75B).

As previously mentioned, secondary glaucoma may result from the development of diabetic rubeosis iridis with peripheral anterior synechia. Many eyes from diabetic patients will also manifest vacuolization of the iris pigment epithelium. These vacuoles have been demonstrated to contain glycogen and are related to the level of the blood glucose at the time of enucleation, similarly to Armanni–Ebstein nephropathy.[204]

Diffuse uveal melanocytic proliferation

Diffuse uveal melanocytic proliferation, a peculiar paraneoplastic syndrome that is bilateral and can lead to blindness, is associated with a variety of poorly differen tiated extraocular tumors, many of them located in the female genital tract (uterus and ovary).[206]

Tumors and tumorlike conditions

Malignant melanoma

General and clinical features. Melanomas arising from the pigmented or potentially pigment-producing cells of the uvea are the most frequent primary intraocular neoplasms in adults. They can also occur in adolescents, children, and even neonates.[208,210] It has been suggested that most of them arise on the basis of preexisting benign nevi.[251–253] A syndrome has been described in which bilateral diffuse melanocytic uveal tumors are seen in association with systemic malignant neoplasms.[209]

Malignant melanoma may be located at any point in the uveal tract, with the choroid and ciliary body being more frequent locations than the iris. Melanoma of the iris presents as an elevated mass with varying degrees of pigmentation and often with distortion of the pupil and the presence of prominent vessels on the tumor (Fig. 30.76). Choroidal melanoma also may vary in pigmentation but characteristically is an irregular, slate-gray, solid, subretinal tumor producing an overlying retinal detachment and decreased vision (Figs 30.77 and 30.78). It may appear as a discoid, globular, or mushroom-shaped mass. Less commonly, it spreads diffusely and extends out along scleral canals into the orbit[221,240] (Figs 30.79 to 30.81).

Visual disturbance caused by retinal detachment is a much more frequent presenting complaint than the formation of an orbital tumor. Not infrequently the patient remains asymptomatic until the tumor has grown sufficiently to become necrotic and produce complications such as endophthalmitis, massive intraocular hemorrhage, and/or secondary glaucoma.

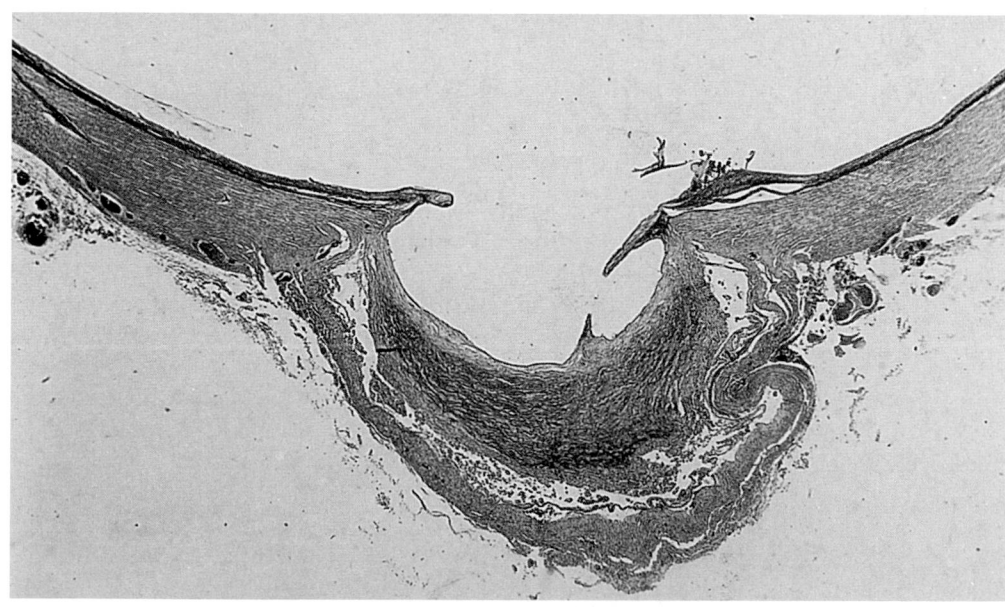

Fig. 30.74 Deep excavation (cupping) of optic disc and severe atrophy of optic nerve, which are important complications of chronic glaucoma.

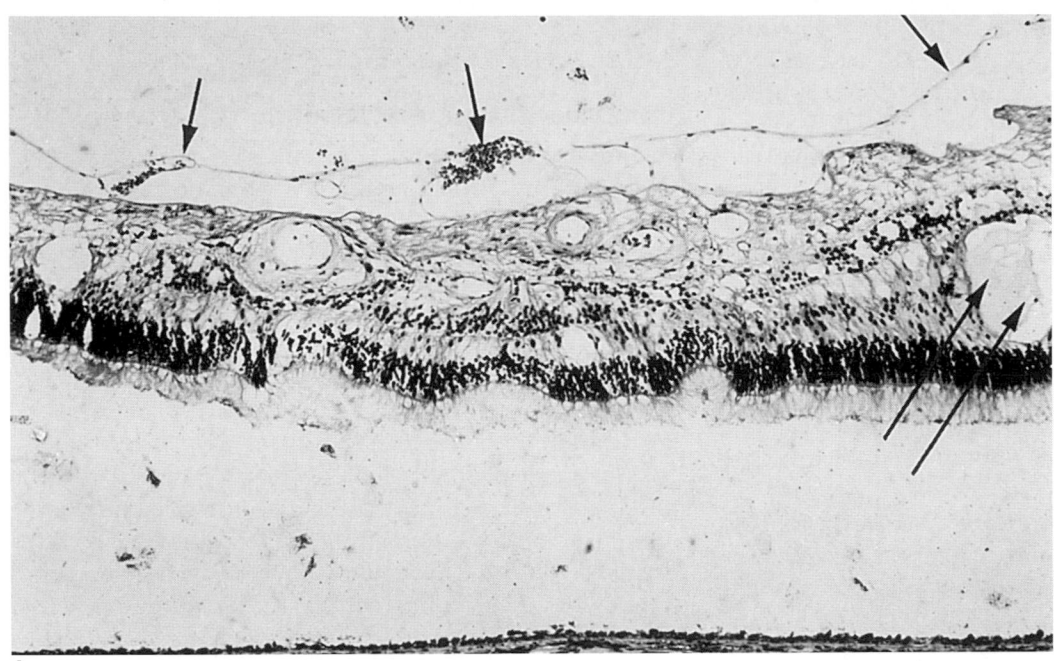

A

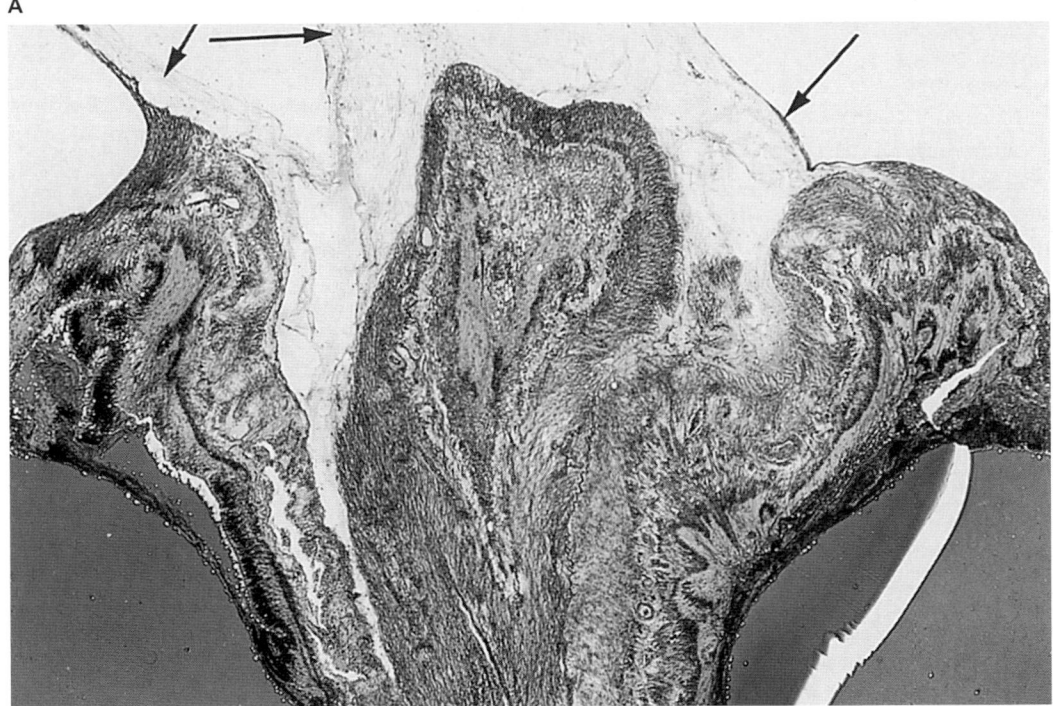

B

Fig. 30.75 A, Diabetic retinopathy with scattered exudates in deep retinal layers (double arrows) and early neovascularization extending from the inner surface of the retina into the vitreous (single arrows). **B,** Diabetic proliferative retinopathy (arrows) has caused complete retinal detachment.

At times, malignant melanomas of the posterior uvea are not discovered until the enucleated eye is examined in the laboratory. Iris tumors are more often recognized early, for they can be seen by the patient and family long before other symptoms appear (Fig. 30.82).

Clinically, there are many lesions that simulate uveal malignant melanoma.[211,218,219,244] The most important are metastatic carcinoma, localized hemorrhage beneath the retina or between the pigment epithelium and choroid (Fig. 30.83), focal areas of proliferation of the retinal pigment epithelium (Fig. 30.84), posterior scleritis, and benign tumors such as nevi and hemangiomas.

Microscopic features. Microscopically, uveal melanomas have been traditionally divided into three types: spindle A, spindle B, and epithelioid, which may occur singly or in combination.[237] Spindle A cells are slender, benign-appearing spindle-shaped cells that have relatively small fusiform nuclei and no nucleoli. The chromatin is frequently arranged in a linear fashion along the central axis of the nucleus.

Spindle B cells are larger and more pleomorphic, merging on the one hand with spindle A cells and on the other with epithelioid cells. They typically possess large ovoid nuclei containing prominent nucleoli (Fig. 30.85).

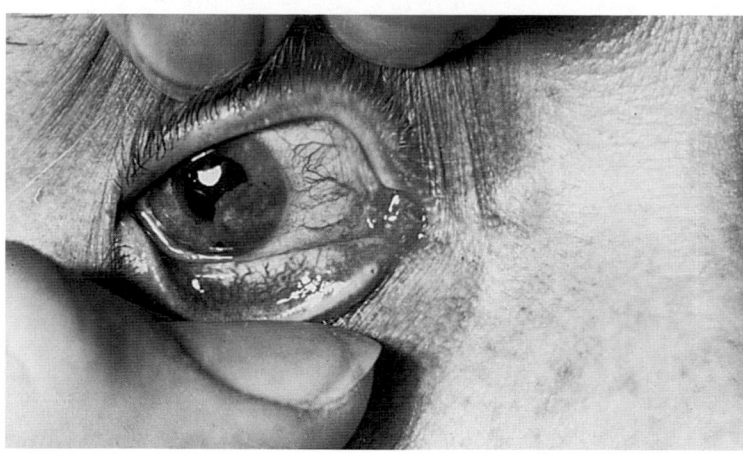

Fig. 30.76 Melanoma of iris that had been observed over a period of 10 years, during which time it became progressively larger and encroached on the pupil. Iridectomy revealed it to be of spindle A cell type. The tumor recurred and necessitated enucleation for secondary glaucoma 15 years after iridectomy. (Courtesy of Dr. ME Nugent, Bismarck, ND)

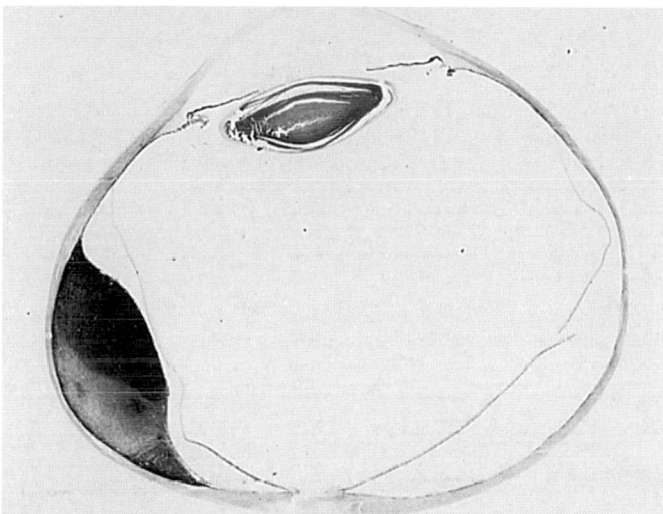

Fig. 30.77 Malignant melanoma of choroid that has not broken through Bruch's membrane but has elevated the retina. Most of the retinal separation observed in this section is artifactual. (From Friedenwald JS, Wilder HC, Maumenee AE, Sanders TE, Keyes JEL, Hogan MJ, Owens WC, Owens EU. Ophthalmic pathology. An atlas and textbook. Philadelphia, 1952, W.B. Saunders)

Fig. 30.78 Malignant melanoma of choroid that, by erupting through Bruch's membrane, has formed a mushroom-shaped subretinal mass.

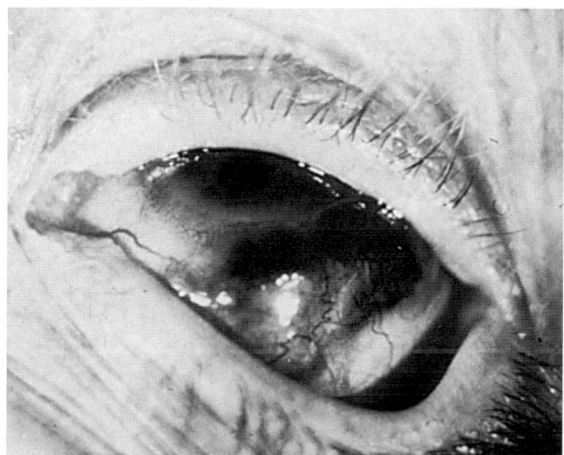

Fig. 30.79 Malignant melanoma of choroid breaking through the sclera and presenting under the conjunctiva. (From del Regato JA, Spjut HJ. Ackerman and del Regato's cancer, ed. 5. St. Louis, 1977, Mosby; courtesy of the Registry of Ophthalmic Pathology, Armed Forces Institute of Pathology, Washington, D.C.)

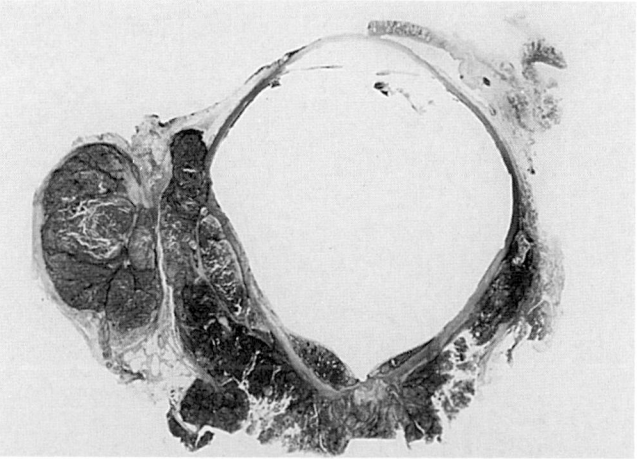

Fig. 30.80 Massive orbital extension from a small choroid melanoma that has occurred as a result of diffuse spread along natural passages through the sclera and optic nerve. (From Friedenwald JS, Wilder HC, Maumenee AE, Sanders TE, Keyes JEL, Hogan MJ, Owens WC, Owens EU. Ophthalmic pathology. An atlas and textbook. Philadelphia, 1952, W.B. Saunders)

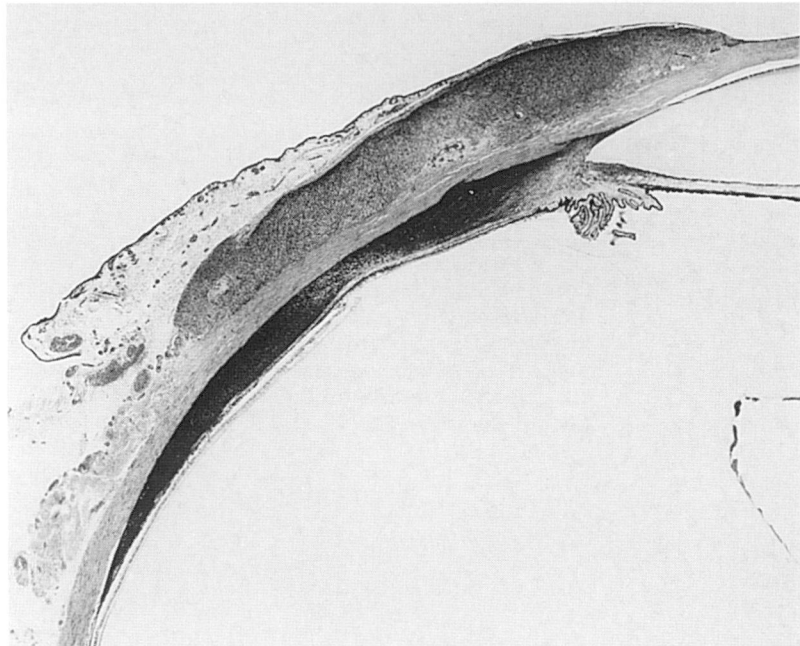

Fig. 30.81 Diffuse malignant melanoma of ciliary body and choroid that extended forward through scleral canals to form a large subconjunctival mass that encroached on the cornea.

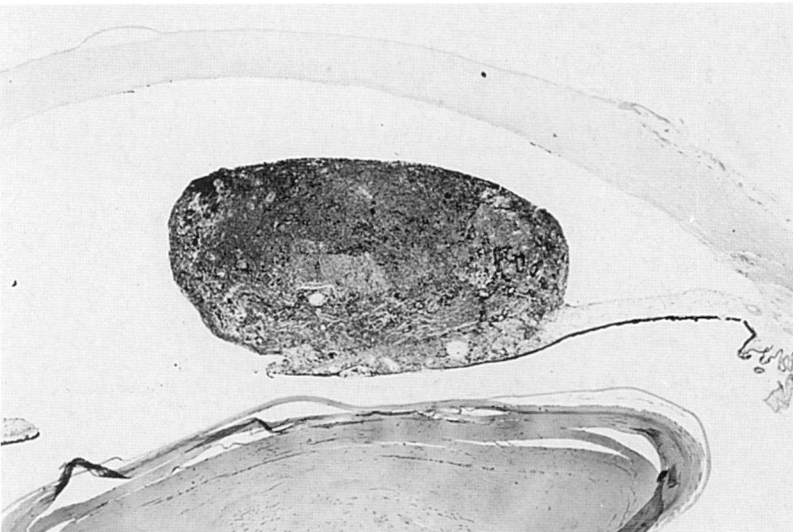

Fig. 30.82 Melanomas of iris are frequently visible through the cornea. Hence, their duration and rate of growth are often known by the patient or family long before other subjective or objective manifestations appear.

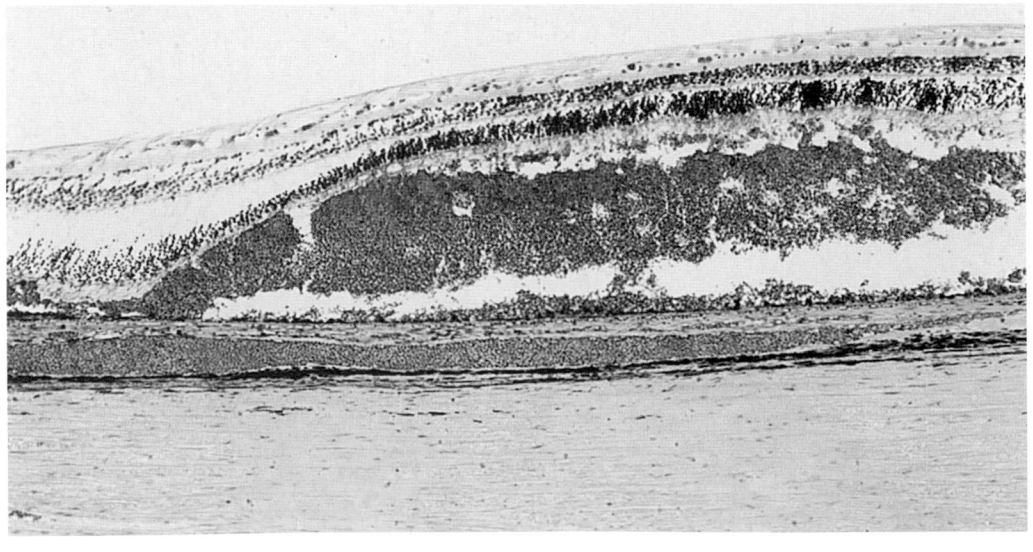

Fig. 30.83 This focal hemorrhage under the retina was clinically mistaken for melanoma.

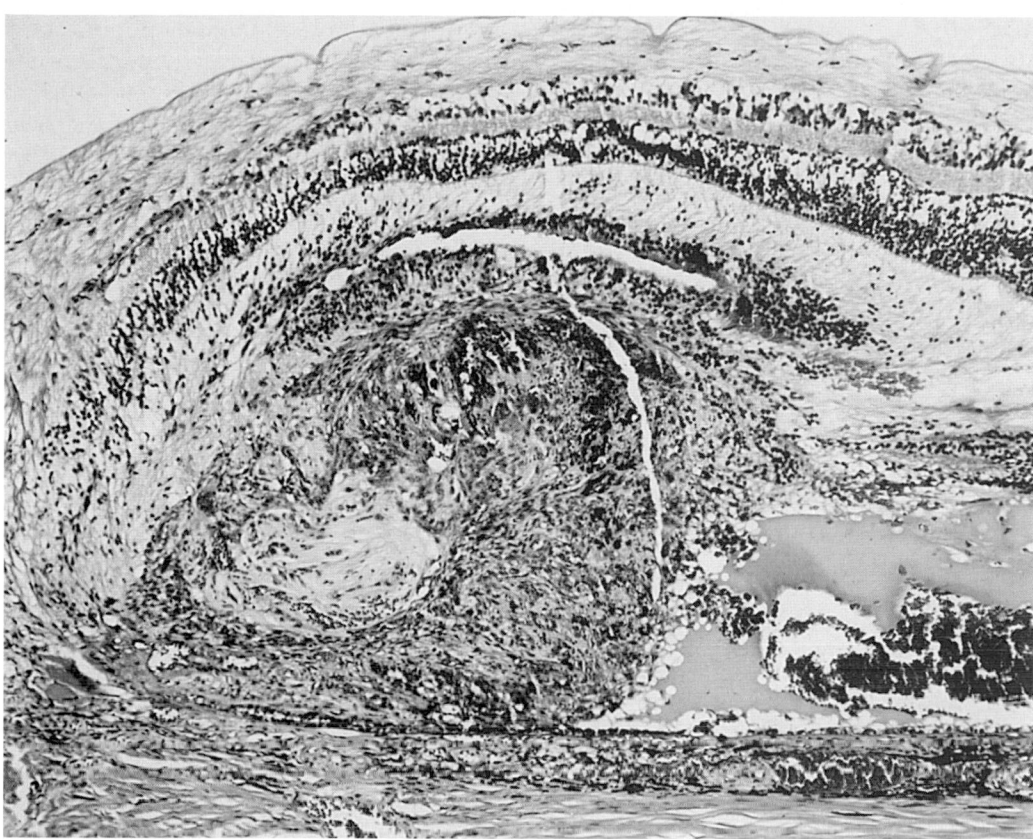

Fig. 30.84 A focal area of proliferation of retinal pigment epithelium that has elevated the retina to simulate melanoma.

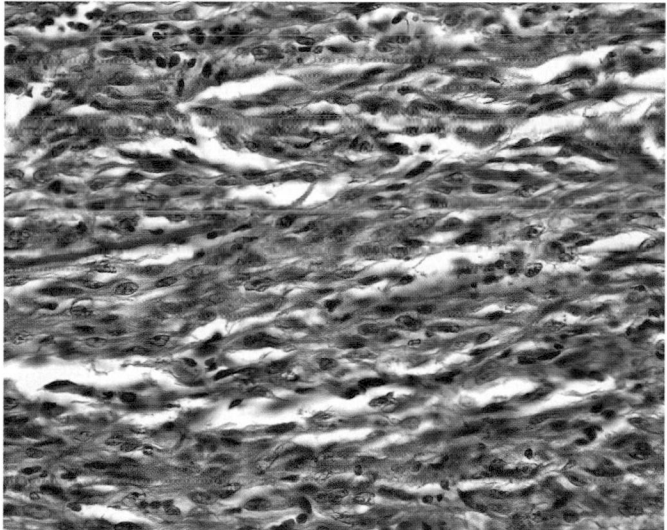

Fig. 30.85 So-called "spindle B melanoma." The tumor cells are spindle-shaped and have conspicuous nucleoli.

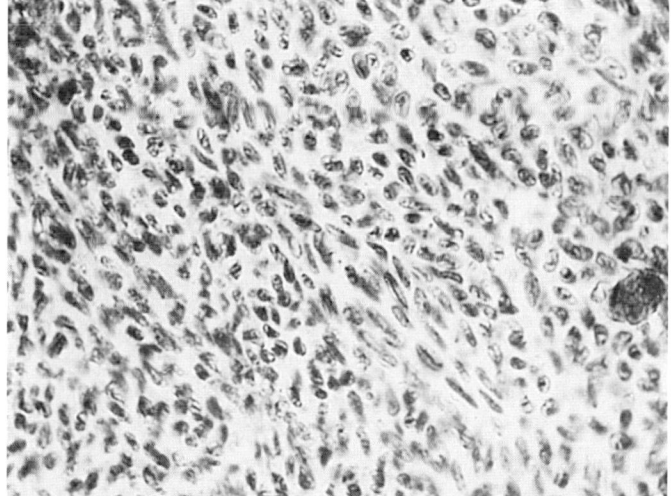

Fig. 30.86 Fascicular type of melanoma composed of spindle cells arranged about dilated capillaries.

Mitotic activity may be more marked. Both spindle A and spindle B tumors tend to be quite cohesive. Some of these tumors have a distinctly fascicular pattern of growth (Fig. 30.86).

Epithelioid cells are still larger and more irregular (Fig. 30.87). They have an abundance of cytoplasm and may be truly gigantic. Multinucleated forms are not unusual. The nuclei are large, and their nucleoli are often strikingly prominent. In some tumors, many bizarre nuclei may be seen. Epithelioid cells are characteristically less cohesive than the spindle cells.

It is rather unusual for these tumors to be composed of a single cell type. Mixtures of spindle A and B cells or mixtures of spindle and epithelioid cells are common.

The microscopic differential diagnosis of primary uveal melanoma includes benign pigmented nevi.[228,243] Along these lines, it has been pointed out that the tumors traditionally designated as spindle A melanomas may actually represent spindle cell nevi (see also p. 2752).

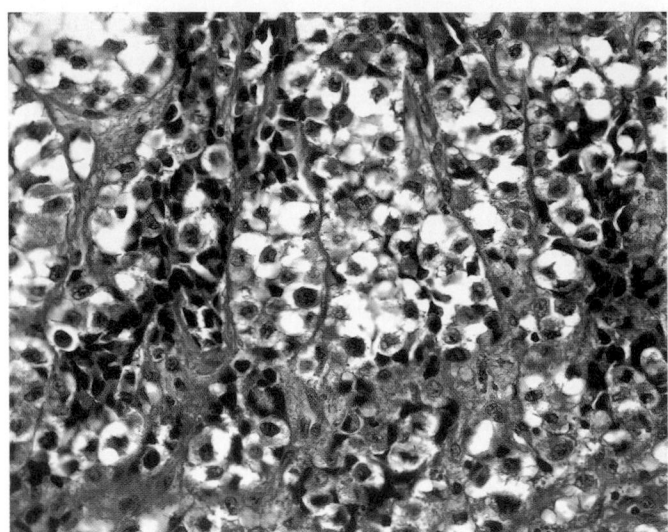

Fig. 30.87 Melanoma of epithelioid type. Some of the tumor cells have a clear cytoplasm, probably of artifactual nature.

Primary uveal melanomas should also be distinguished from intraocular metastases of cutaneous malignant melanoma.[213,215,232] In addition, amelanotic melanomas raise the differential diagnosis with metastatic carcinoma, and spindle cell melanomas with a fascicular pattern of growth may resemble neurofibromas, schwannomas, or leiomyomas. The latter consideration applies particularly to tumors of the ciliary body.

Immunohistochemical and molecular genetic features. Immunohistochemically, malignant melanomas are reactive for S-100 protein and HMB-45. They are also positive for vimentin and often for low-molecular-weight keratins, such as those demonstrated with Cam 5.2.[223] It has been suggested that the melanoma cells exhibiting keratin immunostaining have a greater metastatic potential.[226]

Overexpression of p53 has been observed, but this seems to represent a late event in the course of the disease.[230]

Cytogenetically, the consistent occurrence of monosomy 3 and trisomy 8q, and structural or numerical abnormalities of chromosome 6 have been documented.[227,246]

DNA ploidy studies have shown that all spindle A melanomas are diploid, whereas a varying number of spindle B and epithelioid melanomas are aneuploid.[214]

Spread and metastases. The great tendency of uveal melanoma to spread along the course of the optic nerve has already been mentioned. The most common sites of distant metastatic involvement are the liver, lung, bone, and skin.[231] The liver route is particularly common in uveal melanoma when compared to melanoma of the skin.[233] The skin metastases may simulate blue nevi clinically and pathologically.[250]

Therapy. The standard treatment of melanoma of the choroid has been enucleation of the eye, but several more conservative alternatives have gained in popularity.[244] Small melanomas of the iris can be treated by iridectomy or iridocyclectomy.[222] The suggestion has been made that enucleation may stimulate the development of metastatic disease,[254] but this has not been confirmed in other studies.[242] It is not clear whether the use of adjunctive radiation therapy improves prognosis.[212]

Prognosis. The overall mortality from metastasis of melanoma of the uveal tract 15 years after enucleation is close to 50%.[235] The prognosis of this tumor depends on several factors:

1 *Cell type.* This is an extremely important parameter. There are no deaths with pure spindle A tumors, the proposal having therefore been made for these neoplasms to be regarded as spindle cell nevi rather than melanomas.[237] The 5-year survival rate is 66% to 75% for spindle B melanomas, 50% for mixed (spindle B and epithelioid) melanomas, and 25% to 33% for pure epithelioid melanomas.

2 *Tumor size.* Larger tumors have a worse prognosis than smaller ones.[225,235,238] It has been shown that tumor dimension is a better predictor of prognosis than height or volume.[241]

3 *Location.* Tumors located in the iris have an excellent prognosis.[245] This is in part related to their smaller size at the time of diagnosis and also to their less malignant cytologic features.[207,235] As a matter of fact, it has been suggested that most pigmented lesions of the iris traditionally designated as spindle A melanomas are benign nevi, as indicated previously.[229]

4 *Extension into the optic nerve.* This is said to be associated with a decreased survival, but there are conflicting data in this regard. A juxtapapillary location for the tumor does not result in significantly different survival rates if the optic nerve is not involved.[249]

5 *Extension into the sclera.* Extrascleral extension occurs in 10% to 28% of patients with choroidal melanoma.[238,239] In one series the 5-year mortality was 66% for patients with extrascleral extension and 33% for those with no extension.[248]

6 *Necrosis.* This is a sign of poor prognosis; it is usually associated with epithelioid type tumors.

7 *Lymphocytic infiltration.* The presence of a large number of lymphocytes in the tumor stroma has been found to be significantly associated with decreased survival.[216]

8 *Neovascularization.* Melanomas with "closed vascular loops" behave more aggressively than others, but this morphologic feature is associated with other unfavorable morphologic indicators, such as epithelioid cells.[220]

9 *Nucleolar prominence.* Nucleolar large size and pleomorphism are associated with aggressive behavior in uveal melanoma. Various methods have been

devised to quantify this determination, including automated image capture and analysis of AgNOR-stained sections.[224,234,236,247]

10 *Amount of pigmentation.* This feature does not have independent prognostic significance.

11 *DNA ploidy.* Most studies have found no significant correlations between DNA ploidy status and prognosis once the melanomas have been stratified into the major morphologic subtypes.[214]

12 MDR1 *expression.* Expression of the *MDR1* gene and its product P-glycoprotein seem to correlate with an adverse prognosis.[217]

Retinoblastoma and related lesions

General features. Retinoblastoma is the most common intraocular neoplasm of children. It is generally believed to be congenital and derived from primitive neuroectodermal cells exhibiting retinal differentiation.[277,283,284] However, retinoblastomas are seldom recognized until considerable growth has taken place and are usually diagnosed between the ages of 16 months and 2 years. Approximately 60% of the cases are sporadic, and the other 40% are familial, the predisposition to tumor development being transmitted in an autosomal dominant pattern. Retinoblastoma will develop in 80% to 90% of persons who carry any one of a variety of mutant alleles associated with a predisposition to the tumor.[296]

The gene responsible has been located in chromosome 13q14 and designated the retinoblastoma (*Rb*) gene.[285] Gene mutations in both alleles are necessary to produce inactivation of the Rb protein, which is a negative regulator of cell growth.[270,297,300] Patients with hereditary retinoblastoma have a germ cell mutation in one allele and develop the retinoblastoma as a result of a somatic mutation in the second allele, whereas in patients with sporadic retinoblastoma both mutations are somatic.[266,298]

This model, known as Knudson's "two-hit hypothesis," has become a paradigm of tumorigenesis.[274]

Clinical features. Retinoblastomas characteristically present as a leukocoria (white pupillary reflex; Fig. 30.88) or less often as a strabismus when the tumor is in the macula. Rarely, extraocular extension with the formation of an orbital mass is the presenting manifestation.

Retinoblastomas may be flat and diffuse or elevated and may show multicentric foci of origin, especially in the hereditary type. They may protrude into the vitreous (endophytic type; Fig. 30.89) often with vitreous seeding, or they may grow between the retina and the pigment epithelium (exophytic type). Since the tumors tend to outgrow their blood supply, necrosis is often extensive and many minute foci of calcification are often present in these areas of necrosis (Fig. 30.90). In fact, these areas of calcification may be appreciated by x-ray examination prior to enucleation.

Bilaterality is present in 30% of all cases and in over 90% of the familial cases (Fig. 30.91). Some patients have presented with bilateral retinoblastoma and a morphologically similar intracranial neoplasm localized in the region of the pineal gland, in keeping with the "third eye" nature of the latter structure.[277] These are referred as *trilateral retinoblastomas*[261,269] and are associated with a particularly dismal prognosis.[281]

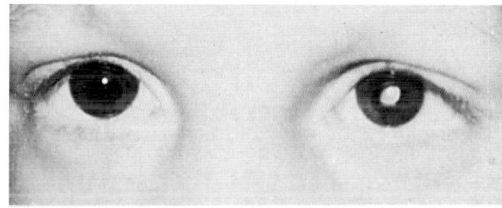

Fig. 30.88 Prominent white reflex attributed to retinoblastoma present in the dilated pupil of the left eye.

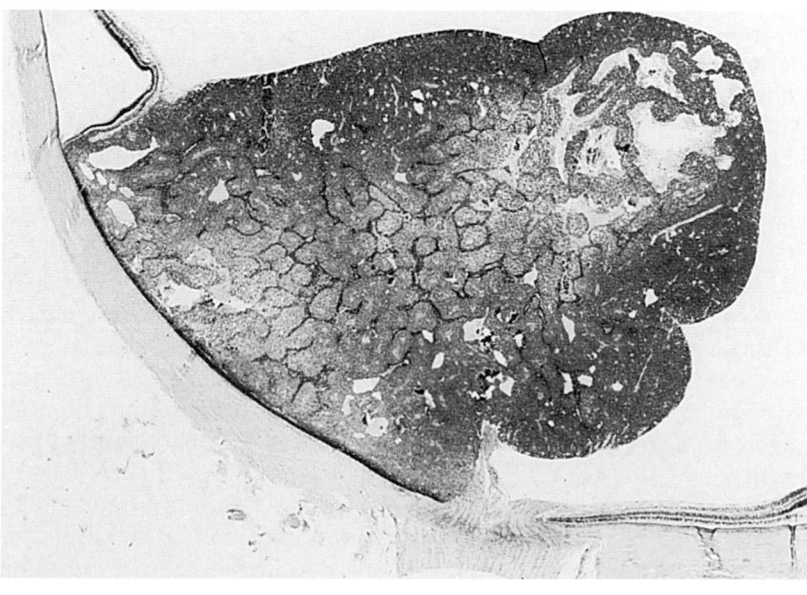

Fig. 30.89 Retinoblastoma presenting as a highly cellular neoplasm with scanty stroma. The tumor tends to outgrow its blood supply, and irregular areas of necrosis are commonly observed.

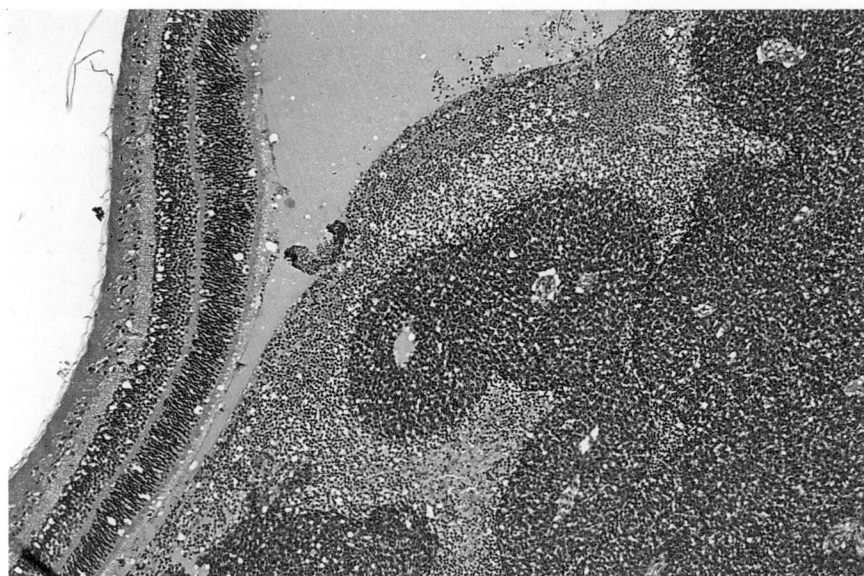

Fig. 30.90 Low-power view of retinoblastoma. There is a collar of viable cells about nutrient vessels. The normal retina is seen on the left.

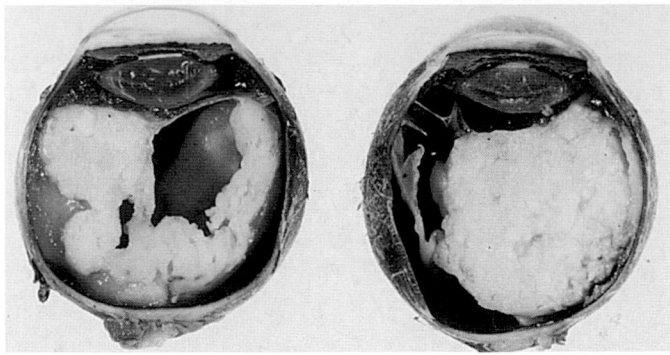

Fig. 30.91 Bilateral retinoblastoma showing a white mass consisting of detached retina and neoplastic tissue immediately behind the lens in each eye.

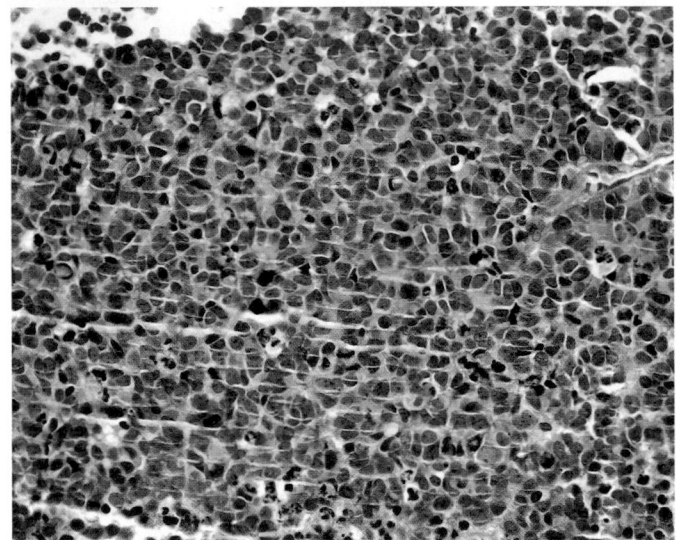

Fig. 30.92 Poorly differentiated retinoblastoma. The appearance is that of a malignant small round cell tumor.

The clinical differential diagnosis of retinoblastoma includes any disease process that leads to retinal detachment or a retrolental mass in a child under 6 years of age.[271,275] Lesions in this category include traumatic or idiopathic retinal detachments, retrolental fibroplasia, persistent hyperplastic primary vitreous, massive retinal gliosis, Coats' disease, nematodiasis, astrocytomas of tuberous sclerosis, and medulloepitheliomas. Some of these disorders are discussed elsewhere in this chapter.

Microscopic features. Microscopically, the tumors are composed of dense masses of small round cells with hyperchromatic nuclei and scanty cytoplasm[278] (Fig. 30.92). Trabecular and nesting formations are common.[289] Hematoxyphilic deposits in and around blood vessel walls are often seen in necrotic areas, similar to those found in pulmonary small cell carcinomas.[262] A sign of differentiation toward retinal structures is provided by the presence of so-called "Flexner–Wintersteiner rosettes" and fleurettes (Fig. 30.93). *Differentiated neuroblastoma* is characterized by the presence of a bipolar-like cell element.[268] Tumors showing an extreme degree of differentiation are designated as *retinocytomas* and

regarded as benign.[280] These lesions carry the same genetic implications as conventional neuroblastomas; they present as small placoid, noninvasive lesions composed entirely of benign-appearing cells with numerous fleurettes, lacking necrosis or mitotic activity.[280]

Electron microscopic, immunohistochemical, and molecular genetic features. Ultrastructurally, evidence of photodifferentiation has been found in the tumor cells of retinoblastoma[291,292] (Fig. 30.94). Immunohistochemically, there is reactivity for neuron-specific enolase, synaptophysin, S-100 protein, GFAP, myelin basic protein, and Leu7, in keeping with an origin from a pluripotential neuroectodermal cell that retains neuronal and glial features.[289,290,294,299] In addition, allegedly specific markers of retinal differentiation such as retinal-binding protein, retinal S-antigen, interphotoreceptor retinal-binding protein, cone opsin, rod opsin, and MLGAPC (a mucin-like

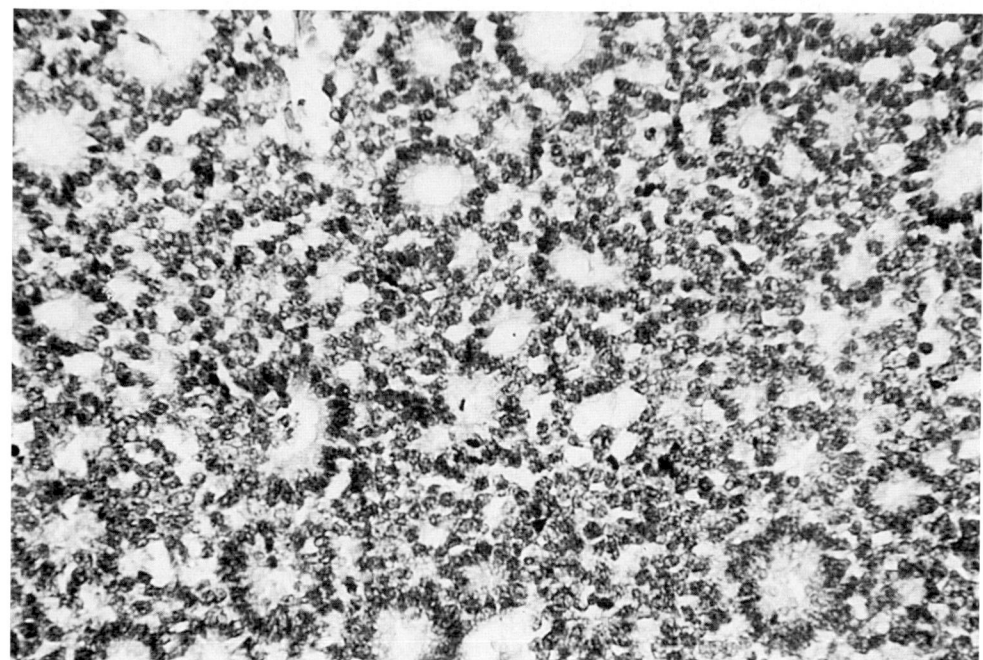

Fig. 30.93 Retinoblastoma with typical rosettes. (From Ackerman LV, del Regato JA. Cancer, ed. 6. St. Louis, 1985, Mosby)

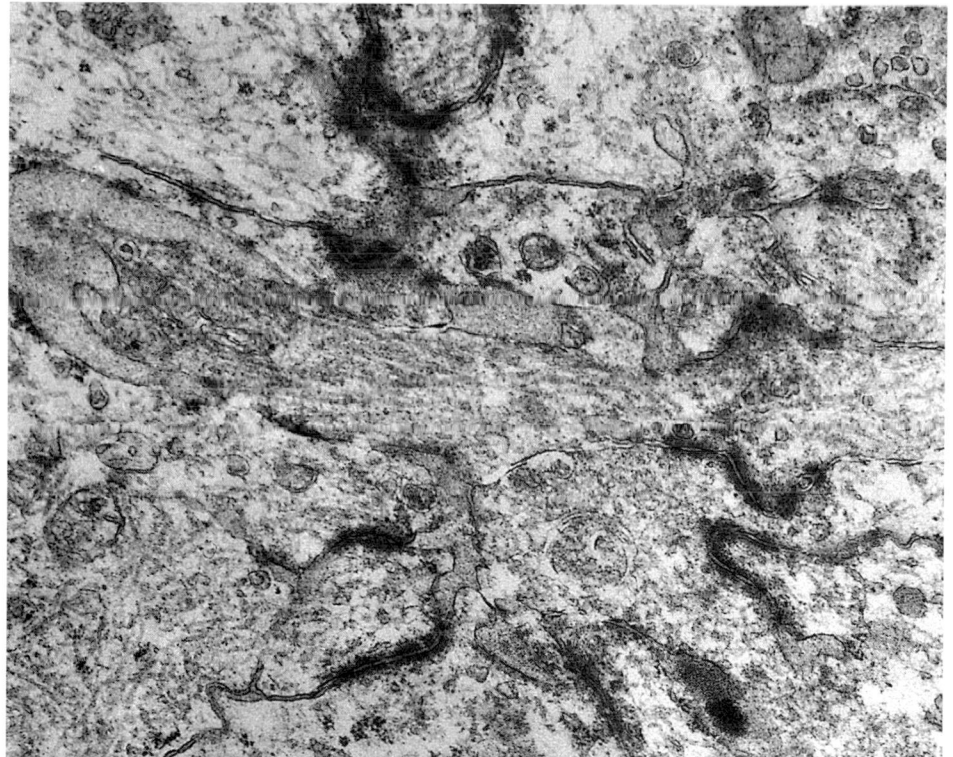

Fig. 30.94 Electron micrograph of retinoblastoma. A portion of the center of a rudimentary Flexner–Wintersteiner rosette illustrating a bulbous apical microtubule-containing cytoplasmic process and numerous cell junctions. (×20,800; courtesy of Dr. Robert A Erlandson, Memorial Sloan-Kettering Cancer Center)

glycoprotein associated with photoreceptor cells) have been found in these tumors.[265,267,282] Interestingly, retinal S-antigen has also been detected in tumors of the pineal gland and in cerebellar medulloblastomas.[276,282] Further evidence of the retinal nature of this tumor has been obtained in vitro, where differentiation toward photoreceptors has been observed spontaneously or after the addition of differentiating agents.[293]

The MIB-1 labeling index is extremely high. Limited p53 immunostaining is present in over half of the cases.

In contrast to Ewing's sarcoma/PNET, most neuroblastomas are negative for CD99.[286]

Spread and metastases. Retinoblastoma has a tendency to invade the optic nerve, from which it can extend to the brain or be carried there by the subarachnoid fluid[288] (Fig. 30.95). Large exophytic tumors with secondary glaucoma are at highest risk for optic nerve invasion.[288] Retinoblastoma can also invade the uveal tract. Distant metastases can be limited to the cranial vault or involve distant sites, particularly the skeletal system.[279]

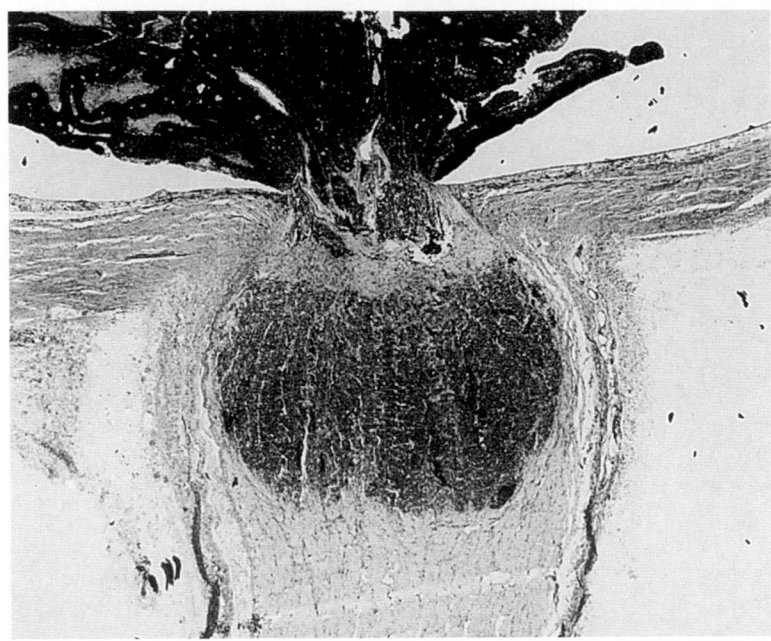

Fig. 30.95 Retinoblastomas exhibit a definite tendency to spread out of the globe by way of the optic nerve. It is therefore of utmost importance for the surgical pathologist to determine whether such optic nerve extension has occurred and, if it has, to what extent.

Treatment. The treatment depends on the extent of the disease.[287] Early cases can be managed with conservative measures aimed at preserving the vision, such as unilateral radiation, cryopexy, or xenon arc photocoagulation.[258] When the tumor is so large that the eye is no longer salvageable, enucleation should be performed.[302] If tumor has extended to the surgically cut end of the nerve, irradiation of the orbit and systemic chemotherapy are performed. In patients with bilateral retinoblastoma, the less affected eye is treated with radiotherapy, at times in combination with chemotherapy. Bilateral cases can also be treated with simultaneous bilateral irradiation.[255,256,260] The success rate for life of the patient and for preservation of vision is quite good. If tumor recurrences develop, they are treated with photocoagulation, cryotherapy, and cobalt discs. Chemotherapy is administered to disseminated cases, but so far with disappointing results.[266a]

Prognosis. The 5-year survival of unilateral retinoblastoma following adequate treatment is over 90% and slightly less for the bilateral cases.[301,302] Features that correlate with prognosis in retinoblastoma are:

1 *Invasion of optic nerve.* In an operation for suspected neuroblastoma, the surgeon will attempt to obtain a long segment of optic nerve attached to the globe. Transverse sections of this nerve should be examined by the pathologist at the prelaminar and retrolaminar levels, including the surgical margin.[259] The levels of invasion of the optic nerve by retinoblastoma have been divided into prelaminar and retrolaminar, the latter further subdivided into lesions with or without resection line involvement. The prognosis decreases with each of these levels.[273,284]

2 *Invasion of meninges.* This is often associated with invasion of the optic nerve.[284]

3 *Invasion of the uveal tract.* Massive invasion of the uveal tract by retinoblastoma is an unfavorable prognostic sign.[273]

Long-term survivors have a greater incidence of development of malignant tumors. The incidence has ranged from 6% to 20% after 10 years, and in one series has reached 90% at 30 years. The most common types have been osteosarcoma and rhabdomyosarcoma, but several other types have been encountered, including rhabdoid tumors.[257,295] This predisposition for a second malignancy, which should be distinguished from a recurrence of the retinoblastoma,[264] is seen almost exclusively with the hereditary form of the disease.[263]

Massive retinal gliosis. Massive retinal gliosis is a relatively uncommon condition in which a large elevated scar develops near the disc and posterior pole following hemorrhage (e.g., in the newborn) or inflammation.

Coats' disease. Coats' disease is an exudative retinopathy associated with retinal detachment and foci of telangiectatic retinal vessels. It is usually unilateral and occurs in young children, more often in males.

Lymphoid tumors and tumorlike conditions
Abnormalities of intraocular tissues are present in approximately 50% of patients with leukemia at autopsy.[303] These are in the form of leukemic infiltrates and hemorrhages, particularly in the choroid and retina.[303,308]

Intraocular **malignant lymphoma** is a rare disease. In over 90% of the cases the eye lesion heralds the presence or development of extraocular lymphoma, which is located in the central nervous system in one half or more of the cases.[305] Sometimes the lymphomatous process preferentially involves the optic nerve.[304]

Reactive lymphoid hyperplasia can also occur within

the ocular globe[306,307]; the criteria for distinguishing it from lymphoma are similar to those applied elsewhere.

Other primary tumors

Fuchs' adenoma (benign ciliary epithelioma, Fuchs' epithelioma, coronal adenoma) is a benign tumor of the ciliary body usually found incidentally in a surgically enucleated eye or on post mortem examination. Microscopically, it is formed by interlacing trabeculae of uniform, nonpigmented ciliary epithelial cells surrounded by an amorphous, hyaline, PAS-positive material.[315]

Medulloepithelioma, also known as *diktyoma*, is a rare tumor that histologically resembles the embryonal retina; most cases arise from the ciliary epithelium, but a few have been found in the optic nerve or retina.

Leiomyomas can develop in the ciliary body or the iris. Some of these tumors are regarded as of possible neural crest origin and designated as mesectodermal leiomyomas.[309a] **Hemangiomas, hemangioblastomas** (as a component of von Hippel–Lindau disease), **neurofibromas, astrocytomas**, and **pleomorphic xanthoastrocytomas** are sometimes found in the retina.[311,312,314,316]

Juvenile xanthogranuloma can occur in the iris and result in spontaneous hyphema and/or secondary glaucoma.[310] It occurs almost exclusively in young children and is associated with skin lesions of similar microscopic appearance.[317]

Glioneuroma has been described in the iris and ciliary body,[309] and **malignant mesenchymoma** (containing rhabdomyosarcomatous and liposarcomatous areas) has been reported involving the entire uveal tract.[313]

Metastatic tumors

The intraocular tissues can be involved by metastatic carcinoma and, less commonly, by metastatic cutaneous melanoma and metastatic sarcoma. In fact, if one were to do serial sections routinely on all autopsy eyes, cases of

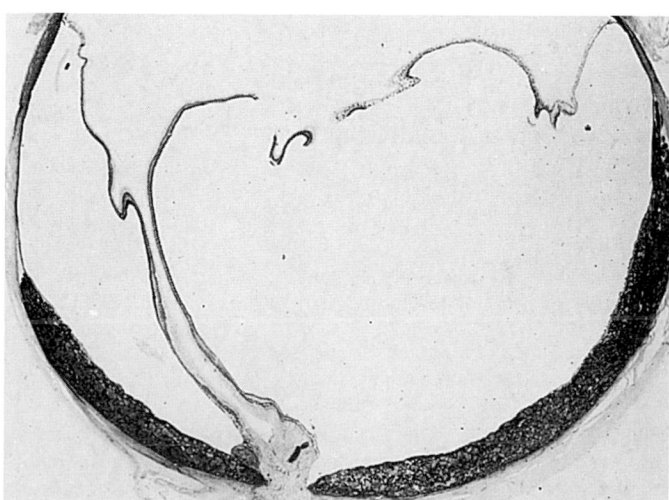

Fig. 30.96 Metastatic carcinoma from breast producing diffuse thickening of the choroid posteriorly.

metastatic carcinoma would outnumber the primary tumors. The difference, of course, is that most of the patients were asymptomatic for ocular symptoms while alive. The most common primary lesions involved are in the breast in the female and in the lung in the male, with the gastrointestinal tract next in frequency.[318–322] The ocular metastasis occasionally may be the initial manifestation of the disease, and the primary lesion is discovered only after the eye has been enucleated.

The posterior choroid is the most common site for these metastases[318a] (Fig. 30.96). Anterior uveal involvement is much less common, and retinal metastases are rare. Diffuse thickening of the choroid along both sides of the optic nerve is the most common presentation, but bulky tumor masses resembling malignant melanomas also may be observed.

Cytology

In certain cases the pathologist may be called on to examine material that has been aspirated from either the aqueous or the vitreous and has been passed through a Millipore filter. Cases in which this has proved useful include large cell lymphoma,[323] retinoblastoma,[325] and phacolytic glaucoma.[324]

References

Introduction
Normal anatomy

1 Duane T (ed.). Clinical ophthalmology, rev ed. New York, 1988, Harper & Row.
2 Harry J, Misson G. Clinical ophthalmic pathology: Principles of diseases of the eye and associated structures. Oxford, 2001, Butterworth Heinemann.
3 Hogan MJ, Zimmerman LE. Ophthalmic pathology. An atlas and textbook, ed. 2. Philadelphia, 1962, W.B. Saunders.
4 Hogan MJ, Alvarado JA, Weddell JE. Histology of the human eye. An atlas and textbook. Philadelphia, 1971, W.B. Saunders.
5 Jakobiec FA. Ocular and adnexal tumors. Birmingham, AL, 1978, Aesculapius.
5a Klintworth K, Scroggs MW. Normal eye and ocular adnexa. History for pathologists 1997, **2:** 315–336.
6 McLean IW, Burnier MN, Zimmerman LE, Jakobiec FA. Tumors of the eye and ocular adnexa. Atlas of tumor pathology, series 3, fascicle 12. Bethesda, 1994, Armed Forces Institute of Pathology.
7 Reese AB. Tumors of the eye, ed. 3. New York, 1976, Harper & Row.
8 Sassani JW (ed.). Ophthalmic pathology with clinical correlations. Philadelphia, 1997, Lippincott-Raven.
9 Spencer WH. Ophthalmic pathology: an atlas and textbook. Philadelphia, 1996, W.B. Saunders.
10 Yanoff M, Fine BS. Ocular pathology, ed. 5. Philadelphia, 2002, Mosby.

Eyelids
Inflammation

11 Codère F, Lee RD, Anderson RL. Necrobiotic xanthogranuloma of the eyelid. Arch Ophthalmol 1983, **101:** 60–63.
12 Riddle PJ, Font RL, Johnson FB, McLean IW. Silica granuloma of eyelid and ocular adnexa. Arch Ophthalmol 1981, **99:** 683–689.
13 Ross MJ, Cohen KL, Peiffer RL Jr, Grimson BS. Episcleral and

orbital pseudorheumatoid nodules. Arch Ophthalmol 1983, **101:** 418–421.

Tumors and tumorlike lesions

Tumors and tumorlike lesions of surface epithelium

14 Aurora AL, Blodi FC. Lesions of the eyelids. A clinicopathologic study. Surv Ophthalmol 1970, **15:** 94–104.

15 Boniuk M. Tumors of the eyelids. Int Ophthalmol Clin 1962, **2:** 239–317.

16 Boniuk M, Zimmerman LE. Eyelid tumors with reference to lesions confused with squamous cell carcinoma. II. Inverted follicular keratosis. Arch Ophthalmol 1963, **69:** 698–707.

17 Boniuk M, Zimmerman LE. Eyelid tumors with reference to lesions confused with squamous cell carcinoma. III. Keratoacanthoma. Arch Ophthalmol 1967, **77:** 29–40.

18 Caya JG, Hidayat AA, Weiner JM. A clinicopathologic study of 21 cases of adenoid squamous cell carcinoma of the eyelid and periorbital region. Am J Ophthalmol 1985, **99:** 291–297.

19 Chaflin J, Putterman AM. Frozen section control in the surgery of basal cell carcinoma of the eyelid. Am J Ophthalmol 1979, **87:** 802–809.

20 Donaldson MJ, Sullivan TJ, Whitehead KJ, Williamson RM. Squamous cell carcinoma of the eyelids. Br J Ophthalmol 2002, **86:** 1161–1165.

21 Giacomin AL, di Pietro R, Steindler P. Merkel cell carcinoma: a distinct lesion of the eyelid. Orbit 1999, **18:** 295–303.

22 Kwitko ML, Boniuk M, Zimmerman LE. Eyelid tumors with reference to lesions confused with squamous cell carcinoma. I. Incidence and errors in diagnosis. Arch Ophthalmol 1963, **69:** 693–697.

23 Searl SS, Boynton JR, Markowitch W, di Sant' Agnese PA. Malignant Merkel cell neoplasm of the eyelid. Arch Ophthalmol 1984, **102:** 907–911.

Adnexal tumors

24 Doxanas MT, Green WR. Sebaceous gland carcinoma. Review of 40 cases. Arch Ophthalmol 1984, **102:** 245–249.

25 Hassan AS, Nelson CC. Benign eyelid tumors and skin diseases. Int Ophthalmol Clin 2002, **42:** 135–149.

26 Hidayat AA, Font RL. Trichilemmoma of eyelid and eyebrow. A clinicopathologic study of 31 cases. Arch Ophthalmol 1980, **98:** 844–847.

27 Howrey RP, Lipham WJ, Schultz WH, Buckley EG, Dutton JJ, Klintworth GK, Rosoff PM. Sebaceous gland carcinoma: a subtle second malignancy following radiation therapy in patients with bilateral retinoblastoma. Cancer 1998, **83:** 767–771.

28 Langel DJ, Yeatts RP, White WL. Primary signet ring cell carcinoma of the eyelid: report of a case demonstrating further analogy to lobular carcinoma of the breast with a literature review. Am J Dermatopathol 2002, **23:** 444–449.

29 Langer K, Konrad K, Smolle J. Multiple apocrine hidrocystomas on the eyelids. Am J Dermatopathol 1989, **11:** 570–573.

30 Pantanowitz L, Lyle S, Tahan SR. Fibroadenoma of the eyelid. Am J Dermatopathol 2002, **24:** 225–229.

31 Rao NA, Hidayat AA, McLean IW, Zimmerman LE. Sebaceous carcinomas of the ocular adnexa. A clinicopathologic study of 104 cases, with five-year follow-up data. Hum Pathol 1982, **13:** 113–122.

32 Rodgers IR, Jakobiec FA, Krebs W, Hornblass A, Gingold MP. Papillary oncocytoma of the eyelid. A previously undescribed tumor of apocrine gland origin. Ophthalmology 1988, **95:** 1071–1076.

33 Russel WG, Page DL, Hough AJ, Rogers LW. Sebaceous carcinoma of meibomian gland origin. The diagnostic importance of pagetoid spread of neoplastic cells. Am J Clin Pathol 1980, **73:** 504–511.

34 Shintaku M, Tsuta K, Yoshida H, Tsubura A, Nakashima Y, Noda

K. Apocrine adenocarcinoma of the eyelid with aggressive biological behavior: report of a case. Pathol Int 2002, **52:** 169–173.

35 Snow SN, Reizner GT. Mucinous eccrine carcinoma of the eyelid. Cancer 1992, **70:** 2099–2104.

36 Tomasini C, Soro E, Pippione M. Eyelid swelling: think of metastasis of histiocytoid breast carcinoma. Dermatology 2002, **205:** 63–66.

37 Wolfe JT III, Yeatts RP, Wick MR, Campbell RJ, Waller RR. Sebaceous carcinoma of the eyelid. Errors in clinical and pathologic diagnosis. Am J Surg Pathol 1984, **8:** 597–606.

38 Wright JD, Font RL. Mucinous sweat gland adenocarcinoma of eyelid. A clinicopathologic study of 21 cases with histochemical and electron microscopic observations. Cancer 1979, **44:** 1757–1768.

Melanocytic tumors

39 Esmaeli B. Advances in the management of malignant tumors of the eyelid and conjunctiva: the role of sentinel lymph node biopsy. Int Ophthalmol Clin 2002, **42:** 151–162.

40 Henkind P, Friedman A. External ocular pigmentation. Int Ophthalmol Clin 1971, **11:** 87–111.

41 Pomeranz GA, Bunt AH, Kalina RE. Multifocal choroidal melanoma in ocular melanocytosis. Arch Ophthalmol 1981, **99:** 857–863.

42 Vaziri M, Buffam FV, Martinka M, Oryschak A, Dhaliwal H, White VA. Clinicopathologic features and behavior of cutaneous eyelid melanoma. Ophthalmology 2002, **109:** 901–908.

Lymphoid tumors and tumorlike conditions

43 Stenson S, Ramsay DL. Ocular findings in mycosis fungoides. Arch Ophthalmol 1981, **99:** 272–277.

Mesenchymal tumors and tumorlike conditions

44 Fett DR, Putterman AM. Primary localized amyloidosis presenting as an eyelid margin tumor. Arch Ophthalmol 1986, **104:** 584–585.

45 Hassan AS, Nelson CC. Benign eyelid tumors and skin diseases. Int Ophthalmol Clin 2002, **42:** 135–149.

46 Smith ME, Zimmerman LE. Amyloidosis of the eyelid and conjunctiva. Arch Ophthalmol 1966, **75:** 42–56.

47 Sorenson RL, Spencer WH, Stewart WB, Miller WW, Kleinhenz RJ. Intravascular papillary endothelial hyperplasia of the eyelid. Arch Ophthalmol 1983, **101:** 1728–1730.

Metastatic tumors

47a Hood CI, Font RL, Zimmerman LE. Metastatic mammary carcinoma in the eyelid with histiocytoid appearance. Cancer 1973, **31:** 793–800.

Lacrimal passages

Canaliculitis and dacryocystitis

48 Harris GJ, Williams GA, Clarke GP. Sarcoidosis of the lacrimal sac. Arch Ophthalmol 1981, **99:** 1198–1201.

Tumors

49 Kuwabara H, Takeda J. Malignant melanoma of the lacrimal sac with surrounding melanosis. Arch Pathol Lab Med 1997, **121:** 517–519.

50 Lamping KA, Albert DM, Ni C, Fournier G. Oxyphil cell adenomas. Three case reports. Arch Ophthalmol 1984, **102:** 263–265.

51 Lee HM, Kang HJ, Choi G, Chae SW, Kim CH, Hwang SJ, Lee SH. Two cases of primary malignant melanoma of the lacrimal sac. Head Neck 2001, **23:** 809–813.

52 Leung SY, Chung LP, Ho CM, Yuen ST, Wong MP, Kwong WK. An Epstein-Barr virus positive undifferentiated carcinoma in the lacrimal sac. Histopathology 1996, **28:** 71–76.

53 Nakamura K, Uehara S, Omagari J, Kunitake N, Kimura M, Makino Y, Ishigami K, Masuda K. Primary non-Hodgkin's lymphoma of the lacrimal sac: a case report and a review of the literature. Cancer 1997, **80**: 2151–2155.

54 Ni C, Wagoner MD, Wang W-J, Albert DM, Fan CO, Robinson N. Mucoepidermoid carcinomas of the lacrimal sac. Arch Ophthalmol 1983, **101**: 1572–1574.

55 Ryan SJ, Font RL. Primary epithelial neoplasms of the lacrimal sac. Am J Ophthalmol 1973, **76**: 73–88.

Lacrimal gland
Mikulicz's disease

56 Font RL, Yanoff M, Zimmerman LE. Benign lymphoepithelial lesion of the lacrimal gland and its relationship to Sjögren's syndrome. Am J Clin Pathol 1967, **48**: 365–376.

57 Godwin JT. Benign lymphoepithelial lesion of the parotid gland (adenolymphoma, chronic inflammation, lymphoepithelioma, lymphocytic tumor, Mikulicz's disease). Cancer 1952, **5**: 1089–1103.

58 Meyer D, Yanoff M, Hanno H. Differential diagnosis in Mikulicz syndrome, Mikulicz's disease, and similar disease entities. Am J Ophthalmol 1971, **70**: 516–524.

Tumors

59 Cho NH, Kie JH, Yang WI, Jung WH. Solitary fibrous tumour with an unusual adenofibromatous feature in the lacrimal gland. Histopathology 1998, **33**: 289–290.

60 DeRosa G, Zeppa P, Tranfa F, Bonavolonta G. Acinic cell carcinoma arising in a lacrimal gland. First case report. Cancer 1986, **57**: 1988–1991.

61 Forrest AW. Pathologic criteria for effective management of epithelial lacrimal gland tumors. Am J Ophthalmol 1971, **71**: 178–192.

62 Gamel JW, Font RL. Adenoid cystic carcinoma of the lacrimal gland. The clinical significance of a basaloid histologic pattern. Hum Pathol 1982, **13**: 219–225.

63 Iwamoto T, Jakobiec FA. A comparative ultrastructural study of the normal lacrimal gland and its epithelial tumors. Hum Pathol 1982, **13**: 236–262.

64 Ludwig ME, LiVolsi VA, McMahon RT. Malignant mixed tumor of the lacrimal gland. Am J Surg Pathol 1979, **3**: 457–462.

65 Morgan MB, Truitt CA, Romer C, Somach S, Pitha JV. Ocular adnexal oncocytoma: a case series and clinicopathologic review of the literature. Am J Dermatopathol 1998, **20**: 487–490.

66 Paulino AFG, Huvos AG. Epithelial tumors of the lacrimal glands: a clinicopathologic study. Ann Diagn Pathol 1999, **3**: 199–204.

67 Pecorella I, Garner A. Ostensible oncocytoma of accessory lacrimal glands. Histopathology 1997, **30**: 264–270.

68 Perzin KH, Jakobiec FA, LiVolsi VA, Desjardins L. Lacrimal gland malignant mixed tumors (carcinomas arising in benign mixed tumors). A clinico-pathologic study. Cancer 1980, **45**: 2593–2606.

69 Sabet SJ, Tarbet KJ, Lemke BN, Smith ME, Albert DM. Granular cell tumor of the lacrimal sac and nasolacrimal duct: no invasive behavior with incomplete resection. Ophthalmology 2000, **170**: 1992–1994.

70 Sanders TE, Ackerman LV, Zimmerman LE. Epithelial tumors of the lacrimal gland. A comparison of the pathologic and clinical behavior with those of the salivary glands. Am J Surg 1962, **104**: 657–665.

71 Yazici B, Setzen G, Meyer DR, Williams EF, McKenna BJ. Giant cell angiofibroma of the nasolacrimal duct. Ophthal Plast Reconstr Surg 2001, **17**: 202–206.

72 Zimmerman LE, Sanders TE, Ackerman LV. Epithelial tumors of the lacrimal gland. Prognostic and therapeutic significance of histologic types. Int Ophthalmol Clin 1962, **2**: 337–367.

Orbit

73 Char DH. Management of orbital tumors. Mayo Clin Proc 1993, **68**: 1081–1096.

74 Shields JA, Bakewell B, Augsburger JJ, Flanagan JC. Classification and incidence of space-occupying lesions of the orbit. A survey of 645 biopsies. Arch Ophthalmol 1984, **102**: 1606–1611.

75 Zajdela A, Vielh P, Schlienger P, Haye C. Fine-needle cytology of 292 palpable orbital and eyelid tumors. Am J Clin Pathol 1990, **93**: 100–104.

Dysthyroid ophthalmopathy

76 Bahn RS, Heufelder AE. Pathogenesis of Graves' ophthalmopathy. N Engl J Med 1993, **329**: 1468–1475.

Inflammatory processes

77 Blodi F, Gass D. Inflammatory pseudotumor of the orbit. Trans Am Acad Ophthalmol Otolaryngol 1967, **71**: 303–323.

78 Eshaghian J, Anderson RL. Sinus involvement in inflammatory orbital pseudotumor. Arch Ophthalmol 1981, **99**: 627–630.

79 Foucar E, Rosai J, Dorfman RF. The ophthalmologic manifestations of sinus histiocytosis with massive lymphadenopathy. Am J Ophthalmol 1979, **87**: 354–367.

80 Frohman LP, Kupersmith MJ, Lang J, Reede D, Bergeron RT, Aleksic S, Trasi S. Intracranial extension and bone destruction in orbital pseudotumor. Arch Ophthalmol 1986, **104**: 380–384.

81 Garner A. Pathology of "pseudotumors" of the orbit. A review. J Clin Pathol 1973, **26**: 639–648.

82 Grimson BS, Simons KB. Orbital inflammation, myositis, and systemic lupus erythematosus. Arch Ophthalmol 1983, **101**: 736–738.

83 Harris GJ. Subperiosteal abscess of the orbit. Arch Ophthalmol 1983, **101**: 751–757.

84 Maalouf T, Trouchaud-Michaud C, Angioi-Duprez K, George JL. What has become of our idiopathic inflammatory pseudo-tumors of the orbit? Orbit 1999, **18**: 157–166.

85 McCarthy JM, White VA, Harris G, Simons KB, Kennerdell J, Rootman J. Idiopathic sclerosing inflammation of the orbit. Immunohistologic analysis and comparison with retroperitoneal fibrosis. Mod Pathol 1993, **6**: 581–587.

86 Parke DW II, Font RL, Boniuk M, McCrary JA III. "Cholesteatoma" of the orbit. Arch Ophthalmol 1982, **100**: 612–616.

Primary tumors
Mesenchymal tumors and tumorlike conditions

87 Cai Y-C, McMenamin ME, Rose G, Sandy CJ, Cree IA, Fletcher CD. Primary liposarcoma of the orbit: a clinicopathologic study of seven cases. Ann Diagn Pathol 2001, **5**: 255–266.

88 Croxatto JO, Font RL. Hemangiopericytoma of the orbit. A clinicopathologic study of 30 cases. Hum Pathol 1982, **13**: 210–218.

89 Dei Tos AP, Seregard S, Calonje E, Chan JK, Fletcher CD. Giant cell angiofibroma. A distinctive orbital tumor in adults. Am J Surg Pathol 1995, **19**: 1286–1293.

90 Dorfman DM, To K, Dickersin GR, Rosenberg AE, Pilch BZ. Solitary fibrous tumor of the orbit. Am J Surg Pathol 1994, **18**: 281–287.

91 Font RL, Hidayat AA. Fibrous histiocytoma of the orbit. A clinicopathologic study of 150 cases. Hum Pathol 1982, **13**: 199–209.

92 Font RL, Zimmerman LE. Nodular fasciitis of the eye and adnexa. A report of ten cases. Arch Ophthalmol 1966, **75**: 475–481.

93 Font RL, Jurco S III, Zimmerman LE. Alveolar soft-part sarcoma of the orbit. A clinicopathologic analysis of seventeen cases and a review of the literature. Hum Pathol 1982, **13**: 569–579.

94 Font RL, Wheeler TM, Boniuk M. Intravascular papillary endothelial hyperplasia of the orbit and ocular adnexa. A report of five cases. Arch Ophthalmol 1983, **101**: 1731–1736.

95 Forrest AW. Tumors following radiation about the eye. Int Ophthalmol Clin 1962, **2**: 543–553.

96 Ganesan R, Hammond CJ, Van Der Walt JD. Giant cell angiofibroma of the orbit. Histopathology 1997, **30**: 93–96.

97 Goldsmith JD, van de Rijn M, Syed N. Orbital hemangiopericytoma and solitary fibrous tumor: a morphologic continuum. Int J Surg Pathol 2003, **9**: 295–302.

98 Guillou L, Gebhard S, Coindre JM. Orbital and extraorbital giant cell angiofibroma: a giant cell-rich variant of solitary fibrous tumor? Clinicopathologic and immunohistochemical analysis of a series in favor of a unifying concept. Am J Surg Pathol 2000, **24**: 971–979.

99 Hasegawa T, Matsuno Y, Niki T, Hirohashi S, Shimoda T, Takayama J, Watanabe C, Kaneko A, Sano T, Sato M, Suzuki J. Second primary rhabdomyosarcomas in patients with bilateral retinoblastoma: a clinicopathologic and immunohistochemical study. Am J Surg Pathol 1998, **22**: 1351–1360.

100 Henderson JW, Farrow GM. Primary orbital hemangiopericytoma. An aggressive and potentially malignant neoplasm. Arch Ophthalmol 1978, **96**: 666–673.

101 Hufnagel T, Ma L, Kuo T-T. Orbital angiosarcoma with subconjunctival presentation. Report of a case and literature review. Ophthalmology 1987, **94**: 72–77.

102 Jacobs JL, Merriam JC, Chadburn A, Garvin J, Housepian E, Hilal SK. Mesenchymal chondrosarcoma of the orbit. Report of three new cases and review of the literature. Cancer 1994, **73**: 399–405.

103 Knowles D, Jakobiec F, Potter G, Jones IS. Ophthalmic striated muscle neoplasms. Surv Ophthalmol 1976, **21**: 219–261.

104 Krohel GB, Rosenberg PN, Wright JE, Smith RS. Localized orbital neurofibromas. Am J Ophthalmol 1985, **100**: 458–464.

105 Mikami Y, Shimizu M, Hirokawa M, Manabe T. Extraorbital giant cell angiofibromas. Mod Pathol 1997, **10**: 1082–1087.

106 Polito E, Tosi M, Toti P, Schurfeld K, Caporossi A. Orbital solitary fibrous tumor with aggressive behavior. Three cases and review of the literature. Graefes Arch Clin Exp Ophthalmol 2002, **240**: 570–574.

107 Sciot R, Goffin J, Fossion E, Wilms G, Dom R. Solitary fibrous tumour of the orbit. Histopathology 1996, **28**: 188–191.

108 Shields JA, Kapustiak J, Arbizo V, Augsburger JJ, Schnitzer RE. Orbital neurilemoma with extension through the superior orbital fissure. Arch Ophthalmol 1986, **104**: 871–873.

109 Weiner JM, Hidayat AA. Juvenile fibrosarcoma of the orbit and eyelid. A study of five cases. Arch Ophthalmol 1983, **101**: 253–259.

110 Westra WH, Gerald WL, Rosai J. Solitary fibrous tumor. Consistent CD34 immunoreactivity and occurrence in the orbit. Am J Surg Pathol 1994, **18**: 992–998.

111 Wilson WB, Roloff J, Wilson HL. Primary peripheral neuroepithelioma of the orbit with intracranial extension. Cancer 1988, **62**: 2595–2601.

112 Wojno T, Tenzel RR, Nadji M. Orbital leiomyosarcoma. Arch Ophthalmol 1983, **101**: 1566–1568.

113 Yamasaki T, Handa H, Yamashita J, Paine JT, Tashiro Y, Uno A, Ishikawa M, Asato R. Intracranial and orbital cavernous angiomas. A review of 30 cases. J Neurosurg 1986, **64**: 197–208.

Glioma of optic nerve

114 Borit A, Richardson EP Jr. The biological and clinical behaviour of pilocytic astrocytomas of the optic pathways. Brain 1982, **105**: 161–187.

115 Dosoretz DE, Blitzer PH, Wang CC, Linggood RM. Management of glioma of the optic nerve and/or chiasm. An analysis of 20 cases. Cancer 1980, **45**: 1467–1471.

116 Marquardt MD, Zimmerman LE. Histopathology of meningiomas and gliomas of the optic nerve. Hum Pathol 1982, **13**: 226–235.

117 Pierce SM, Barnes PD, Loeffler JS, McGinn C, Tarbell NJ. Definitive radiation therapy in the management of symptomatic patients with optic glioma. Survival and long-term effects. Cancer 1990, **65**: 45–52.

Meningioma

118 Karp L, Zimmerman LE, Borit A, Spencer W. Primary intraorbital meningiomas. Arch Ophthalmol 1974, **91**: 24–28.

119 Marquardt MD, Zimmerman LE. Histopathology of meningiomas and gliomas of the optic nerve. Hum Pathol 1982, **13**: 226–235.

119a Adley BP, Cubbon R, Oltvai Z, Bryar D, Variakojis D. Ocular lymphoma: a clinical, histological, immunophenotypic and molecular analysis of 40 patients. (Abstract) Mod Pathol 2003, **16**: 224a.

Lymphoid tumors and tumorlike conditions

120 Astarita RW, Minckler D, Taylor CR, Levine A, Lukes RJ. Orbital and adnexal lymphomas. A multiparameter approach. Am J Clin Pathol 1980, **73**: 615–621.

121 Bennett CL, Putterman A, Bitran JD, Recant W, Shapiro CM, Karesh J, Kalokhe U. Staging and therapy of orbital lymphomas. Cancer 1986, **57**: 1204–1208.

122 Brisbane JU, Lessell S, Finkel HE, Neiman RS. Malignant lymphoma presenting in the orbit. A clinicopathologic study of a rare immunoglobulin-producing variant. Cancer 1981, **47**: 548–553.

123 Knowles DM II, Jakobiec FA. Orbital lymphoid neoplasms. A clinicopathologic study of 60 patients. Cancer 1980, **46**: 576–589.

124 Knowles DM II, Jakobiec FA. Cell marker analysis of extranodal lymphoid infiltrates. To what extent does the determination of mono- or polyclonality resolve the diagnostic dilemma of malignant lymphoma *v* pseudolymphoma in an extranodal site? Semin Diagn Pathol 1985, **2**: 163–168.

125 Knowles DM, Jakobiec FA, McNally L, Burke JS. Lymphoid hyperplasia and malignant lymphoma occurring in the ocular adnexa (orbit, conjunctiva, and eyelids). A prospective multiparametric analysis of 108 cases during 1977 to 1987. Hum Pathol 1990, **21**: 959–973.

126 Lazzarino M, Morra E, Rosso R, Brusamolino E, Pagnucco G, Castello A, Ghisolfi A, Tafi A, Zennaro G, Bernasconi C. Clinicopathologic and immunologic characteristics of non-Hodgkin's lymphomas presenting in the orbit. A report of eight cases. Cancer 1985, **55**: 1907–1912.

127 McNally L, Jakobiec FA, Knowles DM II. Clinical, morphologic, immunophenotypic, and molecular genetic analysis of bilateral ocular adnexal lymphoid neoplasms in 17 patients. Am J Ophthalmol 1987, **103**: 555–568.

128 Mannami T, Yoshino T, Oshima K, Takase S, Kondo E, Ohara N, Nakagawa H, Ohtsuki H, Harada M, Akagi T. Clinical, histopathological and immunogenetic analysis of ocular adnexal lymphoproliferative disorders: characterization of MALT lymphoma and reactive lymphoid hyperplasia. Mod Pathol 2001, **14**: 641–649.

129 Medeiros LJ, Harris NL. Lymphoid infiltrates of the orbit and conjunctiva. A morphologic and immunophenotypic study of 99 cases. Am J Surg Pathol 1989, **13**: 459–471.

130 Medeiros LJ, Harris NL. Immunohistologic analysis of small lymphocytic infiltrates of the orbit and conjunctiva. Hum Pathol 1990, **21**: 1126–1131.

131 Morgan G, Harry J. Lymphocytic tumours of indeterminate nature. A 5-year follow-up of 98 conjunctival and orbital lesions. Br J Ophthalmol 1978, **62**: 381–383.

132 Neri A, Jakobiec FA, Pelicci P-G, Dalla-Favera R, Knowles DM II.

Immunoglobulin and T cell receptor β chain gene rearrangement analysis of ocular adnexal lymphoid neoplasms. Clinical and biologic implications. Blood 1987, **70:** 1519–1529.

133 Peterson K, Gordon KB, Heinemann MH, De Angelis LM. The clinical spectrum of ocular lymphoma. Cancer 1993, **72:** 843–849.

134 Shome DK, Gupta NK, Prajapati NC, Raju GM, Choudhury P, Dubey AP. Orbital granulocytic sarcomas (myeloid sarcomas) in acute nonlymphocytic Leukemia. Cancer 1992, **70:** 2298–2301.

135 Tewfik HH, Platz CE, Corder MP, Panther SK, Blodi FC. A clinicopathologic study of orbital and adnexal non-Hodgkin's lymphomas. Cancer 1979, **44:** 1022–1028.

136 White VA, Gascoyne RD, McNeil BK, Chang WY, Brewer LV, Rootman J. Histopathologic findings and frequency of clonality detected by the polymerase chain reaction on ocular adnexal lymphoproliferative lesions. Mod Pathol 1996, **9:** 1052–1061.

137 Wotherspoon AC, Diss TC, Pan LX, Schmid C, Kerr-Muir MG, Lea SH, Isaacson PG. Primary low-grade B-cell lymphoma of the conjunctiva. A mucosa-associated lymphoid tissue type lymphoma. Histopathology 1993, **23:** 417–424.

Metastatic tumors

138 Freedman MI, Folk JC. Metastatic tumors to the eye and orbit. Patient survival and clinical characteristics. Arch Ophthalmol 1987, **105:** 1215–1219.

139 Reifler DM, Kini SR, Liu D, Littleton RH. Orbital metastasis from prostatic carcinoma. Identification by immunocytology. Arch Ophthalmol 1984, **102:** 292–295.

140 Riddle PJ, Font RL, Zimmerman LE. Carcinoid tumors of the eye and orbit. A clinicopathologic study of 15 cases, with histochemical and electron microscopic observations. Hum Pathol 1982, **13:** 459–469.

141 Zimmerman LE, Stangl R, Riddle PJ. Primary carcinoid tumor of the orbit. A clinicopathologic study with histochemical and electron microscopic observations. Arch Ophthalmol 1983, **101:** 1395–1398.

Conjunctiva
Degeneration

142 Austin P, Jakobiec FA, Iwamoto T, Hornblass A. Elastofibroma oculi. Arch Ophthalmol 1983, **101:** 1575–1579.

Graft-versus-host disease

143 Jabs DA, Hirst LW, Green WR, Tutschka PJ, Santos GW, Beschorner WE. The eye in bone marrow transplantation. II. Histopathology. Arch Ophthalmol 1983, **101:** 585–590.

Inflammation

144 Bornstein J, Frank M, Radnec D. Conjunctival biopsy in the diagnosis of sarcoidosis. N Engl J Med 1962, **267:** 60–64.

145 Chambers J, Blodi F, Golden B, McKee A. Ligneous conjunctivitis. Trans Am Acad Ophthalmol Otolaryngol 1969, **73:** 996–1004.

146 Hidayat AA, Riddle PJ. Ligneous conjunctivitis. A clinicopathologic study of 17 cases. Ophthalmology 1987, **94:** 949–959.

147 Raphael M, Bellefqih S, Piette JC, Le Hoang P, Debre P, Chomette G. Conjunctival biopsy in Sjögren's syndrome. Correlations between histological and immunohistochemical features. Histopathology 1988, **13:** 191–202.

148 Steffen C. Actinic granuloma of the conjunctiva. Am J Dermatopathol 1992, **14:** 253–254.

149 Stenson S. Adult inclusion conjunctivitis. Clinical characteristics and corneal changes. Arch Ophthalmol 1981, **99:** 605–608.

Tumors and tumorlike conditions
Tumors of surface epithelium

150 Blodi FC. Squamous cell carcinoma of the conjunctiva. Doc Ophthalmol 1973, **34:** 93–108.

151 Gamel JW, Eiferman RA, Guibor P. Mucoepidermoid carcinoma of the conjunctiva. Arch Ophthalmol 1984, **102:** 730–731.

152 Irvine AR Jr. Epibulbar squamous cell carcinoma and related lesions. In Ferry AP (ed.): Ocular and adnexal tumors. Int Ophthalmol Clin 1972, **12:** 71–83.

153 McDonnell JM, Mayr AJ, Martin WJ. DNA of human papillomavirus type 16 in dysplastic and malignant lesions of the conjunctiva and cornea. N Engl J Med 1989, **320:** 1442–1446.

154 McDonnell PJ, McDonnell JM, Kessis T, Green WR, Shah KV. Detection of human papillomavirus type 6/11 DNA in conjunctival papillomas by in situ hybridization with radioactive probes. Hum Pathol 1987, **18:** 1115–1119.

155 Searl SS, Krigstein HJ, Albert DM, Grove AS Jr. Invasive squamous cell carcinoma with intraocular mucoepidermoid features. Conjunctival carcinoma with intraocular invasion and diphasic morphology. Arch Ophthalmol 1982, **100:** 109–111.

156 Waring GO III, Roth AM, Ekins MB. Clinical and pathologic description of 17 cases of corneal intraepithelial neoplasia. Am J Ophthalmol 1984, **97:** 547–559.

Melanocytic tumors and tumorlike conditions

157 Ackerman AB, Sood R, Koenig M. Primary acquired melanosis of the conjunctiva is melanoma in situ. Mod Pathol 1991, **4:** 253–263.

158 Brownstein S, Jakobiec FA, Wilkinson RD, Lombardo J, Jackson WB. Cryotherapy for precancerous melanosis (atypical melanocytic hyperplasia) of the conjunctiva. Arch Ophthalmol 1981, **99:** 1224–1231.

159 Folberg R, McLean IW. Primary acquired melanosis and melanoma of the conjunctiva. Terminology, classification, and biologic behavior. Hum Pathol 1986, **17:** 652–654.

160 Folberg R, Jakobiec FA, McLean IW, Zimmerman LE. Is primary acquired melanosis of the conjunctiva equivalent to melanoma in situ? Mod Pathol 1992, **5:** 2–8.

161 Folberg R, McLean IW, Zimmerman LE. Primary acquired melanosis of the conjunctiva. Hum Pathol 1985, **16:** 129–135.

162 Folberg R, McLean IW, Zimmerman LE. Malignant melanoma of the conjunctiva. Hum Pathol 1985, **16:** 136–143.

163 Guillén FJ, Albert DM, Mihm MC Jr. Pigmented melanocytic lesions of the conjunctiva. A new approach to their classification. Pathology 1985, **17:** 275–280.

164 Jakobiec FA, Zuckerman BD, Berlin AJ, Odell P, MacRae DW, Tuthill RJ. Unusual melanocytic nevi of the conjunctiva. Am J Ophthalmol 1985, **100:** 100–113.

165 Jay B. Naevi and melanomata of the conjunctiva. Br J Ophthalmol 1965, **49:** 169–204.

166 Jeffrey IJM, Lucas DR, McEwan C, Lee WR. Malignant melanoma of the conjunctiva. Histopathology 1986, **10:** 363–378.

167 Kabukcuoglu S, McNutt NS. Conjunctival melanocytic nevi of childhood. J Cutan Pathol 1999, **26:** 248–252.

168 Liesegang TJ. Pigmented conjunctival and scleral lesions. Mayo Clin Proc 1994, **69:** 151–161.

169 McLean IW. Differential diagnosis of the conjunctival melanoses. Ann Diagn Pathol 1998, **2:** 264–270.

170 Mihm MC Jr, Guillén FJ. Classification of non-nevoid pigmented lesions of the conjunctiva (letter to the editor). Hum Pathol 1985, **16:** 1078.

171 Reese AB. Precancerous and cancerous melanosis. Am J Ophthalmol 1966, **61:** 1272–1277.

172 Werschnik C, Lommatzsch PK. Long-term follow-up of patients with conjunctival melanoma. Am J Clin Oncol 2002, **25:** 248–255.

Lymphoid tumors and tumorlike conditions

173 Morgan G. Lymphocytic tumours of the conjunctiva. J Clin Pathol 1971, **24:** 585–595.

Other tumors

174 Hufnagel T, Ma L, Kuo T-T. Orbital angiosarcoma with subconjunctival presentation. Report of a case and literature review. Ophthalmology 1987, **94**: 72–77.

175 Jaimovich L, Calb I, Kaminsky A. Kaposi's sarcoma of the conjunctiva. J Am Acad Dermatol 1986, **14**: 589–592.

176 Patrinely JR, Green WR. Conjunctival myxoma. A clinicopathologic study of four cases and a review of the literature. Arch Ophthalmol 1983, **101**: 1416–1420.

177 Truong L, Font RL. Intravenous pyogenic granuloma of the ocular adnexa. Report of two cases and review of the literature. Arch Ophthalmol 1985, **103**: 1364–1367.

Cornea
Endothelial decompensation

178 Waring C, Rodrigues M, Laibson P. Corneal dystrophies. II. Endothelial dystrophies. Surv Ophthalmol 1978, **23**: 147–168.

Fibrosis and vascularization

179 Green WR, Zimmerman LE. Granulomatous reaction to Descemet's membrane. Am J Ophthalmol 1967, **64**: 555–558.

Intraocular tissues
Developmental anomalies

180 Zimmerman LE, Font RL. Some recent advances in the pathogenesis and histopathology of congenital malformations of the eye. JAMA 1966, **196**: 684–696.

Congenital glaucoma

181 Reese AB, Ellsworth RM. The anterior chamber cleavage syndrome. Arch Ophthalmol 1968, **75**: 307–318.

Retrolental fibroplasia

182 Reese AB (moderator). Symposium on retrolental fibroplasia. Trans Am Acad Ophthalmol Otolaryngol 1955, **59**: 7–41.

Phakoma

183 Font RL, Ferry AP. The phakomatoses. In Ferry AP (ed.): Ocular and adnexal tumors. Int Ophthalmol Clin 1972, **12**: 1–50.

Persistent hyperplastic primary vitreous

184 Jensen OA. Persistent hyperplastic primary vitreous. Acta Ophthalmol 1968, **46**: 418–429.

Retinal dysplasia

185 Cogan DG, Kuwabara T. Ocular pathology of the 13–15 trisomy syndrome. Arch Ophthalmol 1964, **72**: 246–247.

186 Hunter WS, Zimmerman LE. Unilateral retinal dysplasia. Arch Ophthalmol 1965, **74**: 23–30.

Other developmental anomalies

187 Boniuk M, Zimmerman LE. Ocular pathology in the rubella syndrome. Arch Ophthalmol 1967, **77**: 455–473.

188 Font RL, Fine BS. Ocular pathology in Fabry's disease. Histochemical and electron microscopic observations. Am J Ophthalmol 1972, **73**: 419–430.

189 Miller RW, Fraumeni JF Jr, Manning MD. Association of Wilms' tumor with aniridia, hemihypertrophy, and other congenital malformations. N Engl J Med 1964, **270**: 922–927.

190 Zimmerman LE. The histopathologic basis for ocular manifestations of the congenital rubella syndrome. Am J Ophthalmol 1968, **65**: 837–862.

Inflammation
Acute inflammation

191 Fishman LS, Griffin JR, Sapico FL, Hecht R. Hematogenous *Candida* endophthalmitis. N Engl J Med 1972, **286**: 675–681.

192 Levine R, Williamson DE. Metastatic carcinoma simulating a postoperative endophthalmitis. Arch Ophthalmol 1970, **83**: 59–60.

193 Michelson PE, Stark W, Reeser F, Green WR. Endogenous *Candida* endophthalmitis. Report of 13 cases and 16 from the literature. Int Ophthalmol Clin 1971, **11**: 125–147.

194 Sugar S, Mandell G, Shaler J. Metastatic endophthalmitis associated with injection of addictive drugs. Am J Ophthalmol 1971, **71**: 1055–1058.

Chronic nongranulomatous inflammation

195 Chan C-C, Fujikawa LS, Rodrigues MM, Stevens G Jr, Nussenblatt RB. Immunohistochemistry and electron microscopy of cyclitic membrane. Report of a case. Arch Ophthalmol 1986, **104**: 1040–1045.

196 Naumann G, Gass D, Font R. Histopathology of herpes zoster ophthalmicus. Am J Ophthalmol 1968, **65**: 533–541.

Granulomatous inflammation

197 Margo C, Zimmerman LE. Idiopathic solitary granuloma of the uveal tract. Arch Ophthalmol 1984, **102**: 732–735.

198 Parke DW II, Font RL. Diffuse toxoplasmic retinochoroiditis in a patient with AIDS. Arch Ophthalmol 1986, **104**: 571–575.

199 Wilder HC. Toxoplasma chorioretinitis in adults. Arch Opthalmol 1952, **48**: 127–136.

200 Wilkinson C, Welch R. Intraocular *Toxocara*. Am J Ophthalmol 1971, **71**: 921–930.

Post-traumatic uveitis

201 Easom H, Zimmerman LE. Sympathetic ophthalmia and bilateral phacoanaphylaxis. Arch Ophthalmol 1964, **72**: 9–15.

Degeneration
Glaucoma

202 Fenton R, Zimmerman LE. Hemolytic glaucoma. Arch Ophthalmol 1963, **70**: 236–239.

203 Flocks M, Littwin CS, Zimmerman LE. Phacolytic glaucoma. Arch Ophthalmol 1955, **54**: 37–45.

Diabetes

204 Smith ME, Glickman P. Diabetic vacuolation of the iris pigment epithelium. Am J Ophthalmol 1975, **79**: 875–877.

205 Yanoff M. Ocular pathology in diabetes mellitus. Am J Ophthalmol 1969, **67**: 21–38.

Diffuse uveal melanocytic proliferation

206 Chahud F, Young RH, Remulla JF, Khadem JJ, Dryja TP. Bilateral diffuse uveal melanocytic proliferation associated with extraocular cancers: review of a process particularly associated with gynecologic cancers. Am J Surg Pathol 2001, **25**: 212–218.

Tumors and tumorlike conditions
Malignant melanoma

207 Ashton N, Wybar K. Primary tumours of the iris. Ophthalmologica 1966, **151**: 97–113.

208 Barr CC, McLean IW, Zimmerman LE. Uveal melanoma in children and adolescents. Arch Ophthalmol 1981, **99**: 2133–2136.

209 Barr CC, Zimmerman LE, Curtin VT, Font RL. Bilateral diffuse melanocytic uveal tumors associated with systemic malignant neoplasms. A recently recognized syndrome. Arch Ophthalmol 1982, **100**: 249–255.

210 Broadway D, Lang S, Harper J, Madanat F, Pritchard J, Tarawneh M, Taylor D. Congenital malignant melanoma of the eye. Cancer 1991, **67**: 2642–2652.

211 Chang M, Zimmerman LE, McLean I. The persisting pseudomelanoma problem. Arch Ophthalmol 1984, **102**: 726–727.

212 Char DH, Phillips TL. The potential for adjuvant radiotherapy in choroidal melanoma. Arch Ophthalmol 1982, **100**: 247–248.

213 Cole EL, Zakov ZN, Meisler DM, Tuthill RJ, McMahon JT. Cutaneous malignant melanoma metastatic to the vitreous. Arch Ophthalmol 1986, **104**: 98–101.

214 Coleman K, Baak JPA, van Diest PJ, Curran B, Mullaney J, Fenton M, Leader M. DNA ploidy status in 84 ocular melanomas. A study of DNA quantitation in ocular melanomas by flow cytometry and automatic and interactive static image analysis. Hum Pathol 1995, **26**: 99–105.

215 de Bustros S, Augsburger JJ, Shields JA, Shakin EP, Pryor CC II. Intraocular metastases from cutaneous malignant melanoma. Arch Ophthalmol 1985, **103**: 937–940.

216 de la Cruz PO Jr, Specht CS, McLean IW. Lymphocytic infiltration in uveal malignant melanoma. Cancer 1990, **65**: 112–115.

217 Dunne BM, McNamara M, Clynes M, Shering SG, Larkin AM, Moran E, Barnes C, Kennedy SM. MDR1 expression is associated with adverse survival in melanoma of the uveal tract. Hum Pathol 1998, **29**: 594–598.

218 Ferry AP. Lesions mistaken for malignant melanoma of posterior uvea. Arch Ophthalmol 1964, **72**: 463–469.

219 Ferry AP. Lesions mistaken for malignant melanoma of iris. Arch Ophthalmol 1965, **74**: 9–18.

220 Folberg R, Pe'er J, Gruman LM, Woolson RF, Jeng G, Montague PR, Moninger TO, Yi H, Moore KC. The morphologic characteristics of tumor blood vessels as a marker of tumor progression in primary human uveal melanoma. A matched case-control study. Hum Pathol 1992, **23**: 1298–1305.

221 Font RL, Spaulding A, Zimmerman LE. Diffuse malignant melanoma of the uveal tract. A clinicopathologic report of 54 cases. Trans Am Acad Ophthalmol Otolaryngol 1968, **72**: 877–895.

222 Forrest A, Keeper R, Spencer W. Iridocyclectomy for melanomas of the ciliary body. A follow-up study of pathology and surgical morbidity. Am J Ophthalmol 1978, **85**: 1237–1249.

223 Fuchs U, Kivela T, Summanen P, Immonen I, Tarkkanen A. An immunohistochemical and prognostic analysis of cytokeratin expression in malignant uveal melanoma. Am J Pathol 1992, **141**: 169–181.

224 Gamel JW, McLean I, Greenberg RA, Naids RM, Folberg R, Donoso LA, Seddon JM, Albert DM. Objective assessment of the malignant potential of intraocular melanomas with standard microslides stained with hematoxylin-eosin. Hum Pathol 1985, **16**: 689–692.

225 Gamel JW, McLean IW, McCurdy JB. Biologic distinctions between cure and time to death in 2892 patients with intraocular melanoma. Cancer 1993, **71**: 2299–2305.

226 Hendrix MJ, Seftor EA, Seftor RE, Gardner LM, Boldt HC, Meyer M, Pe'er J, Folberg R. Biologic determinants of uveal melanoma metastatic phenotype: role of intermediate filaments as predictive markers. Lab Invest 1998, **78**: 153–163.

227 Horsman DE, White VA. Cytogenetic analysis of uveal melanoma. Consistent occurrence of monosomy 3 and trisomy 8q. Cancer 1993, **71**: 811–819.

228 Howard GM, Forrest AW. Incidence and location of melanocytomas. Arch Ophthalmol 1967, **77**: 61–66.

229 Jakobiec FA, Silbert G. Are most iris "melanomas" really nevi? A clinicopathologic study of 189 lesions. Arch Ophthalmol 1981, **99**: 2117–2132.

230 Janssen K, Kuntze J, Busse H, Schmid KW. p53 oncoprotein overexpression in choroidal melanoma. Mod Pathol 1996, **9**: 267–272.

231 Kath R, Hayungs J, Bornfeld N, Sauerwein W, Hoffken K, Seeber S. Prognosis and treatment of disseminated uveal melanoma. Cancer 1993, **72**: 2219–2223.

232 Letson AD, Davidorf FH. Bilateral retinal metastases from cutaneous malignant melanoma. Arch Ophthalmol 1982, **100**: 605–607.

233 Luyten GPM, Mooy CM, Post J, Jensen OA, Luider TM, de Jong PT. Metastatic uveal melanoma: a morphologic and immunohistochemical analysis. Cancer 1996, **78**: 1967–1971.

234 McCurdy J, Gamel J, McLean I. A simple, efficient, and reproducible method for estimating the malignant potential of uveal melanoma from routine H & E slides. Pathol Res Pract 1991, **187**: 1025–1027.

235 McLean IW, Foster WD, Zimmerman LE. Uveal melanoma. Location, size, cell type, and enucleation as risk factors in metastasis. Hum Pathol 1982, **13**: 123–132.

236 McLean IW, Sibug ME, Becker RL, McCurdy JB. Uveal melanoma: the importance of large nucleoli in predicting patient outcome – an automated image analysis study. Cancer 1997, **79**: 982–988.

237 McLean IW, Zimmerman LE, Evans R. Reappraisal of Callender's spindle A type of malignant melanoma of choroid and ciliary body. Am J Ophthalmol 1978, **86**: 557–564.

238 Miller MV, Herdson PB, Hitchcock GC. Malignant melanoma of the uveal tract. A review of the Auckland experience. Pathology 1985, **17**: 281–284.

239 Pach JM, Robertson DM, Taney BS, Martin JA, Campbell RJ, O'Brien PC. Prognostic factors in choroidal and ciliary body melanomas with extrascleral extension. Am J Ophthalmol 1986, **101**: 325–331.

240 Sassani JW, Weinstein JM, Graham WP. Massively invasive diffuse choroidal melanoma. Arch Ophthalmol 1985, **103**: 945–948.

241 Seddon JM, Albert DM, Lavin DT, Robinson N. A prognostic factor study of disease-free interval and survival following enucleation for uveal melanoma. Arch Ophthalmol 1983, **101**: 1894–1899.

242 Seigel D, Myers M, Ferris F III, Steinhorn SC. Survival rates after enucleation of eyes with malignant melanoma. Am J Ophthalmol 1979, **87**: 761–765.

243 Shields JA, Karan DS, Perry HD, Donoso LA. Epithelioid cell nevus of the iris. Arch Ophthalmol 1985, **103**: 235–237.

244 Shields JA, Shields CL, De Potter P, Singh AD. Diagnosis and treatment of uveal melanoma. Semin Oncol 1996, **23**: 763–767.

245 Singh AD, Shields CL, Shields JA. Prognostic factors in uveal melanoma. Melanoma Res 2001, **11**: 255–263.

246 Singh AD, Wang MX, Donoso LA, Shields CL, De Potter P, Shields JA. Genetic aspects of uveal melanoma: a brief review. Semin Oncol 1996, **23**: 768–772.

247 Sorensen FB, Gamel JW, McCurdy J. Stereologic estimation of nucleolar volume in ocular melanoma. A comparative study of size estimators with prognostic impact. Hum Pathol 1993, **24**: 513–518.

248 Starr HJ, Zimmerman LE. Extrascleral extension and orbital recurrence of malignant melanomas of the choroid and ciliary body. Int Ophthalmol Clin 1962, **2**: 369–385.

249 Weinhaus RS, Seddon JM, Albert DM, Gragoudas ES, Robinson N. Prognostic factor study of survival after enucleation for juxtapapillary melanomas. Arch Ophthalmol 1985, **103**: 1673–1677.

250 Wieselthier JS, White WL. Cutaneous metastasis of ocular malignant melanoma: an unusual presentation simulating blue nevi. Am J Dermatopathol 1996, **18**: 289–295.

251 Yanoff M, Zimmerman LE. Histogenesis of malignant melanomas of the uvea. I. Nevi of choroid and ciliary body. Arch Ophthalmol 1966, **76**: 784–796.

252 Yanoff M, Zimmerman LE. Histogenesis of malignant melanomas of the uvea. II. The relationship of uveal nevi to malignant melanomas. Cancer 1967, **20**: 493–507.

253 Yanoff M, Zimmerman LE. Histogenesis of malignant melanomas of the uvea. III. The relationship of congenital ocular melanocytosis and neurofibromatosis to uveal melanomas. Arch Ophthalmol 1967, **77**: 331–336.

254 Zimmerman LE, McLean IW, Foster W. Does enucleation of the eye containing a malignant melanoma prevent or accelerate the dissemination of tumor cells? Br J Ophthalmol 1978, **62**: 420–425.

Retinoblastoma and related lesions

255 Abramson DH, Ellsworth RM, Tretter P, Adams K, Kitchin FD. Simultaneous bilateral radiation for advanced bilateral retinoblastoma. Arch Ophthalmol 1981, **99**: 1763–1766.

256 Abramson DH, Ellsworth RM, Tretter P, Javitt J, Kitchin FD. Treatment of bilateral groups I through III retinoblastoma with bilateral radiation. Arch Ophthalmol 1981, **99**: 1761–1762.

257 Abramson DH, Ellsworth R, Zimmerman L. Nonocular cancer in retinoblastoma survivors. Trans Am Acad Ophthalmol Otolaryngol 1976, **81**: 454–457.

258 Abramson DH, Marks RF, Ellsworth RM, Tretter P, Kitchin FD. The management of unilateral retinoblastoma without primary enucleation. Arch Ophthalmol 1982, **100**: 1249–1252.

259 Albert D, Syed N, for the Members of the Cancer Committee, College of American Pathologists. Protocol for the examination of specimens from patients with retinoblastoma: a basis for checklists. Arch Pathol Lab Med 2001, **125**: 1183–1188.

260 Amendola BE, Lamm FR, Markoe AM, Karlsson UL, Shields J, Shields CL, Augsburger J, Brady LW, Woodleigh R, Miller C. Radiotherapy of retinoblastoma. A review of 63 children treated with different irradiation techniques. Cancer 1990, **66**: 21–26.

261 Amoaku WMK, Willshaw HE, Parkes SE, Shah KJ, Mann JR. Trilateral retinoblastoma: a report of five patients. Cancer 1996, **78**: 858–863.

262 Bunt AH, Tso MOM. Feulgen-positive deposits in retinoblastoma. Incidence, composition, and ultrastructure. Arch Ophthalmol 1981, **99**: 144–150.

263 DerKinderen DJ, Koten JW, Nagelkerke NJD, Tan KEWP, Beemer FA, Den Otter W. Nonocular cancer in patients with hereditary retinoblastoma and their relatives. Int J Cancer 1988, **41**: 499–504.

264 Dickman PS, Barmada M, Gollin SM, Blatt J. Malignancy after retinoblastoma: secondary cancer or recurrence? Hum Pathol 1997, **28**: 200–205.

265 Donoso LA, Hamm H, Dietzschold B, Augsburger JJ, Shields JA, Arbizo V. Rhodopsin and retinoblastoma. A monoclonal antibody histopathologic study. Arch Ophthalmol 1986, **104**: 111–113.

266 Gallie BL, Squire JA, Goddard A, Dunn JM, Canton M, Hinton D, Zhu XP, Phillips RA. Mechanism of oncogenesis in retinoblastoma. Lab Invest 1990, **62**: 394–408.

266a Antoneli CBG, Steinhorst F, Riberio K, Novaes PE, Chojniak MM, Arias V, de Camargo B. Extraocular retinoblastoma: a 13-year experience. Cancer 2003, **98**: 1292–1298.

267 Gonzalez-Fernandez F, Lopes MB, Garcia-Fernandez JM, Foster RG, De Grip WJ, Rosemberg S, Newman SA, Vanden Berg SR. Expression of developmentally defined retinal phenotypes in the histogenesis of retinoblastoma. Am J Pathol 1992, **141**: 363–375.

268 He W, Hashimoto H, Tsuneyoshi M, Enjoji M, Inomata H. A reassessment of histologic classification and an immunohistochemical study of 88 retinoblastomas. A special reference to the advent of bipolar-like cells. Cancer 1992, **70**: 2901–2908.

269 Holladay DA, Holladay A, Montebello JF, Redmond KP. Clinical presentation, treatment, and outcome of trilateral retinoblastoma. Cancer 1991, **67**: 710–715.

270 Horowitz JM, Park SH, Bogenmann E, Cheng JC, Yandell DW, Kaye FJ, Minna JD, Dryja TP, Weinberg RA. Frequent inactivation of the retinoblastoma antioncogene is restricted to a subset of human tumor cells. Proc Natl Acad Sci U S A 1990, **87**: 2775–2779.

271 Howard GM, Ellsworth RM. Differential diagnosis of retinoblastoma. A statistical survey of 500 children. Am J Ophthalmol 1965, **60**: 610–612.

272 Johnson DL, Chandra R, Fisher WS, Hammock MK, McKeown CA. Trilateral retinoblastoma. Ocular and pineal retinoblastomas. J Neurosurg 1985, **63**: 367–370.

273 Khelfaoui F, Validire P, Auperin A, Quintana E, Michon J, Pacquement H, Desjardins L, Asselain B, Schlienger P, Vielh P, et al. Histopathologic risk factors in retinoblastoma: a retrospective study of 172 patients treated in a single institution. Cancer 1996, **77**: 1206–1213.

274 Knudson A. Alfred Knudson and his two-hit hypothesis. (Interview by Ezzie Hutchinson.) Lancet Oncol 2001, **2**: 642–645.

275 Kogan L, Boniuk M. Causes for enucleation in childhood with special reference to pseudogliomas and retinoblastomas. Int Ophthalmol Clin 1962, **2**: 507–524.

276 Korf H-W, Czerwionka M, Reiner J, Schachenmayr W, Schalken JJ, de Grip W, Gery I. Immunocytochemical evidence of molecular photoreceptor markers in cerebellar medulloblastomas. Cancer 1987, **60**: 1763–1766.

277 Kyritsis AP, Tsokos M, Triche TJ, Chader GJ. Retinoblastoma. Origin from a primitive neuroectodermal cell? Nature 1984, **307**: 471–473.

278 Lueder GT, Smith ME. Retinoblastoma. Semin Diagn Pathol 1994, **11**: 104–106.

279 MacKay CJ, Abramson DH, Ellsworth RM. Metastatic patterns of retinoblastoma. Arch Ophthalmol 1984, **102**: 391–396.

280 Margo C, Hidayat A, Kopelman J, Zimmerman LE. Retinocytoma. A benign variant of retinoblastoma. Arch Ophthalmol 1983, **101**: 1519–1531.

281 Paulino AC. Trilateral retinoblastoma: is the location of the intracranial tumor important? Cancer 1999, **86**: 135–141.

282 Perentes E, Rubinstein LJ. Recent applications of immunoperoxidase histochemistry in human neuro-oncology. An update. Arch Pathol Lab Med 1987, **111**: 796–812.

283 Rubinstein LJ. Embryonal central neuroepithelial tumors and their differentiating potential. A cytogenetic view of a complex neuro-oncological problem. J Neurosurg 1985, **62**: 795–805.

284 Sang DN, Albert DM. Retinoblastoma. Clinical and histopathologic features. Hum Pathol 1982, **13**: 133–147.

285 Schubert EL, Hansen MF, Strong LC. The retinoblastoma gene and its significance. Ann Med 1994, **26**: 177–184.

286 Schwimer CJ, Prayson RA. Clinicopathologic study of retinoblastoma including MIB-1, p53, and CD99 immunohistochemistry. Ann Diagn Pathol 2001, **5**: 148–154.

287 Shields CL, Shields JA, Baez K, Cater JR, De Potter P. Optic nerve invasion of retinoblastoma. Metastatic potential and clinical risk factors. Cancer 1994, **73**: 692–698.

288 Shields JA, Shields CL. Current management of retinoblastoma. Mayo Clin Proc 1994, **69**: 50–56.

289 Shuangshoti S, Chaiwun B, Kasantikul V. A study of 39 retinoblastomas with particular reference to morphology, cellular differentiation and tumour origin. Histopathology 1989, **15**: 113–124.

290 Terenghi G, Polak JM, Ballesta J, Cocchia D, Michetti F, Dahl D, Marangos PJ, Garner A. Immunocytochemistry of neuronal and glial markers in retinoblastoma. Virchows Arch [A] 1984, **404**: 61–73.

291 Ts'o MO, Fine BS, Zimmerman LE. The nature of retinoblastoma. II. Photoreceptor differentiation. An electron microscopic study. Am J Ophthalmol 1970, **69**: 350–359.

292 Ts'o MO, Zimmerman LE, Fine BS. The nature of retinoblastoma. I. Photoreceptor differentiation. A clinical and histopathologic study. Am J Ophthalmol 1970, **69**: 339–349.

293 Tsokos M, Kyritsis AP, Chader GJ, Triche TJ. Differentiation of human retinoblastoma in vitro into cell types with characteristics observed in embryonal or mature retina. Am J Pathol 1986, **123**: 542–552.

294 Tsuji M, Goto M, Uehara F, Kaneko A, Sawai J, Yonezawa S, Ohba N. Photoreceptor cell differentiation in retinoblastoma demonstrated by a new immunohistochemical marker mucin-like glycoprotein associated with photoreceptor cells (MLGAPC). Histopathology 2002, **40**: 180–186.

295 Walford N, Deferrai R, Slater RM, Delemarre JF, Dingemans KP,

Van den Bergh Weerman MA, Voute PA. Intraorbital rhabdoid tumour following bilateral retinoblastoma. Histopathology 1992, **20**: 170–173.

296 Wiggs J, Nordenskjöld M, Yandell D, Rapaport J, Grondin V, Janson M, Werelius B, Petersen R, Craft A, Riedel K, Liberfarb R, Walton D, Wilson W, Dryja TP. Prediction of the risk of hereditary retinoblastoma, using DNA polymorphisms within the retinoblastoma gene. N Engl J Med 1988, **318**: 151–157.

297 Wiman KG. The retinoblastoma gene. Role in cell cycle control and cell differentiation. FASEB J 1993, **7**: 841–845.

298 Yandell DW, Campbell TA, Dayton SH, Petersen R, Walton D, Little JB, McConkie-Rosell A, Buckley EG, Dryja TP. Oncogenic point mutations in the human retinoblastoma gene. Their application to genetic counseling. N Engl J Med 1989, **321**: 1689–1695.

299 Yuge K, Nakajima M, Uemura Y, Miki H, Uyama M, Tsubura A. Immunohistochemical features of the human retina and retinoblastoma. Virchows Arch 1995, **426**: 571–575.

300 Zacksenhaus E, Bremner R, Jiang Z, Gill RM, Muncaster M, Sopta M, Philips RA, Gallie BL. Unravelling the function of the retinoblastoma gene. Adv Cancer Res 1993, **61**: 115–141.

301 Zelter M, Damel A, Gonzalez G, Schwartz L. A prospective study on the treatment of retinoblastoma in 72 patients. Cancer 1991, **68**: 1685–1690.

302 Zelter M, Gonzalez G, Schwartz L, Gallo G, Schvartzman E, Damel A, Muriel FS. Treatment of retinoblastoma. Results obtained from a prospective study of 51 patients. Cancer 1988, **61**: 153–160.

Lymphoid tumors and tumorlike conditions

303 Allen R, Straatsma B. Ocular involvement in leukemia and allied disorders. Arch Ophthalmol 1961, **66**: 490–508.

304 Kline LB, Garcia JH, Harsh GR III. Lymphomatous optic neuropathy. Arch Ophthalmol 1984, **102**: 1655–1657.

305 Qualman SJ, Mendelsohn G, Mann RB, Green WR. Intraocular lymphomas. Natural history based on a clinicopathologic study of eight cases and review of the literature. Cancer 1983, **52**: 878–886.

306 Ryan S, Zimmerman LE, King FM. Reactive lymphoid hyperplasia. An unusual form of intraocular pseudotumor. Trans Am Acad Ophthalmol Otolaryngol 1972, **76**: 652–671.

307 Shields JA, Augsburger JJ, Gonder JR, MacLeod D. Localized benign lymphoid tumor of the iris. Arch Ophthalmol 1981, **99**: 2147–2148.

308 Vogel M, Font RL, Zimmerman LE, Levine R. Reticulum cell sarcoma of the retina and uvea. Am J Ophthalmol 1968, **66**: 205–215.

Other primary tumors

309 Addison DJ, Font RL. Glioneuroma of iris and ciliary body. Arch Ophthalmol 1984, **102**: 419–421.

309a Alenda C, Aranda FI, Payá A, Córdoba C. Mesectodermal leiomyoma of ciliary body. Int J Surg Pathol 2002, **10**: 309–312.

310 Bruner WE, Stark WJ, Green WR. Presumed juvenile xanthogranuloma of the iris and ciliary body in an adult. Arch Ophthalmol 1982, **100**: 457–459.

311 Ehlers N, Jensen OA. Juxtapapillary retinal hemangioblastoma (angiomatosis retinae) in an infant. Light microscopical and ultrastructural examination. Ultrastruct Pathol 1982, **3**: 325–333.

312 Messmer E, Font RL, Laqua H, Höpping W, Naumann GOH. Cavernous hemangioma of the retina. Immunohistochemical and ultrastructural observations. Arch Ophthalmol 1984, **102**: 413–418.

313 Pe'er J, Neudorfer M, Ron N, Anteby I, Lazar M, Rosenmann E. Panuveal malignant mesenchymoma. Arch Pathol Lab Med 1995, **118**: 844–847.

314 Ulbright TM, Fulling KH, Helveston EM. Astrocytic tumors of the retina. Differentiation of sporadic tumors from phakomatosis-associated tumors. Arch Pathol Lab Med 1984, **108**: 160–163.

315 Zaidman GW, Johnson BL, Salamon SM, Mondino BJ. Fuchs' adenoma affecting the peripheral iris. Arch Ophthalmol 1983, **101**: 771–773.

316 Zarate JO, Sampaolesi R. Pleomorphic xanthoastrocytoma of the retina. Am J Surg Pathol 1999, **23**: 79–81.

317 Zimmerman LE. Ocular lesions of juvenile xanthogranuloma. Nevoxanthoendothelioma. Trans Am Acad Ophthalmol Otolaryngol 1965, **69**: 412–442.

Metastatic tumors

318 Albert DM, Rubenstein R, Scheie H. Tumor metastasis to the eye. Part I. Incidence in 213 adult patients with generalized malignancy. Am J Ophthalmol 1967, **63**(Pt I): 724–726.

318a D'Abbadie I, Arriagada R, Spielmann M, Lê MG. Choroid metastases: clinical features and treatments in 123 patients. Cancer 2003, **98**: 1232–1238.

319 Ferry AP. Metastatic carcinoma of the eye and ocular adnexa. Int Ophthalmol Clin 1967, **7**: 615–658.

320 Ferry A, Font R. Carcinoma metastatic to the eye and orbit. Arch Ophthalmol 1974, **92**: 276–286.

321 Freedman MI, Folk JC. Metastatic tumors to the eye and orbit. Patient survival and clinical characteristics. Arch Ophthalmol 1987, **105**: 1215–1219.

322 Merrill CF, Kaufman DI, Dimitrov NV. Breast cancer metastatic to the eye is a common entity. Cancer 1991, **68**: 623–627.

Cytology

323 Barr CC, Green WR, Payne JW, Knox DI, Jensen AD, Thompson RL. Intraocular reticulum-cell sarcoma. Clinicopathologic study of four cases and review of the literature. Surv Ophthalmol 1975, **19**: 224–239.

324 Goldberg MF. Cytological diagnosis of phacolytic glaucoma utilizing Millepore filtration of the aqueous. Br J Ophthalmol 1967, **51**: 847–853.

325 Wolter JR, Naylor B. A membrane filter method used to diagnose intraocular tumor. J Pediatr Ophthalmol 1968, **5**: 36–38.

31 Ear

Introduction

Nearly all the diseases that can involve the ear also occur in other sites of the body. However, some of these diseases either have a predilection for the ear or pose special problems when occurring at this site. Only the features of these lesions as they pertain to their location in the ear will be discussed here. The general features of the respective entities are dealt with in the respective chapters.

The reader is referred to the specialized books on the subject for an authoritative discussion of the specific diseases of this structure.[1-4]

Normal anatomy

The ear is divided into the external, middle, and inner segments. The external ear consists of the auricle (pinna) and the external auditory canal, which is further divided into an outer (cartilaginous) portion and an inner (osseous) portion. Microscopically, both the auricle and the canal are covered by skin that differs little from that of the skin elsewhere, except for the fact that in the inner half of the canal the epidermis is very thin and lacks rete pegs. Adnexal structures are present in both areas; they are represented by hair follicles, sebaceous glands, and eccrine sweat glands in the auricle and by hair follicles, sebaceous glands, and a special type of apocrine sweat gland (known as ceruminous glands) in the canal, most of which are located in the outer third of this structure.

The inner portion of the canal is separated from the middle ear by the *tympanic membrane*, a thin fibrous structure lined by an attenuated layer of keratinizing squamous epithelium on the outer surface and by a single layer of cuboidal cells on the inner surface.

The middle ear (tympanic cavity) contains the three auditory ossicles (malleus, incus, and stapes); it connects with the pharynx through the eustachian tube and with the mastoid cavity and its contiguous pneumatic spaces. The middle ear proper and the mastoid are lined by a layer of flat epithelium; the eustachian tube is covered by tall ciliated epithelium, with smooth transitions between the two types.[5,5a]

The inner ear, which is located in the medial portion of the temporal bone, contains the *cochlea* and the *vestibular labyrinth*. These structures are supplied by the eighth cranial nerve, which enters the region through the internal auditory canal together with the seventh nerve. The vestibular labyrinth includes the blind *endolymphatic sac*, which is located in the middle of the posteromedial plate of the petrous bone. It has an intraosseous *rugose* portion and a *distal* portion that lies within the dura. It is lined by a flat to low columnar epithelium resting on a well-vascularized stroma.[6] The sac is connected to the *utricle* and *saccule* (the two main membranous structures of the vestibule) by the *endolymphatic duct*, which passes across the petrous bone.

Diseases of external ear

Non-neoplastic disorders

Congenital abnormalities of this region are common. *Preauricular sinuses, cysts,* and *fistulas* are derived from the first or second branchial clefts.[21,25,28] They are lined by squamous or respiratory epithelium and often contain lymphoid tissue in the wall. Cartilage and skin adnexa may also be present. Secondary inflammatory features are common.[21,28] The treatment is surgical, and recurrences are common.[10] *Accessory tragi* are unilateral or bilateral nodules present at birth, located anteriorly to the auricle in the pretragal area.[7] Like the previous lesions, they are the expression of a branchial cleft anomaly. Sometimes they are seen as a component of the oculoauriculovertebral syndrome (Goldenhar's syndrome).[14] Microscopically they are composed of a covering of skin, numerous tiny, mature hair follicles, and a core of fibrofatty tissue that may contain cartilage.[24] Depending on the relative amounts of these components, these lesions can be variously misdiagnosed as papillomas, fibromas, or soft tissue chondromas. *Ectopic salivary gland tissue* is not uncommon in the region of the middle ear; it can also be found in the external auditory canal.[19]

Keratinous cysts are common in and around the ear. Some are probably developmental anomalies related to the branchial cleft (see preceding discussion), and others are equivalent to those seen elsewhere in the skin and, as such, are either of infundibular hair follicle derivation or of epidermal inclusion type. They are all lined by keratinized squamous epithelium and filled by keratin of epidermal type. Keratinous cysts of pilar type are common in the periauricular area but not in the ear itself.

Cholesteatoma of the external auditory canal is composed of a cystic mass of keratinized squamous epithelium overlying an area of bone sequestration in the inner half of the canal.[22] This rare condition should not be confused with cholesteatoma of the middle ear spaces (see p. 2775) or with *keratosis obturans*, a disorder characterized by a diffuse acanthosis and hyperkeratosis of the skin of the canal associated with underlying chronic inflammation.[20,22]

Epithelioid (histiocytoid) hemangioma (also known as angiolymphoid hyperplasia with eosinophilia) has a predilection for the skin of the ear, external auditory canal, and periauricular region[26] (see Chapter 4).

Malignant external otitis, also known as necrotizing granulomatous otitis, is usually caused by *Pseudomonas aeruginosa* and affects mainly elderly patients who have diabetes. It can also be due to fungi, particularly *Aspergillus*. Microscopically, it is characterized by a necrotizing inflammatory reaction involving skin, soft tissue, cartilage, and bone, with invasion of the skull base.[30]

Chondrodermatitis nodularis chronica helicis (Winkler's disease) usually involves the upper portion of the helix in older patients, but it can also occur in the antihelix and in younger individuals. Clinically, it presents as a painful, small, round nodule often covered by a crust.[16] It is often thought clinically to be squamous cell carcinoma or actinic keratosis. Microscopically, there is marked hyperkeratosis and parakeratosis, acanthosis, and hyperplasia of the epidermis, which can reach pseudoepitheliomatous degrees (Fig. 31.1). The center is usually ulcerated and covered by granulation tissue. The underlying inflammation reaches the perichondrium and is characterized by a mononuclear infiltrate and vascular proliferation. The latter may be so pronounced as to simulate a vascular neoplasm, particularly glomus tumor.[8]

Idiopathic cystic chondromalacia (pseudocyst) results from degeneration of the auricular cartilage and is more commonly seen as a painless localized ear enlargement (sometimes bilaterally) in young males. Grossly, a cystic formation within the external auricular cartilage is filled by a watery fluid. Microscopically, the cyst has no lining, and there is no associated inflammation.[11]

Relapsing polychondritis is characterized by episodic painful inflammation of cartilage, most commonly in the

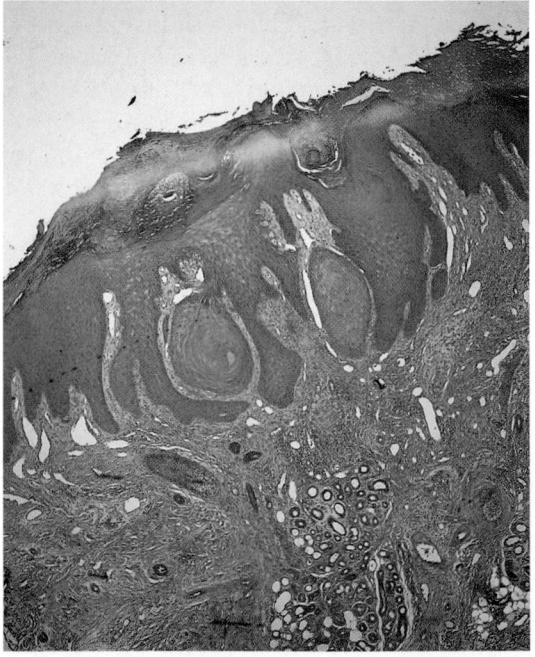

Fig. 31.1 Chondrodermatitis nodularis helicis. There is fibrosis and vascular proliferation in the dermis, accompanied by pseudoepitheliomatous hyperplasia of the overlying epithelium.

outer and inner ear, nose, costochondral junctions, a variety of joints, and sometimes the cartilage of the respiratory tract.[29] Aortic insufficiency is a life-threatening complication. The external ear is affected in almost 90% of the patients, and it represents the initial site of involvement in one third of the cases.[13,18]

Microscopically, there are degenerative changes in the cartilage (decrease in basophilic staining, loss of lacunae, and eventual replacement of collagen) and an inflammatory infiltrate that is neutrophilic initially and mononuclear in the late stages.[13] The etiology is unknown, but the detection in these patients of antibodies to type II collagen suggests an autoimmune mechanism.[12,15]

Nodular fasciitis can involve the external ear region; its morphologic appearance is similar to that seen at other soft tissue sites (see Chapter 25).

Localized disorders of the external ear formed by the accumulation of extracellular material include *keloid* (see Chapter 4), localized *amyloidosis*, the uric acid tophi of *gout*, *elastotic nodules*, and *collagenous papules*. Elastotic nodules are small papules and nodules most commonly noted on the antihelix as a result of actinic damage. Microscopically, they are composed of dermal clumps of elastic tissue.[9,27] Collagenous papules are smooth, firm, small papules, located bilaterally on the inner aspects of the aural pinnae and in rare cases, in the external auditory canal. Microscopically, there is a dense collagenous mass in which dilated vessels and scattered fibroblasts are identified.[73] It has been suggested that auricular lesions with the microscopic features of *granuloma annulare* may be a consequence of trauma.[17]

Tumors and tumorlike conditions

Keratotic lesions

The external ear is a common site for *seborrheic keratosis* and *actinic keratosis* (see Chapter 4). Some ear lesions designated as fibroepithelial papillomas or squamous papillomas are probably variants of seborrheic keratosis. Other *squamous papillomas* present as branching complex polypoid structures in the external auditory canal. Additional types of keratotic lesions that can occur at this site are *keratoacanthoma, inverted follicular keratosis, verruca vulgaris*, and *molluscum contagiosum*. It has been estimated that 8.5% of all keratoacanthomas involve the skin of the external ear.[31] All of these entities are discussed in Chapter 4.

Basal cell carcinoma

Basal cell carcinoma is a common tumor of the auricle and external auditory canal, the ratio between the two sites being 5:1. In the auricle, basal cell carcinoma predominates over squamous cell carcinoma (although not as much as in the rest of the head and neck area[32]), the ratio being reversed in the external auditory canal. The microscopic features and behavior of this lesion are described in Chapter 4. If untreated, basal cell carcino-

mas of the canal may extend into the middle ear, mastoid, or even the cranial cavity.[34] These tumors may be treated with surgery or radiation therapy, the choice depending on the size and location.[33]

Squamous cell carcinoma

Squamous cell carcinoma of the external ear comprises one fourth of all squamous cell cutaneous carcinomas of the head and neck region.[35] Most patients are elderly. The tumors are more common in the auricle (particularly the helix) than in the canal.[37,43,48] Many of the latter present clinically with symptoms of otitis.[45] Grossly and microscopically, they do not differ significantly from those seen elsewhere in sun-exposed skin (Fig. 31.2). Some are of the *adenoid (pseudoglandular)* variant, others belong to the *verrucous* type, and still others to the *spindle cell (sarcomatoid)* variant[42a,41,47] (see Chapter 4). The pattern of local spread varies depending on the initial location of the tumor, a finding that also applies to basal cell carcinomas. Tumors of the helix spread initially along the helix and then anteriorly to the antihelix and posteriorly to the posterior surface of the ear; tumors of the antihelix spread concentrically; tumors of the posterior surface of the ear spread to the helix and along that structure.[36] Tumors of the canal tend to invade bone and often destroy the tympanic membrane to penetrate into the middle ear. Like their basal cell counterparts, squamous cell carcinomas can be treated by either surgery of radiation therapy, the choice being determined by the size, location, and degree of invasiveness of the lesion.[41,42]

The prognosis is much better for tumors of the auricle than for those in the canal, a fact that is at least partially related to the earlier diagnosis of the former type of tumor.[36,40] In one series, tumor-related deaths occurred in only 1 of 17 patients with tumors of the auricle but in 11 of

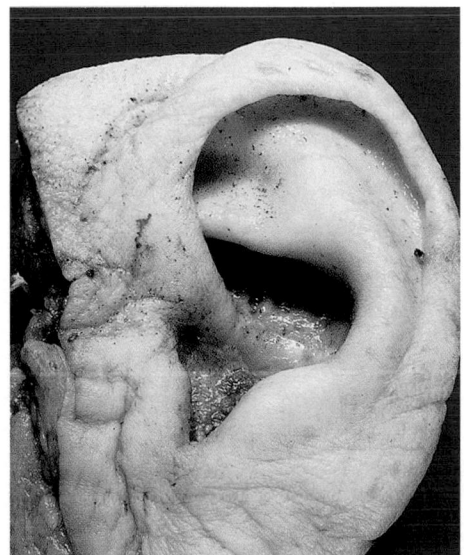

Fig. 31.2 This squamous cell carcinoma required the removal of the entire external ear.

21 patients with tumors of the canal.[38] The survival is directly correlated with the tumor stage, the staging system generally used being that proposed by the University of Pittsburgh.[44] The prognosis is particularly ominous for tumors of the inner portion of the canal exhibiting deep involvement of the temporal bone and beyond.[39,46,49]

Adnexal tumors

Almost any type of adnexal tumor can involve the skin of the external ear.[60] One of the most common is *pilomatrixoma*, often seen in children and sometimes confused microscopically with basal cell carcinoma. Other reported cases of adnexal tumors of this region include other types of *hair-follicle neoplasms*[52] and *sebaceous adenoma*.[59]

Adnexal tumors of the external auditory canal are generally assumed to be of ceruminous gland origin, and the generic term *ceruminoma* has been used for them.[50] The clinical presentation is similar, although the malignant tumors are more often painful and ulcerated.[55] Four major categories are recognized[62]:

Adenoma is sharply demarcated but not encapsulated. Variously sized glandular formations lined by apocrine cells are seen microscopically (Fig. 31.3).[51] A myoepithelial layer can be discerned at the base. Mitotic figures, pleomorphism, necrosis, and invasiveness are lacking.

Benign mixed tumor (pleomorphic adenoma) has an appearance similar to that of its cutaneous or salivary gland counterpart.[53] In some cases, the epithelial component exhibits apocrine features similar to those of adenoma.[61]

Syringocystadenoma papilliferum is morphologically equivalent to the tumor occurring elsewhere in the skin, particularly in the scalp (see Chapter 4). Connection with the surface of the canal is characteristic.

Adenocarcinoma may be well differentiated and therefore difficult to distinguish from adenoma. The presence of more than occasional mitotic activity, pleomorphism, the absence of a myoepithelial layer, necrosis, and invasiveness are the main identifying features.[56,56a] The main problem with this tumor is local recurrence; nodal or distant metastases are exceedingly rare.[58]

Adenoid cystic carcinoma has an appearance similar to that of its more common equivalent in the salivary glands (see Chapter 12) (Fig. 31.4). Like the latter, it has a great tendency for local (including perineural) invasion and distant (rather than nodal) metastases, particularly to the lungs[57] but also to brain.[54] The death rate is approximately 50%.

The differential diagnosis of these tumors includes direct invasion from so-called adenomas and paragangliomas of the middle ear and adnexal tumors of the auricle. It is particularly important to distinguish the benign eccrine dermal cylindroma arising from the conchal portion of the auricle from adenoid cystic carcinoma arising from the canal.

Melanocytic tumors

Nevi of any of the known microscopic types can occur in the auricle or, less commonly, in the canal.[64a]

Malignant melanomas of the external ear comprise about 10% of all melanomas of the head and neck region.[63] Nearly all are located in the auricle rather than in the canal.[64] The most common type is superficially spreading. Nodal metastases are to the upper cervical, intraparotid, or occipital groups, depending on the exact location of the tumor in the auricle.

Other tumors

Osteoma of the external auditory canal presents as a solitary pedunculated osseous mass attached by a narrow

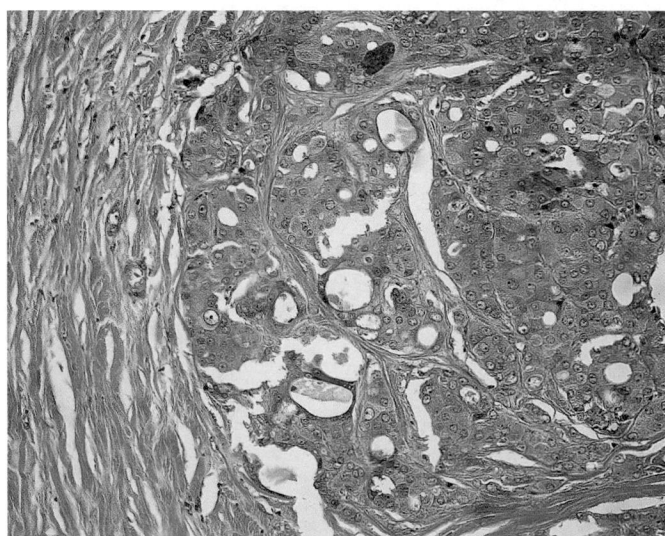

Fig. 31.3 Ceruminous adenoma. The cytoplasm of the tumor cells has an apocrine appearance.

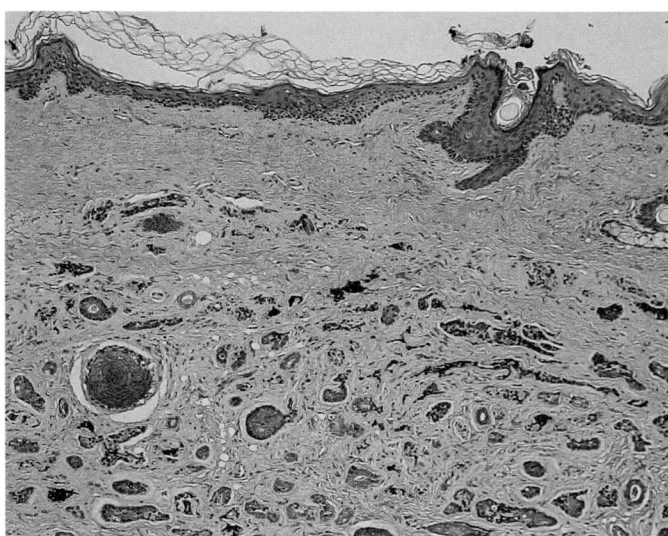

Fig. 31.4 Adenoid cystic carcinoma growing beneath the epidermis of the external ear canal.

pedicle to the tympanosquamous or tympanomastoid suture line.[67] Microscopically, it is formed by mature lamellar bone containing bone marrow and covered by keratinized squamous epithelium.[69]

Exostoses are sessile, often multiple and bilateral masses that seem to be particularly common in swimmers. Microscopically, the appearance is similar to that of osteoma except for the absence of bone marrow spaces.[69]

Myxomas of the external ear occur in patients with Carney's syndrome, sometimes bilaterally. Microscopically, they are nonencapsulated circumscribed nodules composed of scattered stellate and spindle cells set in a myxoid, capillary-rich matrix.[68]

Other primary tumors of the external ear include *Merkel cell carcinoma*[71] and various types of soft tissue neoplasms, including *vascular leiomyoma* (angioleiomyoma),[65] *rhabdomyosarcoma* (see p. 2777), *myxoid chondrosarcoma*,[72] and *peripheral nerve sheath tumors*.[70] As already mentioned, the canal can be secondarily involved by tumors of the middle ear or salivary gland. Exceptionally, *malignant lymphoma* will present initially as an ear lesion.[66]

Diseases of middle and inner ear

Non-neoplastic disorders

Developmental anomalies of the middle ear include encephalocele[83,95] and ectopic salivary gland tissue (sometimes designated as choristoma).[90]

Inflammatory polyp ("otic polyp") arises in the middle ear on the basis of a chronic otitis but often presents in the external auditory canal following perforation of the tympanic membrane. Microscopically, the appearance is that of chronically inflamed stroma, sometimes with the features of granulation tissue. The overlying mucosa may be of columnar ciliated type (consistent with its middle ear origin) or squamous (as a result of metaplasia). Cystically dilated glands may be seen embedded in the stroma.

Inflammations of the middle ear are usually of a nonspecific nature microscopically.[80,81,91] This structure can also be involved by specific conditions such as tuberculosis, aspergillosis, malakoplakia, and Wegener's granulomatosis.[74,75,78,82,88]

Cholesteatoma usually presents during the third or fourth decade, but it may appear at any age. It is the result of chronic otitis media and may involve the middle ear, peritympanic space, mastoid cavities, and petrous portion of the temporal bone. In rare cases, it has been found to extend into the soft tissues of the neck or the intracranial region.[73,84] Grossly, the appearance is that of a cyst filled with a granular waxy material. Microscopically, the membrane that bounds the lesion peripherally is made up of keratinizing squamous epithelium, and the content

is composed of keratin squames.[86] Chronic inflammatory cells, cholesterol clefts, and foreign body-type giant cell granulomas are common. It should be noted that although *cholesterol granulomas* are often seen in the middle ear as a consequence of cholesteatoma, they may also occur independently from it as a result of hemorrhage or otitis media.

The pathogenesis of cholesteatoma is controversial; origin of the squamous epithelium from metaplasia of middle ear mucosa, migration from the external auditory canal, migration from the external surface of the tympanic membrane following a perforation, or retraction of the tympanic membrane into the middle ear have all been considered.[85,89,92,93] In the congenital form, the disease is thought to be the result of inclusions of squamous epithelium in the temporal bone. The matrix-degrading cysteine proteinase cathepsin K may be involved in the bone erosion often seen in this entity.[82a]

The treatment is surgical and aimed at removal of the entire lesion, including the limiting membrane.[87]

Otosclerosis is a disorder of abnormal bone remodeling of unknown etiology. Genetic factors are clearly involved, but measles virus infection and autoimmunity may play contributory roles.[76,94] The typical and apparently unique site of involvement is the temporal bone. It is characterized by an initial bone resorption (otospongiosis) followed by bone production (otosclerosis).[86] This results in the formation of Paget's disease-like woven bone with prominent cement lines.[77] The disease causes hearing loss because of fixation of the stapes footplate in the oval window. Usually, the only specimens received in the pathology laboratory are portions of the stapes head and crura, which are almost always unaffected by the disease.[77] Microscopic studies done on temporal bones at autopsy have revealed cases of "histologic otosclerosis" that were asymptomatic, but the incidence of this finding seems much lower (about 2.5%) than previously claimed.[79]

Presbycusis (hearing loss) is a very common condition but not one likely to generate a surgical specimen. In any event, the morphologic changes described by Michaels[86] in this disorder are hair cell degeneration of the cochlea and a process that he calls giant stereociliary degeneration.

Tumors and tumorlike conditions

Paraganglioma

Paraganglioma of the glomus jugulare or glomus tympanicum is the most common neoplasm of the middle ear.[96] The general features of this tumor are discussed in Chapter 16. It can be found in the jugular bulb area, within the middle ear, in the external auditory canal, or around the eustachian tube.[98] In contrast to paragangliomas of other sites, those of the middle ear region have a marked predilection for females.[99] They can be familial, bilateral, or associated with paragangliomas elsewhere. Clinically, the typical presentation is that of a red mass protruding behind the tympanic membrane or extending in the canal. Profuse bleeding may be encountered at the time of biopsy. This tumor has a tendency to infiltrate adjacent bone; a few cases associated with distant metastases are on record. The initial treatment usually takes the form of local excision, but the incidence of local recurrence is over 50%.[99] Radiation therapy has also been used as an adjunct to surgery or as the primary treatment.[97]

Meningioma

Approximately 6% of all meningiomas arise from the surface of the petrous bone, from which they may invade this structure and reach the middle ear.[100] In addition, meningiomas seemingly localized to the middle ear have been described.[101,102] The tumor may involve the external ear canal, mastoid cavity, or jugular fossa.[102a] The microscopic appearance is described in Chapter 28 (Fig. 31.5). The treatment is surgical. The prognosis is substantially better for meningiomas limited to the middle ear than for those reaching this site through invasion of the petrous bone.

Schwannoma (acoustic neuroma)

The tumor traditionally known as acoustic neuroma is simply a schwannoma arising from the eighth (or sometimes the seventh) nerve, which grows within the internal auditory canal and can reach the middle ear. Its features are described in Chapters 25 and 28. These tumors are bilateral in 8% of the cases and associated with type II Recklinghausen's disease in 16%.[103] The treatment is surgical.

So-called middle ear adenoma and carcinoid tumor

Middle ear adenoma is the term that has been traditionally used for a distinctive tumor of the middle ear mostly

seen in patients between 20 and 40 years of age. Grossly, the lesion is grayish white and firm, not as vascular as paraganglioma, and relatively well circumscribed. Microscopically, the pattern of growth may be solid, glandular, or trabecular (Fig. 31.6).[109,116] The tumor cells are uniform, cuboidal or cylindrical, with a moderately abundant acidophilic cytoplasm that sometimes acquires plasmacytoid features.[107,115] Mitoses are exceedingly rare, pleomorphism is minimal, and necrosis is absent.

Histochemically, there may be intraluminal positivity for mucin and intracytoplasmic argyrophilia. Ultrastructurally, the tumor cells exhibit desmosomes and microvilli; in addition, membrane-bound dense-core granules are present in many of the tumor cells.[105] Immunohistochemically, positivity for keratin and lysozyme has been described.[112,113]

The histogenetic problem posed by middle ear adenoma mainly concerns its possible neuroendocrine nature and relationship with the reported cases of **carcinoid tumors** of the middle ear.[114,119] The latter tumors have many cytoarchitectural features in common with middle ear adenoma but also exhibit undeniable evidence of neuroendocrine differentiation.[111] Some authors like to view middle ear adenomas and carcinoid tumors as separate entities and regard the former as tumors of the middle ear mucosa.[113,114] However, a large number of studies performed in recent years have convincingly shown that these two tumors merge imperceptibly, in the sense of showing various degrees of combined exocrine and neuroendocrine differentiation.[104,108,117,118,120] As such, they could be regarded as analogous to adenocarcinoids or amphicrine neoplasms of other sites.[106,110] The presence of a neuroendocrine component is supported by the previously mentioned argyrophilia, presence of dense-core granules ultrastructurally, and reported immunoreactivity for neuron-specific enolase, chromogranin, serotonin, and numerous peptide hormones (such as pancreatic polypeptide, glucagon, cholecystokinin, and

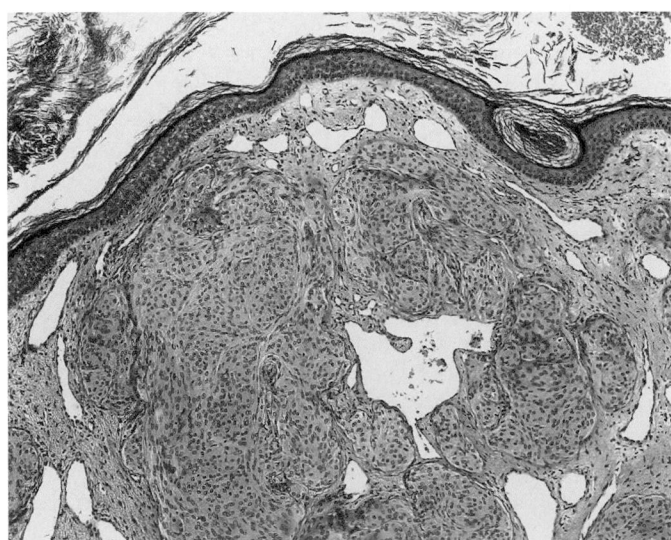

Fig. 31.5 Meningioma of ear. The appearance is identical to that of its counterpart in the central nervous system.

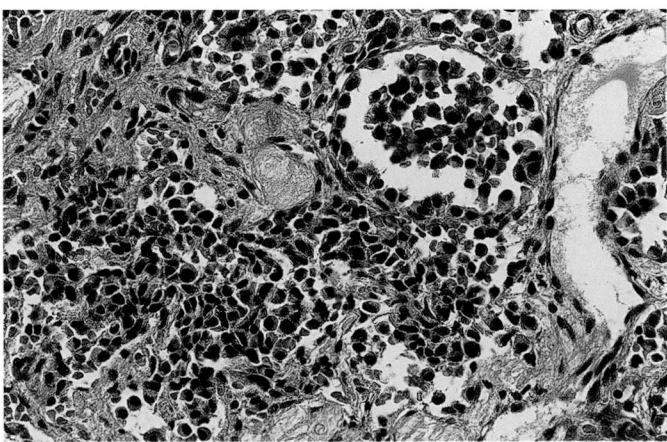

Fig. 31.6 So-called "middle ear adenoma." This tumor is closely related and perhaps identical to carcinoid tumor of the ear.

leucine-enkephalin).[108,119] Cases associated with systemic manifestations are also on record.[111]

The treatment of choice of middle ear adenoma/carcinoid tumor is surgical excision. The prognosis is excellent, with only an occasional example of local recurrence.[108,118,120]

Adenocarcinoma

Adenocarcinoma of the middle and inner ear is a somewhat confusing and controversial entity.[124,128–130] The term has sometimes been used for adenocarcinomas of the external auditory canal secondarily invading the ear and for so-called "middle ear adenoma."[121] However, there is a distinct form of primary adenocarcinoma of this site that is different from the entities previously mentioned. This is a *papillary adenocarcinoma* composed of uniform cuboidal cells with clear to acidophilic cytoplasm forming papillary structures that rest on a vascular stroma (Fig. 31.7). Cystic dilatation of the glands often occurs, leading to a follicle-like appearance that is very reminiscent of that seen in thyroid tumors (Fig. 31.8).[129,131,132]

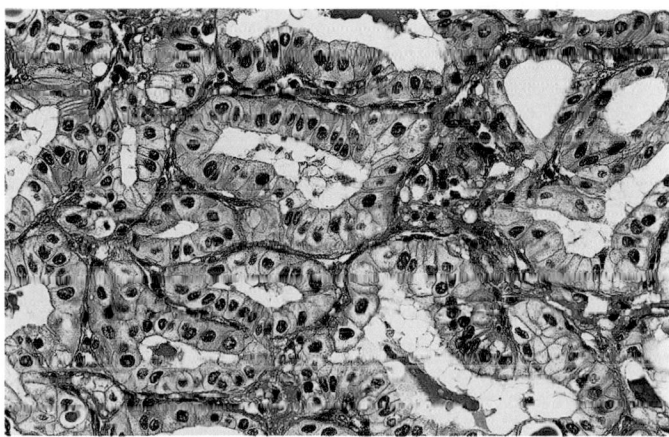

Fig. 31.7 Aggressive papillary middle ear tumor. The tumor forms glandular structures lined by clear cells. In other areas the pattern of growth was papillary.

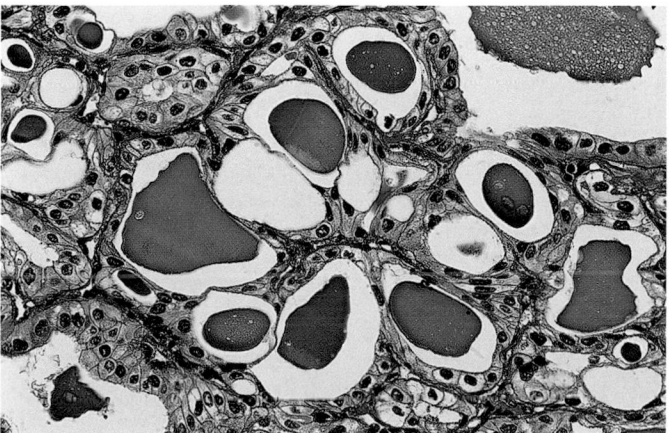

Fig. 31.8 Same case as Fig. 31.7. The cystic dilatation of the glands and the presence of a colloid-like material in the lumen results in an appearance strongly reminiscent of thyroid tissue.

Tumors with prominent cytoplasmic clearing simulate metastatic renal cell carcinoma. Gaffey et al., who refer to this neoplasm as *aggressive papillary middle-ear tumor* (APMET), favor an origin from middle ear/mastoid epithelium.[123] In a subsequent article, they have shown that this lesion can occur in the setting of von Hippel–Lindau disease, sometimes in association with a microscopically similar tumor in the broad ligament of presumed wolffian (mesonephric) origin.[122] APMET is closely related if not identical to the *low-grade adenocarcinoma of probably endolymphatic sac origin* reported by Heffner[126] and known to some as *Heffner tumor*.[127,134] As the name indicates, the author favors an origin from endolymphatic sac epithelium. Regarding the differential diagnosis, it is well to remember that so-called "middle ear adenoma" does not exhibit papillary formations. Cases of this tumor occurring in the setting of von Hippel–Lindau disease are associated with a germline mutation of the *VHL* gene combined with loss of function of the wild-type allele through genetic deletion. Interestingly, mutations or allelic deletions of the same gene have also been found in some sporadic tumors.[125,133]

Papillary adenocarcinoma has a tendency to invade bone, from which it may spread to the cranial cavity. The treatment is surgical, but achievement of local control is difficult.[123,124]

Squamous cell carcinoma

Squamous cell carcinoma of the middle ear typically presents in older patients with a history of longstanding ear discharge, which may be hemorrhagic and is usually associated with pain and hearing loss.[135,138,140] Rarely, the process is bilateral.[139] An etiologic role for chronic otitis media has long been suspected.[137] Jin et al.[136] found HPV16 genetic material in 11 of 14 cases of squamous cell carcinoma of the middle ear they studied. Grossly, the tumor fills the middle ear spaces, from where it may invade the bony walls of the mastoid ear cells, the bone septum that separates the ear from the carotid canal, the internal auditory meatus, the eustachian tube, and the external auditory canal. Eventually, it may reach the intracranial cavity and the soft tissues of the neck.[138] Microscopically, the tumor is an ordinary squamous cell carcinoma of various degrees of differentiation; in rare cases, it may be of *verrucous* type.[141] The differential diagnosis includes secondary invasion of the middle ear by squamous cell carcinomas of the external auditory canal and the eustachian tube. The preferred form of treatment is a combination of surgery and radiation therapy. In the series by Michael and Wells,[138] the 5-year survival rate was 39%.

Rhabdomyosarcoma

Rhabdomyosarcoma of the middle ear occurs almost exclusively in children. At the time of diagnosis, the tumor has often invaded the external canal, mastoid, and meninges.[146] CT scan is the best method to delineate the tumor and to detect intracranial spread. Microscopically, the neoplasms can be of embryonal or botryoid type.[144,145] The microscopic features are described in Chapter 25 (Fig. 31.9). The treatment is a combination of surgery, radiation therapy, and multidrug chemotherapy.[143,145]

A few cases of rhabdomyosarcoma apparently localized to the external auditory canal have been reported.[142,145]

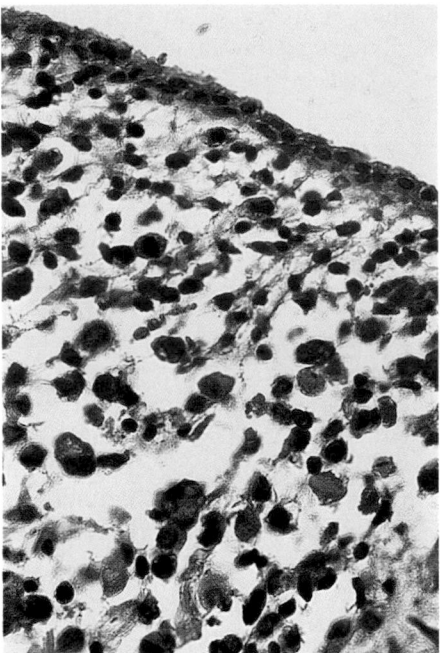

Fig. 31.9 Embryonal rhabdomyosarcoma of the middle ear. Neoplastic tumor cells are seen growing beneath a flattened epithelium. Most of the cell population is small, but there are larger elements with more abundant fibrillary acidophilic cytoplasm.

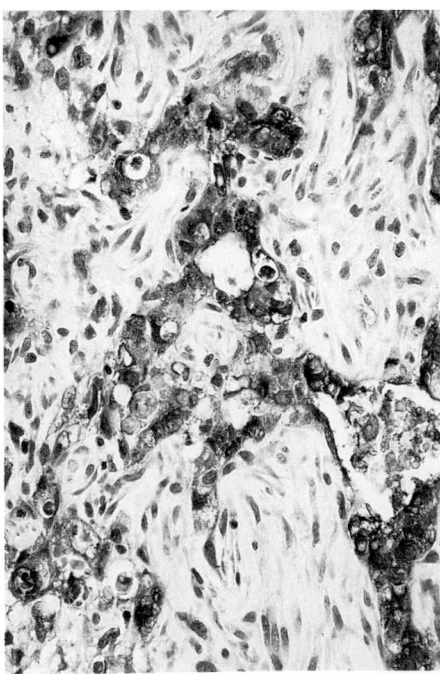

Fig. 31.10 Yolk sac tumor of the middle ear immunostained for α-fetoprotein.

Other primary tumors

Rare benign primary tumors of the middle ear region include *lipoma, hemangioma, osteoma, ossifying fibroma, dermoid cyst* (in the eustachian tube), *teratoma,* and *"glioma."*[147–151,153] The middle ear can also be secondarily involved in cases of *Langerhans' cell histiocytosis.* A middle ear tumor with the histologic and immunohistochemical features of *yolk sac (endodermal sinus) tumor* has been reported[152] (Fig. 31.10), and another with the features of an amelanotic *malignant melanoma.*[154]

Metastatic tumors

The temporal bone can be involved by malignant tumors arising elsewhere. This involvement can be in the form of direct extension from tumors of the pharynx, salivary glands, or central nervous system, or as blood-borne distant metastases. In the latter instance, the most common sites of the primary are breast, lung, and kidney.[155,156]

References

Introduction

1 Friedmann I. Pathology of the ear. Edinburgh, 1993, Churchill Livingstone.
2 Jackler RK, Driscoll CLW (eds). Tumors of the ear and temporal bone. Philadelphia, 2000, Lippincott Williams & Wilkins.
3 Nager GT. Pathology of the ear and temporal bone. Baltimore, 1993, Williams & Wilkins.
4 Schuknecht HF. Pathology of the ear. Philadelphia, 1993, Lea & Febiger.

Normal anatomy

5 Lim DJ. Functional morphology of the mucosa of the middle ear and eustachian tube. Ann Otol Rhinol Laryngol 1976, **85:** 36–43.
5a Michaels L. The Ear. In Sternberg S (ed.): Histology for pathologists, ed. 2. Philadelphia, 1997, Lippincott-Raven Publishers: 337–336.
6 Schindler RA. The ultrastructure of the endolymphatic sac in man. Laryngoscope 1980, **21:** 1–39.

Diseases of the external ear
Non-neoplastic disorders

7 Brownstein MH, Wanger N, Helwig EB. Accessory tragi. Arch Dermatol 1971, **104:** 625–631.
8 Calnan J, Rossatti B. On the histopathology of chondrodermatitis nodularis helicis chronica. J Clin Pathol 1959, **12:** 179–182.
9 Carter VH, Constantine VS, Poole WL. Elastotic nodules of the antihelix. Arch Dermatol 1969, **100:** 282–285.
10 Ellies M, Laskawi R, Arglebe C, Altrogge C. Clinical evaluation and surgical management of congenital preauricular fistulas. J Oral Maxillofac Surg 1998, **56:** 827–830.
11 Heffner DK, Hyams VJ. Cystic chondromalacia (endochondral pseudocyst) of the auricle. Arch Pathol Lab Med 1986, **110:** 740–743.
12 Herman JH, Dennis MV. Immunopathologic studies in relapsing polychondritis. J Clin Invest 1973, **52:** 549–558.
13 Hughes RAC, Berry CL, Siefert M, Lessof MH. Relapsing polychondritis. Three cases with a clinico-pathological study and literature review. QJM 1972, **41:** 363–380.
14 Jansen T, Romiti R, Altmeyer P. Accessory tragus: report of two cases and review of the literature. Pediatr Dermatol 2000, **17:** 391–394.

15 McCune WJ, Schiller AL, Dynesius-Trentham RA, Trentham DE. Type II collagen-induced auricular chondritis. Arthritis Rheum 1982, 25: 266–273.

16 Metzger SA, Goodman ML. Chondrodermatitis helicis. A clinical re-evaluation and pathological review. Laryngoscope 1976, 86: 1402–1412.

17 Mills A, Chetty R. Auricular granuloma annulare. A consequence of trauma? Am J Dermatopathol 1992, 14: 431–433.

18 Moloney JR. Relapsing polychondritis. Its otolaryngological manifestations. J Laryngol Otol 1978, 92: 9–15.

19 Morimoto N, Ogawa K, Kanzaki J. Salivary gland choristoma in the middle ear: a case report. Am J Otolaryngol 1999, 20: 232–235.

20 Naiberg J, Berger G, Hawke M. The pathologic features of keratosis obturans and cholesteatoma of the external auditory canal. Arch Otolaryngol 1984, 110: 690–693.

21 Olsen KD, Maragos NE, Weiland LH. First branchial cleft anomalies. Laryngoscope 1980, 90: 423–436.

22 Piepergerdes JC, Kramer BM, Behnke EE. Keratosis obturans and external auditory canal cholesteatoma. Laryngoscope 1980, 90: 383–391.

23 Sanchez JL. Collagenous papules on the aural conchae. Am J Dermatopathol 1983, 5: 231–233.

24 Satoh T, Tokura Y, Katsumata M, Sonoda T, Takigawa M. Histological diagnostic criteria for accessory tragi. J Cutan Pathol 1990, 17: 206–210.

25 Skau NK, Eriksen KD. Pre-auricular fistula communicating with the external auditory meatus, combined with second branchial cleft anomalies. J Laryngol Otol 1986, 100: 203–206.

26 Thompson JW, Colman M, Williamson C, Ward PH. Angiolymphoid hyperplasia with eosinophilia of the external ear canal. Treatment with laser excision. Arch Otolaryngol 1981, 107: 316–319.

27 Weedon D. Elastotic nodules of the ear. J Cutan Pathol 1981, 8: 429–433.

28 Work WP. Newer concepts of first branchial cleft defects. Laryngoscope 1972, 82: 1581–1593.

29 Yetiser S, Inal A, Taser M, Ozkaptan Y. Otolaryngological aspects of relapsing polychondritis: course and outcome. Rev Laryngol Otol Rhinol (Bord) 2001, 122: 195–200.

30 Zaky DA, Bentley DW, Lowy K, Betts RF, Douglas RG Jr. Malignant external otitis. A severe form of otitis in diabetic patients. Am J Med 1976, 61: 298–302.

Tumors and tumorlike conditions

Keratotic lesions

31 Patterson HC. Facial keratoacanthoma. Otolaryngol Head Neck Surg 1983, 91: 263–270.

Basal cell carcinoma

32 Ahmad I, Das Gupta AR. Epidemiology of basal cell carcinoma and squamous cell carcinoma of the pinna. J Laryngol Otol 2001, 115: 85–86.

33 Avila J, Bosch A, Aristizabal S, Frias Z, Marcial V. Carcinoma of the pinna. Cancer 1977, 40: 2891–2895.

34 Goodwin WJ, Jesse RH. Malignant neoplasms of the external auditory canal and temporal bone. Arch Otolaryngol 1980, 106: 675–679.

Squamous cell carcinoma

35 Avila J, Bosch A, Aristizábal S, Frías Z, Marcial V. Carcinoma of the pinna. Cancer 1977, 40: 2891–2895.

36 Bailin PL, Levine HL, Wood BG, Tucker HM. Cutaneous carcinoma of the auricular and periauricular region. Arch Otolaryngol 1980, 106: 692–696.

37 Barnes L, Johnson JT. Clinical and pathological considerations in the evaluation of major head and neck specimens resected for cancer. Part II. Pathol Annu 1986, 21(Pt 2): 83–110.

38 Chen KTK, Dehner LP. Primary tumors of the external and middle ear. Arch Otolaryngol 1978, 104: 247–252.

39 Goodwin WJ, Jesse RH. Malignant neoplasms of the external auditory canal and temporal bone. Arch Otolaryngol 1980, 106: 675–679.

40 Johns ME, Headington JT. Squamous cell carcinoma of the external auditory canal. A clinicopathologic study of 20 cases. Arch Otolaryngol 1974, 100: 45–49.

41 Johnson WC, Helwig EB. Adenoid squamous cell carcinoma (adenoacanthoma). Cancer 1966, 19: 1639–1650.

42 Kinney SE, Wood BG. Malignancies of the external ear canal and temporal bone. Surgical techniques and results. Laryngoscope 1987, 97: 158–164.

42a Koso-Thomas K, Thompson LDR. Spindle cell (sarcomatoid) carcinoma of the ear: a clinicopathological study of 57 cases. (Abstract) Mod Pathol 2003, 16: 220A.

43 Lewis JS. Cancer of the ear. CA Cancer J Clin 1987, 37: 78–87.

44 Moody SA, Hirsch BE, Myers EN. Squamous cell carcinoma of the external auditory canal: an evaluation of a staging system. Am J Otol 2000, 21: 582–588.

45 Paaske PB, Witten J, Schwer S, Hansen HS. Results in treatment of carcinoma of the external auditory canal and middle ear. Cancer 1987, 59: 156–160.

46 Pfreundner L, Schwager K, Willner J, Baier K, Bratengeier K, Brunner FX, Flentje M. Carcinoma of the external auditory canal and middle ear. Int J Radiat Oncol Biol Phys 1999, 44: 777–788.

47 Proops DW, Hawke WM, van Nostrand AW, Harwood AR, Lunan M. Verrucous carcinoma of the ear. Case report. Ann Otol Rhinol Laryngol 1984, 93: 385–388.

48 Shiffman NJ. Squamous cell carcinomas of the skin of the pinna. Can J Surg 1975, 18: 279–283.

49 Stell PM, McCormick MS. Carcinoma of the external auditory meatus and middle ear. Prognostic factors and a suggested staging system. J Laryngol Otol 1985, 99: 847–850.

Adnexal tumors

50 Batsakis JG, Hardy GC, Hishiyama RH. Ceruminous gland tumors. Arch Otolaryngol 1967, 86: 66–69.

51 Cankar V, Crowley H. Tumors of ceruminous glands. A clinicopathological study of 7 cases. Cancer 1964, 17: 67–75.

52 Cohen C, Davis TS. Multiple trichogenic adnexal tumors. Am J Dermatopathol 1986, 8: 241–246.

53 Collins RJ, Yu HC. Pleomorphic adenoma of the external auditory canal. An immunohistochemical and ultrastructural study. Cancer 1989, 64: 870–875.

54 Conlin PA, Mira JL, Graham SC, Kaye KS, Cordero J. Ceruminous gland adenoid cystic carcinoma with contralateral metastasis to the brain. Arch Pathol Lab Med 2002, 126: 87–89.

55 Lynde CW, McLean DI, Wood WS. Tumors of ceruminous glands. J Am Acad Dermatol 1984, 11: 841–847.

56 Michel RG, Woodard BH, Shelburne JD, Bossen EH. Ceruminous gland adenocarcinoma. A light and electron microscopic study. Cancer 1978, 41: 545–553.

56a Nelson BL, Thompson LDR, Barnes L. Ceruminal gland carcinomas: a clinicopathologic study of 17 cases. (Abstract) Mod Pathol 2003, 16: 221A.

57 Perzin KH, Gullane P, Conley J. Adenoid cystic carcinoma involving the external auditory canal. A clinicopathologic study of 16 cases. Cancer 1982, 50: 2873–2883.

58 Pulec JL. Glandular tumors of the external auditory canal. Laryngoscope 1977, 87: 1601–1612.

59 Raizada RM, Khan NU. Aural sebaceous adenomas. J Laryngol Otol 1986, 100: 1413–1416.

60 Senturia BH, Marcus MD, Lucente SE. Disease of the external ear, ed. 2. New York, 1980, Grune & Stratton.

61 Tang X, Tamura Y, Tsutsumi Y. Mixed tumor of the external auditory canal. Pathol Int 1994, 44: 80–83.

62 Wetli CV, Pardo V, Millard M, Gerston K. Tumors of ceruminous glands. Cancer 1972, **29:** 1169–1178.

Melanocytic tumors

63 Byers RM, Smith JL, Russell N, Rosenberg V. Malignant melanoma of the external ear. Review of 102 cases. Am J Surg 1980, **140:** 518–521.

64 Pack GT, Conley J, Oropeza R. Melanoma of the external ear. Arch Otolaryngol 1970, **92:** 106–113.

64a Saad A, Patel S, Mutasim D. Nevi of auricular region: possible diagnostic errors. (Abstract) Mod Pathol 2003, **16:** 99a.

Other tumors

65 Choe KS, Sclafani AP, McCormick SA. Angioleiomyoma of the auricle: a rare tumor. Otolaryngol Head Neck Surg 2001, **125:** 109–110.

66 Darvay A, Russell-Jones R, Acland KM, Lampert I, Chu AC. Systemic B-cell lymphoma presenting as an isolated lesion on the ear. Clin Exp Dermatol 2001, **26:** 166–169.

67 Deguine C, Pulec JL. Large osteoma of the external auditory canal. Ear Nose Throat J 2001, **80:** 8.

68 Ferreiro JA, Carney JA. Myxomas of the external ear and their significance. Am J Surg Pathol 1994, **18:** 274–280.

69 Graham MD. Osteomas and exostoses of the external auditory canal. Ann Otol Rhinol Laryngol 1979, **88:** 566–572.

70 Tran Ba Huy P, Hassan JM, Wassef M, Mikol J, Thurel O. Acoustic schwannoma presenting as a tumor of the external auditory canal. Case report. Ann Otol Rhinol Laryngol 1987, **96:** 415–418.

71 Virtaniemi J, Hirvikoski P, Pukkila M, Kumpulainen E, Johansson R, Kosma VM. Merkel cell carcinoma of the auricle. Eur Arch Otorhinolaryngol 2000, **257:** 558–560.

72 Worley GA, Wareing MJ, Sergeant RJ. Myxoid chondrosarcoma of the external auditory meatus. J Laryngol Otol 1999, **113:** 742–743.

Diseases of middle and inner ear
Non-neoplastic disorders

73 Arkin CF, Millard M, Medeiros LJ. Giant invasive cholesteatoma. Report of a case with cerebellar invasion. Arch Pathol Lab Med 1985, **109:** 960–961.

74 Azadeh B, Dabiri S, Moshfegh I. Malakoplakia of the middle ear. Histopathology 1991, **19:** 276–278.

75 Barnes L, Beel PL. Diseases of the external auditory canal, middle ear and temporal bone. In Barnes L (ed.): Surgical pathology of the head and neck, ed. 2. New York, 2001, Marcel Dekker.

76 Chole RA, McKenna M. Pathophysiology of otosclerosis. Otol Neurotol 2001, **22:** 249–257.

77 Davis GL. Pathology of otosclerosis. A review. Am J Otolaryngol 1987, **8:** 273–281.

78 Davis GL. Tumorous and inflammatory conditions of the ear. In Gnepp DR (ed.): Pathology of the head and neck, vol. 10. Contemporary issues in surgical pathology. New York, 1988, Churchill Livingstone.

79 Declau F, Van Spaendonck M, Timmermans JP, Michaels L, Liang J, Qiu JP, Van de Heyning P. Prevalence of otosclerosis in an unselected series of temporal bones. Otol Neurotol 2001, **22:** 596–602.

80 Friedmann I. Pathology of the ear. Edinburgh, 1993, Churchill Livingstone.

81 Friedmann I. Pathology of the ear. Selected topics. Pathol Annu 1978, **13**(Pt 1): 363–410.

82 Friedmann I. Nose, throat and ears. In Symmers W St C (ed.): Systemic pathology, ed. 3, vol. 1. New York, 1986, Churchill Livingstone.

82a Hansen T, Unger R, Gaumann A, Hundorf I, Maurer J, Kirkpatrick CJ, Kriegsmann J. Expression of matrix-degrading cysteine proteinase cathepsin K in cholesteatoma. Mod Pathol 2001, **14:** 1226–1231.

83 Kamerer DB, Caparosa RJ. Temporal bone encephalocele. Diagnosis and treatment. Laryngoscope 1982, **92:** 878–882.

84 Kreutzer EW, DeBlanc GB. Extra aural spread of acquired cholesteatoma. Arch Otolaryngol 1982, **108:** 320–323.

85 Linde RE. Cholesterol granuloma. Ear Nose Throat J 1982, **61:** 186–189.

86 Michaels L. The temporal bone. An organ in search of a histopathology. Histopathology 1991, **18:** 391–394.

87 Palva T. Surgical treatment of cholesteatomatous ear disease. J Laryngol Otol 1985, **99:** 539–544.

88 Ramages LJ, Gertler R. Aural tuberculosis. A series of 25 patients. J Laryngol Otol 1985, **99:** 1073–1080.

89 Sade J. Pathogenesis of attic cholesteatomas. J R Soc Med 1978, **71:** 716–732.

90 Saeger KL, Gruskin P, Carberry JN. Salivary gland choristoma of the middle ear. Arch Pathol Lab Med 1982, **106:** 39–40.

91 Schuknecht HF. Pathology of the ear. Philadelphia, 1993, Lea & Febiger.

92 Soldati D, Mudry A. Knowledge about cholesteatoma, from the first description to the modern histopathology. Otol Neurotol 2001, **22:** 723–730.

93 Swartz JD. Cholesteatomas of the middle ear. Diagnosis, etiology, and complications. Radiol Clin North Am 1985, **22:** 15–35.

94 Van Den Bogaert K, Govaerts PJ, Schatteman I, Brown MR, Caethoven G, Offeciers FE, Somers T, Declau F, Coucke P, Van de Heyning P, Smith RJ, Van Camp G. A second gene for otosclerosis, OTSC2, maps to chromosome 7q34-36. Am J Hum Genet 2001, **68:** 495–500.

95 Williams DC. Encephalocele of the middle ear. J Laryngol Otol 1986, **100:** 471–473.

Tumors and tumorlike conditions
Paraganglioma

96 Alford BR, Guilford FR. A comprehensive study of tumors of the glomus jugulare. Laryngoscope 1962, **72:** 765–787.

97 Konefal JB, Pilepich MV, Spector GJ, Perez CA. Radiation therapy in the treatment of chemodectomas. Laryngoscope 1987, **97:** 1331–1335.

98 Larson TC III, Reese DF, Baker HL Jr, McDonald TJ. Glomus tympanicum chemodectomas. Radiographic and clinical characteristics. Radiology 1987, **163:** 801–806.

99 Reddy EK, Mansfield CM, Hartman GV. Chemodectoma of glomus jugulare. Cancer 1983, **52:** 337–340.

Meningioma

100 Nager GT. Meningiomas involving the temporal bone; clinical and pathological aspects. Springfield, Ill., 1964, Charles C Thomas.

101 Prayson RA. Middle ear meningiomas. Ann Diagn Pathol 2000, **4:** 149–153.

102 Salama N, Stafford N. Meningiomas presenting in the middle ear. Laryngoscope 1982, **92:** 92–97.

102a Thompson L, Bouffard JP, Sandberg G. Primary ear and temporal bone meningiomas: a clinicopathologic study of 36 cases with a review of the literature. Mod Pathol 2003, **16:** 236–245.

Schwannoma (acoustic neuroma)

103 Erickson LS, Sorenson GD, McGavran MH. A review of 140 acoustic neurinomas (neurilemmoma). Laryngoscope 1965, **75:** 601–626.

So-called middle ear adenoma and carcinoid tumor

104 Davies JE, Semeraro D, Knight LC, Griffiths GJ. Middle ear neoplasms showing adenomatous and neuroendocrine components. J Laryngol Otol 1989, **103:** 404–407.

105 El-Naggar AK, Pflatz M, Ordôñez NG, Batsakis JG. Tumors of the middle ear and endolymphatic sac. Pathol Annu 1994, 29(Pt 2): 199–231.

106 Faverly DR, Manni JJ, Smedts F, Verhofstad AA, van Haelst UJ. Adeno-carcinoid or amphicrine tumors of the middle ear. A new entity? Pathol Res Pract 1992, 188: 162–171.

107 Friedman I. Middle ear adenoma. Histopathology 1998, 32: 279–280.

108 Hosoda S, Tateno H, Inoue HK, Isojima G, Kondo S, Konishi T. Carcinoid tumor of the middle ear containing serotonin and multiple peptide hormones. A case report and review of the pathology literature. Acta Pathol Jpn 1992, 42: 614–620.

109 Hyams VJ, Michaels L. Benign adenomatous neoplasm (adenoma) of the middle ear. Clin Otolaryngol 1976, 1: 17–26.

110 Ketabchi S, Massi D, Franchi A, Vannucchi P, Santucci M. Middle ear adenoma is an amphicrine tumor: why call it adenoma? Ultrastruct Pathol 2001, 25: 73–78.

111 Latif MA, Madders DJ, Barton RP, Shaw PA. Carcinoid tumour of the middle ear associated with systemic symptoms. J Laryngol Otol 1987, 101: 480–486.

112 McNutt MA, Bolen JW. Adenomatous tumor of the middle ear. An ultrastructural and immunocytochemical study. Am J Clin Pathol 1985, 84: 541–547.

113 Mills SE, Fechner RE. Middle ear adenoma. A cytologically uniform neoplasm displaying a variety of architectural patterns. Am J Surg Pathol 1984, 8: 677–685.

114 Murphy GF, Pilch BZ, Dickersin GR, Goodman ML, Nadol JB Jr. Carcinoid tumor of the middle ear. Am J Clin Pathol 1980, 73: 816–823.

115 Ribe A, Fernandez PL, Ostertarg H, Claros P, Bombi JA, Palacin A, Cardesa A. Middle ear adenoma (MES): report of two cases, one with predominant 'plasmacytoid' features. Histopathology 1997, 30: 359–364.

116 Riches WG, Johnston WH. Primary adenomatous neoplasms of the middle ear. Light and electron microscopic features of a group distinct from the ceruminomas. Am J Clin Pathol 1982, 77: 153–161.

117 Ruck P, Pfisterer EM, Kaiserling E. Carcinoid tumour of the middle ear. A morphological and immunohistochemical study with comments on histogenesis and differential diagnosis. Pathol Res Pract 1989, 185: 496–503.

118 Sakurai M, Mori N, Horiuchi O, Matsuura N, Kobayashi Y. Carcinoid tumor of the middle ear. An immunohistochemical and electron microscopic study. Report of a case. Acta Pathol Jpn 1988, 38: 1453–1460.

119 Stanley MW, Horwitz CA, Levinson RM, Sibley RK. Carcinoid tumors of the middle ear. Am J Clin Pathol 1987, 87: 592–600.

120 Wassef M, Kanavaros P, Polivka M, Nemeth J, Monteil JP, Frachet B, Tran Ba Huy P. Middle ear adenoma. A tumor displaying mucinous and neuroendocrine differentiation. Am J Surg Pathol 1989, 13: 838–847.

Adenocarcinoma

121 Fayemi AO, Toker C. Primary adenocarcinoma of the middle ear. Arch Otolaryngol 1975, 101: 449–452.

122 Gaffey MJ, Mills SE, Boyd JC. Aggressive papillary tumor of middle ear/temporal bone and adnexal papillary cystadenoma. Manifestations of von Hippel-Lindau disease. Am J Surg Pathol 1994, 18: 1254–1260.

123 Gaffey MJ, Mills SE, Fechner RE, Intemann SR, Wick MR. Aggressive papillary middle-ear tumor. A clinicopathologic entity distinct from middle-ear adenoma. Am J Surg Pathol 1988, 12: 790–797.

124 Glasscock ME III, McKennan KX, Levine SC, Jackson CG. Primary adenocarcinoma of the middle ear and temporal bone. Arch Otolaryngol Head Neck Surg 1987, 113: 822–824.

125 Hamazaki S, Yoshiba M, Yao M, Nagashima Y, Taguchi K, Nakashima H, Okada S. Mutation of von Hippel–Lindau tumor suppressor gene in a sporadic endolymphatic sac tumor. Hum Pathol 2001, 32: 1272–1276.

126 Heffner DK. Low-grade adenocarcinoma of probable endolymphatic sac origin A clinicopathologic study of 20 cases. Cancer 1989, 64: 2292–2302.

127 Kempermann G, Neumann HP, Volk B. Endolymphatic sac tumours. Histopathology 1998, 33: 2–10.

128 Mills SE, Gaffey MJ, Frierson HF. Tumors of the upper aerodigestive tract and ear. Atlas of tumor pathology, series 3, fascicle 26. Washington D.C., 2000, Armed Forces Institute of Pathology.

129 Pallanch JF, Weiland LH, McDonald TJ, Facer GW, Harner SG. Adenocarcinoma and adenoma of the middle ear. Laryngoscope 1982, 92: 47–54.

130 Schuller DE, Conley JJ, Goodman JH, Clausen KP, Miller WJ. Primary adenocarcinoma of the middle ear. Otolaryngol Head Neck Surg 1983, 91: 280–283.

131 Siedentop KH, Jeantet C. Primary adenocarcinoma of the middle ear. Report of three cases. Ann Otol Rhinol Laryngol 1961, 70: 719–733.

132 Stone HE, Lipa M, Bell RD. Primary adenocarcinoma of the middle ear. Arch Otolaryngol 1975, 101: 702–705.

133 Vortmeyer AO, Huang SC, Koch CA, Governale L, Dickerman RD, McKeever PE, Oldfield EH, Zhuang Z. Somatic von Hippel–Lindau gene mutations detected in sporadic endolymphatic sac tumors. Cancer Res 2000, 60: 5963–5965.

134 Wenig BM, Heffner DK. Endolymphatic sac tumors: Fact or fiction? Adv Anat Pathol 1996, 3: 378–387.

Squamous cell carcinoma

135 Barnes L, Johnson JT. Clinical and pathological considerations in the evaluation of major head and neck specimens resected for cancer. Part II. Pathol Annu 1986, 21(Pt 2): 83–110.

136 Jin YT, Tsai ST, Li C, Chang KC, Yan JJ, Chao WY, Eng HL, Chou TY, Wu TC, Su IJ. Prevalence of human papillomavirus in middle ear carcinoma associated with chronic otitis media. Am J Pathol 1997, 150: 1327–1333.

137 Kenyon GS, Marks PV, Scholtz CL, Dhillon R. Squamous cell carcinoma of the middle ear. A 25-year retrospective study. Ann Otol Rhinol Laryngol 1985, 94: 273–277.

138 Michaels L, Wells M. Squamous cell carcinoma of the middle ear. Clin Otolaryngol 1980, 5: 235–248.

139 Milford CA, Violaris N. Bilateral carcinoma of the middle ear. J Laryngol Otol 1987, 101: 711–713.

140 Morton RP, Stell PM, Derrick PP. Epidemiology of cancer of the middle ear cleft. Cancer 1984, 53: 1612–1617.

141 Woodson GE, Jurco S III, Alford BR, McGavran MH. Verrucous carcinoma of the middle ear. Arch Otolaryngol 1981, 107: 63–65.

Rhabdomyosarcoma

142 Angervall L, Dahl I, Ekedahl C. Embryonal rhabdomyosarcoma in the external ear. Acta Otolaryngol 1972, 73: 513–520.

143 Hawkins DS, Anderson JR, Paidas CN, Wharam MD, Qualman SJ, Pappo AS, Scott Baker K, Crist WM. Improved outcome for patients with middle ear rhabdomyosarcoma: a children's oncology group study. J Clin Oncol 2001, 19: 3073–3079.

144 Jaffe BF, Fox JE, Batsakis JG. Rhabdomyosarcoma of the middle ear and mastoid. Cancer 1971, 27: 29–37.

145 Raney RB Jr, Lawrence W Jr, Maurer HM, Lindberg RD, Newton WA Jr, Ragab AH, Tefft M, Foulkes MA. Rhabdomyosarcoma of the ear in childhood. A report from the Intergroup Rhabdomyosarcoma Study—I. Cancer 1983, 51: 2356–2361.

146 Tefft M, Fernandez C, Donaldson M, Newton W, Moon TE. Incidence of meningeal involvement by rhabdomyosarcoma of the head and neck in children. A report of the Intergroup Rhabdomyosarcoma Study (IRS). Cancer 1978, 42: 253–258.

Other primary tumors

147 Cremers CW. Osteoma of the middle ear. J Laryngol Otol 1985, **99:** 383–386.

148 Gourin CG, Sofferman RA. Dermoid of the eustachin tube. Otolaryngol Head Neck Surg 1999, **120:** 772–775.

149 Roncaroli F, Scheithauer BW, Pires MM, Rodrigues AS, Pereira JR. Mature teratoma of the middle ear. Otol Neurotol 2001, **22:** 76–78.

150 Shaida AM, McFerran DJ, da Cruz M, Hardy DG, Moffat DA. Cavernous haemangioma of the internal auditory canal. J Laryngol Otol 2000, **114:** 453–455.

151 Singh SP, Cottingham SL, Slone W, Boesel CP, Welling DB, Yates AJ. Lipomas of the internal auditory canal. Arch Pathol Lab Med 1996, **120:** 681–683.

152 Stanley RJ, Scheithauer BW, Thompson EI, Kispert DB, Weiland LH, Pearson BW. Endodermal sinus tumor (yolk sac tumor) of the ear. Arch Otolaryngol Head Neck Surg 1987, **112:** 200–203.

153 Stegehuis HR, Guy AM, Anderson KR. Middle-ear lipoma presenting as airways obstruction. Case report and review of literature. J Laryngol Otol 1985, **99:** 589–591.

154 Uchida M, Matsunami T. Malignant amelanotic melanoma of the middle ear. Arch Otolaryngol Head Neck Surg 2001, **127:** 1126–1128.

Metastatic tumors

155 Hill BA, Kohut RI. Metastatic adenocarcinoma of the temporal bone. Arch Otolaryngol 1976, **102:** 568–571.

156 Schuknecht HF, Allam AF, Murakami Y. Pathology of secondary malignant tumors of the temporal bone. Ann Otol Rhinol Laryngol 1968, **77:** 5–22.

Appendix A
ADASP position papers

The Association of Directors of Anatomic and Surgical Pathology (ADASP) was founded in 1989. The membership is made up largely of directors of anatomic and/or surgical pathology from academic institutions. Originally all members were from American institutions, but subsequently the membership was enlarged to include academic centers in Canada and selected institutions from overseas.

The purposes of the Association are (1) to promote expertise, effective administration and productive education in the practice of administering anatomic pathology laboratories; (2) to sponsor and promote the education of pathologists and others in health care related to administration of anatomic pathology and its branches; (3) to establish and maintain appropriate relationships with other societies and groups of physicians and other scientists who share professional interests with the Association.

The main activities of the Association consist of an annual meeting and the publication of position papers, editorials and recommendations regarding various aspects of the practice of anatomic pathology. Some of these documents are reproduced below.

Standardization of the surgical pathology report

(This document was prepared by an ad hoc committee of ADASP chaired by Richard L. Kempson, M.D. From Am J Surg Pathol 1992, **16**: 84–86.)

The Association of Directors of Anatomic and Surgical Pathology (ADASP) has concluded that a more standardized surgical pathology report may contribute positively to patient care. As the first step toward achieving this goal, ADASP has prepared the following recommendations and urges pathologists to consider adopting these for their own surgical pathology reports. The recommendations concern not only the format of the report but also provide suggestions for information to be included in the report. Widespread adoption of these recommendations should make information transfer from surgical pathology laboratories to clinicians more efficient and complete and also improve communication among surgical pathology laboratories when histologic sections are sent from one institution to another.

Demographic and specimen information

ADASP recommends the following:

1 Placing all demographic information in the top portion of the report.
2 Including in the demographic information the patient's name, location, gender, age and/or date of birth, and race, as well as the requesting physician's name, the attending physician's name (if different from the requesting physician), and the medical record or unit number.
3 Printing the name, address, telephone number, and FAX number of the laboratory at the top of the surgical pathology report.
4 Placing the surgical pathology number in the top portion of the report on every page, set off from other

information so that it can be easily and quickly identified.

5 Including a summary of the pertinent clinical history as part of every surgical pathology report.

6 Including a separate "specimens submitted" section in every report in which each separately identified tissue submitted for individual examination and diagnosis is clearly identified and listed as a separate specimen.

Gross description

ADASP recommends the following:

1 Including an adequate gross description as every surgical pathology report. Prerecorded gross descriptions are satisfactory, provided they include specific information about the particular specimen. Each separately identified tissue specimen submitted for individual examination and diagnosis should have its own gross description. Whether "part" or "all" of the specimen has been submitted for microscopic examination should always be recorded in the gross description.

2 Identifying each block with a unique number or letter. Giving multiple blocks the same identification number or letter is discouraged. A summary listing the sites from which each identified block is taken should be placed at the end of the gross description.

3 Augmenting the identification of block selections of complex specimens, when appropriate, by drawings, photographs, xerographs, etc.; but these pictorial records should *not* replace the printed block identification summary recommended in no. 2 above. Ideally, the pictorial record should accompany the chart copy, the physician copy, and the surgical pathology laboratory copy of the report.

4 Recording in the gross description the fact that margins are inked.

5 Recording the distribution of tissue for special studies in the gross description.

6 Including in the pathology report, when slides or blocks or tissues are received from another laboratory, the numbers of the slides and blocks, the referring hospital's identification numbers or letters, and the referring hospital's demographic data.

Microscopic description and comment section

For purposes of these recommendations, a microscopic description is defined as a description of the cytologic features and the architectural arrangement of the cells in a histologic section. A comment refers to all other pertinent information.

ADASP recommends the following:

1 Recording microscopic features whenever the responsible pathologist deems it appropriate, but a microscopic description need not be a part of every report.

2 Placing comments into the report whenever the responsible pathologist considers they are indicated, but a comment need not be written for every case.

3 Making it optional to place microscopic descriptions and comments in separate sections or to combine them.

4 Designating that "special" stains have been performed, listing each stain and the results of the staining in the microscopic or comment section.

5 Listing, when immunohistochemical stains have been performed, each antibody tested and the results of the staining in the microscopic or comment section of the surgical pathology report in a separate immunohistochemical report, or both.

6 Grading all tumors for which grading has been shown to be a significant prognostic variable. When a grade is given, the grading criteria or scheme should be recorded in a comment or in the diagnosis line unless the grading scheme is standard and well understood by all clinicians.

7 Using a "checklist" approach for recording information needed for patient treatment and prognosis. A statement relating whether each item on the checklist is positive or negative should be made. The checklist is used to ensure that all pertinent information has been included in the pathology report. Such information includes but is not limited to grade, depth of invasion, presence or absence of vascular invasion, size of the tumor, type of tumor, etc., and it is often different for different types of resection specimens. The condition of resection margins should be recorded here if clinically indicated. These checklists may be in manuals, on separate sheets, in computers, etc. It is also recommended that there be routine periodic checks of pathology reports to ensure that this information is present and summarized in an easy to find area of the comment or in the diagnosis section.

8 All information needed to formulate the pathologic state of a cancer be present in the report, but this information need not be recorded by a number or letter per se. If a stage number or letter is recorded, then the system used should be specified.

Intraoperative consultation

ADASP recommends that the intraoperative consultation report be incorporated verbatim into the final report. The persons responsible for the intraoperative report should be identified. If there is a discrepancy between the intraoperative diagnosis and the final diagnosis, this discrepancy should be recorded and discussed in a comment.

Final diagnosis

ADASP recommends the following:

1 Specifying the organ, site, and procedure as well as the

diagnosis in the diagnosis section. These can be set off from the diagnosis by a dash or a colon.

2 Standardizing the format of diagnoses within each pathology department.

3 Setting off anatomic diagnoses so that they can be quickly and easily identified.

4 Listing each separately identified tissue submitted for individual examination and diagnosis in the diagnosis section along with the anatomic diagnosis for that specimen.

General considerations

ADASP recommends the following:

1 Clearly separating and identifying specimen(s) submitted, clinical information, clinical diagnosis, intraoperative diagnosis, gross description, microscopic description, comments (when they are not combined with the microscopic description), and anatomic diagnoses in such a way as to be found readily and easily in the report. Printing should be of sufficient quality to be read easily.

2 Doing a search for prior histologic and cytologic accession numbers for each case and recording pertinent prior specimen numbers in the current surgical pathology report.

3 Incorporating the results of special studies such as electron microscopy, immunohistochemistry, flow cytometry, receptor status, data, etc., into the surgical pathology report whenever possible. If this information is not a part of the surgical pathology report, the fact that tissue has been sent for the study should be recorded in the surgical pathology report.

4 Recording in the pathology report any information regarding procedures other than routine handling of tissue, such as gross photography, decalcification, specimen x-ray, freezing of samples, and placing specimens in a tissue bank.

5 Documenting intradepartmental consultations in the surgical pathology report, either by identifying the consultant in the comment section or at the end of the surgical pathology report or by having the consultant cosign the report.

6 Noting when external consultation is initiated by the pathologist in the pathology report. When the consultant's report is received, a supplemental report containing the consultant's interpretation and opinions should be issued.

7 Conveying to clinicians any clinically significant unexpected findings and documenting immediately in the surgical pathology report the fact that a call was made.

8 Citing references in the surgical pathology report when pertinent.

9 It is acceptable for the responsible pathologist to make suggestions for additional studies or procedures in the surgical pathology report if the pathologist thinks they will contribute to the case. Such information can be incorporated in the surgical pathology report as long as it is emphasized that they are only suggestions.

10 Note clearly and prominently when an amended report is issued. Changes that have been made in the report should be specified if the new report is a complete one; if only changes are recorded in the amended report, that fact should be specified.

11 Including the date the specimen was received and the date of the final report in all surgical pathology reports.

Incorporation of immunostaining data in anatomic pathology reports

(This document was prepared by an ad hoc committee of ADASP chaired by Peter M. Banks, M.D. From Am J Surg Pathol 1992, **16**: 808.)

The Council of ADASP has reviewed issues in the application of immunostains to diagnostic anatomic pathology. In selected cases this means adding the specificity of immune mechanisms to visual microscopic appearances has become an essential adjunctive method for accurate diagnosis. It has also become evident that no immunologically defined marker is entirely specific for a disease entity. Rather, immunologically defined cellular constituents provide a dimension of resolution regarding cellular differentiation that is additive to that deriving from morphologic observations. As is the case with other ancillary methods, such as special histochemical stains or electron microscopy, immunostaining results must be integrated into a diverse mixture of data, including clinical information, gross and conventional microscopic pathologic findings and, in some cases, other types of ancillary study. It is the responsibility of the pathologist to select appropriate immunostain reagents and to render an informed interpretation of the results of these studies, based on the supplier's description of the reagents' activities, on personal experience, and on reported observations and cumulative experience in the professional literature.

For the purposes of the clarity and exchange of information among pathology laboratories and physicians, the following recommendations are offered for reporting immunostain results.

1 Immunostaining results should always be reported, regardless of perceived significance. Ideally such information should be included in the original main report (surgical, cytology, or autopsy); however, because of time constraints, it may be necessary to report immunostaining separately. When the latter

method of reporting is used, it is essential that the initial report state that such studies are pending, and likewise, it is essential that the separate report refer to or even include the original report.

2 A differential diagnosis justifying immunostaining methods should be provided in the report. Reference to differential diagnosis may be very brief or general, for example, "anaplastic large-cell neoplasm of uncertain differentiation" or "epithelial versus lymphoid nature."

3 In the report, or portion of the report, dealing with immunostains the following should be included:

a The nature of the studied sample—paraffin sections, frozen sections, aspiration biopsy smears, cellular imprints, cytocentrifuge preparations, etc.

b The immunoreagents used. These should be specifically described—"HMB-45" rather than simply "melanoma-related antigen." It may be desirable with less commonly encountered reagents to provide a generic designation as well as the specific designation—muscles-specific actin ("HHF-35").

c Results of the staining for each antibody should be reported in detail sufficient to justify the interpretation—in some cases simply *positive* or *negative*, but in others, cellular patterns of staining or localization of some stain reactivity to certain cellular compartments.

4 Detailed technical information regarding the immunostaining procedures, including fixation, enhancing methods such as enzyme predigestion, and so on, need not be included in the diagnostic report but should be available in permanent laboratory records.

Consultations in surgical pathology

(This document was prepared by an ad hoc committee of ADASP chaired by Stephen G. Silverberg, M.D. From Am J Surg Path 1993, **17**: 743–745.)

Consultations are easier to obtain in pathology than in most other medical specialties because of the ability to cut duplicate histologic slides and forward them to any destination. Although this process has been taking place—usually with satisfactory results—for decades, there are numerous steps in the consultation process at which problems can and frequently do arise. Accordingly, ADASP has developed recommendations for consultations in anatomic pathology. Consultations may be generated for many reasons, including (but no limited to) the following:

1 Uncertainty of the referring pathologist about the diagnosis.

2 An internal disagreement between two or more pathologists in a group about the diagnosis.

3 The patient's request for a second opinion.

4 A clinician's request for a second opinion.

5 Quality assurance documentation.

6 Transfer of the patient to a different hospital or clinic, with a need for diagnosis by a pathologist at the new institution.

This section of the appendix consists of two parts: The first considers *personal consultations*, defined as consultations sent to a specific pathologist, usually for one of the first four reasons listed above. The second part deals with *institutional consultations*, in which the sixth reason is generally operative. Specifically excluded are consultations for legal purposes. ADASP recommends that the reason for the consultation be specified in the accompanying letter to the consultant.

Personal consultations

The ideal pathologic consultation proceeds from one pathologist to another; however, consultant pathologists also receive cases for consultation from clinicians, patients, patients' families, and others. ADASP makes the following recommendations:

1 The pathologist whose opinion is being solicited has the right to refuse to accept a case for consultation, if he or she believes that the interests of the patient will not be served by its acceptance.

2 The consultant who accepts a case and renders an opinion should always transmit the report to the pathologist in whose laboratory the initial diagnosis was made.

The pathologist sending a case for consultation has certain responsibilities to the consultant, and ultimately to the patient. ADASP makes the following recommendations:

1 An accompanying letter should provide the reason for the consultation, specific questions to be answered, the referring pathologist's working diagnosis or differential diagnosis, and appropriate billing information.

2 A copy of the surgical pathology report (or as much of it as has been completed) should accompany the letter and the slides; this should include pertinent demographic and clinical data and a gross description, as well as identification of the exact site of origin of each slide submitted.

3 Adequate material to solve the diagnostic problem should be submitted; in some instances, this material may consist of a single hematoxylin and eosin-stained slide, whereas in others all material available in the case—including special stains, electron micrographs, flow cytometric data, x-ray films, paraffin blocks, frozen or fixed tissue, or other special material or information—may be required. If it is anticipated that immunohistochemical stains or other additional

procedures will be needed, the pertinent blocks or appropriately prepared unstained slides should be sent. Previous pathology specimens and reports from the same patient, if pertinent, should be included. If the referring pathologist has a question about a particular area on one or more slides, this question should be clearly indicated in the consultation letter and marked on the slide. The decision as to what to send should be made initially by the referring pathologist, but the consultant may request more material before making a diagnosis.

The referring pathologist should personally assure that the material sent to the consultant is adequate to demonstrate the lesion in question and that this material is packaged to avoid breakage (Rosen PP, Am J Clin Pathol 1989, **91**: 348–354). In particular, recut slides should be inspected to ensure that they are representative. If paraffin blocks and glass slides are sent in the same container, a duplicate set of slides should be retained by the referring pathologist.

4 The referring pathologist may state the time frame in which a diagnosis is requested and in this situation attempt to determine that this schedule can be met. This may require telephoning in advance to ensure that the consultant is available, sending the consultation by an express delivery service, providing a telephone or fax number for rapid transmission of the consultant's report, and providing names and contact numbers for other physicians familiar with the case, should the referring pathologist not be available.

5 If the case is sent to more than one consultant, each should be informed of that fact, as well as of the other consultants' diagnoses.

6 If original material must be sent because no duplicates are available (for example, in the case of paraffin blocks or cytologic material), their return should be requested in the consultation letter. Whenever recut slides will suffice, they should be used and the consultant allowed to retain the slides.

7 The opinion of the consultant should be made part of the referring pathologist's report. The referring pathologist has the responsibility of making the final diagnosis and may agree or disagree with the consultant.

The consultant pathologist also has responsibilities to fulfill to optimize the consultation process. ADASP recommends the following:

1 If a case is accepted for consultation, a written report providing a diagnostic impression should be issued to identify the exact source of all material reviewed. This policy ultimately protects everyone involved in the process, including the patient.

2 Reports should be issued as expeditiously as possible. If the consultant cannot provide at least a preliminary opinion within 1 week of receipt, arrangements should be made to notify the referring pathologist.

3 When the consultant pathologist's diagnosis may alter immediate patient management, this fact should be communicated to the referring pathologist in a timely fashion.

4 If the consultant cannot make a diagnosis on the basis of the material submitted, he or she may either issue a provisional report on the basis of what is available, with suggestions for further studies to be performed by the referring pathologist, or request more or better material to perform the additional studies in the consultant's laboratory. Such a request is best made by telephone. Occasionally, the consultant may recommend a second consultant who might be more appropriate or, with permission of the referring pathologist, send the case directly to the second consultant.

5 If doing additional studies in the consultant's laboratory would generate additional charges, these charges should be authorized by the referring pathologist before the studies are undertaken.

6 Although the consultant may be asked to make recommendations for therapy and may choose to do so, it should be understood by all concerned that therapeutic recommendations made on the basis of a brief clinical summary and pathologic material alone may not always be applicable to the clinical situation.

7 The consultant should return to its source material that cannot be duplicated (e.g. paraffin blocks, cytologic slides, histologic slides showing lesions that do not persist on other cuts, original x-ray films) and otherwise should be allowed to retain and file all consultation material. The retained slides, whether placed in an institutional or a personal file, should be clearly identified and kept available for subsequent review, as should all written records related to the consultation.

8 It should be assumed that a case sent to a consultant may be published as part of a series by the consultant and that the referring pathologist can be acknowledged if permitted by the journal in which the report is published. We further recommend that publication of individual case reports by a consultant should be undertaken only with the express approval of the referring pathologist. In either of these situations, the referring pathologist may be asked by the consultant or a collaborator to contribute additional information, including follow-up, on the contributed case.

Institutional consultations

Many pathologic consultations are transmitted from one laboratory or hospital to another because the patient has been transferred to, or is seeking a second clinical opinion at, a second institution. In most such cases, the clinical consultant or the second institution (or both) will request that pertinent pathology reports and slides be reviewed by the local pathologist. Indeed, ADASP

potentially embarrassing, may violate privacy rights, and requires renewed specific patient consent for its use and/or transferral.

Third, who should have access to the information contained in the genetic material in these blocks? Who should have access to family data? The National Institutes of Health is currently evaluating these questions. Obviously, this situation will have to be looked at again as new legal challenges are brought and decisions rendered. Until these issues are resolved, we believe it is prudent for institutions to not release blocks for repository use.

A final issue arises: What happens when the repository is no longer funded, as funding for collaborative studies may be reduced or eliminated. Once there is not funding, how will the blocks be returned to the original institution—or will they? Will they just be lost, never to be retrieved? The legal implications of this have not been addressed. Until the many questions reviewed here are resolved, it appears inappropriate to demand that tissue blocks be stored in a repository.

Advances in computer technology will allow for an electronic repository—rather than a physical one—so that the location of specific blocks can be known. When and if specific research protocols are designed to use the tissue, unstained sections from the paraffin block for each case could be provided by the pathology department of origin (these could be provided as sections on slides or free in small tubes). The block would be maintained by the original department of pathology. With advances in polymerase chain reaction (PCR) technology, DNA and even RNA could be recovered for studies from the slides. Experienced molecular biologists have used archival material in this manner. The availability of this type of material from pathology departments should not pose a problem and certainly would conform to the legal requirements for maintaining the blocks at the institution of origin. However, the budget of the study should include funds to cover the cost of providing this material.

This position statement is not intended to oppose, and should not be interpreted as indicating that we oppose, the borrowing of blocks on a specific case as needed for an individual patient's care. An alternative of sending unstained sections, is also appropriate as long as it does not completely deplete the diagnostic material. We believe that, with respect to individual patient care issues, the questions reviewed here need to be examined more fully by regulatory agencies and interested medical organizations.

Quality control and quality assurance in anatomic pathology

(This document was prepared by the ad hoc Committee of ADASP chaired by Juan Rosai, M.D. From Am J Surg Pathol 1991, **15**: 1007–1009.)

ADASP has prepared the following recommendations regarding Quality Control and Quality Assurance (QC/QA) in surgical pathology and autopsy pathology. This document does not include QC/QA issues as they apply to cytopathology and to specialized anatomic pathology laboratories such as immunohistochemistry or electron microscopy.

ADASP wishes to emphasize that the recommendations contained in this document were made taking into consideration the structure, responsibilities, and needs of academic anatomic pathology laboratories that have an active pathology residency or fellowship program. It also wishes to point out that they are to be viewed as being of a generic nature and suitable for modification depending on the specific circumstances of the individual laboratories and the respective institutions.

I   It is recommended that each Department of Pathology prepare a written QC/QA plan for surgical pathology and autopsy pathology specifically devised for that Department and the respective institution. This document should be updated on a yearly basis. It should be part of the Departmental QC/QA program and, as such, should be structured along the lines of the JCAHO ten-step monitoring process as detailed in *The Accreditation Manual for Hospitals*.

II It is recommended that each Department establish a QC/QA Committee. The Committee should be appointed by the Chairman on a yearly basis. It should meet monthly, be chaired by a senior pathologist, and have as members representatives from the principal sections or divisions of the Department.

III It is recommended that the QC/QA plan for surgical pathology and autopsy pathology include the components ("indicators") listed below. The first of these indicators is of a prospective nature—i.e. to be carried out before the final report is issued. All others are of a retrospective nature—i.e. to be carried out in a regular fashion independently from the timing of the final report and usually after this has taken place.

Intradepartmental consultation

This function is to be carried out through one or both of the following mechanisms:

1 Review of selected cases by the diagnostic staff as a group, either through a periodic session ("consensus conference") or a written consultation form. The fact that this exercise has taken place should be indicated in the pathology report.

2 Review of selected cases by a second staff pathologist ("consultant"). For those cases in which the entire case is evaluated by the consultant, it is recommended that both pathologists sign the report; for cases in which only a portion of the cases has been reviewed, it is recommended that a note to that effect be added to the report.

Intraoperative consultation

It is recommended that all cases in which an intraoperative consultation has been carried out be reviewed on a regular (i.e. weekly) basis and be placed according to their final disposition in one of the following categories:

1 Agreement
2 Deferral—Appropriate
3 Deferral—Inappropriate
4 Disagreement—Minor
5 Disagreement—Major

For all cases in the "Disagreement—Major" and "Deferral—Inappropriate" categories, it is recommended that the reason for this occurrence be categorized as one of the following:

1 Interpretation
2 Block sampling
3 Specimen sampling
4 Technical inadequacy
5 Lack of essential clinical or pathologic data
6 Other (indicate)

It is further recommended that the medical consequences of the cases included in the "Disagreement—Major" or "Deferral—Inappropriate" categories be listed as one of the following:

1 None
2 Minor/questionable
3 Major

ADASP estimates that an acceptable accuracy threshold for intraoperative consultations (as measured by the number of "Disagreement—Major" cases and determined per case) is 3%; an acceptable threshold for "Deferred—Inappropriate" cases is 10%.

ADASP believes that it is important for each laboratory to establish its own time thresholds for intraoperative consultation, using as a standard unit the time threshold for the performance of a "basic" frozen section, as defined by a case with a single block, with no other cases being performed by the intraoperative consultation team at the same time.

Random case review

It is recommended that the following cases be reviewed on a random basis:

1 Surgical pathology: 1% or 25/month, whichever is larger.
2 Autopsy: 10% or two/month, whichever is larger.

The review on the randomly selected cases should include all material related to them, including final report, microscopic slides, turnaround time, and special procedures, if any.

Clinical indicators

It is recommended that a Clinical Indicator be selected on a regular basis on the basis of organ/lesion (i.e. carcinoma of endometrium) or procedure (i.e. TUR), and that *all* cases belonging to that indicator in a given period be evaluated by checking them against a list of predetermined criteria. This activity should be rotated among surgical pathology and autopsy cases.

Intradepartmental and interdepartmental conferences

For all cases presented at intradepartmental and interdepartmental conferences, it is recommended that the diagnosis as listed in the final report be compared with that made by the presenter when reviewing the case for the conference.

Interinstitutional review

For cases in which an outside review has been carried out at the request of the patient, the clinician or other institution, or as part of a cooperative study, it is recommended that the diagnosis as listed in the final report be compared with that made at the outside institution. The Association estimates that an acceptable threshold for clinically significant disagreement following arbitration is 2%, as applied to those cases in which it is decided that the correct interpretation is that from the outside institution.

Surgical pathology turnaround times

ADASP believes that the following are acceptable turnaround times for surgical pathology reports, as measured in working days from the time the specimen is accessioned in the laboratory to the time the verbal report is available or the final report is signed.

Type of specimen	Verbal report	Written report
Rushes	1	2
Biopsies	2	3
Surgicals	2	3

Extra time should be allowed for the following procedures, to be measured in days from the time the procedure is initiated or ordered and independently from each other:

1 Overnight fixation, 1
2 Decalcification, 1
3 Resubmission, 1–2
4 Recuts, 1
5 Immunocytochemistry, 1–2
6 Electron microscopy, 2–3
7 Intradepartmental consultation, 1

ADASP estimates that an acceptable threshold for these turnaround times is 80%.

Autopsy turnaround time

ADASP believes that the following are acceptable turnaround times for autopsy reports, as measured in working days:

1 Provisional report: 1
2 Final report: 30

ADASP estimates that an acceptable threshold for the provisional report is 90%; acceptable threshold for the final report is 80%.

Specimen adequacy

It is recommended that the adequacy of submission of specimens to the laboratory be monitored in terms of fixation, safety requirements, and proper identification.

Lost specimen

This is defined as the irretrievable loss of a surgical pathology specimen that has occurred after the case has been accessioned in the laboratory and that prevents an adequate pathologic examination of that specimen. ADASP estimates that an acceptable threshold for lost specimens is one in 3000 cases.

Histology QC

It is recommended that the QC related to the histology lab include:

1 Record of time of delivery of slides.
2 Evaluation of slide quality as performed by the pathologist.
3 Evaluation of tissue adequacy as performed by the histotechnologist.

Isolated event report

It is recommended that isolated events not contemplated in any of the foregoing categories be documented through the issuing of an "Isolated Event Report." All such reports should be kept in a permanent log.

Appendix B
Quality control and quality assurance in surgical pathology

The main goals of an Anatomic Pathology Departmental Quality Control/Quality Assurance (QC/QA) program are to ensure (1) accuracy, (2) completeness, and (3) timeliness of all the reports generated by the Division of Anatomic Pathology. These goals are achieved by the continuous monitoring of the following indicators:

Prospective:

1 Intradepartmental consultation (IDC)

Retrospective:

2 Frozen section review (FSR)
3 SP cases random review (SPRR)
4 Autopsy cases random review (ARR)
5 AP clinical indicators (CI)
6 Intradepartmental and interdepartmental conferences (CONF)
7 Interinstitutional review (IIR)
8 Specimen adequacy record (SAR)
9 Lost specimen record (LSR)
10 Single event report (SER)
11 Histology slides delivery (SD)
12 Quality control to histology (TO-H)
13 Quality control from histology (FROM-H)
14 AP turnaround times (TAT)

This activity is usually carried out by a Department Committee appointed by the Chairman, which ideally should have at least one representative from outside the Department. The Chairman of this Committee usually functions as the departmental representative to the institutional Quality Control and Quality Assurance Committee (or whatever synonym may be used for the activity at the time).

National pathology organizations such as the College of American Pathologists have published quality assurance and quality improvement manuals to assist pathologists in setting up individualized programs in their own departments.[1]

What follows is a description of the QC/QA program as it was set up in the Department of Pathology at Yale University some years ago. The elaborated printed forms that were developed on the occasion have been replaced there and elsewhere by electronic versions, but the basic procedures remain the same. This version is offered as a guideline, with the understanding that its application in other laboratories may require some modifications depending on the number of type of specimens, size of staff, and whether there is a residency and/or fellowship program or not. The program as presented here does not include cytopathology or special laboratories, such as immunohistochemistry or electron microscopy.

The meetings of the QC/QA committee are divided in two sessions: (1) one primarily concerned with QC issues, in which all committee members participate, (2) one primarily concerned with QA issues, in which only the attendings participate.

The collection and some of the analysis of the data, organization of the monthly meetings, and all correspondence related to the QC/QA committee are carried out by a QC/QA manager working under the supervision of the Committee Chairman and having secretarial assistance.

1   Nakhleh RE, Fitzgibbons PL: Quality improvement manual in anatomic pathology, 2nd Ed., Northfield, IL, College of American Pathologists, 2002.

Intradepartmental consultation (IDC)

Purpose

To provide a prospective system by which all difficult, controversial, and otherwise problematic cases can be presented by any attending for review and discussion before they are signed out.

Frequency

This collegial session is held daily using a multiheaded microscope. The collegial session is run by the director of anatomic or surgical pathology. The other participants are the anatomic pathology attendings, particularly those on service rotations. Residents, students, and visitors do not participate.

Procedure

1   The date of the conference and the names of all the attendings present should be recorded.
2   The attendings participating at the conference present for discussion cases of their choice. These cases may be selected on the basis of any of the following criteria:

   a   Diagnostic difficulty
   b   Controversy in interpretation among attendings and/or residents
   c   Discrepancy between frozen section diagnosis and intended final diagnosis
   d   Discrepancy between provisional diagnosis and intended final diagnosis
   e   Management purposes, such as performance of additional biopsies, special studies, or therapeutic recommendations
   f   Request on the part of the clinician or patient
   g   Interesting or unusual nature of the case.

3   The material presented should include all pertinent microscopic slides, a summary of the clinical data, and when indicated, gross specimens or gross photographs, x-rays, and electron micrographs.
4   The individual presenting the case should state their diagnostic impression and reason for presentation.
5   The case is examined simultaneously by all participants, the director of anatomic or surgical pathology leading the discussion.
6   Upon completion of the presentation and discussion of each case, the director of anatomic or surgical pathology will enter in the corresponding form the following information:

   a   Pathology number
   b   Name of presenter

   c   Diagnostic impression of presenter and reason for presentation
   d   Consensus reached.

7   If indicated, the nature of the discussion having taken place and the recommendations made.
8   All cases presented at these conferences should be so identified by entering "Case presented at the Departmental Collegial Session of ____(date)." in the final report, immediately following the diagnosis.

Frozen section review (FSR)

Purpose

To monitor the adequacy in the performance of intra-operative consultations ("frozen sections") in surgical pathology in terms of diagnostic accuracy, timing of the procedure, and consequences of the diagnosis rendered.

Frequency

Weekly.

Procedure

1   The copy of the frozen section forms filed in surgical pathology or available through the AP information system should include the following information: time at which the specimen was received, time at which the frozen section diagnosis was given, frozen section diagnosis, and final diagnosis.
2   The QC/QA manager should collect the above information weekly and evaluate it with regard to time employed to perform the procedure and concordance between frozen section and final diagnosis. In cases in which a discordance exits (including deferred cases), the following information should be entered:

   a   Pathology number
   b   Frozen section diagnosis
   c   Initials of resident(s) and attending(s) who performed the frozen section
   d   Final diagnosis, including initials of attending
   e   Final disposition, according to the following categories:
       1   Agreement
       2   Deferment—Appropriate
       3   Deferment—Inappropriate
       4   Disagreement—Minor
       5   Disagreement—Major
   f   For categories 3 to 5, explanation for the lack of agreement according to the following categories:
       1   Interpretation
       2   Block sampling
       3   Tissue sampling
       4   Technical inadequacy
       5   Lack of important clinical or previous pathologic information

g For categories 3 to 5, consequences to the patient according to the following categories:

1 None
2 Minor/questionable
3 Major

h Notes, if indicated
i Action taken

Steps **e** through **i** of this procedure should be completed by the QC/QA committee chairman. When indicated, the FS and permanent slides should be reviewed. In addition, the QC/QA manager should record the above information in a separate form, divided according to the attending who performed the procedure.

Review

1 All FS forms from the preceding month should be presented and discussed at the monthly QC/QA meeting.
2 A formal review of the FS forms should be carried out by the QC/QA committee chairman on a quarterly basis, according to the general review procedure. The results of the review are to be presented at the monthly QC/QA meeting.

SP cases random review (SPRR)

Purpose

To monitor on a random basis the adequacy of the surgical pathology report in all of its aspects.

Frequency

Weekly.

Procedure

1 The QC/QA manager should collect on a random basis one of every 50 surgical pathology cases for the purposes of this review. The material collected should consist of:

a Copy of requisition form
b Copy of final surgical pathology report
c All microscopic slides
d All material from special studies (immunohistochemistry, electron microscopy, etc.), if any
e All gross photographs and specimen x-rays, if any

2 This material will be given to the QC/QA committee chairman, who will evaluate it for the following criteria:

a Clinical history
b Gross description
c Gross photographs, if any
d Sampling for histology
e Quality of slides
f Diagnosis

g Note, if any
h SNOMED (topography and morphology) coding
i Special studies, if any
j Turnaround time
k Other

If indicated, assistance for the evaluation should be requested from other members of the pathology department or from outside consultants. Cases in which an important deficiency is detected, especially regarded the diagnosis, should be immediately brought to the attention of the director of anatomic pathology.

Review

1 All SP forms in which deficiencies have been entered should be presented and discussed at the monthly QC/QA meeting.
2 A formal review of the SP forms should be carried out by the QC/QA chairman quarterly, according to the general review procedure. The results of the review are to be presented at the monthly QC/QA meeting.

Autopsy cases random review (ARR)

Purpose

To monitor on a random basis the adequacy of the autopsy report in all of its aspects.

Frequency

Monthly.

Procedure

1 The QC/QA manager should collect on a random basis one of every 10 autopsy pathology cases for the purposes of this review. The material collected should consist of:

a Copy of autopsy requisition
b Copy of final complete autopsy report
c All microscopic slides
d All material from special studies (immunohistochemistry, electron microscopy, etc.), if any
e All gross photographs and specimen x-rays, if any

2 This material will be given to the QC/QA committee chairman, who will evaluate it for the following criteria:

a Patient identification and history
b Gross description
c Gross photographs, if any
d Sampling for histology
e Quality of slides
f Diagnosis
g Clinicopathologic correlation and bibliography
h SNOMED (topography and morphology) coding

i Special studies, if any
j Turnaround time
k Other

If indicated, assistance for the evaluation should be requested from other members of the pathology department or from outside consultants. Cases in which an important deficiency is detected, especially regarding the diagnosis, should be immediately brought to the attention of the director of anatomic pathology.

Review

1 All AUT forms in which deficiencies have been entered should be presented and discussed at the monthly QC/QA meeting.
2 A formal review of the AUT forms should be carried out by the QC/QA chairman on a quarterly basis, according to the general QC/QA review procedure. The results of the review are to be presented at the monthly QC/QA meeting.

AP clinical indicators (CI)

Purpose

To monitor the completeness and consistency of the information provided in the pathology report for specific specimens or diseases, and to correct any deficiencies encountered.

Frequency

Monthly.

Procedure

1 The QC/QA committee chairman should identify, on a monthly basis, a specimen or disease to be evaluated. The selection can be made on the basis of tissue received regardless of the pathology present in it (e.g. transurethral prostatectomy) or on the basis of a specific disease entity (e.g. carcinoma of large bowel). It should include, on a rotational basis, cases from surgical pathology and autopsy pathology.
2 The QC/QA manager should retrieve all consecutive reports from cases corresponding to the selected specimen/disease that had been accessioned for a predetermined period, which may vary from 2 to 12 months depending on the frequency of the selected item.
3 The reports should be given to the attending designated by the QC/QA committee chairman for this purpose, who will review them for completeness, accuracy, and consistency by cross-checking them with a predetermined list of required items. The results of the review should be tabulated, and the information obtained should be submitted to the QC/QA manager.

Review

1 The results of the review should be presented at the monthly QC/QA meeting.
2 If significant deficiencies are encountered in the review, a follow-up study should be carried out in 3 to 12 months depending on the nature of the material.

Intradepartmental and interdepartmental conferences (CONF)

Purpose

To monitor the degree of agreement between the final diagnosis as expressed in the pathology report (surgical, cytology, or autopsy) and the consensus reached at the intradepartmental or interdepartmental conference(s) in which the case is presented.

Frequency

Monthly.

Procedure

Attendings who present and/or discuss anatomic pathology cases at intradepartmental or interdepartmental conferences should review the diagnostic material on those cases and compare their diagnostic impressions and the consensus reached at the conference with the diagnosis as stated in the official report. This information should be entered in the CONF form. In any case in which a discrepancy exists, the nature and importance of the problem should be stated, and the case should be discussed with the attending who signed the pathology report.

Review

1 All CONF forms should be presented and reviewed at the monthly QC/QA meeting.
2 A formal review of the CONF forms should be carried out by the QC/QA chairman quarterly, according to the general review procedure. The results of the review are to be presented at the monthly QC/QA meeting.

Interinstitutional review (IIR)

Purpose

To monitor the degree of diagnostic agreement rate among cases that have been sent to other institutions for one of the following reasons:

1 At the clinician's or patient's request.
2 At the request of another institution in which the patient is being seen.
3 Because the case has been entered in a cooperative study

If a significant discrepancy between the two diagnoses exits, the director of anatomic or surgical pathology should resolve it by subjecting the case to inside or outside arbitration and submit an addendum report with the final resolution.

Procedure

The QC/QA manager should collect and record the diagnoses made at other institutions and compare those diagnoses with those made on the same cases at our institution. All the cases in which a major discrepancy exits should be recorded, including the arbitration outcome.

Review

1 All IIR from the preceding period should be presented at the monthly QC/QA meeting.
2 A formal review of the IIR forms should be carried out by the QC/QA committee chairman bi-annually, according to the general review procedure. The results of the review should be presented at the monthly QC/QA meeting.

Specimen adequacy record (SAR)

Purpose

To monitor the adequacy of submission of specimens to the pathology laboratory in terms of fixation, safety requirements, and proper identification and to correct any deficiencies encountered.

Frequency

Daily.

Procedure

1 The SP accessioner should examine all material received in the laboratory for the deficiencies listed below and record them in the SAR form if present:

   a Specimen not bagged or bagged inadequately
   b Requisition placed inside bag
   c Staples in bag
   d Lid not sealed properly and/or fluid spill contamination
   e Inadequate amount of fixative fluid
   f No clinical history
   g Requisition form missing
   h No physician name
   i No physician signature
   j No specimen
   k Discordant information between requisition form and container
   l Radioactivity detected in specimen

If deficiencies **g** to **l** were encountered, the specimen should not be accessioned. A pathologist or pathologist assistant should be contacted to resolve the matter.

2 The QC/QA manager should review the SAR form weekly and contact the appropriate services, for correction of the problem whenever indicated.

Review

1 The completed SAR forms should be filed in the SP office.
2 The QC/QA manager should review the SAR forms quarterly, tabulate the findings according to type of problem and service, and present the results at the monthly QC/QA meeting.

Lost specimen record (LSR)

Purpose

To document all incidents in which a specimen is lost, destroyed, misidentified, or otherwise mishandled so as to make impossible its pathologic interpretation, to determine their cause, and to prevent their further occurrence.

Frequency

Monthly.

Procedure

All "lost specimen" incidents should be recorded in the LSR form, which should be sent to the QC/QA files.

Review

The review of the LSR forms should be carried out by the QC/QA chairman monthly, according to the general review procedure. The results of the review are to be presented at the monthly QC/QA meeting.

Single event report (SER)

Purpose

1 To document the occurrence of single events that could reflect on the delivery of care by the division of anatomic pathology and that are brought to the attention of the QC/QA chairman through a notification by any member of the medical or technical hospital staff, either within or outside the department.
2 To evaluate the event, and to take a corrective measure if indicated.

Frequency

Monthly.

Review

The review of the SER form should be carried out monthly, and the results of the review should be presented at the monthly QC/QA meeting.

Histology slides delivery (SD)

Purpose

To monitor the time of delivery of microscopic slides by the histology laboratory to surgical pathology, and to correct any deficiencies encountered.

Frequency

Daily.

Procedure

1 A pathology attending or resident should record the time at which the microscopic slides from biopsies and surgical cases are delivered from the histology laboratory. If there is more than one delivery of any of the categories, each should be recorded. Comments regarding any departures from the norm should be made, such as explanations for undue delays.

2 At the end of each month, the completed form should be given to the QC/QA manager, who will send copies to the director of anatomic or surgical pathology and to the histology manager. The original should be kept in the QC/QA files.

Review

1 All SD forms from the preceding month should be presented and discussed at a monthly meeting held between the supervisor of the histology laboratory and the director of anatomic or surgical pathology. Minutes from this meeting should be sent to the QC/QA manager.

2 A formal review of the SD forms should be carried out by the QC/QA committee chairman on a monthly basis, according to the general review procedure. The results of the review are to be presented at the monthly QC/QA meeting.

Quality control to histology (TO-H)

Purpose

To monitor the quality of microscopic slides produced by the histology laboratory for surgical pathology and autopsy pathology, and to correct any deficiencies encountered.

Frequency

Daily.

Procedure

1 Attendings signing out surgical and autopsy pathology material should fill out one TO-H form per diagnostic session regardless of the number of cases examined. The form should be completed even if the technical quality of all the material examined is deemed to be satisfactory. In the cases thought to be of inadequate quality, the following information should be entered: pathology number, block identification, and type of problem. An attempt should be made to be as specific as possible about the nature of technical deficiency and the time of the preliminary slide. Each attending should complete a separate form.

2 Depending on the nature of the problem, the attending may elect to submit the problem slide(s) or a photocopy of the slide(s) to the histology laboratory in conjunction with the TO-H form.

3 Once completed, the forms (and any accompanying material) should be placed by the pathologist in the histology mailbox in order for them to be had delivered daily to the supervisor of the histology laboratory.

4 The supervisor of the histology laboratory should review the submitted forms within 48 hours of reception, evaluate independently the problem, identify the cutter if indicated, and record in the form any comments and corrective action taken. If necessary, the histology supervisor should examine personally the microscopic slides and discuss the problem with the corresponding attending. The form should be signed, dated, and filed in the histology office. A copy should be sent to the QC/QA manager.

Review

1 All TO-H forms from the preceding period should be presented and discussed at the monthly meeting held between the supervisor of the histology laboratory and the director of anatomic pathology. Minutes from this meeting should be sent to the QC/QA manager.

2 A formal review of the TO-H forms should be carried out by the QC/QA committee chairman on a monthly basis, according to the general review procedure. The results of the review should be presented at the monthly QC/QA meeting.

Quality control from histology (FROM-H)

Purpose

1 To monitor the appropriateness of the material and information supplied by the pathologists to the histology laboratory (e.g. case and block identification, size and thickness of samples, decalcification, special fixation, procedures).

2 To monitor the appropriateness of the requests made to the histology laboratory (e.g. recuts, special stains, re-embedding).

3 To correct any deficiencies encountered.

Procedure

The histology supervisor should send memos through the electronic mail system to the individuals involved. A copy should be sent to the director of anatomic or surgical pathology, and another copy should be filed in the office of the histology supervisor.

Review

1. All FROM-H forms from the preceding period should be discussed at the monthly meeting held between the supervisor of the histology laboratory and the director of anatomic or surgical pathology. Minutes from this meeting should be sent to the QC/QA manager.
2. A formal review of the FROM-H forms should be carried out by the QC/QA committee chairman monthly, according to the general review procedure. The results of this review should be presented at the monthly QC/QA meeting.

Anatomic pathology turnaround times (TAT)

Purpose

To monitor the timely reporting of surgical and autopsy pathology specimens, and to correct any deficiencies encountered.

Frequency

Daily.

Procedure

1. A computer printout should be obtained daily listing overdue cases, according to the following criteria:

   a Biopsies not finalized within 2 days of receipt
   b Surgical specimens (routines) not finalized within 3 days of receipt
   c Autopsies in which a provisional diagnosis has not been sent out in 2 days
   d Autopsies not finalized within 30 days of receipt

2. Additional time will be allowed for special procedures according to the schedule recommended by the Association of Directors of Anatomic and Surgical Pathology (see Appendix A). These extra times will be calculated by the AP information system in a non-cumulative fashion and taking into account the day in which those special procedures were ordered.
3. An individual assigned to the task by the QC/QA manager should determine and record in each case the reason for the delay by checking the corresponding record as entered in the AP information system and, if necessary, by communicating with the pathologist(s) assigned to the case.
4. Once the information has been collected on all cases, the completed form should be given to the director of anatomic or surgical pathology, and a copy should be filed in the QC/QA office.
5. The director of anatomic or surgical pathology will take remedial action on the overdue cases for which no justifiable delay (i.e. waiting for a special study) has been identified.

Review

The formal review of the TAT forms should be carried out by the QC/QA chairman monthly, according to the general review procedure. The results of the review are to be presented at the monthly QC/QA meeting.

Appendix C
Staging of cancer

The stage of a malignant tumor, as determined by the size of the primary tumor and the extent of local and distant spread if any, represents the single most important determinator of prognosis at most sites. The majority of the hundreds of prognostic factors that have been described in the various forms of malignancy lose most, if not all, of their significance once they are evaluated within the confines of a single stage. Because of the powerful nature of this determination, it is of the utmost importance that the criteria employed are the most pertinent and that there is uniformity throughout institutions and countries. The system now universally used, which carries the familiar TNM abbreviation (**T** for tumor, **N** for node, and **M** for metastasis), was originally developed by Pierre Denoix in France in the 1940s and adopted by the International Union Against Cancer (IUCC) in the 1950s.[2] For more than four decades the American Joint Committee on Cancer (AJCC) has played a leadership role in the USA. The joint publication of this effort (now in its sixth edition) by IUCC and AJCC has been a major scientific and political achievement in this regard.[1]

During the 1990s, the importance of TNM staging of cancer in the USA was heightened by the mandatory requirement that Commission on Cancer-approved hospitals use the UICC/AJCC TNM system as the major language for cancer reporting. Before going into the specifics, a tribute is due to the pathologists who have played a vital role in this effort. Among the many, I thought of mentioning W.A.D. Anderson (also the editor of a once very influential general pathology book), Leslie H. Sobin, Donald E. Henson, Carolin C. Comptom, David L. Page and most particularly Robert V. P. Hutter, to whom the latest version of this effort was deservedly dedicated.

1   Sobin LH, *TNM: Principles, History and relation to other prognostic factors.* Cancer 2001, Suppl. **91**: 1589–1593.
2   Greener FL et al (eds), AJCC Cancer Staging Manual, 6th Edn, New York, 2002, Springer-Verlag; Sobin LH, Wittekind (eds), TNM Classification of Malignant Tumors, 6th Edn, New York, 2002, Wiley-Liss.

TNM system of cancer staging

(AJCC and UICC)

(Extracted from AJCC Cancer Staging Manual, 6th Ed, New York, 2002, Springer.)

General rules of the TNM system

The TNM system is an expression of the anatomic extent of the disease and is based on the assessment of three components:

T   The extent of the primary tumor
N   The absence or presence and extent of regional lymph node metastasis
M   The absence or presence of distant metastasis

Definitions of TNM

Primary tumor (T)

TX   Primary tumor cannot be assessed
T0   No evidence of primary tumor
Tis   Carcinoma in situ
T1, T2, T3, T4 Increasing size and/or local extent of the primary tumor

Regional lymph nodes (N)

NX   Regional lymph nodes cannot be assessed
N0   No regional lymph node metastasis
N2, N2, N3 Increasing involvement of regional lymph notes

Note: Direct extension of the primary tumor into a lymph node(s) is classified as a lymph node metastasis.
Note: Metastasis in any lymph node other than regional is classified as a distant metastasis.

Distant metastasis (M)

MX   Distant metastasis cannot be assessed
M0   No distant metastasis
M1   Distant metastasis

Note: For pathologic Stage grouping, if sufficient tissue to evaluate the highest T and N categories has been removed for pathologic examination, M1 may be either clinical (cM1) or pathologic (pM1). If only a metastasis has had microscopic confirmation, the classification is pathologic (pM1) and the stage is pathologic.

Histologic grade (G)

GX   Grade cannot be assessed
G1   Well differentiated
G2   Moderately differentiated
G3   Poorly differentiated
G4   Undifferentiated

Skin—carcinoma

Definitions for clinical (can) and pathologic (pin) classifications are the same.

Primary tumor (T)

TX   Primary tumor cannot be assessed
T0   No evidence of primary tumor
Tis   Carcinoma in situ
T1   Tumor 2 cm or less in greatest dimension
T2   Tumor more than 2 cm, but not more than 5 cm, in greatest dimension
T3   Tumor more than 5 cm in greatest dimension
T4   Tumor invades deep extra dermal structures (i.e. cartilage, skeletal muscle, or bone)

Note: In case of multiple simultaneous tumors, the tumor with the highest T category will be classified and the number of separate tumors will be indicated in parentheses, e.g. T2 (5).

Regional lymph nodes (N)

NX   Regional lymph nodes cannot be assessed
N0   No regional lymph node metastasis
N1   Regional lymph node metastasis

Distant metastasis (M)

MX   Distant metastasis cannot be assessed
M0   No distant metastasis
M1   Distant metastasis

Stage grouping			
Stage 0	Tis	N0	M0
Stage I	T1	N0	M0
Stage II	T2	N0	M0
	T3	N0	M0
Stage III	T4	N0	M0
	Any T	N1	M0
Stage IV	Any T	Any N	M1

Skin—melanoma

Patients with melanoma in situ are categorized as Tis. Those patients with melanoma presentations that are indeterminate or cannot be microstaged should be categorized as TX. The T category of melanoma is classified primarily by measuring the thickness of the melanoma as defined by Dr Alexander Breslow. The T category thresholds of melanoma thickness are defined in whole integers (i.e. at 1.0, 2.0, and 4.0 mm). Melanoma ulceration is the absence of an intact epidermis overlying the primary melanoma, assessed by histopathologic examination. The level of invasion, as defined by Dr Wallace Clark, is used to define subcatagories of T1 melanomas but not for thicker melanomas (i.e. T2, T3, or T4).

Regional metastases most commonly present in the regional lymph nodes. The actual number of nodal metastases identified by the pathologist must be reported for staging purposes. A second staging definition is related to tumor burden: microscopic versus macroscopic. Thus those patients without clinical or radiologic evidence of lymph node metastases, but who have pathologically documented nodal metastases *and* pathologic examination documenting the number of nodal metastases (after therapeutic lymphadenectomy) are defined by convention as having "macroscopic" or "clinically apparent" nodal metastases. Regional metastases also include intralymphatic metastases, defined as the presence of clinical or microscopic satellites around a primary melanoma, and/or in-transit metastases between the primary melanoma and the regional lymph nodes.

Distant metastases are staged primarily by the organ or site(s) in which they are located. A second factor in staging is the presence or absence of an elevated serum lactate dehydrogenase (LDH). An elevated serum LDH should be used only when there are two or more determinations obtained more than 24 hours apart, because an elevated serum LDH on a single determination can be falsely positive as a result of hemolysis or other factors unrelated to melanoma metastases.

Primary tumor (T)

TX Primary tumor cannot be assessed (e.g. shave biopsy or regressed melanoma
T0 No evidence of primary tumor
Tis Melanoma in situ
T1 Melanoma ≤ 1.0 mm in thickness with or without ulceration
T1a Melanoma ≤ 1.0 mm in thickness and level II or III, no ulceration
T1b Melanoma ≤ 1.0 mm in thickness and level IV or V or with ulceration
T2 Melanoma 1.01–2.0 mm in thickness with or without ulceration
T2a Melanoma 1.01–2.0 mm in thickness, no ulceration
T2b Melanoma 1.01–2.0 mm in thickness, with ulceration
T3 Melanoma 2.01–4.0 mm in thickness with or without ulceration
T3a Melanoma 2.01–4.0 mm in thickness, no ulceration
T3b Melanoma 2.01–4.0 mm in thickness, with ulceration
T4 Melanoma > 4.0 mm in thickness with or without ulceration

T4a Melanoma > 4.0 mm in thickness, no ulceration
T4b Melanoma > 4.0 mm in thickness, with ulceration

Regional lymph nodes (N)

NX Regional lymph nodes cannot be assessed
N0 No regional lymph node metastasis
N1 Metastasis in one lymph node
N1a Clinically occult (microscopic) metastasis
N1b Clinically apparent (macroscopic) metastasis
N2 Metastasis in two to three regional nodes or intralymphatic regional metastasis without nodal metastasis
N2a Clinically occult (microscopic) metastasis
N2b Clinically apparent (macroscopic) metastasis
N3 Metastasis in four or more regional nodes, or matted metastatic nodes, or in-transit metastasis or satellite(s) *with* metastasis in regional node(s)

Distant metastasis (M)

MX Distant metastasis cannot be assessed
M0 No distant metastasis
M1 Distant metastasis
M1a Metastasis to skin, subcutaneous tissues or distant lymph nodes
M1b Metastasis to lung
M1c Metastasis to all other visceral sites or distant metastasis at any site associated with an elevated serum lactic dehydrogenase (LDH)

Stage grouping

Patients with primary melanomas with no evidence of regional or distant metastases (either clinically or pathologically) are divided into two stages: Stage I for early-stage patients with "low risk" for metastases and melanoma-specific mortality and Stage II for those with "intermediate risk" for metastases and melanoma-specific mortality. There are no substages for clinical Stage III melanoma, because criteria for subgrouping can be inaccurate. Pathologic Stage III patients with regional metastases make up a very heterogeneous group that has been divided into three subgroups according to prognostic

Clinical Stage grouping			
Stage 0	Tis	N0	M0
Stage IA	T1a	N0	M0
Stage IB	T1b	N0	M0
	T2a	N0	M0
Stage IIA	T2b	N0	M0
	T3a	N0	M0
Stage IIB	T3b	N0	M0
	T4a	N0	M0
Stage IIC	T4b	N0	M0
Stage III	Any T	N1	M0
	Any T	N2	M0
	Any T	N3	M0
Stage IV	Any T	Any N	M1

risk. Stage IIIA patients who have up to three microscopic nodal metastases arising from a nonulcerating primary melanoma and have an "intermediate risk" for distant metastases and melanoma-specific survival. Stage IIIB patients have up to three macroscopic nodal metastases arising from a nonulcerating melanoma, or have up to three microscopic nodal metastases arising from an ulcerating melanoma, or have intralymphatic metastases without nodal metastases. They constitute a "high-risk" group prognostically. The remaining patients are Stage IIIC and are at "very high risk" for distant metastases and melanoma-specific mortality. The presence of melanoma ulceration "upstages" the prognosis of Stage I, II, and III patients compared to patients with melanomas of equivalent thickness without ulceration or those with nodal metastases arising from a nonulcerating melanoma. There are no subgroups of Stage IV melanoma.

Note: Clinical staging includes microstaging of the primary melanoma and clinical/radiological evaluation for metastases. By convention, it should be used after complete excision of the primary melanoma with clinical assessment for regional and distant metastases.

Pathologic Stage grouping			
Stage 0	Tis	N0	M0
Stage IA	T1a	N0	M0
Stage IB	T1b	N0	M0
	T2a	N0	M0
Stage IIA	T2b	N0	M0
	T3a	N0	M0
Stage IIB	T3b	N0	M0
	T4a	N0	M0
Stage IIC	T4b	N0	M0
Stage IIIA	T1–4a	N1a	M0
	T1–4a	N2a	M0
Stage IIIB	T1–4b	N1a	M0
	T1–4b	N2a	M0
	T1–4a	N1b	M0
	T1–4a	N2b	M0
	T1–4a/b	N2c	M0
Stage IIIC	T1–4b	N1b	M0
	T1–4b	N2b	M0
	Any T	N3	M0
Stage IV	Any T	Any N	M1

Oral cavity and lip

Primary tumor (T)

TX Cannot be assessed
T0 No evidence of primary tumor
Tis Carcinoma in situ
T1 Tumor 2 cm or less in greatest dimension
T2 Tumor more than 2 cm but not more than 4 cm in greatest dimension

T3 Tumor more than 4 cm in greatest dimension
T4a (lip) Tumor invades through cortical bone, inferior alveolar nerve, floor of mouth, skin of face, i.e. chin or nose
T4a (oral cavity) Tumor invades adjacent structures (e.g. through cortical bone, into deep [extrinsic] muscle of tongue [genioglossus, hyoglossus, palatoglossus, and styloglossus], maxillary sinus, skin of face)
T4b: Tumor invades masticator space, pterygoid plates, skull base and/or encases internal carotid artery

Note: Superficial erosion alone of bone/tooth socket by gingival primary is not sufficient to classify a tumor as T4.

Regional lymph nodes (N)

NX Regional lymph nodes cannot be assessed
N0 No regional lymph node metastasis
N1 Metastasis in a single ipsilateral lymph node, 3 cm or less in greatest dimension
N2 Metastasis in a single ipsilateral lymph node, more than 3 cm but not more than 6 cm in greatest dimension; or in multiple ipsilateral lymph nodes, none more than 6 cm in greatest dimension; or in bilateral or contralateral lymph nodes, none more than 6 cm in greatest dimension
N2a Metastasis in a single ipsilateral lymph node more than 3 cm but not more than 6 cm in greatest dimension
N2b Metastasis in multiple ipsilateral lymph nodes, none more than 6 cm in greatest dimension
N2c Metastasis in bilateral or contralateral lymph nodes, none more than 6 cm in greatest dimension
N3 Metastasis in a lymph node more than 6 cm in greatest dimension

Distant metastasis (M)

MX Distant metastasis cannot be assessed
M0 No distant metastasis
M1 Distant metastasis

Stage grouping			
Stage 0	Tis	N0	M0
Stage I	T1	N0	M0
Stage II	T2	N0	M0
Stage III	T3	N0	M0
	T1	N1	M0
	T2	N1	M0
	T3	N1	M0
Stage IVA	T4a	N0	M0
	T4a	N1	M0
	T1	N2	M0
	T2	N2	M0
	T3	N2	M0
	T4a	N2	M0
Stage IVB	Any T	N3	M0
	T4b	Any N	M0
Stage IVC	Any T	Any N	M1

Pharynx (including base of tongue, soft palate, and uvula)

Primary tumor (T)

TX   Primary tumor cannot be assessed
T0   No evidence of primary tumor
Tis   Carcinoma in situ

Nasopharynx

T1   Tumor confined to the nasopharynx
T2   Tumor extends to soft tissues
T2a   Tumor extends to the oropharynx and/or nasal cavity without parapharyngeal extension*
T2b   Any tumor with parapharyngeal extension*
T3   Tumor involves bony structures and/or paranasal sinuses
T4   Tumor with intracranial extension and/or involvement of cranial nerves, infratemporal fossa, hypopharynx, orbit, or masticator space

Note: Parapharyngeal extension denotes posterolateral infiltration of tumor beyond the pharyngobasilar fascia.

Oropharynx

T1   Tumor 2 cm or less in greatest dimension
T2   Tumor more than 2 cm but not more than 4 cm in greatest dimension
T3   Tumor more than 4 cm in greatest dimension
T4a   Tumor invades the larynx, deep/extrinsic muscle of tongue, medial pterygoid, hard palate, or mandible
T4b   Tumor invades lateral pterygoid muscle, pterygoid plates, lateral nasopharynx, or skull base or encases carotid artery

Hypopharynx

T1   Tumor limited to one subsite of hypopharynx and 2 cm or less in greatest dimension
T2   Tumor invades more than one subsite of hypopharynx or an adjacent site, or measures more than 2 cm but not more than 4 cm in greatest diameter without fixation of hemilarynx
T3   Tumor more than 4 cm in greatest dimension or with fixation of hemilarynx
T4a   Tumor invades thyroid/cricoid cartilage, hyoid bone, thyroid gland, esophagus, or central compartment soft tissue*
T4b   Tumor invades prevertebral fascia, encases carotid artery, or involves mediastinal structures

Note: Central compartment soft tissue includes prelaryngeal strap muscle and subcutaneous fat.

Regional lymph nodes (N)

Nasopharynx

The distribution and the prognostic impact of regional lymph node spread from nasopharynx cancer, particularly of the undifferentiated type, are different from those of other head and neck mucosal cancers and justify the use of a different N classification scheme.

NX   Regional lymph nodes cannot be assessed
N0   No regional lymph node metastasis
N1   Unilateral metastasis in lymph node(s), 6 cm or less in greatest dimension, above the supraclavicular fossa*
N2   Bilateral metastasis in lymph node(s) 6 cm or less in greatest dimension, above the supraclavicular fossa*
N3   Metastasis in a lymph node(s)* >6 cm and/or to supraclavicular fossa
N3a   Greater than 6 cm in dimension
N3b   Extension to the supraclavicular fossa**

Note: Midline nodes are considered ipsilateral nodes.
**Supraclavicular zone or fossa is relevant to the staging of nasopharyngeal carcinoma and is the triangular region originally described by Ho. It is defined by three points: (1) the superior margin of the sternal end of the clavicle, (2) the superior margin of the lateral end of the clavicle, (3) the point where the neck meets the shoulder. Note that this would include caudal portions of Levels IV and V. All cases with lymph nodes (whole or part) in the fossa are considered N3b.

Oropharynx and hypopharynx

NX   Regional lymph nodes cannot be assessed
N0   No regional lymph node metastasis
N1   Metastasis in a single ipsilateral lymph node, 3 cm or less in greatest dimension
N2   Metastasis in a single ipsilateral lymph node, more than 3 cm but not more than 6 cm in greatest dimension, or in bilateral or contralateral lymph nodes, none more than 6 cm in greatest dimension
N2a   Metastasis in a single ipsilateral lymph node more than 3 cm but not more than 6 cm in greatest dimension

Stage grouping: nasopharynx			
Stage 0	Tis	N0	M0
Stage I	T1	N0	M0
Stage IIA	T2a	N0	M0
Stage IIB	T1	N1	M0
	T2	N1	M0
	T2a	N1	M0
	T2b	N0	M0
	T2b	N1	M0
Stage III	T1	N2	M0
	T2a	N2	M0
	T2b	N2	M0
	T3	N0	M0
	T3	N1	M0
	T3	N2	M0
Stage IVA	T4	N0	M0
	T4	N1	M0
	T4	N2	M0
Stage IVB	Any T	N3	M0
Stage IVC	Any T	Any N	M1

N2b Metastasis in multiple ipsilateral lymph nodes, none more than 6 cm in greatest dimension

N2c Metastasis in bilateral or contralateral lymph nodes, none more than 6 cm in greatest dimension

N3 Metastasis in a lymph node more than 6 cm in greatest dimension

Distant metastasis (M)

MX Distant metastasis cannot be assessed
M0 No distant metastasis
M1 Distant metastasis

Stage grouping: oropharynx and hypopharynx			
Stage 0	Tis	N0	M0
Stage I	T1	N0	M0
Stage II	T2	N0	M0
Stage III	T3	N0	M0
	T1	N1	M0
	T2	N1	M0
	T3	N1	M0
Stage IVA	T4a	N0	M0
	T4a	N1	M0
	T1	N2	M0
	T2	N2	M0
	T3	N2	M0
	T4a	N2	M0
Stage IVB	T4b	Any N	M0
	Any T	N3	M0
Stage IVC	Any T	Any N	M1

Nasal cavity and paranasal sinuses

Primary tumor (T)

TX Primary tumor cannot be assessed
T0 No evidence of primary tumor
Tis Carcinoma in situ

Maxillary sinus

T1 Tumor limited to maxillary sinus mucosa with no erosion or destruction of bone

T2 Tumor causing bone erosion or destruction including extension into the hard palate and/or middle nasal meatus, except extension to posterior wall of maxillary sinus and pterygoid plates

T3 Tumor invades any of the following: bone of the posterior wall of maxillary sinus, subcutaneous tissues, floor or medial wall of orbit, pterygoid fossa, ethmoid sinuses

T4a Tumor invades anterior orbital contents, skin of cheek pterygoid plates, infratemporal fossa, cribriform plate, sphenoid or frontal sinuses

T4b Tumor invades any of the following: orbital apex, dura, brain, middle cranial fossa, cranial nerves other than maxillary division of trigeminal nerve (V_2), nasopharynx, or clivus

Nasal cavity and ethmoid sinus

T1 Tumor restricted to any one subsite, with or without bony invasion

T2 Tumor invading two subsites in a single region or extending to involve an adjacent region within the nasoethmoidal complex, with or without bony invasion

T3 Tumor extends to invade the medial wall or floor of the orbit, maxillary sinus, palate, or cribriform plate

T4a Tumor invades any of the following: anterior orbital contents, skin of nose or cheek, minimal extension to anterior cranial fossa, pterygoid plates, sphenoid or frontal sinuses

T4b Tumor invades any of the following: orbital apex, dura, brain, middle cranial fossa, cranial nerves other than (V_2), nasopharynx, or clivus

Regional lymph nodes (N)

NX Regional lymph nodes cannot be assessed
N0 No regional lymph node metastasis
N1 Metastasis in a single ipsilateral lymph node, 3 cm or less in greatest dimension
N2 Metastasis in a single ipsilateral lymph node, more than 3 cm but not more than 6 cm in greatest dimension, or in multiple ipsilateral lymph nodes, none more than 6 cm in greatest dimension, or in bilateral or contralateral lymph nodes, none more than 6 cm in greatest dimension
N2a Metastasis in a single ipsilateral lymph node, more than 3 cm but not more than 6 cm in greatest dimension
N2b Metastasis in multiple ipsilateral lymph nodes, none more than 6 cm in greatest dimension
N2c Metastasis in bilateral or contralateral lymph nodes, none more than 6 cm in greatest dimension
N3 Metastasis in a lymph node, more than 6 cm in greatest dimension

Stage grouping			
Stage 0	Tis	N0	M0
Stage I	T1	N0	M0
Stage II	T2	N0	M0
Stage III	T3	N0	M0
	T1	N1	M0
	T2	N1	M0
	T3	N1	M0
Stage IVA	T4a	N0	M0
	T4a	N1	M0
	T1	N2	M0
	T2	N2	M0
	T3	N2	M0
	T4a	N2	M0
Stage IVB	T4b	Any N	M0
	Any T	N3	M0
Stage IVC	Any T	Any N	M1

Distant metastasis (M)

MX   Distant metastasis cannot be assessed
M0   No distant metastasis
M1   Distant metastasis

Larynx

Primary tumor (T)

TX   Primary tumor cannot be assessed
T0   No evidence of primary tumor
Tis   Carcinoma in situ

Supraglottis

T1   Tumor limited to one subsite of supraglottis with normal vocal cord mobility
T2   Tumor invades mucosa of more than one adjacent subsite of supraglottis or glottis or region outside the supraglottis (e.g. mucosa of base of tongue, vallecula, medial wall of pyriform sinus) without fixation of the larynx
T3   Tumor limited to larynx with vocal cord fixation and/or invades any of the following: postcricoid area, preepiglottic tissues, paraglottic space, and/or minor thyroid cartilage erosion (e.g. inner cortex)
T4a   Tumor invades through the thyroid cartilage and/or invades tissues beyond the larynx (e.g. trachea, soft issues of neck including deep extrinsic muscle of the tongue, strap muscles, thyroid or esophagus)
T4b   Tumor invades prevertebral space, encases carotid artery, or invades mediastinal structures

Glottis

T1   Tumor limited to the vocal cord(s) (may involve anterior or posterior commissure) with normal mobility
T1a   Tumor limited to one vocal cord
T1b   Tumor involves both vocal cords
T2   Tumor extends to supraglottis and/or subglottis, and/or with impaired vocal cord mobility
T3   Tumor limited to the larynx with vocal cord fixation and/or invades paraglottic space, and or minor thyroid cartilage erosion (e.g. inner cortex)
T4a   Tumor invades through the thyroid cartilage and/or invades tissues beyond the larynx (e.g. trachea, soft tissues of neck including deep extrinsic muscle of the tongue, strap muscles, thyroid, or esophagus)
T4b   Tumor invades prevertebral space, encases carotid artery, or invades mediastinal structures

Subglottis

T1   Tumor limited to the subglottis
T2   Tumor extends to vocal cord(s) with normal or impaired mobility
T3   Tumor limited to larynx with vocal cord fixation
T4a   Tumor invades cricoid or thyroid cartilage and/or invades tissues beyond the larynx (e.g. trachea, soft tissues of neck including deep extrinsic muscles of the tongue, strap muscles, thyroid, or esophagus)
T4b   Tumor invades prevertebral space, encases carotid artery, or invades mediastinal structures

Regional lymph nodes (N)

NX   Regional lymph nodes cannot be assessed
N0   No regional lymph node metastasis
N1   Metastasis in a single ipsilateral lymph node, 3 cm or less in greatest dimension
N2   Metastasis in a single ipsilateral lymph node, more than 3 cm but not more than 6 cm in greatest dimension, or in multiple ipsilateral lymph nodes, none more than 6 cm in greatest dimension, or in bilateral or contralateral lymph nodes, none more than 6 cm in greatest dimension
N2a   Metastasis in a single ipsilateral lymph node, more than 3 cm but not more than 6 cm in greatest dimension
N2b   Metastasis in multiple ipsilateral lymph nodes, none more than 6 cm in greatest dimension
N2c   Metastasis in bilateral or contralateral lymph nodes, none more than 6 cm in greatest dimension
N3   Metastasis in a lymph node, more than 6 cm in greatest dimension

Distant metastasis (M)

MX   Distant metastasis cannot be assessed
M0   No distant metastasis
M1   Distant metastasis

Stage grouping			
Stage 0	Tis	N0	M0
Stage I	T1	N0	M0
Stage II	T2	N0	M0
Stage III	T3	N0	M0
	T1	N1	M0
	T2	N1	M0
	T3	N1	M0
Stage IVA	T4a	N0	M0
	T4a	N1	M0
	T1	N2	M0
	T2	N2	M0
	T3	N2	M0
	T4a	N2	M0
Stage IVB	T4b	Any N	M0
	Any T	N3	M0
Stage IVC	Any T	Any N	M1

Lung

Primary tumor (T)

TX   Primary tumor cannot be assessed, or tumor proven by the presence of malignant cells in sputum or bronchial washings but not visualized by imaging or bronchoscopy

T0   No evidence of primary tumor

Tis   Carcinoma in situ

T1   Tumor 3 cm or less in greatest dimension, surrounded by lung or visceral pleura, without bronchoscopic evidence of invasion more proximal than the lobar bronchus* (i.e. not in the main bronchus)

T2   Tumor with any of the following features of size or extent:
More than 3 cm in greatest dimension
Involves main bronchus, 2 cm or more distal to the carina
Invades the visceral pleura
Associated with atelectasis or obstructive pneumonitis that extends to the hilar region but does not involve the entire lung

T3   Tumor of any size that directly invades any of the following: chest wall (including superior sulcus tumors), diaphragm, mediastinal pleura, parietal pericardium; or tumor in the main bronchus less than 2 cm distal to the carina; or associated atelectasis or obstructive pneumonitis of the entire lung

T4   Tumor of any size that invades any of the following: mediastinum, heart, great vessels, trachea, esophagus, vertebral body, carina; or separate tumor nodules in the same lobe; or tumor with malignant pleural effusion**

*Note: The uncommon superficial tumor of any size with its invasive component limited to the bronchial wall, which may extend proximal to the main bronchus, is also classified T1.

**Note: Most pleural effusions associated with lung cancer are due to tumor. However, there are a few patients in whom multiple cytopathologic examinations of pleural fluid are negative for tumor. In these cases, fluid is nonbloody and is not an exudate. Such patients may be further evaluated by videothoracoscopy (VATS) and direct pleural biopsies. When these elements and clinical judgment dictate that the effusion is not related to the tumor, the effusion should be excluded as a staging element and the patient should be staged T1, T2, or T3.

Regional lymph nodes (N)

NX   Regional lymph nodes cannot be assessed

N0   No regional lymph node metastasis

N1   Metastasis to ipsilateral peribronchial and/or ipsilateral hilar lymph nodes, and intrapulmonary nodes including involvement by direct extension of the primary tumor

N2   Metastasis to ipsilateral mediastinal and/or subcarinal lymph nodes(s)

N3   Metastasis to contralateral mediastinal, contralateral hilar, ipsilateral or contralateral scalene, or supraclavicular lymph nodes(s)

Distant metastasis (M)

MX   Distant metastasis cannot be assessed

M0   No distant metastasis

M1   Distant metastasis present

Note: M1 includes separate tumor nodule(s) in a different lobe (ipsilateral or contralateral).

Stage grouping			
Occult carcinoma	TX	N0	M0
Stage 0	Tis	N0	M0
Stage IA	T1	N0	M0
Stage IB	T2	N0	M0
Stage IIA	T1	N1	M0
Stage IIB	T2	N1	M0
	T3	N1	M0
Stage IIIA	T1	N2	M0
	T2	N2	M0
	T3	N1	M0
	T3	N2	M0
Stage IIIB	Any T	N3	M0
	T4	Any N	M0
Stage IV	Any T	Any N	M1

Pleural mesothelioma

IMIG staging system for diffuse malignant pleural mesothelioma

Primary tumor (T)

TX   Primary tumor cannot be assessed

T0   No evidence of primary tumor

T1   Tumor involves ipsilateral parietal pleura, with or without focal involvement of visceral pleura

T1a   Tumor involves ipsilateral parietal (mediastinal, diaphragmatic) pleura. No involvement of the visceral pleura

T1b   Tumor involves ipsilateral parietal (mediastinal, diaphragmatic) pleura, with focal involvement of the visceral pleura

T2   Tumor involves any of the ipsilateral pleural surfaces with at least one of the following: confluent visceral pleural tumor (including fissure), invasion of diaphragmatic muscle, invasion of lung parenchyma

T3*   Tumor involves any of the ipsilateral pleural surfaces, with at least one of the following: invasion of the endothoracic fascia, invasion into mediastinal fat, solitary focus of tumor invading the soft tissues of the chest wall, nontransmural involvement of the pericardium

T4**   Tumor involves any of the ipsilateral pleural surfaces, with at least one of the following: diffuse or multifocal invasion of soft tissues of the chest wall, any involvement of rib, invasion through the diaphragm to the peritoneum, invasion of any mediastinal organ(s), direct extension to the contralateral pleura, invasion into the spine, extension to the internal surface of the pericardium, pericardial effusion with positive cytology, invasion of the myocardium, invasion of the brachial plexus

*T3 describes locally advanced but potentially resectable tumor.

**T4 describes locally advanced, technically unresectable tumor.

Regional lymph nodes (N)

NX Regional lymph nodes cannot be assessed
N0 No regional lymph node metastases
N1 Metastases in the ipsilateral bronchopulmonary and/or hilar lymph node(s)
N2 Metastases in the subcarinal lymph node(s) and/or the ipsilateral internal mammary or mediastinal lymph node(s)
N3 Metastases in the contralateral mediastinal, internal mammary, or hilar lymph node(s) and/or the ipsilateral or contralateral supraclavicular or scalene lymph node(s)

Distant metastasis (M)

MX Distant metastases cannot be assessed
M0 No distant metastasis
M1 Distant metastasis

Stage grouping

Stage	T	N	M
Stage I	T1	N0	M0
Stage IA	T1a	N0	M0
Stage IB	T1b	N0	M0
Stage II	T2	N0	M0
Stage III	T1, T2	N1	M0
	T1, T2	N2	M0
	T3	N0, N1, N2	M0
Stage IV	T4	Any N	M0
	Any T	N3	M0
	Any T	Any N	M1

Thyroid

Primary tumor (T)

Note: All categories may be subdivided: (a) solitary tumor, (b) multifocal tumor (the largest determines the classification).

TX Primary tumor cannot be assessed
T0 No evidence of primary tumor
T1 Tumor 2 cm or less in greatest dimension limited to the thyroid
T2 Tumor more than 2 cm but not more than 4 cm in greatest dimension limited to the thyroid

T3 Tumor more than 4 cm in greatest dimension limited to the thyroid or any tumor with minimal extrathyroid extension (e.g. extension to sternothyroid muscle or perithyroid soft tissues)

T4a Tumor of any size extending beyond the thyroid capsule to invade subcutaneous soft tissues, larynx, trachea, esophagus, or recurrent laryngeal nerve

T4b Tumor invades prevertebral fascia or encases carotid artery or mediastinal vessels

Stage grouping

Separate stage groupings are recommended for papillary or follicular, medullary, and anaplastic (undifferentiated) carcinoma.

Papillary or follicular
Under 45 years

Stage	T	N	M
Stage I	Any T	Any N	M0
Stage II	Any T	Any N	M1

Papillary or follicular
45 years and older

Stage	T	N	M
Stage I	T1	N0	M0
Stage II	T2	N0	M0
Stage III	T3	N0	M0
	T1	N1a	M0
	T2	N1a	M0
	T3	N1a	M0
Stage IVA	T4a	N0	M0
	T4a	N1a	M0
	T1	N1b	M0
	T2	N1b	M0
	T3	N1b	M0
	T4a	N1b	M0
Stage IVB	T4b	Any N	M0
Stage IVC	Any T	Any N	M1

Medullary carcinoma

Stage	T	N	M
Stage I	T1	N0	M0
Stage II	T2	N0	M0
Stage III	T3	N0	M0
	T1	N1a	M0
	T2	N1a	M0
	T3	N1a	M0
Stage IVA	T4a	N0	M0
	T4a	N1a	M0
	T1	N1b	M0
	T2	N1b	M0
	T3	N1b	M0
	T4a	N1b	M0
Stage IVB	T4b	Any N	M0
Stage IVC	Any T	Any N	M1

Anaplastic carcinoma
All anaplastic carcinomas are considered Stage IV.

Stage	T	N	M
Stage IVA	T4a	Any N	M0
Stage IVB	T4b	Any N	M0
Stage IVC	Any T	Any N	M1

All anaplastic carcinomas are considered T4 tumors

T4a Intrathyroidal anaplastic carcinoma—surgically resectable

T4b Extrathyroidal anaplastic carcinoma—surgically unresectable

Regional lymph nodes (N)

Regional lymph nodes are the central compartment, lateral cervical, and upper mediastinal lymph nodes.

NX Regional lymph nodes cannot be assessed

N0 No regional lymph node metastasis

N1 Regional lymph node metastasis

N1a Metastasis to Level VI (pretracheal, paratracheal, and prelaryngeal/Delphian lymph nodes

Distant metastasis (M)

MX Distant metastasis cannot be assessed

M0 No distant metastasis

M1 Distant metastasis

Stage grouping			
Stage 0	Tis	N0	M0
Stage I	T1	N0	M0
Stage IIA	T2	N0	M0
	T3	N0	M0
Stage IIB	T1	N1	M0
	T2	N1	M0
Stage III	T3	N1	M0
	T4	Any N	M0
Stage IV	Any T	Any N	M1
Stage IVA	Any T	Any N	M1a
Stage IVB	Any T	Any N	M1b

Esophagus

Primary tumor (T)

TX Primary tumor cannot be assessed

T0 No evidence of primary tumor

Tis Carcinoma in situ

T1 Tumor invades lamina propria or submucosa

T2 Tumor invades muscularis propria

T3 Tumor invades adventitia

T4 Tumor invades adjacent structures

Regional lymph nodes (N)

NX Regional lymph nodes cannot be assessed

N0 No regional lymph node metastases

N1 Regional lymph node metastasis

Distant metastasis (M)

MX Distant metastases cannot be assessed

M0 No distant metastasis

M1 Distant metastasis

Tumors of the lower thoracic esophagus:

M1a Metastasis in celiac lymph nodes

M1b Other distant metastasis

Tumors of the midthoracic esophagus:

M1a Not applicable

M1b Nonregional lymph nodes and/or other distant metastasis

Tumors of the upper thoracic esophagus:

M1a Metastasis in cervical nodes

M1b Other distant metastasis

Stomach

Primary tumor (T)

TX Primary tumor cannot be assessed

T0 No evidence of primary tumor

Tis Carcinoma in situ: intraepithelial tumor without invasion of the lamina propria

T1 Tumor invades lamina propria or submucosa

T2 Tumor invades muscularis propria or subserosa*

T2a Tumor invades muscularis propria

T2b Tumor invades subserosa

T3 Tumor invades serosa (visceral peritoneum) without invasion of adjacent structures**,***

T4 Tumor invades adjacent structures**,***

Note: A tumor may penetrate the muscularis propria with extension into the gastrocolic or gastrohepatic ligaments, or into the greater or lesser omentum, without perforation of the visceral peritoneum covering these structures. In this case, the tumor is classified T2. If there is perforation of the visceral peritoneum covering the gastric ligaments or the omentum, the tumor should be classified T3.

**Note:* The adjacent structures of the stomach include the spleen, transverse colon, liver, diaphragm, pancreas, abdominal wall, adrenal gland, kidney, small intestine, and retroperitoneum.

***Note:* Intramural extension to the duodenum or esophagus is classified by the depth of the greatest invasion in any of these sites, including the stomach.

Regional lymph nodes (N)

NX Regional lymph node(s) cannot be assessed

N0 No regional lymph node metastasis*

N1 Metastasis in 1 to 6 regional lymph nodes

N2 Metastasis in 7 to 15 regional lymph nodes

N3 Metastasis in more than 15 regional lymph nodes

Note: A designation of pN0 should be used if all examined lymph nodes are negative, regardless of the total number removed and examined.

Distant metastasis (M)

MX Distant metastases cannot be assessed
M0 No distant metastasis
M1 Distant metastasis

Stage grouping			
Stage 0	Tis	N0	M0
Stage IA	T1	N0	M0
Stage IB	T1	N1	M0
	T2a/b	N0	M0
Stage II	T1	N2	M0
	T2a/b	N1	M0
	T3	N0	M0
Stage IIIA	T2a/b	N2	M0
	T3	N1	M0
	T4	N0	M0
Stage IIIB	T3	N2	M0
Stage IV	T4	N1–3	M0
	T1–3	N3	M0
	Any T	Any N	M1

Small bowel

Primary tumor (T)

TX Primary tumor cannot be assessed
T0 No evidence of primary tumor
Tis Carcinoma in situ
T1 Tumor invades lamina propria or submucosa
T2 Tumor invades muscularis propria
T3 Tumor invades through the muscularis propria into the subserosa or into the nonperitonealized perimuscular tissue (mesentery or retroperitoneum) with extension of 2 cm or less*
T4 Tumor perforates the visceral peritoneum or directly invades other organs or structures (includes other loops of small intestine, mesentery, or retroperitoneum more than 2 cm, and abdominal wall be way of serosa; for duodenum only, invasion of pancreas)

Note: The nonperitonealized perimuscular tissue is, for jejunum and ileum, part of the mesentery and, for duodenum in areas where serosa is lacking, part of the retroperitoneum.

Regional lymph nodes (N)

NX Regional lymph nodes cannot be assessed
N0 No regional lymph node metastasis
N1 Regional lymph node metastasis

Distant metastasis (M)

MX Distant metastasis cannot be assessed
M0 No distant metastasis
M1 Distant metastasis

Stage grouping			
Stage 0	Tis	N0	M0
Stage I	T1	N0	M0
	T2	N0	M0
Stage II	T3	N0	M0
	T4	N0	M0
Stage III	Any T	N1	M0
Stage IV	Any T	Any N	M1

Large bowel

The same classification is used for both clinical and pathologic staging.

Primary tumor (T)

TX Primary tumor cannot be assessed
T0 No evidence of primary tumor
Tis Carcinoma in situ: intraepithelial or invasion of lamina propria*
T1 Tumor invades submucosa
T2 Tumor invades muscular propria
T3 Tumor invades through the muscularis propria into the subserosa or into the nonperitonealized pericolic or perirectal tissue
T4 Tumor directly invades other organs or structures, and/or perforates visceral peritoneum**,***

Note: Tis includes cancer cells confined within the glandular basement membrane (intraepithelial) or lamina propria (intramucosal) with no extension through the muscularis mucosae into the submucosa.
**Note:* Direct invasion in T4 includes invasion of other segments of the colorectum by way of the serosa; for example, invasion of the sigmoid colon by a carcinoma of the cecum.
***Tumor that is adherent to other organs or structures, macroscopically, is classified T4. However, if no tumor is present in the adhesion, microscopically, the classification should be pT3. The V and L substaging should be used to identify the presence or absence of vascular or lymphatic invasion.

Regional lymph nodes (N)

NX Regional lymph nodes cannot be assessed
N0 No regional lymph node metastasis
N1 Metastasis in 1 to 3 regional lymph nodes
N2 Metastasis in 4 or more regional lymph nodes

Note: A tumor nodule in the pericolorectal adipose tissue of a primary carcinoma without histologic evidence of residual lymph node in the nodule is classified in the pN category as a regional lymph node metastasis if the nodule has the form and smooth contour of a lymph node. If the nodule has an irregular contour, it should be classified in the T category and also coded as V1 (microscopic venous invasion) or as V2 (if it was grossly evident), because there is a strong likelihood that it represents venous invasion.

Distant metastasis (M)

MX Distant metastasis cannot be assessed
M0 No distant metastasis
M1 Distant metastasis

*Dukes B is a composite of better (T3 N0 M0) and worse (T4 N0 M0) prognostic groups, as is Dukes C (Any T N1 M0) and Any T N2 M0). MAC is the modified Astler-Coller classification.
Note: The y prefix is to be used for those cancers that are classified after pretreatment, whereas the r prefix is to be used for those cancers that have recurred.

Stage grouping					
Stage	T	N	M	Dukes*	MAC*
0	Tis	N0	M0	–	–
I	T1	N0	M0	A	A
	T2	N0	M0	A	B1
IIA	T3	N0	M0	B	B2
IIB	T4	N0	M0	B	B3
IIIA	T1–T2	N1	M0	C	C1
IIIB	T3–T4	N1	M0	C	C2/C3
IIIC	Any T	N2	M0	C	C1/C2/C3
IV	Any T	Any N	M1	–	D

Anal canal

Primary tumor (T)

TX Primary tumor cannot be assessed
T0 No evidence of primary tumor
Tis Carcinoma in situ
T1 Tumor 2 cm or less in greatest dimension
T2 Tumor more than 2 cm but not more than 5 cm in greatest dimension
T3 Tumor more than 5 cm in greatest dimension
T4 Tumor of any size invades adjacent organ(s), e.g. vagina, urethra, bladder*

Note: Direct invasion of the rectal wall, perirectal skin, subcutaneous tissue, or the sphincter muscle(s) is not classified as T4

Regional lymph nodes (N)

NX Regional lymph nodes cannot be assessed
N0 No regional lymph node metastasis
N1 Metastasis in perirectal lymph node(s)
N2 Metastasis in unilateral internal iliac and/or inguinal lymph node(s)
N3 Metastasis in perirectal and inguinal lymph nodes and/or bilateral internal iliac and/or inguinal lymph nodes

Distant metastasis (M)

MX Distant metastasis cannot be assessed
M0 No distant metastasis
M1 Distant metastasis

Stage grouping			
Stage 0	Tis	N0	M0
Stage I	T1	N0	M0
Stage II	T2	N0	M0
	T3	N0	M0
Stage IIIA	T1	N1	M0
	T2	N1	M0
	T3	N1	M0
	T4	N0	M0
Stage IIIB	T4	N1	M0
	Any T	N2	M0
	Any T	N3	M0
Stage IV	Any T	Any N	M1

Major salivary glands

Primary tumor (T)

TX Primary tumor cannot be assessed
T0 No evidence of primary tumor
T1 Tumor 2 cm or less in greatest dimension without extraparenchymal extension*
T2 Tumor more than 2 cm but not more than 4 cm in greatest dimension without extraparenchymal extension*
T3 Tumor more than 4 cm and/or tumor having extraparenchymal extension*
T4a Tumor invades skin, mandible, ear canal, and/or facial nerve.
T4b Tumor invades skull base and/or pterygoid plates and/or encases carotid artery

Note: Extraparenchymal extension is clinical or macroscopic evidence of invasion of soft tissues. Microscopic evidence alone does not constitute extraparenchymal extension for classification purposes.

Regional lymph nodes (N)

NX Regional lymph nodes cannot be assessed
N0 No regional lymph node metastasis
N1 Metastasis in a single ipsilateral lymph node, 3 cm or less in greatest dimension
N2a Metastasis in a single ipsilateral lymph node, more than 3 cm but not more than 6 cm in greatest dimension
N2b Metastasis in multiple ipsilateral lymph nodes, none more than 6 cm in greatest dimension
N2c Metastasis in bilateral or contralateral lymph nodes, none more than 6 cm in greatest dimension
N3 Metastasis in a lymph node more than 6 cm in greatest dimension

Distant metastasis (M)

MX Distant metastasis cannot be assessed
M0 No distant metastasis
M1 Distant metastasis

Stage grouping			
Stage I	T1	N0	M0
Stage II	T2	N0	M0
Stage III	T3	N0	M0
	T1	N1	M0
	T2	N1	M0
	T3	N1	M0
Stage IVA	T4a	N0	M0
	T4a	N1	M0
	T1	N2	M0
	T2	N2	M0
	T3	N2	M0
	T4a	N2	M0
Stage IVB	T4b	Any N	M0
	Any T	N3	M0
Stage IVC	Any T	Any N	M1

Liver

Primary tumor (T)

TX Primary tumor cannot be assessed
T0 No evidence of primary tumor
T1 Solitary tumor without vascular invasion
T2 Solitary tumor with vascular invasion or multiple tumors none more than 5 cm
T3 Multiple tumors more than 5 cm or tumor involving a major branch of the portal or hepatic vein(s)
T4 Tumor(s) with direct invasion of adjacent organs other than the gallbladder or perforation of visceral peritoneum

Regional lymph nodes (N)

NX Regional lymph nodes cannot be assessed
N0 No regional lymph node metastasis
N1 Regional lymph node metastasis

Distant metastasis (M)

MX Distant metastasis cannot be assessed
M0 No distant metastasis
M1 Distant metastasis

Stage grouping			
Stage I	T1	N0	M0
Stage II	T2	N0	M0
Stage IIIA	T3	N0	M0
IIIB	T4	N0	M0
IIIC	Any T	N1	M0
Stage IV	Any T	Any N	M1

Gallbladder

Primary tumor (T)

TX Primary tumor cannot be assessed
T0 No evidence of primary tumor
Tis Carcinoma in situ
T1 Tumor invades lamina propria or muscle layer (Fig. 15.1)
T1a Tumor invades lamina propria
T1b Tumor invades muscle layer
T2 Tumor invades perimuscular connective tissue; no extensions beyond serosa or into liver
T3 Tumor perforates the serosa (visceral peritoneum) and/or directly invades the liver and/or one other adjacent organ or structure, such as the stomach, duodenum, colon, or pancreas, omentum or extrahepatic bile ducts
T4 Tumor invades main portal vein or hepatic artery or invades multiple extrahepatic organs or structures

Regional lymph nodes (N)

NX Regional lymph nodes cannot be assessed
N0 No regional lymph node metastasis
N1 Regional lymph node metastasis

Distant metastasis (M)

MX Distant metastasis cannot be assessed
M0 No distant metastasis
M1 Distant metastasis

Stage grouping			
Stage 0	Tis	N0	M0
Stage IA	T1	N0	M0
Stage IB	T2	N0	M0
Stage IIA	T3	N0	M0
Stage IIB	T1	N1	M0
	T2	N1	M0
	T3	N1	M0
Stage III	T4	Any N	M0
Stage IV	Any T	Any N	M1

Extrahepatic bile ducts

Primary tumor (T)

TX Primary tumor cannot be assessed
T0 No evidence of primary tumor
Tis Carcinoma in situ
T1 Tumor confined to the bile duct histologically
T2 Tumor invades beyond the wall of the bile duct
T3 Tumor invades the liver, gallbladder, pancreas, and/or unilateral branches of the portal vein (right or left) or hepatic artery (right or left)

T4   Tumor invades any of the following: main portal vein or its branches bilaterally, common hepatic artery, or other adjacent structures, such as the colon, stomach, duodenum, or abdominal wall

Regional lymph nodes (N)

NX   Regional lymph nodes cannot be assessed
N0   No regional lymph node metastasis
N1   Regional lymph node metastasis

Distant metastasis (M)

MX   Distant metastasis cannot be assessed
M0   No distant metastasis
M1   Distant metastasis

Stage grouping			
Stage 0	Tis	N0	M0
Stage IA	T1	N0	M0
Stage IB	T2	N0	M0
Stage IIA	T3	N0	M0
Stage IIB	T1	N1	M0
	T2	N1	M0
	T3	N1	M0
Stage III	T4	Any N	M0
Stage IV	Any T	Any N	M1

Exocrine pancreas

Primary tumor (T)

TX   Primary tumor cannot be assessed
T0   No evidence of primary tumor
Tis   Carcinoma in situ*
T1   Tumor limited to the pancreas, 2 cm or less in greatest dimension
T2   Tumor limited to the pancreas, more than 2 cm in greatest dimension
T3   Tumor extends beyond the pancreas but without involvement of the celiac axis or the superior mesenteric artery
T4   Tumor involves the celiac axis or the superior mesenteric artery (unresectable primary tumor)

Regional lymph nodes (N)

NX   Regional lymph nodes cannot be assessed
N0   No regional lymph node metastasis
N1   Regional lymph node metastasis

Distant metastasis (M)

MX   Distant metastasis cannot be assessed
M0   No distant metastasis
M1   Distant metastasis

*This also includes the "PanInIII" classification

Stage grouping			
Stage 0	Tis	N0	M0
Stage IA	T1	N0	M0
Stage IB	T2	N0	M0
Stage IIA	T3	N0	M0
Stage IIB	T1	N1	M0
	T2	N1	M0
	T3	N1	M0
Stage III	T4	Any N	M0
Stage IV	Any T	Any N	M1

Ampulla of Vater

Primary tumor (T)

TX   Primary tumor cannot be assessed
T0   No evidence of primary tumor
Tis   Carcinoma in situ
T1   Tumor limited to ampulla of Vater or sphincter of Oddi
T2   Tumor invades duodenal wall
T3   Tumor invades pancreas
T4   Tumor invades peripancreatic soft tissue or other adjacent organs or structures

Regional lymph nodes (N)

NX   Regional lymph nodes cannot be assessed
N0   No regional lymph node metastasis
N1   Regional lymph node metastasis

Distant metastasis (M)

MX   Distant metastasis cannot be assessed
M0   No distant metastasis
M1   Distant metastasis

Stage grouping			
Stage 0	Tis	N0	M0
Stage IA	T1	N0	M0
Stage IB	T2	N0	M0
Stage IIA	T3	N0	M0
Stage IIB	T1	N1	M0
	T2	N1	M0
	T3	N1	M0
Stage III	T4	Any N	M0
Stage IV	Any T	Any N	M1

Kidney

Primary tumor (T)

TX   Primary tumor cannot be assessed
T0   No evidence of primary tumor
T1   Tumor 7 cm or less in greatest dimension, limited to the kidney

T1a Tumor 4 cm or less in greatest dimension, limited to the kidney

T1b Tumor more than 4 cm but not more than 7 cm in greatest dimension, limited to the kidney

T2 Tumor more than 7 cm in greatest dimension, limited to the kidney

T3 Tumor extends into major veins or invades adrenal gland or perinephric tissues but not beyond Gerota's fascia

T3a Tumor directly invades adrenal gland or perirenal and/or renal sinus fat but not beyond Gerota's fascia

T3b Tumor grossly extends into the renal vein or its segmental (muscle-containing) branches, or vena cava below the diaphragm

T3c Tumor grossly extends into vena cava above diaphragm or invades the wall of the vena cava

T4 Tumor invades beyond Gerota's fascia

Regional lymph nodes (N)*

NX Regional lymph nodes cannot be assessed
N0 No regional lymph node metastasis
N1 Metastasis in a single regional lymph node
N2 Metastasis in more than one regional lymph node

*Laterality does not affect the N classification.
Note: If a lymph node dissection is performed, then pathologic evaluation would ordinarily include at least eight nodes.

Distant metastasis (M)

MX Distant metastasis cannot be assessed
M0 No distant metastasis
M1 Distant metastasis

Stage grouping			
Stage I	T1	N0	M0
Stage II	T2	N0	M0
Stage III	T1	N1	M0
	T2	N1	M0
	T3	N0	M0
	T3	N1	M0
	T3a	N0	M0
	T3a	N1	M0
	T3b	N0	M0
	T3b	N1	M0
	T3c	N0	M0
	T3c	N1	M0
Stage IV	T4	N0	M0
	T4	N1	M0
	Any T	N2	M0
	Any T	Any N	M1

Renal pelvis and ureter

Primary tumor (T)

TX Primary tumor cannot be assessed

T0 No evidence of primary tumor
Ta Papillary noninvasive carcinoma
Tis Carcinoma in situ
T1 Tumor invades subepithelial connective tissue
T2 Tumor invades the muscularis
T3 (For renal pelvis only) Tumor invades beyond muscularis into peripelvic fat or the renal parenchyma
T3 (For ureter only) Tumor invades beyond muscularis into perureteric fat
T4 Tumor invades adjacent organs, or through the kidney into the perinephric fat

Regional lymph nodes (N)*

NX Regional lymph nodes cannot be assessed
N0 No regional lymph node metastasis
N1 Metastasis in a single regional lymph node, 2 cm or less in greatest dimension
N2 Metastasis in a single lymph node, more than 2 cm but not more than 5 cm in greatest dimension: or multiple lymph nodes, none more than 5 cm in greatest dimension
N3 Metastasis in a lymph node, more than 5 cm in greatest dimension

*Note: Laterality does not affect the N classification.

Distant metastasis (M)

MX Distant metastasis cannot be assessed
M0 No distant metastasis
M1 Distant metastasis

Stage grouping			
Stage 0a	Ta	N0	M0
Stage 0is	Tis	N0	M0
Stage I	T1	N0	M0
Stage II	T2	N0	M0
Stage III	T3	N0	M0
Stage IV	T4	N0	M0
	Any T	N1	M0
	Any T	N2	M0
	Any T	N3	M0
	Any T	Any N	M1

Urinary bladder

Primary tumor (T)

TX Primary tumor cannot be assessed
T0 No evidence of primary tumor
Ta Noninvasive papillary carcinoma
Tis Carcinoma in situ: "flat tumor"
T1 Tumor invades subepithelial connective tissue
T2 Tumor invades muscle
pT2a Tumor invades superficial muscle (inner half)
pT2b Tumor invades deep muscle (outer half)
T3 Tumor invades perivesical tissue

pT3a microscopically
pT3b macroscopically (extravesical mass)
T4 Tumor invades any of the following: prostate, uterus, vagina, pelvic wall, abdominal wall
T4a Tumor invades prostate, uterus, vagina
T4b Tumor invades pelvic wall, abdominal wall

Regional lymph nodes (N)

Regional lymph nodes are those within the true pelvis; all others are distant lymph nodes.

NX Regional lymph nodes cannot be assessed
N0 No regional lymph node metastasis
N1 Metastasis in a single regional lymph node, 2 cm or less in greatest dimension
N2 Metastasis in a single lymph node, more than 2 cm but not more than 5 cm in greatest dimension: or multiple lymph nodes, none more than 5 cm in greatest dimension
N3 Metastasis in a lymph node, more than 5 cm in greatest dimension

Distant metastasis (M)

MX Distant metastasis cannot be assessed
M0 No distant metastasis
M1 Distant metastasis

Stage grouping			
Stage 0a	Ta	N0	M0
Stage 0is	Tis	N0	M0
Stage I	T1	N0	M0
Stage II	T2a	N0	M0
	T2b	N0	M0
Stage III	T3a	N0	M0
	T3b	N0	M0
	T4a	N0	M0
Stage IV	T4b	N0	M0
	Any T	N1	M0
	Any T	N2	M0
	Any T	N3	M0
	Any T	Any N	M1

Urethra

Primary tumor (T)

TX Primary tumor cannot be assessed
T0 No evidence of primary tumor
Ta Noninvasive papillary, polypoid, or verrucous carcinoma
Tis Carcinoma in situ
T1 Tumor invades subepithelial connective tissue
T2 Tumor invades any of the following: corpus spongiosum, prostate, periurethral muscle
T3 Tumor invades any of the following: corpus caver-

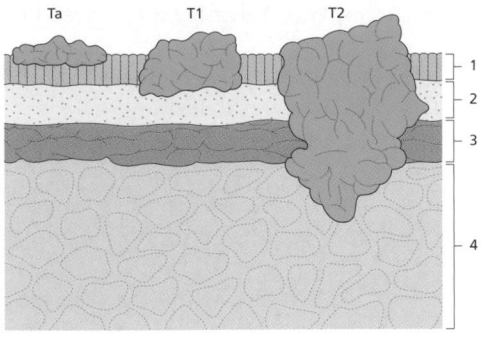

Fig. Appendix C.1. Definition of primary tumor (T). 1–epithelium, 2–subepithelial connective tissue, 3–urethral muscle, 4–urogenital diaphragm.

nosum, beyond prostatic capsule, anterior vagina, bladder neck
T4 Tumor invades other adjacent organs

Urothelial (transitional cell) carcinoma of the prostate

Tis pu Carcinoma in situ, involvement of the prostatic urethra
Tis pd Carcinoma in situ, involvement of the prostatic ducts
T1 Tumor invades subepithelial connective tissue
T2 Tumor invades any of the following: prostatic stroma, corpus spongiosum, periurethral muscle
T3 Tumor invades any of the following: corpus cavernosum, beyond prostatic capsule, bladder neck (extraprostatic extension)
T4 Tumor invades other adjacent organs (invasion of the bladder)

Regional lymph nodes (N)

NX Regional lymph nodes cannot be assessed
N0 No regional lymph node metastasis
N1 Metastasis in a single regional lymph node, 2 cm or less in greatest dimension
N2 Metastasis in a single lymph node more than 2 cm but not more than 5 cm in greatest dimension or

Stage grouping			
Stage 0a	Ta	N0	M0
Stage 0is	Tis	N0	M0
	Tis pu	N0	M0
	Tis pd	N0	M0
Stage I	T1	N0	M0
	T2	N0	M0
Stage II	T1	N1	M0
	T2	N1	M0
	T3	N0	M0
	T3	N1	M0
Stage IV	T4	N0	M0
	T4	N1	M0
	Any T	N2	M0
	Any T	Any N	M1

multiple nodes none more than 5 cm in greatest dimension

Distant metastasis (M)

MX Distant metastasis cannot be assessed
M0 No distant metastasis
M1 Distant metastasis

Prostate

Primary tumor (T)

Clinical

TX Primary tumor cannot be assessed
T0 No evidence of primary tumor
T1 Clinically inapparent tumor neither palpable nor visible by imaging
T1a Tumor incidental histologic finding in 5% or less of tissue resected
T1b Tumor incidental histologic finding in more than 5% of tissue resected
T1c Tumor identified by needle biopsy (e.g. because of elevated PSA)
T2 Tumor confined within prostate*
T2a Tumor involves one-half of one lobe or less
T2b Tumor involves more than one-half of one lobe but not both lobes
T2c Tumor involves both lobes
T3 Tumor extends through the prostate capsule**
T3a Extracapsular extension (unilateral or bilateral)
T3b Tumor invades seminal vesicle(s)
T4 Tumor is fixed or invades adjacent structures other than seminal vesicles: bladder neck, external sphincter, rectum, levator muscles, and/or pelvic wall

*Note: Tumor found in one or both lobes by needle biopsy, but not palpable or reliably visible by imaging, is classified as T1c.
**Note: Invasion into the prostatic apex or into (but not beyond) the prostatic capsule is classified not as T3 but as T2.

Pathologic (pT)
pT2* Organ confined
pT2a Unilateral, involving one-half of one lobe or less
pT2b Unilateral involving more than one-half of one lobe but not both lobes
pT2c Bilateral disease
pT3 Extraprostatic extension
pT3a Extraprostatic extension**
pT3b Seminal vesicle invasion
pT4 Invasion of bladder, rectum

*Note: There is no pathologic T1 classification.
**Note: Positive surgical margin should be indicated by an R1 descriptor (residual microscopic disease).

Regional lymph nodes (N)

Clinical
NX Regional lymph nodes were not assessed
N0 No regional lymph node metastasis
N1 Metastasis in regional lymph node(s)

Pathologic
pNX Regional nodes not sampled
pN0 No positive regional nodes
pN1 Metastasis in regional node(s)

Distant metastasis (M)*

MX Distant metastasis cannot be assessed (not evaluated by any modality)
M0 No distant metastasis
M1 Distant metastasis
M1a Nonregional lymph node(s)
M1b Bone(s)
M1c Other site(s) with or without bone disease

*Note: When more than one site of metastasis is present, the most advanced category is used. pM1C is most advanced.

Stage grouping				
Stage I	T1a	N0	M0	G1
Stage II	T1a	N0	M0	G2, 3–4
	T1b	N0	M0	Any G
	T1c	N0	M0	Any G
	T1	N0	M0	Any G
	T2	N0	M0	Any G
Stage III	T3	N0	M0	Any G
Stage IV	T4	N0	M0	Any G
	Any T	N1	M0	Any G
	Any T	Any N	M1	Any G

Testis

Primary tumor (T)

The extent of the primary tumor is usually classified after radical orchiectomy, and for this reason, a *pathologic* stage is assigned.

Pathologic
*pTX Primary tumor cannot be assessed
pT0 No evidence of primary tumor (e.g. histologic scar in testis)
pTis Intratubular germ cell neoplasia (carcinoma in situ)
pT1 Tumor limited to the testis and epididymis without vascular/lymphatic invasion; tumor may invade into the tunica albuginea but not the tunica vaginalis
pT2 Tumor limited to the testis and epididymis with vascular/lymphatic invasion, or tumor extending through the tunica albuginea with involvement of the tunica vaginalis

pT3 Tumor invades the spermatic cord with or without vascular/lymphatic invasion

pT4 Tumor invades the scrotum with or without vascular/lymphatic invasion

Note: Except for pTis and pT4, extent of primary tumor is classified by radical orchiectomy. TX may be used for other categories in the absence of radical orchiectomy.

Regional lymph nodes (N)

Clinical

NX Regional lymph nodes cannot be assessed

N0 No regional lymph node metastasis

N1 Metastasis with a lymph node mass 2 cm or less in greatest dimension; or multiple lymph nodes, none more than 2 cm in greatest dimension

N2 Metastasis with a lymph node mass more than 2 cm but not more than 5 cm in greatest dimension; or multiple lymph nodes, any one mass greater than 2 cm but not more than 5 cm in greatest dimension

N3 Metastasis with a lymph node mass more than 5 cm in greatest dimension

Pathologic (pN)

pNX Regional lymph nodes cannot be assessed

pN0 No regional lymph node metastasis

pN1 Metastasis with a lymph node mass 2 cm or less in greatest dimension and less than or equal to 5 nodes positive, none more than 2 cm in greatest dimension

pN2 Metastasis with a lymph node mass more than 2 cm but not more than 5 cm in greatest dimension; or more than 5 nodes positive, none more than 5 cm; or evidence of extranodal extension of tumor

pN3 Metastasis with a lymph node mass more than 5 cm in greatest dimension

Distant metastasis (M)

MX Distant metastasis cannot be assessed

M0 No distant metastasis

M1 Distant metastasis

M1a Nonregional nodal or pulmonary metastasis

M1b Distant metastasis other than to nonregional lymph nodes and lungs

Serum tumor markers (S)

SX Marker studies not available or not performed

S0 Marker study levels within normal limits

S1 LDH $< 1.5 \times N$* **AND**
hCG (mIu/ml) < 5000 **AND**
AFP (ng/ml) < 1000

S2 LDH 1.5–$10 \times N$ **OR**
hCG (mIu/ml) 5000–$50,000$ **OR**
AFP (ng/ml) 1000–$10,000$

S3 LDH $> 10 \times N$ **OR**
hCG (mIu/ml) $> 50,000$ **OR**
AFP (ng/ml) $> 10,000$

*N indicates the upper limit of normal for the LDH assay.

Stage grouping				
Stage 0	PTis	N0	M0	S0
Stage I	PT1–4	N0	M0	SX
Stage IA	PT1	N0	M0	S0
Stage IB	PT2	N0	M0	S0
	PT3	N0	M0	S0
	PT4	N0	M0	S0
Stage IS	Any pT/Tx	N0	M0	S1–3
Stage II	Any pT/Tx	N1–3	M0	SX
Stage IIA	Any pT/Tx	N1	M0	S0
	Any pT/Tx	N1	M0	S1
Stage IIB	Any pT/Tx	N2	M0	S0
	Any pT/Tx	N2	M0	S1
Stage IIC	Any pT/Tx	N3	M0	S0
	Any pT/Tx	N3	Mo	S1
Stage III	Any pT/Tx	Any N	M1	SX
Stage IIIA	Any pT/Tx	Any N	M1a	S0
	Any pT/Tx	Any N	M1a	S1
Stage IIIB	Any pT/Tx	N1–3	M0	S2
	Any pT/Tx	Any N	M1a	S2
Stage IIIC	Any pT/Tx	N1–3	M0	S3
	Any pT/Tx	Any N	M1a	S3
	Any pT/Tx	Any N	M1b	Any S

Penis

Primary tumor (T)

TX Primary tumor cannot be assessed

T0 No evidence of primary tumor

Tis Carcinoma in situ

Ta Noninvasive verrucous carcinoma

T1 Tumor invades subepithelial connective tissue

T2 Tumor invades corpus spongiosum or cavernosum

T3 Tumor invades urethra or prostate

T4 Tumor invades other adjacent structures

Regional lymph nodes (N)

NX Regional lymph nodes cannot be assessed

N0 No regional lymph node metastasis

N1 Metastasis in a single superficial, inguinal lymph node

N2 Metastasis in multiple or bilateral superficial inguinal lymph nodes

N3 Metastasis in deep inguinal or pelvic lymph node(s) unilateral or bilateral

Distant metastasis (M)

MX Distant metastasis cannot be assessed

M0 No distant metastasis

M1 Distant metastasis

Additional descriptor

The **m suffix** indicates the presence of multiple primary tumors and is recorded in parentheses—e.g. pTa(m) N0 M0.

Vulva

The definitions of the T categories correspond to the stages accepted by the Fédération Internationale de Gynécologie et d'Obstétrique (FIGO). Both systems are included for comparison.

Primary tumor (T)

TMN Categories	FIGO Stages	
TX		Primary tumor cannot be assessed
T0		No evidence of primary tumor
Tis	0	Carcinoma in situ (preinvasive carcinoma)
T1	I	Tumor confined to vulva or vulva and perineum, 2 cm or less in greatest dimension
T1a	IA	Tumor confined to vulva or vulva and perineum, 2 cm or less in greatest dimension, and with stromal invasion no more than 1 mm
T1b	IB	Tumor confined to vulva or vulva and perineum, 2 cm or less in greatest dimension, and with stromal invasion greater than 1 mm
T2	II	Tumor confined to vulva or vulva and perineum, more than 2 cm in greatest dimension
T3	III	Tumor of any size with contiguous spread to the lower urethra and/or vagina or anus
T4	IVA	Tumor invades any of the following: upper urethra, bladder mucosa, rectal mucosa, or is fixed to the pubic bone

Note: The depth of invasion is defined as the measurement of the tumor from the epithelial stromal junction of the adjacent most superficial dermal papilla to the deepest point of invasion.

Regional lymph nodes (N)

NX		Regional lymph nodes cannot be assessed
N0		No regional lymph node metastasis
N1	III	Unilateral regional lymph node metastasis
N2	IVA	Bilateral region lymph node metastasis

Every effort should be made to determine the site and laterality of lymph node metastases. However, if "regional lymph node metastases, NOS" is the final diagnosis, then the patient should be staged as N1.

Distant metastasis (M)

MX		Distant metastasis cannot be assessed
M0		No distant metastasis
M1	IVB	Distant metastasis (including pelvic lymph node metastasis)

Stage grouping

Stage grouping			
Stage 0	Tis	N0	M0
	Ta	N0	M0
Stage I	T1	N0	M0
Stage II	T1	N1	M0
	T2	N0	M0
	T2	N1	M0
Stage III	T1	N2	M0
	T2	N2	M0
	T3	N0	M0
	T3	N1	M0
	T3	N2	M0
Stage IV	T4	Any N	M0
	Any T	N3	M0
	Any T	Any N	M1

Vagina

The definitions of the T categories correspond to the stages accepted by the Fédération Internationale de Gynécologie et d'Obstétrique (FIGO). Both systems are included for comparison.

Primary tumor (T)

TMN Categories	FIGO Stages	
TX		Primary tumor cannot be assessed
T0		No evidence of primary tumor
Tis	0	Carcinoma in situ
T1	I	Tumor confined to vagina
T2	II	Tumor invades paravaginal tissues but not to pelvic wall
T3	III	Tumor extends to pelvic wall*
T4	IVA	Tumor invades mucosa of the bladder or rectum and/or extends beyond the true pelvis (bullous edema is not sufficient evidence to classify a tumor as T4)

*Pelvic wall is defined as muscle, fascia, neurovascular structures, or skeletal portions of the bony pelvis.

Regional lymph nodes (N)

NX		Regional lymph nodes cannot be assessed
N0		No regional lymph node metastasis
N1	IVB	Pelvic or inguinal lymph node metastasis

Distant metastasis (M)

MX		Distant metastasis cannot be assessed
M0		No distant metastasis
M1	IVB	Distant metastasis

Stage grouping			
Stage 0	Tis	N0	M0
Stage I	T1	N0	M0
Stage IA	T1a	N0	M0
Stage IB	T1b	N0	M0
Stage II	T2	N0	M0
Stage III	T1	N1	M0
	T2	N1	M0
	T3	N0	M0
	T3	N1	M0
Stage IVA	T1	N2	M0
	T2	N2	M0
	T3	N2	M0
	T4	Any N	M0
Stage IVB	Any T	Any N	M1

Cervix uteri

The definitions of the T categories correspond to the stages accepted by the Fédération Internationale de Gynécologie et d'Obstétrique (FIGO). Both systems are included for comparison.

Primary tumor (T)

TMN Categories	FIGO Stages	
TX		Primary tumor cannot be assessed
T0		No evidence of primary tumor
Tis	0	Carcinoma in situ
T1	I	Cervical carcinoma confined to uterus (extension to corpus should be disregarded)
*T1a	IA	Invasive carcinoma diagnosed only by microscopy. Stromal invasion with a maximum depth of 5.0 mm measured from the base of the epithelium and a horizontal spread of 7.0 mm or less. Vascular space involvement, venous or lymphatic, does not affect classification
T1a1	IA1	Measured stromal invasion 3.0 mm or less in depth and 7.0 mm or less in horizontal spread
T1a2	IA2	Measured stromal invasion more than 3.0 mm and not more than 5.0 mm with a horizontal spread 7.0 mm or less
T1b	IB	Clinically visible lesion confined to the cervix or microscopic lesion greater than T1a/IA2
T1b1	IB1	Clinically visible lesion 4.0 cm or less in greatest dimension
T1b2	IB2	Clinically visible lesion more than 4.0 cm in greatest dimension

T2	II	Cervical carcinoma invades beyond uterus but not to pelvic wall or to lower third of vagina
T2a	IIA	Tumor without parametrial invasion
T2b	IIB	Tumor with parametrial invasion
T3	III	Tumor extends to the pelvic wall and/or involves lower third of vagina, and/or causes hydronephrosis or nonfunctioning kidney
T3a	IIIA	Tumor involves lower third of vagina, no extension to pelvic wall
T3b	IIIB	Tumor extends to pelvic wall and/or causes hydronephrosis or nonfunctioning kidney
T4	IVA	Tumor invades mucosa of bladder or rectum, and/or extends beyond true pelvis (bullous edema is not sufficient to classify a tumor as T4)

*All macroscopically visible lesions – even with superficial invasion – are T1b/IB.

Regional lymph nodes (N)

NX	Regional lymph nodes cannot be assessed
N0	No regional lymph node metastasis
N1	Regional lymph node metastasis

Distant metastasis (M)

MX		Distant metastasis cannot be assessed
M0		No distant metastasis
M1	IVB	Distant metastasis

Stage grouping			
Stage 0	Tis	N0	M0
Stage I	T1	N0	M0
Stage II	T2	N0	M0
Stage III	T1-T3	N1	M0
	T3	N0	M0
Stage IVA	T4	Any N	M0
Stage IVB	Any T	Any N	M1

Uterine corpus

The definitions of the T categories correspond to the stages accepted by FIGO. FIGO stages are further subdivided by histologic grade of tumor – for example, Stage IC G2. Both systems are included for comparison.

Primary tumor (T) (surgical–pathologic findings)

TMN Categories	FIGO Stages	
TX		Primary tumor cannot be assessed
T0		No evidence of primary tumor
Tis	0	Carcinoma in situ

T1I		Tumor confined to corpus uteri
T1a	IA	Tumor limited to endometrium
T1b	IB	Tumor invades less than one-half of the myometrium
T1c	IC	Tumor invades one-half or more of the myometrium
T2	II	Tumor invades cervix but does not extend beyond uterus
T2a	IIA	Tumor limited to the glandular epithelium of the endocervix. There is no evidence of connective tissue stromal invasion
T2b	IIB	Invasion of the stromal connective tissue of the cervix
T3	III	Local and/or regional spread as defined below
T3a	IIIA	Tumor involves serosa and/or adnexa (direct extension or metastasis) and/or cancer cells in ascites or peritoneal washings
T3b	IIIB	Vaginal involvement (direct extension or metastasis)
T4	IVA	Tumor invades bladder mucosa and/or bowel mucosa (bullous edema is not sufficient to classify a tumor as T4)

Regional lymph nodes (N)

NX		Regional lymph nodes cannot be assessed
N0		No regional lymph node metastasis
N1	IIIC	Regional lymph node metastasis to pelvic and/or para-aortic nodes

Distant metastasis (M)

MX		Distant metastasis cannot be assessed
M0		No distant metastasis
M1	IVB	Distant metastasis (includes metastasis to abdominal lymph nodes other than para-aortic, and/or inguinal lymph nodes; excludes metastasis to vagina, pelvic serosa, or adnexa)

Stage grouping			
Stage 0	Tis	N0	M0
Stage I	T1	N0	M0
Stage IA	T1a	N0	M0
Stage IA1	T1a1	N0	M0
Stage IA2	T1a2	N0	M0
Stage IB	T1b	N0	M0
Stage IB1	T1b1	N0	M0
Stage IB2	T1b2	N0	M0
Stage II	T2	N0	M0
Stage IIA	T2a	N0	M0
Stage IIB	T2b	N0	M0
Stage III	T3	N0	M0
Stage IIIA	T3a	N0	M0
Stage IIIB	T1	N1	M0
	T2	N1	M0
	T3a	N1	M0
	T3b	Any N	M0
Stage IVA	T4	Any N	M0
Stage IVB	Any T	Any N	M1

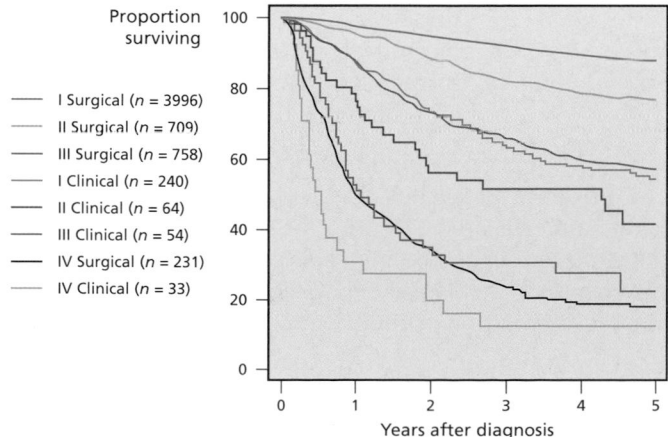

Fig. Appendix C.2 Carcinoma of the corpus uteri, patients treated 1993–1995. Survival by mode of staging, n = 6085. (Reprinted with permission from Creasman W, Odicino F, Maisonneuve P et al: Carcinoma of the corpus uteri. FIGO Annual Report. Jepid Biostat 2001, **6:** 45–86.)

Proportion surviving 100

— I Surgical (n = 3996)
— II Surgical (n = 709)
— III Surgical (n = 758)
— I Clinical (n = 240)
— II Clinical (n = 64)
— III Clinical (n = 54)
— IV Surgical (n = 231)
— IV Clinical (n = 33)

Years after diagnosis

Fallopian tube

Primary tumor (T)

TMN Categories	FIGO Stages	
TX		Primary tumor cannot be assessed
T0		No evidence of primary tumor
Tis	0	Carcinoma in situ (limited to tubal mucosa)
T1	I	Tumor limited to the fallopian tube(s)
T1a	IA	Tumor limited to one tube, without penetrating the serosal surface; no ascites
T1b	IB	Tumor limited to both tubes, without penetrating the serosal surface; no ascites
T1c	IC	Tumor limited to one or both tubes with extension onto or through the tubal serosa, or with malignant cells in ascites or peritoneal washings
T2	II	Tumor involves one or both fallopian tubes with pelvic extension
T2a	IIA	Extension and/or metastasis to the uterus and/or ovaries

T2b	IIB	Extension to other pelvic structures
T2c	IIC	Pelvic extension with malignant cells in ascites or peritoneal washings
T3	III	Tumor involves one or both tubes, with peritoneal implants outside the pelvis
T3a	IIIA	Microscopic peritoneal metastasis outside the pelvis
T3b	IIIB	Macroscopic peritoneal metastasis outside the pelvis 2 cm or less in greatest dimension
T3c	IIIC	Peritoneal metastasis more than 2 cm in greatest dimension

Note: Liver capsule metastasis is T3/Stage III; liver parenchymal metastasis M1/Stage IV. Pleural effusion must have positive cytology for M1/Stage IV.

Regional lymph nodes (N)

NX		Regional lymph nodes cannot be assessed
N0		No regional lymph node metastasis
N1	IIC	Regional lymph node metastasis

Distant metastasis (M)

MX		Distant metastasis cannot be assessed
M0		No distant metastasis
M1	IV	Distant metastasis (excludes metastasis within the peritoneal cavity)

Stage grouping			
Stage 0	Tis	N0	M0
Stage I	T1	N0	M0
Stage IA	T1a	N0	M0
Stage IB	T1b	N0	M0
Stage IC	T1c	N0	M0
Stage II	T2	N0	M0
Stage IIA	T2a	N0	M0
Stage IIB	T2b	N0	M0
Stage IIC	T2c	N0	M0
Stage III	T3	N0	M0
Stage IIIA	T3a	N0	M0
Stage IIIB	T3b	N0	M0
Stage IIIC	T3c	N0	M0
	Any T	N1	M0
Stage IV	Any T	Any N	M1

Ovary

The definitions of the T categories correspond to the stages accepted by the Fédération Internationale de Gynécologie et d'Obstétrique (FIGO). Both systems are included for comparison.

Primary tumor (T)

TMN Categories	*FIGO Stages*	
TX		Primary tumor cannot be assessed
T0		No evidence of primary tumor
T1	I	Tumor limited to ovaries (one or both)
T1a	IA	Tumor limited to one ovary; capsule intact, no tumor on ovarian surface. No malignant cells in ascites or peritoneal washings*
T1b	IB	Tumor limited to both ovaries; capsule intact, no tumor on ovarian surface. No malignant cells in ascites or peritoneal washings*
T1c	IC	Tumor limited to one or both ovaries with any of the following: capsule ruptured, tumor on ovarian surface, malignant cells in ascites or peritoneal washings
T2	II	Tumor involves one or both ovaries with pelvic extension and/or implants
T2a	IIA	Extension and/or implants on uterus and/or tube(s). No malignant cells in ascites or peritoneal washings
T2b	IIB	Extension to and/or implants on other pelvic tissues. No malignant cells in ascites or peritoneal washings
T2c	IIC	Pelvic extension and/or implants (T2a or T2b) with malignant cells in ascites or peritoneal washings
T3	III	Tumor involves one or both ovaries with microscopically confirmed peritoneal metastasis outside the pelvis
T3a	IIIA	Microscopic peritoneal metastasis beyond pelvis (no macroscopic tumor)
T3b	IIIB	Macroscopic peritoneal metastasis beyond pelvis 2 cm or less in greatest dimension
T3c	IIIC	Peritoneal metastasis beyond pelvis more than 2 cm in greatest dimension and/or regional lymph node metastasis

*The presence of nonmalignant ascites is not classified. The presence of ascites does not affect staging unless malignant cells are present.

Note: Liver capsule metastasis T3/Stage III; liver parenchymal metastasis M1/Stage IV. Pleural effusion must have positive cytology for M1/Stage IV.

Regional lymph nodes (N)

NX		Regional lymph nodes cannot be assessed
N0		No regional lymph node metastasis
N1	IIC	Regional lymph node metastasis

Distant metastasis (M)

| MX | | Distant metastasis cannot be assessed |

M0		No distant metastasis	
M1	IV	Distant metastasis (excludes peritoneal metastasis)	

M1		Distant metastasis
M1a	III	Lung metastasis
M1b	IV	All other distant metastasis

Pathologic classifications

The pT, pN, and pM categories correspond to the T, N, and M categories.

Stage grouping			
Stage I	T1	N0	M0
Stage IA	T1a	N0	M0
Stage IB	T1b	N0	M0
Stage IC	T1c	N0	M0
Stage II	T2	N0	M0
Stage IIA	T2a	N0	M0
Stage IIB	T2b	N0	M0
Stage IIC	T2c	N0	M0
Stage III	T3	N0	M0
Stage IIIA	T3a	N0	M0
Stage IIIB	T3b	N0	M0
Stage IIIC	T3c	N0	M0
	Any T	N1	M0
Stage IV	Any T	Any N	M1

Gestational trophoblastic tumors

Primary tumor (T)

TMN Categories	FIGO Stages	
TX		Primary tumor cannot be assessed
T0		No evidence of primary tumor
T1	I	Tumor confined to uterus
T2	II	Tumor extends to other genital structures (ovary, tube, vagina, broad ligaments) by metastasis or direct extension

Distant metastasis (M)

MX	Metastasis cannot be assessed
M0	No distant metastasis

Stage grouping			
Stage	T	M	Risk factors
Stage I	T1	M0	Unknown
Stage IA	T1	M0	Low risk
Stage IB	T1	M0	High risk
Stage II	T2	M0	Unknown
Stage IIA	T2	M0	Low risk
Stage IIB	T2	M0	High risk
Stage III	Any T	M1a	Unknown
Stage IIIA	Any T	M1a	Low risk
Stage IIIB	Any T	M1a	High risk
Stage IV	Any T	M1b	Unknown
Stage IVA	Any T	M1b	Low risk
Stage IVB	Any T	M1b	High risk

Breast

Primary tumor (T)

Definitions for classifying the primary tumor (T) are the same for clinical and pathologic classification. If the measurement is made by physical examination, the examiner will use the major headings (T1, T2, or T3). If other measurements, such as mammographic or pathologic measurements, are used, the subsets of T1 can be used. Tumors should be measure to the nearest 0.1 cm increment.

TX	Primary tumor cannot be assessed
T0	No evidence of primary tumor
Tis	Carcinoma in situ
Tis (DCIS)	Ductal carcinoma in situ
Tis (LCIS)	Lobular carcinoma in situ
Tis (Paget's)	Paget's disease of the nipple with no tumor

Note: Paget's disease associated with a tumor is classified according to the size of the tumor.

T1	Tumor 2 cm or less in greatest dimension
T1Mic	Microinvasion 0.1 cm or less in greatest dimension
T1a	Tumor more than 0.1 cm but not more than 0.5 cm in greatest dimension
T1b	Tumor more than 0.5 cm but not more than 1 cm in greatest dimension
T1c	Tumor more than 1 cm but not more than 2 cm in greatest dimension
T2	Tumor more than 2 cm but nor more than 5 cm in greatest dimension
T3	Tumor more than 5 cm in greatest dimension
T4	Tumor of any size with direct extension to (a) chest wall or (b) skin, only as described below
T4a	Extension to chest wall, not including pectoralis muscle
T4b	Edema (including peau d'orange) or ulceration of the skin of the breast, or satellite skin nodules confined to the same breast
T4c	Both T4a and T4b
T4d	Inflammatory carcinoma

Regional lymph nodes (N)

Clinical

NX	Regional lymph nodes cannot be assessed (e.g. previously removed)
N0	No regional lymph node metastasis
N1	Metastasis to movable ipsilateral axillary lymph node(s)
N2	Metastases in ipsilateral axillary lymph nodes fixed or matted, or in clinically apparent* ipsilateral

internal mammary nodes in the *absence* of clinically evident axillary lymph node metastasis

N2a Metastasis in ipsilateral axillary lymph nodes fixed to one another (matted) or to other structures

N2b Metastasis only in clinically apparent* ipsilateral internal mammary nodes and in the *absence* of clinically evident axillary lymph node metastasis

N3 Metastasis in ipsilateral infraclavicular lymph node(s) with or without axillary lymph node involvement, or in clinically apparent* ipsilateral internal mammary lymph node(s) and in the *presence* of clinically evident axillary lymph node metastasis; or metastasis in ipsilateral supraclavicular lymph node(s) with or without axillary or internal mammary lymph node involvement

N3a Metastasis in ipsilateral infraclavicular lymph node(s)

N3b Metastasis in ipsilateral internal mammary lymph node(s) and axillary lymph node(s)

N3c Metastasis in ipsilateral supraclavicular lymph node(s)

Clinically apparent is defined as detected by imaging studies (excluding lymphoscintigraphy) or by clinical examination or grossly visible pathologically.

Pathologic (pN)*

pNX Regional lymph nodes cannot be assessed (e.g. previously removed, or not removed for pathologic study)

pN0 No regional lymph node metastasis histologically, no additional examination for isolated tumor cells (ITC)

Note: Isolated tumor cells (ITC) are defined as single tumor cells or small cell clusters not greater than 0.2 mm, usually detected only by immunohistochemical (IHC) or molecular methods but which may be verified on hematoxylin and eosin stains. ITCs do not usually show evidence of malignant activity, e.g. proliferation or stromal reaction.

pN0(i–)   No regional lymph node metastasis histologically, negative IHC

pN0(i+)   No regional lymph node metastasis histologically, positive IHC, no IHC cluster greater than 0.2 mm

pN0(mol–) No regional lymph node metastasis histologically, negative molecular findings (RT-PCR)**

pN0(mol+) No regional lymph node metastasis histologically, positive molecular findings (RT-PCR)**

*Classification is based on axillary lymph node dissection with or without sentinel lymph node dissection. Classification based solely on sentinel lymph node dissection without subsequent axillary lymph node dissection is designated (sn) for "sentinel node," e.g. pN0(i+) (sn).

**RT-PCR: reverse transcriptase/polymerase chain reaction.

pN1 Metastasis in 1 to 3 axillary lymph nodes, and/or in internal mammary nodes with microscopic disease detected by sentinel lymph node dissection but not clinically apparent**

pN1mi Micrometastasis (greater than 0.2 mm, none greater than 2.0 mm)

pN1a Metastasis in one to three axillary lymph nodes

pN1b Metastasis in internal mammary nodes with microscopic disease detected by sentinel lymph node dissection but not clinically apparent**

pN1c Metastasis in one to three axillary lymph nodes and in internal mammary lymph nodes with microscopic disease detected by sentinel lymph node dissection but not clinically apparent.** (If associated with more than three positive axillary lymph nodes, the internal mammary nodes are classified as pN3b to reflect increased tumor burden)

pN2 Metastasis in four to nine axillary lymph nodes, or in clinically apparent* internal mammary lymph nodes in the *absence* of axillary lymph node metastasis

pN2a Metastasis in four to nine axillary lymph nodes (at least one tumor deposit greater than 2.0 mm)

pN2b Metastasis in clinically apparent* internal mammary lymph nodes in the *absence* of axillary lymph node metastasis

pN3 Metastasis in 10 or more axillary lymph nodes, or in infraclavicular lymph nodes in the *presence* of one or more positive axillary lymph nodes; or in more than three axillary lymph nodes with clinically negative microscopic metastasis in internal mammary lymph nodes; or in ipsilateral supraclavicular lymph nodes

pN3a Metastasis in 10 or more axillary lymph nodes (at least one tumor deposit greater than 2.0 mm), or metastasis to the infraclavicular lymph nodes

pN3b Metastasis in clinically apparent* ipsilateral internal mammary lymph nodes in the *presence* of one or more positive axillary lymph nodes; or in more than three axillary lymph nodes and in internal mammary lymph nodes with microscopic disease detected by sentinel lymph node dissection but not clinically apparent**

pN3c Metastasis in ipsilateral supraclavicular lymph nodes

Clinically apparent is defined as detected by imaging studies (excluding lymphoscintigraphy) or by clinical examination.

**Not clinically apparent* is defined as not detected by imaging studies (excluding lymphoscintigraphy) or by clinical examination.

Distant metastasis (M)

MX Distant metastasis cannot be assessed
M0 No distant metastasis
M1 Distant metastasis

Stage grouping			
Stage 0	Tis	N0	M0
Stage I	T1*	N0	M0
Stage IIA	T0	N1	M0
	T1*	N1	M0
	T2	N0	M0
Stage IIB	T2	N0	M0
	T3	N0	M0
Stage IIIA	T0	N2	M0
	T1*	N2	M0
	T2	N2	M0
	T3	N1	M0
	T3	N2	M0
Stage IIIB	T4	N0	M0
	T4	N1	M0
	T4	N2	M0
Stage IIIC	Any T	N3	M0
Stage IV	Any T	Any N	M1

*T1 includes T1mic

Bone

Primary tumor (T)

TX Primary tumor cannot be assessed
T0 No evidence of primary tumor
T1 Tumor 8 cm or less in greatest dimension
T2 Tumor more than 8 cm in greatest dimension
T3 Discontinuous tumors in the primary bone site

Regional lymph nodes (N)

NX Regional lymph nodes cannot be assessed
N0 No regional lymph node metastasis
N1 Regional lymph node metastasis

Note: Because of the rarity of lymph node involvement in sarcomas, the designation NX may not be appropriate and could be considered N0 if no clinical involvement is evident.

Distant metastasis (M)

MX Distant metastasis cannot be assessed

M0 No distant metastasis
M1 Distant metastasis
M1a Lung
M1b Other distant sites

Stage grouping					
Stage IA	T1	N0	M0	G1,2	Low grade
Stage IB	T2	N0	M0	G1,2	Low grade
Stage IIA	T1	N0	M0	G3,4	High grade
Stage IIB	T2	N0	M0	G3,4	High grade
Stage III	T3	N0	M0	Any G	
Stage IVA	Any T	N0	M1a	Any G	
Stage IVB	Any T	N1	Any M	Any G	
	Any T	Any N	M1b	Any G	

Soft tissue sarcoma

Primary tumor (T)

TX Primary tumor cannot be assessed
T0 No evidence of primary tumor
T1 Tumor 5 cm or less in greatest dimension
   T1a Superficial tumor
   T1b Deep tumor
T2 Tumor more than 5 cm in greatest dimension
   T2a Supercicial tumor
   T1b Deep tumor

Note. Superficial tumor is located exclusively above the superficial fascia without invasion of the fascia; deep tumor is located either exclusively beneath the superficial fascia, superficial to the fascia with invasion of or through the fascia, or both superficial yet beneath the fascia. Retroperitoneal, mediastinal, and pelvic sarcomas are classified as deep tumors.

Regional lymph nodes (N)

NX Regional lymph nodes cannot be assessed
N0 No regional lymph node metastasis
N1* Regional lymph node metastasis

Note: Presence of positive nodes (N1) is considered Stage IV.

Distant metastasis (M)

MX Distant metastasis cannot be assessed
M0 No distant metastasis
M1 Distant metastasis

Stage grouping						
Stage I	T1a, 1b, 2a, 2b	N0	M0	G1–2	G1	Low
Stage II	T1a, 1b, 2a	N0	M0	G3–4	G2–3	High
Stage III	T2b	N0	M0	G3–4	G2–3	High
Stage IV	Any T	N1	M0	Any G	Any G	High or low
	Any T	N0	M1	Any G	Any G	High or low

Eye—carcinoma of the eyelid

The following definitions apply to clinical and pathologic staging.

Primary tumor (T)

TX Primary tumor cannot be assessed
T0 No evidence of primary tumor
Tis Carcinoma in situ
T1 Tumor of any size, not invading the tarsal plate or, at the eyelid margin, 5 mm or less in greatest dimension
T2 Tumor invades tarsal plate or, at the eyelid margin, more than 5 mm but not more than 10 mm in greatest dimension
T3 Tumor involves full eyelid thickness or, at the eyelid margin, more than 10 mm in greatest dimension
T4 Tumor invades adjacent structures, which include bulbar conjunctiva, sclera and globe, soft tissues of the orbit, perineural space, bone and periosteum of the orbit, nasal cavity and paranasal sinuses, and central nervous system

Regional lymph nodes (N)

NX Regional lymph nodes cannot be assessed
N0 No regional lymph node metastasis
N1 Regional lymph node metastasis

Distant metastasis (M)

MX Distant metastasis cannot be assessed
M0 No distant metastasis
M1 Distant metastasis

Stage grouping

No Stage grouping is presently recommended.

Eye—carcinoma of the lacrimal gland

This classification applies to both clinical and pathologic staging of lacrimal gland carcinomas.

Primary tumor (T)

TX Primary tumor cannot be assessed
T0 No evidence of primary tumor
T1 Tumor 2.5 cm or less in greatest dimension, limited to the lacrimal gland
T2 Tumor more than 2.5 cm but not more than 5 cm in greatest dimension, limited to the lacrimal gland
T3 Tumor invades the periosteum
T3a Tumor not more than 5 cm invades the periosteum of the lacrimal gland fossa
T3b Tumor more than 5 cm in greatest dimension with periosteal invasion

T4 Tumor invades the orbital soft tissues, optic nerve, or globe with or without bone invasion; tumor extends beyond the orbit to adjacent structures, including brain

Regional lymph nodes (N)

NX Regional lymph nodes cannot be assessed
N0 No regional lymph node metastasis
N1 Regional lymph node metastasis

Distant metastasis (M)

MX Distant metastasis cannot be assessed
M0 No distant metastasis
M1 Distant metastasis

Stage grouping

No Stage grouping is presently recommended.

Eye—sarcoma of the orbit

Primary tumor (T)

TX Primary tumor cannot be assessed
T0 No evidence of primary tumor
T1 Tumor 15 mm or less in greatest dimension
T2 Tumor more than 15 mm in greatest dimension, without invasion of globe or bony wall
T3 Tumor of any size with invasion of orbital tissues and/or bony walls
T4 Tumor invasion of globe or periorbital structure, such as eyelids, temporal fossa, nasal cavity and paranasal sinuses, and/or central nervous system

Regional lymph nodes (N)

NX Regional lymph nodes cannot be assessed
N0 No regional lymph node metastasis
N1 Regional lymph node metastasis

Distant metastasis (M)

MX Distant metastasis cannot be assessed
M0 No distant metastasis
M1 Distant metastasis

Stage grouping

No Stage grouping is presently recommended.

Eye—carcinoma of the conjunctiva

These definitions apply to both clinical and pathologic staging.

Primary tumor (T)

TX   Primary tumor cannot be assessed
T0   No evidence of primary tumor
Tis   Carcinoma in situ
T1   Tumor 5 mm or less in greatest dimension
T2   Tumor more than 5 mm in greatest dimension, without invasion of adjacent structures
T3   Tumor invades adjacent structures, excluding the orbit
T4   Tumor invades the orbit with or without further extension
T4a   Tumor invades orbital soft tissues, without bone invasion
T4b   Tumor invades bone
T4c   Tumor invades adjacent paranasal sinuses
T4d   Tumor invades brain

Regional lymph nodes (N)

NX   Regional lymph nodes cannot be assessed
N0   No regional lymph node metastasis
N1   Regional lymph node metastasis

Distant metastasis (M)

MX   Distant metastasis cannot be assessed
M0   No distant metastasis
M1   Distant metastasis

Stage grouping

No Stage grouping is presently recommended.

Eye—malignant melanoma of the conjunctiva

Primary tumor (T)

Clinical

TX   Primary tumor cannot be assessed
T0   No evidence of primary tumor
T1   Tumor of the bulbar conjunctiva
T2   Tumor of the bulbar conjunctiva with corneal extension
T3   Tumor extending into the conjunctival fornix, palpebral conjunctiva, or caruncle
T4   Tumor invades the eyelid, globe, orbit, sinuses, or central nervous system

Pathologic

pTX   Primary tumor cannot be assessed
pT0   No evidence of primary tumor
pT1   Tumor of the bulbar conjunctiva confined to the epithelium
pT2   Tumor of the bulbar conjunctiva not more than 0.8 mm in thickness with invasion of the substantia propria

pT3   Tumor of the bulbar conjunctiva more than 0.8 mm in thickness with invasion of the substantia propria or tumors involving the palpebral or caruncular conjunctiva
pT4   Tumor invades the eyelid, globe, orbit, sinuses, or central nervous system

Regional lymph nodes (N)

Clinical

NX   Regional lymph nodes cannot be assessed
N0   No regional lymph node metastasis
N1   Regional lymph node metastasis

Pathologic

pNX   Regional lymph nodes cannot be assessed
pN0   No regional lymph node metastasis
pN1   Regional lymph node metastasis

Distant metastasis (M)

Clinical

MX   Distant metastasis cannot be assessed
M0   No distant metastasis
M1   Distant metastasis

Pathologic

pMX   Distant metastasis cannot be assessed
pM0   No distant metastasis
pM1   Distant metastasis

Stage grouping

No Stage grouping is presently recommended.

Eye—malignant melanoma of the uvea

These definitions apply to both clinical* and pathologic staging.

Primary tumor (T)

All uveal melanomas

TX   Primary tumor cannot be assessed
T0   No evidence of primary tumor

Iris
T1   Tumor limited to the iris
T1a   Tumor limited to the iris not more than 3 clock hours in size
T1b   Tumor limited to the iris more than 3 clock hours in size
T1c   Tumor limited to the iris with melanomalytic glaucoma
T2   Tumor confluent with or extending into the ciliary body and/or choroid
T2a   Tumor confluent with or extending into the ciliary body and/or choroid with melanomalytic glaucoma

T3   Tumor confluent with or extending into the ciliary body and/or choroid with scleral extension

T3a   Tumor confluent with or extending into the ciliary body with scleral extension and melanomalytic glaucoma

T4   Tumor with extraocular extension

Ciliary body and choroid

T1*   Tumor 10 mm or less in greatest diameter and 2.5 mm or less in greatest height (thickness)

T1a   Tumor 10 mm or less in greatest diameter and 2.5 mm or less in greatest height (thickness) without microscopic extraocular extension

T1b   Tumor 10 mm or less in greatest diameter and 2.5 mm or less in greatest height (thickness) with microscopic extraocular extension

T1c   Tumor 10 mm or less in greatest diameter and 2.5 mm or less in greatest height (thickness) with macroscopic extraocular extension

T2*   Tumor 10 mm to 16 mm in greatest basal diameter and between 2.5 and 10 mm in maximum height (thickness)

T2a   Tumor 10 mm to 16 mm in greatest basal diameter and between 2.5 and 10 mm in maximum height (thickness) without microscopic extraocular extension

T2b   Tumor 10 mm to 16 mm in greatest basal diameter and between 2.5 and 10 mm in maximum height (thickness) with microscopic extraocular extension

T2c   Tumor 10 mm to 16 mm in greatest basal diameter and between 2.5 and 10 mm in maximum height (thickness) with macroscopic extraocular extension

T3*   Tumor more than 16 mm in greatest diameter and/or greater than 10 mm in maximum height (thickness) without extraocular extension

T4   Tumor more than 16 mm in greatest diameter and/or greater than 10 mm in maximum height (thickness) with extraocular extension

*Note: When basal dimension and apical height do not fit this classification, the largest tumor diameter should be used for classification. In clinical practice, the tumor base may be estimated in optic disc diameters (dd) (average: 1 dd = 1.5 mm). The height may be estimated in diopters (average: 3 diopters = 1 mm). Techniques such as ultrasonography, visualization, and photography are frequently used to provide more accurate measurements.

Regional lymph nodes (N)

NX   Regional lymph nodes cannot be assessed
N0   No regional lymph node metastasis
N1   Regional lymph node metastasis

Distant metastasis (M)

MX   Distant metastasis cannot be assessed
M0   No distant metastasis
M1   Distant metastasis

Stage grouping			
Stage I	T1	N0	M0
	T1a	N0	M0
	T1b	N0	M0
	T1c	N0	M0
Stage II	T2	N0	M0
	T2a	N0	M0
	T2b	N0	M0
	T2c	N0	M0
Stage III	T3	N0	M0
	T4	N0	M0
Stage IV	Any T	N1	M0
	Any T	Any N	M1

Eye—retinoblastoma

Primary tumor (T)

Clinical

The classification that follows was extensively revised from the last publication. In T1 eyes, the tumor is confined to the retina, the tissue of origin. The classification below reflects a decade's experience with the response to chemotherapy followed by focal consolidation. The likelihood of salvaging good vision and the eye goes down progressively from T1 through T2. There is a corresponding increase in the morbidity and intensity of therapy from T1 through T2.

TX   Primary tumor cannot be assessed

T0   No evidence of primary tumor

T1   Tumor confined to the retina (no vitreous seeding or significant retinal detachment). No retinal detachment or subretinal fluid >5 mm from the base of the tumor

T1a   Any eye in which the largest tumor is less than or equal to 3 mm in height **and** no tumor is located closer than 1 DD (1.5 mm) to the optic nerve or fovea

T1b   All other eyes in which the tumor(s) are confined to the retina regardless of location or size (up to half the volume of the eye). No vitreous seeding. **No** retinal detachment or subretinal fluid >5 mm from the base of the tumor

T2   Tumor with contiguous spread to adjacent tissues or spaces (vitreous or subretinal space)

T2a   *Minimal tumor spread to vitreous and/or subretinal space.* Vitreous seeding and/or subretinal implantation may consist of lumps, clumps, snowballs, or avascular tumor masses. Retinal detachment may be total. Tumor may fill up to 2/3 the volume of the eye

T2c   Unsalvageable intraocular disease. Tumor fills more than two thirds of the eye **or** there is no possibility of visual rehabilitation **or** one or more of the following are present:

- Tumor-associated glaucoma, either neovascular or angle closure
- Anterior segment extension of tumor
- Ciliary body extension of tumor
- Hyphema (significant)
- Massive vitreous hemorrhage
- Tumor in contact with lens
- Orbital cellulitis-like clinical presentation (massive tumor necrosis)

T3   Invasion of the optic nerve and/or optic coats
T4   Extraocular tumor

Regional lymph nodes (N)

Clinical

NX   Regional lymph nodes cannot be assessed
N0   No regional lymph node involvement
N1   Regional lymph node metastasis involvement (preauricular, submandibular, or cervical)
N2   Distant lymph node involvement

Pathologic

There is one major difference in the pathologic classification from the last edition. No differentiating pathologic separation is proposed for those eyes in which the tumor may vary in size but is confined to the retina, vitreous, or subretinal space.

pTX   Primary tumor cannot be assessed
pT0   No evidence of primary tumor
pT1   Tumor confined to the retina, vitreous or subretinal space. No optic nerve or choroidal invasion
pT2   Minimal invasion of the optic nerve and/or optic coats
pT2a   Tumor invades optic nerve up to, but not through, the level of the lamina cribrosa
pT2b   Tumor invades choroid focally
pTc   Tumor invades optic nerve up to, but not through, the level of the lamina cribrosa and invades the choroid focally
pT3   Significant invasion of the optic nerve and/or optic coats

pT3a   Tumor invades optic nerve through the level of the lamina cribrosa but not to the line of resection
pT3b   Tumor massively invades the choroid
pT3c   Tumor invades the optic nerve through the level of the lamina cribrosa but not to the line of resection and massively invades the choroid
pT4   Extraocular tumor extension that includes:
Invasion of optic nerve to the line of resection
Invasion of orbit through the sclera
Extension both anteriorly or posteriorly into the orbit
Extension into the brain
Extension into the subarachnoidal space of the optic nerve
Extension to the apex of the orbit
Extension to, but not through, the chiasm
Extension into the brain beyond the chiasm

Pathologic

pNX   Regional lymph nodes cannot be assessed
pN0   No regional lymph node metastasis
pN1   Regional lymph node metastasis

Distant metastasis (M)

Clinical

MX   Distant metastasis cannot be assessed
M0   No distant metastasis
M1   Metastasis to central nervous system and/or bone, bone marrow, or other sites

Pathologic

pMX   Distant metastasis cannot be assessed
pM0   No distant metastasis
pM1   Distant metastasis
pM1a   Bone marrow
pM1b   Other sites

Stage grouping

No Stage grouping is presently recommended.

Appendix D
Standardized surgical pathology reporting for major tumor types

Association of Directors of Anatomic and Surgical Pathology (ADASP) recommendations for the reporting of major tumor types

Bladder—carcinoma
Breast—carcinoma (invasive)
Breast—carcinoma (in situ)
Esophagus—carcinoma
Extra-adrenal paragangliomas
Eye and adnexa—common malignancies
Large bowel—carcinoma
Larynx—carcinoma
Liver—malignant tumors
Lung—carcinoma
Lymph nodes with metastatic disease
Major salivary glands
Nasal cavity and paranasal sinuses—carcinoma
Oral cavity and oropharynx—carcinoma
Pancreas and periampullary region—carcinoma
Parathyroid glands
Prostate—carcinoma
Skin—melanoma
Skin—nonmelanocytic neoplasms
Testis and adnexa
Thyroid gland—carcinoma
Uterine cervix—carcinoma

College of American Pathologists (CAP) checklists for the reporting of major tumor types (01/2003)

Adrenal cortical carcinoma—resection
Ampulla of Vater—ampullectomy
Ampulla of Vater—Whipple's resection
Anus—polypectomy
Anus—local excision (transanal disk excision)
Anus—resection
Bone marrow—blood film, aspirate, cell block, trephine biopsy, touch imprint
Brain/spinal cord—biopsy/resection
Breast—excision less than total mastectomy (including wire-guided localization excisions), total mastectomy, modified radical mastectomy, radical mastectomy
Colon and rectum—polypectomy
Rectum—local excision (transanal disk excision)
Colon and rectum—resection
Endometrium—biopsy
Endometrium—hysterectomy, with or without other organs or tissues

Esophagus—biopsy
Esophagus—resection
Extrahepatic bile ducts—resection
Fallopian tube—unilateral salpingectomy, salpingo-oophorectomy, or hysterectomy with salpingo-oophorectomy
Gallbladder—resection/cholecystectomy
Gastrointestinal lymphoma—resection
Heart—resection
Hodgkin's lymphoma—biopsy/staging procedure
Non-Hodgkin's lymphoma—biopsy/resection
Kidney—biopsy
Kidney—nephrectomy, partial or radical
Liver—resection
Major salivary glands—resection
Ovary—oophorectomy, salpingo-oophorectomy, subtotal oophorectomy or removal of tumor in fragments, hysterectomy with salpingo-oophorectomy
Pancreas (endocrine)—resection
Pancreas (exocrine)—resection
Peritoneum—resection
Pleura/pericardium—biopsy
Pleura/pericardium—resection
Prostate gland—needle biopsy, transurethral prostatic resection (TUR), enucleation specimen
Prostate gland—radical prostatectomy
Retinoblastoma—enucleation, partial or complete exenteration
Skin—carcinoma—resection
Small intestine—polypectomy, segmental resection, Whipple procedure (pancreaticoduodenectomy, partial or complete, with or without partial gastrectomy)
Stomach—biopsy
Stomach—resection
Testis—radical orchiectomy
Testis—retroperitoneal lymphadenectomy for malignant testicular tumor
Trophoblast—dilation and curettage/resection
Upper aerodigestive tract and minor salivary glands—incisional and excisional biopsy/resection
Uterine cervix—cone biopsy
Uterine cervix—colpectomy, hysterectomy, pelvic extenteration
Uveal melanoma—resection
Vagina—biopsy
Vagina—resection/excisional biopsy
Vulva—excisional biopsy/resection

The informational content of the surgical pathology report has increased almost exponentially during the course of the last 50 years. At the time that the first edition of this book was written, a pathology report of a mastectomy specimen that read "Invasive scirrhous carcinoma of the breast with three metastatic lymph nodes" was regarded as entirely acceptable. At present, sending out a report with only that amount of information would be almost an invitation to a malpractice suit. Many are the reasons for the need of additional pieces of information, but essentially they boil down to one fact, of which we surgical pathologists are largely responsible and should be proud: this information is clinically significant for prognostic and therapeutic reasons, which of course is the raison d'être of surgical pathology. Dr. Lauren V. Ackerman would have been very happy with this development, in the sense that he thought that the most important question a pathologist had to ask himself after making a morphologic observation was: "What does it mean for the patient?" Many of the determinations we make mean a lot to the patients and to the clinicians treating them, and therefore it is our duty to document them in a precise, clear, and consistent fashion. This becomes mandatory for patients who have been entered in protocols and for whom recording a particular piece of information becomes a requirement. Because it is virtually impossible for most individuals (except for savants of one type or another) to remember to put down all this information in the same order and with the same terminology, in every instance, the use of standardized forms to be used as checklists has become an urgent necessity.[4] An objective corroboration of this was provided by a College of American Pathologists (CAP) sponsored study on the adequacy of the surgical pathology report for colorectal carcinoma among 532 pathology laboratories in the United States and Canada. Review of almost 16,000 reports showed that the single most important factor for the production of a complete report was not whether the institution in question was an academic or community type, whether it had a residency program or not, or whether its workload was light or heavy, but whether it used checklists or not.[6] Analysis of reports of other tumor types, such as lung carcinoma, has produced similar findings and led to similar conclusions.[3]

The necessity for this kind of approach has also received the strong imprimatur of the American College of Surgeons Commission on Cancer, which, beginning January 1, 2004, will require that pathologists in their approved programs include *all* scientifically validated or regularly used data in their reports for each site and specimen.[1] Not everybody is happy with this trend, the point having been made that pathology reports generated with the use of these forms are impersonal and sometimes fail to transmit some unique feature of the case in the way that an old-fashioned narrative report did.[5] Fortunately, one can have it both ways, in the sense that there is no reason why a checklist-generated report could not be followed by a "Comment" section in which the pathologist could elaborate in his own language what it is about this case that the checklist has failed to capture or highlight.

An early attempt at report standardization was published by the members of the Pathology Department of Memorial Sloan-Kettering Cancer Center in the 1990s.[5] Currently, two major pathology organizations—the Association of Directors of Anatomic and Surgical Pathology (ADASP) and the College of American Pathologists (CAP)—are at an advanced stage of production of guidelines accompanied by checklists for the major tumor types. Those produced by ADASP are formatted according to Dr. Ackerman's precept, in the sense that they are divided into two portions: one containing the information that has proved clinically useful and therefore necessary, and the other containing information that can be of interest for one reason or another but that has no proven clinical significance. The forms produced by CAP tend to be more comprehensive. Condensed versions of both recommendation sets are included in this chapter, so that the pathologist can compare them and decide which one best suits him or her. Those interested in going over the bibliography and background information that provides the rationale for these recommendations, as well as the names and affiliations of the various committee members, can consult the official printed versions listed below or access them at the websites of the respective organizations:

Association of Directors of Anatomic and Surgical Pathology (ADASP): www.panix.com/-adasp/
College of American Pathologists (CAP): www.cap.org

References

1   Connolly JL, Fletcher CDM. What is needed to satisfy the American College of Surgeons Commission on Cancer requirements for the pathological reporting of cancer specimens? Hum Pathol 2003, **34**: 111.

2   Compton CC, Ed. Reporting on cancer specimens: Case summaries and background documentation 2003 edition. Northfield, IL, College of American Pathologists, 2003.

3   Gephardt GN, Baker PB. Lung carcinoma surgical pathology report adequacy: a College of American Pathologists Q-Probes study of over 8300 cases from 464 institutions. Arch Pathol Lab Med 1996, **120(10)**: 922–927.

4   Kempson RL. The time is now. Checklists for surgical pathology reports. Arch Pathol Lab Med 1992, **116**: 1113–1119.

5   Rosai J and Members of the Department of Pathology, Memorial Sloan–Kettering Cancer Center. Standardized reporting of surgical pathology diagnoses for the major tumor types. A proposal. Am J Clin Pathol 1993, **100**: 240–255.

6   Zarbo RJ. Interinstitutional assessment of colorectal carcinoma surgical pathology report adequacy. A College of American Pathologists Q-Probes study of practice patterns from 532 laboratories and 15,940 reports. Arch Pathol Lab Med 1992, **116**: 1107–1108.

Association of Directors of Anatomic and Surgical Pathology (ADASP) recommendations for the reporting of major tumor types

In the following report, "Recommended features" have been defined as those features that should be included in the final report because they are generally accepted as being of prognostic importance, required for staging or therapy, and/or traditionally expected. Other features are deemed "Optional features" because they represent specific institutional preferences or are of inconclusive prognostic significance.

Bladder—carcinoma

Final report—recommended features

Gross description

1. **Specimen identification:** labeled with name, medical record number, etc.
2. **Specimen condition:** e.g., fresh, in fixative, on ice, opened, unopened, with Foley catheter still inserted, etc.
3. **Good overall description** including nature of the specimen (chips, partial cystectomy, radical cystectomy, etc.), weight, three-dimensional measurements, etc.
4. **Describe recognizable features** if identifiable (gross evidence of carcinoma, etc.)
5. **Description of other organs:** prostate, ureters, urethra, uterus, vagina, etc.
6. **Paraffin block key** (best listed at end rather than incorporated into narrative)
7. **If ink is used,** give code

Diagnostic information

1. **Topography:** The type of specimen should be specified: bladder, bladder and prostate, bladder with vagina and uterus, etc.
2. **Procedure:** The type of surgical procedure should be stated: transurethral resection of bladder (TURB), partial cystectomy, total cystectomy, radical cystoprostatectomy, anterior exenteration, etc.
3. **Tumor type:** The type of carcinoma should be stated. If transitional cell carcinoma is the diagnosis, state whether it is papillary or not
4. **Tumor grade:** Use WHO or Murphy's grading system outlined in the *Third Series AFIP Fascicle #11*
5. **Tumor extent** in bladder (degree of invasion):
   - No invasion
   - Invasion of lamina propria
   - Invasion of muscularis propria
   - Invasion of paravesicular tissue
   - Presence or absence of lymphatic/vascular invasion
   - Tumor arising in diverticulum (state whether muscularis is present or not)

   Note 1: Presence of fibroadipose tissue is not an indication of paravesicular/adventitial involvement as fibroadipose tissue may be present in the lamina propria and/or between muscle bundles of the detrusor. If one is unsure whether muscle fibers associated with an invasive tumor represent invasion of the muscular wall or the muscularis mucosae of the lamina propria then a comment explaining the problem should be included in the report

6. **Intraepithelial abnormalities**
   - Report focality or multifocality
   - If intraepithelial abnormalities are not contiguous with papillary or invasive neoplasm or are of different degrees of anaplasia, separate diagnoses are indicated
   - Report presence of pagetoid spread of carcinoma in situ

(CIS) in urothelial mucosa. This is not dysplasia even though cells do not occupy the full thickness of the mucosa

7. **Tumor extent in other organs** attached to the bladder (radical cystoprostatectomies, radical cystectomies, anterior exenterations):
   - Prostate
     - Direct extension into prostate from carcinoma in bladder neck
     - Involvement of prostatic urethra
     - Involvement of prostatic ducts with or without stromal involvement
   - Ureter and urethra
     - Report any dysplastic/neoplastic change of the mucosa, including pagetoid spread of CIS
     - Report invasion into adjacent lamina propria or muscularis propria
   - Seminal vesicles
     - Report spread of carcinoma in these organs either through epithelium or by direct extension of infiltrative tumor
   - Vagina/uterus
     - Report direct extension of metastases to any of these organs

8. **Surgical margins**

   Report status of ureteral margins, indicate which side (R or L) if one is positive
   Report status of urethral margin
   Report paravesicular margin involvement

9. **Report important associated conditions, e.g., adenocarcinoma of the prostate**

10. **Lymph node metastases**
    - Report presence/absence of metastases. If metastases are present, state number and size of largest one, i.e., <20 cm, 21–5 cm, or >5 cm

Final report—optional features

1. **Invasion of muscularis mucosae, if present**
2. **Genetic abnormalities**
3. **Cytometry**
4. **Morphometry**
5. **Growth factors and receptors**
6. **Stage: There are two staging systems**
   - The Marshall modification of the Jewett and Strong system (A–D)
   - The AJCC/TNM system (T1–T4, M, N)

Checklist

Specimen type
— Biopsy
— TURB
— Radical cystectomy
— Partial cystectomy
— Pelvic exenteration

Diagnosis section

Pathology report should address all applicable items
— Tumor type and grade (TCC only) (with note or comment, if necessary)
— Other mucosal abnormalities (CIS, etc.)

— Other abnormalities (e.g., changes c/w previous surgical site, cystitis glandularis et cystica)
— Pathology in other organs
> Prostate
> Ureters
> Urethra
> Seminal vesicles
> Vasa deferentia
> Uterus
> Vagina
> Rectum
> Other
— Lymph nodes (usually submitted separately)

Muscular wall
— present
— Not identified

Invasion
— Specimen entirely tumor
— No invasion
— Lamina propria[a]
— Muscular wall
> Inner half
> Outer half
— Paravesicular tissue
— Vascular
— Perineural
— Seminal vesicles
— Prostate
> Glands
> Stroma

Specimen involvement
— None
— Urethra
— Ureters
> Left
— Right
— Paravesicular soft tissue
— Other (specify)

Lymph nodes
— No. of tumor/total nodes
— Size of largest metastasis   cm

TURB, transurethral resection of bladder; TCC, transitional cell carcinoma; CIS, carcinoma in situ; c/w, consistent with; L, left; R, right
[a]Distinguish muscularis mucosae if desired (optional)

Breast—carcinoma (invasive)

Final report—recommended features
Gross description
1. **Specimen identification:** labeled with (name, number), designated as breast (right or left)
2. **Specimen condition:** fresh, in formalin, intact, cut, margins inked or not, etc.
3. **Type of procedure:** core biopsy, incisional biopsy, excisional biopsy (lumpectomy), re-excision, quadrantectomy, simple mastectomy, modified mastectomy, other

4. **Size:** the overall size of the excised specimen should be measured in three dimensions
5. **Tumor description**

Presence of mass(es) or absence of mass(es)
Margins of the mass(es) (circumscribed, infiltrative)
Distance of the mass(es) from nearest surgical margins (measured and recorded)
Location of the mass(es) (e.g., quadrant if the specimen is a mastectomy)
Size of the mass(es) (at least greatest diameter should be recorded, three dimensions are preferable), texture of the mass(es) (e.g., soft, fleshy, hard, gritty, etc.)

6. **Description of prior biopsy site,** if present
7. **Description of the remainder of the breast tissue,** nipple, and skin, if present
8. **Number and appearance of lymph nodes** if received
9. **Special investigations:** It is recommended that tissue submitted for special investigation (e.g., ER/PR, flow cytometry, etc.) be specified if this information is known
10. Whether a **diagnostic frozen section** was performed and the diagnosis that was made

Diagnostic information
1. **Laterality** of the breast and procedure
2. **Histological type**
   - Ductal [usual, no special type, not otherwise specified (NOS)]
   - Lobular (specify subtype)
     – Classic
     – Variant (alveolar, solid, pleomorphic, tubulolobular)
   - Tubular
   - Medullary
   - Mucinous
   - Secretory
   - Infiltrating papillary
   - Adenoid cystic
   - Metaplastic
   - Infiltrating cribriform
   - Other (specify)
3. **Histologic grade:** all ductal (NOS) carcinomas should be graded; some also advocate grading lobular carcinomas. The histologic type for the others (e.g., tubular, medullary) replaces the grade. The Scarff–Bloom–Richardson grading scheme, which evaluates the following three parameters, is recommended: degree of tubule formation; nuclear grade; and mitotic rate. Points are assigned to each parameter as follows:
   - Tubules: 75% or more of the tumor is composed of tubules = 1; 10–75% of the tumor is composed of tubules = 2; <10% of the tumor is composed of tubules = 3
   - Nuclei: small and uniform = 1; moderate variability in size and shape = 2; marked increase in size and marked irregularity = 3
   - Mitotic rate: the mitotic rate is dependent upon the area of the field selected. For a ×40 objective with a diameter of 0.33 mm (area of 0.152 mm^2), scoring of the number of mitoses per 10 fields (at the tumor edge) is as follows: 0 to 5 = 1; 6 to 10 = 2; >11 = 3. The field of the

microscope used should be measured and the counts adjusted proportionately.

The histologic grade is determined by summing the points: grade I, 3 to 5 points; grade II, 6 to 7 points; grade III, 8 to 9 points.

4. **Margins of resection:** the Association recognizes that, at the present time, the clinical relevance of a positive margin is not clear, and further recognizes that there is no standard definition of what constitutes a positive or negative margin. Margin involvement is, however, used by many clinicians in forming therapeutic recommendations.

   In reporting the margins of resection, state: (a) whether sections of the margins have been taken parallel (shaved) or perpendicular to the surgical margin and (b) whether tumor is at margin (grossly or microscopically). If tumor is not present at a shaved margin or at an inked margin, the distance from the margin should be specified.

5. **Lymph node status:** given as numbers of nodes involved and the total number of nodes. If metastases are <2 mm, this fact and the size should be recorded. If any node is larger than 2 cm, it should be recorded. The presence or absence of perinodal extension of tumor into axillary fat should be recorded. If the nodes are fixed to one another or other structures, it should be recorded. The Association does not recommend immunoperoxidase techniques to detect micrometastases.

6. **Peritumoral angiolymphatic invasion:** whether tumor cells involve peritumoral vascular spaces or not should be recorded. If vascular spaces in the skin are involved, this should be recorded. Although some prefer to separate lymphatic from blood vessel invasion, it is prognostically not necessary to distinguish between lymphatic vessels and blood vessels. The Association does not recommend the routine use of immunohistochemical stains to detect intravascular invasion.

7. **Size of the carcinoma:** even though this is recorded in the gross description, the Association recommends it be reported again in the diagnosis line because of the prognostic importance of this parameter.

8. **In situ component:** the presence or absence of an in situ component should be recorded. If the in situ component is ductal and is prominent within the main tumor mass *and* is present outside the mass *or* the tumor is primarily intraductal with only focal invasion, the in situ ductal carcinoma is considered to be "extensive" and the Association recommends recording this if the patient is to be treated by less than total mastectomy. When ductal carcinoma in situ is present, the distance of the in situ process from the nearest margin should be recorded as at the margin, or the specific distance from the margin even if the specimen also contains invasive carcinoma. Because lobular carcinoma in situ is often multifocal, the Association recommends that no specific comments on margin involvement be made.

9. **Microcalcifications:** if present on the mammogram, their presence in the sections should be sought (to be sure a calcified lesion was not missed) and a statement made about their presence and location or their absence.

10. **Other significant disease:** atypical hyperplasias, papillomas, Paget's disease of the nipple, biopsy site changes, etc.

11. **Specify** in the report if information required for prognosis or therapy is not available or cannot be adequately assessed (e.g., no nodes submitted with a mastectomy specimen, margins not assessable because specimen was cut before inking, etc.)

Final report—optional features

1. **Stage:** the data provided above should provide sufficient information for clinicians to determine stage. The Association does not consider inclusion of a specific tumor stage in the pathology report to be required.
2. **Results of ancillary investigations** (e.g., flow cytometry, ER/PR, oncogenes, p53)
3. **Specific level or location of axillary lymph nodes** unless marked and specific identification is requested by the surgeon
4. **Identification of specific margins** unless the surgeon precisely identifies them
5. **Perineural infiltration**
6. **Microvessel quantification**

Breast—carcinoma (in situ)

Final report—recommended features

Gross description

1. **Specimen condition:** fresh, in formalin, intact, cut, margins inked or not, etc.
2. **Specimen identification:** labeled with (name, number), designated as breast (right or left)
3. **Type of procedure:** core biopsy, incisional biopsy, excisional biopsy (lumpectomy), re-excision, quadrantectomy, simple mastectomy, modified mastectomy, other
4. **Size:** the overall size of the excised specimen should be measured in three dimensions
5. **Tumor description**
   - Presence of mass(es) or absence of mass(es)
   - Margins of the mass(es) (circumscribed, infiltrative)
   - Distance of the mass(es) from nearest surgical margins (measured and recorded)
   - Location of the mass(es) (e.g., quadrant if the specimen is a mastectomy)
   - Size of the mass(es) (at least greatest diameter should be recorded, three dimensions are preferable), texture of the mass(es) (e.g., soft, fleshy, hard, gritty, etc.)
6. **Description of prior biopsy site, if present**
7. **Description of the remainder of the breast tissue,** nipple, and skin, if present
8. **Number and appearance of lymph nodes,** if received
9. **Special investigations:** it is recommended that fresh tissue should not be submitted for special investigation because the most important information is the presence or absence of invasion. Blocks may be sectioned for special investigation if that information is desirable in an individual case.
10. **Whether a diagnostic frozen section** was performed and the diagnosis that was made

Diagnostic information

1. **Laterality** of the breast and procedure

2. **Histological type:** the Association recognizes that different terms are sometimes used for microscopically identical lesions (e.g., the term "lobular neoplasia" includes cases of atypical lobular hyperplasia). Moreover, ADASP recognizes that although the majority of cases of in situ carcinoma are readily categorized, there are borderline lesions. The criteria for diagnosing the small borderline lesions as either lobular carcinoma in situ (LCIS) or ductal carcinoma in situ (DCIS) vary. Different authors use different qualitative and quantitative criteria in arriving at the diagnosis of LCIS or DCIS in these circumstances.

   The Association realizes that the classification system for DCIS (intraductal carcinoma) is in a state of flux; because of this, it is recommended that the lesion be graded using the traditional system based primarily upon architectural pattern, as well as assigning a specific nuclear grade.

3. **Architectural type:** ductal carcinoma in situ (intraductal carcinoma) (specify subtype):
   - Cribriform
   - Micropapillary
   - Solid (microacinar)
   - Papillary (includes most cases of intracystic)
   - Comedo (requires high-grade nuclei; necrosis usually present)

4. **Nuclear grade:** because the architectural pattern may vary from area to area in the individual case, and because nuclear grade may be important in regard to the potential for recurrence, the Association recommends that the ductal carcinoma in situ be divided into high, low, or intermediate nuclear grade in addition to providing type. Lobular carcinoma in situ is not routinely graded

5. **Margins of resection:** the Association recognizes that, at the present time, the clinical relevance of a positive margin is not clear, and further recognizes that there is no standard definition of what constitutes a positive or negative margin. Margin involvement is, however, used by many clinicians in forming therapeutic recommendations

   In reporting the margins of resection, state: (a) whether sections of the margins have been taken parallel (shaved) or perpendicular to the surgical margin and (b) whether tumor is at margin (grossly or microscopically). If tumor is not present at a shaved margin or at an inked margin, the distance from the margin should be specified. Assessment of margins for lobular carcinoma is not recommended

6. **Size:** if a mass is present, obtain this from the gross; if not, several methods can be used to measure the size of an in situ process:
   - Sectioning the biopsy from one end of the specimen to the other at 3- to 4-mm intervals and submitting the sections in sequence, thus allowing for an estimate of the size of the lesion based on the sections in which the lesion is present
   - In small lesions, a measurement of size of the lesion may be obtained directly from the slide

7. **Microcalcifications:** if the specimen was removed because of mammographic identification of microcalcifications, these should be identified in the tissue sections and the fact they are found should be reported. A correlation with the location of the microcalcifications in the mammogram should be reported. It should be stated in which lesion the calcifications were identified (DCIS, adenosis, etc.). If they are not found or if the microcalcifications in the sections are not in the location indicated by the mammogram, this should be reported

8. **Other significant disease:** atypical hyperplasias, papillomas, Paget's disease of the nipple, biopsy site changes, etc.

9. **State specifically if information required for prognosis or therapy** is not available or cannot be adequately assessed (margins not assessable because specimen was cut before inking, etc.)

Checklist

Laterality
— Breast
   —— Left   —— Right

Specimen type
— Excisional (for palpable mass)
— Mammographic Loc.
— Incisional (includes core needle and FNA)
— Re-excisional
— Mastectomy
— Chest wall

Specimen size

Tumor size(s)

Tumor type
— DCIS
— Mixed NOS/ILC
— Papillary LCIS
— LCIS
— Tubular
— Cribriform
— Infiltrating ductal (NOS)
— Mucinous other (specify)
— Infiltrating lobular
— Medullary

Grade of invasion
   —— I   —— II   —— III

Gross margin
— Free (specify distance)
— Involved

Margins invasive (specify type of margin evaluation)
— Free (specify distance)
— Focal
— >Focal
— Nonevaluable

Margins DCIS (specify type of margin evaluation)
— Free (specify distance)
— Focal
— >Focal
— Nonevaluable

DCIS nuclear morphology
— High grade
— Intermediate grade
— Low grade

DCIS patterns (specify all that apply)
— Large areas of central necrosis (comedo)
— Small areas of central necrosis
— Cribriform
— Solid
— Micropapillary
— Papillary

Calcification in in situ
— Absent
— Prominent in DCIS
— Focal in DCIS
— In LCIS
— Prominent in benign breast tissue
— Focal in benign breast tissue

Peritumoral lymphatic invasion:
— Absent
— Present
— Dermal

Peritumoral vascular invasion
— Absent
— Present

Extent DCIS within invasive tumor
— Absent
— Slight
— Moderate marked
— Tumor primarily DCIS with focal invasion

Extent DCIS adjacent to invasive tumor
— Absent
— Slight
— Moderate marked

EIC status
— Negative
— Positive
— Indeterminate

> *Note 1:* If a tumor is primarily DCIS with focal invasion or has a moderate or marked amount of DCIS within the infiltrating tumor and any in the adjacent tissue, it is EIC-positive

Skin
— Not sampled
— Free
— Invasive
— Dermal lymphatic

Nipple
— Not sampled
— Free
— Invasive
— Dermal lymphatic
— DCIS
— Paget's

Muscle
— Not sampled
— Free
— Involved

Mastectomy tumor location
— Central
— UOQ
— UIQ
— LOQ
— LIQ

Multiple areas involved
— Central
— UOQ
— UIQ
— LOQ
— LIQ
— Only one area involved

Lymph nodes (number of involved nodes in relation to total number examined)
— Total
— Level I
— Level II
— Level III
— Other (specify)

Extranodal extension
— Absent
— Present

Metastatic cancer in

Nature of nontumorous breast tissue (describe)

Comments

Ancillary studies (results and methodology used)

Esophagus—carcinoma

Final report—recommended features

Gross description
1. **Specimen identification:** labeled with patient name, medical record number, source of specimen, etc.
2. **Specimen condition:** fresh, in fixative (specify type), unopened, opened, etc., and how designated
3. **Appropriate overall gross description,** including nature of the specimen (segmental esophagectomy, esophagogastrectomy, etc.), measurements (including overall length of specimen, length of esophagus, length of stomach), and amount and nature of periesophageal tissue included
4. **Description** of opened specimen including neoplasm (gross appearance, measurement in three dimensions, etc.), mucosal surface away from neoplasm (evidence of Barrett's esophagus, other abnormalities), and distance of neoplasm from proximal and distal margins

   > *Note 1:* If the lesion arises in the gastroesophageal junction region and involves both the esophagus and stomach, it should be classified as (1) an esophageal carcinoma, if the epicenter of the lesion is in the esophagus; (2) a gastric carcinoma, if the epicenter is in the stomach; (3) a gastroesophageal junction primary, if the epicenter coincides with the esophagogastric junction. For this purpose, the gastroesophageal junction is defined as the junction between the tubular esophagus and the saccular stomach

5. **Description of any additional structures included:** stomach, pericardium, etc.
6. **Paraffin block key:** ideally at end rather than incorporated into narrative

7. **If margins are inked** (proximal, distal, radial), provide code

Diagnostic information

1. **Topography:** the type of specimen should be specified (esophagus, esophagus and proximal stomach, etc.)
2. **Procedure:** the type of surgical procedure should be stated (total or segmental esophagectomy, esophagogastrectomy); as well as how the procedure was performed, if known (transhiatal or transthoracic)
3. **Histologic type:** use of the World Health Organization (WHO) classification is recommended
   - Squamous cell carcinoma (including pseudosarcomatous)
   - Adenocarcinoma
   - Adenoid cystic carcinoma (basaloid squamous)
   - Mucoepidermoid carcinoma
   - Adenosquamous carcinoma
   - Undifferentiated carcinoma
   - Other
4. **Histologic grade:** use of the American Joint Committee on Cancer grading system is recommended:
   GX Grade cannot be assessed
   G1 Well differentiated
   G2 Moderately differentiated
   G3 Poorly differentiated
   G4 Undifferentiated
5. **Extent of invasion** of neoplasm in the esophagus, using TNM system:
   Tis None (Tis) (see Note 2)
   T1a Limited to lamina propria (intramucosal carcinoma)
   T1b Into submucosa
   T2   Into muscularis propria
   T3   Into adventitia
   T4   Into adjacent structures (see Note 3)

   Note 2: Although Tis refers to carcinoma in situ, the authors prefer the term high-grade dysplasia for this lesion

   Note 3: In specimens resected after radiation or chemotherapy, or both, a comment should be made regarding whether viable-appearing neoplastic tissue remains. If none is identifiable, a comment regarding the extent of the radiation/chemotherapy-induced injury should be made, i.e., its depth of extension into the esophageal wall as an indication of the probable depth of invasion of the neoplasm

6. **Mucosal abnormalities away from carcinoma:**
   - Squamous epithelial dysplasia
   - Presence of Barrett's metaplastic epithelium
   - Dysplasia in Barrett's metaplastic epithelium
   - Other
7. **Surgical margins:**
   - Status of proximal and distal surgical margins
   - Status of radial (adventitial) margin
   - If Barrett's esophagus, nature of mucosa at proximal margin (squamous *versus* Barrett's); if Barrett's, comment on presence or absence of dysplasia
   - If distal mucosal margin is stomach, comment on any gastric abnormalities (*Helicobacter pylori* gastritis, etc.)
8. **Lymph nodes:** report total number of nodes/number containing metastatic carcinoma

Final report—optional features

1. **Genetic abnormalities**
2. **Flow cytometric analysis**
3. **Growth factors and receptors**
4. **Staging** using American Joint Committee on Cancer TNM system (0-IVB)

Checklist

Site of neoplasm
— Cervical esophagus (from lower border of cricoid to thoracic inlet (suprasternal notch)
— Intrathoracic esophagus (definitions given are from the AJCC manual)
— Upper portion (thoracic inlet to tracheal bifurcation)
— Mid portion (tracheal bifurcation to just above esophagogastric junction)
— Lower thoracic portion (includes intra-abdominal portion of esophagus and esophagogastric junction)
— Not specified

Type of resection
— Transthoracic
— Transhiatal
— Not specified

Resection specimen
— Esophagectomy
— Esophagogastrectomy
— Other (specify)

Dimensions of neoplasm
———— cm × ———— cm × ———— cm

Distance to surgical margins
———— cm to proximal margin;
———— cm to distal margin

Macroscopic depth of penetration of neoplasm
— Into submucosa
— Into muscularis propria
— Through esophageal wall
— Into adjacent structures (specify: trachea, pericardium, etc.)
— Uncertain

Barrett's esophagus
— Present grossly
— Present at proximal margin grossly
— Not apparent grossly
— Uncertain

Histologic type of neoplasm
— Squamous cell carcinoma (including pseudosarcomatous)
— Adenocarcinoma
— Adenoid cystic carcinoma (basaloid squamous)
— Mucoepidermoid carcinoma
— Adenosquamous carcinoma
— Undifferentiated carcinoma

Histologic grade of carcinoma
— Grade cannot be assessed
— Well differentiated
— Moderately differentiated
— Poorly differentiated
— Undifferentiated

Depth of infiltration of neoplasm
— High-grade dysplasia only

— Limited to lamina propria
— Into submucosa
— Into muscularis propria
— Into adventitia
— Into adjacent structures (specify)

Mucosal abnormalities away from carcinoma
— Squamous epithelial dysplasia
— Barrett's metaplastic epithelium
    With dysplasia
    Without dysplasia
— Other (for example, heterotopic gastric mucosa in cervical esophagus ("inlet patch")

Status of surgical margins
— Proximal margin free of carcinoma
    —— Yes   —— No
— Proximal margin composed of squamous epithelium
    —— Yes   —— No
  With dysplasia
    —— Yes   —— No

Proximal margin composed of Barrett's metaplastic epithelium
    —— Yes   —— No
  With dysplasia
    —— Yes   —— No

Distal margin free of carcinoma
    —— Yes   —— No

Status of lymph nodes
— Total number of lymph nodes
— Total number involved by metastatic carcinoma

Tissue submitted for special investigative studies
— Flow cytometry
    —— Yes   —— No
— Tissue frozen
    —— Yes   —— No
— Other (specify)

Extra-adrenal paragangliomas

Guidelines

Extra-adrenal paragangliomas are rare neoplasms that arise in a wide variety of anatomic sites. Knowledge of the widespread anatomic distribution of the tumors and familiarity with variations in their histologic patterns will help in achieving accurate histopathologic diagnosis of these tumors. The following guidelines are offered to facilitate generation of a comprehensive surgical report, realizing of course that minor or major modifications are appropriate depending upon the features of an individual tumor. Pheochromocytomas are arbitrarily regarded as adrenal medullary paragangliomas and recommendations for reporting of adrenal tumors are covered elsewhere. Explanatory notes are appended.

Gross description
1. **Specimen identification:**
   - Name, sex, age, date of birth and medical record number
   - Attending physician and/or surgeon
   - Date of surgery and date of receipt of the surgical specimen in the laboratory
   - History and/or endocrinologic data, and preoperative as well as postoperative diagnosis
2. **Specimen condition:** The date, time and state (fresh or in fixative) of specimen should be noted on receipt in the laboratory. It may be desirable to indicate in the report the approximate time elapsed between surgical removal of the specimen and receiving it for examination in the surgical pathology laboratory
3. **Tumor site:** The precise anatomic location of the tumor should be stated. Terminology of the extra-adrenal paragangliomas should be based upon anatomic site of origin (e.g., urinary bladder paraganglioma, gallbladder paraganglioma, carotid body paraganglioma). Information regarding multicentricity or bilaterality should be included (e.g., bilateral carotid body paragangliomas—familial or sporadic occurrence)
4. **Type of procedure:** The report should indicate whether the surgical specimen was a biopsy, partial excision or complete excision of the lesion or part of a more extended surgical procedure, whether a biopsy or subtotal excision was performed (or if resection was done by laparoscopy)
5. **Description of other organs:** Ideally, the specimen should be given to the pathologist by the surgical team with appropriate orientation of the specimen and identification of any relevant attached tissues or organs
6. **Measure:** Record tumor size (three dimensions in cm) and weight (g) following removal of extraneous tissue
7. **Specify** any other tissue or organs present
8. **Accurate and complete overall description** of the external and internal (cut) surface of the tumor, noting its color and presence of necrosis or hemorrhage
9. **Special investigations:** Specimen photography, special studies and tumor dispersal (tumor bank, immunohistochemistry, electron microscopy, DNA quantitation, cytogenetics or others) should be recorded
10. **Record** results of intraoperative consultation including frozen section and/or smear/imprint preparations

Diagnostic information
1. **Histologic type** of tumor with brief reference to clinical and/or endocrinology data if pertinent
2. **Presence and estimated extent of tumor necrosis**
3. **Presence and approximate quantitation of mitotic activity**
4. **Prognostic features** as appropriate, e.g., invasion of adjacent tissue or organs, presence of vascular/lymphatic invasion. Record status of surgical margins
5. **Status of regional lymph nodes** where pertinent, e.g., total number with metastatic tumor, if present
6. **Record** whether outside consultation is requested or desired and indicate source of consultation
7. **Record** in rare instances whether tumor has composite features with component of ganglioneuroma or malignant peripheral nerve sheath tumor. Some tumors may have areas focally resembling ganglioneuroblastoma or even neuroblastoma

Checklist

Anatomic site
— Pathologic diagnosis, with terminology based upon anatomic site of origin

— Type of resection

Tumor size (cm) and weight (g)

— Gross description, external and cut surfaces

Results of intraoperative consultation

— Microscopic examination: presence and quantitation of mitotic figures
— Presence and approximate extent of necrosis
— Invasive growth (blood vessels, adjacent tissues/organs)
— Special studies, EM, frozen tissue, immunohistochemistry
— DNA quantitation, cytogenetics, other
— Unusual pathologic features

Eye and adnexa-common malignancies

For recommendations on the reporting of tissue removed as part of the surgical treatment of common malignancies of the eye and its adnexa, see:

Folberg R, Salomao D, Grossniklaus HE, Proia AD, Rao NA, Cameron JD. Recommendations for the reporting of tissues removed as part of the surgical treatment of common malignancies of the eye and its adnexa. Am J Surg Pathol 2003; **27**: 999–1004; Mod Pathol 2003; **16**: 725–730.

Large bowel—carcinoma

Final report—recommended features

Gross description

1. **Specimen condition:** fresh, in formalin, opened, unopened, etc.
2. **Specimen identification:** labeled with (name, number) and designated as (e.g., right colon)
3. **Part(s) of intestine included, length of each segment, other structures included**—terminal ileum, appendix, anal canal, attached/adherent organs, identified vessels
4. **Tumor description**
   - Site within intestine
   - Proximity to nearest margin
   - Gross subtype (e.g., polypoid, annular, constricting, ulcerating, infiltrative, plaque, linitis plastica)
   - Dimensions (three if possible)
   - Macroscopic depth of penetration
   - Appearance of serosa adjacent to tumor (e.g., retracted)
5. **Presence of features of obstruction** (proximal dilatation)
6. **Presence of perforation**
7. **Status of residual bowel:** polyps, inflammatory bowel disease, diverticula, ulcers, strictures
8. **Lymph nodes identified**
9. **Tissue submitted for special investigation (e.g., flow cytometry) should be specified**

Diagnostic information

1. **Site** of tumor and part of bowel resected
2. **Histologic type:** the WHO classification of invasive carcinoma is recommended
   - Adenocarcinoma, NOS
   - Mucinous (colloid) carcinoma (>50% mucinous)
   - Signet ring cell carcinoma (>50% signet ring cells)
   - Adenosquamous carcinoma
   - Small cell undifferentiated (oat cell) carcinoma
   - Undifferentiated carcinoma
   - Other (specify)

3. **Histologic grade:** a modification of the WHO classification is recommended for adenocarcinoma NOS only
   - Well differentiated—complex or simple tubules, easily discerned nuclear polarity, uniform sized nuclei
   - Moderately differentiated—complex, simple or slightly irregular tubules, nuclear polarity just discerned or lost
   - Poorly differentiated—highly irregular glands or an absence of glandular differentiation with loss of nuclear polarity

   Note 1: Data reported suggest strongly that the most significant prognostic information is derived from the category of poorly differentiated carcinoma versus more differentiated tumors. An alternate suggestion from the WHO is to divide adenocarcinoma into a high and low grade on this basis

4. **Depth of infiltration:** our recommendations are based on those in the TNM classification
   - Into the submucosa but not into the muscularis propria (T1)
   - Into but not through the muscularis propria (T2)
   - Through the muscularis propria and into the subserosal fat or pericolonic or perirectal adipose tissue (T3)
   - Reaching the serosa or peritoneal surface (T4)
   - Into adjacent organs (T4)
   - With perforation if present

   Note 2: although the TNM classification includes a level **Tis** to represent in situ carcinoma, we recommend against the use of this term for the following reasons:

   - We prefer the term *high-grade dysplasia* rather than *carcinoma in situ/severe dysplasia* (Tis in the TNM classification)
   - Intramucosal carcinoma is present when invasion of the lamina propria is present. This is also included within the category Tis. Because carcinoma of the large intestine has not been shown to have metastasizing potential until the submucosa is invaded, many individuals do not use this term in surgical pathology reports or, if they do, they state that provided the lesion has been excised completely locally no further treatment is required for that lesion

5. **Lymph node metastases:** stated as number of involved nodes and total number of nodes
6. **Presence of mesenteric deposits:** these are likely to be the equivalent of a nodal metastasis although this has not been confirmed
7. **Other sites biopsied for metastatic disease:** peritoneum, adjacent organs, liver, ovary
8. **Adequacy of local excision:** radial/proximal/distal resection margins. Assessment of proximal and distal margins is routine in the bowel as in other organs. In the rectum the deep margin (radial [lateral] margin) should be assessed. The radial margin is defined as the point at which the tumor reaches closest to a deep (lateral, circumferential) resected margin and is usually the deepest point of invasion in the rectum. Inking of the radial margin is highly recommended. For the large intestine outside of the rectum, the "lateral" surgical resection margin is the mesenteric border of resection and

is usually widely free of tumor unless dissection has deliberately been carried out close to the bowel wall. The antimesenteric serosal surface of the non-rectal large intestine is *not* a radial resection margin

9. **Other significant disease:** e.g., inflammatory bowel disease, other tumors, polyps, familial adenomatous polyposis, diverticular disease and its complications, ulcers, strictures

10. **If information required for prognosis or therapy** is not available or cannot be adequately assessed (e.g., no nodes found, radial margin not assessable) this should be stated specifically in the report

Final report—optional features

1. **Stage:** the required data provided above should provide sufficient information for application of most staging systems. We in general do not recommend inclusion of a specific tumor stage in the pathology report; however, if a stage is to be included in the report the staging system used should be specified (e.g., Astler–Collier modification of Dukes' stage) rather than using the misnomer "Dukes' stage" as a generic term. We believe that the AJCC/UICC (TNM) classification is the least ambiguous and currently embodies most criteria required for prognosis and therapeutic decisions. However:
   - We suggest that the stage Tis be replaced by high-grade dysplasia or intramucosal carcinoma as described above (see Depth of invasion, above)
   - We note that the derogatory effect on prognosis of perforation is not included in this system
   - We are uncertain of the significance or practicality of the N3 stage (see below)

2. **Results of ancillary investigations (e.g., flow cytometry)**

3. **Specific lymph nodes:**
   - Apical node if the Gabriel and Dukes modified stage or other modification requiring evaluation of this node is used
   - Nodes along a named vessel if the AJCC/UICC(TNM) classification is used and nodes along a named vessel are identified

   Based on the TNM classification:
   N0 No regional lymph node metastases
   N1 1–3 perirectal or pericolonic nodes involved
   N2 4 or more pericolic or perirectal nodes involved
   N3 Nodes specifically identified to be along the course of a named vascular trunk (e.g., ileocolic, etc.) are involved with tumor

   Note 3: While prognosis is related to the absolute number of nodes involved there is as yet little evidence that N3 has a worse prognosis than N2: some studies suggest that this division is of little prognostic value

   In most centers there is little or no attempt by the surgeon to identify these vessels and no indication that therapy is modified

4. **Nature of the advancing edge:** regular, irregular/infiltrative

5. **Inflammatory infiltrate:** e.g., Crohn's-like, lymphocytic, eosinophilic

6. **Lymph vessel infiltration**

7. **Perineural infiltration**
8. **Venous infiltration** (extramural veins only)
9. **Residual adenoma at the edge of the carcinoma**

Checklist

Tumor site
— Terminal ileum
— Transverse colon
— Descending colon
— Rectum
— Cecum
— Ascending colon
— Sigmoid colon
— Anus
— Not specified

Resection specimen
— Left hemicolectomy
— Right hemicolectomy
— Proctocolectomy
— Low anterior resection
— Not specified

Proximity to nearest margin
— ——— cm
 Dimensions ——— cm × ——— cm × ——— cm

Macroscopic depth of penetration of tumor
— Into submucosa
— Into muscularis propria
— Through muscularis propria
— Uncertain
— With retraction of underlying serosa

Obstruction (proximal dilatation)
 ——— Yes ——— No

Histologic tumor type
— Adenocarcinoma, NOS
— Signet ring cell cancer
— Small cell undifferentiated cancer
— Mucinous (colloid) cancer
— Adenosquamous cancer
— Undifferentiated cancer
— Other (specify)

Histologic grade
— Well differentiated
— Moderately differentiated
— Poorly differentiated

Depth of infiltration
— into the submucosa but not into the muscularis propria (T1)
— into but not through the muscularis propria (T2)
— through the muscularis propria and into the subserosal fat or pericolonic or perirectal adipose tissue (T3)
— reaching the serosa or peritoneal surface (T4)
— into adjacent organs (T4)

Perforation
 ——— Yes ——— No

Lymph node metastases
— Number of involved nodes
— Total number of nodes

Presence of mesenteric deposits
 ——— Yes ——— No

Metastatic disease in other sites biopsied
— Yes
— No
— Specify site

Adequacy of local excision
— Proximal margin free of tumor
—— Yes —— No
— Distal margin free of tumor
—— Yes —— No
— One margin involved with tumor (cannot determine proximal or distal)
—— Yes —— No
— Radial margin free of tumor (rectal tumors only)
—— Yes —— No

Tissue submitted for special investigation
— Flow cytometry
—— Yes —— No
— Other (specify)

Larynx—carcinoma

Final report—recommended features

General

1. **Topography:** type of specimen(s) received (e.g., total or partial larynx, neck contents)
2. **Type of procedure:** total or partial laryngectomy, e.g., supraglottic (horizontal) or hemilaryngectomy (vertical), radical neck dissection
3. **Exact site of tumor:** supraglottic, subglottic, glottic (see Note 1)
4. **Histologic type:** WHO classification recommended (see Note 2); comment on no tumor present post therapy
5. **Histologic grade** as appropriate: check grading systems
6. **Tumor extent:** depth of invasion with respect to landmarks. Comment on neural, vascular, cartilage, pre-epiglottic space and extralaryngeal soft tissue (muscle soft tissue, cartilage) or tracheostomy involvement as well as multifocal growth
7. **Status of surgical margins**
8. **Lymph node metastases:**
   • Size of metastatic node
   • Number of involved nodes
   • Level of node involvement (diagram)
   • Comment whether or not extranodal spread of tumor is found
   • Comment on keratin debris as evidence of previous tumor
9. **Preoperative treatment effects on nodes**

   Note 1: The American Joint Committee on Cancer divides the larynx into the following three regions: supraglottis, glottis, and subglottis. The supraglottis comprises the epiglottis (both its lingual and laryngeal aspects), arytenoepiglottic folds (laryngeal aspect), arytenoids, and ventricular bands (false cords). The inferior boundary of the supraglottis is a horizontal plane passing through the apex of the ventricle. The glottis comprises the true vocal cords, including the anterior and posterior commissures.

The lower boundary is the horizontal plane, 1 cm below the apex of the ventricle. The subglottis is the region extending from the lower boundary of the glottis to the lower margin of the cricoid cartilage.

Note 2: Histologic type (World Health Organization Classification, modified)

1. Squamous cell carcinoma, typical, keratinizing or nonkeratinizing, invasive or in situ
2. Spindle cell squamous (sarcomatoid) carcinoma
3. Verrucous carcinoma
4. Basaloid squamous carcinoma
5. Undifferentiated carcinoma (including lymphoepithelioma)
6. Salivary gland type tumors
7. Adenoid cystic carcinoma
8. Mucoepidermoid carcinoma
9. Adenosquamous carcinoma
10. Others
11. Neuroendocrine carcinoma
12. Well differentiated (carcinoid tumor)
13. Moderately differentiated (atypical carcinoma tumor)
14. Poorly differentiated (small cell carcinoma)
15. Adenocarcinoma, non-salivary gland type
16. Other malignancies (sarcoma, melanoma, etc.)

Note 3: It is generally recognized that most masses greater than 3 cm in diameter are not single lymph nodes but represent confluent nodes or tumor in soft tissues of the neck

Gross description

1. **Specimen condition:** fresh, in formalin, opened by surgeon or pathologist, unopened, etc.
2. **Specimen identification:** labeled (with name, number) and anatomic site designation as, e.g., right partial vertical laryngectomy, modified neck dissection, etc.
3. **Describe** portions of the larynx included with specimen including other structures that may be attached: hyoid bone, adjacent pharynx, thyroid and parathyroid glands and tracheal rings
4. **Tumor description:**
   • Size (give in three dimensions)
   • Shape (ulcerating, exophytic, polypoid)
   • Color
   • Necrosis
   • Multifocal growth
5. **Location of tumor:** describe all anatomic structures involved including ventricles, which cords, right and/or left, true and/or false cord (specify clearly). Distance above and/or below false and true cords respectively. Involvement of aryepiglottic folds. Does tumor cross midline or extend more than 1 cm from below true vocal cord? If tumor crosses the midline, estimate the percentage of tumor on right and left sides. Is there submucosal spread?
6. **Depth of invasion, involvement of cartilage:** note specific cartilages involved
7. **Involvement of extralaryngeal structures,** thyroid soft tissue, prelaryngeal (Delphian) lymph node, and parathyroid glands
8. **Describe tracheotomy site,** if present. Presence or absence of tumor

9. **Lymph node dissection, if included:**
   - Type: extended radical, radical, or modified radical or selective
   - Inclusion of sternomastoid muscle/submandibular and/or parotid gland/jugular vein
   - Palpable mass (solitary, matted)
   - Size and location of gross invasion of adjacent soft tissues, muscle, and jugular vein
   - Measure and describe sternomastoid muscle, major salivary glands, and internal jugular vein
   - Label lymph nodes as to levels according to anatomic location in neck dissection

Final report—optional features

1. **Interface with stroma:** infiltrating, pushing, superficial or deep invasion
2. **Extent of and location of any dysplasia:** including grade/CIS
3. **Results of ancillary investigations:** i.e., flow cytometry
4. **Type or density of inflammatory infiltrate**
5. **Distance from surgical margins**

Checklist

Topography
— Larynx
— Partial larynx
— Neck dissection

Procedure
— Total laryngectomy
— Partial laryngectomy
  Supraglottic (horizontal)
  Hemilaryngectomy (vertical)
— Radical neck dissection
— Partial neck dissection

Exact site of tumor:
— Supraglottic
— Glottic
— Subglottic
— Transglottic

Histologic type:
— CIS/severe dysplasia only
— Squamous cell carcinoma
  Keratinizing
  Nonkeratinizing
— Undifferentiated carcinoma
— Salivary gland carcinoma (specify)
— Neuroendocrine carcinoma
  Well differentiated (carcinoid)
  Moderately differentiated (atypical carcinoid)
  Poorly differentiated (small cell carcinoma)
— Papillary (exophytic) squamous cell carcinoma
— Spindle cell carcinoma
— Verrucous carcinoma
— Basaloid squamous carcinoma
— Adenosquamous carcinoma
— Adenocarcinoma, nonsalivary type
— Other malignancy (specify)

Histologic grade:
— Well differentiated
— Moderately differentiated
— Poorly differentiated
— Undifferentiated

Tumor extent
— Commissure
  —— Anterior   —— Posterior
— Ventricle
  —— Right   —— Left
— False cord
  —— Right   —— Left
— True cord
  —— Right   —— Left
— Subglottic region
  —— Right   —— Left
— Aryepiglottic fold
  —— Right   —— Left
— Vallecula
— Pyriform sinus
  —— Right   —— Left
— Epiglottis
  —— Right   —— Left

Extralaryngeal structures
— Thyroid
— Soft tissue
  Prelaryngeal (Delphian) lymph node
— Tumor invades cartilage
  —— Yes   —— No
— Vascular invasion
  —— Yes   —— No
— Neural invasion
  —— Yes   —— No
— Tracheostomy invasion
  —— Yes   —— No
  Multicentric tumor
  —— Yes   No
— CIS/dysplasia present
  —— Yes   —— No
— Verrucous hyperplasia present
  —— Yes   —— No

Status of surgical margins (specify specimen margins or margins separately submitted)
— Free of tumor
— Involved by tumor (specify)

Lymph node metastases
— Number of nodes removed—right
— Number of nodes involved—right
— Number of nodes removed—left
— Number of nodes involved—left
— Extracapsular invasion present
— Jugular vein invasion present
— Muscle invasion present
— Keratin debris present

Preoperative treatment effects on nodes
  —— Yes   —— No

Special investigations performed
— Flow cytometry
— Electron microscopy
— Image analysis
— Molecular diagnostics
— Gross photograph

Liver—malignant tumors

Final report—recommended features

Gross description

1. **Specimen identification:** labeled with name, medical record number, surgical pathology number, etc.
2. **Specimen condition:** fresh or in fixative
3. **Type of procedure:** segmentectomy, trisegmentectomy, partial lobectomy, complete resection
4. **Tumor site:** exact anatomic site of the tumor in the liver
5. **Weigh** the specimen and give the dimensions in length × width × thickness
6. **Measure and describe** the lesion(s):
   - Mark the resection margin with ink
   - Description of the distribution of lesion(s)
   - Measure the lesion(s) in their greatest dimensions
   - Is the lesion(s) single or multiple, superficial or deep?
   - Does it involve the liver capsule, hepatic vein or portal vein or inferior vena cava?
   - Is the biliary tract and/or the hilum invaded? (Can the involved liver segment be identified?)
7. **Measure** the distance between the inked resection margin and the nearest lesion
8. **Is there preexisting liver disease or cirrhosis?**
9. **Is there evidence of prior chemo-embolization?**
10. **Evidence of locoregional lymph node metastasis?**
11. **Is the gallbladder attached?: describe it**

Diagnostic information

1. **Histologic type:** state whether the tumor is a primary hepatocellular or cholangiocarcinoma, or is metastatic. Describe microscopic peritumoral satellites, if present

    A satellite is defined as a tumor nodule in the same segment or less than 2 cm from a lesion and less than 50% the diameter of the larger lesion and less than 4 cm in size even if escorting a large mass.
2. **Histologic grade:** state the grade of the hepatocellular tumor (Grade I–IV)
3. **Other organs:** document lymphovascular invasion, if present
4. **Margins:** document whether the resection margin is free of tumor or not and how close tumor is to the inked resection margin
5. **Describe lymph node involvement** and the site of the lymph nodes: hilar nodes, celiac nodes or juxtaregional (periaortic-pericaval/other intra-abdominal)
6. **Describe further foci** of small cell dysplasia
7. **Document underlying hepatic disease,** if present, and state the type—cirrhosis, etc., with determination of etiology (i.e., hepatitis B, hemosiderosis, α_1-antitrypsin, etc.

Final report—optional features

1. **Ancillary immunostaining**
   - Cytokeratins: high/low molecular weights—specify results
   - Carcinoembryonic antigen: polyclonal or monoclonal—specify, pattern—canalicular, etc.
   - Epithelial membrane antigen and α_1-fetoprotein
2. **Special stains:** mucicarmine
3. **Proliferation and ploidy results**

Checklist—Primary liver tumors

Site

Procedure
— Wedge resection
— Segmentectomy
— Trisegmentectomy
— Lobectomy
— Complete hepatectomy

Lesion is confirmed as primary
—— Yes   —— No

Tumor type
— Hepatocellular carcinoma
— Fibrolamellar carcinoma
— Cholangiocarcinoma
— Other (specify)

Histologic grade
— Grade I—Well differentiated liver-like
— Grade II—Larger cells with abnormal nuclei. Glandular structures may be present
— Grade III—Numerous giant cells with pleomorphism
— Grade IV—Marked anaplasia, loss of trabecular pattern

Microscopic peritumoral satellites
—— Yes   —— No

Lymphovascular invasion
—— Yes   —— No
— Is it intrahepatic or extrahepatic?

Liver capsular invasion
—— Yes   —— No

Resection margin
— Distance from tumor to inked resection margin
— Involved
— Uninvolved

Lymph node groups
— Hilar
— Celiac
— Juxtaregional periaortic/pericaval/intra-abdominal

Distant metastasis

TNM Stage—UICC System

Underlying liver disease
—— Yes   —— No
— Type
— Etiology

Checklist—metastatic carcinoma involving liver

Site

Procedure
— Segmentectomy
— Lobectomy
— Wedge resection

Lesion is confirmed as metastasis
— Specify site of origin

Differentiation (grade) of malignancy

Vascular invasion
— Present
— Not present

Liver capsular invasion
— Present

— Not present

Resection margin
— Involved
— Uninvolved

Distance to the inked resection margin

Lymph nodes
— Specify site and if involved

Lung—carcinoma

Final report—recommended features

Gross description

1. **Specimen condition:** fresh, in formalin, opened, unopened etc.
2. **Specimen identification:** labeled with (name, number) and designated as (e.g., right upper lobe)
3. **Part(s) of lung included:** including measurements in three dimensions and weights, and description of other attached structures (i.e., parietal pleura, hilar lymph nodes, etc.)
4. **Tumor description**
   - Tumor location, including relationship to lobe(s), segment(s), and, if pertinent, major airway(s), and pleura. Involvement of lobar or mainstream bronchus should be specified
   - Proximity to bronchial resection margin, and to other surgical margins (i.e., chest wall soft tissue, hilar vessels) as appropriate
   - Tumor size (three dimensions if possible)
   - Presence or absence of satellite tumor modules
5. **Description of nontumorous lung,** i.e., presence or absence of postobstructive changes or other abnormalities (e.g., bronchiectasis, mucus plugs, obstructive pneumonia, atelectasis)

Diagnostic information

1. **Tumor site:** i.e., side, lobe, specific segment if appropriate
2. **Type of procedure:** i.e., segmentectomy, lobectomy, pneumonectomy, including portion of lung resected
3. **Histologic type:** i.e., a modified World Health Organization (WHO) classification is recommended. Although the WHO classification is based on light microscopic criteria, the results of ancillary studies (i.e., histochemistry, immunohistochemistry, electron microscopy) should be reported when appropriate (e.g., large cell neuroendocrine carcinoma)
   - Squamous cell carcinoma (keratinization and/or intercellular bridges). Variant: spindle cell (squamous carcinoma)
   - Small cell carcinoma (uniform small cells, dense round or oval nuclei, diffuse chromatin, inconspicuous nucleoli, sparse cytoplasm). Variants can be mixed small cell/large cell carcinoma (spectrum of cell types ranging from typical small cells to large cells with prominent nucleoli and resembling large cell carcinoma) or combined small cell carcinoma (typical small cell carcinoma intimately admixed with areas of squamous cell carcinoma or adenocarcinoma)
   - Adenocarcinoma (tubular, acinar, or papillary growth pattern, and/or mucus production; acinar adenocarcinoma (i.e., adenocarcinoma, not otherwise specified [NOS]); papillary adenocarcinoma; solid carcinoma with mucus formation; and variants including bronchioalveolar adenocarcinoma and spindle cell (adeno)carcinoma
   - Large cell carcinoma (large nuclei, prominent nucleoli, abundant cytoplasm, without characteristic features of squamous cell, small cell, or adenocarcinoma) including variants of giant cell carcinoma and clear cell carcinoma (large cell carcinomas composed extensively [>90%] of large cells with clear or foamy cytoplasm without mucin; clear cell features also can be prominent in squamous cell carcinomas and adenocarcinomas and in metastatic renal cell carcinoma)
   - Adenosquamous carcinoma
   - Non-small cell neuroendocrine carcinomas, including carcinoid tumor; atypical carcinoid tumor (well-differentiated neuroendocrine carcinoma); large cell neuroendocrine carcinoma (large polygonal cells, coarse nuclear chromatin, frequent nucleoli, neuroendocrine differentiation by immunohistochemistry or electron microscopy). Classification of neuroendocrine carcinomas remains controversial, and therefore use of the category "large cell neuroendocrine carcinoma" should be considered optional until sufficient data are available to clarify the clinical significance of this subset of large cell carcinomas
   - Bronchial gland carcinomas, adenoid cystic carcinoma, mucoepidermoid carcinoma
   - Other (specify)
4. **Histologic grade:** World Health Organization (WHO) classification (i.e., well, moderately, and poorly differentiated) recommended for squamous cell carcinoma and adenocarcinomas of acinar (i.e., adenocarcinoma, NOS) or papillary type
5. **Histologic assessment of surgical margins:** include comment regarding involvement of lobar or mainstem bronchi by invasive or in situ carcinoma, and microscopic relationship of tumor to bronchial and/or vascular margin(s)
6. **Pleural involvement:** specify whether tumor invades into but not through visceral pleura without involving parietal pleura (T2), or into parietal pleura (T3) (elastic tissue stains can be helpful in defining the limiting elastic layer of visceral pleura)
7. **Lymph node metastases:** indicate the number of involved nodes and the total number of nodes received. (Precise node counts may be difficult for fragmented specimens such as those received from mediastinoscopy.) The nodal groups (N) should be specifically identified using the American Joint Committee on Cancer intraoperative staging system for regional lymph nodes. N2 lymph nodes (with the exception of level 11 interlobar nodes) are generally received separately and must be appropriately identified by the submitting surgeon; these are to be reported separately. Pneumonectomies are usually accompanied by attached N2 lymph nodes which should be specifically identified by location. If the nodal involvement is only by direct extension, this feature should be noted
8. **Non-neoplastic lung:** any significant abnormalities (e.g., granulomas, pneumonia, etc.) should be recorded

Final report—optional features

1. **Stage:** surgical pathology reports containing the previously listed information will contain all of the necessary data to establish the International TNM Staging System for lung carcinoma. It should be emphasized that pathologic tumor stage may be based on incomplete information and therefore may differ from clinical tumor stage
2. **Angiolymphatic invasion:** whenever possible, it should be specified whether the structures involved are blood vessels or lymphatic vessels, and whether the involved blood vessels are muscular arteries, elastic arteries, or veins
3. **Perineural invasion**
4. **Presence or absence of perinodal (extracapsular) tumor invasion**
5. **Results of ancillary investigations:** e.g., flow cytometry

Checklist

Topography
— Right lung
    RUL
    RML
    RLL
— Left lung
    LUL
    LLL
— Segment (specify)

Procedure
— Pneumonectomy
— Lobectomy
— Bilobectomy
— Segmentectomy
— Wedge excision
— Other (specify)

Tumor type

Tumor histologic grade
— Well differentiated
— Moderately differentiated
— Poorly differentiated/undifferentiated

Tumor location

Tumor size (greatest diameter)

Angiolymphatic invasion

Perineural invasion

Mainstem bronchus

Bronchial margin

Visceral pleural margin

In situ carcinoma

Non-neoplastic lung
— Atelectasis
— Pneumonia
— Other (specify)

Lymph nodes with metastatic disease

This is a set of recommendations for lymph node biopsies, lymph node dissections, sentinel node biopsies, and lymph node fine needle aspiration (FNA) and core needle biopsies, intended specifically for lymph nodes being studied for metastatic neoplasms, and not to be applied to lymph nodes being evaluated for lymphoma, infections, and other disease processes. They are, however, formulated generically enough to apply regardless of whether the primary tumor is a carcinoma of the breast, carcinoma of the prostate, melanoma, or any other malignant, potentially metastasizing tumor.

Lymph node biopsies

1. In the presence of gross tumor in a biopsy of a single lymph node, one or several routine sections to demonstrate the tumor and its possible extranodal extension will suffice
2. In the absence of gross tumor, the entire node should be submitted for microscopic examination, cut into 3- to 4-mm slices in the longitudinal or transverse plane. If the node is so small that it cannot be sliced in this manner, it may be submitted as one piece in toto. If the node is sliced, care should be taken to process different surfaces for microscopic examination. The Association recommends the examination of several levels of each slide, stained with hematoxylin and eosin (H&E) only

Lymph node dissection

1. **Processing and staining**
   - As mentioned above, the principles presented here are generic, and may vary by site or by institution
   - Lymph node dissections are best processed fresh, although other techniques (such as fixation in Bouin's solution) may be used
   - No clearing of adipose tissue is necessary, although it may represent an institutional or individual preference
   - Submit every node for microscopic examination
   - Submit the entire nodes cut as described in the preceding section unless they contain grossly visible tumor, in which case fewer slices are required, or if they are grossly largely replaced by adipose tissue, in which case processing is optional
   - Lymph node levels in a dissection specimen should be specified and submitted separately where clinically appropriate (for example, neck dissections, colectomy specimens)
   - The summary of the sections in the surgical pathology report should include how many sections of how many nodes are submitted in each cassette. Different color inks may be used to distinguish different nodes submitted in a single cassette
   - One H&E slide per cassette is recommended
   - Immunohistochemistry and other specialized techniques may be used as part of a research study or for differential diagnosis, but are not considered mandatory at present

2. **Reporting**
   - The number of lymph nodes positive for metastatic disease and the total number of lymph nodes examined microscopically should be reported, with specific levels mentioned when appropriate
   - The size of the largest metastasis (measured on the slide) should be reported if clinically indicated
   - The presence of extracapsular extension may be reported, depending upon the primary site and institutional preference
   - If the tumor is seen in extranodal vessels, this should be stated

- Deposits of tumor not associated with any structure recognizable as a lymph node should be separately designated
- In rare situations, the grading of nodal metastases may be important
- After preoperative chemotherapy and/or radiotherapy, the notation of necrotic *versus* non-necrotic tumor is recommended

Sentinel node biopsy

1. The adequacy of the sentinel node dissection depends upon the skill and experience of the surgeon. At the present time, the clinical utility of this technique is still controversial. In many institutions, this is still considered an experimental procedure
2. Where this factor has been studied, the level of radiation associated with sentinel node biopsy has not been demonstrated to pose any danger to pathologists or histotechnologists from radioactivity. However, protocols should conform to institutional and state guidelines
3. Intraoperative examination, whether by frozen section or scrape/imprint cytology or both, is appropriate only in those clinical situations in which the results will influence immediate therapeutic management. Examination of the intraoperative specimen by other than routine (H&E) stains is experimental at the present time
4. The number of nodes received and their sizes should be noted in the gross description of the report. Each node should be processed grossly as mentioned earlier under Dissections. If any portion of the sentinel node(s) is not submitted for routine sectioning, this should be specified
5. ADASP recommends that more than one section be performed on each block in these cases, if the node or nodes are not positive grossly or at intraoperative pathologic consultation. However, it is not currently clear how many sections (and from what levels of the block) are optimal. It is also unclear whether immunostains add clinically relevant information and whether they should be substituted for additional H&E-stained sections. It should be remembered that false positive immunostains occur, and these stains should be interpreted in the context of standard histopathology
6. If metastases are identified only by immunostains, this should be stated in the final report. Other statements on reporting provided in this document are also applicable

Fine needle aspiration and core needle biopsy

1. A negative result for tumor does not definitely exclude the presence of a metastatic tumor. Results should be correlated with the clinical situation
2. If only FNA is performed, a cell block may be useful for special studies in positive cases
3. If only a core needle biopsy is performed, all tissue should be submitted. The number of cores received should be specified in the gross description, and should be correlated with the slides received and examined
4. In many cases, it may not be possible to document on an FNA or core needle biopsy specimen that a metastatic tumor is indeed within a lymph node. In such a situation, a comment should be made to that effect

Major salivary glands

Final report—recommended features

Gross description

1. **Specimen identification:** labeled with name or medical record number
2. **Specimen condition:** fresh, in saline, or in formalin or other fixative
3. **Anatomic site and side of tumor:** parotid, submandibular or sublingual gland; left, right, or undesignated
4. **Type of procedure:** needle biopsy, open (incisional or excisional) biopsy, lobectomy, complete excision of gland, wide or radical excision
5. **Describe and measure** the entire surgical specimen (three dimensions). Identify and measure each component (i.e., total parotidectomy with attached radical neck dissection and overlying skin)
6. **Tumor characteristics:** size (three dimensions); solitary or multifocal; localized or diffusely involves the gland; confined to gland or extraglandular extension; margins (encapsulated, circumscribed, or poorly defined); color, consistency, necrosis; cyst formation; presence of apparent cartilage, calcific deposits or hyalinization
7. **Paraffin block key:** i.e., block A is from center of tumor, etc.
8. **When ink is used,** give code (i.e., black ink is inferior resection margin, blue ink is superior resection margin, etc.)

Checklist

Location
— Parotid
— Submandibular
— Sublingual

Side
— Right
— Left
— Not indicated

Procedure
— Needle
— Open biopsy (incisional or excisional)
— Lobectomy
— Complete excision of gland

Histologic type
— Benign epithelial tumors
    Pleomorphic adenoma
    Warthin's tumor
    Basal cell adenoma
    Canalicular adenoma
    Oncocytoma (oncocytic adenoma)
    Myoepithelioma (myoepithelial adenoma)
    Sebaceous adenoma/lymphadenoma
    Cystadenoma
    Intraductal papilloma
    Sialadenoma papilliferum
    Other
— Carcinomas
    Acinic cell carcinoma

Mucoepidermoid carcinoma
Adenoid cystic adenoma
Polymorphous low-grade adenocarcinoma (terminal duct adenocarcinoma)
Epithelial–myoepithelial carcinoma
Clear cell carcinoma
Basal cell adenocarcinoma
Salivary duct carcinoma
Oncocytic carcinoma (malignant oncocytoma)
Adenocarcinoma, NOS
Malignant myoepithelioma (myoepithelial carcinoma)
Malignant mixed tumor
 In situ/intracapsular carcinoma
 Carcinoma ex pleomorphic adenoma
 True malignant mixed tumor (carcinosarcoma)
 Metastasizing pleomorphic adenoma
Cystadenocarcinoma
Mucinous adenocarcinoma
Squamous cell carcinoma
Small cell carcinoma
Undifferentiated carcinoma
Lymphoepithelial carcinoma
Sebaceous carcinoma/lymphadenocarcinoma
Sialoblastoma
Other
— Malignant lymphoma (specify type)
— Soft tissue neoplasms
 Benign (specify type)
 Malignant (specify type)
— Metastatic tumor
 Indicate primary if known
— Other (specify)

Histologic grade[a]

— Low (well differentiated)
— Intermediate (moderately differentiated)
— High (poorly differentiated)
— Undifferentiated

[a]Grading of salivary malignancies is not standardized and may vary according to histologic type. In some instances, histologic type defines the grade; for example, epithelial–myoepithelial carcinoma and basal cell adenocarcinoma are low grade while salivary duct carcinoma is usually high grade

Tumor extent

— Confined to gland of origin
 Intraglandular lymphatic invasion
 Intraglandular vascular invasion
 Intraglandular perineural invasion
— Extraglandular extension
 Cervical lymph nodes
 Major nerve (facial, etc.)
 Major blood vessel (jugular vein, etc.)
 Bone
 Skin
 Other (specify)

Status of surgical margins

— Free of tumor
— Close, but technically free (specify margin and distance to margin)
— Involved by tumor (specify margin)

Lymph node metastasis

— Applies only to cervical lymph nodes. Other than for metastatic tumors, involvement of intraparotid lymph nodes by primary parotid tumors does not appear to have clinical relevance
— Cervical
 ——— Right ——— Left
 Number examined
 Number positive
 Extranodal spread
 Size of largest positive lymph node (necessary for "N" staging in section 9 below)
— Level of lymph nodes (optional)
 Level I (submental, submandibular)
 Level II (upper jugular)
 Level III (middle jugular)
 Level IV (lower jugular)
 Level V (posterior triangle)
 Level VI (anterior compartment)
 Preauricular
 Postauricular
 Suboccipital
 Other

Pathologic stage

Special features

— Gross photographs
— Electron micrography
— Immunohistochemistry
— Flow cytometry
— Image analysis
— Genetic (chromosomal) analysis
— Molecular diagnostics
— Tumor tissue bank

Comments

Nasal cavity and paranasal sinuses—carcinoma

Final report—recommended features

Gross description

1. **Specimen identification:** how the specimen was labeled or identified (name, medical record number), and anatomic site designation, e.g., left maxillary sinus, left neck dissection, etc.
2. **Specimen condition:** how the specimen was received: fresh or in formalin, oriented by the surgeon, etc. Note any anatomic identifiers such as sutures or accompanying drawings
3. **Type of procedure:** maxillectomy, ethmoidectomy, etc. Describe the portions of tissue included with the specimen, including other structures that may be attached, e.g., maxillary sinus and attached tissues, such as teeth, hard palate, rim of orbit
4. **Measure** the overall dimensions of all specimens received
5. **Tumor description:** size (three dimensions), shape, color
6. **Tumor location:** anatomic site. Describe the presumed epicenter of the tumor and all the major anatomic

structures involved such as sinus wall, nasal cavity, orbital rim, etc.

7. **Tumor extent:** size and depth of invasion with respect to adjacent structures, including involvement of cartilage, bone, or soft tissues

8. **Lymph node dissection,** if included: type, e.g., radical, modified, or selective; inclusion of sternocleidomastoid muscle or submandibular or parotid gland; jugular vein; measure and describe each. Describe lymph nodes—multiple solitary nodes or matted. Measure size of largest lymph node mass. Label lymph nodes as to levels according to anatomic location in the neck dissection, i.e., levels 1 through 5

Diagnostic information

1. **Topography:** what is included in the specimen(s) received
2. **Procedure:** e.g., total or partial rhinectomy, radical neck dissection
3. **Site of tumor:** e.g., lateral wall of nasal cavity, anteroinferior maxillary sinus
4. **Size**
5. **Histologic type**
6. **Histologic grade,** as appropriate
7. **Tumor extent:** size and depth of invasion with respect to adjacent structures (refer to checklist for site-specific descriptions). Note vascular, lymphatic, perineural, bone invasion
8. **Status of surgical margins**
9. **Lymph node metastases:** nodes removed and number of nodes positive, for each level examined; size of largest metastasis. Comment on whether extracapsular extension of tumor is present or absent

Final report—optional features

1. **Extent and location** of CIS or any dysplasia including grade
2. **Distance from surgical margins**
3. **Results of ancillary investigations:** immunohistochemistry, flow cytometry

Checklist

Topography
— Nose
    Sphenoid
    Orbital contents
— Maxillary sinus
    Frontal
    Soft palate
— Ethmoid sinus
    Hard palate

Procedure
— Rhinectomy
    —— Total —— Partial
— Maxillectomy
— Ethmoidectomy
— Frontal sinus excision
— Sphenoid sinus excision
— Radical neck dissection
— Partial neck dissection

Site of tumor
— Nasal cavity
    Lateral wall
    Floor
    Septum
    Roof
— Maxillary sinus
    Anteroinferior
    Superoposterior
    Ethmoid
    Sphenoid
    Frontal

Size of tumor
— ——— cm × ——— cm × ——— cm

Histologic type
— Carcinoma in situ only
— Squamous cell carcinoma
    Keratinizing
    Nonkeratinizing
— Lymphoepithelial carcinoma
— Sinonasal undifferentiated carcinoma
— Neuroendocrine carcinoma
    Well differentiated (carcinoma)
    Moderately differentiated (atypical carcinoid)
    Poorly differentiated (small cell)
— Salivary gland carcinoma (specify)
— Adenocarcinoma, nonsalivary type
— Inverted (and all Schneiderian) papillomas
— Carcinoma ex Schneiderian papilloma
— Olfactory neuroblastoma
— Angiofibroma
— Chondrosarcoma
    Osteosarcoma
— Hemangiopericytoma
— Ameloblastoma
— Sarcoma
— Other malignancy

Histologic grade
— Well differentiated
— Moderately differentiated
— Poorly differentiated
— Undifferentiated

Tumor extent
— Nose/nasal cavity
— Involvement of:
    Limited to mucosa with no destruction of bone
    Skin
    Columnella
    Septum
    Lateral wall
    Roof (cribriform plate)
    Ethmoid sinus involvement
    Maxillary sinus involvement
    Nasopharynx
    Hard palate
    Soft palate

Maxillary sinus
— Involvement of:
    Limited to mucosa with no erosion or destruction of bone
    Middle nasal meatus

Subcutaneous tissues or skin of cheek
Posterior wall of maxillary sinus
Orbital floor
Medial wall of orbit
Anterior ethmoid sinus
Orbital contents invasion
Cribriform plate
Posterior ethmoid sinus
Sphenoid sinus
Nasopharynx
Soft palate
Hard palate
Pterygomaxillary fossa
Temporal fossa
Base of skull

Ethmoid sinus
— Limited to sinus
— Involvement of:
  Nasal cavity
  Anterior orbit
  Maxillary sinus
  Intracranial
  Skin of nose
  Apex of orbit
  Sphenoid sinus

Sphenoid
— Limited to mucosa
— Invasion beyond sinus

Other
— Vascular invasion
— Lymphatic invasion
— Perineural invasion
— Bone invasion

Status of margins
— Margins free of tumor or estimated free margin distance from tumor
— Margins involved by tumor, list

Lymph node metastases
— Nodes removed, no. nodes positive
  Level I
  Level II
  Level III
  Level IV
  Level V
  Level VI
— Extracapsular extension present
— Size of largest metastasis

Special studies
— Photographs
— Electron microscopy
— Flow cytometry
— Image analysis
— Molecular studies

Oral cavity and oropharynx—carcinoma

Final report—recommended features

Gross description
1. **Specimen identification:** labeled (with name, medical record number) and anatomic site designation, e.g., right partial glossectomy, modified neck dissection
2. **Specimen condition:** fresh, in formalin, oriented by surgeon, etc.
3. **Describe:** portions of oral cavity or oropharynx included with specimen, including other structures that may be attached, e.g., cortical bone or jaws, palate, tongue, skin of neck, maxillary sinus
4. **Measure** the overall dimensions of all specimens received
5. **Tumor description:** size (give in three dimensions), shape (ulcerating, exophytic, polypoid), color, necrosis, multifocal growth
6. **Location of the tumor:** anatomic sites and subsites
   - External upper lip (vermillion border)
   - External lower lip (vermillion border)
   - Commissures
   - Buccal mucosa
     - Mucosa of upper and lower lips
     - Cheek mucosa
     - Retromolar areas
     - Bucco-alveolar sulci, upper and lower (vestibule of mouth)
   - Upper alveolus and gingiva (upper gum)
   - Lower alveolus and gingiva (lower gum)
   - Hard palate
   - Tongue
     - Dorsal surface and lateral borders anterior to vallate papillae (anterior two-thirds)
     - Inferior (ventral) surface
   - Floor of mouth
   - Oropharynx
     - Anterior wall (glosso-epiglottic area)
       ○ Base of tongue (posterior to the vallate papillae or posterior third)
       ○ Vallecula
     - Lateral wall
       ○ Tonsil
       ○ Tonsillar fossa and tonsillar (faucial) pillars
       ○ Glossotonsillar sulci (tonsillar pillars)
     - Posterior wall
     - Superior wall
       ○ Inferior surface of soft palate
       ○ Uvula
7. **Tumor extent:** based on tumor classification (AJCC, UICC) (applicable only to carcinomas of the vermillion surfaces of the lips and of the oral cavity and oropharynx, including those of minor salivary glands)
   - All sites
     Tis Carcinoma in situ
     T1   Tumor 2 cm or less in greatest dimension
     T2   Tumor more than 2 cm but not more than 4 cm in greatest dimension
     T3   Tumor more than 4 cm in greatest dimension
     T4
       ○ Lip—tumor invades adjacent structures, e.g., through cortical bone, inferior alveolar nerve, floor of mouth, skin of face
       ○ Oral cavity—tumor invades adjacent structures, e.g., through cortical bone, into deep (extrinsic) muscle of tongue, maxillary sinus, skin (superficial

erosion alone of bone/tooth socket by gingival primary is not sufficient to classify a tumor as T4)

   ○ Oropharynx—tumor invades adjacent structures, e.g., pterygoid muscles, mandible, hard palate, deep muscle of tongue, larynx

Note 1: The extrinsic musculature of the tongue includes musculi hypo-, stylo-, genio-, and palatoglossus. Invasion of the intrinsic muscle alone (musculi longitudinales superior and inferior, transversus linguae and verticalis linguae) is not classified T4

Note 2: In cases of doubt regarding the invasion through cortical bone, Paragraph 4 of the General Rules of the TNM System (TNM Booklet, p. 6) should be applied. If there is doubt concerning the correct T, N, or M category to which a particular case should be allotted, the lower (i.e., less advanced) category should be chosen. This will also be reflected in the stage grouping. If scintigraphy is feasible and the resultant finding is conclusive the tumor must be classified as T4

8. **Lymph node dissection** if included: type (extended radical, radical or modified radical or selective); inclusion of sternomastoid muscle/submandibular and/or parotid gland/jugular vein; palpable mass (solitary, matted); size and location of gross invasion of adjacent soft tissues, muscle, and jugular vein; measure and describe sternomastoid muscle, major salivary glands, and internal jugular vein; measure size of lymph nodal masses (see Notes 3a and 3b); label lymph nodes as to levels or according to anatomic location in neck dissection

Note 3a: It is generally recognized that most masses greater than 3 cm in diameter are not single lymph nodes but represent confluent nodes or tumor in soft tissues of the neck

Note 3b: Histologic examination of a selective neck dissection specimen will ordinarily include 6 or more lymph nodes. Histologic examination of a radical or modified radical neck dissection specimen will ordinarily include 10 or more lymph nodes (depending on previous RT)

Diagnostic information

1. **Topography:** type of specimen(s) received, e.g., simple excision, composite resection, neck contents
2. **Procedure:** e.g., total or partial glossectomy, radical neck dissection
3. **Exact site of tumor:** lip, oral cavity, oropharynx (see Checklist, Anatomic site of tumor)
4. **Histologic type:** World Health Organization classification recommended (see Note 4) (comment on no tumor present post therapy)

Note 4: Histologic type (World Health Organization Classification, modified) includes squamous cell carcinoma, typical, keratinizing or nonkeratinizing, invasive or in situ; spindle cell squamous (sarcomatoid) carcinoma; verrucous carcinoma; basaloid squamous cell carcinoma; papillary squamous cell carcinoma; undifferentiated carcinoma (including lymphoepithelioma); salivary gland-type tumor (adenoid cystic carcinoma, mucoepidermoid carcinoma, adenosquamous carcinoma, and others); neuroendocrine carcinoma [well-differentiated (carcinoid tumor), moderately differentiated (atypical carcinoid tumor), poorly differentiated (small cell carcinoma)]; adenocarcinoma, nonsalivary gland type; other malignancies (sarcoma, melanoma, etc.)

5. **Histologic grade** as appropriate
6. **Tumor extent:** size and depth of invasion with respect to adjacent structures (e.g., tonsillar pillar, soft palate, nasal cavity, pterygoid muscles) extrinsic muscle of tongue, skin and soft tissue of neck and face. Distinguish extending to or overlying bone from gross erosion of bone and radiographic destruction of bone. Note tracheostomy involvement, as well as multifocal growth
7. **Status of surgical margins**
8. **Lymph node metastases:** size of metastatic node, number of involved nodes, level of node involvement, comment whether extranodal spread of tumor is found, comment on keratin debris and/or foreign body giant cell reaction as evidence of previous tumor
9. **Preoperative treatment:** effects on nodes

Final report—optional features

1. **Extent and location** of any dysplasia (including grade)
2. **Vascular/lymphatic invasion**
3. **Perineural invasion**
4. **Depth of invasion**
5. **Interface with stroma:** infiltrating, pushing, superficial or deep invasion
6. **Inflammatory infiltrate:** type of density
7. **Results of ancillary investigations:** i.e., flow cytometry
8. **Distance** from surgical margins

Checklist

Topography
— Lip
— Oral cavity
— Oropharynx
— Neck dissection

Procedure
— Incisional biopsy
— Excisional biopsy
— Resection

Anatomic site of tumor
— External upper lip (vermillion border)
— External lower lip (vermillion border)
— Commissures
— Buccal mucosa
    Mucosa of upper and lower lips
    Cheek mucosa
    Retromolar areas
    Bucco-alveolar sulci, upper and lower (vestibule of mouth)
— Upper alveolus and gingiva (upper gum)
— Lower alveolus and gingiva (lower gum)
— Hard palate
— Tongue
    Dorsal surface and lateral borders anterior to vallate papillae (anterior two-thirds)
    Inferior (ventral) surface

— Floor of mouth
— Oropharynx
— Anterior wall (glosso-epiglottic area)
    Base of tongue (posterior to the vallate papillae or
       posterior third)
    Vallecula
— Lateral wall
    Tonsil
    Tonsillar fossa and tonsillar (faucial) pillars
    Glossotonsillar sulci (tonsillar pillars)
— Posterior wall
— Superior wall
    Inferior surface of soft palate
    Uvula

Histologic type

CIS/severe dysplasia only
— Squamous cell carcinoma
    Keratinizing
    Nonkeratinizing
— Undifferentiated carcinoma
    Papillary (exophytic) squamous cell carcinoma
    Spindle cell carcinoma
    Verrucous carcinoma
    Basaloid carcinoma
— Neuroendocrine carcinoma
    Well differentiated (carcinoid)
    Moderately differentiated (atypical carcinoid)
    Poorly differentiated (small cell carcinoma)
— Salivary gland carcinoma (specify type)
    Adenosquamous carcinoma
    Adenocarcinoma, nonsalivary type
    Other malignancy (specify)

Histologic grade

— Well differentiated
— Moderately differentiated
— Poorly differentiated
— Undifferentiated

Tumor extent (see text definition)

— Tis: Carcinoma in situ
— T1: Tumor 2 cm or less in greatest dimension
— T2: Tumor more than 2 cm but not more than 4 cm in
greatest dimension
— T3: Tumor more than 4 cm in greatest dimension
— T4: Tumor invades adjacent structures, e.g., through
cortical bone, mandible, inferior alveolar nerve, skin or
soft tissues of neck, deep (extrinsic) muscle of tongue,
pterygoid muscles, maxillary sinus, hard palate, larynx
— Multicentric tumor

**Status of surgical margins (specify specimen margins or
margins separately submitted)**

— Free of tumor
— Involved by tumor (specify)

Lymph node metastases (specify right or left)

— Number of nodes removed
— Number of nodes involved
— Size of largest involved node
— Extracapsular invasion present
— Jugular vein invasion present
— Muscle invasion present
— Keratin debris and/or foreign body giant cell reaction present

Preoperative treatment effects on nodes
    —— Yes   —— No

Special investigations performed

— Flow cytometry
— Electron micrography
— Image analysis
— Molecular diagnostics
— Gross photograph

Pancreas and periampullary region— carcinoma

Final report—recommended features

Gross description

1. **Specimen identification:** labeled with information such
as name and medical record number
2. **Specimen condition:** e.g., fresh, in fixative
3. **Site:** the exact anatomic site of the tumor
4. **Type of procedure:** biopsy, local excision, standard
pancreaticoduodenectomy (Whipple's procedure),
pylorus-preserving pancreaticoduodenectomy, total
pancreatectomy, distal pancreatectomy stating specifically
which organs have been removed
5. **Describe and measure** (three dimensions) the entire
surgical specimen, e.g., biopsy, local excision, standard
pancreaticoduodenectomy (Whipple's procedure),
pylorus-preserving pancreaticoduodenectomy, total
pancreatectomy, distal pancreatectomy. Describe and
measure each component of the specimen
6. **Describe the gross features** of the tumor: color,
consistency, size, location within the pancreas (head,
body, tail, or diffusely throughout the gland);
encapsulated or nonencapsulated; relationship to the
pancreatic and bile ducts, multicentricity; abnormalities
of the pancreatic ducts including stricture, ductal
dilatation; grossly visible mucin; unilocular or
multilocular neoplastic cysts; cyst contents; non-
neoplastic cysts in pancreatic tissue adjacent to tumor;
secondary cyst formation due to tumor necrosis
7. **Describe:** for Whipple distal or total pancreatectomy
specimens, describe all applicable items, e.g., status of
the main pancreatic duct, accessory ducts, common bile
duct, cystic duct, ampulla of Vater, duodenum, stomach,
spleen, portal, superior mesenteric and splenic veins,
common hepatic artery. Describe duct extension to
duodenum, stomach, spleen, or colon. Report
involvement of vessels, portal, superior mesenteric, and
splenic veins; common hepatic artery; any other large
vessels adjacent to tumor. Identify and describe surgical
margins for adequacy of excision. Comment if the
tumor is grossly identifiable at the margins. Describe
the localization, number, and consistency of lymph
nodes
8. **Paraffin block key**

Diagnostic information

1. **Type of malignancy** should be recorded. The following
classification of pancreatic malignant tumors is
recommended:

- Type of neoplasm
  - Carcinoma in situ
  - Infiltrating ductal carcinoma
  - Adenosquamous carcinoma
  - Mucinous noncystic carcinoma
  - Signet ring cell carcinoma
  - Undifferentiated carcinoma
  - Spindle and giant cell type
  - With osteoclast-like giant cells
  - Small cell carcinoma
  - Mucinous cystadenocarcinoma
  - Mucinous cystic neoplasm of low malignant potential (borderline)
  - Mucinous cystic neoplasm with sarcomatous transformation of the stroma
  - Intraductal mucinous papillary carcinoma with an invasive component
  - Intraductal mucinous papillary carcinoma without an invasive component
  - Serous cystadenocarcinoma
  - Solid pseudopapillary and cystic carcinoma (malignant solid papillary and cystic tumor)
  - Acinar cell carcinoma
  - Acinar cell cystadenocarcinoma
  - Endocrine neoplasm (e.g., insulin, glucagon, somatostatin, gastrin, pancreatic polypeptide and vasoactive-intestinal peptide secreting, multihormonal)
  - Mixed acinar and endocrine carcinoma
  - Mixed ductal and endocrine carcinoma
  - Pancreatoblastoma
- Mesenchymal tumors
  - Leiomyosarcoma
  - Osteosarcoma
- Lymphoma
- Others

2. **Tumor grade:** the following grading system is suggested for infiltrating ductal carcinomas:
   - Grade 1   Well differentiated, more than 95% of the tumor is composed of glands
   - Grade 2   Moderately differentiated, 50% to 95% of the tumor is composed of glands
   - Grade 3   Poorly differentiated, 5% to 49% of the tumor is composed of glands
   - Grade 4   Undifferentiated, less than 5% of the tumor is composed of glands

For papillary intraductal carcinomas, grading is optional. The grading system designed by Albores-Saavedra et al.[1] is recommended. It is based on nuclear atypia and mitotic figures. High-grade tumors are characterized by cells with vesicular or hyperchromatic nuclei and prominent nucleoli. Mitotic figures are common (more than 5 per 10 high-power fields). Low-grade neoplasms are composed of cuboidal or columnar pseudostratified cells with ovoid or elongated vesicular or hyperchromatic nuclei but without nucleoli and without mitotic activity. Tumors with moderate nuclear atypia and very few mitotic figures (<5 per 10 high-power fields) are included in the intermediate category. Because of the poor correlation of cytologic features, pattern of growth, and biologic behavior in most endocrine tumors, they are not graded

Checklist

Specimen type
— Biopsy
— Local excision
— Distal pancreatectomy
— Standard pancreaticoduodenectomy
— Pylorus-preserving pancreaticoduodenectomy
— Total pancreatectomy

Diagnosis section
— Pathology report should address all applicable items
— Tumor type
— Grade
— No stromal invasion
— Invasion confined to the pancreas (include size)
— Invasion of (check all applicable):
    Peripancreatic soft tissues
    Common bile duct
    Cystic duct
    Adjacent large vessels
    Portal vein
    Mesenteric
    Common hepatic artery
— Invasion of any or all of the following (check all applicable)
    Ampulla of Vater
    Duodenum
    Stomach
    Colon
    Spleen
— Invasion of:
    Small vessels
    Large vessels
    Perineural invasion
— Other pancreatic epithelial abnormalities, such as atypical ductal hyperplasia and papillary hyperplasia, should be recorded

Pathology in other organs
— Common bile duct
— Cystic duct
— Ampulla of Vater
— Duodenum
— Stomach
— Spleen

Involvement of surgical margins
— Common bile duct
— Pancreas neck
— Pancreas uncinate
— Posterior (retroperitoneal) pancreas
— Other soft tissue margins
— Duodenum
— Stomach

Lymph nodes
— Number of lymph nodes sampled and number of lymph nodes with metastasis
— Extent of tumor
    Tumor size
    No stromal invasion present
    Invasion confined to the pancreas (include size)
    Direct extension into ampulla

Invasion of peripancreatic soft tissues, common bile duct, cystic duct, duodenum, or invasion of adjacent large vessels (e.g., portal vein, mesenteric, or common hepatic artery)

Invasion of spleen, colon, stomach

Presence or absence of lymphatic or microvascular invasion

Perineural invasion

— Intraductal lesions. Report papillary hyperplasia, ductal hyperplasia, or carcinoma in situ adjacent to tumor. Report dysplasia or carcinoma in situ in common bile duct or ampulla of Vater

— Other lesions

Acute or chronic pancreatitis

Pancreatic cysts

Calculi

Other

— Surgical margins: Report involved or uninvolved surgical resection margins of the pancreas (e.g., neck, uncinate, posterior), bile duct, duodenum, stomach, and soft tissues, including retroperitoneal margin

— Lymph nodes: Report presence or absence of metastases in regional lymph nodes. State the number of lymph nodes sampled and the number of lymph nodes involved. Report separately submitted lymph nodes

— Report results of immunoperoxidase stains and electron microscopy in endocrine and acinal neoplasms and in combined exocrine and endocrine tumors.

Optional features

— Ploidy
— Nuclear morphometry
— Genetic abnormalities
— Growth factors
— Receptors
— Stage

1. Albores-Saavedra J, Henson DE, Milchgrub S. Intraductal papillary carcinoma of the main pancreatic duct. Int J Pancreatol 1994, **16**: 223-224.

Parathyroid glands

Final report—recommended features

Primary hyperparathyroidism is a common disease, the incidence of which has increased rather dramatically over the past several decades. As a result, surgical exploration of the parathyroid has become a relatively commonplace procedure at most large institutions. Most parathyroid tumors represent either adenomas or hyperplasia. The distinction between these two entities is problematic, and usually requires pathologic examination of more than one gland as well as clinical data. This, together with the rarity of other parathyroid neoplasms, focuses this protocol on defining the information necessary to distinguish parathyroid adenoma from hyperplasia, and the features most useful in the diagnosis of parathyroid carcinoma

Gross description

1. **Specimen identification:** precisely designated site (e.g., left upper parathyroid) and whether biopsy or whole gland

2. **Specimen condition:** whether the specimen was received fresh *versus* in fixative (type)

3. **Describe and measure** the specimen:
   - Weight (include estimate from surgeon of percentage of gland removed, if available)
   - Size in three dimensions
   - Color and consistency
   - Presence of capsule
   - Adherence to other structures
   - Cystic elements
   - Hemorrhage
   - Necrosis
   - Nodularity

4. **Specify** when frozen section or touch imprint performed

5. **Paraffin block key**

6. **When ink is used,** so specify

7. **Special investigations:** note following if done
   - Gross photography
   - Tissue processed for ancillary studies or stored for such potential

Diagnostic information

1. **Surgical procedure**

2. **Histologic classification**
   - Hyperplasia
   - Adenoma
   - Atypical adenoma
   - Carcinoma

   Several studies have defined histologic features important in the diagnosis of parathyroid carcinoma, including thick fibrous bands, trabecular growth pattern, and high mitotic rate. Similarly, criteria have been developed to distinguish adenoma from hyperplasia

3. **Characteristics of carcinoma**
   - Features present to make diagnosis
   - Grade (no grading currently available)
   - Extent
   - Margins

4. **Lymph nodes**

Final report—optional features

1. **Subtyping tumor:** e.g., chief cell *versus* clear cell

2. **Results of ancillary studies**
   - DNA ploidy
   - Proliferative activity (e.g., MIB-1, p27)
   - Nuclear morphometry
   - Genetic abnormalities
   - Growth factors and receptors

3. **Pathologic stage—proposed system** (see below)

4. **Clinical data**
   - Patient history, including family history
   - Endocrine testing results
     - Serum Ca^{2+}
     - Serum PTH
     - Other
   - Pre- and postoperative diagnoses

Proposed staging system for parathyroid carcinoma

Primary tumor (T)

T1   <3 cm

T2 >3 cm

T3 Tumor of any size with invasion of the surrounding soft tissues, such as the thyroid gland, strap muscles, etc.

T4 Massive central compartment disease invading the trachea and esophagus, or recurrent parathyroid carcinoma

Nodal involvement (N)

N0 No regional lymph node metastases

N1 Regional lymph node metastases

Metastatic involvement (M)

M0 No evidence of distant metastases

M1 Evidence of distant metastases

Checklist

Topography, procedure, and gross features

— Site

    Left upper

    Right upper

    Left lower

    Right lower

    Other

— Procedure

    Left upper

    Right upper

    Left lower

    Right lower

    Other

— Size

    Left upper

    Right upper

    Left lower

    Right lower

    Other

— Weight (estimated % of entire gland)

    Left upper

    Right upper

    Left lower

    Right lower

    Other

Histologic classification

— Hyperemia

— Adenoma

— Carcinoma

— Other

Prostate—carcinoma

Final report—recommended features

Gross description

1. **Specimen identification:** labeled with name, medical record number, etc.
2. **Specimen condition:** fresh, in fixative, opened, unopened, etc.
3. **Topography:** the type of specimen should be specified: prostate, prostate and seminal vesicles, bladder and prostate, etc.
4. **Type of procedure:** the type of surgical procedure should be stated: radical prostatectomy, transurethral resection of prostate (TURP), supra/retropubic prostatectomy, needle biopsy, etc.
5. **Good overall gross description** including weight and three-dimensional measurements, etc.
6. **Description of recognizable features:** gross evidence of carcinoma, nodular hyperplasia, necrosis, etc.
7. **Description of other organs or structures:** bladder, seminal vesicles, vas deferens, etc.
8. **Paraffin block key**

Diagnostic information

1. **Tumor type:** The type of carcinoma should be stated. The following classification of prostate carcinoma is suggested:
   - Adenocarcinoma, NOS
   - Adenocarcinoma, acinar type
   - Ductal (endometrioid) carcinoma
   - Mucinous carcinoma
   - Signet ring cell carcinoma
   - Neuroendocrine carcinoma
   - Small cell (oat cell) carcinoma
   - Undifferentiated non-small cell carcinoma
   - Transitional cell carcinoma
   - Squamous and adenosquamous carcinoma
   - Sarcomatoid carcinoma (carcinosarcoma)
   - Others
2. **Tumor grade:** It is recommended that the Gleason system be utilized. The Gleason system proposes that any given prostate carcinoma may show one or several of five histologic patterns ranging from the lowest grade (grade 1) to the highest grade (grade 5). Taking the two predominant patterns, one can arrive at a score (for instance 2+3=5; 3+4=7), which has prognostic significance

   The following rules apply to this system:
   - When there are more than two patterns, pattern #1 is the predominant pattern, and pattern #2 is the second predominant pattern
   - When there is only one pattern, for instance in a needle biopsy, duplicate that pattern to arrive at the correct score (example: 3+3=6)
   - In a needle biopsy, when there are more than two patterns and the worst grade is neither the predominant nor the secondary pattern, choose the predominant pattern and the highest grade to arrive at the correct score (for instance, the patterns are: grade 3 is 60%, grade 1 is 30%, and grade 4 is 10%; the score should be 3+4=7)
3. **Tumor amount:** The amount of carcinoma present in the specimen should be recorded:
   - For radical prostatectomy specimens: percentage of the prostate involved by carcinoma in relation to the weight of the specimen. (Note: Computer-assisted methods of measurements are desirable, but at the present time are time-consuming and impractical for routine usage)
   - For transurethral resections of prostate, and suprapubic or retropubic prostatectomies, the amount of carcinoma present should be in terms of: (a) percentage of carcinoma found in relation to the amount of noninvolved prostatic tissue, (b) number of microscopic foci of carcinoma

ulcer to the deepest contiguous tumor cell, excluding tumor sheathing skin appendages) (see Note 4)

5. **Assess the depth of penetration** of the dermis relative to standard anatomic landmarks, when possible

6. **Assess the frequency of mitotic figures** per millimeter squared in the vertical growth phase (invasive nodule), if present. This is regarded as a prognostically important observation, although other authors disagree, and not all pathologists record this information

7. **Record whether there is obvious evidence of invasion** of dermal blood vessels or lymphatics. Immunohistochemical confirmation using the agglutinin of *Ulex europaeus* I or antibody to factor VIII-related antigen is optional

8. **Record desmoplasia or stromal myxoid change,** if present

9. **Report neurotropism,** if present

10. **Report whether melanoma (invasive or radial growth phase) is present** at or near the peripheral or deep "surgical" margin and record in millimeters (using a micrometer) the minimum distance between the tumor nearest the peripheral and deep margins

11. **Record whether there is evidence of regression** subjacent to the radial growth phase or within the vertical growth phase. Regressive changes comprise foci of fibrosis that are variably cellular and variably infiltrated by lymphoid cells and macrophages and that are not due to previous surgical intervention

Note 1a: The radial growth phase is the usually flat pigmentary abnormality that lies peripheral to the vertical growth phase (invasive component) of most primary melanomas

Note 1b: Microscopically, a radial growth phase shows an increase in invariably atypical melanocytes, singly or in small colonies, in a basal or suprabasal position, with or without the presence of single melanoma cells in the upper papillary dermis

Note 2: If the lesion is nonprimary, items C2, C3, C4, C5, C7, and C8 in the text are not relevant

Note 3: It is useful to attempt to separate ulceration that is post-traumatic, i.e., secondary to a shave or punch biopsy or self-inflicted damage from ulceration that is "nontraumatic" or "spontaneous." This determination requires detailed clinical information and correlation

Note 4: It is now common to include satellites in the Breslow measurement, although some authors argue against their inclusion. If microsatellites are included in this measurement, it is important to record that the measurement has been made in this way

Note 5: We have not included mucosal lentiginous melanoma because these recommendations refer to cutaneous melanoma

Final report—optional features

1. **Record the degree of pigmentation:** All kinds of melanomas may be amelanotic, so absence of pigment does not constitute a histogenetic subclass

2. **If a radial growth phase is present,** state whether it is pagetoid, lentiginous, or unclassifiable

3. **Record the dominant cell type:** epithelioid (round–oval) *versus* spindle (elongated) *versus* spitzoid *versus* nevocytoid *versus* balloon *versus* other. List other cell types that are present

4. **Record whether there is a nevus contiguous to the melanoma:** Is this adjacent to the melanoma? Record the type of nevus (common congenital *versus* common acquired *versus* dysplastic *versus* Spitz *versus* blue *versus* cellular blue *versus* combined nevus

5. **Record the density and distribution** of any lymphoreticular cell infiltrate that is present
   • Within the vertical growth phase (invasive component) and disrupting nests of melanoma cells (intratumor)
   • Peripheral to the invasive component as a band-like infiltrate

6. **Record whether necrosis is present**
   • Multicellular necrosis

7. **Record the presence of unusual features,** such as heterologous elements, e.g., bone, cartilage

Checklist

— Site
— Procedure
— Excision
— Incision biopsy (including punch)
— Shave biopsy
— Other (specify)
— Lesion is confirmed as primary
　　—— Yes　　—— No
— Ulceration
— No ulceration
— Histogenetic pattern: see Note 5 above
　　Malignant melanoma, no adjacent component (AC)[a] (nodular)
　　With AC, superficial spreading melanoma type
　　With AC, lentigo maligna type
　　With AC, acral lentiginous type
　　Desmoplastic
　　Of the type that simulates Spitz, nevocytic nevus, other lesions
　　Unclassifiable
— Clark level
　　—— I　　　—— II　　　—— III
　　—— IV　　—— V
— Breslow thickness
　　—— ×　　　—— mm
— Mitotic rate
　　—— /mm^2
— Regressive fibrosis present
　　—— Yes　　—— No
— Excision
　　Complete
　　Not complete peripherally (indicate affected margin)
　　Not complete in depth
　　Not complete peripherally and in depth
— Vascular invasion
　　Absent
　　Blood vessels

Lymphatic vessels
Blood and lymphatic vessels
— Microsatellites
—— Present   —— Absent
— Neurotropism
—— Present   —— Absent
— Lymph node involvement (complete as appropriate)
Number of nodes containing tumor/total no. of nodes
Not applicable

ªAdjacent component is synonymous with radial growth phase

Skin—nonmelanocytic neoplasms

Final report—recommended features

Gross description

1. **Specimen identification:** how was specimen labeled
2. **Specimen condition:** received fresh or in fixative
3. **Specimen type:** i.e., excision, punch, shave, curetting: clinical orientation (if supplied) and measured in three dimensions
4. **Describe** the epidermis and the dermis, if present. Describe grossly identifiable lesions, their size and their extent with regards to the edges of the specimen. Note the presence or absence of subcutaneous fat and gross extent of lesion into fat
5. **If specimen is inked,** note color(s). If multiple colors are used to designate specific margins, give a key
6. **Describe** sectioning and indicate whether or not the entire specimen was submitted for histologic examination
7. **Supply paraffin block key**

Diagnostic information

1. **Tissue:** list types included in the specimen (i.e., stratum corneum only, epidermis only, skin, skin and subcutaneous tissue)
2. **Specimen type:** see Gross description
3. **Location:** as supplied by clinician
4. **Diagnosis:** there is no universally accepted classification of nonmelanocytic skin tumors. The most recent (Second Edition) WHO Classification is recommended as a general guide for the classification of epithelial and mesenchymal neoplasms which primarily arise in the skin. This can be supplemented with the more complete listing of soft tissue tumors found in *Soft Tissue Tumors* by Enzinger and Weiss

The classification of lymphoproliferative diseases is still evolving rapidly. In addition to the Kiel and REAL classifications, the European Organization for Research and Treatment of Cancer (EORTC) has reached consensus on a new classification for primary cutaneous lymphomas. It has the advantage of combining clinical, histologic and immunophenotypical criteria for well-defined disease entities

The skin is frequently the site of metastasis. Whenever possible, the histology of the metastatic lesion should be compared with that of the primary (if known). In the case of an occult primary, an attempt should be made to develop a differential diagnosis and to focus it through the use of special stains, immunocytochemistry or other ancillary studies. In the case of secondary involvement of the skin by leukemic infiltrates or by extracutaneous lymphoma, the cutaneous lesion(s) should correlate with the material upon which the original diagnosis was made, and if appropriate, classified in like fashion.

5. **Tumor grade:** degree of differentiation (e.g., Broder's) should be indicated for invasive squamous cell carcinomas and adnexal adenocarcinomas. Basal cell carcinomas should be subtyped so as to alert the clinician to the presence of an aggressive pattern of growth. Sarcomas should be graded as low grade or high grade. Mitotic index (preferably reported as mitoses per mm^2) should be reported for tumors in which such data are useful for assessing malignant potential (e.g., smooth muscle tumors)
6. **Tumor behavior:** include the presence or absence of skin ulceration, lymphovascular involvement, perineural invasion, involvement of skin adnexa (by squamous cell carcinoma in situ), etc. Where the clinician is unlikely to be familiar with the biologic behavior of a particular tumor, such information should be reported in a comment
7. **Tumor extent:** tumor size, extent with regards to anatomic/histologic landmarks (e.g., extension into subcutis) should be noted
8. **Surgical margins:** these should be reported for those specimen types for which margins can be reliably assessed. Measurement by (calibrated) ocular micrometer is indicated for those instances in which the tumor approaches, but cannot be demonstrated to actually involve a surgical margin
9. **Lymph nodes:** report the presence or absence of metastatic lesions in any lymph nodes included in the specimen. If a node dissection was performed, state the number of nodes sampled and the number of nodes involved. The presence or absence of extranodal involvement should be noted
10. **Histochemistry, immunocytochemistry, ancillary studies:** results of these studies should be included either in the "diagnosis" section or in a separate microscopic comment
11. **Additional comments:** information relating to tumor behavior (metastatic potential), if pertinent, or association of a particular tumor with a defined clinical syndrome should be included in a comment

Testis and adnexa

Final report—recommended features

Gross description

1. **Specimen identification:** patient's name, case number, laterality, specimen identification ("labeled as")
2. **Specimen condition:** fresh, in formalin, intact, incised by surgeon or pathologists, etc.
3. **Number of specimen containers**
4. **Structures attached to testis:** epididymis, spermatic cord, tunica vaginalis
5. **Dimensions of all the specimens**
6. **Tumor description**

- Site in testis/paratestis—central, inferior pole, superior pole, testicular hilum, epididymis, paratesticular soft tissue, spermatic cord
- Tumor size, shape, consistency, color, cysts, scar, necrosis, hemorrhage, calcifications
- Relationship to tunica albuginea
- Relationship to epididymis and spermatic cord
- If spermatic cord involvement, distance of tumor to cord, margin. It is recommended that sections of the spermatic cord be obtained before incision of the main tumor to avoid contamination
- Satellite tumors, if present

7. **Other lesions of the testis**
8. **Tissue submitted for special study**

Diagnostic information

1. **Topography:** left or right testis
2. **Procedure:** as designated by surgeon, e.g., radical or simple orchiectomy
3. **Histologic type:** a modified classification of the World Health Organization (WHO) is recommended:
   - Germ cell tumors
     - Intratubular germ cell neoplasia
       - Unclassified type (IGCNU)
       - Other forms (specify)
     - Tumors of one histologic type
       - Seminoma: variant—seminoma with syncytiotrophoblastic cells
       - Spermatocytic seminoma: variant—spermatocytic seminoma with a sarcomatous component (specify type and grade of sarcoma)
       - Embryonal carcinoma
       - Yolk sac tumor
       - Choriocarcinoma: variant—"Monophasic" choriocarcinoma
       - Placental site trophoblastic tumor
       - Teratoma
         - Mature
         - Immature
         - With a secondary malignant component ("teratoma with malignant transformation") (specify type)
         - Monodermal variants
     - Carcinoid
     - Primitive neuroectodermal tumor
     - Other
       - Tumors of more than one histologic type
         - Mixed germ cell tumor (specify components and provide an estimate of percentage composition)
         - Polyembryoma
         - Diffuse embryoma
       - "Burnt-out" germ cell tumor
   - Sex cord–stromal tumors
     - Leydig cell tumor
     - Sertoli cell tumor
       - Not otherwise specified type
       - Large cell calcifying type
       - Sclerosing type
     - Sertoli–Leydig cell tumor
     - Granulosa cell tumor
       - Adult type
       - Juvenile type
   - Mixed sex cord–stromal tumor
   - Unclassified sex cord–stromal tumor
   - Mixed germ cell–sex cord–stromal tumor
     - Gonadoblastoma
     - Others
   - Miscellaneous
     - Lymphoma (classify according to guidelines for nodal lymphoma)
     - Plasmacytoma and multiple myeloma
     - Granulocytic sarcoma and multiple myeloma
     - Sarcoma (specify type and grade)
     - Carcinomas and borderline tumors of ovarian type (specify type and, for carcinomas, grade)
     - Adenocarcinoma of the rete testis
     - Adenocarcinoma of the epididymis
     - Melanotic neuroectodermal tumor (retinal anlage tumor)
     - Malignant mesothelioma (specify type)
     - Desmoplastic small round cell tumor
     - Others
   - Secondary tumors

4. **Other features:** for tumors in the sex cord–stromal category (with the exception of the juvenile granulosa cell tumor) specify if adverse prognostic features are present or absent. The following are included:
   - Lymphovascular space invasion
   - Coagulative tumor cell necrosis
   - Significant cytologic atypia
   - High mitotic rate (specify number of mitotic figures per 10 high-power fields, averaged from 40 high-power fields)
   - Infiltrating borders
   - Extratesticular growth (see Note 1)
   - Large tumor size

   Note 1: According to the revised TNM staging system of the American Joint Committee on Cancer, only involvement of paratesticular soft tissue, tunica vaginalis, or spermatic cord are features of extratesticular spread that merit designation as pT2 tumors; cases with rete testis or epididymal spread or tunica albuginea invasion without penetration remain pT1 lesions in the absence of vascular invasion

5. **Other organs:** for tumors in categories other than the sex cord–stromal group, specify if there is lymphovascular space invasion or (for testicular tumors) extratesticular extension (see above-mentioned Note)
6. **Adequacy of local excision:** assessment of resection margins
7. **Other significant testicular disease**

Final report—optional features

1. **Stage:** the data specified should facilitate application of most staging systems. In most circumstances, the pathologist will not be aware of the nodal status or other studies to permit an assignment of stage; however, accurate local staging of the testicular tumor can be accomplished, either by providing all of the requisite information (as indicated above) or by specifying a local AP stage according to the revised system of The American Joint Committee on Cancer Staging

2. **Results of ancillary studies**
3. **Association of germ cell tumors with intratubular germ cell neoplasia of the unclassified type**
4. **Presence and type of inflammatory infiltrate**
5. **Multifocal tumor**

Thyroid gland—carcinoma

Final report—recommended features

Gross description

1. **Specimen identification**
2. **Specimen condition:** how received (fresh or fixed, intact or previously sectioned, etc.)
3. **Type of procedure**
4. **Size:** overall dimensions and weight
5. **Outer shape, color, symmetry, and consistency** of entire specimen; presence and appearance of extrathyroid tissues
6. **Tumor description:** number, location, size, shape, consistency, color, encapsulation, secondary changes (fibrosis, calcification, cystic degeneration, hemorrhage), and distance to surgical margins
7. **Appearance of thyroid gland away from tumor;** presence of tumor multicentricity
8. **Number and appearance** of parathyroid gland(s), if any
9. **Lymph node dissection,** if included
   - Type—extended radical, radical, modified radical, selective
   - Presence of sternomastoid muscle/submandibular and/or parotid gland/jugular vein
   - Presence of a palpable mass, and whether solitary or matted
   - Size and location of gross tumor invasion of soft tissues, muscle, and jugular vein adjacent to involved lymph nodes
   - Dimensions and appearance of sternomastoid muscle, major salivary glands, and internal jugular vein
   - Size of lymph nodal masses (masses greater than 3 cm in diameter are to be regarded as confluent nodes or as extension into soft tissues)

Final report—optional features

The histologic grade can be listed as such (despite the fact that some tumor grading is implicit in the diagnosis of tumor type, i.e., poorly differentiated or undifferentiated), or the features evaluated in a grading system (such as mitotic activity or necrosis) can be listed separately. In other words, the use of "Histologic grade" in the listing below is an alternative to using the option "Presence and degree of mitotic activity" or "Presence and amount of tumor necrosis"; yet another alternative is not exercising any of these options.

1. **Histologic grade**
2. **Presence and degree of mitotic activity**
3. **Presence and amount of tumor necrosis**
4. **Presence of ancillary tumor features:** such as squamous metaplasia, cytoplasmic clear cell change, mucinous features, psammoma bodies, other types of calcification, stromal (desmoplastic or "scirrhous") reaction, and amyloid deposition

Checklist (see Note 1)

Type of specimen (see Note 2)
— Nodulectomy
— Lobectomy
— Subtotal thyroidectomy
— Total thyroidectomy
— Other

Tumor type (and subtype)
— Papillary carcinoma
   Classical type
   Other type
— Follicular carcinoma
   Minimally invasive
   Widely invasive
— Hürthle cell carcinoma
   Minimally invasive
   Widely invasive
— Poorly differentiated carcinoma
   Insular type
   Other type
— Undifferentiated (anaplastic) carcinoma
   Without residual well-differentiated component
   With residual well-differentiated component of type
— Medullary carcinoma
   Classical type
   Other type
— Mixed medullary—follicular carcinoma
— Mixed medullary—papillary carcinoma
— Other

Tumor location
— Right lobe (and isthmus)
— Left lobe (and isthmus)
— Both lobes (and isthmus)
— Isthmus

Tumor largest diameter
— —— cm (see Note 3)

Encapsulation
— Absent
— Partial
— Complete

Capsular invasion
— Absent
— Present (minimal)
— Present (extensive)

Lymph vessel invasion
— Absent
— Present (minimal)
— Present (extensive)

Blood vessel invasion
— Absent
— Present (minimal)
— Present (extensive)

Extrathyroid extension
— Absent
— Present (gross)
— Present (microscopic)

Surgical margins (see Note 4)
— Negative

— Positive

Tumor multicentricity (see Note 5)
— Negative
— Positive

C cell hyperplasia (for cases of medullary carcinoma only)
— Absent
— Present

Other pathology
— None
— Adenoma(s) (specify number, location, and size)
— Nodular hyperplasia
— Lymphocytic thyroiditis
— Hashimoto's thyroiditis
— Atrophy
— Fibrosis

Parathyroid gland (see Note 6)
——— Yes ——— No
— Number
— Location
— Normal

Lymph nodes
——— Yes ——— No
— Number
— Location (right, left, central) and level
— Negative
— Positive

Positive (metastatic) lymph nodes
— Size of largest involved node: cm
— Perinodal (extracapsular) extension
——— Yes ——— No

Note 1: If the thyroid is located ectopically (mediastinal, lingual, in a thyroglossal duct cyst, or in a teratoma), this should be indicated in the report

Note 2: For nodulectomy or lobectomy specimens, the report should indicate whether the specimen is from the right or left side. (Nodulectomy is rarely, if ever, performed at present, but it is included in the checklist for the sake of completeness.) If the lobectomy specimen includes the isthmus (as is often the case), the report should make reference to this fact. For subtotal thyroidectomy specimens, the report should indicate which lobe was completely removed and which lobe was excised only partially

Note 3: Provide a size estimate for tumor bulk if the tumor is multifocal. For cases of papillary microcarcinoma (less than 1 cm in diameter), indicate in the report the exact diameter of the tumor

Note 4: If positive, specify location (capsular or isthmic), number (single or multiple), and extent (minimal/microscopic or extensive), whenever feasible

Note 5: Specify approximate number of foci and whether these foci have the same or a different appearance. If the specimen is from a subtotal or total thyroidectomy, indicate whether the tumor foci involves one lobe or both lobes. In a case of papillary carcinoma, indicate whether psammoma bodies are present elsewhere in the gland or not, the former suggesting the presence of tumor multicentricity

Note 6: Whenever possible, the location of the gland(s) should be specified; if this gland is intrathyroidal, this fact should be noted

Uterine cervix—carcinoma

Final report—recommended features
Gross description
1. **Specimen identification:** labeled with patient name, medical record number, organ identified, etc.
2. **Specimen condition:** fresh, in fixative (formalin, Bouin's, etc.), on ice, opened (by pathologist or surgeon), unopened, etc.
3. **Number of specimen containers**
4. **Type of procedure:** the type of surgical procedure should be stated (simple hysterectomy, radical hysterectomy, anterior exenteration, etc.)
5. **Topography:** the exact type of specimen should be specified (uterus, cervical cold knife core biopsy, cervical loop electrosurgical excision procedure, etc.)
6. **Brief but precise overall description:** focusing on the site and extent of the lesion and its relationship to surrounding structures
   • Accurate overall dimensions of each specimen received
   • Exact anatomic location of cervical tumor (anterior or posterior lip, portio or endocervical canal, the "o'clock" location, etc.)
   • Size of tumor
   • Gross estimation of depth of invasion, if any, into the cervical wall
   • Grossly apparent extension to adjacent organs and tissue, e.g., the parametrium, upper vagina, the uterine corpus, or the bladder or bowel (in exenteration specimens)
   • Comment on the proximity of the tumor to pertinent resection margins
7. **Special investigations:** flow cytometry, etc.
8. **If ink is used** for marking resection margins, provide a section code for subsequent interpretation of the microscopic findings

Diagnostic information
1. **Histologic type:** the histopathologic tumor type should be stated. The following modified terminology, as revised and adopted by the ISGP under the auspices of the WHO, is recommended
   • Squamous lesions
     – Squamous intraepithelial lesions (SIL)
       ○ Cervical intraepithelial neoplasia (CIN)
         • CIN 1: mild dysplasia, low-grade SIL
         • CIN 2: moderate dysplasia, high-grade SIL
         • CIN 3: severe dysplasia/carcinoma in situ, high-grade SIL

Note 1: In the Bethesda system for cytologic classification, squamous intraepithelial lesions are divided into low-grade and high-grade. CIN 1 (mild dysplasia) and lesions showing clear-cut evidence of papillomavirus effect are classified as low-grade lesions. CIN 2 (moderate dysplasia) and CIN 3 (severe dysplasia and carcinoma in situ) are classified as high-grade lesions

- Squamous cell carcinoma
  - Keratinizing type
  - Nonkeratinizing type—large cell (optional); small cell (optional)
  - Verrucous carcinoma
  - Warty (condylomatous) carcinoma
  - Papillary squamous cell (transitional) carcinoma
  - Lymphoepithelioma-like carcinoma

Note 2: Keratinizing tumors require the presence of keratin pearls. The morphologic spectrum is wide for nonkeratinizing tumors, including those having individual cell keratinization, tumor cells with clear cytoplasm, and tumor cells with eosinophilic cytoplasm and distinct cell borders. Small cell poorly differentiated carcinomas with light microscopic, immunohistochemical, and ultrastructural features of neuroendocrine differentiation are classified in the category of small cell (neuroendocrine) carcinomas

- Glandular lesions
  - Adenocarcinoma in situ
  - Adenocarcinoma
    - Mucinous adenocarcinoma—endocervical type; intestinal type
    - Endometrioid adenocarcinoma—endometrioid adenocarcinoma with squamous metaplasia
    - Clear cell adenocarcinoma
    - Minimal deviation adenocarcinoma (adenoma malignum)—endocervical type; endometrioid type
    - Well-differentiated (papillary) villoglandular adenocarcinoma
    - Serous carcinoma
    - Mesonephric carcinoma
- Other epithelial tumors
  - Adenosquamous carcinoma
  - Glassy cell carcinoma
  - Adenoid cystic carcinoma
  - Adenoid basal carcinoma (epithelioma)

Note 3: Some workers consider adenoid basal carcinoma to be nonmalignant and have instead proposed the term adenoid basal epithelioma

- Neuroendocrine tumors
  - Carcinoid tumor
  - Atypical carcinoid tumor
  - High-grade neuroendocrine carcinoma—small cell type; large type
- Undifferentiated carcinoma
- Mesenchymal tumors
  - Leiomyosarcoma
  - Endocervical stromal sarcoma
  - Sarcoma botryoides (embryonal rhabdomyosarcoma)
  - Alveolar soft-part sarcoma
- Mixed epithelial and mesenchymal tumors
  - Adenosarcoma
  - Malignant mixed mesodermal tumor (MMMT)
  - Wilms' tumor
- Miscellaneous tumors
  - Malignant melanoma
  - Lymphoma and leukemia
  - Tumors of germ cell type
  - Yolk sac tumor

2. **Tumor grade**
   - Squamous cell carcinoma: several studies have shown that histopathologic grading systems, including the most commonly used modification of Broder's system, fail to correlate reliably with prognosis. Consequently, histopathologic grading is optional
   - Adenocarcinoma—cervical adenocarcinomas may be graded by architectural (the percentage of solid growth, excluding squamous) and cytologic (nuclear) criteria:
     - **Grade 1:** well-differentiated (10% or less solid growth). The tumor contains well-formed regular glands with papillae. The cells are elongate and columnar with uniform oval nuclei; there is minimal stratification (fewer than three cell layers in thickness). Mitotic figures are infrequent
     - **Grade 2:** moderately differentiated (11% to 50% solid growth). The tumor contains complex glands with frequent bridging and cribriform formation. Solid areas are more common, but these make up less than half of the tumor. The nuclei are more rounded and irregular; micronucleoli are present. Mitoses are more frequent
     - **Grade 3:** poorly differentiated (over 50% solid growth). The tumor contains sheets of malignant cells; few glands are discernible. The cells are large and irregular with pleomorphic nuclei. Occasional signet cells are present. Mitoses are abundant, with abnormal forms. Desmoplasia is pronounced, and necrosis is common

3. **Degree of invasion:** the maximum depth of invasion by tumor into the cervical stroma, in millimeters, or the proportion of the wall involved should be recorded. For purposes of staging, the International Federation of Gynecology and Obstetrics (FIGO) and the Society of Gynecologic Oncologists (SGO) subdivide squamous cell carcinomas into microinvasive and frankly invasive carcinoma
   - An early squamous cell carcinoma with 3 mm or less of invasion from its point of origin and without angiolymphatic space invasion is classified as a microinvasive squamous cell carcinoma by SGO criteria
   - An early squamous cell carcinoma with 5 mm of less of invasion from its point of origin and no greater than 7 mm in greatest horizontal dimension is classified as a microinvasive squamous cell carcinoma by FIGO criteria. Only invasive carcinoma should be included in the measurement. Vascular space invasion is noted, if present, but does not in itself exclude a tumor from being placed in the microinvasive category
   - No consensus has been reached for the histopathologic criteria that define a "microinvasive" cervical adenocarcinoma. The maximal deep and lateral dimensions of tumor extension, plus the presence or absence of angiolymphatic invasion, should be carefully recorded

4. **Extent of tumor:** the extent of invasion into extracervical tissues and metastases to both pelvic and extrapelvic organs should be recorded

5. **Angiolymphatic vascular space invasion:** the presence of tumor within blood vessels and/or lymphatic vessels should be noted and an attempt made to distinguish, when possible, between them

6. **Status of lymph nodes:** report the presence or absence of metastases in each submitted group of lymph nodes, recording the total number of involved lymph nodes in relation to the total number of lymph nodes identified
7. **Status of resection margins:** the adequacy of local excision should be assessed by careful examination of resection margins, the latter preferably marked by the use of ink. The distance from the deepest point of stromal invasion to the closest (inked) margin of resection may be noted in the report

Final report—optional features

1. **Stage** (see below)
2. **Glandular intraepithelial lesions:** the natural history and histopathologic criteria to define endocervical glandular lesions with atypia less than that of adenocarcinoma in situ are controversial; their reporting, therefore, is considered optional
3. **Definitions:** the following definitions are slightly modified from the *Histological Typing of Female Genital Tract Tumors,* Second Edition:
   - An *endocervical glandular atypia* is one that does not fulfill the criteria for glandular dysplasia–adenocarcinoma in situ, and may be associated with inflammation
   - *Glandular dysplasia* is characterized by significant nuclear abnormalities that are more striking than those encountered in glandular atypia but do not fulfill the criteria for adenocarcinoma in situ
   - In *adenocarcinoma in situ*, normally situated glands are lined by cytologically malignant glandular epithelium.

College of American Pathologists (CAP) checklists for the reporting of major tumor types (01/2003)

(From Compton CC, Ed. Reporting on cancer specimens: Case summaries and background documentation, 2003 edition, Northfield, IL, College of American Pathologists, 2003).

Data elements with asterisks are not required for accreditation purposes for the Commission on Cancer. These elements may be clinically important, but are not yet validated or regularly used in patient management. Alternatively, the necessary data may not be available to the pathologist at the time of pathologic assessment of this specimen

Adrenal cortical carcinoma—resection

Applies to adrenal cortical carcinoma. Pheochromocytoma, neuroblastoma, and other adrenal medullary tumors of childhood are excluded.

Macroscopic
— Specimen type
    Subtotal adrenalectomy
    Total adrenalectomy

    Other (specify):
    Not specified
— Laterality
    Right
    Left
    Not specified
— Tumor size
    Greatest dimension: —— cm
    Additional dimensions: — × —— cm
    Cannot be determined (fragmented specimen)
— Tumor weight: — g

Microscopic
— Extent of invasion
— Primary tumor
    I: Confined to gland, 5 cm or less
    II: Confined to gland, greater than 5 cm
    III: Extraglandular extension without other organ involvement
    IV: Distant metastasis or extension into other organs
    Cannot be determined
— Regional lymph nodes
    Cannot be assessed
    No regional lymph node metastasis
    Regional lymph node metastasis
    Specify: Number examined:
    Number involved:
— Distant metastasis
    Cannot be assessed
    Distant metastasis
    Specify site(s), if known:
— Margins
    Margins uninvolved by tumor
    Margin(s) involved by tumor
    Site(s) of involvement:
    Involvement by tumor cannot be determined
— Venous (large vessel) invasion (V)
    Absent
    Present
    Indeterminate
— Additional pathologic findings (check all that apply)
    None identified
    Tumor necrosis
    Hyperplasia
    Adenoma
    Other (specify):
— Comment(s)

Ampulla of Vater—ampullectomy

Applies to all intra-ampullary, peri-ampullary, and mixed intra- and peri-ampullary carcinomas

Macroscopic
— Tumor site
    Intra-ampullary
    Peri-ampullary
    Junction of ampullary and duodenal mucosa
    Not specified

Microscopic
— Histologic type

Adenocarcinoma (not otherwise characterized)
Papillary adenocarcinoma
Adenocarcinoma, intestinal type
Adenocarcinoma, gastric foveolar type
Mucinous adenocarcinoma
Clear cell adenocarcinoma
Signet ring cell carcinoma
Adenosquamous carcinoma
Other (specify):
Carcinoma, type cannot be determined
— Histologic grade
Not applicable
GX: Cannot be assessed
G1:   Well differentiated
G2:   Moderately differentiated
G3:   Poorly differentiated
G4:   Undifferentiated
Other (specify):
— Tumor size: —— cm
Cannot be determined (see Comment)
— Extent of invasion
— Primary tumor (pT)
pTis: Carcinoma in situ
PT1:   Tumor limited to ampulla of Vater or sphincter
of Oddi
PT2:   Tumor invades duodenal wall
— Margins (check all that apply)
Not applicable
Cannot be assessed
Uninvolved by invasive carcinoma
Distance of invasive carcinoma to closest margin:
mm
Uninvolved by carcinoma in situ/adenoma
Involved by carcinoma in situ/adenoma
Involved by invasive carcinoma
— Additional pathologic findings (check all that apply)
None identified
Dysplasia/adenoma
Ampullitis
Adenomyosis
Other (specify):
— Comment(s)

Ampulla of Vater—Whipple's resection

Applies to all intra-ampullary, peri-ampullary, and mixed intra- and peri-ampullary carcinomas.

Macroscopic
— Specimen type
Pancreaticoduodenectomy
Pancreaticoduodenectomy (pylorus sparing)
Other (specify):
Not specified
— Tumor site
Intra-ampullary
Peri-ampullary
Junction of ampullary and duodenal mucosa
Not specified

— Tumor size
Greatest dimension: —— cm
Additional dimensions —×   —— cm
Cannot be determined (see Comment)
Microscopic
— Histologic type
Adenocarcinoma (not otherwise characterized)
Papillary adenocarcinoma
Adenocarcinoma, intestinal type
Adenocarcinoma, gastric foveolar type
Mucinous adenocarcinoma
Clear cell adenocarcinoma
Signet ring cell carcinoma
Adenosquamous carcinoma
Other (specify):
Carcinoma, type cannot be determined
— Histologic grade
Not applicable
GX: Cannot be assessed
G1:   Well differentiated
G2:   Moderately differentiated
G3:   Poorly differentiated
G4:   Undifferentiated
Other (specify):
— Extent of invasion
— Primary tumor (pT)
pTX: Cannot be assessed
pT0:   No evidence of primary tumor
pTis: Carcinoma in situ
PT1:   Tumor limited to ampulla of Vater or sphincter
of Oddi
PT2:   Tumor invades duodenal wall
pT3:   Tumor invades pancreas
pT4:   Tumor invades peripancreatic soft tissues or
other adjacent organs or structures
— Regional lymph nodes (pN)
pNX: Cannot be assessed
pN0:   No regional lymph node metastasis
pN1:   Regional lymph node metastasis
Specify
Number examined:
Number involved:
— Distant metastasis (pM)
pMX: Cannot be assessed
pM1: Distant metastasis
Specify site(s), if known:
— Margins (check all that apply)
Cannot be assessed
Margins uninvolved by invasive carcinoma
Distance of invasive carcinoma to closest margin:
mm
Specify margin (if possible):
Carcinoma in situ absent at pancreatic duct margin
Carcinoma in situ present at pancreatic duct margin
Carcinoma in situ absent at common bile duct
margin
Carcinoma in situ present at common bile duct
margin
Margins involved by invasive carcinoma
Specify location(s) (if possible):
Not applicable

— Venous/lymphatic (large/small vessel) invasion (V/L)
    Absent
    Present
    Indeterminate
— Perineural invasion
    Absent
    Present
— Additional pathologic findings (check all that apply)
    None identified
    Dysplasia/adenoma
    Ampullitis
    Adenomyosis
    Chronic pancreatitis
    Acute pancreatitis
    Gastritis
    Other (specify):
— Comment(s)

Anus—polypectomy

Applies to all invasive carcinomas.

Macroscopic
— Tumor site
    Specify, if known:
    Not specified
— Polyp size
    Greatest dimension: —— cm
    Additional dimensions: —×   —— cm
    Cannot be determined (see Comment)
— Polyp configuration
    Pedunculated, with stalk
    Stalk length: —— mm
    Pedunculated, no stalk, narrow-based
    Sessile/broad-based
    Cannot be determined

Microscopic
— Histologic type
    Squamous cell carcinoma
    Adenocarcinoma
    Mucinous adenocarcinoma
    Small cell carcinoma
    Undifferentiated carcinoma
    Other (specify):
    Carcinoma, type cannot be determined
— Histologic grade (if applicable to tumor type)
    Not applicable
    GX: Cannot be assessed
    G1: Well differentiated
    G2: Moderately differentiated
    G3: Poorly differentiated
    G4: Undifferentiated
— Extent of invasion
    Epithelium only (no invasion)
    Invasion (deepest)
        Cannot be determined
        Into lamina propria
        Into muscularis mucosae
        Into submucosa

— Polyp resection margin
    Cannot be assessed
    Uninvolved by invasive carcinoma
    Distance of invasive carcinoma from margin: mm
        Carcinoma in situ absent at mucosal margin
        Carcinoma in situ present at mucosal margin
    Involved by invasive carcinoma
    Not applicable (specify reason):
— Venous/lymphatic (large/small vessel) invasion (V/L)
    Not applicable
    Absent
    Present
    Indeterminate
— Additional pathologic findings (check all that apply)
    None identified
    Active colitis
    Other (specify):
— Comment(s)

Anus—local excision (transanal disk excision)

Applies to all invasive carcinomas.

Macroscopic
— Specimen type: Transanal disk excision
    Intact
    Fragmented
        Number of pieces:
    Other (specify):
    Not specified
— Tumor site
    Unknown
    Specify, if known:
— Tumor size
    Greatest dimension: —— cm
    Additional dimensions: —×   —— cm
    Cannot be determined (see Comment)
— Tumor configuration
    Polypoid
    Infiltrative
    Ulcerating
    Other (specify):

Microscopic
— Histologic type
    Cannot be determined
    Squamous cell carcinoma
    Adenocarcinoma
    Mucinous adenocarcinoma
    Small cell carcinoma
    Undifferentiated carcinoma
    Paget's disease
    Other (specify):
    Carcinoma, type cannot be determined
— Histologic grade
    Not applicable
    GX: Cannot be assessed
    G1: Well differentiated

G2:   Moderately differentiated

G3:   Poorly differentiated

G4:   Undifferentiated

Other (specify):

— Extent of invasion

Primary tumor (pT)

pTX: Cannot be assessed

pT0:   No evidence of primary tumor

pTis: Carcinoma in situ

pT1:   Tumor 2 cm or less in greatest dimension

pT2:   Tumor more than 2 cm but not more than 5 cm in greatest dimension

pT3:   Tumor more than 5 cm in greatest dimension

pT4:   Tumor of any size with invasion of adjacent organ(s); e.g., vagina, urethra, bladder (involvement of sphincter muscles alone is not classified as T4)

— Margins (check all that apply)

Cannot be assessed

Margins uninvolved by invasive carcinoma

Distance of invasive carcinoma from closest lateral margin: mm

Specify margin (if possible):

Carcinoma in situ absent at lateral mucosal margin

Carcinoma in situ present at lateral mucosal margin

Margin(s) involved by invasive carcinoma

Not applicable (specify reason):

— Venous/lymphatic (large/small vessel) invasion (V/L)

Absent

Present

Indeterminate

— Perineural invasion

Absent

Present

— Additional pathologic findings

None identified

Crohn's disease

Condyloma acuminatum

Dysplasia

Associated rectal carcinoma (Paget's disease)

Other (specify):

— Comment(s)

Anus—resection

Applies to all invasive carcinomas.

Macroscopic

— Specimen type

Abdominoperineal resection

Other (specify):

Not specified

— Tumor site (check all that apply)

Anterior wall

Anal margin

Not specified

— Tumor size

Greatest dimension: —— cm

— Additional dimensions × —— cm

Cannot be determined (see Comment)

— Tumor configuration

Polypoid

Infiltrative

Ulcerating

Other (specify):

Microscopic

— Histologic type

Squamous cell carcinoma

Adenocarcinoma

Mucinous adenocarcinoma

Small cell carcinoma

Undifferentiated carcinoma

Paget's disease

Other (specify):

Carcinoma, type cannot be determined

— Histologic grade

Not applicable

GX   Cannot be assessed

G1   Well differentiated

G2   Moderately differentiated

G3   Poorly differentiated

G4   Undifferentiated

— Extent of invasion

— Primary tumor (pT)

pTX   Cannot be assessed

pT0   No evidence of primary tumor

pTis   Carcinoma in situ

pT1   Tumor 2 cm or less in greatest dimension

pT2   Tumor more than 2 cm but not more than 5 cm in greatest dimension

pT3   Tumor more than 5 cm in greatest dimension

pT4   Tumor of any size with invasion of adjacent organ(s): e.g., vagina, urethra, bladder (involvement of sphincter muscles alone is not classified as T4)

— Regional lymph nodes (pN)

pNX   Cannot be assessed

pN0   No regional lymph node metastasis

pN1   Metastasis in perirectal lymph nodes

pN2   Metastasis in unilateral internal iliac and/or inguinal lymph node(s)

pN3   Metastasis in perirectal and inguinal lymph nodes and/or bilateral internal iliac and/or inguinal lymph nodes

Specify

Number examined

Number involved

— Distant metastasis (pM)

pMX   Cannot be assessed

pM1   Distant metastasis

Specify site(s), if known

— Margins (check all that apply)

Cannot be assessed

Proximal margin

Uninvolved by invasive carcinoma

Carcinoma in situ absent at mucosal margin

Carcinoma in situ present at mucosal margin

Involved by invasive carcinoma
Distal margin
    Uninvolved by invasive carcinoma
        Carcinoma in situ absent at mucosal margin
        Carcinoma in situ present at mucosal margin
    Involved by invasive carcinoma
    Circumferential (radial) margin
    Uninvolved by invasive carcinoma
    Involved by invasive carcinoma
    Distance of invasive tumor from closest margin:
    mm
    Specify margin
— Perineural invasion
    Absent
    Present
— Venous/lymphatic (large/small vessel) invasion (V/L)
    Absent
    Present
    Indeterminate
— Additional pathologic findings (check all that apply)
    None identified
    Crohn's disease
    Condyloma acuminatum
    Dysplasia
    Associated rectal carcinoma (Paget's disease)
    Other (specify):
— Comment(s)

Bone marrow—blood film, aspirate, cell block, trephine biopsy, touch imprint

Applies to acute leukemias, myelodysplastic syndromes, myeloproliferative disorders, chronic lymphoproliferative disorders, malignant lymphomas, plasma cell dyscrasias, histiocytic and dendritic cell neoplasms and mastocytosis.

Macroscopic

— Specimen type
    Aspirate
    Biopsy
    Both aspirate and biopsy
    Blood film
    Cell block (clot section)
    Not specified
— Biopsy site
    Not applicable
    Right posterior iliac crest
    Left posterior iliac crest
    Other (specify):
    Not specified
— Aspirate site
    Not applicable
    Right posterior iliac crest
    Left posterior iliac crest
    Sternum
    Other (specify):
    Not specified

— Adequacy of specimen
    Satisfactory
    Limited
    Unsatisfactory
— Phenotyping
    Performed, see separate report
    Performed
        Specify method and results
    Not performed
— Cytogenetics
    Performed (see separate report)
    Performed (specify results)
    Not performed
— WHO classification (check all that apply)
    Chronic myeloproliferative diseases
        Chronic myelogenous leukemia
        Chronic neutrophilic leukemia
        Chronic eosinophilic leukemia/hypereosinophilic
            syndrome
        Polycythemia vera
        Chronic idiopathic myelofibrosis
        Essential thrombocythemia
        Myeloproliferative disease, unclassifiable
    Myelodysplastic/myeloproliferative diseases
        Chronic myelomonocytic leukemia
        Atypical chronic myeloid leukemia
        Juvenile myelomonocytic leukemia
        Myelodysplastic/myeloproliferative disease,
            unclassifiable
    Myelodysplastic syndromes
        Refractory anemia
        Refractory anemia with ringed sideroblasts
        Refractory cytopenia with multilineage dysplasia
        Refractory cytopenia with multilineage dysplasia
            and ringed sideroblasts
        Refractory anemia with excess blasts (RAEB)
        RAEB-1
        RAEB-2
        Myelodysplastic syndrome, unclassified
        Myelodysplastic syndrome associated with isolated
            del(5q)
    Acute myeloid leukemias (AMLs)
        AML with recurrent genetic abnormalities
            AML with t(8;21)(q22;q22)
            AML with abnormal bone marrow eosinophils
            inv(16) or t(16;16)
            Acute promyelocytic leukemia t(15;17) or
            variant
            AML with 11q23 (MLL) abnormality
            Acute myeloid leukemia with multilineage
            dysplasia
            Following a myelodysplastic syndrome or
            myelodysplastic syndrome/myeloproliferative
            disorder
            Without antecedent myelodysplastic syndrome
        Acute myeloid leukemia and myelodysplastic
            syndromes, therapy-related
            Alkylating agent-related
            Topoisomerase type II inhibitor-related (some
            may be lymphoid)
            Other types (specify)

AML not otherwise categorized
    AML minimally differentiated
    AML without maturation
    AML with maturation
    Acute myelomonocytic leukemia
    Acute monoblastic and monocytic leukemia
    Acute erythroid leukemia
    Acute megakaryoblastic leukemia
    Acute basophilic leukemia
    Acute panmyelosis with myelofibrosis
    Myeloid sarcoma
  Acute leukemia of ambiguous lineage
    Undifferentiated acute leukemia
    Bilineal acute leukemia
    Biphenotypic acute leukemia
Precursor B cell and T cell neoplasms
  Precursor B lymphoblastic leukemia/lymphoblastic lymphoma
  Precursor T lymphoblastic leukemia/lymphoblastic lymphoma
Mature B cell neoplasms
  Chronic lymphocytic leukemia/small lymphocytic lymphoma
  B cell prolymphocytic leukemia
  Lymphoplasmacytic lymphoma
  Splenic marginal zone lymphoma
  Hairy cell leukemia
  Plasma cell myeloma
  Monoclonal gammopathy of undetermined significance (MGUS)
  Solitary plasmacytoma of bone
  Extraosseous plasmacytoma
  Primary amyloidosis
  Heavy chain disease
  Extranodal marginal zone B cell lymphoma of mucosa-associated lymphoid tissue (MALT lymphoma)
  Nodal marginal zone B cell lymphoma
  Follicular lymphoma
    Grade 1
    Grade 2
    Grade 3
  Mantle cell lymphoma
  Diffuse large B cell lymphoma
  Mediastinal (thymic) large B cell lymphoma
  Primary effusion lymphoma
  Burkitt's lymphoma/leukemia
B cell proliferations of uncertain malignant potential
  Lymphomatoid granulomatosis
  Post-transplant lymphoproliferative disorder, polymorphic
Mature T cell and NK cell neoplasms
  Leukemic/disseminated
    T cell prolymphocytic leukemia
    T cell large granular lymphocytic leukemia
    Aggressive NK cell leukemia
    Adult T cell leukemia/lymphoma
  Cutaneous
    Mycosis fungoides
    Sézary syndrome

    Primary cutaneous anaplastic large cell lymphoma
    Lymphomatoid papulosis
  Other extranodal
    Extranodal NK/T cell lymphoma, nasal-type
    Enteropathy-type T cell lymphoma
    Hepatosplenic T cell lymphoma
    Subcutaneous panniculitis-like T cell lymphoma
  Nodal
    Angioimmunoblastic T cell lymphoma
    Peripheral T cell lymphoma, unspecified
    Anaplastic large cell lymphoma
Neoplasm of uncertain lineage and stage of differentiation
  Blastic NK cell lymphoma
Hodgkin's lymphoma
  Nodular lymphocyte predominant Hodgkin's lymphoma
  Classical Hodgkin's lymphoma
    Nodular sclerosis classical Hodgkin's lymphoma
    Lymphocyte-rich classical Hodgkin's lymphoma
    Mixed cellularity classical Hodgkin's lymphoma
    Lymphocyte-depleted classical Hodgkin's lymphoma
Histiocytic and dendritic-cell neoplasms
  Histiocytic sarcoma
  Langerhans' cell histiocytosis
  Langerhans' cell sarcoma
  Interdigitating dendritic cell sarcoma/tumor
  Follicular dendritic cell sarcoma/tumor
  Dendritic cell sarcoma, not otherwise specified
Mastocytosis
  Indolent systemic mastocytosis
  Systemic mastocytosis with associated clonal, hematologic non-mast cell lineage disease
  Aggressive systemic mastocytosis
  Mast cell leukemia
  Mast cell sarcoma
  Malignant neoplasm, type cannot be determined
— Additional pathologic findings
  Specify
— Comment(s)

Brain/spinal cord—biopsy/resection

Applies to all neoplasms of the brain/spinal cord. Excludes neoplasms of the pituitary gland.

Macroscopic
— Specimen type
  Open biopsy
  Stereotactic needle core biopsy
  Subtotal/partial resection
  Total resection
  Other (specify):
  Not specified
— Specimen size
  Greatest dimension: ——— cm
  Additional dimensions: × ——— cm
— Tumor site (check all that apply)

Cerebral meninges
Cerebrum (specify lobe(s), if known)
Basal ganglia
Thalamus
Hypothalamus
Suprasellar
Pineal
Cerebellum
Cerebellopontine angle
Ventricle
Brain stem
Spinal cord
Nerve root
Other (specify)
Not specified
— Tumor size
    Largest dimension: —— cm
    Additional dimensions: × —— cm
    Cannot be determined (see Comment)

Microscopic
— Histologic type
Astrocytoma
    Not otherwise characterized
    Diffuse
    Pilocytic
    Pleomorphic xanthoastrocytoma
    Anaplastic
    Other (specify)
Glioblastoma
Gliosarcoma
Oligodendroglioma
    Not otherwise characterized
    Anaplastic
Oligoastrocytoma
    Not otherwise characterized
    Anaplastic
Ependymoma
    Not otherwise characterized
    Tanycytic
    Myxopapillary
    Anaplastic
    Other (specify)
Subependymoma
Choroid plexus papilloma
Choroid plexus carcinoma
Ganglioglioma
Dysembryoplastic neuroepithelial tumor
Desmoplastic infantile ganglioglioma/astrocytoma
Pineocytoma
Pineoblastoma
Medulloblastoma
    Not otherwise characterized
    Desmoplastic
    Large cell
    Melanotic
    Other (specify)
Primitive neuroectodermal tumor (PNET)
Neuroblastoma
Atypical teratoid/rhabdoid tumor
Schwannoma
    Not otherwise characterized

    Cellular
    Plexiform
    Melanotic
    Other (specify)
Neurofibroma
    Not otherwise characterized
    Plexiform
Malignant peripheral nerve sheath tumor (MPNST)
    Not otherwise characterized
    Epithelioid
    Melanotic
    Other (specify)
Meningioma
    Not otherwise characterized
    Atypical
    Papillary
    Rhabdoid
    Chordoid
    Clear cell
    Anaplastic
    Other (specify)
Hemangioblastoma
Craniopharyngioma
    Not otherwise characterized
    Adamantinomatous
    Papillary
    Other (specify)
Germinoma
Embryonal carcinoma
Yolk sac tumor
Choriocarcinoma
Teratoma
    Mature
    Immature
    With malignant transformation
Mixed germ cell tumor (specify)
Other(s) (specify)
Malignant neoplasm, type cannot be determined
— Histologic grade
    Not applicable
    Cannot be determined
    WHO Grade I
    WHO Grade II
    WHO Grade III
    WHO Grade IV
    Other (specify)
— Margins
    Cannot be assessed
    Not applicable
    Uninvolved by tumor
    Involved by tumor
        Specify which margin(s)
— Additional studies (check all that apply)
    None performed
    Electron microscopy
    Cytogenetics
    Molecular testing (specify):
    Other (specify):
— Additional pathologic findings
    Specify:
— Comment(s)

Breast—excision less than total mastectomy (includes wire-guided localization excisions), total mastectomy, modified radical mastectomy, radical mastectomy

Applies to all invasive carcinomas of the breast.

Macroscopic
— Specimen type
    Excision
    Mastectomy
    Other (specify)
    Not specified
— Lymph node sampling
    No lymph node sampling
    Sentinel lymph node(s) only
    Sentinel lymph node with axillary dissection
    Axillary dissection
— Specimen size (for excisions less than total mastectomy)
    Greatest dimension: cm
— Additional dimensions: ×   cm
    Cannot be determined (see Comment)
— Laterality
    Right
    Left
    Not specified
— Tumor site (check all that apply)
    Upper outer quadrant
    Lower outer quadrant
    Upper inner quadrant
    Lower inner quadrant
    Central
    Not specified

Microscopic
— Size of invasive component
    Greatest dimension: —— cm
— Additional dimensions: ×   —— cm
    Cannot be determined (see Comment). *The size of the tumor, as measured by gross examination, must be verified by microscopic examination. If there is a discrepancy between gross and microscopic tumor measurement, the microscopic measurement of the invasive component takes precedence and should be used for tumor staging.*
— Histologic type (check all that apply)
    Noninvasive carcinoma (NOS)
    Ductal carcinoma in situ
    Lobular carcinoma in situ
    Paget's disease without invasive carcinoma
    Invasive carcinoma (NOS)
    Invasive ductal carcinoma
    Invasive ductal carcinoma with an extensive intraductal component
    Invasive ductal carcinoma with Paget's disease
    Invasive lobular
    Mucinous
    Medullary
    Papillary
    Tubular
    Adenoid cystic
    Secretory (juvenile)
    Apocrine
    Cribriform
    Carcinoma with squamous metaplasia
    Carcinoma with spindle cell metaplasia
    Carcinoma with cartilaginous/osseous metaplasia
    Carcinoma with metaplasia, mixed type
    Other(s) (specify):
    Carcinoma, type cannot be determined
— Histologic grade (one grading system required)
    Nottingham Histologic Score (if not used, see Other Grading System below)
      Tubule formation:
        Majority of tumor greater than 75% (score = 1)
        Moderate 10% to 75% (score = 2)
        Minimal less than 10% (score = 3)
      Nuclear pleomorphism:
        Small regular nuclei (score = 1)
        Moderate increase in size, etc. (score = 2)
        Marked variation in size, nucleoli, chromatin clumping, etc. (score = 3)
      Mitotic count (for a 25× objective with a field area of 0.274 mm^2)
        Less than 10 mitoses per 10 HPF (score = 1)
        10 to 20 mitoses per 10 HPF (score = 2)
        Greater than 20 mitoses per 10 HPF (score = 3)
      Mitotic count (for a 40× objective with a field area of 0.152 mm^2)
        0 to 5 mitoses per 10 HPF (score = 1)
        6 to 10 mitoses per 10 HPF (score = 2)
        Greater than 10 mitoses per 10 HPF (score = 3)
    Total Nottingham Score:
      Grade I: 3–5 points
      Grade II: 6–7 points
      Grade III: 8–9 points
      Score cannot be determined
    Other Grading System
      Specify grading system:
        Grade 1
        Grade 2
        Grade 3
        Grade cannot be determined
— Extent of invasion
— Primary tumor (pT)
    pTX Cannot be assessed
    pT0 No evidence of primary tumor
    pTis Ductal carcinoma in situ
        pTis Lobular carcinoma in situ
        pTis Paget's disease without invasive carcinoma
    pT1 Tumor 2.0 cm or less in greatest dimension
        pT1mic Microinvasion 0.1 cm or less in greatest dimension
        pT1a Tumor more than 0.1 cm but not more than 0.5 cm in greatest dimension
        pT1b Tumor more than 0.5 cm but not more than 1.0 cm in greatest dimension
        pT1c Tumor more than 1.0 cm but not more than 2.0 cm in greatest dimension

pT2   Tumor more than 2.0 cm but not more than 50 cm in greatest dimension

pT3   Tumor more than 5.0 cm in greatest dimension

pT4   Tumor of any size with direct extension to chest wall or skin, but only as described below[a]

  pT4a   Extension to chest wall, not including pectoralis muscle

  pT4b   Edema (including peau d'orange) or ulceration of the skin of the breast or satellite skin nodules confined to the same breast

  pT4c   Both T4a and T4b

  pT4d   Inflammatory carcinoma

[a]Clinical information may be required to designate a tumor as pT4 Dermal invasion alone (without ulceration, satellite nodules, or inflammatory breast cancer) does not alter T category. Such cases are classified as T1, T2, or T3, depending on tumor size

— Regional lymph nodes (pN)

— Choose a category based on data supplied with specimen. Immunocytochemistry and molecular studies are not required

  pNX   Cannot be assessed (previously removed or not removed for pathologic study)

  pN0   No regional lymph node metastasis histologically (i.e., none greater than 0.2 mm), no additional examination for isolated tumor cells

    pN0(i-)   No regional lymph node metastasis histologically, negative immunohistochemistry (IHC)

    pN0(i+)   No regional lymph node metastasis histologically, positive IHC, no IHC cluster greater than 0.2 mm

    pN0(mol-)   No regional lymph node metastasis histologically, negative molecular findings

    pN0(mol+)   No regional lymph node metastasis histologically, positive molecular findings

  pN1

    pN1mi   Micrometastasis (greater than 0.2 mm, none greater than 20 mm)

    pN1mi(i+)   Micrometastasis detected only by IHC

    pN1a   Metastasis in one to three axillary lymph nodes (at least one tumor deposit greater than 2.0 mm)

    pN1b   Metastasis in internal mammary lymph nodes with microscopic disease detected by sentinel lymph node dissection but not clinically apparent

    pN1c   Metastasis in one to three axillary lymph nodes and in internal mammary nodes with microscopic disease detected by sentinel lymph node dissection but not clinically apparent

  pN2

    pN2a   Metastasis in four to nine axillary lymph nodes (at least one tumor deposit greater than 2.0 mm)

    pN2b   Metastasis in clinically apparent internal mammary lymph nodes in the *absence* of axillary lymph node metastases

  pN3

    pN3a   Metastasis in 10 or more axillary lymph nodes (at least one tumor deposit greater than 2.0 mm), or metastasis to the infraclavicular lymph nodes

    pN3b   Metastasis in clinically apparent ipsilateral internal mammary lymph nodes in the *presence* of one or more positive axillary lymph nodes; or in more than three axillary lymph nodes and in internal mammary lymph nodes with microscopic disease detected by sentinel lymph node dissection but not clinically apparent

    pN3c   Metastasis in ipsilateral supraclavicular lymph nodes

  Specify

    Number examined

    Number involved

— Distant metastasis (M)

  pMX   Cannot be assessed

  pM1   Distant metastasis

  Specify site(s), if known

— Margins (check all that apply)

  Margins cannot be assessed

  Margins uninvolved by invasive carcinoma

    Distance from closest margin: mm

    Specify which margin

  Margins uninvolved by DCIS (if present)

    Distance from closest margin: mm

    Specify which margin

  Margin(s) involved by invasive carcinoma

    Specify which margin

  Margin(s) involved by DCIS

    Specify which margin

  Extent of margin involvement for invasive carcinoma

    Cannot be assessed

    Unifocal

    Multifocal

    Extensive

    Other (specify):

  Extent of margin involvement for DCIS

    Cannot be assessed

    Unifocal

    Multifocal

    Extensive

    Other (specify):

— Venous/lymphatic (large/small vessel) invasion (V/L)

  Absent

  Present

  Indeterminate

— Microcalcifications (check all that apply)
  Not identified
  Present in DCIS
  Present in invasive carcinoma
  Present in non-neoplastic tissue
  Present in both tumor and non-neoplastic tissue
— Additional pathologic findings
— Comment(s)

Colon and rectum—polypectomy

Macroscopic
— Tumor type
  Cecum
  Right (ascending colon)
  Hepatic flexure
  Transverse colon
  Splenic flexure
  Left (descending colon)
  Sigmoid colon
  Rectum
  Not specified
— Polyp size
  Greatest dimension: —— cm
  Additional dimensions: ×   —— cm
    Cannot be determined (see Comment)
— Polyp configuration
  Pedunculated with stalk
    Stalk length: —— cm
  Pedunculated, no stalk
  Sessile
  Fragmented

Microscopic
— Histologic type
  Adenocarcinoma
  Mucinous adenocarcinoma (greater than 50%
    mucinous)
  Medullary carcinoma
  Signet ring cell carcinoma (greater than 50% signet
    ring cells)
  Small cell carcinoma
  Undifferentiated carcinoma
  Other (specify):
  Carcinoma, type cannot be determined
— Histologic grade
  Not applicable
  Cannot be determined
  Low-grade (well to moderately differentiated)
  High-grade (poorly differentiated to undifferentiated)
— Extent of invasion
  Cannot be determined
  Invasion (deepest):
    Lamina propria
    Muscularis mucosae
    Submucosa
    Muscularis propria
— Margins (check all that apply)
  Margins cannot be assessed
  Deep margin

Uninvolved by invasive carcinoma
    Distance of invasive carcinoma from margin:
      mm
  Involved by invasive carcinoma
    Mucosa/lateral margin
  Not applicable
    Uninvolved by invasive carcinoma
    Involved by invasive carcinoma
    Involved by in situ carcinoma/adenoma
— Lymphatic (small vessel) invasion (L)
  Absent
  Present
  Indeterminate
— Venous (large vessel) invasion (V)
  Absent
  Present
  Indeterminate
— Additional pathologic findings (check all that apply)
  None identified
  Active colitis
  Other (specify)
— Comment(s)

Rectum—local excision (transanal disk excision)

Applies to all invasive carcinomas. Carcinoid tumors, lymphomas, and sarcomas are excluded.

Macroscopic
— Specimen integrity
  Intact
  Fragmented
  Number of pieces
— Tumor site
  Distance from anal verge (per clinical report): cm
  Distance from anal verge unknown
— Tumor configuration
  Exophytic (polypoid)
  Infiltrative
  Ulcerating
  Other (specify)
— Tumor size
  Greatest dimension: —— cm
  Additional dimensions: ×   —— cm
  Cannot be determined (see comment)

Microscopic
— Histologic type
  Adenocarcinoma
  Mucinous adenocarcinoma (greater than 50%
    mucinous)
  Medullary carcinoma
  Signet ring cell carcinoma (greater than 50% signet
    ring cells)
  Small cell carcinoma
  Undifferentiated carcinoma
  Other (specify)
  Carcinoma, type cannot be determined
— Histologic grade
  Not applicable

Cannot be assessed
Low-grade (well to moderately differentiated)
High-grade (poorly differentiated to undifferentiated)
— Extent of invasion
— Primary tumor (pT)
  pTX Cannot be assessed
  pT0 No evidence of primary tumor
  pTis Carcinoma in situ, intraepithelial (no invasion)
  pTis Carcinoma in situ, invasion of lamina propria
  pT1 Tumor invades submucosa
  pT2 Tumor invades muscularis propria
  pT3 Tumor invades through the muscularis propria
       into the subserosa or the nonperitonealized
       pericolic or perirectal soft tissues
       pT3a/b Tumor invades through the
               muscularis propria into the subserosa
               or the nonperitonealized pericolic or
               perirectal soft tissues, invades 5 mm
               or less beyond the border of the
               muscularis propria
       pT3c/d Tumor invades through the
               muscularis propria into the subserosa
               or the nonperitonealized pericolic or
               perirectal soft tissues, invades greater
               than 5 mm beyond the border of the
               muscularis propria
  pT4 Tumor directly invades adjacent structures
— Regional lymph nodes (pN)
  pNX Cannot be assessed
  pN0 No regional lymph node metastasis
  pN1 Metastasis in one to three lymph nodes
  pN2 Metastasis in four or more lymph nodes
  Specify
    Number examined
    Number involved
— Margins (check all that apply)
  Margins cannot be assessed
  Lateral margin
    Uninvolved by invasive carcinoma
      Distance of invasive carcinoma from closest
        lateral margin: mm
      Specify location, if possible
    Involved by carcinoma in situ/adenoma
  Deep margin
    Uninvolved by invasive carcinoma
      Distance of invasive carcinoma from margin:
        mm
    Focal involvement by invasive carcinoma
    Multifocal involvement by invasive carcinoma
— Lymphatic (small vessel) invasion (L) (check all that
apply)
  Absent
  Present
    Intramural
    Extramural
  Indeterminate
— Perineural invasion
  Absent
  Present
— Tumor border configuration
  Pushing

Infiltrating
— Intratumoral/peritumoral lymphocytic response
  None
  Mild to moderate
  Marked (including Crohn-like response)
— Additional pathologic findings (check all that apply)
  None identified
  Adenoma(s)
  Chronic ulcerative proctocolitis
  Crohn's disease
  Dysplasia
  Other polyps (type[s])
  Other (specify)
— Comment(s)

Colon and rectum—resection

Applies to all invasive carcinomas of the colon and rectum.
Carcinoid tumors, lymphomas, sarcomas, and tumors of the
vermiform appendix are excluded.

Macroscopic
— Specimen type
  Right hemicolectomy
    Length: ——— cm
  Transverse colectomy
    Length: ——— cm
  Left hemicolectomy
    Length: ——— cm
  Sigmoidectomy
    Length: ——— cm
  Rectal/rectosigmoid colon (low anterior resection)
    Length: ——— cm
  Total abdominal colectomy
    Length: ——— cm
  Abdominoperineal resection
    Length: ——— cm
  Other (specify)
    Length: ——— cm
  Not specified
— Tumor type
  Cecum
  Right (ascending colon)
  Hepatic flexure
  Transverse colon
  Splenic flexure
  Left (descending) colon
  Sigmoid colon
  Rectosigmoid
  Rectum
  Cannot be determined (see Comment)
— Tumor configuration
  Exophytic (polypoid)
  Infiltrative
  Ulcerating
  Other (specify)
— Tumor size
  Greatest dimension: ——— cm
  Additional dimensions: — ×   ——— cm
  Cannot be determined (see Comment)

— Mesorectum
  Not applicable
  Complete
  Near complete
  Incomplete

Microscopic
— Histologic type
  Adenocarcinoma
  Mucinous adenocarcinoma (greater than 50% mucinous)
  Medullary carcinoma
  Signet ring cell carcinoma (greater than 50% signet ring cells)
  Small cell carcinoma
  Undifferentiated carcinoma
  Other (specify)
  Carcinoma, type cannot be determined
— Histologic grade
  Not applicable
  Cannot be assessed
  Low-grade (well to moderately differentiated)
  High-grade (poorly differentiated to undifferentiated)
  Other (specify)
— Extent of invasion
— Primary tumor (pT)
  pTX Cannot be assessed
  pT0 No evidence of primary tumor
  pTis Carcinoma in situ, intraepithelial (no invasion)
  pTis Carcinoma in situ, invasion of lamina propria
  pT1 Tumor invades submucosa
  pT2 Tumor invades muscularis propria
  pT3 Tumor invades through the muscularis propria into the subserosa or the nonperitonealized pericolic or perirectal soft tissues
    pT3a/b Tumor invades through the muscularis propria into the subserosa or the nonperitonealized pericolic or perirectal soft tissues, invades 5 mm or less beyond the border of the muscularis propria
    pT3c/d Tumor invades through the muscularis propria into the subserosa or the nonperitonealized pericolic or perirectal soft tissues, invades greater than 5 mm beyond the border of the muscularis propria
  pT4a Tumor directly invades adjacent structures
  PT4b Tumor penetrates the visceral peritoneum
— Regional lymph nodes (pN)
  pNX Cannot be assessed
  pN0 No regional lymph node metastasis
  pN1 Metastasis in 1 to 3 regional lymph nodes
  pN2 Metastasis in 4 or more regional lymph nodes
  Specify
    Number examined
    Number involved
— Distant metastasis (pM)
  pMX Cannot be assessed
  pM1 Distant metastasis
  Specify site(s)
— Margins (check all that apply)

Proximal margin
  Uninvolved by invasive carcinoma
  Involved by invasive carcinoma
  Carcinoma in situ/adenoma absent at proximal margin
  Carcinoma in situ/adenoma present at proximal margin
Distal margin
  Uninvolved by invasive carcinoma
  Involved by invasive carcinoma
  Carcinoma in situ/adenoma absent at distal margin
  Carcinoma in situ/adenoma present at distal margin
Circumferential (radial) margin (CRM)
  Not applicable
  Uninvolved by invasive carcinoma
  Involved by invasive carcinoma (tumor present 0–1 mm from CRM)
Distance of tumor from closest margin   mm
  Specify margin
— Lymphatic (small vessel) invasion (L) (check all that apply)
  Absent
  Present
    Intramural
    Extramural
  Indeterminate
— Venous (large vessel) invasion (V) (check all that apply)
  Absent
  Present
    Intramural
    Extramural
  Indeterminate
— Perineural invasion
  Absent
  Present
— Tumor border configuration
  Pushing
  Infiltrating
— Intratumoral/peritumoral lymphocytic response
  None
  Mild to moderate
  Marked (including Crohn-like response)
— Additional pathologic findings (check all that apply)
  None identified
  Adenoma(s)
  Chronic ulcerative proctocolitis
  Crohn's disease
  Dysplasia
  Other polyps (type[s]):
  Other (specify):
— Comment(s)

Endometrium—biopsy (Use of checklist for biopsy specimens is optional)

Applies to all carcinomas of the endometrium.

Macroscopic
— Specimen type
  Biopsy

Curettage
Other (specify):
Not specified

Microscopic
— Histologic type
Endometrioid adenocarcinoma
Not otherwise characterized
Secretory (variant)
Ciliated cell (variant)
With squamous metaplasia
Adenosquamous carcinoma
Serous adenocarcinoma
Clear cell adenocarcinoma
Mucinous adenocarcinoma
Squamous cell carcinoma
Mixed carcinoma (specify types and percentages):
Undifferentiated carcinoma
Other (specify)
Carcinoma, type cannot be determined
— Histologic grade, if applicable
Grading system below applies primarily to
endometrioid carcinoma
Not applicable
GX   Cannot be assessed
G1   5% or less nonsquamous solid growth
G2   6% to 50% nonsquamous solid growth
G3   More than 50% nonsquamous solid growth
Other (specify)
— Additional pathologic findings (check all that apply)
None identified
Hyperplasia
Simple
Complex (adenomatous)
Atypical hyperplasia
Simple
Complex (adenomatous)
Other (specify)
— Comment(s)

Endometrium—hysterectomy, with or without other organs or tissues

Applies to all carcinomas of the endometrium.

Macroscopic
— Specimen type
Hysterectomy
Radical hysterectomy (includes parametria)
Pelvic exenteration
Other (specify)
Not specified
— Tumor site
Specify location(s), if known:
Not specified
— Tumor size
Greatest dimension: —— cm
— Additional dimensions: ×   —— cm
Cannot be determined (see Comment)
— Other organs present (check all that apply)

None
Right ovary
Left ovary
Right fallopian tube
Left fallopian tube
Urinary bladder
Vagina
Rectum
Other(s) (specify)

Microscopic
— Histologic type
Endometrioid adenocarcinoma
Not otherwise characterized
Secretory (variant)
Ciliated cell (variant)
With squamous metaplasia
Adenosquamous carcinoma
Serous adenocarcinoma
Clear cell adenocarcinoma
Mucinous adenocarcinoma
Squamous cell carcinoma
Mixed carcinoma (specify types and percentages):
Undifferentiated carcinoma
Other (specify)
Carcinoma, type cannot be determined
— Histologic grade, if applicable
Grading system below applies primarily to
endometrioid carcinoma
Not applicable
GX   Cannot be assessed
G1   5% or less nonsquamous solid growth
G2   6% to 50% nonsquamous solid growth
G3   More than 50% nonsquamous solid growth
Other (specify)
— Myometrial invasion
No invasion
Invasion present
Specify depth of invasion: mm
Specify myometrial thickness: mm
— Extent of invasion
— Primary tumor (pT)
TNM (FIGO)
pTX (—)   Primary tumor cannot be assessed
pT0 (—)   No evidence of primary tumor
pTis (0) Carcinoma in situ
pT1 (I)   Tumor confined to corpus uteri
pT1a (IA)   Tumor limited to endometrium
pT1b (IB)   Tumor invades less than one-half of the myometrium
pT1c (IC)   Tumor invades one-half or more of the myometrium
pT2 (II) Tumor invades cervix, but does not extend beyond uterus
pT2a (IIA) Endocervical glandular involvement only
pT2b (IIB) Cervical stromal invasion
pT3 (III) Local and/or regional spread as specified in T3a, T3b, N1, and FIGO IIIA, IIIB, and IIIC
pT3a (IIIA) Tumor involves serosa, parametria, and/or adnexa (direct extension or metastasis)

*pT3a (IIIA) Tumor involves serosa, parametria, and/or adnexa (direct extension or metastasis) and/or cancer cells in ascites or peritoneal washings

pT3b (IIIB) Involvement of vagina (direct extension or metastasis), rectal or bladder wall (without mucosal involvement), or pelvic wall(s) (frozen pelvis)

pT4 (IVA) Tumor invades bladder mucosa and/or bowel mucosa

— Regional lymph nodes (pN)
  TNM (FIGO)
  pNX   Cannot be assessed
  pN0   No regional lymph node metastasis
  pN1 (IIIC)   Regional lymph node metastasis
  Specify
    Number examined
    Number involved
— Distant metastasis (pM)
  TNM (FIGO)
  pMX   Cannot be assessed
  pM1 (IVB)   Distant metastasis
    Specify site(s), if known
— Margins
  Cannot be assessed
  Uninvolved by invasive carcinoma
    Distance of invasive carcinoma from closest margin: mm
    (Specify margin):
  Involved by invasive carcinoma
    (Specify margin[s]):
— Venous/lymphatic (large/small vessel) invasion (V/L)
  Absent
  Present
  Indeterminate
— Additional pathologic findings (check all that apply)
  None identified
  Hyperplasia
    Simple
    Complex (adenomatous)
  Atypical hyperplasia
    Simple
    Complex (adenomatous)
  Other (specify)
— Comment(s)

Esophagus—biopsy (Use of checklist for biopsy specimens is optional)

Applies to all invasive carcinomas of the esophagus.

Macroscopic
— Specimen type
  Incisional biopsy
  Excisional biopsy
— Tumor type
  Specify, if known
  Not specified

Microscopic
— Histologic type
  Squamous cell carcinoma
  Adenocarcinoma
  Adenosquamous carcinoma
  Small cell carcinoma
  Undifferentiated carcinoma
  Other (specify)
  Carcinoma, type cannot be determined
— Histologic grade
  Not applicable
  GX Cannot be assessed
  G1 Well differentiated
  G2 Moderately differentiated
  G3 Poorly differentiated
  G4 Undifferentiated
— Extent of invasion
  Cannot be assessed
  Epithelium only (no invasion)
  Lamina propria
  Submucosa
  Muscularis propria
— Additional pathologic findings (check all that apply)
  None identified
  Intestinal metaplasia
  Dysplasia
  Esophagitis (type)
  Other (specify)
— Comment(s)

Esophagus—resection

Applies to all invasive carcinomas of the esophagus.

Macroscopic
— Specimen type
  Esophageal resection
  Esophagogastrectomy
  Other (specify)
  Not specified
— Tumor type
  Specify, if known
  Not specified

Microscopic
— Histologic type
  Squamous cell carcinoma
  Adenocarcinoma
  Adenosquamous carcinoma
  Small cell carcinoma
  Undifferentiated carcinoma
  Other (specify)
  Carcinoma, type cannot be determined
— Histologic grade
  Not applicable
  GX Cannot be assessed
  G1 Well differentiated
  G2 Moderately differentiated
  G3 Poorly differentiated
  G4 Undifferentiated
— Extent of invasion

— Primary tumor (pT)
  pTX   Cannot be assessed
  pT0   No evidence of primary tumor
  pTis   Carcinoma in situ
  pT1a   Tumor invades lamina propria or submucosa
  pT1b   Tumor invades lamina propria
  pT1c   Tumor invades submucosa
  pT2   Tumor invades muscularis propria
  pT3   Tumor invades adventitia
  pT4   Tumor invades adjacent structures
— Regional lymph nodes (pN)
  pNX   Cannot be assessed
  pN0   No regional lymph node metastasis
  pN1   Regional lymph node metastasis
  pN1a   1 to 3 nodes involved
  pN1b   4 to 7 nodes involved
  pN1c   More than 7 nodes involved
  Specify
    Number examined
    Number involved
— Distant metastasis (pM)
  pMX   Cannot be assessed
  pM1   Distant metastasis, cannot further subclassify
    pM1a   Lower thoracic esophagus: metastasis
            in celiac lymph nodes
    Mid-thoracic esophagus: not applicable
    Upper thoracic esophagus: metastasis in cervical
      nodes
    pM1b   Lower thoracic esophagus: other
            distant metastasis
    Mid-thoracic esophagus: non-regional lymph nodes
      and/or other distant metastasis
    Upper thoracic esophagus: other distant metastasis
    Specify location of other distant metastases, if
      possible
— Margins (check all that apply)
  Cannot be assessed
  Proximal margin
    Uninvolved by invasive carcinoma
    Involved by invasive carcinoma
    Carcinoma in situ absent at proximal margin
    Carcinoma in situ present at proximal margin
  Distal margin
    Uninvolved by invasive carcinoma
    Involved by invasive carcinoma
    Carcinoma in situ absent at distal margin
    Carcinoma in situ present at distal margin
  Circumferential (adventitial) margin
    Uninvolved by invasive carcinoma
    Involved by invasive carcinoma
  Distance of invasive carcinoma from closest margin:
    mm
  Specify margin:
— Venous (large vessel) invasion (V)
  Absent
  Present
  Undetermined
— Lymphatic (small vessel) invasion (L)
  Absent
  Present
  Undetermined

— Additional pathologic findings (check all that apply)
  None identified
  Intestinal metaplasia
  Dysplasia
  Esophagitis (type)
  Gastritis (type)
  Other (specify
— Comment(s)

Extrahepatic bile ducts—resection

Applies to all invasive carcinomas of the extrahepatic bile ducts. Sarcomas and carcinoid tumors are excluded.

Macroscopic
— Specimen type
  Pancreaticoduodenectomy
  Segmental resection of bile duct(s)
  Choledochal cyst resection
  Other (specify):
  Not specified
— Tumor site (check all that apply)
  Right hepatic duct
  Left hepatic duct
  Junction of right and left hepatic ducts
  Cystic duct
  Common bile duct
    Proximal
    Middle
    Distal
  Not specified
Microscopic
— Histologic type
  Adenocarcinoma (not otherwise characterized)
  Papillary adenocarcinoma
  Adenocarcinoma, intestinal type
  Mucinous adenocarcinoma
  Clear cell adenocarcinoma
  Signet ring cell carcinoma
  Adenosquamous carcinoma
  Other (specify)
  Carcinoma, type cannot be determined
— Histologic grade
  Not applicable
  GX   Cannot be assessed
  G1   Well differentiated
  G2   Moderately differentiated
  G3   Poorly differentiated
  G4   Undifferentiated
— Extent of invasion
— Primary tumor (pT)
  pTX   Cannot be assessed
  pT0   No evidence of primary tumor
  pTis   Carcinoma in situ
  pT1   Tumor confined to the bile duct histologically
  pT2   Tumor invades beyond the wall of the
         gallbladder, pancreas, and/or unilateral
         branches of the portal vein (right or left) or
         hepatic artery (right or left)

pT4   Tumor invades any of the following: main portal vein or its branches bilaterally, common hepatic artery, or other adjacent structures such as the colon, stomach, duodenum, or abdominal wall
— Regional lymph nodes (pN)
   pNX   Cannot be assessed
   pN0   No regional lymph node metastasis
   pN1   Regional lymph node metastasis
   Specify
      Number examined
      Number involved
— Distant metastasis (pM)
   pMX   Cannot be assessed
   pM1   Distant metastasis
      Specify site(s), if known
— Margins (check all that apply)
   Cannot be assessed
   Margins uninvolved by invasive carcinoma
      Distance of carcinoma from closest margin: mm
      Specify margin
   Margins involved by invasive carcinoma
      Proximal bile duct margin
      Distal bile duct margin
      Other (specify)
   Carcinoma in situ absent at bile duct margin
   Carcinoma in situ present at bile duct margin
— Perineural invasion
   Absent
   Present
   Indeterminate
— Venous (large vessel) invasion (V)
   Absent
   Present
   Indeterminate
— Lymphatic (small vessel) invasion (L)
   Absent
   Present
   Indeterminate
— Additional pathologic findings (check all that apply)
   None identified
   Dysplasia
   Cholangitis
   Stones
   Other (specify)
— Comment(s)

Fallopian tube—unilateral salpingectomy, salpingo-oophorectomy, or hysterectomy with salpingo-oophorectomy

Applies to all invasive carcinomas of the fallopian tube.

Macroscopic
— Specimen type
   Right salpingectomy
   Left salpingectomy
   Right salpingo-oophorectomy
   Left salpingo-oophorectomy
   Hysterectomy with salpingo-oophorectomy
   Other (specify)
   Not specified
— Primary tumor site (check all that apply)
   Right fallopian tube
      Relationship to ovary
         Not fused
         Fused
      Status of fimbriated end
         Open
         Closed
   Left fallopian tube
      Relationship to ovary
         Not fused
         Fused
      Status of fimbriated end
         Open
         Closed
   Not specified
— Specimen integrity
   Specify side
   Intact
   Ruptured
   Fragmented
   Not specified
— Tumor location
   Fimbria(e)
   Ampulla
   Infundibular portion
   Isthmus
   Combination
— Tumor size
   Greatest dimension: —— cm
   *Additional dimensions: ×   —— cm
   Cannot be determined (see Comment)
— Other organs (if applicable)
   None
   Other(s) (specify)
Microscopic
— Histologic type
   Carcinoma in situ
   Serous carcinoma
   Mucinous carcinoma
   Endometrioid carcinoma
   Clear cell carcinoma
   Transitional cell carcinoma
   Squamous cell carcinoma
   Undifferentiated carcinoma
   Other (specify)
   Carcinoma, type cannot be determined
— Histologic grade
   Not applicable
   GX   Cannot be assessed
   G1   Well differentiated
   G2   Moderately differentiated
   G3   Poorly differentiated
— Extent of invasion
— Primary tumor (pT)
   TNM (FIGO)
   pTX (—)   Primary tumor cannot be assessed
   pT0 (—)   No evidence of Primary tumor

pTis (0)   Carcinoma in situ (limited to tubal mucosa)
pT1 (I)   Tumor limited to fallopian tube(s)

    pT1a (IA)   Tumor limited to one tube without penetrating the serosal surface; no ascites

    pT1b (IB)   Tumor limited to both tubes without penetrating the serosal surface; no ascites

    pT1c (IC)   Tumor limited to one or both tube(s) with extension into or through the tubal serosa; or with malignant cells in ascites or peritoneal washings

pT2 (II)   Tumor involves one or both tube(s) with pelvic extension

    pT2a (IIA)   Extension and/or metastasis to the uterus and/or ovaries

    pT2b (IIB)   Extension to other pelvic structures

    pT2c (IIC)   Pelvic extension (T2a or T2b/IIA or IIB) with malignant cells in ascites or peritoneal washings

pT3 and/or N1 (III)   Tumor involves one or both tube(s) with peritoneal implants outside the pelvis and/or regional lymph node metastasis

    pT3a (IIIA)   Microscopic peritoneal metastasis beyond pelvis

    pT3b (IIIB)   Macroscopic peritoneal metastasis beyond pelvis 2 cm or less in greatest dimension

    pT3c/NI (IIIC)   Peritoneal metastasis beyond pelvis more than 2 cm in greatest dimension and/or regional lymph node metastasis

Any T/Any N and MI (IV)   Distant metastasis including presence of malignant cells in pleural fluid or parenchymal hepatic metastasis

— Regional lymph nodes (pN)
    pNX   Cannot be assessed
    pN0   No regional lymph node metastasis
    pN1   Regional lymph node metastasis
    Specify
        Number examined
        Number involved

— Distant metastasis (pM)
    TNM (FIGO)
    pMX   Cannot be assessed
    pM1 (IV)   Distant metastasis
        Specify site(s), if known:

— Summary of organs/tissues involved by tumor
    Fallopian tube only
    Other organs/tissues
        Specify all:

— Venous/lymphatic (large/small vessel) invasion (V/L)
    Absent
    Present
    Indeterminate

— Additional pathologic findings (check all that apply)
    None identified
    Salpingitis (type)
    Dysplasia
    Other (specify)
— Comment(s)

Gallblabder—resection/cholecystectomy

Applies to all invasive carcinomas of the gallbladder, including those showing focal endocrine differentiation.

Macroscopic
— Specimen type
    Cholecystectomy
    Cholecystectomy with partial hepatectomy
    Other (specify):
    Not specified
— Tumor site
    Fundus
    Body
    Neck
    Indeterminate
    Not specified
— Tumor size
    Greatest dimension: ——— cm
    Additional dimensions: ×   ——— cm
    Cannot be determined (see Comment)

Microscopic
— Histologic type
    Adenocarcinoma
    Papillary adenocarcinoma
    Adenocarcinoma, intestinal type
    Clear cell adenocarcinoma
    Mucinous carcinoma
    Signet ring carcinoma
    Squamous cell carcinoma
    Adenosquamous carcinoma
    Small cell carcinoma
    Large cell neuroendocrine carcinoma
    Undifferentiated carcinoma
    Other (specify):
    Carcinoma, type cannot be determined
— Histologic grade
    Not applicable
    GX   Cannot be assessed
    G1   Well differentiated
    G2   Moderately differentiated
    G3   Poorly differentiated
    G4   Undifferentiated
    Other (specify):
— Extent of invasion
— Primary tumor (pT)
    pTX   Cannot be assessed
    pT0   No evidence of primary tumor
    pTis   Carcinoma in situ
    pT1   Tumor invades lamina propria or muscle layer
    pT1a   Tumor invades lamina propria
    pT1a   Tumor invades muscle layer
    pT2   Tumor invades perimuscular connective tissue; no extension beyond serosa or into liver

pT3   Tumor perforates serosa (visceral peritoneum and/or directly invades the liver and/or other adjacent organ or structure, such as the stomach, duodenum, colon, or pancreas, omentum of extrahepatic bile ducts

pT4   Tumor invades main portal vein or hepatic artery or invades multiple extrahepatic organs or structures

— Regional lymph nodes (pN)

pNX   Cannot be assessed

pN0   No regional lymph node metastasis

pN1   Metastasis in perirectal lymph nodes

Specify

Number examined

Number involved

— Distant metastasis (pM)

pMX   Cannot be assessed

pM1   Distant metastasis

Specify site(s)

— Margins (check all that apply)

Cannot be assessed

Margins uninvolved by invasive carcinoma

Distance of invasive carcinoma from closest margin: mm

Specify margin:

Margins involved by invasive carcinoma

Specify margin:

Cystic duct margin uninvolved by in situ carcinoma

Cystic duct margin(s) involved by in situ carcinoma

— Venous/lymphatic (large small vessel) invasion (V/L)

Absent

Present

Indeterminate

— Perineural invasion

Absent

Present

Indeterminate

— Additional pathologic findings (check all that apply)

None identified

Dysplasia/adenoma

Acute cholecystitis

Cholelithiasis

Chronic cholecystitis

Other (specify):

— Comment(s)

Gastrointestinal lymphoma—resection

Applies to Hodgkin's and non-Hodgkin's lymphomas of the gastrointestinal tract.

Macroscopic

— Tumor site(s)

Specify, if known:

Not specified

— Tumor size (largest single mass)

Greatest dimension: ——— cm

Additional dimensions: — × ——— cm

Cannot be determined (see Comment)

Microscopic

— Tumor

Immunophenotyping

Performed

Not performed

— Histologic type (WHO Classification) (check all that apply)

Hodgkin's lymphoma

Nodular lymphocyte predominance Hodgkin's lymphoma (NLPHL)

Classical Hodgkin's lymphoma (CHL)

Nodular sclerosis Hodgkin's lymphoma (NSHL)

Mixed cellularity Hodgkin's lymphoma (MCHL)

Lymphocyte-rich classical Hodgkin's lymphoma (LRCHL)

Lymphocyte depletion Hodgkin's lymphoma (LDHL)

Non-Hodgkin's lymphoma

Histologic type cannot be assessed

B cell lymphoma

Subtype cannot be determined

Precursor B lymphoblastic lymphoma/leukemia

Mature B cell chronic lymphocytic leukemia/small lymphocytic lymphoma

B cell prolymphocytic leukemia

Lymphoplasmacytic lymphoma

Hairy cell leukemia

Plasma cell myeloma/plasmacytoma

Extranodal marginal zone B cell lymphoma of MALT type

Follicular lymphoma

Grade 1 (0–5 centroblasts per HPF)

Grade 2 (6–15 centroblasts per HPF)

Grade 3 (greater than 15 centroblasts per HPF)

Cutaneous follicle center lymphoma

Diffuse follicle center cell lymphoma

Mantle cell lymphoma

Diffuse large B cell lymphoma

Burkitt's lymphoma/Burkitt's cell leukemia

T cell lymphoma

Subtype cannot be determined

Precursor T lymphoblastic lymphoma/leukemia

T cell prolymphocytic leukemia

T cell granular lymphocytic leukemia

Aggressive NK cell leukemia

Adult T cell lymphoma/leukemia (HTLV1+)

Enteropathy-type T cell lymphoma

Anaplastic large cell lymphoma

Peripheral T cell lymphoma, not otherwise characterized

Angioimmunoblastic T cell lymphoma

Other (specify)

— Histologic grade

Not applicable

Cannot be determined

High-grade

Low-grade

Other (specify)

— Extent of involvement

Cannot be assessed

Confined to mucosa/submucosa

Involvement of muscular wall/subserosa
Penetration of serosa, perforation present
Penetration of serosa, perforation absent
Direct extension to other organ(s) or structure(s)
   Specify
Noncontiguous tumor involvement of other organ(s)
   or structure(s) absent
Noncontiguous tumor involvement of other organ(s)
   or structure(s) present
   Specify site(s)
— Margins (check all that apply)
   Cannot be assessed
   Uninvolved by lymphoma
   Proximal margin involved by lymphoma
   Distal margin involved by lymphoma
   Circumferential (radial or mesenteric) margin involved
     by lymphoma
— Regional lymph nodes
   Cannot be assessed
   No regional lymph node involvement
   Regional lymph node involvement
   Specify
     Number examined
     Number involved
— Nonregional lymph nodes
   Not applicable
   No nonregional lymph node involvement
     Number present in specimen:
   Nonregional lymph node involvement
     Number present in specimen
     Number involved
— Additional pathologic findings (check all that apply)
   None identified
   Helicobacter pylori gastritis
   Celiac disease (sprue)
   Inflammatory bowel disease
   Other (specify)
— Comment(s)

Heart—resection

Applies to primary malignant cardiac tumors.

Macroscopic
— Specimen type
   Excisional biopsy
   Other (specify)
   Not specified
— Tumor site (check all that apply)
   Pericardium
   Right ventricle
   Left ventricle
   Right atrium
   Left atrium
   Other (specify):
   Not specified
— Tumor size
   Not applicable
   Greatest dimension: cm
   Additional dimensions: ×   cm
   Cannot be determined (see Comment)

Microscopic
— Histologic type
   Angiosarcoma
   Malignant fibrous histiocytoma
   Myxosarcoma
   Fibrosarcoma
   Leiomyosarcoma
   Rhabdomyosarcoma
   Osteosarcoma
   Synovial sarcoma
   Malignant schwannoma (malignant peripheral nerve
     sheath tumor)
   Malignant mesenchymoma
   Other (specify)
   Sarcoma, type cannot be determined
— Histologic grade
   Not applicable
   Cannot be determined
   Low-grade
   High-grade
   Other (specify)
— Extent of invasion (as appropriate)
   Cannot be determined
   No involvement of adjacent tissue(s)
   Involvement of adjacent tissue(s)
   Other organ involvement (specify):
— Margins (as appropriate)
   Not applicable
   Cannot be assessed
   Uninvolved by tumor
   Involved by tumor
     Specify site(s), if known:
— Additional pathologic findings (check all that apply)
   None identified
   Benign tumor (specify)
   Therapy-related changes (specify)
   Inflammation
   Other (specify)
— Comment(s)

Hodgkin's lymphoma—biopsy/staging procedure

Applies to Hodgkin's lymphoma involving any organ system except for the gastrointestinal tract.

Macroscopic
— Specimen type
   Lymphadenectomy
   Staging laparotomy
   Other (specify)
   Not specified
— Tumor site (check all that apply)
   Lymph node(s), site not specified
   Lymph node(s), (specify site[s])
   Other tissue(s) or organ(s) (specify site[s])
— Tumor size (largest single mass)
   Greatest dimension: cm
— Additional dimensions: ×   cm (site)
   Cannot be determined (see Comment)

Microscopic

— Histologic subtype

Nodular lymphocyte predominant
Hodgkin's lymphoma (NLPHL)

Classical Hodgkin's lymphoma (CHL)

Nodular sclerosis Hodgkin's lymphoma (NSHL)

Mixed cellularity Hodgkin's lymphoma (MCHL)

Lymphocyte-rich classical Hodgkin's lymphoma (LRCHL)

Lymphocyte depleted Hodgkin's lymphoma (LDHL)

Other (specify)

Hodgkin's lymphoma, subtype cannot be determined

— Grade (NSHL only)

Not applicable

Grade I

Grade II

— Extent of pathologically examined tumor (check all that apply)

Involvement of a single lymph node region

Specify site

Involvement of multiple lymph node regions

Specify

Splenic involvement

Liver involvement

Bone marrow involvement

Other organ involvement

Specify

— Immunophenotyping

Performed

Specify results

Not performed

— Additional pathologic findings (check all that apply)

Progressive transformation of germinal centers (PTGC)

Castleman's disease

Other (specify)

— Comment(s)

Non-Hodgkin's lymphoma—biopsy/resection

Applies to Hodgkin's lymphoma involving any organ system except for the gastrointestinal tract.

Macroscopic

— Specimen type

Lymphadenectomy

Other (specify)

Not specified

— Tumor site (check all that apply)

Lymph node(s), site unknown

Lymph node(s), (specify site[s])

Other tissue(s) or organ(s) (specify site[s])

Not specified

Microscopic

— Histologic type (WHO classification)

Histologic type cannot be assessed

B cell lymphoma

Subtype cannot be determined

Precursor B lymphoblastic leukemia/lymphoma

Chronic lymphocytic leukemia/small lymphocytic lymphoma

B cell prolymphocytic leukemia

Lymphoplasmacytic lymphoma

Splenic marginal zone lymphoma

Hairy cell leukemia

Plasma cell myeloma/plasmacytoma

Extranodal marginal zone B cell lymphoma of mucosa-associated lymphoid tissue (MALT lymphoma)

Nodal marginal zone B cell lymphoma

Follicular lymphoma, grade 1 (0–5 centroblasts per HPF)

Follicular lymphoma, grade 2 (6–15 centroblasts per HPF)

Follicular lymphoma, grade 3 (>15 centroblasts per HPF)

Follicular lymphoma, cutaneous follicle center subtype

Follicular lymphoma, diffuse follicle center subtype, grade 1 (0–5 centroblasts per HPF)

Follicular lymphoma, diffuse follicle center cell subtype, grade 2 (6–15 centroblasts per HPF)

Mantle cell lymphoma

Diffuse large B cell lymphoma

Mediastinal (thymic) large B cell lymphoma

Intravascular large B cell lymphoma

Primary effusion lymphoma

Burkitt's lymphoma/leukemia

Lymphomatoid granulomatosis

Other (specify)

T cell lymphoma

Subtype cannot be determined

Precursor T lymphoblastic leukemia/lymphoma

T cell prolymphocytic leukemia

T cell large granular lymphocytic leukemia

Aggressive NK cell leukemia

Adult T cell leukemia/lymphoma

Extranodal NK/T cell lymphoma, nasal type

Enteropathy-type T cell lymphoma

Hepatosplenic T cell lymphoma

Subcutaneous panniculitis-like T cell lymphoma

Mycosis fungoides/Sézary syndrome

Primary cutaneous anaplastic large cell lymphoma

Peripheral T cell lymphoma, unspecified

Angioimmunoblastic T cell lymphoma

Anaplastic large cell lymphoma

Lymphomatoid papulosis

Other (specify)

— Extent of pathologically examined tumor (check all that apply)

Involvement of a single lymph node region

Specify site

Involvement of multiple lymph node regions

Specify

Splenic involvement

Liver involvement

Bone marrow involvement

Other organ involvement

Specify

Not specified
— Phenotyping
Performed, see separate report
Performed
Specify method and results
Not performed
— Additional pathologic findings
Specify
— Comment(s)

Kidney—biopsy (Use of checklist for biopsy specimens is optional)

Applies to all invasive carcinomas of renal tubular origin. It excludes Wilms' tumors and tumors of urothelial origin.

Macroscopic
— Specimen type
Incisional biopsy
Needle
Wedge
Other (specify)
Not specified

Microscopic
— Histologic type
Cannot be determined
Conventional (clear cell) renal carcinoma
Papillary renal carcinoma
Chromophobe renal carcinoma
Collecting duct carcinoma
Sarcomatoid carcinoma arising in renal cell carcinoma
Specify subtype
Renal cell carcinoma, unclassified
Other (specify)
Carcinoma, type cannot be determined
— Histologic grade (Fuhrman Nuclear Grade)
Not applicable
GX   Cannot be assessed
G1   Nuclei round, uniform, approximately 10 μ; nucleoli inconspicuous or absent
G2   Nuclei slightly irregular, approximately 15 μ; nucleoli evident
G3   Nuclei very irregular, approximately 20 μ; nucleoli large and prominent
G4   Nuclei bizarre and multilobated, 20 μ or greater, nucleoli prominent, chromatin clumped.
— Additional pathologic findings (check all that apply)
None identified
Inflammation (type)
Glomerular disease (type)
Interstitial disease (type)
Other (specify)
— Comment(s)

Kidney—nephrectomy, partial or radical

Applies to all invasive carcinomas of renal tubular origin. It excludes Wilms' tumors and tumors of urothelial origin.

Macroscopic
— Specimen type
Partial nephrectomy
Radical nephrectomy
Other (specify)
Not specified
— Laterality
Right
Left
Not specified
— Tumor site (check all that apply)
Upper pole
Middle
Lower pole
Other (specify)
Not specified
— Focality
Unifocal
Multifocal
— Tumor size (largest tumor if multiple)
Greatest dimension: cm
Additional dimensions: ×   cm
Cannot be determined (see Comment)
— Macroscopic extent of tumor (check all that apply)
Tumor limited to kidney
Tumor extension into perinephric tissues
Tumor extension beyond Gerota's fascia
Tumor extension into adrenal
Tumor extension into major veins

Microscopic
— Histologic type
Clear cell (conventional) renal carcinoma
Papillary renal cell carcinoma
Chromophobe renal cell carcinoma
Collecting duct carcinoma
Sarcomatoid carcinoma arising in renal cell carcinoma
Specify: subtype   ;   % of sarcomatoid element
Renal cell carcinoma, unclassified
Other (specify)
Carcinoma, type cannot be determined
— Histologic grade (Fuhrman Nuclear Grade)
Not applicable
GX   Cannot be assessed
G1   Nuclei round, uniform, approximately 10 μ; nucleoli inconspicuous or absent
G2   Nuclei slightly irregular, approximately 15 μ; nucleoli evident
G3   Nuclei very irregular, approximately 20 μ; nucleoli large and prominent
G4   Nuclei bizarre and multilobated, 20 μ or greater, nucleoli prominent, chromatin clumped
Other (specify)
— Extent of invasion
— Primary tumor (pT)
pTX   Primary tumor cannot be assessed
pT0   No evidence of primary tumor
pT1   Tumor 7 cm or less in greatest dimension, limited to the kidney
pT1a   Tumor 4 cm or less in greatest dimension, limited to the kidney

pT1b   Tumor more than 4 cm but not more than 7 cm in greatest dimension, limited to the kidney

pT2   Tumor more than 7 cm in greatest dimension, limited to the kidney

pT3   Tumor extends into major veins or invades adrenal gland or perinephric tissues but not beyond Gerota's fascia

     pT3a   Tumor directly invades adrenal gland or perirenal and/or renal sinus fat but not beyond Gerota's fascia

     pT3b   Tumor grossly extends into the renal vein or its segmental (muscle-containing) branches, or vena cava below the diaphragm

     pT3c   Tumor grossly extends into vena cava above diaphragm or invades the wall of the vena cava

pT4   Tumor invades beyond Gerota's fascia

— Regional lymph nodes (pN)

   pNX   Cannot be assessed

   pN0   No regional lymph node metastasis

   pN1   Metastasis in a single regional lymph node

   pN2   Metastasis in more than 1 regional lymph node

   Specify

     Number examined

     Number involved

— Distant metastasis (pM)

   pMX: Cannot be assessed

   pM1:   Distant metastasis

   *Specify site(s), if known

— Margins (check all that apply)

   Cannot be assessed

   Margins uninvolved by invasive carcinoma

   Margin(s) involved by invasive carcinoma

     Renal capsular margin (partial nephrectomy only)

     Perinephric fat margin (partial nephrectomy only)

     Renal vein margin

     Gerota's fascial margin

     Ureteral margin

     Renal parenchymal margin (partial nephrectomy only)

     Other (specify)

— Adrenal gland

   Not present

   Uninvolved by tumor

   Direct invasion (T3a)

   Metastasis (M1)

— Venous (large vessel) invasion (V) (excluding renal vein and inferior vena cava)

   Absent

   Present

   Indeterminate

— Lymphatic (small vessel) invasion (L)

   Absent

   Present

   Indeterminate

— Additional pathologic findings (check all that apply)

   None identified

   Inflammation (type)

   Glomerular disease (type)

   Interstitial disease (type)

   Other (specify)

— Comment(s)

Liver—resection

Applies to hepatocellular carcinoma and cholangiocarcinoma.

Macroscopic

— Specimen type

   Right lobectomy

   Extended right lobectomy

   Medial segmentectomy

   Left lateral segmentectomy

   Total left lobectomy

   Explanted liver

   Other (specify)

   Not specified

— Focality

   Solitary (specify location)

   Multiple (specify location)

— Tumor size

   Greatest dimension: —— cm

   Additional dimensions: ×   —— cm

   Cannot be determined (see Comment)

Microscopic

— Histologic type

   Hepatocellular carcinoma

   Fibrolamellar hepatocellular carcinoma variant (specify)

   Combined hepatocellular and cholangiocarcinoma

   Cholangiocarcinoma, intrahepatic

   Bile duct cystadenocarcinoma

   Undifferentiated carcinoma

   Other (specify)

   Carcinoma, type cannot be determined

— Histologic grade

   Not applicable

   GX   Cannot be assessed

   GI   Well differentiated

   GII   Moderately differentiated

   GIII   Poorly differentiated

   GIV   Undifferentiated/anaplastic

   Other (specify)

— Extent of invasion

— Primary tumor (pT)

   pTX   Cannot be assessed

   pT0   No evidence of primary tumor

   pT1   Solitary tumor with no vascular invasion

   pT2   Solitary tumor with vascular invasion or multiple tumors none more than 5 cm

   pT3   Multiple tumors more than 5 cm or tumor involving a major branch of the portal or hepatic vein(s)

   pT4   Tumor(s) with direct invasion of adjacent organs other than the gallbladder or perforation of visceral peritoneum

— Regional lymph nodes (pN)

   pNX   Cannot be assessed

   pN0   No regional lymph node metastasis

pN1 Regional lymph node metastasis
Specify
  Number examined
  Number involved
— Distant metastasis (pM)
  pMX Cannot be assessed
  pM1 Distant metastasis
    Specify site(s), if known
— Margins (check all that apply)
  Parenchymal margin
    Cannot be assessed
    Uninvolved by invasive carcinoma
      Distance of invasive carcinoma from closest
        margin: mm
      Specify margin
    Involved by invasive carcinoma
  Bile duct margin (cholangiocarcinoma only)
    Cannot be assessed
    Uninvolved by invasive carcinoma
      Carcinoma in situ absent
      Carcinoma in situ present
    Involved by invasive carcinoma
  Other margin (specify)
    Cannot be assessed
    Uninvolved by invasive carcinoma
    Involved by invasive carcinoma
— Venous (large vessel) invasion (V)
  Absent
  Present
  Indeterminate
— Additional pathologic findings (check all that apply)
  None identified
  Hepatocellular dysplasia
  Ductal dysplasia
  Cirrhosis/fibrosis
  Iron overload
  Hepatitis (specify type)
  Other (specify)
— Comment(s)

Major salivary glands—resection

Applies to all carcinomas of major salivary glands.

Macroscopic
— Tumor site
  Resection, submandibular gland
  Resection, sublingual gland
  Superficial parotidectomy
  Total parotidectomy
  Other (specify)
  Not specified
— Laterality
  Right
  Left
  Not specified
— Tumor size
  Greatest dimension: —— cm
  *Additional dimension: ×   —— cm
  Cannot be determined (see Comment)

Microscopic
— Histologic type
  Acinic cell carcinoma
  Adenoid cystic carcinoma
  Adenocarcinoma not otherwise specified (NOS)
  Squamous cell carcinoma
  Carcinoma ex pleomorphic adenoma (malignant
    mixed tumor)
  Carcinosarcoma (true malignant mixed tumor)
  Mucoepidermoid carcinoma, low grade
  Mucoepidermoid carcinoma, intermediate grade
  Mucoepidermoid carcinoma, high grade
  Polymorphous low-grade adenocarcinoma
  Epithelial–myoepithelial carcinoma
  Basal cell adenocarcinoma
  Sebaceous carcinoma
  Cystadenocarcinoma
  Mucinous carcinoma (colloid carcinoma)
  Oncocytic carcinoma
  Salivary duct carcinoma
  Myoepithelial carcinoma (malignant myoepithelioma)
  Small cell carcinoma
  Undifferentiated carcinoma
  Other (specify)
  Carcinoma, type cannot be determined
— Histologic grade (if appropriate)
  Not applicable
  GX Cannot be assessed
  G1 Well differentiated
  G2 Moderately differentiated
  G3 Poorly differentiated
  Other (specify)
— Extent of invasion
— The phrases in italics include clinical findings required for
  AJCC staging. This clinical information may be unknown
  to the pathologist. It is included here only for the sake of
  completeness
— Primary tumor (pT)
  pTX Cannot be assessed
  pT0 No evidence of primary tumor
  pT1 Tumor 2 cm or less in greatest dimension
    without extraparenchymal extension
  pT2 Tumor more than 2 cm but not more than 4 cm in
    greatest dimension without extraparenchymal
    extension
  pT3 Tumor having extraparenchymal extension
    and/or more than 4 cm in greatest dimension
    without seventh nerve involvement
  pT4a Tumor invades skin, mandible, ear canal, facial
    nerve
  pT4b Tumor invades skull, pterygoid plates, carotid artery
— Regional lymph nodes (pN)
  pNX Cannot be assessed
  pN0 No regional lymph node metastasis
  pN1 Metastasis in a single ipsilateral lymph node,
    3 cm or less in greatest dimension
  pN2a Metastasis in a single ipsilateral lymph node,
    more than 3 cm but not more than 6 cm in
    greatest dimension
  pN2b Metastasis in multiple ipsilateral lymph nodes,
    none more than 6 cm in greatest dimension

pN2c   Metastasis in bilateral or contralateral lymph nodes, none more than 6 cm in greatest dimension

pN3   Metastasis in a lymph node more than 6 cm in greatest dimension

Specify
　　Number examined
　　Number involved
Extracapsular extension of nodal tumor
　　Absent
　　Present
　　Indeterminate

— Distant metastasis (pM)
　　pMX: Cannot be assessed
　　pM1: Distant metastasis
　　　　Specify site(s), if known

— Margins
　　Cannot be assessed
　　Margins uninvolved by tumor
　　　　Distance of tumor from closest margin:　　mm
　　　　(Specify margin, if possible)
　　Margin(s) involved by tumor
　　　　(Specify location(s), if possible)

— Venous/lymphatic (large/small vessel) invasion (V/L)
　　Absent
　　Present
　　Indeterminate

— Perineural invasion
　　Absent
　　Present

— Additional pathologic findings
　　Specify

— Comment(s)

Ovary—oophorectomy, salpingo-oophorectomy, subtotal oophorectomy or removal of tumor in fragments, hysterectomy with salpingo-oophorectomy

Applies to all primary borderline and malignant surface epithelial tumors, germ cell tumors, and sex cord–stromal tumors.

Macroscopic

— Specimen type (check all that apply)
　　Right oophorectomy
　　Left oophorectomy
　　Right salpingo-oophorectomy
　　Left salpingo-oophorectomy
　　Subtotal right oophorectomy
　　Subtotal left oophorectomy
　　Removal of tumor in fragments
　　Hysterectomy with salpingo-oophorectomy
　　Omentectomy
　　Other (specify)
　　Not specified

— Tumor site (check all that apply)
　　Right ovary

　　　　Parenchymal growth
　　　　Growth on surface
　　　　Uninvolved
　　Left ovary
　　　　Parenchymal growth
　　　　Growth on surface
　　　　Uninvolved
　　Not specified

— Specimen integrity (specify side)
　　Intact
　　Ruptured
　　Fragmented
　　Unknown

— Tumor size:
　　Greatest dimension:　　—— cm
　　Additional dimensions:　×　—— cm

Microscopic

— Histologic type (check all that apply)
　　Serous
　　　　Borderline
　　　　Carcinoma
　　Mucinous
　　　　Borderline
　　　　Carcinoma
　　Endometrioid
　　　　Borderline
　　　　Carcinoma
　　Clear cell
　　　　Borderline
　　　　Carcinoma
　　Transitional cell
　　　　Borderline
　　　　Carcinoma
　　Mixed epithelial
　　　　Borderline
　　　　　　Specify types
　　　　Carcinoma
　　　　　　Specify types
　　Undifferentiated
　　Granulosa cell
　　Germ cell (specify type[s])
　　Other(s)

— Histologic grade
　　Not applicable
　　GX Cannot be assessed
　　G1 Well differentiated
　　G2 Moderately differentiated
　　G3 Poorly differentiated
　　G4 Reserved solely for tumors in the undifferentiated category (WHO classification)

— Extent of invasion

— Primary tumor (pT)
　　TNM (FIGO)
　　pTX (—)　　Cannot be assessed
　　pT0 (—)　　No evidence of primary tumor
　　pT1 (I)(—)　Tumor limited to ovaries (1 or both)
　　　　pT1a (IA)　Tumor limited to 1 ovary; capsule intact, no tumor on ovarian surface. No malignant cells in ascites or peritoneal washings

pT1b (IB) Tumor limited to both ovaries; capsule intact, no tumor on ovarian surface. No malignant cells in ascites or peritoneal washings

pT1c (IC) Tumor limited to one or both ovaries with any of the following: capsule ruptured, tumor on ovarian surface, malignant cells in ascites or peritoneal washings

pT2 (II) Tumor involves one or both ovaries with pelvic extension and/or implants

pT2a (IIA) Extension and/or implants on uterus and/or tube(s). No malignant cells in ascites or peritoneal washings

pT2b (IIB) Extension to other pelvic tissues. No malignant cells in ascites or peritoneal washings

pT2c (IIC) Pelvic extension and/or implants (T2a or T2b/IIa or IIb) with malignant cells in ascites or peritoneal washings

pT3 and/or N1 (III) Tumor involves one or both ovaries with microscopically confirmed peritoneal metastasis outside the pelvis (including liver capsule metastasis) and/or regional lymph node metastasis

pT3a (IIIA) Microscopic peritoneal metastasis beyond pelvis

pT3b (IIIB) Macroscopic peritoneal metastasis beyond pelvis 2 cm or less in greatest dimension

pT3c and/or N1(IIIC) Peritoneal metastasis beyond pelvis more than 2 cm in greatest dimension and/or regional lymph node metastasis

Any T/Any N and MI (IV) Growth involving 1 or both ovaries with distant metastasis.

Note 1: If pleural effusion is present, there must be positive cytology to assign a case to Stage IV. Parenchymal liver metastasis is classified as Stage IV

— Regional lymph nodes (pN)
  pNX Cannot be assessed
  pN0 No regional lymph node metastasis
  pN1 Regional lymph node metastasis
  Specify
    Number examined
    Number involved
— Distant metastasis (pM)
  pMX Cannot be assessed
  pM1 (IV) Distant metastasis
    Specify site(s), if known
— Implants (only applies to borderline tumors) (check all that apply)
  Not applicable/none sampled
  Noninvasive (epithelial) implants

    Not present
    Present (specify site[s])
  Noninvasive (desmoplastic) implants
    Not present
    Present (specify site[s])
  Invasive implants
    Not present
    Present (specify site[s])
— Summary of organs/tissues microscopically involved by tumor (check all that apply)
  One ovary
  Both ovaries
  Omentum
  Uterus
  Peritoneum
  Other organs/tissues
    Specify all
— Venous/lymphatic (large/small vessel) invasion (V/L)
  Absent
  Present
  Indeterminate
— Additional pathologic findings (check all that apply)
  None identified
  Endometriosis
  Ovarian
  Extraovarian
  Endosalpingiosis
  Other(s)
    Specify site(s) and type(s)
— Comment(s)

Pancreas (endocrine)—resection

Applies to all endocrine tumors of the pancreas, including those with mixed endocrine and acinar cell differentiation.

Macroscopic
— Specimen type (check all that apply)
  Pancreaticoduodenectomy (Whipple resection)
    Partial pancreatectomy
    Total pancreatectomy
  Pylorus-sparing pancreaticoduodenectomy
    Partial pancreatectomy
    Total pancreatectomy
  Partial resection
    Pancreatic body
    Pancreatic tail
  Other (specify)
  Not specified
— Tumor site (check all that apply)
  Pancreatic head
  Uncinate process
  Pancreatic body
  Pancreatic tail
  Indeterminate
  Not specified
— Focality
  Unifocal
  Multifocal
— Tumor configuration (check all that apply)

Infiltrative
Circumscribed
  Solid, entirely encapsulated
  Solid, partially encapsulated
  Cystic, entirely encapsulated
  Cystic, partially encapsulated
— Tumor size
  Greatest dimension: —— cm
  Additional dimensions: × —— cm
  Cannot be determined (see Comment)
— Other organs
  None
  Spleen
  Gallbladder
  Other(s) (specify)

Microscopic
— Functional type
  Cannot be assessed
  Pancreatic endocrine tumor, functional (correlation
    with clinical syndrome and/or elevated serum
    levels of hormone product) (specify type)
  Pancreatic endocrine tumor, nonsecretory
  Pancreatic endocrine tumor, secretory status unknown
— Extent of invasion
— Primary tumor
  Tumor limited to pancreas
  Tumor invades beyond pancreatic capsule, but does
    not invade adjacent structures/organs
  Tumor invades adjacent structures/organs (check all
    that apply):
  Duodenum
  Bile duct
  Stomach
  Spleen
  Colon
  Adjacent large vessels (e.g., portal vein, celiac
    artery, superior mesenteric vessels, common
    hepatic vessels)
  Other (specify)
— Regional lymph nodes
  Cannot be assessed
  No regional lymph node metastasis
  Regional lymph node metastasis
  Specify
    Number examined
    Number involved
— Distant metastasis
  Cannot be assessed
  Distant metastasis
    Specify site(s) if known
— Margins (check all that apply)
  Cannot be assessed
  Uninvolved by tumor
    Distance of tumor from closest margin: mm
    Specify margin
  Proximal pancreatic margin involved by tumor
  Distal pancreatic margin involved by tumor
  Posterior retroperitoneal surface of pancreas involved
    by tumor
  Common bile duct margin involved by tumor
  Other margin involved by tumor (specify)

— Venous/lymphatic vessel invasion (V/L)
  Absent
  Present
  Indeterminate
— Perineural invasion
  Absent
  Present
— Mitotic activity
  Not applicable
  Absent
  Present; less than or equal to 4 mitoses/HPF
  Present; greater than 4 mitoses/HPF
— Additional pathologic findings (check all that apply)
  None identified
  Chronic pancreatitis
  Acute pancreatitis
  Adenomatosis
  Other (specify)
— Comment(s)

Pancreas (exocrine)—resection

Applies to all carcinomas of the exocrine pancreas.

Macroscopic
— Specimen type
  Pancreaticoduodenectomy
    Partial pancreatectomy
    Total pancreatectomy
  Pylorus-sparing pancreaticoduodenectomy
    Partial pancreatectomy
    Total pancreatectomy
  Partial pancreatectomy
    Pancreatic body
    Pancreatic tail
  Other (specify)
  Not specified
— Tumor site (check all that apply)
  Pancreatic head
  Uncinate process
  Pancreatic body
  Pancreatic tail
  Not specified
— Tumor size
  Greatest dimension: —— cm
  Additional dimensions: × —— cm
  Cannot be determined (see Comment)
— Other organs resected
  None
  Spleen
  Gallbladder
  Other(s) (specify)

Microscopic
— Histologic type
  Ductal adenocarcinoma
  Mucinous noncystic carcinoma
  Signet ring cell carcinoma
  Adenosquamous carcinoma
  Undifferentiated (anaplastic) carcinoma
  Undifferentiated carcinoma with osteoclast-like giant cells

Mixed ductal–endocrine carcinoma
Serous cystadenocarcinoma
Mucinous cystadenocarcinoma—invasive
Invasive papillary–mucinous carcinoma
Acinar cell carcinoma
Acinar cell cystadenocarcinoma
Mixed acinar–endocrine carcinoma
Other (specify)
Carcinoma, type cannot be determined
— Histologic grade (ductal carcinoma only)
Not applicable
GX   Cannot be assessed
G1   Well differentiated
G2   Moderately differentiated
G3   Poorly differentiated
G4   Undifferentiated
Other (specify)
— Extent of invasion
— Primary tumor (pT)
pTX   Cannot be assessed
pT0   No evidence of primary tumor
pTis Carcinoma in situ
pT1   Tumor limited to the pancreas, 2 cm or less in
greatest dimension
pT2   Tumor limited to the pancreas, more than 2 cm
in greatest dimension
pT3   Tumor extends beyond the pancreas but without
involvement of the celiac axis or the superior
mesenteric artery
pT4   Tumor involves the celiac axis or the superior
mesenteric artery
— Regional lymph nodes (pN)
pNX   Cannot be assessed
pN0   No regional lymph node metastasis
pN1   Regional lymph node metastasis
N1a   Metastasis in single regional lymph node
N1b   Metastasis in multiple regional lymph
nodes
Specify
Number examined
Number involved
— Distant metastasis (pM)
pMX   Cannot be assessed
pM1   Distant metastasis
Specify site(s), if known
— Margins (check all that apply)
Cannot be assessed
Margins uninvolved by invasive carcinoma
Distance of invasive carcinoma from closest margin:
mm
Specify margin (if possible)
Carcinoma in situ absent at ductal margins
Carcinoma in situ present at common bile duct
margin
Carcinoma in situ present at pancreatic
parenchymal margin
Margin(s) involved by invasive carcinoma
Posterior retroperitoneal (radial) margin: posterior
surface of pancreas
Uncinate process margin (nonperitonealized surface
of the uncinate process)

Distal pancreatic margin
Common bile duct margin
Proximal pancreatic margin
Other (specify)
— Venous/lymphatic vessel invasion (V/L)
Absent
Present
Indeterminate
— Perineural invasion
Absent
Present
— Additional pathologic findings (check all that apply)
None identified
Pancreatic intraepithelial neoplasia (highest grade:
PanIN   )
Chronic pancreatitis
Acute pancreatitis
Other (specify)
— Comment(s)

Peritoneum—resection

Applies to all primary borderline and malignant epithelial
tumors, and malignant mesothelial neoplasms of the peritoneum.

Macroscopic
— Tumor site(s)
Specify, if known
Not specified
— Organ(s) included (if applicable):
Specify
— Size
Greatest dimension: ——cm
Additional dimensions: ×   ——cm
Cannot be determined (see Comment)

Microscopic
— Histologic type
Malignant mesothelioma
Epithelial
Sarcomatous (spindle cell)
Biphasic
Other (specify)
Serous borderline tumor (of low malignant potential)
Serous carcinoma
Other malignant tumor of müllerian type (specify)
Desmoplastic small round cell tumor
Other (specify)
Malignant tumor, type cannot be determined
— Histologic grade
Not applicable (borderline neoplasms and
mesotheliomas)
GX Cannot be assessed
G1 Well differentiated
G2 Moderately differentiated
G3 Poorly differentiated
Other (specify)
— Venous/lymphatic (large/small vessel) invasion (V/L)
Absent
Present
Indeterminate

— Additional pathologic findings (check all that apply)
    None
    Ferruginous bodies
    Endosalpingiosis
    Endometriosis
    Other (specify)
— Comment(s)

Pleura/pericardium—biopsy

Applies to malignant thoracic mesothelioma.

Macroscopic
— Specimen type
    Percutaneous needle biopsy
    Thoracoscopic biopsy
    Open thoracotomy
    Lymph node biopsy
    Other (specify)
    Not specified
— Tumor site (check all that apply)
    Right pleura
    Left pleura
    Pericardium
    Other (specify)
    Not specified

Microscopic
— Histologic type
    Epithelial mesothelioma
    Fibrous (spindle cell) mesothelioma
    Biphasic mesothelioma
    Other (specify)
    Cannot be determined
— Extent of invasion (as appropriate)
    Cannot be determined
    Lung parenchyma
    Endothoracic fascia
    Soft tissue of chest wall
    Diaphragm
    Other (specify)
— Additional pathologic findings (check all that apply)
    None identified
    Ferruginous bodies
    Pleural plaque
    Pulmonary interstitial fibrosis
    Inflammation (type)
    Other (specify)
— Comment(s)

Pleura/pericardium—resection

Applies to malignant thoracic mesothelioma.

Macroscopic
— Specimen type
    Pleural resection
    Pericardial resection
    Other (specify)
    Not specified
— Tumor site (check all that apply)
    Right pleura
    Left pleura
    Pericardium
    Other (specify)
    Not specified
— Tumor configuration and size
    Localized
        Greatest dimension: —— cm
        Additional dimensions: ×   —— cm
    Diffuse
        Maximum thickness: —— cm
    Cannot be determined (see Comment)

Microscopic
— Histologic type
    Epithelioid (epithelial) mesothelioma
    Sarcomatoid mesothelioma
    Biphasic mesothelioma
    Desmoplastic mesothelioma
    Other (specify)
    Mesothelioma, type cannot be determined
— Extent of invasion
— Primary tumor (pT)
    pTX Primary tumor cannot be assessed
    pT0 No evidence of primary tumor
    pT1 Tumor involves ipsilateral parietal pleura, with
         or without focal involvement of visceral pleura
        pT1a Tumor involves ipsilateral parietal
              (mediastinal, diaphragmatic) pleura. No
              involvement of the visceral pleura
        pT1b Tumor involves ipsilateral parietal
              (mediastinal, diaphragmatic) pleura,
              with focal involvement of the visceral
              pleura
    pT2 Tumor involves any of the ipsilateral pleural
         surfaces with at least 1 of the following:
         confluent visceral pleural tumor (including
         fissure), invasion of diaphragmatic muscle,
         invasion of lung parenchyma
    pT3 Tumor involves any of the ipsilateral pleural
         surfaces, with at least 1 of the following:
         invasion of the endothoracic fascia, invasion into
         mediastinal fat, solitary focus of tumor invading
         the soft tissues of the chest wall, nontransmural
         involvement of the pericardium
    pT4 Tumor involves any of the ipsilateral pleural
         surfaces, with at least 1 of the following: diffuse
         or multifocal invasion of soft tissues of the chest
         wall, any involvement of rib, invasion through
         the diaphragm to the peritoneum, invasion of
         any mediastinal organ(s), direct extension to the
         contralateral pleura, invasion into the spine,
         extension to the internal surface of the
         pericardium, pericardial effusion with positive
         cytology, invasion of the myocardium, invasion
         of the brachial plexus
— Regional lymph nodes (pN)
    pNX Regional lymph nodes cannot be assessed
    pN0 No regional lymph node metastases
    pN1 Metastases in the ipsilateral bronchopulmonary
         and/or hilar lymph node(s)

Specify
  Number examined
  Number involved
pN2 Metastases in the subcarinal lymph node(s)
     and/or the ipsilateral internal mammary or
     mediastinal lymph node(s)
  Specify
    Number examined
    Number involved
pN3 Metastases in the contralateral mediastinal,
     internal mammary, or hilar lymph node(s)
     and/or the ipsilateral or contralateral
     supraclavicular or scalene lymph node(s)
  Specify
    Number examined
    Number involved
— Distant metastasis (pM)
  pMX Cannot be assessed
  pM1 Distant metastasis
    Specify site(s), if known
— Venous/lymphatic (large/small vessel) invasion (V/L)
  Absent
  Present
  Indeterminate
— Margins
  Cannot be assessed
  Margins uninvolved by mesothelioma
    Distance of tumor from closest margin: mm
    Specify margin
  Margin(s) involved by mesothelioma
    Specify margin(s)
— Additional pathologic findings (check all that apply)
  None identified
  Ferruginous bodies
  Pleural plaque
  Pulmonary interstitial fibrosis
  Inflammation (type)
  Other (specify)
— Comment(s)

Prostate gland—needle biopsy, transurethral prostatic resection (TUR), enucleation specimen

Applies to invasive carcinomas of the prostate gland.

Macroscopic
— Specimen type
  Needle biopsy
  Transurethral prostatic resection
    Weight: g
  Enucleation
    Weight: g
  Other (specify)
  Not specified

Microscopic
— Histologic type
  Cannot be determined
  Adenocarcinoma (conventional, not otherwise
    specified)

Prostatic duct adenocarcinoma
Mucinous (colloid) adenocarcinoma
Signet ring cell carcinoma
Adenosquamous carcinoma
Small cell carcinoma
Sarcomatoid carcinoma
Other (specify)
  Undifferentiated carcinoma, not otherwise specified
— Histologic grade
  Gleason Pattern: (if 3 patterns present, use most
    predominant pattern and worst pattern of
    remaining 2)
  Not applicable
  Cannot be determined
  Primary Pattern
    Grade 1
    Grade 2
    Grade 3
    Grade 4
    Grade 5
  Secondary Pattern
    Grade 1
    Grade 2
    Grade 3
    Grade 4
    Grade 5
  Total Gleason Score
— Tumor quantitation (needle biopsy specimens)
  Proportion (percent) of prostatic tissue involved by
    tumor: %
  and/or
  Total linear millimeters of carcinoma/length of core(s):
         /   mm
  and/or
  Other quantitation (specify)
  Number cores positive/total number cores: /
— Tumor quantitation (TUR specimens)
  Proportion (percent) of prostatic tissue involved by
    tumor: — %
    Tumor incidental histologic finding in no more than
      5% of tissue resected
    Tumor incidental histologic finding in more than
      5% of tissue resected
  Number of positive chips/total chips: —/
— Tumor quantitation (enucleation specimens)
  Proportion (percent) of prostatic tissue involved by
    tumor: —%
  Tumor size (dominant nodule, if present):
    Greatest dimension: — cm
    Additional dimensions: ×   — cm
— Periprostatic fat invasion (document if identified)
  Not identified
  Present
— Seminal vesicle invasion (document if identified)
  Not identified
  Present
— Perineural invasion
  Not identified
  Present
— Lymphatic (small vessel) invasion (L)
  Absent

Present
Indeterminate
— Additional pathologic findings (check all that apply)
    None identified
    High-grade prostatic intraepithelial neoplasia (PIN)
    Atypical adenomatous hyperplasia
    Benign prostatic hyperplasia
    Inflammation (specify type)
    Other (specify)
— Comment(s)

Prostate gland—radical prostatectomy

Applies to invasive carcinomas of the prostate gland.

Macroscopic (rarely applicable; see Microscopic)

Microscopic
— Histologic type
    Cannot be determined
    Adenocarcinoma (conventional, not otherwise
      specified)
    Prostatic duct adenocarcinoma
    Mucinous (colloid) adenocarcinoma
    Signet ring cell carcinoma
    Adenosquamous carcinoma
    Small cell carcinoma
    Sarcomatoid carcinoma
    Other (specify)
    Undifferentiated carcinoma, not otherwise specified
— Histologic grade
    Gleason Pattern: (if 3 patterns are present, record the
      most predominant and second most common
      patterns; the tertiary pattern should be recorded if
      higher than primary and secondary patterns)
    Not applicable
    Cannot be determined
    Primary pattern
      Grade 1
      Grade 2
      Grade 3
      Grade 4
      Grade 5
    Secondary pattern
      Grade 1
      Grade 2
      Grade 3
      Grade 4
      Grade 5
    Tertiary pattern
      Grade 3
      Grade 4
      Grade 5
    Total Gleason Score
— Tumor quantitation
    Proportion (percent) of prostate involved by tumor:
      —%
    Tumor size (dominant nodule, if present):
      Greatest dimension: ——cm
      Additional dimensions: × —— cm
— Extent of invasion

— Primary tumor (pT)
    Not identified
    pT2 Organ confined
      pT2a Unilateral, involving one-half of 1 side
            ("lobe") or less
      pT2b Unilateral involving more than one-half
            of 1 side ("lobe") but not both sides
            ("lobes")
      pT2c Bilateral disease
    pT3 Extraprostatic extension
      pT3a Extraprostatic extension
      pT3b Seminal vesicle invasion
    pT4 Invasion of bladder and/or rectum
— Regional lymph nodes (pN)
    pNX Cannot be assessed
    pN0 No regional lymph node metastasis
    pN1 Metastasis in regional lymph node or nodes
    Specify
      Number examined
      Number involved
— Distant metastasis (pM)
    pMX Distant metastasis cannot be assessed
    pM1 Distant metastasis
      pM1a Distant metastasis, non-regional lymph
            node(s)
      pM1b Distant metastasis, bone(s)
      pM1c Distant metastasis, other site(s)

Note 1: When more than 1 site of metastasis is present,
the most advanced category (pM1c) is used

— Margins (check all that apply)
    Cannot be assessed
    Benign glands at surgical margin
    Margins uninvolved by invasive carcinoma
    Margin(s) involved by invasive carcinoma
      Unifocal
      Multifocal
      Apical
      Bladder neck
      Anterior
      Lateral
      Posterolateral (neurovascular bundle)
      Posterior
      Other(s) (specify)
— Extraprostatic extension (check all that apply)
    Absent
    Present
      Unifocal
      Multifocal
    Indeterminate
— Seminal vesicle invasion (invasion of muscular wall
required)
    Absent
    Present
    No seminal vesicle present
— Perineural invasion
    Absent
    Present
— Venous (large vessel) invasion (V)
    Absent
    Present

Indeterminate
— Lymphatic (small vessel) invasion (L)
    Absent
    Present
    Indeterminate
— Additional pathologic findings (check all that apply)
    None identified
    High-grade prostatic intraepithelial neoplasia (PIN)
    Inflammation (specify type)
    Atypical adenomatous hyperplasia
    Benign prostatic hyperplasia
    Other (specify)
— Comment(s)

Retinoblastoma—enucleation, partial or complete exenteration

Applies to retinoblastoma only.

Macroscopic
— Specimen type
    Enucleation
    Limited exenteration
    Complete exenteration
    Other (specify)
    Not specified
— Laterality
    Right
    Left
    Not specified
— Specimen size
    For enucleation
        Anteroposterior diameter: —— mm
        Horizontal diameter: —— mm
        Vertical diameter: —— mm
        Length of optic nerve: —— mm
        Diameter of optic nerve: —— mm
            Cannot be determined (see Comment)
    For exenteration:
        Greatest dimension: —— cm
        Additional dimensions: ×   —— cm
        Cannot be determined (see Comment)
— Tumor site (macroscopic examination/transillumination) (check all that apply)
    Cannot be determined
    Superotemporal quadrant of globe
    Superonasal quadrant of globe
    Inferotemporal quadrant of globe
    Inferonasal quadrant of globe
    Anterior chamber
    Extrascleral extension
    Optic nerve
— Tumor basal dimensions on transillumination
    Cannot be determined
    Size: ×   —— mm
— Tumor dimensions after sectioning
    Cannot be determined
    Base at cut edge: —— mm
    Height at cut edge: —— mm

Maximal tumor height: —— mm
— Tumor location after sectioning:
    Cannot be determined
    Distance from anterior edge of tumor to limbus at cut edge: mm
    Distance of posterior margin of tumor base from edge of optic disc: mm
— Tumor involvement or gross pathology of other ocular structures (check all that apply)
    Cannot be determined
    Optic disc
    Choroid, minimal (Bruch's membrane destroyed by 3 or less microscopic cell clusters without deeper penetration)
    Choroid, massive (anything beyond minimal)
    Vitreous
    Retinal detachment
    Ciliary body
    Iris
    Lens
    Anterior chamber
    Angle
    Sclera
    Cornea

Microscopic
— Histologic features (check all that apply)
    Cannot be determined
    Undifferentiated
        Differentiated
        Homer Wright rosettes
        Flexner–Wintersteiner rosettes
        Fleurettes
    Necrotic
— Growth pattern
    Cannot be determined
    Endophytic
    Exophytic
    Combined exophytic/endophytic
    Diffuse
— Extent of optic nerve invasion
    Cannot be determined
    None
    Anterior to lamina cribrosa
    At lamina cribrosa
    Posterior to lamina but not to end of nerve
    To cut end of optic nerve
— Involvement of other structures (check all that apply)
    Cannot be determined
    Choroid
    Vitreous
    Sclera
    Vortex vein
    Iris
    Other(s) (specify)
— Extent of invasion
— Primary tumor (pT)
    pTX   Primary tumor cannot be assessed
    pT0   No evidence of primary tumor
    pT1   Tumor confined to the retina, the vitreous, or subretinal space. No optic nerve or choroidal invasion

pT2 Minimal invasion of the optic nerve and/or optic coats
    pT2a Tumor invades optic nerve up to, but not through, the level of the lamina cribrosa
    pT2b Tumor invades choroid focally
    pT2c Tumor invades optic nerve up to, but not through, the level of the lamina cribrosa and invades the choroid focally
pT3 Significant invasion of the optic nerve and/or optic coats
    pT3a Tumor invades optic nerve through the level of the lamina cribrosa but not to the line of resection
    pT3b Tumor massively invades the choroid
    pT3c Tumor invades the optic nerve through the level of the lamina cribrosa but not to the line of resection and massively invades the choroid
pT4 Extraocular tumor extension that includes any of the following: invasion of optic nerve to the line of resection; invasion of orbit through the sclera; extension both anteriorly or posteriorly into the orbit; extension into the brain; extension to, but not through, the chiasm; extension into the brain beyond the chiasm
— Regional lymph nodes (pN)
  pNX Regional lymph nodes cannot be assessed
  pN0 No regional lymph node metastasis
  pN1 Regional lymph node metastasis
— Distant metastasis (pM)
  pMX Cannot be assessed
  pM1 Distant metastasis
    pM1a Bone marrow
    pM1b Other sites
    *Specify, if known
— Margins
  Cannot be assessed
  No tumor at margins
  Tumor present at surgical margin of optic nerve
  Extrascleral extension (for enucleation specimens)
  Other margin involved (specify)
— Additional pathologic findings (check all that apply)
  None identified
  Calcifications
  Mitotic rate: Number of mitoses per 40× objective with a field area of 0.152 mm^2
  Necrosis
  Apoptosis
  Basophilic vascular deposits
  Inflammatory cells
  Hemorrhage
  Neovascularization (specify site)
  Other (specify)
— Comment(s)

Skin—carcinoma—resection

Excludes eyelid, vulva, and penis. Excludes melanoma, sarcoma, and hematopoietic malignancy.

Macroscopic
— Specimen type
  Ellipse
  Shavings†
  Curettings
  Other (specify)
  Not specified
— Tumor site
  Specify, if known
  Not specified
— Tumor size
  Greatest dimension: ——— cm
  Additional dimensions: × ——— cm
  Cannot be determined (see Comment)
— Tumor features
  Raised
  Flat
  Ulcerated
  Unpigmented
  Pigmented
  Necrosis
  Hemorrhage
  Indeterminate

Microscopic
— Histologic type (check all that apply)
  Basal cell carcinoma (BCC) (Note: not routinely staged or reported to cancer registries)
    Superficial BCC
    Nodular BCC (solid, adenoid cystic)
    Infiltrating BCC
    Sclerosing BCC (desmoplastic, morpheic)
    Fibroepithelial BCC
    BCC with adnexal differentiation
      Follicular BCC
      Eccrine BCC
    Basosquamous carcinoma
    Keratotic BCC
    Pigmented BCC
    BCC in basal cell nevus syndrome
    Other (specify)
  Squamous cell carcinoma (SCC) (Note: not routinely staged or reported to cancer registries)
    Spindle cell (sarcomatoid) SCC
    Acantholytic SCC
    Verrucous SCC
    SCC with horn formation
    Lymphoepithelial SCC
    Papillary SCC
    Clear cell SCC
    Small cell SCC
    Post-traumatic (e.g., "Marjolin ulcer")
    Metaplastic ("carcinosarcomatous") SCC
    Keratoacanthoma
    Other (specify)
  Paget's disease
    Mammary Paget's disease
    Extramammary Paget's disease (specify site)
  Adnexal carcinoma
    Eccrine carcinoma
      Sclerosing sweat duct carcinoma (syringomatous carcinoma, microcystic adnexal carcinoma)

Malignant mixed tumor of the skin (malignant chondroid syringoma)
Porocarcinoma
Malignant nodular hidradenoma
Malignant eccrine spiradenoma
Mucinous eccrine carcinoma
Adenoid cystic eccrine carcinoma
Aggressive digital papillary adenoma/adenocarcinoma
Apocrine carcinoma
Sebaceous carcinoma
Tricholemmocarcinoma
Malignant pilomatricoma (matrical carcinoma)
Other (specify)
Merkel cell carcinoma
Mitotic activity: fewer than 10 mitotic figures per 10 HPF
Mitotic activity: 10 or more mitotic figures per 10 HPF
Other (specify)
Carcinoma, type cannot be determined
— Histologic grade
Not applicable
GX Cannot be assessed
G1 Well differentiated
G2 Moderately differentiated
G3 Poorly differentiated
G4 Undifferentiated
— Extent of invasion
— Primary tumor (pT)
pTX Primary tumor cannot be assessed
pT0 No evidence of primary tumor
pTis Carcinoma in situ
pT1 Tumor 2 cm or less in greatest dimension
    pT1a Limited to dermis or 2 mm or less in thickness
    pT1b Limited to dermis and more than 2 mm in thickness, but not more than 6 mm in thickness
    pT1c Invading the subcutis and/or more than 6 mm in thickness
pT2 Tumor more than 2 cm but not more than 5 cm in greatest dimension
    pT2a Limited to dermis or 2 mm or less in thickness
    pT2b Limited to dermis and more than 2 mm in thickness but not more than 6 mm in thickness
    pT2c Invading the subcutis and/or more than 6 mm in thickness
pT3: Tumor more than 5 cm in greatest dimension
    pT3a Limited to dermis or 2 mm or less in thickness
    pT3b Limited to dermis and more than 2 mm in thickness, but not more than 6 mm in thickness
    pT3 Invading the subcutis and/or more than 6 mm in thickness
pT4 Tumor invades the deep extradermal tissue (e.g., cartilage, skeletal muscle, bone)
    pT4a 6 mm or less in thickness
    pT4b More than 6 mm in thickness

— Regional lymph nodes (pN)
pNX Regional lymph nodes cannot be assessed
pN0 No regional lymph node metastasis
pN1 Regional lymph node metastasis
Specify
    Number examined
    Number involved
— Distant metastasis (pM)
pMX Presence of distant metastasis cannot be assessed
pM1 Distant metastasis
    Specify site(s), if known
— Margins (check all that apply)
Lateral margins
    Cannot be assessed
    Uninvolved by invasive carcinoma
        Distance of invasive carcinoma from closest lateral margin: mm
        Specify location(s), if possible
    Involved by invasive carcinoma
        Specify location(s), if possible
    Uninvolved by carcinoma in situ
        Distance of carcinoma in situ from closest margin: mm
        Specify location(s), if possible
    Involved by carcinoma in situ
        Specify location(s), if possible
Deep margin
    Cannot be assessed
    Uninvolved by invasive carcinoma
        Distance of invasive carcinoma from margin: mm
        Specify location(s), if possible
    Involved by invasive carcinoma
        Specify location(s), if possible
— Lymphatic (small vessel) invasion (L)
    Absent
    Present
    Indeterminate
— Venous (large vessel) invasion (V)
    Absent
    Present
    Indeterminate
— Perineural invasion
    Absent
    Present
    Indeterminate
— Additional pathologic findings
    Specify
— Comment(s)

Small intestine—polypectomy, segmental resection, Whipple procedure (pancreaticoduodenectomy, partial or complete, with or without partial gastrectomy)

Applies to all invasive carcinomas of the small intestine, including those with focal endocrine differentiation. Excludes carcinoid tumors, lymphomas, and stromal tumors (sarcomas).

Macroscopic
— Specimen type
   Polypectomy
   Segmental resection
   Whipple procedure
   Other (specify)
   Not specified
— Tumor site
   Duodenum
   Jejunum
   Ileum
   Not specified
— Tumor configuration
   Exophytic (polypoid)
   Infiltrative
   Ulcerating
   Other (specify)
— Tumor size
   Greatest dimension: —— cm
   Additional dimensions: × —— cm
   Cannot be determined (see Comment)
— Other organs received
   None
   Other (specify)

Microscopic
— Histologic type
   Adenocarcinoma (not otherwise characterized)
   Mucinous adenocarcinoma (greater than 50%
      mucinous)
   Signet ring cell carcinoma (greater than 50% signet
      ring cells)
   Small cell carcinoma
   Squamous cell carcinoma
   Adenosquamous carcinoma
   Medullary carcinoma
   Undifferentiated carcinoma
   Mixed carcinoid–adenocarcinoma
   Other (specify)
   Carcinoma, type cannot be determined
— Histologic grade
   Not applicable
   GX   Cannot be assessed
   G1   Well differentiated
   G2   Moderately differentiated
   G3   Poorly differentiated
   G4   Undifferentiated
   Other (specify)
— Extent of invasion
— Primary tumor (pT)
   pTX   Cannot be assessed
   pT0   No evidence of primary tumor
   pTis   Carcinoma in situ
   pT1   Tumor invades lamina propria or submucosa
   pT2   Tumor invades muscularis propria
   pT3   Tumor invades through the muscularis propria
         into the subserosa or the nonperitonealized
         perimuscular tissue with extension of 2 cm or
         less
   pT4   Tumor perforates the visceral peritoneum or
         directly invades other organs or structures
— Regional lymph nodes (pN)

pNX   Cannot be assessed
pN0   No regional lymph node metastasis
pN1   Metastasis in regional lymph nodes
Specify
   Number examined
   Number involved
— Distant metastasis (pM)
   pMX   Cannot be assessed
   pM1   Distant metastasis
      Specify site(s), if known
— Margins (check all that apply)
— Polypectomy specimens only
   Cannot be assessed
   Mucosal margin
      Uninvolved by carcinoma
      Involved by carcinoma
      Involved by adenoma
   Deep margin
      Uninvolved by carcinoma
         Distance of carcinoma from margin: mm
      Involved by carcinoma
— Segmental resection or pancreaticoduodenectomy
   (Whipple)
   Proximal (small bowel or stomach) margin
      Cannot be assessed
      Uninvolved by invasive carcinoma
      Involved by invasive carcinoma
      Carcinoma in situ/adenoma absent at proximal
         margin
      Carcinoma in situ/adenoma present at proximal
         margin
      Carcinoma in situ/adenoma not applicable (gastric
         margin)
   Distal (bowel) margin
      Cannot be assessed
      Uninvolved by invasive carcinoma
      Involved by invasive carcinoma
      Carcinoma in situ/adenoma absent at distal margin
      Carcinoma in situ/adenoma present at distal
         margin
   Circumferential/radial (mesenteric or retroperitoneal)
      margin
      Cannot be assessed
      Uninvolved by invasive carcinoma
      Involved by invasive carcinoma
   Bile duct margin
      Not applicable
      Cannot be assessed
      Margin uninvolved by invasive carcinoma
      Margin involved by invasive carcinoma
   Pancreatic margin
      Not applicable
      Cannot be assessed
      Margin uninvolved by invasive carcinoma
      Margin involved by invasive carcinoma
   If margins are uninvolved, distance of invasive
      carcinoma from closest margin: mm
   Specify margin (if possible)
— Venous/lymphatic (large/small vessel) invasion (V/L)
   Absent
   Present

Indeterminate
— Perineural invasion
    Absent
    Present
    Indeterminate
— Additional pathologic findings (check all that apply)
    None identified
    Adenoma(s)
    Crohn's disease
    Celiac disease
    Epithelial dysplasia
    Other polyps (type[s])
    Other (specify)
— Comment(s)

Stomach—biopsy (use of checklist for biopsy specimens is optional)

Applies to all carcinomas of the stomach.

Macroscopic
— Specimen type
    Incisional biopsy
    Excisional biopsy (polypectomy)
    Other (specify)
    Not specified
— Tumor site
    Specify, if known
    Not specified

Microscopic
— Histologic type
    Adenocarcinoma, intestinal type
    Adenocarcinoma, diffuse type
    Papillary adenocarcinoma
    Tubular adenocarcinoma
    Mucinous adenocarcinoma (greater than 50% mucinous)
    Signet ring cell carcinoma (greater than 50% signet ring cells)
    Other (specify)
    Carcinoma, type cannot be determined
— Histologic grade
    Not applicable
    GX   Cannot be assessed
    G1   Well differentiated
    G2   Moderately differentiated
    G3   Poorly differentiated
    G4   Undifferentiated
    Other (specify)
— Extent of invasion (deepest)
    Cannot be determined
    Lamina propria
    Muscularis mucosae
    Submucosa
    Muscularis propria
— Margins (polypectomy only)
    Not applicable
    Cannot be assessed
    Mucosal margin

    Uninvolved by invasive carcinoma
    Involved by invasive carcinoma
    Involved by adenoma
  Deep margin
    Uninvolved by invasive carcinoma
      Distance of invasive carcinoma from margin: mm
    Involved by invasive carcinoma
— Additional pathologic findings (check all that apply)
    None identified
    Intestinal metaplasia
    Dysplasia
    Gastritis (type)
    Other (specify)
— Comment(s)

Stomach—resection

Applies to all carcinomas of the stomach.

Macroscopic
— Specimen type
    Partial gastrectomy
      Proximal
      Distal
      Other (specify)
    Total gastrectomy
    Other (specify)
    Not specified
— Tumor site (check all that apply)
    Cardia
    Fundus
      Anterior wall
      Posterior wall
    Body
      Anterior wall
      Posterior wall
      Lesser curvature
      Greater curvature
    Antrum
      Anterior wall
      Posterior wall
      Lesser curvature
      Greater curvature
    Other (specify)
    Not specified
— Tumor configuration
    Exophytic (polypoid)
    Infiltrative
    Diffusely infiltrative (linitis plastica)
    Expansile (noninfiltrative)
    Ulcerating
    Annular
— Tumor size
    Greatest dimension: ———— cm
    Additional dimensions: × ———— cm
    Cannot be determined (see Comment)

Microscopic
— Histologic type
    Adenocarcinoma

Intestinal type
Diffuse type
Papillary adenocarcinoma
Tubular adenocarcinoma
Mucinous adenocarcinoma (greater than 50%
    mucinous)
Signet ring cell carcinoma (greater than 50% signet
    ring cells)
Other (specify)
Carcinoma, type cannot be determined
— Histologic grade
    Not applicable
    GX   Cannot be assessed
    G1   Well differentiated
    G2   Moderately differentiated
    G3   Poorly differentiated
    G4   Undifferentiated
    Other (specify)
— Extent of invasion
— Primary tumor (pT)
    pTX   Cannot be assessed
    pT0   No evidence of primary tumor
    pTis   Carcinoma in situ
    pT1   Tumor invades lamina propria or submucosa
        pT1a   Tumor invades lamina propria
        pT1b   Tumor invades submucosa
    pT2 Tumor invades muscularis propria or subserosa
        pT2a   Tumor invades muscularis propria
        pT2b   Tumor invades subserosa
    pT3   Tumor penetrates serosa (visceral peritoneum)
        without invasion of adjacent structures
    pT4   Tumor directly invades adjacent structures
— Regional lymph nodes (pN)
    pNX   Cannot be assessed
    pN0   No regional lymph node metastasis
    pN1   Metastasis in 1 to 6 perigastric lymph nodes
    pN2   Metastasis in 7 to 15 perigastric lymph nodes
    pN3   Metastasis in greater than 15 perigastric lymph
        nodes
    Specify
        Number examined
        Number involved
— Distant metastasis (pM)
    pMX   Cannot be assessed
    pM1   Distant metastasis
        Specify site(s), if known
— Margins (check all that apply)
    Cannot be assessed
    Proximal margin
        Cannot be assessed
        Uninvolved by invasive carcinoma
        Involved by invasive carcinoma
        Carcinoma in situ/adenoma absent at proximal
            margin
        Carcinoma in situ/adenoma present at proximal
            margin
    Distal margin
        Cannot be assessed
        Uninvolved by invasive carcinoma
        Involved by invasive carcinoma
        Carcinoma in situ/adenoma absent at distal margin

Carcinoma in situ/adenoma present at distal
    margin
Omental (radial) margins
    Cannot be assessed
    Uninvolved by invasive carcinoma
    Lesser omental margin involved by invasive
        carcinoma
    Greater omental margin involved by invasive
        carcinoma
    Distance of invasive carcinoma from closest margin:
        mm
        Specify margin
— Lymphatic (small vessel) invasion (L)
    Absent
    Present
    Indeterminate
— Venous (large vessel) invasion (V)
    Absent
    Present
    Indeterminate
— Perineural invasion
    Absent
    Present
— Additional pathologic findings (check all that apply)
    None identified
    Intestinal metaplasia
    Dysplasia
    Gastritis (type)
    Polyp(s) (type[s])
    Other (specify)
— Comment(s)

Testis—radical orchiectomy

Applies to all malignant germ cell and malignant sex cord–stromal tumors of the testis, exclusive of paratesticular malignancies.

Macroscopic
— Serum hormone levels
    (see optional Serum Tumor Marker Classification [S] in
        Microscopic section)
    Unknown
    Serum marker studies within normal limits
    α-Fetoprotein (AFP) elevation
    Beta-subunit of human chorionic gonadotropin
        (β-hCG) elevation
    Lactate dehydrogenase (LDH) elevation

Macroscopic
— Laterality
    Right
    Left
    Both
    Not specified
— Focality
    Unifocal
    Multifocal
— Tumor size
    Greatest dimension of main tumor mass: —— cm
    Additional dimensions: ×   —— cm

Greatest dimensions of additional tumor nodules:
___ cm, ___ cm, etc.
Cannot be determined (see Comment)

Microscopic
— Histologic type
    Intratubular germ cell neoplasm, unclassified only
    Seminoma, classic type
    Seminoma with syncytiotrophoblastic cells
    Mixed germ cell tumor (specify components and percentages)
    Embryonal carcinoma
    Yolk sac tumor
    Choriocarcinoma, biphasic
    Choriocarcinoma, monophasic
    Placental site trophoblastic tumor
    Teratoma
        Mature
        Immature
    With a secondary malignant component (specify type)
    Monodermal teratoma
        Carcinoid
        Primitive neuroectodermal tumor
        Other (specify)
    Polyembryoma
    Diffuse embryoma
    Spermatocytic seminoma
    Spermatocytic seminoma with a sarcomatous component
    Testicular scar
    Other (specify)
    Mixed germ cell–sex cord–stromal tumors
        Gonadoblastoma
        Others (specify)
    Malignant neoplasm, type cannot be determined
— Extent of invasion
— Primary tumor (pT)
    pTX Cannot be assessed
    pT0 No evidence of primary tumor
    pTis Intratubular germ cell neoplasia only (carcinoma in situ)
    pT1 Tumor limited to the testis and epididymis without vascular/lymphatic invasion (tumor may invade tunica albuginea but not tunica vaginalis)
    pT2 Tumor limited to the testis and epididymis with vascular/lymphatic invasion or tumor extending through tunica albuginea with involvement of tunica vaginalis
    pT3 Tumor invades spermatic cord with or without vascular/lymphatic invasion
    pT4 Tumor invades scrotum with or without vascular/lymphatic invasion
— Regional lymph nodes (pN)
    pNX Cannot be assessed
    pN0 No regional lymph node metastasis
    pN1 Metastasis with a lymph node mass less than 2 cm in greatest dimension and 5 or fewer positive nodes, none more than 2 cm in greatest dimension
    pN2 Metastasis with a lymph node mass greater than 2 cm but not more than 5 cm in greatest dimension, or more than 5 nodes positive, none

greater than 5 cm; or evidence of extranodal extension of tumor
    pN3 Metastasis with a lymph node mass greater than 5 cm in greatest dimension
    Specify
        Number examined
        Number involved
— Distant metastasis (pM)
    pMX Cannot be assessed
    pM1 Distant metastasis present
        pM1a Non-regional lymph nodes or pulmonary metastasis
        pM1b Distant metastasis other than to non-regional lymph nodes and lungs
        Specify site(s), if known
— Serum tumor markers (s), if known
    SX Serum marker studies not available or performed
    S0 Serum marker study levels within normal limits

	LDH	hCG (mIU/mL)	AFP (ng/mL)
S1	$<15 \times nl$	and <5000	and <1000
S2	$15–10 \times nl$	or $5000–50,000$	or $1000–10,000$
S3	$>10 \times nl$	or $>50,000$	or $>10,000$

— Margins (check all that apply)
    Spermatic cord margin
        Cannot be assessed
        Uninvolved by tumor
        Involved by tumor
    Other margin(s)
        Cannot be assessed
        Uninvolved by tumor (specify)
        Involved by tumor (specify)
        Not applicable
— Direct extension of invasive tumor (check all that apply)
    Rete testis
    Epididymis
    Perihilar fat
    Spermatic cord
    Tunica vaginalis
    Scrotal wall
    None of the above
— Venous/lymphatic (large/small vessel) invasion (V/L)
    Absent
    Present
    Indeterminate
— Additional pathologic findings (check all that apply)
    None identified
    Intratubular germ cell neoplasia
    Hemosiderin-laden macrophages
    Atrophy
    Other (specify)
— Comment(s)

Testis—retroperitoneal lymphadenectomy for malignant testicular tumor

Applies to all malignant germ cell and malignant sex cord–stromal tumors of the testis, exclusive of paratesticular malignancies.

— Pre-lymphadenectomy treatment
   Chemo/radiation therapy
   No chemo/radiation therapy
   Unknown
— Serum hormone levels
   Unknown
   Serum marker studies within normal limits
   α-Fetoprotein (AFP) elevation
   Beta subunit of human chorionic gonadotropin
     (β-hCG) elevation
   Lactate dehydrogenase (LDH) elevation

Macroscopic

— Specimen site(s)
— Number of nodal groups present
   Cannot be determined
— Size of largest metastasis
   Greatest dimension: —— cm
   Additional dimensions: ×   —— cm

Microscopic

— Viability of tumor (if applicable)
   Viable tumor present
   Nonviable tumor present
   No tumor present
— Histologic type of metastatic tumor
   Seminoma, classic type
   Seminoma with syncytiotrophoblastic cells
   Mixed germ cell tumor (specify components and
     percentages)
   Embryonal carcinoma
   Yolk sac tumor
   Choriocarcinoma, biphasic
   Choriocarcinoma, monophasic
   Placental site trophoblastic tumor
   Teratoma
     Mature
     Immature
     With a secondary malignant component (specify
       type)
   Monodermal teratoma
     Carcinoid
     Primitive neuroectodermal tumor
   Polyembryoma
   Diffuse embryoma
   Spermatocytic seminoma
   Spermatocytic seminoma with a sarcomatous
     component
   Other (specify)
   Malignant neoplasm, type cannot be determined
— Regional lymph nodes (pN)
   pNX Cannot be assessed
   pN0 No regional lymph node metastasis
   pN1 Metastasis with a lymph node mass less than 2
       cm in greatest dimension and 5 or fewer positive
       nodes, none greater than 2 cm in greatest
       dimension
   pN2 Metastasis with a lymph node mass greater than
       2 cm but no more than 5 cm in greatest
       dimension, or more than 5 nodes positive, none
       greater than 5 cm; or evidence of extranodal
       extension of tumor

   pN3 Metastasis in a lymph node greater than 5 cm in
       greatest dimension
   Specify
     Total number examined
     Total number involved
— Non-regional lymph node metastasis (M1a)
   Not applicable
   Absent
   Present
— Comment(s)

Trophoblast—dilation and curettage/resection

Applies to all gestational trophoblastic malignancies.

Macroscopic

— Specimen type
   Dilation and curettage
   Hysterectomy
   Radical hysterectomy
   Pelvic exenteration
   Other (specify)
   Not specified
— Tumor site
   Specify, if known
   Not specified
— Fetal tissue
   Absent
   Present
— Tumor size
   Greatest dimension: —— cm
   Additional dimensions: ×   —— cm
   Cannot be determined (see Comment)
— Other organs involved by tumor (check all that apply)
   Not applicable
   Specify organ(s) with direct extension
   Specify organ(s) with separate metastasis

Microscopic

— Histologic type
   Hydatidiform mole
     Complete
     Partial
     Invasive
   Choriocarcinoma
   Placental site trophoblastic tumor
   Epithelioid trophoblastic tumor
   Other (specify type)
   Malignant trophoblastic tumor, type cannot be
     determined
— Extent of invasion
— Primary tumor (pT)
   TNM (FIGO)
   pTX (—)   Primary tumor cannot be assessed
   pT0 (—)   No evidence of primary tumor
   pT1 (I)   Tumor confined to uterus
   pT2 (II)   Tumor extends outside of the uterus but is
             limited to the genital structures (adnexa,
             vagina, broad ligament)

— Distant metastasis (pM)
  TNM (FIGO)
  pMX (—)   Metastasis cannot be assessed
  pM1a (III) Tumor extends to the lungs with or
              without genital tract involvement
  pM1b (IV)   Tumor involves all other metastatic sites
      Specify site(s), if known
— Margins
  Cannot be assessed
  Uninvolved by malignant tumor
      Distance of malignant tumor from closest margin:
          mm
      Specify margin
  Involved by malignant tumor
      Specify margin(s)
— Venous/lymphatic (large/small vessel) invasion (V/L)
  Absent
  Present
  Indeterminate
— Additional pathologic findings (check all that apply)
  None identified
  Implantation site
  Fetal tissue (specify type)
  Fetal anomalies (specify)
  Other (specify)
— Comment(s)

Upper aerodigestive tract and minor salivary glands—incisional and excisional biopsy/resection

Applies to all invasive carcinomas of the upper aerodigestive tract: carcinomas of the oral cavity (including lip and tongue), pharynx (oropharynx, hypopharynx, nasopharynx), larynx, paranasal sinuses, and minor salivary glands.

Macroscopic
— Specimen type
  Incisional biopsy
  Excisional biopsy
  Resection (specify type)
  Other (specify)
  Not specified
— Tumor site
  Lip
  Oral cavity
  Pharynx
      Oropharynx
      Hypopharynx
      Nasopharynx
  Larynx
      Supraglottis
      Glottis
      Subglottis
  Paranasal sinus(es)
      Maxillary
      Ethmoid
  Other (specify)
  Not specified

— Tumor size
  Greatest dimension: —— cm
  Additional dimensions: ×   —— cm
  Cannot be determined (see Comment)

Microscopic
— Histologic type
  Carcinomas of the upper aerodigestive tract
      Squamous cell carcinoma, conventional
      Squamous cell carcinoma, variant
          Verrucous squamous cell carcinoma
          Spindle cell carcinoma
          Adenosquamous carcinoma
          Basaloid squamous cell carcinoma
          Papillary squamous cell carcinoma
          Lymphoepithelioma-like carcinoma (non-nasopharyngeal)
      Sinonasal carcinoma
          Keratinizing sinonasal carcinoma
          Nonkeratinizing sinonasal carcinoma (transitional type)
          Undifferentiated sinonasal carcinoma (SNUC)
      Nasopharyngeal carcinoma
          Keratinizing nasopharyngeal carcinoma
          Nonkeratinizing nasopharyngeal carcinoma, differentiated
          Undifferentiated nasopharyngeal carcinoma, (lymphoepithelioma)
          Nonkeratinizing nasopharyngeal carcinoma, mixed differentiated and undifferentiated
          Adenocarcinoma, salivary gland type (specify type)
      Adenocarcinoma, non-salivary gland type
          Papillary adenocarcinoma
          Intestinal-type adenocarcinoma
          Adenocarcinoma, not otherwise specified (NOS)
      Neuroendocrine carcinoma
          Typical carcinoid tumor (well differentiated neuroendocrine carcinoma)
          Atypical carcinoid tumor (moderately differentiated neuroendocrine carcinoma)
          Small cell carcinoma (poorly differentiated neuroendocrine carcinoma)
          Other (specify)
          Carcinoma, type cannot be determined
  Carcinomas of minor salivary glands
      Acinic cell carcinoma
      Adenoid cystic carcinoma
      Adenocarcinoma not otherwise specified (NOS)
      Adenosquamous carcinoma
      Squamous cell carcinoma
      Carcinoma ex pleomorphic adenoma (malignant mixed tumor)
      Carcinosarcoma (true malignant mixed tumor)
      Mucoepidermoid carcinoma, low grade
      Mucoepidermoid carcinoma, intermediate grade
      Mucoepidermoid carcinoma, high grade
      Polymorphous low-grade adenocarcinoma
      Epithelial–myoepithelial carcinoma
      Basal cell adenocarcinoma
      Sebaceous carcinoma
      Cystadenocarcinoma

Mucinous carcinoma (colloid carcinoma)
Oncocytic carcinoma
Salivary duct carcinoma
Myoepithelial carcinoma (malignant
    myoepithelioma)
Small cell carcinoma
Undifferentiated carcinoma
Other (specify)
Carcinoma, type cannot be determined
— Histologic grade
Not applicable
GX Cannot be assessed
G1 Well differentiated
G2 Moderately differentiated
G3 Poorly differentiated
Other (specify)
— Extent of invasion (see appropriate site below)

Note 1: The phrases in italics include clinical findings
required for AJCC staging. This clinical information may
be unknown to the pathologist. It is included here only
for the sake of completeness

— Primary tumor (pT): lip and oral cavity
    pTX   Cannot be assessed
    pT0   No evidence of primary tumor
    pTis Carcinoma in situ
    pT1   Tumor 2 cm or less in greatest dimension
    pT2   Tumor more than 2 cm but not more than 4 cm in
          greatest dimension
    pT3   Tumor more than 4 cm in greatest dimension
    pT4a Lip: Tumor invades through cortical bone,
          inferior alveolar nerve, floor of mouth, skin
    Oral cavity: Tumor invades through cortical bone,
          deep/extrinsic muscle of tongue, maxillary sinus,
          skin
    pT4b: Tumor invades masticator space, pterygoid
          plates, skull base, internal carotid artery
— Primary tumor (pT): Oropharynx
    pTX   Cannot be assessed
    pT0   No evidence of primary tumor
    pTis Carcinoma in situ
    pT1   Tumor 2 cm or less in greatest dimension
    pT2   Tumor more than 2 cm but not more than 4 cm in
          greatest dimension
    pT3   Tumor more than 4 cm in greatest dimension
    pT4a Tumor invades larynx, deep/extrinsic muscle of
          tongue, medial pterygoid muscles, hard palate
          or mandible
    pT4b Tumor invades lateral pterygoid muscle,
          pterygoid plates, lateral nasopharynx, skull base,
          carotid artery
— Primary tumor (pT): Hypopharynx
    pTX   Cannot be assessed
    pT0   No evidence of primary tumor
    pTis Carcinoma in situ
    pT1   Tumor limited to one subsite of hypopharynx
          and 2 cm or less in greatest dimension
    pT2   Tumor invades more than one subsite of
          hypopharynx or an adjacent site, or measures
          more than 2 cm but not more than 4 cm in
          greatest dimension, *without fixation of hemilarynx*

pT3   Tumor measures more than 4 cm in greatest
      dimension, *or with fixation of hemilarynx*
pT4a Tumor invades thyroid/cricoid cartilage, hyoid
      bone, thyroid gland, esophagus, central
      compartment soft tissue
pT4b Tumor invades prevertebral fascia, carotid artery,
      mediastinal structures
— Primary tumor (pT): Nasopharynx
    pTX   Cannot be assessed
    pT0   No evidence of primary tumor
    pTis Carcinoma in situ
    pT1   Tumor confined to nasopharynx
    pT2a Without parapharyngeal extension
    pT2b Tumor extends to soft tissue of oropharynx
          and/or nasal fossa with parapharyngeal
          extension
    pT3   Tumor invades bony structures and/or
          paranasal sinuses
    pT4   Tumor with intracranial extension and/or
          involvement of cranial nerves, infratemporal
          fossa, hypopharynx, orbit, and masticator space
— Primary tumor (pT): Supraglottis
    pTX   Cannot be assessed
    pT0   No evidence of primary tumor
    pTis Carcinoma in situ
    pT1   Tumor limited to one subsite of supraglottis *with
          normal vocal cord mobility*
    pT2   Tumor invades mucosa of more than one
          adjacent subsite of supraglottis or glottis or
          adjacent region outside the supraglottis (mucosa
          of base of tongue, vallecula, medial wall of
          pyriform sinus) *without fixation of the larynx*
    pT3   Tumor limited to larynx *with vocal cord fixation*
          and/or invades any of the following: postcricoid
          area, pre-epiglottic tissues, paraglottic space,
          thyroid cartilage
    pT4a Tumor invades through thyroid cartilage,
          trachea, soft tissues of neck, deep/extrinsic
          muscle of tongue, strap muscles, thyroid,
          esophagus
    pT4b Tumor invades prevertebral space, mediastinal
          structures, carotid artery
— Primary tumor (pT): Glottis
    pTX   Cannot be assessed
    pT0   No evidence of primary tumor
    pTis Carcinoma in situ
    pT1a Tumor limited to one vocal cord (may involve
          anterior or posterior commissure) *with normal
          mobility*
    pT1b Tumor involves both vocal cords
    pT2   Tumor extends to supraglottis and/or subglottis,
          and/or with impaired vocal cord mobility
    pT3   Tumor invades paraglottic space, erodes thyroid
          cartilage, *with vocal cord fixation*
    pT4a Tumor invades through thyroid cartilage,
          trachea, soft tissues of neck, thyroid, esophagus
    pT4b Tumor invades prevertebral space, mediastinal
          structures, carotid artery
— Primary tumor (pT): Subglottis
    pTX   Cannot be assessed
    pT0   No evidence of primary tumor

pTis Carcinoma in situ
pT1 Tumor limited to subglottis
pT2 Tumor extends to vocal cord(s) *with normal or impaired mobility*
pT3 Tumor limited to larynx *with vocal cord fixation*
pT4a Tumor invades through cricoid or thyroid cartilage trachea, soft tissues of neck, thyroid, esophagus
pT4b Tumor invades prevertebral space, mediastinal structures, carotid artery

— Primary tumor (pT): Maxillary sinus
pTX Cannot be assessed
pT0 No evidence of primary tumor
pTis Carcinoma in situ
pT1 Tumor limited to the antral mucosa with no erosion or destruction of bone
pT2 Tumor causing bone erosion or destruction into hard palate and/or middle nasal meatus
pT3 Tumor invades any of the following: bone of posterior wall of maxillary sinus, subcutaneous tissues, floor or medial wall of orbit, pterygoid fossa, ethmoid sinuses
pT4a Tumor invades anterior orbit, cheek, skin, pterygoid plates, infratemporal fossa, cribriform plate, sphenoid sinus, frontal sinus
pT4b Tumor invades orbital apex, dura, brain, middle cranial fossa, cranial nerves other than V2, nasopharynx, clivus

— Primary tumor (pT): Nasal cavity and ethmoid sinus
pTX Cannot be assessed
pT0 No evidence of primary tumor
pTis Carcinoma in situ
pT1 Tumor confined to one subsite
pT2 Tumor involves two subsites or adjacent nasoethmoidal site
pT3 Tumor invades medial wall/floor orbit, maxillary sinus, palate, cribriform plate
pT4a Tumor invades anterior orbit, skin of nose/cheek, anterior cranial fossa, pterygoid plates, sphenoid and/or frontal sinus
pT4b Tumor invades orbital apex, dura, brain, middle cranial fossa, cranial nerves other than V2, nasopharynx, clivus

— Regional lymph nodes (pN): All aerodigestive sites except nasopharynx
pNX Cannot be assessed
pN0 No regional lymph node metastasis
pN1 Metastasis in a single ipsilateral lymph node, 3 cm or less in greatest dimension
pN2a Metastasis in a single ipsilateral lymph node, more than 3 cm but not more than 6 cm in greatest dimension
pN2b Metastasis in multiple ipsilateral lymph nodes, none more than 6 cm in greatest dimension
pN2c Metastasis in bilateral or contralateral lymph nodes, none more than 6 cm in greatest dimension
pN3 Metastasis in a lymph node more than 6 cm in greatest dimension
Specify
Number examined

Number involved
— Regional lymph nodes (pN): Nasopharynx
pNX Cannot be assessed
pN0 No regional lymph node metastasis
pN1 Unilateral metastasis in lymph node(s) 6 cm or less in greatest dimension, above supraclavicular fossa
pN2 Bilateral metastasis in lymph node(s) 6 cm or less in greatest dimension, above supraclavicular fossa
pN3a Metastasis in lymph node(s) more than 6 cm in greatest dimension
pN3b Metastasis in lymph node(s) residing wholly or in part in the supraclavicular fossa
Specify
Number examined
Number involved
Extracapsular extension of nodal tumor
Absent
Present
Indeterminate
— Distant metastasis (pM)
pMX Cannot be assessed
pM1 Distant metastasis
Specify site(s), if known
— Margins (check all that apply)
Cannot be assessed
Margins uninvolved by tumor
Distance of tumor from closest margin: mm
Specify margin (if possible)
Carcinoma in situ absent
Carcinoma in situ present
Carcinoma in situ, not applicable
Margin(s) involved by tumor
Specify location(s) (if possible)
Not applicable
— Venous/lymphatic (large/small vessel) invasion (V/L)
Absent
Present
Indeterminate
— Perineural invasion
Absent
Present
— Additional pathologic findings (check all that apply)
None identified
Carcinoma in situ
Inflammation (specify type)
Epithelial hyperplasia
Epithelial dysplasia
Other (specify)
— Comment(s)

Uterine cervix—cone biopsy

Applies to all invasive carcinomas of the cervix.

Macroscopic
— Tumor site
Right superior quadrant (12 to 3 o'clock)
Right inferior quadrant (3 to 6 o'clock)

Left inferior quadrant (6 to 9 o'clock)
Left superior quadrant (9 to 12 o'clock)
Not specified

Microscopic
— Tumor size
   Dimensions: ×   ×   mm

Note 1: all dimensions important; see definition for "microinvasive carcinoma" under T1a1/IA1

   Cannot be determined (see Comment)
— Histologic type (check all that apply)
   Squamous cell carcinoma
      Keratinizing
      Nonkeratinizing
      Other (specify)
   Adenocarcinoma
      Mucinous
         Endocervical type
         Intestinal type
      Endometrioid
      Clear cell
      Other (specify)
   Other (specify)
   Carcinoma, type cannot be determined
— Histologic grade
   Not applicable
   GX   Cannot be assessed
   G1   Well differentiated
   G2   Moderately differentiated
   G3   Poorly differentiated
   G4   Undifferentiated
— Stromal invasion
   Depth: —— mm
   Horizontal extent: —— mm
   Extent cannot be assessed
— Margins (check all that apply)
   Margins cannot be assessed (e.g., obscuring
      electrocautery artifact)
   Endocervical margin
      Uninvolved by invasive carcinoma
         Distance of carcinoma from margin: mm
         Specify location, if possible
      Involved by invasive carcinoma
         Specify location, if possible
            Focal
            Diffuse
      Uninvolved by intraepithelial neoplasia
      Involved by intraepithelial neoplasia
         Specify grade
   Exocervical margin
      Uninvolved by invasive carcinoma
         Distance of carcinoma from margin: mm
         Specify location, if possible
      Involved by invasive carcinoma
         Specify location, if possible
            Focal
            Diffuse
      Uninvolved by intraepithelial neoplasia
      Involved by intraepithelial neoplasia
         Specify grade
   Deep margin

   Uninvolved by invasive carcinoma
      Distance of carcinoma from margin: mm
      Specify location, if possible
   Involved by invasive carcinoma
      Specify location, if possible
   Uninvolved by intraepithelial neoplasia
   Involved by intraepithelial neoplasia
      Specify grade
— Additional pathologic findings (check all that apply)
   None identified
   Koilocytosis
   Inflammation
   Other (specify)
— Comment(s)

Uterine cervix—colpectomy, hysterectomy, pelvic exenteration

Applies to all invasive carcinomas of the cervix.

Macroscopic
— Specimen type
   Colpectomy
   Hysterectomy
   Radical hysterectomy
   Pelvic exenteration
   Not specified
— Tumor site (check all that apply)
   Right superior quadrant
   Right inferior quadrant
   Left superior quadrant
   Left inferior quadrant
   Not specified
— Tumor size
   Greatest dimension: —— cm
   Additional dimensions: ×   —— cm
   Cannot be determined (see Comment)
— Other organs present
   None
   Right ovary
   Left ovary
   Right fallopian tube
   Left fallopian tube
   Uterine corpus
   Vagina
   Urinary bladder
   Rectum
   Other(s) (specify)

Microscopic
— Histologic type (check all that apply)
   Squamous cell carcinoma
      Keratinizing
      Nonkeratinizing
      Other (specify)
   Adenocarcinoma
      Mucinous
         Endocervical type
         Intestinal type
      Endometrioid

Clear cell
Other (specify)
Other (specify)
Carcinoma, type cannot be determined
— Histologic grade
Not applicable
GX Cannot be assessed
G1 Well differentiated
G2 Moderately differentiated
G3 Poorly differentiated
G4 Undifferentiated
— Extent of invasion
— Primary tumor (pT)
TNM (FIGO)
pTX (—)   Cannot be assessed
pT0 (—)   No evidence of primary tumor
pTis (0) Carcinoma in situ
pT1 (I)   Cervical carcinoma confined to uterus (extension to corpus should be disregarded)
pT1a (IA)   Invasive carcinoma diagnosed by microscopy only. All macroscopically visible lesions (even with superficial invasion) are pT1b/1B.
pT1a1 (IA1)   Stromal invasion 3.0 mm or less in depth and horizontal spread 7.0 mm or less ("microinvasive carcinoma")
pT1a2 (IA2)   Stromal invasion more than 3.0 mm but not more than 5.0 mm in depth and horizontal spread 7.0 mm or less
pT1b (IB)   Clinically visible lesion confined to the cervix or microscopic lesion greater than T1a2/IA2
pT1b1 (IB1)   Clinically visible lesion 4.0 cm or less in greatest dimension
pT1b2 (IB2)   Clinically visible lesion more than 4.0 cm in greatest dimension
pT2 (II)   Tumor invades beyond the uterus but not to pelvic wall or to lower third of vagina
pT2a (IIA)   Tumor without parametrial invasion
pT2b (IIB)   Tumor with parametrial invasion
pT3 (III)   Tumor extends to the pelvic wall and/or involves the lower third of the vagina and/or causes hydronephrosis or nonfunctioning kidney
pT3a (IIIA)   Tumor involves lower third of vagina, but not pelvic wall
pT3b (IIIB)   Tumor extends to pelvic wall and/or causes hydronephrosis or nonfunctioning kidney

pT4 (IVA)   Tumor invades the mucosa of bladder or rectum and/or extends beyond true pelvis (bullous edema is not sufficient evidence to classify a tumor as pT4)
pM1(IVB)   Distant metastasis
— Regional lymph nodes (pN)
pNX Cannot be assessed
pN0 No regional lymph node metastasis
pN1 Regional lymph node metastasis
Specify
Number examined
Number involved
— Distant metastasis (pM)
pMX   Cannot be assessed
pM1 (IVB)   Distant metastasis
Specify site(s), if known
— Margins (check all that apply)
Cannot be assessed
Margins uninvolved by invasive carcinoma
Distance of tumor from closest margin: mm
Specify margin (if possible)
Carcinoma in situ absent at distal margin
Carcinoma in situ present at distal margin
Margin(s) involved by invasive carcinoma
Specify location(s) (if possible)
Not applicable
— Venous/lymphatic (large/small vessel) invasion (V/L)
Absent
Present
Indeterminate
— Additional pathologic findings (check all that apply)
None identified
Intraepithelial neoplasia (specify type and grade)
Other (specify)
— Comment(s)

Uveal melanoma—resection

Applies to malignant melanoma of the uvea.

Macroscopic
— Specimen type
Enucleation
Limited exenteration
Complete exenteration
Other (specify)
Not specified
— Tumor site
Right
Left
Unspecified
— Specimen size
For enucleation
Anteroposterior diameter   —— mm
Horizontal diameter   —— mm
Vertical diameter   —— mm
Length of optic nerve   —— mm
Diameter of optic nerve   —— mm
Cannot be determined (see Comment)

For exenteration:

    ×   ×   mm

Cannot be determined (see Comment)

— Tumor location (check all that apply) (macroscopic examination/transillumination)

Cannot be determined

Superotemporal quadrant of globe

Superonasal quadrant of globe

Inferotemporal quadrant of globe

Inferonasal quadrant of globe

Anterior chamber

Extrascleral extension

Optic nerve

— Tumor basal dimensions on transillumination

Cannot be determined

Specify: ×   ——— mm

— Tumor dimensions after sectioning

Cannot be determined

Base at cut edge: —— mm

Height at cut edge: —— mm

Maximal tumor height: —— mm

— Tumor location after sectioning

Cannot be determined

Distance from anterior edge of tumor to limbus at cut edge: mm

Distance of posterior margin of tumor base from edge of optic disc: mm

— Tumor involvement or gross pathology of other ocular structures (check all that apply)

Cannot be determined

Sclera

Vortex vein(s)

Optic disc

Vitreous

Choroid

Ciliary body

Iris

Lens

Anterior chamber

Angle/Schlemm's canal

Cornea

Retinal detachment

— Growth pattern

Cannot be determined

Solid mass

Ciliary body ring

Diffuse

Microscopic

— Histologic type

Cannot be determined

Spindle cell type

    Spindle A

    Spindle B

Epithelioid cell type

Mixed cell type

Necrotic

Balloon cell

— Tumor location

Cannot be determined

Anterior margin located anterior to equator of globe

Within 1 mm of optic disc

None of above

— Scleral involvement

Cannot be determined

None

Extrascleral

Intrascleral

— Involvement of other structures (check all that apply)

Cannot be determined

Vortex vein

Optic nerve

Vitreous

Retina

Angle/Schlemm's canal

Other(s) (specify)

— Extent of invasion

— Primary tumor (pT): Iris

pTX   Primary tumor cannot be assessed

pT0   No evidence of primary tumor

pT1   Tumor limited to the iris

    pT1a   Tumor limited to the iris not more than 3 clock hours in size

    pT1b   Tumor limited to the iris more than 3 clock hours in size

    pT1c   Tumor limited to the iris with melanomalytic glaucoma

pT2   Tumor confluent with or extending into the ciliary body and/or choroid

    pT2a   Tumor confluent with or extending into the ciliary body and/or choroid with melanomalytic glaucoma

pT3   Tumor confluent with or extending into the ciliary body and/or choroid with extrascleral extension

    pT3a   Tumor confluent with or extending into the ciliary body with extrascleral extension and melanomalytic glaucoma

pT4   Tumor with extraocular extension

— Primary tumor (pT): Ciliary body and choroid

pTX   Primary tumor cannot be assessed

pT0   No evidence of primary tumor

pT1   Tumor 10 mm or less in greatest diameter and 2.5 mm or less in greatest height (thickness)

    pT1a   Tumor 10 mm or less in greatest diameter and 2.5 mm or less in greatest height (thickness) without microscopic extraocular extension

    pT1b   Tumor 10 mm or less in greatest diameter and 2.5 mm or less in greatest height (thickness) with microscopic extension

    pT1c   Tumor 10 mm or less in greatest diameter and 2.5 mm or less in greatest height (thickness) with macroscopic extraocular extension

pT2   Tumor greater than 10 mm but not more than 16 mm in greatest basal diameter and between 2.5 and 10 mm in maximum height (thickness)

    pT2a   Tumor 10 to 16 mm in greatest basal diameter and between 2.5 and 10 mm in maximum height (thickness) without microscopic extraocular extension pT2b Tumor 10 to 16 mm in greatest basal diameter and between 2.5 and 10 mm in maximum height (thickness) with microscopic extraocular extension

pT2c Tumor 10 to 16 mm in greatest basal diameter and between 2.5 and 10 mm in maximum height (thickness) with macroscopic extraocular extension

pT3 Tumor more than 16 mm in greatest diameter and/or greater than 10 mm in maximum height (thickness) without extraocular extension

pT4 Tumor more than 16 mm in greatest diameter and/or greater than 10 mm in maximum height (thickness) with extraocular extension

Note 1: When dimension and elevation show a difference in classification, the highest category should be used for classification

— Regional lymph nodes (pN)
  pNX Regional lymph nodes cannot be assessed
  pN0 No regional lymph node metastasis
  pN1 Regional lymph node metastasis
— Distant metastasis (pM)
  pMX Cannot be assessed
  pM1 Distant metastasis
    *Specify site(s), if known
— Margins
  Cannot be assessed
  No melanoma at margins
  Extrascleral extension (for enucleation specimens)
  Other margin involved (specify)
— Additional pathologic findings (check all that apply)
  None identified
  Mitotic rate: Number of mitoses per 40× objective with a field area of 0.152 mm^2
  Necrosis
  Microvascular patterns
  Vascular invasion (tumor vessels or other vessels)
  Degree of pigmentation
  Inflammatory cells/tumor-infiltrating lymphocytes
  Drusen
  Retinal detachment
  Invasion of Bruch's membrane
  Nevus
  Hemorrhage
  Neovascularization
  Other (specify)
— Comment(s)

Vagina—biopsy (use of checklist for biopsy specimens is optional)

Applies to all invasive carcinomas of the vagina.
Macroscopic
— Specimen type
  Incisional biopsy
  Excisional biopsy
  Other (specify)
  Not specified

— Tumor site
  Upper third
  Middle third
  Lower third
  Not specified
— Tumor size (excisional biopsy only)
  Greatest dimension: ——— cm
  Additional dimensions: × ——— cm
  Cannot be determined (see Comment)
Microscopic
— Histologic type (check all that apply)
  Squamous cell carcinoma
  Adenosquamous carcinoma
  Adenocarcinoma
    Mucinous
    Clear cell
    Not otherwise specified
  Other (specify)
  Carcinoma, type cannot be determined
— Histologic grade
  Not applicable
  GX Cannot be assessed
  G1 Well differentiated
  G2 Moderately differentiated
  G3 Poorly differentiated
  G4 Undifferentiated
  Other (specify)
— Extent of invasion
  Cannot be assessed
  Stromal invasion (specify if present)
  Muscle invasion (specify if present)
— Margins
  Not applicable
  Cannot be assessed
  Uninvolved by tumor
  Involved by tumor (specify site):
— Additional pathologic findings (check all that apply)
  None identified
  Dysplasia
  Condyloma acuminatum
  Adenosis
  Other (specify)
— Comment(s)

Vagina—resection/excisional biopsy

Applies to all invasive carcinomas of the vagina.

Macroscopic
— Specimen type
  Excisional biopsy
  Partial vaginectomy
  Radical vaginectomy
  Other (specify)
  Not specified
— Tumor site (check all that apply)
  Upper third
    Circumferential
    Anterior
    Posterior

Left lateral
Right lateral
Middle third
Circumferential
Anterior
Posterior
Left lateral
Right lateral
Lower third
Circumferential
Anterior
Posterior
Left lateral
Right lateral
Not specified
— Tumor size
Greatest dimension: —— cm
Additional dimensions: — × —— cm
Cannot be determined (see Comment)

Microscopic
— Histologic type (check all that apply)
Squamous cell carcinoma
Adenosquamous carcinoma
Adenocarcinoma
Mucinous
Clear cell
Not otherwise specified
Other (specify)
Carcinoma, type cannot be determined
— Histologic grade
Not applicable
GX Cannot be assessed
G1 Well differentiated
G2 Moderately differentiated
G3 Poorly differentiated
G4 Undifferentiated
Other (specify)
— Extent of invasion
— Primary tumor (pT)
TNM (FIGO)
pTX (—) Cannot be assessed
pT0 (—) No evidence of primary tumor
pTis (0) Carcinoma in situ
pT1 (I) Tumor confined to vagina
pT2 (II) Tumor invades paravaginal tissues but not to pelvic wall
pT3 (III) Tumor extends to pelvic wall
pT4 (IVA) Tumor invades mucosa of bladder or rectum and/or extends beyond true pelvis
— Regional lymph nodes (pN)
TNM (FIGO)
pNX Cannot be assessed
pN0 No regional lymph node metastasis
pN1 (III) Pelvic or inguinal lymph node metastasis (pT1–pT3)
pN1 (IVA) Pelvic or inguinal lymph node metastasis (pT4)
pN1 (IVB) Pelvic or inguinal lymph node metastasis (pT1–pT4, pM1)
Specify
Number examined

Number involved
— Distant metastasis (pM)
TNM (FIGO)
pMX Cannot be assessed
pM1 (IVB) Distant metastasis
Specify site(s), if known
— Margins (check all that apply)
Cannot be assessed
Margins uninvolved by invasive carcinoma
Distance of invasive carcinoma from closest margin: mm
Specify margin (if possible)
Carcinoma in situ absent at margin
Carcinoma in situ present at margin
Margin(s) involved by invasive carcinoma
Specify location(s) (if possible)
— Venous/lymphatic (large/small) vessel invasion (V/L)
Absent
Present
Indeterminate
— Additional pathologic findings (check all that apply)
None identified
Dysplasia
Condyloma acuminatum
Adenosis
Other (specify)
— Comment(s)

Vulva—excisional biopsy/resection

Applies only to invasive carcinomas of the vulva.

Macroscopic
— Specimen type
Local excision
Wide excision
Partial vulvectomy
Total vulvectomy
Radical vulvectomy
Other (specify)
Not specified
— Lymphadenectomy
Not applicable
Sentinel lymph node biopsy
Inguinal–femoral nodes
Pelvic nodes
Other (specify)
— Tumor site (check all that apply)
Right vulva
Labia major
Labia minor
Left vulva
Labia major
Labia minor
Clitoris
Other (specify)
Not specified
— Tumor size
Greatest dimension: —— cm
Additional dimensions: × —— cm
Cannot be determined (see Comment)

Microscopic
— Histologic type (check all that apply)
    Squamous cell carcinoma
        Vulvar intraepithelial neoplasia 3 (VIN3: severe
           dysplasia/carcinoma in situ)
        Keratinizing
        Nonkeratinizing
        Basaloid
        Warty (condylomatous)
        Other (specify)
    Verrucous carcinoma
    Adenocarcinoma
        Bartholin's gland carcinoma (specify type)
        Carcinoma resembling breast carcinoma
        Eccrine carcinoma
        Other (specify)
    Paget's disease
    Other (specify)
    Carcinoma, type cannot be determined
— Histologic grade
    Not applicable
    GX   Cannot be assessed
    G1   Well differentiated
    G2   Moderately differentiated
    G3   Poorly differentiated
    G4   Undifferentiated
    Other (specify)
— Extent of invasion
— Primary tumor (pT)
    TNM (FIGO)
        pTX (—)   Cannot be assessed
        pT0 (—)   No evidence of primary tumor
        pTis (0)   Carcinoma in situ
        pT1 (I)   Tumor confined to vulva or vulva and
                perineum, 2 cm or less in greatest
                dimension
            pT1a (IA)   Tumor confined to vulva or
                            vulva and perineum, 2 cm or
                            less in greatest dimension,
                            and with stromal invasion no
                            more than 1 mm
            pT1b (IB)   Tumor confined to vulva or
                            vulva and perineum, 2 cm or
                              less in greatest dimension,
                            and with stromal invasion
                            greater than 1 mm
        pT2 (II)   Tumor confined to vulva or vulva and
                perineum greater than 2 cm in greatest
                dimension
        pT3 (III)   Tumor invades any of the following: lower
                urethra, vagina, anus

        pT4 (IVA)   Tumor invades any of the following:
                bladder mucosa, rectal mucosa, upper
                urethral mucosa; or is fixed to pubic bone
— Regional lymph nodes (pN)
    TNM (FIGO)
        pNX   Cannot be assessed
        pN0   No regional lymph node metastasis
        pN1 (III)   Unilateral regional lymph node metastasis
                (pT1–pT3)
        pN1 (IVA)   Unilateral regional lymph node metastasis
                (pT4)
        pN1 (IVB)   Unilateral regional lymph node metastasis
                (pT1–pT4, pM1)
        pN2 (IVA)   Bilateral regional lymph node metastasis
                (pT1–pT4)
        pN2 (IVB)   Bilateral regional lymph node metastasis
                (pT1–pT4, pM1)
    Specify
        Number examined
        Number involved
— Distant metastasis (pM)
    TNM (FIGO)
        pMX   Cannot be assessed
        pM1 (IVB)   Distant metastasis
        Specify site(s), if known
— Depth of invasion
    Specify: —— mm
    Cannot be determined (see Comment)
— Tumor border
    Pushing
    Infiltrating
— Margins (check all that apply)
    Cannot be assessed
    Uninvolved by invasive carcinoma
        Distance of invasive carcinoma from closest margin:
            mm
        Specify margin, if possible
            Carcinoma in situ absent at margin
            Carcinoma in situ present at margin
    Involved by invasive carcinoma
        Specify margin(s)
— Venous/lymphatic (large/small vessel) invasion (V/L)
    Absent
    Present
    Indeterminate
— Additional pathologic findings (check all that apply)
    None identified
    Dysplasia
    Condyloma acuminatum
    Other (specify)
— Comment(s)

Appendix E
Guidelines for handling of most common and important surgical specimens

Some general guidelines for the procedure, description, and sampling of the most common and important surgical specimens received in the laboratory are set forth in the following pages. They are mainly derived from personal experience, although the *Gross Room Manual* used for years in the Surgical Pathology Laboratory at Barnes Hospital in St Louis and considerably expanded by the surgical pathologists at Stanford University was freely used as a model for many of the procedures. Several other versions of these guidelines have been published over the years, either incorporated into major surgical pathology textbooks or as free-standing manuals.[1-8,10] Of them, the most detailed and up-to-date is the one published by the powerful Surgical Pathology team at Johns Hopkins, edited by William H. Westra et al, with the help of a superb medical illustrator.[9] Of course, there are also innumerable other versions which have been prepared in individual pathology laboratories for domestic use and which have never been published.

The instructions from any of these manuals can be used in a printed form, in a microfiche format or—increasingly—by incorporating them into the AP information system and making them available to the prosecutors through terminals located in the dissection stations.

Naturally, not all types of specimens or eventualities can be covered. The guidelines presented herein and those from any other version will be useful only if they are taken as *general recommendations* for a typical specimen showing a typical lesion. All kinds of modifications need to be made according to the specific circumstances of the case. Each specimen is unique and thus requires variation in the dissection, description, and sampling procedures here recommended. To quote from a high source in connection with a somewhat related matter (i.e. the autopsy procedure)[9]:

> It is scarcely necessary to point out that there are many cases in which deviation from this method are not merely allowable, but also absolutely necessary. The individuality of the case must often determine the plan of the examination. But we must not begin with individualizing, nor make a rule of the exceptions. The expert may allow himself to make alterations, supposing that they are well founded, but he must be able to remember his motive for so doing, and also to state it.

1 Fazzini EP, Waldo E, Weber DL. A manual for surgical pathologists. Springfield, IL, 1972, Thomas
2 Leong AS-Y, James CL, Thomas AC. Handbook of surgical pathology. New York, 1996, Churchill Livingstone
3 Lowe DG, Jeffrey IJM. Macro techniques in diagnostic histopathology. London, 1990, Wolfe Medical Publications
4 Nochomovitz L. Gross room and specimen handling. In Weidner N et al (eds) Modern Surgical Pathology. Philadelphia, 2003, Saunders
5 Pierson KK. Principles of presection: a guide for the anatomic pathologist. New York, 1980, Wiley
6 Rosai J. Manual of surgical pathology gross room procedures. Minneapolis, 1981, University of Minnesota Press.
7 Schmidt WA. Principles and techniques of surgical pathology. Menlo Park, CA, 1983, Addison-Wesley
8 Teloh HA. Methods in Surgical Pathology. Springfield, IL, 1957, Thomas
9 Virchow R. Postmortem examinations and the position of pathology among biological sciences, with an introduction by Putschar WJ: The history of medicine, Series No 37. Published under the auspices of the Library of the New York Academy of Medicine, Metuchen, NJ, 1973, Scarecrow
10 Westra WH, Hruban RH, Phelps TH, Isacson C. Surgical pathology dissection. An illustrated guide, 2nd Ed. New York, 2003, Springer-Verlag

Adrenal gland—adrenalectomy[1]

Procedure

1 Ink the specimen
2 Measure and weigh the organ
3 Cut parallel sections at 5-mm intervals in the transverse plane
4 Look for and sample the adrenal vein

Description

1 Size and weight
2 External surface: smooth? bosselated? shape of gland preserved?
3 Cut surface: color? necrosis? hemorrhage? cystic changes? encapsulation? extension of the disease into the surrounding tissues?

Sections for histology

1 Tumor if present, trying to demonstrate relationship with normal gland, tumor capsule, and surrounding organs
2 Non-neoplastic gland, some including adrenal vein
3 Surgical margins

1 Conran RM. An approach to handling pediatric thyroid and adrenal tumors excluding neuroblastoma. Am J Clin Pathol 1998, **109**: S73–S81

Appendix—appendectomy

Appendectomy consists of the removal of the entire appendix after dividing the mesoappendix and ligating the base of the appendix that connects to the cecum.

Procedure

1 Measure organ (length and greatest diameter)
2 Divide specimen in two by cutting a cross-section 2 cm from tip
3 Cut cross-sections of proximal fragment at 5-mm intervals
4 Divide distal fragment in two by a longitudinal cut

Description

1 Length and greatest diameter
2 External surface: fibrin? pus? hemorrhage? hyperemia? perforation? condition of mesentery?
3 Wall: any localized lesions?
4 Mucosa: hyperemic? ulcerated?
5 Lumen: obliterated? dilated? Content: fecaliths? stones?

Sections for histology

1 Proximal one third, close to surgical margin: one cross-section. If tumor is present in the specimen, paint the surgical margin with India ink and take an additional section from it
2 Mid one third: one cross-section
3 Distal one third: one longitudinal section

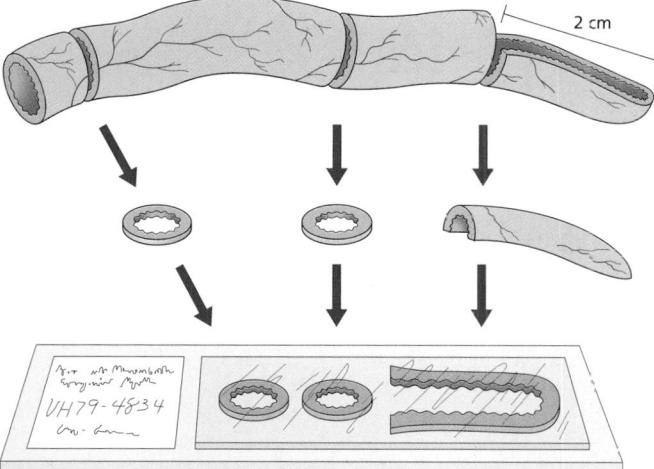

Bladder—cystectomy

Cystectomy consists in removal of the bladder. In most instances the entire organ is removed (total cystectomy). In males this may be accompanied by removal of the prostate and seminal vesicles (cystoprostatectomy). The entire length of the urethra may also be excised (cystourethrectomy). The performance of partial cystectomies for carcinoma has fallen into disfavor.

Procedure

1 Paint the entire external surface (including the prostate, if present) with India ink
2 Two options are available for the dissection depending on the type of lesion present and the status of the organ when received in the laboratory (see accompanying drawings):

   a Open with scissors in a Y shape through the anterior wall, pin on a corkboard, and fix overnight in formalin
   b Fill with formalin, fix overnight and divide into anterior and posterior halves by first cutting the lateral bladder walls with scissors and then sectioning the prostate with a sharp knife, beginning at the bladder neck and being careful to make the cut through the urethra. See instructions for Injection of specimens—general guidelines. The injection can be performed through the urethra with a Foley catheter, with a 50-ml syringe with large-bore needle inserted through the bladder dome after the urethra has been clamped or tied, or by filling the bladder with formalin-soaked cotton

3 Take photographs or photocopies and identify in one of them the site of the sections taken for histology

Description

1 Size of bladder; length of ureters; other organs present
2 Tumor characteristics: size (including thickness), location, extent of invasion, shape (papillary, ulcerated); multifocal lesions?
3 Appearance of non-neoplastic mucosa; thickness of bladder wall away from tumor

Sections for histology

1 Tumor: at least three sections, through bladder wall
2 Bladder neck: one section
3 Trigone: two sections
4 Anterior wall: two sections
5 Posterior wall: two sections
6 Dome: two sections
7 Any abnormal-looking area in bladder mucosa if not included in previous sections

8 Ureteral orifices, including intramural portion
9 Ureteral proximal margins
10 In males: prostate (two sections from each quadrant) and seminal vesicles (one section from each). If a prostatic carcinoma is identified, see instructions for Prostate gland—radical prostatectomy
11 Other organs present
12 Perivesical lymph nodes, if any

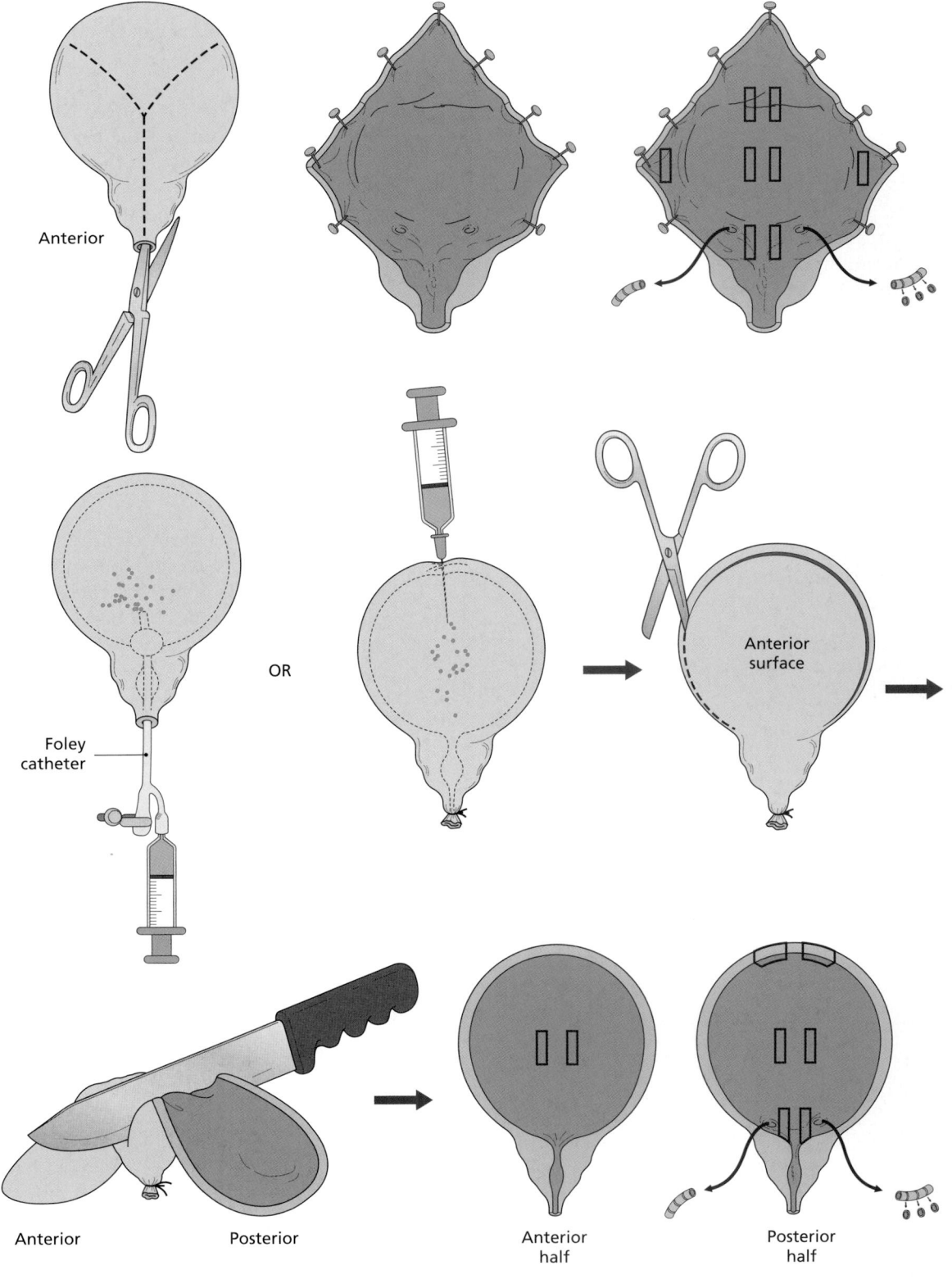

Anterior

OR

Foley catheter

Anterior surface

Anterior   Posterior

Anterior half   Posterior half

Bladder—stone removal

Procedure

1 Take photographs or photocopies of all stones submitted

2 Send a 1- to 2-g sample for crystallographic (often incorrectly referred to as chemical) analysis.[1] Specimens should be rinsed well in water and air dried. Formalin is to be avoided because uric acid is soluble therein. Heat should not be used to hasten drying because it will drive off the ammonium in magnesium ammonium phosphate, changing struvite into newberyite. Specimens should be shipped in protective containers rather than in plain envelopes. They should not be secured with a transparent tape

3 The same procedure applies to stones removed from other portions of the urinary tract, such as the renal pelvis or ureter

Description

1 Number of stones, shape, color, and consistency. *Phosphate* stones are gray or grayish white and may be hard or soft and friable. *Oxalate* stones are usually hard and smooth, rounded, or nodular (resembling mulberries) or irregularly speculated. *Urate* stones are smooth, yellow or brown, and round or oval. *Cystine* stones are hard, smooth, and yellow, with a waxy appearance. Stones associated with local bleeding may be impregnated with blood and acquire a black or dark brown color

Sections for histology

None

1   Several specialized laboratories have offered this service for many years, including the Laboratory for Stone Research, 31 Wyman Street, Newton, MA 02468, USA and Louis C. Herring and Company, 1111 South Orange Avenue, Orlando, FL 32806–1236, USA.

Bone—biopsy

Procedure

1 Trocar or needle biopsy: divide longitudinally with a fine-toothed saw if specimen is over 5 mm in diameter. Look for any soft material, dissect from rest of specimen, and process separately without decalcification.

2 Open biopsy and curettage: divide calcified from noncalcified tissues and process separately

Description

1 Number and size of fragments
2 Consistency, calcification, color, cystic changes, necrosis

Sections for histology

1 Submit all material received, except for unduly large specimens. Send, separately, material to be decalcified from the rest

Bone—femoral head excision

Procedure

1 Examine articular and cut surfaces
2 Measure diameter and thickness
3 Take photographs, if indicated
4 Hold the specimen with a specially devised clamp (a meatball maker works quite well) or in a vice and cut through the center of the articular surface (fovea) with a band saw (see accompanying drawings)
5 Make a parallel cut about 3 mm from the first cut while holding the specimen in the same position
6 Examine a cut section of the slice; take a photograph and roentgenogram. Make parallel cuts through remaining pieces, if indicated

Description

1 Type of excision; side, if known
2 Diameter and thickness
3 Articular surface: smooth or irregular? osteophytic lipping at the periphery?
4 Synovial membrane at edges: hypertrophic? papillary?
5 Cut surface: thickness or articular cartilage; bone exposed? subchondral eburnation? cysts? (if so, size and content); areas of necrosis? (if so, size and appearance); appearance of bone away from the articular surface; evidence of previous fracture?

Sections for histology

1 Take two sections from the most abnormal areas, at least one including the articular surface and synovium (see accompanying drawings)

2 Two options are available for obtaining these sections. The first is more expeditious and quite adequate and is the one to be used in most instances. The second is more time consuming and requires extra care but provides slightly better results

a Cut the sections from the fresh slice with a fine band saw or strong knife, depending on the amount and hardness of the bone; fix thoroughly in formalin and decalcify
b Fix a whole slice in formalin for several hours or overnight; decalcify thoroughly; cut desired sections with a scalpel or submit material in its entirety, if facilities are available

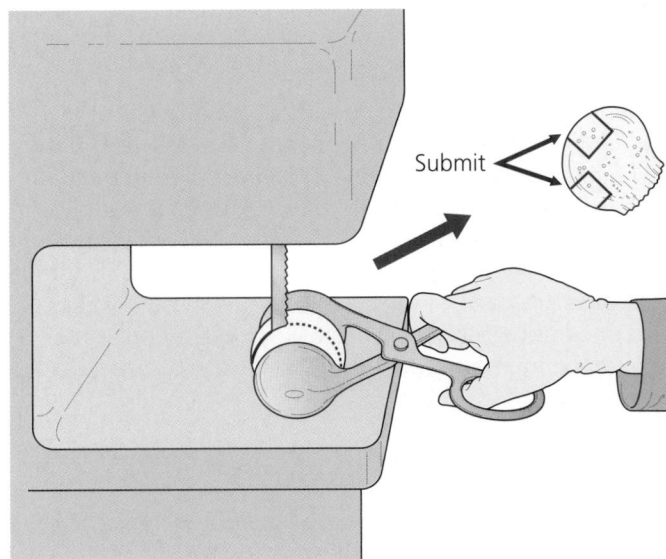

Bone—resection for tumor[1–3]

The procedure here described was written specifically for amputations specimens but it can be easily adapted to the lesser operations that are currently carried out for these neoplasms.

Procedure

1 Review the X-ray studies taken before amputation
2 Measure the length and circumference (including a measure of the circumference at the level of the tumor, if this is apparent or known)
3 Determine the presence, position, and dimensions of biopsy sites
4 Search for the major lymph node groups; identify and place in separate containers
5 Cut a cross-section of the proximal bone margin with a band saw
6 Dissect out all the soft tissues (down to the periosteum) around the involved bone with a scalpel,

forceps, and scissors. Review the clinical and roentgenographic findings before proceeding. If there is any indication (from the roentgenograms or at the time of dissection) of soft tissue extension by the tumor, dissect *around* this area and keep it in continuity with the bone. If, from the X-ray studies, the tumor does not seem to involve the joint, cut through it; if it does, leave the joint intact and make a cross-section with the band saw through the adjacent noninvolved bone, approximately 5 to 10 cm from the joint. If a previous incision site is present, take a sample for histology at this time, along the entire course of the incision

7 Cut the bone specimen thus obtained longitudinally with a band saw. In most cases a section dividing the specimen into an anterior and a posterior half is preferable; in others, sagittal, lateralized, or even oblique cuts are to be recommended. The type of bone involved and the location of the tumor as seen radiographically will determine which plane of section will give the most information

8 Examine the cut section and take photographs or photocopies; identify in one of them the site of the sections to be taken

9 Examine under Wood's light if tetracycline had been administered before amputation (to detect satellite foci)

10 Cut a parallel section with the band saw, producing a slice about 5 mm thick. Use a saw guide for this purpose. Take a roentgenogram of the slice. Make additional cuts of the remaining bone pieces, if indicated. It might be desirable to take additional photographs or photocopies at this time

11 Quickly dissect the soft tissues that had been peeled off the involved bone; cut sagittally with the band saw all major bones that were left in this portion of the specimen and examine carefully for other foci of tumor or other lesions. Open the major joints and examine them

Description

1 Type of amputation; side of extremity
2 Length and circumference of extremity, including circumference at level of tumor
3 Presence, position, and dimensions of biopsy sites
4 Tumor characteristics:

a Location: bone involved; diaphysis, metaphysis, or epiphysis? medulla, cortex, or periosteum? epiphyseal line apparent? (if so, is the tumor crossing it)? does the tumor involve articular cartilage and joint cavity? does it extend into soft tissue? is the periosteum elevated by tumor? (if so, to what extent?) invaded by tumor? if previous incision present, is there evidence of tumor extension along it?

b Features of tumor: size, shape, color, borders, consistency; does it appear to be bone forming, cartilaginous, fibrous, or myxoid? cystic changes, hemorrhage, or necrosis?

c Distance of tumor to osseous margin of resection

5 Appearance of bone away from tumor; satellite lesions? any fluorescent foci seen if examined under Wood's light?

6 Appearance of remaining extremity if abnormal (if not, so state); skin, subcutaneous fat, muscle, major vessels and nerves, other bones, joints

7 Appearance and approximate number of lymph nodes found

Sections for histology

1 Tumor: four sections or more depending on size and extent

All grossly dissimilar areas should be sampled. Wherever possible, sections should be taken to include the periphery of the tumor *and* adjacent cortex, medulla, epiphyseal line, articular cartilage, periosteum, and soft tissues.

2 Previous incision site, if present, taken all along its course

3 Section from grossly non-involved bone, midway between tumor and margin of resection. If the tumor involves upper end of a bone, take this section from midportion of proximally located bone

4 Osseous margin of resection

5 Any abnormal-looking areas elsewhere in bone, soft tissues, or skin

6 Lymph nodes: if grossly normal, only representative ones; if grossly abnormal or if there is clinical suspicion of metastases, all of them

1 Weatherby RP, Unni KK. Practical aspects of handling orthopedic specimens in the surgical pathology laboratory. Pathol Annu 1982, 17(Pt 2): 1–31.
2 Khuu H, Moore D, Young S, Jaffe KA, Siegal GP. Examination of tumors and tumor-like conditions of bone. Ann Diagn Pathol 1999, 3: 364–369
3 Patterson K. The pathologic handling of skeletal tumors. Am J Clin Pathol 1998, 109: S53–S66

Bone marrow—fragments from aspirate

Procedure

1 The material is obtained by aspiration and usually allowed to clot before fixation
2 Alternatively, the marrow particles can be concentrated "by ejecting the aspirate, before it clots, onto a slated slide and into a [fixative] solution. The latter is rapidly filtered, and the residue is processed by usual histologic technics"[1]

Description

1 Approximate amount of material
2 Appearance and relative amount of marrow particles in relation to blood clots

Sections for histology

1 Submit the material in its entirety unless blood clots are excessive
2 If clots are excessive, select areas with largest concentration of marrow particles
3 Decalcification is generally not needed for this material

1 From Rywlin AM, Marvan P, Robinson MJ. A simple technic for the preparation of bone marrow smears and sections. Am J Clin Pathol 1970, **53:** 389–393

Bone marrow—needle biopsy

Procedure

The needle biopsy should be fixed immediately after it is obtained. B–5 or Zenker's fixative are usually employed.

Description

1 Number, length, and diameter of fragments
2 Color and consistency; homogenous?

Sections for histology

1 Submit the material in its entirety
2 If bilateral biopsies were performed, submit them separately.
3 Decalcify only after the tissue is properly fixed and washed and for the shortest time that will allow proper sectioning

Bone marrow—rib from thoracotomy

Procedure

Sometimes a rib is submitted together with a specimen of pneumonectomy or lobectomy. Gross examination alone is adequate if no gross abnormalities are detected. However, an opportunity to study the status of the patient's bone marrow should not be overlooked. Proceed as follows:

1 Measure the length and diameter of the rib
2 With a saw, cut a piece about 2 cm long, having bone marrow at both ends, from the fresh specimen
3 Place between pliers longitudinally and squeeze until bone marrow is expressed from both ends (see accompanying drawing). Let the marrow fall in a container with fixative or scrape it out with a blade
4 Fix and submit for microscopic examination; decalcification is not necessary
5 Cut the remainder of the rib longitudinally along its entire length and examine cut sections

Description

1 Identification of side and number of rib information is provided
2 Length and greatest diameter
3 Appearance of bone marrow on cut section: color, amount; any focal changes?

Sections for histology

1 If no abnormalities are observed, submit only bone marrow preparation as described under Procedure (without decalcifying)
2 If gross abnormalities are present, cut blocks, fix, decalcify, and submit for histology

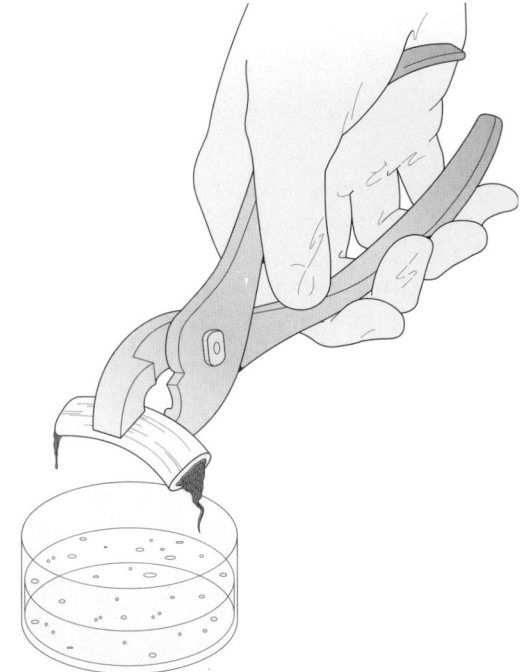

Breast—biopsy and local excision for palpable mass

(Adapted from Schnitt SJ, Connolly JL. Processing and evaluation of breast excision specimens. A clinically oriented approach. Am J Clin Pathol 1992, **98**: 125–137.)

Open breast biopsies are carried out after performing a circumareolar (preferable for cosmetic reasons) or a radial incision and removing the lesion either partially (incisional biopsy) or in its entirety with a rim of surrounding normal tissue (excisional biopsy). Excisional biopsy is essentially synonymous with lumpectomy and is sometimes combined with the sampling of axillary lymph nodes.

Procedure

1 Measure the specimen before cutting. Weigh if amount of material is substantial (over 50 g)
2 Blot dry, apply India ink to surface, and blot dry again.
3 If indicated, take a radiograph of the specimen
4 Section specimen: if specimen is 3 cm or smaller, cut 3- to 4-mm slices; if it is larger, bisect specimen transversely, fix the residual hemispheres for 1 to 2 hours, place cut surface down, and take sagittal blocks through superior and inferior portions
5 If indicated, take a sample for hormone receptor studies (see instructions for Hormone receptor assays— sampling)

Description

1 Dimensions and consistency of specimen
2 Appearance of cut sections: fibrosis, cysts (size, number, content), calcification, tumor masses (size in three dimensions, color, borders, consistency, necrosis, distance from surgical margins)

Sections for histology

1 Small specimens: submit in their entirety (up to five cassettes)
2 Larger specimens: through sampling. At least two thirds of the breast tissue (exclusive of adipose tissue) should be processed. This should include any grossly visible lesions and the inked surgical margins[1-3]

1 Carter D. Margins of "lumpectomy" for breast cancer. Hum Pathol 1986, **17**: 330–332
2 National Cancer Institute. Standardized management of breast specimens. Recommended by Pathology Working Group, Breast Task Force. Am J Clin Pathol 1978, **60**: 789–798
3 Connolly JL, Schnitt SJ. Evaluation of breast biopsy specimens in patients considered for treatment by conservative surgery and radiation therapy for early breast cancer. Pathol Annu 1988, **23**(Pt 1): 1–23

Breast—mammographically directed excision

(Adapted from Schnitt SJ, Connolly JL. Processing and evaluation of breast excision specimens. A clinically oriented approach. Am J Clin Pathol 1992, **98:** 125–137.)

Procedure

1 Obtain through radiograph of intact specimen.
2 Measure specimen before cutting
3 Blot dry, apply India ink to surface, and blot dry again.
4 Slice specimen through the equatorial plane at 1- to 4-mm intervals.
5 Obtain radiograph of sliced specimen. Some authors have found the use of a Perspex grid useful for the subsequent localization of the lesion.
6 Label slices on the radiograph
7 Take a sample for hormone receptor analysis only if tumor is grossly visible and of sufficient size; do not submit tissue for this analysis if there is no grossly evident tumor

Description

1 Dimension and consistency of specimen
2 Appearance of cut sections: fibrosis, cysts (size, number, content), calcification, tumor masses (size in three dimensions, color, borders, consistency, necrosis, distance from surgical margins)

Sections for histology

1 Submit in its entirety. Label cassettes as in the radiograph.

* From: Champ CS, Mason CH, Coghill SB, Robinson M. A Perspex grid for localization of nonpalpable mammographic lesions in breast biopsies. Histopathology 1989, **124:** 311–316
Upper and middle drawings redrawn from National Cancer Institute: Standardized management of breast specimens recommended by Pathology Working Group, Breast Cancer Task Force. Am J Clin Pathol 1973, **60:** 789–798

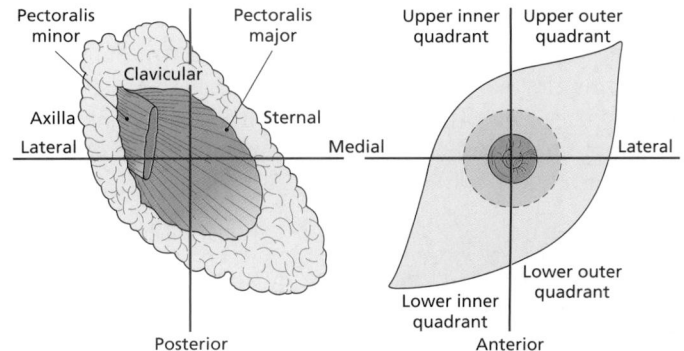

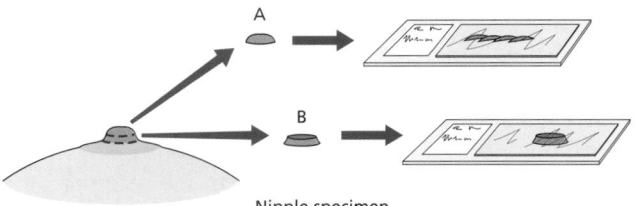

Nipple specimen

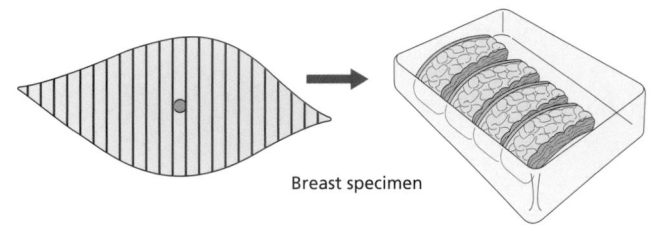

Breast specimen

Breast—mastectomy

(Adapted from National Cancer Institute. Standardized management of breast specimens recommended by Pathology Working Group, Breast Cancer Task Force. Am J Clin Pathol 1973, **60**: 789–798.)

Several types of mastectomy procedures exist. The Halsted's type *radical mastectomy*, which has been all but abandoned, consists of removal of the entire breast parenchyma, the underlying and surrounding adipose tissue, the pectoralis major and minor muscles, and the axillary contents in continuity and en bloc. A *modified radical mastectomy* (also known as extended simple mastectomy and total mastectomy), consists in removal of all the mammary tissue, including the axillary tail, together with the nipple, the surrounding skin, and a variable amount of lymph node-bearing fat from the lower axilla; the pectoralis muscles are preserved. A *simple mastectomy* consists of all or almost all of the mammary tissue, the nipple, and a variable amount of surrounding skin. A *subcutaneous mastectomy* includes most the mammary tissue, without overlying skin or nipple and often without the axillary tail. In a quadrantectomy a portion of the breast roughly corresponding to one of the four anatomic quadrants is excised, often in combination with removal of the axillary content. A *tylectomy* (lumpectomy; excisional biopsy) consists in removal of the entire mass and a variable amount of surrounding breast tissue. A *quadrantectomy* is a form of tylectomy in which the area of excision roughly corresponds to an anatomical quadrant of the breast. Finally, there is the *supraradical mastectomy*, mentioned here only for historical reasons. It contains all the components of a radical mastectomy specimen, plus a resected segment of chest wall, usually the sternal ends of the second, third, fourth, and fifth ribs, an adjacent segment of sternum, and the subpleural connective tissue that contains the internal mammary vessels and nodes; a segment of pleura also may be present.

Procedure

First day

1 Weigh the specimen.
2 Orient the specimen. In radical mastectomy cases, use the axillary fat as a marker for the lateral side and the surgical section of the muscle as a marker for the upper side. Place the specimen on the cutting board, posterior side up, with its most inferior point toward the dissector. The specimen is oriented as if the dissector were standing behind it. Note that at the junction of the upper and middle thirds of the pectoralis major, the muscle fibers run in a nearly horizontal direction
3 Dissect lymph nodes as follows:
   Radical mastectomy (rarely performed at present but included for historical reasons and completeness' sake):

   a Arrange the pectoral muscles and axillary contents in the anatomic positions, using the cut attachments of the pectoral muscle fibers as guides. The axillary contents, which are sometimes partially detached from the muscle during operation, when properly arranged will form a broadly linear fatty mass extending upward and

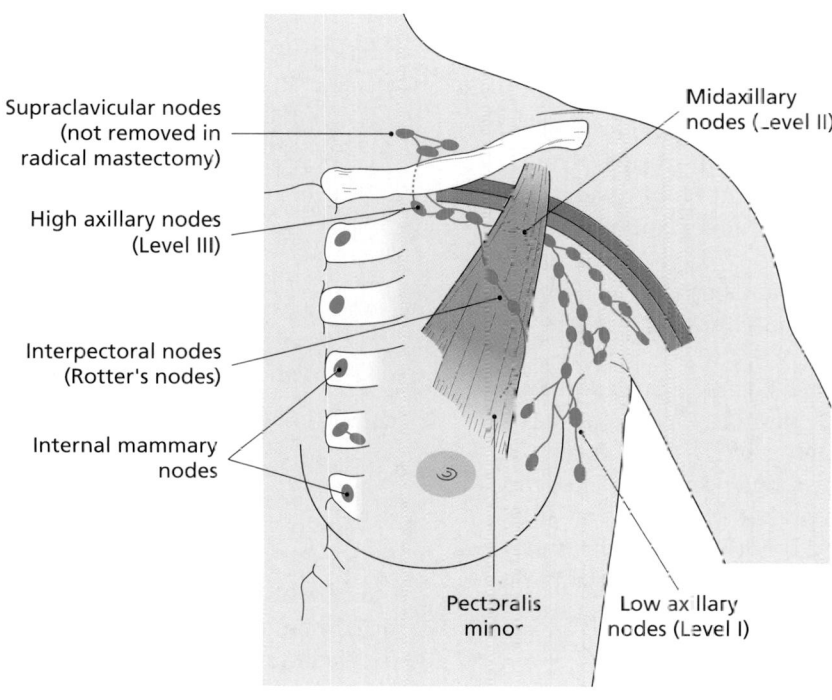

Supraclavicular nodes (not removed in radical mastectomy)

High axillary nodes (Level III)

Interpectoral nodes (Rotter's nodes)

Internal mammary nodes

Midaxillary nodes (Level II)

Pectoralis minor

Low axillary nodes (Level I)

Breast—mastectomy *(continued)*

laterally, crossing the posterior surface of the pectoralis minor muscle

b Using the pectoralis minor muscle as a guide, divide the axilla into three segments (see drawing, p. 2921):

- Level I (low): inferior to lower border of muscle
- Level II (middle): between upper and lower borders of muscle
- Level III (high): superior to upper border of muscle
  Remove each separately and fix overnight; Carnoy's solution is preferred because, besides fixing, it clears the fat somewhat

c Remove the pectoralis minor muscle and search for the interpectoral (Rotter's) nodes; these are usually found near the lateral edge of the posterior surface of the pectoralis major. If no nodes are apparent, submit the adipose tissue from this site

d Remove the pectoralis major muscle and look for evidence of tumor invasion

Modified radical mastectomy:

a Separate the axillary tissue from the breast

b Because the landmarks used in radical mastectomy specimens are not present, divide the axillary tissue into a higher and lower half and fix overnight in separate containers

4 Turn the specimen around, with skin side up and the 6 o'clock position nearest the dissector (i.e. as if the dissector were facing the patient)

5 Evaluate features of the external appearance and measure. Palpate the specimen for masses or nodularity. With a water-resistant marker, draw a vertical line passing through the nipple and another perpendicular to it, also passing through the nipple. This will divide the breast specimen into four quadrants: upper outer, lower outer, lower inner, and upper inner

6 Remove the nipple and areola, using scalpel, forceps, and scissors and fix the specimen thus obtained overnight

7 With a long sharp knife, cut the entire breast longitudinally into slices about 2 cm thick. One of the cuts should be exactly through the level of the nipple, using as a guide the vertical line previously made in the skin; this will allow a precise separation of slices belonging to the inner and outer halves of the breast. Lay out the slices in order on a flat surface, maintaining orientation. Examine each slice carefully; take photographs and X-ray film, if indicated. Take a sample for hormone receptor studies, if indicated (see instructions for Hormone receptor assays—sampling). Fix all the slices overnight, keeping their orientation either by laying them flat sequentially in a long pan (preferable) or by stringing them together (see drawing, p. 2921).

Second day

1 Lymph node specimens (radical or modified radical mastectomies): shred the axillary tissue and dissect out all lymph nodes, which stand out as white modules. A minimum of 20 lymph nodes should be found in the usual radical mastectomy

2 Nipple specimen: if following fixation the nipple is erect, cut as indicated in the accompanying drawing. If it is retracted or inverted, cut several parallel sections, about 2 to 3 mm apart, perpendicular to the skin surface through the nipple and areola

3 Breast specimen: reexamine the slices, make additional cuts, if necessary, and take sections for histology according to instructions that follow

Description

It is preferable to make short notes at the time the specimen is examined the first day and to dictate the whole case the second day.

1 Side (right or left) and type of mastectomy

2 List of structures included in specimen: skin, nipple, breast, major and minor pectoralis muscles, fascia, axillary tissue, chest wall structures

3 Weight and dimensions (greatest length of skin and length perpendicular to it)

4 Features of external appearance:

a Shape and color of skin

b Location and extent of skin changes (scars, recent surgical incisions, erythema, edema, flattening, retraction, ulceration)

c Appearance of nipple and areola (erosions, ulceration, retraction, inversion)

d Location of lesions and other features, which can be designated by stating their distance from nipple and quadrant on their direction in clock face numerals

e Description of abnormalities on palpation, if any

5 Features of cross-sections:

a Relative amounts of fat and parenchyma

b Cysts and dilated ducts: size, number, location, content

c Masses: quadrant and distance from nipple, depth beneath skin, size, shape, consistency, color; necrosis? hemorrhage? calcification? relation or attachment to skin, muscle, fascia, or nipple

d Lymph nodes, if present: number of nodes in each group, size of largest node in each group, and sizes and locations of nodes containing grossly evident tumor

Sections for histology

1 Breast: take three sections of tumor; sample all lesions noted grossly or radiographically; take at least one section from each quadrant (using as guidelines the previously made marks on the skin) in the following order:

- Upper outer quadrant (UOQ)
- Lower outer quadrant (LOQ)
- Lower inner quadrant (LIQ)
- Upper inner quadrant (UIQ)

2 Nipple: see under Procedure
3 Pectoralis major muscle (in radical mastectomies): take one section from any grossly abnormal area or, if none is found, from the area closest to the tumor

4 Lymph nodes: all identified nodes should be processed for histology. Small nodes are submitted entirely; nodes over 0.5 cm in diameter are sliced. If the axillary fat is grossly involved, a representative section should be taken. Label in the following order:

Radical mastectomy:

- Low axillary (Level I)
- Mid axillary (Level II)
- High axillary (Level III)
- Interpectoral (Rotter's) nodes or, if none found, adipose tissue from this site

Modified radical mastectomy:

- Lower half
- Upper half

(For this operation it is better not to use the terms low, mid, and high as these are used for radical mastectomies.)

Cell surface markers—sampling

This technique has become essential for the evaluation of lymphoid proliferations. It is useful in identifying a given proliferation as lymphoid, in distinguishing a reactive from a neoplastic process, and in identifying the specific cell type.

If facilities for the performance of this test are available, it should be used in:

- All specimens from lymph nodes, spleen, or thymus in which the possibility of a proliferative lymphoid process is considered
- All tumors with clinical or gross features suggestive of malignant lymphoma
- All tissues in patients with known malignant lymphoma or leukemia in which the possibility of involvement by the disease exists

Cell surface markers, detected with immunocyto-chemical reagents, can be evaluated quantitatively by flow cytometry or by microscopic examination of frozen sections. In either case the specimen should be received fresh. For flow cytometry a 0.5 m^2 piece of tissue is sufficient. This should be dropped in a bottle containing culture medium (such as RPMI or DMEM) and submitted to the appropriate laboratory. If immediate transportation is not feasible, store temporarily in the refrigerator at 4°C.

For frozen section purposes, a $2 \times 2 \times 1$ cm piece is desirable. This should be placed in a Petri dish having in its bottom a layer of filter paper wet (not overly soaked) with saline solution and submitted to the laboratory immediately. If the specimen is not large enough for a $2 \times 2 \times 1$ cm piece to be taken, sample a fragment as large as feasible.

Chromosomal analysis—sampling

Chromosomal analysis of surgically excised tissues (using direct and indirect techniques) can be useful in the differential diagnosis between reactive and neoplastic processes, and it can demonstrate specific chromosomal defects associated with particular tumor types.

Cut a piece of viable tissue in the fresh state as soon as possible after excision under sterile conditions, drop

in a bottle containing culture medium (such as RPMI or DMEM), and submit to the genetics laboratory. The piece should be about 0.5 to 1 cm in diameter or as large a sample as allowable. If immediate transportation to the laboratory is not feasible, store temporarily in the refrigerator at 4°C.

Cultures—bacterial, fungal, and viral

Whenever a fresh specimen is received in the laboratory and there is some indication (clinical, gross appearance, frozen section) that it may be involved by an infectious process, cultures should be taken, unless this has already been done in the operating room.[1]

Large specimens

Several techniques can be used for large operative specimens (lung, spleen) received intact in the fresh state. In general, technique 1 (following) is recommended over technique 2

1 Technique 1

 a Burn the surface close to the area to be cultured with a red-hot spatula
 b Make a deep cut through this sterilized surface with a sterile blade
 c Cut a portion of tissue from the inside using sterile forceps and scalpel or scissors. A size of $1 \times 1 \times 1$ cm is recommended
 d Put the specimen in a sterile container

2 Technique 2

 a Burn the surface close to the area to be cultured with a red-hot spatula
 b Make a deep cut through this sterilized surface with a sterile blade
 c Introduce a sterile swab stick (such as Culturette) through the opening, push beyond the cut into the tissue, remove, and place in appropriate transport medium

3 For cystic processes that need to be cultured for anaerobic organisms: aspirate with a sterile syringe and needle (about 2 to 4 ml), expel air bubble from the syringe, and inject the sample into an anaerobic vial. If a vial is not available, put a rubber cork on the end of the needle

Small specimens

1 If the specimen is submitted fresh in a sterile container with the request for bacteriologic studies to be carried out:

 a Open the container, cut a portion of tissue with sterile instruments, and transfer to a sterile container
 b Use the rest of the specimen for histologic examination.

2 If the need for culture becomes evident after the fresh specimen has been handled in a nonsterile fashion, proceed as follows:

 a Cut a piece of the tissue (approximately 1 cm × 1 cm × 1 cm) with a sterile blade.
 b Sterilize a pair of clean forceps by dipping them in ethanol and flaming
 c Holding the specimen with the sterilized forceps, wash thoroughly with sterile saline solution
 d Lay specimen in a sterile container. Sterilize the forceps again and pick up the specimen in a different portion
 e Repeat the washing with sterile solution
 f Put the specimen in a sterile container

3 After a sample has been taken for cultures, it is advisable to make a smear from an adjacent area, fix in alcohol, and stain for the microorganisms suspected (Gram's, Ziehl–Neelsen)

1 Braunstein H. The value of microbiologic culture of tissue samples in surgical pathology. Mod Pathol 1989, **2:** 217–221

DNA ploidy and cell proliferation analysis by flow cytometry—sampling

Cut viable tissue into 0.5-cm³ cubes in the fresh state as soon as possible after excision, drop in a bottle containing culture medium (such as RPMI or DMEM), and submit to the appropriate laboratory. If immediate transportation is not feasible, store temporarily in the refrigerator at 4°C

Ear—temporal bone resection

Subtotal or total temporal bone resections can be carried out for carcinoma of the external auditory canal, middle ear, or mastoid

Procedure

1 Review roentgenograms if available and obtain roentgenograms of the specimen if facilities are available
2 Orient the specimen as to anteroposterior, supero-inferior, and mediolateral planes
3 Mark the margins with India ink
4 Section longitudinally in two halves or in parallel cross-sections, depending on location and size of tumor

Description

1 Type of resection: subtotal or total
2 Tumor: size, gross features, and location: external ear, auditory canal, middle ear. If in the canal, does it involve the outer cartilaginous third or the inner osseous two thirds?
3 Location within the canal: floor, walls, roof, circumferential; invasion anteriorly toward the parotid gland? superiorly toward the cranial cavity?
4 Status of tympanic membrane
5 Parotid gland, if present: invaded by tumor?

Sections for histology

1 Tumor: in its entirety
2 Surgical margins
3 Parotid gland, if present

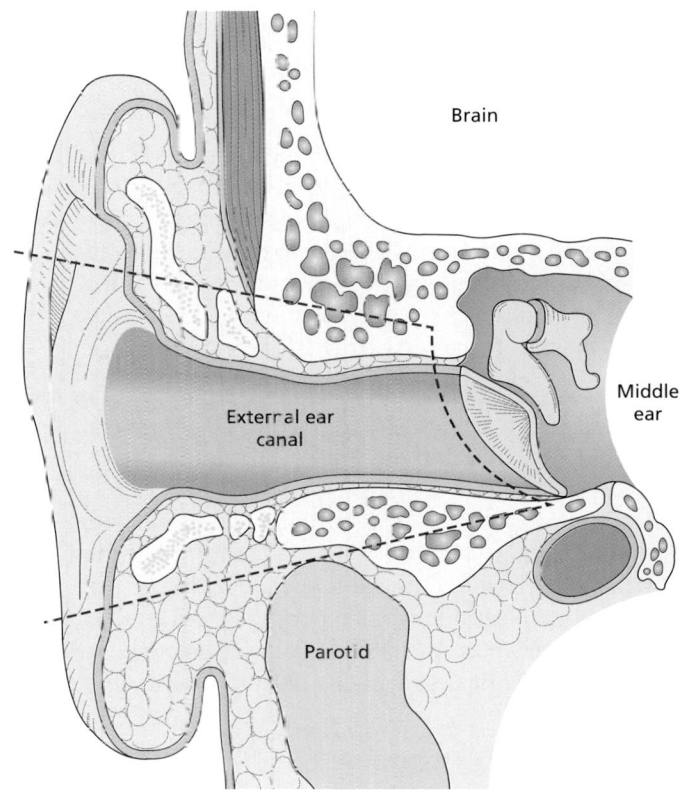

Electron microscopy—sampling

Fixative

Several fixatives are available for electron microscopy. The most commonly used is 2.5% glutaraldehyde in Millonig's phosphate buffer, in amounts of 3 to 4 ml per vial, which is kept refrigerated at 4°C. The working solution can be stored for up to 1 month.

Sampling from fresh tissue

Fresh tissue is highly preferable to routinely fixed material. It is imperative for tissue to be handled *immediately* after excision.

1 Put the specimen on a clear cutting board (such as a heavy plastic card) and cut 1-mm thick slices with a sharp razor blade
2 Place several drops of electron microscopy fixative in another area of the cutting board, place the tissue slice on top, and cover with a few drops of fixative

3 Chop the slide into 1-mm cubes with a sharp razor blade, and immerse them in cold (4°C) fixative. Five to 15 fragments of tissue are adequate. If the specimen has grossly different areas, submit for electron microscopy in separate containers
4 Submit to electron microscopy laboratory for processing; the tissue can remain in the electron microscopy fixative for several days at 4°C

Sampling from routinely fixed tissue

In routinely fixed tissue, there is usually extensive fixation artifact, but at times recognizable diagnostic electron microscopy features are retained (such as desmosomes, neurosecretory granules, melanosomes)

1 Cut a 1-mm slice from an *edge* of the specimen that was in direct contact with the fixative
2 Proceed as for fresh tissues

Esophagus—esophagectomy

The extent of an *esophagectomy* depends on the type and location of the lesion. Most esophagectomies consist of removal of the distal portion of the organ, followed by an esophagogastric anastomosis

Procedure

1 Dissect the specimen in the fresh state; open longitudinally from one end to the other after marking the deep margins with India ink, trying to cut on the side opposite the tumor (see accompanying drawing A). If a portion of the stomach is included, open along the greater curvature in continuity with the esophageal cut (see accompanying drawing B)

 a Dissect the periesophageal fat and look for lymph nodes. Divide into three portions: adjacent, proximal, and distal to the tumor (the latter might include the cardioesophageal nodes)

 b Pin the specimen in a corkboard, mucosal side up, and float in a large formalin container with the specimen on the underside; fix overnight.

 c Take two photographs or photocopies, and identify in one of them the sites of the sections to be taken

d Paint the surgical specimens with India ink after the

specimens are fixed; this includes both mucosal ends and the soft tissue around the tumor

Description

1 Length and diameter or circumference of specimen; proximal stomach included? (if so, indicate length along lesser and greater curvature)

2 Tumor: size, appearance (fungating? rolled edges? ulcerated?); does it involve entire organ circumferentially? depth of invasion; extension into stomach and adjacent organs? distance from both lines of resection and from cardias, if present

3 Mucosa: appearance of non-neoplastic mucosa; recognizable esophageal mucosa *distal* to tumor? evidence of Barrett's esophagus? (if so, length of the segment and appearance of mucosa); lumen dilated proximal to tumor?

4 Wall: thickened? varices?

5 Stomach, if present: features of cardioesophageal junction and gastric mucosa

6 Lymph nodes: number found, size of largest; do they appear grossly involved by tumor?

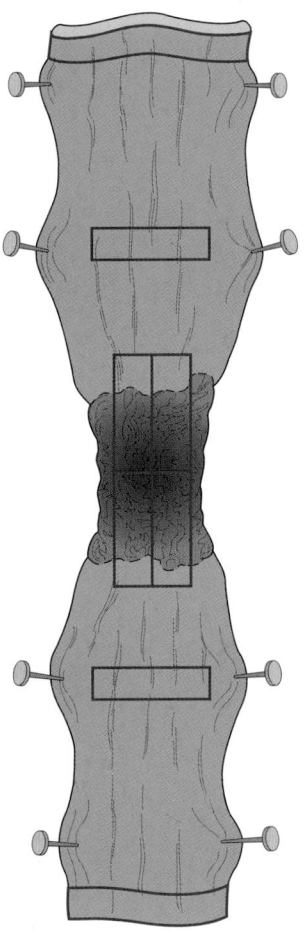

A

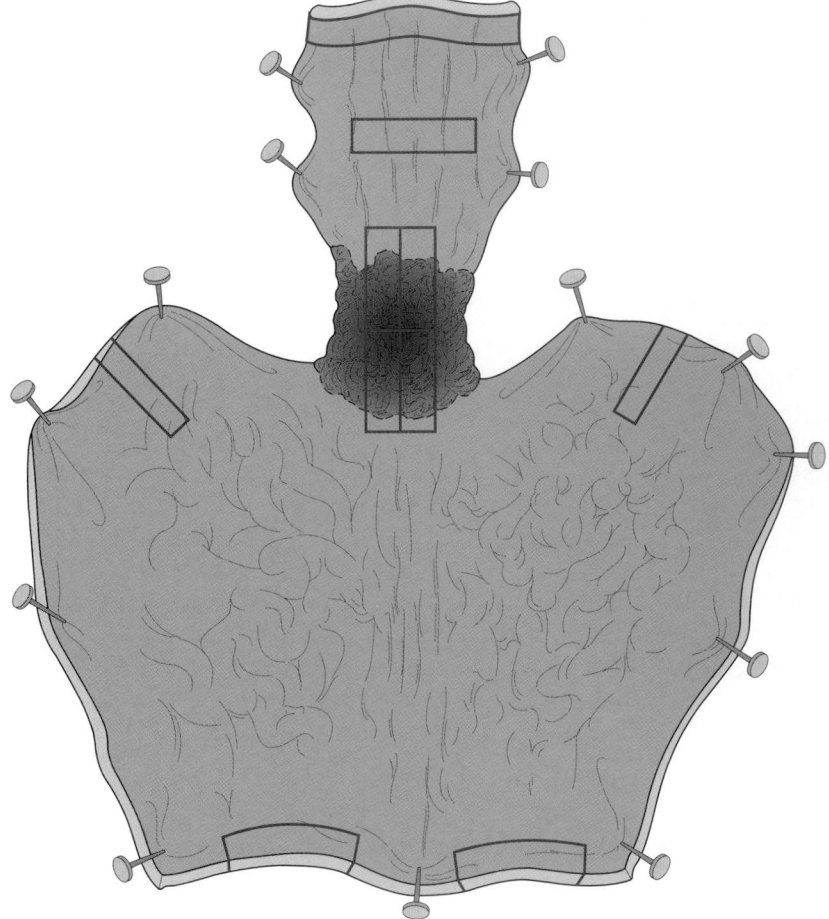

B

Sections for histology

1 Tumor: four longitudinal sections, one including a portion of non-neoplastic mucosa proximal to tumor and another a portion distal to tumor
2 Non-neoplastic mucosa: two to three transverse sections, at different distances from tumor edge, proximally and/or distally, depending on location of tumor

3 Stomach, if present: two sections, one including gastroesophageal junction
4 Proximal line of resection
5 Distal line of resection
6 Lymph nodes:
   a Adjacent to tumor
   b Proximal to tumor
   c Distal to tumor

Extremities—amputation for occlusive vascular disease

(Adapted from Rodriguez-Martinez HA, Cruz-Ortiz H, Alcantara-Vazquez A, Alcorta-Anguizola B, Burgos-Mendivil J. Dissecting technique for gangrenous lower limbs with vascular occlusions. Patologia 1972, **10**: 69–78.)

Procedure

1 Removal of femoral, popliteal, and posterior tibial neurovascular bundles and peroneal vessels:

   a Place the extremity on a dissection board with the posterior surface upward. The dissection will be completed more rapidly if an assistant holds the specimen and helps retract flaps
   b Incise longitudinally the skin over the midline of the popliteal region and the upper two thirds of the posterior tibial region (see accompanying diagram p. 2928
   c Incise obliquely the skin from the lower end of the first incision to 2 cm below the posterior border of the medial malleolus (see accompanying diagram, p. 2928
   d With a scalpel or knife, cut through the subcutaneous tissue and superficial fascia of the entire incision
   e In the posterior femoral and popliteal regions, separate, with blunt and sharp dissection, the semitendinous, semimembranous, and medial head of the gastrocnemius muscles from the biceps femoris and lateral head of the gastrocnemium. This maneuver will expose the sciatic and posterior tibial nerves and the femoral and popliteal vessels
   f Deepen the incisions made in steps b and c in the posterior tibial regions, cutting through the gastrocnemius and soleus muscles and the tendo-calcaneus. This will show, underneath the intermuscular fascial septum, the posterior tibial neurovascular bundle and the peroneal vessels
   g Beginning at their upper end, dissect and excise the sciatic and posterior tibial nerves down to the place where the latter nerve joins the popliteal vessels

   h Beginning at their upper end, dissect and excise the femoral and popliteal vessels down to the place where the latter vessels join the posterior tibial nerve
   i Excise *en bloc* the popliteal vessels and the posterior tibial nerve
   j Continue with the removal of the entire posterior tibial neurovascular bundle, down to the lowest portion of the skin incision, and transect it there. The bundle should be excised together with neighboring portions of muscle fascia
   k Last, remove the peroneal vessels together with contiguous muscle fibers. These vessels are chiefly located behind the fibula and the interosseous membrane and within the muscle fibers of the flexor hallucis longus

2 Removal of the anterior tibial neurovascular bundle:

   a Place the extremity with its anterior surface upward
   b Incise longitudinally the skin from a point located between the head of the fibula and the tibial tuberosity to a joint equidistant between both malleoli (see accompanying diagram)
   c With a scalpel or knife, cut through the subcutaneous tissue and superficial fascia of the whole incision
   d In the middle portion of the incision, cut, with scissors or knife, through the fibers of the tibialis anterior muscle down to the interosseous membrane. This will uncover part of the anterior tibial neurovascular bundle
   e With sharp or blunt dissection, separate partially the regional muscular masses in the upper portion and the tendons in the lower portion, so as to expose lengthwise the anterior tibial neurovascular bundle
   f Cut across the lowest portion of the anterior tibial neurovascular bundle. Pull the bundle downward, and excise it together with portions of adjacent muscles and interosseous membrane. The upper

Extremities—amputation for occlusive vascular disease *(continued)*

end of the bundle becomes loose by just exerting traction downward

3 Removal of the tissue block with dorsalis pedis vessel:

   a Trace a 3- to 4-cm wide rectangle over the dorsum of the foot, extending from the lowest part of the anterior tibial incision to the proximal portion of the first interosseous space

   b Following the sides of the rectangle, cut through the skin, subcutaneous tissue, superficial fascia, regional muscles and tendons, and deep fascia. Actually cut down to the very dorsal surface of the regional bones

   c With a scalpel or knife, excise the whole tissue block, clearing away all the soft tissues from the underlying bones. The vessels lie very keep in this region

4 Removal of the tissue block with the medial and lateral plantar vessels:

   a Place the extremity with the posterior surface upward

   b Trace a rectangle on the sole with the following anatomic landmarks: posterior border of the medial malleolus, medial side of the foot, base of the metatarsal bones, and lateral side of the foot. The transverse limits can also be determined, approximately, dividing the sole in fifths

   c Following the sides of the rectangle, cut through the skin, subcutaneous tissue, plantar aponeurosis and fascia, and regional muscles and tendons. In fact, cut down to the very plantar surfaces of the regional bone

   d With sharp dissection, remove the entire tissue block so as to leave fully exposed the regional bones and ligaments

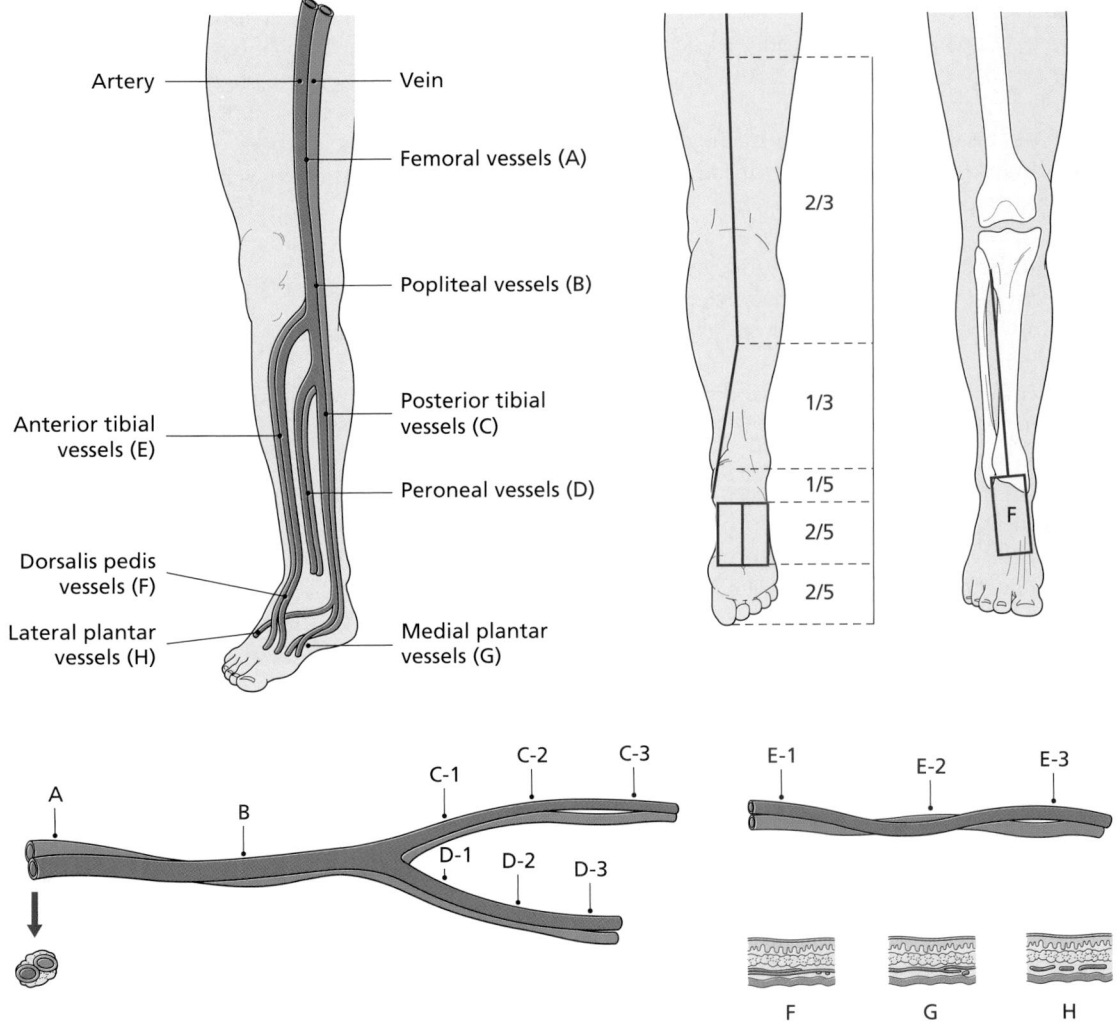

e Bisect longitudinally the tissue block. The medial half represents the tissue block of the medial plantar vessels, whereas the lateral half represents the tissue block of the lateral plantar vessels

5 Take samples of skin and soft tissues from areas of ulceration, necrosis, or infection and from bone, if indicated. Now the extremity can be disposed of

6 Fix all the excised tissues overnight in formalin. The neurovascular bundles should be pinned down on corkboard

7 Once neurovascular bundles are well fixed, cut transversely every 4 to 5 mm and carefully examine the wall and lumen of vessels

Description

1 Type of amputation; side of extremity
2 Length and circumference
3 Appearance of skin: ulcers (size, extent), hemorrhage, stasis dermatitis
4 Subcutaneous tissue; muscle; bone and joints
5 Appearance of major arteries and veins: atherosclerosis (degree), thrombosis

Sections for histology

1 Skin
2 Major arteries, veins, and nerves according to accompanying diagram or an abbreviated version of it
3 Skeletal muscle
4 Bone and joint (when pertinent)

Eyes—conjunctiva

Procedure

Lesions of the conjunctiva are thin and tend to fold into distorted patterns when placed into fixative. To prepare the tissue so that the pathologist can orient it properly, the surgeon should spread the lesion onto a small piece of filter paper and allow it to dry for a few seconds before gently placing the filter paper with the adherent specimen into the jar of fixative. Specimens should never be put onto sponges of any kind since these will expand when placed into the fixative, thus distorting the specimen.

Eyes—enucleation[1-3]

Procedure

1 Fix the intact ocular globe in formalin for 24 hours before sectioning; it is not advisable to open the eye, to cut windows into the sclera, or to inject fixative into the vitreous

2 Wash in running tap water for 1 or more hours and, optionally, place in 60% ethyl alcohol for a few more hours

3 Review the summary of the clinical history and the results of the ophthalmologic examination prior to sectioning

4 Measure anteroposterior, horizontal, and vertical dimensions of the globe, length of the optic nerve, and horizontal dimensions of the cornea

5 Look for sites of accidental or surgical injuries

6 Transilluminate the globe before opening it. A substage microscope lamp in a darkened room is satisfactory. Rotate the globe over the light source; if abnormal shadows are detected, mark them on the sclera with an indelible pencil

7 Examination of the globe with a ×7 objective of a dissecting microscope can be carried out to detect minute lesions

8 If intraocular foreign bodies or retinoblastoma is suspected, take a roentgenogram of the globe before it is opened

9 If choroidal malignant melanoma is suspected, sample at least one of the vortex veins from each of the four quadrants (see accompanying drawing)

10 Open the eye with a sharp razor blade by holding the globe with the left hand, cornea down against the cutting block and the blade between the thumb and middle finger of the right hand. Open the eye with a sawing motion from back to front. The plane of section should begin adjacent to the optic nerve and end through the periphery of the cornea. The plane of section is dependent on whether a lesion

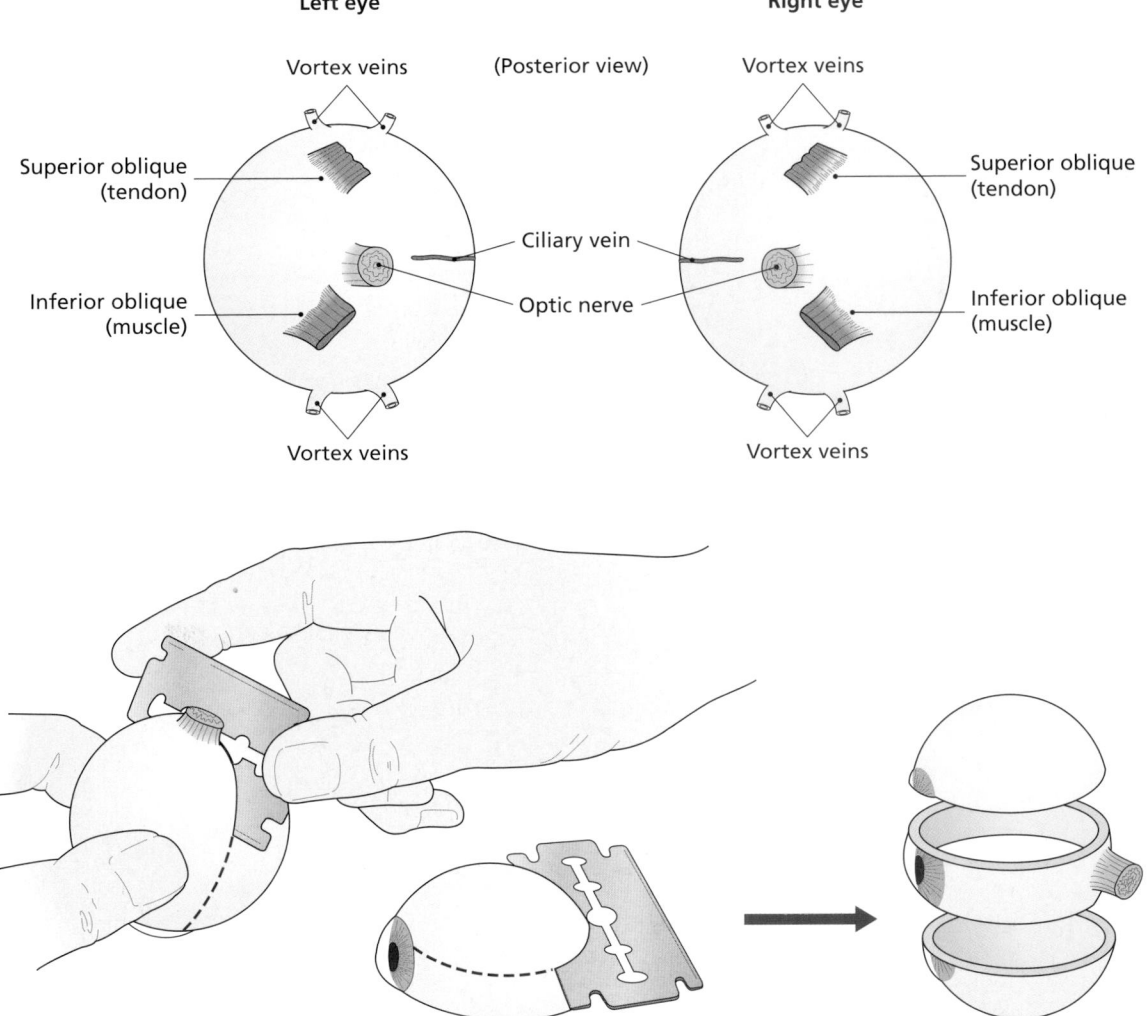

has been detected in the previous steps. If it has not, cut the globe along a horizontal plane, using as surface landmarks the superior and inferior oblique insertions and the long postciliary vein (see accompanying drawing). If a lesion has been found, modify the plane of section so that the lesion will be included in the slab

11 Examine the interior of the globe

12 Place the eye flat on its cut surface, and make a second plane of section, parallel to the first, again passing from back to front

13 Examine carefully the ~8-mm disc-shaped slab thus obtained, which should contain the cornea, pupils, lens, and optic nerve. Take photographs or photocopies, if indicated

Description

Intact eye

1 Side of the globe (see accompanying drawing); anteroposterior, horizontal, and vertical dimensions

2 Length of optic nerve

3 Horizontal and vertical dimensions of cornea

4 Anterior segment: surgical incisions? corneal opacification? iris abnormalities? lens present?

5 Transillumination findings

Slab

1 Corneal thickness; anterior chamber depth; configuration of anterior chamber angle

2 Condition of iris, ciliary body, and lens

3 Condition of choroids, retina, vitreous body, and optic disc

4 If tumor present: location, size, color, edges, consistency, presence of hemorrhage or necrosis, ocular structures involved, extension into optic nerve

Sections for histology

1 Entire eye slab

2 Any (other) abnormal areas

3 In tumors, particularly retinoblastoma: cross-section of surgical margin of optic nerve

4 In suspected malignant melanoma: sample from at least one of vortex veins from each of four quadrants

1   Folberg R, Verdick R, Weingeist TA, Montague PR. The gross examination of eyes removed for choroidal and ciliary body melanomas. Ophthalmology 1985, **93**: 1643–1647

2   Herreman R, De Buen S, Cortés T. Oftalmóun Nuevo apparato para secionarlos ojos en el laboratorio de anatomía patológica. Rev Fac Med (Mexico) 1965, **7**: 157–167

3   Smith ME. A method for immediate gross sectioning of enucleated globes. Am J Ophthalmol 1974, **77**: 413–414

4   Yanoff M, Fine BS. Glutaraldehyde fixation of routine surgical eye tissue. Am J Ophthalmol 1967, **63**: 137–140

Fallopian tubes—ligation

In tubal ligation, an avascular segment in the midisthmic portion of the tube is made into a loop, the base is ligated, and the top of the loop is excised.

Procedure

1 Separate specimens from right and left tubes

2 Measure the length and diameter of each

Description

1 Length and diameter of each specimen

2 Do they appear to be a complete segment of each tube? lumen present?

Sections for histology

1 All tissues received, identified as to right and left tube

2 Very important that tissue be sectioned on end; instructions to histotechnician or embedding in agar may be necessary

1   Robboy SJ, Kraus FT, Kurman RJ. Gross description, processing, and reporting of gynaecologic and obstetric specimens. In: Kurman RJ (ed). Blaustein's Pathology of the Female Genital Tract, 4th Edn. New York, 2002, Springer-Verlag, pp. 1319–1346

Fallopian tubes—salpingectomy

Salpingectomy may be performed by itself in the case of fallopian tube pathology or—more often—as part of a total abdominal hysterectomy with unilateral or bilateral salpingo-oophorectomy.

Procedure

1 Fix the specimen before sectioning. If the tubes are attached to the uterus, they should be fixed in that position
2 Measure the length and greatest diameter
3 If the tube is relatively normal in size, serially section at 5-mm intervals and examine. Make the cuts incomplete so that the pieces remain attached by the serosa
4 If the tube is obviously enlarged, make one complete longitudinal section, followed by parallel sections, if necessary

Description

1 Length and greatest diameter
2 Serosa: fibrin? hemorrhage? fibrous adhesions to ovary or other organs?
3 Wall: abnormally thick? ruptured?
4 Mucosa: atrophic? hyperplastic? appearance of fimbriated end; inverted?
5 Lumen: patent? dilated? content; diameter, if abnormally large
6 Masses: size, appearance, invasion
7 Cysts in paraovarian region: diameter, thickness of wall, content; sessile or pedunculated?
8 In cases of suspected ectopic pregnancy: embryo or placenta identified? amount of hemorrhage; rupture?

Sections for histology

1 For incidental tubes without gross abnormalities: three cross-sections of each tube, taken from the proximal mid, and distal portions, submitted in the same cassette (see accompanying drawing)
2 For tubes with suspected ectopic pregnancy: submit any tissue with gross appearance of products of conception. If none is grossly identified, submit any

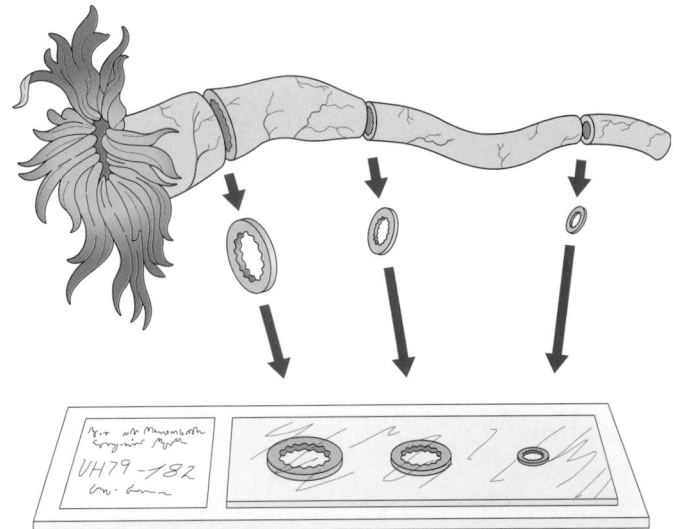

tissue with gross appearance of products of conception. If none is grossly identified, submit several sections from the wall in the area of hemorrhage as well as several from the *intraluminal clot*. If products of conception are not identified microscopically, submit additional sections

3 For tubes with other lesions: as many as needed to adequately examine any abnormal areas. If tumor is present, at least three sections must be taken to include grossly uninvolved mucosa

Procedure

Keep intact, cut sagittally, or dissect, depending on fetus size.

1   Robboy SJ, Kraus TF, Kurman RJ. Gross description, processing, and reporting of gynaecologic and obstetric specimens. In: Kurman RJ (ed). Blaustein's Pathology of the Female Genital Tract, 4th Edn. New York, 2002, Springer-Verlag, pp. 1319–1346

Fetus—abortion

Description

1 Sex; weight; crown-rump (A) or crown-heel length (B) or foot length (C) (see accompanying drawings)
2 Approximate length of gestation (see table, and figure below)
3 General condition: well preserved? macerated?
4 External and internal anomalies and other changes
5 Umbilical cord: appearance, number of vessels
6 Placental tissues accompanying fetuses:

   a Weight
   b Membranes: insertion, color, transparency, completeness; extramembranous pregnancy? marginal or membranous hemorrhage?
   c Umbilical cord: insertion, color, focal changes
   d Chorionic plate: vascular patter, vessel caliber, color; subchorionic hemorrhage?
   e Villi: hydatidiform change? (note proportion of involved villi and size of cysts); focal lesions?

Sections for histology

1 Small embryos: submit whole embryo or one half, depending on size
2 Large fetuses: submit one section from lungs, stomach (including gastric contents), kidneys, and other organs, as indicated
3 Placental tissues:

   a Extraplacental membranes (one section)
   b Umbilical cord (one section)
   c Chorionic plate (one section)
   d Villi from chorion frondosum, including maternal surface (one section)

For a more thorough examination of specimens for fetal malformations and chromosomal abnormalities, see:

1 Klatt, EC. Pathologic examination of fetal specimens from dilation and evacuation procedures. Am J Clin Pathol 1995, **103**: 415–418
2 Robboy SJ, Kraus TF, Kurman RJ. Gross description, processing, and reporting of gynaecologic and obstetric specimens. In: Kurman RJ (ed). Blaustein's Pathology of the Female Genital Tract, 4th Edn. New York, 2002, Springer-Verlag, pp. 1319–1346
3 Szulman AE. Examination of the early conceptus. Arch Pathol Lab Med 1991, **115**: 696–700

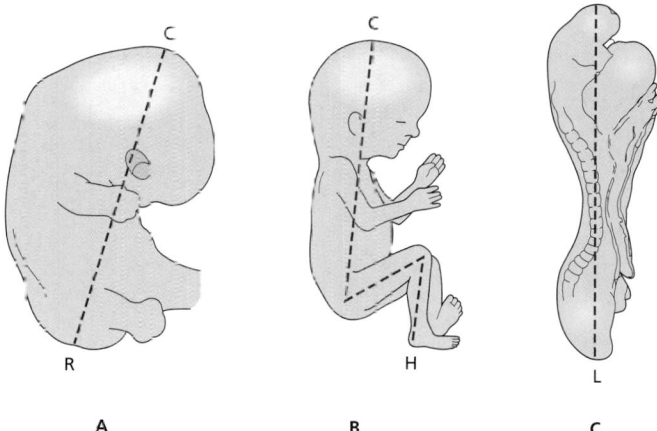

A   B   C

Table App E-1 Relations of age, size, and weight in the human embryo

Age of embryo	Crown-rump (CR) length (mm)	Crown-heel length (mm)	External diameter of chorionic sac (mm)	Weight in grams	Amount of increase each month when value at start of month equals unity	
					CR length	Weight
One week	0.1	—	0.2			
Two weeks	0.2	—	3			
Three weeks	2.0	—	10			
Four weeks	5.0	—	10	.02	49.0	40000.00
Five weeks	8.0	—	25			
Six weeks	12.0	—	30			
Seven weeks	17.0	19.0	40			
Two lunar months	25.0	30.0	50	1	3.6	49.00
Three lunar months	56.0	73.0	—	14	1.4	13.00
Four lunar months	112.0	157.0	—	105	1.0	6.50
Five lunar months	160.0	239.0	—	310	0.43	1.95
Six lunar months	203.0	296.0	—	640	0.26	1.07
Seven lunar months	242.0	355.0	—	1080	0.14	0.69
Eight lunar months	277.0	409.0	—	1670	0.14	0.55
Nine lunar months	313.0	458.0	—	2400	0.13	0.43
Full term (38 weeks)	350.0	500.0	—	3300	0.12	0.38

From Arey LB: Development anatomy, ed 7. Philadelphia, 1965, W.B. Saunders Co, p 104.
*Total length of embryonic disc.

Gallbladder—cholecystectomy

Cholecystectomy consists of removal of the entire gallbladder after dissecting it from the base of the liver and suturing the cystic duct and cystic artery. At present, a high number of cholecystectomies are performed through a laparoscopic route.

Procedure

1 Open the entire organ longitudinally as soon as feasible after excision; otherwise the mucosa will quickly undergo autolytic changes
2 If stones are present, was them, estimate the number and the size of the largest, and cut one or several of them with a scalpel
3 Search for lymph nodes along the bladder neck
4 In cases of carcinoma the organ also can be studied by extracting the bile with a syringe, filling the lumen with formalin, fixing overnight at 4°C, and cutting the specimen with scissors and a scalpel

Description

1 Length and greatest diameter of gallbladder
2 Serosa: thickened? fibrous adhesions? fibrin?
3 Wall: thickened? (if so, focally or diffusely?) hemorrhage?
4 Mucosa: color, appearance, ulcerated? hyperplastic? cholesterosis

5 Cystic duct: dilated? impacted with stones? lymph nodes present? size and appearance
6 Approximate volume, color, and consistency of bile
7 Stones: approximate number, shape, and size range: color and appearance on cross-sections; type of stone (see accompanying table)
8 If tumor present: location, distance from fundus and neck, size; polypoid? ulcerated? infiltrative? serosal involvement?

Sections for histology

1 Three sections including entire wall, one from the fundus, one from the body, and one from the neck; additional sections from any area that appears grossly abnormal
2 In cases of suspected carcinoma in situ, the organ can be studied by embedding the entire specimen by the Swiss roll method. In addition, the bile can be decanted into a breaker or centrifuge tube and studied cytologically[1]
3 Cystic duct and lymph nodes, if they appear grossly abnormal or if the gallbladder contains a tumor

1   Albores-Saavedra J, Henson DE, Klimstra DS. Tumors of the gallbladder, extrahepatic bile ducts, and ampulla of Vater. Washington, DC. Armed Forces Institute of Pathology, 2000; Atlas of tumor pathology. Third series, fasccile 27;365.

Table App E-2 Types of gallstones

Type of stone	Incidence	Composition	Appearance
Pure	10%	Cholesterol Calcium bilirubinate Calcium carbonate	Solitary; crystalline surface Multiple; jet black; crystalline or amorphous Grayish white; amorphous

Mixed	80%	Cholesterol and calcium bilirubinate
		Cholesterol and calcium carbonate
		Calcium bilirubinate and calcium carbonate
		Cholesterol, calcium bilirubinate, and calcium carbonate
			Multiple, faceted or lobulated, laminated, and crystalline on cut surfaces
			Hue:
			    Yellow—cholesterol
			    Black—calcium bilirubinate
			    White—calcium carbonate

Combined	10%	Pure gallstone nucleus with mixed gallstone shell Mixed gallstone nucleus with pure gallstone shell	Largest of gallstones when single Hue depends on composition of shell

Slightly modified from de Schryver-Kecskemet K: Gallbladder and biliary ducts. In Kissane JM, ed: Anderson's pathology, ed 9. St Louis, 1990, Mosby.

Heart—valve replacement

(Adapted from Roberts WC, Morrow AG. Cardiac valves and the surgical pathologist. Arch Pathol 1996, 82: 309–313.)

Traditionally, valve replacement operations have entailed the removal of the entire diseased valve. However, in cases of mitral valve disease, there has been a tendency in recent years to remove only the anterior mitral leaflet during valve replacement and to remove only portions of the valve (usually from the posterior leaflet) during reparative procedures.

Procedure

1 Fix the specimen before sectioning
2 Take photographs or photocopies and a roentgenogram in every case. For atrioventricular valves, photograph from both atrial and ventricular aspects. For aortic valves, photograph from both aortic and ventricular aspects

Description

Atrioventricular valves

1 Leaflets fibrotic, calcified, or normal?
2 Fibrosis or calcification focal or diffuse?
3 Fibrosis or calcification distributed on leaflets? (only at margins? on one surface? on both?)
4 Leaflets immobile, shortened, stretched, or normal?
5 Commissures fused? (if so, to what extent?)
6 Chordae tendineae intact, ruptured, shortened, elongated, fused, or normal?
7 Papillary muscles normal in number, scarred, hypertrophied, or elongated?
8 Valve incompetent, stenotic, or both?
9 If incompetent: because of scanty valvular tissue, dilated annulus, or ruptured chordae or because of ruptured, scarred, or shortened papillary muscle?

Semilunar valves

Same as for atrioventricular valves in most respects plus:

1 Number of cusps present?
2 Cusps of equal or unequal size?

Sections for histology

Several sections, including free edge; decalcify, if necessary

Hormone receptor assays—sampling

(Adapted from Keffer JH. Hormone-receptor assays and cancer of the breast. The pathologist's role [editorial]. Am J Clin Pathol 1978, 70: 719–720.)

Determination of receptors for different steroid hormones (estrogens, progesterone, androgens) has become an established technique for the evaluation of several surgically excised tissues, particularly breast carcinoma. It correlates with clinical response to hormone therapy and, according to some, also with clinical response to chemotherapeutic agents. In some cases of metastatic cancer, it may provide some indication of the site of origin of the primary lesion. Sampling should be taken of recurrent or metastatic carcinoma, even if the original tumor had been previously assayed, to establish the continued presence or absence of the receptor.

Two methods are available for the determination of hormone receptors in tissue: biochemical and immunohistochemical. The former, based on charcoal-dextran assay, has been the standard for many years, but has been largely replaced by the immunohistochemical method. The procedure for procuring tissue for the biochemical assay if still desired is the following:

1 Examine tissue in the fresh state, immediately after excision; select a sample carefully, avoiding areas of necrosis, adipose tissue, and other unsuitable areas
2 Cut a sample measuring approximately 1 cm in greatest diameter (or as large as allowable). The instruments should be clean but not necessarily sterile
3 Freeze quickly in liquid nitrogen (–70°C) in isopentane or with freon spray
4 Store in the deep freeze until the sample is ready to be delivered (in the frozen state) to the appropriate laboratory
5 Submit for histology (for control purposes) a piece of tissue immediately adjacent to the one frozen and identify as such
6 When the lesion is so small that a 1 cm sample for biochemical assay cannot be spared, cut frozen sections and store in the freezer (–70°C) for subsequent immunohistochemical staining for receptor

Imprints (touch preparations)

(Adapted from Berard CW, Bowling MC. Technical factors in evaluation of lymph node biopsies. Tutorial on Neoplastic Hematopathology, Henry Rappaport, MD., Director, Pasadena, California, Feb 5–9, 1979; presented in cooperation with The City of Hope National Medical Center and The University of Chicago Center for Continuing Education.)

1 Cut a block of tissue measure approximately (10 × 10 × 3 mm)
2 Hold the tissue gently with forceps with the freshly cut, flat surface upward
3 With the other hand, lightly touch an alcohol-clean class slide repeatedly in serial adjacent areas with the cut surface of the tissue. Just contact—do not compress the block. If the surface touched is excessively bloody or wet, discard the slide and repeat with another slide until the touch preparations are barely opaque. Prepare an average of four slides in this fashion
4 As each slide is prepared, dry it rapidly by waving it in the air. Do not heat or blow on the slide. It should take no more than 30 to 60 seconds for the slide to dry; if it takes more, it means that the touches are too wet and that the resulting imprints will be unsatisfactory

5 For standard purposes, fix (after drying) in methyl alcohol, and stain two with hematoxylin–eosin and two with Wright's or Giemsa stain
6 After preparation of the imprints, fix and submit for histology the block used for this purpose to correlate its appearance with that of the imprint

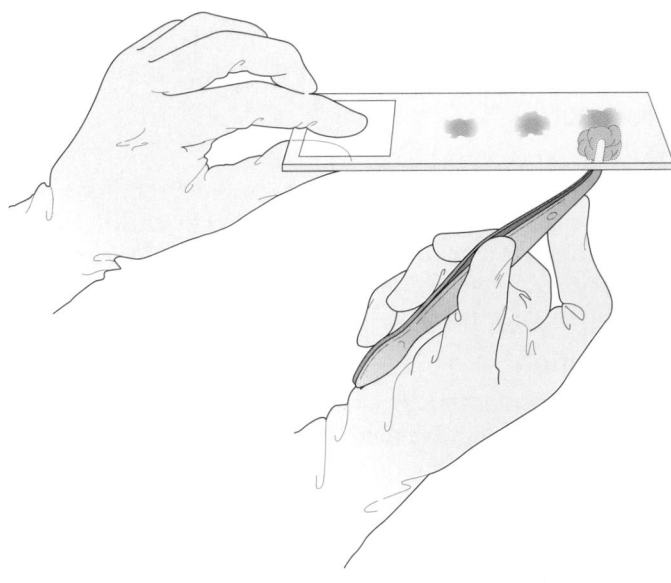

Injection of specimens—general guidelines

When feasible, the injection of surgical specimens may serve to illustrate more clearly the gross pathology present, as well as to ensure proper fixation. The procedure has been found most useful for lobectomies, pneumonectomies, cystectomies, colectomies, and pelvic exenterations.

1 Partially fill a large container with fixative
2 Prepare the specimen properly (see specific instructions for the respective organs)

3 Place in container and inject with formalin
4 Add additional fixative to the container to ensure that the entire specimen is covered by fixative
5 Place a towel or several gauze pads of the free-floating specimen to prevent the surface from drying
6 Cover the container with a lid
7 Fix for 24 hours before dissecting

Jaw resection for tumor—mandibulectomy[1]

Procedure

1 Fix the whole specimen in formalin overnight in the refrigerator at 4°C
2 Paint the surgical margins with India ink
3 For bone tumors: make multiple parallel sections through bone and soft tissue with a band saw, fix further in formalin, and decalcify
4 For mucosal or soft tissue tumors: separate soft tissue from the mandible with a scalpel. The direction of the dissection should be from the inferior to the superior and from the posterior to the anterior aspects
5 Take photographs or photocopies and identify in one of them the site of the sections to be taken
6 If the specimen includes a radical neck dissection, process according to instructions for Lymph node dissection—radical neck

Description

1 Type of resection (partial or total) and side
2 Tumor size, color, appearance, edges; bone invaded?
3 Non-neoplastic mucosa: leukoplakia?
4 Bone: appearance on cross-sections
5 Teeth: number and appearance

Sections for histology

1 Tumor: three sections
2 Non-neoplastic mucosa
3 Mucosal surgical margins
4 Soft tissue surgical margins
5 Bone surgical margins
6 Mandibular nerve (surgical margins)
7 Bone, if grossly involved or suspicious

1   A very detailed set of instructions for surgical specimens from the upper aerodigestive tract is available from: Slootweg PJ, de Groot JAM. Surgical pathological anatomy of head and neck specimens: A manual for the dissection of surgical specimens from the upper aerodigestive tract. London, 1999, Springer

Jaw resection for tumor—maxillectomy[1]

Procedure

1 Fix the specimen in formalin overnight in the refrigerator at 4°C
2 Paint the surgical margins with India ink
3 Take surgical margins (anterior, posterior, external, and superior); cut the specimen with the band saw in parallel slices 0.5 cm thick. Fix them overnight Take photographs and X-ray studies, if indicated
4 Take photographs or photocopies and identify in one of them the site of the sections to be taken

Description

1 Extent of resection
2 Presence of following structures: hard and soft palates; superior, middle, and inferior turbinates; medial and lateral pterygoid plate of sphenoid bone; air cells of ethmoid; bony floor of orbit; orbital contents; zygoma, masseter, temporalis, external, and internal pterygoid muscles

3 Tumor characteristics: location, extent, size; limited to the maxillary sinus? arising from superior, medial, lateral, anterior, posterior, or inferior part of sinus? extending into intratemporal fossa, nasal cavity, ethmoid cells, or any other of aforementioned structures? presence of tumor at surgical margins?
4 Condition of ostium of maxillary sinus and any other sinuses present; fistulae present

Sections for histology

1 Tumor: as many sections as necessary, with minimum of three
2 Surgical margins

1   A very detailed set of instructions for surgical specimens from the upper aerodigestive tract is available from: Slootweg PJ, de Groot JAM. Surgical pathological anatomy of head and neck specimens: A manual for the dissection of surgical specimens from the upper aerodigestive tract. London, 1999, Springer

Kidney—needle biopsy

Procedure

The examination and sampling of this material should be carried out at the bedside or *immediately* after the specimen is received in the pathology laboratory.

1 Measure the length and diameter
2 Try to determine by gross inspection whether the cortex is present; this can be done by identifying glomeruli with a dissecting microscope or magnifying lenses. An experienced observer can do it most of the time with the naked eye on the basis of color
3 If the cortex is grossly identified:

   a Take three pieces (1 mm thick each) from this area and fix in glutaraldehyde for electron microscopic examination
   b Take one additional piece (2 mm thick) from this area and freeze in isopentane cooled with liquid nitrogen for immunofluorescence
   c Place the remainder of the specimen in fixative for routine light microscopy

4 If the cortex cannot be identified with certainty on gross inspection, the operator may decide to perform another needle biopsy. Otherwise, the following should be done with the specimen:

   a Take two pieces (1 mm each) from *each* end and freeze for immunofluorescence

   b Take two additional pieces (2 mm) from *each* end and freeze for immunofluorescence
   c Fix the remainder for routine histology

5 If the amount of tissue is insufficient to divide for all these studies, electron microscopy and immunofluorescence have priority, one of the reasons being that a modified version of the light microscopic evaluation can be carried out on them
6 If the specimen is an open wedge biopsy, the same guidelines apply, except for the fact that the cortex is always readily identifiable and therefore double sampling is not necessary

Description

1 Number of fragments; length and diameter of each
2 Color: homogenous or not?
3 Cortex recognizable? glomeruli; size, color; prominence

Sections for histology

1 See Procedure
2 Needle renal biopsies should be routinely stained with:

   a Hematoxylin–eosin
   b Alcian blue–PAS
   c Jones' silver methenamine
   d Masson's trichrome

Kidney—nephrectomy for nontumoral condition

Procedure

1 Measure and weigh the organ
2 Two options are available depending on the type of abnormality present and the status of the organ when received in the laboratory:

   a Cut the kidney sagittally, strip the capsule, and carefully open the pelvis, calyces, and ureter
   b Inject with formalin through the ureter and, if possible, through the renal artery, ligate the ureter (and artery), and submerge in formalin overnight. Cut sagittally the next day, strip the capsule, and open the pelvis, calyces, and ureter. This technique is especially useful in cases of hydronephrosis

3 Take photographs or photocopies and identify in one of them the sites of the sections to be taken
4 If stones are present, submit for chemical analysis, if indicated

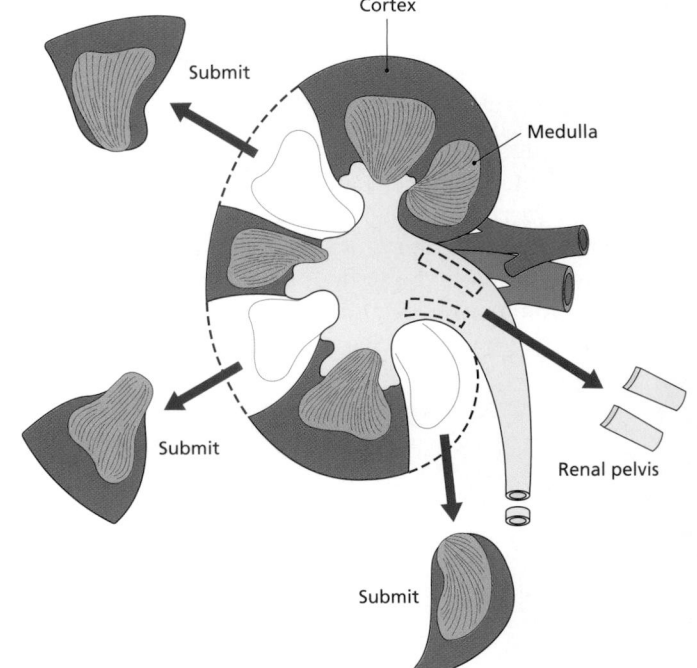

Description

1 Weight and size of kidney
2 Capsule: amount of pericapsular tissue, thickness of capsule, adherence to cortex
3 External surface: smooth? scars: number, size, shape (flat or V shaped?); cysts? (if so, number, size, location, content)
4 Cortex: color, width; glomeruli apparent? striations apparent and orderly?
5 Medulla: color, width; medullary rays apparent and orderly?
6 Pelvis: size; dilated? blunting of calyces? thickened? hemorrhage? crystalline deposits? stones: number, size and shape (see Bladder—stone removal); amount of peripelvic fat
7 Ureter: diameter, length, evidence of dilation or stricture
8 Renal artery and vein; appearance

Sections for histology

1 Kidney: three sections, each including cortex and medulla
2 Pelvis: two sections
3 Ureter

Kidney—nephrectomy for tumor[1]

Procedure

1 Look for and dissect any perirenal lymph nodes
2 Look for and open the renal vein longitudinally
3 Cut the kidney sagittally and open the pelvis, calyces, and ureter
4 Strip the capsule and look for capsular and perirenal tumor extensions
5 If stones are present, submit for chemical analysis
6 Take photographs or photocopies and identify in one of them the sites of the sections to be taken
7 Cut the kidney in thin slices searching for additional cortical or medullary lesions

Description

1 Weight and dimensions of specimen; length and diameter of ureter
2 Tumor characteristics: size, shape, location, extent, homogenicity, necrosis, hemorrhage; invasion of capsule, perirenal tissues, calyces, pelvis, and renal vein
3 Uninvolved kidney: external surface, cortex, medulla; any additional focal lesions?
4 Pelvis: dilated? blunting of calyces? stones?
5 Presence, number, size, and appearance of perirenal lymph nodes

Sections for histology

1 Tumor: for renal cell carcinoma: minimum of three sections (including one with adjacent kidney); for pediatric tumors: minimum of one section for each centimeter of tumor diameter; for carcinoma of renal pelvis: minimum of three sections with adjacent pelvis and/or renal parenchyma
2 Kidney not involved by tumor: two sections
3 Pelvis: one section is cases of renal cell carcinoma or pediatric tumors; two sections in cases of carcinoma of renal pelvis
4 Renal artery and vein
5 Ureter: one section in cases of renal cell carcinoma or pediatric tumors; one section of every centimeter of ureter resected (and any abnormal-looking areas) in cases of carcinoma of renal pelvis
6 Lymph nodes, if present

1 Eble, JN. Recommendations for examining and reporting tumor-bearing kidney specimens from adults. Semin Diagn Pathol 1998, 15: 77–82

Large bowel—colectomy for nontumoral conditions

Procedure

1 Sample a few lymph nodes, and remove the mesentery while the specimen is fresh
2 Two options are available to study the bowel, depending on the type of abnormality present and the status of the specimen when received in the laboratory. The first is the one usually carried out

   a Open the bowel longitudinally, pin on a corkboard, and fix overnight in formalin
   b Inject the specimen (see Injection of specimens—general guidelines). Evacuate gross fecal contents by gentle external massage of the specimen. Further cleansing may be accomplished by the use of a gentle stream of formalin or saline solution (*not* water) into the bowel lumen. One end of the specimen is tied off, the specimen is injected with formalin, and the other end is tied off. If a constricting lesion is present, be sure that adequate fixative can be easily passed through the point of constriction. If this cannot be achieved, the main mass will not be properly fixed; under these circumstances, it is better to open the specimen and fix as noted in **2a** rather than to inject on both sides of the lesion. Injection is especially demonstrative in cases of diverticulosis

3 Take photographs or photocopies and identify in one of them the sites of the sections to be taken
4 In general, take the sections *perpendicular* to the direction of the mucosal folds

Description

1 Part of bowel removed, length of specimen, and amount of mesentery
2 Mucosa: type of lesions, extent, ulceration (linear or transverse), depth, pseudopolyps, hemorrhage, fissures
3 Wall: thickening (focal or diffuse), atrophy, fibrosis, necrosis
4 Serosa: fibrin, pus, fibrosis, adherence of mesentery
5 Diverticular: number, size, location in relation to teniae, content, evidence of inflammation, hemorrhage or perforation

Sections for histology

1 As many as necessary to sample abnormal areas
2 Proximal and distal lines of resection in cases of colitis
3 Appendix, if included in specimen

Large bowel—colectomy for tumor

The major types of large bowel resection are *total colectomy*, *right hemicolectomy* (which includes the colon up to the hepatic flexure, cecum, ileocecal valve, appendix, portion of terminal ileum, and the corresponding mesentery), *transverse colectomy* (from the hepatic to the splenic flexures), *left hemicolectomy* (from the splenic flexure to the sigmoid colon), *low anterior* (rectosigmoid) *resection*, and *abdominoperineal resection* (sigmoid colon, rectum, and anus).

Procedure

1 Dissect the lymph nodes and remove the mesentery while the specimen is fresh
2 Two options are available to study the bowel, depending on the size and location of the specimen when received in the laboratory. The first is the one usually carried out

   a Open the bowel longitudinally through its entire length, trying not to cut through the tumor. Pin the intestine on a corkboard and fix overnight in formalin
   b Inject the specimen (see Injection of specimens—general guidelines and **2b** under Procedure in the preceding section)

3 Take photographs or photocopies and identify in one of them the sites of the sections to be taken
4 In cases with deep penetration by tumor, dissect the veins carefully for possible tumor invasion
5 In general, take the sections *perpendicular* to the direction of the mucosal folds

Description

1 Part of bowel removed, length of specimen, and amount of mesentery
2 a Tumor characteristics: size (including thickness); extent around bowel; shape (fungating, flat, ulcerating; presence of necrosis or hemorrhage; extent through bowel wall; serosal involvement, satellite nodules; evidence of blood vessel invasion; invasion of adjacent organs
   b Distance of tumor to pectinate line, peritoneal reflection, each line of resection

3 Other lesions in bowel and appearance of uninvolved mucosa; if polyps absent, so state
4 Estimate of number of lymph nodes found; whether or not nodes appear involved by tumor; size of largest node

Sections for histology

1 Tumor: at least three sections (extending through the entire wall)
2 Representative section of subserosal connective tissue, fat, and blood vessel around tumor
3 Other lesions of bowel
4 Proximal line of resection
5 Distal line of resection
6 Bowel between tumor and distal line of resection (halfway or 5 cm, whichever suits the case)
7 Appendix, if included in specimen
8 Lymph nodes:

   a Around tumor
   b Distal to tumor
   c Proximal to tumor
   d At high point of resection (areas surrounding ligated vessels)

9 In abdominoperineal resections: anorectal junction

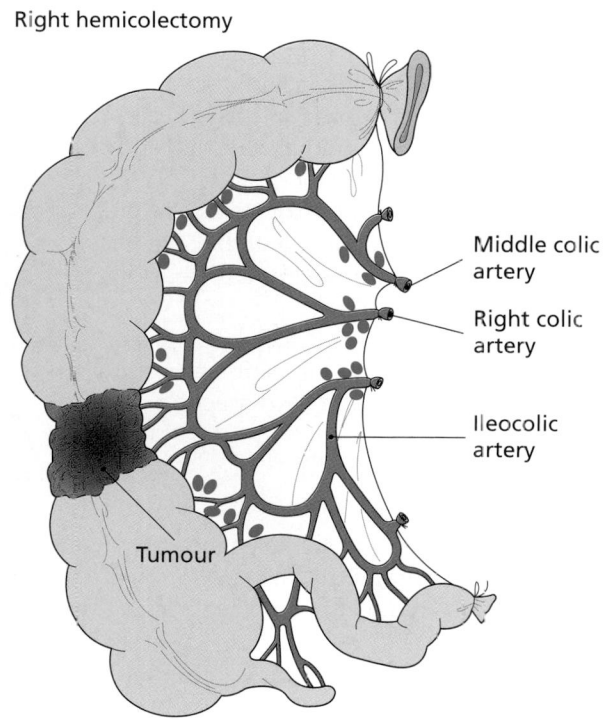

Right hemicolectomy

Middle colic artery

Right colic artery

Ileocolic artery

Tumour

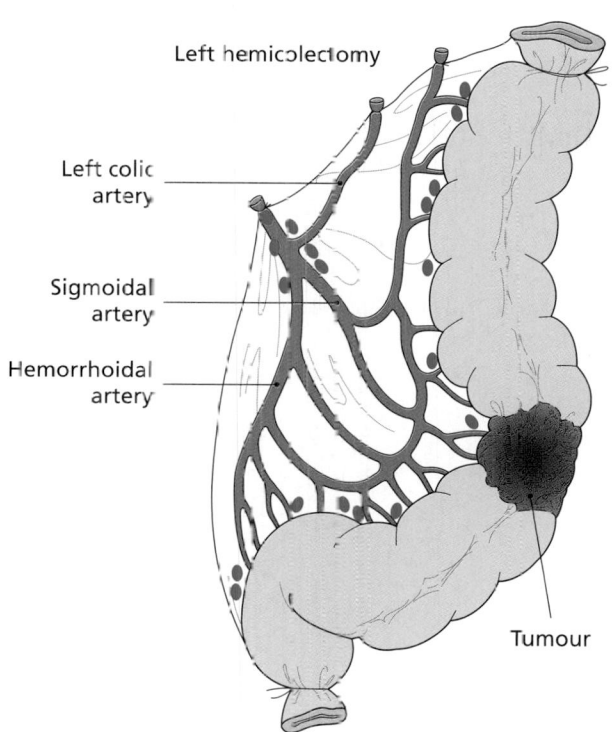

Left hemicolectomy

Left colic artery

Sigmoidal artery

Hemorrhoidal artery

Tumour

Large bowel—polypectomy

Procedure

1 Fix the specimen intact in formalin for several hours
2 Measure the diameter of the head and length of the stalk
3 For polyps with a short talk or no stalk, identify the surgical section and cut in half longitudinally (see accompanying drawing **A**)
4 For polyps with a long stalk (1 cm or more), cut a cross-section of the stalk near the surgical margin and then cut the polyp longitudinally, leaving as long a stalk as will fit in the cassette (see accompanying drawing **B**)
5 If half the polyp head is over 3 mm, trim to this thickness on the convex side

Description

1 Dimensions of polyp; diameter of head and length of stalk
2 Polyp sessile or pedunculated? ulcerated? surface smooth or papillary? any cysts on cross-section? stalk appear normal?

Sections for histology

1 One longitudinal section (including surgical margin in polyps with short stalk or no stalk)
2 One cross-section of base of stalk (in polyps with long stalk)
3 Appendix, if included in specimen

Larynx—laryngectomy[1]

(Adapted from Barnes L, Johnson JT. Pathologic and clinical consideration in the evaluation of major head and neck specimens resected for cancer. Part I. Pathol Annu 1986, **21(Pt 1):** 173–250.)

Three types of laryngectomy are performed: hemilaryngectomy, supraglottic laryngectomy, and total. *Hemilaryngectomy* consists of dividing the thyroid cartilage in the midline and resecting in continuity the thyroid cartilage along with the corresponding true and false vocal cords and ventricle. *Supraglottic laryngectomy* consists of excising the upper half of the larynx horizontally through the ventricle. *Total laryngectomy* consists of removal of the entire larynx, including upper laryngeal rings.

Procedure

1 Separate the larynx from the radical neck dissection if accompanied by the latter
2 In total or supraglottic laryngectomy specimens, open the larynx along the posterior midline and keep it open with wires or by pinning to a corkboard
3 Photograph, if indicated
4 Fix overnight in formalin
5 Remove the hyoid bone, thyroid cartilage, and cricoid cartilage, trying to keep the soft tissue as a single piece even if the bone and cartilage need to be fragmented in the process
6 Take photographs or photocopies and identify in one of them the sites of the section to be taken
7 Paint the surgical margins (lingual, pharyngeal, and tracheal) with India ink
8 Orient as to superoinferior and anteroposterior axis
9 Handle the radical neck dissection according to instructions for Lymph node dissection—radical neck

Description

1 Type of laryngectomy: total laryngectomy, hemilaryngectomy, supraglottic laryngectomy; presence of pyriform sinus, hyoid bone, tracheal rings, thyroid and organs from neck dissection
2 Tumor characteristics: location (glottic, supraglottic, infraglottic, or transglottic?), side involved (wholly unilateral or encroaching on or crossing the midline?), size, pattern or growth (exophytic or endophytic?), ulceration, depth of invasion, presence of extralaryngeal spread, features of non-neoplastic mucosa (especially in true vocal cords)

   a For glottic tumors: length of cord involved; involvement of anterior or posterior commissures, extension to ventricle, and degree of subglottic extension as measured from the superior border of the true cord

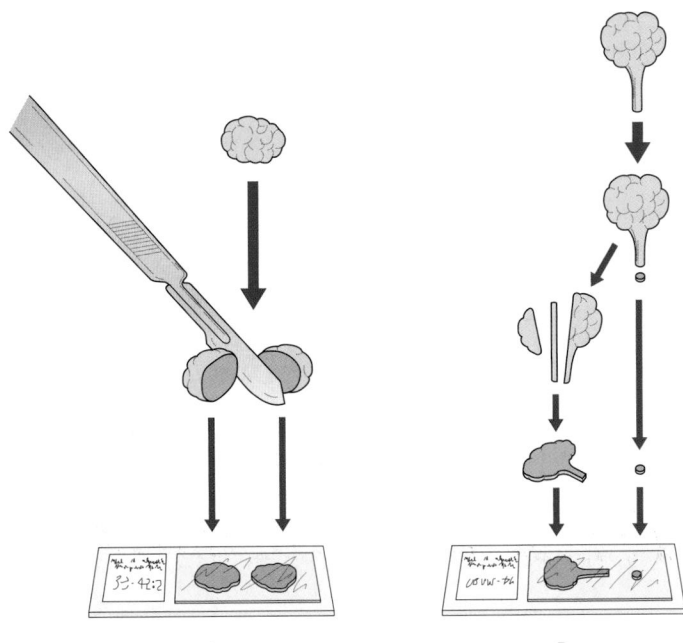

A   B

b For supraglottic tumors: if the hyoid bone is attached, is the tumor suprahyoid or infrahyoid? Does it involve the false cords, aryepiglottic folds, pyriform sinus (if present), or pre-epiglottic space?

c If thyroid is included: weight, measurement, and appearance; invaded by tumor: parathyroid glands or perilaryngeal (delphian) node present? is there a tracheostomy? if so, is there any evidence of tumor involvement?

d If thyroid is included: weight, measurement, and appearance; invaded by tumor? parathyroid glands or perilaryngeal (delphian) node present? is there a tracheostomy? if so, is there any evidence of tumor involvement?

Sections for histology

1 Entire tumor in properly identified longitudinal strips (unless massive, in which case representative sections should be taken)
2 Representative step section of larynx, including epiglottis
3 Thyroid cartilage at the site of maximum tumor invasion, if any
4 Thyroid, parathyroid, and tracheostomy site, if present
5 Lymph nodes (see under Lymph node dissection—radical neck)

1   A very detailed set of instructions for surgical specimens from the upper aerodigestive tract is available from: Slootweg PJ, de Groot JAM. Surgical pathological anatomy of head and neck specimens: A manual for the dissection of surgical specimens from the upper aerodigestive tract. London, 1999, Springer

Lip—V excision

Procedure

1 Fix the specimen for several hours
2 Paint all surgical margins with India ink
3 Cut the specimen as shown in the accompanying drawing

Description

1 Size of specimen
2 Tumor characteristics: size, shape (ulcerated, polypoid), location (vermilion border, skin), distance to margins

Sections for histology

1 Cross-sections through center (see accompanying drawing **A**)
2 Lateral margins, without trimming (see accompanying drawing **B** and **C**)

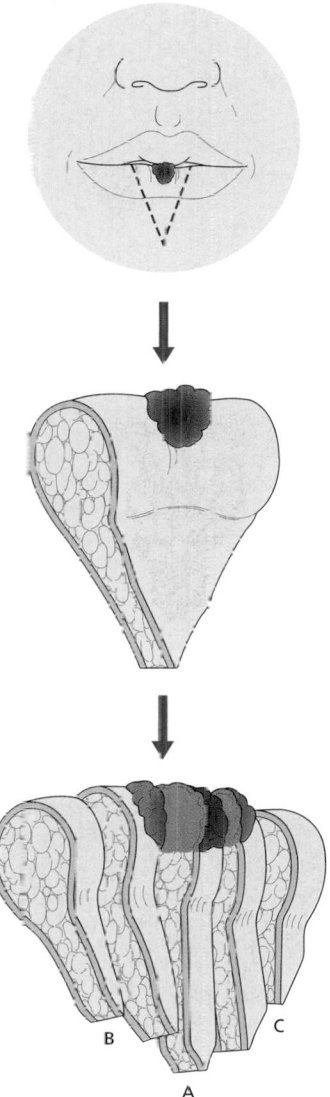

Liver—excision

Operations to remove liver masses include wedge resection, segmental resection, formal and extended right and left lobectomy, trisegmentectomy (which consists of resection of both right lobar segments and the medial segment of the left lobe), and total hepatectomy followed by liver transplant. The delineation of the various hepatic segments is difficult in the excised specimen and need not be attempted unless specifically requested by the surgeon, who may need to be consulted for assistance in the orientation of the specimen.

Procedure

1 Measure and weigh the specimen
2 *For hepatic parenchymal tumors*: paint the hepatic surgical margin and cut parallel 1-cm slices in a plane roughly corresponding to the cut of the CT scan, if one was performed and is available
3 *For tumors of major bile ducts*: identify all of the bile duct and vascular surgical margins (with the help of the surgeon, if necessary), and submit them *en face* (see later section); palpate the bile ducts for areas of induration; open the major bile ducts longitudinally with scissors; after taking photographs, serially section the bile ducts perpendicularly to their long axes; search for hilar lymph nodes

Description

1 Size and weight of specimen
2 Appearance of the capsular surface

3 *For hepatic parenchymal tumors*: size, color; consistency; margins; relationship to capsular surface, major vessels (portal and hepatic veins) and biliary tree; distance to surgical margin; multiplicity; appearance of non-neoplastic liver (congested? signs of biliary obstruction? cirrhosis?)
4 *For tumors of major bile ducts*: same as for hepatic parenchymal tumors, plus: intraductal papillary component? areas of ductal stenosis or dilation? presence of biliary stones?
5 Gallbladder: if present, describe as per instructions in Gallbladder—cholecystectomy; relationship with hepatic parenchymal or bile duct tumor
6 Hilar lymph nodes: number, size, and appearance

Sections for histology

1 Tumor: four sections or more depending on size and extent. All grossly dissimilar areas should be sampled. If several nodules are present, samples of up to five should be taken. Unless excessively large, tumors of major bile ducts should be submitted *in toto*
2 Surgical margins: these should be taken from the areas that appear grossly closer to the tumor. In the case of the tumors of major bile ducts, one of these sections should be an *en face* view of the bile duct and vascular surgical margin
3 Non-neoplastic liver: include portions distal and proximal to the tumor, if feasible
4 Gallbladder, if present; one section
5 Lymph nodes, if present: in their entirety

Lung—biopsy

(Adapted from Brody AR, Craighead JE. Preparations of human lung specimens by perfusion-fixation. Am Rev Respir Dis 1975, **112:** 645–649; Carrington CB, Gaensler EA. Clinical-pathologic approach to diffuse interstitial lung disease. In Thurlbeck WM (ed). The Lung. Baltimore, 1978, Waverly Press, pp 58–87; Churg A. An inflation procedure for open lung biopsies. Am J Surg Pathol 1983, **7:** 69–71.)

Procedure

1 Obtain cultures from lesions suspected of being infectious
2 Take samples for electron microscopy and for deep freezing, if indicated
3 Open biopsies obtained in patients with suspected interstitial lung disease are better evaluated microscopically if specimen has been fixed in the inflated state. This can be achieved by one of three methods:

   a The surgeon should take the biopsy from a lung that is held inflated and maintain inflation by clamping the portion of the lung to be biopsied; the specimen should be placed in formalin immediately after excision

   b The small airways and/or vessels are cannulated under a dissecting microscope. This is a tedious and somewhat complicated procedure
   c The specimen is inflated slowly with formalin or other fixative (using a 25-guage butterfly needle connected to a small syringe), sticking the needle through the pleura and gently infusing fixative until the specimen is well expanded. If specimen is large, several punctures with the needle may be necessary. After inflation, the specimen is dropped in formalin, allowed to fix for at least an hour, and then cut in parallel slices

Description

1 Dimensions: weight, if specimen is large
2 Pleura: thickness; fibrosis? fibrin? other changes?
3 Lung parenchyma: consolidated? diffuse interstitial fibrosis or well-defined nodules?

Sections for histology

1 Submit entire biopsy

Lung—resection for nontumoral condition

Lung resections include *segmentectomy* (removal of one or more of the eighteen segments in which the various pulmonary lobes are divided), *lobectomy* (removal of one or more of the five pulmonary lobes), and *pneumonectomy* (removal of one entire lung).

Procedure

1 Obtain cultures from lesions suspected of being infectious
2 Weigh the specimen
3 Two options are available depending on the type of abnormality present and the status of the organ when received in the laboratory:

   a Open the bronchi longitudinally with scissors and cut the lung parenchyma (including the lesion) in slices with a sharp knife
   b Inject with formalin through the main bronchus, tie off or clamp the bronchus, fix overnight, and section at 0.5- to 1-cm intervals with a sharp knife or meat cutter. The sections should be frontal, perpendicular to the hilum. The slices formed by this procedure can be kept in order by stringing them on a piece of twine

4 For lungs with tuberculosis and other contagious diseases (proven or suspected): fix in formalin for 48 hours; keep the specimen in the same container while dissecting and cutting the sections; send the contaminated instruments for sterilization; carefully wrap the contaminated material in a plastic bag and place in a scrap bucket

5 For lungs with suspected asbestosis: scrape vigorously the cut surface of the lung with a scalpel, layer twenty successive scrapings onto a glass slide, let the preparation dry, stain lightly with toluidine blue or leave unstained, apply a mounting medium and coverslip, and examine microscopically[1]
6 If a rib was submitted as part of the thoracotomy, examine according to instructions under Bone marrow—rib from thoracotomy

Description

1 Weight of specimen and type of resection (pneumonectomy, lobectomy, wedge resection)
2 Pleura: thickness; fibrosis? fibrin? other changes?
3 Bronchi: mucosa, lumen (diameter and content)
4 Parenchyma: appearance; if localized lesion is present: appearance: lobe and, if possible, bronchopulmonary segment in which located; relationships to bronchi, vessels, pleura, and lymph nodes
5 Lymph nodes: number, size, and appearance

Sections for histology

1 Main lesions: three sections
2 Uninvolved lung: one section per lobe
3 Bronchus
4 Lymph nodes, if present: at least one section

1 Mark EJ. The second diagnosis. The role of the pathologist in identifying pneumoconiosis in lungs excised for tumor. Hum Pathol 1981; 12: 585–587

Lung—resection for tumor[1]

Procedure

1 Dissect hilar lymph nodes as a single group and take out a cross section from the bronchial line of resection while the specimen is fresh

2 Two options are available depending on the location of the tumor and the status of the organ when received in the laboratory:

  a Open all major bronchi and their branches longitudinally with scissors and follow this by cutting parallel slices of the lung, including tumor

  b Inject with formalin through the main bronchus, tie off or clamp the bronchus, fix overnight, and section at 0.5- to 1-cm intervals with a sharp knife or meat cutter. The sections should be frontal, perpendicular to the hilum. The slices formed by this procedure can be kept in order by stringing them on a piece of twine

3 If tuberculosis, other infections, or asbestosis is suspected in the non-neoplastic lung, proceed according to instructions listed under Lung—resection for non-tumoral condition

4 If a rib was submitted as part of the thoracotomy, examine according to instructions under Bone marrow—rib from the thoracotomy

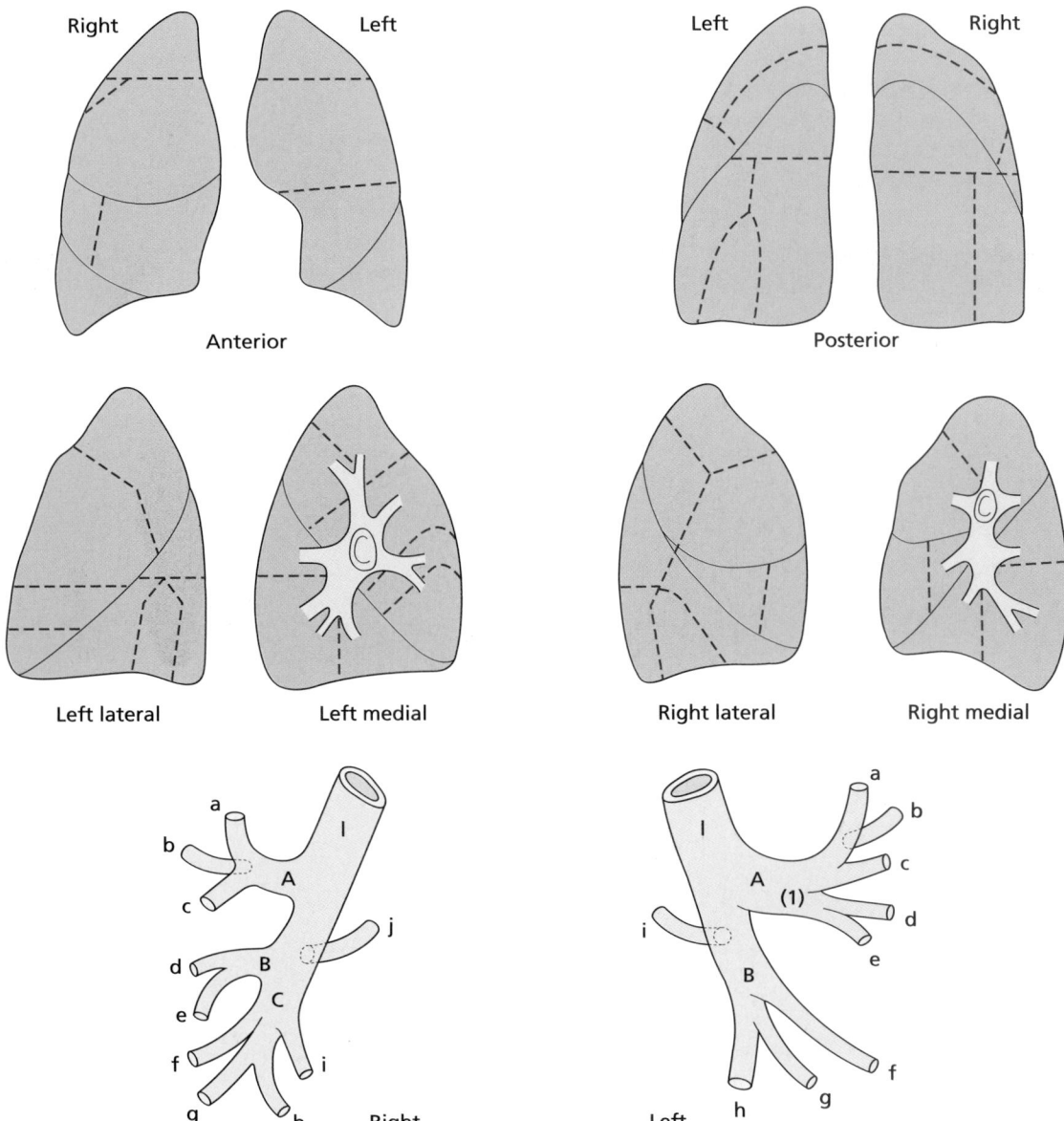

Description

1 Weight of fresh specimen and type of resection (pneumonectomy, lobectomy)
2 Pleura: fibrosis, fibrin, tumor invasion; parietal pleura present (identified by presence of fat)?
3 Tumor characteristics: size, location within lobe and segment, relation with bronchi, hemorrhage, necrosis, cavitation, blood vessel invasion, extension to pleura; distance to bronchial line of resection and pleura
4 Appearance of non-neoplastic lung
5 Number and appearance of regional lymph nodes

Sections for histology

1 Tumor: three sections, including one showing relationship to bronchus, if any
2 Non-neoplastic lung, including pleura: three sections, at least one from lung distal to tumor
3 Bronchial line of resection: one cross section comprising entire circumference
4 Lymph nodes: bronchopulmonary (hilar) and mediastinal
5 If rib submitted, process according to instructions under Bone marrow—rib from the thoracotomy

1 More detailed instructions are available from: Carter D. Pathologic examination of major pulmonary specimens resected for neoplastic disease. Pathol Annu 1983, **18(Pt 2):** 315–332

	Brock's nomenclature			Jackson and Huber's nomenclature	
Right bronchial tree (I, main bronchus; A, upper lobe bronchus; B, middle lobe bronchus; C, lower lobe bronchus)					
a	*Apical* bronchus, upper lobe		a	*Apical* bronchus, upper lobe	
b	*Subapical* bronchus, upper lobe		b	*Anterior* bronchus, upper lobe	
c	*Pectoral* bronchus, upper lobe		c	*Posterior* bronchus, upper lobe	
d	*Medial* division, middle lobe		d	*Medial* division, middle lobe	
e	*Lateral* division, middle lobe		e	*Lateral* division, middle lobe	
f	*Anterior basal* bronchus, lower lobe		f	*Anterior basal* bronchus, lower lobe	
g	*Middle basal* bronchus, lower lobe		g	*Lateral basal* bronchus, lower lobe	
h	*Posterior* bronchus, lower lobe		h	*Posterior basal* bronchus, lower lobe	
i	*Cardiac* bronchus, lower lobe		i	*Medial basal* bronchus, lower lobe	
j	*Apical* bronchus, lower lobe		j	*Superior* bronchus, lower lobe	
Left bronchial tree (I, main bronchus; A, upper lobe bronchus; B, lower lobe bronchus; (1), lingular bronchus)					
a	*Apical* bronchus, upper lobe		a	*Superior division,* upper lobe	
b	*Subapical* bronchus, upper lobe		b	*Apical posterior,* upper lobe	
c	*Pectoral* bronchus, upper lobe		c	*Anterior* bronchus, upper lobe	
d	*Upper division, lingular,* upper lobe		d	*Superior lingular, inferior division,* upper lobe	
e	*Lower division, lingular,* upper lobe		e	*Inferior lingular, inferior division,* upper lobe	
f	*Anterior basal* bronchus, lower lobe		f	*Anterior-medial basal,* lower lobe	
g	*Middle basal* bronchus, lower lobe		g	*Lateral basal,* lower lobe	
h	*Posterior basal* bronchus, lower lobe		h	*Posterior basal,* lower lobe	
i	*Apical* bronchus, lower lobe		i	*Superior bronchus,* lower lobe	

Lymph node—biopsy

Procedure

1 If the lymph node is received in the fresh state, cut 2- to 3-mm slices perpendicular to the long axis and:

a Take a small portion for culture and if an infectious disease is suspected or needs to be ruled out
b Make four imprints of the cut surface on alcohol-cleaned slides, fix in methanol, and stain two with hematoxylin–eosin and two with Wright's stain. See instructions for Imprints (touch preparations)
c Place one of the slices in B5 fixative and submit for histology
d In cases of suspected hematolymphoid disorders, submit tissue for cell markers (by flow cytometry), cytogenetics, and molecular genetics (see respective sections for instructions)

e If additional tissue is available, fix in a formalin, and submit for histology

2 If the specimen is received already fixed in formalin, cut in 3-mm slices and submit representative sections

Description

1 State whether node received fresh or fixed
2 Size of node and condition of capsule
3 Appearance of cut surface: color, nodularity, hemorrhage, necrosis

Sections for histology

Cross-sections of node, including at least portion of capsule: one to three sections depending on size of node.

Lymph node dissection—general instructions

Procedure

1 Dissect the node-containing fat from the organ in the fresh state, using forceps and sharp scissors. Make the fat dissection as close as possible to the wall of the organ; this is where most lymph nodes are located. Divide them in groups according to specific instructions
2 Two options are available

   a Search the fat for nodes while specimen is fresh, under a strong light and with the use of scissors, forceps, and scalpel. Avoid crushing the nodes by rough palpation. If not enough nodes are identified, contact the senior pathologist or surgeon
   b Fix overnight in formalin or Carnoy's solution, and search for nodes the next day. The latter fixative is preferred because it clears the fat somewhat

Description

1 Number of nodes in each group
2 Size of largest node in each group
3 Appearance; obvious involvement by tumor?

Sections for histology

1 *All* lymph nodes should be submitted for histology
2 Small nodes (up to 3 mm in thickness after fat is removed) are submitted as a single piece
3 Several small node groups may be submitted in the same cassette
4 Larger nodes are bisected and, if necessary, further sectioned into 2- to 3-mm slices. A slice as large as will fit the cassette should be submitted for each one of these larger nodes[1]
5 Store the remainder in the formalin container, properly identified as belonging to lymph node group

---

1 The alternative would be to submit the entirety of these large nodes, but the number of additional metastases found seems too small to justify the considerably higher cost involved (Niemann TH, Yilmaz AG, Marsh Jr WL, Lucas JG. A half node or a whole node. A comparison of methods for submitting lymph nodes. Am J Clin Pathol 1998, **109:** 571–576.)

Lymph node dissection—axillary

See under Breast—mastectomy

Lymph node dissection—inguinal

1 All lymph nodes are submitted as a single group unless the surgeon has submitted the superficial and deep groups separately. A minimum of twelve lymph nodes should be found
2 A cross-section of the internal saphenous vein also should be submitted for histology

Lymph node dissection—radical neck

The *standard* radical neck dissection includes removal of cervical lymph nodes, sternomastoid muscle, internal jugular vein, spinal accessory nerve, and submaxillary gland; the tail of the parotid is sometimes also included.

In the *modified* radical neck dissection (also known as functional or Bocca neck dissection, the sternomastoid muscle, spinal accessory nerve, and internal jugular vein are spared.

The *extended* radical neck dissection includes, in addition to the structures removed in the standard operation, the excision of retropharyngeal, paratracheal, parotid, suboccipital, and/or upper mediastinal lymph nodes.

In the *regional* (partial or selective) neck dissection, only the station of lymph nodes thought to represent the first metastatic station is removed.

The instructions following are devised for the standard radical neck dissection and need to be modified for the other three. Because of the lack of anatomic landmarks in the modified and regional procedures, the labelling of the lymph nodes according to groups needs to be done by the surgeon. The same applies to the extra lymph node groups removed in the extended operation.

Procedure

1   Orient the specimen and divide it into submaxillary gland, platysma, sternomastoid muscle, internal jugular veins, and node-containing fat
2   Divide the lymph nodes into six groups depending on whether they are on the upper or lower portion of the specimen and on their relationship with the ster-

nomastoid muscle (see accompanying drawing). A minimum of 40 lymph nodes should be found[1]

Description

1   Site and type of primary neoplasm (see specific instructions)
2   Length of sternomastoid muscle
3   Jugular vein included? length? invaded by tumor?
4   Presence of tumor in lymph nodes, submaxillary gland, soft tissue, or muscle
5   Size of the largest node

Sections for histology

1   Superior anterior cervical lymph nodes
2   Superior jugular cervical lymph nodes
3   Superior posterior cervical lymph nodes
4   Inferior anterior cervical lymph nodes
5   Inferior jugular cervical lymph nodes
6   Inferior posterior cervical lymph nodes
7   Submaxillary gland
8   Jugular vein
9   Sternocleidomastoid muscle
10   Thyroid gland, if present

1   Other pathologists use an alternative scheme in which lymph nodes are divided into five regions: anterior (submental and submandibular), superior jugular, middle jugular, inferior jugular, and posterior (posterior triangle) (Robbins KT, Medina JE, Wolfe GT, Levine PA, Sessions RB, Pruet CW. Standardizing neck dissection terminology. Arch Otolaryngol Head Neck Surg 1991, **117**: 601–605.)

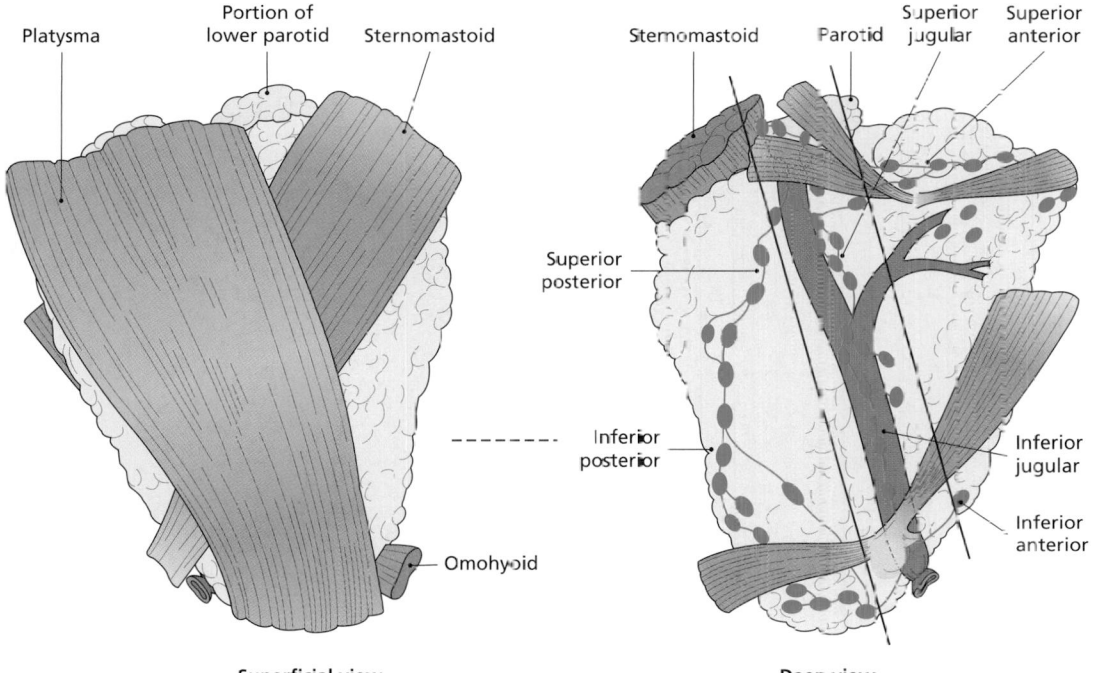

Superficial view   **Deep view**

Lymph node dissection—retroperitoneal

1 For the proper evaluation of this specimen, it is essential for the surgeon to divide the lymph nodes in groups at the time he is doing the dissection and submit them to the laboratory in separate containers. In most institutions, urologic surgeons divide the node groups as follows:

- Suprahilar (above level of renal artery)
- Superior interaortocaval
- Pericaval
- Periaortic
- Common iliac (usually excised only on side of tumor)

2 If the specimen is submitted as a single piece, it is necessary to identify, with the help of the surgeon, the upper and lower borders and the periaortic and pericaval regions. When this is established, the lymph nodes can be divided in the following groups:

- Superior periaortic
- Middle periaortic
- Inferior periaortic
- Superior pericaval
- Middle pericaval
- Inferior pericaval
- Common iliac (specify side)

3 If the surgeon is unavailable or unable to orient the specimen, all lymph nodes are submitted as one group. A minimum of 25 lymph nodes should be found

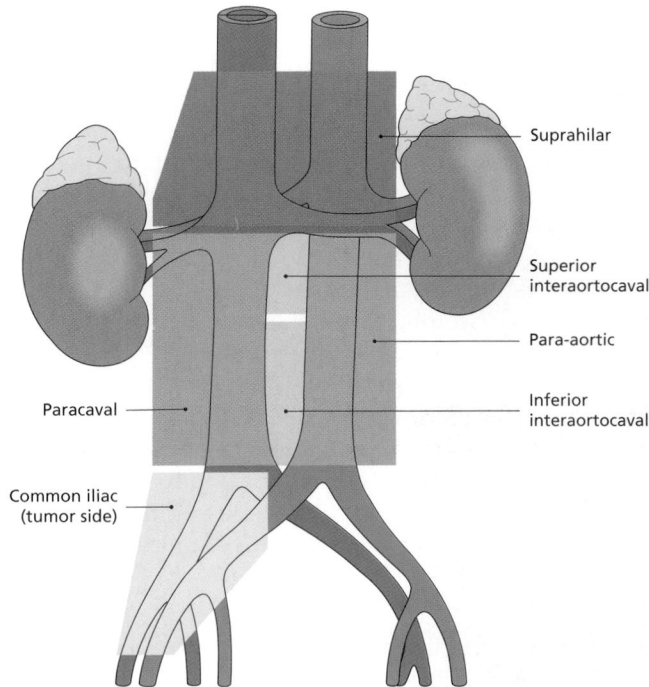

Molecular diagnosis—sampling

Evaluation of tissue using molecular techniques has become a very important diagnostic procedure, particularly for the evaluation of hematolymphoid processes and many solid tumors, particularly of soft tissue type.

Sample 1 cm³ of fresh tumor tissue (or as much as available), drop in Petri dish having in its bottom a layer of filter paper wet (not overly soaked) with saline solution, and submit to appropriate laboratory immediately. If prompt transportation is not feasible, freeze at −70 °C until time of use.

Needle biopsies

Procedure

1 Remove the tissue from the fixative without squeezing it with a forceps; do not use toothed forceps; handle the tissue in such a manner as to keep it intact; do not cut it transversely but rather coil it inside the cassette if overly long
2 Always search the container, including the undersurface of the lid, for tiny fragments of tissue that may be overlooked
3 Carefully wrap the tissue in a tea bag, without squeezing
4 If the amount of the tissue core permits (a core over 1 cm long or two tissues cores) and if it would be anticipated that a fat stain may be useful, save a 3- to 5-mm portion in formalin

Description

1 Length and diameter of core; number of fragments; color
2 Homogeneity or lack of it

Sections for histology

All material received (except if fat stains desired, see under Procedure)

Orbital exenteration

Procedure

1 Pin down the elliptic piece of orbicular skin, and fix overnight at 4°C
2 Paint the surgical margins with India ink
3 Take surgical margins; cutaneous, soft tissue, optic nerve
4 Cut skin, soft tissue, and ocular globe

Description

1 Skin: shape and length; appearance; if lesion present: size, shape, depth of invasion, color
2 Soft tissues
3 Ocular globe: dimensions, appearance, length of optic nerve (see under Eyes—enucleation)

Sections for histology

For skin tumors

1 Tumor: three sections
2 Cutaneous surgical margins (superior, inferior, internal, and external)
3 Soft tissue surgical margins
4 Ocular globe

For ocular tumors

1 Globe with tumor
2 Orbital soft tissue adjacent to tumor
3 Surgical margin of optic nerve

Orientation of specimens with agar

1 Prepare beforehand a 3% solution of "bacteriologic" agar, divide in 1- to 2-ml samples, and place in small test tubes. Keep these samples at 4°C in the refrigerator until the time of use

2 Heat the test tube on a specially prepared hot plate until the agar acquires a semiviscid consistency. The temperature should be around 60°C, and it is important to keep it as close as possible to this figure (otherwise, the agar will not melt or will become too fluid). The melting of the agar should take no more than 1 to 2 minutes. It is convenient to heat as many test tubes in the morning as will be needed during the working day. However, it is advised not to keep the agar at 60°C longer than 24 to 48 hours

3 Pick up the specimen gently with a small forceps and place it in the desired position ("on edge") on top of a glass slide (see accompanying drawing)

4 While holding the specimen in this position with one hand, use the other hand to drop a small amount of melted agar on top of the specimen with a Pasteur pipette. Do not use an excessive amount. The solidifying process can be speeded up by gently blowing in the agar. When the agar has solidified just enough for the tissue to remain in the desired position without support (it should take no more than 1 minute), remove the forceps and wait an additional 1 or 2 minutes

5 Detach the tissue surrounded by the agar from the glass slide by sliding a blade beneath it (see accompanying drawing), and transfer the material to the cassette. If the size is very small, it may be necessary to wrap it in lens paper or a tea bag

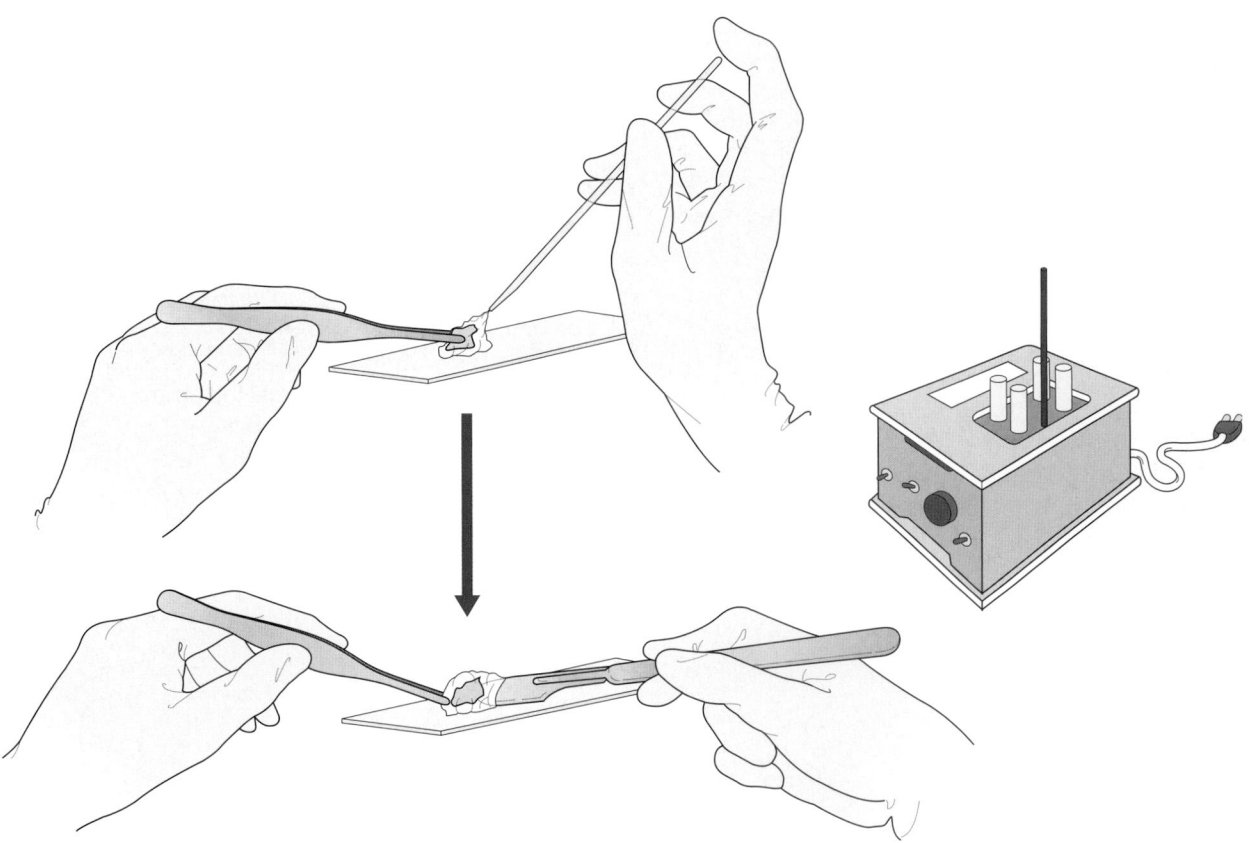

Ovary—oophorectomy

Oophorectomies may be total or partial. The most common type of conservative operation is the removal of an ovarian cyst with preservation of the uninvolved parenchyma (ovarian cystectomy).

Procedure

1 Measure the organ. Weigh it if it is obviously abnormal
2 If the specimen is received fresh:

   a **Normal-sized** or nearly normal-sized organ: bivalve and fix for several hours
   b **Enlarged** organ: make several cuts and fix for several hours

Description

1 Size and shape; weight, if enlarged
2 Capsule: thickened? adhesions? hemorrhage? rupture? external surface smooth or irregular?
3 Cut section: character of cortex, medulla, and hilum; cysts (size and content); corpus luteum? calcification? hemorrhage?
4 Tumors: size; external appearance: smooth or papillary? solid or cystic? content of cystic masses; hemorrhage, necrosis, or calcification?

Sections for histology

1 For incidental oophorectomies: one sagittal section of each entire ovary, labelled as to side
2 For cysts: up to three sections of cyst wall (particularly from areas with papillary appearance)
3 For tumors: three sections or one section for each centimeter or tumor, whichever is greater; also, one section of non-neoplastic ovary, if identifiable

1   Robboy SJ, Kraus FT, Kurman RJ Gross description, processing, and reporting of gynaecologic and obstetric specimens. In: Kurman RJ (ed). Blaustein's Pathology of the Female Genital Tract, 4th Edn. New York, 2002, Springer-Verlag, pp. 1319–1346

Pancreas—pancreatectomy

The *Whipple's procedure* consists of partial pancreatectomy plus partial gastrectomy and duodenectomy.[2] *Total pancreatectomy* consists of removal of the entire pancreas plus partial gastrectomy, duodenectomy, and splenectomy. *Regional pancreatectomy type I* consists of total pancreatectomy plus partial gastrectomy, cholecystectomy, duodenectomy, splenectomy, and resection of portal vein. It may also include transverse colectomy and removal of mesocolon, omentum, and regional lymph nodes. *Regional pancreatectomy type II* includes, in addition to the procedures listed under type I, the resection of mesenteric vessels, celiac axis vessels, and/or a segment of vena cava and aorta. *Distal pancreatectomy* consists in resection of the tail of the pancreas (often with a portion of the body) plus splenectomy.

Procedure

1 Dissect lymph nodes while the specimen is fresh and divide them according to groups (see accompanying drawing)
2 Fill the stomach and duodenum with gauze or cotton impregnated with formalin
3 Pin the whole specimen on a corkboard, trying to preserve the anatomic relationships
4 Place in a large container, cover with formalin, and fix overnight at 4°C
5 Paint with India ink the common bile duct surgical margin, as well as the pancreatic surgical margin in a Whipple's procedure
6 Divide the specimen into anterior and posterior halves as follows: with scissors, cut the lesser curvature of the stomach and the free border of the duodenum; with scissors, cut the gastric greater curvature up to the pancreas, as well as the fourth portion of the duodenum; with a large sharp knife, cut the peripancreatic border or the duodenum; and the pancreas. The orientation of the latter cut can be better controlled by introducing a catheter through the common bile duct and by cutting in front of it. It may be necessary to postfix the two halves overnight before proceeding to further dissection, as indicated

Description

1 Type of operation: Whipple's procedure, total pancreatectomy, regional pancreatectomy type I or II, distal pancreatectomy
2 Organs present in specimen and their dimensions; weight of spleen
3 Tumor characteristics: involvement of ampulla, duodenal mucosa, stomach, common bile duct, pancreatic duct, and pancreas; size, shape (papillary? flat? ulcerated?), color, and consistency; if tumor is in the ampulla: intra-ampullary, periampullary, or mixed?
4 Common bile duct, main pancreatic duct, and accessory pancreatic duct: location and relationship with each other; dilated? stones? tumor?

Pancreas—pancreatectomy *(continued)*

5 Pancreas: tumor invasion? atrophy? fibrosis? ductal dilation?
6 Spleen: tumor invasion? other features
7 Location, number, and appearance of regional lymph nodes

Sections for histology

1 Tumor: up to three sections
2 Pancreas: three sections, one from distal line of resection (or proximal, depending on the type of specimen)
3 Common bile duct: two cross-sections, one from surgical margin
4 Uninvolved duodenum: two sections, one from distal line of resection
5 Stomach: two sections, including proximal line of resection
6 Lymph nodes[1]:

- Peripancreatic (superior and inferior)
- Pancreaticoduodenal (anterior and posterior)
- Common bile duct and pericystic
- Lesser curvature
- Greater curvature
- Splenic
- Other groups, if present (jejunal, midcolic, omental)

7 Other organs, if present (gallbladder, spleen, portal vein, colon, omentum)

Other authors[1] divide these lymph nodes into the following five major groups:

1 Superior: superior margin of head and body of pancreas, common bile duct, and stomach (greater and lesser curvature and pylorus)
2 Inferior: inferior margin of head and body of pancreas, around mesenteric vessels, jejunal, gastrocolonic ligaments, pericolonic, and periaortic
3 Anterior (anterior pancreaticoduodenal): along the anterior surface of the head of the pancreas
4 Posterior (posterior pancreaticoduodenal): along the posterior surface of the head of the pancreas
5 Splenic: splenic hilum

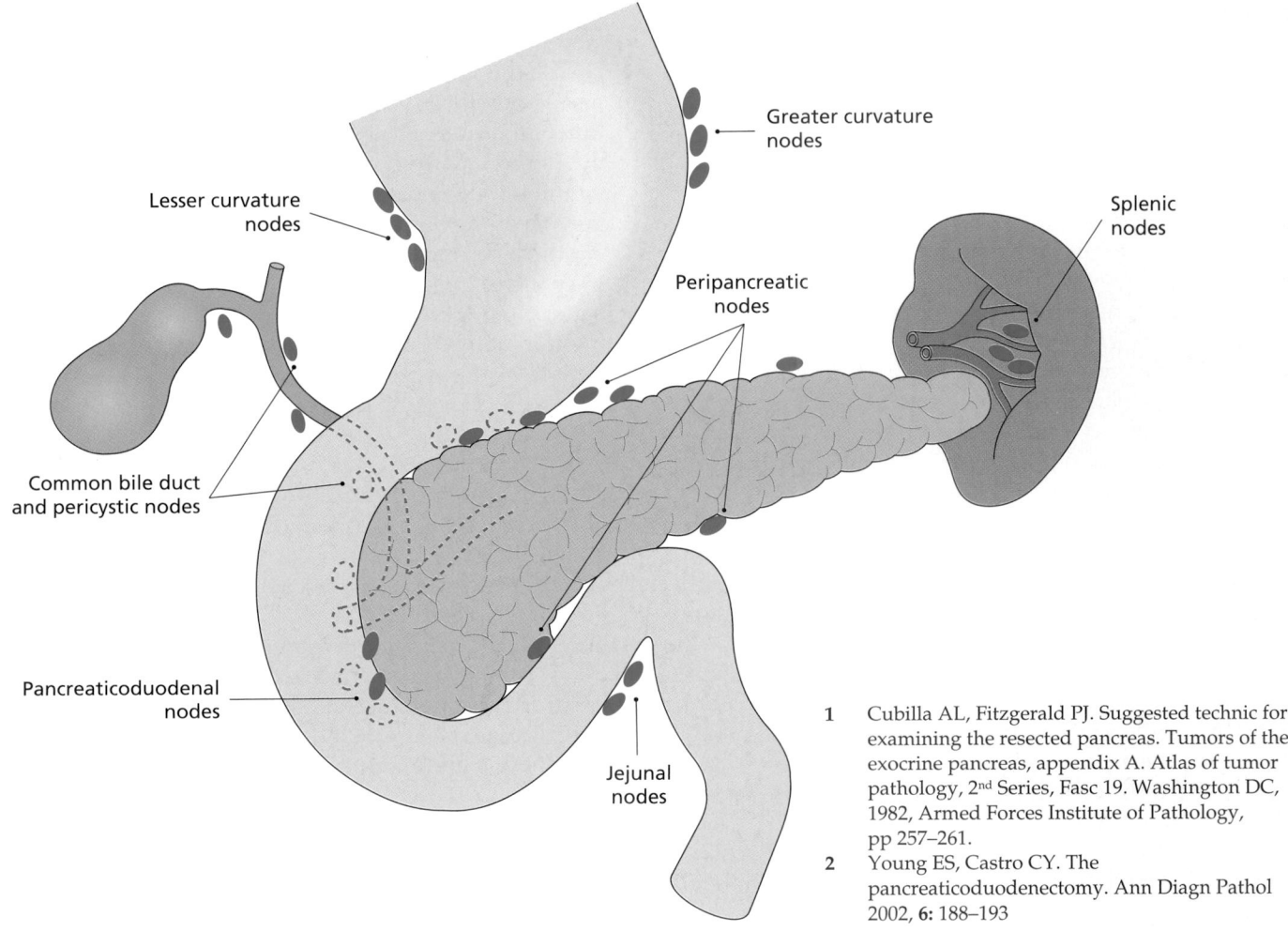

Greater curvature nodes

Lesser curvature nodes

Splenic nodes

Peripancreatic nodes

Common bile duct and pericystic nodes

Pancreaticoduodenal nodes

Jejunal nodes

1 Cubilla AL, Fitzgerald PJ. Suggested technic for examining the resected pancreas. Tumors of the exocrine pancreas, appendix A. Atlas of tumor pathology, 2nd Series, Fasc 19. Washington DC, 1982, Armed Forces Institute of Pathology, pp 257–261.
2 Young ES, Castro CY. The pancreaticoduodenectomy. Ann Diagn Pathol 2002, 6: 188–193

Parathyroid glands—parathyroidectomy

Removal of diseased parathyroid glands is usually complete, but in cases of hyperplasia a portion (approximately one half) of one gland is retained, in situ or implanted in the forearm.

Procedure

1 Accurately weigh each gland on a delicate balance after removing the surrounding fat but *before* removing any parathyroid tissue for frozen or other sections

2 Accurately label each parathyroid gland as to site

Description

Weight, color, consistency. and external appearance of *each* gland

Sections for histology

All parathyroid tissue (except for markedly enlarged gland in which minimum of three sections should be taken) accurately labeled as to site

Pelvic exenteration

Most pelvic exenterations are performed on females because of postradiation persistence of carcinoma of uterine cervix. Anterior pelvic exenteration consists of removal of the vagina, uterus and adnexa, bladder, distal ureters, and urethra. Posterior pelvic exenteration consists of removal of the vagina, uterus and adnexa, and rectum. Total pelvic exenteration is a combination of the two procedures. The operation also includes removal of the pelvic lymph nodes.

Procedure

1 Gently express content from the rectosigmoid, wash with formalin or saline solution, and fill with cotton or gauze impregnated in formalin
2 Fill the vagina with the same material
3 Inject the bladder with formalin with a Foley catheter or syringe after tying the urethra
4 Suspend the specimen in anatomic position in a large container with abundant fixative
5 Inject formalin in the uterine cavity with a syringe through the fundus
6 Fix for 24 hours
7 Removal all cotton and gauze and cut sagittally in equal halves. The sections of large bowel, bladder, and vagina are made with scissors; those of the uterus are made with a knife
8 Take photographs or photocopies and identify in one of them the site of the sections to be taken
9 Remove the lymph nodes in the following groups: right parametrial, left parametrial, retrorectal, and mesosigmoid
10 Paint the surgical margins with India ink

Description

1 Type of exenteration: total, anterior, posterior; organs included; length of ureters
2 Tumor characteristics: location, invasion of other structures, size, color, consistency; fistulae: signs of radiation change?
3 Number and appearance of lymph nodes

Sections for histology

1 Tumor: three sections or one section per centimeter of tumor, whichever is greater
2 Cervix and vagina
3 Cervix and bladder
4 Cervix and rectum
5 Surgical margins (parametrial, vaginal, vesical, and rectal)
6 *In females*: vulva, vagina, cervix endometrium, tubes, ovaries (in addition to sections from tumor)
7 *In males*: prostate
8 Lymph nodes

- Right parametrial
- Left parametrial
- Retrorectal
- Mesosigmoid

1 Robboy SJ, Kraus FT, Kurman RJ. Gross description, processing, and reporting of gynaecologic and obstetric specimens. In: Kurman RJ (ed). Blaustein's Pathology of the Female Genital Tract, 4th Edn. New York, 2002, Springer-Verlag, pp. 1319–1346

Penis—penectomy

Procedure

1 If the specimen is accompanied by inguinal node dissections, separate them and handle according to specific instructions
2 Introduce a catheter through the urethra
3 Fix overnight at 4°C
4 Paint the surgical margins (including the urethra) with India ink
5 Cut longitudinally through the center: the section should cut the urethra in two
6 Take photographs or photocopies and identify in one of them the site of the sections to be taken

Description

1 Type of operation: partial, total, with or without scrotal skin, testicles, inguinal nodes
2 Length and diameter of specimen
3 Tumor: location in relations to glans, prepuce, skin, and urethra; size, color, borders, depth of invasion
4 Glans penis: balanitis? atrophy? leukoplakia?
5 Urethra: invaded by tumor?

Sections for histology

1 Tumor: three sections
2 Glans penis and urethra
3 Surgical margin (including urethra)

1   Cubilla AL, Piris A, Pfannl R, Rodriguez I, Agüero F, Young RH. Anatomic levels: important landmarks in penectomy specimens: a detailed anatomic and histologic study based on 44 cases. Am J Surg Pathol 2001, 25: 1091–1094

Peripheral nerve—biopsy

Procedure

1 The examination and sampling of this material should be carried out at the bedside or *immediately* after the specimen is received in the pathology laboratory. Be careful to avoid stretching or crushing
2 Measure the length and diameter (biopsies of the sural nerve usually measure between 3 and 6 cm)
3 For paraffin embedding, cut a portion 2 to 4 mm long from either end, fix in B5, and postfix in formalin. Divide the specimen so that a cross-section and a longitudinal section are obtained
4 For "thick sections" and electron microscopy, fix a portion in 2.5% glutaraldehyde in 0.05M cacodylate buffer at pH 7.4 (osmolarity ≈340). After 2 hours of fixation, the nerve is placed under a dissecting microscope and divided into 3- to 4-mm segments. Four to five of these pieces are submitted in large blocks, whereas the others are sectioned along a longitudinal plane. Twenty to 30 pieces are thus obtained, each having two to three fascicles. For electron microscopy, 1- to 2-mm³ fragments should be submitted
5 If facilities are available for fiber teasing preparations, a 1- to 2-cm nerve segment should be dissected and, immediately after biopsy, fixed in formalin, postfixed in O_5O_4 in Millonig's buffer at pH 7.4 for 3 to 5 hours at room temperature, and passed through graded glycerine, where it can be kept until time of observation
6 If indicated, a small piece of fresh nerve should be "snap frozen" for biochemical studies, lipid staining, and immunofluorescent techniques

Description

1 Length and diameter
2 Color
3 Irregularities

Sections for histology

1 One cross-section and one longitudinal section for paraffin embedding
2 For other portions of biopsy, see under Procedure

Placenta—singleton

Procedure and description

1 Examine as soon as possible after delivery in the fresh state; handle the specimen with great care, avoiding lacerations

2 Note the amount of blood and clots in the container and search for separate pieces of membranes, cord, or placenta

3 Examine in this order: membranes, cord, fetal surface, and maternal surface

4 Measure the distance from the placental margin to the nearest point of rupture (zero: marginal placenta previa)

5 Examine membranes for completeness (if a portion is missing, notify the obstetrician), insertion, decidual necrosis, edema, extra-amniotic pregnancy, retromembranous hemorrhage, meconium staining, color, and transparency

6 Take a long, 2- to 3-cm wide section of membranes beginning with the point of rupture and extending to and including a small portion of placental margin. Roll the specimen with amniotic surface inward, fix for 24 hours, take a 3-mm section from the center (taking care not to strip the amnion off), and submit for histology. Take a second section including amnion, chorion, and deciduas from the rim of the site rupture (in vaginal deliveries)

7 Trim the remaining membranes from the placental margin

8 Measure the length of the cord and the shortest distance from the cord insertion to the placental margin

9 Examine the cord: insertion (nonmembranous or membranous; if latter, are vessels intact?), number of umbilical vessels (by sectioning the cord transversely at two or more points), color, true knots, torsion, stricture, hematoma, thrombosis

10 Remove the cord from the placenta 3 cm proximal to the insertion, and take a 2- to 4-cm segment from its midpoint; fix this segment for 24 hours, take a 3-mm section, and submit for histology

11 Examine the fetal surface: color, opacity, subchorionic fibrin, cysts (number and size), amnion nodosum, squamous metaplasia, thrombosis of fetal surface vessels, chorangioma

12 Examine the maternal surface: completeness, normal fissures, laceration (extent), depressed areas, retroplacental hemorrhage (size and distance from margin)

13 Measure the maximum diameter, thickness in the center, weight (after trimming cord and membranes), shape

14 Hold the placenta gently with one hand, maternal side up on a flat surface, and make parallel sections with a large sharp knife at 10-cm intervals. The fetal surface will not be cut through and will hold the specimen together

15 Remove four 2-cm pieces that include the fetal surface and intact maternal surface, selecting tissues of the placenta (within 2 cm of placental margins). Take the piece so that the fetal surface vessels are cut at right angles to their long axis; fix for 24 hours, trim a 3-mm section (through and through), and submit for histology. One section should include the chorionic plate in an area with minimal subchorionic fibrin. The other sections should include the maternal surface. Submit similar sections of lesions present

16 Examine all cross-sections for infarcts (location, size, number); intervillous thrombi (number); laminate, perivillous fibrin deposition, pallor, consistency, calcification (extent), cysts, tumors. Describe lesion location (central, lateral, or marginal), depth (parabasal, intermediate, or subchorionic), and age (recent or old)

Sections for histology

1 Placenta (as indicated previously plus abnormal areas, if present)

2 Membranes

3 Cord

1 Driscoll SG, Langston C. College of American Pathologists conference XIX on the examination of the placenta: report of the working group on methods for placental examination. Arch Pathol Lab Med 1991, **115**: 704–708

2 Robboy SJ, Kraus FT, Kurman RJ. Gross description, processing, and reporting of gynaecologic and obstetric specimens. In: Kurman RJ (ed). Blaustein's Pathology of the Female Genital Tract, 4th Edn. New York, 2002, Springer-Verlag, pp. 1319–1346

Placenta—twin

Procedure and description

1 If placentas are separate (nonfused): examine each placenta as a singleton
2 If placentas are fused:

   a Note whether the two cords are labelled twin A and twin B. If not, label them arbitrarily and make a statement to that effect

   b Determine the presence and type of dividing membranes:

     (1) If absent (monochorionic–monoamniotic), so state

     (2) If present:

       (a) Remove a square of the dividing membrane, roll it, fix it for 24 hours, take a 3-mm section, and submit for histology

       (b) Attempt to determine grossly whether the dividing membrane has chorion or not, according to the accompanying tables

       (c) Record the kind and number of vascular anastomoses in monochorionic-diamniotic placentas: artery-to-artery, vein-to-vein, artery-to-vein (arteriovenous shunts). The latter can be better demonstrated by injecting the artery of one twin along the plane of fusion of the placenta with 30 to 50 ml of saline solution containing a dye and noting whether the fluid emerges from the vein of the other twin through one or more common villous lobules. The placenta must be intact to perform this test. Arteries always run over veins

   c Divide the fused twin placenta along the "vascular equator" (rather than through the base of the dividing membrane)

   d Examine each half as a singleton placenta

Sections for histology

1 Placenta from twin A
2 Membranes from twin A
3 Cord from twin A
4 Placenta from twin B
5 Membranes from twin B
6 Cord from twin B
7 Dividing membrane, if present

Table App E-3 Dividing membrane in twin placentas

Features	Dichorionic-diamniotic (fused)	Monochorionic-diamniotic
Appearance	Thick and opaque	Thin and transparent
Separation of membranes by stripping	Difficult	Easy
Point of attachment to fetal surface	Ridge or tearing of chorion	Smooth and continuous, without ridge
Vascular anastomoses	Very rare	Numerous

Type	Incidence	Gross	Twin type
Dichorionic-diamniotic (separate)	35%		Monozygotic or dizygotic
Dichorionic-diamniotic (fused)	34%		Monozygotic or dizygotic
Monochorionic-diamniotic	30%		Monozygotic
Monochorionic-monoamniotic	1%		Monozygotic

1 Driscoll SG, Langston C. College of American Pathologists conference XIX on the examination of the placenta: report of the working group on methods for placental examination. Arch Pathol Lab Med 1991, **115**: 704–708
2 Robboy SJ, Kraus FT, Kurman RJ. Gross description, processing, and reporting of gynaecologic and obstetric specimens. In: Kurman RJ (ed). Blaustein's Pathology of the Female Genital Tract, 4th Edn. New York, 2002, Springer-Verlag, pp. 1319–1346

Prostate gland—radical prostatectomy for tumor

This procedure can be carried out through the retropubic or the perineal route.

Procedure

1 Orient the specimen and paint the surgical margins with India ink
2 Fix the entire specimen overnight or at least for a few hours. Reduction of fixation time can be obtained by microwave treatment
3 Shave the vasa deferentia and the proximal (bladder neck) margins
4 Sample the distal (apical) margins by obtaining a thinly shaved section or amputating the distal 1 cm of the apex and sectioning the cone thus obtained perpendicularly to the cut edge
5 Serially section the prostate at 2- to 3-mm intervals from apex to base
6 Lay the individual slices sequentially and examine them carefully. Using the cross-section of the urethra (U-shaped, with the concavity toward the posterior lobe) as a landmark
7 Take photographs or photocopies of the slices to be submitted to histology and identify in one of them the site of the sections taken

Description

1 Weight and dimensions of specimen
2 Organs present: whole prostate? urethra (length), seminal vesicles, vas, lymph nodes
3 a Prostate: tumor (location in lobes, size, color, borders, capsular and periprostatic extension)
  b Non-neoplastic prostate: nodular hyperplasia?
4 Urethra: patent? impinged by tumor?
5 Seminal vesicles: involved by tumor?

Sections for histology

1 Vasa deferentia margin
2 Proximal (bladder neck) margin
3 Distal (apical) margin, divided into right and left
4 Seminal vesicles: proximal, mid, and distal portions from each side
5 Prostate: there is no consensus on the preferred method of sampling, particularly in the absence of grossly identifiable tumor. At many institutions (particularly academic ones), the entire specimen is submitted. In others a protocol has been devised in which the specimen is partially sampled depending on the gross features of the tumor; the latter strikes the author as a more efficient alternative. The individual slices can be submitted in toto using extra-large cassettes (preferable if resources allow it) or by cutting the slices to fit the standard cassette (right and left halves and, if necessary, anterior and posterior quadrants)

1   Hall GS, Kramer CE, Epstein JI. Evaluation of radical prostatectomy specimens; a comparative analysis of sampling methods. Am J Surg Pathol 1992, **16**: 315–324

Prostate gland—suprapubic prostatectomy for nodular hyperplasia

Procedure

1 Step section the specimen into 3-mm slices, either in the fresh state or after formalin fixation
2 Examine *each slice* carefully for areas suspicious of carcinoma (yellow areas or foci that are harder or softer than the rest of the specimen)

Description

1 Weight of specimen
2 Shape, color, and consistency
3 Presence of hyperplastic nodules, cysts, calculi, areas suspicious of carcinoma

Sections for histology

1 Left lobe: three sections
2 Right lobe: three sections
3 Middle lobe

Prostate gland—transurethral resection (TUR)

Procedure

1 Weight with accurate balance
2 Carefully examine all the fragments. Carcinoma of the prostate is often yellow and/or hard; submit for histology chips with these gross characteristics

Description

1 Weight of specimen
2 Size, shape, and color of chips

Sections for histology

1 *If all fragments received in a single container*

   a All of specimen until four cassettes filled
   b If an excess, one additional cassette for each additional 10 g of tissue (each cassette holds approximately 2 g)

2 *If all fragments received are identified as to lobe from which they were taken*, submit as follows for each specimen (lobe) received:

   a All of specimen until four cassettes filled
   b If an excess, one additional cassette for each additional 10 g of tissue
   c Identify in following order (not all lobes may have been biopsied in some cases):

   • Anterior lobe
   • Middle lobe
   • Posterior lobe
   • Left lateral lobe
   • Right lateral lobe

   d If carcinoma is identified microscopically in a specimen that was not entirely submitted, the remainder of the tissue should be processed in its entirety, regardless of amount

Salivary gland—resection for tumor[1]

The three most common types of operation performed because of salivary gland tumors are *superficial parotidectomy* (also known as lateral lobectomy, consisting of removal of the superficial lobe of the gland with preservation of the facial nerve), *total parotidectomy* (removal of both superficial and deep lobes, usually with sacrifice of the facial nerve), and *total submaxillectomy*.

Procedure

1 Paint surgical margins with India ink
2 Fix *in toto* or bisect in the fresh state, depending on size of specimen
3 Cut parallel sections
4 Look for intraparotid lymph nodes and for major nerves in total parotidectomy specimens
5 If the specimen includes a radical neck dissection, process according to instructions for Lymph node dissection—radical neck

Description

1 Type of specimen: parotid lobectomy, total parotidectomy without facial nerve, total parotidectomy with facial nerve, total submandibulectomy; side of operation
2 Tumor: size, location, shape, distance from closet margin; solitary or multiple? cystic or solid? encapsulated, circumscribed, or poorly defined? hemorrhage or necrosis? extraglandular extension?
3 Appearance of non-neoplastic gland
4 Appearance of intraparotid and other lymph nodes

Sections for histology

1 Tumor: four or more, depending on size; capsule or tumor margins should be included
2 Non-neoplastic gland
3 Surgical margins
4 Facial nerve margins, if included
5 Lymph nodes, if included

1   A very detailed set of instructions for surgical specimens from the upper aerodigestive tract is available from: Slootweg PJ, de Groot JAM. Surgical pathological anatomy of head and neck specimens: A manual for the dissection of surgical specimens from the upper aerodigestive tract. London, 1999, Springer

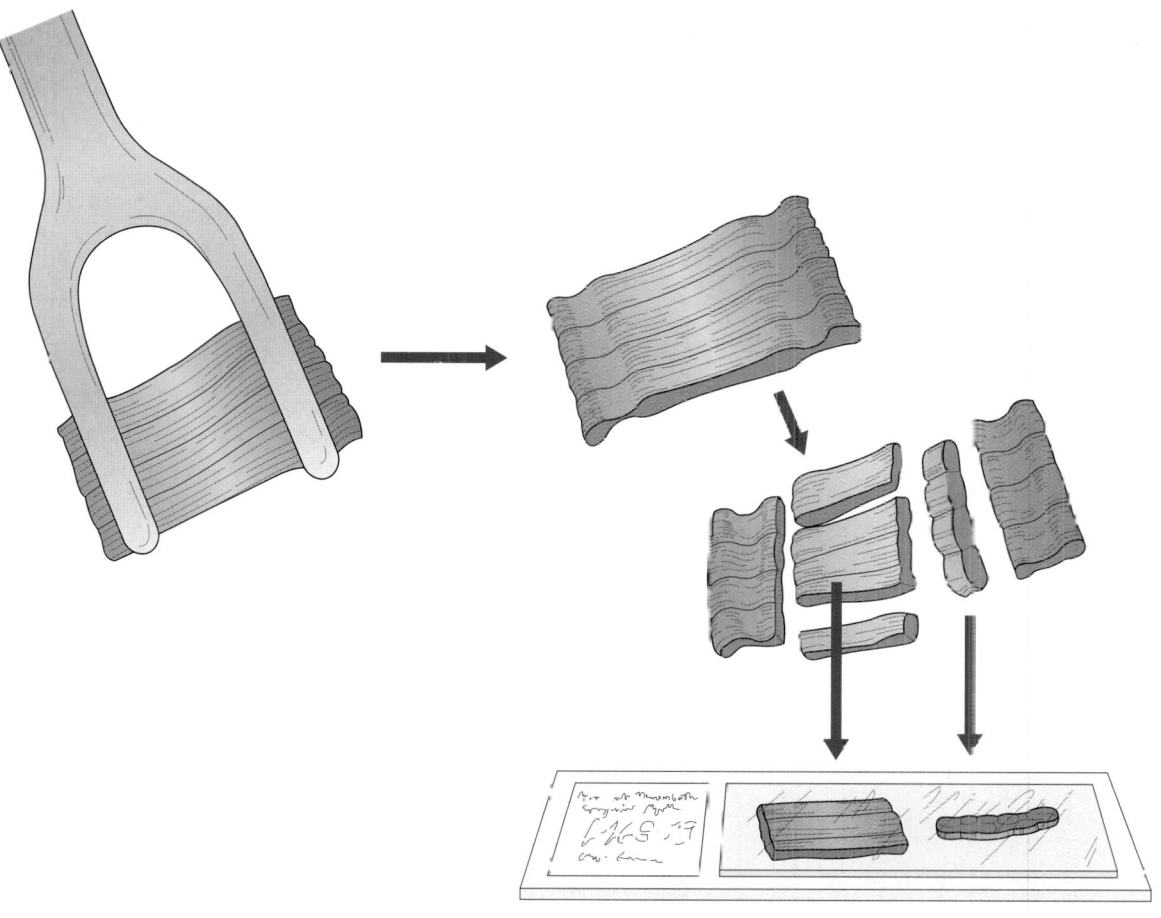

Skeletal muscle—biopsy

Procedure

The proper evaluation of a skeletal muscle biopsy includes routine processing and staining, enzyme histochemistry, and electron microscopic examination.

1 *Routine processing*: The specimen is usually received stretched on a special muscle biopsy clamp. It should remain on the clamp for overnight fixation. If the specimen is received fresh, pin it to a corkboard and fix overnight

2 *Enzyme histochemistry*: Freeze a small fragment in liquid nitrogen. It is important for this to be a cross-section. Freeze also a longitudinal section if enough tissue is available

3 *Electron microscopy*: See instructions under Electron microscopy—sampling

Description

1 Dimensions of specimen
2 Color and consistency; fibrosis? edema? necrosis?

Sections for histology

1 One longitudinal section
2 One cross-section

Skin—excision for benign lesion

Procedure

1 Pigmented nevi, seborrheic keratoses, and other benign skin conditions (as well as small basal cell carcinomas) are usually removed with narrow margins, and the size of the specimen depends mainly on the size of the lesion
2 Fix well before processing
3 If there is any clinical or gross suggestion that the tumor may be malignant, paint margins with India ink

Description

1 Size and shape of specimen; features of surface; lesion present? size, color, other features; margin grossly involved?
2 If specimen transected, description of appearance of cross-section

Sections for histology

Note: In specimens from vesicular diseases, the vesicle should be submitted intact. Do not cut through the vesicle.

1 For specimens measuring 3 mm or less (see accompanying drawing **A**): submit *in toto* without cutting
2 For specimens measuring between 4 and 6 mm in width (see accompanying drawing **B**): cut through the center and submit both halves
3 For specimens with a width of 7 mm or more (see accompanying drawing **C**): cut a 2- to 3-mm slice from the center for histology and save the remainder in formalin
4 Make sure that sections will be embedded on edge

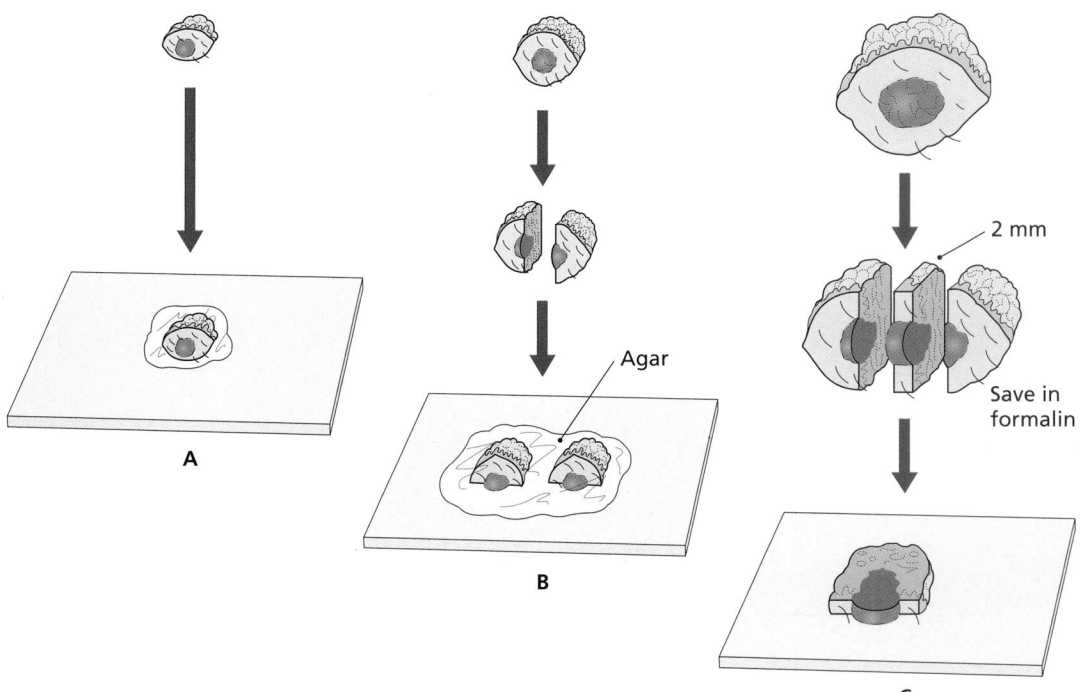

Skin—excision for malignant tumor

Procedure

1 Paint all excision margins with India ink
2 Take photographs or photocopies in cases of large tumors and identify in one of them the site of the sections to be taken

Description

1 Shape and dimensions of specimen
2 Characteristics of lesion: size, shape, color or colors, configuration; elevated or depressed? ulceration? types of margins (sharp or ill-defined? flat or elevated?); distance from margins of resection; satellite nodules?

Sections for histology

1 *Small specimens*—up to 5 cm in greatest length (see accompanying drawing **I**):
Cut parallel 3-mm slices of the entire specimen, making sure that the initial section goes from the center of the lesion to what grossly appears the narrowest surgical margin

2 *Larger specimens* (see accompanying drawing **II**):

  a Tumor: parallel 3-mm slices of the entire lesion (*T*)
  b Surgical margins: tangential sections along the entire edge (*M*)[1-5]

1 For alternative methods to evaluate surgical margins, see: Gormley DE. Evaluation of a method for controlled tissue embedding for histologic evaluation of tumor margins. Am J Dermatopathol 1987, **9**: 308–315
2 Hurt MA. The rule of halves. A method of controlling the uniform "cutting-in" of skin biopsies. Am J Dermatopathol 1991, **13**: 7–10
3 Mondragon G, Nygaard F. Routine and special procedures for processing biopsy specimens for lesions suspected to be malignant melanomas. Am J Dermatopathol 1981, **3**: 265–272
4 Rapini RP. Comparison of methods for checking surgical margins. J Am Acad Dermatol 1990, **23**: 288–294
5 Woods JE, Farrow GM. Peripheral tissue examination for malignant lesions of the skin. Mayo Clin Proc 1991, **66**: 207–209

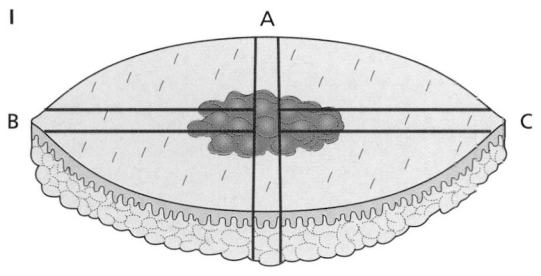

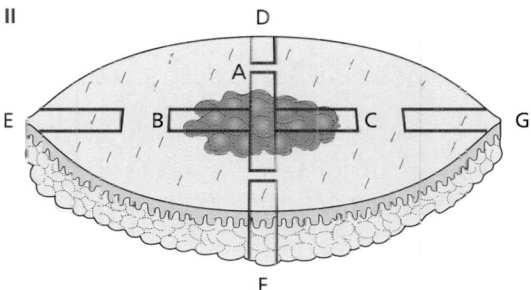

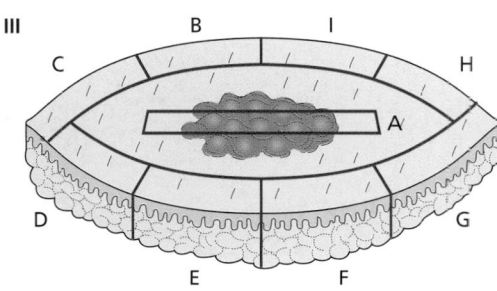

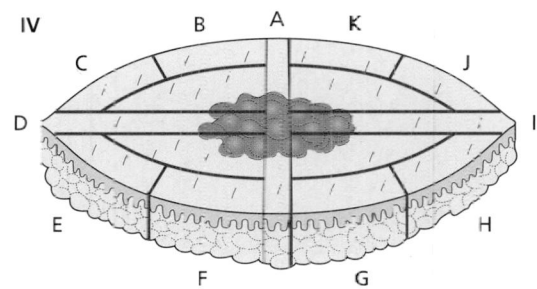

Skin—punch biopsy

Procedure

1 Submit *in toto*, if 4 mm in diameter or smaller (see accompanying drawing **A**). This prevents loss of tissue during the facing-up of the block and allows better microscopic sampling; cut in half longitudinally only if 5 mm or larger, and submit both halves for histology (see accompanying drawing **B**)

2 If the specimen is from a vesicular disease, the vesicle should be submitted *intact* for histology

Description

1 Diameter and thickness of biopsy
2 Appearance of surface; subcutis included?

Sections for histology

1 Entire biopsy (see under Procedure)
2 Make sure section oriented on edge

1   White CR Jr. Laboratory handling of skin biopsy specimens. Lab Med 1982, **13**: 211–217

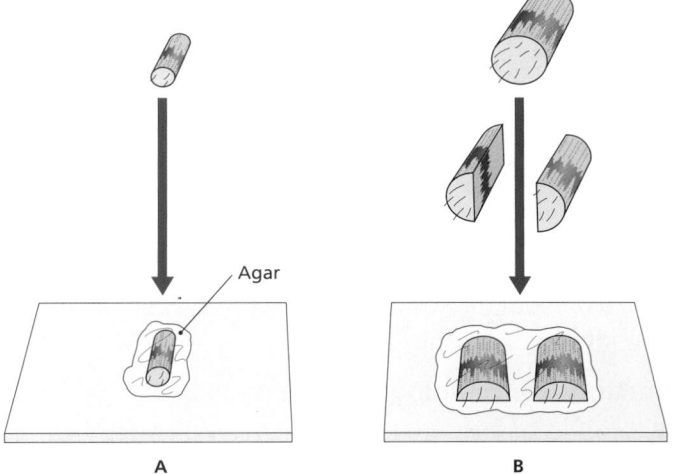

Skin—shave biopsy

Procedure

Shave biopsies of the skin, usually done for keratoses or basal cell carcinomas, can be quite thin, often of round or oval shape.

Description

1 Size of specimen
2 Number of fragments
3 Features of surface

Sections for histology

1 If width is 3 mm or less: submit *in toto* without cutting
2 If width is 4 mm or more: cut in parallel slices, about 2 to 3 mm thick, and submit all for histology
3 Make sure all sections are oriented on edge

1   White CR Jr. Laboratory handling of skin biopsy specimens. Lab Med 1982, **13**: 211–217

Small bowel—biopsy

Procedure

1 The specimen is usually received attached to a piece of filter paper or Gelfoam, mucosal side up; let it fix well before processing

2 Examine with dissecting microscope and determine mucosal pattern; avoid drying of the specimen and traumatizing the mucosa during this procedure. Performance of this step has lost some of the popularity it had years ago, but it still retains some usefulness as a quick predictor of the histologic appearance and as an aid for proper orientation of the specimen

Description

1 Size and color of specimen
2 Mucosal pattern with dissecting microscope (see accompanying drawings)

Sections for histology

1 The entire specimen is submitted. It is essential for it to be oriented on edge
2 If the specimen comes attached to Gelfoam, the latter can be processed together with the specimen

Small bowel—excision

Small bowel resections vary a great deal in length and location depending on the characteristics of the lesion. They include the regional mesentery and are usually followed by an end-to-end anastomosis.

Procedure

1 Two options are available depending on the length of the bowel and the type of pathology present:

  a Cut longitudinally through the antimesenteric border, pin on corkboard, and fix overnight

  b Wash out contents gently with formalin or saline solution (not with water), tie one end, fill the lumen with formalin, and tie the other end. Fix overnight and open longitudinally along the antimesenteric border

Description

1 Length and diameter of specimen
2 Mucosa: appearance; edema? hemorrhage? ulcerations? tumor? (size, location, circumferential involvement? depth of invasion)
3 Wall: thickness, abnormalities
4 Serosa: fibrosis, peritonitis, adhesions
5 Lymph nodes: size and appearance
6 Mesentery; mesenteric blood vessels

Sections for histology

1 Depends on pathology present
1 In cases of infarct: several cross-sections of mesenteric vessels

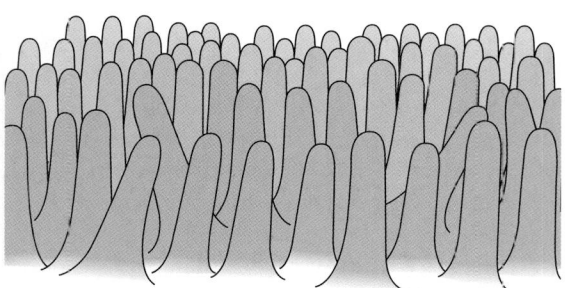

Fingerlike

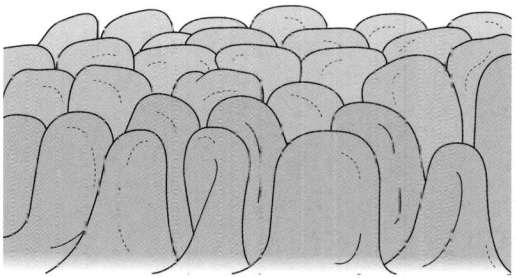

Leaflike

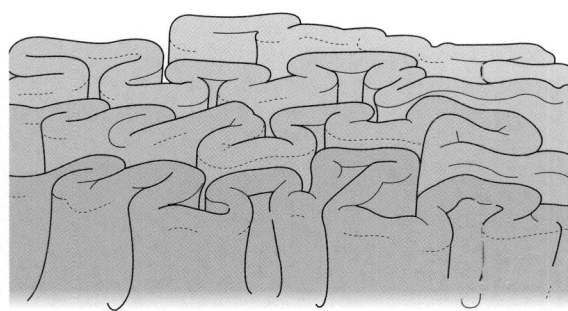

Cerebriform

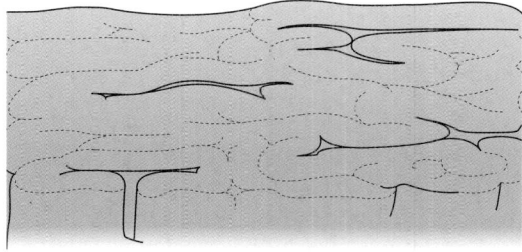

Flat

Soft tissue—resection for tumor

The procedure here described was written specifically for amputations specimens but it can be easily adapted to the lesser operations that are currently carried out for these neoplasms.

Procedure

1 Review any imaging studies (CT scans, MRIs) that may have been taken before amputation
2 Measure the length and circumference of the extremity, including a measure of the circumference at the level of the tumor
3 Determine the presence, position, and dimensions of biopsy sites
4 Search for the major lymph node groups and identify and place in separate containers
5 Cut through the skin and carefully dissect the subcutaneous fat, muscles, and major arteries, veins, and nerves *around* the tumor, avoiding cutting through the latter. Use an anatomy atlas as a guide, if necessary. Try to determine as accurately as possible the relationship of the tumor with the following structures: skin, subcutaneous fat, and specific muscles; arteries, veins, and nerves; and periosteum and bone. Mark some of the major anatomic landmarks with tags, if indicated
6 As soon as all the margins of the tumor have been determined, remove the entire area with a good margin of normal tissues using a scalpel and scissors
7 Two options, outlined later, are available for studying the specimen thus obtained. The first is used in most instances, but the second is preferable in selected cases. In either case, if a previous incision site is present, take a sample for histology at this time along the entire course of the incision

   a Divide the tumor into slices with a large, sharp knife. Continue the dissection with the forceps, scissors, and scalpel to determine the tumor relationship with the structures previously mentioned. Place several pieces from different areas in formalin, fix for several hours or overnight, and trim to place in cassettes
   b Place the entire specimen in a large pan containing formalin, cover with a towel, leave in the refrigerator at 4°C overnight, and cut parallel slices with a large sharp knife. Take X-ray studies, if pertinent. Take photographs or photocopies, and identify in one of them the site of the sections to be taken

8 Quickly dissect the soft tissues from the rest of the extremity, looking for other foci of tumor or other lesions

9 Cut the major bones of the extremities longitudinally with a band saw. Make one of the sections through the area of bone closest to the soft tissue tumor. Examine for tumor extension or other lesions
10 Open the major joints and examine them

Description

1 Type of amputation; side of extremity
2 Length and circumference of extremity, including circumference at level of tumor
3 Presence, position, and dimensions of biopsy sites
4 Tumor characteristics:

   a Primary location: subcutaneous fat; muscle compartment(s) (specify which); fascial planes
   b Tumor extension into and relation with skin, subcutaneous fat, deep fascia, muscle, periosteum, bone, joint vessels, and nerves (specify which); presence of obvious vascular or neural involvement by tumor
   c If previous incision present, is there evidence of tumor extension along it?
   d Size (three dimension), shape, color, borders (encapsulated? pushing? infiltrating?), consistency, secondary changes (cysts? necrosis? hemorrhage?)
   e Presence of myxoid changes, foci of calcification, cartilage, or bone
   f Shortest distance of tumor from margin of resection

5 Appearance of remaining extremity, if abnormal (if not, so state); skin, subcutaneous fat, muscles, major vessels and nerves, bone (tumor invasion? osteoporosis? bone marrow), joints (osteoarthritis?)
6 Appearance and approximate number of lymph nodes found

Sections for histology

1 Tumor: four sections or more, depending on size and extent. All grossly dissimilar areas should be sampled. Whenever possible, sections should be taken to include the periphery of the tumor *and* adjacent fat, muscle, skin, periosteum, vessels, and/or nerves
2 Previous incision site, if present, taken all along its course
3 Lymph nodes: if grossly normal, only representative ones; if grossly abnormal or if clinical suspicion or metastases, all of them
4 Proximal margins of resection: subcutaneous fat and muscle (plus skin and bone, if indicated)

Spleen—splenectomy

Splenectomy consists of removal of the entire spleen after ligating the splenic artery and vein.

Procedure

1 Measure and weigh the specimen
2 Cut parallel slices as thin as possible with a sharp knife or meat cutter while the specimen is fresh and examine each slice carefully for focal lesions; do not wash the cut surface in tap water. Fix each slice flat in a large container
3 Take cultures if an inflammatory condition is suspected
4 Prepare four imprints of the cut surface in all cases in which splenic pathology is suspected; stain two with hematoxylin–eosin and two with Wright's stain
5 If sickle cell disease is suspected, fix a block of tissue in formalin *immediately* after it has been cut from the interior of the organ
6 Look for lymph nodes and accessory spleens in the splenic hilum
7 For the evaluation of the red pulp in diseases associated with hypersplenism, the specimen can be injected with formalin through the splenic artery. A sharp distinction between sinuses and chords will thus be obtained in the microscopic preparations
8 For the spleen removed as part of a staging procedure, see under Staging laparotomy for malignant lymphoma

Description

1 Weight and dimensions
2 Hilum: nature of vessels, presence of lymph nodes, presence of accessory spleens
3 Capsule: color, thickness, focal changes, adhesions, lacerations (location, length and depth)
4 Cut surface: color; consistency; bulging; malpighian corpuscles (size; color; conspicuous?); fibrous trabeculae; nodules or masses; diffuse infiltration?

Sections for histology

1 For incidental splenectomy: one section, including capsule
2 For traumatically ruptured spleen: one section through tear and one away from it
3 For diseased spleen: at least three sections, one to include hilum and two to include capsule

Staging laparotomy for malignant lymphoma

Procedure

1 Spleen: handle as described under Spleen—splenectomy except that *the entire spleen* should be sliced carefully, 3 to 4 mm apart, and each slice should be carefully examined. Any nodules, no matter how small, that differ from the adjacent normal malpighian corpuscles should be processed for histology. Square blocks containing these suspicious nodules, in addition to other obvious lesions, should be cut out and fixed separately for several hours or overnight in formalin
2 Lymph nodes: these will usually include splenic hilar, para-aortic, and possible mesenteric nodes. Dissect carefully the splenic hilum for the former
3 Liver wedge biopsy (right and left lobes): keep separate; trim into several slices, if necessary
4 Open iliac crest biopsy: fix, decalcify, and trim, if necessary

Description

1 Proceed as per instructions for the respective organs
2 Presence or absence of grossly identifiable nodes in the splenic hilum must be noted

Sections for histology

1 Spleen: all grossly abnormal or suspicious areas; if no gross abnormalities seen, four random pieces
2 Lymph nodes: all, properly identified as to site
3 Liver: all, properly identified as to lobe
4 Bone marrow: all

Stomach—gastrectomy for tumor

Gastrectomy for tumor can be *total* (including cardia pylorus), *subtotal* (including the pylorus), and *proximal* or *inverted subtotal* (including the cardia).

Procedure

1 Open the specimen along the greater curvature (unless the lesion is in this location; if it is, open the specimen along the lesser curvature)
2 Dissect the lymph node groups according to the accompanying diagram and remove the omentum
3 If a splenectomy is included, dissect the hilar lymph nodes, measure and weigh the spleen, and cut in 1-cm longitudinal slices
4 Pin the stomach on a corkboard and fix overnight in formalin before sectioning
5 Take photographs or photocopies and identify in one of them the sites of the sections to be taken
6 Paint the surgical margins with India ink
7 In general, take the sections *perpendicular* to the directions of the mucosal folds
8 Another way to examine these specimens is as follows: inject the stomach with formalin (in cases of total gastrectomy) or fill it with gauze or cotton impregnated in formalin (in partial gastrectomies). Fix overnight. Cut the side opposite the tumor with scissors and the tumor side with a long knife
9 If a thorough mapping of the mucosal abnormalities is desired, the entire specimen can be submitted, or the Swiss roll technique can be used (see Chapter 11, Stomach)

Description

1 Type of resection (total or subtotal); length of greater curvature, lesser curvature, and duodenal cuff
2 Tumor characteristics: location, size (including thickness), shape (fungating, spreading, ulcerated); depth of invasion; presence of serosal involvement; blood vessel invasion; extension into duodenum; distance from both lines of resection
3 Appearance of non-neoplastic mucosa

Sections for histology (see accompanying drawings)

1 Tumor: four sections through wall and including tumor border and adjacent mucosa
2 Non-neoplastic mucosa; midstomach, two sections
3 Proximal line of resection along lesser curvature: two sections
4 Proximal line of resection along grater curvature: two sections
5 Distal line of resection (along pylorus and duodenum, if present): two sections
6 Spleen, if present

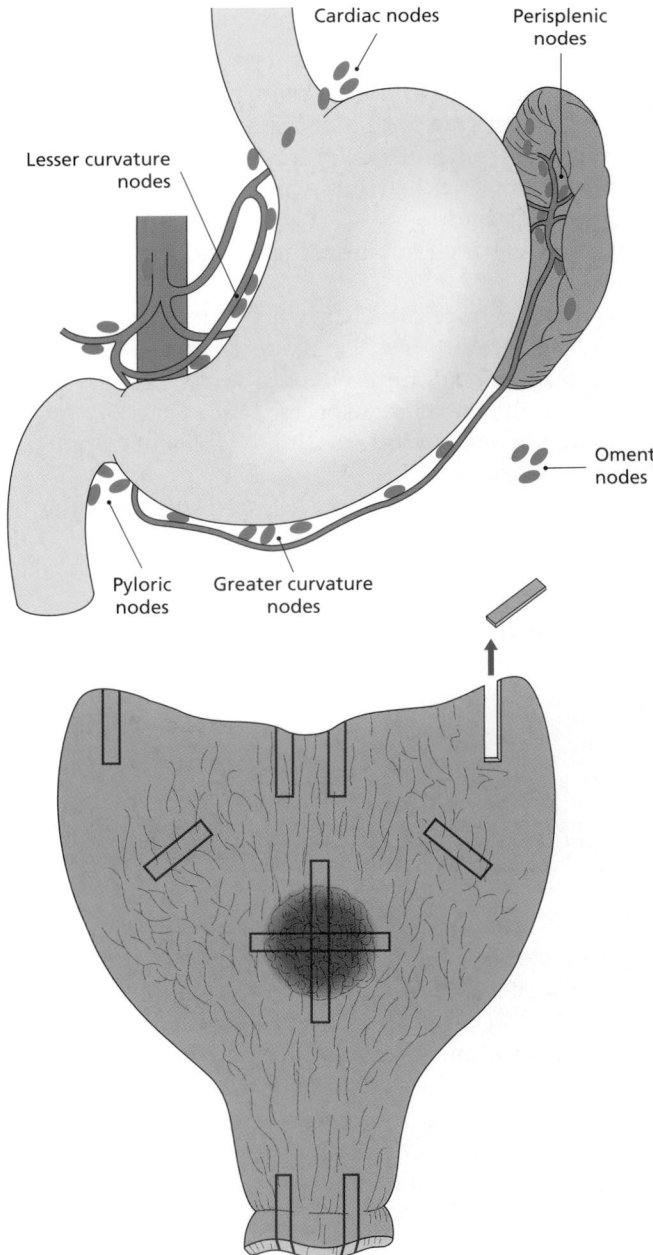

7 Pancreas, if present
8 Lymph nodes:

   a Pyloric
   b Lesser curvature
   c Greater curvature
   d Omentum
   e Perisplenic

Stomach—gastrectomy for ulcer

Gastric resection for peptic ulcer, rarely done at present, includes removal of the antrum with the pylorus and a small portion of the first portion of the duodenum. For duodenal peptic ulcers, this is routinely combined with truncal vagotomy.

Procedure

1 Examine specimen in the fresh state
2 Open the specimen along the greater curvature (unless the lesion is in this location; if it is, open the specimen along the lesser curvature)
3 Dissect the lymph node groups and remove the omentum
4 Look carefully for small mucosal erosions and irregularities and for intramural or subserosal nodules
5 Pin the stomach on a corkboard and fix overnight in formalin before sectioning
6 Take photographs or photocopies and identify in one of them the sites of the sections to be taken

Description

1 Type of resection; length of greater curvature, lesser curvature, and duodenal cuff
2 Ulcer characteristics: location, size, depth of penetration, shape, and color of edges (flat or elevated? converging folds?); presence of large vessels and/or perforation at ulcer base; appearance of serosa. (If the clinicoradiographic diagnosis is peptic ulcer but no ulcer is identified in the specimen, contact the surgeon or assistant to find out whether the ulcer was not resected. Record this information as part of the gross dictation)
3 Appearance of uninvolved mucosa: atrophy, edema, hemorrhage

Sections for histology

1 Ulcer: at least four sections
2 Lesser curvature: two sections cut from proximal margin of excision (Paint line of resection with India ink)
3 Greater curvature: two sections cut from proximal margin of excision (Paint line of resection with India ink)
4 Pylorus and duodenum: two sections, including distal line of resection
5 Other lesions, if present
6 Lymph nodes: up to three sections

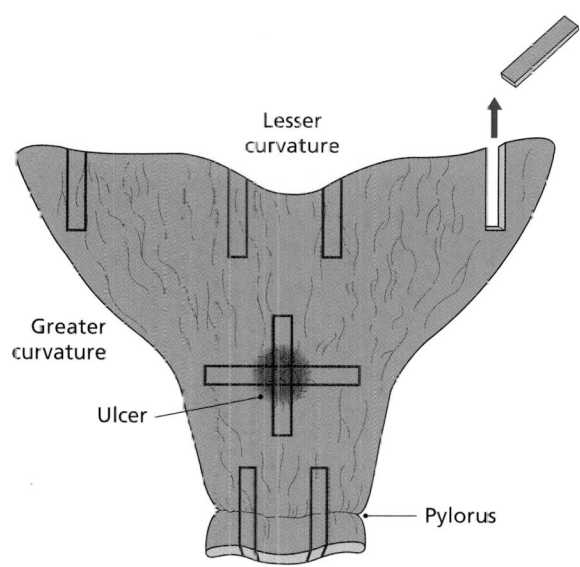

Testicle—orchidectomy

Procedure

1 Open the tunica vaginalis; weigh and measure the testicle
2 Cut the testicle sagittally while it is in the fresh state and fix in formalin
3 Take photographs or photocopies and identify in one of them the sites of the sections to be taken
4 Cut serial slices, about 3 mm thick, of each testicular half, perpendicular to the original section, stopping just at the level of the tunica albuginea (to keep them together), and examine each surface carefully
5 Cut the epididymis longitudinally throughout its entire length
6 Make several cross-sections of the spermatic cord at several levels

Description

1 Weight and dimensions of testicle
2 Length of spermatic cord
3 Features of tumor, if present: size, color; consistency; homogeneity or lack of it; presence of cysts, necrosis, hemorrhage, bone, or cartilage; tumor extension to tunica albuginea, epididymis, cord, and other structures
4 Features of non-neoplastic testicle: atrophy? fibrosis? nodules?

Testicle—orchidectomy (continued)

5 Features of rete testis and epididymis

Sections for histology

1 Tumor: at least three sections or one section for each centimeter of tumor, whichever is greater, at least one of which should include some uninvolved testicle. Most of the sections should include tunica albuginea. (Always submit sections from hemorrhagic or necrotic areas of tumor, as well as from solid or fleshy areas.)

2 Uninvolved testicle: two sections

3 Epididymis

4 Spermatic cord and surrounding soft tissue at point about 1 cm from testicle: one cross-section

5 Spermatic cord and surrounding soft tissue at line of resection: one cross-section

Thymus gland—thymectomy

Procedure

1 Weigh the entire organ. Cut parallel slices, either in the fresh specimen or after formalin fixation

2 Look carefully for lymph nodes around the thymus

Description

1 Weight and dimensions; both lobes identifiable?

2 Relative amount of fat and thymic parenchyma

3 Tumor characteristics: size, shape, external appearance (lobulated or smooth), cut section, color, necrosis, hemorrhage, fibrous bands, calcification, cysts (size, content)

4 Attached structures (pleura, pericardium, lung, lymph nodes)

Sections for histology

1 Tumor: three or more sections, at least two of which should include capsule

2 Uninvolved thymus: two sections

3 Other organs, if present (lung, lymph nodes)

Thyroid gland—thyroidectomy

Operations on the thyroid gland include *nodulectomy* (a procedure largely abandoned that consists of enucleation of a thyroid nodule), *lobectomy* (often combined for cosmetic reasons with removal of the isthmus), *subtotal thyroidectomy* (in which the posterior capsule and a small portion of thyroid tissue—1 to 2 g—are left on the side opposite to the lesion), and *total thyroidectomy* (in which the entire gland—including the posterior capsule—is removed).

Procedure

1 Weigh and measure the specimen

2 Orient the specimen and cut parallel longitudinal slices 5 mm each either in the fresh state or after formalin fixation

3 Search for parathyroid glands in the surrounding fat

Description

1 Type of specimen: lobectomy, isthmectomy, subtotal thyroidectomy, total thyroidectomy

2 Weight, shape, color, and consistency of specimen

3 Cut surface: smooth or nodular? if nodular: number, size, and appearance of nodules (cystic? calcified? hemorrhagic? necrotic?); encapsulated or invasive? distance to line of resection

Sections for histology

1 For diffuse and/or inflammatory lesions: three sections from each lobe and on from isthmus

2 For a solitary encapsulated nodule measure up to 5 cm: entire circumference; take one additional section for each additional centimeter in diameter. Most of these sections should include the tumor capsule and adjacent thyroid tissue, if present

3 For multinodular thyroid glands: one section of each nodule (up to five nodules), including rim and adjacent normal gland; more than one section for larger nodules

4 For papillary carcinoma: block entire thyroid gland and (separately) line of resection

5 For grossly invasive carcinoma other than papillary: three sections of tumor, three of non-neoplastic gland, and one from line of resection

6 For all cases: submit parathyroid glands if found on gross inspection

Uterus—cervical biopsy

Procedure

1 Do not cut the specimen unless the individual pieces are greater than 4 mm in diameter
2 It is essential that *all of the tissue* received be processed, no matter how small
3 Always carefully search the container and the underside of the lid for tiny fragments of tissue

Description

1 Number of pieces received, shape and color
2 Measurement in aggregate
3 Presence or absence of epithelium; epithelial erosions or ulcers? irregularity in epithelial thickness?
4 Any evidence of tumors or cysts?

Sections for histology

1 Submit the material in its entirety
2 If specimens are received with a specific identification (e.g. anterior lip, posterior lip), label and submit them separately
3 If a specimen from endocervical scraping is received, submit as a separate specimen in its entirety (including the endocervical mucus)

Robboy SJ, Kraus FT, Kurman RJ. Gross description, processing, and reporting of gynaecologic and obstetric specimens. In: Kurman RJ (ed). Blaustein's Pathology of the Female Genital Tract, 4th Edn. New York, 2002, Springer-Verlag, pp. 1319–1346

Uterus—cervical conization

Specimens from cervical conizations have the shape of a cone with the base toward the portio. In the *leep procedure* (loop electroexcision procedure), the cone is much smaller than that obtained with the conventional method. Orientation of the specimen is more difficult but just as important.

Procedure

1 Ideally the specimen should be received intact, in the fresh state, and with a suture or other material identifying the 12 o'clock position
2 Open the specimen by inserting a sharp pointed scissors into the cervical canal and cutting it longitudinally along the 12 o'clock position. If the specimen has not been oriented as to position, open at any site
3 Pin on a corkboard with the mucosal side up and fix in formalin for several hours
4 Paint both surgical margins with India ink, taking special care that the epithelial side of the margin is well stained along its entire length
5 Cut the entire cervix by making parallel sections, 2 to 3 mm apart, along the plane of the endocervical canal starting at the 12 o'clock position (or left-hand side of the specimen) and moving clockwise. Sections should be taken in such a way that the epithelium (including the squamocolumnar junction) is present in each section; some trimming of the stroma may be necessary (see accompanying drawing)

Description

1 Size (diameter and depth) and shape of cone; complete cast of cervix or fragmented?
2 Epithelium: color; presence of irregularities, erosions, healed or recent lacerations, masses (size, shape, location), cysts (size, content), previous biopsy sites

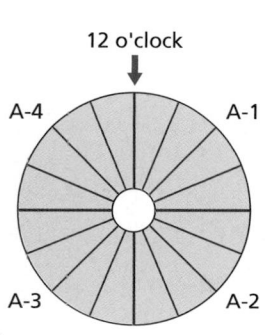
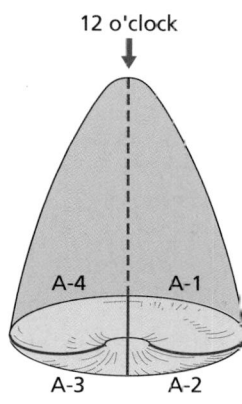
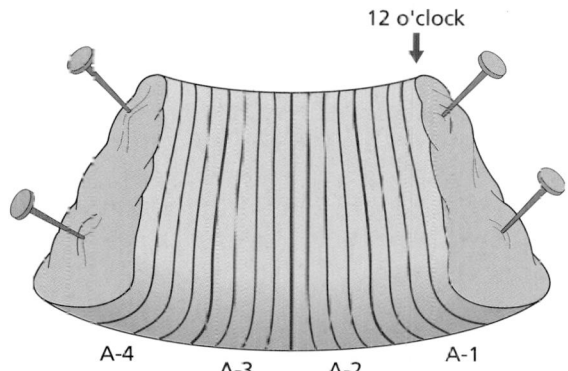

Uterus—cervical conization (continued)

Sections for histology

1 All of the tissue must be submitted (except for trimming of the stroma)
2 If the cone has been oriented to the 12 o'clock position, identify separately:

  a Sections from 12 to 3 o'clock (**A-1** on accompanying drawings)
  b Sections from 3 to 6 o'clock (**A-2** on accompanying drawings)
  c Sections from 6 to 9 o'clock (**A-3** on accompanying drawings)
  d Sections from 9 to 12 o'clock (**A-4** on accompanying drawings)

3 If an accurate mapping of the lesions is desired, identify sequentially each section with a letter, beginning from the 12 o'clock position

1   Robboy SJ, Kraus FT, Kurman RJ. Gross description, processing, and reporting of gynaecologic and obstetric specimens. In: Kurman RJ (ed). Blaustein's Pathology of the Female Genital Tract, 4th Edn. New York, 2002, Springer-Verlag, pp. 1319–1346

Uterus—endometrial curettings or biopsy

Procedure

1 Use of metal strainer or a filter paper in a funnel to collect the specimens
2 In cases of suspected abortion, search for chorionic villi, if necessary, under a dissecting microscope
3 In cases of recurrent abortion, save a sample of villi for possible cytogenetic evaluation. Clean the forceps, other instruments, and the table carefully before handling the next case

Description

1 Measurement in the aggregate
2 Color and consistency; blood clots present? proportion of clots in relation to whole specimen; any unusually large or firm pieces? globular tissue? evidence of necrosis? tissue suggestive of products of conception: if so, describe the appearance of chorionic villi (a dissecting microscope may be necessary); if presence or absence of villous vessels, shape of villi (tubular, clubbed, cystic, hydatidiform); if gestational sac is present, describe as indicated under Uterus—tissue passed

Sections for histology

1 For endometrial biopsy or diagnostic curettage: submit *all* tissue. Do not fill the cassette more than half full
2 For endometrial curettage for incomplete abortion: submit representative sections of tissue with the appearance of placenta, fetal parts, and deciduas unless the entire specimen is small enough to fit into three cassettes. If the microscopic sections do not show products of conception, submit the rest of the material

1   Robboy SJ, Kraus FT, Kurman RJ. Gross description, processing, and reporting of gynaecologic and obstetric specimens. In: Kurman RJ (ed). Blaustein's Pathology of the Female Genital Tract, 4th Edn. New York, 2002, Springer-Verlag, pp. 1319–1346

Uterus—hysterectomy (general instructions)

Hysterectomies can be performed by either the abdominal or the vaginal route, the latter reserved for benign conditions. They consist of removal of the entire organ. Supracervical hysterectomies (in which the corpus is separated from the cervix and the latter is left in place) are no longer performed. Depending on the age of the patient and the nature of the disease, abdominal hysterectomies may be accompanied by unilateral or bilateral adnexectomy and by the removal of regional lymph nodes.

Procedure

1 If operation was done for endometrial hyperplasia, endometrial carcinoma, or cervical (in situ or invasive) carcinoma, read specific instructions before proceeding
2 Measure and weigh the specimen
3 If the uterus is received fresh and intact:

  a Open it by cutting with scissors through both lateral walls, from the cervix to the uterine cornua

b Make a mark as to which half is anterior (e.g. by cutting a small wedge on one side) and, if the tubes are attached, by the fact that their insertion is anterior to that of the round ligament

c Make additional cuts through any large mass in the wall

d Fix for several hours or overnight

e Make parallel transverse sections through each half, about 1 cm apart, beginning at the upper level of the endocervical canal and stopping short of completing them on one side to keep them together, and examine carefully each surface

f Make several sections of the cervix along the endocervical canal

g Make at least one cross section of every myoma present and examine carefully; larger myomas need additional cuts

h If tubes and/or ovary accompanies the specimen, follow instructions for these organs

Description

1 Type of hysterectomy: total? radical? with salpingo-oophorectomy?

2 Shape of uterus: deformed? subserosal bulges?

3 Serosa: fibrous adhesions?

4 Wall: thickness, abnormalities

5 Endometrium: appearance; thickness; polyps? (size, shape); cysts?

6 Cervix: appearance of exocervix, squamocolumnar junction, endocervical canal; erosions? polyps? cysts?

7 Myomas: number, location (subserosal, intramural, submucosal); size; sessile or pedunculated? hemorrhage, necrosis, or calcification? ulceration of overlying endometrium?

Sections for histology

1 Cervix: one section from anterior half and one from posterior half

2 Corpus: at least two sections taken close to fundus and including endometrium, good portion of myometrium, and, if thickness permits, serosa; additional sections from any grossly abnormal areas

3 Myomas: at least one section per myoma, up to three; sections from any grossly abnormal area (e.g. soft, fleshy, necrotic, cystic)

4 Cervical or endometrial polyps: to be submitted in entirety unless extremely large

1 Robboy SJ, Kraus FT. Kurman RJ. Gross description, processing, and reporting of gynaecologic and obstetric specimens. In: Kurman RJ (ed.) Blaustein's Pathology of the Female Genital Tract, 4th Edn. New York, 2002, Springer-Verlag, pp. 1319–1346

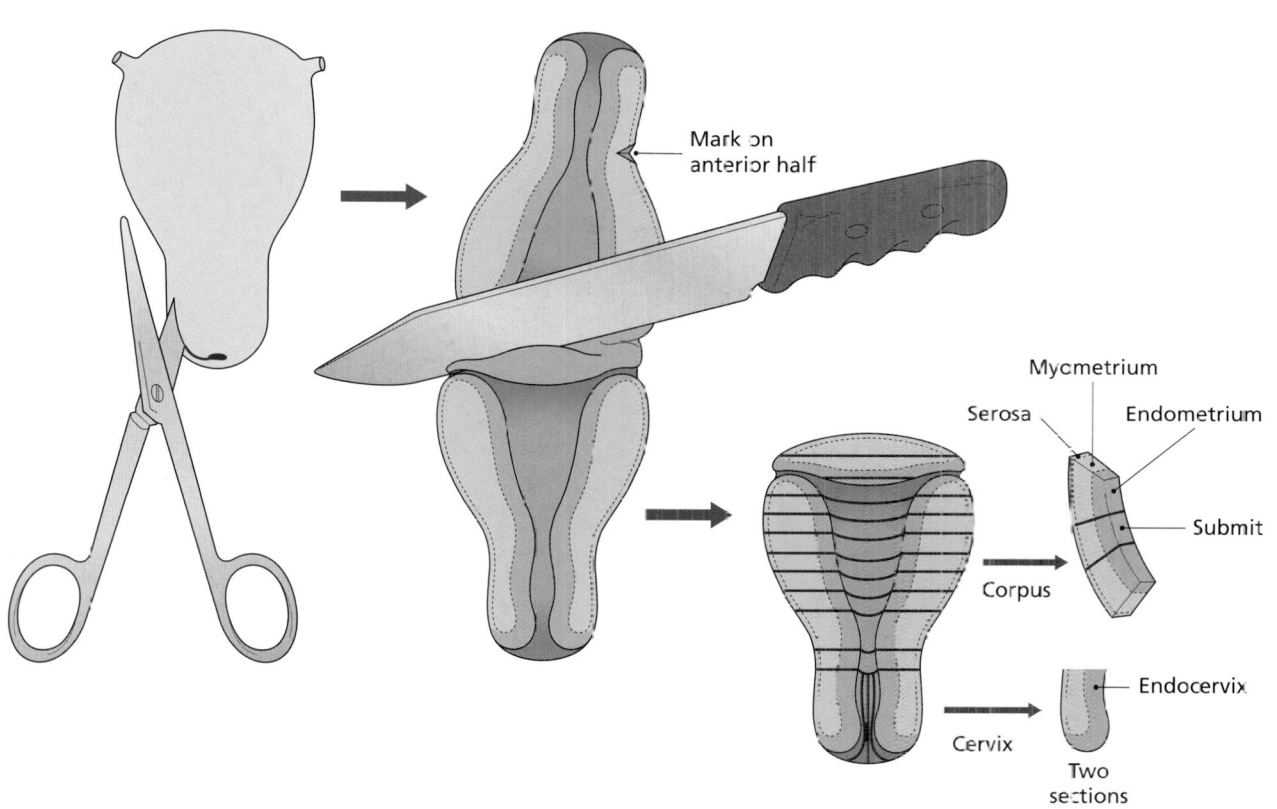

Mark on anterior half

Serosa · Myometrium · Endometrium · Submit · Corpus · Cervix · Endocervix · Two sections

Uterus—hysterectomy for cervical carcinoma (in situ or invasive)

Procedure

1 If lymph nodes are included (radical hysterectomy), dissect while fresh and separate into left and right obturator, interiliac, and left and right iliac (high nodes) groups (not all of these groups will be present in every specimen)
2 Measure and weigh the specimen; orient as to anterior and posterior sides; see under Uterus—hysterectomy (general instructions)
3 Amputate the cervix from the corpus about 2.5 cm above the external os with a sharp knife
4 Handle the uterus as described under Uterus—hysterectomy (general instructions) and the tubes and

ovaries, if present, according to instructions for these organs
5 Open the cervix with scissors through the endocervical canal at the 12 o'clock position and carefully pin stretched specimen on a corkboard with the mucosal side up. Be careful to avoid tearing or rubbing the epithelial surface
6 Fix by floating for several hours or overnight with the tissue on the underside of the corkboard in a formalin container
7 Paint the vaginal surgical margin with India ink
8 Cut the entire cervix by making parallel longitudinal sections, 2 to 3 mm apart, along the plane of the

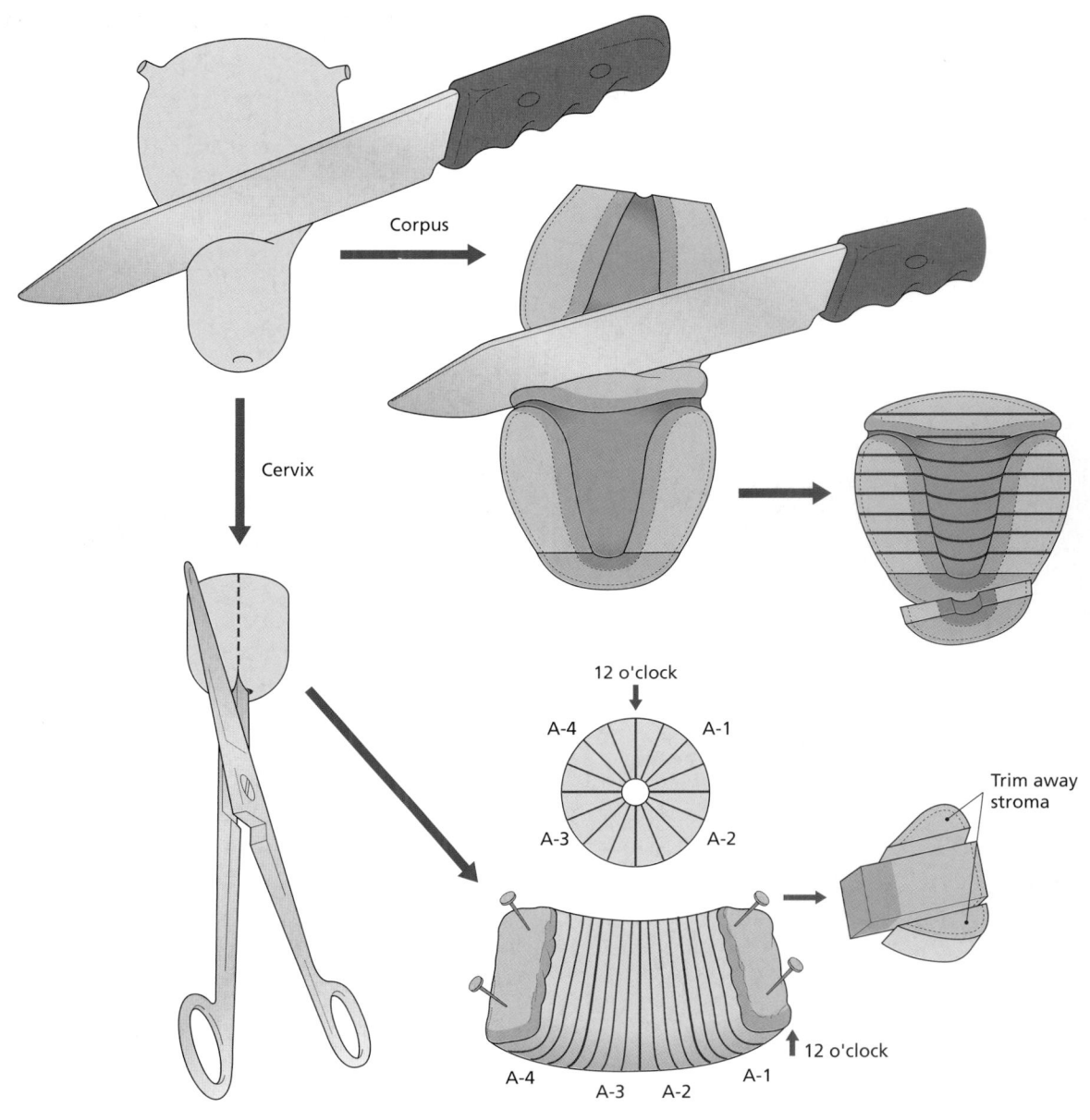

endocervical canal starting at the 12 o'clock position and moving clockwise. Sections should be taken in such a way that the epithelium (including the squamocolumnar junction) is present in each section; some trimming of the stroma may be necessary (see accompanying drawing)

Description

1 Cervix: color of epithelium; presence of irregularities, erosions, healed or recent lacerations, masses (size, shape, location), cysts (size, content), previous biopsy, or conization sites
2 Rest of uterus: see under Uterus—hysterectomy (general instructions)
3 Ovaries and tubes, if present: see instructions for respective organs
4 Lymph nodes, if present: approximate number; gross appearance; seem involved by tumor?

Sections for histology

1 Cervix: all tissue is submitted (except for trimming of stroma) and identified separately as follows:

   a Sections from 12 to 3 o'clock (**A-1** on accompanying drawings)
   b Sections from 3 to 6 o'clock (**A-2** on accompanying drawings)
   c Sections from 6 to 9 o'clock (**A-3** on accompanying drawings)
   d Sections from 9 to 12 o'clock (**A-4** on accompanying drawings) (If an accurate mapping of the lesions is desired, identify sequentially each section with a letter, beginning from the 12 o'clock position)

2 Vaginal cuff (entire line of resection
3 Left soft tissue (for invasive cases only)
4 Right soft tissue (for invasive cases only)
5 Rest of uterus: see under Uterus—hysterectomy (general instructions)
6 Ovaries and tubes: see Instructions for respective organs
7 Lymph nodes, if present

   • Left obturator
   • Right obturator
   • Interiliac
   • Left iliac (high nodes)
   • Right iliac (high nodes)

1   Robboy SJ, Kraus FT, Kurman RJ. Gross description, processing, and reporting of gynaecologic and obstetric specimens. In: Kurman RJ (ed). Blaustein's Pathology of the Female Genital Tract, 4th Edn. New York, 2002, Springer-Verlag, pp. 1319–1346

Uterus—hysterectomy for endometrial hyperplasia or carcinoma

Procedure

1 If lymph nodes are included (radical hysterectomy), dissect while fresh and separate into left and right obturator, interiliac, and left and right iliac (high nodes) groups (not all of these groups will be present in every specimen)
2 Open and fix the uterus as indicated under Uterus—hysterectomy (general instructions)
3 If ovaries and tubes are present, handle according to respective instructions

Description

1 Type of operation: radical? total? with salpingectomy and oophorectomy?
2 Tumor: exact location; size; appearance (solid, papillary, ulcerated, necrotic, hemorrhagic); color; extent of endometrial extensions; presence of myometrial, serosal, parametrial (soft tissue), venous, cervical, or tubal extension
3 Rest of uterus: see under Uterus—hysterectomy (general instructions)
4 Ovaries and tubes: see respective instructions
5 Lymph nodes, if present: approximate number; gross appearance; seem involved by tumor?

Sections for histology

1 If obvious tumor present:

   a Three sections, one of which should be through area of deepest invasion and be complete sections from surface of endometrium through serosa (if too thick for a cassette, divide in half and identify both halves appropriately)
   b Two sections from non-neoplastic endometrium; do not need to be through entire wall

Uterus—hysterectomy for endometrial hyperplasia or carcinoma *(continued)*

2 Soft tissue from left and eighth parametria

3 If no obvious tumor present (previous irradiation, very superficial carcinoma, endometrial hyperplasia):

   a Sample entire endometrium by making complete transverse parallel sections, 2 to 3 mm apart, of both uterine halves; one section should comprise entire thickness of organ, from mucosa to serosa; trim away from all others deepest two thirds of myometrium. Label separately as anterior and posterior halves

   b Rest of uterus: see under Uterus—hysterectomy (general instructions)

   c Ovaries and tubes: see respective instructions

   d Lymph nodes, if present:

- Left obturator
- Right obturator
- Interiliac
- Left iliac (high nodes)
- Right iliac (high nodes)

1 Robboy SJ, Kraus FT, Kurman RJ. Gross description, processing, and reporting of gynaecologic and obstetric specimens. In: Kurman RJ (ed). Blaustein's Pathology of the Female Genital Tract, 4th Edn. New York, 2002, Springer-Verlag, pp. 1319–1346

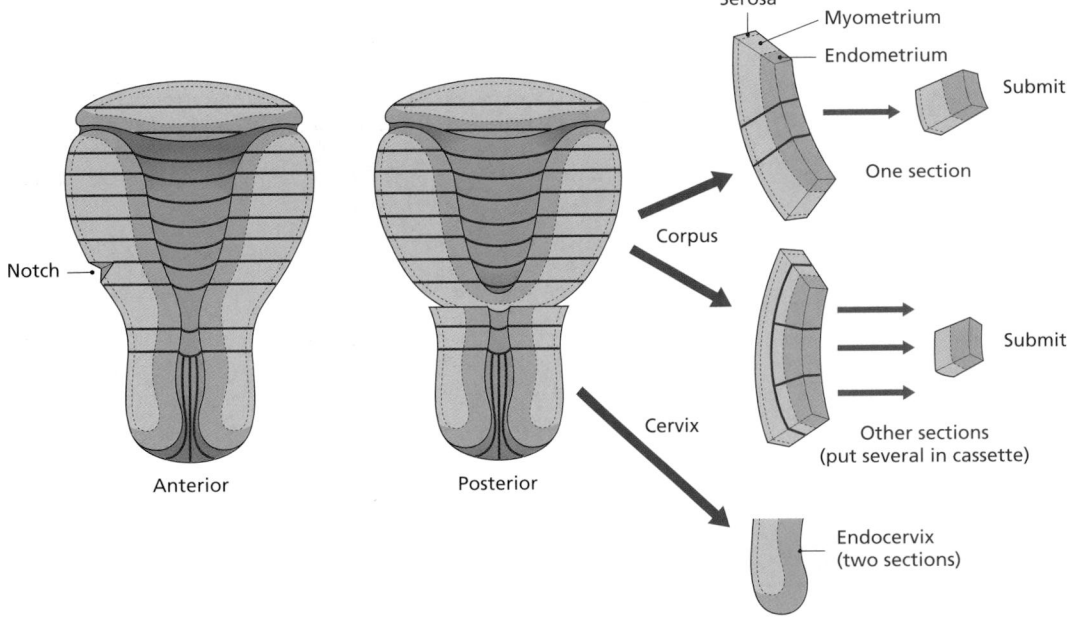

Uterus—tissue passed[1,2]

Procedure

1 Examine for presence of gestational sac and other evidence of conception. Use dissecting microscope, if necessary

Description

1 Measurement in the aggregate; color, consistency, appearance; decidual cast present? if so, note whether intact or ruptured, diameter, presence and size of amniotic sac, yolk sac, and embryo. If latter is present, measure and state whether it appears normal, malformed, or rudimentary, and whether there is evidence of maceration. If only fragments of the fetus are present, try to identify a foot and measure its length to estimate gestational age (see diagram)

Sections for histology

1 If identifiable products of conception are present: submit representative sections of the various components
2 If identifiable products of conception are absent: submit entire material

1 Berry CL (ed). Correlation of foot length with crown-rump length of human fetuses. In: Pediatric Pathology. New York, 1981, Springer-Verlag, p. 3
2 Robboy SJ, Kraus FT, Kurman RJ. Gross description, processing, and reporting of gynaecologic and obstetric specimens. In: Kurman RJ (ed). Blaustein's Pathology of the Female Genital Tract, 4th Edn. New York, 2002, Springer-Verlag, pp. 1319–1346

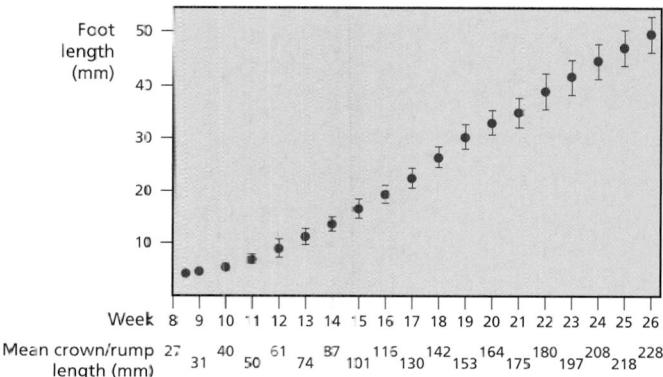

Vulva—vulvectomy

Procedure

1 Measure size of the specimen, including the inguinal region, if present; also measure the size of the lesion
2 In radical vulvectomy specimens, separate lymph nodes into groups and fix overnight in separate jars; Carnoy's fluid is preferable
3 Pin on a corkboard and fix overnight; be careful to pin down the entire external borders and vaginal margins. The latter is better preserved when it is pinned down on a cork placed in the introitus
4 Take photographs or photocopies, and identify in one of them the sites of the sections to be taken

Description

1 Type of vulvectomy: simply, subcutaneous, radical; lymph node groups present

2 Size of specimen
3 Lesion: size, location, extent, invasion into adjacent structures or vessels, color, surface (verrucous? ulcerated?), borders (distinct? rolled?), depth of stromal invasion
4 Appearance of non-neoplastic surface: atrophy, keratosis, ulceration
5 Lymph nodes: size of largest appearing grossly involved?

1 Robboy SJ, Kraus FT, Kurman RJ. Gross description, processing, and reporting of gynaecologic and obstetric specimens. In: Kurman RJ (ed). Blaustein's Pathology of the Female Genital Tract, 4th Edn. New York, 2002, Springer-Verlag, pp. 1319–1346

Index

Page references in *italics* indicate figures. Page references followed by *t* or *b* indicate tables or boxes respectively.

ELSEVIER CD-ROM LICENSE AGREEMENT

PLEASE READ THE FOLLOWING AGREEMENT CAREFULLY BEFORE USING THIS CD-ROM PRODUCT. THIS CD-ROM PRODUCT IS LICENSED UNDER THE TERMS CONTAINED IN THIS CD-ROM LICENSE AGREEMENT ("Agreement"). BY USING THIS CD-ROM PRODUCT, YOU, AN INDIVIDUAL OR ENTITY INCLUDING EMPLOYEES, AGENTS AND REPRESENTATIVES ("You" or "Your"), ACKNOWLEDGE THAT YOU HAVE READ THIS AGREEMENT, THAT YOU UNDERSTAND IT, AND THAT YOU AGREE TO BE BOUND BY THE TERMS AND CONDITIONS OF THIS AGREEMENT. ELSEVIER INC. ("Elsevier") EXPRESSLY DOES NOT AGREE TO LICENSE THIS CD-ROM PRODUCT TO YOU UNLESS YOU ASSENT TO THIS AGREEMENT. IF YOU DO NOT AGREE WITH ANY OF THE FOLLOWING TERMS, YOU MAY, WITHIN THIRTY (30) DAYS AFTER YOUR RECEIPT OF THIS CD-ROM PRODUCT RETURN THE UNUSED, PIN NUMBER PROTECTED, CD-ROM PRODUCT, ALL ACCOMPANYING DOCUMENTATION TO ELSEVIER FOR A FULL REFUND.

DEFINITIONS As used in this Agreement, these terms shall have the following meanings:

"Proprietary Material" means the valuable and proprietary information content of this CD-ROM Product including all indexes and graphic materials and software used to access, index, search and retrieve the information content from this CD-ROM Product developed or licensed by Elsevier and/or its affiliates, suppliers and licensors.

"CD-ROM Product" means the copy of the Proprietary Material and any other material delivered on CD-ROM and any other human-readable or machine-readable materials enclosed with this Agreement, including without limitation documentation relating to the same.

OWNERSHIP This CD-ROM Product has been supplied by and is proprietary to Elsevier and/or its affiliates, suppliers and licensors. The copyright in the CD-ROM Product belongs to Elsevier and/or its affiliates, suppliers and licensors and is protected by the national and state copyright, trademark, trade secret and other intellectual property laws of the United States and international treaty provisions, including without limitation the Universal Copyright Convention and the Berne Copyright Convention. You have no ownership rights in this CD-ROM Product. Except as expressly set forth herein, no part of this CD-ROM Product, including without limitation the Proprietary Material, may be modified, copied or distributed in hardcopy or machine-readable form without prior written consent from Elsevier. All rights not expressly granted to You herein are expressly reserved. Any other use of this CD-ROM Product by any person or entity is strictly prohibited and a violation of this Agreement.

SCOPE OF RIGHTS LICENSED (PERMITTED USES) Elsevier is granting to You a limited, non-exclusive, non-transferable license to use this CD-ROM Product in accordance with the terms of this Agreement. You may use or provide access to this CD-ROM Product on a single computer or terminal physically located at Your premises and in a secure network or move this CD-ROM Product to and use it on another single computer or terminal at the same location for personal use only, but under no circumstances may You use or provide access to any part or parts of this CD-ROM Product on more than one computer or terminal simultaneously.

You shall not (a) copy, download, or otherwise reproduce the CD-ROM Product in any medium, including, without limitation, online transmissions, local area networks, wide area networks, intranets, extranets and the Internet, or in any way, in whole or in part, except for printing out or downloading non-substantial portions of the text and images in the CD-ROM Product for Your own personal use; (b) alter, modify, or adapt the CD-ROM Product, including but not limited to decompiling, disassembling, reverse engineering, or creating derivative works, without the prior written approval of Elsevier; (c) sell, license or otherwise distribute to third parties the CD-ROM Product or any part or parts thereof; or (d) alter, remove, obscure or obstruct the display of any copyright, trademark or other proprietary notice on or in the CD-ROM Product or on any printout or download of portions of the Proprietary Materials.

RESTRICTIONS ON TRANSFER This License is personal to You, and neither Your rights hereunder nor the tangible embodiments of this CD-ROM Product, including without limitation the Proprietary Material, may be sold, assigned, transferred or sublicensed to any other person, including without limitation by operation of law, without the prior written consent of Elsevier. Any purported sale, assignment, transfer or sublicense without the prior written consent of Elsevier will be void and will automatically terminate the License granted hereunder.

TERM This Agreement will remain in effect until terminated pursuant to the terms of this Agreement. You may terminate this Agreement at any time by removing from Your system and destroying the CD-ROM Product. Unauthorized copying of the CD-ROM Product, including without limitation, the Proprietary Material and documentation, or otherwise failing to comply with the terms and conditions of this Agreement shall result in automatic termination of this license and will make available to Elsevier legal remedies. Upon termination of this Agreement, the license granted herein will terminate and You must immediately destroy the CD-ROM Product and accompanying documentation. All provisions relating to proprietary rights shall survive termination of this Agreement.

LIMITED WARRANTY AND LIMITATION OF LIABILITY NEITHER ELSEVIER NOR ITS LICENSORS REPRESENT OR WARRANT THAT THE CD-ROM PRODUCT WILL MEET YOUR REQUIREMENTS OR THAT ITS OPERATION WILL BE UNINTERRUPTED OR ERROR-FREE. WE EXCLUDE AND EXPRESSLY DISCLAIM ALL EXPRESS AND IMPLIED WARRANTIES NOT STATED HEREIN, INCLUDING THE IMPLIED WARRANTIES OF MERCHANTABILITY AND FITNESS FOR A PARTICULAR PURPOSE. IN ADDITION, NEITHER ELSEVIER NOR ITS LICENSORS MAKE ANY REPRESENTATIONS OR WARRANTIES, EITHER EXPRESS OR IMPLIED, REGARDING THE PERFORMANCE OF YOUR NETWORK OR COMPUTER SYSTEM WHEN USED IN CONJUNCTION WITH THE CD-ROM PRODUCT. WE SHALL NOT BE LIABLE FOR ANY DAMAGE OR LOSS OF ANY KIND ARISING OUT OF OR RESULTING FROM YOUR POSSESSION OR USE OF THE SOFTWARE PRODUCT CAUSED BY ERRORS OR OMISSIONS, DATA LOSS OR CORRUPTION, ERRORS OR OMISSIONS IN THE PROPRIETARY MATERIAL, REGARDLESS OF WHETHER SUCH LIABILITY IS BASED IN TORT, CONTRACT OR OTHERWISE AND INCLUDING, BUT NOT LIMITED TO, ACTUAL, SPECIAL, INDIRECT, INCIDENTAL OR CONSEQUENTIAL DAMAGES. IF THE FOREGOING LIMITATION IS HELD TO BE UNENFORCEABLE, OUR MAXIMUM LIABILITY TO YOU SHALL NOT EXCEED THE AMOUNT OF THE LICENSE FEE PAID BY YOU FOR THE SOFTWARE PRODUCT. THE REMEDIES AVAILABLE TO YOU AGAINST US AND THE LICENSORS OF MATERIALS INCLUDED IN THE SOFTWARE PRODUCT ARE EXCLUSIVE.

If this CD-ROM Product is defective, Elsevier will replace it at no charge if the defective CD-ROM Product is returned to Elsevier within sixty (60) days (or the greatest period allowable by applicable law) from the date of shipment.

Elsevier warrants that the software embodied in this CD-ROM Product will perform in substantial compliance with the documentation supplied in this CD-ROM Product. If You report a significant defect in performance in writing to Elsevier, and Elsevier is not able to correct same within sixty (60) days after its receipt of Your notification, You may return this CD-ROM Product, including all copies and documentation, to Elsevier and Elsevier will refund Your money.

YOU UNDERSTAND THAT, EXCEPT FOR THE 60-DAY LIMITED WARRANTY RECITED ABOVE, ELSEVIER, ITS AFFILIATES, LICENSORS, SUPPLIERS AND AGENTS, MAKE NO WARRANTIES, EXPRESSED OR IMPLIED, WITH RESPECT TO THE CD-ROM PRODUCT, INCLUDING, WITHOUT LIMITATION THE PROPRIETARY MATERIAL, AND SPECIFICALLY DISCLAIM ANY WARRANTY OF MERCHANTABILITY OR FITNESS FOR A PARTICULAR PURPOSE.

If the information provided on this CD-ROM contains medical or health sciences information, it is intended for professional use within the medical field. Information about medical treatment or drug dosages is intended strictly for professional use, and because of rapid advances in the medical sciences, independent verification of diagnosis and drug dosages should be made.

IN NO EVENT WILL ELSEVIER, ITS AFFILIATES, LICENSORS, SUPPLIERS OR AGENTS, BE LIABLE TO YOU FOR ANY DAMAGES, INCLUDING, WITHOUT LIMITATION, ANY LOST PROFITS, LOST SAVINGS OR OTHER INCIDENTAL OR CONSEQUENTIAL DAMAGES, ARISING OUT OF YOUR USE OR INABILITY TO USE THE CD-ROM PRODUCT REGARDLESS OF WHETHER SUCH DAMAGES ARE FORESEEABLE OR WHETHER SUCH DAMAGES ARE DEEMED TO RESULT FROM THE FAILURE OR INADEQUACY OF ANY EXCLUSIVE OR OTHER REMEDY.

U.S. GOVERNMENT RESTRICTED RIGHTS The CD-ROM Product and documentation are provided with restricted rights. Use, duplication or disclosure by the U.S. Government is subject to restrictions as set forth in subparagraphs (a) through (d) of the Commercial Computer Restricted Rights clause at FAR 52.22719 or in subparagraph (c)(1)(ii) of the Rights in Technical Data and Computer Software clause at DFARS 252.2277013, or at 252.2117015, as applicable. Contractor/Manufacturer is Elsevier Inc., 360 Park Avenue South, New York, NY 10010 USA.

GOVERNING LAW This Agreement shall be governed by the laws of the State of New York, USA. In any dispute arising out of this Agreement, You and Elsevier each consent to the exclusive personal jurisdiction and venue in the state and federal courts within New York County, New York, USA.